ENCYCLOPEDIC
DICTIONARY
OF RELIGION

ENCYCLOPEDIC

Edited by

Paul Kevin Meagher, OP, S.T.M.
Thomas C. O'Brien
Sister Consuelo Maria Aherne, SSJ

THE SISTERS OF ST. JOSEPH OF PHILADELPHIA

Volume **A-E**

DICTIONARY
OF RELIGION

CORPUS PUBLICATIONS: WASHINGTON, D.C.

Nihil Obstat:

John P. Whalen S.T.D., J.D.
Censor Deputatus

Imprimatur:

✠ William Cardinal Baum
Archibishop of Washington D.C.
February 7, 1978

Prepared by an

Editorial Staff at Corpus Publications, Inc. (1966–1970)
Washington, District of Columbia, and at
Mt. St. Joseph (1973–1979) Chestnut Hill,
Philadelphia, Pennsylvania.

Production Manager: Gerard G. Mayer

Composition: Lexigraphics Inc.
150 Fifth Avenue
New York, N.Y. 10011

Sales Manager: Jack Heraty and Associates, Inc.
P. O. Box 875
Palatine, Illinois 60067

Encyclopedic Dictionary of Religion

Library of Congress Catalog Number: 78-62029

ISBN 0-9602572-0-9 (Volume A-E)   ISBN 0-9602572-3-3 (Set)

TO SISTER ALICE ANITA MURPHY, SSJ

NINTH SUPERIOR GENERAL
OF THE
SISTERS OF ST. JOSEPH OF PHILADELPHIA
1968-1979

Forsan et haec olim meminisse
juvabit.

Foreword

The *Encyclopedic Dictionary of Religion* has been in preparation since 1966. It seems appropriate to describe its history briefly. The editorial staff of the *New Catholic Encyclopedia* completed its work that year; their expertise, developed over five years, seemed too valuable to be allowed to dissipate, and so in 1966 the group formed a religious-book publishing corporation under the title Corpus Instrumentorum. This editorial group, of which Reverend John P. Whalen was President, began as one of its projects the *Dictionary,* under the editorship of Very Reverend Paul Kevin Meagher, OP. In 1973, Corpus donated the incomplete manuscript of the *Dictionary* to the Sisters of St. Joseph of Philadelphia (about 11,000 articles representing half the title list). Sister Consuelo Maria Aherne, as assistant editor for medieval church history for NCE and medieval church history editor for the *Dictionary,* accepted the offer with the concurrence of Sister Alice Anita Murphy, Superior General of the Sisters of St. Joseph, and that of her Council (Sister Loyola Maria Coffey, Sister Mary Thomas Murphy, Sister Clare Michael Keating). This collaboration was continued by the Council elected in 1974: Sister Agnes Marie Gunn, Sister Marie Ellen Hegarty, and Sister St. Ursula Egan. Father Meagher continued as Editor in Chief (until his death on December 31, 1976); Sister Consuelo Maria Aherne served as Senior Editor. Jeanne H. Brady was appointed Managing Editor, and several Sisters of St. Joseph were assigned full-time to the work: Sister Rosalie Marie† Funchion (1973–74), Sister Margaret Rose Brown (1973–79), Sister St. Agnes Heeney (1973–78), Sister Mary Charles Bradley (1974–75), Sister Ann Patrick Hanlon (1975–79), Sister Mary Sarah Dillon (1977–79), Sister Rita Christi Egan (1975–76); also Sister Rita Cliggett, SHCJ (1976–77). Mary T. Hansbury and Maureen Brady worked full-time on the *Dictionary* for about a year and were succeeded by Frances M. Burke. Dr. Thomas C. O'Brien, associate of Father Meagher from the beginning of the project, succeeded as Editor in Chief in 1976.

Feast of St. Joseph
March 19, 1979

Sister Consuelo Maria Aherne, SSJ

Contributing Editors

Area Editors and Consultants

1966-70:

Consuelo Maria Aherne, SSJ (medieval church history).
Mary Julia Daly, SSJ (art and architecture).
Anthony Doherty (music).
Patricia Doherty (music).
Tracy Early (Protestantism; ecumenism).
Richard M. Frank (Islamic studies).
Thomas †Gilby, OP (moral theology; political history; English church
 history).
Norman H. Maring (church history; Protestantism).
Frederick E. Maser (Methodism).
M. Benedict Murphy, RSHM (education).
Jean C. Willke (European history; spirituality).
John F. Woolverton (Anglicanism).

1973-78:

John R. Aherne, OSA (literature; Latin American and American church
 history).
James Dallen (liturgy).
Mary Julia Daly, SSJ (art and architecture).
Edward J. Dillon (biblical studies; hagiography).
Tracy Early (Protestantism; ecumenism).
Joseph F. †Fallon (biblical studies).
Mary Theresa Legge, SSJ (music).
Thomas M. McFadden (ecclesiology; Christology).
Norman H. Maring (church history; Protestantism).
Frederick E. Maser (Methodism).
Ludvik Nemec (Eastern Churches).
Charles J. Noone (liturgy).
J. Roberta Rivello, SSJ (philosophy).

Sisters of St. Joseph
Summer Dictionary Staff
1973-78

Annas, Sister Helen Patrice
Bateman, Sister Kathleen
Boyle, Sister Maria Benedetta
Boyle, Sister Mary Rita
Bradley, Sister Mary Charles
Casey, Sister Mary Agnes
Cooper, Sister Paschal
Coughlin, Sister Rose Clare
Crane, Sister Anne Hélène
Craven, Sister Maria Dolores
Devlin, Sister Grace Elizabeth
Dillon, Sister Mary Sarah
Doherty, Sister Irma Regina
Dunn, Sister Cordata
Esker, Sister George Ann
Feighery, Sister Rose Amadeus
Garvin, Sister Ann Dorothea
Gilligan, Sister Gertrude Marie
Herron, Sister Grace Catherine
Hickey, Sister Agnes Christi
Higgins, Sister Miriam
Higgins, Sister Stella Immaculate
Hoehn, Sister Peter Josephine
Hurlbrink, Sister Susan
Keenan, Sister Carolyn
Kirby, Sister John of the Cross
Lanman, Sister Gertrude Leonore
Lannutti, Sister Maria Rita

Legge, Sister Mary Theresa
Lynch, Sister Lupita
McDonnell, Sister Philothea
Mack, Sister Ann Marie
McKay, Sister Charles Margaret
McMenamin, Sister John Patrice
McVeigh, Sister Anne
Manning, Sister Marie Isabel
Monaghan, Sister Marie Brigid
Morgan, Sister Juanita
Moriarty, Sister Kathleen Thérèse
Mulzet, Sister Mary Ann
Naughton, Sister Maria Bernard
Neal, Sister Pauline
Nolan, Sister Miriam Rose
O'Brien, Sister Frances Gervase
O'Callaghan, Sister Clare Gervase
O'Donnell, Sister Catherine Christi
O'Keefe, Sister Mary Aquin
O'Neill, Sister Agnes Angela
O'Neill, Sister Kathleen
Rein, Sister Gregory Marie
Reilly, Sister Maria Trinita
Ryall, Sister Margaret
Smith, Sister Marie Emily
Todd, Sister Regina Augusta
Wardle, Sister Amata
Willmanns, Sister George Elizabeth

Chestnut Hill College Library Staff

Brimmer, Sister Regina Maria
Gruber, Sister Rita Madeleine
Hayes, Helen M.

Contributors

ABBOTT, NICHOLAS MARIE, SSJ, MA; Villanova University. Teacher, Allentown Central Catholic HS, Pa.

AHERNE, CONSUELO MARIA, SSJ, PhD; The Catholic Univ. of America. Assistant Superior General of the Sisters of Saint Joseph of Philadelphia; Visiting Professor of History at Chestnut Hill College.

AHERNE, JOHN R., OSA, MA, LittD; The Catholic Univ. of America. President Emeritus, Merrimack College.

ALLISON, C. FITZSIMONS, DPhil (Oxon.). Rector of Grace Church, New York City.

ALLWEIN, MARY ESDRAS, SSJ, MS; Fordham University. Coordinator of Curriculum, Nativity HS, Pottsville, Pa.

AMAR, PAULA B., PhD; Medical College of Pennsylvania. Program Administrator, Jefferson Community Mental Health Center; Assistant Professor, Department of Psychiatry, Jefferson Medical College of Philadelphia.

ANNAS, HELEN PATRICE, SSJ, MA; Saint Bonaventure University. Teacher, Queen of Peace HS, North Arlington, N.J.

ARONSTAM; ROBIN A., PhD; Columbia University. Assistant Professor of Theology, Saint Joseph's College, Philadelphia.

AUMANN, JORDAN, OP, STD; Univ. of Salamanca. Professor of Theology, Univ. of St. Thomas Aquinas, Rome. Director, Institute of Spirituality, River Forest, Ill.

BACKMUND, NORBERT, OPraem, DrScHist-Mediaev; Univ. of Munich. Author and Lecturer.

BARR, ROBERT R. (no information available).

BARRETT, DAVID B., PhD, BD (Cantab.); Columbia University. Editor, *World Christian Encyclopedia,* Oxford.

BARRY, M. JUSTIN, OP, MA; The Catholic Univ. of America. Chairperson, Department of Classics, Professor of Greek and Latin, Dominican College of San Rafael.

BARRY, MARY MARTIN, OP, PhD; The Catholic Univ. of America. Professor of English Literature, Dominican College of San Rafael.

BATEMAN, KATHLEEN, SSJ, AB; Chestnut Hill College. Teacher, John Carroll HS, Bel Air, Md.

BAYNE,† RIGHT REVEREND STEPHEN F., JR., STD; General Theological Seminary. Former Professor of Ascetical Theology, General Theological Seminary. Member, Executive Council of the Episcopal Church, New York City.

BEAUREGARD, ERVING EDWARD, PhD; Union Graduate School. Professor of History, Univ. of Dayton.

BEESE, ROGER, STM; Concordia Seminary, St. Louis. Pastor, Bethlehem Lutheran Church, Warrensburg, Mo.

BEIRNE, MARY HELEN, SSJ, MA; The Catholic Univ. of America. Principal and Teacher, Star of the Sea School, Cape May, N.J.

BERDAR, SALOME, OSBM, MA; The Catholic Univ. of America. Co-ordinator for Grade Language Program, Saints Peter and Paul School, Cohoes, N.Y.

BERGMANN, ROSEMARIE L., PhD; McGill University, Montréal. Associate Professor of Art History, McGill University, Montréal.

BERLINSKI, HERMAN, Dr. of Sacred Music; École Normale de Musique, Paris. Music Director, The National Jewish Musical Art Foundation.

BERMEJO, ALOYSIUS M., SJ, STD; Gregorian University, Rome. Professor of Systematic Theology, De Nobili College, Poona, India.

BERNAS, CASIMIR, OCSO, SSD; Pontifical Biblical Institute, Rome. Professor of Sacred Scripture and Theology at Holy Trinity Abbey, Huntsville, Utah.

BIECHLER, JAMES E., JCL, PhD; The Catholic Univ. of America. Univ. of Pennsylvania. Assistant Professor of Religion, La Salle College, Philadelphia.

BILANIUK, PETRO B. T., STD, PhD; Univ. of Munich; Ukrainian Free Univ., Munich. Professor of Theology, Univ. of St. Michael's College; Professor of Religious Studies, Univ. of Toronto; Visiting Professor of Church History, Ukrainian Free Univ., Munich.

BIRD, THOMAS E., MA; Princeton University. Editor, *Queens Slavic Papers;* Professor, Slavic and East European Languages and Literatures, Queens College, Flushing, N.Y.

BLACKLAW, B. (no information available).

BLACKLEY, FRANK D., PhD; Univ. of Toronto; Pontifical Institute of Mediaeval Studies, Toronto. Professor of History, Univ. of Alberta.

BLAIR, JOAN, SSJ, AB; Chestnut Hill College.

BLUM, OWEN J., OFM, PhD; The Catholic Univ. of America. Professor of History, Quincy College, Ill.

BLUM, SHIRLEY N., PhD; Univ. of California, Los Angeles. Professor of Art History, Univ. of California.

BOCK, PAUL J., PhD; Western Reserve Univ., Cleveland, Ohio. Professor of Religion, Heidelberg College, Tiffin, Ohio.

BOURKE, DAVID J. (no information available).

BOYLE, LEONARD E., OP, DPhil (Oxon.). Professor, Pontifical Institute of Medieval Studies, Toronto.

BOYLE, MARIA BENEDETTA, SSJ, MA; Univ. of Delaware, Newark. Teacher and Department Head, Notre Dame HS, Easton, Pa.

BRADY, JEANNE M., AB; Chestnut Hill College. Teacher.

BRADY, RICHARD J., AB; Villanova University. Teacher.

BRADLEY, MARY CHARLES, SSJ, AB; Chestnut Hill College. Teacher, Delone HS, McSherrystown, Pa.

BRIGHAM, FREDERICK H., Jr., MA; Boston College Graduate School of Arts and Sciences. Legislative Analyst, Massachusetts General Court.

BROWN, MARGARET ROSE, SSJ, MA; The Catholic Univ. of America. Assistant Staff Editor, *Encyclopedic Dictionary of Religion*.

BRUCE-MITFORD, RUPERT LEO SCOTT, MA (Oxon.), D Litt, FBA, FSA, FSAS. Former Keeper of Medieval and Later Antiquities in the British Museum, London.

BRUNAUER, DALMA H., PhD; Univ. of Budapest, Hungary. Professor of Humanities, Clarkson College of Technology.

BRYCE, MARY CHARLES, OSB, PhD; The Catholic Univ. of America. Associate Professor in Department of Religion and Religious Education, The Catholic Univ. of America.

BUCHER, OTTO N., OFMCap, SSL; Pontifical Biblical Institute, Rome. Associate Professor of New Testament at Sacred Heart School of Theology, Hales Corners, Wis.

BUCK, FIDELIS, SJ, SSD; Pontifical Biblical Institute, Rome. Professor of Sacred Scripture at the Toronto School of Theology.

BUCKLEY,† CEPHAS, SSJ, MA; Villanova Univ. Former Teacher, Bishop McDevitt HS, Wyncote, Pa.

BULLOUGH, VERN L., PhD; Univ. of Chicago. Professor of History, California State University.

BURNS, ROBERT I., SJ, PhD, D ès ScHist, DLitt; Johns Hopkins University; Univ. of Fribourg, Switzerland. Professor of History, Graduate School, Univ. of California at Los Angeles.

BUSCHMILLER, ROBERT J., STD; Univ. of Fribourg, Switzerland. Pastor of Saint Andrew's Church, Milford, Ohio.

BUSHINSKI, LEONARD A., CSSp., SSL; The Pontifical Biblical Institute, Rome. Professor, Duquesne University.

BYRON, WILLIAM J., SJ, PhD; Univ. of Maryland. President of the University of Scranton.

CABANISS, ALLEN, PhD; Univ. of Chicago. Research Professor of History, Emeritus, Univ. of Mississippi.

CABEY, EDWIN, SVD, SSL; Pontifical Biblical Institute, Rome. Pastoral work at Saint Carthage Church, Chicago, Ill.

CALDER, RALPH F. G., MA; Manchester University. Former Secretary of International Congregational Council and Overseas Appointments Bureau.

CARNEY, EDWARD J., OSFS, MA, STD; Catholic Univ., Fribourg, Switzerland. Professor of Dogmatic Theology, De Sales Hall School of Theology, Hyattsville, Md.

CAROL, JUNIPER BENJAMIN, OFM, STD; Pontifical Univ. of Saint Anthony in Rome. Chaplain, Cor Jesu Center, Tampa, Fla.

CARRILLO, ELISA, PhD; Fordham Graduate School. Professor of History; Chairperson, History Department, Marymount College, Tarrytown, N.Y.

CARROLL, CLAIRE, SSJ, MA; Saint Charles Seminary, Overbrook, Pa. Coordinator of Religious Studies, Saint Anne's School, Bethlehem, Pa.

CARTHY, MARGARET, PhD; The Catholic Univ. of America. Dean of Graduate School, College of New Rochelle.

CARTON, FRANCIS REGIS, SSND, PhD; The Catholic Univ. of America. Professor of Religious Studies, The College of Notre Dame of Maryland.

CASTELOT, JOHN J., SS, STD; Pontifical Biblical Institute, Rome. Professor of Sacred Scripture, Saint John's Provincial Seminary, Plymouth, Mich.

CAWLEY, CATHERINE ROSARII, SSJ, MA; Villanova University. Secretary, Saint Francis of Assisi School, Springfield, Pa.

CEROKE, CHRISTIAN PAUL, OCarm, STD. Associate Professor, Department of Religious Education, The Catholic Univ. of America.

CHANDLER, DOUGLAS, R., DD; Yale University. Professor Emeritus of Wesley Theological Seminary, Washington, D.C.

CHANEY, WILLIAM A., PhD; Univ. of California; Society of Fellows, Harvard University. George McKendree Steele Professor of Western Culture, Lawrence University.

CHOATE, NORMAN L., CR, MA; Univ. of Illinois. Campus Chaplain, Saint Jerome's College, Waterloo, Ontario.

CLANCY, THOMAS H., SJ, PhD; London School of Economics, Oxford Univ. Superior, New Orleans

Province of the Society of Jesus, New Orleans, Louisiana; Author and Lecturer.

CLARK, BAYARD STOCKTON, MD; Virginia Theological Seminary. Education Program Specialist, Division of Adult Education, United States Office of Education, Health Education and Welfare, Washington, D.C.

CLIGGETT, RITA, SHCJ, MA, PdD; The Catholic Univ. of America. Assistant Director of the Overbrook School for the Blind, Philadelphia, Pa.

CODDINGTON, DOROTHY T. (no information available).

CODY, AELRED, OSB, STD, SSD; The Pontifical Biblical Institute, Rome; The Pontifical Oriental Institute, Rome. Professor of Old Testament in the Pontificio Ateneo di Sant'Anselmo and the Pontifical Biblical Institute, Rome; Procurator General of the North American Benedictine Federations.

COLBERT, EDWARD PAUL, PhD; The Catholic Univ. of America. Professor of History, Eastern Illinois University.

CONLAN, M. SAMUEL, OP, PhD; Stanford University. President of Dominican College of San Rafael.

CONNERY, JOHN R., SJ, STD; Gregorian Univ., Rome. Professor of Moral Theology, Loyola Univ. of Chicago.

CONWAY, GEORGE EDWARD, SSJ, PhD; The Catholic Univ. of America. Professor of Classics, Chestnut Hill College.

CONWAY, SUZANNE, MA; Columbia University. Assistant Professor of Art History, Chestnut Hill College.

COOK, GENEVIEVE MARIE, RSM, PhD; The Catholic Univ. of America. Retired.

COOKE, JOHN PETER, SSJ (EILEEN FRANCIS M. COOKE), AB; Chestnut Hill College. Teacher, Nativity School, Philadelphia.

COOPER, PASCHAL, SSJ, MA; Seton Hall University. Teacher and Mathematics Coordinator, St. Gabriel School, Norwood, Pa.

CORBISHLEY,† THOMAS, SJ, MA (Oxon.). Former Superior of Farm Street Church, London, England.

CORCORAN, CHARLES, OP (no information available).

CORDOUE, JOHN, PhD; The Catholic Univ. of America. Assistant Professor, Department of Sociology and Social Work, Briar Cliff College, Sioux City, Iowa.

CORE, ARTHUR C., PhD; Univ. of Nebraska. Professor Emeritus of Church History at United Theological Seminary, Dayton, Ohio.

COSTELLOE, M. JOSEPH, SJ, PhD; Johns Hopkins University. Librarian of the Curia Generalizia della Compagnia di Gesù, Rome.

CRANE, ANNE HÉLÈNE, SSJ, MA; The Catholic Univ. of America, Washington. Coordinator of Vocational–Technical Students, Archbishop Prendergast HS, Drexel Hill, Pa.

CRANE, THOMAS E., SSL; Pontifical Biblical Institute, Rome. Professor of Sacred Scripture, Saint Patrick's Seminary, Manley, Australia.

CRISAFULLI, ALESSANDRO S., PhD; The Ohio State University. Professor Emeritus, The Catholic Univ. of America.

CROWLEY, EDWARD J., SSL; Pontifical Biblical Institute, Rome. Professor and Head of the Department of Religious Studies, University of Windsor, Ontario.

CUNNINGHAM, FRANK J., PhD; Fordham University. Associate Professor of Philosophy, Loyola College, Baltimore.

CUNNINGHAM, JAMES J., OP, SSL; Pontifical Biblical Institute, Rome. Associate Professor of New Testament, Dominican House of Studies, Washington, District of Columbia.

CUTTER, PAUL F., PhD; Princeton University. Professor of Music, Texas Technological University.

DAILEY, ROBERT H., SJ, JCD; Gregorian University, Rome. Professor of Moral and Pastoral Theology.

DALLEN, JAMES, MA, STD; The Catholic Univ. of America. Assistant Professor of Theology, Rosemont College.

DALY, MARY JULIA, SSJ, MA; Univ. of Pennsylvania. Professor Emeritus, Art, Chestnut Hill College.

DAMAZ, PAUL, BArch, AIA, New York.

DAMBORIENA,† PRUDENCIO, SJ, PhD. Former Professor of Church History, Saint Louis University.

DAOUST, JOSEPH, Docteur ès lettres; Univ. of Caen, France. Professor, Faculté des lettres, Université Catholique de Lille, France.

DAVISH, WILLIAM, M., SJ, MA; Georgetown University. Professor of Theology and Associate Dean, Loyola College, Md.

DEEGAN, AGNES PERPETUA, SSJ, MA; Seton Hall University. Teacher at Archbishop Wood High School, Warminster, Pa.

DE LETTER, PRUDENT, SJ, PhD, STD. (no information available).

DENNIS, GEORGE THOMAS, SJ, ScEcclOrD; Pontifical Institute of Oriental Studies, Rome. Professor of History, The Catholic University of America.

DILLON, EDWARD J., STD; Gregorian Univ., Rome. Program Developer, Southwest Community Enrichment Center, Philadelphia, Pa.

DIRSCHERL, DENIS, SJ, PhD; Georgetown University. Chaplain in the United States Air Force Reserve; Author.

DOHERTY, ANTHONY, MusB (no information available).

DOHERTY, PATRICIA (no information available).

DONLON, STEPHEN E., SJ, STD; Weston College. Associate Professor of Theology, Loyola University, Chicago.

DOWDALL, GEORGE W., PhD; Brown University. Associate Professor of Sociology, State University College at Buffalo.

DRESSLER, HERMIGILD, OFM, PhD; The Catholic Univ. of America. Editorial Director, *Fathers of the Church,* published by Catholic University Press.

DRUMMOND, WILLIAM F., SJ (no information available).

DRUSE, JOSEPH L., PhD; Univ. of Chicago, Professor of Humanities, Michigan State University.

DUBAY, THOMAS, SM, PhD; The Catholic Univ. of America. Lecturer and Author.

DUCLOS, VINCENT, OP, STL; Le Saulchoir, France. Religion Teacher.

DUFFY, MARY EDGAR, MA; Marquette University. Continuing Education, Outpost of Malcolm X College, Chicago.

DUGGAN, WILLIAM J., STD; The Catholic Univ. of America. Dean of Graduate Programs, Webster College.

DUNN, ELLEN CATHERINE, PhD; The Catholic Univ. of America. Professor of English and Chairman of the English Department at The Catholic Univ. of America.

DUPRÉ, LOUIS, PhD; Univ. of Louvain, Belgium. T. Lawrason Riggs Professor, Yale University.

DUPRÉ, WILHELM, PhD; Univ. of Vienna, Austria. Professor of Philosophy of Religion, Univ. of Nijmegen, The Netherlands.

DUPUIS, JAMES, SJ (no information available).

DURBIN, PAUL T., PhD (no information available).

EARLY, TRACY, ThD; Union Theological Seminary, New York City. Author.

EBY, CHARLES T., MA; Univ. of Notre Dame. Instructor in History, Saint Joseph's College, Philadelphia.

EENIGENBURG, ELTON M., PhD; Columbia Univ., New York City. Professor of Christian Ethics and Philosophy of Religion, Western Theological Seminary.

EFROYMSON, DAVID P., PhD; Temple University. Associate Professor of Religion, La Salle College.

ELDAROV, GEORGE, OFMConv., STD, OrScD; Pontifical Theological Faculty of Saint Bonaventure, Rome; Pontifical Institute of Oriental Studies, Rome. Professor of Ecclesiology at Pontifical Theological Faculty of Saint Bonaventure; Professor of Oriental Spirituality at Pontifical Athanaeum Antonianum, Rome.

EL-HAYEK, ELIAS, JUD; Saint John Lateran, Rome. Professor of Philosophy of Law at the Law School of the University of Lebanon. Temporarily, Pastor of Saint Maron, Cleveland, Ohio.

ELLWOOD, ROBERT S., PhD; University of Chicago Divinity School. Bishop James W. Bashford Professor of Oriental Studies, School of Religion, University of Southern California.

ENGLERT, CLEMENT, CSSR, SEOL, PhD; Pontifical Oriental Institute, Rome. Spiritual Director, Professor.

ENNIS, ARTHUR J., OSA, HED; Gregorian Univ., Rome. Director, Augustinian Historical Institute; Professor of Ecclesiastical History, Villanova University.

ENO, ROBERT B., SS, STD; Institut Catholique de Paris.

Associate Professor of Church History, The Catholic Univ. of America.

EVERY, GEORGE, AB; University of Exeter. Lecturer at Saint Mary's College, Oscott, Birmingham, England.

FALARDEAU, ERNEST RENÉ, SSS, STD; Gregorian Univ., Rome. National Director of Vocations for the Congregation of the Blessed Sacrament.

FALLON,† JOSEPH F., SSL; St. Thomas Aquinas Univ., Rome; École Biblique, Jerusalem.

FALTEISEK, EDWIN F., SJ, STD; Gregorian Univ., Rome. Associate Professor of Religious Studies, Trinity College, Burlington, Vermont.

FANG, JOSEPHINE RISS, PhD; The Catholic Univ. of America. Professor, School of Library Science, Simmons College.

FARRAHER, JOSEPH J., SJ, MA, STD; Gregorian Univ., Rome. Moral Theologian.

FARRELL, AMBROSE, OP (no information available).

FEATHERSTONE, JEFFREY (no information available).

FEHL, PHILIPP, PhD (no information available).

FEIDT, THORPE (no information available).

FENNINGHAM, MARIE E., SSJ, MA; Villanova University. Teacher, Archbishop Kennedy HS, Conshohocken, Pa.

FICHTNER, JOSEPH A., OSC, STD; St. Thomas Aquinas Univ., Rome. Professor of Systematic Theology, Mount St. Mary's Seminary, Emmitsburg, Md.

FINNEGAN, MARY JEREMY, OP, PhD; Yale University. Professor Department of English, Rosary College, River Forest, Ill.

FINNERTY, D. JOSEPH, MS; Saint Mary's Univ., Baltimore. Associate Pastor, Saint Brendan's Church; Spiritual Director, Saint Brendan's HS, Brooklyn, N.Y.

FLEISCHER, ROLAND EDWARD, PhD (no information available).

FLOOD, JAMES J., STD; Gregorian Univ., Rome. Professor, Faculty of Theology, Saint Charles Seminary, Overbrook, Pa.

FORD, MARY ELLEN, SSJ, MA; Univ. of Virginia. Teacher and Assistant Dean of Students, Allentown Central Catholic HS, Pa.

FORSHAW, BERNARD, DD; Maynooth Univ., Ireland. Parish Priest, Holy Name, Liverpool, England.

FORSYTH, CHARLES, OSB, AB, DD; Holy Cross Abbey, Canon City, Colorado; Fordham University. Director of Campus Ministry Program, Graduate School of Religious Education, Fordham University.

FOSCOLOS, PANAYOTIS, SJ (no information available).

FOULK, REGINA ANN, SSJ, BS; Chestnut Hill College. Teacher, Saint Andrew School, Bayonne, N.J.

FRAGNIÈRE, GABRIEL (no information available).

FRANCAVILLA, JOSEPH F., STL; The Catholic Univ. of America. Pastor, Holy Transfiguration Church, Vienna, Va.

FRANK, RICHARD MacDONOUGH, PhD; Università degli Studi di Rome. Professor of Semitics at The Catholic Univ. of America.

FUNCHION,† ROSALIE MARIE, SSJ, PhD; Univ. of Pennsylvania. Former Teacher, Author, Directress of Education.

GALLAGHER, EUGENE V., MA; Univ. of Chicago. College Teacher.

GALLAGHER, JOHN F., STD (no information available).

GALLIN, MARY ALICE, OSU, PhD; The Catholic Univ. of America. Professor of History, College of New Rochelle.

GARCIA, EMMANUEL, OP, STD; Univ. of St. Thomas Aquinas, Rome. Professor of Theology, Associate Pastor of Our Lady of Mercy Church, Hicksville, N.Y.

GARDINER,† HAROLD CHARLES, SJ, PhD; Cambridge University. Former Staff Editor for Literature, New Catholic Encyclopedia; Literary Editor, America (1940–1962); Author and Lecturer.

GARDNER, MARVIN A., AB, BC (no information available).

GARRIGAN, OWEN WALTER, PhD; The Catholic Univ. of America. Associate Professor of Chemistry, Seton Hall University.

GAST, FREDERICK, OCD, SSL; Pontifical Biblical Institute, Rome; The Catholic Univ. of America.

GATES, ELEANOR M., MA; Cornell University. Freelance Editor and Writer.

GAUGHAN, MOST REVEREND NORBERT, PhD; Univ. of Pittsburgh. Auxiliary Bishop, Diocese of Greensburg.

GENOVESI, VINCENT J., SJ, PhD; Emory University, Atlanta, Georgia. Associate Professor of Theology, St. Joseph's College, Philadelphia.

GEORGIADIS, HELLE E., MSc; University of London. Teacher.

GHANEM, JOSEPH R., PhD; The Univ. of Wisconsin in Madison. Assistant Professor of History at the Lebanese University, Beirut, Lebanon.

GIBBONS, ROBERT J., PhD; Yale University. Former Professor of European History at Yale Univ. and Saint Joseph's College, Philadelphia.

GILBY,† THOMAS, OP, PhD, STM; Saint Thomas Priory, Staffordshire, England; Louvain Univ., Belgium. General Editor of the Latin-English edition of St. Thomas Aquinas, Summa theologiae (60 v., 1965–1976).

GILLEMAN, GÉRARD AUGUSTE, SJ, STD (no information available).

GILLIGAN, VIRGINIA, SSJ, MA; Saint Bonaventure University. Director of Religious Education, Cherry Hill, N.J.

GINGRAS, GEORGE E., PhD; Manhattan College; The Catholic Univ. of America. Associate Professor of French and Chairperson, Department of Modern Languages, The Catholic Univ. of America.

GODBEY, JOHN C., PhD (no information available).

GOLINI, ROLAND K., AB, STL; Univ. of Notre Dame. Pastor, St. George's Church, Milwaukee.

GRAHAM, HOLT H., ThD; Union Theological Seminary in New York. Director of Library Services and Professor of New Testament Studies, United Theological Seminary of the Twin Cities, Minn.

GRAHAM, ROBERT A., SJ, PhD; Graduate Institute of International Studies, Univ. of Geneva, Switzerland. Co-editor, Actes et documents du Saint-Siège relatifs à la Seconde Guerre Mondiale, Vatican City (1965–).

GRANAHAN, MARILYN, SSJ, MM; The Catholic Univ. of America. Chairman of Music Department, Mount Saint Joseph Academy, Flourtown, Pa.

GRASSI, JOHN L., DPhil (Oxon.). Principal Lecturer in History, Trinity and All Saints College, Troy, Horsforth, Nr. Leeds, England.

GRASSI, JOSEPH A., SSL; Pontifical Biblical Institute, Rome. Professor, Department of Religious Studies, The University of Santa Clara.

GRIFFIN, MARIA THERESA, SSJ, MA; Univ. of Notre Dame. Teacher, Mount Saint Joseph Academy, Flourtown, Pa.

GRIFFIN, MICHAEL, OCD, MA; The Catholic Univ. of America. Teacher of Spiritual Theology at the Adult Education Section of The Catholic University of America. Chaplain at the National Institutes of Health, Bethesda, Md.

GRUBAR, FRANCIS S., PhD; Johns Hopkins University. Professor of Art, The George Washington University, Washington, D.C.

GUILLOT, LAWRENCE B. (no information available).

HALLIGAN, NICHOLAS, OP, STD; Univ. of Saint Thomas Aquinas, Rome. Archivist–Secretary at the Apostolic Delegation, Washington, D.C.

HALPIN, JOSEPH LAWRENCE, SSJ, MA; Seton Hall University, Teacher, Queen of Peace HS, North Arlington, N.J.

HALPIN, MARLENE, OP, PhD; The Catholic Univ. of America. Professor of Philosophy at Aquinas Institute of Theology; Coordinator of Continuing Education at Aquinas Institute, Dubuque, Iowa.

HAMBRICK, CHARLES H., PhD; Univ. of Chicago. Associate Professor of Religious Studies, Vanderbilt University.

HANLON, ANN PATRICK, SSJ, MA; Saint Charles Seminary, Overbrook, Pa. Assistant Staff Editor, Encyclopedic Dictionary of Religion.

HANSBURY, MARY T., MA; Temple University.

HARDON, JOHN A., SJ, STD; Gregorian Univ., Rome. Professor of Theology, Institute for Advanced Studies in Catholic Doctrine, Saint John's University, New York City.

HARVEY, JOHN F., OSFS, MA, STD; The Catholic Univ. of America. Professor of Moral and Pastoral

Theology, De Sales Hall of Sacred Theology, Hyattsville, Md.

HAYDEN, J. MICHAEL, PhD; Loyola Univ., Chicago. Professor of History, University of Saskatchewan.

HAYS,† RHŶS W., PhD; Union Theological Seminary, New York. Former Professor of History, Univ. of Wisconsin, Stevens Point.

HEANEY, JOHN J., SJ, STD, Institut Catholique, Paris. Associate Professor of Theology, Fordham Univ., New York City.

HEATH, THOMAS R., OP, PhD; The Catholic Univ. of America. Novice Master, Saint Stephen Priory, Dover, Mass.

HEENEY, ST. AGNES, SSJ, PhD; Univ. of Pennsylvania. Assistant Staff Editor, *Encyclopedic Dictionary of Religion*.

HEFTING, PAULUS H., Doctor, History of Art; Utrecht Univ., Netherlands. Curator of Rijksmuseum Kröller-Müller, Otterlo.

HEKKER, RITA FRANCES, SSJ, MA; Saint Charles Seminary, Overbrook, Pa. Teacher, John Carroll HS, Bel Air, Md.

HENNESSEY, JUSTIN, OP, STD; Research Fellow, Divinity School, Yale University. Pontifical Faculty of the Immaculate Conception, Dominican House of Studies, Washington. Professor of Systematic Theology, Saint Mary Seminary, Cleveland, Ohio; Visiting Professor of Theology, Univ. of Saint Thomas Aquinas, Rome.

HENNESSEY, PATRICIA J., MA; Univ. of Hartford. Laval Univ., Canada. Teacher, Univ. of Quebec.

HENNESSEY, RICHARD E., MA; Univ. of Hartford. Teacher, Laval Univ., Canada.

HENNESSY, EDWARD LEO, SSJ, MS; Univ. of Cincinnati. Associate Professor of Physics, Chestnut Hill College.

HICKERSON, JOSEPH C. (no information available).

HICKEY, JOHN T., MA; Xavier University. Professor of Philosophy, Sinclair Community College.

HIGGINS, MIRIAM, SSJ, MA; The Catholic Univ. of America. Teacher, Our Lady Help of Christians School, Abington, Pa.

HIGGINS, PATRICIA, SSJ, AB; Chestnut Hill College. Teacher, Ascension School, Philadelphia, Pa.

HIGGINS, STELLA IMMACULATE, SSJ, AB; Chestnut Hill College. Retired.

HILL, JANE MARIE, SSJ, MA; Univ. of Notre Dame, Indiana. Principal of Our Lady of the Valley HS, Orange, N.J.

HINNEBUSCH, WILLIAM A., OP, DPhil (Oxon.), STM; The Catholic Univ. of America. Professor Emeritus of Church History; Historian of the Dominican Order.

HOFFMAN, JOHN C., PhD, ThD.; McGill University, Montréal; Union Theological Seminary. Professor of Religious Studies, Univ. of Windsor, Ontario.

HOLBROOK, CLYDE A., PhD, STD; Yale University; Denison Univ. Sometime William H. Danforth Professor of Religion, Oberlin College.

HOPKO, THOMAS, MA; Duquesne University. Assistant Professor of Theology, Saint Vladimir's Orthodox Theological Seminary, Crestwood, Tuckahoe, New York.

HOUSTON, J. RICHARD, PhD; Bryn Mawr College. Professor of Physics, Saint Joseph's College, Philadelphia.

HOVDA, ROBERT W., STL; The Catholic Univ. of America. Editorial Director, The Liturgical Conference, Washington, District of Columbia; Priest of the Diocese of Fargo, N. Dak.

HUBBERT, EILEEN CLARE, SSJ, AB; Chestnut Hill College. Fairfield University. Teacher, Sacred Heart School, Miller Hts., Bethlehem, Pa.

HUGHES, DEBORAH, SSJ, AB, Chestnut Hill College. The Catholic Univ. of America. Teacher, St. Vincent School, Mays Landing, N.J.

HUGHES, JOHN JAY, PhD (no other information available).

HUNT, JOSEPH IGNATIUS, STD, SSL; Pontifical Biblical Institute, Rome. Professor of Old Testament, Nashotah House, Nashotah, Wisconsin.

HURLEY, ROBERT F., Immaculate Conception Seminary, Huntington, N.Y. Presiding Judge, Brooklyn Diocesan Tribunal.

JACK,† HONORA, IHM, PhD, DScEd; LLD; Fordham University. Former President of Marygrove College.

JACOPIN,† ARMAND JOHN, MA; Former Assistant Professor of Art, College of Notre Dame of Maryland.

JEHRING,† JOHN JAMES, MA; The Catholic Univ. of America. Former Director for the Study of Productivity Motivation, Univ. of Wisconsin.

JELLY, FREDERICK M., OP, STLr; Pontifical Faculty of the Immaculate Conception. Member of the Pontifical Faculty of Systematic Theology of the Immaculate Conception, Dominican House of Studies, Washington, D.C.

JOHNSON, DAVID W., SJ, PhD; The Catholic Univ. of America. Senior Research Fellow, Institute of Christian Oriental Research, Washington, District of Columbia.

JOHNSON, STELLA FRANCIS, SSJ, MA; Seton Hall University. Librarian, Good Counsel HS, Newark, N.J.

JOHNSON, VIRGINIA THÉRÈSE, MM, PhD; Univ. of Michigan. Professor of Asian Studies, Saint John's University, N.Y.

JONAS, GERARD, AB; La Salle College. Free-Lance Writer; Television and Radio Producer.

JONSEN, ALBERT R., PhD; Gonzaga University. Associate Professor of Bioethics, Departments of Medicine, History of Health Sciences and Pediatrics, School of Medicine, Univ. of California.

JURGENS, WILLIAM A., HED; Gregorian Univ., Rome. Diocesan Historian, Diocese of Cleveland.

KAISER, EDWIN G., CPPS, STD, DLitt.; Saint John Lateran, Rome. Professor Emeritus of Theology.

KASHUBA, IRMA, SSJ, DML; Moscow State University. Associate Professor of French and Russian at Chestnut Hill College; Chairman of Foreign Language Department, Chestnut Hill College.

KAUFFMAN, ANN VIRGINIA, SSJ, MA; Saint Charles Seminary, Overbrook, Pa. Teacher at Immaculate Conception School, Pen Argyl, Pa.

KAVANAUGH, KIERAN, OCD, STL; Teresianum, Rome. Translating collected works of Saint Teresa of Ávila.

KEARNEY, PETER J., SSL; Pontifical Biblical Institute, Rome. Associate Professor of Sacred Scripture, The Catholic Univ. of America.

KEENAN, CAROLINE, SSJ, BS; Villanova University. Teacher, Saint Matthew's School, Conshohocken, Pa.

KELLEY, FRANCIS E., BLitt (Oxon.), DPhil (Oxon.); Engaged in Research at the Franciscan Institute of Saint Bonaventure University.

KEYSER, C. (no information available).

KING, JAMES P., JCD; The Catholic Univ. of America. Pastor, St. Mel's Church. Flushing N.Y.

KNOX, L. MASON, JCD.; The Catholic Univ. of America. Associate Professor of Canon Law, Sacred Heart School of Theology, Hales Corners, Wis.

KOLLAR, NATHAN, STD (no information available).

KRAHN, CORNELIUS, ThD; Univ. of Heidelberg. Professor of Church History at Bethel College; Editor of *Mennonite Encyclopedia;* Editor of *Mennonite Life,* Bethel College.

KRAMER, NOEL, OFMConv, STL; Le Grand Séminaire de Montréal. Provincial Custos, Custody of Our Lady of Guadalupe; Pastor, Saint Helena Church, Hobbs, New Mexico.

KÜNG, GUIDO, PhD; The University of Fribourg, Switzerland. Professor of Modern and Contemporary Philosophy at the Univ. of Fribourg.

KUTNER, RAYMOND W., JCD; Catholic Univ. of America. Vice Officialis of The Brooklyn Tribunal, New York.

LACKO, MICHAEL, SJ, PhD, HED; Jesuit Philosophical Institute, Zagreb, Yugoslavia; Gregorian Univ., Rome. Professor of History of the Eastern Churches at the Pontifical Oriental Institute.

LANGLINAIS, J. WILLIS, SM, STD; Univ. of Fribourg, Switzerland. Academic Vice-President, Saint Mary's Univ., San Antonio.

LAZENBY, FRANCIS DUPONT, PhD; Univ. of Michigan. Associate Professor of Modern and Classical Languages, University of Notre Dame.

LECLERCQ, JEAN, OSB, STD; Institut Catholique, Paris. Corresponding Fellow of the Medieval Society of America. Professor at the Gregorian University.

LEE, WILLIAM J., SS, PhD; The Catholic Univ. of America. President of Saint Mary's Seminary and University, Baltimore.

LEGGE, MARY THERESA, SSJ, MM; The Catholic Univ. of America. Teacher, Our Lady of the Valley HS, Orange, N.J.

LEITE, LAWRENCE A., PhD; Johns Hopkins University. Professor Emeritus of Art History, The George Washington University.

LEKAI, LOUIS J., SOCist, PhD; Univ. of Budapest. Professor of History, Univ. of Dallas.

LIDDY, MARIE THÉRÈSE, MA; Saint Bonaventure University. Campus Ministry, La Salle College.

LITZ, ROBERT J., MTS; L'Université du Nouveau Monde; Harvard University. Author.

LOUGHERY, BERNARD FRANCIS, SSJ, PhD; The Catholic Univ. of America. Teacher.

LOUGHLIN, J. D. (ELAINE LOUGHLIN SHAW), PhD; The Catholic Univ. of America. Supervisor of Staff Development, San Antonio Independent School District.

LUSSIER, JOSEPH E., SSS, SSL; École Biblique, Jerusalem. Research Professor; Author.

LUZBETAK, LOUIS J., SVD, PhD; Univ. of Fribourg. President, Divine Word College.

LYNCH, CYPRIAN J., OFM, MA; Saint Bonaventure University. Assistant Professor, The Franciscan Institute, Saint Bonaventure University; Archivist, Holy Name Province, OFM, New York.

LYNCH, JOHN E., CSP, PhD; Univ. of Toronto. Professor of History and the History of Canon Law, The Catholic Univ. of America. Chairman of the Canon Law Department.

LYNCH, JOHN J., SJ, STD (no information available).

LYNCH, WILLIAM E., MA; Univ. of St. Thomas Aquinas, Rome. General Family Counselor.

McBRIDE, LETITIA, SSJ, MA; La Salle College. Teacher, Saint Luke's School, Glenside, Pa.

McCAREY, MARIE SAINT JAMES, SSJ, AB; Villanova University. Teacher.

McCARTHY, MARY FRANCES, SND, PhD; Johns Hopkins University. President, Emmanuel College.

McCARTHY, PETER J. (no information available).

McDERMOTT, ROBERT A. (no information available).

McDONALD, CHARLES C., MA; The Catholic Univ. of America. Research Associate.

McEWEN, ROBERT J., SJ, PhD; Boston College. Professor, Department of Economics, Boston College.

McFADDEN, JOHN (no information available).

McFADDEN, MONICA A., MA; New York University. Free-Lance Writer and Editor.

McFADDEN, THOMAS M., STD; Gregorian Univ., Rome. Associate Professor of Theology, Saint Joseph's College, Philadelphia.

MacFARLANE, LESLIE J., PhD, FRHistS, FSA; The Universities of London and Oxford; The Accademia Britannica, Rome. Senior Lecturer in Medieval History, Univ. of Aberdeen.

McGHEE, PHILIP M. (no information available).

McGLYNN, JAMES, OSA (no information available).

McGONAGLE, DOROTHEUS, SSJ, MA; Saint Charles Seminary. Overbrook, Pa. Teacher.

McGOVERN, EILEEN THERESA, SSJ, AB; Chestnut Hill College. Chairperson, History Department, Sacred Heart HS, Vineland, N.J.

McGRATH, CUTHBERT, OFM, PhD (no information available).

McGUCKIN, DENNIS A., OFM, MA; Saint Bonaventure University.

McGUIRE,† MARTIN RAWSON PATRICK, PhD, LHD; The Catholic Univ. of America. Former Professor of Greek and Latin and of Ancient History; Senior Editor, *New Catholic Encyclopedia;* Coeditor, The Catholic Univ. of America Patristic Studies; Coeditor, The Catholic Univ. of America Studies in Mediaeval and Renaissance Latin Language and Literature.

MACK, ANN MARIE, SSJ, MA; Univ. of Virginia, Charlottesville. Teacher, Department Chairperson, Saint Rose HS, Belmar, N.J.

MacKENZIE, J. A. ROSS, PhD; Univ. of Edinburgh. Professor of Church History, Union Theological Seminary in Virginia.

MacMASTER, RICHARD K., MA, PhD; Georgetown University. Associate Professor of History, James Madison University.

McNAMARA, MARIAN F., MA; The Catholic Univ. of America; Johns Hopkins University. Teacher of Latin, Palo Alto Unified School District, Calif.

McNAMARA, MARIE AQUINAS (MARILYN McNAMARA SCHAUB), PhD; Univ. of Fribourg, Switzerland. Professor of Theology, Duquesne University.

McNICHOLL, AMBROSE, OP, DPh; Univ. of Fribourg. Professor, Faculties of Philosophy at Univ. of St. Thomas Aquinas and Lateran University, Rome.

MACOSKEY, ROBERT A., PhD (no information available).

McSHANE, EDWARD D., SJ, HistEcclD; Gregorian University. Professor of Church History, Univ. of Santa Clara and the Collegio Pontificio Beda, Rome.

MADEY, JOHANNES, PhD; Univ. of Munich. Author.

MAHONEY, IRENE, OSU, PhD; The Catholic Univ. of America. Writer-in-Residence, College of New Rochelle.

MOHONEY, WILLIAM B., OP, PhD; University of Saint Thomas Aquinas, Rome. Administrative Assistant, Aquinas Institute, Dubuque, Iowa; Associate Editor, *Cross and Crown.*

MALONE, EDWARD F., MM, STD.; St. Thomas Aquinas Univ., Rome. Assistant Secretary of Federation of Asian Bishops' Conference.

MALONEY, GEORGE A., SJ, SEOD; Pontifical Oriental Institute, Rome. Editor of *Diakonia,* Director of Master's Program of John XXIII Institute of Eastern Christian Studies, Fordham University.

MALTMANN, M. NICHOLAS, OP, PhD; Univ. of California, Berkeley. Professor of English and Chairman of the English Department, Dominican College of San Rafael.

MALY, EUGENE H., STD, SSD; Univ. of St. Thomas Aquinas, Rome; Pontifical Biblical Institute, Rome. Dean of Theology; Professor of Sacred Scripture, Mount Saint Mary's of the West, Ohio.

MANROSS, WILLIAM W., STD, PhD. Former Professor of Church History and Librarian, Philadelphia Divinity School, Philadelphia, Pa.

MANTEUFEL, THOMAS, MDiv; Concordia Seminary, Saint Louis, Mo. Pastor.

MARAS, RAYMOND J., PhD; Univ. of California, Berkeley. Professor of History, Univ. of Dayton.

MARING, NORMAN H., PhD; Univ. of Maryland. Professor of Church History and Dean of the Faculty, Eastern Baptist Theological Seminary.

MARIQUE, JOSEPH, M. F., SJ, DD, PhD; Johns Hopkins University. Director of Institute for Early Iberian Studies; Editor, *Classical Folia.*

MARKS, RICHARD (no information available).

MARR, JOAN CAROL, SSJ, MusB; Chestnut Hill College. Coordinator of Liturgical Music and Teacher of Music, Saint John's School, Severna Park, Md.

MARSHALL, RICHARD H., Jr., PhD; Columbia University. Professor of Russian, Univ. of Toronto.

MARTHALER, BERARD L., OFMConv., STD, PhD; Seraphicum, Rome; Univ. of Minnesota. Chairman and Professor of Religion and Religious Education, The Catholic Univ. of America.

MASER, FREDERICK E., MA; Princeton University. Consultant to the Commission on Archives and History of the United Methodist Church.

MATZERATH, ROGER, STD; Gregorian Univ., Rome. Director of Religious Education.

MAY, ERIC, OFMCap., STD; Pontifical Biblical Institute, Rome. Pontifical Biblical Institute, Palestine. Formation Staff, Capuchin Theological Seminary.

MAZIARZ, EDWARD A., CPPS, PhD; Univ. of Ottawa. Professor of Philosophy, Loyola University of Chicago, Ill.

MEAGHER,† PAUL KEVIN, OP, PhD (Oxon.), STM; Former Editor in Chief, *Encyclopedic Dictionary of Religion;* Coeditor in Chief, McGraw-Hill translation of Saint Thomas's *Summa theologiae;* Staff Editor of Moral Theology, *New Catholic Encyclopedia.*

MECK, JOHN P. (no information available).

MEGIVERN, JAMES JOSEPH, STD (no information available).

MEIJER, JOHAN A., CSSR, SEOD; Pontifical Oriental Institute, Rome. Professor of Liturgy of East and

West, and of Liturgical Theology at The Catholic Univ. of Tilburg, Netherlands.

MEILACH, MICHAEL D., OFM, PhD; Fordham University. Assistant Professor, Philosophy, Siena College.

MERKEL, INGRID, PhD; The Catholic Univ. of America. Associate Professor of German, The Catholic Univ. of America.

MEYENDORFF, JOHN, Docteur ès lettres, MDiv; Orthodox Theological Institute, Paris; Univ. of Paris. Professor of Church History and Patristics, Saint Vladimir's Orthodox Theological Seminary, Tuckahoe, N.Y. Professor of Byzantine History, Fordham University.

MEYER, CHARLES R., STD; Saint Mary of the Lake Seminary, Mundelein, Ill. Academic Dean of the School of Theology, Saint Mary of the Lake Seminary.

MEYER, ROBERT T., PhD, Univ. of Michigan. Emeritus Professor of Celtic, The Catholic Univ. of America.

MISNER, PAUL, STD; Univ. of Munich.

MITCHELL, LYDIA, SSJ, MA; Seton Hall University. Coordinator, Secondary Schools Department of Catholic Education, Arlington, Va.

MITRA, KANA, MA; Calcutta University. Teacher.

MOFFATT, M. ANNE, PhD; Univ. of London. Univ. of Melbourne. Lecturer in Classics, Australian National Univ., Canberra.

MOHRBACHER, AUSTIN, AB; Fordham University. Pastor of Byzantine parish.

MONAGHAN, MARIE BRIGID, SSJ, MA; Saint Bonaventure University. Chairperson Social Studies Department, Allentown Central Catholic HS, Pa.

MONDIN, G., BATTISTA, PhD, Libera Docenzo, Rome; Harvard University. Full Professor and Dean of the Faculty of Philosophy and Director of the Institute for the Study of Atheism, Urbaniana Univ., Rome.

MONTALBANO, FRANK J., OMI, SSL; Pontifical Biblical Institute, Rome. Professor of Holy Scripture, Oblate College of Southwest, San Antonio, Texas.

MOODY, JOSEPH NESTOR, PhD (no information available).

MORGAN, JUANITA, SSJ, MA; The Catholic Univ. of America. Director of Religious Education, Ambler, Pa.

MORLINO, PASCHAL A., OSB, MDiv; University of Pittsburgh. Lecturer in Monastic History, Saint Vincent's College.

MORRIS, J. B., OP (no information available).

MORRISON, JOHN L., PhD; Univ. of Missouri. Professor of History, Mount Saint Mary's College, Emmitsburg, Md.

MORRY, M. FLAVIAN, OP, STD.; College of the Immaculate Conception. Professor of Philosophy and of Christology, Providence College.

MOST, WILLIAM G., PhD; The Catholic Univ. of America. Teacher of Scripture and Classics, Loras College.

MOTHERWAY,† THOMAS J., SJ, STD; Univ. of Rome. Former Professor of Theology, Saint Mary of the Lake Seminary, Mundelein, Ill.

MUELLER, WILLIAM J., FSC, MA (no information available).

MULDOON, JAMES MICHAEL, PhD (no information available).

MULHERN, PHILIP F., OP, STD; Univ. of Fribourg, Switzerland. Professor of Moral and Historical Theology, Providence College.

MÜLLER, LIGUORI, OFM, PhD; The Catholic Univ. of America. Head of Department of Classical Languages and Literature, Siena College.

MURPHY, FREDERICK J., PhD; Gregorian Univ., Rome; Tufts University. Academic Dean, Professor of Latin and Greek and of the History of Religions, Saint John's Seminary College.

MURPHY, JOHN J., PhD; Yale University. Associate Professor of Economics, The Catholic Univ. of America.

MURPHY, M. BENEDICT, RSHM, PhD; Columbia University. Free-Lance Translator.

MURPHY, PATRICK, OSB (DORIS MURPHY), MA; The Catholic Univ. of America. Religious Education Consultant for the Diocese of La Crosse, Wis.

MURPHY, RICHARD T.A., OP, STD., SSD; Univ. of Saint Thomas, Rome; École Biblique, Jérusalem. Associate Pastor, New Orleans, Louisiana; Author.

MURPHY, SHEILA, SSJ, AB; Chestnut Hill College; Saint Charles Seminary, Overbrook, Pa. Teacher, Saint Denis School, Manasquan, N.J.

MURRAY, JOHN C., CSB, STD; Univ. of St. Thomas Aquinas, Rome. Chairman, Department of Religious Studies, Saint John Fisher College.

MURRAY, STEPHEN D. (no information available).

MUSHOLT, SILAS, OFM, SSL; Biblical Institute, Rome. Staff of Franciscan Retiro, Portland, Mo.

NACHBAHR, BERNARD A., PhD; Pontificium Athenaeum Antonianum, Rome. Professor of Philosophy, Loyola College, Md.

NEAL, M. PAULINE, SSJ, MA; Providence College, Rhode Island. Teacher of Religion, Cardinal O'Hara HS, Springfield, Pa.

NEELY, CHARLES (no information available).

NELSON,† KATHERINE B., PhD (no information available).

NELSON, JOHN OLIVER, PhD, DLitt; Yale University. Founder-Director, Kirkridge Retreat.

NEMEC, LUDVIK, PhD, STD; Charles IV Univ. in Prague; The Catholic Univ. of America. Professor of Humanities at Rosemont College. Visiting Professor of Religious Studies, Chestnut Hill.

NEWSOM, JON, MFA.; Princeton University. Head, Reference Section, Music Division, Library of Congress.

NICHOLICH, ROBERT N., PhD; Michigan State University. Associate Professor of French, Department of Modern Languages. The Catholic Univ. of America.

NOONE, CHARLES JOSEPH, MA; Saint Bonaventure University. Teacher, Bishop McDevitt HS, Wyncote, Pa.

NUGENT, DONALD G., PhD; Univ. of Iowa. Associate Professor of History, Univ. of Kentucky.

O'BRIEN, FRANCES GERVASE, SSJ, MA; Seton Hall University. Principal of Our Lady of Good Counsel School, Vienna, Va.

O'BRIEN, THOMAS C., PhD, STD; Univ. of Saint Thomas Aquinas, Rome. Executive Editor, *New Catholic Encyclopedia*, Volume 17.

O'CONNOR, MARY (LADY PATRICK), AB; Saint Anne's College, Oxford. Author.

O'DONNELL, CATHERINE CHRISTI, SSJ, MA; Saint Bonaventure University. Teacher.

O'DONNELL, JOSEPH M., CM, STD.; The Catholic Univ. of America. Hospital Chaplain.

OESTERLE, PAUL DANIEL, SSJ, MS; Johns Hopkins University. The Catholic Univ. of America. Associate Professor of Biology, Chestnut Hill College.

OGDEN, JOAN, MA; Oxford Univ., Saint Anne's College, England. Journalist.

O'HERN, CHARLES, JCD; Lateran Univ. Rome. Pastor of Saint Anne's, Gilbert, Arizona; Vice Officialis, Diocese of Phoenix.

OLIN, JOHN C., PhD; Columbia University. Professor, Fordham University.

O'NEILL, AGNES ANGELA, SSJ, MA; Villanova University. Teacher, Star of the Sea School, Cape May, N.J.

O'NEILL, KATHLEEN, SSJ, MA; Columbia University. Superintendent of Schools, Diocese of Raleigh.

O'ROURKE, JOHN J., SSL; Gregorian Univ., Rome; Pontifical Biblical Institute, Rome. Archdiocesan Theological Consultant, Archdiocese of Philadelphia.

OSBORN, RONALD E., PhD, LittD; Univ. of Oregon. Professor of American Church History, School of Theology at Claremont, Calif.

PALLOZZA, JOSEPH STEPHANIE, SSJ, MM, West Chester State College. Instructor in Music. Chestnut Hill College.

PALMER, PAUL FRANCIS, STD; Woodstock College, Md. Writer and Visiting Lecturer in Sacramental Theology.

PEANO, LUIGI, BS, STD; Urbaniana Univ., Rome. Assistant Professor of Religious Studies, Merrimack College.

PELIKAN, JAROSLAV, PhD, ThD, DD; Univ. of Chicago. Dean of the Graduate School, Sterling Professor of History and Religious Studies, Yale University.

PENN, DONALD ROBERT, PhD; Manhattan College, New York; Univ. of Wisconsin. Professor Emeritus, Georgetown University.

PENNINGTON, M. BASIL, OCSO, JCL; Univ. of St. Thomas Aquinas, Rome. Author.

PETTIT, WALTON S., Jr., MDiv; Virginia Theological Seminary, Alexandria, Va. Acting Rector, Saint Paul's Episcopal Church, Richmond, Va.

PIERCE, JUSTIN A., SDS, SSL; Georgetown University. Associate Professor of Religious Studies, Silver Lake College, Manitowoc, Wisconsin.

POSPISHIL, REV. MONSIGNOR VICTOR J., JCD, ScOrEcclLic; Gregorian Univ., Rome; Papal Institute for Eastern Ecclesiastical Studies. Vicar General and Presiding Judge of the Ukrainian Catholic Archdiocese of Philadelphia.

POWERS, MARY EMILY, SSJ, BS; Chestnut Hill College. Teacher of Religion; Parish Ministry.

PRESTON, ROBERT M., PhD; The Catholic Univ. of America. Associate Professor of History, Department of History and Political Science, Mount Saint Mary's College, Emmitsburg, Maryland.

PRUSAK, BERNARD P., JCD; Lateran Univ., Rome. Associate Professor of Religious Studies, Villanova University, Pennsylvania; Co-Editor, *Horizons,* Journal of the College Theology Society.

QUITSLUND, SONYA A. (no information available).

RANDEL, DON M., PhD; Princeton University. Professor of Music, Cornell University.

READ, WILLIAM J., SJ, STD; Gregorian Univ., Rome, Professor of Spiritual Theology.

REGAN, CAROLE BENNETT, PhD; Univ. of Pennsylvania. Assistant Professor of Psychology, Counseling Psychologist, Saint Joseph's College, Philadelphia, Pa.

REGAN, CRONAN, SP (no information available).

REID, JOHN PATRICK, OP, MA (no information available).

REILLY, MARIA TRINITA, SSJ, MA; Seton Hall University. Teacher, Prendergast HS, Drexel Hill, Pa.; Chairperson, Diocesan Mathematics Curriculum Committee.

REIMER, HENRY FRANCIS, SSJ, MusB; Chestnut Hill College. Teacher of Music, Mount Saint Joseph Academy, McSherrystown, and Sacred Heart School, Conewago, Pa.

RIGHTOR, HENRY H., JD, DD; Harvard Law School; Harvard Divinity School. Professor of Pastoral Care and Canon Law, Virginia Theological Seminary, Alexandria.

RILEY, MARGARET, SSJ, MA; Saint Bonaventure University. Teacher of Religion, Mount Saint Joseph Academy, Flourtown, Pa.

RIVELLO, J. ROBERTA, SSJ, PhD; Temple University. Senior Editor, Research Analyst, Lecturer in Ethics at United States Army Materiel Systems Analysis Activity.

ROCHE, JOHN ANITA, SSJ, MS; Fordham University. Principal of Holy Family Academy, Bayonne, N.J.

RODGERS, JOHN H., ThD; United States Naval Academy, University of Basel, Switzerland. Senior Professor, Trinity Episcopal School for Ministry.

ROHLING, JOSEPH H., CPPS, STD; The Catholic Univ. of America. Chaplain of Holy Family Hospital, New Richmond, Wis.

RÖHRIG, FLORIDUS HELMUT, CRSA, DrPhil, DrTheol (no information available).

RONAN, JAMES L., MA; Fordham University. Pontifical Biblical Institute, Rome.

RONK, ALBERT T., DD (no information available).

ROSATO, PHILIP J., SJ, ThD; The Univ. of Tübingen. Assistant Professor of Theology, Saint Joseph's College, Philadelphia, Pa.

ROSENDALL, BRENDAN C., OFMConv, STD; Univ. of Fribourg, Switzerland. Associate Pastor, Saint Bonaventure Parish, Bloomington, Minnesota.

ROSS, C. D., PhD (Oxon.) (no information available).

RUPPEL,† GEORGE JOSEPH, SM, PhD; The Catholic Univ. of America.

RUSSELL, ROBERT P., OSA, PhD; Gregorian Univ., Rome. Graduate Professor in Philosophy and Theology, Villanova Univ.; Visiting Professor at Lateran Univ., Rome; Editor of *Augustinian Studies*.

RYAN, FRANCIS T., MA; Georgetown University. Pontifical Faculty of the Immaculate Conception, Washington, D.C. Association Executive.

RYAN, THOMAS J., STD; The Catholic Univ. of America. Associate Professor of Theology, Saint Joseph's College, Philadelphia, Pa.

SAGUÉS, MARIE, OP, MA; Univ. of California, Berkeley. Assistant Professor of English, Dominican College of San Rafael.

SAMPSON, VIRGINIA, SUSC, PhD; Saint Louis University. Engaged in Spiritual Development Programs.

SATTERWHITE, JOHN H., ThD, DD; Boston University; Johnson C. Smith University. Professor of Ecumenics; Director of Center for Black Church Studies, School of Religion, Howard University.

SCHEPERS, MAURICE B., OP, STD.; Saint Thomas Univ., Rome. Associate Professor of Religion, La Salle College.

SCHERER, BERNARD F., PhD, JD; Duquesne University; Univ. of Pittsburgh. Assistant to the President of Saint Vincent College; Attorney at Law.

SCHMANDT, RAYMOND H., PhD; Univ. of Michigan. Professor of History, Saint Joseph's College, Philadelphia.

SCHULZ, JOSEPH R. (no information available).

SCHULZ, SIEGFRIED A., PhD; University of Berne, Switzerland. Professor of German and Comp. Philology, The Catholic Univ. of America.

SCHUMACHER, MARY G. (no information available).

SCHÜRMANN, REINER, OP (no information available).

SHARKEY, OWEN NEIL, CP, STD; Univ. of Tübingen.

Professor of Systematic Theology, Saint John's Univ., Long Island, N.Y.

SHEPHERD, MASSEY H., PhD, STD, DD, LittD; Univ. of Chicago, Berkeley Divinity School, Calif.; Anglican Theological College of British Columbia. Hodges Professor of Liturgics, The Church Divinity School of the Pacific, Berkeley, Calif.

SHEERIN, FRANCIS L., SJ, STD (no information available).

SHIRLEY, WAYNE D. (no information available).

SHORT, HOWARD E., PhD, LLD, LittD; Univ. of Marburg. Interim President, Board of Higher Education, Disciples of Christ.

SHUSTER,† GEORGE NAUMAN, PhD, LLD, LittD, LHD; Former President Emeritus, Hunter College New York, Assistant to the President of Notre Dame Univ., Indiana.

SIGER, LEONARD PAUL, PhD (no information available).

SKARDON, ALVIN W., PhD; Univ. of Chicago. Professor of History, Youngstown State University.

SMITH, JEREMIAH J., OFMConv., PhD; The Catholic Univ. of America. Professor, Bellarmine College.

SMITH, PHILIP, OP, MA; Saint Stephen's College, Dover, Mass. Associate Professor of Religious Studies, Caldwell College.

SMUCKER, DAVID J., MA; Hartford Seminary; Boston University.

SMURL, JAMES F. (no information available).

SMYLIE, JAMES H., PhD; Washington University. Professor of American Religious History, Union Theological Seminary, Virginia.

SOMMERFELDT, JOHN R., PhD; Univ. of Michigan. Professor of History, Western Michigan University; President, Cistercian Publications, Incorporated.

STAHL, THERESA CONSILII, SSJ, MA; Saint Charles Seminary, Overbrook, Pa. Teacher, Saint Bartholomew's School, Philadelphia.

STANKIEWICZ, WLADYSLAW J., PhD; The London School of Economics and Political Science. Professor of Political Science, Univ. of British Columbia, Vancouver.

STEIN, K. JAMES, DD, PhD; Westmar College. Union Theological Seminary, New York City; Professor of Church History, Garrett-Evangelical Theological Seminary, Evanston, Ill.

STEINBRUCKNER, BRUNO F., PhD; Univ. of Innsbruck, Austria. Full Professor and Chairman, Department of Language and Foreign Studies, American University.

STENGER, ROBERT L., STD, JD; The Catholic Univ. of America; Univ. of Iowa. Associate Professor of Law, Univ. of Louisville School of Law.

STEVENSON, DWIGHT E., DD; Yale Univ., Divinity School. Dean Emeritus, Lexington Theological Seminary; Coordinator, Theological Education Association of Mid-America.

STEWART, RICHARD L., STL; Gregorian Univ., Rome. Secretary, Roman Catholic Ecumenical Commission of England and Wales.

STEWART, ZEPH, MA; Harvard University. Professor of Greek and Latin, Chairman of the Department of the Classics, Harvard University.

STOCK, MICHAEL E., OP, PhD; Univ. of St. Thomas Aquinas, Rome. Director, Adult Education, Saint Stephen's College, Dover, Mass.

SUELZER, MARY JOSEPHINE, SP, PhD (no information available).

SURRENCY, RIGHT REVEREND SERAFIM, MA; Boston University. Member of the Clergy Staff of Saint Nicholas Russian Orthodox Cathedral in New York City; Personal Secretary to the Vicar Bishop of the Moscow Patriarch in the United States of America.

SVOBODA, CYRIL PAUL, SSC, PhD (no information available).

TAFT, ROBERT, SJ, PhD; Pontifical Oriental Institute, Rome. Associate Professor of Eastern Liturgy, Univ. of Notre Dame, Indiana; Visiting Professor of Eastern Liturgy and Languages, Pontifical Oriental Institute, Rome.

TALLARICO, ROSE CONCETTA, SSJ, MusB; Chestnut Hill College. Teacher and Librarian at Pius X HS, Roseto, Pa.

TANEY, MARY STALLINGS, PhD, Dottoressa in Lettere; The Catholic Univer. of America; Universita Cattolica del Sacro Cuore, Milan. Professor, Department of History, Glassboro State College.

TAPIA, RALPH J., STD.; Gregorian Univ., Rome. Full Professor of Christian Ethics, Fordham University.

TENNELLY, JOHN BENJAMIN, SS, STD; Univ. of St. Thomas Aquinas, Rome. Retired.

TINSLEY, LUCY, SND, PhD; The Catholic Univ. of America. Professor Emeritus.

TKACIK, ARNOLD J., OSB., MA; Governors State Univ., Park Forest, South Ill. Coordinator of External Training Programs, Illinois College of Podiatric Medicine.

TOBIN, WILLIAM J. (no information available).

TODD, REGINA AUGUSTA, SSJ, MSLS; Seton Hall University. Librarian, Our Lady of the Valley School, Orange, N.J.

TOLLES,† FREDERICK B., PhD, DLitt; Harvard University. Former Professor of Quaker History and Research Director, Friends Historical Library, Swarthmore College

TOTON, SUZANNE C., MA; Columbia Univ. Teachers College. Lecturer, Department of Religion, Cabrini College, Radnor, Pa.; Lecturer, Religious Studies Department, Villanova University.

TYLENDA, JOSEPH N., SJ, STD; Gregorian Univ., Rome. Assistant Editor, *Theological Studies*.

VAILLANCOURT, NORMAND LEO, MS (no information available).

VAN ALLEN, RODGER, PhD; Temple University. Professor of Religious Studies, Villanova University.

VANDERHAAR, GERARD A., STD; Univ. of St. Thomas Aquinas, Rome. Associate Professor of Humanities and Religion, Christian Brothers College, Memphis, Tenn.

VEROSTKO, ROMAN J., MFA; Pratt Institute, Brooklyn. Academic Dean, Minneapolis College of Art and Design.

VIARD, ANDRE, OP (no information available).

VOLL, W. URBAN, OP, STD.; Pontifical Faculty of the Immaculate Conception, Washington, D.C. Rector; President of Major Seminary, Saint Vincent de Paul, Miami, Fla.

VON FALKENHAUSEN, VERA (no information available).

WALGRAVE, JAN HENRICUS, OP, STD; Univ. of Louvain, Belgium. Professor of Fundamental Theology.

WALKER, ANSELM C., MA; John XXIII Center, Fordham University. Professor of Early Church History, Patrology and Eastern Orthodox Theology, Saint Mary's Seminary, Univ. of Saint Thomas, Houston, Texas.

WALSH, JAMES J., MA; Syracuse University; Johns Hopkins University. Teacher, Walter Johnson High School, Bethesda, Md.; Music Director of Convivium Musicum, Saint Thomas Apostle Choir, Washington, D.C.

WARDLE, M. AMATA, SSJ, MA; The Catholic Univ. of America.

WATHEN, M. ANTONIA, OSU, PhD; The Catholic Univ. of America. Director of Education, Mount Saint Joseph Ursuline Sisters, Maple Mount, Ky.

WEINLICK, JOHN R., PhD; Columbia University. Dean Emeritus, Moravian Theology Seminary, Bethlehem, Pa.

WEIS, EARL AUGUST, SJ, STD; Gregorian Univ., Rome. Professor and Chairman, Department of Theology, Loyola Univ., of Chicago.

WEISHEIPL, JAMES A., OP, PhD, DPhil (Oxon.); Univ. of Saint Thomas, Rome. Professor of the History of Medieval Science, University of Toronto. Fellow of the Pontifical Institute of Mediaeval Studies, Toronto.

WHALEN, JOHN P., STD, JD; The Catholic Univ. of America; The George Washington University. Executive Director, Consortium of Universities of the Washington Metropolitan Area.

WHALEN, WILLIAM J., MS; Northwestern University. Director of Publications and University Editor, Purdue University; Director of the Purdue University Press; Associate Professor of Communication.

WILCOCK, FEODOR, SJ, PhD; Gregorian Univ., Rome. Ecumenical Commission, Interreligions Council, Los Angeles, California; Pastor, Russian Catholic Church, Los Angeles.

WILLIAMS, BRUCE A., OP, PhD; Saint John's Univ.,

New York. Assistant Director, Institute for Advanced Studies in Catholic Doctrine, Saint John's University.

WILLIAMS, CORNELIUS, OP, STD; Fribourg Univ., Switzerland. Professor of Moral Theology, Maynooth College, County Kildare, Ireland.

WILLIAMS, SCHAFER S., PhD (no information available).

WILLIMAN, JOSEPH P., PhD; Univ. of North Carolina. Associate Professor of Modern Languages, The Catholic Univ. of America, Washington, D.C.

WILLKE, BARBARA, BS; Univ. of Cincinnati. Author and Lecturer.

WILLKE, JEAN C., PhD; The Catholic Univ. of America. Academic Dean, Trinity College.

WILLKE, JOHN C., MD; Univ. of Cincinnati College of Medicine. Physician, Author, Lecturer.

WILLS, MARY M., PhD; Univ. of Southern California, Los Angeles. Emeritus Professor of English, Central Michigan University.

WINKELMANN, ANNE, SSND, PhD; Saint Louis University.

WIPPEL, JOHN F., PhD; Louvain Univ., Belgium. Professor, School of Philosophy, The Catholic Univ. of America.

WITTY, FRANCIS J., PhD; The Catholic Univ. of America. Professor, School of Arts and Sciences, The Catholic Univ. of America.

WOLF, NORBERT G., MA; Saint Mary's College, Baltimore, Md.; The Catholic Univ. of America. Pastor, Saint Michael's Parish, Emlenton, Pa.

WOOD, THOMAS O., MA; Seattle University. Administrator, Health Department, State of Maryland.

WOOLVERTON, JOHN F., PhD; Columbia University. Professor of Church History, Episcopal Theological Seminary, Alexandria, Va.

WRATHER, EVA JEAN, AB; Vanderbilt University. Writer in Church History.

WRIGLEY, JOHN E., PhD; Univ. of Pennsylvania. Professor of History; Chairman, Department of History, Univ. of North Carolina.

ZEENDER, JOHN K., PhD; Yale University. Professor of Modern European History, The Catholic Univ. of America.

ZINK, ANNA REGINA, SSJ, AB; Chestnut Hill College. Teacher, St. Ursula's School, Baltimore, Md.

ZUREK, JEROME R., Jr., PhD; Bryn Mawr College. Chairperson, Department of English and Communications, Cabrini College.

Encyclopedic Dictionary of Religion
Abbreviations of Titles of Reference Books

AAS	*Acta Apostolicae Sedis*. Rome 1909–
Abbo	J. Abbo and J. Hannan, *The Sacred Canons*. Rev. ed. 2 v. St. Louis 1960.
Abbott	W. M. Abbott, *Documents of Vatican II*, tr. ed. J. Gallagher. New York 1966.
Abel GéogrPal	F. M. Abel, *Géographie de la Palestine*. 2 v. Paris 1933–38.
ABR	*American Benedictine Review*. Newark, N. J. 1950–
ACPA	*American Catholic Philosophical Association*. Proceedings of the Annual Meeting. Baltimore 1926–
ACW	*Ancient Christian Writers: The Works of the Fathers in Translation*, ed. J. Quasten et al. Westminister, Md.–London 1946–
ADB	*Allgemeine deutsche Biographie*. Leipzig 1875–1910. Superseded by *Neue deutsche Biographie*. Berlin 1953–
AER	*American Ecclesiastical Review*. Washington 1889–
AFH	*Archivum Franciscanum historicum*. Quaracchi/Florence 1909–
AFP	*Archivum Fratrum Praedicatorum*. Rome 1931–
AHSJ	*Archivum historicum Societatis Jesu*. Rome 1932–
Algermissen[7]	K. Algermissen, *Konfessionskunde*. 7th ed. Celle 1957.
Altaner	B. Altaner, *Patrology*, tr. Hilda Graef from 5th German ed. New York 1960. 7th German ed. by A. Stuiber. Freiburg 1966.
AMS	repr. series, no dates available.
AnalBoll	*Analecta Bollandiana*. Brussels 1882–
AnalCap	*Analecta Ordinis Fratrum Minorum Cappucinorum*. Rome 1884–
AnalFranc	*Analecta Franciscana*. Quaracchi/Florence 1885–
AnalGreg	*Analecta Gregoriana*. Rome 1930–
AnalHymn	*Analecta hymnica*. Leipzig 1886–1922.
AnalOCarmC	*Analecta Ordinis Carmelitarum Calceatorum*. Rome 1909–
AnalOCarmD	*Analecta Ordinis Carmelitarum Discalceatorum*. Rome 1926–
AnalOCist	*Analecta Sacri Ordinis Cisterciensis*. Rome 1945–
AnalOP	*Analecta Sacris Ordinis Praedicatorum*. Rome 1892–
AnalPraem	*Analecta Praemonstratensia*. Tongerloo-Saint-Norbert, Belgian Congo 1925–
Andrieu OR	M. Andrieu, *Les 'Ordines Romani' du haut moyen-âge*. 5 v. Louvain 1931–61.
ANF	*The Ante-Nicene Fathers*, ed. A. Roberts et al. Am. reprint of the Edinburgh ed., rev. A. Coxe. 10 v. Grand Rapids 1951–
AnnDom	*L'Année Dominicaine*, 24 v. New ed. Lyons 1883–1909.
AnnPont	*Annuario pontificio*. Rome 1912–
AOF	*Archiv für Orientforschung*. Berlin-Graz 1923–
Apel GregCh	W. Apel, *Gregorian Chant*. Bloomington, Ind. 1958.
Apel HDMus	W. Apel, *Harvard Dictionary of Music*. Cambridge, Mass. 1958.
ARC	*Acta reformationis catholicae ecclesiam Germaniae concernentia saeculi XVI*, ed. G. Pfeilschifter. Regensburg 1959–
ArchLit	*Archiv für Liturgiewissenschaft*. Regensburg 1950– . Supersedes *Jahrbuch für Liturgiewissenschaft*. Münster 1921–41.
ARG	*Archiv für Reformationsgeschichte*. Gütersloh 1903–
Arndt-Gingrich	W. F. Arndt and F. W. Gingrich, *A Greek-English Lexicon of the New Testament and Other Early Christian Literature*, tr. and adap. of W. Bauer's *Griechisch-Deutsches Wörterbuch*. Chicago 1957.
AS	*Acta sanctorum*. Antwerp 1643– ; Venice 1734– ; Paris 1863–
ASS	*Acta Sanctae Sedis*. Rome 1865–1908.
Attwater CCE	D. Attwater, *The Christian Churches of the East*. 2 v. rev. ed. 1961–62.
Aurenhammer	H. Aurenhammer, *Lexikon der christlichen Ikonographie*. Vienna 1959–
Ayrinhac–Lydon	H. A. Ayrinhac and P. J. Lydon, *Marriage Legislation in the New Code of Canon Law*. 3d ed. New York 1957.

BAC — *Biblioteca de autores cristianos*. Madrid 1945–

Backmund — N. Backmund, *Monasticon Praemonstratense*. 3 v. Straubing 1949–56.

Baker — *Baker's Biographical Dictionary of Musicians*. Rev. N. Slonimsky. 5th ed. New York 1958.

Balt II — *Concilii plenarii Baltimorensis II. . . acta et decreta*. Baltimore 1863.

Balt III — *Acta et decreta concilii plenarii Baltimorensis III*. Baltimore 1884, 1886.

Bardenhewer — O. Bardenhewer, *Geschichte der altkirchlichen Literatur*. 5 v. Freiburg 1913–32.

BASOR — *The Bulletin of the American Schools of Oriental Research*. New Haven 1919–

Baudot-Chaussin — J. L. Baudot and L. Chaussin, *Vies des saints et des bienheureux selon l'ordre du calendrier avec l'historique des fêtes*, by the Benedictines of Paris. 12 v. Paris 1935–56; v. 13 suppl. and table général, 1959.

Beck — H. G. Beck, *Kirche und theologische Literatur im byzantinischen Reich*. Munich 1959.

BHG — *Bibliotheca hagiographica Graeca*, ed. F. Halkin. 3 v. Brussels 1957.

BHL — *Bibliotheca hagiographica latina antiquae et mediae aetatis*. 2 v. Brussels 1898–1901. Suppl. 1911.

BHO — *Bibliotheca hagiographica orientalis*. Brussels 1910.

BiblFranSchMA — *Bibliotheca Franciscana scholastica medii aevi*. Quaracchi/Florence 1903–

BiblSanct — *Bibliotheca sanctorum*. 12 v. Rome 1961–69.

Bihlmeyer–Tüchle — K. Bihlmeyer and H. Tüchle, *Church History*. 3 v. Westminster, Md. 1958–66. v. 1 *Christian Antiquity*, tr. V. Mills, 1958; v. 2 *The Middle Ages*, tr. V. Mills and F. Muller, 1963; v. 3 *Modern and Recent Times*, tr. V. Mills and F. Muller, 1966.

Bilan du Monde — *Bilan du Monde. Encyclopédie catholique du monde chrétien*. 2d ed. 2 v. Tournai 1964.

Blaise-Chirat — A. Blaise, *Dictionnaire Latin-Française des auteurs chrétiens*, rev. H. Chirat. Turnhout 1954.

Bouscaren-Ellis–Korth — T. L. Bouscaren, A. C. Ellis and N. Korth, *Canon Law*. 4th ed. Milwaukee 1966.

Bouscaren-O'Connor — T. L. Bouscaren and J. I. O'Connor, comps., *Canon Law Digest*. Milwaukee 1934–

Bréhier HistPhil — É. Bréhier, *History of Philosophy*, tr. J. Thomas and W. Baskin. 5 v. Chicago 1963–67.

Bremond — H. Bremond, *Histoire littéraire du sentiment religieux en France depuis la fin des guerres de religion jusqu'à nos jours*. 12 v. Paris 1911–36. Index 1971.

BrevRom — *Breviarum Romanum ex decreto sacrosancti Concilii tridentini restitutum*. 2 v. Tours 1961.

BukMusB — M. F. Bukofzer, *Music in the Baroque Era* (1947).

BullRom — *Bullarium romanum*, ed. F. Gaude et al. 24 v. Rome 1857–72. 2 suppl. 1867, 1885.

BullThom — *Bulletin thomiste*. Paris 1924.

Butler — A. Butler. *The Lives of the Saints*, rev. ed. H. Thurston and D. Attwater. 4 v. New York 1956.

BVC — *Bible et vie chrétienne*. Paris 1953–

BZ — *Biblische Zeitschrift*. Freiburg 1903–29; Paderborn 1931–33; 1957–

CAH — *The Cambridge Ancient History*. 12 v. London and New York 1923–39.

CAH² — *The Cambridge Ancient History*. Rev. ed. Cambridge, Eng. 1961–

Cappello IC — F. M. Cappello, *Summa iuris canonici*. Rome v. 1, 6th ed. 1961; v. 2, 5th ed. 1951; v. 3, 4th ed. 1955.

Carol Mariol — J. B. Carol, ed., *Mariology*. 3 v. Milwaukee 1954–61.

CathEdRev — *The Catholic Educational Review*. Washington 1911–

Catholicisme — *Catholicisme. Hier, aujourd'hui et demain*, ed. G. Jacquemet. Paris 1947–

Cavallera — F. Cavallera, comp., *Thesaurus doctrinae catholicae ex documentis magisterii ecclesiastici*. Paris 1920.

CBE — *Catholic Biblical Encyclopedia*, ed. J. E. Steinmueller and K. Sullivan. 2 v. in 1. New York 1956. v. 1 OT 1956; v. 2 NT 1950.

CBEL — *The Cambridge Bibliographies of English Literature*, ed. F. W. Bateson. 5 v. Cambridge, Eng. 1940–57.

CBQ — *The Catholic Biblical Quarterly*. Washington 1939–

CCL — *Corpus Christianorum. Series latina*. Turnhout, Belg. 1953–

CCTSD — *Proceedings of the Society of Catholic College Teachers of Sacred Doctrine*. Washington 1955–

CDT — *A Catholic Dictionary of Theology*, ed. H. F. Davis et al. London 1962–

CE — *The Catholic Encyclopedia*, ed. C. G. Herbermann et al. 16 v. New York 1907–14. Suppl. 1922.

CharlesAPOT — R. H. Charles, *The Apocrypha and Pseudepigrapha of the Old Testament*. 2 v. 1913.

Chevalier H. — U. Chevalier, *Repertorium hymnologicum*. 6 v. Louvain-Brussels 1892–1921.

CHGMP	*The Cambridge History of Later Greek and Early Medieval Philosophy*, ed. A. H. Armstrong. New York 1967.
CHR	*American Catholic Historical Review.* Washington 1916–
CIC	*Codex iuris canonici.* Rome 1918. Reprint Graz 1955.
CiT	*Ciencia tomista.* Madrid 1910–
CivCatt	*La civiltà cattolica.* Rome 1950– (Florence 1871–87).
ClerSanc	Pius XII, *Motu proprio,* "Cleri sanctitati," AAS 49 (1957) 433–603.
ClergyRev	*Clergy Review.* London 1931–
CMedH	*Cambridge Medieval History.* 8 v. London-New York 1911–36.
CMedH²	*Cambridge Medieval History.* 2d ed. 8 v. London-New York 1964–
CModH	*Cambridge Modern History.* London-New York 1902–12.
CModH²	*New Cambridge Modern History.* 2d ed. London-New York 1957–
CollFran	*Collectanea Franciscana.* Rome 1931–
CollLac	*Collectio Lacensis: Acta et decreta sacrorum conciliorum recentiorum,* ed. Jesuits of Maria Laach. 7 v. Freiburg 1870–90.
CollOCR	*Collectanea ordinis Cisterciensium Reformatorum.* Rome–Westmalle 1934–
CollRit (Eng)	*Collectio Rituum: The 1964 English Ritual.* Collegeville, Minn. 1964
ComRel	*Commentarium pro religiosis.* Rome 1920–
ConcTrid	*Concilium Tridentinum. Diariorum, actorum, epistularum, tractatum nova collectio,* ed. Görres-Gesellschaft. 13 v. Freiburg 1901–38.
Connelly Hymns	J. Connelly, *Hymns of the Roman Liturgy.* Westminster, Md. 1957.
ConOecDecr	*Conciliorum oecumenicorum decreta.* Bologna-Freiburg 1962.
Conte Coron Sac	M. Conte a Coronata, *Institutiones iuris canonici: De sacramentis.* 3 v. Turin-Rome 1949–57. v. 1, 2, 2d ed.; v. 3, 3d ed.
Copleston	F. C. Copleston, *History of Philosophy.* Westminster, Md. 1946– . v. 1 Greece & Rome. 1946, 2d ed. 1950; v. 2 Medieval Philosophy, Augustine to Scotus, 1950; v. 3 Ockham to Suárez, 1953; v. 4 Descartes to Leibniz, 1958; v. 5 Hobbes to Hume, 1959; v. 6 Wolff to Kant, 1960; v. 7 Fichte to Nietzsche, 1963; v. 8 Bentham to Russell, 1966.
CorpApol	*Corpus apologetarum,* ed. J. C. T. von Otto. 9 v. Jena 1847–72.
CorpIurCan	*Corpus iuris canonici,* ed. E. Friedberg. Leipzig 1879–81. Reprint Graz 1955.
Cosenza	M. E. Cosenza, *Biographical and Bibliographical Dictionary of the Italian* Humanists and the World of Classical Scholarship in Italy, 1300–1800. 2d ed. 5 v. Boston 1962.
Cottineau	L. H. Cottineau, *Répertoire topo-bibliographique des abbayes et prieurés.* 2 v. Mâcon 1935–39.
CouS	H. Coussemaker, *Scriptorum de musica medii aevi nova series.* 4 v. Paris 1864–76.
CQR	*Church Quarterly Review.* London 1875–
CR	*Corpus reformatorum.* Halle 1834–52; Braunschweig 1852–96; Berlin 1900–1906; Leipzig 1906–
Creusen	J. Creusen, *Religious Men and Women in Church Law.* 6th ed. Milwaukee 1958.
CrossCrown	*Cross and Crown.* St. Louis 1949–
CSCO	*Corpus scriptorum Christianorum orientalium.* Paris-Louvain 1903–
CSEL	*Corpus scriptorum ecclesiasticorum latinorum.* Vienna 1866–
CSHB	*Corpus scriptorum historiae Byzantinae.* 50 v. Bonn 1828–97.
CTS	*Catholic Theological Society of America. Proceedings.* New York 1946–
CUA CLS	Catholic University of America. *Canon Law Studies.*
CUA PatrSt	Catholic University of America. *Patristic Studies.*
CUA StAmChHist	Catholic University of America. *Studies in American Church History.*
CUA StMRLLL	Catholic University of America. *Studies in Medieval and Renaissance Latin, Language, and Literature.*
D	H. Denzinger, *Enchiridion symbolorum,* ed. A. Schönmetzer. 32d ed. Freiburg 1963.
DAB DAB (1957)	*Dictionary of American Biography,* ed. A. Johnson and D. Malone. 20 v. New York 1928–36; Index 1937; Suppl. 1 1944; 2 1958. Re-issued in 1957, 10 v. Suppl. 1958.
DACL	*Dictionnaire d'archéologie chrétienne et de liturgie,* ed. F. Cabrol and H. Leclercq, 15 v. Paris 1907–53.
DAFC	*Dictionnaire apologétique de la foi catholique,* ed. A. d'Alès. 4 v. Paris 1911–22; Table analytique 1931.
Dahlmann-Waitz	F. C. Dahlmann and G. Waitz. *Quellekunde der deutschen Geschichte.* 10th ed. Stuttgart 1965.
Daniélou-Marrou	J. Daniélou and H. Marrou, *The First Six Hundred Years,* tr. V. Cronin, v. 1 of *The Christian Centuries.* New York 1964–
Dansette	A. Dansette, *Religious History of Modern France,* tr. J. Dingle. 2 v. New York 1961.

Davis MorPastTh
H. Davis. *Moral and Pastoral Theology*, rev. and enl. L. W. Geddes. New York 1958.

Davison-Apel
A. T. Davison and W. Apel, eds., *Historical Anthology of Music*. Rev. ed. 2 v. Cambridge, Mass. 1957.

DB
Dictionnaire de la Bible, ed. F. Vigouroux. 5 v. Paris 1895–1912.

DBF
Dictionnaire de biographie française. Paris 1929–

DBSuppl
Dictionnaire de la Bible. Suppl., ed. L. Pirot et al. Paris 1928–

DBT
X. Léon-Dufour et al., *Dictionary of Biblical Theology*. Tr. P. J. Cahill, 1967.

DCB
A Dictionary of Christian Biography, ed. W. Smith and H. Wace. 4 v. London 1877–87.

DDC
Dictionnaire de droit canonique, ed. R. Naz. 7 v. Paris 1935–65.

DE
Dizionario ecclesiastico, ed. A. Mercati and A. Pelzer. 3 v. Turin 1954–58.

Dekkers CPL
Clavis Patrum latinorum, ed. E. Dekkers. 2d ed. Steenbrugge 1961.

Delacroix
S. Delacroix, ed., *Histoire universelle des missions catholiques*. 4 v. Paris 1956–59.

Denifle-Ehrle Arch
H. Denifle and F. Ehrle. eds., *Archiv für Literatur- und Kirchengeschichte des Mittelalters*. 7 v. (Berlin) Freiburg 1885–1900.

Deutsches Archiv
Deutsches Archiv für Erforschung des Mittelalters. Cologne-Graz 1950– ; supersedes ed. Weimar 1937–43 and Neues Archiv.

De Vaux AncIsr
R. de Vaux, *Ancient Israel, Its Life and Institutions*, tr. J. McHugh. New York 1961.

DHGE
Dictionnaire d' histoire et de géographie ecclésiastiques, ed. A. Baudrillart et al. Paris 1912–

DictEd
C. V. Good, *Dictionary of Education*. 2d ed. New York 1959.

DictLangPhil
P. Foulquié and R. Saint-Jean, *Dictionnaire de la langue philosophique*. Paris 1962.

DictLetFranç
G. Grente et al., *Dictionnaire des lettres françaises*. v. 1 Le XVIIe siècle, v. 2 Le XVIIIe siècle. Paris 1954–60.

DivThomF
Divus Thomas. Fribourg 1914–54. Superseded by *Freiburger Zeitschrift für Philosophie und Theologie*, 1954–

DivThomP
Divus Thomas. Piacenza. v. 1–6, 1880–1900; Series 2, v. 1–6, 1900–05; Series 3. 1924–

DizBiogItal
Dizionario biographico degli Italiani, ed. A. M. Ghisalberti. Rome 1960–

DNB (year)
DNBSuppl
The Dictionary of National Biography from the Earliest Times to 1900. 63 v. London 1885–1900; reprinted, with corrections, in 21 v. 1908–09, 1921–22, 1938; suppl. 1901–

DNBConc
The Concise Dictionary of National Biography. 2 v. Oxford 1961. v. 1, From the Beginnings to 1900; v. 2, 1901–1950.

DownRev
Downside Review. Yeovil, Eng. 1880– Suspended during 1920.

DSAM
Dictionnaire de spiritualité ascétique et mystique. Doctrine et histoire, ed. M. Viller et al. Paris 1932–

DTC
Dictionnaire de théologie catholique, ed. A. Vacant et al. 15 v. Paris 1903–50. Tables générales 1951–

DublinRev
Dublin Review (Wiseman Review 1961–65). London 1836–

Duchesne FÉ
L. Duchesne. *Fastes épiscopaux de l'ancienne Gaule*. 2d ed. 3 v. Paris 1907–15.

Duchesne LP
Liber pontificalis, ed. L. Duchesne. Paris. v. 1–2, 1886–92; v. 3, 1958–

EB (year)
Encyclopedia Britannica. 23 v. Index and atlas. Chicago-London-Toronto.

ECQ
The Eastern Churches Quarterly. Ramsgate 1936–

EDB
Encyclopedic Dictionary of the Bible, tr. and adap. L. Hartman from A. Van den Born's *Bijbels Woordenboek*. New York 1963.

EETS
Early English Text Society. London 1864–

EHR
English Historical Review. London 1886–

Ehrhard
A. Ehrhard, *Überlieferung und Bestand der hagiographischen und homiletischen Literatur der griechischen Kirche von den Anfängen bis zum Ende des 16.Jh.* Leipzig-Berlin 1937–52 (v. 50, 51, 52 of TU).

Eisenhofer Lit
L. Eisenhofer and J. Lechner, *The Liturgy of the Roman Rite*, tr. A. J. and E. F. Peeler from the 6th Ger. ed., ed. H. E. Winstone. New York 1961.

Eisler
R. Eisler, *Wörterbuch der philosophischen Begriffe*. 4th ed. 3 v. Berlin 1927–30.

Emden Camb
A. B. Emden, *Biographical Register of the University of Cambridge before 1500*. Cambridge, Eng. 1963.

Emden Ox
A. B. Emden, *Biographical Register of the University of Oxford to A.D. 1500*. 3 v. Oxford 1957–59.

EncCatt
Enciclopedia cattolica, ed. P. Paschini et al. 12 v. Rome 1949–54.

EncFil
Enciclopedia filosofica. 4 v. Venice-Rome 1957.

EnchAscet
Enchiridion asceticum, comp. M. J. Rouët de Journel. 4th ed. Barcelona 1947.

EnchBibl⁴
Enchiridion biblicum. 4th ed. Rome 1961.

EnchPatr | *Enchiridion patristicum*, comp. M. J. Rouët de Journel. 21st ed. Freiburg 1960.

EncIslam¹ | *Encyclopedia of Islam*, ed. M. T. Houtsma et al. 4 v. Leiden 1913–38.

EncIslam²
see Gibb-Kramers
SEI | *Encyclopedia of Islam*, ed. B. Lewis et al. 2d ed. Leiden 1954–

EncIt | *Enciclopaedia Italiana di scienze, lettere, ed arti.* 36 v. Rome 1929–39; suppl. 1938–

EncJewRel | *Encyclopedia of the Jewish Religion*, ed. R. J. Zwi Werblowsky and G. Wigoder. New York 1966.

EncJud | *Encyclopaedia Judaica: Das Judentum in Geschichte und Gegenwart.* 10 v. Berlin 1928–34. Incomplete.

EncLuthCh | *The Encyclopedia of the Lutheran Church.* ed. J. Bodensieck. 3 v. Minneapolis 1965.

EncModChrMiss | *The Encyclopedia of Modern Christian Missions*, ed. B. L. Goddard. Camden, N. J. 1967.

EncPhil | *The Encyclopedia of Philosophy.* 8 v. New York 1966.

EncRelCat | *Enciclopedia de la religión católica*, ed. R. D. Ferreres et al. 7 v. Barcelona 1950–56.

EncRelKnow | S. M. Jackson, ed., *The New Schaff-Herzog Encyclopedia of Religious Knowledge.* 13 v. Grand Rapids, Mich. 1951–54. Supplement titled *Twentieth Century Encyclopedia of Religious Knowledge*, ed. L. A. Loetscher. 2 v. 1955.

EncSocSc | *Encyclopedia of the Social Sciences*, ed. E. R. Seligman and A. Johnson. 15 v. New York 1930–35.

EncWA | *Encyclopedia of World Art.* New York 15 v. 1959–68.

Englebert-Brady-Brown | O. Englebert. *Saint Francis of Assisi: A Biography*, tr. E. M. Cooper. 2d augm. ed. I. Brady and R. Brown. Chicago 1966.

ÉO | *Échos d'Orient.* Paris 1897–

EphemIC | *Ephemerides iuris canonici.* Rome 1945–

EphemLiturg | *Ephemerides liturgicae.* Rome 1887–

EphemThLov | *Ephemerides theologicae Lovanienses.* Bruges 1924–

Espasa | *Enciclopedia universal ilustrada Europeo-Americana.* 70 v. Barcelona 1908–30. Suppl. 1934–

EspSagr | *España sagrada*, ed. H. Flórez et al. 54 v. Madrid 1741–1957.

Farrar-Evans | C. P. Farrar and A. P. Evans, *Bibliography of English Translations from Medieval Sources.* New York 1946.

FathCh | *The Fathers of the Church: A New Translation*, ed. R. J. Deferrari et al. New York 1947–60; Washington 1961–

Fellerer | K. G. Fellerer, *The History of Catholic Church Music*, tr. F. A. Brunner. Baltimore 1961.

Fliche-Martin | A. Fliche and V. Martin. eds. *Histoire de l'église depuis les origines jusqu'à nos jours.* Paris 1935–

FrancStudies | *Franciscan Studies.* St. Bonaventure, N.Y. 1940–

FranzStud | *Franziskanische Studien.* Münster-Werl 1914–

FreibZPhilTh | *Freiburger Zeitschrift für Philosophie und Theologie.* Fribourg 1954– . Supersedes *Jahrbuch für Philosophie und spekulative Theologie.* Berlin 1887–1913 and *Divus Thomas* 1914–1953.

Fries | H. Fries, ed., *Handbuch theologischer Grundbegriffe.* 2 v. Munich 1962–63; Fr. tr. *Encyclopédie de la foi.* 4 v. Paris 1965–

GallChrist | *Gallia christiana.* Paris. v. 1–13, 1715–85; v. 14–16, 1856–65.

GallChristNov | *Gallia christiana novissima*, ed. J. H. Albanès, continued by U. Chevalier. Montbéliard 1899–1921.

Gams | P. Gams, *Series episcoporum ecclesiae catholicae.* Regensburg 1873. Suppl. 1879–86. Repr. Graz 1957.

Garraghan | G. J. Garraghan, *Jesuits of the Middle United States.* 3 v. New York 1938.

GCS | *Die griechischen christlichen Schriftsteller der ersten drei Jahrhunderte.* Leipzig 1897–

Gebhardt-Grundmann | B. Gebbhardt, *Handbuch der deutschen Geschichte*, ed. H. Grundmann. 8th ed. 4 v. Stuttgart 1954–60.

GeistL | *Geist und Leben.* Munich-Würzburg 1947– Supersedes *Zeitschrift für Aszese und Mystik* 1926–46.

GerbertS | M. Gerbert, *Scriptores de musica sacra potissimum.* 3 v. Milan 1931.

Ghellinck Essor | J. de Ghellinck, *L'Essor de la littérature latine au XIIe siècle.* 2 v. Brussels-Paris 1946.

Ghellinck Litt | J. de Ghellinck, *Littérature latine au moyen-âge.* 2 v. (*Bibliothèque catholique des sciences religieuses* 85–86) Paris 1939. v. 1 Depuis les origines jusqu'à la fin de la renaissance carolingienne. v. 2 De la renaissance carolingienne à saint Anselme.

Ghellinck Mouv | J. de Ghellinck, *Le Mouvement théologique du XIIe siècle.* Sa preparation lointaine avant et autour de Pierre Lombard, ses rapports avec les initiatives des canonistes. 2d ed. Bruges 1948.

Ghellinck Patr | J. de Ghellinck, *Patristique et moyen-âge: Études d'histoire littéraire et doctrinale.* v. 1 2d ed. Paris 1949; v. 2 and 3 Brussels 1947–48.

Gibb-Kramers SEI — H. A. R. Gibb and J. H. Kramers, *Shorter Encyclopedia of Islam* Leiden, 1953.

Gillow BDEC — J. Gillow, *A Literary and Biographical History or Bibliographical Dictionary of the English Catholics from 1534 to the Present Time,* 5 v. London-New York 1885–1902. Repr. New York 1961.

Gilson HCP — É. H. Gilson, *History of Christian Philosophy in the Middle Ages.* New York 1955.

GKW — *Gesamtkatalog der Wiegendrucke.* Leipzig 1925.

Glorieux L — P. Glorieux, *La Littérature quodlibétique.* 2 v. (v. 5 and 21 of *Bibliothèque Thomiste*). v. 1, Kain 1925; v. 2, Paris 1935.

Glorieux R — P. Glorieux, *Répertoire des maîtres en théologie de Paris au XIIIe siècle.* (v. 17–18 of *Bibliothèque Thomiste*). Paris 1933–34.

Graf GCAL — G. Graf. *Geschichte der christlichen arabischen Literatur.* 5 v. Vatican City 1944–53 (ST 118, 133, 146, 147, 172).

Greg — *Gregorianum.* Rome 1920–

Grill-Bacht Konz — A. Grillmeier and H. Bacht, *Das Konzil von Chalkedon: Geschichte und Gegenwart* 3 v. 1951–54.

Grove DMM — *Grove's Dictionary of Music and Musicians,* ed. E. Blom 9 v. 5th ed. 1954.

Gründler — J. Gründler. *Lexikon der christlichen Kirchen und Sekten.* 2 v. Vienna 1961.

Guibert — J. de Guibert. *The Jesuits: Their Spiritual Doctrine and Practice, a historical study,* tr. W. J. Young, ed. G. E. Ganss. Chicago 1964.

Guilday — P. Guilday, *A History of the Councils of Baltimore, 1791–1884.* New York 1932.

Guthrie — W. K. C. Guthrie. *A History of Greek Philosophy.* 2 v. Cambridge U. Press 1962.

Hardouin — J. Hardouin, *Acta conciliorum et epistolae decretales ac constitutiones summorum pontificum* (34–1714). 11 v. in 12. Paris 1715.

Hastings DB
Hastings DB (1963) — J. Hastings and J. A. Selbia. eds., *Dictionary of the Bible.* 5 v. Edinburgh 1942–50. Rev. in 1 v. ed. F. C. Grant and H. H. Rowley. New York 1963.

Hastings ERE — J. Hastings, ed., *Encyclopedia of Religion and Ethics.* 13 v. Edinburgh 1908–27.

HAT — *Handbuch zum Alten Testament,* ed. O. Eissfeldt. Tübingen 1934–

Hauck — A. Hauck, *Kirchengeschichte Deutschlands.* 9th ed. 5 v. Berlin-Leipzig 1958.

HBS — *Henry Bradshaw Society.* London 1891–

Hefele-Leclercq — C. J. von Hefele, *Histoire des conciles d'après les documents originaux,* tr. and continued. H. Leclercq. 10 v. in 19. Paris 1907–38.

Heimbucher — M. Heimbucher. *Die Orden und Kongregationen der katholischen Kirche.* 3d ed. 2 v. Paderborn 1932–34.

HeythropJ — *Heythrop Journal.* Oxford 1960–

Hinnesbusch HDO — W. A. Hinnebusch, *The History of the Dominican Order.* Staten Island, N.Y. 1966– . 5 v. planned.

HistAmMeth — *The History of American Methodism,* ed. E. S. Bucke et al. 3 v. New York 1964.

HistRecStud — *Historical Records and Studies of the U.S. Catholic Historical Society of New York.* 1900–

HistRel — *History of Religions:* An international Journal for Comparative Historical Studies. Chicago 1961–

Hocedez — E. Hocedez, *Histoire de la théologie au XIXe siècle.* 3 v. Brussels-Paris. v. 1 (1800–31) 1948; v. 2 (1831–78) 1952; v. 3 (1878–1903) 1947.

HPR — *Homiletic and Pastoral Review.* New York 1900–

HTR — *Harvard Theological Review.* Cambridge, Mass. 1908–

Hughes HC — P. Hughes, *A History of the Church.* 3 v. New York 1947–49; v. 1–2, 2d ed. 1949; v. 3 1947.

Hughes RE — P. Hughes, *The Reformation in England.* 5th ed. 3 v. in 1. New York 1963.

Hugo — C. L. Hugo, *S. Ordinis Praemonstratensis annales.* 2 v. Nancy 1734–36.

Hurter — H. Hurter, *Nomenclator literarius theologiae catholicae.* 5 v. in 6. 3d ed. Innsbruck 1903–13; v. 1, 4th ed. 1926.

HZ — *Historische Zeitschrift.* Munich 1859–

ICC — *International Critical Commentary,* ed. S. R. Driver et al. Edinburgh-New York 1895–

IER — *The Irish Ecclesiastical Record.* Dublin 1863–

InterB — *The Interpreters' Bible,* ed. G. A. Buttrick et al. 12 v. New York 1951–57.

InterDB — *The Interpreters' Dictionary of the Bible,* ed. G. A. Buttrick et al. 4 v. Nashville 1962. Suppl. 1 v. 1976.

ITQ — *The Irish Theological Quarterly.* Dublin 1906–22; 1951–

Jaffé — P. Jaffé, *Regesta pontificum romanorum ab condita ecclesia ad annum post Christum natum 1198,* ed. S. Löwenfeld et al. 2d ed. 2 v. Leipzig 1881–88. Repr. Graz 1956. (For continuation see Potthast Reg.)

James ApocNT — M. R. James, *The Apocryphal New Testament.* Oxford 1924. Corrected repr. 1953.

Janssen-Pastor — J. Janssen, *Geschichte des deutschen Volkes seit dem Ausgang des Mittelal-*

ters, continued by L. von Pastor. 8 v. Freiburg. v. 1–3, 19th–20th ed. 1913–17; v. 4–6, 17th ed. 1924; v. 7–8, 15th ed. 1924. Eng. tr. of earlier eds. by M. A. Mitchell and A. M. Christie. 16 v. London-St. Louis 1906–10. Index 1925.

JB   *Jerusalem Bible*, ed. A. Jones. Garden City, N.Y. 1966.

JBC   *Jerome Biblical Commentary*, ed. R. E. Brown et al. 2 v. in 1 Englewood Cliffs, N.J. 1968.

JBL   *Journal of Biblical Literature*. Boston 1881–

JbLit   *Jahrbuch für Liturgiewissenschaft*. Münster 1921–41. Superseded by *Archiv für Liturgiewissenschaft* 1950–

JE   *The Jewish Encyclopedia*, ed. J. Singer. 13 v. New York 1901–06.

Jedin-Baus   K. Baus, *From the Apostolic Community to Constantine*, with a "General Introduction to Church History" by H. Jedin, tr. from 3d rev. Ger. ed. New York 1965 (v. 1 of *Handbook of Church History*, ed. H. Jedin and J. Dolan). v. 2 published in Germany 1967. v. 3.1 1966. v. 3.2 1968.

JEcclHist   *The Journal of Ecclesiastical History*. London 1950–

Jedin Trent   H. Jedin, *History of the Council of Trent*, tr. E. Graf. v. 1–2 St. Louis 1957–60. *Geschichte des Konzils von Trient*. 2 v. Freiburg 1949–57; v. 1, 2d ed. 1951.

JHI   *Journal of the History of Ideas*. New York 1937–

JQR   *Jewish Quarterly Review*. London 1888–1908. Philadelphia 1910–

JR   *Journal of Religion*. Chicago 1921–

JTS   *Journal of Theological Studies*. London 1900–05; Oxford 1906–49; NS 1950–

Jugie   M. Jugie, *Theologia dogmatica christianorum orientalium ab ecclesia catholica dissidentium*. 5 v. Paris 1926–35.

Julian   J. Julian, ed., *A Dictionary of Hymnology*. 2d ed. 2 v. London 1907; reprint New York 1957.

Kapsner BB   O. L. Kapsner, *A Benedictine Bibliography: An Author-Subject Union List*. 2d ed. 2 v. Collegeville, Minn. 1962. v. 1 author part; v. 2 subject part.

Kenney   J. F. Kenney, *The Sources for the Early History of Ireland*. v. 1 Ecclesiastical. New York 1929.

Kirch   K. Kirch, *Enchiridion fontium historiae ecclesiasticae antiquae*, ed. L. Ueding. 6th ed. Barcelona 1947.

Kittel TD   G. Kittel, *Theological Dictionary of the New Testament*. 9 v. Grand Rapids 1964–73.

Knowles-Hadcock   D. Knowles and R. N. Hadcock, *Medieval Religious Houses: England and Wales*. New York 1953.

Knowles MOE   D. Knowles, *The Monastic Order in England, 943–1216*. 2d ed. Cambridge, Eng. 1962.

Knowles ROE   D. Knowles, *The Religious Orders in England*. 3 v. Cambridge, Eng. 1948–60.

KnoxEnth   R. A. Knox, *Enthusiasm*. Oxford 1957.

Koch JL   L. Koch, *Jesuitenlexikon: Die Gesellschaft Jesu einst und jetzt*. Paderborn 1934. Photo-duplicated with rev. and suppl. 2 v. Leiden 1962.

König Christus   F. König, ed., *Christus und die Religionen der Erde: Handbuch der Religionsgeschichte*. 2d ed. 3 v. Vienna 1961; Span. tr. R. Valdes del Toro, *Cristo y las religiones de la tierra: Manual de historia de la religión*. 3 v. Madrid 1960–61 (BAC).

LACT   *Library of Anglo-Catholic Theology*. 97 v. Oxford 1841–63.

Laistner   M. L. W. Laistner, *Thought and Letters in Western Europe, A.D. 500 to 900*. 2d ed. New York 1957.

Lampe   G. W. H. Lampe, ed., *A Patristic Greek Lexicon*. Oxford 1961–

Landgraf   A. M. Landgraf, *Dogmengeschichte der Frühscholastik*. 4 v. Regensburg 1952–56.

Latourette   K. S. Latourette, *A History of the Expansion of Christianity*. 7 v. New York 1937–45.

Latourette CRA   K. S. Latourette, *Christianity in a Revolutionary Age: A History of Christianity in the Nineteenth and Twentieth Centuries*. 5 v. New York 1958–62.

Lenssen   S. Lenssen, *Hagiologium cisterciense*. 2 v. Tilburg 1948–49. Suppl. 1951.

Léonard HistProt   E. Léonard, *History of Protestantism*, ed. H. H. Rowley, tr. J. M. H. Reid. v. 1, New York 1968.

Le Quien   M. Le Quien, *Oriens Christianus*. 3 v. Paris 1740; Reprint Graz 1958.

LexAW   *Lexikon der alten Welt*. Zurich 1965.

LibCC   *Library of Christian Classics*. Philadelphia 1953–

LibF   *Library of the Fathers*. 43 v. Oxford 1838–74.

Loeb   *Loeb Classical Library*. London-New York-Cambridge, Mass. 1912–

LTK   *Lexikon für Theologie und Kirche*, ed. M. Buchberger. 10 v. Freiburg. New ed. by J. Höfer and K. Rahner, 1957–65. Suppl. 1966, Vatican II.

LumV   *Lumen Vitae*. Brussels 1946–

LW   J. Pelikan and W. A. Hansen, *Luther's Works*, 56 v. 1957–

Mabillon AS	J. Mabillon, *Acta sanctorum ordinis S. Benedicti*. 9 v. Paris 1668–1701. 2d ed. 6 v. Venice 1733–40.
Mai NPB	A. Mai, ed., *Nova Patrum bibliotheca*. Rome. v. 1–7, 1852–57; continued by J. Cozza-Luzi v. 8–10, 1871–1905.
Mai SR	A. Mai, *Spicilegium romanum*. 10 v. Rome 1839–44.
Mai SVNC	A. Mai, *Scriptorum veterum nova collectio e Vaticanis codicibus edita*. 10 v. Rome 1825–38.
Manitius	M. Manitius, *Geschichte der lateinischen Literatur des Mittelalters*. 3 v. Munich 1911–31.
Mann	H. K. Mann, *The Lives of the Popes in the Early Middle Ages from 590 to 1304*. 18 v. London 1902–32.
Mansi	J. D. Mansi, *Sacrorum Conciliorum nova et amplissima collectio*. 31 v. Florence-Venice 1757–98. Repr. and continued by L. Petit and J. B. Martin. 53 v. in 60. Paris 1889–1927; repr. Graz 1960–
Manuscripta	*Manuscripta*. St. Louis 1957–
MartRom	*Martyrologium romanum*, ed. H. Delehaye. Brussels 1940 (v. 68 of *Acta sanctorum*).
Martyrs	H. Leclercq, *Les Martyrs*. 15 v. Paris 1902–24.
Mayer RB	F. E. Mayer, *The Religious Bodies of America*. 4th ed. rev. A. C. Piepkorn. St. Louis 1961.
MedRenSt	*Mediaeval and Renaissance Studies*. London 1949–
MedSt	*Mediaeval Studies*. New York-London 1939–
MélSciRel	*Mélanges de science religieuse*. Lille 1944–
MennEnc	*The Mennonite Encyclopedia*. 4 v. Hillssboro, Kans.-Scottdale, Pa. 1955–59.
Merkelbach	B. H. Merkelbach, *Summa theologiae moralis*. 8th ed. 3 v. Paris 1949.
MGG	*Die Musik in Geschichte und Gegenwart*, ed. F. Blume. 1949– .
MGH	*Monumenta Germaniae historica*. Berlin 1826–

MGHAuct.ant.	=	Auctores antiquissimi
MGHCap.	=	Capitularia
MGHConc.	=	Concilia
MGHConst.	=	Constitutiones
MGHDD.	=	Diplomata
MGHEp.	=	Epistolae
MGHEp.sel.	=	Epistolae selectae
MGHLib.lit.	=	Libelli de lite
MGHLL.	=	Leges
MGHNecr.	=	Necrologia
MGHPoetae	=	Poetae
MGHS	=	Scriptores
MGHS rer.Germ.	=	Scriptores rerum Germanicarum
MGHS rer.Germ. NS	=	Scriptores rerum Germanicarum, NS
MGHS rer.Lang.	=	Scriptores rerum Langobardicarum
MGHS rer.Mer.	=	Scriptores rerum Merovingicarum

Miller	J. H. Miller, *Fundamentals of the Liturgy*. Notre Dame, Ind. 1960.
MissCattol	*Le missioni cattoliche: Storia, geographia, statistica*. Rome 1950.
ModSchoolm	*The Modern Schoolman*. St. Louis 1925–
MonHistSJ	*Monumenta historica Societatis Jesu*. Madrid 1894– ; Rome 1932–
MonOPraed	*Monumenta Ordinis Fratrum Praedicatorum historica*, ed. B. M. Reichert. Rome-Stuttgart-Paris 1896–
Month	*The Month*. London 1864–
MoyerWWW	*Who Was Who in Church History*, ed. E. S. Moyer. Chicago 1962.
MQ	*Musical Quarterly*. New York 1915–
NCE	*New Catholic Encyclopedia*. 15 v. New York 1967. Suppl. v. 16 1974.
NDB	*Neue deutsche Biographie*. Berlin 1953– . Supersedes *Allgemeine deutsche Biographie*. Leipzig 1875–1910.
NED	*New English Dictionary*. Oxford 1888–1928.
NewSchol	*New Scholasticism*. Washington 1927–
Nilsson	M. P. Nilsson, *Geschichte der griechischen Religion*. 2 v. 2d ed. Munich 1955–61.
NOHM	*New Oxford History of Music*, ed. J. A. Westrup, 11 v. 1957–
Noldin	H. Noldin, *Summa theologiae moralis*, rev. A. Schmitt and G. Heinzel. 3 v. Innsbruck 1961–62. v. 1 contains complementa *De castitate*, and *De poenis ecclesiasticis*, separately paged.
NovTest	*Novum Testamentum*. Leiden 1956–
NPNFC	*A Select Library of the Nicene and Post-Nicene Fathers of the Christian Church*, ed. P. Schaff. 14 v. New York 1886–1900; 2d series, ed. P. Schaff and H. Wace 1890–1900.
NRT	*Nouvelle revue théologique*. Tournai-Louvain-Paris 1869–
NTS	*New Testament Studies*. Cambridge, Eng.-Washington 1954–

Numen
: *Numen*. International Review for the History of Religions. Leiden 1954–

NZM
: *Neue Zeitschrift für Missionswissenschaft*. Beckenried 1945–

OC
: *Oriens Christianus*. Leipzig-Wiesbaden 1901–

OCD
: *The Oxford Classical Dictionary*, ed. M. Cary et al. Oxford 1949.

ODCC
: F. L. Cross, *The Oxford Dictionary of the Christian Church*. London 1957. Repr. with corrections, 1961, 1966.

OED
: *The Oxford English Dictionary*, ed. J. A. H. Murray et al. 13 v. New York 1933.

Olmstead
: C. E. Olmstead, *History of Religion in the United States*. Englewood Cliffs, N.J. 1960.

OrChr
OrChrAnal
: *Orientalia Christiana Analecta*. Rome 1935– . Supersedes *Orientalia Christiana* 1923–34.

Orchard
: *Catholic Commentary on Holy Scripture*, ed. B. Orchard et al. London-New York 1957.

OrFrat
: *Orate Fratres*. Collegeville, Minn. 1926–51. Superseded by *Worship* 1951–

Orientalia
: *Orientalia*, ed. Pontifical Biblical Institute. Rome 1920–30; NS 1932–

OrientCatt
: *Oriente Cattolico*. Vatican City 1962.

OssRom
: *L'Osservatore romano*. Rome 1849–

Ostrogorsky
Ostrogorsky-Charanis
: G. Ostrogorsky, *History of the Byzantine State*, tr. J. Hussey from 2d German ed., Oxford 1956; American ed. by P. Charanis. New Brunswick, N.J. 1957.

Pastor
: L. Pastor, *The History of the Popes from the Close of the Middle Ages*. 40 v. London-St. Louis 1938–61; v. 1, 6th ed.; v. 2, 7th ed.; v. 3–6, 5th ed.; v. 7–8, 11–12, 3d ed.; v. 9-10, 4th ed.; v. 13–40 no ed. statements. *Geschichte der Päpste seit dem Ausgang des Mittelalters*. 16 v. in 21. Freiburg 1885–1933. Repr. 1955–

Periodica
: *Periodica de re morali canonica liturgica*. Rome 1912–

Pfister
: L. Pfister, *Notices biographiques et bibliographiques sur les Jésuites de l'ancienne mission de Chine 1552–1773*. 2 v. Shanghai 1932–34.

PG
: *Patrologia graeca*, ed. J. P. Migne. 161 v. Paris 1857–66.

PL
: *Patrologia latina*, ed. J. P. Migne. 217 v., indexes 4 v. Paris 1878–90.

PLSuppl
: *Patrologiae cursus completus, series latina*. Suppl., ed. A. Hamman. Paris 1957–

PO
: *Patrologia orientalis*, ed. R. Graffin and F. Nau. 10 v. Paris 1903–15.

Podhradsky
: G. Podhradsky, *New Dictionary of the Liturgy*. Staten Island, N.Y. 1966.

Potthast Reg
: A. Potthast, *Regesta pontificum romanorum inde ab a.1198 ad a. 1304*. 2 v. Berlin 1874–75. Repr. Graz 1957. (Continuation of Jaffé).

PRE
: J. J. Herzog and A. Hauck, eds., *Realencyklopädie für protestantische Theologie*. 3d ed. 24 v. Leipzig 1896–1913.

Prümm
: K. Prümm, *Religionsgeschichtliches Handbuch für den Raum der altchristlichen Umwelt*. 2d ed. Rome 1954.

Prümmer
: D. M. Prümmer, *Manuale theologiae moralis*, ed. E. M. Münch. 12th ed. 3 v. Freiburg-Barcelona 1955.

PS
: *Patrologia syriaca*, ed. R. Graffin et al. 3 v. Paris 1894–1926.

PSO
: I. Ortiz de Urbina, *Patrologia syriaca*. Rome 1958.

PW
: *Paulys Realenzyklopädie der klassischen Altertums wissenschaft*, ed. G. Wissowa et al. Stuttgart 1893–

Quasten
: J. Quasten, *Patrology*. 3 v. Westminster, Md. 1950–60.

Quasten Init
: J. Quasten, *Initiation aux Pères de l'Église*. v. 1–3 Paris 1955– . Tr. of his *Patrology* with text additions and bibliographies brought up to date.

Quasten MonE
: J. Quasten, ed., *Monumenta eucharista et liturgica vetustissima*. Bonn 1935–37 (*Florilegium Patristicum* 7).

QLP
: *Questions liturgiques et paroissiales*. Louvain 1921–

Quétif–Échard
: J. Quétif and J. Échard, *Scriptores Ordinis Praedicatorum*. 5 v. Paris 1719–23; continued by R. Coulon, Paris 1909– . Reprint 2 v. in 4. New York 1959.

Raby CLP
: F. J. E. Raby, *A History of Christian Latin Poetry from the Beginnings to the Close of the Middle Ages*. 2d ed. Oxford 1953.

Raby SLP
: F. J. E. Raby, *A History of Secular Latin Poetry in the Middle Ages*. 2d ed. 2 v. Oxford 1957.

RAC
: *Reallexikon für Antike und Christentum*, ed. T. Klauser. Stuttgart 1941 (1950)–

RACHS
: *Records*, American Catholic Historical Society of Philadelphia. Philadelphia 1887–

Rahner-Vorgrimler
: K. Rahner and H. Vorgrimler, *Theological Dictionary*, ed. C. Ernst, tr. R. Strachan. New York 1965.

Rahner ThInvest
: K. Rahner, *Theological Investigations*, tr. C. Ernst. 1961.

RAM
: *Revue d'ascétique et de mystique*. Toulouse 1920–

Razón y Fe
: *Razón y Fe*. Madrid 1901–

RechSR
: *Recherches de science religieuse*. Paris 1910–

RechTAM	*Recherches de théologie ancienne et médiévale.* Louvain 1929–
Reese MusMA	G. Reese, *Music in the Middle Ages.* New York 1940.
Reese MusR	G. Reese, *Music in the Renaissance.* Rev. ed. 1959.
RevBén	*Revue bénédictine.* Maredsous 1884–
RevBibl	*Revue biblique.* Paris 1892–
RevScPhilTh	*Revue des sciences philosophiques et théologiques.* Paris 1907–
RevScRel	*Revue des sciences religieuses* Strasbourg 1921–
RevT	*Revue thomiste.* Paris 1893–
RevTP	*Revue de théologie et de philosophie.* Lausanne 1868–
RFHMA	*Repertorium fontium Historiae medii aevii,* ed. A. Potthast. v. 1, Series collectionum. Istituto Storico Italiano per il Medio Evo. Rome 1957–
RGG	*Die Religion in Geschichte und Gegenwart.* 3d ed. 6 v. Tübingen 1957–63; Index 1965.
RHE	*Revue d'histoire ecclésiastique.* Louvain 1900–
Rice ByzArt	D. T. Rice, *Byzantine Art.* Oxford 1935.
Righetti	M. Righetti, *Manuale di storia liturgica.* 4 v. Milan, v. 1, 2d ed. 1950; v. 2, 2d ed. 1955; v. 3, 1949; v. 4, 1953.
Robert-Feuillet	A. Robert and A. Feuillet, eds., *Introduction à la Bible.* Tournai-New York. v. 1 *Introduction générale. Ancien Testament.* 2d ed. 1959; v. 2 *Nouveau Testament* 1959. *Introduction to the New Testament,* tr. P. W. Skehan et al., 1965.
Robert-Tricot	A. Robert and A. Tricot, *Guide to the Bible,* tr. E. P. Arbez and M. P. McGuire. 2 v. Tournai-New York 1951–55; v. 1 rev. and enl., 1960.
Roberti–Palazzini	F. Roberti et al., comps., *Dictionary of Moral Theology,* ed. P. Palazzini et al., tr. H. J. Yannone et al. from 2d Ital. ed. Westminster, Md. 1962.
RollsS	*Rerum britannicarum medii aevi scriptores,* 244 v. London 1858–96. Repr. New York 1964– . Ordinarily called Rolls Series.
RQ	*Römische Quartalschrift für christliche Altertumskunde und für Kirchengeschichte.* Freiburg 1887–
RSV	*The Oxford Annotated Bible with the Apocrypha. Revised Standard Version,* ed. H. G. May and B. M. Metzger, New York 1965.
SacMund	*Sacramentum Mundi, an Encyclopedia of Theology,* ed. K. Rahner et al. 6 v., 1968–70. New York.
Sbaralea	J. H. Sbaralea, *Supplementum et castigatio ad scriptores trium ordinum S.*

	Francisci a Waddingo. 2 v. Rome 1806; new ed. in 4 v. Rome 1906–36.
SC	*Sources chrétiennes,* ed. H. de Lubac et al. Paris 1941–
Schaff Creeds	P. Schaff, *The Creeds of Christendom.* 3 v. 6th ed. Reprint Grand Rapids 1966.
Schanz	M. Schanz, C. Hosius, and G. Krüger, *Geschichte der römischen Literatur.* 4 v. in 5. Munich 1914–35.
Schroeder DD	H. J. Schroeder, *Disciplinary Decrees of the General Councils.* St. Louis 1937.
Schroeder T	H. J. Schroeder, tr., *Council of Trent: Canons and Decrees, 1545–63.* St. Louis 1941.
Schottenloher	K. Schottenloher, *Bibliographie zur deutschen Geschichte im Zeitalter der Glaubensspaltung, 1517–85.* 6 v. Leipzig 1933–40. Reprint Stuttgart 1956–58. v. 7 *ibid.* 1962–
Seppelt	F. X. Seppelt, *Geschichte der Päpste von den Anfängen bis zur Mitte des 20. Jh.* v. 1, 2, 4, 5, Leipzig 1931–41; v. 1, 2d ed. Munich 1954; v. 2, 2d ed. 1955; v. 3, 1956; v. 4–5, 2d ed. 1957.
Smith-Jamison	J. W. Smith and A. L. Jamison, eds., *Religion in American Life.* 4 v. Princeton, N. J. 1961–63. v. 4 is *A Critical Bibliography of Religion in America,* by N. R. Burr. 2 v. 1961.
Sommervogel	C. Sommervogel et al., *Bibliothèque de la Compagnie de Jésus.* 11 v. Brussels-Paris 1890–1932. Suppl. v. 12 1960.
SPCK	Society for Promoting Christian Knowledge. London 1698–
Speculum	*Speculum. A Journal of Mediaeval Studies.* Cambridge, Mass. 1926–
SSL	*Spicilegium sacrum Lovaniense.* Louvain 1922–
ST	*Studi e testi.* Rome 1900–
StA	*Studia anselmiana.* Rome 1933–
Stammler	W. Stammler and K. Langosch, eds., *Die deutsche Literatur des Mittelalters: Verfasserlexikon.* 5 v. Berlin-Leipzig 1933–55.
StC	*Studia catholica.* Roermond 1924–
Stegmüller RB	F. Stegmüller, *Repertorium biblicum medii aevi.* 7 v. Madrid 1949–61.
Stegmüller RS	F. Stegmüller, *Repertorium commentariorum in Sententias Petri Lombardi.* 2 v. Würzburg 1947.
Stein-Palanque	E. Stein, *Histoire du Bas-Empire,* tr. J. R. Palanque. 2 v. in 3. Paris 1949–59.
StGreg	*Studi gregoriani,* ed. G. B. Borino. Rome 1947–
Stickler	A. M. Stickler, *Historia iuris canonici latini.* v. 1, Historia fontium. Turin 1950.
StL	*Staatslexikon,* ed. Görres-Gesellschaft. 6th enl. ed. 8 v. Freiburg 1957–63.

StLit	*Studia liturgica.* An international ecumenical quarterly. Rotterdam 1962–
Strack-Billerbeck	H. L. Strack and P. Billerbeck, *Kommentar zum Neuen Testament.* 4 v. Munich 1922–28.
Streit-Dindinger	R. Streit and J. Dindinger, *Bibliotheca missionum.* 23 v. Freiburg 1916–64.
STS BAC	*Sacrae theologiae summa,* ed. Fathers of the Society of Jesus, Professors of the Theological Faculties in Spain. 4 v. BAC 61,90,62,73. Madrid. v. 1, 5th ed. 1962; v. 2, 3d ed. 1958; v. 3, 4th ed. 1961; v. 4, 4th ed. 1962.
SubsidHag	*Subsidia hagiographica.* Brussels 1886–
Syntopicon	J. M. Adler, ed., *The Great Ideas: A Syntopicon of Great Books of the Western World.* 2 v. Chicago 1952. (Great Books of the Western World, v. 2 and 3).
Szövérffy	J. Szövérffy, *Die Annalen der lateinischen Hymnendichtung.* Ein Handbuch. 2 v. Berlin 1964–65.
Taurisano Cat	I. Taurisano, *Catalogus hagiographicus ordinis praedicatorum.* Rome 1918.
Taurisano Hier	I. Taurisano, *Hierarchia Ordinis Praedicatorum.* Rome 1916.
TCEC	*Twentieth Century Encyclopedia of Catholicism,* ed. H. Daniel-Rops. 150 v. 1958–71.
ThAq ST (Lat-Eng)	Thomas Aquinas, *Summa theologiae,* ed T. Gilby et al. 60 v. New York 1965–76. Bilingual: Latin and English.
TheolDig	*Theology Digest.* Kansas City, Mo. 1953–
Thieme-Becker	U. Thieme and F. Becker, eds., *Allgemeines Lexikon der bildenden Künstler von der Antike bis zur Gegenwart.* 37 v. Leipzig 1907–38.
Thomist	*The Thomist.* Washington 1939–
Thorndike	L. Thorndike, *A History of Magic and Experimental Science.* 8 v. New York 1923–58.
ThQ	*Theologische Quartalschrift.* Tübingen 1819– ; Stuttgart 1946–
ThSt	*Theological Studies.* Woodstock, Md. 1940–
TL	*Theology Library,* ed. A. M. Henry, tr. W. Storey et al. 6 v. Chicago 1954–58. v. 1 Introd. to Theology, 1954; v. 2 God and His Creation, 1955; v. 3 Man and His Happiness, 1956; v. 4 Virtues and the States of Life, 1956; v. 5 The Historical and Mystical Christ, 1958; v. 6 Christ and His Sacraments, 1958.
TLL	*Thesaurus linguae Latinae.* Leipzig 1900–
Traditio	*Traditio.* New York 1943–78.
TU	*Texte und Untersuchungen zur Geschichte der altchristlichen Literatur.* Berlin 1882–
Turner EOMIA	C. H. Turner, ed., *Ecclesiae occidentalis monumenta iuris antiquissima. Canonum et conciliorum Graecorum interpretationes Latinae.* Oxford 1899–1939.
Ueberweg	F. Ueberweg, *Grundriss der Geschichte der Philosophie,* ed. K. Praechter et al. 11th–12th ed. 5 v. Berlin 1923–28.
UNESCO WSEd	UNESCO, *World Survey of Education.* 4 v. New York 1955–65.
UnivJewishEnc	*Universal Jewish Encyclopedia.* 10 v. New York 1939–44.
Ursprung	O. Ursprung, *Die katholische Kirchenmusik.* Potsdam 1931.
Vasari	G. Vasari, *The Lives of the Painters, Sculptors and Architects,* ed. W. Gaunt, tr. A. B. Hinds. 4 v. New York 1963.
Vermeersch-Creusen	A. Vermeersch and J. Creusen, *Epitome iuris canonici.* 3 v. Rome. v. 2, 7th ed. 1954; v. 3, 7th ed. 1956; v. 1, 8th ed. 1962.
VC	*Vigiliae christianae.* Amsterdam 1947–
VieI	*La Vie intellectuelle.* Paris 1928–39. Superseded by *La Vie intellectuelle et la revue des jeunes.* 1939–
VieIRJ	*La Vie intellectuelle et la revue des jeunes.* Paris 1939–56. Superseded *Revue des jeunes* and *La Vie intellectuelle.* 1928–39.
VieS	*La Vie spirituelle.* Paris 1919– (title varies).
Vorgrimler	H. Vorgrimler, ed. *Commentary and Documents of Vatican II.* 5 v. tr. L. Adolphus and K. Smyth. New York 1968.
VT	*Vetus Testamentum.* Leiden 1951–
Wadding Ann	L. Wadding, *Annales Ordinis Minorum.* 86 v. Lyons 1625–54. 2d ed. and continuation by J. M. Fonseca et al. 25 v. Rome 1731–1886. 3d ed. and continuation by A. Chiappini. Quaracchi/Florence 1931–
Wadding S	L. Wadding, *Scriptores Ordinis Minorum.* Rome 1650; 3d ed. 1906.
Wattenbach-Holtzmann	W. Wattenbach, *Deutschlands Geschichtsquellen im Mittelalter. Deutsche Kaiserzeit,* ed. R. Holtzmann. 3d ed. v. 1–4 Tübingen 1948 (repr. of 2d ed. 1938–43).
Wattenbach-Levison	W. Wattenbach, *Deutschlands Geschichtsquellen im Mittelalter. Vorzeit und Karolinger.* Heft 1–4, ed. W. Levison and H. Löwe. Weimar 1952–63.
WCH	*World Christian Handbook, 1968,* ed. H. W. Coxill and K. Grubb. Nashville 1967.
Weissenbäck	A. F. Weissenbäck, *Sacra Musica: Lexikon der katholischen Kirchenmusik.* Klosterneuburg 1937.

Wellesz	E. Wellesz, *A History of Byzantine Music and Hymnography.* 2d ed. Oxford 1961.
Wernz-Vidal	F. X. Wernz and P. Vidal, *Ius canonicum.* 7 v. in 8. Rome. v. 1, 2d ed. 1952; v. 2, 3d ed. 1943; v. 3, 1933; v. 4.1, 1934; v. 4.2, 2d ed. 1936; v. 5, 3d ed. 1946; v. 6, 2d ed. 1949; v. 7, 2d ed. 1951.
Wikenhauser NTI	A. Wikenhauser, *New Testament Introduction,* tr. J. Cunningham. New York 1958.
Willis	J. R. Willis, ed., *The Teachings of the Church Fathers.* New York 1966.
WoordBoek Oudheid	*Woordenboek der Oudheid,* ed. G. Bartelink et al. Roermond-Maaseik 1965.
Worship	*Worship.* Collegeville, Minn. 1951– Supersedes OrFrat 1926–51.
Woywod-Smith	S. Woywod, *A Practical Commentary on the Code of Canon Law,* rev. and enl. C. Smith. New York 1963.
YBACC	*Yearbook of American and Canadian Churches.* New York 1932–
YBLS	*Yearbook of Liturgical Studies,* ed. J. H. Miller. Notre Dame, Ind. 1960–
Young CT	P. M. Young, *The Choral Tradition.* New York 1962.
ZAM	*Zeitschrift für Aszese und Mystik.* Würzburg 1926–46. Superseded by *Geist und Leben* 1947–
ZATW	*Zeitschrift für die alttestamentliche Wissenschaft.* Giessen-Berlin 1881–
Zimmermann	A. M. Zimmermann, *Kalendarium Benedictinum: Die Heiligen und Seligen des Benediktinerordens und seiner Zweige.* 4 v. Metten 1933–38.
ZKG	*Zeitschrift für Kirchengeschichte.* Stuttgart 1876–
ZKT	*Zeitschrift für katholische Theologie.* Vienna 1877–
ZMR	*Zeitschrift für Missionswissenschaft und Religionswissenschaft.* Münster 1911– (title varied: *Zeitschrift für Missionswissenschaft* 1911–27, 1935–37; *Missionswissenschaft und Religionswissenschaft* 1938–41, 1947–49).
ZNTW	*Zeitschrift für die neutestamentliche Wissenschaft und die Kunde älteren Kirche.* Giessen-Berlin 1900–

Vatican Council II Documents

Vat II SacLit	Constitution on the Sacred Liturgy (*Sacrosanctum Concilium*)	Vat II EastCath	Decree on Eastern Catholic Churches (*Orientalium ecclesiarum*)
Vat II ChrEduc	Declaration on Christian Education (*Gravissimum educationis*)	Vat II Ecum	Decree on Ecumenism (*Unitatis redintegratio*)
Vat II NonChrRel	Declaration on the Relationship of the Church to Non-Christian Religions (*Nostra aetate*)	Vat II SocComm	Decree on the Instruments of Social Communication (*Inter mirifica*)
Vat II RelFreed	Declaration on Religious Freedom (*Dignitatis humanae*)	Vat II MinLifePriests	Decree on the Ministry and Life of Priests (*Presbyterorum ordinis*)
Vat II ApostLaity	Decree on the Apostolate of the Laity (*Apostolicam actuositatem*)	Vat II PriestForm	Decree on Priestly Formation (*Optatam totius*)
Vat II RenRelLife	Decree on the Appropriate Renewal of the Religious Life (*Perfectae caritatis*)	Vat II DivRev	Dogmatic Constitution on Divine Revelation (*Dei Verbum*)
Vat II BpPastOff	Decree on the Bishops' Pastoral Office in the Church (*Christus Dominus*)	Vat II ConstChurch	Dogmatic Constitution on the Church (*Lumen gentium*)
Vat II MissAct	Decree on the Church's Missionary Activity (*Ad gentes*)	Vat II ChurchMod-World	Pastoral Constitution on the Church in the Modern World (*Gaudium et spes*)

Example: Vat II ConstChurch 22 = Vatican II, Dogmatic Constitution on the Church, #22

Books of the Bible

Acts	Acts of the Apostles	1 Kg	1 Kings (formerly 3 Kings in Vulg)
Am	Amos	2 Kg	2 Kings (formerly 4 Kings in Vulg)
Bar	Baruch	Lam	Lamentations
1 Chr	1 Chronicles [1 and 2 Paralipomenon in LXX (Septuagint) and Vulgate]	Lev	Leviticus
		Lk	Luke
2 Chr	2 Chronicles	Mal	Malachi
Col	Colossians	1 Macc	1 Maccabees
1 Cor	1 Corinthians	2 Macc	2 Maccabees
2 Cor	2 Corinthians	Mic	Micah
Dan	Daniel	Mk	Mark
Dt	Deuteronomy	Mt	Matthew
Ec	Ecclesiastes	Nah	Nahum
Eph	Ephesians	Neh	Nehemiah (2 Esdras in LXX and Vulg)
Est	Esther	Num	Numbers
Ex	Exodus	Ob	Obadiah
Ezek	Ezekiel	1 Pet	1 Peter
Ezra	Ezra (Esdras B in LXX; 1 Esdras in Vulg)	2 Pet	2 Peter
		Phil	Philippians
Gal	Galatians	Philem	Philemon
Gen	Genesis	Pr	Proverbs
Hab	Habakkuk	Ps	Psalms
Hag	Haggai	Rev	Revelation
Heb	Hebrews	Rom	Romans
Hos	Hosea	Ru	Ruth
Is	Isaiah	1 Sam	1 Samuel (formerly 1 Kings in Vulg)
Jas	James	2 Sam	2 Samuel (formerly 2 Kings in Vulg)
Jdt	Judith	Sir	Sirach (Ecclesiasticus in LXX and Vulg)
Jer	Jeremiah		
Jg	Judges	S of S	Song of Solomon
Jl	Joel	Tob	Tobit
Jn	John	1 Th	1 Thessalonians
1 Jn	1 John	2 Th	2 Thessalonians
2 Jn	2 John	1 Tim	1 Timothy
3 Jn	3 John	2 Tim	2 Timothy
Job	Job	Tit	Titus
Jon	Jonah	Wis	Wisdom
Jos	Joshua	Zech	Zechariah
Jude	Jude	Zeph	Zephaniah

Biblical Versions and Texts

Apoc	Apocrypha	LXX	Septuagint Version
ARV	American Standard Revised Version	MT	Masoretic Text
ARVm	American Standard Revised Version, margin	NAB	New American Bible
AT	American Translation (Smith-Goodspeed)	NEB	New English Bible
		NT	New Testament
AV	Authorized Version (King James Bible)	OT	Old Testament
CCD	Confraternity of Christian Doctrine Version	RSV	Revised Standard Version
		RV	Revised Version
DV	Douay-Challoner Version	RVm	Revised Version, margin
ERV	English Revised Version	Syr	Syriac
ERVm	English Revised Version, margin	Vulg	Vulgate
EV	English Version (s) of the Bible	WNT	Westminster New Testament
JB	Jerusalem Bible	WOT	Westminster Old Testament

Dead Sea Scrolls

1QS	Manual of Discipline	4Q T. Levi	The Testament of Levi from Cave IV
1QSa, 1QSb	Adjuncts to the Manual of Discipline	4Q Flor	The further testimonia
pap4QSe	Papyrus exemplar of the Manual of Discipline from Cave IV	4QExa	An Exodus manuscript from Cave IV
		4QDeut. 32	32d chapter of Deuteronomy
1QH	Hodayoth, or Thanksgiving Psalms	4QExa	Exodus manuscript from Cave IV
1QM	The War Scroll	4QSama	Manuscript of 1 and 2 Samuel from Cave IV
1QIsa	The Isaiah Scroll from Cave I		
1QIsb	The incomplete Isaiah Scroll from Cave I	4QSamb	Manuscript of 1 and 2 Samuel from Cave IV
		CD	The Damascus Document from Cave VI
1QpHab.	The Habukkuk Commentary	4Q Prayer of Nabonidus	The Daniel Document
1Q Apoc.	The Genesis Apocryphon		
4QpNah.	The commentary on Nahum	Jubilees (Q)	Jubilees (Qumran text)
4Q Testimonia	The testimonia from Cave IV	Enoch (Q)	Enoch (Qumran text)

N.B. For the citation of Qumran material not herein listed, see the data on abbreviations in the article by J. Fitzmyer, *New Catholic Encyclopedia*, v. 4: 678–680.

Miscellaneous Abbreviations

abbr.	abbreviated; abbreviations
abp.	archbishop (not invariably used)
abr.	abridged
acc.	according
A.D.	*Anno Domini*
adap.	adaptation; adapted by
Afr.	Africa; African
al.	alias; aliases
Ala.	Alabama
A.M.	*Artium magister,* Master of Arts; usually M.A.
Am.	America, American
anon.	anonymous (in citations)
Ap	Apocalypse or Rev (Revelation)
Apoc.	Apocrypha
app.	appendix, appendixes
Arab.	Arabic (in giving Arab. form of a word)
Aram.	Aramaic (in giving Aram. form of a word)
Arg.	Argentine; Argentina
Ariz.	Arizona
Ark.	Arkansas
art.; arts.	article; articles
ARV	American Standard Revised Version
ARVm	American Standard Revised Version, margin
AS	Anglo-Saxon
Asia M.	Asia Minor
AT	American translation
A.U.C.	*ab urbe condita*
augm.	augmented, augmented by
Aus.	Austria; Austrian
Austl.	Australia; Australian
auth.	author (in citations)
AV	Authorized Version (King James)
b.	born (only in connection with life dates)
B.A.	Bachelor of Arts
Babyl.	Babylonia; Babylonian
B.C.	Before Christ
BCP	*Book of Common Prayer*
B.D.	Bachelor of Divinity
Belg.	Belgium; Belgian
betw.	between
bibliog.	bibliography; bibliographer; bibliographical
biog.	biography; biographer; biographical (in citations)
bk., bks.	book; books
Bl.	Blessed
Bol.	Bolivia
bp., bps.	bishop; bishops (not invariably used)
Braz.	Brazil; Brazilian
B.S.	Bachelor of Science
Bulg.	Bulgaria; Bulgarian
BVM	Blessed Virgin Mary (not invariably used)
Byz.	Byzantine; Byzantium
c.	*circa; circum,* about (e.g., *c.*750.)
c.; cc.	canon; canons (in canon law citations only)
Calif.	California
can.	canon (in other than canon law citations).
card.	cardinal (only with a name)
Carib.	Caribbean
CCD	Confraternity of Christian Doctrine Version
cent.	century; centuries
cf.	confer; compare
ch.	chapter; chapters
Chin.	Chinese (only in giving Chin. form of a word)
chron.	chronology; chronological (used sparingly)
cod.	codex
C of E	Church of England
col., cols.	column; columns
Colo.	Colorado
Colom.	Colombia; Colombian
comment.	commentary (used sparingly)
comp., comps.	compiler; compilers; compiled; composer (in citations)
Conn.	Connecticut
const.	*constitutio;* constitution (in citations)
crit.	critical (edition)
Czecho.	Czechoslovakia
C.Z.	Canal Zone
d.	died (only with death date)
D.C.	District of Columbia
D.D.	Doctor of Divinity
Del.	Delaware
Den.	Denmark
dept.	department (sparingly)
dict.	dictionary (in citations)
diss.	*dissertatio,* dissertation (in citations)
DV	Douay-Challoner Version
E	East; eastern
eccl.	ecclesiastical; ecclesiastic (rarely used)

ed., eds.	editor; editors; edition; editions; editorial, edited by (in citations)
e.g.,	*exempli gratia,* for example
encyc.	encyclopedia (in citations)
encycl.	encyclical (in citations)
Eng.	England; English (in giving Eng. form of a word)
enl.	enlarged (as in ''enl. ed.''); enlarged by (in citations)
ep., epp.	*epistola; epistolae,* letter; letters (in citations)
ERV	English Revised Version
ERVm	English Revised Version, margin
esp.	especially
est.	estimated (in population figures)
et al.	*et alii,* and others
etc.	*et cetera,* and so forth
Eur.	Europe; European
EV	English Version(s) of the Bible
fac.	facsimile (in citations)
fasc.	fascicle
ff.	following (pages)
fig., figs.	figure; figures (in citations)
Fin.	Finland; Finnish
fl.	*floruit,* flourished; lived
Fla.	Florida
Flem.	Flemish (in giving Flem. form of a word)
fn.	footnote; footnotes
fol.	folio (in citations)
Fr.	France; French; Father (title)
front.	frontispiece (in citations)
Ga.	Georgia
Ger.	Germany; German (in giving Ger. form of a word)
Gr.	Greece, Greek (in giving Gr. form of a word)
Guat.	Guatemala
H.	*Heft,* number of a periodical
Heb.	Hebrew (in giving Heb. form of a word)
hist.	history; historian; historical (in citations)
Hon.	Honorable (as title only)
Hung.	Hungary; Hungarian (in giving Hung. form of a word)
ibid.	*ibidem,* in the same place
Ice.	Iceland; Icelandic (in giving Ice. form of a word)
id. (or *idem*)	*idem,* the same (in citations)
i.e.	*id est,* that is
Ill.	Illinois
illus.	illustration (in citations); illustrated
Ind.	Indiana
inst.	institute, institution (sparingly)
introd.	introduction (in citations)
Ire.	Ireland
isl., isls.	island; islands
Isr.	Israel
Ital.	Italy; Italian (in giving Ital. form of a word)
Jap.	Japanese (in giving Jap. form of a word)
JB	Jerusalem Bible
J.C.D.	*Juris Canonici Doctor,* Doctor of Canon Law
Jr.	junior
J.U.D.	*Juris Utriusque Doctor,* Doctor of Canon and Civil Law
Kans.	Kansas
Ky.	Kentucky
l.	line; lines (in citations)
La.	Louisiana
Lat.	Latin (in giving Lat. form of a word)
leg.	legend; legendary (in citations)
lib.	*liber,* book (in citations)
LL	Late Latin
loc. cit.	*loco citato,* in the place cited
LXX	Septuagint Version
m.	married (in dates only)
M.A.	Master of Arts
Mass.	Massachusetts
mag.	magazine (in citations)
Md.	Maryland
M.D.	Doctor of Medicine
ME	Middle English
M.E.Ch.	Methodist Episcopal Church
med.	medieval
Mex.	Mexico; Mexican
MHG	Middle High German
Mich.	Michigan
Minn.	Minnesota
Miss.	Mississippi
Mme.	Madame
Mo.	Missouri
mod.	modern (in citations)
Mont.	Montana
Msgr.	Monsignor
MS; MSS	manuscript; manuscripts
MT	Masoretic Text of the Bible
mt., mts.	mount, mountains
myth.	mythology; mythological (in citations)
N	North; northern
n.; nn.	note; notes
N.A.	North America (sparingly)
natl.	national (in citations)
N.C.	North Carolina
NCWC	National Catholic Welfare Conference

N.D.	North Dakota
n.d.	no date of publication (in citations)
NE	northeast
NEB	New English Bible
Neb.	Nebraska
Neth.	Netherlands
Nev.	Nevada
newsp.	newspaper (in citations)
N.H.	New Hampshire
N.J.	New Jersey
N. Mex.	New Mexico
No.	*numero,* number (in citations)
Nor.	Norway; Norwegian
nr.	near (in locating a place)
NS	New Series; used for periodicals
NT	New Testament
NW	northwest
N.Y.	New York
N.Z.	New Zealand
OE	Old English
OF	Old French
OHG	Old High German
Okla.	Oklahoma
Ont.	Ontario
o.p.	out of print (in citations)
op. cit.	*opere citato,* in the work cited
Ore.	Oregon
orig.	original; originally (in citations)
OT	Old Testament
p.; pp.	page; pages
Pa.	Pennsylvania
pa.	paper; paperback (in citations)
Pal.	Palestine
pam.	pamphlet (in citations)
Pan.	Panama
par.; pars.	paragraph; paragraphs (in citations)
passim	throughout the work; here and there
period.	periodical (in citations)
Ph.D.	Doctor of Philosophy
philol.	philology; philological (in citations)
philos.	philosophy; philosophical (in citations)
pl.	plural
Pol.	Poland; Polish (in giving Pol. form of a word)
pop.	population
Port.	Portugal; Portuguese (in giving Port. form of a word
P.R.	Puerto Rico
pref.	preface (in citations)
proc.	proceedings (in citations)
prof.	professor; professorial
Prot.	Protestant (in citations)
prov.	province; provincial
pseud.	pseudonym (in citations)
psych.	psychology; psychologist; psychological (in citations)
pt., pts.	part; parts (in citations)
pub.	publication; publishing; publisher; published (in citations)
q.v.	*quod vide,* which see
r.	ruled
RC	Roman Catholic
ref.	reference
rel.	religion (in citations)
repr.	reprint; reprinted (in citations)
rev.	revision; revised; revised by (in citations)
Rev.	Reverend
R.I.	Rhode Island
RSV	Revised Standard Version
Rt. Rev.	Right Reverend
Rom.	Romania; Romanian (in giving Rom. form of word)
Russ.	Russian (in citations)
RV	Revised Version
RVm	Revised Version, margin
S	South; southern
S.	San, São
S.A.	South America (in locating places only)
S.Afr.	South Africa
S.C.	South Carolina
Scand.	Scandinavian (in giving Scand. form of word)
Scot.	Scotland; Scottish; Scotch
S.D.	South Dakota
SE	southeast
sec.	section; sections (in citations)
ser.	series (in citations)
sic	thus; so
sing.	singular
Sl.	Slavic (in giving Sl. form of word)
sociol.	sociology; sociologist; sociological (in citations)
Sp.	Spain; Spanish (in giving Sp. form of word)
Sr.	Sister (title); senior
SS.	Saints; Sanctissimus, Santissimo (most holy)
S.S.L.	Licentiate in Sacred Scripture
St.	Saint
Sta.	Santa
S.T.B.	Bachelor of Sacred Theology
S.T.D.	Doctor of Sacred Theology
Ste.	Sainte
S.T.L.	Licentiate in Sacred Theology
S.T.M.	Master of Sacred Theology

s.v.	*sub. verbo; sub voce,* under the word or heading (in citations)
SW	southwest
Swed.	Sweden; Swedish (in giving Swed. form of word)
syn.	synonym; synonymous (in giving a synonymous form)
Syr	Syriac Versions of the Bible
Syr.	Syria; Syrian (in giving Syr. form of word)
Tenn.	Tennessee
Tex.	Texas
theol.	theology; theologian; theological (in citations)
tom.	*tomus;* volume (in citations)
tr.	translation; translator; translated by (in citations)
U.K.	United Kingdom
univ.	university, universities
U.S.	United States
U.S.C.C.	United States Catholic Conference
U.S.S.R.	Union of Soviet Socialist Republics
v.	volume; volumes
v	verse; verses
Va.	Virginia
Ven.	Venerable
V.I.	Virgin Islands
viz	*videlicet,* namely
vs.	versus, against; but *v.* for ''versus'' in legal citations
Vt.	Vermont
Vulg	Vulgate
W	West; western
Wash.	Washington
Wis.	Wisconsin
wks.	works (in citations)
WNT	Westminster New Testament
WOT	Westminster Old Testament
W. Va.	West Virginia
Wyo.	Wyoming
Yugo.	Yugoslavia

Editorial Preface

Paul Kevin Meagher, OP, conceived the plan and set the editorial tone for the *Encyclopedic Dictionary of Religion* out of his comprehensive learning and dedication to dispassionate communication in the field of religious studies. The plan has resulted in a coverage that is as extensive as the vast subject of religion requires; that is compact without being cryptic; and that provides for the individual reader's desk or bookshelf a ready and sound reference work. The tone that Fr. Meagher intended—and by his article-by-article editorial guidance up to the time of his death, December 31, 1976—achieved, is one of reportorial fidelity devoid of rhetoric or doctrinaire judgments. Developed under Roman Catholic auspices and inspiration, the *Encyclopedic Dictionary of Religion* bears the marks of a broad ecumenicity and respect for the human search for truth that were among the noble ideals inspiring and inspired by Vatican Council II. The work's choice and proportion of topics, the choice as well of scholar-contributors to deal with them, aimed at the basic objective of providing faithful and accurate information. Even concept or thematic entries are as far as is humanly possible expository statements of the author's unbiased perceptions, not polemical or exhortatory tracts. The editorial tone of the work reflects a desire to serve the reader's need for information and a convinced respect for the reader's right and power of interpretation in the use of that information. The volumes contain much that is of perennial interest from past centuries; the time-frame of development for the volumes also coincides with a period of major religious events and trends. Vatican II and its implementation are one major phenomenon that symbolizes the cross-denominational and cross-cultural awareness of the present age. The *Encyclopedic Dictionary of Religion* will admirably serve the need for knowledge that such awareness generates.

The system of cross-references in the work serves economy and conciseness by indicating supplementary material on specific points. The cross-references also enable the reader to pursue the correlations underlying the planning of areas and choice of entries. Cross-references are either internal to an entry or external. The internal are indicated either by an asterisk (*) attached to a term or name or by a parenthetical "see" reference to a title printed in small capitals, e.g., (see FAITH, ACT OF). The external cross reference is printed after the text (and bibliography) of an entry with an asterisked term in small capitals, e.g., *FLORENCE, COUNCIL OF.

As the closest associate of Fr. Meagher since the inception of this work, I know well, and share, his appreciation for those who have aided in the planning and development of these volumes: the members of Corpus Instrumentorum Inc. and adjunct editors during both periods of the work's development, and the contributors. Since 1973 both Editors in Chief have been especially indebted to the high competence and immense labors of Jeanne Helen Brady, Managing Editor.

Feast of St. Thomas Aquinas
January 28, 1979

THOMAS C. O'BRIEN

A

A CAPPELLA (Ital., in the manner of the [Sistine] chapel), choral music unaccompanied by instruments. The term has also been applied, by somewhat inaccurate extension, to all polyphonic choral music of the 15th and 16th centuries, which era has even been termed the "*a cappella* period." In common performance practice instruments accompanied the voices or even replaced them in one or more *parts. Many churches employed instrumentalists, and the performances at St. Mark's in Venice were esp. lavish (see VENETIAN SCHOOL). The noteworthy exception was the Sistine Chapel, where the choir gallery was too small to accommodate instrumentalists. Composers of the *Roman School, esp. after Palestrina, cultivated the *a cappella* style, and by the 19th cent. it was thought to be the only correct way to perform Renaissance polyphony. BIBLIOGRAPHY: P. A. Scholes, *Oxford Companion to Music* (10th ed., 1970) 154; Apel HDMus (1969) 3.

[J. J. WALSH]

A JURE (Lat., from the law), the designation of a specific ecclesiastical penalty or censure fixed by the law itself. The term is used in CIC c. 2217 in contrast to *ab homine* penalties which are inflicted by a judge. An *a jure* penalty may be either *latae sententiae* or *ferendae sententiae*. BIBLIOGRAPHY: Woywod-Smith 533.

[T. M. MCFADDEN]

AACHEN (Aix-la-Chapelle), historic city in west central Germany, scene of many treaties, partly destroyed in World War II (1944), site of Early Christian graves and chapel (5th cent.) and center of the Carolingian Renaissance. Charmagne here built a palace and chapel (*c*.786) in which 30 German kings were subsequently crowned (936–1531). From Pepin's time most important relics were objects of pilgrimage. Cathedral treasures include the throne of Charlemagne, Carolingian and Ottonian gospels, cross of Lothair, and bronze corona chandelier of Frederick I Barbarossa. Aachen has been the site of the origin of many spiritual institutions up to the 20th century. BIBLIOGRAPHY:

W. Henry, DACL 1.1:1039–42; W. Schöne, "Die künstlerische und liturgische Gestalt der Pfalzkapelle Karls des Grossen in Aachen," *Zeitschrift für Kunstwissenschaft* 15 (1961) 97–148; J. Ramackers, NCE 1:1–2.

[M. J. DALY]

AACHEN, PALATINE CHAPEL OF, a centralized building consisting of an ambulatory of 16 bays enclosing an octagonal domed space, built by Odo of Metz *c*.792, as part of Charlemagne's palace complex and probably dedicated July 17, 800. San Vitale, Ravenna, almost certainly visited by Charlemagne, served as a model, but at Aachen the masonry is heavier and the spatial concept less sophisticated. Gothic side chapels with hall choir were completed in 1414. BIBLIOGRAPHY: K. J. Conant, *Carolingian and Romanesque Architecture 800–1200* (1939).

[S. D. MURRAY]

AALTO, ALVAR (1898–1976), great architect of Northern Europe. His buildings of international significance characterized by a dynamic flow in undulating walls and ceilings merge with their sites through a dramatic use of wood with brick and concrete. His plans for towns, buildings, and furniture are distinguished by a unique sensitivity to human scale. Notable are his Finnish Pavilion, N.Y. World's Fair (1939), dormitory at M.I.T. (1947), and town hall, Säynätsalo, Finland (1953). BIBLIOGRAPHY: A. Aalto, *Alvar Aalto* (ed. K. Fleig, 2d ed., 1965); F. Gutheim, *Alvar Aalto* (1960).

[M. J. DALY]

AARON, son of Amran and Jochebed (Ex 6.18, 20), brother of Moses and Miriam. In the OT Aaron is described as Moses' associate, whether as his spokesman (Ex 4.14; 7.1), aide (Ex 7.19; 8.1, 12; 18.12), replacement (Ex 24.14), or companion (Ex 7.10, 22; 8.8, 19, 21; 19.24). He was also high priest (Ex 28.1–2; Lev 8.1–9, 24). His judgments in the two incidents in which he figures, the making of the golden calf (Ex 32.1–6) and Moses' marriage to a Cushite woman

1

(12.1–10) were not to his credit, although the OT is never critical of his conduct. According to OT tradition, he and his family established the Israelite priesthood, always held by the clan of Aaron (2 Chr 26.18; 29.21; 31.19; 35.14; Neh 10.39). The Aaronic priesthood is upheld in Num 16.1–18 to be the divinely established priesthood in Israel. Aaron died on Mount Hor, the location of which is uncertain (Num 20.22–29), before the Israelites entered Canaan. Before his death he was stripped of his high-priestly robes, which were placed on his son, Eleazar, thus inaugurating the transfer, within the family of Aaron, of the Israelite priesthood. Heb 7.11 noted the inferiority of the Aaronic priesthood by comparison to the priesthood of Christ. BIBLIOGRAPHY: A. S. Kapelrud, EB (1971) 1:4–5; T. M. Mauch, InterDB 1:1.

AB AEGYPTIIS, an apostolic letter of Gregory IX (July 7, 1228) to the theologians of Paris, some of whom were allegedly giving novel interpretations to traditional theological teachings, attempting to reduce them to merely philosophical truths naturally knowable by human reason, thus rendering faith useless and devoid of meaning. The Pope calls such a procedure rash and impious and insists that human reason must be subordinate to divine faith as is indicated by such scriptural injunctions as 2 Cor 10.4; Gal 4.9; Heb 13.9; and 1 Tim 6.20. BIBLIOGRAPHY: D 824.

[J. H. ROHLING]

AB HOMINE (Lat., from a man), a designation applied to those ecclesiastical censures or penalties that are inflicted either by a special precept or by a condemnatory juridical sentence. The term is used in CIC c. 2217 in contrast to *a jure* penalties which are fixed by the law itself. BIBLIOGRAPHY: Woywod-Smith 533.

[T. M. MCFADDEN]

ABAD Y SÁNCHEZ, DIEGO JOSÉ (1727–79), Mexican Jesuit educator, writer, humanist. Ordained in 1751, A. taught in Jesuit schools in Mexico until the Jesuits were expelled from the Spanish Empire (1767). He then went to Ferrara, Italy, where he devoted himself to writing verse (his *De Deo Deoque homine heroica* was much admired by contemporaries) and treatises in his teaching fields. BIBLIOGRAPHY: N. F. Martin, NCE 1:3–4.

[H. JACK]

ABADDON, Hebrew word meaning "destruction," "perdition," found in the OT only in the Wisdom literature (Pr 15.11; Job 26.6; 28.22; 31.12; Ps 88.12). Here it is used simply as a synonym for *Sheol, the abode of the dead. In rabbinic literature the term came to mean a place of punishment for the wicked, conceived to be located within the earth. In this sense, Abaddon appears in Rev 9.11 under the figure of an angel. The author of Rev correctly translates the term into Greek to mean "destroyer," the leader of God's avenging angels who punish the wicked on the earth. BIBLIOGRAPHY: T. H. Gaster, InterDB 1:3; A. Romeo, EncCatt 1:7–8.

ABANDONMENT, SPIRITUAL, an ascetico-mystical term with several not entirely related meanings. (1) In an active sense, it signifies the yielding of self to God's will, not so much as this is expressed in commandment (for abandonment goes beyond simple obedience) but rather as it is discerned in the unfolding of events manifesting God's *will of good pleasure. These events abandonment accepts not only with passive *resignation but with positive, even joyful acquiescence. Spiritual writers discern different degrees of acceptance, from patient but reluctant submission, to ardent conformity; from a single act, "God's will be done," to a habitual state. See J. P. de Caussade, *Abandonment to Divine Providence* (tr. A. Thorold, 1959); M. Villier, DSAM 1:2–25. (2) In a passive sense, abandonment signifies the dereliction of man by God. This may be real, as when God leaves the sinner in punishment for his sin; or it may be only apparent, as in the experience of passive *purification. Again this admits of degrees from the feeling that God is far away or hiding to the experience of total dereliction. See K. Kavanaugh, NCE 1:5; St. John of the Cross, *The Dark Night*. (3) In an objectionable sense, abandonment means the complete repudiation of all self-interest, including hope of salvation, such as was advocated by *quietism. See P. Pourrat, DSAM 1:25–49. BIBLIOGRAPHY: E. Underhill, *Mysticism* (1970) 380–412; *Index to the Writings of St. Francis de Sales* (comp. M. L. Lynn and M. G. Glynn; 1968).

[U. VOLL]

ABBA, a transliteration of *abbā* from Aramaic into Greek; emphatic form of *ab,* meaning "father." *Abbā* was used at the time of Jesus in the family circle as the familiar title for one's father. In the Gospels it appears explicitly only in Mk 14.36, where it is used by Jesus to address God as his father. Some scholars think that the Greek put on the lips of Jesus by the evangelists as the name he used to speak of his relationship to God (e.g., Mt 7.21; 11.25; Lk 2.49; Jn 2.16) reflects the *abbā* he actually used. *Abbā* appears elsewhere in the NT Rom 8.15 and Gal 4.6 as the name of God upon which Christians have a special claim in virtue of their solidarity with Jesus. It is also used as a title of honor in addressing priests in the Ethiopian Church. BIBLIOGRAPHY: J. L. McKenzie, *Dictionary of the Bible* (1965) 1; A. Wikgren, InterDB 1:3.

ABBA SALAMA (Aram., father of peace), a title originally accorded to St. Frumentius (d. *c*.383), apostle of Christianity in Ethiopia. It is still used as one of the titles of the head of the Ethiopian Church, the metropolitan of Axum. BIBLIOGRAPHY: EB (1971) 9:974. *ABUNA; *ETHIOPIAN CHURCH.

[A. J. JACOPIN]

ABBADIE, JACQUES (Abadie; *c*.1654–1727), French *Reformed apologist. A. was pastor of the Huguenot refugees in Berlin, 1680–88, then of the Savoy Church in London, 1690–99; he was dean of Killaloe, Ireland, 1699–1726. His most important apologetic treatise, *Traité de la vérité de la religion chrétienne* (3v., 1684–89; Eng. tr.,

2v., 1694), was a defense of Christian teaching based on principles of reason and was popular in France. Other apologetic works were written to support Reformed against RC teaching, but in a temperate tone. He also wrote a moral treatise, *L'Art de se connaître soi-même* (1682; Eng. tr. and abridgment, 1694). BIBLIOGRAPHY: DHGE 1:19–22; DNB 1:1–3.

[T. C. O'BRIEN]

ABBASIDS, the name of the second great dynasty of the Mohammedan empire (750–1258), derived from the name of Mohammed's uncle, al-Abbas (566–652), from whom the Abbasid caliphs claimed their descent. In 747 a rebellion broke out among the Arabs and Persians in Khurasan against the Omayyad dynasty. The Khurasanian armies defeated the Omayyad caliph Mirwan II in 750 and named Abu'l-Abbas, great-grandson of al-Abbas, caliph. The Abbasids established a new capital at Baghdad. Owing to the sense of community that already existed between the Arabs and Persians in Iraq and Khurasan, the Abbasids were enabled to develop a common Muslim civilization that gradually spread over their whole empire. The Arab language and religion became accepted throughout the empire, while Persian traditions were retained at the court and in administration. The rule of the Abbasids fostered commerce and liberal arts and strengthened the Muslim faith as the basis of culture and administration. The high points were reached in the reigns of Harun al-Rashid (786–809) and al-Ma'mun (813–833), when the Abbasid empire attained its apex of power, prosperity, and cultural development. Rivalries and jealousies at court and a series of revolts throughout the empire gradually weakened Abbasid rule, until the caliph Radi (934–941) and his successors were compelled to place more and more political power in their armies. The Abbasid dynasty endured until the capture of Baghdad by the Mongols in 1258. BIBLIOGRAPHY: B. Lewis, *Arabs in History* (1950); EncIslam² 1:15–23; M. Fakhry, *History of Islamic Philosophy* (1970) 287–288.

[C. P. CEROKE]

ABBATINI, ANTONIO MARIA (1595–1680), baroque theorist and composer. A student of Nanino, he expanded the *polychoral style of his church music which consisted of several volumes of Masses, motets, psalms, *sacre canzoni* and antiphons. He held appointments at various Roman churches, including St. John Lateran and St. Mary Major. His 14 discourses on music theory are preserved in a Bolognese edition. BIBLIOGRAPHY: K. G. Fellerer, MGG 1:15–16; BukMusB.

[P. MURPHY]

ABBÉ, derived from the same root as abbot, French title for a member of the secular clergy and, by extension, for anyone entitled to wear clerical dress even though he may not yet have received major orders. It is applied esp. to clerics unassigned to any specific ecclesiastical office. Thus "M. le curé," from the point of view of ecclesiastical rank, is more

honorific than "M. l'abbé." BIBLIOGRAPHY: CModH² (1968) 3:51.

ABBELEN, PETER (1843–1917), priest controversialist. An emigrant from Germany, A. attended St. Francis Seminary, Milwaukee, Wis., and was ordained there (1868). During the controversy between German- and English-speaking Catholics, A. supported P. *Cahensly's program to protect the rights of Catholic immigrants to their native language and customs. In his *Memorial on the German Question . . .* , A. petitioned Rome (1886) for recognition of national churches and establishment of foreign-language parochial schools. The petition was unacceptable to the so-called liberal and Americanizing members of the U.S. hierarchy and increased the tensions that culminated in the end-of-the-century *Americanism controversy. The Holy See's belated response to the *Memorial* was generally regarded as unfavorable to Abbelen. BIBLIOGRAPHY: C. J. Barry, *Catholic Church and German Americans* (1953).

[M. CARTHY]

ABBESS, the female superior of a community of nuns in certain orders, notably those of the Benedictine tradition. The title is also applied to superiors of certain other orders, esp. to those of the Poor Clares (Second Order of St. Francis). The first known use of the term abbess dates back to an inscription of the year 514 at Rome. The abbess is elected by the choir sisters and is entitled to the ring and staff. Except in the Franciscans, she is elected for life. Only those 40 years old and 10 years professed are eligible for election. In the medieval period, abbesses often exercised quasi-episcopal powers and jurisdiction both civil and ecclesiastical. All such external powers have disappeared, but the abbess retains control of her abbey according to the constitution and rules of her order. BIBLIOGRAPHY: M. F. Laughlin, NCE 1:6–7; S. Cita-Malard, *Religious Orders of Women* (tr. G. J. Robinson, 1964) 33.

[R. B. ENO]

ABBEVILLE, CLAUDE D' (d. 1616), French Capuchin who worked on the missions in Maranhão (Brazil) in the years 1612–14. His most significant service to the cause of the missions, however, was his writing. He published letters on French conquests in Brazil (1612) and his *Histoire de la mission des Pères Capucins en l'îsle de Maragnan et terres circonvoisines* (1614). BIBLIOGRAPHY: M. de Pobladura, NCE 1:7.

ABBEY, EDWIN AUSTIN (1852–1911), American artist. Born in Philadelphia, Pa., A. studied at the Pennsylvania Academy of the Fine Arts and became one of the foremost illustrators of his time with Harper and Brothers, N.Y. He went to England where his drawings for writings of Herrick, Goldsmith, and Shakespeare, together with his water colors and pastels, established his reputation. He painted murals in the Boston Public Library and the official coronation portrait of Edward VII (1902). A. was elected to many societies; his work hangs in New York, Boston, and London, with a large collection at Yale University. BIBLIOGRAPHY: G. H. Hamilton, "Edwin Austin Abbey Show," *Carnegie Magazine,* v. 15, no. 3 (1941) 83–86.

[M. J. DALY]

ABBEY, the word used in certain religious orders (monks, canons regular, or nuns) to designate their major monastic communities that enjoy the highest degree of status and recognition. An abbey is usually autonomous and is governed by an abbot or abbess, assisted by a council of seniors, and a conventual chapter. It is distinguished from a *priory, a monastery governed by a prior or a prioress. The abbey may constitute an independent territorial jurisdiction *(abbatia nullius)* or simply enjoy exemption of its members from the jurisdiction of the local diocesan ordinary, or even be subject to him (esp. in the case of the nuns or in the East). The name also denotes the buildings in which a monastic community ordinarily resides. An abbey usually comprises several buildings (church, chapterhouse or meeting hall, refectory, scriptorium, dormitories or cells, infirmary, etc .) joined together by a covered walk (usually rectangular in form and called the cloisters) surrounding an enclosed garden. An abbey may also be distinguished from a *laura, a monastic colony comprised of many separate buildings and cells, and a charterhouse, which includes many individual cottages or hermitages connected to the common buildings by the same cloister walk. BIBLIOGRAPHY: J. M. Besse, DACL 1.1:25–39; G. Jacquemet, *Catholicisme* 1:7–14.

[M. B. PENNINGTON]

ABBO OF FLEURY, ST. (*c*.945–1004), Benedictine abbot, scholar, reformer, and writer. A. entered the Benedictines at Fleury, studied at Paris, Reims, and Orléans, and was ordained in England where, at the invitation of Oswald, abp. of York, he directed a school at Ramsey 982–988. He then returned to his own monastery and on the death of the abbot was elected to take his place. He worked to promote peace at a time when conflicts were numerous and violent, yet he took a strong stand against the encroachment of royal upon ecclesiastical, and of episcopal upon monastic, authority. His correspondence, a valuable source for the history of his period, indicates his interest and part in monastic reform in England and France. He died of a wound he received while trying to quell a tumultuous brawl between the French and Gascons at the abbey of La Réole, a monastery whose reform he had undertaken. Many of his writings have survived, most of them written in connection with the contemporary events and issues in which he was involved. Some of his spiritual writings may have been lost. His cult (he was honored as a martyr) can be traced back as far as 1031. BIBLIOGRAPHY: Butler 4:333–334; A. Tessarolo, BiblSanct 1:37–38; Zimmerman 3:299–301; J. Huijben, DSAM 1:61–63.

ABBO OF METZ, ST. (Goericus; d. 647), bp. of Metz. Abbo or Goericus succeeded St. Arnulf in the See of Metz in

629 and built St. Peter's in Metz. The information in the medieval life of A., the *Vita Goerici,* is untrustworthy. A letter of A. to St. Desiderius of Cahors is extant. He is named Abbo in the will of King Dagobert. BIBLIOGRAPHY: AS Sept. 6:48–55; Butler 3:597.

[J. M. O'DONNELL]

ABBOT, EZRA (1819–84), American biblical scholar, professor of NT textual criticism at the Harvard School of Divinity. He was the foremost American textual critic of the 19th cent.; exercised a major influence on the Revised Version of the Bible; contributed, without seeking acknowledgment, to the works of many biblical scholars. Part of the *Prolegomena* to the 8th ed. of Tischendorf's Greek NT, edited by the American C. R. Gregory in 1890, was A.'s work. He also wrote an able defense of the Johannine authorship of the Fourth Gospel and was responsible for the bibliographical excellence of Smith's *Bible Dictionary* (1867–70). BIBLIOGRAPHY: EB (1971) 1:11.

[T. C. O'BRIEN]

ABBOT, GEORGE (1562–1633), abp. of Canterbury After his academic career had led him to the vice-chancellorship of the Univ. of Oxford, A. won royal favor by his defense of hereditary monarchy (1606). His reputation was increased by his success in inducing Scotland to accept the idea of *episcopacy, which prepared the way for the union of the Scottish and English Churches. He was appointed bp. of Lichfield and Coventry (1609), was transferred later in the same year to London, and became abp. of Canterbury in 1611. From early life his convictions were markedly *Puritan and anti-Roman, and this put him in opposition to high churchmen generally (whose influence was growing while that of the Puritans was declining), and particularly to W. *Laud, whom he antagonized by an accusation of "popish" sympathies. He was among those chosen to prepare the Authorized Version of the Bible. BIBLIOGRAPHY: life by P. A. Welsby (1962); DNB (1885) 1:5–20.

ABBOT (Aram. *abba, father), the official title in the Western Church of the superior of a large monastery in orders of the Benedictine tradition and in certain orders of canons regular. In Egyptian monasticism the title *apa* was given to one who acted as a guide for other monks. According to the Rule of St. Benedict, the superior of monks should be the father and ruler of all in his monastery. He has charge of both the spiritual and temporal affairs of the monastery. In the Middle Ages the abbots of certain monasteries exercised important roles in the political and economic, as well as religious, life of their areas. The abbot is elected by the monks, usually for life, although a fixed period of years (6,8, or 12) is stipulated in some congregations. To be eligible, a monk must be at least 30 years old and 10 years professed. When the election has been confirmed by higher authority, the abbot must receive the abbatial blessing from a bishop. While usually not in episcopal orders, abbots are allowed to wear the garb of prelates and to celebrate *pontifical Mass. BIBLIOGRAPHY: P. Salmon, *L'Abbé dans la tradition monastique* (1692); P. Volk, NCE 1:8–10; *Heads of Religious Houses, England and Wales 940–1216* (ed. D. Knowles, 1972).

[R. B. ENO]

ABBOT, BLESSING OF. According to CIC c. 625, an *abbot must receive a solemn blessing within three months of his election. This blessing is a *sacramental and is normally conferred by the bishop of the diocese in which the abbey is found. Although the ceremony outwardly resembles episcopal consecration, it confers no grace of itself. The Congregation of Rites in 1970 issued a new blessing (AAS 63:710).

[R. B. ENO]

ABBOT, LAY, an *abbot who has not received holy orders. The title generally refers to an 8th–11th-cent. abuse, chiefly in the Frankish Empire, whereby a king or someone in authority assigned an abbey to a favored layman so that he might oversee its finances and share in its revenues. But since the first men to receive the title abbot in monastic tradition were holy solitaries, almost always laymen who acted as spiritual fathers for a group of disciples, lay abbot may also refer to them. The Congregation for Religious and Secular Institutes at present requires that all abbots be priests. BIBLIOGRAPHY: M. B. Pennington, "Monastic Autonomy," *Cistercian Studies* 3 (1968) 24–25. *ABBOT, SECULAR; *COMMENDATORY ABBOT.

[T. M. MCFADDEN]

ABBOT, SECULAR, a cleric who held the title and benefice of an extinct monastic foundation but who was not a member of the monastic order. After the suppression of the monastery, its benefices would be secularized, i.e., transferred to other churches and placed under the administration of a secular cleric. The privileges of the secular abbot in regard to dress, choir precedence, etc., vary. BIBLIOGRAPHY: CModH² 3:51. *ABBOT, LAY; *COMMENDATORY ABBOT.

[T. M. MCFADDEN]

ABBOT, TITULAR, an honorary title found in the Western Church (parallel to the title of Archimandrite in the Eastern Churches), usually given to a priest in recognition of some special service to a monastic order. It carries with it the right to receive the abbatial blessing from a bishop or someone else empowered to give it, to wear the garb of prelates including a jeweled cross and ring, and to celebrate pontifically in certain places and circumstances. Although in the past it was attached to certain offices, such as that of procurator general of a monastic order, today it is relatively rare. BIBLIOGRAPHY: P. Salmon, *L'Abbé dans la tradition monastique* (1962); P. Volk, NCE 1:8–9.

[M. B. PENNINGTON]

ABBOT GENERAL, the head of certain monastic orders and congregations (e.g., the Cistercian Orders, certain Ben-

edictine Congregations) and the superior general of the orders of canons regular (e.g., the Norbertines). The Code of Canon Law does not employ the title but speaks of superiors of monastic congregations (*Superior congregationis monasticae* CIC c. 501.3). While the abbot general of the *Cistercians of the Strict Observance is simply an *abbot president of a monastic congregation or federation, the abbot general of the Sacred Order of Cistercians appears more comparable to the *abbot primate of the Benedictine Confederation since he has under him a definitory of abbots president who head the 13 congregations which make up the order. BIBLIOGRAPHY: P. Salmon, *L'Abbé dans la tradition monastique* (1962); J. De Punet, DSAM 1.1:49–57.

[M. B. PENNINGTON]

ABBOT NULLIUS (DIOECESIS), an abbot with quasi-episcopal jurisdiction over his abbey and a certain area around it. Thus this area is not within any diocese (hence the title), and the abbot is directly responsible to the Holy See. Those abbots *nullius* who are entirely exempt have most of the rights and privileges, as well as the obligations, of bishops. In future no more abbots *nullius* will be appointed (*motu proprio, Cum ecclesia,* Oct. 23, 1976).

ABBOT PRESIDENT, a title sometimes given to the head of a monastic congregation, esp. among the *Benedictines and the *Cistercians of the Common Observance (Sacred Order of Cistercians). According to canon law, apart from some judiciary power as a court of appeal, he has only those powers that are given him by the constitutions of his respective congregation (CIC c. 501.3). These are usually powers of visitation and of temporary provision between chapters of the congregation. The office is usually temporary, lasting from 3 to 12 years according to the law of each congregation. In some congregations the office is conjoined with that of regular abbot of a particular monastery (e.g., Solesmes, Zirc, etc). and in these cases the tenure is usually for life. BIBLIOGRAPHY: P. Salmon, *L'Abbé dans la tradition monastique* (1962).

[M. B. PENNINGTON]

ABBOT PRIMATE, the supreme moderator of the Benedictine Confederation of Monastic Congregations. He is also regular abbot of St. Anselm's Abbey, Rome, and president of the Pontifical Academy of St. Anselm. The Benedictine Confederation and the office of abbot primate, established by Leo XIII (1893), received a complete new code of legislation from Pius XII (*Lex propria,* 1952). The abbot primate has only the powers that are given to him by the *Lex propria,* largely those of visitation and coordination (CIC c. 501.3). He is elected by the Congress of Abbots for a 10-year term. BIBLIOGRAPHY: A. Di Vincenzo, *Lex propria confederationis congregationum monasticarum Ordinis Sancti Benedicti: commentarium, historia, fontes* (1955); F. Cimetier, *Catholicisme* 1:20.

[M. B. PENNINGTON]

ABBOTT, LYMAN (1835–1922), Congregational preacher and editor. Before being ordained (1860), he had practiced law. He served as pastor in Terre Haute, Ind. (1860–65), New York City (1865–69), and in Brooklyn, where he succeeded (1887) Henry Ward *Beecher as pastor of the Plymouth Church and won acclaim for his clear, practical sermons. With Beecher he edited the *Christian Union* (1876; named *Outlook* in 1893). His sermons and writings reflected and popularized 19th-cent. *liberal theology, with emphasis on social reform and adaptation of evolutionary theory to Christian ideas. His works included *Christianity and Social Problems* (1896), *The Evolution of Christianity* (1892), and *Theology of an Evolutionist* (1897). BIBLIOGRAPHY: J. V. Brown, *Lyman Abbott: Christian Evolutionist* (1953); R. T. Handy, *Christian American, Protestant Hopes and Historical Realities* (1971) 126–127, 151.

[T. C. O'BRIEN]

ABBREVIATORS, certain officials of the apostolic chancery who were responsible for the drafting of acts and letters to be issued in the name of the pope. The office existed as early as the beginning of the 13th century. It grew in importance and under Pius II in 1463 a college of abbreviators was established. This was suppressed by Pius X in 1908 in the reorganization of the apostolic chancery. BIBLIOGRAPHY: L. A. Voegtle, NCE 1:13.

[P. K. MEAGHER]

'ABDALLĀH ZĀHIR (1680–1748), a native of Aleppo, Syria, who became attached to the monastery of Mar Hannā. Living as a lay deacon, he built one of the earliest printing presses for Arabic in the East and devoted himself to the publishing of religious writings, some of which he composed himself. He was firmly opposed to attempts being made at the time to Latinize the Melchite Church. BIBLIOGRAPHY: L. Malouf, NCE 1:13.

[P. K. MEAGHER]

ABDIA, BOOK OF, see OBADIAH, BOOK OF.

ABDIAS OF BABYLON, ST. (2d cent.?) who acc. to legend was named first bp. of Babylon by SS. Simon and Jude and was erroneously credited with a compilation of several legends now ascribed to two unknown 6th-cent. authors, describing the martyrdoms and virtuous lives of the Apostles. A 5th-cent. epitaph in Henchir Djezza, Tunisia, records the martyrdom of an A. probably a victim of the Vandals. BIBLIOGRAPHY: A. Audollent, DHGE 1:62–63; A. Frutaz, EncCatt 1:56. *APOCRYPHA (NT) 1.

[F. H. BRIGHAM]

ABDIAS, APOSTOLIC HISTORY OF, see APOCRYPHA (NT), 1.

ABDICATION (Lat., disowning), here considered as the renunciation of an ecclesiastical office, esp. by a pope or patriarch who is normally elected or appointed for a life term. Abdication should be distinguished from resignation, e.g., the resignation of a bp. from his diocese, since a bishop would permanently maintain his episcopal character but would surrender his administrative rights and duties, whereas a pope would give up that title itself. Abdication by a pope is of theological significance since it explains something of the nature of papal authority. Although other occurrences are ambiguous the case of Pope *Celestine V is clear. Contemporary canonists maintained that a pope could not resign but Celestine issued a constitution (Potthast Reg, 24019) declaring that popes could abdicate then and in the future, and immediately gave up his office. Boniface VIII, his successor, upheld the legality of papal abdication, referring to Celestine as "formerly pope"; this is maintained by present Catholic legislation (CIC c. 221). The significance of the fact of abdication is that just as the cessation of papal power can depend on the free will of the pope so does its beginnings. In other words, after papal election and the provided period of deliberation, the newly elected pope assumes universal jurisdiction even if he is not a priest (AAS 38:97). This also means that the pope does not derive his power from the electing *college of cardinals but is designated by them, receiving his actual authority from Christ. Abdication by patriarchs in the various Eastern Churches has occurred more frequently than in the Roman Church but they do not necessarily lose the title "patriarch," although their jurisdiction is surrendered. Patriarchs of the Eastern Catholic rites must have their renunciation accepted by the pope. BIBLIOGRAPHY: J. Leclercq, *Revue de l'histoire de l'église de France* (1939) 25:183–192; ClerSanc cc. 306, 468.1; J. H. Crehan, CDT 4–5.

[F. T. RYAN]

ABDINGHOF, ABBEY OF, a monastery in Westphalia, founded in 1015 by Meinwerk, bp. of Paderborn. It was an important cultural center in the 11th and 12th cent., but suffered a decline in the 13th and again in the 16th century. After this last period, the abbey was restored with some difficulty and thereafter remained vigorous until its suppression in 1803. BIBLIOGRAPHY: U. Berlière, DHGE 1:64–65.

[S. A. HEENEY]

'ABDISHO IV (Ebediesu; d. 1567), Chaldean patriarch. He was patriarch of East Assyria from 1555 to 1567. A. succeeded John *Sulaqua, the first patriarch after the Nestorian union with Rome of 1553 and received the pallium from Pope Pius IV (1562). Invited to be a participant in the Council of Trent, he declined but made a profession of faith at its 22d session (1562). BIBLIOGRAPHY: E. Tisserant, DTC 11.1:228–230; F. X. Murphy, NCE 1:14. *CHALDEAN CHURCH.

[F. H. BRIGHAM]

'ABDISHO BAR BERĪKĀ (also Ebedjesu; d. 1318), Nestorian writer and metropolitan of Nisibis whose *Catalogue of*

Writers lists his writings in Syriac. His *Book of the Pearl* and *Introduction to the Trinity and the Incarnation* are a reliable statement of Nestorian theology of the 14th century. BIBLIOGRAPHY: J. Parisot, DTC 1.1:24–27; F. X. Murphy, NCE 1:14.

[F. H. BRIGHAM]

ABDON AND SENNEN, SS. (3d cent.). According to their unreliable *passio,* A. and S. were Persian kings brought to Rome in the persecution of Diocletian and there slain by gladiators in the amphitheater after the beasts had refused to touch them. It is more probable that they were slaves or freedmen from the East martyred in Rome in the late 3d or early 4th cent. and buried in the cemetery of Pontian on the road to Porto. Some of their relics were later sent to Arles-sur-Tech. BIBLIOGRAPHY: W. Böhne, LTK 1:12; C. van Hulst, EncCatt 1:58.

[R. B. ENO]

ABDUCTION, as understood in canon law, is the forcible removal of a woman from a place in which she is free and her forcible retention with a view to marriage. The present law of the Church, in practically the same words as those used by the Council of Trent, provides that no valid marriage is possible between the woman and her abductor as long as she remains in his power (CIC c. 1074.1–3). Thus the fact of abduction, to which forcible detention alone is equivalent, constitutes an invalidating impediment to marriage. The impediment is a conclusive presumption of law that the consent of the woman under such circumstances is insufficient for valid marriage. The impediment ceases when the woman is released from detention and is secure in a place in which she can act freely. BIBLIOGRAPHY: B. F. Fair, *Impediment of Abduction,* CUA CLS (1944); E. Jombart, *Summary of Canon Law* (1960) 137–138.

[U. VOLL]

ABECEDENARIANS, a name that in its religious reference refers to a part of the Anabaptist movement in Wittenberg *c.*1522. The *Zwickau Prophets, particularly N. *Storch, proclaimed that the sole rule of faith is interior illumination by the Holy Spirit. The Bible is a dead letter; all human learning, esp. theology, is to be despised; the ABCs are the most learning that anyone should have. In keeping with these ideas, *Karlstadt renounced the doctorate, gave up teaching for a time, and became a manual laborer. BIBLIOGRAPHY: S. Roddy, *Baker's Dictionary of Theology* (1960) 15.

[T. C. O'BRIEN]

ABECEDARIUM, list of letters of the alphabet esp. Greek and Latin, so called from its first four letters and found on both pagan and Christian monuments. There are some indications that some stones of the catacombs so marked may have had a didactic purpose for young students, but many of the arrangements have yet to be fathomed by scholars. Its liturgical use is treated separately. BIBLIOGRAPHY: H. Leclercq, CE 1:35; DACL 1:45–61. *ALPHABET

ABEGHA (ABEL'AY), i.e., celibate, an Armenian unmarried priest, who in the Gregorian Armenian Church is juridically classified as a monk.

[A. CODY]

ABEL, see CAIN AND ABEL.

ABEL, CARL AUGUST VON (1788–1859), Bavarian statesman, Catholic activist. In 1837, he became minister of the interior and a key advisor to King Ludwig I, furthered the foundation of monasteries, championed Catholic traditions against Prussian hostility, but was generally extreme in his emphasis upon monarchical authority and opposition to German unification. A. was friendly toward J. *Döllinger, inviting him to teach at the Univ. of Munich (1838) and urging Döllinger to write a universal history and manual of religion. A. lost his position as minister of the interior (1847) because of his opposition to E. von Lasaulx and the citizenship of Lola Montez. BIBLIOGRAPHY: H. Rall, LTK 1:14; EB (1971) 3:304, 14:334.

[T. M. MCFADDEN]

ABEL, FÉLIX MARIE (1878–1953), Dominican scholar of the École Biblique in Jerusalem, preeminent authority on Palestinian geography. He published his 2-v. masterwork, *Géographie de la Palestine* in 1932, and collaborated with L. H. *Vincent on the monumental *Jérusalem: Recherches de topographie, d'archéologie et d'histoire* (8 v., 1912–26). BIBLIOGRAPHY: R. T. A. Murphy, NCE 1:15.

[T. C. O'BRIEN]

ABELARD, PETER (Abailard; 1079–1142), philosopher and theologian. Born at Le Pallet, near Nantes, in Brittany, he was baptized Peter; the accurate form and the origin of the name Abelard are unknown. In passionate pursuit of learning, he became a student in philosophy of the celebrated masters *William of Champeaux and *Roscelin; later in theology, of *Anselm of Laon. He soon won renown as a teacher himself, by his brilliant opposition on the problems of universals to the primitive realism of William and the no less primitive nominalism of Roscelin; Anselm he ridiculed for uncritical authoritarianism. By 1115 at Notre Dame in Paris A. was lecturing to more than 5,000 students from all over Europe. As he himself later stated, out of passion for Héloïse he had her entrusted to his tutorship by her uncle, Fulbert, a canon of Notre Dame. The course of their tragic love affair ended in the savage emasculation of A. ordered in vengeance by Fulbert. A. became a monk at St.-Denis; Héloïse, at his command, a nun at Argenteuil. In a short time he was teaching again. Rivals arranged the condemnation of a short treatise of his on the Trinity at the Council of Soissons in 1121. Soon, however, near Nogent-sur-Seine A. was surrounded again by hundreds of students at the school he had built and named the Paraclete. In 1125 he was sent as abbot to the monastery of St.-Gildas de Rhuy in Brittany, where for 10 years he struggled to rule the barbarous and recalcitrant monks. In 1129 he arranged for Héloise to be installed at the Paraclete as abbess with her community of nuns; by correspondence and visits he became her spiritual guide. By 1136 he was again teaching in Paris at Ste.-Geneviève. His final tribulation came through the zeal of St. *Bernard of Clairvaux. A. was summoned to a council of French bps. in June 1140 (1141?); ordered to retract 19 propositions allegedly drawn from his writings, A. refused, and was condemned as a heretic. En route to appeal to the pope, he stopped at Cluny, and there learned that on July 16, 1140 (1141?), Innocent II, at the urging of Bernard, had confirmed the condemnation. Comforted by the kindness and counsel of *Peter the Venerable, who helped reconcile A. and Bernard, he spent the remainder of his life at Cluny. When he died, his body was sent to Héloise for burial at the Paraclete. The remains of the two were entombed together in Paris in the 19th century.

A. stands as a tragic romantic figure in literature through his correspondence with Héloise (tr. C. K. Scott Moncrieff, 1926; the authenticity of the letters is questionable), and the autobiographical letter *Historia calamitatum* (tr. J. T. Muckle, 1954). His surviving philosophical treatises are in logic; the *Theologia christiana* (J. K. McCallum, tr., *Abailard's Christian Theology*, 1948) and *Theologia scholarium* were cited against him by Bernard; the *Sic et non* is a compilation of authoritative texts contradicting each other; the *Scito teipsum* (J. K. McCallum tr., *Abailard's Ethics*, 1935) is a moral treatise emphasizing intention as decisive of the moral goodness or evil of any act. The 1848–59 ed. by V. *Cousin of A.'s *Opera* was reprinted in 1969. A. exercised his formative influence above all as a teacher. By his keen and critical mind, and bold personality, he was the leader of the progressive spirits of his age. In particular, he refined the philosophic problem of universals, and with few textual resources, grasped the elements of Aristotle's theory of cognition, esp. abstraction. To theology he communicated a spirit of confidence in and a need for critical judgment of authorities as well as the analysis of ideas and terms in order to clarify the understanding of revelation. A. was condemned for the dangers to devout faith that Bernard saw in this, but the spirit that A. embodied led to the perfecting of the scholastic method and the theological progress of the 13th century. BIBLIOGRAPHY: T. Gilby, EncPhil 1:3–6, bibliog; E. Gilson, *Héloise and Abelard* (tr. L. K. Shook, 1951); J. G. Sikes, *Peter Abailard* (1932); A. V. Murray, *Abelard and Saint Bernard: A Study in 12th-Century Modernism* (1967); D. E. Luscombe, *School of Peter Abelard* (1969).

[T. C. O'BRIEN]

ABELL, ROBERT (1792–1873), native Kentuckian missionary priest ordained in 1818, who worked in various places throughout Kentucky and contributed notably to the establishment and development of the Catholic faith in that area. Illness forced him into semi-retirement in 1860, from which he emerged when his health permitted to give occasional assistance to pastors of the diocese. BIBLIOGRAPHY:

J.H. Schauinger, NCE 1:17–18; RACHS 13:212; 27:131; 29:53–57.

[H. JACK]

ABELL, THOMAS, BL. (d. 1540), English martyr. For his defense of the marriage bond of Henry VIII with *Catherine of Aragon, whom he served as chaplain and emissary to Charles V, A. was imprisoned in the Tower (1532), but later released; he was rearrested (1534) and after 6 years in prison was attainted for high treason and died on the scaffold at Smithfield (1540). Beatified 1886. BIBLIOGRAPHY: J. H. Pollen, *Lives of the English Martyrs* (ed. B. Camm, 2 v., 1904–05) 1:461–483; Butler 3:219.

ABELLY, LOUIS (*c*.1603–91), French theologian, probabilist. Consecrated bp. of Rodez in 1664, he resigned 3 years later. He was a disciple of St. Vincent de Paul, whose life he wrote, along with a formidable number of theological works. Scholar and man of prayer, A. was a foe of Jansenism and Gallicanism. BIBLIOGRAPHY: DTC 1.1:55–57.

[E. A. WEIS]

ABENDMUSIK (Ger. evening music), a concert of sacred music performed in Protestant churches in Lübeck and other North German cities in the 17th and 18th centuries. *Abendmusiken* were begun by F. Tunder at St. Mary's Church, Lübeck, in 1641, and under D. Buxtehude, who succeeded Tunder in 1668, became famous throughout northern Europe. These hour-long concerts of music for organ, choir, and orchestra followed the afternoon service on the last 2 Sundays after Pentecost and the 2d, 3d, and 4th Sundays of Advent (both the morning and evening services on the 1st Sunday of Advent had elaborate musical programs). Later they were given on the 5 Sundays preceding Christmas. Besides the music written for them by Buxtehude and others, they are important as an early instance of the concert performance of sacred music outside of an actual liturgy or service. BIBLIOGRAPHY: W. Stahl, MGG 1:32–35; P. A. Scholes, *Oxford Companion to Music* (1970) 10:232.

[A. DOHERTY]

ABERCIUS, EPITAPH OF, the epitaph of Abercius, bp. of Hieropolis in Phrygia, composed by himself at the end of the 2d cent. for his tomb, and discovered in 1883. It relates in symbolic and metaphorical language how Abercius has been led by the ''Chaste Shepherd'' (Christ) on his journey to Rome to see the ''Queen with golden robe and golden shoes,'' i.e., the Church of Christ, his Bride. He describes the Christian Eucharist using the famous word *ICHTHUS* (see FISH, SYMBOLISM OF). Then he refers to the seal of baptism and the divinity of Christ. The epitaph is now at the Lateran Museum. BIBLIOGRAPHY: Quasten 1:171–173; J. Quasten, NCE 1:18–19.

[P. FOSCOLOS]

ABERCROMBY, JOHN (d. 1561?), Scottish martyr. Thomas Dempster, in his *Historia ecclesiastica gentis*

Scotorum (1627), lists A. as a martyr, and adds that he was probably a Benedictine and apologetical writer. BIBLIOGRAPHY: J. Pollen, CE 1:41; DNB 1:41.

[T. M. MCFADDEN]

ABERCROMBY, ROBERT (1532–1615), Jesuit. A. studied for the priesthood and became a Jesuit on the Continent. After 23 years of teaching and assisting refugee Catholics, he was recruited for the Scottish Catholic underground and was notably successful in converting a number of prominent persons. Under his direction Anne of Denmark, the wife of James VI, became a Catholic in 1600. The King appointed him superintendent of the royal falconry to keep him accessible to the queen for Mass and the sacraments. When the Jesuits fell under suspicion on discovery of the Gunpowder Plot in 1605, James put a price on A.'s head. This drove him from Scotland to Braunsberg, East Prussia, where he died. BIBLIOGRAPHY: J. D. Hanlon, NCE 1:19; *Essays on the Scottish Reformation 1513–1625* (ed. D. McRoberts, 1962).

[H. JACK]

ABGAR, LEGEND OF, see APOCRYPHA (NT), 2.

ABGARUS, EPISTLES OF CHRIST AND, see APOCRYPHA (NT), 2.

ABIATHAR, the only son of Ahimelech, priest in the sanctuary at Nob, a town lying probably to the north of Jerusalem. He was sole survivor of Saul's massacre of Ahimelech and the priests of Nob (1 Sam 22.6–23) in revenge for the unwitting aid given David at the sanctuary during his escape from Saul (1 Sam 21.2–10). Because David was the occasion of the massacre, A. was retained by him as one of his priests (1 Sam 22.23; 2 Sam 20.25). In 1 Chr 27.34 he is mentioned as one of David's councilors. A. incurred Solomon's displeasure because of his support of Adonijah and upon Solomon's accession was deprived of his priesthood and confined to his estate. (see also 2 Sam 15.24–29). BIBLIOGRAPHY: R. W. Corney, InterDB 1:6–7.

[C. P. CEROKE]

ABIDING IN CHRIST, a scriptural formula expressive of the new grace-life of the Christian in virtue of his union with Christ and, through Christ, with the heavenly Father. Emphasis on the persevering character of the grace-life is given by the choice of the verb "to abide," *menein,* favored by St. John in the Greek NT: "Abide in me, and I in you" (Jn 15.4); "He who eats my flesh and drinks my blood abides in me and I in him" (Jn 6.56). Source of the grace-life and cause of its imperishableness is indicated by the words "in Christ." The Christian's life of grace is a new life brought to him in virtue of his union with Christ; of its nature it is calculated to endure not merely in this life but throughout eternity. The formula is sometimes reversed (see above: ". . . and I in him") or paraphrased with added meaning and effect: "He who has the Son has the life" (1 Jn 2.12).

BIBLIOGRAPHY: A. Robert and A. Feuillet, *Introduction to the New Testament* (tr. P. W. Skehan et al., 1965) 866–889; R. Bultmann, *Gospel of John, A Commentary* (tr. G. R. Beasley-Murray, 1971) 236, 534–536.

[E. A. WEIS]

ABILENE, the district, mentioned in Lk 3.1, under the rule of Lysanias at the beginning of Jesus' public life. It was located about 20 miles NW of Damascus, and the city of Abila was its capital. An inscription discovered in the area indicates that it was made into a tetrarchy after 4 B.C. BIBLIOGRAPHY: RevBibl NS 9 (1912) 533–540; G. M. Perrella, EncCatt 1:80–81.

[C. P. CEROKE]

ABIMELECH. (1) King of Gerar in Canaan. He is associated with Abraham in Gen 20.1–18. Led by Abraham to think that Sarah was Abraham's sister, he took her into his harem. Discovering that Sarah was Abraham's wife, Abimelech strongly objected to the subterfuge, freed Sarah, and bestowed valuable gifts on Abraham. For a variant of the same story about A. in connection with Isaac, see Gen 26.1–11. (2) Son of Gideon. He appears in the biblical account of the judges of Israel (Jg 8.31; 9.57). Having persuaded the leading citizens of Shechem to accept him as their king, he murdered the other sons of Gideon, his half-brothers (some 70 in all), except for Jotham, who escaped. But the leaders of Shechem revolted against him after 3 years of his rule. A. broke the back of the insurrection by routing the force of its leader, Gaal. He followed this success with a slaughter of the city's inhabitants, the razing of the city, and the pursuit of its leading citizens, whom he also slew. Approaching a tower during the siege of Thebez, a town near Shechem, he was struck on the head by a millstone thrown by a woman. At his own request he died by the sword of his armor-bearer. BIBLIOGRAPHY: H. Cazelles, DBSuppl 4:1394–1414.

[C. P. CEROKE]

ABINAL, ANTOINE (1829–87), French Jesuit missionary to Madagascar, who wrote an account of his experiences and translated into Malagasy many books of the Old and New Testaments and the *Imitation of Christ.* He also collaborated in the publication of a French-Malagasy dictionary. BIBLIOGRAPHY: Sommervogel 1:14.

[U. VOLL]

ABINGDON, ABBEY OF, Benedictine monastery, Berkshire, England. Abingdon was founded about 675, but was ruined by the Danes in the 9th century. St. Ethelwold restored it about 954 and it became a center of monastic revival. It had 80 monks in the 12th cent. and was known for its generosity to the poor. It was dissolved in 1538; its church was destroyed, but its guesthouse survives. BIBLIOGRAPHY: *Chronicon monasterii de Abingdon* (ed. J. Stevenson, 2 v., 1858); C. H. Lawrence, NCE 1:22–23.

[J. R. SOMMERFELDT]

ABINGTON, THOMAS (1560–1647), a recusant of Elizabethan days, twice saved from death by the influence of friends. Son of Elizabeth's treasurer, A. studied at Oxford and on the Continent, where he became a Catholic. On his return to England he involved himself in the cause of Mary, Queen of Scots. With his brother Edward he was accused of having part in the Babington Plot; Edward was executed (1586) and Thomas sentenced to the Tower, from which he was released after 6 years of imprisonment. Later he was arrested again when four Jesuits were found in his house. The Jesuits were executed for alleged complicity in the Gunpowder Plot, but A. was released, though forbidden thereafter to leave Worcestershire. His *History of Edward V* was published posthumously (1638) and he left two MSS on local antiquities. BIBLIOGRAPHY: R. I. Bradley, NCE 1:22–23.

[H. JACK]

ABIOGENESIS, see SPONTANEOUS GENERATION.

ABJURATION, the solemn disavowal of errors that until 1972 was required, along with a profession of faith, of baptized Christians being received into the RC Church. Implementing Vatican Council II's affirmation of the positive ecclesial elements in other Christian communions, (Vat II ConstChurch 15) the Congregation of Divine Worship in 1972 in issuing a new Rite for Receiving Baptized Christians into Full Communion with the Church instructed that it was inappropriate to call such Christians "converts" or *neo-conversi* (these terms are restricted to those turning from unbelief, for whom an abjuration was never required). Conditional baptism is not permitted in the reception, unless there is grave, irresolvable doubt about the person's baptism. Two former requirements, the abjuration and an absolution from censures or excommunication, are suppressed. The reception simply consists in the person's profession of faith and the declaration of the bp. or his delegate that the person is a member of the church community. The reception should take place at Mass, in which the one received shares for the first time in Eucharistic communion with the community (confession of sins would normally have preceded). The reason for the ritual reception is that it outwardly express that the faith is to be lived within the ecclesial community. The one received is thus also accompanied by a sponsor.

ABLUTION, a means of ritual purification, generally accomplished by washing with water or sprinkling with blood. Among primitives, water was considered effective in cleansing from evil considered as material pollution, warding off demons, or freeing from the stain of moral guilt. Thus water ablutions are often connected with childbirth, puberty, removal of taboos, and death. The practice has continued into the more developed religions. Among the Babylonians ablutions with pure water, esp. water drawn from the confluence of the Tigris and Euphrates Rivers, were the first requisite for pardon for an offense against the gods. Immediately before his coronation, the Egyptian pharaoh washed his face in the water of the River Nun (in which the sun god was thought to have washed), thereby purifying the pharaoh for his filial relationship with the gods. The Hebrews also stressed ritual purity through ablutions, e.g., each priest who was to participate in the Day of Atonement services in the Temple was required to undergo ritual immersion. In particular, the Passover lamb's blood is seen as purificatory (Ex 12.7; Heb 9.22). BIBLIOGRAPHY: Hastings ERE 10:455–505.

[T. M. MCFADDEN]

ABLUTIONS, the ritual cleansing of the fingers, mouth, or instruments that the eucharistic elements touch. The Roman rite practice of washing the fingers and chalice after communion began in the 10th or 11th cent. as an outgrowth of contemporary eucharistic devotion. The Roman Missal of 1970 calls for one ablution after communion; it may be done with either wine and water or water alone; it may be left till after Mass. BIBLIOGRAPHY: W. Lockton, *Treatment of the Remains at the Eucharist after Holy Communion and the Time of the Ablutions* (1920).

[N. KOLLAR]

ABNEGATION, a word of frequent occurrence in spiritual literature signifying the act or practice of denying oneself or the readiness to do so. The word is taken from the Vulgate reading of Mt 16.24: "Si quis vult post me venire, *abneget* seipsum (If anyone would come after me, let him deny himself). . . ." In one sense this precept calls for something necessary as a precondition for sanctifying grace. A man must be prepared to give up every attachment that is essentially incompatible with grace, for grace is the pearl of great value for which one must be ready to sacrifice anything else (Mt 13.46). Often, however, the word is used for the renunciation of self satisfactions not incompatible with grace, but which might retard one's spiritual development. *SELF-DENIAL.

[P. K. MEAGHER]

ABNER, uncle to Saul and commander of Saul's army. After Saul's suicide at Gilboa (2 Sam 2.8–9), A. remained loyal to the House of Saul, supporting his son, Ishbaal, as king over Israel. Meanwhile, David had been made king of Judah (2 Sam 2.7). A. incurred the implacable enmity of Joab, commander of David's army, when he reluctantly killed Joab's brother, Asahel (2 Sam 2.17–23). Motivated by the growing strength of David and by the weakness of Ishbaal's position, he used his influence to turn Israel over to the rule of David (2 Sam 3.12–19). After his negotiations with David he was met by Joab and treacherously murdered in revenge for the killing of Asahel (2 Sam 3.22–27).

[C. P. CEROKE]

ABNER OF BURGOS (*c*.1270–1346), Jewish rabbi and physician converted to Christianity in 1295. From then on A. was known as Alfonso of Burgos. He took up the Christian cause, wrote in Hebrew a refutation of Rabbi Kimchi's attack on the Christians, and was the first to produce apologetic works in Spanish. BIBLIOGRAPHY: P. Sicart, DHGE 2:696–697; F. deSola Mendes, JE 1:72.

[H. JACK]

ABOMINATION OF DESOLATION. This biblical phrase occurs in slightly different forms in Dan 9.27; 11.31; 12.11, the source of its use in Mk 13.14 and Mt 24.15. The general sense of the Hebrew phrase, *šiqqūṣ m^e šōmēm*, is "the desolating abomination." It evokes the religious repugnance felt among the Jews at the profanation of the temple in 168 B.C. by Antiochus IV, Epiphanes, who apparently erected an altar to Zeus in the temple (2 Macc 6.2). Some scholars think that the Hebrew phrase is a pejorative allusion to the Syrian god, Baal Shamem, "Lord of the heavens." The term *šiqqūṣ*, "abomination," that the Hebrews used of pagan idols replaced *ba'al*, and the vowels of the word *bōšet*, "shame," were used for *šāmēm*, "heavens." The desolating abomination of Dan was the honor paid in the temple to Baal Shamem, the Syrian god. In 1 Macc 1.54 the Hebrew phrase is translated by *bdelugma erēmōseōs*, the phrase used in Mk and Mt, where it has an apocalyptic meaning in reference to the threat to the temple that was the sign of Jesus' prophecy of its coming destruction.

[C. P. CEROKE]

ABONDANCE, MONASTERY OF (Abbey of Sainte-Marie d'Abondance), a religious house located in the valley of the Drance in Haute-Savoie, France. The origin of Abondance is uncertain, but it is known that Louis of Féterne established Canons Regular of St. Augustine there in 1080. Abondance flourished spiritually and materially for several centuries, and was given the status of an abbey in the 12th century. After monastic observance at Abondance declined, Francis de Sales sought and achieved its reform, and Pope Paul V transferred the abbey to the Cistercian Feuillants (1607). Once more religious life declined and the abbey was suppressed in 1761. Today, the abbey church, which serves as the parish church, and the remaining portion of the monastery are designated as historical monuments. BIBLIOGRAPHY: J. Garin, DHGE 1:144–153; J. Daoust, NCE 1:27.

[S. A. HEENEY]

ABORTION

History of. Abortion is the expulsion from the uterus of a non-viable fetus. The product of an abortion may be a dead fetus, but this is no concern of the moralist, since it offers no moral problem. Similarly, a distinction must be made between the spontaneous and the induced abortion. The spontaneous abortion usually results from either disease or accident, and consequently presents no moral problem. The concern of the moral theologian is rather with the voluntary or induced abortion which is the result of deliberate human interference in the progress of pregnancy.

The crime of abortion has been well known from pre-Christian days. The Sumerian code (*c*.2000 B.C.) contains the most ancient law prescribing penalties for abortion. Statutes against abortion are also found in the code of Hammurabi, the Assyrian code, the Hittite code, the Vendidad of Persia, as well as Greek and Jewish law. Plato and Aristotle allowed for abortion in certain cases, but Aristotle permitted it only if procured before life and sensation were present. For Aristotle life was present only when the fetus was formed, 40 days after conception for the male, and 90 days for the female.

In the Mosaic legislation reference is made to abortion in Exodus 21. 22–23. Curiously enough, there are two different versions of this text. According to the Hebrew text, if by striking a pregnant woman someone caused her to lose her child, he was required to pay a fine. But if the woman died, he was to pay the death penalty. In the Septuagint version the distinction is not between the death of the child and the death of the woman, but rather between the formed and unformed fetus. If the fetus was unformed, the one responsible for the blow was to pay a fine, but if the fetus was formed, he had to give life for life. This Septuagint version became very important in the Christian tradition. In demanding the death penalty for the destruction of the formed fetus, it evaluated the formed fetus as a human being. The Palestinian school, however, and the common rabbinical teaching said nothing about murder in relation to abortion. The accepted Talmudic law considered the child to be part of the mother as long as it was in the womb.

The earliest Christian reference to abortion is found in the terse commandment of the Didache (80-100): "Thou shalt not kill the fetus by abortion." Christian writers of both the East and the West were unanimous in condemning abortion during the first millennium of the Church. The practice was also condemned in several local councils, first at Elvira in the West (305) and then at Ancyra in the East (314). Elvira imposed a very severe penance on women who committed abortion; they were forbidden communion for the rest of their lives. Ancyra reduced this penance to 10 years.

Augustine and Jerome both condemned abortion without qualification, but both fell back on the distinction of the Septuagint between the formed and unformed fetus. Only abortion of the formed fetus must be classified as homicide. Abortion of an unformed fetus, while wrong, they did not consider to be homicide. This distinction was generally accepted until the 19th cent. when theories of immediate animation began to prevail.

Until the 14th cent. references to abortion were relatively brief and no attempt was made at a detailed treatment of the subject. At this time a more thorough treatment was presented by John of Naples, OP, who taught at the Univ. of Paris. He makes use of the distinction between the animated and unanimated fetus and allows the abortion of the unanimated fetus to save the life of the mother, the so-called therapeutic abortion.

This allowance was accepted by St. Antoninus, abp. of Florence, and in this way became the basis of a difference of opinion among moralists for the next 5 centuries. Moralists who made this allowance tended to argue either that the unanimated fetus was an unjust aggressor or that it was part of the mother and could be disposed of, like any other part, for the good of the whole. Others simply argued that since the unanimated fetus was not yet a human being, aborting it would not result in the death of a human being; on the other hand, the life of a human being, the mother, would be saved.

A few minor moralists tried to extend this allowance to cover the abortion of an unanimated fetus to save the reputation of the mother or to save her life from some extrinsic threat, e.g., an angry husband, but most reputable moralists, while hard put to show the distinction between these cases and the therapeutic abortion, rejected this extension. The opinion was finally condemned by Innocent XI on March 2, 1679. At the same time another extreme opinion that no fetus has a human soul while in the uterus and that animation takes place only at birth was condemned. But the opinion that the fetus was not animated until it was formed was left untouched. Prior to this, in 1588, Sixtus V in the Bull *Effraenatam* attached an ecclesiastical penalty to the abortion of an unanimated fetus, but this lasted only 3 years. In 1591 Gregory XIV limited these penalties to the abortion of an animated fetus.

During the 17th cent. some members of the medical profession began to have doubts about the theory of delayed animation, maintaining that it probably took place on the first, second, or third day after conception. This opinion met initially with opposition from the theologians because it was contrary to practically unanimous theological opinion, and esp. to Scripture (the Septuagint version of Exodus 21. 22–23). Gradually, however, it won acceptance. In revising the list of censures in 1869 Pius IX made no distinction between the animated and the unanimated fetus in the penalty for those procuring abortion.

Long before this, however, the distinction between the animated and unanimated fetus began to give way in importance to another distinction, that between direct and indirect abortion. While this terminology was not altogether fixed in meaning, at least in the earlier days, it did become very basic. Many moralists outlawed all direct abortion, whether the fetus was animated or not. But they were willing to allow indirect abortion, even of an animated fetus, under the proper conditions. They argued that the direct abortion of an unanimated fetus was illicit either because it was anticipated homicide or because it was worse than direct pollution (it was worse to destroy *semen duplex* or *conceptum* than *semen simplex*) which was never permitted, even to save a life.

What was consistent during the first 18 centuries was the almost unanimous opposition of theologians to the direct abortion of an animated fetus. It is curious, however, that in the 19th cent. for the first time some moral theologians began to argue in favor of direct abortion of an animated fetus to save the life of the mother. A possible explanation of this may be the fact that general acceptance of the theory of immediate animation outmoded the opinion allowing the abortion of the unanimated fetus to save the life of the mother. But this is not clear. At any rate three of the best moralists of the 19th cent., Ballerini, D'Annibale, and Lehmkuhl held as probable the opinion that allowed the direct abortion of the fetus to save the life of the mother. A series of church responses beginning in 1882 and ending with Vatican Council II and Paul VI in *Humanae vitae* make its opposition to any kind of direct attack on the fetus, including abortion, quite clear.

It is fortunate that in this country and the more developed countries throughout the world the medical profession has all but eliminated the necessity of therapeutic abortion.

[J. R. CONNERY]

Contemporary problem. Today popular opinion has been led to favor abortion. Some argue that a woman should be free to have a child or not, and that the fact that she is pregnant should not prejudice this freedom. Increased agitation for abortion in current society has produced cogent arguments that support benign liberalized abortion. In fact, recent developments in the 1970s broaden justification for abortion to include what is essentially the convenience of the mother and protection of society against the dangers of overpopulation. Presently, it seems that the decision to abort can be based solely on an assessment of the quality of life likely to be lived by the human organism. Numerous and monumental studies of biological, social, legal, and moral issues that determine abortion decision and practice show widespread norms based on social worthiness or social costs, genetic potential, or developmental potential.

The crucial question of ethics, "When does fully protectable human life begin?" or "When does a human infant acquire a right to life?" has been answered legally in some states, e.g., New York, which permits abortion on demand. The 1973 U.S. Supreme Court 7-2 decision (Jan. 22) favoring abortion declared that the only moderately compelling state interest lies in protecting "viable" fetuses in the last trimester or even the last ten weeks of pregnancy. The reason given for this legal protection of life is that after viability the fetus may have the capability of "meaningful" life outside the mother's womb. Furthermore, state funds must be granted to any woman on welfare, for a requested abortion. Since the U.S. Supreme Court decision cited above, a conference of medical men on the West Coast has argued against abortion, but obviously not on ethical or moral grounds. They favor allowing all infants to live three days before a decision to kill or let live on the basis of physical and social potential.

Legalization of abortion seems the most striking manifestation in America and other civilized countries of a morally permissive attitude pervading society, with the dignity of human life at stake. The Catholic Church's vigorous battle against abortion shows the measure of her present vitality. With no relaxation of objective moral standards, the Church through teaching, preaching, writing, through pro-life and anti-abortion groups, maintains that the moral malice of abortion lies in the fact that it is a directly intended, wholly indefensible destruction of innocent human life. The presupposition that a fetus is not human until after it has been delivered and has its existence completely separate from the mother is inadmissible legally, physiologically, philosophically, and theologically. As long as it is probable that embryonic life is human from the first moment of conception, the deliberate purposeful termination of any pregnancy violates man's most fundamental human right—the right to life itself. The medical profession exists to protect life. Both Pope Pius XII and Pope Paul VI have condemned the destruction of innocent human life through direct abortion.

In 1968 through the Human Life Foundation, the bishops of the U.S. responded to Pope Paul VI's appeal in *Humanae vitae* for the initiation of scientific research to improve methods of child spacing. The foundation, totally independent and self-governing, with a board of 12 lay scientists, sponsors investigation and analysis of the generation of human life and reproductive physiology as these affect family life—medically, psychologically, socially, economically. Educational programs on scientific knowledge are provided by this foundation in cooperation with other organizations. Initial studies sponsored by the Human Life Foundation focused almost exclusively on child spacing by means of periodic abstinence. Remarkably, this foundation and the population research center of the National Institute of Child Health and Human Development co-sponsored (Jan. 24–26, 1972) a conference on natural family planning. Co-sponsorship by this institute marked the first specific participation of federal government in rhythm research.

Meanwhile, with approval and funding from state and federal government, widespread dissemination of "family planning" information encouraging birth control through abortion and other artificial means is slowly liberalizing attitudes at all age levels in the U.S. Fortunately, pro-life associations, representing many religious and social groups, accelerate their articulate defense of the integrity of human life, esp. the defenseless unborn infant.

Regarding abortion as a simple matter of routine, a simple medical operation, the one way to end an unwanted pregnancy as claimed by the abortion lobby, has not solved the problem. Worldwide passionate controversy about abortion shows that the most stringent legislation against the practice does not reduce the escalating number of abortions. Total rejection of abortion is probably the chief point of ethical difference between Catholics and many contemporary thinkers. In the abortion debate it is not merely two ethics facing each other, but the world views of two epochs, two cultures. If abortion becomes a way of life, a matter of unexceptional, indifferent routine, then we will have changed our view of man and society. The future of society is really at stake. The main practical aim of Catholic policy is to make the moral issue clear (sometimes achieved by rhetorical overkill in propaganda) and to make abortion as unnecessary as possible. Diocesan institutions have launched programs to aid girls with unwanted pregnancies, esp. young unmarried girls or women who are still minors or students. All recommendations will be designed to mitigate the evil rather than elimi-

nate it. BIBLIOGRAPHY: "Abortion and the Court," *Christianity Today* 17 (1973) 32–33; R. F. Collins, "Abortion: An Ethical and Moral Appraisal," *Louvain Studies* III: #1, 17–30; R. F. Drinan, "The Abortion Decision," *Commonweal* 97 (1973) 438–440; J. R. Nelson, "What Does Theology Say about Abortion?" *Christian Century* 90 (1973) 124–128; P. Ramsey, "Abortion—A Review Article," *Thomist* 37 (1973) 174–226.

[J. MORGAN]

ABOTH (Heb., patriarchs or fathers), the first blessing of the Amidah, the main section of all obligatory Jewish prayers. It extols the greatness of the God of the Jewish patriarchs; Abraham is its legendary author. The term is also linked with the Pirke Aboth *(Sayings of the Fathers)*, a Mishnaic tract which is the most popular collection of Jewish proverbs. It contains the proverbial sayings of 63 rabbis, arranged chronologically from 300 B.C. to 200 A.D.. Its chief emphasis is on the value of Torah study and the observance of Jewish ethical ideals. BIBLIOGRAPHY: *Encyclopedia of the Jewish Religion* (eds. R. J. Zwi Werblowsky and G. Wijoder, 1966) 51.

[T. M. MCFADDEN]

ABRA DE RACONIS, CHARLES FRANÇOIS D' (*c.*1580–1646), convert, along with his whole family, in 1592, from Calvinism. Philosopher and anti-Jansenist theologian and writer, A. was appointed chaplain and preacher to the royal court, and then bp. of Lavaur in 1637. Among other points of Catholic belief, A. defended the primacy of the Holy See against Martin de Barcos, who held that SS. Peter and Paul were both heads of the Church. BIBLIOGRAPHY: DTC 1.1:93–94; Bremond 2:244–251.

[E. A. WEIS]

ABRABANEL (ABRAVANEL), ISAAC (1437–1508), Jewish statesman, biblical scholar, and philosopher. A. was minister of finance to Alfonso V of Portugal and later to Ferdinand V of Castile, but when the Jews were expelled from Spain, A. was driven into exile in Italy, where he eventually settled in Venice. His writings include a commentary on the Bible much esteemed by Christian scholars of the 17th and 18th centuries. His writings on the Messiah contributed to the Jewish messianic movements of the 16th and 17th centuries. BIBLIOGRAPHY: B. Netanyahu, *Don Isaac Abravanel, Statesman and Philosopher* (1953).

[P. K. MEAGHER]

ABRAHAM, in the Book of Genesis, the originator of Hebrew religion. His name Abram (Gen 11.27), meaning the "father is exalted," is changed in Gen 17.5 to Abraham and given a popular etymology meaning "the father of a multitude." According to Gen 11.31, A. migrated with his father, Terah, and other members of the family from Ur in

Chaldea to Haran in Turkey. Upon Terah's death A. left Haran to settle in Canaan. Whether in Haran or in Canaan (the text of Gen is unclear on this point), he received a divine promise of a great posterity, despite the fact that his wife, Sarah, was sterile (Gen 11.30–12.5). At Shechem in Canaan, a second divine promise granted the land of Canaan to his descendants (Gen 12.6–9). After settling near Bethel, he moved on to the Negeb, then down into Egypt because of famine in Canaan.

The Book of Genesis conserves a number of family traditions about A. that recount his adventure in Egypt (12.10–20); his kindness to his nephew, Lot (13.1–13); his rescue of Lot from kidnappers (14.1–16); the honor paid him by Melchizedek, king of Salem (14.17–20); and an adventure in the Negeb with Abimelech similar to the one with Pharaoh in Egypt (Gen 20.1–8). The destruction of Sodom and Gomorrah, probably an ancient tradition that antedated A.'s settlement in Canaan, is associated with him and given a theological explanation of the anger of Yahweh against the sinful inhabitants of those cities (Gen 18.16–19.29). The most important theme in the story of A. is Yahweh's promise to him of the birth of a son from the barren Sarah (Gen 15.1–6; 17.15–22; 18.1–15) in fulfillment of the divine pledge of a great posterity for A. (Gen 12.1–3). A. already had an heir, a son born of Hagar, Sarah's slave, in accordance with the custom of the time in the case of a sterile wife. Upon the birth of Isaac (Gen 21.1–6), Abraham consented to Sarah's urging that his first son, Ishmael (probably named by later Israelite tradition), together with his mother, Hagar, be expelled from the family circle (Gen 16.1–16; 21.8–21). A.'s attempted sacrifice of Isaac is difficult to account for from the circumstances of his life. The story was probably developed as a catechetical lesson against child sacrifice, teaching A.'s obedience in faith to Yahweh. In order to prevent Isaac from marrying a Canaanite woman, A. secured Rebecca for him from his own kinsmen in Mesopotamia (Gen 24.1–67). A. was buried at Hebron in the same plot of ground he purchased for the burial of Sarah (Gen 25.7–11; 23.1–20).

The portrait of A. in Gen depicts him as affable in his dealings with men and staunchly convinced of his unique relationship to God. As evidence of his faith he sealed this relationship in a covenant rite (Gen 15.6–18; cf., 17.1–8), to which probably later tradition added the rite of circumcision (17.9–14). Throughout Israel's history Yahweh's covenant with A. over the land of Canaan was ever retained as the foundation of its faith (Ex 32.13; Num 32.11; Dt 1.8; 2 Kg 13.23; Ps 104–105.9). A. became the symbol of Yahweh's saving acts on behalf of Israel (Is 29.22) and the person in whose privileges it participated (Is 51.1–2). By the time of Jesus he was given the title "father of Israel," as if mere physical descent from him guaranteed salvation (Mt 3.9; Jn 8.39), a point of view that most likely explains the difficulty of Nicodemus in understanding Jesus' teaching (Jn 3.3–4). This strong conception of Israel's relationship to A. was used by the Judaizers in the Galatian communities founded by St.

Paul to urge the observances of Judaism as part of the Christian life (Gal 5.7–12). Paul not only accepted the concept of the Christian's relationship to Abraham, but argued that the apostolic teaching of justification through faith in Christ rather than through the observance of the Law was the actual fulfillment of the promise God made to A. concerning the blessings to stem from him for the Gentiles (Gal 3.6–9; Rom 4.1–25). God's salvific paternity over Israel, reflected in the figure of A., is revealed through Christ to be his salvific paternity over the entire human race. BIBLIOGRAPHY: P. Hinnebusch, "Abraham and St. Joseph," CrossCrown 24 (1972) 6–11.

[C. P. CEROKE]

ABRAHAM OF CLERMONT, ST. (Abraham of St.-Cyr; d. between 474 and 481), hermit, abbot. Born in Persia and reared a Christian, A. was arrested in the persecution of the Christians by Kings Yazdagird I and Varahran V. After 5 years in prison he made his way to Gaul and settled at Clermont. His virtuous way of life attracted disciples. He became abbot of the monastery of St.-Cyr and was ordained a priest. A. was invoked during the Middle Ages by those suffering from eye diseases. BIBLIOGRAPHY: AS June 3:534–536; V. Ermoni, DHGE 1:161; P. Sfair, BiblSanct 1:119–120.

[J. M. O'DONNELL]

ABRAHAM ECCHELLENSIS (1605–64), Maronite scholar who participated in the revision of the Arabic translation of the Bible, assisted C. Le Jay as an editor of the *Polyglot Bible, taught Syriac and Arabic in Pisa and Rome, and was made scriptor for Arabic and Syriac at the Vatican Library by Pope Alexander VII. BIBLIOGRAPHY: L. Petit, DHGE 1:169–171.

[F. H. BRIGHAM]

ABRAHAM OF EPHESUS, ST. (fl. 550) bishop. Founder of two monasteries, one in Constantinople and another in Jerusalem, A. became bp. of Ephesus and metropolitan in 542 (553?). Two homilies by Abraham are extant, on the Presentation and the Annunciation. The latter is the earliest testimony to the feast of the Annunciation which replaced another older Marian feast celebrated on the Sunday before Christmas. BIBLIOGRAPHY: AS Oct. 12:757–769; PO 16:429–452; G. Morelli, BiblSanct 1:117–118.

[J. M. O'DONNELL]

ABRAHAM OF SANCTA CLARA (secular name Johann Ulrich Megerle; 1644–1709), Discalced Augustinian preacher and author of popular devotional works. Most of his career was in Vienna where he was preacher to the imperial court while simultaneously acting as superior in his own order. Although criticized by contemporaries for buffoonery and excessive dramatics in the pulpit, he was admired, not only by the people but by discerning critics such as Schiller, for his vast erudition, scintillating wit, and literary charm, all of which he used with effective oratory. His collected works begin with a dramatic description of the plague that devastated Vienna in 1679 and continue with an appeal for the Christian world to battle against the Turks. They range from the sober *Grammatica religiosa,* a compendium of moral teaching, to a group of sketches on the fools of the world entitled *Huy! und Pfuy der Welt* (Hey, Phooey with the World). His masterpiece is the 4-volume work on Judas the Arch-Knave, which adorns an apocryphal work with moral applications. BIBLIOGRAPHY: A. J. Clark, NCE 1:35.

[U. VOLL]

ABRAHAM THE SIMPLE, ST. (fl. 4th cent.), an Egyptian hermit called "the Simple," or "the Child" *(pais)* because of his innocence and simplicity of character. He was referred to by Cassian *(Collationes* 15, 24) but his identity is otherwise uncertain. He was remarkable for his austerity of life, some of it undertaken to remedy the pangs of homesickness from which he suffered, and for his miraculous powers. BIBLIOGRAPHY: M. V. Brandi, BiblSanct 1:121.

ABRAHAM OF SMOLENSK, ST. (d. 1221), a monk in Smolensk who devoted himself to biblical studies and also to preaching a very stern and austere doctrine which earned him a large following among the people. But he aroused the jealousy of the clergy, who brought serious charges against him. As a result the bishop took disciplinary action but later exonerated him. The rest of his life was spent as abbot of a small monastery. BIBLIOGRAPHY: Butler 3:377–379.

[G. T. DENNIS]

ABRAHAM, APOCALYPSE OF, a Jewish apocryphal work, written about A.D. 100 apparently out of reflection upon the destruction of Jerusalem and the Temple in A.D. 70 and the effect of this disaster upon the Jewish people. The work contains an imaginative construction of Abraham's youth influenced by Genesis and rabbinic tradition, that emphasizes his faith in monotheism. It then depicts Abraham as brought to heaven, where he is allowed to view human history, past and future, including the sin of Adam and Eve and the destruction of the Temple. These evils are ascribed to the influence of a satanic being, Azazel, who is identified with the serpent of Gen 3. A real dominion over the earth is conceded to Azazel. Thus the thought of the work tends to be dualistic: the life of man is ruled by one God whose justice cannot be impugned and by a powerful evil being able to influence man's decisions. The text of the work, originally written in Hebrew or Aramaic, exists only in a Slavonic version which in turn is a translation of a Greek version of the original. BIBLIOGRAPHY: L. Ginzberg, JE v.1.

[C. P. CEROKE]

ABRAHAM, TESTAMENT OF, a Jewish apocryphal work, written probably in the 1st cent. A.D. in Hebrew or Aramaic and now extant only in two Greek versions of different length. The work is a mythical story built around Abraham's death. Abraham refuses to surrender his soul in death to the angel Michael, requesting a vision of all creation before he dies. When in the vision he sees the earth filled with sin, he curses the sinners, who expire at his word. Abraham also sees souls in judgment and succeeds by his prayers in effecting a favorable verdict upon those whose guilt is balanced by their good works. At length Abraham reluctantly surrenders to death and is borne to God. Ginzberg, JE v.1.

[C. P. CEROKE]

ABRAHAMITES (Bohemia), an 18th-cent. sect, also called Israelites. They were mostly peasants of Jewish and Protestant background in the vicinity of Pardubice near Prague. Their name came from their claim to be followers of the patriarch Abraham. While denying all Christian teachings, they made use of baptism and Christian wedding services to avoid legal reprisals. Their whole scripture was the Lord's Prayer and the Ten Commandments. When, after the Edict of 1780, they did not identify themselves as either Protestant or Catholic, the Emperor Joseph II expelled them and the sect soon scattered and disappeared. BIBLIOGRAPHY: E. Winter, *Der Josephinismus und seine Geschichte* (1943); A. Molnar, RGG 1:72–73.

ABRAHAMITES (Syria), a 9th-cent. sect named from Ibraham (Abraham), their leader. They denied the divinity of Christ. Some associate them with the *Paulicians or the Samosatenes.

[T. C. O'BRIEN]

ABRAHAMS, ISRAEL (1858–1925), English Hebraist and writer who with the collaboration of his friend C. Montefiore founded and edited (1889–1908) the *Jewish Quarterly Review.* Among his more important writings were: *Jewish Life in the Middle Ages* (1896; rev. ed. 1932) and *Judaism* (1907). BIBLIOGRAPHY: *Jewish Studies in Memory of Israel Abrahams* (ed. J. A. Kohut, 1928).

[P. K. MEAGHER]

ABRAHAM'S BOSOM. This figure of speech appears in the parable of the Rich Man and Lazarus, Lk 16.22–23, where Lazarus is described as residing in Abraham's bosom while the rich man abides in torments. In rabbinic literature, "rest in Abraham's bosom" sometimes suggested fellowship with the Patriarch, while at other times it referred to sharing in the messianic banquet (Mt 8.11). In any case the figure was used at the time of Jesus for the happy lot of the just after death.

[C. P. CEROKE]

ABRANTOVIC, FABIJAN (1884–1940), Byzantine-Slavonic rite exarch. After studying for the priesthood at St.

Petersburg and Louvain, A. was ordained in 1908. He taught theology at the Catholic Academy in St. Petersburg, taking prominent part in all Byelorussian Christian activities. Under Bp. Z. Losinski, he organized the Catholic seminary at Minsk, capital of the Byelorussian Republic, remaining with the seminary as it was moved from Minsk to Navahradak and then to Pinsk. He joined the Marian Fathers in 1926 and was sent by Pius XI to organize and govern the first Byzantine-Slavonic diocese at Harbin, Manchuria. Within 10 years the diocese was firmly established, with a Catholic church, a boarding school for boys, and a house of the Marian Fathers. In 1938 he attended a general chapter of his congregation in Rome and reported to the Holy See. Stopping in Byelorussia on his return, he was seized by the Communists. It is uncertain whether he was executed or died after transportation to Siberia. BIBLIOGRAPHY: C. Sipovič, NCE 1:36–37.

[H. JACK]

ABRAXAS, a magico-mystical word found in Hellenistic papyri, and often inscribed on ancient Roman, Greek, and Egyptian (as well as medieval) amulets. The word's origin is obscure: perhaps it is a Greek corruption of the Aramaic *abhadda kedhābra* which survives in the modern term, abracadabra. The term was used by the Gnostics, probably because the numerical value assigned to its Greek letters totals 365, to refer to the Supreme Being and ultimate source of the 365 heavens. Tertullian maintains (*De praescriptione haereticorum*, 4) that the gnostic *Basilides uses the term for God, but this is disputed. BIBLIOGRAPHY: H. Leclercq, DACL 1.1:127–155; A. S. Peake, Hastings ERE 2:429. *GNOSTICISM.

[T. M. MCFADDEN]

ABREACTION, a psychiatric term referring to the release of a repressed emotion by re-experience and consequent catharsis with or without intellectual insight. Sigmund *Freud first discovered this possibility by the use of hypnosis, but later achieved the same effect by free association. The later process was the cause of some confusion of abreaction with the relief achieved by confession or "ventilation" of the mind. Successive hypotheses have been advanced about the therapeutic value of abreaction; since World War II, it has proved useful in the treatment of amnesia cases, where barbiturates were used instead of hypnosis to effect the reaction. Moralists, uncertain of the nature of the phenomenon, have hesitated to pronounce with certainty; some have had recourse to the principle of the *double-effect or the idea of material sin to defend its use. Morality appears involved because abreaction is frequently libidinous or aggressive in character. Since the conscious ego does not produce the abreaction, but is involved at most by permitting its occurrence, it is sometimes argued that the issue of moral consent in the full sense does not arise. But moral consent and the influence of abreaction on subsequent life are in fact the moral problem. Both therapist and patient are bound to take

into consideration the perils of the process, but viewing it positively in the reconstruction-context of the entire personality toward moral values freely chosen. BIBLIOGRAPHY: Pius XII, OssRom, April 16, 1953; J. Nuttin, *Psychoanalysis and Personality* (tr. G. Lamb, 1962) 168–174; A. Snoek, "Moral Reflections on Psychiatric Abreaction," ThSt 13 (1952) 173–189; M. E. Stock, "Some Moral Issues in Psychoanalysis," *Thomist* 23 (1960) 176–188; G. F. Mahl, *Psychological Conflict and Defense* (1971) 13, 15.

ABRIKOSSOV, ANNA IVANOVA (1882–1936), Russian Orthodox convert to Catholicism, foundress of a religious community in which she was known as Mother Catherine. Born into a Russian Orthodox family, A. studied at Cambridge and married her cousin Vladimir Vladimirovic in 1903. While traveling in Italy she became familiar with the writings of St. *Catherine of Siena which led her to convert to Catholicism in 1908 as did her husband the following year. In 1910 they entered the Third Order of St. Dominic and established a small religious community in Moscow under the Dominican rule. Because of pastoral demands, and in accord with Oriental canon law, Vladimir was ordained a priest in 1917 by A. *Szeptycky, Metropolitan of Lvov. In 1923 A. was arrested with about 20 sisters of her community. Having bravely endured imprisonment in several places, she died in the Butyski prison in Moscow. BIBLIOGRAPHY: Attwater CCE 1:126; P. de Regis, "Ste. Catherine de Sienne à Moscow," *Unitas* Sept. (1946) 7–31.

[F. T. RYAN]

ABROGATION, the total suppression of a law by legislative authority through the enactment of a new law. As such, abrogation is a relatively modern legal phenomenon; in the earlier Byzantine and Roman tradition useless laws were generally allowed to lapse through desuetude. The CIC c. 6 gives the criteria for judging whether the Code has changed laws existing before its promulgation (1918); canon 22 gives the general principles regarding abrogation: the former law is abrogated if the new law explicitly says so, or if it is directly contrary to the old law, or if it readjusts the entire subject matter of the former law. BIBLIOGRAPHY: Woywod-Smith 17–18.

[T. M. MCFADDEN]

ABS see AMERICAN BIBLE SOCIETY.

ABSALOM, son of David by his wife Maacah. He engineered the murder of his half-brother, Amnon (2 Sam 13.23–29), in revenge for Amnon's rape of Tamar, Absalom's sister (2 Sam 13.1–22). Through the intervention of Joab he was recalled from exile by David after 3 years and admitted into the King's presence 2 years later (2 Sam 13.39–14.33). From this time on he won popular favor against his father by his criticism of the administration of justice at the King's court (2 Sam 15.1–6). On the pretext of fulfilling a vow at Hebron, he proclaimed himself king there and led a revolt against David (2 Sam 15.7–12). His forces were defeated by David's army; and contrary to the express orders of the King (2 Sam 18.1–8), he was killed by Joab and his armor-bearers as he hung entangled by his long hair in an oak tree (2 Sam 18.9–14).

[C. P. CEROKE]

ABSALON OF LUND (1128–1201), abp., founder of Copenhagen, considered the most brilliant and effective Scandinavian prelate of the Middle Ages. A. graduated from the Univ. of Paris, was ordained there, and adopted the Latin culture of the European continent. When he returned to Denmark, he founded the monastery at Sorø, became bp. of Roskilde (1158), and abp. of Lund and primate of Denmark (1178). He exercised significant influence upon the Danish Kings Valdemar I and Canute VI and introduced Western monasticism and other religious practices into Denmark (e.g., tithing, clerical celibacy). BIBLIOGRAPHY: L. Musset, NCE 1:38–39.

[T. M. MCFADDEN]

ABSOLUTE, THE (Lat., *absolutum* unrestricted, which also means 'abstract' that is, not caught up in particularities of existence), a term referring to that which is perfect, independent, unitary, unchanging, and the principle of all things. Thus it stands in contrast to the contingent and relative, and in various philosophical systems has been identified with being, truth, goodness, mind, humanity, or God. The religious experience of the "Other" as unconditional power in Hindu mysticism becomes the Universal One while the world is an illusory appearance. In Plato the Good, the highest form, is the absolute, and for Aristotle it is the unmoved mover, the first cause standing apart from the material constituents of the world. Influenced by *Neoplatonism, St. Augustine identified subsistent truth, the *Logos,* with absolute being. Scholasticism added the notion of necessity to the absolute: it is that which of itself has no dependence on any other for its being. For St. *Thomas Aquinas God's essence is his existence and, in fact, the plurality characteristic of creatureliness points toward a unitary Creator.

B. *Spinoza denied a multiplicity of substances and affirmed a monism in which God is the one substance of which created existents are attributes. I. *Kant sought to "find the conditioned knowledge of the Understanding the Unconditioned that completes its unity" (*Critique of Pure Reason,* A307), and postulated God's existence and human freedom on practical rather than theoretical grounds. The philosophy of J. *Fichte asserted the ego or self in its freedom as the basic principle from which all other categories of experience were derived. God as process is the absolute ego of which finite individual egos are expressions. F. *Schelling, an exponent of absolute *idealism, tried to overcome the dualism of nature and ego that remained in Fichte, maintaining that nature and mind are moments in the unfolding of the absolute ego, i.e., the absolute does not already exist but historically evolves. G. *Hegel proposed a philosophy of the absolute in which the real is rational and the rational is real. The absolute is not substance but an ongoing process whose purpose is complete self-consciousness. For him the absolute develops as society progresses toward higher expressions of freedom in history. In 1893 F. H. Bradley argued that appearances are self-contradictory and that the absolute must be consistent, and, therefore, a supra-relational harmony of experience rather than a self or God. The constant reaction to philosophies of the absolute has been to prevent the total absorption of the many into the one and to preserve individuality in the midst of identity. Yet the absolutist tendency toward favoring unity has, at the very least, increased understanding of the relationship between mind and reality. BIBLIOGRAPHY: Copleston 7; H. B. Acton, EncPhil 1:6–9; M. C. Chill, *Absolute and the Relative in Modern Philosophy* (1939); T. A. Burkhill, *Evolution of Christian Thought* (1971) 382–397.

[F. T. RYAN]

ABSOLUTES, MORAL. The term "absolute" is not so flat as contemporary usage might suggest. The Latin *absolutus* (*absolvere,* to loose from) has a long history in law, grammar, politics, philosophy, and theology, and is recapitulated in English, with the addition of metaphorical shades of meaning. In moral theory, though the notions are cognate, it is useful to distinguish between what (1) is unconditional, (2) is disengaged, and (3) can be viewed without relation to context.

In meaning (1), namely absolute in contrast to conditional or hypothetical, the term comes easily to the lips of an ethical formalist: moral value is revealed to a moral sense or insight and is not arrived at by considerations of expediency nor complemented by those of satisfaction; it is uplifted above them, and in fact their introduction if anything serves to spoil it. The *categorical imperative, duty for duty's sake, is enunciated, and applied to human vicissitudes, sometimes heroically, often nobly, but always with some strain on the facts of life. Since the central tradition in Catholic moral thought is eudaemonian and lies nearer to *utilitarianism, we need not linger here over the proclamation of absolute values as though this meant they were sheerly self-contained or even self-supporting, though they may so appear in rhetoric, and on occasion justly: *fiat justitia et ruat coelum* (let justice be done though the world perish).

Nor should meaning (2), namely the absolute as abstract, in contrast to concrete, present much difficulty. For whenever there is rational discourse about the principles and implications of morality in general, the topic is disengaged from individual cases, though these are respected; in fact they are consulted as bases for induction and appealed to for exemplification. Only through ideas can we communicate at large, and not be restricted to making sensible signs and images with those who happen or are disposed to be in personal sympathy with us, or to *ad hoc* counseling with a penitent or patient face to face. An abstract standard of reference is assumed in all ethical writings which are not merely records of case histories or statements of the author's own affective attitude: you find this, with differences of degree, of detail, and of tone, in the theological manuals, some more stiffly-minded than others, in the good-advice columns of the newspapers, in warmly evangelical homilies, in existentialist protests against a maze of meanings, and in personalist manifestos against impersonal categories. Any claim to more than fugitive and contingent validity is absolute in the sense that it is abstract.

The problem arises with meaning (3), absolute as meaning isolated, in contrast to relative; particularly when a moral value seems to be put forward as a kind of idol, which devours human lives in the present though it may have been innocuous in the past when people were allegedly less tender to human living. The affirmation of absolutes is accused of doing violence to the principle that conduct is not static; morals are made for man, not man for morals, and his activity has to be adaptive, and not fixed upon obsolete values. The absolute in meaning (2) is every bit as freely flung about by critics as by defenders of traditional morality, and rather more freely in meaning (1), notably when love is proclaimed as its own justification without exploration of its content. Clearly the questions need to be sorted out.

It can be said quite simply that the whole moral order is relative, and so, therefore, is any value within it. It does not form a frame like a chessboard or a Euclidean system; it is all open and outgoing. Only the theological *virtues, which are not moral virtues, break out of the scene composed of creaturely challenges, opportunities, occasions, or objects which face us; only they are engaged directly with God, and not with things subordinate (ea quae sunt ad finem); and of them only charity, which loves God for himself and neighbor as finally as one loves oneself, is uncompromising and never passes away, for faith expects to be displaced by vision, and hope by comprehension. Yet admitting that moral values are relative, one still has to ask, to what are they relative? If this be stated as a subjective optimum, it will make a deal of difference whether the subject be regarded as merely expressive of himself—to which no theory or practice of Christian morals will subscribe—or as responsive to some objective reality other than himself, without at this stage claiming that our environment is not itself also relative to us or to another order of reality or to both.

Ultimately, however, there is God, and he is not really relative to us as we are to him. Though Christian philosophy may arrive at its concept of him by way of causality, heightening the values it discovers in his effects and eliminating their imperfections, he is affirmed as the absolute good. Moreover, our commitment to him by faith and charity is even more unqualified. He is the summum bonum transcending all moral categories. All the same he is the last end to which all right action is relative, above all in virtue of the will's intention. Nevertheless, moral values consist not only in being teleologically right in this respect, but also in being rightfully adapted to circumstances; they are disclosed in

events, which are never exactly repeated in the history of individuals and communities, and their worth is to be estimated also as relative to the exigencies of a situation. On both counts, namely the moral determinants of right intention and due circumstances, fully recognized by the classical Catholic authors, moral values are relative; the first is a response to a post-moral absolute, the second an accommodation to a condition of fluidity in which positions can be fixed only provisionally and approximately. Must it then be left at that, with the conclusion that the moral picture can be adequately drawn in terms of personalism and situationalism? Or are there also true moral values which are absolute according to meaning (3)?

Let us take as an illustration the grammatical clause known as the ablative absolute. It makes some sense when considered apart; it makes complete sense only when carried along with the whole sentence. Creatures themselves are like ablative absolutes; they have meaning in themselves, they are beings and causes, yet they have full meaning only when they are seen also as wholly from and to God. They certainly engage us for their own sake, and are therefore ends: witness any devoted scientist or person who has fallen in love. They also provide moral objects for our activity, which can be classified according to their kind. Comforting somebody in a state of shock is a type of action, as real as administering oxygen or a pain-reliever, and is accordingly dealt with in the appropriate books of instruction. Few would hesitate to approve of it, and there is a moral quality, at least implicit, in their judgment without anticipating the actual surroundings of an incident or weighing the motives at work. The circumstances can be infinitely variable—a sailor burnt from an explosion between decks, a child whose father has just deserted her, indeed any sudden loss, and the comfort may be given by crooning, hugging, or just sitting alongside in companionable silence. And as for intentions, the deed is still good when done in despair of God's providence or, as happens not rarely with emergencies, with an exasperation that does nothing to color with insincerity the instant kindness.

There are absolutes here within a relative framework of thought, nor are they artificial, like the Greenwich meridian, but forms of action shaped in the nature of things with real objects, some of which are morally good of their kind, and some are bad. As such they are not just transitory items of biography, but express values that are constant. That they but partially represent the complex of human factors released should be appreciated, for they are absolutes according to meaning (2); also that all should not be equally emphasized, for while some are primary, others are secondary, sometimes being conclusions arrived at by narrow and exacting ways of proof. Consequently they can be graded among themselves, and as men enter new socio-psychological dimensions may be progressively manifested or in their details revised: here, or course, statements which are pure period pieces may become dead letters. BIBLIOGRAPHY: ThAq ST (Lat-Eng) v. 18 and 28; P. E. Hutchings, *Kant on Absolute Value* (1972);

R. W. Sellers, *Principles, Perspectives and Problems of Philosophy* (1970) 442–446; H. Allard, "Questions of Moral Absolutes," *Theology* 75 (1972) 32–37.

[T. GILBY]

ABSOLUTION, the forgiveness extended by an offended party, generally the Supreme Being, to a wrongdoer; in particular, the pardon granted by the priest in the name of Christ within the sacrament of penance (see PENANCE, SACRAMENT OF; ABSOLUTION, SACRAMENTAL). The term is also used in other contexts with some difference of meaning: e.g., absolution from censures (see CENSURES, ECCLESIASTICAL); absolution after a requiem Mass (see ABSOLUTION OF THE DEAD); absolution in the Divine Office, i.e., the short prayer said before the lessons at Matins; and absolution from the temporal punishment due to sins (see INDULGENCES). Here we are concerned with the term only in its general sense.

Those religions that maintain belief in a personal God also acknowledge the evil that man can do before him, and the need he therefore has upon occasion to restore an amicable relationship. Thus the Babylonian creation myths, ritually recited at the start of each year, seek to effect a return to the time of purity at creation's beginning. By symbolically participating in the re-creation of the world, man too begins a new life absolved from past faults (see ENUMA ELISH). The ancient Chinese religions held the emperor responsible for natural disorders, and he had to subject himself to atonement ceremonies to achieve divine forgiveness. In Islam, Allah is said to remain silent about man's sins not because of forgetfulness but because of his mercy. Among the Jews also, there is a strong sense of man's need for forgiveness from the all-holy God. Israel was convinced that God did not will the death of the sinner (Jer 18.1–10; Ezek 18.21–22; 33.11); since man is weak, God will exercise mercy toward him (Ps 78.38; 89.47–49). Christianity has continued this Jewish emphasis, as indicated in the articles cited above. BIBLIOGRAPHY: H. Von Glasenapp, *Non-Christian Religions* (tr. E. Protter, 1963); B. Häring, *Shalom: Peace, the Sacrament of Reconciliation* (1969) 77–85.

[T. M. MCFADDEN]

ABSOLUTION, CONDITIONAL, the conferral of absolution in the sacrament of penance with the proviso that it is intended to be effective only if some specified condition, necessary to the reception of the sacrament, is verified in fact. The imparting of absolution in this manner is of relatively recent origin. The practice was first defended as certainly legitimate by J. *Gerson (15th cent.); it was attacked by Cajetan; today it is universally accepted by sacramental theologians. But such absolution is valid only if the condition concerns either the past (e.g., I absolve you if you have been baptized) or the present (e.g., I absolve you [say, the victim of a traffic accident] if you are still alive). But if the condition concerns the future, RC theologians hold that it invalidates the absolution, for the efficacy of the sacrament cannot be

suspended in this way. A condition may licitly be attached to absolution when the confessor judges that to do so is the best way, in a given case, of preserving the dignity of the sacrament without depriving the penitent of the sacramental grace he may be capable of receiving. BIBLIOGRAPHY: Davis MorPastTh 3:255–256; B. Häring, *Shalom: Peace, the Sacrament of Reconciliation* (1969) 82–83.

[T. M. MCFADDEN]

ABSOLUTION, FORMS OF, the manner of expressing sacramental absolution, i.e., in either a declaratory or deprecatory form. The declaratory form (I absolve you . . .) is used in the Latin rite and reflects the Western emphasis upon the confessor's juridic powers. The deprecatory form, traditionally used in the Eastern Churches, may either mention the priest's power to absolve (May God, through me a sinner, pardon you . . .) or omit it entirely. Thus the Eastern Orthodox formula is, ". . . I, miserable sinner, do not have the power to absolve a sin upon earth; only God can do that. . . . But what you have confessed to my extreme lowliness, . . . may God forgive you in this world and the next." These formulas vary greatly among the Eastern Churches, and today some (e.g., the Russian Orthodox) use a typically Western, declaratory form. In the early Church, the forms were deprecatory; it is only in the 11th cent. that the tendency toward the indicative form begins. In the 13th cent., Thomas Aquinas denied the validity of the deprecatory form, and his opinion was generally followed in the 14th and 15th centuries. The Councils of Florence (D 1323) and Trent (D 1673) declared that only the declaratory formula is to be used since the sacramental form should express the priest's authority to pardon sins, an essential quality of the sacrament. Contemporary theologians agree, however, that the deprecatory form is valid, provided that it does not positively exclude the idea of the minister's judicial role. BIBLIOGRAPHY: A. Vacant, DTC 1.1:244–252; E. Hanna, CE 1:64–65; E. Benz, *Eastern Orthodox Church. Its Thought and Life* (tr. R. and C. Winston, 1963).

[T. M. MCFADDEN]

ABSOLUTION GENERAL, a term used to indicate both the sacramental forgiveness granted to a group of penitents without private auricular confession and the apostolic blessing given to those in danger of death. In the first sense the term has been extended to include an absolution granted in a penitential service to the group of penitents who participate in it. After Vatican Council II many theologians, esp. liturgists, have advocated the giving of a more liturgical character to the sacrament of penance by holding of special penitential services in which not single individuals but whole groups participate. The instruction "Pastoral Norms concerning the Administration of General Sacramental Absolution," issued by the Sacred Congregation for the Doctrine of Faith on June 16, 1972, approved and encouraged the practice but held that for the valid and complete reception of the sacrament those guilty of mortal sin had to follow up their participation in the general rite by private auricular confession of their grave sins. The norm enunciated by the Council of Trent with respect to necessity of the integral confession of one's mortal sins according to their kind and number, has always been understood to admit of some exceptions—cases where intelligible communication between penitent and confessor is physically or morally impossible, cases of urgent necessity, cases where one has no access to confessor but cannot without grave difficulty defer his reception of the Eucharist, etc. Some contemporary theologians have expressed dissatisfaction with the new Pastoral Norms, and prefer to understand that the exceptions can legitimately be interpreted to include participation in a communal penitential service. Moreover, some are also disposed to deny the obligation of a penitent to mention, when he has the opportunity to make a private confession, the sins forgiven in the general absolution but not yet specifically confessed. However, this is a matter of private theological opinion and in practice the Norms of the Congregation for the Doctrine of Faith remain in effect. BIBLIOGRAPHY: J. Gallen, ThSt (March 1973) 114–121; "Document on General Absolution; press conference," OssRom (Eng.) no. 30 (226) 7. *CONFESSION, INTEGRITY OF; *PENITENTIAL SERVICES.

[P. K. MEAGHER]

ABSOLUTION, SACRAMENTAL, actively understood, the granting of a judicial pardon by the priest, the minister of the sacrament of penance, in the name of Christ; passively understood, the forgiveness effected by the sacrament. According to the Thomist school, sacerdotal absolution (i.e., sacramental absolution actively understood) is the form of the sacrament, or part of the sacramental sign; according to the Scotist school, it is the total sign. Theologians now emphasize the churchly aspect of absolution, whereby the sinner is reconciled to the mystical body of Christ and thus again made a sharer in divine friendship; B. Häring, *Shalom: Peace, the Sacrament of Reconciliation* (1969) 84–85.

[E. A. WEIS]

ABSOLUTION FROM CENSURES, see CENSURES, EC-

ABSOLUTION OF AN ACCOMPLICE, see ACCOMPLICE.

ABSOLUTION OF THE DEAD, a name given to the liturgical prayers for the dead that include petitions that the deceased may be absolved, freed by God from his sins. In the Roman rite such prayers for the dead are recited at the coffin or catafalque after a requiem Mass. The term is also applied sometimes to the sacramental absolution administered conditionally and within a short interval after death to a person who has died without any opportunity of receiving the sacrament of penance. This is absolution of the dead in an improper sense because it is given not to a dead person as such, but to one in whom, it is hoped, there is still some flicker of life,

despite apparent death. The absolution is given conditionally in these circumstances because it is effective only on condition that the person is still alive and capable of receiving the sacrament. Ignorance of other necessary dispositions on the part of the recipient may cause the minister of the sacrament to amplify the conditionality.

[E. A. WEIS]

ABSOLUTISM, a political regime in which the governing authority, usually vested in one person, is not dependent on the voice of a *democracy or the counsel of an effective *aristocracy. It degenerates into *tyranny, and produces an insolent vulgarity quite its own when the despot pursues his private advantage, not the common good; it is prone to produce the same effect when, twisting the old Roman maxim, "That which pleases the prince has the force of law," he acknowledges no higher rule than his own will. Nevertheless when subject to divine law and responsive to the checks of customary law, benign or paternal despotism, though not to the medieval temper or to that of English constitutionalism later, has proved at periods tolerable, not unpopular, and even an admirable system of government. Recent dictatorships, however, have usually lacked the requisite aplomb, good manners, high style, humanity, practical wisdom, and efficiency. BIBLIOGRAPHY: O. Köhler, SacMund 1:5–8.

[T. GILBY]

ABSTINENCE, see FAST.

ABSTINENCE, TOTAL, see TOTAL ABSTINENCE.

ABSTINENTES (3d.–4th. cent.), a communal sect of the East also known as the *Apotactics.

[F. T. RYAN]

ABSTRACT ART, term describing art characterized by forms separated from nature by the invention of the artist or wholly created without reference to external appearances. The term nonobjective was later used for works without reference to visible nature. Though many early cultures evidenced nonfigurative forms, 20th-cent, visual experiments conceived these as a new art content. Abstract expressionism developed in 1960 a "perceptual abstraction" in which paint film on bare canvas effected a sensuous tactility. The "optical" painters achieved visual shock through afterimages of repetitive geometric forms. BIBLIOGRAPHY: G. Nordland, NCE 1:42–44; V. Seitz, *Responsive Eye* (1965). *ABSTRACT EXPRESSIONISM.

[M. J. DALY]

ABSTRACT EXPRESSIONISM, American art movement of the 1940s and 1950s, effecting an international style. Concerned with personal symbols it emphasized the artist's intuition and innermost responses to his world. This ideology affirmed the aesthetic absolute of pure color and free form. In

1958 the style became internationally known as New American Painting. Key examples were Pollock's "drip paintings," de Kooning's brutal human content, and Kline's massive calligraphic imagery. Out of such "action painting" have come assemblage, pop and optical art, happenings, environments, and hard-edge painting. BIBLIOGRAPHY: R. L. Wickiser, NCE 1:54–56; B. Heller, "Roots of Abstract Expressionism," *Art in America* 49.4 (1961) 40–49.

[T. FEIDT]

ABSURD, THEATER OF THE, see THEATER OF THE ABSURD.

ABSURDITY, in older usage irrationality; in some contemporary circles, nonrationality, or being without reason. Like nonsense, with which it merges, calculated absurdity —which is not a contradiction in terms—can produce great works of art, easier to recognize than to define or classify, such as the works of Edward Lear and Lewis Carroll, shaggy dog stories, and some pieces of the Theater of the Absurd. Always they have their own logic, even if rather mad, like that of the Marx brothers; and always they suppose some point of reference to reason and good sense; otherwise they degenerate into drivel, either frivolous or slimy, cheerful or sad. Nor can they be appreciated if the whole of life is held to be meaningless, as is the case with other pieces of the Theater of the Absurd; for then there is no real communication or dialogue, but at best a polite waiting for the other's soliloquy to finish so that you may begin your own. We cannot even begin to be absurd if all is absurd, just as we cannot begin to be vicious except against a background of virtue.

The benignly and laudably absurd, which calls for great art to contrive, can be divided into the gay and the grave, or rather differently and more profoundly, into the comic and the tragic. In all cases, though their purpose is not to point a moral but just to be themselves, when they are well done, these works throw down a challenge to contentment with didactic and explanatory reasons and the safer shores of love. When they are fun, they are salutary reminders that life is too serious to be taken solemnly: even St. Thomas Aquinas in his somewhat prim and Aristotelean treatment of the virtue of playfulness *(eutrapelia)* ends by citing Seneca in support of the occasional aptness of being ridiculous. Sometimes the absurd springs from agony, and then it is a salutary reminder that we cannot save ourselves and are all in the situation of *Waiting for Godot*.

Theological evaluation, which should always remain respectfully tentative, cannot fail to see the connection with the following doctrines: God creates us and saves us only in the play of his own sheer generosity, and any reasons we may advance do no more than skirt round the fact; all our present speech about him is, as St. Gregory says, only stammering; and we reach to him by the theological virtues which extravagantly surpass the reasonable measures, the right reason, *orthos logos,* of the moral virtues. In this sense things are nonreasonable, first, last, and best. BIBLIOGRAPHY: R.

Nogar, *Lord of the Absurd* (1968); D. Marano "Two Faces of the Absurd," *Philosophy Today* 16 (1972) 254–267.

[T. GILBY]

ABŪ'L-BARAKĀT (d. 1324), Coptic priest and writer in Cairo. He collaborated on a history of Islam, and among his independent works were a Coptic-Arabic dictionary and a theological encyclopedia for the instruction of priests and laity.

[T. C. O'BRIEN]

ABŪ'L-FADL (FAZL) 'ALLĀMĪ (1551–1602), Indian historical and religious writer, whose principal work *Akbar Nāma* is a unique source on Hindu philosophy and literature, as well as on the political history of the Mogul Emperor Akbar (1556–1605).

[T. C. O'BRIEN]

ABŪ'L-FARA'J ABDALLAH IBN AṬṬAYIB (d. 1043), a priest and secretary of the patriarch in Baghdad, who wrote commentaries on Aristotle's works and on Scripture, as well as treatises in theology and canon law.

[T. C. O'BRIEN]

ABU, MOUNT, a mountain of granite peaks in South Rajasthan, India, for 2000 years a place of pilgrimage to elaborately sculptured Jain shrines, temples, and tombs, as mentioned in *Mahabharata*. The two principal temples, preeminent as baroque Gujarati architecture are Tejpal (A.D. 1197–1247) unrivaled in delicacy of rich detail; and that built earlier by Vimala under a Solanki monarch (A.D. 1032) in simpler and bolder style—the oldest and most complete example of Jain architecture. BIBLIOGRAPHY: EB (1971) 1:53.

[M. J. DALY]

ABU SIMBEL, site of two temples of Ramses II (*c*.1250 B.C.) in Aswan governate of Egypt (ancient Nubia), hewn in sandstone cliffs on the W bank of the Nile. The principal one was discovered by J. Burckhardt in 1812. Recessed to form façade are four, seated colossi of the King (65 feet high). Dedicated to the sun gods and so oriented to the E, the morning sun penetrated 185 feet through the great halls to the innermost sanctuary. Graffiti evidences Greek mercenaries in Egyptian army (5th cent. B.C.). Plans for the Aswan dam threatening the temples' complete submergence, in 1955 an international team of archeologists recorded scenes and transcriptions. In 1968 the seated colossi were cut out of the rock face and precisely reconstructed on a cliff 200 feet above the river bed, through funds of 50 nations, in response to a drive sponsored by UNESCO. BIBLIOGRAPHY: W. A. Fairservis, *Ancient Kingdom of the Nile and the Doomed Monuments of Nubia* (1962); R. Keating, *Nubian Twilight* (1963).

[M. J. DALY]

ABUNA (Arab., our father), a general term in use among Arabic-speaking Christians equivalent to the Western title of address for priests, "father." It also has a specific sense in the Ethiopian Church, in which the metropolitan of Axum is styled abuna. Elected from the monastic clergy, he was always formerly a Copt (Egyptian), the only bp. in Ethiopia, and was directly under the jurisdiction of the Coptic patriarch of Alexandria. Since 1948 the abuna has been Ethiopian; he has the right to consecrate Ethiopian bps. and the holy chrism, and although still consecrated by the Coptic patriarch, retains only a nominal submission to the Egyptian Church. The abuna now often uses the title "katholikos-patriarch" and resided at the royal court in Addis Ababa until the overthrow of 1974.

[A. J. JACOPIN]

ABUNDIUS OF COMO, ST. (d. 469?), bp. of Como from 449. Sent by Pope Leo the Great as legate to the imperial court at Constantinople, A. succeeded in obtaining the signatures of the Eastern bishops met in synod in the Hagia Sophia to the papal condemnation of the doctrine of Nestorius and Eutyches (450). After returning to Italy he represented the Pope on a like mission, equally successful, to the See of Milan (452). His remaining years were spent in pastoral work in his own diocese, esp. in the evangelization of the pockets of paganism that still remained. BIBLIOGRAPHY: P. Gini and M. C. Celletti, BiblSanct 1:23–32.

[H. JACK]

ABUSE, understood not in the sense of using up and consuming (found in Roman law and therefore in the early canonists), nor in the sense of disuse, but in its bad sense of misuse, the privative of use. This meaning appears from its opposite, *use, which in moral theology has a double sense. Thus abuse can refer to a man's perverting the nature of a thing to which he applies himself, or to denying it or loading it with a value it does not possess. The former is the ordinary meaning; the latter is more recondite and perhaps more questionable. To take them in order:

(1) In the moral scene one is required to respect the nature of things as they are made by God and not to live and act in a world of make-believe. Accordingly one should lay hold of them in accordance with what they really are. If he tries to manipulate them merely to fit his private whim, he is abusing them. Abuse in this sense indicates disharmony with the objective world.

(2) In the human environment some things are for enjoyment and some for use. According to St. Augustine's canon a man should not use what should be enjoyed, nor enjoy what should be used. Enjoyable things are too good to be used; in fact when a man treats them as utilities, he abuses them. Making love for reasons of hygiene is as bad as, or worse than, going to a funeral just for the ride. The second arm of the canon is more doubtful. But then, St. Augustine's theology lacked the metaphysical pluralism of St. Thomas' and also the recognition that subordinate ends are not just utilities, so that a man of great virtue may aspire to a state when there are no disagreeable things to be done and when he is never bored by whatever he is doing.

[T. GILBY]

ABYDOS, Greek form of Egyptian Abdu ("hill of the reliquary"), one of the most important archeological sites in Egypt. Pit tombs discovered by E. Amélineau (19th cent.) and further excavated by Sir Flinders Petrie are with some doubt held as 2d dynasty necropolis. Temple of Seti I, excavated by A. Mariette (1859) is one of the most beautiful of antiquity, having seven sanctuaries and two hypostyle halls. A relief of great delicacy shows Seti and his son Ramses near cartouches of 76 predecessors—the "Abydos list of kings." A remarkable *Osireion*—an underground vaulted hall with 10 monolithic pillars surrounded by water—may have cosmological inferences. BIBLIOGRAPHY: M. F. Broome, *Temple of King Sethos I at Abydos* (4 v., 1933–39).

[M. J. DALY]

ABYSS (in the Bible), in the NT a concept of the underworld where evil spirits dwell (Lk 8.31; Rev 9.1–11; 11.7; 17.8; 20.3) and the dead reside (Rom 10.7), expressed in the Greek word *abyssos* meaning "bottomless." The concept derived from the OT *tehōm*, the primeval, chaotic ocean imagined to lie under the earth, thought to be a source of the earth's water (Gen 7.11; Is 51.10) over which God alone had power (Gen 1.2; Is 63.13).

[C. P. CEROKE]

ABYSSINIA, see ETHIOPIA.

ACACIAN SCHISM (484–519), the rupture with Rome caused by Acacius, Patriarch of Constantinople (471–489). Acacius used the doctrinal differences between Catholics and Monophysites to gain spiritual leadership of the Eastern Church. He co-authored the *Henoticon* with Peter Mongus, Monophysite patriarch of Alexandria. Imposed on all by the Emperor *Zeno, this implicit rejection of *Chalcedon was neither Catholic nor Monophysite and alienated all (see ACEPHALI). Excommunicated by Pope *Felix III, first in 484, again in 485, Acacius reacted by striking the Pope's name from the diptychs and thus began the Acacian Schism, presage of *Photius' break with Rome. The schism was important also as the occasion for the *Gelasian Letter on the two powers, spiritual and temporal. After Acacius' death (489) Popes *Gelasius and *Anastasius II insisted on a condemnation of Acacius by his successors Fravita (490) and Euphemius (490–494). Both, though faithful to Chalcedon, refused, yielding to the anti-Chalcedonian Emperor Anastasius. With the accession of Justin I as emperor, Pope *Hormisdas proposed a formula of reunion that was accepted (519). The names of both Zeno and Acacius were struck from the diptychs by John, patriarch of Constantinople.

BIBLIOGRAPHY: PL 58:41–60, letters of Pope Simplicius; 58:893–967, letters of Felix III; E. Marin, DTC 1:288–290; Bardenhewer 4:218; P. Charanis, *Church and State in the Later Roman Empire* (1939); L. Sabaville, DTC 6:2153–78.

[T. C. O'BRIEN]

ACACIANS, a moderate Arian sect, also called *homoeans, that stemmed from Acacius, bp. of Caesarea in Palestine (340–*c*.366). They held that the Son was not consubstantial with, but merely similar to, the eternal Father. *ARIANISM.

[A. J. JACOPIN]

ACACIUS, PATRIARCH OF CONSTANTINOPLE (d. 489). At the beginning of his patriarchate, A. demonstrated his allegiance to the bp. of Rome by refusing to sign the encyclical of the Emperor Basiliscus which rejected the teaching of Chalcedon. When Zeno became Emperor and the Monophysite Peter Mongus was endeavoring to seize Alexandria from John Talaia (482), A. used the occasion to enhance the prerogatives of the patriarchate of *Constantinople. Under the semblance of effecting union in the East, A. drew up a proposal which was both a creed and a statement of reunion called the *Henoticon. It reaffirmed the Nicene-Constantinopolitan creed, condemned Eutyches and Nestorius, accepted the anathemas of Cyril of Alexandria, and ignored the formula of Chalcedon. Despite his excommunication by Pope Felix, A., with Zeno's endorsement of the *Henoticon,* was able to maintain his ascendancy in the East until his death. He was the occasion of the *Acacian Schism (484–519). BIBLIOGRAPHY: C. Clifford, CE 1:82–83.

[F. H. BRIGHAM]

ACACIUS OF BEROEA (*c*.322-after 433), a monk of Gindarus near Antioch who was consecrated bp. of Beroea in 378 and sent by Meletius of Antioch to Rome to end the Antiochian schism. He participated in the Council of Constantinople (381) and in the Synod of the Oak (403) but was prevented by old age from attending that of Ephesus (431). His interventions on behalf of orthodoxy at the time of the Nestorian controversy eventually led to the restoration of peace between Alexandria and Antioch in 433. BIBLIOGRAPHY: V. Ermoni, DHGE 1:241–242; Quasten 3:482–483; C. Clifford, CE 1:80–81.

[M. J. COSTELLOE]

ACACIUS OF CAESAREA (d. 366), successor to Eusebius as bp. of Caesarea in 340. A man of great learning and intelligence, he became the leader of the Homoean Arians and a favored counselor of Emperor Constantius. Condemned by the orthodox synod of Sardica in 343, he later became a bitter opponent of St. Cyril of Jerusalem, whom he deposed at the Council of Antioch (358). He was himself temporarily deposed the following year at the Council of Seleucia. In 360 he directed the approval of the creed of Nice at the Synod of Constantinople which proclaimed that the Son is "like" the Father. Later, under the orthodox Emperor Jovinian, A. subscribed to the Nicene Creed, but then returned to his Arian beliefs under Valens. He was condemned by the Semi-Arian synod of Lampsacus in 365 but retained his see until his death about a year later. BIBLIOGRAPHY: V. Ermoni, DHGE 1:240–241; Quasten 3:345–346.

[M. J. COSTELLOE]

ACADEMY OF AMERICAN FRANCISCAN HISTORY, a society of Franciscan scholars founded in 1944 to foster interest in, and to promote historical research concerned with, the work done by Spanish and Portuguese Franciscans in the development of the New World. Headquarters are in Bethesda, Maryland. BIBLIOGRAPHY: C. Tallararico, "Silver Jubilee of the Academy of American Franciscan History," *Americas* 26 (1970) 447–449.

ACARIE, BARBE, see MARIE DE L'INCARNATION, BL.

ACATHIST HYMN (Gr. *akathistos hymnos,* in the Byzantine liturgy the hymn during which one does not sit; Sl. *akafist*), a term with two meanings. (1) An office of thanksgiving in honor of the Mother of God which is sung standing (thus its name). One legend ascribes the Patriarch Sergius I as its author either *c*.620 during a Persian attack on Constantinople or in 626 when the Slavs and Avars were assailing the city. The inhabitants strongly believed the city was spared and the enemy routed through the intercession of the Holy Virgin and repaired to Hagia Sophia, where the patriarch composed the new prayer as a thanksgiving service. Others claim Patriarch Germanus as its author after the lifting of the Muslim siege of 718. The origins of the hymn, therefore, remain obscure. The Acathist is now sung in the Byzantine liturgy with great solemnity during Lent. The text is based upon gospel narratives of the Nativity and poetical praises of God and the Virgin and consists of 24 stanzas, each beginning with one of the 24 letters of the Greek alphabet. It is divided into four parts, and one section is sung each Friday evening for the first 4 weeks of Lent, the hymn being repeated in its entirety on the vigil of the 5th Saturday (Acathist Saturday). The poetry of the text is unrivaled as one of the most famous examples of Byzantine religious literature. (2) An office, celebrated in some churches, honoring a particular mystery of faith or a certain saint based on the pattern of the original Acathist Hymn to the Mother of God. BIBLIOGRAPHY: G. V. Shann, *Euchology, Manual of Prayers of the Holy Orthodox Church* (1969) 19.

[A. J. JACOPIN]

ACATHISTUS, see AKATHISTOS.

ACCA, ST. (*c*.660–740), successor in 709 to Wilfrid, his friend and adviser, as bp. of Hexham, England. He carried

carried forward the diocesan works begun by Wilfrid, and on his own fostered learning, founded a library, introduced the psalmody of Gregory the Great, and was a generous patron of scholars, notably Bede, whose commentaries on the Scriptures he stimulated. In 732, he was, for unrecorded reasons, expelled from his diocese. His return before his death is uncertain, but he was buried at Hexham. BIBLIOGRAPHY: M. A. Calabrese, BiblSanct 1:150; Butler 4:156–157.

[H. JACK]

ACCADEMIA PLATONICA (FLORENCE), the leading institute for Platonic studies in Italy. It was established by Cosimo de'Medici at the suggestion of the Byzantine Neoplatonist, George Gemistus *Plethon, who was sent from Byzantium together with John Bessarion of Trebizond to the Council of Florence (1438–45). John Argyropoulos (d.1486), who held the chair of Greek (1456–71) and later was the teacher of J. *Reuchlin at Rome, continued the Neoplatonic tradition. Rejecting Aristotle because of his naturalistic bias, they proposed the positive elements of Neoplatonism in a Christian context as a more effective means of promoting the Christian renewal of Church and State. BIBLIOGRAPHY: Copleston 3:207–216; S. Pasquazzi, EncCatt 1:176–177.

ACCADEMIA ROMANA, a learned society of archeologists that traces its beginnings to Pomponio Leto (1428–97). Its modern development was initiated by Pope Benedict XIV (1740), given formal recognition by Pius VII (1816), and pontifical status by Pius VIII (1829–30). Under the leadership of G. de Rossi during the pontificate of Pius IX (1846–78) it achieved outstanding prominence in the world of scholarship as the most significant international archeological society of the 19th century. With the support and cooperation of the popes and civil officials of Rome it has continued to maintain its scholarly traditions, which have influenced archeological research in the major universities of the world. It has 30 honorary and distinguished members, all residents of Rome, and 120 corresponding members, 30 of whom are residents of Rome. The pope is the honorary president and the society meets once a month from November through June. It publishes *Rendiconti* and *Le Memorie.* BIBLIOGRAPHY: U. Begnini, CE 1:83–89; S. Pasquazzi, EncCatt 1:178.

ACCARON, see EKRON.

ACCELERATION OF BIRTH, an expression used in RC moral theology for the induced premature delivery of a viable fetus, i.e., a fetus which, though immature, has a reasonable hope of surviving outside the maternal womb. The term is used in opposition to abortion, in which reasonable hope of survival does not exist. The acceleration of birth is considered legitimate when it is necessary in the interests of the mother (e.g., when pregnancy cannot continue without endangering her life) or of the fetus (e.g., when the possibility

of safe delivery will be lessened if the fetus is not delivered before it comes to maturity). The more questionable the viability of the fetus, the more urgent must be the reasons for inducing premature delivery.

[P. K. MEAGHER]

ACCELERATION OF DEATH, see DEATH, HASTENING OF.

ACCELLINI, GIROLAMO, see BALBI, GIROLAMO.

ACCENTUS, (1) the portions of liturgical chanting performed by the celebrant or other ministers rather than by the schola or choir; (2) the simple musical style characteristic of such chants, i.e., the inflected monotone of liturgical recitative and Gregorian psalmody. BIBLIOGRAPHY: P. A. Scholes, *Oxford Companion to Music* (1970) 5. *CONCENTUS.

[P. DOHERTY]

ACCEPTANCE OF PERSONS, see FAVORITISM.

ACCEPTANTS, members of the clergy in France and the Netherlands who, during the controversies over *Jansenism, accepted the bull *Unigenitus* (1713) of Clement XI. The bull was a condemnation of 101 propositions (D 2401–2501) from P. *Quesnel's *Nouveau testament avec des réflexions morales sur chaque verset.* Acceptance of the bull was imposed by Louis XIV on the Sorbonne and on parliament in 1714. A majority of the clergy accepted it, but were opposed by a strong minority. At the heart of the bitter controversy that ensued was the issue of the pope's personal infallibility; in accord with the second of the four *Gallican Articles, the minority appealed to a general council in 1717 (see APPELLANTS). During these conflicts the *Schism of Utrecht took place (1723). The Acceptants achieved a victory in 1730, when adherence to the bull *Unigenitus* was made obligatory by royal decree; still, resistance to the bull lingered for many decades. See bibliog. for Jansenism.

[E. A. WEIS]

ACCESS, a word that appears in religious contexts in several different senses. (1) It was the proper term for the right formerly enjoyed by cardinals at a papal election to change their vote after a ballot had been taken. This was usually exercised for the purpose of establishing the two-thirds majority needed for election. This privilege was abolished by Pius X in 1904. (2) It was used in canon law for the right given to a person to obtain at some future time a benefice temporarily held in abeyance because some necessary condition (e.g., sufficient age) has not yet been satisfied. (3) In the RC Church prayers of access are the prayers recommended to the priest for recitation before Mass. (4) In Churches of the Anglican communion the prayer of humble access is a special prayer placed in different Prayer Books either before or after the prayer of consecration.

ACCESSION, a term used in law and moral theology to signify a special mode of acquiring ownership, namely, by addition to property already owned through growth, increase, or labor.

[P. K. MEAGHER]

ACCESSION SERVICE, in the C of E, the special forms of prayer for use on the anniversary day of the accession of the British sovereign.

ACCIAIUOLI (also spelled Acciaioli or Acciajuoli), a celebrated Florentine family, originally from the foothills of the Alps (where they dealt in steel, *acciaio*), of merchants, bankers, statesmen, and patrons of the arts. Cardinal Angelo (1340–1408) was an effective supporter of the Roman pontiffs during the *Great Western Schism. Cardinal Niccolò (1630–1719) was one of the *zelanti* cardinals of his period, though his clumsy immuring in a convent of a widow to prevent her marriage to his nephew embarrassed his chances as a *papabile*. Cardinal Filippo (1700–76) was nuncio to Portugal and, doing his best to defend the Jesuits, was declared *persona non grata* by *Pombal and ordered out of the country.

[T. GILBY]

ACCIDENT, an Aristotelian term in general designating something nonessential or adventitious; it is used in philosophy and theology in three different senses. (1) In metaphysics it signifies one of the two kinds of actual being (predicamental accident). One distinguishes in the complex beings of experience between the essentially constituted, permanent subject (*substance) and its nonessential modification (accident). Being is primarily substance; accident is being only in a secondary, though real, sense. An accident has being by inhering in a subject; it exists only in the sense that through it a substance has an accessory and modifying type of existence. Nine of the ten *categories into which being is divided represent the different kinds of accident. The substance-accident composition is a consequence of the variableness and perfectibility of the creature and so cannot be found in God. An accident's need to inhere in a subject poses a problem for the theologian, who must explain the existence of the eucharistic accidents or *species after *transubstantiation. (2) In logic, accident (predicable accident) is a classification of predicates, applicable to a predicate that expresses not the substance but an attribute or condition of a subject. (3) In moral science the term is applied to *circumstances of a moral action, the action itself being regarded as comparable to a substance, or to a consequence of moral action not directly intended by the person acting. BIBLIOGRAPHY: H. Reith, *Metaphysics of St. Thomas Aquinas* (1958); V. E. Smith, *Elements of Logic* (1957).

[T. C. O'BRIEN]

ACCIDIE, a corruption through the Medieval Latin (*accidia*) and Norman French of the Late Latin *acedia,* which transliterated the Greek *akedia,* a term indicating a state of not caring. In the late Middle Ages, before the revival of Greek learning, the transformation undergone by the word blurred the general appreciation of its derivation and meaning as it had been used in earlier ecclesiastical literature. BIBLIOGRAPHY: OED 1:56. *ACEDIA.

[U. VOLL]

ACCLAMATION (Lat., to exclaim), a term expressing unanimous vocal approval or sometimes denunciation; it has been used with some variety of meaning in civil, ecclesiastical, liturgical, and musical contexts. (1) Originally an Eastern practice, acclamation became common in the Roman republic, e.g., the senate would ratify decrees by this method or emperors were occasionally elected by common acclamation. (2) By extension, bishops were approved and deposed in the early Church by this process; acclamation is even now considered a valid form of electing a pope, should the cardinal-electors be so inspired (ASS 38 [1946] 85–86). (3) Christian liturgical acclamations, probably influenced both by secular practice and Jewish ritual, commonly refer to invocations used in divine worship such as litanies and the reproaches in the old Good Friday liturgy. In the Byzantine rituals for ordination and consecration the candidate is presented to the congregation while the ordaining prelate asks if they deem the candidate worthy. The people respond *Axios* ("he is worthy") three times in approval. (4) In a very specific sense, acclamations refer to musical salutations addressed on state occasions to the Byzantine emperor, or to Church dignitaries. The emphasis in the acclamations was on the dignity of the one acclaimed, and the wishing of long life and good health. Gradually the music for these acclamations became standardized and was normally antiphonal in form. After the Byzantine empire fell (1453) the musical form of acclamation was restricted to the lauding of ecclesiastical dignitaries, usually during the Divine Liturgy. A Western version of the imperial acclamation is the *laudes regiae* (royal praises) which appeared in the Gallican ritual in the 8th cent. and is similar to the *Litany of the Saints. This formulary had a variety of uses and traces of it remain today in ceremonial acclamations for popes and certain secular rulers. BIBLIOGRAPHY: J. H. Crehan, CDT 21–22; Wellesz; E. H. Kantorowicz, *Laudes Regiae: A Study in Liturgical Acclamations and Medieval Ruler Worship* (1946); F. Cabrol, DACL 1:240–265.

[F. T. RYAN]

ACCO, coastal city of Palestine, the medieval Acre, the modern Akka. In the Bible Acco is mentioned in Jg 1.31; elsewhere it is referred to as *Ptolemais, the name it received under Ptolemy II Philadelphus (285–246 B.C.).

[T. C. O'BRIEN]

ACCOLTI, MICHAEL (1807–78), Jesuit missionary. An Italian of noble birth and a Jesuit from 1830, A. was assigned (1843) to the American Indian missions (Oregon); during the

Gold Rush (1849) the need for priests for the mission took him to San Francisco. A few months later he was back in Oregon as superior of the Northwest missions. By 1854 he had obtained from his general superior a decree assigning the responsibility for the Oregon and California missions to the Province of Turin. From 1855 until his death his services were divided between the Jesuit universities of San Francisco and Santa Clara. BIBLIOGRAPHY: J. B. McGloin, NCE 1:80; G. J. Garraghan, *Jesuits in the Middle United States* (3v., 1938).

[H. JACK]

ACCOLTI, PIETRO (1455–1532) and **BENEDETTO** (1497–1549), cardinals, uncle and nephew, of a noble Tuscan family. Pietro became bp. of Ancona in 1505 and was made cardinal by Julius II in 1511. During Leo X's pontificate, he was in charge of papal letters. He held seven bishoprics and one archbishopric. Benedetto was abp. of Ravenna and papal secretary. He succeeded to several of his uncle's bishoprics and in 1527 Clement VII named him a cardinal. BIBLIOGRAPHY: J. G. Gallagher, NCE 1:80; G. K. Brown, *Italy and the Reformation to 1550* (1933).

[H. JACK]

ACCOMMODATION, here understood as the adaptation of a communication to the person to whom it is given, is a concept with important application in both systematic and practical theology. (1) It is used in the study of divine revelation, for God must adapt or accommodate the expression of his truths to man's capacities, limited as they are by many factors, such as his nature, state of development, place in time, and cultural background. (2) Accommodation is also an important aspect of the communication of divine truth from one human being to another, whether it be effected by preaching, liturgical rite, catechesis, or missionary activity. Such communication, accommodated in and with the aid of faith to the one who receives it, further develops understanding. Although the practice of accommodation is justified by reflection on the nature of God, man, and communication, it also has explicit scriptural warrant; for example, St. Paul wrote: "And I, brethren, could not speak to you as to spiritual men but only as carnal, as to little ones in Christ. I fed you with milk, not with solid food, for you were not yet ready for it, for you are still carnal" (1 Cor 3.1–2).

[E. A. WEIS]

ACCOMPLICE, in moral theology, one who cooperates in the evil act of another. The morality of abetting another in sin is discussed elsewhere (see COOPERATION IN ANOTHER'S SIN; RESTITUTION). The term accomplice *(complex)* is also used in canon law, often with reference to complicity in sexual sin. The constitution *Sacramentum poenitentiae* (1741) decreed that a confessor who has seriously sinned against chastity with another is deprived of his jurisdiction to absolve his accomplice of that sin, except in danger of death when no other confessor is available. If, despite the fact that he has no jurisdiction, a confessor attempts to absolve his accomplice, he incurs *ipso facto* the penalty of excommunication reserved in a most special way to the Holy See (CIC c. 2367.1,2). It is understood that the sin in question involves an external act that is gravely sinful on the part of both participants.

[T. M. MCFADDEN]

ACCUSATION, in general, the act of charging self (*CONFESSION) or another with fault. In moral theology accusation may be either evangelical, i.e., *fraternal correction, or judicial. Public officials, such as the ecclesiastical promoter of justice or a civil district attorney, are bound by their office, more or less gravely as the offense itself and the danger to the common good are more or less grave, to accuse criminals. A private person may also be bound to accuse when the peace of society or the rights of a third person are seriously threatened. Another special obligation to accuse occurs when the precept of a superior, e.g., in canonical visitation, demands it. Accusation in these instances flows from charity, justice, or obedience to a superior and is distinct from *denunciation, an obligation that comes from some law. BIBLIOGRAPHY: ThAq ST 2a2ae, 68; J. Fearon, NCE 1:83; Prümmer 2:159.

[U. VOLL]

ACCUSATION, FALSE, in a forensic context, a crime and affront to the public justice of a community, which, according to 13th-cent. jurisprudence, should rightly be visited with the very penalties it sought to procure. When a false accusation has no forensic context, it is simply the moral offense called calumny.

ACEDIA, more generally called sloth through confusion with its most outstanding effect, is a disgust with the spiritual because of the physical labor involved. If the spiritual good from which acedia recoils has the necessary connection with the Divine Good which is the subject of Christian joy, it can be sinful and even seriously so. Moreover, acedia is one of the *capital sins, a common distraction from virtue, producing other, even quite distinct, sins. The word is found not only in the Septuagint Bible, e.g., Sir 6.26, but in Greek and Latin pagan authors. Whatever its possible Stoic origins, the psychology of acedia received careful attention from the desert Fathers of the 4th century. Evagrius Ponticus in 383 seems to be the first to have written a description of acedia (PG 40:1274), obviously drawing more from actual experience than scriptural exegesis. John Cassian faithfully reported this fairly common trouble to Western monasticism in his *On the Spirit of Acedia* (PL 49:359–369). St. Gregory the Great changed the expression to "sadness" *(tristitia),* but the tradition of acedia prevailed in the Middle Ages. See ThAq ST 2a2ae, 35; *De malo,* 11. While theological commentators remain faithful to the Thomist synthesis, a popular tendency to confuse acedia with its principal external effect, sloth *(pigritia),* developed. Those aware of more profound interior implications attempted the spiritualization of acedia by "baptizing" it as spiritual sloth. This terminology has the distinct advantage of making acedia appear exotic and reserved for the spiritual elite, whereas tradition and experience show it to be a very common difficulty. BIBLIOGRAPHY: PL 49:359–369; ThAq ST 2a2ae, 35; *De malo*, 11; G. Bardy, DSAM 1:166–169; U. Voll, NCE 1:83–84; E. Waugh, "Sloth," *Seven Deadly Sins* (ed. I. Fleming, 1962); S. Wenzel, *Sin of Sloth* (1960, 1967).

[U. VOLL]

ACEPHALI, from the Greek word *acephaloi* (headless), a strict Monophysite, anti-Chalcedonian sect in Alexandria with several subdivisions, so called because its members, who had initially separated from the Patriarch Timothy Aleurus for his leniency toward clerics conforming to Chalcedon, later rejected the Patriarch Peter Mongus when he endorsed the *Henoticon* of the Emperor Zeno (482). BIBLIOGRAPHY: Bihlmeyer-Tüchle 1:299; Daniélou-Marrou 1:361–368. *ACTISTAE.

[F. H. BRIGHAM]

ACHAB, see AHAB.

ACHAIA (also Achaea), originally a section of Greece including SE Thessaly and the N coast of the Peloponnesus bordered by Elis and Sicyon, but after its conquest by Rome (146 B.C.) and as Roman senatorial province (27 B.C.) it embraced all of Ancient Greece together with a section of S Epirus, the Ionian Islands, the Cyclades, Euboea, Sycros, Peparethos, Sciathos, and Icos. The cities of Athens, Corinth, and Cenchraea were prominent during NT and early Christian history. Elevated to the rank of an imperial province by Tiberius (15), it became again a senatorial province under Claudius (44). Initially, the Romans disbanded the Greek regional leagues but then reactivated them, allowing a limited exercise of executive powers over the cities within each federation. No group of delegates actually represented all of Achaia, but the Achaian league claimed this prerogative in establishing the cult of the emperor. Under Roman rule, the land of this province was apportioned to its many cities whose rights and standing were varied. Athens and Sparta were practically autonomous, though Trajan and his successors assigned overseers of their internal affairs. Nicopolis, Patrae and Corinth, the capital and largest city, all prospered. St. Paul witnesses the extensive Christian community in Achaia (2 Cor. 1.1; 1 Th 1.8) and Luke correctly names Gallio Proconsul (51–53) in his account of Paul's arrest for sedition (Acts 18.12–21). BIBLIOGRAPHY: J. Keil, CAH 11:556–565; T. Dumbabin, OCD 2; H. Leclerq, DACL 1:321–340.

[F. H. BRIGHAM]

ACHARD, BL. (Aichardus; d. *c.*1170) monk of Clairvaux, which he entered possibly in the year 1124. Under St. Bernard he was architect of several Cistercian monasteries; the Romanesque abbey of Himmerod (consecrated 1178) in the

Rhineland is among these. As novice master at Clairvaux he wrote "On the Seven Deserts" and "On All the Saints," both extant in MS (Montfaucon, 1299). He has been extolled, somewhat exaggeratedly, by Herbert of Torres, a pupil of his, as a "great philosopher and theologian." BIBLIOGRAPHY: A. Schneider, NCE 1:85; *idem,* NCE 6:1120–21; G. Venuto, BiblSanct 1:147.

[J. R. RIVELLO]

ACHARD OF SAINT VICTOR (d. 1171–72), theologian, canon, and later (1155) abbot of Saint-Victor, Paris. He was bp. of Avranches, France, from 1162 and author of the treatises *De Trinitate* and *De discretione animae, spiritus et mentis.* BIBLIOGRAPHY: J. Châtillon, "Achard de Saint-Victor. . .," *Mélanges F. Cavellera* (1948) 317–337; *idem,* NCE 1:85.

[J. L. GRASSI]

ACHARIUS OF NOYON, ST. (Aighardus; d. *c.*640), bishop. A. was a disciple of St. Eustace of Luxeuil, the successor of St. Columban. He participated in the synod of Clichy (626–627) as bp. of Tournai-Noyon and summoned Audomar to preach the gospel in Thérouanne. He commissioned St. Amandus, apostle of Belgium, to evangelize Tournai. The report that King Dagobert I forced pagans to receive baptism at A.'s request is suspect. BIBLIOGRAPHY: R. Desreumaux, BiblSanct 1:148–149.

[J. M. O'DONNELL]

ACHAZ, see AHAZ.

ACHEIROPOIETOS, a Greek term meaning "made without hands", having direct reference to the *Image not made by hands.

[F. T. RYAN]

ACHERON, a river in Thesprotia, upper Epirus, which, according to legend, with its murky gorges and underground channels, was a waterway to Hades and a likely location for the oracle of the dead mentioned by Herodotus (*Histories* 5:92). P. Devambez, *Praeger Encyclopedia of Ancient Greek Civilization* (1966) 9.

ACHILLI, GIACINTO, apostate Italian Dominican. Suspended by the Holy Office for immorality, A. became an anti-Catholic propagandist in Malta, Italy, and England. At a public meeting (1851), J. H. *Newman accused him of certain offenses against morality. A. responded with a libel suit. In the judgment of the court, only the fact of A.'s suspension for immorality was sufficiently established; it had been impossible to assemble and bring from abroad enough evidence to constitute legal proof of the other charges. But the fine imposed, slight in view of the gravity of the alleged injury, showed that the court had no high regard for A.'s moral character. He thereafter fell into obscurity, no longer able to find a market for his propaganda. BIBLIOGRAPHY:

N. Wiseman, "Authentic Brief Sketch of the Life of Dr. Giacinto Achilli" DublinRev 56 (1856) 13–21; W. Ward, *Life of John Henry Newman* (2 v., 1912), 1:275–304.

ACHIOR, see AHIKAR.

ACHRON, JOSEPH (1886–1943), violin virtuoso and composer. Lithuanian by birth, A. belongs to a group of Russian-Jewish composers who, under the influence of the Russian nationalistic school of music (Rimsky-Korsakov, Mussorgsky, Liadov, and others) turned towards the secular aspects of *Jewish music. He was one of the founders of the Society for Jewish Folk Music organized in St. Petersburg in 1908. A great number of Jewish composers such as Joel Engel, Lazare Saminsky and Michael Milner were either members or came under the influence of this society. A.'s works composed in Russia reflect these folkloristic trends. He left Russia in 1922 and settled in the U.S. in 1925. In 1932 A. wrote his only major liturgical work for the synagogue, *Evening Service for the Sabbath.* In this work, commissioned by Temple Emanu-El, N.Y.C., he shows an understanding of the asymmetrical rhythmic structure of the Hebrew language and develops a harmonic style which evolves logically from the modal characteristics of Hebrew liturgical music. BIBLIOGRAPHY: A. Weisser, *Modern Renaissance of Jewish Music* (1954); P. A. Scholes, *Oxford Companion to Music* (1970) 6.

[H. BERLINSKI]

ACINDYNUS, GREGORY (fl. first half of 14th cent.), Greek monk and theologian. Very little is known about his life. Although strongly influenced by Western scholasticism, his first writings were directed against one of its protagonists, Barlaam of Calabria. But he devoted most of his theological work, some six books, to attacking Gregory Palamas and the hesychast teachings. After his death he was condemned, together with Barlaam, by the Palamite council of 1351 under Emperor John VI Cantacuzenus. Almost all of his writings remain unedited. BIBLIOGRAPHY: M. Jugie, DHGE *HESYCHASM. 1:339–340.

[P. FOSCOLOS]

ACKERMANN AUS BÖHMEN, DER *(The Bohemian Plowman),* masterpiece of German humanism, written in Prague *c.*1400 by Johannes von Tepl (von Saaz; *c.*1350–*c.*1414), as a lament for his deceased wife. In form, the work is a legalistic debate between the Plowman (Man, confronted by the riddle of Death) and Death (God's representative), in which God, as Judge, awards the victory to Death. The author's learning is evident in the numerous references to ancient and medieval sources; his craftsmanship, in the sustained tension, the variety of moods evoked, and the inherent power and rhetorical beauty of the language. BIBLIOGRAPHY: *Death and the Plowman* or *The Bohemian Plowman* (tr. E. N. Kirrmann, 1958).

[M. F. MCCARTHY]

ACMEISM, popular name for the Guild of Poets, founded in 1912 by Gumilyov and Gorodetski. As a literary movement, it opposed clarity of diction and imagery to the vague mysticism of Symbolism. Acmeism did not survive World War I. BIBLIOGRAPHY: R. Poggioli, *Poets of Russia: 1890–1930* (1960) 105–111; G. Donchin, *Influence of French Symbolism on Russian Poetry* (1958) 74–75.

[M. F. MCCARTHY]

ACOEMETAE, originally the monks of a monastery founded in Constantinople by the abbot Alexander (*c.*350–*c.*430) after a considerable experience of monastic life coupled with evangelical preaching in Syria and Mesopotamia. They practiced an absolute poverty, made no point of manual labor, stressed charity and apostolic activity, and dedicated themselves to uninterrupted choral prayer. Their continuous chanting was carried on by the monks in relays, and because it went on day and night, the monks were called *akoimetos,* i.e., the sleepless ones. Because of the hostility of the patriarch Nestorius and others, they were expelled from Constantinople and took refuge at Goman in Bithynia, later moving to Tchiboukli. They were stout defenders of orthodoxy against the Monophysites and *Eutychians but later lapsed into *Nestorianism and were excommunicated by Pope *John II (534). Little is recorded of them in later times, though they were still in existence in the late 12th and early 13th centuries. BIBLIOGRAPHY: E. Marin, DTC 1:304–308; J. Pargoire, DACL 1:312–313; S. Vailhé, DHGE 1:274–282; H. Bacht, LTK 1:244–245.

[G. T. DENNIS]

ACOLYTE, in the Latin Church only, formerly a minor order (first mentioned by Pope Cornelius in 251; also mentioned by St. Cyprian); but since Paul VI's *motu proprio, Ministeria quaedam* in 1972 the office of acolyte has been a lay ministry, along with that of reader. These ministries are restricted to men; choice is made by the bp. or by the major superior of religious. The acolyte's ministry is to assist at the Eucharistic liturgy, and he may be an *extraordinary minister of the Eucharist. There is a special rite of initiation at Mass, with the bp. presenting the bread or wine to the candidate as he confers the office. The ordinary altar boy or server, also referred to as an acolyte, exercises some of the functions, but is not instituted into this ministry, since the ministry is for those of mature age.

[T. C. O'BRIEN]

ACOSTA, GABRIEL (1590–1640), Jewish rationalist and religious skeptic. A. was born into a wealthy Portuguese, *Marranos family (sometimes called Da Costa), came to doubt Christian doctrine, fled to Amsterdam with his mother and four brothers (*c.*1617), and professed the Jewish faith openly, taking the name Uriel. But he soon came to be dissatisfied also with Judaism, which seemed to emphasize rituals and external observances to the neglect of the OT prophetic spirit. He began to write against Jewish and Christian doctrines—personal immortality, a resurrection, divine reward or punishment—and was condemned by the Jewish rabbis of Venice, Hamburg, and Amsterdam as well as by the Dutch courts (1618). He lived as an outcast for 15 years, but compelled by poverty and isolation, he finally agreed to recant (1633). A. again came under suspicion and was condemned a second time. Near despair, he recanted 7 years later, was flogged and forced to do public penance. His spirit broken by these humiliations, he committed suicide. Shortly before his death, he wrote a bitter autobiography, *Exemplar humanae vitae.* BIBLIOGRAPHY: N. J. Cohen, NCE 1:87–88 with bibliog; S. Shepard, "Background of Uriel da Costa's Heresy," *Judaism* 20 (1917) 341–350.

[T. M. MCFADDEN]

ACOSTA, JOSÉ DE (1539–1600), Jesuit missionary, ethnologist, historian, and theologian. Born at Medina del Campo, Spain, A. was a missionary superior in what is now Peru and Chile. He is best known for his writings, among them *Historia natural y moral de las Indias,* praised by Humboldt and translated into various languages; a number of manuals for pastoral work; and his now famous *De procuranda Indorum salute,* one of the first systematic treatises on missiology. He was often consulted by his Roman superiors and by officials of the *Consejo de Indias* on matters pertaining to the Church in Latin America. BIBLIOGRAPHY: Sommervogel 1:15–16; L. Lopetegui, *El P. José de Acosta S.J. y las misiones* (1942).

[P. DAMBORIENA]

ACQUAVIVA, prominent Neapolitan family, several of whose members rendered significant service to the Church from the 16th to 18th centuries. (1) Francesco (1665–1723), cardinal. F. held important positions under several popes; Clement XI named him cardinal and bp. of Sabina. (2) Giulio (1546–74), cardinal, papal nuncio. On Pius V's request, he intervened in the controversy between Charles Borromeo and the governor of Milan (1568), and bore the Pope's condolences to Philip II of Spain upon Queen Elizabeth of Valois' death (1570). (3) Ottavio (the elder, 1560–1612), cardinal, abp. of Naples. He was the legate of Gregory XIII to Campania; represented Clement VIII at Avignon, where he reorganized the juridical processes, and perhaps was instrumental in Henry IV's conversion. (4) Ottavio (the younger, 1608–74), cardinal. He was governor of Jesi (1638), Orvieto (1642), and Ancona (1643), defended the latter two cities against Parma and the French, and was papal legate in Bologna. (5) Trojano (1695–1747), cardinal, diplomat. T. held a variety of posts under several popes: governor of Ancona, majordomo of the Vatican Palace; titular abp. of Larissa; abp. of Toledo and Monreale. He was friendly with Charles III, was Spain's ambas-

sador to Rome, and helped to achieve the concordat of 1741. BIBLIOGRAPHY: E. J. Thomson, NCE 1:89.

[T. M. MCFADDEN]

ACQUAVIVA, CLAUDIUS (1543–1615), an Italian of noble birth who became the fifth superior general of the Society of Jesus, and whose term of office (1581–1615) has never been exceeded in length. So extended a generalate in the early years of the Society's existence exerted an important formative influence on the nature of the Jesuit organization. Providentially his talents were equal to the task; in fact, after St. *Ignatius of Loyola he is considered to have no equal as administrator in the history of the order, which during his tenure grew from about 5,000 members to more than 13,000. Among the gravest problems A. faced within the order was a threatening Spanish schism; from outside the order, he was confronted with the fierce opposition of the Dominican theologians to the Jesuit teaching on the nature of efficacious grace—a controversy *(de auxiliis)* never in theory resolved. Under A. the famed *Ratio studiorum,* the Jesuit plan of humanistic education, was composed; from him came also the *Directory* of St. Ignatius' *Spiritual Exercises,* a guide for making and conducting the latter, as well as his *Industria,* a guide for superiors in dealing with the spiritual problems of their subjects. All his writings were for the members of the Society. BIBLIOGRAPHY: P. Dudon, DSAM 1:829–834; Guibert 230–280.

[E. A. WEIS]

ACQUAVIVA, RODOLFO, BL., see RUDOLF ACQUAVIVA, BL.

ACROPOLITES, GEORGIOS (*c.*1217–82), Byzantine diplomat and historian, one of the most outstanding students of N. Blemmydes. In 1233 G. was appointed to the court of John III of Nicaea and in 1244 became the logothete (chancellor) of Emperor Michael Paleologus III. The latter chose A. to conduct the negotiations at the Council of *Lyons (1274), which achieved temporary reunion with the Western Church. He also wrote an accurate and objective history of the Byzantine Empire from the time of its capture by the Crusaders in 1204 until its restoration by Paleologus in 1261. BIBLIOGRAPHY: A. A. Vasiliev, *History of the Byzantine Empire* (v. 2, 1964).

[F. T. RYAN]

ACROSTIC, an arrangement of words, lines, or verses in which letters or syllables occurring in certain key positions (e.g., first or last) make up, when taken together, a word, name, phrase, or alphabetical sequence. Many examples are found in classical antiquity, and the device is used also in the Bible (e.g., in the *Alphabetic Psalms and in Lam 1–4). In the Byzantine liturgy this form appears in the first letters of a troparion and other prayers such as the division of the *acathist hymn into 24 stanzas each beginning with a letter of the Greek alphabet. The most famous Christian acrostic is the *ICHTHUS. BIBLIOGRAPHY: H. Leclercq. DACL 1:356–372; M. R. P. McGuire, NCE 1:90.

[F. T. RYAN]

ACT, a term widely used in scholastic theology and philosophy. From the sense in which it is understood as the operation or activity of a being, or organ, or faculty, it came to signify the being, the perfection, or realization, or fulfillment of a thing, thus translating Aristotle's *energeia,* and its verbal form, "actuate," accordingly means the perfecting of a thing. Act in this sense is the correlative of *potency or what is merely potential *(en dynamei).* Before being perfected, a thing must somehow have the perfection it is to receive in its potential, i.e., it must be in potency to that perfection. Thus a stone from which a statue is to be carved must be in potency to being cut into that shape. In scholastic philosophy, act and potency are transcendentally related constituents of all created being as well as the metaphysical conditions for all change. No change can occur unless a thing has both the capacity to be changed and some positive perfection or actuality, since potency cannot exist in itself but only in a subject that has some measure of actuality. All finite things are composed of act and potency. The act is called first act if it is the perfection by which a thing exists as a specific kind of substance; it is second act when the reference is to an accidental perfection or determination that is added to a being already having a first act. Since act is perfection, nothing in its notion, simply as act, connotes imperfection or limitation. But because perfection manifestly exists in the world in many different degrees and forms, some explanation must be found for its actual limitation in created being. What explains the limitation is the fact that act exists in created things only as actuating a finite essence which, as a passive potency, limits the act it receives to its own capacity for being perfected. Thus the act of existence is limited by the essence that it actuates. Such is the Thomistic ontology that postulates a real distinction between essence (passive potency) and existence (act). God, who is pure (unlimited) act, has in himself no element of potentiality whatever, but all creatures are composed of potency and an act of existence limited by that potency. BIBLIOGRAPHY: J. D. Robert, NCE 1:90–92, O. Schwemmer, SacMund 1:8–11.

[B. FORSHAW]

ACT, FIRST, a term with three meanings in scholastic theology and philosophy. (1) It is the completely underivative act that is the absolutely independent principle of its own actuality and at the same time gives actuality to all else that is. In this sense the first act is God, who is also called pure act inasmuch as actuality in him is unmixed with potentiality of any kind. The derivative actuality of the creature is always in some way combined with potency. (2) Philosophical usage also styles as first act an essence or form that itself is actuated by an *esse* (or act of existence), the two being thus related as first and second acts. (3) Finally, the term is applied to an

agent who is in being (first act) prior to its operation (second act).

[E. A. WEIS]

ACT, HUMAN, see HUMAN ACT.

ACT OF CONTRITION, see CONTRITION, ACT OF.

ACT OF FAITH, see FAITH, ACT OF.

ACT OF SUPREMACY, in England the law enacted by Parliament in 1534 under *Henry VIII, renewed (it had been repealed by Mary Tudor) and revised in 1559 under Elizabeth I, constituting the reigning sovereign earthly head of the Church of England. The Elizabethan version declared the monarch to be the supreme governor, "as well in all spiritual or ecclesiastical things or causes as temporal." All ecclesiastical jurisdiction for the visitation, reformation, and correction of the ecclesiastical state and persons, and of all manner of errors, heresies, schisms, etc., was forever united and annexed to the crown. The Elizabethan act also renewed the 1534 Annates Statute of Henry, which had put all appointments of bishops in the royal hands (SEE CONGÉ D'ÉLIRE). An oath acknowledging the royal supremacy and rejecting all foreign powers was imposed on all ecclesiastics, public officials, and candidates for holy orders and academic degrees. The effect of the act was to end communion with Rome and to make the C of E a *national Church. BIBLIOGRAPHY: Hughes RE 1:247–281; 2:21–35.

[T. C. O'BRIEN]

ACTA ALEXANDRINORUM, a name given to 22 papyrus fragments from various sites in Egypt, the first of which was discovered in 1839, describing the trials of Greek patriots before the Roman governors of Alexandria. The papyri written at different times between the first and the second half of the 3d cent. A.D. are based directly or indirectly upon, or composed in imitation of, court records extending from the reign of Tiberius, or even Augustus, to that of Commodus. Their glorification of Hellenic laws, life, and education, their anti-Semitic and anti-Roman prejudices, indicate that they probably originated among prominent individuals associated with the Alexandrian clubs and *gerousia,* whose 2 centuries of opposition to Roman rule was ultimately overcome by their reception of a senate in 199–200 and of Roman citizenship in 212. Though they are not of a religious nature, these acts are important for the light which they throw on ancient "martyr literature." BIBLIOGRAPHY: H. A. Musurillo, *Acts of the Pagan Martyrs* (1954); *Acta Alexandrinorum* (1961).

[M. J. COSTELLOE]

ACTA APOSTOLICAE SEDIS (AAS), official periodical for the Holy See since 1909. Under the care of the secretary of State and edited primarily in Latin by the Libreria Vaticana, the AAS is usually published monthly; an index is issued yearly. Each monthly fascicle contains: the acts of the Holy Father (encyclicals, constitutions, addresses, etc.); the decrees and decisions of the Roman congregations, tribunals, pontifical commissions, and curia; papal audiences with heads of state or their representatives; honors, decorations granted, and appointments made by, the pope; and a necrology of bps. and cardinals. Publication in the AAS is a necessary condition for the promulgation of Church law (CIC c. 9); the new law takes effect 3 months after the date of publication unless a different period of time is specified. BIBLIOGRAPHY: Woywod-Smith 1:9. *ACTA SANCTAE SEDIS.

[T. M. MCFADDEN]

ACTA ARCHELAI, an anti-Manichaean polemic composed by an otherwise unknown Hegemonios in the first half of the 4th century. A few Greek fragments and a very imperfect Latin translation of this work are still extant. It is cast in the form of two disputations which Archelaus, bishop of Kashkar in Mesopotamia, had with Manes *c*.270 A.D. Though the dialogues are obviously fictitious and the person of Archaelaus is probably so, these acts are of great importance for the history of Manichaeism. Text: PG 10:1405–1528. BIBLIOGRAPHY: P. de Labriolle, DHGE 3:1542; E. Stommel, LTK 1:115–116.

[M. J. COSTELLOE]

ACTA SANCTAE SEDIS (ASS), a monthly periodical begun at Rome in 1865 which contained the most important texts, addresses, and decisions of the Holy Father and the Roman curia. It ceased publication (1908) with the foundation of the *Acta Apostolicae Sedis.* The ASS was not an official publication until the Congregation for the Propagation of the Faith declared it to be "official and authentic" from May 1904. BIBLIOGRAPHY: P. Ciprotti, EncCatt 1:254–255.

[T. M. MCFADDEN]

ACTA SANCTORUM (AS), a famous collection of the lives of the saints arranged according to the order of their feasts in the ecclesiastical year, edited and published by the *Bollandists. They now comprise 67 folio volumes covering the days from January 1 to November 10. The first two appeared in 1643 and the last in 1940. The various lives of the saints are prefaced by introductions and accompanied by notes, the quality of which varies according to the state of hagiographical studies at the time of their publication and the critical acumen of their editors. Since 1882 the Bollandists have published the *Analecta Bollandiana* containing articles on, and reviews of, lives of the saints, and since 1886 the *Subsidia Hagiographica,* monographs dealing with hagiographical problems. BIBLIOGRAPHY: H. Delehaye, *Work of the Bollandists* (1922); P. Peeters, *L'Oeuvre des Bollandistes* (new ed. 1961); R. Aigrain, *L'Hagiographie* (1953) 329–350.

[M. J. COSTELLOE]

ACTION and **ACTIVITY,** from the Latin *agere,* terms equivalent to the Greek *prasso,* hence "practice." Christian theology has seen being and acting as identical in God. Some "action" philosophies regard them as identical in man also, but more generally action is looked upon as the complement of being. Though "action" and "activity" are often used interchangeably, even by the most exact scholastics, it is useful to draw a distinction between them in some contexts. In a narrow sense action is one of the correlatives in an *actio-passio* (an acting-and-being-acted-upon) type of situation in which a physical effect of some kind is produced outside the agent, whereas activity *(operatio)* may remain or be "immanent" in the agent and be unproductive of any extrinsic physical change (such, e.g., are the activities of knowing and loving). Aristotle and St. Thomas Aquinas draw a distinction, not unimportant for the philosophy of art—and, it may be added, for the theology of justification, in the distinction it may make between "deeds" and "works"—between "doing" and "making." Morality is concerned with the quality of the doing, art with the quality of the making, irrespective of the moral temper of the maker. Thus a "good" thief may be understood to mean either a thief who has reformed and become prudent, or an unregenerate thief who is yet an artist in the practice of his profession. BIBLIOGRAPHY: J. Maritain, *Art and Scholasticism and the Frontiers of Poetry* (tr. J. F. Scanlan, 1930).

[T. GILBY]

ACTION FRANÇAISE, French monarchists. The committee occasioned by the Dreyfus affair in 1898 became a League in 1905 with biweekly (1899) and daily (1908) periodicals. Its leaders were Charles Maurras, Leon Daudet, Maurice Pujo, and Jacques Bainville. It sought what was called integral nationalism for France with the support of the Catholic Church, traditional guardian of order and of French civilization. Despite atheist leaders, Action recruited many Catholic students and clergy. Opposed to centralization and parliamentary government, it did not offer candidates for election but instead sought power by the energetic action of zealots. It taught a naturalist view of man, society, and religion—all subordinate to integral nationalism. The Republic reacted against the movement, as did Rome. But papal condemnation was withheld 1914–26 because of war and Action's attacks against French anticlericals. Action reacted against the papacy with bitter antipapal and anticlerical attacks. It then lost recruits, including the pretender to the throne of France in 1937. In 1939 Action submitted to the new pope, Pius XII. Association with the Vichy government during World War II ruined Action Française, whose postwar heirs regrouped around the weekly *Aspects de la France.*

[E. P. COLBERT]

ACTION MASS, recent term to designate a Mass in which the forms for the congregation's active participation would be extensive. These forms usually stress spontaneity and improvisation, e.g., dialogue sermons, dancing, newspaper readings, and are sometimes contrary to official liturgical legislation. *UNDERGROUND CHURCH.

[T. M. MCFADDEN]

ACTION PAINTING, critical term for the spontaneous painting of *Abstract Expressionism, an American art movement of the 1940s and 1950s. The term was used first in 1952 by Harold Rosenberg, whose thesis was that the artist's life-encounter culminating in spontaneous action on the canvas constituted an event in itself most meaningful. The act of painting had validity beyond subject matter or other traditional references. BIBLIOGRAPHY: R. L. Wickiser, NCE 1:54–55, s.v. "Abstract Expressionism."

[T. FEIDT]

ACTISTAE (Actistetae), members of a strict Monophysite sect, and a later subdivision of the *Acephali, who opposed Severus of Antioch and were so called because they believed that the body of the Lord was "uncreated." BIBLIOGRAPHY: Daniélou-Marrou 1:363.

[F. H. BRIGHAM]

ACTIVE LIFE, that form of living whose predominant operation and principal intent is the ascetic activity of the moral virtues and effective charity, particularly, though not exclusively, through the corporal works of mercy. Although Christian writers used the blear-eyed Leah and the busy Martha as biblical symbols and exemplars of the active life, the teaching of Augustine, Gregory, and Aquinas may owe more to Platonic and Aristotelian reflection on the *bios practicos.* The active life is generally opposed to the *contemplative life. The term is obviously analogous. In a non-spiritual sense it would be the opposite of the quiet of contemplation. However, it may mean either the preparation for the contemplative life, or the life that flows from contemplation. BIBLIOGRAPHY: J. F. Conwell, NCE 1:98–99; T. Camelot, TL 4; E. Coreth, "Contemplative in Action," TheolDig 3 (1955) 37–45; ThAq ST (Lat-Eng) v. 46, J. Aumann, ed., *Action and Contemplation.*

[U. VOLL]

ACTIVE ORDERS, religious orders or congregations whose purpose and daily life entail external activities, esp. the temporal and spiritual works of mercy, such as the pastoral ministry, teaching, nursing, and social work. These orders are often contrasted with contemplative orders and sometimes with mixed orders which unite the active and contemplative life. Thomas Aquinas maintains that the highest form of spirituality is "the active life which flows from the fullness of contemplation" (ThAqST 2a2ae, 188.6). BIBLIOGRAPHY: A. Bride, DTC 13.2:2168–69.

[T. M. MCFADDEN]

ACTIVISM, a doctrine or tendency emphasizing action as opposed to passivity. Thus in philosophy the functionalism promoted by John Dewey is called activism. So also in education the Montessori method of teaching children which so emphasizes learning by doing is called activism. As a general philosophic notion activism is opposed to the speculative search for essences and gives precedence to commitment and activity over theorizing. In this sense contemporary *existentialism is activism. However in Catholic circles, esp. in America, activism means an excessive apostolic activity which is detrimental to the spiritual life. The external works of the apostolate so absorb interest that the interior life suffers. This activism is also called naturalism. While not a formal teaching but rather a tendency of human nature, it is called the "heresy of action" and may be said to be the opposite extreme to *quietism. Pius XII, in *Menti nostrae,* refers to activism as that spiritual activity prompted by an indiscreet zeal lacking a spiritual foundation: "that kind of activity not based on divine grace and not making constant use of the aids provided by Jesus Christ for the attainment of holiness." At times authors, esp. Europeans, refer to activism as *Americanism. The spiritual pragmatism condemned by Leo XIII in *Testem benevolentiae* of 1899 warns the American people not to place too great an emphasis on externals and outward activity to the detriment of the spiritual life. BIBLIOGRAPHY: J. B. Chautard, *Soul of the Apostolate* (tr. J. A. Moran, 1941); J. Aumann, "Heresy of Action," CrossCrown 3 (1951) 25–45; J. L. F. Bacigalupo, NCE 1:99–100.

[U. VOLL]

ACTON, CHARLES (1803–47), cardinal. After a preparatory education at Westminster School, A., son of Sir John Francis Acton, studied at Magdalene College, Cambridge (1819–23), then at the Academy of Noble Ecclesiastics in Rome. After some experience in the diplomatic service, he was made secretary of the Congregation of Regulars (1831), then auditor of the Apostolic Camera, and, in 1842, a cardinal. He was present as interpreter at the meeting of Gregory XVI with Nicholas I (1845) and later, at the request of the Pope, published a report of that event. He opposed the restoration of the RC hierarchy in England. BIBLIOGRAPHY: C. S. Isaacson, *Story of the English Cardinals* (1907); B. Fothergill, NCE 1:101.

[G. RUPPEL]

ACTON, JOHN EMERICH EDWARD DALBERG (first Lord Acton; 1834–1902), English journalist and historian. The only child of Sir Richard Acton, A. was educated at St. Nicholas preparatory school near Paris and St. Mary's College, Oscott. Denied admission to Cambridge, he became pupil and companion of Johannes Ignaz von *Döllinger, with whom he traveled in Europe and the U.S. (1855) and under whose tutelage he acquired a proficiency in languages and critical scholarship. After returning to England, he became a Whig member of Parliament (1859–65) and a friend of W. E. Gladstone. In 1859 he became editor of *The Rambler* and was responsible for it until 1864. A stout opponent of every restriction of freedom, he took a stand against papal temporal power, Pius IX's *Syllabus,* and the definition of papal infallibility. Although he gave up Catholic journalism after the appearance of the *Syllabus,* he continued to write on historical matters in the *Chronicle* (1867–68) and the *North British Review* (1867–71). He was also a founder of the *English Historical Review* (1886) and first editor of the *Cambridge Modern History.* In 1895 he was appointed professor of history at Cambridge. BIBLIOGRAPHY: J. L. Altholtz, *Liberal Catholic Movement in England* (1962); G. Himmelfarb, *Lord Acton: a Study in Conscience and Politics* (1952); H. A. MacDougall, NCE 1:101–102.

[G. RUPPEL]

ACTS, NOTIONAL, see NOTIONAL ACTS.

ACTS OF THE APOSTLES, the fifth book of the NT. It presents a broad survey of the origin and spread of Christian communities from the resurrection of Jesus, *c.* A.D. 30, to *c.* A.D. 60, when St. Paul arrived in Rome as a prisoner. As its prologue indicates (Acts 1.1–5), Acts is a sequel to the third Gospel; early Christian tradition ascribed it to Luke. It pursues a loose geographical plan (Acts 1.8), tracing the origin of the Church from Jerusalem (ch. 1–7) to Judea and Samaria (ch. 8–9), and elsewhere throughout the Roman empire to Rome (ch. 10–28). Although the title, "Acts of the Apostles," is very ancient, its Lucan origin is not beyond doubt. Although Luke insists upon the fundamental importance of the Twelve as the witnesses to the ministry and resurrection of Jesus (1.21–22; 3.15; 4.20; 10.41–42), he provides no detailed information concerning their activity except for Peter, whom he characterizes as the spokesman and leader of the community in Jerusalem. Otherwise his chief personage is Paul (his Roman name; Saul his Jewish name), originally persecutor of the community led by Peter, converted and appointed an Apostle by the risen Jesus appearing to him near Damascus (9.1–19; 22.1–21; 26.1–23). The predominance of Peter and Paul in Acts coheres with Luke's historical portrait of the origin of Christianity: after a short period of success among the Jews of Palestine (2.1–8.1), it met with the popular opposition of Palestinian Judaism (12.1–3) and the rejection of Diaspora Judaism (13.44–46). This situation led it to turn to the gentiles. According to Gal 2.9 Peter bore the chief responsibility for the Judaeo-Christian communities, while Paul led the mission to the gentiles, the same general picture drawn by Luke in Acts.

Despite deficiency of detail and lacunae in the data out of which Luke created Acts, his book supplies information of inestimable value for both the theological and historical understanding of the origin of Christianity. The kerygmatic speeches proclaiming the resurrection of Jesus and its religious significance (2.14–36; 3.12–26; 4.8–12; 5.29–32; 10.34–43; 13.17–41), in substance the earliest form of Christian preaching, stand at the center of the development of Christian thought that ultimately crystallized into the books of the NT. The kerygma implied the divine validation of the historical ministry of Jesus (Acts 2.22), and thus his deeds and sayings entered into the mainstream of Christian faith through the creation of material about him and his activity that provided the data for the four Gospels. The doctrine of the parousia, likewise implicit in the kerygma (Acts 3.21; 17.31) and associated with the early Christian Eucharist (Lk 24.30–31), focused attention on the person of Jesus (1 Th 1.10), gradually understood through the deepening insights of faith to be divine (Phil 2.5–11; Col 1.15–20; Eph 1.3–10; Jn 1.1–14). The low-key Christology of the kerygma in Acts constitutes a vital connecting link between the historical Christology detectable in the Synoptic Gospels and the high Christology of Pauline and Johannine literature.

Acts contains valuable historical information concerning the primitive Christian community in Jerusalem, its characteristics and its vicissitudes there (1.15–8.3), the expansion of the Christian movement outside Jerusalem (8.4–11.30), its gradual independence of Judaism, and the missionary activity of Paul (12.1–28.31). Nonetheless, Acts is primarily a theological history, ascribing the origin and spread of Christian communities to the action of the Holy Spirit upon Peter (2.14–18; 4.8; 15.8) and Paul (13.2–4; 16.6; 20.22–23). The theological character of the book reveals that it was written for a Christian audience, and therefore not mainly as a brief to defend Christianity against the suspicions of non-Christians in the Roman empire. Luke shows that the origin and spread of Christianity was due to the divine power, operative esp. in the activity of Peter and Paul. Latent in his material is evidence that the Christian movement was not found by civil authority to be a threat to the Roman Empire, but Luke does no more than present the non-political orientation of Christianity as a simple fact. He acknowledges that social disturbances were connected with the movement, not only because of Jewish opposition to it (13.50; 14.2; 17.5; 21.27–28), but also because of its threat to the cult of idolatry (19.23–28). In the MS tradition Acts is represented in a second text, called the "Western Text" or Codex D. This text generally contains longer readings and some additional minor facts not present in the classical text of the MS tradition. Although some scholars have accepted Codex D as Luke's original work, later abridged by him, the better opinion is that Codex D is the result of Christian editorial additions to Acts made in the 2d century.

[C. P. CEROKE]

ACTS OF THE MARTYRS, a rather large body of Christian literature composed betwen the 2d and 7th centuries describing the trials and executions of the early Christians for their faith. The Acts may be conveniently divided into three different categories: (1) The Acts proper (*acta* or *gesta martyrum),* transcriptions of the official court record of a martyr's trial, usually with the addition of an introduction and conclusion so that the account could be read at a liturgical function; (2) the written reports of eyewitnesses (*passiones, martyria*) of a martyr's arrest, trial, and execution; (3) legends (*legenda*) composed long after a martyr's death for the edification of the faithful and into which a great deal of fiction is mingled with a few, even very few facts.

The proceedings of a Roman criminal court, including the questions of the judge and the responses of the defendant, were regularly taken down in shorthand by professional notaries and then transcribed and deposited in the provincial archives *(instrumentum provinciae)*, where they could be consulted years later (cf. Eusebius *Hist. Eccl.* 5.18.9; 7.11.6; St. Augustine, *Contra Cresconium* 3.70; Lydus, *De magistratibus* 3.29). Copies of these could be obtained for private circulation (cf. Cyprian, *Epist.* 77.2), though bribery in times of persecution was probably required. Actual transcripts of this sort, however, are quite few. These would include the *Acts of St. Justin and his Companions,* who were executed in Rome about 164 A.D., the *Acts of the Martyrs of Scilli,* condemned at Carthage on July 17, 180, and the *Proconsular Acts of Cyprian,* executed on Sept. 14, 258, though these last contain two separate protocols and the evidence of eyewitnesses.

Among the more famous Acts (Passions) of the second class are the *Martyrdom of Polycarp,* who was put to death at Smyrna probably in A.D. 156, the *Letter of the Churches of Vienne and Lyons to the Churches of Asia and Phrygia,* describing the sufferings of the Christians at Lyons in 177, and the *Passion of SS. Perpetua and Felicitas,* executed at Carthage in 202. To this same type may be ascribed the *Acts of Saints Carpus, Papylus, and Agathonice,* of *Apollonius,* of *Pionius,* of *Marion and James,* and of *Montanus and Lucius,* though all of these have been more extensively edited.

The third type of Acts (Legends) is by far the most numerous and embraces (1) historical romances, in which there is a kernel of fact such as a saint's name, the date of his martyrdom, and a cult at his place of burial; (2) imaginative tales in which not only the events but the characters themselves are fictitious; and (3) deliberate forgeries. To the first of these belong the accounts of the martyrdoms of SS. Agnes, Cecilia, Lawrence, and many other Roman martyrs. To the second may be ascribed the legends connected with SS. Barbara, Catherine of Alexandria, and Genesius, the comedian who was converted on the stage while ridiculing baptism. Among the hagiographical forgeries which were written to enhance the prestige of different sees may probably be classed the legends telling of the founding of the Gallic Churches. The trivial character of many of the legendary acts led to a prohibition of their being read in the churches in Rome towards the end of the 5th cent., according to the so-called *Gelasian Decree 1* (PL 59:171–172).

The Acts of the Martyrs give testimony to many traditional beliefs and practices in the early Church, such as a reverence for Scripture, the veneration of relics, prayers for the departed, the observance of fasts, the practice of infant baptism, and the conviction that a martyr is an imitator of Christ in his passion. Even today the authentic Acts and Passions have an apologetic value for the divine character of the truths for which the martyrs died (see Justin *2 Apology*

13; Tertullian, *Apologeticum* 50). BIBLIOGRAPHY: H. Leclercq, DACL 1.1:373–446; M. J. Costelloe, NCE 1:106–108; W. H. C. Frend, *Martyrdom and Persecution in the Early Church* (1965).

[M. J. COSTELLOE]

ACTS OF UNIFORMITY. Successive revisions of the Book of Common Prayer were accompanied by Acts of Uniformity requiring conformity to its prescribed rites. The first such Act was adopted in 1549, making the new Prayer Book mandatory in all religious services. Intended to replace the varied former uses with a single order of worship, it was prepared by *Cranmer and other bishops and theologians. Its distinctive features were the use of the vernacular, communion in both kinds, and transformation of the Mass into a communion service. Severe penalties were prescribed for any priest refusing to use the Prayer Book, or for anyone ridiculing the new rites, with life imprisonment being imposed for a third conviction. The second Act of Uniformity was passed in 1552, accompanying the revised Prayer Book, which reflected Cranmer's changed views of the Eucharist. Expressing a Zwinglian interpretation of the Lord's Supper, it also omitted the requirement of wearing ecclesiastical vestments in services of worship. The provisions and penalties of the 1549 Act were declared to be still in force, and a section was added providing similar punishments for persons attending religious services in which any forms other than those of the Prayer Book were used. Since the Prayer Book and the Act of Uniformity were revoked during Mary's reign, a third Act of Uniformity was passed in 1559, at the accession of Elizabeth I. In accord with her desire for a *via media,* the Prayer Book was modified to make it more widely acceptable. References to the body and blood of Christ were added, the *Black Rubric denying the Real Presence was omitted, and wearing alb and cope was required. The early Stuarts enacted no new Acts of Uniformity during their reigns, but by special proclamations and rigorous enforcement, they tried to achieve religious uniformity. After the suspension of the Act of Uniformity during the Civil Wars and the Cromwellian era, Charles II was faced with the settlement of the religious problem. Presbyterians desired a comprehensive Church that would include them; Independents, Baptists, and Quakers wanted freedom of worship. Parliament settled the question by the Act of Uniformity of 1662, accompanied by a modified Book of Common Prayer. More elaborate than its predecessors, the new Act required the clergy publicly to declare their "unfeigned assent and consent" to use the Prayer Book. Teachers in the universities, as well as private tutors, were also to subscribe a similar declaration. The earlier Acts of Uniformity were stated to be still in effect. This Act resulted in ejection of about 2,000 clergy from their churches and in making *Dissenters of Presbyterians. Heavy penalties for nonconformity and strict enforcement of the Act failed to achieve religious uniformity, however, and in 1689 the *Toleration Act exempted Protestant Dissenters from its requirements.

The Acts of Uniformity were important both to the establishment of the C of E as the national Church, and to the difficult progress toward religious toleration of Nonconformists. BIBLIOGRAPHY: H. Gee and W. H. Hardy, *Documents Illustrative of English Church History* (1921); R. S. Bosher, *Making of the Restoration Settlement* (1951); A. G. Dickens, *English Reformation* (1964). *BOOK OF COMMON PRAYER.

[N. H. MARING]

ACTUALISM, a tendency among certain theologians to stress the gracious activity of God toward man to the neglect of any created effect of such activity. It is rather an attitude than a body of doctrine.

Two factors are to be considered in every phase of God's activity toward man. There is God's gracious activity, which is uncreated grace, and there is the effect of that activity, which is a created thing, transient or permanent, produced in man himself, more commonly designated by the term grace.

The gracious activity of God toward man may be described as event, insofar as it is a transient activity, but it can not be adequately understood without some effect, transient or enduring, resulting from it in man. This effect is what is known among Catholic theologians as created grace. The created effect resulting in man from God's gracious activity, and which is properly called grace, is neglected by actualism, which distrusts the Catholic notion of sanctifying grace as a continuing possession of the justified person. It sees in this concept only the projection of an abstract mental image in the place of God. Actualism regards the religious relationship between God and man to be always an event, an encounter between God and man. Catholic theology, in the actualist mind, by interposing created reality between God and man, misinterprets divine action. There is this much truth in the actualist doctrine that the relationship between God and man is a continual event, or encounter; nevertheless, God's action terminates outside God in a created effect transient or permanent. BIBLIOGRAPHY: A. Halder and H. Volk, LTK 1:260–262; F. L. Sheerin, NCE 1:108; M. J. Buckley, *Motion and Motion's God* (1971) 254–265.

[F. L. SHEERIN]

ACTUS FIDEI, see AUTO-DA-FÉ.

ACTUS PURUS, see PURE ACT.

ACUÑA, CRISTOBAL DE (1597–1670), Spanish Jesuit missionary. He engaged in missionary work in Peru, Chile, and Ecuador, where he was rector of the college at Cuenca. In 1639 he took part in an expedition exploring the Amazon and made a report of his findings to the King and the Council of the Indies in Spain (1640). His experiences and conclusions are recorded in *Nuevo descobrimiento del Gran Río de las Amazonas* (1641). Political developments put an end to the missionary and colonizing possibilities opened up by

his discoveries. After several years in Rome and Spain, he returned to South America.

[H. JACK]

A.D., abbreviation for the Latin *anno Domini,* year of the Lord. Dionysius Exiguus (d. *c*.526) began the practice of computing dates from the year of Christ's birth but reckoned incorrectly, assigning the Nativity to the year 754 *A.U.C.,* a date at least 4 years too late. BIBLIOGRAPHY: L. E. Boyle, NCE 2:1062–64.

[T. M. MCFADDEN]

AD BEATISSIMI APOSTOLORUM, the first encyclical letter of Pope Benedict XV (Nov. 1, 1914). In it he pleaded for peace between nations, between social classes, and between Catholic schools of thought. Without mentioning the Integralists, though evidently having them in mind, he declared that in discussing matters not settled by the Church moderation should prevail and not rash suspicion about the orthodoxy or good morals of opponents, and that Catholic writers and speakers should not presume to usurp the function of the Church's magisterium. BIBLIOGRAPHY: AAS 6(1914) 576–578; D 3625–26; G. J. O'Brien, NCE 7:552–553 s.v. "Integralism."

[J. H. ROHLING]

AD BESTIAS, condemnation to death by exposure to wild beasts. Spectacles in which armed or unarmed persons fought ravenous beasts were perhaps of Etruscan origin. From the 2d cent. B.C. Romans gave special training for this sport to slaves, captives, and even paid freemen. At times individuals convicted of such crimes as parricide and treason incurred *damnatio ad bestias.* For them the sentence was equivalent to a death warrant, whereas trained performers often survived. Christians often suffered the penalty *ad bestias* because their refusal to worship the emperor was looked upon as treasonous. BIBLIOGRAPHY: A. Pillet, *Étude sur la "damnatio ad bestias"* (1902).

[M. J. SUELZER]

AD CAUTELAM, Latin phrase meaning "for precaution," frequently used in canon law when the necessity of obtaining a dispensation is only probable, e.g., before a mixed marriage when the validity of the non–Catholic baptism is in doubt, a dispensation from the impediment of disparity of cult would be granted *ad cautelam.*

[T. M. MCFADDEN]

AD LIMINA VISIT, a visit to the tombs (literally "to the threshold") of the Apostles Peter and Paul in Rome. Such pilgrimages were common in the Middle Ages, and were often made to fulfill a vow. Today, as a technical term, it denotes the obligation of a RC diocesan bp. or vicar apostolic to visit Rome either personally or by deputy every 5 years if his see is in Europe; otherwise every 10 years. (CIC cc. 299, 341, 342). The obligation involves (1) a visit to the tombs,

(2) a personal visit to the Supreme Pontiff, (3) the submission of a written report (quinquennial report) on the condition of the Church in his diocese. BIBLIOGRAPHY: F. Cappello, *De Visitatione SS. Liminum* (1912); J. Carroll, *Bishop's Quinquennial Report* (1956); Bouscaren–Ellis–Korth 179.

[L. M. KNOX]

AD MAJOREM DEI GLORIAM (A.M.D.G.), Christian motto generally connected with the Society of Jesus (see JESUITS). Translated as "To the Greater Glory of God," the phrase with some variations appears over 1,000 times in the *Constitutions* and letters of St. *Ignatius of Loyola, founder of the Jesuits. BIBLIOGRAPHY: W. J. Young, NCE 1:109 with bibliography.

[T. M. MCFADDEN]

AD METALLA, short for *damnatio ad metalla,* condemnation to the mines, one of the severest penalties meted out by Roman courts and considered to be only a little short of execution. Those condemned to work in the mines, which were state-owned under the Empire, lost their citizenship, were kept in chains, and were at times branded or mutilated in some other way. There is ample evidence that this was a punishment frequently inflicted upon the early Christians during times of persecution (see, e.g., Eusebius, *Hist. Eccl.* 4.23.10; Hippolytus, *Philosophoumena* 9.7; Cyprian, *Ep.* 76). BIBLIOGRAPHY: H. Leclercq, DACL 1.1:467–474.

[M. J. COSTELLOE]

AD NUTUM, an expression used to signify that an individual's tenure in an ecclesiastical office is not regulated by the nature of the office itself or by law, but is at the pleasure of a higher official, usually the one who made the appointment.

AD SANCTAM BEATI PETRI SEDEM, bull of Alexander VII (Oct. 16, 1656), confirming the condemnation by Innocent X in *Cum occasione* (1653) of C. *Jansen's celebrated five propositions (D 2010–12). A. Arnauld, Jansenist leader, had insisted that the first proposition—"Some commandments of God are impossible to just men"—excerpted almost verbatim from Jansen's *Augustinus,* was not heretical and that the other four were not Jansen's doctrine. The bull declared that all five propositions were drawn from *Augustinus* and were condemned in Jansen's meaning. Parlement reluctantly registered the bull, the Sorbonne revoked Arnauld's doctorate, and a royal declaration demanded the clergy's assent. BIBLIOGRAPHY: F. Mourret, *History of the Catholic Church* (tr. N. Thompson, 8 v., 1931–57) 6:400–407.

[W. DAVISH]

ADA, SCHOOL OF, one of the two chief stylistically opposed schools producing illuminated MSS which were the finest achievements of the Carolingian Renaissance. Themes include figures of the Evangelists, royal portraits, historiated initials, and ornamental borders in classical style modified by Celtic and Near Eastern influences. The Ada group, contrary to the Palace School of vital linear expression, is characterized by monumental figures in solid color and gold. Important are the Gospels of the scribe Godescalc for Charlemagne (*c.*781, Bibliothèque Nationale, Paris), the Ada Gospels by Godescalc (*c.*800, Trier Cathedral), and the Gospel Charlemagne gave to Abbot Angilbert of St. Riquier (*c.*800, Abbeville).

[M. J. DALY]

ADALAR, ST. (d. 754), Benedictine monk who shared the missionary labors of St. Boniface in Frisia and his martyrdom at Dokkum. BIBLIOGRAPHY: A. M. Zimmermann, BiblSanct 1:172–173.

[H. JACK]

ADALARD (ADALHARD), ST. (*c.*751–*c.*827), abbot, cousin of Charlemagne. After his early education at court, A. became a monk at *Corbie (771) where 4 years later he became abbot. His cousin used him as one of his chief counselors, but after Charlemagne's death Louis the Debonair banished him (814) for suspected complicity in the revolt of Bernard, son of Pepin. When Louis recognized his innocence, A. returned to Corbie (821). The following year he founded the monastery of Corvey (New Corbie) in Westphalia to provide missionaries to work for the conversion of the northern nations. A zealous promoter of learning and religious discipline in his monasteries, A. has been venerated as a saint since the 11th century. BIBLIOGRAPHY: Butler 1:22–23; C. Lefebvre, BiblSanct 1:170–171.

[P. K. MEAGHER]

ADALBALD, ST. (d. 652), a nobleman venerated as a martyr, although his claim to martyrdom appears to be based either on an excess of French national feeling, or perhaps upon the fact that he died by violence in a region then still largely pagan. A., a grandson of St. Gertrude, fought with the French against the Gascons. He chose a Gascon, (St.) Rictrude, for his wife; they had four children, all of whom were later venerated as saints. He was slain, probably by an agent of his father-in-law who was still unreconciled to his daughter's marriage to an enemy. BIBLIOGRAPHY: Butler 1:236; R. Wasselynck, BiblSanct 1:173.

ADALBERO OF AUGSBURG, BL. (d. 910), monk, bishop. Educated probably at Sankt Gallen, A. became a monk sometime after 850. The reform of the abbey of Lorsch was due to his zeal for monastic observance. In 887 he became bp. of Augsburg. BIBLIOGRAPHY: P. Bertocchi, BiblSanct 1:173–174.

[H. DRESSLER]

ADALBERO OF METZ, the name of two bps. of the See of Metz. Adalbero I (d. 962), bp., political figure, reformer. Brother of Duke Frederick, A. was given the See of Metz in

929. The attempt to turn Lorraine over to France, to which he was party, ended in failure, but he managed to re-establish friendly relations with the German court. As bp. he was active in the reform of monasteries, not neglecting his own, Saint-Frond. BIBLIOGRAPHY: R. H. Schmandt, NCE 1:111.

Adalbero II (d. 1005), bp., monastic reformer, ascetic, educator. A. was made bp. of Verdun in 984 but was promptly translated to the See of Metz. There he devoted himself to promoting education and learning and to raising the level of spiritual life in the monasteries of both men and women. His political activity was minimal for the period, esp. as compared to that of his uncle Adalbero I. BIBLIOGRAPHY: C. Lefebvre, BiblSanct 1:177.

[H. JACK]

ADALBERO OF REIMS (d. 989), Benedictine, abp., reformer. Accused of treason for supporting the Ottonian emperors against the Carolingian kings of France, he was saved by Hugh Capet. After the death of the Carolingian Louis V in 987, A. persuaded the nobles to make the succession elective, not hereditary, and to bestow the crown of France on Hugh Capet rather than on the Carolingian claimant. BIBLIOGRAPHY: M. Sepet, DHGE 1:433–436.

[M. F. MCCARTHY]

ADALBERO OF WÜRZBURG, ST. (Adalbert; c.1010–90), a man of noble birth who studied at Paris, was a canon at Würzburg, and in 1045, was consecrated bp. of Würzburg by royal designation. He supported the Emperor in his dealings with the papacy until Henry IV attempted to depose Gregory VII; then turned actively against him. Driven from his diocese in 1085, he found refuge in the monastery at Lambach. BIBLIOGRAPHY: P. Bertocchi, BiblSanct 1:175–177.

[H. JACK]

ADALBERT OF BREMEN (c.1000–72), a man of noble birth who was successively canon, subdeacon to the abp., provost of the cathedral, and finally by royal favor, abp. of Bremen-Hamburg. He refused the papacy. He failed to achieve his ambition to establish a Scandinavian missionary patriarchate, but used his political power to the advantage of his diocese. Rival nobles finally managed to have him exiled from court. BIBLIOGRAPHY: E. N. Johnson, "Adalbert of Hamburg-Bremen: a Politician of the Eleventh Century," Speculum 9 (1934) 147–149; R. Kay, NCE 1:112.

[H. JACK]

ADALBERT THE DEACON, ST. (Adalbert of Egmond; d. c.705), a Northumbrian monk who volunteered for missionary work among the Frisians under the leadership of St. Willibrord. According to late and undependable sources, his efforts met with great success and he was made archdeacon of Utrecht. His cult can be traced back to the 10th cent.; it was centered in Egmond, the site of a chapel he had built and the place of his burial. Later a monastery dedicated under his name was built there. BIBLIOGRAPHY: W. Lampen, BiblSanct 1:182–183; Butler 2:641–642.

ADALBERT OF MAGDEBURG, ST. (d. 981), missionary and archbishop. Sent by Otto II in 961 to evangelize the Russians, he was forced by maltreatment to return to Germany in 963. While abbot of Weissenburg in Alsace (966–968), he may have completed the Chronicon of Regino of Prüm. As abp. of Magdeburg (968–981) he continued his missionary endeavors for the Slavs. BIBLIOGRAPHY: Butler 3:590; P. Bertocchi, BiblSanct 1:183–185; Zimmermann 2:337.

[M. F. MCCARTHY]

ADALBERT OF MAINZ (d. 1137), chancellor and faithful servant of Henry V who rewarded his complicity in the Treaty of Sutri by naming him abp. of Mainz in 1111. He suddenly experienced a change of heart, became a defender of the pope and promulgated the excommunication of Henry (1112). The Emperor retaliated by locking him in a dungeon. When the people forced his release, he was consecrated and participated in the Council of Worms (1122) which ended the investiture strife. He was responsible for the election of Lothair II as Henry V's successor. BIBLIOGRAPHY: P. Acht, LTK 1:122.

[H. JACK]

ADALBERT OF PRAGUE, ST. (also known by his Czech name, Vojtěch; c.956–997), bp. and martyr. A. completed his studies at Magdeburg and was consecrated second bishop of Prague in 983. His skill as an organizer enabled him to expand his diocese to include the territory of Moravia. His zealous reforms were concentrated on the eradication of pagan customs, but the rivalry between the reigning Przemyslides and the Slavnik family to which he belonged inhibited his work. In 990 he took solemn vows as a Benedictine monk at the Abbey of SS. Alexis and Boniface on the Aventine. In response to a Czech delegation's appeal to Pope John XV, A. returned to Prague; but dynastic conflict again impelled him to depart for Rome. At the request of the Polish Duke, Boleslaw the Great, Bp. Adalbert accepted a mission to the Prussians and was martyred in 997. He is honored as a patron of the Poles, Czechs, and Hungarians. BIBLIOGRAPHY: F. Dvornik, Sv. Votěch, II biskup pražský (1950); Making of Central and Eastern Europe (1949) 97–135; L. Nemec, "New Historical Portrait of St. Adalbert," Polish Review 7, No. 2 (1962) 41–64; Butler 2:152–153; G. D. Gordini, BiblSanct 1:185–189.

[L. NEMEC]

ADALBERT OF WEISSENBURG, see ADALBERT OF MAGDEBURG.

ADALBERT OF WOLLIN (d. 1162), companion of Otto of Bamberg on a mission to western Pomerania (1124–25), appointed bp. of Wollin in 1140 by Innocent II. He tried to Christianize the Slavs, but at first made little headway because of the hatred provoked by the crusade of 1147. With the arrival of a group of Premonstratensians (1155) the tide turned, and with their help A. made progress in his apostolic mission till his death. BIBLIOGRAPHY: P. David, *La Pologne et l'evangélisation de la Poméranie aux XIe et XIIe siècles* (1928).

ADALBERT AND CLEMENT, see ALDEBERT AND CLEMENT.

ADALDAG, ST. (*c*.900–988), imperial chancellor, archbishop. He served Otto the Great and became abp. of Bremen-Hamburg (937–988). He founded the suffragan Dioceses of Schleswig, Ribe, Aarhus, and Odense for the extension of missionary activities among the Danes. The Diocese of Oldenburg in Holstein was established in 967 or 968 for the conversion of the Wends. BIBLIOGRAPHY: Adam of Bremen, *History of the Archbishops of Hamburg-Bremen* (ed. and tr. F. J. Tschan, 1959) 54–74 and *passim*.

[M. F. MCCARTHY]

ADALGAR OF BREMEN, ST. (d. 909), a monk of Corbie who was sent by his abbot to assist the abp. of Bremen. He became the abp.'s coadjutor and successor. He divided his activity between the court and his diocese, saw Bremen reduced to a suffragan bishopric by Cologne, but lived to see it restored to its former status by Pope Sergius III. BIBLIOGRAPHY: Adam of Bremen, *History of the Archbishops of Hamburg-Bremen* (ed. and tr. F. J. Tschan, 1959); A. M. Zimmermann, BiblSanct 1:192.

ADALGIS OF NOVARA, ST. (d. 850), probably a canon of Novara who became bp. there *c*.830. He is praised in inscriptions, but nothing is known in detail of his life except that he made generous provision for the canons charged with carrying out divine services in his cathedral church and in the basilica of S. Gaudenzio. BIBLIOGRAPHY: V. G. Gremigni, BiblSanct 1:194–196.

ADALGOTT, SS. There were two abbots of Disentis, Switzerland, with this name. The first was abbot from 1016 to 1031; and the second, a disciple of St. Bernard of Clairvaux, was abbot of Disentis and bp. of Chur, 1150–60. BIBLIOGRAPHY: P. Delhaye, LTK 1:124; Zimmermann 3:133, 135, 222, 224; C. Vens and G. Venuta, BiblSanct 1:196–197, esp. for bibliog.

[J. L. GRASSI]

ADALHARD, ST., see ADALARD (ADALHARD), ST.

ADAM. The heretofore prevalent understanding of Adam in Catholic theology is under pressure as being related to an excessively literal interpretation of biblical revelation. Consequently it is being reappraised, esp. in its relationship with the teaching on *original sin, to which teaching scientific considerations are also relevant. According to the traditional position, Adam was a proper name, not merely in its occurrence in Gen 4.25 but in its first mention (2.19). He was created by God in the divine image and likeness, his body possibly by evolution, but his soul by God's action (2.7); he was created as the crown of the material world with dominion over it. His state of original justice included: sanctifying grace (represented by his friendly relationship with God); preternatural gifts (represented by the happiness of his lot in Eden); immortality, because death was a curse laid on him by God (Gen 3.19; Rom 5.12); and integrity (Sir 17.5–12). He also had a special knowledge (Gen 2.20). He lost God's friendship by an act of disobedience described in Gen ch. 3. The result for Adam himself was the loss of original justice. He was said by the scholastics to have "been despoiled of supernatural and wounded in natural ability" to live his life as he should. These disabilities he acquired not only for himself but also for his descendants. As the fountainhead of all humanity (any pre-Adamites had no part in fathering the human race Christ saved). Adam acted in the name of all mankind, so that his sinful act involved all humanity. His descendants are not culpable, yet this failure is in some way voluntary in them. This original sin is passed on to them by physical descent. This is not unfair, since what his descendants lost was supernatural (or preternatural), and therefore they had no right to it. Adam, as the source of humanity's sinfulness, is contrasted with Christ, who as the second Adam (Rom ch. 5; 1 Cor 15.21–22) is the source of its salvation. This typology entails the individual personality of Adam no less than that of Christ. This reference to Adam as an individual transmitting original sin by physical heredity is the Church's normal way of propounding its teaching on this point, as seen most notably at Trent, session 5 (D 1510–16).

Because Pius XII's statement in *Humani generis* (1950) was not definitive, further study was undertaken and this has shed additional light on the question. The Pope wrote: "Christians cannot admit a theory that the word Adam means some group of our primordial ancestors, granted that it does not now appear how such a view can be reconciled with what the revealed sources of truth and the acts of the teaching authority lay down on the subject of original sin, which is the result of a sin really committed by one individual, Adam, and which is passed on to all men by generation and so is in each of us and belongs to each of us." In fact the difficulty of reconciliation to which the Pope refers seems now to be somewhat diminished. Both biblical and scientific considerations come together to help on this new theological understanding of Adam. Exegetically, the reference in Gen ch. 2–3 is not to a man referred to by his proper name but simply to the common noun "man." Karl Rahner, when still holding to the view that Adam was an individual man, which he abandoned in *Consilium,* June, 1967, gave an etiological explanation of the Genesis narrative of the Fall; i.e., this description of the first sin is a mental reconstruction based on sins known to the author as effects of causes conditioned by previous sins. The Genesis narrative, even as exegeted by many Catholic scholars, indicates a law of spiritual inheritance (i.e., all men are conditioned to sin by being born into a sinful world) rather than a clearly defined sin of an individual. This does not make it merely a parable, Adam standing for everyman; it in fact takes into account the biblical teaching that sin is not merely an individual affair but a social heritage identifiable with the "sin of the world" with which the biblical writers are so much concerned. Many writers, however, still feel that even if Adam is not the biological head of mankind, an explanation is necessary that allows for an individual sin committed by one man. Others, however, take Adam as merely everyman who fails in his response to God and who through Christ, the second Adam, will eventually make a perfect response to God. BIBLIOGRAPHY: T. R. Heath, NCE 1:114–115; C. J. Peter, *ibid.* 10:777–781; A. M. Dubarle, *Biblical Doctrine of Original Sin* (tr. E. M. Stewart, 1965); J. Deretz and A. Nocent, *Dictionary of the Council* (1968) 1.

[B. FORSHAW]

ADAM OF BREMEN (11th cent.), German historian and geographer. While still a young man, A. went to Bremen at the invitation of Abp. *Adalbert in 1068. He wrote *Gesta Hammabergensis Ecclesiae Pontificum,* a history of the See of Hamburg and of the missions to the northern lands from 788 to 1072. This is the chief source of information about the northern countries before the 13th century. A. gathered his material from written sources—the archives at Bremen, official documents, preceding chroniclers—but he also drew heavily upon what was told him orally by Adalbert, the Danish King Svein Estridsson, and by traders and missionaries. The fourth book of his work, a geographical appendix entitled *Descriptio insularum Aquilonis,* contains the earliest known mention in any geographical work of a place called Vinland (or Wineland), which in the judgment of scholars was located on the coast of North America. BIBLIOGRAPHY: Adam of Bremen, *History of the Archbishops of Hamburg* (ed. and tr. F. J. Tschan, 1959).

[P. K. MEAGHER]

ADAM OF BUCKFIELD (c.1200–betw. 1279 and 1292), English commentator on Aristotle, Oxford secular master of arts (1243). He glossed all the works of Aristotle, with the exception of the Logic, Ethics, and *De animalibus.* His usual method of exposition, a literal explanation of each subdivision of a work, remarkable for its clarity, perfected the technique and reflects the interpretation of Averröes. His works give us some knowledge of the Arts curriculum at mid-13th-cent. Oxford. A.'s popularity is attested by the survival of many MSS of his works. BIBLIOGRAPHY: A. Maurer, *Nine Mediaeval Thinkers* (ed. R. J. O'Donnell, 1955), 99–144; Gilson HCP 261, 662.

[F. D. BLACKLEY]

ADAM EASTON (c.1330–97), English theologian, cardinal. A monk of Norwich priory, A. became an Oxford master of theology in 1366. His later writings evidence his scriptural scholarship. In 1368 he went to the curia at Avignon where he wrote a *Defensorium ecclesiasticae potestatis,* a refutation of the antipapal works of Marsilius and Wycliffe, a work that occasioned the papal condemnation of Wycliffe. He stood for the validity of the election of Urban VI. In 1381 he was named cardinal. His *Office of the Visitation of the BVM* and his *Defensorium S. Brigittae* were works of contemporary importance. BIBLIOGRAPHY: L. Macfarlane, *Life and Writings of Adam Easton* (1955).

ADAM OF EBRACH, BL. (d. 1161), abbot. A Cistercian, A. was made abbot of Morimond in 1121. He was founder and first abbot of Ebrach near Mannheim (1127) as well as founder of Reun (1129), Heilsbrom, and Langheim (1133), Nepomuk (1145), Alderspach (1146), and Bildhausen (1158). BIBLIOGRAPHY: R. Trilhe, DHGE 1:461–463; L. Hoffmann-Erbrecht, LTK 1:131–132; J. L. Grassi, NCE 1:116; G. Venuta, BiblSanct 1:226–227, esp. for bibliog.

[J. L. GRASSI]

ADAM OF FULDA (c.1445–1505), German monk, musical theorist, and composer. His surviving works include a treatise *De musica* (in GerbertS 3:329–381), 12 liturgical works, and three secular polyphonic lieder, one of which, "Ach hülf mich leid," was praised by Glareanus in his *Dodecachordon.* BIBLIOGRAPHY: W. Ehmann, MGG 1:79–81; Reese MusR.

[A. DOHERTY]

ADAM OF HOUGHTON (d. 1389), bishop. Oxford doctor of civil law, A. was canon of St. David's, archdeacon of Chichester, object of royal favors in the form of numerous benefices, and in 1361, appointed bp. of St. David's by the pope. He represented Edward III in diplomatic relations with France, was active in Parliament, and served as chancellor 1377–78. BIBLIOGRAPHY: G. Williams, NCE 1:117; Emden Ox 2:272–273.

[H. JACK]

ADAM MARSH (c.1200–85), English Franciscan. He studied at Oxford under *Robert Grosseteste, entered the Franciscan Order at Worcester (1232 or 1233), accompanied Bp. Grosseteste to the Council of Lyons II (1245). He was the first Franciscan to receive his masterate in theology at Oxford (c.1247). He is buried in Lincoln Cathedral next to Grosseteste. BIBLIOGRAPHY: J. A. Weisheipl, NCE 1:117; Emden Ox 2:1225–26.

[J. A. WEISHEIPL]

ADAM OF ORLETON (d. 1345), English ecclesiastic and politician. He was bp. of Hereford (1317), Worcester (1327), and Winchester (1345). Able but unscrupulous and opportunist, he sided with the rebellious Mortimers, played a leading role in securing Edward II's abdication (1327), and served Edward III in various capacities both before and after Roger Mortimer's fall (1330). BIBLIOGRAPHY: R. W. Hays, NCE I:117.

[R. W. HAYS]

ADAM OF PERSEIGNE (d. 1221), Cistercian abbot, papal diplomat, spiritual writer. Ordained a secular priest, A. first became chaplain to the Count of Champagne, then successively joined the Canons Regular, the Benedictines of Marmoutier, and the Cistercians at Pontigny. Elected abbot of Perseigne in 1188, he was commissioned (1195) by Celestine III to reason with *Joachim of Fiore. Innocent III repeatedly employed him as peacemaker in disputes between England and France; in 1200–01 he helped organize the Fourth Crusade. In his writings he seems to follow St. Bernard's spirituality. BIBLIOGRAPHY: *Lettres* (SC No. 66; ed. J. Bouvet, 1960); sermons and other fragmentary works: PL 211:699–754.

[L. J. LEKAI]

ADAM PULCHRAE MULIERIS (fl. 1230–45), a master at Paris, whose curious name is probably a Latinization of something like Adam Bellefemme. His work *De intelligentiis,* cited by St. Thomas Aquinas, was well known in the 13th century. BIBLIOGRAPHY: P. Glorieux, NCE 1:118.

[P. K. MEAGHER]

ADAM OF SAINT-VICTOR (d. between 1177 and 1192), hymnographer and, in the estimation of many, the greatest poet of the Middle Ages. Called Brito by his near contemporaries (Breton, or possibly Briton), A. studied in Paris and entered the monastery of Saint-Victor c.1130. Although a number of works of other kinds have been attributed to him (among which is a biblical dictionary), A.'s fame depends chiefly upon the many *sequences he wrote. These, combining splendor of form with doctrinal precision and depth of conception, came into liturgical use throughout the Latin Church and were much imitated. With A. the form of the sequence became defined and fixed. He composed three admirable proses in honor of St. Thomas Becket, who had visited the monastery of Saint-Victor 16 months before his martyrdom. BIBLIOGRAPHY: P. Delhaye, NCE 1:118; Raby CLP 345–375; E. Misset and P. Aubry, *Les proses de Adam de Saint-Victor, texte et musique, précedées d'une étude critique* (1969).

[P. K. MEAGHER]

ADAM SCOTUS (Adam of Dryburgh; d. c.1212), preacher, scripture writer. A. joined the Premonstratensians and was probably the abbot at Dryburgh where he wrote voluminously and became noted as a preacher. About 1188 he entered Witham, the only Carthusian monastery in England. His writings include sermons, a history of the Premonstratensians, a commentary on the rule of St. Augustine, one on Carthusian life, along with mystical and ascetical works.

BIBLIOGRAPHY: J. Bullock, *Adam of Dryburgh* (1958); A. Versteylen, DSAM 1:196–198.

[H. JACK]

ADAM WODHAM (c.1295–1358), English Franciscan who lectured at London, Paris, and Oxford. He studied under William of Ockham and has sometimes been classified as an Ockhamist. However, though Ockham dedicated his *Summa logicae* to him, he was too critical of his master to be called an Ockhamist without qualification. BIBLIOGRAPHY: A. G. Little, *Grey Friars at Oxford* (1892).

[P. K. MEAGHER]

ADAM, KARL (1876–1966), Roman Catholic theologian whose writings presaged many of the theological orientations of Vatican Council II. After his ordination in 1900, A. began his academic career at Strasbourg University. In 1919, he transferred to the University of Tübingen where he did his major work and contributed extensively to the revival of German Catholic theology. As an engaging seminary teacher, a reflective author whose books were quickly translated into several languages, and a pioneer in the theological formation of the laity. A. was imbued with the new progressive vitality of German theology after World War I. Although he believed at first that the Church in Germany should accommodate itself to Hitler and so urged the German bishops in 1938, A. soon came to realize the true nature of Nazism and publicly changed his position. He retired in 1949, but was named (1959) a member of the Preparatory Commission on Seminaries and Universities of Vatican Council II although his advanced age did not permit his attendance at any of the Council sessions.

Adam's theology was kerygmatic and Christocentric. He saw the theologian's task as "interpreting the Church in its self-consciousness," and only the person who is inwardly attached to that self-consciousness, who is a believer, can engage in theology properly so-called. Yet faith is not a logical conviction, but an inward emotion founded on humanity's natural attraction for God and confirmed by God's revelation in Jesus Christ. At the center of Adam's thought, therefore, is the figure of Jesus as the Lord through whose humanity redemption has been effected. Thus "Christianity is Christ," and other Christian doctrines have meaning only in relation to the Incarnation. In his books, *The Christ of Faith, The Son of God,* and *Christ our Brother,* Adam uses the techniques of biblical theology to show the full humanity of Jesus united with a complete divinity. For Adam, Jesus combined the Isaianic notion of a suffering servant and the later Jewish proclamation of the glorious Son of Man to forge a new image of the Messiah.

The Church as the one body of Christ, his effective presence in time and space, is also a central idea in Adam's theology. Like Augustine, whose thought he deeply appreciated, Adam insisted upon the solidarity of all persons both in sin and in grace. The Church is the gathering of those who have accepted that grace of God in Christ. This notion was the impetus behind Adam's ecumenical activity, esp. as set forth in his *One and Holy.* BIBLIOGRAPHY: J. Laubach, "Karl Adam" in *Theologians of Our Time* (1964), 92–108; "Theological Pioneer," *Tablet* 220 (1966), 473–474.

[T. M. MCFADDEN]

ADAM, ROBERT (1728–92), British architect. Born in Scotland, A. broke with current ponderous Palladian forms introducing a neoclassical style which determined architectural design both exterior and interior for the next 30 years. Employing a repertoire of classical and Renaissance motifs from his Roman sketchbooks, A. introduced festoons, vines, and arabesques formerly used by Wren, Gibbs, and Kent but refined to a delicacy and elegance by attenuating proportions giving to the classical a "picturesque" quality and grace unknown until the Georgian age. The Adam style dominated Great Britain, Russia, and Sweden, spreading to the U.S. in works of C. Bulfinch and S. McIntyre. Imitation in papier-mâché discredited the style (1780), but its revivals confirm its unsurpassed elegance in the history of architecture. BIBLIOGRAPHY: H. Honour, *Neoclassicism* (1968); D. Stillman, *Decorative Work of Robert Adam* (1966).

[M. J. DALY]

ADAM AND EVE, LIFE OF. Most of the numerous versions of the life of Adam and Eve are early Christian in origin, but one in particular, *Vita Adae et Evae,* is a Latin translation of a Greek story that may in turn be based on a Hebrew original, and is in any case of Jewish provenance. It is closely paralleled by, and indeed in large sections virtually identical with, another Jewish apocryphal work, the inappropriately named *Apocalypse of Moses,* though each of the two contains some material not included in the other. The *Life of Adam and Eve* in particular alludes to the temple of Herod as still standing, and this, together with certain other factors, suggests that is was written between 20 B.C. and A.D. 70. The contents may be summarized as follows:

Adam and Eve do penance for their fall, but Eve is interrupted by a fresh attempt by Satan to beguile her (Life only, 1–17). Accounts of the birth of Cain and Abel, Abel's death, and the birth of Seth and other children to Eve follow (Life, 18–24; Apoc., 1–5). Adam receives a vision of his approaching death, which he relates to Seth (Life only, 25–29). Adam falls sick and Eve and Seth try vainly to obtain the "oil of life" which flows from the tree of mercy in Paradise in order to cure him (Life, 30–44; Apoc., 5–14). Eve gives her version of the Fall (Apoc. only, 15–30). Adam dies (Life, 45–46; Apoc., 31–32). The entire angelic host implores pardon for him (Apoc. only 33–36). God has compassion on Adam (Life, 46–47; Apoc., 37). The angels ask that his body may be buried (Apoc. only, 33–36), and there follows a description of the funeral rites for him and Abel in Paradise (Life, 48; Apoc., 40–42). Finally Eve's death and burial are described (Life, 49–51; Apoc., 42–43).

The work is strongly haggadic throughout, i.e., it elaborates upon and interprets the original Bible story in such a way as to edify and to inculcate moral values. In particular it appears to convey a message of the value of penance and ascetical practices, the dangers of temptation and, in some vaguely adumbrated sense, the hope of future resurrection.

Many curious details have been singled out by scholars in their analysis of this apocryphal work. The tree of life is identified, for example, as an olive tree, and the oil of the olive is described as having curative powers for Adam's illness. The repentance of Adam and Eve is marked by a penitential exercise peculiar to the Celtic Church and Celtic monasticism, standing in neck-deep water for long periods of time. The dialogue of Adam with the devil incorporates a Jewish teaching on angels, namely that they were created in the image and likeness of God, a doctrine repudiated by many early Christian writers. The account of Adam's death and burial, on the other hand, reflects the burial customs of the early Christians; the idea of Adam's ascension or assumption is also more akin to Christian thinking. St. Epiphanius makes mention of Gnostic apocalypses of Adam, but the *Life of Adam and Eve* in its various versions has nothing in common with Gnostic teaching.

[T. M. MCFADDEN]

ADAMANTIUS (early 4th cent.) Greek writer who wrote a dialogue in five books, *De recta in Deumfide,* translated into Latin by Rufinus, in which A. emerges the victor in a debate with the followers of the Gnostics Marcion, Bardesanes, and Valentinus. Internal and theological evidence of this work dating its composition within the period of Nicaea and the testimony of Theodoret (*Haeretic. fabular. compendium,* PG 83:339, 377) and Photius (PG 103:1090) disprove the claim made by SS. Basil and Gregory Nazianzus that Origen is its author. BIBLIOGRAPHY: V. Ermoni, DHGE 1:500.

[F. H. BRIGHAM]

ADAMITES, a Christian sect of the 2d cent. mentioned by Epiphanius (PG 41:953) and Augustine (PL 42:31). Its members attended their religious assemblies in the nude. They may perhaps be identified with the Carpocratians described by Clement of Alexandria (PG 8:1112–13), a group that practiced sexual promiscuity and community of wives. Sects with similar beliefs and practices appeared in later times in The Netherlands, France, and Bohemia (SEE PICARDIANS). BIBLIOGRAPHY: G. Bareille, DTC 1:391–392; H. Grundmann, RGG 1:91–92.

[G. T. DENNIS]

ADAMNAN OF IONA, ST. (c.625–704), abbot, scholar. A. left Donegal for the abbey of Iona where he became abbot in 679. On a trip to England in 685, he became an advocate of the Roman Easter calendar and tonsure, but Iona would endure no change. He wrote the life of St. Columba, a celebrated example of medieval biography, and preserved in *De locis sanctis* a detailed record of Arculfus's journey through the Holy Land and adjacent places. Bede and his contemporaries esteemed A. as a scholar. BIBLIOGRAPHY:

J. T. Gilbert, DNB 1:392–393; C. McGrath, Bibl-Sanct 1:199–201.

[H. JACK]

ADAMS, HENRY (1838–1918), American writer, novelist, historian. Descended from distinguished New England ancestors (two were presidents of the U.S.), A. rejected his complacent Protestant orientation but through a lifetime of inquiry recovered the religious instinct. Influenced by Louis Agassiz of Harvard, he devoted himself to the intellectual life. He served as secretary to his father (congressman and minister to Great Britain), became professor of medieval history at Harvard (1870) and editor of the *North American Review* (1870–76). From 1877 he wrote prolifically, the most important work of that period being the monumental *History of the U.S. during Administrations of Jefferson and Madison* (9 v. 1889–91), hailed by some as the greatest work of its kind since that of Gibbon. After the death of his wife he traveled extensively with his close friend, the artist John LaFarge, visiting the Far and Near East and Russia (1890–1900). His two most important books *Mont Saint Michel and Chartres* (1902)—a poetic and passionate study of 12th-cent. medievalism contrasting the "unity" of the Middle Ages with the "multiplicity" of 20th-cent. forces—and *The Education of Henry Adams* (1906) were acclaimed after his death. BIBLIOGRAPHY: J. Schwartz, NCE 1:119–120; E. Samuels, *Henry Adams* (4 v., 1948–64); J. C. Levenson, *Mind and Heart of Henry Adams* (1957).

[M. J. DALY]

ADAPTATION, LITURGICAL, the process whereby the liturgy as worship is adjusted to the cultural requirements of different times and places. It includes the idea of improvisation by which the president of the liturgical assembly exercises the freedom allowed him to construct or change the ritual prayers reserved to him (collects, prefaces, anaphoras). Liturgical adaptation can be general, adapting the liturgical norms of the universal Church to a new cultural era; or particular, making the adjustments required within a particular racial or national setting; or individual, accommodating a specific liturgical celebration to the immediate cultural demands peculiar to the assembled group. The first two types invariably involve some sort of liturgical reform. The aim of liturgical adaptation is to achieve active, intelligent, and fruitful participation of the people in worship. It recognizes that while liturgical tradition must be maintained, the liturgy must also be made relevant to men of the changing world. In the early Church, both adaptation and improvisation were more frequent than in succeeding ages. Since Vatican Council II, which elaborated principles of liturgical adaptation (SacLit 37–40), adaptation has been rapid and significant. BIBLIOGRAPHY: J. Gaillard, *Catholicisme* 5:1377–79; A. Tegels, "Liturgy and Culture: Adaptation or Symbiosis?", *Worship* 41 (1967) 364–372; J. Deretz and A. Nocent, *Dictionary of the Council* (1968) 3.

[B. ROSENDALL]

ADAPTATION, MISSIONARY, the reinterpretation of Christian beliefs, values, and practices in light of cultural variations. This policy, originally regarded as a special concession to newer Churches in non-Western lands to facilitate evangelization, has been increasingly viewed not only as a missiological accommodation but as a theological necessity extending to all cultures and subcultures, including those of Christianized countries in Europe and America. In this extended form, it is identical with the Church's pluralism and transcultural nature. This accommodation to the needs of local Churches is traceable to apostolic times (1 Cor 9; Tit 1.5), and underlies the circumcision controversy at the Council of Jerusalem (Acts 15). It is evident also in the writings of the Church Fathers, particularly in their attitude toward pagans whose virtue and wisdom they regarded as fundamentally Christian (see ANIMA NATURALITER CHRISTIANA). It is reflected in the historical accounts of the great apostles to the Germanic, Slavic, and English peoples as well as in the apostolic approaches of such great 16th- and 17th-cent. missionaries as M. *Ricci and R. de *Nobili. Missionary accommodation has been the consistent policy of the Sacred Congregation of the Propagation of the Faith during its several centuries of existence. The policy is further evidenced in many present-day RC liturgical symbols and usages which are unquestionably of pagan origin, e.g., incense, candles, holy water. It has been repeatedly emphasized in papal documents, esp. those of more recent times (*e.g.,* Benedict XV, *Maximum illud;* Pius XI, *Rerum ecclesiae;* Pius XII, *Evangelii praecones;* and John XXIII, *Princeps pastorum*). The policy is applied in various documents of Vatican II and is reflected in such postconciliar developments as the geographical diversification of liturgical forms, and the growing decentralization of Church authority in favor of regional and cultural norms.

Various theological justifications might be suggested for the policy, but the cardinal reason is the incarnational nature of the Church. The pilgrim Church is but an extension of the mission of the Incarnate Word. As Vat II MissAct 10 notes, "The Church, in order to be able to offer all (peoples) the mystery of salvation and the life brought by God, must implant herself into these groups for the same motive which led Christ to bind himself, in virtue of his Incarnation, to certain social and cultural conditions of those human beings among whom he dwelt." The mission of the Church is to make Christ present not to an imaginary man, but to the man of today, as he is, where he is. Her mission is to proclaim the gospel, and to form the Christian community in such a way that every man would be able to respond to Christ in symbols, values, and a style of life that are truly his. Adaptation is required also because the Church must communicate the Word as effectively as possible. As modern social sciences have shown, the most effective communication is the one tailored to the ways and values of a people. Unity in diversity is demanded of the Church because it is intimately associated with the Church's effectiveness and relevancy. Indeed, the very nature of the Church's unity presupposes and implies a multiplicity of local Churches, each with its peculiar qualities, liturgical variations, ecclesiastical order, and theological orientations. Only in the various communities' recognition of each other as legitimate representations of the one Church of Christ is the full meaning of "the Church" guaranteed. Finally, nativization is also a question of justice, for one of the most basic rights of any society is its right to its own distinct character and culture, a right demanded by the laws of human freedom and nature itself. BIBLIOGRAPHY: L. J. Luzbetak, NCE 1:120–122; id., *Church and Cultures: An Applied Anthropology for the Religious Worker* (2d ed., 1970); E. A. Nida, *Message and Mission: The Communication of the Christian Faith* (1960); J. Boberg, NCE 16:294–295.

[L. J. LUZBETAK]

ADAPTATION, RELIGIOUS, the adjustment made by religious communities to adapt their manner of living, praying, and working to contemporary cultural, social, and economic circumstances and the requirements of their apostolate (see Vat II RenRelLife, 3). The term should be distinguished from religious renewal: adaptation is concerned with changes demanded by contemporary needs and outward circumstances; renewal refers to the continual interior conversion to Christ, which forms the basis of any exterior modification. Although the very nature of religious adaptation obviates a specific, definitive list of changes, Vatican Council II indicated several general principles: appropriate adaptation requires conformity to the gospels and the evangelical counsels; adaptation is the responsibility of the community, and the observations of all its members should be considered; there should be a return to the purposes for which the religious community was founded; provinces and religious houses should share personnel and financial resources; superiors should consult with their subjects before reaching decisions; nuns devoted to external apostolic work may be exempt from papal cloister; religious habits should be suited to circumstances of time, place, and activity; the educational and professional development of the members should be provided for. BIBLIOGRAPHY: L. Orsy, *Open to the Spirit* (1968); L. J. Suenens, *Nun in the World* (tr. G. Stevens, 1963); J. B. Tse, *Perfectio christiana et societas christiana iuxta magisterium Pii Papae XII* (1963); Pope Paul VI, *Apostolic Exhortation on the Renewal of Religious Life* (June 29, 1971).

[T. M. MCFADDEN]

ADDAI, DOCTRINE OF, a 4th-cent. apocryphal account of the Christianization of Edessa. This Syriac MS recounts how King Abgar V (4 B.C.–50 A.D.) heard of Jesus and his miracles and sent a letter asking him to come and heal his incurable disease. Jesus declined, but promised to send a disciple after his Ascension. According to the legend, the Apostle Thomas sent Addai (Thaddeus), one of the 72 Disciples of the Lord, to heal the King and convert Edessa to Christianity. The legend also records that Ananias, the King's messenger, painted a portrait of Christ which was given a place of honor in the royal palace. This tradition was generally accepted in the East but was rejected by the West. BIBLIOGRAPHY: Quasten 1:140–143; *Doctrine of Addai* (ed. and tr. G. Phillips, 1876); E. Peterson, EncCatt 1:290–292.

[F. T. RYAN]

ADDAI AND MARI, SS., founders of the Church in Syria and Persia, said to have been two of the Lord's 72 Disciples. A. is mentioned in the *Acta Edessana* (SEE APOCRYPHA [NT] n. 62) quoted in part by Eusebius (*Hist. Eccl.* 1.13) and the 4th-cent. apocryphal *Doctrine of *Addai;* he was allegedly sent by St. Thomas to Edessa to heal King Abgar V and to baptize his subjects. M., his disciple, according to legend established the Church in Persia at Kōkē near Seleucia-Ctesiphon. The East Syrian Church has traditionally called the anaphora most frequently used in its liturgy the Liturgy of SS. Addai and Mari. BIBLIOGRAPHY: Quasten 1:140–143; G. Proja, BiblSanct 1:230–233; E. Amann, DBSuppl 1:510–512. *ADDAI AND MARI, ANAPHORA, OF.

[F. H. BRIGHAM]

ADDAI AND MARI, ANAPHORA OF SS., the most frequently used of the three anaphoras proper to the *East Syrian Church which calls it the "Anaphora of the Apostles," i.e., of SS. *Addai and Mari, the legendary evangelizers of Mesopotamia. It is also used with some revisions by the *Malabar Christians. A primitive anaphora, dating possibly from the 2d cent., it may be the one abbreviated by the Catholicos Īshŏ 'yahb III in the 7th century. As it is now known, it is peculiar in having no words of institution, in its *epiclesis interrupting the *anamnesis and as an anaphora that is addressed not to the Father but to Christ alone. On the basis of internal and comparative evidence, Dom Botte has suggested that its primitive form provided for words of institution, perhaps said from memory, just before the present anamnesis. The present epiclesis is certainly out of place. Until recently no known MSS earlier than the 15th cent. contained the anaphora, but recently W. F. Macomber has discovered two from the 12th cent., and one of either the 9th or 10th. This anaphora has been commonly referred to as the "Liturgy of Addai and Mari," but this designation is inaccurate because a liturgy, strictly speaking, is composed of a common order along with the anaphora proper. BIBLIOGRAPHY: the text in Eng. (intermingled with prayers from the common order) in E. F. Brightman, *Liturgies Eastern and Western,* 1 (1896) 283–288; D. Botte, *L'Orient syrien* (1965) 10:89–106; W. F. Macomber, OrChrAnal (1966) 32:335–371; G. Dix, *Shape of the Liturgy* (1945) 177–187.

[F. T. RYAN]

ADDICTION, a compulsive propensity. Usually the term is used in connection with an habituation to something harmful. In proportion to the degree in which addiction operates compulsively, it diminishes freedom and hence moral responsibility. BIBLIOGRAPHY: DRUG ADDICTION; ALCOHOLISM.

ADELA, ST. (Adola, Adula; *c*.675–*c*.734), abbess. Perhaps the daughter of Dagobert II, King of Austrasia, A. is said to have founded, after the death of her husband Alberic, the Benedictine Abbey of Pfalzel near Trier. (*c*.690). St. *Gregory of Utrecht was her grandson. BIBLIOGRAPHY: A. M. Zimmermann, BiblSanct 1:237–238.

[M. F. MCCARTHY]

ADELAIDE (ADELHEID), ST. (931–999), empress, daughter of Rudolph II, King of Burgundy. A war between her father and Hugh of Provence for the crown of Italy was settled (933) with the stipulation that A. should marry Hugh's son, Lothair. The marriage took place 14 years later. Lothair, nominally king but under the power of Berengarius of Ivrea, died apparently of poison administered by Berengarius, who then attempted to force A. into marriage with his own son. She fled to Otto I who was then invading Italy; the two were married in 951 and the union facilitated Otto's subjugation of the peninsula, for A. was very popular in Italy, as she came to be also in Germany. She acted as regent for her grandson Otto III. She was noted for her generosity in the foundation and restoration of monasteries and her concern for the conversion of the Slavs. She was never formally canonized but has been venerated as a saint in several dioceses of Germany. BIBLIOGRAPHY: Butler 4:572–573; The *Epitaphium* of St. Odilo of Cluny, the best source of information about A., can be found in PL 143:967–992; C. Egger, BiblSanct 1:233–235.

[P. K. MEAGHER]

ADELAIDE OF ST. TERESA (secular name Adelaide Frances O'Sullivan; 1817–93), Discalced Carmelite nun. Born in New York City of Protestant parents, A. was converted to Catholicism and entered Carmel in Guatemala (1843). With the suppression of religious communities she was expelled from that country (1874). Enduring this as well as much calumny and persecution with patience, she established a new foundation at Grajal de Campos in Spain (1881). She is much esteemed for the holiness of her life, and appears to have enjoyed remarkable supernatural gifts. The first steps in the promotion of her cause have been taken (1940). BIBLIOGRAPHY: A. F. Valerson, *Life of Mother Adelaide of St. Teresa* (1928).

[P. K. MEAGHER]

ADELAIDE OF SCHAERBEEK, see ALEYDIS, ST.

ADELAIDE OF TURIN (*c*.1020–91), daughter of Count Manfredi of Turin, at whose death (1035), she assumed the regency of his lands. She played a part in imperial and papal politics, was alternately in and out of favor with Emperor and Pope. After Canossa she helped arrange a reconciliation between Henry IV (her son-in-law) and the Pope. BIBLIOGRAPHY: W. M. Plöchl, NCE 1:125–126.

[H. JACK]

ADELAIDE OF VILICH, ST. (d. *c*.1015), abbess. Daughter of Megingoz, count of Guelder, A. became a nun in Cologne, but when her parents founded a monastery at Vilich she became its first abbess. Her reputation for sanctity and the report of miracles came to the attention of St. Heribert, abp. of Cologne, who, through the intervention of the Emperor, prevailed upon her to take the monastery of St. Mary in Cologne also under her rule. Her veneration as a saint has been local. BIBLIOGRAPHY: Butler 1:258; AS Feb. 1:721–727; A. Amore, BiblSanct 1:236–237.

[P. K. MEAGHER]

ADELARD OF BATH (Adelhard, Aethelhard; 12th cent.), one of the English scholars active in spreading Arab learning in the 12th cent. He taught at Paris and Laon and traveled extensively in Italy, Sicily, Greece, Asia Minor, and probably Spain. He translated into Latin Euclid's geometry, as well as mathematical and astronomical works of Arabian authors, and made a contribution of his own to philosophy with his *De eodem et diverso*, a dialogue on the theme of unity and diversity. BIBLIOGRAPHY: Gilson HCP 625–626; P. Delhaye, *Medieval Christian Philosophy* (tr. S. J. Tester, 1960).

[P. K. MEAGHER]

ADELELM, ST. (Sp. Lesmes; d. 1097), patron saint of Burgos, Spain. A French soldier on a pilgrimage to Rome, A. became a Benedictine at Chaise-Dieu and was famous for asceticism and cures of sicknesses by means of blessed bread and water. Royal request brought him to Burgos *c*.1081 to do hospital work; he also played a role in the reconquest of Toledo in 1085. A contemporary monk of Chaise-Dieu wrote the vita (EspSagr 27:87–98). BIBLIOGRAPHY: Butler 1:205–206; G. P. Altabella, BiblSanct 1:239–240.

[E. P. COLBERT]

ADELGERUS OF LIÈGE, see ALGER OF LIÈGE.

ADELGUNDE, ST., see ALDEGUNDIS, ST.

ADELHELM, ST. (d. 1131), abbot. He was the first abbot of Engelberg in Switzerland, *c*.1122. Almost nothing is known of his life, but he was reputed to be saintly and was venerated from the mid-12th century. Though his relics were translated in 1744, his cult is now almost extinct. BIBLIOGRAPHY: M. Besson, DHGE 1:528; Zimmermann 1:252–254; J. L. Grassi, NCE 1:127; S. Mottironi, BiblSanct 1:239–240.

[J. L. GRASSI]

ADELINUS, see HADALINUS, ST.

ADELMANNUS (Almannus; d. *c*.1061), bp. of Brescia from *c*.1050. A cleric from Liège, a disciple of Fulbert of Chartres, A. taught at Liège and Speyer. Some of his verse and letters have survived.

ADELOPHAGITES (Gr. *adēlōs,* secretly; *phagein,* eat), a 4th-cent. Christian sect. Alleging the example of the prophets (see 3 Kg 13.9), they taught that a Christian must eat in secret. Filaster (PL 42:44) states that they also denied the divinity of the Holy Spirit.

[G. T. DENNIS]

ADELPHUS OF METZ, ST. (d. 5th cent.), bp. of Metz. Little is known of him except that his cult existed at Metz from an early date. Believed to have succeeded St. Rufus as bishop, A. converted many pagans during his 17-year episcopate. His relics, translated (836) to Neuweiler, were restored to the abbey church at Metz during the Reformation. BIBLIOGRAPHY: M. B. Ryan, NCE 1:127; C. Lefebvre 1:242–243.

[G. M. COOK]

ADÉMAR, see ADHÉMAR.

ADEN, the name given to both the former British crown colony (75 sq mi; pop. 250,000 [U.N. est. 1966]) and the former Aden protectorates in Arabia (112,000 sq mi; pop. 1 million [1964 est.]), now in the People's Democratic Republic of Yemen. The official language of the regions is Arabic; Islam is the religion of the majority. Capuchins and Servites opened missions in the territories in the 19th century. A vicariate apostolic was created there in 1888. Conflict first occurred when misioners liberated several hundred children from slavery. Conversions continue to be few because of Muslim opposition. Protestants have been working in Aden for about 80 years. There are good mission hospitals in Bashra, Barein, Mascate, Matrah, Kuweit, and Katar. The Reformed Church of America, Anglicans, Danish Lutherans, Presbyterians, and Adventists are the chief denominations at work, but statistics are unavailable. BIBLIOGRAPHY: D. Van Ess, *History of the Arabian Mission* (1959); *Bilan du Monde* 2:21–23.

[P. DAMBORIENA]

ADENAUER, KONRAD (1876–1967), German statesman and chancellor. After receiving his education at Freiburg, Munich, and Bonn, A. held public positions of trust. He was a member of the Center Party and lord mayor of Cologne from 1917 to 1933, when he was dismissed by the Nazi government. For political reasons he was temporarily imprisoned in 1934 and again in 1944. When the constitution for the new Federal Republic of Germany went into effect in 1949, the 73-year-old A. was made chancellor. In this position he distinguished himself as a statesman, made his government respected nationally and internationally, and aligned West Germany with the democracies and the free world. He led his country to a phenomenal recovery: within 10 years Germany was leading Western Europe in productivity. During the last years of his chancellorship he suffered some loss of influence and prestige because of several un-popular political moves. He resigned his position in 1963 and lived in retirement until his death. BIBLIOGRAPHY: R. Hiscocks, *Adenauer Era* (1966); K. Adenauer, *Memoirs 1945–53* (tr. B. R. Oppen, 1966); T. Prittie, *Konrad Adenauer, 1876–1967* (1972).

[M. A. WATHEN]

ADENULF OF ANAGNI (d. 1289), a nephew of Pope Gregory IX, canon of Saint-Victor, who studied under St. Thomas Aquinas in Paris. Despite having refused at first to accept the See of Paris, he appears to have held that ofiice for a time, although he died in retirement at Saint-Victor. BIBLIOGRAPHY: M. Grabmann, ''Adenulf von Anagni, Propst von Saint-Omer, ein Freund und Schüller des hl. Thomas von Aquin,'' *Traditio* 5 (1947) 269–283.

ADEODATUS, POPE, see DEUSDEDIT, POPE.

ADEODATUS (*c.*372–389), the son of St. Augustine and the woman with whom he lived before his conversion. Baptized with Augustine and Alypius at Milan, A. gave promise of a brilliant future, but died shortly after his return with Augustine to Africa. Reference to him can be found in the *Confessions* (PL 32:769), the *De beata vita* (PL 32:962, 966, 968), and the *De magistro* (PL 32:1193–1220). BIBLIOGRAPHY: A. Audollent, DHGE 1:247–249.

ADHÉMAR OF CHABANNES (998–1034), Benedictine monk of the monastery of Saint-Cybard. He gained renown by his goodness and his writing, which included sermons, pieces on the liturgy, chronicles of his order, and a history of France up to 1028.

[H. JACK]

ADHÉMAR OF PUY (d. 1098), bp. of Le Puy. Lineage of the Counts of Valentinois, A. became bp. sometime in 1080; in that capacity he reclaimed lands taken from his see by surrounding noblemen. Responding to Urban II's call for a crusade (made at Clermont, 1095) he set out for the Holy Land as papal legate and deputy with Raymond IV, count of Toulouse. Before his death at Antioch, he acted as military adviser during the battle of Dorylaeum; he was instrumental in preventing defections of rival Western leaders in Asia Minor and Syria, and in reconciling Eastern and Western clergy. More importantly, he helped maintain the religious character of the crusade. It is believed that had he reached Jerusalem, the organization of the Holy Land would have been very different. BIBLIOGRAPHY: A. Fliche, *Catholicisme* 1:141–142; L. M. Tocci, EncCatt 1:306; S. Runciman, *History of the Crusades* (1951) v. 1; *History of the Crusades* (ed. K. M. Setton, 1955) v. 1.

[J. R. RIVELLO]

ADI-GRANTH, the sacred book of the Sikh religion. It was compiled by Arjun, the fifth Sikh guru (1581–1606), from the hymns and poems of the preceding gurus, esp. those of Nānak, founder of Sikhism. It is written in ancient Hindi and Punjab verse, and is extremely difficult to understand for present-day Sikhs. The Songs in Praise of God form the largest part of the book and are frequently employed as cultic prayers. Extensive sacred commentaries on the Adi-Granth have grown up, but are not regarded as canonical. BIBLIOGRAPHY: M. A. MacAuliffe, *Sikh Religion: Its Gurus, Sacred Writings and Authors* (6 v., 1909); Hastings ERE 6:389–390. *SIKHISM.

[T. M. MCFADDEN]

ADIAPHORA (Gr., indifferent things), a term first used in Reformation times among Protestants to signify certain Catholic doctrines and practices that could, it was claimed, be admitted or rejected without prejudice to Protestant belief (see INTERIMS). In later Protestant controversy the term was used in reference to worldly pleasures (alleged to be neither good nor evil in themselves) in which a Christian could legitimately indulge. In both cases there were those who denied that the adiaphora were truly matters of indifference. *ADIAPHORISTS.

[P. K. MEAGHER]

ADIAPHORISTS, Melanchthon's followers in the 16th-cent. controversy in Germany precipitated by a compromise attempted in the Augsburg *Interim (1548) as interpreted in Melanchthon's modification of it known as the Leipzig Interim (1548). According to Melanchthon a number of Catholic ceremonies and rites were "adiaphora," i.e., morally indifferent in themselves, and could be admitted without sacrifice of Protestant principles for the sake of peace. M. *Flacius Illyricus opposed this, declaring that such concessions would bring a return of "popery." The controversy was brought to an unsatisfactory close with Article 10 of the *Formula of Concord (1577), which stated that ordinarily anything not explicitly covered in the Scriptures was a matter for individual churches to decide, but that in times of persecution no such concessions should be made. The term was also applied to a party in a 17th-cent. controversy between Pietists (see PIETISM) and their adversaries. Anton Reiser (1628–86) declared the opera to be anti-Christian, and Pietists generally took the position that amusements and the arts were not compatible with the dignity of a Christian and ought to be condemned. Their opponents held that such things were indifferent in themselves. F. D. E. *Schleiermacher proposed a compromise that many found satisfactory: he denied the concept of indifference but declared that ordinary pleasures were part of the whole of human life and as such were not only permissible to a Christian but could very well be a matter of duty. BIBLIOGRAPHY: A. Baudrillart, DTC 1:396–398; Schaff Creeds 1:298–302.

[P. K. MEAGHER]

ADJURATION, a solemn command using the authority of the divine name or some holy person or thing. As an *oath or *vow binds him who takes it, and an *obsecration pleads with a superior, adjuration takes the divine name to command a subject. The classical example is that of the high priest in the Passion narrative (Mt 26.63): "I adjure thee by the living God that thou tell us whether thou art the Christ." The *exorcism is a form of adjuration invoking the divine name to compel the demon to leave, e.g., in the exorcism of salt, or of the catechumen himself. Another form of adjuration is the formal precept under the vow of obedience whereby the superior invokes not only obedience of the subject but the power of the Holy Spirit. BIBLIOGRAPHY: ThAq ST 2a2ae. 90; Davis MorPastTh 2:48.

[U. VOLL]

ADJUTOR, ST. (Adjutor of Vernon; d. 1131), crusader, hermit. A., born of a noble and devout family of Vernon (Eure), joined the First Crusade (1095), spent 17 years as a prisoner of the Saracens, and upon his liberation and return to France became a monk at the abbey of Tiron. He lived his last years as a hermit near Vernon. BIBLIOGRAPHY: C. Lefebvre, BiblSanct 1:255.

ADJUTOR FRATRIS (Brother's Helper), a consortium of priests formed to provide spiritual assistance to parishes and dioceses, incorporated with the approval of the abp. of San Francisco in 1966 as a non-profit organization. The assistance primarily given is a priests' placement service. It is sometimes necessary for a priest to obtain a substitute to take his place during a temporary absence (e.g., for a vacation). Priests, esp. in remote areas, are often unable to take a vacation because available substitutes cannot be found, although other priests, able and willing to supply, are unaware of the need. The central office of Adjutor Fratris offers help in establishing contact between priests having such need and others who might be willing to substitute for them. For the address of the central office, see the miscellaneous listings under the heading "San Francisco" in the *Official Catholic Directory*.

[C. O'HERN]

ADLER, ALFRED (1870–1937), Austrian psychiatrist, founder of individual psychology, who settled in the U.S. in 1934. An early associate of Freud, A. broke with his distinguished colleague on several critical points. He rejected the primacy Freud assigned to sex and the libido as the source of psychic disorder and proposed the will to power as the more dominant driving force in human nature. When this is too powerful or too frustrated, the outcome is neurosis. Because the frustration of the will to power comes from the outside world, A.'s thought on mental disorder is more sociologically and less biologically oriented than that of Freud. BIBLIOGRAPHY: P. Bottome, *Alfred Adler* (1939; 2d ed. 1946); H. Ansbacher and R. Anshacker, *Individual Psychology of Alfred Adler* (1964); J. Dominian, *Psychiatry and the Christian* (1962); H. Orgler, *Alfred Adler* (1972).

ADLER, FELIX (1851–1933), founder of the Society for *Ethical Culture. He was born in Alzey, Germany, the son of a rabbi who came with his family to the U.S. when A. was six. After graduation from Columbia in 1870, A. studied at Berlin and Heidelberg preparing for the rabbinate; but through his study, particularly of Kant and biblical criticism, he came to reject traditional religion. He became professor of Hebrew and Oriental literature at Cornell in 1874, but in 1876 resigned to found the New York Society for Ethical Culture, a movement of ethical humanism. From 1903 till his death he was professor of political and social ethics at Columbia, while continuing to play a leading role in the society and various movements of social reform. BIBLIOGRAPHY: D. Muzzey, *Ethics as a Religion* (1951).

[T. EARLY]

ADLER, SAMUEL (1928–), composer of liturgical music for the synagogue. Born in Germany, A., son of cantor-composer Hugo Chayim Adler, was brought to the U.S. in 1939. He received his music education at Boston and Harvard Univ., where he studied with Walter Piston, Randall Thompson, and Paul Hindemith. A.'s most significant contribution towards synagogal music are his oratorios "The Vision of Isaiah," "Lament of Jeremiah," "The Binding of Isaac," and music for the Sabbath liturgy. At present he teaches composition at the Eastman School of Music, Rochester, New York. BIBLIOGRAPHY: A. M. Rothmuller, *Music of the Jews* (rev. ed. 1967); S. Adler, *Choral Conducting: An Anthology* (1971).

[H. BERLINSKI]

ADMINISTRATOR, one to whom authority is given to manage ecclesiastical affairs until the usual executive is designated. In church law, the Holy See may appoint an administrator to govern a diocese or a religious institution (see ADMINISTRATOR, APOSTOLIC); the diocesan consultors or cathedral chapter must elect an administrator within 8 days to provide for a diocese without a bp. (See ADMINISTRATOR, DIOCESAN [VICAR CAPITULAR]); and a bp. may appoint a priest as administrator of a parish when it is without a pastor.

[T. M. MCFADDEN]

ADMINISTRATOR, APOSTOLIC, a cleric to whom the government of a diocese is entrusted by the Holy See as an extraordinary measure. He may be appointed when the resident bp. is incapacitated by illness, exile, the imposition of a canonical penalty, or other cause, or when the see is vacant and requires extraordinary supervision. He governs the diocese with vicarious power as deputy of the Roman Pontiff in whose supreme power he shares. The present discipline in the CIC cc. 312–318 is based on the Constitution *Sapienti consilio* of Pius X (1908), although the office has roots in the interventors and papal visitators of the early Middle Ages. BIBLIOGRAPHY: T. J. McDonough, *Apostolic Administrators* (1941); DDC 1:181–192; Abbo 1:342–345.

[L. M. KNOX]

ADMINISTRATOR, DIOCESAN (Vicar Capitular), a priest elected by the cathedral chapter (vicar capitular) or the board of diocesan consultors (diocesan administrator) to provide temporarily for the needs of a vacant see. In the late Middle Ages the cathedral chapter (see CHAPTER, CATHEDRAL) as a college governed the vacant see; the Council of Trent insisted on the election of an administrator within 8 days of the occurrence of the vacancy. The administrator must be a priest and at least 30 years old (CIC c. 434). During the vacancy he governs the diocese with ordinary jurisdiction, but may not make any innovations tht would prejudice the rights of the diocese or bishop (CIC c. 436). The office ceases with the installation of the newly appointed bishop. BIBLIOGRAPHY: L. A. Jaeger, *Administration of Vacant and Quasivacant Dioceses in the United States* (1932); Abbo 1:417–439.

[L. M. KNOX]

ADMIRATIO POPULI (popular astonishment), a phrase used in moral and canonical literature for the shocking effect one's behavior may have upon the public at large. The expression takes on this fidgety meaning in the manualists who treat *admiratio populi* as a category that should impose a check upon one's conduct, even when on other counts it is right and proper. Hence the warnings against "causing *admiratio*" which still linger in some RC vernaculars. That one should take care not to shock people is, up to a point, an imperative of good manners, friendliness, urbanity, and this is largely a matter of the circumstances. It is analogous to the lowest category among the notes of theological censure, namely, that of being "offensive to pious ears," and—like it—needs to be treated respectfully yet robustly. People often deserve better than to have their prejudices echoed. "Shocking" should not be confused, as it often is, with "giving scandal."

[T. GILBY]

ADMONITION, see WARNING.

ADMONITION TO PARLIAMENT, a document of the English Puritans (1572), demanding esp. abolition of *episcopacy.

[T. C. O'BRIEN]

ADMONT, ABBEY OF, Benedictine foundation in Styria, diocese of Graz-Seckau, mentioned in a document of 859. It reached its first peak under abbots Gottfried and Irimbert (1138–77) with a scriptorium famous for illumination. After plunderings by Protestants, Turks, Bonapartists, and Nazis, Admont started rebuilding (1945) and restoring its art treasures. The ornate library has seven ceiling frescoes by B. Altomonte (1776) and baroque carvings by J. T. Stammel (d. 1765). Important are a natural history museum of insects and an art museum with a 1000-year-old collection. The neo-Gothic abbey church (1869) boasts a Christmas crib by Stammel (1745) and precious 17th- and 18th-cent. vestments.

BIBLIOGRAPHY: A. Krause, NCE 1:133; P. A. Krause, *Das Blasiusmünster in Admont* (1965).

[M. J. DALY]

ADO OF VIENNE, ST. (*c*.800–875), a man of noble family who was educated and became a monk at the abbey of Ferrières. After teaching briefly at Prüm, he went to Lyons, was appointed to the church of St. Romanus, and in 859 was made archbishop. He worked at reform in his diocese and vigorously opposed Lothair II's divorce. His historical writing left much to be desired by way of accuracy, esp. his martyrology through which many errors crept into the Roman Martyrology, and his chronicle of world events up to 869. BIBLIOGRAPHY: Butler 4:571–572; Zimmermann 3:439–440; I. Checchetti, BiblSanct 1:258–265.

[H. JACK]

ADOLA, ST., see ADELA, ST.

ADOLESCENCE, the stage of life between childhood and early adulthood, whose beginning is marked by the onset of puberty (about 12th year in girls, 14th in boys). It may be considered terminated by society's recognition of the individual's rights and duties as an adult. Adolescence is characterized by physical (particularly sexual), emotional, intellectual, and behavioral developments, qualitatively distinct enough to constitute a definite phase of life. Sexually the reproductive organs mature for function, and secondary sex characteristics are produced by secretions of male and female hormones. Growth in stature and weight, which has been progressing at a decreasing rate since birth, now accelerates rapidly for a brief period until the individual reaches adult height. Intellectually the adolescent changes from a classifying, accumulative, and absorptive mentality to a questioning, hypothesizing, and theorizing mentality. Emotionally, the adolescent begins to feel less dependence on the family and more on the peer group, besides the new qualities of emotion introduced by sexual maturation. He also feels a need for independent and responsible self-determination in matters of study, work, and recreation. All of these changes proceeding rapidly in different spheres of life tend to produce uncertainty, insecurity, and self-consciousness. In behavior, the adolescent becomes more experimenting, restless under authority, involved in activities with his own age group, and concerned about problems of sexuality, morality, and religion, and his future responsibilities as an adult. The problem or task of adolescence is to integrate the new drives, capacities, and needs into a stable personality structure acceptable to himself, his family, and his peers, and effective in the social and economic structure of which he is a part. This involves achieving one's sexual identity, control of sexual drives, and eventually making the choice of a compatible, permanent marital partner. It involves the understanding and personal assimilation of traditions, goals, and ideals acceptable to the larger social group, and forms of interpersonal relations facilitating identification and cooperation with de-sired social subgroups. Finally it involves the perfecting of knowledge and skills useful to society, and the choice of an occupational role enabling the individual to support himself economically.

In societies that are stable rather than rapidly evolving, monolithic rather than pluralistic, and that mark off the stages of adolescence by definite rituals and observances, the passage through adolescence tends to be less stressful for the individual. Moreover, if the family is understanding, willing to offer both support and freedom, and bound by ties of genuine love easily expressed, the adolescent makes the transition to adulthood more smoothly. In every society, however, there is evidence that adolescence presents some crisis, even if minimal, and most societies recognize the need for special measures to assist maturing youth. In the complex, rapidly changing, pluralistic societies of Western culture, more and more of the energies, time, and resources of religious, educational, psychological, psychiatric, and social organizations are being devoted to solving problems of the adolescent crisis. On the other hand, since adolescence is also a period of high enthusiasm, energy, and idealism, society is paying more attention today to tapping these resources for its own renewal and reform. BIBLIOGRAPHY: A. A. Schneiders, *Counselling the Adolescent* (1967); B. G. Lambert et al., *Transition from Childhood to Maturity* (1972); D. Elkind, *Sympathetic Understanding of the Child 6 to 16* (1971).

[M. E. STOCK]

ADOMNAN, ST., see ADAMNAN OF IONA, ST.

ADONAI (Canaanite and Hebrew *'ādôn*) my lords, in the plural of majesty. Jews before the Christian era did not pronounce the holy name of God (J H V H) and used Adonai for God. When later Jews wanted to read Adonai they put vowel markings under J H V H, and it was misunderstood as Jehovah by the Christians. The Septuagint translates J H V H as *kyrios* (lord); hence in English versions J H V H is put as "the Lord," and the Jews read these consonants as "Adonai." In the Christian liturgy the term refers to the Second Person of the Trinity. BIBLIOGRAPHY: ODCC 18.

[M. C. BRADLEY]

ADONIJAH, fourth son born to King David at Hebron by Haggith, one of his wives. When David was old A. claimed the throne as the eldest remaining son, although neither law nor custom required this. He had the support of Joab, David's general, and Abiathar the priest, but not that of the priest Zadok, Benaiah of the royal army, or the prophet Nathan. A. had himself crowned king at En-Rogel. However, Solomon's mother, Bathsheba, supported by Nathan, reminded the dying king of his promise to make Solomon, divinely chosen to be the successor to David, the rightful king. David thus proclaimed Solomon king. In the midst of A.'s feasting, fear came upon him, and he fled to the altar for protection. He was pardoned by Solomon, but later when A.

wished to take David's young concubine, Abishag, as his wife, Solomon believed A. was again aiming to secure the throne and he ordered A. put to death. BIBLIOGRAPHY: F. E. Gigot, CE 1:146–147; B. McGrath, NCE 1:136.

[M. C. BRADLEY]

ADOPTING ACT, a provision in 1729 by Presbyterian clergy at Philadelphia that every entering clergyman or candidate for the ministry should declare the *Westminster Confession and the *Westminster Catechisms to be ''in all the essential and necessary articles, good forms of sound words and systems of Christian doctrine.'' To counter tendencies within Presbyterianism toward Arianism and Unitarianism, clergy of Scottish and Irish origin had been advocating subscription to the Confession as a requisite for membership in the *presbytery and *synod. Those, like Jonathan *Dickinson, with origins in England and New England resisted such a measure as being contrary to Scripture and even to the spirit of the Confession. The Adopting Act was a compromise. A clergyman who could not accept some point in the Confession or Catechisms was obliged to state his scruples to the presbytery or synod for a decision as to whether the matter was so essential or necessary as to warrant exclusion from the ministry. The act made American Presbyterianism a confessional body permitting a broad liberty in interpretation of doctrine. Tension, explicit in the compromise, has also been a cause of disruption throughout the history of the denomination. BIBLIOGRAPHY: E. A. Smith, *Presbyterian Ministry in American Culture: A Study in Changing Concepts, 1700–1900* (1962).

[J. H. SMYLIE]

ADOPTION, the legal and social process whereby a child becomes a member of a family other than that of his natural parents. The practice was known in the ancient Near East and is found in the OT, esp. in the stories of the Patriarchs, insofar as a slave could be made an heir in the absence of a natural son (Gen 15.2–3) or a concubine bear a child that would be adopted into the patriarchal family (Gen 16.2–5). The Egyptian practice is testified to in the story of Moses (Ex 2.10). Although English common law does not provide for it, Roman law embodies certain adoption procedures, reflecting a primary concern for the adoptive family's continuity and rights of inheritance. The earliest U. S. legislation reflected the Roman law emphasis, but in 1850 Massachusetts became the first state to require juridical proceedings for adoption in order to secure the child's welfare. Today every state has legislation dealing with adoption procedures, although their variation is significant. The natural parents must consent to the adoption except in cases of abandonment, moral or mental unfitness, etc., and there is usually a probationary period of 1 year before the adoption becomes final. The legal effect of adoption in the great majority of states is that the adopted child has the same rights and obligations as the natural child, and all legal bonds with his natural parents are broken. In regard to marriage, church

law follows the civil statutes; adoption constitutes an impediment to marriage only and to the degree that it is such according to the civil law of the region (CIC cc. 1059; 1080). In the Oriental code, it is a minor impediment (CrebAllat c. 31.5).

Beyond its legal ramifications, adoption is an important social process and one that has been steadily increasing in the U. S. In 1960, there were c.107,000 adoptions (57,800 by non-relatives); in 1965, c.142,000 adoptions (76,700 by non-relatives); in 1967, c.158,000 adoptions (83,700 by non-relatives). Adoption most often involves a social welfare agency which assists each person involved in the process: a complete range of social services for the natural parents, esp. in the case of an unwed mother, physical and psychological care of the child, as well as evaluation and postadoption counseling for the adoptive parents. Most agencies attempt to match the parent and child ethnically and racially, although some do not follow this policy where there is a disproportion between adoptive parents and children of a particular race or ethnic background. Religion is also a factor; both Catholic and nonsectarian agencies try for religious matching except in those cases where the natural parents specify otherwise. Catholic adoption agencies have stressed that the spiritual needs of a baptized child can be most adequately fulfilled in a Catholic home. BIBLIOGRAPHY: *Readings in Adoption* (ed. I. E. Smith, 1963); Child Welfare League of America, *Study of Adoptive Practice* (3 v., 1956); S. N. Katz, NCE 1:136–138; C. T. Dwyasuk, *Adoption–Is It for You?* (1973).

[T. M. MCFADDEN]

ADOPTION, SUPERNATURAL, the assumption of man into divine sonship. Man was created in the image and likeness of God. The Fathers of the Church see God reflected esp. in human reason, freedom, and creativity. The divine Logos is the pattern after which man was fashioned. But modern writers like P. Teilhard de Chardin and K. Rahner teach that the Logos precisely in his humanity is the prototype of visible creation. When man is divinized through grace by the surrendering of himself in faith and charity to God's special offer of personal love, he becomes in the fullest sense a replica of the Logos-made-man. Through faith and charity man invests his freedom in and identifies with the free project of God that is Christ. He receives the projection, or seal (Gr. *sphragis*) of the Spirit of God's love, which is precisely the image of the God-man, divinity as well as humanity. The Christian's identity with Christ is proclaimed in the liturgy where the believer finds himself acting out Christ's paschal mystery. Bread and wine, symbolizing the very life of the Christian, are converted into the body and blood of Christ. He is reminded that what takes place ritually on the altar already happened in his life through baptism. He is truly a son of God because he is identified with the Son of God and lives not only his own human life but also a participated divine life communicated to him through Christ. The Christian becomes a member of the divine family only by means of the supernatural action of God. Christ alone is by nature the Son of the heavenly Father. So those who bear his image are called supernatural or adopted sons and daughters of God. As such they are co-heirs with Christ of his own patrimony. BIBLIOGRAPHY: R. Gleason, *Grace* (1962).

[C. R. MEYER]

ADOPTIONISM (Adoptianism), the teaching that Jesus is the Son of the Father by adoption, not naturally. The term has been used to designate Monarchianism, Nestorianism, and the 12th-cent. teaching of the Abelardian school that the humanity of Jesus had no substantial entity of its own (D 750). As an explicit doctrine Adoptionism refers to the Christology of certain Spanish bps. in the 8th and 9th centuries. As human, Jesus was son of God by adoption, in virtue of exceptional grace; as divine, he was naturally the son of God. Elipandus of Toledo, who well knew the difference between person and nature, is quoted as saying that Christ is adoptive in humanity and not at all adoptive in divinity (PL 96:918); but he avoided saying that Christ was an adopted person. A favored term of Elipandus for the Redeemer is *Dei simul et hominis filius* (at once the son of God and of man). He may have been led into his difficult position by his earlier condemnation of *Migetius's statement that the second person of the Trinity is that made from the seed of David according to the flesh and not that begotten by the Father. His stand may also have been influenced by his having to deal with Moors and Mozarabs under Muslim and Nestorian influence. His fellow bps. supported him, and the Mozarabic liturgy did refer to the Redeemer as *homo adoptivus,* although probably in a metaphorical sense.

The works of *Felix of Urgel, ally of Elipandus, are lost, and his position is given in his adversaries' texts. Brought to account by both Charlemagne and Pope Adrian I (D 595, 610–611), Felix died (818) in the custody of Bp. Agobard of Lyons, who proceeded to refute Adoptionist views discovered among Felix's papers. Alcuin in a long disputation pointed out to Felix that the issue came down to a need to say that concrete human nature was "assumed" by the Word and not "adopted." Spanish Adoptionists were regarded as a threat not only by Alcuin, who with Benedict of Aniane waged an intensive campaign to keep monks on the Spanish frontier orthodox, but also by the papacy, in supporting the Carolingians against Felix and in the Council of Frankfurt (794; D 612, 615), and by Albar of Córdoba, who *c.*850 charged that Elipandus had afflicted Mozarab Spain with the evil. BIBLIOGRAPHY: É. Amann, *Histoire de l'Église* 6:129–152; FlicheMartin 6:129–152; ThAq ST 3, 23.4.

[E. P. COLBERT]

ADOPTIONISTS, proponents of the teaching that Jesus as man is not the Son of the Father naturally, but by adoption. They may be grouped into three historical periods, although the position of its adherents is by no means identical. The early adoptionists belong to the period of intense Christological controversy from the 2d cent. to the Council of *Chalcedon (451); they strove to uphold Jesus' true humanity which they thought would be compromised by the "one person, two natures" doctrine. Among them are *Theodotus the Tanner, *Paul of Samosota, *Lucian of Antioch, and by implication *Nestorius and *Origen (see Monarchianism). Adoptionism properly so-called arose in the 8th cent., esp. in Spain, and was proposed by *Elipandus of Toledo and *Felix of Urgel (see ADOPTIONISM). The controversy appeared again in the 12th and 14th centuries. *Abelard erroneously understood the hypostatic union and wrote, "God is neither flesh, nor is he man properly so-called" (PL 178:1107). In the 14th cent., *Durandus of Saint-Pourçain defended the formula, "Jesus Christ as man is the adopted son of God"; his position seems to be based on the fundamental error of applying filiation to Christ's divine or human nature rather than to him as a person. BIBLIOGRAPHY: E. Portalié, DTC 1.1:403–421; Schaff Creeds 1:48–50.

[T. M. MCFADDEN]

ADORATION (WORSHIP), the intellectual, volitional, and physical homage rendered to God by which man acknowledges and subjects himself to God's infinite grandeur. In this sense, it is employed in the Second Commandment (Dt 6.13), although the term was also used in a wider sense by Eastern peoples and in the OT to signify respect or dependence, e.g., Joseph's brothers are said to adore him (Gen 43.26). Christ taught that adoration be rendered to God alone (Mt 4.10), and was himself the recipient of adoration (Jn 9.38). The early Christians recognized the adoration due uniquely to God as a central point of their belief, and many of the Roman persecutions were based upon the Christians' refusal to worship the emperor. Controversy quickly arose in the Church whether the same adoration rendered to the Father should be extended to the Son and Holy Spirit (SEE Arianism), but *Nicaea I (325) defining that the Son was of the substance of the Father virtually affirmed the Son's claim to the worship due to God. Similarly, the Councils of *Ephesus (431) and *Constantinople II (553) declared that Christ in his humanity and not only insofar as he possessed a divine nature was worthy of adoration, since the object of worship is a person not an abstract principle. In 787, *Nicaea II confronted the problem of *iconoclasm and taught that adoration or *latria was reserved to God, but could be rendered to him indirectly through reverence for his images.

The Christian adores God primarily through the eucharistic liturgy, uniting himself to the perfect adoration of the Son. Prayer is also an act of adoration, in which God's perfection and his relationship with man through Christ is the primary consideration. In addition, the believer's constant openness to God in all his existential manifestations is a genuine adoration in spirit and in truth (Jn 4.23). BIBLIOGRAPHY: A. Molien, DSAM 1:210–222; M. Gaucheron, *Catholicisme* 1:157–159; B. Neunheuser, NCE 1:141–142; ODCC 19. *ADORATION OF THE BLESSED SACRAMENT.

[T. M. MCFADDEN]

ADORATION, NOCTURNAL, the RC practice of worshiping Christ as present in the Blessed Sacrament exposed upon the altar or reserved in the tabernacle, during the night hours. Aside from the religious communities dedicated to perpetual adoration, the practice grew up in connection with the *Forty Hours Devotion. Since Church practice, established by law in Clement VIII's bull *Graves et diuturnae* (1592), does not permit exposition without adoration, the continuous exposition during the Forty Hours Devotion required nocturnal adoration. The practice is also fostered independently of Forty Hours by the Nocturnal Adoration Society, founded by Giacomo Sinibaldi in Rome (1810), and raised to the rank of archconfraternity in 1858. BIBLIOGRAPHY: E. R. Falardeau, NCE 1:142. *ADORATION OF THE BLESSED SACRAMENT.

[T. M. MCFADDEN]

ADORATION, PERPETUAL, the continual worship of the Blessed Sacrament solemnly exposed on the altar or present in the tabernacle. Although there have been instances dating back to the 12th cent., the practice became popular in the 16th cent., largely as a reaction against Protestant eucharistic beliefs. In the thought of its Milanese originators, Christians should render special homage to the Blessed Sacrament for 40 consecutive hours, commemorating the 40 hours between Christ's Crucifixion and Resurrection. Thus the Host was solemnly exposed, and various prayers and ceremonies were provided (see FORTY HOURS DEVOTION). The practice quickly spread throughout Italy, and was introduced to Rome by St. *Philip Neri. But its adherents were not satisfied to have the devotion only once a year (usually immediately before Lent); archconfraternities were formed; the first and third Sundays of the month were set aside for perpetual adoration in Rome; and Clement VIII asked (1592) that "public prayer ascend without intermission before the face of the Lord" to make reparation for a sinful world. The devotion grew until the time of the French Revolution when it gradually died out, only to be revived in the 19th cent. with even greater force. Perpetual adoration continues today through many eucharistic confraternities, the Forty Hours Devotion, and religious orders of men and women dedicated to reparation through the uninterrupted worship of the Blessed Sacrament. BIBLIOGRAPHY: T. Ortolan, DTC 1.1:442–445; G. Vassali, et al., DSAM 4.2:1637–48. *ADORATION OF THE BLESSED SACRAMENT.

[T. M. MCFADDEN]

ADORATION OF THE BLESSED SACRAMENT, worship of the eucharistic species, extending to them as the body and blood of Christ the adoration rendered to God alone. Although always practiced in the Church, its external forms have varied in time. In the early Church, there was no specific adoration of the Blessed Sacrament except that implied in the liturgy and in certain customary observances such as the use of a low voice at the consecration, the bowing of heads, the covering of ciboria with a veil. These practices were introduced only gradually after the 4th century. After a more precise theology of the Real Presence developed, however, a strong eucharistic cult emerged in the 12th cent.: Urban IV instituted the feast of Corpus Christi (1264) with its various eucharistic processions, monstrances were used for reservation of the Blessed Sacrament, and the *Forty Hours Devotion appeared. It was also at this time that the practice of elevating the Host at Mass began, probably when Odo, bp. of Paris (1196–1208), ordered his priests to elevate the Host so that it could be seen by all. Many abuses grew up alongside of this development. So much emphasis on the awesome majesty of the consecrated species tended to cause people to satisfy their devotion by gazing upon them rather than by consuming them sacramentally. The Protestant Reformation forcefully condemned these abuses, and most Protestant Churches do not reserve the eucharistic species. RC practice continues to encourage adoration of the Blessed Sacrament, but insists that it be related to the Mass. BIBLIOGRAPHY: L. Bouyer, *Liturgical Piety* (1955); A. Molien, *Catholicisme* 1:160–163; M. Burbuch, NCE 5:615–617. *ADORATION, PERPETUAL; *ADORATION, NOCTURNAL.

[T. M. MCFADDEN]

ADORATION OF THE CROSS, a term with a liturgical and theological significance: liturgically, it refers to a section of the *Good Friday services in the Latin rite in which the cross is venerated, or a similar service in some Eastern churches, e.g., the Greeks on the third Sunday of Lent; theologically, it applies to the homage which Christians have given to relics or images of the cross. In the Good Friday service, the crucifix is gradually unveiled while the ministers chant *Behold the wood of the cross*. The congregation then venerates the cross by a kiss, and the choir sings the reproaches, concluding with the *Pange lingua* (O faithful cross). There are several feasts commemorating the cross in the East; in the West, the Exaltation and Finding of the True Cross are observed. Although iconoclastic movements have at times sought to discourage it, such veneration has been consistently present among Christians. Thomas Aquinas defended the practice, but maintained that it should be described as relative adoration to distinguish from the homage due directly only to God (ThAq ST 3a, 25.3–4). BIBLIOGRAPHY: H. Quilliet, DTC 3.2:2339–2363.

[T. M. MCFADDEN]

ADRAGNA, ANTONIO MARIA (1818–90), influential theologian at Vatican Council I. Born in Sicily, A. entered the Conventual Franciscans (1834) and taught at Würzburg, Assisi, Perugia, and Palermo. Pius IX made him a consultor to the Holy Office (1861), and one of the eight members of the dogmatic commission preparing for Vatican Council I. He prepared a schema on the temporalities of the Church; his influence on the Council was generally conservative. BIBLIOGRAPHY: L. Di Fonzo, EncCatt 1:331.

[T. M. MCFADDEN]

ADRIAN, see HADRIAN.

ADRIAN, ST. (Hadrian; fl. 9th-cent.), missionary. He was born into the Hungarian royal family and went to the British Isles as a missionary. He went later to Scotland with 6,602 companions of many nationalities, possibly refugees from the Danish invasion of Ireland. A. founded a monastery on the Isle of May (Firth of Forth). Those Scots martyred in the Danish attack (875) on this monastery are commemorated in the Aberdeen Breviary. BIBLIOGRAPHY: Butler 1:480–481; W. F. Skene, *Celtic Scotland* (2d ed. 1886–90) 2:311–316; M. A. Calabrese, BiblSanct 1:267–268.

[R. T. MEYER]

ADRIAN I (d. 795), **POPE** from 772. A Roman of noble birth, A. served the Holy See in the pontificates of Paul I and Stephen III. On the death of the latter he was elected pope by acclamation of clergy and people. Troubled by the meddling in ecclesiastical affairs of the Lombards and their seizure of papal properties, A. appealed to Charlemagne for help. Twice Charlemagne came with troops; the capitulation of Desiderius, King of the Lombards, after the siege of Pavia, finally put an end to Lombard power. Charlemagne assumed the title ''King of the Franks and Lombards,'' and ultimately fulfilled the promises of his father, *Pepin, regarding the Patrimony of St. Peter. This put the Pope in control of a substantial part of central Italy, which came to be known as the *States of the Church. A. gave Charlemagne a collection of canon law based on the 6th-cent. *Dionysiana collectio* but brought up to date. Its circulation in the West was important to the developing concept of papal authority. A. also beautified the city of Rome and organized an agricultural project to help feed the poor. He collaborated with Charlemagne on the reform of the Church, succeeded in countering the Adoptionist heresy in Spain, and cooperated with the plan of the Empress Irene to convoke the Council of *Nicaea II, which condemned Iconoclasm. A poor translation of the acts of this council caused some consternation in the West, and it was condemned by a council in Frankfurt, but Adrian explained and approved the acts. BIBLIOGRAPHY: J. E. Bresnahan, NCE 1:144–145; Bihlmeyer–Tüchle 2:48–49.

[P. F. MULHERN]

ADRIAN II (d. 872), **POPE** from 867. Of a prominent Roman family from which two earlier popes, Stephen IV and Sergius II, had come, A. married in his youth, and his wife and a daughter were still living when at the age of 75 he was elected pope, the compromise choice of those who favored and those who opposed the strong policies of his predecessor, *Nicholas I. His daughter was carried off by Eleutherius, who later killed her and her mother also. Anastasius the Librarian, brother (or cousin) of Eleutherius and adviser and secretary to the Pope, was for a time under suspicion of complicity in the crime, but was apparently exonerated, for he was shortly restored to favor. A. attempted in the main to follow in the course marked out by Nicholas. He forced Lothair II, King of Lorraine, to acknowledge his lawful wife and abandon the idea of a divorce. He upheld against Hincmar of Reims the right of suffragan bishops to appeal to Rome. In a Roman synod in 869 and again at the Council of Constantinople IV, over which his legates presided, he condemned *Photius. He did not succeed in retaining the Bulgarians in the patriarchate of the West, but he fared better with the Slovak people of central Europe, encouraging the mission of *Cyril and Methodius, and permitting the use of Slavic liturgy. BIBLIOGRAPHY: A. J. Ennis, NCE 1:145; A. Noyon, DHGE 1:619–624.

[P. F. MULHERN]

ADRIAN III, ST. (d. 885), **POPE** from 884. Of Roman family and birth, A. reigned briefly in the disturbed generation that marked the breakup of the Carolingian Empire. He recognized *Photius and was conciliatory in his attitude toward the Byzantine Empire generally. But he dealt with factional opposition and intrigue in Rome with a ferocity understandable only when measured against the grave disorders of the time. He died at Modena while en route to a diet at Worms called by Charles the Fat to discuss the succession in the empire and the growing menace of the Saracens. A. was buried in a local monastery, in the vicinity of which he has been venerated from antiquity. His public cult in Rome and Modena was approved by Leo XIII in 1892. BIBLIOGRAPHY: A. J. Ennis, NCE 1:146; Butler 3:41; F. Caraffa, BiblSanct 1:271–272.

[P. F. MULHERN]

ADRIAN IV (d. 1159), **POPE** from 1154, known as Nicholas Breakspear before he was elected to the papacy, the only Englishman ever to achieve that distinction. In early youth he left England, probably as a wandering scholar in the fashion of the times, and became a canon regular in Valence, France, where he eventually was elected abbot of the monastery of St. Rufus. When he visited Rome on some business connected with his office, he attracted the attention of Eugene III (1145–53), who made him cardinal bishop of Ostia in 1149. As Eugene's legate to Scandinavia, A. established Trondheim as the independent archiepiscopal see for Norway (1152) and instituted other reforms affecting the Scandinavian Church. On the death of Anastasius IV (1154), he was elected without opposition. His was a stormy reign of 5 years but significant for the future of the Church. The independence of the Holy See was threatened variously by the dictatorial *Frederick I Barbarossa, the rebellious Roman populace led by *Arnold of Brescia, and the grasping aims of William the Norman, King of Sicily. A. faced these forces, at times singly, at times with the help of others, with resolution, skill, and a consciousness of destiny. With him the term Vicar of Christ came into use as a title for the Pope. Barbarossa he fought to the end; Arnold he saw go to the gallows; of William he made an ally. His chief contribution is that he established a line of action that his successors would follow in achieving freedom for the Church in the tumultuous generations that lay ahead. In his disputed but probably authentic bull *Laudabiliter* and letter of investiture, A. granted Ireland (considered to belong to the dominion of the Church) to the rule of the English King Henry II. This grant, known as the *Donation of Adrian, was solicited not by Henry, but by *John of Salisbury, as the latter testifies in a passage (most probably genuine) of his *Metalogicon* (PL 199:945). BIBLIOGRAPHY: W. Ullman, NCE 1:146; A. U. Clerigh, CE 1:156–159; E. M. Almedingen, *English Pope* (1925); Mann 9:231–340.

[P. F. MULHERN]

ADRIAN V (d. 1276), **POPE** from July 11 till Aug. 18, 1276, but never ordained, consecrated, or crowned. Born Ottobuono Fieschi, of an influential Genoese family, A. was made cardinal deacon of S. Hadriano in 1251 by his uncle, *Innocent IV. Under *Clement IV, he distinguished himself on a mission to England to compose the quarrel between Henry III and his barons. He ascribed what proved to be his final illness to the meager diet served in the conclave in which he was elected, and which was held according to the stringent decrees the Council of Lyons (1272) had made to hasten the choice of a pope. He planned to repeal these decrees but, within 5 weeks, while preparing for ordination, he died in Viterbo where his tomb remains. BIBLIOGRAPHY: B. J. Comaskey, NCE 1:146–147; R. Graham, "Letters of Cardinal Ottoboni," EHR 15 (1900) 87–120.

[P. F. MULHERN]

ADRIAN VI (1459–1523), **POPE** from 1522. Born Adrian Florensz Dedal, son of a Utrecht shipwright, A. was the first pope in 200 years to retain his baptismal name, and the last non-Italian to be pope. He received his early education from the Brothers of the Common Life and later attended the university at Louvain, where he became, in turn, professor, chancellor, and rector. In 1507 he was made tutor to the future Charles V, and after 1515 his rise to eminence was rapid. Within 2 years he was administrator of the Kingdom of Castile, bp. of Tortosa, viceroy of Spain, and finally cardinal. On the death of Leo X (1521), A., absent from the conclave, was elected unanimously, as a compromise candidate, probably because of his personal influence with the newly-elected Emperor Charles V. A man of simplicity, with no taste for pomp and luxury, A. was disgusted with the religious situation he found in Rome, where he mistook for laymen the foppishly dressed cardinals who welcomed him. His attempts at the reform long overdue at the papal court were ill-received. He tried to reduce expenses but succeeded only in getting himself accounted a miser. His efforts to deal with the Lutheran crisis came to nothing. His call for arms against the threatening Turks was unheeded. Exhausted and overwhelmed by the opposition shown him in the office he had not sought, he died within 20 months of his election. BIBLIOGRAPHY: K. M. Saum, NCE 1:148; EphemThLov 35 (1959), 520–629 (commemorative issue); J. F. Loughlin, CE 1:159–160.

[P. F. MULHERN]

ADSO OF MONTIER-EN-DER (d. 992), a monk at Luxeuil, abbot at Montier-en-Der, and finally, abbot at Dijon, who wrote hymns, lives of the saints, and some theological treatises.

[H. JACK]

ADUARTE, DIEGO FRANCISCO (1569–1636), Dominican bishop, missionary. He was sent to the Philippines in 1594, where he worked as a missionary and recruited for the missions in the Philippines and the Far East. He was named bishop of Nueva Segovia in 1632. His history of the Dominican province in the Philippines, Japan, and China has been reprinted several times, most recently in 1962. BIBLIOGRAPHY: E. Gómez Tagle, NCE 1:148–149.

[H. JACK]

ADULA, see ADELA, ST.

ADULATION, servile flattery, excessive praise beyond merit, feigned devotion which may or may not be done out of self-seeking motives. Because of the dishonesty and deceit it involves, it is morally against the virtue of truthfulness.

[J. R. RIVELLO]

ADULT BAPTISM, the rite whereby an adult participates in the sacraments of Christian initiation has varied significantly within the history of Christianity. Scripture and other 1st- and 2d-cent. documents indicate that one prepared for Christian initiation by hearing the word of God, repenting, and being converted. *The *Apostolic Tradition* (c.215) witnesses to the *catechumenate, a period of remote and proximate preparation for baptism. The remote preparation, usually lasting for 3 years, was a period of intellectual and moral instruction and scrutiny during which the catechumen was introduced to the life and beliefs of the Christian community, and examined regarding his ability to live the Christian life. If the catechumen then decided to be baptized and was accepted by the community, he entered a second stage of preparation, beginning during Lent and culminating in the baptismal rite itself at the *Easter Vigil service. Although local Churches had considerable variations, the full rite encompassed a renunciation of Satan, the candidate's profession of faith, entry into the baptismal pool, an anointing, kiss of peace, and a procession to the altar in white robes while carrying a lighted candle. It was only later (at Rome, between the 6th and 8th centuries) that the minister's declarative statement that the person is baptized in the name of the Trinity was used. After the 6th cent., however, the baptism of adults became less frequent, and the ritual for adults came to be a compilation of prayers and ceremonies intended for infant baptism. Thus features crept into the baptismal rite which rendered its nature and purpose far from clear (Vat II SacLit 62).

Vatican Council II called for significant reforms in the administration of these rites of Christian initiation, esp. that "the period of the catechumenate, properly spaced, should be sanctified by sacred rites celebrated at successive periods" (*op. cit.* 64). The new Roman ritual proposes four stages: the enrollment of the candidates as catechumens, their election to be baptized (properly during Mass on the first Sunday of Lent), the scrutinies and presentation to the community (on the third, fourth, and fifth Sundays of Lent), and the rite of immediate preparation through prayer and fasting on Good Friday and Holy Saturday. The baptism itself is celebrated during the Easter Vigil service, and if possible is immediately followed by the conferral of confirmation. Finally, the Sundays after Easter are designated as a period of *mystagogia*, i.e., a time during which the community extends its warm support to the newly baptized and celebrates with them the mystery of their incorporation into Christ (see MYSTAGOGY). In those cases where serious reasons demand that baptism be celebrated outside of the Lenten-Easter season, Sunday should be chosen in preference to other feasts for the celebration of baptism. BIBLIOGRAPHY: C. Davis, *Sacraments of Initiation* (1964); J. D. Fisher, *Christian Initiation: Baptism in the Medieval West* (1965); E. Whitaker, "History of the Baptismal Formula," JEcclHist 16 (1965) 1–42; B. Neunheuser, *Baptism and Confirmation* (1964); *Adult Baptism and the Catechumenate* (ed. J. Wagner, Concilium 22, 1967); K. Rahner, *Holy Baptism* (pa. 1970).

[T. M. MCFADDEN]

ADULT BASIC EDUCATION, a program designed to explore educational resources and to encourage establishment of programs of adult basic education and of continuing education to the level of completion of secondary school. It also includes teacher training, the development of new instructional media and materials, and vocational training for the disadvantaged. Initiated in 1966, the project has attracted religious groups—sisters, brothers, and priests—and laymen of all faiths in both summer and year-round programs. Originally administered by the Office of Education of the Department of Health, Education and Welfare (HEW), but financed by the Office of Economic Opportunity, through funds provided to state educational agencies, in 1967 the program became the full responsibility of the U.S. Office of Education. For fiscal 1975, $67,500,000 was provided for the program. BIBLIOGRAPHY: A. W. Cass, *Basic Education for Adults* (1971).

[M. B. MURPHY]

ADULT RELIGIOUS EDUCATION, the various programs which promote a deepened awareness of the faith and its mature lived expression in adults. For the past 30 years, the RC Church in the U.S. has placed increasing stress upon continuing adult religious formation, but Vatican Council II's emphasis on renewal, deepening of the faith, and lay apostolicity gave rise to new and varied educational programs during the latter half of the 1960s. There arose the basic conviction that the faith of the child and adolescent depends upon the faith of the adult community. Applied sociological research, such as the Greeley-Rossi report (see bibliography), stressed the primary educational role of the family community. Adult religious education programs tend to follow a twofold thrust: to reach large groups of adults esp. through group conferences and the news, radio, and television media, and to work with smaller group units in a more intensive fashion. Liturgical renewal with its greater awareness of the catechetical implications of the homily and liturgy of the word has played an important role in this small group formation. Among the many programs that have been devised, there has been an expansion in lecture series, and in comprehensive adult religious education centers, usually situated in colleges, high schools, or large central parishes where a number of sequentially structured courses are offered over a two-semester period similar to non-credit college courses. The courses generally deal with theology, scriptural studies, liturgy, ecumenism, community and social relations, and lay spirituality. In addition, the centers also may be involved in catechist training and development. In many areas closed-circuit television programs have been produced for adult audiences. Correspondence courses, esp. those conducted by the Knights of Columbus and the National Council of Catholic Men, continue to reach large numbers. Discussion-action groups have also increased in number. As in the Catholic Family Movement, these groups are usually composed of couples who meet regularly to discuss the basic issues of contemporary society and try to formulate an appropriate and effective response. These discussions have acquired an ecumenical dimension through the use of *Living Room Dialogues* (ed. W. Greenspun and W. Norgren, 1965). Among the most frequently discussed topics are morality, ecclesiastical authority, and the formation of Christian conscience.

Educators involved in developing adult religious education programs have stressed that they must begin with the dilemmas of the people involved. They should aim at fostering the development of Christian attitudes, admit of a legitimate plurality of views, help develop the ability to make moral decisions responsibly and freely, and present a comprehensive view of contemporary Christian belief in the light of its authentic tradition. Ultimately adult religious education programs promote the growth of the Christian family; hence great stress has been placed upon involving parents in the religious formation of their children, esp. at first communion and penance. Locally adapted family learning centers, geared to stress parish-family cooperation, flexibility, and the developmental quality of religious education are also being promoted. BIBLIOGRAPHY: A. M. Greeley and P. H. Rossi, *Education of Catholic Americans* (1966); G. Moran, "Christianity: A Religion for Adults," *Catholic World* 204 (1966) 135–148; M. P. Ryan, "Growing Up in All

Things—Reflections on the Religious Education of Adults Today,'' *Living Light* 3 (1966) 67–77; M. Farren, "A Family Learning Center," *Living Light* 6 (1969) 62–72; P. Bergevin and J. McKinley, *Adult Education for the Church* (2d ed., 1974 pa.).

[W. J. TOBIN]

ADULTERY, from the Lat. *adulterium,* a word that has displaced the earlier "advowtry," though this survived until the end of the 17th century. It is defined as the voluntary sexual intercourse of a married person with one of the opposite sex, whether unmarried (single adultery), or married to another (double adultery). Condemned in Scripture and consistently by the Church, the sin, a special type of unchastity or *luxuria,* adds to the wrong of *fornication the special injustice of violating marriage vows and sometimes of spuriously tampering with lawful inheritance. The obligation of making restitution, though often delicate and difficult to fulfill, cannot be dismissed. The fact that the injured party or parties are indifferent to the violation of their rights, or perhaps even consent to it, may mitigate but cannot excuse the unfaithfulness. The OT, like the Roman law, takes a rather one-sided view; a woman can violate only her own wedlock, a man only the wedlock of another man. But the term is extended to include all impurity. The term is also used in a figurative sense; spiritual or metaphorical adultery, as it is called, is the adulteration present in all sin, an unfaithfulness to God, a whoring after strange gods, for which the whole community was reproached in the prophets (Hos 2.4; Jer 2.2.; 3.8; 5.7; 9.1; 13.22; Ezek 16; 23). The usage continues in the NT (Mt 12.39; 16.4; Mk 8.38; Jas 4.4; Rev 2.22) BIBLIOGRAPHY: ThAq ST 2a2ae, 154.8. esp. in ed. Lat-Eng v. 43, ed. T. Gilby (1968); EDB 37–39.

[T. GILBY]

ADVAITA (Sanskrit, nondualism), monistic Hindu philosophy of S(h)ankara (788–820), one of the three principal forms of *Vedanta. Sankara denied that Brahman (God, Being, the Absolute) and the world exist separately. Nothing exists but the impersonal Brahman. The personal God (Isvara) and the world are but appearance, created by maya (illusion). The soul attains knowledge by looking within and realizing its oneness with Brahman.

[T. EARLY]

ADVENA, (Lat., a newcomer) a term used in RC canon law (CIC c. 91) in its classification of the different statuses of persons in a place with reference to local ecclesiastical jurisdiction. An *advena* has not yet acquired stable local residence (*domicile), but is more stably located than a *peregrinus* (a visitor who has residence elsewhere) or a *vagus* (a visitor who has residence nowhere).

ADVENT (Lat. *adventus,* coming), a season approximately 4 weeks in length of liturgical and ascetical preparation for Christmas. In the Latin Church it begins on the Sunday nearest the feast of St. Andrew (Nov. 30); since the 9th cent. this Sunday marks the beginning of the liturgical year. It drew something from the analogous season of preparation for the feast of the Epiphany observed in Spain as early as the 4th cent., and in Gaul a century later, as the baptismal feast of Christ. This preparatory observance was mainly ascetical in character in memory of Christ's preparation for baptism and lasted from 3 to 6 weeks in different locales. But as the observance appeared in Rome (6th cent.), it was primarily a liturgical preparation for Christmas; its rites were developed by Pope *Gregory I. The Church in Gaul in the 9th cent. adopted the Roman observance and enriched it, esp. by bringing out the thought of Christ's Second Coming. Thus Advent became a time of expectation not only of the anniversary of Christ's first appearance among men but also of his future coming in glory. Between these two comings, one past and one future, there is, as Christian piety has noted, a third, namely, his present coming through grace to the hearts of men. Since the 12th cent. Advent observance in the West has been shaped by these three themes. BIBLIOGRAPHY: W. J. O'Shea, NCE 1:152–153; A. G. Martimort, *L'Église en prière* (3d ed., 1965) 734–738; A. C. McArthur, *Evolution of the Christian Year* (1953) 70–76; "Avent, Noël, Epiphanie," *La Maison-Dieu* 59 (1959). H. Van Zeller, "Advent Mystery," *Tablet* 226 (1972) 1220.

[N. KOLLAR]

ADVENT, SECOND, see PAROUSIA

ADVENT CHRISTIAN CHURCH, a Church formed in 1860 by adherents of the *Adventism of W. *Miller and previously named Advent Christian Association and Advent Christian Conference. Those who organized the Church were led by Jonathan Cummings (1785–1867), a follower of Miller, who preached that Christ's second coming would be in 1853 or 1854. At the foundation of the Church, particular stress was laid upon *conditional immortality as taught by Charles F. Hudson and George Storrs. While accepting Adventism, the Church differs from *Seventh-day Adventists by Sunday observance, by disregarding OT prohibitions on unclean foods, and by rejecting the prophetic gifts of Ellen G. *White. The Church is *congregational in polity; five regional conferences and other church agencies are coordinated in the Advent Christian General Conference of America. In 1973 there were 31,947 members in 391 churches in the U.S. and Canada. Missionary work was begun in 1891 and continues in India, Japan, Malaysia, Mexico, the Philippines, and Nigeria, with 2,056 members in 64 mission churches. The Church supports two colleges, Aurora in Ill. and Berkshire Christian College in Lenox, Massachusetts. In 1964 the Life and Advent Union merged with the Advent Christian Church.

[W. J. WHALEN]

ADVENT OF THE LORD, see SECOND COMING.

ADVENT WREATH, evergreens intertwined into a circular shape and suspended from the ceiling or placed on a table as an Advent observance. Fastened to the wreath are four candles standing upright and at equal distances from one another. The candles represent the four weeks of Advent. Where the custom is observed, the family gathers daily for a short religious exercise in which prayers are recited and hymns sung. A candle is lit for each Sunday of Advent. The practice originated among the Lutherans of Eastern Germany and spread rapidly among all Christians. BIBLIOGRAPHY: F. X. Weiser, *Handbook of Christian Feasts and Customs* (1958) 54–55; H. McLoughlin, *Family Advent Customs* (1967).

[N. KOLLAR]

ADVENTISM, the belief that Christ's second coming, or advent, is at hand to inaugurate the millennium in which the wicked will be annihilated and the kingdom of the saints established. In this generic sense *chiliasm, *apocalypticism, or *millenarianism, as seen in the Montanists, Anabaptists, Fifth Monarchy Man, Jehovah's Witnesses, and many other bodies, are forms of adventism. The term has a particular historical connection, however, with the Adventist groups arising in the 19th cent., esp. as the result of the preaching of W. *Miller. Concentrating on the books of Daniel and of Revelation, Miller not only announced the nearness of the millennium, but computed the exact date (see TIME SETTING). Christians from various Churches accepted his ideas, but many abandoned Adventism when his predictions went unfulfilled. From those who remained unshaken the various Adventist Churches were formed. BIBLIOGRAPHY: E. Clark, *Small Sects in America* (1949); K. Algermissen *Christian Sects* (tr. J. R. Foster, 1962) 55–75; *7th-Day Adventist Fact Book* (1967). *ADVENT CHRISTIAN CHURCH; *CHURCH OF GOD (ABRAHAMIC FAITH); *SEVENTH DAY ADVENTISTS.

[W. J. WHALEN]

ADVERTENCE, a term used in moral theology to signify the actual awareness of what one is doing that is necessary to full human responsibility in the performance of a human act. Inadvertence, or the lack of such awareness, is a momentary form of *ignorance, generally inculpable, and its effect on the morality of what one does while under its influence is the same as that of ignorance.

[P. K. MEAGHER]

ADVERTISEMENTS, BOOK OF, see BOOK OF ADVERTISEMENTS.

ADVERTISING, the public announcement, generally made enticingly, that certain opportunities, properties, goods, or services are available. Industry's need to find a market and the public's need for industry's products make it useful or even necessary. Competition between producers has provided the incentive, and the development of the modern media of communication has supplied the means, of bringing the art of advertising to a high level of effectiveness. It is probable that free enterprise in a highly industrialized society could not survive without it.

There is nothing inherently objectionable in informing the public how its legitimate needs and desires can be satisfied. This notification, advantageous to buyer and seller alike, can be considered a public service of genuine value. But certain questions of cultural and moral importance can be raised about advertising as it is actually practiced and these make any blanket approval of its objectives and methods impossible.

On the cultural side, it can be argued that advertising tends to produce a regrettable standardization of taste, a sheep-like uniformity of desire and behavior, a concentration upon tinsel or snob values, a preoccupation with matters of artificial concern, a hypersensitivity to negligible discomforts, and an intensification of the materialism to which human nature is already too prone.

On the moral side, the most obvious questions concern justice, for much advertising is in some degree false or misleading. Apart from the glaring examples of this, which continue to crop up despite the vigilance of governmental authorities, almost all advertising holds out the promise of greater satisfaction than the buyer of a product is likely to experience. Advertisers—and some moralists—discount the dishonesty of this by classifying it as "puffery," a kind of exaggeration which the public expects and which therefore causes no actual deception.

A more profound question concerns the legitimacy of creating, or intensifying beyond relation to natural need, the desire for material things. Much advertising seems to encourage a kind of anxiety and solicitude in fundamental discord with the doctrine of the Sermon on the Mount (Mt 6.25–33). This awkward point of conflict is by no means easy to resolve. BIBLIOGRAPHY: T. M. Garrett, *Introduction to Some Ethical Problems of Modern American Advertising* (1961); *idem*, NCE 1:154; D. Lowery, NCE 1:154–156.

[P. K. MEAGHER]

ADVOCATE, see LAWYER.

ADVOCATUS ECCLESIAE, a layman charged with the temporal affairs of ecclesiastical institutions. The need for such an official was suggested by 2 Tim 2.4; the actual institution of the *advocatio,* or *advocatia,* as it was called, dates from the 4th or 5th cent., the role of the official being patterned after that of similar functionaries who had acted for pagan religious institutions. In Carolingian times every diocese and abbey was required to have an *advocatus,* and during the feudal period generally he was looked upon as a military protector. Revenues came to be attached to the office, which frequently was hereditary. The *advocati* were most often feudal lords, many of whom became predators rather than protectors. English law translated the concept into the institution known as *advowson. The abuse of *ad-

vocatia ecclesiae recurs in *Febronianism and Josephinism. BIBLIOGRAPHY: R. Laprat, DHGE 5:1220–41; R. Naz, DDC 1:1561–78; A. Stiegler, LTK 1:164.

[T. C. O'BRIEN]

ADVOWSON, in English law a proprietary, often hereditary, right of presenting a cleric for an ecclesiastical benefice. The advowson is the form that the feudal institution called *advocatio* or *advocatia* took in England where the *advocatus ecclesiae* signified one enjoying this right. The Statutes of Provisors of 1351 resisted papal interference with advowson. The right was acquired originally by one who built, or was patron of, a church or abbey; then advowson became attached to the manor on which the establishment stood. Thus, in current law an advowson is either appendant, attached to an estate, or in gross, detached and possessed by itself. A presentative advowson is one in which presentation is submitted to a bishop for approbation of the presentee; a collative advowson is one exercised by the bishop himself. BIBLIOGRAPHY: R. Laprat, DHGE 5:1220–41.

AEDESIUS (d. *c*.335 A.D.), Neoplatonic philosopher, founder of the Pergamene School. He was a pupil of Iamblichus and was a specialist in theurgy. Among his pupils was the Maximus who taught theurgy to the Emperor Julian. Ueberweg 1:618–620.

[M. R. P. MCGUIRE]

AEDHAN, ST., see AIDAN OF LINDISFARNE, ST.

AEGIDIUS, see GILES, ST.

AEGIDIUS ALBORNOZ, see ALBORNOZ, GIL ÁLVAREZ CARRILLO DE.

AEGINA, TEMPLE OF (*c*.500–480 B.C.), supreme example of Doric style of the late archaic severe period, dedicated to Athena Aphaia, who according to Pausanias is related to the Cretan goddess Britomartis. The superb pedimental sculptures (substantial fragments are now in Munich) rank in importance with those of the Parthenon and the Temple of Zeus at Olympia. Here are evident first solutions to compositional problems posed by the triangular shape of the pediment. Figures here are successfully contrived to fill the field, though the articulation at times does violence to the grace of the image. BIBLIOGRAPHY: G. M. A. Richter, *Handbook of Greek Art* (1959); W. G. Forrest, EB (1971) 1:193–194.

[M. J. DALY]

AELFRIC OF CANTERBURY, ST. (d. 1005), a monk of Abington who became abbot of St. Alban's, bp. of Ramsbury and Wilton (990), and was promoted to the archbishopric of Canterbury (996). He may have been responsible for establishing the Benedictines at Canterbury Cathedral. Certain writings (PL 139, 1469–76) have been attributed to him, but scholars think these may have been the work of *Aelfric

the Grammarian. BIBLIOGRAPHY: S. Mottironi, BiblSanct 1:863; Zimmermann 2:630–632.

AELFRIC THE GRAMMARIAN (950 or 955–1020), first abbot of the Benedictine monastery of Eynsham, outstanding prose scholar of 10th-cent. England. He was an important figure in English monastic reform at a time when Danish invasions were weakening moral and cultural values of clergy and people. He labored to strengthen both groups by book learning. He first made accessible in English an account of and commentary on the origin and doctrines of Christianity, its development, and its saints. His Latin *Grammar*, *Glossary*, and *Colloquy* were educational works for monastic schools. His Anglo-Saxon writings include *Lives of the Saints*, two series of homilies, and a treatise on the Old and New Testaments. BIBLIOGRAPHY: C. L. White, *Aelfric: A New Study of His Life and Writings* (1898); P. Clemoes, "Chronology of Aelfric's Works," *Anglo-Saxons* (ed. Clemoes, 1959); S. B. Greenfield, *Critical History of Old English Literature* (1965); W. A. Chaney, NCE 1:156.

[M. M. BARRY]

AELFRYTH, ST., see ETHELDRITA, ST.

AELIA CAPITOLINA, the name given by Hadrian to the city of *Jerusalem, which he rebuilt *c*.130 after the second revolt of the Jews. The name derives from his family (Publius Aelius Hadrianus) and from Jupiter Capitolinus, to whom was dedicated a shrine built on the site of the Jewish temple. A shrine to Venus was erected on the spot which Christian tradition assigns to the tomb of Jesus. Jews were forbidden under pain of death to live in the city. In the long peace of the 3d cent. Aelia Capitolina became a place of pilgrimage and a center of monasticism. The Council of Chalcedon elevated it to an independent patriarchate with all of Palestine dependent on it. BIBLIOGRAPHY: H. Vincent and F. M. Abel, *Jerusalem* (1914–26) 2:1–39.

[M. J. SUELZER]

AELRED, ST. (1109 or 1110–67), Cistercian abbot and spiritual writer. A. was born of a noble Northumberland family, studied in England and Scotland, and spent much of his youth at the court of King David I of Scotland, son of St. Margaret. He entered the Cistercians at Rievaulx (*c*.1134), was imbued with the teachings of St. *Bernard of Clairvaux through Abbot William (Bernard's former secretary) and Simon of Clairvaux, his novice master. He became the first abbot of Rievaulx's daughterhouse at Revesby (1143) and finally abbot of Rievaulx (1147), then the most important Cistercian abbey in England. A. worked indefatigably, visiting monasteries throughout England, advising King Henry II in affairs of state, and writing ascetical and historical works. His writings reflect a warm, sensitive spirit, and an enthusiasm for the *Cluniac reforms. His most important works are *Speculum caritatis*, an excellent practical treatise on Christian perfection, and *De spirituali amicitia*, a dialogue based on Cicero's *De amicitia* but imbued with the realization that Christian spiritual friendship has its source and finality in Christ. He has been called the "Bernard of the North," accomplishing for English monasticism what Bernard of Clairvaux had brought about on the Continent. BIBLIOGRAPHY: W. Daniel, *Life of Ailred of Rievaulx* (ed. and tr. F. M. Powicke, 1950); A. Hoste, NCE 1:157–158; A. Le Bail, DSAM 1:225–234; M. A. Calabrese, BiblSanct 1:276–279, bibliog.; M. N. Holmes, *De vita eremitica of Aelred of Rievaulx* (Villanova Univ., 1944).

[T. M. MCFADDEN]

AEMILIAN, SS. The martyrologies list a number of saints who bore this name. Among them were: (1) A., a soldier who suffered martyrdom at Cirta in 258. SEE P. Palazzini, BiblSanct 1:307–313. (2) A. of Colgolla (Aemilian Cucullatus; d. 574), a shepherd-turned-hermit whose life was written by Braulio (PL 80:699–714) and who came to be honored as patron of Spain. SEE Butler 4:321–322; M. Sotomayor, BiblSanct 4:1186–88. (3) A. of Lagny (Eminian; d. c.660), an Irishman who founded the abbey at Lagny and became its abbot. See J. Marilier, BiblSanct 4:1189–90. (4) A. of Nantes, known also as Emiland, martyr and possibly bp. of Nantes, who lost his life in a Saracen invasion c. 730. See J. Marilier, BiblSanct 4:1190–91. (5) A., an Irish bishop who died at Faenza on his return journey after visiting Rome. (6) A., bp. of Cyzicus (fl. 800–830) who vindicated the cult of images against Emperor Leo V, the Armenian, and as a result suffered exile and death. BIBLIOGRAPHY: A. Amore, BiblSanct 4:1185.

AENEAS OF GAZA (d. 518), Neoplatonic philosopher, convert to Christianity, who had studied at Alexandria under the Platonist Hierocles. His dialogue *Theophrastus* (PG 85:865–1004) attempted to reconcile the Platonic concept of the immortality of the soul with the Christian doctrine of the resurrection of the body. In addition to *Theophrastus*, 25 of his letters are extant. BIBLIOGRAPHY: *Epistolographi Graeci* (ed. R. Hercher, 1873) 24–32.

AENEAS SYLVIUS PICCOLOMINI, see PIUS II, POPE.

AENNON. The exact location of Aennon (the Springs), near Salim (Jn 3.23), is unknown. It must have been in the western Jordan valley, perhaps about 8 miles S of Bethshan (Scythopolis). Ain Farah is also a possibility.

[J. E. LUSSIER]

AEOLIAN, also *nonus tonus*, ninth mode, the *mode or scale equivalent to a white-key scale beginning on A. Its existence was not recognized in theory until the 16th cent. (see GLAREANUS), and modern chant books classify pieces whose *final is A as *dorian. It is identical in form to the modern minor scale. Its *plagal form is termed hypoaeolian (*decimus modus*, tenth mode). BIBLIOGRAPHY: Apel HDMus 165–168.

[J. J. WALSH]

AEONIUS OF ARLES, ST. (d. c.502), bp. of Arles from 494 until 500 when he resigned in favor of St. Caesarius of Arles. During his episcopate he contributed to the development of monasticism and secured the rectification of the status of his diocese and its boundaries. BIBLIOGRAPHY: P. Viard, BiblSanct 4:1251.

AËR (Gr. for air; Sl. *vozdukh*), in the Byzantine liturgy the large outer veil which covers both *diskos (paten) and poterion (chalice). Often made of the same material as the vestments, it is usually marked with a cross in the middle. Originally it was probably made of a light silken material, hence its name. At the table of preparation the priest first covers the diskos and poterion with their own veils and then places the aër over both. At the great *entrance he puts the veil over the shoulders of the deacon or, if there is no deacon, the priest places it on his own shoulders, or in Slavic usage, over his left forearm. Arriving at the altar, he holds the aër while it is incensed and then places it over the diskos and poterion, their own veils being laid aside. At the Creed he gently shakes it over the offerings to symbolize the descent of the Holy Spirit; at the words, "He ascended into heaven," he lays it aside. In Slavic usage the aër is generally not used after this, but the Greeks fold it and at the beginning of the *anaphora it is used to bless the offerings and the people. The veil is used again before and after the consecration to fan the gifts in a circular fashion.

[A. J. JACOPIN]

AËRIANS, followers of Aërius of Pontus (4th cent.) once a member of a group of ascetics whose leader was Eustathius of Sebaste, onetime disciple of Arius. After Eustathius's election to the bishopric. Aërius, candidate for the same bishopric, broke with Eustathius and established his own sect. Epiphanius (*Panar.* 75) states that he became an Arian, adding errors of his own: bishops and priests are equal; Easter is to be abolished as a Jewish celebration; prayers and alms for the dead are useless; laws of fasting are relics of the Old Law. BIBLIOGRAPHY: H. Hemmer, DTC 1:515–516.

[L. G. MÜLLER]

AËRIUS (4th cent.), priest of Pontus, associated in early life with *Eustathius of Sebaste in the practice of asceticism and ordained by him after he had become bp. of Sebaste. A rift developed between the two when A., embittered by frustrated ambition, began denouncing Eustathius for abandoning ascetical practices. A. also espoused doctrines unacceptable to Eustathius, i.e., that there was no difference of rank or function between bishops and priests, that Easter was a superstitious Jewish observance, that obligatory fasts were wrong, and that it was useless to pray for the dead. Epiphanius, to whom we are indebted for most of what is known of A., accused him of Arianism. A. attracted some followers, but the sect that bore his name did not long survive him. BIBLIOGRAPHY: Epiphanius, *Haeres.* 75.1, PG 62:504–508; V. Ermoni, DHGE 1:663.

AERTNYS, JOZEF (Aertnijs; 1828–1915), Dutch Redemptorist moral theologian who taught at Wittem, Holland, 1860–98. His *Theologia moralis juxta doctrinam S. Alphonsi* (1886–87) ran through many editions, the 9th-16th under the editorship of A. Damen. Other popular works from A.'s pen included a ceremonial, a compendium of liturgy, and a manual of pastoral theology.

[P. K. MEAGHER]

AERTSEN (AERTSZEN), PIETER (1508–75), northern Netherlandish painter of history and genre, active in Antwerp and Amsterdam. His realistic statements blending genre elements with large areas of still life eventually led to the rise of independent still-life painting in Holland and Flanders. A.'s rendering of religious subjects with a dominance of homely objects was unique, e.g., *Christ in the House of Mary and Martha* (1553; Boymans-Van Beuingen Museum, Rotterdam).

[M. J. DALY]

AESCULAPIUS, see ASCLEPIUS.

AESOP (fl. 550 B.C.), a Greek author credited with writing a body of fables, stories based on incidents from animal life with a didactic moral application. According to Herodotus (2.174) A. was a slave from Samos. Initially written in prose, his work later became a vehicle for rhetorical exercise. Its use in this form eventually resulted in the medieval collection called Aesop. In Latin, it found particular expression in satire, esp. that of Horace, but Ennius and Lucilius had both used it before him. The first Latin collection is that of Phaedrus, a freedman of Augustus who coupled material from Aesop with that of his own imagination. BIBLIOGRAPHY: W. Edwards, OCD 355; EB 1:263 (good bibliog.).

[F. H. BRIGHAM]

AESTHETICS, a word that comes from the Gr. *aisthanesthai,* to perceive by feeling, and means the science and art of appreciating, perhaps enhancing, our response to beauty. In ancient and medieval philosophy it was not a separate discipline; take care of truth and goodness, said Eric *Gill, and beauty will take care of itself. Nevertheless the dense and difficult chapters on the beautiful by Dionysius (*On the divine names*) are classical, if little-studied, texts. Partly in reaction to the trim and formal concepts of the late 17th cent., and the echoes of Cartesianism and Newtonianism in literature, the 18th cent. witnessed a revival of sensibility and feeling manifested in the cultivation of taste for the sublime and picturesque, a fashion for the noble savage and *chinoiserie,* a prelude to the wilder and less genteel romantic mood of the 19th. The transition to that from the classical cannot, however, be simplified into a series of discontinuous stages, and the pulse of aesthetic experience beats steadily through all art not exclusively didactic in burden. It was the German philosopher A. G. Baumgarten, a pupil of Leibniz and Wolff and master of Kant, who established aesthetics as a distinct discipline and gave it its name, *Aesthetica,* 2 v.

(Frankfort 1750, 1758). However the main force of the movement before his time came from England, and so it was to continue until over the turn of the century.

Indeed Coleridge's *Kubla Khan* may be taken as the signature of the aesthetic enterprise, which is to break through the notional and deliberate constructions in which the prose of our life is necessarily written and to get into contact with concrete things, more rounded, real, and richer. Its practice has sometimes deserved to be laughed at as a somewhat precious pastime, thus in Gilbert and Sullivan, but it should keep the robust and earthy sense indicated in its very name. Though tending to concentrate on artistic beauty, and even to reserve this to the "fine arts" and sometimes to an esoteric gnosis, it has developed a vast and varied modern literature, some of which has not lost the tang of humanity. This baffles summary, for many of the differences shade off into one another. A rough division might lie between emphasis on the objective and on the subjective conditions of beauty. The first and older interest is now being recovered in theories of "pure form," of the singleness in diversity of beauty, or better, of "a beauty"; the study also of representation, mimesis, and symbol may be ranged under this heading. The second goes in for more psychological, and even epistemological analysis, and considers art as expression, lonely or communicated, and sometimes even tests it by its social usefulness.

Aesthetics may be called the search for a natural mysticism, so long as this does not convey the *suggestio falsi* that there can be a "true delight" (which is what beauty is) not proceeding from the Holy Ghost. In this connection it is not straining the facts to say that the saints have been better critics than the poets, if not in watching, then at least in describing their processes. The philosophy of aesthetics does well to go to mystical theology, and not for its grammar alone. Such is the theme of H. Bremond's *Poésie et prière* (1925), a small but important work of devout humanism. Cardinal points will be the interaction of the "intake" of knowledge and the "outgoing" of love and their fusion when a thing is held in itself, not just in intention, the role of analogy in the build-up of symbols preceding the union, and the touch of divine genius, the good fortune adumbrated in the *Eudemian Ethics.* Without the paradigms found in high theology, aesthetic philosophy can sometimes look like jottings at an art exhibition. It remains for divines to be less confessional in their imagery, and for lovers of beauty to glimpse that there is no real profane without a sacred. BIBLIOGRAPHY: *Theories of Beauty* (E. F. Carritt, ed. selected texts, 1931); S. K. Langer, *Feeling and Form* (1954); M. C. Beardsley, *Aesthetics* (1958); R. C. Zaehner, *Mysticism Sacred and Profane* (2d printing, 1961); T. Gilby, *Poetic Experience* (2d printing 1968).

[T. GILBY]

AETERNI PATRIS, an encyclical letter of Leo XIII, Aug. 4, 1879 (to be distinguished from an apostolic letter by the same name of Pius IX, by which he convoked Vatican Council I, June 29, 1868), expressing the Church's concern for Christian philosophy because so many errors flow from false philosophy. He points out that, although human reason has its limitations, true philosophy can prepare the mind for the acceptance of divine faith and for its deeper understanding and more intelligent defense. To this end he strongly urges the restoration of the philosophy of St. Thomas Aquinas. BIBLIOGRAPHY: D 3135–40; W. F. Hogan, NCE 1:165–166.

[J. H. ROHLING]

AETHERIA, see ETHERIA.

AËTIANS, followers of Aëtius (d. *c*.370). After the Catholic faith on the nature of the Son had been formulated and crystallized by the Council of Nicaea (325) in the term *homoousios* (consubstantial), Aëtius brought Arianism to its logical conclusion. The more moderate Arians sought to liken the Son to the Father, using the term *homoiousios;* Aëtius maintained that the Son is in no way like the Father, employing the term *anomoios.* Hence, he and his followers the Aëtians, were also known as the Anomoeans. BIBLIOGRAPHY: X. Le Bachelet, DTC 1:516–517.

[L. G. MÜLLER]

AËTIUS (1st or 2d cent. A.D.), an eclectic philosopher whose *sunagōgē peri àreschontōn* usually cited under the Latin title, *Placita,* constitutes an important source for our knowledge of the opinions of the Greek philosophers on natural philosophy. His *Placita* are preserved in Pseudo-Plutarch, *Epitome,* and in the *Eclogae* of *Stobaeus. In many cases the *Placita* are the only extant remains of the works of the philosophers in question. BIBLIOGRAPHY: OCD 17; H. Diels, *Doxographi Graeci* (1879) 273–444.

[M. R. P. MCGUIRE]

AETOS (Gr. for eagle; Sl. *orletz*), in the Byzantine Church a name for either: (1) a small round or oval rug depicting a walled city with an eagle soaring above it. This rug is used by Byzantine bishops at the ceremony of their consecration, although in Russian usage the bishop stands on it for all functions. The city represents the eparchy or territory that the bishop rules, while the eagle symbolizes his lofty spirituality and his eagle-eyed vigilance for the faithful under his care. Or (2) the marble slab fixed in the pavement of a Byzantine church where formerly the throne of the emperor was set up. It was usually engraved with the crowned double-headed eagle of Byzantium. The imperial eagle is now used on the seal of the ecumenical patriarch, and in the Greek Orthodox Church it is often seen as a decorative motif, sometimes carved over the royal doors of the iconostasis.

[A. J. JACOPIN]

AEVIA, an abbreviation for *alleluia occasionally used in medieval liturgical MSS, formed from the vowels of the word. BIBLIOGRAPHY: Apel HDMus 16. *EUOUAE.

[A. DOHERTY]

AFFABILITY, a word often used by RC moral theologians for the virtue of *courtesy.

AFFAIRE DES PLACARDS, L', in the history of French Protestantism, the name given to the events of the night of Oct. 17–18, 1534, when the Huguenot Reformers in Paris and other cities put up printed posters attacking the Mass. In offensive language, the handbills also attacked all, including Lutherans, who taught the Real Presence. Since a poster was even affixed to the bedchamber of Francis I at Amboise, the incident, which erupted in a period of relative calm and revealed Huguenot power and boldness, marked a change in the King's moderate policy toward the Reformers. A period of severe repression followed until the Declaration of Coucy (July 16, 1535). BIBLIOGRAPHY: A. Bailly, *La Réforme en France jusqu'à l'Édit de Nantes* (1960) 121–133; Léonard HistProt 1:233.

[R. N. NICOLICH]

AFFECTIVE KNOWLEDGE, see KNOWLEDGE, CONNATURAL.

AFFECTIVE PRAYER, a type of mental prayer in which a primarily affective relationship with God is elicited. Through confidence, penitence, humility, and love, affective prayer seeks to respond more fully to the living God. It differs from discursive mental prayer, characterized by a predominance of reasoning and intellectual considerations, and from contemplative prayer in which the sole affection sought is love. Since the 17th cent., spiritual writers have spoken of affective prayer, and it figures strongly in Carmelite and Franciscan spirituality. BIBLIOGRAPHY: G. Lercaro, *Methods of Mental Prayer* (tr. T. F. Lindsay, 1957); K. J. Healy, NCE 11:675–676; O. Steggink, "*La integración de la afectividad en la vida espiritual de santa Teresa de Jesús,*" *Carmelus* 18 (1971) 122–141.

[T. M. MCFADDEN]

AFFINITY, the relationship created by marriage between a person and the blood relatives of his/her spouse. It is distinct from consanguinity, the relationship existing among blood relatives. According to canon law (cc. 97 and 1077), affinity arises from any valid marriage, does not cease upon death, and in some instances constitutes a diriment impediment to subsequent marriage. Affinity does not apply to blood relations themselves; thus two brothers may marry two sisters. Canon law forbids marriage in the direct line (the husband's mother-in-law, grandmother-in-law, or stepmother; daughter-in-law, granddaughter-in-law, or stepdaughter) in any degree. In the collateral line, the marriage is invalid in both the first degree (sister-in-law and wife's aunt), and in the second degree (the wife's first cousin and niece). The Church can dispense from affinity in any degree of the direct or collateral line, although such dispensation is rarely granted in the direct line.

Affinity was regarded as an impediment to marriage in the

Mosaic law (esp. Lev 18. 8–15) as well as in Roman law. It is mentioned twice in the NT (Mt 14. 3–4; 1 Cor 5.1). Many states retain affinity as a marriage impediment; the reasons can be traced to the respect and reserve due to near relatives. BIBLIOGRAPHY: F. Wahl, *Matrimonial Impediments of Consanguinity and Affinity* (1934); C. Henry, NCE 1:167–170.

[T. M. MCFADDEN]

AFFIRMATION, AN, see AUBURN AFFIRMATION.

AFFLIGEM, ABBEY OF (*Affligenium*), Benedictine monastery located at Heckelgem, near Alost (Belgium), founded by six converted knights who in 1083 adopted the Rule of St. Benedict. Its first two abbots were Fulgentius (d. 1122) and Franconius (d. 1135), the author of *De gratia Dei*. Under their rule many foundations were made from Affligem: Maria-Laach in the Rhineland (1093), Saint-André-les-Bruges (1105), Vlierbeek near Louvain, and several others. In 1146 St. Bernard visited the abbey and praised the fervor of its monks. It adopted the reform of Bursfeld in 1519; but it was incorporated into the archiepiscopal property of Malines and after 1569 was governed by a provost. Affligem was destroyed in 1534 and 1536 in the course of a war between Flanders and Brabant, burned by the Gueux in 1580, and suppressed in 1796. The monks who survived reassembled in 1847 at Termonde. In 1870 they restored Affligem, which again became an abbey in 1887. A center of the liturgical movement, the monastery edited a missal in Dutch (1916) and publishes a liturgical review, *Tijdschrift voor Liturgie*. The most famous writer of Affligem was the provost Benedict Haeften (d. 1648), the author of *Sanctus Benedictus illustratus* (1640) and other ascetical works. The historians of the abbey are Jean van der Meeren (d. 1556), Hubert du Falais (d. 1636), and Odon Cambier (d. 1808). BIBLIOGRAPHY: Cottineau 1:23–24; N. N. Huyghebaert, NCE 1:170.

[J. DAOUST]

AFFUSION, or *infusion, a method of baptizing whereby the water is poured over the head of a candidate in the form of a cross. It is the method in general use now in the Western Church, and it is contrasted with aspersion and immersion (submersion). It is generally considered to be a later development from the primitive usage in baptism, but was sanctioned as early as the 2d cent. in the *Didache in cases where immersion was not possible.

[R. B. ENO]

AFGHANISTAN, a mountainous country in central Asia (250,966 sq mi; pop. 17,481,000) that shares extensive boundaries with Russia, Kashmir, and Pakistan. Pathans are the principal ethnic group and make up 60% of the population. Many of the inhabitants lead a nomadic life. The official language is Persian; the government is monarchical; almost 90% of the population is illiterate. Owing to its strategic position, the favor of Afghanistan is sought by

foreign powers of antagonistic ideologies. Kais, a disciple of Mohammed, introduced Islam into the land, and this remains the faith of the overwhelming majority of the people. Catholicism has never been permitted to establish a foothold in the country. It was visited by Marco Polo and by a few Jesuits called from Goa in the 17th cent. by Emperor Akbar to the court at Kabul, but they were unable to start a mission. Nestorians at one time had communities in cities along the caravan route, but they disappeared without leaving a trace. Groups of Armenian merchants who professed the Catholic faith were expelled in 1888. Pope Pius XI, profiting by the visit of the Afghan monarch to Rome, obtained permission to have a chaplain stationed in Kabul to care for the Catholic foreign colony. Christian instruction is forbidden and missionaries are denied admission. Afghanistan signed the charter of the United Nations. Protestants do some work through their border organizations. The few Catholics in the country are foreign embassy and technical personnel.

[P. DAMBORIENA]

AFRA, SS. Two martyrs have been venerated under this name. (1) A. of Augsburg (d. *c*.304), who died during the persecution of Diocletian in Augsburg, a Roman *municipium* in the province of Rhetia. No doubt exists concerning her existence or the fact of her martyrdom. Venantius Fortunatus in the 6th cent. testified to the veneration in which she was held in Augsburg. However, the *acta* of her martyrdom appear to be a compilation of two different accounts. One, dating probably from Merovingian times, makes her out a prostitute before her conversion, and associates three of her servants—Digna, Eunomia (Eumenia), and Euprepia—with her in her martyrdom. The other account, dating perhaps from the 4th cent., is considered more reliable. It declares that she was a woman condemned to the flames because she professed herself a Christian and refused to participate in pagan rites. See Butler 3:267–268; C. Egger, BiblSanct 1:283–287. (2) A. of Brescia, a woman whose martyrdom was linked with that of SS. Faustinus and Jovita (2d cent.). Her name and identity are obscure in the earliest chronicles of the church at Brescia, but a *passio* that goes back to the 8th cent. names her and gives the circumstances of her martyrdom. Delehaye thought the identification stemmed from a confusion of this person with A. of Augsburg. BIBLIOGRAPHY: M. V. Brandi, BiblSanct 1:279–283.

AFRAHAT, see APHRAATES.

AFRICA, EARLY CHURCH IN ROMAN. The history of Roman Africa reflects the growth of Roman power in the West after the fall of Carthage (146 B.C.). Originally the province included only Carthage and its environs (modern Tunisia) but after the battle of Thapsus (46 B.C.) Caesar annexed Numidia and under Augustus (40 B.C.) a proconsul was appointed with the third Augustan legion assigned to his command. From the reign of Gaius (A.D. 40) the *legatus* of the legion was independent of the proconsul and eventually his territory (Numidia) became a separate province (198). After Claudius had reorganized the two provinces of Mauretania and Septimius had expanded the frontiers to the south, Roman holdings reached their limit of growth under Caracalla (188–217). At this time Roman Africa included what is now Tunisia, Tripoli, Algeria, and Morocco.

With relatively few Roman immigrants to assist growth in government and commerce, Roman Africa achieved economic independence by its extensive use of natural resources. Agriculture and stock breeding supplied the province with its livelihood. Industry was relatively insignificant because Africans showed little aptitude for it and also because Rome depended primarily on Africa for food supply. Romanization was more widespread in Proconsular Africa than in the provinces of Numidia and the two Mauretanias. The predominant Berber natives maintained their native customs and language together with those of Punic origin which they had inherited by intermarriage, even though Roman urbanization made Latin the official language of government, and Roman law prevailed in the larger cities and towns and in those areas joined by Roman roads.

Fundamentally a religious people, the Berbers adopted Greco-Roman religious cults, the observance of the imperial cult, and Oriental religions without abandoning their native primitive cults which survived barely disguised by Latin names, e.g., Punic deities, Saturn for Baal of Carthage. By the 2d cent. of the Empire, African towns and cities became centers of Roman culture with an increasing number of Berbers enjoying full Roman citizenship and the advantages of upper-class living. Carthage became well known for its schools of rhetoric and Proconsular Africa produced a tradition of excellence in the Latin literature of the 2d cent., e.g., Apuleius, Fronto, Florus, and Aulus Gellius.

Christianity probably came to Africa from Rome at the end of the 1st cent. but the earliest records are the acts of the Scillitan martyrs (180) and the passion of SS. Perpetua and Felicity (203). Tertullian (197–220) said that the population of the cities was almost entirely Christian and that even the small towns had bishops (*Ad scap.* 2). By the time of St. Cyprian, there were over 100 bishops. In the 2d and 3d centuries the African Church was using a Latin version of the Scriptures and of the liturgy, although Greek was still the official language for the Church of Rome.

Amid the three severe persecutions of Decius (250), Valerian (258), and Diocletian (303) and the resulting conflicts of readmission of the *lapsi* (lapsed), the Novatian schism, and later Donatism, the African Church produced the leading Latin ecclesiastical writers and theologians of the West, e.g., Minucius Felix, Tertullian, Cyprian, Arnobius, Lactantius, Tyconius, Optatus, and St. Augustine. Under the leadership of *Augustine, the African Church strongly opposed pagan traditions and teaching, established monasticism, and bequeathed a rich intellectual legacy to the West. The Councils of *Carthage raised questions and established precedents that proved a significant contribution in the

medieval canonical definitions of local and papal ecclesiastical jurisdiction. With the invasion of the Vandals and their Arian kings (429), orthodox Christians were restricted and persecuted until the victory of Justinian's general, Belisarius (534). Notable writers of this time included Victor Titensis, Dracontius, Vigilius of Thapsus, Fulgentius of Ruspe, and Facundus. Monasticism continued to grow and more Berber tribes were converted. Pope Gregory I carried on extensive correspondence with the African bishops (590–604). With the victory of the Arabs and the fall of Carthage (698), the African Church became but a remnant of its 6 centuries of ascendancy in the West. BIBLIOGRAPHY: E. Albertini, CAH 11:479–490; Fliche-Martin 2:136–210; H. Leclercq, CE 1:191–194; W. Marschall, *Karthago und Rom* (1972).

[F. H. BRIGHAM]

AFRICAN CHRISTIANITY (Contemporary), one of the most massive and variegated responses to the Christian faith in the history of Christian missions. After the extinction of the Church in North Africa by the year A.D. 1000, RC missions began south of the Sahara early in the 16th cent.; Protestant missions began three centuries later. After 1800 almost every variety of European and North American Christianity was introduced somewhere onto the African scene and left its imprint. By the year 1900 missioners had begun work with about 400 of the 750 tribes south of the Sahara and had translated the NT into about 100 vernacular tongues. The Christian population in sub-Saharan Africa grew from virtually zero in 1800 to about 98 million in 1974, about 34 million Catholics in 315 dioceses, about 46 million Protestants in 600 national Churches or missions, 6 million Orthodox (almost entirely in Ethiopia), and 8 million adherents of the *African Independent Church Movement (AICM). By 1970 the majority of these dioceses and Churches had come under strong African leadership. National and international *Bible societies, again with predominantly African leadership, had brought about one of the greatest intellectual achievements of Christian missions in all times, namely the translation of the Holy Scriptures, in whole or in part, into 395 languages in sub-Saharan Africa. In almost all of these translations a traditional African religious vocabulary has been used to express Christian concepts. Despite strong African leadership, Christianity has still been regarded by many in Africa as a foreign religion, heavily influenced by Western ecclesiastical traditions and patterns, with Western denominational rivalry imposed on the African response to the Gospel. But in many areas the Church has now entered the third or fourth generation of its existence, and strong indigenous expressions of Christianity are beginning to emerge. These may be reviewed under four heads as follows.

Renewal and Revival Movements within the Churches. Within the RC and Protestant Churches in Africa about 1,000 popular religious movements of renewal, revival, protest, or dissidence had crystalized sufficiently to possess distinct names and membership by 1967. Most of these movements were begun on African initiative, or in a few cases under missionary leadership with strong African backing, e.g., the *Jamaa* (Family) movement within the RC Church in Katanga, Congo-Kinshasa, which was begun after World War II among the Luba tribe, under the inspiration of the Belgian missionary Placide Tempels, and by 1967 had about 20,000 adult members throughout the Congo. Other such renewal movements have been the East African Revival, or *Balokole* (Saved Ones), mainly within the Anglican Church, which had spread to about 70 East African tribes. A similar movement in Madagascar is the *Fifohazana* (Those Who Have Woken Up) Revival, which has affected some 100,000 members of the Lutheran and other Protestant Churches. All such renewal movements have spread spontaneously, usually on lay initiative. A considerable number of renewal movements have sprung up within the RC Church since the liberal reforms of Vatican II. Lay leaders have become bolder, to the point where clashes with the clergy occur. In central Africa the canonization of the Uganda martyrs by Paul VI in 1964 touched off a wave of enthusiastic movements, not among the Ganda themselves but among tribes in adjoining territories. In the Tanzanian Dioceses of Bukoba and Rulenge arose the movement called *Banyakaroli* (Followers of Charles; named after the Ganda protomartyr Charles Lwanga, who was murdered in 1885). Under the zealous leadership of a RC lay prophet of the Haya tribe, Bernardo, the *Banyakaroli* went about preaching in blood-red *kanzus* (cassocks) and traveled to distant dioceses to conduct lay retreats. By 1967 they were in serious difficulties with the hierarchy. In the Congolese Dioceses of Kabinda and Luluabourg, a similar movement, Bena Nzambi wa BaMartyre ya Baganda (Children of God of the Uganda Martyrs), had actually broken off and become a separatist body by 1966. But in 1967 the vast majority of such RC movements were still inside the Church.

Beginning with the first feeble stirrings of reaction in the early days of Christian missions, such movements within the Churches have gradually increased with each succeeding decade until by 1967 they had reached astonishing proportions. Exact enumeration of the total of all such movements over the whole period is clearly impossible; the records do not exist, and in any case the phenomena themselves were only barely discernible and often short-lived. But even if a majority of them were very small, sometimes a grouping of only 10 or 20 church members, a rough assessment yields some startling figures. To begin with, there are the 5,000 separatist Churches in the AICM, virtually all of which were at one time movements within the mission Churches. Next, for every successful attempt to form a separatist body there have been several that fell short of schism; hence, it is possible that at least an additional 5,000 attempts at forming dissident movements have failed. Then there has been the mass of similar movements, large or small, that have not attempted to secede but have been able to exist as renewal movements within the Churches. Therefore, about 10 to 20 thousand distinct groupings of renewal or dissidence, suc-

cessful or frustrated, have arisen within the Churches in Africa during the last 2 centuries of the missionary era. By 1967 all such existing movements still within the Churches probably embraced several million persons in the Protestant, RC, and Orthodox communities across the continent. The ensemble represents a vast reservoir of religious unrest and a fertile field for indigenous reformers intent on creating a truly African Christianity, having a spirit that is conformed to nationalist aspirations and native culture.

Leader Figures. A large number of charismatic leader figures have been thrust up by such movements within the Churches. Many have been seers, visionaries, or prophets, coexisting in varying degrees of tension with foreign missionaries and African church leaders. Others have been renowned healers; still others have been pioneer missionaries to unevangelized areas, such as John Tsizehena, a Malagasy Anglican youth who evangelized and became bp. of the Northern Church of Madagascar. In addition, countless African musicians, male and female, have supplied traditional African tunes with Christian words, e.g., in Tanzania Christians of the Wagogo tribe sing whole chapters of the Gogo Bible to Gogo music in their evangelistic work. Other leaders have been preachers of great power, employing traditional African techniques of public speaking—question and answer, responsive singing, dialogue preaching, dual staccato preaching (one preacher speaking rapidly for a few minutes, then the second taking over without a pause, then the first, etc.), and even preaching out of doors to huge crowds while running up and down long avenues.

The African Independent Church Movement (AICM). This phenomenon, unprecedented for size and importance in the entire history of the expansion of Christianity, is dealt with in the article African Independent Church Movement.

Complex of New Religious Forms. In movements both within the historical churches and in the AICM, there are at least 200 varying new emphases in Christian belief and practice, representing a genuinely African response to the Christian faith. All center around the basic African concept of the people of God as a community and the legitimacy of Christianizing African traditional concepts and practices. They represent a creative response on the part of African Christianity to the turmoil and disruption that followed the breakdown of traditional patterns of life as a result of contact with the Western world. A selection of these new forms or emphases is given below, divided for convenience into nine categories.

Community Structure. Under this heading are included small face-to-face communities, based often on traditional social structure, characterized by fellowship, agape, and philadelphia; communal life; communities of love; prominence of women; strong lay leadership; the desacralization of politics.

Land and Property. Included are centers of religious innovation called holy villages or renewal centers; houses of prayer; prayer plots; holy places for vigils; open-air worship sites; communal ownership of land and agricultural or commercial enterprises; "The Lord's Acre" plots for church crops; and a stress on philanthropic funds, burial societies, and mutual-help societies.

Laws and taboos. These include sabbatarianism; tithing and fasting; personal austerity; prohibition of tobacco, alcohol, and pork; often a rejection of European medicine; a marked legalism in church affairs; spiritual vagrancy or fluidity of membership; experimental membership; occasional dual or plural membership (in mission and separatist Churches); and random borrowing from various historical denominations.

Religious concepts. Among these concepts are a supernatural view of life; the divinity of the Holy Spirit; God as the Living God, the God of Power, the God of Miracles, the God of the Impossible, the God of the Ancestors; theories of mythological eras in church history; and a claimed indigenous or African theology.

Religious leadership. A wide range of leadership is seen: corporate leadership; decisions made by the group rather than by individuals; prophets and prophetesses; healers, faith healing; titled officials; differentiated leadership systems; evangelists; judges; dialogue preaching; lay involvement; mothers-in-God; traditions of prophets' miracles; new holy books; stress on spiritual gifts, pneumatic phenomena, trances, visions, and dreams; and revelation on sacred mountains. Polygamists are accepted as members but not as officials.

Religious symbolism. Included under this heading are symbolic colors revealed in dreams; blue and white as sacred colors; new forms of dress, e.g., white robes for all participants, and uniforms; symbolic letters or embroidery; monograms; large red crosses; special headwear; beards, shaven heads; removal of shoes; indigenous craftmanship; carrying of holy staffs, banners, or flags as symbols of pilgrimage; and the use of candles and candelabra in revelation.

Magical Concepts. The reality of magic is recognized but all its forms are opposed, whether benevolent or malevolent. Also noted are destruction of all fetishes and rejection of charms and nostrums.

Rituals. Various forms of ritual are: special greetings with prayer and ritual; ritual postures during prayer; blessing of medicines; blessing of newly bought articles; ritual dancing; anointing with oils; footwashing; use of holy water; purification rites; communal weeping for sins; ringing of handbells; exorcism of devils; millennial release from sorcery; and mass confession of witches.

Worship. The following practices are observed: sealing of doors and windows during worship; indigenous liturgies; praying bands; mass *glossolalia; multilingual praying ensemble; religious grunting, hiccoughing, or humming; religious joy and ecstasy; long prayers; testimonies; stress on the name of Jesus; drums or flutes in worship; use of megaphones, hand clapping, rhythmic movement, and antiphonal responses; annual conventions or festivals; processions; incessant religious itineration; vernacular hymns; indigenous tunes in worship; and the use of vernacular names of endearment for Jesus.

Although many of these features have occurred in other eras and areas of the Christian world mission, their intensity and proliferation in Africa accentuate both the African genius for religion and religious creativity and also the rapidity with which Christianity is becoming rooted in African culture and society. BIBLIOGRAPHY: C. P. Groves, *Planting of Christianity in Africa* (1958) v.4; D. B. Barrett, *Schism and Renewal in Africa* (1968).

[D. B. BARRETT]

AFRICAN INDEPENDENT CHURCH MOVEMENT. Widespread Christian missionary activity in sub-Saharan Africa began around the year 1800, and since 1819 schisms and other religious movements have grown in number each decade. By 1967 there were 5,100 distinct bodies among 290 different tribes in 33 African nations and colonies (and Madagascar), with an estimated total of 6,900,000 adherents (total nominal community). By 1973 the number of adherents had increased to 8 million. An average of seven hitherto uninvolved tribes became part of the movement each year as well. In ecumenical circles the emergence of these Churches is designated as the African Independent Church Movement (AICM), though in fact the vast majority of these bodies do not know of each other's existence and are in no sense a consciously organized movement. Of the more than 1,500 books, reports, and articles in 20 languages written on the AICM, most deal with a single body or area, but a handful attempt an overall description and analysis of the whole movement. A wide range of terminology is used: some of the classifications are favorable, e.g., spiritual movements, renewals, revivals; others indicate characteristics, e.g., charismatic, prophetic, separatist, schismatic; others are derogatory, e.g., syncretistic, neopagan, non-Christian.

Geographical and Historical Scope. The AICM is spread across the whole of sub-Saharan Africa, but with particularly large concentrations in the Union of South Africa (3,000), Nigeria (500), Congo-Kinshasa (500), Ghana (200), and Kenya (160). In the sub-Saharan regions, western, central, and eastern Africa each has a total of about 1 million adherents, while southern Africa has well over 3 million. In northern Africa, almost entirely Muslim in religion, there are about 12,000 adherents of separatist bodies. The first of these independent church movements occurred in 1819 in western Africa, where in 1967 about 800 separatist ecclesiastical bodies existed, each with its own distinct name and organization. In northern Africa the first schism took place in 1869; subsequently seven bodies in Egypt have separated from Protestant missions. Since 1872 southern Africa has produced at least 3,200 such secessions, the greatest proliferation being among the Zulu of South Africa. In central Africa about 570 movements have arisen since 1888, almost all in French-speaking territories; in Congo-Kinshasa alone, 200 bodies have emerged since independence in 1960. The last region to become involved was eastern Africa in 1894; although it had in 1967 the smallest number of groups (350), these groups included dynamic religious leaders and were growing as rapidly as anywhere else on the continent. At least 90% of all the 5,000 secessions over the last century and a half still existed in 1967 as organized bodies with gradually increasing memberships. The Berlin Conference for the partitioning of Africa (1885) marked an upsurge of the AICM; since then expansion has been at a remarkably even rate. Some 10% of all bodies formed since the start have rejoined their parent Church, been suppressed, or have otherwise disbanded. The average size of a body is only 1,370 adherents, but many have more than 50,000 members, and the largest (Église de Jésus-Christ sur la terre par le prophète Simon Kimbangu, or ÉJCSK, in Zaire has about 200,000 adult members.

A Single Phenomenon. The AICM may give a preliminary impression of a mass of disparate and unrelated movements, with causes as numerous and different as are the prophets who lead them. Observers have naturally tended to emphasize local causes, which vary widely from case to case—personal friction, racial incidents, ambition, missionary paternalism, political and economic crises. Closer analysis, however, has revealed a correlation between separatism and the following elements, less visible but common to all tribes involved: a strong traditional African society, e.g., polygamous structure and ancestral cult; strong colonial impact, e.g., high literacy and the presence of white settlers; strong missionary impact, e.g., high missionary concentration and vernacular translations of the Scriptures. The correlation suggests that the underlying cause of the whole AICM is the clash of African culture with colonial and missionary cultures. A further common feature is the diffusion, unparalleled in previous Christian expansion, of the vernacular Scriptures in a total of 411 African languages. One may speak, therefore, of the AICM as a single phenomenon; and one unique in history. Granted the spectrum of types, ranging from the ultraorthodox to the definitely syncretistic, almost all these bodies are nevertheless characterized by a clear acceptance, often under new and original African forms, of the centrality of the historical Jesus as Lord. In varying degrees there are in virtually every movement: a central confession of Christ as *Kyrios* (using the traditional vernacular term for chiefship); a marked resurgence of traditional African custom and world view; and a strong affirmation of their right to be both fully Christian and fully African, independent of foreign pressures. All over the continent the African Churches, working quite spontaneously and in the main independently, seem to be engaged in an attempt to synthesize the apostolic kerygma with genuinely African insight, based on ideas derived from the vernacular translations of the Bible. Beyond the tragic spectacle of schism after schism, therefore, a renewal of Christianity, truly indigenous in form, is emerging.

Civil and Ecumenical Status. There are three developments in recent years that indicate a fundamental shift in the relations between the AICM on the one hand and governments and ecumenical Christianity on the other. First, determined efforts have recently been made by the independent Churches to secure government recognition through application to register as legitimate societies. In the case of most of the larger bodies, this has already been successful. In Kenya, Nigeria, and Zaire, particularly, there were recorded so many applications during the 1960s that the movement as a whole is being treated with a new and marked respect. Further, a similar determination is being shown to win ecumenical recognition and to work toward Christian unity. Here a definite strategy—almost certainly unorganized and spontaneous—seems to be in process. In the first place, importunate applications for membership have been made in increasing numbers since 1955 to national Christian councils across the continent; but in only a handful of cases, notably in Kenya, Cameroon, and Rhodesia, has this membership been granted. When such efforts prove fruitless, bodies have bypassed national councils and applied directly to the major ecumenical bodies. Here, their reception has been equally cautious; by 1966 the All-Africa Conference of Churches had accepted into membership only four of the many applying bodies—the African Church (Nigeria), the African Brotherhood Church (Kenya), the African Methodist Church (Rhodesia), and the Église Protestante Africaine Baptiste (Congo). Among the applications received by the World Council of Churches in 1966 were those of the Église Harriste (Ivory Coast) and of the ÉJCSK. (The latter's application was approved by the World Council's Central Committee in 1969, and membership became final in Feb. 1970).

The next step of the separatist bodies has been to form federations with assistance from liberal elements in the historical Churches. The happiest examples of this today are the African Independent Churches Association (AICA) and the Assembly of Zionist and Apostolic Churches, both in South Africa, which receive assistance (particularly with theological education) from the Christian Institute of Southern Africa and the Christian Council of South Africa. But, lastly, if all such ecumenical feelers are rebuffed, the separatist Churches have shown that they can organize powerful rival Christian councils: the East African United Churches in 1967 organized 40 constituent members, and COSSÉUJCA (Conseil Supérieur des Sacrificateurs pour les Églises-Unies de Jésus-Christ en Afrique), from Luluabourg, claims to act on behalf of about 50 bodies.

Membership statistics for 17 of the largest Churches of the AICM are listed in order of size in the following table. "Adherents" is the term used for the total nominal community of a body, including adult members, fringe members, and children.

Missionary Character. One final development of major significance for the evangelization of Africa is that independency has now taken on a distinctively missionary character. In at least 16 nations separatist Churches are growing faster than their Protestant or RC counterparts. In western Africa, where the historical Churches are making little headway in the Muslim north, separatist congregations have been established in most of the major Muslim towns and cities. Elsewhere in Africa, numerous bodies have commenced missionary work far distant from their home areas, e.g., the ÉJCSK has worked in southwest Africa, the African Apostolic

Body and Nation	Date Founded	Adherents
Église de Jesus-Christ sur la terre par le prophète Simon Kimbangu, Zaire	1921	500,000
Zion Christian Church, South Africa	1914	200,000
Church of Christ, South Africa	1910	200,000
Society of the One Almighty God, Uganda	1914	110,000
Lumpa Church, Zambia	1954	100,000
Divine Healer's Church, Ghana	1954	100,000
Christ Apostolic Church, Nigeria	1931	94,000
Église Déimatiste, Ivory Coast	1923	90,000
Church of Christ in Africa, Kenya	1957	75,000
Mai Chaza Church, Rhodesia	1952	70,000
Église Harriste, Ivory Coast	1913	68,000
Apostolic Revelation Society, Ghana	1939	60,000
Legio Maria, Kenya	1963	60,000
African Israel Church Nineveh, Kenya	1942	60,000
Église du Réveil, Malagasy	1955	50,000
Eternal Sacred Order of the Cherubim and Seraphim, Nigeria	1925	50,000
African Apostolic Church of Johane Maranke, Rhodesia	1932	50,000

SOURCE: D. B. Barrett, *Schism and Renewal in Africa: An Analysis of Six Thousand Contemporary Religious Movements* (1968).

NOTE: The date of these estimates is the period 1964–67, except for the Lumpa Church and Église Déimatiste (1958) and the Society of the One Almighty God (1921).

Church of Johane Maranke (Rhodesia) has spread as far west as Luluabourg and Zaire, and Zionists have moved out from South Africa to all adjoining nations including Mozambique. The major concern behind this development of expansion seems to be genuine evangelization rather than mere proselytizing.

Significance. From many points of view the AICM is a phenomenon unique in the entire history of Christian missions. There is first the immense number of schisms and adherents involved (one-fifth of the entire Christian community in Africa); second, a remarkably uniform spread across a third of Africa's tribes in the last 100 years; and third, for the first time in history the paradoxical coexistence of four elements—strong animistic traditional societies, mass movements into the historical Churches, formidable missionary assaults of traditional religion and society, and

the widespread provision of vernacular Scriptures, which have been interpreted as vindicating much of the traditional African way of life. The AICM has therefore a significance equal to the encounter of the post-apostolic Church with the Gnostic movement in the 2d cent., the East-West schism, and the fragmentation of Christendom in Europe during the Reformation. In most cases AICM bodies attempt to Christianize traditional African customs, and this has inevitably led to charges of *syncretism. An ecumenical assessment of their theological character, however, would have to acknowledge that, although in many respects they fall short of recognized Christian orthodoxy, their almost universal claim to confess Jesus as Lord, Savior, and God establishes them as genuine Christian Churches. BIBLIOGRAPHY: R. C. Mitchell and H. W. Turner, *Bibliography of Modern African Religious Movements* (1966); D. B. Barrett, *Schism and Renewal in Africa: Analysis of Six Thousand Contemporary Religious Movements* (1968); H. W. Coxill, et al., *World Christian Handbook 1968* (1967) 227–228. *LEGIO MARIA; *AFRICAN CHRISTIANITY; *ANCESTOR CULT.

[D. B. BARRETT]

AFRICAN LITURGY, the liturgy used in N Africa from *c*.150 to the 8th cent., probably the oldest Latin liturgy in the Church. It is an important link in tracing liturgical development, although precise information is limited since none of its liturgical books have survived, and scholars are forced to depend upon citations, esp. in Tertullian, Cyprian, and Augustine. Consideration of the African liturgy is usually divided into 2 periods: the relatively unstructured and simple Christian observances prior to Nicaea I (325), and a more developed, extensive, and stylized liturgy in the post-Nicene period. The Eucharistic Liturgy of the earlier period was celebrated on Sundays as well as on the "station days," Wednesdays and Fridays. The Mass was divided into that of the catechumens and the faithful; a vigil with psalms and scripture readings preceded the Sacrifice; there was a Preface, Sanctus, Consecration using Christ's words of institution, the Our Father, kiss of peace, a litany, and communion under both species. The liturgical calendar was sparse, including only Good Friday, Easter, Pentecost, and feasts of local martyrs. Baptism, public penance, ordination, a rite of marriage, and ceremonies connected with the burial of the dead are also mentioned. In the post-Nicene liturgy, the Eucharistic Celebration seems to have been quite similar to the Roman rite Mass. It was celebrated daily, and frequent communion was the practice. The calendar was greatly expanded; Lent appears as a penitential season, and Holy Thursday, Christmas, Epiphany, Pentecost, and the feasts of several nonlocal saints are commemorated. The other sacraments were also administered with the greater solemnity that an emerging Christian culture and freedom from persecution would allow. BIBLIOGRAPHY: J. F. Goggin, CE 1:194–199; F. Cabrol, DACL 1:591–657. *COPTIC RITE; *ETHIOPIA, CHURCH IN.

[T. M. MCFADDEN]

AFRICAN METHODIST EPISCOPAL CHURCH, a denomination founded in the 1790s by members of the Methodist Society of Philadelphia who seceded from their congregation because of racial discrimination. One of their number, Richard Allen, erected a separate place of worship for them on his own ground at his own expense. For a few years it was served by pastors ordained by an Anglican bishop. In 1799, however, Francis *Asbury, bp. of the mother Church, after futile attempts to win back the Negroes made Allen their bishop. In 1816 the new Church invited Negro Methodists of Baltimore and other cities, who were likewise on the verge of seceding from their congregations, to attend a *general conference with a view to forming a connection. The new Church grew rapidly in the North and was soon sending missionaries to Liberia (1824) and to Haiti (1827). After the Civil War it added numerous southern Negro congregations to its membership. It now conducts institutions of higher education in seven states and Liberia. Two seminaries supply its preachers, and it publishes five periodicals. Since the late 1920s the African Methodist Episcopal (AME) Church has been plagued with internal dissension, esp. over the issue of episcopacy. It has also suffered from litigation with former members. Since its doctrines and form of worship are similar to those of the other African church bodies in the U.S., a merger with the Christian Methodist Episcopal Church and the AME Zion Church seemed imminent early in the 20th cent. but interest waned. In 1974, however, renewed efforts were being made for such a union. The Consultation on Church Union also includes these three Churches. The AME is the largest of the Negro Methodist bodies in the U.S.; in 1951 its census reported 5,878 churches and 1,166,301 members. BIBLIOGRAPHY: HistAmMeth 3:581–583.

[J. H. SATTERWHITE]

AFRICAN METHODIST EPISCOPAL ZION CHURCH, denomination founded in 1796 by members of the John Street Methodist Episcopal Church of New York City in protest against racial discrimination. The first place of worship of the new Church was built in 1800 and named Zion; but only in 1848 was the word added to the church title to distinguish it from the other *African Methodist Episcopal (AME) Church. The Church was originally supplied with unordained pastors by the Methodist Episcopal Church. The first ordained minister was assigned in 1821. The AME Zion Church is the second largest of the African Methodist bodies in the U.S. Its 1970 census reported 4,500 churches and 940,000 members. It conducts missions in Liberia, the Bahamas, Ghana, Nigeria, and South America. Its chief college is Livingstone in N.C., with which Hood Theological Seminary is connected. It publishes three periodicals besides other literature. A member of the World Council of Churches, it participates also in the *Consultation on Church Union. In 1974 negotiations for a union with the African Methodist Episcopal Church and the Christian Methodist

Episcopal Church were progressing. BIBLIOGRAPHY: HistAmMeth 3:585–586.

[J. H. SATTERWHITE]

AFRICAN MISSIONS, SOCIETY OF THE, a religious society of pontifical right, founded in France (1856) by Bp. Melchior de Marion-Bresillac, for the evangelization of Africa and its native emigrants. The society began its work in Sierra Leone, Dahomey, and along the W coast of Africa, and today labors in seven African countries. It has houses throughout Europe and the U.S., and in 1973 numbered 1,643 members. In 1904, a mission was established in Savannah, Georgia. The society grew rapidly in the U.S., and an American province was canonically erected (1941) in Tenafly, New Jersey. BIBLIOGRAPHY: E. J. Biggane, NCE 1:186; J. M. Todd, *African Mission* (1962).

[T. M. MCFADDEN]

AFRO-AMERICAN MUSIC, the sacred music of the black race in America, insofar as it differs from the standard repertory of worship music. Besides the *spiritual and voodoo cult music, the two principal forms of Afro-American sacred music are the intoned sermon and a style called "gospel music," or occasionally "black gospel music." The intoned sermon, less a musical form than a manner of delivery, may begin with spoken discourse, rise to a half-sung, half-spoken delivery punctuated by remarks ("Amen!" "Tell it, brother!") from members of the congregation, and end as a series of fully sung phrases answered by the entire gathering. A similar use of song is the occasional sung "witness speech" or testimonial to the Lord from a member of the congregation; this, however, usually takes the form of a known song rather than an impromptu sung speech. While gospel music evolves from the same roots as the spiritual, it draws on a later corpus of material. A few of the old spirituals survive, and it shares some hymns with the white gospel tradition; but most of its songs stem from the present century, having been written by black gospel composers such as W. Herbert *Brewster and Kenneth *Morris. These songs may be sung by an entire church as a form of worship—in some churches, the only form—or may be performed by soloists or a small group of chosen singers. The fast songs almost always involve *antiphonal singing, the slow songs, a heavily ornamented style; both encourage congregational participation, by antiphonal singing, clapping, and, when the spirit truly descends, by dancing. There is considerable cross-fertilization between sacred and secular styles of black music, several leading gospel singers, such as Thomas A. *Dorsey, being converted bluesmen. Some gospel singers such as Mahalia *Jackson and Clara *Ward have become internationally famous musical figures, while others like Roberta *Martin and James *Cleveland command an equal respect within the black community. While many of the *jazz Masses and other attempts at creating a popular liturgy are Afro-American only in remote ancestry if at all, a few black composers whose background is jazz, most notably Duke

*Ellington, have turned to the writing of sacred works. BIBLIOGRAPHY: L. Hughes, *Tambourines to Glory* (1963); L. Zenetti, *Peitsche und Psalm* (1963); C. J. Rivers, *Soulful Worship* (1974).

[W. D. SHIRLEY]

AFTERLIFE, the continuity of existence after death. The topic is here considered under three divisions: primitive, biblical, and Greco-Roman thought. The developed Christian theology on the afterlife is treated in several separate entries (see ETERNAL LIFE; ETERNAL PUNISHMENT; HEAVEN; HELL; HOLY SOULS; etc.).

Primitive Thought. A general explanation of the multiform primitive thought on the afterlife is best obtained through the notion of eternal return. In the primitive mind, there is both a spacial center of the world and a temporal point at which the world emerged from a totally chaotic state. This spacial and temporal heart of the universe is the point at which the gods inaugurated their contact with the earth. The gods are real, indeed they are the ultimate basis of reality in the sense of an ordered, comprehensible, and inhabitable sphere of life; they are also immortal, and hence the source of life, youth, and immortality. In his myth and ritual, primitive man sought to live in a real and sacred cosmos through his relationship with this primordial center, this contact point between himself and the source of life. In many primitive myths, immortality could be attained by returning to that sacred time of cosmic beginnings at the center of the world. A clear pattern in these myths is discernible: primeval man searches for immortality (sometimes perpetual youth or a tree of life) which is always difficult to obtain and usually guarded by a monster or serpent. Only by overcoming the hazardous difficulties of his quest and vanquishing the monster does he return to the source of life and thus conquer death. This is not to say, however, that the hero's immortality was the only primitive concept of the afterlife. Rather, it establishes the world view within which the continuity of existence was conceived. In the primitive mind, man did not perdure because he began a totally new or supraterrestrial life as would the hero, nor did he cease to exist upon death. Rather, the life cycle was seen to be continuous, and after the spirit sheds one body which can no longer house it, it seeks another. Although the notion of reward was present and the level of future existence depended upon the type of life lived in the present, primitive thought did not imagine a separate sphere of existence unrelated to the experiential world. See M. Eliade, *Myth of the Eternal Return* (2d ed., tr. W. R. Trask, 1965); *Sacred and the Profane* (tr. W. R. Trask, 1959; pa. 1961); P. Radin, *World of Primitive Man* (1953).

In the Bible. According to OT Jewish thought, at least during all but the latest period, all the dead reside in a single place, called *sheol. It is usually localized in the depths of the earth, and Job describes it as the deepest place in creation (11.8). It is spoken of as having gates and guards (Ps 9.14; 107.18; Jb 38.17), totally dark and silent (Jb 10.21-23; Ps 88.7), a realm of dust. The dead may not return from sheol, and all human activity, power, and vitality cease there. It is, therefore, not an affirmation of an afterlife, but its denial. Scholars disagree as to when this univocal classification of the dead began to break down; some (e.g., M. Dahood) see intimations of immortality and resurrection in the Psalms, but the more general opinion is that notions of divergent retribution for the good and evil appear only by the post-exilic period (Ez 32.17–32; Is 24.22; 26.19; Sir 21.10; Dan 12.2). Because of the Jewish rejection of any Platonic duality in man, this belief in an afterlife necessarily encompasses a resurrection of the body. This conception is also found in the NT, e.g., Lk 16.22–23 speaks of Lazarus at rest in Abraham's bosom and Lk 23.43 mentions paradise as the abode of the just. See M. Dahood, *Psalms 1–50* (Anchor Bible 16, 1966); JBC 765–767; EDB 508–510.

Greco-Roman. The traditional Greek and Roman concept of afterlife is varied, at times contradictory, but in all its forms reflects a deep unconscious intuition toward survival after death whether it be the cult of the dead, the songs of epic or lyric poetry, the teaching and ritual of the mystery religions, or the insights of philosophy.

In early Greece, archeological evidence indicates a belief in an earthly mode of existence in the grave. To survive, the dead man required furniture, food, clothing, weapons, and entertainment in accord with his economic and social status. Mycenaean family cult of the dead eventually included a special cult for the dead heroes outside the family. Homer established the basic popular understanding of the dreary underworld life for all the dead, as the ghost of Achilles speaks to Odysseus, ". . . Don't talk to me of death, glorious Odysseus! I had rather work in the fields as a hired hand for a man who has little land and less means than be king of all the dead in the world below . . ." (*Odyssey* 11.488–491), and this had a variety of literary expressions culminating in book 6 of Virgil's *Aeneid*. Even though Homer made the distinction between the corpse and its ghost when the mother of Odysseus speaks to her son in his visit to the underworld (*Odyssey* 11.216–224), he failed to dislodge the more popular primitive belief of the shadowy survival of the whole person after death. As archeological evidence shows, the people continued to dress the dead in expensive garments, much to the dismay of Solon and later Plato (*Laws* 959).

Homer also provides a description of the ancient Minoan religious belief in the Isle of the Blessed, Elysium, " . . . the plain at the ends of the earth where fair-haired Rhadamanthus is; where life is most easy for men; neither snow nor great storm nor rain is there but ever as the shrill West wind blows, Ocean sends forth breezes to refresh men . . ." (*Odyssey* 4.563); but the writers of a later period assigned Elysium and the lot of the fortunate dead to the more traditional Homeric vision of the underworld. Thus while the influence of Homer was profound in determining conventional Greek attitudes toward the afterlife, his eschatological descriptions are not consistent and do reveal more primitive beliefs at variance with his own.

In early Rome, on the other hand, the ghosts of the dead

became identified with the vast impersonal underworld of the *Manes* or *Lemures* (departed spirits) only to return on particular occasions, e.g., feast of Lemuria in May. There is no evidence for the primitive Roman belief in punishment after death. But these native concepts were gradually Hellenized and by the time of the Late Republic, Greek and Roman belief about afterlife were not noticeably different.

Pythagorean and Orphic belief in transmigration and *apotheosis loosely constructed from many sources, gave some hope to the individual with his fears about the afterlife and its potential punishments for those who were not purified. The most popular expression of these attitudes was found in Greece after the 7th cent. in the Eleusinian mysteries with their attendant rites of purification.

After Pindar had immortalized the ethical conclusions of Pythagorean and Orphic teaching, it was left to Plato to develop a philosophical basis for immortality of the soul in his theory of recollection, theory of ideas, and moral principles (*Phaedr* 245–257b, *Laws* 893b–900, *Rep*. 608–611). More far reaching than these metaphysical arguments were the vision and hope generated by his great myths, e.g., the confidence of Socrates facing death (*Phaedo* 114–118), the striking picture of the fearful soul before the judgment of Rhadamanthus (*Gorg*. 524 d-e) and the believable account of judgment in the tale of Er (*Rep*. 614–621). After Aristotle, who granted immortality to the mind of man alone, the Hellenistic period saw some members of the Academy adopt a position of skepticism toward immortality; the Epicureans and some Stoics rejected it altogether, while other Stoics accepted it with limitations. In the 1st cent. B.C., the Stoic Posidonius effected new philosophical interest and confidence in the afterlife throughout Greece and Rome.

While the teaching of philosophers had a limited audience, the Greco-Oriental mystery religions of Dionysius, Sabazius, Attis, Isis, and Mithras promised salvation to their adherents in the traditional Homeric underworld or in the spheres of the heavens and appealed to a greater cross section of the population in the Late Republic and Early Empire. This partially explains the interest in *Neopythagoreanism (1st and 2d cent. B.C.) with its eclectic and varied synthesis of the ascetical elements of Greco-Oriental mystery religion, Pythagorean and Orphic ritual, and the philosophical vision of Plato, Aristotle, and the Stoics. It taught that apotheosis was achieved after death when souls passed through the atmosphere and cleansing winds to their final dwelling place among the stars. It remained for *Neoplatonism (3d to 6th cent. A.D.) to effect a more substantial synthesis and describe the afterlife in terms of the One and the Many; man must go beyond the corrosive limitations of the sensible to the simplicity and unity of the immortal spirit. To the extent that these religious and philosophical movements of the Empire spoke to the increased desire for a more personalized religion and philosophy of life and death, they flourished. But the fears and longing for the peace of a trouble-free eternity survived the popularity of mystery religions and the sophisticated solutions of the philosophers as the cryptic epitaphs of Greek

and Roman sarcophagi attest. BIBLIOGRAPHY: E. Rhode, *Cult of Souls and Belief in Immortality among the Greeks* (tr. W. B. Hillis from 8th Germ. ed. 1925); L. R. Farnell, *Greek Hero Cults and Ideas of Immortality* (1921); E. R. Dodds, *Greeks and the Irrational* (1951) 136–178; H. J. Rose, *Religion in Greece and Rome* (1959) 157–197; W. K. G. Guthrie, *Greeks and Their Gods* (pa. 1955), 307–374; G. Sanders, NCE 1:118–192; *MYSTERY RELIGIONS (GRECO–ORIENTAL); *CRETAN–MYCENAEN RELIGION; *ELEUSINIAN MYSTERIES; *IMMORTALITY; *ETRUSCAN RELIGION; *GREEK RELIGION; *ROMAN RELIGION; *ORPHISM.

[T. M. MCFADDEN; F. H. BRIGHAM]

AGA KHAN, title of the spiritual head of the *Nizari branch of the Ismailis in India. *FATIMIDS.

[R. M. FRANK]

AGABUS, NT prophet from Jerusalem. At Antioch he foretold a great famine affecting the world (Acts 11.27–28), which occurred during the reign of Claudius (41–54 A.D.). Later at Caesarea he told by symbolic action of Paul's imprisonment (Acts 21.10–11).

[J. J. O'ROURKE]

AGAGIANIAN, GREGORY PETER XV (Lazarus; 1895–1971), cardinal and Catholic Armenian patriarch. Born in Akhaltsikhe, Russia, A. was educated from the age of 11 at the Pontifical Armenian College at Rome. Ordained priest in 1917, he obtained doctorates in philosophy, theology, and canon law. He became rector of the college (1932) and was consecrated titular bp. of Comana (1935). That same year he was named to the Commission for the Codification of Oriental Canon Law. A. was elected patriarch of the Catholic Armenians and catholicos of Cilicia in 1937. An outstanding patriarch, he was created a cardinal by Pope Pius XII (1946) and served on numerous and diverse Vatican congregations and commissions, notably as proprefect and then prefect of the Congregation for the Propagation of the Faith (later the Congregation for the Evangelization of Peoples) from 1958 to 1970. The demands of this position which necessitated extensive travel throughout the world, together with his numerous other functions, led to his resigning as patriarch in 1962. A. acted as a presiding officer of Vatican Council II and played an important role in drawing up the missionary decree *Ad gentes*.

[A. H. CRANE]

AGAPE, SS. Name of several early Christian martyrs. (1) A., daughter of St. Sophia mentioned with SS. Faith and Hope, was martyred during the persecution of Hadrian according to a 7th– or 8th–cent. *Passio* by John the Priest. See A. Amore, BiblSanct 11:1278–79. (2) A. of *Thessalonica* was martyred on April 1, 304 together with her sisters Chionia and Irene after a trial under the Roman Prefect Dulcitius. The acts of the trial have been preserved. See A. Palmieri, DHGE 1:876. (3) A., companion of St. Marina, who was put to death at Antioch on March 11, 411, according to the Syrian martyrology. See S. Salaville, DHGE 1:875–876. (4) A. of Terni, according to the Roman Martyrology, was a virgin martyred on Feb. 15, 273, a victim of the persecution of Aurelian. Her existence and martyrdom are questionable. BIBLIOGRAPHY: Butler 1:341; G. Lucchesi, BiblSanct 1:301–302.

[F. H. BRIGHAM]

AGAPĒ (Greek word for love or charity), very rare in secular Greek, it is used occasionally by the LXX, twice in the Synoptics, and frequently in the Johannine and Pauline writings. Coined from the old Gr. verb *agapan,* which often conveys the idea of a respectful and unselfish love, as between parents and children or friends, it must have been chosen by the authors of the NT to avoid the implication of selfishness and passionate emotions often found in the usual word for love, *eros. Agapan* was used by the LXX in such sentences as: "God *loved* the people he has chosen" (Dt 4.37); "*Love* God with all your heart" (Dt 6.5); "*Love* your neighbor as yourselves" (Lev 19.18). The Jews were not asked to love their enemies, but to help them in some of their difficulties (Ex 23.4; Pr 25.51). Later some rabbis may have had broader views. But in the rule of the Qumran community, its members were asked "to hate all the sons of Darkness" (1Q1 1.10). In the NT the commandments of the love of God and neighbor are put together as the most important commandments of the Law (Mt 22.37–40). The neighbor to be loved is not only a member of the Jewish community but every man, even enemies and persecutors (Mt 5.43–48; Rom 12.14–19; Gal 6.10). This universality of love is founded on a new understanding of the relations between God and man revealed in Jesus Christ. God is not the God of only one people, but of the whole world. He "wants everyone to be saved" (1 Tim 2.5). Since he "is love" (1 Jn 4.8), "he loved so much the world that he gave his only Son so that everybody who believes in him may have eternal life" (Jn 3.16). Jesus, his Son, manifested this love when "he loved his own to the end. . . . laying down his life for them" (Jn 15.13). He asked his disciples to love one another as he has loved them (Jn 13.34). Such love, asking men to work for the fulfillment of the will of God for true happiness and the salvation of all men, cannot be a mere human love. It is possible because "the love of God has been poured into our hearts by the Spirit given to us" (Rom 5.5); and it is the proof that we really love God and that his love is complete in us (1 Jn 4.12). As principle and rule of the whole Christian life, it abides forever (1 Cor 13). *Agapē* was also the name given to Christian "love-feasts" (Jude 12), community meals with or without Eucharist. BIBLIOGRAPHY: EDB 1377–85; A. Nygren, *Agape and Eros* (tr. P. S. Watson, 1953); C. Spicq, *Agape in the New Testament* (tr. M. A. McNamara and M. H. Richter, 1963); G. Outka, *Agape: An Ethical Analysis* (1972).

[A. VIARD]

AGAPEMONE, CHURCH OF THE, see CHURCH OF THE AGAPEMONE.

AGAPETAE (Gr. *agapētai,* darlings), a term applied in sarcasm to consecrated virgins who lived with men also dedicated to chastity. A council at Antioch in 268 spoke of *suneisaktai,* Latinized as *subintroductae* (women brought in by stealth), referring to women living with clerics in "white" or "spiritual" marriages. In support of such unions 1 Cor 9.5, together with 1 Cor 7.36–38, was sometimes cited, and it has been suggested that they were an accepted phenomenon in early Christian life. But this is not borne out by the evidence, for they were severely condemned by a number of the Fathers and by various councils of the 3d and 4th centuries. A practice similar to that of the *agapetae* seems to have existed in 5th-cent. Irish monasticism and was also condemned. In 6th-cent. Brittany there were *conhospitae* (female guests), with the added abuse that they administered the chalice for holy communion; this also met with episcopal prohibition. BIBLIOGRAPHY: H. Achelis, *Virgines subintroductae, ein Beitrag zu I Cor. VII* (1902); E. Magnin, DDC 1:311–315, who gives the patristic and conciliar texts; R. Kugelman, NCE 14:698; F. X. Murphy, NCE 14:698–699.

[T. C. O'BRIEN]

AGAPETUS (AGAPITUS) I, ST. (d. 536), **POPE** from 535. A., a Roman archdeacon, was elected to the papacy on the death of John II, with the support of those opposed to allowing a pope to name his successor, a practice John had attempted to make the rule. After his election, A. summoned a council which condemned this uncanonical procedure. At the request of King Theodatus (Theodahad), A. went to Constantinople to deflect the Emperor, Justinian I, from his avowed purpose of recovering the western provinces of the empire from the sway of the Ostrogoths. He was well received and strengthened ties between Christians of East and West; but he was unable to win the Emperor to a peaceful policy toward Italy. He did, however, secure the deposition of Anthimus, a Monophysite who had been made patriarch of Constantinople through the influence of the Empress Theodora, and consecrated the orthodox Mennas in his place. A. died in Constantinople, and his remains were returned to St. Peter's for burial. He is noted for having planned a university, in cooperation with Cassiodorus, and gave his ancestral home as a library for this project. He is honored as a saint in East and West. Extant letters: PL 66:35–80. BIBLIOGRAPHY: J. Chapin, NCE 1:194–195; Butler 2:145; I. Daniele, BiblSanct 1:316–318.

[P. F. MULHERN]

AGAPETUS II (d. 955), **POPE** from 946. A Roman, A. became pope at the time when the papacy and the Roman Church were controlled by the Duke of Spoleto, *Alberic II, who had wrested the temporal power in central Italy from his mother, the infamous Marozia. Thus when A. was installed in 946, he was virtually without authority, except in spiritual matters. He is credited with promoting a renewal of fervor and discipline in the monasteries and with promoting the evangelization of northern Europe. He took an active interest in the Church in France and cooperated with the Emperor Otto I in settling a bitter struggle for the important See of Reims. He welcomed Otto's intervention to quiet disorder in Italy, but refused him the imperial crown, probably at the insistence of Alberic. The ultimate indignity A. was obliged to endure from Alberic was to see the clergy and nobles of Rome forced to swear that they would choose Alberic's own illegitimate son, Octavian, pope after A.'s death. He was buried in the Lateran. BIBLIOGRAPHY: C. M. Aherne, NCE 1:195; Mann 4:224–240.

[P. F. MULHERN]

AGAPIOS OF HIERAPOLIS, 10th-cent. historian and bp. of Hierapolis (Manbij) in Syria. He is noted for a general history of the world to his time (c.942), the *Book of the Title (Kitāb Al-'Unwān),* which presents material often unavailable in other sources, such as lists of Eastern metropolitans.

[A. J. JACOPIN]

AGAPITUS AND FELICISSIMUS, SS., see FELICISSIMUS AND AGAPITUS, SS.

AGAR, see HAGAR.

AGATHA, ST. (d. c.251?) a martyr who according to her 6th-cent. legend was allegedly put to death during the persecution of Decius at Catania, Sicily, by the Roman Senator Quintian for her faith in Christ and her defense of chastity. Apart from the fact of her death, there is no historical support for the details of this account. But the martyrologies of Carthage (530) and St. Jerome, two churches in Rome dedicated in her honor in the 6th cent., the inscription of her name in the Canon of the Mass, and her presence in the procession of saints in Sant' Apollinare Nuove in Ravenna indicate her early and extensive cult outside of Sicily. She is the patroness of nurses, against eruptions of Mt. Etna and outbreak of fire, of bell-founders, and of Catania, Italy. BIBLIOGRAPHY: J. Kirsch, CE 1:203–204; Butler 1:255–256; G. Gordini, BiblSanct 1:320–327.

[F. MURPHY]

AGATHANGE (AGATHANGELUS) OF VENDÔME, BL. (secular name François Noury; 1598–1638), French Capuchin missionary and martyr. Sent to the mission at Aleppo after his ordination (1628), he worked there till 1633, when he went with *Cassian of Nantes to Cairo to labor for the reunion of the Copts with the Holy See. On their way to Ethiopia to establish a mission, they were seized and condemned to death. They died at Gondar Aug. 7, 1638, hanged with their own cinctures and stoned by the crowd. They were beatified Jan. 1, 1905. BIBLIOGRAPHY: L. de Vannes, *Deux martyrs capuchins* (1905); R. da Cesinale, *Storia delle mis-*

sioni dei Cappuccini (1867–73) 3:747; B. d'Arenzano, BiblSanct 1:336–337.

[P. K. MEAGHER]

AGATHANGELOS, the supposed early Armenian historian responsible for the Life of St. *Gregory the Illuminator, the Apostle of Armenia, whose contemporary he claimed to be. Probably the name Agathangelos is simply a pen name used by an author whose identity is otherwise unknown. The writer indicated the work was written at the command of King Trdat (c.248–314) but some textual critics claim it cannot be earlier than c.450.

[A. J. JACOPIN]

AGATHO, ST. (d. 681), **POPE** from 678. Like all the popes of this period, A. was absorbed in the struggle of the Church against the Monothelites. He promoted the Council of Constantinople III (The Sixth Ecumenical Council) and sent three delegates to preside. In a letter to the Emperor Constantine IV, he declared that the Holy Spirit kept the pope from error in matters of doctrine. He stood by Wilfrid of York against the Archbishop of Canterbury's division of Wilfrid's diocese. Also, he sent a legate, John, to win the English Church to the liturgical practices of Rome. BIBLIOGRAPHY: C. M. Aherne, NCE 1:197; J. S. Brusher, *Popes through the Ages* (1959); Mann 1.2:22–48; I. Daniele, BiblSanct 1:341–342.

[P. F. MULHERN]

AGDE, COUNCIL OF, a council convened at Agde in S France in 506 under the leadership of St. Caesarius of Arles and with the endorsement of the Arian Visigoth King Alaric. This proved to be the first significant gathering of all bishops from that part of Gaul under the rule of the Visigoths. Its 47 authentic statutes, written by St. Caesarius, clarified several matters of ecclesiastical discipline, e.g., clerical celibacy, administration of church property by bps., canonical age for ordination to major orders, obligation of the laity to receive the Eucharist on Christmas, Easter, and Pentecost, and several regulations concerning monastic life. BIBLIOGRAPHY: A. Rastoul, DHGE 1:929–930; F. Cabrol, DACL 1:871–877.

[F. H. BRIGHAM]

AGE, CANONICAL. In the RC and Eastern Catholic Churches rights are recognized and duties are imposed upon their subjects with a view to their moral and physical stage of development. Hence, for various provisions of law certain different stages are recognized: infancy, which embraces those who have not completed their 7th year; the age of reason, which is presumed to be achieved at the completion of infancy; puberty, which is presumed to be achieved by the female at the age of 12, and by the male at 14; adulthood, which is attained under the Latin code at 21 and in Oriental legislation at 18; and old age is attained at 65. Marriage contracted before the age of puberty is considered invalid by reason of the diriment impediment of insufficient age.

According to the 1966 revision of the law requiring abstinence and fast, the law of fasting begins to oblige a person when he becomes 21, and ceases to oblige at the completion of his 60th year; the law of abstinence begins to oblige when one is 14 and continues to oblige as long as its observance involves no serious difficulty or threat to health. With the attainment of adulthood, one enjoys the full exercise of his rights; as long as an individual is a minor, he is subject to the authority of his parents, except in certain matters in which the law regards minors as exempt from parental authority. Before an individual, male or female, has reached the age of 14, he is not subject to ecclesiastical censures *latae sententiae*. To become a novice in a religious institute, one must be at least 16. Certain ecclesiastical offices are regarded by the Church as requiring more than a minimum maturity. Thus, unless one is dispensed from this age requirement, a man may not be ordained deacon before he is 22, a priest before he is 24, a bishop before he is 30. He must be 35 before being appointed novice master, and 40 before being named a regular confessor for female religious.

[P. K. MEAGHER]

AGE, CANONICAL (Impediment to Marriage). There are 13 diriment impediments to marriage in the Code of Canon Law that render a person incapable of making a valid contract of marriage. Defect of age or nonage is one of them. According to Roman law the legal age for marriage was for a male 14 years and for a female 12 years. This calculation was followed by the previous canon law, and by English civil law, till the rule was changed in 1929 by The Age of Marriage Act, which makes the marriage void if either party is under sixteen. In the U.S. the legal age is variable according to different states. In the Code of Canon Law it is laid down: "A male before the completion of the 16th year and a female before the completion of the 14th year cannot marry validly." (CIC c. 1067, par. 1.) This enactment goes on the assumption that the young people under the minimum age are too immature in mind and body to take on the responsibilities of a marriage partnership. It would however be rash to suppose that young people above the legal age are necessarily sufficiently mature to give a valid marriage consent. Otherwise fewer marriages would be before matrimonial tribunals, where the plea for annulment is increasingly being brought on the grounds of lack of due discretion, or insufficient natural judgment in either party. And this problem cannot be resolved as in former jurisprudence with reference to the capacity to perform the marriage act alone. Also, there are increasing numbers of pathological personalities who are incapable of accepting the burdens of the married state. This mental condition may be curable or not; and some people remain retarded.

A word of warning is offered to the effect that although marriage contracted above the minimum legal age may be valid, "pastors of souls shall take care to deter from it young people who have not reached the age at which, according to the customs of the country, marriage is usually contracted." (CIC c. 1067, par. 2).

[A. FARRELL]

AGE OF REASON, as understood here, is the age at which a person has advanced in his mental development to the point that he is capable of forming and applying to his own actions true moral judgments at least in some matters. It does not mean that he is yet aware of the whole content of the moral law, but simply that he is able to distinguish some right from wrong, and hence has become capable of some morally good action on the one hand, and of some sin on the other. In canon law this capacity is presumed to be attained at the age of seven. However, this is merely a presumption of law and, like other presumptions, ought in particular cases to yield to fact. It is possible that a child of seven, or even older, has not in fact reached that point of development; or it is possible in other cases that some children achieve the capacity for moral judgment at earlier ages. Individual cases must be judged on their own merits, and blanket assertions that all children of seven, or that no children of that age, are capable of some sin and hence ready to be introduced to the practice of confession, are to be avoided.

[P. K. MEAGHER]

AGED, CARE OF. The aged are identified as those over 65. With the proliferation of advanced drugs and medication, many of the aged are able to survive the ills and pains of old age. What is less likely, however, is that they will survive the loneliness that our economic and social arranging has imposed on them. Formerly, the care of the aged was a family affair. The Christian family esp. saw in them an added opportunity to show its love. In the Middle Ages the elderly were cared for by monasteries, convents, and guilds. After the suppression of these, the charitable work done by them was neglected. English poor laws of the 16th and of the 19th cent. merely reflect the common notion that poverty was a result of voluntary acceptance on the part of the poor and aged. In America, esp. among Catholics, homes for the aged multiplied during the late 19th cent. and during the mid-50s of the 20th. The governments of nations have a responsibility toward their elderly citizens. What forms this responsibility takes will depend largely on the prior realization they have of their moral obligations toward the elderly. This is not to say that persons and families are free from an obligation to care for the aged. If one speaks of the rights of the elderly, one must speak as well of the obligations such rights impose on some other group. BIBLIOGRAPHY: M. A. McBride, NCE 1:198–200.

[J. R. RIVELLO]

AGEN, suffragan diocese to Bordeaux (suffragan to Toulouse 1802–22) whose cathedral bears the name of the martyr St. Capracius (d. *c*.300). Its Christian population suffered continued persecution from the Romans and Arian Visigoths until the 6th century. Plundered successively by the Saracens (732) and Normans (848), it witnessed both the ascendancy of the Albigensians who built a church there (1145–55) and their decline. It was the scene of many battles of the Hundred Years War between the French and English. Though repeatedly disturbed by local religious and civil discord and beleaguered by the influence of Jansenism and Gallicanism, its population remains predominantly Catholic today. BIBLIOGRAPHY: E. Jarry, *Catholicisme* 1:203–205.

[F. H. BRIGHAM]

AGENDA, in its primary sense, liturgical uses or the books prescribing them. The Council of Carthage (390) applied the term to the entire eucharistic service; some early African liturgies limit it to the anaphora. Throughout the Middle Ages the word designated the liturgical practices and books proper to particular places; after the Reformation the term fell into disuse among Roman Catholics. Among the German Lutherans the word has always signified the prescribed forms of service and the service book itself (see CHURCH ORDER). In another sense the 17th-cent. English theologians distinguished between *agenda*, matters of religious practice, and *credenda*, essentials of belief. BIBLIOGRAPHY: Enc-RelKnow 1:84–86.

[N. KOLLAR]

AGENDA CONTROVERSY, the polemics that arose when King Frederick William III of Prussia, seeking to promote a union of Reformed and Lutheran Churches in Prussia, introduced in 1822 and later forcibly imposed new liturgical agenda that had been drawn up by himself.

AGENDE (Ger., from Lat. *agenda*, things to be done), the liturgical orders of worship, esp. in the German Lutheran Church (corresponding to the *ordo missae*, etc.), and the liturgical books containing them. BIBLIOGRAPHY: C. Mahrenholz, MGG 1:137–148.

[A. DOHERTY]

AGENNĒTOS, Greek adjective meaning uncreated or self existent, but spelled with two n's it could mean unbegotten as distinct from *agenetos* (uncreated). Arius and his followers used the term without distinguishing its two meanings, stressing that God the Father alone is unbegotten and uncreated. Therefore they concluded that because the Son is begotten, he is therefore created, for there cannot be two self existent principles *(duo agennetous archas)*. The Council of Nicaea declared that the Son was uncreated *(ou poiethenta)* but begotten *(genethenta)*. In his discourses against the Arians, St. Athanasius uses *agennetos* in the sense of uncreated in his defense of the Nicene Creed to affirm the unity of essence between the Father and the Son. BIBLIOGRAPHY: J. N. D. Kelly, *Early Christian Doctrine* (2d ed. 1960) 226–237; Quasten 3:8, 26, 195, 306, 308.

[F. H. BRIGHAM]

AGENT, from Lat. *agere,* to act, in Scholastic philosophy as deriving from Aristotle, one of the four causes. The explanation of change includes the subject undergoing it (the material cause), the determinant perfection acquired (formal cause; form) the initiator of change (the mover, efficient or agent cause) and the aim of the agent's action (final cause). The idea of the initiator or mover is transferred to include every cause that by an action based on the cause's perfective power produces an effect. Thus an agent is a thing or person bringing about an effect by a transitive, externalized action, or one bringing about an inward, immanent, action whether cognitive or affective. Theology considers God to be the first principal agent, the universal cause of being in its initiation and continuance; creatures, both by transitive and immanent action, to be principal causes of particular modes of being, and as subordinated to God's agency. A principal agent produces an effect proportionate to its own power; an instrumental agent (e.g., a sacrament) produces an effect proportionate to the user's power. In moral theology the moral agent is the person whose action is a reasoned choice, for which the agent is thus responsible.

[J. R. RIVELLO]

AGERICUS (AIRY), ST. (*c.* 521–591), bp. of Verdun from *c.* 554, friend of Gregory of Tours and Venantius Fortunatus, a builder of churches, esteemed for his virtuous life and generosity toward the poor. He enjoyed the favor of King Sigibert I and his son Childebert, though he strove manfully, if not very successfully, to put an end to the barbarous practice in vogue among those of princely rank of murdering their opponents and rivals. BIBLIOGRAPHY: C. L.-R. Desreumaux, BiblSanct 1:351–352; Butler 4:454–455.

AGES, SPIRITUAL, stages identified by spiritual writers in the growth of the soul as it moves onward toward God. These stages are given different names by different writers, and sometimes the classification appears based on the practice of virtue, and sometimes upon the type of prayer that is markedly characteristic of, but not the exclusive preoccupation of, each stage. These two different points of view, however, imply no contradiction, because growth in virtue goes hand in hand with development in one's prayer life. The number commonly assigned to these stages is three, and many writers identify them as the stages (ages, or ways) of purgation, illumination, and union (or perfection), the first being proper to beginners, the second to those who have achieved some progress (proficients), the third to those who have attained a notable degree of perfection. The beginner is dependent, but not exclusively, on vocal prayer, the proficient on meditation, and those who have achieved perfection on contemplation. St. Teresa of Avila enumerates not three but four stages of development in the life of prayer, using the metaphor of the different methods by which a garden may be watered. In the first stage, the water is drawn from a well and carried to the garden; in the second, a windlass and bucket are employed; in the third, water is supplied by irrigation coming from a river or stream; in the fourth, the water is, like rain, obtained not by one's own effort but by God's gifts. BIBLIOGRAPHY: R. Garrigou-Lagrange, *Three Ages of the Interior Life* (2 v., tr. M. T. Doyle, 1947).

[P. K. MEAGHER]

AGESANDER (Hagesandros), a Rhodian mentioned by Pliny in his *Natural History* with Polydorus and Athenodorus as sculptors of the Laocoön. (Inscriptions found at Lindus in Rhodes date A. and Athenodorus 42-21 B.C.) The Laocoön (50 B.C., though some date it as late as 25 B.C.) is the most significant example of Hellenistic baroque characterized by emphatic descriptive realism in minute anatomical detail, pathos, and violent contortion.

[M. J. DALY]

AGGAI, BOOK OF, see HAGGAI, BOOK OF.

AGGEUS, BOOK OF, see HAGGAI, BOOK OF.

AGGIORNAMENTO (Ital., updating), a term popularized by Pope John XXIII. The word is now used to indicate the attempt to modernize the RC Church's teachings and practices so that contemporary men will better understand and accept them. It is an ongoing process that has only begun to take shape; yet certain distinctive trends have gradually emerged, indicating the probable trend of Catholic thought in the immediate future.

Theology before Vatican II was largely characterized by a systematic approach that highly valued the integration of reality into a comprehensive world-view based on a comparatively few, solid theological principles. Now, proponents of desystematization argue that contemporary reality is too rich and manifold to be limited by any current or past world-view. Desystematization, they think, enlarges the possibility of genuine and meaningful progress, since the development of doctrinal and moral thought would not be left exclusively to the explicitation of formerly implicit principles. Newer principles could be deduced from the knowledge available today. Desystematization is a reaction to the extreme forms of systematic theology that tended to reject new thought and the new stirrings of the Spirit in the Church. Still, desystematization itself has the endemic danger of becoming not only iconoclastic but also anarchic.

A second trend is the stress laid on personal, usually at the expense of legal, natural, or institutional values. Allied to the philosophic position loosely termed personalism, exponents of this movement severely condemn the encroachment of man-made restrictions upon the rights and dignity of human persons. They oppose various political, economic, social, educative, and religious systems that have been tolerated in the past because of ignorance or necessity. There are differences of opinion as to what institutional stresses can be abandoned or lessened, and also as to whether evolution or revolution, a gradual and nonviolent or a quick and violent change, offers the better method of establishing the primacy of personal values.

The coming of age of the layman is still another recognizable trend. In an updated Church he should no longer be taken as a passive, voiceless, spiritually incompetent follower. He should be accorded his right to be heard both in theology and in church affairs. The new emphasis on the role of the laity in the life of the Church gives the movement toward *aggiornamento* a "secular," as opposed to a more "sacred," direction.

Aggiornamento also stresses *ecumenism. Vatican II officially designated non-Catholic Christian bodies as separated Churches and communions. There is no longer talk of reunion with Rome, with its connotation of the return of prodigal sons to an unerring father. This is now replaced by emphasis on the common Christian search for the activity of the Spirit with each tradition contributing, according to its capacity, insights gained since the scandalous divisions of Christianity, with the hope that eventually the mutual mistakes of the past will cease to influence the present and the future.

There are many other features to be observed in this movement. In addition to its original denotation of updating, it is acquiring the humbling connotation of "catching up with" the knowledge of reality (esp. regarding human existence and behavior) already available from nontheological sources. RC theology takes all this seriously and is at the present time suffering some of the crises and the inevitable uncertainties of a new movement.

[C. NEELY]

AGGRAVATION, a term often used in RC moral theology in reference to the increased malice an evil act may have by reason of some attendant circumstance. A circumstance is usually called aggravating, however, only if it adds no new specific kind of malice but merely intensifies the kind of malice that characterizes the act apart from the circumstance. It is, other things being equal, more wicked to steal a larger than a smaller sum of money, yet in either case the act would be theft. The larger quantity stolen in one, as compared with the other theft, would constitute an aggravating circumstance.

[P. K. MEAGHER]

AGGRESSIVE DRIVE, in general psychology, the competitive, pugnacious, belligerent urges in men and animals, esp. if, in people, it is habitual. In Freudian psychology the aggressive drive is one of the two basic instinctual drives (the other being the sexual or libidinal drive). This aggressive drive is conceived as a source of continually generated aggressive energies which cause increasing psychic tension which must be discharged in hostile, destructive, or hurtful activities. The aggressive drive always operates in conjunction with the libidinal drive, providing, for example, the sadistic element in libidinal activity. When turned against the self, the aggressive drive is conceived as provoking suicidal tendencies. BIBLIOGRAPHY: W. W. Meissmer, "Toward a Theology of Human Aggression," *Journal of Religion and Health* 10 (1971) 324–332.

[M. E. STOCK]

AGGRESSOR, UNJUST, a term used in moral theology to designate one who without justifying cause attacks the person, good name, or belongings of another. The term appears most frequently in questions that involve the right to self-defense in the face of attack. It is commonly held that natural justice entitles a man to defend himself with force proportionate to the attack, to kill if necessary a would-be murderer, but not a pickpocket. Aggression is constituted by the use of violence or by immediate preparation for it. Its injustice consists in the violation of the rights of the intended victim; thus it is not present in the forcible arrest of a criminal or the good soldier who shoots his way into an enemy stronghold. BIBLIOGRAPHY: J. McHugh and C. Callan, *Moral Theology,* (rev. and enlg. E. Farrell, 1958) 2:109–112.

[T. GILBY]

AGGREY, JAMES EMMAN KWEGYIR (1875–1927), African educator. Born in Ghana, then known as Gold Coast, A. was educated in Methodist mission schools and at Livingstone College, Salisbury, North Carolina. After teaching at Livingstone College, he returned to Africa and became vice-principal of University College, Achimoto. He made a notable contribution to education and religious development in his native land. BIBLIOGRAPHY: E. W. Smith, *Aggrey of Africa. A Study in Black and White* (1930).

[P. K. MEAGHER]

AGHTAMAR, CATHOLICATE OF. When in 1137 Gregorios III Pahlavouni was elected Armenian catholicos of Sis, Bp. David of Aghtamar (a small island in Lake Van), refused to recognize him; it was David's claim that Aghtamar had been the see of the Armenian catholicos from 931 until its patriarch Vahan was unjustly deposed at a synod in Ani in 969. David's position was strengthened by the fact that he was in possession of important relics—right hand, staff, and girdle—of St. Gregory the Illuminator, founder of the Armenian Church. A synod at Kara Dagh deposed and excommunicated David, but he continued to govern his see. The Persians, in an effort to foster disunity among the Armenians, bestowed the title Catholicos of All Armenia upon a successor of David in 1461. The tiny catholicate continued in existence until the troubles of 1917. Its jurisdiction was limited to the island of Aghtamar and a few villages around Lake Van, but it contained 300 churches and 50 monasteries.

[J. MEIJER]

AGIL, ST. (*c*.590–*c*.650), abbot, missionary. A. was educated and became a monk at the abbey of Luxeuil. He was ordained before going to Bavaria as a missionary. He refused the see of Langres, and became the first abbot of Rebais in 636. BIBLIOGRAPHY: C. Lefebvre, BiblSanct 1:361–362

[H. JACK]

AGILITY, one of the four qualities with which the glorified bodies of the risen just will be endowed, according to scholastic theology's amplification of St. Paul's doctrine on the risen body (1 Cor 15.42–44). It is commonly interpreted as ability to respond with swift movement and action to the soul's desire.

[P. K. MEAGHER]

AGILULF OF COLOGNE, ST. (d. 750 or 751), bishop. He supported the reforms of Boniface, attending the Frankish synod of 747. He has been wrongly identified with the martyr Agilulf (d. March 31, 716) and with the Benedictine monk Agilulf, erroneously said to have been simultaneously abbot of Stavelot and bp. of Cologne (after 745). BIBLIOGRAPHY: M. F. McCarthy, NCE 1:203; A. M. Zimmermann, BiblSanct 1:362–363.

[M. F. MCCARTHY]

AGIOS O THEOS (HOLY GOD), ancient Greek hymn, so called from its first three words and common to several Eastern liturgies. Since the 11th cent., the Roman liturgy has included it among the *reproaches sung during the veneration of the cross on Good Friday until recently.

[F. H. BRIGHAM]

AGLIPAY, GREGORIO (1860–1940), first bp. of the *Philippine Independent Church, sometimes popularly called the Aglipayan Church. He was ordained a RC priest in 1889. During the Philippine Revolution (1898) against Spanish rule, the Filipino rebel leaders made him a military vicar general in order to take over government of the RC Church. He was excommunicated (1899) by the abp. of Manila and became a guerrilla fighter. After the U.S. took over the Philippines, the nationalist leader, Isabelo de los Reyes, Sr. (1864–1938), set up the Philippine Independent Church (1902), and A. was elected supreme bishop. He received consecration from 12 priests, but never from a bishop. Until his death he remained head of his Church, which dwindled in numbers after an initial success. In 1935 he ran unsuccessfully for president of the Philippines. BIBLIOGRAPHY: P. S. de Achútegui and M. A. Bernad, *Religious Revolution in the Philippines: The Life and Church of Gregorio Aglipay* (2v., 1960–66).

[T. C. O'BRIEN]

AGLIPAYANS, members of the *Philippine Independent Church, popularly named for Gregorio *Aglipay.

[T. C. O'BRIEN]

AGNELLI, GIUSEPPE (1626–1706), Italian Jesuit writer. He entered the Society in 1637 and was successively professor and rector in several Jesuit colleges. The last half of his religious life he spent in catechetical writing along with devotional materials, sermons, and commentaries on the Exercises. BIBLIOGRAPHY: Sommervogel 1:65–68.

[H. JACK]

AGNELLUS OF PISA, BL. (d. 1232), led the Franciscans into England in 1224, was the first superior of the order there, and began their connection with study of science at Oxford. BIBLIOGRAPHY: Thomas of Eccleston, *De adventu Fratrum Minorum in Angliam* (ed. A. G. Little, 2d ed., 1951); C. Mariotti, *Il beato Agnello da Pisa ed i Frati Minori in Inghilterra* (1895); L. Hardick, NCE 1:203–204; G. V. Sabatelli, BiblSanct 1:367–369; Butler 1:589–590.

[J. L. GRASSI]

AGNELLUS OF RAVENNA (805–*c*.846), a secular priest in Ravenna, possibly a titular abbot of St. Mary's and St. Bartholomew, author of a history of Ravenna that was antipapal on all crucial questions. BIBLIOGRAPHY: A. Ferrua, EncCatt 1:465–467.

[H. JACK]

AGNES, ST., (d. *c*.304), virgin and martyr executed at Rome. Though her name appears in the Roman Canon, in the various martyrologies of the East and West, and in the writings of Pope St. Damasus, St. Ambrose, and Prudentius, very little is known about her life or manner of death. According to a 6th-cent. legend she was a beautiful young girl who rejected the suitors for her hand. Accused of being a Christian, she was sent to a house of prostitution. One who looked lustfully upon her lost his sight but regained it through her prayers. Condemned and executed, she was buried in a catacomb on the Via Salaria. A still extant basilica was built over her tomb, where two lambs, from whose wool archiepiscopal pallia will be woven, are blessed each year on her feast. In the 4th century, St. Agnes is represented with her arms outstretched in prayer. From the 6th cent. on she is represented with a lamb, no doubt because of the similarity of her name "Agnes" (from the Greek *agnē*, pure or holy) and *agnus* (Latin for lamb). BIBLIOGRAPHY: E. Josi, BiblSanct 1:382–407; Butler 1:133–137.

[J. COSTELLOE]

AGNES OF ASSISI, ST., (1197–1253), Poor Clare abbess. Soon after her sister Clare decided to follow Francis of Assisi, A. joined her at San Damiano and assisted in organizing the Poor Ladies. Francis sent her as abbess to Monticelli because the Benedictine nuns there had asked tó join the new order. In 1253 she returned to San Damiano in time to witness Clare's death, and died soon after. BIBLIOGRAPHY: *Legend and Writings of St. Clare of Assisi* (ed. I. Brady and M. F. Laughlin, 1953); Butler 4:358–359; A. Brunacci, BiblSanct 1:369–370; for iconography, P. Bruzzichelli, BiblSanct 1:370–374.

[O. J. BLUM]

AGNES OF BOHEMIA, BL. (*c*.1205–*c*.1282), abbess. Of royal blood, A. was destined for marriage, but succeeded in keeping her freedom. She and her brother established, among other benefactions, a convent of Poor Clares in Prague where she received the veil in 1236. By nomination of Gregory IX, she was abbess for a brief term. BIBLIOGRAPHY: Butler 1:462; G. Cerafogli, BiblSanct 1:374–375.

[H. JACK]

AGNES OF JESUS, VEN. (1602–34), mystic. A. became first a lay, then a choir sister, and finally prioress of the Dominicans at Langeac. Her life was marked by mystical phenomena, including the stigmata. J. *Olier saw her many times in vision during her lifetime and after her death; she encouraged his work, made predictions that eventually proved true, and aided in his spiritual development. BIBLIOGRAPHY: AS 8 (1853) 381; M. M. Gorce, DSAM 1:252–253; the basic biog. was by M. de Lantages (1655); S. Mattei, BiblSanct 1:413–414.

[P. K. MEAGHER]

AGNES OF MONTEPULCIANO, ST. (*c*.1268–1317), Dominican nun, patroness of Montepulciano. She entered the Sisters of the Sack at the age of 9, became bursar when 14, and later abbess of a monastery at Proceno, which she had helped to found. In 1306 she became prioress of, and had incorporated into the Dominican Order, a monastery that the citizens of Montepulciano, impressed by her holiness, built for her. Simplicity, ardor, and austerity marked her spirituality. She was favored by apparitions of the Christ Child, the Virgin Mary, and the angels. Cross-shaped particles "like manna" often fell upon her while she was praying. She died after a painful illness. BIBLIOGRAPHY: Raymond of Capua, *Vita*, AS April 2:790–810; AnnDom 23:519–546; A. Walz, *Die hl. Agnes v. Montepulciano* (1922); G. Di Agresti, BiblSanct 1:375–381.

[W. A. HINNEBUSCH]

AGNES OF POITIERS, ST. (d. *c*.589), abbess. She was an adopted daughter of Chlotar I and Radegunda. Radegunda founded the convent of the Holy Cross in Poitiers; A. was named the first abbess. Her saintly character was attested to by Venantius Fortunatus in letters and in verse. BIBLIOGRAPHY: C. Lefebvre, BiblSanct 1:412–413.

[H. JACK]

AGNETS, the Slavonic word for the square piece cut from the round cake of bread at the *prosphora* or preparation of the liturgy in the Byzantine rite. The cutting symbolizes the sacrifice of the lamb of God.

[F. H. BRIGHAM]

AGNI, Vedic god of fire who represents not only earthly fire but that of lightning and of the sun as well. Because sacrificial fire consumes man's offerings to the gods, Agni was conceived as a priest-god, a mediator between heaven and mankind, and to him were attributed the functions of forgiveness and punishment.

[P. K. MEAGHER]

AGNOETAE (Gr. for ignorant), a Monophysite sect founded by Themistius, a deacon of Alexandria. Basing their doctrine on Mk 13.32 and Jn 11.35, they attributed an ignorance in some matters to the human mind of Christ. They were condemned by Eulogius, patriarch of Alexandria (580–607) and by Pope Gregory I. The name *Agnoetae* has also been applied to Arians and Nestorians for their derogation of the perfection of Christ. BIBLIOGRAPHY: A. Vacant, DTC 1:586–596; V. Ermoni, DHGE 1:992–995. *KENOSIS.

[G. T. DENNIS]

AGNOSTICISM, in general, not knowing about religious truth; more specifically, not having rational certitude about it. The term is not derived from the Latin *agnoscere,* but from the Greek *agignosko,* the alpha being privative. It was first used by T. H. Huxley in 1869 at a meeting of what was later called the Metaphysical Society. There are two accounts of its original meaning, one given by Huxley and the other by R. H. Hutton. According to Huxley the word was designed as antithetic to the "Gnostic" of early church history, and was intended to be opposed not simply to theism and Christianity, but also to atheism and pantheism. He meant the word to cover with a mantle of respectability not so much ignorance about God but the strong conviction that the problem of his existence is insoluble. Hutton's recollection was that Huxley borrowed it from St. Paul's reference to the inscription on the altar to the unknown god (Acts 17.23). Both explanations show a want of precision: the Gnostics opposed their spiritual knowledge to the historical revelation of the Church, and the altar of which St. Paul spoke was dedicated to an unknown rather than an unknowable god.

Taken in its broadest sense, agnosticism should always be defined in a given system of reference. It may concern the so-called natural truths of religion: the existence and nature of God, the immortality of the soul, the moral law. Thus as a rationalist a man may be skeptical about these matters and yet as a believer be an ardent Christian. Or it may concern specifically Christian truths of faith, at various stages or periods of articulation: thus a believer may be agnostic about an institutional Church, a Presbyterian about episcopacy, an Anglican about the pope, or a Roman Catholic about a current usage concerning indulgences.

Agnosticism admits differences of degree as well as of object. The absence of certitude that characterizes the agnostic may range from having no more than a merely opinionative judgment to a condition of doubt, either just negative or more positive, that stops short of a definite rejection of religious truth.

Agnosticism has several styles. The reverent agnosticism that hesitates before anthropomorphism or cocksureness about divine things is nobly represented by Moses Maimonides, and indeed by the *theologia negativa* of a high mystical tradition in Christianity. Then there is the wistful agnosticism of earnest thinkers who would like to believe but cannot honestly bring themselves to do so; they were prominent in the Victorian era, when the term first came to be widely used. Finally there is the complacent agnosticism of those who do not bother or do not care to make the effort required to find out about eternal truths. Culpability enters, if at all, only with these last; it may be assessed in accordance with the rules governing the influence of ignorance on moral responsibility, as when one is too lazy to discover what is important, or fears to discover it, lest it prove awkward.

Philosophical agnosticism is traceable to nominalism. *William of Ockham explicitly denied that the human intellect can with certainty demonstrate the existence of one infinite God. For Ockham and other nominalists the abstraction to universality is not part of the structure of being but only of the signification of words. Later the central emphasis of the empiricism of Hume was that all knowledge came through sense experience. This led him to the affirmation that necessity and causality are purely mental rather than objectively real, and hence the human mind can never reason with certitude to God's existence. Kant subscribed to Hume's critique of causality, but viewed the construction of its critical philosophy as a synthesis of empiricism and rationalism. The importance of Kant, esp. in Protestant circles, cannot be overstressed. Kant's *Critique of Pure Reason* in the minds of most Protestants—and others—has given the *coup de grâce* to any possible proof of God's existence. Even though Kant attempts to restore the idea of God as a postulate of moral consciousness, and may have intended to defend religion against rationalism, his idea of reason as purely theoretical ultimately leads to skepticism and, more specifically, to agnosticism.

Comte saw the theological and metaphysical explanations of the world as superseded stages of human thought. His "positivism" would not connect phenomena by the principle of causality since only sequences and resemblances can be empirically observed. Under the same influence philosophical agnosticism took the form of the theory of "the unconditioned" in the works of W. Hamilton (*Philosophy of the Unconditioned,* 1829) and Herbert Spencer (*Principles,* 1862). These works were widely read and accepted in the 19th century. Their theory of knowledge was based on the major principle that an object which cannot be conditioned by either classification or relation is unknowable. Since God, by all accounts, is infinite and absolute, he cannot be known.

Protestant theologians generally, moved perhaps by implicit Kantianism and by the failure to make any, or at least any sharp, distinction between natural and supernatural knowledge, and devoted to the absolute primacy of God's Word and the response of faith, could be classified as believing agnostics. RC thinkers, on the other hand, following Aquinas (ThAq ST 1a, 2), have asserted that God's existence can be proved, even though they admit that this may be possible only to a few over a long time and with admixture of error. Vatican Council I paid what Chesterton called a high compliment to the power of human reason by insisting as of faith that God's existence can be proved by human reason (Wis 13; Rom 1.20; D 2853, 3004, 3026, 3475, 3538, 3892). BIBLIOGRAPHY: H. de Lubac, *Drama of Atheistic Humanism* (1949); J. Collins, *God in Modern Philosophy* (1959); R. Jolivet, *God of Reason* (tr. D. M. Pontifex, 1959).

[T. GILBY; U. VOLL; P. K. MEAGHER]

AGNOSTOS THEOS (Greek for unknown god), used by St. Paul in Acts 17.23 when he said he had seen an altar in Athens with the inscription in Greek "to an unknown god." Honor was often paid to gods whose names were not known to the worshiper but who may have done favors for him and so must not be overlooked.

[C. C. O'DONNELL]

AGNUS DEI, the Latin of the title *Lamb of God given to Jesus by John the Baptist (Jn 1.29). The term has three uses: (1) It stands for the verse employed in the Roman rite at the conclusion of litanies and at the *Fraction at Mass, "Lamb of God, who take away the sins of the world, have mercy on us." This was introduced into the Roman Mass by Pope Sergius I (687–701), probably as a replacement of a variable chant. With the disappearance of the multiple fraction in the 9th cent., the petition was made no more than three times. The conclusion of the third petition, "grant us peace," was introduced in the 10th or 11th cent., either as a preparation for the kiss of peace, or because of the calamities of the time. The chant was reserved to the clerics from the 8th cent. until the modern liturgical movement. The repetitive chanting of the verse was reintroduced in 1967. (2) The term also refers to a wax medallion bearing the figure of a lamb. It is blessed by the pope in the first year of his pontificate and every seventh year afterwards. It is made of the remnants of the previous year's paschal candle. This custom first is referred to in the 9th century. (3) It is the name given to the image of a lamb when used as a symbol either of the Blessed Sacrament or of Christ as victim. Generally the lamb is haloed and bears a cross or pennon. BIBLIOGRAPHY: J. A. Jungmann, *Mass of the Roman Rite* (tr. F. A. Brunner, 2 v., 1951–55) 2:332–340; J. Froger, *Les Chants de la Messe aux VIIIe et IXe siècles* (1950).

[N. KOLLAR]

AGNUS DEI (music), the last sung section of the Mass Ordinary, based on Jn 1.29. This three-fold supplication was added to the Mass during the reign of Pope Sergius I (687–701), though it and the *Kyrie Eleison were reported to have been used long before in the litanies of the rogation days. As with the other sections of the ordinary except for the Credo, the Agnus Dei was originally intended to be sung by the congregation. But W. Apel cites a direction in the *Ordo Romanus Primus* (PL 78:946) "*Archidiaconus . . . respicit in scholam et annuit eis ut dicant agnus dei*" (The archdeacon looks toward the schola and nods to them to sing the Agnus Dei). The result of this take-over by the schola was the introduction of more elaborate melodies. The three part structure of the Agnus Dei permits a variety of formal schemes. The similarity of the tripartite structure of the opening Kyrie and the closing Agnus Dei led composers to close the form of the polyphonic settings of the ordinary by using the same music for both sections, while in chant the Agnus Dei is usually an independent composition. BIBLIOGRAPHY: B. Stäblein, MGG 1:148–156; P. Wagner, *Einführung in die gregorianischen Melodien* (3 v., 1901–21); Apel GregCh; L. M. O. Duchesne, *Christian Worship: Its Origin and Evolution* (1931).

[P. J. MCCARTHY]

AGOBARD OF LYONS, (769–840), bishop. Consecrated *chorepiscopus* of Lyons (804), he succeeded Leidrad in 816. He vigorously opposed judicial ordeal, the heresy of Felix of Urgel, influence of Jews at court, the machinations of Empress Judith, weather magic and other superstitions, increasing centralization of government, its encroachment on the Church, and the liturgical allegories of Amalarius. He approved the first and joined the second baronial revolt against Louis I. After brief exile in Italy, he returned to his see. Reconciled to Louis, he died on a mission for him. Although he was virtually ignored during the Middle Ages, his works were rediscovered in 1605. His cult, recognized in Lyons, has never been ratified by the Roman Church. BIBLIOGRAPHY: A. Cabaniss, *Agobard of Lyons: Churchman and Critic* (1953); I. Cecchetti, BiblSanct 1:414–422.

[A. CABANISS]

AGONISTICI, roving bands of Donatist terrorists more commonly known as *Circumcellions. The name is derived from the Greek word *agon*, used to designate a martyr's contest. They also called themselves *milites Christi*. BIBLIOGRAPHY: Optatus, *De schism. Donat.* 3.4; Augustine, *Enarr. in Psalm.* 132.6. *DONATISTS.

[M. J. COSTELLOE]

AGONY IN THE GARDEN. The passages in Mk 14.32–42; Mt 26.36–46; Lk 22.40–46 that give the Synoptics' account of Jesus' agony in the garden. Mark's version is substantially the same as Matthew's. Luke's is shorter and different. Mark and Matthew mention Peter, James, and John, the three eye witnesses to the suffering of Jesus. It is Mark who calls the place Gethsemani (oil press), a place at the foot of the Mount of Olives which Jesus and his disciples visited frequently. All three Synoptics speak of Jesus' chalice of woe. Luke gives the most vivid portrayal of the agony when he says "his sweat fell to the ground like great drops of blood." (Lk. 22.44). Jesus removes himself a short distance and prays to the Father. The substance of his prayer is his acceptance of the Father's will. Luke alone speaks of an angel from heaven coming to give Jesus strength. Mark and Matthew mention that Jesus returns three times to the sleeping disciples. Luke gives only one time when Jesus returned. All three Synoptics tell of Jesus' counsel to his Disciples to pray that they not be put to the test. In this scene of the agony of Jesus his humanity is portrayed very realistically. He is one with us in this fear of death, one in all things except sin. John says Jesus crossed the Valley of Kidron and went into a garden there; probably Jesus and his disciples were well known to the owner who allowed them the use of it when they were looking for a quiet place. John does not mention any prayer or suffering here. He emphasizes the kingship of Christ during all of the Passion but he has carried the message of the agony to other places in his Gospel, esp. in chapter 12.

[C. C. O'DONNELL]

AGONY OF DEATH, the suffering of body and soul that sometimes accompanies one's passage from this life. Real suffering at the time of death is by no means a universal or necessary phenomenon. In some cases death occurs instantaneously and unexpectedly. In others, suffering is often dulled by coma or drugs. In many instances the dying person welcomes release from his physical troubles, and in a few at least he may long to be dissolved and to be with Christ. Thus what to the healthy may appear an unmitigated horror, may be viewed quite differently by a dying person. Still, there do exist cases in which death is difficult, and the Christian heart will reach out with compassion to those who have such a death to suffer, as well as to those who are not spiritually prepared for the trial. BIBLIOGRAPHY: K. Rahner, LTK 10:224–226.

[P. K. MEAGHER]

AGOSTINI, PAOLO (1593–1629), Italian composer and organist of the baroque period. A son-in-law and student of *Nanino, he provided music for several Roman churches and was *maestro di cappella* at St. Peter's from 1626 until his death. His sacred music—Masses, psalms, magnificats and motets—combines the *polychoral writing with authentic *stile antico* counterpoint. He was regarded by some as among the most ingenious musicians of the century because of his skill in harmonic, contrapuntal, and canonic writing; some of his works are composed in as many as 48 parts. Fourteen books of his liturgical pieces were published; much more is preserved in MS in the Vatican and other Roman libraries. BIBLIOGRAPHY: BukMusB; E. H. Pember, Grove DMM 1:70–71.

[P. MURPHY]

AGRAPHA (Gr., unwritten), designates words of Jesus not recorded in the four canonical Gospels. The NT itself refers to such sayings (Acts 20.35; 1 Th 4.15–17). Other sources include the NT MS *Codex Bezae,* which departs occasionally from the usual gospel text; the apocryphal gospels (esp. the gnostic Gospel of Thomas and other related papyri discovered in Egypt); the works of the Church Fathers; the Talmud; and Mohammedan writings. Much of the material is regarded as dependent in some way upon texts found in the canonical Gospels, and little historical value is attributed to most of the other sayings; however, a small number of them may well represent authentic traditions parallel to those that preserved the canonical words of Jesus. BIBLIOGRAPHY: J. Jeremias, *Unknown Sayings of Jesus* (tr. R. H. Fuller, rev. ed., 1964); J. Fitzmyer, "Oxyrhynchus *Logoi* of Jesus and the Coptic Gospel according to Thomas," ThSt 20 (1959) 505–560.

[P. KEARNEY]

AGREDA, MARY OF (also known as Mary of Jesus; 1602–65), Spanish Poor Clare mystic, much esteemed by Philip IV with whom she corresponded, and author of a controversial work called *Mystical City of God and the Divine History of the Virgin Mother of God* (3 v. 1670). In this she recorded what she claimed had been revealed to her in vision. The work was put on the Index in 1681, but the condemnatory decree was suspended later in the same year. Controversy concerning the book has continued. BIBLIOGRAPHY: H. Thurston, *Surprising Mystics* (ed. J. H. Crehan, 1955); Bremond 9:273–276.

[P. K. MEAGHER]

AGRICIUS OF TRIER, ST. (Agrecius, Agritius, Agroetius; d. c.335). Beyond the fact that he was a bishop and attended the Council of Arles (314), little is known of A. His name figures prominently in the legend of the Holy Coat of Trier. According to the story, A. was patriarch of Antioch, but was sent to Germany to restore Christianity at the request of St. *Helena. To facilitate his task, he took with him many relics, including the seamless robe of the Lord. Pope *Sylvester allegedly granted A. primacy over Gaul and Germany. BIBLIOGRAPHY: Butler 1:74–75; P. Bertocchi, BiblSanct 1:619–620.

[R. B. ENO]

AGRICOLA, ALEXANDER (c.1446–1506), Renaissance composer. A. held posts at Milan (1471–75), Cambrai (1476), the court of Charles VIII of France (1476–91), Mantua (c.1491), and finally the court of the Duke Philip the Fair (1500–06). His works include Masses, motets, and secular songs in French, Flemish, and Italian. His work resembles that of his predecessor Johannes Ockeghem in its concentration on detail, esp. in the interplay of rhythmic motives. Instead of song-like melodies, A. preferred long, rhythmically intricate lines made up of short fragments. He treated the *cantus firmus* with great freedom and often used the same music for sacred *motets and secular chansons. O. Petrucci published five of A.'s Masses in 1504, and included other works of A. in his various collections. BIBLIOGRAPHY: P. Müller, MGG 1:158–160; M. Picker, "Letter of Charles VIII of France Concerning Alexander Agricola," *Aspects of Medieval and Renaissance Music* (ed. J. LaRue, 1966) 665–672; Reese MusR; N. Bridgeman, "Age of Ockeghem and Josquin," NOHM 3:277–279.

[P. MURPHY]

AGRICOLA, JOHANN (*c*.1494–1566), German Reformer whose family name was Schneider (Schnitter), known also as Magister Islebius. A native of Eisleben, A. studied under Martin Luther at Wittenberg. He preached Lutheran doctrine in Frankfurt and Eisleben and in 1536 taught theology in Wittenberg. He came into bitter conflict with Luther by maintaining that the believer was freed from observance of the law of God. The *Formula of Concord rejected this view in its articles (5 and 6) on *law and gospel.

AGRICOLA, MICHAEL OLAVI (1508–57), Finnish Reformer. While studying at Wittenberg he was won over to Protestantism by reading the works of Luther and Melanchthon. He became Lutheran bp. of Turku and translated the NT and parts of the Old into Finnish. He was moderate in his doctrinal position and tolerated the continuance of many old beliefs and practices.

[P. K. MEAGHER]

AGRICOLA, RODOLPHUS FRISIUS HUYSMAN (1444–85), Dutch humanist and educator. He studied at Groningen, Erfurt, Cologne, and Louvain. At Pavia and Ferrara he perfected his Latin style, esp. in poetry, and achieved proficiency in Greek, without disdaining his native German. He promoted classical studies at Heidelberg. He belonged to the second generation of German humanists who prepared the way for Erasmus and others. His main works are *De inventione dialectica* and *De formando studio*. BIBLIOGRAPHY: J. Pietsch, DHGE 1:1025–26.

[J. E. LYNCH]

AGRICOLA, STEPHAN (KASTENBAUER, BOIUS; 1491–1547), Protestant theologian. A. studied at Vienna, becoming chaplain and preacher there in 1515; in 1519 he received a doctorate in theology. He joined the Augustinians at Regensburg, becoming prior in Rattenburg. Because he sympathized with Luther, he was jailed (1522), but escaped. After 1524, he was openly a Lutheran, and he preached at Augsburg, translated Bugenhagen's *Contra novum errorem de sacramentis*, which sharply rejected Zwingli's eucharistic teaching. He was one of the signers of the Schmaldkaldic Articles. BIBLIOGRAPHY: D. Albrecht, LTK 1:208–209; J. Pietsch, DHGE 1:1026.

[N. F. GAUGHAN]

AGRIPPA I AND II, the last two Jewish kings of Palestine. Agrippa I (*c*.10 B.C.–44 A.D.). He was the grandson of Herod the Great and was educated in Rome, where he developed friendships among the nobles. In A.D. 37 Caligula gave him the northeast territories that Herod, Philip, and Lysanias had ruled. Caligula gave him the additional territories of Galilee and Peraea (39 A.D.) and added Samaria and Judea in 41 A.D. To win the favor of the Pharisees he persecuted the Christians in Palestine. He was responsible for the death of the Apostle James and the imprisonment of Peter (Acts 12.1–6). He was one of the cruelest members of his family. He died suddenly at a public event (Acts 12.20–23). Agrippa II (A.D. 27–*c*.93). He was only 17 years old when his father Herod Agrippa I died. Because he was so young the Roman emperor Claudius placed the whole kingdom under a Roman procurator. Jewish religious affairs, however, were given over to Agrippa's uncle, Herod. In A.D. 50, 2 years after his uncle's death, Claudius appointed Agrippa in his uncle's place. He was consistently on the side of the Romans. Asked by the Roman procurator Porcius Festus to listen to St. Paul's appeal to the emperor, A. said Paul could have been set free by Festus if he had not appealed to Caesar. He remained king until his death, after which his territory was put under Roman administration. BIBLIOGRAPHY: C. Fabro, EncCatt 1:580–583.

[C. C. O'DONNELL]

AGRIPPA VON NETTESHEIM, HEINRICH CORNELIUS (1486–1535), philosopher, humanist, theologian, and reputed magician. His was an active life: he taught theology at Dôle and Cologne; was syndic (town orator) at Metz; physician at Geneva, Freiburg, and Lyons; and archivist and historiographer to Charles V. Openly interested in theosophy and magic, he defended magic as supreme wisdom by which men might arrive at knowledge of God and nature in his *De occulta philosophia* (1533). His *De . . . vanitate scientiarum* (1530) harshly criticized contemporary science and pretentious scholars. Though charged with heresy and with being sympathetic to the Reformation, A. remained Catholic throughout his life. BIBLIOGRAPHY: DE 1:70; C. G. Nauert, NCE 1:220–221.

[F. D. LAZENBY]

AGUADO, PEDRO DE (1538–1609?), Franciscan missionary. He first worked among the Indians in Cartagena, Colombia, then became guardian in the Bogotá monastery. He continued in Latin America in various capacities and wrote there his chronicle of the conquest of Venezuela and Colombia, *Recopilación historial*. BIBLIOGRAPHY: D. Ramos, NCE 1:221.

AGUESSEAU, HENRI FRANÇOIS D' (1668–1751), twice (1717–18 and 1720–22) chancellor of France, a man of considerable dignity of character who contributed to legal reform and, as a conscientious Gallican, opposed the bull *Unigenitus*.

[P. K. MEAGHER]

AGUIAR Y SEIYAS, FRANCISCO (d. 1698), archbishop. First as bishop of Michoacán and later abp. of Mexico City (1682), A. proved to be zealous and capable. Devoting himself to all the needs of his diocese, he built churches and convents and established a seminary.

[H. JACK]

AGUILAR, NICOLÁS (1741–1818), secular priest who studied under the Jesuits in Guatemala and in 1769 was ordained in San Salvador, where he became a pastor. In 1811 and again in 1814, he directed uprisings against the governor; both failed through mismanagement and vacillation. One of his brothers was deported; one, imprisoned; both were good priests and loyal. BIBLIOGRAPHY: S. Malaina, NCE 1:221–222.

[H. JACK]

AGUIRRE, JOSEPH SAENZ D', see SAENZ D'AGUIRRE, JOSEPH.

AGUSTÍN, ANTONIO (1517–86), humanist, scholar, bp., reformer. He took a degree in law at Bologna (1541), was appointed auditor of the Roman Rota (1544), sent as nuncio to England (1555), and became bp. of Alife (1556) and later of Lérida (1561). At the sessions of the Council of Trent (1562–63) he distinguished himself as an independent thinker. In consideration of his zealous efforts to carry out the reforms of Trent he was appointed to the see of Tarragona (1576). His writings include works on theology, classical philology, history, and Roman and canon law. His *De emendatione Gratiani dialogorum libri duo* laid the foundation for the history of the sources of canon law. BIBLIOGRAPHY: L. Serrano, DHGE 1:1077–80; E. Magnin, DDC 1:628–630; C. L. Hohl, NCE 1:222.

AGYMNIANS, Manichees of the 7th cent. who opposed intercourse with women on the grounds that marriage was evil and not of divine origin. Their way of life, without women (Gr. *a gune*), occasioned their name.

[F. H. BRIGHAM]

AHAB (ACHAB), the son of Omri; king of Israel, 869–850 B.C. His marriage to Jezebel, daughter of the king of Tyre, was an arrangement probably made by Omri to ally Israel with Tyre (1 Kg 16.29–31). Ahab allowed Jezebel considerable freedom to encourage the fertility cult of Baal and Asherah. He met with strong resistance from Elijah and other prophets, in the light of whose opposition the account of his reign is recorded in 1 Kg 17.1–22.38. He allowed himself to be duped by Jezebel into an immoral possession of Naboth's vineyard (1 Kg 21.1–24). He died bravely from an arrow wound in a battle against the Aramaeans, as the prophet Micaiah had foretold. The biblical author does not mention Ahab's extensive building program, which excavations in Samaria have disclosed. His liberal religious policy seems to have been partly dictated by a widespread lack of faith in Yahwism. BIBLIOGRAPHY: J. Bright, *History of Israel* (1959).

[C. P. CEROKE]

AHAZ (ACHAZ), son of Jotham; king of Judah, 735–715 B.C. Early in A.'s reign King Rezin of Damascus and King Pekah of Israel besieged Jerusalem in an effort to force him to ally with them against Assyria (2 Kg 16.5; 2 Chr 28.5–8). The prophet Isaiah counseled A. to stand alone against the two kingdoms. But he appealed to Assyria for aid even at the price of becoming its vassal (2 Kg 16.7–8), a policy that provoked the famous *Emmanuel prophecy (Is 7.1–14). Although freed from his enemies by the military might of Assyria, A. fell under its domination. He fostered idolatrous practices in Judah, for which he is heavily scored by the inspired writers (2 Kg 16.10–18; 2 Chr 28.20–25).

[C. P. CEROKE]

AHAZIAH (Ochozias), name of two OT kings. (1) Ahaziah, King of Israel c.850–849 B.C., succeeded his father Ahab (1 Kg 22.40–53; 2 Kg 1; 2 Chr 20.35–37). In rebuke for his reliance on Baal-zebub, Elijah sent word to him that he would die. His brother Jehoram succeeded him. (2) Ahaziah, King of Judah c.842 B.C., succeeded his father Jehoram (2 Kg 8.25–29; 9.16–29). After he was killed by Jehu's archers, his mother Athaliah seized the throne and ruled until c.837, when his son Joash was proclaimed king.

[T. EARLY]

AHIJAH (Ahias), prophet who encouraged Jeroboam to rebel against Solomon (1 Kg 11.29–39). A prophet of Shiloh, he encountered Jeroboam outside Jerusalem and told him that because Solomon had worshiped foreign gods 10 tribes would be taken from his son and given to Jeroboam. A. symbolically tore his garment in 12 pieces and gave 10 of them to Jeroboam. Later disappointed with Jeroboam, he predicted the destruction of his house (1 Kg 14).

The name was also borne by several other OT men. BIBLIOGRAPHY: 1 Sam 14.3; 1 Kg 4.3; 15.27; J. Dheilly, *Prophets* (tr. R. Attwater, 1960).

[T. EARLY]

AHĪKĀR (Achior; Aram., *Aḥia-iaqar*, the little brother is precious, dear), a character of folklore whose story is woven into Scripture, as in the Book of Tob 1.21–22, 2.10, and 11.18 (the one allusion to A. in the Vulgate). The Eastern tale of the "dear little brother" lends color to Bible literature: A.'s lore with its detective theme of the adopted nephew's conspiracy with false letters that disrupt relations of his uncle with the king, and A.'s rescue by the hangman's substituting another prisoner, with exposure and execution of the villain, named variously Naman, Naban, Nadan, Nadin; involvement of three generations in the elements that appear both in Tobit's counsel to his nephew A., and in a punitive series of 95 maxims or wise sayings before Nadan's execution.

Influence on Hellenistic literature is shown by A.'s appearance in writings of Menander and of the "laughing philosopher" Democritus. A. is found moreover in the *Arabian Nights* and in the Koran. A. H. Krapp asks: "Is the story of A. the wise of Indian origin?" (Journal of the American Oriental Society 67 [1941] 280–284). In the OT A. is also in Jdt which with Tob is in the Deuterocanonical grouping; familiar with him was the author of Dan, in part also a disputed text; in the NT some think to detect A. in the parable of the wicked servant (Mt 18.32). Though some scholars held that A. depends on the Book of Tob (after 500 B.C.), A.'s story was well-known in Eastern folklore (*c*.650 B.C.). Possibly based on an Assyrian court personage, the history and maxims of A. the Assyrian entered into Eastern writings; a 5th-cent. Aramaic version was discovered by the German mission in the *Elephantine papyri and first published in 1906. Some evidence indicates that the Aramaic writing must cede to an earlier Akkadian text. F. Nau in *Histoire et sagesse d'Ahikar l'Assyrien* (1909) gives a basic study with bibliog.; RevBibl 21 (1912) 68–79 treats of A. and the Elephantine papyri. BIBLIOGRAPHY: N. M'Lean, EB 21:721, s.v. "Syriac Literature"; A. Romero, EncCatt 1:589–590.

[M. R. BROWN]

AHIMSA, a Sanskrit word meaning nonviolence, the Indian doctrine opposing injury to animal life, which is regarded as sacred because of the possibility of reincarnation. Different religious groups practice it—Jainism most rigorously, and Buddhism more strictly than Hinduism. Mahatma Gandhi adopted it as the basic principle of political and social life.

[P. K. MEAGHER]

AHITHOPHEL (Achithophel), the counselor of Absalom in the latter's revolt against David. When A.'s advice that David be slain was not followed, he hanged himself (See 2 Sam 15–17).

[T. C. O'BRIEN]

AHMADIYA, an Islamic sect and religious movement. It originated in the preaching of Mirza Ghulam Ahmad (1839–1908), the son of a well-to-do family of the village of Kadiyan in the Punjab (India), who beginning in 1899 claimed to receive revelations from God; he identified himself as an incarnation of Christ *(al-Masîh)*, the *Mahdî, and Krishna. After the death of Ghulam Ahmad, his son (b. 1889), Mirza Bashir al-Din Mahmud Ahmad (The Second Masîh) became caliph of the movement. Following the partition of India (1947) the center of the movement was transferred to Pakistan where the sect founded a new city, Rabwa (SEE Koran 2.265). At present the sect claims some half a million adherents, chiefly in Pakistan and East Africa. Though insisting that Ghulam Ahmad is a prophet and calling those who do not recognize him as such unbelievers *(kâfir)*, they nonetheless allow that Mohammed was the Seal of the Prophets (SEE Koran 33.40). The doctrine of the sect is fundamentally Muslim with a few notable aberrations in the direction of Indian religion. The movement, under the highly centralized control of its caliph, is well financed and extremely energetic in missionary activities, doing considerable publishing and operating many schools. At the death of

Ghulam Ahmad, a group broke off from the community of Kadiyan and moved to Lahore. This smaller branch of the Ahmadiya, led by Mohammed Ali up to his death (1951), has been remarkably active in the dissemination of Islamic literature, particularly translations of the Koran, throughout the world. They do not consider Ghulam Ahmad as a prophet but rather as a reformer. BIBLIOGRAPHY: EncIslam² s.v. "Ahmadiya."

[R. M. FRANK]

AHRIMAN, see AHURA MAZDA (OHRMAZD) AND AHRIMAN.

AHURA MAZDA (OHRMAZD) AND AHRIMAN (earlier, *Ahra Manyu*), in ancient Persian religion the Wise Lord or highest God, and the Evil Spirit, respectively. *Ahura Mazda* seems to be identical with the early Indo-Iranian god *Varuna* under another name. In the teaching ascribed to *Zoroaster and in the inscriptions of Darius I the Archaemenid (521–486), he is the Wise Lord, the Creator of good and evil, and of light and darkness. Zoroaster seems to have recognized him as a unique, supreme god, but in the more popular form of Persian religion there were other divinities besides him. The *Amesha Spenta, "the Beneficent Immortals," are the attendants or helpers of *Ahura Mazda* in all his activities, but particularly in his conflict against Ahriman, the Prince of Darkness, the Lie. Every man has to decide whether he wishes to be a follower of *Ahura Mazda* or *Ahriman* and will be rewarded or punished accordingly for his conduct when he dies. At the end of time *Ahura Mazda* will triumph completely and *Ahriman* and his adherents will be destroyed. The origins of *Ahura Mazda* and *Ahriman*, and of the opposition between them are obscure. In the latter speculation found in Zervanism, *Zervan* or "Time," after offering sacrifice for 1,000 years for offspring, has two sons born to him, *Ahura Mazda* and *Ahriman*—the latter because he had begun to despair about the efficacy of his sacrifice. BIBLIOGRAPHY: J. Duchesne-Guillemin, NCE 1:223; *id.*, *La Religion de l'Iran ancien* (1962).

[M. R. P. MCGUIRE]

AI, see HAI.

AIBERT, ST. (1060–1140), a monk who began a life of austere penance as a hermit near the abbey of Crespin in the diocese of Cambrai. After 20 years he entered the monastery and became a monk, but later was given permission to resume his life as a hermit. People came in such great numbers to receive his counsel that he was ordained priest so that he could give them sacramental absolution. BIBLIOGRAPHY: C. Lefebvre, BiblSanct 1:623–624.

[P. K. MEAGHER]

AIBLINGER, JOHANN KASPAR (1779–1867), German church composer, scholar and conductor. Recalled in 1819 from Italy, where he had cofounded the Odeon Institute in Venice, he became, for a time, Kapellmeister of the Italian

Opera at Munich and, later, court conductor for the king of Bavaria. In 1833, he returned to Italy to collect ancient and church music, which is now in the Munich State Library. His involvement, with others, in the revival of polyphony in Italy became the focal point for its restoration in all countries. He was highly regarded by church musicians of his time for his effective combining of Renaissance and contemporary techniques. BIBLIOGRAPHY: K. G. Fellerer, *History of Catholic Church Music* (tr. F. A. Brunner, 1961) 182–183; C. F. Pohl, Grove DMM 1:76.

[M. T. LEGGE]

AICHINGER, GREGOR (1564–1628), German priest, organist and composer. Strongly influenced by Lassus, A.'s style reflects many of the traits of the *Roman school, esp. *Palestrina. A.'s music is distinguished by harmonic richness without excessive chromaticism. He was the first composer to publish a printed continuo score (1607). BIBLIOGRAPHY: E. F. Schmid, MGG 1:177–183; ReeseMusR.

[J. J. WALSH]

AIDAN OF LINDISFARNE, ST. (d. 651), bp. of Lindisfarne (635) who made many journeys from that island to do missionary work among the English. Educated at Iona, A. favored practices of the schismatic Celtic Church esp. the date of Easter. Many of his pupils, e.g., Chad, Eata, Hild, later became leaders in the English Church. BIBLIOGRAPHY: M. Creighton, DNB 1:182–183; Butler 3:451–452; C. McGrath, BiblSanct 1:625–627 (bibliog.)

[R. T. MEYER]

AIGUANI, MICHELE (Michael of Bologna; 1320–1400), Carmelite theologian. He studied at Paris, taught theology at Bologna, and became one of the most esteemed among the early Carmelite schoolmen. After holding important administrative positions in the Bologna province of the Carmelites, he became vicar-general, then prior general, of the entire order. Urban VI, probably because his loyalty to the Holy See was called into question, removed him from office, but he was exonerated by Boniface IX, who made him vicar-general of the Bologna province. BIBLIOGRAPHY: H. Spikker, NCE 1:224.

AIGUILLON, DUCHESSE D' (Marie Madeleine Thérèse de Wignerod; 1604–75), niece of Cardinal Richelieu, friend and benefactress of St. Vincent de Paul and J. J. Olier. When she was widowed at the age of 18, she wished to enter the Carmelites, but at Richelieu's insistence accepted an appointment as lady-in-waiting to the Queen. She avoided the splendid parties of the court and gave what time she could spare from her duties to works of charity. When Richelieu died (1642) she withdrew from court and gave herself entirely to charitable activities. She helped to establish St. Vincent de Paul's hospital for foundlings and the general hospital in Paris and others in the provinces. She was also a patroness of letters and aided Corneille in defending himself in the quarrel touched off by his *Le Cid*. BIBLIOGRAPHY: A. Bonneau-Avencant, *La Duchesse d'Auiguillon . . .* (2d ed., 1882); P. Coste, *Life and Works of St. Vincent de Paul* (tr. J. Leonard, 1952); J. Calvet, *St. Vincent de Paul* (1948).

AIGULF OF LÉRINS, ST. (*c.* 630–674), a monk of the monastery of Fleury (St.-Benoît-sur-Loire), in 671 elected abbot of Lérins. His strict reform of the rule resulted in his martyrdom at Capri. BIBLIOGRAPHY: R. Aigrain, *Catholicisme* 1:244–245; C. Lefebvre, BiblSanct 1:633–634.

[H. JACK]

AIJALON (AJALON), a town of ancient Palestine NW of Jerusalem, near the Philistine border (1 Sam 14.31). It was originally an Amorrite town and continued in their hands until David conquered it. There are numerous biblical references to this town: Jos 10.12, 19.42, 21.24; 1 Kg 4.9; 1 Chr 6.54, 6.69, 8.13; 2 Chr 11.10, 28.18.

[C. C. O'DONNELL]

AIKENHEAD, MARY (1787–1858), foundress. A convert to Catholicism at the age of 16, she founded, under the direction of Abp. Murray of Dublin, the Irish Sisters of Charity, whose fourth vow is service to the poor. The congregation was canonically erected in 1816. During her life, she established 10 houses, including St. Vincent's Hospital, the first Catholic hospital in Ireland. The congregation has spread to England, the U.S., Australia, and South Africa. BIBLIOGRAPHY: M. B. Butler, *A Candle Was Lit: the Life of Mother Mary Aikenhead* (1953).

[H. JACK]

AIMERIC OF ANGOULÊME (fl. late 11th cent.), poet. Born in Gastinaux, France and educated at Senlis, A. is known for his work on Latin metrics and for having proposed in his *Ars lectoria* (1086) rules for liturgical and other spoken forms of Latin. BIBLIOGRAPHY: M. M. McLaughlin, NCE 1:225; Manitius 3:180–182.

[J. R. RIVELLO]

AIMERIC OF PIACENZA (*c.* 1250–1327), 12th Dominican master general (1304–11). He entered the Dominicans at Bologna (1267) and was active in organizing studies, but is best known for his favorable treatment of the Knights Templar. Although summoned to Council of Vienne (1312), he did not attend and resigned his generalate May 30, 1311, rather than take part in the process against the Templars. BIBLIOGRAPHY: P. M. Starrs, NCE 1:225; Quétif-Échard 1.2:494–496.

[J. A. WEISHEIPL]

AIMERIC OF SANTA MARIA NUOVA (d. 1141), cardinal and ecclesiastical diplomat. Burgundian by birth, A. was appointed cardinal by Pope Callistus II in 1120. He served as chancellor from 1123 until his death. His friends included

Bernard of Clairvaux, Guigo I, and Peter the Venerable. BIBLIOGRAPHY: PL 182; Fliche-Martin 9:50–53; M. M. McLaughlin, NCE 1:225.

[J. R. RIVELLO]

AIMERICH, MATEO (1715–99), Spanish Jesuit and classical philologist. He taught in several Jesuit colleges and served in turn as rector and chancellor. When the Jesuits were expelled from Spanish territory (1767), he went to Ferrara and devoted the rest of his life to writing. He is distinguished for his philological writing and research, e.g., *Novum lexicon historicum et criticum antiquae romanae literaturae* (1787). BIBLIOGRAPHY: É. Van Cauwenbergh, DHGE 5:1298.

[H. JACK]

AIMO, see HAYMO.

AIMOIN OF FLEURY (*c*.960–*c*.1010), French chronicler. His chief work is a history of the Franks from prehistory to 663, *Historia Francorum*. It was later continued by others and brought to the mid-12th century. A. also wrote a life of *Abbo, abbot of Fleury, and bks. 2 and 3 of the *Miracula S. Benedicti*. His *Historia* is printed in MGS 26; the *Vita* and *Miracula* in Mabillon AS. BIBLIOGRAPHY: G. Hocquard, *Catholicisme* 1:247; P. Fournier, DHGE 1:1185–87.

AĬNALOV, DMITRIĬ VLAS'EVICH (1826–1939), Russian Byzantine art historian and student of N. Kondakov. He changed the orientation of Byzantine art studies with his book *The Hellenistic Origins of Byzantine Art* by establishing the origins of Byzantine style in the Near East rather than in Rome as previously accepted. His work has become the basis for the standard historical texts on early Byzantine and Christian art. His theory concerning the relation of 14th-cent. Byzantine style to the Italian Duecento is not supported. BIBLIOGRAPHY: *Hellenistic Origins of Byzantine Art* (tr. E. and S. Sobolevitch, 1961).

[F. T. RYAN]

AINAY, ABBEY OF, former Benedictine monastery of St. Martin, founded in the 6th cent. in what is now Lyons, France. It declined in the 9th cent., was restored by Benedictines and prospered during the 12th to 14th centuries. At its height, its jurisdiction extended over 190 parishes. Gradually it declined once more and was secularized in 1685 and the community transferred to a chapter of canons. In 1907 the abbey was elevated to the rank of minor basilica, marking the 800th anniversary of its consecration. BIBLIOGRAPHY: R. Gazeau, *Catholicisme* 1:248–249.

[S. A. HEENEY]

AINOI (Gr., praises), the last section of Orthros, the morning office of the Byzantine Church. It receives its name from the psalms of praise recited in it.

[A. J. JACOPIN]

AION (Gr. *aion,* Lat. *aeon*), a segment of time or an undetermined extent of time personified and divinized. A festival at Alexandria in his honor, a late Greek embodiment of Egyptian ideas, marked the beginning of the new year by celebrating his birth as the son of the maiden Kore. He was also honored by a late Orphic cult and in Mithraic theology by his possible identification with Boundless Time, sometimes called *aion, aeon, saeculum, chronos,* Saturnus, or after the Iranian god, Zervan Akarana. For Plato, *aion* is eternity, the opposite of chronos (*Tim.* 37d) a given segment of time. In Gnostic literature, the theory of emanation equates *aeon* with immaterial beings belonging to a noumenal world which together with their source constitute the fullness of being. BIBLIOGRAPHY: H. J. Rose, OCD 27; A. Nock, HTR 27 (1934) 53; F. Cumont, *Mysteries of Mithra* (pa. 1956) 104–149. *GNOSTICISM; *EVITERNITY.

[F. H. BRIGHAM]

AIRVAULT, ABBEY OF (Aurea Vallis), a house of Canons Regular of St. Augustine near Poitiers, France. Founded in the 2d half of the 10th cent. by Audéarde, wife of Aubert, as a collegiate chapter, which adopted *c*.1095 the rule of St. Augustine, Airvault was destroyed by the Calvinists in 1568 and was never rebuilt; but the community continued, never joining any reformed congregation. In 1768 it was ordered suppressed, but continued to exist until 1791. The monumental church still stands. BIBLIOGRAPHY: N. Backmund, NCE 1:226–227; P. de Monsabert, DHGE 1:1219–23.

[F. N. BACKMUND]

AIRY, ST., see AGERICUS, ST.

AISLE, the passage between rows of pews or chairs; a division of a church separated from the nave by arches along its complete length; it may be on one or both sides of the whole length.

[S. A. HEENEY]

AISTULF (d. 756), king of the Lombards from 749. Attempting to bring all Italy under Lombard control, A. seized Ravenna (751) and a number of papal towns. In 753 he threatened Rome itself. The Byzantine Emperor sent no aid, though Italy was nominally his. Pope Stephen II appealed to the Frankish King Pepin I. Two Frankish campaigns forced the Lombards to relinquish their conquests. These lands became the nucleus of the Papal States when Pepin handed them over to the Pope. BIBLIOGRAPHY: T. Hodgkin, *Italy and Her Invaders* (7v., 1899); K. F. Drew, NCE 1:227; H. J. Magoulias, *Byzantine Christianity: Emperor, Church and the West* (1970) 93–94.

[G. M. COOK]

AITESIS (Gr., supplication), in the Byzantine liturgy a series of litany-like invocations recited before the Creed and repeated again in the same form directly before the Lord's

Prayer. The invocations ask peace, forgiveness of sin, and repentance; they express hope for a painless and Christian death as well as a good defense at the judgment tribunal. Each concludes with the words, "Let us ask the Lord," to which the people respond, "Grant this, O Lord!"

[A. J. JACOPIN]

AITKEN, JOHN (1745?–1831), American musician and music publisher. Born in Scotland, A. settled in Philadelphia, where he published *A Compilation of the Litanies and Vespers, Hymns and Anthems, as They Are Sung in the Catholic Church, Adapted to the Voice or Organ* (1787; facs. ed. 1954). This collection contains a variety of English and German hymns, Mass and Vespers ordinaries set to elaborations of Gregorian melodies, and other items ranging from a Handel aria ("Let the Bright Seraphim," from *Samson*) to a brief chapter on the rudiments of music. No composers' names are given, and it is uncertain what, if any, of the music is A.'s own. One of the four clergy signing the statement of approbation at the front of the work was John *Carroll, later the first abp. of Baltimore.

[A. DOHERTY]

AIX (*Aquensis in Gallia*), metropolitan see since 445 in SE France, 20 miles N of Marseilles embracing Arles and Embrun, known for baths (*Aquae Sextiae* after Consul Sextius 123 B.C.). Important historic sites are: the 12th-cent. cloister of Saint-Sauveur, the composite 5th- to 16th-cent. Cathedral of Saint-Sauveur with 5th-cent. tomb of St. Mitrias (d. *c.*300), and Sainte-Madeleine. Arles boasts the most impressive church and cloister of Saint-Trophime (11th-15th cent.) and the Romanesque Church of Saint-Honorat.

[M. J. DALY]

AIX-LA-CHAPELLE, see AACHEN.

AJANTA, ancient Buddhist site in Maharashtra State, West Central India. Here a series of 30 rock caves, cut into a crescent cliff 60 miles NE of Aurangābād, are world famous for extensive and beautifully executed paintings (2d cent. B.C. to A.D. 700). A monastic retreat during the rainy season these caves—some *caitya* halls, others *viharas*—are the greatest examples of Gupta painting in existence. BIBLIOGRAPHY: R. S. Gupta and B. D. Mahajan, *Ajantā, Ellora and Aurangābād Caves* (1962).

[M. J. DALY]

AKAKIOS, see ACACIUS.

AKATHISTOS (Gr., without sitting down), famous *kontakion* of the Greek Church. Sung on the eve of the fifth Sunday of Lent, it is one of the most impressive works of the Byzantine rite still performed. An ode of 294 lines based on the gospel account of the Annunciation, it contains two narrative sections, separated by a salutation to the Virgin and an Hallelujah. Time and composer are uncertain. In the style

of Romanos, evidence seems to favor Sergios (Sergius) who supposedly wrote it as a thanksgiving hymn to Mary for her defense of Constantinople. BIBLIOGRAPHY: G. Dévai, "Akathistos-Prooemia in Byzantine Musical MSS in Hungary," *Studies in Chant* (1966) 1:1–3; Reese MusMA 80.

[M. T. LEGGE]

AKBAR (Jalal-ud-din Mohammed; b. 1542), Mughal (Mogul) Emperor, called the Great, reigned 1556–1605. He restored and increased the territories of the Mughal Empire in NW India and carried out a thorough reorganization of its administration. A man of remarkable ability and wide interests, he was esp. concerned with religion. He instituted religious debates for Muslims in 1575, and 3 years later he opened these debates to Hindus, Jains, Parsees, and Sabaeans. Having heard of Christianity, in 1579 he invited the Jesuits Rudolph Acquaviva, Hieronymus Xavier, and Emmanuel Pineira to his court, where they remained until 1595. They built a church at Agra (1575) and an ecumenical house of "dialogue." A. found it impossible, however, to accept the Christian doctrines of the Trinity and Incarnation. Not being fully satisfied with Hinduism, Parsism, or Islam, he developed a personal syncretistic religion, *Din Ilāhi* (Divine Faith). Despite the opposition of his advisers, he continued his policy of religious toleration. His *Din Ilāhi* died with him, and his successors abandoned his policy of toleration.

Profoundly interested also in the arts, he effected the golden age of Hindu-Muslim cultural synthesis, drawing architects and painters to his court. The Jesuits presented him with an illustrated Bible which was copied by Indian artists adopting Western perspective and chiaroscuro. Mughal architecture of the period evidences an elegance and simplicity foreign to Indian taste. A. built the tomb of his father Humayun at Delhi, the mosque of Agra, and the city of Fatehpur Sikri (1569). Startling scale and richness of material characterize the Mughal turreted palaces, arcades, pavilions, pools, immense stables, and magnificent mosques with partial Indianization in *caitya* arches. A.'s successors continued as ardent patrons of the arts (their greatest triumph the Taj Mahal by Shah Jahan) until the violence of the fanatical Aurangzeb (1658–1707), who persecuted painters, destroyed temples, and caused finally the overthrow of Mughal rule. BIBLIOGRAPHY: L. Kilger, LTK 1:236; A. Schimmel-Tari, RGG 1:208–209; W. Bingham et al., *History of Asia* (1964) 1:233–243; E. Maclagan, *Jesuits and the Great Mogul* (1932); A. B. Pandey, *Later Medieval India: A History of the Mughals* (1963).

[M. R. P. MCGUIRE; M. J. DALY]

AKHMATOVA, ANNA (Anna Andreyevich Gorenko; 1888–1966), important Russian poet of the Acmeist movement. In 1940, she broke her long silence (1922–40) under the Soviet regime with the volume *A Selection from Six Books,* which contained all her earlier poems and some new ones. She was expelled from the Union of Soviet Writers in

1946 on charges of corrupting Soviet youth with "bourgeois" poems about love and disillusionment in love. Many of her poems are also in a religious or prophetic vein. The volume *In Praise of Peace* (1950), containing chauvinistic poems of poor quality, is perhaps not her work. BIBLIOGRAPHY: L. I. Strakhovsky, *Craftsmen of the Word: Three Poets of Modern Russia* (1949 repr. 1970); R. Poggioli, *Poets of Russia: 1890–1930* (1960) 105–111; J. Lavin, EB (1971) 1:478.

[M. F. MCCARTHY]

AKHMIN FRAGMENT, a discovery made in 1886 by the Frenchman Bauriant in Upper Egypt. This fragment gives us the conclusion of the Passion narrative including the entire story of the Crucifixion and the Resurrection. It claimed special credit by using the name of St. Peter. Scholars have examined this fragment and shown its faults. It is a radical recasting of the gospel narratives. However, scholars agree there is no trace of doctrinal error. It is an interesting early attempt at Christian theology at the beginning of the second century. It is characterized by its unfortunate anti-Jewish polemic and its eagerness to defend the divinity of Christ.

[C. C. O'DONNELL]

AKHNATON (Amenhotep IV), Egyptian pharaoh of the 18th Dynasty, mid-14th cent., B.C. Son of Amenhotep III and his wife Tiye, he ascended the throne at the age of 13 during his father's incapacity. He discarded his original name, Amenhotep IV, because of his increasing conflict with the powerful priesthood of Amun. A. developed his own monotheistic theology, based on the exclusive worship of the sun's disk, Aton. He was the new religion's chief prophet, priest, and poet. Effecting a complete break with the past, he moved the court from Thebes—where it was deeply intertwined with temple politics—to virgin ground closer to Memphis, the ancient capital, and Heliopolis, seat of the sun-god Ra. The new capital, which he called Akhetaten, became the center of a new and revolutionary school of art ("Amarna art") characterized by grotesque forms and showing A.'s family in intimate attitudes and with emotional expressions. Among this school's hallmarks are individualized but stylized portraits, iconoclastic rejection of traditional distinctions between sexes, (men are represented with feet together, women striding,) and the ubiquitous sun-disk with rays ending in hands blessing the royal family. A.'s "Hymn to the Sun" is found inscribed throughout the ruins of Akhetaten. A.'s political career was catastrophic. A pacifist, he found even defensive wars repugnant. The famous Tell el-Amarna letters record his viceroys' concern about Egypt's waning power. The warlike Kabiru of these letters have been tentatively identified with Hebrew tribes. The final years of his reign are shrouded in mystery, but the outcome is plain. His capital was abandoned, the worship of Aton declared heretical, the former *status quo* in religion restored. More than any pharaoh before or since, A. has fascinated posterity; he is the subject of such diverse works of scholarship and imagination as Freud's *Moses and Monotheism*, Velikovsky's *Oedipus and Akhnaton*, and Mika Waltari's novel *The Egyptian*. BIBLIOGRAPHY: J. A. Wilson, *Culture of Ancient Egypt* (1956); A. H. Gardiner, *Egypt of the Pharaohs* (1961); J. Vergote, NCE 1:229–230; A. E. P. B. Weigall, *Life and Times of Aknaton, Pharaoh of Egypt* (1971).

[D. H. BRUNAUER]

AKIBA BEN JOSEPH (Akiva, Agiba; *c.*A.D. 50–135), the leading rabbi of his time; one of the founders of Talmudic Judaism. A. was the first to make a systematic collection of the halakic traditions of the Tannaim (rabbis of the first 2 Christian centuries), who transmitted the Oral Law. A. also taught that the Oral Law was not immutable but could be adapted to the situation of the time. Because of this teaching he is regarded as the father of the Talmud.

[C. C. O'DONNELL]

AKOIMETOS LYCHINA (Gr., watchful light), in a Byzantine church the lamp that usually hangs above or before the royal doors of the iconostasis. Whether the Eucharist is reserved or not, this lamp should never be allowed to go out. It may be fed with oil or, as is commonly the case today, may be electrified.

[A. J. JACOPIN]

AKOLOUTHIA (Gr. for the natural flowing of things, sequence), a Byzantine term used to indicate: (1) The prescribed order of religious rites and ceremonies, esp. the parts of the canonical hours (Psalms, lessons, hymns, etc.) in their successive order. (2) Any Byzantine liturgical ceremony. (3) The canonical hours of the Byzantine Church. These correspond closely to the Western hours of the Divine Office but are entirely different in their construction and are of great length. Their Greek and Slavonic names are as follows: Matins—*Mesonyktikon, Polunoschtchnitza* (midnight office); Lauds—*Orthros* (dawn); Prime—*Hōra prōtē, Tchas pierve;* Terce—*Hōra tritē, Tchas trietie;* Sext—*Hōra hektē, Tchas shiestie;* None—*Hōra enatē, Tchas devyatie;* Vespers—**Hesperinon, Vetchernya;* Complini —*Apodeipnon, Nediela.* Technically, only the hours of the day, i.e., Prime to None, are termed hours. At certain feasts these hours are greatly lengthened and during the fasts preceding Christmas and the feast of SS. Peter and Paul, *Mesoria* (mid-hours) are recited between the usual day hours. Monks are obligated to recite the whole Office in choir, and when this is sung properly it takes about 8 hours, but frequently it is shortened. Secular priests are urged to recite as much as possible, esp., before the Divine Liturgy. In the ordinary parish church at least Vespers and Matins for Sundays and feasts are celebrated.

[A. J. JACOPIN]

AKROTELEUTAION (Gr. for the end of a verse), in the Byzantine liturgy a term that may refer either to the last words of a solo hymn sung by the cantor, which are then repeated by the entire choir and congregation as a refrain, or to the repetition after the first part of the doxology of the last words of the preceding troparion.

[A. J. JACOPIN]

AKSUM (AXUM), a village in the northern Ethiopian province of Tigre, once the capital and spiritual center of Ethiopia. According to Ethiopian legend, Aksum was the city of the biblical Queen of Sheba, Makeda, who bore Solomon a son, Menelik, the founder of the Ethiopian royal dynasty. The city emerged into Christian history when St. Frumentius arrived there (c.320) and began to convert the kingdom. Inscriptions attest to the conversion of King Ezana who appears in one as a pagan and in a later one as a worshiper of the true God. Ezana made Christianity the official religion of the kingdom. The cathedral of St. Mary of Zion is said to have contained the Ark of the Covenant brought to Ethiopia by Menelik. Of this ancient building only the foundations remain. Ahmed Gran, a Muslim invader, destroyed the original in the 16th century. The most remarkable ancient remains in Aksum are the steles, the largest standing one measuring 70 feet in height. These were long considered pagan relics connected with the religion of South Arabian invaders, but recent investigations indicate that they are Christian and that Aksum grew into a city under the influence of Christianity. The Aksumite Kingdom, surrounded by Islam from c.640, rapidly declined when political power moved south to Shoa province in 1289. BIBLIOGRAPHY: G. W. van Beek, ''Monuments of Axum in the Light of South Arabian Archeology,'' *Journal of the American Oriental Society* 87 (1967) 113–122.

[D. W. JOHNSON]

ALABADO (Span., from *alabar*, to praise, to give glory to), Spanish hymn or motet sung in praise of the Blessed Sacrament, esp. when it is being returned to the tabernacle after Benediction, often beginning ''*Alabado sea . . .*'' (Glory be to . . .). Also a devotional song sung in certain parts of rural Mexico at the beginning and end of the day's work. BIBLIOGRAPHY: Apel HDMus 26.

[A. DOHERTY]

ALABAMA, a southeastern state, admitted to the Union as the 22d state (1819). Inhabited by Creek, Cherokee, Choctaw, and Chickasaw Indians, the area was first explored by the Spanish in the 16th cent. but the French made the first permanent settlement at Mobile (1702). The first Catholic parish was erected there the following year. Unsettled political conditions prevailed until the Florida Purchase (1819). The states of Alabama and Florida were then erected into a vicariate apostolic, and in 1829 the Diocese of Mobile (Mobile-Birmingham since 1954) was established. When John Quinlan was consecrated as second bp. of Mobile in 1859, the diocese contained almost 10,000 Catholics. With the aid of Irish priests Quinlan doubled this number and

guided the Church through the difficulties of Reconstruction. After a period of financial retrenchment, Bp. Edward Patrick Allen served from 1897 to 1927, when Thomas Joseph Toolen was consecrated as sixth bp. of Mobile. Under his direction the Church adapted to the growing urbanization of the state. Alabama's population of 3,373,006, over 55% of it urban, makes it the 21st most populous state. In 1972 Catholics numbered 86,218 or 2.56% of the total state population. Baptists and Methodists have long been the major Protestant sects, their prominence dating from the missionary visits of George *Whitefield and John *Wesley and from the effective use of the circuit rider in pioneer days. In 1971 the Southern Baptist Convention embraced 30.6% of the population and the Methodist Church 8.0%. The Jewish population of the state, as of 1968, was 9,465, or 0.27%. There are 10 church-related colleges in Alabama, 3 of which are Catholic affiliated. Five Catholic high schools enroll more than 3,114 students, while 53 Catholic elementary schools serve some 13,865 pupils. BIBLIOGRAPHY: A. B. Moore, *History of Alabama* (1934); M. T. A. Carroll, *Catholic History of Alabama and the Floridas* (1908); J. H. Parks and R. E. Moore, *Story of Alabama* (1952). L. B. Griffith, *Alabama: A Documentary History to 1900* (1972).

[J. L. MORRISON; R. M. PRESTON]

ALABASTRON (Gr. for an alabaster vessel in which to place perfume; Sl. *alavastr*), in the Byzantine Church a vessel of alabaster, glass, or precious metal used to contain the holy *myron (chrism). It is usually kept in the sanctuary area and is similar to the Western ampulla.

[A. J. JACOPIN]

ALACOQUE, MARGARET MARY, ST. (1647–90), Visitation nun at Paray-le-Monial, whose revelations experienced 1673–75 greatly contributed to the propagation of devotion to the Sacred Heart, esp. to the widespread adoption of the practice of receiving communion on first Fridays and to the establishment of the Feast of the Sacred Heart. Jansenists caused delay in her process of beatification and canonization which was set in motion in 1715. She was beatified in 1864 and canonized in 1920. BIBLIOGRAPHY: L. Gauthey, *Vie et oeuvres de Sainte Marguerite–Marie* (3 v., 1920), the basic study; H. Marduel, *Sainte Marguerite-Marie, sa physionomie spirituelle* (1964); R. Darricau, BiblSanct 8:804–809; A. Haman, DSAM 2:1033–35; Butler 4:134–138.

[P. K. MEAGHER]

ALAIN (ÉMILE AUGUSTE CHARTIER; 1886–1951), philosopher, educator, essayist; of Norman ancestry, teacher of foremost French philosophers at Henri Quatre and other *lycées*. As teacher he influenced A. Maurois, his biographer (*Alain*, 1949). A.'s daily *propos* (discourse or observation), begun in 1908, continued in brilliant essays, many gathered later into books, of which one was *Propos sur l'éducation*. A.'s intent was that the pupil achieve excellence; to this end he preferred Napoleonic control over education to parental rights. Always shy of dogma, the writer of *Les Dieux* (1934) contributed not at all to growth in French schools of the Christian ideal. In the year of his death, *Mercure de France* published seven articles on his life and teaching (v. 313, 581–661). BIBLIOGRAPHY: A. Maurois, EB 1:494; H. Mondor, *Alain* (1953).

[M. R. BROWN]

ALAIN CHARTIER (*c.* 1390–*c.* 1440), French diplomat and author. He served Charles VI and Charles VII in the crises of the Hundred Years' War. His *Book of the Four Ladies* (1416) mourns the defeat at Agincourt; the brilliant *Quadrilogue invectif* (1422) exhorts France, nobility, Church, and people to unite the nation. His most famous work is *La Belle dame sans Merci* (1424), a short poem free of political concern. His works show a rhetoric and imagination foreshadowing French humanism.

[J. P. WILLIMAN]

ALAIN OF LILLE, see ALAN OF LILLE.

ALAIN, JEHAN (1911–40), French composer and organist. He was a pupil of Marcel Dupré, and was organist at the Church of Saint-Nicholas de Maisons Lafitte, Paris, prior to World War II, when he was killed in action. His works include piano and choral pieces as well as chamber music, but it is for his organ works that he is chiefly known. In these A. added an independent and original style, particularly in his use of rhythm and form, to the tradition of French organ music. His father Albert gave him his first organ lessons, and his sister Marie-Claire is a concert organist of international reputation. BIBLIOGRAPHY: B. Gavoty, *Jehan Alain, musicien français* (1945); N. Dufourcq, *La Musique d'orgue française de Jehan Titelouze à Jehan Alain* (2d ed. 1949).

[A. DOHERTY]

ALAIN-FOURNIER (pseudonym of Henri Alban Fournier; 1886–1914), French writer. Refused entrance to L'École Normale Supérieure, he abandoned a projected teaching career to work at journalism and as a businessman's private secretary. Although reared in a Catholic milieu and called by his classmates "Fournier the pious," by 1906 he had lost his faith. Nostalgia for asceticism and the will to believe periodically drew him toward a renewed commitment to Catholicism: in 1907 when first influenced by Claudel's works and personality; in 1909 when Dostoevski's *Idiot* seemed to afford "perhaps the bridge so long sought between the Christian world and my own"; in 1911 when he made a second pilgrimage to Lourdes. Although lost in battle before resolving his attitude toward the Church, his belief in Providence is confirmed by a fellow soldier Pierre Maury, a Protestant pastor. His only novel, *Le Grand Meaulnes* (1913, Eng. tr. *The Wanderer*), has exercised great spiritual influence on young Frenchmen, and Catholic critics interpret its symbolic quest for purity, idealism, and lost childhood as a yearning for the absolute. The vicissitudes of his religious disquiet are best reflected in his correspondence with his brother-in-law Jacques Rivière. His earlier writings, some of which develop the quest theme in more explicitly religious terms, were collected and published as *Miracles* (1924). BIBLIOGRAPHY: A. Becker, *Itinéraire spirituel d'Alain-Fournier* (1946); R. Gibson, *Quest of Alain-Fournier* (1954).

[G. E. GINGRAS]

ALAMANNI (ALEMANNI), the name given by neighboring tribes to a confederation of Swabian tribes (*alle Männer*). In 213 they first opposed Caracalla, broke through the Roman lines by 259, and flowed steadily into SW Germany, Gaul, Raetia, and Italy. Clovis defeated them in 496, and soon Alamannia became a Frankish province; but uprisings occurred for centuries. The Alamanni retained their own customs and language as well as a certain autonomy. Their evangelization began in the 6th century. The missioners Columban, Gall, Fridolin, Pirin, Landelin, and others founded influential monasteries, among which were the abbeys of Sankt Gallen and Reichenau. BIBLIOGRAPHY: H. Tüchle, *Kirchengeschichte Schwabens* (1950).

[M. J. SUELZER]

ALAN OF LILLE (Alain, Alanus ab [de] Insulis; d. 1202), French theologian and poet known as the "universal doctor." Little detail is known of his early life. He studied and taught at Paris, then at Montpellier, before retiring as a lay brother at Cîteaux. He is venerated in the Cistercian Order as a Blessed. A. represented the Platonico-Aristotelian tradition that dominated Christian thinking in Europe before the works of the Arabian commentators became known. His works show the influence of Boethius and Plotinus. His *Contra haereticos* (i.e., Cathari, Jews, and Saracens) is an early example of medieval polemic against those who could be reached only through an appeal to reason. But another rational apologetical work, *De arte [articulis] catholicae fidei,* once attributed to him, is now thought to be the work of Nicholas d'Amiens. A. made much use of definitions, axioms, postulates, and aphorisms and contributed notably to the development of theological terminology. His *Anticlaudianus,* an epic poem dealing with nature's production of perfect man, is said to have inspired Chaucer and Dante. Works: PL 210. BIBLIOGRAPHY: Gilson, HCP 172–178; A. M. Zimmermann, BiblSanct 1:649–651; P. Glorieux, NCE 1:239–240; G. Crispin, "Alan of Lille and Jacob ben Reuben," *Speculum* 49 (1974) 34–47.

ALAN DE LA ROCHE (Alanus de Rupe; *c.* 1428–75), founder of the Confraternity of the Rosary. A. entered the Dominican Order at Dinan in Brittany and belonged to the reformed Congregation of Holland. He studied at Paris

(1453–60) and was master of novices at Lille in 1460. Subsequently he lectured at Paris (1461), Lille (1462), Douai (1464–65), and Ghent (1468–69). He commented on the *Sentences* of Peter Lombard at Rostock (1470–74), and took the masterate in theology there (1474). He was then assigned to Zwolle. In 1475 he took part in a chapter of the Congregation of Holland at Lille, where he composed his *Apologia* for the rosary. Alan preached the rosary widely, seeing it as an instrument of reform. He founded the first Confraternity of the Rosary at Douai in 1470. The confraternity, with its obligation of reciting the 15 mysteries weekly (at Douai Alan required their daily recitation), did much to popularize the rosary. His rosary revelations are without historical foundation and are to be judged as a type of medieval literary genre. BIBLIOGRAPHY: Quétif-Échard 1:849–852; B. de Boer, "De Souter van Alanus de Rupe," *Ons Geestelijk Erf* 29 (1955) 358–388; 30 (1956) 156–190; 31 (1957) 187–204; 33 (1959) 145–193.

[W. A. HINNEBUSCH]

ALAN OF TEWKESBURY (d. 1202), English Benedictine abbot, writer. A former canon of Benevento, Italy, A. became a monk at Canterbury (1174), and prior in 1179. He supported Abp. Thomas Becket, writing an account of his life and compiling a collection of Becket's correspondence. His objection to Baldwin as abp. of Canterbury led to his translation to Tewkesbury abbey as abbot (1186). BIBLIOGRAPHY: *Materials for the History of Archbishop Thomas Becket* (ed. J. C. Robertson, 7 v. 1875–85); J. B. Mullinger, DNB 1:214–215.

[F. D. BLACKLEY]

ALAN OF WALSINGHAM (d. 1364), English Benedictine monk, sacristan (1321), prior (1341) and twice unsuccessful bishop-elect of Ely (1345, 1361). Reputedly the architect of Ely's famous central octagonal tower with its timber "lantern," built after the Norman central tower collapsed (1322), A. probably inspired the work but William Hurle, a master carpenter, perhaps designed it. BIBLIOGRAPHY: *Sacrist Rolls of Ely* (ed. F. R. Chapman, 2 v., 1907).

[F. D. BLACKLEY]

ALANS, a nomadic, Iranian people in the South Russian steppes during the early Christian era. Moving westward they came under the domination of the Huns and Visigoths, but in the 5th cent. most of them wandered back to the steppes, and some settled in the central Caucasus where they became known as Ossets. Their conversion to Christianity took place early in the 10th cent. under the guidance of the monk Euthymius, sent from Constantinople. A metropolitan see of Alania was then established, which lasted to the end of the 16th century. BIBLIOGRAPHY: S. Vailhé, DHGE 1:1334–38; B. S. Bachrach, *History of the Alans in the West* (1973).

[G. T. DENNIS]

ALANUS ANGLICUS (fl. 1200–15), an English canonist of Welsh origin who taught canon law at Bologna and contributed to the then developing curialist concept of papal sovereignty. BIBLIOGRAPHY: L. E. Boyle, NCE 1:241.

[P. K. MEAGHER]

ALANUS AB INSULIS, see ALAN (ALAIN) OF LILLE.

ALAPA, the light touch or pat upon the cheek given by the confirming bishop to the person confirmed after anointing him on the forehead. As the accompanying words "Peace be with you" suggest, this is probably a stylized version of the kiss of peace in use before the 12th century. There is nothing to support its alleged derivation from the sword blow by which a young Teutonic warrior was dubbed a knight.

[N. KOLLAR]

ALASKA, the largest but least populous state, admitted to the Union as the 49th state (1959). Formed by a large peninsula and a series of islands in northwest North America, the area was discovered (1741) by Vitus Bering, a Danish explorer in command of a Russian expedition. Two Franciscan missionaries visited the region in 1779, and Russian Orthodox priests established the first churches after 1794. Until the U.S. acquired Alaska (1867), Episcopalians from Canada were the most active Protestant missionaries, although Lutherans had established the first Protestant parish at Sitka (1853). Presbyterians became the most successful proselytizers after 1878. Climate, vast area, and sparse population have compounded the difficulties of missionary work in Alaska. The efforts of Jean Sequin in 1862, of Émile Petitot in 1870, and of August Lecorre and Bp. Isidore Clut in 1872 to establish a mission at Fort Yukon all ended in failure. Although missions were founded at St. Michael and other points along the coast, it was not until 1887 that Jesuit missions could be established in the interior, at Nulato and Nukluroyit. Anchorage is the metropolitan see of Alaska; Joseph T. Ryan was consecrated as its first abp. in 1966. Its suffragan sees are Fairbanks, covering the north central area, and the southern Diocese of Juneau. Fairbanks, traditionally administered by the Jesuits, became a prefecture apostolic in 1894, with Paschal Tosi, SJ, as prefect apostolic. In 1916 Raphael Crimont, SJ, was appointed as vicar apostolic, and when the vicariate became a diocese in 1962, Francis Gleeson, SJ, became its first bishop. The southern suffragan of Juneau was established as a diocese in 1951, and Dermot O'Flanagan was named as its first bishop. Alaska's population of 296,120 is more than 70% rural. In 1974 Catholics numbered 42,112 or 14% of the total state population. There are no Catholic colleges in the state, but four elementary schools and two Catholic high schools have been established. About half of these educational facilities are located in the Diocese of Fairbanks. In 1974, Bp. Robert L. Whelan of Fairbanks accepted a proposal by the Jesuit Order to open a seminary (the first to be established in the state of

Alaska) for diocesan priests. BIBLIOGRAPHY: E. Gruening, *State of Alaska* (1954); G. G. Steckler, "Diocese of Juneau, Alaska," HistRecStud 47 (1959) 234–254; B. Cooper, *Alaska* (1973). RACHS 29:98–130.

[J. L. MORRISON; R. M. PRESTON]

ALASKA, ORTHODOX CHURCH IN. In 1794 Russian monks built the first Orthodox church in North America on Kodiak Island. The liturgical books were translated into the native dialects very early. Canonically established in 1840 as the Diocese of Kamchatka, the Kuriles, and Aleutians under Bp. Innocent Veniaminov, Alaska was a diocese of the Russian Metropolia of America with its own ruling bishop and numerous native clergy. Canonical status of independence was granted by its Mother Church, the Russian Orthodox Church, in 1970. It is now known as The Orthodox Church in America. BIBLIOGRAPHY: R. Stephanopoulos, *Encyclopedia of Modern Christian Missions* (1967) 237; YBACC (1974) 76.

[T. BIRD]

ALB, a tunic extending from neck to ankles and gathered at the waist by a cincture, worn at most liturgical functions, generally as an undergarment, by the principal officiating clergy. Originally it was the ordinary Greco-Roman ankle-length tunic *(tunica talaris)* of daily use. When the long tunic became outmoded, it was retained for liturgical wear and has continued in use down to the present time, surviving some vicissitudes of fashion. During the Gothic period colored albs were sometimes used; from the 16th cent. they were often made ornate with lace. Under the influence of the liturgical movement of the 20th cent. the plain white linen alb has returned to general favor. BIBLIOGRAPHY: H. Norris, *Church Vestments* (1950); E. A. Roulin, *Vestments and Vesture* (tr. J. McCann, 1950); R. Lesage, *Vestments and Church Furniture* (tr. F. Murphy, 1960).

[N. KOLLAR]

ALBA JULIA, UNION OF, the union with the Roman Church of a portion of the Romanian Orthodox Church in Transylvania in 1698. After Transylvania became part of the Austro-Hungarian empire in 1690, some Catholic military chaplains, chiefly Jesuits, established themselves in Alba Julia and proved influential with the Orthodox clergy. In 1697 under Bp. Theophilus and in 1698 under Bp. Athanasius the clergy decided on union with Rome. A synod in 1700, composed of over 2,000 priests and many of the laity, ratified the union and accepted the four doctrinal points of the Council of *Florence (1439): papal primacy, the existence of purgatory, the legitimacy of unleavened bread, and the *filioque*. They set down the conditions that the Eastern clergy receive the same civil immunities and privileges as the Latin, that their rite and use of the vernacular be preserved, and that they elect their own bishop. Despite many difficulties the union flourished, and in 1853 an ecclesiastical province was erected, but in 1948 the Com-

munist government dissolved it by force. BIBLIOGRAPHY: W. de Vries, *Rom und die Patriarchate des Ostens* (1963) 132–180.

[G. T. DENNIS]

ALBA, FERNANDO ÁLVAREZ DE TOLEDO, DUKE OF, see ALVA, DUKE OF.

ALBAN, ST. (d. 287?), protomartyr of Britain. According to legend his conversion was due to sheltering a priest in time of persecution. Miracles attended his execution near Verulamium, later renamed St. Albans. The date is doubtful: Bede says under Diocletian, but it may be as early as Decius (*c.*250). BIBLIOGRAPHY:C. Testore and R. Ruocco, BiblSanct 1:656–659; Butler 2:612–614.

[J. L. DRUSE]

ALBANEL, CHARLES (1616–96), French Jesuit missionary and explorer. A. entered the Jesuits in France in 1633 and arrived at the Canadian missions in 1649. He was probably the first white man to reach Hudson Bay from Quebec by land as a member of the French expedition of 1670–71. On a second trip in 1674, he was seized by the British and sent to England for imprisonment, but returned to Canada in 1676. BIBLIOGRAPHY: G. L. Gilsdorf, NCE 6:751.

[H. JACK]

ALBANENSES, one of the larger 13th-cent. bodies of *Cathari in Italy. Adherents were numerous in Lombardy, especially in the vicinity of Verona. The founders probably migrated from Albania, which may account for the name. The Albanenses professed absolute dualism, insisting on the eternal coexistence and complete equality of the principles of good and evil. Christ, they held, had a human body in appearance only. BIBLIOGRAPHY: S. Runciman, *Medieval Manichee* (1961) 126–127.

[C. J. LYNCH]

ALBANI, the name of a prominent Umbrian family of Urbino, the most important of whom was Pope *Clement XI (1700–21). Other distinguished members included: (1) Annibale (1682–1751) papal nuncio to Vienna, Dresden, and Frankfort, cardinal (1711), bp. of Sabina (1730). He was influential in the election of Popes Innocent XIII and Benedict XIV; his writings include an edition of the works of his uncle Clement XI. (2) Alessandro (1692–1779) brother of Annibale, cardinal (1721). He is best known for his scholarly pursuits as director of the Vatican Library (1761), and his collection of Greek and Roman sculpture in the Villa Albani. (3) Giovanni Francesco (1727–1803) cardinal bp. of Ostia and dean of the Sacred College, who played an important role in the election of Pope *Pius VII. (4) Giuseppe (1750–1834) cardinal and secretary of state to Pope *Pius VIII. BIBLIOGRAPHY: P. Richard, DHGE 1:1369–73; M. DeCamillis, EncCatt 1:638–641.

[F. H. BRIGHAM]

ALBANIA, a republic of SE Europe, the smallest in the Balkan Peninsula, one-fifth the size of England, bounded on the N and E by the Yugoslavian lands of Macedonia and Montenegro, on the S by Epirus, Greece, and on the W coast by the Adriatic sea.

Of pure Aryan descent, Albanians have been divided since antiquity into Ghegs in the N (Illyria) and the Tosks in the S (Epirus). Those in the N speak a native language with Slavic influence; those in the S use Greek words with their native tongue. The dividing line is the Skumbi River. Assigned to the eastern section of the Roman Empire by Gratian (379), Albania later was absorbed by the Byzantine Empire. In medieval times, the Slavs, Avars, Serbs, Bulgaro-Macedonians, Normans, and Venetians were its rulers at different times until the Turks took it over in the 15th century. Their rule extended to 1912 when it was made a principality. A republic (1925) and a kingdom (1928), it has been a Communist people's republic since 1946. Its present allegiance is to Communist China.

The history of its Christian origins shows both a Latin and Byzantine influence. The presence of five bps. from Epirus Nova and Dardania at the Council of Sardica (343–344) establishes the presence of the Church before that date. After the Slavonic invasions (7th-11th cent.) those who moved S toward Greece adopted the Byzantine rite whereas those in the N kept the Latin rite. After the invasion of Turkey, the majority of Albanians became Muslims. Yet some secretly maintained Christian traditions and practices e.g., baptism, veneration of saints, fasting and abstinence, etc. Shkodër is presently the Metropolitan See for Latin rite Catholics. Most Byzantine rite Catholics are Orthodox and reside in S Albania. With the Turkish invasion (1512) several from this area emigrated to Southern Italy where a number eventually joined the Latin rite. Until 1912, the Orthodox Church in Albania used the Greek rite and language. At that time Noli, an Albanian priest, introduced the vernacular and made the Albanian Church autonomous. This was approved by the patriarch of Constantinople (1937). The four dioceses of the Albanian Orthodox Church are under the Metropolitan of Tirana. In 1967 the government closed over 2000 mosques and churches and claimed to be the first atheist state in the world. In Greece, Albanians have retained the Greek rite and language. BIBLIOGRAPHY: H. Leclercq, DACL 7.1:89–180, s. v. "Illyricum"; M. Lacko, NCE 1:246–247.

[F. H. BRIGHAM]

ALBANIA, ORTHODOX CHURCH OF, the autocephalous Orthodox Church of Albania. Christianity entered Albania from Rome by way of the Latin rite and from Greece by way of the Byzantine rite. Details regarding the manner and date of evangelization are lacking but it was prior to the mid-4th century. The Slavic invasions of the 7th cent. disrupted ecclesiastical organization and successive invaders extended this decline. After the 11th cent., groups migrated southward into Greece where they adopted the Byzantine rite and followed Constantinople. Northern Albania, however,

remained Catholic and retained the Latin rite. In spite of strong opposition, the Turks captured the country and maintained control from 1468 to 1912. Thus the majority of the country gradually became Muslim until today Islam claims 68% of the population. Many Albanians escaped to southern Italy and contributed to the formation of the *Italo-Albanian Rite. For centuries the Orthodox Church in Albania was Greek dominated but when independence was proclaimed in 1912, the Orthodox of Albania, under the leadership of the priest Fan Noli, declared itself autocephalous. This was not accepted by the patriarch of Constantinople until 1937. Although the Orthodox Church has adapted itself by recognizing the Communist government, religious conditions are extremely poor. The liturgy is Byzantine and in 1912 the vernacular replaced Greek as the ritual language. The Orthodox Church of Albania numbers approximately 321,000 in four dioceses under the metropolitan see of Tirana.

[F. T. RYAN]

ALBANIAN RITE, one of the 18 Eastern Catholic rites. Byzantine influence was one of the original factors in the Christianizing of Albania. The Orthodox Church of *Albania developed with the acceptance of the Byzantine separation from Rome, but union with the Holy See persisted in the mountain districts until the 17th century. Requests for clergy were made and in 1628 the Congregation for the Propagation of the Faith sent priests from the Greek College in Rome and Basilian monks from S Italy. In 1660, Athanasius II, Abp. of Ochrid, having taken refuge in Chimarra, united with Rome and consecrated one of the missionaries as bp. of the Byzantine rite. The mission was forced to close in 1765 but later enjoyed a temporary restoration (1938–45). In 1939, an apostolic administration of S Albania was established for Catholics of the Byzantine rite and the apostolic delegate held this position until his expulsion in 1945. The Catholic Church of this rite was virtually destroyed by Communist persecution; the last statistics (c.1945) recorded only 400 Albanian rite Catholics. The Latin rite, prevalent in the North, survived in spite of the execution and banishment of its pastors. There are five Eastern dioceses with the Metropolitan See at Shkodër. Three Catholic bishops were residing in the country in 1969 and Albanians of the Latin rite numbered 143,500.

[F. T. RYAN]

ALBAR OF CÓRDOBA (9th cent.), layman and Latin author; his works appear in a single MS. The *Indiculus luminosus* (854) defends the ideals of the Martyrs of Córdoba and is one of the earliest polemics to accuse Islam of immorality. A vita of *Eulogius of Córdoba and the *Confessio,* a manual for penitence, are valuable spiritual works; a correspondence of 20 letters deals mostly with religious disputes. He wrote 540 lines of verse for the Latin renaissance in Córdoba. BIBLIOGRAPHY: E. P. Colbert, *Martyrs of Córdoba, 850–859* (1962); idem, NCE 1:249–250.

[E. P. COLBERT]

ALBELDA, ABBEY OF, former Benedictine monastery of St. Martin in the Diocese of Calahorra, Spain, renowned in 951 as a center of learning. Its scriptorium was famous for the exquisite illumination of the *Codex Albedensis* and for session of other valuable codices. BIBLIOGRAPHY: M. Alamo, DHGE 11:327–333; J. Pérez de Urbel, NCE 1:250.

[S. A. HEENEY]

ALBER, MATTHÄUS (1495–1570), Protestant Reformer, known as "the Luther of Swabia." He stood for moderation amid the religious strife of Germany. After the Augsburg *Interim he labored in the cause of the reform at Württemberg and Stuttgart. He was the first Protestant head at the monastery school of Blaubeuren, near Ulm, where he died. BIBLIOGRAPHY: M. Miller, LTK 1:274; D. Hermann, RGG 1:213–214.

ALBERDI, JUAN BAUTISTA (1810–84), Argentinian lawyer and political theorist. Born at Tucumán, A. studied law and at first supported and then opposed the policies of Rosas. As diplomat in Paris, Madrid, and Washington, he pleaded for the recognition of the South American republics. His ideas on democracy, tolerance, and anticlericalism greatly influenced the Argentina constitutional assembly of 1835. With the advent of Mitre to power, A. went into exile and lived mostly in Paris. His main political treatise was *Bases y puntos de partida para la organización política de la República Argentina* (1852). A.'s political influence in his homeland and in other parts of the Southern Hemisphere has been considerable. BIBLIOGRAPHY: A. Santillan, *Gran Enciclopedia Argentina* 1:91–92; A. Pelliza, *Alberdi, su vida y sus obras* (1877); R. Ravene, *Lecciones de historia Argentina* (1919) v.2.

[P. DAMBORIENA]

ALBERGATI, NICCOLÒ, BL. (1375–1443), a graduate in law from the Univ. of Bologna, who became a Carthusian (1395). After holding administrative positions of importance in his order, he was elected bp. of Bologna (1417) and was made cardinal (1426). He served Martin V and Eugene IV with conspicuous success in delicate diplomatic missions and participated in the Councils of Basel and Ferrara-Florence. He was a patron of learning and after his death was greatly venerated by the Carthusians and the Augustinians, whose protector he was. BIBLIOGRAPHY: P. de Toth, *Il beato cardinale Niccolò Albergati e i suoi tempi* (2 v., 1934); Butler 2:262–263; C. Di Fonsega, BiblSanct 1:662–668.

[N. G. WOLF]

ALBERIC, ST. (d. *c.* 1109), 2d abbot of *Cîteaux, companion of *Robert of Molesme and *Stephen Harding. He assisted with the founding of the abbey of *Molesme and became its first prior (1075). His effort to establish austerity in a time of monastic laxity aroused the hostility of the monks, and he was imprisoned (1090). Liberated, he left the abbey to join Robert and a small group of monks who had left

earlier that year. They eventually formed the core of the new *Cistercian Order founded at Cîteaux, living according to early Benedictine tradition. Robert of Molesme was the first abbot, but A. replaced Robert when the latter returned to Molesme; A. was in turn succeeded by Stephen Harding. BIBLIOGRAPHY: Butler 1:173–174; AS Jan. 2:753; J. B. Dalgairns, *Life of St. Stephen Harding* (new ed., 1946); J. Canivez, DSAM 1:276–277.

ALBERIC OF MONTE CASSINO, a name under which two, possibly three, distinct persons have been confused. (1) Alberic, a monk of Montecassino (*c.* 1101–40), a native of Settefrati, who before entering the monastery (*c.* 1115) had a vision of heaven, hell, and purgatory, which later was written up and came to be accepted as genuine because of A.'s holy life. Many critics believe this to have been one of Dante's main sources. (2) Alberic the Deacon (d. 1088), also a monk of Montecassino, author of treatments in verse of the pains of hell and the joys of heaven. That this A. was born in the same place as the foregoing, or that either is identifiable with the following A., is doubtful. (3) Alberic, cardinal (from *c.* 1057) whose titular church was the SS. Quatro Coronati, and who wrote a treatise *Liber de corpore Domini* against *Berengarius. He appears to have been present at the Roman synod of 1079 before which Berengarius was obliged to sign a formula confessing faith in the substantial conversion of the bread and wine at Mass into the body and blood of Christ. BIBLIOGRAPHY: F. Tinello, EncCatt 1:664–665.

ALBERIC OF OSTIA (1080–1148), Cluniac Benedictine who became abbot at Vézelay and was made cardinal-bishop of Ostia by Innocent II (1138). A. was sent to England as legate and there he visited the sees and monasteries of England and Scotland, introduced Gregorian reform at the Synod of Westminster, and supervised the election of Theobald, abbot of Bec, as abp. of Canterbury. He attended Lateran Council II and a synod at Jerusalem, then worked with St. Bernard against heresy in S France. BIBLIOGRAPHY: O. J. Blum, NCE 1:252.

ALBERIC OF ROSCIATE (1290–1360), a jurist of Bergamo, Italy, who practiced law in that city, in which he was a leading figure. He revised the city's civil statutes and several times served it as an ambassador to the pope at Avignon. Two of his works were of special importance: his *Quaestiones statutorum* because it contained one of the earliest theoretical studies of international law, and a dictionary of civil and canon law because it was the most complete work of the kind attempted up to that time.

[P. K. MEAGHER]

ALBERIC OF SPOLETO (Alberic of Rome; *c.* 905–954). Son of Alberic I, Marquess of Spoleto, and *Marozia, he made himself master of Rome in 932 by expelling the powerful Hugh of Provence, his step-father, and imprisoning his mother and his half-brother, Pope *John XI. A despot, he gave Rome 22 years of relative peace, broken mainly by efforts of Hugh to regain the city and by several punitive expeditions against the Saracens. In 936 he married Alda, daughter of Hugh of Provence. Under A. the temporal power of the papacy was greatly weakened, as John XI and his four successors "cooperated" with the *princeps*. On his deathbed he secured the election of his young son Octavian to the papacy. BIBLIOGRAPHY: C. B. Fisher, NCE 1:252–253; CMedH 3:154–161.

[M. A. WINKELMANN]

ALBERIC OF TROIS FONTAINES (d. *c*.1251), Cistercian monk. A member of the abbey of Trois Fontaines, A. wrote a universal *Chronicle* of events of his own time. Though somewhat uncritical, it is valuable because it included references to records and documents that are no longer extant. BIBLIOGRAPHY: MGS 23:631–950; U. Berlière, DHGE 1:1413–14.

[V. BULLOUGH]

ALBERIC OF UTRECHT, ST. (d. 784), Benedictine monk, abbot, bp. of Utrecht from 780, who reorganized the teaching in the school at Utrecht and continued the missionary work begun by St. Willibrord, sending out St. Ludger to clear away the last traces of paganism among the Frisians. BIBLIOGRAPHY: W. Lampen, BiblSanct 1:671.

[H. JACK]

ALBERIONE, GIACOMO (1884–1971), Italian priest, writer, and founder of numerous religious institutes. Keenly aware of the signs of the times, A. chose communications as a special apostolate. In Alba, Italy, he established (1914) the Society of St. Paul for the Apostolate of Communications (Pauline Fathers) and (assisted by Teresa Merlo, later Mother Thecla) the Daughters of St. Paul (1915), both of which flourish at the present time in 26 countries, including the U.S., and on all continents. Three other sisterhoods likewise owe their inception to A.: Sisters of the Good Shepherd, Sisters of Queen of Apostles, and the Pious Disciples of the Divine Master. Adding also to the 10,000 total membership of his foundations (known collectively as the *Famiglia Paolina*), is a triad of secular institutes: Jesus the Priest (for diocesan clergy), St. Gabriel (for men), and Annunciationists (for women). A.'s own publications were initiated (1958) with two Marian books; in 1964 appeared the development of this ideal in *Woman, the Influence of Her Zeal*. His decade of spiritual writing culminated in 1968 with *Living Our Commitment: Cardinal and Moral Virtues for Religious* and *Paschal Mystery and Christian Living*.

[M. R. BROWN]

ALBERONI, GIULIO (1664–1752), statesman, cardinal. Educated by the Jesuits and Barnabites, A. was a canon at Parma by 1698 and acted as agent of the Duke of Parma on various diplomatic missions (1703–15), including one to

Spain (1711–15), where he became prime minister to the Spanish crown (1716) and was made cardinal (1717). His domestic policies were sound and worked to the national benefit, but his disastrous foreign policy led to his expulsion from Spain (1719). The Spanish invasion of Sicily and Sardinia he had ordered as prime minister caused him to be charged with treason in Italy, and for a time he lived in hiding to escape arrest. Ultimately he was cleared of the charge by Innocent XIII (1723) and made bp. of Malaga. Twice thereafter he served on important papal missions. BIBLIOGRAPHY: E. J. Thomson, NCE 1:253–254.

[H. JACK]

ALBERT OF AIX (Aachen; fl. *c*.1100), canon, custodian of the church at Aix-la-Chapelle, and historian. A. wrote a history of the First Crusade and of the Latin Kingdom of Jerusalem to 1221, *Historia Hierosolymitanae expeditionis*, or *Chronicon Hierosolymitanum de bello sacro*, in 12 books. This was used by William, Abp. of Tyre, as the first six books of his *Belli sacri historia*. The first edition of A.'s work was published at Helmstadt in 1584; another good edition is found in *Recueil des historiens des croisades* (1880) 4:20.

ALBERT THE BEAR (*c*.1100–70), margrave of Brandenburg. A. inherited the Saxon estates of his father (1123) and half those of his mother (1142). He had received (*c*.1123) the margraviate of Lusatia from Lothair, Duke of Saxony, but was deprived of it (1128) when he attacked the Saxon North Mark. He finally received the North Mark in 1134, and, by prearrangement with the duke, secured Brandenburg at the duke's death, assuming the title "margrave of Brandenburg." Henry the Proud drove A. from Saxony and his mark (1137), forcing him to take refuge in Southern Germany until peace was secured (1142). A. had to renounce his Saxon dukedom but received the counties of Weimar and Orlamunde. The greater part of his life was spent in struggles to convert the Slavs; he quelled disorders in the territory of the Wends (1136–37), and from 1134 worked with missionaries to colonize and improve the economy of the lands E of the Elbe. BIBLIOGRAPHY: L. von Heinemann, *Albrecht der Bär* (1864); K. Hampe, *Das Hochmittelalter; Geschichte des Abendlandes von 900 bis 1250* (1932).

ALBERT OF BRANDENBURG (1490–1545), cardinal, abp., and elector of Mainz. A. studied at Frankfurt-an-der-Oder, became abp. of Magdeburg (1513) and of Mainz as well (1514), and was made cardinal in 1518. Commissioned by Leo X (1517) to publish the indulgence for St. Peter's in Saxony and Brandenburg, A. gave an important impetus to the Reformation by inviting J. *Tetzel to preach the indulgence. It was in response to Tetzel's preaching that Luther published his theses in 1517. At first A. showed some favor to Reformers, but at Dessau in 1525 he cleared himself and confirmed his loyalty to the papacy. He granted freedom of religion in his territory and advocated moderation in the treatment of Protestants. He was one of the most liberal Church princes of the time, a patron of art and learning, and a friend of Erasmus. Because of his friendship with Peter *Faber, whom he met in 1542, he gave warm support to the Jesuits. BIBLIOGRAPHY: W. Delius, RGG 1:218; P. Redlich, *Kardinal Albrecht von Brandenburg neue Stift zu Halle* (1900); W. G. Tillmanns, *World and Men around Luther* (1959) 333–335.

[P. K. MEAGHER]

ALBERT THE GREAT, ST. (also known as Albertus Magnus, Albert of Lauingen [on the Danube where he was born of a military family], Albert of Cologne [where he taught and died], and Albert the German [Albertus Teutonicus]; *c*.1200–80), scientist, philosopher, theologian, bp., Doctor of the Church. As an undergraduate at Padua he was received into the Dominicans by Bl. *Jordan of Saxony, and became professor at the Univ. of Paris, provincial of the German Dominicans, and bp. of Regensburg. He was the master of St. Thomas Aquinas, but in his own right is eminent in the history of Western thought. He established the study of nature as a legitimate interest in the Christian tradition. He was credited with exceptional authority by his contemporaries, became the object of continuous devotion in Germany, and was legendary as a benign magician. He was canonized in 1931 and afterwards declared patron of those who cultivate the natural sciences. A true Suabian, he was energetic, strong, rather stocky, with eyes open to minerals, plants, and animals. He was less composed and tranquil than St. Thomas and could be irascible in a scholarly way about humbug or obscurantism in the name of piety. He was not credulous in matters of natural science, but conducted various curious and extensive observations and experiments for himself. He was among the first to assimilate the revived Aristotelianism of the 13th cent., though in philosophy he was more semi-Platonist and influenced by *Avicenna than St. Thomas, and his theology is less interiorly consistent than his disciple's. His thought is distinctive, so much so that his followers (who included Ulrich of Strasbourg, Theodoric of Freiburg, Berthold of Mosburg, and Meister Eckhart) formed a characteristic group of Dominicans called Albertists rather than Thomists; though the two have since coalesced, the two streams are still discernible. His works (38 v., ed. Borgnet, 1890–99) are the monument of the greatest encyclopedist of the Middle Ages. BIBLIOGRAPHY: A. Walz, BiblSanct 1:700–716, with extensive bibliography; J. A. Weisheipl, NCE 1:254–258; M. Albert, *Albert the Great* (1942); H. Wilms, *Albert the Great* (tr. and ed. A. English and P. Hereford, 1938); R. F. Waskell, *"Logic, Language, and Albert the Great,"* JHI 34(No. 3, 1973) 445–450.

[T. GILBY]

ALBERT OF JERUSALEM, ST. (1149–1214), canon regular who became bp. of Bobbio (1184), was transferred to Vercelli (1185), acted as mediator between Clement III and Frederick Barbarossa, was made prince of the empire by Henry IV, and elected patriarch of Jerusalem by the Canons Regular of the Holy Sepulcher (1205). He was greatly esteemed by Innocent III, whom he served as legate first in N Italy and later in Jerusalem. As patriarch he effectively promoted peace in the Near East and took prominent part in civil as well as ecclesiastical affairs in that troubled area. He composed *c*.1208 a set of rules for a group of hermits living on Mt. Carmel, at the request of their prior Burchard (Brocard), which became the first Carmelite rule. A. was assassinated at Akka by a hospitaller he had deposed for his scandalous life. BIBLIOGRAPHY: Butler 3:638–639; A. Staring, BiblSanct 1:686–690.

ALBERT OF LIÈGE (LOUVAIN), ST. (*c*.1166–92), bp. and martyr. Younger son of Godfrey III, Duke of Brabant, A. was canonically elected bp. of Liège in 1191. At that time, though he held the office of archdeacon and provost, he had not advanced in orders beyond the subdiaconate. The Emperor Henry VI opposed the choice and gave the see to Lothaire, provost of Bonn. A., protesting this violation of the Church's rights, went to Rome to appeal to the Holy See. Celestine III confirmed A.'s election, ordained him deacon, and ordered that the abp. of Cologne, or in his default, the abp. of Reims, should ordain him priest and consecrate him. Because of fear of the Emperor, Bruno, Abp. of Cologne, refused, and A. went to Reims where he was ordained and consecrated. There he remained for some weeks because of the turbulent situation in Liège. One day when he was outside the walls of the city he was waylaid and slain by German knights. Henry was forced by the threat of censure to do penance for this crime; and Lothaire, excommunicated, fled to Rome. After the translation of what were supposed to be A.'s relics from Reims to Liège in 1612, Paul V granted to Reims and Brussels a Mass and Office of St. Albert, Bishop and Martyr. The cathedral in Reims was damaged by bombardment in World War I. When in 1919 the debris was being cleared up, it was discovered that the wrong relics had been sent to Liège in 1612. The mistake was rectified ceremoniously in 1921. BIBLIOGRAPHY: MGS 25:137–168; E. de Moreau, *St. Albert de Louvain* (1946); Butler 4:400–402.

[P. K. MEAGHER]

ALBERT OF PARIS (also called Felix; d. 1727), Capuchin preacher. A. entered religious life in 1665. He was active as a preacher of parish missions, at which, as is clear from his manual of missions (1702), he introduced the idea of closed retreats and instruction in mental prayer for those qualified. His *Visite du très saint Sacrement . . .* (1693) inculcated the practice of visits to the Blessed Sacrament spent in scriptural and liturgical meditation. BIBLIOGRAPHY: J. de Blois, DSAM 1:286–287.

[P. K. MEAGHER]

ALBERT OF PISA (d. 1240), Franciscan minister general 1239–40. Received into the order probably by Francis of

Assisi in 1211, he was successively appointed provincial minister to Germany, Spain, Hungary, to various provinces of Italy, and to England. At the deposition of Elias of Cortona in 1239, Albert was elected in his stead. Constitutions passed under his leadership permanently affected the order's government and development. BIBLIOGRAPHY: R. B. Brooke, *Early Franciscan Government* (1959).

[O. J. BLUM]

ALBERT OF PONTIDA, ST. (d. 1095), monastic reformer. A. began life as a soldier, but a cure led him to enter the Benedictines after a pilgrimage to Santiago de Compostela. At Pontida, near Bergamo, he founded the monastery of St. James (*c*.1080) and, as its first prior, governed it according to Cluniac reforming principles until his death. BIBLIOGRAPHY: K. Nolan, NCE 1:258 (bibliog.).

[G. E. CONWAY]

ALBERT OF PRUSSIA (1490–1568), last grand master of the Teutonic Order (1511–25) and first Hohenzollern duke of Prussia (1525–68). A. was converted to Protestantism by Luther, who counseled him to make Prussia a hereditary duchy. This was accomplished in 1525, but A. was obliged to make his duchy a fief of the Polish king. In 1549 A. appointed *Osiander to the Univ. of Königsberg, founded by A. in 1544, and gave him support in the controversy with Melanchthon over justification by faith. As a consequence of this, strict Lutheranism came to prevail in Prussia. BIBLIOGRAPHY: K. Lohmeyer, *Herzog Albrecht von Preussen* (1890); E. Joachim, *Die Politik des letzten Hochmeisters in Preussen, Albrecht von Brandenburg* (1892); for full bibliog., see Schottenloher 3:412–420.

[P. K. MEAGHER]

ALBERT I OF RIGA (*c*.1165–1229), bishop. Perhaps the strongest personality in Baltic history, A. was born near Bremen, ordained priest, and made canon at Bremen after 1189. His uncle, Abp. Hartwig II of Bremen, appointed him the third bp. of Uexküll, in Livonia, then a missionary outpost. During the next 30 years, A. established Livonia and Estonia as Christian lands, but much less as a missionary than as a prince, diplomat, and empire builder. He founded the city of Riga on the Duna in 1200, and by 1208 had established a Livonian principality with the aid of military forces of Saxon Knights of the Sword and his own crusaders, the Brotherhood of the Cross. After 1208 A. absorbed Estonia with equal success. Traveling incessantly he sought Pope Innocent III's help, attended Lateran Council IV, and worked for diplomatic ties with Denmark, Saxony, Finland, and Westphalia. BIBLIOGRAPHY: *Chronicle of Henry of Livonia* (tr. J. A. Brundage, 1961); H. Nolfram, NCE 1:258–259.

[N. F. GAUGHAN]

ALBERT II OF RIGA (late 12th cent.–1272), archbishop. Albert was a German from Cologne, who in 1229 was a canon at Bremen. Abp. Gerard II of Bremen named him (1229) to succeed Albert I at Riga (d. 1229), but the chapter there, claiming independence, chose instead Nicholas, a Premonstratensian, approved by Gregory IX. In 1240, Albert was sent as bp. of Armagh and primate of Ireland to support Henry III of England: here Albert promoted the canonization of Edmund Rich of Abingdon. He was at the Council of Lyons I (1245), and Innocent IV appointed him (1246) abp. of Prussia, Livonia, and Estonia, and apostolic delegate to the adjoining territories. Once again hindered from occupying his see, he administered only Lübeck during the years 1247–53. When Nicholas died (1253), the chapter at Riga elected Albert archbishop. His rule there was clouded by controversies with the Knights of the Sword. BIBLIOGRAPHY: M. Hellman, LTK 1:281; P. M. Starrs, NCE 1:259.

[N. F. GAUGHAN]

ALBERT OF SARTEANO, BL. (1385–1450), Franciscan missionary and papal legate. He accompanied St. Bernardine of Siena as a preacher in the Holy Land (1435–37). Eugene IV sent him (1439–41) as an envoy to Greece and the Near East where his successful meetings with the Coptic patriarch, John of Alexandria, proved to be a significant contribution in the reunion of the Greek Church with Rome at the Council of Florence (1442). BIBLIOGRAPHY: B. Neri, *La vita e i tempi del beato Alberto da Sarteano* (1902); A de Sérent, DHGE 1:1554–56; M. Habig, *Franciscan Book of Saints* (1959); R. Pratesi, BiblSanct 1:696–697.

[J. J. SMITH]

ALBERT OF SAXONY (1316–90), philosopher, bishop. He was a master in the faculty of arts in Paris (1351–60), and was rector in 1357 and in 1362; he was also first rector of the Univ. of Vienna (1365), and became bp. of Halberstadt in 1366. His writings on logic indicate that he was a nominalist; in his physical and mathematical works he developed the physical theories of *John Buridan on the motion of bodies and on gravity. BIBLIOGRAPHY: Gilson HCP 516–520; J. Weisheipl, NCE 1:259.

[T. C. O'BRIEN]

ALBERT OF TRAPANI, ST. (Albert of Abati, or of Sicily; d. 1307), Carmelite. He entered the Carmelite monastery at Trapani, was ordained, and in 1296 became superior of the Sicilian province of his order. He preached successfully throughout Sicily and was credited with the miraculous relief of Messina from famine when it was under siege in 1301. BIBLIOGRAPHY: Butler 3:276–277; L. Saggi, R. Ruocco, BiblSanct 1:676–681.

ALBERTI, LEANDRO (1479–1551), Italian Dominican historical writer. Socius to two masters general of his order, Cajetan and Francesco Silvestri, A. held the office of inquisitor general at Bologna from 1532 and wrote a history of Bologna, lives of illustrious Dominicans, and a description of the whole of Italy. BIBLIOGRAPHY: Quétif-Échard 2:137–139.

[H. JACK]

ALBERTI, LEONE BATTISTA (1404–72), Renaissance architect and theoretician. Brilliantly educated humanist and antiquarian, A. held with Aristotle and St. Thomas Aquinas that art imitates nature—architecture in its material and structure, painting *(istoria)* in its truth to the nature of the subject. Examining classical articulation in nonclassical Renaissance structures, he conceived the "ideal church"—centralized and completely symmetrical—which became supreme in the High Renaissance. He created the Palazzo Ruccelai, Florence (1446), the Tempio Malatestiano (1447) at Rimini, and San Andrea, Mantua (1470). Following his treatise *On Painting* (1435), and *Della famiglia* (1437–41) proposing that children develop according to their natures, his treatise *On Architecture* (1450) established a "divine proportion," A. having deduced a cosmic significance of divine origin from the arithmetical ratios found in musical harmony and seen throughout the universe. A.'s architectural ideals governed 16th-cent. Palladian forms, though falsified by a certain strictness, and are revived in the 20th-cent. "divine proportions" of Le Corbusier's *modulor*. BIBLIOGRAPHY: *Ten Books on Architecture* (ed. J. Rykwert, 1955); *On Painting* (tr. J. R. Spencer, 1956); I. Galantic, *Sources and Analysis of Alberti's Theory of Art* (Harvard Univ. 1965).

[M. J. DALY]

ALBERTINUS OF FONTE AVELLANA, ST. (d. *c.*1294), Camaldolese hermit. A. entered the monastery of Fonte Avellana and *c.*1250 was elected prior general of his congregation. He exercised a pacifying influence on neighboring communities, served several times as papal legate, and refused the offer of a bishopric rather than forsake his eremitical way of life. BIBLIOGRAPHY: C. Somigli, BiblSanct 1:675.

[H. JACK]

ALBERTO CASTELLANI (*c.*1459–1552), Dominican writer, editor, of Venetian origin. The major part of the historical writing by which he is known is devoted to his order. His editing included the Dominican constitutions and various manuals in use in the order; a concordance of the Bible; ascetical, patristic, and apologetical works; and a revision of the Roman Pontifical. BIBLIOGRAPHY: Quétif-Échard 2:48–49.

[H. JACK]

ALBERTUS MAGNUS, ST., see ALBERT THE GREAT, ST.

ALBIGENSES, the *Cathari in S France named from the city of Albi, one of their centers, by the Council of Tours (1169). In spite of repeated condemnations by church councils (Reims, 1148; Verona, 1184), the Albigenses continued to increase, especially in Languedoc and Provence. Among the contributing factors were the protection of an indulgent nobility, the laxity and negligence of an effete clergy, and the common people's admiration for the rigorous asceticism practiced by the *perfecti,* as the full-fledged devotees called themselves. The Albigenses taught a literal Manichaean dualism. Two equal and coeternal principles competed for control of the universe: the principle of good, which created the spiritual world, and the principle of evil, which created the material world. Human souls were created good, but some of them were enticed to rebellion by the evil principle and were punished by being imprisoned in material bodies. Christ, who had a human body in appearance only, was a perfect spirit, who could not die or rise and was not divine. He came only as a teacher to announce a salvation that consisted in total liberation of the soul from matter. This liberation was to be accomplished through asceticism or *consolamentum,* a ceremony by which one was admitted to the ranks of the *perfecti.* If the soul were not completely purified at death, it would be imprisoned in yet another body.

Albigensian dogmatic teachings were a denial of the most fundamental Christian beliefs. They were bitterly against the Church, for its corrupting NT teaching and for using material things in its rituals. Their moral precepts, if carried out on any large scale, would have completely disrupted the Christian social order. The *perfecti* were obliged to abandon their spouses, while ordinary believers were allowed almost complete sexual liberty. Sacred suicide, called *endura,* was advocated as the highest act of virtue. Oaths, military service, capital punishment, and even self-defense were proscribed. The profession of faith of Lateran Council IV was against their teachings (D 800–802).

By the beginning of the 13th cent. the Albigenses had become a threat to the very existence of the Church in S France. Innocent III at first attempted to convert the heretics by sending Cistercian and later Dominican preachers into the infected area, but sermons and disputations proved generally ineffective. When the Papal Legate Peter of Castelnau was murdered in 1208, the Pope decided that the use of force was justified and launched a crusade against the recalcitrant Albigenses. During the next 10 years the army led by Simon de Montfort forced the surrender of the most important heretical strongholds, employing in the process methods that were cruel even by medieval standards. Fighting continued until 1229, but its purpose became political, the incorporation of Languedoc into France. Once deprived of baronial protection, the Albigenses found it necessary to flee or go underground. Their final extirpation was accomplished by the Inquisition established by Gregory IX in 1233. By the end of the 14th cent. their power was completely broken. BIBLIOGRAPHY: M. Lignières, *L'Hérésie albigeoise et la croisade* (1964); E. G. A. Holmes, *Albigensian or Catharist Heresy* (1925); S. Runciman, *Medieval Manichee* (1961) 116–170; H. Söderberg, *La Religion des Cathares: Études sur le gnosticisme de la basse antiquité et du moyen-âge* (1949); H. J. Warner, *Albigensian Heresy* (2v., 1922–28); *Inquisition at Albi, 1299–1300* (ed. G. N. Davis, 1948).

[C. J. LYNCH]

ALBINUS (2d cent. A.D.), Middle Platonist philosopher. He distinguished formally the First God *(prōtos theos)*, mind *(nous)*, and soul *(psychē)*. The First God is unmoved, but operates through the *nous* or world-intellect. Ideas of Plato are interpreted as the eternal ideas of God and as the patterns or exemplary causes of things. Ascent to God is attained through the various degrees of beauty. All this reflects a fusion of Platonic, Aristotelian, and Neo-Pythagorean concepts. In his psychology and ethics he likewise combines Platonic, Aristotelian, and Stoic notions in a strikingly eclectic manner. In his fusion of Platonic and Aristotelian elements he is precursor of Neoplatonism. BIBLIOGRAPHY: Copleston 1:455; CHGMP 64–70 (best treatment).

[M. R. P. McGUIRE]

ALBINUS, see ALCUIN.

ALBINUS OF ANGERS, ST. (469–550), abbot, bishop. A. entered the monastery of Tincillac and became its abbot in 504; in 529 he reluctantly consented to be made bp. of Angers. He distinguished himself by his generosity to the poor, his ransoming of captives, and his vigorous attack, which had the support of St. Caesarius of Arles, upon the incestuous marriages not uncommon between people of noble rank at that time. BIBLIOGRAPHY: Butler 1:452; C. Lefebvre, BiblSanct 1:720–721.

[H. JACK]

ALBIZZESCHI, BERNARDINO DEGLI, see BERNARDINE OF SIENA, ST.

ALBO, JOSEPH (*c.*1380–*c.*1435), Spanish-Jewish religious philosopher. A., who had studied under Ḥasdai Crescas, defended Judaism at the Disputation of Tortosa (1413–14). Seeing the need of a better presentation of Jewish religious thought, he produced a work called *Sepher ha-Ikkarim* (Book of Dogmas). In this he indicated three basic and essential principles (*shorashim*, roots) that cannot be denied without heresy: the existence of God, divine revelation, and reward and punishment. Other teachings, including that concerning an expected Messiah, are branches *(anaphim)* and can be called into question without prejudice to orthodoxy. Although his apparent indifference to messianic doctrine gave offense to some, his work achieved wide popularity.

[P. K. MEAGHER]

ALBORNOZ, GIL ÁLVAREZ CARILLO DE (*c.*1295–1367), Spanish prelate who brought order to the Papal States in preparation for the return of *Urban V. As abp. of Toledo (1338–50) he crusaded against the Moors in Andalusia and helped unify Castile with the Ordenamiento de Alcalá (1348). The rejection of his policies by Peter I drove him to Avignon, where he was made cardinal (1350). By skillful use of negotiation and military force (1353–67) and with no aid from Emperor Charles IV or Cola di Rienzo, he brought one petty tyrant after another to recognize the popes as overlords, meanwhile fostering communal rights.

His Constitutions (1357) governed the Papal States until 1816. His political gains, tenaciously opposed by Bernabò Visconti and all but undone by an inept successor, were set back by the Western Schism. BIBLIOGRAPHY: E. P. Colbert, NCE 1:264, P. Partner, *Lands of St. Peter—the Papal States in the Middle Ages and Early Renaissance* (1972).

[E. P. COLBERT]

ALBRECHTSBERGER, JOHANN GEORG (1736–1809), Austrian church musician, whose career culminated in Vienna with appointments as court organist (1772) and director at St. Stephen's Cathedral (1792). His reputation as a master of counterpoint brought him many pupils, most notably Beethoven, who evidently received excellent instruction from A. Only a few of A.'s compositions, which number more than 250, have been published; thus his numerous church works including 26 Masses plus many Graduals, Offertories, hymns, psalms, etc., are unfortunately little known. BIBLIOGRAPHY: H. Goos, MGG 1:303–307; F. Gehring, Grove DMM 1:97; P. A. Scholes, *Oxford Companion to Music* (1970).

[A. DOHERTY]

ALBRIGHT, JACOB (Albrecht; 1759–1808), evangelical preacher and church founder. Born at Fox Mountain, Pa., of immigrant parents from the German Palatinate, A. received little schooling; he was confirmed into the local Lutheran church. After service in the Continental Army, he married, settled, and prospered at Reamstown, Lancaster Co., Pennsylvania. The impression left by itinerant revivalists, and the sudden death of several of his children, moved him to reflect on his own spiritual condition. Following a conversion experience in 1791, he united with a nearby Methodist *class and was later licensed as a lay preacher. He began in 1796 to preach the gospel of personal salvation and pious Christian living to his spiritually slumbering neighbors, moving some to antagonism, others to conversion. By 1800 three small classes totaling 20 persons had been organized. In 1803 he experienced a lay ordination by representatives of these classes. His adherents became known as Albright People, or Albright Brethren, or German Methodists. His plan for a German branch of Methodism was not accepted by Methodist bishops; but in 1807 at the first annual conference with his lay preachers A. adopted an organization patterned after the Methodist Episcopal Church; this was the beginning of the Evangelical Church. *EVANGELICAL UNITED BRETHREN.

[K. J. STEIN]

ALBRIGHT, WILLIAM FOXWELL (1891–1971), a distinguished scholar in the field of Near Eastern and biblical studies. Born in Chile to Methodist missionary parents and educated in the U.S., A. received his Ph.D. from Johns Hopkins in 1916. By 1919 he was a fellow of the American School of Oriental Research, becoming its acting-director (1920) and subsequently director (1921–29). He was professor of Semitic language at Johns Hopkins (1929–58), but his association with the American School in Jerusalem continued. A. served a second term as its director 1933–36, and this school was renamed Albright Institute of Archeological Research in 1970.

A.'s immense productivity as orientalist, archaeologist, biblical scholar, Palestinologist, philologian, linguist, and philosopher of history can scarcely be measured: in the 60 years following his first scholarly article in 1911, the total number of his books, articles, and reviews exceeded 1,000. Universally acclaimed for his contribution to learning, he was recipient of countless honors from academic institutions and societies. A. remained active in research, lecturing, and teaching after his retirement until 2 months before his death in Baltimore, Md. A volume of essays in his honor signalized both his retirement and his 80th birthday. The blossoming of Catholic biblical and Near Eastern scholarship was enhanced by A.'s teaching career in which he influenced many modern Scripture scholars. As historian and synthesist, he is best known through the stimulating study *From the Stone Age to Christianity* (1940). A. established the fundamental chronology of Palestinian archeology by publishing the results of excavations in *The Excavations of Tell Beit Mirsim* (3 v., 1932–43). A popular treatment of the subject is found in *Archaeology of Palestine* (1949; rev. ed. 1960).

A. combined control of data with daring, breadth, penetration, and a sense of the expanding limits of his field of study. New societies and new journals sought constantly the work of this archaeologist and Christian humanist. Among his major works is also *Yahweh and the Gods of Canaan* (1968). BIBLIOGRAPHY: "Essays in Honor of W. F. Albright," *Bible and the Ancient Near East* (ed. G. E. Wright, 1961) bibliog. of Albright 1911–58; *Near Eastern Studies in Honor of William Foxwell Albright* (ed. H. Goedicke, 1971).

[J. MORGAN]

ALBRIGHT BRETHREN, see ALBRIGHT, JACOB.

ALBUIN (ALBWIN) OF SÄBEN-BRIXEN, ST. (d. *c*.1005), bishop. Born of an aristocratic family in Carinthia, Albuin was educated at Brixen. He became bp. of Säben (*c*.977) and transferred the episcopal residence to Brixen. Active in political life, Albuin counted Otto II and Henry II among his benefactors. BIBLIOGRAPHY: A. W. A. Leeper, *History of Medieval Austria* (1941); R. Schmandt, NCE 1:266.

[M. J. FINNEGAN]

ALCALÁ, UNIVERSITY OF, an institution of higher learning that developed from a *studium generale* whose establishment at Alcalá de Henares (a town 19 miles NE of Madrid known as Complutum before the Moorish occupation) was authorized by King Sancho IV of Castile in 1293. Nothing is known of the early history of this studium. In 1459 Pius II granted permission to Abp. Alonso Carrilo y Acuña to establish there three professorships for the teaching of grammar and the arts. Card. Ximenez de Cisneros in 1499 erected the College of San Ildefonso and incorporated into it the pre-existing studium. This marked the beginning of the institution as a university with faculties of liberal arts, philosophy, canon law, and the classical and biblical languages. Because it was intended primarily for clerical students, it did not at first have faculties of medicine and civil law, but these were added later. In the beginning the university consisted of one major college (San Ildefonso) and 18 minor colleges. The number of its colleges was 27 when the university was at its peak; one of these, operated by the Franciscan sisters, was for women. The student population at its greatest was about a third of the size of Salamanca's. The university was distinguished for its cultivation of the scholarly interests awakened by the Renaissance. Its study of the biblical languages bore fruit in the publication of the celebrated *Complutensian Polyglot Bible* (6 v., 1514–17), and its achievement in scholastic philosophy and theology was hardly less distinguished. The professors of the Discalced Carmelite college of St. Cyril published in the 17th cent. a frequently edited and reprinted course in scholastic philosophy, the *Complutensis artium cursus*. Among the great names associated with the university either as professors or students were Ignatius of Loyola, Thomas of Villanova, Melchior Cano, John of Avila, Luis de Molina, Francisco Suárez, and Diego Laínez. The transfer of the university from Alcalá to Madrid was seriously considered several times during the 17th cent. because of trouble between town and gown and other disorders. After reform measures instituted in the 18th cent. by royal visitors had robbed the university of its autonomy, its vitality declined. In 1836 it was transferred to Madrid and was later replaced by the Central Univ. of Madrid. BIBLIOGRAPHY: H. Rashdall, *Universities of Europe in the Middle Ages* (ed. F. M. Powicke and A. B. Emden, new ed., 1936); J. Urriza, NCE 1:266–267.

[M. B. MURPHY]

ALCALÁ DE HENARES, Renaissance center of 16th-cent. Spain. It is located 19 miles NE of Madrid, on the Henares River in New Castile. Alcalá, an Arabic name, replaced the Latin Complutum, from which derives the name of the *Complutensian Polyglot produced there under Ximenez. Alcalá had bps. at least from 579 (Novelus) to 851 (Venerius). After the Reconquest it came under Toledo, the Spanish primatial see. Abps. of Toledo often resided in Alcalá, and several councils met there. Ximenez (abp. 1495–1517) founded a university at Alcalá that opened in 1508 and became celebrated as a center of the new learning and a force for church reform. Its faculty included noted theologians, and among its illustrious alumni was St. Ignatius. In 1836 the university moved to Madrid, and Alcalá now forms part of the Madrid archdiocese. It was the birthplace of Cervantes, Emperor Ferdinand I, and Henry VIII's first wife, Catherine.

[T. EARLY]

ALCANTARINES, the Franciscan Observants in Spain with whom St. Peter of Alcántara became associated and among whom he achieved a position of leadership. They were commonly known by this title until it was suppressed in 1897.

[P. K. MEAGHER]

ALCHEMIST HERETICS. John XXII's condemnation of alchemists in 1317 seems directed against the fraudulent pretensions of many practitioners of the art rather than against any clearly identifiable doctrinal eccentricity inherent in their teachings. Still the esoteric jargon and the flights of mystical allegory in which alchemists commonly indulged exposed many of them to the charge of heresy. The 14th cent. saw many clerics brought to trial for the practice of alchemy and other occult arts. The inquisitor Nicholas Emeric (d. 1399) prosecuted many alchemists as heretics. The 15th-cent. *Adamites in Bohemia found a place for alchemy in their thinking and inspired the painter Hieronymus Bosch to take an interest in the art. BIBLIOGRAPHY: J. E. Grennen, NCE 1:268–270.

[P. K. MEAGHER]

ALCHEMY, in the strict sense, a pseudoscience concerned with attempts to transform base metals (such as lead or copper) into silver or gold. Since such attempts presumed chemical concepts, alchemy for most of its history was indistinguishable from chemistry. It therefore attracted some of the greatest intellects of medieval times. As late as the 16th cent. practically all rulers patronized alchemists even though their activities were often pervaded by a spirit of secrecy, greed, and extravagant mysticism. Its beginnings are usually traced to the Hellenistic period (after 323 B.C.) in Alexandria, where various elements of Greek philosophy, Egyptian technology, and Middle Eastern mysticism coalesced. It was picked up by the Arabs who expanded it and transmitted it to Latin Europe. Alchemists invented and used many types of laboratory apparatus such as the still, furnaces, water baths, flasks, and beakers now used in chemistry, developed scientific procedures, and discovered a few basic chemical processes like sublimation. Nevertheless, their achievements were minor as compared with the degree of intellectual effort which the Middle Ages unfortunately devoted to the science. Displaying obscurantist tendencies, perhaps partly in defense of trade secrets, alchemy appealed to many by the aura of mystery with which it surrounded itself, and mystically minded adherents made it quasitheological and allegorical. The best known medieval Latin writer on alchemy was Geber whose *Summa perfectionis* was a summary of Arabic practices and concepts. St. Thomas Aquinas and other medieval theologians accepted the possibility of transmutation of metals, but alchemists often were the subject of satire by Petrarch, Chaucer, Erasmus, Ben Jonson, and others. With the development of the science of chemistry in the 18th cent., alchemy moved from the main stream of science to join astrology, numerology,

and other pseudosciences. BIBLIOGRAPHY: E. J. Holmyard, *Alchemy* (1954); M. Eliade, *Forge and the Crucible* (tr. S. Corrin, 1962); J. Lindsay, *Origins of Alchemy in Greco-Roman Egypt* (1970) bibliog. 433–440; G. B. Kauffman and Z. A. Payne, "Contributions of Ancients and Alchemists," *Chemistry* 46 (1973) 6–10.

[V. L. BULLOUGH]

ALCHER OF CLAIRVAUX (fl. 11th cent.), Cistercian monk of Clairvaux, contemporary of St. Bernard, friend and correspondent of Peter of Celle and Isaac of Stella. Attributed to him are the *De spiritu et anima,* once thought to be the work of St. Augustine, and also the pseudo-Augustinian *De deligendo Deo.* The *De spiritu et anima* is of some importance in the history of both psychology and of spiritual literature. These writings are in large part compilations of thoughts of St. Augustine and other writers of earlier times. BIBLIOGRAPHY: J. M. Canivez, DSAM 1:294–295.

[H. JACK]

ALCIBIADES OF APAMEA (fl. 220), a member of the Gnostic sect, the *Elkesaites who according to Hippolytus brought the Book of Elkesai to Rome from Syria. BIBLIOGRAPHY: Bihlmeyer-Tüchle 1:144.

[F. H. BRIGHAM]

ALCIMUS (Alkimos), Hellenized form of Hebrew 'elāqīm, "God will raise up." A. belonged to the Oniad priestly family (1 Macc 7.14; 2 Macc 14.7) and was a Jewish leader of the pro-Hellenistic party in Judea. A. was prevented from taking the office of high priest by Judas Maccabeus. He appealed for aid to Demetrius I, who gave him an army to take into Judea. A. was routed from Judea by Judas Maccabeus. Again he applied for help to the Syrian King Demetrius. A. finally came into power in 160 B.C. He died while tearing down the wall in the Temple area which separated the Jews from the Gentiles.

[C. C. O'DONNELL]

ALCOBAÇA, ABBEY OF, the greatest Cistercian abbey in Portugal, founded by monks from Clairvaux in 1153. It was rebuilt after its destruction by the Moors in 1195. Its monumental Gothic church, the largest in Portugal, was consecrated in 1252. The abbey, housing 300 monks at the peak of its development in the 14th century, played an important part in the religious, cultural, and economic development of medieval Portugal. From it came Portugal's first college (1269), first pharmacy, and an early printing press. It did important work in agricultural education through model farms, and it developed techniques in metallurgy, ceramics, glasswork, and weaponry. The monastery was suppressed in 1834; its buildings are now a national monument. BIBLIOGRAPHY: M. Cocheril, *Études sur le monachisme en Espagne et au Portugal* (1966); L. J. Lekai, NCE 1:271–272.

ALCOCK, JOHN (1430–1500), English bishop. After doctorates in civil and canon law at Cambridge (before 1459), A. became rector of St. Margaret's, Fish Street, London (1461). Bishop of Rochester in 1472 and keeper of the great seal, he was successively bp. of Worcester (1476) and Ely (1486). Chiefly known for his educational interests and for the setting up of Jesus College, Cambridge, he is the author of some works of devotion, notably *Mons perfectionis* (printed by Wynkyn de Worde 1496–97) and *Abbay of the Holy Gost* (a commentary in English on the penitential psalms). BIBLIOGRAPHY: Emden Camb 5–6, 669.

[L. E. BOYLE]

ALCOHOLICS ANONYMOUS (AA), a society of recovered alcoholics who assist each other in achieving and maintaining sobriety. It was founded in the U.S. in 1935 by Bill W., a former New York stock broker, and Dr. Bob S. (1879–1950), an Akron, Ohio, surgeon. The two became acquainted through participation in the *Oxford Groups. The tradition that members maintain anonymity in print or on the air is designed to assure potential members that their membership will not be publicly revealed, and also to preclude any member's using his association with AA for personal gain.

The society receives general direction from a General Service Board (composed of both recovered alcoholics and nonalcoholics), which since 1951 has reported to an annual General Service Conference. The society currently reports about 15,000 groups with some 400,000 members in more than 90 countries. It is totally self-supporting, and insistent upon devoting itself exclusively to its one purpose without involvement in other causes.

Early members of AA listed 12 steps toward their recovery, and they remain fundamental in the society's work. The first is, "We admitted we were powerless over alcohol—that our lives had become unmanageable." AA is not connected with any religious group but puts strong emphasis on the spiritual. Its third step is, "Made a decision to turn our will and our lives over to the care of God *as we understood him.*" BIBLIOGRAPHY: Bill W., *Alcoholics Anonymous Comes of Age* (1957); "Anonymous Ally," *Time* 97 (1972) 52.

[T. EARLY]

ALCOHOLISM, the disorder of being so addicted to the drinking of fermented liquor or distilled spirits that bodily, mental, and moral health are sapped or broken down, usually with grave damage to others. Starting with this rough nominal definition, we should note that it is, in the strictest sense, a medical category, to be distinguished from drunkenness, which is a moral category. Therefore alcoholism, as opposed to drunkenness, is in itself a "physical evil," or a pathological condition, a disease or at least a symptom of mental illness, to be pitied. It is not in this sense a "moral evil," or a fault to be blamed. However, in the criss-cross of individuality the two shade into one another, and alcoholism does involve its victim in grave issues of right and wrong.

An outline of a matter so complicated and still controversial must proceed cautiously. Different criteria are proposed by different authorities to distinguish the alcoholic from other drinkers. Although the alcoholic's drinking is marked by excess, it should be observed that the measures of quantity and repetition and protractedness are quite relative. There are redoubtable drinkers who cannot be classified as alcoholics who might regard the intake of some alcoholics as scarcely enough to moisten the human clay. The indulgences of such drinkers may require forgiveness as sins but not treatment by a doctor; they may even acquire a hobnailed liver or die of drink without qualifying as alcoholics. On the other hand, a person may suffer from alcoholism without ever having been completely drunk. One man's drink is another man's poison, a saying that is perfectly exemplified in this matter, for we are faced with a difference in kind, not merely in degree.

In the effort toward definition analysis seems to come upon two notes that are more decisive than others, namely *addiction and fixation.

In the development of a human act from necessary volitions to irreversible consequences, there is between them a patch of indeterminancy which is normally resolved by the agent's making up his own mind. This moment of choice in normal drinking, whether virtuous or vicious, lies within the drinking episode and from the moment of lifting the glass. Though control may tend to slacken as the session goes on, so that a man may not know when to stop, the drinking is imputed to him because he did decide for himself to start and did continue in the grip of no insuperable compulsion. An alcoholic, on the other hand, must never start; for him there can be no moment of poise within the drinking episode, and if his freedom is to operate, then this must be thrown back well beforehand. If he toys with a sip, he is lost, for because of his physiological condition, as some hold, or because of a psychological compulsion, a train of mechanisms will be started off which he is quite unable to check. For him the moment of choice comes in his firm resolve to be a total abstainer.

Next, whereas ordinary drinking is prompted by a complex of motives—thirst, sociability, appropriate surroundings, historical associations, labels evocative sometimes of ancient and assured cultures, and even of self-pampering —the alcoholic drinks to be relieved of his anxiety, to escape from his insecurity, and he drinks for the most part sadly, in the end to drink away the symptoms of his drinking. His preoccupation centers and is fixed on the alcoholic content of his drink, and in extreme cases he is prepared to isolate that in some noxious liquid, e.g., from the bowl of a magnetic compass. Even the most abandoned drinker who is not an alcoholic never takes alcohol abstract, but a much more companionable *Gestalt.*

There is no cure for alcoholism, for a sufferer will always react abnormally if he starts drinking again, even after years of abstinence. The remedy lies in the all or nothing principle. Sufferers can be rehabilitated, and various methods, chemical, psychological, and spiritual have been used with success. In particular the work of *Alcoholics Anonymous deserves to be signalized. Prevention by the enactment of universal and total prohibition would probably be as ineffective as it was when tried before in the U.S., and it would bring about other evils. Yet the price of freedom is high when, as has been calculated, about 1 in 20 of the drinking population of the U.S. has passed beyond being a problem drinker and has become an alcoholic. It hits some racial groups—e.g., the Chinese, Italians, and Jews—less than others. In assessing responsibility each case must be judged separately. Though the governing rules look alike, drunkenness is a condition which lacks *temperance in pleasure, whereas what sin there may be in cases of alcoholism seems rather to lie in a lack of fortitude about fears. BIBLIOGRAPHY: E. H. Jellinek, *Disease Concept of Alcoholism* (1959); J. C. Ford, *Depth Psychology, Morality and Alcoholism* (1951); *idem, Man Takes a Drink* (1956).

[T. GILBY]

ALCUIN (*c*.735–804), educator, theologian, liturgist, friend and adviser of Charlemagne, leading figure in the *Carolingian Renaissance. An Anglo-Saxon, A. was educated at the cathedral school of York under Aelbert, whom he succeeded as teacher and librarian (778). At the invitation of *Charlemagne he went to the Frankish court to serve as adviser in religious and educational matters (782). There he became head of the palace school, established a library of importance, and organized and systematized Charlemagne's educational program. His system centered about the traditional seven liberal arts, and he employed the dialogue method for instruction; Boethius, Augustine, and the grammarians were the principal subjects of his academic concern. Among his more famous pupils were *Amalarius of Metz and *Rabanus Maurus. More than 250 of his letters are extant, valuable for the view they provide of Carolingian society. He wrote poetry, improved some vitae of the saints by putting them into better Latin, wrote and edited textbooks on grammar, rhetoric, dialectic, and orthography, and commented upon various books of the Bible. None of these works are of great literary or scholarly merit; his chief contribution to learning lay less in his own works than in the impetus and practical direction he gave to education. Circumstances compelled him to take an interest in theology. He refuted the Adoptionism of *Felix of Urgel and *Elipandus of Toledo in three apologetical treatises, denounced heretical doctrines at synodal meetings, and composed the Frankish episcopate's *Synodica*, as well as Charlemagne's letter from the Council of Frankfort to Spain in 794. The authorship of the *Libri Carolini* has been attributed to him, but this is regarded as questionable by many authorities. To revise the Roman liturgy in Gaul he edited a lectionary and revised and supplemented the Gregorian Sacramentary to adapt it to certain Gallican customs. The influence of Alcuin and his circle of friends upon Charlemagne's coronation has been recognized by recent scholarship. Works: PL v. 100, 101; additions can be found in P. Jaffé, *Monumenta Alcuiana* (ed.

W. Wattenbach and E. L. Dümmler, *Bibliotheca Rerum Germanicarum* 6; 1873). BIBLIOGRAPHY: E. S. Duckett, *Alcuin, Friend of Charlemagne: His World and His Work* (1951); G. Ellard, *Master Alcuin: Liturgist* (1956); L. Wallach, NCE 1:279–280; A. F. West, *Alcuin and the Rise of the Christian Schools* (1971).

[M. S. TANEY]

ALDEBERT AND CLEMENT (fl. mid-8th cent.), early medieval examples of religious frauds. The former of Gallic, the latter of Irish, origin, they imposed on the credulity of Gallic bishops to get themselves ordained. With extravagant claims of spiritual gifts they managed to convince many simple folk of their sanctity. They were condemned at several councils in the 740s and the Roman Council of 745 degraded them and imposed severe penalties. Nothing is known of their later history. BIBLIOGRAPHY: C. P. Loughran, NCE 1:280.

[H. JACK]

ALDEGUNDIS, ST. (Aldegunda, Adelgunda; *c*.630–684 [or d. between 695 and 700]), abbess. She founded and governed the convent of Maubeuge. Her cult began early and spread widely; her help was invoked for protection against cancer, the disease from which she died. BIBLIOGRAPHY: A. D'Haenens, BiblSanct 1:737–739.

[H. JACK]

ALDEIAMENTO SYSTEM, a method used in evangelizing and educating Indians in Brazil. In this plan Indians were gathered into mission-settlements (*aldeias*) and thus kept separated from their pagan fellow tribesmen. This method, which had some success, was introduced after other plans had been tried and found ineffective. It was analogous to the system of reductions employed by the Jesuits elsewhere in South America.

[P. K. MEAGHER]

ALDEMAR, ST. (fl. 982), Benedictine abbot. First a monk at Monte Cassino, later in charge of the monastery of San Lorenzo at Capua, after ordination to the priesthood he became the founder of monasteries in the region of Chieti and in Piceno. He is buried at Bucchanico. BIBLIOGRAPHY: AS March 3:487–490; Mabillon AS 6.2:625–630.

[W. A. JURGENS]

ALDENBURG ABBEY, see OUDENBURG ABBEY.

ALDERICH, ST. (d. *c*.1200), Premonstratensian lay brother. Born of a noble family, he served his monastery at Füssenich as a swineherd. His story is remarkably similar to that told of Alexander of Foigny, a Cistercian; this has given rise to the suspicion of legendary duplication.

[H. JACK]

ALDETRUDE, ST. (d. *c*.696), daughter of SS. *Vincent Maldegarius and Waldetrude. A. succeeded her aunt, St. Aldegundis as abbess of Maubeuge. Much of what is recorded of her is obviously legendary. BIBLIOGRAPHY: AS (1865) Feb. 3:514–516; A. D'Haenens, BiblSanct 1:750–751.

[H. JACK]

ALDHELM, ST. (639–709), first bp. of Sherborne, earliest Anglo-Saxon writer whose works have survived. Related to West-Saxon royalty and educated at the church school of Canterbury, A. passed on to the West-Saxon Church a mixed Roman and Celtic tradition. His Latin works are: *De virginitate* (prose); *Carmina ecclesiastica* (religious poems); a treatise on grammar. He also wrote letters of literary and historical importance and popular vernacular verses. *Works*, ed. R. Ehwald (MGH Auct. Ant. 15). BIBLIOGRAPHY: Bede, *Ecclesiastical History* (tr. J. Stevenson, rev. L. C. Jane, 1954) 5:18; S. B. Greenfield, *Critical History of Old English Literature* (1965); *Riddles of Aldhelm* (tr. J. H. Pitman, 1970); V. Lagorio, "Aldhelm's Aenigmata in Codex Vaticanus Palatinus Latinus 1719," *Manuscripta* 15 (1971) 23–27.

[M. M. BARRY]

ALDOBRANDINI, a celebrated Florentine family prominent in Vatican affairs in the 16th and 17th centuries. The family, now extinct, produced a pope, several cardinals, archbishops, bishops, and men of learning. *Silvestro* (1499–1558) was a distinguished jurist who, when banished from Florence in 1531, entered the service of Pope Paul III in Rome and established the fortunes of the family. Four of his sons held high office in the Church. One of them, *Ippolito*, became pope as Clement VIII (1592–1605). He encouraged the apostolate of St. Francis de Sales, took counsel with St. Philip Neri, and reconciled Henry IV of France with the Church. BIBLIOGRAPHY: J. C. Willke, NCE 1:282.

[D. NUGENT]

ALDRED, see EALDRED.

ALDRIC OF SENS, ST. (d. 836 or 841), Benedictine abbot, abp. of Sens (from 829). Brought by Louis the Pious from the abbey of Ferrières to Aachen to direct the palace school, A. was elected abbot of Ferrières (821) and consecrated abp. of Sens. He reformed several monasteries, among them Saint-Denis. At the Council of Thionville (835), he and the other bishops voted unanimously to restore King Louis, who had been deposed by his own sons. BIBLIOGRAPHY: P. Cousin, NCE 1:283; H. Stein, DBF 1:1361.

[G. M. COOK]

ALEANDRO, GIROLAMO (1480–1542), Italian humanist, papal envoy, cardinal (from 1538). A. studied in Padua, lectured in Venice, Orleans, and Paris, and was well acquainted in humanistic circles. Sent to Germany in 1520 as nuncio to Charles V, he failed to secure Luther's arrest, but succeeded in bringing about his condemnation at the Diet of Worms (1521). He was strongly in favor of Paul III's desire for a general council, left an unfinished treatise on the subject, but died before the council's convocation. BIBLIOGRAPHY: E. Santovito, EncCatt 1:741–742.

[V. SAMPSON]

ALEGAMBE, PHILIPPE (1592–1652), Jesuit biographer. Born in Belgium, A. studied in Rome, taught in Austria, and served as tutor to the Prince of Eggenberg. He was called back to Rome in 1638 as secretary in the Jesuit generalate. There he brought Ribadeneira's *Bibliotheca scriptorum S.J.* up to date, published a number of biographies, and in his *Heroes et victimae caritatis Soc. Jesu* (1658) reported the apostolate of service to the plague-stricken in which many 17th-cent. Jesuits distinguished themselves. BIBLIOGRAPHY: T. J. Campbell, CE 1:281; Bremond 1:67.

ALEGRE, FRANCISCO JAVIER (1729–88), Jesuit historian. For 10 years he taught the classics, philosophy, and theology in Havana and Mérida, and in 1764 was called to Mexico City to write the history of the Jesuits in New Spain; before the expulsion of the Society from Mexico (1767), he had mastered the contents of hundreds of original documents and had the history well under way. He spent the remainder of his life in Bologna in study and writing. BIBLIOGRAPHY: F. Zubillaga, NCE 1:284; F. Bandelier, CE 1:281.

[H. JACK]

ALEIJADINHO (Antônio Francisco Lisboa; 1730 or 1738–1814), major exponent of Brazilian rococo style in sculpture and architecture. At Congonhas do Campo, in Minas Gerais, a state rich in diamonds and gold, is the series of *Twelve Prophets* in stone (1800–05)—his most famous pieces—on the square of the Church of Nosso Senhor Bom Jesus de Matazinhos, one of his two major architectural works, the other being the Church of São Francisco de Assis (1766) in Ouro Preto, his birthplace. His architectural style of elliptical curves and sensuous rhythms, though derived from Borromini through works of Italian architects in Portugal in the 17th and 18th centuries, in its unusual emotional intensity and distinctive elegance is more related to 18-th cent. rococo of Germany and Austria. Lisbôa, crippled by disease (probably leprosy) was called Aleijadinho (Little Cripple). BIBLIOGRAPHY: G. Bazin, *Aleijadinho et la sculpture baroque au Brésil* (1963).

[M. J. DALY]

ALEIPTRON (Gr. ointment box), in the Byzantine Church an instrument for anointing the foreheads of the people with oil or anointing the walls of the church in the rite of consecration. It is sometimes merely a stick tipped with cotton but also may be especially made of metal with a small ball at the end for applying the oil. In the latter form its handle may be decorated and may form a matched set with the communion spoon and lance. *ANOINTING.

[A. J. JACOPIN]

ALEKSANDR, see ALEXANDER.

ALEMANNI, see ALAMANNI.

ALEMANY, JOSEPH SADOC (1814–88), Spanish Dominican who became bp. of Monterey, California, and later first abp. of San Francisco. He came to the U.S. in 1840, became a U.S. citizen, and worked with the Dominicans of the Ohio-Kentucky-Tennessee area. As provincial of the U.S. Dominicans he attended a general chapter of the order in Rome and while there was consecrated bp. of Monterey (1850). His appointment to the archdiocesan see of San Francisco came in 1853; he resigned and retired to Spain in 1884. BIBLIOGRAPHY: J. B. McGloin, *Life of Joseph Alemany* (1965); RACHS 17:130–133.

[P. K. MEAGHER]

ALEMBERT, JEAN LE ROND D' (1717–83), a *philosophe* linked with *Diderot in editorship of the *Encyclopédie*, to which he contributed a noteworthy introductory essay. He enjoyed high esteem as a scientist, esp. as a mathematician. His two great passions, it is said, were for mathematics and against priests, although A.'s anticlericalism was, during his lifetime, carefully disguised. In 1759 he published a work of popular science: *Elements de la philosophie*. He rejected revealed religion as absolutely foreign to the sciences of man in its object, character, and the kind of conviction it produces. Religion is made rather for the heart than for the mind; but reason must examine the ground of belief, and the historical evidence of religion must be criticized by the rules of evidence. Christianity is pure deism, Jesus Christ a kind of philosopher. D'Alembert died a skeptic in religion. BIBLIOGRAPHY: R. Grimsley, *Jean D'Alembert* (1963); J. Bertrand, *D'Alembert* (1889); M. Muller, *Essai sur la philosophie de Jean d'Alembert* (1926); J. N. Pappas, *Voltaire and d'Alembert* (1962); EncPhil 1:68–69.

[J. P. REID]

ALEN (ALLEN), JOHN (1476–1534), last old Catholic abp. of Dublin. A graduate of Cambridge, A. studied law in Rome where he also acted as agent for the abp. of Canterbury. He served as commissary to Wolsey in the suppression of the small monasteries (1524), was granted a number of benefices, and was made abp. of Dublin in 1528. He was also chancellor of Ireland, 1528–32. Because of his earlier association with Wolsey, he was hated by the Irish house of Kildare, and when the false word spread that Gerald Fitzgerald, its ninth earl, then imprisoned in the Tower, had been put to death, A. was murdered by two retainers of the earl's son. BIBLIOGRAPHY: J. Gairdner, DNB 1:305–307; T. J. Shahan, CE 1:321–322.

[P. K. MEAGHER]

ALENI, GIULIO (1582–1649),Italian Jesuit, missionary to China. He taught humanities before he sailed for China in 1609, and in Macao he taught mathematics until he could enter China in 1613. He converted some 20,000 Chinese before he was expelled in 1638 during the Chinese rites controversy. On his return 1639–49 he had less success. "Confucius of the West" to Chinese scholars, he wrote some 50 volumes in Chinese, most on religious topics (reprinted in Chinese several times and sometimes translated into Korean). Also noteworthy are a World Geography and biographies of M. Ricci and two eminent Chinese converts. BIBLIOGRAPHY: E.-M. Rivière, DHGE 2:99–100; G. H. Dunne, *Generation of Giants* (Notre Dame, Ind. 1962).

[E. P. COLBERT]

ALEPPINES (from Aleppo in Syria), a name applied to two Eastern Catholic religious communities. (1) A Maronite community of Antonian monks is known as the Antonian Aleppine Order. It is an offshoot of the older Lebanese Antonian Order. A bitter controversy between the Syrian (Aleppine) and Lebanese factions in the order resulted in a split at the general chapter of 1747. Efforts to heal the breach, even those of Pope Benedict XIV, were unavailing, and the separation became final in 1768. Today the order engages in the apostolic ministry and since 1955 has been considered non-monastic. (2) A Melchite community of Basilian monks is known as the Aleppine Basilian Order. It was also the product of a nationalistic split. Its separation from the Shuwairite Basilians began in 1824 and became definitive in 1829. Rome approved the new foundation in 1832, and since then the terms Aleppine (Syrian) and Shuwairite (Lebanese) have been fixed. Since 1952 the Aleppines have been considered a non-monastic order. Its members conduct parishes, missionary centers, and schools. *ANTONIANS; *SHUWAIRITE ORDER.

[A. J. JACOPIN]

ALEPPO (Arab., Haleb), city in Syria second only to Damascus. Its name occurs early in the 2d millennium B.C. It is situated in 38°68′5″ E. and 40°12′ N., and at an altitude of 1275 feet at the NW of the extreme inland Syrian plateau. It has a sub-desert climate. Wheat, cotton, olive, vines, market gardens, and sheep rearing are its basic resources. In ancient times Aleppo was a kingdom that witnessed the invasions of Babylonian, Hittite, Egyptian, Mitani, Hurrian, Aramean, Persian, Greek, Roman, and Byzantine troops. In A.D. 636 it surrendered to the Muslim Arabs and has stayed in Muslim hands of different races until now. Its geographical location has kept it an important center of commerce. It has over half a million inhabitants; 30% are Christians of different rites and denominations, a few thousand are Jews, and the rest are Muslims. There are an American College and a National one. Its museum and monuments are very important. BIBLIOGRAPHY: Soubhi Saouaf, *Aleppo Past and Present* (English ed. by G. F. Miller (1958); J. Sauvaget, EncIslam², s.v. "Alep."

[J. R. GHANEM]

ALER, PAUL, (1656–1727), Jesuit theologian. He studied the humanities, philosophy, and theology at Trier, Münster, Aachen, and Cologne. He was admitted to the Jesuit novitiate in 1676 and later taught at Tricoronatum College, Cologne, where he was also rector. He wrote a number of theological tracts, a *Philosophia tripartita*, prepared a German-Latin dictionary, and did some educational writing. He had some fame as a dramatist, preparing a number of theatrical pieces for use in the colleges, even building a theater for their presentation. BIBLIOGRAPHY: C. Sommervogel, DTC 1:707; M. Monaco, NCE 1:287. *JESUIT DRAMA.

[N. F. GAUGHAN]

ALERDING, HERMAN JOSEPH (1845–1924), church historian; bp. of Fort Wayne, Ind. A. came to America from Germany in his infancy. He was ordained for the diocese of Vincennes, (1868), and was consecrated bp. of Fort Wayne in 1900 where he advanced the parochial school system and secondary education in a growing population of Catholic steel workers. A. is noted among church historians for his *History of the Catholic Church in the Diocese of Vincennes* (1883) because of the vast information it contained. In 1907 he published *Diocese of Fort Wayne*. BIBLIOGRAPHY: M. C. Schroeder, NCE 1:287.

[M. C. BRADLEY]

ALÈS, ADHÉMAR D' (1861–1938), French Jesuit theologian and patrologist. He joined the theological faculty of the Catholic Institute of Paris in 1907, becoming its dean in 1925. A. published numerous studies in the field of historical theology, the best known of which concern Tertullian (1905), Hippolytus (1906), the Edict of Callistus (1914), Cyprian (1922), and Novatian (1925). A. was also director of the *Dictionnaire apologétique de la foi catholique* (4 v., 1911–28). BIBLIOGRAPHY: E. Lamalle, EncCatt 1:752, F. X. Murphy, NCE 1:287–288; Bremond 7:7–13.

[R. B. ENO]

ALESIUS, ALEXANDER (Aless, Alane; 1500–65), Scottish Lutheran theologian who published many exegetical and polemical works. He studied at St. Andrews in Edinburgh and was converted to Lutheranism through the arguments and example of P. *Hamilton. An attack he made upon the morals of the clergy led to his arrest. Escaping, he made his way to Germany, where he met Luther and Melanchthon and signed the *Augsburg Confession. As an emissary from Melanchthon to Henry VIII, he became friendly with T. *Cranmer and T. *Cromwell, and lectured in theology at Cambridge for a time. After Cromwell's execution A. withdrew to Germany but revisited England to work under Cranmer during the reign of Edward VI. He translated sections of the 1549 *Book of Common Prayer into Latin for the benefit of M. *Bucer and *Peter Martyr Vermigli. He died at Leipzig where he had been twice rector of the university. BIBLIOGRAPHY: DNB (1885) 1:254.

[J. P. WHALEN]

ALETHIANS, see SHAKERS.

ALEXANDER, MARTYR (2d cent.?). According to legend, A. was one of seven brothers martyred with their mother, St. Felicity, under Publius, prefect of Rome, for professing Christianity and inspiring others to do the same. When the family was called before the prefect, all stood firm in the faith under questioning, punishment, and imprisonment. Finally they were sent to different judges and condemned to die in various ways: one was scourged to death, two beaten with clubs, one thrown into the Tiber, and Felicity and Alexander, with the remaining two were beheaded. They were buried in three or four different cemeteries, but one of the "brothers" is buried beside the tomb of St. Felicity in the catacomb of Maximus. It is certain that a woman named Felicity suffered martyrdom. But the information concerning her supposed sons' suffering martyrdom with her depends on *acta* of dubious historical value. Some scholars have thought that seven martyrs were associated by popular piety with St. Felicity under the influence of the biblical account of the mother of the Maccabees and her sons (2 Macc ch. 7). Nevertheless the cult has existed in Rome since the mid-4th century. BIBLIOGRAPHY: Butler 3:62–64.

[P. K. MEAGHER]

ALEXANDER, ST. (*c.* 250–328), **PATRIARCH OF ALEXANDRIA** who vigorously attacked Arianism and at a synod of the Alexandrian clergy *c.* 321 excommunicated Arius, one of his priests. Together with his deacon, St. Athanasius, he attended the Council of Nicaea. BIBLIOGRAPHY: B. Piault, *What Is the Trinity?* (tr. R. Haughton, 1959) 106–107.

[A. J. JACOPIN]

ALEXANDER I, ST. (d. *c.* 115), **POPE** from *c.* 105. According to Eusebius, his pontificate lasted 10 years, but little is known of him, and even the duration and dates of his reign are uncertain. The *Liber pontificalis* attributes to him the insertion of the *Qui pridie* in the Canon of the Mass and the blessing of houses with holy water and salt, but neither ascription is reliable. The martyrology of St. Jerome and a fragmentary inscription discovered in 1855 link the name of a martyred Alexander with those of Eventius and Theodulus, but the identification of that Alexander with the sixth pope rests on an unreliable *passio*. It is not known that this pope died a martyr. The *acta* attributed to A. are not authentic, but the letters ascribed to him by the Pseudo-Isidore are to be found in PG 5:1057. BIBLIOGRAPHY: E. G. Weltin, NCE 1:288; J. S. Brusher, *Popes through the Ages* (1959); T. J. Shahan, CE 1:285–286; Butler 2:223; AS May 1:371–380, for the *passio*.

[P. F. MULHERN]

ALEXANDER II (Anselm of Baggio; d. 1073), **POPE** from 1061. Sympathetic to the Patarine movement in Milan, strongly opposed to the prevalent simoniacal practices that kept ecclesiastical benefices in the hands of unworthy clerics,

A. became bp. of Lucca (1057) and as legate of Nicholas I was associated with *Peter Damian and Hildebrand (*Gregory VII) in the Pope's program of reform. On the death of Nicholas I, A. was elected by the first conclave to be governed by the Lateran decree of 1059 limiting the papal electors to the Roman cardinals, with no voice accorded the Emperor. A dissident Roman faction, encouraged by the German court, elected an antipope, Honorius II. Imperial forces moved into Italy to impose the rule of Honorius, and Rome became a battleground between Henry's forces and the Normans, who came to A.'s support. The schism lost most of its adherents by the general acceptance of A. by the Council of Mantua (1064), and ended definitively with the death of Honorius (1072). A. campaigned strenuously for reform, using a system of personal legates sent to all parts of the Western Church. His efforts to heal the rift between East and West came to nothing, but the conquest of Muslim territory in Italy and Spain by allies of the Pope prepared the way for the first crusades. A. followed a policy of friendship for the Normans, both in Britain and Italy. Two of his legates presided over a great council of the British Church, held in Winchester in 1070, and the forces of the Norman *Robert Guiscard helped the Holy See achieve independence of the German court. However, the deterioration of relations with the German court was to lead to the investiture quarrel under A.'s successor, Hildebrand. BIBLIOGRAPHY: J. J. Ryan, NCE 1:288; Bihlmeyer-Tüchle 2:147; J. F. Loughlin, CE 1:286.

[P. F. MULHERN]

ALEXANDER III (Rolando Bandinelli; c.1105–81), **POPE** from 1159. A native of Siena, A. became a prominent canonist in the school of Bologna, and was made cardinal (1150), then chancellor of the Roman Church (1153), under Eugene III. As legate of Eugene and later of Adrian IV, he strongly influenced papal policy in European politics, winning the special disfavor of *Frederick Barbarossa for his able defense of the Pope's rights. On Adrian's death (1159), A. was elected by a majority who saw him as the one to keep the Church free from German domination. Frederick attempted to control the Church through a succession of pro-German antipopes, Victor IV, Paschal III, Callistus III, and Innocent III, and was able to keep A. out of Rome from April 1162 to November 1165. But this did not prevent the Pope from ruling the Church. A. presided in person over the Council of Tours (1163) and administered church affairs from Sens, France. He worked for reconciliation with Frederick, as he tried to achieve peace between Henry II of England and Thomas Becket. Eventually, he generously pardoned the German king (1177) and received the English monarch to penance for his part in the death of Becket (1174). Despite the turmoil of his reign, A. was able to make significant contributions to the Church. He promoted the beginnings of schools that were to develop into universities, sent missionaries to Scandinavia, and posted legates in France to arrest the growing influence of Albigensian doctrines. Many of A.'s decisions found their way into the canon law of the Church after his death, and the decrees of the Lateran Council III held at the end of his reign (1179) are a testimony to his legal genius. During his academic career he wrote a commentary, *Summa (Stoma) magistri Rolandi*, on the *Decretum* of Gratian, as well as a theological work, *Sententiae Rolandae Bononiensis magistri*. BIBLIOGRAPHY: M. W. Baldwin, *Alexander III and the 12th Century* (1966); NCE 1:288–290; Bihlmeyer-Tüchle 2:175–176; J. F. Loughlin, CE 1:286–287.

[P. F. MULHERN]

ALEXANDER IV (Rainaldo dei Conti di Segni; d. 1261), **POPE** from 1254. Of the same family as Innocent III and Gregory IX, A. was made a cardinal in 1227 and bp. of Ostia in 1231. Noted for his virtue, he was an old man when elected to the papacy, and he ruled the Church wisely in spiritual affairs. But his commitment to Innocent IV's policy of implacable antagonism to the progeny of Emperor Frederick II was disastrous to the temporal power of the papacy. He looked for help from the French and English to overcome the Hohenstaufens, offering the crown of Sicily to Henry III of England for his second son, Edmund of Lancaster, in order to circumvent the growing power of Manfred. The offer was withdrawn when Henry could not meet the financial obligations he had assumed in accepting it, but not before the English clergy and people were embittered by the attempts to raise the money. Manfred established his control of southern Italy, made helpful alliances in the North, and had himself crowned king of Sicily. With the States of the Church overrun by the forces of Manfred and his allies, the Pope was forced to spend much of his time outside Rome. His attempts to unite Greek and Latin Churches met with failure. Many privileges were granted to the Franciscans during his pontificate. He died and was buried in Viterbo. BIBLIOGRAPHY: J. A. Brundage, NCE 1:290; J. M. Powell, NCE 9:149–150; J. F. Loughlin, CE 1:287–288.

[P. F. MULHERN]

ALEXANDER V (Peter of Candia, Pietro Philarghi; d. 1410), more commonly considered an antipope from 1409. As a homeless child, A. was befriended by Capuchins of Crete, who gave him a home and an elementary education. He joined the Franciscans, who sent him to Italy and later to Oxford to study. As a master he lectured at Paris. He became tutor to the children of the Visconti, a powerful family of Lombardy through whose patronage he was successively bishop of several Italian sees and finally abp. of Milan (1402). Under Innocent VII he became a cardinal and was later made papal legate to Lombardy. He used his mounting influence to urge the holding of a council to heal the schism that had divided the Church since 1378 and to elect a pope who would be acceptable to all. To punish him for this effort *Gregory XII deposed him from his see and deprived him of his cardinalate, but he remained a leading figure in the convocation of the Council of *Pisa (1409). Respected for his great learning and devotion to the Church, he was elected pope by the council and presided over its remaining sessions.

He enjoyed at first the hopeful support of most of Christendom, but the schism was not healed, and the result was now three instead of two claimants to the papacy. A.'s distribution of privileges and gifts, censured by some as extravagant, was probably a well-intentioned effort to secure unity. A. died and was buried in Bologna. His magnificent tomb was restored at the direction of Leo XIII in 1889. The assumption of the name John XXIII by Angelo Roncalli on the occasion of his election (Oct. 28, 1958) has been taken by some as a rejection of the legitimacy of the claim not only of John XXIII (1410–15), but also that of A., who was John's predecessor. BIBLIOGRAPHY: B. Tierney, *Foundations of Conciliar Theory* (1955); A. Franzenen, "Council of Constance: Present State of the Problem," *Concilium* 7:29–68; L. Salembier, DTC 1:722–724; F. J. Gray, NCE 11:213 (Peter of Candia). *WESTERN SCHISM.

[P. F. MULHERN]

ALEXANDER VI (Rodrigo Borja [Borgia]; *c*. 1431–1503), **POPE** from 1492, elected not without simony, and not the only one of his family to achieve eminence. The Borgias were riddled with nepotism and favoritism, and during the lifetime of Rodrigo Borja—Borgia is the Italian form of the name—he could muster nearly 20 cardinals who were kin or familiars. Aragonese by origin, Valencian by settlement, Catalan and Neapolitan by affiliation, this powerful clan, the emblem of which was a bull, produced characters at both extremes of the holiness-villainy continuum; they were rarely middle of the road. A.'s uncle was the personally austere Callistus III, and his great-grandson, Francis *Borgia, became general of the Jesuits and was later canonized. A. himself was not altogether the monster he was made out to be by hostile publicists soon after his death and later. In this he bears comparison with some other popes. Still he was bad enough in all conscience, loose-living and unscrupulous. From numerous illegitimate children his blood now flows through many of the princely families of Europe. He was a capable administrator and his political talent was called for in the imbroglios of contemporary Italy. He was a patron of the arts (Michelangelo created the *Pietà* for him; Pinturrichio painted his portrait in the frescos of the Borgia apartments in the Vatican) and not without piety (he encouraged the recitation of the Angelus and liked to listen to good sermons) and humanity (despite pressure, he would not abandon his policy of tolerance toward the Jews). When the history of his struggle with *Savonarola is studied, one is left not altogether without sympathy for him; he had provocation enough, and the condemnation was not of reforming zeal, but of schism. He mellowed toward the end of his life. All in all, one might say of him that he was not one of the bad bad popes, and he was certainly not one of the good good popes. Nor was he one of the good bad popes, who have probably done more harm than the bad good popes, of whom, perhaps, he is the choicest specimen. BIBLIOGRAPHY: G. Portigliotti, *I Borgia* (1921); Hughes HC, v. 3; M. Batllori, NCE 1:290–292; C. Fusero, *Borgias* (1972).

[T. GILBY]

ALEXANDER VII (Fabio Chigi; 1599–1667), **POPE** from 1655. A grandnephew of Pope Paul V. A. obtained a doctorate in theology at Siena, entered the papal diplomatic service, became nuncio to Cologne and then the Pope's envoy-extraordinary to the peace conference at Münster. His promotion of papal policy in the negotiations of the Peace of Westphalia (1648) led to his appointment as secretary of state and cardinal. On the death of Innocent X he was elected in a stormy conclave that lasted 80 days. During his pontificate B. *Pascal's *Provincial Letters,* attacking Jesuit *probabilism, was put on the Index, and propositions taken from G. Pirot's *L'Apologie des casuistes,* defending the laxist position, were condemned. A.'s constitution *Ad sanctam* (1656) affirmed that the five propositions taken from the *Augustinus* of C. Jansen and condemned by Innocent X (1653) were condemned in the sense in which Jansen had understood them (see L. J. Cognet, NCE 7:820–824). In his condemnation of Jansenism A. had the full support of the French crown, but in other issues he fared less felicitously and was obliged to contend with much opposition from Mazarin. A clash between A.'s Corsican guards and the French embassy was used by Louis XIV as an excuse for seizing Avignon and Venaissin and for threatening to invade the States of the Church. A. was obliged to submit to humiliating peace terms (1664). With few visible results A. tried to moderate the quarrels between Spain and Portugal, but he did succeed in giving effective help to Venice against the Turks. Although he was personally a man of virtuous life, his reputation was tarnished somewhat by relatives whom he advanced to lucrative positions. He did much to embellish Rome, was a patron of G. L. Bernini, and encouraged learning by adding to the Vatican Library, modernizing the Roman University, and promoting the work of the *Bollandists. His tomb by Bernini is in St. Peter's Basilica. BIBLIOGRAPHY: J. S. Brusher, NCE 1:292–293; J. B. Peterson, CE 1:294–295; for A.'s condemnation of the Jansenist propositions, see A. Vacant, DTC 1:729–747; CModH² (1970) 5:426–427.

[P. F. MULHERN]

ALEXANDER VIII (Pietro Ottoboni; 1610–91), **POPE** from 1689. A. was son of the chancellor of the Republic of Venice. A brilliant student, he earned doctorates in canon and civil law, and then filled a variety of posts in the service of the papacy under Alexander VII, Clement IX, Clement X, and Innocent XI. The last-named he succeeded in 1689. He was nearly 80 when elected, and his pontificate lasted only 16 months. Despite the cajolery of Louis XIV, A. forthrightly condemned the Gallican Liberties which had been in existence since 1682. Also, he proscribed a number of erroneous Jansenist propositions, including the doctrine of "philosophical sin." His diplomacy improved relations with the court of France but occasioned strained ties with the Emperor Leopold I. A. was an able administrator, but a generous nature led him to extravagance in dispensing papal monies and offices, esp. to members of his own family. His condemnations of errors may be found in D 2290–93;

2301–32. BIBLIOGRAPHY: S. V. Ramge, NCE 1:293; CModH² (1970) 6 (Index).

[P. F. MULHERN]

ALEXANDER I, EMPEROR OF RUSSIA (1777–1825).

Two major efforts dominated A.'s attention during the first half of his reign: internal reforms, idealistically conceived, but largely impractical and unsuccessful in execution; and the Napoleonic wars, with their political and military involvements, out of which Russia emerged as the leading power of Europe. Religion was an important administrative problem for A. He supported the Orthodox Church, recognized the Synod of Russian Churches, but was usually just in his dealings with Latin Christians. Upon accession to the throne (1801), he established diplomatic relations with the Vatican, but fostered the Roman Catholic Ecclesiastical College, which was supposed to administer Catholic church affairs under strict state control and did not have the approval of the Holy See. He obtained from Pius VII a brief formally authorizing the presence of the Jesuits, but later expelled them from St. Petersburg (1815) and from Russia (1820). He guaranteed freedom of worship and education to the Jews (1804), though they had to suffer economic strictures. In 1812, he abandoned his rationalistic deism through an intensive reading of the Bible, and a latent mystical emotionalism became a force in his life. He required strict conformity to the Bible in all courses at the newly reorganized universities. Influenced by Mme. De Krüdener, a revivalist and evangelical preacher, as well as by his own visionary nature, A. was the moving force behind the *Holy Alliance in which he, with the rulers of Prussia and Austria, pledged to promote religion, peace, and justice and to regard the commandments as the highest norms of Government. The Alliance provided, at least for the public, an aura of sanctity to the Congress of Vienna (1815). Despite Russia's continued mistreatment of the Polish and Ruthenian Uniat Church, A. maintained peaceful relations with the Holy See to the end of his reign. BIBLIOGRAPHY: L. I. Strakhovsky, *Alexander I of Russia* (1947, repr. 1970); R. E. Byrnes, NCE 1:293–294; J. D. Clarkson, *History of Russia* (1961) 253–266; V. A. Kluchevsky, *History of Russia* (1960) 5:130–157.

[H. JACK]

ALEXANDER OF ABONOTEICHOS (fl. 150), religious

pretender whose exploits are described by *Lucian of Samosata in his *Pseudomantis* (The False Prophet). A. established a temple in honor of Asclepius in Paphlagonia where he delivered as many as 80,000 answers from the oracle to people from Greece and Italy. He blamed his erroneous predictions on the presence of Christians in the community. Otherwise a strong opponent of the Christians, Lucian comes to their defense in his critical evaluation of Alexander. BIBLIOGRAPHY: S. Dill, Hastings ERE 1:306; G. W. MacRae, NCE 1:294–295.

[F. H. BRIGHAM]

ALEXANDER OF APHRODISIAS (lectured at Athens

between 198 and 211 A.D.), Peripatetic philosopher, and the ablest and most influential of the ancient commentators on Aristotle. His commentaries on the *Anal. pr.* (Bk. 1), *Metaph., Meteor.,* and *Top.* are extant. Of the other extant works attributed to him the following may be regarded as genuine: *De anima, De mixtione,* and *Problemata.* In his commentaries and in the development of his own thought he was influenced by his teacher, the Peripatetic Aristocles (2d half of 2d cent. A.D.), who, to some degree at least, combined Stoicism with his Aristotelianism. Though an "orthodox" Aristotelian, Alexander deviates from Aristotle on some points. He takes a nominalist position regarding universals, is much more positive than Aristotle in denying the immortality of the human soul, and distinguishes more clearly than his master between the passive and active intelligence. His restatement of Aristotle's noetics and his own treatment of noetics exercised a strong influence on Plotinus. Despite his criticism of Plato, he was closer to Plato on many points than is usually assumed. BIBLIOGRAPHY: OCD; P. Merlin, CHGMP 116–122.

[M. R. P. McGUIRE]

ALEXANDER OF COMANA, ST. (d. 250), martyr,

bishop. Called the "Charcoal Burner" because he gave his wealth to the poor to follow Christ by a life of labor and deprivation, he is said to have been named by Gregory Thaumaturgus to the newly erected see of Comana in Pontus. BIBLIOGRAPHY: G. Eldarov, BiblSanct 1:776–777; Butler 3:303.

[H. JACK]

ALEXANDER OF FIESOLE, ST. (d. between 833 and

841), martyred bishop. As bp. of Fiesole, he persuaded Emperor Lothair I to restore despoiled ecclesiastical property. On his return from this mission he was waylaid by those forced to surrender these possessions and was drowned near Bologna. BIBLIOGRAPHY: G. Raspini, BiblSanct 1:781–782.

[J. E. LYNCH]

ALEXANDER THE GREAT (356–323 B.C.), emperor of

Macedonia from 336. At 13 Alexander received as his tutor Aristotle, the man who did more than any other Greek to round Hellenic culture into an organic whole. He instilled into the youth a lasting love of literature and of all things Greek. Alexander was left in charge of Macedonia in 338 by his father, Philip II. When Philip was assassinated in 336, A. (III) took over his projected conquest of the Persian Empire, which at that time included all of western Asia and Egypt. His victories at Granicus (334), Issus (333), and Gaugamela (Arbela, 331), and his subsequent capture of Babylon, Susa, Persepolis, and Pasargadei broke the Persian might. In his progress Alexander founded more than 70 cities, cells of Greek culture. To further the union of Hellenes and Orientals he married two eastern princesses and presided over the wedding feast of 10,000 of his troops who had taken Oriental brides. He constantly had with him on his campaigns Greek scientists and men of letters. In 327 he advanced into India and conquered the Punjab, but a mutiny of his soldiers forced him to withdraw to his capital, Babylon. He was about to attempt the conquest of Arabia when he was stricken with a fatal fever. Within 11 years his vast empire was dismembered, but the distinctive blend of the Greek and Oriental genius he had fostered endured until the end of antiquity. One of its consequences, the spread of Greek as the language of government and commerce, was destined four cent. later to aid the diffusion of Christianity. BIBLIOGRAPHY: W. W. Tarn, *Alexander the Great* (2 v., 1948); *Hellenistic Civilization* (3d ed., 1952); C. A. Robinson, *History of Alexander the Great* (1953); P. Green, *Alexander the Great* (1970).

[M. J. SUELZER]

ALEXANDER OF HALES (c.1185–1245), English Franciscan scholastic at the Univ. of Paris. Born at Hales Owen, Shropshire, he was a master of arts at Paris c.1210, a regent master of theology c.1220. He became a Friar Minor in 1236 and until his death served Church and order as teacher, director of studies, and conciliar *peritus*. A. is an important figure in the flowering of 13th-cent. theology. He was the first master at Paris to lecture on the *Sentences* of Peter Lombard rather than on Scripture. He was an innovator in content and method in many of the questions and tractates he discussed, esp. in moral theology. The first systematic treatment of synderesis, for example, appears to have been made by A. rather than Philip the Chancellor. A. was acquainted with the Aristotelian corpus, by then available in translation, but he read Aristotle in an Augustinian light, never fully achieving a synthesis of the new theology with traditional theology. His authentic works (or at least student reports of his lectures) include a number of disputed questions and a gloss on Lombard's *Sentences*. These show a fidelity to the tradition of Augustine, to Boethius, and to the master of St. Victor. The *Summa Fratris Alexandri*—"that book as big as a horse," as Roger Bacon querulously characterized it—is certainly not from his hand. The original schema was probably his, and he served as compiler, editor, and, in part, author. For the next 70 years other Franciscan masters were to add to it, which accounts to some extent for the diffuseness, internal contradictions, and eclecticism which mark it. Its general thrust is traditional Augustinianism; it represents the thought of the Franciscan school and might well be called, as one author has remarked, the *Summa minorum*. A. had as direct disciples John of Rochelle (whose hand is large in the work) and St. Bonaventure. His influence may be seen in Scotus. BIBLIOGRAPHY: I. Brady, EncPhil 1:73–75; B. Piault, *What Is a Sacrament?* (tr. A. Manson, 1963) 115–116.

[W. B. MAHONEY]

ALEXANDER OF HIERAPOLIS (5th cent.), bishop. An unwavering opponent of Cyril of Alexandria and supporter of Nestorius before, during, and after the Council of Ephesus in 431, he joined with John of Antioch and some 30 other bps. in a struggle against Cyril and his followers for papal and imperial support. When in the end Nestorius was condemned, Alexander held out alone against the "abomination of Egypt." Holy, learned, beloved by his people, his stiff conscience condemned him, via imperial edict, to the Egyptian mines where he died. BIBLIOGRAPHY: T. J. Shahan, CE 1:285; H. Ouilliet, DTC 1:766–769.

[H. JACK]

ALEXANDER OF JERUSALEM, ST. (d. 250 or 251), bp. and martyr. A pupil of Clement of Alexandria and friend of Origen, he was bp. of a see in Cappadocia (c.200), was imprisoned (c.204–211) in the Severan persecution, became bp. of Jerusalem (222), and died in prison during the Decian persecution. He founded a library used by Eusebius at Jerusalem. BIBLIOGRAPHY: G. Bareille, DTC 1.1:763–764; T. Špidík, BiblSanct 1:783–784; B. Bagatti, *Church from the Gentiles in Palestine* (1971) 13–17.

[J. L. GRASSI]

ALEXANDER OF LYCOPOLIS (late 3d or early 4th cent.), author of a treatise against Manichaeism, *Pros tas Manichaion Doxas* (PG 18:411–448). It is probable that he was himself a Manichaean for some time, and his work, despite its occasional obscurity of thought and style, is valuable as a source for the history of Manichaeism. Because his work praises the logic and practicality of Christian philosophy in contrast to the irrationality and inconsistency of Manichaean doctrine, it has been commonly assumed that Alexander was a convert to Christianity, and Photius even declared that he was a bishop (*Contra Manichaeos* 1–11; PG 102). Nevertheless, some scholars have doubted that he was in fact a Christian. BIBLIOGRAPHY: G. Bareille, DTC 1:785–786; A. Brinkmann, *Alexandri Lycopolitani contra Manichaei opiniones disputatio* (1895).

[T. C. O'BRIEN]

ALEXANDER NECKHAM (1157–1217), English Augustinian Canon, whose numerous writings included encyclopedic compilations, scriptural commentaries, and theological treatises. BIBLIOGRAPHY: A. Emmer, NCE 1:297–298.

[T. C. O'BRIEN]

ALEXANDER NEVILLE (c.1332–92), abp. of York. After being archdeacon of Durham (1369–71) A. was enthroned at York (1374) where he promptly involved himself in quarrels with the citizens, chapter, and various ecclesiastics. At court (from 1386) he actively engaged in political conflict with Gloucester and Arundel. With certain other supporters of King Richard II, A. was charged with treason (1387–88) and deprived of his see. He escaped to Louvain where he died. BIBLIOGRAPHY: W. Hunt, DNB 14:243–244; M. McKisack, *Fourteenth Century* (1959); A. B. Steel, *Richard II* (1963).

ALEXANDER NEVSKI (1220–63), Grand Duke of Vladimir and Kiev, negotiated with the Mongols for the survival of Russia. As prince of Novgorod in northern Russia, A. recognized the impossibility of withstanding the Mongol invasion after their armies had overrun southern and a great part of eastern Russia. He insured the protection of his people by becoming a loyal vassal of the Great Khan who appointed him Grand Duke and, in effect, primal prince of Russia. The Russian Church venerates A. as a saint. BIBLIOGRAPHY: V. O. Klîuchevskiĭ, *History of Russia* (5 v., tr. C. J. Hogarth, 1911–31).

[B. SCHERER]

ALEXANDER OF ROES (fl. 13th cent.), canon of a Cologne convent. In 1281 as a cleric of a Colonna cardinal in Italy he wrote a *Memoriale* on the rights of the Holy Roman Empire that was still popular among conciliarists and early printers. Against French denials, he defended the German right to the empire and the Roman right to the papacy, with the French right to university life; the three constituted the historical Christian society. A 1284 poem describes a council of birds where the peacock pope and French rooster king depose the German eagle emperor.

[E. P. COLBERT]

ALEXANDER THE VALENTINAN (fl. 175), Gnostic writer of the Italian or Western school of Valentinus whose book on syllogisms mentioned by Tertullian (*De carne Christi*, 17), stresses the psychic nature of Christ's body. *GNOSTICISM.

[F. H. BRIGHAM]

ALEXANDER OF VILLA DEI (*c.*1170–*c.*1250), grammarian; born Villedieu, Normandy. As tutor to the nephews of the bp. of Dol in Brittany, A. wrote the poem (2,645 hexameter verses) *Doctrinale puerorum*, or the *Grammatica versibus descripta*, based on such grammarians as Prician and Donatus and contemporaneous Peter Riga, which served as a grammar for more than 3 centuries. One purpose of the *Doctrinale* was to reject such pagan poets as Maximianus, a 6th-cent. poet. *Ecclesiale*, important for the history of liturgy, was written with a like purpose; it was also an attack against the humanists of Orléans. A. intended to write a great encyclopedia *Alphabetum maius;* however, only parts of a metrical glossary exist. Other works which are ascribed to him are *Computus* and the *Algorismus*. BIBLIOGRAPHY: R. T. Meyer, NCE 1:298–299.

[M. C. BRADLEY]

ALEXANDER, ARCHIBALD (1772–1851), American Presbyterian theologian, founder of Princeton Theological Seminary. Born at Lexington, Va., he studied at Washington College, Chestertown, Md., and was ordained in 1794. From 1796 to 1807 A. served as president of Hampden-Sydney College, the first Presbyterian college in Virginia. In 1807, as *moderator of the *General Assembly, Alexander strove to convince Presbyterians of the need for a theological seminary. In 1812 Princeton Theological Seminary was authorized and he became its first professor, remaining there until his death. He was one of the principal Old School Presbyterian theologians, basing his courses on Turretine (see TURRETINI) and other Calvinist theologians. A.'s *Brief Outline of the Evidences of the Christian Religion* (1825) was a standard apologetic work. He defended verbal inspiration and inerrancy of Scripture in his *Canon of the Old and New Testaments* (1826). In *Thoughts on Religious Experience* (1841) he defended a moderate Calvinism against the *revivalism of the New School. BIBLIOGRAPHY: J. W. Alexander, *Life of Archibald Alexander* (1854); H. T. Kerr, *Sons of the Prophets* (1963). *PRINCETON THEOLOGY.

[R. K. MacMASTER]

ALEXANDER, MICHAEL SOLOMON (1799–1845), Anglican bishop. Born in Poland and brought up in orthodox Judaism, he came to London, was suspended from his duties as a rabbi, was baptized, and ordained in the Church of England (1827). He joined the London Society for Promoting Christianity among the Jews and was sent to Danzig as a missionary for 3 years. In 1832, he was appointed professor of Hebrew in King's College. He collaborated in revising the Hebrew NT and the translation of the BCP into Hebrew. In 1841 a bishopric was set up in Jerusalem by the joint efforts of the British and Prussian governments, and he was appointed the first holder. He was not unsuccessful in his brief charge, but the scheme, which provided for Anglicans and Lutherans alternately, foundered before the end of the century, objected to on both sides and having proved the occasion of stepping up the flow of Oxford men to Rome. BIBLIOGRAPHY: A. H. Grant, DNB 1:273.

[H. JACK]

ALEXANDER, NATALIS (Fr., Noël Alexandre; 1639–1724), French Dominican historian, theologian, and controversialist. Regent of studies at the Jacobins, he threw himself into the current disputes about *Jansenism and *Gallicanism, and was critical of papal interventions in both matters, suspecting *Molinism in the first, and unwarranted curial pretensions in the second. His view that both might be met with "respectful silence" was not enough for Rome, where he was not *persona grata*. However, he died at peace with the authorities, and his voluminous writings were much esteemed in the 18th century. BIBLIOGRAPHY: P. Mandonnet, DTC 1.1:769–772.

[T. GILBY]

ALEXANDER, SAMUEL (1859–1938), Australian realist metaphysical philosopher, educated at Wellesley in Melbourne, and later at Balliol College, Oxford, where he had a scholarship. A. was the recipient of the Green prize for his contribution to moral philosophy, *Moral Order and Progress* (1889). He developed his theories with the aid of knowledge acquired through the empirical sciences, esp. biology and psychology, and considered what he produced to be an empirical metaphysics. He viewed metaphysics as the integrating science in philosophy, and for this reason he was able to carry his study and research toward a deeper insight into the psychological aspects of man's experiencing and his understanding of that experience. Some of this research and theory development was done at Freiburg where he studied, and also at Victoria Univ. in Manchester where he taught until his retirement in 1924. A. was influenced by idealist ethics; probably a great deal of this influence came from G. E. *Moore. He was equally influenced by the realism of B. *Russell and the theory of psychic evolution developed by A. N. *Whitehead. An interesting aspect of A.'s theory is similar to a strand developed by European phenomenologists today—the mind as emergent. For A., the mind is the organizing structure whose neural processes, when organized in a certain way, yield newer and exciting probabilities for man. He identifies the urge to move to a newer emergent as the nisus. These newer emergents then become the nisus for further development. Through his rational consciousness (and in ethics and morality, his rational self-consciousness) he organizes further insights and the nisus into another higher integration of knowledge. In this way every integration in man is a probable exigent for future knowledge. The pattern of such emergents is not the subject for prior appropriation since it is only when the mind itself organizes and appropriates the structure of such knowledge that the true emergent is yielded. In some ways, his theory is similar to Piaget's integrations. A second interesting concept in his philosophy is his idea about the spatio-temporal continuum. While the theory offers some interesting analogues to *Kant's spatio-temporal manifold, it lacks the precisions and explicitness of a Kantian construct. For A., the interrelationship between the complexities of motion is really a manifold of relations which have as their limitations "point instants." Such a theory is demonstrated by him with the concentric rings of a tree. But the model fails to take account of the historical perspective of the "point instants," which surely have a fuller relationship with one another than mere concentric rings. Rather, these events (of which the concentric ring is model) singly and together form a larger spatio-temporal pattern discernible in their interrelations and in their distinct causal relations.

A. was also concerned with the relation between ethics and aesthetics. From this concern he moved toward a development of a theory of value. The basic values of life he viewed as always in the making and as coming into fuller existence. Ultimately all finite beings are, in such a schema, elements in a process, and thus they gain their significance in that process by the place they hold in it. BIBLIOGRAPHY: D. M. Emmet, EncPhil 1:69–73; Copleston 8.2:153–160; R. J. Nogar, NCE 1:299–300.

[J. R. RIVELLO]

ALEXANDER ROMANCES, legendary medieval poems and stories based on the fictional Greek history of Alexander by the pseudo-Callisthenes (c.300) and its Latin translation by Julius Valerius. These works appeared in various vernaculars and enjoyed considerable popularity from the 11th to the 16th century. They tell of Alexander's journey to the East, his visit to paradise, his excursions into the air and under the sea, and his letter to his old tutor, Aristotle, describing the wonders of India. BIBLIOGRAPHY: G. Highet, *Classical Tradition* (pa. 1957); C. S. Baldwin, *Medieval Rhetoric and Poetic* (1928).

[F. H. BRIGHAM]

ALEXANDRIA, Egyptian city and Mediterranean seaport. The Egyptian village of Rhakote existed on the site of the present city from c.1500 B.C. In 332 B.C. Alexander the Great began the construction there of a great seaport; after his death the work was carried on by the Ptolemies, his successors on the throne of Egypt, who made the city their capital (304–30 B.C.). It became a great trade mart, larger even than Carthage, within 100 years of its foundation. It was the Hellenistic center of Egypt and contained a large Jewish population as well. It grew into one of the pre-eminent centers of learning in the ancient world, having two great libraries, one in the temple of Zeus and the other in the museum. Scholars gathered there in great numbers during the Hellenistic period, and its reputation as a seat of learning continued into the Roman Period. Its Jewish community produced the Septuagint, and *Philo Judaeus, the most noted exponent of a Jewish-Hellenistic synthesis in philosophy, was a native of the city. Alexandria's intellectual tradition was upheld by the Christians for whom it became a center of a developing theology. Clement and *Origen were among the outstanding Christian thinkers of the early period. The city was also a focal place for heresy in the early Church. It was the chief center of Gnosticism, and the city of Arius, founder of Arianism. But Athanasius, indefatigable foe of Arianism, was its bp. from 328 till 373. The patriarchs Theophilus, Cyril, and Dioscurus wielded great power in the city and consequently throughout Egypt. With the triumph of *Monophysitism the city became isolated from the Christian mainstream. In the year 616 it was captured by the Persians and 30 years later was definitively taken and held by the Muslim Arabs. This brought its prominence in Christendom, apart from history, to an end. The city declined steadily through the Middle Ages and early modern times. Its revival can be traced to the efforts of Mohammed Ali, who developed the city as a modern seaport in the 19th century. BIBLIOGRAPHY: E. M. Forster, *Alexandria: A History and a Guide* (pa., 1961); H. R. Willoughby, InterDB 78–81.

[R. B. ENO]

ALEXANDRIA, CATHOLIC-COPTIC PATRIARCHATE OF, primatial see for Coptic Rite Catholics. In 1824 Pope Leo XIII restored the Catholic-Coptic Patriarchate of Alexandria particularly because of the influence of Khedive Mohammed Ali who had supported religious freedom in Egypt. Ecclesiastical difficulties prevented the

Catholic patriarchate from being operative until 1895 when Cyril II Makarios was officially proclaimed patriarch. The patriarch resides in Cairo and governs about 107,000 Catholic Copts in three jurisdictions. *COPTIC RITE.

[F. T. RYAN]

ALEXANDRIA, CATHOLIC-MELCHITE PATRIARCHATE OF. From an ecclesiastical viewpoint, the patriarchate of Alexandria for Catholic Melchites is subsumed under the Greek-Melchite Catholic Patriarchate of *Antioch. In 1772, the Melchite patriarch of Antioch was given jurisdiction over Melchites in Alexandria and Jerusalem, but in 1838 Patriarch Maximos III Mazlūm (1833–55) was given the personal title of patriarch of Antioch, Alexandria, Jerusalem, and the whole East. This title has been handed down to his successors but a patriarchal vicar actually governs Alexandria. At present there are about 26,000 Melchite Catholics in this patriarchate. *MELCHITE RITE.

[F. T. RYAN]

ALEXANDRIA, COPTIC PATRIARCHATE OF, primatial see of the Coptic Church (Monophysite). The condemnation of *Monophysitism that came from the Council of *Chalcedon (451) brought a division within the Egyptian Church. For a time, the patriarchate passed between the Orthodox Melchites and the monophysitic Copts, but since 567 there has been a distinct line of Coptic patriarchs. The patriarch resides in Cairo and has jurisdiction over 2,500,000 faithful in 23 eparchies. *COPTIC CHURCH.

[F. T. RYAN]

ALEXANDRIA, LITURGY OF, the Greek source of all Egyptian and Ethiopian eucharistic liturgies. Traditionally the liturgy of Alexandria is attributed to St. Mark the Evangelist but with little foundation. The liturgy of St. Mark in its final version was probably completed under St. Cyril of Alexandria in the 5th century. The Coptic liturgy is often referred to as that of St. Cyril as well as of St. Mark. The earliest MSS of the complete liturgy date from the 12th and 13th centuries. Reconstructions have been made of 5th-cent. St. Mark by comparisons of existing texts. Up until the 5th cent., the Greek liturgy of Alexandria was in a state of evolution. An extant fragment of the anaphora of St. Mark, although dated from the 4th cent., probably represents an earlier usage. It contains the prayer of intercession and is significant in representing the Egyptian liturgy prior to Byzantine influences. A part of an early Egyptian Sacramentary from the monastery of Der-Balizeh is also extant. It is debated whether it reflects the usage of the 6th cent. or the 3d and 4th cent., but the latter seems more probable. It also contains the prayer of intercession and places the epiclesis before the institution. The *Sacramentary of Serapion of Thmuis* probably dates from the early 4th century. It consists of a series of prayers, 18 devoted to the eucharistic liturgy. The preface ends with the *Sanctus,* an innovation. The epi-

clesis is the Logos, and the prayer of intercession is between the consecration of the bread and the wine. Other early fragments exist in the works of Egyptian Church Fathers. The Greek Alexandrian liturgy was replaced by the Byzantine liturgy in the 12th century. BIBLIOGRAPHY: F. E. Brightman, *Liturgies Eastern and Western* (1896); I.-H. Dalmais, *Eastern Liturgies* (tr. D. Attwater, 1960) 12 and *passim;* S. A. B. Mercer, *Ethiopic Liturgy* (AMS ed. 1970) 79–81.

[D. W. JOHNSON]

ALEXANDRIA, PATRIARCHATE OF, one of the four eminent patriarchates of the Eastern Church. At its height it included the bishoprics of Egypt, the Pentapolis, Libya, Nubia, and Ethiopia and ranked second in honor only to Rome. St. Mark is considered the apostle of Egypt, but the tradition, found no earlier than Eusebius, is doubtful. The Alexandrian Church, already well-established, emerged into history c. 190 under Patriarch Demetrius. In 320 Alexandria became embroiled in the controversy brought on by Arius, one of the presbyters of the city. St. Athanasius was chiefly instrumental in the condemnation of Arianism at the Council of Nicaea (325), but as patriarch he suffered a series of exiles because of his action. By 389 Christianity had become strong enough to launch a campaign against paganism under Patriarch Theophilus. St. Cyril ruled (412–444) during the conflict with *Nestorius of Constantinople, whom he had condemned at Alexandria and at the Council of *Ephesus (431). Since Constantinople had tried to usurp Alexandria's rank among the patriarchates, it was a double victory for Cyril. He had the full support of the Coptic monks. When Eutyches was condemned at the Council of *Chalcedon, Patriarch Dioscorus opposed the condemnation because he erroneously thought it attacked the theology of St. Cyril. The monks again supported the patriarch but this time against Chalcedon. Dioscorus was exiled and became a national hero and martyr. The patriarchate passed back and forth between the Dyophysites (called Melchites or King's men) and Monophysites (Copts) until Emperor Justin II recognized both patriarchates (567). From the reign of Peter III to the present there has been an unbroken line of Coptic patriarchs. Ecclesiastical independence was the first step the Egyptians took toward ridding themselves of Greek oppression, which had lasted almost 8 centuries. In 619 they helped the invading Persians drive out the Greeks. In 640 the Arabs invaded Egypt for the first time, and in 645, with Egyptian help, they ended Graeco-Roman rule in Egypt. The Arabs made their headquarters at El Fustat, and in the 11th cent. the Fatimids built their capital, El Qahira (Cairo), toward the north. The Coptic patriarch had moved into the Nitrian desert in the 6th cent. and in the 11th cent., while retaining the title patriarch of Alexandria, he moved his residence to Cairo. The Orthodox patriarch, presiding over a small flock of Greeks and Syrians, remained in Alexandria. His see became more and more dependent on Constantinople and by the 12th cent. the Orthodox Melchites took the Byzantine liturgy in place of the Alexandrian. Because the *Coptic Church has been the strongest Christian group in Egypt, the Orthodox have never really flourished. Further, the Orthodox have suffered internal dissent because of conflicting Greek and Syrian factions. The recent rise of Arab nationalism has also caused an emigration of non-Egyptians, thus bringing the total of faithful under the Orthodox patriarch to about 35,000. Besides the Coptic patriarchate there is also one for the Catholic Coptic and the Catholic-Melchite jurisdictions. BIBLIOGRAPHY: D. Attwater, *Christian Churches of the East* (2 v., rev. ed. 1961–62); G. Downey, ''Coptic Culture in the Byzantine World,'' *Greek and Byzantine Studies* 1 (1958) 119–135; O. F. A. Meinardus, *Christian Egypt: Faith and Life* (1970) 89–141.

[D. W. JOHNSON]

ALEXANDRIA, SCHOOL OF, a term applied to both the catechetical school for the Christian community of the city and the philosophical and theological school of thought, both pagan and Christian, which originated in Alexandria, the chief cultural center of the Hellenistic world and a clearinghouse for ideas from both East and West. The school for training catechists grew in this cosmopolitan atmosphere. Its first known director was Pantaenus (d. *c*.200), who was succeeded by his pupil, *Clement of Alexandria (150–215). The greatest leader of the school was *Origen (185–253), Clement's successor and probably the most important representative of the Christian Alexandrian school of thought. Under Origen the school became a decisive cultural force that moved beyond catechetics into general education. The era of Clement and Origen marked a turning point in Christian development. After an initial period of defensive apologetics, Christianity became well enough established to meet pagan philosophy on its own ground and to begin to lay the foundation for scientific theological thought. The Alexandrian Christian school attracted pagans, and Origen himself attended the classes of the Father of Neoplatonism, Ammonius Saccas, in the company of Ammonius's most famous pupil, Plotinus. This contact between Christianity and Neoplatonism was decisive for Christian thought. Among the Alexandrian theologians the tendency to emphasize the transcendence of God and an inclination toward the subordination of the Son and the Holy Spirit owes much to Neoplatonism. Another outside influence on Alexandrian Christianity was Hellenistic Judaism, esp. as exemplified by Philo (*c*.25 B.C.–*c*.40 A.D.). This influence was esp. strong in biblical interpretation where the Jews adapted the pagan method of interpreting the classics to the Bible. The allegorical method, which helped Christians to explain the OT in relation to the NT became a characteristic of the Alexandrian school. Philo's attempt to recast biblical theology in Greek categories also inspired the Alexandrian theologians to do the same and to try to demonstrate that the teachings of Jesus represent the highest human knowledge and the grounds for the greatest possible human achievement. The work begun by Clement and Origen was carried on by their successors,

Dionysius (*c*.190–265), Theognostus (d. 282), and Peter (d. 311) being the most noteworthy. By the 4th cent. speculative theology was an accepted fact among Christians. This era also made it clear that, while speculation on matters of faith made its content more intelligible, it also generated corruptions of the faith. Alexandria found itself confronted with the teaching of *Arius (256–336), a presbyter of the city. It took the patient work of Patriarch Alexander and his successor, St. Athanasius, at the Council of Nicaea (325) to expose Arius's errors and have them condemned. During Athanasius' patriarchate the catechetical school was under the learned and capable Didymus the Blind (*c*.313–*c*.398). The Nestorian controversy followed Arianism, and another Alexandrian, St. Cyril, defended orthodoxy at Ephesus (431). Ironically it was St. Cyril who set the stage for the destruction of the Alexandrian school. When Eutyches was condemned at Chalcedon (451), the Alexandrian patriarch, Dioscorus, interpreted this erroneously as an attack on St. Cyril's definition of Christ as the ''one nature of the Word incarnate,'' and Alexandria became Monophysite. This struggle tore apart the Alexandrian Church and its school, and what little remained was destroyed by the Arabs when they invaded Egypt (640). BIBLIOGRAPHY: C. Bigg, *Christian Platonists of Alexandria* (1913); Quasten 1:1–120; F. Norman, SacMund 6:16–19.

[D. W. JOHNSON]

ALEXANDRIA, SCHOOL OF (ART). Hellenistic Alexandria, wealthy and cultivated, developed a distinctive, sophisticated style emphasizing realism and individuality foreign to the classical Greek expressions. Christian artists worked in the local style, frescoes of the catacombs of Karmuz influencing Roman painting. In early images Christ is portrayed as a youthful Hermes with short curly hair (the bearded Oriental image derives from Syria and Palestine). Christian artists exported textiles, glass, gold, silver, and ivory. Coptic art of the rest of Egypt is always differentiated from the Hellenic tradition of Alexandria.

[M. J. DALY]

ALEXANDRIAN TEXT, see BIBLE TEXTS.

ALEXANDRINE BULLS, the name given two bulls promulgated in 1493 by *Alexander VI (1492–1503) to establish the areas discovered during Columbus' first voyage in which Spain and Portugal had exploratory and colonizing rights. Addressed to the Catholic kings of Europe, the bulls fixed a line 100 maritime leagues W and S of the Azores and the Cape Verde Islands, and provided that Spain possess the lands to the west of the line and Portugal, the lands to the east. When Portugal complained, a compromise solution was agreed upon in the Treaty of Tordesillas (1494), moving the line 370 leagues to the W of the Azores. These rights were granted on the condition that Spain and Portugal Christianize the natives of the territories in question. Alexander's

action was based upon the commonly accepted "omni-insular" theory, according to which the pope possessed all newly discovered "islands" by virtue of the Donation of Constantine. BIBLIOGRAPHY: H. Vander Linden, "Alexander VI and the Demarcation of the Maritime and Colonial Domains of Spain and Portugal," *American Historical Revue* 22 (1916–17) 1–20; L. Weckmann, NCE 1:306.
*PAPAL LINE OF DEMARCATION.

[T. M. MCFADDEN]

ALEXEI, PATRIARCH OF MOSCOW (Sergei Vladimirovich Simansky; 1877–1970). He was elected patriarch of Moscow and all of Russia in 1945. A. followed a policy of cooperation with the Soviet government, promoted intra-Orthodox relations by his travels, and in 1948 convened the representatives of world Orthodoxy in Moscow. BIBLIOGRAPHY: P. B. Anderson, "Patriarch Aleksii of Moscow" *Eastern Churches Review* 3 (Autumn 1970) 193–199.

[T. BIRD]

ALEXIAN BROTHERS, a congregation founded in Germany to work among the victims of the Black Death and the needy of 14th-cent. Europe. In Belgium they were known as Poor Brothers, Bread Brothers, or Cellite Brothers. The society in Germany took vows according to the Augustinian rule; in the latter part of the 15th cent. the society was raised to a religious order with St. Alexius as patron. They have since been known as Alexian Brothers. At its peak the congregation had several thousand members. In the 19th cent. vocations increased and the order had papal approval. In the U. S. the congregation conducts modern medical establishments and in 1974 numbered 229. BIBLIOGRAPHY: J. Brosch, LTK 1:326–327; A. Sanford, NCE 1:306–307.

[M. C. BRADLEY]

ALEXIS, ST. (5th cent.), an ascetic and mendicant who lived in Edessa during the episcopate of Rabbula (d. 436), and who revealed before his death that he was of a noble Roman family. As this story was carried westward, details were added that grew into the popular legend. He was given the name Alexis, though the venerable beggar of Edessa was known only as the Man of God. Having fled from Rome on his wedding day, he traveled to the East and lived there 17 years as a beggar. When a statue of the Blessed Virgin Mary spoke, making known his holiness, he took flight once more, this time to escape popular veneration. Returning to Rome, he was unrecognized. He found employment as a servant in his father's house and lived in a corner under a stairway, enduring privation and ill-treatment at the hands of the other servants for another 17 years. After his death his true identity was discovered to the great wonder of all. There is no evidence that the legend was known at Rome before the late 10th century. For a more detailed account and for the bibliog. of the legend, see Butler 3:123–124.

[P. K. MEAGHER]

ALEXIUS I COMNENUS (1048–1118), **BYZANTINE EMPEROR,** from 1081. The nephew of Emperor Isaac I Comnenus, A. came of a distinguished military family of Asia Minor. In April 1081 he seized the throne and by his brilliant diplomatic and military maneuvers was able to avert the disaster threatening the empire from the Seljuk Turks, the Normans, and the Patzinaks. But his protection of wealthy landowners and his granting of extensive commercial privileges to Venice greatly weakened the empire. To obtain military aid against the Turks he negotiated with Popes Gregory VII and Urban II; the result was the *Crusades, not at all what Alexius had in mind. Intimately connected with these negotiations was the question of reunion between the Eastern and Western Churches. A. was interested in theology and took part in disputations; he also took very strong action against the *Bogomils. BIBLIOGRAPHY: Ostrogorsky, 315–333.

[G. T. DENNIS]

ALEXIUS THE STUDITE, PATRIARCH OF CONSTANTINOPLE (1025–43). He was archimandrite of the Studite monastery (SEE STUDIUS, MONASTERY OF), who was not elected patriarch by the permanent synod but instead was appointed to that office by the dying Emperor Basil II. This fact marred his reign and several unsuccessful attempts were made to depose him. He is noted as a reformer and for his administrative policies as exemplified in his summoning of several synods and his issuance of edicts and laws, esp. regarding marriage. In 1034 A. founded a Studite monastery dedicated to the *Theotokos*, which was later named after him. BIBLIOGRAPHY: PG 119:744–748; 827–850.

[F. T. RYAN]

ALEYDIS (ALICE), ST. (Alix, Adelaide of Schaerbeek; d. 1250). Born at Schaerbeek, near Brussels, A. was given into the care of the Cistercian nuns in a nearby convent at the age of 7. Humble, retiring, zealous in the service of others, she contracted leprosy at an early age and had, to the grief of all, to live in seclusion. Communion under both kinds, which was then in practice, was denied her for fear of contagion. This was a sore trial, but she was comforted in a revelation by the words: "Where there is part, there also is the whole." She became blind and endured other great sufferings in the last year of her life. Her cult under the title of *Saint* was approved by Pius X in 1907. BIBLIOGRAPHY: AS June 2 (1717) 476–483; Butler 2:549–550; K. Spahr, LTK 1:142, bibliog.

[P. K. MEAGHER]

ALFANO, see ALPHANUS.

ALFĀRĀBĪ (Fārābī, Al-; full name Abū-Nasr Muhammad al-Fārābī; *c*.873–950), Muslim philosopher. Also known as Alfarabius, he was rated highly by other Arabian philosophers. Among his teachers is Abū-Bishr Mattā ibn-Yūnus, the famous Aristotelian Christian philosopher of

Baghdad. A. was accomplished in music, philosophy, physics, and other sciences. He lived frugally: indeed he might be better described as an ascetic. His philosophy is similar to other Arabic philosophers insofar as he sees no essential difference between Aristotle and Plato. He was, however, absorbed in Aristotelian metaphysics. He believed Plato was superior to Aristotle only when it came to the practical implementation of philosophy. Perhaps the best word to describe A.'s philosophy is methodological, since it develops a system of thought rather than a content. There are, of course, ample provisions in that content for philosophical matter on which to speculate. One such provision is that which holds that the order in the world relates to God through various levels in a hierarchically devised system. Furthermore, he made significant contributions to the formulation of the distinction between essence and existence. Dante is said to be in debt to him for the former's theory of Intelligences, the influence of celestial spheres, and the light-doctrine of God. A. viewed philosophy as distinct from theology. For him, logic was the propaedeutic and preparation for philosophy. Works: *Ideal City* (Ger. tr. F. Dieterici, 1900; Fr. tr. R. P. Jaussen et al., 1949); *Short Commentary on Aristotle's Prior Analytics* (tr. N. Rescher, 1963). BIBLIOGRAPHY: J. Finnegan, NCE 1:308–309; W. M. Watt, EncPhil 3:179–180; Copleston 2.1:220–221, 3.2:183.

[J. R. RIVELLO]

ALFERIUS, ST. (d. 1050), monk and hermit. A member of the Pappacarbone family, A. served the Duke of Salerno as ambassador. He entered the monastery of Cluny in 1003 but was soon recalled to Salerno to reform its monasteries. In 1011 he retired to the hermitage of La Cava (SS. Trinità) which became the motherhouse of many dependent churches and abbeys. BIBLIOGRAPHY: R. Grégoire, NCE 1:309; Butler 2:80; I. Mannocci, BiblSanct 1:828–831.

[M. A. WINKELMANN]

ALFIERI, PIETRO (1801–63), Camaldolese monk, musicologist, and composer, and professor of music at the English College, Rome. He contributed greatly to the mid-19th-cent. revival of interest in *Palestrina and others through his scholarly articles and esp. his editions of music. *Raccolta di musica sacra* (7 v. 1841–46) contained many important works of Palestrina; he also published pieces by Victoria, Allegri, and Anerio. BIBLIOGRAPHY: K. G. Fellerer, MGG 1:316.

[P. DOHERTY]

ALFIERI, VITTORIO (1749–1803), Italian dramatist. His writings include odes, lyrics, essays, and political treatises, but his tragedies are the great work of his life. His ideals were those of Neoclassicism rather than of the Enlightenment; he combined enthusiasm for the early principles of the American and French Revolutions with an aristocratic severity against progressivist "levelling." He was one of the progenitors of the *Risorgimento and of tragic Latin opera.

Deeply religious, he swung between attachment to the Church and the contrary. His autobiography, completed in 1803, is a candid account of his personal, political, and literary ideas and goals as they evolved through the checkered experiences that brought him back at the end. BIBLIOGRAPHY: M. Apollonio, NCE 1:309–310; G. Megaro, *Vittorio Alfieri, Forerunner of Italian Nationalism* (1972).

[H. JACK]

ALFONSO X (El Sabio; 1221–84), **KING OF CASTILE** from 1252. Son of Frederick III, A.'s reputation as scholar and patron of the arts dims his somewhat doubtful reputation as ruler. He petitioned unsuccessfully for the title of Emperor of the Holy Roman Empire and suffered from enemies without and disloyalty within his own family. A. sponsored such valuable translations as *Las siete partidas,* primarily a legal work. This translation embodied the first educational code of its kind in Europe. Alfonso established schools in Seville, Murcia, and Toledo, and three chairs in civil and canon law at the Univ. of Salamanca. His *Grande e General Estoria* includes an OT translation (the so-called *Alfonsonian),* one of the oldest Spanish versions. *Cantigas de Sancta Maria* consists of 420 lyrics concerning miracles of the Blessed Virgin. BIBLIOGRAPHY: E. S. Procter, *Alfonso X of Castile, Patron of Literature and Learning* (1951); J. E. Keller, *Alfonso X, El Sabio* (1967).

[R. M. FUNCHION]

ALFONSO OF BURGOS, SEE ABNER OF BURGOS.

ALFONSO DE CASTRO (1495–1558), Franciscan theologian. Besides teaching at Salamanca, A. authored several works: *Adversus omnes haereses lib. XIV* (1534), *De justa haereticorum punitione* (1547), and the most noted, *De potestate legis poenalis* (1550), which is one of the first works of its kind dealing with punishment and penal justice. He served as theologian at the Council of Trent and participated in the controversy (1530) over one of Henry VIII's marriages. BIBLIOGRAPHY: B. Cavanaugh, NCE 1:311; V. Heynck, LTK 1:330.

[J. R. RIVELLO]

ALFONSO OF MADRID (c. 1475–after 1521); Franciscan spiritual writer. His writings include a treatise on spiritual perfection, meditations on the life of Jesus and on Holy Week. One work, *Arte para servir a Diós* (1521), is one of the first works on asceticism written in the vernacular, and it was highly esteemed by Teresa of Avila. BIBLIOGRAPHY: B. Cavanaugh, NCE 1:311.

[J. R. RIVELLO]

ALFONSO EL SABIO, SEE ALFONSO X, KING OF CASTILE.

ALFONSUS BONIHOMINIS (De Buenhombre; 14th cent.), Spanish Dominican Hebraist and Arabist. A. was bp. of Marrakech in Morocco (1344–53). He translated into

Latin two Arabic dialogues of Christian apologetics as well as *Historia Joseph* and *Legenda S. Antonii abbatis Thebaidis.* BIBLIOGRAPHY: Quétif-Échard 1:594–595; M. J. Finnegan, NCE 1:311.

[M. J. FINNEGAN]

ALFORD, MICHAEL (pseudonym for Michael Griffith; 1587–1652), English Jesuit missionary and historian. A. joined the Jesuits in Louvain (1607), studied philosophy in Seville, theology in Louvain, and after his ordination was stationed in Naples and Rome. In 1628 he was assigned to the English mission. Being mistaken for a bp. whom the authorities were watching for, he was arrested and imprisoned upon his arrival in Dover. After his release he settled in Leicestershire, where, along with his missionary labors, he did some historical writing, producing two works, *Britannia illustrata* (1641) and the posthumous *Annales ecclesiae Brittanicae* (4 v., 1663). BIBLIOGRAPHY: T. Cooper, DNB 1:284; T. J. Campbell, CE 1:309; Gillow BDEC 3:58–61.

ALFRED THE GREAT (849–899), king of England from 871, soldier, educator, jurist. Son of King Aethelwulf and Osburh, A. twice visited Rome as a boy. He defeated the Danes in 878 and 885, united the English, and successfully defended the southern coast against Danish marauders. He developed an educational plan for clergy and laity with the help of scholars, particularly St. Grimbald of France, John of Saxony, and John *Asser of Wales. With them he began a systematic program of translation from Latin works into English. The best known are Pope Gregory I's *Pastoral Care*, Bede's *Ecclesiastical History of the English People*, Orosius' *Universal History*, and Boethius's *Consolation of Philosophy*. These works mark the beginning of English prose, especially in the prefaces written by the King and in passages where he abridges the Latin works. Through books Alfred hoped to give to his people an education at once practical and liberal and so to rebuild the once flourishing Christian civilization ruined by the Danish invasions. The *Old English Annals (Anglo-Saxon Chronicle)* begun before Alfred's rule is associated with him and was continued by his orders. BIBLIOGRAPHY: *Anglo-Saxon Chronicle* (tr. D. Whitelock et al., 1961); John Asser, *Life of King Alfred* (ed. W. H. Stevenson, 1904; Eng. tr. L. C. Jane, 1924); E. S. Duckett, *Alfred the Great* (1956); C. Plummer, *Life and Times of Alfred the Great* (1970).

[M. M. BARRY]

ALFRED OF SARESHEL (fl. 1210), English scientist, an intermediary between Arabic and Western knowledge, who visited Spain. He glossed Aristotle's *Parva naturalia, De anima,* the pseudo-Aristotelian *De vegetabilibus* and translated the appendix *(Liber de congelatis)* to Avicenna's *Meteorology.* His *De motu cordis,* dedicated to Alexander Neckham, shows a knowledge of physiological writings and postulates the heart as the basic organ. BIBLIOGRAPHY: C. H. Haskins, *Studies in the History of Medieval Science* (1927),

128–129; Gilson HCP 235, 260, 658, 661; P. Delhaye, *Medieval Christian Philosophy* (tr. S. J. Tester, 1960) 100.

[F. D. BLACKLEY]

ALFRED JEWEL, late 9th-cent., flat, oval, gold, enamel and crystal jewel with openwork sides shaped at one end into an animal head from the mouth of which protrudes a small socket. Probably mounted originally on a bone pointer, it has inscribed in Anglo-Saxon round the sides "ALFRED HAD ME MADE." Found at Athelney, Somerset, it is associated with King Alfred, who effected the Christian intellectual renaissance of his people. The cloisonné-enamel figure under a rock-crystal sheet represents Sight. BIBLIOGRAPHY: D. J. A. Matthew and C. L. Wrenn, NCE 1:312.

[R. L. S. BRUCE-MITFORD]

ALFREDA, ST., see ETHELDRITA, ST.

ALFREDUS ANGLICUS, see ALFRED OF SARESHEL.

ALGAZEL (Arabic, al-Ghazzālī; 1058–1111), Muslim theologian, jurist, reformer, and mystic. Born near Tūs in Khorāsān, Persia, A. was a student of al-Juwaynī (see Ash-ʿarites) and in 1091 was appointed to a professorship by Niẓām al-Mulk in Baghdad but gave up his teaching 4 years later for reasons not fully known. Having undergone a crisis of faith, he turned to mysticism and went into a long seclusion, during which he wrote his most important work, the *Iḥyā ʿulum ad-dīn (Revival of the Religious Sciences).* In 1106 he returned to his teaching and composed his autobiography, *Deliverance from Error,* which has been compared to Augustine's *Confessions.* A. was a prolific writer on all religious subjects. Above all he attempted to restore interior depth and honesty to the observance of the law. Although he attacked philosophy, esp. that of Avicenna, as incompatible with revealed religion, the Latin West considered him to be an Aristotelian, since it knew him only through the translation of his *Intentions of the Philosophers,* a work wherein he set himself to outline that philosophy to which he was opposed. Paradoxically A. used reason or dialectic to refute the rational methods of philosophy, a fact the Spanish-Arab philosopher, Averroës (d. 1198), later seized upon in telling rebuttal. Although A.'s assault undoubtedly lowered the prestige of Islamic philosophy in some degree, it is probable that he did not intend to reject the philosophic quest completely. It is in great part through the work of A. that Sufism gained respectability in orthodox Islam and he is considered one of the great restorers *(mujadidūn).* BIBLIOGRAPHY: W. Montgomery Watt, *Islamic Philosophy and Theology* (1962); *idem,* EncIslam² s.v. "al-Ghazali." *ISLAMIC MYSTICISM; *ISLAMIC THEOLOGY.

[J. T. HICKEY; R. M. FRANK]

ALGER OF LIÈGE (Albert of Cluny; Algerus Magister; d. *c.*1131), canon of Liège, later monk of Cluny, theologian and canonist. As a theologian he wrote on the sacraments, esp. baptism, holy orders, and the Eucharist, and on the Sacrifice of the Mass. His *De misericordia et iustitia* was an important source for Gratian's *Decretum*. Works: PL 180:739–972. BIBLIOGRAPHY: U. Berlière, DTC 1:827–828; N. M. Haring, "*Sententiae Magistri A.* and the School of Laon," MedSt 17 (1955) 1–45; *idem,* NCE 1:315–316.

[P. K. MEAGHER]

ALI ('Alî ibn abî Ṭâlib, d. 661), the cousin of the Prophet Mohammed and fourth caliph of Islam. Ali, the son of Mohammed's uncle abû Talib, though very young, became one of the first and most devout of Mohammed's followers. At *Medina he participated in nearly all the Prophet's military expeditions and married his daughter Fatima. Later he was, on seemingly religious grounds, more or less openly opposed to the caliphate of Uthmân, the third caliph, and was accused by some of having complicity in the death of the latter. Ali's election as Uthmân's successor (June 656) caused a major rift in the Muslim community, and some, including Aisha, Mohammed's wife, refused to recognize his election. After his death various groups insisted that rightly the caliphate belonged only to the family of the Prophet and supported the candidacy of Ali's sons, first Hasan and then Husayn (both by Fatima), and thereafter of Mohammed, his son by a Hanafite woman. Quite early certain of the movements in support of the Alid cause turned into heterodox religious movements, spawning the many sects and subsects of the Shiites with the passage of time. BIBLIOGRAPHY: L. Vecia Vaglieri, EncIslam², s.v. " 'Alî ibn abî Ṭâlib"; M. G. S. Hodgson, "How Did the Early Shî'a Become Sectarian," *Journal of the American Oriental Society* 75 (1955) 1–13.

[R. M. FRANK]

ALICE, ST., see ALEYDIS, ST.

ALIEN IMMERSION, among Baptists, signifies a baptism correctly performed, but by a minister authorized in a different denomination, hence an "alien." Such a baptism is recognized by more liberal Baptist groups; conservatives reject it as invalid, but differ as to which ministers are to be considered alien.

[T. C. O'BRIEN]

ALIENATION, a belief that affirms the state of estrangement; used in science and philosophy. It is used also in the social sciences; one distinguishes its everyday usage from other uses such as its legal, psychological, sociological, and philosophical uses. It was first used by F. Hegel, L. Feuerbach, and K. Marx. Presently, alienation is said to refer to God, man, and animals. Some see no logical reason for the term's being used except in regard to man. There is a tendency today to see alienation in five possible categories: powerlessness, meaninglessness, social isolation, normlessness, and self-estrangement. Whatever the content, history, or cause of it, it is something with which man must deal if he

is to negotiate his own future. BIBLIOGRAPHY: G. Petrović, EncPhil 1:76–81.

[J. R. RIVELLO]

ALIPIUS, ST. (b. *c.*360–d. after 429), bp. of Tagaste, friend of St. *Augustine. He was a fellow student of Augustine in their home town of Tagaste in North Africa and deviated with him into Manichaeism in Carthage. As a law student in Rome, A. became addicted to gladiatorial spectacles. In 384 he was baptized with Augustine by St. *Ambrose in Milan. He participated in the dialogues of Cassiciacum and followed Augustine back to Africa, where he lived in the quasi-monastic community of Hippo under his friend. On a journey to the Holy Land he made the acquaintance of St. *Jerome (*c.* 393). The next year he was elected bp. of Tagaste and there spent the rest of his life, taking part in the same councils as Augustine and fighting the same battles against *Donatists and Pelagians. BIBLIOGRAPHY: St. Augustine, *Confessions,* passim; A. Frutaz, LTK 1:410; R. Poetzel, NCE 1:317–318; C. Testore, EncCatt 1:888–889.

[R. B. ENO]

ALITURGICAL DAYS, days on which the Eucharist is not celebrated. In the present Roman rite only Good Friday is an aliturgical day. Documentary evidence is lacking to show that in the early Church Mass was commonly offered on weekdays; Sunday was liturgical, i.e., the day for assembly and the Eucharist, and other days were aliturgical. Gradually other liturgical days were added. In the Eastern Church many days have remained aliturgical. BIBLIOGRAPHY: J. J. von Allmen, *Worship: Its Theology and Practice* (1965) 213–229.

[N. KOLLAR]

ALKINDI, see KINDI, AL-.

ALKMAAR, MARTYRS OF, eight Franciscans who were tortured and hanged in Alkmaar near Amsterdam, Holland, by partisans of the Prince of Orange. Called "Sea Beggars" because they refused to deny the Real Presence, the six who were put to death on June 20, 1572, included Daniel of Arendonck, Cornelius of Diest, John of Naarden, Louis of Arguennes, Adrian of Gouda, and Engelbert of Terborg. The following year Nov. 12, 1573, Eylard Dirksz of Waterland and David Leendertsz were martyred. Reports of miraculous lights which appeared on the seacoast where their bodies were abandoned have been recorded. The process for their beatification has been initiated but has yet to be completed. BIBLIOGRAPHY: W. Lampen, LTK 1:338–339.

[F. H. BRIGHAM]

ALL SAINTS, FEAST OF, the feast honoring all the saints, observed in the West on Nov. 1. A similar feast was celebrated in the East from the 4th cent.; originally it commemorated all martyrs, but later was extended to include nonmartyrs as well and was most commonly observed on the first Sunday after Pentecost. In the West the dedication of the Roman Pantheon as a Christian basilica under the title *S. Maria ad Martyres* (c.610) led to an annual commemoration of the event on May 13. Some regard this as the original feast of all saints (or martyrs) in the West, but others hold that this observance was no more than an anniversary feast of the dedication. Some scholars trace the feast as celebrated on Nov. 1 to an Irish feast kept on that day, holding that from Ireland the observance spread through England to the Continent and to Rome. The celebration of the feast on Nov. 1 in Rome goes back at least to the pontificate of Gregory VII (d. 1085). BIBLIOGRAPHY: C. Smith, NCE 1:318–319; J. Hennig, ''Meaning of All the Saints,'' MedSt 10 (1948) 147–161; P. Jounel, ''Le Sanctoral romain du 8e au 12e siècles,'' *Maison-Dieu* 52 (1957) 59–88.

[N. KOLLAR]

ALL SAINTS OF RUSSIA, FEAST OF (June 15), a feast established by the Great Church Sobor of Moscow in 1917 as an appeal to national solidarity during a time of crisis. The feast has particular significance for exiles from Russia. Its object is to honor all the saints revered by the Russian Church. The original icon of the feast executed in 1947 hangs in the Ascension Cathedral in the Bronx, New York.

[T. BIRD]

ALL SOULS' DAY, the commemoration of all the faithful departed observed on Nov. 2 in the Latin Church or on Nov. 3 when the 2d falls on a Sunday. The Byzantine rite has a similar observance on the Saturdays before Septuagesima and Pentecost; the Armenians, on Easter Monday. A commemoration for the dead was celebrated in various localities on different dates from the 7th cent. onward. Odilo of Cluny is generally credited with the fixing of Nov. 2 as the day for the commemoration in the West. He ordered c.1030 that the commemoration be celebrated on that day at Cluny and at all its dependent houses. From Cluny the practice spread to many dioceses and was adopted in Rome in the 14th century. The custom of priests' celebrating three Masses on this day originated with the Spanish Dominicans at Valencia; Benedict XIV in 1748 extended the privilege to priests throughout the Spanish dominions. In 1915 Benedict XV made the permission general, specifying, however, that one of these Masses must be offered for all the faithful departed and another for the pope's intention. BIBLIOGRAPHY: Butler 4:240–242; A. Cornides, NCE 1:319.

[P. K. MEAGHER]

ALLAH, Arabic name for God, associated primarily with Islam but also used by Arab Christians. The term is formed by joining *al,* the definite article, with Ilah, a pre-Islamic name for God in North Arabia, corresponding to Hebrew El and Babylonian Bel. The Quraysh tribe to which Mohammed belonged was devoted to Allah, but allowed worship of other gods in the Ka'bah until Mohammed removed them. In the faith taught by Mohammed the first of the Five Pillars of religious practice is making the credal affirmation: *la ilaha illa Allah* (there is no god but the God). The second part of the declaration is *Muhammad rasul Allah* (Mohammed is the messenger of the God). Earlier prophets, including Abraham, Moses, and Jesus, are held to have revealed A., but for Muslim thought Mohammed was the last and greatest of the prophets. Against Arab polytheism and Christian trinitarianism Mohammed insisted rigorously on the absolute oneness of Allah. But in many ways his teaching about Allah corresponds with Christian belief—that God is the omnipotent creator and that he demands ethical behavior, rewarding or punishing man in the life to come. As in Christianity, stress on God's power leaves questions about predestination and human freedom.

[T. EARLY]

ALLAMANO, GIUSEPPE (1851–1926), founder of the Consolata Missionary Fathers and Consolata Missionary Sisters. A. studied at the seminary in Turin and was ordained (1873). In 1880, he became rector of the Santuario della Consolata in Turin, a popular Marian shrine with a residence for priests attached. In 1883 he was made a canon of Turin and was a famous preacher and confessor. Strong in the Salesian tradition passed on through St. John Bosco and St. Joseph Cafasso, the latter A.'s uncle, he founded in 1901 the Institute of the Consolata for Foreign Missions, and in 1910 the Missionary Sisters of the Consolata. He directed these until his death. In 1960 a decree in his cause for beatification was issued. BIBLIOGRAPHY: U. Viglino, EncCatt 1:892–893.

[M. C. BRADLEY]

ALLARD, PAUL (1841–1916), French archeologist and historian. Journeying through Europe (1861–68), introduced to ancient Roman Christian antiquities by G. B. De Rossi and further influenced by E. Le Blant (d. 1897) recorder of Christian epigraphy in Gaul, A. wrote *L'Art päien sous les empereurs chrétiens* (1879) and *Histoire des persécutions* (1885–90). He translated and annotated De Rossi's *Roma sotteranea* (1872) and wrote three volumes on Julian the Apostate (1900–02). From 1904 he was director of *Revue des questions historiques*. In addition to his historical work, A. was greatly interested in the Christian social apostolate and wrote extensively on social questions. BIBLIOGRAPHY: G. Bardy, *Catholicisme* 1:326–327.

[M. J. DALY]

ALLATAE SUNT, encyclical letter issued in 1755 by Pope Benedict XIV addressed to missionaries in the Near East, reminding them that they were not to make Latins of the Eastern Christians but to have them maintain their own rites. Its famous phrase, ''We desire most intensely that all people should be Catholics but not all Latins,'' is often repeated. The encyclical traces the consistent efforts of the popes in this regard since the 11th cent. and urges the missionaries to work with, rather than attempt to dominate the native Eastern clergy.

[A. J. JACOPIN]

ALLATIUS, LEO (1586–1669), Byzantine scholar, theologian, and historian. Born on the island of Chios and reared as a Roman Catholic, A. was a zealous advocate of reunion between the Eastern and Western Churches. Among his more important works are: *De Ecclesiae occidentalis atque orientalis perpetua consensione libri III* (1648), which attempts to establish the primacy of the pope and gives a history of relations between the East and West after the Schism; and *Graeciae orthodoxae scriptores* (2 v., Rome 1652, 1659), a collection of Byzantine writings favorable to Catholic doctrine on the procession of the Holy Spirit. BIBLI-OGRAPHY: E. le Grand, *Bibliographie hellénique du XVIIᵉ siècle* (1895) 3:435–471 (includes a list of his works). Writings listed in Hurter 4:122–130. L. Petit, DTC 1:830–833.

[G. T. DENNIS]

ALLEGIANCE (PLEDGE), see LOYALTY.

ALLEGORY (IN THE BIBLE) in general, a hidden meaning that is attained through a tendency to cancel out the more obvious sense of the text (e.g., 1 Cor 9.9). In the entire Bible, the Greek root for allegory appears only in Gal 4.24, where Sarah and Hagar are symbols of the two covenants. However, elements of allegory are widespread through the Scriptures, with a variety of form that defies neat classification. Occasionally the language and thought of the deeper sense will even disturb that of the surface meaning (note the difficult sequence in Mt 22.1–14; cf. also Ezek 17.7 and 1 Cor 10.2). Often, the link between the two levels of meaning is effected through a series of corresponding details and is evident only to those who already understand the hidden meaning. Allegorical form is often complex and its appeal highly intellectual. When used as an interpretive device, it attempts to make older texts relevant (cf. Ex 13.21 and Wis 10.17; Ezek 31.3–14 and Dan 4; Jer 25.11–12 and Dan 9; Gen 14.17–20 and Heb 7.1–10), but it does so by an appeal to the aesthetic sense, without historical criticism. Such allegorical interpretation probably underwent Greek influence, but it is most likely native to Palestine. Elements of allegory are found in the dreams of Joseph (Gen 37.5–10) and Pharaoh (Gen 47.17–24); somewhat more developed are Ezek 16, 17, 19, 23, 31, 34; the visions of Dan ch. 2, 4, 7, 8 and Zech 1–6 are partially allegorical; the S of S has been retouched with explicit allegory (e.g., 8.9); Ec symbolizes old age through varied brief allusions (12.1–6); Wis, despite its Greek influence, has only a very simple form of allegory (10.17; 16.6, 18.24).

NT material ranges from the very brief examples of 1 Cor 9.9 and Gal 3.16 and the simple forms of 1 Cor (3.12; 5.6–8; 11.17–24; 12.12–30), through the more developed Eph 6.13–17, the partially allegorical visions of Rev, and the allegorical parables of Jn 10 and 15. As for Mt, Mk, and Lk,

there is widespread agreement that their parables were mostly free from allegory when spoken by Jesus. The originally simple message was then allegorized, as the early Church, including the evangelists, adapted them to new circumstances. Thus, e.g., a parable illustrating the urgency of God's demand (Lk 14.15–24, already partially allegorized) was transformed into a history reaching from the prophets to the Last Judgment (Mt 22.1–14). There is a current tendency to admit occasional allegory in Jesus' own words. In some cases, scholars are unwilling to discount an origin later than Jesus for parables which may be originally allegorical (e.g., Mk 4.1–9; Mt 13.24–30). BIBLIOGRAPHY: J. Jeremias, *Parables of Jesus* (1963); B. Gerhardsson, "Parable of the Sower and Its Interpretation," NTS 14 (1968) 165–193.

[P. KEARNEY]

ALLEGRANZA, JOSEPH (1713–85), Dominican of the Enlightenment. Born in Milan, he taught theology when not researching Christian antiquities in South France and Italy, esp. Lombardy. A planned Universal Encyclopedia was abandoned when his partner died. In a multitude of brief articles he has left many valuable archeological studies. He catalogued two libraries for Maria Theresa. BIBLIOGRAPHY: R. Coulon, DHGE 2:489–493.

[E. P. COLBERT]

ALLEGRI, GREGORIO (1582–1652), Roman church musician and priest, chiefly known for his famous *Miserere* in nine parts traditionally sung during Holy Week in the Sistine Chapel. Its copying was for a time forbidden under pain of excommunication, but it was in circulation by the end of the 18th century. Mozart, for one, copied it out from memory. Most of A.'s numerous other works are in MS in various Roman archives. Four collections were published during his lifetime. BIBLIOGRAPHY: E. H. Pember, Grove DMM 1:114–115; K. G. Fellerer, MGG 1:329–330.

[A. DOHERTY]

ALLELUIA, (Hebrew for Praise Yahweh, but one Jewish tradition casts some doubt on whether the original meaning contained the divine name). It has been regarded as a very ancient acclamation, the surviving basic core of Hebrew hymn singing; but others, citing its infrequency in Ps (it appears first in Ps 104.35), regard it as a late development. In some psalms, it appears at the beginning (Ps 111; 112) or end (Ps 104; 105; 115–117) and sometimes in both places (Ps 106; 113; 135; 146–150). Some scholars regard it as originally an opening invitation, while another opinion sees its origin at the end of the psalm, marking the concluding response of the entire congregation. In any event, at its final development, alleluia occurs, sometimes together with amen, as an independent congregational acclamation in both Jewish and Christian liturgy (cf. Ps 106.48; 1 Chr 16.36; Tob 13.22; Ap 19.4). In all the Eastern liturgies except the Ethiopian, two or more alleluias are sung after the Epistle and before the Gospel; they are accompanied by a verse or verses from the Psalms similar to the Gradual in the Roman rite. In the Byzantine liturgy it is also found at the end of the Cherubic Hymn after the great entrance and again after the Communion anthem and in most of the offices. The Eastern tradition as opposed to that of the West retains the alleluia during Great Lent and even at funeral services giving a joyful spirit to these more somber events. The Lenten suppression of the alleluia during the Middle Ages in the Western Church was for a long time one of the principal subjects of debate between East and West. BIBLIOGRAPHY: J. Hempel, InterDB 2:514–515; A. Cabiniss "Alleluia: A Word and Its Effect," *Liturgy and Literature* (1970) 114–121.

[P. KEARNEY AND A. J. JACOPIN]

ALLELUIA VERSE, the third chant of the Mass proper in the Roman rite, sung (or recited) immediately after the gradual, between the epistle and gospel lessons. It consists of the word alleluia sung twice, followed by a verse from a psalm or other text, then a final repetition of alleluia. Musically it is one of the most florid chants, containing as a rule one or more melismas within the verse, in addition to the elaborate *jubilus sung on the last syllable of the word alleluia itself. In performance the first alleluia is sung by a cantor up to the beginning of the jubilus. It is then repeated by the choir, with the jubilus added. The cantor sings the verse up to the last word or so, at which point the choir re-enters. In almost all cases the melody at the end of the verse is the same as that for the alleluia, or at least the jubilus. Finally the cantor begins the alleluia again, and the choir enters at the jubilus. When a sequence is to be sung, the final alleluia is omitted. The alleluia verse, like all liturgical use of the word alleluia, is suppressed during the seasons of Septuagesima and Lent.

The history of the alleluia verse is complicated. There are conflicting views as to when it was added to the Roman Mass, but its use was evidently extended during the pontificate of St. Gregory the Great. Early writings would indicate that the verse was a later addition, probably after Gregory's time, and that the original form was simply the word alleluia sung with the florid jubilus. The alleluia verse remained for some time independent of the rest of the Mass proper. The earliest sources show fixed alleluia verses only for Masses from Advent to Septuagesima, plus one or two other days such as Easter and Pentecost. There is reason to believe that these fixed verses are the oldest, an opinion supported by an analysis of their musical style. MSS through the 12th cent. often group alleluia verses for Sundays after Pentecost in a separate section from which the cantor could freely choose. It was common for a single melody to be used to set as many as 10 different alleluia verses. As a group the alleluia verses are unique in the chant repertory for the use of melodic repetition within single pieces: not only does the alleluia and jubilus melody often reappear within the verse, but melodic phrases within melismas are sometimes repeated. BIBLIOGRAPHY: Apel GregCh; K. H. Schlager, *Thematischer Katalog der ältesten Alleluia-Melodien (Erlanger Arbeiten zur Musikwissenschaft* 2; 1965).

[A. DOHERTY]

ALLEMAND, JEAN-JOSEPH (1772–1836), director of youth. A native of Marseilles and a Priest of the Sacred Heart from 1798, A. chose the youth apostolate for his life's work. His youth society (Oeuvre de la jeunesse) was designed for the young of middle-class family status. It was impeded in its early development by political events, but after 1814 it expanded quickly. Its program of play and prayer stressed religious formation and spiritual development. A. met with the young evenings and weekends, and arranged spiritual exercises to help them toward Christian perfection. The main group was located in Marseilles, but branches in other cities and towns were affiliated with it in A.'s lifetime. BIBLIOGRAPHY: F. Gibon, DHGE 2:494–495; A. Gaduel, *Le Directeur de la jeunesse . . . Jean-Joseph Allemand* (1855; new ed. 1934).

[T. C. O'BRIEN]

ALLEN, FRANCES MARGARET, SISTER (1784–1819), nurse. A. was the daughter of Ethan Allen, patriot of the American Revolution, and his second wife, Frances Buchanan. Mrs. Allen, after the death of her husband, married Dr. Jabez Penniman, who like Ethan Allen was averse to religion. A. grew up in a period of religious revival, and although a Protestant, she asked to attend the school of the Sisters of Notre Dame in Montreal where she became a Catholic. Later she entered the nursing order of the Hôtel Dieu of St. Joseph and worked as a pharmacist. She died at the Hôtel Dieu at the age of 35, having brought converts to the Catholic Church. BIBLIOGRAPHY: L. Gibson, NCE 1:323; J. J. a'Becket, CE 1:320–321.

[M. C. BRADLEY]

ALLEN, GEORGE (1808–76), educator, writer. A. was sent by his parents to learn French in Canada where he lived in the house of a Catholic priest. He graduated from the Univ. of Vermont and later was admitted to the bar. As an Episcopalian he studied theology, becoming rector of St. Albans, Vermont (1834–37). Upon returning to teaching, A. was professor of ancient languages at Delaware College, Newark, and afterward occupied the chair of Latin and Greek at the Univ. of Pennsylvania. A. became a Catholic in 1847. He wrote several books, among which were *Remains of W. S. Graham* (1849) and *Life of Philidor* (1863). BIBLIOGRAPHY: J. L. Morrison, NCE 1:323; J. J. a'Becket, CE 1:321.

[M. C. BRADLEY]

ALLEN, ROLAND (1869–1947), English missionary, who worked for many years in the north of China, then in England for the World Dominion Movement, and finally in Kenya. He considered the chief goal of mission labors to be the establishment of native Churches which with the help of the Spirit would spread in complete independence. He wrote three treatises on the subject, the most important of which was *Missionary Methods: St. Paul's or Ours* (1912). His works continue to be read. BIBLIOGRAPHY: E. J. Bingle, RGG 1:240–241.

[M. J. SUELZER]

ALLEN, WILLIAM, (1532–94), English cardinal. Born at Rossall, Lancashire, he studied at Oriel College, Oxford (1553) and later became Principal of St. Mary's Hall, Oxford (1556) and canon of York (1558). Because of his opposition to the Elizabethan Settlement, he was forced to leave England in 1565. In 1568 he established the college at Douai, France, which became the most important educational center for English Catholics, and he later established English colleges at Rome (1575–78) and Valladolid (1589). The Douay Bible was produced under his inspiration. King Philip II of Spain interceded with Sixtus V to get A. made a cardinal in 1587, anticipating his role as abp. of Canterbury had the Armada succeeded. A.'s support of the invasion created difficulties for Catholics in England. His last days were spent in Rome. BIBLIOGRAPHY: M. Haile, *Elizabethan Cardinal* (1914); B. Camm, *Cardinal William Allen* (1909); M. P. McCarthy, *Catholicism in English-Speaking Lands* (1964) 31.

[T. EARLY]

ALLERS, RUDOLF (1883–1963), RC philosopher and psychiatrist. Born in Vienna, A. received his M.D. from the Univ. of Vienna, where he studied under S. *Freud. He specialized in psychiatry from 1908 and in 1913 became an instructor in psychiatry at Munich. After service with the Austrian army during World War I, he taught at Vienna 1918–38. During that period he also engaged in laboratory research and private practice and studied philosophy at Milan, receiving his doctorate in 1934. He became professor of psychology at The Catholic Univ. of America in 1938 and in 1948 professor of philosophy at Georgetown. He had a special interest in *phenomenology and *existentialism, and emphasized the continuity of the modern period with the medieval. Notable among his writings is *Psychology of Character* (1929).

[T. EARLY]

ALLGEIER, FRANZ ARTHUR (1882–1952), German biblical scholar. Appointed instructor in biblical languages in 1915 at Univ. of Freiburg, A. succeeded G. Hoberg as professor of OT literature (1919) at the same university. Because of his training in classical and Semitic languages he chose as his chief field of endeavor working on the Greek and Latin versions of the Bible. His publications, all of them in German, reflect his research on bible versions, esp. of *Psalms*. Made a papal domestic prelate in 1941 and also a consultor of the Pontifical Biblical Commission, in 1945 he became rector of the Univ. of Freiburg.

[C. C. O'DONNELL]

ALLIANCE OF THE REFORMED CHURCHES throughout the World Holding the Presbyterian Order, formed in 1875, one of the strongest of several ecumenical denominational organizations dating from that era. The Alliance involves over 65 constituent church bodies, from more than 45 countries, representing over 40 million adherents. The General Council, a delegated body that has the responsibility for governing the Alliance, has held meetings since the first one in Edinburgh (1877). It has always been federative and advisory, existing to promote the common interests of the member bodies. It has no power to obligate or to interfere in the internal affairs of a member body. With headquarters in Geneva, the general secretary coordinates the work of the Alliance in various geographical areas under area secretaries. At the General Council meetings considerable attention has been given to theological discussion, problems of religious liberty, and ecumenical relations. During World War II the organization did much to continue fellowship among Christians on both sides of the conflict. While the Alliance covers a wide range of national and linguistic differences, its greatest support has come from Europe and North America. In 1959 it held a historic meeting in São Paulo, Brazil, on "The Servant Lord and His Servant People," at which time it noted the existence of strong Churches holding Reformed doctrine and the Presbyterian system in Hispanic America and other parts of the world. In 1954 the Alliance revised its constitution. In 1968 final plans were made for the International Congregational Council to merge with the Alliance of Reformed Churches. Representatives of the Alliance and the RC Church engaged in formal discussions in 1969 on issues of common interest. BIBLIOGRAPHY: *Report of Proceedings* (1877–); M. Pradevand, "Leaves from the Alliance History," *Reformed World* 32 (June 1972) 73–78.

[J. H. SMYLIE]

ALLIES, THOMAS WILLIAM (1813–1903), English writer, educated at Bristol Grammar School, Eton College, and at Wadham College where he received his M.A. degree. In 1838 he became an Anglican minister. Convinced that A.'s views were influenced by the Oxford Movement, the bp. changed him to a small rural parish. There his study of the Fathers of the Church led ultimately to his conversion to Roman Catholicism (1850). He later (1853) held the post of secretary to the Catholic Poor School Committee to which Card. Wiseman appointed him. Of his many writings, *Journal in France* (1849) and the *Formation of Christendom* (8 v., 1861–95) are the most important. BIBLIOGRAPHY: G. Donald, *Men Who Left the Movement* (1933); T. W. Allies, *Life's Decision* (1880).

[S. A. HEENEY]

ALLIOLI, JOSEPH VON (1793–1873, scripture scholar. Ordained at Regensburg, Germany (1816), A. completed his studies in Oriental languages, archeology, and exegesis at Vienna, Rome, and Paris (1818–20). He was professor at the Univ. of Landshut but had to resign from his position because of a weak throat. He was made canon at Regensburg (1835) and was dean of the chapter at Augsburg from 1838. Among his many works on the biblical sciences, the most important was his German translation of the Bible (1830–32), which received a papal commendation (1830). For a century it was the most widely used Catholic German Bible. BIBLIOGRAPHY: K. Staab, LTK 1:352; J. Pietsch, DHGE 2:617–618.

[C. C. O'DONNELL]

ALLO, ERNEST BERNARD (1873–1945), Dominican biblical scholar who applied his learning in the history of religions to show that the Gospel transcended the mystery religions of the Mediterranean world. Professor at the Univ. of Fribourg (1905–38), he published commentaries on the Apocalypse (1921) and the Epistles to the Corinthians (1935–37), both esteemed for their critical exegeses.

[T. C. O'BRIEN]

ALLOCUTION, PAPAL, an address by the pope to the cardinals in private consistory on a matter of contemporary relevance. It is published if the subject matter is of general interest. Often it states papal policy concerning dealings with civil powers. In the 20th cent. the term has been extended to include addresses by the pope of a less formal nature.

[S. A. HEENEY]

ALLOGENES SUPREME, see APOCRYPHA (NT), 3.

ALLOUEZ, CLAUDE JEAN (1622–89), Jesuit missionary. He became a Jesuit in the Toulouse province of the Society (1639). After his ordination (1655) he was sent to Canada (1658), and from 1660 served as superior of the Jesuit residence at Trois Rivières. A. was primarily active in missionary labors in the Great Lakes area of Wisconsin, Michigan, and Ontario. He established a station at Pointe du St. Ésprit on Georgian Bay (1665) and reached Lake Nipagon, Ontario (1667). For the rest of his life he was constantly engaged in missionary journeys. BIBLIOGRAPHY: T. J. Campbell, *Pioneer Priests of North America* (1919) 3:147–164; RACHS 6:167, 18:132–133, 21:141, 243.

[R. K. MacMASTER]

ALLOWIN, ST., see BAVO, ST.

ALLSTON, WASHINGTON (1779–1843), American painter. One of the most intelligent artists of his generation, A. marked the turn to a new poetic romanticism, imbuing works with mood, mystery, and magic in religious, literary, and landscape themes. He studied with B. West in London (1801–03). Coleridge wrote that A. alone of his time understood nature as "revealed in the Phaenomenon." Deeply impressed by Venetian painters, A. (called the American Titian, in Rome) early perceived the "expressive" language of color per se, thus presaging the 20th-cent. schools of

Symbolisme. His portraits are studies of a state of soul: *Dead Man Restored to Life by Touching the Bones of the Prophet Elisha* (1811–13) and the tragically unfinished *Belshazzar's Feast* are notable. BIBLIOGRAPHY: E. P. Richardson, *Washington Allston* (1948); J. B. Flagg, *Life and Letters of Washington Allston* (1969).

[M. J. DALY]

ALMAH, a Hebrew word by which Isaiah (7.14) designates the mother of Emmanuel: "Therefore the Lord himself will give you this sign: the virgin (*'ălmah*) shall be with child, and bear a son, and shall name him Emmanuel." Elsewhere in the OT (apart from Ps 45.8 and 1 Chr 15.20 where the word seems to have musical connotations), *'ălmah* is used for a young girl of marriageable age—presumably a virgin (cf. Gen 24.43; Ex 2.8; Pr 30.19; S of S 1.3; 6.8; Ps 68.26). In Is 7.14 the meaning is controverted. Here the LXX translated *'ălmah* as *parthenos* (virgin). Mt 1.22 understood the text of Isaiah as referring to the virginal conception and birth of Christ. In explaining Is 7.14 most non-Catholic authorities today reject the messianic interpretation. Most Catholic scholars agree in seeing the text as a prophetic reference to the virgin birth of Christ, but differ on details and on the literary and historical context of the passage. BIBLIOGRAPHY: J. Prado, *Enciclopedia de la Biblia* (1963) 1:371–376; C. Lattey, "Term Almah in Is 7.14," CBQ (1947) 89–95.

[E. MAY]

ALMAIN, JACQUES (c. 1480–1515), Gallican theologian who attempted to refute Thomas de Vio's (later Cardinal Cajetan) defense of the superiority of the pope to a general council of bishops. A. was educated at the Univ. of Paris, the intellectual center for conciliarist theories, and taught theology at the Univ. of Navarre. Although the faculty at Paris refused to attack Cajetan's *De comparatione auctoritatis papae et concilii* (1511), A. acquiesced to King Louis XII's request and published *De auctoritate ecclesiae et conciliorum generalium adversus Thomam de Vio* (1512), in which he maintained that only a general council is the full and adequate representation of the Church. BIBLIOGRAPHY: DTC 1:895–897; G. M. Grabka, NCE 1:327.

[T. M. MCFADDEN]

ALMANNUS, see ADELMANNUS.

ALMOHAD ARCHITECTURE, 12th- and 13th-cent. architectural style of the Muslim dynasty on the Barbary coast of North Africa, reflected in great mosques of Spain (Seville). BIBLIOGRAPHY: G. Marçais, *Manuel d'art musulman* (v. 1, 1926).

[M. J. DALY]

ALMOHADS (Arabic al-*Muwaḥḥidûn*), an Islamic dynasty. The Almohad movement was begun by Ibn Tûmart (d. 1128 or 1130), a native of Sus in North Africa. Ibn Tûmart studied in Córdoba and in the Orient and following his return to

North Africa began a concerted campaign against what he considered the corruption of Western Islam, insisting on a return to the *Koran and the *ḥadîth. Under the influence of *Ash 'arite theology he attacked the crass fundamentalism of the Malikite (SEE ISLAMIC LAW) school then dominant in North Africa, declaring that to attribute anthropomorphic qualities to God was unbelief *(kufr)*. It is from this "declaration of the transcendent unity of God" *(tawḥîd)* that his followers were called *muwaḥḥidûn* (or *mu'aḥḥidûn*). Ibn Tûmart proclaimed himself *mahdi in 1121 and supported by a large group of Berbers began a "holy war" (SEE JIHÂD) against the *Almoravids whom he considered unbelievers because of their fundamentalist doctrines. Following his death the movement was led by his disciple 'Abd al-Mu'min (d. 1163) who took the title *caliph. The Almohads conquered Tangiers and Morocco in 1146 and not long thereafter held control of all North Africa from Egypt to the Atlantic and of southern Spain. Culturally the Almohad period was one of the richest in the history of Muslim Spain and 'Abd al-Mu'min's successor, abû Yûsuf Ya'qûb (d. 1184) was the patron of the philosophers Averroës and Ibn Tufail (see ISLAMIC PHILOSOPHY). From the early 13th cent. Almohad power began to weaken with the decline of their military effectiveness under renewed attacks by the Christians in Spain and Muslim princes in North Africa. The last Almohad caliph died in 1269. BIBLIOGRAPHY: W. M. Watt, *History of Islamic Spain* (1965) 103–111; E. Lévi-Provençal, *Islam d' occident* (1948) 257–280.

[R. M. FRANK]

ALMOND, JOHN, ST. (c. 1576–1612), English martyr. A native of Lancashire, A. studied in Ireland (1585–97), then at the English College in Rome, where he was ordained (1598). He went on the English mission (1602), was imprisoned (1608), but either escaped or was released, for he was working in Staffordshire in 1609. Again arrested in 1612, he was committed to Newgate. He was a man of ingenuity and ready speech, as appears in the account of his interrogation by Bp. King of London. Although no proof was brought against him, he was found guilty when he refused to take the oath of allegiance in the unacceptable form in which it was proposed to him, and was executed at Tyburn. He was beatified in 1929 and canonized in 1970. BIBLIOGRAPHY: W. J. Steele, *Blessed John Almond* (1961); G. B. Proja, BiblSanct 1:881; Butler 4:502–503.

[V. SAMPSON]

ALMONER, an official in charge of distributing alms in the court of a king, a prince, or a royal house. The office of Grand Almoner in France (14th cent.) became important because that minister had the charge of the king's ecclesiastical patronage. Army chaplains are known as almoners in France. BIBLIOGRAPHY: ODCC 38.

[M. C. BRADLEY]

ALMORAVIDS (Arabic, *al-Murâbiṭûn*) an Islamic sect and dynasty. The term *murâbiṭ* designates one who lives in

ribâṭ: a kind of fortified monastery on the borders of *Islam to which some zealous Muslims would retire to carrry out the *jihâd against the infidel (SEE MARABOUT). The movement originated with Ibn Yâsîn (d. 1059), a "holy man" who had founded a *ribâṭ* in Senegal. Under his influence, the Sanhâja, a major group of Berber tribes, were organized as troops for the spread of Islam, calling themselves *murâbiṭûn*. In a short time they gained control over most of North Africa, founding the city of Morocco (Arabic, *Marrâkuš*) in 1062. They were subsequently called by the Muslim princes of Spain to aid them in their struggle against Alfonso VI of Leon and after a time, supported by the *ulema became masters of Andalusia. The last commander of the Almoravids, Tâfshîn, died in Oran in 1145 fighting against the rising power of the *Almohads. Because of their narrow and rigid orthodoxy, the rule of the Almoravids in Spain was oppressive to Muslims and Christians alike. BIBLIOGRAPHY: W. M. Watt, *History of Islamic Spain* (1965) 95–102; E. Lévi-Provençal, *Islam d'occident* (1948) 239–256.

[R. M. FRANK]

ALMSGATHERING (CANON LAW), the activity of orally requesting or personally collecting alms—as distinct from receiving the spontaneous offerings of the faithful—to fund some religious purpose or to assist an ecclesiastical institution. The Code of Canon Law (c. 1503) establishes norms for such requests. Private persons, whether clerical or lay, may solicit alms only with the permission of the Holy See or their ordinary, and that of the local ordinary. Members of mendicant orders may solicit funds, solely with the permission of their superiors, in the diocese where their religious house is situated; elsewhere they need the permission of the local ordinary. Permission for almsgathering is readily granted to mendicants; other religious would have to demonstrate a pressing financial need that could not otherwise be met. The law applies to the solicitation of alms from many persons, rather than from a few or only those personally known to the person seeking alms; an oral request rather than one conducted through the mails; and does not apply to collecting money in a church since such gifts are considered voluntary offerings. BIBLIOGRAPHY: L. Meyer, NCE 1:331–332.

[T. M. MCFADDEN]

ALMUCE, a cope lined with fur worn by canons and by religious of certain orders during choral services. It came into use during the 13th cent. as a means of keeping the head and neck warm. In more recent times canons in France carried it over their left arms as a mark of ecclesiastical dignity. It has also been called amess or amice, though it is not to be identified with the linen piece of that name worn under the liturgical garments. BIBLIOGRAPHY: H. Norris, *Church Vestments* (1950); R. Le Sage, *Vestments and Church Furniture* (tr. F. Murphy, 1960) 101.

[N. KOLLAR]

ALNWICK, WILLIAM, see WILLIAM OF ALNWICK.

ALOGOI (Gr., not-worders), a term of double meaning: it may be understood to signify either (1) those without reason, or (2) more specifically, those denying the Logos, applied to certain heretics in Asia Minor c. 170. Not all of their teaching is known, but they certainly rejected the Gospel, Epistles, and Apocalypse of St. John the Apostle and denied the doctrine of the Logos presented by him as not in agreement with the rest of Scripture. They are mentioned in the writings of Eusebius, Irenaeus, and Epiphanius.

[A. J. JACOPIN]

ALOYSIUS GONZAGA, ST. (1568–91), beatified 1605, canonized 1726, patron of youth (esp. students) since 1729. His father prepared him for the military nobility from 5 years of age, but as a Medici page of 7 Aloysius made a vow of virginity and at 12 became devoted to the Eucharist after receiving first communion from Charles Borromeo. As a page of Philip II in Spain at 13 he was influenced by reading Louis of Granada to practice mental prayer as much as 5 hours a day, meanwhile studying philosophy at Alcalá. Renouncing his inheritance to a younger brother, he entered the Jesuits in 1585 despite his father's objections. Humble and obedient as a novice, he cared for the sick and catechized the poor. He died in Rome tending the sick in a plague. BIBLIOGRAPHY: F. Baumann, BiblSanct 8:348–353.

[E. P. COLBERT]

ALPAIS, BL. (c.1153–1211). A simple peasant girl accustomed to work in the fields at Cudot in France, A. was stricken with what was possibly leprosy. Resigning herself to the affliction and offering her suffering to God, she experienced a vision of the Bl. Virgin during which she was completely cured of her disease, but lost all power of movement. Paralyzed thereafter, but otherwise in good health, she subsisted for a long time on the eucharistic species alone and was almost continuously in ecstasy. The abp. of Sens appointed a commission to investigate the truth of her fast, and when this was confirmed, had a priory built adjacent to her lodging and put Augustinian friars in charge of the church. A.'s cult was confirmed in 1874 by Pius IX. BIBLIOGRAPHY: L. H. Tridon, *La Vie merveilleuse de Ste. Alpais de Cudot* (1886); Butler 4:253.

ALPHA AND OMEGA (first and last letters of the Greek alphabet), used by St. John (e.g., Rev 1.8; 22.13) to denote the infinite majesty of the eternal Father or the transcendent dignity of the Son, who is equal in all things to the Father. Since ancient times these letters have been used together in both Eastern and Western Christian symbolism to denote the divinity of Christ and are usually placed in conjunction with the monogram of Christ. They symbolize Christ as the beginning and end of all things.

[A. J. JACOPIN]

ALPHABET, a system of writing by consonantal symbols. The earliest writing was pictographic. From such picture writing the Egyptians developed from the 4th millenary B.C. a system of writing called hieroglyphic (i.e., sacred carving), a name suggesting that its use was at first assimilated to magic or religion and that those skilled in writing were privileged persons. During the 2d millenary B.C. a system of writing was developed in the Syria-Palestine region that simplified written communication by replacing pictographic writing with the representation of consonants by signs. This reached a final determination c. 10th cent. B.C. in the Phoenician alphabet, from which the Hebrew, Greek, and Latin alphabets are derived. BIBLIOGRAPHY: D. Diringer, *Alphabet: A Key to the History of Mankind* (1948); W. F. Albright, *Archeology of Palestine* (1949) 177–203; C. H. Gordon, "Accidental Invention of the Phonemic Alphabet," *Near Eastern Studies* 29 (July 1970) 193–197.

[J. E. LUSSIER]

ALPHABET, LITURGICAL USE OF. The Greek, Roman, and Hebrew alphabets are used in the Tenebrae Office, calendars, and in symbolic representations of Christ. The most significant use is in the dedication of a church. The bishop traces with his crozier the letters of the Greek and Latin alphabet on the floor within two diagonal lines which cross in the center of the Church. This ceremony probably arose from the ancient Roman methods of field measurement where the surveyor traced two transverse lines and connected them to form a perimeter. The use of the alphabet is probably an expansion of this, placing an alpha and omega to signify that this church belongs to Christ.

[N. KOLLAR]

ALPHABETIC PSALMS, psalms in which the parts begin consecutively with one of the 22 letters of the Hebrew alphabet. The part so begun may be a verse, a half verse, or a strophe. Examples are psalms 9, 25, 34, 37, 145, 111, 119. (See also Sir 51.13–30; Pr 31.11–31 and Lam). The device was perhaps employed as an aid to memory; it is useful for the literary and textual study of the Bible.

[T. C. O'BRIEN]

ALPHABETOS (Gr., alphabet), *troparia whose initial letters are placed in alphabetical order.

[A. J. JACOPIN]

ALPHANUS OF SALERNO (Alfano; c.1015–1085), Benedictine abbot and archbishop. Before becoming a monk at Monte Cassino, then a center of humanistic learning, A. taught at the Univ. of Salerno where he fostered the study of medicine. A theologian, hagiographer, and writer of hymns, he gave refuge to Gregory VII, fleeing to Salerno from Emperor Henry IV (1085). BIBLIOGRAPHY: B. D. Hill, NCE 1:336.

[M. A. WINKELMANN]

ALPHEGE OF CANTERBURY, ST. (d. 1012), arch-bishop, martyr. A. was bp. of Winchester, 984–1006 and was transferred to the See of Canterbury in 1006. The Danes, who captured him in 1011, murdered him in a drunken rage when he refused to allow himself to be ransomed. BIBLIOG-RAPHY: W. Hunt, DNB 1:150–152; Knowles MOE *passim;* Butler 2:129–131; R. Van Doren, BiblSanct s.v. "Elfego" 4:1017–18, esp. for bibliog.

[J. L. GRASSI]

ALPHEGE OF WINCHESTER, ST. (Aelfheah; "the Bald"; d. 951), bp. of Winchester from 934. He was chap-lain and secretary to his kinsman King Athelstan, and as bp. promoted the English monastic revival. He ordained his fellow-reformers Dunstan and Tehelwold as priests, proph-esying their future episcopates. BIBLIOGRAPHY: E. Duckett, *Saint Dunstan of Canterbury* (1955); E. Watkin, BiblSanct 4:1018.

[W. A. CHANEY]

ALPHERIUS, ST., see ALFERIUS, ST.

ALPHONSA, MOTHER, see EPPINGER, ELISABETH.

ALPHONSUS LIGUORI, ST. (1696–1787), founder of the Redemptorists, bp., moral theologian, Doctor of the Church. Born of an ancient Neapolitan family, he received his doctorate in laws at the Univ. of Naples, and practiced at the bar before becoming a priest (1726). After a pastoral ministry, he formed an association of priests and brothers living a common life, formally approved by Benedict XIV in 1749 as the Congregation of the Most Holy Redeemer, which despite the anti-clerical policies of the Tanucci gov-ernment, flourished and spread. He was elected superior general for life, and was busied in administration, in giving missions, and in writing. Consecrated bp. of Sant' Agata dei Gothi (1762), he added the charges of the diocese to his other work, but resigned in 1777 on account of ill health. He was canonized in 1839.

No man contributed more to the devotion, mentality, and working morality of the Church in the 19th century. His thought was practical rather than speculative and cast in concrete terms, his character was good-humored and gentle, and he was devoted to those in need. He was a talented musician and an admired composer in the great Neapolitan style of the period. His literary productions were numerous. He wrote on preaching, his sermons were admired by New-man, and his spiritual teaching, which was utterly opposed to Jansenism, breathed an ardent love toward the person of Our Lord, the Blessed Sacrament, and Our Lady in terms more extravagant than stilted.

Above all it is as a moral theologian that he is widely famous. Here his main work is the *Moral Theology* (1748) begun as an annotation of H. *Busenbaum; the 3d ed. began to take on a more personal shape, and he himself regarded the 8th edition (1779) as definitive. There were more than 60 editions before the critical edition of L. Gaudé (4 v., 1905–12). His moral writings, which make up a third of his literary output, express his characteristic method, called *equiprobabilism. He had begun as a *probabiliorist but practical experience had persuaded him to probabilism, until a vigorous controversy with a Dominican, Giovanni Vin-cenzo Patuzzi, a disciple of *Concina, led him to a restate-ment of his own proper position. His citations from other authors are exceedingly numerous, and in the manner of most works of the genre are frequently not at first-hand. Many of the manuals of moral theology which were used in seminaries throughout the world either belong to his school or are strongly marked by his influence. BIBLIOGRAPHY: C. Henze, BiblSanct 1:837–859, with excellent bibliog; for A.'s theological authority, P. Palazzini, *op. cit.* 1:860–861; L. Vereecke, NCE 1:336–341; D. F. Miller and L. X. Aubin, *Saint Alphonsus* (1940); A. Berthe, *St. Alphonsus de Ligouri* (2 v., tr. H. Castle, 1905); L. Colin, *Alphonse de Liguori, doctrine spirituelle* (2v., 1971).

[T. GILBY]

ALPIRSBACH, ABBEY OF, former Benedictine monas-tery in Württemberg, Germany; at present in the Diocese of Rottenburg. In 1099 the extant Romanesque church was dedicated. In 1101 Pope Pascal II confirmed Alpirsbach as an abbey with free election of abbot and bailiff. The abbey felt the impact of the Reformation by being alternately Catholic and Protestant. Today the church is Lutheran; the refectory, a Catholic chapel. BIBLIOGRAPHY: G. Allmang, DHGE 2:765–768.

[S. A. HEENEY]

ALT, ALBRECHT (1883–1956) German biblical scholar who, applying the form criticism method, devised a classification of biblical law that became standard, with his distinction between casuistic and apodictic laws, in the Pen-tateuch. Professor at the Univ. of Leipzig, he was an expert in epigraphy, philology, and the history and topography of biblical lands. BIBLIOGRAPHY: his *Essays on Old Testament History and Religion.* (tr. R. A. Wilson, pa. 1968); J. L. McKenzie, JBC 2:751–752.

[T. C. O'BRIEN]

ALTAMIRA, paleolithic caves near Santillana del Mar, in Santander Province, Spain, explored by Marcelino de San-tuola, scholar of prehistory in 1875. His small daughter Maria noted bison on the ceiling of the so-called Great Hall (1879). The beauty and vigor of these paintings are recog-nized as the supreme expression of the Magdalenian Age (10th millennium B.C.). More than 150 forms of bison, horses, deer, and boars, evidencing keen observation with a grasp of the spirit of the animal, were executed with great skill in black, yellow, red, and purple colors with frequent emphases of engraving. BIBLIOGRAPHY: S. Giedion, *Eternal Present* (v. 1, 1962); E. A. Lord, *McGraw-Hill Dictionary of Art* 1:68–70.

[M. J. DALY]

ALTAMIRANO, DIEGO FRANCISCO DE (1625–1715), Spanish Jesuit missionary. His active life was spent in South America where he held various offices: rector, provincial, visitor, and procurator; his assignments acquainted him thoroughly with Argentina, Paraguay, Ecuador, Colombia, and Peru. He founded a reduction for the Chaco Indians, translated a catechism, planned for, promoted, and protected the missions wherever he was located. His two historical studies of the work of the Jesuits in Peru are based on his personal investigation and experience.

[H. JACK]

ALTANER, BERTHOLD (1885–1964), church historian and patristic scholar. After receiving a doctorate in theology at the Univ. of Breslau he began in 1919 to teach church history there, becoming in time ordinary professor of patrology, church history, and Christian archeology. During the Nazi regime he was deprived of his professorship. After World War II he was appointed to the chair of patrology and history of liturgy at the Univ. of Würzburg, where he taught till his retirement (1950). Although he produced important studies in Dominican history, A. is most widely known for his *Patrologie,* which went through 17 editions and has been translated into six languages. The English translation appeared in 1960. BIBLIOGRAPHY: J. Quasten, CHR 50 (1964) 92–93.

[H. DRESSLER]

ALTAR, in Christian usage, the table at which the central sacrament or liturgy of the community of faith is celebrated. That liturgy—called the Eucharist, or the Mass, or the Lord's Supper, or the Service of Holy Communion—is essentially a sacrificial meal involving readings, preaching, witnessing, and prayer. The community of faith sees and celebrates in the constituents of the meal the body and blood of the Lord; hence the need of a table, an altar, for bread and wine and book (prayer-texts). Normally the altar is a fixed table in a building or hall devoted exclusively to worship. It may, however, be movable and temporary. The primary determinant of the sacred for Christians is not the place or altar but the celebrating community. It is the community (the Church) that makes the altar sacred, not vice versa. Christian liturgy, therefore, can be celebrated in homes or multipurpose halls, using any suitable table as the altar. Since it is the central location of the eucharistic action, the altar *mensa* (table-top) should be visible to all in the assembly. It should be large enough to comfortably support the bread and wine and book. Made of wood in the earliest Christian centuries, the fixed altar is now more commonly of stone. Its original square shape is returning to favor under the impetus of the 20th-cent. liturgical renewal, after decadence and distortion transformed it into a long bench for the support of relics, tabernacle, gradines, candles, etc. Originally, one altar for each eucharistic hall was a principle of liturgy—one table-symbol of the one Christ and his sacrament of unity, to be placed in a central position in the hall. Periods of liturgical decadence, however, encouraged a multiplication of altars and the removal of the principal one to the far end of the hall. Current reform has brought the altar again to a central position, has separated it from the place of reservation, and has eliminated secondary altars, at least in principle.

As a symbol of Christ, the altar in a church building is reverenced by a bow or genuflection as one enters or leaves the hall. Since the first part of the Eucharist is a celebration of the word of God, for which *ambo and presider's chair are the relevant furnishings, action at the altar begins with the bringing of the gifts of bread and wine and ends with the sharing of holy communion. The altar, therefore, should be bare, except for a cloth, until the gifts are brought, and should be bared again after holy communion is distributed. Candles and cross may be placed upon the floor about the altar, defining its space, and need not rely on the table itself for their support. The custom of celebrating the Eucharist occasionally at grave sites (of martyrs), and then of building churches and altars over the tombs of martyrs, developed into the practice of enclosing relics of saints in the base or *mensa* of an altar. By the end of the 16th cent., church law required such a "sepulcher" in every altar, and portable altars had to be fitted with an altar-stone or corporal (cloth) reliquary. This law is no longer in force so far as movable altars or tables on which Mass is to be celebrated outside a sacred place are concerned. (SEE "General Instruction of the Roman Missal," as found in *The Sacramentary* of 1974, ch. 5, n. 265). Formerly, in a technical sense the movable altar of church law consisted precisely in this stone. The fixed altar is now considered to be one attached to the floor so that it cannot be moved. (*ibid*. n. 260). The table of a fixed altar should be of natural stone, but other solid, becoming, and skillfully constructed material may be used if the conference of bishops permits this. In fixed altars it is still considered fitting to have relics enclosed in the altar, or placed under the altar (*ibid*. 266).

The place of reservation (tabernacle) became a permanent fixture of the altar in the 16th century. Liturgical renewal and post-conciliar documents have made it clear that the altar is the place of eucharistic action, and totally distinct from the place of static reservation, so the anomaly of that custom is now obvious. The Holy See's "Instruction on Eucharistic Worship" (May 25, 1967) articulates this position: "Consequently because of the sign, it is more in keeping with the nature of the celebration that the eucharistic presence of Christ, which is the fruit of the consecration and should be seen as such, should not be on the altar from the very beginning of the Mass through the reservation of the sacred species in the tabernacle" (n. 55). BIBLIOGRAPHY: F. X. Redmond, NCE 1:347–351; A. M. Roguet, "L'Autel," *Maison-Dieu* 63 (1960) 96–113; *ibid,* 70 (1962); J. Jungmann, "New Altar," *Liturgical Arts* 37 (1969) 36–40; C. Napier, "Altar in the Contemporary Church," *Clergy Review* 57 (1972) 624–632.

[P. K. MEAGHER]

ALTAR, GREGORIAN, the privileged altar in the Church of St. Gregory on the Coelian Hill in Rome. All altars enjoying the same privilege are called Gregorian altars *ad instar*. BIBLIOGRAPHY: T. Bouscaren and A. Ellis, *Canon Law, A Text and Commentary* (3d ed., 1961) 392.

[N. KOLLAR]

ALTAR, HIGH, the principal altar in the church. In North America this is usually called the main altar. This altar gives symbolic expression to the unity of the Church in life and worship. This unity is the basis of the custom of having one central, free-standing altar in each church. The multiplication of altars began in the 6th cent. in the West and reached its apex in the 14th century. Vatican Council II reaffirmed the symbolic value of one altar and one celebration. BIBLIOGRAPHY: K. Seasoltz, *House of God* (1964); Podhradsky.

[N. KOLLAR]

ALTAR, PAPAL, the altar upon which only the Pope or his special delegate may celebrate Mass. The greater basilicas of Rome have such an altar.

[N. KOLLAR]

ALTAR, PRIVILEGED, an altar at which the celebration of Mass may gain a plenary indulgence in favor of a soul in purgatory. This privilege either belongs to any priest celebrating at a particular altar; or to a particular priest, at any altar; or to certain priests, at certain altars. The concept of privileged altars was modified by the apostolic constitution *Indulgentiarum Doctrina* (Jan. 30, 1967) in regard to the conditions and emphasis of indulgences. BIBLIOGRAPHY: "A Revision of the Rules on Indulgences," *Pope Speaks* 12 (1967) 124–135; T. Bouscaren and A. Ellis, *Canon Law, A Text and Commentary* (3d ed. 1961) 379.

[N. KOLLAR]

ALTAR BOY, a boy or young man who assists the celebrant at liturgical functions. At Mass he acts as *acolyte, even though he is not formally a lay minister. This arrangement is permitted by ecclesiastical law (CIC c. 813) and is commonly necessary. The lay ministry of acolytes is restricted to males. There has been some movement toward permitting "altar girls," but the Holy See has not yet sanctioned the practice.

[N. KOLLAR]

ALTAR BREADS, the pieces of bread intended for consecration at Mass. In the West since the 11th cent. only unleavened bread (azyme) has been used for the purpose. It is made of pure wheaten flour that is mixed with water and baked. Commonly the breads are pressed thin between baking irons; they are round in shape and are made in larger and smaller sizes, the larger for consumption by the celebrant or celebrants and the smaller for distribution to the faithful. In

the East round cakes of leavened bread (*prosphora) are used. BIBLIOGRAPHY: F. Amiot, *History of the Mass* (tr. L. C. Sheppard, 1958) 64, 98.

[N. KOLLAR]

ALTAR CARDS, memory aids introduced into the furnishings of the altar in the 16th century. There were three: at the epistle side, one containing the prayers at the washing of the fingers; at the gospel side, one containing the Prologue of St. John's Gospel (the Last Gospel); at the center, one containing parts of the Ordinary recited there. The reform of the liturgical rites and books has made altar cards obsolescent.

[T. C. O'BRIEN]

ALTAR CLOTHS, three blessed white linen cloths that cover the altar during the celebration of Mass, the uppermost of which commonly hangs down nearly to the floor at either end of the altar. Precisely when it became customary to cover the altar with cloths is not known, but their use goes back to the early centuries of the Church. They serve the useful purpose of presenting the altar to the faithful as the Lord's table, kept in appropriate cleanliness; they also provide an absorbent material to soak up any drops of consecrated wine that may be spilled. The thought that they are representative of Christ's burial shroud is an unnecessary, and perhaps even a positively misleading, example of symbolism. From the 17th to the 20th cent. the uppermost cloth was often elaborately ornamented with lace, but this practice has gone out of favor in consequence of the current trend toward architectural and artistic simplicity in churches and their appointments. In earlier times it was customary to spread the altar cloths immediately before Mass and to remove them after its completion, and thus the present *corporal can be seen as a development of the uppermost altar cloth. In modern times the cloths are usually left on the altar after Mass, but they are often covered, when the altar is not in use, to prevent the dust from settling on them. BIBLIOGRAPHY: J. B. O'Connell, *Church Building and Furnishing* (1955) 133–218.

[N. KOLLAR]

ALTAR CROSS, the crucifix placed on the altar behind or above the tabernacle. Since the gradual implementation of Vat II SacLit, the altar cross is more often located near the altar rather than on it.

ALTAR OF INCENSE, a small altar made of precious wood plated with gold on which incense was burned as an offering to God. This "golden altar" was situated in the Holy Place of the Temple. It was alongside this altar that the Angel of God appeared to Zechariah to tell him of the marvelous birth of his son, John, and of John's mission (Lk 1.5–23).

[J. E. FALLON]

ALTAR OF REPOSE, the altar where the Eucharist to be distributed on Good Friday is reserved from Holy Thursday to Good Friday. It was the custom in the early Church to put aside, in the sacristy or elsewhere, the consecrated hosts for consumption on days when Mass was not celebrated. Such days gradually dropped from the calendar until Good Friday was left as the only surviving instance. The reservation of the Eucharist for Good Friday began to be surrounded with greater solemnity, the more so because during the Middle Ages the observance came to be viewed allegorically as a symbol of Christ's burial. After Pius XII's reform of Holy Week (1955) the adventitious association of the reservation with the burial of Christ and the altar of repose with the tomb was de-emphasized. BIBLIOGRAPHY: W. J. O'Shea, NCE 7:105–107; id., *Meaning of Holy Week* (1958).

[N. KOLLAR]

ALTAR SOCIETIES, organizations whose members' aim is to assist in the maintenance of the altar and of the accessories used in the liturgy, by contributing their services and yearly dues.

[S. A. HEENEY]

ALTAR STONE, a term that may refer to either: (1) the single unbroken slab of stone that constitutes the entire top portion *(mensa)* of a fixed altar; or (2) a square piece of natural stone about an inch in thickness and large enough to allow a host and chalice to rest upon it; this is laid upon or preferably set into the surface that serves as a movable altar's *mensa.* Since 1596 Church law in the West has required that the altar stone must contain a repository or *sepulcher with relics cemented into it. In the Byzantine rite the *antimension,* into which a packet containing relics is sewn, is used as an altar stone. In recent years permission was granted to many priests of the Latin rite to use the Greek *antimension,* but now church law does not require a repository of relics in a movable altar (see "General Instruction of the Roman Missal," as found in *The Sacramentary* of 1974, ch. 5, n. 265), nor indeed does it require an altar stone for such altars.

[N. KOLLAR]

ALTAR STRIPPING, the removal of the linen and movable objects, except the cross, from the altar on Holy Thursday. This is performed in a brief ceremony after the Holy Thursday Mass by a priest, wearing an alb and purple stole, while Psalm 21 is chanted. This is probably a survival in ceremonious form of the removal of the altar cloths, once commonly performed after the celebration of Mass on any day. The bare altar after the Holy Thursday Mass calls attention to the suspension of Mass until the Easter Vigil, and some have looked upon it as a reminder of Christ stripped of his garments. BIBLIOGRAPHY: W. J. O'Shea, NCE 7:107.

[N. KOLLAR]

ALTARPIECE, a religious representation, usually a painting or frescoed picture on the wall behind an altar, or hung above an altar, or sometimes a structural part of the altar itself. BIBLIOGRAPHY: Podhradsky 25.

[N. KOLLAR]

ALTDORF, ABBEY OF, former Benedictine monastery in the diocese of Strasbourg, France. The first monastery was founded in 974 by Count Hugo III of Nordgau and dedicated to St. Bartholomew. Before 1049 Pope Leo IX, a member of the founder's family, donated the relics of St. Cyriacus and consecrated the altar. During the 12th cent. the abbey was a double monastery. The Romanesque church was built c.1200; its choir and transept were rebuilt in the Baroque style by Peter Thumb (1724–27). Altdorf cultivated the spirit of Cluny and was later connected with Sankt Gallen and Bursfeld. The Peasants War damaged it severely, and the French Revolution destroyed its monastic life in 1791. BIBLIOGRAPHY: A. Sieffert, *Altdorf* (1946); G. Spahr, NCE 1:352.

[F. RÖHRIG]

ALTDORFER, ALBRECHT (*c*.1480–1530), Bavarian painter, printmaker, and architect in Regensburg and Vienna. His biblical and historical subjects show figures dwarfed by the immensity and variety of the landscape. In religious works (*Nativity,* Vienna) this contrast adds an affecting intimacy to the story. In *Lot and His Daughters* (Vienna) he attempted heroic nudes with unfortunate results. A. was also a pioneer in copperplate etching. BIBLIOGRAPHY: L. von Baldass, *Albrecht Altdorfer* (1941).

[P. P. FEHL]

ALTENBERG, ABBEY OF, Cistercian abbey near Cologne, Germany, founded (1133) by monks from Morimond. Its community numbered 107 choir monks and 138 lay brothers by 1200. After an earthquake had destroyed much of the earlier Romanesque structures, the abbey was magnificently rebuilt in Gothic. It survived the Reformation but was secularized in 1803. Devastated by fire in 1815, the church was restored in 1847 by Frederick William IV of Prussia for both Catholic and Lutheran services. Since 1922 it has been a center for the German Catholic Youth Movement. BIBLIOGRAPHY: H. Mosler, *Die Cistercienserabtei Altenberg* (1965).

ALTENBURG, ABBEY OF, Benedictine monastery in the diocese of St. Pölten. It was founded in 1144 by Countess Hildburg of Rebgau-Poigen with monks from St. Lambrecht in Styria. Despite the calamities it has suffered at various times in its history at the hands of Hussites, Protestants, Nazis, and the Russian army, the abbey still survives. Rebuilt 1729–42 by Joseph Munggenast, it is one of the most splendid Baroque monuments in Europe, with painting by P. Trogers and valuable stucco by J. Holzinger and M. Flor.

BIBLIOGRAPHY: F. Endl, *Stift Altenburg* (1929); G. Scheighofer, *Stift Altenburg* (1963); *idem*, NCE 1:352–353.

[F. RÖHRIG]

ALTENSTAIG, JOHANNES (*c*. 1480–*c*.1525), German humanist, educator, and theologian. He studied poetry and rhetoric under H. *Bebel at Tübingen. He taught Latin at Mindelheim, Bavaria, his birthplace. A correspondent of John Eck and other humanist theologians, he criticized ecclesiastical abuses but stopped short of joining the Reformation. Among his writings are *Dialectica* (1514), *Vocabularius theologiae* (1517), and *Opusculum de amicitia* (1519). BIBLIOGRAPHY: M. Monaco, NCE 1:353.

[J. E. LYNCH]

ALTERNATION, the practice of substituting a short organ piece for every other verse of choral sections of the Mass ordinary, or the hymn or Magnificat at Vespers. *ORGAN MASS; *VERSET.

[A. DOHERTY]

ALTHERR, HEINRICH (1878–1947), Swiss painter who studied in Munich and Rome. Through the architect Karl Moser A. was commissioned to do mosaics in St. Paul's, Basel. Turning to architectural painting, he executed monumental figures of symbolic subject (Zurich Univ. and the Cantonal Archives, Basel). BIBLIOGRAPHY: Ueberwasser and Braun, *Der Maler Heinrich Altherr* (1938).

[M. J. DALY]

ALTMANN OF PASSAU, ST. (1015–91), bishop. A. was among the greatest German reformers and supporters of Gregory VII. He served as a canon and teacher at Paderborn, provost at Aachen, chaplain to the Empress Agnes, and became bp. of Passau in 1065. He imposed the Rule of St. Augustine on the clergy in several churches and founded two Augustinian houses at Rottenbuch and Reichersberg. He vigorously supported the papal position against married clergy and in 1076 was the first to announce the excommunication of Henry IV. He continued his pastoral and political duties until his death in spite of Henry's persecution. BIBLIOGRAPHY: A. M. Zimmermann, BiblSanct 1:891–893; Butler 3:282–283.

[S. WILLIAMS]

ALTO, ST. (d. *c*.770), abbot. A. came *c*.758 to the region of modern Dachau and lived an eremitical life on land granted by Pepin III. He probably built the monastery of Alto-münster, and St. Boniface probably consecrated the monastic church. Othloh of Sankt Emmeran wrote the life of Alto. BIBLIOGRAPHY: A. M. Zimmermann, BiblSanct 1:893–894; H. Dressler, NCE 1:354.

[H. DRESSLER]

ALTO (It. high), one of the four major subdivisions of the human singing voice, the lower range of the female voice, with a characteristic range of f to f''. The individual female voice in this range is usually termed mezzo-soprano or contralto (the middle and low female ranges respectively), while in a choir alto refers to either the section or the part in the music itself, the second highest in four-part writing. It is also applied to musical instruments (e.g., the alto saxophone) that employ the alto range and quality, and is the French name for the viola. Until the introduction of women to choirs the alto part was sung by male voices, either boys (still the practice in England), *countertenors, or *castrati. BIBLIOGRAPHY: P. A. Scholes, *Oxford Companion to Music* (1970) 27.

[J. J. WALSH]

ALTÖTTING, the most famous shrine of Our Lady in Bavaria. In what was originally a royal residence a collegiate chapter with an abbot was established in 876. It declined later and was rebuilt in 1228. Suppressed in 1803, it was restored with a mitred provost in 1930. In the 15th cent. it became a popular center of Marian pilgrimage and was served first by the Jesuits, later by Franciscans, and finally by Capuchins. About half a million pilgrims annually visit the nearby Capuchin church of St. Anne, a basilica since 1913, the shrine also of Brother Konrad of Parzham (d. 1894). BIBLIOGRAPHY: C. J. König, *Dreimal Chorherrnstift Altötting* (2 v., 1950); M. A. König, LTK 1:404–405.

ALTRUISM, a term coined by A. *Comte from the Italian *altrui* ("others"; cf. Lat. *alter*) to denote devotion to the interests of others, rather than a concern for self, as the principle of moral action. The rejection of self-interest as a motive of moral worth has been a recurrent theme in modern ethical thought. *Utilitarianism, taking the greatest happiness of the greatest number as the foundation of morality, proposed an altruistic form of *hedonism. Kant in his insistence upon duty for duty's sake as the sole motive of morally worthy action stressed the value of disinterestedness. The tension between self-interest and unselfishness has also been a matter of major interest to Christian thinkers, esp. from the time of *Abelard. Some have been inclined to base all man's appetitive striving upon his desire for his own proper good; others have sought to empty love of all self-reference. *Quietism and *semi-quietism represent an extreme exaltation of disinterested love. More orthodox thinkers, such as Bernard of Clairvaux and Thomas Aquinas, resolved the antinomy by seeing the true love of self realized in the love of God. BIBLIOGRAPHY: É. Gilson, *Mystical Theology of St. Bernard*; id., *Spirit of Mediaeval Philosophy*.

[P. K. MEAGHER]

ALUMBRADOS, name for the adherents of a form of religious *illuminism in 16th-cent. Spain. Their history is obscured by polemical charges against them. The name was apparently first applied (1492) to a group led by Antonio de Pastrana, religious of Ocaña, who was accused of immorality. The divine mission he professed was a renewal of pure contemplation that merges the human being in the divine essence and makes him incapable of sin. In 1529 a secret community of Alumbrados was uncovered at Toledo, grouped around Fray Alcazar and Isabel de la Cruz. Claiming visions and uttering prophecies, they followed strange practices of piety, and undertook spectacular mortifications. After similar incidents throughout Spain, involving fraudulent miracles, levitations, and stigmata, the Alumbrados were proscribed by the Inquisition (1568, 1574, 1623). Not all Alumbrados went to extremes; many, however, were credulous regarding the marvelous and were eager to make the extraordinary the normal in the life of prayer. Many theologians reacted with an extreme intellectualism. Thus the *Sinner's Guide* and the *Treatise on Prayer and Meditation* by Louis of Granada were put on the Index. Teresa of Avila, John of the Cross, and Ignatius of Loyola all came under suspicion because of the anti-illuminism of the period. BIBLIOGRAPHY: J. Vincke, LTK 1:407; L. Cognet, *Post-Reformation Spirituality* (tr. P. H. Scott, 1959) 27–30; Bremond 8:194; 8:80; 11:296.

[P. DELETTER]

ALUMNUS, a term that may mean: (1) an ecclesiastical college student; (2) a child reared and educated in a monastery, usually wearing the habit and taking part to a degree in the monastic life, but with no commitment to become a monk; or (3), esp. in the U.S., a graduate or at least a former student of some school or college.

[S. A. HEENEY]

ALVA, DUKE OF (Fernando Álvarez de Toledo; 1508–82), Spanish military leader. For 57 years he was a *caudillo* in Spain's wars. At 17 he joined the campaign that drove France out of Spain. After service against Turks in Hungary and North Africa, he commanded Charles V's armies against German Protestants, with much success until the failure to capture Metz 1552–53. His successes in Italy against France and Pope Paul IV were halted by Philip II's prudent decision not to take Rome in 1556. But A. helped conclude the Treaty of Cateau-Cambrésis with France in 1559; and, having assisted at Philip's marriage to Mary Tudor in 1554, he now stood proxy for Philip in the marriage to Isabelle of France. Best known of A.'s efforts is his 1567–73 rule of the Netherlands, a program of hard Castilianization (centralization). His Council of Troubles executed hundreds of rebels, nobles, and burghers. Until Alkmaar (1573) he had no trouble crushing rebel armies invading from France and Germany, but his efforts against the Sea Beggars were no more successful than the Armada of 1588. His attempt to finance the war by local taxes, esp. a 10% sales tax, caused bad feeling; Philip II solved this problem by his 1575 bankruptcy. Philip's switch to the rival Federationist policy in the appointment of Requesens to succeed A. proved no more successful than Castilianization. In 1580 when Federationists intrigued to keep Philip off the throne of Portugal, A. was one of a few reliable supporters of the King. He defeated the Portuguese army almost effort-

lessly in the last of his masterly campaigns. A. personified one side of Philip II's character. BIBLIOGRAPHY: L. Berra, EncCatt 1:631–633.

[E. P. COLBERT]

ALVA Y ASTORGA, PEDRO DE (d. 1667), a Franciscan of the Province of the Twelve Apostles of Peru. A. is known for his contribution to the history of his order by publishing his *Bullarium* (10 v.). He is most noted for his writings on the Immaculate Conception, the most important of which is his *Armentarium Seraphicum pro tuendo Immaculatae Conceptionis titulo* (1648). Next to Duns Scotus he is credited with the development of the belief in the Immaculate Conception. BIBLIOGRAPHY: A. Eguiluz, NCE 1:358; E. Longpré, *Catholicisme* 1:361–362.

[M. C. BRADLEY]

ALVARADO, FRANCISCO DE (d. 1603), missionary. A. was born in Mexico, joined the Dominicans, and became a missionary among the Mixtec Indians. He wrote a dictionary of Mixtec based, probably, on the work of other Dominican missionaries.

[H. JACK]

ÁLVARES, FRANCISCO (d. *c.*1540), missionary, chaplain to the Portuguese embassy to Ethiopia which left Lisbon for Massawa, via Goa, in 1517 and arrived in 1520. The Portuguese started their return 6 years later with Emperor David II's ambassador to Portugal on board, and with A. commissioned to convey the pledge of Ethiopian loyalty to the Holy See, which was rendered after a forced delay of 5 years to Clement VII at Bologna. The news of this event was rapidly circulated, but the opportunity for formal reunion was missed. A. left an account of Ethiopia and its people in his *Verdadera informaçam das terras do Preste Joam*. BIBLIOGRAPHY: F. M. Rogers, NCE 1:358–359.

[H. JACK]

ÁLVAREZ OF CÓRDOBA, BL. (*c.*1360–1430), Dominican, confessor-counselor to Henry III, John II, and Queen Catherine of Castile, apostle of Andalusia. A. swung Castile against antipope Pedro de Luna. Vicar for Spain's Observants (1427), he founded Córdoba's Scala Coeli priory (1413) and its earliest stations of the cross. BIBLIOGRAPHY: A. Walz, *Compendium historiae O.P.* (1948); G. Cappelluti, BiblSanct 1:900–901.

[R. I. BURNS]

ÁLVAREZ, BALTASAR (1533–80), Jesuit spiritual writer. A. was engaged in the active ministry of the Jesuits; rector of Salamanca, Medina del Campo, and Villagarcía. Eventually, he was named provincial of Toledo. For a time he was counselor and confessor to St. Teresa of Avila. His devotion and dedication to contemplation, vis à vis the apostolic work of the Jesuits, was looked upon with disfavor by some within the order. His works include commentaries, sermons, and treatises on prayer. BIBLIOGRAPHY: I. Iparraguirre, NCE 1:359; J. Carreras y Artau, LTK 1:408.

[J. R. RIVELLO]

ÁLVAREZ, DIEGO (d. 1631), Spanish Dominican theologian; abp. of Trani in southern Italy from 1606. As a professor in *studia* of his order in Spain, he became prominently involved in the controversies with the Jesuits on the issue of grace and free will. He was sent to Rome in 1596 and appointed, with Tomás de Lemos, to speak for the Dominican side in the **Congregatio de auxiliis*, debates ordered by the Pope in an effort to resolve the dispute. A.'s published works, most of which are concerned with efficacious grace and freedom, evidence his theological acumen. BIBLIOGRAPHY: R. Coulon, DHGE 2:872–873, for a list of A.'s works.

[T. C. O'BRIEN]

ÁLVAREZ, FELIX ALEJANDRO CEPEDA, see CEPEDA ALVAREZ FELIX ALEJANDRO.

ÁLVAREZ, FRANCISCO, see ÁLVARES, FRANCISCO.

ÁLVAREZ DE PAZ, DIEGO (1560–1620), Jesuit spiritual writer. A. served as professor of philosophy and theology and provincial of the Jesuits in Peru from 1616 until he died. The influence of philosophy is seen in his works on moral theology, esp. those dealing with sin, vice, and virtue. Another of his works, one dealing with types of asceticism and mysticism, is vast in both content and scope and is considered one of the first treatises on infused contemplation by a Jesuit. BIBLIOGRAPHY: I. Iparraguirre, NCE 1:359–360; J. Carreras y Artau, LTK 1:408.

[J. R. RIVELLO]

ÁLVAREZ DE TOLEDO, FERNANDO, see ALVA, DUKE OF.

ALVARO PELAYO (c.1275–c.1349), Spanish Franciscan reformer. He sided with the Fraticelli on the poverty issue but defended John XXII against Marsilius, Ockham, and others at the court of Louis IV. His erudite *De statu et planctu ecclesiae* (1330–40) is theocratic but hard on clerical abuses; A. also wrote a Mirror for the King of Castile c.1341 and an Exposé of Heresies in 1344. A lawyer trained at Bologna by 1304 and papal penitentiary (1330–32), he tried to reform his See of Silves in Portugal after 1332, but King and clerics drove him to Seville.

[E. P. COLBERT]

ALVASTRA, ABBEY OF, the first and most notable Cistercian abbey in Sweden. Founded near Lake Vättern (1143) by monks of Clairvaux, it in turn founded three other Swedish abbeys: Varnhem, Julita, and Husby. From it came many of Sweden's prominent churchmen, among whom were Stephen (d. 1185), first abp. of Uppsala, and Petri

Olaus (d. 1390), St. Bridget's confessor and biographer. The remarkable abbey church, consecrated in 1185, was the burial place of Swedish royalty. Alvastra was secularized in 1527 by Gustavus I Vasa. BIBLIOGRAPHY: O. Odenius, NCE 1:360.

[L. J. LEKAI]

ALVELT, AUGUSTINE OF (born Alfred Hildesheim; 1480–1535), Franciscan of the Saxony province. A. lectured in Holy Scripture at Leipzig (1520) and in Italy (1523 and 1526). From 1524 he was prior at Halle and served later as provincial (1529–32). In central Germany A. defended Catholic beliefs at a time of their rejection by the leaders of the reform movement. He published countless writings, among them *Super apostolica sede* and *Salve Regina*. BIBLIOGRAPHY: V. Heynck, LTK 1:410.

[M. C. BRADLEY]

ALVEQUIN, MARIE (1564–1648), French Benedictine nun. A. entered the convent at Montmartre, and though tempted to transfer to another community because of the disorder and laxity of the house, she stayed on and aided the abbess, Marie de Beauvilliers, in restoring discipline and fervor in the community. Her role in the reformation of convent life in 17th-cent. France is considered important. With Marguerite d'*Arbouze, her friend, she ranks among the earliest of the mystics of Montmartre. Her life was written by M. de Lacout, *sieur de Marivaut* (1697). BIBLIOGRAPHY: Bremond 2:449, 455–458, 501.

[P. K. MEAGHER]

ALVERNIA (La Verna), a mountain in the Tuscan Apennines between Arezzo and Florence. It became a popular place of pilgrimage following St. Francis of Assisi's stigmatization there in the chapel of St. Mary of the Angels (1224). Here also, he probably wrote his well-known blessing to Brother Leo. In 1263, a Church of the Stigmata was built and a third church, Chiesa Maggiore, was begun in 1348 and completed in 1459. This church was designated a minor basilica in 1921 by Benedict XV and is under the supervision of the Franciscans. BIBLIOGRAPHY: R. M. Huber, *Documented History of the Franciscan Order* (1944); V. Facchinetti, *La Verna nel Casentino. . .*, v. 1 of *I Santuarii francescani,* (3 v., 1925–27); J. J. Smith, NCE 1:360–361.

[J. J. SMITH]

ALYPIUS, ST., see ALIPIUS, ST.

ALZOG, JOHANN BAPTIST (1808–78), church historian and patrologist. A native of Silesia, A. was ordained in 1834. He taught church history and patrology in Posen, Hildesheim, and finally at Freiburg from 1853 until his death. His *Lehrbuch der Kirchengeschichte* (1841) became a standard text in its field and was translated into many languages (first U.S. ed. by F. J. Pabisch and T. S. Byrne,

Manual of Universal Church History, 3 v., 1874). His *Handbuch der Patrologie* (1866) was also widely used. As one of the leading scholars of his day A. took part in the preparations at Rome for Vatican Council I. BIBLIOGRAPHY: F. X. Murphy, NCE 1:362; S. Furlani, EncCatt 1:956.

[R. B. ENO]

ALZON, EMMANUEL D' (1810–80), French founder of two religious congregations, educational administrator, theologian. Ordained in 1834, A. became vicar-general of the diocese of Nîmes. In 1845 he founded the Augustinians of the Assumption whose threefold purpose was teaching, the Catholic press, and the conducting of Byzantine-rite residences in Eastern Europe. Other apostolates were later added to their activities. The congregation flourished and established houses in many places in the world. A. served as college president, vicar-general, and superior-general of the Assumptionists till his death. He co-founded (1865) the Oblate Sisters of the Assumption.

[S. A. HEENEY]

AMADEO, GIOVANNI ANTONIO (1447–1522), Italian architect and sculptor. A. assisted in the terra-cotta and marble decoration of the Certosa, Pavia (1466–1501), built the memorial chapel of Bartolomeo Colleoni in Bergamo (1470–76), executed the tomb of Colleoni's daughter (d. 1470), which was removed to the chapel in 1842, and assisted in the construction of the Cathedral of Milan (1491). His early work shows a mixture of Gothic and classical motifs. Later, influenced by the Mantegazzas (1474), his style became more realistic. BIBLIOGRAPHY: J. Pope-Hennessy, *Italian Renaissance Sculpture* (1958).

[M. J. DALY]

AMADEUS OF CLERMONT, BL. (d. *c.*1147), Seigneur of Hauterive (Drôme), Cistercian monk. About 1119 A. retired to the abbey of Bonnevaux with six vassal lords and his son, St. *Amadeus of Lausanne. A. was noted for his austerity; he took part in founding the abbeys of Montpeyroux (*c.*1126), Tamié (1134), and Léoncel (1137). BIBLIOGRAPHY: P. Fournier, DHGE 2:1147; G. Venuta, BiblSanct 1:998–999.

AMADEUS OF LAUSANNE, ST. (1110–59), Cistercian abbot of Hautecombe, in Savoy; bp. of Lausanne from 1144. He became a monk in 1125. His positions as abbot (from 1139), counsellor to the counts of Savoy, envoy to the papal court, were undertaken at the behest of St. Bernard of Clairvaux. His Marian sermons (SC 72, ed. G. Bavaud, 1960) were cited in the dogmatic declaration of the Assumption. A.'s cult was confirmed by Pius X.

[J. R. RIVELLO]

AMADEUS VIII OF SAVOY (Felix V, Antipope; 1383–1451). Having declared Eugenius IV deposed, the Council of Basel elected A., the Duke of Savoy, as pope (1440) but he received little support, abdicated (1449), and submitted to Eugenius' successor, Nicholas V. BIBLIOGRAPHY: J. Gill, *Eugenius IV* (1961); J. G. Rowe, NCE 1:363.

[J. MULDOON]

AMADEUS IX OF SAVOY, BL. (1435–72), duke, husband of Yolanda, daughter of Charles VII of France. He lived an austere and devout life, was generous to the poor, and readily forgave his enemies. His able administration prevented his open-handed liberality from depleting the treasury, but his tolerance of troublemakers, in the view of some historians, encouraged strife. The epilepsy from which he suffered eventually wore him down and he put authority in the hands of his wife. BIBLIOGRAPHY: Butler 1:706–707.

[N. G. WOLF]

AMALAKA, a flattened, fluted, ring stone crowning the curvilinear tower *(śikhara)* of Hindu temples in northern India and surmounted by a finial with vase *(kalaśa)*.

[M. J. DALY]

AMALARIUS OF METZ (*c.*755–*c.*850), a prominent figure in the Carolingian renaissance whose liturgical scholarship stemmed from studies under Alcuin. He is sometimes identified with the Amalarius who was abp. of Trier (809–813), but this has been questioned by some scholars. He did, however, administer the See of Lyons (835–838) but was removed from that office by the Synod of Quiercy (838) because of his theological opinions. His *De ecclesiasticis officiis* and his *De ordine antiphonarii* are sources of prime importance for the history of the liturgy. He led the way to the practice so common in medieval times of explaining the liturgy in terms of allegory. BIBLIOGRAPHY: J. A. Cabanniss, *Amalarius of Metz* (1954).

[N. KOLLAR]

AMALBERGA, SS., two Amalbergas, whose legends are intertwined. One (7th cent.) seems to have been wife of Count Witger (later a monk at Lobbes) and mother of SS. Gudula, Reinelde, and Bp. Emebert of Cambrai. Following Witger's example, she entered the Benedictines at Maubeuge. The other Amalberga (8th cent.) was probably a nun at Münsterbilzen (Belgium). Legend says she was sought, because of her beauty, as a wife for Charlemagne. BIBLIOGRAPHY: Butler 3:64–65; J. F. Fahey, NCE 1:364.

[G. M. COOK]

AMALEKITES (Amalecites), a tribe or group of tribes, the perennial enemy of Israel (see Dt 25.17–19). They harassed the Israelites during the Exodus (Ex 17.8–16) and in the promised land itself (Jg 3.13; 6.3; 7.12). Victories by Saul and David over them (1 Sam 15.4–9, 33; 30.1–18) led to their extinction (see 1 Chr 4.42–43).

[T. C. O'BRIEN]

AMALRIC AUGERIUS (d. after 1362), historian and theologian. Perhaps an Augustinian, A. was chaplain to the Avignonese Pope, Urban V (1362–70). His chronicle, *Actus romanorum pontificum a primo usque ad Johannem papam XXII sive annum 1321,* has been edited by L. A. Muratori, *Rerum italicarum scriptores* (1734) 3.2. BIBLIOGRAPHY: A. J. Ennis, NCE 1:364.

[J. E. WRIGLEY]

AMALRIC OF BÈNE (Amalricus, Amaury, Amauri de Chartres; d. 1206 or 1207), inspirer of the Amalricians. Professor of logic and theology at the Univ. of Paris, A. apparently followed the teaching of John Scotus Erigena. In 1209 clerics and laymen calling themselves Amalricians were discovered in Paris teaching pantheism, proclaiming the age of the incarnation of the Holy Spirit in every man, and that those who were so deified were like Christ incapable of sinning. A.'s teaching was condemned by a synod in Paris in 1210 and by Lateran Council IV in 1215 (D 808). The errors of the Amalricians seem to have occasioned a proscription of Aristotle's writings on natural philosophy in 1215. BIBLIOGRAPHY: Bihlmeyer-Tüchle 2:306; Gilson HCP 240–241, 654; F. Vernet, DSAM 1:422–425.

[T. C. O'BRIEN]

AMALRICIANS, a name for those who, in the early 13th cent., followed the pantheistic and antinomian teachings of *Amalric of Bène.

[T. C. O'BRIEN]

AMAN, JACOB, see AMMANN, JAKOB

AMANA CHURCH SOCIETY, one of the oldest and most successful American communal bodies. It originated under the influence of *Pietism in western Germany when Johann Rock and Eberhard Grüber organized the Community of True Inspiration in 1714. Calling for a return to pure Christianity and a life of simplicity, members held that God deals directly with man through inspiration and revelation. After initial success, the group declined until 1817, when it was revived by Christian Metz and Barbara Heineman, who again claimed the charism of inspiration. Difficulties with the German government over their pacificism and opposition to oaths led the group in 1842 to immigrate to the U.S.; near Buffalo, N.Y., they adopted a pure communist form of living in order to pursue more effectively their ideal of Christian simplicity. When additional land and greater isolation became desirable, they migrated in 1854 to Iowa, where they founded the town of Amana and several adjacent villages. Communal forms were followed until 1932, when the members voted a reorganization of community life. All property and control of temporal affairs was vested in a joint stock corporation, the Amana Society, which today farms the original 25,000 acres and also manages a variety of business enterprises. The Amana Church Society, governed by elected elders, handles all ecclesiastical matters.

The doctrine of the society is basically that of the evangelical tradition, along with the distinguishing belief that God "even now operates audibly through the instruments of true inspiration." There is no paid ministry and services consist mainly of prayer, testimony, and readings from the works of the inspired. Baptism by water is rejected in favor of the concept of baptism as a purely spiritual occurrence. The rite of confirmation is observed at the age of 15. The Lord's Supper with footwashing is celebrated rarely. Older regulations governing simplicity of dress, house, and amusements have been relaxed, as has been the ban on participation in warfare. In 1973 there were 1500 members in the 7 congregations.

[J. C. WILLKE]

AMANDUS, ST. (Amandus of Maastricht; d. after 676), bp., apostle of Belgium. From the MS *Vita prima* and a letter (649) of Pope Martin I, one learns that, after a visit to Rome, A. began a missionary career that led him to northern Frankish areas, Ghent, the region of the Danube, south to the Pyrenees, to Narbonne, north again to the North Sea. Founder of monasteries and probably bp. of Tongres-Maastricht, he wrote his testament at his monastery of Elnone. BIBLIOGRAPHY: "La vita Amandi prima," AnalBoll 67 (1949) 447–464; *Book of Saints* by the Benedictine Monks of St. Augustine's Abbey (1966); H. Platelle and D. Misonne, BiblSanct 1:918–923.

[M. E. DUFFY]

AMANDUS OF WORMS, ST. Doubtful evidence points to two persons of this name, one of the 4th cent., and another said to have been bp. of Worms during the reign of Dagobert I. It has been plausibly suggested that the Bp. Amandus venerated at Worms was in fact Amandus of Maastricht, the apostle of Belgium, whose body was for a time at Worms before its translation to Salzburg. It seems likely that some relics were left which legend in time came to associate with a person of local identity. BIBLIOGRAPHY: I. Polc, BiblSanct 1:924–925.

[H. DRESSLER]

AMANN, ÉMILE (1880–1948), early church historian and theologian. A. studied at Nancy, where he was ordained, and at the Institut Catholique of Paris. He later (1919) held the chair of ancient church history at the Univ. of Strasbourg. In 1910, he inaugurated the collection *Apocryphes du Nouveau Testament* with his *Protoévangile de Jacques,* to which he added *Actes de Paul et ses lettres apocryphes* (1913), and *Actes de Pierre* (1920). He was on the editorial staff of the *Dictionnaire de théologie catholique* from 1913, and its director from 1922, during which time he contributed over 100 articles and edited nearly 20 volumes of that collection. BIBLIOGRAPHY: C. R. Meyer, NCE 1:366.

[T. M. MCFADDEN]

AMANTIUS OF RODEZ, ST., bp. of Rodez in South France in 481 when the Arian Visigothic king occupied it. Gregory of Tours (d.594) praises his anti-Arian pro-Frankish successor Quinctian, who housed A.'s relics in a basilica. A., perhaps the first bp. of Rodez, was a miracle worker. His vita (7th or 9th cent.) is not reliable. BIBLIOGRAPHY: F. Caraffa, BiblSanct 1:933.

[E. P. COLBERT]

AMARĀVATĪ, coastal city on the Krishna River in southern India, famous for Buddhist stupa of the 1st and 2d cent. A.D., an object of study since 1816. Almost completely sculptured with scenes from the life of Buddha, its attenuated, elegant, and lively figures showing greater sophistication than its counterparts in northern Mathura will reappear at Badami and Aihole (6th cent.) and at Mamallapuram (7th cent.). The Buddha figure at Amarāvatī is a synthesis of Indian physical, fluid movement and Roman style (Madras) though different from the Gandhāra type. The Amarāvatī Buddha (4th cent.) influenced forms in Ceylon and Thailand. BIBLIOGRAPHY: P. Stern and M. Bénisti, *Évolution du style indien d' Amarāvatī* (1961).

[M. J. DALY]

AMARCIUS (fl. 1043–92), medieval Latin poet. He was a cleric of uncertain nationality with some medical knowledge, who styled himself Sextus Amarcius Gallus Piostratus. His main work, surviving in a single MS, the *Sermones,* was based on one by Odo of Cluny. BIBLIOGRAPHY: *Sexti Amarcii . . . sermonum libri IV* (ed. M. Manitius, 1888) for its text; J. L. Grassi, NCE 1:367.

[J. L. GRASSI]

AMARNA LETTERS, clay tablets in cuneiform script, discovered in 1887 at Tel El Amarna, *c.*190 miles S of Cairo. Their content, correspondence between *Amenhotep III and the rulers of the cities of Palestine and Syria, provides historical background for the century prior to the biblical account of the Exodus. The Akkadian language of the tablets reveals features of the Canaanite language, from which biblical Hebrew derived. There are 377 extant tablets, 82 of which are in the British Museum, 2 in the Metropolitan Museum in New York City. BIBLIOGRAPHY: W. Moran, NCE 1:368–369.

[T. C. O'BRIEN]

AMASIA, see AMAZIAH.

AMAT, THADDEUS (1810–78), missionary, educator, bp. of Monterey and Los Angeles. He entered the Congregation of the Missions in Barcelona and was ordained in 1837. Coming to the U.S., he was active as a teacher and an administrator. In 1848 he became rector of St. Charles Seminary, Philadelphia. His Spanish and American cultures were made use of when he was named bp. of Monterey, Califor-

nia. BIBLIOGRAPHY: G. E. O'Donnell, *St. Charles Seminary, Philadelphia* (1964); N. C. Eberhardt, NCE 1:369–370.

[M. C. BRADLEY]

AMATOR, SS. (1) Amator of Auxerre (d. 418), bishop. His historical existence is certain, but little else is known. See AS May 1:51–61. (2) Amator (d. 855), priest and martyr, was killed by the Mohammedans at Córdoba, according to Eulogius (PL 115:814). See AS April 3:815. (3) Amator of Lucca is venerated as a saint at San Michele in Borgo San Lorenzo. He is perhaps to be identified with the Amator venerated in Quercy and the Limousin. The historical existence of either is improbable. BIBLIOGRAPHY: AS Aug. 4:16–25; AnalBoll 28 (1909) 57–90.

[W. A. JURGENS]

AMATUS OF MONTE CASSINO (d. before 1105), poet and historian, monk at Monte Cassino who flourished there in the time of Abbot Desiderius (Pope Victor III). He appears to have been a bp., but whether this was before or after becoming a monk, and the place of his see are not known. He wrote the first history of the Normans, a work no longer extant in its original Latin. BIBLIOGRAPHY: A. Potthast, *Bibliotheca historica medii aevi* 1:39–40; Manitius 3:449–454; W. Smidt, "Die Historia Normannorum von Amatus," StGreg 3 (1948) 173–231.

[W. A. JURGENS]

AMATUS OF NUSCO, ST. (*c.*1104–93), bp. and Benedictine abbot. There are two versions of his life; the later and more reliable makes him bp. of Nusco from 1154; the earlier, bp. from 1048 (or 1071) to 1093. BIBLIOGRAPHY: A. Palmieri, DHGE 2:993–994; Zimmermann 2:642, 644; J. L. Grassi, NCE 1:370; A. Balducci, BiblSanct 1:937–938.

[J. L. GRASSI]

AMATUS OF OLORON (d. 1101), papal legate, active in promoting the reforms of Gregory VII. Elected bp. of Oloron in 1073, he was named legate in Aquitaine the following year. His legation was soon extended to Spain, Gaul, and Gascony (1077), where he continued the struggle against simony and investiture begun by *Peter Damian and *Humbert of Silva Candida. In 1089 he was elected bp. of Bordeaux and again appointed papal legate, this time for Urban II. BIBLIOGRAPHY: R. Biron, DHGE 2:973–977.

[P. K. MEAGHER]

AMATUS OF REMIREMONT, ST. (*c.*565–*c.*628), abbot. He entered the monastery at Agaunam *c.*581 and in 614 went to Luxeuil. With his friend Romaric, whom he persuaded to become a monk, he founded (*c.*620) a double monastery at Remiremont, one of the most fruitful of the foundations from Luxeuil. BIBLIOGRAPHY: Butler 3:549–550; A. Codaghengo, BiblSanct 1:938–939.

[G. E. CONWAY]

AMAURISTS, see AMALRIC OF BÈNE.

AMAZIAH (Amasia), the name of two OT personages. (1) Amaziah, king of Judah 800–783 B.C., challenged Jehoash of Israel, was defeated, and slain (2 Kgs ch. 14; 2 Chr ch 25). (2) Amaziah, priest of the sanctuary at Bethel, who tried to prevent Amos from prophesying there, and Amos pronounced a curse on him (Am ch. 7).

[T. C. O'BRIEN]

AMBA (Coptic, father), a title of address for a bishop in the Coptic Church, e.g., Amba Cyril VI. It is also used in the same Church as a title for saints.

[A. J. JACOPIN]

AMBARACH, PETER (also called Benedictus and Benedetti, Lat. and It. equivalents of his name; 1663–1742), Maronite, Orientalist. From Gusta in Syria, A. studied in Rome (1672–85), then served as a priest in his native land. Returning to Rome (1693), he was asked by Cosimo de'Medici III to supervise the printing of Oriental MSS at Florence. A. became a Jesuit in 1708 and served on a papal commission for editing the *Septuagint. He translated the works of St. *Ephrem into Latin (*S. Ephraemi Syri opera omnia*, 3 v., 1737–43; 3d v. by Stephen Assemani). BIBLIOGRAPHY: Sommervogel 1:1295–98.

[T. C. O'BRIEN]

AMBIGUITY, an obfuscation of meaning that renders a statement or proposition open to conflicting interpretations. B. Russell, G. Frege, L. Wittgenstein, and others of the analytic school expand at length on ridding propositions of ambiguity. BIBLIOGRAPHY: H. A. Nielsen, NCE 1:371; J. van Heijenoort, EncPhil 5:45–51 s.v. ''Logical Paradoxes.''

[J. R. RIVELLO]

AMBITION. Understood as the desire for advancement, in English the term has come to have no moral implication in itself, and indeed may be applied to the energetic prosecution of laudable purposes even without gain to self. In Latin moral theology, however, which keeps close to the etymology, *ambire,* with its suggestion of lobbying for favor, the unqualified term stands for a vice, and one against the cardinal virtue of courage, and, more precisely, against that part of it called *magnanimity. The hero of the *Nicomachean Ethics* is the high-souled man, *megalopsychos,* who on proper occasions disdains, as it were, the jog-trot mean of virtue and goes all out despite the difficulties. It is because personal pushfulness (*praesumptio*), vaingloriousness (*inanis gloria*), and greed for prestige (*ambitio*) indicate an inordinate appetite for honor as an end in itself and out of its social context, that they are caricatures of lofty virtue by exceeding due sense of proportion, and, like pusillanimousness at the opposite extreme, are condemned. Ambition, however, is one of the high-spirited faults, as St. Thomas

Aquinas observes, that are less shameful (though perhaps no less wicked) than the low-spirited. There is more panache about holding up a stagecoach than picking a pocket. BIBLIOGRAPHY: ThAqST (Lat-Eng), v. 42 (ed. A. Ross and P. G. Walsh, 1966).

[T. GILBY]

AMBITUS (Lat., range, scope, extent), the octave range of the various Gregorian chant modes. When a chant melody exceeds the ambitus of its mode by more than one note it is regarded as having changed modes. This usually occurs between the authentic and plagal form of the same mode.

[J. J. WALSH]

AMBIVALENCE, opposition of an individual's emotional response to the same object, as when one is simultaneously attracted and repulsed by the same person. The conflict may or may not be consciously perceived; the repression of one emotion or the other into the unconscious happens in consequence of an individual's inability to face the fact of his unpleasant or discreditable feelings. To enforce the repression, he may exaggerate the more desirable emotion that remains in consciousness, but the conflict continues and may become the source of psychic and moral disorder. Conscious ambivalence may also be troublesome. When a person is drawn in opposite directions, decision is hampered, and the inability to resolve the resultant dilemma often causes mental anguish. In the normal maturing process a child needs to learn how to find a solution to the conflicts that life is bound to impose. Otherwise he is liable to become indecisive, shifting back and forth from one opposing value to another. The ability to direct oneself to a decision in the presence of ambivalent feelings is important for the formation of conscience, which must dictate action in moral matters. BIBLIOGRAPHY: J. Ford and G. Kelly, *Contemporary Moral Theology* (1958) 174–200; E. Synan, ''Demands of the Present: Education of the Emotions,'' *New Morality* (ed. W. Dunphy, 1967) 141–157; R. P. Vaughan, NCE 1:371.

[P. F. MULHERN]

AMBO, a raised platform for the reading of the scriptures, chanting, and preaching. Originating in the East, Roman sources first refer to it in the 7th century. One ambo was customary at this time. As a result of allegorical interpretation during the late Middle Ages two ambos were built; one for reading, one for preaching. The result was the development of an elaborate platform for preaching called the pulpit. By the 14th cent., the ambo was replaced by the pulpit in the West. BIBLIOGRAPHY: J. A. Jungmann, *Mass of the Roman Rite* (tr. F. A. Brunner, 2 v., 1951–55) 1:391–461; H. Leclercq, DACL 1.1:1330–47.

[N. KOLLAR]

AMBOISE, FRANÇOISE D', see FRANCES D'AMBOISE, BL.

AMBROS, AUGUST WILHELM (1816–76), eminent musicologist and one of the pioneers of modern musical historiography. Trained as a lawyer, he held civil posts in Prague and Vienna, but taught music history at the same time. His fame is chiefly due to his *Geschichte der Musik* (3 v., 1862–68; v. 4 ed. from A.'s incomplete material by C. F. Becker and G. Nottebohm, 1881; sequel *Geschichte der Musik des 17., 18., und 19. Jahrhunderts* by W. Langhans, 2 v., 1882–87) in which he strove to relate music to the cultures which produced it. Although he was incapable of understanding music before 1400, he based his history on original research, and in four trips to Italy turned up some 800 pieces of 15th–17th-cent. music. Later editions of his history were considerably altered by editors. A. also wrote on musical aesthetics and composed. His religious works include a *Missa Solemnis* in A minor (1857). BIBLIOGRAPHY: G. Adler, MQ 17 (1931) 360–373; F. Blume, MGG 1:408–413.

[A. DOHERTY]

AMBROSE, ST. (A.D. *c*.334–397), bp. of Milan and one of the four great Doctors of the Latin Church. He was born in Trier, the son of the prefect of Gaul or at least of a high functionary in the prefecture. Apparently after the death of his father, *c*.340, he and his elder sister and brother, Marcellina and Satyrus, were taken by their mother back to Rome. There he studied grammar, Greek and Latin literature, rhetoric, and law. On the feast of the Epiphany, 353 or 354, his sister dedicated herself to a life of virginity, taking the veil from Pope Liberius in the Vatican Basilica. A. and his brother left Rome for Sirmium *c*.365 to begin their public careers as lawyers at the tribunal of the prefect of the praetorium. There they became members of the prefect's council. About the year 370 A. was named governor of the province of Aemilia-Liguria with its headquarters in Milan. Accompanied there by his brother, he gained the esteem of the people by his honesty and fairness. When Auxentius, the Arian bp. died in 374, the rivalry between the Catholics and Arians over the election of a successor was so intense that it threatened the peace of the city. When A. entered the church to calm the people, a child allegedly cried out, and the congregation immediately took up the refrain: "Ambrose, bishop!" Only a catechumen at the time, the governor vainly tried to refuse the honor. Then, realizing it was a divine call, he was baptized, ordained, and consecrated bishop (Dec. 7, 374) within 8 days. After his consecration, he devoted himself to the study of theology under the guidance of the priest Simplicianus, who was to succeed him. He renounced his fortune in favor of the Church of Milan and began to lead a life of prayer and penance. His preaching, which was extraordinarily efficacious, and his example, being always ready to receive rich and poor alike, did much to revive the religious fervor of his flock. He was strongly opposed to paganism and any form of heresy and championed the freedom of the Church in the face of secular opposition, insisting that "the Emperor is within the Church, not above the Church" (*Con-*

tra Auxentium 36). Under his influence Gratian renounced the title of *pontifex maximus*, refused to restore the statue of Victory to the senate (as had been requested by Symmachus), withdrew state subsidies from the pagan priests and vestals, and passed a number of laws restricting pagan worship. A. prevented the Empress Justina from seizing one of the Milan churches for Arian services. He was a guiding spirit at the Councils of Aquileia and Rome (381, 382). The friend and adviser of three emperors, he found it necessary after the massacre of 7,000 people in Thessalonica to demand a public penance of the Emperor Theodosius (390).

Despite the many cares of his office, A. was a prolific writer. He drew much from Philo, Origen, Basil of Caesarea, and other writers of the East and is justly credited with bringing Greek thought to the West. Most of his works were first given as sermons to his people. These were of an exegetical, moral, and dogmatic nature. He composed commentaries on Scripture, particularly on the OT, a treatise modeled on a work of Cicero on the duties of clerics, and a number of essays on virginity and widowhood. In his *De mysteriis* he discusses baptism, confirmation, and the Eucharist. In his *De paenitentia* he opposes the rigorism of the Novatianists and the claim of heretics to have the power of forgiving sins. In his *De sacramentis* he quotes from the early Roman Canon of the Mass. He introduced antiphonal singing into the churches of the West and composed a number of hymns. His letters are of great historical interest. His defense of the rights of the Church laid the foundation for Church-State relations that were to prevail in later centuries. He was the greatest ecclesiastic of his age, and it is to his lasting credit that his preaching and instructions effected the conversion of one who was destined to be even greater than himself, St. Augustine. BIBLIOGRAPHY: A. Paredi, *Saint Ambrose: His Life and Times* (1964); G. D. Gordini, Bibl-Sanct 1:945–966.

[M. J. COSTELLOE]

AMBROSE OF ALEXANDRIA, ST. (d. *c*.250), deacon. Of noble family, A. was converted from Gnosticism by Origen (*c*.212). He became a friend, disciple, and patron of the teacher after his conversion, furnishing him with copyists as well as with the necessities of life. During the persecution of Maximin (*c*.235), A. was arrested and imprisoned, and was set at liberty only when the persecution ended. A number of Origen's works are dedicated to A., and the *Contra Celsum* owes its existence to him: it was A., who gave a copy of the *True Discourse* of Celsus to Origen, asking him to refute it. BIBLIOGRAPHY: S. Salaville, DHGE 2:1086–90; Quasten 2:52–57.

[P. K. MEAGHER]

AMBROSE OF CAHORS, ST. (8th cent.?). According to a doubtful tradition he held his episcopal office under Pepin the Short (714–768). It is impossible to sort out any certain historical information in the accounts that have come down. Because of a veneration that goes back to at least the 10th cent., the existence of a saintly bp. who died near Bourges after ruling the Church at Cahors may prudently be admitted. BIBLIOGRAPHY: J. E. Lynch, NCE 1:375; C. Lefebvre, BiblSanct 1:943

[J. E. LYNCH]

AMBROSE OF LOMBEZ (1708–78), Capuchin, spiritual director, ascetic author. Called the "Francis de Sales of the 18th cent.," A. became a Capuchin in 1724. As the years passed, his reputation for sanctity grew and he was sent (1765) to reform the convent at Saint-Honoré in Paris. As spiritual director, he based his work on the principle of interior peace; Queen Marie Leczinska was among those who visited him regularly for guidance. His best-known works are: *Traité de la paix intérieure* (1756); *Lettres spirituelles,* 90 in number; and *Traité de la joie de l'âme.* His *Oeuvres complètes* were edited by F. de Benejac (3 v., 1881). BIBLIOGRAPHY: Sigismond, DSAM 1:430–432; U. d'Alençon, DHGE 2:1120–21; J. Bénac, *Vie de Père Ambroise de Lombez* (1908); *Lexicon Capuccinum* (1951) 56, bibliog.

[P. K. MEAGHER]

AMBROSE OF MASSA, VEN. (d. 1240), Franciscan. A diocesan priest in Tuscany, he reformed his life and entered the Franciscan Order in 1225. During the last 15 years of his life in Orvieto, he devoted himself to penance and works of charity. Miracles at his tomb in the church of St. Francis, Orvieto, led to a petition for his canonization. In the Franciscan martyrology he is honored with the title of blessed, but this has not been definitively confirmed by the Church. BIBLIOGRAPHY: R. Pratesi, BiblSanct 1:945; M. Bihl, DHGE 2:1121

[O. J. BLUM]

AMBROSE SANSEDONI (OF SIENA), BL. (1220–86), Italian Dominican, a student with Thomas Aquinas at Paris under Albert the Great, under whose direction he began his teaching career at Cologne (1248). Recalled to Italy *c.* 1271 by the pope, he served the Holy See on various missions and occupied himself with teaching and preaching. He is chiefly remembered for his holiness of life, which so impressed Honorius IV that he ordered that A.'s life be written. No early evidence supports the story that A. destroyed his own writings, considering them unworthy in comparison with those of Thomas Aquinas. His cult was recognized in 1443, and he was formally beatified in 1622. BIBLIOGRAPHY: AS March 3 (1865) 179–250; Quétif-Échard 1:401–403; R. Coulon, DHGE 2:1124–26; Butler 1:644–646.

[P. K. MEAGHER]

AMBROSIAN CHANT, see MILANESE CHANT.

AMBROSIAN HYMN, a title sometimes given to the *Te Deum* of the Divine Office on the supposition, once common, that it was written by St. Ambrose.

[R. B. ENO]

AMBROSIAN RITE, see MILANESE RITE.

AMBROSIANS, the name of several religious congregations who took their name from St. Ambrose but were not founded by him. They included: (1) the 14th-cent. Order of St. Ambrose at Milan, an order of men founded by three Milanese noblemen and canonically erected by Pope Gregory XI (1375) who directed them to follow the rule of St. Augustine and the liturgical rite of St. Ambrose, and an order of women founded by Blessed Catarina Morigia and granted canonical approval by Sixtus IV (1474); (2) the Sisters of St. Marcellina or the Nuns of St. Ambrose (Annunciatae of Lombardy) who claimed many convents in Lombardy and Venetia but were united as a single cloistered congregation by Pope Pius V under the rule of St. Augustine; they were suppressed by Napoleon; (3) the Oblates of St. Ambrose, a society of priests organized by St. Charles Borromeo (1578) and approved by Pope Gregory XIII. Suppressed by Napoleon (1810), it was reinstated by Abp. Romilli (1854). In England, Card. Wiseman approved the congregation and called it the Oblates of St. Charles (1857). BIBLIOGRAPHY: J. Besse, CE 1:403–406; P. Fournier, DHGE 3:412; F. Bertoglio, EncCatt 5:1705.

[F. H. BRIGHAM]

AMBROSIASTER, the name given by *Erasmus to the unknown author of a commentary on 13 Pauline Epistles, a work attributed throughout the Middle Ages to St. *Ambrose. It is now admitted by all that this attribution was erroneous because the work employs a biblical text, a style, and a method of exegesis that differ markedly from those used by Ambrose. The commentary appears to have been written during the pontificate of *Damasus (366–384). It is highly probable that the pseudo-Augustinian *Quaestiones veteris et novi testamenti* is also the work of Ambrosiaster. As an exegete he is superior to many of his contemporaries, and an important witness to the Old Latin text of the Bible and to the pre-Augustinian teaching on grace. His identity has been much discussed. One of the more common opinions is that he was a converted Roman Jew known simply as Isaac. PL 17:45–508. BIBLIOGRAPHY: C. Martini, *Ambrosiaster* (1944); Altaner 457–458; A. Souter, *Earliest Latin Commentaries on the Epistles of Saint Paul* (1927).

[R. B. ENO]

AMBROSIUS CATHARINUS (Lancelloto de' Politi; *c.* 1484–1553), Italian Dominican theologian, bp. of Minori (1546), abp. of Conza (1552). He was one of the first theologians to engage in anti-Lutheran polemics (1520–21). He incurred some disfavor among his brethren for defending the doctrine of the Immaculate Conception. More eclectic philosophically than was common among Dominicans, A. inclined to Scotism on some points, and in the matter of predestination his position foreshadowed that of L. Molina. He was influential in the development of the juridico-moral explanation of the transmission of original sin. BIBLIOGRAPHY: M. M. Gorce, DTC 12.2:2418–34.

[P. K. MEAGHER]

AMBRY (ARMARIUM; var. aumbry), a cabinet or niche in a wall, usually doored, in which objects are stored or exhibited. In ecclesiastical use ambries have served to contain bread and wine for Mass, sacred vessels, relics, the holy oils, and even the Blessed Sacrament. The eucharistic ambry passed out of use in the 16th cent. and gave place to tabernacles on altars. In modern usage the term is usually reserved to designate the doored niche in the church in which the holy oils are kept. BIBLIOGRAPHY: S. J. P. Van Dijk and J. H. Walker, *Myth of the Ambry: Notes on Medieval Reservation Practice and Eucharistic Devotion* (1957) 15–66; S. J. P. Van Dijk, NCE 1:377.

[N. KOLLAR]

AMBULATORY, (1) the continuation of the aisles around the back of the high altar, thus effecting an unbroken processional path; (2) a covered passageway, one of the walks of a cloister.

[S. A. HEENEY]

A.M.D.G., see AD MAJOREM DEI GLORIAM.

AMELINE, CLAUDE (1635–1707), French Oratorian. As a student for the priesthood, A. knew and was much influenced by Malebranche. In the controversies of his time A.'s sympathies were with the Jansenists and he was strongly opposed to Quietism. When Fénelon's *Maximes des Saints* appeared in 1697, A. added a chapter to a work he was in process of composing against the doctrine of *Molinos—Traité de l'amour du souverain bien* (1699). BIBLIOGRAPHY: C. Toussaint, DTC 1.1:1041–42; Bremond 4:591.

[P. K. MEAGHER]

AMELOTE, DENIS (1609–79), French Oratorian. In 1643 he published a biography that was a spiritual and psychological portrait of C. de Condren, whose beloved disciple he had been. A.'s translation with notes of the NT into French (3 v., 1666–70) was highly esteemed and frequently reprinted. He wrote other scriptural, theological, and devotional works, and a defense of the constitutions of Innocent X and Alexander VII against Jansenism. BIBLIOGRAPHY: A. Molien, DSAM 1:473–474; Bremond, *Index* (repr. 1971) 6.

[T. C. O'BRIEN]

AMELRY, FRANCIS (*c.* 1498–*c.* 1552), Belgian Carmelite spiritual writer whose treatises, *What the Love of God Can*

Do and *The Loving Soul*, rank among the classics of spiritual literature in the Low Countries. BIBLIOGRAPHY: B. Cavanaugh, NCE 1:378.

[P. K. MEAGHER]

AMEN, THE (Heb. *'āmēn*, to trust), a word received into Christian use through the example of Jesus. In the OT it denotes true, faithful, certain, assent to an administered oath (note a variant meaning in Is 65.16), as also acceptance, approval, asseveration. Of frequent appearance in the NT in the sense of: yes, surely, so be it, so may it be, it intensifies in significance. Christ (as in John's Gospel) doubled the Amen as in OT doxologies adding a new note of authority, a guarantee of truth on his Word. Jesus was himself called (Rev 3.14) "the Amen," i.e., the reliable one.

In anticipation of the heavenly liturgy where all answer Amen (Rev 5.14) Christians in worship respond: Ah'men' (in Latin and when sung) or Aye' men' (in English). BIBLIOGRAPHY: J. Jungmann, *Public Worship* (tr. C. Howell, 1957) 20; EDB, 67–68.

[M. R. BROWN]

AMENDE HONORABLE, an obsolete provision of ecclesiastical discipline and of some systems of civil law by which a person guilty of wrongdoing could be required at the bidding of a magistrate to make reparation to an injured party by an acknowledgment of his offense, coupled with an apology. (For examples of eccl. use see V. Ermoni, DACL 1:1573–74). The reparation could be effected either in appropriate penitential ceremony (*amende honorable in figuris*), or privately (*amende honorable sèche*). The term has continued in devotional use, esp. among the French, to signify prayers of the kind usually called acts of reparation in English, which are intended to make satisfaction to God's honor for sins such as blasphemy, sacrilege, and profanation, e.g., *Amende honorable au très saint Sacrement de l'autel*.

[P. K. MEAGHER]

AMENDMENT, PURPOSE OF, see PURPOSE OF AMENDMENT.

AMEN-EM-OPE, WISDOM OF, an Egyptian didactic work containing counsel intended to prepare a young man for a good, respected, and prosperous life. The entire work, less materialistic and more altruistic in tone than other Egyptian works of the same genre, is found on a papyrus roll now in the British Museum, a portion of it having been detected also on a writing tablet now in Turin. In its extant form it comes from some time between the 11th and 6th cent. B.C.; it cannot be dated more precisely. The similarity of its contents to those of Pr 22.17–24.22 (a text originally existing independently of the Book of Proverbs) is too great, quantitatively and qualitatively, to be a matter of coincidence. Scholars have, on the whole, considered the *Wisdom of Amen-em-Ope* to be the direct source of much material in Pr 22.17–24.22, but dissenting voices have been raised by R. O. Kevin and E. Drioton—Kevin suggesting that the Egyptian text was the work of an Egyptian drawing upon the present Book of Proverbs; Drioton holding the Egyptian work to be a literal translation of a Hebrew text, which was also the basis of what is now 22.17–24.22. These theories of a dependence of the Egyptian work on a Hebrew source continue to be rejected by the great majority of both Egyptologists and biblical scholars. BIBLIOGRAPHY: F. L. Griffith, ''Teaching of Amenophis the Son of Kanakht,'' *Journal of Egyptian Archaeology* 12 (1926) 191–231; E. Drioton, ''Sur la Sagesse d'Aménémopé,'' *Mélanges bibliques rédigés en l'honneur de André Robert* (1957) 254–280; R. J. Williams, ''Alleged Semitic Origin of the Wisdom of Amenemope,'' *Journal of Egyptian Archaeology* 47 (1961) 100–106; *Wisdom of Amen-em-ope* (Eng. tr. J. Wilson in J. B. Pritchard ed., *Ancient Near Eastern Texts*, 2d ed., 1955) 421–425.

[A. CODY]

AMENHOTEP III, of the Eighteenth Dynasty. He consolidated Egyptian supremacy over Palestine, reconquered by his predecessors, and fostered commerce throughout the Mediterranean basin. His religious devotion to the sun-god Aton foreshadowed the monotheistic-type cult of his more famous son, Akhnaton (Amenhotep IV).

[J. E. FALLON]

AMENHOTEP IV, see AKHNATON.

AMENTIA, a term used in some psychiatric literature to describe a state of subnormal mental development such as idiocy, imbecility, as distinguished from dementia, which is understood as a mental derangement occurring after a relatively normal development has been achieved. Less commonly among some European writers amentia is also used to designate acute mental confusion or hallucination. As the word occurs in the writings of canonists and moral theologians, it designates a state or condition of a person whose mental condition is such that he is incapable of responsible human action.

AMERBACH, JOHANNES AND BONIFACE. (1) Johannes (*c*.1440–1513), Basel printer. By 1461 M.A. at the Univ. of Paris, where he learned printing, he moved to Basel (1475) where his shop became famous for editions of Ambrose (1492), Augustine (1506), and the Bible. His sons merged his business with Johannes Froben, who printed A.'s Jerome in 1516. (2) Bonifatius (1495–1562), son of Johannes, studied law in Freiburg and Avignon before teaching it in Basel, where he was rector of the university. Erasmus named him his sole heir; Holbein painted his portrait. BIBLIOGRAPHY: G. J. Donnelly, NCE 1:379.

[E. P. COLBERT]

AMERBACH, VIET (1503–57), humanist scholar. He studied at Wittenberg from 1522 and taught there from 1530; but patristic authors and Eck led him to break with Luther and Melanchthon in 1543 and return to Ingolstadt, where he had studied as a child. He never wrote against Protestantism; most of his many writings deal with classical items. BIBLIOGRAPHY: J. Pietsch, DHGE 1198–99.

[E. P. COLBERT]

AMERICAN BAPTIST ASSOCIATION, fundamentalist body with historical and theological antecedents in *Landmarkism. As early as 1850, Landmarkists posed a threat to cooperation at the denominational level among Southern Baptists: they rejected a move to transfer control of the mission enterprise from local churches to denominational boards and formed a separate missionary program. The continuing drift of the Southern Baptist Convention away from an ecclesiology based on the *local church toward associations of churches resulted in the organization of the American Baptist Association at Texarkana, Tex., in 1902. The heaviest population of these churches is to be found in the SW; in 1974 there were 3,336 churches with 955,900 members. Because of the strong emphasis on the autonomy of the local church, the denomination receives the name Church Equality Baptists.

[R. A. MACOSKEY]

AMERICAN BAPTIST CHURCHES IN U.S.A., a large denomination, organized in 1907 as the Northern Baptist Convention. Although defending congregational polity and local church autonomy, prerevolutionary Baptists formed themselves into voluntary associations to develop fellowship, mutual concern, and more effective service. The most formal of these was the Philadelphia Association, founded in 1707 and composed of 25 churches scattered from N.Y. to Virginia. As a result of an inspiring report of missionary opportunities in Burma, several associations of churches met at Philadelphia in 1814 to organize in what was soon called the Triennial Convention. Its activities expanded rapidly and resulted in the formation of additional boards with special interest in home missions and Christian education. All the Baptists in the U.S. continued to work harmoniously until 1845, when regional passions surrounding the question of slavery led to separate organizations in the North and the South (SEE SOUTHERN BAPTIST CONVENTION). Instead of an overall denominational organization in the North, a multiplicity of agencies conducted missionary, educational, and social work, until need for better coordination led to the formation of the Northern Baptist Convention (1907). The name was changed in 1950 to the American Baptist Convention. Several reorganizational steps were taken after 1950, resulting in 1961 in doubling the size of the general council of the denomination to include all executive ministers of state conventions, heads of agencies, and staff persons. The heads of each separate society became associate general secretaries of the Convention. National offices were moved from New York City to Valley Forge, Pennsylvania.

In 1972 the Convention's name was changed to American

Baptist Churches in U.S.A. Membership at that time was reported to be 1,472,478 in 6090 churches. While adhering to traditional Baptist teaching and polity, it is theologically more progressive than some other Baptist groups: it accepts *open communion and participates in ecumenical endeavors. Missionary work, increasingly ecumenical and cooperative, is done in 12 foreign and 11 home mission fields. Among the most active Protestant denominations in the field of higher education, it founded, and still maintains ties with, 25 colleges, 11 junior colleges, 4 preparatory schools, and 8 seminaries. Among the great universities historically connected with it are Brown Univ., Bucknell Univ., and the Univ. of Chicago. BIBLIOGRAPHY: O. K. and M. M. Armstrong, *Indomitable Baptists* (1967).

AMERICAN BAPTIST CONVENTION see AMERICAN BAPTIST CHURCHES IN U.S.A.

AMERICAN BIBLE SOCIETY (ABS), an organization founded in New York City in 1816 for the purpose of distributing faithful translations of the Scriptures, in all languages, at low cost or free, throughout the world. ABS works in 150 countries and distributes Scripture translations in more than 1,300 languages and dialects. Most translations are made by missionaries in the field, working with Christian nationals. ABS also supplies Bibles for the blind, in Braille and on "Talking Bible" records. To avoid theological controversy or rivalry with commercial publishers, its Bibles are limited to the text alone, without notes or comments. From its inception till 1970 the ABS distributed more than 800 million complete or partial Bibles, with an annual average, in the 1960s, of 43 million. In 1973 ABS announced its plan for distributing an additional 725 million Bible selections by 1985. BIBLIOGRAPHY: "Bibles for Millions," *America* 129 (1973) 269–270; YBACC (1973) 8–9.

[D. CODDINGTON]

AMERICAN BOARD OF CATHOLIC MISSIONS, begun in 1919 for the purpose of gathering contributions for the missions, with Abp. Henry Moeller of Cincinnati as chairman. The ABCM thus gives support to missions in the U.S. and its territories, which are not aided by the Society for the Propagation of the Faith. The board gives grants to the missions, esp. for Spanish-speaking Catholics in the Southwest and the Negroes of the South. Recently, financial aid may be applied for by the Latin-American missions also. BIBLIOGRAPHY: R. Trisco, NCE 1:398.

[M. C. BRADLEY]

AMERICAN BOARD of Commissioners For Foreign Missions (ABCFM), the first missionary society in the U.S. to send missionaries overseas. The ABCFM was formed in 1810 by a group of Congregationalists who had experienced a call to the missions while students at Williams College at a famous "haystack meeting" in 1807. It was incorporated legally in Mass. 2 years later. From the beginning the policy was not narrowly denominational; the board served not only the Congregational but also Reformed (1826–66) and Presbyterian Churches (1812–70). Even after these arrangements were terminated, the ABCFM continued to sponsor Christian missionaries of many denominations. First missionaries, among them L. Rice and A. Judson, were sent to India in 1812. The field was extended throughout the Near East, the Far East, and Africa. From 1868 onward three Woman's Board of Missions worked in conjunction with ABCFM, and were amalgamated with it in 1927. Various mergers of the Congregational Churches have resulted in the ABCFM's becoming part of the United Church Board for World Ministries, formed in 1961, one of the instrumentalities of the *United Church of Christ. BIBLIOGRAPHY: RACHS 2:185, 193–194.

[F. E. MASER]

AMERICAN CATHOLIC PHILOSOPHICAL ASSOCIATION, professional society for the study of philosophy organized in 1926 at The Catholic University of America. Its aims include the promotion of philosophical scholarship and the improvement of the teaching of philosophy. It publishes a quarterly journal, *New Scholasticism*, the *Proceedings of the American Catholic Philosophical Association* containing material from its annual 3-day convention, and periodic volumes of "Philosophical Studies."

[J. C. WILLKE]

AMERICAN CATHOLIC PSYCHOLOGICAL ASSOCIATION, see PSYCHOLOGISTS INTERESTED IN RELIGIOUS ISSUES.

AMERICAN COUNCIL OF CHRISTIAN CHURCHES (ACCC), a body made up of 15 conservative fundamentalist Churches. The founder and until 1968 the dominant personality was Carl McIntire (b. 1906). It was organized in 1941 to provide a means of cooperative effort by Churches whose members felt that the Federal Council of Churches (now National Council of Churches) gave too wide a latitude to theological liberals and economic socialists. There are no official figures available on ACCC membership. The *Southern Methodist Church and the Bible Presbyterian Church (Collingswood Synod) are among the member Churches. Headquarters are maintained in New York City. In 1968 Dr. McIntire's influence was challenged, and a strain in relations with his *International Council of Christian Churches developed. The ACCC should not be confused with the *National Association of Evangelicals, which represents a wider spectrum than the politically conservative American Council of Christian Churches, with its right-wing activism.

[R. K. MacMASTER]

AMERICAN EVANGELICAL LUTHERAN CHURCH, one of four Churches that entered a union forming in

1962 the *Lutheran Church in America. It had been established for Danish immigrants in the Midwest in 1872; the name Danish Evangelical Lutheran Church in America, which was adopted in 1874, was changed in 1954 to American Evangelical Lutheran Church. BIBLIOGRAPHY: EncLuth Ch 2:1367–68.

[T. C. O'BRIEN]

AMERICAN FEDERATION OF CATHOLIC SOCIETIES developed from Pope Pius IX's recommendation that unions of Catholic societies be formed throughout the world in line with the work of the Belgian Catholic Union in 1871. Attempts were made over a period of years to federate the societies into a national organization until a loose union of organizations was formed, known as the American Federation of Catholic Societies. The federation rendered extensive service for 18 years by helping to mold an informed Catholic public opinion and by acting as a watchdog over pending legislation. Eventually, the National Council of Catholic Men and Women (NCWC) replaced the federation. BIBLIOGRAPHY: A. F. Gorman, NCE 1:400.

[M. C. BRADLEY]

AMERICAN GUILD OF ORGANISTS (founded 1896), professional society for church musicians in the U.S. Members who pass the appropriate Guild examinations are awarded certificates as Fellows (F.A.G.O.), Associates (A.A.G.O.), or Choirmasters (Ch.M.), which represent a high degree of professional competency. There are local chapters throughout the country as well as student groups at a number of colleges; these hold regular meetings in addition to the Guild's national and regional conventions. Information and news about the organ and church music are published in its periodical *Music: The A.G.O. Magazine*. Other A.G.O. activities include competitions in organ playing and composition, interfaith music programs, and the drawing up of such material as a code of ethics for church musicians, standard dimensions and specifications for organ consoles, etc.

[A. DOHERTY]

AMERICAN LUTHERAN CHURCH, one of the three principal bodies of the Lutheran Church in North America, the others being the Lutheran Church in America and the Lutheran Church—Missouri Synod. The American Lutheran Church was created in 1961. It brought together four groups that had previously been distinct bodies, although they were involved together in many forms of cooperation and fellowship: the American Lutheran Church (formed in 1930 from the Iowa, Ohio, and Buffalo Synods), the Evangelical Lutheran Church (a body uniting various synodical groups of Norwegian background), the United Evangelical Lutheran Church (a Danish-American body), and the Lutheran Free Church (a Norwegian-American group). Geographically, the American Lutheran Church is strongest in the Midwest and upper Midwest, with considerable rep-

resentation also in the Pacific Northwest. Theologically, it combines a variety of emphases within the Lutheran tradition, including both orthodox and Pietist theologies in its heritage (SEE ORTHODOXY; PIETISM). This combination has tended to cast it in a mediating role between the Lutheran Church in America and the Lutheran Church—Missouri Synod. With both it had established full fellowship of pulpit and altar by 1969. It has been neither as vigorous in its ecumenical role as the former of these synods nor as aloof from other, non-Lutheran groups as the latter. Characteristic of the American Lutheran Church has been a strong interest in the Christian world mission. From its Pietist roots in both Germany (esp. as represented by the work of Wilhelm Löhe) and Scandinavia it has inherited the general concern for evangelization and a specific interest in certain fields of mission work, including Africa. In the U.S., too, the Pietist heritage has stimulated a greater attention to the evangelistic task of the Church than has sometimes characterized Lutheranism. The headquarters of the American Lutheran Church are in Minneapolis, Minnesota. Its seminaries are: Luther Seminary, Saint Paul, Minnesota; Wartburg Seminary, Dubuque, Iowa; and Capital Seminary, Columbus, Ohio. Its total membership of baptized and confirmed Lutherans is approximately one-third of the eight million total of American Lutheranism as a whole, numbering (1973) 2,521,930 baptized souls. BIBLIOGRAPHY: F. Meuser et al., EncLuthCh 1:44–59.

[J. PELIKAN]

AMERICAN ORGAN, see HARMONIUM.

AMERICAN PRAYER BOOK, the authorized liturgical book of the Protestant Episcopal Church. The Anglican churches in the American colonies used the BCP in its Jacobean (1604) and Caroline (1662) editions. After the Revolution a revision of the BCP was adopted as the norm of liturgical worship by the first General Convention of the Protestant Episcopal Church in 1789. In addition to necessary alterations in the prayers for civil rulers, the principal change made in this first American Prayer Book was the form of holy communion, derived from the 1764 Liturgy of the Scottish Episcopalian nonjurors, who had consecrated the first American bp. in 1784, Samuel Seabury of Connecticut. The rite, in distinction to the BCP form, included in the consecration of the Eucharist an oblation of the elements and an invocation of the Holy Spirit. Major revisions were completed in 1892 and in 1928, with enrichments from ancient and modern sources, and with more flexible rubrical adaptations for varied occasions of public worship. The General Convention of 1967 authorized a new revision, now in trial use of proposed forms prepared by the Standing Liturgical Commission. Final acceptance awaits the decision of the 1979 General Convention.

Canon law of the Episcopal Church requires all public

services to conform to the text of a standard book in the charge of an official custodian. Alterations may be made only by vote of two successive general conventions, which meet triennially. Diocesan bps. may authorize forms for special occasions not provided by the Prayer Book. BIBLIOGRAPHY: E. L. Parsons and B. H. Jones, *American Prayer Book, Its Origins and Principles* (1937); M. H. Shepherd, Jr., *Oxford American Prayer Book Commentary* (1950).

[M. H. SHEPHERD]

AMERICAN PROTECTIVE ASSOCIATION (APA), an organization founded to oppose the RC Church and its parochial schools. The APA was established on March 13, 1887, in Clinton, Iowa, by Henry F. Bowers and seven other men. It carried on the tradition of nativism and Know-Nothingism and sought to limit the growth of Roman Catholicism in the U.S. by restricting immigration. APA activities centered in the mid-western states; membership grew when it was announced that Abp. F. Satolli would arrive in 1892 as first apostolic delegate to the U.S. By 1896 the APA claimed 1 million members and achieved a measure of influence in Republican politics. It had recognized chapters in 24 states, published more than 70 periodicals, and sponsored lectures by former priests and former nuns warning against the Roman menace. Some Protestants, such as Washington Gladden, branded the APA as bigoted and un-American. W. J. H. Traynor, editor of the *American Patriot,* succeeded Bowers as president of the APA in 1894. Political errors led to a rapid decline after 1900, but the organization lingered on until 1911. BIBLIOGRAPHY: D. L. Kinzer, *Episode in Anti-Catholicism: The American Protective Association* (1964).

[W. J. WHALEN]

AMERICAN RESCUE WORKERS, an organization that developed by separation from the *Salvation Army. Maj. Thomas E. Moore was appointed commander of the American Salvation Army forces by William Booth a few months after the first Salvationists landed in the U.S. in 1880. Under Moore's direction the work expanded rapidly (1881–84), and beginnings were made in Canada. Following Booth's directions, Moore held all property in his own name and was responsible only to Booth. He sought to incorporate the Salvation Army as a religious body to own property in its own right and to make it more democratic in its polity. Moore was dismissed and in 1885 organized his following under the name Salvation Army in America, and under the direction of five trustees. In 1889 a second split led to reunion of one group with the British parent body; the other remained loyal to Moore (who died in 1898 as pastor of a Baptist church in Kansas). In 1913 the Moore group changed its name to American Rescue Workers. In 1973 it numbered 46 churches with 5,410 members. Its beliefs, type of organization, and fields of dedication are indistinguishable from

those of the Salvation Army. BIBLIOGRAPHY: YBACC (1973) 28.

[R. K. MacMASTER]

AMERICAN SABBATH UNION, see LORD'S DAY ALLIANCE OF THE UNITED STATES.

AMERICAN SCHOOLS OF ORIENTAL RESEARCH (ASOR), a society having two schools, one located in Jerusalem (founded in 1900), the other in Baghdad (1921). A new school in Beirut is in the planning stage. The society's purpose is to promote the study of biblical literature, specifically by research in the archeology, geography, history, and the languages, ancient and modern, of the Middle East regions. The organization undertakes explorations and excavations, and subsidizes the studies of qualified students at its schools. The corporate members of ASOR number about 130 American and Canadian institutions on an interdenominational basis. The individual associate members are about 800. Professors William F. Albright and Nelson Glueck are among the better known and influential long-term directors of the Jerusalem school, which was renamed Albright Institute of Archeological Research in 1970. Representatives of this school have been prominent in the research involved in the recent discovery of the Dead Sea Scrolls. Publications include a *Bulletin,* an *Annual,* the *Biblical Archaeologist,* and the *Journal of Cuneiform Studies.*

[J. E. LUSSIER]

AMERICAN STANDARD VERSION, a variant of the *Revised Version of the Bible. When the latter was being prepared in England, a group of American scholars was invited to make recommendations. In 1901 the American Standard Version incorporating the work of this American committee was published. This version was a basis for the Revised Standard Version.

[T. C. O'BRIEN]

AMERICAN TRACT SOCIETY, an organization founded in New York City in 1825 for the dissemination of Protestant literature. The society was interdenominational and received strong financial support. It published and distributed not only "tracts," or leaflets, but also Sunday school literature and volumes of Protestant devotion, history, and biography. It was the publisher for temperance movements and *Bible societies, and helped in the evangelization of immigrants and of settlers in places where there was no church.

[T. C. O'BRIEN]

AMERICAN UNITARIAN ASSOCIATION, see UNITARIAN UNIVERSALIST ASSOCIATION; UNITARIANISM.

AMERICANISM, a term associated with the debate within Roman Catholicism in the U.S. in the late 19th cent. concerning the extent to which traditional RC practices should be adapted to the American milieu. In the effort to relate Roman Catholicism to American society, the open-minded approach of some bps., e.g., James Gibbons, John Ireland, and John J. Keane, was viewed with suspicion by the more conservative members of the Church led by Abp. Michael A. Corrigan of N.Y., who feared that such efforts threatened the integrity of RC doctrine. Controversy between the two groups over parochial schools and the language question (whether, as a protection to faith, to preserve the native language and customs of the immigrants or to Americanize them as quickly as possible) was further exacerbated by such incidents as the participation of Gibbons, Keane, and others in the Parliament of Religions held in conjunction with the Chicago Columbian Exposition (1893); differences of opinion with regard to Catholic membership in the Knights of Labor and other societies; and debate over the single tax proposal of Henry George. When a French translation of W. Elliott's *Life of Father Hecker* led to an exaggerated interpretation of the author's ascetical principles and apologetical practices, the issues of Americanism were hotly debated in France, where the progressives and conservatives were already at odds over the *ralliement*, a movement inspired by the pope for Catholic acceptance and participation in the French Republic.

In his apostolic letter *Testem benevolentiae* addressed to Gibbons (Jan. 22, 1899), Leo XIII referred to the controversy aroused by the *Life of Father Hecker*, esp. in the interpretations given in European reviews, and he condemned as false doctrines certain new ideas concerning the manner of leading a Christian life. Based on the principle that the Church should relax its ancient rigor and develop more effective ways of attracting converts, the condemned errors maintained that in an era of liberty external guidance was less necessary in the search for Christian perfection; that the natural virtues were better suited to modern times than the supernatural; that the active virtues were more important than such "passive" virtues as humility and obedience; and that religious vows were opposed to the spirit of the present time and that religious life was of little use to the Church.

In his letter, the Pope did not say that anyone held the condemned propositions, and he made it clear that he exempted those laudable political and social qualities of the American people that were also sometimes called Americanism. In the U.S., the more conservative prelates thanked the Pope for saving the American Church from the danger of heresy, while the followers of Gibbons maintained that no American Catholicism, and the subsequent censure of *Modernism that had acquired the name of Americanism were caricatures of the real ideas of Father Hecker and of American Catholicism as it actually existed. The papal condemnation tended to accentuate the generally conservative cast of American Catholicism, and the subsequent censure of *modernism (1907) contributed further to the theological silence characteristic of the RC Church in the U.S. in the succeeding decades. BIBLIOGRAPHY: T. T. McAvoy, *Americanist Heresy in Roman Catholicism* (1963); R. D. Cross, *Emergence of Liberal Catholicism in America* (1958); A. M. Greeley, *Catholic Experience* (1967) 150–215.

[M. CARTHY]

AMERICANS UNITED for Separation of Church and State, a shorter form of title used by *Protestants and Other Americans United for Separation of Church and State (POAU).

AMES, WILLIAM (1576–1633), English Calvinist theologian and moralist. Educated at Cambridge, A. developed strong Puritan convictions. From 1610 he lived, lectured in theology, and engaged in polemical writing in Holland. He is esp. notable as one of the few Protestant divines who wrote expressly on moral theology and casuistry. BIBLIOGRAPHY: DNB 1:355.

[P. K. MEAGHER]

AMESHA SPENTA, the "Beneficent Immortals," or "archangels," of Zoroastrianism. They reflect functions or adaptations of functions connected with the Indo-Iranian social or class structure and the Indo-Iranian concept of the world and its government. They are *Arta* (True Order), *Vohu Manah* (Good Mind), *Khshathra* (Dominion), *Ārmaiti* (Devotion), *Haurvatāt* (Health), *Ameretāt* (Non-Death). The god *Vāyu* (Cosmic Wind), is represented in the Zoroastrian system by the two Mainyus or Spirits, *Spenta Mainyu* (Beneficent or Holy Spirit), and *Anra Mainyu* (Destructive Spirit). BIBLIOGRAPHY: J. Duchesne-Guillemin, NCE 1:445; *id.*, *La Religion de l'Iran ancien* (1962).

[M. R. P. MCGUIRE]

AMETTE, LÉON ADOLPHE (1850–1920), cardinal, abp. of Paris. A. studied at St. Sulpice, was ordained (1873), worked in the Évreux diocese (1873–99), was consecrated bp. of Bayeux (1899), became abp. of Paris (1908), and cardinal (1911). A. helped to relieve tensions between civil and ecclesiastical authorities and often acted as intermediary between France and the Vatican. He participated in relief efforts during World War I and, throughout his entire episcopate, was effective in his championship of labor, the organization of the hierarchy, the establishment of parish committees and unions, and the provision of free elementary education. He was responsible for the building of 50 new churches and chapels. BIBLIOGRAPHY: G. Jacquemet, *Catholicisme* 1:459–460; CE Suppl 1:40.

[H. JACK]

AMICE, the first liturgical garment a minister puts on when he is vesting for certain functions. It is a square or oblong linen cloth that is worn around the neck and shoulders and is held in place by two strings or tapes. The amice goes over the cassock but under the alb (in modern usage). Originally it was used to prevent the soiling of the outer liturgical garments where they came into contact with the wearer's face or neck. In certain religious orders in which the habit is fitted with a cowl or capuce, the amice is worn over the head, but is laid back when the minister comes to the altar. BIBLIOGRAPHY: E. A. Roulin, *Vestments and Vesture* (tr. J. McCann, 1950).

[N. KOLLAR]

AMICO, FRANCESCO (1578–1651), Italian Jesuit theologian who taught at the Univ. of Graz. He produced a *Cursus theologicus* (9 v., 1640–49), the fifth volume of which (*De jure et justitia*) was placed on the Index in 1651 for questionable views concerning the killing of a calumniator (D 2037) and the killing of one who unjustly stands in the way of one's coming into property (D 2132–33). In subsequent editions these opinions were corrected. BIBLIOGRAPHY: Sommervogel 1:280–282.

[P. K. MEAGHER]

AMICUS AND AMELIUS, SS. These two saints, venerated as martyrs in Lombardy, are first mentioned in the *Speculum historiale* of *Vincent of Beauvais (13th cent.). He makes of them Frankish warriors killed in battle by the Lombards *c*.773. Their cult is late and built on the shakiest of foundations. BIBLIOGRAPHY: P. Richard, DHGE 2:1235–36; C. Carletti, BiblSanct 1:1003–04.

[R. B. ENO]

AMIDA BUDDHA, GREAT (*DAIBUTSU*). In the Nara period the principal icon of the Todaiji, the Great Buddha (*Daibutsu Vairocana*) was a Mahayana conception of the cosmic Buddha—massive but mystical, of great dignity and sublime beauty. Made by order of Emperor Shōmu in 752, the Todaiji *Daibutsu*, the largest ever made and taking over 15 years to construct, has not survived in its original form.

The Great Buddha of Kamakura, a gigantic Japanese bronze statue 49 feet high, cast *c*.1252 for the Kotokuin temple, probably emulating the Todaiji Buddha, retains traces of the style of Kaikei showing the influence of Nara ideals in calmness, gentleness, and elegant pose. The temple having been destroyed by fire, this heroic Buddha remains, serene and majestic, conveying the supreme compassion of the Amida Buddha.

[M. J. DALY]

AMIDISM, a branch of Mahayana Buddhism teaching salvation through faith in the Buddha of Unlimited Light (Sanskrit, *Amitabha*; Jap. *Amida*), rather than by works. Known as Pure Land Buddhism, it is based on the Pure Land Sutra written in India *c*.1st cent. A.D. It reached China in the 3d cent. and became the most popular form of Buddhism. It became a separate school, Jodo, in Japan by the 13th century. Later a more radical form, Shin, became the largest Buddhist sect in Japan. It stresses invoking Amitabha, who presides over the Western Paradise, or the Pure Land. Adherents seek rebirth in the Pure Land rather than Nirvana.

[T. EARLY]

AMIENS, an ecclesiastical center of N France. It is a suffragan see to Reims, and lies on the Somme about 40 miles from the Channel. Historically it served as the capital of Picardy, and today is the capital of the Somme department. Two saints named Firmin are traditionally regarded as the first Christian apostles of Amiens, though some scholars speculate that they were the same person. According to documents written centuries later, the first Firmin was a native of Navarre who, after some years in the S of France became the first bp. of Amiens and was martyred there during the reign of Maximian and Diocletian (284–305). The second Firmin, also a bp., is said to have been the son of a senator converted by the first Firmin. A St. Honoratus, who according to a late biography was bp. of Amiens *c*.575–600, became patron of bakers. Peter the Hermit (*c*.1050–1115), preacher of the First Crusade, came from Amiens or its vicinity. In 1185 Philip II added Amiens to his domains. Under the Treaty of Arras (1435) it was given to Philip the Good of Burgundy, but in 1477 it reverted to France. The Cathedral of *Amiens is particularly noteworthy, representing the culmination of High Gothic style. Another church at Amiens marks the site where St. Martin of Tours is said to have divided his cloak with a beggar.

[T. EARLY]

AMIENS, CATHEDRAL OF (1220–75), one of the finest monuments of High Gothic in 13th-cent. France, ranking with Chartres and Reims. None of the great Gothic cathedrals displays greater homogeneity of style and iconography. Built by Robert de Luzarches, Amiens cathedral boasts a nave of quite extraordinary beauty of proportion. There are two towers 215 feet high and an elegant flèche at the crossing. With five monumental portals richly adorned, the *trumeau* of the central portal supporting the *Beau Dieu* (1200–50, the finest of classic Gothic figures), the *trumeau* of the later elegant Gothic door of the south transept (1250–75) adorned by the equally famous *Vierge Dorée* echoing the Joseph Master of Reims, Amiens marks the apogee of Gothic art. BIBLIOGRAPHY: M. Aubert and S. Goubet, *Gothic Cathedrals of France and Their Treasures* (1959).

[M. J. DALY]

AMILLENARIANISM (Amillennialism), the studied disbelief in millenarianist doctrine, whether of the premillenarian or postmillenarian variety. Those characterized as amillenarianists generally base their position on the claim that the scriptural passages on which millenarianists rely, esp. Rev ch. 20, are figurative and allegorical and hence cannot reasonably be taken in a literal sense. *MILLENARIANISM.

[P. K. MEAGHER]

AMIOT, JEAN JOSEPH MARIE (1718–93), French Jesuit missionary to China. Soon after ordination he arrived in Macao 1750 and Peking 1751. The Manchus esteemed him for his many talents, linguistic and scientific; and Europe prized his translations, grammars, and dictionaries, studies of Asian peoples, treatises on Confucius and Chinese history, on warfare and music. BIBLIOGRAPHY: J. A. Otto, LTK 1:439.

[E. P. COLBERT]

AMIS DE L'HOMME (Friends of Man), a sect founded in Switzerland by Alexandre Freytag (1870–1947). It is sometimes called the Army of the Eternal, and sometimes also the Church of the Kingdom of God. Freytag was a disciple of C. T. *Russell from c.1898 and in 1916 was a prominent member of the coterie of Bible Students at Geneva. Disappointed with the unfulfillment of prophecies credited among the Bible Students, he began to develop a doctrine of his own. He published three books: *Divine Revelation* (1918); *Message to Humanity* (1922); and *Life Eternal* (1923). More than a million copies of his writings have been sold. He claimed to be the messenger announced in Mal 3.1 and the faithful servant of Mt 24.45. Denying the immortality of the soul, he taught that eternal life is something man could enjoy here on earth if only he could free himself from the sin of egoism, the one sin to which all evils and sickness are reducible. The achievement of pure altruism was therefore to be the cardinal objective of believers. This positive aspect of their doctrine and the benevolent activities in which it is expressed throw a friendlier light on the Amis than their somber millennial inheritance would cause one to expect. But like the Bible Students and the Jehovah's Witnesses, they hold other religions, and esp. the Roman Catholic, in abomination. Their methods of spreading their message have much in common with those of the Jehovah's Witnesses. With imperturbably courteous persistence they go methodically from door to door with their literature. After Freytag's death there was a division among his followers. One segment, led by M. Ruffner, carried on with headquarters at Cartigny in Switzerland, and some French groups have been faithful to this allegiance. Most of the French groups, however, accepted the leadership of Bernard Sayerce, who was already head of the movement in France during Freytag's lifetime. He claimed that Freytag had destined him to succeed to leadership of all the Amis. Headquarters of this segment are in Paris. There are Amis groups in Belgium, Germany, and Italy. BIBLIOGRAPHY: H. C. Chéry, *L'Offensive des sectes* (1961) 198–232.

[P. K. MEAGHER]

AMISH MENNONITES, those Mennonites, commonly called simply the Amish, named after J. *Ammann. They separated from the main body of Mennonites in Switzerland and Alsace (1693–97). The main issue was a desire for strict enforcement of *Meidung,* i.e., the avoidance or "shunning" of the excommunicated, and for a more rigid separation from worldly ways. This practice of nonconformity remains their main characteristic; their basic beliefs are Mennonite. There are no longer any Amish in Europe; most migrated to N.A.; the rest rejoined the main body of Mennonites. In the 18th cent. migration to Pa. took place, and there Amish customs

and language still reflect the "Pennsylvania Dutch" culture developed by German-speaking Lutherans, Mennonites, Moravians, Reformed, and others. The Amish also have most consistently retained the cultural features that sprang up around Anabaptist-Mennonite beliefs in Switzerland. The Amish continued not only in Pa. but also in Ohio, Ind., Ill., Iowa, Neb., and Kans. and in the Province of Ontario, Canada. As they moved westward, they lost some of their rigidity and adjusted more readily to their environment.

The *Old Order Amish are the most conservative group, and because of their disapproval of a gradual acculturation, numerous splinter groups arose. The Central Conference of Mennonites, or Stuckey Amish, belong to the General Conference Mennonite Church. The Egli Amish separated in 1864 under the influence of a revival movement, which led to the founding of the Defenseless Mennonites, later called the Evangelical Mennonite Church. The "New Amish" (Neutäufer) started in Ohio in 1846; they also came under the influence of revivalism and formed the majority in the organization of the Apostolic Christian Church. A separation in 1927 led to the formation of the Beachy Amish Mennonite Churches. In general, there has been a tendency for separating Amish groups to join one of the larger Mennonite conferences. BIBLIOGRAPHY: J. A. Hostetler, *Annotated Bibliography on the Amish* (1951); *id., Amish Society* (1970); MennEnc 1:93–98.

[C. KRAHN]

AMITABHA BUDDHA, the Buddha of Boundless Light represented seated in meditation holding a begging bowl. Devoutly worshiped in China and Japan, Amitabha is the Buddha of boundless compassion who welcomes all who call his name into the Western Paradise or Pure Land. BIBLIOGRAPHY: W. Willets, *Foundations of Chinese Art* (1965).

[M. J. DALY]

AMMANATI, BARTOLOMMEO (1511–92), Italian mannerist sculptor and architect, who studied with Bandinelli in Florence and with Sansovino in Venice. A. executed Benavides' tomb (Eremitani) with classical Sansovinesque allegories. At the Del Monte Chapel of S. Pietro, Montorio, A. reflects Vasari's "mannerism" and in the Nymphaeum of the garden of the Villa Giulia echoes Vignola's villa plan. In Florence (1555) as chief architect to Cosimo I de' Medici, A. added the garden façade with rusticated orders at Palazzo Pitti (1558–70) and carved the colossal Neptune of the fountain in Piazza della Signoria (1563–75). A. worked on the Jesuit church of S. Giovannino, Florence (1579) until failing health restricted his activities. BIBLIOGRAPHY: A. Prandi, EncCatt 1:1078–79; H. V. Niebling, NCE 1:449.

[M. J. DALY]

AMMANATI DE PICCOLOMINI, JACOPO (1422–79), humanist, bishop, cardinal. Having mastered classical studies at Florence, he became secretary of briefs for Callistus III. He was adopted into the Piccolomini family by Pius II who made him bp. of Pavia in 1460, and cardinal in 1461. Transferred to Lucca in 1471, he also served as papal legate to Umbria and Perugia. BIBLIOGRAPHY: G. Calamari, *Il confidente di Pio II*. (2 v., 1932); N. G. Wolf, NCE 1:449.

[N. G. WOLF]

AMMANN, JAKOB (fl. 17th cent.), founder of the *Amish Mennonites. He was a Mennonite elder in the Canton of Bern, Switzerland, when in 1693 he excommunicated all the other elders of Switzerland. His grievance was their refusal to impose *Meidung*, or avoidance of the excommunicated. The action caused the separation of his followers, the Amish, as a distinct body of Mennonites. His conservatism extended to other practices, e.g., simple uniformity in dress, that remain typical of the Amish. He also introduced footwashing into the Swiss Mennonite congregations. He resided in Alsace, possibly as elder of a congregation, probably from 1694 to 1708, but little else is known of him. BIBLIOGRAPHY: MennEnc 1:98–99.

[T. C. O'BRIEN]

AMMIANUS MARCELLINUS (*c*.330–*c*.395 A.D.), Roman historian. Born of a good pagan family in Antioch, he served in the East and West under Ursicinus, Constantius' *magister equitum*, accompanied Julian on his ill-fated Persian expedition, and then retired from public life. His history of the Roman Empire was a continuation of the work of Tacitus, covering the years from 96 (death of Domitian) to 378 (death of Valens) in 31 books. Only the last 18, narrating the events of the years 353–378, are still extant. A.'s native intelligence, impartiality, wide experiences, and extensive readings enabled him to become one of the greatest historians of the ancient world. Despite an obscure and affected style resulting largely from the fact that he wrote in Latin rather than in his native Greek, his pages are never dull. BIBLIOGRAPHY: E. A. Thompson, *Historical Work of Ammianus Marcellinus* (1947); G. B. Pighi, RAC 1:386–394.

[M. J. COSTELLOE]

AMMON, see AMUN, ST.

AMMONAS (fl. 350), hermit. As one of the early disciples of St. Anthony and later his successor at Pispir, his letters (7 in Greek and 15 in Syriac) are an important witness to early desert monasticism and mysticism. BIBLIOGRAPHY: Quasten 3:153–154.

[H. JACK]

AMMONIAN SECTIONS, divisions noted in the margins of nearly all Greek and Latin MSS of the four Gospels to facilitate comparison of parallel passages of different Gospels and so named because Ammonius Saccas was reputed to be their author. Recent opinion has attributed them to Eusebius of Caesarea. Prior to the 13th-cent. division by

chapter, they were very useful for identifying passages. BIBLIOGRAPHY: F. Bechtel, CE 1:431.

[F. H. BRIGHAM]

AMMONITES, Aramaic tribe that settled in Palestine at the same time as the Israelites. Accounts of their warfare with Israel appear in the books of Judges, 1 and 2 Samuel (David sent Uriah, husband of Bathsheba, to his death in a campaign against the Ammonites), 2 Kings, and 1 Maccabees. The prophets Jeremiah, Ezekiel, Amos, and Zepheniah uttered vengeance against the Ammonites. Their name survives in the modern city of Amman, capital of Jordan.

[T. C. O'BRIEN]

AMMONIUS, ANDREAS (1478–1517), humanist, author. Ammonius acquired literary distinction in Rome. From 1504 until his death he lived in England, a promoter of humanism, a papal representative, and a friend of Thomas More and correspondent of Erasmus. Henry VIII named him secretary of Latin letters in 1511. He wrote a volume of Latin poetry and a panegyric of Henry. BIBLIOGRAPHY: M. Monaco, NCE 1:450; C. Pizzi, *Un amico di Erasmo, l'umanista Andrea Ammonio* (1956).

[N. G. WOLF]

AMMONIUS HERMION (*c*.445–517 or 526), Neoplatonist philosopher. The son-in-law of *Syrianus, he had studied under Proclus at Athens before his appointment to a chair at Alexandria. Like the Alexandrian philosophers in general, he was primarily concerned with the assimilation of Aristotelian psychology and logic into Neoplatonism. He is esp. important as the teacher, among others, of *Ioannes Philoponus, *Simplicius, Olympiadorus, and *Damascius. BIBLIOGRAPHY: CHGMP 316–317; Ueberweg 1:643–644.

[M. R. P. MCGUIRE]

AMMONIUS SACCAS (1st half of 3d cent. A.D.), the teacher of Plotinus at Alexandria and the founder, or one of the founders, of Neoplatonism. He wrote nothing, but seems to have taught that Plato and Aristotle were in basic agreement and that the soul was immaterial. There is no solid foundation for the view widely held until recently that he was brought up a Christian and became a convert to pagan philosophy. He must have been a man of unusual intellectual depth and attractive personality, for Plotinus adopted him as his master and was his pupil for 11 years (232–243). BIBLIOGRAPHY: CHGMP 196–200.

[M. R. P. MCGUIRE]

AMNESIA, an abnormal loss of memory with regard to past experience. Its victim may be unable to recall a small portion of that experience, or it may be so extensive that one suffers a loss of his own identity. It can happen as a consequence of organic injuries or of toxic conditions, or it may be brought on by a psychoneurotic process of dissociation. In the latter case it is a defense mechanism by which one dissociates himself from the memory of painful emotional experience. The duration of a condition of amnesia may be brief, or it may be extended over a long period of time. BIBLIOGRAPHY: E. J. Ryan, NCE 1:450–451.

[J. R. RIVELLO]

AMNESTY, pardon and immunity from prosecution granted by sovereign authority, to individuals or groups that have violated the law, esp. in cases of prolonged civil disorder or insurrection. The amnesty demanded by many for draft evaders, deserters, and violent anti-war activists during the unpopular war in Vietnam has raised in the U.S. in its postwar period a practical moral problem of considerable magnitude. This problem is aggravated by various considerations favoring or contraindicating some form of general amnesty: the vast number of individuals involved, whose prosecution and punishment would require enormous trouble and expense; the inadequacy of the existing judicial and penal systems for the accomplishment of the task; the want of indisputable evidence concerning the morality of the war itself; the impossibility of establishing generally acceptable criteria for distinguishing true conscientious objectors from those whose motives were selfish or disloyal; the inequity of leaving those who served at the cost of much personal sacrifice in no better case than those who refused to serve; the impracticality of alternative means of public service proposed for conscientious objectors. The intensity of feeling accompanying the pro and con positions as these polarized during the war itself has carried over into the ensuing debate on amnesty, and until this abates it seems unlikely that any widely acceptable solution to the problem can be achieved. BIBLIOGRAPHY: *America* 128 (1973) 10a. *CONSCIENTIOUS OBJECTION.

[P. K. MEAGHER]

AMNOS (Gr. for lamb; Sl., *agnetz*), the large square portion of bread cut from the first loaf at the office of preparation before the Byzantine Divine Liturgy. It roughly coincides with the seal stamped on the loaf bearing the cross with the Greek letters $\overline{IC}$ $\overline{XC}$ $NIKA$ (Jesus Christ conquers). The amnos has come to signify "the Lamb of God, who rids the world of sin, and is sacrificed for the life and salvation of the world," and hence its name and the highly elaborate and symbolic ritual associated with its preparation. As the priest cuts the "lamb" from the loaf with five strokes of the *lance, he quotes Is 53.7–8, "Like a lamb led to the slaughter . . ."; then removing it, he places it inverted on the paten, carves a cross with the lance and then places it aright while piercing the upper left hand section (Jn 19.34–35). The "lamb" now remains on the paten surrounded by smaller particles cut from four other loaves symbolizing the Mother of God, the saints, the living, and the dead. It is consecrated during the *anaphora, and after the Lord's prayer the priest elevates it while intoning, "Holy things are for the holy!" He then breaks the "lamb" into four sections saying, "Broken and shared is the Lamb of God; though broken, he is not divided;

though ever eaten, he is never consumed: but sanctifies those who eat him." Each piece is then arranged on the paten; the part marked $\overline{IC}$ is placed at the upper edge, $\overline{XC}$ at the bottom, NI at the left, and KA at the right. The section marked $\overline{IC}$ is then placed into the chalice while the $\overline{XC}$ section is consumed by the priest and deacon. The faithful receive from the remaining two quarters of the "lamb" marked NI and KA. *POSPHORA; PROTHESIS.

[A. J. JACOPIN]

AMOLO (Amulo, Hamulus; d. 852), writer on predestination. A. succeeded (841) St. *Agobard as abp. of Lyons. He is chiefly remembered for his *Epistola ad Gothiscalcum, de gratia et praescientia Dei* (PL 116:77–104). A kindred work attributed to him (PL 116:105–184) belongs to *Florus of Lyons. A. also wrote on the veneration of relics and on relations with Jews. AS Oct. 12 (1867) 701 ff. refers to a cult. BIBLIOGRAPHY: PL 116:77–184; Fliche Martin 6:320–333; J. B. Martin, DTC 1:1126; C. Charlier, *Mélanges Podechard* (1945) 79ff.

[T. C. O'BRIEN]

AMON (or Amun, probably "Hidden One"), originally one of the eight primordial gods constituting the Ogdoad worshiped in Hermopolis; then, from the beginning of Dynasty XII in Egypt (*c*.1992 B.C.), the principal god of Thebes, and hence, Thebes having become the capital of all Egypt, the supreme god of the Egyptian pantheon. The solar theology of On (Heliopolis), with its already supreme sun god Re, was then the prevailing Egyptian theological system, and a Theban theological construction blended Amon with Re as "Amon-Re, King of the Gods." Amon's quality of hiddenness and his original nature as a wind or air god evolved in Dynasty XVIII (*c*.1567–1320 B.C.) into his quality of a life-giving breath serving as the vital principle of all living things. This, strengthened by the solar force of Re, made Amon-Re not only a national but a universal god as well. However Kurt Sethe's view of a transcendent, vital Amon as the origin of the Israelite Yahweh is received skeptically by Orientalists, who point out that germinal notions of transcendence in Egypt were not limited to Amon and that early Israelite notions of Yahweh as a storm god had little in common with sophisticated Egyptian notions of Amon. Amon is usually represented with a human head wearing a crown topped by two long, stylized feathers. He is mentioned with "No" (Thebes) in Jer 46.25 and Nah 3.8. His main sanctuary is the magnificent temple at Karnak. BIBLIOGRAPHY: K. Sethe, *Amun und die acht Urgötter von Hermopolis* (1929); H. Frankfort, *Kingship and the Gods* (1948) 160–161; H. Bonnet, *Reallexikon der ägyptischen Religionsgeschichte* (1952) 31–37.

[A. CODY]

AMORAIM, Heb. pl. of Aramaic word for speaker, explainer, specifically ancient Jewish scholars who interpreted the Tannaim (the teachers of the Mishnah and other ancient

Jewish moral and doctrinal teachings). They could not go beyond the texts in their interpretation, a limitation that led them to twist meanings to suit their own needs and purposes. There were five Palestinian and seven Babylonian generations of Amoraim, whose compilations of opinions were added to the Mishnah and bear the name Gemarah (completion), the whole process resulting in what are now called the Jerusalem Talmud and the Babylonian Talmud.

[J. F. FALLON]

AMORALISM, a system of belief that is lacking in, or indifferent to, moral responsibility; one in which the agent is freed (by choice) from the restraint of norms and criteria by which actions can be judged. Perhaps it is best described as a system wherein the ultimate norm is that there are no prescriptions against which one's actions can be judged—at least morally.

[J. R. RIVELLO]

AMORBACH, ABBEY OF, Benedictine monastery in Lower Franconia founded at the beginning of the 8th cent. by St. Pirmin. After a period of decline the abbey prospered and in the 18th cent. celebrated the millennium of its foundation. The abbey came to an end with a decree of secularization in 1803. A magnificent church, which exists today, is now in Protestant hands, and the library was sold in 1851. BIBLIOGRAPHY: J. Pietsch, DHGE 2:1324–25.

[M. C. BRADLEY]

AMORITES, a Canaanite tribe that in the Bible belong to the history of Abraham (see Gen 14.13). They are also mentioned in the books of Numbers, Joshua, and Judges. Hebrew ancestry partly derives from the Amorites (Ez 16.3). From secular records the Amorites are known to have figured in Babylonian history from the 21st century B.C.

[T. C. O'BRIEN]

AMORT, EUSEBIUS (1692–1775), moral theologian. A Bavarian Canon Regular of the Lateran, he was a copious writer on religious subjects; his best-known works are the four folios on "Theology, eclectic, moral, and scholastic" (1752), which were admired and re-edited by Benedict XIV. He took a middle way between rigorism and laxism, and anticipated the *equiprobabilism of St. Alphonsus Liguori. A. attacked the revelations of Mary of *Agreda in 1744 and became involved in a controversy on the subject. His work, though a valuable statement of the principles to be observed in the theological criticism of private revelation, was marred, so far as the Agredan revelations were concerned, by his imperfect understanding of the Spanish text. A. also made an important contribution to the controversy concerning the authorship of the *Imitation of Christ, which he held to be the work of *Thomas à Kempis. BIBLIOGRAPHY: L. Hertling, DSAM 1:530–531.

[T. GILBY]

AMOS, OT prophet. The first whose oracles were preserved in a book, A. began a new era in Hebrew prophecy. A. was not a professional prophet, but a shepherd and dresser of sycamore trees (Am 7.14). A native of Tekoah in Judah (1.1), his recorded oracles were apparently spoken at Bethel (7.10), a shrine of the northern kingdom, during the time of Jeroboam II (c.786–746 B.C.). They condemned the sins of Israel and the surrounding nations, and exalted justice above ritual (5.21–24).

[T. EARLY]

AMOS, BOOK OF. The earliest of the "writing prophets," Amos probably delivered the substance of these oracles between 760 and 750 B.C. in the northern kingdom, having been summoned by Yahweh from his normal work in the south as a herdsman and fig-dresser specially for this purpose. His outlook is intensely Judahite. It is at Zion that Yahweh dwells (1.2), and it is his will to rebuild the fallen hut of David (9.11–12). But the northern kingdom, by rebelling against the Davidic monarchy and setting up a rival shrine, has made itself in Yahweh's eyes merely one of the nations, no more favored than any other (cf. 9.7). Indeed it is worse than all the rest because Yahweh has "known" it and not the others, and so its punishment will be correspondingly greater. All its present prosperity and luxury will be swept away. Instead of the increase in prosperity the rich northerners expect there will be total destruction. The corrupt shrines and cult on which they confidently rely will be swept away together with their priests. Only a pitiful remnant of survivors will be left to flee to the southern kingdom (3.12). This, though so much poorer now, will be renewed and re-endowed with paradisal fertility (ch. 9). BIBLIOGRAPHY: A. Neher, *Amos. Contribution à l'étude du prophétisme* (1950); T. H. Sutcliffe, *Book of Amos* (2d ed., 1955); V. Maag, *Text, Wortschatz und Begriffswelt des Buches Amos* (1951); R. S. Cripps, *Critical and Exegetical Commentary on the Book of Amos* (2d ed., 1955); R. Fey, *Amos und Jesaja* (1963); A. S. Kapelrud, *Central Ideas in Amos* (1961); J. D. W. Watts, *Vision and Prophecy in Amos* (1958).

[D. BOURKE]

AMPHILOCHIUS (c.340–395), bp. **of ICONIUM** in Asia Minor. A cousin of *Gregory Nazianzus and a friend of Basil, A., after studying in Antioch, practiced law in Constantinople. He abandoned the city c.371 to lead a hermit's life, but reluctantly, at Basil's request, accepted his bishopric in 373. As metropolitan of Lycaonia he was active in the cause of orthodoxy and played an important role in the Council of Constantinople I (381). He presided over the Council of Side (390), which condemned the *Messalians, and he campaigned vigorously against puritanical and extremist cults. Only the following of his writings are extant: a synodal letter defending the divinity of the Holy Spirit; a poem known as *Iambics for Seleucus*, preserved among the works of Gregory Nazianzus (PG 37:1577–1600); parts of a Coptic version of a treatise against the Apotactites and Gemellites; and eight homilies. Works: PG 39:35–130, and *Amphilochiana* (ed. G. Ficher, 1906) v. 1. BIBLIOGRAPHY: Quasten 3:296–300.

[R. B. ENO]

AMPHION (Gr., dress, clothing), the sacred vestments of the deacon, priest, and bishop; also the cloths or vesture of the altar table.

[A. J. JACOPIN]

AMPHITHEATER (COLOSSEUM) the *Amphitheatrum Flavianum*, constructed in Rome between 72 and 80 A.D. by the emperors Vespasian and Titus for gladiatorial contests, beast fights, and mock sea battles. The name Colosseum, current since the 9th cent., derives most probably from the huge statue of Nero erected in the vicinity before 68. The elliptical marble building is four stories high where best preserved. Estimates of the amphitheater's capacity range from 50,000 to 87,000, with standing room for an additional 15,000 persons. The structure remained practically intact until the end of the 11th century, but it has since been damaged by earthquakes and by the removal of travertine for re-use. Excavations which began in 1864 have laid bare an elaborate system of underground rooms. It is popularly supposed that many martyrs perished in the Colosseum, but no authentic text exists to prove any particular martyrdom. BIBLIOGRAPHY: S. B. Platner, *Topographical Dictionary of Ancient Rome* (ed. T. Ashby, 1929).

[M. J. SUELZER]

AMPLEFORTH, ABBEY OF (St. Lawrence's), Benedictine monastery at Ampleforth, near York, England. It was founded as a priory of the English Benedictine Congregation in 1802, but claims descent from Westminster Abbey. It became an abbey in 1900 and is the largest monastic community in England. It is famous also for its boys' school which is noted for its high standards and is the largest RC boarding school in England. BIBLIOGRAPHY: *Ampleforth and Its Origins* (ed. J. McCann and C. Cary-Elwes, 1952); C. Cary-Elwes, NCE 1:456.

[J. R. SOMMERFELDT]

AMPULLAE, small, two-handled flasks of clay or glass found fastened or embedded in tomb walls of catacombs, carrying oil or perfume used to anoint the dead. Ampullae, holding oil for lamps at shrines of martyrs during the Middle Ages, carried the image or symbol of the saint from whose tomb they were taken. *Ampullae chrismatis* of clay, glass, or metal, hold oils consecrated by the bishop. Chemical analysis has disproved that the red sediment in *ampullae sanguinis* of the catacombs is the blood of martyrs. Though some ampullae probably did contain blood, such coloring is found in burials of the late 4th cent.—long after the era of persecution. Ampullae have been found in Jewish catacombs (*Via Labicana*) fastened to tombs as in Christian burials.

BIBLIOGRAPHY: H. Leclercq, DACL 1.2:1722–78; ODCC 45.

[M. J. DALY]

AMPUTATION, see MUTILATION.

AMRAPHEL, King of Shinar, one of four foreign kings said to have launched a punitive expedition against South Palestine to control the trade routes to Egypt and South Arabia (Gen 14). His identification with Hammurabi of Babylon is exceedingly doubtful.

[J. F. FALLON]

AMRI, see OMRI.

AMSDORF, NIKOLAUS VON (1483–1565), German Lutheran theologian. While a professor at Wittenberg (1511–24), A. became a close friend and disciple of Martin Luther, assisted him in translating the Bible, and later supervised the Jena edition (1555–58) of Luther's works. Luther and the elector of Saxony named A. bp. of Naumburg-Zeitz (1542–47), but the Imperialists expelled him during the Schmalkaldic War. A. urged the high Lutheran party to separate from *Melanchthon (1557) and fought ceaselessly for Luther's teachings, though in doing so he was maneuvered into the extreme position of declaring that *good works are actually detrimental to salvation, a teaching repudiated by Article IV of the *Formula of Concord (1577). BIBLIOGRAPHY: P. Brunner, *Nikolaus Von Amsdorf als Bischof von Naumburg* (1961); A. Kawerau, EncRelKnow 1:159. *SYNERGISTIC CONTROVERSY; *MAJORISTIC CONTROVERSY.

[M. J. SUELZER]

AMSTERDAM ASSEMBLY, first general assembly of the *World Council of Churches (WCC), Aug. 22–Sept. 4, 1948. It had as its theme "Man's Disorder and God's Design," and was attended by 351 delegates from 44 countries and 147 Churches, plus alternates, consultants, observers, and visitors. Membership was based on the formula, later revised: "The World Council of Churches is a fellowship of churches which accept the Lord Jesus Christ as God and Saviour." The WCC was formally constituted Aug. 23. The Assembly adopted a constitution, designated Geneva as headquarters, and elected W. A. Visser 't Hooft general secretary. The following were to serve jointly as presidents: Pastor M. Boegner (Reformed, France), Abp. G. Fisher (Anglican, England), Prof. T. C. Chao (Anglican, China), Bp. G. B. * Oxnam (Methodist, U.S.), Abp. S. Germanos (Orthodox, Greece), and Abp. E. Eidem (Lutheran, Sweden). BIBLIOGRAPHY: *Man's Disorder and God's Design* (ed. W. A. Visser 't Hooft, 5 v., 1949).

[T. EARLY]

AMULETS, objects worn for magical use to protect against all conceivable dangers or maladies. Traced to remote prehistoric times, belief is undoubtedly rooted in the primordial concept of mana. Of stone, bone, wood, metal, and even the parts of animals, these signs, symbols, figures, engraved magic formulas, and anagrams secure potency through rituals of consecration, place of origin, or fabrication. The object itself possesses magical power.

Christians assign no magical powers to their *sacramentals. Their efficacy is precisely the promotion of a religious habit of mind which influences the Christian's life through the power of Christ in his Church. Amulets of other beliefs are held to possess and exercise power regardless of awareness in the one carrying or using them. Mere contact with the object causes operation of its powers. BIBLIOGRAPHY: H. Leclercq, DACL 1.2:1784–1860; A. Closs and M. Hain, LTK 1:462–464; T. A. Brady, NCE 1:457–458.

[M. J. DALY]

AMUN, ST. (also Ammon; d. c.350), an Egyptian monk, reputed founder of monasticism in the Nitrian desert (Wâdi el Natrûn). He is said to have left his wife to become a hermit. Disciples gathered around him, and on the advice of his friend St. *Anthony he organized them into a loose confederation. BIBLIOGRAPHY: AS Oct. 2:413–422; Butler 4:32–33.

[D. W. JOHNSON]

AMUSEMENTS, see RECREATION.

AMYOT, JACQUES (1513–93), French humanist and bishop. Professor of Latin and Greek at Bourges, A. received from Francis I the Premonstratensian abbey of Bellozane-en-Bray (1547), probably as an encouragement to translate Plutarch's *Lives*. He traveled to Italy to study texts in Venice (1548–50) and at the Vatican (1550–51), and undertook a diplomatic mission to the Council of Trent. Back in France, he was made tutor to Henry II's sons, was appointed grand almoner of France by Charles IX (1560), and was named by Henry III almoner of the Order of the Holy Spirit (1578). Made bp. of Auxerre (1570), he spent his last years under constant attack by the Holy League, particularly for his participation in the Estates of Blois (1589). Besides his translation of Plutarch's *Lives*, a model of style, which was translated into English by Sir Thomas North (1579) and used by Shakespeare, A. translated Plutarch's *Oeuvres morales* (1572), Heliodorus's *Histoire éthiopique* (1547), seven books of history by Diodorus Siculus (1554), and Longus's *Daphnis et Chloé* (1559). His translations of Plutarch, esp., greatly influenced French literature and ethical thought. Among his original works, now lost, were several important sermons. BIBLIOGRAPHY: A. Cioranescu, *Vie de Jacques Amyot d'après des documents inédits* (1941); Bremond, *Index* (repr. 1971) 7.

[R. N. NICOLICH]

AMYOT, JOSEPH MARIE, see AMIOT, JEAN JOSEPH MARIE.

AMYRAUT, MOÏSE (1596–1684), French Calvinist theologian, proponent of a theory on *predestination called after him Amyraldism. From 1633 he was a professor at the theological academy in Saumur and was a respected representative of the Reformed Church in France. In an era of sharp conflict A.'s works were notably pacific and moderate. BIBLIOGRAPHY: R. Stauffer, *Moïse Amyraut: Un Précurseur français de l'oecuménisme* (1962).

[T. C. O'BRIEN]

ANABAPTISTS (rebaptizers; Gr. *ana*, again), diverse Reformation groups named from the practice of repeating baptism. The more essential, subjectivist content of the Anabaptist religious message was similar to teachings of such medieval groups as the *Beghards, *Brothers and Sisters of the Free Spirit, *Waldenses, and *Taborites, but no historical connection has been proved. The Anabaptists were inspired by the extreme interpretations of Reformation doctrine developed in Germany and in Switzerland. In both places religious ideas became intermingled with sociopolitical currents, and Anabaptists became the object of ferocious persecution by civil and ecclesiastical authority, both Protestant and Catholic, and were slaughtered by the thousands. The Anabaptists of German origin were revolutionaries, prominent among them the *Zwickau Prophets, N. *Storch, and T. *Münzer. The *apocalypticism of Münzer was brought to Holland by M. *Hofmann; persecution there led to the flight of *John of Leiden, and Jan *Matthys and to the establishment of the theocratic kingdom of Münster. This episode of religious and moral extravagance, ending in bloodshed, put an end to the revolutionary side of the Anabaptist movement (1555).

In Switzerland leaders of the *Swiss Brethren (see GREBEL, C.; BLAUROCK, G.; HUBMAIER, B.; MANZ, F.), breaking with H. *Zwingli c.1520, stressed more the Anabaptist religious vision and practiced nonviolent resistance toward secular authority. The central religious message of such Anabaptists was that saving faith is essentially a freely accepted inner experience of Christ and that the rule of faith is no external authority, not even the Bible, but the inspiration of the Holy Spirit given to the individual believer. One consequence was that baptism is meaningful only as the adult's outward profession of personal faith. (see BELIEVER'S BAPTISM; INFANT BAPTISM.) Another was the social equality of all believers and their freedom from any subjection to, or involvement with, civil authority.

The Anabaptist religious message was taken up by *Menno Simons, and J. *Huter and continues among *Mennonites and *Hutterian Brethren. Emphasis on inner experience influenced H. *Niclaes (see FAMILISTS), S. *Franck, and C. *Schwenkfeld. Further, the religious ideals of the Anabaptists affected subsequent religious history in Holland and England and so in the U.S. This influence included rejection of rigid Calvinism (see ARMINIANISM; EPISCOPIUS, S.), and opposition to an *established Church, stress on inner religious experience, human brotherhood and equality, nonviolence and pacifism. Such ideas helped form the religious milieu in which the Religious Society of Friends and the Baptists came into being. BIBLIOGRAPHY: R. S. Armour, *Anabaptist Baptism* (1966); H. S. Bender, *Anabaptist Vision* (pa. 1955); F. Blanke, *Brothers in Christ* (tr. J. Nordenhang, pa. 1961); G. W. Forell, NCE 1:459–460; *Bibliography of Anabaptism 1520–1630* (ed. H. J. Hillerbrand, 1962); MennEnc 1:113–116, 532–534; and the series of Anabaptist sources published by Herald Press, Mennonite Publishing House, Scottsdale, Pennsylvania.

[T. C. O'BRIEN]

ANABATHMOI (Gr. for a flight of steps), a liturgical term that may signify: (1) the gradual psalms (Ps 119–133) sung successively by Jewish pilgrims as they mounted the steps of the Temple of Jerusalem; or (2) in Greek liturgical books, a series of troparia occurring in the office of Orthros. There are eight series of this type, and each is sung according to one of the eight modes of liturgical music. They are probably termed anabathmoi since they are similar to the Jewish gradual psalms, being steps in a series, although they may have received their name simply because they "elevate" the soul.

[A. J. JACOPIN]

ANACLETUS, ST., see CLETUS, ST.

ANACLETUS II, ANTIPOPE (Pietro Pierleoni; d. 1138), Benedictine cardinal deacon who was chosen as pope by a group of cardinals after the death of Honorius II and crowned on the same day as Innocent II, the choice of the electoral commission named before the death of Honorius. A. had the support of Roger of Sicily, the people of Rome, and a majority of the college of cardinals, and a strong case could be made for the legitimacy of his claim. But his position was challenged by the Christian powers of France and Germany under the influence of SS. Norbert and Bernard. He held Castel Sant' Angelo and compelled Innocent II to withdraw from Rome to Pisa after the departure of his protector, the Emperor Lothair (1131). The 8-year schism ended with A.'s death (1138) when the Roman people, moved by the persuasive arguments of St. Bernard, accepted Innocent II as pope and rejected Roger of Sicily's antipope Victor IV. BIBLIOGRAPHY: Hughes HC 2:293–295; J. Loughlin, CE 1:447.

[F. H. BRIGHAM]

ANADOCHOS (Gr. for security), in the Byzantine Church the sponsor at the sacrament of baptism who presents the child at the font and guarantees that he will receive a religious education. One sponsor suffices although often two are used.

[A. J. JACOPIN]

ANAGNOSIS (Gr. for the act of reading), in the Byzantine liturgy the act of reading at a liturgical office.

[A. J. JACOPIN]

ANAGNOSMA (Gr. for that which one reads), in the Byzantine liturgy a passage extracted from Holy Scripture, the writings of the Fathers, or the lives of the saints which is read during a liturgical office.

[A. J. JACOPIN]

ANAGNOSTES (Gr. for reader; Sl., *tchetz, lektor*) in the Byzantine Church the order of reader, the first of the minor orders. Tonsure, although given at the same ceremony, is not an order but a prerequisite to the order of anagnostes. The bishop confers the order outside the sanctuary before the beginning of the Divine Liturgy. The chief function of the anagnostes is to read the apostol (Epistle) and any other lessons that might occur in the Liturgy except the Gospel, which is reserved to a priest or deacon. The term acolyte is also sometimes applied to this office, since the anagnostes assists by bearing the candle in processions, placing incense on the lighted coals, and by bearing the cross or *ripidia*. The vestment proper to this order is the long tunic or *sticharion*. As in Western parish churches, the office of anagnostes is often not carried out by one in orders but by laymen or boys.

[A. J. JACOPIN]

ANAGOGIC SENSE OF SCRIPTURE, one of the spiritual senses of Scripture, as the realities contained in Scripture are seen to foreshadow the future consummation of all things in heaven. For example, the Promised Land in the OT is a type of the new world which, according to Hebrews, Christ has already entered and where the blessed will follow him. The anagogic sense was one of the spiritual senses stressed in medieval exegesis. *SENSES OF SCRIPTURE.

[T. C. O'BRIEN]

ANAKIM (Enacim), Canaanite tribe living in Palestine prior to the coming of the Israelites under Joshua (Jos 11.21–22). The term means people of the neck, and they were feared for their height (Dt 2.21; 9.2). They were called descendants of the Nephilim (Num 13.28–33; Gen 6.4). Arba was said to be the father of Anak (Jos 15.13) and the greatest man among the Anakim (Jos 14.15). But the name may be a shortening of Kiriath-arba, an earlier name for Hebron, where the Anakim were concentrated.

[T. EARLY]

ANAKOMIDĒ (Gr. for the act of returning), the ceremony in the Byzantine Church of the translation of the bodies or relics of the saints from one place to another.

[A. J. JACOPIN]

ANALABOS (Gr. for put on top of; Sl., *analov*), the scapular-like part of the Eastern monastic *angelic habit. It is composed of two rectangular pieces of brown or black wool joined at the shoulders and falling down front and back. Because it symbolizes the cross and the penance of the yoke of Christ, it is usually ornamented with crosses, the skull of Adam, and the instruments of the passion. BIBLIOGRAPHY:

N. F. Robinson, *Monasticism in the Orthodox Churches* (1971) 42–44.

[A. J. JACOPIN]

ANALECTA BOLLANDIANA, the annual publication of the *Bollandists.

[F. H. BRIGHAM]

ANALEPSIS (Gr. for taking up; Sl., *voznesenia*), the Eastern feast of the Ascension recalling the day on which the Savior left the earth and ascended into heaven. It is celebrated on the 40th day after Easter, i.e., the Thursday of the 6th week after Easter.

[A. J. JACOPIN]

ANALGESIA, see PAIN.

ANALOGION (Gr. for lectern; Sl., *analoy*), in the Eastern liturgies a high lectern-like stand upon which the gospel book is placed as it is solemnly read during the Divine Liturgy. Analogia are also used as stands for the service books of the chanters and for icons offered for the veneration of the faithful. In Russian usage a small analogion stands at the left of the altar table to hold the liturgical books. Analogia are usually draped with silk or brocade. An elaborate form of the analogion is sometimes used by the chanters, consisting of a foursided, revolving desk mounted on a base that serves as a storage cabinet for the service books.

[A. J. JACOPIN]

ANALOGY, among its many different meanings, has three that are most important: a form of reasoning, i.e., reasoning by analogy, also called argument from convenience; a mode of explanation (the parable); and a mode of predication, i.e., analogous predication. The present article is concerned with analogy as a form of predication and with its use in theology.

Aristotle, who has been called the father of analogy, was the first to deal systematically with analogy as a form of predication. He taught that all the basic metaphysical and ethical concepts, such as being, substance, cause, and good are predicated neither univocally nor equivocally but according to a certain analogy *(kat' analogian)*. However, he did not go so far as to elaborate a systematic theory of theological language. Philo and Clement of Alexandria were the first to do this. But in their theories about the value of theological language they put greater stress upon the negative than upon the positive value of man's theological concepts. Thus they laid the foundations of negative theology, the theology that was due to find so many supporters among the Greek Fathers. The doctrine of analogy received its final shape from St. Thomas Aquinas. He distinguished three kinds of predicative analogy. There is (1) attributive analogy, e.g., when "healthy" is predicated of Peter, medicine, food, climate, color, etc. In attributive analogy a quality is predicated properly and intrinsically of the first analogate, and it is predicated of the other analogates because of the relation that they have to the first analogate. There is also (2) metaphorical analogy, e.g., when "to smile" is predicated of Peter and of the meadow. In metaphorical analogy a quality is predicated properly only of the first analogate; of the others it is predicated only because of some similarity between their situations and the situation of the first analogate. There is also (3) proportional analogy, e.g., when substance, nature, being, cause are predicated of man, animals, trees, stones, etc. In proportional analogy a perfection is predicated properly and intrinsically of each analogate. According to St. Thomas all three kinds of analogy may be used in theology. Metaphorical analogy helps one to talk about God's dynamic perfections. Proportional analogy enables one to talk about God's entitative perfections, i.e., about God's nature as it is in itself. Attributive analogy allows one to talk about both his dynamic and entitative perfections (ThAq CG 1.30–34; ThAq ST 1, 13).

On the correct interpretation of Aquinas's doctrine of analogy his disciples have never been able to reach an agreement. Whereas in the past Cajetan's interpretation, according to which Aquinas gives preference to proportional analogy, received more support, today many Thomists believe that his preference goes to attributive analogy. But, apart from this hermeneutical problem, all Catholic theologians agree that analogy is the only doctrine capable of safeguarding both God's transcendence and immanence, and, therefore, that it is the only adequate interpretation of theological language. They start from the fact that man applies his concepts to God. One says, e.g., that God is good, omnipotent, intelligent, father, spirit. What do these concepts mean when applied to God? If one asserts that the meaning is altogether the same as when they are applied to creaturely realities, he falls into anthropomorphism. If he asserts that the meaning is entirely different, he falls into agnosticism. To avoid these two pitfalls it is necessary to say that the meaning is partly the same and partly different, i.e., it is analogous: it is the same with regard to content (the *res praedicata*); it is different with regard to the mode (the *modus praedicandi*).

No systematic historical study of the teaching of Protestant theologians on the subject of analogy has yet been made, with the exception of a sketchy outline drawn by B. Mondin in his book *Principle of Analogy in Protestant and Catholic Theology* (2d ed., 1967). Three periods can be distinguished in Protestant thought on the subject: (1) the period of the Reformers and orthodoxy, during which Protestant theologians were still attached to Catholic tradition and kept considering analogy as the only proper way of talking about God; (2) the period of Hegelian and Kierkegaardian theology, during which analogy was replaced by dialectics; and (3) the period of the modern theologians—K. Barth, P. Tillich, and R. Bultmann—during which a notable revival of interest in analogy has taken place. These theologians recognize that analogy is the only proper way of talking about God but do not agree about its nature: Tillich conceives it as symbolic; Barth, as an analogy of faith *(analogia fidei)*;

Bultmann, as an existential analogy. Both classical and modern Protestant theologians have tried to elaborate a theory of analogy coherent with their doctrine of the relationship between nature and grace, which are conceived as two opposites that can never be reconciled. Sin has caused a corruption of human nature that cannot be healed; it has raised between God and man an infinite qualitative difference that will last forever. This principle of the infinite qualitative difference is reflected in the Protestant theories of theological language: in the theory of analogy of extrinsic attribution of Luther and Calvin, in the Hegelian theory of dialectics, in Tillich's theory of symbolic analogy, in Barth's theory of analogy of faith, and in Bultmann's theory of existential analogy. While in the Catholic theory of analogy it is legitimate to use human concepts and human language, when one talks about God, because of a permanent similarity between God's being and man's being (since man is *imago Dei*), according to the Protestant theories of analogy any such use is illegitimate, because after the Fall there is no longer an analogy between God and man, man no longer being *imago Dei*. Therefore man's words are such that they can never, of themselves, be properly predicated of God. They can express divine reality either by a purely extrinsic attribution, or dialectically, or symbolically, or mythically, or by a divine choice. The radical theologians (or death-of-God theologians) have repudiated the doctrine of analogy most emphatically, since it contradicts their rejection of theology. BIBLIOGRAPHY: J. F. Anderson, *Reflections on the Analogy of Being* (1967); G. P. Klubertanz, *St. Thomas Aquinas on Analogy* (1960); E. L. Mascall, *Existence and Analogy* (1949).

[B. MONDIN]

ANALOGY OF BEING, in general a semantic procedure in Catholic theology whereby the meaning of words applied to God is determined. The terminology "analogy of being" *(analogia entis)* is not very old: it goes back to the 1930s, when K. Barth in building his theological system abandoned the method of dialectics in favor of the method of analogy. While doing this, he made it clear that his theory of analogy was different from the Catholic one, which he considered to be "an invention of the antichrist." To keep them distinct he called the Catholic doctrine *analogia entis* (analogy of being), and his own *analogia fidei* (analogy of faith).

In Catholic theology, words applied to God are taken from ordinary language, i.e., the language used to describe natural beings *(entia)*, e.g., good, faithful, strong, father, spirit. But, before applying them to God, one must subject them to close scrutiny, which is made up of several steps. (1) It must be determined whether the term in question indicates an imperfection or a perfection; in the first case it has to be rejected. (2) It must be determined whether the name indicates a simple or a mixed perfection. Simple perfections are those qualities that can exist without matter (e.g., goodness, wisdom, grace); mixed perfections are those that exist only in matter (e.g., sensation, passion). Names of mixed perfections cannot be applied to God except by way of metaphor. Finally, (3) in the case of terms indicating simple perfec-

tions, the substance of the idea indicated by the term *(res praedicata)* must be distinguished from the manner in which it is predicated *(modus praedicandi)*. Only the former can be predicated of God, and the more properly, the more it is magnified. Catholic theologians believe that this procedure is legitimate for two reasons. (1) Creatures are created by God and consequently resemble him; therefore one may know God through them. (2) All man's concepts come from below, from creatures. Therefore he must start from these if he is to know God. Barth's charges against analogy of being started fruitful discussion between Catholic and Protestant theologians. Catholic theologians have reached the conclusion that in their work they need both the *analogia entis* and *analogia fidei;* the former operates within the latter and is corrected and improved by it. BIBLIOGRAPHY: E. Przywara, *Analogia entis* (1932); J. F. Anderson, *Reflections on the Analogy of Being* (1967); B. Mondin, *Principle of Analogy in Protestant and Catholic Theology* (2d ed., 1967); J. Splett and L. B. Puntel, SacMund 1:21–25.

[B. MONDIN]

ANALOGY OF FAITH, an expression that goes back to St. Paul, who in Rom 12.6 warns Christians who are endowed with the charism of prophecy to use it according to their degree of faith (Gr.: *kata tēn analogian tēs pisteōs;* Vulg: *secundum rationem fidei*). The analogy of which the Apostle is speaking is to be understood charismatically rather than theologically. In RC theology the expression analogy of faith is generally used to signify a theological norm; in this sense it is another name for *regula fidei*, rule of faith. This rule, or the supreme norm of theological investigation, is the Catholic truth as it is taught and interpreted by the official authority of the Church. The expression is also used to designate methods of theological investigation: (1) biblical—a scriptural text is interpreted in the light of other scriptural texts and of the teaching of the Church; (2) dogmatic—dogmas are compared with other dogmas in order to discover their mutual relationships and to clarify them. These methods are legitimate because scriptural texts have one and the same author, God; consequently they cannot contradict each other. The Church, moreover, has been established by Christ as the supreme and infallible teacher of all revealed truth; hence any interpretation that contradicts the teaching of the Church is to be rejected as incorrect and false (see Leo XIII, *Providentissimus Deus;* D 3283).

According to the teaching of the Catholic Church (Vatican Council I; D 3016) theology, in seeking to understand and explain the Word of God, is to make use not only of analogy of faith but also of being *(analogia entis):* "If reason enlightened by faith searches prudently, piously, and conscientiously, it will reach with God's help a fruitful insight into the mysteries, both through the analogy of the things that it naturally knows *(ex eorum, quae naturaliter cognoscit, analogia)* and through the relationships of the mysteries among themselves and with the final end of man *(e mysteriorum ipsorum nexu inter se et cum fine hominis ultimo)*."

Against this theology based on two kinds of analogy (of being and of faith) K. Barth leveled strong objections. In the use of analogy of being he saw a trait so characteristic of Catholic theology that he accused of Catholicism and Thomism all those who accepted some sort of analogy of being, esp. E. Brunner, because of his doctrine on the *Anknüpfungspunkt* (point of contact). According to Barth the doctrine of a twofold analogy is untenable, because there is no analogy of being. *Analogia entis* is impossible for two reasons: (1) it eliminates the infinite qualitative difference between God and man by bringing man and God under the same category of being, namely, an idea, a genus in which God and man are comprehended together; (2) it turns the divine-human relationship upside down and, instead of starting with God in order to descend to man, it starts with man in order to ascend to God. Against the teaching of the Catholic Church, according to which man's nature and reason remain substantially incorrupted even after the Fall and preserve the possibility of acquiring a truthful knowledge of God, Barth, interpreting Calvin and Luther, asserts that the Fall caused a substantial corruption in human nature and reason. These of themselves can no longer acquire any truthful knowledge of God but only by means of his grace. Man's concepts are suitable for predication of God, not because they are imposed on God by man but because they are chosen by God. "To the question how we come to know God by means of our thinking and language, we must give the answer that of ourselves we do not come to know him, that on the contrary this happens only as the grace of the revelation of God comes to us and therefore to the means of our thinking and language, adopting us and them, pardoning, saving and protecting, and making good. We are permitted to make use, and a successful use at that, of the means given to us. We do not create this success. Nor do our means create it. But the grace of God's revelation creates it" (*Church Dogmatics* 2.1:223). By God's grace alone, then, human language can be used to speak about God.

What then can human language say of God. According to Barth human language can express God only in a veiled, hidden way. And the reason for this is obvious. Since man remains always man even with revelation, he will never be able fully to understand God's word or to grasp the entire meaning of his own word when attributed to God. Human language when employed by God or for God is, therefore, always something hidden, veiled, and ambiguous to man's understanding. God's word is and always remains God's word, unbound, unattachable to this thesis or to that antithesis. A sketch of the concept as the philosopher would like it has not arisen and cannot arise. God alone conceives himself, even in his Word. Man's concept of him and his Word can only point to the limits of his conceiving (*Church Dogmatics* 1.1:186–187).

The lively discussion that ensued upon Barth's charges against the analogy of being was fruitful for both Catholic theologians and for Barth himself. Catholic theologians have come to see that *analogia entis* and *analogia fidei* cannot be conceived as two floors of the same house, the former as the lower and the latter as the upper floor. They are not two separate floors nor is there any continuity between them. Consequently, it is not possible to ascend from *analogia entis* to *analogia fidei*. The theologian does not start from the analogy of being and then proceed to the analogy of faith. It is the other way around. He starts from faith and moves toward reason; he tries to clarify faith by means of reason: *fides quaerit intellectum*. Barth also has received some profit from the discussion. He has abandoned his drastic opposition to analogy of being and his exclusivist support of analogy of faith. He has seen that the theologian can understand and clarify the word of God only by means of reason. Reason, however, according to the author of *Church Dogmatics*, does not achieve its understanding of revelation through *analogia entis* but through *analogia relationis*. For instance the statement, "Man is an image of God," does not mean that there is some resemblance between man's and God's natures, but that "as the addressing I in the divine nature is related to the addressed divine Thou, so also in human existence the I is related to the Thou" (*Church Dogmatics* 3.1:320). BIBLIOGRAPHY: S. A. Matczak, *Karl Barth on God* (1962); B. Mondin, *Principle of Analogy in Protestant and Catholic Theology* (2d ed., 1967); H. G. Poehlmann, *Analogia entis oder analogia fidei?* (1965); L. Scheffczyk, SacMund 1:25–27.

[B. MONDIN]

ANALYTICAL PSYCHOLOGY, the theoretical and therapeutic system of depth psychology originated and developed by C. G. Jung, an early disciple of *Freud. For Jung, the goal and major problem of human life is the discovery of self, i.e., the development and integration of all of the dimensions of the human psyche around and into that authentic center of the psyche which he termed the self. Man's mind has a conscious ego and unconscious spheres; the creation of the self involves the emergence from the unconscious into the conscious of the great symbolic forms, principally the *archetypes, which contain meaning for the person and which, when interpreted and consciously assimilated, constitute his personal significance. Every one has a personal unconscious containing repressed and unassimilated materials from his individual history, which must eventually be brought into consciousness; but this is not as important as his *collective unconscious, which he shares as a heritage with the whole human race and which contains the archetypes that symbolically represent the great issues in life he must confront to fulfill himself as human. This collective unconscious is the most powerful and influential system in the psyche; the archetypes it contains are the deposit of human racial experiences over countless generations in the form of predispositions to think about and respond to the major themes of life in definite patterns. In addition the psyche contains the shadow, an archetype which comprises the animal instincts man possesses as derivatives of his evolutionary past. There is also the persona or mask, which is the social front the individual presents to the group in response to its demands. Moreover, the individual possesses animus and anima, the male and female sides of personality, which are archetypes or products of the racial experiences of man with woman and woman with man. A man's feminine side is his anima, a woman's masculine side is her animus; in virtue of these archetypes men and women apprehend and respond to each other. The final establishment of the self involves, therefore, the conscious assimilation and integration of sexual and social relations, of instinctual drives and personal experiences, under the aegis of the great themes of life as represented in the archetypes. This achievement of self is not usually accomplished until middle age. If in the course of maturing, any particular dimension of the psyche is prevented from being developed, i.e., remains unconscious and unassimilated, a tension is generated that leads to neurosis. For Jung, neuroses are not the resultants of undischarged instinctual energies but the strivings of unfulfilled potentials; his psychology has a definite teleological cast. Besides psychic systems and a theory of neurosis, analytical psychology proposes a typology. The two basic types are extraverts and introverts; the former is characterized by an attitude oriented toward objective reality; the latter, toward the inner, subjective world. These types are subdivided according to tendencies toward one or another of the four basic functions. Thinking is the intellectual function; feeling, the value-making function; sensing, the reality-oriented function; and intuiting, the mystical function. Given the several systems and prevailing attitudes and functions in a personality, there will be complex interactions. Systems, attitudes, and functions may compensate when the weakness of one is balanced off by strength in another, or they may oppose and compete with one another, or they may fuse into a synthesis. There is constant conflict and resolution of conflict, and out of this the personality is formed.

Although Jung's analytical psychology has been criticized severely for postulating the collective or racial unconscious, which depends on the as yet unproven hypothesis of the inheritance of acquired characteristics and for the archetypes which are possibly explainable simply in terms of personal experience, it has had value in treating neuroses, esp. those of middle age, when the crisis of the meaning of life may become acute. Jung has also gathered great quantities of material to illustrate his ideas, from sources as disparate as clinical experience and experimental research, myths and fairy tales, religions, alchemy and astrology, anthropology, and the arts. Nevertheless, his system has not been as widely studied nor as influential as that of Freud, which is considered the major depth psychology. It has attracted some followers because it gives religion a place in the human psyche as an authentic dimension, unlike Freud's system, which makes religion a universal neurosis; but even in this respect many claim that Freud's contribution is more valuable in explaining aberrations of religious behavior. Jung's major contributions to scientific psychology are the concepts of introversion and extraversion, and the word-association tests he devised to explore unconscious complexes. BIBLIOG-RAPHY: V. White, *Soul and Psyche* (1960); G. D. Wilson, *Encyclopedia of Psychology* (1972) 1:52–53.

[M. E. STOCK]

ANAMNESIS, a term referring to the commemoration of the Passion, Resurrection, and Ascension of Christ. In the older Roman liturgy, it referred to the prayer following the consecration called *Unde et memores*. This prayer is an essential part of the entire Eucharistic Prayer (anaphora, Canon). Not all ancient liturgies included a mention of Christ's Passion, Resurrection, and Ascension. The Gallican included only the Passion; Hippolytus mentioned the Resurrection; and Ambrose in his *De sacramentis* mentioned the Ascension. The Eucharistic Prayers in present use all contain mention of the Passion and Resurrection, and all, with the exception of Eucharistic Prayer II, include mention of the Ascension as well. There are various translations of the word *anamnesis:* recall, memory, remembrance, commemoration. Yet all of these are in some degree misleading. They emphasize the subjective element, while the word itself has both an objective and a subjective significance. It has the meaning not merely of remembering something absent, but of recalling and representing before God an event of the past so that it becomes present and operative. BIBLIOGRAPHY: N. A. Dahl, "Anamnesis mémoire et commémoration dans le Christianisme primitif," *Studia Theologica* (1948) 69–95; J. A. Jungmann, *Eucharistic Prayer: a Study of the Canon Missae* (tr. R. L. Batley, 1956) 1–14; A. Schlitzer, "Protestant Ecumenical on the Eucharist," YBLS (1962) 119–135.

[N. KOLLAR]

ANAMPHIASIS, the Eastern Orthodox term for stripping the altar prior to the liturgical washing of Holy Thursday.

ANANIAS, a Hebrew name meaning "Yahweh is gracious." In the OT it occurs as the name of a relative of Tobias (Tob 5.12), and an ancestor of Judith (Jdt 8.1). Several persons of importance in the NT bore this name. (1) A Judaeo-Christian in the early years of the Church in Jerusalem, who with his wife, Sapphira, attempted to deceive the Christian community in Jerusalem into believing that, out of faith in the proximity of the Lord's parousia, they had turned over to the community for the care of the poor the entire proceeds of their sale of personal property. They were punished with death for their duplicity (Acts 5.1–11). (2) A Judaeo-Christian of Damascus, who baptized St. Paul after his experience of seeing the risen Jesus (Acts 9.10–17; 22.12–16). (3) A Jewish high priest before whom St. Paul was arraigned in Jerusalem (Acts 23.2–5). He was also among Paul's accusers at a hearing before the Roman governor, Felix (Acts 24.1). According to Josephus, this A. was murdered by the Jewish populace because of his collaboration with the Romans.

[C. P. CEROKE]

ANAPAUSIMOS (Gr. for relating to repose, at death), in the Byzantine liturgy a special Canon in which mercy and a place of peace and repose in the celestial kingdom are asked of the Lord for the faithful departed.

[A. J. JACOPIN]

ANAPHORA (Gr. for offering), liturgical term in the Eastern liturgies referring to that part of the liturgy which extends from the dialogue of the Preface to the great doxology. As a prayer form it is similar to the Western Canon. Here Canon and anaphora will be used interchangeably. The anaphora is a development of the Jewish cult blessing known as the berakah. The basic structure of the berakah consisted of the following: an exclamation of praise and thanks of God, a recall of the deeds of God which are the source of this praise-thanksgiving, and a concluding doxology. This form of prayer with its corresponding theology was adopted and adapted by the Christians in the form known as the anaphora. It was directed to the Father as a proclamation of praise-thanksgiving. Every anaphora contains the following elements: (1) an introductory dialogue between the president of the assembly and the people; (2) a narrative recalling the wondrous deeds of God, the sending of his Son who took flesh, suffered, died, rose, ascended, and gave us his own body and blood; (3) an *anamnesis and oblation; (4) an *epiclesis; (5) a *doxology. Some would also include the "intercessions" as an essential part of the present anaphora structure. The effect of this anaphora prayer is twofold: (1) it joyfully thanks the Father for his wondrous deeds; (2) it results in the consecration of the gifts of bread and wine into the body of Christ, and the deepening of the community's being in that same body.

There are many anaphoras in the Churches. Prior to recent changes the Latin rite since the 12th cent., has had only one which is the Roman Canon, whereas the Eastern Church liturgies always used various anaphoras. The Eastern liturgies are characterized by their fixed anaphoras and the position of the included intercessory prayers and epiclesis. The intercessory prayers for the living and dead are at the end of the Antiochene liturgies, while these prayers come immediately before the Sanctus in the Egyptian liturgies. The epiclesis is found after the words of institution and the anamnesis in the Syrian liturgies, whereas it is divided in the Egyptian liturgies: one part before the words of institution, and another after the anamnesis. The development of these various anaphoras was a process of centuries, going from a stage of diversity (1st to 4th cent.) to one of relative uniformity (12th century). BIBLIOGRAPHY: M. Collins, "Eucharistic Proclamation of God's Presence," *Worship* 41 (1967) 531–541; G. Every, *Basic Liturgy: A Study in Structure of Eucharistic Prayer* (1961); W. Frere, *Anaphora* (1938); R. Ledogar, "Eucharistic Prayer and the Gifts over Which It Is Spoken," *Worship* 41 (1967) 578–596. *CANON.

[N. KOLLAR]

ANARCHISM, the theory that the state should be abolished and human society ordered by agreements freely made without coercion. The term is from the Gr. *anarchos,* rulerless. It usually is opposed to private property, but differs from socialism in that it considers the state intrinsically evil. It holds that man is good by nature but corrupted by government, which is an agency of exploitation and oppression.

Zeno of Citium (*c*.320–*c*.250 B.C.), the founder of Stoic philosophy, is generally considered the father of anarchism. In modern times it has been developed as a political program by such thinkers as W. Godwin (1756–1836) and P. J. Proudhon (1809–65), who was the first to use the term. M. Bakunin (1814–76) was expelled from the First International by Marx in 1872 because of his advocacy of anarchism. Through Bakunin's influence anarchism is generally associated with violent rebellion against the State, though P. Kropotkin (1842–1921) and L. Tolstoy (1828–1910) developed more peaceful theories of anarchism. Anarchism was suppressed in Russia by the Bolsheviks.

Anarchism was advocated in the U.S. by J. Warren (1798–1874) and others, and was associated with the formation of cooperatives and utopian communities. Following the 1886 Haymarket riot in Chicago and the 1901 assassination of President McKinley, however, a law was passed excluding anarchists from the U.S. BIBLIOGRAPHY: R. E. Westmeyer, *Modern Economic and Social Systems* (1940); A. Carter, *Political Theory of Anarchism* (1972); J. Folliet, *Man in His Environment* (tr. M. Murphy, 1963) 77–78.

[T. EARLY]

ANARCHY, from Greek, *an,* privative, and *archos,* leader, chief; the lack of government, the lawlessness or disorder due to failure of supreme power, and, by transference, the nonrecognition or rejection of authority in any sphere. The term is usually applied to social life in Church and State. Antinomian theories and practices play a turbid and not ignoble part in Christian history, and though their extremes are way out of the authentic tradition, an appreciation of their ideals should qualify a reading of Church teaching on the obligation of moral and positive laws. BIBLIOGRAPHY: Knox Enth, *passim.*

[P. F. MULHERN]

ANARGYROS (Gr. for one who receives no money; Sl., *bezsredrenneke*) A title given to certain saints who worked without accepting money or payment for their labors. The doctor-saints Cosmas and Damian are of this type and in the East represent the whole grouping.

[A. J. JACOPIN]

ANASTASIA, SS., the name of several early martyrs and saints. (1)A martyr (fl. 250?) probably during the persecution of Diocletian at Sirmium, Pannonia (Yugoslavia), where her cult originated. Her relics were transferred to a church with her name at Constantinople in the 5th century. The mention of A. in the Canon of the Mass and in the second Mass of Christmas indicate a cult at Rome. (2) A woman (fl. 60–70?) who, according to legend, buried the bodies of SS. Peter and Paul together with a Basilissa and who was later martyred during the persecution of Nero. (3) Since the 6th cent. a person of uncertain identity whose name has been used in the title of a Roman basilica erected by Pope Damasus in 4th century. No conclusive evidence connects this A. with the cult of either of the above. BIBLIOGRAPHY: Butler 2:98; 4:613–614; M. Brandi, BiblSanct 1:1040–46.

[H. JACK]

ANASTASIMON (Gr. for pertaining to the Resurrection), in the Byzantine liturgy a *troparion in which the Resurrection of the Lord is celebrated.

[A. J. JACOPIN]

ANASTASIMOS (Gr. for pertaining to the Resurrection), in the Byzantine liturgy a special *anaphora in which the Resurrection of the Lord is celebrated.

[A. J. JACOPIN]

ANASTASIS, THE (Gr. for resurrection), a term that may signify either (1) the Resurrection of Christ from the dead and with him that of all mankind; or (2) the great Church of the Holy Sepulcher in Jerusalem, commonly referred to as the Church of the Resurrection of the Lord. Another famous church of the Resurrection was found in Constantinople, and perhaps the Church of St. Anastasia in Rome was originally dedicated to the Resurrection.

[A. J. JACOPIN]

ANASTASIUS I, ST. (d. 401), **POPE** from 399. With A.'s election to the papacy, *Jerome, who had been thwarted during the pontificate of *Siricius in his efforts to secure the condemnation of *Rufinus and *Origenism, renewed the campaign, with the help of several influential friends. Though A. did not condemn Rufinus personally, he did condemn a number of Origen's doctrines, and thus earned the praise of Jerome and *Paulinus of Nola for his blameless life and apostolic solicitude. A. also wrote to Africa encouraging the bishops there to vigilance against Donatism. BIBLIOGRAPHY: P. T. Camelot, NCE 1:478–479; T. J. Campbell, CE 1:454; Butler 4:584.

[P. F. MULHERN]

ANASTASIUS II (d.498), **POPE** from 496. The central issue of A.'s pontificate was the restoration of normal relations with the Eastern Church after the *Acacian schism. A. sent legates to Constantinople exhorting Emperor Anastasius I to support church unity by striking Acacius' name from the diptychs (signifying a rupture of communion). Although A. made the concession of recognizing the baptisms and ordinations performed by Acacius, the Emperor refused, hoping that the Pope would eventually accept the *Henoticon. A.'s efforts were misunderstood by some of the

Roman clergy who renounced communion with the Pope, declaring him to be heretical. Their action, unsupported by facts, gave rise to the medieval legends of A.'s heresy and Dante's consignment of A. to the sixth circle among the heretics. (*Inferno* 11.6–9). BIBLIOGRAPHY: H. Leclercq, DACL 13.1:1212–13; G. Bardy, Fliche-Martin 4:340–341.

[T. M. MCFADDEN]

ANASTASIUS III (d. 913), **POPE** from 911, a Roman esteemed for his rectitude of life. Nothing is known of his election and little more of his brief reign. During his pontificate Rome was under the control of the House of *Theophylactus, which probably prevented him from exercising any effective influence. The patriarch of Constantinople addressed a letter to A. denouncing the approval given by *Sergius III to the fourth marriage of the Byzantine Emperor, *Leo VI. No response is extant. BIBLIOGRAPHY: Mann 4:143–147; A. J. Ennis, NCE 1:479.

[P. F. MULHERN]

ANASTASIUS IV (Conrad de Suburra; 1073–1154), **POPE** from July 8, 1153 to Dec. 3, 1154. Born in Rome, he was named cardinal bishop of the suburbicarian diocese of Sabina (Rome). He was elected pope on the day his predecessor, Eugene III, died. In policy he was conciliatory, restoring St. William Fitzherbert (deposed by Eugene) as abp. of York and acquiescing in the contested translation of *Wichmann to Magdeburg. Sweden began paying *Peter's Pence during the reign of A.

[T. EARLY]

ANASTASIUS I (431–518), **BYZANTINE EMPEROR** from 491. After serving in the imperial administration, A., at heart a Monophysite, was named emperor but was forced to sign a profession of faith in the doctrine of Chalcedon before the patriarch would crown him. An able and efficient emperor, his attempts at compromise in religious matters proved unsuccessful. BIBLIOGRAPHY: P. Charanis, *Church and State in the Later Roman Empire: The Religious Policy of Anastasius* (1939).

[G. T. DENNIS]

ANASTASIUS, PATRIARCH OF CONSTANTINOPLE (d.754) chosen by Emperor Leo III to succeed Germanus, the vigorous opponent of *iconoclasm (730). He was excommunicated by Popes Gregory II and Gregory III as heretic and pretender. Politically an opportunist, A. modified his strong iconoclastic policies which had aroused the hatred of the people to win the favor of the usurper to the throne, Artabasdus (741). When Emperor Constantine V (742–775) regained the throne, he publicly reprimanded A. and demanded the patriarch's renewed support of iconoclasm as the price of retaining the patriarchate. BIBLIOGRAPHY: R. Janin, DHGE 2:1465–66.

[F. H. BRIGHAM]

ANASTASIUS, PATRIARCHS OF ANTIOCH, SS.,
(1) Anastasius I (d.599), monk of Sinai, who was *apocrisiarius* of Alexandria before becoming patriarch of Antioch (559). Deposed by Emperor Justin II for his outspoken defense of orthodoxy and opposition to Emperor Justinian, A. was sent to Jerusalem but restored to his see by Emperor Maurice at the request of St. Gregory the Great (593). Of his writings, five important treatises on Christological and Trinitarian questions have survived in Latin translation (PG 89:1309–62) together with a compendium of Christian doctrine in the original Greek (PG 89:1399–1404).

(2) Anastasius II, St. (d.*c*.609), successor to Anastasius I as patriarch of Antioch (599), he translated Gregory the Great's *Liber regulae pastoralis (Pastoral Care)* into Greek. Gregory's letter to A. acknowledging him as patriarch of Antioch and accepting his profession of faith has survived (MGH ep. 7:48). He met death during the violence of the Jewish rebellion against the Emperor Phocas (609). BIBLIOGRAPHY: A. Raes, BiblSanct 1:1064–65; R. Janin, DHGE 2:1460; Altaner 559, 619.

[F. H. BRIGHAM]

ANASTASIUS OF CLUNY, ST. (d. *c*.1085), Benedictine and hermit. Born at Venice, A. became a monk at Mont-Saint-Michel, but left the abbey to live in solitude at Tombelaine when the abbot was found guilty of simony. About 1066 he joined the monastery at Cluny and was later (1073) sent with Hugh Candidus by Gregory VII as a missionary to the Moors in Spain. After returning to Cluny, he received the abbot's permission to live a hermit's life near Toulouse (*c*.1080). Recalled by his abbot (*c*.1085), he died on the journey to Cluny. A letter on the Eucharist (PL 149:433) has been attributed to A. BIBLIOGRAPHY: life by Galterius, AS Oct. 7:1125–36; P. Fournier, DHGE 2:1469; B. Heurtebize, DTC 1:1166; Butler 4:130.

[P. K. MEAGHER]

ANASTASIUS OF HUNGARY, ST. (d. between 1036 and 1039), apostle of the Magyars and Hungary's first prelate. He has been variously identified as a Roman monk who followed St. Adalbert to Prague, or as abbot of Břewnow near Prague, or as a Croatian or Czech who studied at Magdeburg with Adalbert of Prague. He was consecrated bp. in 1001. He spent himself with great zeal in the evangelization of the Magyars. The story that he was sent by King Stephen to bring the royal crown from the Pope is probably legendary. BIBLIOGRAPHY: Butler 4:325–326; E. Mihályi, BiblSanct 1:1053–54.

[S. WILLIAMS]

ANASTASIUS THE LIBRARIAN (d. *c*.878), a learned, often troublesome, and very influential person who became papal librarian, playing an important role in formulating papal letters, esp. those dealing with the Byzantine Church. Sent to Constantinople by the Frankish Emperor Louis II on what proved an unsuccessful mission, he attended some sessions of the synod of 869–70 there which deposed the patriarch *Photius, to whom he was strongly opposed. He translated the acts of the synod into Latin. He is noted for his intense literary activity, most of which consisted of translations from Greek into Latin notably of works by or on Pseudo-Dionysius. BIBLIOGRAPHY: P. Devos, NCE 1:480–481.

[G. T. DENNIS]

ANASTASIUS THE MONK, ST. (d. 662), disciple of St. Maximus the Greek in the monastery of Chrysopolis with whom he was exiled to Lazia in Colchis, together with Anastasius Apocrisiarius, where he was tortured and put to death for his opposition to Monothelitism. A Latin version of his letter on the two wills of Christ is extant (PG 90:131–136), but his alleged compilation *Doctrina patrum*, a valuable florilegium of various lost writings against Monophysitism and Monothelitism, is ascribed by some to St. Anastasius of Sinai. BIBLIOGRAPHY: Altaner 630–633; S. Salaville, DHGE 2.1461–62; C. Vona, BiblSanct 9:41–47, s.v. "Massimo il Confessore."

[F. H. BRIGHAM]

ANASTASIUS THE PERSIAN, ST. (d. 628), martyr. A. became interested in Christianity while a soldier in the Persian army invading Palestine (*c*.614). After returning to Persia, he went again to Jerusalem where he was baptized and later entered a monastery (*c*.621). After some years of thirsting for martyrdom, he appeared boldly before the Persian governor in Palestinian Caesarea, confessed his conversion to Christianity, and patiently endured the torment inflicted upon him in a vain attempt to make him offer sacrifice to the Persian deities. Transferred to the royal court at Bethsaloe in Assyria, he underwent further torture and finally died by strangulation, together with 68 other Christians, by order of Chosroës. His remains were later taken to Palestine, thence to Constantinople, and finally to Rome, where they were kept in the church of St. Vincent, thereafter known as the church of SS. Vincent and Anastasius. BIBLIOGRAPHY: Butler 1:144–146 for a more detailed account and bibliog.

[P. K. MEAGHER]

ANASTASIUS OF SENS, ST. (d.976), abp. of Sens from 967. His principal accomplishments were the reconstruction of the cathedral of Sens and the restoration of monastic life at St.-Pierre-le-Vif. BIBLIOGRAPHY: AS Jan. 1:389.

[P. K. MEAGHER]

ANASTASIUS OF SINAI, ST. (d. *c*.700), abbot of St. Catherine's Monastery on Mt. Sinai, a champion of orthodoxy against the Egyptian and Syrian *Monophysites. Against this heresy he published a florilegium of patristic texts known as the "Guide." He also published an allegorical exegesis of the *Hexaemeron* in 12 books, as well as a collection of questions and answers on various theological themes. Works: PG 89:35–1288. BIBLIOGRAPHY: Altaner 633–634; F. de Sa, NCE 1:481.

[R. B. ENO]

ANATHEMA (Gr. for a curse, an accursed thing), the cursing or expelling of a serious offender from the Church, synonymous with excommunication. The word is used in the canons of a council to indicate that the doctrine described in the canon is erroneous and is condemned, and that the proposition contradictory to it is to be held as true.

[P. FOSCOLOS]

ANATHEMAS OF CYRIL (12 in number), condemnations of Nestorius' doctrine about Christ drawn up by St. Cyril of Alexandria (d. 444) and attached by him and an Alexandrian synod to a letter sent to Nestorius of Constantinople the year before the Council of Ephesus (431). The saint, commissioned by Pope Celestine to ask Nestorius to retract his Christological error (centering in the denial that Mary is *Theotokos*, the mother of God), exceeded his mandate by drawing up what might be considered a new profession of faith. The tone of this summary, the rejection of which was proposed as denial of the faith, the suspect derivation and ambiguous nature of certain concepts (the *mia physis*, or one nature, in Christ and the analogy of body-soul relation in man to the human and divine in Christ) could not fail to arouse opposition at a time when the Christological terminology was still fluid. As intended and later explained by Cyril, the propositions are undoubtedly orthodox; their study should contribute to a more profound insight into the unity of Christ and the communication of idioms. Nevertheless, their imprecision coupled with their use by so great a spiritual leader as Cyril favored the stubborn misuse of the anathemas by the Monophysites in proof of their error. Their presence in the acts of the Council of Ephesus and of the Council of Constantinople II cannot be taken as solemn definition, though they should not be disregarded in repudiation of Cyril's theology. BIBLIOGRAPHY: W. J. Burghardt, NCE 4:571–576.

[E. G. KAISER]

ANATHOTH, a priestly town in Benjamin's territory, a short distance N of Jerusalem. Jeremiah was a native of Anathoth, although he was not honored by his fellow townsmen (Jer 11.21–23). That Jeremiah was willing to buy back his cousin's land there was a hopeful sign of rebirth for Jerusalem's territory despite all his predictions of doom (Jer 32.6–25).

[J. F. FALLON]

ANATOLIUS, PATRIARCH OF CONSTANTINOPLE (c.400–458), disciple of St. Cyril of Alexandria and chosen to succeed Flavian as bp. of Constantinople after the Robber Synod of Ephesus (449). Before he could be recognized as the lawful bp., however, Pope Leo I obliged him to rehabilitate the bps. deposed at Ephesus in 449, condemn

Eutyches and Nestorius, and subscribe to Leo's *Tome to Flavian*. He played an important role at the Council of Chalcedon in 451 and promoted the famous canon 28 of the Council which declared the See of Constantinople second after Rome. BIBLIOGRAPHY: M. Jugie, DHGE 2:1497–1500; P. T. Camelot, NCE 1:482–483.

[P. FOSCOLOS]

ANATOLIUS OF LAODICEA, ST. (d.283) philosopher, scientist, and mathematician who founded a school of Aristotelian philosophy in Alexandria. With the Alexandrian district of Bruchium under seige, he successfully negotiated with the Roman military for the escape of the noncombatants (261–262). Shortly after being appointed coadjutor to the bp. of Caesarea in Palestine, A. was named bp. of Laodicea by popular acclamation (268). Eusebius quotes his treatise on the date of Easter (*Hist. Ecc.* 7.32). BIBLIOGRAPHY: J. Quasten, LTK 1:497; G. Eldarov, Bibl-Sanct 1:1084–85.

[H. JACK]

ANAXAGORAS OF CLAZOMENAE (c.500–c.428 B.C.), one of the most distinguished representatives of Ionian philosophy, and especially important for his introduction of Mind *(nous)* into Greek philosophy. After spending 30 years at Athens as the teacher and friend of Pericles, he was accused of impiety by the latter's enemies and had to flee to Lampsacus in Asia Minor. Although his *Physica* was still extant in the 6th cent. A.D., when *Simplicius made excerpts from it, it is very difficult to reconstruct his system with certainty because of our fragmentary knowledge of it and the conflicting views expressed by ancient writers. His cosmic "Sphere is a 'mixture' containing 'seeds' of every qualitatively distinct natural substance, organic and inorganic, . . . infinitely divisible into parts like each other and the whole" (OCD 50). "In everything there is a portion of everything except Mind" *(nous;* Fragment 11). He introduces Mind as the source of cosmic motion and the life principle of plants and animals, characterizing it "as infinite and self-ruled, and mixed with nothing, but alone, itself by itself" (Frg. 12). While recognizing the great importance of Anaxagoras' concept of Mind, Socrates and Plato criticized him for not realizing its significance as a teleological principle. He recognized the limitation of the senses, but did not discredit them in the manner of *Parmenides. His doctrine on matter is more subtle and penetrating in many respects than the more familiar and influential theory of the Atomists. He adhered to the Ionian notion of the earth as a flat disk and regarded the heavenly bodies as red-hot stones. However, he was the first to explain solar eclipses correctly. BIBLIOGRAPHY: OCD 50–51; Copleston 1:66–71; Guthrie 2:266–338.

[M. R. P. MCGUIRE]

ANAXIMANDER OF MILETUS (c.610–c.546 B.C.), Ionian natural philosopher and astronomer, a younger contemporary and friend of *Thales, writer of a work *peri*

physeōs (On Nature), the first Greek treatise in prose, which was still extant in the 2d cent. B.C. Our knowledge of his thought and writings is based essentially on the information furnished by *Aristotle, *Aëtius, *Plutarch, *Simplicius, and *Hippolytus. He asserted that the origin *(archē)* of all things is the Infinite or the Boundless *(to apeiron).* He regarded the Boundless as divine, "eternal and ageless," and "surrounding and governing innumerable worlds." Each world is made up of opposites: hot and cold, moist and dry, etc. They are separated out of the Boundless by an eternal world motion and must atone for their mutual "injustice" by being absorbed again into the Boundless. He thus formulated a general cosmic law. All life, he thought, came from the sea, and he held that man—because of his helplessness in infancy—was born from animals of another species. He considered that the earth was a cylinder and that the planets and stars circle it at fixed distances. He drew the first map of the earth and is said to have introduced the gnomon to the Greeks. His teaching on opposites and his emphasis on the *how* as well as on the *why* exercised an important influence on Greek philosophy. BIBLIOGRAPHY: Copleston 1:24–26; LexAW s.v.; Guthrie 1:72–115.

[M. R. P. MCGUIRE]

ANAXIMENES OF MILETUS (*c.*585–*c.*525 B.C.), Ionian natural philosopher, a pupil of *Anaximander. None of his writings are preserved, and information on his teachings must be based on data furnished by *Theophrastus, *Aëtius, Pseudo-*Plutarch, and *Hippolytus. He held that the origin *(archē)* of all things is to be found in air *(aēr)* through a process of condensation and rarefaction. On being rarefied, air becomes fire, but, when condensed, becomes, in order, wind, cloud, water, earth and stone. He conceived the Earth as a thin flat disk floating on air, and the planets and stars as leaves of fire carried around it by the air. For him air is living, eternal, and divine, and the human soul itself is air. "Just as our soul, which is air, holds us together, so breath and air surround the whole cosmos." He thus seems to have introduced the distinction between microcosm and macrocosm into Greek philosophy. Through his theory of condensation and rarefaction he was the first to think of the Earth's being governed by a physical rather than by a moral law. BIBLIOGRAPHY: OCD 51; LexAW s.v.; Copleston 1:26–27; Guthrie 1:115–139.

[M. R. P. MCGUIRE]

ANCESTOR CULT (Africa), veneration for family ancestors, also called currently "remembrance of the living dead." South of the Sahara Desert, the ancestor cult is still important in the religion of 70% of the 700 African tribes on the continent; but it is completely absent from the remaining 30%. As an expression of family and clan continuity and solidarity, the recently deceased ancestors (esp. illustrious persons or those who died with a grievance) are regarded as still inhabiting the family land. They exercise absolute control over the living; all life exists under their surveillance.

They are treated with fear and reverence; they are venerated and, occasionally, worshiped. Special shrines may be built for them or masks worn for them to speak through.

In contemporary Africa the ancestor cult is still a force to be reckoned with. Among the Bantu peoples in particular, it represents the hierarchical social system carried over into the spirit world; it validates the traditional political structure; it ensures fertility, health, prosperity, and the continuity of past and future in family life; and it is a sanction for the respect of living elders. To attack it, therefore, as Protestant and RC missionaries almost without exception have done, was to attack something basic in tribal and family structure.

In reaction to this attack, the *African Independent Church Movement across the continent has reasserted the ancestor cult to some extent. Some bodies actually mention the ancestors in their name: Dini ya Msambwa (Religion of the Ancestors) in Kenya, Église de Nos Ancêtres in the Congo, now Zaire, and Calici ca Mokolo (Church of the Ancestors) in Malawi. In South-West Africa, the Herero Church combines ancestral worship with the holy communion service. Hence, although most similar bodies across Africa hold the basic doctrines of Christian faith, they have attempted to Christianize, with varying success, this deep-rooted belief of traditional societies in their solidarity with the ancestors.

[D. B. BARRETT]

ANCESTOR WORSHIP, the cult of tribal ancestors or of the dead in general. Already Apollodoros of Athens in the 2d cent. B.C. put forth theories concerning ancestor worship. Euhemeros (330–260 B.C.) propounded a theory, Euhemerism, that the gods were really prominent men of old days. In modern times, this theory was embraced by Herbert Spencer who declared, "ancestor-worship is the root of every religion." W. Schmidt, on the other hand, maintains that "there is not a single religion which consists of ancestor worship alone . . . this is never more than one element of religion." Schmidt points to the following types of ancestor worship in the various cultural strata of his classification: (1) Ancestors in Primitive Cultures. The Supreme Being, who has neither wife nor family, created the primal pair from whom the tribe is descended. (Pygmies, some Australians, north central Californians, Algonkians, and, to a certain extent, Koryaks and the Ainu.) The First Father and First Mother are considered the ancestors of the tribe; initiation ceremonies are designed to teach their example. In the primitive cultures, dead ancestors are loved rather than feared, their bony remains preserved lovingly; for the ordinary dead, burial is the norm. (2) In the so-called boomerang culture, there is only a First Father, who is "at once the first mortal and also risen from the dead," equated with the moon and symbolized by lunar animals. Often he coalesces with the Supreme Being into a single figure and receives the combined cult of both. (Old Man of the Blackfeet.) Often he is characterized by a wounded or withered knee. (Oedipus and Odysseus.) There is no cult of the individual dead, the predominant mode of burial being the niche-grave. (3) In primary cultures, the worship of the Primal Pair or of First Father is replaced by worship of numerous dead ancestors or even of other dead persons. Among patrilineal nomads, e.g., Mongols, Turkomans, the father of the race acquired the cults of the Supreme Being; sometimes his cult is connected with sorcery. The memory of the departed heroes receives separate worship, in ballads and other cultic forms. Burial is in barrows of earth. (4) In patrilineal totemistic cultures—S and E Australia, New Guinea, India, large parts of Africa and North and South America—the First Father becomes a sun-figure, symbolized by solar animals (lion, wolf, eagle, hawk, falcon) and these animals themselves may be considered the ancestors. Ordinary mortals may also be identified with the solar First Father and gain immortality (Osiris). Mummification is typical; the chief magician, here and elsewhere, is buried with special ceremonies. (5) In exogamous matrilineal horticultural societies, the mother of the race is identified with the moon or Mother Earth, or both; she has two sons, tribal culture-heroes, representing the full and dark moon. In self-defense, the men of such groups form secret societies, worshiping ghosts and honoring individual male ancestors, skull worship and masked dances being typical practices. Animism appears here and leads to a cult of the dead in general. (6) In later, nonexogamous forms of mother-right, headhunting is engaged in, to get the skulls, hands, feet, etc., of strangers, used chiefly in magical rites of fertility. (7) Later combinations of these forms result from cultural cross-fertilization, often leading to a division of society into classes, one above another. The royal house then develops the cult of ancestors into a cult of departed kings and chiefs, possibly deifying them in their lifetimes. BIBLIOGRAPHY: W. Schmidt, *Origin and Growth of Religion* (tr. H. J. Rose, 1931). *MATRIARCHY

[D. H. BRUNAUER]

ANCHARANO, PETRUS DE (*c*.1330–1416), a canonist of high repute who taught at Bologna, Siena, and other universities. He wrote important commentaries on canon law and numerous studies of special points of law. His advice, sought by the cardinals at the Council of Pisa, at first favored but later, as the situation became more complicated, opposed the position of Gregory XII.

[P. K. MEAGHER]

ANCHIETA, JOSÉ DE (1534–97), Brazilian missionary and linguist. Born of Basque parents in Laguna in the Canary Islands, A. sailed for Brazil in 1553 to work in evangelizing the Puru and Guarani Indians. On the spot where he offered the first Mass, the city of São Paulo was founded. A. wrote grammars and dictionaries as well as catechetical and pastoral manuals. His knowledge of biology was considerable; he was an authority on poisonous snakes. A.'s poetical work includes *Cantiones sacrae, Dramma ad extirpanda Brasiliae vitia,* and *De b. virgine Maria.* Credited with miraculous power, he is called "the apostle of Brazil."

BIBLIOGRAPHY: H. G. Dominian, *Apostle of Brazil: The Biography of Padre José Anchieta, S.J., 1534–1597* (1958).

[P. DAMBORIENA]

ANCHIN, ABBEY OF, former Benedictine abbey near Douai, France, founded in 1079 by two knights, Walter and Figer Anchin. The monastery was famous and prosperous throughout the whole of its history. Its church, dedicated in 1230, was 350 feet in length. Yearly revenues of the abbey and its three priories amounted to more than 200,000 livres. It was suppressed in 1791 and the buildings were completely razed. BIBLIOGRAPHY: M. G. Blayo, DHGE 2:1516–24; P. Cousin, NCE 1:485–486.

[N. BACKMUND]

ANCHOR, a Christian symbol for spiritual safety, salvation, and hope. Employed as early as the NT (Heb 6.19), it was used in the early centuries of the Church on funeral monuments and jewelry, often with a cross. The symbol fell into disuse during the medieval period, but later reappeared, associated particularly with patrons of seamen such as St. *Nicholas of Myra and with ports. BIBLIOGRAPHY: G. Ferguson, *Signs and Symbols in Christian Art* (2d ed., 1955); V.-H. Debidour, *Christian Sculpture* (tr. R. Cunningham, 1968) 38.

[T. EARLY]

ANCHOR CROSS, symbol of hope and spiritual security, used in the catacombs and on jewelry in ancient times. It was formed with the central shaft of the anchor in the form of a cross. The anchor was considered a Christian symbol as early as the NT (Heb 6.19).

[T. EARLY]

ANCHORAGE, the house or cell in which an *anchorite or anchoress dwells.

ANCHORESS, or ancress, a female *anchorite.

ANCHORHOLD (ankerhold), the cell of an *anchorite.

ANCHORITE (Gr., *anachōrein,* to retire, withdraw), in the Eastern Church, a person who has retired into solitude to lead a religious life. Often anchorites would live in cells adjacent to a monastic community, and this is the prevailing custom today e.g., on Mt. Athos.

[G. T. DENNIS]

ANCHORITES, spiritual ascetics who retire into a solitude to live a life of penance, prayer, and contemplation. The term is derived from the Greek *anachōrites* from *anachōrein* (to withdraw, retire), and is analogous with the Latin *eremita,* or hermit. Anchorites lived close to a community but hermits retired completely from the company of others. In the early Church an anchorite ordered his life according to his own discretion, but this later became subject to ecclesiastical rules. One of the most famous of the early anchorites was St. *Anthony of Egypt (c.250–356). Though anchorites as such have disappeared from the Western Church, their ascetical ideal and peculiar manner of life have been continued in religious orders such as the Carthusians and Camaldolese. BIBLIOGRAPHY: C. Lialine, DSAM 4.1:936–953; R. M. Clay, *Hermits and Anchorites of England* (1914).

[M. J. COSTELLOE]

ANCIAU DE SENS, master of medieval MS illumination, who with Jacquet Mahiet collaborated with the renowned 14th-cent. illuminator Jean *Pucelle (Bible of Billyn, Breviary of Belleville), whose workshop rather enjoyed a monopoly in France during that period, bringing international fame to the school of Paris through graceful and elegant MS illuminations. BIBLIOGRAPHY: L. Huyghe, *Larousse Encyclopedia of Byzantine and Medieval Art* (ed. R. Huyghe, 1958).

[M. J. DALY]

ANCIEN RÉGIME (the old order), a French expression designating the political and social organization of France from approximately the end of the feudal period (16th cent.) to the 1789 Revolution. In this period of "absolute" and "divine right" monarchy, esp. as it was shaped by the Bourbons, the king was considered the image of God and answerable to God alone, since he had been anointed with the legendary holy oils brought to earth by an angel at the baptism of Clovis. Society was divided into three orders: the nobility, clergy, and the third estate. BIBLIOGRAPHY: C. B. A. Behrens, *Ancien régime* (1967).

[R. N. NICOLICH]

ANCIENT OF DAYS (Aram. *Attik Yomin*), a name of God that occurs three times in the Book of Dan, an apocalyptic term that occurs often in postbiblical writing and was taken up by cabalistic literature. BIBLIOGRAPHY: R. Fuller et al., *New Catholic Commentary on Holy Scripture* (1960), 533g-i, 676k.

[M. R. BROWN]

ANCREN RIWLE (Ancren Wisse), a medieval code of rules for three anchoresses or recluses (not nuns) written probably in the early 13th century. The date, authorship, place of composition, and names of the women for whom the rule was written are unknown. It is divided into eight parts: Divine Service, Keeping the Heart, Moral Lessons and Examples, Temptation, Confession, Penance, Love, and Domestic Matters. The author shows scholarly interests in his references to the Bible, to lives of the Fathers, Cassian, works of Anselm and Bernard. His advice to the three women is practical, kindly, and full of piety. The rule throws light on religious aspirations of late 12th-cent. England, and

also reflects secular life of the times. It gives the daily *horarium,* advice about speaking to visitors and about abuses arising from much outside contact. Daily life consisted of prayer (chiefly oral), spiritual reading, sewing, religious instruction to the "maiden" who looked after material needs of the recluses, and two meals eaten in silence. Seven copies of the text are extant in English. Two French and several Latin versions show its popularity. The *Ancren Riwle* belongs to a group of six prose treatises called the Katherine Group written in the same dialect and in a similar style. BIBLIOGRAPHY: *Ancren Riwle,* Parts 6,7 (ed. G. Shepperd, 1960); *Manual of the Writings in Middle English* (ed. J. E. Wells, 1916–41); CBEL.

[M. M. BARRY]

ANCUS, in Gregorian chant, one of the liquescent neumes, variants of the basic neumes characterized by the use of a smaller head for the last note. The ancus is a liquescent climacus (⌒ ⌐⌐ ⌐⌐.). Also called semivocales, the liquescents always occur on a diphthong or where there are two consonants in succession, and were designed to facilitate correct pronunciation: in the case of two consonants, by the insertion of a mute *e* and, in the case of a diphthong, by the separation of the two vowels, the second of which was made weak. BIBLIOGRAPHY: Apel GregCh 104–105; Apel HDMus 572 s.v. "Neumes."

[M. I. LEGGE]

ANCYRA, the name of two ancient cities of Asia Minor, both important in early church history. (1) Ancyra in Galatia (today Ankara, Turkey) was distinguished for the number of its martyrs, but its religious history was marked from apostolic times by heretical movements, and was, in particular, a center of Montanism. A number of important synods met there in the 3d and 4th cent., one of which (358) dealt with Christological controversies and adopted the Homoiousian formula; and another (375), Arian dominated, deposed Gregory of Nyssa. In the 7th cent. Ancyra was still an important city, ranking fourth in the Byzantine Empire, but with the Arab invasions its prominence declined. Armenians settled there in the 13th cent., and the bishopric at Ancyra, established in the 18th cent., was restored to the Catholic Armenians by Pius IX in 1850, but the massacre of 1917 and the Treaty of Lausanne in 1923 effectively put an end to Catholicism in that region. (2) Ancyra in Phrygia, a city of Laodicaea. Its first bishop was Florentius; it had two Latin bishops in the 15th century. BIBLIOGRAPHY: C. Karalevsky, DHGE 2:1538–48; OCD (1970) 62.

[P. FOSCOLOS]

ANCYRA, SYNOD OF, a plenary synod of the Churches of Asia Minor and Syria convened in Ancyra (modern Ankara) in 314. Its 25 canons deal chiefly with the admittance of the lapsed to communion and with certain moral problems.

[E. EL-HAYEK]

ANDACHTSBILD, term for late 13th-cent. Gothic religious images of great emotional appeal. Characteristic is the tragic Pietà (pity). Often in wood, painted with grotesque realism, these agonized faces, limbs rigid and lean, and blood-encrusted wounds arouse in the beholder overwhelming pity for the grief-stricken Mother of Sorrows.

[M. J. DALY]

ANDECHS, ABBEY OF, Benedictine abbey on Lake Ammer in Upper Bavaria. In the 12th cent. it was the seat of a noble family, and it became a center of pilgrimage (Sacer Mons) because of the impressive collection of relics the family had gathered. It was a Benedictine abbey 1455–1803; in 1846 it was restored as a dependent priory of the Abbey of St. Boniface in Munich. BIBLIOGRAPHY: J. Hemmerle, *Die Benediktinerklöster in Bayern* (1951) 18–20; W. Fink, NCE 1:488.

[N. BACKMUND]

ANDERSON, LARS (Laurentius, Lorenz Andreae; *c*.1480–1522), Swedish theologian and Reformer. After study at Rostock, Leipzig, and Greifswald, A. became a canon at Strägnäs and secretary to Bp. Mattias. He was converted to Lutheranism by Olavus Petri whom he helped to introduce the Reformation into Sweden. When the Swedish estates chose Gustavus Vasa as king, A. was appointed chancellor (1523). He had a major part in the proceedings of the Council of Örebro (1529), which gave political status to the new Church, but for opposing Vasa's later attempt to give the Swedish Church a presbyterian polity, he was convicted of treason and sentenced to death along with Olavus Petri. The penalty, however, was commuted to a heavy fine and deprivation of office; A. spent the rest of his life in retirement. BIBLIOGRAPHY: J. Wordsworth, *National Church of Sweden* (1911).

[M. J. SUELZER]

ANDERTON, English recusant family in 17th-cent. Lancashire. Among its representatives were: (1) Roger (d.1640). Son of Christopher Anderton of Lostock and cousin of Lawrence, he probably supported a secret Catholic press in Lancashire (Birchley Hall Press, 1615–21). (2) Lawrence (*c*.1575–1643). After ordination on the Continent, he became a Jesuit (1604) and labored as a missionary in Lancashire, London, and S England. He wrote several controversial works. BIBLIOGRAPHY: T. Cooper, DNB 1:396–397; Gillow BDEC 1:34–41.

[V. SAMPSON]

ANDLAUER, MODESTE, BL. (1847–1900), French Jesuit martyred during the Boxer Rebellion in China.

[P. K. MEAGHER]

ANDORRA, miniature state of 175 square miles between France and Spain. Virtually the entire population is Catholic, as is the state officially. Located in high mountain valleys of the East Pyrenees, Andorra has been able to maintain a separate identity while most other small principalities of the feudal period were being incorporated into modern nation states. Though it is largely self-governing, through an elected Council General of the Valleys, sovereignty is held by the president of France and the Catholic bp. of Urgel, Spain. According to tradition, Charlemagne gave a charter to Andorra in return for help against the Moors. In 843 Charles II placed it under the Spanish count of Urgel. In 1208 it passed to the Foix family, and through Henry of Navarre, Count of Foix, became attached to the French crown in 1589. Ecclesiastically Andorra was under the bp. of Urgel and an agreement, the *Pareatges* of 1278, recognized his joint sovereignty. From early times Andorra has been divided into six parishes. It has numerous churches, some dating to the pre-Romanesque period and carrying historical interest. Our Lady of Meritxell, patroness since 1873, has a shrine with Romanesque image. The language and primary cultural tradition of Andorra are Catalan.

[T. EARLY]

ANDRADE, ANTONIO DE (1580–1634), Portuguese Jesuit missionary. He was sent to India in 1600; in 1624 he crossed the Himalayas into Tibet and in the following year founded a mission on the Sutlej River with the help of six other Jesuits. Believing Tibet to be Cathay, he wrote an account of his journey, *Novo descubrimento do gram Cathayo,* which was read in Europe with considerable interest. BIBLIOGRAPHY: Sommervogel 1:329–331.

[P. K. MEAGHER]

ANDRÉ, BERNARD (Andreas; *c*.1450–after 1521), Augustinian poet, historiographer. A doctor of civil and canon law, he lived from *c*.1485 in England, becoming poet laureate and historiographer to Henry VII, of whom he wrote a life (incomplete; ed. by J. Gairdner, 1858). BIBLIOGRAPHY: J. Gairdner in DNB 1:398–399; F. Roth, *History of English Austin Friars, 1249–1538* (1962) 2:nn. 893, 947, 972, 1010, 1015, 1029.

[L. E. BOYLE]

ANDRÉ, BROTHER (1845–1937), a brother of the Congregation of the Holy Cross, born in the Province of Quebec, Canada. Because of recurring poor health in his youth, A. did not receive any education and was unable to read or write. He was assigned for years as doorkeeper at the College of Notre Dame, Montreal. Here he endeared himself to the students and their parents by his piety and desire to help those who were in any kind of distress. Later he interviewed the pilgrims who came to the Oratory of St. Joseph from all parts of the world. A.'s passionate love for St. Joseph made possible the first humble wooden chapel and eventually the present great basilica in Montreal dedicated to St. Joseph. BIBLIOGRAPHY: W. H. Gregory, *Brother André* (1925); A. Hatch, *Miracle of the Mountain* (1959).

[M. C. BRADLEY]

ANDREÄ, JAKOB (1528–90), German Lutheran theologian. He was also called by the German name *Schmidlin* and the Latin *Faber* from the fact that his father was a blacksmith. Ordained in 1546, A. helped introduce the Lutheran reform teachings and church order in many places in Germany. He was counselor of Duke Christopher of Württemberg at the Diets of Regensburg (1557) and Augsburg (1559); attended several theological colloquies with Reformed theologians; and was made (1561) professor of theology and chancellor at the Univ. of Tübingen. From 1568 onward he worked to rescue Lutheranism from the divisions caused by disputes between Gnesiolutherans and Crypto-Calvinists. Six sermons that he preached in 1572 on these controversies began a process of conciliation culminated by the *Formula of Concord (1577). One of its co-authors and signers, he wrote the *Epitome* to the Formula. BIBLIOGRAPHY: A. Piepkorn, EncLuthCh 1:73–74.

[M. J. SUELZER]

ANDREA, MIGUEL DE, see DE ANDREA, MIGUEL.

ANDREAE, LAURENTIUS, see ANDERSON, LARS.

ANDREAS CAPELLANUS (André Le Chapelin; fl. 12th cent.). A. is believed to have served as chaplain at the French court—hence his surname. His famous treatise, *Liber de arte honeste amandi et de reprobatione inhonesti amoris,* treats of medieval manners and morals, as well as of courtly love. It was translated into French twice during the 13th century. The most important MSS are those of the 13th-cent. MS in the Vatican, the 14th-cent. MS at the Bibliothèque Nationale de Paris, and the 15th-cent. MS in the Ambrosian library, Milan. It was translated into English *(Art of Courtly Love)* by J. J. Parry in 1941. BIBLIOGRAPHY: J. F. Benton, NCE 1:493; F. J. Warne, EB 1:910.

[J. R. RIVELLO]

ANDREAS DE ESCOBAR, see ESCOBAR, ANDRÉS DE.

ANDREIS, FELIX DE (1778–1820), superior of the band of Italian Vincentians who came to the U.S. in 1816 in response to the appeal of Bp. L. Dubourg of New Orleans. After helping for a time in Bardstown, Ky., they settled first in St. Louis, Mo., then at the Barrens, Perryville, a little to the NW of Cape Girardeau in the same state. A. found the rugged life of a missionary too much for his frail health and soon died; he left behind him a reputation for holiness. His cause was formally introduced in 1918. BIBLIOGRAPHY: RACHS 9:206, 20:7–8.

[P. K. MEAGHER]

ANDREONI, JOÃO ANTONIO, see ANTONIL, ANDRÉ JOÃO.

ANDRES STEFAN (1906–70), German author, deeply rooted in Catholic faith. His vivacious, but also somber novels and short stories reflect his Rhenish background, his experience of Greece and Italy, and the tragic aberrations of totalitarianism. In the first book of his trilogy, *Die Sintflut (The Great Flood),* a defrocked priest and former moral theologian, ''the animal from the abyss,'' becomes the *tyrannos auros* and ''standardizer'' of the pseudo-religious party with headquarters in South Italy. A. is less successful in his dramatic and lyrical creations. BIBLIOGRAPHY: E. Baum, *Stefan Andres: Eine Einführung* (1962); *International Who's Who* (1971–72) 43–44.

[S. A. SCHULZ]

ANDREW, ST., APOSTLE (Gr. *andreas,* manly), brother of Simon Peter (Mk 1.16), and with him Disciple and Apostle (Mt 10.5–42); he was in the Cenacle when the Spirit came upon them (Acts 1.13). Born in Bethsaida of Galilee (Jn 1.44), A. would live later at Capharnaum (Mk 1.29); he and his brother were fishermen of the Sea of Galilee. John who was close to A. records in his Gospel (1.35–44) the occasion when A. was of the first two to meet Jesus. Both (perhaps one was John himself) had been present when John the Baptist proclaimed Jesus as Lamb of God (Jn 1.37), and they followed him. A. brought Simon to Jesus, and later when ''certain Gentiles'' came to Philip, fellow townsman of A. and his brother in Bethsaida, he brought them to A. who told Jesus of their desire to see him (Jn 12.20–22). These texts have caused A. to be named ''introducer to Christ.''

Not only was A. present at the multiplication of the loaves and fishes (Jn 6.8), but he answered Jesus' question with another and told him of the boy with the five barley loaves and two fishes, ''but what is that among so many?'' Half-informing, half-questioning in faith and love while leaving his reply open-ended, A. would again be with Peter, James, and John, listening to Christ tell of what was to come hereafter (Mk 13).

During the rest of Jesus' life on earth, save in the awful hour when the Apostles fled, A. remained with him. After Acts 1.13 Scripture records nothing further of A.

An apocryphal work, *Acts of Andrew* (see APOCRYPHA [NT], 4) has survived; H. Delahaye cautions about ancient hagiographers by reference in his *Legends of the Saints* (tr. D. Attwater, 1962, p. 80) to *Passio S. Andreae, n. 1.* Artists, too, have been hagiographers as was Eusebius, representing the legend of A. in great sculpture and painting (see R. Aprile, BiblSanct 1:1100–13) that pass on the strong tradition of A.'s cross shaped as an X, believed the mode of his crucifixion (unconfirmed) at Patras in Greece, his limbs nailed to the four arms of the cross.

A.'s cult spread to Rome where St. Gregory the Great procured for his monastery the arm of the Apostle, and his head was placed in St. Peter's Basilica; from there the cult spread to France and to England. Dear to the Eastern Church where he is believed to have evangelized, A. was chosen patron of Russia, but Scotland likewise chose him as patron. BIBLIOGRAPHY: G. D. Gordini, BiblSanct 1:1094–1100;

E. Josi and E. Peterson, EncCatt 1:1183–88; Benedictines of Ramsgate, *Book of Saints* (3d ed., 1942) 22.

[M. R. BROWN]

ANDREW ABELLON, BL. (1375–1450), Dominican preacher, reformer, artist. Having joined Dominicans at Saint-Maximin-la-Saint-Baume, France, A. taught in various Dominican houses and made a great name as a preacher in South France between 1408 and 1419. He introduced many reforms while prior of Saint-Maximin, Toulouse (1419–22), Aix (1438–42), and Marseilles (1446–50). A. was beatified in 1902. BIBLIOGRAPHY: The best life is that of H. M. Cormier, *Le Bienheureux André Abellon* (2d ed., 1902).

[L. E. BOYLE]

ANDREW BOBOLA, ST., see BOBOLA, ANDREW, ST.

ANDREW CACCIOLI, BL., (1194–1254), Franciscan preacher celebrated for miracles. In 1223 A. received the habit from Francis himself. He was presumably the first priest to join the group, and Francis commissioned him in writing, to preach. Among others of the original band, he was present at Francis' death in 1226. His rigid interpretation of the rule twice earned him imprisonment during the administration of Elias of Cortona, but in each case he was released. In 1233 he attended the general chapter at Soria in Spain. BIBLIOGRAPHY: G. Odoardi, BiblSanct 1:1155–56.

[O. J. BLUM]

ANDREW OF CAESAREA (6th or 7th cent.), abp., commentator on the Apocalypse. His work (PG 106), difficult to date with precision, is valued by exegetes less for its originality or the profundity of its insights than for its abundant compilation of ancient opinion on the Apocalypse. Its method is eclectic, often setting forth various opinions without choosing between them. It attached great weight to the spiritual sense. The popularity of the work is attested by its influence upon later treatments of the subject. BIBLIOGRAPHY: E. B. Allo, *L'Apocalypse* (1933) ccxliv-ccxlv; H. Rahner, LTK 1:516.

[T. C. O'BRIEN]

ANDREW CONTI, BL., (de Comitibus; *c*.1240–1302), Franciscan brother. A member of the noble Conti family, he was a close relative of Popes Innocent III, Gregory IX, Alexander IV, and Boniface VIII. Boniface wished to create him cardinal, but Andrew refused the dignity. A treatise, *On the Birth of the Bl. Virgin Mary*, now lost, is ascribed to him. BIBLIOGRAPHY: G. Odoardi, BiblSanct 1:1156–57.

[O. J. BLUM]

ANDREW CORSINI, ST. (1302–73), Carmelite, bishop. He entered the Carmelites in 1317 and became provincial for Tuscany in 1348. He energetically combated the effects of the plague of 1348 striving to restore the fervor and discipline of religious communities. Elected bp. of Fiesole in 1349, he was an active and capable administrator. BIBLIOGRAPHY: P. Caioli, *S. Andrea Corsini carmelitano* (1929); P. Caraffo, BiblSanct 1:1158–67.

[N. G. WOLF]

ANDREW OF CRETE, ST. (660–740), theologian and hymn writer. A native of Damascus, he became abp. of Gortyna in Crete *c*.692. In 712 he accepted Monothelitism but retracted in the following year. He is regarded by the Greek Church as one of its greatest hymn writers. Byzantine hagiography ascribes to him the invention of the "kanon," the new genre of hymnography consisting of nine odes in strophic form, each of them sung to a different melody. His most famous piece, the Great Canon for Thursday in the 5th week of Lent, contains no less than 250 strophes. A considerable number of his homilies have also survived. He is not to be confused with St. Andrew of Crete the Colybite. BIBLIOGRAPHY: Beck 500–501; F. Caraffa, BiblSanct 1:1142.

[P. FOSCOLOS]

ANDREW DOTTI, BL. (1256–1315), Servite preacher. Having entered the Servite Order at Florence in 1278, after ordination he was sent to a convent near San Sepolcro. Later he joined with a group of hermits near Vallucola, uniting them to the Servite Order in 1294. Buried at San Sepolcro, his cult was approved by Pope Pius VII in 1806. BIBLIOGRAPHY: C. Battini, *Vita del beato Andrea Dotti dei Servi di Maria,* (1866); G. M. Roschini, EncCatt 4:1899.

[W. A. JURGENS]

ANDREW OF FIESOLE, ST. (d. *c*.877), archdeacon of Fiesole near Florence, Italy. According to his highly fictional 14th and 15th cent. *acta,* he was a native of Ireland who made a Roman pilgrimage in the company of his teacher Donatus. On their return journey their visit to the cathedral of the then vacant see of Fiesole occasioned the miraculous ringing of bells and lighting of candles, signs to the people that Donatus was to be their next bishop. After his election, Donatus ordained A. deacon. Later A. founded a monastery and rebuilt the church of San Martino di Mensola where his relics were discovered (1285) and are still preserved. BIBLIOGRAPHY: Butler 3:382, R. Aigrain, DHGE 2:1615; S. Mottironi, BiblSanct 1:1130–39.

[F. H. BRIGHAM]

ANDREW FRANCHI (1335–1401), Dominican preacher, bishop. Born of the noble Franchi-Boccagni family, A. became a Dominican *c*.1357 and distinguished himself as a preacher, teacher, and director of souls. He was made bp. of Pistoia *c*.1380 but resigned his see in 1400. He spent himself for the poor and for sinners. BIBLIOGRAPHY: I. Taurisano, *B. Andrea Franchi* (1922); W. A. Hinnebusch, NCE 1:495.

ANDREW OF LONGJUMEAU (d. *c*.1270), Dominican missionary, papal ambassador. In 1238 he was commissioned by Louis IX to bring the Crown of Thorns to France from Constantinople. Because of his fluency in languages, he was sent on missions to Jacobite and Nestorian churches by Innocent IV. He accompanied King Louis on the Crusades (1248–1254). BIBLIOGRAPHY: The best account of A. is that of A. Duval, *Catholicisme* 1:530–531.

[L. E. BOYLE]

ANDREW OF NEUFCHÂTEAU (of Newcastle; 14th cent.), philosopher and theologian, cited by several authors as a Dominican, but most probably a Franciscan (see R. Couloy, DHGE 2:1685). He enjoyed a limited authority as a nominalist in Parisian intellectual circles of the late Middle Ages and is credited as the author of a commentary on the first book of the *Sentences* of Peter Lombard. BIBLIOGRAPHY: Quétif-Échard 1:740; C. Toussaint, DTC 1:1185.

ANDREW OF PESCHIERA, BL. (1400–85), Dominican preacher. Born of a family of Greek origin, A., after taking the Dominican habit at Brescia, was sent to Florence for his studies. For almost 45 years he preached in Valtellina and neighboring districts where heresy and general moral deterioration caused the people to receive him coldly. Undaunted by this challenge, he preached tirelessly and won many converts not only by his words but also by his humble and austere way of life and his great charity for the poor. His cult began immediately upon his death and was confirmed in 1820. BIBLIOGRAPHY: Butler 1:123–124; G. M. Fusconi, BiblSanct 1:1142–44.

ANDREW OF RINN, BL. (1459–62), alleged child martyr. The traditional account claims that the two-year-old A. was sold by his insane uncle to Jews and put to death. His mother found his body suspended from a tree and interred him in the cemetery of Ampass without investigation or legal action. In 1475 the city of Trent honored the youth, Simon, who was also allegedly a victim of ritual murder at the hands of Jews; the inhabitants of Rinn, imitating Trent's example, solemnly brought A.'s body to the cemetery of Rinn and interred it near the church of St. Andrew. Devotion to A. spread throughout the Tyrol. Equivalent beatification of A. was sanctioned by Benedict XIV who declared canonization impossible. Reputable authorities have unquestionably ascribed the boy's death to his deranged uncle. BIBLIOGRAPHY: E. Vacandard, DHGE 2:1700–02; M. Mayer, LTK 1:519; M. G. McNeil, NCE 1:496; Butler 3:86–87; BiblSanct 1:1148–49.

[J. M. O'DONNELL]

ANDREW OF SAINT VICTOR (*c*.1110–75), English exegete. A. entered the monastery of the Canons Regular at Saint-Victor in Paris; while there he studied under Hugh of Saint-Victor and later succeeded him. A. became the first abbot of Wigmore *c*. 1147. He returned to Saint-Victor as a teacher and was again abbot of Wigmore from *c*.1161–63 until his death. He was the first medieval Scripture commentator who used Jewish sources in his exegesis of the OT. His commentaries on the OT were influential.

[C. C. O'DONNELL]

ANDREW OF STRUMI, BL. (b. early 11th cent.–d.1097? 1106?) abbot, church reformer. With the deacon Arialdo and the "Pataria" he strove to rescue the Milanese clergy from simony and concubinage, but was opposed by Abp. Guido who instigated the death of Arialdo. Andrew entered the Vallombrosans about 1069, and became abbot of the former Benedictine Monastery of Strumi *c*.1085. BIBLIOGRAPHY: Butler 1:549–550; A. Rimoldi, BiblSanct 1:1152–53. *PATARINES.

[G. E. CONWAY]

ANDREW, ACTS OF, see APOCRYPHA (NEW TESTAMENT), 4.

ANDREW, FRAGMENTARY STORY OF, see APOCRYPHA (NEW TESTAMENT), 5.

ANDREW, LEGEND OF THE APOSTLE, a legend originating in the 4th cent. to the effect that St. Andrew the Apostle preached Christianity in Scythia, that is, the region around the Crimea in southern Russia (perhaps the most likely part of the legend), in Asia Minor, Thrace, and Achaia and was martyred in Patras. In the 4th cent. his reputed relics were placed in the church of the Holy Apostles in Constantinople. The legend was expanded *c*.8th cent. to include a visit of Andrew to Byzantium, where he was supposed to have ordained its first bp., St. Stachys, one of the 72 Disciples of Christ. Only during the 10th cent. did this aspect of the legend come to be generally accepted among the Byzantines. From the 13th cent. the legend was used in polemics against Rome in an effort to assert the apostolicity of the See of Constantinople. BIBLIOGRAPHY: F. Dvornik, *Idea of Apostolicity in Byzantium and the Legend of the Apostle Andrew* (1958).

[G. T. DENNIS]

ANDREW AND MATTHIAS (MATTHEW), ACTS OF, see APOCRYPHA (NEW TESTAMENT), 6.

ANDREW AND PAUL, ACTS OF, see APOCRYPHA (NEW TESTAMENT), 7.

ANDREWE, RICHARD (d.1477), English cleric trained in civil and canon law who held various benefices, including the deanship of York (1452–77), and served as secretary (1442–55) to Henry VI. BIBLIOGRAPHY: Emden Ox 1:34–35.

ANDREWES, LANCELOT (1555–1626), Anglican bp., theologian, preacher. Educated at Pembroke Hall, Cambridge, A. was elected to a fellowship there (1576), took orders (1580), and as a prebendary of St. Paul's (from 1589) came to prominence as a preacher. Twice he refused offers of a bishopric, but was finally persuaded by King James I, who esteemed him greatly, to accept appointment to the See of Chichester (1605). He later was transferred to Ely (1609), and thence to Winchester (1613). A. was one of the translators of the Authorized Version of the Bible; the Pentateuch and historical books of the OT are in large part his work. His exposure to Puritan influence during his Cambridge days in no way shook his fundamental conservatism. Although firmly antipapal and an able defender of the English Church against the attack of Robert Bellarmine, A. was in many respects (e.g., in his view of the Eucharist) theologically nearer to the traditional Catholic than to the Protestant position. This appeared also in his attachment to older liturgical forms. He had a marked aversion to Calvinism and is regarded as a representative of distinctively Anglican theology, upon which he had a strong formative influence. His literary fame rests primarily upon his sermons, which are perhaps too intricate and erudite for modern taste, but are yet rewarding in the delicacy and power of their language and in the rich meaning A. never fails to extract from his texts. In his personal life he was ascetical and saintly. His *Preces privatae (Manual of Private Devotions)*, a collection of prayers composed for his own use, is a classic of devotional literature. Works: II v., ed. J. P. Wilson and J. Bliss (LACT, 1841–54). BIBLIOGRAPHY: R. W. Church, "Lancelot Andrewes," *Masters of English Theology* (ed. A. Barry, 1877); T. S. Eliot, *For Lancelot Andrewes* (1928).

[P. K. MEAGHER]

ANDRIESSEN, HENDRIK (1892–1964), prominent Dutch composer and choral conductor, one of a family of musicians including his brother Willem (1887–1964), their father Nicolas Hendrik (1845–1913), the latter's brother Cornelius (Kees) (1865–1947), and Hendrik's son Juriaan (1925–). A.'s sacred works include Masses, motets, organ works, and a *Te Deum*, many of which are known internationally, as are his numerous secular works. In 1936 he went from his native Haarlem to Utrecht to become director of the conservatory and cathedral organist. BIBLIOGRAPHY: H. Antcliffe, Grove DMM 1:153–154.

[A. DOHERTY]

ANDRIEU, MICHEL (1886–1956), French Oratorian and liturgical scholar. As a member of the Catholic theological faculty at Strasbourg, A. devoted his energies and critical scholarship to the study of Ordinals and Pontificals. His monumental editions of these—*Ordines Romani* (5 v., 1931–61) and *Pontifical Romain* (5 v., 1938–63)—are important landmarks in the historical study of the liturgy. They show the gradual development and evolution of the Roman rite as this was modified by various influences, especially Gallican, between the 6th and the 15th centuries. He also contributed many articles on the liturgy to the *Revue des sciences religieuses*. BIBLIOGRAPHY: R. T. Callahan, NCE 1:497–498.

[N. KOLLAR]

ANDRIVEAU, LOUISE APPOLINE ALINE (Sister Appoline; 1810–95), Daughter of Charity and foundress of the devotion to the scapular of the Passion. Born at Saint-Pourçain, A. entered the Daughters of Charity at Paris (1833), was sent to Troyes the following year, to Caen in 1872, and finally to Montolieu (1887). In 1846 in the chapel at Troyes she experienced a vision in which she saw Jesus Christ holding in his hand a scapular in color and design like that which has since been popularized through the devotion. The superior general of the Daughters of Charity reported this to Pius IX, and the following year the wearing of the scapular was approved and indulgenced as an act of devotion to the Passion. A request, based also on Sr. Appoline's vision, that a feast in honor of the Passion be established for Easter Week was not granted. BIBLIOGRAPHY: F. Combaluzier, DSAM 1:558–560.

[P. K. MEAGHER]

ANDROIN DE LA ROCHE (d. 1369), abbot of Cluny, twice papal legate in Italy. Neither of A.'s missions in strife-torn Italy entrusted to him by the Avignon Popes, Innocent VI and Urban V (1357–58; 1363–68), was successful, but the peace negotiations he conducted between France and England resulted in the treaty signed at Calais ending the Hundred Years' War. He was made cardinal at the instance of the grateful kings of France and England (1361). BIBLIOGRAPHY: G. Mollat, *Les Papes d'Avignon* (1947); G. Mollat, DHGE 2:1770–73, for more complete bibliography.

ANDRONICUS II PALAEOLOGUS, BYZANTINE EMPEROR (1256–1332), son of the Emperor Michael VIII Palaeologus and Theodora Ducas. A. severed relations with Rome by reinstating Joseph, Patriarch of Constantinople, in place of John XI Beccus and attempted clerical and monastic reform through the Patriarchs Athanasius (1289–93; 1304–12) and John Comus (1295). His rule, marked by continued military encroachments from the West and Turkey, together with local, civil, and religious controversy, ended with his defeat by his grandson Andronicus III (1328). BIBLIOGRAPHY: L. Béhier, DHGE 2:1782–92; CMedH 4:613–614.

[F. H. BRIGHAM]

ANDRONICUS III PALAEOLOGUS, BYZANTINE EMPEROR (1296–1341), eldest son of Michael IX Palaeologus. Together with John Cantacuzenus he defeated and deposed his grandfather Andronicus II in a civil war precipitated by the latter's refusal to accept him as a successor to the throne (1328). Pressed by constant attacks of the Turks, A. enlisted the assistance of Pope Benedict XII and later made conciliatory overtures for Church reunion through legates at Avignon (1339) who discussed the possibility of an ecumenical council. BIBLIOGRAPHY: L. Bréhier, DHGE 2:1792–97.

[F. H. BRIGHAM]

ANDRONICUS OF RHODES (1st cent. B.C.), Peripatetic philosopher, and 10th or 11th head of the Lyceum after Aristotle. He performed an invaluable service for philosophy by collecting, arranging, and editing the treatises of Aristotle, and he did much similar philosophical work on Theophrastus. He wrote commentaries on Aristotle, showing a special interest in logic. For him logic was the instrument or tool (*organon*) of philosophy, and mastery in its use was an indispensable preliminary condition for entering upon the study of philosophy proper. The corpus of Aristotle's works as we know it goes back to him. BIBLIOGRAPHY: OCD 53; Ueberweg 1:559.

[M. R. P. MCGUIRE]

ANDROUTSOS, CHRESTOS (1869–1937), Greek philosopher and theologian who taught dogmatic and moral theology at the Univ. of Athens 1912–18 and 1925–37. He wrote a number of theological works in which he maintained the traditional anti-Latin theses and vigorously attacked Catholic dogma, with which, however, he was not very intimately acquainted. He appears on some points to have been influenced by Protestant theology. BIBLIOGRAPHY: Jugie v. 2–4 for an exposition of his theology.

[P. K. MEAGHER]

ANEIROS, LEÓN FEDERICO (1828–94), abp. of Buenos Aires from 1873. A. was a zealous man who strove somewhat ineffectively to stem the mounting tide of secularism in his country by promoting education and the Catholic press. His difficulties were aggravated by troublemaking clerics he had admitted to his archdiocese from abroad.

[P. K. MEAGHER]

ANERIO, two brothers, Italian Renaissance composers. (1) Felice (c.1560–1614), student of and successor to *Palestrina as composer to the papal chapel, and whose style is so similar to that of his predecessor that several of his compositions were for some time attributed to Palestrina. Felice's style is, however, somewhat more chromatic and some of his works require organ accompaniment. (2) Giovanni Francesco (c.1567–c.1621), priest and composer, whose most important musical posts were in Rome. His sacred works are, like his brother's, in the Palestrina style and surpass his attempts at secular music in the then-new baroque manner. BIBLIOGRAPHY: K. G. Fellerer, MGG 1:470–474.

[J. WALSH; A. DOHERTY]

ANESTHESIA, distinguished from analgesia, a loss of the perception of feeling and sensation. It is induced muscle relaxation to relieve pain of sickness or prolonged operative pain. From the earliest history of man herbs and alcohol were used for pain relief. Then ether and nitrous gas were introduced. These gave way to modern methods of anesthesia. Christian forbearance of pain and suffering is not to be overlooked nor are the supererogatory effects of such forbearance. But the use of anesthesia does not create moral problems, except the term be extended to the abuse of amphetamines, barbiturates, and other types of tranquilizers. BIBLIOGRAPHY: T. J. O'Donnell, NCE 1:499–500.

[J. R. RIVELLO]

ANFREDUS GONTERI (b. c.1270), Franciscan theologian. A. was born in Brittany and studied at Paris where he was a follower of Duns Scotus. He was involved in transactions against Boniface when the latter fought with Philip the Fair. Apparently A. was recognized by his contemporaries as an able theologian—one of whom, at least, referred to him as an "outstanding disciple of Scotus." He also holds the honorific title, *Doctor providus*. BIBLIOGRAPHY: A. Emmen, NCE 1:500–501.

[J. R. RIVELLO]

ANGEL, GUARDIAN, see GUARDIAN ANGEL.

ANGEL OF INCENSE, a descriptive title based on Rev 8.3. The iconography of the angels in the Western Church frequently depicts them as thurifers. In the Roman high Mass, the blessing of incense alludes to the celestial altar of incense in Rev 8.3, and identifies the angel as Michael. Medieval missals often named the angel Gabriel, because of Lk 1.11.

[T. C. O'BRIEN]

ANGEL OF SACRIFICE, a description based on the prayer of the Roman Canon, *Supplices te rogamus,* which petitions that the sacrifice be borne by the hands of God's holy angel to the heavenly altar. The imagery, based on Rev 8.3–5, is found in many Eastern liturgies, in the writings of Irenaeus, Origen, Augustine, and other Fathers, and in Christian iconography. Commentators speculate on whether the angel of sacrifice is one angel, e.g., Michael, or a figure of the intercessory ministrations of the angelic host.

[T. C. O'BRIEN]

ANGEL OF THE LORD, an expression found esp. in the Pentateuch and the historical books of the OT. The Angel of Yahweh or Angel of Elohim (Gen 31.11) seems at times to be identical with God himself or a personification of some divine attribute; at other times the angel seems to be a distinct, personal being, the messenger of God. There is no biblical speculation on the nature of such a being. The expression is also found in the NT, Mt 1.20; Acts 5.19.

[T. EARLY]

ANGEL OF THE SCHOOLS, a title, perhaps a variant of Angelic Doctor, given to St. Thomas Aquinas.

[P. K. MEAGHER]

ANGELA OF FOLIGNO, BL. (c.1249–1309), Franciscan mystic. A. married at an early age, had several children, and lived a worldly and frivolous life until 1285 when she experienced a sudden conversion. After some time the deaths of her husband and children left her free to become a third order Franciscan. In a pilgrimage to Assisi she put herself under the protection of St. Francis, and upon her return sold her property, giving the proceeds to the poor, and entered upon a life of prayer and penance in company with another devout woman. She quickly reached a state of mystical union with God, enduring in the process great suffering and temptation. Disciples, men and women, gathered about her. Her spiritual doctrine was in the orthodox Franciscan tradition, despite the fact that she made a great impression on Umberto of Casale and favored, without endorsing its exaggerations, the position on poverty taken by the Spirituals. What is known of her life and mystical experience was recorded by her confessor and spiritual director, a Franciscan named Arnold. Her experiences and doctrine, acknowledged by such respected authorities as SS. Philip Neri, Francis de Sales, Alphonsus Liguori as well as by Bossuet, Fénelon, and Benedict XIV, have won her a high place among the great Catholic mystics. BIBLIOGRAPHY: P. Doncoeur, DSAM 1:570–571; H. Graef, NCE 501–502; Butler 1:440–444; A. Blasucci, BiblSanct 1:1185–90.

[P. K. MEAGHER]

ANGELA MARIA OF THE IMMACULATE CONCEPTION, VEN.

(1649–90), Trinitarian reformer. Born in the diocese of Salamanca, Spain, A. entered the Discalced Carmelites at 21 but left before profession. She was then received into the Order of the Holy Trinity at Medina del Campo and made her profession. Some years later, desiring a more austere way of life, she took with her a number of young companions and established a convent at Toboso (1681). The constitutions of these Trinitarians of the Primitive Observances were approved by Innocent XI. The cause for her beatification was introduced in 1912. Two of her writings have been published, an autobiography written in obedience to her spiritual director (1691), and *Riego espiritual para nuevas plantas* (1691) a treatise on perfection, which contains an excellent treatment of meditation and contemplation. BIBLIOGRAPHY: J. de Guibert, DSAM 1:569–570; T. della S. Famiglia, BiblSanct 1:1190–91.

[P. K. MEAGHER]

ANGELIC BRETHREN

(Ger. Engelsbrüder), a spiritualistic group called also Gichtelians, after the founder Johann Georg Gichtel (1638–1710). He was a lawyer who claimed to have visions and mystical dreams. He came in conflict with the Lutheran Church over his mysticism and agitation for church reform and was expelled from Regensburg as a heretic. After a period of wandering, he settled in Amsterdam. Deeply impressed by the writings of J. *Boehme, he edited their first complete edition (1682). The Angelic Brethren were not members of any Church, but held their own gatherings of silent worship and of testimony to their own visionary experiences. The name connotes their imitation of angels by the renunciation of marriage (Mt 22.30) and devotion to quiet contemplation; they also practiced voluntary poverty. Small communities in The Netherlands, Germany, and Russia survived into the 20th century. BIBLIOGRAPHY: Gründler 1:454; M. Schmidt, RGG 2:1568–69.

[T. C. O'BRIEN]

ANGELIC DOCTOR,

an honorific title used in reference to St. Thomas Aquinas.

[P. K. MEAGHER]

ANGELIC HABIT,

called also by Byzantine monks, the great habit, a habit given to a monk only after he has been tried and tested over a period of many years of monastic life. It is considered a sign of great holiness of life, and many additional prayer obligations are imposed upon the one who wears it. This garment is frequently embellished with the symbols of the Passion and Death of Christ.

[P. MORLINO]

ANGELIC HYMN,

one of the names given to the *Gloria in excelsis* hymn. It is so called because the opening phrases are taken directly from the angelic song heard by the shepherds at the time of Christ's birth (Lk 2.13–14).

[P. K. MEAGHER]

ANGELIC LIFE,

a metaphor comparing the monastic life to the life of the angels. This comparison has been in use from the earliest times of monasticism. The foundation for this theme of angelic life is to be found in St. Luke's Gospel 20.34–36. Monastic life already anticipates this state inasmuch as it is free of purely temporal preoccupation. In a broader sense the angelic state is a dimension of the life of every Christian, for the life of grace is already the life of heaven in a germinal state.

[P. MORLINO]

ANGELIC SALUTATION, see HAIL MARY.

ANGELICO, FRA (GIOVANNI DA FIESOLE,

1378–1455), Florentine painter and Dominican friar (known also as Guido da Vicchio) whose early work (1418–30) in International Gothic style, with tooled gold grounds and elegant delicate figures, shows the influence of a Neoplatonic mysticism. Great examples from his mature period include *The Deposition from the Cross* (1433) and frescoes in the monastery of S. Marco (1437), where figures set in flowery Tuscan meadows evidence a new positive mysticism. A. began a Last Judgment fresco in Orvieto cathedral (1447) but was called to Rome by Nicholas V to decorate the Nicholas Chapel in the Vatican. A. demonstrated there his command of contemporary Renaissance investigations in form and perspective. In 1449 A. became prior of S. Domenico at Fiesole for 3 years, after which he returned to Rome where he is buried in the church of S.

Maria sopra Minerva. BIBLIOGRAPHY: J. Pope-Hennessy, *Fra Angelico* (1952); M. Salmi, *Il beato Angelico* (1958).

[L. P. SIGER]

ANGELICUM, see ST. THOMAS AQUINAS, PONTIFICAL UNIVERSITY OF.

ANGELINA, ST. (d. 1516), despot of Serbia. A relative of Prince Ivan Tsrnoievič, she married Stephen Branovič, who became despot of Serbia upon the death of his brother (1458). Her husband died in 1477, and after the death of Vunk (1485 or 1486), who succeeded him, A. herself assumed the title and carried on the struggle against the Turks. She was a devout woman and has been venerated in Yugoslavia down to the present time both for her piety and her patriotism. BIBLIOGRAPHY: A. Moreschini, BiblSanct 1:1232.

[P. K. MEAGHER]

ANGELINA OF MARSCIANO, BL. (known also as A. of Corbara and A. of Foligno; 1377–1435), considered the foundress of the Franciscan Third Order Regular for women. Married and widowed at an early age, A. adopted the dress of a Franciscan tertiary and turned her household into a kind of religious community. She went about encouraging young women to a life of virginity with such success that she was accused of sorcery and heresy. She was exiled by King Ladislaus of Naples. After a visit to Assisi, she and her companions went to Foligno where they took the vows of religion and founded their first monastery (1397). Another house was founded in Foligno (1399), which was followed by others at Assisi, Viterbo, Florence, Spoleto, etc. Pope Martin V united the 16 houses existing in 1430 in a single congregation and made A. superior general. The congregation was put under the jurisdiction of the Friars Minor. BIBLIOGRAPHY: G. Cerafogli, BiblSanct 1:1231–32.

ANGELO OF ACRI, BL. (baptized Luca Antonio Falcone; 1669–1739), Capuchin preacher, whose simple mission talks, void of all ornate rhetoric, were eminently successful among the country folk of southern Italy. He was beatified in 1825. BIBLIOGRAPHY: B. da Anrenzano, BiblSanct 1:1234–35; Butler 4:228–229.

[P. K. MEAGHER]

ANGELO CARLETTI DI CHIVASSO, BL. (baptized Antonio Carletti; 1411?–1495 or 1496), Franciscan theologian, canonist, preacher. A. took a degree in law at Bologna and made a promising start upon a secular career, but at the age of 30 abandoned it to become a Franciscan. He held high administrative positions in his order, preached a crusade against the Turks who had occupied Otranto (1480–81), worked as apostolic commissary to win back the Waldensians of Piedmont and Savoy, encouraged the establishment of *montes pietatis* for the relief of the poor, gave spiritual direction to individuals, and wrote as a practical guide for confessors his *Summa casuum conscientiae*, a work

that enjoyed wide popularity for many years. It was commonly known as the *Summa angelica*. A. was beatified in 1753. BIBLIOGRAPHY: Butler 2:81–82; P. K. Meagher, NCE 1:505; G. V. Sabatelli, BiblSanct 1:1235–37.

[P. K. MEAGHER]

ANGELO DEL PAZ (del Pas; 1540–96), Franciscan theologian. In 1555 A. became a Franciscan at Perpignan, then a part of Catalonia, and studied at Alcalá. His office as guardian of the Catalan Recollect houses took him to Rome in 1581, and the rest of his life was spent in Italy, first at Genoa, then at Rome (1584). Sixtus V commissioned A.'s commentaries on the Gospels; two of these were published posthumously, *In Marci evangelium* (1623), *In Lucae evangelium* (1625). So also was an Italian translation of one of A.'s spiritual treatises, *Breve trattato del cognoscere ed amare Iddio* (1596). His cause of beatification was introduced in 1625 and resumed in 1890. BIBLIOGRAPHY: J. Guyens, DSAM 1:567; Hurter 3:246–247.

[P. K. MEAGHER]

ANGELOLOGY, the organized body of teaching concerning angels. The various truths it comprises were first systematized by *Pseudo-Dionysius (c.600) in his work *On the Heavenly Hierarchy*. He holds that there are nine choirs of angels divided into three orders of three choirs each; he obtained their names by collating Eph 1.21 with Col 1.16 to which he added angels, archangels (Jude 9), seraphim (Is 6.2), and cherubim (Ezek 1.5; 10.1–17). This classification was accepted although it has no foundation in revelation. St. Thomas systematically worked out the implications of the spiritual nature of angels. This angelology is denied by those who regard angels as either a personification of God's activity or a mythological representation of natural forces. Such an interpretation of them does not satisfy biblical theologians and is contrary to the constant belief of the Church, which has, however, defined its belief in no more than the existence of angels and their spiritual nature. BIBLIOGRAPHY: J. Michl and T. Klauser, RAC 5:53–322; K. Rahner, SacMund 1:28–31.

[B. FORSHAW]

ANGELS, spiritual messengers of God whose appearances are recorded in the Old and New Testaments, whose nature was extensively discussed in patristic and medieval theology, and whose existence was defined by the Church at Lateran Council IV (1215) and Vatican Council I in 1870 (D 800 and 3002). In the OT, angels are mentioned frequently as a group in Yahweh's service; Hebrew monotheism did not forestall the acknowledgment of these sacred powers present in the divine court and yet clearly subject to God's rule. Their principal activity was to praise God, although they could be sent by God to intercede in human affairs at which time they usually appeared in human, male form. In the NT, angels are related to the central mystery of Christ's lordship over all creation. They are frequently engaged in events connected with the birth of Christ, but also serve a ministering function during the public life of Jesus and as messengers of the Resurrection. In the Pauline Epistles, the significance of the angels is subordinated to the unique mediation of Christ, and Paul is careful to assert the supremacy of Christ over all spiritual powers. The Apocalypse extends significantly the role of angels, esp. in connection with the end of the world, although this must be interpreted within the literary genre of that book.

In patristic theology (esp. that of Pseudo-Dionysius and Gregory the Great), angels came to be regarded as incorporeal, free and therefore able to sin, and of service to God in his care over each human being. Thus devils were regarded as fallen angels, and the notion that God appointed a guardian angel for every person came to be accepted. Nine choirs or groups of angels were designated: archangels (notably those mentioned in Scripture: Gabriel, Michael, and Raphael), angels, the five classes named in the Pauline epistles (virtues, powers, principalities, dominations, and thrones), cherubim, and seraphim. Medieval theology repeated these patristic ideas, and often used angels as a basis for speculation on the immateriality of thought. In contemporary theology the attention paid to angels seems to be quite scant. When they are directly considered, their existence is related to Christ's saving relationship to the world and angels assume the role of being truly the "principalities and powers" of the cosmos. Their nature is to be related to the coming-to-be of Christ in a world dynamically open to spiritual presence and influence. BIBLIOGRAPHY: H. Schlier, *Principalities and Powers in the New Testament* (1961); K. Rahner, SacMund 1:27–35; T. L. Fallon et al., NCE 1:506–519.

[T. M. MCFADDEN]

ANGELS, FALL OF THE, see FALL OF THE ANGELS.

ANGELS OF THE CHURCHES, those to whom the seven letters in Rev ch. 2–3 were addressed. They appeared in John's vision as stars (1.13–16). Interpreters disagree as to whether they were guardian angels, the pastors of the Churches, or whether the term bears some other symbolic meaning.

[T. EARLY]

ANGELUS CLARENUS (Peter of Fossombrone; c.1245–1337), a leader of the Franciscan *Spirituals in Italy. Born Peter at Fossombrone, he entered the Friars Minor in 1270. He was a cleric but not a priest, and gained fame as a preacher, moralist, and translator of the Greek Fathers. Opposing all mitigations of the Franciscan rule in regard to poverty, he held that neither pope, nor council, nor general chapter could change it because, like the Scriptures, it was inspired. He was imprisoned (1275) for his intransigent advocacy of Spiritual doctrines. After his release (1289) he joined a group of like-minded friars who were going as missionaries to Armenia. Peter took the name Angelus, and

the group became known as *Celestines in 1294, when Celestine V granted them immunity from the jurisdiction of the Franciscan minister general. When the immunity was revoked by Boniface VIII, the group retired to the Island of Trixonia in the Gulf of Corinth. At the death of Liberatus of Macerata (1307) A. assumed leadership of the fugitive company, which thereafter was known as *Clareni. In 1311 he was summoned to Avignon to answer charges of heresy but was protected by Card. Colonna. After the bull of John XXII, *Sancta Romana* (1317), A. was excommunicated and imprisoned, but he succeeded in getting his freedom through a letter of appeal to the Pope.

Returning to Italy, he reorganized his followers and proclaimed them the true Friars Minor and the authentic Church of Christ. After a period of security until 1334, A. had to flee to Basilicata, farther south in Italy, and there he died. His most influential writing was *Historia septem tribulationum*. A. has been accused of *Joachimism, but C. Pesaro and others have attempted to establish his great sanctity. BIBLIOGRAPHY: L. Bernardini, *Frate Angelo da Chiarino alla luce della storia* (1964); V. Doucet, "Angelus Clarenus ad Alvarum Pelagium," AFH 39 (1946) 63–200; D. Douie, *Nature and Effects of the Heresy of the Fraticelli* (1932) 49–80; L. Oliger, *Expositio Regulae Fratrum Minorum auctore Angelo Clareno* (1912) ix–lxxvii; C. Pesaro, *Il Clareno* (1921); L. von Auw, *Angelo Clareno et les Spirituels franciscains* (1952).

[C. J. LYNCH]

ANGELUS DE SCARPETIS, BL. (Angelus of Borgo San Sepolcro; d. 1306), hermit. Born in Borgo San Sepolcro (Umbria) of the noble family of Scarpetti, A. entered the Augustinian Order c.1254, and it is believed he was sent to England where he founded several houses. He was noted for his humility, poverty, and childlike innocence. A.'s body was preserved intact, and his life was said to be written by the Augustinian, John of St. William. BIBLIOGRAPHY: J. E. Bresnahan, NCE 1:520; A. Palmieri, DHGE 3:16; A. M. Giacomini, BiblSanct 1:1245.

[M. C. BRADLEY]

ANGELUS SILESIUS (Johannes Scheffler; 1624–77), German mystical poet, polemicist. He was physician to the Duke of Oels in Silesia when he left the Lutheran for the RC Church (1653), abandoning his career and family name. He was ordained in 1661, and in seclusion at Breslau devoted his life to writing. A.'s mystical works are marked by sweetness and tenderness; his polemics, by bitterness and vituperation. Drawn to mysticism through his acquaintance, while a student at Leyden, Holland, with the writings of J. *Boehme, A. deeply studied the Fathers and the medieval mystics. His mystical works are *Heilige Seelenlust* (1657) and *Der Cherubinische Wandersmann* (1675; first published in 1657 under a different title). He employed the Alexandrine verse form to write in antithetical epigrams on the descent of God to the soul in mystical experience. His poetic works are esteemed not only for their literary quality, but for their sublimity and devotion, which led to their adoption in both RC and Protestant, esp. Pietist, prayers and hymns. His polemics, both defending himself against ridicule at his conversion and attacking Reformation bodies, were matched in bitterness only by those of his opponents. They were a mine for the controversialists of the 17th and 18th cent.; of more than 50, mostly pseudonymous, some 30 were published in his *Ecclesiologia* (1677). BIBLIOGRAPHY: S. Schulz, NCE 1:520–521, bibliog.; W. Dürig, LTK 1:542.

[T. C. O'BRIEN]

ANGELUS, a Catholic devotional practice performed in the early morning, at noon, and in the evening, usually, in places where the custom is generally observed, during the ringing of a bell. The name is taken from the first word of the versicle with which it begins, *Angelus Domini nuntiavit Mariae* (The angel of the Lord declared unto Mary). It consists of three versicles with their responses, each followed by a Hail Mary, and it concludes with a prayer. A similar devotion appeared in Germany in the 13th century. It was said at night, and the morning and midday usage developed later. The Angelus came into general use in the 17th century. BIBLIOGRAPHY: H. Graef, *Devotion to Our Lady* (1963) 57–58.

[T. EARLY]

ANGER, an emotional reaction against an injury inflicted by another or against the threat of such injury. It prompts one to take action to overcome the injury or its threat and the physical changes it brings about mobilize the body's forces for aggression. The injury or threatened harm may be seen as directed against oneself or against what is in some way identified with oneself. It can occur in varying degrees. It is not per se an evil or sinful reaction, for in the Gospels we are told that Jesus was angered on some occasions. It becomes sinful, however, when it is unreasonable or excessive. Anger can be an extremely forceful drive and learning to keep it under reasonable control is very important to one's emotional training. Anger has been classified as a *capital sin because it can easily be the source from which many different sins arise.

[P. K. MEAGHER]

ANGER OF GOD, see WRATH OF GOD.

ANGERS, CATHOLIC UNIVERSITY OF, a coeducational institution of higher learning at Angers in France, established in 1875 as a restoration of a university that had flourished at Angers from medieval times down to its suppression during the French Revolution. This ancient university was the outgrowth of a celebrated cathedral school that had existed at Angers from the early 11th century. The faculty of law in the new university gained official recognition in 1875, letters in 1876, science in 1877, and theology in 1879. At the time of its foundation the university was intended to train teachers to staff the seminaries and colleges of Western France, but as time went on the need for a broader

objective became apparent and a number of schools and colleges were added to the original four faculties. The faculty of theology grants the baccalaureate, licentiate, and doctorate, but the other faculties are not permitted by French law to confer university degrees and diplomas; these are awarded by the state to students of the university who fulfill the necessary requirements. Enrollment, including both French and foreign students, averages about 1,800; the teaching staff, 200. The university's Lamoricière library contains approximately 100,000 volumes. The university is governed by a council of bishops of the region which it serves. In civil matters it is subject to the jurisdiction of the Ministry of Education. BIBLIOGRAPHY: International Handbook of Universities (ed. H. M. R. Keyes, 1966); E. Bricard, NCE 3:336–337.

[M. B. MURPHY]

ANGILBERT, ST. (d. 814), poet and official at the court of Charlemagne; lay abbot of Saint-Riquier (781–814). Taught by Alcuin, A. became tutor of Charlemagne's son Pepin, and for more than 20 years he held important court positions. His poems caused him to be called "Homer" in the court circle. He rebuilt and endowed Saint-Requier with a fine library and introduced continuous choir service *(laus perennis)*. He wrote two treatises on his monastic work. BIBLIOGRAPHY: V. Gellhaus, NCE 1:524; Butler 1:371.

[G. M. COOK]

ANGILRAMNUS OF METZ (d. 791), canonist, abbot of Sens, bp. of Metz (768–791), chaplain at Charlemagne's court from 784. His historical importance derives from the *Capitula Angilramni*, a part of the psuedo-Isidorian decretals bearing his name. This collection contains 71 capitularies, concerned mostly with the prosecution of clerics, esp. bps., and purports to have been sent by Pope Adrian I to A. and afterward to have been dispatched by the latter to Adrian II as a defense of his own administration at Metz. BIBLIOGRAPHY: P. L. Hug, NCE 1:524.

[G. M. COOK]

ANGKOR THOM (12th–13th cent.). A synthesis of Hindu and Buddhist iconography, this colossal, magnificent temple was built by the great Khmer king, Jayavarman VII (1181–1220). The central Bayon or sanctuary rises high above the complex of five gateways, continuous corbel galleries, and pavilions, its avenues of approach lined by 54 giant gods and demons clasping the Hindu serpent (naga) Vaṣuki in the allegory of creation, its reflecting moat more than 10 miles long and 100 yards wide. Unique carvings on each side of the square towers are the colossal, ever-watchful nine-foot heads of the king *(devarāja)* symbolizing his power in all directions, remarkable for that enigmatic mystic 'Angkor smile' of the compassionate Lokeśvara and determined by Mus, Coedes, and Prsyluski to be likenesses of Jayavarman himself. Overwhelming in expanses of sculptured walls two miles long on each side, Angkor Thom, executed in haste and therefore lacking the synthesis and sublimity of *Angkor Wat, establishes the incredibly magnificent Khmer civilization as the most brilliant of the Indochina peninsula. BIBLIOGRAPHY: B. P. Groslier, *Art of Indochina* (1962).

[M. J. DALY]

ANGKOR WAT (1113–50), temple complex. The highest expression of Khmer genius and last of Cambodian pure Hindu art forms, this prime example of colossal agglomeration was built by the Khmer king Suryavarman II (1112–52) to Viṣnu and to himself as god-king *(devarāja)*, evidencing his power and ambition. This divine cosmic mountain, surrounded by a reflecting moat 2 1/2 miles long and more than 200 yards wide, its approach flanked by the long serpent *(naga)* balustrade, one of the most beautiful inventions of Khmer civilization, its gateways, continuous galleries (corbel vaulted) surmounted by a profusion of towers and pavilions, rises to the Bayon (sanctuary) at its summit. The miles of colored and gilded sculptured reliefs, characterized by the mystic 'Angkor smile' of deep compassion, depicting the legend of creation, the avatars of Viṣnu, the Rāmāyana and Mahabharata, are among the noblest in the history of man. Angkor Wat is the apogee of Khmer art in grandeur, unity, and balance. BIBLIOGRAPHY: B.P. Groslier, *Art of Indochina* (1962).

[M. J. DALY]

ANGLÈS, HIGINI (1888–1969), Catalan priest and musicologist. A. studied musicology with F. Pedrell, W. Gurlitt, and F. Ludwig, later became head of the music section of the Biblioteca de Catalunya, Barcelona (1917), professor of music history at the Barcelona Conservatory (1927) and University (1933), director of the Instituto Español de Musicologia (1943), and president of the Pontifical Institute of Sacred Music Rome (1947). His publications include editions of important Spanish sources of medieval and Renaissance music, such as the Las Huelgas codex, the Cantigas of Alfonso X, and the *Cancionero del Palacio*, the collected organ works of Cabanilles, and articles in MGG and elsewhere. BIBLIOGRAPHY: MGG 1:482; A. Doherty, NCE (1974) 16:9.

[A. DOHERTY]

ANGLESEY, PRIORY OF, Cambridgeshire, England. Anglesey was a hospital in the 12th cent. which was converted into a priory of Canons Regular of St. Augustine (*c.*1212). The community usually numbered nine members. The priory was suppressed in 1536. BIBLIOGRAPHY: E. Hailstone, *History and Antiquities of . . . the Priory of Angelsey* (1873); S. Wood, NCE 1:524–525.

[J. R. SOMMERFELDT]

ANGLICAN CHANT, music employed for the unmetrical texts of the Anglican liturgy. Used first in England and still popular in the U.S., it developed, in the 16th cent., directly from the Gregorian psalm tones. It is a harmonized recita-

tion, on one note, with cadential formulas, differing from the Gregorian tones in the elimination of the intonation and in the use of English, of four-part harmony and of metrical divisions. Each chant (single) has seven measures in a partially free 2/2 time. (There exist also double, triple, and quadruple chants.) The example below will best illustrate the chant and show its derivation from the Gregorian tones:

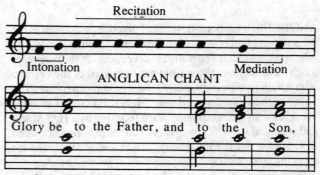

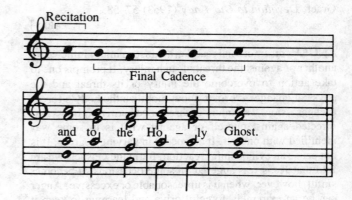

The effect of this type of chant is a sort of musically delivered speech, almost entirely syllabic.

Since the ancient Gregorian tones remained in universal use as late as the 17th cent., it was not until *c.*1660 that musicians such as James Clifford and Edward Lowe, in addition to Gregorian settings, gave some four-part harmonizations, inspired, no doubt, by the falso-bordones of composers Tallis, Byrd, etc. The number composed since then is very great, but their quality is variable. BIBLIOGRAPHY: *Oxford Companion to Music* (ed. P.A. Scholes, 1970) 34–36; E. Dickinson, *Music in the History of the Western Church* (1925) 336–342; Grove DMM 2:172–174.

[M. T. LEGGE]

ANGLICAN CHURCH, the *Church of England; also used commonly of any of the Churches of the *Anglican Communion.

[T. C. O'BRIEN]

ANGLICAN CHURCH MUSIC, music used for the services of the Church of England. In the period immediately following the break with Rome, pre-Reformation musical practices survived in the C of E, with minimal changes necessitated by the introduction of the vernacular. The development of English church music in the 400 years that followed, however, has reflected the continuing controversies over matters of dogma and liturgy (Anglicanism vs. Puritanism, conformity vs. independence, etc.) which troubled the Church. Musical schools have tended, to some extent, to identify with particular schools of "churchmanship."

Notable among the developments in Anglican music are the following: the adaptation of the Gregorian Missal and Breviary to all parts of the *Prayer Book* by John Marbecke in 1550 (settings which are still in use); the development of Anglican chant and more elaborate figured settings of the *anthem* and *service;* the incorporation, in the 17th cent., of continental vocal style and technique; the early 19th-cent. Oxford Movement, which aimed at a restoration of the ancient principles of vocal worship, including a restoration of Gregorian chant; and the foundation of several excellent societies, such as the Royal School of Church Music.

The ritual of the C of E is contained, basically, in the *Book of Common Prayer*, which comprises matins and evensong, the liturgy of holy communion, the rites of confirmation, ordination, etc. The liturgy contains constant and variable parts, including prayers, special psalms to be sung, canticles, the ordinary parts of the Mass, etc.

Aside from the 16th-cent. composers Tallis, Byrd, Tye, and Gibbons, the 17th-cent. John Blow and Henry Purcell, and the contemporary Vaughan Williams and Benjamin Britten, English church music has never risen above a certain mediocrity in composition. However, by reason of the creditable average excellence it has maintained for over 400 years, it has won an honorable position in the total volume of church music. BIBLIOGRAPHY: W. Douglas, *Church Music in History and Practice* (1937); E. Dickinson, *Music in the History of the Western Church* (1925); Grove DMM 35–39.

[M. T. LEGGE]

ANGLICAN CHURCH OF CANADA, since 1893 an autocephalous Church of the *Anglican Communion. Third largest of Canadian religious bodies, it has about 1 million members in its 28 dioceses, grouped in four ecclesiastical provinces. The Church shares a common origin with the Protestant Episcopal Church in the U.S. Prior to the American Revolution, political consideration both in England and in the colonies prevented the establishment of the episcopate in N.A., and Anglican jurisdiction was loosely vested in the bp. of London. With the coming of independence to the U.S. the C of E in the remaining provinces of British N.A. began developing its own separate tradition. The emigration of the continuing loyalists from the U.S. following the Revolution added strength to the scattered Anglican population, esp. in Ontario and Nova Scotia. In 1787 Charles Inglis (1734–1816), sometime rector of Trinity parish in New York City, was consecrated bp. of Nova Scotia, the first Anglican bp. appointed outside the British Isles. Aided by the British missionary societies, the Anglican Church moved westward with the nation. The confederation of four civil provinces to form the Dominion of Canada (1867) and the later addition of other provinces stimulated parallel action by the Anglican ecclesiastical provinces; in 1893 a national general synod was established and Canada's first primate elected.

The Church remained the Church of England in Canada until 1955, when the title Anglican Church of Canada was adopted, the first use of "Anglican" in such a manner.

Growth in Canadian national unity and self-awareness in the 19th and 20th cent. has been echoed in the life of the Anglican Church. Relations with the Episcopal Church in the U.S. became increasingly strong in the mid-20th cent., culminating in the establishment of the Regional Council of North America in 1968. The Anglican Church of Canada (ACC) has in the past maintained strong ties with the C of E and continues to uphold the faith and order of that Church; it uses in its worship the *Book of Common Prayer, revised in 1918 and again in 1959. Conversations between the Anglican and United Churches of Canada led in 1965 to the publication and formal acceptance of *The Principles of Union Between the Anglican Church of Canada and the United Church of Canada*. In 1967 consultations and negotiations looking toward organic union were begun, with a third group, the Christian Church, Disciples of Christ, joining the Commission on Union in 1969. A *Plan of Union* produced by that Commission in 1973 was received for study and consideration by the Anglican Church of Canada, and a Committee on Union and Joint Mission was set up to continue and facilitate work toward union and unity in mission among the three denominations.

A member of the World Council of Churches and the Canadian Council of Churches, the Anglican Church of Canada endeavors to work ecumenically wherever possible. A Canadian Anglican theologian has been a member of the Anglican/Roman Catholic International Commission since its inception in 1967, and there has been Canadian participation in international dialogue with the Lutheran and Orthodox Churches. BIBLIOGRAPHY: P. Carrington, *Anglican Church in Canada* (1963); *idem, Christian Unity and the Anglican Communion* (1965); G. Lane, "New Canadian Hymnal Brings Anglican-UCC Union a Step Closer," *Christian Century* 89 (1972) 18–19; YBACC (1974) 117–118.

[S. F. BAYNE]

ANGLICAN COMMUNION, "a fellowship, within the One Holy Catholic and Apostolic Church, of those duly constituted Dioceses, Provinces, or Regional Churches in communion with the See of Canterbury" (1930 Lambeth Conference, Resolution 49). The definition adds that these Churches "uphold and propagate the Catholic and Apostolic faith and order as it is generally set forth in the Book of

Common Prayer''; ''are particular or national churches, and, as such, promote within each of their territories a national expression of Christian faith, life and worship''; and ''are bound together not by a central legislative and executive authority, but by mutual loyalty sustained through the common counsel of the Bishops in conference.'' The name seems to have been used first in 1851. ''Anglican'' refers not to language or culture but to common ancestry in the Church of England.

In this fellowship 21 Churches are included. Four are in the British Isles—the Church of England, the Church in Wales, the Church of Ireland, and the Episcopal Church in Scotland. Next oldest in separate existence are the Protestant Episcopal Church in the U.S. and the Anglican Church of Canada. Following (in the Lambeth order of seniority) are the Church of India, Pakistan, Burma, and Ceylon; the Church of England in Australia; and the Churches of the Provinces of New Zealand, of South Africa, and of the West Indies. Founded by Anglican missionary effort are Nippon Sei Ko Kai (Holy Catholic Church of Japan) and Chung-Hua Sheng Kung Hui (Holy Catholic Church of China). More recently organized Churches are those of the Provinces of West Africa and Central Africa, the Archbishopric in Jerusalem, the Province of East Africa, and the Church of Uganda, Rwanda, and Burundi. The first autocephalous Church in Latin America is the Igréja Episcopal do Brasil. There are also 11 extraprovincial dioceses under the abp. of Canterbury; and finally the Iglésia Episcopal de Cuba, an extraprovincial diocese under its own metropolitan council. About 46 million Christians are included (1974) in the membership of the various Churches, gathered in 364 dioceses in 35 ecclesiastical provinces.

The unity of the Anglican Communion is neither constitutional nor confessional. The prayer books of the various Churches differ increasingly as revision and liturgical development continue; nevertheless, there is still unity in the central matters of faith and order among the Churches, and the lack of a ''central legislative and executive auhority'' has thrown correspondingly greater weight on various voluntary and informal but significant inter-Anglican agencies and gatherings. The *Lambeth Conference is the oldest and most important of these. Second only to it is the Anglican Congress, a decennial gathering of bishops, priests, and lay people from all Anglican dioceses. The abp. of Canterbury holds a preeminent position of honor among the Anglican metropolitans and in many ways plays a patriarchal role. Administrative liaison is supplied by the Anglican executive officer, who is responsible for the coordination of many practical matters. BIBLIOGRAPHY: G. W. C. Wand, *Anglicanism in History and Today* (1962); H. G. G. Herklots, *Church of England and the American Episcopal Church* (1966); idem, *Frontiers of the Church* (1961); S. Neill, *Anglicanism* (1958); G. F. Fisher, ''Resolutions of the Lambeth Conference of 1968 concerning Church Relations,'' *Theology* 73 (1970) 395–398; G. Tavard, *Protestantism* (tr. R. Attwater, 1959) 91–106; R. H. Fuller, ''Worship, Sacraments and the unity of the church,'' *Anglican Theological Review* 52 (1970) 214–227; H. C. Snape, ''Can the church be saved?'' in *Modern Churchman* 15 (1972) 132–135.

[S. F. BAYNE]

ANGLICAN ORDERS, as a point of dispute, orders in the C of E derived from Matthew Parker, Abp. of Canterbury. He was consecrated Dec. 17, 1549, by two bps. who had been consecrated with the rite of the Roman Pontifical under Henry VIII and two others consecrated with the Edwardine Ordinal under Edward VI. This Ordinal was also used at Parker's consecration; all four consecrators joined in the imposition of hands and in uttering the essential form. A further link connecting Anglican orders with the Latin hierarchy is provided by M. de Dominis, a former abp. of Spalato (Split, Yugo.), who came to England in 1616 and who, like Parker, appears in the table of consecration of all Anglican bps. today. The ''Nag's Head Fable,'' first published in 1604 and asserting that Parker's only consecration was a mock ceremony in a Cheapside tavern, lived on for 3 centuries despite numerous refutations. This and all other attempts to dispute the historical succession of Anglican orders were passed over in silence when their invalidity was reaffirmed in the bull *Apostolicae curae* (1896). The unbroken historical succession of these orders is now admitted by all competent authorities. Beginning in the 1930s the constituent Churches of the *Anglican Communion have entered into intercommunion with the Old Catholic and Polish National Catholic Churches, the orders of which are recognized as valid by the Holy See. The mutual participation of bps. of each of these Churches in the episcopal consecrations of the other Churches has introduced a new valid line of succession into Anglican orders. In 1960 the Holy See took practical cognizance of this changed situation by granting to a converted Anglican priest in the U.S. a matrimonial dispensation from the diriment impediment of the major orders he had received from Anglican bps. of the above succession. On Jan. 27, 1968, Bp. Joseph Höffner of Münster, Germany, gave conditional ordination as deacon and priest to J. J. Hughes, a former priest of the Protestant Episcopal Church, in view of the Old Catholic succession of the Anglican bps. from whom he had previously received the same orders.

Rejection of purely Anglican orders in *Apostolicae curae* is based upon defects of intention and form in the 16th century. (The bull avoids a direct judgment about the validity of the expanded forms of ordination in use among Anglicans since 1662.) In 1956 F. Clark classified no less than seven different interpretations of the intention by those seeking to show why it was rightly condemned. Clark himself presents the most thorough and scholarly reasoning on why the intention was declared invalid; yet the authorities he cites do not, when read in context, support him.

Of greater weight is the papal argument from defect of form. This asserts that the English Reformers rejected the sacrifice of the Mass and drew up their new ordination rites to express this rejection, carefully eliminating from the elements retained from the old rites all references to any priestly power of offering sacrifice in the Mass. These rites were therefore incapable, it is argued, of passing on what opponents of Anglican orders invariably call "the sacrificing priesthood."

Defenders of Anglican orders admit the English Reformers' rejection of eucharistic sacrifice but point out that valid orders can be conveyed and received by those whose theology of orders is heretical. They assert that the denial of the sacrifice of the Mass must be judged in the light of mistaken ideas about eucharistic sacrifice said to have been current in the 16th century. Opponents reply that the ideas of eucharistic sacrifice prevalent on the eve of the Reformation were sound and orthodox and that the English Reformers deliberately rejected this body of traditional teaching. The counterreply asserts that the vast multiplication of Masses in the late medieval period had produced a highly questionable theology: the idea of a limited value of every Mass with the quantitative conception of grace that this implied, and the widespread idea that each Mass added something to Calvary. They maintain that the Reformers' protest, though exaggerated, was thus occasioned by real theological abuses that are rejected by RC theologians today. The controversy involves a fundamental judgment about the nature of the Reformation and remains unsettled.

Critics of *Apostolicae curae* also argue that it reflects a narrow and polemically colored theology of the ministry that is not fairly representative of the full RC tradition. Contemporary attempts to break the impasse include the 1971 Windsor Statement and the 1973 Canterbury Statement on the Eucharist and on ministry by the Anglican-RC International Consultation cast new light and raise hope on the issue of mutual recognition of ministry. BIBLIOGRAPHY: F. Clark, *Anglican Orders and Defect of Intention* (1956); *idem, Eucharistic Sacrifice and the Reformation* (2d ed., 1967); J. J. Hughes, *Absolutely Null and Utterly Void* (1968), with bibliog.; *idem, Stewards of the Lord* (1969); E. Mascall, "Anglican Orders after Vatican II," *Tablet* 225 (1971) 78–80; H. B. Porter, "Theology of Ordination and the new Rites," *Anglican Theological Review* 54 (1972) 69–81; E. P. Echlin, "Anglican Orders; a case for validity," *ibid.*, 52 (1970) 67–76.

[J. J. HUGHES]

ANGLICAN ORDINALS, the four formularies for conferring orders in the C of E, important in the history and nature of Anglicanism. The Ordinals have been printed with the *Book of Common Prayer, although not properly a part of it. The four Ordinals appeared respectively in 1550, 1552, 1559, and 1662; the last remains in use. The 1550 Ordinal, the work of T. *Cranmer and other bishops and theologians, was modeled on the Pontifical of the Sarum rite. M. *Bucer's revision of the ordination formula and exhortation to ordinands reflected a pastoral rather than a sacrificial accep-

tance of the priesthood. The 1552 Ordinal omitted the ceremony of handing the chalice with the bread to the ordinand. The 1559 Ordinal contained only minor revisions. The formula was: "Receive the Holy Ghost. Whose sins thou dost forgive they are forgiven; whose sins thou dost retain they are retained. And be thou a faithful dispenser of the Word of God and of His Holy Sacraments. In the name of the Father and of the Son and of the Holy Ghost. Amen." The significant modifications in the 1662 Ordinal were the insistence in the preface on the requirement for episcopal consecration or ordination prior to acceptance as a lawful bishop, priest, or deacon; the revision of the formula of ordination, i.e., with the laying on of hands the bishop was to say, "Receive the Holy Ghost for the office and work of a priest in the Church of God, now committed to thee by the imposition of our hands. Whose sins thou dost forgive they are forgiven; whose sins thou dost retain they are retained. And be thou a faithful dispenser of the Word of God and His Holy Sacraments. In the Name of the Father and of the Son and of the Holy Ghost. Amen." The Ordinal printed in the American Prayer Book substantially conforms in preface and in the actual text to that of 1662. There is, however, an alternate form, which omits mention of the forgiveness of sins. BIBLIOGRAPHY: J. J. Hughes, *Absolutely Null and Utterly Void* (1968) with bibliog.; J. A. Hardon, *Spirit and Origins of American Protestantism* (1968) 191–200; bibliog. for Book of Common Prayer. *ANGLICAN ORDERS.

[T. C. O'BRIEN]

ANGLICAN—ROMAN CATHOLIC INTERNATIONAL COMMISSION (ARCIC), the group of Anglican and RC bps. and theologians engaged since 1969 in a study and discussion of doctrine with the ecumenical intent of reconciling the viewpoint of each Church. Its most important achievements to date are the Windsor Statement of 1971 on the Eucharist and the Canterbury Statement of 1973 on ministry. Both have brought the cause of unity dramatically forward; they are not official church teaching, but they have been submitted to and received by the ruling authorities of each body. The statements acknowledge that differences remain between the two Churches, but that they are documents of doctrinal agreement in which each communion on such vital topics can recognize its own beliefs. The Windsor Statement agrees that the Eucharist when celebrated is an *anamnesis* (memorial) of Jesus' Paschal Mystery; that it makes present the historic reality of Christ's sacrifice; that Christ becomes really present in virtue of the celebration, not simply by reason of the faith of the assembly. The Canterbury Statement, while excluding from its scope the issues of authority, primacy, and mutual recognition of ministries, agrees that the ordained ministry of deacons, presbyters, and bishops serves the priesthood of all the faithful, but is itself a separate ministry in the Church, related to Christ and commissioned by him. It is a ministry in continuity with apostles' ministry and that succession is expressed in the ordination rite. The ordained ministry is Eucharistic and in the sense that, following the Windsor Statement, the Eucharist is memorial and sacrifice. A moving witness to the achievements of the ARCIC was the joint prayer service led by the abp. of Canterbury and the pope together in 1977.

ANGLICANISM, the tradition and practice of the *Anglican Communion, that worldwide body of Christians in communion with the abp. of Canterbury. National Churches, which are found in six continents, possess a wide range of autonomy. The bps. gather each decade in England for their *Lambeth Conferences; the resolutions, though not binding, are significant expressions of the opinions of the Anglican episcopate. The hierarchy possesses a minimum of coercive authority; Anglicans are bound together, most importantly, through their use of the *Book of Common Prayer (BCP), variously amended and revised through the centuries. Lex orandi, lex credendi is a most important principle of Anglicanism and places great weight upon worship and its forms, which still largely follow those of T. *Cranmer (1489–1556). The distinctive formularies and the basis for the historical claims of Anglicanism are to be found in the reign of Elizabeth I (1558–1603) and not that of Henry VIII or Edward VI. Elizabeth's decisions, along with those of Parliament and *Convocations in regard to the ecclesiastical settlement, are to be seen in the BCP of 1559, which largely follows Cranmer's second Book of 1552, and in the *Thirty-Nine Articles, issued in the same year as the closing of the Council of *Trent. The BCP and the Articles, together with the careful retention of continuity with the medieval Church through ordination and polity, form the basis for the Anglican claim to be "truly Catholic and truly Reformed."

The writings of John *Jewel (1522–71) have been traditionally regarded as indicating the Anglican posture toward Roman Catholicism. On the critical differences in doctrine and practice he appealed to Scripture, the first four general councils, and the Fathers of the first 6 centuries of undivided Christendom. He sought to prove that the necessary reformation could not be accomplished by the Council of Trent and that national Churches have a right to legislate through provincial synods. John *Whitgift (1530–1604) and Richard *Hooker (1554–1600) provide in their writings the lines between Anglicanism and the demands of the Puritans in regard to ceremonials, polity, and doctrine. Hooker's *The Laws of Ecclesiastical Polity* generally has been accepted as the most central and balanced view of the distinctive Anglican positions, esp. in regard to his appeal to Scripture, reason, and tradition in questions of authority. Hooker's three headings conveniently schematize the often perplexing spectrum of emphases within historical Anglicanism. Though each of the three basic emphases accepts the judgment of Scripture as primary, the evangelicals' emphasis upon Scripture leads them esp. to put strong weight upon preaching, the doctrines of the Fall, justification, and atonement and to stress *kerygmatic theology. Charles *Simeon (1759–1836) is an example of this emphasis within Anglicanism.

Those whose emphasis is upon reason are referred to as latitudinarian, liberal, or modernist. Their appeal is most frequently to toleration and freedom, with stress upon apologetics, historical and biblical criticism, and the atonement as exemplary, not substitutionary. Abp. John *Tillotson (1630–94) is an example of this emphasis.

The emphasis upon tradition has produced men of deep commitment to institutional continuity, polity, liturgy, and conformity, with stress upon the doctrines of the Church, sacraments, and the incarnation. Abp. William *Laud (1573–1645) has always been regarded as personifying much of this heritage. More central figures illustrating the nature of Anglicanism, in addition to Cranmer and Hooker, are John Donne (1571 or 72–1631), Frederick Denison *Maurice (1805–72), and Abp. William *Temple (1881–1944). BIBLIOGRAPHY: Works of figures mentioned above; E. J. Bicknell, *Theological Introduction to the Thirty-Nine Articles* (3rd ed., 1955); *Doctrine in the Church of England: The Report of the Commission on Christian Doctrine Appointed by the Archbishops of Canterbury and York in 1922* (1938); P. E. More, F. L. Cross, *Anglicanism* (1951); S. Neill, *Anglicanism* (pa. 1958); E. James, "Can the Church of England Be Renewed?" *Christian Century* 88 (1971) 313–315; J. Simpson and E. Story, *Long Shadows of Lambeth X* (1969). *CHURCH OF ENGLAND; *PROTESTANT EPISCOPAL CHURCH.

[C. F. ALLISON]

ANGLO-CATHOLIC CONGRESSES, rallies held in London in 1920, '23, '27, '30, '33, and again in '48, to further the cause of Catholicism within the *Anglican Communion. They were often stirring occasions in the best tradition of meetings at the Albert Hall. In 1934 the Congresses were united with the English Church Union to form the Church Union. BIBLIOGRAPHY: *Reports,* esp. 1920 and 1933.

ANGLO-CATHOLICISM, the group or movement within Anglicanism seeking to stress the continuity of the *Anglican Communion with the pre-Reformation Church and to move toward the closest possible agreement in faith and practice with the RC and Orthodox Churches. This use of the name dates only from the *Oxford movement, and did not become popular until the late 19th century. In rare earlier usage, now obsolete, it referred simply to the C of E or the Anglican Communion (as in the 1865 appeal by the metropolitan of the ecclesiastical province of Canada, which led to the first *Lambeth Conference, in which he described the Canadian bps. as "representatives of the Anglo-Catholic branch of the Christian Church").

Anglo-Catholicism (like the earlier *high-church or *low-church groups) is a spirit, a school of thought, a movement, sometimes a party, but never an organized Church in itself. It sees its role as that of recalling the Anglican Churches to fresh awareness of their Catholic nature, as witnessed by apostolic order, sacramental life, creedal continuity, and the like. Its roots lie in the Oxford movement (sometimes called *Tractarianism or the Catholic Revival), the explosive awakening within the C of E, starting in 1833 in the famous sermon of John *Keble on "National Apostasy." The immediate occasion was the plan of Parliament to abolish 10 Anglican dioceses in Ireland. But the burden of the Oxford movement was rediscovery, not merely protest—a vigorous restatement of the essentially Catholic character of the C of E. The early years of the movement were intense and often divisive. Among the first leaders some, John Henry *Newman among them, became Roman Catholics; this increased the sharpness of the conflict. In later years, as ceremonial enrichment became characteristic of the movement, there was often bitter hostility on the *ritualism issue. The more lasting monuments of Anglo-Catholicism, however, are two—a strong and adventurous ecumenical spirit and a powerful renewal of concern for the Church's social witness. The 20th-cent *Faith and Order movement, for example, was to owe much of its inspiration to Anglo-Catholic leadership, both in England and elsewhere. On the social side the influence of the Anglo-Catholic Summer School of Sociology during the 1920s and 30s was notable in developing relevant and virile Anglican witness in social and political affairs. BIBLIOGRAPHY: G. Tavard, *Protestantism* (1959) 99–105; S. A. Quitslund, "'United not absorbed, does it still make sense?" *Journal of Ecumenical Studies* 8 (1971) 255–285; "Doctrinal Agreement and Christian Unity," *Catholic Mind* 70 (1972) 61–64.

[S. F. BAYNE]

ANGLO-SAXON ART, art in the British Isles embracing a pagan pre-Christian idiom of Scandinavian and Germanic provenance, which with Christian modifications pervaded Europe through Irish and Anglo-Saxon missionaries to enrich Carolingian, Romanesque, and Gothic art forms. Contacts with Rome after 597 led to a great flowering of all the arts esp. in N England (the "Northumbrian renaissance"). Contributing to it was the Hiberno-Saxon development, a fusion of Celtic and Germanic impulses and themes. Developing from an earlier established excellence in applied arts (*Sutton Hoo ship-burial) and timber architecture (Yeavering), MS illumination, metalwork, architecture, and sculpture all achieved great heights. From the 7th–8th-cent. climax Anglo-Saxon art continued to develop, making contributions to the Carolingian renaissance, and influencing Scandinavian art through Viking raiders and settlers (*Winchester School). BIBLIOGRAPHY: R. L. S. Bruce-Mitford, EncWA 1:446–463; T. D. Kendrick, *Anglo-Saxon Art to* A.D. *900* (1972).

[R. L. S. BRUCE-MITFORD]

ANGLO-SAXON CHURCH, the Church in England as established and directed by St. *Augustine of Canterbury (d. c.605) and his successors up to the Norman Conquest (1066). After the coming of the Angles, Saxons, and other Germanic invaders (c.450–500), destroying Christianity in

E and S England, two movements of evangelization were carried out. One stemmed from Augustine, who had been sent by Gregory the Great and was closer to Roman traditions. The other was led by St. *Aidan (d. 651), who came from *Iona and represented the *Celtic Church. Roman usage was decreed by the Synod of *Whitby (664), but Celtic traditions continued in many places, and the abps. of Canterbury struggled throughout the period to establish their authority. Romanization of the Scottish Church was only completed by Queen Margaret (d. 1093). Considerable disruption was caused by the Danish invaders of the 9th cent., but they accepted Christianity after defeat by King Alfred. Outstanding figures of the Anglo-Saxon Church included St. *Boniface and other missionaries to the Continent, the Venerable *Bede who provides much of our knowledge of the period, and Theodore of Tarsus, abp. of Canterbury from 669 to 690. In the 10th cent. the reforms of St. *Dunstan led to closer ties with the Continent. At the Norman Conquest most of the Anglo-Saxon bps. were removed, but the most outstanding of them, St. *Wulfstan, continued at Worcester till his death in 1095. BIBLIOGRAPHY: J. Godfrey, *Church in Anglo-Saxon England* (1962); J.-R. Palanque, *Dawn of the Middle Ages* (tr. D. F. Murphy; 1960) 92–95.

[T. EARLY]

ANGLO-SAXONS. The Roman withdrawal from Britain (410) was followed by Angle, Saxon, and Jute colonization from Germany. They either expelled the Britons, thus destroying Christianity, or submerged the older culture. Earlier the invaders had been exposed to Christianity but it remained for Irish monks from Iona and the Roman mission of St. Augustine in 597 to convert them. By 660 the hierarchy was established, monastic life flourished, and by 690 England was sending missionaries to Germany. Success brought a struggle between Irish and Roman traditions. The triumph of Roman Christianity produced great cultural by-products: Bede and Aldhelm writing Latin; the great hymns in Anglo-Saxon; in sculpture the stone crosses; in illumination the Hiberno-Saxon school. Laxity weakened the monastic backbone of the culture and Viking invasions in the 9th and 10th centuries destroyed both Church and culture. *Alfred (d. 899) restored order and began monastic reform. The new cultural wave was terminated by the Norman Conquest of 1066. BIBLIOGRAPHY: S. J. Crawford, *Anglo-Saxon Influence on Western Christendom* (1966); M. Deansley, *Pre-Conquest Church in England* (1961); F. M. Stenton, *Anglo-Saxon England,* (2v., 1947; repr. 1971); C. P. Loughran, NCE 1:537–540; *Anglo-Saxon England* (ed. P. Clemoes, 1972).

[J. DRUSE]

ANGOI (Gr. for cups), in the Byzantine Church three vessels, usually resting on the same base, used to contain the wheat (in Slavic usage, five loaves), wine, and oil that are blessed at Vespers on certain feasts.

[A. J. JACOPIN]

ANGOULÊME, city on a promontory between the valleys of Charente and Anguienne. Excavations (19th cent.) uncovered ancient pagan and Christian sepulchers, engraved vessels, and *stelae*. The Cathedral of St. Pierre (*c*.1105; 19th-cent. restoration by Abadie) distinctively Périgord-Romanesque, has a single nave with massive piers engaged to walls that carry four domes on pendentives, their "Oriental silhouettes" peculiarly French (not Byzantine). Its magnificent façade shows 75 decorative sculptures. Historic sculptures of Jean of Angoulême and Marguerite of Valois (born here 1492), the Church of St. André (12th-cent. porch; 15th-cent. nave), and the Hôtel St. Simon (Renaissance) are noteworthy. The ruins of an Augustinian abbey (1122) and the Château La Rochefoucauld beyond Angoulême are likewise important. BIBLIOGRAPHY: J. de Martinière, DHGE 3:242–257; H. Saalman, *Medieval Architecture* (1962); M. J. Daly, NCE 1:541.

[M. J. DALY]

ANGRIANA, MICHELE, see AIGUANI, MICHELE.

ANGUANI, MICHELE, see AIGUANI MICHELE.

ANGST, traditionally described by philosophers and theologians as a sense or feeling of dread and anxiety in the awareness of the human condition. Aristotle, Aquinas, as well as other ancient and medieval philosophers have described it. Yet, to give ample evidence to its more recent meaning one ought to distinguish it as a candidate for serious reflection in the fields of psychology and psychiatry, along with its meaning for philosophy and theology. In philosophy, recent philosophers like Kierkegaard and Heidegger have opened the concept to a fuller meaning, one which opens up to man—as he comes closer and closer to its true meaning—the possibilities of his existence, of his being. One ought not to omit its connotations in literature either, since consideration of it is characteristic of a whole generation of writers, esp. those of the Existential school. They have centered attention upon the moral ambience that angst creates. BIBLIOGRAPHY: H. Rombach, LTK 1:556–557; P. Matussek, *ibid*. 1:599; V. M. Martin, NCE 1:649–651.

[J. R. RIVELLO]

ANGUANI, MICHELE, see AIGUANI, MICHELE.

ANI, city and district in Armenia on the right bank of the Arpa-chay flowing into the Araxes from the north. It was named capital during the reign of Ashot III, the Merciful (952–977), but after suffering countless internal civil dissensions, the attacks of the Byzantine emperor, the king of Lori, and the Shaddadib amir of Dovin, its Christian king, Gagik II, yielded to the threats of the Byzantine emperor, Constantine IX, and abdicated his throne at Constantinople (1045). Harassed by the Emperor's excessive taxation and the continued attacks of the Seljuks, Ani finally capitulated to the Turkish leader, Alp Arslan (1046). BIBLIOGRAPHY: C.

Toumanoff, CMedH 14:609, 619–621; A. Saruxan, "City of Ani," *Handes Amsorga* (1940) 14.

[F. H. BRIGHAM]

ANIANE, ABBEY OF *(Anianensis),* former Benedictine monastery dedicated to the Holy Savior. A. was founded *c*.785 by St. Benedict of Aniane in lower Languedoc, in the diocese of Maguelone (now Montpellier). Its customs were imposed on all monasteries of the Empire by the Council of Aachen in 817. A. declined in the 16th century. The Maurists took it over in 1635 and rebuilt the church, which is now the parish church of the village of Aniane. The abbey was suppressed in 1790. At present its buildings are used as a school for delinquents. BIBLIOGRAPHY: Cottineau 1:115–117.

[J. DAOUST]

ANIANUS, MONK OF ALEXANDRIA (5th cent.), an Egyptian who wrote a chronography from Adam down to *c*.407 A.D. According to A., Christ was born in the year 5500 after creation. He also held that the creation, the Incarnation, and the Redemption all took place on March 25. BIBLIOGRAPHY: S. Salaville, DHGE 3:282.

[P. K. MEAGHER]

ANIANUS, DEACON AT CELADA (5th cent.), a writer who produced a work, now lost, in defense of the doctrine of Pelagius. He also translated patristic writings, esp. homilies of St. John Chrysostom, into rhythmic Latin prose, and may have helped Pelagius in the compilation of his works. The "Celada" associated with his name has not been identified. BIBLIOGRAPHY: F. di Capua, EncCatt 1:1287–88; Altaner 441–442.

[P. K. MEAGHER]

ANIANUS OF CHARTRES, ST. (fl. first half of 5th cent.), fifth bp. of Chartres. His cult goes back at least to the 11th century. His vita is legendary. Twice his relics were saved when fire destroyed the church bearing his name in which they were preserved (1136 and 1262). BIBLIOGRAPHY: A. Clerval, DHGE 1:1111–14; C. Vens, BiblSanct 1:1258.

ANIANUS OF ORLÉANS, ST. (d. *c*.453), bishop. Sidonius of Apollinaris and Gregory of Tours concur in claiming that Orléans was preserved by A. from the devastation of the Huns under Attila in 451. A.'s part probably consisted in mobilizing the citizens to defend the city and urgently requesting assistance from the Roman general Aëtius. In Orléans, the church of St. A. contains his relics. A congregation of sisters in Orléans, the Sisters of St. Anianus, was approved in 1852. BIBLIOGRAPHY: M. Besson, DHGE 1:1110–11; Butler 4:367; G. Mathon, BiblSanct 1:1258–59.

[J. M. O'DONNELL]

ANIANUS AND MARINUS, SS., 7th-cent. hermits. Anianus, a deacon, and Marinus, a bishop, established a hermitage at Wilparting in the Bavarian Alps. They were martyred by the Vandals or Wends, and their still-active cult derives historical support from a 12th-cent. Sacramentary as well as an 8th-cent. vita. BIBLIOGRAPHY: A. M. Zimmermann, BiblSanct 8:1180–81.

[M. S. TANEY]

ANICETUS, ST. (d. *c*.166), **POPE** from *c*.155. As in the cases of the other popes of this period, exact verification of the dates on which A.'s pontificate began and ended is impossible, but he was pope before the martyrdom of Polycarp (*c*.155?) and is said to have ruled the Church from 9 to 11 years. Polycarp came to confer with him about the difference between Eastern and Western observance of the date of Easter. The matter was discussed in a friendly spirit, but no settlement of the difference was attempted. Hegesippus, too, came to Rome during his pontificate, and he includes A. in his list of popes. Irenaeus reports that Marcion with his rival Church was flourishing at Rome while A. was pope. A. is credited with martyrdom, but nothing is known of the circumstances of his death. He is thought to have built a sepulchral monument to St. Peter. BIBLIOGRAPHY: E. G. Weltin, NCE 1:544; T. J. Campbell, CE 1:514; Butler 2:112.

[P. F. MULHERN]

ANICONIC ART, a nonimage, nonobjective, nonfigurative, abstract art which speaks through the pure elements of visual language (space, light, form, color, texture) without allusion (reference to nature), without illusion (scientific, academic determinants that deceive the eye), and without symbolism (extensions of the image through iconographic or imaginative concepts). As in 'absolute' music which is a pure tonal language aniconic 'absolute' art exists as a most pure visual statement—an entity in itself and, as with all art forms whether in sound or shape, enjoys an essential being in itself which is presented for man's contemplation. This relation alone constitutes the aesthetic experience. Nor is this a new aesthetic of the 20th cent. since such address to the art form has been true since Lascaux. For the aniconic artist space, light, form, color, texture are no longer descriptive accidents but essences. The key concept is to experience the art form immediately and not through reference which often bypasses the art work. The choice of image or nonimage in church art is not a matter of dogma but of judgment. Though the Church affirmed images (787) it did not advocate images. (St. Bernard demanded an aniconic art for his monasteries to counteract the distraction of natural forms.) After World War II directives of the German bishops (1947) for the use of contemporary art in a Church which for some time had separated itself from contemporary art expression resulted in the beautiful, postwar churches of Germany. Assy, Audincourt, Ronchamp, and Vence further witness to the specific beauty of 20th-cent. expression.

Abstract art seeks to *signify*—in a technological age which communicates incessantly in a system of allegories, signs, and devices. A 20th-cent. literate society is no longer moved by didactic, iconographic expressions or Renaissance scientific deceptions. We must create a 'worship environment' through the visual language of contemporary aniconic style so that transcending the palpable and experiencing intuitively man may come finally through contemplation to truth.

[M. J. DALY]

ANIMA CHRISTI (*Soul of Christ*), prayer listed in the RC Missal and Breviary among prayers to be said after Mass. It begins, "Soul of Christ, sanctify me." It was recommended by St. *Ignatius, but though commonly called *Aspirationes Sancti Ignatii,* it dates from prior to his time. Authorship and exact origin are unknown. It was current in the 14th cent., when John XXII granted an indulgence for its recitation, but has not been found in any 13th cent. MS.

[T. EARLY]

ANIMA NATURALITER CHRISTIANA, phrase used by Tertullian (*Apol.* 17) to express man's spontaneous awareness of one God following upon a basic consideration of the universe and the interior dispositions of the human soul. According to Tertullian the soul of the pagan, independently of revelation or any philosophical instruction, is naturally Christian insofar as it witnesses to the existence of God, his attributes, and a life of punishment or reward after death (the testimony of the soul). As used by theologians the phrase has a variety of related meanings. Basically it signifies the fundamental harmony between human nature and the supernatural order. Man is capable of forming some idea of God through reason and seeks to express a relationship with the numinous (however vaguely conceived and expressed) by cultic rites, and is open to divine revelation through word and event. Man is also dynamically inclined to the transcendent as his unique existential finality. BIBLIOGRAPHY: Quasten 2; K. Rahner, LTK 1:564–565. *SUPERNATURAL EXISTENTIAL; *SUPERNATURAL ORDER.

[T. M. MCFADDEN]

ANIMAL SCROLLS, a set of Japanese monochrome (ink) *emaki* (horizontal narrative scrolls) of animal caricatures in the Kozanji, near Kyoto, made at different times by diverse artists at the end of the Heian period (12th cent. and later). Attributed in part to the abbot *Toba Sōjō (though positive proof is lacking), the scrolls without text depict with masterful draftsmanship in settings of decorative foliage the frolics of frogs, monkeys, and hares in a whimsical satire of Buddhist practices, exposing the follies and absurdities of man. BIBLIOGRAPHY: H. Okudairo, *Emaki (Japanese Picture Scrolls)* 1962.

[M. J. DALY]

ANIMAL STYLE, the highly imaginative and sophisticated arrangement of the animal as decorative and symbolic form—naturalistic, abstract, or fantastic—found over vast areas of the world from China through the Asiatic steppes to Central and Western Europe, from Iran to Scandinavia, with reference particularly to portable bronze objects of nomads' gear (bridles and bits for horses, belt buckles, pendants, weapons, tools, bowls) which being small were widely diffused.

The bronzes of Luristan (9th-7th cent. B.C.), linked through Kassite and Akkadian origins with ancient fantastic winged beasts of Assyria, are characterized by a most sophisticated dynamic line, inventive distortion in elongated necks and horns—often fantastic, heraldic in their addorsed or affronted forms, and exquisite in gold and silver inlay linking them to the metalwork of the Asiatic steppes. The fabulous "Scythian gold treasure" (8th-4th cent. B.C.) of the Hermitage, Leningrad, the carnivores, birds of prey with curious curved beak (ubiquitous from China's Ordos desert to South Russia) add a new and violent syntax in the "animal attack," the convulsively writhing, twisted, and inverted forms seen also at Noin-ula in North Mongolia in the textiles of the Huns who were in conflict with the Chinese in the Ordos region (800 B.C.), moving westward to South Russia by the last century B.C. The work of the Scyths (7th-4th cent.), later replaced by the Sarmatians, was modified by the naturalism of the Ionian Greek goldsmiths on the shores of the Black Sea (550 B.C.). At Hallstatt (500 B.C.) the Celts in contact with Scyths show a strong rectilinear style which in La Tène (5th cent.-2d cent. B.C.) becomes distinctively curvilinear.

In the 5th cent. A.D. Germanic animal style, esp. that of the Ostrogoths, shows highly abstracted, geometric, fantastic animal forms in fibulae of gold and silver, with enamel, paste, glass, and stone inlaid in a cloisonné technique.

The Anglo-Saxons (5th-7th cent. A.D.) produced objects of great splendor in gold and silver, boldly inlaid with garnets, colored glass, and shell in a cloisonné technique that surpassed that of the Germanic world, in filigree, niello, and enameling (654 A.D. gold and enamel purse cover of Sutton Hoo). The carnivore and victim, the "fabulous" beasts with tails, legs, and jaws elongated enter a maze of interlaced bands and borders which "migrate" into stone and wood (Oseberg Viking ship 825 A.D., south Norway).

Hiberno-Saxon style (Celtic and Germanic), 600–800 A.D., shows sinuous, tightly wrought, infinitely complex, entangled bodies in "S" or "Ribbon style" meanders of coiling tails, legs, and jaws, yet never so labyrinthine as to deny precise clarity of division between organic and geometric details, engaging the patient eye in arduous but ever-logical interlace which would point to proto-types of weaving in reed, thread or leather thong which gave rise to the phrases "tapestried," "carpet pages" (Book of Durrow c.665 A.D., the Lindisfarne Gospels, c.700 A.D.). The monogram page of the Book of Kells (c.800 A.D.) is reminiscent of jewel inlay.

The animal style moves from book covers in ivory and metal to monumental work in stone (balustrade at Cividale, 762 A.D.). In the fantastic interlocked lions of the *trumeau* of the south portal at Moissac and cloister capitals of interlaced "monster" basilisks and lizards, the entire "fantastic animal" vocabulary engages in a late synthesis with Christian iconography. In the Romanesque portals of France and Spain, the caryatids of Lombardy porches, the camels in Persian lozenges at St. Gilles du Gard, winged dragons in 12th-cent. Cistercian illuminations, the *cynocephaloi* of Isidore of Seville at Autun, the "animal style" which earlier evidenced the intangibles locked in the dark recesses of the barbaric mind proves itself perennially viable to express for man in all ages those hieratic, abstract concepts to which the tangible percept can neither aspire nor attain. BIBLIOGRAPHY: M. J. Daly, *Ordos Bronzes in the University of Pennsylvania Museum* (Univ. of Penna., 1959).

[M. J. DALY]

ANIMAL WORSHIP, a general designation covering the different types of reverence, superstition, or cult afforded to animals. There are pastoral cults in which a domestic animal is revered as a species, e.g., the Hindu respect for cattle, or one animal is selected as a representative of the species and declared sacred. In hunting communities, the animal upon which the group depends for its sustenance is often represented by an individual animal which receives divine honors before being slain. The cult of dangerous animals is characterized by various taboos, and by ceremonies to propitiate the spirit of the slain animal, e.g., the cult of the leopard, lion, and tiger in Africa and India. In other cultures, reverence is shown to animals because they are regarded as the abode of deceased humans. Thus some of the Celebes tribes conduct a ceremony in honor of crocodiles since they believe that their deceased relatives take that form. Totemism is a frequent form of animal worship in which a totem animal is never injured. In Greek and Roman mythology, there are a number of woodland deities (Pan, the Satyrs) which are spirits of the woods in animal form. The widespread cult of snakes is open to various interpretations: their association with ancestor cults, or their extreme dangerousness, or their connection with water and the formlessness of the primordial chaotic mass. BIBLIOGRAPHY: N. W. Thomas, Hastings ERE 1:485–491; V. Preston, *Divine Names and Attributes of Animals* (1953). *ANIMALS, SACRED; *ANIMALS, SYMBOLISM OF.

[T. M. MCFADDEN]

ANIMALS, living beings whose existence is endowed with sensation and voluntary motion; sometimes referred to as "brute animal"; creatures who share the processes of feeding, growing, maturing, and reproducing with man, yet distinct from him by lower intelligence and lack of a rational soul. Although one speaks of animal "spirit" and animal "soul," it is usually in the context of distinguishing that capacity in brute animals which directs them to make responses to other animals and to man. These responses lack the self-conscious appropriation that marks man's responses. One is unable to imagine any civilized, moral society that does not recognize the need for humane treatment of animals.

Furthermore, while it is highly unusual to speak of moral behavior in relation to animals, it is not unusual that treatment of animals surely makes a moral demand on man—a demand recognized, it seems, by Aquinas and Aristotle, since both saw in animals an opportunity for man to exercise his moral superiority. In Aquinas esp., the animal is viewed as a creation of God and deserving of our respect. In his monumental work, *Theory of Justice,* John Rawls speaks of our duties of compassion and humanity toward animals. This work is representative of recent philosophy and the consideration it gives to animals. BIBLIOGRAPHY: A. E. Manier, NCE 8:734–737.

[J. R. RIVELLO]

ANIMALS, CRUELTY TO, see CRUELTY.

ANIMALS, SACRED. The history of religions shows that many animals have been considered sacred, either because of their symbolic value (SEE ANIMALS, SYMBOLISM OF), or as objects of worship (SEE ANIMAL WORSHIP). Perhaps the best known example is the Hindu attitude toward the cow. The beast is not actually worshiped, but actions harmful to it are prohibited, originally, it seems, because of the fact that products of the cow were necessary for exorcism and magic, and because it was believed that the cow's function was to carry the Hindu across the river of death. Several American Indian tribes have considered the eagle a sacred animal, and the same bird has also occupied an important place in classical mythology, according to which it was associated with Zeus. The cult of the leopard is extensive in W Africa; a man who kills one is liable to death, and a stuffed leopard is an object of worship. In Thailand many think that a white elephant may contain the soul of a Buddha; it is kept by the king, baptized, feted, and upon death mourned like a human being. Many other examples of the sacred status of certain animals could be given. Although different explanations account for the status in the cases of different animals, several fairly common factors are discernible. Often the motive seems to be the material benefits that the animal is thought to confer upon its worshipers, or the fear of the consequences of refusing reverence. In some cases, the wrath of a god is thought to be aroused by maltreatment of a particular animal; in other cases, the abuse of an animal may seem to involve the rejection of an ancestor's spirit which is believed to dwell in it. BIBLIOGRAPHY: N. W. Thomas, Hastings ERE 1:483–535; G. Manzini, *Animali sacri e profani* (1953); V. Preston, *Divine Names and Attributes of Animals* (1953).

ANIMALS, SYMBOLISM OF. The similarity between animals and men as well as their distinction in being and action renders the animal kingdom an inexhaustible storehouse of symbols. Animal behavior becomes a mirror of human characteristics, filled with metaphorical content (e.g., associations such as lion—strength, fox—cleverness, snake—caution, etc.) and an excellent tool to moralize about individuals and society by fables and fairy tales. Also, since the death of an animal often offers life to man, the human-animal relationship underlines the mystery of life and death in a way that turns the animal into the foremost figure of mythology. Consequently animal symbols can be found in all religions with the scale of reference reaching from the deployment of mere metaphors to the actual sanctification and worship of animals as representatives of the godhead. Thus the animal serves religion in two basic ways. It offers symbols to describe sacred reality, and/or is a medium for the realization of hierophanies, thereby assuming significance as an object of worship and cult. Christianity makes wide use of animals as symbols. Christ is represented by the paschal lamb; the Holy Spirit is commonly symbolized by a dove, thus maintaining the imagery used at Christ's baptism (Mk 1.10–12); the pelican represents Christ's self-sacrifice for the redemption of others; the fish is an early symbol for Christ since the Greek word forms an acrostic for Jesus Christ, Son of God, Savior (see ICHTHUS). Other animal symbols are also employed to represent evil, e.g., the serpent, the devil; the hydra, heresy; and the hyena, impurity. BIBLIOGRAPHY: G. Manzini, *Animali sacri e profani* (1953); K. Rathe, EncCatt 1:1345–47; T. J. Allen, NCE 1:547–548.

[W. DUPRÉ]

ANIMISM AND ANIMATISM, attribution of consciousness, spirit, or soul to material objects and natural phenomena. Animism generally implies a conception of more individualized spirits. In anthropological studies, the origin of religion has sometimes been located in animism, a theory associated particularly with E. B. Tylor (1832–1917). Others have postulated an earlier stage of belief in a generalized, pervasive force such as mana, while still others have found the beginnings of religion in the social context of totemism or in certain psychological reactions to interpersonal relationships. BIBLIOGRAPHY: E. B. Tylor, *Primitive Culture* (1873); *Reader in Comparative Religion* (ed. W. A. Lessa and E. Z. Vogt, 1969).

[T. EARLY]

ANIMUCCIA, GIOVANNI (d. 1571), Florentine composer who succeeded *Palestrina as choirmaster of the Julian Chapel in 1555, and became choirmaster for St. Philip Neri's Oratory in 1570. For the latter's use he published two successful books of *laudi.* A. was among those who submitted scores to the commission of cardinals appointed by the Council of Trent to study the question of retaining polyphonic music at Mass. His Mass compositions, although based on plainsong melodies, are ornate and brilliant polyphonic works which reflect Franco-Netherlandish influence. His brother Paolo (*c.*1500–63), also a church musician, was *maestro di cappella* at St. John Lateran. BIBLIOGRAPHY: K. G. Fellerer, MGG 1:483–485; Reese MusR.

[J. J. WALSH]

ANIZAN, JEAN ÉMILE (1853–1928), founder of a congregation called the Sons of Charity (Fils de la Charité). Under the influence of Bp. F. Dupanloup, A. studied for the priesthood. Ordained in 1877, he entered the Brothers of St. Vincent de Paul in 1886 to whom he was attracted by their interest in work among youth. He became superior general of the congregation in 1907 but was deposed from office in 1914 under the charge that his social thinking was tinged with Modernism. Dispensed from his vows, he served as chaplain in World War I. After the war he gathered together a group of priests who wished to devote themselves to the parochial ministry, esp. in poor parishes. The congregation was encouraged by Benedict XV and received definitive approval in 1934. BIBLIOGRAPHY: G. Bard, *Jean Émile Anizan* (1945).

[P. K. MEAGHER]

ANJOU, a former province in western France (now dept. Maine-et-Loire), whence the name ''Angevin'' of two ruling families celebrated in medieval history. The first, descended from the original count, inherited the crown of England in the person of *Henry II, son of Geoffrey, eleventh count (surnamed Plantagenet from his habit of wearing a sprig of broom—*planta genista*—in his cap) by his marriage (1128) with Matilda, heiress of Henry I. The kings of England kept Anjou in their possession until 1203, when it was seized by Philip Augustus of France. The next Angevin family descended from the younger brother of St. Louis IX: he received Anjou as an appanage, and as Charles I established his dynasty on the throne of Naples (1266) on the downfall of the Hohenstaufer. His daughter brought Anjou as a dowry to the *Valois kings, and later (1480) it was annexed to the French crown.

[T. GILBY]

ANJOU, HOUSE OF, French house figuring prominently in political history of the late Middle Ages. In 1246 Louis IX of France gave Anjou to his youngest brother, Charles, who, favored by Clement IV, established Angevin rule in Italy. His plans to gain power in the E Mediterranean were foiled by political interventions; then definitely terminated by the Sicilian Vespers. He died in 1285. Under Charles II, Sicily was lost to the house but papal favor kept it in influential power. Robert the Wise, third son of Charles, attempted to recover Sicily but failed. After his death in 1343, his granddaughter, Joanna I, succeeded him. Four times married, she survived a war waged by Louis I of Hungary, a relative of the Angevin House. Restored to the throne, she sold Avignon to Clement VI. She supported the antipope Clement VII when the Western Schism began; as a result, Urban VI excommunicated her and gave Naples to her cousin, Charles III, who successfully claimed the throne of Hungary when Louis I died. Murdered in 1386, Charles was succeeded by his son, Ladislaus, who gained control of Naples in 1399. Joanna II (1414–35), a most licentious woman, was the last Angevin ruler. She bequeathed Naples to Louis III's brother, René the Good. The Two Sicilies were then united under Aragon and

later under Spain. BIBLIOGRAPHY: E. J. Smyth, NCE 1:548–550; A. Nitshke, LTK 1:566–567.

[F. D. LAZENBY]

ANNA COMNENA (1083–1148), Byzantine princess, daughter of Emperor Alexius I Comnenus (1081–1118). She engaged in intrigue in an unsuccessful effort to prevent the succession of her brother John to the throne after her father's death. John put her in a convent where she wrote her father's biography, a work known as the *Alexiad*. Despite its panegyrical tone it is a valuable source for the reign of Alexius I and for the First Crusade. Text: Anna Comnena, *Alexiad* (tr. E. Dawes, 1928). BIBLIOGRAPHY: G. Buckler, *Anna Comnena: A Study* (1929).

[P. K. MEAGHER]

ANNA, CANTICLE OF, see CANTICLE OF ANNA.

ANNALES ECCLESIASTICI, the 12-v. church history published (1588–1607) by Baronius as a RC reply to the *Magdeburg Centuries,* a Lutheran history.* BARONIUS, CAESAR, VEN.

[T. C. O'BRIEN]

ANNALS, a brief historical record of public events arranged year by year. The Hittites and Assyrians recorded their military expeditions in this form and Roman historians also employed it.

Medieval annalists used the *Chronographer of 354* as model and when the consular system of dating went out of use, the Paschal Tables had added significance in their chronology of the West. These tables included pages for each year which were set apart by large blank spaces. These spaces were used by monks to note the important events of the year. The notations were first separated from the Paschal Tables and compiled as annals by Anglo-Saxon monks of the 7th century. Brought to the Continent by missionaries of Britain and Ireland, they became the accepted means of recording history during the Carolingian period. The golden age of annals (650–1100) included the Annals of Einhard, of Lorsch, the Bertinian, all of which record the important events of the Rule of Charlemagne and his successors. After this, annals become interchangeable with *chronicles their more detailed counterpart. BIBLIOGRAPHY: M. R. P. McGuire, NCE 1:551–556; Altaner 278–284.

[F. H. BRIGHAM]

ANNAPHÛRŌ (Arab. *nâfûr),* a name given to (1) the large veil spread over the offerings from the preparation until the end of the preanaphora in West Syrian and Maronite liturgies; also called, '*aimō* (cloud) or, generically, *shûsheppō* (veil); (2) in Maronite usage it designates a small piece of cloth, the ''little annaphûrō,'' also called *kûssōyō* or (Arab.) *gitâ,* used to cover the chalice or the paten. It is the West Syrian *hûpōyō.*

[A. CODY]

ANNAS (Greek form of Hebrew name Hananiah), Jewish high priest according to Lk 3.2, Jn 18.13–24, Acts 4.6. He was appointed in 6 A.D., deposed in 15 A.D., but the Gospels and Acts speak of him as virtually remaining in office, since he had five of his sons and Caiphas his son-in-law appointed to the high priesthood.

[T. C. O'BRIEN]

ANNAT, name of two 17th-cent. French theologians, uncle and nephew. (1) FRANÇOIS (1590–1670), Jesuit theologian and controversialist. From 1654 until his death he lived in Paris and was confessor to King Louis XIV. He began engaging in polemics with the Jansenists c.1644, producing a number of notable works in defense of orthodox thought against both Jansenism and Gallicanism. Though he was a formidable controversialist, his character was esteemed even by his adversaries, among whom were *Pascal, *Arnauld, and Nicole. His most important work was *Opuscula theologica ad gratiam spectantia* (1666), a 3-v. work containing several earlier treatises. SEE C. Sommervogel, DTC 1:1320–21; J. Dutilleul, DHGE 3:299–306. (2) PIERRE (1638–1715), nephew of preceding, philosopher, and theologian. A member of the Congregation of Christian Doctrine, A. published a valuable introduction to positive theology, *Methodicus ad positivam theologiam apparatus* (2 v., 1700). This work was put on the Index in 1713 but was removed the following year when corrections had been made. BIBLIOGRAPHY: C. Toussaint, DTC 1:1321; R. Aigrain, DHGE 3:307.

[P. K. MEAGHER]

ANNATES, a tax on the first year's revenue of an ecclesiastical *benefice (from the Lat. *annus*, year). From the 11th cent. various church officials and some kings took annates from benefices they controlled. The first pope to do so was Clement V, and under John XXII the payment of annates to the popes became general. The development resulted from the increased frequency of papal nominations to church offices, combined with the financial needs of the *Avignon papacy. Only slight vestiges of the practice now remain. BIBLIOGRAPHY: W. E. Lunt, *Papal Revenues in the Middle Ages* (2 v., 1934).

[T. EARLY]

ANNE AND JOACHIM, SS. (Anne, grace, graciousness; Joachim, preparation of the Lord), names accorded in the apocrypha to the parents of the Blessed Virgin Mary. Other than the Heli of Luke's genealogy (2.23) which some take to be the name of Mary's rather than Joseph's father (SEE EDB 967), their names are not in the NT. In the apocryphal gospels A. appears, and J. in the *Protoevangelium of James*. P. Parsch writes, "The feast is not primarily one in honor of a saint" but in honor of Jesus Christ, the Redeemer, of whom they are the grandparents.

First source for their story is the *Protoevangelium* in whose "legend" is the scorn of childlessness long suffered by the fervent Jewish couple, and their charity (their income was divided into three: provision for the poor, for the upkeep of the Temple, for their own needs). In other sources J. is named variously Sadoch, Jonachir, Eliacim, Cleopas, Heli.

In the Middle Ages the two were much honored; in the East the cult of J. is immemorial; that of A. is traced likewise in the East to the 6th cent. when in 550 a church in Constantinople was given her title and one a little later in Jerusalem; only in 1584 was A's feast extended to the whole Church.

The name of A. was borne likewise by the mother of Samuel, echo of whose thanksgiving at his birth (1 Sam 1.9–28; 2.1–11) permeates Mary's Magnificat and may, conceivably, be the reason, in absence of counter testimony, for choice of the name Anne for Mary's own mother.

Scripture eulogies applicable to Mary's parents have traditionally been found in the OT: for J. the text of the just man (Ps 111) and that of almsgiving in another just man's story (Tob 4 and 12) while A. is represented as "the perfect wife, the valiant woman" (Pr 31.10–31), a woman of dedication without reserve whose zeal for God's kingdom is seen in fulfillment of the duties of her state as mother of a household. For the Divine Office Epiphanius provided a text in their praise: "Joachim and Anne earned divine favor by an irreproachable life and merited that their union should bear for its beautiful fruit the Blessed Virgin Mary, the temple and Mother of God. . . ."

The cult of Anne in the West, which took root in Brittany and France, was much encouraged by the interest of Queen Anne of Austria, Louis XIV's mother; the devotion was brought across the water by French settlers in Canada and thus into the U.S. BIBLIOGRAPHY: E. Croce, BiblSanct 1:1269–95; P. Asselin, NCE 1:558–560; M. Faulhaber, *Women of the OT* (1938; ed. B. Keogh, 1955) 13–25, 51–73.

[M. R. BROWN]

ANNE OF DENMARK (1574–1619), queen of James I of England and VI of Scotland, daughter of the King of Denmark and Norway. She was married without dower at the age of 15 but she brought the final settlement of the claims of Scotland to the Orkneys and Shetlands. In 1603 she was crowned in England; it was not known whether her refusal to take the sacrament according to the Anglican ordinal was due to her Lutheran upbringing or her flirtation with Roman Catholicism, which encouraged the hopes of the Recusants. Her extravagance was not grudged, for her passion for dresses, jewels, and building was carried off in great style; she threw herself into theatricals devised by Jonson and Decker and made her court "a constant maskerado" and "the night more glorious than the day." She was admired for her wit, tact, and liveliness; moreover she was faithful to her shambling husband, devoted to her children, and staunch to her friends. BIBLIOGRAPHY: D. W. Willson, *King James VI and I* (1956).

[T. GILBY]

ANNE OF JESUS, VEN. (Anna di Lobera; 1545–1621), Discalced Carmelite nun from 1570. She aided St. Teresa of Avila in the establishment of monasteries in Andalusia and Granada and after Teresa's death wrote a biography of her and began the editing of her works. In response to the invitation of Cardinal de Bérulle, she went to France where, with the help of Bl. Anne of St. Bartholomew and four other nuns, she founded Reformed Carmelite houses at Paris and Pontoise. She also established a convent at Brussels. BIBLIOGRAPHY: S.N.D. *Life of Anne of Jesus* (1932); V. di S. Maria, BiblSanct 1:1303–05; L. Van den Bossche, *Anne de Jesus, coadjutrice de Ste-Thérèse d'Avila* (1958).

[P. K. MEAGHER]

ANNE OF ST. BARTHOLOMEW, BL. (Anna Garcia; 1549–1626), Carmelite nun. She entered the Discalced Carmelites as a lay sister (1570) and was the first to be received under the Reform; later (1604) her status was changed to that of a choir nun. She assisted St. Teresa, accompanied her on her travels, and held her in her arms as she was dying. She was associated with *Anne of Jesus in the establishment of the Carmelite Reform in France and founded the convent at Antwerp. Under obedience she wrote an autobiography and also left an instruction for novices and exercises for each day of the week. BIBLIOGRAPHY: Elisée de la Nativité, DSAM 1:676–677; V. di S. Maria, BiblSanct 1:1307–09.

[P. K. MEAGHER]

ANNE OF SAVOY (d. 1360), Byzantine empress. Daughter of Amadeus V of Savoy, A. married Andronicus III, at whose death (1341) she named *John VI Cantacuzenus regent for her 9-year-old son, John V. But the regent proclaimed himself emperor the same year, and there was civil war for the next 6 years. A temporary reconciliation was effected in 1347, when John V married Cantacuzenus' daughter, but lasting peace was never really achieved. While regent, A. had deposed the Patriarch John Calecas and begun a series of negotiations for reunion with Rome. Although her son continued these, they proved fruitless. The regency of A. and the reign of John V marked a major decline in Byzantine power that was to eventuate in the fall of the empire in the next century. BIBLIOGRAPHY: L. Brehier, DHGE 3:350–352; Ostrogorsky-Charanis 454, 458, 462–464, 469, 477.

[P. K. MEAGHER]

ANNECY, MONASTERY OF, a priory of the Canons Regular of the Holy Sepulchre, founded in Annecy, France, in the 12th century. In the 14th cent. the canons built a Gothic church, much of which still exists beneath subsequent construction work. Destroyed by fire in 1590, the priory was not rebuilt. Community life consequently suffered; relaxation set in, and the lack of religious spirit led to the suppression of the order in the 18th century. BIBLIOGRAPHY: A. Gavard, DHGE 3:363.

[S. A. HEENEY]

ANNIBALE, GIUSEPPE D' (1815–92), Italian moralist, canonist, and cardinal. His compendium of moral theology, *Summula theologiae moralis* (3 v. 1881–83), a concise, well-documented work, was widely used at the end of the 19th and the early part of the 20th century. He also wrote a commentary on the constitution *Apostolicae sedis*. BIBLIOGRAPHY: A. Beugnet, DTC 1.2:1322.

[P. K. MEAGHER]

ANNIHILATION, the reduction of something to nothing. When God has brought a thing into existence by creation, he maintains it in existence by his continuing creation, or conservation. When it is destroyed, it does not totally cease to be but begins to exist in a different way or ways inasmuch as God still conserves its elements. Were God to desist from conserving it, the thing would simply cease to be. Just as God alone can create and conserve finite being, so he alone can annihilate it. There is no evidence that God ever annihilates anything, although the view of Arnobius the Elder (d. *c*.327) and Edward White, the Congregationalist minister, in his *Life in Christ* (1846), and of Adventists generally, that man's immortality is conditional on his moral behavior involves God's annihilation of the unworthy (see CONDITIONAL IMMORTALITY). BIBLIOGRAPHY: M. R. E. Masterman, NCE 1:561–562; C. Ferro, "Annientamento," EncFil 1:255.

[B. FORSHAW]

ANNIHILATIONISM, see CONDITIONAL IMMORTALITY.

ANNIUS (NANNI), JOHN (*c*.1432–1502), Italian Dominican humanist, historian, and archeologist. Among many writings he composed a 17-volume history of antiquities (1498), which contained many texts questionably attributed to classical authors. In 1499 A. was appointed master of the sacred palace. BIBLIOGRAPHY: Quétif-Échard 2.1:4–7.

[J. A. WEISHEIPL]

ANNIVERSARY (liturgical), the annual remembrance, or "keeping in mind," in liturgical celebration of an event in the Mystical Body, thereby releasing "the grace of the time" for present efficacy. Liturgy for days of special dedication: coronation of a pope, consecration of a bp., religious profession, marriage; for remembrance of death, of diocesan or parish centenary, etc., is applied to the yearly recurrence, inviting real participation in the happening. In Christ is accomplished what the sacrifices of the Old Law were not capable of doing (Heb ch. 10). BIBLIOGRAPHY: E. Loehr, *Year of Our Lord: The Mystery of Christ in the Liturgical Year* (1937), esp. A. Vonier, pref., and O. Casel, introd.; G. Diekmann, *Come, Let Us Worship* (pa. 1966) 142.

[M. R. BROWN]

ANNO II OF COLOGNE, ST. (*c*.1010–75), abp., reformer. Chancellor of the empire under Henry III, he was briefly regent and guardian of Henry IV. In 1062 A. supported Pope Alexander II against the antipope Cadalus, bp. of Parma (d. *c*.1071). Ousted by the people of Cologne in 1074, A. was restored to his see, but soon retired to the monastery of Siegburg, where he died. His *vita* (*c.* 1106; see Pertz, MGS 11:462–514) is not reliable, nor is the *Annolied* (*c*.1100). BIBLIOGRAPHY: P. Bertocchi, Bibl-Sanct 1:1317–21; Butler 4:490–491.

[M. F. MCCARTHY]

ANNO DOMINI (Lat. for in the year of the Lord), a term referring to the numbering of years in the Christian era from the birth of Christ. The system was devised by Dionysius Exiguus (d. *c*.550), who dated the birth of Christ in 753 A.U.C., apparently a miscalculation since Herod's death is now dated 4 B.C.

[T. EARLY]

ANNO SANTO, see HOLY YEAR.

ANNOLIED, medieval German world chronicle, composed *c*.1100, first edited by Martin Opitz (1639). The original MS is lost. In 49 strophes the poet (perhaps a monk of Siegburg) traces salvation and world history, the history of Cologne, and the life, death, and miracles of Anno II, abp. of Cologne (1065–1075), in whom he finds the perfect synthesis of spiritual and secular power. BIBLIOGRAPHY: J. Schwietering, *Die deutsche Dichtung des Mittelalters* (1957); K. Fristchi, *Das Annolied* (1957).

[M. F. MCCARTHY]

ANNONCIADES, a penitential order for women founded by St. Joan of Valois. The rule was approved in 1501. Before the French Revolution the order had 45 houses in France and the Low Countries. Of these two have survived, one in Villeneuve-sur-Lot and the other at Thiais in France. BIBLIOGRAPHY: S. Cita-Malard, *Religious Orders of Women* (tr. G. J. Robinson, 1964) 49.

[P. K. MEAGHER]

ANNUAL CONFERENCE (Methodist), the administrative body for the churches in a particular district, as well as the group of churches in that district. *CONFERENCE (METHODIST).

[T. C. O'BRIEN]

ANNUARIO PONTIFICIO, a volume of statistics and data concerning personnel of the Roman curia, and bishops throughout the world, published yearly in Vatican City. It includes the statistics of each diocese concerning such items as churches and chapels open to the public, priests, seminarians, religious—male and female—hospitals, schools, clinics, and many other religious institutions and activities.

[S. A. HEENEY]

ANNULMENT OF MARRIAGE, the determination that a putative marriage has been from its inception nonexistent. In RC church law, three general categories of causes may lead to a declaration of nullity: defect of form, presence of a diriment impediment, or an essential defect in matrimonial consent. Such declarations are classified as formal or informal depending upon whether the procedure used to determine the grounds for an annulment entails an actual trial or simply an administrative procedure. An informal declaration of nullity is granted in three instances: defect of form, documentary evidence of a diriment impediment and cases of presumed death. Defect of form applies if a Catholic attempts marriage without the assistance of a duly authorized priest or minister. If a diriment impediment arising from disparity of cult, sacred orders, prior marriage, consanguinity, affinity, et al., is sufficiently demonstrated by documents, the marriage can be annulled informally. A case of presumed death occurs when only circumstantial evidence of the death is available; in such a situation, moral certitude of the spouse's death must be reached by evaluating the evidence presented. A formal declaration of nullity is granted in two instances: lack of consent and the presence of some types of diriment impediment. For a valid marriage, both parties must freely and knowingly enter into the marriage contract. Several factors may effectively eliminate that consent and thus invalidate the marriage, e.g., insanity, force and fear, or ignorance that marriage is a permanent union between a man and woman for the procreation of children. Some diriment impediments that require a formal ecclesiastical trial are impotence, abduction, and public propriety. BIBLIOGRAPHY: R. P. Roberts, *Matrimonial Legislation in Latin and Oriental Canon Law* (1961); W. J. Tobin, *Homosexuality and Marriage* (1964); C. A. Ropella, NCE 9:284–286.

[T. M. MCFADDEN]

ANNUNCIATION (IN THE BIBLE), (Lat. *annuntiatio,* declaration, announcement; OE, *hal,* salutation), a word that concerns not only the most important message ever sent, that of God the Father to the Virgin Mary at Nazareth espoused to Joseph, but the act of the Incarnation at that very moment that Gabriel's word was spoken and Mary responded in her fiat and was overshadowed by the Holy Spirit. Appropriate to the Spirit was the "work of grace and love" accomplished in Mary (Mt 1.21, Jn 1.14), the event foretold in Dan 7.14–27; Is 7.14; 9.5–6; Mic 4.7; Ps 89.20–29; 2 Sam 7.16. Together in Luke's first chapter are related the annunciation to the Virgin (26–38) and the preparative annunciation made to Zechariah of the coming birth of John to his wife Elizabeth (5–25) foretold in Is 40.3. Mary set forth in haste to their home in the hill country when the Angel of the Incarnation, Gabriel, advised her that her cousin was in her 6th month; St. Ambrose comments on Elizabeth's greeting, "Hail, full of grace," that it was reserved alone for Mary (Lk 1.39–58). The OT records yet another annunciation with which God prepared the kingdom of his Son, that to Elkanah and Hannah to whom God spoke through the priest Eli (1 Sam

1.9–18) and later to the child Samuel "who had as yet no knowledge of Yahweh" (1 Sam 3.7); Hannah's *Canticle of Thanksgiving* (1 Sam 2.1–10) is woven into the Magnificat. In the mystery of the Annunciation we are met by the astounding fact of the *Incarnation: God himself enters into the human sphere, takes on man's form, and joins his divine nature to our human mortality.

The mystery has been the motivation of man's actions, the subject of his pondering, the object of his contemplation through two millennia. The weighing in prayer of the OT and gospel texts that foretell or memorialize the event, the preaching of God's generosity, of his Son's humbling himself to our lowliness, the liturgical celebration of the Annunciation Feast, are universal in intent, according to the Word of him who was announced.

Benedict XIV, supported by St. Augustine, affirmed March 25 as "the actual day of the Incarnation." Church observance of the Annunciation is universal and perhaps of apostolic origin; Gregory Thaumaturgus in 5th-cent. homilies documents its celebration. The Council in Trullo (692) mentions the feast, though in this 7th cent., Spain not accepting the date March 25, the Council of Toledo ordered it kept on Jan. 18, not to fix the actual date but to avoid its falling in Lent when Christians must restrain their jubilation. In the U.S. celebration of the Annunciation as a holyday of obligation on March 25 was abrogated by the Third Council of Baltimore (1884).

Beyond the vast theological tomes written on the Annunciation, archeology, architecture, music, painting, sculpture, literature (particularly poetry since Dante honored it in his *Purgatorio*) are headings that indicate the abundant influence of the scripture versicles and responses of the evangelical salutation and Annunciation doctrine; above all, the celebrations of the whole liturgical year, at whose core is embedded the Annunciation, proclaim the tidings brought to Mary. BIBLIOGRAPHY: I. Cecchetti et al., EncCatt 1:1382–96; J. Jungmann, *Public Worship: A Survey* (tr. C. Howell, 1957) 185; L. J. Suenens, *Mary, the Mother of God* (1959). 39–44.

[M. R. BROWN]

ANNUNCIATION, see EVANGELISMOS.

ANNUNCIATION, SUNDAY OF, in the *East Syrian Church, any one of the four Sundays preceding Christmas; in the *West Syrian Church, any one of the six Sundays preceding Christmas, but esp. the first two (Sunday of the Annunciation of Zachary, Sunday of the Annunciation of the Mother of God), the other four having other titles proper to themselves.

[A. CODY]

ANNUNZIO, GABRIELE D', see D'ANNUNZIO, GABRIELE.

ANOINTING. In the ancient Near East oil was considered to have refreshing, and even healing properties, and to anoint the head of someone with oil was considered a mark of favor and esteem, such as a host might bestow upon an honored guest (cf. Ps 23.5; Lk 7.46). In the case of an overlord anointing a subordinate it was an effective way of establishing him in authority. Thus in the Tel el-Amarna letters a subordinate king of a Canaanite city-state relates how the Pharaoh "established (Taku) my grandfather as king in Nuhashshe and set oil upon his head." Hittite coronations too included the rite of anointing "with the fine oil of kingship," and "anointed one" (equivalent to the Hebrew *mᵉsiah* or Messiah) was one of the titles of the Hittite king. In the OT this secular significance is retained. Thus David is twice anointed at Hebron, first by the men of Judah (cf. 2 Sam 2.4) and second by all the elders of Israel (cf 2 Sam 5.3). But here it acquires a sacral significance and is applied primarily by the prophets in the name of Yahweh as a sign that he has not only established the individual concerned in authority but also consecrated him to his service and bestowed upon him the charisms of the spirit. Thus Samuel anoints Saul (1 Sam 10.1) and David (cf. 1 Sam 16.12–13), and Elisha anoints Jehu (cf. 2 Kg 9.6) etc. Thereby the king received divine life-force into his own person, enabling him to perform extraordinary feats on behalf of his people. Henceforward he was made over to Yahweh in roughly the same sense that a sacred cult object, a sacred stone or altar, was conceived to belong to him. These too were consecrated by anointing and were pregnant with the divine life-force of Yahweh's presence and use. In a similar way and for a similar reason the anointed king was "untouchable." Anointing is also used for the consecration of the high priest (cf. Ex 40.13; Lev 21.10; Ps 133.2, etc.) and also for that of Elisha (cf. 1 Kg 19.16) with a similar significance. The only anointing ritual prescribed in the NT is that prescribed for the sick (cf. Jas 5.14), and here it is plainly thought of as a medicinal remedy capable of acquiring a sacramental significance as well. BIBLIOGRAPHY: De Vaux AncIsr.

[D. J. BOURKE]

ANOINTING OF THE LORD, the story of the Lord's anointing at Bethany which appears in all four Gospels. In Matthew and Mark the host is Simon the leper and the woman is neither named nor identified as a sinner. John's version mentions Judas's complaint. Mark identifies the perfume as nard but Matthew says only that it was expensive. It was the custom to anoint the head generously at banquets; in Luke's account the host did not do this. The perfume was kept in a small sealed alabaster vase which could only be used by breaking it. Jesus accepts the gesture graciously and excuses the extravagance by referring to his death and burial. This permits him to accept it. It is the only action in the Gospel that is promised an everlasting remembrance.

[C. C. O'DONNELL]

ANOINTING OF THE SICK, a term now often used for the sacrament formerly known as extreme unction. The older term is now considered objectionable because it fostered a once common objection to the use of the sacrament in many instances because of its tendency to frighten people by conveying the suggestion that they were upon the brink of death. Here the sacrament is treated under the heading, *SICK, SACRAMENT OF THE.

[P. K. MEAGHER]

ANOIXIS (Gr. for the act of opening), in the Byzantine Church the opening of a church building for liturgical worship for the first time after its consecration, and also of the reopening of a church closed by profanation after its reconciliation.

[A. J. JACOPIN]

ANOMOEANS, a name given to the followers of Aëtius and Eunomius who maintained, in opposition to the Council of *Nicaea (325), that the Son is in no way like *(anomoios)* the Father. BIBLIOGRAPHY: X. Le Bachelet, DTC 1:516–517.

[L. G. MÜLLER]

ANOMY (*anomie;* from the Gr. *anomia,* without law), a word used in 17th-cent. religious literature for disregard of law, esp. divine law; in modern usage it indicates a state or condition of a society in which moral standards have disappeared, or of an individual who, through frustration or otherwise, has given up the moral standards commonly honored in the society in which he lives. *ANTINOMIANISM.

[P. K. MEAGHER]

ANONYMOI (Gr. for those who are nameless), in the Byzantine liturgy a term applied to those saints who do not have a proper *apolytikion or *kontakion for their festal offices but rather use those common to their class or category. The common of the saints lists the following divisions: angels, a prophet, several prophets, an apostle, several apostles, a martyr, several martyrs, a priest or bishop martyr, a bishop, several bishops, a monk, a monk who had not struggled in the desert, several monks, a woman martyr, a virgin.

[A. J. JACOPIN]

ANONYMOUS IV (*c.*1275), a theorist, probably an Englishman, who appears to have studied in France. He is referred to as the Anonymous of the British Museum (because a burnt fragment of his MS lies there) or as Anonymous IV (title used in Coussemaker, *Scriptorum de musica medii aevi*). He describes, in his valuable treatise, the nature and practice of the polyphonic art. To him we owe our knowledge of the leaders of the Notre Dame school: Magister Leoninus (Léonin), a great composer of organa, and Magister Perotinus (Pérotin), who exhibited a great perfection of musical technique in his adding of a third and fourth part to

the works of the former. BIBLIOGRAPHY: Reese MusMa 264; A. Hughes, *Early Medieval Music up to 1300 (The New Oxford History of Music,* 1954) 2:306.

[M. T. LEGGE]

ANONYMOUS OF YORK, a collection of 31 tracts in Corpus Christi College, Cambridge, MS 415, representing both papal and anti-papal views of the immediate post-Gregorian reform period. Put together probably at York, England, the collection appears to have had little or no influence. Its chief interest is for the historian of medieval political theory. BIBLIOGRAPHY: edition by H. Böhmer in MGH Lib. lit. 3:642–687; G. H. Williams, *Norman Anonymous of 1100* A.D. (1951).

[L. E. BOYLE]

ANONYMOUS CHRISTIANS, those people who, according to K. Rahner and some other contemporary RC theologians, believe in the Incarnation of the Word of God whether they explicitly realize this or not. The designation would apply to those who accept that God has given man the ultimate and decisive expression of himself in Jesus Christ, even if that person denies the orthodox formulas of the Church. Indeed, a person who is still far from any explicit and properly formulated acceptance of Christian revelation but who accepts his own humanity as a mystery of God's love, accepts the Son of Man contained in the depths of every truly human openness to reality. BIBLIOGRAPHY: K. Rahner, SacMund 3:208–209; *idem, Theological Investigations* 4 (1966) 118–120; A. Roper, *Anonymous Christians* (1966).

[T. M. MCFADDEN]

ANONYMOUS LETTERS, communications without an identifiable subscription. A common form for a public manifesto, e.g., a letter to a newspaper, these are less tolerable in private interchanges, even when done with good intention, e.g., to warn a friend. They are quite intolerable in their general connotation as poison-pen publications written to make mischief or vent personal spite. Often the result of mental or emotional disturbance, they are grave wrongs against charity, justice, and the social virtues of truthfulness and friendliness.

[T. GILBY]

ANOVULANTS, pharamceutical products that inhibit ovulation. When it was discovered in the 1950s that the female hormone, progesterone, influenced ovulation, the way opened to the development of an effective contraceptive drug. This led to a spirited controversy among RC moral theologians, some of whom maintained that, in some circumstances at least, such drugs could legitimately be used for contraceptive purposes, while others, though conceding the probability that certain uses of the drugs were morally unobjectionable, nevertheless denied that they could be lawfully employed by married persons for the specific purpose of preventing conception. Although Pius XII supported the latter view, the debate continued. John XXIII in March 1963 set up an advisory commission to look into questions concerning the regulation of birth, and the deliberations of this commission were continued under Paul VI. Although the discovery of contraceptive drugs had precipitated the debate, the reports of the commission, written in May-June 1966, made no distinction between mechanical and chemical forms of contraception, but it was clear that antifertility pills were included under the general heading of contraception, to which the majority reports wanted to give some limited measure of approval, while the minority report opposed any change in the earlier teaching of the magisterium. On July 25, 1968, Paul VI issued the encyclical *Humanae vitae* in which he declared that from the licit means of regulating birth was to be excluded "every action which, either in anticipation of the conjugal act, or in its accomplishment, or in the development of its natural consequences, proposes, whether as an end or as a means, to render procreation impossible." *CONTRACEPTION.

[P. K. MEAGHER]

ANQUETIL, LOUIS PIERRE (1723–1806), French Canon of St. Augustine, historical writer, brother of A. H. *Anquetil-Duperron. His *Histoire de Reims* (3 v., 1756–59) is a work of some merit, but his *L'Esprit de la Ligue (3 v., 1767) and his *Histoire de France* (14 v., 1805), though popular at the time, suffer from a want of critical scholarship. BIBLIOGRAPHY: P. Calendini, DHGE 3:422–423.

[P. K. MEAGHER]

ANQUETIL DUPERRON, ABRAHAM HYACINTHE (1731–1805), French Orientalist. He went to India (1755) to learn what the Parsees could teach him about the language and religion of the ancient Zoroastrians. He returned to Paris in 1762 with many ancient texts he had copied. His *Zend-Avesta, ouvrage de Zoroastre* (3 v., 1771) and his translation of the Vedic Upanishads (2 v., 1801–02) won him a considerable reputation in the scholarly world and opened the way to further studies. BIBLIOGRAPHY: R. Schwab, *Vie d'Anquetil-Duperron* (1934); E. P. Colbert, NCE 1:579–580.

[P. K. MEAGHER]

ANSBALD ST. (d.886), abbot of Prüm from 860. Under his guidance the abbey became famous for its regular observance. His correspondence with Lupus of Ferrières reveals A.'s concern for improving the holdings of the monastic library. BIBLIOGRAPHY: A. M. Zimmermann, BiblSanct 1:1336.

[H. DRESSLER]

ANSCHLUSS, the union of Germany and Austria, usually referring to the annexation of Austria by Germany, March 13, 1938. Great interest in the union between the two countries was stirred after World War I, when Austria was stripped of her vast possessions which had comprised the Habsburg Empire. With the coming of the German revolution in the early 1930s, the tempo of interest increased in Germany, and the Austrian government began to suspect Nazi strategy. On Jan. 30, 1933, Adolf Hitler was appointed Chancellor of Germany by von Hindenburg and soon began to arouse the populace by relentlessly exploiting his theme of the persecution of Germans outside the fatherland. He fomented agitation in Austria through pro-Nazi sympathizers and blamed Chancellor Kurt von Schuschnigg for permitting the alleged atrocities. On Feb. 12, 1938, Schuschnigg met with Hitler to discuss relations between the two countries, at which time the German leader made excessive demands on Austria, amounting to the surrender of its independence. Rather than submit, the Chancellor called for a plebiscite to ascertain the will of his country. Hitler, stunned by this measure, demanded the cancellation of the plebiscite and the resignation of Dr. Schuschnigg in favor of pro-Nazi Artur von Seyss-Inquart. Austria failed to receive the support of the European democracies, and German soldiers occupied the country on March 12. The following day Austria "announced" its new status as a province of the German Reich. On March 14, 1938, Hitler triumphantly entered Vienna. The *Anschluss* was complete. BIBLIOGRAPHY: K. von Schuschnigg, *Austrian Requiem* (1946); M. A. Wathen, *Policy of England and France toward the "Anschluss" of 1938* (1954); J. Gehl, *Austria, Germany, and the Anschluss 1931–1938* (1963).

[M. A. WATHEN]

ANSE, COUNCILS OF. The first of several medieval councils held at Anse, near Lyons, was convened in 994. Besides regulating the property of Cluny and the lives of the clergy, it called for Sunday rest to begin at None (3 P.M.) on Saturday; and it laid the obligation on priests of carrying viaticum to the sick. Councils held in Anse in 1070, 1076, 1100, 1112, and 1300 were also primarily disciplinary. BIBLIOGRAPHY: A. Condit, NCE 1:580 for bibliog.

[B. L. MARTHALER]

ANSEGIS, ST. (c.770–833), abbot. A monk of Fontenelle, A. became one of Charlemagne's advisers and administrative officials and was named by him abbot of Saint-Germer-de-Flay, which he restored spiritually and materially. Louis the Pious made him abbot of Luxeuil (817) and of Fontenelle (823), to both of which monasteries he restored discipline, prosperity, and a dedication to learning evident in Fontenelle's famous library and scriptorium. His collection of Carolingian capitularies (827) became the authority on ecclesiastical law (bks. 1–2) and civil law (bks. 3–4) in the Frankish Empire. Several chapters were later incorporated into Gratian's *Decretum*. BIBLIOGRAPHY: P. Cousin, NCE 1:580–581; Butler 3:155; C. Lefebvre, BiblSanct 1:1339–40.

[G. M. COOK]

ANSELM OF BAGGIO, see ALEXANDER II, POPE

ANSELM OF CANTERBURY, ST. (*c*.1033–1109), theologian and abp. of Canterbury. A. was born at Aosta in N Italy, the son of a Lombard landowner. He entered the monastic school of Bec in 1059, coming under the influence of its prior *Lanfranc, and took monastic vows there in 1060. When Lanfranc became abbot of St. Stephen's, Caen, in 1063, A. succeeded him as prior, and in 1078 succeeded Herlwin, the founding abbot.

Extensive properties of the monastery in England involved A. in English life, and he made visits to Lanfranc, who had become abp. of Canterbury in 1070. Upon Lanfranc's death in 1089 A. was chosen as his successor, but his assumption of the post was delayed by a dispute with King William II (Rufus), over lay investiture. The dispute was resolved in 1093, and A. took the *pallium from the legate of Urban II. Conflict over church independence arose again, however, and A. went to Rome in 1097 seeking support. The King meanwhile seized the properties of the see. While away from England at this time A. defended the *filioque creed against the Greeks at the Council of Bari (1098), and also wrote his classic work on the atonement, *Cur Deus Homo* (Why God Became Man).

Upon the accession of Henry I in 1100, A. was recalled to England, where he helped arrange the King's marriage to Matilda of Scotland and aided him in gaining baronial support against Henry's elder brother, Robert II of Normandy. The conflict over lay investiture also arose under the new King, however, when A. refused to consecrate bishops and abbots nominated by the King. A. again went to Rome for support. Henry then surrendered the right of lay investiture, establishing supremacy of the papacy over the English Church. In his later years A. introduced many reforms, including the encouragement of regular synods, enforcement of clerical celibacy, and suppression of the slave trade. He was canonized in 1163, and in 1720 Clement XI declared him a Doctor of the Church.

Though he did not write a *Summa*, A. is often called the father of the schoolmen and is generally considered the outstanding theologian between St. Augustine and St. Thomas. He asserted the harmony of faith and reason, contending that faith preceded reason but that what was held by faith could be demonstrated by reason and did not rest merely on the authority of Scripture and tradition. Expressions central to his approach included, I believe that I may understand (*credo ut intelligam*), and, faith seeking understanding (*fides quaerens intellectum*). He was the first successfully to incorporate Aristotelian dialectics into theology.

In his *Proslogium* he set forth several converging proofs for the existence of God, and in the *Monologium* presented his famous proof known since Kant's time as the ontological argument. That proof runs: I have an idea of that than which there could be nothing greater; it must therefore exist, because if it did not, it would not be the greatest conceivable entity, since that which exists in reality is greater than that which exists only in the mind. In his own lifetime the argument was rejected by Gaunilo, and later by St. Thomas and Kant. It has been defended by Bonaventure, Descartes, and others, including more recently K. Barth in his *Anselm: Fides Quaerens Intellectum* (2 ed., 1958).

A.'s doctrine of the atonement has been widely accepted as the classic expression of what is known as the objective theory. In contrast with the subjective theory, expressed by Abelard and others, it asserted the necessity of an objective act of atonement for man's sin. In contrast, too, with some patristic theories of the devil having a claim on sinful man, A. said that satisfaction was paid to God, not the devil. Since the offense was against God, A. added, it was infinite and could not be paid by sinful man. Since the offense had been committed by man, however, the infinite satisfaction must be paid by man. The only solution was the satisfaction paid by the God-man, who was sinless and so owed no penalty, and by his suffering on the Cross could give infinite satisfaction.

A. was an advocate of realism in the conflicts of medieval philosophy regarding the existence of universals against the nominalism of Roscelin (fl. 1092–1119). BIBLIOGRAPHY: R. W. Southern, *Saint Anselm and His Biographer* (1963); J. Clayton, *Saint Anselm* (1933); J. McIntrye, *St. Anselm and His Critics* (1954); B. Calati, BiblSanct 2:1–19.

[T. EARLY]

ANSELM OF HAVELBERG (d.1158), bp. of Havelberg, later abp. of Ravenna. A. served as envoy of Emperor Lothair III to Constantinople where he took part in ecumenical dialogues with the Byzantine clergy, defending the Western Church against charges of doctrinal novelty. Later at the request of Frederick I Barbarossa, he helped arrange a treaty with Pope Eugene III. He is the author of important doctrinal works. BIBLIOGRAPHY: PL 188:1087–1248; Mann 9:143–147; J. R. Sommerfeldt, NCE 1:583–584.

[M. A. WINKELMANN]

ANSELM OF LAON (*c*.1050–1117), theologian. One of the most respected teachers of the late 11th and early 12th cent., A. directed the cathedral school at Laon and had both William of Champeaux and Abelard among his pupils. His *Sentences* was one of scholasticism's earliest attempts to systematize theological thought. The biblical *Glossa ordinaria*, once attributed to Walafrid Strabo, is now believed to have been compiled by glossators under his direction. BIBLIOGRAPHY: B. Guillemain, *Early Middle Ages* (tr. S. Taylor, 1960) 85.

ANSELM OF LIÈGE (d. 1056), chronicler. Born in the late 10th cent., A. studied at Liège with Poppo of Stavelot, became a canon and dean of St. Lambert's. He was highly esteemed, and chronicled the activities of the bps. of Tongres, Utrecht, and Liège, using carefully the materials at hand and his own knowledge. BIBLIOGRAPHY: T. A. Carroll, NCE 1:584.

[S. WILLIAMS]

ANSELM I OF LUCCA, see ALEXANDER II, POPE.

ANSELM II OF LUCCA, ST. (1036–86), one of the most learned men of his time, nephew of Pope Alexander II (whom he succeeded as bp. of Lucca), staunch supporter of Gregory VII. His *Collectio canonum* provided a useful juridical basis for the Gregorian reform and is an important source for the history of the reform movement. BIBLIOGRAPHY: Butler 1:628–629; G. M. Fuscone, BiblSanct 2:26–36.

[P. K. MEAGHER]

ANSELM OF NONANTOLA, ST. (d.803), soldier, Lombard duke, abbot. He founded a monastery and hospital at Fanano (750). Entering the Benedictines (753), he became abbot of Nonantola which he had founded *c*.752, building a hospital and hospices for pilgrims. Banished to Monte Cassino by the Lombard King Desiderius, he was later restored to his flourishing monastery by Charlemagne. BIBLIOGRAPHY: Butler 1:470; G. Lucchesi, BiblSanct 2:22–25.

[G. E. CONWAY]

ANSELME, ANTOINE (1651–1737), preacher. Son of a doctor, A. was educated by a priest-uncle and later became tutor to the De Montespan family. Having established a reputation as a preacher, he was invited by the Académie Française to preach the panegyric for St. Louis at the Louvre chapel (1681). Through the favor of Louis XIV he was given the abbey of St.-Sever (1699), where he eventually retired (1724). His sermons are noteworthy for their sound morality and for the personal manner, uncharacteristic of his time, in which he treated his topics. His works may be found in J. P. Migne's *Collection intégrale et universelle des orateurs sacrés* (102 v., 1844–66) v. 20–21.

[P. K. MEAGHER]

ANSELMIANUM (PONTIFICIO ATENEO DI S. ANSELMO), an institution that had its origin in the college erected by Innocent XI by his apostolic constitution *Inscrutabili* (1687) for the Cassinese Benedictines in the monastery of St. Paul-Outside-the-Walls. It included faculties of philosophy, theology, and canon law. The theologians were directed to follow the guidance of St. Anselm of Canterbury. The institution suffered adversities in the 19th cent. when it was suppressed for a time by Napoleon (1810) and suspended in 1837 because of a plague. It was restored by Pius IX but had to be closed again on account of political disturbances (1870). Leo XIII reconstituted it (1887) for all the black Benedictines. Meanwhile it had become a pontifical institute.

[S. A. HEENEY]

ANSELMO DEDICATA, COLLECTIO, a canonical collection discovered near the end of the 9th cent. dedicated by its anonymous author to Anselm, abp. of Milan (II, 882–896). Its goal was the distributing of a large number of works into a systematic form. The contents were divided into 12 books of 3 sections: canonical works; works derived from the letters of St. Gregory the Great; and works of Roman sources. Its impact was great for more than a century, esp. on Italian and German canonical life.

[S. A. HEENEY]

ANSFRID, ST. (d. *c*.1010), Benedictine monk, bishop. Count of Brabant, A. was educated at the imperial school at Cologne. He was a loyal supporter of the Emperor and strove to suppress brigandage. In 992 he became a monk and was made bp. of Utrecht, an office he filled until he lost his sight in 1006 and retired to Heiligen, which he had founded. BIBLIOGRAPHY: Butler 2:273; W. Lampen, BiblSanct 2:39.

[S. WILLIAMS]

ANSGAR, ST. (Anskar, Anschar, Scharies; *c*.801–865), abbot, abp., "Apostle of the North." A Benedictine of Corbie and teacher at Corvey, he engaged in missionary activities in Denmark and later in Sweden, where he converted Heriger, governor and councilor to King Björn. Emperor Louis I the Pious named him abbot of Corvey and bp. of Hamburg in 831, and in 832 Pope Gregory IV made him both abp. and papal legate to Scandinavia. When Hamburg was destroyed by the Normans (845), King Louis the German gave A. the then-vacant See of Bremen. Pope Nicholas I subsequently confirmed A. as abp. of Hamburg and bp. of Bremen (864). Renewing missionary activities he converted King Haarik in Denmark and King Olaf in Sweden. His vita by his successor, Rembert, is an important historical source for the 9th century. BIBLIOGRAPHY: P. Manns, *Die Heiligen in ihrer Zeit* (1966) 1:435–438; S. A. Schulz, NCE 1:586; Butler 1:242–243; P. Maarschallkerweerd, BiblSanct 1:1337–39.

[M. S. TANEY]

ANSHELM, VALERIUS (1475–1546 or 47), Swiss chronicler. After studying in Cracow, Tübingen, and Lyons, A. taught school in Bern (1505–09), then became the city physician. In 1525 he was expelled from Bern for his zeal in promoting Zwinglianism, continued his activities in Rottweil, and was brought back to Bern in 1529 by the victorious Reformers. He then wrote the chronicles of Bern from 1477 to 1526, and with discriminating use of the archives and earlier annals, produced a good, if slanted, picture of the Reform movement in Switzerland. BIBLIOGRAPHY: T. Schwegler, LTK 1:598; D. McAndrews, NCE 1:586.

[H. JACK]

ANSTRUDIS, ST. (*c*.645–*c*.709), abbess of Laon, probably the daughter of SS. Blandinus and Salaberga. Her mother founded the abbey; A. faithfully followed her work and succeeded her mother as abbess. When A.'s brother was treacherously murdered, she was accused to Ebroin, the mayor of the palace, of taking sides against his interest. An attempt was made on A.'s life; amid many difficulties her virtue and innocence were proved. Her relics were venerated

at St.-Jean of Laon until after the French Revolution. BIBLI-
OGRAPHY: E. Brouette, NCE 1:586; M. A. Calabrese, Bibl-
Sanct 2:44–45.

[M. C. BRADLEY]

ANSUERUS, ST. (c.1040–66), abbot and martyr. A. became a Benedictine monk and an early and zealous missionary among the pagan Slavic tribes still powerful in W
Germany. He was stoned to death with some companions by
pagan Wends or Obotrites at Ratzeburg. BIBLIOGRAPHY:
A. M. Zimmermann, BiblSanct 2:45–46.

ANTELAMI, BENEDETTO (c.1150–c.1230), greatest
Romanesque sculptor in N Italy. A.'s only documented
works are the signed architrave of the north portal of the
Parma baptistery, and a *Deposition from the Cross* (Parma
Cathedral, 1178) with style and iconography relating to
Provencal Romanesque (St. Gilles and St. Trophime,
Arles). As architect and sculptor of the Parma baptistery
(1196–1270), his greatest work shows novel and complex
iconography with interesting antique and eastern relevances.
Extensive sculpture infers numerous assistants but unity of
design proves A.'s supervision. Attributed to him as ar-
chitect are the cathedral of Borgo San Donnino (1179) and S.
Andrea, Vercelli (1219–27) with carved tympanum by
Antelami. BIBLIOGRAPHY: G. de Francovich, *Benedetto
Antelami* (1952).

[M. J. DALY]

ANTELMI, JOSEPH (1648–97), French church historian.
His published works include an account of the beginnings of
the Church at Fréjus, studies on the writings of SS. Leo the
Great and Prosper of Aquitaine, and on the life and times of
St. Gregory of Tours. He also produced a number of hagiographical works. BIBLIOGRAPHY: F. Bonnard, DHGE
3:515–516.

[P. K. MEAGHER]

ANTEPENDIUM, a veil or hanging used to cover the entire
front of the altar. It varies in color according to the ecclesiastical season or feast. Its use goes back to the 4th cent. in the
East and to the 5th in the West. It serves to protect the altar
from dirt and may have developed as an extension of the altar
covering. In the RC Church its use has now become obsolete. BIBLIOGRAPHY: J. B. O'Connell, *Church Building and
Furnishing* (1955), 192–196; P. Radó, *Enchiridion litur-
gicum* (2 v., 1961), 2:1410.

[N. KOLLAR]

ANTERION (derived from Lat. *anterium;* Sl., *podryasnik),*
the Eastern cassock worn under the *rason as the ordinary
dress of all orders of clergy and monks. It is sometimes called
the inner rason but is better termed anterion to distinguish it
from the outer rason usually called the rason. It is preferably
black, but any color may be used, and grey, deep violet, and
dark blue are often seen. The front has no buttons but laps

over from right to left and is fastened by a button at the side.
Among the Russians the collar is closed with small buttons at
the left side, but among the Greeks it is often left open,
similar to the collar on the Roman cassock. Monks universally gird the anterion with a leather belt while other clergy
either leave it loose or use the belt, or a cloth cincture (sash)
that is never tasseled as in the West. Many Eastern Catholics
have adopted the Roman or semi-Jesuit style cassock for the
sake of convenience, but this practice is not favored.

[A. J. JACOPIN]

ANTERUS, ST. (d. 236), **POPE** from 235. His election
followed upon the resignation of his predecessor, St.
*Pontian, who gave up his office when sent to Sardinia in
exile. His pontificate lasted only 43 days (Nov. 21 to Jan 3).
He is credited in the *Liber pontificalis* with collecting copies
of official proceedings against the martyrs for preservation.
He was the first to be buried in the papal crypt in the
catacomb of Callistus. It is not certain that he died a martyr.
Letters credited to him by Pseudo-Isidore are found in
PG 10:165–168. BIBLIOGRAPHY: E. G. Weltin, NCE
1:590–592; J. P. Kirsch, CE 1:553; J. S. Brusher, *Popes
through the Ages* (1959); Butler 1:26.

[P. F. MULHERN]

ANTHELM OF CHIGNIN, ST. (1107–78), Carthusian
bishop. As a young priest A. visited the Carthusians at
Portes and chose to remain among them (1137). He was sent
to Grande Chartreuse, became the seventh prior after the
resignation of Hugh I (1139), and later became the first
minister-general of the order. After 12 years as prior, he
returned to Portes, but 2 years later was back at Grande
Chartreuse, where he supported Alexander III against antipope Victor IV. In 1163 he became bp. of Belley and was
energetic in the reform of the clergy. He was to be papal
legate to England in the controversy between Henry II and
Becket, but was prevented by circumstances from going.
BIBLIOGRAPHY: C. Marchal, *Vie de Saint Anthelme* (1878);
C. Vens, BiblSanct 2:48–50; Butler 2:650–652.

[N. F. GAUGHAN]

ANTHEM (ME, *antem, antefn,* fr. Lat. *antiphona,* antiphon), a sacred choral composition used exclusively by the
Anglican Church, deriving from and corresponding to the
Latin motet of the Roman Catholic Church. Although authorized, anthems are not considered liturgical in the sense of
being an integral part of a particular service. The basic
difference between an anthem and a motet is the language of
the text. The anthem came to be written in the vernacular as a
result of the Act of Uniformity (1549), which established
English as the liturgical language. Among the composers of
that time who made significant contributions for the Anglican service were Tye, Tallis, Gibbons, Tompkins, and
William Byrd whose Catholicism did not diminish the quality or integrity of his Anglican works. The style of these early
pieces was somewhat simpler and more homophonic than

contemporary motets, principally because of the need of the text to be understood.

Toward the end of the 16th cent. there began to appear short selections for solo voice with an independent accompaniment. This type of anthem came to be called "verse," while those that used choir throughout were called "full" anthems. By the 17th cent. verse anthems far outnumbered full anthems. Instrumental ritornellos were employed by such composers as Humfrey, Blow, and Purcell. With these composers the anthem began to take on the aspect of a cantata, with its several movements and the use of solos, duets, etc. Much has been made of the influence of Lully and the French overture on composers of this period, and one can see traces of this in the frequency of dotted rhythms, especially in the final "Halleluia." This device became a mannerism, precipitating a style change in the 18th cent. which resulted in a closing choral fugue, reportedly borrowed from the oratorio. The anthem in the 18th cent. came to serve more as an occasional piece. Handel's 12 Chandos Anthems of 1720 (using Purcell as a model), the coronation anthem for George II, and the Foundling Hospital Anthem serve as examples of this development. Theatrical music began to exert a strong influence on all church music of this period, and its force was felt throughout the late 18th and the 19th cent., resulting in less than great religious music. Composers of some merit who contributed to the repertory of anthems during that time were Maurice Greene and S. S. Wesley. Their works would never equal the quality of the Masses of Haydn, Mozart, and Schubert, but served a purpose during a generally bleak period in the history of English music. A new flourishing of the latter in general and of church music in particular from the late 19th cent. on resulted in numerous fine anthems by such composers as Stanford, Parry, Vaughan Williams, and Rubbra, as well as the younger generation of English composers. It is interesting to note Britten's "Antiphon" (1957). In the U.S. the term anthem has come to mean any choral composition with a sacred text, esp. when performed in the course of a Protestant service.

[P. J. MCCARTHY]

ANTHEM OF PUY, a name often given in medieval times to the *Salve Regina* because of its popularity at the shrine of Our Lady at Le Puy in the Middle Ages. The composition of the antiphon has been attributed, among others, to Adhemar of Puy.

[P. K. MEAGHER]

ANTHEMIUS. Among the notable persons who bore this name were: (1) A statesman (fl. 400–414) who was master of the offices, a patrician, praetorian prefect of the Orient (406), and regent of the empire upon the accession of the 7-year-old Emperor Theodosius II. Praised for his statesmanship by St. John Chrysostom (PG 52:699), he harmonized relations between Ravenna and Constantinople, made peace with Persia, reorganized the empire's financial system, halted the advance of King Uldin and the Huns and prevented future attacks by improving the fleet on the Danube and constructing the land wall west of Constantinople. In her 16th year the Empress Pulcheria succeeded him as regent. SEE J. Bury, *History of the Later Roman Empire* (1958) 212–213. (2) A bp. of Constantia (ancient Salamis) during the 5th century. Alexander, a monk of the 6th cent, reported that A. claimed to have discovered the body of St. Barnabas in 488, and on that basis alleged the apostolicity of the See of Cyprus and petitioned the Emperor Zeno to confirm its ecclesiastical independence from the patriarchate of Antioch. In granting the request the Emperor upheld the decision of the Council of Ephesus (431) against the challenge of Peter the Fuller, patriarch of Antioch. SEE R. Aigrain, DHGE 3:526–527. (3) A saint (Anthemus, Attenius, Aptemius; d. c. 400) whom the sometimes inaccurate episcopal lists of Poitiers name as that city's 13th bishop. His feast day has been celebrated since the 17th cent. in Poitiers and Saintes, but no existing record confirms his alleged death at Saintonge and burial at Jonzac. SEE C. Lefebvre, BiblSanct 2:50–51; R. Aigrain, *Catholicisme* 1:626.

[F. H. BRIGHAM]

ANTHEMIUS OF TRALLES, Byzantine mathematician and architect. Born in Lydia, he turned his knowledge of geometry to practical use in 532 when he and *Isidore of Miletus were commissioned by the Emperor Justinian to design the new church of Holy Wisdom (*Hagia Sophia, 532–537) in Constantinople, masterpiece of early Christian Byzantine architecture, its dome construction a triumph surpassing all Roman predecessors, and establishing a pattern for all Byzantine architecture except in Greece and Macedonia. BIBLIOGRAPHY: R. Krautheimer, *Early Christian and Byzantine Architecture* (1965); T. F. Matthews, NCE 3:780–784.

[R. C. MARKS]

ANTHIMUS, the name of several early martyrs. (1) A., martyred in Rome under Diocletian, whose acts emphasize fortitude and miracles. (2) A., bp. of Nicomedia who was martyred in the same persecution. He did not tell the soldiers sent to arrest him who he was until they had enjoyed his hospitality overnight. They converted and offered him liberty, but he declined. Likewise he declined an offer of pagan priesthood and relief from torture before he was beheaded. A letter attributed to him refers to events 50 years later. (3) A., (fl. 450), a hymnographer. With Auxentius, he belonged to the imperial guard and to a group of lay ascetics. As a priest later, he wrote strophes and hymns and psalmody for choirs of men and women. (4) A., bp. of Tyana who quarreled with his friend St. Basil (c. 372) over episcopal jurisdiction in Cappadocia and Armenia.

Seven patriarchs of Constantinople were named Anthimus. One owed his position to the Empress Theodora, who had him transferred uncanonically from Trebizond. But Pope Agapetus had him deposed from both sees and deprived of sacerdotal functions. BIBLIOGRAPHY: I. Daniele, Bibl-Sanct 2:62–65.

[E. P. COLBERT]

ANTHOLOGION (Gr. for a collection of choice flowers; Sl., *prazdichnaya mineya*), a Byzantine liturgical book composed at the end of the 16th cent. containing an abridgement of several other books, principally the Menaia.

[A. J. JACOPIN]

ANTHONY, PATRIARCHS OF CONSTANTIN-OPLE, (1) Anthony I (d. 837) Kassimatas, Iconoclast and patriarch, who was successively hegumen (abbot) of the Monastery of Metropolitou in Petrion (*c*.815), bp. of Sylaion, an active supporter of the Iconoclastic policies of Emperor Leo V (813–821) by his opposition to Patriarch Nicephoras I and his role in the Iconoclastic Synod (815), and patriarch of Constantinople (821–837). (2)A. II (d. 901) patriarch, who was first a monk and then hegumen (abbot) of the Monastery of the Mother of God (later Kalliou Kauleos) until he became patriarch of Constantinople (893–901). (3) A. III (d. 983) the Studite, patriarch, who was syncellus to Patriarch Basil I and appointed his successor by Emperor John Tzmices (974). A. favored the antipope, Boniface VII, over Pope Benedict VII and was allegedly removed from the patriarchate by Emperor Basil II for his sympathy with Bardo Sclerus. Well known for his austere life, he was responsible for the first collection of the lives of the saints of the Oriental Church. (4) A. IV (d. 1399) patriarch and diplomat, who was first appointed patriarch (1389), deposed (1390), and reappointed after regaining the Emperor's favor (1391). His diplomatic efforts enhanced the internal strength of the Byzantine rite Churches, maintained the ecclesiastical sovereignty of Constantinople over Alexandria, and united the Kings of Poland, Hungary, and Kiev against the power of the Turks. BIBLIOGRAPHY: R. Janin, DHGE 3:746, 796–797.

[F. H. BRIGHAM]

ANTHONY OF BOLOGNA (d.*c*.1403), Dominican preacher. His Lenten sermons were published anonymously (1501), but other sermons for Sundays and feasts of saints are still in manuscript.

[E. P. COLBERT]

ANTHONY BONFADINI (1402–82), a Franciscan missionary whose distinguished preaching and teaching were well known throughout Italy and the Holy Land. The discovery of his incorrupt body (1483) and the reports of miracles at his tomb in Cotignola, Romagna, the place of his death, occasioned his cult which Pope Leo XIII eventually confirmed (1901). BIBLIOGRAPHY: J. Campbell, NCE 1:594; Butler 4:460–461; L. Oliger, DHGE 3:763.

[J. J. SMITH]

ANTHONY OF THE CAVES, ST. (983–1073), hermit who after several years at Mt. Athos returned to Russia, settling in a cave in Kiev on the banks of the Dnieper River. Followers gathered about him to form the first purely Russian monastery, that of the Caves (Pecherskaya Lavra). An austere and uncompromising ascetic, he soon left Kiev to seek greater solitude. *CAVES, MONASTERY OF THE (KIEV).

[G. T. DENNIS]

ANTHONY OF EGYPT, ST. (*c*.251–356), hermit and father of anchoritic monasticism. He was a Coptic-speaking Christian born at Coma in Middle Egypt. He disposed of his possessions *c*.269 and began an ascetical life near his home. In 285 he retired into solitude near Pispir. There he went through various personal trials, his famous "temptations." Disciples were attracted to his refuge, and in 305 he emerged to give them a rule, the first recorded attempt to organize anchoritic life. He retired *c*.310 into solitude again but reemerged to lend his support to St. *Athanasius during the Arian conflict. Thus began a tradition of monastic support of the Alexandrian patriarchate that grew into a movement for Coptic national self-determination. It reached its climax in the schism between the *Coptic Church and the supporters of the Council of *Chalcedon (451). A. died at the age of 105 near the Red Sea. The monastery of St. Anthony survives in that region today. BIBLIOGRAPHY: Quasten 3:39–45; Butler 1:104–109; Athanasius, *Vita Antonii* (tr. and ed. R.T. Meyer, ACW 10, 1950).

[D. W. JOHNSON]

ANTHONY OF FUSSALA, a 5th-cent. African bp. raised to this dignity by St. Augustine, who was later forced to remove A. when he was convicted of neglect of the spiritual needs of his flock. Permitted by a weak superior, he appealed to Rome. He was then absolved and sent back to his see.

[S. A. HEENEY]

ANTHONY OF THE HOLY GHOST (1618–74). Born at Monte Morovelho, Portugal, he entered the Discalced Carmelites at Lisbon (1636), becoming prior and later (1673) named bp. of Angola in Africa. Renowned as a preacher, he composed five volumes of spiritual and canonico-moral works, among which was his *Directorium mysticum* (1967). BIBLIOGRAPHY: B. Cavanaugh, NCE 1:595; P. Marie-Joseph, DHGE 3:810–811.

[R. I. BURNS]

ANTHONY OF LÉRINS, ST. (d. before 521), hermit. After his father's death, which occurred when A. was 8 years old, he was cared for by Severinus of Noricum (d. *c*.482), then by Constantius of Lauriacum, and prepared for a monastic life. About 488 he became a hermit near the tomb of Felix of Como at Lake Como, where he lived a life of prayer, penance, and solitude. When fame came to him by reason of his exposure of a murderer who came to him posing as a solitary, he fled across the Alps to Southern Gaul and set up a hermitage at Lérins. BIBLIOGRAPHY: Butler 4:628–629; Ennodius of Padua (chief authority for his life), MGH Auct. ant. 7:185–190.

[P. K. MEAGHER]

ANTHONY MARY CLARET, ST., see CLARET, ANTHONY MARY, ST.

ANTHONY OF NOVGOROD (Dobrynia Jadrejkovič; fl. 1211–38), abp. honored as a saint in the Russian Church. A. was a monk when he was chosen by the people of Novgorod (1211) to be their metropolitan in place of Metrophane, whom they had expelled. When the people repented their act and wanted Metrophane back, A. was put in charge of another diocese, but was later restored to Novgorod after Metrophane's death. Two years later he was again expelled from his see and retired to his monastery. He wrote an account of a journey to Constantinople which is important for its description of Constantinople's churches, relics, images, etc. BIBLIOGRAPHY: A. Palmieri, *Nomenclator litterarius theologiae orthodoxae* 1:86–87; *idem*, DHGE 3:768–769.

[P. K. MEAGHER]

ANTHONY OF PADUA, ST. (1195–1231), Franciscan theologian, preacher, Doctor of the Church. Born of a noble and illustrious family at Lisbon, Portugal, he was given the name Ferdinand at baptism. At age 15 he joined the Canons Regular of St. Augustine, and in 1212 he was transferred to the house of studies in Coimbra. There for 8 years he devoted himself to the practice of piety and the study of Scripture. In 1220, moved at the sight of the bodies of the first Franciscan martyrs of Morocco brought back for burial at Coimbra, he was seized with a desire to become a Franciscan missionary, to preach the gospel in Africa, and to suffer a martyr's death. Given permission to enter the Franciscan Order, he changed his name to Anthony and within a year was sent to work in Morocco. Serious illness forced his return, but his ship, driven by gales and storms, carried him to Sicily. He proceeded to Assisi, where St. Francis had convoked a general chapter in 1221. He was assigned to the Romagna province and sent to a convent near Forlì. There his reputation for learning and preaching was established, and he was sent to preach against the heretics in northern Italy and southern France. Then, appointed by St. Francis as the first theologian of the order, he taught at Montpellier, Bologna, Padua, and Toulouse. Before his death in 1231 at Padua, he held the offices of guardian and provincial. He was canonized by Gregory IX in 1232 and declared a Doctor of the Church by Pius XII in 1946. Many miracles have been attributed to his intercession; hence he is called the Wonder Worker and is esp. revered as the Finder of Lost Things. BIBLIOGRAPHY: S. Clasen, *St. Anthony, Doctor of the Gospel* (tr. I. Brady, 1961); M. Purcell, *Saint Anthony and His Times* (1960).

[D. A. MCGUCKIN]

ANTHONY PAVONIUS, BL. (1326–74), Dominican inquisitor and martyr who was assigned as inquisitor general in Liguria, Piedmont, and upper Lombardy where his preaching and exercise of his office reduced the numbers of the Waldensians. Their resulting hatred of him occasioned his murder as he left his church. The following year Gregory IX (1375) eulogized him as a holy martyr in a letter to the Count of Savoy. Pius IX approved his beatification (1856). BIBLIOGRAPHY: X. Faucher, DHGE 3:802–803.

[F. H. BRIGHAM]

ANTHONY OF STRONCONE, BL. (1381–1461), Franciscan lay brother. Like St. Francis he refused the dignity of the priesthood and remained a lay brother in his order. A. was assistant novice master in Fiesole (1411–20) under Thomas Bellaci with whom he was assigned to counter the heretical Fraticelli in Siena and Corsica (1420–35). The last 25 years of his life were spent at the Carceri hermitage near Assisi. BIBLIOGRAPHY: R. Brown, NCE 1:596; Butler 1:272–273; L. Canonici, *Antonio Vici principe conteso* (1961); R. Pratesi, BiblSanct 2:197–198.

[J. J. SMITH]

ANTHONY, RULE OF ST., a spurious work allegedly written by the holy Egyptian anchorite. It is extant in two Latin translations. The Maronite scholar Abraham of Ekel (Abraham Echellensis, Al-Haquelâní) published a translation from an Arabic text in 1646. Lukas Holste (Holstenius) edited another version in 1661. Careful study shows that both versions are a compilation based in part on the vita of the saint and produced by at least two persons. St. Athanasius, Anthony's biographer, makes no mention of a rule. Text: PG 40:1065–74. BIBLIOGRAPHY: Bardenhewer 3:82; G. Bardy, DSAM 1:705; Quasten 3:152–53.

[H. DRESSLER]

ANTHROPOCENTRISM (Gr., *anthropos*, man + *kentron*, center), any view that accords human beings a position of central importance or interprets the world in terms of human concerns and values. In theological contexts the term is generally used in contrast to either *theocentrism or *Christocentrism to indicate that a doctrine or system of doctrines accords undue importance to man and not enough to God or Christ. Anthropocentrism in an absolute sense is equivalent to atheism. Thus the view of T. J. J. Altizer, that God has so emptied himself into the man-centered world as no longer to maintain a transcendent existence, is rightly, if somewhat inconsistently, called Christian atheism. A limited or relative type of anthropocentrism is found in two contexts in the history of Christian thought: one doctrinal, and the other moral and spiritual. In doctrinal theology, Scotistic authors used the term anthropocentrism as a pejorative characterization of the Thomistic view that excluded the Incarnation from God's "primitive" creative plan. Scotists called their own view Christocentric because it maintained that Christ was from the first intended to be the center of creation, independently of sin. Orthodoxy was never in question in this discussion, and today there is general agreement that, although Christ is the head of creation, neither he nor mankind can be understood, in the actual order of things, apart from one another. Orthodoxy is very much involved, however, in the moral and spiritual type of anthropocentrism. It was taught in a Christian context by Pelagius; hence every Christian approach to morality and spirituality that places undue emphasis on man's role in his own salvation is said to be Pelagian in inspiration. The alternative in this case is a theocentrism that accords God the initiative in every saving act and insists on the need for divine grace in the sustenance and completion of all such human activities. BIBLIOGRAPHY: T. J. J. Altizer, *Gospel of Christian Atheism* (1966); J.-F. Bonnefoy, "Raison de l'Incarnation et primauté du Christ," *Divus Thomas* 46 (1943) 105–121; G. de Plinval, *Pélage: Ses écrits, sa vie et sa réforme* (1943); E. Borne, *Atheism* (tr. S. J. Tester, 1961) 90–96.

[M. D. MEILACH]

ANTHROPOLOGY, the science of man and his works which is both (1) cultural: the study of man's social behavior, beliefs, and languages, i.e., his methods of doing, thinking, and making things, and (2) physical: the study of man as a biological organism. This article will be limited to a brief description of some aspects of cultural anthropology.

In this branch of anthropology, culture is understood as the plans, forms, designs, patterns, or structures that are evident in man's behavior or the products of his behavior. Such patterns are organized around a number of summative principles known as themes. According to Opler, a theme is a postulate or position declared or implied and usually controlling behavior or stimulating activity which is tacitly approved or promoted in society. Very often such prevalent patterns are matched by a theme which demonstrates a contrasting direction, e.g., De Tocqueville's observation of the principle of equality in conflict with the principle of freedom in the United States. These themes are most often not at work on the conscious level of man's experience in society and are difficult to unravel.

Culture is transmitted from one generation to another by forms of learning and to a significant degree by the symbolism of language. Through it the past lives on and is available for invention and adaptation. The same themes tend to be shared by all or by specifically designated members of a group within society. Major divisions of cultural anthropology include: (1) anthropological archeology which is limited to the study of man's past as revealed by the remains of man and his artifacts before recorded history; (2) ethnology which directs its attention to a comparative study of existing cultures and those which are preserved through written records; social anthropology, a subdivision of ethnology, is concerned with a comparative study of social systems; (3) linguistics which is both descriptive (an analysis of sound systems, grammar, and vocabulary of languages of a particular era) and comparative (an analysis of the relationships between languages); (4) applied anthropology which isolates existing problems in definable terms for public administrators, mass communication, public health programs, improvement of race relations, and interpersonal relationships affecting business and industry. Cultural anthropology's direct relationship to history, economics, psychology, sociology, and missiology together with the generally accepted theory of the natural origin of religion have established sound working relationships between it and theology. BIBLIOGRAPHY: F. M. Keesing, *Cultural Anthropology* (1958); R. L. Beals and H. Hoijer, *Introduction to Anthropology* (2d ed., 1959).

[F. H. BRIGHAM]

ANTHROPOLOGY, THEOLOGICAL, the systematic study of what the Christian message of salvation and theological reflection on it teach about man's nature, history, and destiny; of its own it constitutes a science of man. Such a theology is possible because God reveals himself as savior of men: the message is an economy before being a theology and so includes a doctrine on man. Man, both as individual and as community, is created in the image of God, called to sonship of God and to sharing in the life of the Triune God, even after the Fall with its consequent sinfulness and insufficiency before God; he is redeemed in Christ for the life of grace now, and later for the life of glory at the fulfillment of salvation history. Theological anthropology may not replace theology, as though the Christian message were first or exclusively a message about man and subordinately a revelation about God. Some contemporary trends incline to this one-sidedness. Nor does theological anthropology set aside the philosophy and sciences of men such as anthropology proper, psychology, and sociology. Theology does not replace these; rather it draws on them for a deeper understanding of man. BIBLIOGRAPHY: J. Schmid et al., LTK 1:604–627; *Christian Anthropology* (tr. I. Richards, pa. 1973); H. U. Von Balthasar, *Theological Anthropology* (1967); J. Fichtner, *Theological Anthropology* (1963).

[P. DeLETTER]

ANTHROPOMORPHISM (Gr., *anthropos*, man, and *morphe*, form), a process of man's myth-making faculty by which he ascribes human characteristics to the deity. The myth-making faculty is man's intelligence as it attempts to describe the mysterious in human conceptual constructs and language forms, e.g., the Genesis description (Gen 2.7) of creation in which God is pictured as an oriental potter who molds and shapes the human figure and breathes into it the breath of life. Such examples abound in the OT and illustrate man's response to the mystery of God's presence in language forms derived from human experience. In this sense, anthropomorphism is indispensable to religious thought and imagery. But anthropomorphism can also be carried to an extreme when the transcendence of God or the specifically "other" of the numinous is vitiated. Thus the Greek mythologies which pitted angry, petty, and vengeful gods against man and each other are examples of an extreme anthropomorphism. Theology is continually involved in the attempt to penetrate further into the mystery of God by negating the specifically human, limiting characteristics of its judgments about God. BIBLIOGRAPHY: B. Lonergan,

Insight: A Study of Human Understanding (1957); E. L. Mascall, *Words and Images: A Study of Theological Discourse* (1957); J. Macquarrie, *God-Talk* (1967).

[W. J. DUGGAN]

ANTHROPOMORPHITES, another designation for the *Audians. From a literalist interpretation of Gen 1.26, they held a rigid form of anthropomorphism, describing God to be exactly like man, his image. BIBLIOGRAPHY: G. Bareille, DTC 1:2265–67.

[L. G. MÜLLER]

ANTHROPOPATHISM (Anthropopathy), the attribution of human feelings to objects or non-human beings. The sentimentalist school of English poetry carried this idea to an extreme, eventually provoking Ruskin's essay on the "pathetic fallacy" which belittled the use of anthropopathism in relation to inanimate nature.

[P. K. MEAGHER]

ANTHROPOSOPHY, a form of *theosophy developed by Rudolf *Steiner in several books published between 1902 and 1925. The central idea of Steiner's system is to see the history of mankind's evolutionary development in its relation to the Christ-Event. Steiner broke with the Hinduism of Annie *Besant and the Theosophical Society and in 1912 founded the Anthroposophical Society. Anthroposophy is based on man's spiritual origin and his historic evolution. Steiner posited a stage of prehistory, which he identified as Lemuria, in which mind evolved and man gained self-consciousness under the influence of Ahrimanic spirits. At a later stage, which he called Atlantis, man became aware of the material universe through the inspiration of Luciferic spirits. Both of these early stages saw the rise of a higher consciousness through oracles and mystery centers. Man progressed through the evolutionary stages represented by the Indian, Persian, Assyrian-Babylonian, Egyptian, and Greco-Roman civilizations, which culminated in the Christ-Event. Christ wrought for all mankind what the mysteries had done for individuals; he gave them a knowledge of their true higher self. In Steiner's view, the cosmic centrality of the Christ-Event is crucial. He held the divinity of Christ and believed that Gnosticism had erred in failing to give equal recognition to his humanity. Steiner saw the future of man as requiring a threefold social order in a delicate balance of his economic, judicial, and religious character. The role of Anthroposophy is to assist man to attain the needed Higher Knowledge, or direct perception of reality as spiritual fact, which was unperceived at the conscious level. This Higher Knowlege is also threefold. It consists of Imagination, by which we perceive material realities, Inspiration, by which awareness of the spiritual or astral world and of reincarnation is attained, and finally Intuition, by which we have direct knowledge of the Higher Worlds. Sources on Steiner's theories are his *Christianity As Mystical Fact* (1902), *Know-*

ledge of the Higher Worlds (1904), and *An Outline of Occult Science* (1909).

[R. K. MacMASTER]

ANTICAMERA, the private room next to the pope's workroom; a waiting room for cardinals and other distinguished people who are scheduled for an audience with the pope.

[S. A. HEENEY]

ANTI-CATHOLICISM, an attitude of suspicion or hostility toward the beliefs and practices of Roman Catholics. As an historically significant phenomenon, anti-Catholicism has been present in many sections of the world, including Great Britain, Europe, Mexico, Latin America, and the U.S. In Europe, anti-Catholicism often took the form of anti-clericalism, esp. during the 18th and 19th cent. when the emergence of the various nation states (esp. France and Italy) pitted conservative church interests against liberal nationalistic concerns. Thus the ascendant factions in the French Revolution (1789–99) sought to demolish the traditional ecclesiastical structure of that country by abolishing the privileges of the clergy, nationalizing church property, dissolving religious congregations, and installing the "Goddess Reason" in place of prior beliefs. In Italy, too, the drive toward national unity in the latter half of the 19th cent. frequently combined attacks against religion and diminution of the Church's temporal power and territory. The Kulturkampf in Germany proceeded from a different type of anti-Catholicism in which the Protestant majority distrusted RC loyalties and viewed the Church as a "state within the state." Allegiance to Germany was seen as the equivalent of Protestantism and Prussianism, and Catholic preference for a federation of German states rather than one centralized government was regarded with suspicion.

Anti-Catholicism in Great Britain was a significant factor in that nation's history from the formation of the C of E in the 16th cent., and this attitude was carried over into the colonial period in North America. Thus a strong anti-Catholic animus was one of Puritanism's legacies to Anglo-American civilization. This first instance of hostility toward Roman Catholicism in N.A. which can be conveniently dated from 1692 until the American Revolution, has come to be known as the Penal Period for American Catholics. In addition to its basis in English history, this type of anti-Catholicism was augmented by the expansionist ambitions of Great Britain against the French and Spanish (traditionally RC) colonial empires. The so-called French and Indian wars left, understandably enough, an enduring legacy of RC bias in the 13 Colonies. In the Massachusetts Bay Colony, for instance, laws were passed in 1647 and again in 1700 prohibiting the presence of priests; in 1685, the celebration of Pope's Day was authorized as a public expression of hostility toward the Church. From 1691 until 1776, RC liberties were denied in New York: the celebration of Mass was prohibited,

Catholics were denied the right to vote and hold office, and no priests were permitted in the colony. Laws of this type prevailed in 7 of the 13 original colonies, so that during this period the Church existed in a small, private, and nearly clandestine basis.

The American Revolution, however, inaugurated a new day of religious freedom. Yet in the 1820's the situation changed significantly and a new kind of anti-Catholic mood appeared—a mood largely caused by the xenophobia of "native Americans" toward a Church that had ceased to be numerically insignificant. Several factors combined in this nativist movement to give it its anti-Catholic bias: a heritage of traditional Protestant English hostility toward Continental Catholicism, the growth of an American Protestant "establishment" in contrast with immigrant Catholic groups, and the concentration of Catholics in cities seemed to challenge the traditional patterns of American life and presage a political power base that could destroy a conservatively structured society. The nativist movement declined in the 1840s as Americans concentrated on territorial expansion, the Mexican-American war, and an era of general prosperity. Anti-Catholicism resurrected, however, with the appearance of the Know-Nothing Party whose basic principles were the same as the earlier nativists and whose name derived from their insistence upon secretiveness. The Know-Nothings did extremely well in the elections of 1854 but their hopes for a presidential victory in 1856 were short-lived. The party declined rapidly, its principles rejected as contrary to a national ideal of equality. While that ideal was often compromised in the succeeding years, such a blatant rejection of it as in the Know-Nothing movement did not in fact survive as a national force.

The nomination of Alfred E. Smith as the Democratic party's presidential candidate in 1928 was a significant occasion for anti-Catholic prejudice, a prejudice that in previous decades had taken the form of restrictive immigration legislation and the activities of bigoted groups like the Ku Klux Klan. Smith's defeat, even though he gained more popular votes than the Democratic party had ever before received, was due to several factors; one of them was undoubtedly the suspicion that the Catholic faith and an unreserved political commitment to national interests were not always compatible. The subsequent Depression and outbreak of World War II contributed to the significant diminution of anti-Catholicism. Catholics came to be accepted in public life, the Church felt free to speak on national issues, and the socio-economic situation of American Catholics was no longer identified with that of the newly arrived immigrant. The presidential election of John F. Kennedy in 1960 seems to have signaled the widespread acceptance of Catholic participation in American life. BIBLIOGRAPHY: E. Ahlstrom, *Religious History of the American People* (1972); R. A. Billington, *Protestant Crusade, 1800*–1860 (1938); J. T. Ellis, *American Catholicism* (2d rev. ed., 1969); L. H. Fuchs, *John F. Kennedy and American Catholicism* (1967).

[T. M. MCFADDEN]

ANTICHRIST, literally, the antagonist of Christ. The term itself occurs only four times and only in the Johannine Epistles (1 Jn 2.18, 22; 4.3; 2 Jn 7). Those references indicate that a conception of the antichrist as a single figure was current, though the author applied the term to false teachers generally. The background of the NT idea can be traced in Jewish apocalyptic literature, and interpreters often identify the antichrist with other superhuman figures personifying an evil opposition that the Messiah must destroy before he can decisively establish his kingdom. The concept usually includes the combination of opposition and a deceptive likeness to the Christ. In the "Little Apocalypse" (Mk ch. 13) Jesus spoke of false Christs who would appear as deceivers prior to the end of the age. Paul wrote in similar fashion of the "man of lawlessness" (2 Th, ch. 2), who proclaims himself to be God, deceives those who are to perish, and is then destroyed at the second coming. The two beasts of Rev, ch. 13, may reflect the same concept. The first beast, which has features of the four beasts in Dan, ch. 7, is an incarnation of Satan and perhaps symbolizes the Roman Empire. The second is a pseudo-Christ, with horns like a lamb but speaking like a dragon (13.11). The antichrist is probably intended not as a historical person, but as a figure of the forces of evil. Though the interpretation of the various symbolic concepts is obscure, the idea of the antichrist has been prominent in the history of Christian thought, and has been applied to heretics or wicked popes, and to political rulers notably hostile to Christianity. BIBLIOGRAPHY: P. Misner, "Newman and the Tradition concerning the Papal Antichrist," *Church History* 42 (1973) 377–395.

[T. EARLY]

ANTICIPATION, the practice not uncommon under the arrangement of the Divine Office before the conversion of the Church's prayer into the Liturgy of the Hours, as the Office is now known, of reciting Matins and Lauds on the evening before the day to which those hours were properly attached. A major concern of the revision was to make it possible for the different hours to be recited at the time of day they are intended to sanctify. This is always observed, to the extent that this is possible, in the public or choral recitation of the hours. Ideally, the same correspondence of the liturgical hour with the proper time of day ought to be observed even in the private recitation of the hours, though this may not always be practicable, but at least the older practice of anticipation, even in the private recitation of the hours, has become obsolete.

[P. K. MEAGHER]

ANTIDICOMARIANITES a general term meaning adversaries of Mary. The *Ebionites, for example, maintained that she lost her virginity before the birth of Jesus through natural processes of generation. Helvidius, Bonosus of Sardica, and Jovinian taught that she lost her virginity after the birth of Jesus by bearing other children to Joseph. According to Epiphanius (*Panar.* 78) a sect in Arabia (4th cent.) that held suppositions similar to those advanced by Bonosus and Helvidius were the first to be called antidicomarianites. BIBLIOGRAPHY: H. Quilliet, DTC 1:1378–82.

[L. G. MÜLLER]

ANTIDOGMATISM, the rejection of truths considered by others to be revealed either because these truths are not sufficiently grounded in the original source of revelation or because of a fundamental prejudice against any proposition that would attempt to formulate the word of God. Antidogmatism can be legitimate when it requires theology to go beyond the mere repetition of past authoritative dogmatic statements. It is inadequate when it denies legitimacy to any authentic expression of revealed truth. BIBLIOGRAPHY: W. Kern, SacMund 2:111–112.

[T. M. MCFADDEN]

ANTIDORON (Gr. for a gift given in place of another; Sl., *antidor*), the blessed bread *(eulogia)* distributed by the priest to the faithful at the conclusion of the Byzantine Divine Liturgy on Sundays and festivals. The pieces of bread are remnants of the loaves *(*prosphora)* from which the particles to be used at the consecration were taken. During the singing of the hymn to the Mother of God after the consecration, a server brings these remnants in a basket to the priest at the altar who makes with them a sign of the cross over the consecrated bread and wine. The basket is then placed aside until after the Liturgy is concluded. Originally the antidoron was probably a substitute given to those not able to receive Holy Communion in an attempt to convey to them something of the spiritual blessings of the sacred banquet. In modern times, however, it is received by all, even those who have partaken of the Eucharist. It is generally consumed immediately, although sometimes taken home as a sacramental. The giving of the antidoron is also found in the Armenian, Coptic, and Chaldean liturgies and was formerly a custom in the West. BIBLIOGRAPHY: W. Jardine Grisbrooke, *Dictionary of Liturgy and Worship* (comp. and ed. J. G. Davis, 1972) 21. *EULOGIA.

[A. J. JACOPIN]

ANTIGONISH MOVEMENT, a detailed program in the early 20th cent. designed to improve social and economic conditions in the Diocese of Antigonish, E Nova Scotia, in places of disadvantage. The aim was to make people aware of their own deficiencies and the self-help possible with the aid of adult education and cooperatives. The program served as a model for others in many parts of the world, and the area has since attracted visitors who make use of the training in social action for community leaders and cooperatives. BIBLIOGRAPHY: M. E. Schirber, NCE 1:620–621.

[M. C. BRADLEY]

ANTILEGOMENA, Greek term for disputed works of the Bible. It was first used by Eusebius of Caesarea (*Hist. Eccl.* 3.25) to distinguish such works from those which were universally accepted in the canon. In present usage the term refers to works included in the canon but which were contested prior to its definition. According to Eusebius there are two classes of antilegomena (1) those disputed but generally known, e.g., Jas, Jude, 1–2 Pet, 2–3 Jn and (2) spurious works, e.g., Acts of Paul, Shepherd of Hermas, Epistle of Barnabas, the teaching of the Apostles, the Apocalypse of Peter, and possibly Revelation. BIBLIOGRAPHY: G. Jacquemet, *Catholicisme* 1:643.

[F. H. BRIGHAM]

ANTI-MARCIONITE PROLOGUES, prefaces to Mk, Lk, and Jn that were originally written in Greek, but are now extant in 38 MSS of the *Vulgate. The only one to survive in the original Greek is that of Lk. The Anti-Marcionite prologue to Mt has been lost. These prologues must have been composed between 160 and 180 A.D., and are therefore, according to A. von Harnack and others, the earliest prologues to the gospels that we possess. They purport to give brief accounts of the three evangelists concerned, and of the circumstances under which they wrote, and thus have an important contribution to make to the question of the origin of the gospels. BIBLIOGRAPHY: A. Huck et al., *Synopsis of the First Three Gospels* (1936); E. de Bruyne, "Les plus anciens prologues latins des évangiles", RevBibl 40 (1928) 193–214.

[D. J. BOURKE]

ANTIMENSION (a compound of Greek *anti-*, "in place of" and Latin *mensa* "table"), a square or rectangular piece of cloth measuring 18 to 24 inches on a side. It has a small pocket of relics sewn on to the lower surface, and an upper surface decorated with variable designs, most frequently centered around the entombment of Christ. The cloth antimension, whose existence is not directly attested until *c.*800, was originally a variant of the wooden tablet used as a portable altar in the East. Among the Byzantines, the wooden tablet disappeared from use long ago, leaving only the cloth antimension, and the latter has come to be used on consecrated altars themselves, lying unfolded on top of the corporal *(eilēton)* during the liturgy of the faithful and folded within the *eilēton,* on the altar, at all other times. It is most properly consecrated by a bishop in the rite of consecration of the altar on which it is to lie, but the *eucologion* contains formulae for the consecration of an antimension separately. In other Eastern churches the cloth antimension is unknown, but the portable wooden slab underwent a development similar to that of the antimension, being placed (without relics) on all West Syrian and Ethiopian altars and inserted into the surface of Coptic altars. The Gregorian Armenians alone continue to use the wooden tablet exclusively on surfaces not consecrated as altars; the same could be said for the Nestorian *dapâ,* which seems, however, to be obsolete. The Catholic counterparts of these two churches have adopted the Latin altar stone, called by the Armenians *vem,* by the Chaldeans *saḵrâ.* BIBLIOGRAPHY: S. Petrides DACL 1:2319–26; A. Raes, "Antimension, Tablit, Tabot", *Proche-Orient chrétien* 1 (1951) 59–70.

[A. CODY]

ANTINOMIANISM (Gr. *anti,* against, *nomos,* law), the theory that human actions are not subject to moral law or that actions usually considered sinful are not so for true Christians. Luther used the term in opposing J. Agricola, but the idea has been recurrent in Christian history, although with varying bases; it has often been expressed in sexual license. The teaching that grace frees man from the bondage of the law was distorted into the antinomianism reproved by St. Paul (1 Cor 6.12–20; Eph 4.19). Opposition between the God of the Jews and the God of the Christians or between the OT and NT was held as grounds for licentiousness among the Gnostics (Carpocratians, Adamites, Cainites, Ophites) and the rejection of all law by *Marcion (see G. Bareille 1398–99). The theory that marriage and the body are evil led to the practice of sexual abuses among the Manichaeans, ancient and medieval (*Albigenses, *Cathari, *Waldenses). Perfectionism and reliance on inner experience and personal inspiration included antinomianism in theory and sometimes in practice among the *Brothers and Sisters of the Free Spirit, *Beghards, *Anabaptists, and *Familists. The Antinomian Controversy (1527–60) in which Luther was involved arose from an extreme interpretation of his teaching on faith without works, and grace vs. law (see LAW AND GOSPEL); the controversy dragged on until 1577 and the *Formula of Concord (art. 4–6; cf. D 1536, 1570). The Calvinist theology of the divine decree of election was interpreted by some in Puritan England, and in the 19th cent. by certain of the *Plymouth Brethren, to mean that the actions of the elect could not possibly be sinful. The Antinomian Controversy in colonial New England concerned the spiritual teaching of Anne *Hutchinson. In modern times some view existentialist ethics, situation ethics, and moral relativism as forms of antinomianism because they either reject or diminish the normative force of moral law. BIBLIOGRAPHY: G. Bareille, DTC 1:1391–99; J. Fletcher, *Situation Ethics* (1966); Knox Enth; J. L. Witte, LTK 1:646–647; Bihlmeyer-Tüchle 3:71.

ANTINOMY, in philosophy a proposition whose truth function leads to contradiction and one in which the truth of its denial leads to contradiction. The contradiction may be real or apparent. Such propositions have always yielded a manifold of speculation—from Socrates to the present. The development of further philosophical systems since the Greeks has provided newer inquiry and speculation and even newer "candidates" for that investigation. Among the philosophers contributing to that candidacy is Kant, who, in his attempt to demonstrate the futility of metaphysical inquiry in critical reasoning, describes several antinomies: the infinity and finiteness of the universe, the infinite divisibility of matter, freedom and necessity. Others who deserve mention are G. Leibniz, G. Frege, B. *Russell, and L. Wittgenstein. BIBLIOGRAPHY: A. Brody, EncPhil 5:70–71, s.v. "paradox"; H. A. Nielsen, NCE 1:621–623; W. A. Schaaf, EB (1974) 13:356.

[J. R. RIVELLO]

ANTIOCH, (modern Antakya, Turkey), ancient city on the Orontes river, 17 miles from its port city, Seleucia. Founded by Seleucus in 300 B.C., it was named after his father Antiochus, and became one of the more influential cities of the Roman Empire, possessing a notable Jewish population. Known as a center of commerce and culture, it was selected by Rome as the capital of Syria (64 B.C.). The OT speaks of Antioch only in 1–2 Macc in connection with the campaigns against the Jews. In the NT Acts 11.19–30 speaks of Christians coming to Antioch to escape the persecutions that followed St. Stephen's martyrdom. Barnabas brought Paul from Tarsus to evangelize Antioch and there the term "Christian" (Acts 11.26) was first used. Here Paul's first two missionary journeys began and also ended. The episode of Gal 2.11 concerning Peter's withdrawal from association with Gentiles took place at Antioch and this community sent a delegation to attend the Council of Jerusalem. As a Christian center, Antioch promoted one of the important theological schools esp. involved with Arianism and Monophysitism. The ensuing Christological debates brought great division to the patriarchate of Antioch, thus giving rise to several Eastern Churches. Because of its wealth and location, the city underwent several political changes. It fell to the Persians in 538, to the Arabs in 637, to the Byzantine Empire in 969, to the Turks in 1058, to the Crusaders in 1098, to the Mamelukes in 1268, and to the Ottoman Turks in 1516. It was transferred to Syria in 1920 after the defeat of Turkey in World War I and was returned to Turkey in 1939. The present population is about 46,000.

[F. T. RYAN]

ANTIOCH, COUNCIL OF, known also as *Concilium in Encaenis* (Dedicatory Council), the most influential of several early councils held in Antioch because of its disciplinary canons. Held in 341 on the occasion of the consecration of Constantine's Golden Church in Antioch, it was attended by 97 Eastern bishops. According to tradition, the council promulgated 25 canons and proposed 4 different creeds to supplant that of Nicaea, all of which came under suspicion of heresy because of their avoidance of the key word "consubstantial" *(homoousios).* But the orthodoxy of what the canons positively stated is seemingly inconsistent with the reputed Arian tendencies of the council. This, together with the allusion in the canons to historical details of an earlier date, has caused Ballerini, L. Duchesne, C. Turner, and more recently G. Bardy to assign them to an earlier council of 330 or 332. C. J. Hefele, on the other hand, held that they were actually the work of the council of 341. Although he admitted the strong Arian influence of the council under the direction of Eusebius of Nicomedia, he believed that the majority of the bps. were orthodox, that they condemned Athanasius through ignorance rather than malice, and that the creeds adopted actually refute the main points of Arianism, despite their omission of the much disputed *homoousios.* BIBLIOGRAPHY: L. Duchesne, *Early History of the Christian Church*

(1912, repr. 1957) 2:165–168; Hefele-Leclercq 2:56–82; G. Bardy, DTC 1:590–598.

[M. J. COSTELLOE]

ANTIOCH, GREEK-MELCHITE CATHOLIC PATRIARCHATE OF, primatial see of the Melchite rite.

Although this patriarchate traces its foundation to the first Christian community at Antioch (Acts 8–11), it was not definitely distinguished from the Melchite Orthodox Patriarchate until 1724 (SEE ANTIOCH PATRIARCHATE OF) The jurisdiction of the Catholic patriarch limited originally to Antioch, was extended by the Holy See in 1772 over the Catholic Melchites in Jerusalem and Alexandria. Various conflicts over jurisdiction have marred the relationship between the Holy See and the Melchite hierarchy. The Synods of Qarqofel (1806) and of Jerusalem (1849), aimed at making the Melchite rite a self-governing body, were not recognized by Rome. Patriarch Maximos III Mazlūm established official residence at Damascus in 1834 and received civil approval in 1848. Gregory II Jusof appeared at Vatican Council I to oppose papal primacy and accepted it only on condition that patriarchal rights were recognized. At Vatican Council II, Patriarch Maximos IV Saigh upheld the traditions of the Oriental Churches and of the patriarchs. The Byzantine liturgy in the vernacular of the country is followed. (SEE ANTIOCH, LITURGY OF) The patriarch presides over 17 dioceses with 250,000 Catholic Melchites in his territory and 150,000 overseas.

[F. T. RYAN]

ANTIOCH, LITURGY OF, the liturgical rites of the patriarchate of *Antioch now observed by some Syrians.

Tradition maintains that the liturgical formula of thanksgiving employed at Antioch was adopted in Jerusalem where it was translated from Greek to Aramaic and eventually became the model for most of the Eastern liturgies. Because of the rapid growth of Christianity supervision of the liturgy became necessary. This led to written formulae and these circulated quickly. In this way, the ritual of the patriarchate of Antioch developed into the Antiochene liturgy. The influence of Antioch on the Byzantine liturgy of St. John Chrysostom is clear, for he was a priest at Antioch before becoming bp. of Constantinople (370–397). Tradition maintains that St. Mark introduced the Antiochene ritual into Egypt, where it became the liturgy of Alexandria.

The *Apostolic Constitutions (Book 8) records the following order of the early Antiochene liturgy: (1) readings with antiphonal response, (2) homily, (3) dismissal of catechumens and public penitents, (4) prayer of the faithful, (5) kiss of peace, (6) preparation of the gifts, (7) Preface, (8) Sanctus, (9) eucharistic prayer with epiclesis, (10) intercessory prayers, (11) preparation for communion, (12) communion, (13) recitation of Ps 33, and (14) blessing with dismissal. The Antiochene ritual was used by both Catholic and Monophysite Syrians until the 7th cent. but, with the rise of Constantinople, the *Byzantine liturgy came to dominate the entire East. The liturgy of Antioch is sometimes known as the *West Syrian liturgy which developed independently after the condemnation of Nestorius (431). Christians following this rite who reunited with Rome developed what is known as the Chaldean rite. Antioch also influenced Christian India, for the members of the Malankar rite claim West Syrian origins and those of the Malabar rite recognize East Syrian origins. At present, the Liturgy of St. *James, a modified form of the Antiochene rite, survives among the Catholics and Jacobites of Iraq and Syria. BIBLIOGRAPHY: I. H. Dalmais, *Eastern Liturgies* (tr. D. Attwater, 1960) 36–47; H. Leclercq DACL 1.2:2432–39.

[F. T. RYAN]

ANTIOCH, MARONITE PATRIARCHATE OF, primatial see of the Maronite Rite.

Because the patriarchate of *Antioch was vacant 702–742 the monks of St. Maron elected a patriarch from their monastery. Official recognition of the Maronite Patriarch is not recorded before the bull of Pope Innocent III convening Lateran Council IV (1215). Because a Latin patriarch of Antioch was appointed during Crusader occupation, the Maronite patriarch was reduced to a subordinate position. With the withdrawal of the Crusaders and the Latin hierarchy, Rome granted the Maronite patriarch full recognition as Patriarch of Antioch for the Maronites. His official residence is at Bkerke, Lebanon, with 600,000 faithful in the patriarchate and 350,000 or more abroad. *MARONITE RITE.

[F. T. RYAN]

ANTIOCH, PATRIARCHATE OF, one of the four eminent patriarchates of the early Church, presently claimed as principal see by five Eastern Churches.

The founding of the Christian community at Antioch is ascribed to St. Peter, and with the destruction of Jerusalem in 70 A.D. it became the focal point of Christianity in the East. Its original authority claimed Syria, Phoenicia, Arabia, Palestine, Cilicia, Cyprus, and Mesopotamia; the Council of *Nicaea I (325) recognized Antioch after Rome and Alexandria as one of the apostolic patriarchates. Division began when the Council of Ephesus (431) condemned *Nestorius, bp. of Antioch, who was residing in Constantinople. He and his followers founded the *East Syrian (Nestorian) Church. The Council of Chalcedon (451) by establishing the patriarchate of Jerusalem removed 58 dioceses from Antiochene jurisdiction.

The council's condemnation of *Eutyches for *Monophysitism left Antioch divided into two camps because of Christological differences. Christians faithful to Chalcedon, who became known as *Melchites, tended to dominate the Hellenized coastal cities, whereas the Monophysites occupied the towns and rural areas of inner Syria. Control over the patriarchate fluctuated between the two groups. However, *Jacob Baradai (c.543), with the support of Empress *Theodora, consecrated a Monophysite hierarchy, whose adherents became known as *Jacobites in his honor. After 550, the patriarchate of Antioch was divided between Jacobites and Melchites. The Arab invasion of the 7th cent. did not weaken the status of Christianity although the Muslims showed preference to the Jacobites. Because the Antiochene patriarchate was vacant (702–742) the monks of St. Maron used this opportunity to establish their own Maronite patriarchate of Antioch. After Byzantine forces recaptured Syria in 960, the Melchite patriarchs accepted the Byzantine rite and canon law. Antioch increasingly depended on Constantinople and joined Michael Cerularius in separation from Rome (c.1054). The Crusaders set up a Latin patriarchate of Antioch to rival that of the Melchites. After the Crusaders' kingdom of Antioch fell to the Turks (1268) the Melchite patriarch returned, but because the city was nearly destroyed his see was changed to Damascus in 1366. Capuchin, Jesuit and Carmelite missionaries began to work for reunion in the 16th cent. and made no distinction between Orthodox and Catholic communities. Although members of the hierarchy and faithful were occasionally reconciled to Rome, organic union was beyond reach. In 1724, Cyril VI of Turov was chosen patriarch in an election that included the Orthodox. However, the Ecumenical Patriarch refused to recognize him and appointed another. From this point on there have been two distinct Melchite patriarchates of Antioch, one Orthodox and one Catholic. Besides the Jacobite and Maronite patriarchates already mentioned, in 1662 there evolved a *Syrian-Catholic patriarchate begun by former Jacobites who reunited with Rome. The Orthodox patriarch continues to reside in Damascus with 285,000 faithful in 18 eparchies and 150,000 in the Americas. BIBLIOGRAPHY: G. A. Maloney, NCE 1:626–627; OrientCatt 247–282.

[F. T. RYAN]

ANTIOCH, SCHOOL OF, a disciplined approach to biblical exegesis used in Antioch, but not an institution or a specific doctrine. Perhaps influenced by Jewish schools, Antioch reacted against the allegorical interpretation that found favor in Alexandria c.300 and again c.400. The rationalist traditions of Aristotle and of Paul of Samosata appeared in Antioch before the exegete Lucian of Samosata (martyred 312), whose many disciples included Arius and Arians. But Bp. Eustathius of Antioch refuted Arius; and in his clear distinction between the divine Logos and the human nature of Christ, he foreshadowed the dualist Christology of Diodore of Tarsus. Diodore wished to distinguish the Word of God, which dwells in the Flesh, from the Son of Mary, who is not Mother of God; he did not accept the Incarnation. The orthodox John Chrysostom and Theodoret of Cyr followed Diodore's strict method, as did Nestorius and Theodore of Mopsuestia. But Alexandrine allegory prevailed after the Council of Ephesus 431 drove the School of Antioch to Edessa, from where Emperor Zeno drove it into Persia in 489. Antioch can claim to have begun scientific exegesis.

[E. P. COLBERT]

ANTIOCH, SYNOD OF, another name for *Concilium in Encaenis* (Dedicatory Council). *ANTIOCH, COUNCIL OF.

ANTIOCH, SYRIAN-CATHOLIC PATRIARCHATE OF, primatial see of the Syrian Rite. Formed by former members of the *West Syrian (Jacobite) Church who united with Rome, the patriarchate was officially confirmed by Rome in 1783. The patriarch resides in Beirut with 79,000 in the patriarchate and 10,000 abroad. *SYRIAN RITE

[F. T. RYAN]

ANTIOCH, SYRO-JACOBITE PATRIARCHATE OF, primatial see of the West Syrian Church. The Church originated at Antioch with those Christians who rejected the Council of *Chalcedon (451) and were named Jacobites after *Jacob Baradai. The residence of the patriarch has been at Damascus since 1959. He rules 115,000 faithful in 10 Eastern eparchies and the *Syrian Church of Antioch in the U.S. *WEST SYRIAN CHURCH

[F. T. RYAN]

ANTIOCH IN PISIDIA, ancient city of S Asia Minor, the remains of which lie close to modern Yalovatch, Turkey. Founded in 280 B.C., it was made a free city by the Romans in 189 B.C. By 11 B.C. Augustus named it a colony with the title of Caesarea. St. Paul preached to the Jewish and Gentile population there on two occasions (Acts 13.14, 14.21, 16.6, 18:23). Several of Antioch's bps. contributed to the formation of the early Church. In 1097 its walls provided the Crusaders with shelter. BIBLIOGRAPHY: R. Janin, DHGE 3:704–705.

[F. T. RYAN]

ANTIOCHENE RITE, liturgy of the Antioch patriarchate. As a flourishing city of the Roman Empire, with a Church of apostolic origins, Antioch (Turkish Antakya) early assumed an important place in the Christian world. At Nicaea (325) it was recognized as a patriarchate, and other Churches of its area guided their liturgies according to its practices. While the influence of the Antiochene Rite on other Eastern rites is a subject of scholarly debate, it is generally believed to have been substantial. Sometimes called the Syrian or West Syrian Rite, it continues in use among some Christians of the Syrian tradition, both Jacobites and Catholics.

[T. EARLY]

ANTIOCHUS OF ASCALON (betw. c.130 and 120–c.68 B.C.), founder of the so-called Fifth Academy. He followed his teacher, Philo of Larissa, as head of the Academy (88–68). Cicero attended his lectures in the winter of 79–78. A. broke completely with the skepticism of Carneades and returned to the dogmatism of the Old Academy. He maintained that Stoicism was based essentially on the Old Academy, that Aristotle was in part a Platonist, and that, in spite of its modification of Plato's ethics, the teachings of the

Lyceum were essentially identical with those of Plato. While he claimed that he was returning to pure Platonism, Antiochus actually incorporated Aristotelian and Stoic elements into his thought—his Stoic elements, moreover, reflecting the Stoic eclecticism of Panaetius and esp. of Posidonius. He was really an eclectic, and more Stoic than Platonist. It is possible that Antiochus was the first to hold that ideas are God's thoughts. BIBLIOGRAPHY: W. D. Ross, OCD 61; P. Merlan, CHGMP 53–58; Ueberweg 1:470.

[M. R. P. McGUIRE]

ANTIOCHUS EPIPHANES IV (reigned 175–164 or 163 B.C.), son of Antiochus the Great (223–187) and usurper of the throne of the Seleucid dynasty, whose ineptness caused the Hasmonean uprising. After he had been held for 15 years a prisoner at Rome after the Battle of Magnesia in year 190, A.'s admiration for the Hellenistic river cults and the pressure of the Jewish movement to adapt Greek culture, set on foot already in his father's reign, led his unstable character into much excess; despised as a tyrant, he has in the light of his unfortunate background, been more favorably treated by recent scholarship. The Scriptures tell his unhappy tale (Dn 11.25–30; ch. 7–9; 1 Macc 1.11–16, 21–29, 43–53; 2 Macc 1.13–16; 4.7–9, 29), one of war, frustration, and sacrilege; the Samaritans, according to Josephus (Ant. 12, 5, 5), actually addressed A. as God made manifest.

In an expedition against the Persian city of Elymais (1 Macc 6.1–16), A. met strong resistance and retreated disconsolate toward Babylon. News reached him while yet in Persia that enemies, in particular Lysias, had come in great strength but had been overcome by the Jews who, by resupplying their own troops with the gear of those they had slain, had overthrown the "abomination," the Olympian Zeus that A. had set up in the Temple. At last A. realized that the despondency that had overcome him was the result of his own wrongdoing, and why he was "dying of melancholy in a foreign land" (1 Macc 6.13). A. placed his friend Philip in the regency, charging him to educate and train his son for the throne; A. was succeeded by his son Antiochus V Eupator. BIBLIOGRAPHY: M. R. P. McGuire, EDB 99–101.

[M. R. BROWN]

ANTIOCHUS OF LYONS, ST. (d. early 5th cent.), bishop. As a priest of Lyons, A. was sent to Egypt to bring back *Justus, Bp. of Lyons, who was living there as a monk. Unsuccessful in this, he would have stayed as a companion to Justus in his solitude, but Justus would not permit it. Upon the death of Justus, A. returned to Lyons, bringing the remains of the venerable solitary with him, and later was himself made bp. of Lyons, where he is venerated as St. Andéol. BIBLIOGRAPHY: AS Oct. 7:17–18; H. Leclercq, DACL 10:191–193.

[P. K. MEAGHER]

ANTIOCHUS OF PTOLEMAÏS (d. no later than 408), bp. of Ptolemaïs in Phoenicia, an eloquent orator, promi-

nent among the foes of John Chrysostom at Constantinople. He took part in the Synod of the *Oak (403) and thus contributed to Chrysostom's second exile by the Emperor Arcadius (404). He was severely criticized by several early writers for his jealousy. BIBLIOGRAPHY: Quasten 3:483–484, with bibliog.

[P. K. MEAGHER]

ANTIOCHUS OF ST. SABAS (of Palestine; 7th cent.), a monk of the St. Sabas laura near Jerusalem, remembered chiefly for his *Pandect of Holy Scripture* (PG 89:1411–1856). This work begins with an account of the capture of Jerusalem by the Persians (614), followed by a manual of morality based on the Bible and early Christian writers, and ends with a list of heresies and heresiarchs from Simon Magus to the Monophysites. The work as a whole is valuable for the fragments it contains of the lost works of other writers. The authorship of the historical portion of the *Pandect* has been called into doubt. BIBLIOGRAPHY: S. Vailhé, DTC 1:1440; Altaner 627; H. Rahner, LTK 1:655, bibliog.

[P. K. MEAGHER]

ANTIPASCHA (Gr., opposite to Easter), in the Byzantine liturgy the Sunday following Easter, also known as "the Sunday of the touching of the wounds of the Lord by St. Thomas" or simply "Thomas Sunday" because the Gospel of this day relates the memorable meeting of the Lord and that Apostle after the Resurrection.

[A. J. JACOPIN]

ANTIPATER, son of Alexander Jannaeus's governor in Idumea, prefect of the palace under Hyrcanus II, and father of Herod the Great. His marriage to Cyprus, a Nabataean princess, assured him of a power base. He championed the cause of Hyrcanus, the legitimate heir, against his usurper brother Aristobolos after the death of Queen Alexandra in 67 B.C. Sensing the future Roman domination in Palestine, he ingratiated himself first with Pompey and then with successive Roman leaders. He was murdered in 43 B.C. after having his sons Phasael and Herod appointed governors of Jerusalem and Galilee respectively. BIBLIOGRAPHY: A. H. M. Jones, *Herods of Judaea* (1938) 15–34.

[J. J. O'ROURKE]

ANTIPATHY, a settled attitude of dislike and incompatibility, generally for some person, but sometimes also place or thing. Usually considered more emotional than intelligent, it may be the result of a recognized experience or rooted in feelings whose genesis is not known. Spiritual theology as well as psychiatry is very interested in finding the true cause. Self-examination may reveal that it is a reflection of some wickedness in self, or a bad relationship of envy, anger, or hatred for another. If it is deliberately cultivated and/or expressed, it may be sinful as an offense against charity or even justice. An antipathy which does not go beyond feelings is not sinful; practically everyone experiences such antipathies, which, when recognized and brought into rational control, may contribute to virtue and the maturation of the personality. BIBLIOGRAPHY: J. A. McHugh and C. J. Callan, *Moral Theology* (rev. E. P. Farrell, 2 v., 1958).

[P. F. MULHERN]

ANTIPHON, something said in response to something else, esp. in its earliest Christian usage, the response of one choir or part of a choir to the singing of another in the alternate chanting of the Psalms, a practice that began in the East and spread to the West. In the liturgy of the West the term now most commonly indicates the refrain sung before and after a psalm or canticle. Such verses were probably first used to announce the melody, but in later times their function has been rather to direct attention to the thought that should be dominant in the singing of the Psalm. During the Middle Ages certain chants sung antiphonally, i.e., by alternating choirs or voices but independently of any Psalm began to be called antiphons (e.g., processional antiphons, Marian antiphons). In the East the term refers to anthems chanted antiphonally in the celebration of the Eucharist and at other liturgical functions. BIBLIOGRAPHY: A. Robertson, *Dictionary of Liturgy and Worship* (ed. J. G. Davis, 1972) 21.

[N. KOLLAR]

ANTIPHONAL CHANTS, chants performed antiphonally, i.e., by alternating choirs or voices. The term is applied specifically to the Introit, Offertory, and Communion chants of the Mass in distinction to the Gradual and Alleluia, which are responsories, or responsorial chants.

[P. K. MEAGHER]

ANTIPHONAL SINGING, in the Byzantine rite, a cathedral, or popular, nonmonastic method of psalmody in which the psalm verses are sung by a soloist (or alternately by two soloists), to which the people, in two choirs, alternately respond with a refrain or verse of a refrain. Although monastic influence later obscured the structure of antiphonal psalmody, the usual understanding of antiphonal as the alternate singing of psalm verses by two choirs is erroneous. In the Byzantine rite the psalm always ends with a doxology. Sometimes the final repetition of the refrain, called *perissē*, appendix, is replaced by another refrain. For example, the *kontakion* of the third antiphon of the Divine Liturgy on some feast days is, when properly executed, a *perissē*. Antiphon initially referred to the refrain, but now designates the psalm with its refrains. The refrain, variously designated in the Byzantine rite as *troparion, kontakion, hupakoē, hirmos*, etc., has its parallels in other rites (e.g., the Chaldean *qānōnā, hepaktā, 'ōnītā*). BIBLIOGRAPHY: J. Mateos, "La Psalmodie dans le rite byzantin," *Proche-Orient Chrétien,* 15 (1965) 107–126.

[R. F. TAFT]

ANTIPHONALE MISSARUM, a liturgical book containing the sung portions of the proper of the Mass. The term is earlier than *graduale,* book of graduals, the name most commonly applied to a book of this kind, and means simply chant-book for the Mass, in contradistinction to *antiphonale officii,* chant-book for the Office. It is also the title for the *official Mass-chant book of the* *Milanese rite published in 1934 under the editorship of Dom G. Sunyol. A few of the chants were centonized or even newly composed by Sunyol for texts or feasts not found in the sources.

[A. DOHERTY]

ANTIPHONALE MONASTICUM, the liturgical book of the monastic rite (i.e., the Divine Office as celebrated by Benedictines) equivalent to the **Antiphonale Romanum.* The chants as given in this edition, published 1934, incorporate more recent researches by the monks of *Solesmes than those in the *Antiphonale Romanum* and so present more authentic forms of the melodies, as well as notational nuances not incorporated in chant books of the *Editio vaticana.* Most noteworthy is the use of the old form of the third mode with a reciting-tone on B instead of C.

[A. DOHERTY]

ANTIPHONALE ROMANUM (full title: *Antiphonale Sacrosanctae Romanae Ecclesiae pro diurnis horis . . .*), the official liturgical book of the Roman rite providing the texts and their Gregorian chant settings for all of the *Divine Office except Matins. The present edition, incorporating the researches of the monks of *Solesmes, was first published in 1912. *ANTIPHONARY; *ANTIPHONALE MONASTICUM.

[A. DOHERTY]

ANTIPHONARY (also antiphonal, antiphoner; Lat. *antiphonarium),* a liturgical book containing antiphons, and by extension, all the chants for the *Divine Office (as opposed to Mass chants). Medieval antiphonaries usually contained antiphons, invitatories, responsories, and *hymns of the office. Modern editions (SEE ANTIPHONALE ROMANUM; ANTIPHONALE MONASTICUM) contain the entire texts of the hours of the Office, including psalms, lessons, and collects. The chants and texts for Matins are omitted, however, since this hour is rarely sung. BIBLIOGRAPHY: K. Gamber, *Codices liturgici latini antiquiores* (1963).

[A. DOHERTY]

ANTIPHONS OF OUR LADY, SEE MARIAN ANTIPHONS.

ANTIPODES, in ancient usage, the inhabitants of a region diametrically opposite to a given place on earth; in contemporary usage, more generally, the opposite region itself. Ancient philosophers and astronomers were in fairly common agreement that the earth was spherical in shape (e.g., SEE Pliny, *Hist. Nat.* 2.65). Fabulous creatures, including human beings, were thought by some to inhabit the antipodal regions. St. Augustine held that these stories were untrue, or, if such regions were inhabited by human beings, these were in fact descendants of Adam (SEE *City of God,* 16.9). However, since unnavigable bodies of water were thought to separate those regions from the known habitable portions of the earth, the hypothesis of descent from Adam appeared untenable. Accordingly, it became the common view of Christian thinkers that belief in the unity of the human race, its common inheritance of original sin, and its redemption by Christ made it necessary to deny that the antipodal regions were inhabited by men. *VIRGIL (FERGAL) OF SALZBURG, ST.

[P. K. MEAGHER]

ANTIPOPE, one who makes an illegitimate claim to the papacy. Incomplete records make it impossible now to establish the merits of certain claims to the papacy in early and medieval periods. Lists of antipopes vary. Some 25–35 persons are so classified on most lists, and in addition to these, the claims of some, usually listed among the rightful popes, are open to question. The problem of antipopes became esp. serious during the *Western Schism. The last antipope was *Amadeus VIII of Savoy (Felix V), who yielded his claims to Nicholas V in 1449.

[T. EARLY]

ANTIREMONSTRANTS, strict Calvinist opponents of *Arminianism; also called Contra-Remonstrants.

ANTISECTARIANISM, a spirit that deplores party divisions among Christians, as opposed to *sectarianism in its narrow sense. Today greater awareness of what Christians share, and of the need for unity, fosters antisectarianism. As sectarianism is used to designate *denominationalism, antisectarianism also connotes opposition to any centralized form of church polity or organization.

[N. H. MARING]

ANTI-SEMITISM, term of 19th-cent. origin, now commonly signifies the mysterious, irrational hatred of the Jews by non-Jews since they became a noticeable, ethnic, and cultural group in the Persian empire (Bks. of Est and Tobit). Persecution of Jews and Judaism continued in the Hellenistic period esp. at Antioch in Syria and Alexandria in Egypt. Roman persecution became severe in the middle of the 1st cent. A.D. Jewish rebellions against Roman oppression in the late 60s and the 130s were mercilessly put down and Jewish history as a separate nation was ended until 1948. In the Mediterranean diaspora new religious and legal restrictions were imposed on Jews when Christianity became the Roman Empire's religion under Constantine, and, later, through the Theodosian and Justinian codes. In the Byzantine period Jews were forced en masse to accept baptism. In the Middle Ages more virulent anti-Judaism, provoked by the Crusades and intemperate, bigoted preachers led to massacres and expulsions of Jews throughout Europe. Jews were banned from trades and forced to become peddlers, moneylenders, and royal tax collectors. Fantastic, folklorish accusations of Jewish maliciousness led to further slaughters and expulsions, until Jews became a hated, embittered, fearful mass of Christian-haters, living in urban ghettoes or, in Eastern Europe, in completely Jewish rural towns.

With the political emancipation of the 19th cent., Jews received more freedom, but, when they began to prosper in commerce, finance, and journalism, a new wave of anti-Semitism was provoked in Germany by Hegelian idealists who attacked the Jews as a race apart, unassimilable into the "more noble" Aryan race. This erroneous doctrine eventually unleashed the greatest of all persecutions against any single people in the history of human savagery. Hitler's attempt at genocide as the final solution to the "Jewish problem" caused the death of about 6 million European Jews, and, added to the pogroms in Russia, brought to the most dire culmination the deep-seated xenophobia of non-Jews against Jews that had begun over 2,000 years before.

No explanation of the hatred of Jews can be completely satisfying. The facts are known; the reasons escape adequate analysis. Although Christians were not the first nor the last to oppress and savage the Jews (Hitler's persecution was also anti-Christian), the failure of Christianity to bring into being the ideal of love for all men, which the Jew, Jesus Christ, demanded of it, can be quite accurately measured by the hatred and injustice of Christians against Jewry throughout history. Perhaps Hitler gave one of the most profound reasons for anti-Semitism when he said that he hated them because they had invented conscience. BIBLIOGRAPHY: J. Katz, *Out of the Ghetto: The Social Background of Jewish Emancipation: 1770–1870* (1973); R. Reuther, *Faith and Fratricide* (1974); Vat II NonChrRel; Commission for Religious Relations with the Jews, *Guidelines and Suggestions for Implementing "Nostra aetate"* (1974 [Oss Rom, No. 375, 1975, 3–4]).

[J. F. FALLON]

ANTI-SLAVERY MOVEMENTS. With the exception of movements to remedy unscrupulous exploitation by Europeans in the South Sea and the Amazon basin, these have mainly been directed against the enforced bondage of Africans. Their history may be considered in two stages: first, the suppression of the slave trade, second, the abolition of slavery itself as an institution.

Toward the end of the 18th cent. the traffic in human lives, which had already run into millions, was predominantly in the hands of the British, followed by the Dutch, French, Portuguese, Danes, and Swedes. Slaves, procured through the rapacious barbarity of native chiefs, were shipped into the American colonies of the European powers; the circumstances of horror were increased later, when slave-running began to be outlawed, and profits demanded a tightly-packed and quickly disposable human cargo. The trade was repugnant to the sentiments alike of Christianity and of the Enlightenment, of which the former were the more effectively deployed in Great Britain and the United States, and the latter in countries swayed by the French Revolution and by Napoleon. The Quakers took the lead, and after patient and determined political action, the importation of slaves was prohibited in 1807 by the Americans, and in the same year the act abolishing the slave-trade was passed in the British Parliament and strengthened with severe sanctions in 1811. Even earlier the humanitarianism released by the French Revolution had worked to the same effect, so that by the end of the Napoleonic Wars (1815) the great powers were able to take concerted action, and by the application of naval power, above all of the British, the slave-trade was substantially extinguished by 1830, when the Spanish and Portuguese had been indemnified.

The institution of slavery, however, still remained. Already in 1772 it had been decided that as soon as a slave set foot on British soil he became free. The movement against it grew, and in 1833, largely by the pressure of Christians, Whigs, and Liberals, it was abolished throughout the British dominions. This example was followed by the French in 1848; it had already been anticipated by some Latin-American states, and the same action was followed by other countries, most gradually by Brazil and Cuba. There remained the slave system in the United States, the principles of which had been reprobated by the Founding Fathers. Moral factors worked strongly for its abolition, esp. among the Unitarians and Congregationalists of New England; the Baptists and Methodists were split by their position north and south of the Mason-Dixon line, and the Catholics as a body were neutral, though belligerently so, since most of them were Irish. There were socio-economic forces at work against it, thus the Free Soil Party which opposed the extension of the plantation system in the new lands being opened up beyond the Mississippi. Nevertheless, it acted rather for the restriction of slavery to the Southern States rather than for its total abolition. However, the wave of feeling associated with *Uncle Tom's Cabin,* less a novel than one of the most powerful political manifestos of all time, and with the myth of John Brown, swept the country, complicated the debate on state rights, and occasioned the Civil War which resulted in the ratification (1865) of the constitutional amendment abolishing and forever prohibiting slavery throughout the United States. BIBLIOGRAPHY: RACHS 8:220–221. *SLAVERY.

[T. GILBY]

ANTISTES, a Latin word for overseer or president. It was applied sometimes in pagan antiquity to the high priest of a temple and in the OT Vulgate to priests. It came into use among Christians as a designation for a bishop. It was used in the Reformed State Church of Basel (1530–1911), Zürich (1532–1895), and Schaffhausen (1536–1915) as the title of the rector of a cathedral church.

[F. H. BRIGHAM]

ANTISTHENES OF ATHENS (c.455–c.360 B.C.), a devoted follower of Socrates and reputed founder of Cynicism. He held that happiness (eudaimonia) is founded on virtue (aretē), and that virtue, through being based on knowledge, can be taught. Knowledge is obtained by the investigation of the meaning of words (onamatōn episkepsis). If one knows a word's meaning, he knows also the thing signified by the word. Knowledge of virtue of necessity leads to right conduct. As regards pleasures, only the pleasure that requires exertion (ponos) is enduring and good. He reverenced Hercules as a model of the life of virtue and effort. He rejected Plato's theory of Ideas, maintained that self-contradiction is impossible, and challenged the traditional views on the State, Law, and religion. He would seem to have exercised a definite influence on *Diogenes of Sinope (c.400–c.325), the true founder of Cynicism. Only fragments of his dialogues and other works are extant. BIBLIOGRAPHY: OCD 62; LexAW s.v.; Copleston 1:118.

[M. R. P. McGUIRE]

ANTISTITA, the common feminine form of *antistes,* a word used in canon law to designate the superior of a monastery of nuns, or the superior general of a congregation of religious sisters.

[P. K. MEAGHER]

ANTITACTES (*antitactae;* Gr; those opposing), a 2d-cent. antinomian Gnostic sect named by Clement of Alexandria (*Stromata* 3.4) which held that a created demiurge, identified with the God of the OT, caused evil to enter into creation. Basing themselves on Mal 3.15 they contended that those who resist the prohibitions of the Decalogue are the ones who will be saved. BIBLIOGRAPHY: G. Bareille, DTC 1.2:1441.

[P. K. MEAGHER]

ANTITRINITARIANISM, any interpretation of Christian belief that rejects the doctrine of the Trinity. Its more important ancient forms were Modalism and Arianism. In the era of the Reformation, *Socinianism was antitrinitarian; *Unitarianism is one modern form of antitrinitarianism, and the Jehovah's Witnesses strongly reject the Trinity as "the devil's doctrine." The interpretations given to trinitarian doctrine by Mormons and Christian Scientists bear little resemblance to the traditional Christian meaning. Apart from official teachings of religious bodies, such theological trends as rationalism and *liberal theology have diminished serious belief in the Trinity in many of the Churches. Once the divinity of Christ is rejected, there is little meaning left in the doctrine of a triune God.

[T. C. O'BRIEN]

ANTITYPE, a term indicating something that fulfills a previous foreshadowing. The usage is based on Paul's description of OT realities as types pointing toward the NT (1 Cor 10.6; Rom 5.14). This manner of interpretation led eventually to naming the fulfilling reality an "antitype," that which "corresponds" (1 Pet 3.21). This is the common meaning of the term today. A somewhat different NT usage, independent of Paul's influence, connotes an inferiority of the antitype. It is regarded as the mere earthly counterpart of a more perfect heavenly reality (Heb 9.24). In this usage, it is the superior reality which is called the type (Acts 7.44; cf. Ex 25.40). Such an outlook reflects the mythical thought of the ancient Near East as well as the Platonic distinction between the world of substantial ideas and the world of mere appearances. BIBLIOGRAPHY: Kittel TD s.v. *typoi*.

[P. J. KEARNEY]

ANTOINE, CHARLES (1847–1921), economist. A. held a degree in engineering and had taken specialized work in chemistry at the Collège de France before he joined the Jesuits in 1869. He taught theology (1887–1906) and in 1896 he published his *Cours d' économie sociale,* an economics text, in which he emphasized the relationship between theology and the science of economics. He lectured at the Semaines Sociales (1905–13), wrote the "Social Chronicle" for *Études* (1897–1906), and published monographs and numerous articles on economics. He withdrew from the Society of Jesus in 1913. BIBLIOGRAPHY: J. Villain, NCE 1:641.

[H. JACK]

ANTOINE, LOUIS, the founder of *Antoinism.

[P. K. MEAGHER]

ANTOINE, PAUL GABRIEL (1678–1743), French Jesuit moral theologian and spiritual writer. His *Theologia moralis universalis* (1726), which was immensely popular and went through many editions, was considered overly severe in its doctrine by St. Alphonsus Liguori. A.'s name appeared prominently in the *Spiritual Instructions* (1741) written by J.-P. de Caussade but published anonymously; it seems probable that A. edited the work. BIBLIOGRAPHY: P. Klug, DSAM 1:723–724.

[P. K. MEAGHER]

ANTOINETTE OF JESUS (1612–78), a Canoness of St. Augustine at the royal abbey of Ste.-Perrine near Paris, which she entered in 1637 after the death of her husband (1636). Her mystical writing is contained in letters and in a few pages written for her directors. These were not destroyed after her death, as she had ordered; they reveal, according to H. Bremond, a cloistered Mme. de Sévigné (Bremond 6:347). BIBLIOGRAPHY: J. Duhr, DSAM 1:724; Bremond, *Index* (repr. 1971) 11.

[P. K. MEAGHER]

ANTOINISM, the cult founded by Louis Antoine (1846–1912), a Belgian laborer who, after his retirement at Jemeppes-sur-Meuse, started conducting spiritistic séances and from that advanced to faith healing. He attracted followers who came to accept him as the "Healer," the "Father." Being semiliterate, he did not personally put his doctrine in writing, but words uttered by him in trancelike states were taken down by his followers and gathered in a collection known as *The Teachings of the Father;* this became the gospel of the cult. At Antoine's "disincarnation" in 1912,

leadership of the cult was assumed by his wife (the "Mother") and held until she in turn was "disincarnated" in 1940. Antoinism denied being a religion, declaring its followers free to worship as they pleased. Nevertheless it propounded a doctrine, a mixture of spiritism, *theosophy, and vague mysticism that was presented as a new revelation. Antoinism does not deny the reality of physical evil, but calls for faith (in its understanding of the term) to remedy the disease of the soul upon which all bodily affliction depends. Antoinism survived World War II and in the late 1950s had several thousand adherents. The cult's claim to a greater membership is regarded as greatly exaggerated. BIBLIOGRAPHY: H. C. Chéry, *L'Offensive des sectes* (1961) 256–267.

[P. K. MEAGHER]

ANTOLÍNEZ, AGUSTÍN (1554–1626), Spanish Augustinian theologian and spiritual writer, bp. of Rodrigo (1623), abp. of Santiago from 1624. His commentary on the *Spiritual Canticle* of St. John of the Cross suggests that A. used St. John of the Cross' own interpolated revision of the text, a matter of some importance for the question it raises regarding the authenticity of the text of the *Canticle* as edited by the Carmelites. BIBLIOGRAPHY: F. Lang, DSAM 1:724; M. Ledrus, NCE 1:641.

[P. K. MEAGHER]

ANTONELLI, GIACOMO (1806–76), Italian cardinal and diplomat ordained deacon (1840) but never priest, A. was elevated to the cardinalate by Pius IX (1847), became pro-secretary (1848), and finally secretary, of state (1852–76). He helped formulate and administer the liberal reforms of Pius IX (1848), arranged the temporary papal residence at Gaëta when violence arose in the Papal States (1848), and became head of the papal government in exile. He reduced dependence on Austria, but later looked to France to protect the Papal States after 1859. A. opposed the calling of Vatican Council I lest it adversely affect relations with France. Through his efforts the invasion of Rome (1870) took place with a minimum of violence. He was accused of nepotism by Msgr. de Mérode and others, but Pius IX retained his services. A. advised Pius IX to remain in Rome (1870) and successfully rearranged the papal finances in accord with the reduction of papal temporal sovereignty. BIBLIOGRAPHY: E. E. Y. Hales, *Pio Nono* (1954); R. Aubert, NCE 1:641–642; P. Richard, DHGE 3:832–837.

ANTONELLO DA MESSINA (1430–79), Italian painter developing a Flemish style under Colantonio (Naples) and showing in early works a Spanish influence also. His Venetian period (1475–78) shows a synthesis of Flemish realism, Tuscan formal composition, and abstracted forms related to Piero della Francesca and Francesco da Laurana. A.'s most important "Venetian" work is the Altarpiece of S. Cassiano (fragments recently discovered in Vienna). A.'s paintings may be seen in Venice, Dresden, Antwerp, and London.

BIBLIOGRAPHY: S. Bottari, *Antonello da Messina* (tr. G. Scaglia, 1955); I. Galantic, NCE 1:642.

[M. J. DALY]

ANTONIA OF BRESCIA (1407–1507), saintly Dominican prioress. Born at Brescia of the noble family of Guaineri, she lived a life of gentleness and austerity and died in the cloister of Ferrara where she had worked for reform. BIBLIOGRAPHY: G. Gieraths, LTK 1:663.

[M. C. BRADLEY]

ANTONIA OF FLORENCE, BL. (d. 1472), a Florentine widow who entered the Franciscan Third Order Regular at Florence in 1429, was prioress at Foligno (1430–33), and, acting on the counsel of St. John Capistran, founded at Aquila in 1447 a monastery under the first rule of the Poor Clares. Her body, still whole and flexible, is kept in the monastery of St. Clare of the Eucharist in Aquila. BIBLIOGRAPHY: G. Cerafogli, BiblSanct 2:74–75.

ANTONIA, a fortress which stood at the NW corner of the Temple area, built by Herod the Great and renamed Antonia in honor of Mark Antony. It stood on a precipice nearly 75 feet high, and had four strong towers at its four corners. Many scholars locate here the Praetorium where Jesus was tried before Pilate, mocked, and scourged (Mk 15.1–20). The only remnant of ancient construction still existing above ground is the so-called *ecce-homo* arch which, however, has no relation to the Antonia citadel or the life of Jesus. It was part of the triumphal entry-way to the new city erected by Hadrian (A.D. 117–138). Much of the pavement that once covered the court of the Antonia can still be seen. The paving stones are large blocks of hard limestone, about 1 foot thick and 3 feet square covering an area approximately 165 feet square. This pavement has special interest because it probably is the one mentioned in Jn 19.13. Scratched on the stone slabs in more than one place are patterns for games which evidently were enjoyed by the Roman soldiers. BIBLIOGRAPHY: J. Finegan, *Light from the Ancient Past* (2d ed., 1959) 320; G. E. Wright, *Biblical Archeology* (rev. ed., 1962) 226.

[J. E. LUSSIER]

ANTONIANO, SILVIO (1540–1603), Italian humanist called to Rome by Pius IV. He later served also under Sixtus V and Clement VIII (who made him a cardinal in 1599). With the encouragement of St. Charles Borromeo he wrote an important pedagogical work on the Christian and political education of youth.

[P. K. MEAGHER]

ANTONIANS, a small sect in the Swiss cantons of Aargau and Zurich, named for the founder Anton Unternährer (1759–1824). He was a Catholic who turned preacher, proclaiming a doctrine of absolute antinomianism as the way to God; he died in prison for his denunciation of civil authority.

Antonians no longer oppose authority, and they interpret love to mean brotherly love, not the sexual liberty advocated by their founder.

[T. C. O'BRIEN]

ANTONIĬ (ALEKSEĬ PAVLOVICH KHRAPOVITSKIĬ, see KHRAPOVITSKY, ANTONY.

ANTONIL, ANDRE JOÃO, literary pseudonym of João António Andreoni (1649–1716), Jesuit missionary in Brazil from 1681. His *Cultura e opulenza do Brasil* (1711) gives a valuable account of Brazil as it appeared in the early 18th century.

[P. K. MEAGHER]

ANTONINES (ANTONIANS), the generic title for several Catholic religious congregations of the Eastern Church that have adopted St. *Anthony of Egypt as their patron. The so-called rule of St. Anthony is dated after the latter's death but is based on authentic and apocryphal writings of Anthony including a compilation known as the *Apophthegmata Patrum*. The systematic organization of Antonines only began in the 17th cent. and the various congregations may be classified as follows: (1) The Lebanese Maronite Order of St. Anthony, begun in 1695 by Maronite monks, approved by the Maronite Patriarch of Antioch Al-Douaihi in 1700 and whose rules were later revised by Clement XII in 1732. With headquarters in Beirut they number about 500 and are devoted to teaching and pastoral work. A female contemplative branch has some 95 members. (2) The Aleppian Maronite Order of St. Anthony branched from the above in 1758 and with 80 members engages in teaching and missionary work. (3) The Maronite Order of St. Isaiah was established in 1700, approved by Patriarch Al-Douaihi in 1703 and confirmed by Pope Clement XII in 1740. The 80 members are engaged in the educational and pastoral apostolates, and their female branch numbers 140. (4) The Chaldean Antonian Order of St. Hormisdas established in Iraq in 1808, received final approbation from Rome in 1845 and now numbers about 42. (5) Armenian Antonines, established at Kreim in 1705, first tried to unite with the Mechitarists, but this failing, modeled themselves after the Maronite Antonines. They never exceeded 60 members and gradually went out of existence, esp. after a schism during the politico-religious difficulties of 1869–80. (6) Ethiopian-Coptic Antonines never existed precisely as a religious order. In the 15th cent. Pope Sixtus IV designated the hospice of St. Stefano dei Mori in Vatican city for Ethiopian pilgrim monks and the so-called rule of the hospice was merely intended for internal regulation. In 1731 Clement XII gave St. Stefano's to the care of Ethiopian and Coptic monks of the "Order of St. Anthony." In 1919 the hospice became the Ethiopian College under the administration of the Capuchins. BIBLIOGRAPHY: R. Janin and K. Hofmann, LTK 1:676–677; OrientCatt 560–565, 606–608.

[F. T. RYAN]

ANTONINUS, ST. (1389–1459), Dominican, abp. of Florence, reformer, theologian, historian. He entered the Dominican Order in 1405. His ascetical life, prudence, knowledge, pastoral zeal, and gifts as director of souls earned him the confidence of the people and the title "Antoninus the Counselor." Deep compassion for the unfortunate led him to found (1442) the still-existing charitable organization, the Buonomini di San Martini (1442). He served as vicar-general of the Tuscan Dominican priories of strict observance and successively as prior of Dominican houses at Cortona, Fiesole, Naples, Rome, and Florence. As abp. of Florence (1446), he was concerned for civic liberties in face of the Medici. His zeal for his clergy and people is attested by his episcopal visitations and writings, all of which had a pastoral intent: the *Opera a ben vivere* and *Specchio di coscienza,* guides to the Christian life; the three-part *Confessionale* for confessors and penitents; the *Chronicon,* a world history showing the lessons of the past; and the *Summa moralis.* The *Summa* was probably the first, and certainly the most comprehensive, pastoral treatment of Christian ethics and asceticism of the Middle Ages. It gives abundant insight into the financial activity, the political life, and the condition of the professional and working classes of 15th-cent. Italy. BIBLIOGRAPHY: R. Morcay, *Saint Antonin, fondateur du Couvent de Saint-Marc, archevêque de Florence, 1389–1459* (1914); B. Jarrett, *S. Antonino and Medieval Economics* (1914); J. B. Walker, *"Chronicles" of St. Antoninus: A Study in Historiography* (1933); W. T. Gaughan, *Social Theories of Saint Antoninus from His Summa Theologica* (1951).

[W. A. HINNEBUSCH]

ANTONINUS OF PIACENZA, ST. (*c*.303?), martyr, patron of Piacenza. The antiquity of A.'s cult in Piacenza, which is traceable to the 4th cent., seems to put his existence and martyrdom beyond doubt. But the earliest source for information about the circumstances of his life is a 9th-cent. document which contains much evidently legendary material, and it is not certain even that he belonged to the Theban Legion, as is claimed. BIBLIOGRAPHY: A. Wilmart, DHGE 3:852–853; G. Tammi, BiblSanct 2:83–86.

ANTONIUS ANDREAS (*c*.1280–*c*.1320), Spanish Franciscan who studied in Paris under Duns Scotus and became a dedicated proponent of his master's doctrine, esp. in logic and metaphysics. BIBLIOGRAPHY: M. Bihl, DHGE 2:1633–34; Gilson HCP, 768.

[P. K. MEAGHER]

ANTONIUS DE BUTRIO (1338–1408), lay professor of law at Bologna, Perugia, and Florence. He acted at Marseilles for Gregory XII in 1407 in negotiations with the antipope Benedict XIII to put an end to the schism. BIBLIOGRAPHY: A. Amanieu, DDC 1:630–631.

[P. K. MEAGHER]

ANTWERP, Belgian city historically prominent as a commercial and artistic center. It is located on the Scheldt (Schelde) River, about 55 miles from the North Sea, and serves as capital of Antwerp province. Its population of almost one million is predominantly Catholic. Antwerp lies in the Flemish-speaking part of Belgium, and is a sort of unofficial capital of Flanders. Christianity was first preached there by St. Eligius, bp. of Noyon, France (*c*.590–*c*.660). In the 13th cent. its port began to develop, and subsequently banking and other forms of commercial life also became important. With the arrival of Jewish craftsmen expelled from Portugal in the 15th cent., Antwerp became a diamond center, and Jewish immigrants of later centuries continued the trade. In 1576 a riot of Spanish troops in Antwerp, the Spanish Fury, led to its coming under the Protestant William of Orange. But it was retaken by A. Farnese in 1585, and the Counter Reformation triumphed. The work of the Brueghels and Rubens brought artistic fame. C. *Plantin made Antwerp a printing center. The Cathedral of Notre Dame, built in the 14th and 15th cent., is the largest church in Belgium (see of Antwerp suppressed 1801–1961).

[T. EARLY]

ANU, in Babylonian religion, the sky god, king and father of the gods, head of the divine triad—Anu, Bel or Enlil (earth god) and Ea, water god. Anu was also the name of a goddess in Celtic religion, possibly identified with Danu.

[P. K. MEAGHER]

ANUBIS, in Egyptian religion, the jackal-headed god of the dead. He was supposed to preside over embalming and to conduct the dead to the hall of judgment.

[P. K. MEAGHER]

ANURĀDHAPURA, famous capital of ancient Sinhalese kings on the island of Ceylon, established in the 5th cent. B.C. and converted to Buddhism by Mahinda, son of Aşoka. Most remarkable archeological remains are the huge *dagobas* (Buddhist relic shrines or *stupas*), *viharas* (monasteries), and palaces with *pokunas* (bathing pools). It is believed that the famous Bo (pipal) tree under which Buddha attained enlightenment at Bodh Gaya was miraculously transplanted and now grows at Anurādhapura. Rediscovered by the British in the 19th cent., Anurādhapura is today an important archeological site and place of Buddhist pilgrimage. BIBLIOGRAPHY: H. Zimmer, *Art of Indian Asia* (2 v., 1955).

[M. J. DALY]

ANXIETY, in psychiatry today, a feeling of uneasiness or apprehension for which one can find no immediate apparent cause. Probably everyone experiences anxiety at times, but it can be persistent and distressing, occasionally erupting into panic feelings, accompanied by rapid heart beat, difficulty in breathing, sweating, and faintness. In more acute forms, it is a symptom in all neuroses, and one form of neurosis is simply anxiety reaction. Generally anxieties are caused by the threatened emergence into conciousness of hostile, destructive, obscenely sexual or otherwise unacceptable urges and feelings that are sensed as dangerous to personal peace and order. The threat is signaled by a feeling of anxiety which is then followed by a repressive reaction safeguarding the conscious ego. When a person is unable to control the urges sufficiently by repression, the anxiety signals become persistent and intense, and a more or less chronic condition of anxiety ensues. One kind of anxiety stems from the ego's fear of being overwhelmed by violent urges, another from the guilt feelings that arise when instinctual urges conflict with unconscious superego norms, i.e., norms of good and bad behavior inherited from childhood. Anxieties can be controlled by avoiding as far as possible situations that precipitate them, and by the use of tranquilizing drugs. Milder anxieties can be alleviated by the support and reassurance afforded by sympathetic counseling; but anxieties that arise from more deep-seated conflicts require skilled *psychotherapy, in which the patient obtains some insight into his immature, repressed needs and attitudes, and assistance in relinquishing his ineffective modes of coping with them. Since the clergy meet anxieties in penitents and counselees, it is important that they understand something of the psychological roots of anxiety in order to help these people. It is useless or worse to advise anxious people to relax or to get a grip on themselves. On the other hand, sympathetic listening, moral support, and judicious advice are helpful. When anxieties attach themselves to moral issues, scruples and the feeling that past confessions were bad are likely to occur. Some people assuage anxieties by excessive drinking or by autoerotic activities. Anxieties make people insecure in their vocation. In all such cases, the moral and spiritual issues cannot be properly handled unless the psychological problem of the anxiety itself is resolved.

[M. STOCK]

ANXIOUS BENCH (Anxious Seat; Mourner's Bench), a feature of the revivalistic new measures practiced by C. G. *Finney. It was a pew at the front of the room to which those who were repentant and eager to turn to God were invited for guidance from the preacher.

[T. C. O'BRIEN]

AN-YANG, important Chinese archeological site of ancient *Shang dynasty (1766–1122 B.C.) in northern Honan. Excavations by *Academia Sinica* in 1928–37 (resumed in 1950) revealed about 300 burials which have yielded magnificent ritual bronze vessels (some of zoomorphic shape) evidencing masterly technique in *cire perdue* casting, their walls covered with unique symbolic decoration (e.g., cicada, *t'ao t'ieh*) rich with patinas of green, red, blue, and silvery tones due to alloys of malachite, cuprite, azurite, and tin. Sculptured forms, inscribed oracle bones, tortoise shells, ceremo-

nial jade, ivory, and protoporcelainous ware establish the Shang as a period of supreme artistic achievement.

[M. J. DALY]

ANZENGRUBER, LUDWIG (1839–89), dramatist, following the tradition of the Austrian popular play (*Volksstück*), depicting peasant life and its moral and social implications in a realistic manner. Born in Vienna, son of a government official, he began as an apprentice in a bookstore, then tried unsuccessfully to be an actor, and finally became a police clerk. His first drama, *Der Pfarrer von Kirchfeld* (*The Pastor of Kirchfeld*, 1870), an appeal for marriage of the clergy, was a great success. Important among his 23 other dramas were: *Der Meineidbauer* (1871), a tragedy of peasant avarice; the comedies *Der G'wissenswurm* (1874) and *Die Kreuzelschreiber* (1872); and the tragedy of the sins of the fathers revealed through the crimes of their children, *Das vierte Gebot* (*The Fourth Commandment*, 1877). His village tales, *Der Schandfleck* (1876) and *Der Sternsteinhof* (1884), are considered realistic masterpieces.

[B. F. STEINBRUCKNER]

APÁCZAI, JOHANN (Csere of Apahza; 1626–59), distinguished puritan Protestant Hungarian scholar, writer of *Magyar logikácska*, first philosophic compendium in his tongue; outstanding was his *Magyar Encyclopedii* (1655) in which he attempted to encompass the knowledge of his own period, an important advance in the growth of technical vocabulary. BIBLIOGRAPHY: P. Ruzicska, EncCatt 12:780, s.v. "Ungheria."

[M. R. BROWN]

APAMEA, the name of several cities in Western Asia; (1) Apamea in Bithynia, originally called Myrleia, was named Apamea by Prusias I of Bithynia (230?–183 B.C.) in honor of his wife after he rebuilt it and Julia Concordia Augusta Apamea by Julius Caesar. According to a letter of Pliny the Younger to Trajan (10.96) it contained numerous Christians by the 2d century (113). A suffragan see of Nicomedia, it became a metropolitan see in 536 and a titular see in the 14th century. (2) Apamea in Syria on the Orontes River, originally Pharnake, later Pella, was named Apamea by Seleucis I Nicator for his wife. It may have been a bishopric during apostolic times but did become a metropolitan see under Theodosius II (408–450) and remained so until the invasion of the Arabs (650). It was revived as a Latin metropolitan see at the insistence of the victorious Tancred (1111) but became a titular see in 1238. (3) Apamea in Phrygia (or more recently referred to as Apamea in Pisidia) also known as Apamea Cibotus (the Ark), the legendary landing place of Noah's ark, was founded by Antiochus Soter (223–187 B.C.). As a Roman city (120 B.C.) it became an important Greco-Roman-Jewish trade center in the Roman Province of Asia Minor. Along the great road between Cilicia and Apamea there were several Jewish settlements in communion with the Jews of Tarsus. St. Paul preached there on his three missionary journeys. The apocryphal acts of Paul and Thecla give some idea of the attitudes and circumstances of the Christians in this area at the end of the 2d cent. After the 3d cent., a new trade route through Constantinople hastened its decline as a commercial center. Captured and razed by the Turks (1010), it was occupied by the Muslims after the 13th century. The ruins of the ancient city have preserved several significant Greco-Roman inscriptions. BIBLIOGRAPHY: J. Keil, CAH 14:580–602; W. M. Ramsay, *Cities and Bishoprics of Phrygia* (2 v., 1895–97) 2:396–483; R. Janin, DHGE 3:916–920.

[F. H. BRIGHAM]

APARICIO, SEBASTIÁN DE, BL. (1502–1600), Spanish-born worker who emigrated to Puebla, Mexico, in 1533. There he farmed, built roads, and engaged in other works by way of service and instruction for the Indians. After the death of his second wife he entered the Franciscans at the age of 72. He was assigned to begging to support various convents and ended his days at Puebla where he was held in great repute for the holiness of his life. BIBLIOGRAPHY: I. da Villapadierna, BiblSanct 11:773–776; J. Escobar, *Vida del Beato Sebastián de Aparicio* (1958).

[H. JACK]

APARTHEID, a system for maintaining white supremacy and separation of the races in South Africa. The term, coined *c*.1943, is from the Afrikaans, meaning apartness. The generally prevailing system since the Dutch colonists settled in the 17th cent., Apartheid became a central political issue in 1948 when D. F. Malan included it in the Nationalist Party platform, with the party winning a parliamentary majority. The policy has since been carried out with increasing rigor, and in 1961 South Africa withdrew from the British Commonwealth rather than modify its racial policies. Three Dutch Reformed bodies withdrew from the World Council of Churches over the issue the same year. Apartheid has been staunchly defended by most whites in South Africa, esp. those of Dutch descent, despite opposition from the UN, church bodies, rising African nationalism, and some liberal white forces within the country. Supporters of Apartheid insist that "separate development" under white direction is the only way all races can live in peace, achieve progress, and maintain respect for the distinctive culture of each group. Nonwhites are divided into Bantus (African Negroes), Asiatics (Indians), and coloreds (mulattoes), with separate schools and other facilities provided for each. A limited degree of autonomy for the nonwhite groups is allowed under the authority of the national government, which is totally white. BIBLIOGRAPHY: E. H. Brookes, *Apartheid: A Documentary Study of Modern South Africa* (1968); UNESCO, *Apartheid: Its Effects on Education, Science, Culture and Information* (1972); H. MacMillan, "Change

of Heart in South Africa," *Tablet* 226 (1972) 468, 493–494.

[T. EARLY]

APATHEIA, a term used in Greek philosophy to designate the Stoic ideal of freedom from emotion. Literally the term means impassibility, dispassion, or passionlessness. As a technical term in Eastern Christian asceticism, it signifies the state of man in contemplation of God, who, although still in the midst of the world of passions (classically listed as gluttony, fornication, covetousness, anger, sadness, accidie-despondency, vainglory, and pride), remains unmoved by them. Although *apatheia* follows the stage of *praxis* or action in the description of spiritual stages and is described as peace, immobility, serenity, and stability, it is not to be confused with any sort of Western "quietism." *Apatheia* is not a passive state. Neither is it a condition of the absence of, or total insensitivity to, attacks of passion. It is rather the state of one who remains unmoved by such passionate forces because of the positive condition of inner peace, joy, and active love. As such, *apatheia* is not in itself "perfection" understood as unending growth in living union with God and through him with all creation.

[T. HOPKO; M. R. P. MCGUIRE]

APATHY, the state of mind making activity repulsive. While it may often be a condition caused by physical illness, perhaps as yet undiagnosed, it can also be a spiritual ailment closely related to the classical vice of *acedia. The general despondency and disgust with any spiritual activity requiring a personal effort may even exist in people who are otherwise quite energetic. In fact energetic action in areas other than religious may be escape from spiritual obligation. Therefore apathy can be sinful when it disposes a person to act contrary to reason in avoiding the fulfillment of religious duties. Like acedia it is seriously sinful when it leads a man to hate the object of charity, God, and anything directly related to him. Cure is not easy since it involves a direct attack by the acts it finds repulsive. Perhaps limited objectives, e.g., small religious observances, may be a beginning. But most helpful might be the reading of reflective works showing the value of religious practice for full human development. BIBLIOGRAPHY: T. Moore, *Life of Man With God* (1956) 136–146.

[P. F. MULHERN]

APELLES (*c*.350–300 B.C.), Greek painter from Colophon. Foremost in Sicyonian school, perhaps the most famous painter in antiquity, A.'s style is characterized by unequalled grace. No works remain but Lucian's literary descriptions of his famous *Aphrodite Rising from the Sea* and the allegorical *Calumny* provided inspiration for many later works, noteworthy being Botticelli's two great paintings of the same names. As court painter A. is famed for portraits of Alexander and other Hellenistic rulers. BIBLIOGRAPHY: M. Swindler, *Ancient Painting* (1929).

[M. J. DALY]

APELLES (2d cent. A.D.), founder of an heretical Gnostic sect. A. was an important Roman disciple of *Marcion but was expelled from the sect for incontinence. In Alexandria, he was influenced by a pseudoprophetess, Philoumena, whose visions he recorded in his *Phanerōseis* (Manifestations). He returned to Rome late in life and debated Gnostic doctrine with Rhodon—an event that A. von *Harnack called "the most important religious discussion of church history." A. differs from Marcion significantly: there is only one First Principle, who is totally good but entirely removed from human events; creation and providence are attributed to a variety of angels, some of whom are evil; Christ was truly a man, born of Mary, but also the supreme son of God who came to rekindle the divine element in man. BIBLIOGRAPHY: G. Bareille, DTC 1:2.1455–1457; Quasten 1:272–274. *GNOSTICISM.

[T. M. MCFADDEN]

APELLITES, a sect founded by a disciple of *Marcion, Apelles, who lived in Rome in the 2d century. Apelles was closely associated with a female visionary, Philoumena, whose revelations he recorded. In opposition to Marcion's theory of a God of the OT and a God of the NT, Apelles maintained that there was only one divine principle, the God of the NT who revealed himself in Jesus, and who lived and died in a real body formed of cosmic matter. In his *Syllogisms* he rejected the OT more strongly than had Marcion. He maintained moreover that all that was necessary for salvation was hope in Jesus crucified and good works. BIBLIOGRAPHY: G. Bareille, DTC 1:1455–57; Bihlmeyer-Tüchle 1:153.

[L. G. MÜLLER]

APER OF TOUL, ST. (Evre; d. *c.* 507), bp. of Toul. A late vita states that he served 7 years as bishop, miraculously freed 3 prisoners of the common law of Chalon-sur-Saône, and built a basilica in honor of St. Maurice at the gates of Toul. The basilica was later better known as the Abbey of Saint–Aper. A.'s cult is popular in the ancient See of Toul and its environs. BIBLIOGRAPHY: J. Choux, NCE 1:653.

[M. S. TANEY]

APHAIA, TEMPLE OF, see AEGINA, TEMPLE OF.

APHRAATES (Syr. *Afrahàt;* fl. first half of 4th cent.), earliest of the Syriac Fathers, called "The Persian Sage." A. was a monk, probably also a bp. in the Persian Empire. Apart from this, little is known of him except what can be gleaned from his 23 treatises, mistakenly termed homilies, written during the years 336–345. The first 22 are arranged as an *acrostic and give an exposition of the Christian faith with strong emphasis on ascetical practices. Contemporary Western influence, such as Nicene theology, is conspicuously lacking in this work, a defect that is evidence of the isolation of the Persian Church because of both persecution and differences of language. Works: ed. J. Parisot, PS 1:1–2. BIBLIOGRAPHY: Altaner 400.

[R. B. ENO]

APHRODISIACS, stimulants used to stir up experience of sexual excitement. These have not been a subject for organized scientific research, although aphrodisiacs have wide use. Actually, there are two types: the psychophysiological and the internal. Traditionally, their power is somewhat exaggerated; this may be due to the influence of folklore and myths. Those identified in myths and folklore are certain exotic foods and spices. Certain drugs, such as alcohol and marijuana, are however conducive to increased sexual excitation sometimes, not so much by actual stimulation as by the dulling of inhibitions they produce. BIBLIOGRAPHY: EB (1974) 1:443, 939.

[J. R. RIVELLO]

APHTHARTODOCETISTS (Gr. *aphthartos,* incorruptible; *dokeo,* seem, consider). A group of *Monophysites of the 5th century. They were *Julianists or Gaianists to whom this name was applied for teaching that the body of Christ was inherently incorruptible, immune to suffering and death, but that in fact, by a continual miracle, he allowed himself to be as other men. The name is pejorative, unjustly attached by the *Severian Monophysites; the Julianists were not docetist. BIBLIOGRAPHY: M. Jugie, DTC 5:1608.

APIARIUS OF SICCA (fl. 420), African priest. When A. appealed his excommunication, by his bp. for misconduct, to Popes Zosimus and Celestine and was reinstated (417 and 422) in virtue of the canons of Sardica, he was the occasion of a prolonged controversy in which the African bps. maintained their right to jurisdiction in all disciplinary cases of Africans (418 and 423). Papal use of the canons of Sardica in this case prepared the way for the eventual acceptance of the right of appeal throughout the Church and its further clarification in canon law. BIBLIOGRAPHY: Bihlmeyer-Tüchle 1:313–314.

[H. JACK]

APION (fl. 190–220), the author, according to Eusebius (*Hist. eccl.* 5.27), of a commentary, now lost, on the *Hexaemeron* esp. directed against *Apelles, the Gnostic disciple of Marcion. BIBLIOGRAPHY: G. Bardy, *Catholicisme* 1:688.

[H. JACK]

APOCALYPSE, BOOK OF, the only NT book of prophecy, titled likewise the Book of *Revelation.

[M. R. BROWN]

APOCALYPSE, ICONOGRAPHY OF THE, monumental, transcendent, and inexhaustible imagery and symbolism of the Apocalypse of St. John, which, through numberless commentaries has been the source of such major themes in art as Christ in Majesty (Sta. Maria Maggiore,

432–440), the Adoration of the Lamb by the 24 Elders (5th cent., St. Paul-outside-the-Walls), the Lamb enthroned among seven lamps—"the seven Spirits of God" (Apoc 4.5) subjects repeated in Carolingian MSS (Evangeliary of St.-Médard of Soissons and the *Codex aureus* of 870).

The 12 books of commentaries by *Beatus of Liébana (d. 798) were recopied until the 15th cent. and influenced 24 MSS (MSS 429 and 644 in Pierpont Morgan Library, N.Y.) and stone capitals at Fleury showing the Son of Man in the midst of seven candlesticks, the Four Horsemen, and the Dragon in chains. É. *Mâle determined that the Beatus MS inspired the sculptured tympanum at Mhoissac showing the Elders beneath Christ enthroned amidst the Evangelists (symbols) and two six-winged Seraphs. The 11th-cent. frescoes at St. Savin-sur-Gartempe gesture to the Apocalypse in scenes of locusts appearing as battle horses, the Woman attacked by the Dragon, the new Jerusalem.

The *Hortus deliciarum* of Abbess Herrade de Landsberg (c.1180) shows Byzantine iconography in the *Etimasia* and Greek influence in the *eptazephalus*. Interesting is the Abbess's representation of Philosophy as a woman from whose bosom flow the seven rivers of the seven arts in the forms of seven young women. The MS was destroyed by fire (1870).

The Apocalypse cycles of the Gothic period appear no longer in the tympanum but in voussoirs at Paris and Amiens and in the rose window of the south transept at Chartres. Apocalyptic themes are seen in Franco-English and English MSS (13th and 14th cent.) the most beautiful of the latter being that illustrated c.1230 at St. Albans. Nicholas *Bataille of Paris wove 98 scenes in the monumental and magnificent tapestry *Apocalypse of Angers* (1375–81) for the Duke of Anjou.

Faded frescoes of *Cimabue in the upper church of *Assisi show the seven seals and the fall of Babylon. The frescoes of the baptistery, *Padua (1375–78) by Giusto de Menabuoi relate to the Pentecost theme in the choir and the All Saints subject of the cupola (Apoc 7.9). Second in scope only to the program at Padua is the immense east window of York Minster, depicting 90 scenes of the Apocalypse in 1700 square feet of colored glass, by Thornton of Coventry (1405–08). The theme of antichrist is introduced in *Signorelli's 15th-cent. Last Judgment frescoes in *Orvieto. The famous polyptych *Adoration of the Lamb* by Jan and Hubert van *Eyck (1432) shows an overwhelming vision of the Heavenly Jerusalem and choirs of the blessed with the Lamb (Apoc 9.2–12), an exposition of the liturgy (adopted 835) for All Saints Day.

Dürer's woodcuts of the Apocalypse with Latin and German texts (1498) were copied in Protestant Bibles (Lutheran, 1522) and appeared in the Catholic idiom at Antwerp (1530), Lyons (1541), and in the idiom of the school of Fontainebleau in the magnificent windows of the chapel at Vincennes (1558). Dürer's work was the model for Byzantine painting on Mt. Athos (1547).

The apocalyptic destruction of World War II inspired moving graphic interpretations as late as 1955. A most dramatic emulation of the Apocalypse of Angers is seen in the huge tapestry in the apse of Notre-Dame-de-Toute-Grâce at *Assy by Jean Lurçat (1948). BIBLIOGRAPHY: P. Verdier, NCE 1:659–663; J. *Lurçat, *L'Apocalypse d'Angers* (1955).

[M. J. DALY]

APOCALYPSE OF ANGERS (TAPESTRY; 1375–81), a tapestry executed by the Parisian master Nicolas Bataille from the cartoons of Jean Bondol de Bruges for Louis I, Duke of Anjou (d. 1384). Designed for the château, the tapestry is in 7 sections, each divided into 14 subjects against alternate blue and red backgrounds. This gigantic cycle of 98 scenes, 800 square meters when intact, is now in the *Musée des Tapisseries,* Angers. Monumental and heraldic in appearance, it constitutes one of the best surviving examples of late medieval French tapestry. BIBLIOGRAPHY: A. Lejard, *Les Tapisseries de l'apocalypse de la cathédral d'Angers* (1942); R. A. Weigert, *French Tapestry* (1962).

[S. D. MURRAY]

APOCALYPSE OF ASSY, the monumental and dramatically decorative tapestry hanging in the apse of Notre-Dame-de-Toute-Grâce (1950) at *Assy, depicting the confrontation of the Beast and the Woman clothed with the Sun, designed by Jean *Lurçat who, inspired (1938) by the magnificent *Apocalypse of Angers, exerted tremendous influence in the renaissance of French tapestry and indeed in the universal revival of creative weaving. The Apocalypse of Assy is a most impressive work in a church which, planned by *Couturier, leader of the *art sacré* movement, is rich in the works of the greatest contemporary French artists. BIBLIOGRAPHY: R. J. Verostko, NCE 1:979–981; W. S. Rubin, *Modern Sacred Art and the Church of Assy* (1961); P. Verlet et al., *Great Tapestries* (1965).

[M. J. DALY]

APOCALYPSE OF BEATUS OF LIÉBANA, see BEATUS OF LIÉBANA.

APOCALYPSE OF MOSES, the title inappropriately given by K. von Tischendorf to a Greek MS similar in content to the Life of *Adam and Eve. It is also a title given sometimes to the Book of Jubilees.

[T. C. O'BRIEN]

APOCALYPSE OF SAINT-SEVER. This masterpiece of the Southern French school, signed by Stephanus Carsia (mid-11th cent.), illustrating the *Commentary on the Apocalypse* by *Beatus of Liébana in Asturias, shows a distinctly Mozarabic influence.

[M. J. DALY]

APOCALYPTIC MOVEMENTS, vogues having some popularity that have occurred in both NT and OT times concerning coming events of an eschatological nature. These have been commonly based on supposed revelation and have derived their strength from the commanding personality of their leading figures. Such movements existed among the Jews from the 2d cent. B.C. to the 2d cent. A.D. In the history of the Church, movements of a similar kind have generally centered about the proximate expectation of the second coming of Christ, or the advent of a new era in which the Holy Spirit would replace the centrality of Christ. In the early Church, movements of this kind appear in the case of the Ebionites and the Montanists. The end of the first millennium of Christianity gave impetus to a variety of apocalyptic movements, prominent among which is that of Joachim of Fiore (c.1120–1202). In later times the Anabaptists, the Seventh-Day Adventists, the Jehovah's Witnesses have kept the apocalyptic current alive. BIBLIOGRAPHY: Knox Enth, corrected editions 1951 and 1957, *passim.*

[P. K. MEAGHER]

APOCALYPTICISM, a term with two meanings: (1) A type of literature, prominent in Judaism from *c.*250 B.C. and in the 1st cent. of Christianity. Couched in symbolic language, using such elements as visions, figures, numerology, the invention of grotesque animals, and pseudonymity, this type of literature portrayed the evil of present days, but judgment and better days to come. The Book of Daniel in the OT was the first great apocalyptic work; Revelation (the Apocalypse) in the NT is of the same genre. Other examples are the Books of Enoch, Baruch, I and II Esdras, the Shepherd of Hermas, and the Apocalypse of Peter. (2) An attitude equivalent or akin to *millenarianism. Apocalypticism in this sense has been a perennial basis for the formation of new Christian bodies. It is characterized by appeal to apocalyptic literature, expectation of Christ's second coming and the righting of grievances, and insistence on penitence and poverty. The *Montanists in the early Church; the *Fraticelli inspired by *Joachimism in the Middle Ages; the *Taborites in the 15th cent.; the Münster *Anabaptists in the left-wing Reformation; and in modern times *Seventh-Day Adventists and *Jehovah's Witnesses exemplify apocalypticism. BIBLIOGRAPHY: W. G. Rollins, "New Testament and Apocalyptic," NTS 17 (1971) 454–476.

[N. MARING]

APOCATASTASIS (Gr. for restoration or reestablishment), in Christian theological history, the term denoting the doctrine of a final restoration of the whole creation (including fallen angels, men, and demons) to harmony with God. The Greek word *apokatastasis* appears in Acts 3.21, in the phrase "till the time for the universal restoration." Clement of Alexandria, Origen, and Gregory of Nyssa were early advocates of the doctrine. The fifth ecumenical council at Constantinople (A.D. 553) implicitly condemned the doctrine in its condemnation of Origen (D 433), whose restorationism had been explicitly condemned at the Synod of Constantinople in 543 (D 409, 411). John Scotus Erigena affirmed the

doctrine. In the Reformation era some Anabaptists proposed it, and their teaching was condemned by Article 17 of the *Augsburg Confession. In the 17th cent. Jane Lead and Johann W. Petersen of the *Philadelphians proclaimed the apocatastasis; in the 18th cent. the Pietists J. A. Bengel and F. C. Oetinger cautiously considered it. F. *Schleiermacher (*The Christian Faith,* Appendix: "On eternal Damnation") and his followers gave the doctrine wider influence. Karl *Barth clearly admitted the possibility of an apocatastasis (*Church Dogmatics* 2.2:295). In the U.S. the Universalists (SEE UNITARIAN-UNIVERSALIST ASSOCIATION) have been its chief advocates. BIBLIOGRAPHY: R. Eddy, *Universalism in America* (2 v., 1884–86); D. P. Walker, *Decline of Hell* (1964); G. Müller, "Idea of an *Apokatastasis Ton Panton* (Universal Salvation) in European theology from Schleiermacher to Barth," *Annual Journal of the Universalist Historical Society* 6 (1966) 47–64. *RESTORATIONISM.

[J. C. GODBEY]

APOCRISIARIOS (Gr. for one who gives replies), in the East an envoy or representative of a patriarch or a bp. to another patriarch or to the Byzantine emperor. The Western equivalent would be that of nuncio or delegate. BIBLIOGRAPHY: Beck 103.

[G. T. DENNIS]

APOCRYPHA (Gr., hidden things), classification of writings which, though purporting to be Scripture, are excluded from the canon of the Bible. The classification has two different interpretations. (1) In Jewish and Protestant usage the apocrypha are the parts of the Greek Septuagint that are not found in the Hebrew Bible, i.e., books or parts of books that were not originally written in Hebrew. The RSV prints the following as apocrypha: the books of Tob, Jud, Wis (Wisdom of Solomon), Sir, Bar and the Letter of Jeremiah, 1 and 2 Macc, additions to Est, and parts of Dan (Prayer of Azariah, Song of the Three Young Men, Bel and the Dragon, Susanna), 1 and 2 *Esdras, the *Prayer of Manasseh. (2) RC usage agrees regarding the last two writings as apocrypha; the rest are contained in the RC biblical canon, and are designated *deuterocanonical. The RC designation of a work as apocryphal may simply mean noncanonical as in the case of parts of the LXX not accepted in the canon; parts of these apocrypha are quoted in the NT and in the liturgy. In other cases the designation means that the works are of spurious origin or are unorthodox and esoteric in content. This usage dates from the early Christian centuries. RC scholars divide apocrypha, because of origin or subject matter into OT and NT apocrypha. Nonscriptural writings contained in the *Dead Sea Scrolls may also be classified as apocrypha. BIBLIOGRAPHY: J. Michl, SacMund 1:52–66.

[T. C. O'BRIEN]

APOCRYPHA (NT). **1. Abdias, Apostolic History of,** extant Lain collection of legends earlier circulated separately in Greek on the eleven Apostles and Paul. The contents are drawn chiefly from the canonical Gospels and Acts, from the Clementine literature and from heretical Acts. It was put together not earlier than 6th or 7th cent., probably in France. The preface asserts that Julius Africanus took the material from books written in Hebrew by Abdias (Obadiah), Bishop of Babylon, about the Apostles.

2. Abgarus, Epistles of Christ and, a work Eusebius (*Histories* 1.13) claims to have found in the archives of Edessa, and to have translated into Greek from Syriac. It consisted of two short letters: one from King Abgar V Ukkama to Christ, asking him to come and heal him, recognizing his divinity, and offering a safe city; a second, in which Christ replies that he will send someone after his ascension. No one today defends their authenticity. The letters (probably early 4th cent.) form part of the *Acts of Thaddeus.* In a similar account in Syriac, the *Doctrina Addaei (c.*400 A.D.) Jesus replies only orally via Ananias, who brings a portrait of Jesus he had painted.

3. Allogenes Supreme, a Gnostic work, in Coptic, found at Chenoboskion, Egypt, in 1946, probably written early in the 3d century. Porphyry reports that Plotinus the great Neoplatonist, fought against five apocalypses. This work may be one of the five.

4. Andrew, Acts of, an apocryphon telling of the travels, wonders, discourses, and martyrdom of Andrew. Scant remains of the original Greek are extant, dating from 2d or 3d century. There is also a shortened Latin form edited by Gregory of Tours. It is likely that Gregory pruned out unorthodox thoughts, such as the sweeping ascetic attack on marriage. Eusebius (*Hist. eccl.* 3:25.6-7) puts it among the "forgeries of heretics." Epiphanius (*Heresies* 47) reports it was liked by the Encratites, the Apostolics, and the Origenians. Scholars disagree on Gnostic influence in these Acts. The account of the martyrdom also circulated independently. It includes an address to his cross in a long sermon.

5. Andrew, Fragmentary Story of, an extant Coptic fragment, an incident from one of the oriental Acts of the Apostles. A dog tells Andrew that a woman in the desert killed her illegitimate child and fed it to him. Andrew causes the dog to disgorge, the fragments are joined, and the child lives again.

6. Andrew and Matthias (Matthew), Acts of, an apocryphon telling how Jesus appeared to Andrew, told him to go to rescue Matthias who was then in his 27th day of captivity by cannibals who planned to eat him on the 30th day. Andrew boards a ship piloted by Jesus himself (whom Andrew does not then recognize) and so tells Jesus of his own earlier exploits. Andrew rescues Matthias, works many miracles, is tortured, cured by Jesus, nearly submerges the city by a miracle, saves it when the people repent, then baptizes them. The story is extant in Greek and Syriac and also in a Latin version prefixed by Gregory of Tours to his Latin edition of the *Acts of Andrew.* The Acts probably originated in Egypt. Matthias and Matthew are confused in the account.

7. Andrew and Paul, Acts of, an extant Coptic tale of fantastic adventures. Paul dives into the sea, reaches the underworld, visits with Judas. Andrew and Paul come to a city, find the gates locked, and cause them to disappear into the ground. They convert some 27,000 Jews.

8. Apostles, Epistle of the, the most important of the apocryphal epistles, completely unknown until 1895 when a Coptic version was found at Cairo. It probably originated in Asia Minor or Egypt in mid-2d century. It tells of the birth, miracles, and Resurrection of Jesus; then the epistle form is discontinued, and the apocalyptic form used: Jesus answers questions on the date of the parousia, the universal resurrection, judgment, and signs. Finally, the Ascension is described. The writer used the NT, esp. St. John, and also the *Apocalypse of Peter, the Epistle of Barnabas,* and the *Shepherd of Hermas.* A few Gnostic tinges appear, but on the whole it is anti-Gnostic.

9. Arabic Gospel of the Infancy, a late compilation, heavily emphasizing the miraculous, on the infancy of Jesus. The first part depends on the *Protoevangelium of James,* the second part on the *Gospel of Thomas,* with the addition of many new and strange incidents in intervening chapters. The original was probably Syriac. Existing copies depend on an Arabic MS first published in 1697.

10. Armenian Gospel of the Infancy, a late apocryphon, drawing heavily on the *Protoevangelium of James* and the *Gospel of Thomas.* Its stories are very wordy, containing dialogues of unusual length.

11. Assumption of the Virgin, a group of apocryphal works, probably from the 4th cent., though the nucleus may go back to 3d, perhaps originating in Egypt. There are two chief forms. In the Coptic version, Jesus appears before the Apostles depart and tells Mary of her coming death and assumption. In the form found in Greek, Latin, and Syriac, the Apostles have already left, but at her request are transported back on clouds. Pope Pius XII defining the Assumption did not rest at all on these dubious accounts; rather, he ignored them in his survey of the development of the belief, and appealed instead to a facet of the virtually unanimous patristic New Eve tradition.

12. Barnabas, Acts of, a brief apocryphal work, extant in Greek, not earlier than the 5th cent., telling of the travels of Barnabas with Paul, and later without Paul, and of his martyrdom. It pretends to have been composed by Mark. It is largely an imaginative expansion of parts of the canonical Acts, much more sober than most apocrypha.

13. Bartholomew, Gospel of, a work mentioned by St. Jerome (Prologue to Matthew) and the Gelasian Decree. It is not sure that either knew the book. If it exists, it is probably to be identified with the *Questions of Bartholomew,* extant in Greek, Latin, and Slavonic. It is not earlier than the 5th cent., though perhaps based on much earlier materials, perhaps Gnostic. It contains answers made by Jesus after the Resurrection, by Mary and by Satan, in reply to Bartholomew. They deal chiefly with Christ's descent into hell, the annunciation to Mary, a vision of the bottomless pit given to the Apostles, Satan's replies on the sin and fall of the angels, and a short passage on the deadly sins.

14. Bartholomew the Apostle, Book of the Resurrection of Christ by, a Coptic apocryphon, probably from the 5th or 6th cent., a loosely strung together set of fanciful narratives mostly on the Resurrection of Christ and his descent into hell. Stories from canonical Gospels are expanded, altered, and combined. It contains strange inconsistencies: Jesus is twice buried; Thomas, who had raised his own son from the dead and made him bp., later on the same day doubts the Resurrection of Jesus.

15. Basilides, Gospel of, an apocryphal gospel known to Origen (*Homily on Luke* 1), Jerome, and Ambrose. Eusebius (*Hist. eccl.* 4:7.6–7) mentions 24 books on the Gospel by Basilides. Clement of Alexandria (*Stromata* 4.12) cites several passages from an *Exegetica* of Basilides. Hegemonius (*Acta Archelai* 67.4–11) also cites such a passage. According to Irenaeus (*Heresies* 1:24.3–4) Basilides was an Egyptian Gnostic of the early 2d century. Perhaps he revised the canonical Gospels to make them conform to his view, then commented on his work.

16. Corinthians, Third Epistle to the, apocryphon contained in the *Acts of Paul*. It is supposedly an answer to a letter sent by the Corinthians to Paul in which they reported that the heretics Simon and Cleobius taught that we must not use the prophets, that God is not almighty, that there will be no resurrection, that man was not made by God, that Christ did not become incarnate, that the world was made by angels, not by God.

17. Dositheus, Apocalypse of, a Gnostic work written in Coptic, found at Chenoboskion, Egypt, in 1946. It has the subtitle, ''The Three Great Steles of Seth.'' It has not yet been published or sufficiently studied.

18. Ebionites, Gospel of the, an apocryphal gospel, probably of the first half of the 2d or early 3d cent., probably written E of the Jordan. Fragments are quoted by Epiphanius (*Heresies* 30.13, 14, 16, 22). The confused and unclear state of ancient testimony leaves modern scholars divided on how many Jewish-Christian gospels there may have been. Probably there were three: *of the Nazareans, of the Ebionites, of the Hebrews.* Some believe the last two are identical works; others identify the *Gospel of the Ebionites* with the *Gospel of the Twelve Apostles* mentioned by Origen (*Homil. in Luke* 1). The *Gospel of the Ebionites* seems to have denied the virgin birth, averring that the union of a heavenly being with the man Jesus resulted in the Christ, the Son of God (a Gnostic trait). Jesus was to annul sacrifices. The work also appears to teach vegetarianism.

19. Egyptians, Gospel According to the, an apocryphal Greek gospel current in Egypt in the 2d cent., cited by Clement of Alexandria (*Stromata* 3.6, 9, 13). The citations show Gnostic opposition to marriage. It is also mentioned, unfavorably, by Origen, Hippolytus, and Epiphanius. Only fragments are extant. It seems to be unrelated to a *Book of the*

Great Invisible Spirit or Gospel of the Egyptians, found at Chenoboskion in 1946.

20. Eugnostos, Letter of, a Gnostic work, written in Coptic, found at Chenoboskion, Egypt, in 1946. Soter, the bisexual creator, and Sophia Pangeneteira, the feminine counterpart of Soter, produce six bisexual spirits. The sixth of these is Archigeneter (male) – Pistis Sophia (female). Another Chenoboskion work, ''Wisdom of Jesus'' is based on this letter. In the former, Pistis Sophia is one of the aeons.

21. Hebrews, Gospel according to the, an apocryphal Gospel, probably from the first half of the 2d cent., perhaps from Egypt. Ancient testimony is not entirely clear. Some would identify it with the *Gospel of the Ebionites.* Jerome (*De viris illustribus* 2) says he translated it into Greek and Latin, and observes (*On Matthew* 12.13) that the Nazareans and Ebionites used it, and that many considered it the original of Matthew. The fragments do indicate some close relation to Matthew: it may have been a reworking and extension of Matthew, yet is probably a totally different book. Quotations by Hegesippus, Origen, and Eusebius seem to show it came from a writer of Ebionite tendency, e.g., James is placed above Peter and is depicted as hostile to Paul.

22. James, Apocalypse of, a Gnostic apocryphon, found at Chenoboskion in 1946, in Coptic codices. It is not yet certain if the work is correctly styled an apocalypse; further study is needed.

23. James, Ascents of, an apocryphon known only from Epiphanius (*Heresies* 30.16). He says that the Ebionites used this book. It told how James spoke against the Temple and sacrifices. It is strongly against St. Paul, who is called a Greek proselyte and who is said to have written against the law and circumcision. It is likely that James is described as making ''Ascents'' of the Temple steps and speaking from there (cf. *The Clementine Recognitions* 1.66–71).

24. James, Protoevangelium of, the earliest of the apocryphal infancy gospels, the chief source of several other similar infancy gospels, probably written in the mid-2d century. It is extant in many MSS, in Greek as well as in translations. Most of the work is taken up in retelling the birth of Mary, her being brought up in the Temple, her betrothal to Joseph (from whose rod a dove flew out and lit on his head), the annunciation of the birth of Jesus, Joseph's fears, the trip to Bethlehem, the birth of Jesus, the midwife's testimony to Mary's continuing virginity, the episode of the Wise Men, the escape of John the Baptist from Herod, the murder of Zacharias by officers of Herod. It is certainly not by the Apostle James. Discrepancies seem to point to more than one author, who show considerable ignorance of the geography of Palestine. The style is sober, restrained, even artistic.

25. James the Great, Acts of, an apocryphon, the same as Book 4 of the *Apostolic History of Abdias*. It is a romance, a tale of magical wonders, the adventures and martyrdom of James, son of Zebedee. It pictures James as in frequent conflict with Hermogenes the magician and his follower

Philetus. James converts the latter and gives him miraculous power. It exists only in Latin. Clement of Alexandria seems to quote a probable Greek original in his lost *Hupotoposes* (Eusebius, *Hist. eccl.* 2:9.1–3).

26. Jesus, Wisdom of, a Gnostic writing found at Chenoboskion in 1946. It represents Jesus after his resurrection as speaking with 12 disciples and 7 holy women. Mary Magdalen asks him about the origin and role of the disciples. It is based on another work found at Chenoboskion, the *Letter of Eugnostos.*

27. John, Acts of, probably the earliest extant apocryphal Acts, composed *c.* 150–180 A.D. About 70% of the whole work is in Greek, supplemented in some parts by the Latin version. From the 5th cent. it was ascribed to a certain Leucius, also regarded as author of all five apocryphal Acts used by the Manichaeans instead of the canonical Acts. Strong Docetic tendencies appear: the body of Christ sometimes seems material to John, at other times immaterial. A tone of ascetic hostility to marriage and everything sexual is evident. The extant portion contains no mention of John's miraculous escape from boiling oil (reported by Tertullian, *De praescriptione* 26). The work has had a considerable influence on literature and art, and is important as the oldest source on Eucharist for the dead.

28. John, Acts of (Prochorus), an apocryphon, a Greek work of romantic genre, from the 5th cent., extant in Greek and several versions. It pretends to record the acts of John, chiefly in his 15 years in Patmos. The author has used material freely molded from the earlier Leucian *Acts of John.* Byzantine art represents John as dictating these acts to Prochorus (Acts 6.5), a Jerusalem deacon.

29. John, Apocryphon and Secret Book of, two distinct apocryphal works written under the name of John the Apostle. The *Apocryphon* is a 2d cent. Gnostic work, whose contents were long known in part only from the partial resumé of it given by Irenaeus *(Heresies* 1.29) without mention of its name. Today it is available in four MSS: a Berlin Papyrus 8502 (5th cent.; found in late 19th cent. near Akhmim, Egypt) and Codices I, III, and VIII found about 1945 at Chenoboskion. The latter three date from 3d to 5th centuries. It opens with a narrative of a vision and the teaching is imparted, first in continuous discourse, then in a dialogue in which John questions Christ. The *Secret Book* has sometimes been considered as a later remolding of the *Apocryphon.* Though the two works deal in general with the same themes, they have nothing more in common, The *Secret Book* was the *Interrogatio Iohannis et apostoli et evangelistae in cena secreta regni coelorum de ordinatione mundi istius et de principe et de Adam,* brought from Bulgaria to N Italy *c.* 1190 by a Bp. Nazarius of a Cathar community.

30. Joseph the Carpenter, History of, an apocryphal narrative of the life and death of Joseph, and the eulogy spoken over him by Jesus. It was written not earlier than 4th, not later than 5th cent. and is extant in Arabic and Bohairic. It is heavily dependent on the *Protoevangelium of James* and

also on the *Gospel of Thomas.* It is aimed at the glorification of Joseph and the promotion of his cult, popular in Egypt.

31. Laodiceans, Epistle to the, a short (247 words) apocryphon, occasioned by Paul's statement (Col 4.16) that he wrote to the Laodiceans. It is a patchwork of phrases from the canonical epistles, esp. that to the Philippians. It was in existence in the 4th cent. as is seen from warnings against it that then began, though Gregory the Great thought it authentic (not canonical). It exists only in Latin, but there may have been a Greek original. The *Muratorian Fragment* mentions an *Epistle to the Laodiceans* as a Marcionist forgery, which probably was a different work.

32. Lentulus, Epistle of, a medieval apocryphon, purporting to be a letter to the Roman senate by Lentulus, a Roman official in Judea. The date is uncertain, probably 13th–14th century. It describes the physical appearance of Christ. *LENTULUS, LETTER OF

33. Marcion, Gospel of, an apocryphal book developed by Marcion from an earlier tradition or by the heretical sect he founded. Marcion and his followers rejected the OT and accepted only Luke and 10 Pauline Epistles of the NT. His gospel seems to have consisted of an abridgment of Luke, dropping the first two chapters, modifying other parts to suit his Gnosticism, Docetism, Encratism, hostility to Judaism and the OT. A few have claimed Marcion used an earlier version of Luke; some think he also made occasional use of the other three Gospels.

34. Mary, Gospel of the Birth of, a Latin infancy gospel, drawing its substance from the first part of the gospel of Pseudo-Matthew. It tells of Mary's birth at Nazareth, the giving of her name by an angel, her life in the Temple, the miraculous selection of Joseph as her husband, and the birth of Christ. It has been traditionally but wrongly attributed to Jerome. It is not the same work as the Gnostic *Birth of Mary.*

35. Matthew, Martyrdom of, a late story, extant in Greek and Latin, of how Matthew was sent by Christ to the king of the cannibals. He plants a rod which grows into a tree and produces marvels. He is martyred by fire and buried in an iron coffin in the sea. The coffin rises, the king is converted, and becomes a bishop. The writer is interested in wonders, not in religion or dogma. Dependent on *Acts of Andrew and Matthias,* but confused.

36. Matthias, Gospel of. A work mentioned by Origen *(Homily 1 on Luke).* Clement of Alexandria cites the *Traditions of Matthias (Stromata* 2.9; 3.4; 7.13). Some think the two may be one work; others are doubtful.

37. Messos, Apocalypse of, a Gnostic writing in Coptic, found at Chenoboskion in 1946. Messos was probably a Gnostic seer or prophet, not Moses, nor a mystic mediator. This work is probably one of the five apocalypses against which Plotinus fought, according to Porphyry.

38. Nazarenes, Gospel of the, a Gospel mentioned by Hegesippus, Eusebius, Epiphanius, and Jerome, written in Syriac or Aramaic (perhaps translated from Greek), probably composed in the first half of the 2d century. Fragments are extant. It seems to be not a proto-Matthew, but a development of the Greek Matthew, quite similar in narratives and discourse matter, but involving some fictional development of the tradition in the narratives. It was in use, according to Jerome, among the Nazarenes and Syrian Jewish Christians.

39. Oxyrhynchus Sayings of Jesus, from six small fragments of papyrus, found, among many others, at Oxyrhynchus (now Behnesa) about 125 miles S of Cairo, Egypt. In the Grenfell and Hunt edition they are numbered 1;654;655;840;1081;1224;1384. Papyrus 1 dates from soon after 200 A.D.; 654 from end of 2d or start of 3d cent.; 655, 2d or 3d cent.; 840 seems to have been in an amulet of the 4th to 5th cent.; 1081 dates from 3d or early 4th cent.; 1224, from early 4th cent.; 1384, 5th to 6th century. They contain fragments of "sayings of Jesus," probably mostly from apocryphal gospels. Papyrus 1081 seems to be a fragment of the Gnostic gospel *Sophia Iesu.* Most of them seem to show knowledge of and dependence on the canonical Gospels.

40. Paul, Acts of, an extant romance, written probably 185–200 A.D. in Asia Minor. A Coptic MS found in 1894 has proved that the *Acts of Paul and Thecla,* the apocryphal correspondence between Paul and the Corinthians, and the story of the *Martyrdom of Paul* are all parts of these Acts. Thecla, converted by Paul, breaks her engagement, escapes death in the arena, baptizes herself, is sent by Paul to preach and baptize. In the correspondence, the Corinthians write to Paul of false preachers. Paul refutes them. There is much stress (some unorthodox) on continence and the resurrection. The Acts clearly reject Docetism and Gnosticism. Most but not all the theological views in the Acts are orthodox. They contain the most famous ancient description of the appearance of Paul, which has influenced ecclesiastical art.

41. Paul, Apocalypse of, an apocryphal work that may have existed in several forms. Epiphanius (*Heresies* 38.2) mentions an *Ascent Anabastikon of Paul,* a forgery by Cainites, which is surely not to be identified with the extant Apocalypse, although it may be related to it. A Gnostic Coptic *Apocalypse of Paul* was found at Chenoboskion in 1946, but this has not yet been studied. The extant *Apocalypse of Paul* was written in the 4th or perhaps even the 3d century. The introduction asserts that it was found under the house of Paul at Tarsus during the reign of Theodosius. Sozomen (*History* 7.9) mentions the story, and adds that an aged priest of Tarsus in his day said no such find was known there. The Apocalypse expands on 2 Cor 12.2: Paul is sent by Christ to preach penance to men, against whom all creation complains. He hears the reports of guardian angels, then is shown the death and judgment of one just and one wicked man. He sees paradise, is given a tour of hell, begs Christ for mercy for the damned, and obtains a 1-day-per-week respite for them as a permanent commemoration of Jesus' Resurrection. Finally, he has a second vision of paradise.

42. Paul, Passion of, a later Latin revision of the *Martyrdom of Paul* (which is part of the *Acts of Paul*). It is attributed to Linus. It adds several stories and a paragraph about Seneca's admiration for Paul and says that Seneca read part of Paul's letters to Nero.

43. Paul and Seneca, Epistles of, a set of apocryphal correspondence of Paul and Seneca, eight letters by the latter, six replies by the former, still extant. Seneca praises the sublimity of content of Paul's Epistles and asks him to be more careful of style. It was composed not later than the 3d century. Jerome (*De viris illustribus* 12) lists Seneca as a Christian writer because of these.

44. Peter, Acts of, an apocryphal romance (there is no evidence that it preserves historical tradition), composed probably before A.D. 200, perhaps in Asia Minor or Rome. We have about two-thirds of the whole. A large part, the Vercelli Acts, in Latin, probably written before A.D. 200. tells of Paul's departure to Spain, the arrival in Rome of Simon Magus who by wonders causes many to fall away, Peter's trip from Jerusalem to counter Simon, the latter's attempted ascension from the Forum, foiled by Peter, Peter's martyrdom (including the *Quo vadis* incident). Several other episodes, seemingly part of the Acts, are also extant. The work is probably not by a Gnostic but shows heavy Gnostic influence in places, as also Encratite and Docetic influences. Paul uses bread and water for the Eucharist. Peter moves his hearers to avoid sexual intercourse. The original complete form may have attacked marriage more strongly.

45. Peter, Apocalypse of, an apocryphal work extant in a number of versions: (1) a Gnostic apocalypse found in 1946 at Chenoboskion in Egypt; (2) an *Apocalypse of Peter* translated from the Arabic (cf. *Woodbrooke Studies,* Cambridge, 1931, 3.2). (3) an older apocalypse, probably dating from 125–150 A.D. It exists in two forms, an Ethiopic translation and a fragment in Greek from the tomb of Akhmim (found in Upper Egypt, 1887). The former seems closer to the original. The content is mainly imaginative visions of heaven and hell, probably borrowing imagery from Orphic-Pythagorean eschatology and oriental religions. Clement of Alexandria (Eusebius, *Hist. eccl.* 6.14.1) seems to have considered it canonical. The Muratorian Canon lists it, but notes that "some will not have it read in church." Jerome and Eusebius consider it uncanonical. Sozomen (7.19) reports it was still used in the Good Friday liturgy in some churches in Palestine in the 5th cent. Its use in later apocrypha shows its popularity.

46. Peter, Gospel of, an apocryphal gospel of which a large fragment was found in 1886 in the tomb of Akhmim in Upper Egypt. The scribe seems not to have known any more of it, since he puts ornaments at both ends of the copy. It begins with Pilate washing his hands and ends with the appearance of Jesus at the Sea of Tiberias. It certainly depends heavily on the canonical Gospels. It is debatable how much Gnostic or Docetic influence is to be seen in it: at least, it prepares the way for later Gnostic work. A strong apologetic and also anti-Jewish interest is apparent. It was formerly known through a part of a refutation made by Serapion, quoted by Eusebius (*Hist. eccl.* 6.12). Serapion calls it Docetic. Origen also mentions such a work. Theodoret says it was in use among the Nazarenes, but probably refers to a different work, in view of the anti-Jewish bias in the Gospel of Peter.

47. Peter, Passion of, a late Latin revision of the account of the martyrdom of Peter from the *Acts of Peter,* attributed to Linus, Peter's successor as bishop of Rome, but probably written not earlier than the 6th century. It adds some details to the story of the Acts, such as the names of Peter's jailers and a vision at the time of his crucifixion. It is purely legendary.

48. Peter, Preaching of, a nonexistent apocryphon, professing to be a handbook of the preaching of Peter. A number of quotations from it exist, perhaps amounting to an epitome, in Clement of Alexandria's *Stromata* (6.5, 6, 15). He accepted it as genuine, while Eusebius (*Hist. eccl.* 3:3.1–4) rejected it. The several warnings against the worship of animals suggest it may have originated in Egypt. It does not seem to be the same as the preachings of Peter found in the Clementine *Homilies and Recognitions*.

49. Peter, Slavonic Acts of, a late, grotesque, apocryphal romance, with some Gnostic coloring, pretending to narrate Peter's experiences on the way to and in Rome and his death. A young child urges him to go. On the way Peter buys the child from the ship's captain. The child works miracles in Rome; the dead are raised and returned to their graves by Peter. After the crucifixion of Peter, the child appears, the nails fall from Peter, the child reveals he is Jesus. Extant only in Slavonic, it seems to have no connection with the Leucian *Acts of Peter*.

50. Peter and Andrew, Acts of, a short series of wonder stories with no seeming interest in doctrine, extant in Greek and Slavonic, a sequel to the *Acts of Andrew and Matthias*. Among other things: Andrew rides a cloud from the cannibal land to a mountain where Peter is preaching. Jesus appears as a child, orders Peter and Andrew to go to the land of the barbarians. Peter converts the hostile Onesiphorus by causing a camel to go through the eye of a needle.

51. Peter and Paul, Acts of, an apocryphon recounting Paul's journey from the island of Gaudomelete to Rome, and the work, close association, and deaths of Peter and Paul in Rome. Except for the early chapters, its content is essentially the same as the *Passion of Peter and Paul* that is arbitrarily ascribed to Marcellus. Extant only in Greek.

52. Peter and Paul, Passion of, the title of two apocrypha: (1) a late (not before 5th cent.) but quite orthodox apocryphon, extant in Latin and Greek. It is in substance identical to the *Acts of Peter and Paul* except for the early chapters. It is often, but without reason, attributed to Marcellus. (2) A quite different work extant only in Latin. Peter and Paul stay at the home of a relative of Pilate; reply to the claims of Simon Magus to be the Christ. The account of their deaths is brief.

53. Peter and the Twelve Apostles, Acts of, a Gnostic work found in 1946 at Chenoboskion, Egypt, to be distinguished from the *Acts of Peter,* the Ebionite *Acts of the Apostles,* and the Manichaean *Acts of the Twelve Apostles*.

54. Philip, Acts of, a late (not earlier than 4th or 5th cent.) romance, pretending to narrate the adventures, miracles, and death of Philip (by crucifixion, head down) at Hierapolis. Extant are 9 of the 15 acts, plus the martyrdom of Philip.

55. Philip, Gospel of, a gospel forged by Egyptian Gnostics (*Heresies* 26.13). Epiphanius quotes it, telling how the soul must reveal proper knowledge as it goes up to heaven and must be able to say it has not begotten children. The *Pistis Sophia* also seems to refer to this work. In 1945 a *Gospel of Philip* was found in the Gnostic library at Chenoboskion. Study of it is not yet completed, but it seems to be a different work, for it does not have the form of a gospel, and the citation by Epiphanius does not seem to occur in it.

56. Pilate, Acts of, an extant passion gospel consisting of two parts: (1) many fanciful and imaginative details on the trial and death of Jesus (1-11) and acts of the Sanhedrin that led to proofs of his Resurrection and Ascension (12–16); (2) the garish account of the two sons of Simeon who, being dead, had seen Christ's descent into hell and had returned to life (17–19). The present form of the first part probably dates to c. A.D. 350, though it is highly likely that a previous work on which this is based was known to Justin Martyr (*First Apology* 35; 48). This work seems to have originated as a reply to a pagan forgery, the *Memoirs of Pilate,* which Epiphanius (*Hist.* 9:5.1) says was full of blasphemy against Christ. A prologue in many MSS attributes this work to Nicodemus; composition is never attributed to Pilate. The relative age of the two parts is uncertain: probably they were not joined before the 5th century. Later appendices were added, esp. a letter from Pilate to Claudius on the trial of Jesus.

57. Pistis Sophia, a late title given to a group of works whose primitive title was "Books (Rolls) of the Savior." They are found in a Coptic parchment MS of the second half of the 4th century. In the first 3 of the 4 sections, probably composed 250–300 A.D., Jesus, 12 years after his Resurrection, replies to questions of Mary Magdalene, gives to her and the disciples information on the fate, fall, and redemption of Pistis Sophia (faith-wisdom), a being of the world of Gnostic aeons. The *Epistle of Eugnostos* calls Pistis Sophia the name of the consort of the Savior, who seems to be bisexual. The fourth section (probably first half of 3d cent.) tells things recounted by Jesus right after his Resurrection and does not mention Pistis Sophia.

58. Pseudo-Matthew, Gospel of, a late Latin infancy gospel of 8th or 9th century. Our earliest MSS are of the 11th century. When certain infancy gospels had been condemned by Popes Damasus, Innocent I, and the Gelasian Decree, popular interest seems to have motivated the writing of the Pseudo-Matthew. It is substantially a rewrite, with additions, omissions, changes of the *Protoevangelium of James* and the *Gospel of Thomas*. It seems also to have aimed at the veneration of Mary as Queen of Virgins. It had great influence on medieval literature and art.

59. Savior, Dialogue of the, a Gnostic writing found at Chenoboskion, Egypt, in 1946. In it Jesus holds a dialogue with his disciples on cosmogony.

60. Silvanus, Teachings of, a Gnostic writing found at Chenoboskion, Egypt, in 1946, attributed to Silvanus (almost certainly the same as Silas), a companion of Paul, and the one through whom the *First Epistle of Peter* was sent, who probably put Peter's thoughts into words.

61. Stephen, Revelation of, an apocryphal apocalypse, now lost, known through its condemnation in the so-called Decree of Gelasius (early 6th cent.) along with the Apocalypse of Paul and that of Thomas. Some have conjectured, with scant reason, that the *Revelation of Stephen* has the same substance as the story of the discovery of the bodies of Stephen, Nicodemus, Gamaliel, and Gamaliel's son by Lucian (415 A.D.) a priest of Kaphargamala, near Jerusalem.

62. Thaddeus, Acts of, a set of Edessene legends, taking as its starting point the *Epistles of Christ and Abgarus* (extant), this work recounts how Thomas the Apostle after Christ's Ascension was divinely led to send one of the 70 Disciples, Thaddeus, to King Abgarus of Edessa. Thaddeus heals him and converts the entire community. The letters probably date from early 4th century. There is also another form of these Acts, the *Doctrina Addaei,* extant in Syriac, probably composed *c.*400 A.D.

63. Thomas, Acts of, an apocryphal acts, probably originally written in Syriac in the first half of the 3d cent. at Edessa. They recount how Thomas was assigned to India, refused, and was forced by Christ, who sold him to a merchant, to serve Indian King Gundephorus as a carpenter. After many marvelous incidents, Thomas is martyred. The extant Greek is probably closer to the original than the Syriac text, which seems to have been much revised to purify it of Gnostic tendencies: Thomas is represented as the twin of Christ, like him both in appearance and in redeeming work. Thomas specializes in urging renunciation of marriage. All attempts to prove the historicity of Thomas's mission to India have failed.

64. Thomas, Apocalypse of, formerly known only through its condemnation in the so-called Gelasian decree (6th cent.), found in the early part of the 20th cent. in two versions, the longer in MSS dating from 8th and 9th cent., the shorter in MSS of 5th and 11 or 12th centuries. The first part of the longer version is probably an interpolation from the 5th century. The second corresponds to the shorter version and is probably earlier than the 5th century. In it Christ is pictured as describing to Thomas the events of the 7 days that precede the final consummation of the world.

65. Thomas, Gospel of, a title given to two apocryphal gospels: (1) the infancy *Gospel according to Thomas,* extant in Greek, Syriac, and other versions, which recounts the childhood of Jesus between the ages 5 to 12. It is a welter of tasteless (and worse) wonder stories, e.g., a child running dashes against Jesus; Jesus strikes him dead; Jesus is found making clay birds on the Sabbath, is rebuked, brings them to life. The present form is probably later than 6th cent., but it may go back to the late 2d cent.; (2) the *Gospel of Thomas* found at Chenoboskion in 1946. It contains hardly any narrative, is a collection of 114 sayings of Jesus. It seems to be the Manichaean gospel mentioned by Cyril of Jerusalem (*Catecheses* 6.31). Hippolytus attributes such a gospel to the Gnostic Naasenes, probably this one (*Heresies* 5.2). Perhaps the Manichaeans reworked the Gnostic gospel. It may go back to the mid-2d cent., but it is not later than the beginning of the 3d century.

66. Titus, Apocryphal Epistle of, an apocryphon of uncertain date, discovered in an 8th-cent. Latin MS in 1896. It is really an address on virginity and a denouncement of "spiritual marriages" in which ascetics of both sexes lived under one roof, with no sexual contacts. It perhaps originated in Priscillianist circles in Spain. The original may have been Greek; the style is barbarous.

67. Virgin, Apocalypse of. There are two such apocalypses, of late origin. One, extant in Greek, relates how the Virgin Mary asks Michael to see the tortures of the damned. She is moved to pity, obtains from her son a respite for them on all subsequent Pentecost days. The other apocalypse, now extant only in Ethiopic (perhaps originally Greek), retells chapters 13–44 of the *Apocalypse of Paul* with some alterations and additions. BIBLIOGRAPHY: V. R. Gold, "Gnostic Library of Chenoboskion" *Biblical Archeologist,* 15 (1952) 70–88; E. J. Goodspeed, *Modern Apocrypha* (1956); *idem, Strange New Gospels* (1931); R. M. Grant and David N. Freedman, *Secret Sayings of Jesus* (1960); E. Hennecke, *New Testament Apocrypha* (ed. W. Schneemelcher; tr. R. McL. Wilson, v. 1, 1963; v. 2, 1964); M. R. James, *Apocryphal New Testament* (1953); Quasten (1950) v. 1.

[W. G. MOST]

APOCRYPHA, ICONOGRAPHY OF THE. From late Hellenistic times apocryphal literature constantly provided artists with a rich source of imagery. The *Ascensio Jesaiae* is the only book known today for iconography of the OT. Apocryphal NT literature was used to complete narrative cycles of the lives of Christ, the Virgin Mary, the Apostles, and other saints. The *Protoevangelium Jacobi, Evangelium Pseudo-Matthaei* and *Evangelium Infantiae Salvatoris arabicum* are sources for the infancy of Christ and the life of the Virgin. Apocryphal books of the *Acts of Paul, Acts of Peter,* and *Acts of Andreas,* etc., are sources of miraculous deeds and martyrdoms of the Apostles. BIBLIOGRAPHY: S. Tsuji, NCE 1:665; *Reallexikon zur byzantinischen Kunst* (ed. K. Wessel, 1963) v.i.

[M. J. DALY]

APODEIPNON (Gr. for after supper), the hour of the Byzantine Office that follows the evening meal. The Great Rule of St. Basil gives the first clear reference to such an Office, called Compline in the West. It probably originated with Basil because it was unknown in Asia Minor and Egypt before his time. He specified that Ps 90, a characteristic of Compline in every rite, was to be recited, and determined the end of the Office as prayer for a night without trouble or strain, tranquillity in repose free from evil dreams, themes still expressed in today's apodeipnon. In contemporary practice, already witnessed to by Symeon of Thessalonica at the beginning of the 15th cent., there are two kinds of Compline: Great Compline, which follows the tradition of St. Sabas, is really a series of three Offices, each with its own introductory and concluding prayers. As this Office gradually came to be reserved to Lent, Lesser Compline, a selection of elements from Great Compline, became the Office for the rest of the year. Oriental Compline has not yet been adequately studied. In general, one can say that in the different rites this hour manifests no common schema (except for Ps 90), and is not completely autonomous, being often attached to another hour or omitted entirely, as in the Byzantine Vigil Service. BIBLIOGRAPHY: A. Raes, "Les Complies dans les rites orientaux," *Orientalia Christiana Periodica*, 17 (1951) 133–145; J. Pargoire and S. Pétrides, DACL 1.2:2579–89.

[R. F. TAFT]

APODERMA, in Byzantine chant, a subsidiary rhythmical sign having a definite time value. In the Round System of notation (in use *c*.1100–1450), the subsidiaries of this type are called *hypostases*. Used sparingly in earlier times, they are found more frequently in the MSS from the 13th cent. to the 15th. Like the *Diple* and the *Kratema*, the Apoderma (⁀ ⁀) lengthens a quaver (eighth note) to a crotchet (quarter note). BIBLIOGRAPHY: H. J. W. Tillyard, *Byzantine Music and Hymnography (Church Music Monographs*, 1923) 6:48–49.

[M. T. LEGGE]

APODOSIS, the conclusion of a feast that lasts several days in the Byzantine rite. Whereas the West has the fixed octave, the length of Eastern feasts varies, that of Easter lasting to the vigil of the Ascension, for example.

[E. P. COLBERT]

APOLLINAIRE, GUILLAUME (1880–1918), pseudonym of Wilhelm Apollinaris Kostrowitsky, pioneer of modern poetry and art criticism. His career began with translations into French from several languages, and journalistic miscellanea; fiction and poetry followed, in a postSymbolist vein. His poems *Alcools* (1913) abandoned punctuation and espoused personal and psychological imagery; *Calligrammes* (1918) were poems in visual patterns. A. was the first interpreter of the cubists; a friend of Cocteau and Picasso, he introduced the term "surrealism" in his play *The Breasts of Tiresias* (1918), written with their collaboration. BIBLIOGRAPHY: biog. by F. Steegmuller (1964); D. G. Sullivan, "On Time and Poetry: A Reading of Apollinaire," *Modern Language Notes* 88 (1973) 811–837.

[J. P. WILLIMAN]

APOLLINARIANISM, the first great Christological heresy, the doctrine (forerunner of *Monophysitism) that Christ had no human soul. Apollinaris of Laodicea (310?–390?), friend of St. *Athanasius of Alexandria, collaborated with him and with the great Cappadocian St. *Basil the Great in the reduction of *Arianism, and was the bulwark of orthodoxy in Arian Syria. But his zeal to safeguard the absolute divinity of Christ led him to teach that the divine Word replaces the human soul in the hypostatic union and performs all its functions. He alleged two reasons. First, God and man are each complete beings; hence the union of God and a complete man in a single being would be an absurdity, since two beings cannot be one being. Second, a human soul has the liberty to sin, but Christ could not sin. A. is the originator of St. *Cyril of Alexandria's great Christological formula, "One nature, incarnate, of the Word of God." But whereas Cyril was to understand "nature" in the sense of a concrete personal unity (hence the formula as used by Cyril is orthodox, however ambiguous), A. understood it in the sense of "essence" or "substance"; hence the formula as used by A. is monophysitical. The foremost antagonists of Apollinarianism are probably the great Cappadocians, SS. *Gregory of Nazianzus and *Gregory of Nyssa. BIBLIOGRAPHY: Quasten 3:377–383.

[R. R. BARR]

APOLLINARIANS, a late 4th cent. sect named after their founder, Apollinaris, bp. of Laodicea (d.392) who held that the human nature of Christ included a body (*sōma*), an animating soul (*psyche*), and divine nature (*Logos*) with no capacity for sin in place of a rational soul (*nous*) with its inherent tendency for evil. *APOLLINARIANISM.

[F. H. BRIGHAM]

APOLLINARIS OF HIERAPOLIS, ST. (fl. 170), bishop, apologist. A. was bp. of Hierapolis in Phrygia during the reign of Marcus Aurelius (161–180). Of his numerous writings no longer extant, Eusebius lists five books against the Greeks, two against the Jews, two on truth; a discourse on the faith addressed to Marcus Aurelius and treatises against the Phrygians (Montanists). His refutations of these early Montanists were highly esteemed by Serapion of Antioch. But A. could not be the author of anti-Montanist passages quoted by Eusebius *(Hist. eccl.* 5. 16–19) since they were written after his death. BIBLIOGRAPHY: G. Bardy, *Catholicisme* 1:704; Quasten 1:228–229; P. de Labriolle, DHGE 3:959–960; P. Burchi, BiblSanct 2:232–233.

[F. H. BRIGHAM]

APOLLINARIS OF LAODICEA (*c*.300–*c*.390), also known as Apollinaris the Younger, bp. of Laodicea and originator of *Apollinarianism. A. was the son of Apollinaris the Elder, with whom he collaborated in classical paraphrases of the Bible. He was an anti-Arian, a firm supporter of the teaching of the Council of *Nicaea I (325), and a friend of *Athanasius. In 361 A. was elected bp. of Laodicea by the

Nicene community there. He was a noted theologian and lectured at Antioch, one of his auditors being St. *Jerome. The departure from orthodoxy that bears his name and was the first Christological heresy was first suspected on the occasion of the Council of Alexandria in 362, but became overt in 371. A. left the Church *c.*375. His teaching was condemned by Roman synods in 374 and 380 and by the Council of Constantinople I in 381. (See APOLLINARIANISM.) A.'s anticipation of *Monophysitism is known chiefly through *Gregory of Nyssa's *Antirrheticus contra Apollinarem* (PG 45:1156), since only fragments of his writings survived. His disciples circulated his teachings under the names of Pope *Julius, Athanasius, and other orthodox writers. BIBLIOGRAPHY: Bihlmeyer-Tüchle 1:268–269; G. L. Prestige, *Fathers and Heretics* (1940) 195–246; Quasten 3:377–383.

[T. C. O'BRIEN]

APOLLINARIS OF MONTE CASSINO, ST. (d. 828), Benedictine abbot of Monte Cassino 817–828. As a young child A. was entrusted to the abbey as an oblate. During his reign the abbey reached a high point of development, materially and spiritually. He himself was reputed a saint. His relics, placed under an altar in the abbey, survived the World War II bombing. BIBLIOGRAPHY: A. Lentini, NCE 1:668; B. Cignitti, BiblSanct 2:233–234.

[M. A. WINKELMANN]

APOLLINARIS OF VALENCE, ST. (d. *c.*520), bishop. Son of St. Hesychius and brother of St. Avitus, successively bps. of Vienne. A. labored to reestablish discipline in the Diocese of Valence and to convert the Burgundians from Arianism. Exiled by Sigismund shortly after his return from the Synod of Epaon (517), he was restored to his see in 518. BIBLIOGRAPHY: G. M. Cook, NCE 1:668; Butler 4:36; G. Mathon, BiblSanct 2:249–250; for his correspondence with Avitus, PL 59:231–232, 273.

[G. M. COOK]

APOLLO BELVEDERE, Roman copy of the Hellenistic Apollo (Vatican Museum, Rome). The original is ascribed to Leochares (mid-4th cent. B.C.) The striding Apollo with cloak draped from extended left arm and face finely modeled, greatly admired by *Winckelmann, established a Hellenistic norm for 18th-cent. Neoclassicism. BIBLIOGRAPHY: M. Bieber, *Sculpture of the Hellenistic Age* (rev. ed., 1961).

[M. J. DALY]

APOLLODORUS OF ATHENS (b. *c.* 180 B.C.), Greek grammarian and historian. His *Chronicle,* which contained condensed historical and literary data from the fall of Troy to his own time, was the most important ancient work in its field. The literary criticism he incorporated in his commentary on the Homeric catalogue of ships became a mine for later writers. It contained in addition numerous quotations from earlier authors. A. also wrote commentaries on

Epicharmus' mimes and Sophron's comedies. His most influential work was a rationalistic account of Greek religion, *On the Gods.* The lengthy summary of myths and heroic legends ascribed to him under the title *The Library* is certainly spurious. BIBLIOGRAPHY: F. Jacoby, *Die Fragmente der griechischen Historiker* 2 B (1919) 1022–1128; J. F. Lockwood, OCD 69–70.

[M. J. SUELZER]

APOLLONIA, ST. (d. 249), virgin and martyr who was put to death in the anti-Christian disturbances in Alexandria toward the end of the reign of the Emperor Philip the Arabian. Her martyrdom is well attested. An account of it was written in a letter by *Dionysius, bp. of Alexandria at the time (cited by Eusebius, *Hist. eccl.* 6.41). Although Christian art always pictures A. as a young maiden, she was in fact an elderly deaconess at the time of her death. Honored as patroness of dentists and of those suffering from toothache because her teeth were broken when she was mauled by the crowd before her martyrdom, she is usually depicted with a pair of pincers or with a golden tooth suspended from her neck. The fact reported of her, that she threw herself voluntarily into the flames with which she was threatened because of her refusal to blaspheme, has given some trouble to moralists. St. Augustine suggested that the act would not have been suicidal in any objectionable sense of the word if it were performed under the direct inspiration of the Holy Spirit. BIBLIOGRAPHY: M. Costelloe, NCE 1:668–669; M. Scaduto et al., EncCatt 1:1645–48; Butler 1:286.

[R. B. ENO]

APOLLONIOS (mid-1st cent. B.C.), Greek sculptor, son of Nestor, whose signature is on the *Belvedere Torso* in the Vatican Museum and on the bronze *Boxer* in the Terme Museum, Rome—two of the most powerful works of the late Hellenistic period.

[M. J. DALY]

APOLLONIUS OF CITIUM, scholar during the intellectual renaissance of the 9th-cent. Byzantine golden age, who produced an illustrated "surgical treatise" in an age of "Hellenism" which studied, recopied, collated, and chose extracts imitating both the language and form of works of classical antiquity, producing voluminous encyclopedic collections leading to the knowledge and dissemination of writings of the ancient past. BIBLIOGRAPHY: S. der Nersessian, *Larousse Encyclopedia of Byzantine and Medieval Art* (ed. R. Huyghe, 1958) s.v. "Later Byzantine Empire."

[M. J. DALY]

APOLLONIUS OF EPHESUS (fl. 195) apologist. A strong anti-Montanist, A. was praised by Jerome and Eusebius who quoted his written indictments of the teaching and practice of Montanus (*Hist. eccl.* 5.18), but was criticized by Tertullian. BIBLIOGRAPHY: G. Bardy, *Catholicisme* 1:710.

APOLLONIUS OF TYANA (fl. 1st cent. A.D.). Neopythagorean philosopher and reputed wonder-worker. The chief source for his career is the *Life of Apollonius* written in Greek by Philostratus II (fl. *c*.200). He is described as a wandering ascetic, teacher, and miracle worker. Philostratus wished apparently to present him as an ideal representative of Pythagoreanism. It is possible that he was acquainted with the Gospel and was influenced by it to depict A. as a kind of pagan Christ. A. was undoubtedly an historical person and a Pythagorean teacher. The *Life* was very popular among pagans in the 3d and 4th cent. and was employed by the pagan Sossianus Hierocles under Diocletian to make an unfavorable comparison between the life and miracles of Christ and the life and miracles of Apollonius. BIBLIOGRAPHY: M. R. P. McGuire, NCE 1:669; RAC s.v.; P. de Labriolle, *La Réaction païenne: Étude sur la polémique antichrétienne du I*er *au VI*e *siècle* (6th ed., 1942) 175–189.

[M. R. P. McGUIRE]

APOLLONIUS OF TYRE, the most notable piece of late Old English secular prose. It is of interest and importance for giving the first evidence of a desire for a prose in English that would primarily please and entertain. An anonymous romance of classical antiquity, it was rightfully popular in the Middle Ages; and though it underwent many medieval rearrangements, it kept its form. Only a fragment of the Old English translation has survived. The oldest extant version (5th-6th cent. A.D.) is in Latin—*Historia Apollonii regis Tyri;* but matter and style suggest that there was a Greek original of the 2d to 3d cent. A.D. The earliest mention of it is in the *Carmina* of Venantius Fortunatus in the second half of the 6th century. Shakespeare used the story—with little change—for his play, *Pericles, Prince of Tyre.* BIBLIOGRAPHY: *Apollonius of Tyre* (ed. P. Goolden, 1958).

[S. A. HEENEY]

APOLLOS, an Alexandrian Jew educated in Greek eloquence and the OT probably under the influence of Philo. After becoming a member of the Baptist's sect he was converted to Christianity by Prisca and Aquila at Ephesus. He preached at Corinth; then some set up a party in opposition to Paul, but Apollos remained a friend of Paul's and refused to return to Corinth from Ephesus (Acts 18.24–19.1; 1 Cor 1.12; 3.4–6.22; 6.6; 16.12). About his later life nothing is known. Many attribute Heb to him. BIBLIOGRAPHY: H. Montefiore, *Epistle to the Hebrews* (1965).

[J. J. O'ROURKE]

APOLOGETICS, the theological discipline that deals with the reasons for believing God and accepting the faith presented by the Christian Church. The NT is only indirectly concerned with such a reasoned justification of Christian belief insofar as it presents faith in Jesus as linked with the OT prophecies which he fulfilled and the signs which he performed. But the Scriptures are not an apologetic treatise in the sense of a reasoned argument leading to an act of faith.

The term apologist is applied to the early Christian writers, e.g., *Justin Martyr, *Origen, *Irenaeus, and *Tertullian, who defended Church teaching against its critics by an appeal to the moral effects of Christianity, its antiquity when joined with the OT, Christ's fulfillment of prophecies and his miraculous acts. Even up to the time of the Reformation, apologetics retained this general orientation toward showing the coherence and intelligibility of Christian doctrine.

The rise of *rationalism in the 17th cent. greatly influenced the future development of apologetics. Because of the general emphasis on strict proof and scientific procedures, a new criterion for the assent of faith was introduced—that faith should be justified by at least an implicit, antecedent, and speculative knowledge of divine revelation. Thus apologetics came to be separated from the rest of theology and treated as an independent and preliminary field of study. In the 19th cent., naturalism and the appearance of more scientific scriptural studies which raised fundamental questions concerning the reliability of the gospels as an historical source caused a reaction in both Protestant and Catholic theological circles. Much effort was spent to build up an argument to demonstrate the existence of the supernatural, the nature of revelation, and the NT as a true historical document. The miracles of Christ came to have an increasingly important role to play in establishing the *motive of credibility. During this period the so-called quest for the historical Jesus was the key theological problem, largely identified with thinkers such as D. Strauss, M. Kähler, A. Schweitzer, and ultimately R. Bultmann. Such a strictly rationalistic approach was mitigated by the RC theologians J. H. *Newman who stressed the role of conscience in coming to a faith decision, and M. *Blondel's immanence apologetics. According to the Blondelian school, experience indicates that existence has a meaning, that this meaning is dependent upon an Absolute, and finally that this Absolute has been historically realized in the process of revelation which the Church serves.

Apologetics is of its nature the most fluid branch of theological study. Being a defense of the faith, it must, to be effective, vary its approach, its major emphases, its methods and procedures, to meet whatever attacks upon the faith are most in vogue in any given age. In the contemporary period there have been many developments and changes in apologetics made necessary by trends of thought rooted in the prevailing pluralism in philosophy and in the wide differences in the fundamental values that tend to be held in honor at the present time. The advances in the study of Scripture and history account for other changes. In consequence apologetics has moved away from the strongly rationalistic approach that characterized it in the 19th and early 20th centuries. Today it stresses the unity of man, the believer, to whose faith commitment a characteristically human mixture of affective factors contributes. Diversity of approach is stressed with the recognition that different men are impelled by different arguments. Contemporary apologetics perceives more clearly that the desired product of any viable apologetic is a loving affirmation of God's revelation in Jesus Christ; a merely intellectual grasp of doctrine is not faith. Hence there is both an objective and a subjective pole in apologetics. Objectively it considers the possibility and nature of revelation as such and of the Judaeo-Christian revelation in particular. Subjectively, apologetics considers the mystery of the individual before God, the dynamics of faith, and the relationship of faith and reason. Finally, contemporary apologetics tends to be addressed less exclusively to the unbeliever who attacks the faith from the outside, but to believers themselves, the substructure of whose faith may be threatened by the welter of philosophical and theological opinion to be found in contemporary society. BIBLIOGRAPHY: J.-B. Metz, SacMund 1:66–70; P. J. Cahill, NCE 1:669–674; D. L. Balas, NCE 16:13–14; H. Bouillard, *Logic of Faith* (1967).

[T. M. MCFADDEN]

APOLOGETICS, MISSIONARY, the special theory and practice of apologetics concerned with placing the faith in the best possible light for those who are non-Christians and live in a culture in which Christianity forms a relatively minor part. Vat II ChurchModWorld 91 notes that the gospel message must be adapted to individual nations and mentalities. It is contrary to the Christian mission to preach to all nations that the gospel should be identified with any particular philosophical or cultural stance. The missionary is faced with the task of so formulating the Christian message that it responds to the religious needs of those with whom he is working. Those religious needs must be evaluated within the context of cultural values, past religious formation, and social attributes. BIBLIOGRAPHY: H. R. Schlette, SacMund 4:81–84; H. W. Law, *Winning a Hearing* (1968); H. van Straelen, *Catholic Encounter with World Religions* (1966). *ADAPTATION, MISSIONARY.

[P. MISNER]

APOLOGETICS, PRACTICAL, the application of the principles attained through scientific *apologetics to the individual who is seeking religious truth. Practical apologetics is the process whereby a Christian attempts to understand the inquirer's religious psychology and the depth of his intellectual search so that he may adopt that approach to Christian truth that will be intellectually convincing and emotionally appealing. The history of Christianity attests to wide diversification in practical apologetics: Paul spoke to the Areopagites of the unknown God (Acts 17.22–24); *Irenaeus tried to demonstrate that Jesus fulfilled the OT prophecies; *Francis Xavier and Matteo *Ricci adopted different approaches in their missionary endeavors in the East; B. *Pascal's dependence upon religious experience differs considerably from the highly rational approach of much early 20th-cent. apologetics. Today emphasis is placed on an apologetic that responds to the needs of the total person seeking the faith; that presents the Gospel as religious testimony; that respects human freedom; and that admits the

mysterious quality of the personal encounter with God that is at the heart of faith. BIBLIOGRAPHY: P. L. Berger, *Rumor of Angels* (1969); *Faith, Reason, and the Gospels* (ed. J. J. Heaney, 1961); C. S. Lewis, *Mere Christianity* (1952); G. K. Chesterton, *Orthodoxy* (1908). *ADAPTATION, MISSIONARY; *APOLOGETICS, MISSIONARY.

[T. M. MCFADDEN]

APOLOGIAE SACERDOTIS, the prayers said by the celebrant in some older Eucharistic Liturgies to implore divine pardon for his own sins. These prayers did not have a fixed position in the liturgy, but were most frequently recited during the chanting of the Introit or Offertory psalms. They were principally composed from the 9th to the 11th centuries. Their function is achieved through the Confession of Sins in the contemporary liturgy. BIBLIOGRAPHY: F. Cabrol, DACL 1.2:2591–2601.

[T. M. MCFADDEN]

APOLOGIES (LITURGICAL), prayers begging God's forgiveness for personal guilt and unworthiness. They are said at Mass, usually by the celebrant. They first appeared in the Gallican rite of the 6th and 7th centuries and reached their apex between the 10th and 11th century. The Confiteor and Offertory prayers, both prescribed by Pius V's Missal of 1570, are examples of the apologies. BIBLIOGRAPHY: F. Cabrol, DACL 1.2:2591–2601; E. J. Gratsch, NCE 1:677; J. A. Jungmann, *Mass of the Roman Rite* (tr. F. Brunner, 2 v., 1951–55) 1:78–80. *MISSA ILLYRICA.

[N. KOLLAR]

APOLOGISTS, a term applied to a group of early Christian writers, mainly of Greek origins, who flourished *c*.120–220 A.D. They had three principal objectives: to refute false charges made by their non-Christian contemporaries, e.g., that Christianity was a danger to the State; to expose absurdities and immoralities in pagan myths and cults; and to show the superiority of Christian teachings over pagan philosophy. The Greek writers in this category are Quadratus, Aristides of Athens, Aristo of Pella, Justin Martyr, Tatian, Miltiades, Apollinaris of Hierapolis, Athenogoras of Athens, Theophilus of Antioch, and Melito of Sardes. The outstanding Latin apologists are Tertullian and Minucius Felix. BIBLIOGRAPHY: Quasten 1:186–248; 2:155–161, 255–269; Altaner 114–137.

[H. DRESSLER]

APOLOGY OF THE AUGSBURG CONFESSION, one of the confessional documents of Lutheranism, included in the Book of Concord. After the presentation of the *Augsburg Confession to the imperial Diet on June 25, 1530, three RC theologians, J. *Eck, J. *Faber, and J. *Cochlaeus, were asked to prepare a response. This they did in the *Confutatio,* a rebuttal, which on Aug. 3 was read to the assembly. The Lutherans were obliged to respond in turn. They did so in the Apology of the Augsburg Confession.

Philipp *Melanchthon, chief author of the Augsburg Confession, also undertook its defense, and a first draft was ready on Sept. 22, 1530. When this was rejected, Melanchthon undertook a more ample defense, which was published in the spring of 1531 and forms the present text of the Apology. Both the irenic language (even and esp. on the Eucharist) and the polemical sharpness of the Augsburg Confession appear in the Apology, which thus forms an authoritative commentary on the Confession itself. BIBLIOGRAPHY: *Book of Concord: The Confessions of the Evangelical Lutheran Church* (ed. T. G. Tappert, 1959).

[J. PELIKAN]

APOLOGY OF THE TRUE CHRISTIAN DIVINITY, statement of Quaker belief by Robert *Barclay. He published it first in Latin, *Theologiae verae Christianae apologia* (1676), then in English, *Apology of the True Christian Divinity as the Same is Set Forth and Preached by the People Called in Scorn "Quakers"* (1678). While the Society of Friends in principle has never adhered to a *confession of faith, the *Apology* has been recognized as an authentic declaration of beliefs, although modern Quakers regard it with reservations. Barclay was a theologian, and the *Apology* is written in a scholastic style. It consists of 15 propositions on the following: (1) the need for true knowledge of God; (2) the need of inner revelation as source of faith; (3) the Scriptures; (4) the Fall; (5) redemption by Christ, the true light; (6) the saving and spiritual light by which every man is enlightened; (7) justification, Christ formed within us; (8) perfection; (9) perseverance and the possibility of falling from grace; (10) the ministry, based on God's gift, not a human commission; (11) spiritual worship; (12) spiritual baptism, and the rejection of *infant baptism; (13) spiritual sharing in the body and blood of Christ; (14) civil magistrates and religious matters; (15) hat-doffing and similar salutation, and worldly recreations. The doctrine of the *Apology* on the *Inner Light became particularly celebrated. BIBLIOGRAPHY: L. Eeg-Olafson, *Conception of the Inner Light in Robert Barclay's Theology* (1954); D. Freiday, *Barclay's Apology in Modern English* (1967).

[T. C. O'BRIEN]

APOLOUSIS, the Eastern Orthodox rite of washing the anointed parts of the child's body 8 days after the Baptism; it is followed by the tonsure or cutting of the hair in the form of a cross.

[F. H. BRIGHAM]

APOLYSIS, the leave taking of the faithful at the end of liturgical services in some Eastern rites. The blessing of the priest is accompanied by prayers, either brief or lengthy.

[E. P. COLBERT]

APOLYTIKION, a trope at the end of the Byzantine liturgical Office which recapitulates the day's mystery or the virtues of the saint of the day.

[E. P. COLBERT]

APONIUS (fl. 410), the author of an allegorical commentary on the Song of Songs which stresses the primacy of the Church of Rome. BIBLIOGRAPHY: Altaner 544.

[F. H. BRIGHAM]

APOPHATIC THEOLOGY (Gr., *apophatikos,* negative), theology that proceeds to the knowledge of God by way of negations, by way of unknowing. It is opposed to cataphatic theology, which proceeds by positive, propositional assertions about God. In this sense, apophatic theology may be called a mystical theology as opposed to theology understood as a scholastic, rationalistic science.

Eastern Christianity is fundamentally characterized by the apophatic spirit in its theology, liturgy, and spirituality. In the Eastern tradition, apophaticism is not merely considered as a corrective to cataphaticism, nor is there a dialectical balance between the two theologies as two possible and valid approaches, nor is there a possibility of their synthesis into a single mode of knowledge. On the contrary, apophatic theology is considered as superior to cataphatic theology since God is essentially unknowable by creatures and, strictly speaking, may never be the object of conceptual knowledge. All positive assertions about God are necessarily inadequate, and, if taken literally, are simply untrue. Apophatic theology, which proceeds by unknowing, is not irrational. It involves the conscious overcoming of concepts and propositions. As a knowledge of God, and not merely about God, apophatic theology requires faith, prayer, sacraments, liturgical experience, and ascetic purification. It offers the knowledge of mystical union rather than that of philosophical speculation. In this sense, the Eastern Fathers claim that apophatic theology is truly biblical, the genuine overcoming of Platonic-Hellenistic metaphysical and epistemological rationalism. BIBLIOGRAPHY: V. Lossky, *Mystical Theology of the Eastern Church,* (1957).

[T. HOPKO]

APOPHTHEGMATA PATRUM, a collection of sayings of the Fathers. Among the Coptic monks of the 4th and 5th cent. instruction was commonly given by older monks and ascetics to their disciples by word of mouth in terse form. These sayings were sometimes written down, and various collections of them were made in the 5th and 6th centuries. The recording and gathering of such sayings was generally done in Greek by literate monks rather than in the original Coptic in which they had been spoken. The best known collection is that published by J. B. Cotelier in *Ecclesiae Graecae monumenta* I (1677; repr. PG 65:71–440). This collection of sayings and stories is extant in Greek, Latin, Coptic, Armenian, Ethiopic, and Syriac forms. It is valuable as a source for the history of monasticism. BIBLIOGRAPHY:

A. Wand, NCE 1:678; Quasten 3:187–189; F. Cavallera, DSAM 1:766–770.

[R. B. ENO]

APORIA (Gr., *aporia*) a term used in Greek philosophy to indicate perplexity in the face of a difficult question, which is to be resolved by finding the right approach or explanation. It plays an essential role in the Socratic method of questioning as exemplified in Plato's *Apology* and especially in the Platonic dialogues in which Socrates is a major character. It is used likewise in the later polemic of the New Academy against the Stoics and Epicureans. Its Platonic employment is usually ironic in tone. Aristotle, however, made *aporia* an essential part of his methodology in his preliminary approach to a new field of knowledge and its problems. BIBLIOGRAPHY: LexAW 223.

[M. R. P. MCGUIRE]

APOSTASY (Gr., revolt), the renunciation of a previous loyalty, ordinarily religious. Like its antonym, *conversion, it is a complex human reality involving a change in the principle(s) that control the synthesis and direction of life. In fact what may be objectively apostasy both from moral and canonical considerations may psychologically and subjectively appear as a conversion in its primordial sense of a change *from* something to something else. Nevertheless the pejorative connotation of such "de-conversion" remains strong, since reasons for it are quite often of a somewhat weak value from an objective and critical perspective. In its theological sense, apostasy represents a departure from God in varying degrees according as the apostate was previously united with God by faith and profession alone, by the living of faith in obedient love, or by some special connection, e.g., vows or sacred orders. Thus RC canon law deals with apostates from the religious life and sacred orders as well as those who are apostates in the complete sense, i.e., from the faith. Such disbelief does not entail a transfer to a non-Christian religion or even transfer to another Christian Church; apostasy is essentially a departure. (ThAq ST 2a2ae, 12.1).

[U. VOLL]

APOSTATE, one who stands apart or who abandons his beliefs (Acts 21.21 and Th 2.3). These two strands embody both the Greek and Hebrew understanding of the word. Its usage became general around the time of Julian the Apostate (see Augustine *Civ Dei* 5:21). It can also mean abandonment of religious life or of orders (ThAq ST 2a2ae, 12.1). A baptized believer who abandons faith totally or who rejects an essential truth is labeled an apostate. Under Justinian even civil penalties were administered because of apostasy. The Vatican Council II decree on religious liberty gives a response to the questions of previous generations about liberty. Earlier, 19th-cent. German theologians had raised questions about the subjective and objective aspects of apostasy. The magisterium of the Church as represented in Vat II RelFreed,

rejects coercion and affirms the obligation of fidelity of truth.

[J. R. RIVELLO]

APOSTLE (from the Gr. *apostellein,* to send), a title commonly given to the 12 principal followers of Christ. According to Matthew (10.2–4), they were Simon Peter and his brother Andrew, James and John of Zebedee, Philip and Bartholomew, Thomas and Matthew, James of Alphaeus and Thaddaeus, Simon and Judas Iscariot. Acts (1.13–14) gives the same list, minus Iscariot, and substitutes the name Jude for Thaddaeus. After the Ascension, Matthias was chosen by lot to succeed Judas Iscariot (Acts 1.26). Paul is regularly called an Apostle in the Acts and Epistles. Although Barnabas is sometimes given the title, tradition does not consider him an Apostle in the same sense as the rest.

Christ conferred on the Apostles the threefold office he had received from the Father: to teach, to rule, and to sanctify. Thus he told them to "make disciples of all the nations" (Mt 28.19). He gave them such authority that "whatever you bind on earth shall be considered bound in heaven; whatever you loose on earth shall be considered loosed in heaven" (Mt 18.18). He communicated to them, among other gifts, the ability to reenact what he had done at the Last Supper: "Do this as a memorial of me" (Lk 22.19); and the power of remitting sins: "As the Father sent me, so I am sending you . . . . For those whose sins you forgive, they are forgiven; for those whose sins you retain, they are retained" (Jn 20.21,23).

These apostolic prerogatives were not merely functional but inherent in the sacramental powers they received from Christ. The Apostles, therefore, were not only commissioned to carry on his work, but consecrated to do so. Their right to teach, govern, and sanctify was intrinsic to their office and included the reception of all the graces necessary to exercise their apostolate effectively for the people of God. They were also empowered by Christ to transmit the essentials of this threefold office to their successors in the ministry by laying on of hands. This is the basis for the historical episcopate and presbyterate, and the fundamental reason why the Church is called apostolic.

The apostles were not only individually called by Christ and sent into the world in his name; they were also a collegial community, bound together by their common loyalty to him and intended by him to work together, under Peter, as the nucleus of his Church.

Among the special privileges generally ascribed to the Apostles were individual infallibility in matters of faith and morals, personal confirmation in grace, and universal jurisdiction, at least implicitly subject to Peter. All but John are believed to have died martyrs.

Among the conditions for being an Apostle, those mentioned by Peter before the election of Matthias were crucial: "We must therefore choose someone who has been with us the whole time that the Lord Jesus was traveling with us, someone who was with us right from the time when John was baptizing until the day when He was taken up from us—and he can act with us as witness to His Resurrection'' (Acts 1.21–22). By this norm Paul was an exception, as he admitted, yet valid because of a special call from Christ (1 Cor 9.1; 15.9–10).

In a wider sense, the term apostle is applied to those leaders who first planted the Church in various countries, e.g., Patrick in Ireland, Boniface in Germany, Cyril and Methodius among the Slavs.

Apostle is the name given to the epistle read in the liturgy of the Eastern Churches. In the East this is from one of the Apostles or the Acts, and never from the OT. The book containing such readings is likewise an apostle.

In several denominations, apostles are church officials of high rank, e.g., among the Latter-Day Saints and in the Catholic Apostolic Church. BIBLIOGRAPHY: F. Klostermann, *Das Christliche Apostolat* (1962); M. L. Held and F. Klostermann, NCE 1:679–682.

[J. A. HARDON]

APOSTLE, THIRTEENTH, a title used on occasion by certain patriarchs in the Eastern Church. The Melchite patriarch of Antioch on solemn occasions is styled ''The most blessed, holy and venerable chief and head, Patriarch of the great cities of God, Antioch, Alexandria, and Jerusalem, of Cilicia, Syria and Iberia, of Arabia, Mesopotamia and the Pentapolis, of Ethiopia, Egypt, and all the East, (N.), Father of fathers, Shepherd of shepherds, High Priest of high priests, and Thirteenth Apostle.'' Attwater CCE 1:107.

[A. J. JACOPIN]

APOSTLES, COUNCIL OF, the meeting of the Apostles in Jerusalem held *c*.52 A.D. described in Acts 15. It was there determined that converts to Christianity from paganism were not to be bound by the prescriptions of the Jewish law, particularly circumcision. But they were simply obliged to abstain from meat offered to idols, fornication, meat of strangled animals, and blood. By the acts of this council the infant Church broke out of the narrow confines of Judaism and assured the Gentiles and all men of their admission as full members of the Christian fellowship.

[P. FOSCOLOS]

APOSTLES, ICONOGRAPHY OF THE. In Early Christian art the establishment of the Church is shown by the Apostles seated to the left and right of Christ; the expansion of the Church by standing Apostles converging toward Christ. At times the Apostles gather around Christ who holds the victorious cross. On sarcophagi fragments crowns are held by the hand of God over the heads of the Apostles, or a crown is presented by the Apostles to Christ as Roman provinces sent the *aurum coronarium* to the head of State.

The Apostles as 12 lambs converge on the *Agnus Dei* on a mount or as 12 doves surround the monogram of Christ. Above the heads of the Apostles were written at times the names of their missions (''Spania'' above St. James). The Apostles' mission and Pentecost are fused in Romanesque

Apocalyptic MSS and portals where with the 24 Elders the Apostles attend the *Majestas Domini*. The 12 columns of early rotund churches and columns in naves signified the Apostles as supports of the Church. The Apostles in Ottonian art are placed on the shoulders of the Prophets, noting the inspiration of their preaching. In the Renaissance Giotto and other masters presented the Apostles historically, often in narrative panels. Apostle figures were used decoratively in the Renaissance and 17th century (e.g., spoons).

The symbols of individual Apostles are considered in their biographies. BIBLIOGRAPHY: P. Verdier, NCE 1:682–687.

[M. J. DALY]

APOSTLES, DISPERSION OF THE, see DISPERSION OF THE APOSTLES.

APOSTLES, EPISTLE OF THE, see APOCRYPHA (NEW TESTAMENT), 8.

APOSTLES, EQUAL OF THE, see ISAPOSTOLOS.

APOSTLES, LITURGY OF THE, see ADDAI AND MARI, ANAPHORA OF SS.

APOSTLES, SUCCESSORS OF, see APOSTOLIC SUCCESSION.

APOSTLES, TROPHIES OF, the tombs of the Apostles Peter and Paul, at Rome. The expression was used by a Roman priest Gaius in a controversy in the early 3d century (see Eusebius, *Hist. eccl.* 2.25; 3.31). The tomb of St. Peter, as it existed at that time, is sometimes called the *trophaeum Gaii*.

[P. K. MEAGHER]

APOSTLES' CREED, a *creed, authorship of which was for centuries attributed to the Apostles, and which enjoys a high degree of authority in Churches of the West. References to a *Symbolum Apostolorum* occur from the 4th cent., and Rufinus of Aquileia, writing in 404, relates that the Apostles composed a creed. The first known written version of the Apostles' Creed as we have it is in the *Scarapsus* by Priminius of Reichenau, written between 710 and 724. Rufinus wrote of the creed in use at Aquileia (S Italy), which differed only slightly from the ancient *Roman Creed. This formulary achieved stability only by the 4th cent., but in substance it can be clearly traced to *c*.190 in both Greek and Latin texts. The legend of apostolic authorship does reflect the witness by Justin Martyr, Irenaeus, and Tertullian to a ''rule of faith'' handed down by the Apostles. Actual creedal formularies were devised for candidates for baptism, as, e.g., the *Apostolic Tradition* of Hippolytus (*c*.170–*c*.236) indicates. The creeds were passed down orally in the era of persecution. The Apostles' Creed slightly amplifies the Roman Creed, and is in fact a link with the faith of the primitive Church.

Many authorities see the emphasis of this creed upon Jesus Christ as an elaboration of St. Peter's confession in Mt 16.16; and its arrangement according to the Three Divine Persons as the development of the baptismal formula in Mt 18.19. The articles of the Apostles' Creed are simple statements, admitting of ready substantiation in Scripture. Criticism or difficulties blocking its acceptance are those inherent in the Bible itself and in the whole Christian message. Early in the Middle Ages this creed became part of the baptismal ritual, of daily liturgical offices, and even of private prayers. At the time of the Reformation, it was accepted as a *doctrinal standard by the main Protestant traditions; it continues to be used widely in worship. It remains the principal *ecumenical creed in the West, because of its widespread acceptance, and because, as the *Lambeth Conference of 1920 and the *Lausanne Conference (1929) of *Faith and Order suggested, it provides a possible basis for agreement among Christians. BIBLIOGRAPHY: D 10–36; J. N. D. Kelly, *Early Christian Creeds* (2d ed., 1960); W. Pannenberg, *Apostles' Creed: In the Light of Today's Questions* (1972).

[T. C. O'BRIEN]

APOSTLESHIP OF PRAYER, RC Association emphasizing special devotion to the *Sacred Heart of Jesus. Founded at Vals, France in 1844 by F. X. Gautrelet, SJ, it received formal statutes from Leo XIII in 1879 (revised in 1896 and 1951). The general of the Society of Jesus serves as director, and American headquarters are in New York City. The association reported about 40 million members in 1969, with three degrees of membership according to the rule of devotion undertaken.

[T. EARLY]

APOSTLESHIP OF THE SEA (*Opus Apostolatus Maris),* international RC association for ministry to seamen. Founded in 1920 in Glasgow, Scotland, by RC laymen, it received approval from Pius XI 2 years later. A general secretariat was established at Rome in 1952, and in 1957 Pius XII promulgated a series of laws and statutes for the organization. Chaplains of the apostleship serve seafarers both on ship and in port, particularly those in ports away from their own country. BIBLIOGRAPHY: T. McDonough, "Apostolatus Maris. What's That?" OssRom (Eng.) no. 23 (219) 8 (1972).

[T. EARLY]

APOSTOLATE, a generic term to describe the Church's function of "extending the kingdom of Christ throughout the world for the glory of God the Father . . . and to direct the whole universe to him [Christ] through the instrumentality of men" (Vat II ApostLaity 2). Essentially it is an extension of Christ's commission to the Apostles, sending (cf. Gr. *apostellein,* to send) them into the world to preach the gospel to all nations. Its object, therefore, is to bring Christ to others; its purpose is the greater glory of God; its scope is the whole world; and its means is every form of human agency by which the life of grace may be infused or increased in the souls of men.

Bringing Christ to others implies the possession of Christ, by faith, in the apostle and its absence or deficiency in someone else. Apostolic effort is thus based on the Pauline principle that there is no spontaneous generation in the spiritual life any more than in biology. Christians reproduce other Christians, since "faith comes from what is preached" (Rom 10.17); and, as St. Paul told the Corinthians, "it was I who begot you in Christ Jesus by preaching the Good News" (1 Cor 4.15). Besides preaching of the Word, the apostolate includes bringing Christ to others in the sacraments, either by actual administration or by due preparation of those who are to receive.

The goal of the apostolate is to advance the glory of God. Every sinner converted, every unbeliever brought to the faith, every believer deepened in his knowledge and love of the Creator and Redeemer increases the loving recognition that is the external glory of God.

The apostolate is Catholic, i.e., universal by the will of him who "wants everyone to be saved" (1 Tm 2.4). It is moreover universal in the duty it imposes. Those who bind themselves by special dedication to the Church's service, as in the priesthood or religious life, are gravely obligated to be apostles to their fellowmen. Yet all Christians are bound, in virtue of their baptism, to share with others the spiritual riches that they have received.

Finally, the apostolate is almost infinite in the variety of ways available to Christians to bring Christ and his message into the lives of others. Vatican Council II particularly stressed the opportunities currently open to the laity to join forces with the hierarchy in advancing the kingdom of Christ both in the Church and in the world. In the first area, "their activity is so necessary within church communities that without it the apostolate of the pastors is normally unable to achieve full effectiveness" (Vat II ApostLaity 10). On the second level, "the layman is called by God to burn with the spirit of Christ and to exercise his apostolate in the world as a kind of leaven" (*ibid.* 2), since he is in the world, knows its problems and needs, and the world knows him.

Essential to the Catholic apostolate is the mandate from the Church. A person cannot be an apostle of himself. He must have received in some appropriate way the Church's authorization that gives him the right to evangelize, and the assurance of divine assistance in his apostolic labors. BIBLIOGRAPHY: F. Klostermann, NCE 1:688; M. L. Held and F. Klostermann, NCE 1:679–682; F. Klostermann, *Das Christliche Apostolat* (1962).

[J. A. HARDON]

APOSTOLATE AND SPIRITUAL LIFE. In a strict and somewhat antiquated sense of the word, apostolate refers to all ecclesial activity directed to man's spiritual perfection. Within this frame of reference, the apostolate was seen to be exercised almost exclusively by religious and was often thought of as an activity distinct from the search for spiritual perfection. The dedicated religious had to avoid the trap of excessive activism, even in apostolic concerns, in order to assure his growth in the spiritual life. Thus a false dichotomy was established between the apostolate and the spiritual life. This estimate has radically changed in recent years through two new perspectives: a deeper appreciation of a nonmonastic spirituality which stresses sanctification through the active apostolate, and a wider notion of apostolic activity itself. Thus, esp. in regard to the diocesan priest, many contemporary spiritual writers emphasize that the following of Christ is achieved in the ministry itself and not only through specifically spiritual activities. In addition, the apostolate itself is now seen to include all activity that would extend the kingdom of God, contribute to the amelioration of social institutions, and insure a more fully human life. Thus, as Vat II ApostLaity notes, every Christian is called to the apostolate since the duty and right to exercise the apostolate derives from union with Christ and is imparted through the sacraments of baptism, confirmation, and the Eucharist. As Christian faith, hope, and love grow, the need of living for the cause of Christ becomes more intense. On the other hand, as one attends to the duties of his state in life, the need to remain close to Christ and to live by the light of the gospels should increasingly grow. The apostolate and spiritual life, therefore, mutually presuppose and aid one another. BIBLIOGRAPHY: J. B. Chautard, *Soul of the Apostolate* (tr. J. A. Moran, 1941); G. Thils, *Diocesan Priest* (tr. A. J. LaMothe, 2d ed., 1964); F. Cuttaz, DSAM 1:773–790; F. Klostermann, Vorgrimler 3:273–405.

[T. M. MCFADDEN]

APOSTOLATE OF THE SICK. The term is applicable to the sick themselves as well as to those who minister to the sick. In the first sense the sick have the opportunity to offer the pain and loneliness they sustain as a form of reparation, not so much for themselves (though not exclusive of this either) as for the community of the faithful. In another sense, there is a discreet and unique apostolate that beckons all Christians to fulfill the commitment of their confirmation and the challenge of the Sermon on the Mount. Historically, the visitation of God to someone through affliction of sickness was looked upon as retribution and divine punishment, at least in the OT. There still is evidence of this in the NT (Jn 9.2). That sickness is an evil to be overcome and for the cure of which man must strive is attested to by Christ himself who worked countless miracles for the cure of illness (Mk 2.1–12; Jn 5.1–15) in compassion for the sick. In reference to the OT belief that sickness is believed by some to be a divine punishment, one is directed to Christ's response in the NT to his Disciples that neither the man blind from birth nor his parents have sinned. In any case, the occurrence of sickness or physical disability is not to be taken as a retribution, since to do so would free the Christian from the responsibility of ministering to the sick and, at the same time, it would ascribe to God a motive which is clearly an absurdity. On the other hand, to say that sickness is an evil denotes, quite

straightforwardly, that all are subject to the effect of evil and wrongdoing and, as such subjects, are candidates for the redemptive and salvific merits of Christ. Without these elemental insights into the meaning and existence of suffering and its possibility in his own life, man is bound and helpless in a Nietzschean absurdity that holds the Christian exigence of oblatory sickness as nothing more than glorification of weakness through acceptance of it. BIBLIOGRAPHY: M. Scaduto, NCE 3:483b, 490c, s.v. "Charity, Works of"; J.-C. Didier, SacMund 3:98–100 s.v. "Illness"; L. M. Weber, LTK 6:593–595 s.v. "Krankheit."

[J. R. RIVELLO]

APOSTOLIC, an adjective used to indicate that something (e.g., a time, a community, a spirit, a doctrine) is closely related to the Apostles. The term has been used differently in different places, and the meaning, esp. in its more or less technical application, has not always been the same. The earliest recorded use was by Ignatius of Antioch (d. *c*.107 A.D.), who greeted the Trallians as having an apostolic character. In the East the term was commonly applied from the late 2d cent. to Churches, persons, or writings that had some historical connection with the Apostles. By extension, the term was also applied to Churches that were orthodox in their teaching. Among Western writers, at least since Tertullian (*c*.160–*c*.220), those Churches were generally called apostolic that were actually founded, or at least had somehow been governed, by an Apostle. They consequently enjoyed special dignity and acquired apologetic importance when the authentic apostolic faith was being controverted with the Gnostics, Arians, Pelagians, and Donatists. After some of these historically apostolic Churches had lapsed from orthodoxy in the 4th and 5th cent., the term shifted from local communities to the Church at large, and this designation has remained constant to the present day. One exception is the Church of Rome, the apostolic character of which was commonly recognized throughout the patristic age, e.g., in Vincent of Lérins (d. before 450), who speaks of Rome as the Apostolic See (*Commonit.* 6). Apostolic was the touchstone of orthodoxy of doctrine in the early centuries, even as apostolicity later became the mark of genuineness of the Church when challenged by competitive ecclesial communities. In Tertullian's classic statement, "We have to show whether our doctrine . . . is derived from apostolic teaching and whether, therefore, other doctrines have their origin in a lie" (*De praescr. haer.* 21). At the present time, apostolic has become a generic adjective in Christian literature to describe a person, place, doctrine, or institution that either derives from the Apostles or reflects their spirit, e.g., in the work of evangelization. BIBLIOGRAPHY: H. Bacht, LTK 1:758–759; F. Klostermann, NCE 1:689.

[J. A. HARDON]

APOSTOLIC AGE, a term in use since Tertullian's *De praescriptione haereticorum* and Pseudo-Justin's *Quaestiones et responsiones ad orthodoxos* to designate the period that coincides with the activity of the Apostles and their close associates. It is generally considered to begin with Pentecost, probably in A.D. 30, and to end about the close of the 1st century. The Christian community at Jerusalem was for a time the focal point from which missionary activity extended to various sectors of the Mediterranean area. The second coming of Christ was regarded as imminent. Many Christian communities held all worldly possessions in common. Though eyewitnesses of the life and ministry of Christ were still alive, false prophets and heretical teachings appeared. Information gleaned from the NT points to urban-centered Christian communities in this period. BIBLIOGRAPHY: J. Daniélou, H. Marrou, *Christian Centuries* (1964) 1:3–16.

[H. DRESSLER]

APOSTOLIC BLESSING, the blessing given by the pope, usually at Mass, on certain special occasions, e.g., at Easter, on the feast of SS. Peter and Paul, or immediately after his election. Bishops may give the apostolic blessing twice a year; priests may bestow it upon the dying or at the end of a mission or retreat. A plenary indulgence is attached.

[T. M. MCFADDEN]

APOSTOLIC CAMERA, see CAMERA, APOSTOLIC.

APOSTOLIC CANONS, a collection of 85 canons found in the last part of the eighth book of the *Apostolic Constitutions. These canons, like the Constitutions themselves, were falsely attributed to the Apostles. Most of the canons concern the duties and conduct of the clergy; 20 of them are based on the decrees of the Council of *Antioch (341). The last canon gives a list of the canonical books of Scripture, including the two epistles of Clement and the Apostolic Constitutions. Through a 6th-cent. Latin translation, the first 50 of these canons were widely known in the West in early medieval times. Text: ed. F. X. Funk, *Didascalia et Constitutiones Apostolorum* (1905) 1:564–593.

[R. B. ENO]

APOSTOLIC CHURCH ORDER, a document from the early Church containing moral precepts and canonical legislation. It was originally in Greek *c*. 300, probably in Egypt, but the Greek text was not published until 1843. The treatise claims apostolic authorship, its first section (4–14) being based on the moral doctrine of the Two Ways as set forth in the *Didache. The second half (15–29) regulates the elections of bishops, priests, and other church officers. Besides the Greek text, early versions have survived in Latin and in several Eastern languages. Greek text: *Die Allgemeine Kirchenordnung* (ed. T. Schermann, 1914) 1:12–34. Coptic text with Eng. tr. and Arabic-Ethiopic texts with Eng. tr. ed. G. Horner, *Statutes of the Apostles* (1904). BIBLIOGRAPHY: V. G. Bartlet, *Church Life and Church Order during the First Four Centuries* (1943); Quasten 2:119–120.

[R. B. ENO]

APOSTOLIC CHURCHES, a term often used to designate churches founded or governed by one of the Apostles, e.g., the Apostolic See of Rome founded by St. Peter, Alexandria (St. Mark), Antioch (St. Peter), Jerusalem (St. James the Less), Athens (St. Paul), Cyprus (St. Barnabas).

APOSTOLIC COLLEGE, a phrase with two meanings: the 12 Apostles considered as a particular entity or body, holding a special place in the Church as witnesses to the Resurrection and original proclaimers of the Gospel; those Roman institutions (e.g., Collegio Propaganda Fidei) which are under the immediate care and direction of the Holy See.

[T. M. MCFADDEN]

APOSTOLIC CONSTITUTION, a type of papal decree concerning the faith and/or important concerns of the Church. It is more universal in scope than a papal *bull, but not addressed to all bps. as an *encyclical. An apostolic constitution is signed by the pope if it concerns a dogmatic definition, or by an official of the Roman Congregation to whose jurisdiction its contents pertain. BIBLIOGRAPHY: J. A. Forgac, NCE 1:689.

[T. M. MCFADDEN]

APOSTOLIC CONSTITUTIONS, a collection in eight books of ecclesiastical law from the early Church. The document as a whole, and esp. in the 85 *Apostolic Canons with which it ends, is supposed to be of apostolic origin, but it is in fact a 4th-cent. compilation made by a Syrian writer who was probably a Semi-Arian. It derives from various early sources, some of which are clearly recognizable: the *Didascalia Apostolorum*, the *Didache*, the *Apostolic Tradition* of Hippolytus, and the Antiochene liturgy. It was suggested by J. Ussher that the compiler of this collection was also the author of the spurious epistles in the corpus of Ignatius of Antioch. The chief value of the work lies in the witness it gives to early ecclesiastical discipline and worship. Text: PG 1:555–1156. BIBLIOGRAPHY: Altaner 57–59.

[R. B. ENO]

APOSTOLIC DATARY, see DATARY, APOSTOLIC.

APOSTOLIC DELEGATION IN THE U.S., the official representative body for the Holy See in its religious dealings with the Church in the U.S. Such a delegation usually exists in those countries that have no nunciature, i.e., an agency that provides a channel for regular diplomatic and political relations between a particular country and the Vatican. In general, the apostolic delegate serves as a liaison between the Holy See and the U.S. Church; he informs the Holy See of ecclesiastical affairs, and conveys papal decisions to the persons concerned. More specifically, the delegate advises the Holy See on the establishment or division of dioceses, the status of religious orders, the qualifications of those considered for the episcopacy, the granting of dispensations, and may be asked to act as an intermediary in disputes between religious superiors and their subordinates. There have been nine delegates to the U.S. since 1893.

The first attempts (1853) to establish an apostolic delegation in the U.S. were rejected by the American bps., in spite of an affirmative recommendation by Abp. Gaetano Bedini. The bps. feared that accusations of foreign allegiance would harm the American Church if diplomatic representatives were exchanged (see KNOWN-NOTHINGISM). In succeeding decades, various visitators served as apostolic delegates for specific purposes, and petitions were made by several churchmen for a permanent delegation, but the general attitude among the U.S. hierarchy was negative. The matter came to a climax in the 1890s. The bps. opposed a delegation for fear of a diminution of their authority, and the prospect of a foreign observer reporting on matters that would be difficult for him to understand seemed both inevitable and undesirable. The Holy See, on the other hand, wished to establish a more direct connection with the U.S. Church and did not feel that this could be done impartially by an American observer. In addition, the Vatican wished to oversee the neglected observance of juridical procedure in various dioceses, and to adjudicate the major disagreement regarding the establishment of religious schools. In view of these reasons, Pope Leo XIII appointed Abp. Francesco *Satolli as the first apostolic delegate to the U.S. BIBLIOGRAPHY: R. Trisco, NCE 1:690–693 with bibliography.

[T. M. MCFADDEN]

APOSTOLIC FATHERS, a term that designates a group of early Christian writers who actually or reputedly had personal contacts with the Apostles. In this meaning the term in the 17th cent. included Clement of Rome, Ignatius of Antioch, Polycarp of Smyrna, the authors of the *Shepherd of Hermas* and of the *Epistle of Barnabas.* Subsequently the *Letter to Diognetus,* fragments of Papias of Hierapolis, of Quadratus, the so-called presbyter sections of Irenaeus, and the *Didache* were added. Since 1956 the term has come to be restricted to Clement of Rome (*I Epistle to the Corinthians*), Ignatius of Antioch (seven *Letters*), Polycarp of Smyrna (two *Letters*), and the Quadratus fragment. The works of these Fathers closely resemble the Epistles of the Apostles, being occasional writings rather than systematic doctrinal treatises. Nevertheless, they are important witnesses to the life and thought of the Christian communities of the subapostolic age. They present a Christological doctrine that clearly shows belief in Christ as the Son of God, existing before all time, collaborating in the creation of the world, whose second coming is considered imminent. Some of these writings were so highly esteemed by the early Christians that they were for a time considered to belong to the inspired writings of the NT. BIBLIOGRAPHY: Altaner 97–113; J. Fischer, NCE 1:693–694; *Early Christian Writings: The Apostolic Fathers* (tr. M. Staniforth, 1973).

[H. DRESSLER]

APOSTOLIC KING, a title given by Pope Sylvester II to St. Stephen I, King of Hungary, in sending him the royal crown he had requested. The title was regarded as the hereditary privilege of the successors of St. Stephen and was used also by the Austrian emperors in their capacity as kings of Hungary.

[P. K. MEAGHER]

APOSTOLIC LETTERS, both a specific and generic title for several forms of papal communication. As a specific form, apostolic letters may be either composed in the pope's name, usually by the Roman Curia, or signed by the pope himself. As a generic title, other types of papal documents such as *encyclicals and *motu proprio's* fall within this classification.

[T. M. MCFADDEN]

APOSTOLIC SEE, in a general sense, a local church or diocese that was, or was thought to have been, founded (organized or directed) in apostolic times by the Apostles themselves or by men closely associated with the Apostles in the work of evangelization. In postapostolic times when disputes arose about doctrine and discipline, such Churches and their bishops were often appealed to as esp. conspicuous guarantors of the apostolic tradition. In the course of time, as is evident in the writings of Cyprian, Optatus, Jerome, and others, the title was accorded in a special sense to the Roman Church because it possessed the chair or see of Peter. Thus the Roman see came to be called *the* Apostolic See (e.g., in the writings of Pope Damasus I), and this usage has been maintained down to the present time in the RC Church. In this sense the term is used abstractly to designate the power and authority of the pope as the present occupant of the chair of Peter as this is exercised, not only by the Roman pontiff personally but also through the congregations, tribunals, and offices that the pope has named to assist him in conducting the affairs of the universal Church (CIC c. 7; the names and duties of the agencies are catalogued under *CURIA, ROMAN. BIBLIOGRAPHY: H. Leclercq, DACL 15.1:1427–31; R. A. Graham, *Vatican Diplomacy* (1959).

[S. E. DONLON]

APOSTOLIC SUCCESSION, in RC teaching, the relationship of the bishops of the Church to the Apostles, to whom Christ gave the commission summarized in Mt 28.18–20. The development of a theory of apostolic succession was preceded by its acceptance in practice. In the 2d cent., Gnostic claims to a secret doctrinal tradition provided the first occasion for conscious reflection on the existing practice. The historians Papias and Hegesippus argued that the doctrinal agreement of all local Churches having an uninterrupted line of bishops going back to the Apostles authenticated their teaching against Gnostic claims. Similar agreements were given by Irenaeus (*Adv. haer.* 3.3.1) and Tertullian, who first used the expression *ordo episcoporum* (*Adv. Marc.* 4.5.2). The position that only a minister incorporated into the apostolic succession through valid ordination can validly administer certain sacraments was developed by medieval scholastics, reflecting on the existing practice of the Church. They also developed a distinction between "material" apostolic succession (valid reception of the sacrament of orders) and "formal" apostolic succession (valid orders, plus communion with the college of bishops under the pope, successor of Peter and center of the unity of the episcopal college). RC theologians have considered the relationship of bishops belonging to the material apostolic succession but separated from the bishops in communion with the pope to be analogous to the relationship of non-Roman Christians to the RC Church. Both cases present a host of questions that are controverted in RC theology.

The older view of apostolic succession emphasized the uninterrupted chain of episcopal consecrations, which in theory permits every bishop (and through him the clergy he has ordained) to trace his commission back to one of the Apostles. Since Vatican Council II apostolic succession has been viewed more in terms of incorporation into a collegial body, the original members of which were the Apostles (Vat II ConstCh, 21). Although the bishops are collectively the successors of the Apostles (*ibid.*, 20), the Apostles had a unique status because of their special personal relationship with Christ, the one foundation of the Church (SEE I Cor 3.11). The Apostles were appointed to build up the Church on the foundation Christ had laid (SEE Eph 2.2; Rev 21.14; Mt 16.18). They passed on their commission to others, who came to be called bishops. The Pastoral Epistles teach that the bishop's first task is to transmit faithfully to others the apostolic teaching, thus maintaining the *local Church in the foundation laid down by its apostolic founder (SEE 2 Tim 1.6 and 13; 2.2; 1 Tim 3.2; Tit 1.9).

The 16th-century Reformers fought not so much for or against apostolic succession as such, as for the true Church, which, according to the *Augsburg Confession, was to be found only where God's word was rightly preached. Luther taught that the only true bishops were those who succeeded the Apostles not locally or historically but in teaching the apostolic gospel. In his *Institutes of the Christian Religion (4.7.23) Calvin recognized apostolic succession in theory but said that it was necessary to abandon it in practice because the bishops had erred from the truth. Anglicanism has preserved an intact historical succession with the pre-Reformation hierarchy and insists on the necessity of the *historic episcopate, while refusing to impose any doctrine about this episcopate or to condemn the ministries of Protestant Churches that, because of historical circumstances, lack episcopacy. Though contemporary Anglican teaching about apostolic succession often approximates the RC doctrine (while denying the papal primacy and infallibility as defined at Vatican Council I), more Protestant views enjoy equal

rights in Anglicanism. In practice Anglican insistence on episcopacy has proved a major barrier to reunion with Protestant Churches.

The question of the ministry is a crucial dogmatic difficulty in contemporary ecumenical discussion (SEE CONSULTATION ON CHURCH UNION), but a certain reconciliation of views is discernible since Vatican Council II. RC theologians are striving to soften the rigid juridical positions of the past, and many Protestants show a certain awareness of the value of apostolic succession and episcopacy in constituting and guarding doctrinal and sacramental unity. BIBLIOGRAPHY: *L'Épiscopat et l'église universelle* (ed. Y. Congar and D. Depuy, 1962); H. Küng, *Structures of the Church* (1965); *idem, Church* (1968); K. Rahner and J. Ratzinger, *Episcopate and Primacy* (tr. K. Barker, 1962); *Apostolic Ministry* (ed. K. E. Kirk, 1957); A. Ehrhardt, *Apostolic Ministry* (1958).

[J. J. HUGHES]

APOSTOLIC TRADITION, an early Church order written *c.*215 and generally considered the work of *Hippolytus. It gives valuable information about the Christian community at Rome and new insights into the history of its liturgy. Only excerpts of the original Greek are extant through quotations in later documents. There are translations of the complete text in Coptic, Arabic, Ethiopic, and Latin. The work consists of three parts. The first treats of the consecration of bishops, the Eucharistic Liturgy, ordination of priests and deacons, and various blessings. The second lists laws for the laity, and the third deals with ecclesiastical practices. The *Apostolic Tradition* exerted its greatest influence in the East where it played an important role in the development of the liturgy and canon law. BIBLIOGRAPHY: Altaner 55; J. Daniélou and H. Marrou, *Christian Centuries* (1964) 144–151; B. Botte, *La Tradition apostolique de Saint Hippolyte* (1963).

[H. DRESSLER]

APOSTOLIC UNION, an association of secular priests founded by Ven. Bartholomew Holzhouser of Bavaria in the 17th cent., reorganized in France in the 19th cent. by Canon Lebeurier, and authorized by papal brief of Pius IX (1862). The observance of its simple rule, which reflected the ordinary responsibilities and spirit of the priestly state, was intended to promote the faithful fulfillment of priestly duties. Pius X, himself a member of the association, commended its advantage and its growth throughout Europe, America, and Asia. BIBLIOGRAPHY: J. McMahon, CE 1:643–644; L. Piovesana, "Apostolic Union from Pope Leo XIII to Pope Paul VI," OssRom (Eng.) No. 15 (263) 9 (1973).

[F. H. BRIGHAM]

APOSTOLICAE CURAE, the bull issued by Leo XIII on Sept. 13, 1896, which confirmed the existing RC practice of treating the orders of convert Anglican clergy as invalid by declaring that "ordinations carried out according to the Anglican rite have been and are absolutely null and utterly void." The document was occasioned by a reunion campaign started in the 1890s (with astonishing initial success) by the Anglican Lord *Halifax and the Abbé *Portal, and aimed at initiating a theological dialogue between their two Churches. An eight-man papal commission was set up in the spring of 1896 to investigate Anglican orders. In 1910 Card. Merry del Val, who had been secretary of the commission, stated in a private letter that at the end of the secret proceedings the case for validity had been lost by one vote. Heavy pressure for a negative verdict was brought on the Holy See by F. A. (later Card.) Gasquet acting on behalf of Card. Vaughan and the English RC hierarchy. On July 16, 1896, the cardinals of the Holy Office in the presence of Leo XIII unanimously passed the negative verdict subsequently promulgated in *Apostolicae curae*. The Secretary of State, Card. Rampolla, who had been friendly to the Anglicans in the preceding reunion campaign, absented himself from this meeting. The bull was drafted by 31-year-old Merry del Val. Beginning at Vatican II demands have been raised by RC theologians that the case be reopened. BIBLIOGRAPHY: J. J. Hughes, *Absolutely Null and Utterly Void* (1968). *ANGLICAN ORDERS.

[J. J. HUGHES]

APOSTOLICI (Apostolics), a name used by the following groups: (1) Apostolici was an alternate name for the Apotactics, a 3d–4th-cent. communal group in the East. (2) The Apostolici in 12th-cent. France and the Rhineland were obscurely connected with eastern Manichaeism. Members often outwardly conformed to the Church, but their aim was antihierarchical; in the Rhineland they apparently attracted many followers, including clerics. St. Bernard of Clairvaux preached and wrote against the Rhineland Apostolici (PL 183:1088–1102). The Apostolici practiced vegetarianism and celibate cohabitation but without a marriage contract; they rejected oaths, veneration of saints, prayers for the dead, and infant baptism. Some claimed that the power of eucharistic consecration was shared by all and was to be exercised at every meal. (see E. W. McDonnell, NCE 1:698–699; S. Runciman, *Medieval Manichee* [1961] 119–20) (3) The Apostolici of the 13th and 14th cent. were adherents of a lay evangelical movement begun at Parma by Gerard *Segarelli as a return to the apostolic life of poverty, penance, and preaching. The founder's attacks on the clergy and the institutional Church stirred rebellion against ecclesiastical authority. Members adopted a distinctive garb but followed no rule and took no vows, being bound together by what Segarelli called interior obedience. Their way of life combined mendicancy, vagabondage, and idleness. Their doctrinal views seem to have been somewhat imprecise until Fra *Dolcino assumed leadership in 1300. A man of considerable talent and a degree of education, he gave the movement a semblance of organization and a doctrine combining

*Joachimism and his own form of *millenarianism. The sect was condemned by a number of popes and councils, and in 1305 Nicholas V finally summoned a crusade to extirpate it. Fra Dolcino was captured and later executed. Small pockets of these Apostolici lingered on into the 15th cent. but exercised no significant influence. BIBLIOGRAPHY: E. Anagnine, *Dolcino e il movimento ereticale all'inizio del trecento* (1964); E. W. McDonnell, NCE 1:698–699; J. M. Vidal, DHGE 3:1038–48.

APOSTOLICI REGIMINIS, a bull published in 1513 by Leo X during the Fifth Lateran Council. Designated as heretical, three propositions were cited: the soul is mortal; all humanity shares a common soul; truth may be double. The bull explicitly states that each man has an individual soul. Because of the influence of pagan ideas gleaned from classical studies, the bull specified that any clergy intending to study advanced philosophical and literary works should first devote 5 years to theology and canon law.

[S. A. HEENEY]

APOSTOLICITY, the abstract nominal form of the adjective "apostolic," one of the four terms used by the Nicene Creed in qualification of the Church. RC theologians have commonly taken the designation as applicable to the Church by reason of its origin, its mission, its doctrine, and its continuity in ministerial succession. As applied to origin it means that the Church is identical with the Church established by the Apostles. In reference to mission, it signifies that like—and through—the Apostles the Church is commissioned by divine mandate to proclaim the person and doctrines of Christ until the end of time. It is apostolic in doctrine because it preserves the deposit of revealed doctrine committed to the Apostles. Its ministerial succession is apostolic because the lineage of the *historic episcopate reaches back in uninterrupted sequence to the Apostles. RC apologetics, which counts apostolicity among the four distinguishing notes or marks of the Church, has developed these themes extensively. It cannot be claimed, however, that apostolicity has proved to be an easily applicable test of the true Church. The scarcity of documentary evidence relating to the primitive Church, and the ambiguity of much that has survived, make the continuity of doctrine, practice, and institutions difficult to prove or disprove. The fact of the historical continuity of the episcopate is perhaps easier to deal with, but this lies outside the concept of apostolicity as understood by many Protestant theologians.

While in Anglicanism the historic episcopate is regarded as essential to the Church, the Protestant Churches long rather ignored apostolicity. Calvin acknowledged the possibility of apostolic succession but abandoned it because in fact the bishops had erred (*Institutes of the Christian Religion*, 4.7.23). The Lutheran view became general, that apostolicity meant fidelity to the witness of the Apostles to the true gospel, not a historical or local succession to them. The rejection of a teaching authority or ministerial priesthood includes a rejection of apostolicity as continuity in a special office of the Church. Generally, apostolicity as "lineal descence," in the words of the *Scots Confession (Art. 18), has had no relevance in Protestantism. Rather it was regarded as one of the claims of Rome from which the Church must be purged. Apostolicity, however, is professed by the historical Protestant Churches. (To Quakers and others who have replaced the historical dimension of Christian faith with inner spiritual experience, this fidelity is not essential.) The desire to keep the preaching of the gospel true to the teaching and witness of the Apostles was one of the motivations of the Reformation. The ideal of restoring the Church to the life of the apostolic Church has motivated the foundation of new Churches. Protestant Churches, as well, share in the acceptance of apostolicity as signifying the Church's continuance of the mission and witness of the Apostles.

As noted above, in RC apologetics, apostolicity is one of the four traditional marks of the Church, as stated in the Nicene Creed, which says, "I believe in one, holy, catholic, and apostolic Church." While the earlier creeds, e.g., the Apostles', do not include the term apostolic, it was already part of the baptismal formula of Epiphanius (c.374). The scriptural basis is St. Paul, who stressed the necessity of a divinely established mission. "How can men preach," he asked, "unless they are sent (apostalōsin)?" (Rom 10.15).

As the need arose for validating the Church's teachings, the norm of apostolicity was first applied to doctrine and then to the Church itself. Applied to doctrine, it meant that a given teaching was orthodox if it had been held since apostolic times. Applied to the Church, it meant that the Catholic Church was the true Church of Christ because it had an unbroken apostolic succession that made it one with the Church of the Apostles in origin, teaching, and divinely authorized mission.

Apostolic origin is verified in the historic episcopate and Roman primacy. Both trace their lineage, respectively, in uninterrupted sequence to the Apostles and to Peter as their appointed head. This lineage is not only individual but corporate, so that the bishops under the pope are not only inheritors of apostolic powers in virtue of their consecration, but the episcopate is apostolic as an organic unity. As expressed by the Vatican Council II: "Just as in the Gospel, the Lord so disposing, St. Peter and the other Apostles constitute one apostolic college, so in a similar way the Roman pontiff, the successor of Peter, and the bishops, the successors of the Apostles, are joined together" (Vat II ConstChurch 22).

The Church's apostolicity is further discernible in the teaching office committed to the Apostles and their successors accurately to preserve, interpret, and proclaim the Person and doctrines of Christ until the end of time. Viewed in this way, the Church is apostolic in the hierarchy to whom Christ gave the right and the duty "to preach the Gospel to every creature, so that all men may attain to salvation by faith, baptism, and the fulfillment of the commandments"

(ibid. 24). In order to insure that this teaching be authentically that of Christ, he endowed his Church with immunity from error in matters essential to salvation. Infallibility is therefore a function of apostolicity.

Finally, the Church is apostolic because, like the Apostles and through them, it has a divine mandate to communicate the good news to all people "until the Lord comes." Christianity is unique among the world's religions in the commission it considers itself to have received to preach Christ to all mankind. More than once the Apostles were given the imperative to go and preach, to baptize and sanctify. St. Paul felt under obligation to share what he had received. "It is a duty which has been laid on me," he believed. "I should be punished if I did not preach it (the gospel)" (1 Cor 9.16).

Accordingly, "the pilgrim Church is missionary by its very nature," seeing itself "divinely sent to the nations of the world to be unto them 'a universal sacrament of salvation' " (Vat II MissAct). In this sense the Church's *mission* (Latin) is the Church's *apostolate* (Greek): to implement the mission of the Son and the Holy Spirit, which is to bring creatures to share, by divine grace, in the Trinitarian life of God. BIBLIOGRAPHY: G. Thils, NCE 1:699–700; id., *Les Notes de l'église dans l'apologétique catholique depuis la réforme* (1937); J. Pelikan, *Riddle of Roman Catholicism* (1950).

[J. A. HARDON]

APOSTOLIKI DIAKONIA, the modern Gr. equivalent of Apostolic Diaconate.

APOSTOLIS, ARSENIOS (1468–1535), Byzantine humanist. The son of Michael Apostolis, he came to the West from Crete and was a teacher of Greek at Florence and Rome, and, for a time, was employed by the famous painter Manutius at Venice. He was only partially successful in his ambition to become abp. of Monemvasia in the E Peloponnesus. In addition to his influence as a teacher of Greek in the West, he is esp. important for his copying of Greek MSS and for his editions of Greek texts, in particular the *scholia* of Euripides (1534). BIBLIOGRAPHY: D. J. Geanakoplos, NCE 1:700–701; id., *Greek Scholars in Venice: Studies in the Dissemination of Greek Learning from Byzantium to Western Europe* (1962) 167–200.

[M. R. P. McGUIRE]

APOSTOLIS, MICHAEL (c.1422–c.1486), Byzantine scholar. Following the sack of Constantinople in 1433, he settled in Candia in Crete. In 1454, he went to Italy where he met the great Byzantine scholar, Card. Bessarion. He was commissioned by the latter to return to the East and search for Greek MSS. He was a successful teacher of Greek and produced some literary work, but he is particularly important for his copying of Greek MSS. He has well been described as a significant connecting link between Byzantine Hellenism in Crete and the rising interest in Greek studies in Venice and elsewhere in Italy. BIBLIOGRAPHY: D. J. Geanakoplos, NCE

1:701; *id., Greek Scholars in Venice: Studies in the Dissemination of Greek Learning from Byzantium to Western Europe* (1962) 73–110.

[M. R. P. MCGUIRE]

APOSTOLOS (Gr. for apostle; Sl., *apostol*), a term with different uses in the Eastern Churches. It may signify: (1) One of the twelve apostles. (2) The first lesson in the Byzantine liturgy taken from the Acts of the Apostles or one of the Epistles chanted directly after the prokimenon verses by the reader. (3) The liturgical book containing extracts of the Acts of the Apostles and the Epistles divided for reading during the ecclesiastical year. It also contains the chants before and after the epistle reading. It owes its name to the fact that the bulk of the readings are selected from St. Paul, "the Apostle." The *Apostolos* is sometimes kept on the altar with the Gospel Book but more usually at the table or shelf on the S side of the altar. The cover of the book, esp. among the Greeks, is sometimes ornamented with metal plates depicting the Apostles and St. Paul supporting a church edifice or a throne. (4) The term is also used to indicate SS. Stachys, Apelles, Amplias, Urban, Aristobulus, and Narcissus, six of the holy persons mentioned by St. Paul in Romans ch. 16.

[A. J. JACOPIN]

APOSTROPHA, in *Gregorian chant notation, a sign used for repeated notes on a single pitch. The neums resulting from two or three of these are termed *bistropha* and *tristropha*, respectively. They indicate a repeated, rather than held, note. The written form in early MSS was a dot with a hook, like a comma or apostrophe, but the modern printed chant books, except for the Milanese books and the *Antiphonale monasticum,* inaccurately replace it with the punctum.

[A. DOHERTY]

APOSTROPHOS, in *Byzantine chant notation, the sign indicating a note one scale step lower than the previous note. Two apostrophos signs together termed *dyo apostrophoi,* double the length of the note rather than indicate two successive descending steps.

[A. DOHERTY]

APOTACTICS (Gr. *apotacticae,* Renuntiants), a sect, also called *Apostolici,* reported to be widespread in the East during the 3rd and 4th centuries. Epiphanius (*Penar.,* 61) is the sole source of information about them. They also called themselves Renuntiants because of their extreme ascetical practices, which included the rejection of marriage and of private property. They probably held other beliefs similar to those of the Tatians, Encratites and Novatians. BIBLIOGRAPHY: G. Bareille, DTC 1:1631–32; M. Bodet, DHGE 3:1037.

[L. G. MÜLLER]

APOTHEOSIS (from the Gr. *theos,* God), signifies the deification of the human. In pagan Greek and Roman thought, eminent heroes or rulers were said to be apotheosized, to be deified, or to be given divine status. Thus Hercules of mythology, Alexander the Great, Julius and Augustus Caesar, were said to have become divine. Even in his lifetime the Emperor Domitian (d. 96) was called divine. Some scholars have tried to find an expression of this pagan conception in the worship of the risen Lord by the primitive Christian community. They attribute this idea chiefly to the Apostle Paul and to Hellenic Christianity. Other scholars (e.g., O. Cullmann) have shown that the notion of the Lordship of Jesus had Jewish-Christian roots and was not merely Hellenic. Furthermore, the preexistence and deity of Christ were part of the primitive Christian faith; early Christians did not believe in a hero who was deified because of his deeds. Neither can any convincing argument be given to show that the Greek notion of apotheosis is the background of the Christian idea of the canonization of the saints. In Catholic thought the saint never loses his status as a human being. Nor is the term ever used of the saints to indicate that they are made divine, although it is used—but rarely—to imply a kind of union with God. BIBLIOGRAPHY: O. Cullmann, *Christology of the New Testament,* (tr. S. Guthrie and C. A. M. Hall, 2d ed., 1963) esp. 193–237, 270–314; M. Boismard, "Divinity of Christ in St. Paul," *Son and Savior* (2d ed., ed. A. Gelin, 1962) 95–124.

[J. HENNESSEY]

APPAREL, a small, oblong, embroidered panel on the cuffs and at the bottom, front and back, of an alb, and along the top of an amice. The purpose of apparels is to strengthen and protect the linen where it is most subject to wear.

[S. A. HEENEY]

APPARITION, a sensible manifestation of God, an angel, or a saint to a person on earth. The distinctive feature of such visitations is that they are sensible and thus differ from visions and revelations that are purely intellectual in nature and content. The one who experiences the visitation is convinced that there is real contact, an actual dialogue between himself and the heavenly person. The phenomenon is known in most of the world's religions, from the most primitive to the more highly developed. Apparitions are narrated in the Bible, although they occupy a relatively small place. They figure in the stories of the patriarchs and esp. of Moses (Ex 3). Within the history of Christianity, biblical exegetes have interpreted these apparitions in various ways, but modern scholars generally see them as a touch of anthropomorphic realism added to the message itself which is centrally important. Visions and apparitions are commonly narrated by the later prophets and become a literary vehicle for rich imagery and symbolism, although the prophetic emphasis on revelation as the Word of God is never lost. In the NT, angelic appearances are fairly frequent, esp. in the infancy narratives, probably because of the contemporary Jewish tendency to regard angels as mediators between God and man. Their purpose in the NT also seems to be the proclamation of a revealed truth in concrete symbolic form. In addition to the biblical apparitions, the Church has at times recognized certain apparitions of a private nature, the most famous being the apparitions of the Blessed Virgin at *La Salette, *Fatima, and *Lourdes.

A characteristic common to these apparitions is always an appeal for a more vital awareness of the message of Jesus. Hence a particular apparition may be a call to work for the solution of the problems of the Church or the world; a summons to the Church for a better understanding of a revealed doctrine; an appeal to action; or a call to practice penance, conversion, and expiation for the sins of the world. The Church's approval of such private revelations never enjoins anyone to accept them with the certitude of divine faith. Such approval does attest that the message involved is not harmful or contrary to the truths of faith, and (in some cases of ecclesiastical approbation) that the apparition and the message connected to it are worthy of credibility, reverence, and the devotion of the faithful. BIBLIOGRAPHY: L. Volker, *Visions, Revelations and the Church* (1963); K. Rahner, *Visions and Prophecies* (1963); J. McKenzie, *Dictionary of the Bible* (1965) 914–916.

[M. GRIFFIN]

APPARIZIO, SEBASTIÁN DE, BL., see APARICIO, SEBASTIÁN DE, BL.

APPEAL, the act whereby a contested juridical decision is referred to a higher court. The right of appeal is generally considered an essential aspect of a judicial system. In the RC Church, most cases are first heard by a diocesan tribunal from which appeal may be made to the tribunal of the metropolitan see. Appeal from the metropolitan tribunal is made to the Roman Rota, the ordinary court of appeal for cases directed to the Holy See. In ecclesiastical law, courts of appeal do not review lower court decisions but inaugurate a new hearing of the case. BIBLIOGRAPHY: R. W. O'Brien, NCE 14:284–286, s.v. "Trials, Ecclesiastical."

[T. M. MCFADDEN]

APPEAL AS FROM AN ABUSE (APPEL COMME D'A-BUS), juridical recourse to civil authority from an ecclesiastical court or administrative act when that act or decision seemed to be in violation of civil law or beyond the competence of the ecclesiastical court or official. The practice began in France in the 15th cent. and spread, under different names, throughout Europe. In the 16th cent., such appeals were efficacious ways of restricting the freedom of the Church to decide matters within its competence. The separation of Church and State and/or the existence of various concordats has made such appeals unnecessary today. BIBLIOGRAPHY: C. B. DuChesnay, NCE 1:702.

[T. M. MCFADDEN]

APPEAL TO A FUTURE COUNCIL, the practice of declaring that a papal decision will be submitted for final judgment to the next ecumenical council. Such an appeal implies that a council is superior in authority to the pope (see CONCILIARISM). Although scholars differ concerning the origins of the practice, it was common in 15th-cent. France and figured prominently in the theories of Gallicanism. Pius II condemned this type of appeal and excommunicated those who invoked it (1460). Succeeding popes repeated this condemnation; the Code of Canon Law forbids an appeal even to a council in session (c.228.1), and excommunicates the appellant (c.2332). BIBLIOGRAPHY: C. B. Du Chesnay, NCE 1:702–703.

[T. M. MCFADDEN]

APPEAL TO CAESAR, St. Paul's famous recourse to the Roman emperor during his imprisonment in Palestine under Roman jurisdiction (Acts 21.27–26.32). The Apostle had been arrested by the Roman authority when a tumult occurred against him in Jerusalem because of the suspicion that he was disloyal to the tenets of Judaism. When Paul was asked by the Roman governor, Festus, if he would agree to be tried by the Sanhedrin in Jerusalem, the Apostle made a formal appeal for a trial before the imperial tribunal in Rome (Acts 25.9–11). The assumption of Acts is that Paul could make this appeal as a Roman citizen (Acts 22.25–28). Pliny's *Letter to Trajan,* in which he speaks of sending Christians to Rome for trial offers substantiating evidence for this right of Roman citizens. Festus honored Paul's appeal (Acts 25.12) and sent him under guard to Rome (Acts 27.1); but Acts does not report the outcome of Paul's appeal.

[C. P. CEROKE]

APPELLANTS, a term with two historical usages: (1) the secular priests in England who in 1599 appealed to Rome against the pro-Jesuit policies of George Blackwell, who had been given the title archpriest and been put in charge of RC priests in England; (2) members of the French clergy who, in their resistance to the bull *Unigenitus,* appealed (1717) to a general council. Pope Clement XI's condemnation of 101 propositions from a work of P. *Quesnel (D 2401–2501) was opposed (1714) by a strong minority; a bitter controversy with a flood of polemical literature against the *Acceptants of the bull ensued. The minority held that by censuring what was really true Catholic doctrine, the Pope had demonstrated that he was not personally infallible. The Appellants acquired their name by reason of the formal public act of appeal made at the Sorbonne by four bps. to a general council (March 5, 1717), an act conforming to the spirit of the *Gallican Articles. Excommunication by Clement in 1718 of the 12 bps., 3,000 priests, and countless laymen numbered among the Appellants had little effect since they had strong support in Parlement and from the regent, Philip of Orléans. He eventually turned against them, used force to make them submit, and in 1730 made acceptance of *Unigenitus* mandatory. Not all Appellants were Jansenists, but many did join the *Schism of Utrecht, and Jansenists in France never relinquished their opposition to *Unigenitus*. See bibliog. for Jansenism.

[T. C. O'BRIEN]

APPETITE, Lat. *appetitus*, tr. of Aristotle's term, *orexis*, a tendency toward what is good and away from what is harmful. The term includes, for St. Thomas Aquinas, the inner order of every being to be fully itself and to resist its own contradiction. Such a "natural appetite" is the reason that the good is a *transcendental property of being, and is the *finality innate in being. In a knowing being knowledge serves the natural bent towards the good and away from the harmful: to the perception of each corresponds an "elicited appetite," a specific kind of power or faculty. As the knowledge is either sensory or intellective, the appetites corresponding are the sensory and the intellective. The first, designated by the general term "sensuality," is divided into the "mild" (concupiscible) and the "emergency" (irascible) appetites; their responses and reactions are the eleven *passions or *emotions. The intellective or rational appetite is the will, whose responses to good and evil are not emotions, but are analogously parallel. The moral life in its over-all shape as good or evil is largely determined by the way the drives of appetite develop. The primary orientation of the will is towards the true human good. That sets a measure for the particular goods and evils to which both the will itself and the sensory appetites respond: such objectives have a hierarchized value as they are meant to contribute to the total and integrated good of the person. A disordered appetite is one that responds to its objective absolved from the subordinated value of that objective. The disorderly moral life is one in which the true human good is displaced by what should be a relative, measured good, become absolutized. Because appetitive dispositions color the practical, moral evaluation of the mind, an orderly moral life requires moral virtues. These are the habituated amenability of appetite so that appetitive responses are moderated in relation to the measured value of their objectives for the full and true good of the whole person. BIBLIOGRAPHY: ThAq ST 1a, 5.1, 19.1, 80, 81, 82; 1a2ae, 69, 65. BIBLIOGRAPHY: G. P. Klubertanz, *Philosophy of Human Nature* (1953); T. V. Moore, *Driving Forces of Human Nature* (1948).

[T. C. O'BRIEN]

APPROPRIATION, attributing an activity which is common to the three Persons of the *Trinity to an individual Person because of some connection between that activity and what is conceived to be characteristic of the divine Person. Appropriation is used in reference to the divine operations that are extrinsic to the Trinity, and not to describe the

Trinitarian *relations themselves. The NT employs appropriation when describing the history of salvation, e.g., the Father is acknowledged as the creator (Mt 3.9), the Son as the source of wisdom and order in the world (Col 1.15–20), and the Spirit as the agent of sanctification (Rom 5.5). The liturgy also uses appropriation when it addresses prayers to the Father whose power is exercised through the Son, bringing about a unity of love in the Holy Spirit. The basis for this practice is the resemblance that obtains between an attribute and the person. Appropriation is, therefore, a means of understanding the mystery of three Persons in one God, even though their external actions proceed as from one principle. It is, in fact, God who creates, redeems, and sanctifies man. This is not to say, however, that the Incarnation is common to all three Persons, or that grace does not establish a special relation between each divine Person and the believer. Only the Word became incarnate and only the Spirit is sent since these actions are the temporal effect of the Trinitarian *processions. Similarly, it is not appropriation when we state that the First Person of the Trinity is our Father or that the Spirit abides in man as the source of love since each Person communicates his own relational mode of being through grace. BIBLIOGRAPHY: J. B. Endres, NCE 1:708–709; A. Chollet, DTC 1.2:1708–17. *MISSIONS, DIVINE.

[T. M. MCFADDEN]

APRINGIUS (6th cent.), bp. of Beja (Pax Julia) in central Portugal. He lived under the Visigothic King Theudis (531–548) and wrote a commentary on the Book of Revelation, of which his interpretation of only the first 5 and the last 5 chapters has survived. Even in ancient MSS this gap was filled in by taking excerpts from the commentary of *Victorinus of Pettau. The work is important for the history of the allegorical exegesis of the Bible. BIBLIOGRAPHY: F. de Almeida, DHGE 3:1072; Altaner 591–592; A. Amatucci, EncCatt 1:1714.

[R. B. ENO]

APSARAS, Sanskrit term (moving in the water) for a Hindu female nymph in Vedic times. *Apsarases*, carrying as a standard a sea monster, attend Kāma the Indian Eros who carries a bow of sugarcane strung with a row of bees, and arrows that are flowers. Later *apsarases* were translated from water to Indra's heaven. BIBLIOGRAPHY: A. L. Basham, *Wonder That Was India* (1959).

[M. J. DALY]

APSE, semicircular architectural extension in Roman basilicas (law courts) becoming in early Christian basilicas (churches) the sacred area of sanctuary and altar. Whereas the Roman law court was a latitudinally oriented building, the apse or raised area for the judge's seat being to the far side as one entered, the Christian basilica opened its door on the narrow side, orienting the building longitudinally toward the altar in the apse now reached by the long approach of a nave.

[M. J. DALY]

APSIDAL CHAPELS, the Gothic proliferation of the apse into many floriated, semicircular, small chapels which with an ambulatory form an architectural complex termed the *chevet.*

[M. J. DALY]

APULEIUS OF MADAURA (*c*.124–after 170), Latin rhetorician and Middle Platonist philosopher. A typical representative of the Latin *Second Sophistic, A. wrote and spoke on a variety of subjects and enjoyed a great reputation, esp. in Africa. His *Apologia* was written to refute the charge of employing magic that was made against him. His most famous work, the *Metamorphoses* or *Golden Ass,* relates the adventures of a certain Lucius, who had been turned into an ass by magic. It contains a full description of the mysteries of Isis and Osiris and is thus a valuable source for our knowledge of the Greco-Oriental mystery religions. His philosophical writings, and, in particular, his *De deo Socratis* have a pronounced mystical character. His teaching on the *daimones* corresponds closely to that of Plutarch. The "demons" are the intermediaries between God and man, and every man has a guardian spirit during life. St. Augustine employs Apuleius as a source on demons (*De civ. Dei* 8–9). BIBLIOGRAPHY: M. R. P. McGuire, NCE 1:709–710; H. E. Butler, OCD 73–74; R. Hanslik, LexAW 232–233; CHGMP 70–72; A. J. Festugière, *Personal Religion among the Greeks* (1954).

[M. R. P. McGUIRE]

AQIBA, RABBI, see AKIBA BEN JOSEPH.

AQUAMANILE, fascinating medieval (12th-13th cent.) bronze water containers for the ritual washing of the priest's hands in the Mass. Shaped as lions, dragons, birds, griffins, likely symbolic, the handles inventively designed from tails or second animals, the German ewers adeptly cast in zinc and copper with beautifully incised textural patterns of feather or fur in polished *auricalcum* glisten like gold. BIBLIOGRAPHY: T. Hoving, *Medieval Treasury* (1965).

[M. J. DALY]

AQUARIANS, called also from the Gr. Hydroparastatae, early Christian heretical sect(s). Various authors such as Clement of Alexandria, Cyprian, and Augustine mention groups of the 2d cent. and later who substituted water for wine in the Eucharist. This was characteristic of the *Ebionites, the followers of *Marcion and *Tatian, the *Manichaeans, and, in general, of dualistic sects that considered material things to be the work of the evil principle in the universe. BIBLIOGRAPHY: A. Giamboni, EncCatt 1:238–239.

[R. B. ENO]

AQUARIUS, MATTIA DEI GIBBONI (d. 1591), Italian Dominican theologian who taught at Milan, Turin, Rome, and Naples. He was a staunch Thomist, much influenced by *Capreolus. BIBLIOGRAPHY: P. Mandonnet, DTC 1.2:1725; Quétif-Échard 2.302.

[P. K. MEAGHER]

AQUAVIVA, see ACQUAVIVA.

AQUEI (Hydrotheitae), a group referred to without name by Augustine (*Haer.* 75), relying on Filaster (*Haer.* 96). Augustine states that they believed water was uncreated and co-eternal with God. The name Aquei (Lat. *aqua,* water) was invented by Danaeus in his edition of Augustine's *De haeresibus* (1576; PL 12:1203). The author of *Praedestinatus* (*c*.75) calls the same group Hydrotheitae (Gr., *hydor,* water; *theos,* God).

[L. G. MÜLLER]

AQUILA AND PRISCILLA (Lat., *Aquila,* eagle; *Priscilla,* diminutive of *Prisca,* venerable), a Jewish couple of Pontus in Asia Minor who came to Rome, where probably they were baptized. Their removal to Corinth was due to the edict of Emperor Claudius against the Jews (Acts 18.1–2), and there they met the Apostle Paul to whose service they dedicated themselves (Rom 16.3–4). Paul lived with them in Corinth, sharing their trade of canvas making, and later with them went to Ephesus (Acts 18:18–19). The Christians met there in their home (1 Cor 16.19; Rom 16.5), where later Paul would greet them from his Roman prison (2 Tim 4.19). Card. Faulhaber in *Women in the Bible* (1938; 1955 ed. B. Keogh, 198–204) states that Priscilla must be reckoned as "a pattern of the feminine workers in the Apostolic mission-field." He notes likewise that in mention of the couple in Acts, Rom, 2 Tim, she is named first, indicative of her role as "soul of the house" and spiritual leader in her sphere.

[M. R. BROWN]

AQUILA, VERSION OF, literal translation of OT original Hebrew into Greek by Aquila (117–138), a Jewish proselyte and native of Sinope in Pontus. Fragments have survived in writers quoting the *Hexapla of Origen and palimpsests discovered in Cairo. BIBLIOGRAPHY: Robert-Tricot, 1:622–632.

[F. H. BRIGHAM]

AQUILEIA, a Roman military colony *c*.180 B.C. Archeological excavations at Aquileia have uncovered an imperial villa under the ancient church, which after the peace of Constantine was enlarged and decorated with mosaics (Good Shepherd, etc.). Destroyed by fire (5th cent.) there followed new constructions with baptistery under *Justinian I and a campanile (11th cent.).

[M. J. DALY]

AQUILEIA (RITE OF), early liturgy used by the now-suppressed patriarchate of Aquileia (located at the head of the Adriatic Sea). Its details are largely unknown, but the limited evidence available indicates resemblances to the *Milanese rite. A lectionary of *c*.700, the oldest documentary evidence, shows such features as five Advent Sundays, absence of Septuagesima, and observance of St. Stephen's Day on the Eastern date (Dec. 27). Use of the rite spread to various other places, including Verona and Trent. From the Carolingian period it began conforming closer to the Roman rite and its use as a distinct rite was ended in 1596. BIBLIOGRAPHY: A. A. King, *Liturgies of the Past* (1959); F. Cabrol, DACL 1.2:2683–91.

[T. EARLY]

AQUILINUS, ST. (*c*.970–*c*.1015), priest, martyr. A. was born in Würzburg, Germany. He studied at Cologne but left there when his associates chose him as successor to the bishop. He went to Paris and left there for the same cause. After a short time at Pavia he established himself as a canon at S. Lorenzo, Milan. Because of his ardor in combating the Arian errors, A. made himself an enemy of the heretics and was martyred. His body was taken to S. Lorenzo where a special chapel was raised in his honor. He is revered by the churches of Cologne, Würzburg, and Milan and by the canons of the *Lateran. BIBLIOGRAPHY: N. M. Riehle, NCE 1:711–712; A. Rimoldi, BiblSanct 2:331–332.

[M. C. BRADLEY]

AQUINAS, PHILIPPUS (Juda Mordechai; *c*.1575–1650), Hebraist. Born of a Jewish family, A. became a rabbi, but *c*.1610 was baptized a Roman Catholic at Aquino in Italy. He became professor of Hebrew at the College of France, worked on the Paris Polyglot, and contributed to the development of Hebrew lexicography.

[P. K. MEAGHER]

AQUINAS, THOMAS, see THOMAS AQUINAS, ST.

ARA COELI, the title since the 14th cent. of the Church of St. Mary on the Capitoline in Rome. According to an apocryphal legend the Emperor Augustus there erected an altar (*ara*) to the Redeemer of whose coming he knew through the Sibyline prophecies. The church was given to the Franciscans by Innocent IV in 1250 and houses in its sacristy a celebrated wood carving of the Bambino.

[P. K. MEAGHER]

ARA PACIS (Altar of Peace; 13th-9th cent. B.C.), altar dedicated to Augustus, that stood on the Campus Martius, Rome. Raised on a podium, the altar enclosed by a wall carries a processional frieze depicting Augustus as *Pontifex Maximus* (high priest) with members of the imperial family, *flamines,* and senators. Decorative reliefs show masterly floral (*rinceau*) patterns, mythological panels of the Earth goddess Tellus with Air and Water, and sacrificial themes. The *Ara Pacis* is significantly Roman in depicting the actual historical event. BIBLIOGRAPHY: L. Budde, *Ara Pacis Augustae* (1957).

[M. J. DALY]

ARABA, from the Hebrew *hā 'ărābāh,* meaning desert or plain, the name of the rift valley in which the river Jordan and the Dead Sea lie. It extends from the Sea of Galilee to the head of the gulf of Aqaba and is part of a great geological fault that reaches through the Red Sea all the way to Lake Nyasa in E Africa. It includes the long Jordan valley, the Dead Sea, called the Salt Sea of Arabah in Dt 3.17, and the modern *wadi el-Araba,* the wilderness extending from the Dead Sea to the gulf of Aqaba. The width of the valley varies from 5 to 25 miles. At the Sea of Galilee it is about 700 feet below sea level; it sinks to 1286 feet below at the Dead Sea, and rises above sea level in the southern wadi. In ancient times the wadi area was a N-S travel route; it was used by some of the Israelites on their way to Palestine after the exodus from Egypt (Dt 2.8). Traces of ancient mining and smelting of iron and copper have been explored in the Araba, esp. near Asiongaber, by N. Glueck and dated back to Solomonic times. BIBLIOGRAPHY: N. Glueck, *Rivers in the Desert* (1959); D. Baly, *Geography of the Bible* (1957) 198–217; R. Blanchard, *Promised Land* (tr. R. Hunt, 1966) 67–68.

[J. E. LUSSIER]

ARABACI, a 3d-cent. sect that maintained that the soul perishes with the body; yet both will experience resurrection at the end of time. This doctrine was a type of materialism, ascribing to the body the principal role in human personality. John of Damascus (*Orat. ad Graec.* 13) calls them *Thnetopsychitae* (Gr. *thnētos,* mortal; *psychē*, soul). The sect was described and located in Arabia by Eusebius (*Hist. eccl.* 6.37). Hence Augustine (*Haer.* 83) calls them *Arabaci.* BIBLIOGRAPHY: A. Audino, EncCatt 1:1749; F. Hort, DCB 1:151.

[L. G. MÜLLER]

ARABESQUE (Ital. *arabesco*), a pattern of endless geometric interlace in Islamic art, and of intricate curvilinear plant and animal design used in late Roman and Renaissance work.

[M. J. DALY]

ARABIA, predominantly desert and wilderness peninsula of SW Asia. In the Bible Arabia and its people appear as recurrent influences on Israelite history, and in Islam the peninsula holds special significance as the birthplace of the faith and location of its holiest cities, Mecca and Medina.

An area of about 1 million square miles, the largest peninsula in the world, Arabia is bounded on the W by the Red Sea, the S by the Gulf of Aden and the Arabian Sea and on the E by the Gulf of Oman and the Persian Gulf. The arid area extends above the peninsula proper, and historically this region too has been called Arabia, as was the Sinai peninsula in the time of Paul (Gal 4.25). Most of Arabia today is ruled by Saudi Arabia, but the area also includes Yemen Arab Republic, People's Democratic Republic of Yemen (Southern Yemen), Oman, Trucial States, Qatar, Bahrain (archipelago off the E coast of Arabia) and Kuwait.

Though Arabia may have had greater precipitation in the remote past, from the time its history can be traced the rainfall has been slight, not enough to keep rivers flowing. The Empty Quarter and some other areas are sandy desert where virtually nothing grows. However, in much of Arabia small amounts of rainfall produce enough pasturage to allow the maintenance of animal herds by moving them about from one spot to another. This has given rise to the characteristic pattern of nomadic, bedouin life of tent dwellers. In limited areas agriculture is possible and settled communities have long existed as another component of the population. Coastal areas have also had fishing and trading communities. Particularly important was the caravan route running up western Arabia, an area known in its upper regions as the Hejaz and the area where Islam was born. This trade route connected India with the Mediterranean world and carried a valuable commerce in spices, incense, and other goods. The modern discovery of oil in immense quantities (1932) brought Arabia a new importance in the world economy, and consequently in world politics. This factor was particularly prominent in its bearing on the Arab-Israeli struggle.

Numerous references to Arabia appear in the Bible. Ezekiel refers to Tyre's importing sheep and goats, characteristic produce, from Arabia (27.21), and in another context prophesies the fall of Arabia along with Egypt and other countries (30.1–5). A prophetic vision sees a multitude of camels bringing two frequently mentioned products of Arabia, gold and frankincense, to Jerusalem (Is 60.6). Paul says he went into Arabia after his conversion, but does not indicate which part (Gal 1.17).

From early times Arabia was touched by Egyptian, Mesopotamian, Greco-Roman, and other outside cultures, as well as the Hebrew. From its coastal areas ships went to Africa, Persia, and India. But the interior of Arabia was little affected and remained relatively isolated. In the late Middle Ages the West began to forget even the small amount antiquity had known about Arabia, and in the 19th cent. the peninsula was discovered anew by missionaries, French and British officials, and explorers who reported their findings in works such as C. M. Doughty's notable *Arabia Deserta* (1888).

Little documentary evidence from ancient Arabia has survived, if it ever existed, and most of the available knowledge comes from references in the literature of other peoples. From this evidence it appears that inhabitants of Arabia were raiding the Fertile Crescent as early as the 4th millennium B.C., often apparently remaining to become part of these societies. Early in the 2d millennium B.C. an alphabet was developed in Arabia. About the same time the camel was domesticated, a pre-eminent factor making possible the human habitation of Arabia. (Somewhat later came the fam-

ous Arabian horse, a luxury for display, sport, or raiding rather than a necessity for survival as the camel was.)

The South is the most fertile part of Arabia and has numerous inscriptions reflecting its position as the most advanced civilization of Arabia during the pre-Islamic period. Toward the end of the 3rd cent. A.D. the Himyarite kingdom became dominant in the South. By the 5th cent. it had expanded into central Arabia, and a monotheistic faith in the "lord of Heaven and Earth" became the religion of the state. A mission from Byzantium introduced Christianity into South Arabia in the latter half of the 4th cent., and Judaism may have been introduced about the same time. Various tribes held north and central Arabia. One of them, the Lakhmids, bordering on Mesopotamia, became the first to adopt Arabic as an official language.

In 25 B.C. Aelius Gallus, prefect of Egypt, failed in the only Roman attempt to conquer Arabia. But in 106 A.D. Trajan was able to incorporate the kingdom centered at Petra in NW Arabia into the empire. Into this area, along the trade routes and in various other parts of Arabia Christianity and Judaism began to make limited penetrations. Such Christian influences as entered were primarily Nestorian and Monophysite. In 525 Christian Abyssinians overthrew the Himyarite king, who had converted to Judaism. The Abyssinians received backing from Byzantium, but were expelled when the Himyarites received Persian support in the late 6th century. When Islam arose, it built on the knowledge of Judaism and Christianity that was current in Arabia, but this was limited and not based on the more definitive forms of the religions as found in their principal centers.

The birth of Mohammed at Mecca *c*.570 and his divine call *c*.610 to proclaim a strictly monotheistic faith proved decisive for the subsequent history of Arabia. The existing religion of Arabia found stones to be the dwelling places of gods, and pre-eminent in pre-Islamic Arabia was the black stone (a meteorite) of the Ka'bah (cube) temple in Mecca. This city, on the Hejaz caravan route, was already a center of trade and religious pilgrimage to the Ka'bah (then apparently serving several cults). It was ruled by Mohammed's tribe, the Quaraysh (or Kuraish), which traced its descent to Ishmael and worshipped Allah but apparently made political agreements allowing the cults of other tribes. When he began receiving his revelations, Mohammed found his fellow citizens unsympathetic, and in 622 he moved north to Medina. When the Jews there took sides against Mohammed, he killed 600 of them, expelled the others and took over their date plantations. He also stopped praying toward Jerusalem and started facing Mecca. Mohammed became theocratic head of the Medina tribal confederation and in 630 was able to take Mecca. On his death in 632 a large segment, though not all, of Arabia had been united under the faith in the one God and his Prophet. The united Arab tribes then began moving out of the peninsula on a career of conquest that brought them dominance over a large part of the civilized world, but the development of Arabia itself was largely neglected. Nevertheless, Islam soon spread throughout

Arabia. Medina, capital of the Hejaz for three centuries after Mohammed, and Mecca, capital for a millennium thereafter, grew rich on foreign income. The practice of facing Mecca while praying and inclusion of a pilgrimage to Mecca among the primary religious practices of Islam gave Arabia a permanent importance for Muslims of all lands.

The political center of Islam soon moved out of Arabia to Damascus and then Baghdad, and the unity it had given was soon ended by divisions within the new faith. In the division between Shiites, who favored limiting the caliphate to Mohammed's family, and the Sunnites, who did not, Arabia followed the Shiites, and at the end of the 9th cent. Arabia was further divided by the emergence of the *Ismailis and Carmathians. Then Saladin imposed Sunnite rule toward the end of the 12th century.

After the decline of the Baghdad caliphate, Arabia came under general overlordship of the *Mamelukes, who remained dominant until their overthrow by the Ottoman Turks. In the 18th cent. a puritanical movement to reform Sunnite Islam, the Wahabi movement, developed in the Saud tribe of Arabia. After some temporary victories in the 19th cent., the Saud tribe finally came to control Arabia when Sharif Husayn threw off Turkish rule after World War I and Ibn-Sa'ud then defeated Husayn. On his death in 1953 he was succeeded by his oldest son, Saud, who was deposed in 1964 by King Faisal. Assassinated in 1975, Faisal was succeeded by a half-brother, Khalid bin Abdul Aziz. Islam remains the state religion of Saudi Arabia, and as custodian of the holy sites of Mecca and Medina, the king has the role of chief defender of Islam. The other states of Arabia also give official favor to Islam, and their populations are overwhelmingly Muslim, though small Christian and Hindu communities exist in Yemen. BIBLIOGRAPHY: P. K. Hitti, *History of the Arabs* (10th ed., 1970); John B. Glubb, *Short History of the Arab Peoples* (1969).

[T. EARLY]

ARABIA, CHRISTIANITY IN. Historically, the name Arabia has been used to designate: (1) the old Roman Province of Arabia (modern Western Transjordan and southern Syria); (2) the Arab tribes in the desert of east central Syria, (modern eastern Transjordan, and southwest Iraq); and (3) the Arabian peninsula. The "Arabs" of the Roman province were mostly the Aramaicized *Nabataeans, and that area will not be considered here.

Of the semi-nomadic tribes in the north, some lived on the Roman side of the imperial frontier, others on the Persian side. On the Roman side, the Christians already found at the end of the 4th cent. were augmented by tribal conversions in the 5th and 6th. These tribes were mostly Monophysite, and the most important were the Ghassanids; their tribal chieftains were made vassal rulers (phylarchs) of the Byzantine state, which otherwise could not cope with the unsettled tribes. The phylarch Al-Ḥarith ibn Jabala did much to help *Jacob Baradai organize the Syrian Monophysite Church.

On the Persian side of the frontier there were Christian Arabs in what is now southwestern Iraq and the Arabian coast of the Persian Gulf, but no tribe was entirely Christian. Some were settled in the Arab Lakhmid capital, Ḥira. Ḥira and the other Arab bishoprics of the region were dependent on the Church of Persia, with which they became Nestorian in the 5th century. In southwest Arabia (modern Yemen) an ephemeral mission by the Arian Theophilus of Dibous c.356 was followed by a more durable implantation of Christianity c.500, with Najrān and Ṣan'ā' its most important centers. The area was in the Ethiopian sphere of influence when the Church was organized (this probably explaining its original Monophysite traits) but came (again) under Persian rule in 572. The rest of Arabia seems to have had no organized Christianity, although there were Christians, mostly Syrian tradesmen and craftsmen or Ethiopian and Coptic slaves, in Western Arabia (the Tihama and the Hejaz) when that area was the setting for Mohammed's career.

Already under 'Umar, the second caliph, the principle was enunciated that only Muslims were to be tolerated in Arabia, but there were still Christians in the Hejaz itself under the early caliphs. The Nestorian Arabs along the Persian Gulf fell away quickly, but the Nestorian and Monophysite bishoprics for the Arabs in the north survived into the 10th century. The Monophysites of Najrān in Yemen were deported to the Ḥira area under 'Umar; yet, there is good evidence of Christians in Yemen, with a bishopric, by then Nestorian, at Ṣan'ā' in the 9th century. There were also South Arabian Nestorians on the island of Socotra in the Arabian Sea as late as the 13th century. Today Christianity is excluded from Saudi Arabia and Yemen. Catholic and Protestant missions exist in Aden and Kuwait. BIBLIOGRAPHY: R. Aigrain, DHGE 3:1158–1339; F. Nau, *Les Arabes chrétiens de Mésopotamie* (1933); H. Charles, *Le Christianisme des Arabes nomades* (1936); J. A. Devenny, NCE 1:721–722; R. N. Bellah, *Beyond Belief* (1970) 149–156.

[A. CODY]

ARABIC GOSPEL OF THE INFANCY, SEE APOCRYPHA (NEW TESTAMENT), 9.

ARABIC LANGUAGE IN LITURGY. Arabic has long been the vernacular language of Christians in Egypt and the Near East, except for the Armenians and a number of Syrians. Its use in the liturgy has gradually increased since its first introduction in the 11th century. Today the Copts employ it for almost everything, including the Divine Office, although some Monophysite Copts increase the amount of Coptic used. The Maronites and Syrian Catholics use it for large parts of the eucharistic and sacramental rites, but not at all in the Office. The Jacobites, Nestorians, and Chaldeans are much more retentive of Syriac, using Arabic, where it is the vernacular language, only for readings and a few liturgical prayers. The Orthodox patriarchates of Jerusalem, Antioch, and Alexandria use Arabic exclusively where clergy and people are Arabic-speaking, but Greek where clergy or people are Greek. The Catholic Melchites, having no Greek members, use Arabic almost exclusively.

[A. CODY]

ARABIC PHILOSOPHY, SEE ISLAMIC PHILOSOPHY

ARABIC STUDIES, PONTIFICAL INSTITUTE OF,
founded in 1926 in Tunisia. Under the direction of the White Fathers, the institute came to be regarded highly by Muslim intellectuals for its profound and sympathetic knowledge of the country. It was moved to Rome in 1964.

[M. C. BRADLEY]

ARABS, originally nomads, a name applied to inhabitants of *Arabia, particularly the bedouin of N Arabia, but now often used more widely of all those peoples of the Middle East and Northern Africa who speak Arabic, including some Christian groups.

Little is known of the earliest Arabs, and much of that comes at second hand from the impact they made on other peoples of the surrounding area. A distinction has been drawn from ancient times between those of the North, 'Adnani, and those of the South, Qahtani. Arabs of the south, a more fertile area supporting permanent settlements, had developed an outstanding civilization by c. 1200 B.C. In the NW a later notable culture was maintained by the Nabateans with their capital at Petra, in the biblical Edom. Northern Arabs were characteristically nomadic, bedouins, living in tents and moving about to find pasture for their flocks. They present the most typical form of Arab life, and their language became the classical Arabic.

Arabs are Semitic, and Hebrew acknowledgment of kinship appears in the genealogical table of Gen 10, where Eber's two sons are Peleg, ancestor of Abraham, and Joktan, ancestor of various Arab peoples. In the Gen 25 genealogy, other Arab groups are descendants of Abraham by his wife Keturah and the servant Hagar.

The Israelites were perpetually in contact with the Arabs—known under such tribal names as Ishmaelites, Midianites, Sabeans, etc. Often the relation was hostile. In a description reflecting a common view of the Arab, Ishmael is called "a wild ass of a man, his hand against every man and every man's hand against him" (Gen 16.12). Job's friends were Arabs, but so were the Sabeans who killed his herdsmen and took his cattle. The Gideon story tells of destructive Arab raids on Israel as a recurrent experience (Jg 6). In a more positive vein, the story of Solomon records a visit by an admiring queen from Sheba (1 Kg 10), generally thought to lie in SW Arabia, though some scholars suggest the North. In recounting her visit, the Bible speaks of Solomon's receiving gold from "all the kings of Arabia" (10.15). According to 2 Chr, Jehoshaphat received tribute of sheep and goats from Arabs (17.11), but during the reign of his son Jehora the Arabs and Philistines sacked Judah and took away members of the royal family (21.16–17). Arabs were among those opposing the rebuilding of Jerusalem (Neh 4.7).

Arabs, presumably converts to Judaism, were in Jerusalem at Pentecost (Acts 2.11).

Destruction by Arabs of almost everything reflecting pre-Islamic paganism has made study of their religion before Mohammed difficult. But it was apparently more advanced in the South than among the bedouin. And apart from limited influences by Judaism and Christianity it apparently centered on astral deities, sacred stones and wells, pilgrimages, festivals and sacrifices, with priests relatively unimportant.

Traditionally Arabs lived in tribal units and had little political unity. But Mohammed was able to provide a unifying faith that sustained a campaign of conquest giving them not only Damascus (635), Jerusalem (638), and Alexandria (641) but also taking them E into central Asia and W across North Africa and into Spain, to be stopped only in southern Gaul by Charles Martel (732). Arabs also provided the language in which Greco-Roman culture was preserved until western Europe was ready to receive it in the High Middle Ages.

[T. EARLY]

ARADITES, SEE ARVAD.

ARAM, OT name of an important Semitic people, the Arameans, and of the land in which they lived, esp. Syria. Gen 10.22 lists Aram as a son of Shem, the father of Semites, while in Gen 22.20 Aram is a grandson of Nahor, the brother of Abraham. Dt 26.5 refers to Jacob as "a wandering Aramean." The origin of the Arameans is obscure, but they seem to have been part of a nomadic invasion of the fertile Crescent from the Arabian Peninsula in the 2d millennium B.C. In the 10th-9th cent. B.C., they formed several city-states in the upper Euphrates region. That at Damascus was often at war with Israel during the period of the monarchy, yet with the Assyrian conquests of the 8th cent. B.C. both were swept away.

[O. N. BUCHER]

ARAMAEANS, an ancient tribe of nomads who first invaded the Assyrian Empire during the reign of Tiglath-pileser I (1115–1076 B.C.) and established a series of federated states in Syria in the vicinity of the upper Euphrates also known as Aram (Num 23.7). In Southern Babylonia, they merged with the Chaldeans sometime during the 10th cent. B.C. Yet they maintained their political and commercial independence in Syria until taken over by the Assyrians under Tiglath-pileser III (740–732 B.C.). At this time, some of the more important states included Arpad (2 Kg.18.34); Hamath in the center of Syria (2 Kg.18.34) in the South, Damascus (1 Kg 11.23, 25); north of Damascus, Zobah (2 Sam 8.3–8); Beth-Rohob, east of the Jordan and north of Ammon (2 Sam 10.6); and Geshur (2 Sam 3.3) east of the Sea of Galilee. There is evidence that the Israelites had close economic and cultural ties with the Aramaeans of Syria from the time of the patriarchs (Dt 26.5; Gen 25.20; 28.5; 31.20; 24). They were absorbed by the Persian empire in the 6th cent. B.C.; there is no further existing record of the Aramaeans as a distinct political entity.

Influenced in their religion by the beliefs of the Canaanites and the peoples of Mesopotamia, they were polytheistic in their worship. Their chief deity was Haddad, the storm god and called by various epithets, e.g., Remman, the god Wer, the lord of the heavens. They also worshiped Tammuz, the god of fertility, Sin and Nikkal, the lunar god and goddess.

The Aramaeans spoke Aramaic, a NW Semitic language of the same family as Hebrew and Phoenician. Significantly, it served as an international language from 700 to 300 B.C. when it was superseded by Greek.

Later descendants of the Aramaeans flourished in the Nabataean kingdom of Petra in S Transjordan and the Palmyrene kingdom of Palmyra in the Syrian desert, both of them thriving caravan centers. The more important members of the Nabataean dynasty are mentioned in both OT and NT beginning with Aretas I (2 Mac 5.8; Mt 3.4; 2 Cor 11.32). When Petra was conquered by the Romans (106) Palmyra became a prosperous trade center whose political structure oscillated between that of a Hellenized kingdom and a Roman colony until its final defeat by the Emperor Aurelian (272). BIBLIOGRAPHY: M. F. Unger, *Israel and the Aramaeans of Damascus* (1957); J. A. Fitzmyer NCE 1:735–736.

[F. H. BRIGHAM]

ARAMAIC, a northwest Semitic language that gets its name from the Aramaeans, whose wide trading activities carried their language throughout Palestine, Syria, Assyria, and Babylonia. The Jews adopted it during the Babylonian Captivity, and it remained their ordinary language for centuries. It was thus Jesus' native tongue, and according to early tradition was used by Matthew in his original Gospel.

[J. J. CASTELOT]

ARAMAIC LANGUAGE IN LITURGY. Usually the term Aramaic in this context is used inaccurately for Syriac, a language of the Eastern branch of the Aramaic family, distinct from that Western type of Aramaic spoken in ancient Palestine. Orientals who use Aramaic for the more exact Syriac often do so tendentiously, claiming that their liturgical language is that of Christ. Until the 13th cent. a Western Aramaic dialect (Christian Palestinian) was used liturgically in certain places in the Orthodox patriarchates of Jerusalem and Antioch. *SYRIAC LANGUAGE IN LITURGY.

[A. CODY]

ARANDA, FELIPE (1648–95), Spanish Jesuit theologian who taught philosophy at Huesca and theology at Saragossa. Among his theological commentaries, that on the *Prima pars* of the *Summa* of St. Thomas, subtitled *Schola scientiae mediae,* is a defense of *Molina's theory of *scientia media.* BIBLIOGRAPHY: Sommervogel 1:501–503.

[T. C. O'BRIEN]

ARARAT, a mountainous region of Armenia in which the ark of Noah came to rest (Gen 8.4), located around Lake Van where modern Turkey, Russia, and Iran converge. In ancient times it was known as Urartu; its people were a constant threat to the Assyrian Empire. Sennacherib's sons fled there after murdering their father (2 Kg 19.37). Jer 51.27 lists Ararat among the enemies who would bring about the destruction of Babylon.

[O. N. BUCHER]

ARATCHNORD, in the *Armenian Church, the head of a diocese. He is usually a bishop but may also be a major vardepet, and is, in either case, subject to the catholicos or patriarch on whose jurisdiction the diocese depends.

[A. CODY]

ARATOR (6th cent.), Christian poet. Orphaned at an early age, he was educated by Lawrence, bp. of Milan, and the poet Ennodius. After pursuing for a time a legal career at the court of the Ostrogothic kings at Ravenna, he was ordained subdeacon c.540 by Pope *Vigilius. In Rome in 554 he wrote his epic on the Acts of the Apostles in 2336 hexameters; the Pope allowed him to introduce it by a public reading in the Church of St. Peter in Chains. The poem was admired in the Middle Ages, but its inferior verse and its flights of extravagant allegory have not been much acclaimed in later times. PL 68:45–252; crit ed. A. McKinlay, CSEL 72 (1951). BIBLIOGRAPHY: F. di Capua, EncCatt 1:1769–70; V. Declercq, NCE 1:738–739.

[R. B. ENO]

ARAÚJO, ANTÔNIO DE (1566–1632), Jesuit missionary, linguist. Born in the Azores, A. entered the Jesuits in 1582 in Bahia, was ordained, and taught for a short time before he was sent to live and work with the Tupí Indians. Zealous, practical, and gifted, he provided catechetical material in Tupí and wrote several treatises compiled from the geographical and ethnographical information gathered during Pero Domingues' expeditions into N Brazil.

[H. JACK]

ARAÚJO, FRANCISCO DE (1580–1664), Dominican theologian, bp. of Segovia (1648–56). Highly reputed for piety and learning, A. commented on most of the parts of St. Thomas Aquinas's *Summa theologiae*. A passage in his commentary on the 1a2ae that is Molinist, is now known to be an interpolation. BIBLIOGRAPHY: T. C. O'Brien, ''El Enigma de Francisco de Araújo,'' *Ciencia Tomista* 282 (1962):221–226; 285 (1963):3–79.

[P. K. MEAGHER]

ARBELA, CHRONICLE OF, a Syrian history of the Church in the region of Adiabene, whose capital at the time was Arbela. A. Mingana discovered and published the document in 1907. It was written by a Nestorian named

Mesihazeka, who, although he undoubtedly had access to many excellent sources now lost, made liberal use also of legendary material. BIBLIOGRAPHY: "Chronica ecclesiae Arbelensis" (ed. F. Zorell), OrChrAnal 8 (1926–27) 145–204.

[P. K. MEAGHER]

ARBIOL Y DIEZ ANTONIO (1651–1726), Franciscan spiritual writer. His background is predominantly philosophical and theological. Perhaps the rare combination of excellence in both coupled with his intense quest for holiness led him to write several works in the varied fields of theology, homiletics, asceticism, and mysticism. Notable among these are: *Desengaños místicos* (1706); *Novenarios espirituales*, published posthumously; *La familia regulada* (1715). His mystical theology shows the influences of SS. Bonaventure, Teresa of Avila, and John of the Cross. BIBLIOGRAPHY: G. Gál, NCE 1:740.

[J. R. RIVELLO]

ARBOGAST (d.394), general, statesman who was successively master of the horse in the Western Roman army under Gratian; master of both armies after his campaigns in Thrace, Italy, and Gaul under Theodosius; and regent of Gaul (391). After the suspicious death of the Emperor Valentinian II, A. declared the rhetorician Eugenius emperor of the West and with the substantial support of many at Rome initiated a revival of paganism (392). After leading several successful campaigns against the Ripuarian Franks, the Chamavi and the Chatti along the Rhine, A. together with Eugenius was defeated by Theodosius in the battle of the Frigidus (394). His endeavor to renew ancient Roman religion was the result of his interest in the Roman republic and his disenchantment with the Arian controversy of Christendom. BIBLIOGRAPHY: N. Baynes, CMedH 1:244–247.

[F. H. BRIGHAM]

ARBOGAST OF STRASBOURG, ST. (d. mid-6th cent.), bishop. According to later sources, A. became bp. of Strasbourg *c.*673 through the influence of King Dagobert II of Austrasia (d. 679) but catalogues of the diocese and inscriptions on the 6th cent. cathedral of Strasbourg assign his episcopate to *c.*550. A. was noted for his humility and is venerated as the patron of the diocese of Strasbourg. BIBLIOGRAPHY: Butler 3:158–159; G. Allmang DHGE 3:1462–63; G. Mathon, BiblSanct 2:344.

[M. S. TANEY]

ARBOUZE, MARGUERITE D' (1580–1626), Benedictine abbess. In 1589 she entered a Lyons convent and took vows in 1599. By 1611, when she transferred to Montmartre, she had learned Italian and Spanish to read mystics. As novice mistress 1613 and prioress 1614, she promoted a strict Benedictine rule. In 1619 she became abbess of the restored Val-de-Grâce, thanks to the Queen, Anne of Austria who, with other high persons, paid her frequent visits. Marguerite died on a journey in which she reformed two convents. BIBLIOGRAPHY: G. Marsot, *Catholicisme* 1:758–760.

[E. P. COLBERT]

ARBROATH, ABBEY OF, former Benedictine abbey located in Angus, Scotland. Founded by King William II in 1078. Arbroath was richly endowed by William and his successors, and became one of the wealthiest abbeys in the kingdom. After the Reformation, the abbey was made into a temporal lordship for the Marquis of Hamilton and the revenues bestowed on him. It is now a ruin. BIBLIOGRAPHY: R. L. Mackin and S. Cruden, *Arbroath Abbey* (1954).

[S. A. HEENEY]

ARBUÉS, PETER, ST., see PETER ARBUÉS, ST.

ARC DE TRIOMPHE DE L'ÉTOILE, Paris, largest triumphal arch in the world and the magnificent focus of the Champs Elysées built by Chalgrin and others (1806–36) for Napoleon I, with some figures by Rude, Cortot, and Etex.

[M. J. DALY]

ARC DE TRIOMPHE DU CARROUSEL, Paris (1806–08), triumphal arch, by Percier and Fontaine, formerly the gateway from the Tuileries, in delicate proportion and decorativeness contrasting strongly with the Arc de Triomphe de l'Étoile. Earlier bronze horses atop the arch —taken from St. Mark's, Venice—were replaced (1828) by the bronze group by Bosio.

[M. J. DALY]

ARCADELT, JACOB (*c.*1504–67), Flemish composer active in Florence and in Rome where he formed the Sistine Choir (1539). His secular madrigals, which were widely popular, combine Flemish contrapuntal devices with Italian melodic style. In 1553 he returned to France, where he served as *maître de chapelle* for the cardinal of Lorraine, and devoted his talents to the composition of chansons. The famous *Ave Maria* attributed to him is a 19th-cent. adaptation of one of his secular chansons, which were very successful despite their generally serious tone. BIBLIOGRAPHY: Reese MusR; J. Schmidt-Görg, MGG 1:603–607.

[J. J. WALSH]

ARCADIUS (*c.*377–408), first **ROMAN EMPEROR** of the East from 395. His father, Theodosius I, proclaimed him Augustus when he was only 6 years old and left him in Constantinople in 394 as sole ruler of the eastern half of the Empire. Upon his father's death Arcadius kept the East while his younger brother Honorius obtained the West. Arcadius was weak in body and in character and governed largely through his ministers Rufinus and Eutropius. He confiscated the chief pagan temples and forbade heretics from assembling; but his championship of orthodoxy was dictated by reasons of state. It was his wife Eudoxia who brought about the exile of St. John Chrysostom. BIBLIOGRAPHY: J. B. Bury, *History of the Later Roman Empire I* (1923); C. Baur, *John Chrysostom and His Time* (tr. M. Gonzaga, 2 v., 1960–61).

[M. J. SUELZER]

ARCADIUS OF CAESAREA, ST. (d. 304?), martyr, probably legendary despite the inclusion of his *passio* in the *Acta sincera* of T. *Ruinart. This story is that in the persecution of Diocletian he fled his city (Caesarea in Mauritania?), but hearing that a kinsman had been seized in his place, he returned and presented himself to the judge. When he refused to sacrifice, he was condemned to a lingering death; his limbs were cut off, joint by joint, till only his torso remained. He died encouraging his companions to keep their faith. BIBLIOGRAPHY: Butler 1:70–71; A. P. Frutaz, LTK 1:821, bibliog.

[P. K. MEAGHER]

ARCANGELO DI COLA DA CAMERINO (*c*.1390–*c*.1440), Italian painter and talented follower of Gentile da Fabriano. In Florence (1420) A. executed an altar-piece for S. Lucia de' Magnoli (1421) and began frescoes in St. John Lateran, Rome (1422), continued later by Pisanello and Gentile da Fabriano. There is a small diptych by A. in the Frick collection, N.Y. BIBLIOGRAPHY: R. Longhi, "Fatti di Masolino di Masaccio," *Critica d'arte* 5 (1940).

[M. J. DALY]

ARCANGELO OF CALATAFIMI, BL. (1380–1460), Sicilian Franciscan. He longed for solitude but had difficulty in finding it because of his reputation for sanctity and miraculous power. He revived a hospice for the poor at Alcama. When Pope Martin V ordered hermits to return to lay life or join an approved religious order, A. became a Franciscan of the Observance at Palermo and was later provincial for Sicily. BIBLIOGRAPHY: G. Morabito, BiblSanct 2:373.

ARCANI DISCIPLINA, see DISCIPLINE OF THE SECRET.

ARCANUM, an encyclical letter of Pope Leo XIII (ASS 1879, 385–402) in which he defends the indissolubility of the marriage bond and the exclusive right of the Church to determine the legal implications of its sacramental contract. He acknowledges the limited prerogatives of the State in those aspects of marriage which pertain to civil order. But in areas of conflicting jurisdiction, he upholds the priority of the Church's authority. He reminds Christian spouses that fulfillment of their responsibilities must be based on conjugal love. BIBLIOGRAPHY: J. Husslein, *Social Well-Springs* (1940–42) 1:24–46.

[F. H. BRIGHAM]

ARCES, JEAN D' (d. 1454), abp. of Tarentaise from 1438, cardinal. At the Council of Basel (1440) A. supported Duke Amadeus of Savoy, antipope under the name Felix V, against Eugene IV, and was involved in the ensuing schism. His cardinalate, received in 1444 from the council, was confirmed by Nicholas V at the termination of the schism. During his archbishopric A. was engaged in a power struggle with the house of Savoy over the Tarentaise domain. BIBLIOGRAPHY: J. Garin, DHGE 3:1525–26.

[P. K. MEAGHER]

ARCESILAUS OF PITANE (*c*.316–240 B.C.), founder of the Middle Academy and of logical skepticism. He was head of the Academy from 268 to his death and, though leaving no writings, was a very influential teacher. He attacked the Stoic theory of apprehension and elaborated a theory of logical skepticism: nothing is certain, not even the fact of uncertainty. Suspension of judgment *(epochē)* is the only position that can be justified. Unlike the Stoics and Pyrrhon, he approached the problem of knowledge primarily from the viewpoint of logic, and not from that of ethics. Henceforth logical skepticism, if in the modified form of the New Academy, became a permanent feature of Platonic epistemology. BIBLIOGRAPHY: OCD 79; Copleston 1:414.

[M. R. P. MCGUIRE]

ARCH, TRIUMPHAL, erected over a roadway or street to honor a personage or commemorate an important event; the archway of sculptured decoration, with *attic* carrying an inscription, permits procession through single or triple opening. Popular in ancient Rome, the triumphal arch was prevalent in the Neoclassical movement (19th cent.) throughout Europe and America. In China such honorary forms were often erected for widows of virtue.

[M. J. DALY]

ARCH OF CONSTANTINE (312–315 A.D.), last great triumphal Roman arch of triple opening, commemorating Constantine's victory over Maxentius. Beneath medallions, in reliefs of Constantine addressing the people, nonclassical figures in low relief with incised detail mark a decline in the realization of form. Free-standing figures in the *attic* align with the Roman Corinthian columns of the lower zone, and carved reliefs wing the center area of inscription.

[M. J. DALY]

ARCH OF TITUS (81 A.D.), Roman triumphal arch of single opening flanked by Corinthian piers on pedestals in Roman style with a dynamic string course and superstructure *(attic)* bearing the commemorative inscription. On one wall of the passageway are deeply carved relief panels of Titus's conquest of Jerusalem (66–70 A.D.). The opposite panel of the *Triumph of Titus* shows Vespasian and Domitian in the historic realism of Roman style.

[M. J. DALY]

ARCHABBOT, a title of honor given to abbots of certain distinguished Benedictine monasteries; e.g., Monte Cassino.

[S. A. HEENEY]

ARCHAIC ART, art in an early stage of development characterized by fullness of meaning or intent ("thought form") but limited in technical facility. This crudity of execution enhances the integrity of the work as contrasted with works which though technically facile engage in virtuoso surface effects emphasizing "seen form" but having a dearth of inner meaning. An archaic age is usually followed by a golden age in which technique and intention or meaning are balanced. According to A. Toynbee's "cycle", following the golden age is an age of decline in which artists appropriating only the solutions of the golden age with amazing virtuosity express insignificant ideas or instinctive, purely naturalistic images with a decline in meaning.

[M. J. DALY]

ARCHAMBAULT, PAUL (1883–1950), French Catholic writer. A native of Orléans, A. became professor of philosophy at Ste-Croix de Neuilly (1910), director of *La Nouvelle journée,* a monthly review (1914), and contributed notably to the popularization of M. Blondel with his *Vers un réalisme intégral: L'Oeuvre philosophique de Maurice Blondel* (1930) and his *Initiation à la philosophie blondélienne . . .* (1942). He was also an outspoken defender of Christian democracy, as appears in his *Essai sur l'individualisme* (1910) and his *Pierres d'attente pour une cité meilleure* (1935).

[P. K. MEAGHER]

ARCHANGEL, literally a high or chief angel, hence one that differs from other angels in power or in degree of importance. The term is not used in the OT, and in the NT it is found only twice (Jude 9 and 1 Th 4.16). The Church's liturgy honors three archangels: Michael, captain of the heavenly host and called archangel in Jude 9; Gabriel, angel of the annunciation; and Raphael, traditionally considered the angel that moved the water at the pool of Bethzatha (Jn 5.1–4). Often Uriel, and less frequently Raguel, Sarial, and Jeramial (names taken from Hebrew angelology and occurring in the apocryphal book of Enoch) have been numbered among the archangels by Christian writers. In the hierarchy of the angels that developed under the influence of Pseudo-Dionysius, archangels constitute a distinct heavenly choir ranking above that of the angels but below the seven other choirs. BIBLIOGRAPHY: P.-R. Régamey, *What Is an Angel?* (tr. D. M. Pontifex, 1960).

[T. EARLY]

ARCHANGEL OF PEMBROKE (c.1568–1632), Capuchin. Born William Barlow, of a prominent Catholic family, he moved to France when he could not practice his religion as he wished in England. In 1587 he joined the Capuchins and became a noted reformer (Port-Royal) and spiritual adviser to Angelique Arnaud. He led a group of missionary Capuchins to Brazil in 1614, and he contributed to an effort to convert Hugo Grotius in 1624. BIBLIOGRAPHY: C. Reel, NCE 1:742.

[E. P. COLBERT]

ARCHBISHOP, a term that generally designates a bp. of a diocese who has jurisdiction over an ecclesiastical province. In the Western Church, the title is practically equivalent to *metropolitan. The word first occurs in the 4th cent. when Athanasius, bp. of Alexandria, refers to himself and his predecessor as archbishops. It was also applied to the *patriarchs and bps. of other important sees, but does not appear in the West until the 9th century. In the Middle Ages, abps. had wide jurisdiction within their regional group of dioceses. They could summon provincial councils, judge suffragan bps. as a court of the first instance, and hear appeal cases from their suffragan sees. Today, their power is quite limited: they are obliged to summon a provincial council at least every 20 years; to receive certain appeals from the ecclesiastical courts of the suffragan dioceses; and to observe the doctrine and discipline throughout the province and report any abuses to the Holy See. In addition to metropolitans, the title may be granted *ad personam* to other ordinaries and nonresidential bishops. It is also applied to an ordinary of a diocese outside any ecclesiastical province but not itself a metropolitan center. BIBLIOGRAPHY: S. E. Donlon, NCE 1:742–743; 745–746.

[T. M. MCFADDEN]

ARCHBISHOP MAJOR, a hierarch independent of any patriarch, and as such the head of an Eastern Church or rite; he might have subject metropolitans over their own ecclesiastical provinces. The first such hierarch was the abp. of New Justiniana and of all the Island of Cyprus when the Council of Chalcedon (451) recognized his independence from the patriarch of Antioch and his jurisdiction over emigrants from Cyprus who had settled in other parts of Asia Minor. The abp. of Athens and All Greece is also an archbishop major. In the Catholic Church there is at the present time one archbishop major, the Byzantine rite archbishop-metropolitan of Lvov (Western Ukraine), recognized as such by a decree of Dec. 23, 1963, when Abp. Joseph Slipyj was released after 18 years of Soviet imprisonment. An archbishop major enjoys patriarchal rights in nearly all respects with the exception of those that are an immediate reflection of the patriarchal dignity (ClerSanc cc. 324–339). He appoints the bishops with his synod, erects dioceses, governs with a permanent synod, and exercises similar supraepiscopal authority.

[V. J. POSPISHIL]

ARCHCHANCELLOR, a title bestowed in the Middle Ages on a high ecclesiastical official who also directed the royal chancery.

[S. A. HEENEY]

ARCHCONFRATERNITY, a religious society authorized canonically to affiliate with other societies of the same kind and to confer on them its privileges and indulgences.

[S. A. HEENEY]

ARCHCONFRATERNITY OF PRAYER FOR IS-RAEL, a spiritual association whose purpose is to promote better understanding between Jews and Christians, founded (1905) by the Congregation of Notre Dame de Sion at the request of the laity who wished to join their prayers with those of the sisters. In 1909 Pius X erected it to the rank of an archconfraternity. The canonical headquarters are located in Jerusalem, with branches in many countries in the world. In conjunction with local Jewish communities, these organize libraries specializing in biblical studies. Since 1934, 55,390 members have been enrolled in the U.S.

[S. A. HEENEY]

ARCHDEACON, originally a deacon chosen by the bp. to assist in liturgical and administrative functions in the diocese. The office is known to have existed from the 3d cent.; the title, from the 4th. Often the archdeacon in practice had right of succession to the see. Growth and abuse of the power of the office led to its curtailment after the 12th cent., and after the Council of Trent the title became largely honorary in the RC Church. In the C of E and some other Anglican Churches, however, the office and title continue. The archdeacon must be a priest ordained for at least 6 years; he supervises the discipline and temporalities of a fixed territory (archdeaconry), may also induct both vicars and *churchwardens into their offices, and examines and presents candidates for ordination. BIBLIOGRAPHY: A. Amanieu, DDC 1:948–1004; G. W. O. Addleshaw, *Beginnings of the Parochial System* (1953). *ARCHPRIEST.

[T. C. O'BRIEN]

ARCHDIOCESE, see DIOCESE.

ARCHELAUS, son of Herod the Great and Malthace and brother of Herod Antipas. He ruled Judea, Samaria, and Idumea as ethnarch from 4 B.C. to A.D. 6. He was despised by both Jews and Samaritans and finally was deposed by Augustus and exiled to Vienne in Gaul where he died. BIBLIOGRA-PHY: A. H. M. Jones, *Herods of Judaea* (1938).

[J. J. O'ROURKE]

ARCHEOLOGY, the study of the material remains of the past including the things man made and the things man used. Materials are obtained either by surface collecting or excavation. Things made or artifacts include villages, buildings, tools, ornaments, weapons, art pieces, and monuments.

Things used or nonartifacts include bones of animals eaten, plants used as food, charcoal burned as fire, everything of nature man employed. The study of the bones of ancient man himself is matter for the physical anthropologist or human paleontologist. The deciphering and interpretation of ancient writings and inscriptions is the work of the epigraphist or the philologist. However, epigraphy as a science in itself is closely involved with Near Eastern archeology, esp. that which concerns the Bible and Greco-Roman antiquity. Before the 19th cent. archeology was looked upon more as an art which dealt with the broad study of antiquity in all its existing records. This article is limited to a brief consideration of biblical and early Christian archeology.

In biblical archeology, the site which rises above the ground as a mound is called a *tell* (Arab. mound) within which are strata of several different civilizations. These mounds are explored either by removing one stratum at a time or by excavating vertical trenches so that the various levels can be compared. Sites are chosen because of chance discovery, their proximity to known biblical locations, or because their very antiquity seems to offer some knowledge of the past. One of the most difficult problems for the biblical archeologist is chronology. At present, the study of ancient pottery has provided the most accurate identification of the various strata uncovered. Noteworthy in this development is the study of Mt. Carmel by Dorothy Gerrard (1929–34). Through pottery, Palestinian strata can be dated with respectable accuracy as far back as 3000 B.C. Beyond this period, archeologists date objects and levels according to culture, e.g., the Stone Age (Paleolithic, Mesolithic, and Neolithic); the Bronze Age (3000 B.C.–1200 B.C.; Early, Middle, Late); and the Iron Age (1200 B.C.–). The value of biblical archeology is that it complements what we know of biblical history from the Bible and other sources, has resolved long standing mysteries, raised new questions, and broadened the scope of our understanding of the literary forms in which the Bible was composed. Thus the excavation at Gibeah is the only direct evidence we have of the Age of Saul (1020 B.C.–1000 B.C.). The discovery of the remains of his palace which was built as a fort is in accord with the stories about him in I Sam; the city of Megiddo in the N plain of Esdraelon gives the best example of Solomonic building which has been excavated (I Kgs 9:15–19). The plan of the whole gateway as discovered here is quite similar to that described by Ezek 8.5–16. In matters literary, archeology has discovered literary parallels and background to biblical works, e.g., Sumerian proverbs, Sumerian discussion of the problem of evil; ancient inscriptions which have enhanced our understanding of the texts, e.g., Hebrew, Ugaritic inscriptions; Canaanite religious inscriptions at Ras Shamra; and ancient biblical MSS which have expanded our limited knowledge of the Hebrew, e.g., Dead Sea Scrolls.

Among the more important archeological discoveries of Palestine at the time of Christ are those made by Father H. Vincent of the Dominican School of Jerusalem. These include that of Herod's Tower of Antonia in the NW corner of the temple area and the pavement of the Court of Antonia where Pilate judged Jesus (Jn 19.13). Again the discovery of the Dead Sea Scrolls has shed much light on the Essenes.

Early Christian archeology is mainly concerned with the study of ancient Christian monuments made for or by Christians, e.g., paintings, mosaics, medals, gems, inscriptions, and papyri. Its beginnings were in the 16th cent. with the excavations of the catacombs by Antonio Bosio (1575–1629). While many of his descriptions of the paintings are inaccurate, his approach was critical and his method sound. This was followed by the important study of the hierarchy, organization, calendar, and liturgy of the early Church by the Anglican Joseph Bingham (1668–1723). But it was G. B. De Rossi, who in the 19th cent., made Christian archeology a science. To refine his dating, he used 7th and 8th cent. *itineraria,* early Christian inscriptions, and martyrologies. He discovered the tomb of Pope Cornelius, the crypt of the popes of the 3rd cent. in the catacomb of St. Callistus (1854), the basilica of Nereus and Achilleus in the tomb of St. Domitilla (1873), and the tomb of the antipope Hippolytus (1882).

His work *Roma sotterranea christiana* (3 v., 1864–77) details the topography of early Christian cemeteries. The 20th cent. saw the organizing of systematic excavations, several international congresses on Christian archeology, the founding of academies and chairs of Christian archeology at major universities. With the excavations at Dura Europos in Syria, more attention has been given to the possibility that Christian art began in the East rather than at Rome. Comparative studies in the fields of classical and Christian art as well as the history of religions have been advantageous for all three disciplines. These studies have shown that there are no known Christian paintings before the 2d cent. (*c.*220). The most important excavations of the 20th cent. include the rediscovery of the *Memoria Apostolorum* with several hundred graffiti and inscriptions in honor of SS. Peter and Paul. But the most significant have been the excavations below St. Peter's and the discovery of an early Christian and pagan necropolis containing several highly decorated mausoleums of pre-Constantinian times and a memorial of the Apostle mentioned by the priest Caius (180) at the burial place of St. Peter. Several early basilicas were discovered in Palestine and Syria, e.g., the Basilica of the "Multiplication of Loaves" on the Lake of Galilee (1932); at Gerasa, 11 chapels built between the 2d half of the 4th cent. and the year 611, by Yale University and the American University School of Oriental Research; the Christian house church at Dura-Europos (1931–1932) by Yale University and the French Academy under M. Rostovtzeff. BIBLIOGRAPHY: G. Wright, *Biblical Archeology* (1957); J. Gray, *Archeology and the Old Testament World* (1962); J. Quasten, NCE 1:761–769.

[F. H. BRIGHAM]

ARCHEOLOGY, CHRISTIAN. The Greek word *archaiologia* like the Latin *antiquitates* originally meant "the science of ancient things." It made use of any available source of information, whether formal (written documents), or material (non-written objects made by men for their own use or pleasure), to reconstruct the past. Since the 16th cent., however, the term archeology has been more and more restricted to the study of the nonformal, i.e., the material remains of past cultures. It uses literary sources as means of interpreting these remains, but does not study them as such, with the possible exception of ancient writings on durable materials such as bronze and stone. These are the objects of study for epigraphy, which is by convention included under the science of archeology. Archeology may thus be defined as the science of the material remains of antiquity. As a science comprising a systematized body of knowledge, it collects, classifies, compares, studies, and interprets man-made objects such as roads, towns, temples, houses, statues, weapons, altars, paintings, and pottery of the distant past in order to know something about the life and thought of those who made them. Because of the vast field which it embraces, archeology must be divided into different categories. These divisions may be made according to geographical areas, the objects themselves, or the religion or culture which they represent. We thus have Egyptian and Near Eastern archeology, the study of paintings and sculpture as a part of classical archeology, and American Indian and Early Christian archeology. The latter may be defined as the science of the material remains of Christian antiquity. It studies such objects as religious edifices, cemeteries, liturgical instruments, paintings, sculptures, mosaics, lamps, and gold glasses that can throw some light upon the early Christians as individuals and as members of a community. The period it embraces extends from Apostolic times down to the beginning of the Middle Ages, which may be dated from the death of St. Gregory the Great (A.D. 604). Christian archeology as a science had its origins in the 16th cent. and may be traced back to the Renaissance interest in the past, the discovery of a number of lost catacombs near Rome, and, esp., to the religious controversies arising from the Reformation. Both Catholics and Protestants were keenly interested in finding proofs in Scripture, in the Fathers, and in the remains of Christian antiquity to support their own theological positions. Because of its surpassing wealth in early Christian churches and cemeteries, Rome has been the leading center for such studies. Among the great pioneers in this field were the Augustinian Onofrio Panvinio (1529–68), who wrote on the basilicas and cemeteries of Rome, Pompeo Ugonio (*c.*1613), and Antonio Bosio (1575–1629), whose main work *Roma sotterranea* was not published until after his death (3 v., 1632).

A new epoch in Christian archeology began with the work of Giuseppe Marchi, S.J. (1795–1860), and his great disciple Giovanni Battista De Rossi (1822–94), who devoted his life to the rediscovery and exploration of the Roman catacombs. In recent centuries the popes have been strong supporters of archeological studies. In 1757 a Museum of Christian Archeology was added to the Vatican; in 1816 Pius VII founded the Pontificia Accademia Romana di

Archeologia; in 1852 Pius IX, the Pontificia Commissione di Archeologia Sacra; and in 1925 Pius XI, the Pontificio Istituto di Archeologia Cristiana for the conferring of academic degrees. In his *motu proprio* of Dec. 11, 1925, with which the Pope established the institute, he noted that the treasures of early Christian Rome "constitute for the Holy Roman Church a sacred patrimony of incomparable value and importance. They are indeed witnesses as venerable as they are authentic to the faith and religious life of antiquity and, at the same time, are sources of the first rank for the study of Christian institutions and culture from the times nearest to the apostles" (AAS 17 [1925], 619). The evidence of the early Christian monuments taken alone is of course limited since they were not made to convey information. Nonetheless they do provide concrete support for the doctrines handed down from antiquity through the direct magisterium of the Church. They bear witness to a belief in the particular judgment, the communion of saints, the value of prayers for the living and the dead, the necessity of Baptism, the celebration of the Eucharist, and the role of Peter as the visible head of the Church. Though Rome has far more early Christian remains than any other site, there are many other areas in N Africa, the Near East, and in Europe that are of great significance for their Christian antiquities. From a scientific point of view these remains are frequently as important as those of classical antiquity. For the faithful they can be, in addition, places of pilgrimage and devotion where they can put themselves in tangible contact with their spiritual predecessors of the distant past. BIBLIOGRAPHY: J. Quasten, NCE 1:761–768; P. Testini, *Archeologia Cristiana* (1958); I. Mancini, *Archaeological Discoveries Relative to Judaeo-Christians* (1970).

[M. J. COSTELLOE]

ARCHES, COURT OF, the court for the administration of ecclesiastical law within the Province of Canterbury; it also serves as a court of appeals from diocesan courts within the province. The court formerly met in St. Mary of the Arches, from which it derived its name. BIBLIOGRAPHY: ODCC 79.

[T. M. MCFADDEN]

ARCHETYPES (Jungian *analytical psychology), the structural elements of the *collective unconscious. They are not fully formed symbols but predispositions to think and feel in a certain way about important objects met in life experience, e.g., the infant has an unconscious thought form of mother-in-general which emerges in conjunction with his actual experiences of his mother, and fuses with them in his perception of her. Archetypes originate in the historical experiences of the race repeated through countless generations; they are inherited memory traces of these experiences, and common to all men. Examples are mother, father, hero, Satan, God, magic, birth, rebirth, etc. Archetypes reveal themselves in *dreams, myths, neurotic and psychotic symptoms, art and literature, religions, etc. Archetypes significant enough to be rated a personality system are the persona, the anima and animus, and the shadow. The entire concept has been criticized because it presupposes the possibility of inheriting acquired characteristics. BIBLIOGRAPHY: H. N. Genius, *Encyclopedia of Psychology* (ed. H. J. Eysenck et al., 1972) 1:78–79; M. R. Gamman, "Window into Eternity: Archetype and Relativity." *Journal of Analytical Psychology* 18: No. 1 (1973) 11–24.

[M. E. STOCK]

ARCHIEREUS (Gr. high priest), bishop of any Orthodox or Eastern-rite Catholic diocese; also used for chief priests of the Jews.

[F. WILCOCK]

ARCHIMANDRITE (Gr. head of the fold), in the Eastern Church the superior of a large monastery; nowadays also an honorary title often given to priests for distinguished service.

[F. WILCOCK]

ARCHINTO, FILIPPO (1495–1558), a diplomat who served the papacy and aided in Catholic reform. Born of a distinguished family of Milan, he was educated at the Univ. of Pavia and Bologna. To prepare for his role of reformer, he studied theology and published *De fide et sacramentis* and *Oratio de nova christiani orbis pace habita*. As a doctor of law, A. was talented in diplomacy and was made in succession governor of the city of Rome, vice-chamberlain apostolic, bp. of the Holy Sepulchre, and of Saluzzo. He was also sent by Pope Paul III to represent him at the Council of Trent. BIBLIOGRAPHY: T. Walsh, CE 1:695–696; B. Richard, DHGE 3:1550–53.

[M. C. BRADLEY]

ARCHIPENKO, ALEXANDER (1887–1964) American sculptor. Studying in Russia (1902–08), visiting Paris, and exhibiting in Berlin (1910), A. created cubist forms in concave and convex shapes with innovative *hollows*. Having exhibited in the Armory Show (1913), A. founded an art school in N.Y. (1923), became an American citizen (1928), and taught at the Univ. of Washington (1937). One of the most influential teachers in modern sculpture, A.'s work hangs in the Guggenheim and other important museums throughout the world. BIBLIOGRAPHY: M. Seuphor, *Sculpture of This Century* (1960).

[M. J. DALY]

ARCHITECTONIC, term from architectural design, applied to paintings concerned with form and space. Poussin and Cézanne, in monumental arrangements, examine and express such formal spatial relationships.

[M. J. DALY]

ARCHITECTURE, ECCLESIASTICAL, see CHURCH ARCHITECTURE.

ARCHIVES. Almost from the beginning ecclesiastical authorities sought to preserve records in addition to the Sacred Books. According to the *Liber pontificalis* (1:123) Pope

Clement (c.90 A.D.) assigned notaries to compile accounts of the Roman martyrs. Records of the actual court proceedings against martyrs were available to Christians (Eusebius, *Hist. eccl.* 5:18.9); the *Acts* of Justin and his companions (c.164) are the earliest. Eyewitness accounts, *passiones,* were circulated among various churches; Polycarp of Smyrna (c.156) is the first to be so immortalized. Eusebius (*op. cit.,* 5.1.1), copied a letter about the martyrs in Gaul (c.177), as well as many other early documents. Decisions of early councils were communicated to distant communities (*ibid.* 5:23). The *Acta* of the Councils of Ephesus (431 A.D.) and the Council of Chalcedon (451) have been preserved. Material in the Vatican Archives does not go back much beyond 1200. Pope Paul V in 1612 sought to consolidate papal records. In 1727 Pope Benedict XIII legislated for ecclesiastical archives in Italy. Present canon law (CIC, cc. 372–384, 470) regulating diocesan, capitular, and parochial archives derives largely from 18th–cent. prescriptions. BIBLIOGRAPHY: K. A. Fink, NCE 1:769–770.

[J. E. LYNCH]

ARCHIVES (CIC), the collection of documents relating to the temporal and spiritual affairs of dioceses and parishes (cc. 375–384; 470). Bishops are required to retain the documents, records, and important papers dealing with the origin, history, and official acts of a diocese in a safe place and to maintain a current catalogue of this material. Access to these archives is permitted for an appropriate reason and for a specified period of time, but only with the permission of the bp. or vicar general, and the diocesan chancellor. In addition, secret archives are to be kept for matters of conscience (c. 379). The strict privacy of these secret archives is described in Canon Law; only the bp. or an apostolic administrator may open and inspect these records. Parishes are also required to maintain archives pertaining to its origin, history, and finances. Registers listing the baptism, confirmations, marriages, and deaths of parishioners are also to be kept, as well as a record of their spiritual practices, e.g., reception of sacraments, Easter duty. In November 1974, the National Conference of Catholic Bishops issued "A Document on Ecclesiastical Archives," which urges that each U.S. diocese appoint a qualified archivist so that a "nationwide effort to preserve and organize all existing records and papers" be undertaken. BIBLIOGRAPHY: W. F. Lewis, *Diocesan Archives* (CUA CLS 137, 1941); J. A. Fink, NCE 1:769–770.

[T. M. MCFADDEN]

ARCHONTICS (from *arkōn,* ruler). A Gnostic sect of the 4th cent., known only from the writings of St. *Epiphanius (*Adversus haereses* PG 41:67ff). Peter, a Gnostic anchorite of Palestine, imparted the teachings to Eutachtus who spread them in Armenia. The Archontics rejected all Christian truths. Their bizarre teaching centered upon a system of *archons* ruling over the seven heavens under the mother of light in the eighth. The god of the Jews, called Sabaoth, presides over the seventh; his son is the devil, who from Eve begot Cain and Abel. The quest of the soul is to reach the gnosis, then ascend past Sabaoth through the heavens until it reaches the mother of light. The practices of the sect were vilely licentious. They relied heavily on the apocrypha, esp. the *Assumption of Isaia.* Their history was brief. BIBLIOGRAPHY: G. Bareille, DTC 1:1.2:1769–70.

ARCHPOET (c.1130–c.1164), pseudonym of the greatest of the medieval satirical poets. A client of Rainald of Dassel, Abp. of Cologne, he wrote much of his surviving poetry (10 poems, c.850 lines in all; the last of these c.1164) in Italy. His *Confessio Goliae,* regarded as the masterpiece of medieval secular Latin verse, is remarkable for its metrical and rhythmical virtuosity. It is found in the *Carmina Burana* and was the principal influence in the spread of what is now known as the Goliardic strophe. BIBLIOGRAPHY: H. J. Waddell, *Wandering Scholars* (1932; repr. 1955); Raby SLP 2; P. Pascal, NCE 1:772.

[M. S. TANEY]

ARCHPRIEST, a title applied in several senses: (1) From the 4th or 5th cent. it designated a priest (presbyter) chosen to assist the bp. directly, and esp. by substituting for him in specifically priestly functions (see ARCHDEACON). There were cathedral or urban archpriests and from the 4th cent. rural archpriests, similar to the present-day rural deans or vicars forane (SEE CIC. c. 217). Rural archpriests were important to the development of the parish system. The title survives as honorific, attached to some principal churches in France and Italy. In the Eastern Churches the office in some cases carries with it territorial jurisdiction. (2) The superior over secular priests in England, 1598–1621, was called archpriest. (3) By custom, an older priest assisting one newly ordained at his first Mass was sometimes unofficially designated as archpriest. BIBLIOGRAPHY: A. Amanieu, DDC 1:1004–26; G.N.O. Addleshaw, *Beginnings of the Parochial System* (1953).

[T. C. O'BRIEN]

ARCHPRIEST CONTROVERSY (1598–1602), the dispute between the pro-Jesuit and anti-Jesuit RC clergy in England after the death of Card. Allen in 1594. Not considering the time appropriate to appoint a bishop, Clement VIII appointed George Blackwell archpriest with 12 assistants to rule the secular priests on the missions. Appeals to Rome by the appellants met with disfavor, and the appointment of Blackwell was confirmed. Some of his powers, however, were restricted: Blackwell was rebuked, was disassociated from the Jesuits, and was ordered to have three appellant priests on his council. In 1608 he was superseded by George Birkhead. In 1611 he was suspended for recommending the faithful to take an oath of allegiance to James I in a form condemned by the Holy See.

[S. A. HEENEY]

ARCIMBOLDI, GIOVANNANGELO (1485–1555), papal legate. His father served the Sforza dukes, and his uncles were abps. of Milan, Giovanni (1468–88) and

Guidantonio (1489–97). In 1514 Giovannangelo became legate for indulgences from the Rhone to the Rhine and in Scandinavia. Association with rebels in Scandinavia and abuses in Germany made his mission a failure and set the stage for the success of Lutheranism, but did not hurt his career. Sforza made him ambassador to the popes from 1522, and he later became bp. of Novara 1526–50 and abp. of Milan (1550–55) where he introduced reforms.

[E. P. COLBERT]

ARCIMBOLDO, GIUSEPPE (c.1527–93), Italian painter of cartoons of the life of St. Catherine (in glass, Cathedral in Milan, 1549). As court painter to Emperor Maximilian, A. is renowned for uniquely curious and bizarre "heads" composed of fruits, vegetables, etc., both amusing and satiric. BIBLIOGRAPHY: F. Sluys and F. C. Legrand, *Arcimboldo et les arcimboldesques* (1955).

[M. J. DALY]

ARCOSOLIUM, elaborate 3d-cent. Roman catacomb grave (the burial litter of antiquity was called a *solium;* by extension the tomb came to be so called [Suetonius, *Nero,* 50]). An *arcosolium* was an elegant wall excavation closed horizontally by a slab above which was a stucco arch frequently decorated with a fresco. Earlier *arcosolia* were excavated to the floor to receive sarcophagi. Although some *arcosolia* are along catacomb passages, greater numbers are located in *cubicula.* BIBLIOGRAPHY: P. Testini, *Archeologia cristiana* (1958).

[M. J. DALY]

ARCOVERDE DE ALBUQUERQUE CAVAL-CANTI, JOAQUIM (1850–1930), Brazilian cardinal. Ordained in 1874, he was made bp. of Goias (1890), coadjutor, then bp. of São Paulo (1894), abp. of Rio de Janeiro (1897), and first cardinal of Brazil and Latin America (1905). His entire career was directed toward a revitalization of the Church in Brazil and toward improved Church-State relations. After 1901 he met annually with his suffragan bps. in an effort to implement better the directives of the Latin American Plenary Council (1899). These meetings also prepared the way for the Brazilian Plenary Council of 1939. BIBLIOGRAPHY: I. Silveira, NCE 1:774.

[H. JACK]

ARCUDIUS, PETER (1562–1633), Greek Catholic theologian. A native of Corfù, A. was the first to become a doctor (1591) at the newly formed Greek College in Rome. Shortly thereafter he was sent to Poland, where he fostered the newly achieved reunion of the Ruthenians with Rome as professor of theology in the Greek College of Vilna. His chief work appeared at this time, *Antirrhesis* (1600), a response to an anti-Catholic polemic by the Calvinist Bronski. Returning to Rome (1609), A. spent the rest of his life in study and writings at the Greek College. His controversial works are often rhetorical and not altogether free of exaggeration. BIBLIOGRAPHY: L. Petit, DTC 1:1771–73, with descriptive list of A.'s works; E. Legrand, *Bibliographie hellénique du XVIIe siècle* (1895) 3:209–232.

[T. C. O'BRIEN]

ARCUEIL, MARTYRS OF. A school for boys was opened by the Dominicans at Arcueil in 1863. During the insurrection of the Commune (1871), religious and lay teachers of the school were arrested and imprisoned, 12 eventually being martyred (May 25, 1871). *COMMUNE, MARTYRS OF THE.

[P. K. MEAGHER]

ARDAGH CHALICE, example of 8th cent. apogee of Hiberno-Saxon art in technical perfection and color-splendor of decoration. The cup of beautiful proportions, low-lying and broad, free from barbaric sumptuousness, consists of two semi-spheres of sheet silver joined by a large rivet masked by a band of chased gilt bronze, handles covered with glass plaques, and two medallions on either side of the chalice rich in filigree and enamel; on the foot are small blue glass beads encrusted with gold. Studs of enameled bosses mounted in a plait of gold wire which punctuate the chalice are neither cloisonné nor champlevé technique but formed by an old Celtic method in clay molds fitted with metal grills, or glass encrusted with gold filigree made brilliant by several gold wires of different granulations soldered one above the other forming interlace linear or animal as in Celtic MSS. The silver cup was engraved with names of the Apostles—now half-effaced—in stately lettering with animal interlace similar to that of the Lindisfarne gospels. The chalice is in the National Museum, Dublin. BIBLIOGRAPHY: F. Henry, *Irish Art* (1970).

[M. J. DALY]

ARDALION, ST. (3d or 4th cent.), martyr, probably legendary. The story is that he was a Greek mime who, after a dramatic portrayal of the death of a Christian, was suddenly given the gift of faith; speaking out before his audience, he declared himself to be a Christian. Brought before a magistrate, he could not be induced to apostatize and was burned alive. A similar story is told of SS. Gelasius, Genesius, and Porphyrus. BIBLIOGRAPHY: AS April 2:213; Butler 2:91.

[P. K. MEAGHER]

ARDANT, GEORGES MAURICE (1866–1946), French priest, educator, and journalist. Born at Limoges, A. studied at the Facultés catholiques de l'Ouest, at St-Sulpice, and in Rome. He served as military chaplain during World War I, was a frequent contributor to various journals, and enjoyed a considerable reputation as a speaker. For a list of his works, see G. Jacquemet, *Catholicisme* 1:804.

ARDBRACCAN, ABBEY OF (Áird Breccáin), ancient Celtic monastery near Navan, County Meath, Ireland. It had as abbot-bishop the distinguished Patrician scholar Ultán moccu Conchobuir (fl. before 670). Another Patrician scholar, Tírechán, disciple of Ultán, seems to have studied there. The abbey was frequently plundered by Northmen; it had passed to the bishopric of East Meath by the end of the 12th century. BIBLIOGRAPHY: J. F. Kenney, *Sources for the Early History of Ireland* (1966); J. Ryan, NCE 1:774.

[C. MCGRATH]

ARDCHATTAN PRIORY OF, one of three Valliscaulian houses in Scotland, located on Loch Etive, Argylle, founded by Duncan Mackoull (1230). It declined in the 16th cent., was dissolved by James VI (1602), and is at present a ruin. BIBLIOGRAPHY: S. Cruden, *Scottish Abbeys* (1960).

[S. A. HEENEY]

ARDEN, EDWARD (1542–83), Catholic victim of Elizabeth's persecution. He was high sheriff of Warwickshire where his family had held land from the time of Edward the Confessor. His son-in-law was arrested for plotting to kill the Queen and implicated Arden and a priest living in disguise at Arden's house. The enmity of the Earl of Leicester may have brought on Arden's hanging. BIBLIOGRAPHY: R. Harrison, DNB 1:546.

[E. P. COLBERT]

ARDENNE, MONASTERY OF, a former Premonstratensian abbey near Caen, France. It began as a hermits' cell (1138), came into the possession of the Premonstratensians (1144), and was made an abbey in 1150. It was suppressed in 1790. The church, destroyed in 1944, was rebuilt in 1960. Little remains of the original structures. BIBLIOGRAPHY: N. Backmund, NCE 1:775.

[N. BACKMUND]

AREDIUS, ST. (Aridius, Arigius, Yrieix; d. 591), abbot. Born at Limoges, of a well-known family, A. was instructed in letters and sent to Trèves to the court of Théudebert. He became one of the clergy under Bp. Nicetius who commended A. for his holiness. After his father's death he returned to Limoges and used his patrimony to build churches; later he founded the Abbey of Attane, subsequently called St. Yrieix in his honor, and became the first abbot there. His friend, Fortunatus, celebrates A. in his poems. St. Gregory of Tours relates that miracles were performed through his intercession. BIBLIOGRAPHY: M. C. McCarthy, NCE 1:775; R. Aigrain, *Catholicisme* 1:806.

[M. C. BRADLEY]

AREMBERG, CHARLES D', (1593–1669), Capuchin historical and ascetical writer, iconographer. A., from a noble Flemish family, became a Capuchin (1616), and held the offices of definitor general and provincial in Flanders. His writings defended the Capuchins as authentic Friars Minor and presented their early history, life, and customs. He produced two collections of engravings to accompany his historical works. BIBLIOGRAPHY: T. MacVicar, NCE 1:775.

[H. JACK]

ARENA CHAPEL, PADUA, see GIOTTO DI BONDONE.

ARENDT, HANNAH (1906–75), American writer and social scientist. Born in Germany, A. was educated at the Universities of Marburg, Freiburg, and Heidelberg. She emigrated to the U.S. (1941) and was naturalized in 1950. Her book, *Origins of Totalitarianism* (1951), established her as a major political thinker. *Human Condition* (1958) furthered her reputation. She was the director of various Jewish agencies in the U.S.; was lecturer and Guggenheim fellow (1952–53), Rockefeller fellow (1958–60); held professorships at the Univ. of California (Berkeley), Princeton (where she was the first woman to be given a full professorship), Univ. of Chicago, and the New School for Social Research, N.Y. Among her other works are *Men in Dark Times* (1968) and *Crises of the Republic* (1972). She edited K. *Jaspers' The Great Philosophers* (1962) and W. Benjamin's *Illuminations* (1968). BIBLIOGRAPHY: *International Who's Who* (1973) 55.

[J. R. RIVELLO]

ARENDT, WILHELM (1808–65), German convert to Catholicism, savant, antiquarian, archeologist, publicist. A. was a Berliner. As a Protestant, he was a student of *Schleiermacher and *Hegel, later instructor in theology at the Univ. of Bonn (1831). Shortly after he embraced Catholicism (1832), his masterwork, *Leo der Grosse und seine Zeit,* appeared (1835). A. was appointed to a newly established chair at the Univ. of Louvain, where he labored with distinction and versatility. His writings on antiquity include a *Manuel des antiquités romaines* (1837). A. also published much on the contemporary political issue between Belgium and Germany. BIBLIOGRAPHY: G. Allmang, DHGE 3:1643; J. Forget, DTC 1:1773–74.

[T. C. O'BRIEN]

AREOPAGUS, the name of a rocky hill in Athens NW of the Acropolis and of the oldest council of Athens which met there. Areopagus means "hill of Ares (Mars)." In ancient times the council was politically powerful, but when Paul spoke before it (Acts 17.16–34), its influence was confined to educational and religious affairs. Seemingly it was in this capacity that Paul was brought before it, although the place of its meeting was probably not on the ancient site but farther north on the Agora.

[O. N. BUCHER]

ARESO, JOSÉ (1797–1878), Franciscan Observant, restorer of his order in France. A native of Navarre, A. became a Franciscan in 1824 and went to France during the Spanish Revolution in 1833, working with Spanish people at Bayonne until 1848. Charged with restoring the Franciscan Observants in France, he founded the first house at Saint-Palais, then several others, and served as provincial of the restored French province (1860–63). BIBLIOGRAPHY: E. Longpré, *Catholicisme* 1:807–808, with full bibliog.

[T. C. O'BRIEN]

ARETAS, dynastic name borne by kings of Nabatea. (1) Aretas I was king during the Maccabean period and is mentioned in 2 Macc 5.8 as punishing the high priest Jason, who sought to gain control of the government by violent means. (2) Aretas IV (9 B.C.–40 A.D.), called Philodemos, apparently had jurisdiction as far as Damascus, since Paul said that his governor tried to seize him there (2 Cor 11.32–33). He defeated Herod Antipas in a conflict caused in part by Herod's divorcing the daughter of Aretas to marry Herodias (Josephus, *Antiquities,* 17. 10.9), the marriage condemned by John the Baptist (Mk 6.17–18).

[T. EARLY]

ARETE, a Greek word with a variety of meanings. In relation to a person it can denote any excellence of mind or body; in a moral sense: virtue, moral integrity, or a virtuous way of thinking, acting, or feeling or a specific virtue, e.g., modesty, courage, purity. In relation to God, it denotes his power (2 Pet 1.3) but in the plural his perfections (1 Pet 2.9).

[F. H. BRIGHAM]

ARETHAS OF CAESAREA (d. *c*.944), biblical exegete, bishop. An outstanding figure in the intellectual and literary flowering of 9th and 10th cent. Byzantium, A. made full use of his encyclopedic, heavily philological training in his commentaries on Scripture. He is also noted for his polemical, apologetic, and rhetorical writings as well as a number of revealing letters. Very much involved in the *Tetragamy controversy, as an ecclesiastic he showed himself to be a complete opportunist. BIBLIOGRAPHY: Beck 591–594.

[G. T. DENNIS]

ARETHAS OF NAJRAN, ST., see NAJRAN, MARTYRS OF.

ARETINO, PIETRO (1492–1556), Italian literary tyrant. Poor but noble, he gained notoriety with scurrilous attacks on important people. He had to leave Rome in 1522 for the protection of a condottiere, upon whose death in 1526 he found refuge in Venice, where he became rich by literary blackmail. Vulgar, pornographic, and essentially negative, he wrote better burlesque than serious work. He was the first person to publish his own letters (6 v. 1537–57), valuable for insight into his society. Saints' lives and other Counter Reformation works (1534–43) are shallow and failed to win for him a coveted cardinalate. He lived in licentious opulence but gave to the poor. Titian painted his portrait. At his death, which was sudden, publication of his works was prohibited.

[E. P. COLBERT]

AREVALO, RODRIGO SÁNCHEZ DE (1404–70), Spanish bp. and scholar. A graduate of Salamanca (1428) and a Castilian delegate to the Council of Basel 1434–39, he defended the papacy against conciliarism in five treatises and in diplomatic service. Popes secured four Spanish bishoprics in turn for him before he went to Rome to serve the king and

pope 1460–70. Other works include a Latin treatise on ecclesiastical reform, a Latin history of Spain that follows a chronology of papal reigns, Latin correspondence with Italian humanists, and early vernacular Castilian essays. BIBLIOGRAPHY: A. Lambert, DHGE 3:1657–1661.

[E. P. COLBERT]

AREZZO, Italian city important as a religious and cultural center in the Middle Ages; birthplace of Petrarch. Arezzo is capital of Arezzo province in Tuscany, central Italy, and has been the seat of a bp. since the 4th century. St. Satyrus was the first known bishop. The diocese includes the site where St. Francis received the stigmata. Arezzo had been an Etruscan city before becoming a Roman military station, Arretium, on the Via Cassia. In the 11th century it became a free commune. But Arezzo was Ghibelline and in 1289 the Guelf city of Florence gained a dominance over it that was continued until formation of the kingdom of Italy. Arezzo is one of the dioceses directly subject to Rome, and by action of Clement XII (1730–40) its ordinary holds the rank of archbishop. In addition to its notable Gothic cathedral, dating from the 13th cent., Arezzo has the 14th-cent. Church of St. Francis with frescoes by Piero della Francesca. Near Arezzo is the Camaldoli monastery founded by St. Romuald (*c*.950–1027) and the original abbey of the Olivetans founded in 1319 by St. Bernard Tolomei.

[T. EARLY]

AREZZO, SAN FRANCESCO, see PIERO DELLA FRANCESCA.

ARFE, JUAN DE Y VILLAFANE (1535–1603), son of goldsmith Antonio de Arfe, A. was the most important Spanish High Renaissance goldsmith. His major works are towering elaborate silver custodials. BIBLIOGRAPHY: F. J. Sánchez Cantón, *Los Arfes* (1920).

[M. J. DALY]

ARGENTAN, LOUIS FRANÇOIS D' (family name Jean Yver; 1615–80), Capuchin ascetical writer. Having in his possession some of the writings of J. de *Bernières-Louvigny, he published these under the title *Le Chrestien intérieur ou la conformité intérieure que doivent avoir les chrestiens avec Jésus-Christ* (1660). The work was extraordinarily successful, going through many editions, and was translated into other languages. In 1689 it was condemned by the Holy Office because its doctrine on certain points appeared too close to *Quietism, or at least could be viewed as favoring Quietism. Probably the work would not have fallen under suspicion had it not been for the heat of the antiquietist reaction. Among A.'s other writings, *Les Exercises du chrestien intérieur* (2v., 1664) was proscribed by the Congregation of the Index in 1728. BIBLIOGRAPHY: E. de Alençon, DTC 9:961–963.

[P. K. MEAGHER]

ARGENTEUIL, MONASTERY OF, a religious house founded near Versailles (c.660) by a nobleman, Emeric, and his wife, for religious women. Charlemagne installed his daughter Theodrade there as abbess. At the time of the dispersion of religious, decided by a council of Paris in 1129, Héloise was abbess, or at least superior. The religious were replaced by monks. The monastery was ruined by the Hundred Years War, sacked by the troops of the Prince of Condé in 1587, and restored only about 1625. The Revolution suppressed the monastery in 1791. It was at Argenteuil during the Middle Ages that the holy tunic of the Infant Jesus, thought to be his seamless robe, was venerated. It is actually preserved in the parish church. BIBLIOGRAPHY: A. Lesort, DHGE 4:23–39.

[S. A. HEENEY]

ARGENTI, EUSTRATIUS (1687–1756), Greek theologian and polemicist. A native of Chios, he studied in Germany and Italy before becoming the official theologian of Patriarch Matthew of Alexandria (1746–66). He devoted himself to arguing against Roman missionaries in the Middle East. His writings are characterized by their polemical, anti-Latin tone and include such titles as: *On Rebaptism, Against the Unleavened Bread, Fire of Purgatory, Characteristics of the Antichrist, Against the Pope.* He died in Chios as member of the fraternity of St. John of the Mound. BIBLIOGRAPHY: T. Ware, *Eustratius Argenti* (1964).

[P. FOSCOLOS]

ARGENTINA, country in S America, a republic since 1810 (1,072,157 sq mi; pop. c.23 million). The present pop., largely of Spanish and Italian descent, includes some Indians, Mestizos, and Negroes. Religious communities number over 22 million Roman Catholics, 500,000 Orthodox, 1 million Protestants, and 1 million Jews (the largest Jewish community in Latin America). In 1516 Díaz de Solís discovered the Plata Estuary; in 1536 Pedro de Mendoza founded Buenos Aires; the first Franciscans arrived in 1538, one of whom (Juan de Lezcano) opened schools for the Indians. The first diocese, Río de la Plata (now Asunción), embracing the territories of Argentina, Paraguay, Uruguay, and the south of Brazil, was created in 1547. During the colonial period the Church was governed under the *Patronato Real, and with independence (1810) had to adapt itself to the new situation. The Congress of Tucumán reestablished contact with the Holy See, many of the signatories being clerics. Under Rivadavia (1824–27) there was some danger of a national Church. Religious freedom was decreed and Protestant denominations were admitted; there was a great shortage of priests and profound religious ignorance among the masses. The Vatican named a few bps. *in partibus.* From 1865 until 1897 the situation was in flux; Buenos Aires became an archbishopric; Freemasonry was active and anti-Catholic; schools were secularized; the nuncio was expelled (1884); civil marriage was made a prerequisite to the religious ceremony. In 1897 through the influence of promi-

nent laymen, a *modus vivendi* was agreed upon with Rome. Efforts were multiplied to increase the number of parishes and to provide a system of Catholic education. These goals began, at least in part, to be realized after 1910. Catholic Action was organized and there was a thorough diocesan restructuralization under Pius XI; from Europe came religious of many orders, men and women; a great Eucharistic Congress was held in Buenos Aires in 1934; there were new ventures in the fields of education and communication. From 1952 to 1955 the Perón government showed hostility to the Church: laws opposed to Catholic doctrine were enacted, divorce was made legal, and attempts were made to take control of the Church's institutions. When these failed there was persecution culminating in the burning of churches and religious buildings (1955). This became a national issue and precipitated the end of the regime. Since then Church-State relations have become stable. The nation was subdivided (1961–63) into numerous ecclesiastical circumscriptions: 12 archdioceses (Buenos Aires, Bahía Blanca, Córdoba, Corrientes, La Plata, Mendoza, Paraná, Rosario, Salta, San Juan de Cuyo, Santa Fe, and Tucumán) and 38 dioceses. Efforts have been made to increase the number of educational institutions at all levels (there are at present six Catholic universities); through Catholic Action, Workers' Unions, management groups, sodalities, the Christian Family Movement, cursillos, etc. Laymen have been taking an increasing part in the apostolate; much attention is being devoted to the liturgical and social aspects of the life of the Church; Catholic opinion is fairly well represented in the press as well as on radio and television; the bishops show in general an awareness of renewal; and there has been a fostering of ecumenical contact with other Christian groups and with the Jewish community. By an agreement between the government and the Holy See (Nov. 1966) the Church has recovered full freedom in the nomination of bishops. Among the more pressing problems confronting the Church in Argentina are: the great numbers, esp. of the urban population, who are deprived of the priestly ministry and the sacraments; the scarcity of vocations to the priesthood and the religious life; and the need of adaptation to a population increasingly influenced by powerful secularist opinion. BIBLIOGRAPHY: A. P. Whitaker, *Argentina* (1964); G. Furlong, NCE 1:779–785.

[P. DAMBORIENA]

ARGENTRÉ, CHARLES DU PLESSIS D' (1673–1740), bp. and historian of theology. After studies at the Sorbonne, A. was ordained (1699), named vicar-general of Treguiers (1707), and consecrated bp. of Tulle (1725) where he was noted for his personal holiness and erudition. He helped develop a syncretic doctrine of grace, through which he hoped to avoid the extremes of both the Molinist and Bañezian schools. Most significant among his theological works is the valuable *Collectio judiciorum de novis erroribus,* a three-volume compilation of papal and other ecclesiastical and academic documents relative to theological controversies since the 12th century. BIBLIOGRAPHY: DTC 1:1777–78.

[T. M. MCFADDEN]

ARGON, in Byzantine chant, a subsidiary rhythmical sign (⌐) called a "slow sign." In the Round System of notation, it indicates a slight rallentando, but was rarely used. In present usage, it is a character that divides and augments the value of notes. It is used only above a note called the *oligon* (▬) having a *kentimata* (ۦۦ) below it. In the example below, the argon divides the first note, an *ison* (◡) and the *kentimata* (ۦۦ) into quavers (eighth notes) and augments the *oligon* (▬), making it a minim (half note).

BIBLIOGRAPHY: S. I. Savas, *Byzantine Music in Theory and Practice,* (1965) 17; H. J. W. Tillyard, "Byzantine Music and Hymnography," *Church Music Monographs* (1923) 6:48–49.

[M. T. LEGGE]

ARGYROPOULOS, JOHN (1415–87), one of the most famous Byzantine scholars who went to Italy in the 15th century. He was a member of the Greek delegation to the Council of Florence (1438–39). In the years immediately following, he taught Greek at Venice and Padua. He then returned to Constantinople as a teacher of Greek literature. After the fall of Constantinople, he fled to the Peloponnesus. In 1456 he was invited to Florence by Cosimo de' Medici to take the chair of Greek studies at the Univ. of Florence. Following the plague in Florence in 1471, he went to Rome where he taught for the rest of his life. He is esp. important for his influence as a teacher, numbering among his pupils Politian, Reuchlin, Palla Strozzi, and Lorenzo de' Medici, and for his translations of many works of Aristotle, including the *Physics, Metaphysics,* and *Nicomachean Ethics.* BIBLIOGRAPHY: D. J. Geanakoplos, NCE 1:789–790; *idem, Greek Scholars in Venice: Studies in the Dissemination of Greek Learning from Byzantium to Western Europe* (1962) 75–79, and *passim.*

[M. R. P. MCGUIRE]

ARGYROS, ISAAC (d. *c.*1375), Greek monk. He wrote several works against the Hesychasm of Gregory Palamas. Moreover, he left scientific works in MS on geometry and astronomy.

[E. P. COLBERT]

ARGYRUS, MARIANUS (*c.*1005–68), Byzantine *Dux Italiae.* Argyrus, son of Melo, a Lombard, was held as a hostage in Constantinople (1010–29). He fought against Byzantine domination on his return and in 1042 was chosen leader of the Normans. However, he transferred his allegiance to Byzantium, helping to re-establish its authority in S Italy, and to drive out the Normans. Agreement between papacy and Byzantium on this policy alarmed the patriarch Michael Cerularius who fostered misunderstandings that grew into the schism in 1054. When Pope Nicholas II abandoned the Byzantine alliance, Argyrus retired to Bari. BIBLIOGRAPHY: P. Charanis, NCE 1:790; F. Chalandon, *Histoire de la domination normande en Italie* I (1907).

[G. E. CONWAY]

ARHAT, (Chinese, *Lo-han;* Japanese, *Rakan*), class of disciples or holy men (not deities) who have reached perfection of the Eightfold Path by rigorous discipline but refrain from nirvāna in order to sustain others in the law. As Lohans in the Chinese Buddhist imagery of Sung (960–1279), they reached cult proportions.

[M. J. DALY]

ARIA (It., from Lat. *aer* air), an accompanied solo song, lyric, or dramatic in style. Its length, non-strophic form, and emphasis on musical design distinguish it from related shorter forms such as the air, song, or *lied.* Although generally associated with opera, where it has held a place of prominence until contemporary times, the concert aria, usually quite dramatic in tone, is a well-established musical form, Mozart and Beethoven having composed in this vein. The aria is also an important part of the *oratorio and the *cantata, musical forms which developed along with the opera during the Baroque era in music, as well as related forms such as the musical passion. In such works the dramatic exposition, whether narration or dialogue, is accomplished through *recitatives, while the aria is used for subjective expression of a mood or emotion. During the 17th and 18th centuries the aria was inevitably in ABA form; that is, an opening section, followed by a contrasting middle section, then the opening section repeated, usually with much musical ornamentation added by the singer. The text was usually quite short, only one or two lines per section, and the emphasis was on musical development and, esp. in secular works, vocal display. In later works the ABA form came to be abandoned, and the aria took on a freer form.

[J. J. WALSH; A. DOHERTY]

ARIADNE, ST. (early 4th cent.) martyr. Legend and tradition are probably accurate in recording the fact of A's. martyrdom at Primnesso, Phrygia, during the persecution of Diocletian. The legendary circumstances of her death are repeated in the account of a St. Mary of Phrygia. BIBLIOGRAPHY: R. Aigrain DHGE 4:97–99; G. Gordini, BiblSanct 2:406–407.

[H. JACK]

ARIALDO, ST. (*c.*1000–66), reformer and martyr. Assisted by the laymen Landulph and Erlembald Cotta, A., a deacon, led the Milanese *Patarines in their attempted reform of the Milanese clergy. Excommunicated by the anti-reforming Abp. Guido of Velate, A. appealed to the Holy Father, who upheld him and condemned Guido. He was assassinated by two antireformers. BIBLIOGRAPHY: N. M. Riehle, NCE 1:791; A. Rimoldi, BiblSanct 2:408–410.

[M. A. WINKELMANN]

ARIAN BAPTISTERY, RAVENNA, domed octagonal building erected by Goths (c.500 A.D.), the plain exterior in sharp contrast to the brilliant mosaics (Baptism of Christ) in gold and colored glass on the interior of the dome. The mosaics of early hieratic iconography influenced the later Orthodox Baptistery of Ravenna. BIBLIOGRAPHY: F. W. Derchmann, *Frühchristliche Bauten und Mosaiken von Ravenna* (1958).

[M. J. DALY]

ARIANISM, the important Trinitarian heresy, named after its originator *Arius, that profoundly disturbed both the Church and the Empire in the 4th and 5th centuries. The heresy was condemned by the Council of Nicaea (325), where 300 bps. drew up the Nicene Creed as an expression of orthodox Trinitarian faith. Arius' basic error was his attempt to give a rationalistic explanation to the mystery of the Blessed Trinity, combining Neoplatonic convictions as to the need of intermediaries between God and the world with the *Subordinationism of earlier Christian writers, particularly Origen and Lucian of Antioch. Though only fragments of his few writings remain, from these and other sources the basic outline of his teaching may be drawn: (1) God is unique, uncreated and unbegotten (agennesia). (2) The Son of God, the Logos, cannot therefore be true God. Though the first of God's creatures, he is still a creature, produced like the rest out of nothingness. There was therefore "a time when the Word was not." (3) Since the Word does not proceed from the Father, he is Son only by adoption. (4) Though inferior to God, the Logos, the instrument of creation who later became the Incarnate Word (Christ), is to be worshiped as Ruler and Redeemer and one exalted above every other creature. This doctrine had a great appeal since it gave an easy answer to the difficult problem of the relation existing between the Father and the Son. In fact it solved nothing, since it attributed the redemption to one who was not truly God and thus deprived the redemption of its essential character.

A few years after the condemnation of Arius, a small but resolute group of sympathizers mounted an attack upon his adversaries. Through the decrees of local synods they were able to bring about the deposition of the staunchest supporters of Nicaea, including Eustathius of Antioch, Marcellus of Ancyra, and Athanasius of Alexandria. They were able to do this by appealing to the fears of a large number of Eastern bps. who were essentially orthodox but feared that the key phrase of the council, that the Son was "consubstantial (*homoousios) with the Father," failed to safeguard the real distinction of persons in the Trinity. After the death of Constantine in 337, the exiled bps. were allowed to return to their sees, but the peace did not last long. In the West the Emperor Constans favored the followers of Nicaea, but Constantius II in the East supported the Arians. After the death of Constans in 350 and of Pope Julius I in 352, Constantius, through a series of councils, was able to Arianize the West, driving the orthodox bishops into exile and receiving the submission of the less valiant.

Soon, however, the Arians were themselves divided in their attempts to find a definitive substitute for "consubstantial" of Nicaea. Three main factions emerged, each receiving its name from the attribute given to the Son to designate his relation with the Father: (1) the radical Arians who held that the Son was unlike (anomois) the Father and were thus called *Anomoeans; (2) the moderate Semi-Arians, who held that the Son was "of like substance with" (*homoiousios) the Father and were known as Homoiousians; (3) the uncommitted Arians, who rejected ousia and all its compounds and simply maintained that the Son was "like" (homoios) the Father. These were called Homoeans. The heresy waxed and waned largely in consequence of political developments and the religious convictions of the individual emperors. Valens (364–378) was an ardent defender of Homoeism. Gratian and Theodosius I, on the other hand, vigorously supported Nicaea and by decrees in 380 and 381 denounced Arianism and deprived the Arians of their offices and churches. In the latter year the Council of Constantinople I reaffirmed the faith of Nicaea and condemned the Macedonians, Semi-Arians who had denied the full divinity of the Holy Spirit.

Though checked within the Roman empire, Arianism was by no means dead, particularly among the Germanic tribes in the north who had been converted to this type of Christianity by Wulfila and his successors. During their invasions into Roman lands, they frequently persecuted the native Christians, but they were themselves eventually destroyed or converted. Thus it was the armies of Justinian I that destroyed Arianism among the Vandals in Africa (533) and the Ostrogoths in Italy (540). The Visigoths in Spain were brought into the Church through the conversion of their king, *Reccared, in 587. But it was only a century later that the Lombards under Kings Aribert and Perctarit renounced their Arianism. BIBLIOGRAPHY: Quasten 3:7–13; X. le Bachelet, DTC 1.2:1779–1863.

[M. J. COSTELLOE]

ARIAS, FRANCIS (1533–1605), Jesuit theologian and spiritual writer. A. taught moral philosophy at the Univ. of Córdoba and held the rectorship at two universities. He is known more for his self-discipline and exemplary life than he is for teaching. What is known about his personal life of the spirit is largely gathered from his own spiritual writings, esp. from *Exhortación al aprovechamiento espiritual*, a work in which he unfolds his own inner growth and development. Francis de Sales mentions him as an ascetic in his own work, *Introduction to a Devout Life*. BIBLIOGRAPHY: D. M. Barry, NCE 1:794; J. De Guibert, DSAM 1:844–855.

[J. R. RIVELLO]

ARIAS MONTANUS, BENITO (1527–98), Spanish Orientalist and biblical scholar. He studied at Seville and Alcalá, was a priest by 1559, a member of the influential Order of Santiago in 1560, and a theologian at the Council of Trent (1562–64). Known as an ascetic hermit and master of Hebrew, Syriac, and Arabic, he collected Latin and Oriental MSS for Philip II's Escorial. Philip sent him to Flanders with the Duke of Alva to supervise the edition of the *Complutensis* as the Royal Polyglot Bible (1568–72); papal approval required two trips to Rome. A. also supervised in Antwerp the printing of standard liturgical books for Philip's lands, and he drew up there an Index of Prohibited Books. He returned to Spain via Rome and became the first librarian of the Escorial, for which he had continued to collect MSS of all kinds. From 1584 he lived mostly in Seville. His incomplete commentary on the Bible is literal and depends on rabbinical scholarship; also incomplete is his humanist synthesis of the Bible. He wrote Latin and Spanish poetry all his life. Some of his numerous scattered letters have been published. BIBLIOGRAPHY: A. Romeo, EncCatt 1:1893–94; A. Lambert, DHGE 4:129–145.

[E. P. COLBERT]

ARIBO OF MAINZ (*c*.990–1031), archbishop. Before he became abp. of Mainz and archchaplain of the Empire (1021), Aribo founded a convent at Goss (1020) and a church at Hasungen. His interest in education led him to invite Ekkehard IV of Sankt Gallen to direct the cathedral school of Mainz. Aribo participated in a number of synods as a theologian and canonist. Although he was a brilliant man, an organizer, and a writer, his rigorist attitude nevertheless complicated the problems of Church and State that confronted him. He attended a Lateran Council in 1027, and died while returning from a later trip to Rome. BIBLIOGRAPHY: H. Wolfram, NCE 1:794.

[G. E. CONWAY]

ARIDITY, a state in which the soul is without the consolation or satisfaction that one normally derives from prayer. Traditionally, there are various reasons offered to account for such dryness: lukewarm or half-hearted prayer, and/or service to God, sin, sensuality, excessive activity, and esteem for the goods of the world. One cannot rule out, however, such other causes as physical ailments, sleeplessness, and mental anxiety. Neither can one dismiss the fact that it may be an act of God, in which case one is encouraged to see in it a way of purification for the soul, and thus it may be the liberating force, divinely inspired, to rid the soul of excessive attachment to the world, before the soul is finally brought to a closer, more loving prayer and contemplation of him. The reader is referred to the works of John of the Cross, Francis de Sales, Teresa of Avila, Rodriquez, and other mystics and ascetics for a fuller account of the actual experience of aridity. One is cautioned to forestall ascribing purificatory aridity to one's failure at prayer; it may be that such dryness is a simple extension of a failure to take seriously the evangeli-

cal norms for living totally in the Father, through the Son and Spirit. BIBLIOGRAPHY: K. Kavanaugh, NCE 1:794–795.

[J. R. RIVELLO]

ARIEL, biblical name: (1) one of the leading men summoned by Ezra (8.16); (2) possibly the name of a clan (2 Sam 23.20; 1 Chr 11.22; meaning of the term here is uncertain); (3) name used in Isaiah for Jerusalem (29.1–2, 7)—perhaps referring to the presence of the altar there—translated as mountain of God, lion of God, or hearth of God; (4) water demon in occult medieval literature. In Milton's *Paradise Lost* it is the name of one of the fallen angels. The term also appears on the *Moabite Stone, possibly as a proper name.

[T. EARLY]

ARIMATHEA, the home of Joseph of Arimathea (Mt 27.57 and parallels), generally identified with modern Rentis, 10 miles NE of Lydda, and with OT Ramathaim-zophim, the home of Samuel (1 Sam 1).

[O. N. BUCHER]

ARIMINUM, see RIMINI AND SELEUCIA, SYNODS OF.

ARINTERO, JUAN GONZÁLEZ, (1860–1928), Dominican natural scientist, born in Spain. A.'s special interest was the study of the relationship between the natural sciences and philosophy and theology. After 1908 he was more interested in ascetical and mystical theology than in philosophy. His later years were spent in involvement in controversy over the question of true contemplation. His major work is *Desenvolvimiento y vitalidad de la Iglesia* (*c*.1905); in 1920 he founded *La vida sobrenatural*, a Spanish review of spirituality, published by the Dominicans. BIBLIOGRAPHY: J. Aumann, NCE 1:795; J. Carreras y Artau, LTK 1:851.

[J. R. RIVELLO]

ARIOSTO, LUDOVICO (1474–1533), poet of the Italian Renaissance, author of the first significant Italian dramas, and a leading force in the development of European drama. His great work, a vast epic poem, *Orlando Furioso*, a retelling of the Roland story, was published in final form—46 cantos—in 1532. It has been acclaimed as the greatest work of the Italian Renaissance. BIBLIOGRAPHY: E. G. Gardner, *King of Court Poets* (1906).

[S. A. HEENEY]

ARISTARCHUS OF SAMOS (*c*.310 B.C.–230 B.C.), Greek mathematician and astronomer. A. anticipated Copernicus' theory that the earth revolves about the sun. His statement survives only in a quotation by Archimedes in *The Sandreckoner:* "The fixed stars and the sun remain unmoved, and the earth revolves about the sun in the circumference of a circle, the sun lying in the middle of the orbit." A. combined with this hypothesis the rotation of the earth about its own axis. Vitruvius (9.8) credits him with the invention of an improved semicircular sundial. Only one of Aristarchus's treatises is extant, *On the Sizes and Distances of the Sun and Moon,* which is based, however, on the geocentric theory. BIBLIOGRAPHY: T. L. Heath, *Aristarchus of Samos,* the *Ancient Copernicus* (1913), a work which includes the Greek text; OCD 89.

[M. J. SUELZER]

ARISTARCHUS OF THESSALONIKE, companion and co-worker of St. Paul who traveled with him on his last journey from Troas to Jerusalem (Acts 19.29;20.4), was his fellow prisoner in Caesarea (Col 4.10) and apparently left him at Rome after a harrowing sea voyage (Acts 27.2; 2 Tim 4.11). The 5th cent. Pseudo-Dorotheus and Pseudo-Hippolytus list him with the 70 disciples and say that he was bp. of Apamea in Syria. The former also claims that he was martyred under Nero at Rome together with Pudens and Trophimus. BIBLIOGRAPHY: R. Aigrain, DHGE 4:185–186.

[F. H. BRIGHAM]

ARISTEAS, LETTER OF, a letter supposedly written by one Aristeas to a certain Philocrates, an officer at the court of Ptolemy Philadelphus (283–247 B.C.) which told of the translation of the Hebrew Scriptures into Greek by 72 learned men. This legend accounts for the name, the Septuagint (Latin, seventy), by which the translation is known. There is no doubt about the legendary character of the letter. The date of its composition is uncertain; it was probably written some time between 130 and 70 B.C. Although the letter is apocryphal, it does provide evidence that the Pentateuch was translated from Hebrew into Greek at Alexandria during the 3d cent. B.C. BIBLIOGRAPHY: Charles APOT, (Eng. tr. H. T. Andrews, 1963) 2:83–122; JBC 2:540.

[J. E. LUSSIER]

ARISTIDES (2d cent., A.D.), an Athenian philosopher and early Christian apologist. His *Apology* addressed to the Emperor Hadrian, though known through mention in Eusebius and Jerome, was long considered lost. In 1878 part of the *Apology* in an Armenian translation was published at Venice. A complete Syriac translation was discovered at the Monastery of St. Catherine on Mt. Sinai in 1889 by J. Rendel Harris. In two unequal sections the *Apology* points out the inadequacies of pre-Christian concepts of the Godhead and shows that Christians have come into possession of truth in the fullest measure. BIBLIOGRAPHY: J. R. Harris and J. Robinson, *Apology of Aristides* (1893); Altaner 118–119; C. Tresmontant, *Origins of Christian Philosophy* (tr. M. Pontifex, 1965).

[H. DRESSLER]

ARISTIPPUS OF CYRENE (*c*.425–*c*.355 B.C.), Cyrenaic philosopher. It is disputed whether the philosopher Aristippus or his grandson of the same name is to be identified as the friend of Socrates. More probably, however, the elder Aristippus is the philosopher in question and the founder of the Cyrenaic School. Influenced perhaps by the teachings of Protagoras, he declared that our sensations alone give us certain knowledge; that sensation consists in movement; that, according to the gentle or violent nature of the movement, sensation is pleasurable or painful; and that, in the absence of movement, there is neither pleasure nor pain. Therefore, having ruled out pain and the absence of pleasure or pain, he held that the end of life should be pleasure, stressing the pleasure of the moment as the only true reality, and that this pleasure is physical rather than intellectual. On the basis of experience and judgment, however, the wise man will restrain his desires and thus keep his independence and happiness. BIBLIOGRAPHY: LexAW 305–306; Copleston 1:121–122; Ueberweg 1:171–176.

[M. R. P. MCGUIRE]

ARISTO OF PELLA (2d cent.), early Christian apologist. Although his work is lost, his name is mentioned by *Eusebius and by John of Scythopolis; John links him with the lost Christian apology known as the *Discussion between Jason and Papiscus.* This work, a Christian apology directed to the Jews, is mentioned (without the author's name) by *Origen in his reply to Celsus, who attacked its allegorical interpretation of the OT. In the Dialogue, Jason, a Jewish Christian, uses the allegorical method to convince the Jew Papiscus that Jesus is the predicted Messiah. Works: ed. M. Férotin (1900). BIBLIOGRAPHY: E. Peterson, EncCatt 1:1911–12; Quasten 1:195–196.

[R. B. ENO]

ARISTOBULUS (fl. *c*.169 B.C.) a Jewish philosopher and teacher at Alexandria under the Ptolemies who attempted to reconcile Greek philosophy and Judaism. Eclectic, he used Peripatetic as well as Platonic and Pythagorean traditions in his interpretation of Greek philosophy and poetry as dependent upon Jewish thought. Some of the early Church Fathers considered him the founder of Jewish philosophy at Alexandria. His *Commentary on the Mosaic Law* is preserved only in fragments quoted in Eusebius's *Ecclesiastical History* and in the *Miscellanies* of Clement of Alexandria.

There is also an Aristobulus mentioned by Paul (Rom 16.10) about whom little is known. Various traditions, however, associate him as one of the 70 Disciples who are mentioned in Lk 10:1. BIBLIOGRAPHY: ODCC 83.

[M. G. SCHUMACHER]

ARISTOCRACY, from Gr. *aristos,* best, and *kratos,* rule, a form of government in which ruling power is exercised by an ideally superior class of persons. This was the regime admired in Plato's *Republic,* St. Thomas More's *Utopia,* and Tommaso Campanella's *City of the Sun,* and, sometimes more priggishly, by many later philosophers. In its purity it has been historically realized only briefly and intermittently, for the intelligence and ability of an oligarchy are more to be relied on than its virtue, though the converse might be charitably hazarded about a democracy; the results, however, are worse, for the commonwealth usually suffers more from fools than from wicked men. Strictly speaking in social and political theory an aristocracy is not composed of "aristocrats," for aristocrat has another and cadet lineage from French usage at the time of the Revolution and means a person of an hereditary social class, an *aristo* who is not one of the people. Yet the two, though not necessarily connected, do go together when it is allowed that birth and breeding have something to do with a talent for government. All the same, aristocracies seem to prove more vigorous when they allow for the infusion of fresh blood and recruit themselves from outside: a closed caste has more pride of ancestry than hope of posterity. The fine arts seem to enjoy their best patronage under an aristocracy. It is right that a certain magnificence should attend the honorable conduct of affairs. Ordinary people are appreciative of glitter, both in the worship of God and the service of the state, and are less grudging about its privileged display than levelers think. Still, there are limits to a mystique, and aristocracy often presents its deviation-forms. There are three. Oligarchy, already alluded to, or government by the few, as such has little more to recommend it than government by the majority as such; it may be more efficient here and now, but its basis of popular consent is more precarious. Plutocracy (Gr. *ploutos,* riches) has much to discommend it, though when conducted without avarice, there is more of a swagger about it than about bureaucracy, which may be regarded as an etiolated form of aristocracy.

[T. GILBY]

ARISTOTELIANISM, the term used in the strict sense to designate the philosophy of Aristotle himself. In a broader sense it is employed to designate the teachings of the philosophers who modified in many ways Aristotle's doctrines and who incorporated into their philosophy elements borrowed from Platonism, Stoicism, and Neoplatonism.

[M. R. P. MCGUIRE]

ARISTOTLE (384–322 B.C.), Greek philosopher. His father was a physician and as a result he apparently developed an early interest in science. At the age of 18 he went to study at Plato's Academy, where he remained for 19 years. After the death of Plato he left the Academy. In 343 B.C. Philip of Macedon invited A. to undertake the education of his son Alexander, and he accepted. Eight years later, upon the death of Philip, A. returned to Athens. It was at this time that he founded his own philosophical school, the Lyceum. Besides engaging in philosophical and scientific research, A. began at this time to collect a large number of MSS, thus creating at the Lyceum one of the first great libraries. When Alexander died in 323 B.C., A. was the object of strong anti-Macedonian feelings and he fled from Athens so that the city might not "sin twice against philosophy."

Of all A.'s works, the most important and those of the greatest lasting value are the following: the *Organon* (a collection of his writings on logic); the *Physics;* the *Metaphysics;* the *Politics;* the *Nicomachean Ethics;* the *Eudemian Ethics;* the *De Anima* (his treatise on the soul); and the *Poetics.*

The project which A. sets for himself in his *Metaphysics,* and in particular in Books Z, E, and Θ, is a description of what it means *to be.* We may immediately distinguish two senses in which the question is asked, and so discover two entirely different answers in the *Metaphysics.* In Books Z and E the question appears to be a question of what it means to be something that can be talked about, and in Book Θ the question becomes what it means to be something that comes into being and passes away. The central question of the *Metaphysics* thus distinguishes the two major preoccupations of A.'s entire philosophical enquiry: namely, a consideration of *logos* (talking) and a consideration of *kineseis* (natural processes).

A. begins the consideration of the question of being as subject of discourse by specifying immediately that to ask what it means to be is to ask what it means to be a substance *(ousia)* (Metaph. 1028b2). In other words, the proper question to ask concerning an individual being is "what is it as this particular individual." A. insists that this question is not to be answered in terms of matter or form (see below), since neither of these specifications addresses itself to the question of what something is precisely insofar as it is this individual. Rather, both matter and form address themselves to the more general question of what it means to be this kind of thing.

It is important to note that there are several reasons why A. considers the question of substance to be of central importance to his metaphysical investigations. He expresses these reasons in terms of the priority of the notion of substance. Substance in A. may be said to be prior in three ways. (1) It has priority of existence because substance can exist alone, whereas all other categories which might be considered in metaphysics rely upon substance for their existence. (2) It has a priority of definition, in the sense that to define anything correctly it is necessary to define the substance in which the characteristics of the thing are grounded. (3) It has a priority in knowledge, in the sense that knowing what something is is superior to knowing about its relations (i.e., quality, quantity, place, etc.). Thus the question of substance is conceived to be central to any questions dealing with being, or with logic, or with knowledge.

Now there are several senses in which the notion of substance may be understood. It may be seen to refer to matter, as that which distinguishes one individual from another having the same form. It may be conceived as that which defines a particular genus of individuals. It may be understood as a universal possessed by individuals. Finally, it may be conceived of in terms of essence. Of these alternatives, only the last defines substance in any primary sense.

For A. the precise answer to the question of what it means to be this particular thing is to possess this particular essence *(to ti ēn einai).* Essence is to be conceived as that which is identical with the thing itself, insofar as the thing is to be understood as individual thing. It is the intelligible structure of anything, which intelligible structure is expressed in language when we attempt to say of anything what it is. It is that which is knowable about a thing; that which language formulates or depicts about an individual. Essence itself is not to be conceived of as a formula or definition, but rather as that which makes such formulation by language possible. Essence is that which everything that is possesses, insofar as we can speak of its being at all. But, because of the distinction between essence and substance (essence explains what it means to be in terms of speaking) it remains true for Aristotle that what is known is always something different from what is. What is is substance, and what is spoken about, and therefore known, is essence.

In arriving at the notion of substance explainable in terms of essence, A. also introduces and considers the notions of matter and form. Although these categories ultimately fail to answer the question of substance, they are none the less central to A.'s analysis of what it means to be. The concepts of matter and form may be seen as an attempt to view substance in a static state, in order to see what composes it and makes it this individual thing.

Matter is seen as that which is presupposed in any change; that which preserves the identity of a being through change. It is therefore to be found in all substances which change. There are four different ways in which things can change according to A., and so substances may be implicated in matter in four ways: (1) locomotion; (2) change in quality; (3) change in size; and (4) generation and corruption. Everything that is involved in change is implicated in matter in some way, and so every substance (except rational mind) involves matter. A. also posits what he calls intelligible matter, over and above the matter which defines these changes, as that which characterizes extension.

Now when we abstract from a given substance all matter (including intelligible matter) that which remains is form. Form thus becomes an abstract, universal category which serves the function of specifying of an individual what type of individual it is. It is a class specification, and as such has no separate existence apart from the members of the class which it specifies. It is, of course, still to be considered as a real determination of an individual, but not as a self-sufficient determination. Neither matter nor form, then, answer to the question of what it is to be insofar as one is this particular concrete individual. However, the matter-form complex, which A. considers to be a way of speaking about essence, does define the individual as what it is.

When A. turns from a consideration of what it is to be as a subject of discourse to what it is to be as something which comes into existence and passes away, he moves from the relatively static concepts of essence, form, and matter, and considers the questions of causality, potentiality, and action.

Things, A. realizes, are constantly becoming other things. He was too much of a realist to deny this empirical fact, and so he is faced with the problem of accounting for change and for identity throughout change. Change, he suggests, can be accounted for in terms of a series of questions, the answers to which specify all possible causes of a thing's changing. The questions are: (1) what is it (what is its formal cause); (2) who made it (what is its efficient cause); (3) out of what was it made (what is its material cause); and (4) why was it made (what is its final cause). In any process of change, A. suggests, all four answers, and thus all four causes are discoverable. These four answers are precisely the answer to the question of what is necessary to understand the production and change of substances.

Although the four causes define change with respect to substances, they fail to explain how an individual can preserve his individuality through change. In order to handle this problem in terms of dynamic categories, A. proposes the notions of potentiality and actuality. Potentiality is said to be the ability of an individual to change in a particular way, which ability must be part of his nature. Actuality, on the other hand, is conceived as the actual state in which something is existing. Thus, nothing passes from one thing to another with no reason for change and with no preparation. If there is change, we must be able to discover in that which changes the seeds of the change itself. This renders change orderly instead of catastrophic, and insures the preservation of identity in some sense, since change is the actualization of a potentiality already present, and not the total annihilation of one individual and the instantaneous creation of another.

It would be well to consider briefly, at the end of a discussion of A.'s metaphysics, the notion of God or the Unmoved Mover as it occurs in A. In Book Lambda of the *Metaphysics* A. is concerned with a description of that which is the cause of all things. This ultimate cause must have certain characteristics in terms of which it may be said to be the cause of everything else. It is an immaterial substance, which exists eternally in a state of act, and is itself unmoved. Such a substance would be the cause of all other things in the sense of being the final cause which causes in terms of attraction. As A. puts it: "... the object of desire and the object of thought move in this way; they move without being moved." (Metaph. 1072a25).

A few brief words are necessary about Aristotle's conception of the soul, as described in the *De Anima*. A. distinguishes three types of souls: the nutritive, the sensitive, and the rational; these are arranged in ascending order of importance, the higher requiring the lower as part of its nature, but the lower not implying the higher. The nutritive soul is found in all living beings, and is regarded as the principle of orderly and symmetrical growth. The sensitive soul is found in some animals and is the principle in terms of which perception is possible. In a discussion of the sensitive soul, A. distinguishes not only the five senses, but also the *sensus communis,* or "common sense," which is that faculty of the sensitive soul which enables a being to perceive that which is common to more than one sense, that which is incidental to sense, and that which distinguishes between senses. Imagination is distinguished as a by-product of the sensitive soul. Finally the rational soul, which is found only in man, is the receptacle of rational form and is the principle in terms of which thought and judgment are possible. In the rational soul, A. distinguishes between active and passive reason, or between the efficient and material causes of thought. Reason does not create its thoughts out of nothing, and so there must be a material for rational thought (passive reason) and an efficient cause of the thought (active reason). Passive reason is that out of which all thoughts are made, or that which becomes all thoughts, and active reason is that which makes all thoughts.

Aristotle's consideration of ethics centers around the question of what is the good for man. This good for man is that which he seeks according to his nature. A. calls it *eudaimonia* or happiness. This is to be distinguished from what a particular man might wish for, since *eudaimonia* is what is good by nature, and not what man happens to think is good. The entire thrust of the ethics is the discovery of this natural good.

In his analysis of good, A. distinguishes two different classes of virtues. These two types of virtue are: (1) moral virtue, which is involved with the rational control of desires; and (2) intellectual virtue, which is involved either with the contemplation of unchanging and eternal truths (theoretical wisdom) or with the contemplation of objects which are subject to change (practical wisdom). Practical wisdom is concerned with the good in action, with discovering specific ends and relating means and ends so that desire can be brought into conformity with reason. This A. considers to be inferior to theoretical wisdom, which does not concern itself with the adjustment of means to ends but merely with the contemplation of the ends themselves. It is in theoretical wisdom that A. ultimately discovers *eudaimonia*. The end of man is the contemplation of unchanging truths, and that which is a good or virtuous action is one which is directed toward this end.

There is a sense in which it is impossible to specify the influences which A. has had upon contemporary philosophy since his influence has been so pervasive. Of course, it is possible to distinguish certain obvious influences. Thomas Aquinas was profoundly influenced by A. and insofar as there are still Thomists in contemporary philosophy, A.'s influence is obvious. But there are more subtle influences which A. exerts, and these are not easily specified. A. N. Whitehead, for example, quotes A. with approval and seems to oscillate in his own philosophy between A. and Plato. P. Weiss, in his *Modes of Being*, shows tendencies which could be considered Aristotelian. In general we might say that anyone doing metaphysics today in some way comes under the influence of A. BIBLIOGRAPHY: G. R. G. Mure, *Aristotle* (1932); W. D. Ross, *Aristotle* (5th ed., 1949.)

[F. J. CUNNINGHAM]

ARIUS (256?–336), originator and chief proponent of *Arianism, a major 3d-cent. Trinitarian heresy. A. was born in Libya, studied under Lucian of Antioch, and was ordained a priest in Alexandria c.312. Some years later his orthodoxy came under suspicion. Condemned by a synod of 100 bps. in 320 or 323, he left Alexandria and found powerful allies in Eusebius of Nicomedia and Eusebius of Caesarea. While in Nicomedia he wrote his principal work, the *Thalia* (Banquet), partly in prose and partly in verse so that it would have more appeal for the common people. Only fragments of this work are still extant. Through the intercession of Arius' friends, Constantine summoned the Council of Nicaea (325) to examine his doctrine. There the 300 assembled bps. condemned Arius and formulated a creed to quash the errors he had been promulgating. Rehabilitated by a profession of faith judged to be orthodox by his own followers at the Council of Jerusalem in 335, he died suddenly in Constantinople, the day before he was to have been formally reconciled by the order of the Emperor. BIBLIOGRAPHY: T. E. Pollard, "Origins of Arianism," JTS (1958) 9:103–111; X. Le Bachelet, DTC 1.2:1779–1806. L. W. Barnard, "What Was Arius' Philosophy?" *Theologische Zeitschrift* 28 (1972) 110–117.

[M. J. COSTELLOE]

ARIUS, KING OF SPARTA (309–265 B.C.), son of Acrotates of the family of Agiades and an ally of the Egyptian rulers Ptolemy Ceraunos (280 B.C.) and Ptolemy Philadelphus (267 B.C.) against Antigonus Gonatas, the Macedonian. According to 1 Macc 12.7, A. concluded a treaty of friendship with Onias I, the Jewish highpriest. The Hebrew version of A.'s letter is quoted by Jonathan Maccabee (1 Macc 12.19–23) in his effort to renew this ancient bond of friendship (143 B.C.). BIBLIOGRAPHY: J. C. Swain, InterB 1:222.

[F. H. BRIGHAM]

ARIZONA, one of the Rocky Mountain states, admitted to the Union (1912) as the 48th state. Artifacts discovered there have an age of 20,000 years, and early inhabitants included such anthropologically significant tribes as the Hopi Pueblo Indians. The first white explorer, the Franciscan Fray Marcos de Niza, crossed over into Arizona from New Spain during an official expedition in 1539. He was followed by Francisco Vásquez de Coronado, who led military expeditions against the Zuni and Hopi tribes. Missionary activity from Mexico brought Catholicism to Arizona. Eusebio Francisco *Kino, a scholarly Italian Jesuit, left his base in Sonora in 1687 to establish Mission Dolores in southern Arizona. Kino founded numerous missions, baptized thousands of Pimas, promoted cattle raising, and explored and mapped the region around the Gila and Colorado rivers. After his death (1711), his work was continued by German Jesuits under the direction of Mexican superiors. The expulsion of the Jesuits by Charles III of Spain left the Arizona missions without priests, but other orders, particularly the Franciscans and Dominicans, gradually filled the gap.

Arizona was made a vicariate apostolic in 1868. Its first bishop, Jean B. Salpointe, together with six French priests, administered to Catholics in the vast area between the Colorado River and the Rio Grande. Salpointe's successor as vicar was Peter Bourgade, who became the first bp. of Tucson when that diocese was erected in 1897. In 1936, under Bp. Daniel Gercke, the diocese joined the new metropolitan Province of Los Angeles, and 3 years later the new Diocese of Gallup was created to administer the northern half of the state. Arizona's pop. of 1,824,534, now more than 55% urban, makes it the 33d most populous state in the Union. In 1971 Catholics numbered 408,996, or 3.1% of the total state population. The major Protestant sects are the Church of Jesus Christ of Latter Day Saints (Mormons), comprising in 1971 6.0% of the state's population, and the Southern Baptist Convention, with 4.8%. The Jewish population (1968) was 20,485, or 1.1%. Although there are no Catholic colleges in Arizona, there are 10 Catholic high schools with an enrollment of 4,452 students, as well as 52 Catholic elementary schools with more than 14,000 pupils. BIBLIOGRAPHY: H. H. Bancroft, *History of Arizona and New Mexico* (1889); P. M. Dunne, *Jacobo Sedemayr: Missionary, Frontiersman, Explorer in Arizona and Sonora* (1955); R. K. Wyllys, *Arizona: The History of a Frontier State* (1950).

[J. L. MORRISON; R. M. PRESTON]

ARK, vessel in which Noah, his family, and representatives of each animal species survived the Flood (Gen 6–8). Noah built the ark at God's command and according to God's instructions. Made of ''gopher'' wood (the kind of wood is uncertain), it had three decks and measurements equivalent to about 450 feet in length, 75 in width, and 45 in height. Some scholars think the biblical description was likely patterned after the ark of Utnapishtim of the Babylonian Flood. Since it was the means through which Noah and his family were saved from God's judgment on the sinful world, the ark became a symbol of salvation (1 Pet 3.20). *FLOOD.

[T. EARLY]

ARK (Coptic Church; Coptic, *pitote;* Arabic, *kursi' l-kas*), in the *Coptic Liturgy a cubical box which rests on the altar. The chalice with paten is placed in the ark through a hole in the top before the consecration and remains there until the communion. The sides are covered with paintings. The ark is never used outside the Liturgy to reserve the Eucharist. Among the Ethiopians, the ark *(tabot)* is solemnly placed on the altar when a church is consecrated. Its origin is unknown and it has no function in the liturgy, although a wooden board on which the sacred gifts rest during the liturgy is also called *tabot,* as is sometimes the whole altar. BIBLIOGRAPHY: A. J. Butler, *Ancient Coptic Churches of Egypt* (2 v., 1884).

[D. W. JOHNSON]

ARK OF THE COVENANT. The Hebrew word *'ărōn* by which the ark is expressed means a chest. The ark is described in Ex 25.10–22; 37.1–9. It was made of setim wood (an incorruptible acacia) and measured about 4 feet long, 2½ feet wide, and 2½ feet high. It was overlaid within and without with plates of gold and a golden rim ran around it. At the four corners, toward the upper part four golden rings were cast; through them passed two bars of setim wood overlaid with gold. This was the way the ark was carried. These two bars always remained in the rings even when the ark was in the Temple of Solomon. Over the ark was a gold plate the same size as the ark called in Hebrew the *kappōret,* which served as a cover or lid to the ark. Upon this were two cherubim of beaten gold, one at each end looking toward the other. The ark, the cherubim, and eventually even the *kappōret* were all symbols of God's providential presence with his chosen people. The tablets on which the Ten Commandments were written were placed in the ark (Ex 25.16; 40.20; Dt 10.1–5). Moses was also commanded to put into the tabernacle, near the ark, a golden vessel containing an omer of manna (Ex 16.34) and the rod of Aaron which had blossomed (Num 17.10). The holiest part of the ark was the oracle, the very heart of the sanctuary, the place where Yahweh gave his prescriptions to Israel, from the midst of the two cherubim. The ark was both receptacle and a sign of God's presence. The Jewish rabbis avoided pronouncing the names expressing the Divinity such as El, Elohim, etc., and still less Yahweh, the ineffable name; instead they used expressions referring to the divine attributes. The word *Shekinah* became popular; it meant The Divine Presence. The ark was a place above which his presence would in some mysterious way be localized, and in such a way the ark represented the footstool of his royal throne. The ark needed a tent to protect it from weather and profanation. The ark and the tent came to express the distinctive faith of Israel. Yahweh was worshipped as the transcendent God who dwells in heaven and who is also present in the midst of his people as their leader. The tent represented a theology of manifestation and the ark a theology of presence. The tent was associated with the Southern group, esp. Judah, while the Ark became identified with the Northern group, esp. the Joseph tribes. During David's time the tent and the ark were reunited. One of the oldest fragments of the Pentateuch is the ''Song of the Ark.'' The ark was carried by the Levites (Dt 10.8). When the Israelites left Sinai the ark went before them and showed them their resting places (Num 10.33–36). Josue (ch.3–6) states that the ark led the way into the Promised Land. It was carried into battle at Aphec, captured by the Philistines (1 Sam 4.3–7), and then returned to the Israelites at Beth-Sames. The most important center of cult was the sanctuary at which the ark of the convenant was reserved. At first this was at Gilgal near Jericho, then at Shiloh, Shechem, Shiloh again, and for a period at Bethel. David brought the ark to Jerusalem. It was placed in the Temple Holy of Holies by Solomon (1 Kg 6.19; 8.1–9). It was probably destroyed with the Temple in 587 B.C. The Fathers of the Church have considered the ark of the covenant as one of the richest symbols of the realities of the New Law. It signifies the Incarnate Word of God. St. Bonaventure has seen in the ark a mystical representation of the Holy Eucharist. It might well be regarded also as a mystical figure of the Blessed Mother.

[C. C. O'DONNELL]

ARKANSAS, a south central state, admitted to the Union (1836) as the 25th state. After the area was explored (1541) by Hernando de Soto, it was not entered again by white men until 1673, when it was visited by Jacques *Marquette and Louis Jolliet. In 1682 the whole Mississippi Valley was claimed by France and named Louisiana by Sieur de *La Salle. The Arkansas area was acquired by the U.S. as part of the Louisiana Purchase in 1803. Jesuits and Vincentians conducted Catholic missionary work in Arkansas. Because of the small number of Catholics and the fluctuating political situation, local ecclesiastical jurisdiction was not established until the Diocese of Little Rock was created (1843). The first bishop was Andrew Byrne, an Irish-born prelate who began his work (1844) with only two priests as assistants. Byrne died in 1862 but because of the Civil War, Edward Fitzgerald was not named as his successor until 1867. Fitzgerald's episcopacy began with only five priests and 1,600 Catholics, but by the time of his death (1907) the Benedictines, Holy Ghost Fathers, and seven orders of nuns had established themselves in Arkansas. John B. Morris, the third bp. of Little Rock, served for nearly 40 years. He supported publication of the *Guardian,* a Catholic weekly, and convoked (1909) the first synod in the diocese. An ambitious building program resulted in such institutions as St. John's Home Missions Seminary and St. Joseph's Orphanage. Albert L. Fletcher, bishop from 1946–72, continued the institutional growth of the diocese, founding Catholic High School and St. Vincent's Infirmary. Arkansas' pop. of 1,923,295, more than two-thirds rural, makes it the 32d most populous state in the Union. In 1971 Catholics numbered 55,025, or 2.9% of the total state population. The major Protestant sects are the Southern Baptist Convention, with 22.6% of the pop. (1971), and the Methodist Church, with 9.6%. The Jewish pop. (1968) was 3,306 or 0.16%. There are six church-related colleges in Arkansas, but none are affiliated with the Catholic Church. There are 7 Catholic high schools and 40 Catholic elementary schools with enrollments of 2,220 and 6,757 respectively. BIBLIOGRAPHY: J. G. Fletcher, *Arkansas* (1947); Historical Commission of the Diocese of Little Rock, *History of Catholicity in Arkansas* (1925).

[J. L. MORRISON; R. M. PRESTON]

ARLEGUI, JOSÉ (1685–*c*.1750), Franciscan historian. A. was born and educated in Spain, became a Franciscan (1701), and was sent to Zacatecas in Mexico where he was successively professor of theology, regent of studies, guardian, and provincial. He was a zealous mission worker, influential preacher, builder, and educator. He wrote treatises on theology, but his most important work is the history of the Zacateca province of the Franciscans which incorporates some unique information on Indian life and Franciscan catechetical efforts. BIBLIOGRAPHY: E. Gómez-Tagle, NCE 1:820.

[H. JACK]

ARLES, former ecclesiastical center of S France. Located near the mouth of the Rhone and controlling access to and from the Mediterranean, Arles was an important city from Roman times and became noted in Christian history as the site of an archbishopric and several councils. For a time from the 10th cent. it was the capital of a Kingdom of Arles.

According to statements by Pope Zosimus (d. 418) and St. Gregory of Tours (*c*.540–594), the first bp. of Arles was St. Trophimus. He is perhaps to be dated in the 3rd cent., though in the MA he was identified with Paul's companion Trophimus (Acts 20.4). Other prelates who served at Arles included SS. Honoratus (*c*.350–429), founded of Lérins abbey; Hilary (403–449), Caesarius (*c*.470–542) and Aurelian (d. 551). Before the honor passed to Lyons, Arles was at times the primatial see of Gaul, and its abps. often played key roles in church affairs. From a reference in Bede, it appears that St. Augustine of Canterbury received episcopal consecration in Arles, presumably from St. Virgilius (d. *c*.610). The last abp. of Arles, J. M. Du Lau, was a victim of the Paris massacre of Sept. 2, 1792. The 1801 concordat abolished Arles as an episcopal see, and today it is an archdeanery under Aix-en-Provence.

The first and most noted of the councils held in Arles was called by Constantine in 314 to deal with the Donatist controversy. In addition to taking a stand against Donatism, the assembled prelates dealt with the Easter question and other matters of discipline. A list of the churchmen present at the council gives evidence of the state of the church hierarchy at the dawn of the Constantinian era. Among some 15 other councils held in Arles were an Arianizing council in 353 and one in 1234 that acted against the Albigensians. The last council of Arles was in 1275, though numerous diocesan synods were held there in later centuries.

Arles became a center of Jewish scholarship in the MA, but Jews were expelled in 1494 and did not return until after the French Revolution.

[T. EARLY]

ARLES, ARCHITECTURE OF. Trading post of the Ionians (6th cent. B.C.) the port was designated Arelate (4th cent. B.C.). Julius Caesar gave his name to a colony of veterans at Arles and in 104 B.C. the Romans linked Arles to the Mediterranean Sea by canal. Impressive Roman ruins are an amphitheater, forum, and theater (all of the Augustan Age), baths (Constantinian), and city walls (late Empire). In 353 A.D. the city was named Constantia in honor of Constantius II (350–361) who resided there. Famed is the Alyscamps, avenue of Merovingian stone sepulchers (*Falling Leaves* by Van Gogh, Metropolitan Museum, N. Y. City). Early Christian archeology presents difficulties, scholars disagreeing regarding foundations. H. G. J. Beck states that the ancient pavement underlying Saint-Trophime (latter 12th cent.) probably belonged to the basilica Constantia mentioned in *Vita s. Hilarii* (13). *Arles is most renowned for the beautiful Romanesque church of Saint-Trophime. Several museums house antique art, Christian sarcophagi (4th-5th cent.), Byzantine ceramics and coins, and Romanesque and Gothic sculpture from the Abbey of Montmajour. BIBLIOGRAPHY: H. G. J. Beck, NCE 1:820–821. *ARLES, SAINT-TROPHIME.

[M. J. DALY]

ARLES, SAINT-TROPHIME, a great ensemble of noble Provençal Romanesque, Saint-Trophime, in a region rich in Roman remains, is distinguished for its classical portal. Built after 1150 in a spirit foreign to French, quiet, dignified as a Roman triumphal arch, the portal carries a Greek pedimental gable supported by a French corbelled table. The archivolt of the tympanum presents a series of Roman string courses in dramatically measured bands, framing the serene and monumental Christ of the Last Judgment, surrounded by symbolic forms of the Evangelists. At Christ's feet are the Apostles beneath whom range right and left the saved and the damned in a synthesis of garment and form reminiscent of the frieze on the Arch of Constantine. Corinthian columns on animal pedestals (Lombardy) define niches where saints, gravely classical, stand in draped robes. The magnificently imaginative cloister bears a pillar inscription (1180), and carved out of the angle (a device from Languedoc) are figures of Peter, John, and Trophimus, the last, one of the finest creations of Provençal Romanesque in the local character of the face. Characteristic of the Provençal School is the theme of the women purchasing perfumes for anointing the dead Christ. Legend tells of the noble beauty of the women of Arles (*L'Arlésienne* by Van Gogh). Saint-Trophime (with Saint-Gilles du Gard) evidences classical and derivative forms foreign to the eccentric genius of other French Romanesque centers. BIBLIOGRAPHY: C. R. Morey, *Medieval Art* (1942); H. Focillon, *Art of the West* (1963) v.1.

[M. J. DALY]

ARMADA, the great Spanish fleet sent by Philip II of Spain against England in 1588. The expedition was organized by Philip of mixed Spanish and Portuguese sails, partially at the urging of Pope Sixtus V. The objectives of the enterprise were to unseat the Protestant Queen Elizabeth of England, restore Catholicism there, and facilitate the suppression of the Dutch rebels, who had been receiving the support of Elizabeth. Philip approached the enterprise with great caution. Because of political considerations, he had been reluctant to undertake it until the execution of Mary Stuart in 1587. Mary bequested her claim to the English throne to Philip, and it now became a matter of honor. Philip's action was in many respects a defensive one. English seamen like Sir Francis Drake had, with the covert encouragement of Elizabeth, long been raiding Spanish shipping, and Elizabeth had been supporting the Dutch rebels. In consequence, by 1585 there was an undeclared state of war between England and Spain. Contrary to a long-held popular

view, the Armada itself was the underdog, for Elizabeth was "mistress of the most powerful navy Europe had ever seen" (Mattingly). Everything went wrong for Spain. The stores were short, the winds were contrary, and the English Catholics were loyalist. The Armada was destroyed not so much by the English navy as by the storms at sea. Half the fleet returned to Spain, but the vessels were no longer seaworthy. The significance of the Armada has been exaggerated, but it did seem to indicate that the Counter-Reformation would not triumph throughout Europe. BIBLIOGRAPHY: G. Mattingly, *Armada* (1959).

[D. G. NUGENT]

ARMADIUM, from the Latin *armarium* a term derived from the Italian *armadio* and the English *ambry or aumbry. To its original meaning of "cupboard" there was added, even in classical Latin, the connotation of a repository for books. The librarian in medieval monasteries was called the *armarius*. Later the *almorie* was a cupboard or closed recess in the wall of a church for sacred books, vestments, or altar vessels. Today only the holy oils are kept in the ambry. BIBLIOGRAPHY: E. E. Malone, NCE 1:822–823.

[J. E. LYNCH]

ARMAGEDDON, scene of the final battle between good and evil (Rev 16.16, only occurrence of the word in the Bible). After the sixth angel poured out his bowl of wrath, John saw three foul spirits gathering the kings "of the whole world" for battle on the "great day of God," and assembling them at Armageddon. John said the place was called Armageddon in Hebrew, but the word has not been found in any extant Hebrew literature. Some scholars suggest that it is a Greek transliteration of the Hebrew *har-magedon,* mountain of Megiddo, designating the part of Mount Carmel near which Megiddo lay. Many battles of Israel's history were fought on the plain of Esdraelon, which is in that area (Jg 5.19; 2 Kgs 23.29), but no Mount Megiddo is known. Other scholars consider the term a corruption of the Hebrew *har mo'edh,* mount of assembly, given by Isaiah as the place where the pagan gods would assemble (14.13).

[T. EARLY]

ARMAGNAC, GEORGES D' (*c.*1500–85), cardinal, diplomat, humanist. He was made bp. of Rodez (1530), ambassador to Venice (1536–38) and Rome (1540–45), cardinal (1544), abp. of Tours (1545), abp. of Toulouse and lieutenant-general of Languedoc (1552), and governor of Avignon (1565–85). He was a defender of civil and religious orthodoxy and worked against the Huguenot disturbance in S France. A. was also a noted patron of letters. BIBLIOGRAPHY: C. Samaran, DHGE 4:263–267.

[V. SAMPSON]

ARMAND DE BELVÉZER (de Beauvoir; fl. early 14th cent.), French Dominican, early Thomist. He wrote a commentary on St. Thomas Aquinas's *De ente et essentia* (1326–28), and as master of the sacred palace at Avignon (1328–34) he opposed John XXII's teaching on the beatific vision. BIBLIOGRAPHY: A. Duval, NCE 1:824–825.

[T. C. O'BRIEN]

ARMAND, IGNACE (1562–1638), French Jesuit theologian and controversialist. A Jesuit from 1579, A. taught philosophy and theology and held administrative positions of high responsibility in the Society in France. He disputed with the Protestant D. Chamier at Tournon (1599) and persuaded Henri IV at Metz that the Jesuits should be re-established in France (Edict of Rouen, 1603); when parliament attacked the works of A. Santarelli and demanded their burning, as well as the signing of certain propositions Gallican in content, A. intervened, and with the aid of Richelieu, produced orthodox propositions to replace those of parliament. BIBLIOGRAPHY: Sommervogel 1:553ff; Bremond 1:567–568; 2:87.

[T. C. O'BRIEN]

ARMARIUM, see ARMADIUM.

ARMELLINI, MARIANO (1662–1727), Benedictine historian. A. entered the Benedictines in Rome; completed his studies at Monte Cassino; and taught philosophy in various Cassinese monasteries (1687–95). He then devoted himself to preaching and was noted throughout Italy for his pastoral zeal and eloquence. He was successively abbot at Siena, Assisi, and St. Felician near Faligno. He wrote extensively on the Cassinese congregation: a two-volume biographical bibliography of Cassinese writers; appendices, additions to and corrections of earlier works; and listings of the lives and works of members of his congregation. BIBLIOGRAPHY: N. R. Skvaria, NCE 1:825; CE 1:736.

[H. JACK]

ARMENIA, the name of two geographical areas. Greater Armenia is the plateau around Mt. Ararat in the U.S.S.R. Lesser Armenia lies in Turkey and Persia between Trebizond, Melitene, and the Upper Euphrates. Greater Armenia was originally an independent Roman protectorate but has been subject to foreign rule since 430 A.D. Through the efforts of St. *Gregory the Illuminator, who converted King Trdat III in the late 3d cent. Armenia was the first nation formally to accept Christianity. Gregory established his see at Etchmiadzin and the office of *catholicos remained in his family for some time. From 390 Armenia was divided between the Persian Empire of the Sassanides and the Roman Empire. The tension between Byzantium and Persia made it impossible for the Armenian kingdom to stay in contact with the rest of Christianity. Because of political and ecclesiastical difficulties the Armenians gradually separated to form an independent national Church. (see ARMENIAN CHURCH.) Until the 13th cent. the country was the victim of Persian and Arab persecutions, but the creation of a new kingdom in

Lesser Armenia opened the way for contact with the West. In 1198, during the Crusades, a temporary reunion with Rome was established, and another attempt was made at the Council of Florence (1439) through the *Decree for the *Armenians.* During recent times the country has suffered further persecution under the Turks and Soviets, and in 1923, after a short-lived independence, Armenia was incorporated into the U.S.S.R. The capital is at Yeravan with a population of about 2,493,000; a significant number of Armenians live outside the country in Syria, Egypt, Persia, France, South America and the U.S. BIBLIOGRAPHY: L. Arpee, *History of Armenian Christianity* (1946); N.M. Setian, NCE 1:825–830.

[J. MEIJER]

ARMENIAN ART. Armenian church forms include the basilica and, thereafter, the square, cross-in-square, and a variety of polygonals. The churches also abound in sculpture, and the 10th-cent. Church of Aght'amar is the first example of a church decorated on all its exterior walls by carved reliefs. The 10th and 11th centuries were rich in MS illumination, and the traditions of Armenian miniaturists were continued in the brilliant work of Cilician artists during the 13th and 14th centuries. BIBLIOGRAPHY: G. Tschubinaschwili, EncWA 1:716–728.

[L. P. SIGER]

ARMENIAN CHANT, the liturgical chant of the *Armenian rite, used by both the Apostolic Armenian Church and Roman Catholics of the Armenian rite. Just as the rite itself was a development from both the Byzantine and *Syrian rites, so its chant shows the influence of its mixed lineage. It is organized, like *Byzantine chant, in eight modes (see OKTOECHOS), and the greater part of its repertory is made up of hymns. A neumatic notation resembling that of Byzantine chant was introduced in the 13th century; its development in following years coincided with flourishing compositional activity at centers such as the monasteries of Naregh and Arkagaghin. Unfortunately the key to this notation was lost, and the medieval melodies remain indecipherable. There is some question as to the extent to which elements of the ancient chant are preserved in the chants of present day Armenian churches. The eight modes, as they are now sung, differ a great deal from the scales of Western music, or the Gregorian or Byzantine modes, and, to the Western ear, sound distinctly oriental. Many of the hymns are very florid and of great beauty. Modern practice in Armenian churches admits the organ (uniquely among Eastern churches) as well as more or less Westernized choral harmonizations. BIBLIOGRAPHY: G. Kaftangian, ''Il canto liturgico armeno,'' *Atti del Congresso Internazionale di Musica Sacra Rome, 1950* (1952) 149–151; L. Dayan, ''I canti armeni attraverso la tradizione dei secoli,'' *op. cit.* 152–154.

[A. DOHERTY]

ARMENIAN CHURCH, the national Church of Armenia. The original Church is often called Gregorian to distinguish it from the Catholic Armenian rite, but its own members call it the Armenian (Apostolic) Church. The origins of Christianity in Armenia are shrouded in legend. Historically the first Armenian Christians seem to have been in Roman Lesser Armenia (NW of the Upper Euphrates) and S of Lake Van. The establishment of Christianity as the national religion of Greater Armenia, through the conversion of King Trdat (Tiridates) III c.300, was the work of St. *Gregory the Illuminator. Gregory was sent to Cappadocian Caesarea for episcopal consecration, and on returning he organized the Armenian Church on Caesarean models under the primacy of a bishop (after 427 or 428 titled "catholicos") at first loosely dependent on the bishop of Caesarea, and from Armenia the (Caucasian) Albanians and Georgians were evangelized. It was in the reign of the catholicos Isaac (Sahak) I (387–438) that the monk Mesrop Mashtotz invented the Armenian alphabet, saw to the translation of the Bible and the liturgy into Armenian, and promoted the beginning of a native Armenian religious literature, thus making possible a deepening of the official but superficial conversion effected by Gregory the Illuminator. In 387 most of Armenia was absorbed by the Persian Empire (the rest becoming Byzantine). The Armenian Arsacids continued to rule as vassal Christian kings until 427/428, when the Persians began a policy of imperial unification which led them to attempt to force the Armenians to accept the Zoroastrian state religion or at least the Syro-Persian form of Christianity which was basically Nestorian. For this reason the Armenian Church was not represented in the Council of Chalcedon in 451. It accepted the conciliatory Henoticon of Zeno in the First Synod of Dvin (505–506) but did not become officially Monophysite or break with the Byzantine Church until the Second Synod of Dvin in 555. The five reunions with Constantinople effected between 572 and 690 were ephemeral. The establishment of the Armenian kingdom of Cilicia or "Little Armenia" in S Asia Minor in the 11th cent. was soon followed by the transfer of the catholicos' residence to Cilicia (fixed at Hromkla in 1150, at Sis in 1292), where relations with the Church of Rome began to develop, and from 1198 one can speak of actual union, not sealed by formal decree, however, until the Synod of Sis of 1307. Opposition to the union on the part of the lower clergy and the people, encouraged by monks. esp. in Greater Armenia, was never lacking, and the excessive Latinizing efforts represented by the Armenian Dominican *Fratres Unitores* added to the tension. Another Synod of Sis in 1345 took a strongly independent and Monophysite (though not schismatic) stand, and the union was broken by a third Synod of Sis in 1361. The Armenian delegates to the Council of Florence in 1439, acting on the decision made by the catholicos Constantine VI just before his death, submitted entirely to the Pope, but despite the adherence of the next catholicos, Gregory IX, the union had no lasting effect. The anti-Roman, nationalist Armenian majority insisted on the return of the catholicate from Cilicia to Greater Armenia, and upon Gregory IX's refusal elected another catholicos in 1441, installing him in Echmiadzin. The problem of jurisdiction between Echmiadzin and Sis was further complicated by the existence of an Armenian patriarchate of Jerusalem from 1311, of a catholicate on the Isle of Aghtamar in Lake Van from 1113, and esp. by the creation of a patriarchate in Constantinople by the Sultan Mehmet II in 1461 (or 1458) for civil jurisdiction over all Armenians of the Ottoman Empire. A synod held in Jerusalem in 1652 determined the religious primacy of Echmiadzin and limited the supreme catholical jurisdiction of Sis to Cilicia, Cyprus, and N Syria, but recognized the civil jurisdiction of Constantinople over all Armenians of the Empire. The rivalries between Echmiadzin and Sis have never been totally resolved. The 18th cent. saw the definitive separation of Gregorian and Catholic Armenians, the 19th, the rise of Armenian Protestantism and the struggle over increased lay participation in ecclesiastical affairs, and the 20th, the massive persecutions and massacres by the Turks. Of the 3½ million Armenians today, it is estimated that some 2 million belong to the Gregorian and some 375,000 to the Catholic Church. The formerly Cilician catholicate of Sis, with jurisdiction limited to Lebanon, Syria, and Cyprus, is now at Antelias in Lebanon as a result of the Turkish massacres. The minor catholicate of Aghtamar perished in the massacres. The Armenian patriarch of Constantinople exercises jurisdiction (now exclusively religious) over the single Gregorian diocese remaining in Turkey, and the patriarch of Jerusalem has jurisdiction over the Gregorians of Jordan and Israel. All other Gregorians are under the jurisdiction of Echmiadzin. BIBLIOGRAPHY: M. Ormanian, *Church of Armenia* (tr. G. M. Gregory, 1912; later editions in Eng., though statistically more up-to-date, have been altered in the text); F. Tournebize, DHGE 4:290–391; Attwater CCE 2:219–231; I. H. Dalmais, *Eastern Liturgies* (tr. D. Attwater, 1960) 22–23. *ARMENIAN RITE.

[A. CODY]

ARMENIAN CHURCH OF NORTH AMERICA, the American branch of the Armenian Church having two dioceses under the Catholicate of Echmiadzin of Soviet Armenia. Both the eastern and western dioceses have their own bishops with a total membership of 136,000 in 43 parishes. BIBLIOGRAPHY: *Handbook of Armenian Orthodoxy* (1972) 169–173. *ARMENIAN CHURCH.

[F. T. RYAN]

ARMENIAN GOSPEL OF THE INFANCY, see APOCRYPHA (NEW TESTAMENT), 10.

ARMENIAN LITURGY, the rites and ceremonies of the Armenian Church. When the Armenian Church was organized in the early 4th cent., the liturgical practice of Cappadocian Caesarea was introduced along with a certain amount of Syrian practice; only in the reign of the catholicos Sahak I (387–438) were the texts translated into Armenian from Greek and Syriac. The liturgical calendar and the lectionary system reflect the usages of 5th cent. Jerusalem. The texts of several translated anaphoras are extant in Armenian, but it is doubtful that most of them were ever used except for study by liturgical compilers and reformers. The most ancient anaphora (and the only one in use today), was long ascribed to St. Gregory the Illuminator; then, from the Middle Ages on, to St. Athanasius. In its original form it seems to have been a primitive, pre-Byzantine form of the anaphora of St. Basil. The Byzantine anaphoras of SS. Basil and John Chrysostom were also translated into Armenian, perhaps in the 8th cent., and were actually used in the liturgy; a MS dated 1287 notes the days on which they were to be celebrated. The Eucharistic Liturgy (*patarag,* "offering" or "oblation"), which by 1177 had attained basically the form it has today, consists of: (1) a rite of preparation; (2) an office of readings (the *djashou*), comprising the entrance of the clergy, readings, songs, and the creed; (3) an offertory with entrance of the gifts and kiss of peace; (4) the anaphora; (5) a rite of blessing and dismissal. The influence of the Byzantine rite is evident in the rite of preparation, while the prayers of intercession after the epiclesis show affinities with Antiochene Syrian usage. In the age of the Crusaders certain Roman elements entered the liturgy (the *confiteor* in the rite of preparation, the reading of the Prologue to the Fourth Gospel before the dismissal). The liturgy is not celebrated on ordinary days, but a modified form of the Office of *Djashou* ("noon-meal") is then the Midday Office in choir among the Gregorian Armenians. The Gregorians retain their ancient custom of not adding water to the chalice. Both Gregorians and Catholics use unleavened bread. An ordinary priest-celebrant wears the crown *(saghavart),* while an episcopal celebrant wears the mitre (another adopted Latin usage).

In the 5th cent. the canonical hours were six: the Night Office, the Dawn Office, Tierce, Sext, None, and Vespers. In the 8th cent. were added the Offices of Sunrise (Prime) and Repose (Compline), and still later another hour, of Peace, to be said privately before retiring. In certain places Tierce and None were suppressed and Sext replaced by the Office of *Djashou* by the 13th cent., and this arrangement is largely followed by the modern Gregorian Armenians. The core of the Office is made up of psalms, but the lengthy canons of psalmody in the Night Office have fallen out of use.

Baptism (normally by immersion) is always followed by the anointings of confirmation, and the newly baptized is then taken to the sanctuary to receive Communion; if he is an infant, the priest dips his finger in the Precious Blood and with it makes the Sign of the Cross on the infant's lips. Communion is received under both species (by intinction) among the Gregorians but not necessarily by the Catholics. The system of major and minor orders in both Armenian churches resembles that of the Roman Church. A cleric in major orders may continue to live with a wife married before the subdiaconate, but he may not be ordained bishop or named vardapet. Married priests among the Catholics are

now almost nonexistent. All liturgical texts remain in Classical Armenian. BIBLIOGRAPHY: V. Hatzuni, EncCatt 1:1976–1980; [Tiran Nersoyan], *Divine Liturgy of the Armenian Apostolic Orthodox Church* (1950).

[A. CODY]

ARMENIAN RITE, one of 18 Eastern Catholic rites. A number of Armenian catholicoses, with many of the clergy and people, were in communion with Rome in the 13th and 14th cent. and even later, but by the 18th cent. the catholicoses and the official Armenian Church had become generally quite hostile to Rome. The Catholic Armenians were organized with their own hierarchy in 1740 when Abraham Ardzivian, bp. of Aleppo and a Catholic, was elected catholicos of *Sis. His election was confirmed by the Holy See in 1742, but meanwhile the non-Catholic bps. had elected another incumbent, and Abraham took up residence in Lebanon, first at Kraim, then at Bzommar, as Catholic catholicos of Sis, with jurisdiction over all Armenian Catholics of Syria, Cilicia, Mesopotamia, and Egypt. In 1759 the Holy See erected an Armenian vicariate in Constantinople, subject to the Latin apostolic delegate, with ecclesiastical jurisdiction over the Armenian Catholics of Asia Minor (except Cilicia) and Greater Armenia. When the Catholic Armenians of the Ottoman Empire had been emancipated civilly from the *Gregorian Armenians by the Treaty of Adrianople (1829), Rome elevated the Constantinopolitan vicariate to a primatial archbishopric (1830). The Turkish government insisted that a patriarchate be established to exercise over Catholic Armenians of the Empire that civil jurisdiction exercised over the Gregorian Armenians by their own patriarchate of *Constantinople, and thus Rome named the archbishop-primate Anthony Hassoun (or Hassounian) patriarch in 1846. The anomaly of having the double ecclesiastical jurisdiction of the catholicos in Bzommar and the patriarch in Constantinople, with a single civil jurisdiction in the hands of the latter, was resolved after the death of the incumbent of the catholicate in 1866 when the patriarch Hassoun was himself elected catholicos. The following year the two ecclesiastical jurisdictions were united in a single Patriarchate of Cilicia of the Armenians, with patriarchal residence in Constantinople.

The Catholic Armenians were troubled throughout the 19th cent. by the same movement toward lay participation in ecclesiastical affairs that beset the Gregorians in the same period. In 1870, 5 bishops, 45 priests, and a number of laymen were excommunicated for their resistance to the procedures for hierarchical appointment insisted upon by Rome, and to what they considered the excessive Romanization of their Church. The matter reached another crisis after the Armenian synod held in Rome in 1911. Catholic Armenians, like other Christians, suffered heavy losses in the Turkish massacres of 1915–22. In the reorganization that followed, the patriarchal residence returned to Bzommar in 1921 before being fixed in Beirut in 1928. Of the 18 patriarchal dioceses before the massacres, only 5 remain, with 2 others added in 1954. Outside the patriarchal jurisdiction are the Armenian bishopric of Lwow in Poland, united with Rome in 1635, and the Armenian apostlic administrature of Romania established in 1930, both vacant since the Communist seizure of power. The Armenian Catholics of France have their own exarch, while the parishes in the Western Hemisphere are under the jurisdiction of the Latin local ordinaries. There are about 375,000 Catholic Armenians. BIBLIOGRAPHY: F. Tournebize, DHGE 4:338–344; D. Attwater, *Christian Churches of the East* (2d ed., 1962) 1:175–180; J. Mécérian, *Histoire et institutions de l'Église arménienne* (1965) 134–139.

[A. CODY]

ARMENIANS, DECREE FOR, the bull *Exultate Deo* of Pope Eugene IV published at the Council of Florence (Nov. 22, 1439) in promulgation of the reunion of the Armenian and Catholic Churches. It had little practical result, because the Armenian representatives at Florence returned home to find their patriarch had died and the union was never put into effect. The decree speaks about the Niceno-Constantinopolitan Creed (with the *filioque*), the teachings of Pope Leo the Great and the Councils of Chalcedon (451) and Constantinople (680–681) on the two natures of Christ. But its main importance lies in its teaching on the sacraments which was drawn in large part from St. Thomas Aquinas's opusculum *De fidei articulis et septem sacramentis*. It gives a compendium of the then current Catholic sacramental theology. Dealing with each of the seven sacraments in particular, it states their matter, form, minister, and effects. With regard to the conferring of the priesthood, it made the handing over of the chalice and paten the most important and central act instead of the imposition of the hands, which older tradition had seen as the central act. This led to a theological controversy which was resolved only in 1947 when Pius XII restored the earlier tradition.

[J. MEIJER]

ARMENTIA, NICOLÁS (1845–1909), Franciscan missionary, explorer, and bishop. Though born in Spain, he was ordained in La Paz, Bolivia, and became a dedicated missionary. From his missions along the Beni River, he made expeditions into the jungle to gather the aborigines to established centers and explored unknown territory to reach new forest tribes. At government request he undertook (1884–85) a greater exploration of the regions of the Beni and the Madre de Dios, and during a later expedition reached the Purus and Amazon rivers. The result was the knowledge of new tribes, the founding of new missions, and the publication of his multiple discoveries. In 1902 he was made bp. of La Paz in Sucre. BIBLIOGRAPHY: H. Sanabria Fernández, NCE 1:839.

[H. JACK]

ARMINIAN, characterized by adherence to *Arminianism, as this is either a specific theological system or simply a doctrinal emphasis on human cooperation with grace.

ARMINIANISM, primarily the theological system inspired by J. *Arminius, and by extension any similar theological position. Historical Arminianism belongs to 17th-cent. Holland where it was condemned by the Synod of *Dort (1618–19) and given systematic formulation by S. *Episcopius. Its basic, anti-Calvinist tenets were contained in the "Remonstrance" (1610; see REMONSTRANTS): (1) predestination is conditioned by God's foreknowledge of man's belief; (2) Christ died for all and all can benefit by his atonement; (3) although fallen and in need of grace, man cooperates in his regeneration; (4) grace is not irresistible; (5) grace can be lost and hence final perseverance is not assured. The Remonstrant Church survived persecution and continues to exist in Holland. There in the 18th cent. Arminianism became associated with Socinianism and other rationalist tendencies.

In its wider use, designating a theological viewpoint, the term Arminianism applies first of all to an emphasis on the freedom to accept grace. The latitudinarians of 17th-cent. England were anti-Calvinist and were called "Arminians," but had no close link with Dutch Arminianism. The theology of John *Wesley was Arminian, not because of his opposition to Calvinism, but because of his *perfectionism. Arminianism is taken as an anthropocentric theological emphasis in the accepted classification of *Reformed Churches into "Calvinist" and "Arminian." Arminianism characterizes all Wesleyan Methodist groups, the Holiness Churches, the United Brethren, the Evangelical Alliance, and the Salvation Army; the Mennonites and the General Baptists, while older than historic Arminianism, also classify their own theology as Arminian. Finally, simply on the basis of their being liberal, rationalist, or "enlightened," many other theological trends have been labelled Arminian. This was the broader sense Arminianism had in Jonathan *Edwards's polemics; and in which it was a prominent feature of the *Great Awakening, a part of *revivalism, and a formative element in American Universalism and Unitarianism. Often singled out as characteristic of American Protestant theology, Arminianism has had a broad influence upon the history of Protestantism in America. BIBLIOGRAPHY: A. W. Harrison, *Arminianism* (1937); Mayer RB 199–200, 283–342; *Man's Faith and Freedom* (3d. G. O. McCulloh, 1962); Smith-Jamison 1:242–251; Schaff Creeds 1:509–519.

[T. C. O'BRIEN]

ARMINIUS, JACOBUS (Jakob He[a]rmandszoon, or He[a]rmann, etc.; 1560–1609), Dutch theologian for whom *Arminianism is named. A. studied at Marburg, Leiden, Geneva, Basel, Padua, and Rome. He was ordained as a pastor at Amsterdam in 1588. His theological training was in Calvinist orthodoxy; but his mind was formed also by humanist learning, the philosophy of Peter Ramus, and esp. at Leiden by liberalizing attitudes toward religions and political freedom. Designated in 1589 to debate against D. V. Coornheert's denial of the orthodox Calvinist doctrine on predestination, A. came instead to reject it himself. His subsequent life was one of controversy, esp. with F. *Gomarus, who contested his appointment to the faculty of Leiden in 1603. A. was charged with *Socinianism and *Pelagianism; political considerations added acrimony to the debates. But A. gradually clarified his own criticisms of strict Calvinism and his defense of human freedom under grace and achieved renown as a theologian of moderation. His works (Eng. tr. J. Nichols and W. R. Bagnall, 3v., 1956) were not a systematized exposition of Arminianism, but were patterned to the exchanges of controversy. Nor were his efforts to modify the *Belgic Confession or the *Heidelberg Catechism successful. Nevertheless, the liberal and humane theological trend he inspired had a considerable influence upon the subsequent history of Protestantism. BIBLIOGRAPHY: Bihlmeyer-Tüchle 3:202; A. W. Harrison, *Beginnings of Arminianism to the Synod of Dort* (1926); *idem, Arminianism* (1937); *Man's Faith and Freedom* (ed. G. O. McCulloh, 1962).

[T. C. O'BRIEN]

ARMOR OF GOD, a phrase that occurs twice in Eph ch. 6, in the metaphorical sense of a Christian's spiritual resources against the wiles of the devil. Paul links truth, justice, the gospel of peace, faith, salvation, and the word of God to the various pieces of a fully armed soldier. The image of a battle for the eschatological struggle between God and Satan is common in the Bible, as is the figure of God's spiritual armor (Is 59.16–18; Wis 5.17–23).

[O. N. BUCHER]

ARMORY SHOW, THE, first showing of avant-garde European and American art in the Armory, N.Y. (1913). This International Exhibition of Contemporary Art, meeting with protest and ridicule, confronted 300,000 Americans with modern art, forcefully demonstrating the right of the independent artist to exhibit outside academically controlled boundaries. The Armory Show permanently changed the nature of private collecting and other patronage in the U.S. BIBLIOGRAPHY: L. Goodrich, *Pioneers of Modern Art in America* (1963).

[M. J. DALY]

ARMS, JOHN TAYLOR, foremost etcher of medieval French cathedrals and churches of Spain (1923), Italy (1925), and England (1937), in most precise and dramatic detail, light, and shade. BIBLIOGRAPHY: C. Zigrosser, *Artist in America* (1942).

[M. J. DALY]

ARNALDUS AMALRICI (Arnaud Amauri; *c.*1150–1225), abp. of Narbonne; Cistercian monk, and later abbot of Poblet in Catalonia and Grandselve in Languedoc; in 1221 he was elected abbot-general of the Cistercians. The Cistercians, traditionally involved in the controversy between the Church and the Albigenses, responded to Innocent

III's commission by sending the monks Raoul and Peter of Castelnau, as legates to Languedoc. In 1206 A. joined them; A. responded to the murder of Peter (Jan. 14, 1208), believed to have been perpetrated by Raymond VI of Toulouse, leader of the opposing clergy and nobility, by leading a crusade against the Albigenses. After a bloody battle that culminated in the capture of Béziers (July 22, 1209) Innocent III rejected any further attempts to confront Raymond. He did, however, appeal personally to Raymond; when the latter refused reconciliation Innocent III excommunicated him. The Moors were later defeated by A. at the battle of Navas de Tolosa, July 16, 1212. He died at the abbey of Fontfroide (1225) and his body was taken to Cîteaux for burial. BIBLIOGRAPHY: A. Posch, LTK 1:888; A. Sabarthès, DHGE 4:420; H. Wolfram, NCE 1:840.

[J. R. RIVELLO]

ARNAUD, HENRI (1641–1721), Waldense leader. Pastor after studies in Geneva and Basel 1662–66, he fled Louis XIV in 1685 and in 1686 led 3,000 followers to Switzerland away from the king of Savoy. His defiance of French forces in the Alps with 900 men (1689–90) was heroic, but Savoy again expelled him in 1696. His church then received land to clear in Wurtemberg, which it kept after 1703 when allowed back in Savoy. Arnaud made two trips to London during these war years.

[E. P. COLBERT]

ARNAULD FAMILY (Arnaut; Arnault), French family distinguished for its near monopoly of the Jansenist movement (see JANSENISM). The father, Antoine II (1560–1619), further enhanced the established family name in the practice of law and left a legacy of anti-Jesuitism, in his *Plaidoyer . . . contre les Jésuites* (1594–95), for the 10 of his 20 children who reached maturity. The six girls entered the Cistercian convent of *Port-Royal. Catherine (1588–1651), the eldest, entered after a marriage that gave Antoine and Isaac Le Maistre as theologians for the Jansenist cause. Two sisters, Anne (1594–1653) and Madeleine (1607–49), were relatively undistinguished, but Marie Claire (1607–42) had her brief moment of importance by opposing the Abbé de *Saint-Cyran, imperiling family as well as conventual unity. Jeanne, Mère Agnès (1593–1672), is overshadowed by her sister Jacqueline, Mère Angélique, but she wrote, besides valuable source material for history, a mystical work, *Le Chapelet secret du Saint Sacrement* (1627), which played its part in the controversies. Among the brothers it was Antoine, the 20th child, who became "le Grand Arnauld."

The temper of the Arnaulds, despite their theological and ascetic preoccupations, was legalistic. While they concerned themselves with the grand issues of predestination and grace, they did so in a legalistic manner. Moreover, they delighted in controversy and perhaps injured their cause by their implacable hatred for Jesuits. Their endless legal debate and devices, such as Antoine's distinction between law and fact, and their "respectful silence" in the face of papal decisions did much to discredit their claims of evangelical simplicity.

Mère Angélique (Jacqueline; 1591–1661). She had succession to the abbacy of Port-Royal assured her at the age of 7, although she was close to 11 when she assumed office. At first she drifted with the relaxed discipline of the convent, but she was converted at 16 and began a series of ruthless reforms that extended even beyond Port-Royal. A brief contact with St. Francis de Sales, to which she ever afterward made reference, almost led to her joining the Visitandines, but in 1622 she was back at Port-Royal with her mother and four sisters. In 1625, at the age of 34, she moved the entire convent to the influential Faubourg Saint-Jacques in Paris. Although she was replaced by her sister Agnès as abbess in 1630, she retained her great influence. She was in her 40s when she came under the influence of Saint-Cyran, under whom the community became Jansenist in principle and practice. She was abbess again, 1642–54, and died shortly after signing the formulary of 1661 at the age of 70. Her three volumes of memoirs, conferences, and writings are still extant.

Antoine (1612–94). His father died when Antoine was only 7; through his mother and his Port-Royal sisters, he came under the influence of Saint-Cyran. After studying law he entered the Sorbonne, where his bachelor's thesis on the doctrine of grace (1635) was a brilliant success. While still prominent in intellectual circles of Paris, he received sacred orders and entered into even closer association with the Port-Royal circle of Jansenism. Under the direction of Saint-Cyran he wrote *De la fréquente communion* (1643), which stressed the need for careful preparation for communion and which, according to St. Vincent de Paul, kept at least 10,000 people from the sacrament. Antoine was the real popularizer of Jansenism, for he went beyond the teachings on predestination and grace to elaborate practical conclusions on sacraments, not only the Eucharist but particularly penance, for which he demanded perfect contrition. While a brilliant theologian, he injured his cause by his bitter polemics. The Jesuits protested so vigorously that Antoine was stripped of his titles (1656) by the Sorbonne even though he sought the support of the Dominicans and of *Pascal, who defended him magnificently in the first of the *Provincial Letters. In reply to Alexander VII's *Ad sanctam beati Petri sedem,* published in France in 1657, and condemning five propositions attributed to C. *Jansen's *Augustinus,* A. formulated the distinction between *droit* and *fait.* Accepting the pope's right to condemn heresy, he denied the fact that the five propositions condemned were present in *Augustinus.* Although A. was reinstated at the Sorbonne by Louis XIV in 1669, he imposed exile in Holland on himself from 1679. He wrote against the Calvinists, against Malebranche, on *Gallicanism, on various biblical subjects, as well as on philosophy, science, and mathematics. While less radical than the original Jansenists in his teaching, he was the main source for the diffusion of Jansenist principles. BIBLIOGRAPHY: J. Q. C. Mackrell, NCE 1:840–843; Bremond, *Index* (repr. 1971) 7–15.

[U. VOLL]

ARNDT, ERNST MORITZ (1769–1860), German poet and pamphleteer, professor of history at Griefswald (1805) and Bonn (1818–20; 1840–54), rector of the University of Bonn (1840–41). The spirited prose work *Geist der Zeit* (4 v., 1806–18) and the stirring lyrics (e.g., "Vaterlandslied," "Was ist des Deutschen Vaterland?") were written to awaken German patriotism during the Napoleonic era. His hymns and lyrics are couched in biblical language and reflect his strong Lutheran piety. BIBLIOGRAPHY: Julian 1:79–80.

[M. F. MCCARTHY]

ARNDT, JOHANN (Arnd; 1555–1621), German Lutheran theologian and ascetical writer. After studying theology at Wittenberg, Strassburg, and Basel, A. became pastor at Badeborn in 1538 but was deposed in 1590 by Duke John George for opposing the order to remove pictures from churches and to omit exorcism rites from baptism. He served churches in Quedlinburg, Brunswick, and Eisleben. In 1611 he was made superintendent for Lüneburg through the good offices of Johann *Gerhard, whom he had befriended. A.'s chief works, *Vier Bücher vom wahren Christentum* (4v., 1606–09) and *Paradiesgärtlein aller christlichen Tugenden* (1612), were inspired by St. Bernard, Tauler, and Thomas à Kempis and were widely used as devotional reading. They stress the theme of Christ working in the heart of the believer. Through P. *Spener and *Pietism, his influence on Lutheran theology, hymnody, and devotional life extended into the 19th century. BIBLIOGRAPHY: I. Ludolphy, EncLuthCh 1:105–106; M. Braure, *Age of Absolutism* (1963) 73–74.

[M. J. SUELZER]

ARNHEM LAND, region of N central and N coastal Australian aboriginal art, mostly religious in origin. These ancient rock engravings, paintings on rock and bark in a native technique, and incised polychromed wooden ancestor figures in a native technique are superior among Australian carvings. BIBLIOGRAPHY: F. D. McCarthy, *Australian Aboriginal Decorative Art* (1952).

[M. J. DALY]

ARNIM, LUDWIG ACHIM VON (1781–1831), romantic novelist. With C. M. *Brentano he edited *Des Knaben Wunderhorn* (3 v., 1806–08), one of the chief products of Heidelberg romanticism. He is also author of some plays (e.g., *Halle und Jerusalem,* 1811), but his greatest success is as a writer of prose fiction (e.g., the fragmentary historical novel *Die Kronenwächter,* v. 1, 1817; v. 2, 1854, and the novella *Der tolle Invalide auf dem Fort Ratonneau,* 1818). BIBLIOGRAPHY: O. Walzel, *German Romanticism* (tr. A. E. Lussky 1932) *passim.*

[M. F. MCCARTHY]

ARNO (Arn, Aquila; 746–821), abp. of Salzburg, responsible for the preservation of a portion of the correspondence of *Alcuin, whose associate and (probably) disciple he had been. He was also on familiar terms with Charlemagne, through whose influence he received the pallium. He was a patron of art and letters and promoted clerical reforms within his jurisdiction. BIBLIOGRAPHY: G. Hocquard, *Catholicisme* 1:847–848; T. Schieffer, LTK 1:887

[P. K. MEAGHER]

ARNOBIUS THE ELDER (d. *c*.330), Christian apologist. St. *Jerome states that A. was a rhetorician at Sicca in Proconsular Africa; one of his pupils was *Lactantius. At first anti-Christian, A. was converted and wrote his *Adversus nationes* (PL 5:349–1374; Eng. tr. G. E. McCracken, ACW, 1949) as a pledge to the bp. of Sicca, skeptical of the sincerity of this conversion. The work was a hurriedly composed counterattack against pagan objections, but A.'s own theological grasp of Christianity was tenuous. His principal sources are pagan, and he explicitly rejects the OT. His notion of God is deistic; the pagan deities are secondary gods, as is Christ; the soul is not created by God, nor is it immortal by nature, but solely through good deeds. BIBLIOGRAPHY: Altaner 205–207; Quasten 2:383–392, with bibliog. and list of editions.

[T. C. O'BRIEN]

ARNOBIUS THE YOUNGER (5th cent.), African monk and writer. A. was at Rome from *c*.432 onward. His attacks on the Augustinian anti-Pelagian doctrines are themselves *Semipelagian. A.'s teaching on grace is found in his commentaries on the Psalms. The *Praedestinatus* (PL 53:579–692), similar to these commentaries in teaching and style, is also attributed to him. BIBLIOGRAPHY: PL v. 53; Altaner 546; G. Bardy *Catholicisme* 1:853.

[T. C. O'BRIEN]

ARNOLD OF BONNEVAL (Arnold of Marmoutier; d. *c*.1156), monk of Marmoutier, abbot of Bonneval, friend and biographer of St. Bernard of Clairvaux (he wrote Book 2 of the *Vita Bernardi* begun by William of Saint-Thierry). He was also the author of spiritual and exegetical works. BIBLIOGRAPHY: J.-M. Canivez, DSAM 1:888–890.

[P. K. MEAGHER]

ARNOLD OF BRESCIA (d. 1155), medieval reformer. A., who had studied at Paris under Peter Abelard, was ordained in Brescia and became a canon regular and prior of his monastery. A man of extreme austerity, he denounced clerical licentiousness and simony and became a leader of the populace against the political power of the bishop. He denied the right of Church or clergy to own property, urging the people not to receive the sacraments from priests who owned property. He was condemned at Lateran Council II (1139). Exiled from Italy, he took refuge in Paris; in 1141 he was condemned again, with Abelard, at the Council of Sens. He was banished from France, passed through Switzerland and Bohemia, and was reconciled for a time with Pope Eugene III in 1145 at Verona. In Rome he led a revolt of the populace against papal temporal power; after 9 years as virtual ruler of

Rome, he was condemned and executed. The Council of Verona (1184), in condemning lay groups' challenging clerical power, listed Arnoldists (D 760), but it is doubtful that A. ever actually formed a sect. BIBLIOGRAPHY: J. A. Brundage, NCE 1:844; Hughes HC 2:233–234.

[W. A. JURGENS]

ARNOLD OF HILTENSWEILER, BL. (d. after 1127), layman, monastic founder. He founded a convent at Langnan near Berne, left all his property to the house of All Saints at Schaffhausen on the Rhine, and was buried at the oratory he founded at Hiltensweiler. BIBLIOGRAPHY: W. Müller, LTK. 1:893; P. Volk, DHGE 5:565; J. L. Grassi, NCE 1:844.

[J. L. GRASSI]

ARNOLD OF LÜBECK (d. between 1211 and 1214), abbot and chronicler. He was first abbot of the Benedictine monastery of St. John in Lübeck and compiled the *Chronica Slavorum* (begun by Helmold) for the years 1172–1209. Despite errors and interpolations, his work is a valuable source of information for the era of Henry the Lion, Henry VI, Philip of Swabia, Otto IV. BIBLIOGRAPHY: M. F. McCarthy, NCE 1:845.

[M. F. MCCARTHY]

ARNOLD OF VILLANOVA (*c*.1240–1311), physician, theologian, and church reformer. A. studied theology and medicine under the Dominicans at Montpelier and Barcelona, and with Arabic physicians in Valencia. He was considered the leading alchemist and physician of his day, and frequently ministered to popes and kings. Several of his medical works were important in placing medicine and pharmacy on a scientific basis. Although a layman, A. wrote extensively but rather fantastically on theological matters, and was declared heretical by the Inquisition in Spain and Paris. His religious writings never became well known; he is most famous for his 70 scientific works reflecting his contact with the Arabic scientific tradition. BIBLIOGRAPHY: Thorndike 2:841–861.

[T. M. MCFADDEN]

ARNOLD, EBERHARD (1883–1935), the founder of the Society of Brothers (*Bruderhof). Born at Königsberg July 26, 1883, he attended the Univ. of Breslau. As executive of the Student Christian Movement in Germany, scholar of the NT, and follower of Christophe F. Blumhardt, he drew together in 1920 a Society of Brothers, first on a farm in Sannerz, then on a large farm-estate in the Rhoen hills. His ideal was the Sermon on the Mount: agape, nonviolence, common possession. He later found Hutterite settlements in Dakotas to be like those of the Society, and he briefly joined one of these communes. A prolific writer in German, he is best known in English translation for *Salt and Light* (1967), which gives most of the principles of the Bruderhof. He died in Darmstadt in 1935; his influence is ably carried on by members of his family.

[J. O. NELSON]

ARNOLD, GOTTFRIED (1666–1714), German Lutheran writer on mysticism. After studying theology at Wittenberg (1685–89), A. came in contact with the Pietist P. *Spener and experienced a conversion. For the most part, until his marriage in 1701, he devoted himself to writing. In *Die erster Liebe* (1696) and his chief work, important for the wealth of sources it quotes, *Unparteriensche Kirche—und Ketzerhistorie* (1699–1700), he maintained that the Church had fallen away from the early ideals and that those mystics who had been classified as heretics were alone representatives of true Christianity. In 1702 he accepted a pastorate, and his later works, mostly devotional, avoided earlier extremes. His novel views on the Church and Christian history impressed many literary figures of the *Enlightenment. Some of his hymns came into popular use. BIBLIOGRAPHY: R. Fischer, NCE 1:845.

[T. C. O'BRIEN]

ARNOLD, MATTHEW (1822–88), son of Thomas Arnold of Rugby; English poet and critic, national inspector of schools (1851–53), professor of poetry at Oxford (1857–67). Poetry was his expression in early life, prose in his maturity. As a critic, literary and social, he asked for trained, close, impartial examination of the literary work or of the political or social institution, and thus the development of moderation and open-mindedness. In the religious debates of his time, A. was a liberal Protestant who applied rationalizing criticism to contemporary orthodoxy but whose personal spiritual and ethical purpose was undeniable. He tried to bridge the gap between Christianity and the modern world by a stress on culture, which would result from education, from a knowledge of "the best that has been thought and said in the world." BIBLIOGRAPHY: L. Trilling, *Matthew Arnold* (1939); E. K. Brown, *Matthew Arnold: A Study in Conflict* (1948); M. H. Quinn, *Critical Essays of Matthew Arnold* (Villanova Univ., 1936).

[M. M. BARRY]

ARNOLD, THOMAS (1795–1842), English educator and historian, headmaster of Rugby (1828–42) where he set the modern pattern for the English public school system, which aims to train its pupils not only intellectually in classical general learning but also morally and religiously for the responsibilities of adult life. He lectured for one term in the chair of modern history at Oxford in 1842. His outspoken criticism of certain aspects of the C of E arose from his intensely religious character and his lofty view of duty. His interest in ecclesiastical questions and in social and moral improvement of the working class remained active throughout his life. BIBLIOGRAPHY: T. Walrond, DNB 2:113–117;

L. Strachey, *Eminent Victorians* (1918); A. Whitridge, *Dr. Arnold of Rugby* (1928).

[M. M. BARRY]

ARNOLDI, BARTHOLOMAEUS (1465–1532), Catholic apologist. At Erfurt as student (1484–91) and nominalist professor of philosophy (1491–1514), he taught Luther, who induced him to join the Augustinians in 1512. Theologian from 1514, he preached in Erfurt until expelled by Lutherans in 1525. Thereafter he preached and promoted reforms for the bp. of Würzburg. He was one of 20 theologians who examined the Lutheran confession at Augsburg in 1530. Arnoldi's writings, in Latin, were frequently published; in 1522 he abandoned philosophy textbooks for treatises and sermons against Lutheranism. BIBLIOGRAPHY: C. Bertola, EncCatt 1:2013; L. Boiteux, DHGE 4:583–586.

[E. P. COLBERT]

ARNOLDI, HENRI (1407–87), Carthusian spiritual writer. A. studied in Rome and was a notary at the Council of Basel (1431) where he gained a great reputation. In 1437 he entered the Chartreuse du Val-Ste-Marguerite at Basel, which he governed from 1450 to 1480. A. wrote the *Chronique de la chartreuse de Bâle,* which was later finished by two religious of this house. BIBLIOGRAPHY: A. Musters, EncCatt 1:2014; H.-M. Féret, *Catholicisme* 1:854.

[M. C. BRADLEY]

ARNOLDISTS, see ARNOLD OF BRESCIA.

ARNOLFO DI CAMBIO (*c.*1245–before 1310), Italian architect and sculptor, designer of the Florence Cathedral. His tomb of Card. de Braye (Orvieto, San Domenico, 1282), with its arched canopy beneath which the effigy of the deceased lies on a bier below a representation of the Madonna enthroned, set the type of the wall tomb for more than a century. BIBLIOGRAPHY: M. Salmi, EncWA 1:755–764; J. Pope-Hennessy, *Italian Gothic Sculpture 1* (1958).

[L. A. LEITE]

ARNON, stream, now known as the Wadi Mojib, flowing through a deep canyon into the Dead Sea at about the middle of its eastern shore. It was the border between the Amorite kingdom of Sihon and Moab (Num 21.13, 26), and later the southern border of the Reubenite territory (Dt 3.16).

[T. EARLY]

ARNOU, NICOLAS (1629–92), Dominican theologian. Born near Verdun, A. entered the Dominicans (1644), and after studying and teaching at various houses of his order in Catalonia and Roussillon, was called to Italy where he taught at Rome (1675) and later at the Univ. of Padua (1679). Much esteemed in his own time, A. defended the Thomistic tradition, publishing a *Clypeus philosophiae thomisticae* (1672) and a commentary on the first 19 questions of the *Summa theologiae* of St. Thomas. Less felicitously he ventured into prophecy and published a book predicting the imminent downfall of the Ottoman Empire (1681). BIBLIOGRAPHY: Quétif-Échard 2:703; P. Mandonnet, DTC 1:1889.

ARNULF (c.850–899), German Emperor from 896; King of the East Franks (887–899); last Carolingian ruler of Germany. At the request of Pope Formosus A. led an expedition against Guy of Spoleto in 894 and took Rome in 895, where he was crowned emperor by Formosus (896). He was stricken with paralysis and died shortly after his return to Germany. BIBLIOGRAPHY: CMedH 3:58–68.

[M. F. MCCARTHY]

ARNULF, PORTABLE ALTAR OF, see CAROLINGIAN ART.

ARNULF OF BEAUVAIS (1040–1124), Benedictine abbot, bishop. A student at the Abbey of Bec, A. became prior in Canterbury, abbot of Peterborough (1107), and bp. of Rochester (1115). He is known for his historical writings, esp. a history of the see of Rochester and a study of transubstantiation. BIBLIOGRAPHY: S. Hilpisch, LTK 1:899.

[B. SCHERER]

ARNULF OF GAP, ST. (d. between 1070 and 1079), Benedictine monk, bishop. Born near Vendôme, France, he became a Benedictine monk at Holy Trinity, Vendôme, and went to Rome in 1061; there he was detained by Alexander II, who consecrated him bp. of Gap in 1063. He was a zealous supporter of the reform movement. BIBLIOGRAPHY: P. Villette, BiblSanct 2:445–446.

[S. WILLIAMS]

ARNULF OF LISIEUX (d. 1184), bp. of Lisieux. As a youth A. studied at Séez where he received a fine literary education and later became archdeacon. In 1130 he wrote a polemical work attacking the antipope, Anacletus II. Elevated to bp. of Lisieux in 1141, A. was active in various controversies both within the Church and between the Church and Henry II of England, who was bitterly attacking Thomas Becket. The latter was defended by A., but his efforts were interpreted as self-serving rather than mediative. In the Synod of Tours (1163) he again defended the supremacy of the Apostolic See against the antipope, Victor IV, and Frederick Barbarossa. After the Becket affair he retired to a monastery, remaining until his death. BIBLIOGRAPHY: A. Fliche, *Catholicisme* 1:855; M. Maccarone, EncCatt 2:6–7; A. Noyon, DHGE 4:609–611; H. Wolter, LTK 1:900.

[J. R. RIVELLO]

ARNULF OF METZ, ST. (c.582–641). Of a prominent Austrian family, A. served King Theodebert II, possibly as mayor of the palace. He was the father of Ansegis and St. Cloud, the first of whom married Begga, the daughter of Pepin (I) of Landen, whose son was Pepin (II) of Herstal,

father of Charles Martel. A. is thus the progenitor of the Carolingian dynasty. In 614 A.'s wife entered a convent at Trier, and he was promoted to the see of Metz, which he served 15 years. He assisted at councils in Metz (626), Clichy (626–627), and Reims (627–630). He retired to Remiremont, where he passed his remaining years. BIBLIOGRAPHY: O. J. Blum, NCE 1:848; G. Mathon, BiblSanct 2:446–447.

[O. J. BLUM]

ARNULF OF MILAN (d. after 1077), historian of the abps. of Milan. The little that is known of him must be gleaned from his own writings. He was of the aristocracy and probably a cleric. About the year 1072 he began the five books of the *Gesta archiepiscoporum Mediolanensium*, which remains a very valuable source for the period it covers, 925–1077. BIBLIOGRAPHY: PL 147:279–332; MGS 8:1–13; Manitius 3:507–509.

[W. A. JURGENS]

ARNULF OF SOISSONS ST. (c.1040–87), monastic reformer, bp. of Soissons. After a brief military career, A. became a monk at St. Médard (Soissons) where, because of his personal asceticism, he was elected abbot, and later bp. of the diocese. When his efforts at reform among the monks and the clergy were repulsed, he founded a Benedictine monastery at Oudenbourg in Flanders where he died. BIBLIOGRAPHY: H. Roeder, *Saints and their Attributes* (1955); Butler 4:335–336; Benedictine Monks of St. Augustine's Abbey, *Book of Saints* (1966); H. Platelle, BiblSanct 2:449.

[M. E. DUFFY]

ARON, PIETRO (c.1470–1545), Italian monk and music theorist. Of his five treatises, which establish him as one of the most significant and forward-looking theorists of his day, the most important is his *Toscanello in musica* (1523 and four later eds.), an excellent compendium of the then current rules of counterpoint. In it A. advocates that written accidentals (sharps and flats) be used regularly and that conflicting key signatures be avoided. The *Toscanello* is thus an important source on the controversial question of *musica ficta*, although A. himself later tempered his position as a result of criticism from other theorists. In his other treatises he discusses the nature of the modes and gives the earliest report on the practice of composing all parts of a piece at once (simultaneous counterpoint) rather than one at a time (successive counterpoint). A. wrote only the first of his works in scholarly Latin, the rest being in vernacular Italian. BIBLIOGRAPHY: Reese MusR; D. P. Walker, MGG 1:665–667; L. Lockwood, "Sample Problem of *musica ficta:* Willaert's *Pater noster,*" *Studies in Music History: Essays for Oliver Strunk* (ed. H. Powers, 1968).

[P. DOHERTY]

ARP, JEAN (Hans; 1887–1966), studied at Weimar and Académie Julian, Paris, exhibited with *Blaue Reiter* (1912), contributed to *Der Sturm* (1913), and founded Dadaists

(1916), composing abstract collages according to "laws of chance." In 1950 A. did mural reliefs for Harvard Univ. and in 1958 copper reliefs for the UNESCO building, Paris, with wit and insight. A.'s abstract, biomorphic curvilinear shapes of bright color raised the creative practice of free association, chance, and automatism to a high level. BIBLIOGRAPHY: J. T. Soby, *Arp* (1953).

[M. J. DALY]

ARRAS, city of N France, capital of the old province of Artois, ruled through the MA by counts of Flanders, dukes of Burgundy, and the Hapsburgs, passing to the French in 1659. Through the energetic Countess Mahaut of Artois (purchases 1311, 1313) and rich Burgundian dukes (Philip the Bold, 1387) Arras attained a golden age as woolen textile center, weaving finest tapestries (*fin fil d'Arras*) in an area renowned for facility and skill in the preparation and dyeing of wool. Weavers of the 14th cent. used gold, silver, and silk threads with finer wool. The most important tapestry, signed Pierre Fère, 1402, hangs in the cathedral of Tournai. BIBLIOGRAPHY: J. Bountry, *Arras: Son histoire et ses monuments* (1890).

[M. J. DALY]

ARRAS, COUNCILS OF. In 1025 Gerhard, bp. of Cambrai, summoned a council at Arras to deal with a Manichaean outbreak. The council reaffirmed traditional doctrine and practice in regard to baptism, the Eucharist, marriage, Christian burial, and other rites. Councils in 1097 and 1128 were primarily concerned with monastic discipline. Later synods in Arras were held in the 15th, 16th, and 17th centuries. BIBLIOGRAPHY: H. G. J. Beck, NCE 1:849 for bibliog.

[B. L. MARTHALER]

ARRAS, MARTYRS OF, four Sisters of Charity martyred at Arras during the French Revolution. Madeleine Fontaine, directress, Jeanne Gérard, Marie Lanel, and Thérèse-Madeleine Fantou, while working with the poor and sick, were arrested in Arras. The revolutionary tribunal in Cambrai convicted them for refusing the oath upholding liberty and equality and for presumed concealment of counter-revolutionary pamphlets and newspapers. The sisters, convinced in conscience that the oath was serving the de-Christianization movement, preferred to give their obedience and loyalty to God. National and local laws dealt relentlessly with suspects and counter-revolutionaries. On June 26, 1794 the sisters walked to the scaffold. They were beatified in 1920. BIBLIOGRAPHY: A. Lovat, *Sisters of Charity Martyred at Arras in 1794* (1920); M. Lawlor, NCE 1:849.

[R. J. MARAS]

ARREGUI, ANTONIO MARÍA (1863–1942), Spanish Jesuit moralist whose *Summarium theologiae moralis* (1918) has enjoyed wide favor among theology students because of its clarity and concision.

[P. K. MEAGHER]

ARRIAGA, PABLO JOSÉ DE (1564–1622), Jesuit missionary, writer. Born in Spain, he was sent to Peru (1585) where he spent his life as professor or rector in Jesuit colleges. He worked with and for the Indians of Peru, esp. in urban areas, wrote and translated spiritual works, and published his experiences as visitor to the Incas in the Quechua area. BIBLIOGRAPHY: A. de Egañá, NCE 1:850.

[H. JACK]

ARRIAGA, RODRIGO DE (1592–1667), Jesuit; philosopher, theologian. His *Cursus philosophicus* was published at Antwerp (1632). In one way he was influenced by Suárez, esp. in the latter's thinking that metaphysics need not include rational psychology and that it be treated in its own distinct category. BIBLIOGRAPHY: B. Schneider, LTK 1:904; J. C. Willke, NCE 1:850.

[J. R. RIVELLO]

ARRICCIO, first rough plaster coat on a wall in preparation for fresco painting. The finishing coat of plaster (*intonaco*), on which color is applied, is laid on a base of *arriccio*.

[M. J. DALY]

ARRICIVITA, JUAN DOMINGO (1720–94), Franciscan missionary and chronicler. A. was born in Querétaro, Mexico, entered the Franciscans there (1735), and worked at various missions in NW Mexico and SW United States. He is noted for completing the chronicle of the Mission College of the Holy Cross in Querétaro (1791), a valuable, often first-hand report of the Franciscan missionary efforts. BIBLIOGRAPHY: L. G. Canedo, NCE 1:850.

[H. JACK]

ARRIETA, FRANCISCO SALES DE (1768–1843), Franciscan of Lima who reluctantly became that city's archbishop. His main efforts were directed at the reform of the clergy, the improvement of religious education, and the combating of Peruvian liberalism. BIBLIOGRAPHY: F. B. Pike, NCE 1:850–851.

[H. JACK]

ARRILLAGA, BASILIO (1791–1867), Mexican Jesuit. He held various offices within the order, including that of provincial, and was active as an educator, becoming rector of the Univ. of Mexico (1844–49). His political efforts made him a member and president of congress (1830s), one of Santa Anna's junta (1842), and an honorary councilor of state for Maximilian. He spoke and wrote vigorously as an able and energetic defender of the Church during a troubled period of Church-State relations. BIBLIOGRAPHY: F. Zubillaga, NCE 1:851.

[H. JACK]

ARROGANCE, a type of pride that reveals itself in haughty, insolent, overbearing words or behavior that show disdain for others and an exaggerated assumption of one's own claims to rank, dignity, or esteem.

[P. K. MEAGHER]

ARROWSMITH, EDMUND, ST. (1585–1628), Jesuit priest and martyr. Educated at English College, Douai, A. was ordained in 1612 and sent to England (1613) where he labored in his native Lancaster. He entered the Society of Jesus (1623) and in 1628 was betrayed and sentenced to death. He was beatified in 1929 and canonized in 1970. BIBLIOGRAPHY: H. Foley, *Records of the English Province of the Society of Jesus,* II (1875) 24–74.

[V. SAMPSON]

ARS ANTIQUA (Lat. the ancient art), in music history, the period comprising the late 12th and esp. the 13th cent., chiefly in the French-speaking area of Europe and centered at Paris. The term was first applied to late 13th-cent. music by musicians of the early 14th cent. to distinguish it from their own works, which they labeled *ars nova,* after the treatise of Philippe de Vitry. The musical style of the *ars antiqua* began with the Notre Dame school, whose chief figures were Leonin and Perotin. Leonin composed the *Magnus liber organi,* a collection of two-part organa which represented the highest development of this form. Perotin edited Leonin's repertory and added additional organa in three and even four parts. The increased number of parts necessitated greater rhythmic organization by means of the rhythmic *modes employed throughout a composition. For the sections of Leonin's organa based on chant melismas Perotin (and presumably others) wrote substitute pieces called clausulae. These were self-contained compositions which in turn gave rise to the most important musical form of the 13th cent., the motet. This was essentially a three-part clausula, with texts added to the two upper parts. The texts might be Latin or French, sacred or secular, or both. Notable composers of the middle and late 13th cent. were *Franco of Cologne and Petrus de Cruce. The compositional procedure followed throughout the *ars antiqua* period was successive counterpoint, in which the lowest part (tenor) is laid out first, then the upper parts (duplum, triplum) are added one at a time, as opposed to writing all the parts at once (simultaneous counterpoint). Thus two-part motets are sometimes found in other sources with a third voice added. BIBLIOGRAPHY: G. Reese, *Music in the Middle Ages* (1940).

[P. DOHERTY]

ARS DICTAMINIS, the art of letter-writing as taught in schools from the 11th to 16th cent., and expounded in books known as *Artes dictaminis* or *dictandi.* Beginning in the 11th cent. at Monte Cassino, chiefly under the influence of Alberic, the *ars* spread all over Europe, to clergy and laity alike. Practiced in particular at the papal curia, where Thomas of Capua (d. 1243) produced a fine *Summa dictaminis c.*1200. A typical *summa* contains the theory in the first part, then gives practical examples of letters in the second. The greater treatises are printed in L. von Rockinger, *Briefstette und Formelbücher des elften bis vierzehnten Jahrhunderts* (1863). BIBLIOGRAPHY: C. H. Haskins, *Studies in Mediaeval Culture* (1929); J. J. Murphy, *Medieval Rhetoric: A select bibliography* (1970).

[L. E. BOYLE]

ARS MORIENDI, "the art of dying," literary genre of the late Middle Ages concerned with the spiritual preparation for death. Originally intended as manuals for the clergy, they were soon translated into the vernacular languages and achieved a wide popularity. The text of Jean Gerson (d.1429), the reformer, conciliarist, and mystic, is an outstanding example. There were numerous block-printed books of this type before 1500. BIBLIOGRAPHY: F. Dressler, NCE 1:852–853.

[J. E. LYNCH]

ARS NOVA (Lat., the new art), the music of the 14th cent., esp. the first half. The period is characterized by the sharpening of the dichotomy between sacred and secular music, the use of a greater variety of musical forms as well as generally longer pieces, and the invention of a means of notating time-values exactly. This last development freed music from the limitations of the rhythmic modes and resulted in the exploitation by composers of the expanded rhythmic possibilities. Much of the information about the *ars nova* comes to us from the writings of contemporary music theorists. Philippe de Vitry, whose treatise *Ars nova* gave the period its name, discusses current notational procedures; Jacobus of Liège's *Speculum musicae* is an excellent though reactionary comparison of the *ars antiqua* and *ars nova.* Marchettus de Padua also treats of notational questions in a comparison of French and Italian practice. It was during this era that the papal court was established at Avignon, and, while it patronized dazzling displays of secular music, Pope John XXII in his bull *Docta sanctorum* (1324) attacked innovation in church music. The resulting pressure, coupled with growing disillusionment with ecclesiastical foibles, forced church music into a conservative mold, while secular music made rapid advances. The technique of isorhythm was used in both sacred and secular pieces, and Guillaume de Machaut employed it as well as recurring melodic motives to unify the movements of his *Messe de Notre Dame,* the first complete polyphonic setting of the Mass ordinary by a single composer. If Machaut is the most renowned composer of the *ars nova,* he is also prototypical for this period, esp. in France. Making the usual allowances for genius, his great Mass and motets are less forward-looking than his secular works, the virelais, rondeaux, and ballades which, with the madrigal, were the chief secular forms of the period. Like other *ars nova* composers, Machaut used dissonance and syncopation freely, esp. in his non-sacred works. He also ceased using the *cantus firmus* as a basis of composition, and tended toward accompanied melody rather than successive counterpoint. The musical style of the Italian *ars nova,* of which Francesco

Landini was the chief figure, was characterized by a concentration on melody, rather than the contrapuntal complexities of the French. This difference in the two styles was mirrored in their respective notations: the Italian notation simply did not lend itself to the rhythmic intricacies which were so readily handled by French notation. Italian composers also concentrated almost exclusively on secular music. Sacred polyphony in Italy was normally improvised to the existing Gregorian chant. Toward the end of the 14th cent. the fascination with complex notational procedures, including tricks and puzzles, superseded true musical development, and represents the decline of medieval music, in anticipation of the Renaissance period of music history. BIBLIOGRAPHY: Reese MusMA; H. Besseler, MGG 1:702–729.

[P. DOHERTY]

ARS PRAEDICANDI, literally, "the art of preaching"; but commonly used to denote a literary genre which began *c*.1200 and was popularized by the friars. As outlined in the *summae* and manuals, preaching should be along thematic lines. There should be, first of all, a theme from scripture, followed by an introduction (protheme) aimed at capturing the good will of the audience; then the theme was to be reintroduced and treated at length, with citations from scripture, the Fathers, philosophy, and theology, and with a liberal use of pointed moral stories *(exempla)*. The method, which was widely known but not always followed to the letter in the Middle Ages, is still the basis of many preaching techniques. Examples of the *artes praedicandi* of the Middle Ages are edited in T. M. Charland, *Artes praedicandi,* (1936); and there are lists of published and unpublished *artes* in H. Caplan, *Medieval Artes praedicandi: A Hand-list* (1934), *Medieval Artes praedicandi: A Supplementary Hand-List* (1936). BIBLIOGRAPHY: in general R. R. Owst, *Preaching in Medieval England* (1926).

[L. E. BOYLE]

ARSENITE SCHISM, the withdrawal of the followers of the deposed Patriarch of Constantinople. Arsenius Autorianos, from the Patriarchate of Constantinople when the Emperor Michael VIII Palaeologus appointed Germanus, bp. of Adrianople, as Patriarch (1264) and the latter decided to absolve the emperor from the excommunication which he had received from Arsenius (1267). The schism ended through the conciliatory efforts of Patriarch Niphon (1315). BIBLIOGRAPHY: A. A. Vasiliev, *History of the Byzantine Empire* (2d Eng. ed., 1952) 544–661.

[F. H. BRIGHAM]

ARSENIUS AUTORIANOS, PATRIARCH OF CONSTANTINOPLE (d.1273), successively hegumen (abbot) of a monastery in Nicaea, an envoy of the Emperor John Vastatzes to Pope Innocent IV, and successor to Manuel as Patriarch of Constantinople (1255). When he excommunicated the usurper Michael Palaeologus (who had blinded John the son of Emperor Theodore II to preclude his lawful

succession to the throne,) and demanded his abdication, A. was exiled to the convent of St. Nicholas on the island of Proconnessus and died there. BIBLIOGRAPHY: A. A. Vasiliev, *History of the Byzantine Empire* (2d Eng. ed., 1952) 544–661; L. T. Petit, DTC 1.2:1992–1994.

[F. H. BRIGHAM]

ARSON, in statute law it is described as a crime in which one destroys, through fire, the property of another without his consent. Such destruction is malicious and voluntary. English common law makes a distinction between fires that endanger human life and those that do not. In all countries, except England, death resulting from arson is considered murder. Legally, the concept of arson has been refined to such an extent that it now provides for distinctions among arson with intent to conceal evidence or hide a crime, arson for destruction of property, and arson with intent to kill. Within the U.S. penalties for arson vary from state to state. Arson resulting from a pyromaniac condition is considered as a special category wherein the arsonist may plead insanity for defense purposes. From the moral point of view, arson involving the destruction of property is grievously sinful.

[J. R. RIVELLO]

ART, BEURONESE, SEE BEURONESE ART.

ART NOUVEAU, an art style influenced by Japanese forms, and, more generally, by organic wave-like shapes from nature. Like the psychedelic art of the 1960s, which revived many of its forms, *art nouveau* was anti-industrialist in character. Henri de Toulouse-Lautrec and Paul Gauguin influenced this style. BIBLIOGRAPHY: *Art and Design at the Turn of the Century* (ed. P. Selz and M. Constantine, 1959); S. T. Madsen, *Sources of Art Nouveau* (1956).

[L. P. SIGER]

ARTAUD DE MONTOR, JEAN ALEXIS FRANÇOIS (1772–1849), diplomat, biographer. After a diplomatic career, during which he had published works on medieval painting and the catacombs as well as a translation of the *Divine Comedy,* A. concentrated upon historical biography. He wrote an eight-volume history of the popes, lives of Pius VII, Leo XII, Pius VIII, Dante Alighieri, and an historical estimate of Machiavelli. BIBLIOGRAPHY: G. Goyau, CE 10:544–545; R. Limouzin-Lamothe, NCE 1:917.

ARTAXERXES, name of three Persian rulers. Artaxerxes I, known as Macrocheir or Longimanus, was the son of Xerxes I and ruled 465–425 B.C. He authorized Nehemiah's two missions to rebuild Jerusalem, the first in 445 B.C. (Neh ch. 2). Artaxerxes II, known as Mnemon, was the son of Darius II and the grandson of Artaxerxes I, and ruled 404–359 B.C. He was succeeded by his son Artaxerxes III

(Ochus). Scholars disagree as to whether Ezra went to Jerusalem under Artaxerxes I or Artaxerxes II (Ezra 7).

[T. EARLY]

ARTEMIS, the Greek name for the goddess Diana. The Artemis of the Ephesians, a mother-goddess, is mentioned in Acts 19.23–41. Paul and his companions are set upon by silversmiths who made idols of Artemis, because of the threat to their trade they feared in Christian conversions. As huntress in Arcadia, A. was a popular theme of the Renaissance world, particularly in the French court of Louis XIII. *DIANA OF THE EPHESIANS.

[T. EARLY]

ARTEMIS OF THE EPHESIANS, see DIANA OF THE EPHESIANS.

ARTEMISIUM, ZEUS (God from the Sea), Greek bronze statue found in the sea off Cape Artemisium (1928), now in the National Archaeological Museum, Athens. The over-life-size statue of the majestic god in striding pose with arms outstretched as if throwing an object in his right hand is interpreted as Zeus with his thunderbolt or Poseidon throwing a trident. Dated $c.460$–450 B.C., the statue is one of the few great Greek bronzes extant.

[M. J. DALY]

ARTHURIAN LEGENDS, one of the two major cycles of medieval legends that center in an historical person. They furnish the "matter of Britain," while Charlemagne is the center of the "matter of France" (see CAROLINGIAN LEGENDS). The Arthurian stories in their full development (12th to 15th cent.) portray the world of chivalry, love, and adventure. Historically Arthur was a leader of the Britons against the Saxons and won a series of battles $c.500$. The early chronicler Gildas refers to the Battle of Mount Badon (*De Excidio et Conquestu Britanniae*, $c.500$). Nennius (*Historia Britonum*, $c.800$) names Arthur and calls him *dux bellorum*. William of Malmesbury (*Gesta Regum Anglorum*, 1125) speaks of the great leader Arthur. *Geoffrey of Monmouth (*Historia Regum Britanniae*, 1137) gives a full, imaginative account of the history of Britain derived from legends, early chronicles, and Welsh genealogies, and covers the history of Britain from Brutus, a descendant of Aeneas of Troy to Arthur and the fall of the kingdom before the Germanic conquerors. Geoffrey includes in his account Merlin, Arthur's father Uther Pendragon, Guinevere, the traitor Modred, Arthur's wars, and his departure for Avalon. Translations of Geoffrey into French poetry by Wace (1155) and into English by Layamon ($c.1190$) add the story of the Round Table. The French Arthurian romances (1150 and later) use additional oral Breton legends and join what were originally independent stories to the Arthurian cycle. *Chrétien de Troyes (12th cent.) gives literary polish and courtly ideals to his romances, making Lancelot forever the model of knightly perfection. The Vulgate Cycle (5 long French prose romances, 13th

cent.) spread the Grail story and the concept of chivalry throughout Western Europe, and was a main source for Sir Thomas Malory's *Le Morte D'Arthur* (1469–70; ed. and printed by Caxton in 1485). Arthurian stories have held interest until the present day. Spenser, Milton, Tennyson, Wagner, William Morris, E. A. Robinson, Mark Twain, and T. W. White look at them for points of view which are sympathetic, seriously interested, or mocking. The central catastrophe as Malory (or Caxton) presents it shows the moral struggles of the major characters in the face of human passions and contradictory human allegiances. Politically the stories may have helped to build up the national background of Britain under the Norman kings; later they were used to support Tudor claims to the throne. BIBLIOGRAPHY: K. Chamber, *Arthur of Britain*, (1927); *Arthurian Literature* (ed. R. S. Loomis); *Arthurian Legends in the Middle Ages* (1959); *Development of Arthurian Romances* (1963).

[M. M. BARRY]

ARTICLES DECLARATORY (Church of Scotland), the statement setting forth the distinctive claims of the *Church of Scotland as a *national Church. The "Articles Declaratory of the Constitution of the Church of Scotland in Matters Spiritual" was recognized by Parliament in 1921 and enacted by the General Assembly of the Church in 1926. The Church declares itself to be part of the Holy Catholic or Universal Church, adheres to the Scottish Reformation, and receives the word of God as its supreme rule of faith and life (Art. I). Its principal subordinate standard is the *Westminster Confession; its *polity is presbyterian; its system and principles of worship, orders, and discipline are in accordance with the *Westminster Standards (Art. 2). This Church is in historical continuity with the Church of Scotland that was reformed in 1560 and acknowledges its distinctive call and duty to bring the ordinances of religion to the people in every parish through a territorial ministry (Art. 3). It receives from its Divine King and Head the right and power, subject to no civil authority, to legislate and to adjudicate finally in all matters of doctrine, worship, government, and discipline (Art. 4). It has the right to frame or modify its subordinate doctrinal standards, "always in agreement with the Word of God" (Art. 5). It acknowledges the divine appointment and authority of the civil magistrate within his own sphere, and the duty of the nation to render homage to God (Art 6). It recognizes the obligation to seek and promote union with other Churches (Art. 7) and claims the right to interpret, modify, or add to its Declaratory Articles, subject to the conditions of the first article (Art. 8). BIBLIOGRAPHY: J. R. Fleming, *History of the Church in Scotland, 1875–1929* (1933) 310–312, text.

[J. A. R. MACKENZIE]

ARTICLES OF FAITH, those revealed truths which have a specific and proper identity, yet are broad enough to subsume other revealed truths so as to form an organic unity within Christian doctrine. These truths must be revealed for themselves, and are comparable to fundamental principles within the various branches of science. Thus the Passion and Resurrection of Jesus are distinct articles of faith, whereas the suffering and death of Jesus would be incorporated into the Passion as an article of faith. Other revealed truths, such as the miracles described in Scripture, are not articles of faith since they have not been revealed for themselves but insofar as they have a connection with a broader truth, e.g., the divinity of Christ.

The phrase is not found in the writings of the early Church Fathers. In the Middle Ages, the word *sententia* was first used to designate these truths but, esp. due to the influence of Thomas Aquinas, article of faith came to be the more common designation. Aquinas defines an article of faith as a truth revealed for itself and so distinct from other truths of the same nature as to offer our intelligence a special difficulty (ThAqST 2, 2.1,6), and regards the division of revealed truth into several articles—and ultimately into a creed—making explicit faith's search for understanding. Contemporary theologians differ concerning the precise meaning of the phrase: some reserve the phrase to that which is contained in the creeds, others to truth defined by the Church. BIBLIOGRAPHY: DTC 1.2:2023–25.

[T. M. MCFADDEN]

ARTICLES OF WAR (Salvation Army), a statement of the doctrinal position of the Salvation Army, drawn up by William Booth in 1878. They affirm the inspiration of the Bible, the only rule of Christian faith and practice, the Unity and Trinity of God, the humanity and divinity of Christ, the Fall, the atonement by the suffering and death of Jesus on the Cross, the necessity of repentance for salvation, faith in Christ, and regeneration by the Holy Spirit, justification by faith, *sanctification by the Holy Spirit as a second blessing, the immortality of the soul, eternal happiness, and eternal punishment.

[R. K. MACMASTER]

ARTIFICIAL INSEMINATION, method of implanting male semen into the female genital tract by use of a syringe or other device. Where the woman's husband is the donor, permissible means may be postulated for obtaining the sperm, but Pius XII ruled out as nonmarital this manner of injecting the sperm and therefore rejected the procedure. Theologians do not agree on the means that may legitimately be used to assist insemination by the husband, when it cannot be accomplished in the ordinary manner. Artificial insemination by a donor not the woman's husband is altogether ruled out, whether the husband consents or not, as contrary to the nature and significance of marriage. BIBLIOGRAPHY: J. F. Dedeck, *Human Life* (1972) 98–118.

[T. C. O'BRIEN]

ARTOPHORION, in the Eastern Church, a container for the Eucharist when it is reserved.

[M. C. BRADLEY]

ARTOTYRITES (Gr. *Artos tyros,* bread-cheese), members of a Montanist sect in Phrygia during the 2d century. They employed bread and cheese in the celebration of their mysteries. BIBLIOGRAPHY: G. Bareille, DTC 1:2035–36.

[L. G. MÜLLER]

ARTUSI, GIOVANNI MARIA (*c.*1540–1613), Italian music theorist and composer, a pupil of Zarlino. He wrote a treatise on counterpoint (*L'arte del contrapunto,* 1586–89), then devoted himself to a reactionary defense of the strict contrapuntal style of the *prima prattica* through polemical attacks on Monteverdi (*L'Artusi, overo delle imperfettioni della musica moderna,* 1600–03), Bottrigari, V. Galilei, and, posthumously, his teacher, Zarlino. BIBLIOGRAPHY: H. F. Redlich, MGG 1:747–749.

[P. DOHERTY]

ARUNDEL, 12TH EARL OF, see FITZALAN, HENRY.

ARUNDEL, JOHN (1291–1331), son of first earl of Arundel. He began his studies in 1317 and was at Oxford from 1323–25. By papal indult he held several benefices. He was warden of the King's free chapel, canon of Lincoln, Salisbury, and St. Paul's, London. At the time of his death he was a papal chaplain. BIBLIOGRAPHY: Emden OX 1:48.

[A. WARDLE]

ARUNDEL, THOMAS (1352–1414), English prelate, bp. of Ely (1373–88), abp. of York (1388–96), abp. of Canterbury (1396–97, 1399–1414), foe of Lollardy. He also served as chancellor of England (1386–89, 1396–97, 1407–10, 1412–13). Under suspicion of implication in a plot against Richard II, who procured his translation to the schismatic see of St. Andrews (1397), he fled into exile and supported the usurpation of Henry IV, whose trusted adviser he became. He was strongly opposed to Lollardy and obtained state support for anti-heretical legislation (1401–1406), issued constitutions regulating preaching (1407–09), and intervened to purge Oxford of heresy (1411–12). BIBLIOGRAPHY: M. E. Aston, *Thomas Arundel* (1967); J. Gairdner, DNB 2:137–141; R. D. Davies, "Thomas Arundel as Archbishop of Canterbury, 1396–1414," J EcclHist 24 No. 1 (1973) 9–21.

ARUNDELL, JOHN (d. 1477), physician, bishop. A. was a fellow of Exeter College, Oxford, who took a degree in medicine after his ordination. He served as physician and chaplain to Henry VI who recommended him for the see of Durham in 1457. Although this was not granted, he later (1459) became bp. of Chichester by papal provision. BIBLIOGRAPHY: Emden Ox 1:49–50; W. P. Courtney, DNB 1:618.

[A. WARDLE]

ARUNDELL, JOHN (d. 1504), bishop. A native of Cornwall, A. was educated at Oxford where he took several degrees. He was chaplain to Edward IV in 1479 and was sent on diplomatic missions that required skill and strength. By papal provision A. became bp. of Lichfield and Coventry (1496) and was translated to the see of Exeter in 1502. His biographers note his love of learning and his generosity to the poor. BIBLIOGRAPHY: Emden Ox 1:50–51; W. P. Courtney, DNB 1:618.

[A. WARDLE]

ARUNDELL, THOMAS (1560–1639), first Baron of Arundell of Wardour; soldier and statesman. A. was the son of Sir Matthew Arundell of Wardour Castle, Wiltshire, and grandson of Sir John Arundell, of a Norman family, dating from the 13th cent., that settled in Cornwall. A. entered the Austrian service under Archduke Matthias, brother of Emperor Rudolph II. He distinguished himself by fighting against the Ottomans in Hungary; at the siege of Gran he was the first to plant the imperial standard. When A. returned to England, James I recognized his loyalty and made him Baron Arundell of Wardour in 1605. He commanded the English regiment that served the Archduke Albert in Flanders against the Dutch. A. was active in several committees in Parliament and took the oath of allegiance in 1610. Charles I at the beginning of his reign forbade A. to bear arms because he was a Catholic, but A. was later pardoned. BIBLIOGRAPHY: F. W. Grey, CE 1:765; F. Edwards, NCE 1:927–928.

[M. C. BRADLEY]

ARVAD, Phoenician city-state on a small island just off the coast of Syria opposite Cyprus, about 125 miles north of Tyre. The Table of Nations lists Arvadites as descendants of Canaan (Gen 10.18), and Ezekiel said they served Tyre as oarsmen and warriors (27.8, 11). It is the Aradus of 1 Macc 15.23. The modern name is Ruad.

[T. EARLY]

ARX, ILDEFONS VON (1755–1833), Benedictine scholar, archivist. A. was director of the Sankt Gallen Abbey archives and prevented their despoliation by revolutionaries after the Swiss Directory secularized religious institutes and confiscated their property (1798). He discovered the Sankt Gallen palimpsests and wrote a three-volume history of the abbey. He was G. H. Pertz's first collaborator (1826–29) on the *Monumenta Germaniae Historica.* BIBLIOGRAPHY: E. Studer, LTK 1:912.

[H. JACK]

ĀRYA-SAMĀJ, the society of the noble, an Indian religious organization founded by Swami Dagan and Sarasvatī (1824–83) for the purpose of reforming Indian religious, political, and social life. Because they believed that the Vedas are God's only revealed word and therefore the source of all knowledge and science, it is their duty to direct India's attention to the Vedic books and proclaim their teaching to the world. BIBLIOGRAPHY: H. Griswold, Hastings ERE 2:57–62.

[F. H. BRIGHAM]

ARZUGES, native Africans living along the coast of the Roman province of Tripolitana, which embraced the important cities of Leptis Magna, Oea, and Sabratha. The Arzuges were slow to adopt Christianity and in the 4th cent. partially accepted Donatism. BIBLIOGRAPHY: Orosius 1.2: Augustine, *Ep.* 46.1; 93.24; I. Daniele, EncCatt 2:74.

[M. J. COSTELLOE]

ÅS (ASYLUM), ABBEY OF, a former Cistercian monastery located in Halland, Sweden. It was founded in 1194, probably by Waldemar, a son of King Canute V of Denmark. Very little is known of the history of the abbey. Ravaged by fire in 1397, it was not fully restored by 1441. In 1536 the abbey was sold. During the reign of terror in Halland, the monastery was pillaged and devastated by the Swedes, who left only a heap of ruins. BIBLIOGRAPHY: J.-M. Canivez, DHGE 4:865–867.

[S. A. HEENEY]

ASA, third king of Judah, ruling c.913–873 B.C. In contrast with his father Abijah, whom he succeeded, he is praised for loyalty to Yahweh (1 Kgs 15.9). Under attack from Baasha of Israel, however, he sent the Temple treasures to Benhadad of Syria to gain his aid and was condemned by Hanani for not relying on Yahweh (2 Chr ch. 16).

[T. EARLY]

ASAM, COSMAS DAMIAN (1686–1739) and **EGID QUIRIN** (1692–1750), Bavarian brothers, important in the development of south German late Baroque and early Rococo architecture and decoration with its exploitation of optical illusions. Collaborating, Cosmas Damian executed the ceiling paintings and altarpieces while Egid Quirin determined the architecture, stucco work, and figural sculpture. Among their works may be named the monastery church of Weingarten, Württemberg (1718–20), Rohr near Regensburg (1718–25), and the castle at Bruchsal (1729). Their masterpiece is the tiny church of St. John Nepomuk, Munich (1733–c.1750), where architecture and lighting are superbly coordinated. BIBLIOGRAPHY: L. Faison, Jr., EncWA 1:814; E. Hanfstaengl, *Die Brüder Cosmas und Egid Quirin Asam* (1955).

[L. A. LEITE]

ASAPH, biblical name: (1) father of Joah (2 Kg 18.18); (2) eponymous ancestor of one of the three chief families of temple musicians (1 Chr 6.31–48; 25.1–2). He is mentioned only by the Chronicler and in superscriptions to Ps 50 and 73–83, perhaps the hymnal of the Asaphite choir. Participants in almost every temple celebration recorded by the Chronicler, the Asaphites are called singers, though they also sound the cymbals (1 Chr 15.19; Ezra 3.10); (3) official under Artaxerxes (Neh 2.8).

[T. EARLY]

ASARHADDON, see ESARHADDON, KING OF ASSYRIA.

ASBURY, FRANCIS (1745–1816), second bp. of the Methodist Episcopal Church, the first ordained in the United States. A native of Handsworth, Staffordshire, England, A. left school at 12 to serve as an apprentice. Hearing Methodist preaching at Wednesbury, he was converted at the age of 14 and later became an itinerant preacher under John *Wesley. He answered Wesley's call for service in America and preached his first American sermon at Philadelphia, Oct. 28, 1771. A. traveled extensively among the Methodist *societies in America, enforcing Methodist discipline and securing allegiance to John Wesley. In 1772 Wesley appointed him "General Assistant in America." During the Revolutionary War most of Wesley's itinerants returned to England; A. remained in America, although he was forced into hiding for suspected English sympathies. The Methodist societies in the Colonies had been regarded as part of the Church of England. Since their own preachers were not ordained, and many Anglican ministers had fled, after the Revolution the societies asked Wesley to provide for their having the sacraments. Wesley ordained Thomas *Coke in England as general superintendent (bp.) of American Methodism, sending him with two others to the U.S. to ordain Asbury. Asbury, however, desired appointment by election, and the Methodist preachers elected him at Lovely Lane Chapel, Baltimore (1784). There he was ordained general superintendent, and the Methodist Episcopal Church in America was organized. During his administration he traveled widely, kept a *Journal,* now invaluable to historians, wrote hundreds of letters, and preached constantly. There were about 1,200 Methodists when he came to America; 214,000 at his death. BIBLIOGRAPHY: L. C. Rudolph, *Francis Asbury,* (1966); *Journal and Letters of Francis Asbury* (ed. E. T. Clark, 1958); F. E. Maser, *Dramatic Story of Early American Methodism* (1965) 62–65, 78–83, 93–94.

[F. E. MASER]

ASCALON, see ASHKELON.

ASCELLINO (Asselino, Anselmo; fl. 1245–48), Lombard Dominican sent by Pope Innocent IV on a mission to the Tartars. He reached mid-Persia, established contact with a Tartar general, but was not permitted to see the Grand Khan because of his unwillingness to conform to court ceremonial. He returned without favorable response to any of the Pope's proposals. BIBLIOGRAPHY: Quétif-Echard 1:122.

[P. K. MEAGHER]

ASCENSION, FEAST OF, the commemoration of Christ's final historical departure from his disciples (see Acts 1.1–11), his entry into heaven so as to manifest his victory to the good and evil spirits who did not dwell on earth, and his exaltation in glory at the right hand of the Father. It is celebrated on the 40th day after *Easter as a universal *holy day of obligation. At first, the A. was commemorated on the same day as *Pentecost. By c.350, however, it gained an independent status in the liturgical calendar. The paschal candle was once extinguished on this day to mark Christ's departure; now it is lighted at baptisms, funerals, etc. as a sign of the *Passion, *Resurrection, and Ascension. BIBLIOGRAPHY: G. Lefebvre, *Spirit of Worship* (tr. L. C. Sheppard, 1959) 71–73. *ASCENSION OF CHRIST; *PENTECOST CYCLE.

[T. M. MCFADDEN]

ASCENSION OF CHRIST, the mystery of the manifest return to the Father of the risen Christ, of his enthronement as Messiah and Lord and as sender of the Spirit. Thus it is a moment in the historical unfolding of the one redemptive paschal mystery; it is in the whole of this mystery that Christ redeems mankind and becomes the source of life to all. In a sense his passover to the Father is perfected in the exaltation of his death and Resurrection, but the paschal mystery involves so many elements that their manifestation and revelation have to occur successively. The Resurrection reveals Christ as conqueror of death, a victim whose sacrifice is accepted by the Father. The Ascension complements this by showing (1) the end of Christ's visible mission on earth, (2) his return in his whole glorified humanity to the Father, and so (3) his enthronement as Lord at the Father's side, an eternal state from which (4) at Pentecost he sends the Spirit, through whom men are to find union with his saving mysteries, and from which (5) he is eventually to come to judge the living and the dead. Because of the varied themes involved, it is not surprising to find a twofold trend in the NT allusions to the Ascension. First at times the sacred writers seem to consider it as an event that occurred, if not simultaneously with the Resurrection, at least on the evening of Easter Day (see Jn 20.17; the penetration of the High Priest to the Holy of Holies; Heb 1.4; 4.14; 6.19–20; also Acts 2.32–34; Eph 4.8–10; 1 Tim 3.16; 1 Pet 3.22). Second, they speak elsewhere of an interval in which Christ completed his earthly work of teaching and of establishing his Church; only after 40 days did he visibly ascend before his Apostles (Mk 16.19; Lk 24.50–51; Acts 1.2, 9, 22). There is no real contradiction here. Christ's return to the Father in his total humanity occurs ontologically in the Resurrection itself, but the very nature of the Incarnation economy demands both the clear attestation of the Resurrection, with all its implications, and the manifest glorious completion of his earthly mission. The cosmological aspects of the Ascension need not detain one: the physical going up of God-made-man is a reality, but it is a sign of his return to the Father rather than an indication of where the Father is to be found. The cloud that receives him is not just a natural phenomenon; in accord with Scriptural usage (e.g., the narratives of the Transfiguration), this itself is a manifestation of that divine glory into which Christ is now wholly received. In this as in the other moments of the paschal mystery Christ is our head. In the Ascension mankind makes its return to the Father in and through Christ; just as God has raised us with him, so he has "made us sit with him in the heavenly places" (Eph 2.6). But this process has to be implemented over the successive centuries until the last day, when Christ's lordship will be fully manifested, the very crown of a redeemed humanity. BIBLIOGRAPHY: F. X. Durrwell, *Resurrection* (1960); E. Schillebeeckx, *Christ the Sacrament* (1963); P. Benoit, "Ascension of Christ," *TheolDig 8* (1960) 105–110.

[R. L. STEWART]

ASCETIC one who does battle with himself while he remains faithful to the exigence of that battle, i.e., his humanness. While it is true to say that the ascetic looks after the things of the spirit, it is neither the necessary nor sufficient reason to say that he is freed from the human contingents and from the limitless liabilities of his humanness. It is, rather, within that tension between the two that he does battle with the world, himself, and the devil. While we may speak of the "new asceticism" it is important not to undervalue asceticism as it has appeared in the past. It is well also to consider that no asceticism is possible, at least in the Christian context, without a prior moral conversion. In this sense, it is reasonable to see ascetical living as an expectation for all Christians rather than as a conceptual modality to be lived out by elitist monastic groups. BIBLIOGRAPHY: B. Häring, NCE 1:942–944; K. Rahner, *Theological Investigations* (tr. D. Bourke, 1971) 7:19ff.

[J. R. RIVELLO]

ASCETICAL THEOLOGY, that branch of the science of theology which deals with the attainment of salvation through the disciplined renunciation of personal desires and impulses for religious motives. Thus ascetical theology is distinct from moral theology which treats of those acts that are essential for salvation; since the 17th cent., the study of asceticism has also been distinguished from mystical theology which treats of those moral acts resulting from an extraordinary grace leading to infused contemplation. Some contemporary theologians, however, reject any clear distinction between asceticism and mysticism, and prefer to speak of a spiritual theology that flows out of a truly existential and nonrationalistic dogmatic theology.

As any science, ascetical theology has several fundamental principles which direct its approach. (1) Asceticism is not merely self-discipline performed so that the individual can control his inclinations and desires. Asceticism is a grace, a free gift of God to which the Christian is called to respond. Care must be exercised to free asceticism from Pelagian theories. (2) Asceticism entails both a positive and a negative element: a turning toward God and neighbor, and from sinful inclinations. Emphasis on the negative element alone robs asceticism of its proper élan. (3) All too frequently in the past, asceticism has been predicated upon a dualistic anthropology, i.e., a supposition that mind or soul or spirit is good and that materiality and the body are evil. Contemporary theology insists upon the essential unity of spirit and body, and denies the value of Neoplatonic theories for a proper understanding of human nature. (4) The motive for

Christian asceticism must be Christocentric. Asceticism becomes Christian only when it is done in the consciousness of human guilt as manifest in the cross of Christ. Thus all Christian asceticism becomes a participation in Jesus' asceticism. (5) Faith is the first ascetical act insofar as it is the individual's acceptance of a Word which comes to him from another and not from his own intellectual operations. Faith is self-transcendence, the surrender of the self to God's will; the asceticism of faith is this radical openness to the divine command. (6) Asceticism is eschatological. Because the kingdom has not yet arrived, the Church remains a pilgrim people awaiting the final realization of salvation in a world where God often seems removed. In such a situation, patient watchfulness is an essential remedy for despair. The asceticism of accepting the experience of the absence of God rests upon the Christian's eschatological hope. (7) As with all Christian virtues, asceticism has an important reference to service within the Church. An asceticism that would be unmindful of the community's needs in an exclusive search for perfection disregards the communal nature of Christian life. (8) In order to distinguish fruitful ascetical practices from those that might be obsessive or extreme, ascetical theology must be in consistent dialogue with other disciplines, esp. psychology. (9) It is obvious from the previous principles that the call to asceticism is universal and not the obligation of the clergy alone. Asceticism is not a legalistic imposition but a response beyond any legal norms to the presence of the kingdom. (10) Since acts of renunciation play a decisive role in the development of moral holiness and the way toward Christian perfection admits of various stages, various levels of ascetical practices are recognized. A three-fold division has been common since St. Thomas Aquinas' classification of the purgative, illuminative, and unitive stages or ways to God (ThAqST 2a2ae, 24.9; 183.4). The purgative way emphasizes purification of the soul from all serious sin; the illuminative way directs the soul to the positive exercise of Christian virtue; and the unitive way, sometimes assigned to mystical theology, aims toward habitual and intimate union with God. BIBLIOGRAPHY: J. Lindworsky, *Psychology of Asceticism* (1936); *Christian Asceticism and Modern Man* (tr. W. Mitchell et al., 1955); K. Rahner, *Theology of the Spiritual Life* (1967); F. Wulf, SacMund 1:110–116.

[T. M. MCFADDEN]

ASCETICISM, the disciplined renunciation of personal impulses and desires for religious motives. The word is derived from the Greek *askēsis,* meaning exercise or athletic training, and it is in this context that St. Paul presents Christian renunciation, "Athletes deny themselves all sorts of things. They do this to win a crown of leaves that withers, but we a crown that is imperishable" (1 Cor 9.25). In its broadest sense, asceticism also refers to the practice of virtues like temperance, chastity, and patience when these virtues would be performed simply out of a desire for self-mastery. In this sense, asceticism was often practiced in human history—notably in the classical and Hellenistic Greek cultures. In the earliest Jewish religious traditions, asceticism was not valued: material goods enhanced the quality of life and were accepted in simple thankfulness as a sign of Yahweh's graciousness. Cultic fasting and sexual abstinence out of reverence for the holy was practiced, but otherwise only extreme indulgence would have occasioned any rebuke against the enjoyment of material things, e.g., in the Book of Amos. In later Judaism, however, a growing sense of abstinence and penance accompanies a developed consciousness of individual and communal guilt. Penitential practices and vows of abstinence were not infrequent, as for instance with the Essenes, Nazarites, and Rechabites. Late Hellenistic Judaism regarded asceticism highly; for Philo, the Patriarch Jacob was the model ascetic since he was the spiritual wrestler (Gen 32.24ff.).

In the NT, Jesus proclaimed the joyfulness of the messianic kingdom and came "eating and drinking" (Mt 11.19), yet his life was also full of renunciation. He came to do the will of the Father, he renounced possessions and family, and he accepted a criminal's torturous death. Jesus enjoined a similar willingness to take up one's cross upon his followers (Mt 10.34–38), described entrance into the kingdom of God as a passage through a narrow gate (Mt 7.13), and asked various followers for the renunciation of possessions or complete celibacy (Mt 19.12). St. Paul strongly urges bodily and spiritual self-discipline and renunciation. Christians should "crucify their flesh with its passions and desires" (Gal 5.24), and "put to death whatever in your nature is rooted in earth" (Col 3.5). But the distinguishing motive for Christian asceticism is all-important: conformity to the sufferings of Christ out of the desire for unity with him and service to the community. Thus rejection of marriage and the imposition of dietary restrictions are condemned in the Pastoral Epistles (1 Tim 4.1–5; Titus 1.14ff.).

In the first centuries of the Christian era, the principal ascetical discipline was the willingness to accept martyrdom, although fasting and virginity were also widely practiced. The excessive asceticism of the Gnostics and Manichaeans was rejected, and the early Church was consistently challenged to distinguish its doctrine of spiritual discipline from any condemnation of the physical as such. With the institutional acceptance of the Church in the Roman Empire, ascetical forms changed significantly: in the 4th cent., monastic life was begun and with it a communal and systematic asceticism. Religious superiors instructed their communities in the ways of self-denial for the attainment of perfect charity, and monasteries and convents were organized around the triple vows of poverty, celibacy, and obedience. Various rules inculcating ascetical practices were formulated, such as those of Pachomius, St. Basil, St. John Chrysostom, and St. Benedict. Increasing devotion to the humanity of Christ, esp. to his Passion, led to a shift in emphasis in the Middle Ages. The earlier cenobitic stress on progress in spiritual contemplation through the mastery of physical needs was altered in favor of a desire to conform to the sufferings of Christ—at

times through self-inflicted punishments. The formation of the mendicant orders also gave a significant direction to ascetical ideals; in contrast to the frequent worldliness of the secular clergy, the mendicants championed the ideal of voluntary poverty and encouraged an ascetical life for the Christian layman as well as the monk. In the 15th cent. a further development, emphasizing the search for perfection through the acceptance of Christ as the model for the Christian's inner life, gained widespread acceptance esp. through the use of Thomas à Kempis' *Imitation of Christ*.

Reformation and Renaissance thought entailed a marked reaction against prior ascetical ideals. Martin Luther wrote strong polemics against monasticism and asceticism on the grounds that they disregard the total gratuity of salvation and produce a doctrine of justification by good works. A response in favor of the medieval type of asceticism is common to the counter-Reformation. St. Ignatius of Loyola (1495–1556) in particular outlined a universally applicable asceticism based on renunciation and loving disregard for the self and all created things so that the soul could be delivered from any improper attachments and enabled to direct itself entirely to God. Through prayer and a precise examination of conscience the individual is disposed to discover the true will of God. The Church continues to insist upon the value of asceticism as a free response to a gracious God revealed in Christ. The three traditional vows of the religious life continue to be lived; voluntary poverty is chosen as an aid to the ministry of the Word; prayer and fasting are recommended as freely chosen exercises in expectation of the final coming of the kingdom of God. The rationale behind Christian asceticism continues to be acknowledged: in order to grow into union with Christ, the individual must die to egocentricity and a debilitating concern for his own material comfort. Through ascetical exercises, such a death is embraced in order to come to new life. BIBLIOGRAPHY: L. Bouyer, *Spirituality of the New Testament and the Fathers* (1964); K. Rahner, *Theology of the Spiritual Life* (1967), esp. pp. 47–86; R. Schnackenberg, *Moral Teaching of the New Testament* (1965); DSAM 1:936–1010; DTC 1:2038–77.

[T. M. MCFADDEN]

ASCETICISM (EASTERN). Although some ascetical practices have been present in almost all religions, Hinduism and Buddhism have been esp. concerned with the problem of physical and psychological denial in order to attain a distinctive spiritual purpose. Since asceticism does not hold a significant place in Chinese and Japanese religions (except in the form of Buddhism), this article will consider only the first two religions mentioned. The fundamental concept that gives direction to the Hindu ascetical ideal is the desire to escape from *samsāra*, the circle of continuous rebirth in which all finite beings are involved, and finally to enjoy *mokṣā* or unity with the One beyond all change and materiality. Through self-denial, ranging in form from the traditional practices of fasting, sexual abstinence, and renunciation of physical comforts to the infliction of extreme pain practiced by some Indian yogas, the ascetic attempted to break away from the hopeless procession of life, hardship, and death. This attitude does not seem to have been prevalent among the early Aryan invaders of India and is only peripherally reflected in the Vedic literature. But the synthesis of Aryan and Dravidian beliefs which is at the heart of Hinduism soon gave rise to an ascetic ideal in the Upanishads. In these spiritual meditations, the existence and validity of ascetical practices are accepted as a matter of course even though the main thrust of Upanishadic literature is the exaltation of knowledge as the most efficacious means toward spiritual insight. In the Laws of Manu and the later Dharmasutras or law books, specific regulations for an ascetic are set forth: "Let him live without a fire, without a house, wholly silent, subsisting on roots and fruit, chaste, sleeping on the bare ground, dwelling at the roots of trees. . . . Thus an ascetic gains bliss after death" (*Laws of Manu*, ch. 6, 80–85). The doctrine of the ashramas or stages of life which was also developed at this time has made asceticism an established part of Hindu life: after the stages of student and householder, a man ideally becomes a hermit and finally an absolute ascetic. Although the Bhagavad Gita adopts a reforming tack in Hindu thought when it teaches that the essence of ascetical practice is not bodily mortification but the abnegation of selfish desire in loving devotion to Lord Krishna, asceticism remains a strong influence and positive ideal for the Hindu.

The origins of Buddhism can be at least partly traced to the Buddha's selection of a "middle path" between the extremes of sensual indulgence and harsh asceticism. After his own lengthy experiments in self-denial, the Buddha reveals in his famous Sermon at Deer Park that moderation is the key to existence. Since rigid asceticism is far from moderation, it is unprofitable for the soul. Thus the Buddha encouraged proper care of the body and the uselessness of suffering and painful penance. Nevertheless, Buddhism is thoroughly ascetical if asceticism is taken to mean discipline, psychological control, and the mastery of selfishness in the effort to attain compassion. In this sense, the Eightfold Path of Buddhism whereby the disciple escapes the continually renewed cycle of life's sufferings through ethical conduct is properly regarded as the epitome of ascetical discipline. BIBLIOGRAPHY: G. van der Leeuw, *Religion in Essence and Manifestation* II (1963), esp. ch. 96; Hastings ERE 2:69–71, 87–96; O. Hardman, *Ideals of Asceticism; an Essay in the Comparative Study of Religion* (1924).

[T. M. MCFADDEN]

ASCHAM, ROGER (c.1515–68), English scholar and educator. After studying at St. John's College, Cambridge (B.A., 1533; M.A., 1537), A. became a Greek reader at St. John's. His *Toxophilus* (1545), a treatise on archery, brought him some fame as a prose stylist, and he served briefly as tutor to Princess (later Queen) Elizabeth in 1545. As secretary to Sir Richard Moryson, English ambassador to Charles V, he traveled extensively on the Continent. Despite his

outspoken Protestant views, he was appointed Latin secretary to Queen Mary (1553) and later served Elizabeth in the same capacity. The *Scholemaster*, his best-known work, presents his views on the psychology of learning and the importance of educating the whole man by persuasion rather than by force. In it he explains his famous method of teaching Latin prose composition, which was widely adopted. This work was published posthumously in 1570. BIBLIOGRAPHY: L. V. Ryan, *Roger Ascham* (1964).

[M. B. MURPHY]

ASCHERICH, see ANASTASIUS OF HUNGARY, ST.

ASCITES (*Ascodrugitae*), a sect in Galatia described by Filaster (*Haer*. 75) under the name *Ascodrugitae* (Gr. *askos*, meaning wine-skin), whose adherents danced around an inflated wine-skin much as the pagans danced to Liber. The name *Ascodrugitae* was abbreviated by Augustine to Ascites (*Haer*. 62). Filaster erroneously ascribed the practice to an interpretation of Mt 9.17 or Lk 5.37. The rite may have been a relic of the earlier worship in Asia Minor of Marsyas, the musician in Greek mythology who was defeated in a contest and slain by Apollo. BIBLIOGRAPHY: F. Hort, DCB 1:175.

[L. G. MÜLLER]

ASCLEPIUS (Latin, *Aesculapius*), Greek hero and god of healing. In Homer he is still a mortal, a Thessalian prince and "blameless physician." In Hesiod and Pindar he has become the son of Apollo and Coronis, the daughter of Phlegyas. His cult probably originated in Thessaly and passed from there to Phocis, Boeotia, and the Peloponnesus. Through his association with Apollo Maleatas, his cult became prominent at Epidaurus and passed from there to Athens, Pergamum, and other cities. After a plague in 293 B.C. and a consultation of the Sibylline Books, his cult was officially introduced to Rome and a temple erected to him in 291 B.C. on the island in the Tiber. The cures he was presumed to have effected were largely associated with the rite of *incubation. The number of his temples and the quantities of votive offerings erected in his honor attest his popularity. BIBLIOGRAPHY: F. R. Walton, OCD 106–107; W. A. Jayne, *Healing Gods of Ancient Civilization* (1925) ch. 7; A. Hus, *Greek and Roman Religion* (1962) 63–64.

[M. J. COSTELLOE]

ASCODRUGITAE, see ASCITES.

ASEITY (Lat. *aseitas*, i.e. "from himselfness"), name given in scholastic theology and philosophy to the primary divine attribute whereby God's being is of and from his own self without dependence upon any other being. In this he is distinguished from all creatures, who are not *a se* (from themselves) but *ab alio*, i.e., their being is from another.

[P. K. MEAGHER]

ASENATH, see JOSEPH AND ASENATH.

ASER (ASHER), eighth son of Jacob and Zilpah, Leah's maid (Gen 30.12–13), ancestor of one of the tribes of Israel. Their territory extended from the W end of the mountains of Galilee westward to the Mediterranean and from near Tyre southward to Mt. Carmel. Though described as prosperous in the Blessings of Jacob and Moses (Gen 49.20; Dt 33.24–25), the tribe's part in Israelite history was small. It formed part of an administrative region under Solomon (1 Kg 4.16) and according to 2 Chr 30.11 took part in the special passover celebration in Jerusalem under Ezechia. The prophetess Anna is identified as belonging to the tribe of A. (Lk 2.36). BIBLIOGRAPHY: EDB 150–151.

ASFELD, JACQUES VINCENT BIDAL D' (d. 1745), French priest who was won over to the teachings of P. *Quesnel, became a leader among Jansenists, and a prominent appellant against the bull *Unigenitus*. For a time he gave support to, but later detached himself from, Jansenist extremists who were attaching great importance to ''miracles'' and convulsions. BIBLIOGRAPHY: J. Dedieu, DHGE 4:926.

[P. K. MEAGHER]

ASH WEDNESDAY, the first day of *Lent, so named because it is the day on which ashes are blessed and imposed on the heads of the faithful. In the earlier observance Lent began on Quadragesima Sunday, the 6th Sunday before Easter. But because no fast was kept on Sunday, 4 extra days were added to bring the number of fasting days to 40 in imitation of Christ's fast, and the beginning of Lent was moved back to the Wednesday before Quadragesima Sunday. When Lent began, public penitents in Rome were once obliged to begin their penance, but this practice was abandoned between the 8th and 10th cent., and by the 10th or 11th cent. it became customary for all the faithful to be sprinkled with ashes on this day and to begin a season of penance in preparation for Easter. BIBLIOGRAPHY: F. Cabrol, DACL 2.2:3037–44; E. J. Johnson, NCE 1:948–949.

[N. KOLLAR]

ASHANTI GOLD WEIGHTS, small weights used by the Ashanti tribe of Ghana, W African Gold Coast, since the 18th cent. for weighing gold dust (which is plentiful), cast in bronze, brass, or copper by *cire perdue* method perfected by Ife and Bini peoples. Subjects are joyously lively commentaries on daily life, showing the African as storyteller, humorist, nature lover, and sage, with inferences of etiquette and customs, proverbs and legends. Since the method of casting destroyed each wax model, new designs were needed constantly, giving free scope to originals. Minute in scale the forms are simplified emphasizing action. The lightest weight known is a short lizard (5.974 grams); an intriguing peanut form weighs about 13 grams. Fascinating correlations can be drawn with early, though much larger, intimate bronze rocking figures of the contemporary British sculptor, H. Moore.

BIBLIOGRAPHY: J. Battiss and F. Grossert, *Art of Africa* (1958).

[M. J. DALY]

ASH'ARÎ, 'AL-, abû l-Ḥasan 'Alî ibn Ismâ'il al-Ash'ari (A.D. 847–935), a Muslim theologian. A student of the *Mu-'tazilite abû 'Alî al-Jubbâ'î, A. broke with his master in 912 on several theological questions, chiefly those of the reality of the divine attributes, the reality of the vision of God by the blessed, the uncreatedness of the *Koran and God's creation of human acts. His teaching formed the basis for the principal orthodox school of speculative theology in *Islam, known as the Ash'arites (Arab. *al-Aš'arîya* or *al-Ašâ'ira*). In law the Ash'arites are associated with the school of al-Shâfi'î (see ISLAMIC LAW). The teaching of the school evolved considerably, esp. from the end of the 11th cent. with the introduction of a number of elements taken over from the Aristotelian philosophical tradition. The most important masters of the school are al-Bâqillânî (d. 1013), Ibn Fûrak (d. 1015), al-Baghdâdî (d. 1037), al-Juwainî, known as Imâm al-ḥaramayn (d. 1085), al-Gazâlî (d. 1111), al-Shahrastânî (d. 1153), *Fakhr al-Dîn al-Râzî (d. 1210), al-Ijî (d. 1355), and al-Jurjânî (d. 1413). BIBLIOGRAPHY: Fuat Szgin, *Geschichte des arabischen Schrifttums* (1967) 1:602–604.

[R. M. FRANK]

ASHBURNHAM GOSPELS, see LINDAU GOSPELS.

[M. J. DALY]

ASHBURNHAM PENTATEUCH, Merovingian illuminated MS in the National Library, Paris. *Early Christian Art and Architecture.

[M. J. DALY]

ASHERAH (ASERA; meaning originally perhaps ''she who treads the sea''), a Canaanite goddess whose cult influenced many Israelites. In the Ugarit texts A. is the wife of the supreme god El. She was often confused with the goddesses of fertility Ishtar (Astarte) and Anath, the sister of Baal. A. appears in the OT as the consort of Baal (Jg 3.7). The names of these godesses also appear in Phoenician texts. During the reign of Ahab and Jezabel (1Kg 18.19) this cult was popular. Her idol was set up in the Temple at Jerusalem (2Kg 21.7). She is connected with cultic prostitution. It was also the name given to the wooden pole or post planted near the altars of the various gods. This pole was found near the altar of Baal and down to the days of Josiah near those of Yahweh also, not only at Samaria (2Kg 13) and Bethel (2 Kg 23.15) but even at Jerusalem (2 Kg 23.6). This name is most associated in the Bible with the pillars that in the primitive days served at once as a representation of the god and as an altar. BIBLIOGRAPHY: W. L. Reed, *Asherah in the OT* (1949), M. Du Buit, *Biblical Archeology* (tr. K. Pond, 1960) 74–79.

[C. C. O'DONNELL]

ASHES, sometimes produced by the burning of specific substances, have been used for religious, magical, or medical purposes by many peoples. In the OT, often in conjunction with dust, they signify mortality, mourning, and penance and in that sense were employed in various symbolic actions. The use of ashes in Christian liturgy is grounded upon this scriptural symbolism. In earlier times they were sprinkled upon penitents, private or public. The practice of putting ashes on the heads of all the faithful at the beginning of Lent began at the latest in the 10th cent. and has been observed throughout the Western Church from the 11th century. Ashes have also been used from the 8th cent. in the ritual of the consecration of a church. They are strewn upon the floor and in them the bishop traces with his pastoral staff the Latin and Greek alphabets so that they intersect in the form of the Greek letter chi (X, for Christ). This probably symbolizes Christ's taking possession of his Church. Moreover, ashes are used in the preparation of the Gregorian water with which the interior of the church is sprinkled in the same ceremony. BIBLIOGRAPHY: F. Cabrol, DACL 2:3037–44; R. J. Johnson, NCE 1:948–949.

[N. KOLLAR]

ASHKELON (Ascalon), one of the five principal cities (pentopolis) of the Philistines; modern Khirbet Askalan, on the coast between Ashdod and Gaza. The Israelites did not conquer the area during the Conquest (Jos 13.1–3), and the report that Judah conquered it (Jg 1.18) is considered unhistorical (see 2 Sam 1.20 and Am 1.8). The city was destroyed when it rebelled against Assyria (Jer 47.5). According to one tradition, Herod the Great was born there, but Ashkelon is not mentioned in the NT.

[T. EARLY]

ASHRAMA (asrama), a word which in Hindu religious usage may have several meanings: (1) a place or hermitage in which austerities are practiced; (2) the actual performance or practice of austerities; (3) the four stages in the ideal life, to each of which appropriate austerities are attached. These stages are: Brahman student; householder; hermit; and homeless mendicant.

[P. K. MEAGHER]

ASHTAROTH, the Hebrew plural form of the Canaanite fertility goddess Astarte. The singular, Ashtoreth, is a deliberate misvocalization of Ashtaroth, the form found at Ras Shamra, to link the sound to the Hebrew word *bosheth,* "shame." More common in the plural, it is found in conjunction with the Baals as examples of Israel's apostasy to fertility rites (Jg 2.13; 10.6). In Palestine she apparently was the consort of Baal. Her cult flourished at Beth-shan at the end of the 2d millennium B.C. The Philistines placed the armor of Saul in the temple of Ashtaroth and fastened his body to the walls of Beth-shan (1 Sam 31.10). Clay figurines of a naked goddess found even in Israelite levels of sites perhaps indicates the popularity of her cult.

[O. N. BUCHER]

ASHTEROTH (Ashteroth Karnaim; Ashtaroth–Carnaim), scene of Ched-or-laomer's victory over the Rephaim (Gen 14.5). Ashteroth and Carnaim were twin cities in Gilead, east of the sea of Galilee. Excavations indicate the two seldom flourished simultaneously. King Og of Bashan, last of the Rephaim, lived at Ashteroth (Dt 1.4; 3.11); it was given to the Gershomites as a city of refuge (1 Chr 6.71). Amos mentioned Karnaim (6.13); Judas Maccabeus attacked it and its temple to Atargatis (1 Macc 5.26, 43–44; 2 Macc 12.21–26). "Ashteroth Karnaim" means Ashtaroth of the Horns, perhaps referring to twin peaks nearby or to the goddess Astarte, often represented with a horned headdress.

[T. EARLY]

ASHUR (ASSYRIA), Mesopotamian empire in what is now Iraq. It received its name from its capital city on the Tigris River. Assyria began to achieve importance c.2000 B.C. with extensive commercial activity, including trade in textiles and bronze. Its history was continuously interwoven with that of Babylonia to the south, sometimes as a conquered province (as in the time of Hammurabi, 1728–1686 B.C.), sometimes as conqueror. Assyria reached a peak under Tukulti-Ninurta I (1244–08 B.C.), who devastated Babylonia, but soon afterward Assyria again became subordinated to Babylonia, and then later regained its dominance. Throughout its history, it tended to receive its cultural forms from Babylonia. Its polytheistic religion resembled that of Babylonia, except for its worship of the national god Ashur, a warrior deity.

Assyria was the major outside influence during 2 centuries of Israel's history, and Isaiah saw it as God's unconscious agent (10.5–11). Shalmaneser V (727–722 B.C.) of Assyria laid siege to Samaria, and his brother and successor Sargon II (722–705 B.C.) captured it, deporting many Israelites to Assyria (2 Kgs 17.6). Sargon's son Sennacherib (704–681 B.C.) unsuccessfully besieged Jerusalem during the reign of Hezekiah (2 Kgs 19.35). Israel's consciousness of being the kingdom of God manifested itself during the period of Assyria's self-assertion as a world state.

Sennacherib moved the capital from Ashur to Nineveh, and the history of Assyria ended with the destruction of Ashur in 614 B.C. and Nineveh in 612 B.C. It was defeated by an alliance of Chaldeans-Babylonians, under Nabopolassar, and Medes, under Cyaxares. Dominance then passed to Babylonia. A wealth of material on Assyrian history has become available through excavations. Of special importance is the library of Ashurbanipal (668–629 B.C.), which was discovered at Nineveh.

[T. EARLY]

ASHURBANIPAL, the last great king of Assyria (668–629? B.C.), the son of Esarhaddon. He destroyed Thebes in 663 and Susa, the Elamite capital in 640. His name does not appear in the Bible, but he was king when Manasseh of Juda paid tribute to Assyria (2 Chr 33). A revolt by his brother, Shamashshumukin, ended in the destruction of Babylon in 648 and helped to weaken the empire, which collapsed soon after his death. His library at Nineveh with thousands of cuneiform tablets is his greatest memorial.

[O. N. BUCHER]

ASHURNASIRPAL (ASSURNASIRPAL) II, see ASSURNASIRPAL (ASHURNASIRPAL) II.

ASIA, largest and most populous of the world's continents and birthplace of all the major world religions.

Though Europe can be viewed geographically as a peninsula of the Eurasian land mass, conventionally it is considered a separate continent. The generally recognized border between Asia and Europe runs along the Ural Mountains, then to the Caspian and Black Seas, and through the Bosporus to the Mediterranean. Africa is separated from Asia by the Suez Canal, though culturally Egypt and some of the adjacent area are normally included in the Asian area known as the Near East. On its eastern side Asia reaches almost to Alaska, separated only by the Bering Strait. In addition to the non-European part of the U.S.S.R., Asia includes the islands of Japan, the Philippines, Indonesia, and Ceylon, as well as the Near East area from Suez and the Bosporus eastwards and Iran, Afghanistan, Pakistan, India (with Sikkim), Nepal, Bhutan, Bangladesh, Burma, China (with Tibet, Manchuria, and Taiwan), Mongolia, Korea, Vietnam, Laos, Cambodia, Thailand and Malaysia. The land area amounts to 17 million sq mi, about 30 per cent of the world's total land mass, and contains more than half the human race.

Migrations of Asian peoples have constituted one of the primary activating factors of world history. These include the *Aryan migrations from ancient Turkistan to India, Persia, and elsewhere, as well as various Asian invasions into Europe. In the 7th cent. A.D. an explosion of Arab energy resulted in widespread conquest. The Indians of North and South America are thought to be descended from Asians who crossed the Bering Strait.

Among the most ancient world cultures are those of the Tigris-Euphrates area of Mesopotamia, the Indus and Ganges Rivers of India, and the Yellow and Yangtze Rivers of China. Civilizations developed there have been determinative in world history, and their religious practices, concepts, and writings form the background for all the world's major religions.

Hinduism, the oldest of these, developed in India through the interaction of Aryan religion of the *Vedas with the religion of pre-Aryan peoples of the region. It has remained the dominant religion of India, but has not spread widely abroad. Jainism developed in the 6th cent. B.C. as a reform movement within Hinduism, and continues to draw a following in India today. Developing about the same time was a more far-reaching reform movement based on teachings of the Buddha (the enlightened one). It denied the sanctity of the Vedas and rejected the caste system. Buddhism, in varying forms, spread rapidly throughout most of Asia and remains a dominant Asian religion today. But in India it virtually disappeared, partly absorbed by Hinduism and partly destroyed by hostile invaders.

In China, about the time of the Buddha, Confucius was teaching the ethical philosophy that became known as Confucianism and which later developed a religious component. It competed with Taoism, which emerged about two centuries after Confucius and had a more mystical and emotional character. Both Buddhism and Confucianism exercised influence on Shintoism, the ancient national religion of Japan.

The ancient religion of Mesopotamia and *Arabia formed the historical background from which emerged Judaism, from it Christianity and then Islam, drawing to some extent on both. All three of these monotheistic faiths profess descent from Abraham, who, according to the Genesis account, left the Tigris-Euphrates area to settle in Canaan. The definitive figure in the development of Judaism was Moses, who led the Exodus from Egypt, traditionally dated in the 15th cent. B.C. but placed by many modern scholars in the 13th. Part of Asia, including Asia Minor (Anatolia) and Palestine, was conquered by Alexander the Great, and much of this area was subsequently incorporated into the Roman Empire. During this period Christianity arose in Palestine, and by the 4th cent. A.D. it had become the official religion of the empire. In the area of its origin, however, it was challenged in the 7th cent. by a new religion from Arabia. Based on teachings of the Arab prophet Mohammed, Islam proved effective in welding political unity and inspiring zeal. At one time its adherents controlled about half of what had been the Christian world, and in the East, Islam virtually eliminated Zoroastrianism (it survives in a small community of Parsis).

During the Middle Ages contact of the West with Asia primarily involved Asia Minor, long a part of Byzantium, and what European Christians came to call the Holy Land. However, there was some contact through trade across Near East trade routes, limited missionary activity, and such travelers as Marco Polo. Crusaders sought to regain control of the Holy Land from the Muslims, and for a time enjoyed some success but eventually had to give up the effort.

Beginning with Jesuit activity in the 16th cent., Western Churches devoted increasing efforts to missionary work in Asia. Jesuits gained some success in China and Japan, but also met severe opposition. The refusal of Rome to allow certain adaptations of Christianity to traditional national culture hampered work in China. William Carey, the English Protestant pioneer of the modern missionary movement, went to India in the late 18th century. The movement subsequently sent thousands of Western missionaries all over the Asian continent. As the largest and most populous Asian country, China received more missionary attention than any other area of the world. But all missionary work was stopped after the Communist revolution (1949), and only limited forms of church life continued.

Europe secured political dominance over much of Asia in the modern period. Czarist Russia extended its empire to the Pacific and down into central Asia. The Dutch controlled Indonesia. France held Indo-China. Britain secured Hong

Kong, Burma, Ceylon, and India, and shared power in the Near East with France. Spain held the Philippines until replaced by the United States. Portugal held the enclaves of Goa and Macao. Though China never became a colony, it was effectively under Western dominance. At the beginning of the 20th cent. Western powers exercised control over virutally the entire continent of Asia. But since World War II Asia has become politically independent of the West. And concurrently, Christians of Asia have begun to assume a position of greater equality in the world Christian community. The association of Western missionaries with the geopolitical expression of Western power brought advantages to the Christian movement, but handicapped it in the minds of Asians resentful of Western penetration.

In the West the concept of Asia has exercised a fascination on many minds. Lack of knowledge and understanding has led Westerners to speak of the "mysterious" East, and to posit some basic dichotomy in the culture and spiritual outlook of Occident and Orient. But such theories as those contrasting the "materialistic" West with the "spiritual" East remain dubious. And whether the immensely diverse peoples and cultures of Asia share any principle of unity remains debatable. BIBLIOGRAPHY: A. Dudley, *History of Eastern Civilization* (1973); *Changing Map of Asia* (5th ed., W. G. East et al. eds., 1971); J. M. Kitagawa, *Religions of the East* (1968).

[T. EARLY]

ASIA, ROMAN PROVINCE OF, a rich and fertile area in central and western Anatolia (Asia Minor), formerly ruled over by the kings of Pergamum; its name was derived from the fact that the Romans had known the Attalids as the kings of Asia. It became a Roman province after the death of Attalus III (133 B.C.) who without an heir and fearing a war of succession bequeathed his kingdom to Rome in his will. As originally constituted, the province of Asia comprised Mysia, Lydia, Ionia, Caria, and a number of important islands in the eastern Aegean. In 116 B.C. Phrygia, which had originally been given to Mithridates Eupator of Pontus was incorporated into it. About A.D. 297 Diocletian divided Asia into seven different provinces, keeping the original name for the coastal areas and lower river valleys in the west.

As a senatorial province, Asia was ruled over by a governor with the title of proconsul appointed by the Senate. Before the time of Augustus its capital was transferred from Pergamum to the more convenient and important city of Ephesus. According to Cicero the province of Asia surpassed all other lands "in the richness of its soil, the variety of its products, the extent of its pastures, and the number of its exports" (*De imp. Cn. Pomp.* 14). During the Republic it became the prey of greedy Roman officials, but under the Empire it fared much better and enjoyed a great deal of prosperity, as is evidenced by the extensive ruins to be seen at Pergamum, Ephesus, Izmir (the ancient Smyrna), and numerous other sites.

As is indicated by his epistles to the Ephesians and to the Colossians, Asia was an important field of missionary labors

for St. Paul. It was also the center of interest for the author of the Apocalypse. The seven Churches which he addresses —Ephesus, Smyrna, Pergamum, Thyatira, Sardis, Philadelphia, and Laodicea—were all in the western part of the province (*Rev* 1.11). Among its better known martyrs are Polycarp and Pionius of Smyrna, and Carpus, Papylus, and Agathonica of Pergamum. BIBLIOGRAPHY: D. Magie, *Roman Rule in Asia Minor* (1950, repr. 1966); W. M. Calder, OCD 108; J. Keil, CAH 14:580–588.

[M. J. COSTELLOE]

ASIA MINOR, a geographical term for the peninsula which embraces modern Turkey and is bounded on the W by the Aegean Sea, the Mediterranean in the S, the Black Sea to the N, the Armenian Plateau on the E, and separated from Europe by the Dardanelles and the Bosphorus. In classical times its territory included Pontus, Bithynia, and Paphlagonia in the N; Mysia, Lydia, Caria in the W; Lycia, Pamphylia, Pisidia, and Cilicia in the S; Phrygia was in the interior E and Lycaonia SE of Lydia with Cappadocia further to the East. Its most important ports were Ephesus, Cos, Miletus, Smyrna, Pergamum, and Troas. Along its inland waterways were Thyatira, Sardis, and Philadelphia on the Hermes; and Laodicea, Colossae, and Hierapolis on the Maeander (Menderes). First called Asia Minor by Horosius, a 5th-cent. writer (PL 31:679), its first known settlers were Hittites in NW Cappadocia whose kingdom went beyond Asia to Carchemish on the Euphrates and S toward Syria where the OT records their meeting the Jews. The earliest written evidence of their history and culture is in a variety of languages on cuneiform tablets (1300 B.C.). With the Mycenaean migrations from Europe to Asia Minor (1200 B.C.) the Hittite power ended. About this time Greek chieftains of Homer's Iliad were victorious over Phrygian newcomers to the territory. This occasioned a massive movement of peoples from Greece to the E shores of the Aegean. The Aeolians settled the N coast near Troy together with the island of Lesbos; the Dorians came to the S in Halicarnassus and Cnidus; the Ionians took over the West. In the 7th cent. B.C.; the Lydians were a dominant empire, but they were conquered by Cyrus the Great of Persia (546 B.C.), and the Greek cities henceforth played a subordinate role. Before this, they had expanded Greek culture as far as Sicily and Spain in the W and maintained thriving commerce with Egypt in the South. The intellectual legacy which developed in the Ionian cities spread to Athens and thence to the West. After a period of decline during the rise and fall of Athens (479–404 B.C.), Asia Minor returned to the power of Persia until the victory of Alexander the Great (334 B.C.). When he died (332 B.C.), it became a pawn in the hands of his successors Perdiccas, Antigonus, and Seleucus. But in 301 B.C., Seleucus controlled Phrygia; Lysimachus of Thrace took over the new Smyrna and Ptolemy of Egypt had the Greek towns on the coast. It was an era notable for building important cities named after members of royal households, e.g., Antioch, Seleucia, Apamea, Laodicea, etc.

Roman power asserted itself in Asia Minor with the defeat

of Antiochus III (190 B.C.). When Attalus III died (113 B.C.), Rome formed the province of Asia (see ASIA, ROMAN PROVINCE OF).

The varied culture of the territory is evident from the presence of its many religions. Its numerous Jewish communities of the Diaspora were eventually disposed to accept Christian teaching. The record of much of St. Paul's activity (Acts 13–16, 18) and the greetings of St. John to the seven Churches (Apoc. 1.11; 2.3) of Ephesus, Taurus, Smyrna, Pergamum, Thyatira, Sardis, Philadelphia, and Laodicea indicate the growth of Christianity in the cities. In the postapostolic age, its vitality was enhanced by the leadership of Ignatius of Antioch and Polycarp and tested by the rise of Montanism in Phrygia and Monarchianism in Smyrna. At the beginning of the 3d cent. Bp. Firmilian of Cappadocia led a strong mission effort throughout the area. But much suffering and the problem of the *lapsi* (Lat. for lapsed) resulted from the Decian persecution and later from that of Diocletian. Constantine I provided the freedom necessary for the strong development of the great urban centers of Christianity in Asia Minor, chief of which was Antioch with its constant influence on the Churches of Cilicia, Isauria, Phoenicia, Palestine, Cyprus, Arabia, and Mesopotamia. BIBLIOGRAPHY: G. Bardy, DHGE 4:966–988; H. Dressler, NCE 1:955–957.

[F. H. BRIGHAM]

ASIANIC RELIGION, a term denoting the beliefs and practices of non-Semitic, non-Indo-European cultures in the ancient Near East. Drioton, Contenau, and Duchesne-Guillemin define the area as consisting of Mesopotamia including Sumer; to the east of Sumer, Elam (the SW of modern Iran); the kingdom of Urartu or Van to the NE bordered by Lake Sevan; Syria and Asia Minor to the N and NW (later the sphere of Hurrite and Hittite powers); the Mediterranean coast, divided into Phoenicia and Palestine. They observe, "As far back as one may care to inquire, traces are to be found in these areas of a religion based on fertility and fecundity, while all the languages of this vast region are of a particular type, known as agglutinative. This appears sufficiently characteristic to warrant these peoples a special name; they have been called Asianic, a term meaningless in itself but convenient for the purpose of distinguishing them from Semites and Indo-Europeans." The unity of these peoples was disturbed by Semitic settlers and/or invaders even before the historic period; eventually, Semites triumphed over them, though accepting the superior civilization of the Sumerians. The Indo-Europeans appeared in the area much later and, according to Drioton and his coworkers, "there is much less difference between the Asianic religions and the religions of the Indo-European group than between the former and Semitic religions." Written documents and monuments, temple ruins and decorations, statues, bas-reliefs, small religious objects and jewelry, esp. cylinder-seals, abound, giving us information about worship, liturgy, and the pantheon. The principle of fertility is expressed in the divine couple, the High God of the moun-

tains, the High Goddess, and their sacred marriage. A young god, and sometimes a young goddess as well, round out the family. The influence of this religion on the history of religion is incalculable, for it has served directly or indirectly as the basis of most high religions. The chief features of the High God survived in, or became amalgamated to, the figures of Olympian Zeus, Baltic Dievs, Roman Jupiter, etc.; the High Goddess is Ishtar-Astarte-Cybele-Ephesian Artemis-Hera-Juno; the young god is Dumuzi-Tammuz-Dionysos-Bacchus; the virgin goddess is Inanna, Virgin Artemis, Diana, etc., to mention just the best-known names. However, all of these divinities, once adopted by non-Asianic cultures, show certain corruptions. They become capricious, blood-thirsty, immoral, etc. I. Bobula's treatise presents compelling arguments to show that the purest survivals and true heirs of Sumer are the Finno-Ugric religions. (The book, *Sumerian Affiliations,* also revives the arguments, contemporaneous with the discovery of Sumerian culture in the second half of the 19th cent., that the agglutinative Finno-Ugric languages are the closest relatives of Sumerian living today.) Adducing new linguistic and ethnological data, the book shows how the Magi, exiled from Sumer, could have spread the chief tenets of Sumerian religion throughout the area. It also adduces many examples of its survival within the Finno-Ugric heritage, e.g., a reference to a god called Damasek mentioned in two Hungarian chronicles in the 16th cent. (cf. Sumerian Dumu-zig: "risen son"). On the basis of these data, it is possible that, in examining Asianic religion, we are dealing, not with several related religions, but rather with the dissemination, adaptations, and survival of one religion, that of the ancient Sumerians. BIBLIOGRAPHY: E. Drioton et al. *Religions of the Ancient East* (tr. M. Loraine 1959); Y. Rosengarten, *Trois aspects de la pensée religieuse sumérienne* (1971); I. Bobula, *Sumerian Affiliations* (1959). *BALTIC RELIGION, *FINNO-UGRIC RELIGION, *GERMANIC RELIGION, *SLAVIC RELIGION, *CELTIC RELIGION, *DRUIDS AND DRUIDISM.

[D. H. BRUNAUER]

ASIARCH, the title of a kind of official in the Roman province of Asia, some of whom befriended Paul at Ephesus (Acts 19.31). Apparently they were men of wealth and influence but not part of the regular Roman structure.

[O. N. BUCHER]

ASÍN PALACIOS, MIGUEL (1871–1944), Spanish archbishop. A learned student of Islamic philosophy and mysticism, of philology and Muslim literature, he wrote among other works: *The Christianization of Islam* and *The Muslim Eschatology in the Divine Comedy,* a fundamental work which destroyed the idea of Dante's fecund imagination and showed that he was influenced by early Muslim works. This opinion was confirmed by Munog Sendino with the discovery in Oxford and Paris of two MSS of Halmoereig in which he found some general scenes similar to

Dante's creations. BIBLIOGRAPHY: J. M. Sola-Sole, NCE
1:957.

[C. C. O'DONNELL]

ASIONGABER (EZIONGEBER), a port city and industrial center in Edom, at the head of the gulf of Aqaba (1 Kg
9.26; 22.48), founded by Solomon. It is identified with
modern Tell el-Khalaifeh. Elath was near Asiongaber (Dt
2.8; 1 Kg 9.26) and later was confused with it (2 Kg 12.22).
Important excavations were directed here by Nelson Glueck
(1938–40). The project revealed the remains of ancient
(10th-9th cent. B.C.) refineries for smelting copper. The spot
was favored with a strong, steady N wind, and was ideally
located on the seashore and near the mineral deposits of the
Araba. It was from Asiongaber that Solomon's ships carried
on a lively gold trade with Arabia (1 Kg 9.28). His successors were not always as successful as he was (1 Kg 22.49). A
signet seal ring of King Jotham (742–735 B.C.) was found
here. BIBLIOGRAPHY: N. Glueck, *Other Side of the Jordan*
(1940) 89–113.

[J. E. LUSSIER]

ASKE, ROBERT (d. 1537), the Yorkshireman who led the
*Pilgrimage of Grace. He was condemned and executed for
treason. BIBLIOGRAPHY: Hughes RE 1:303–319.

ASKER, JOHN, see ASSER, JOHN.

ASKETERION (Latinized, *asceterium;* Gr. *askētērion*), a
hermitage or monastic house.

ASKLEPIOS, see ASCLEPIUS.

ASMATIKON, a small group of 13th-cent. MSS, which
contain the melismatic repertoire of choral chants for the
Byzantine rite. Though modest in size, they are important
since, apart from a few chants found in the Psaltikon, the
Asmatikon contains all the earliest known chants for the
Byzantine Mass. Here are found the *koinonika,* or commun-
ion chants, in their earliest surviving form, several of them
with six or more different melodies. Proof exists that the
Asmatikon repertoire was generally used throughout the
Byzantine world, though its original distribution was very
uneven. BIBLIOGRAPHY: S. Harris, "Communion Chants in
Thirteenth-Century Byzantine Musical MSS," *Studies in
Western Chant* (ed. M. Velimirovič, 1971) 2:51–53.

[M. T. LEGGE]

ASMODEUS, the evil being, known in Jewish tradition as
king of the demons, sometimes identified with Beelzebub

(see MK 3.22) and with Aeshma-Daeva, an evil spirit of the
Persians. Frequently mentioned in the Talmud, he is prominent in the book of Tobit. With the help of Raphael, Tobit's
son Tobias is able to drive A. away and marry Sarah (3.8;
8.2–3).

[T. EARLY]

AŚOKA COLUMNS, commemorative, sacred, symbolic
edict pillars erected in various parts of India by the benign
Emperor Aśoka (*c*.273–236 B.C.), Mauryan conqueror and
ruler in N India, convert from militaristic violence to Buddhism and known as the Constantine of Buddhism. The tall
monolithic pillar shafts of polished sandstone (60 or 70 feet
high) carry 3-zoned capitals: (1) an inverted lotus (symbol of
the pure Buddha), (2) a frieze showing the "wheel of the
law," and (3) an animal symbolic of the Buddha—a lion for
Buddha Sākyamuni (lion of the Sākya tribe), bull, or
elephant. Carved on the shaft is a teaching of the compassionate Buddha, as edicts by Aśoka, who also planted fruit
trees along India's roads to shade and feed the traveler.

[M. J. DALY]

ASOLA, GIOVANNI MATTEO (1550–1609), cleric and
composer who was active in the region of Venice. A pupil of
Ruffo, A. composed in a conservative style but wrote *basso
continuo* organ parts for his choral works which are among
the earliest examples of this device. Among his numerous
works are *falso bordone* psalm settings (in collections published in 1575, 1587, and 1592), three passions, a requiem
Mass, and a set of introits and alleluia verses (1565). BIBLI-
OGRAPHY: Reese MusR.

[P. DOHERTY]

ASOR, see AMERICAN SCHOOLS OF ORIENTAL RESEARCH.

ASPERGER, SEGISMUNDO (Aperger; 1687–1772),
Jesuit missionary among the Guaraní Indians in South
America. He attained some renown for his knowledge of
medicinal herbs.

[P. K. MEAGHER]

ASPERGES, the ceremony of sprinkling with holy water,
especially the sprinkling of the altar, ministers, and the
people at the principal Mass on Sundays. The name is the
first word of the antiphon chanted in the Latin liturgy (except
during the Paschal season) while the sprinkling takes place:
Asperges me, Domine, etc. (Ps. 51.7). The practice appears
to have begun after the 8th cent. in the monasteries, from
which it spread to parish churches. The ceremony reminds
the participants of their baptism and of the inner spiritual
purification by which they should be prepared for the celebration of the Eucharist. The rite is also observed in the visitation of the sick, the consecration of churches, and the blessing of houses. BIBLIOGRAPHY: G. Goeb, "Asperges," Or-
Frat 3 (1927–28) 338–342; F. Amiot, *History of the Mass*
(tr. F. Murphy, 1958) 32.

[N. KOLLAR]

ASPERGILLUM, a short rod with a small brush or a perforated metal bulb at the end used for sprinkling holy water as in the *asperges and blessings. It is also called aspersorium, aspergill, or goupillon.

[N. KOLLAR]

ASPIRATION (EJACULATION), a short prayer that can be said in one breath or aspiration, e.g., the exclamation of Thomas the Apostle upon seeing the risen Christ, "My Lord and my God." Indulgences are often attached to them, and they are frequently used in times of temptation or danger when longer prayers would be impossible.

[T. M. MCFADDEN]

ASSASSINATION, a term applied to *murder when this is performed with treachery or secretly, esp. when its object is a public figure. To it attaches all the malice of murder, and usually it is accompanied by aggravating circumstances.

[P. K. MEAGHER]

ASSASSINS (from Arab. *ḥašîšîya),* a name given in the Middle Ages to the *Nizaris a sect of the Ismaili *Shiïtes in Syria, where a few adherents of the sect yet remain. The term—taken from their custom of drinking hashish *(cannabis indica)*—was used as an equivalent of *fidâ'î,* one who sacrifices himself (i.e., a zealot). The bloodthirsty character of the sect so impressed the crusaders that by the 14th cent. the word passed into use in Europe in the present English sense of murderer. BIBLIOGRAPHY: B. Lewis, *Assassins, a Radical Sect in Islam* (1967).

[R. M. FRANK]

ASSAULT, in moral theology, the unjust infliction of bodily hurt, harm, or damage on another, in law called battery. As an offense against commutative justice, which regulates rights between individuals, it sets up an obligation to make restitution. BIBLIOGRAPHY: J. A. McHugh and C. J. Callan, *Moral Theology* (rev. E. P. Farrell, 2 v., (1958).

[T. GILBY]

ASSEMANI, JOSEPH ALOYSIUS (1710–82), nephew of Joseph Simon *Assemani, professor of Syriac and liturgy at the Sapienza in Rome. He produced scholarly works on liturgical, canonical, and historical topics.

[P. K. MEAGHER]

ASSEMANI, JOSEPH SIMON (1687–1768), Syriac scholar, prefect of the Vatican Library and titular abp. of Tyre. A native of Tripoli in Lebanon, he studied for the priesthood in the Maronite college in Rome. Instead of returning to his homeland, in 1710 he was appointed editor of Syriac MSS in the Vatican Library, a scholarly activity that occupied the rest of his life. On visits to the Near East in 1715 and 1735, he collected many more such MSS for the Vatican Library. Among his numerous scholarly publications were a 6-volume edition of *Ephrem the Syrian and the 4-volume *Bibliotheca Orientalis,* a collection of documents on the history of the Eastern Churches. His two nephews, S. E. and J. A. Assemani continued his work of editing MSS. BIBLIOGRAPHY: L. F. Hartman, NCE 1:959; P. Sfair, EncCatt. 2:159–160.

[R. B. ENO]

ASSEMANI, STEPHEN EVODIUS (1707–82), Lebanese scholar, Orientalist. He studied at the Maronite college in Rome, and after spending some time in the Orient, was appointed to the Vatican Library where he assisted his uncle, J. S. Assemani, and eventually succeeded him as prefect of the library. A. catalogued the Oriental MSS in the Laurentine and Palatine Medici Library in Florence and collaborated with his uncle on a complete catalogue of MSS in the Vatican Library. This latter series was planned to run to 20 v. but only the first 3 were completed. A. also edited the *Acta Sanctorum Martyrum Orientalium et Occidentalium* (1748), and the sixth volume of the Syrian and Latin works of St. Ephrem (1743). A. was made titular abp. of Apamaea. BIBLIOGRAPHY: M. Morseletto, DE 1:240; A. Schall, LTK 1:943; G. Oussani, CE 1:795.

[H. JACK]

ASSEMBLAGE, term introduced by Jean Dubuffet to distinguish in pictorial art a conglomeration of real objects whole or fragmented from the cubist collages (1912–20) of Picasso, Braque, etc. It describes developments such as Kurt Schwitter's Merz constructions, the Dada "readymades" of M. Duchamp, and Joseph Cornell's surrealistic boxes. In the U. S. of the 1950s and 60s assemblage was the reintegration of art and environment, often satirical or violent, as seen in the use of hypnotic images from popular culture in the painting-constructions of Rauschenberg and Jasper Johns, and in Jean Tinguely's "self-destroying" machines. BIBLIOGRAPHY: W. C. Seitz, *Art of Assemblage* (1961).

[M. J. DALY]

ASSEMBLIES OF GOD, the largest Pentecostal body in the U.S.; 1973 membership, 1,078,332 in 8,799 churches; headquarters, Springfield, Mo. The name and organization date from a "General Council of Pentecostal (Spirit Baptized) Saints from local Churches of God in Christ, Assemblies of God and various Apostolic Faith Missions and Churches, and Full Gospel Pentecostal Missions and Assemblies of like faith in the U.S.A., Canada, and Foreign lands" (K. Kendrick, 84), held in April 1914 at Hot Springs, Arkansas. The aim was to overcome the lack of organization characteristic of early Pentecostalism and to express doctrines in which Pentecostals were agreed. In a "Statement of Fundamental Truths" issued in a subsequent general council (St. Louis, 1916), the Assemblies affirmed the teachings of Pentecostalism and of *fundamentalism, including an emphasis on *premillenarianism. The Assemblies reject *sacramentalism and *infant baptism; affirm separation from the world and *entire sanctification, but as gradual, not instantaneous. Polity combines *presbyterian and *congregational elements. The local church retains autonomy and the power to accept or reject policies of higher bodies. Supreme legislative and executive power resides in the General Council; the working administrative body is the General Presbytery, composed of 16 presbyters. Local churches are united in district councils for their region. The denomination, at least in the U.S., is making an effort to work out a systematic body of doctrine; this theological reflection is still at its beginning but promises to bear fruit. In the U.S., also, worship services and those in which *glossolalia and *divine healing take place have become more restrained than in early Pentecostalism. There are signs that the Assemblies might become a link between conservative Pentecostals and other Christian Churches. The Assemblies have more than 900 missions in 75 lands; the *Assembléias de Deus* in Brazil is the largest of all Pentecostal denominations, with a total membership (1968) exceeding 1½ million, and a phenomenal 230% rate of growth each decade. BIBLIOGRAPHY: C. Brumback, *Suddenly from Heaven* (1961); K. Kendrick, *Promise Fulfilled: A History of the American Pentecostal Movement* (1961); J. T. Nichol, *Pentecostalism* (1966); W. A. Menzies, *Anointed to Serve: Story of the Assemblies of God* (1971).

[T. C. O'BRIEN]

ASSEMBLIES OF THE FRENCH CLERGY, regular representative meetings of bishops and elected clergy holding royal benefices that determined the subsidy of the clerical estate to the king of France. They also dealt with heresy, Protestantism, Jansenism, intrusion of Parlement into religion, impiety; the extraordinary assembly of 1682 supported Louis XIV's Gallicanism against the pope. The reliability of the clergy to produce their lump sum "free gift" from 1561 on made the assemblies welcome to the king. And the clergy were glad to have a tax system free of the royal bureaucracy and were willing to finance religious wars. From the end of Louis XIV's wars, however, they had to borrow (at low interest) to make the payments. The assemblies met every five years, for 4-19 months of daily sessions. Their electoral system was usually free of royal interference; but the king determined the town of assembly, whose archbishop was President of the Assembly, a powerful official who appointed committees. A general agent represented the assembly when not in session; Talleyrand and others gained good political experience from this office. Contrary to regulations, the assemblies almost always sat in Paris. The French Revolution put an end to the assemblies. BIBLIOGRAPHY: M. Marion, DHGE 4:1103–14; R. Chalumeau, *Catholicisme* 1:916–918.

[E. P. COLBERT]

ASSEMBLY, GENERAL, see GENERAL ASSEMBLY (PRESBYTERIAN).

ASSENT, the mind's acceptance of some truth or proposition. This agreement can be grounded in immediate evidence or logical proof, but in many cases the strict logical dependence of the assent upon evidence or proof is wanting.

[P. K. MEAGHER]

ASSER, JOHN (d. *c*.909), English chronicler. *Alfred persuaded A., a learned Welsh monk of St. David's, to spend half of each year at his court as tutor (*c*.885). A. received the monasteries of Congresbury and Banwell (887) and later the bishoprics of Exeter and Sherborne. He aided in Alfred's writings; but his primary achievement was *De rebus gestis Aelfredi,* which described Alfred's career to 887. It was used, with interpolations, by Florence of Worcester and Simeon of Durham. Its authenticity has been challenged, e.g., by V. H. Galbraith (*Introduction to the Study of History,* 1964), who dates the work after the 10th-cent. revival. BIBLIOGRAPHY: *Asser's Life of King Alfred* (ed. W. H. Stevenson, 1904), introd.

[W. CHANEY]

ASSES, FEAST OF, a medieval mock festival celebrated generally on Jan. 1. It was more commonly called the Feast of *Fools. BIBLIOGRAPHY: E. K. Chambers, *Mediaeval Stage* (1903) 1:274–335.

ASSISI, Italian town where St. *Francis was born (1181 or 1182) and found his first followers, including St. *Clare. Located in the Perugia province of Umbria, central Italy, Assisi has a history going back to the ancient Umbrians and Romans. A surviving temple of Minerva is used as a church. Though Assisi perhaps had bps. from the 3rd cent., the first one known by name was Aventius, who served during the time the Ostrogoth King Totila took Assisi (*c*.545). Assisi belonged to the Lombard Duchy of Spoleto from *c*.800 until the 12th century. From 1160 until a revolt of 1198 it was under the Hohenstaufen and ruled by German counts. The subsequent history of Assisi was often stormy. St. Francis was captured and held prisoner while fighting with its army against Perugia. But Assisi reached its peak in the time of St. Francis. Later it suffered from internal conflict and was several times sacked by outsiders. From 1535 to 1860 it was part of the Papal States. The Church in Assisi was a prominent force during the time of St. Francis, under Bp. Guido II (1204–28) coming to own half the commune. In the 20th cent. Assisi has achieved renewed importance as a center of world pilgrimage. Paul *Sabatier and other writers spent much of their time there and helped bring it increased attention. St. Francis is entombed in the crypt of the church of S. Francesco. (See ASSISI, SAN FRANCESCO BASILICA.) Another church holds the tomb of St. Clare. Near Assisi is Portiuncula, the little chapel where the Franciscan Order began and where St. Francis welcomed "Sister Death" in 1226, subsequently enclosed by the huge Basilica of S. Maria degli Angeli (1569). Also nearby is the Church of San Damiano where St. Francis heard Christ speaking from the crucifix.

[T. EARLY]

ASSISI, SAN FRANCESCO BASILICA, Umbrian-Romanesque-Gothic basilica designed by Brother *Elias of Cortona. To the single-naved upper and lower churches with transept and sanctuary (1228–53) were added chapels in the lower church (14th cent.) and crypt (1818). Frescoes in the upper and lower churches are of the greatest significance as an invaluable record of 13th- and 14th-cent. painting in central Italy. The nave of the lower church was painted by the 13th-cent. Master of St. Francis (pupil of Giunta *Pisano); the Madonna Enthroned with St. Francis in the right transept is the work of *Cimabue. From workshops of *Giotto and *Lorenzetti are four allegories of the life of St. Francis with the life of Christ. The St. Martin Chapel was decorated by Simone *Martini. The entire wall surface of the upper church is covered with 13th-cent. frescoes—those in the sanctuary and transept by Cimabue, the upper half of the nave walls with OT and NT paintings by the Roman school. The lower register of the nave walls showing 28 scenes of the life of St. Francis by Giotto are the climax of the whole decoration. BIBLIOGRAPHY: L. Tintori and M. Meiss, *Painting of the Life of St. Francis in Assisi* (1962).

[M. J. DALY]

ASSISTANT PRIEST, (1) a curate who aids the parish priest; (2) in pontifical functions, the chief of the ministers serving the bishop by holding the books open, by transmitting the kiss of peace to the choir, etc.; (3) abbots and protonotaries are permitted an assistant priest when they sing Mass pontifically. A newly ordained priest is also permitted an assistant priest when celebrating his first Mass; likewise certain regular prelates at high Mass may have an assistant priest.

[S. A. HEENEY]

ASSISTANTS AT THE PONTIFICAL THRONE, patriarchs, abps. and bps. who have been summoned to Rome by the pope, to become a part of the Papal Chapel, ranking after the cardinals. In ceremonies they have a specially designated place around the papal throne.

[S. A. HEENEY]

ASSIZES OF JERUSALEM, a 13th-cent. compilation of laws and legal treatises that to some extent reflect the customs and procedures of law in the Kingdom of Jerusalem in the 11th and 12th cent. but are actually a more complete record of those of the 13th century. While the *Livre au roi* (c.1197–1205) and the *Livre des assises de la cour des bourgeois* (c.1215) probably include legal customs that precede the fall of Jerusalem (1187), the *Livre de Philippe de Novare, Livre de Jean d'Ibelin, Livre de Geoffroi le Tort, Livre de Jacques d'Ibelin,* and *La Clef des assises de la haute cour au royaume de Jérusalem* were written in the 13th cent. or later and contain the existing legal practices for the Kingdom of Jerusalem, which at that time had been restricted to a small section along the sea near Acre and to the Island of Cyprus. Thus, they tend to stress the rights of local barons in

their struggle with Frederick II. BIBLIOGRAPHY: Philip de Novare, *Wars of Frederick II against the Ibelins in Syria and Cyprus* (tr. J. L. LaMonte and M. J. Hubert, 1936); CMedH² 5:303; *ibid.,* 870–871; M. Grandclaude, *Étude critique sur les livres des assises Jérusalem* (1923).

[F. H. BRIGHAM]

ASSMAYER, IGNAZ (1790–1862), Austrian composer and organist, a pupil of Michael *Haydn; his career was spent first at Salzburg, then at Vienna, where he held appointments as imperial organist and court conductor. Among his many sacred works are 3 oratorios, 15 Masses, and 2 requiems; he also wrote over 50 secular pieces.

[A. DOHERTY]

ASSOCIATION (BAPTIST), an agency of Baptist *polity. Recognizing both the right of every congregation to be self-governing and the obligation of each church to the others, Baptists have expressed their sense of interdependence though associations. An early English association (1625) expressed the "associational principle" thus: "There is the same relation between particular churches . . . as there is betwixt particular members of one church, for the churches do all make up but one body or church in general under Christ their head." The Philadelphia Association, organized in 1707, illustrated the purposes of such a body. It sought to promote doctrinal unity, helped to provide a suitable ministry, offered assistance in settling disputes, occasionally sent representatives on missions to the South, and after the advent of the foreign missions movement raised funds to help W. *Carey's mission in India. The Association never had juridical power over churches, but it could exclude uncooperative members. By the mid-20th cent. the functions of the Association had largely been taken over by other agencies, and its usefulness was being questioned. BIBLIOGRAPHY: N. H. Maring and W. S. Hudson, *Baptist Manual of Polity and Practice* (rev. ed., 1966).

[N. MARING]

ASSOCIATION, RIGHT OF, a nonabsolute natural right which safeguards individual personal rights as well as the collective corporate rights of all individuals. It is tied in with civil rights such as freedom of religion, freedom of speech, and freedom of movement. Certain regulative norms adopted by countries support and affirm these natural rights. Such is the case with the Bill of Rights (1791). Sometimes these rights are violated under the shibboleth of promoting more freedom. Such was the case when the Jesuits were excluded from Germany (1871). The right of association has been acclaimed by many Pontiffs in recent years, esp. Pope Pius XII in *Sertum laetitiae* (*Acta apostolicae sedis* 31, 1939) and John XXIII in *Mater et Magistra* (1961) and *Pacem in Terris* (1963). The United Nations has also declared these rights on behalf of man (*Declaration of Human Rights,* 1948). The moral right of association is the right all men share, and one from which flows a responding effort to achieve one's good and that of the community to which one belongs. BIBLIOGRAPHY: J. Rawls, *Theory of Justice* (1971); J. Feinberg, *Social Philosophy* (ed. E. and M. Beardsley, 1973).

[J. R. RIVELLO]

ASSOCIATION FOR SOCIAL ECONOMICS (formerly the *Catholic Economic Association*), professional society organized in 1942 to promote consideration of economic problems in the light of both economic principles and Christian social philosophy. It encourages research and scholarly endeavor, publishes the *Review of Social Economy*, and meets annually with the American Economic Association. Its members numbered 1,000 in 1974.

[J. C. WILLKE]

ASSOCIATION FOR THE PROMOTION OF THE UNITY OF CHRISTENDOM, a society founded Sept. 8, 1857, in London to unite Anglicans, Orthodox, and Roman Catholics in daily prayer for the restoration of visible unity to Christendom. The climate was prepared in an irenical pamphlet, "On the Future Unity of Christendom," by a lay RC convert from Anglicanism, A. Lisle Phillips (1809–78; in the latter part of his life he took the name A. Phillips De Lisle), who in 1838 had founded the Association of Universal Prayer for the Conversion of England. He and the architect A. W. Pugin (1812–52) were the RC leaders in the project, joining with the Anglicans, Bp. A. P. Forbes (1817–75) and F. G. Lee (1832–1902), who converted to Catholicism near the end of his life. Members of the Association recite each day the Lord's Prayer followed by a designated prayer for unity. By 1864 the Association had over 5,000 Anglican, 1,000 Catholic, and 300 Orthodox members. In that year, allegedly through the intervention of the future Cardinal H. E. Manning (1808–92), it was condemned by Rome. The RC members were required to withdraw, bringing the Association to an end in its original form, though it continued to function in some ways. Its publication, the *Union Review*, begun in 1863, continued until 1875. For a connection between the Association and the current *Week of Prayer for Christian Unity, see *History of the Ecumenical Movement 1517–1948* (eds. R. Rouse and S. C. Neill, 2d ed., 1967) 348. BIBLIOGRAPHY: H. R. T. Brandreth, *Dr. Lee of Lambeth* (1951).

[T. EARLY]

ASSOCIATION FOR THE SOCIOLOGY OF RELIGION (formerly the *American Catholic Sociological Society*), professional association organized in 1938. Its aims include the promotion of study and research among Catholic sociologists and the explication of the sociological implications of Catholic thought. It holds annual conventions and publishes a quarterly journal, *Sociological Analysis* (formerly the *American Catholic Sociological Review*). Headquarters are located at Loyola Marymount Univ., Los Angeles, Cal.

[J.C. WILLKE]

ASSOCIATION OF CATHOLIC TRADE UNIONISTS, see TRADE UNIONISTS, ASSOCIATION OF CATHOLIC.

ASSOCIATIONS, PIOUS, organizations of lay people or clerics within the Church usually formed to achieve a specific Christian goal or encourage a particular type of devotion. They are subject to the CIC and fall into three classifications: secular *third orders (lay people joined to a religious order such as the Dominicans or Franciscans), *confraternities (e.g., the Priests' Eucharistic League, or the Confraternity of the Rosary), and pious unions (the Knights of the Blessed Sacrament).

[T. M. MCFADDEN]

ASSUMPTION OF MARY, the doctrine, defined by the Roman Catholic Church as a dogma of faith, that Mary, the Mother of God, was taken body and soul into heavenly glory after the course of her earthly life (Pius XII, *Munificentissimus Deus* [hereafter, MD], Nov. 1, 1950; D 3903). The scriptural basis for this belief is more indirect, or oblique, than for the dogmas of the Immaculate Conception, the virginity, and the holiness of Mary. Paul's "If the dead are not raised . . ." (1 Cor 15.14–22) is the assurance of the Christian's resurrection from the dead; it will be like Christ's Resurrection. Paul's "now the sting of death is sin. . ." (1 Cor 15.56) is evidence that every man's death is linked with sin, as was Adam's death (Gen 3.19). The exceptional and anticipatory application to Mary of this universal law is seen as an example of her uniqueness as described in Luke's "Rejoice, so highly favored!" (1.28, JB trans.; cf. *gratia plena* of the Vulg and "full of grace" of the DV). She was said to be of all women the most blessed (Lk 1.42 [JB]; cf. MD 27). In Pauline logic, as it would be applied to Mary, (1) her sinlessness would have dispensed her from death and its consequences: "We are dead to sin. . . . as Christ was raised from the dead by the Father's glory, we too might live a new life" (Rom 6.2–4). New life for Mary would be not only participated divine life in Christ but also an immediate enjoyment of "body and soul in heavenly glory" (MD 44). Furthermore, (2) "If . . . we have imitated his death, we shall also imitate him in his resurrection" (Rom 6.5). Mary imitated Christ so truly that she not only never sinned but was also intimately and actively cooperative in his Incarnation (Lk, ch. 1–2) and in his life work, the Redemption of mankind (Jn 2.1–12). She was, moreover, surely present at his death and burial, possibly present at his apparitions after the Resurrection and at his Ascension. Finally, (3) her dissociation from sin (and death, its consequence according to the Scriptures) is implied by her close association with the founding of the Church on Pentecost (Acts 1.12–14; 2.1–4) and by her resemblance to the Church (cf. Revelation, ch. 12). These elements of the Marian mystery indicate a preeminent holiness, like Christ's, that would set her apart from the human conditions of sin, death, and corruption.

Tradition has continued the exaltation of Mary begun in the Scripture. Paul's parallel between Christ and Adam (Rom 5.18–19) inspired Irenaeus's (d. 202) comparison (*Haer*. 3.32.1) of the superlative and positive characterizations of Mary and the disparaging characterizations of Eve. This eventually evolved into the one basic contrast between Mary and Eve, Mary's cooperation with the goodness of God and his gift of new life (and the logic of her enjoying its glory immediately with the risen Christ), and Eve's cooperation with the evil of Satan and the introduction of sin into human existence (and the punishment of suffering its consequences, esp. death). Pius XII three times in the apostolic constitution proclaiming the Assumption (MD 27, 30, 39) alludes to this Mary-Eve comparison as an explanation for Mary's justly being the first person, as the New Eve, to join the New Adam in glory. But the principal theological reason for the Assumption, as for all the other mysteries of Mary, is that she is the Mother of Jesus, who is the Son of God (MD 6, 14, 21, 22, 25). Because of that fact she was conceived sinless (MD 14), was a virgin-mother (and spared the birth pangs that are the punishment of sin, Gen 3.16), and was exempt from death (but accepted it in order to be, again, one with her Divine Son)—giving a new meaning to Hosea's "Where is your plague, Death?" (13.14), Ezechiel's "Only the one who sins shall die" (18.4), and Paul's "Death is swallowed up in victory" (1 Cor 15.54). The death of Mary is taken for granted by many writers who speak of her Assumption. The earliest documents, e.g., the apocryphal *Transitus Mariae*, and later the feast of the Dormition (5th cent.) imply her death. But Pius XII's solemn declaration uses the ambiguous phrase, *expleto terrestris vitae cursu*, leaving the question open to mortalists and immortalists. To Protestants the Assumption is the least acceptable of the Roman Catholic Church's teachings on Mary because of its lack of clear scriptural basis. The Eastern Churches can be said to have given this belief to the West and they still cherish it faithfully. BIBLIOGRAPHY: J. W. Langlinais, NCE 1:971–975; L. Everett, "Mary's Death and Bodily Assumption," C. Mariol 2:461–475; *Thomist* 14.1 (1951), text of MD, 8 articles, bibliog; C. Decelles, "Fresh Look at the Assumption of Mary," AER 167 (1973) 147–163.

[J. W. LANGLINAIS]

ASSUMPTION OF THE VIRGIN, see APOCRYPHA (NEW TESTAMENT), 11.

ASSUMPTUS-HOMO THEOLOGY, the theology of the man who is exalted or assumed, a theological approach to the mystery of the Incarnation. In its earlier, less orthodox form it proposed that a man was assumed and united to the Word of God. The expression had defenders among Catholic theologians against Apollinarian or other unsatisfactory *Logos-sarx* Christologies and was useful in stressing the reality and integrity of Christ's humanity. Frequently, however, the formula was understood in an adoptionist or Nestorian sense. Peter Lombard included the man-assumed

theory among his famous three opinions, but this position was sharply criticized by St. Thomas Aquinas (ThAq ST 3a, 2.6) and other scholastics. Deodat de Basly, OFM (d. 1937) revived the *assumptus-homo* theology in a more nuanced, but orthodox fashion. He stressed the obvious advantages of this notion in expressing Christ's humanity and argued that his view was in accord with Antiochene and Scotistic Christology. This position, while it recognizes that the *homo-assumptus* is not completely autonomous, tries to express the integrity of Christ's humanity in terms of a human psychological (but not ontological) ego. A number of Catholic theologians, e.g., Amann, Galtier, Gaudel, Glorieux, have defended this theory frequently with their own additions or qualifications. L. Seiler's extreme form of this theory, which spoke of the human being Jesus Christ as "someone" distinct from the Word, was condemned by the Holy See (AAS 43 [1951] 561). Pius XII (*Sempiternus Rex,* D 3905) did not condemn the notion but implied the need for caution in its use. BIBLIOGRAPHY: H. F. Dondaine, "Bulletin de théologie dogmatique," *RevTP* 35 (1951) 609–613.

[J. HENNESSEY]

ASSURANCE OF SALVATION, the Christian's certitude that because his life is based on faith, he is saved from sin and numbered among the elect. Luther's strong emphasis on faith as the sole principle of salvation gave prominence to this assurance. By faith the true believer is comforted with the conviction that God is faithful to his promises; the assurance is absolute. Calvinism grounded such assurance in the sovereign absoluteness of divine *election. RC teaching in the Council of Trent denied the possibility of an absolute certitude of one's salvation (D 1566). Both RC and classical Protestant views recognize that salvation does remain an object of hope, and that certitude of salvation is modified by the believer's capacity to fall away or be unfaithful to God's love.

John *Wesley stressed the idea of assurance as a conscious factor in Christian living. In his understanding, assurance is the experience of being able to live without voluntary sin (see PERFECTION, CHRISTIAN). The idea was developed in the U.S. in *revivalism and the *Holiness movement, and assurance in this sense is a characteristic teaching of many of the Churches originating in these movements. *ENTIRE SANCTIFICATION; *PERFECTIONISM.

[M. B. SCHEPERS]

ASSURBANIPAL, see ASHURBANIPAL.

ASSURNASIRPAL (ASHURNASIRPAL) II, King of Assyria from 884–860 B.C. He was the son and successor of Tukulti-Ninurta II. The son followed the example of his father in his conquest of the Hurrians and Aramaeans. He also obtained tribute from the cities of Tyre, Sidon, and

Byblos. Inscriptions record the cruelties he inflicted on the places he conquered. His use of the cavalry for the first time explains his success. Among the excavations found at Nimrud are extensive bas-reliefs of this king at war and worship. He is not mentioned in the Bible but was a contemporary of Kings Asa and Josaphat of Juda and Amri (Omri) and Achab of Israel. His son Salmansar (Shalmaneser) III was able to demand tribute from Israel under Jehu because of the powerful army inherited from his father. BIBLIOGRAPHY: *Ancient Records of Assyria and Babylonia* (2 v., ed. D. D. Luckenbill, 1926–27) 1:138–199.

[C. C. O'DONNELL]

ASSY, NOTRE-DAME-DE-TOUTE-GRÂCE (1950), a parish church serving convalescents in the French Alps. It was early a focal point of post-World War II controversies concerning modern religious art. Impressive for outstanding artists engaged rather than for the architecture of M. Novarina, the church includes works by: Rouault, Lurcat, Matisse, Lipchitz, Braque, Bazaine. A highly expressionistic crucifix by G. Richier drew prominent figures and reactionary French Catholics into public controversy. This led to a censure by C. Constantini (OssRom June 10, 1951) and eventually to a more conciliatory directive by a French Episcopal Commission (see P. Régamey, "Directives de l'épiscopat", *L'Art sacré*, May, 1952). The Assy controversies served to clarify the role of modern art in the Church. BIBLIOGRAPHY: W. S. Rubin, *Modern Sacred Art and the Church of Assy* (1961); F. and D. Getlein, *Christianity in Modern Art* (1961) 108–113.

[R. J. VEROSTKO]

ASSYRIA, the name of the ancient country of NE Mesopotamia surrounded on the N by the Armenian mountains, on the S by the alluvial plain of Babylonia, on the W by the Middle Tigris and on the E by the Kurdestan Mountains; also the name of the empire of the Assyrian kings which at different and extended periods of time included Mesopotamia, Babylon, and Syria as well as sections of N Palestine, Egypt, and Asia Minor.

Though their ethnic origin is Semitic, closely related to the Akkadians, Chaldeans, Arrapachians, Sutians, Lulubians, Amorites, Aramaeans, Hebrews, and Arabs, the Assyrians displayed a distinctive national character.

The chief god of the Assyrians was Assur. In the beginning a local deity, with the growth of the Empire, he became the national god. His symbol was an archer with a winged disk, the exemplary soldier. Next to him, Ishtar was worshiped at Arbela as goddess of war. Other gods such as Samesu, the sun god, and Sin, the moon god, were worshiped throughout the Semitic world. Forms of worship and festivals were quite similar in Babylonia and Syria.

The legacy and influence of Assyria included a significant rule of Israel for almost two centuries. Though culturally dependent on Babylonia, the Assyrian Empire was responsible for the spread of Babylonian culture. The library of Ashurbanipal preserved Akkadian literature and ancient grammatical aids indispensable for interpreting Sumerian and Akkadian texts. Their chronology, set by the Limmu lists which indicate each year by the royal officer's name, is the most accurate tool available for computing the date of happenings in the Near East (9th–7th cent. B.C.). The Royal Annals' distinctive literary form supplements the more limited record of the OT for the history of this period. Their ideal of world kingdom influenced Babylonia, Persia, Alexandria, and Rome in their political and military achievements and was the indirect occasion of the Hebrew clarification of the concept of the kingdom of God. BIBLIOGRAPHY: W. F. Albright, *Encyclopedia Americana* 2:426–432; A. T. E. Olmstead, *History of Assyria* (1923); W. L. Moran, NCE 9:698–707.

[F. H. BRIGHAM]

ASSYRIAN CHURCH, the contemporary Nestorian Church. The title Assyrian was first applied to the Church by Englishmen in the early 20th cent., the Archbishop of Canterbury's 19th-cent. mission of aid to the Nestorians having already been known as the "Assyrian Mission," a name chosen as more likely to encourage popular contributing support. Today the Nestorians have come to call themselves Assyrians and their Church the Assyrian Church in Western languages, but in their own vernacular Arabic or Soureth, as well as officially in classical Syriac, they continue to speak of "the (Apostolic) Church of the East." BIBLIOGRAPHY: J.-M. Fiey, *L'Orient syrien* 10 (1965) 141–160. *EAST SYRIAN CHURCH.

[A. CODY]

ASSYRIOLOGY, the study of the civilization of ancient Assyria and Babylonia, but in its more restricted and generally accepted meaning, the study of the written texts of the Akkadian (Assyro-Babylonian) language. It had its beginning as a science with the discovery by P. E. Botta (1842–43) of the inscriptions at Kuyunjik (Ancient Ninive) and at the palace of Sargon II in Khorasbad and by A. M. Layard (1845) of several palaces at Nimrud (Ancient Calah) and of the royal library of Ashurbanipal (668 B.C.–627 B.C.). Since that time, major archeological excavations of Mesopotamia have continued. Decipherment of Akkadian cuneiform began with studies of G. Grotefend who noted the differences between Babylonian and Assyrian cuneiform script in his discovery (1815) of the Persian kings listed in a trilingual (Old Persian-Elamite-Babylonian) inscription at Persepolis, was continued by Hincks who properly named 80 cuneiform signs and noted the syllabic dimensions of the script (1846–50), and finalized by H. C. Rawlinson who published the *Behistun inscription together with his statement of the principle of polyphony (1857)—one sign with many different phonetic values. Challenged by Renan and Sir Cornwall Lewis, Rawlinson, Hincks, Oppert, and Fox Talbot presented essentially the same translation of a unilingual Babylonian text working independently of one another and thus confirmed the accuracy of their decipherment and the acceptance of Assyriology as a science.

Oppert developed the first Assyrian grammar (1860) and Norris the first detailed Assyrian dictionary (1868–72). The most recent dictionaries of note are the *Assyrian Dictionary of the Univ. of Chicago* (1956–) and the *Akkadisches Handwörterbuch* of Van Soden (1959–). The standard grammar is Van Soden's *Grundriss der Akkadischen Grammatik* (1952).

With the continued discovery of new inscriptions, it is difficult for scholars to close the gap which divides published from unpublished cuneiform texts.

As a result of the refinement of the science of Assyriology, hitherto unsolved mysteries of Oriental history have been clarified. Exact dates are now established from these inscriptions which are a continuous record of events going back at least to 4500 B.C. Valuable comparisons can now be made between the account of Genesis and the earlier Babylonian epic of the Deluge, between the records of the Assyrian and Babylonian kings and the OT Books of Kings, e.g., the records of Shalmaneser II, Tiglath-pileser III, and Sennacherib, Assyrian Kings, have direct references to Hebrew history. Such comparison has confirmed the historical validity of some biblical accounts and established the fact that the writers of biblical events had consulted contemporary documents. BIBLIOGRAPHY: S. A. Pallis, *Antiquity of Iraq* (1956); S. Lloyd, *Foundations in the Dust* (pa. 1955).

[F. H. BRIGHAM]

ASTARTE (ISTART), Greek equivalent name of the Babylonian goddess of love, fertility, and war, associated with the planet Venus. These elements she kept in her Mesopotamian guise as Ishtar. In Ugaritic mythology she receded into the background, her principal functions being assumed by Anat. In Palestine she was prominent as a fertility goddess, although the fact that the Philistines put in her temple the armor of Saul and his sons after their defeat (1 Sam. 31:10) suggests her association with war in Southern Canaan, too. A number of plaques representing a nude goddess have been found throughout Canaan, but it is difficult to determine whether the goddess represented in a given instance is Astarte, Anat, or Qadesh, or a blending of them in a single figure. The OT takes an unequivocally negative attitude toward her cult. *ASHERAH.

[A. CODY]

ASTATIANS (Gr. *Astatoi,* the homeless), a group of 9th-cent. *Paulicians. The Astatians received their name because they became fugitives after assassinating two emissaries of the Emperor Leo V the Armenian, persecutor of the Paulicians. The Astatians fled to Melitene in the Arab-held sector of Armenia. Outwardly they became Mohammedans, but secretly maintained Paulician belief and worship. BIBLIOGRAPHY: C. Verschaffel, DTC 1:2141.

[T. C. O'BRIEN]

ASTERICUS, see ANASTASIUS OF HUNGARY, ST.

ASTERISK (Gr. *asteriskos,* star; Sl. *zvyezditza*), in the Byzantine liturgy a practical accessory instrument to the *diskos* (paten) made of two intersecting, collapsible, and bent metal bands meeting at right angles and held together by a screw. It is placed on top of the diskos to prevent the veil (*diskokalymma*) covering the *diskos* from touching the bread placed beneath. The Greek form is usually rounded and forms two intersecting arches while the Slavs often prefer a more squared shape. A metal star is often suspended beneath the intersecting arch. During the rite of preparation (prothesis) the asterisk is incensed by holding it open over the fuming censer and then placing it over the bread with the words, "and the star came and stood over the place where the child was." This connection of the asterisk with the star of Bethlehem is a late addition to the practical use of this instrument. At the end of the preface before the Holy, Holy, Holy, at the words, "singing, shouting, proclaiming the hymn of victory and saying" the priest or deacon lifts the asterisk and strikes the four sides of the *diskos* with it, folds it, kisses it and lays it aside. It is not used in the liturgy after this point.

[A. J. JACOPIN]

ASTERIUS, OF AMASEA, ST. (d. *c*.410), bp. of Amasea in Pontus. Practically nothing is known of his life except that he was probably a lawyer before becoming a bishop between 380 and 390. His 16 extant homilies show him to have been a man well versed in the learning and culture of his time. The 11th homily, on the martyrdom of St. Euphemia, contains a description of a painting of the saint; this text was used by Nicaea II against the Iconoclasts. Works: PG 40:155–480. BIBLIOGRAPHY: Butler 4:221–222; S. McKenna, NCE 1:984; Quasten 3:300–301.

[R. B. ENO]

ASTERIUS THE SOPHIST (d. *c*.342), Arian theologian. A native of Cappadocia, A., like *Arius, was a student of *Lucian of Antioch. He seems to have apostatized during the persecution of Maximinus, in which Lucian was martyred. This lapse barred him from ordination, but during the post-Nicene controversies he was among the first theologians to write in defense of Arius. He is mentioned among the participants in the Council of Antioch of 341. Some of his works survive: 31 homilies, 27 fragments of his commentaries on the Psalms, and part of a treatise called the *Syntagmation*. BIBLIOGRAPHY: Quasten 3:194–197.

[R. B. ENO]

ASTORGA, PEDRO DE ALVA Y, see ALVA Y ASTORGA, PEDRO DE.

ASTRAIN, ANTONIO (1857–1928), Jesuit historian, editor of the *Mensajero del Sagrado Corazón* from 1890, and staff member of the *Monumenta historica Societatis Iesu* from 1893. In 1895 he began to write the history of the Spanish Jesuits from the beginning to 1767, but after publishing seven volumes (1902–25) he died with his total project uncompleted. The work includes a life of Ignatius of Loyola and an extensive history of the Spanish Jesuits in the Americas, Pacific Islands, and the Philippines. BIBLIOGRAPHY: J. F. Bannon, NCE 1:984–985; B. Schneider, LTK 1:962–963.

ASTRAL RELIGION, the worship of the celestial bodies, the sun, moon, planets, stars, and constellations, a widespread practice among primitive peoples and those of higher cultures. It may be ascribed to man's theopoetic tendency to ascribe preternatural and even divine powers to natural phenomena, esp. those intimately connected with his own welfare, but whose origins and movements are shrouded in mystery. Among primitive tribes the sun and moon are almost universally regarded as being alive and possessing a quasi-human nature. Their sex differs from race to race, but the moon is more commonly regarded as male and the sun as female. Countless myths have been invented to explain their origin as well as that of the stars, e.g., the belief of the Mantras, that the sun and moon are women who brought forth many children, the stars.

Among more advanced civilizations similar animistic beliefs are to be found. In former times the Chinese, for example, held that the heavenly bodies were the dwelling places of spiritual beings with superhuman powers who were, however, subordinate to Tien, Shang-ti, or God, the sole possessor of sovereign might. Sacrifices if not actual worship were offered to these luminaries, to the sun at the vernal equinox, and to the moon at the autumnal. The ancient Egyptians worshiped a Sun-god Re at Heliopolis along with numerous other divinities. Towards the end of the 15th cent. B.C., Amenhotep IV changed his name to *AKHNATON and attempted to establish a new solar theology and worship centered upon Aton, an ancient name for the physical sun, but his efforts to introduce this new, more monotheistic form of worship proved to be ineffectual.

Astral religion found its fullest development among the Babylonians, and it passed from there to the peoples of the West, where it prepared the way for Greco-Roman acceptance of astrology as a science with religious overtones. Though they worshiped all of the celestial bodies as "gods," their principal deities were the sun, moon, and the five visible planets. The sun was Shamash, the moon Sin, Venus Ishtar, Jupiter Marduk, Saturn Ninib (a war god), Mercury Nebo (a herald), and Mars Nergal (a god of the dead). When the Greeks and Romans became acquainted with the Babylonian pantheon, they adopted it for their own use, identifying with some modifications their own deities with those of the East. The seven gods so honored by the Romans were Sol (the sun), Luna (the moon), Mars, Mercury, Jupiter, Venus, and Saturn, names which have survived in the Romance languages as those of the 7 days of the week.

The ancestors of the Hebrews were, like other Semites,

worshipers of the sun, moon, and stars, but such worship is condemned in the OT as idolatrous. Though the stars are at times personified in the OT this was done to stress the sovereignty of the one true God (cf. Ps 18; Is 14). In interpreting the beliefs of ancient peoples it is not always easy to distinguish between their knowledge of astronomy, a legitimate science; astral religion, a false though not debased form of worship; and astrology, a pseudo-science and art used to interpret human events from the varied movements of the stars. BIBLIOGRAPHY: F. von Oefele et al., Hastings ERE 12:48–103; N. Turchi, EncCatt 2:229–30.

[M. J. COSTELLOE]

ASTROLOGY (Gr. *astrologia,* science of the stars), a term employed in ancient times for the study both of the real or apparent motions of the sun, moon, planets, and stars, and of their presumed influence upon human and terrestrial affairs. The former, now known as astronomy, was specified as natural astrology, and the latter, now simply designated as astrology, was called judicial astrology.

Astrology is one of the oldest and most widespread pseudo-sciences in the world and is found in various forms among most primitive peoples, who use it to insure a successful hunt or fruitful crops, and among many peoples of a higher culture such as the ancient Hindus, Chinese, Egyptians, and Etruscans. It has its origins in a belief in the divine or at least preternatural character of the stars and in a kind of universal sympathy that binds the ever changing positions of the heavenly bodies with the transient activities of men. One of the most basic beliefs is in the existence of "lucky" and "unlucky" days. Though astrology has evolved as an independent phenomenon in many parts of the world, the astrology of the West is indebted almost exclusively to the astrological beliefs and practices of the ancient peoples of Mesopotamia, some of which may be traced to the Sumerians of the 3d millennium B.C. Babylonian astrology was concerned with the interpretation of both terrestrial and celestial phenomena such as earthquakes, meteors, comets, and halos about the moon. Predictions from such data referred originally to the country or to the king and were concerned with such things as wars, plagues, droughts, and floods. With the passage of time more subtle phenomena were examined and the conclusions applied to private individuals as well. In its developed form Babylonian astrology made use of the twelve signs of the zodiac and more than 200 different constellations to arrive at its conclusions. Much of this lore has been recovered in the thousands of astrological documents and fragments discovered during the last cent. in the library of King Assurbanipal (668–626 B.C.) at Nineveh.

During the Hellenistic Age great strides were made in astrology in Egypt through the amalgam of Greek science with Eastern astronomical observations and the general religious anxieties of the time. From there it spread throughout the Greco-Roman world despite occasional suppressions of *mathematici* (astrologers) by Roman authorities. With the adoption of the Julian calendar in 46 B.C. even the poorest people could afford what had formerly been a luxury of the rich. Astrology came to be regarded as a perfectly legitimate science and commanded the allegiance of some of the ablest minds of the ancient world, particularly those imbued with Stoicism. It had a profound effect on medicine; it found poetical expression in the *Astronomica* of Manilius and architectural embodiment in such buildings as the Roman Pantheon; and it contributed to the development of the concept of Natural Law.

Since astrology permeated the whole culture of the period, references to it may be found in the NT (Gal 4.9–11; Rom 8.38; Col. 2.8). Through the strong opposition of the Church Fathers (e.g., St. Augustine, *De Civ. Dei* 5.1–8), astrology was eventually suppressed in the Roman empire, but during the Middle Ages it was reintroduced into the West through Jewish and Arabic scholars. The presumption that the stars could influence the lives of men created a moral problem which was resolved by St. Thomas in the following manner: Since the will is an entirely spiritual and incorporeal faculty, it can only be indirectly influenced by the heavenly bodies. Men thus remain free and responsible for their actions. (ThAq ST 1a2ae, 9.5).

During the Renaissance astrology reached its apogee in the Christian West. Pope Julius II employed it to fix the day for his coronation, and Pope Leo X, following the trend of the times, even founded a chair of astrology at the Sapienza. The invention of the telescope, the general increase in scientific knowledge, and the skepticism of the 18th cent. did much to destroy the credibility of this ancient divinatory art. But that it is by no means dead is clearly indicated by the daily horoscopes printed today in countless papers throughout the world. BIBLIOGRAPHY: M. Camozzini et al. EncCatt 2:232–242; F. von Oefele et al., Hastings ERE 12:48–103; F. Cumont, *Oriental Religions in Roman Paganism* (pa. 1956).

[M. J. COSTELLOE]

ASTROS, PAUL THÉRÈSE DAVID D' (1772–1851), bp. of Bayonne (1820–30), abp. of Toulouse from 1830, cardinal (1850). Earlier in his career he opposed Napoleon, was accused of publishing Pius VII's bull of excommunication, and was imprisoned 1811–14. He energetically promoted the condemnation of De *Lamennais, and also opposed P. Guéranger's attack upon the diversity of local Gallican usages in the liturgy of France. BIBLIOGRAPHY: J. Dedieu, DHGE 4:1253–55.

[P. K. MEAGHER]

ASTRUC, JEAN (1684–1766), French physician, pioneer in the textual criticism of the Bible. In his *Conjectures* (1753) on the composition of Genesis, A. indicated his discovery of the distinction between the *Elohistic and Yahwistic passages of Genesis to support the hypothesis of diverse documents embodied in its composition. He thus became the initiator of the documentary theory that was developed in

19th-cent. textual criticism. BIBLIOGRAPHY: A. M. Malo, NCE 1:992–993. *GENESIS, BOOK OF.

[T. C. O'BRIEN]

ASTURIAN ART. In the 9th cent. under king Ramiro I, small important churches of S. Maria de Naranco and S. Miguel de Liño near Oviedo (848) show strong Moorish influence in windows, cusped arches, and decorations, with sculpture of Visigothic style. Hall churches of strong vertical emphasis carry down the walls transverse ribs culminating in disks excitedly decorated with low relief sculpture of Teutonic origin. BIBLIOGRAPHY: *Ars Hispaniae II* (1947); K. J. Conant, *Carolingian and Romanesque Architecture 800 to 1200* (1959).

[M. J. DALY]

ASURA (Sanskrit term for divine), used in earliest Vedas for Supreme Spirit, yet later in India meaning demon.

[M. J. DALY]

ASYLUM, ABBEY OF, see ÅS (ASYLUM), ABBEY OF.

ASYLUM, CITIES OF, six cities, three on either side of the Jordan set aside by the Mosaic law to safeguard the unintentional killer from blood vengeance (Num 35.9–34); in the earlier legislation, in the Book of the Covenant (Ex 21.13–14) apparently any altar offered such refuge. Asylum did not dispense from investigation and trial, and in case of an unfavorable verdict the refuge was denied. In Jos 20 are found the names of Kedesh, Shechem, and Hebron for the west bank of the Jordan; Bezer, Ramoth in Gilead, and Golan for Transjordan. It is probable that each of these cities was chosen because it possessed a notable place of worship. Scholars also believe that the institution of the cities of refuge should be attributed to the reign of David. BIBLIOGRAPHY: De Vaux AncIsr 160–163.

[J. E. LUSSIER]

ASYLUM, RIGHT OF, claim to refuge and safety from enemies accorded to fugitives in certain places. The Mosaic code made certain cities places of asylum for murderers (Ex 21.12–14; Num 35.11–29; 19.1–13), and under Greco-Roman influence temples were treated as places of asylum. In 431 A.D., Theodosius II extended the privilege to all Christian sanctuaries and environs. Right of asylum became attached to holy places during the Christian ages and found its way into canon law in the 12th century. With the rise of the monarchies and the decline of church authority, the custom lost common recognition. Today, right of asylum is sometimes granted in a purely political context. BIBLIOGRAPHY: M. M. Sheehan, NCE 1:994; J. Hennessey, "Right of Asylum—Then and Now," *America* 125 (1971) 482–483.

[P. F. MULHERN]

ATARAXY (ataraxia), a term used in Greek philosophy to designate the Epicurean ideal of calmness, imperturbability of mind, or serenity of soul. BIBLIOGRAPHY: Copleston 1:407.

[M. R. P. MCGUIRE]

ATELIER, L' (Sept. 1840–July 1850), journal "devoted to the moral and material interests of the workers," founded by followers of Philippe Buchez who had been converted to Catholicism from Saint-Simonianism in 1829. Its writers were generally craftsmen who defended their cause with courage and intelligence when social conditions were particularly harsh. They described their doctrine as Christian Socialism with Christianity the moral guarantee essential to their system. Their "democratic spiritualism" meant more than the proclamation by some secular socialists that Christ was a humanitarian and a socialist. For L'Atelier Christ was the Word of God, and the Gospels, genuinely revealed documents. While the degree of commitment to religion varied, the journal and the association connected with it reduced working-class anticlericalism and stimulated several conversions. It condemned charity as degrading and remained absolutely anticapitalistic, rejecting rent, interest, and wages. Its objective was worker dignity and independence with full democracy and the full fruit of the work to the laborer.

[J. N. MOODY]

ATELIERS DE CHARITÉ, centers organized in France in 1770 by Abbé Terray, comptroller general, to enable the unemployed to find work. The term charité was used to dispel the impression left by earlier comparable institutions that they existed to punish rather than to help. These centers were several times suppressed and revived, and in 1848 became the Ateliers nationaux, the vicissitudes of their history being attributable to the difficulty of giving necessary aid without fostering laziness or giving scope to agitators. BIBLIOGRAPHY: Catholicisme 1:973.

[P. K. MEAGHER]

ATHALA OF BOBBIO, ST. (d. 627), abbot. He succeeded Columban as Abbot of Bobbio (c.615). According to a contemporary account by the Abbot Jonas of Bobbio, he was born in Burgundy, spent some time in the monasteries of Lérins and Luxeuil before going to Italy. He combated Arianism among the Lombards and supported the papacy in the controversy over the *Three Chapters. BIBLIOGRAPHY: B. Krusch, MGHS rer. Mer. 4:113–119; C. Poggi and A. M. Raggi, BiblSanct 2:565–567.

[J. E. LYNCH]

ATHALIAH (Athalia), wife of King Jehoram of Judah, daughter of Ahab and Jezebel, and mother of Ahaziah (2 Kg 8.18, 26; 11). After the death of Ahaziah, she seized the throne and ruled 6 years (c.842–837 B.C.) until the priest Jehoiada deposed her and crowned the young Joash. She was then killed.

[T. EARLY]

ATHANASIAN CREED, a creed, called also the Quicumque vult from the initial words of the Latin text, thought until the 17th cent. to have been composed by St. Athanasius. In 40 rhythmic statements it clearly, if not gracefully, expresses the belief in the Trinity and the Incarnation that is necessary for salvation. The author remains a mystery, but the name of St. Ambrose among others has been suggested. The formulary is not Athanasian in content or style; it was composed between 434 and 542, and was possibly a compilation from many sources. Written in Latin, it was later translated into Greek (earliest Gr. MSS are of the 14th cent.); its use seems to have begun in Arles in the 6th cent. and spread. From the 9th cent. it appeared in the liturgy. Its former frequent recitation in the Roman liturgy at Prime on Sundays ceased when that canonical hour was suppressed by Vatican Council II in 1963 (Vat II SacLit 89). The Athanasian Creed, retained by the great Reformers, was esp. esteemed by Martin Luther. Acknowledged in the Anglican *Thirty-Nine Articles, it retains its place, in spite of some opposition in the C of E, as part of Morning Prayer in the Book of Common Prayer on certain days. The Protestant Episcopal Church, however, in its adaptation of the Articles and the BCP dropped this creed. In the East it is not one of the doctrinal standards, but from the 17th cent. it has been part of the Russian liturgy. BIBLIOGRAPHY: G. Owens, NCE 1:995–996.

[T. C. O'BRIEN]

ATHANASIUS, ST. (c.295–373), Father and Doctor of the Church, defender of the Nicene faith, friend of St. Anthony of Egypt. He was ordained deacon by Bp. Alexander (318), accompanied him as secretary to the council of Nicaea and became patriarch of Alexandria (328). Influenced by the intrigues of Eusebius of Nicomedia, the Arians, and the partisans of the Meletian schism, Constantine banished A. to Trier. He was reinstated after a successful appeal to Pope Julius I. Persistent opposition from his enemies forced A. from his see four more times so that he spent more than 17 years in exile between 335 and 366. His most important authentic works, written after he became bishop, fall into four categories: dogmatic, historical-polemical, and ascetical treatises, and letters. Of the dogmatic works the three Discourses against the Arians are the most important. The historical-polemical category contains three apologies of which the Apology against the Arians is the most valuable because of the official documents it incorporates. His History of the Arians is extant only in fragments. The principal ascetical work of A. is his Life of St. Anthony. This work profoundly influenced subsequent Greek and Latin hagiography. The Athanasian authorship of the treatise On Virginity is still disputed. The correspondence of A. is of prime importance for the history of Arianism and the development of Christian doctrine in the 4th cent. The following extant letters are the most noteworthy. The Festal Letters, primarily annual messages to the bps. of Egypt, announce the beginning of Lent and the date for Easter. The letter of 367 is most widely known for its list of the canonical books of

Sacred Scripture. The *Synodal Letters* requested by synods held in Alexandria are chiefly doctrinal in content explaining the Nicene faith and warning against Arian errors. The four *Letters to Serapion of Thmuis* are in reality a unified dogmatic treatise setting forth the correct doctrine on the Holy Spirit. The *Letter on the Decrees of the Council of Nicaea* is unique for its description of the proceedings of the council. It incorporates a letter of Eusebius of Caesarea which dates from the year of the council. The exegetical writings of A. are known mostly through fragments preserved in *catenae*. From these meager remains it seems that the allegorical explanation of Scripture predominated. The numerous homilies attributed to A. still await further study to determine their authenticity. The so-called Athanasian Creed usually called *Quicumque* from its opening word, was associated with A. till the 17th cent. This document, written in Latin, most probably dates from the mid-5th cent., and may well embody the teaching of several local synods held in Gaul. BIBLIOGRAPHY: Quasten, 3:20–79; P. Camelot, LTK 1:976–981; V. De Clercq, NCE 1:996–999.

[H. DRESSLER]

ATHANASIUS I, PATRIARCH OF CONSTANTINOPLE (1230–1310), a native of Adrianople who changed his name from Alexius to Athanasius when he entered the monastery of Thessalonica. Named patriarch of Constantinople by Emperor Andronicus II (1289) after his life as a monk at Esphigmenou on Mt. Athos, as a hermit at St. Lazarus on Mt. Galesios, and establishing a monastery at Ganos in Thrace, he initiated several regulations restricting the travel of monks and bishops. Opposition to this reform resulted in his resignation and assignment to the monastery of Xerolophus (1293). Reinstated at the request of the people of Constantinople (1304) he returned to this same monastery where he died after his second resignation of the patriarchate (1310). Of his writings, 126 unedited letters dealing with matters of ecclesiastical discipline, two catechetical instructions, and an anthem in praise of the Mother of God have survived (PG 142:471–528). BIBLIOGRAPHY: K. Baus, LTK 1:981.

[F. H. BRIGHAM]

ATHANASIUS OF ANAZARBA (fl. 325) bp., disciple of Lucian of Antioch and teacher of the Arian Aetius, who wrote a letter in defense of Arian teaching to Alexander, bp. of Alexandria, prior to the Council of Nicaea. St. Athanasius summarizes this statement as a clear example of Arian teaching (*De synodis,* 17; PG 26:712). A. probably took part in the council of Nicaea but is not listed with those who attended. BIBLIOGRAPHY: J. Mécérian, DHGE 4:1351; G. Bardy, *Catholicisme* 1:980.

[F. H. BRIGHAM]

ATHANASIUS THE ATHONITE, ST. (*c*.920–1003), the founder of organized monasticism on Mt. Athos. A native of Trebizond, A. became a teacher in Constantinople,

then a monk in Bithynia, and in 958 settled on Mt. Athos. The peninsula had been populated by hermits and, despite their opposition, he established the first monastery there, known simply as the Laura, which is still in existence and which was followed by other monasteries. BIBLIOGRAPHY: L. Petit, ''Vie de Saint Athanase l'Athonite,'' AnalBoll 25 (1906) 5–89; Butler 3:20–22.

[G. T. DENNIS]

ATHANASIUS OF NAPLES, ST., (832–872), bp. The son of Duke Sergius of Naples, A. chose the clerical state in early youth, and at the age of 18 was made bp. of Naples by Pope St. Leo IV. In an age of great difficulties, he was a most exemplary cleric, renowned for personal austerity and compassion for others, while proving his abilities as an administrator and peacemaker. His relics have been twice translated and are venerated now in the cathedral at Naples. BIBLIOGRAPHY: AS July 4 (1867) 72–89; MGHS rer. Lang. 433–435, 439–452, 1065–76; A. P. Frutaz, EncCatt 2:263–264.

[W. A. JURGENS]

ATHANASIUS OF PAROS (*c*.1725–1813), Greek Orthodox theologian and preacher. A native of the Greek island of Paros, A. studied theology at the academy at Mt. *Athos under the renowned Eugenius Bulgaris, whom he succeeded after achieving prominence as teacher and preacher. For a time A. was under a cloud, excommunicated, and deposed for his stand in the dispute about the *colybai* (1776–81). Once reinstated, he resumed his career and in 1792 became director of the school at Chios, where he died. A. wrote many theological works, biographies, and manuals. He took an anti-Western position against both Roman Catholics and Protestants. BIBLIOGRAPHY: L. Petit, DTC 1:2189–90, with descriptive list of A.'s theol. works; ''La Grande controverse des colybes,'' ÉO 2:321–331.

[T. C. O'BRIEN]

ATHEISM (literally, godlessness, the elimination or rejection of God from one's thoughts and affections and the denial of his existence) as a modern phenomenon, *unbelief in its most articulate and dramatic version. It may be a personal choice, expressing the life-stance of an individual, or it may be an end product, the residue of a long indifference to God and the things of God, which terminates in effective denial of him. In contemporary life acquaintance with the phenomenon comes through its literary expression in novels and drama and its theoretical elaboration in philosophy. Atheism has not yet appeared in a pure form in political life on any extensive basis, hence it is difficult to see clearly the reach and impact it may exercise in either cultural institutions or individual lives. It is much easier to define atheism in the abstract than to account for its various, complex manifestations. When it is a conscious option, atheism is often intellectually serious and always morally serious; it is, in any case, the position on which a man stakes his integrity as a human being and, as such, deserves respect. The atheist is not merely negative; he can develop explicit, positive ideal systems and can apply his unbelief to the most weighty metaphysical and ethical questions. Atheism enjoys a relatively concealed existence because atheists do not ordinarily organize or band together in groups or associations. This, too, tends to hide its real extent and influence. It would be misleading to think of atheism only or primarily as a highly sophisticated reflection, a thoroughly rationalized attitude; as a conviction it may be sincerely and strongly held, but in fact it is most commonly practical, undercover, shifting, restless, and not deeply thought out. Atheism remains, nevertheless, a permanent possibility, both theoretical and lived.

Atheism has become an all-purpose word for many forms of rejection of God that are designated variously as misbelief, disbelief, nonbelief, and unbelief. When it closes itself to all concern for the divine, atheism succeeds in rooting out God and the idea of God from human existence, denying both his transcendence of the world and his action in history. Because it is surrounded by beliefs in gods and by social forces imbued, however imperfectly, with religious values, atheism must be antitheist and antireligious. Militant atheism is not uncommon among secular humanists, and is not restricted to the ranks of Communism. Atheism is more than an intellectual position and a spiritual attitude; it is a historical event and occurs only where there has been some recognition and acceptance of the reality of God. Unbelief in the strong sense is denial, explicit and conscious, and presupposes belief, at least in the social ambiance. From a purely historical perspective atheism has the aspect of an accidental development; evidence points to a pervasive and usually predominant belief in a world other than this one and in some sort of deity. As a culturally defined and respectable stance, atheism is a newcomer on the scene, with a past as yet rather short. This is not an argument against atheism, which could be conceived as a cultural achievement of modern man, the final victory of man over his anxiety and as a sign of his coming of age.

When atheism is intensely bitter, hostile, bent on the utter extermination of every vestige of religion, it witnesses in spite of itself to the depth and reality of the religious impulse. What M. Marty calls "closed atheism" rules out a priori the very possibility of revelation or divine intervention in human affairs. But the atheist may construct distinct views of the meaning and direction of history, even after the elimination of God. In recent times there have appeared an atheism of solitude, aristocratic, skeptical, and an atheism of human solidarity, popular in appeal, enthusiastic. Nietzsche, as an example of the first, calls for the rejection of God on the ground that man cannot be free, cannot be a man, if he must accept a Being superior to himself, to whom he is answerable and indebted for all that he is and has. Marx, an example of the second, also embraces atheism in the name of freedom, but the freedom of the collectivity, conditioned historically and by social forces, the freedom of mankind to discover and conform to the laws of nature. There is a third type of atheism, nonintegral in the form of pantheism, and integral in the version worked up by Sartre, for whom the most decisive proof against God is the universal absence of order. From the alleged experience of absolute evil, all-pervasive discord, the opposition between value and reality, the atheistic existentialist argues to the impossibility of God. It is important to note that atheism must reject not just any God but one to whom infinite wisdom, power, and goodness are attributed. Whatever the motives for sustaining a posture of unbelief, the arguments for atheism are basically two: one from a completely self-sufficient universe, intelligible on its own right and needing no principle of being or explanation outside itself; and one from a radically disordered universe, shot through with absurd and unredeemed evil. God, then, is metaphysically superfluous in the first instance and ethically repugnant in the second.

It is difficult to incarnate and institutionalize integral or closed atheism; there is small prospect of a religion of atheism, in any proper sense, for each man rejects God on his own responsibility. There is, on the other hand, an atheistic dimension, or at least the threat of one, in religion itself, to the extent that men use religious involvement to mask their flight from God. The failures and betrayals of Christianity have a guilty connection with much of the prehistory of modern atheism. Only where God has been radically proclaimed and believed is he denied and rejected with an absolute finality. As it grows self-confident and self-understanding, atheism takes on new forms, and esp. that of a dogmatic humanism, a straightforward affirmation without reference to Christianity. As the secular order achieves total autonomy, the unbeliever will have to exploit and reap the benefit on his own terms of values and forces developed under the aegis of religion. BIBLIOGRAPHY: É. Borne, *Atheism* (1960); J. Lacroix, *Meaning of Modern Atheism* (1965); W. Luijpen, *Phenomenology and Atheism* (1964); Q. Lauer, "Problems of Unbelief," *Thought* (Winter, 1967) 505–518; A. MacIntyre and P. Ricoeur, *Religious Significance of Atheism* (1968). C. Fabro, *God in Exile: Modern Atheism* (1968).

[J. P. REID]

ATHEISM, CHRISTIAN, see CHRISTIAN ATHEISM.

ATHELNEY, Abbey of, former Benedictine monastery, Somerset county, England. The foundation by King Alfred (888) failed; the abbey was refounded *c*.960. It was poor and had few monks, and survived in a position of quasi-dependence on Glastonbury. Athelney was dissolved in 1539. BIBLIOGRAPHY: Knowles MOE; Knowles-Hadcock; F. R. Johnston, NCE 1:1004.

[J. R. SOMMERFELDT]

ATHENA, virgin goddess of wisdom and defensive warfare, armed with helmet, spear, shield, and cuirass, thought to have introduced the olive to ancient Greece. As the

Roman Minerva she was patroness of spinning. Known as *Pallas Athena,* she was protectress of Athens.

[M. J. DALY]

ATHENAGORAS (2d cent.), early Christian apologist. Educated in Athens in Greek philosophy, the arts, and rhetoric, A. was converted to Christianity and thereafter used his learning in defense of Christian truth. Founder of a school of philosophy in Alexandria, he is known for two works: *Supplication for the Christians* and *On the Resurrection from the Dead.* The former, addressed to Marcus Aurelius and Commodus, exonerates Christians from the pagan accusation of atheism, cannibalism, and incest and demonstrates the philosophical basis for monotheism. The latter presents a rational argument for belief in the resurrection of the dead. BIBLIOGRAPHY: Quasten 1:229–236; G. Bardy, *Catholicisme* 1:991–992.

ATHENAGORAS I (1886–1972), patriarch of Constantinople. Called Aristokles Spirou as a layman, A., the son of a physician, was born in Epirus, Greece. After graduating from the seminary of Halki, he was ordained deacon in 1910 and took the name Athenagoras. In Athens he served as archdeacon to Abp. Meletios (later to become ecumenical patriarch), where he was ordained deacon and received the title of archimandrite. He was consecrated bp. in 1922 and was appointed metropolitan of Corfu and Paxos. In 1931 he was made abp. of the Greek Orthodox archdiocese of North and South America. During his incumbency in this office he established many new parishes and parochial schools as well as a seminary for the training of Greek-American priests. Elected ecumenical patriarch in 1948, he used his influence as senior patriarch of the Orthodox Church to promote two causes of deep concern to him: closer cooperation among the Orthodox patriarchates and autocephalous Churches with a view to a Pan-Orthodox Great Synod, and friendship with the RC Church to heal the schism and restore communion between the two Churches. His meeting with Pope Paul VI in Jerusalem in 1964 took place on his initiative. Other milestones toward unity have been the lifting of the anathemas of 1054 by simultaneous ceremonies held in St. Peter's, Rome, and in A.'s patriarchal church (1965), and the visits exchanged between Paul VI and A. in 1968. At the time of his death Pope Paul VI mourned him as "a great protagonist of the reconciliation of all Christians."

[H. GEORGIADIS]

ATHENAÏS, see EUDOCIA.

ATHENODORUS, ST. (3d cent.), bp., younger brother of *Gregory Thaumaturgus. Born in Neocaesarea in Pontus of a distinguished family, he was orphaned at an early age. He and his brother studied law and rhetoric at Berytus before going on to Caesarea in Palestine, where they spent about 5 years as disciples of *Origen (233–238). Some time after their return home, A. was elected bp. of an unknown city in Pontus. In this capacity he took part in the Council of Antioch (264–265). Little else is known of his life. BIBLIOGRAPHY: M. Disdier, DHGE 5:43–44; T. Niggl, LTK 1:996.

[R. B. ENO]

ATHENS, capital of Greece. In the 5th cent. B.C. it took hegemony of the Aegean away from Persian-dominated Ionia, and in the 4th cent. it boasted schools (Plato, Aristotle) that lasted until A.D. 529. St. Paul had few converts in Roman Athens. The bishopric was transferred *c.*733 from the jurisdiction of Rome to Iconoclast Constantinople and became a metropolitanate with 10 suffragans by the 10th century. Many churches were built 900–1200. Pillage of churches and monasteries by crusaders was a bad way to introduce after 1204 a Latin hierarchy, which was never accepted by Greeks, despite the rule of France, Aragon, Florence, and Venice. Greek metropolitans were titular from 1204 until they returned under Turkish rule, whereupon the Latin abps. became titular. But the Church of Athens, metropolitanate and monasteries, was subject to the Turkish-dominated Patriarch of Constantinople. After Greek independence in 1821, the metropolitan of Athens became independent of Constantinople in 1833 and now presides over a holy synod of 13 bishops that governs the Church of Greece. BIBLIOGRAPHY: R. Janin, DHGE 5:15–42. G. Hofmann, EncCatt 2:287–299.

[E. P. COLBERT]

ATHENS, THEOLOGICAL SCHOOL OF, a school of theology that began with the foundation of the Univ. of Athens in 1837 by King Otto. Although its faculty is noted for its more conservative theology as compared to that of the Univ. of Thessalonika, the Athenian school still exerts great influence as the center of Orthodox theological thought in Greece, esp. through the training of future bishops and many teachers of theology. Until 1964 there was no postgraduate theological study in Greece, so that most of the Athens faculty have had to study abroad, principally in Protestant-oriented German universities. Since 1945 many have studied also at Catholic universities in France, Germany, Switzerland, and Italy. The 4-year course of studies includes no specialization but exposes the present 250 students to an encyclopedic knowledge of OT and NT, dogma, patristics, canon law, church history, archeology, ethics, liturgy, catechetics, homiletics, and pastoral theology. Some of the outstanding theologians of this faculty are: Chresto Androutsos (d. 1935), Demetrios Balanos (d. 1948), Grigorios Papamichail (d. 1956), Hamilcar Alivisatos, Panayotes Bratsiotis, Panayotes Trembelas, and John Karmires.

[G. A. MALONEY]

ATHINGANOI (Gr., not touching [anything unclean]), a religious sect that flourished in central Asia Minor in the 9th and 10th cent. Often regarded as a branch of the Paulicians, they were really quite distinct. They apparently practiced an exaggerated levitical purity, observed the Sabbath, held to adult baptism, and indulged in astrology and black magic. Their reputation for magic and fortune telling caused the name of the sect to be used for the gypsies (Gr., *athinganoi*, It., *zingari*, Fr., *tsiganes*, etc.) when they first appeared in the Byzantine Empire. BIBLIOGRAPHY: J. Starr, "Eastern Christian Sect: the Athinganoi," *HTR* 29 (1936) 93–106.

[G. T. DENNIS]

ATHONITE, a monk of Mount *Athos.

[G. T. DENNIS]

ATHOS, MOUNT, an autonomous monastic district that occupies Akte, the northernmost of three prongs that project from the peninsula Chalcidice in NE Greece into the Aegean Sea. It takes its name from the mountain 6670 feet in height at its SE end. The district is a theocratic republic under the protection of Greece and ecclesiastically under the jurisdiction of the patriarch of Constantinople. Its central governing body, the Holy Synod, consists of 20 members chosen from the 20 main monasteries of which 17 are Greek, 1 Russian, 1 Bulgarian, and 1 Serbian. Eastern monasticism finds here a sanctuary that has made Mt. Athos synonymous with the glories of early Christian monasticism. Besides the cenobitic rule written by St. Athanasius the Athonite (*c*.925–1002), the idiorrhythmic rule is also followed. This latter, however, which allows each monk greater freedom in disposing of his own time and property, has also ushered into Athonite monasticism a breakdown in monastic discipline. Besides the larger monasteries, the peninsula is dotted with numerous smaller houses called *sketes, kalyves* or *kellia*. Asceticism centers chiefly around the liturgical recitation of the Byzantine Office, vigils, fasts, and manual labor. The main monasteries possess rich collections of icons, frescoes, and ancient MSS. Before the Russian Revolution there were more than 9,000 monks, but a crisis in monastic vocations has reduced the total number of monks on Mt. Athos to 1,238. BIBLIOGRAPHY: J. J. Norwich and R. Sitwell, *Mount Athos* (1966); E. Amand de Mendieta, *Mount Athos* (tr. M. R. Bruce, 1972).

[G. A. MALONEY]

ATHOS, MOUNT (FRESCOES), the Paleologan renaissance (14th and 15th cent.) a last efflorescence of Byzantine creative power replaced the glowing mosaics of the great Empire by frescoes, not monumental and grandiose but delicate and detailed in dramatic, dynamic friezes or narrative cycles in which expressive figures gesticulate in more lyrical landscapes. However, the transcendental idea dominates. In the schools at Mount Athos and Mistra, Greek painters continued the tradition but opposed by Hesychasm the humanistic Hellenistic style of Theophanes the Great in Constantinople (*c*.1330–1405), emphasizing the occult, iconic art of the East. Important painting at Mount Athos (16th and 17th cent.) showed few innovations, artists using old formulae in the *Painter's Guide* by the 14th-cent. monk Dionysios of Fourna for decoration and iconography. Since World War II Greek scholars attribute to the famous Manuel Panselinos the frescoes at the Monastery of Protaton (first quarter of the 14th cent.) but this is questioned. Frescoes at Chilander and Vatopedi are overpaintings on 14th-cent. work. The lofty transcendental expression appears for the last time at Mount Athos before the 16th-cent. decline in Byzantine art. Among many impressive examples of Byzantine art treasures at Mount Athos, a bible cover in the Monastery of the Lavra with a *repoussé* Christ in *orfèvrerie cloisonnée* and precious stones was probably the treasure of Emperor Nicephorus II Phocas (963–969). BIBLIOGRAPHY: F. Fichtner, *Wandmalereien der Athos–Klöster* (1931); *Reallexikon zur byzantinischen Kunst* (1966) 1:411; E. Amand de Mendieta, *Mount Athos* (tr. M. R. Bruce, 1972).

[M. J. DALY]

ATIENZA, JUAN DE (1542–92), Jesuit educator and canonist. He joined the Jesuits in Spain (1564) and was sent to Peru in 1581. A. founded the Colegio de San Martín in Lima and was rector of the major seminary. He served as provincial of the order and as a valued collaborator of Toribio de *Mogrovejo, abp. of Lima. BIBLIOGRAPHY: A. de Egaña, NCE 1:1010.

[H. JACK]

ATKINSON, MATTHEW (PAUL OF ST. FRANCIS; 1656–1729), English Franciscan missionary. In 1698 he was sentenced to life imprisonment for being a priest. After complaints against liberties allowed him, he voluntarily confined himself to his cell in Hurst Castle prison, Hampshire, for his last 30 years. BIBLIOGRAPHY: T. Cooper, DNB 1:697.

[E. P. COLBERT]

ATLANTES, male human figures used as pillars in Greek architecture, and counterparts of female caryatids (Porch of Maidens, Erechtheum), called telamones in Roman architecture.

[M. J. DALY]

ATMAN, Hindu term for the self or soul. It is used in the *Upanishads, which teach the unity of ātman with Brahman (God, Being, the Absolute). Ultimate reality is known through the soul's intuition of itself, and intuition of the soul's identity with the source and substance of all being.

[T. EARLY]

ATOMIC WARFARE, see NUCLEAR WEAPONS.

ATOMISM, a Greek philosophical system founded by *Leucippus of Miletus (fl. *c*.440 B.C.), elaborated by Democritus of Abdera (*c*.460–*c*.370 B.C.), continued with some modifications and popularized by Epicurus (341–270 B.C.) and the Latin poet *Lucretius (94–55 B.C.). Owing to the unsatisfactory character of the ancient sources, it is impossible in practice to distinguish sharply between the respective contributions of Leucippus and Democritus. Accordingly, the features of Atomist philosophy are treated in detail in the article LEUCIPPUS AND DEMOCRITUS. Atomism may be characterized as the logical development of the philosophy of *Empedocles (*c*.493–*c*.423 B.C.), but with the doctrine of the particles worked out in detail. It offered a formal comprehensive explanation of life in terms of mechanical materialism. In Democritus, Epicurus, and Lucretius, not only cosmology, but psychology, theology, epistemology, and ethics are described and interpreted in terms of the Atomist theory. As is noted in the article EPICURUS, Epicurean philosophy was primarily concerned with ethics, but an ethics founded on Atomist physics and its implications. The influence of Atomism in antiquity has often been exaggerated. It was far less influential, for example, than *Platonism or *Stoicism. With the development of physical science in modern times, mechanistic materialism not only was revived but has acquired a fundamental significance in modern thought. BIBLIOGRAPHY: Copleston 1:72–75; Guthrie 2:382–507; Ueberweg 1:104–111.

[M. R. P. MCGUIRE]

ATONEMENT, a word prominent in the theology of the Redemption. It is used in two senses: first, as practically synonymous with reconciliation. This is the primitive sense of the Anglo-Saxon word: the work of Jesus is the at-one-ment; He sets "at one" God and sinful humanity. Thus the word "atonement" translates the Greek *katallagē* in Rom 5.11 (KJV). The second sense of the word is synonymous with expiation, satisfaction, compensation: Jesus' Passion and death are atonement for mankind's rebellion. Thus it is taken in most satisfaction-oriented theologies of the Redemption. All Christian theology agrees on these positions in understanding the atonement: (1) all mankind existed in a state of estrangement from God; (2) the estrangement is the result of man's sin, which is an offense against God; (3) reconciliation or at-one-ment is accomplished through Jesus Christ. Through the centuries many approaches have been taken to explain how the work of Jesus accomplishes mankind's reconciliation. The meaning given to the word atonement will vary accordingly. Some have emphasized the offensiveness of man's sin. If reconciliation was to be effected, man must make up for his sin; he must placate an injured God, whose justice requires satisfaction. Atonement came to connote the idea of undergoing punishment for sin. Since the sinner was incapable of doing enough to atone for the infinite offense that sin is, God sent his Son to make worthy atonement through his death. This idea found early development in the writings of SS. Irenaeus, Ambrose, and Peter Damian. St. Anselm of Canterbury built into a system the idea of vicarious atonement in his *Cur Deus homo*. St. Thomas Aquinas carefully eliminated from this view any tendency to imagine Christ's atonement for sin as meaning that He became the object of God's wrath, innocently undergoing punishment in man's stead.

However, in the pessimism of the age of the Reformers, along with the concept of a purely juridic imputation of men's sins to Christ, there appeared the idea of an atonement for sin by a purely penal substitution. This distortion still affects some popular writing and preaching in all the Christian Churches. A defective theology of sin and the demands of God's justice and an excessive stress on man's cooperation in the work of atonement, have given rise to harsh rigorism like that of the Jansenists. Others see the work of Christ in the framework of the biblical concept of covenant. God is in Christ seeking out his faithless covenant partner to return him to at-one-ment (2 Cor 5.19). Jesus, the one mediator between God and men (1 Tim 2.5), summing up in himself the whole of mankind, is perfectly responsive to the overtures of his Father. He is perfectly one with man, sharing the consequences of man's sinful condition (esp. that of death) without any guilt of his own. His life and death express an unwavering love of and obedience to his Father. Through the mystery of death, his humanity passes over to a perfect at-one-ment with God that is proclaimed in God's raising him from the dead. Through this event, the whole of creation is reconciled in principle. Whether it be seen as laborious satisfaction for sin, or as perfect reconciliation with God, the atonement is purely God's gift to man. In Christ it has been fully accomplished. Catholic theology speaks of man's need for atonement. It invites men to respond to grace and to show their gratitude for God's work by renouncing whatever is the source of pride and sin, thus restoring the harmony of creation that has been disrupted by man's sin. Trends in contemporary Lutheran theology of justification show a remarkable agreement with this view of the need of man's cooperation. BIBLIOGRAPHY: K. F. Dougherty, NCE 1:1024–26; *EDB* 167–175; L. Richard, *Mystery of the Redemption* (tr. J. Horn, 1965); L. Sabourin, *Rédemption sacrificielle* (1961). M. Van Caster, *Redemption–A Personalist View* (tr. E. O'Gorman and O. Guedatarian, 1965).

[C. REGAN]

ATONEMENT, DAY OF, see DAY OF ATONEMENT.

ATONEMENT, LIMITED, see LIMITED ATONEMENT.

ATONEMENT, SOCIETY OF THE, a society of friars and sisters in the Franciscan tradition, founded by Fr. Paul James Francis (Lewis T. Wattson, 1843–1940) and Mother Lurana (Lurana Mary White, 1870–1935), at Graymoor, New York, in 1898. The order now operates internationally, its principal purposes being ecumenical, missionary, and charitable works. The headquarters remain at Graymoor, hence the order is frequently identified by that name.

Wattson and the Atonement Society, originally Episcopalian, were received into the RC Church in 1901. He did much to establish and advance the Chair of Unity Prayer Octave (Jan. 18–25) and was a cofounder of the Catholic Near East Welfare Association. The Society began *The Lamp* magazine in 1903 and the English edition of the ecumenical review *Unitas* in 1948.

In conjunction with the ecumenical orientation of Vatican

II, the society revamped its style of work for Christian unity, and established a new *Centro pro Unione* in Rome and the Ecumenical Institute at Graymoor. Both sponsor lectures, theological meetings, retreats, and prayer movements with special concern for unity. BIBLIOGRAPHY: T. Cranny, *Father Paul, Apostle of Unity* (2d ed., 1965); M. Celine, *Woman of Unity* (1956).

[L. B. GUILLOT]

ATREUS, TREASURY OF (Tomb of Agamemnon), in Mycenae. Dated 1250 B.C. on the basis of ceramics and figurines found there, Atreus is the most-developed and best-preserved beehive tomb, known also as *tholos* tomb, a form found earlier in Crete (*c*.2700–2000 B.C.). A passageway (*dromos*) 118 feet long by 20 feet wide of ashlar masonry leads to a lintel doorway formerly carrying a carved triangular decorative stone distinctive of Mycenae (e.g., Lion's Gate); within is a domed chamber 48 feet in diameter and 44 feet high, corbel-vaulted with a side room hewn out of rock. BIBLIOGRAPHY: G. E. Mylonas, *Ancient Mycenae* (1957).

[M. J. DALY]

ATRIUM, room of early Roman house, partly covered by a roof shedding rain into the *impluvium*. It became a forecourt in Christian basilicas (Sant' Ambrogio, Milan, and *St. Paul–outside–the–Walls).

[M. J. DALY]

ATTACHMENT, a term used by spiritual writers to indicate an unreasonable tie of affection or sympathy which a person can build up with respect to another person or thing.

[P. K. MEAGHER]

ATTAINGNANT, PIERRE (d. 1553), Parisian music publisher (1528–49), the first in that city to employ Pierre Haultin's newly developed movable type. Among his numerous publications are some 2,000 chansons, in addition to songs, motets, and Masses. He was probably the first printer to insist on the careful placing of words under their appropriate notes. Prior to the Haultin system, staff and notes were printed separately. A., who published all the leading composers of his era including *Arcadelt, Gombert, Jannequin, and Josquin des Pres, issued the first prints of polyphonic music in France (1528). BIBLIOGRAPHY: Reese MusR; V. Fedorov, MGG 1:766–770.

[J. J. WALSH]

ATTALEIATES, MICHAEL, see MICHAEL AT-TALEIATES.

ATTAVANTE DI GABRIELLO DI VANTE DI FRANCESCO DI BARTOLO (1452–1517), Italian miniature painter connected with Verrocchio, Ghirlandajo, and Pollaiuolo. A. produced illuminated books, religious and secular, for patrons throughout Europe (Bible for Duke Federico of Urbino, Vatican Library; Missal now in Lyons Cathedral). A.'s compositions were crowded, his colors glaring, but he was adept in classical ornament.

[M. J. DALY]

ATTENDANCE AT MASS, see MASS, ATTENDANCE AT.

ATTENDANCE AT OTHER THAN CATHOLIC SERVICES. The principles and norms for Roman Catholics' attendance at other than Catholic services enunciated in Vatican II's *Decree on Ecumenism* and in the *Directory,* published in 1967 by the Secretariat for Promoting Christian Unity for the application of the conciliar decisions, differ greatly from those in effect previous to the council. The 1917 Code (cf. CIC c. 1258) declared it illicit for Catholics to assist actively in the services of non-Catholics. Merely passive or material presence was allowed for reasons of civil courtesy or respect. The theological reasoning was that to share (*"communicatio in sacris"*) in what was false worship would be cooperation in an evil act and was forbidden by divine and natural law.

The conciliar *Decree on Ecumenism* (esp. nn 3–4, 8, 15, 22, and also the *Decree on Eastern Churches,* nn. 24–29) recognizes more positively the religious endowments and activities of other Churches as coming from Christ and leading back to him. The diversity of Orthodox, Anglican, Protestant, and other religious traditions is to be taken into account, along with such factors as local and cultural diversity, reciprocity, the possible dangers of indifferentism and proselytism, and the patience necessary for growth in ecumenical harmony, when drawing up norms for Catholics attending other services.

Taking into consideration this greater variety of kinds of services and of ways in which Catholics may worship with others and not compromise their faith, the *Directory* deals first with the possibilities of sharing in others' spiritual activities and resources (*"communicatio in spiritualibus"*). This includes joint prayer services and the common use of church buildings and objects, as well as the strictly liturgical and sacramental practices of a given Church or worshiping community. Catholic participation in services of prayer for unity or for common concerns, and in services of national or community interest, is generally encouraged, in accordance with norms laid down by the local ordinary (cf. *Directory,* nn. 32–37).

When there is a question of Catholics sharing in the liturgical worship, i.e., that celebrated according to the liturgical books or defined norms, or in the sacramental actions of a particular Church or worshiping community, this is to be considered *"communicatio in sacris"* in the strict sense and the principles of the *Decree on Ecumenism* (no. 8) are to be followed. The *Directory* interpreted this as allowing Catholics to attend occasionally the liturgical services of others. They may join in the prayers and hymns as long as such are in harmony with Catholic faith. Up to the present, practically speaking, communion has not been allowed. A

Catholic may be a witness in Christian baptismal services, where there is a godparent as a representative of that community. Catholics may be witnesses, as well as attend, other than Catholic wedding services. (see *Directory*, nn. 55–60) BIBLIOGRAPHY: J. Prah, NCE 1:1028–29, for a summary of pre-Vatican II norms; for the arguments behind changing the norms, see T. Ambrogi, ''Roman Catholics and Intercommunion: Changing Perspectives'' in *Experiments in Community: North American Liturgical Week* (1968) 147–158, and G. Baum, *''Communicatio in sacris''* in *Ecumenist* 2 (1964) 60–62, and '' 'Communicatio in Sacris' in the Decree on Ecumenism,'' *One in Christ* 3 (1967) 417–428.

[L. B. GUILLOT]

ATTENTION, a cognitive process involving the focussing of mind upon something. It is important in the use of the sacraments, as well as in prayer and other religious activities. It differs from intention insofar as the latter is concerned with one's purpose. It may be well to caution the reader that such ascriptions as ''internal'' and ''external'' are not made to pertain to the essence of attention, but rather to the fullness, or lack of it, in a given action. BIBLIOGRAPHY: C. I. Litzinger, NCE 1:1029–30.

[J. R. RIVELLO]

ATTICUS (A.D. *c*.150–200), Middle Platonist philosopher. He is much more orthodox as a Platonist than *Albinus. He attacks Aristotle for rejecting Divine Providence, for maintaining the eternity of the world, and for his denial or weak presentation of immortality. In emphasizing Divine Immanence and the all-sufficiency of virtue, he reflects Stoic influence. He, like his Middle Platonist contemporaries, interprets the Platonic ideas as the thoughts of God. He identifies the Demiurge of Plato's *Timaeus* under the form of the Good. Finally, like Plutarch, he holds that matter has an evil soul as its principle. BIBLIOGRAPHY: Copleston 1:455–456; P. Merlan, LexAW 393; CHGMP 73–78 (best treatment).

[M. R. P. McGUIRE]

ATTICUS OF CONSTANTINOPLE, ST. (d. 425) patriarch of Constantinople (406–425) who testified against St. John Chrysostom at the Synod of the Oak (403) and later persecuted his followers. The schism created by this policy was healed when he restored Chrysostom's name to the diptychs (421). His efforts to equalize the jurisdiction of the patriarch of Constantinople in the East with that of the bp. of Rome in the West met with some success when Theodosius II approved a law requiring the consent of the patriarch of Constantinople for episcopal consecration in the Hellespont, Bithynia, and Asia Minor. But the Emperor revoked a law giving A. jurisdiction over appeals from Illyricum when Pope Boniface I objected (421). The Councils of Ephesus (431) and Chalcedon (451) recognized him for his defense of orthodox teaching against the Pelagians and the Novatians. His extant writings include letters to St. Cyril of Alexandria

and Callipes of Nicaea, portions of a treatise against Nestorius, and homilies. He is listed with the saints of the Greek Church. BIBLIOGRAPHY: G. Bardy, *Catholicisme* 1:1002–03; M. T. Disdier, DHGE 5:161–166.

[F. H. BRIGHAM]

ATTIGNY, COUNCILS OF. A residence of the Carolingian kings situated at Attigny near Vouziers in the diocese of Rheims accounts for the number of councils held there in the 8th and 9th cent. None is of major importance, although two were scenes of important events: in 785 or 786 the forced baptism of Widukind; in 865 a council there decreed that Lothair II take back his repudiated wife. BIBLIOGRAPHY: A. Condit, NCE 1:1031.

[B. L. MARTHALER]

ATTILA (d. 453), last and most famous king of the Huns. On the death of an uncle, *c*.435, A. and his brother Bleda became kings of the Huns, perhaps governing different regions. About a decade later A. murdered his brother and began ruling alone. In the years up to 450 A. raided the Balkan provinces from his home base in Pannonia (in the Danube area of east-central Europe), forcing tribute from Emp. Theodosius II. When Marcian, successor to Theodosius in 450, stopped paying tribute and Valentinian III did likewise in the West, A. sought to compensate by conquering Gaul. In 451 at the Mauriac Plain near Troyes he was stopped by the Roman general Aetius. The following year A. led a raid into Italy. Pope Leo I led an embassy to negotiate with A., an encounter later celebrated in legend. A. returned home, but perhaps more because of food shortages, disease among his troops, and the strength of imperial armies than the papal appeal. After his death in 453 his kingdom was torn by feuds among his sons, and the Huns as a people were dispersed. In European Christian tradition, A. became notorious—perhaps unjustly—for ferocity and was called the *flagellum Dei* (scourge of God). BIBLIOGRAPHY: J. Otto Maenchen-Helfen, *World of the Huns* (1973).

[T. EARLY]

ATTILANUS, ST. (d. 916), disciple of St. *Froilán and his fellow worker in the organization of monastic life in NW Spain. He became bp. of Zamora *c*.900. Information concerning him derives from cartularies. When the see was restored *c*.1109 after destruction by the Moors *c*.986, his cult and a Cistercian vita became popular. It is claimed that his relics were miraculously discovered in 1260. He was included in the Roman Martyrology in 1583. BIBLIOGRAPHY: Butler 4:18–19; AS Oct. 5., E. P. Colbert, NCE 1:1031.

[E. P. COLBERT]

ATTO OF MILAN (d. 1085), card. and canonist who, though elected successor to Abp. Wido of Milan (1072) with the approval of Pope Gregory, never took possession of the see due to local disturbances and the opposition of King Henry IV. Named cardinal priest of the title of St. Mark, he wrote *Brevarium,* a summary of disciplinary canons of some importance in the early reform measures of Pope Gregory VII. BIBLIOGRAPHY: A. Fliche, DHGE 5:184–185. *ATTO, COLLECTION OF.

[F. H. BRIGHAM]

ATTO OF VERCELLI (*c*.885–961), bp., canonist. Born into a distinguished Lombard family, A. received a fine education which helped him to preserve the culture of the ancients in an area of mounting barbarism. Bishop of Vercelli in 924, he later served as grand chancellor to Hugh of Provence, King of Italy (d. 947), Lothair II (d. 950), and Berengar II (d. 966). A.'s literary work includes a voluminous *Commentary on the Epistles of Paul,* which proves his competence in exegesis; a *Libellus de pressuris ecclesiasticis* (*c*.940), a canonical treatise in three books, by which he endeavored to combat abuses arising from religious-lay relations; *Polypticum,* an abridgment of moral philosophy; *Canones statutaque Vercellensis ecclesiae,* in which he summarizes ecclesiastical legislation in his diocese; and numerous letters and pastoral sermons. BIBLIOGRAPHY: W. C. Korfmacher, NCE 1:1032 (good bibliog.)

[G. E. CONWAY]

ATTO, COLLECTION OF, the *Brevarium,* a compilation of disciplinary canons in 500 unnumbered chapters arranged by *Atto of Milan, cardinal priest of the title of St. Mark (1075). Based on the False Decretals of Dionysius Exiguus, the letters of Pope Gregory I, and including the lesser known canons from Pope Gelasius I, it summarizes the discipline of the Roman Church reflected in ancient papal decrees and the disciplinary canons of councils. BIBLIOGRAPHY: Hughes HC 2:287–289; DDC 1:1330–31.

[F. H. BRIGHAM]

ATTRIBUTES, in painting accessories with figures, establishing characteristics or identification. The attributes in portrayal of saints are associated with their lives (alabaster box of Magdalen) or the manner of their martyrdom (wheel of St. Catherine).

[M. J. DALY]

ATTRITION, sorrow for sin rising from a consciousness of its hatefulness as such or from a fear of its connected punishment. The contrast is with contrition, which rises rather from a benevolent love of God that causes the penitent to regret his sins because they are evidences of a rupture with a loving God. Such sorrow for sin is generally called perfect contrition whereas attrition is called imperfect contrition. Contrition was always considered central in the forgiveness of sin. The early Fathers of the Church were aware that sorrow for sin may rise from different motives and be experienced in different degrees. They emphasized that only reconciliation with God through repentance is the certain and complete sign of forgiveness. Further, they noted that a person's dispositions influenced justification from sin. It was only in the 12th cent., however, that ecclesiastical writers began to distinguish between contrition and attrition, and to incorporate the distinction into Catholic theology. Some considered attrition a kind of incomplete contrition which became contrition through God's grace. For St. Thomas, in the 13th cent, attrition and contrition differ as to the intensity of sorrow and the presence of grace; attrition is a genuine form of repentance, but imperfect, a disposition not yet ready for grace. While attrition does not "become" contrition, one who has attrition achieves contrition by means of the sacrament of penance. The Council of Trent noted that attrition which excludes the intention of sinning again disposes the sinner to receive God's grace in the sacrament of penance (D 1678). There followed tedious and what may be considered pointless disputes between the "contritionists" and the "attritionists" on the sinner's dispositions when he turns toward God. Today, most theologians grant that there must be some initial degree of love in attrition. The distinction between it and contrition should not be magnified to make the sacrament an external substitute for genuine conversion, metanoia. Verification in experience of the acceptance by divine grace is not required. The ordinary and reliable sign of contrition and forgiveness is the sacrament itself. BIBLIOGRAPHY: P. Anciaux, *Sacrament of Penance* (1962) 88–111, 145–62; J. M. T. Barton, *Penance and Absolution* (1961) 54–62.

[P. F. MULHERN]

ATTWATER, DONALD (1892–1977), English lay scholar, hagiographer, lexicographer, translator, and authority on ancient Churches of the East. Born of Puritan stock in Kent, A. was educated at Alderham School, from which he went on to the study of law. He was received into the RC Church in 1911, and from 1920 on he gave himself to scholarly work, specializing in works of introduction and reference. Among his principal works are *Christian Churches of the East* (2 v., 1948 and 1961); *Catholic Dictionary* (first published as *Catholic Encyclopaedic Dictionary,* 3d ed., 1961); *St. John Chrysostom* (1959); *Cell of Good Living* (a biography of Eric Gill) which appeared in 1968. He translated the early works of N. A. Berdyaev from the French, and Y. Congar's *Laity* and contributor to *Worship* (formerly called *Orate Fratres*) from its first number until 1966. He collaborated with Herbert Thurston in the revision, scholarly updating, and supplement of Butler's *Lives of the Saints* (v. 7–12 in Butler; v. 3–4 in the Thurston-Attwater edition). This work was completed by A. in 1956, 17 years after the death of Thurston; it provided English-speaking Catholics with the most complete collection of lives of the saints available in their own language. A. was one of the earliest advocates of liturgy in the vernacular and an enthusiastic ecumenist years before the term came into use.

[J. C. WILLKE]

ATWATER, WILLIAM (1440–1521), English ecclesiastic. At Oxford Univ. he probably tutored Wolsey, who seems to have helped him accumulate benefices and offices for the rest of his life. Several times vice-chancellor of Oxford, he succeeded Wolsey as bp. of Lincoln in 1514. BIBLIOGRAPHY: S. Lee, DNB 1:713.

[E. P. COLBERT]

AUBARÈDE, JEAN MICHEL D'ASTORG D' (1639–92), French cleric. On the death of Bp. Caulet of Pamiers in 1680, Aubarède as vicar general of the cathedral chapter renewed episcopal laws against the regalism of Louis XIV, who kept Aubarède imprisoned in Normandy for the rest of his life.

[E. P. COLBERT]

AUBENAS, MARTYRS OF, two Jesuits, James Salès and William Saultemouch, a priest and a lay brother (both b. 1556) who were brutally slain by Huguenot raiders at Aubenas in the French diocese of Viviers on February 7, 1593 and were beatified (1926) as "Martyrs of the Eucharist." In 1592 Fr. Salès had been invited by the mayor of Aubenas to come there to preach the series of sermons during Advent. As a result of his successful preaching, he was asked to stay on until Easter. During this period there were open discussions with Calvinist ministers. Unexpectedly, in early February, Huguenot raiders burst in: the Jesuits rushed to the chapel and consumed the eucharistic hosts before they were forcibly dragged away and soon killed. BIBLIOGRAPHY: F. De S. Boran, NCE 1:1034.

[M. G. SCHUMACHER]

AUBERT OF AVRANCHES, ST. (d. 725), bp. of Avranches. Tradition says that A. was told in a dream to erect a church on Mont Tombe and dedicate it to St. Michael the Archangel, which the bp. undertook to do. The church was dedicated in 709 and entrusted to a chapter of canons. These were later replaced by Benedictines. The body of A. was transported to Mont Tombe c.1009. The French Revolution dispersed the bones; only the head is preserved at Saint-Gervais in Avranches. BIBLIOGRAPHY: E. Dupont, DHGE 5:222; G. J. Donnelly, NCE 1:1034.

[M. C. BRADLEY]

AUBIGNÉ, JEAN HENRI MERLE D' (1794–1872), Protestant ecclesiastical historian. A., the son of French émigrés in Geneva, was educated and ordained in Berlin; he served as pastor of the French Protestant church in Hamburg (1819), pastor and court preacher in Brussels (1823), and president of the consistory of French and German Protestants. Upon returning to Geneva (1830), he wrote, taught church history, and worked toward an all-Protestant union. To insure a ministry Calvinist in principle but evangelical and mission-minded, he founded and was president of the College of Geneva. He wrote an important five-volume history of the Reformation in the 16th cent., and eight volumes on the Reformation at the time of Calvin. BIBLIOGRAPHY: F. De S. Boran, NCE 1:1034.

[H. JACK]

AUBIGNÉ, THÉODORE AGRIPPA D' (1552–1630), French Huguenot writer and soldier. While still a child, upon seeing the Protestant victims of the aborted "conspiracy of Amboise" (1560), he swore to his father to avenge the Huguenot cause. Receiving a Protestant education, he fled from his guardian's house (1568) to join the Huguenot armies in the French Wars of Religion and became companion to Henry of Navarre (the future Henry IV). After Henry's abjuration of Protestantism, A. withdrew to his estates, opposed the regency of Marie de' Medici, took up arms again under Louis XIII, and sought refuge in Geneva where he died. His son Constant, who abjured Protestantism during his father's last years, was the father of Françoise d'Aubigné, the future Madame de Maintenon, who was to play a role in the Revocation of the Edict of Nantes (1685). A.'s greatest work is his religious epic poem, *Les Tragiques* (pub. 1616), inspired by the St. Bartholomew's day massacre (1572) and by a personal "vision," and begun while he was recovering from battle wounds received at Casteljaloux (1577). It is a glorification of God avenging the persecuted Protestants and contains many powerful, poetic passages of apocalyptic dimension despite its irregular quality and extreme sectarian bias. His other works include *La Confession catholique du sieur de Sancy* (1660), against the Protestants who, emulating Henry IV, abjured; *Les Aventures du baron de Faeneste* (1617), against court frivolities; *L'Histoire universelle 1550–1601* (1616–1626), containing valuable accounts of the Protestant forces; *Le Printemps* (pub. 1874), a collection of A.'s youthful love poetry. BIBLIOGRAPHY: J. Galzy. *Agrippa d'Aubigné* (1965); A. Garnier, *Agrippa d'Aubigné et le parti protestant*, (3 v., 1928).

[R. N. NICOLICH]

AUBIN, ST., see ALBINUS OF ANGERS, ST.

AUBRAC, ORDER OF, religious community founded in the 12th cent. by Viscount of Flanders, Adalard, at Aubrac, to aid travelers. The Rule of St. Augustine given to the community by the bp. of Rodez was adapted to the circumstances of their works and was confirmed by Pope Alexander III. The membership consisted of five groups: priests, knights, lay brothers, oblates, and helpful women. Some dependent hospitals were established by Aubrac. By the end of the 17th cent. the hospitalers were in full decadence and were replaced by the Reformed Canons of Chancelade. Aubrac was suppressed by the French Revolution. BIBLIOGRAPHY: R. Chalumeau, *Catholicisme* 1:1013–14; J. Cambell, NCE 1:1035.

[M. C. BRADLEY]

AUBRY, PIERRE (1874–1910), French musicologist and author of numerous pioneering studies of medieval music. His most significant contributions were editions of important 13th-cent. musical sources and studies of the rhythm of late medieval music, esp. secular monody. BIBLIOGRAPHY: H. Besseler, MGG 1:778–780.

[A. DOHERTY]

AUBURN AFFIRMATION (1924), a document whose full title is *An Affirmation Designed to Safeguard the Unity and Liberty of the Presbyterian Church in the United States of America*. Signed by almost 1,300 Presbyterian ministers, the document, drafted primarily by church leaders of the Synod of New York, protested loyalty to evangelical Christianity and adherence to the *Westminster Confession during the height of the fundamentalist-modernist controversy. The *Affirmation* held, however, that the constitutional system of the Presbyterian Church allowed clergymen to hold differing theories concerning the interpretation of Christian faith and that the General Assembly of the denomination acted unconstitutionally in 1910 in defining "essential and necessary" doctrines, thus amending the *doctrinal standards without the concurrence of two-thirds of the presbyteries. The *Affirmation* was sent to every minister in the denomination and aroused great interest. It indicated that many men who were not fundamentalists were evangelical believers. A special commission appointed in 1925 to study the causes of unrest in the Church confirmed the constitutional contention of the Affirmationists about the organization of the denomination. With the adoption of the commission's report, the General Assembly attempted to preserve liberty of its members and unity of the denomination amid the theological ferment of the period. BIBLIOGRAPHY: L. A. Loetscher, *Broadening Church* (1954).

[J. H. SMYLIE]

AUBUSSON, PIERRE D' (1423–1503), cardinal and grand master of the Order of St. John of Jerusalem. Under his leadership the knights defeated an attempt by the Turks to conquer Rhodes (1480). Though he was an effective diplomat and able soldier, A.'s reputation has been somewhat clouded by his willingness to accept subsidies from the Turkish Sultan to neutralize Jem, a Turkish claimant to the throne who had sought refuge on Rhodes, as well as by his efforts to eliminate Judaism on Rhodes by expelling all adult Jews and forcibly baptizing their children. The letters and documents of A. can be found in *Codice diplomatico del sacro militare ordine Gerosolimitano* (v. 2, ed. S. Paoli, 1737). BIBLIOGRAPHY: V. L. Bullough, NCE 1:1035–36.

[V. BULLOUGH]

AUCTOR OF METZ, ST. (fl. *c*.451), bp., contemporary of Attila the Hun. There is extant a life of Auctor written by *Paul the Deacon. Auctor of Trier is an unhistorical personage whose vita probably derives from that of Auctor of Metz. BIBLIOGRAPHY: AS Aug. 2:536–538 (Auctor of Metz); AS Aug 4:37–53 (Auctor of Trier); J. Clauss, *Die Heiligen des Elsass* (1935) 41, 194.

[W. A. JURGENS]

AUCTOREM FIDEI, a bull of Pius VI (Aug. 28, 1794) condemning the acts of the diocesan Synod of *Pistoia (1786), after thorough study by a papal commission. Impelled by Scipione de' Ricci, Bp. of Pistoia-Prato, the syn-od had enacted Gallican-Jansenist reforms subsequently rejected by the assembled bishops of Tuscany, but its decrees were widely disseminated. *Auctorem fidei* censures verbatim, each in a carefully specified sense and with an individual theological note, 85 propositions on the Church, the hierarchy, grace, sacraments, worship, and religious orders (see D 2600–2700). Suppressed in several countries, the bull nevertheless ultimately disabled *Jansenism and *Gallicanism. BIBLIOGRAPHY: J. Carreyre, DTC 12.2:2202–30; Pastor 39:127–156.

[W. DAVISH]

AUDACITY, see BOLDNESS.

AUDENARDE, old Belgian town on the Scheldt River in E Flanders, a prosperous textile and tapestry-making center in the late MA and the Renaissance. The town hall incorporates the old cloth hall and a museum houses paintings by Jacob van Ruisdael and Jan Breughel the Elder. Of interest are the Béguinage, royal fountain (1676), and episcopal palace.

[M. J. DALY]

AUDENTIUS (d. *c*.393), Spanish bp. (of Toledo, according to Ildefonsus), whom Gennadius credits with a treatise (not extant) against "Manichaeans, Sabellians, Arians, and Photinians, now called Bonosians"; probably the heretics were Priscillianists, a term Gennadius does not use. A senator named Audentius (d. 435 in Milan), venerated as a confessor, is buried in Novara. A bp. of Die in France, also called Audentius, known from 439, subscribed to a petition to Pope Leo I in 450 to restore the metropolitanate of Arles. BIBLIOGRAPHY: F. Baix and A. Lambert, DHGE 5:301–303.

[E. P. COLBERT]

AUDIANS, rigorist sect of the 4th cent. founded by Audius, a Mesopotamian, reacting against the worldliness of the clergy. He officially broke with the Church by rejecting the decree of the Council of *Nicaea on Easter. Illegally consecrated bishop, Audius was exiled to Scythia where he engaged in missionary activities among the Goths. After his death the sect dwindled rapidly, although there were still evidences of it in the next cent. If it began as a schism, it adopted certain heretical tenets tinged with Gnosticism. BIBLIOGRAPHY: E. Peterson, EncCatt 2:389–390; H. Puech, RGG 1:688.

[R. B. ENO]

AUDIENCE, PAPAL, in general, any reception given by the pope to one person or to a group of people. Non-Catholics who wish to participate are welcomed equally with Catholics provided that they are willing to observe Catholic courtesies.

[S. A. HEENEY]

AUDIENTES also *auditores*, the hearers, groups of catechumens and penitents in the early Church who were so named because they were allowed to remain for the service of the word until the conclusion of the homily when the deacon ordered their dismissal.

[F. H. BRIGHAM]

AUDIO-VISUAL MEDIA, the artificial means for sharing aesthetic experience or transmitting information to eye and ear. They are being used increasingly by parishes for religious instruction and in liturgy, esp. in homilies. They are also an important tool of missionaries of mobile units in India and elsewhere in Asia, in the Philippines, and in several countries of Africa and Latin America.

AUDITOR, an official who hears and draws up a record of an ecclesiastical cause and reports to his superior. He may not deliver judgment without special authorization. An auditor of the Rota is one of the college of judges of that body. An auditor of the pope has charge of the department dealing with the appointment of bishops.

[S. A. HEENEY]

AUDRAN, CLAUDE III (1658–1734), French painter who transformed the style of Louis XIV into Regency *rocaille* and was the teacher of Watteau (his assistant 1707–09). Gobelin tapestries in A.'s designs are most beautiful. His drawings are in the Louvre and Cooper Union Museum, N. Y. BIBLIOGRAPHY: S. F. Kimball, *Creation of the Rococo* (1943).

[M. J. DALY]

AUERSPERG, FRANZ JOSEPH (1734–95), Austrian ecclesiastic. He became bp. of Lavant (1763), Gurk (1772), and Passau (1783). During most of his years as bp., Joseph II was Emperor of Austria and A. was compliant with the Emperor's interference in ecclesiastical matters. Upon his appointment to Passau, the Emperor divided and reorganized the diocese without papal consent. Still he was appointed cardinal in 1789. BIBLIOGRAPHY: J. Oswald, LTK 1:1027; Pastor 29:269–270.

AUFKLÄRUNG, see ENLIGHTENMENT.

AUGER, EDMOND (1530–91), Jesuit preacher. Ignatius himself received A. into the Jesuits and was his teacher in Rome in 1558. A. taught Latin in Italy until 1559, when he began a career of great success in preaching and catechizing against Calvinists in S France. He attracted the notice of Charles IX and Catherine de Medicis in 1563 and in 1564 became the first Jesuit provincial of Aquitaine. He was the close adviser and confessor of Henry III (1574–87), after having been chaplain of his army from 1568. His enmity with the Catholic League made him leave France after Henry's assassination in 1589. Most important of his writings are his long (1563) and his short (1568) French catechisms, which were translated into Latin. His apostolic life included care of the sick and preaching in hospitals. BIBLIOGRAPHY: E.

Lamalle, EncCatt 2:393; J. Dutilleul, DHGE 5:378–383.

[E. P. COLBERT]

AUGIER, ÉMILE (1820–89), French realistic dramatist. An exponent of utilitarian theater, he employed Eugène Scribe's techniques of the well-made play to create the modern comedy of manners, in which he flayed romantic idealism and defended bourgeois mores and values. His political plays, like *Les Effrontés* (1861) and *Lions et renards* (1869), expressed the liberal bourgeoisie's anticlericalism, and in *Le Fils de Giboyer* (1862) he attacked the Ultramontane party's intervention on the Roman Question and created the journalist Déodat as a caricature of Louis Veuillot. His social comedies include *Le Gendre de M. Poirier* (1854), *Le Mariage d'Olympe* (1855), and *Madame Caverlet* (1876). BIBLIOGRAPHY: H. Gaillard, *Emile Augier et la comédie sociale* (1910).

[G. E. GINGRAS]

AUGOUARD, PROSPER (1852–1921), missionary, called sometimes the Bishop of the Cannibals. After a brief service in the Papal Zouaves (1870), A. joined the Holy Ghost Fathers, was sent to Gabun, Africa (1876), then to the Congo (1880), where he was named vicar apostolic (1890). During the years 1883–1920 he founded 11 mission posts, explored the Congo River, mapped the area, and penetrated the region of the Baroumbis and Bandjos. He cooperated in opening Africa to French civilization and colonization. BIBLIOGRAPHY: U. Milliez, *Catholicisme* 1:1024.

AUGSBURG, German town associated with several events of the Reformation and the birthplace of the Holbeins. Located on the Lech River in Bavaria, it was founded in 15 B.C. under Augustus and named Augusta Vindelicorum. In the 6th cent. Augsburg became an episcopal see, and in 1276 an imperial city, which later formed part of the Swabian League. It reached a peak in the 15th and 16th cent. when commercial eminence came to the Fuggers, a Catholic family whose loans proved vital to Catholic forces in the Reformation era.

In 1518 Luther appeared in Augsburg before the papal legate, Cajetan, but they were unable to resolve the dispute over indulgences. A 1527 meeting of Anabaptists in Augsburg came to be called the Martyrs Synod because it sent evangelists out to many places and most of them suffered martyrdom. In 1530 Lutheran princes stated their position to Emperor Charles V at the Diet of Augsburg in what is known as the *Augsburg Confession. It has since been the principal confession of Lutheranism. A Protestant statement with Zwinglian overtones, the Tetrapolitan Confession, was presented to the Diet on behalf of four S German cities. In 1548 the Diet approved the Augsburg Interim, an effort by Charles to secure a truce between Catholics and Protestants. It was rejected by Protestants in 1552.

Augsburg is noted for its thermae, temples, and statuary from Roman times; a cathedral from the Ottonian period

(10th-11th cent.), boasting bronze doors of elegant simplicity, with early German stained glass (1130–40) and a nave and choir from the 14th and 15th centuries. The city is also famous for its stately monuments along Maximillianstrasse, ecclesiastical building, and exquisite gold and silverwork until the end of the 18th century. Most of the great German painters and sculptors worked for Augsburg patrons. *AUGSBURG, RELIGIOUS PEACE OF.

[T. EARLY]

AUGSBURG, RELIGIOUS PEACE OF, an agreement aimed at "a continual, firm, unconditional peace" between Lutherans and Catholics reached by the Emperor Ferdinand I and the German electors at Augsburg, Sept. 25, 1555. The treaty marked the establishment of *territorialism in the sanctioning of the principle *cuius regio, eius religio. It was a victory for Lutheranism to the extent that Lutheran Churches were granted civil recognition equal to that of the Roman Church, and the right to all properties taken over before the Treaty of Passau (1552). For Catholicism it was at least acceptable because it ensured protection in the states of Catholic princes and provided against further losses of property in sees whose bishops might become Protestants. The agreement regulated the religious situation until the Peace of Westphalia (1648) concluding the Thirty Years' War, a conflict intensified by the concession of tolerance by the Peace of Augsburg to Lutherans alone among Protestants. BIBLIOGRAPHY: Léonard HistProt 1:285–286.

[J. DAMBORIENA]

AUGSBURG CONFESSION (*Confessio Augustana*), the chief particular Lutheran *confession of faith, presented to the imperial Diet held at Augsburg on June 25, 1530, and published in 1531. The principal issue before the Diet was the continuing threat of the Turks, but the religious questions that divided Roman Catholics and Protestants were also urgent. The spokesmen for the Lutheran cause, under the leadership of the elector of Saxony, wanted to set forth a defense of the Reformation as they had been carrying it out in their lands. To this end they commissioned Philipp Melanchthon (Martin Luther was under the ban of the Empire and could not appear at Augsburg) to draw up a statement of Lutheran doctrine—both the doctrines that Lutherans shared with Roman Catholics and those distinctively Lutheran. Basing his composition on earlier formulations of Lutheran teaching (most notably the so-called *Schwabach Articles and *Torgau Articles) and employing J. *Jonas, G. *Spalatin, and J. *Agricola as consultants, Melanchthon summarized the principal articles of Luther's positive position as well as the "abuses which have been corrected." Luther gave his approval to the document.

The Augsburg Confession consists of 28 articles. The First Part (1-21) is on the chief articles of faith; on God, original sin, and the person of Christ; Articles 1–3 affirm fidelity to the orthodox Catholic tradition. Article 4 states the Lutheran doctrine of justification, which is followed by articles on the office of the ministry; (5) and "the new obedience"; (6). Articles 7–15 deal with the doctrine of the Church and of the sacraments, including the matter of ecclesiastical order and rites. Article 16 treats of civil government. The remaining articles of the First Part take up certain controverted questions: the return of Christ as judge (17); free will (18); the cause of sin (19); the relation of faith and good works (20); and the cult of saints (21). The "corrected abuses" enumerated in the Second Part (22–28) include reception of both kinds in the Eucharist, the marriage of priests, the Mass, confession, the distinction of foods, monastic vows, and the power of bishops.

Despite the sharpness of some of its polemics, the Augsburg Confession strove wherever possible to stress the common ground with Roman Catholicism and to state its own position irenically. It was subscribed by seven German princes and two free cities and was intended as a confession of the entire Lutheran community, not just of its theologians. The accepted text of the confession is the so-called *Invariata, prepared for the *Book of Concord (1580). The other confessions in the Book of Concord are taken by Lutherans to be explanations of the Augsburg Confession, just as it in turn claims to be an explanation of the Catholic creeds. BIBLIOGRAPHY: *Book of Concord: The Confessions of the Evangelical Lutheran Church* (ed. T. G. Tappert, 1959); E. Schlink, *Theology of the Lutheran Confessions* (tr. P. F. Koehneke and H. J. A. Bowman, 1961). *APOLOGY OF THE AUGSBURG CONFESSION; *VARIATA.

[J. PELIKAN]

AUGSBURG CONFESSION, APOLOGY OF THE, see APOLOGY OF THE AUGSBURG CONFESSION.

AUGSBURG INTERIM, see INTERIMS.

AUGURY, the Roman art of discerning the will of the gods with respect to a certain course of action through the interpretation of the *auguria,* or "signs." These could be of a casual nature (*oblativa*), or they could be deliberately sought (*impetrativa*). They consisted of such diverse things as the creaking of a chair, the spilling of salt, the movement of animals, the sound of thunder, or the flash of lightning. The most significant, however, were those given by birds, either in their cry, their course of flight, or in their manner of eating. To assist the magistrates in taking the auspices there was an official college of augurs at Rome. Originally 3 in number, this was increased to 16 under Caesar. The taking of the auspices was necessary before every important public action. Though a magistrate was not bound to follow the advice given by the augurs, failure to do so could have dire political consequences if he proved unsuccessful in his endeavors. BIBLIOGRAPHY: G. Wissowa, *Religion und Kultus der Römer* (1912²) 523–534.

[M. J. COSTELLOE]

AUGUSTANA EVANGELICAL LUTHERAN CHURCH (AELC), one of the four church bodies that merged in 1962 to form the *Lutheran Church in America. It was founded in Wisconsin in 1860 by 36 Swedish and 13 Norwegian congregations. The title, which refers to the unaltered *Augsburg Confession (*Confessio Augustana*) indicates the confessional conservatism to which the Church was committed. In 1870 the Norwegians withdrew to form a synod of their own. At the time of the merger in 1962, AELC membership numbered more than 500,000. BIBLIOGRAPHY: G. E. Arden, EncLuthCh 2:1368–73.

[T. C. O'BRIEN]

AUGUSTINE, ST. (354–430), bp. of Hippo, Father of the Church, the single most influential theologian in the history of the Church in the West.

Life. Born of a Christian mother, Monica, and a pagan father, Patricius, at Tagaste in the African province of Numidia, A., while pursuing rhetorical studies in Carthage (371–374), underwent an intellectual and moral crisis. A reading of Cicero's *Hortensius* awakened in him a burning desire for wisdom, which led him on a long and tortuous search for truth. He first turned to the Scriptures but was quickly repelled by the inelegance of their style and language. He next joined the Manichaean sect, to which he was powerfully attracted both by its professed rationalism and its facile dualistic solution to the problem of evil, remaining in it in the lower rank of "hearer" *(auditor)* for nearly 9 years. About this same time he formed a concubinary relationship from which was born a son, Adeodatus, who later figured as interlocutor in A.'s short dialogue, *The Teacher*. While professor of rhetoric in Carthage (376–383), he had serious doubts on basic Manichaean teachings which led to alienation from the sect that culminated in his disappointing encounter with Faustus, the most celebrated representative of the sect at that time. A new and more dangerous intellectual crisis arose during Augustine's brief sojourn in Rome (383–384) when, discouraged by his failure to discover truth, he began to adhere somewhat to the philosophy of the New Academy, which denied the possibility of human certitude. He left for Milan late in 384, having successfully competed for the municipal chair of rhetoric in that city, where he was soon joined by Monica. Two influences there gradually prepared the way for his return to the Catholic faith. First, the Sunday preaching of Ambrose, to which he was attracted by professional curiosity, introduced him to an allegorical interpretation of the Scriptures and to an exposition of Catholic teaching that belied many of the doctrines advanced by the Manichaeans. Second, his first acquaintance with the spiritualistic philosophy of neoplatonism, represented by Plotinus and Porphyry, helped to free his mind from the residue of Manichaean materialism and from the skepticism of the New Academy. Augustine's intellectual conversion to the Catholic faith was largely inspired by his abiding belief in a Divine Providence that could not fail to provide a sure way of salvation and by the growing conviction that the unique authority and prestige enjoyed by the Church pointed to it as a divinely appointed instrument to achieve this purpose. His moral and final conversion, which was delayed some time by the burden of sensuality and worldly ambition, reached its dramatic climax in the summer of 386; in response to a mysterious voice, he read a passage from St. Paul (Rom 13.13–14), which led to his decision to dedicate himself completely to the love and service of God (see *Conf.* 8.12.30).

In order to prepare for baptism, A. withdrew to the villa Cassiciacum near Milan (probably the present-day Cassago in Brianza). His first Christian writings, composed in dialogue form, belong to this period and represent his first efforts to construct a Christian philosophy, namely, a kind of rational inquiry inspired and guided by revealed truth. Early the following year (387) he was enrolled as a candidate for baptism, and during the Easter Vigil (April 24–25) he received the sacrament from the hands of Ambrose, together with his friend Alypius and Adeodatus. While awaiting embarkation to Africa at the Roman port of Ostia, Monica was seized with a fatal illness. The ecstatic experience shared by mother and son during Monica's last days is described by A. in his *Confessions* (9.10–11). After Monica's death he spent a year in Rome, making an extensive study of the numerous monastic communities. Soon after his return to Tagaste in Africa he set up his first monastery, a kind of lay institute devoted to study, prayer, and above all to the strict practice of the common life. During a visit to the basilica in Hippo in 391, where the aged Bp. Valerius was pleading for the services of a priest, A. was presented by the people for ordination, which he accepted, though reluctantly, as a manifestation of God's will. At A.'s request, Valerius provided a portion of the church property for a monastery, where he continued to live in community. The new foundation, and later the episcopal residence, became a center of ecclesiastical training that provided numerous clergy for the Church in N Africa, including some 10 bishops. In 396 A. was consecrated auxiliary bp. to Valerius, whom he succeeded within the year as bp. of Hippo.

A.'s remaining 34 years were filled with activity, both pastoral and polemical. Like other bps. of that day, he spent considerable time hearing and adjudicating cases of litigation, civil and religious. Despite delicate health, he was an indefatigable preacher, not only in Hippo but also in Carthage and other cities to which he was frequently invited. Even as a priest he played a conspicuous role in councils and synods of the African Church. At the invitation of bps. assembled in plenary council in 393, he pronounced a discourse on the Creed, later published under the title *Faith and the Creed*. He figured prominently as bp. at the councils held at Carthage between 397 and 419, and at the Council of Milevis in 416. As a pioneer of monasticism in Africa and author of a religious rule still widely used by male and female institutes, he has had a lasting influence upon the history of spirituality in the West. A.'s polemical efforts, which occupied most of his ecclesiastical career, were the occasion for a vast theological literature that has decisively affected the thought and life of the Church down to the present time. Of the church Fathers and Doctors, he is the one most frequently cited in the documents of Vatican Council II; in the important *Dogmatic Constitution on the Church* he figures no fewer than 25 times.

A. was successively engaged in three main controversies, which roughly cover the following periods: Manichaeism (388–405). Donatism (394–411), and Pelagianism (412–430). During his second sojourn in Rome as a layman, A. undertook a refutation of Manichaeism in a work entitled *The Catholic and Manichaean Ways of Life*. In Africa he successfully engaged in public debate with the foremost Manichaean spokesmen. His reply to one of them, *Contra Secundinum,* A. himself regarded as the most effective of his anti-Manichaean treatises. It was mainly through A.'s polemical efforts and influence that the Donatist schism, which had seriously threatened the Church in Africa for nearly a century, was finally terminated. Although he at first urged and pursued a policy of leniency and persuasion, later, because of increasing atrocities perpetrated by the Donatists, he invoked the repressive measures enacted against the schismatics by the imperial laws. In the course of this polemic he had occasion to articulate important points of doctrine on the nature of the Church and on the objective efficacy of the sacraments against tenets that had given rise to the Donatist schism. Toward the end of this controversy A. was confronted with a "new heresy" propagated by the "enemies of God's grace." In essence, Pelagianism was a kind of Christian Stoicism that exaggerated human freedom and moral self-sufficiency while denying original sin and any strict need for grace. By A.'s personal influence and numerous writings in defense of grace, Pelagianism was condemned by three African councils whose action was confirmed by Pope Zosimus in 418. The error reappeared during Augustine's last years in a form later known as Semi-Pelagianism. In two complementary works, *The Gift of Perseverance* and *The Predestination of the Saints,* he defended the gratuitousness of grace with special reference to the "beginning of faith" *(initium fidei)* and to final perseverance.

Works and Teachings. Augustine's writings have, with few exceptions , been preserved in their entirety. They include more than 100 books, in addition to some 240 letters and more than 500 sermons. His books, which include such masterpieces as the *Confessions, The Trinity,* and *The City of God,* cover a wide range of topics, philosophic, apologetic, moral, and exegetical. His dogmatic works comprise in large part the numerous polemical treatises directed against Manichaeism, Donatism, and Pelagianism. The doctrinal synthesis achieved by A. is neither a theological nor philosophical system, strictly speaking. It is more properly described as a Christian wisdom whose content and spirit have variously exercised a profound influence upon the intellectual history of the West for more than 1,500 years. In its essence, authentic Augustinianism aims at a progressive comprehension of

revealed truth by reason illuminated by faith and with the resources of philosophic principles and method at its disposal *(fides quaerens intellectum).* Faith and reason thus cooperate as two distinct but inseparable sources of knowledge. The following doctrines are characteristic of this Augustinian dialectic:

The Primacy of Faith. The priority of faith is emphatically affirmed even in A.'s earliest works, where the respective roles of faith and reason are assessed with respect to the pursuit of truth (see *C. Acad.* 3.20.48; *De Ord.* 1.5.16). For A., the final and supreme authority is Christ, whereas for reason, his express preference is the philosophy of Platonism insofar as this is not at variance with revealed truth. From the primacy accorded to faith God becomes at once the principal source of knowledge and the central object of human inquiry. Accordingly, God is comprehensively viewed as the cause of being, the source of truth, and the ultimate norm of moral life (see *De Civ. Dei* 8.4).

God and the Soul. The theocentric character of Augustinian speculation readily explains his concentration on the soul and why the soul and God comprise the two principal objects of human inquiry (see *Solil.* 1.15.27). Since the soul's spiritual nature brings it into closer proximity with God, its progress in knowing God is largely determined and measured by its advance in self-knowledge. This so-called "metaphysics of internal experience" imparts to Augustinianism its distinctive mark of "interiority," which in turn makes possible A.'s exploration of the triune God through the analogous manifestations that appear within the life and activities of the soul. In contrast to the Greek theologians who sought to discover "vestiges" of the Trinity in physical nature, A. turns rather to the divine image of the soul in his effort to unfold in human language the inscrutable mystery of God's inner life. The soul as "image" is not only the most authentic reflection of the triune God but is also the cornerstone of A.'s theology of the spiritual life. Actually, religious perfection consists essentially in the progressive restoration of the soul's image, defiled by sin, to its true and proper condition. The method of interiority is further reflected in A.'s epistemology, where the basic certitudes spring from the indisputable evidence of the thinking subject and from changeless and necessary truths within the soul. The quest for certitude is, in effect, the search for God, since to discover an order of changeless truth transcending the mind itself is to perceive an absolutely unchanging reality reducible to God himself.

Augustinian Illumination. Although it manifests biblical and neoplatonic influences. A.'s explanation of the origin of intellectual knowledge cannot, at least in its final and definitive expression, be reduced to any of the classical epistemologies of Greek philosophy. For A., the source of such knowledge must be sought within the soul, whose spiritual nature brings it into a habitual and connatural relationship with the higher world of intelligible reality illumined by the participated light of God's uncreated light. And since the perception of truth is essentially realized by the inner activity of the mind, the senses can do no more than prompt (*admonere*) the soul to turn its attention to the truth within. As a logical corollary to this epistemological doctrine. A. draws the significant pedagogical conclusion that learning is essentially autodidactic. Teachers exercise a role analogous to that played by the senses since they merely direct the pupil to discover for himself the truth that is present within.

Seminal Reasons. A.'s notion of seminal reasons, adopted in part from Platonic and Stoic sources, was devised in an attempt to harmonize the revealed doctrine of the uniqueness of God's creative act with the successive appearance of new forms of life. His theory, sometimes referred to as "virtual creation," reveals a tendency already observed in his explanation of intellectual knowledge to exalt divine causality by minimizing the dynamic quality of secondary causes operating in nature. According to A.'s view, while all things were created at once, some came into being in their actual state while the rest were virtually created, namely, produced in a seminal or potential state. BIBLIOGRAPHY: G. Bonner, *St. Augustine of Hippo* (1963); E. Portalié, *Guide to the Thought of Saint Augustine* (tr. R. J. Bastian, 1960). For a listing of the more important Latin editions of A.'s works, see NCE 1:1049–51; H. Marrou, *St. Augustine and His Influence through the Ages* (tr. P. Hepburne-Scott, 1957).

[R. P. RUSSELL]

AUGUSTINE OF ANCONA (Triumphus; *c.*1241–1328), Augustinian theologian and philosopher. After *Giles of Rome, founder of the Augustinian school, A. is the most versatile and voluminous writer of his order. Although possessed of a critical and independent spirit, his philosophy remains basically within the tradition of Aquinas and Giles. Unfortunately, most of his writings, which include treatises on Scripture, canon law, and a celebrated commentary on Aristotle's *Metaphysics,* have remained unpublished. He was the first to undertake a concordance of St. Augustine's writings, *Milleloquium S. Augustini,* though its implementation was principally the work of his pupil Bartholomew of Urbino. He is also credited with having composed the first scientific treatise on the nature and scope of papal authority. In this work, *Summa de ecclesiastica potestate,* Augustine not only defends the theocratic doctrine of Giles and James of Viterbo but carries them to their extreme conclusions. According to Augustine, all authority, civil and ecclesiastical, derives solely from the Roman pontiff, who alone possesses absolute and direct power in both the religious and civil domains. BIBLIOGRAPHY: B. Ministeri, "De A. vita et operibus," *Analecta Augustiniana* 7 (1952), 7–56, only reliable study of A. and his works; M. J. Wilks, *Problem of Sovereignty in the Later Middle Ages: The Papal Monarchy with Augustinus Triumphus and the Publicists* (1963).

[R. P. RUSSELL]

AUGUSTINE OF CANTERBURY, ST. (d. 604), first abp. of Canterbury (597). As prior of St. Andrew's in Rome he was a fellow monk of Pope Gregory I who dispatched him

and 30 monks on the mission to the Anglo-Saxons in 596. He was received by Ethelbert and Bertha, the Kentish sovereigns; his preaching was fulfilled in the conversion of many including the King. He established his cathedral seat with a monastic chapter in Canterbury and consecrated bps. for other English cities. His attempts at rapprochement with the Celtic bps. failed. He may have influenced the composition of Ethelbert's "Dooms." BIBLIOGRAPHY: A. Amore BiblSanct 1:426–427; Butler 2:407–408.

[J. L. DRUSE]

AUGUSTINE KAŽOTIĆ, BL. (*c.* 1260–1323). Dominican bp. He founded convents in Dalmatia and undertook missions in Italy, Bosnia, and Hungary. In 1303 A. became bp. of Zagreb, Croatia. He was persecuted by Miladin, governor of Dalmatia, whose tyranny he opposed until his transfer to the See of Lucera in 1317. He was venerated for charity to the poor and for the gift of healing. BIBLIOGRAPHY: Butler 3:255–256; M. J. Finnegan, NCE 1:1058; C. Sisto, BiblSanct 1:428.

[M. J. FINNEGAN]

AUGUSTINE NOVELLUS, BL. (d. 1309), jurist and Augustinian prior general. Professor of jurisprudence at the Univ. of Bologna, chancellor to King Manfred of Sicily, he had entered Augustinian Order as a lay brother, but was ordained priest after his identity became known. He was confessor to Nicholas IV, papal legate in Siena under Boniface VIII, and helped revise the constitutions of his order. BIBLIOGRAPHY: A. J. Ennis, NCE 1:1059; Butler 2:353; A. M. Giacomini, BiblSanct 1:601–607.

[M. A. WINKELMANN]

AUGUSTINE, RULE OF ST., an ancient monastic rule, in 12 brief chapters, attributed to St. *Augustine of Hippo (d.430). It has been and continues to be employed by very numerous groups of religious, both male and female. Its appeal is based not only on its antiquity and brevity, but also on its sound principles of charity, discretion, and community living. The authenticity and historicity of the rule have been the object of much study and difference of opinion. More recent scholarship indicates that the rule was written by Augustine for his first monastery at Hippo, founded in 391. Scholarly discussion has centered about several documents: *Disciplina monasterii* (DM), a very brief rule in 11 sections; a rule of men (RV), considered to be the original work of Augustine; and *Regula puellarum* (RP), a feminine form of RV, found in Augustine's Letter 211 and preceded by a prologue in four sections. Because of the presence of the feminine text in the Letter 211, and certain internal arguments, RP has been considered by many to be the original form of the rule. This viewpoint was put forth as early as the 12th cent. and was defended by Erasmus. More recently, however, scholarly opinion favors the authenticity of RV, while RP is thought to be a later adaptation, perhaps done in Spain in the 6th century. The arguments in favor of RV are based chiefly on its older and more substantial MS tradition (6th or 7th cent.). RV, moreover, is cited in other ancient rules, e.g., that of St. Caesarius of Arles, in c.512. The origin and authorship of DM remain an unsolved problem. It is suggested that DM was written by Augustine for the original monastic foundation at Tagaste in 388, and that he later added RV by way of a spiritual commentary. Internal arguments about the authenticity of DM cause the question to remain undecided. The Rule of St. Augustine as employed today is made up of the first sentence of DM followed by the text of RV. BIBLIOGRAPHY: L. Verheijen, *La Règle de saint Augustin* (2v., 1967). For contrasting viewpoints about the authenticity of the rule, cf. J. J. Gavigan, NCE 1:1059–60 and M. C. McCarthy, *Rule for Nuns of St. Caesarius of Arles* (1960).

[A. J. ENNIS]

AUGUSTINIAN NUNS, those religious women who were founded by, are under the jurisdiction of, or participate in the privileges of the *Augustinians. In a wider sense, the title could refer to all orders or congregations of women who follow the rule of St. Augustine, e.g., the *Dominicans, *Bridgettines, and Visitation nuns. Convents of Augustinian nuns came into existence first in Germany (1264, at Oberndorf am Neckar) and were soon found in Italy, Spain, and France. The first convents were strictly cloistered, but by the 15th cent. members of the noncloistered third order regulars came to be more typical. Notable among the Augustinian saints of this period are *Clare of Montefalco (d. 1308) and *Rita of Cascia (d. 1447). Following the reforms of the Council of Trent, most of the existing convents came under the jurisdiction of the local ordinaries, but in recent years many of them have returned to Augustinian jurisdiction. The confederated houses of Italy are organized in one congregation and those of Spain in four congregations, of which two pertain to the *Augustinian Recollects. In 1970 the number of convents of Augustinian nuns dependent on the Augustinian Order was 29 in Italy, 47 in Spain, and 8 in other countries, including one in Michigan. BIBLIOGRAPHY: F. Roth, NCE 1:1060–61.

[A. J. ENNIS]

AUGUSTINIAN RECOLLECTS, a religious order of men, originating in the 16th cent. out of a desire for stricter discipline and a dedication to eremitical ideals among Spanish *Augustinians under the leadership of Luis de León (d. 1591). The movement began in the Augustinian province of Castile which became independent (1602) of the provincial and directly subject to the prior general, and in 1912 was established as an independent order by Pius X. The Recollects early expanded into three provinces in Spain and one in the Philippines where they had been appointed as missionaries by the Spanish crown in 1605. Missions were also established in Colombia, and briefly in Japan. In 1917 three Recollect friars from Colombia established the first foundation in the U.S., a parish in the diocese of Omaha, Nebraska.

A province, with headquarters in Kansas City, Kansas, was formed in 1943, embracing all the houses in the U.S., Puerto Rico, and the Dominican Republic. The order in 1969 comprised 1,580 priests, brothers and professed religious, who are engaged in teaching, and in parish and mission work. BIBLIOGRAPHY: G. LaMountain, NCE 1:1061–62.

[A. J. ENNIS]

AUGUSTINIAN SPIRITUALITY, the spiritual teachings and traditions of the *Augustinian and other religious groups who, related to them, base their traditions on the teachings and example of St. *Augustine of Hippo (d. 430). Apart from the Scriptures and other sources common to all Christian spirituality, Augustinian spiritual writers have relied chiefly on both the authentic and spurious works of Augustine, esp.: his rule (see Augustine, Rule of St.), the *De opere monachorum,* his sermons and letters, and the *Vita* by St. Possidius. Numerous commentaries on the rule have been written; one that has gone through many editions and translations is that of Bl. Alfonso de Orozco (d. 1591), although several recent commentaries are available. The Constitutions of the Augustinian Order—the oldest extant text is that of Ratisbon (1290)—are another source of Augustinian spirituality, in which the harmonious blending of prayer, studies, and apostolate is spelled out. Further contributors to this spirituality were Augustinian theologians and saints, such as *Giles of Rome (d. 1316), St. Thomas of Villanova (d. 1555), Girolamo Seripando (d. 1563), Henry *Noris (d. 1704), and Giovanni *Berti (d. 1766). Some of the characteristic notes of Augustinian spirituality are the following: the defining of theology as an affective science ordered toward love; the tendency to unite doctrine and piety; the defense of the primacy of grace in man's encounter with God; and the emphasis on the centrality of Christ and his mystical body in the order of salvation. The attempt to single out one key characteristic of Augustinian spirituality has given rise to numerous opinions. These may be reduced to two principal ideas, one of which is more speculative, while the other is more practical. According to the former, the fundamental note is interiorness, that is, the pursuit of wisdom through retirement from the world and dedication to the interior life, esp. in the loving contemplation of the Holy Trinity. According to the latter, it is perfect common life, a holy community of love, epitomized in Augustine's maxim, *"anima una et cor unum ad Deum."* Both opinions agree, however, in their emphasis upon charity. BIBLIOGRAPHY: A. J. Ennis, NCE 1:1062–63, D. Gutiérrez, *DSAM* 4.2:983–1018; A. Orozco, *Rule of St. Augustine: Commentary* (tr. T. A. Hand, 1956); C. Vaca, *La vida religiosa en S. Augustín* (4v., 1955–64).

[A. J. ENNIS]

AUGUSTINIANISM, a school of philosophical and theological thought claiming fidelity to the doctrine of St. Augustine of Hippo. For the 8 cent. following his death in 430, the authority and influence of St. Augustine were predominantly theological in nature. Nevertheless, in the development and formulation of his theology, based mainly upon Scripture and ecclesiastical tradition, he had consciously appropriated and assimilated much of the prevailing philosophy of his time. This was the neoplatonic philosophy of Plotinus and Porphyry, which may already have been modified by Christian influence by the mid-4th cent.

Medieval Augustinianism. Medieval Augustinianism began to appear soon after the 13th-cent. introduction of Aristotelian metaphysics into the Univ. of Paris. As an intellectual movement, it was mainly a reaction against the "new learning," which was viewed as a serious threat to Catholic orthodoxy. To the traditional mind this was an attempt to replace the Christian wisdom of Augustine with the pagan wisdom of Aristotle. To meet this challenge, a new doctrinal synthesis emerged that, while remaining Augustinian in its theological content, appropriated a number of philosophical notions ascribed to St. Augustine, though several of these were derived from a neoplatonism influenced by Avicenna and Avicebron. Because of its dubious authenticity, some historians have preferred to describe the movement as either a pre-Thomistic school or as an eclectic Aristotelianism.

The principal doctrinal tenets of this school were: (1) There is no autonomous philosophy independent and separate from theology. (2) The will enjoys a primacy over intellect, with the resulting voluntarist view that beatific vision is formally constituted by man's highest affective power rather than through an act of intellectual contemplation. (3) The soul knows itself directly and is really identified with its various powers or faculties. (4) Every created reality, spiritual as well as corporeal, is ultimately constituted of matter and form, with the result that the soul, being a complete substance, is individuated by its own spiritual matter. (5) To achieve its higher forms of knowledge, including God, the soul requires a special divine "illumination." (6) Within the structure of every composite reality there are several substantial forms hierarchically ordered, including the form of corporeity, identified with light. (7) The notion of "seminal reasons," or of a "virtual creation," to describe the causal or potential mode of being imparted at creation to living things that appear progressively in the course of time. (8) The absolute impossibility of an eternally existing world.

Proponents of this doctrine pertained for the most part to the Franciscan Order, though several, including Peter of Tarentaise (later Innocent V) and Richard Fishacre belonged to the earlier Dominican school. Notable among the Franciscan representatives of this movement were Alexander of Hales, John Peckham, Bonaventure, Roger Marston, Matthew of Aquasparta, William de la Mare, and Richard Middleton. The famous condemnation issued by Abp. Tempier at Paris in 1277, which included several Thomistic doctrines, provided the Augustinian traditionalists with a decisive but short-lived victory. Within a few years, largely owing to the basic eclecticism of the period, the main body of Augustinianism was gradually absorbed into the mainstream of the new scholastic movements, both Thomistic and non-

Thomistic. see F. Van Steenberghen, *Aristotle in the West* (tr. L. Johnston, 1955).

Augustinianism and Grace: Reformation Era. In their theology of grace the Augustinians of the period continue the tradition of their early school, particularly the tendencies introduced into it in the 14th cent. by Gregory of Rimini (d.1358). These include a greater preoccupation with the problem of grace and a wider use of the writings and authority of St. Augustine. The new doctrinal controversies of the 16th cent. concerning original sin, *concupiscence, and justification occasioned a more thorough and detailed study of the saint's anti-Pelagian works in an effort to present his teachings on grace in terms suitable to meet the challenges posed by Luther and the new theology. The principal exponent and defender of the Augustinian school at the Council of Trent was Girolamo *Seripando, who also served for a time as papal legate. His teaching on grace, as related to baptism and justification, is deeply rooted in a notion of concupiscence inherited from Gregory of Rimini. Concupiscence is viewed as sinful not only as a result and penalty of original sin, as well as a source of personal sin, but also because its persistence, even after baptism, renders it impossible for man to accomplish the full and perfect observance of God's law. Augustine is invoked to support the view that man cannot fully observe the commandment forbidding evil desires since concupiscence remains in active opposition to the precept; he can, at best, only fulfill the injunction not to follow these evil desires. Since, according to the Augustinians, such a condition is necessarily displeasing to God, they tried unsuccessfully to have removed from the final form of Trent's decree on justification the statement that "God finds nothing hateful in the reborn." Like Seripando, they were convinced that this notion of concupiscence, as well as the related doctrine of *"double justice," were Pauline and Augustinian in origin. The double justice theory had already been proposed as a doctrinal compromise to reconcile RC and Lutheran teaching on justification, though Luther himself found it unacceptable. As viewed by Seripando, the justice effected in man, enabling him to perform good works, remains incomplete owing to concupiscence and must be further complemented by a second justice, the justice of Christ, in order to merit eternal life. This application of Christ's justice is made possible by man's incorporation into the mystical body through a previous grace that enables him to believe and trust in Christ the head. The culminating and decisive role of this two-fold justice can be seen in the following steps traced out by Seripando in the process of justification: (1) the first grace, or call to the faith; (2) a second grace, which enables man to accept the first and to turn from sin through penance; (3) the remission of sin by incorporation into the mystical body by acts of faith and trust in Christ its head; (4) infusion of charity and gifts of the Holy Spirit enabling man to keep the commandments; (5) application of the justice of Christ to complement the justice of his members, which remains incomplete by reason of concupiscence.

The central doctrine of concupiscence, which underlies the doctrine of justification, was to play an equally important role in the explanation of efficacious grace by the Augustinian theologians of the 17th and 18th centuries. See H. Jedin, *Papal Legate to the Council of Trent: Cardinal Seripando* (tr. F. C. Eckhoff, 1947).

Augustinianism and Grace: 17th and 18th centuries. The Augustinian theologians of this later school, also known as *Augustinenses* and the school of H. Noris, endeavor to present an authentic and timely statement of Augustine's teachings on grace in order to rehabilitate his authority against interpretations that resulted in the condemnation of the doctrines of Calvin, Baius, and Jansen. Accordingly, Augustinians of this period are principally preoccupied with such questions as the original state of justice, predestination, and the necessity and nature of efficacious grace vis-à-vis man's free will. Basic to the development of their theology of grace is the notion already defended by the early school and inspired by St. Augustine's doctrine of the soul as "image," that man's spiritual nature is naturally ordered toward beatific vision. Hence, these later theologians emphatically deny the possibility of a purely natural state for man and at the same time endeavor to safeguard the gratuity of the supernatural order by introducing a distinction current at the time between God's "absolute" and "ordered" power, the latter being his power as directed by his essential attributes of wisdom and goodness. Consequently, not only sanctifying grace, but also such preternatural endowments as knowledge, immortality and integrity, were owing to man because of a certain fittingness on the part of the Creator. Because of the quasi-natural character of these latter, the Fall entailed both the loss of grace and an impairment to full natural human integrity. Hence the special necessity for a "medicinal" grace to remedy this impairment, and the further conclusion that concupiscence results from original sin alone and constitutes its material element.

The Augustinian teaching on the divine economy of grace is thus based upon a strictly concrete and historical view of man considered in the successive states of innocence and sin. Even before the Fall man needed and received a grace that conferred upon his will the "power" (*posse*) to do good but that did not guarantee either the consent of the will (*velle*) or the consummation of the good work (*perficere*). Characterized as "indifferent" (*gratia versatilis*), such a grace, sufficient for man in his innocent condition, was one that man could either accept or resist, so that in the performance of good the will played the principal role. Because of his fallen state this grace is no longer sufficient and there is required an efficacious grace (*gratia efficax*), which, though leaving freedom intact, infallibly produces its effect.

The same historical view of man likewise underlies the Augustinian theology of predestination. Predestination before the Fall, as well as reprobation, resulted from God's foreknowledge of man's future merits (*post praevisa merita*), while, in consequence of Adam's sin, predestination to grace and glory is absolutely gratuitous on the part of God, prior to, and independent of any foreknowledge of man's merits (*ante praevisa merita*). Reprobation, understood in a negative sense, is the direct result of original sin and embraces those who, in accordance with the "just judgment of God," comprise the so-called *massa perditionis*. While acknowledging God's salvific will, these theologians think it at least probable that sufficient grace is not given to all, citing in support of this view infants who die unbaptized and adults who have no knowledge of Christian revelation. In explaining the nature of efficacious grace, these later Augustinian theologians adduce what is perhaps the most celebrated and controversial point of doctrine in their entire theology, namely, the *delectatio victrix*, which the early school of Giles of Rome (d. 1316) had appropriated from St. Augustine without further development. As outlined by Noris, the will of man in his fallen condition is drawn by two opposed forces of attraction, concupiscence (*cupiditas mali*) and grace (*cupiditas boni*), and inevitably yields to the stronger attraction. Only when grace exercises the stronger attraction and effectively overcomes the contrary delight of concupiscence is such grace efficacious, though in accepting this grace, as G. L. Berti insists, the will is acting with complete freedom (*liberrima voluntate*). Grace remains "inefficacious" when the power conferred is insufficient to overcome the attraction of concupiscence and leaves the will in a "weak" and "feeble" state, as Augustine had pointed out in one of his later anti-Pelagian works (see *De Grat. et lib. arb.*, 17). Augustinians acknowledge no essential difference between these two kinds of grace; grace becomes efficacious by reference to the relative intensity of the present evil attraction and to the moral condition of the recipient. Consequently, one and the same grace may prove efficacious for some but inefficacious for others. See W. Bocxe, *Introduction to the Teaching of the Italian Augustinians of the 18th Century on the Nature of Actual Grace* (1958).

Recent Augustinianism. Although contemporary Augustinianism is represented by no particular school or system, theological or philosophical, its influence is apparent both in the nature of the problems posed and in the various approaches adopted toward a solution. Contemporary thought shares with Augustine its concern for problems that arise in exploring the mysterious complexity of the human person or in describing man's destiny in its fuller existential dimensions. In particular, current spiritualistic and existential movements show a marked preference for the spirit and form of dialectic initiated by Augustine. In France and Italy the Augustinian "metaphysics of internal experience" is the point of departure for the several forms of the "philosophy of the spirit" represented by Lavelle, Sciacca, and Carlini. Augustine's impact upon the existential movement can be traced back to its origin with S. *Kierkegaard, who credited Augustine with having discovered the "dialectic of existence" to solve the mystery of human existence by assigning a priority to faith over reason. The Augustinian primacy of faith is stressed even further by Karl Jaspers, who regarded Augustine as the founder of true philosophy. Since, according to the German philosopher, reason cannot reach beyond mere phenomena, faith alone can grasp reality, including not only God's existence but even one's personal identity. Finally, the prominent role given to the teachings of Augustine in Vatican Council II, where he is cited more frequently than any other Father or Doctor of the Church, suggests not only a fuller exploration of his theology but also new possibilities for fruitful dialogue between Catholics and those Protestant communities that historically have revered his authority. BIBLIOGRAPHY: J. Guitton, *Modernity of St. Augustine* (tr. A. V. Littendale, 1959); T. J. Livernois, ''Approaches to God in Continental Theology; An Augustinian Emphasis,'' *Susquehanna Univ. Studies* 8, no. 4 (1970).

[R. P. RUSSELL]

AUGUSTINIANS. The Order of St. Augustine (OSA), formerly called Hermits of St. Augustine and commonly known as the Augustinians, a mendicant order that was canonically organized in 1256, but which traces its spiritual heritage back to St. *Augustine of Hippo (d.430). Its constitutions, newly revised in 1968, are based on the rule and other writings of St. Augustine (see AUGUSTINE, RULE OF ST.), and the order's tradition has been characterized by constant study of and devotion to its spiritual father. The order was formed at the ''Great Union'' (1256) when several semi-eremitic or penitent groups, mostly Italian, were brought together, under the guidance of the Holy See, and directed toward the apostolate of preaching and teaching in the expanding cities and towns of the 13th cent. Like the other mendicant orders the Augustinians experienced a rapid growth throughout Europe; by the beginning of the 14th cent. the order was divided into 22 provinces with about 8,000 members. Despite the decline and the losses in the 15th and 16th cent., the Augustinians continued to expand (they counted about 20,000 friars in the 17th cent.), esp. through extensive mission activity. In the New World they arrived first in Mexico in 1533 and thence expanded to other parts of Latin America and to the Far East. In the U.S. the first foundation was made in 1796 at Philadelphia by Thomas M. Carr (d.1820), an Augustinian from Ireland. Villanova Univ., founded in 1843, became the center from which the order in the U.S. gradually grew into three provinces (East, Mid-West and Calif.) and one vice-province, with a total membership of about 760. Throughout the world (1975), the order possesses 419 houses and 3,780 friars, distributed among 26 provinces. Among the Augustinian saints, the best known are *Nicholas of Tolentine (d.1305), Thomas of Villanova (d.1555) and *Rita of Cascia (d.1447). BIBLIOGRAPHY: D. Gutiérrez, DSAM 4.2:983–1018; A. C. Shannon, NCE 1:1071–76.

[A. J. ENNIS]

AUGUSTINIS, AEMILIO DE (1829–99), educator, theologian. Born in Naples, Italy, A. studied law, served in the army, and later entered the Society of Jesus. He was transferred to Laval, France, where he studied theology and was ordained. In 1869 A. taught at the new scholasticate of the Jesuits in the U.S. at Woodstock, Md. and was a founder and editor of the *Woodstock Letters*. He was recognized by Leo XIII for his contribution to theology, was professor of dogma at the Gregorian Univ. in Rome, and rector of that institution from 1891–95. BIBLIOGRAPHY: F. G. McMenamin, NCE 1:1076.

[M. C. BRADLEY]

AUGUSTINUS, Cornelius *Jansen's treatise on grace, source work for *Jansenism, published posthumously and secretly at Louvain, July 14, 1640. It was written in Latin in three books. Book I is a historical introduction on the persistence of *Pelagianism. Book II depicts man as angelic before his Fall, demonic afterward. Book III concludes that fallen man is radically evil and capable only of sin; redemption reaches only a predestined few. Jansen denies sufficient grace; he admits freedom of will only as freedom from coercion. This he claimed as St. Augustine's definitive teaching; he documents his propositions with isolated texts of Augustine, some used earlier by Luther and Calvin. Jesuits and some others saw this as moderated Calvinism, reviving *Baianism, which had been condemned by Pius V and Gregory XIII. Like Cardinal Richelieu, they sought papal condemnation of *Augustinus*. Urban VIII complied on March 6, 1642, with *In eminenti,* not published until June 19, 1643. BIBLIOGRAPHY: F. Mourret, *History of the Catholic Church* (tr. N. Thompson, 8v., 1931–57) 6:384–389; H. Daniel-Rops, *Church in the Seventeenth Century* (tr. J. J. Buckingham, 1963) 339–346; Pastor 29:62–130.

[W. DAVISH]

AUGUSTUS, ROMAN EMPEROR (b. Gaius Octavius, 63 B.C.-A.D. 14). After his adoption by his great-uncle Julius Caesar, his name became Gaius Julius Caesar Octavianus. The religious title Augustus was conferred on him by the senate because of his great services to the state. Upon Caesar's assassination Augustus became by war and diplomacy, as he said, ''master of all things.'' He kept the old forms of government where possible but changed Rome from a republic to a principate. As *princeps* (first citizen), he theoretically held authority along with the senators; but since he commanded the armies, his power was superior to the senate's. Augustus vastly extended Roman territory and established the long peace which became a factor in the spread of Christianity. He revived religious traditions, built or restored numerous temples, and fostered the imperial cult that posed a threat to Christianity until the age of Constantine. BIBLIOGRAPHY: M. P. Charlesworth et al., CAH (1934) 10:1–606; J. Buchan, *Augustus Caesar* (1937).

[M. J. SUELZER]

AULARD, FRANÇOIS ALPHONSE (1849–1928), historian of the French Revolution. Educated at the École Normale Supérieure, he taught history in three universities before he went to the Univ. of Paris, where he taught until 1922. In 1888 A. founded the Société de l'histoire de la révolution française and a review, *La Révolution française*. His *Histoire politique de la révolution française: Origines et développement de la démocratie et de la république: 1789–1804* (1901) earned him a position of leadership in the field. His chief work on the religious aspect of the Revolution was *Le Christianisme et la révolution française* (1927). He is credited with making a major contribution to the study of the Revolution by his research and his use of the most advanced historical techniques. BIBLIOGRAPHY: A. Martin, *Dictionnaire de biographie française* (1929–) 4:583–585.

[S. A. HEENY]

AULÉN, GUSTAF (1879–1959), bp. of Strangnas, Swedish Lutheran theologian, professor at the Univ. of Lund. With Anders *Nygren, A. was a leader of the *Motivforschung* (see *MOTIF RESEARCH) school, which stressed the essential truth of Christian doctrine rather than the form of presentation. The school also emphasized the connection between the early Christian Fathers and the Reformation. A.'s important works are *Den allmänneliga kristna tron* (1923; Eng. tr., *The Faith of the Christian Church*, 1954); *Den kristna gudsbilden* (1927); and the Olaus Petri lectures of 1930, *Den kristna försoningstanken* (abridged Eng. version by A. G. Hebert, *Christus Victor*, 1931).

[P. K. MEAGHER]

AULNAY, SAINT-PIERRE (1150–70), French church in the center of a Roman cemetery, boasting superb, luxuriant, sculptural decoration in a labyrinth of ornament, close-knit and continuous on archivolts of the W front and S transept. Rich and magnificent undercutting of the *voussoirs* indicate Moorish influence on the art of Aquitaine, and ornamentation and fantasy inspired by Muslim ivories and jewels attest to the participation of the counts of Poitou in the Spanish Crusades. One of the finest examples of Romanesque art is the carving of *Virtues and Vices* from *Psychomachia* of Prudentius; of impressive mastery are the architectural configurations of human forms with the moldings, and intricate frets reminiscent of ivory or iron work. Aulnay is one of the handsomest monuments linking the art of Poitou, Aquitaine, and Saintonges. BIBLIOGRAPHY: H. Facillon, *Art of the West* (1963) v.1; Y. Labande-Maelfert, *Poitou roman* (1957).

[M. J. DALY]

AULNE-SUR-SAMBRE, ABBEY OF *(Alne, Alna)*, former monastery founded *c*.656 in the Diocese of Liège, now Tournai (Hainaut, Belgium), either by St. Landelin, who had established the neighboring monastery of Lobbes, or by St. Ursmer. In 1144 the monastery adopted the Rule of St. Augustine, but after 1147 the monastery was given over to St. Bernard. The Cistercians kept up regular observance until the 13th cent. Laxness then set in until a reform was effected by Jean de Gesves (d. 1420). From a material viewpoint, the 18th cent., which witnessed the reconstruction of the abbey by Dom Louant (d. 1753), was the most brilliant. The revolutionary troops under Gen. Charbonnier set fire to Aulne in 1794. The last abbot, Dom Herset, gave to the poor what he had saved from the abbey's wealth. The buildings still standing include a hospice bearing the name of this charitable monk, imposing ruins of the church (13th cent.), and some monastic buildings (18th cent.). BIBLIOGRAPHY: Cottineau 1:202–203; M. Standaert, NCE 1:1077–78.

[J. DAOUST]

AUMBRY, see (1) AMBRY; (2) ARMADIUM.

AUMONT, JEAN (d. 1689), spiritual writer. Nothing is known of his life except that he was a vinedresser at Montmorency. In *L'Ouverture intérieure du royaume de l'Agneau occis dans nos coeurs* (1660) he set himself to describe at length what takes place in the mystical life. He made much of "pure love" and the prayer of the heart, which he tried to show as possible to all. He concerned himself with the practical details of the life of prayer and tried to work out a method useful to ordinary people. The work, an abridgment of which appeared in 1669, helped those for whom more technical books were unintelligible to gain some understanding of the mystical life. BIBLIOGRAPHY: P. Pourrat, DSAM 1:1136–38; Bremond 7:321–373.

[P. K. MEAGHER]

AUNARIUS OF AUXERRE, ST. (Aunacharius; d. *c*.605); bp. of Auxerre. After spending his youth at the royal court of Burgundy, A. renounced the world and was ordained by Syagrius, bp. of Autun. He was elected to the See of Auxerre and attended the Councils of Paris and Mâcon. He himself held synods at Auxerre, enacting 45 canons which give interesting light on the mode of living when pagan superstition and abuse of Christian practices still persisted. A. encouraged the faithful by providing biographies of his two distinguished predecessors, St. Amator and St. Germain, and also arranged liturgical prayer. His relics, seized by the Calvinists, were retrieved and are believed authentic. BIBLIOGRAPHY: H. Claude, BiblSanct 2:592–593; P. Cousin, NCE 1:1078.

[M. C. BRADLEY]

AUNEMUND, ST. (d. 658), abp. Reared at the court of Dagobert I and Clovis II, A. probably held civil office before becoming abp. of Lyons. He was murdered by Ebroin, mayor of the palace of Neustria. A.'s cult began in the 9th century. BIBLIOGRAPHY: C. Lefebvre, BiblSanct 1:1311; Butler 3:667–668.

[H. DRESSLER]

AUPIAIS, FRANCIS (1877–1945), Fr. missionary. A. joined the Society of African Missions of Lyons and began work in Dahomey in 1903. He became superior of the mission and vicar general of Dahomey in 1919. On his return to France he was the provincial of his congregation

(1928–31, 1937–45). Shortly before his death he took part in the constituent assembly of Dahomey. BIBLIOGRAPHY: U. Milliez, *Catholicisme* 1:1066.

[M. J. SUELZER]

AURAEUS, ST., 5th-cent. bp. The oldest sources place his martyrdom, along with that of his sister, Justina, in the time of Attila (*c*.451). More recent research suggests he was martyred by the Vandals in 406. Medieval sources unite his name with that of a certain St. Justinus, a deacon or sub-deacon. BIBLIOGRAPHY: AS June 4:37–79; H. Leclercq, DACL 11.1:26.

[W. A. JURGENS]

AURANGĀBĀD, city near Ellora and Ajantā, India, site of 9 or 10 important Buddhist caves, the earliest a *Caitya* hall (1st or 2d cent. A.D.). Other 7th cent. caves except one are *vihāras* relating stylistically to Ajantā and early Hindu caves at Ellora. Cave III adorned with columns complex and elabo-rate, shows life-size worshiper-figures carved *in situ* in deep relief. In Cave VII the shrine, moved to the center of the cave, provides an ambulatory. Dancers and musicians wor-ship the Buddha and a litany of Avalokiteśvara illustrates the Amitābha Sūtras of the Pure Land cult. A later cave shows a Hindu-Buddhist synthesis. Aurangzeb built here a Muslim tomb for his mother which, though imitating the Taj Mahal, fails in classic repose because of crowded domes and kiosks. BIBLIOGRAPHY: R. S. Gupte and B. D. Maha-jan, *Ajantā, Ellora and Aurangābād Caves* (1962).

[M. J. DALY]

AUREA OF CÓRDOBA, ST. (d. 856), martyr. After the martyrdom (825 or 826) of her two brothers, Adolph and John, she lived with her Christian mother in a monastery in a suburb of Córdoba. Under Moorish law she was technically subject to the penalty for apostasy, for her father had been a Muslim, but for some time she escaped persecution because of her noble birth. Nevertheless, when relatives denounced her, the authorities felt obliged to take action. Under threats she weakened and agreed to abandon Christianity. Back with her mother, she repented and did penance. Again she was denounced, and this time she held firmly to her purpose and was put to death. BIBLIOGRAPHY: P. A. Gracia, BiblSanct 2:594–596.

[E. P. COLBERT]

AUREA CATENA HOMERI, see GOLDEN CHAIN.

AURELIAN OF ARLES, ST. (d. *c*.553), bp. of Arles and papal vicar for Gaul from 546. A. established two monasteries, one for men and the other for women, and provided them with a rule adapted from that of St. Caesarius (d. 543). He exchanged letters with Pope Vigilius concern-ing the stand the Pope was taking with regard to the *Three Chapters, a matter that caused some anxiety in the West for fear the validity of the Council of Chalcedon might be brought into question. BIBLIOGRAPHY: R. Aigrain, *Catholicisme* 1:1070; Butler 2:554–55.

[R. B. ENO]

AURELIAN (LUCIUS DOMITIUS AURELIANUS) ROMAN EMPEROR from 270 A.D. (*c*.213–274). Born in Pannonia, A. had a distinguished military career, and was proclaimed emperor by his troops after the death of Claudius II. In a few short years he succeeded in earning the title *restitutor orbis* (restorer of the world). He first brought to a conclusion the current war against the Goths by driving them out of Moesia across the Danube, and in campaigns against several Germanic tribes, secured the Rhine frontier. In 271 he marched East against Zenobia, queen of Palmyra, and after defeating her armies at Antioch, Emesa, and Palmyra, secured the full allegiance of the Eastern provinces. In 274 he moved against the usurper Tetricus, who had ruled Gaul, Spain, and Britain undisturbed since the death of Gallienus, and defeated him in battle near Chalons. Then as *Restorer of East and West* he celebrated a triumph in Rome in which he paraded both Zenobia and Tetricus. A. then devoted himself to the many internal problems of Rome by assisting the poor and moving against informers and embezzlers. He intro-duced a new system of coinage, and continued the restoration and enlargement of the city walls begun in 271. He inaugu-rated the cult of *Sol dominus imperii Romani* (the Sun, Lord of the Roman Empire) as the focus of a revived paganism. The tolerance he manifested toward Christianity earlier in his reign was abandoned toward the end and persecution was renewed. While on a campaign against the Persians, he was assassinated by some of his officers through the treachery of his secretary (274). BIBLIOGRAPHY: H. Mattingly, CAH 12:297–311.

[F. J. MURPHY]

AURELIAN OF RÉOMÉ (9th cent.), Benedictine monk and musical theorist. His treatise *Musica disciplina* (Ger-bertS 1:27–63) discusses the nature of *Gregorian chant and in particular the modes; it is the earliest treatment of the melodic formulas of chant with respect to their modal impli-cations. A. regarded the beginning of a piece, rather than its end, conclusive for determining its mode. The treatise is also valuable for its evidence on chant performance practice dur-ing the Carolingian era. BIBLIOGRAPHY: Reese MusMA; H. Hüschen, MGG 1:858–859. *MODE.

[A. DOHERTY]

AURELIUS OF ARMENIA, ST. (d. 475). The 9th-cent. vita, now lost, stated that he brought the relics of St. Dionysius, Bp. of Milan (355), from Cappadocia, where he had been exiled, to Milan. In 830 Bp. Noting of Vercelli removed his bones to Hirsau and erected a church in his honor. He is the patron or copatron of Hirsau. BIBLIOGRA-PHY: BHL 1:819–822; R. Browning, NCE 1:1079; M. Mil-ler, LTK 1:1108.

[M. R. P. McGUIRE]

AURELIUS OF CARTHAGE, ST. (d. *c*.430), bp. of Carthage from *c*.391, close friend of St. *Augustine. Although not a theologian or a scholar, he was praised by Augustine for the many practical measures he took to advance the cause of Christianity in his city. As leader of the African bishops, he presided over many synods, most of them at Carthage. These councils dealt with the principal doctrinal and disciplinary problems of the day, esp. *Donatism and *Pelagianism. The most important of these were two Councils of Carthage (411 and 418), the first of which condemned Donatism, and the second *Pelagius and *Celestius. A. was in communication with most of the great figures in the Church of his day. BIBLIOGRAPHY: A. Bigelmair, LTK 1:1108–09; Butler 3:153–154; G. Corti, EncCatt 2:409.

[R. B. ENO]

AURELIUS, SABIGOTONA, AND COMPANIONS, SS. (d. 852), martyrs. A., born of a noble Muslim father and a Christian mother, was orphaned at an early age, and was brought up by a Christian aunt. He married Sabigotona (Sabigoto, known later also as Natalia), a Christian. They practiced their religion secretly at first, but, inspired by the courage of the Christians they saw suffering under Moorish persecution, they resolved to let it be known that they were Christians. Another couple, Felix and Liliosa, joined with them in their decision, as did also a monk from Jerusalem named George. All five were beheaded. BIBLIOGRAPHY: M. Sotomayor, BiblSanct 6:544.

[E. P. COLBERT]

AUREOLE (nimbus; *aureolus,* of gold, golden), a field of radiating light surrounding the entire figure of a holy person. The Italian name *mandorla* applies to the clearly defined almond shape. In Christian art the aureole is a symbol of divinity, though it has been extended to the figure of the Virgin at times. A blaze of glory around a figure has biblical origins (e.g., the Transfiguration), whereas halos (light surrounding the head alone) were often used in pre-Christian pagan art. Christian halos, more or less ornate, may be triangular, circular, or diamond shaped within an accepted iconography. BIBLIOGRAPHY: M. Collinet-Guérin, *Histoire du nimbe* (1961); E. E. Malone, NCE 1:1079–81.

[S. D. MURRAY]

AURICULAR CONFESSION, see CONFESSION, AURICULAR.

AURIGNACIAN ART, beginning of paleolithic art made possible by the invention of a blade tool (knife). Carvings in wood, bone, horn, and incised stone, cave art (e.g., *Altamira, Spain) show keenly observed contours and silhouettes of animals in engraving and painting followed by greater plastic modeling and textural effects. Naturalism increased, reaching a climax in the magnificent polychrome paintings of Lascaux and well-known fertility figurines (Venus of Willendorf) 15,000–10,000 B.C. BIBLIOGRAPHY: H. G. Bandi and J. Maringer, *Art in the Ice Age* (1953).

[M. J. DALY]

AURILLAC, ABBEY OF, a former Benedictine monastery founded *c*.890 by Count Gerald of Aurillac and located in what is now the city of Aurillac. Based on the customs and spirit of Cluny, it became a model abbey. It was also famous as a seat of medieval learning. Decline set in as a result of wars, the loss of fervor, and of the system of commendation—all of which led to secularization in 1561. The abbey then became a collegiate church of secular priests. BIBLIOGRAPHY: P. Fontaine, DHGE 5:757–760.

[S. A. HEENEY]

AURISPA, GIOVANNI (*c*.1369–1459), humanist, collector, translator. From his several trips to Greece, he collected over 200 MSS which he helped to translate. Appointed tutor to the son of the marquis of Este in 1427, he spent his life in their service; he was emissary of the Este to Rome and to the Council of Basel (1433). BIBLIOGRAPHY: E. G. Gleason, NCE 1:1081; R. Sabbadini, *Biografia documentata di Giovanni Aurispa* (1890).

[G. E. CONWAY]

AUSCULTA FILI, a bull of Boniface VIII indicting Philip IV of France and announcing a synod for the reform of the Church in France. Issued Dec. 5, 1301, it was burned publicly by Philip as soon as it reached Paris. It is the most forthright example in practice of Boniface's theory of the direct power of the papacy over the secular. BIBLIOGRAPHY: for English translation and commentary, B. Tierney, *Crisis of Church and State, 1050–1300* (1964) 185–187.

[L. E. BOYLE]

AUSONIUS, DECIMUS MAGNUS (A.D. *c*.310–*c*.396), Roman poet, born at Bordeaux, where he taught grammar and rhetoric for 30 years. Appointed by Valentinian as tutor of his son Gratian, he later became prefect of Gaul, Italy, Illyria, and Africa. Made consul in 379, he retired to his estate near Bordeaux after the assassination of Gratian in 383. There he continued his literary career. Endowed with a great facility but no great originality in composition, Ausonius has left a large number of poems, mostly short, on a wide variety of subjects and in many different meters. His most famous poem is the *Mosella,* in which, with a remarkable feeling for the beauties of nature, he praises the river flowing by Trier, then the capital of the West. Ausonius probably embraced Christianity, but there is little evidence of it in his poems. BIBLIOGRAPHY: F. Marx, RAC 2:2562–80; Altaner 478–479.

[M. J. COSTELLOE]

AUSTERITY, a state or quality of severity or rigor, especially when this involves the practice of the control of self or others in matters of discipline and mortification undertaken to suppress self-indulgence. One may practice austerity for religious, moral, intellectual, or even aesthetic reasons. In modern times it is often practiced for political motives. Some austerity of life is inseparable from the Christian concept of asceticism.

[P. K. MEAGHER]

AUSTIN, JOHN (1613–69), English Catholic author. He left Cambridge Univ. after he became a Catholic and studied law at Lincoln's Inn. From 1650 he belonged to a Catholic literary group in London and was known for his still admired style of writing. He defended Catholicism against bigotry, and his Gospel Devotions with Psalms, Hymns, and Prayers were so popular that non-Catholics adopted them. BIBLIOGRAPHY: T. Cooper, DNB 1:735–736.

[E. P. COLBERT]

AUSTRALIA, earth's smallest continent or largest island, a federal parliamentary state, member of the British Commonwealth (2,967,909 sq mi; pop. [1973] 12,833,667). The land was discovered by the Dutch in the 17th cent. and was explored by Capt. Cook in 1770. The British occupied it 17 years later and used it for half a cent. as a place of exile for criminals, paupers, and political agitators expelled from the British Isles. All colonists were required to attend Anglican services. The first prefect apostolic appointed by Rome was arrested and sent back to England. After the Emancipation Act (1829) the situation improved. W. *Ullathorne, OSB, came as vicar-general in 1833 and 2 years later J. B. Polding, OSB, became Australia's first bishop. He was made abp. of Sydney in 1842. Adelaide and Hobart became suffragan sees. Italian Passionists began a short-lived mission to the aborigines in 1843; Spanish Benedictines who arrived in 1846 were more successful, but missionary progress was slow because of the nomadic character of the people. Trappists, Pallotines, Swiss Missioners of the Sacred Heart, and Missioners of the Divine Word followed. By 1869 the number of sees had increased to seven. The Catholic community grew from 5,000 in 1800 to 475,000 in 1875. After World War II many Catholics from Italy and Central Europe entered Australia, and the Catholic community now makes up one fourth of the total population. The hierarchy now includes 8 archbishoprics and 28 suffragan sees.

The 40th International Eucharistic Congress was held in Melbourne in 1973. This congress was the local climax to a year-long program of spiritual renewal in the host archdiocese. It was considered unique because of its ecumenical dimension and particular emphasis on matters of social concern and ministry.

The chief Protestant denominations active in Australia are Anglicans, Methodists, Presbyterians, Congregationalists, the London Missionary Society, the Rhenish Missionary Society, the Christian and Missionary Alliance, and various branches of Lutherans. BIBLIOGRAPHY: J. G. Murtagh,

Australia: The Catholic Chapter (1959); *Bilan du Monde* 2:101–109; AnnPont (1972).

[P. DAMBORIENA]

AUSTREBERTA, ST. (d. 704), Merovingian abbess. Her father, perhaps of the royal family, was in the court of Dagobert (623–639). Her mother Framehilda (d. c.680), of German royalty, had a cult. Austreberta fled marriage for the veil in 655. Famed for humility, she became prioress in Ponthieu and c.670 abbess of newly founded Pavilly. Her rule combined Benedict and Columban. Protectress against drought and fire, her relics were venerated until destroyed in the French Revolution. BIBLIOGRAPHY: H. Platelle, BiblSanct 1:629–630.

[E. P. COLBERT]

AUSTREGISILUS (OUTRIL), ST. (551–624), bp. After living at the court of King Guntram, A. became a priest and abbot of St. Nicetus. In 612 he was bp. of Bourges. BIBLIOGRAPHY: Butler 2:358; H. Platelle, BiblSanct 2:630.

[H. DRESSLER]

AUSTRIA, predominantly Catholic nation of central Europe; former center of the Austro-Hungarian Empire and seat of the Hapsburgs who served for centuries as emperors of the Holy Roman Empire. Austria was long considered the eastern outpost of Western Christian civilization, a bulwark against non-Christian invaders from the E. Incorporated into the realm of Charlemagne and the Holy Roman Empire, it was the East March or East Realm (Osterreich), from which the name Austria comes. Its role as defender of Christian civilization reached a dramatic peak when Vienna successfully resisted the siege of the Muslim Turks in 1529, and again in 1683.

Under the Hapsburgs (1282–1918) Austria came to form the center of an extensive and powerful, though somewhat ramshackle, polyglot empire, much of it acquired through prudent marriages. Parts were also lost from time to time, and the empire finally expired with World War I, which Austria touched off by its reaction to assassination of the Hapsburg heir apparent. Austria today is a relatively small, land-locked nation of 32,000 square miles, bounded on the E by Hungary, S by Yugoslavia and Italy, W by Switzerland and Lichtenstein and N by Bavaria and Czechoslovakia.

At the rise of Christianity, much of modern Austria stood within the Roman Empire, the Danube generally serving as the boundary, and Christians were present in the area before the time of Constantine. But the Christianity of Roman times was obliterated by the turmoil of tribal invasions. Evangelization then resumed under leadership of churchmen of the Merovingian and Carolingian empires. As in other parts of Europe, monasticism played a key role. Leading the way was St. Rupert, who, with a community of Irish-Celtic monks, established the Abbey of Sankt Peter at Salzburg (Roman Juvavum) c.700, while also founding there the Nonnberg Abbey for women. Later St. Boniface created a diocese at Salzburg with St. Virgilius as bishop. Missionaries then went east from Salzburg to Moravia, where they met SS. Cyril and Methodius coming west from Constantinople. St. Virgilius became the apostle to the Slavs of Carinthia, part of which now forms a province of Austria. In 798 Salzburg became a metropolitan see with the dioceses of Bavaria as suffragans. The Bavarian dioceses were removed from its jurisdiction in 1803, but Salzburg has remained a principal ecclesiastical center of Austria, second only to Vienna. Because of the many notable church buildings erected in Salzburg over the centuries, climaxed by its baroque cathedral, it came to be called the German Rome.

Vienna, a Roman camp from *c*.100 A.D., had a church at the end of the 4th century. After the departure of the Romans, the city declined but was revived under the Babenbergs, who ruled 976–1246. It became a diocese in 1469 and an archdiocese in 1722. Ecclesiastically much of modern Austria was ruled by prelates at Passau (now in Bavaria) and, on the south, Brixen (It. Bressanone) and Trent. Reforming impulses from Gorze and Cluny reached Austria, and Dominicans and Franciscans appeared shortly after their orders were formed in the 13th century. St. Colomon was the first patron saint of Austria. Succeeding him in 1663 was Margrave St. Leopold III (*c*.1075–1136), who brought Cistercians in to found the Abbey of Heiligenkreuz. He also established a monastery at his home near Vienna, Klosterneuburg, which now houses his tomb and the noted Verdun altar.

In 955 Otto I, crowned by Pope John XII in 962 as the first in a new succession of emperors of the Holy Roman Empire, defeated the Magyars (Hungarians) who had invaded from the East. The March (raised to a duchy in 1156 and an archduchy in 1453) was entrusted in 976 to the counts of Babenberg.

In 1273 Rudolph of Hapsburg (a small principality in modern Switzerland) was elected emperor and, with aid from Gregory X, gained possession of Austria by defeating Ottocar II of Bohemia, who had taken the Babenberg territory when their line died out. Rudolf's son, Albrecht, was also elected to the imperial crown, and then after an interval when various other houses held the title, the Hapsburgs were emperors from 1438 until the title became meaningless and Francis I resigned it in 1806.

Hapsburg ties with Rome were strengthened when Frederick III, the last emperor crowned at Rome (1452), supported Eugene IV against anti-pope Felix V and issued the 1448 Concordat of Vienna, returning to his successor, Nicholas V, the revenues and privileges taken by the Council of Basel. In 1451 at the request of Frederick, Nicholas sent St. *John Capistran to aid in the anti-Hussite struggle.

The Reformation drew widespread and powerful support in Austria for a time. But the Hapsburg family, which then had Spanish and Austrian branches, remained Catholic and held their lands loyal to Rome under the Augsburg formula, *cuius regio, eius religio*. From 1526 the Austrian Hapsburg lands included Bohemia and Hungary.

Among Luther's foremost opponents were two bps. of Vienna—J. Faber (1530–41), called the "hammer of the heretics," and F. Nausea (1541–52). Abp. M. Lang of Salzburg also worked effectively against Protestantism. And the newly-established Jesuit Order played a significant role in the Counter Reformation, St. Peter *Canisius (1521–97) arriving in Vienna in 1552 at the invitation of Ferdinand I. Another Counter Reformation force, the Capuchins, came in 1600. Cardinal M. Klesl, who became bp. of Vienna in 1598 and leader of the Counter Reformation in Austria, had been converted from Protestantism by the Jesuit court chaplain, G. Scherer. Maximilian II (1564–76) showed tendencies toward Lutheranism, but imperial pressures finally resulted in a decision to uphold Catholicism. During the Thirty Years War, the Catholic League under Ferdinand II defeated the Prostestant Bohemians under Frederick the Winter King in 1620, a decisive victory that left Austrians with the alternatives of supporting Catholicism or emigrating. The cent. following the Peace of Westphalia brought Austria a period of religious revival, expressed both in piety and in church building.

Though the Hapsburgs defended Catholicism against Protestants and Turks, the 18th cent. brought them into conflict with the papacy over State control of the Church. Empress Maria Theresa (1740–80) began the policy of establishing government dominance of many spheres formerly left to the Church. But it came to be called *Josephinism for her son Joseph II (1765–90), a "benevolent despot" of Enlightenment views who pushed the policy more vigorously. While issuing an edict granting toleration to all religious groups (1781), he dissolved monasteries not engaged in active ministries, increased state control over marriage and education, and interfered with Vatican governance of the Austrian Church. Pius VI visited Vienna in 1782 in an unsuccessful attempt at conciliation, the first time a pope had left Rome in over two centuries. Josephinism declined under Francis I (1804–35), and the Redemptorist St. Clement Hofbauer (1751–1820), called the apostle of Vienna, stimulated a revival of Catholic life.

Napoleon forced Austria to surrender the Holy Roman Empire concept. But at the Congress of Vienna (1815) Metternich secured for Austria leadership in a new German Confederation. This was lost after defeat by Prussia in 1866, and the empire became (1867) the Austro-Hungarian Dual Monarchy, with other nationalities left subordinate.

The Revolution of 1848 returned self-government to the Catholic Church at the price of disestablishment. A concordat (1855) restoring some benefits was abrogated following Vatican Council I. At the 1903 papal conclave Austria became the last power to exercise a veto, blocking election of the Cardinal Secretary of State, M. Rampolla.

In the late 19th cent., Austrian Catholics seeking social reforms organized the Christian Social Party (now People's Party). Anti-Marxist and anti-Semitic, it was in rivalry with the Social Democrats (now Socialists), who were Marxist, anti-clerical, and guided by a leadership including many

Jews. After 1918, former monarchists came into the Christian Social Party. A priest, I. Seipel, led the party in the 1920s and for several years served as chancellor. A third political movement, led by G. Schonerer, based itself on German nationalism and influenced Hitler, born to a Catholic family in Braunau, near the Bavarian border. Using the slogan *Los von Rom,* it sought an end to Vatican ties and favored establishment of union *(Anschluss)* with Protestant Prussia. D. Dollfuss, Christian Social chancellor from 1932, was assassinated by Nazis in 1934, and in 1938 Hitler forced Austria to accept *Anschluss.* Since the war church issues have played less of a political role. BIBLIOGRAPHY: E. Barker, *Austria 1918–72* (1973); K. R. Stadler, *Austria* (1971); V. L. Tapie, *Hapsburg Monarchy* (1971).

[T. EARLY]

AUTARCHY, from Gr. *aut(o),* by oneself, and *archos,* ruler, the quality attaching to an autocrat or ruler who enjoys absolute power (though perhaps subject to God's judgment) or to a political community which enjoys self-government (even though that be democratic). Thus the term can be applied both to the regime of Louis XIV and to the Irish Republic.

[T. GILBY]

AUTARKY, from Gr. *aut(o),* independently, and *arkein,* to suffice, the quality of being self-contained. It is applicable to a closed system of thought or to an economic community that can live on its own resources. Thus, the term can be applied to a science of legal positivism or to an early settlement of Cistercians or Amish.

[T. GILBY]

AUTHENTIC MODE (Ambrosian Mode), one of the two classes into which the eight Gregorian modes are divided, the other being the *plagal.* Each mode is an octave segment of the diatonic (C Major) scale, with one of its tones playing the role of a central tone or tonic. The octave range is called *ambitus,* the central tone *finalis.* There are four *finales:* d, e, f and g. The *ambitus* of the authentic modes starts with the final and extends to its upper octave. The older terminology would classify the authentic modes according to their *finales* as follows: protus authenticus (d–d'); deuterus authenticus (e–e'); tritus authenticus (f–f'); and tetrardus authenticus (g–g'). From the 10th cent. to the present, however, they would simply be called by numbers: modes 1, 3, 5, and 7. In Greek terminology, they would be called the Dorian, Lydian, Phrygian, and Mixolydian Modes. BIBLIOGRAPHY: W. Apel, *Gregorian Modes* (1958) 133–135.

[M. T. LEGGE]

AUTHENTICATION OF RELICS, the process whereby the Church declares that a relic is truly an object connected with the life of Christ or the Blessed Virgin, or part of the remains of a saint. Unless there is cause for grave doubt, relics considered by the faithful to be authentic are not further scrutinized. Canon Law (*c.*2096) requires an examination of the exhumed body of a person whose beatification is being considered, a process entitled recognition of the relics. Public veneration of relics requires authorization from an ecclesiastical official. BIBLIOGRAPHY: F. Chiovaro, NCE 12:239.

[T. M. MCFADDEN]

AUTHORITY, in broadest terms, the office of directing others in a society.

General Theories. The nature and functions of authority have been understood differently by political theorists according to their differing conceptions of society itself. In the voluntaristic outlook man's natural condition is one of complete independence, and society with its organs of authority is an artificial human construction. For some voluntarists (Hobbes, Locke) this construction is necessary to prevent conflict and chaos among men, for others (Rousseau) it is a demoralizing force; either way, authority is conceived as essentially a coercive restraint on man's natural freedom. In Marxist ideology, society is natural to man but the State, again understood as the instrument of coercion (i.e., of economic class exploitation), will disappear when the classless society is evolved. On the other hand, the followers of Aristotle hold that man is by nature a social and political animal. He is not naturally capable of living in complete independence but needs society for his fulfillment as a person; and there is no society without authority, since some person or persons chiefly responsible for the common welfare must have the duty and right to direct others toward that end. For this philosophy, authority is essentially a moral rather than coercive power. Its proper means of directing men are means of the moral order, i.e., commands that carry the force of moral obligation for those to whom they are addressed. Such power does not compromise but presupposes human freedom, since moral obligations can be imposed only on free, responsible agents. Moreover, authority enhances freedom inasmuch as it directs men to the truest exercise of their freedom, i.e., to the performance of acts ordered for their common good. The ability to coerce must belong to authority also, but only as a means of enforcing its moral power on those who cannot be directed as responsible beings, e.g., on children in a family who do not yet understand moral obligation, or on recalcitrant citizens in civil society.

Christian Perspectives. From the Christian viewpoint all authority is seen as coming from God, and this is the ultimate basis of man's moral obligation to obey legitimate rulers (Rom 13.1). Moreover, it follows that no man's authority can be absolute; his commands are null if they exceed the scope of his God-given power or, a fortiori, if they contradict God's own law (cf. Jn 19.11; Acts 5.29). While all Christian thinkers have necessarily subscribed to these principles, their explanations of the role of authority have shown divergences somewhat parallel to the differing philosophical positions discussed above. Augustine, characteristically emphasizing the consequences of man's Fall and also heavily influenced by the political realities of his day, described civil authority chiefly in terms of a coercive force which serves as a punishment and remedy for sin. For Thomas Aquinas, assimilating the Aristotelian tradition, the essential function of human authority is not the correction of sin but the ordering of social life. Authority as a moral directive power would have been present among men even without the Fall; it exists not because Adam sinned but because God, being an infinitely liberal Creator, wishes to communicate a share of his providential lordship to creatures by having some men direct others toward their common destiny. The mainstream of modern Catholic social teaching has favored St. Thomas' approach; popes from Leo XIII through Paul VI have carried forward the idea that government is responsible not only for protecting citizens from unjust harm but for advancing human welfare in a positive way.

Ecclesiastical Authority. Authority in the Church is a unique case, since the Church is unique among societies. It does have the essential features of a society, but the concept of society is clearly insufficient to express her full reality as the Body of Christ, the visible extension of Christ's salvific life and activity in the world. Ecclesiastical authority, therefore, cannot be understood in purely political terms. Christ himself, who insisted that his kingship is not of this world (Jn 18.36), forbids the shepherds of his Church to aspire to lordship in the manner of earthly rulers; those who would be first in his kingdom must be the ministers, slaves, of the others (Mt 20.20–28; Mk 10.35–45; Lk 22.24–27).

Nevertheless, this does not exclude from the Church offices of prelacy which involve power to direct the faithful. The Apostles were conscious of their commission to teach and command with binding force in Christ's name (Mt 16.19, 18.18; 2 Cor 13.10, Gal 1.6–9). In the Church as well as in civil society, therefore, there is an order of directive power which incarnates the universal providence of God; but whereas in the State this order is the supreme principle, in the Church its role is thoroughly subordinate to that of charity and grace which are the essential motive forces of the Christian life. BIBLIOGRAPHY: Y. Simon, *General Theory of Authority* (1962); J. M. Todd, ed., *Problems of Authority* (1962); K. Schmitz, "Scrutinizing the Inscrutable," *Review of Metaphysics* 27 (1973) 346–370. *AUTHORITY, ECCLESIASTICAL; *MAGISTERIUM.

[B. A. WILLIAMS]

AUTHORITY, ECCLESIASTICAL, the right or power to direct community life and action in the Church. As the visible people of God seeking a common end through concerted action, the Church needs some recognized control, some power to determine ways and means, to allot functions, and to redress grievances. In the Catholic view Christ himself provided for this need by selecting and preparing the Twelve as his surrogates and by enabling them to direct the Christian community in his name. As the Gospels testify to the apostolic preparation and commission, the Acts of the Apostles and the Pauline Epistles portray the exercise of this authority during the next generation by those who were "not from men nor through men, but through Jesus Christ and God the Father" (Gal. 1.1). Since the Church is of its nature a doctrinal society, maintaining Christian revelation and living by it, it pertains to the authority of the Apostles and their successors to propose the message of salvation authentically. From the beginning it was to the "doctrine of the Apostles," as well as to "fellowship, the breaking of bread and prayers" (Acts 2.42), that the Christian community devoted itself. Broad and penetrating as the apostolic authority is in the Catholic understanding, it need not smother the activity of those subject to it. The Christian life is not a mere mechanical execution of directives externally received; men and women begotten in the Gospel are children of God and must develop internal precepts of supernatural life by which they continually grow. This healthy growth is not necessarily jeopardized by the intervention of authority, which may sometimes prune the branches "that they may bring forth more fruit" (Jn 15.2) or assert itself to keep the more slowly maturing branches from being stifled by the exuberance of the more rapidly developing ones. BIBLIOGRAPHY: L. Bouyer, *Word, Church and Sacraments in Protestantism and Catholicism* (tr. A. V. Littledale, 1961); E. Dublanchy, DTC 4.2:2175–2207; K. Mörsdorf, LTK 6:218–221; J. Deretz and A. Nocent, *Dictionary of the Council* (1968) 24–28.

[S. E. DONLON]

AUTHORITY PROBLEMS. In the narrow or psychological sense they are problems of an individual's acceptance of and adjustment to outside control and direction of behavior. In the broader or sociological sense, they are problems of the relationship between structure and command on the one hand and individual spontaneity and responsibility on the other. The psychological and sociological dimensions are connected. In every society there must be a balance between organization which produces order, peace, and efficiency, and individual initiative which provides inventiveness, competition, and enthusiasm. An excess of organization produces rigidity and stagnation, an excess of individual initiative permits conflict and chaos. The problem of achieving a healthy balance (which varies with circumstances, e.g., in times of crisis the need for authority increases) is complicated by the tendency of authority to extend its influence without justification, (e.g., once constituted, an organization tends to work for its own continuation regardless of the purposes for which it was established; power tends to accumulate privilege and protect itself), and by the tendencies of individuals to demand more self-determination, more private reward, and less burden in contributing to the common good. Conflicts between authority and individuality generate fear and suspicion in the former, resentment and rebellion from the latter. In this context, individual or psychological authority problems arise. A child reared in a rigid authoritarian pattern serving primarily the needs and interests of the parents, will have difficulty accepting any authority as beneficent and will react by rebellion, or subservience with deep hostility, or deceit. A person regarding larger social structures as self-serving, oppressive, and indifferent to individual needs will react by open or covert delinquency and crime.

[M. E. STOCK]

AUTHORIZED VERSION, English translation of the Bible published in 1611; known in the U.S. as the King James Version. At the Hampton Court Conference (1604) the Puritan John Rainolds (Reynolds) proposed a new translation, and James I ordered one prepared. A group of 47 scholars did the work, though not undertaking a totally new translation but a revision of the *Bishops' Bible, with other versions used for comparison. When it was printed, the words "appointed to be read in churches" appeared on the title page, but no record exists of any official act authorizing its use. It became, however, the standard version of English-speaking Protestants.

[T. EARLY]

AUTO-DA-FÉ (Portuguese, act of faith), the public ceremony wherein the decisions of the Spanish Inquisition were proclaimed. The elaborate event included a procession, a sermon, and a reading of the decisions of the Inquisition, followed by recantations, reconciliations, and the handing over of the obdurate to the secular arm. Popular usage often erroneously connects *auto-da-fé* with the execution of heretics. The first *auto* was held in Seville in 1481; the last, in Mexico in 1850. BIBLIOGRAPHY: H. Kamen, *Spanish Inquisition* (1965); R. I. Burns, NCE 1:1116. *INQUISITION, SPANISH.

[D. NUGENT]

AUTOCEPHALY (from the Gr. *auto*, self, and *kephalē*, head), the independence or self-governing status of an Orthodox Church. The two essential rights proper to an autocephalous Church are the authority to resolve all internal problems without external ecclesiastical interference and the power to name its own bishops including the ruling head of the Church. The term has evolved in Orthodox practice; it is not a canonical term employed in the definitions of the seven Ecumenical Councils recognized by Orthodoxy. Three elements are commonly held to be canonically necessary for autocephalous status: (1) canonical origin, i.e., a region must have belonged to an autocephalous Church in order to claim autocephaly itself; (2) location in a state politically independent of that in which the autocephalous Mother Church is located, although independence is often determined more by cultural and racial unity than by national boundaries; (3) a hierarchy composed of at least three duly appointed bishops, i.e., appointed according to canon 4 of the Council of Nicaea I (325), by at least three other ruling bishops of the original jurisdiction. In addition to the ancient patriarchates of Constantinople, Alexandria, Antioch, and Jerusalem, autoceph-

aly is enjoyed by the later patriarchates of Bulgaria, Serbia, Moscow, and Rumania; the catholicate of Georgia, and the Orthodox Churches of Cyprus, Mt. Sinai, Greece, Poland, Albania, and Czechoslovakia. Among these autocephalous Churches there exists a traditional hierarchy of honor based upon date of establishment rather than present strength. Since the Russian revolution (1917) some of the emigré Churches, e.g., Ukrainian and Russian groups, claim autocephaly but are not necessarily recognized as such by the Mother Church. In the West the Churches of the Anglican and Old Catholic communions are often described as autocephalous to indicate the independence of each member Church from higher ecclesiastical jurisdiction. BIBLIOGRAPHY: L. Herman, DDC 1:1475–80; G. A. Maloney, NCE 10:789–794; *Handbook of American Orthodoxy* (1972) "Autocephalous," 181.

[F. T. RYAN]

AUTOGENIC CHURCHES, a classification for the numerous, small pseudo-Orthodox bodies that have sprung up in the 20th cent., esp. in the U.S. The designation "autogenic" (self-starting) is applied to such Churches to indicate a lack of canonical lineage. They generally claim Old Catholic or Monophysite orders, but in most cases no Old Catholic or Monophysite Church nor any canonical Orthodox jurisdiction recognizes them.

[F. T. RYAN]

AUTOLYCUS, the addressee in the only extant work of Theophilus of Antioch, entitled *To Autolycus,* an apology in three loosely connected books written shortly after 180. This is the earliest extant work to use the word *Trias* to designate the three divine persons. Whether Autolycus is a real person or a literary fiction is uncertain. Resemblances between *To Autolycus* and Irenaeus's *Adversus haereses* have suggested that Irenaeus perhaps used the work of Theophilus. BIBLIOGRAPHY: R. M. Grant, "Theophilus of Antioch to Autolycus," HTR 40 (1947) 227–256; Quasten 1:236–242.

[H. DRESSLER]

AUTOMATISM, a belief in the pre-eminence of control of man through machines. Such a belief holds that man's technological inventiveness finds its fullest expression when man designs the machine that controls man. Before one identifies the theological implications in holding it, one might do well to say something about the philosophical implications. Automation is the cumulative result of man's technological endeavors that finds its final expression in cybernetics. The belief that every human "need" can be satisfied and fulfilled in an ever-increasingly perfect mode is as immoral as it is absurd. There are, it seems clear, some "needs" (neither identified by man as an individual nor expressed by him in that manner) that ought not to be fulfilled. The current trend in society has been toward fulfilling contrived needs and doing so in an ever-increased production of ways to satisfy man. We are, allegedly, a society of consumers. Automation is the helmsman for technology, and it has steered the course from machine-guided to machine-controlled. Man is "liberated" by it from guiding and directing the hardware of his work. Other "needs" are created—some of which result in man's displacement, and thus contribute to an unstable society. The religious and moral issues are obvious. Not so obvious is the response that man himself must make if he is ever to regain control over his life and over the future. The autonomy with which God has endowed him can only find form in a future where man assumes leadership and responsibility for the events and circumstances of his life. BIBLIOGRAPHY: A. C. Hughes, NCE 1:1118–19; R. M. Young, EncPhil 1:126–127 s.v. "Cybernetics"; J. R. Rivello, *Adaptation of Bernard J. F. Lonergan's Heuristic Structure: A Response to Institutional Moral Scotosis* (Temple Univ., 1974).

[J. R. RIVELLO]

AUTOMATISM, a form of modern art related to surrealism, not unlike doodling in its expression of the creative unconscious through free-flowing or uncontrolled movements of the artist's hand. André Masson's work is an exposition of the style. BIBLIOGRAPHY: M. Raynal et al., *History of Modern Painting* (v. 3, *From Picasso to Surrealism,* 1950).

[M. J. DALY]

AUTOMELON, a type of Greek hymn. In Byzantine music, a hymn (*kontakion, kanon, sticheron,* etc.) which has a metrical pattern and melody original with itself is called an idiomelon. An automelon is one of a select group of idiomela whose melody was used for a prosomoion, i.e., a hymn text sung to a borrowed melody. BIBLIOGRAPHY: Apel HDMus 401, s.v., "Idiomelon"; Reese MusMA 78.

[M. T. LEGGE]

AUTONOMY, the status of an Orthodox Church that enjoys a limited right to self-government. The chief restriction upon its independency consists in the fact that its ruling head must be selected or confirmed by an autocephalous Church. Moreover, its right to participation in the community of world Orthodoxy is subject to various limitations. Development within an autonomous Church sometimes reaches a point that justifies the concession to it of the status of autocephaly, as e.g., in the Orthodox Church of Czechoslovakia. At the present time the Orthodox Churches of Finland, Japan, China, Estonia, Latvia, Hungary, and Macedonia are autonomous. The Orthodox Church of America, with approximately 850,000 members, was given independent status by the Patriarchate of Moscow in 1970.

[F. T. RYAN]

AUTOPSY, exploration of the human cadaver for purposes of scientific research or for detection of crime. Moralists regard it as permissible. However, legal permission to perform autopsy must be obtained from those who have legal responsibility for the deceased. In addition, permission, whether legal, moral or ecclesial, does not remove the further obligation of decent Christian burial. BIBLIOGRAPHY: M. B. Walsh, NCE 4:671 s.v. "Dead, Care of the Bodies of the."

[J. R. RIVELLO]

AUTOS SACRAMENTALES, a Spanish play in one act, presented with personified abstractions as characters; an allegorical action on a sacred or biblical subject.

[S. A. HEENEY]

AUTPERT, AMBROSE (d. 784), Benedictine preacher and writer. It is only because of the work of recent scholars that he is known. A.'s works include commentaries on the Apocalypse, an ascetical treatise, and a commentary on the lives of the saints. BIBLIOGRAPHY: M. J. Barry, NCE 1:1120; H. Riedlinger, LTK 1:426 s.v. "Ambrosius Autpertus."

[J. R. RIVELLO]

AUTUN, seat of ancient bishopric now embracing the French Department of Saône-et-Loire, in the Burgundy region. Known in Roman times as Augustodunum, it received Christianity from Lyon and today is a suffragan see to Lyon. According to tradition, a St. Amator became the first bp. of Autun c.250, but the first bp. definitely known was St. Reticius, who attended the Council of Arles in 314. Several monasteries were founded at Autun, and a council under St. Leodegar (c.616–679), bp. of Autun ordered strict observance of the Benedictine Rule. St. Leodegar also involved himself in the power struggles of the Merovingian kingdom after the death of Clotaire III (670) and was expelled from his see, blinded, and finally executed by his opponents. The Autun diocese embraces the site where the monastery of *Cluny was founded in 909. The abbey of Cluny, completed in the 12th cent., was the largest church in Europe until the basilica of St. Peter's in Rome was built. With the legate of Gregory VII presiding, a council at Autun (1077) deposed Abp. Manasses of Reims for defying Gregory's reforms.

[T. EARLY]

AUTUN, CATHEDRAL OF SAINT-LAZARE, a French pilgrimage shrine, Burgundian Romanesque, consecrated in 1130, completed c.1146, with the famous Apocalyptic Last Judgment portal which, covered with bricks and plaster in the mid-18th cent. (removed 1939), was saved from the iconoclasm of the Revolution. The Gothic central towers and chapels were added in the 15th cent. by Nicolas Rolin, chancellor of Burgundy (born in Autun and immortalized as the donor in the Madonna by Van Eyck). One of the greatest masterpieces of Romanesque style the awesome tympanum sculptured in the early 12th cent. by the famed Giselbertus is the *summa* of his achievement, carrying 23 signed originals and the inscription "*Giselbertus Hoc Fecit*" beneath the feet of Christ on the west tympanum. Giselbertus alone was capable of this expressive, highly emotional style, the long slender proportions, and swirling drapery. The greatest carvings are Dream of the Magi, Three Hebrews in Fiery Furnace, and on the lintel of the N door the reclining Eve—sensuous and hauntingly beautiful (Rolin Museum) unparalleled as a nude female form in medieval sculpture. With assistants Giselbertus further carved trumpeting angels, the dead rising from tombs, St. Michael weighing souls against the devil, while roaring demons thrust the lost into the maw of hell. In the 12th cent. Cluny served as model for Autun. Autun in turn influenced Gothic sculpture of the 13th century. BIBLIOGRAPHY: D. Grivot and G. Zarnecki, *Giselbertus, Sculptor of Autun* (1961).

[M. J. DALY]

AUTUN, COUNCILS OF. The many medieval councils held at Autun dealt largely with local problems. The one held *c*.670 insisted on strict observance of the Benedictine Rule; sacramental communion by all Christians at Christmas, Easter, and Pentecost; and priests' knowing the Apostles' and Athanasian Creeds. A council in 1077 promoted the Gregorian reform. BIBLIOGRAPHY: A. Condit, NCE 1:1120.

[B. L. MARTHALER]

AUVERGNE, CHURCHES OF, a peculiarly bold and impressive style of French 12th-cent. Romanesque architecture under the influence of Burgundy and the Loire regions. Varied architectural forms without galleries and aisles, pedimental lintels, cusped arches (Notre-Dame-du-Port) and curling brackets suggest Moorish and Oriental influences. Decoration peculiar to the region (found in no other part of France) shows elaborate geometric appliqués to apse walls of star, diaper, and stripe polychrome designs in red, brown, gray, and black local stone, in a style so vital and dynamic, its very crudity is the basis of its sincerity and depth. The greatest achievement in Auvergne sculpture is at Notre-Dame-du-Port in Clermont-Ferrand. At Le Puy are very fine Romanesque frescoes and dominant Moorish influence. BIBLIOGRAPHY: K. J. Conant, *Carolingian and Romanesque Architecture, 800–1200* (1959).

[M. J. DALY]

AUXENTIUS OF DOROSTORUM (Mecurinus; 4th cent.), Arian bishop. Disciple and biographer of the Arian bp., Ulfilas, A. was deposed by the edict of Theodosius after the Council of Constantinople (381). Named Arian bp. of Milan by Valentinian II at the suggestion of the Empress Justina (385), he took the name of the predecessor of Ambrose. Ambrose thwarted his and Justina's attempts to gain the Basilica of the Apostles and the Basilica Portiana for the use of the Arians. BIBLIOGRAPHY: T. Shahan, CE 2:144; G. Godini, BiblSanct 1:956.

[F. H. BRIGHAM]

AUXENTIUS OF MILAN (d. 374), Arian bishop. A native of Cappadocia, A. was appointed to replace Dionysius, the exiled bp. of Milan (355). Though condemned by the

councils of Rimini (359) and Paris (360), he took advantage of the unwillingness of Valentinian I to become involved in theological disputes and by subscribing to the controversial creed of Rimini maintained his see until his death despite the efforts of orthodox opposition led by Hilary of Poitiers (364–365) and St. Athanasius and Pope Damasus (369). St. Ambrose was his successor by popular acclamation. BIBLIOGRAPHY: T. Shahan, CE 2:144; J. Zeiller, DHGE 5:935–936.

[H. JACK]

AUXERRE, French city and site of a bishopric from the 4th to 18th centuries. A flourishing town from pre-Roman times, it is on the Yonne River and today serves as the capital of Yonne Department in Burgundy, central France. According to tradition, Christian martyrdoms occurred at Auxerre under Aurelian (270–275), and one Peregrinus, perhaps an itinerant, was the first bishop. But a more definite succession begins with Bp. Marcellian of the early 4th century. Later bps. included St. Amator (d. 418) and St. Germanus or Germain (*c*.378–448). St. Patrick perhaps visited Auxerre during their time, but the extent of his association with them remains uncertain. A diocesan synod under St. Aunarius (bp. 561–601) produced canons of historical interest. He also arranged for an important transcription of the Hieronymian Martyrology. During the medieval period, the bps. became feudal lords, and the diocese was often disturbed by wars. Jansenism became strong under Bp. Charles G. de Caylus (1704–54). The diocese was abolished in 1790, and it now forms part of the Archdiocese of Sens.

[T. EARLY]

AUXERRE, SAINT-ÉTIENNE, French Burgundian Gothic cathedral (13th-16th cent.), built on the site of a 5th-cent. sanctuary and over an austere Romanesque crypt with nave, ambulatory, and apsidal chapel (11th cent.) and frescoed vaults (12th cent.). Famous are the 13th cent. windows of the choir and ambulatory, and rare 13th cent. enamels and MSS in its treasury. BIBLIOGRAPHY: R. de Lasteyrie, *L'Architecture religieuse en France à l'Époque gothique*, (2 v., 1926–27).

[M. J. DALY]

AUXERRE, SAINT-GERMAIN, French abbey church on the site of the Merovingian basilica, erected (early 6th cent.) by Queen Clotilda, wife of Clovis, demolished in the 9th century. New construction added an eastern apse and rotunda to the vaulted crypt (*c*.841) which housed the tomb of St. Germain (5th cent. bp.). A. series of frescoes to the west executed under Heribald (857) are the oldest extant wall paintings in France. This complex basilica was dedicated in 864. Further modifications in a beautiful bell tower (12th cent.) and Gothic reconstruction (1277–1398) followed. BIBLIOGRAPHY: J. Vallery-Radot, "St. Germain d'Auxerre, l'Église haut," *Congrès Archéologique de France, 1958* (1959).

[M. J. DALY]

AUXILIARY BISHOP, a coadjutor but without right of succession, given by the Holy See to the person of a residential bishop. Some of the duties required of an auxiliary are to help the ruling bishop who, because of his health, age, or pressures of work, needs assistance. Since no bishop may be consecrated without a title to a see, auxiliary bishops are of necessity titular bishops.

[S. A. HEENEY]

AUXILIARY SAINTS, see FOURTEEN HOLY HELPERS.

AUXILIUS OF NAPLES (fl. 890), Frankish priest whose ordination by Pope Formosus (891–896) was declared invalid by the decrees of the Cadaveric Council (897) which were reaffirmed by Pope Sergius III (904–911). When Sergius demanded reordination, A. defended the legality of the papal election of *Formosus and opposed reordination on the grounds that the validity of orders was not contingent upon the integrity of its minister. His principal writings though polemical in tone reflect a remarkable familiarity with earlier canonical literature and include *De ordinationibus a Formoso papa factis* (PL 129:1059–74), *Infensor et defensor* (PL 129:1073–1102), and *Defensionem sacrae ordinationis papae Formosi* (*Auxilius und Vulgarius* [1866] ed. E. Dümmler), 59–65. BIBLIOGRAPHY: P. Fournier, DHGE 5:971–972; E. Mangenot, DTC 1.2:2622–23; J. P. Kirsch, CE 2:147.

[F. G. O'BRIEN]

AVAGHERETZ, archpriest, in the Armenian Church, the head of a parish church.

[A. CODY]

AVALOKITEŚVARA (Chinese, *Kuan-yin;* Japanese, *Kwannon*) Buddhist deity, the watchful (*Avalokita*) Lord (*Isvara*) or Bodhisattva of Compassion. Tantric forms show 1,000 arms with 5 or 11 heads. At first a male deity, A. in later Chinese and Japanese art is the female *Kuan-yin,* Goddess of Mercy and Compassion. Catholic missionary iconography relates her to the Virgin as Mother of Mercy.

[M. J. DALY]

AVANCINI, NICOLA (1612–86), Jesuit moralist and ascetical writer. Born at Val di Non near Trent, A. joined the Jesuits in 1627, taught at Trieste (1634), Laibach (1635), and Vienna (1641). He held various administrative positions in the Society. He achieved some reputation as an orator, dramatist, and poet, but is best remembered for his *Vita et doctrina Iesu Christi* (Vienna 1665). This was among the most widely diffused collections of meditations of the 17th century. It went through more than 50 eds. and has been translated into most modern European tongues. A modern English translation of it, with some adaptation, was published by R. D. McKenzie (SPCK, 1937). BIBLIOGRAPHY: Sommervogel 1:668–680; B. Duhr, *Geschichte der Jesuiten in den Ländern deutscher Zunge* (6 v., 1921–28) 3:579–581.

[P. K. MEAGHER]

AVARICE, see GREED.

AVARS, Mongol nomads who formed a central European state from *c.*559–796. They were in frequent contact with the Byzantine Empire and organized the Slavs in their southward migrations. In the early 7th cent. the Avars and their Slavic subjects ravaged the Balkans. The Slavs broke away, and Charlemagne effectively ended the Avar power in 796. In the 9th cent. they became Christians and were absorbed into other peoples. BIBLIOGRAPHY: F. Dvornik, *Slavs, Their Early History and Civilization* (1956).

[G. T. DENNIS]

AVATAR(A) (Sanskrit, descent), incarnation of the Hindu god Vishnu. Nine avatars have occurred already—in both human and animal form—and a tenth is yet to come. Identification of the Buddha as the ninth avatar of Vishnu weakened Buddhism as a separate movement in India. Also identified as avatars were Rama and Krishna.

[T. EARLY]

AVE MARIA (Lat. for Hail Mary), the prayer with which Christians honor Mary, the Mother of Jesus, addressing her directly as did Gabriel. The prayer is twofold: the scriptural part, based on the opening chapter of Luke (see ANNUNCIATION), and the prayer of the Church asking Mary's intercession. The first part was in common use toward the end of the 12th cent., and enjoined in 1196 by Odo of Paris; for the second, a 15th cent. Franciscan is credited with composing the supplication for sinners. In the canonical hours the Church is loathe to separate the Ave Maria from the Pater Noster and the Gloria. Tertullian calls the Ave Maria the resumé of the Gospel. It is recited or sung alone or in company, interpreted in pictorial media or in dance or theater; to compose music for it for voice or instrument is a perennial aspiration of Christendom (see C. Gounod, F. Schubert). The "*Ave* bell" is the bell rung for the *Angelus. BIBLIOGRAPHY: R. Steiner, NCE 1:1123; A. A. DeMarco, *ibid.* 6:898.

[M. R. BROWN]

AVE MARIS STELLA, an unrhymed metrical hymn in honor of Our Lady. It has seven strophes of four lines each, written in trochaic dimeter with three trochees to each line. Attributed to various authors, Fortunatus and St. Ambrose, among others, it was first recorded in the Codex Sangallensis 95, and so must date from at least the 9th cent., if not before. One of the most popular Marian hymns of the Middle Ages, it is retained in the Roman Breviary for the Vespers of feasts of the Blessed Virgin, and may be found in the *Liber usualis,* pp. 1259–63, in three versions, one each in the first, fourth and seventh modes.

The hymn addresses Our Lady under the title (also in her litany) "star of the sea," the virgin through whose assent to Gabriel's message, evil was overcome. It begs her maternal protection and assistance and concludes with a doxology.

Being a metrical hymn (one of the few which escaped the

revision of the Breviary under Urban VIII), it has been set many times to hymn tunes, usually harmonized or at least with organ accompaniment, and it still has a place in almost every hymn book. There are also polyphonic settings (Dufay), Masses (Josquin, Morales, Victoria) and organ compositions based on the first melody in the *Liber Usualis*.

Translations are manifold, among the most beautiful being those of G. R. Woodward and of E. Caswall. BIBLIOGRAPHY: B. J. Comaskey, NCE 1:1123–24; M. Britt, *Hymns of the Breviary and Missal* (1922) 317–319.

[M. T. LEGGE]

AVEBURY, Neolithic monument (betw. 1700 and 1500 B.C.), near Avebury, England, relating to Stonehenge, showing an outer earthwork with circular ditch, a Great Circle of upright stones and several smaller circles each *c*.320 feet in diameter. The Great Circle originally contained *c*.100 undressed sarsen blocks, the heaviest weighing over 40 tons. An avenue to the S was added later.

[M. J. DALY]

AVELLANA COLLECTIO, a canonical collection of MSS of emperors and popes. One of the oldest of this ancient collection, acquired by the Vatican Library, was bought for the abbey of Santa Croce Avellana by St. Peter Damian (d. 1073). Dating from about 553, the collection begins with a rescript in the year 368 of Emperor Valentinian I and ends with a letter of Pope Vigilius to Justinian in 553. It is highly regarded because it contains about 200 early canonical documents that are found in no other collection. BIBLIOGRAPHY: P. Ciprotti, EncCatt 2:509–510; J. Gaudemet, NCE 1:1124.

[M. C. BRADLEY]

AVELLINO, ANDREW, ST. (1521–1608), Theatine reformer. Of noble birth, he became a cleric in 1537 and a priest in 1545. He abandoned the study of law for the care of souls in 1548, thanks to the Jesuit Lainez. In 1556 he became a Theatine after recovery from a beating by enemies of his reform. He was spiritual director of several institutions in Milan and Piacenza (1570–82) and spent the rest of his life in Naples. His letters (2 v. 1731–32) and other writings (5 v. 1733–34) were published after his canonization in 1712. BIBLIOGRAPHY: T. Andrew, BiblSanct 1:1118–23; A. Palmieri, DHGE 2:1635–37.

[E. P. COLBERT]

AVEMPACE (Ibn Bājja, Abū-Bakr Mohammed ibn Yahya ibn al-Sāyigh, d. 1138), Islamic philosopher. A.'s philosophy is seen best in his work, *Rule of the Solitary*. The work depicts man's voyage toward a union with the Active Intellect; for A. the only modality of existence for such a movement is one of discipline since the assumption of that modality places a demand for prior reflective action on the subject. The citizen of the ideal state and the perfect city finds his model in such a modality. Ultimately, it is every man's task to find that modality and make its content a viable one for the union of the human soul with the Divine. His development of philosophy is different from that of his contemporaries, but the recognition of the need for a spiritual man capable of choosing that modality is common to other philosophers of his age, e.g., Ibn Arabi and Ibn Masarra. It is alleged that he influenced *Galileo in the formulation of his law of falling bodies. BIBLIOGRAPHY: H. Corbin, EncPhil 4:105–106; s.v. "Ibn Bājja" B. H. Zedler, NCE 1:1125; Copleston 2.1:222.

[J. R. RIVELLO]

AVENDAÑO, DIEGO DE (1594–1688), Jesuit missionary. Born in Spain, he became a Jesuit in Lima, where he taught at Cuzco and Chuquisaca, was rector of the major seminary in Lima, and became provincial (1663–66). His great achievement , however, was his *Thesaurus indicus* in which he applied his knowledge of Canon, civil, and moral law to the solution of legal problems peculiar to the Indian environment.

[H. JACK]

AVENIR, L', a daily newspaper representing the cause of French Liberal Catholics from Oct. 16, 1830 until Nov. 15, 1831. It was founded and edited by F. de *Lamennais in the aftermath of the Revolution of 1830 to defend the Church threatened from association with the deposed Bourbons. Its motto was "God and Liberty"; it rejected all privilege or penalty for any religious belief. At the cost of the loss of state support, the Church would thus gain freedom to choose its officials and direct its affairs (abrogating Napoleon's concordat of 1801). It protested state monopoly of education (Napoleon's univ.) in favor of the right of parents to select schools for their children. It championed the elimination of censorship of press and theater, free association of all groups (contrary to Napoleon's Civil Code), and local self-government. It sponsored a lay association for freedom of education and interested itself in social justice and the liberation of Catholics in Belgium, Poland, and Ireland. Growing hostility to these novelties and a decline in subscriptions led Lamennais, *Lacordaire, and Montalembert to journey to Rome. Their consistent support of the papacy did not prevent the condemnation of their principles by Gregory XVI in *Mirari vos* (Aug 15, 1832). BIBLIOGRAPHY: P. N. Stearns, *Priest and Revolutionary* (1967).

[J. MOODY]

AVENTINUS (Johannes Thurmayr; 1477–1534), historian and humanist. As historian for the dukes of Bavaria, he collected original documents and produced *Annales ducum Boiariae* (1522; pub. 1544), and *Bayerische Chronik* (1533; pub. 1566). He was a virulent anticlerical and social critic, an enthusiastic German nationalist, and a friend of Melanchthon and Lefèvre d'Étaples, but he remained within the Roman Church. BIBLIOGRAPHY: G. Strauss, *Historian in an Age of Crisis: The Life and Work of Johannes Aventinus* (1963).

[V. SAMPSON]

AVERROËS (c.1126–c.1198). Latinized name of Ibn Rushd, physician, theologian, and the most celebrated Islamic philosopher in Spain. Born at Córdoba to a Spanish Arabian family of judges, A. was educated in Islamic studies, particularly theology and law, but also in philosophy, mathematics, astronomy and medicine. A. became *qadi* or judge of Seville in 1169, and 1171 returned to Córdoba where he served as chief *qadi*. In 1182, he was appointed physician to Abu Ya'qūb Yusūf, calif of Marrakesh. After a brief interval of residence in Lucena (c.1195) as a result of a religious controversy, he returned to Marrakesh where his death marked the end of the period of Islam's greatest philosophic tradition from 700 to 1200.

Most of A.'s datable writings fall between 1159 and 1195. In medicine, his *Kitab al-Kulliyyat* (c.1162) served as an authoritative encyclopedia for centuries. In theology, his *Fasl al-Maqal (Divine Treatise)*, supports the right of Muslim scholars to philosophize, whereas in *al-Kashf an Manahij al-Adilla (Exposition of The Method of Proof)*, he provides an exposition of Mohammedan theology. His principal independent work in religious philosophy is the *Tahafut al-Tahafut (Incoherence of the Incoherence)*, rebuttal of *Algazel's attack upon rationalism in theology. But A. is known in philosophy mainly for his commentaries on Aristotle's works, which had a profound influence upon Christian Scholasticism and Jewish thought during the later Middle Ages and the Renaissance. Many of these were translated into Latin and Hebrew in the 13th cent. and were first printed in 1472–74. Because of them, A. is frequently known as *"The Commentator."*

A. regarded philosophical truth and the philosophy of Aristotle as one and the same. His intent was always to set forth authentic Aristotelian teaching. But his approach to Greek philosophy and Aristotle was conditioned by the influence of a work now attributed to Plotinus —*Theology*—which he knew through the commentators Alexander of Aphrodisias and Simplicius. As a consequence, the substance of his philosophy is Aristotelian, but his methodology shows the influence of Plato.

Although the doctrine is not strictly articulated in A.'s writings, Latin-Averroists erroneously inferred from them that there are two species of truth, religious and philosophic, which may be contradictory and yet both true. This trend of interpretation in European universities in the 13th cent. led to the condemnation of A.'s teachings by the Pope in 1277 and for a time tended to retard the acceptance of Aristotle himself (see DOUBLE TRUTH, THEORY OF). BIBLIOGRAPHY: Gilson HCP 216–225 and *passim;* Copleston 2:197–200; S. MacClintock, EncPhil 1:220–226.

[J. T. HICKEY]

AVERROISM, LATIN, a school of thought among medieval Catholics that followed the philosophy of *Averroës (1126–98). Its principal figure was *Siger of Brabant (c.1240–c.1282), a member of the faculty of arts at Paris.

Averroës' commentaries on Aristotle were translated into Latin between 1220 and 1235, and subsequently gained influence with Christian theologians, esp. after the study of Aristotle was prescribed at Paris in 1255. Among the ideas expounded by Averroës in the commentaries were assertions that philosophical truth is derived from reason, not faith, but that faith and reason do not conflict and therefore do not need to be reconciled; that all men share in a single intellect, and that individuals therefore do not have immortality; and that matter is eternal (thus denying the creation and end of the world).

St. *Albert wrote a book against Averroës in 1256, and St. *Thomas wrote one in 1270. Siger, however, though also influenced by the *Neoplatonism of *Avicenna, followed Averroës, reconciling the conflict with Christian doctrine by what appeared to be a theory of the double truth, that a doctrine might be true in philosophy but false in theology. Cited for heresy in 1277, he fled to the papal curia at Orvieto, Italy, where he was killed by an apparently demented secretary. Averroism returned to Paris in the 14th cent., however, and existed in Italy as late as the 17th century. BIBLIOGRAPHY: Gilson HCP.

[T. EARLY]

AVERSA, RAPHAEL (1588–1657), Theatine theologian; noted for his work in Scholastic theology, esp. for *Theologia scholastica universa ad mentem s. Thomae.* BIBLIOGRAPHY: J. C. Willke, NCE 1:1129–30; G. Fussenegger, LTK 1:1146–47.

[J. R. RIVELLO]

AVESTA, the sacred book of ancient Persian religion preserved by the Parsees. The early *Avesta* (writings) and the edition available in the time of the Arsacid kings (249 B.C.-226 A.D.) are lost. The *Avesta* of the Sassanid period (226–651) consisted of 21 books (*nasks*), but only about a fourth of the work is extant. An official edition of the *Avesta* was made under the direction of the Sassanid king, Shappur II (309–379). The extant *Avesta* consists of the *Avesta* proper or the *Large Avesta* and the *Little Avesta*. The *Large Avesta* is divided into three parts: (1) *Yasna* (Sacrifice), texts in verse and prose sung by the priests during sacrifices—among these are the *Gāthās*, hymns and sayings ascribed to Zoroaster, the oldest part of the *Avesta;* (2) *Visprat*, or "All the patrons," containing invocations to all the gods; (3) the *vidēvdat* or Code against the Demons. The *Little Avesta* is composed of the *Yashts* (hymns) to the many divinities, including ancient gods whom Zoroaster opposed or ignored. There are also hymns to the spirits of the dead, to Royal Fortune, etc. An abundant literature in Pahlavi (Middle Persian) serves as a commentary on the *Avesta*. The term *Zand (Zend)* which is sometimes used erroneously in the phrase *Zand (Zend) Avesta* refers actually not to the *Avesta* but to the commentary on the *Avesta*. BIBLIOGRAPHY: J. Duchesne-Guillemin, NCE 1:1130; id., *La Religion de* *l' Iran ancien* (1962); R. C. Zaehner, *Dawn and Twilight of Zoroastrianism* (1962).

[M. R. P. McGUIRE]

AVICEBRON (Solomon ibn Gabriel; *c.* 1021–*c.* 70), Jewish poet and author of the philosophic treatise known to the scholastics in Latin translations by *John of Spain and *Dominic Gundisalvi as *Fons vitae* (*Fountain of life,* Eng. tr. H. E. Wedick, 1962). He was born and lived in Spain, and was influenced by the Arabic culture that flourished there. To medievals A. (also spelled Avicembron, Avicenbrol) was an Arabian philosopher, admired by many for his "Christian" insights; only in the 19th cent., through research by S. Munk, was the identity of the philosopher with the outstanding medieval Hebrew poet Solomon Ibn Gabirol ben Judah, established. The views characteristic of the *Fons vitae* are its Neoplatonic view of the hierarchized emanation of all things from God; the emphasis on the Divine Will (rather than the Logos) as the source of all creation; the universal hylomorphic composition and the plurality of forms in all creatures. The last two points particularly brought the *Fons vitae* into the controversies between medieval Augustinians and Aristotelians. The *Fons vitae* also influenced Spinoza. A. also wrote the *Improvement of Moral Qualities,* and the *Choice of Pearls,* both ethical treatises. Esp. from his *Kether Malkhut* (*Crown of Divine Kingship;* ed. with Eng. tr. J. Leedman, 1960), many of his poems have been incorporated into the Jewish liturgy, because they express the Jewish spirit of reverence for God, submission to his ways, and longing for redemption. BIBLIOGRAPHY: S. Munk, *Mélanges de Philosophie Juive et Arabe* (new ed., 1955); I. Husek, *History of Medieval Jewish Philosophy* (2d ed., 1959) 59–79; Gilson HCP 226–228.

[T. C. O'BRIEN]

AVICENNA (980–1037), Latinization derived from the name Abū 'Ali al-Ḥusayn ibn Abdullah ibn Sīnā—renowned medieval Islamic philosopher, physician, and scientist. Born in Bukhara, A. was educated as a child in the Koran and Arabic grammar and literature, and largely self-taught in his youth, studied logic, the natural sciences, mathematics, philosophy, and medicine. At 18 he was physician to the Samanid court in the library of which he acquired his vast knowledge of Greek philosophy. In 999, the Samanid empire collapsed and A. left Bukhara to wander in the cities of Transoxiana and Iran, serving local princes. About 1020, he was vizier and physician to the ruler of Hamadhān, later migrating to Ispahān where he became physician to the ruler, in whose service he spent the remainder of his life on journeys and military expeditions.

Of a prodigious number of writings, over 100 have survived in philosophy, natural science, medicine, religion, and literature. Some are in Persian e.g., the *Book of Science,* but most are in Arabic. His principal medical work, *Canon of Medicine,* is a voluminous synthesis of the Greek and Arabic

medicine and pharmacology studied in European universities into the 17th century. This and his most detailed philosophical work, *The Healing,* are his most influential writings, the latter being a presentation of the whole of ancient knowledge, divided into logic, natural science, the quadrivium, and metaphysics. But the *Demonstrations and Affirmations* distills the essence of A.'s philosophy and includes his more esoteric and mystical views.

With some major differences, his philosophic thought is built on that of al-Farabi (*c.* 873–950), owes much to Aristotle, and includes many Neoplatonic elements, all in an attempt to harmonize Greek philosophy with Islamic beliefs. Other influences are also present such as Stoicism, Gnosticism, and *Islamic theology and philosophy. For A., religion and philosophy are not different areas of truth but rather one and the same, as long as religion is properly construed in A.'s philosophic terms. Islamism is to be comprehended only through the philosophy of Aristotle and Plotinus (205?–270), the Neoplatonist, as interpreted by A.; thus understood, Islam is the highest mode of human life. A.'s doctrines had a profound impact on Islamic life and were also widely felt throughout the Latin Middle Ages. His philosophic teachings include the immortality of individual human souls; the identity of essence and existence in God; God as the Necessary Existent, the First Cause, Highest Intellect and Love; a hierarchy of separated intellects; and the emanation of all being from God.

There is no collected edition of A.'s works but a series of critical editions of parts of *al-Shifa* is being sponsored by the Egyptian government under the supervision of Ibrahim Madkur. Among English translations of A.'s works are: *Avicenna on Theology* (tr. A. Arberry, 1951); *Avicenna's Psychology* (tr. F. Rahman, 1952). BIBLIOGRAPHY: Y. Mehdawi, *Bibliographie d' Ibn Sina* (1954).

[J. T. HICKEY]

AVIGNON, capital of the French department of Vaucluse, 143 miles S of Lyons on the left bank of the Rhone. With a marshy valley to the N and the S, firm ground in the vicinity of the W bank and a limestone spur on the E bank, which became the foundation of the papal castle and the center of the town, Avignon was not easily accessible and its geography appears to have been a significant factor in its choice as a refuge for the popes (1309).

The city's existing plan still includes the 14th-cent. residence of the popes with its oval wall broken by 12 gateways. The papal residence erected on the Roches-des-Domes (1334–52) is a military structure including a hall of justice, consistory court, several chapels, private apartments, and banquet hall adjacent to the 12th-cent. Cathedral of Notre-Dame-des-Doms.

Its prehistoric village on the Roches-des-Domes became a Gallic tribal center and then a town of some importance in Gallo-Roman times on the Roman road between Arles and Valence.

In the 6th cent. a bishopric was established, but during the

MA Avignon was not part of the kingdom of France until Louis VIII captured the city in his campaign against the Albigensians (*c*.1219–26). Its period of prosperity began when Boniface VIII established a univ. there (1303) and peaked with the residence of Pope Clement V (1305–14) and his successors (1309–78), John XXII (1316–34), Benedict XII (1334–42), Clement VI (1342–52), Innocent VI (1352–62) Urban V (1362–70) and Gregory XI (1370–78). During the Western Schism, Pope Clement VII (1378–94) and Benedict XIII (1394–1411) resided there. The papal palace, the walls of the city, and several religious houses and collegiate churches were completed during the reigns of Popes Benedict XII, Clement VI, and Innocent VI.

After the Western Schism, the city was governed by a papal legate until 1693 when it became the responsibility of a vice legate representing a congregation in Rome. Temporarily occupied by French forces to bolster the prerogatives of French kings in their quarrels with the papacy (1663, 1688, 1768–74) it was annexed by the French constituent assembly during the Revolution (1791). The site of many councils and diocesan synods, it became a metropolitan see under Sixtus IV (1475), an extended bishopric under Aix including the Depts. of Vaucluse and Gard by the Concordat of 1801, and a metropolitan see again in 1822 with its suffragans of Carpentras, Cavaillon, and Vaison. BIBLIOGRAPHY: J. Girard, DHGE 5:1121–52; G. Mollat, *Popes at Avignon* (tr. J. Love, 1963); *id.*, *Catholicisme* 1:1129–30. *PAPACY; *AVIGNON PAPACY.

[F. H. BRIGHAM]

AVIGNON, PIETÀ OF, a painting by an anonymous master from Villeneuve-les-Avignon on the west bank of the Rhone, one of the most memorable renderings of this poignant theme, having elements Italian and Flemish (e.g., Roger van der Weyden), painted on luminous gold ground with tooled halos. The suppressed ornament and simple design are Italian rather than Northern, the monumental forms a "detente" or relaxation of Gothic detail effecting in a simple style of profound significance a masterpiece of serenity and grandeur. The painful accents, the isolation of the figures, the severe Islamic landscape mark a "coastal style" from Barcelona to Naples. BIBLIOGRAPHY: C. R. Morey, *Medieval Art* (1942).

[M. J. DALY]

AVIGNON, SCHOOL OF, in the 15th and the early 16th cent. a school of painting merging Flemish and Italian tradition in an "International Style," characterized by soft, pictorial quality, "realism of particulars" as in Gothic sculpture and *drôleries* of MSS, modeling in atmospheric space integrated panoramas of life in nature, effecting a poetic intimacy. Famous in the "International School" is the altar frontal *Parement de Narbonne* now in the Louvre. Principal masters were *Enguerrand de Charenton, Nicolas *Froment, *Simon de Chalons. Nicolas and Pierre *Mignard were

famous in the 17th cent. when the school showed greater Italian plasticity.

[M. J. DALY]

AVIGNON PAPACY, the papacy during the period 1308–78 when the popes lived at Avignon. The papacy was moved by Clement V due to disturbed conditions at Rome and other political factors. Though Avignon was not formally a part of France at the time, the move was widely construed as an increase in French influence over the papacy and was opposed by those resentful of French power. Other popes of the period were John XXII, Innocent VI, Urban V, and Gregory XI, who yielded to the pleas of St. *Catherine of Siena (1347–80) that he return to Rome. The period of the Avignon papacy almost exactly equalled the period of the Jewish Exile (Jer 25.11) and therefore was sometimes called the Babylonian Captivity. BIBLIOGRAPHY: G. Mollat, *Popes at Avignon* (tr. J. Love, 1963). *WESTERN SCHISM.

[T. EARLY]

ÁVILA, FRANCISCO DE (1573–1647), Peruvian scholar. A. was ordained (1591) in Cuzco and trained in law in Lima. He was known for his crusade against idolatry among the Indians. He wrote extensively and contributed to the development of Quechua literature. BIBLIOGRAPHY: C. D. Valcárcel, NCE 1:1136.

[H. JACK]

ÁVILA Y ZÚÑIGA, LUIS DE (1500–64), soldier, diplomat. A. belonged to the court of Emperor *Charles V, served in the imperial army in Africa, in the war against the German Estates (Schmalkald League), and in France. He was a confidant of the Emperor and was his personal and private emissary to Popes Paul III and Julius III in connection with the Council of *Trent. After the abdication of Charles, he acted as confidential ambassador for Philip II. Because of his intimate association with Charles and his various diplomatic assignments, his *Commentario* on the war in Germany (1546–47) is particularly valuable. BIBLIOGRAPHY: J. Coignet, DHGE 5:1192–94.

[H. JACK]

AVITUS OF BRAGA (d. 5th cent.), a venerable priest exiled by the barbarian invasions from Galicia, Spain, to Jerusalem, where he defended the anti-Origenist zeal of *Orosius (415). He had Lucian write an account of the sensational discovery of the relics of the protomartyr Stephen near Jerusalem, and his Latin translation is the only extant copy of Lucian's original Greek text. The relics of Stephen that A. sent to his bishop by Orosius came to rest in Minorca. BIBLIOGRAPHY: A. Lambert, DHGE 5:1201.

[E. P. COLBERT]

AVITUS OF VIENNE, ST. (*c*.450–*c*.519), Bp. of Vienne from *c*.494 in succession to his father, Isychius. Avitus converted the Arian Burgundian prince Sigismund to the

Catholic faith. He was also instrumental in bringing about closer ties between Rome and the Church in Gaul. He possessed a good classical education for his time. Of his works, 86 letters, 3 complete and many fragmentary homilies, and several poems survive. Works: PL 59:191–388. BIBLIOGRAPHY: Altaner 568–569; Butler 1:256–257.

[R. B. ENO]

AVIZ, ORDER OF, a military order of Portugese knights under Benedictine rule as adapted by John Ziritu, an early Cistercian abbot of Portugal. The order began in Portugal about 1146. Alfonso I gave the order the town of Evora, and the knights were first called Brothers of Santa Maria of Evora. Sometimes the knights were regarded as a branch of the Calatravan Order in Castile. A chief requisite was nobility of birth. The military orders were finally suppressed by Dom Pedro (1834). BIBLIOGRAPHY: C. Moeller, CE 2:161–162; J. Greven, LTK 1:1155.

[M. C. BRADLEY]

AVOIDANCE, also called shunning, the Mennonite practice of ostracizing those who have been placed under the *ban. The Swiss Anabaptists did not observe avoidance. Obbe *Philips introduced the practice among Dutch Anabaptists c.1533, and *Menno Simons continued it. There was continuous difficulty with the problem of applying the penalty without harshness, and with the question of marital avoidance when one spouse was excommunicated. The zeal of Jakob *Ammann to observe shunning was the cause of the separate existence of the Amish. Only the Old Order Amish and a few other conservative groups still enforce this form of discipline. Shunning has been referred to colloquially in the U.S. as an Amish "mite," from the German word for it, *Meidung.* BIBLIOGRAPHY: MennEnc 1:200–201.

[T. C. O'BRIEN]

AVOTH, see PIRKE AVOTH.

AVRANCHES, COUNCILS OF. King Henry II, excommunicated for the murder of Thomas Becket, abp. of Canterbury, was reconciled to the Church at Avranches, May 21, 1172. Thereupon he summoned the bishops of his realm to a council. It met in September of that year; its 12 canons regulate clerical privileges and obligations in regard to benefices. BIBLIOGRAPHY: A. Condit, NCE 1:1139.

[B. L. MARTHALER]

AVRIL, PHILIPPE (1654–98), Jesuit missionary. A novice in 1670, he taught mathematics and philosophy in Paris until 1684, when he tried to reach China by land free of Portuguese interference. He reached Moscow via Syria, Armenia, and the Volga, but was refused further transit and had to return. His account of this six-year journey (1692) was translated into German, English, Flemish, and Polish. His

promised history of Muscovy did not appear. He died in a shipwreck en route to China.

[E. P. COLBERT]

AVVAKUM PETROVITCH, archpriest (c.1620–82), son of a country priest in the district of Nizhni Novgorod (now Gorki). He is one of the most colorful figures in Russian church history because of his courageous, fanatical, and OT cast of mind. Blessed with many talents, including a fine literary style, he became the leader of resistance to ecclesiastical reform inaugurated by Patriarch Nikon. A. opposed the correction of church books by Kievan and Greek scholars and the modification of church rituals such as the proposed change from two to three-fingered sign of the cross. He and his followers' protests led to schism and the formation of the Old Believers, still in existence today. Despite exile (in which he wrote his autobiography), poverty, and prison, A. remained steadfast in his convictions, blurting out accusations against the reforms as he was burned at the stake. BIBLIOGRAPHY: *Life of the Archpriest Avvakum by Himself* (tr. J. Harrison and H. Mirrlees, 1963).

[D. DIRSCHERL]

AWARENESS, a heightened consciousness in man of a given event, condition, circumstance, or experience; usually accompanied by a stress or pressure to do something that the state of awareness has made present to one. Sometimes action under this stress is less effective, and frequently cumulative stress may lead to mental breakdown. While he struggles to maintain a modicum of integrity, man may be subject to a loss of awareness of the cause (s) of stress in the first place. This may, in turn, be due to any of four reasons: introduction of mechanisms, isolation of memory content, fragmentation of memory content, and finally failure to face the goals and motivational forces that either he or someone else has set for him. BIBLIOGRAPHY: D. J. Wack, NCE 1:25–26 s.v. "Abnormal Psychology."

[J. R. RIVELLO]

AXIONICUS (fl. 220), Gnostic teacher, the disciple of Valentinus who represented the Eastern or Anatolian school of the master and held that the body of Christ was pneumatic. His collegium was at Antioch. Both Tertullian(*Adv. Valent.* 4) and Hippolytus (*Adv. Haer.* 6) mention his significant influence. *GNOSTICISM.

[F. H. BRIGHAM]

AXUM, see AKSUM.

AYMARD, BL. (fl. 10th cent.), third abbot of Cluny 942–953, known for humility. He added only three monasteries to the Cluniac system, but he acquired 278 property charters as against 188 by his predecessor Odo; and in 948 he had Cluny's direct ties with the pope confirmed. He relinquished his functions to Majolus in 953 because he was blind. BIBLIOGRAPHY: A. M. Zimmermann, BiblSanct 1:639.

[E. P. COLBERT]

AYMER DE LUSIGNAN (d. 1260), bishop. The younger son of Isabella, widow of King John, and Hugh X, Count of La Marche, A. was half-brother to Henry III of Eng. who secured for him the See of Winchester (1250). Nevertheless, A. joined with other bps. in opposing Henry's taxation of clerical revenues, and in 1253 he ironically petitioned the king to allow free election of bishops. He was forced to flee Eng. when he refused to accept the Provisions of Oxford (1258). BIBLIOGRAPHY: Emden Ox 2:1179–80; H. S. Snellgrove, *Lusignans in England, 1247–58* (1950).

[O. BLUM]

AYMER DE LA CHEVALERIE, HENRIETTE (1767–1834), cofoundress of the Picpus Sisters. Of a royal family, A. and her mother were imprisoned during the French Revolution for harboring two priests. Upon her release, she joined an organization of laywomen in Poitiers dedicated to charitable works and perpetual adoration of the Blessed Sacrament. Prevailed upon by their spiritual director, Abbé Coudrin, A. became cofoundress of the Sisters of the Sacred Hearts and of Perpetual Adoration. In 1800 the congregation was approved by ecclesiastical authorities and A. was confirmed as perpetual superior. Moving to Paris (1804) the community took up residence in Rue Picpus. Papal approval was given in 1817 and the work of the congregation was expanded to include the religious education of children. BIBLIOGRAPHY: P. Heran, NCE 1:1141–42; G. Bourgin, DHGE 5:1289–90.

[S. A. HEENEY]

AYMERICH, MATEO, see AIMERICH, MATEO.

AYSCOUGH, JOHN (pseudonym of Francis Bickerstaffe-Drew; 1858–1928). He was educated at Pembroke College, Oxford, became a domestic prelate, British Army chaplain, and wrote well-regarded stories and sketches in the Edwardian manner, sometimes historical, delicately touching on the tensions of sacred and profane love. *Gracechurch*, which belongs to the genre of *Cranford*, is perhaps the most lasting.

AYTON, JOHN, see JOHN OF ACTON.

AZARIAH, the name of: (1) the king of Judah better known as Uzziah (2 Kg ch. 15); (2) the companion of Daniel whom the Babylonian eunuch called Abednego (Dan 1.6–7). He was one of the three saved from the fiery furnace (Dan 3). Some twenty other OT characters also had this name.

[T. EARLY]

AZAZEL, term of uncertain meaning used in describing the ritual of sending a goat into the wilderness on the Day of Atonement (Lev 16.8). The goat was sent to or for Azazel, which rabbinic exegetes generally considered a place but most modern scholars consider a demon of the desert. In the apocryphal Books of Enoch, Azazel is a leader of rebellious angels.

[T. EARLY]

AZEVEDO, IGNACIO DE, BL. (1527–70), Portuguese Jesuit martyr. Of noble birth, he became a Jesuit in 1548 and was rector of colleges in Lisbon and Braga before Francis Borgia made him visitor of Brazil missions in 1566. He returned to recruit 69 young Spanish and Portuguese for the missions, but a Huguenot corsair captured them at sea and killed A. and 39 of his recruits. He was beatified in 1854. BIBLIOGRAPHY: C. Testore, BiblSanct 3:388–390; J. Despont, *Catholicisme* 5:1192.

[E. P. COLBERT]

AZEVEDO, LUIZ DE, (1573–1634), Portuguese missionary. He entered the Society of Jesus in 1588. He was missioned in India in the early part of his ministry (1592–1604). While here he was master of novices at Goa and rector of the college of Thana. In 1605 he was sent as a missionary to Ethiopia. He worked among the Agaus. He made many converts among the Agaus from the schismatic Church of Ethiopia. Later his fellow missionaries were forced to leave the country and many of his converts returned to the schismatic Church. He was too infirm to leave Ethiopia and died there. He translated a NT catechism, instructions on the Apostles Creed into Ethiopic and compiled an Ethiopic grammar. BIBLIOGRAPHY: L. F. Hartman, NCE 1:1144.

[C. C. O'DONNELL]

AZHAR, AL- (Arab. *al-Jâmi 'al-azhar,* The Bright Mosque), a univ. mosque in Cairo, Egypt. The Azhar was dedicated in 972 by the *Fatimid Caliph, al-Mu'izz, as the cathedral mosque of his new administrative center, Cairo. From the beginning it was a center of *Ismaili teaching and under the Caliph al-'Azîz endowment was granted for the support of 35 jurists who were housed near the mosque. Al-Azhar fell into disuse under the *Sunnite Ayyubids from 1171. Under the Mamluks it was restored, and Friday worship recommenced in 1266 while at the same time the teaching of Sunnite law was begun. Within a cent. it was supporting a large number of students, including many from abroad. During the Ottoman period it came to be the foremost center of religious studies in Egypt and with the 18th cent. the most important in Islam. From the end of the 19th cent., with a process of continual reform, expansion, and modernization of its programs and curricula, al-Azhar has come to take on the character of a true university. In recent years it has grown extensively both within Cairo and without, through affiliation and annexation of numerous educational institutions in Egypt and abroad. Al-Azhar remains today the most important single univ. in the Arabic-speaking area of Islam and, in matters of religious learning, the most prestigious in all Islam. BIBLIOGRAPHY: J. Jomier, s.v. ''Azhar'', in EncIslam².

[R. M. FRANK]

AZOR, JUAN (1535–1603), Jesuit moral theologian. A. taught in Spain and Rome. His concern with moral issues took form in works that are now considered some of the first in moral theology. His work, *Institutiones morales,* was considered by Bossuet a unique one in its class. BIBLIOGRAPHY: R. A. Couture, NCE 1:1144, B. Schneider, LTK 1:1159.

[J. R. RIVELLO]

AZORES, Atlantic island group belonging to Portugal. The population is predominantly Catholic. Located *c*.750 miles west of Portugal, the Azores have a total area of 890 square miles and form three districts of Portugal. Though not unknown, they were uninhabited when Portuguese explorers first arrived (1427), according to one account. Colonization was led by ''Friar'' Goncalo Velho Cabral, a knight of the celibate military Order of Christ, and the order was initially given ecclesiastical jurisdiction over the Azores. In 1514 they came under the Diocese of Funchal, Madeira Islands, and a suffragan diocese was later established at Angra, on the Azorian island of Terceira. Angra, still the seat of a diocese embracing the entire archipelago, has been suffragan to Lisbon since the middle of the 16th century. In 1493 Columbus stopped at the Azores on his return from America, and some of his sailors attended Mass at a chapel there.

[T. EARLY]

AZPILCUETA, MARTINO DE (Doctor Navarrus; 1492–1586), Spanish canon regular, canonist, and moral theologian. A. studied at Alcalá, and after teaching at Cahors, Toulouse, Salamanca, and Coimbra, became a consultor for the Sacred Penitentiary in Rome. His works, esp. his *Manuale confessariorum et paenitentium* (1588), were very popular in their day. Against exaggerations of the tendencies to legalism and speculation, he insisted upon the importance of the internal forum and the necessity of sound casuistry. BIBLIOGRAPHY: A. Lambert, DDC 1:579–583.

[P. K. MEAGHER]

AZTEC ART. Last of the great pre-Columbian Indian cultures in the Valley of Mexico, their capital established (1325) at Tenochtitlán (Mexico City), and destroyed by Cortes (1521), this warring people—of a fierce religion dominated by human sacrifice, serving deities decorated with human heads, hearts, and skulls—built ceremonial temples and palaces ornamented with massive, terrifying, highly stylized sculpture, both anthropomorphic and zoomorphic, of rich iconographic symbolism in coarse lava or fine jadeite. They displayed great ability in engineering, ranging streets, plazas, waterways, and causeways in functional relationship. Smaller objects in onyx, feathers, gold, and leather have been lost but many of the more durable ceramics are extant. Their culture having been absorbed from other peoples, the Aztecs showed no remarkably innovative forms. BIBLIOGRAPHY: I. Marquina, *Arquitectura prehispánica,* 2d. ed. 1964.

[M. J. DALY]

AZTEC RELIGION, the religion of NW Mexican tribe also known as Tenochas. Their name is a derivative of Aztan (white land), their legendary place of origin. Their alternate name Tenochas was in honor of their legendary leader Tenoch. Their empire which was remarkable for its rapid rise in the 14th cent. was matched only by that of the Incas. They achieved their greatness after the dissolution and decline of the advanced civilization of the Toltecs for whom they probably served as mercenaries. They settled what became their capital of Tenochtitlán on a small island on Lake Texoco (1325) in the Valley of Mexico.

Their religion proved to be one of the major factors in their empire's growth. A synthesis of their own tribal traditions and those of the many cultures with which they were familiar, its most important cult was that of Huitzilopochtli, a young war-god and symbol of the sun. He died every evening and was born the next day. Each morning Huitzilopochtli came to power by banishing the moon and the stars with his bright ray of light. At sunset, he returned to the bowels of the earth (Coaticue), his mother, where he recovered his power to battle darkness, i.e., his sisters the stars and his brother the moon. For all life to continue it was imperative that Huitzilopochtli be well fed and in the best of health. His basic nourishment was human blood (chalchiuatl), life's precious liquid. It was therefore the duty of the people of the sun, the Aztecs, to provide human victims through warfare. For this, Huitzilopochtli promised continued life and conquest of the world. The number of victims was enlarged as the empire expanded. During the rule of the most savage of their leaders, Ahuizotl, 80,000 prisoners were sacrificed at the high altar in Tenochtitlán. Victims had their chests slashed, with a stone knife, their hearts torn out by priests who offered them to the god; limbs were served at ritual banquets and mutilated bodies were the food of wild beasts. Blood sacrifices were made by piercing the victims' tongues, ears, or genitals with thorns, and incense was offered.

The Aztecs believed that the world had four stages of development each dominated by different gods. Tezcatlipoca reigned over the age of Four Ocelot; Quetzalcoatl ruled the age of Four Wind; Tlaloc controlled the Age of Four Rain, and Chalchihuitlicue, the age of Four Sun. The unifying cosmic principle was the quality of life and death, darkness and light, male and female, symbolized by the continuing struggle between Quetzacoatl and Tezcatlipoca, the death god.

The calendar was important in setting times of sowing and harvesting and their accompanying festivals. Like the Mayan calendar, the dates of their ceremonial and solar years were in agreement at 52-year intervals. The end of a cycle was observed by the extinction of all fire and the destruction of idols and pottery. This was done to prevent the end of the world. To mark a new era new fires were kindled and temples were redecorated. Divination characterized the ceremonial year and it was a time of great authority for priests as they interpreted omens. Priests also recorded history in picture writing on folded paper or strips of hide. They accompanied their religious ceremonies with gourd rattles, wooden drums, flutes, and pottery whistles. BIBLIOGRAPHY: G. Vaillant, *Aztecs of Mexico* (pa. 1956) 161–181; J. E. Thompson, *Mexico before Cortez* (1933); A. Caso, *Aztecs, People of the Sun* (1958).

[F. H. BRIGHAM]

AZULEJO (from Arab. term *az-zulechi*), a rectangular tile of red clay for paving walls and floors, made in Spain since the Almohade period. Medieval Christian *azulejos* were ornamented with armorial designs from molds pressed into the wet clay, later colored with lead and tin glazes of black, white, green, and yellow.

[M. J. DALY]

AZURITE, or chessylite, known to Pliny as *caeruleum*, a basic copper carbonate of vivid blue color in contrast to emerald green malachite which it usually accompanies, formed by reaction between copper-bearing solutions and limestone, and in the corrosion of bronze. Azurite effects the rich blue patina in ancient bronzes.

[M. J. DALY]

AZYMES (Gr., without yeast), unleavened bread which is used by the Western Church for the Eucharist, whereas the Eastern Church employs leavened bread. In the controversial and polemical writings of Greek and Latin churchmen, this issue played a prominent role out of all proportion to its importance. Apart from arguments based on metaphor and symbolism, the dispute centered on the question of the night of the Last Supper and the type of bread used by Christ, a question to which no satisfactory answer has yet been given. Debate on this quite secondary issue became unusually vitriolic and vehement from the 11th to the 16th cent., and it is extremely difficult to discern any elements of learning or reason in this controversy. In 1439 the Council of Florence decreed that the body of Christ was truly made from wheaten bread, whether leavened or unleavened, and that each Church should follow its own tradition in this matter.

[P. FOSCOLOS]

AZYMES, FEAST OF, the Passover, or Feast of the Unleavened Bread. *Azymos* was the Greek word used to translate the Hebrew. *massôth,* unleavened.

[T. C. O'BRIEN]

AZYMITES, a term of abuse, applied by Greek Christians of the 11th cent. to those who used unleavened bread (*azymos,* unleavened) for the Eucharist.

[P. MORLINO]

B

BAADER, FRANZ XAVER VON (1765–1841), German Catholic social philosopher, theologian. While practicing mining engineering he became interested in the mysticism of Boehme and in contemporary developments in philosophical thought. He was influenced by, and in turn influenced, F. von Schilling. B. was granted an honorary professorship at the Univ. of Munich and lectured in theology and philosophy. Strongly opposed to any ethical system that does not see man's end as the realization in himself of the divine life and to any atheistic or secularist concept of the State, B. vigorously affirmed the need of society to be penetrated by religion and morality. He was disturbed by the increasing division between the proletariat (he was the first German to use that term) and the propertied class, and advocated the substitution of ideal medieval corporations for the laissez-faire capitalism of the modern constitutional State. Though his style was aphoristic and obscure, he exerted a considerable influence upon those who followed him and may indeed be considered the founder of German Catholic social thought and the outstanding pioneer among those who strove to interest the Church and its clergy in modern social problems.

[M. A. WATHEN]

BAAL, a fertility god and the principal deity in the Canaanite pantheon. The name is generic meaning "lord master, owner, or protector." B. is frequently qualified by some epithet when used to designate a person or city. The Israelites often took over these epithets to describe Yahweh. Therefore, Israelites with names combined with B. are not necessarily worshippers of B. However, the worship of this deity in the land of Canaan presented a grave threat to pure Yahwism. It was vigorously attacked by the prophets from the time of Elijah (1 Kg 18.16–40) until the Exile. B.'s representation was an upright stone column or pillar, probably a phallic symbol. Sanctuaries to B. were numerous in Canaan. They were referred to as the "high places."

[F. GAST]

BAALBEK, a site in Lebanon, in Semitic times dedicated to Baal the sun-god, called by the Greeks Heliopolis. Augustus founded here the *Colonia Julia Augusta Felix Heliopolitana*. Nero probably began the Temple of Jupiter of which six gigantic Corinthian columns of the peristyle remain. Caracalla erected later forms. On the south terrace is the Corinthian Temple of Bacchus and to the E the dramatic, small circular Corinthian Temple of Venus (*c*.245), a dynamic, baroque syntax of convex and concave forms.

BĀBAI THE GREAT (*c*.540–628), Syro-Nestorian archimandrite. He served as administrator of the Nestorian Church during the persecution of Chosroes II and was active as a monastic reformer. Of 83 works ascribed to him, a number of those extant have been edited by modern scholars.

[M. R. P. MCGUIRE]

BABEL, TOWER OF, see TOWER OF BABEL.

BABISM, a Muslim sect deriving from Mohammed Ali (1819–50), who was accepted by his followers as Bab-al-Din (gateway to religion) or al-Bab for short. Originating in 1844 as a movement within *Shiite Islam, with some dependence on Shaykhism, Babism advocated the abrogation of certain laws of the Koran. Founded in Shiraz, Persia, it came to be considered a threat to Shiism, the official religion of the state. Persecution of the sect began in 1845, and the Babists revolted in 1848 when Nasir-al-Din became shah. The revolt was crushed, and al-Bab executed in 1850 at Tabriz. In 1863 the remaining Babists were expelled to Constantinople. From the group came Baha-Ullah (1817–92), founder of the *Bahá'í Faith.

BABITS, MIHÁLY (1883–1941), Hungarian poet and man of letters. After completing his studies at the Univ. of Budapest, B. devoted his life to writing, but was also an editor, teacher, and translator. Among his important works are: a collection of lyric poems, entitled *Recitative* (1916); a translation of the *Divina Commedia* (1940); three autobiographical novels (1916–1924), revealing B.'s search for God and meaning in his life; a history of European literature (1934–35), in which, as a Christian humanist, he emphasizes the religious foundations of European culture; and *Jonás Könyve* (Book of Jonas, 1939), a long, quasi-mystical poem. BIBLIOGRAPHY: M. Babits, *Összes versei* (1942), collected poetry; *Összes novellai* (1938), novels; *Összes müvei* (10 v., 1937–38), essays.

BABYLAS, ST. (d. *c*.250), martyr, bp. of Antioch. Eusebius states that the (allegedly) Christian Emperor Philip the Arabian (244–249) was forbidden entry to a church for the Easter Vigil as an unrepentant sinner by a certain bishop, whom *John Chrysostom identified as Babylas. He was martyred in the persecution of Decius. About a cent. later B.'s remains were removed to a church in Daphne, a suburb of Antioch, near a temple of Apollo. This is the first recorded translation of relics. It is said that when the relics were removed by order of the Emperor Julian, the temple was destroyed by lightning. BIBLIOGRAPHY: Butler 1:160; R. Janin, DHGE 6:33.

[R. B. ENO]

BABYLON city on the Euphrates River, near the modern Baghdad; center of the territory known as Babylonia. The history of Babylon touches that of Israel at two main points. First, the institutions of the ancient Babylonian Empire (*c*.1830–1530 B.C.) seem to have been an influence on Israelite thought that is hard to measure and was possibly more indirect than direct. For instance, the ancient Babylonians constructed vast temple-towers or artificial cosmic "mountains" known as *ziggurats,* and thought of these as linking heaven with earth. This is plainly reflected in the story of the Tower of Babel (Gen 11.1–9), and less plainly in that of Jacob's vision (Gen 28.11–19). Again the law-code of Hammurabi, the greatest of the ancient Babylonian kings, contains numerous and striking points of similarity with the early Israelite law-codes, esp. the Book of the Covenant (Ex 20.22–23.33).

Far more important and more direct was the influence of the Neo-Babylonian or Chaldaean Empire (721–550). The Babylonians' victory over the Assyrians at Nineveh (612), and their final overthrow of the Assyrian Empire at Carchemish (605) under Nebuchadnezzar both had strong repercussions in Israelite history. Jerusalem itself surrendered to the Babylonians in 597, though the disastrous attempts at rebellion which Jeremiah vainly strove to prevent resulted in its final destruction by Nebuchadnezzar in 587. The Babylonian Empire was finally overthrown in 539 B.C., the regent Balshazzar (Dan 5.1; 8.1) having succumbed to treachery while his father Nabonidus was absent from Babylon.

Among the wealth of Babylonian literature which has survived, the following documents in particular display important affinities with areas of the OT: the creation epic *Enuma Elish,* the Epic of Gilgamesh (including an account of a cosmic flood), the poem "I will praise the Lord of Wisdom," and the Babylonian psalms of lamentation. In addition to these a number of ritual texts pertaining to the New Year festival in Babylon have been preserved, and many scholars would hold that these throw the most important light of all on the significance of the Israelite cult as celebrated at the temple of Jerusalem, and on the part played by the king in this cult.

In the NT the name is used symbolically of Rome (1 Pet 5.13), often with a connotation of wickedness (Rev 14.8; 16.19; 17.5; 18.2).

[D. J. BOURKE]

BABYLON, PATRIARCH OF, the official title given to the patriarch of the Catholics of the *Chaldean rite. The first Chaldean patriarch, John Sulāqā (confirmed in Rome in 1553), and his successors were styled Patriarch of Mossul or of the East Assyrians. Joseph I, the first of the second series of unionist patriarchs, was made Patriarch of the Chaldean nation in 1681; the title Patriarch of Babylon first appeared with his successor, Joseph II, in 1696.

[A. CODY]

BABYLON OF THE CHALDEANS, PATRI-ARCHATE OF, patriarchate of the Chaldean rite in Baghdad, Iraq, called Chaldean after the name of the Syrian language in the 15th cent. to distinguish Nestorian Christians who were reunited with Rome from other Nestorians known as Assyrians.

The early history of Christianity in the general area of what is now Baghdad witnessed the preaching of the gospel by Christians from Edessa (226); the union of independent Christian bps. under Bp. Mar Papa of Seleucia-Ctesiphon as the bps. of Seleucia (*c*.300); persecution by the Sassanids (340–380); the Council of Seleucia, under Maruthas of Martyropolis, which approved the Canons of the Council of Nicaea I (410); the Synod of Markabta, which proclaimed the independence of the Catholicos of Seleucia-Ctesiphon from the Western bps. (424); the birth of the Nestorian school of theology at Nisibis (457); and the Council of Seleucia which declared the Nestorian Church as the official Church of Persia (486). With the invasion of the Arabs (637), many Nestorians became Muslim. The seat of the caliphate moved to Baghdad (777). Under the favorable encouragement of the Abbasid Caliphate, Nestorian Christianity was extended from Baghdad to Central Asia, India, and China.

After their systematic persecution by the Mongol rulers of Persia, there are few records of Nestorian Christians from the 14th to the 16th cent. when John Sulāqā of Mosul was named patriarch of the Chaldeans by Rome (1553). His successors changed the seat to Kotchanes and the patriarchate was confirmed by the Holy See (1681). After 1780, administrators were named until Rome designated Metropolitan John IX Hormizd of Mosul (d. 1838) as sole patriarch of Babylon of the Chaldeans (1830). The seat of the patriarchate was moved from Mosul to Baghdad (1947) and was erected as a diocese (1960).

[F. H. BRIGHAM]

BABYLONIA, the name of the alluvial plain irrigated by the Tigris and Euphrates Rivers, now the Arab state of Iraq but in ancient times the Southern part of what classical writers termed Mesopotamia. Bordered on the N by Assyria, on the S by the Persian Gulf, on the E by Elam and the foothills of Persia and on the W by the Syrian desert, it maintained its inner division between Sumer in the S and Akkad (Accad) in the N for centuries after Sumerians and Akkadians had merged their identities in Babylonian civilization.

The earliest intelligible records together with archeological evidence mark the beginning of the history of Sumer at about 3000 B.C. In this early dynastic period no single ruler held sway. The Sumerian king list of 2000 B.C. records the local rulers of cities of some importance at different times, but these dynasties were contemporaneous and, apart from the mythical and astronomical reigns of kings before the Flood, can be assigned to a few hundred years of the 3d millennium. History begins with the reign of Mes-ani-padda whose name is in the temple he built at Al Ubaid. The archeology of this time and the list of kings indicate a definite cultural unity throughout Mesopotamia even though political union had not been achieved. Eannatum of Lagash carried his conquests through Ur, Uruk, and Umma to the foothills of Elam, but Lugal-zaggisi avenged his city's defeat soon after by destroying Lagash and setting himself up as king of Uruk. Then came a dynasty of Semitic kings at Kish. The most successful early king in the Akkad kingdom of the N was Sargon (Sharrukin) who made the city of Agade capital and extended the boundaries of his kingdom to the Mediterranean in the N and the Persian Gulf in the South. After the fall of the Sargonid dynasty, a Sumerian king, Ur Nammu, took over and called himself king of Sumer and Akkad. But this dynasty was eventually toppled by a union of Elamites and Amorites, and an Amorite dynasty made Babylon its center. Hammurabi, the sixth king of this dynasty conquered Mari, Malga, and Tirgua, defeated an Elamite coalition, invaded Gutium and with the capitulation of Rim-Sin of Larsa became master of S Mesopotamia (1762 B.C.). He declared the cult of the god Marduk the official state religion, appointed a governor to rule each state, established law and order, compiled a collection of laws engraved in stone in every city, constructed canals, and expanded commerce as far as Egypt and Crete. With the Hittite destruction of Babylon (1595 B.C.) the way was open for the Cassites to assume complete dominance of Babylonia. Their reign extended over a 500-year period. They took over Babylonian civilization, made Dur-Kurigalzu the new capital (1450 B.C.), built temples in palaces in Babylonian style and made Sumerian the official language of religion. The Amarna letters are evidence of trade and diplomatic correspondence between these kings and the Pharoahs Amenhopes III and Akhnaton of Egypt. After border wars with the Assyrians to the N and the invasion of Elamites, the Cassites were succeeded by a native Babylonian dynasty (1171 B.C.). During the next 500 years Babylonia was subject to several periods of Assyrian rule (*Assyria) and the changing fortunes of Chaldean, Elamite, and Aramaean ascendancy in the South. Chaldean power had some success under Marduk-apal-iddin (in the Bible, Merodach-baladan) who in alliance with Elam became ruler of Babylon. But the conquests of the Assyrian Sargon II forced him to abandon the city (710 B.C.). In the next cent. the Chaldean general Nabopolassar (Nabu-apatutsur) in alliance with the Medes and Scythians utterly defeated Assyria and destroyed Nineveh (612 B.C.).

With the neo-Babylonian dynasty, Babylonia reached the apogee of its prosperity and influence. The most important reign was that of Nebuchadnezzar (605 B.C.—562 B.C.). When Jehoiakim of Judah revolted, Nebuchadnezzar attacked Jerusalem, forced the submission of Judah and after a second revolt destroyed Jerusalem (587 B.C.), driving Zedekiah and most of his people into exile. Under Nabonidus, Babylonia fell to Cyrus the Great (539 B.C.). It remained under the sway of the Persian Empire until the death of Alexander the Great when it became part of the Seleucid Empire and the Parthians made Ctesiphon its capital. It resisted Hellenization until the Sassanian dynasty came to power.

The thousands of cuneiform tablets of lists, contracts, letters, accounts, and receipts discovered in the various cities give a comprehensive picture of the economic and social structure of the country. Tax receipts and administrative letters present valuable details of government; omen texts enhance our knowledge of magic and astrology; syllabaries help in grasping the spoken languages of Sumerian, Akkadian, Hurrian, and Elamite. The literary texts of legends, hymns, epics, and prayers, the portions of annals, lists of kings, and building inscriptions are outstanding historical sources.

Babylonian religion took over the complete Sumerian pantheon, in which Anu, Enlil, and Ea are the great gods ruling the universe, heaven, earth, and waters. Marduk became chief god in place of Enlil when Babylon became the capital of Mesopotamia. An earlier mother goddess was superseded by Ishtar, the most worshiped goddess of the country. Ea was the god of magic; Shamash, the sun god, was protector of justice and morality. Sin, the moon god, was worshiped in Abraham's city of Ur. There were also many evil spirits from which priests protected the people by incantations and spells.

The ritual of Babylonian religion was most important. The chief seasonal feast was Akitu, New Year, held in the spring, the month of Nisan. Because of the agricultural life of the people, the ritual acts for the New Year were directed toward securing fertility and were centered around the victory of Marduk over chaos-dragon Tiamot, an epic of creation. Consulting omens was also important to the religious life of the Babylonian, e.g., entrails of victims and flights of birds. Religious literature included hymns, prayers to gods, and myths, e.g., the myth of the deluge in the Gilgamesh epic, the myth of Adapa, the myth of Etana who ascended to Alan on the back of an eagle.

[F. H. BRIGHAM]

BABYLONIAN CAPTIVITY, the deportation of the Jews to Babylonia (598 and 587 B.C.) and their retention there until Babylon fell to the Persians under Cyrus (538 B.C.). In Christian times the term has had two celebrated metaphorical applications. It was used: (1) by Petrarch and others in referring to the residence of the popes at Avignon (1309–77); and (2) by Martin Luther in his treatise *A Prelude Concerning the Babylonish Captivity of the Church* (1520). Luther's reference was to the bondage in which he declared the Church had been kept by Roman teaching on the sacraments, transubstantiation, and the sacrificial character of the Mass and by withdrawal of the chalice from the laity.

[C. P. CEROKE]

BACCHUS, CULT OF, see DIONYSIUS, CULT OF.

BACH, JOHANN CHRISTIAN (1735–82), German composer. Eleventh son of Johann Sebastian *Bach, B. studied under his father until 1750 and then under his brother Carl Philip Emanuel. When the Seven Years' War broke out, B. went to Italy where he became a pupil of G. B. *Martini. Here it was that he became a Roman Catholic. Appointed (1760) organist at Milan cathedral, he composed two Masses, a *Requiem, Miserere, Te Deum* and other religious works. In 1762 he was appointed to the King's Theater, London, and became (1763) music master to Queen Charlotte Sophia, a post he held until his death. Composer also of operas, oratorios, many arias and cantatas, clavier concertos, chamber music, symphonies, and overtures, B. was the first composer who preferred the pianoforte to older keyed instruments, and he introduced the all-important method of emphasizing a change of key to dramatize it.

BACH, JOHANN SEBASTIAN (1685–1750), Lutheran organist and composer. Like another great composer of the high baroque, G. F. *Händel, his artistic forebears included French and Italian as well as German musicians; but the relatively provincial compass of his activity at Arnstadt, Mühlhausen, Weimar, Cöthen, and Leipzig, together with the determination with which he mastered musical forms and techniques considered academic, even archaic, by his more cosmopolitan contemporaries perhaps explains his isolation as a composer during his lifetime. For nearly a century after his death his works were known only to a few: it was as an organist that he had been most esteemed; yet the catalog of his extant compositions includes important examples of nearly every type of secular and sacred composition of the era of high *baroque music which he and Händel epitomize as masters of its final state of development. Even the operatic style is represented in B.'s cantatas, almost all sacred, though he never composed opera.

But his dramatic genius was not essentially operatic; its device was counterpoint. His fugues and chorale preludes, genres which pose rigorous contrapuntal musical problems and present opportunities for solutions both dramatic and lyrical, as well as academic, are found not only among his keyboard works, but within his Passions, Masses, and cantatas.

It was in his cantatas that B. most frequently applied his art to the setting of religious texts. The sensitivity with which he made his music to emphasize the meaning of the word is manifest not only in such audible techniques as melodic contour but in extramusical devices of notational symbolism apparent only on examining his scores, which reveal the delight in musical games he was able to indulge as the privilege of his facility, if not as the essential working method of his genius.

His complete works will never be known: e.g., only the text of a major work, *St. Mark Passion,* survives. But B.'s practice, common in his time, of reworking movements of his own compositions for use in later works has enabled scholars partially to reconstruct its music. Among his extant religious compositions we have the *St. Matthew* and *St. John Passions,* more than 200 sacred cantatas, motets, and several Masses with Latin text, including his famous *High Mass in B minor.* Many organ compositions such as the chorale preludes of the *Orgelbüchlein* or the so-called *Organ Mass (Clavierübung,* part 3) are sacred works; but numerous other organ pieces cannot be considered sacred music.

The monumental biography of B. by Philip Spitta has not been superseded, although a major revision in the chronology of B.'s works, largely the result of a cooperative scholarly project begun about 1950, has produced many surprises. This revision has been based entirely on extramusical evidence: there is little apparent development in B.'s musical style through the course of his career. BIBLIOGRAPHY: P. Spitta, *Johann Sebastian Bach: His Work and Influence on the Music of Germany, 1685–1750* (tr. C. Bell and J. A. Fuller-Maitland, 3 v. in 2, 1883–85, repr. 1951).

[J. NEWSOM]

BACH, JOSEPH VON (1833–1901), German theologian. Ordained in 1856, he taught at the Univ. of Munich. His major work, *Die Dogmengeschichte des Mittelalters* (2 v., 1873–75) is still useful.

BACHA, CONSTANTINE (1870–1948), historian of the Melchite Church. After early studies at Holy Savior Seminary (Saida, Lebanon), B. became a Salvatorian religious (1886) and was ordained in 1893. His greatest work, *History of the Catholic Melchite Community and the Salvatorian Order* (2v., 1938 and 1945), is acclaimed as the authoritative source in its field. This and other works, about 40, which he translated or composed, are preserved in the archives of the library of Holy Savior Monastery where, from 1925, he devoted the remainder of his life to study and to writing.

[T. C. STAHL]

BACHEM, JULIUS (1845–1918), German journalist and politician. B. began his journalistic career by managing the *Kölnische Volkszeitung* (1869), making it the most important voice of Catholicism in Germany. He anonymously wrote many political tracts, arguing for a more equitable respect of citizens' rights, esp. those of northern German Catholics during the *Kulturkampf. B. was a member of the Cologne municipal assembly and, from 1876 to 1891, a representative of the (Catholic) Center Party to the Prussian Parliament (Landtag). During this time, he continued to fight for RC rights and sought to attract members to the Center Party on the basis of its political platform rather than religious principles. B. wrote an important *Staatslexikon,* and was a founding member of the *Görres-Gesellschaft.*

BACHIARIUS (4th cent.), wandering monk and admirer of Priscillian; ties with a heretical region may place him in Galicia, Spain, *c.*380. His extant works (PL 20:1019–1102) consist of a defense of his orthodoxy, evidently before a pope, and an appeal to ''brothers'' for clemency toward a sin of the flesh by a monastic deacon, whom he exhorts to penitence. B. may have composed an exchange of two mystical letters supposedly between two women, important for their description of the religious practices peculiar to Spain in 380. Learned and gifted with a keen and imaginative mind, he has also been identified as Bp. Peregrinus, a compiler of a Priscillianist canon of the Epistles of St. Paul.

[E. P. COLBERT]

BACHOT, JACQUES (1493–1526), sculptor of ornament becoming *imagier* (1513). B. executed the funeral monuments of Henry of Lorraine, Ferry II of Lorraine, Yolande of Anjou—all tombs destroyed in the French Revolution. His major surviving work is *Deposition* (eight Gothic figures) in St. Nicolas-du-Port near Nancy.

BACK TO THE LAND MOVEMENT, a name given, esp. in England, to efforts at relocation of urbanized people on the land as a solution to various evils associated with industrialism. Indications as diverse as the settlement policies of Abp. J. *Ireland of St. Paul and the writings of William Morris mark a common feeling for the country simplicities and the dignity of personal craftsmanship outraged by the inroads of industrialism. During the past 100 years organized groups have translated the protest into action; the inspiration has sometimes been purely ethical and humanitarian, sometimes, and with less ephemeral effect, more toughly religious, after the example of the Cistercians and the Amish. Based on the social philosophy of *Distributism, and on the sacramental and liturgical forms of Catholicism, several groups were established in England and Scotland between 1910 and 1939. The best known was on Ditchling Common in Sussex, where, under the leadership of Hilary Pepler and Eric Gill, a community of Dominican tertiaries was settled. It kept itself by working the land, and by the excellence of its craftsmanship in stone, metal, fab-

rics, wood, and printing. Yet a difficulty for such colonies has been to keep the younger generation born into them in face of the pressures and attractions of mass methods of production and enjoyment, and their tendency is to dissolve into the component families. Those who remain on the land and prosper generally do so by abandoning the more primitive, less industrialized, methods of agriculture to which their original inspiration committed them.

[T. GILBY]

BACKER, AUGUSTIN DE (1809–73), Belgian Jesuit bibliographer. While studying in Louvain, he discovered the incomplete work of Nathaniel Southwell (Bacon), *Bibliotheca scriptorum Societatis Jesu,* which stimulated his interest in bibliography. With the collaboration of his brother, Alois, he published the first edition of his colossal work, *La Bibliothèque des écrivains de la compagnie de Jésus* (1853–61). The second edition, compiled between 1869 and 1876, containing the names of 11,000 Jesuit writers, was broader in scope, giving more space to each author, pointing out important personal information, and citing translations, editions, and critiques. B. died while the final volume of this edition was still in progress. His brother, with the collaboration of C. Sommervogel, continued the work which was published 3 years later. BIBLIOGRAPHY: Sommervogel 1:753–755.

[M. A. WATHEN]

BACKOFFEN, HANS (1460?–1519), German sculptor active in Mainz, producing tomb monuments and crucifixion groups. Unlike his contemporary Riemenschneider, B.'s work is monumental, anticipating baroque.

BACKUS, ISAAC (1724–1806), Baptist pastor, revivalist, and advocate of religious liberty. Reared a Congregationalist, he experienced conversion during the *Great Awakening, joined those who accepted revivalist conversion, called the Separate, or New Light Congregationalists, and soon became a minister. Protesting payment of taxes to support the standing order, he advocated religious freedom. In 1756 he joined the Baptists and traveled over 15,000 miles as a preacher throughout New England. From 1770 he was the Baptist leader in a campaign to disestablish the Congregational Church in Massachusetts, and for this purpose organized the Warren Association in Warren, Rhode Island, with two other ministers. Although influenced by *Enlightenment ideas, his appeal for religious liberty was based primarily on religious grounds. Besides tracts on religious freedom and numerous polemical works, he wrote a three-volume *History of New England, with Particular Reference to the . . . Baptists* (1777), valuable as a source work and as a vindication of religious liberty.

[N. H. MARING]

BACON, DAVID WILLIAM (1813–74), first bp. of Portland, Maine. He studied at the Sulpician College in Montreal and Mount Saint Mary's Seminary at Emmitsburg, Maryland. After serving in New Jersey and New York, he was assigned to Brooklyn to organize a new parish where he served as pastor until he was appointed bp. of Portland. His diocese included Maine and New Hampshire. He met the needs of the Catholics in this area by employing the aid of Jesuits and priests from Quebec, Canada. B. attended Vatican Council I.

[J. HILL]

BAD FAITH, a term that is sometimes taken simply as the opposite of *good faith, i.e., the want of sincerity or integrity in entering an agreement. It is also used sometimes to designate treachery or faithlessness.

BAD WIMPFEN IM THAL, ST. PETER, German church of the Ottonian period, built (979–998) under Bp. Hildebold of Worms. The hexagonal central plan with aisle and galleries and massive westwork façade topped by two towers (remodeled 12th cent.) is a provincial variation on the Palatine Chapel, *Aachen. Gothic modifications were added (13th-15th cent.).

[M. J. DALY]

BADAMI, site of important early Hindu caves and temples in eastern Maharashtra State, India. Cave I is Saivite; Caves II and III, Vaishnavite; later Cave IV is Jain. Some figures are elegant, elongated in the Southern style of Amarāvati; others are heavier in the Gupta style of the North. The Boar avatar of Vishnu is derived from Udayagiri. Cave I exterior shows the earliest and most elaborate example of the multi-armed Siva in India. Opposite the caves are temples (600 A.D.) of which the most important is Malegitti-Sivalaya, southern in type and classically serene.

[M. J. DALY]

BADET, ARNOLD (*c*.1475–1536), Dominican writer, mystical theologian. B. worked mostly in Languedoc, at Toulouse, of which he became Inquisitor in 1531. His friendship with Jean Caturce and other humanists caused an unsuccessful denunciation for heresy by his fellow-Dominicans to the Parlement of Toulouse. Among his writings there is *Destructorium haeresium* (1532). BIBLIOGRAPHY: G. Loirette, DHGE 6:140–141.

[L. E. BOYLE]

BADÍA, TOMMASO(1483–1547), Dominican theologian and cardinal. He was a distinguished teacher at Ferrara, Venice, and Bologna, master of the sacred palace, and friend and advisor to Cardinal Contarini. B. was among the theologians who prepared for the Council of Trent and influenced papal approval of the Jesuits. He became cardinal in 1542 and inquisitor general. His writings have not been published, although he took important part in the doctrinal discussions of his time. BIBLIOGRAPHY: P. Mandonnet, DTC 2.1:33; A. Duval, *Catholicisme* 1:1161–62.

BADILE, ANTONIO (1518–60), Italian painter in Verona of conservative style, whose finest work, *Virgin Enthroned with SS. Peter and Paul* (Verona, Castelvecchio), shows the influence of his great pupil Paolo Veronese. BIBLIOGRAPHY: A. Venturi, *Storia dell' arte italiana* (1929) v. 9, pt. 4.

[M. J. DALY]

BADIN, STEPHEN THEODORE (1768–1853), French missionary, first priest ordained in the U.S. He left France because of the Revolution and became one of the first students at Saint Mary's Seminary, Baltimore. He was ordained by Bp. Carroll in 1793. From 1793 to 1811, B. served in the states of Kentucky, Tennessee, Ohio, Indiana, Illinois, and Michigan. He spent the years 1819-26 in his homeland of France acting as agent for American bishops. Upon returning to the U.S. he worked with the Pottawatomie Indians in Indiana. He was the founder of the first orphan asylum near South Bend and purchased the land on which the Univ. of Notre Dame now stands. B.'s writings include religious tracts, Latin poems, and books on Catholic doctrine. He worked for 60 years on frontier lands; his missionary labors gave him the title, "the Apostle of Kentucky." He is buried in the Badin Chapel of the Univ. of Notre Dame. BIBLIOGRAPHY: J. H. Schauinger, NCE 2:12.

[J. HILL]

BADLAH or *badleh,* Arabic word, used: (1) commonly for the Maronite Latin-style chasuble, also called (Syriac) *shaddōyō;* 2) it is also used sometimes for the West Syrian *phainō.*

BAEGERT, DERICK (1440–1515), German Westphalian painter of large altarpieces (e.g., that in the Probsterkirche, Dortmund, *c*.1480), showing the influence of Dirk Bouts. Other works by B. hang in Antwerp, Munich, and Nürnberg museums.

BAERZE, JACQUES DE (Baerse, Barse; fl. 1375–1400), Flemish sculptor of Termonde. B. executed two altarpieces for the Chartreuse de Champmol (now in Dijon, Fine Arts Museum) modeled on former ones made for the church of Termonde and the Abbey of Biloque. Restored (1841–43), the painted and gilded figures are patterned in graceful International Gothic style. The outer wings show *Life of Christ* by Melchior Broederlam.

[M. J. DALY]

BAEUMKER, CLEMENS (1853–1924), historian of medieval philosophy. Professor at Breslau (1883), Bonn (1900), Strassburg (1903), and Munich (1912), he was prominent in the Neo-Scholastic movement in Germany and pioneered in the editing of medieval texts. He founded and directed the *Beiträge zur Geschichte der Philosophie des Mittelalters* (1891). His most important publication was *Die christliche Philosophie des Mittelalters* (1909, 1913, 1923). BIBLIOGRAPHY: A. A. Bogdanski, *Significance of Clemens Baeumker in Neo-Scholastic Philosophy* (1942).

BAGAWAT, EL-, FRESCOES OF, extensive series of frescoes (4th or 5th cent.) in a mortuary chapel in the Kharga Oasis, 100 miles W of the lower Nile, closely related in style and subject to Early Christian art of Alexandria.

BAGH, village in NW Madhya Pradesh, India, site of several rock-cut caves containing fragments of most important wall paintings of the Gupta period (320–600) in the classical style as at Ajanta. Notable in Cave IV are a procession of elephants and dancing scene around a personage in Kushan or Iranian costume. BIBLIOGRAPHY: B. Rowland, *Art and Architecture of India* (1959).

[M. J. DALY]

BAGHDAD, the capital of Iraq, originally founded as the administrative center of the Abbasid Empire by the Caliph Mansur (762–766) 30 miles from Seleucia Ctesiphon on the W bank of the Tigris. Its original round city expanded gradually SE to its present location. For more than 500 years, Baghdad remained the academic and cultural center of the Arabian empire until it was devastated by the attack of the Mongols under Hulagu (1256). Regained and rebuilt by the Persians (1517), it capitulated to the Sultan Mourad IV as part of the Ottoman Empire (1638). In 1917, it became the capital of the independent state of Iraq. Only three or four buildings have survived from Abbasid times. The city's modern development began under Namik Pasha (1861) and has advanced under the present monarchy as the center of government and commerce containing nine-tenths of the industry of Iraq.

There is evidence that Christians lived in a village in the vicinity of Baghdad as early as 762. The Christian Churches in communion with Rome were named the Babylonian Church because it was mistakenly thought that Baghdad was built on the ruins of Babylon. Established as a Latin diocese by Pope Urban VIII (1638), it became an archdiocese in 1848. It is also the seat of the Chaldean Patriarchate since 1830, of the Syrian Patriarchate since 1862 and of the Armenian Archdiocese since 1954. BIBLIOGRAPHY: R. Janin, DHGE 6:198–201; H. Dressler, NCE 2:13. G. Weit, *Baghdad: Metropolis of the Abbasid Caliphate* (tr. S. Feller, 1971).

[F. H. BRIGHAM]

BAGNOLENSES, one of the principal branches of the *Cathari in Italy in the 13th century. The name probably derives from Bagnola, a town near Mantua, where many of the adherents resided. They taught a mitigated form of dualism according to which the evil principle did not create the material universe but fashioned it from the four primordial elements. They also held that Christ had not a real, but a phantom, human body. BIBLIOGRAPHY: *Un Traité néo-manichéen du XIIIᵉ siècle: Liber de duobus principiis* (ed. A. Dondaine, 1939); I. da Milano, EncCatt 2:689–690; A. Borst, *Die Katharer* (1953) 101, 237.

[C. J. LYNCH]

BAGSHAW, CHRISTOPHER (*c*.1552–*c*.1625), controversialist. Educated at Oxford, he went to Paris where he was converted to Catholicism and ordained. After obtaining his doctorate, he returned to England (1587) "to make converts." He was captured immediately, sent to the Tower for 6 years, then to Wisbeach Castle. In both places he came into conflict with the Jesuits against whom his writings show an unrelenting animosity. After he was freed in 1601, he became rector of the Ave Maria College in Paris. BIBLIOGRAPHY: *The Archpriest Controversy* (ed. T. G. Law, 1896–98); A. H. Bullen, DNB 1:872–873; Gillow BDEC 1:100–101.

[H. JACK]

BAHÁ'Í FAITH, less correctly Bahá'ísm, a belief that recognizes the unity of God and his prophets, teaches that divine revelation is continuous and progressive, and that the founders of all past religions, though different in the nonessential aspects of their teachings, proclaim the same spiritual truth. The Bahá'í Faith is named after Bahá'Ullāh (Glory of God), whom his followers in more than 300 countries and territories believe to be the most recent in a succession of divine educators such as Moses, Christ, and Mohammed. The central principle of this faith is the oneness of mankind. It teaches the necessity and inevitability of an organic change in the structure of present-day society, and the removal of all forms of provincialism and prejudice, recommending the reconstruction and demilitarization of the whole civilized world, anticipating a consummation of human evolution, the coming of age of the entire human race, and attainment to a permanent and universal peace. This pivotal theme revolves around the belief that the fundamental purpose of religion is to promote harmony and conjoins with the principles of an unfettered search after truth, of equal opportunity, rights, and privileges of both sexes. Compulsory education and abolition of extremes of wealth and poverty are advocated; work performed in the spirit of service is regarded as worship.

The Bahá'í Faith grew out of Babism in Persia, a religion founded in 1844 by Mirza Ali Muhammed of Shiraz (1819–50). Taking the name al-Bāb (the Gateway), he proclaimed his twofold mission as an independent prophet and herald of "One greater than himself." Al-Bāb was imprisoned and finally killed as were thousands of his followers. In 1863 while an exile in Baghdad, Mirza Husayn 'Alī Nūri (1817–92) announced that he was the one of whom al-Bāb had spoken. He subsequently wrote, under the title Bahá'Ullāh, more than 100 books and letters in which he enunciated the spiritual and social principles of the new faith and urged the leaders of mankind to establish a world government by mutual agreement.

Bahá'Ullāh appointed his son, 'Abd-al-Bahā (Servant of the Glory; 1844–1921), interpreter and exemplar of his teachings. 'Abd-al-Bahā visited the U.S. in 1912 and laid the cornerstone for the Bahá'í house of worship in Wilmette, Illinois. He appointed his grandson, Shoghi Effendi

(1896–1957), guardian of the Bahá'í Faith. In his *Book of Laws* Bahā'Ullāh provided for administrative institutions, at the head of which is the Universal House of Justice. This supreme body was established in 1963 and has its headquarters in Haifa, Israel. BIBLIOGRAPHY: Shogi Effendi, *World Order of Bahā'u'llāh* (1965).

BAHIRA LEGEND, a well-known medieval story which describes an alleged encounter between Mohammed and a Christian monk named Bahira (Aramaic *bahira,* the chosen or the esteemed) in many Mohammedan versions but also called Sergius-Bahira in several Christian versions. The most familiar Muslim account included in the better-known biographies of Mohammed depicts the prophet at the age of 12 meeting the Christian monk in the Syrian town of Bosra on a caravan trip with his uncle Abu-Talib. Sergius-Bahira then predicts Mohammed's role as prophet warning Abu-Talib to safeguard the boy from the Jews and the Byzantines. In some versions, the monk cites Christian Scriptures in support of his prophecy.

The Christian version first appeared in the 8th cent. and its purpose was to challenge the veracity of Mohammed's teaching. Most earlier versions describe Sergius as an excommunicated Nestorian monk who assisted Mohammed in his literary, religious, and political career. The best-known Christian account, *Apocalypse of Bahira,* a synthesis of earlier Christian and some Muslim versions, claims that Sergius is responsible for all references to Scripture in the Koran. BIBLIOGRAPHY: R. Gottheil, "Christian Bahira Legend," *Zeitschrift für Assyriologie* 13 (1898) 189–242; 14 (1899) 203–268; Ibn Ishâq, *Sîrat rasul allâh (Life of Mohammed,* tr. A. Guillaume, 1955); F. Nau, *Expansion Nestorienne* (1914) 214; A. Mingana, Hastings ERE 10:549.

[F. H. BRIGHAM]

BAHR, HERMANN (1863–1934), Austrian author, dramatist, essayist, and literary critic; next to A. Schnitzler and H. von Hofmannsthal, the leading exponent of Neoromantic Impressionism. Born in Linz, son of a lawyer, B. studied national economy, law, and philology at Vienna and other German universities. As drama critic at the Vienna state theater (Burgtheater, 1892–1912) and editor, he exerted considerable influence on contemporary art and literature. His numerous dramas (e.g., *Das Konzert,* 1910) and novels (e.g., *Himmelfahrt; Der inwendige Garten*) reflect his way from naturalism to religious symbolism after his entering the Catholic Church. BIBLIOGRAPHY: H. Bahr, *Briefweschsel mit seinem Vater* (1971).

[B. STEINBRUCKNER]

BAIANISM, the system Michael *Baius proposed in his treatises on man, his nature and Fall, and grace (1563–66). Condemned in the 79 propositions that state the main erroneous points (see D 1901–79), it has been called an "Augustinism gone astray" (see H. de Lubac, *Augustinisme et théologie moderne,* 1965). Baius wished mainly to explain two points, as Augustine had done: (1) the corruption of man's fallen nature; and (2) his need of divine grace. He took as his starting point the nature of man, who is meant to seek God by keeping the commandments and for that purpose was given the gifts of the original state: grace, the Spirit, subordination of his lower to his higher powers. These gifts belong to his "natural" state, not as resulting from his nature but as required for man to be able to live as he should and keep the law of God. The original state and the gifts involved are natural in this sense (D 1901–07, 1909, 1911, 1978). By keeping the commandments man merits life eternal by a natural merit, as his due for his efforts (D 1904–07, 1911–15). This thorough naturalism or *Pelagianism is the reversal of Augustine's teaching. It confuses nature as historical native state of man (Augustine) and as opposed to supernatural. It reverses the perspective of nature and grace: to Augustine's mind nature is meant for grace; according to Baius grace is at the service of nature and man has a claim to all the gifts needed to keep the law.

The original situation was ruined by the Fall. Original sin means the loss of natural justice; it is a corruption of man's nature. Man no longer understands the things of God. He loves the world instead of God. *Concupiscence dominates (D 1948–50). Unless helped by grace (i.e., a passing help for good actions), fallen man sins in all that he does voluntarily (D 1925, 1927, 1928, 1939, 1946). Sin is what does not conform to the law, even when committed under the compulsion of concupiscence (D 1940, 1946). What man does without love for God, he does for love of self and the world (D 1938). Thus the naturalism of the original state, combined with Baius's legalism, leads to an idea of man's fallen state that, while conforming in some aspects with the letter of St. Augustine's writings, reveals a contrary spirit, esp. regarding love and grace. In Baianism love of God and grace are not inner transformations of man but are passing helps to fulfill the commandments and are unnecessary for meriting life eternal. Righteousness is mere conformity of man's actions with the prescriptions of the law, not an infused gift, or *habitus* (D 1942, 1969). Nor is freedom required for sin or for merit (D 1967). Concupiscence, though not free, is sin (D 1974–75), but in the just it no longer dominates. Every sin is mortal (D 1920). Springing from love of self instead of love of God, it adheres to an evil end.

Against this background appears the inherent ambiguity of Baianism, Augustinian in wording, anti-Augustinian in spirit. Baius's basic naturalism, the starting point of his system, is foreign to Augustine. He distorts the reading of Augustine's teaching on the Fall and its reparation, on grace and charity, by the legalism that pervades his views on justice and merit, sin and freedom. The condemnation of Baianism on the nature of man and grace settled in RC doctrine the points of faith on man's gratuitous call to the supernatural and life eternal, his fall from it through sin, and his restoration by the grace of Christ. BIBLIOGRAPHY: X. Le Bachelet, DTC 2:38–111.

[P. DELETTER]

BAIJ, MARIA CECILIA (1694–1766), Italian Benedictine abbess, mystic. B. received the habit and made profession in 1714 at the abbey of St. Peter in her native Montefiascone. She was elected abbess in 1743. B.'s writings, reluctantly composed at the command of her confessor, bear evidence that by 1736 she was given the grace of *transforming union. Her works, chief of which is *Vita interna di Gesù Cristo* (2 v., 1920–21), were published only in the 1920s. The editor, a priest of Montefiascone, Pietro Bergomaschi, in his introductions and in a biography of B. (2 v., 1923) claims that what she wrote was of supernatural origin, true, private *revelations. Much published discussion of this view ensued. J. de Guibert's critique, while sympathetic to B., (he finds her writings superior to those of Mary of *Ágreda) rejects Bergomaschi's thesis. BIBLIOGRAPHY: P. Bergomaschi, *Vita della serva di Dio Maria Cecilia Baij* (2 v., 1923–25); J. de Guibert, DSAM 1:1190–92.

[T. C. O'BRIEN]

BAILLET, ADRIEN (1649–1706), French writer. After his ordination he became librarian for the advocate general of Lamoignan. He was a talented scholar but an extremist, as his works indicate. His life of Descartes is excessively apologetic; he approves devotion to the Blessed Virgin, but denies the Immaculate Conception and the Assumption; his lives of the saints are Jansenistic and attack historical facts as well as legends. BIBLIOGRAPHY: R. Aigrain, *Catholicisme* 1:1162; C. Toussaint, DTC 2:36–37, Bremond, *Index* (repr. 1971) 19.

[H. JACK]

BAILLY, VINCENT DE PAUL (1832–1912), French Assumptionist and journalist. Grounded in a strong Christian heritage at home, B.'s vocation was undoubtedly fostered by this atmosphere and by his father's active participation in a variety of religious movements. He was ordained in Rome in 1863. He was a versatile and dynamic worker—founder of many organizations, organizer of pilgrimages, the superior of the community's college of Nîmes, chaplain of the French forces defending the Holy See in 1867 and again at Metz in 1870, and founder of many publications. A. was able to defend the Church through the daily *La Croix,* esp. when the Third Republic was making the existence of religious communities very difficult. After the Assumptionists were suppressed in 1899, he left for Rome. Having founded houses in Belgium and England, he returned to Paris in 1906 where he was assistant general of his order until his death. BIBLIOGRAPHY: M. T. Disdier, DHGE 6:266–267; L. Merklen, *Catholicisme* 1:1165–66.

[S. A. HEENEY]

BAINBRIDGE, CHRISTOPHER (*c*.1462–1514), servant of Henry VIII. He was educated at Oxford, Ferrara, and Bologna, served as master of the rolls (1504–07), bp. of Durham (1507–08), abp. of York (1508–14), and cardinal from 1511. He acted as Henry VIII's ambassador to the Roman curia (1509) and papal legate in Italy (1511). He shared Henry's hostility toward France and favored his entry into the Holy League. Wolsey's opposition prevented his appointment as legate *a latere* (1514). He died by poison administered either by Silvestro de Gigli, resident English agent at the Roman curia (though Gigli was acquitted of the charge), or by one of his own chaplains (who had accused Gigli). BIBLIOGRAPHY: D. S. Chambers, *Cardinal Bainbridge in the Court of Rome, 1509–1514* (1965); J. Gairdner, DNB 2:433.

BAINES, PETER AUGUSTINE (1787–1843), founder of a seminary at Prior Park, Bath, England. He received his education at the monastery in Lampspring, Germany, and Ampleforth, England. He made his profession in the Benedictines in 1804. B. took care of the Benedictine mission at Bath and in 1829 was appointed vicar apostolic of the Western District of England. He fell into dispute with the Benedictines because of his plan to establish a seminary in his district. He and four others left the order and put the plans for a seminary into effect at Prior Park. He had hoped for a Catholic Univ. for lay students as well as clerics but Prior Park failed to attain this hoped-for status. BIBLIOGRAPHY: V. A. McClelland, NCE 2:18.

[J. HILL]

BAINVEL, JEAN VINCENT (1858–1937), Jesuit theologian who taught at the Institut Catholique in Paris (1900–25). Three of his courses were published in Latin: *De magisterio vivo et traditione* (1905); *De scriptura sacra* (1910); and *De ecclesia Christi* (1925). His *La Foi et l'acte de foi* (1908) and *Nature et surnaturel* (1920) were important studies in topics of emerging interest. In the field of spiritual theology his *Dévotion au Sacré-Coeur de Jésus* (1919; Eng. tr. ed. G. O'Neill, tr. E. Leahy, *Devotion to the Sacred Heart* [1924]) and *Le Saint Coeur de Marie* (1919) are classical treatments of their topics. BIBLIOGRAPHY: J. Lebreton, *Catholicisme* 1:1168; Bremond *Index* (repr. 1971) 19.

[H. JACK]

BAIRSTOW, EDWARD CUTHBERT (1874–1946), English church musician. Appointed organist of York Minster in 1913, he set high standards for *Anglican Church music through his example of a large and varied repertory excellently performed by his well-trained choir of men and boys. His own compositions, mostly anthems and other service music, are the work of an educated and sensitive musician. BIBLIOGRAPHY: H. Thompson and H. C. Colles, Grove DMM 1:359.

[A. DOHERTY]

BAIUS, MICHAEL (Michel de Bay; 1513–89), the Walloon theologian, best known in theology for the 79 propositions condemned by Pope Pius V in 1567 and listed in D 1901–79 as "errors of Michel de Bay about the nature of man and grace." Born at Meslin l'Évêque (Hainaut), he studied philosophy (1533–36) and theology (1536–41) at the Univ. of Louvain. From 1544 to 1551 he taught philosophy there and meanwhile gained his licentiate (1545) and master's degree in theology (1550). In the following year he became professor of theology and remained so till his death, being also from 1575 dean at St. Peter's and vice-chancellor of the university. B. inaugurated a new method in the study of theology, at the time when the Council of Trent was in session. He anticipated by nearly 4 centuries the "return to the sources" that characterizes contemporary theology. For him, this meant Scripture seen through the eyes of Augustine. A healthy desire for a theology closer to life inspired the new venture, but its antischolastic Augustinianism was not without danger of deviation (see H. de Lubac, *Augustinisme et théologie moderne* [1965], ch. 1). Friction arose between Baius and J. Hessels, the new team, and their older colleagues at the university, R. Tapper and J. Ravesteyn. In 1560 the Sorbonne condemned 18 propositions of Baius, who made ready for a reply, and the conflict came into the open. Pope Pius IV imposed silence; the Council of Trent was to decide the question. Baius and Hessels actually went to the Council, May 1563, but avoided a discussion.

Meanwhile Baius started publishing a first tome appearing in 1563 with three tracts: *De libero arbitrio, De iustitia et iustificatione,* and *De sacrificio.* A second volume followed in 1564–65: *De meritis, De primi hominis iustitia, De virtutibus impiorum, De sacramentis,* and *De forma baptismi.* From these and other unpublished writings of Baius, Ravesteyn drew 28 propositions that, together with many more, were condemned by the Universities of Alcalà and Salamanca (1565), for the Netherlands at the time were under the King of Spain. In a new edition of his first volume Baius included additional tracts, *De peccato originis, De charitate, De indulgentiis,* and *De oratione pro defunctis* (1566). The Louvain faculty turned to Rome for a judgment. After 40 more propositions taken from the new volume had been condemned by Alcalà, a papal commission, at the request of Philip II, took up the case. Of the 120 propositions condemned in Spain, 76 were condemned also by Pius V's bull *Ex omnibus afflictionibus* (1567). Baius submitted to the condemnation at once; after a futile attempt at obtaining a revision of the judgment, he abjured the propositions in the sense meant in the bull. His attitude, however, was not unambiguous. New propositions of his provoked new trouble. Pope Gregory XIII confirmed the condemnation of Pius V, and Baius again submitted, declaring that several of the condemned propositions were found in his works in the sense meant in the condemnation. To put an end to the continuing uneasiness, a summary of the doctrine contrary to the condemned propositions was drawn up and accepted by the Louvain faculty as an obligatory guide (1565). B. died, as he had remained throughout his troubled career as a theologian, a Catholic at heart. His firm conviction that his teaching was not different from that of St. Augustine (which to his mind could not be wrong), and the ambiguity left by the punctuation in Pius V's bull, the so-called *comma pianum,* may explain B.'s hesitancy about submission. BIBLIOGRAPHY: P. J. Donnelly, NCE 2:19–21; P. Smulders, LTK 1:1198–99. *BAIANISM.

[P. DeLETTER]

BAKER, CHARLES, see LEWIS, DAVID, ST.

BAKER, DAVID AUGUSTINE (1575–1641), spiritual writer. B. was reared in Wales as a Protestant, studied law, and after a narrow escape from drowning, turned to religion from what was practical atheism. He was received into the RC Church (1603) and entered the English Benedictines in 1605. He was greatly attracted to contemplative prayer, which seems to have been innate, since he received no formal instructions on it in his novitiate. At one point, he gave himself to internal prayer for 5 and 6 hours daily. At the peak of this period he had some sort of intellectual vision, followed immediately by a period of desolation. At this point he abandoned prayer entirely for about 12 years; he did return to it however, and was faithful to this prayer life for the remainder of his life. In 1624, while chaplain to some English Benedictine nuns, he wrote more than 60 treatises on prayer. His style was diffuse, and his work reflected more his assiduous readings rather than any new or coherent treatment of the spiritual life. His goal was contemplative prayer, and he reacted against methodology in prayer, in favor of affective prayer. BIBLIOGRAPHY: G. Sitwell, NCE 2:21–22; D. McCann, DSAM 1:1205–06.

[M. E. ALLWEIN]

BAKER, FRANCIS ASBURY (1820–65), Paulist missionary. B. was a Methodist who joined the Episcopal Church after his graduation from Princeton. In 1846 he was ordained to the ministry and became an outstanding preacher. He entered the RC Church in 1853, became a Redemptorist and joined four other Redemptorists, Isaac Hecker, Augustine Hewit, George Deshon, and Clarence Walworth in their missionary activities. In 1858 B. was released from his Redemptorist vows and helped in the formation of the Society of Missionary Priests of Saint Paul. He played a major role in establishing the Paulist tradition of ceremony in liturgy. BIBLIOGRAPHY: V. F. Holden, NCE 2:22

[J. HILL]

BAKER, NELSON HENRY (1841–1936), administrator of Our Lady of Victory Homes of Charity, New York. One of the first students at Canisius College, Buffalo, B. spent some time before and after college in business, but finally entered our Lady of the Angels Seminary at Niagara, N.Y., in 1870. After his ordination (1876), he served as assistant pastor at Lackawanna and in Corning. In 1882 he returned to Lackawanna and became superintendent of the institution that carried out varied works of mercy, including an orphanage, an industrial school, a maternity hospital, and a home for infants. In 1902, B. was named vicar-general of Buffalo. The Basilica of Our Lady of Victory was consecrated (1926) and B. administered it and its homes of charity that helped many unfortunate men, women and children. BIBLIOGRAPHY: P. J. Riga, NCE 2:22

[J. HILL]

BAKÓCZ, TAMÁS (1442–1521), Hungarian cardinal, statesman. After studies in Italy, B. returned to Hungary (1470) to become secretary and vice-chancellor to the King, bp. of Győr (1486), chancellor (1490), abp. of Esztergom (1497), cardinal (1500), and titular patriarch of Constantinople (1510). He was deeply and influentially involved in national and ecclesiastical affairs, not always too creditably, until 1516 when his plans for a new crusade failed and he lost his political power. BIBLIOGRAPHY: G. C. Paikert, NCE 2:22–23.

[H. JACK]

BALAAM, seer called by Balak, king of Moab, to curse the Israelites entering Moab on their way from Egypt to Palestine (Num ch. 22–24). Balaam lived near the Euphrates, and on his way to Balak an angel blocked the road, causing Balaam's ass to stop. Unable to see the angel, he beat the ass until it spoke, complaining of the beating. Balaam then saw the angel, who allowed him to proceed with the understanding that he would say only what God told him. On four occasions then with Balak he blessed the Israelites instead of cursing them. He was later blamed for leading the Israelites to serve Baal at Peor (Num 31.8, 16; Rev 2.14).

[T. EARLY]

BALADITES, Arabic for "native," a term applied to Lebanese Melkite and Maronite orders of monks. The former, the Basilian Order of St. John the Baptist, was organized in 1712 in Suwayr, Lebanon, requiring its members to vow poverty, chastity, obedience, and humility. Benedict XIV imposed the Rule of St. Basil in 1742; Constitutions derived from the Maronite Order of St. Anthony were approved in 1757; canonical status was attained in 1955. The order has expanded to other nations including the U.S. with a motherhouse in Khonchara, Lebanon. The Maronite Order of St. Anthony was originally an eremitic congregation whose constitutions were approved (1732) by Clement XII, though later years saw their apostolate expanded from monastic prayer to include teaching and parish work. The motherhouse is in Beirut and the order has fostered several autonomous monasteries of nuns.

[M. E. FORD]

BALAEUS (Balai; fl. late 4th cent.), a Syriac hymn writer who was a disciple of Ephraim and apparently developed the quinquesyllabic meter (five syllable). Probably a chorbishop in the Diocese of Alep, his hymns in honor of Acacius, the bp. of Alep, on the occasion of his death (431) and at the dedication of a new church in the north Syrian village of Zinnasrin are numbered among his extant writings. BIBLIOGRAPHY: G. Leven, DHGE 6:304.

[F. H. BRIGHAM]

BALAWAT, sites of important ruins of the Palace of Assurnasirpal II (880–830 B.C.), most famous for Balawat Gates—masterpieces of ancient bronze—added by Assurnasirpal's son Shalmaneser III (859–824 B.C.), carrying on horizontal reliefs engraved and embossed narrative scenes of the King's campaigns and religious customs, affording a wealth of information concerning the appearance and equipment of Urartians, Tyrians, and Hittites together with cuneiform texts. Portions of the gates are in London, Paris, Istanbul, and Boston. Another pair of gates is in the British Museum, and a third pair (Assurnasirpal II) remain in position. BIBLIOGRAPHY: A. Godard, *L'Art de l'Iran* (1962).

[M. J. DALY]

BALBÁS, GERÓNIMO (Barbás, Balbáz; 1670–1760), Spanish Mexican architectural designer and great retable master. His most ambitious work for the Sargrario Cathedral of Seville (later replaced) was duplicated in the Altar de los Reyes, Cathedral of Mexico City (1718–37; gilded 1743). B. introduced the distinctive mannerist pilaster form (*estípite*) of 18th-cent. Mexico. With Lorenzo Rodríguez, B. created eclectic, mannerist, and baroque forms distinctive of Mexico for 50 years. BIBLIOGRAPHY: E. W. Weismann, *Mexico in Sculpture* (1950).

[M. J. DALY]

BALBI (ACCELLINI), GIROLAMO (1460–1535), humanist, statesman, bishop. When adopted by his maternal grandfather, he relinquished his original family name, Accellini, for his mother's name. He studied at Rome in the school of Pomponius Laetus and also at Padua. As lecturer at the Univ. of Paris (1489), proneness to quarrels so involved him with the humanists that he had to depart suddenly from France. In 1493, similar conflicts in Vienna forced him to leave. After a sojourn in Prague where he was a successful lecturer, he settled in Hungary. There he received the priesthood and also functioned as a diplomat. He was ordained bp. of Gurk in 1523 and resigned in 1529. After 1524 he spent several years in the service of the Holy See. He is more renowned for his contribution to the spread of humanism through Europe than for his ecclesiastical achievements. BIBLIOGRAPHY: F. Seib, LTK 1:1201–02; M. Monaco, NCE 2:23–24; P. S. Allen, "Hieronymus Balbus in Paris," EHR 17 (1902) 417–428.

[J. M. O'DONNELL]

BALBINA, ST. (date unknown), virgin, called the daughter of Quirinus. Nothing certain is known of her. The Acts of Balbina are taken from the legendary *passio* of Alexander, Eventius, and Theodulus, one version of which makes B. a martyr as well as a virgin dedicated to Christ. Scholarly opinion does not identify B. with the Balbina after whom a cemetery bearing that name is called. A church dedicated to her on the Aventine is mentioned for the first time in the records of the Roman synod of 595, but it is not known which Balbina it honors. BIBLIOGRAPHY: Butler 1:707–708; E. Josi, EncCatt 2:726–727; A. Frutaz, LTK 1:1202.

[R. B. ENO]

BALBO, GIROLAMO, see BALBI (ACCELLINI), GIROLAMO.

BALDACHINO (baldachin), a canopy suspended over altars, thrones, statues, or persons as a mark of distinction. Originally baldachinos were made of a rich fabric from the East—hence the name, which derives from the It. *Baldacco,* meaning Baghdad—but later structures of solid material such as wood, stone, or metal came into use; these were supported by columns, or suspended from the ceiling, or projected from a wall, generally to cover a fixed altar or throne. Such canopies are prescribed over the high altars and the altar of the Blessed Sacrament in greater churches. A portable baldachino made of fabric and attached to poles to form a sort of umbrella is carried above the Blessed Sacrament in processions, or in certain circumstances of solemnity above the pope, cardinals, bishops, or abbots. BIBLIOGRAPHY: J. B. O'Connell, *Church Building and Furnishing* (1955), 183–186; *idem,* NCE 2:25.

[N. KOLLAR]

BALDE, JAKOB, (1604–68), German Jesuit, court preacher in Munich, then in Neuburg; satirist; dramatist (*Jephthias,* 1654); author of a no longer extant allegorical poem (*Urania victrix,* 1663), and of some relatively insignificant poems in German; educator of the nephews of Maximilian I. It is, however, as "the German Horace," i.e., as author of neo-Latin lyrics of great technical perfection, that B. distinguished himself. BIBLIOGRAPHY: C. L. Hohl, NCE 2:25; W. Kosch, *Deutsches Literatur-Lexikon* (1963) 24 (bibliog.); R. Berger, *Jakob Balde: Die deutschen Dichtungen* (1972).

[M. F. MCCARTHY]

BALDINI, BACCIO (fl. 2d half 15th cent.), one of the earliest Italian copper engravers. B. worked after designs of *Botticelli. *Coronation of the Virgin,* with probable signature (1460–70), *Crucifixion* with 14 stations of the Passion, and a *Resurrection* (1461) show influence of German engravers. Prior attribution to B. of Florentine editions of Dante (1481) is disputed. BIBLIOGRAPHY: J. G. Phillips, *Early Florentine Designers and Engravers* (1955).

[M. J. DALY]

BALDINUCCI, ANTONIO, BL. (1665–1717), Italian Jesuit home missioner. He was assigned to preach missions in Abruzzi and Romagna. His zeal, coupled with severe penitential practices, achieved remarkable results. He conducted more than 400 missions and wrote innumerable sermons and conferences before he finally collapsed while taking care of famine-stricken peasants. BIBLIOGRAPHY: C. Testore, BiblSanct 722–723; Butler 4:292–293.

[H. JACK]

BALDINUCCI, FILIPPO (1624–96), Florentine historiographer of art, connoisseur, and curator of Card. Leopold de'Medici's drawing collection; author of the *Notizie de'*

professori del disegno da Cimabue in qua (6 v., 1681–1728), a complete documentation of artists—Italian, Flemish, and Dutch—and an authoritative *Life of Bernini* (1682). His rare personal collection of drawings (in the Louvre) is of the highest quality. BIBLIOGRAPHY: Musée National du Louvre, *Dessins florentins de la collection de Filippo Baldinucci* (1958); M. M. Schaefer, NCE 2:25–27.

[L. A. LEITE]

BALDOVINETTI, ALESSO (1425–99), Florentine painter influenced by *Veneziano, *Castagno, *Piero della Francesca, and *Pollaiuolo and an innovator in techniques evident in the deterioration of the *Nativity,* a bold, large-scale fresco in SS. Annunziata (1460–62) noteworthy for a definitive Arno Valley landscape. B. studied and restored mosaics at S. Miniato al Monte (1481) and the Florence Baptistery (1482). A minor artist of first rank, B.'s archaic charm and refinement of draftsmanship influenced many Florentine engravers of the 15th century. BIBLIOGRAPHY: R. W. Kennedy, *Alesso Baldovinetti* (1938).

[M. J. DALY]

BALDUCCIO, GIOVANNI (fl. 1300?), Italian sculptor whose carving in Opera del Duomo, Pisa, and works in Bologna and Milan combine Gothic and classical motifs in a decorative yet restrained manner. BIBLIOGRAPHY: J. Pope-Hennessy, *Italian Gothic Sculpture* (1955).

[M. J. DALY]

BALDUCCIO, GIOVANNI (1550?–1603), Italian fresco painter who executed decorative works for his patron Card. Alessandro de' Medici (later Pope Leo XI).

[M. J. DALY]

BALDUNG-GRIEN, HANS (1480–1545), German painter. B. studied (1504–07) with Albrecht *Dürer in Nürnberg. From 1512–17 B. created his major work for the high altar of Freiburg Cathedral. He was one of the earliest masters of the Upper Rhine working in Renaissance style, creating portraits, altarpieces, unique demonic allegories (examples of which are in museums of Germany and Austria), extensive drawings, woodcuts, and engravings of intense vitality. Stylistically B. combines Dürer's Renaissance classicism and Grünewald's Gothic expressionism. BIBLIOGRAPHY: C. Koch, *Ausstellung Hans Baldung-Grien* (1959).

[M. J. DALY]

BALDWIN, KING OF JERUSALEM, the name of five kings of the Crusaders' Kingdom of Jerusalem. (1) B. I, King of Jerusalem (1100–18), the brother of Godfrey of Bouillon and the founder of the feudal kingdom of Jerusalem who was crowned by Patriarch Daimbert of Pisa, took over the ports of Arsuf, Caesarea, Acre, Beirut, and Sidon, withstood the attacks of Egypt, and advanced the boundaries of the kingdom to the Gulf of Aqaba (2) B. II, King of

Jerusalem (1118–31) count of Edessa and cousin of B. I. He strengthened the feudal structure of the kingdom, commissioned the Knights Templars, armed the Knights of St. John (Knights of Malta), and was acknowledged as the leading ruler by the other crusader states. (3) B. III, King of Jerusalem (1143–63) who was crowned with his mother Melisend since he was only 13 when his father King Fulk died. He was crowned again in 1151 (this time alone), and his rule was marked by continued success. He maintained the balance of power against the Muslims and Egypt with his victory at the port of Ashkelon and prepared the way for alliance with Byzantium by marrying the daughter of Emperor Manuel I Comnenus (1158). (4) B. IV, King of Jerusalem (1174–85), nephew of B. III who also became king at the age of 13. Afflicted with leprosy, his continued ill health required a succession of regents. The resulting internal upheaval and gradual weakening of the kingdom led to his crowning of his 5-year-old nephew, Baldwin V. (5) B. V, King of Jerusalem (1185–86). The end of his brief reign heralded the dissolution of the Kingdom. BIBLIOGRAPHY: S. Runciman, *History of the Crusades* (3 v., 1951–54).

[F. H. BRIGHAM]

BALDWIN OF CANTERBURY (d. 1190), Cistercian abp. of Canterbury, canonist. Educated in Exeter for the secular clergy, B. later joined the Cistercians at Ford. Elected abbot there in 1175, he became bp. of Worcester (1180) and abp. of Canterbury (1184). He helped to organize and joined the third Crusade, dying at Tyre in Syria. Earlier a strong papalist, B. as abp. was friendly with Henry II, who in turn helped him against rebellious monks at Christ Church. He wrote letters, sermons, and numerous treatises; his best known work is *De sacramento altaris,* an early example of eucharistic piety. BIBLIOGRAPHY: *Chronicles and Memorials* (ed. W. Stubbs, 2 v., 1865) for his correspondence; other works PL 202 and 204; DNB 1:952–954; bibliog. in DHGE, 6:1415–16.

[L. J. LEKAI]

BALDWIN, WILLIAM (fl. 1547), English writer, first editor of *Mirror for Magistrates.* He studied at Oxford, entered the printing house of Whitchurch, which published B.'s *Treatise of Moral Philosophy* and his *Canticles,* metrical translations of the songs of Solomon. Whitchurch, a zealous Protestant, sold his business to Wayland, a Roman Catholic, when Mary became queen. Baldwin remained with the printing house. In 1559 he edited *Mirror for Magistrates,* adding four or more original poems in accordance with the plan to bring the account up to date. Other writers failed to keep their agreements. (The original design was finally completed in 1610.) He became a clergyman and schoolmaster, published a verse elegy for Edward VI and a satirical attack, partly on Roman Catholics, in the form of a jest book called *Beware the Cat* (1561). BIBLIOGRAPHY: DNB 3:38.

[M. M. BARRY]

BALE, JOHN (1495–1563), English dramatist. As a Carmelite at Cambridge, B. came under the influence of the Reformers, abandoned his order, married, and devoted himself to the production of miracle plays that made effective if unscrupulous propaganda, esp. against the monastic system. Since he was a partisan of the Reformers, his efforts were rewarded with the Irish See of Ossory (1552). B.'s best known dramatic work, *Kynge Johan (c.* 1540), was one of the earliest English historical dramas. He also made a notable contribution to the bibliography of early English literature. BIBLIOGRAPHY: W. Harris, *Life and Works of John Bale* (1935) and *Select Works* (ed. H. Christmas, Parker Society, 1849); T. B. Blatt, *Plays of John Bale* (1968).

[P. K. MEAGHER]

BALEN, HENDRIK VAN, THE ELDER (1575–1632), Flemish painter of religious and mythological subjects. His altarpiece, Antwerp Cathedral, is important, but his smaller mythological panels in the best mannerist tradition are his finest. BIBLIOGRAPHY: F. C. Legrand, *Les Peintres flamands de genre au XVIIe siècle* (1963).

[M. J. DALY]

BALFOUR, ARTHUR JAMES (1848–1930), British statesman and philosopher. Educated at Eton and Trinity College, Cambridge, B. took an active part in political life, holding at different times from 1891 until 1922 positions of importance, including that of prime minister (1902–05). He is remembered for issuing as foreign secretary the so-called Balfour Declaration (1917), which was a qualified pledge of support to the Zionist cause. His interest in religion found expression in his *Defence of Philosophic Doubt* (1879), a work showing the need of a solution through the non-rational (i.e., religious faith) to the problems left unsolved by the philosophical and natural sciences. He took a stand against both naturalistic positivism and the sort of idealism that would identify man with God, or see in man a necessary manifestation of God. Further development of his thought is to be found in his *Foundations of Belief* (1895) and in his Gifford Lectures, *Theism and Humanism* (1915) and *Theism and Thought* (1923). See biog. by his niece, B.E.C. Dugdale (2v., 1936); BIBLIOGRAPHY: J. Dennis, *Balfour and the British Empire* (1968).

[P. K. MEAGHER]

BALL, FRANCES MARY TERESA (1794–1861), foundress. As a child she left Dublin to study at the Institute of the Blessed Virgin Mary (Ladies of Loretto) in York, England. She entered the York novitiate and returned to Ireland in 1822 to found the Irish branch of the institute. Before her death, she founded 35 Loretto (Loreto) convents in North America, Europe, and India. BIBLIOGRAPHY: H. J. Coleridge, *Life of Mother Frances Mary Teresa Ball* (1881); *Joyful Mother of Children* by a Loreto Sister (1961).

[H. JACK]

BALL, JOHN (d. 1381), English priest of radical views and doubtful sanity. Excommunicated by Abp. Islip (c.1366), he continued to denounce nobles, lawyers, and prelates, and to advocate complete social equality. He incited and took a leading part in the Peasants' Revolt (1381) and after its failure was executed for treason. Although they held similar views, Ball and Wycliffe were personally unconnected. BIBLIOGRAPHY: R. W. Hays, NCE 2:29.

[R. W. HAYS]

BALLA, GIACOMO (1871–1958), Italian painter. As teacher of Boccioni and Severini and exponent of futurist style, B. contributed to the origins and culmination of this important modern movement. His best-known work, *Dynamism of a Dog on a Leash* (1912), does not completely express his deep concern with an abstract synthesis derived from machines expressing velocity, illumination, and sound. B. exhibited in the International Exhibition of Decorative Arts in Paris (1925), in N. Y. (1949). Retrospective shows were hung in Venice (1959) and N. Y. (1961). BIBLIOGRAPHY: J. C. Taylor, *Futurism* (1961).

[M. J. DALY]

BALLERINI, ANTONIO (1805–81), Italian Jesuit theologian. He was professor of church history and then moral theology at the Gregorian Univ. in Rome. A defender of probabilism, he made a significant contribution to the development of moral theology through his *De morali systemate s. Alphonsi M. de Ligorio* (1863), his annotations to J. P. Gury's *Compendium theologiae moralis* (2 v., 1866), and his *Opus theologicum morale in Busembaum medullam* (7 v., 1889–93). BIBLIOGRAPHY: C. Sommervogel, DTC 2.1:130–131; R. Brouillard, DHGE 6:398–399.

[H. JACK]

BALLERINI, PIETRO AND GIROLAMO (1698–1769; 1702–81), Patristic scholars and theologians. Two brothers, natives of Verona, ordained priests in 1722 and 1725 respectively, who in collaboration edited many texts of earlier theologians in addition to writing original works of theology. They produced new editions of the writings of Card. Noris (1729–32), Zeno of Verona (1739), Antoninus of Florence (1740–41), Leo the Great (1753–57), and Ratherius of Verona (1765). Although some of Pietro's published views on usury were condemned (1745) by Pope Benedict XIV, the theological writings of the two brothers supported the Holy See against *Febronianism and *Jansenism. Pietro's research also contributed to the history of canon law. BIBLIOGRAPHY: F. X. Murphy, NCE 2:31; C. Testore, EncCatt 2:751.

[R. B. ENO]

BALLI (BALLO), GIUSEPPE (1567–1640), Italian theologian. B. is notable for his learned *Resolutio de modo evidenter possibili transubtantiationis panis et vini in sacrosanctum Domini Jesu corpus et sanguinem* (1640). In it he advances the thesis that in the Holy Eucharist the species become accidents of Christ's body, this being modified to give the appearances of bread and wine. BIBLIOGRAPHY: Hurter 1:261. *CHIAVETTA.

BALLOU, HOSEA (1771–1852), Universalist minister. Born in Richmond, N.H., he was converted from Calvinism to *Universalism by influences deriving from Caleb Rich and by biblical study. His own views were soon clearly distinguishable from the Relly-Murray interpretation of Universalism. The influence of *Reason the Only Oracle of Man,* by the deist Ethan Allen, is discernible in B.'s major work, *A Treatise on Atonement* (1805); some of his concepts derive from *Thoughts on the Divine Goodness* by Ferdinand Oliver Petitpierre. B.'s *Treatise on Atonement* is the first systematic statement of Universalist teaching; he argues that sin is finite, rejects the doctrine of the Trinity, and interprets atonement as reconciliation, a "renewal of love." Later, embroiled in controversy with the Restorationists (see RESTORATIONISM), he rejected the doctrine of punishment after death. Ballou was the dominant figure in the growth of American Universalism. BIBLIOGRAPHY: R. Eddy, *Universalism in America* (2v., 1884–86); E. Cassara, *Hosea Ballou* (1961).

[J. C. GODBEY]

BALLOU, HOSEA (1796–1861), Universalist minister; grandnephew of the preceding. Born in Guilford, Vt., the son of a Baptist, B. became a Universalist. He served Universalist pastorates in Stafford, Conn., and in Roxbury and Medford, Massachusetts. His major work was *Ancient History of Universalism* (1829). BIBLIOGRAPHY: R. Eddy, *Universalism in American* (2v., 1884–86).

[J. C. GODBEY]

BALLY (BAILLY), PHILIBERT-ALBERT (1605–91), Barnabite theologian and bp. of Aosta. B. joined the *Barnabites (1632) after a career in the royal court of his native Savoy. As preacher and theologian he engaged in controversies with the Protestants, and defended the papacy against the *Jansenists. His writings include: *Disputationes de traditionibus apostolicis contra haereticos* (1643); and ascetical works in the spirit of St. *Francis de Sales. BIBLIOGRAPHY: J. M. Albini, *Mémoire historique sur P.-A. Bally* (1865).

[T. C. O'BRIEN]

BALMACEDA, FRANCISCO (1772–1842), Chilean priest, renowned for his poverty and for his charity to the poor. Of a rich and aristocratic family, B. graduated from the Univ. of Santiago and distinguished himself as a poet. When his wishes to enter the Franciscan Order were opposed by his family and advisors, he became a diocesan priest and was named chaplain of the women's hospital. To assist the needy he sold his estates and even his furniture. Serving the sick in person, he achieved a reputation for sanctity and has been compared with St. Vincent de Paul. BIBLIOGRAPHY: E. Balmaceda Valdés, *La familia Balmaceda* (1919); *Diccionario Enciclopédico Hispano-Americano* 3:114.

[P. DAMBORIENA]

BALMERINO, ABBEY OF, former Cistercian abbey in Fifeshire, Scot. founded and endowed by King Alexander II and his mother, Queen Ermengarde *c.*1227; colonized by monks from Melrose *c.*1229 and dedicated to St. Mary and St. Edward the Confessor. The abbey had a succession of notable superiors and patrons. It was devastated by the English in 1547 and later desecrated by the Reformers. It is now in ruins. BIBLIOGRAPHY: J.-M. Canivez, DHGE 6:411–413; J. Wilkie, *Benedictine Monasteries of Northern Fife* (1927).

[S. A. HEENEY]

BALMES, JAIME LUCIANO (1810–48), Spanish RC priest, apologete, philosopher, and intellectual leader. A native of Vich (Catalonia), he began to establish a reputation as a writer shortly after the completion of his theological studies (1833). In addition to teaching he took an active interest in numerous political and intellectual topics of contemporary interest. His most widely known work was *Protestantism Compared with Catholicity in their Effects upon the Civilization of Europe* (4 v., 1842–44). This was undertaken in reply to F. Guizot's *History of Civilization;* it was quickly translated from the Spanish into other tongues and became a standard work of Catholic apologetics. Influential also were his *Fundamental Philosophy* and *Elementary Philosophy* which contributed to the revival of interest in philosophy in the mid-19th century. Although he held St. Thomas Aquinas in respect, B. was an eclectic and departed from commonly held Thomistic teachings upon some major points. BIBLIOGRAPHY: F. P. Siegfried, CE 2:224–226; M. Batllori, EncCatt 2:753–755; R. Gorman, *Catholic Apologetic Literature in U.S. 1784–1858* (repr. 1974) 165–166.

BALSAM (BALM), an aromatic resinous substance that flows or is drawn from certain plants. It is mixed with olive oil in the preparation of chrism. Its symbolism derives from its natural fragrance and perhaps also from its uses as a medicinal agent for soothing muscles and healing wounds.

[P. K. MEAGHER]

BALSAMON, THEODORE (d. *c.*1200), Byzantine canonist. A deacon of Constantinople, he became chartophylax, one of the chief offices of the patriarchate, and served as legal advisor to the patriarch. He was named patriarch of Antioch (1185–91) but never resided in his see, which was then occupied by the Crusaders. His most important work is his commentary on the Nomocanon of XIV Titles in which he aimed at solving the conflicts existing between civil and ecclesiastical law. This commentary is especially useful since B. cites numerous excerpts from

documents no longer extant. In 1195 he also wrote a series of answers to canonical questions of Patriarch Mark of Alexandria. A number of other canonical works are attributed to him. BIBLIOGRAPHY: E. Herman, DDC 2:76–83.

[E. EL-HAYEK]

BALTHASAR, a legendary name of one of the Magi. The names of the Magi, Caspar, Melchior, and Balthasar make their first appearance in Western tradition in the 8th century. BIBLIOGRAPHY: E. J. Joyce, NCE 9:63; A. Dörrer, LTK 3:567–568; H. Leclercq, DACL 10.1:1061–67.

[M. R. P. MCGUIRE]

BALTHASAR OF ST. CATHERINE OF SIENA (*c.*1597–1673), Discalced Carmelite and mystical writer. B. was attracted to the Teresian reform. He studied at the seminary of La Scala, Rome; after his ordination he rose rapidly to administrative positions—provincial, procurator, general definitor. His important writings include a pastoral letter to the religious of his own Lombardy province, and a commentary on the Mansion of St. Teresa, wherein he harmonized the teachings of St. Teresa with those of St. John of the Cross. Although B.'s style is artificial, his interpretation of the Mansion is known and often quoted in Teresian Carmelite schools. BIBLIOGRAPHY: G. de Sainte Marie Madeleine, DSAM 1.1:1210–17.

[M. E. ALLWEIN]

BALTIC RELIGION, so called for the areas it covers (Latvian, Lithuanian, Yatsyage and Old Prussian), a religion similar to Indo-Iranian but later influenced by Finno-Ugric religion. Extinct for 3 centuries, the tenets of Baltic Religion were reconstructed with the help of folksongs (*dáinos*). Baltic folksongs cover every aspect of life; their chief characteristic is gentleness toward mankind and nature. Even the grass has feelings and should not be thoughtlessly trampled. Absence of aggressive war songs and of bloody sacrifices is noteworthy. Sifting out admixtures of Christian tenets, it appears that the chief god, Dievs (from a root meaning god, cf. *Zeus*), was originally a high god, remote and abstract. The important thunder god, Perkōns or Perkunas, who is associated with fertility, may be another name for him, the sky-god in the process of becoming all-god. Saule, the sun goddess and Mēness the moon god are the heroes of song and myth; their children, the morning and evening twilight, carry on charming and poetic love affairs with "God's sons"—the morning and evening star. Mother Earth, Laima—goddess of fate—and other goddesses appear in many songs; in Christian times they often became confused with the Virgin Mary. Their cults were associated with feasts and ceremonials connected with agriculture and with important phases of human life. Birth and wedding rites as well as the summer solstice and annual harvest were solemnly observed. BIBLIOGRAPHY: L. H. Gray, "Baltic Mythology," in v.3 of *Mythology of All Races* (1918); H. Biezais, *Die Hauptgöttinnen der alten Letten* (1955);

idem, Die Gottesgestalt der lettischen Volksreligion (1961).

[D. H. BRUNAUER]

BALTICUS, MARTINUS (*c*.1532–1600), humanist and educator. Director of the Latin school at Ulm (1559–92), he wrote three books of Latin elegies and epigrams. His unique work is a paraphrase in Latin elegiacs of the Sunday Epistles and Gospels. BIBLIOGRAPHY: A. Roersch, DHGE 6:431; H. Dressler, NCE 2:33.

[H. DRESSLER]

BALTIMORE, BASILICA OF THE ASSUMPTION OF THE BLESSED VIRGIN MARY, see CATHEDRAL.

BALTIMORE, COUNCILS OF. A series of provincial and plenary councils held in Baltimore in the 19th century. These councils established much of the policy and practice that have shaped the RC Church in the U.S. They legislated for the peculiar needs of the Church in the formative years of the American Republic.

   Provincial Councils. Between 1829 and 1869, Baltimore was the site of ten provincial councils. The first seven (1829, 1833, 1837, 1840, 1843, 1846, and 1849) brought together the hierarchy of the entire country, and the legislation passed at these assemblies was operative for most of the U.S. and its territories.

   The first provincial council was convoked by Abp. James Whitfield (1828–34). But it was John England of Charleston, S.C., who is "the father of the conciliar tradition in the U.S." England argued the need for provincial councils and was the author of the pastoral letters issued in 1829, 1833, 1837, and 1840. The first provincial council ordered the publication of the enactments of the diocesan synod held in Baltimore in 1791 and the articles concerning ecclesiastical discipline drawn up by the American hierarchy in 1810, along with the decrees of the council itself.

   The decrees of this and succeeding provincial councils dealt with problems and issues peculiar to the newly emerging nation: church support and church property; the relationship of the clergy, secular and regular, to the bishops; religious education; relationships with non-Catholics and Freemasons; holy days of obligation and laws of fast and abstinence; sacramental practice, esp. governing baptism and marriage, and parasacramental rituals such as the burial service and devotions; the use of the vernacular in the liturgy. Concern was expressed for missionary activity among the Indians and for the emancipated slaves expatriated to Liberia. At the sixth council in 1846 the Blessed Virgin Mary under the title of the Immaculate Conception was chosen as patroness of the U.S.; and at the seventh council the American bps. expressed the view that they thought it opportune to declare the Immaculate Conception a dogma of the Church.

   Plenary Councils. As long as the ecclesiastical province of Baltimore comprised the whole U.S. and its territories, the provincial councils held there were *de facto* assemblies of the national hierarchy. In 1846, however, Oregon City, Oregon (now the archdiocese of Portland), was constituted the second province, and in 1847, St. Louis became the third. In 1849, moreover, the seventh provincial council petitioned that New Orleans, Cincinnati, and New York be constituted metropolitan sees. At the same time the American bps. requested authorization to hold a plenary council which would bring together the abps. and bps. of all the ecclesiastical provinces.

   The first plenary council met May 9–20, 1852, Abp. Kenrick of Baltimore presiding. The council promulgated 25 decrees, most dealing with administrative policies and procedures. It declared that the regulations set down by the seven provincial councils of Baltimore were binding in all the dioceses of the U.S. The bishops praised the government's "hands-off" policy in religious affairs, and at the same time asked that Catholics in military service not be obliged to attend non-Catholic worship services. The decrees were sent to Rome for approval. The prefect of the Propaganda privately warned against the danger of a national Church: the American dioceses were not to push for uniformity in practices that differ from the common law of the Church.

   The second plenary council met in Baltimore October 7–21, 1866, Abp. Spalding presiding. The enactments of this council are listed under 14 headings. In announcing the meeting Spalding referred to the Civil War which had recently ended. Though they deal with administrative, procedural, and ritual questions, the decrees of this council show the markedly pastoral interest of the U.S. hierarchy; the faithful were cautioned against indifferentism, Unitarianism, universalism, transcendentalism, pantheism, and various kinds of spiritism. Guidelines were set down for clerical life. The establishment of both preparatory and major seminaries was urged. Each parish was required to have a school and catechism classes for children attending public schools. Further warnings were issued about printed matter, textbooks and newspapers, which contained material contrary to faith and morals. The council also promulgated many positive directives on preaching, pastoral care, and missionary activities, including efforts for the conversion of Negroes.

   The third plenary council of Baltimore met Nov. 9—Dec. 7, 1884, Abp. Gibbons presiding. It went over much of the same ground covered in the assembly of 1866, formulating a series of decrees that had the force of canon law for the Church in the U.S. Detailed regulations governing the lives and education of clerics were set down. A commission was given the mandate to create a Catholic university under the patronage of the national hierarchy. Another commission was directed to prepare a catechism for general use. The first led to the foundation of The Catholic University of America in Washington, D. C. (1889), and the second to the Baltimore Catechism. The third plenary council fixed the shape of the diocesan organization of the Catholic Church in America. BIBLIOGRAPHY: *History of the Councils of Balti-*

more, 1791–1884 (ed. P. Guilday, 1932); W. H. W. Fanning, CE 2:235–241; J. Hennessey, NCE 2:38–43.

[B. L. MARTHALER]

BALTIMORE CATECHISM, the question and answer text commissioned by the Third Plenary Council of Baltimore (1884) for use in elementary religious instruction throughout the U.S. Prior to its appearance in 1885, a variety of European catechisms had been used. Drawn up by Bp. J. J. Spaulding, and Msgr. J. V. De Concilio, the catechism had 421 entries dealing with the creed, sacraments, prayer, commandments, and the last things. Its basic structure was the same as that of the catechism of the Council of Trent, and it received wide use throughout the early decades of the 20th cent., esp. in the growing parochial school system. Revision of the original catechism began in 1935 under the supervision of the Episcopal Committee on Christian Doctrine of the National Catholic Welfare Conference. Over 200 catechists, pastors, and theologians cooperated with the general authorship of Rev. F. *Connell, and the revised edition was published in 1941. In brief, simple modes of expression, it sought to present RC doctrine with clarity and completeness. This Baltimore Catechism No. 2, intended for use in grades 6 to 8, contained 499 questions and answers as well as a brief apologetics section entitled "Why Am I a Catholic?" Treating the same basic topics in order but differing in presentation, other catechisms were published within a year for first communicants and for primary grade students (Baltimore Catechism No. 1), and in 1949, an expanded edition for high school students (Baltimore Catechism No. 3). Periodic revisions took place over the subsequent years.

Contemporary catechetical experts have raised serious difficulties concerning the general orientation of the Baltimore Catechism. It is objected that the question-and-answer methodology in the catechesis of children does not take into account the child's particular approach to the relevant matter. The organic psychological development of the child and his affectivity do not seem to be sufficiently heeded. Contemporary catechists stress that living faith comes from many interrelating sources such as parental teaching and example, religious observances, pastoral care, etc. In the revised Baltimore Catechism they noted a lack of distinction between simplified doctrinal expression and basic theologizing. Finally, the individualistic emphasis of the Baltimore Catechism seemed at odds with a developing community awareness and commitment on the part of the child in a more Christocentric framework of response. BIBLIOGRAPHY: F. J. Connell, "Catechism Revision," *Confraternity Comes of Age: A Historical Symposium* (1956) 189–201; G. Sloyan, *Modern Catechetics* (1963) 85–101.

[W. J. TOBIN]

BALTZER, JOHANN BAPTIST (1803–71), German theologian. Professor of dogmatic theology at Breslau (1830), B. became a follower of G. Hermes, then of A. Günther. The second he violently defended at Rome (1854).

Eventually suspended, B. later joined the Old Catholic movement. Some of his works were placed on the Index. BIBLIOGRAPHY: R. Bäumer, LTK 1:1214.

[T. C. O'BRIEN]

BALUFFI, GAETANO (1788–1866), cardinal, internuncio. He was bp. of Bagnorea, Italy, when appointed internuncio to New Granada (1837). Also acting for several other South American countries, he unfortunately made the wrong connections and encountered difficulties. By 1841, he was back in Italy as bp. of Camerino, then of Imola, and cardinal. His attempt in his book on Spanish America to explain the Latin American countries to Europeans revealed his lack of knowledge and experience.

[H. JACK]

BALZAC, HONORÉ DE (1799–1850), French writer, creator of *La Comédie humaine,* a collection of more than 90 novels and tales portraying French society under the Restoration and the July Monarchy. He began his literary career in 1819. Although educated under Catholic auspices, B. initially elaborated a materialistic philosophy (*Traité de l'immortalité de l'âme,* 1818; *La Philosophie de la religion,* 1818), and his earliest novels attacked Catholic dogma, ethics, and ritual (e.g., *Le Vicaire des Ardennes,* 1822; *Sténie,* 1821). Favorable views during this period on the civilizing effects of religion and on the contemplative life, found in *L'Histoire impartiale des Jésuites* (1824) and *Traité de la prière* (1824), foreshadow his steady evolution after 1829 toward traditionalist ideas. The *Essai sur la situation du parti royaliste* (1832) marked his formal adherence to Catholicism and legitimism as twin pillars of society; thereafter B. would "write in praise of two eternal truths, Religion and Monarchy" (preface to *La Comédie humaine,* 1842) and elements of a romantically tinged apologetics appear throughout his works. B. distinguished religion from the institutionalized Church. The former, a quasi-primitive sentiment rooted in man's nature, is a creative and ennobling force motivating numerous Balzacian heroines to act uprightly, guaranteeing the stability of institutions like the family and preserving the individual from despair and debauchery; its authentic faith and awesome liturgical mysteries effect many conversions, compelling the fealty even of its enemies. The latter is an ideal bearing the scars of history, at times ill-served by its adherents. Its position in 19th-cent. France he saw as precarious. In his clerical portraits and sketches of Catholic life, B. the realist grasps the currents at work in the French Church—from Ultramontanism to Lamennaisian liberalism—and depicts every shade of priest. Representative works embodying these ideas include *Un Épisode sous la terreur* (1830), *Jésus-Christ en Flandre* (1831), *Le Curé de Tours* (1832), *Le Médecin de campagne* (1833), *Eugénie Grandet* (1833), *Le Père Goriot* (1835), *La Messe de l'athée* (1836), *Le Curé de village* (1839), *L'Envers de l'histoire contemporaine* (1844), and *La Cousine Bette* (1846). Yet his personal commitment to

Catholicism was ambiguous and he held heterodox religious views. Philosophical novels like *Louis Lambert* and *Séraphîta* (1834) reflect his readings in 18th-cent. illuminism and his preoccupation with occultism, mesmerism, and Swedenborgian mysticism. However, B. did marry the Polish countess, Mme. Hanska, in a Catholic ceremony (1850) and received the sacraments on his deathbed. BIBLIOGRAPHY: P. Bertaut, *Balzac et la religion* (1942); G. Atkinson, *Les Idées de Balzac d'après La Comédie humaine* (5 v., 1950); A. Maurois, *Prometheus or the Life of Balzac* (tr. 1966); M. F. Sandars, *Honoré De Balzac: His Life and Writings* (repr. 1970).

[G. E. GINGRAS]

BALZAC, JEAN LOUIS GUEZ DE (*c*.1597–1654), French writer, one of the original members of the French Academy. Educated by the Jesuits, and after a trip to Holland, B. was the representative of Card. de La Valette, Abp. of Toulouse, in Rome (1621–22), where he began writing his celebrated *Lettres*. Published shortly after his return to France and early retirement (1624), they were to influence greatly the development of the French classic prose style. While his *Le Prince* (1631) was a political treatise on the ideal sovereign, his *Socrate chrétien* (1652) concluded his ethical thought with a synthesis of Christianity and stoicism. He was also the author of religious poetry; *Aristippe ou La Cour* (1658); 14 *Dissertations chrétiennes et morales;* and 28 *Dissertations critiques* which include his severe criticism of Heinsius' tragedy, *Herodes Infanticida,* for its mixture of Christianity and mythology. BIBLIOGRAPHY: J.-B. Sabrié, *Les Idées religieuses de J.-L. Guez de Balzac* (1913); Bremond Index 20.

[R. N. NICOLICH]

BAMBERG APOCALYPSE, Ottonian illuminated MS in the State Library, Bamberg, Germany.

BAMBERG CATHEDRAL, church of German High Romanesque architecture dedicated to SS. Peter and George, the old foundations erected 1002–12 and the present church, 1185. Most noteworthy is its sculpture (end of 12th and first part of the 13th cent.), stylistically eclectic, influenced by Naumburg, Reims, Burgundy, and Lombardy. The famous ''prophets'' from the choir screen show great perception in strong characterization. The most significant sculptures are *Bamberg Rider* and *The Last Judgment* tympanum.

[M. J. DALY]

BAMBINO, the Italian word for child or infant. In a religious context it refers to the *Bambino Gesù*, i.e., the Infant Jesus. The cult of the Infant, esp. as associated with the Nativity and the devotion of the *Crib, was popularized largely through the influence of Franciscan spirituality from the 13th cent. onward. The image of the Child in the crib is often called simply the Bambino.

[N. KOLLAR]

BĀMIYĀN, town in north central Afghanistan, center of pilgrimage exerting strong influence on Buddhist art in Turkistan and China. Two colossal Buddhas of chalk, straw, and rope painted in Indian-Iranian style are dated 400 A.D. and 600 A.D. respectively. See J. Hackin, *Nouvelles recherches archéologiques à Bāmiyān* (*Mémoires de la délégation archéologiques française en Afghanistan,* v. 3, 1953).

[M. J. DALY]

BAMPTON LECTURES, an annual series of lectures established under terms of the will of J. Bampton (d. 1751) to be delivered in the university church, St. Mary's, Oxford, in exposition and defense of the Christian faith. The first series was given in 1780; since 1895 the lectures have been given biennially, a change made necessary by depreciation in the value of the fund. The lectureship is restricted to Anglican M.A.s of Oxford or Cambridge. The lectures, always published after delivery, constitute on the whole an important collection of apologetical literature, and individual series over the years have provided notable stimulus to scholarship and theological debate.

BAN (Ger. *Bann*), the term for the form of excommunication practiced particularly by Mennonites. There are two kinds of ban: exclusion from communion *(kleiner Bann)* and complete exclusion from membership in the Church *(grosser Bann)*. The prominence of the ban in Mennonite history rests upon the teaching that the Church must be kept visibly pure; only by discipline of those who have failed to live up to the decision involved in *believer's baptism can this purity be assured. The ban was one of the points of disagreement between the Swiss Anabaptists and Zwingli; its importance to church life was declared in the *Schleitheim Confession (1527) and later in the *Dordrecht Confession (1627). Early Anabaptist leaders stressed the need first to admonish scandalous sinners, then to apply the ban. Repeatedly in Anabaptist and Mennonite history stricter or milder interpretation of the ban, and particularly the complete *avoidance or shunning of the banned, became a cause of division (see AMISH; AMMANN JAKOB). The ban is still recognized as essential to church discipline by modern Mennonites, although not all enforce it. BIBLIOGRAPHY: MennEnc 1:219–223.

[T. C. O'BRIEN]

BANCHIERI, ADRIANO (1567–1634), monk, organist, and composer, later abbot of San Michele, near Bologna. His numerous secular works include many ''madrigal comedies'' and stage works. Among his church compositions his *Concerti ecclesiastici* (1595) for double choir is notable for its written-out organ accompaniment, one of the first of its kind printed. Italianate in melody and strongly rhythmic in character, his works stand in sharp contrast to the music of his contemporaries *Palestrina and Lasso. BIBLIOGRAPHY: Reese MusR; H. F. Redlich, MGG 1:1206–12.

[J. J. WALSH]

BANDAS, RUDOLPH G. (1896–1969), a writer on theological, philosophical, and catechetical subjects. Born in Minnesota, educated at Univ. of Minn., St. Thomas College, and St. Paul's Seminary, and after graduate work at Louvain and at the Angelicum in Rome (with doctorates from both), B. taught at St. Paul's Seminary. Activities included the Archdiocesan Curia, director of CCD, Catholic Youth Council, associate editor of Our Parish Confraternity, rector of St. Paul's Seminary, nonresident professor at the Lateran Univ., member of the Roman Pontifical Academy, consultor of the Sacred Congregations of Seminaries and Universities, pastor of St. Agnes Church, St. Paul, Minn. Besides contributing extensively to *Thought, America,* the *Ecclesiastical Review,* the *Homiletic and Pastoral Review,* B. wrote books helpful to catechists and teachers. BIBLIOGRAPHY: *Master Idea of St. Paul's Epistles* (1925); *Contemporary Philosophy and Thomistic Principles* (1931); *Catechetics in the NT* (1934); *Modern Questions* (6 v., 1941).

[J. MORGAN]

BANDINELLI, BACCIO (1488 or 1495–1560), Italian sculptor at the court of Cosimo de'Medici. B. carved the important *Lamentation over the Dead Christ* in the choir screen of the Cathedral of Florence. While influenced by Michelangelo, he emphasized muscular form at the expense of expressive sculptural qualities. BIBLIOGRAPHY: M. Salmi, *L'Arte italiana* (1946–47).

[M. J. DALY]

BÁÑEZ, DOMINGO (1528–1604), Spanish Dominican theologian, for whom the system of grace called *Bañezianism is named. Born at Valladolid, at the age of 15 he began his philosophical studies at Salamanca, and 3 years later he joined the Dominican convent of San Esteban there. He studied theology under Bartolomé de Medina and Melchior Cano. From 1552 until his death he taught theology in various places: 1552–61 in the Dominican convent at Salamanca; 1561–66 at the newly founded university in Avila; 1567–70 at Alcalá; 1570–73 he was Durandus professor at Salamanca; and after the death of Medina (1581) he held for 20 years the "Chair of Prime" at the university. Báñez was one of the great commentators on the *Summa Theologiae* of St. Thomas Aquinas and a profuse writer. Of his scholastic commentaries, the following were published in modern times through the care of V. Beltrán de Heredia: *In 1am2ae* v.1 *(De fine ultimo et de actibus humanis),* v.2 *(De vitiis et peccatis),* v.3 *(De gratia Dei),* 1942-1948; *In 3am partem* v.1 *(De Verbo incarnato),* v.2 *(De sacramentis),* 1951, 1953. B's theological writings would themselves have given him a place in the history of theology, even apart from

his system of grace. Like the other Spanish theologians of the 16th- and 17th-cent. scholastic revival, B. was highly systematic, essentialist and conceptualist in approach rather than biblical or existential. This makes his profound speculative thought of more historical than vital interest to post-Vatican II theology. While at Avila, B. became the spiritual director of St. Teresa and remained so until her death in 1582. He was the defender of her reform as well as of her writings. His influence, it is said, explains the Thomistic cast of mind underlying her spirituality. For Teresa, B. was a learned, firm, and understanding director. BIBLIOGRAPHY: W. J. Hill, NCE 2:48–50.

[P. DE LETTER]

BAÑEZIANISM, the name given to the system of grace (or explanation of the cooperation between divine grace and free will) constructed by Domingo *Báñez. The historical occasion for its origin was in the controversies on grace between Jesuits and Dominicans in Spain, and particularly over L. *Molina's *Concordia liberi arbitrii cum gratiae donis, divina praescientia, providentia, praedestinatione, et reprobatione* (Lisbon, 1588), which was censured by Báñez for the Inquisition. After Molina's self-defense, the book was approved. When the controversy following on this was delated to Rome, Molina denounced Báñez to the Inquisition in Castile. Báñez replied by publishing (1595), in collaboration with P. Herrera and D. Alvarez, an *Apologia* against certain assertions of Molina, and 2 years later a *Libellus supplex* to Clement VIII. Báñez himself did not take any part in the *Congregatio de auxiliis held in Rome (1598–1607). The problem that both Molinism and Bañezianism seek to solve is this: how do efficacious grace and human free consent go together? Both agree that for a salutary or supernatural act God grants prevenient actual grace intended to be sufficient to bring about man's free consent. They also agree that, when the free consent follows in fact, the grace received is a greater gift of God than was sufficient grace. The point of disagreement regards the difference between a sufficient grace that will remain purely sufficient (i.e., to which man will not freely consent) and one that will become efficacious in fact (i.e., to which man will freely consent). Molina says that there is no objective difference between the two; the difference exists only between a purely sufficient grace and a grace efficacious in the actual event.

Báñez maintains that sufficient grace, or prevenient grace given to arouse the free consent, does not actually bring about this consent unless there is added an efficacious grace, different from merely sufficient prevenient grace. He says so because of his view on God's physical *premotion of all free acts, by which in a mysterious manner and without prejudice to human freedom God brings about man's free consent. Truly efficacious grace is a physical premotion that of its inner nature produces a free consent. It is on God's part a physical predetermination of man's free act on which the free consent infallibly, or of the very nature of efficacious grace, follows as a free consent. This paradox is not a contradiction, because there can be no opposition between the causality of the First Cause and the act of the secondary free cause, since both the act and its freedom are given being, or created, by God. The concept of efficacious grace as physical premotion and physical predetermination is linked with the idea of predestination *ante praevisa merita,* i.e., independent of the foreknowledge of merit and of man's free consent. In fact, God's decree by which he predestines a man for salvation through free cooperation with grace is purely gratuitous and in no way dependent on man, though it does not take effect without man's free cooperation. Bañezianism stresses God's supreme dominion over everything created and the mystery that envelops man's free consent to efficacious grace. Freedom itself appears as a mysterious gift insofar as a divine physical predetermination and physical premotion, which of their nature entail man's free consent, do not destroy but rather constitute that freedom. In fact, created freedom does not mean independence from the Creator and First Cause that gives it being but only from created coercion or necessity. BIBLIOGRAPHY: M. J. Farrelly, *Predestination, Grace and Free Will* (1964).

[P. De LETTER]

BANGKOK, MONASTERIES OF. Noteworthy are the Monastery of the Dawn (at Tonburi) magnificent in glazed tile, lacquer, and gold and the Monastery of the Bo Tree (Wat Po) with paintings of the Buddha; in the west city a giant sculptured Buddha shows cosmic pattern of inlaid mother-of-pearl on the soles of his feet. Banners and frescoes show slight European influence. Themes of *Rāmāyana* in the Thai mode of theater and dance evidence influences from India. BIBLIOGRAPHY: B. P. Groslier, *Art of Indochina* (1962).

[M. J. DALY]

BANGLADESH, predominantly Muslim country located in the delta area of the Ganges and Brahmaputra Rivers, on the Bay of Bengal. Its land boundaries are almost entirely with India, except on the SE where it adjoins Burma. Formerly known as East Pakistan, a province separated from the rest of Pakistan by 1100 miles, Bangladesh won independence in 1971, aided by military forces from India. Bengali constitute the principal ethnic group of the country. Conversion of the eastern Bengali from Hinduism to Islam began after a takeover by Turkic conquerors in the 12th century. Later part of the Mogul empire, the area came under British rule in the colonial period. In 1947 western Bengal, predominantly Hindu, became part of India, and the Muslim area part of Pakistan. Bangladesh also includes a significant number of Hindus and smaller communities of Buddhists, Christians, and animists. With 75 million people and only 55,000 square miles, it is one of the world's most densely populated areas, as well as one of the most poverty stricken. The Catholic population numbers about 120,000 and is cared for by 1 abp., 3 bps., and 133 priests. Bangladesh established diplomatic relations with Vatican City in 1972.

[T. EARLY]

BANGOR, ABBEYS OF, (1.) in Wales, Bangor Caernarvonshire or Bangor Fawr yn Anfron, was founded by St. Deiniol in the 6th cent. It lost its monastic character *c*.1092 and became a diocesan seat. Bangor-on-Dee or Bangor Iscoed, Flintshire, was also probably founded by St. Deiniol. It had at one time 2,100 monks, 1,200 of whom were massacred in the battle of Chester (616). Its abbot, Donatus, was one of the British who had an unfruitful meeting with Augustine of Canterbury. Nothing is known of its later history. (2.) In Ireland, Bangor or Bend-chor in County Down, founded *c*.555 by St. Comgall, played a part in the conversion of the Picts of Scotland, and (through Columban) in restoring religious life in Merovingian Gaul. Its Antiphonary contains the oldest Eucharistic hymn *Sancti venite* (680–691). It declined in 10th cent. but was restored by St. Malachy of Armagh (d.1148). BIBLIOGRAPHY: A. W. Wade-Evans, *Welsh Christian Origins* (1934); J. E. Lloyd, *History of Wales* (2 v., 1948); Kenney (1966); G. Williams, NCE 2:50.

[C. MCGRATH]

BANKAL, in the Armenian Church, a small room opening off the forecourt of a church compound, where devotional business (small contributions, purchase of candles, etc.) is transacted.

[A. CODY]

BANKRUPTCY, a legal provision by which a person, indebted to others and unable to meet his financial obligations, may yield his assets to his creditors and become freed of further obligation for the portion of his indebtedness he has not been able to satisfy. Moralists are generally agreed that the proper declaration of bankruptcy, as approved by civil law, liberates the debtor in conscience as well as before the law, though most think it laudable, should his financial situation improve at a later time to such extent that he could do so without undue strain, to reimburse his erstwhile creditors for the loss they sustained on his account.

[P. K. MEAGHER]

BANNABIKIRA, (Luganda-Daughters of Mary), a religious congregation of African women founded in Uganda by Abp. Henry Streicher (1909). Their mission is to assist the White Fathers in their equatorial missions by nursing, catechetics, teaching, and the social apostolate.

[F. H. BRIGHAM]

BANNER *(vexillum),* in its religious use, a ceremonial ensign consisting of a cloth, generally rectangular in shape and marked with some symbol or pictorial design, fastened to a crossbar at the top of a staff that is often tipped with a cross or statue. The earliest Christian standard was the cross itself, the symbol of Christ's victory, but in Christian art from the 9th cent. the Church and the risen Christ were often depicted holding a banner to symbolize that victory. In later usage the symbolism was broadened, and banners became popular to identify persons or groups, esp. in religious processions. Many blessings of banners are found in medieval Pontificals. Banners and flags of various kinds are still blessed and may be admitted into a church as long as they are not anti-Christian or representative of condemned societies. (CIC c. 1233.2).

[N. KOLLAR]

BANNISTER, HENRY MARRIOTT (1854–1919), Anglican hymnologist. After study at Oxford, B. was ordained in 1878 and served for 5 years in the pastoral ministry. He then devoted the rest of his life to the study of medieval music, doing his research chiefly in Oxford and Rome. He published important Vatican MSS containing medieval musical notation and co-edited v. 40–55 of *Analecta hymnica medii aevi*. His studies showed that the religious sequence originated in northern France. BIBLIOGRAPHY: L. Ellinwood, NCE 2:52.

[M. J. SUELZER]

BANNON, JOHN B. (1829–1913), military chaplain and Confederate commissioner. Ordained in Maynooth, Ireland, (1853), B. came to St. Louis, Mo. and served in St. Louis Cathedral and the Immaculate Conception Church. When the Civil War broke out, B. left his new church and began his service as a chaplain to the Confederate army. After serving as an outstanding chaplain on the battlefields, he was released from the army and sent to Ireland as a Confederate commissioner to elicit aid from the Irish for the Confederate cause. He also accompanied Bp. Patrick Lynch of Charleston to Rome to try to obtain papal recognition of the Confederacy. B. returned to Ireland, joined the Society of Jesus, and served at St. Ignatius Univ. in Dublin. BIBLIOGRAPHY: A. Plaisance, NCE 2:52–53.

[J. HILL]

BANNS (Lat. *bannum* from the Teutonic *bann*). The calling of banns is the public and official announcement or proclamation of names and persons who intend to marry, to discover whether the parties are free to marry, and that there are no hidden impediments to a valid and lawful marriage. The first trace of these proclamations appears to be in the 8th cent. in the Synod of Ratisbon. In 1200 Abp. Hubert Walter, in a council of Lambeth, published a constitution that declared that no marriage was to be celebrated until after a triple publication of the Church's bann. At the Lateran Council of 1215 Innocent III extended over the whole of Western Christendom the practice that had hitherto prevailed in some countries, of publishing the banns of intended marriages, that is of calling upon all to declare any cause or impediment that could be urged against the proposed union. The Council of

Trent (1563) extended the law to a threefold public announcement on three successive feast days. The Code of Canon Law (c. 1024) adds that the proclamation may be made not only at Mass but also at other services frequented by many of the parishioners. By permission of the Ordinary the announcement may be posted on the notice board at the church door. This practice has become very general, particularly since the new order of the Mass. If anyone is aware of an impediment to the marriage announced, he is bound in conscience to disclose the fact to the clergy concerned. The proper Ordinary of one or other of the parties is empowered to dispense from banns for good reasons and if the freedom to marry is otherwise known (CIC c. 1028).

[A. FARRELL]

BAÑOS DE CERRATO, SAN JUAN BAUTISTA (*c.*661), Spanish church near Palencia, example of Early Christian Visigothic architecture. Remaining are three square-ended sanctuaries, horseshoe arches, and evidences of degenerate Roman carvings. BIBLIOGRAPHY: G. G. King, *Pre-Romanesque Churches of Spain* (1924).

[M. J. DALY]

BANZ, MONASTERY OF, former Benedictine monastery near Bamberg, N Bavaria, Germany, founded 1069, secularized in 1803. Fine abbey buildings date from 1695 and the church, 1710–19 by J. Dientzenhofer, with entrance court (1752) by Balthasar *Neumann.

[M. J. DALY]

BAPST, JOHN (1815–87), Jesuit missionary and educator, B. attended St. Michael's College, Fribourg, Switzerland, entered the Society of Jesus (1835), and was ordained in 1846. He came to New York when Jesuits were exiled from Switzerland. Sent to an Indian mission in north central Maine, he and some companions organized missions covering 33 towns and serving 9,000 people, mostly Irish, Canadians, and Indians on reservations. He suffered physical harm at the hands of the Know-Nothings at Ellsworth. This act met with general condemnation and he was honored by Protestants of Bangor. B. was the first superior of Boston College (1864–69) and superior of New York-Canadian missions. BIBLIOGRAPHY: W. L. Lucey, NCE 2:53–54.

[J. HILL]

BAPTISM, the Christian rite of initiation by washing. Both its Christian beginnings and its connection with non-Christian ritual washings (both Jewish and pagan) are obscure. There is in the NT no account of the institution of baptism by Jesus Christ; rather, each time it is referred to it is already taken for granted as a constituent element of Christian faith and life. Christ's words to Nicodemus, "Unless one is born of water and of the Spirit, he cannot enter the kingdom of God" (Jn 3.5), seem to presuppose baptism. Similarly, the command to "make disciples of all nations, baptizing them in the name of the Father and of the Son and of the Holy

Spirit'' (Mt 28.19) does not seem to be an act of instituting baptism but a commission to employ it in the world mission of the Church. Necessary to a valid baptism, according to most theologians, are the use of water (whether by immersion or by sprinkling is a matter of controversy), the invocation of the Holy Trinity (although some passages in the NT do seem to speak of a baptism in the name of Christ only), and the intention that this action be the baptism of the Church (although the validity of the baptism does not depend upon the state of grace of the officiant).

Baptism is usually said to confer three benefits: the remission of sins, the infusion of grace, and incorporation into the Church. When it was administered as part of the process by which one renounced paganism and embraced Christianity, the remission it granted was ordinarily related to the actual sins that the candidate had committed before his conversion. Baptism and repentance are therefore linked in the NT as a break with the sinful past and a renunciation of the dominion of sin. With the advent of *infant baptism as the general practice of the Church the remission was understood to include *original sin as well. Indeed, the practice of infant baptism provided St. Cyprian and above all St. Augustine with powerful evidence for the doctrine of original sin; for if baptism did effect remission, this could not apply to actual sins in the case of an infant but had to apply to what he had inherited. As a means for the infusion of divine grace, baptism has the special importance of emphasizing and documenting the priority of the divine initiative in the establishment of the new relation between God and man. The grace of God is not earned or seized or won but is received when God, through his selected channel, pours it into the baptized. This baptismal grace, once received, marks the baptized unalterably. He may prove unfaithful to it, but he cannot remove it; and if he falls away from the faith and then returns, baptism is not repeated. By remitting sins and infusing grace, baptism becomes the initiation of the new Christian into the community of faith. It is therefore the most fundamental of all the sacraments, for upon it all the others depend, each of them adding its special spiritual endowment to the grace already given in baptism. The solemn repetition of one's baptismal vows, particularly in its modern liturgical form, is a profound reminder of the meaning of baptism.

As has already been indicated, both the mode and the subject of baptism have been issues of doctrinal controversy. There seems to be little question that the primitive Christian practice was a baptism by immersion, usually in flowing water. From this some Protestant groups have concluded that any other method of washing is a violation of the divinely prescribed pattern and therefore not a proper baptism. The same groups have also repudiated the practice of infant baptism as inconsistent with the personal faith and explicit commitment to Christian discipleship that baptism demands. The defenders of the traditional practice have contended that the mode of baptism is an indifferent matter, so long as water and the name of the Trinity are used. The baptism of infants is justified by its apologists either on the grounds that infants can have true faith even though they can neither understand nor express it, or on the grounds that baptism is the initial step of a relationship to Christ and to the Church, of which *Christian nurture, confirmation, and the deepening commitment of the believer are the continuation. Even its defenders are increasingly careful to avoid the magical connotations that have sometimes appeared in the theology of infant baptism, stressing its place in the life of the Church. BIBLIOGRAPHY: G. W. Lampe, *Seal of the Spirit* (1951); K. Barth, *Church Doctrine of Baptism* (1948); J. Jeremias, *Infant Baptism in the First Four Centuries* (1960); ThAq ST 3,66–71; A. R. George, "Christian Initiation." J EcclHist 23 (1972) 65.

[J. PELIKAN]

BAPTISM, ADULT. Vatican Council II called for the revision of the liturgy of baptism, and this was completed with the *Ordo Baptismi parvulorum* (1969) and the *Ordo initiationis Christiane adultorum* (1972). The new rite of Christian initiation for adults includes the three sacraments of initiation—baptism, confirmation, and the Eucharist—but it embraces as well the new rites of the catechumenate arranged in three stages before the reception of the sacraments of initiation and a period of instruction that carries on through the Easter period following the reception of the sacraments. The ritual also provides a less elaborate rite where all the stages are not necessary, and a rite for Christian initiation in danger of death.

[T. LIDDY]

BAPTISM, CONDITIONAL, the baptismal rite performed by a minister whose intention is to confer the sacrament only if the individual he is baptizing is capable of being validly baptized. Doubt about a person's capacity to receive valid baptism occurs: (1) when the baptizand, sufficiently mature to make the choice for himself, is in danger of death (hence the urgency) but is unconscious or otherwise not in possession of his faculties so that his desire to be baptized cannot be ascertained; or (2) when it is possible that a person desiring baptism has already been validly baptized. In the first type of case, if the person in danger of death has given no positive indication of a desire, implicit or explicit, to be baptized, RC theologians commonly hold that he should not be baptized; but if there has been some probable indication of such desire, he should be baptized conditionally. The second type of case occurs most often at the time of conversion from one Christian communion to another. Proper regard for the efficacy of the sacrament among the various Christian communions which invoke the Triune God and confess Jesus as Lord and Savior should prohibit any general policy of conditional baptism. In individual cases in which doubt remains (e.g., concerning the intention of a particular minister of the sacrament), the sacrament is conferred conditionally.

[T. M. MCFADDEN]

BAPTISM, LAY, administration of the sacrament of baptism by someone other than a cleric. In RC theology, the priest is the usual minister of baptism but in case of emergency anyone, even non-Christians, may validly baptize. Three things are generally recognized as necessary for valid administration: (1) the intention of doing what the Church does when baptizing; (2) proper matter, i.e. water flowing on the head of the baptized person; (3) verbal expression of the intention to baptize in the name of the Trinity (usually: I baptize you in the name of the Father and of the Son and of the Holy Spirit).

[T. M. McFADDEN]

BAPTISM, SECOND, see SECOND BAPTISM.

BAPTISM FOR THE DEAD, the vicarious baptizing of a living person for someone who has died. It is possible that this peculiar ceremony, which is condemned by the RC Church, and practiced by the Mormons, developed as a result of a misinterpretation or translation of the original text of 1 Cor 15.29. Until the 16th cent. Biblical scholars were divided into two schools of thought. The Latin writers thought that St. Paul referred to some Corinthians who in good faith were baptized for their friends who died without baptism. The Greek Fathers claimed that Paul meant "baptism" for our dead bodies, baptism received for the resurrection of our dying mortal bodies.

Protestant Scripture scholars proposed other new theories: Luther interpreted baptism of the dead as referring to baptism administered upon sepulchers of martyrs; Calvin taught it as baptism of dying people; Theodore Beza viewed it as the washing of the dead; St. Robert Bellarmine applied it as baptism of tears and penance. BIBLIOGRAPHY: B. M. Foscini, NCE 2:68–69.

[T. C. STAHL]

BAPTISM OF BELIEF, see BELIEVER'S BAPTISM.

BAPTISM OF BLOOD, the martyrdom of an unbaptized person whose faith in Christ, witnessed with such heroism, is believed to obtain for him the grace of justification. The scriptural foundation for the belief is Christ's general statement about the efficacy of martyrdom (Mt 10.32, 39). The term was used frequently in the early Church, e.g., Tertullian *(De Bapt.,* 16), Cyprian *(Epistle* 73), Augustine *(City of God* 13.7). In his *Apostolic Tradition,* Hippolytus of Rome (d. 235) wrote: "If a catechumen should be apprehended for the Name, let him not be fearful of martyrdom. For if he suffers violence and be put to death before baptism, he will be justified through the baptism he has received in his own blood" (19.2). Theologians differ as to whether the efficacy of this baptism is based upon the fact of martyrdom itself or upon the act of perfect love for God implicitly contained in martyrdom. BIBLIOGRAPHY: ThAq ST 2a2ae, 124.

[T. M. McFADDEN]

BAPTISM OF CHRIST, the rite whereby Jesus was baptized by John in the River Jordan. It is narrated in each of the Synoptics (Mt 3.13–17; Mk 1.9–11; Lk 3.21–22), and is presupposed by Jn 1.29–34 without actually being mentioned. The difficulty which the early Church experienced in proclaiming the reception of John's baptism of repentance by the sinless Christ is reflected in the divergent treatment which the event receives in the Gospels. Mark says simply that Christ was baptized by John; Matthew states that Jesus presented himself for baptism; Luke does not mention John and takes the theophany rather than the baptism as his focal point; John has the Baptist speak of his baptism as a prelude to the messianic age. But the theological purpose of the narrative in its earliest Marcan form is relatively clear. According to Mark, the baptism is an apocalyptic vision seen only by Jesus. The "heavens being opened" refers to Is 64.1 where the prophet prays that God would rend the sky and come to inaugurate the new age of salvation. The Spirit's descent recalls Is 63.11,14 where the Spirit's presence among the Israelites during the exodus is remembered as the cause of their formation as a new people for the Lord. The symbolism of the dove here refers to Jesus. The OT frequently speaks of Israel as a dove (Hos 11.11; Ps 68.13; 74.19; 56.1; *et al.*), and the sense of the symbol is that Jesus is ordained as the representative of God's new people according to the Spirit. The voice from heaven is an allusion to Is 42.1, and attests that Jesus is the servant of Yahweh foretold by the prophets. As the Davidic messiah, he too is anointed by the Spirit through the greatest of the prophets. The employment of the voice reflects the Jewish belief that such a device is the new means of revelation after the cessation of prophecy; in the NT a voice from heaven is often a vehicle for indicating God's intentions and determination. In conformity with his evangelical plan, Mark says that only Jesus saw the vision and only he is aware of his true identity. Thus the Marcan narrative indicates that Isaiah's longing for the Messiah has been fulfilled; that this Messiah embodies the new people of God; and that he is the suffering servant rather than a royal warrior-hero.

Matthew's account adds an explanation of why Jesus should be baptized by John: Jesus is a devout Jew who observes the Law and the pious practices of Jewish life. Matthew presents the dove as a symbol of the Spirit of love. Luke quickly disposes of the baptism itself and concentrates on Jesus at prayer at the time of the theophany. But his perspective, as with Mark and Matthew, is also eschatological. He too alludes to Is 63.19 and implies a new exodus, a final saving event whereby God's people may at last advance toward the promised land. Luke also employs the dove as a symbol of this new community, and the phrase "as a dove in bodily form" implies that Jesus could almost reach out and touch the community being formed around him.

Christian tradition has seen the institution of sacramental baptism in Jesus' baptism, at least in the sense that water, through contact with Christ's sacred humanity, was given its sanctifying power. Thus Jesus' baptism is the prototype of all

Christian baptism since through this sacrament the Christian also becomes a child of God, receives the Spirit, and is pleasing to the Father. BIBLIOGRAPHY: JBC 24–25, 68, 128–129; EDB 201; G. R. Beasley-Murray, *Baptism in the NT* (1962); H. Muller, NCE 2:56; O. Cullman, *Baptism in the NT* (tr. J. Reid, 1961).

[T. M. MCFADDEN]

BAPTISM OF DESIRE, the desire, either explicit or implicit, to be baptized, and to know and love God that remits original and actual sin in a person who has not received the sacrament of baptism. As such, it would appear to be the means of salvation for the vast majority of men chosen by God, although it does not bestow the sacramental character peculiar to baptism, enable the person to receive the other sacraments, or perfectly incorporate him into the Church. The scriptural basis for baptism of desire is rooted in God's universal salvific will (2 Cor 5. 15; 1 Tim 2. 4–5) and Christ's words in which he promised justification for those who love him (Jn 14. 21,23). Even though the concerns of the early Church were centered more upon the necessity of sacramental baptism, a theology of baptism by desire is not unknown among patristic writers esp. in regard to catechumens, e.g., Ambrose's funeral oration over the Emperor Valentinian II. In medieval times, and esp. after the discovery of America, the notion of baptism by desire became much more important and explicit. Theologians emphasized that Christ is the unique mediator of salvation and that the invitation to respond to this saving grace is extended to all men, even to those who had never heard of Christ. Some tried to delineate the means and conditions whereby this invitation was made known; others more wisely refused to define the ways in which God might communicate with his creatures. Two recent documents reiterate the Church's teaching. In 1949, Pius XII wrote Cardinal Cushing of Boston, stating that an implicit desire to belong to the Church is sufficient for salvation provided that this desire is inspired by a supernatural faith and love of God. Vatican II treats of the same topic: "Those also can attain to everlasting salvation who through no fault of their own do not know the gospel of Christ or his Church, yet sincerely seek God and, moved by grace, strive by their deeds to do his will as it is known to them through the dictates of conscience" (Vat II Const-Church, 16). BIBLIOGRAPHY: G. Baum, SacMund 1:144–146.

[T. M. MCFADDEN]*

BAPTISM OF HERETICS, the rebaptism of persons wishing to abandon the heresy in which they were originally baptized. For the celebrated controversy concerning the practice, see REBAPTISM. In the RC Church converts from other Christian Churches are not baptized, unless investigation shows that the fact or validity of the earlier baptism is open to doubt, in which case baptism is administered conditionally *BAPTISM, CONDITIONAL.

[P. K. MEAGHER]

BAPTISM OF INFANTS, see INFANT BAPTISM.

BAPTISM WITH THE HOLY SPIRIT (Second Baptism; Spirit Baptism), in Holiness and Pentecostal teaching, the reception, distinct from *justification or *conversion, of Christ's Holy Spirit, usually manifested by some outward sign; the experience of the first Pentecost renewed for the recipient. *Holiness Churches teach it as the means through which *entire sanctification is bestowed. In *Pentecostalism, baptism with the Spirit is central, an instantaneous, ecstatic experience, transcending mere purification from sin and conferring the Holy Spirit himself. Furthermore, it is necessarily accompanied by *glossolalia, and often by other charismatic gifts. Citing Joel 2.23 and many NT texts (e.g., Acts 1.4–8; 10.46; 12.16–18; 19.1–7; 1 Cor 12.14), Pentecostals insist that a continuous experience of Pentecost is essential in the ordinary life of the Church and of the Christian. Even as the first disciples, all must await, but can confidently expect, this baptism as by fire. The purpose of Spirit baptism is considered to be the endowment of the recipient with new understanding, courage, and patience both for his own Christian life and for his share in evangelism. Among Pentecostals the pattern for "receiving the blessing" usually has consisted in a fervent sermon of the minister recounting other "breakthroughs" of the Spirit; the coming forward of the seeker; his cries, trembling, rhythmic movements and trance; the muttering of unintelligible sounds; the imposition of hands by the pastor and elders; and the shouts of joy for the blessing received. Recently among more sophisticated groups such sessions have taken place in a more sedate atmosphere and with less emotionalism. Baptism by the Holy Spirit is connected with Pentecostal *dispensationalism, i.e., the present is the dispensation of the Holy Spirit (the passage on the *latter rain in Joel 2.23 is so interpreted). The experience of baptism with fire is the connotation of "Fire Baptized" in Pentecostal terminology. The term is doctrinally unclear in RC *Neopentecostalism. BIBLIOGRAPHY: J. T. Nichol, Pentecostalism (1966) 8–15 and bibliog.; P. Damboriena, *Tongues as of Fire* (1969). BIBLIOGRAPHY: The term is doctrinally unclear in RC *Neopentecostalism.

[T. C. O'BRIEN]

BAPTISMAL CERTIFICATE, the document issued by the parochial church and recorded in its baptismal register, certifying baptism of the person named. This proof of church membership is necessary for: (1) initial reception of other sacraments, (2) entrance into seminaries and religious institutes.

[T. LIDDY]

BAPTISMAL EUCHARIST, the eucharistic celebration immediately joined to and completing the baptismal ceremony. It is the concretization of the baptized's new life in Christ. The custom of giving the newly baptized Communion was retained in Rome until the 12th cent.; in the Eastern Churches to the present day. *The Apostolic Tradition* (c.217) includes in the baptismal Eucharist the partaking of milk and honey between the reception of the Body and Blood. The new Roman rite of adult Christian initiation concludes with an appropriate Eucharistic celebration at which the neophytes, sponsors, catechists, and relatives receive communion under both kinds. BIBLIOGRAPHY: G. Wainright, "Baptismal Eucharist before Nicaea," StLit (1965) 9–35; J. G. Davies, *Select Liturgical Lexicon* (1965) 27–28; B. Luykx, "Confirmation in Relation to the Eucharist." *Readings in Sacramental Theology* (ed. C. S. Sullivan, 1964) 187–209; A. McCormack, *Christian Initiation* (1969) 116–117.

[N. KOLLAR]

BAPTISMAL FONT, a fixed basin or vessel used in baptism; baptismal water is stored in it, and the person to be baptized bends, or is held, above it while the water is poured. It is sometimes called a baptistery, although this term is more properly applied to the building or the portion of a building in which the font is located. In modern times fonts tend to be designed for use in infant baptisms, but examples from Christian antiquity are often large enough to accommodate adults. The earliest example, from *c*.230, was found at Dura Europos, and is rectangular in shape. Other shapes have also been used—hexagonal, octagonal, cruciform, and circular—most of which can be seen as symbolic of the death of the sinner in baptism, or of the death and resurrection of Christ by which the sinner is born to a new life. BIBLIOGRAPHY: C. H. Meinberg, "Baptistery and Other Spaces," *Worship* 35 (1960) 536–549; J. G. Davies, *Architectural Setting of Baptism* (1962).

[N. KOLLAR]

BAPTISMAL GARMENT, the white garment once worn by the newly baptized during the week following their baptism. There is indication of the custom in the *Apostolic Tradition* (*c*.217), in St. Ambrose's *De mysteriis* (chapter 7), and perhaps also in Rev 3.4. The garment symbolized the innocence of the newly baptized. Because solemn baptism took place on the vigils of Easter and Pentecost, white came to be associated with those feasts and seasons. Thus the Latin name of Low Sunday is *Dominica in Albis (depositis* or *deponendis)*, i.e., the day for laying aside the white garments, and the English name for Pentecost is Whitsunday; i.e., White Sunday. The new baptismal rituals for infants and adults call for the sponsor(s) to clothe the baptized with a garment of a color conformed to local culture. BIBLIOGRAPHY: J. Daniélou, *Bible and the Liturgy* (1856) 49–53; C. Davis, *Sacraments of Initiation* (1964); *L'Église en prière* (ed. A. Martimort, 3d ed., 1965) 552–556.

[N. KOLLAR]

BAPTISMAL NAME, see Name, Baptismal.

BAPTISMAL PROMISES, the promises to renounce Satan and serve God faithfully that are part of the baptismal ritual. The renewal of this baptismal commitment introduced into the liturgy of the Easter Vigil in 1951 has focused attention upon these promises and in so doing deepened in many Christians their appreciation of the significance of the sacrament and rite of baptism. The content of the promises is seen concretely in the Antiochean liturgy when the catechumen turns first to the West and says: "I detach myself from you, Satan, from your pomp, your worship, and your angels." Turning then toward the East he says: "And I attach myself to you, O Christ." BIBLIOGRAPHY: L. Ligier, "Biblical Symbolism of Baptism in the Fathers of the Church and the Liturgy," *Concilium* 22:16–22; T. Maertens, *Histoire et pastorale du catéchuménat et du baptême* (1962).

[N. KOLLAR]

BAPTISMAL SYMBOL, the personal confession of Christ by the recitation of the creed during the baptismal ceremony. The precise sense of the term symbol is disputed, although it is ultimately derived from the Greek *symbolon,* meaning a sign of recognition. Thus the creedal confession of Christ is the sign whereby the Christian may be distinguished. The recitation of a creed within the baptismal liturgy dates from the earliest times (Acts 8.37). The bishop delivered the creed to the *catechumen who would memorize it and then recite it immediately prior to his baptism. Various creeds have been used in the Church's history, ranging from the simple declarative creeds of the early Church to the more nuanced affirmations that began to appear as various Christological and Trinitarian heresies threatened dogmatic orthodoxy. From the 6th cent., the Nicene Creed came to be used almost exclusively in the East. In the West, the Apostles' Creed came to be predominant from the 9th cent. and it is used today. The recitation of the symbol is theologically important as a rejection of magicism and an emphasis on the necessity of faith for sacramental efficacy. BIBLIOGRAPHY: J.N.D. Kelly, *Early Christian Creeds* (2d ed., 1960).

[T. M. MCFADDEN]

BAPTISMAL WATER, water blessed for use in the rite of baptism. Although unblessed water suffices for valid baptism, the custom of the Church from the 2d cent. requires, apart from emergencies, the use of water that has been specially blessed for the purpose. Water was blessed at the Easter Vigil before the baptisms that were to follow. When the paschal baptism disappeared, the blessing of the water remained anomalously separated from the baptismal rite. This separation continued in the Roman rite until Vatican Council II permitted, except during Eastertide, the blessing of the water during the baptismal liturgy (Vat II SacLit 70). During the blessing, oil of *catechumens and *chrism are added to the water. BIBLIOGRAPHY: E. Lengeling, "Blessing of Baptismal Water in the Roman Rite," *Concilium* 22:62–68; T. Maertens, *Histoire et pastorale du* *catéchuménat et du baptême* (1962); *L'Église en prière* (ed. A. Martimort, 3d ed., 1965) 552–556.

[N. KOLLAR]

BAPTIST OF MANTUA (SPAGNOLI), BL.

(1447–1516), theologian, poet, Carmelite general. He became a Carmelite in Mantua, 1464, and was ordained in Bologna. His excellent qualities and holy life secured his election as vicar general for six 2-year terms, 1483 to 1513. From 1513 to his death, he was prior general of the whole Carmelite order. Leo XIII beatified him in 1885. He was friendly with Picco della Mirandola and Erasmus. Zealous for reform he composed his *Fastorum libri duodecim* at the request of Leo X. His works were very popular in the 16th and 17th centuries. Among his poems were the *Eclogues* written in Vergilian style, and *Parthenice Mariana* in honor of Our Lady of Mt. Carmel. His influence is discernible in English literature. BIBLIOGRAPHY: E. Coccia, BiblSanct 11:1340–42, s.v. "Spagnoli."

[J. M. O'DONNELL]

BAPTIST GENERAL CONFERENCE,

a group of Swedish Baptist Churches that began to dissociate from the American Baptist Convention after 1944. Grounds for the separation were the Convention's resistance to a creedal test imposed on denominational leaders, and its participation in the *National Council of Churches. The Baptist General Conference stresses theological conservatism and denominational autonomy. It maintains missions in Assam, Brazil, Burma, Ethiopia, Japan, and the Philippines; it also supports Bethel College and Seminary, St. Paul, Minnesota. There were (in the 1970s) 108,474 members in 681 churches.

[R. A. MACOSKEY]

BAPTIST MISSIONARY SOCIETY (BMS),

the first modern Protestant missionary society, established in 1792 in Kettering, England, through the efforts of William *Carey. He was its first missionary, going in 1793 to India, the first great field for the Society, where it sponsored schools and translations of the Bible. Africa, esp. the Congo, China, the East and West Indies, and South America have all had missionaries from the Society. Since 1901 a Medical Missionary Auxiliary has been part of its program. The Society now supports about 3,000 workers in the mission fields. As of 1973, Baptist Missionary Society in America has 1,404 churches and an inclusive enrollment of 193,439 members. BIBLIOGRAPHY: EncModChrMiss 67–70.

[F. E. MASER]

BAPTIST WORLD ALLIANCE,

a fraternal association uniting Baptist *conventions around the world, established in 1905 in London, with John Clifford as first president. The stated purpose of the Alliance is "more fully to show the essential oneness of Baptist people in the Lord Jesus Christ, to impart inspiration to the brotherhood, and to promote the spirit of fellowship, service and cooperation among its members; but this Alliance may in no way interfere with the independence of the churches or assume the administrative functions of existing organizations." Maintaining headquarters in Washington, D.C., it has an executive secretary and a small staff; an executive committee meets annually to discuss common interests and make necessary decisions. The Alliance gathers information, publishes the *Baptist World*, provides aid in emergencies, and resettles displaced persons. Where religious rights have been denied Baptists, it may use its good offices to seek remedies. It also serves as a means of communication and help for scattered Baptists. BIBLIOGRAPHY: F. T. Lord, *Baptist World Fellowship* (1955).

[N. H. MARING]

BAPTISTERY,

a building or area within a church where the sacrament of baptism is administered. The earliest Christians baptized by immersion in lakes or rivers but, by the 3d cent. separate buildings or adjacent rooms were constructed as evidenced by the earliest extant examples, Dura-Europos and the pools at the Lateran in Rome. Situated to the W of the church and polygonal in shape, the baptisteries were often highly ornamented according to the period. As infant baptism became the rule, only a small font was needed for affusion and the baptisteries were moved into the church, frequently by a door to represent the position of catechumens. The new Ordo places the baptistery in the front of the church to the left of and a trifle lower than the altar in keeping with the current practice of incorporating baptism into the liturgy of the Mass. Another change is the use of running water to symbolize the "living waters" of baptism and to relate more closely with the first baptisteries.

[M. E. FORD]

BAPTISTERY OF SAN GIOVANNI, FLORENCE,

octagonal building faced with colored marbles in present state dating from the 11th and 12th centuries. Impressive are the three pairs of bronze doors—south door by Andrea Pisano (14th cent.), north door, Lorenzo Ghiberti (1403–24), and the most famous gilded bronze east door, *Gates of Paradise* (1425–52), in which Ghiberti broke with traditional Gothic design of earlier doors evidencing the genius of Renaissance form and composition. The cupola is sheathed inside with 13th-cent. mosaics of Byzantine style. BIBLIOGRAPHY: R. Krautheimer, *Lorenzo Ghiberti* (1956).

[M. J. DALY]

BAPTISTS,

those many autonomous Christian bodies that, while exhibiting great diversity, share a similar congregational *polity and the doctrine of *believer's baptism. The largest Protestant denomination in the U.S., the Baptists have a history of outstanding preachers and scholars and of emphasis upon personal religious experience, religious freedom, and the separation of *Church and State.

History. Claims of a continuous Baptist history from the 1st cent., or of links with the *Anabaptists, are not supported by historical evidence. The Baptists were a natural development from English Congregationalism. They shared the *gathered-church theory of the Congregationalists: each local congregation has everything necessary to make it a Church, having, under the headship of Christ, power to elect its own officers, determine membership, and carry out discipline. Baptists, however, maintained that the *visible Church must reflect the invisible Church and so restrict its membership to persons old enough to give credible testimony of conversion; thus infants were ineligible for baptism. Baptists emerged at three distinct points from Congregational backgrounds. The first was in Holland in 1609, when a band of *Separatists, refugees from England, with their pastor, John *Smyth, concluded that *infant baptism had no scriptural warrant. They formed a new Church, Smyth baptizing himself and the others. He soon felt uneasy about his "sebaptism," and the Church became divided; the minority chose Thomas *Helwys pastor and returned to England in 1612. They became the *General Baptists, since, having been influenced by *Arminianism in The Netherlands, they asserted that the atonement of Christ had been for all men. A second Baptist group began around 1638, when several members withdrew from a congregation in London and adopted believer's baptism. Retaining a more consistent *Calvinism, they stressed *predestination and *limited atonement; hence they were called *Particular Baptists. A third emergence of Baptists occurred in America when Roger *Williams helped reorganize the Church at Providence, R.I., on the basis of believer's baptism.

In England during the Civil Wars and the *Commonwealth, Baptists increased in numbers. The repressive legislation of the *Restoration did not halt their growth, although some suffered imprisonment. Granted freedom to worship by the *Toleration Act of 1689, the General Baptists declined because of inroads of *Unitarianism, lack of capable leadership, and an unprogressive spirit; Particular Baptists experienced a century of stagnation resulting from a hyper-Calvinism as expressed in the works of their leading theologian, John Gill (1697–1771). The formation in the late 18th cent. of a New Connexion of General Baptists, and a theological renewal led by Andrew Fuller (1754–1815), led to vigorous evangelism and foreign missionary activity. The 19th cent. witnessed a marked increase in Baptist membership, which reached a peak of about 400,000.

In the U.S. the *Great Awakening gave an impetus to Baptist expansion, and after 1740 their ranks in New England were augmented by the aggressive evangelism of the Separate Congregationalists, hundreds of whom became Baptists. From New England Shubael *Stearns and Daniel *Marshall moved to Sandy Creek, N.C. which became the center for a phenomenal growth (see REGULAR BAPTISTS; SEPARATE BAPTISTS). Spreading into all the neighboring states, these revivalistic Baptists laid the foundations for present Baptist strength in the South. In Pa. and N.J., Baptist work began in 1688, and the Philadelphia Baptist Association was formed in 1707. Numerically small prior to the

American Revolution, the Association exerted considerable influence upon the shape of Baptist faith and practice in America. At the beginning of the 19th cent. Baptists had risen to first place among the denominations in America, and although overtaken by the Methodists by 1860, they subsequently regained the lead. Of the Baptist bodies listed in the *Yearbook of American and Canadian Churches* (1973), the Southern Baptist Convention is the largest (*c*.11,800,000) followed by the National Baptist Convention, U.S.A., Inc. (*c*. 6 million), the National Baptist Convention of America (2,668,779), and the American Baptist Convention (1,562,636).

Emphasis on local autonomy, strong individualistic tendencies, and the lack of common confessional standards have contributed to the fragmentation of Baptists. In the 18th cent. the *Free Will Baptists broke away because of their Arminianism. In contrast, a strong predestinarian group protested against missionary organizations, Bible societies, and *revivalism, and organized separately as the *Primitive Baptists. Northern and Southern Baptists divided over slavery and polity in 1845. The Landmarkists, with an extreme emphasis upon the independence of local Churches and a claim that Baptists are the only true Church, formed about 1850. Negro Baptists organized in 1895 but divided into the National Baptist Convention, U.S.A., Inc. (1915), the National Baptist Convention of America (1916), and the Progressive National Baptist Convention, Inc. (1961). Some Baptist bodies have their basis in ethnic backgrounds, such as the North American Baptist General Conference (German) and Baptist General Conference (Swedish). The General Association of Regular Baptists (1933) and the Conservative Baptist Association (1947) resulted from the fundamentalist-modernist controversy. Lack of a magisterium opened the way to diverse theological developments. Although Baptists originally had *confessions of faith, which served as standards (see NEW HAMPSHIRE CONFESSION; ORTHODOX CREED), these have largely disappeared and it is commonly asserted that Baptists have never had creeds. Partly in reaction against the *liberal theology of their divinity school at the Univ. of Chicago, several more conservative seminaries were organized. Baptists furnished leaders for the *Social Gospel movement (Walter Rauschenbusch, Leighton Williams) and also leaders of the fundamentalists (W. B. Riley, T. T. Shields, J. R. Straton, C. L. Laws). The pluralism of the American Baptist Convention is evident in the persons of William Hamilton, Martin Luther King, Jr., Carl F. H. Henry, and Billy Graham.

Practice. Baptist services of worship have always tended toward informality with emphasis upon preaching. Prior to the 19th cent. they objected to the observance of Christmas and Easter. Their places of worship, called auditoriums, were unadorned except for the Bible, pulpit, baptistery, and Lord's Table. Now, however, there is greater variety, and one may find churches with sanctuaries, crosses, pictures, candles, stained-glass windows, vested choirs, a gowned minister, and even Lenten services in some Baptist churches of the North. Typical emphasis upon simplicity and relatively informal conduct of the service of worship still remains. While always maintaining a congregational polity, Baptists early formed *associations to express their interdependence. The surge of activism in the early 19th cent. led to the formation of societies, esp. to promote and support foreign missions: the Triennial Convention (1814), the American Baptist Publication Society (1824), the American Baptist Home Mission Society (1832), and the American and Foreign Bible Society (1837). State *conventions first were formed in the 1820s in both North and South; larger, more comprehensive, organizations began with the formation of the Southern Baptist Convention (1845), the National Baptist Convention, U.S.A. (1895), and the Northern Baptist Convention (1907). All of these organizations depend upon voluntary cooperation from Churches, as no association or convention has legal power over an autonomous local Church; these larger organizations exist as means for voluntary cooperation in larger tasks. There is no organic connection between the organizations on these different levels, but they cooperate in varying degrees to carry out the programs instituted by their respective national agencies.

Baptists early took an interest in ministerial education, founding Brown Univ. (1764), Colby College (1813), Colgate Univ. (1820), and George Washington Univ. (1821). A great many other academies and colleges sprang up in nearly all states. There are today more than 100 Baptist junior colleges, colleges, and theological seminaries in the United States. While many shared the interest in education, there has always been a tension between the emphasis upon spiritual qualifications and educational preparation of a minister. Consequently, educational standards vary greatly. The American Baptist Convention has adopted minimum standards that require both college and seminary degrees, and most Churches respect these criteria; but a Church may ignore such rules and ordain a person of no formal education.

From England the U.S. Baptist missionaries spread their principles around the world, so that Baptists are found in more than 115 countries. In 1972 the aggregate membership was 31,432,130. Most Baptist bodies belong to the *Baptist World Alliance, and some have regional organizations, such as the European Baptist Federation and the North American Baptist Fellowship. Several American groups help to support the Baptist Joint Committee on Public Affairs in Washington, D.C., which seeks primarily to keep in touch with legislation affecting Church-State relations. Baptists vary as to their attitudes toward the *ecumenical movement. The American Baptist Convention, the National Baptist Convention, the *Seventh-Day Baptists, and the Baptist Union of Great Britain and Ireland are members of the *World Council of Churches as well as of their own national councils, but most other remain aloof. No official observer was sent by the Baptist World Alliance to Vatican II, although many Baptists favored such representation. The American Baptist Convention, through its Commission on Christian Unity, and Southern Baptists hold consultations with Roman Catholics, some of the seminaries have working relations with RC seminaries, and numerous individual theologians are involved in Protestant-Catholic dialogue. BIBLIOGRAPHY: O. K. and M. M. Armstrong, *Indomitable Baptists* (1967); R. G. Torbet, *History of the Baptists* (rev. ed., 1963); N. H. Maring and W. S. Hudson, *Baptist Manual of Polity and Practice* (rev. ed., 1966); *Baptist Bibliography* (ed. E. C. Starr, 3 v., 1947–74).

[N. H. MARING]

BAR, CATHÉRINE DE (Mechtilde du Saint Sacrement; 1614–98), foundress of the Benedictine Nuns of the Blessed Sacrament. B. entered the convent of the Annonciades at Bruyère, was professed in 1633, and was soon named superior. The vicissitudes of the Thirty Years War caused her to move frequently. She and her nuns took shelter with the Benedictines of Rambervillers. On the advice of her directors she asked for a transfer to that order and took her vows as a Benedictine in 1640. Displaced again by war, she founded at Montmartre a congregation to make reparation for offenses against the Eucharist. Before her death 10 houses had been established. She numbered among her advisors Vincent de Paul, John Eudes, and Jean-Jacques Olier. B. wrote on various spiritual topics and left over 2,400 letters, most of which are unpublished. BIBLIOGRAPHY: B. Egan, NCE 2:80.

[M. J. SUELZER]

BAR CURSUS (c.483–538), Joannes Tellenis, bp. of Tella in north Mesopotamia who became ordinary of that diocese (519) and took part in doctrinal debate on Christology at Constantinople (533). An adherent of the Monophysitism of Severus of Antioch, he was banished and put to death in prison for his doctrinal stand. His *Canonical Resolutions,* written and edited in answer to 48 questions of a priest named Sergius, are an important witness for the history of liturgy and the sacraments, e.g., the reception of the Eucharist under one species. BIBLIOGRAPHY: F. Nau, *Les Canons et les résolutions canoniques de Rabboula, Jean de Tella* (1906); T. J. Lamy, *Dissertatio de Syrorum fide et disciplina in re eucharistica* (1859).

[F. H. BRIGHAM]

BAR-DAISĀN, see BARDESANES.

BAR-HEBRAEUS (Abû-l-Faraǧ; 1226–86), Jacobite Syrian bp., whose Hebrew father (hence his name) provided for his education, including medical training in Antioch. Afterwards, he entered the ministry, was consecrated bp. in 1246 (receiving the name Gregory) and was appointed Primate of the East in 1264. In this latter role, he traveled extensively and had access to numerous libraries. His scholarship is attested to by his prolific literary production, most notably *Chronicles, Granary of Mysteries,* and *Cream of Sciences,* an ambitious work revealing strong Aristotelian influence. BIBLIOGRAPHY: M. Jugie, *Catholicisme* 1:1249–50.

[M. E. FORD]

BAR-JESUS, (Aramaic for son of Jesus), a Jewish magician and false prophet who attempted to thwart Paul's preaching before the proconsul Sergius Paulus at Paphos on Cyprus (Acts 13.4–12). At the curse of Paul, he was struck with temporary blindness. Unlike Paul, who had been blinded by light (Acts 9.3), he fell victim to darkness. The theme of darkness surrounding a magician suggests a possible variation on Wis 17. Paul calls him son of the devil, apparently a play on his name. He is also called Elymas, but the relationship of this name to Bar-Jesus is not clear; the explanatory clause of Acts 13.8 may indicate that Elymas means magician or that Elymas was considered, for some unknown reason, the Greek equivalent of Bar-Jesus. BIBLIOGRAPHY: A. Romeo, EncCatt 2:852–853.

[P. KEARNEY]

BAR KOKHBA, SIMON (Bar Cocheba; Aramaic for "Son of the Star"), a variation of the name of Simon bar Coziba, the leader of the second Jewish revolt (A.D. 132-135). Based on Num 24.17 ("A star from Jacob takes the leadership"), this change of name reflects the messianic hope placed in his initially successful attempt to liberate Judea from Roman control; one immediate reason for the uprising was probably the attempt of the Emperor Hadrian to build a Greco-Roman city in Jerusalem, including a temple to Jupiter on the former site of the Jewish temple. Assuming the title Prince of Israel (cf. Ezek 37.25), Simon extended his conquests through guerrilla warfare and administered the land of Judea from headquarters located probably in Jerusalem. As the Roman reconquest spread, many of his followers sought final refuge in caves W of the Dead Sea; some of their hiding places have recently yielded important MSS, including letters of Simon and some biblical texts. Bar Kokhba died during his last stand in Beth-Ter, a fortress about 6 miles SW of Jerusalem. The revolt was crushed; Jerusalem was rebuilt in honor of Hadrian; and the Jews were excluded from free access to the city, a prohibition which remained generally in force until the Israeli capture of old Jerusalem in 1967. BIBLIOGRAPHY: J. Fitzmyer, "Bar Cochba Period," *Bible in Current Catholic Thought* (ed. J. McKenzie, 1962) 133–168; Y. Yadin, *Bar-Kokhba, the Rediscovery of the Legendary Hero of the Second Jewish Revolt against Imperial Rome* (1971).

[P. KEARNEY]

BAR KOKHBA, REVOLT OF, the insurrection against the Romans during the reign of Hadrian (131–135) organized and executed by the Jewish leader, Simon bar Coziba (Aram. for son of the Lie) who may have taken the name Bar Kokhba (son of the star) on the assumption that the prophecy "There

shall be a star out of Jacob" (Num 24.17) applied to him. Among the causes alleged for the revolt, none of which are certain, are the effort of Hadrian to erect a Greco-Roman city on the site of Jerusalem (Dio Cassius, *Roman History* 69.12.1–2) and the edict of Hadrian forbidding circumcision (*Vita Hadriana* 14.2).

After his initial victory in Jerusalem where he forced the Romans to retreat, Bar Kokhba carried the war to the countryside capturing about 50 towns and as many villages. But under Julius Severus the Romans regained their lost territory including Jerusalem and after a long siege overcame the last Jewish fortress, Beth-Ter (135). B. K. was killed in this final decisive encounter which marked the end of a Jewish majority in Southern Palestine. BIBLIOGRAPHY: S. Krauss, JE 2:505–509; J. Fitzmyer, NCE 2:82–83; M. Noth, *History of Israel* (tr. P. Akroyd; 2d ed., 1960).

[F. H. BRIGHAM]

BAR MITZVAH, (Mizwah), literally "the son of command," i.e., a dutiful and responsible man, a phrase applied to a Jewish boy who has completed his 13th year and has entered into an awareness of his religious responsibilities and liabilities for not fulfilling them. The phrase, in a transferred sense, signifies the rite of initiation, which takes place soon after the boy's 14th year begins. In the synagogue he is called upon to read from the Law for the first time or at least to recite a benediction for the reading. A festive banquet follows during which the new adult gives a learned discourse or a prayer before invited friends, receives congratulatory gifts, and a special blessing from the rabbi. Henceforth, he is considered to be an adult Jew for filling the number of 10 men necessary for public worship. This more ancient ceremony (14th cent., with much earlier roots) has been superseded in many progressive Jewish congregations by a rite of confirmation for both young men and women who have completed their religious schooling and who are called upon in public to live as Jews faithful to the Sinai covenant and its sacred moral obligations. BIBLIOGRAPHY: J. Sanders, *Bar Mitzah; Reflections and Remembrances* (1970).

[J. F. FALLON]

BAR SAUMA, see BARSUMAS.

BARABBAS, the criminal whom Pilate presented to the crowd with Jesus that they might choose which one they wanted freed; B. was selected. Matthew 27.16 calls him a notorious prisoner; Mk 15.7, a murderer; Lk 29.13, a rioter and murderer; Jn 18.40, a brigand; Acts 3.14, a murderer. BIBLIOGRAPHY: H. Z. Maccoby, "Jesus and Barabbas", NTS 16 (1969) 55–60.

[J. J. O'ROURKE]

BARABUDUR (Borobudur; 800 A.D.), stupa-like Buddhist structure in central Java, covering mound 500 feet in diameter and 116 feet high in nine levels, the lower rectangular, the upper round. Important are relief carvings of Mahāyāna

Buddhist themes on lower levels and stone figures of the Buddha in stupas of the upper levels. BIBLIOGRAPHY: A. J. Bernet Kempers, *Ancient Indonesian Art* (1959).

[M. J. DALY]

BARADAI, JAMES, see JACOB BARADAI.

BARAGA, FREDERIC (1797–1868), Slovenian missionary priest and first bp. of Sault Ste.-Marie (Marquette), Michigan. While studying law at the Univ. of Vienna he met Clement *Hofbauer who inspired him to become a priest. After preparation at Ljubljana seminary, he was ordained in 1823. He labored as a parish priest in Lower Carniola until 1830 when he came to the U.S. as a missionary to the Indians. His first efforts among the Ottawas at Arbre Croche (now Harbor Springs) Mich. were most successful. From 1833 to 1835 he worked at Grand River; from 1835 to 1843, at LaPointe, Wis., where he baptized 981 Chippewas and whites. He then founded the L'Anse Indian mission, Mich. and was for a long time the only priest in Upper Michigan, traveling almost incessantly and enduring great hardships. When the northern peninsula of Michigan was made a vicariate apostolic, B. was chosen its first bishop. His jurisdiction included also much of the lower peninsula, to northern Wisconsin, and the north shore of Lake Superior. Here he labored for the remainder of his life. Outstanding in American Indian literature B. compiled the first Chippewa dictionary (1853), wrote *Theoretical and Practical Grammar of the Otchipwe (Chippewa) Language* (1850) and many other works, for the most part religious, in Chippewa and in his native Slovenian. BIBLIOGRAPHY: C. Verwyst, *Life and Labours of Rt. Rev. Frederic Baraga* (1900); *id.*, CE 2:282–284; A. Cicognani, *Sanctity in America* (1941).

[M. R. BROWN]

BARANAUSKAS, ANTANAS (1835–1902), Lithuanian bp. and poet. Ordained in 1862, B. taught at the seminary of Kaunas (1867–84), was consecrated auxiliary bp. of Kaunas (1884), and 13 years later was made bp. of Seinai. From 1897 he gave much time and effort to a translation of the Bible into Lithuanian. His literary fame rests chiefly on his poem, *Forest of Anykščiai* (1858; Eng. tr. 1956). BIBLIOGRAPHY: A. Vaičiulaitus, NCE 2:85.

[M. J. SUELZER]

BARAT, MADELEINE SOPHIE, ST. (1779–1865). The daughter of a small vine owner, she was educated in Joigny in Burgundy under the rigid demands of her elder brother Louis, who felt that she must be adequately prepared for the vocation to which he was sure God destined her. Following the fury of the Revolution, she came under the influence of Father Varin, who convinced her to become one of the founders of a religious congregation devoted to the education of girls. In 1800 in Amiens she began her religious training and 2 years later became the superior of the small group, a role which she was to fill for over 60 years. The

group was immediately successful and the next years she spent traveling through France acceding to the requests that came from all sides to found new groups that would fill the educational and religious needs of young French girls. Success was not the only experience of Mother Barat, who weathered a long and stormy battle in which she saw her original goals and methods countered by ambitious forces within her society. Nonetheless, the congregation, now called the Society of the Sacred Heart, flourished not only in France but also in the New World. She died in Paris at the age of 86 and was canonized in 1925. Noteworthy among her biographies are A. Brou, *Saint Madeleine Sophie Barat*, (tr. J. W. Saul, 1963); M. Williams, *St. Madeleine Sophie* (1965); M. Monahan, *Saint Madeleine Sophie* (1925).

[I. MAHONEY]

BARBARA, ST. The name of a martyr who was introduced in the 9th cent. into European martyrologies, from the *Menology* of Simeon Metaphrastes, but there is no evidence she ever existed. According to her spurious 7th-cent. legend, B. was imprisoned in a tower by her father, Dioscorus, to discourage her many suitors. When Dioscorus discovered his daughter had become a Christian, he had her condemned to death, and upon her refusal to recant, he himself beheaded her. For this he was struck by lightning and reduced to ashes. B. is one of the Fourteen Holy Helpers, and patroness of gunners, miners, and those exposed to sudden death. BIBLIOGRAPHY: G. Gordini, BiblSanct 2:760–767; Butler 4:487–488.

[F. J. MURPHY]

BARBARIC STYLE, term covering varieties of decoration and ornament in nonfigural and zoomorphic interlace, which entered Western Europe from the 1st to the 9th centuries through invasions from the East by Huns, Goths, Celts, Norsemen, Scythians, and Sarmatians and influenced pre-Carolingian and Carolingian styles (examples seen in MSS [Lindisfarne, Durrow] and in many objects excavated [fibulae, etc.]). BIBLIOGRAPHY: A. Spiltz, *Styles of Ornament* (1959). *ANIMAL STYLE.

[M. J. DALY]

BARBARIGO, prominent Venetian family which produced several eminent churchmen. (1) St. Gregory (1625–97). Educated in Padua, he attended the Congress of Münster (1648) where he met the future Alexander VII who became his friend and supporter. G. became bp. of Bergamo (1657), cardinal (1660) and bp. of Padua (1664). He was an energetic and zealous pastor who reorganized and improved seminary education, established a six-language printing press, revised catechetical instruction, and used his fortune for charity. (See I. Daniele, BiblSanct 7:387–403.) (2) Marc' Antonio (1640–1706). He was ordained in 1671, studied in Padua, and became bp. of Corfù (1678). Trouble with the admiral of the Venetian fleet forced him to flee to Rome (1685) where Innocent XI cleared him of the charges against him, named him cardinal and bp. of Montefiascone and Corneta. He was known for his efficient administration and pastoral concern. (See G. Löw, EncCatt 2:819–820.) (3) Giovanni Francesco (1658–1730). Cousin to Marc'Antonio and nephew of St. Gregory, he began a diplomatic career but exchanged it for the priesthood. He became bp. of Verona (1697), bp. of Brescia (1714), cardinal (1721), and bp. of Padua (1723). He was a devoted bishop and patron of scholarship. BIBLIOGRAPHY: M. T. Disdier, DHGE 6:578–579.

[H. JACK]

BARBARO, distinguished family of Venice from which came the following distinguished persons:

Francesco (c.1398–1454), statesman and humanist. In 1415 he wrote *De re uxoria libri II* and throughout his life was in contact with Italian humanists. He served as Venetian ambassador to Florence, Verona, Bologna, and to Pope Martin V, and opposed the ambitions of the Duke of Milan. He earnestly strove for religious unity with the Greeks in order to safeguard Constantinople from the Turks.

Niccolo, while ambassador to Constantinople composed an account of the siege and capture of the city in 1453.

Ermolao the Elder (c.1410–71), humanist, churchman, brother of Francesco. He became bp. of Treviso in 1443 and of Verona in 1453. His *Oratio contra poetas* objected to the fulsome approbation of the ancient poets.

Ermolao the Younger (1454–93), patriarch of Aquileia, humanist, statesman, nephew of Ermolao. He taught philosophy at Padua and was Venetian ambassador to Milan and to Pope Innocent VIII. Named patriarch of Aquileia in 1491, he was prevented from taking possession of his see by the Republic of Venice because he had not obtained the consent of the senate. Remaining in Rome, he died of the plague. His main work is *Castigationes* wherein he corrected Pliny's history. His *Compendium scientiae naturalis ex Aristotele* contains some of Aristotle's writings translated into Latin.

Daniele (1513–70), statesman, patriarch of Aquileia. Ambassador to England in 1548, he was appointed (1550) patriarch of Aquileia at the instance of Venice which desired a Venetian in this see. He took part in the latter sessions of the Council of Trent. His last work was *Aurea in quinquaginta priores Davidicos Psalmos...catena.* BIBLIOGRAPHY: H. Jedin, LTK 1:1237–38; W. H. Wallaik, NCE 2:88–89.

[J. M. O'DONNELL]

BARBAROSSA, EMPEROR, see FREDERICK I BARBAROSSA, ROMAN EMPEROR.

BARBASTRO, FRANCISCO (1734–1800), Spanish Franciscan missionary. He entered the order at Saragossa, Spain, attended the missionary college at Querétaro in Mex-

ico, and became director for the missions of Sonora, Mexico. His knowledge and use of Indian tongues contributed to his great success in evangelization. He also assembled valuable notes and reports for the use of other Franciscan missionaries. BIBLIOGRAPHY: F. A. Barbastro, *Sonora hacia fines del siglo XVIII; un informe del misionero franciscano fray Francisco A. Barbastro* (1971).

[H. JACK]

BARBATUS, ST. (d. 682), bp. of Benevento. According to a late and unreliable biography, B. dedicated himself zealously to uprooting pagan superstitions rampant in his diocese. As the story goes, the fulfillment of his prophecy that Constans II's siege of Benevento would fail brought success to his reforming efforts. He died shortly after returning from the the Third General Council of Constantinople (681). BIBLIOGRAPHY: R. E. Geiger, NCE 2:90; Butler 1:375; A. Balducci, BiblSanct 2:770–772.

[G. M. COOK]

BARBEAUX, ABBEY OF, royal Cistercian abbey near Melun, established in 1146 by Louis VII of France, who was buried there. The abbey was richly endowed and magnificently constructed in Gothic. Devastated during the Hundred Years' War, it suffered later from commendatory abbots (1498). It was reformed in 1643 by the Cistercian Strict Observance but had only 11 monks at its dissolution in 1790. Portions of the cloister survive. BIBLIOGRAPHY: L. J. Lekai, NCE 2:90.

[L. J. LEKAI]

BARBELITES, a 2d–cent. Gnostic sect which taught all things came from a female principle Barbelo, the image of the father. BIBLIOGRAPHY: G. Bardy, *Catholicisme* 1:1240.

[F. H. BRIGHAM]

BARBER, the name of a New England family which was converted to the RC faith in the 19th cent. and distinguished itself for its total dedication to the service of the Church. Among these were *Daniel* (1756–1834), once a soldier in the Continental Army, who first converted from the Congregational Church to become an Episcopalian, in which denomination he served as a minister for 24 years. *Virgil Horace* (1782–1847), also an Episcopalian minister and schoolmaster, was converted to Catholicism (1816) even before Daniel, his father; his entire family joined him in his new faith. Receiving permission to enter religious communities, Virgil Horace became a Jesuit, was ordained in 1822, and did missionary work in New Hampshire, Maine, and Georgetown, while his wife, *Jerusha,* became a Visitandine, taking the name Sister Mary Austin. She served her community well in Georgetown, Illinois, Missouri, and Alabama. Before Virgil Horace and his wife separated to pursue their religious vocations, they had had four daughters and one son. Three of the girls *(Abigail, Mary,* and *Susan)* became Ursuline nuns; the son, *Samuel Joseph,* became a

Jesuit priest; and *Josephine,* the youngest of the children, a Visitandine nun. BIBLIOGRAPHY: J. W. Scully, NCE 2:90–91.

[P. K. MEAGHER]

BARBERI, DOMINIC, BL. (1792–1849), Italian Passionist who worked as a missionary in England. Having lectured in theology at Viterbo (1821) and later at Rome (1824), and served as provincial of the Passionists (1833), B. began his mission to England in 1841 at Aston, Staffordshire. He received John Henry *Newman into the RC Church in 1845. B. made many converts among the English, established four Passionist foundations in England, and planned one Passionist house in Ireland. He was beatified on Oct. 27, 1963. BIBLIOGRAPHY: A. Wilson, *Blessed Dominic Barberi* (1966).

BARBERINI, Italian family noted for its prominent churchmen and patronage of art in the 17th century. By the 14th cent. the Barberini (originally Tafani) were established in Florence as a wealthy merchant family. During the pontificate of Paul III, Francesco went to Rome and held various positions in the curia. Through him, his nephew Maffeo (1568–1644) began in 1592 a Vatican-favored career that led to his becoming in 1623 Pope Urban VIII. With his brothers and their families now gathering in Rome, Urban became distinguished for his nepotism. His brother Carlo became governor of the Borgo and a general of the Church. Another brother, Antonio (1596–1646) and two of Carlo's sons, Francesco (1597–1679) and Antonio (1607–71), became cardinals. Carlo's third son, Taddeo (d. 1647), became a prince of Palestrina and held a series of civil and ecclesiastical offices. Two sisters who were Carmelites in Florence also received benefices. The enormous increase in family fortune during the reign of Urban VIII led to an investigation by his successor, Innocent X. Much of their wealth, however, was expended to the benefit and beauty of the Church and the city of Rome. The Barberini library and the Palazzo Barberini by Bernini evidence their munificence. In the next generation two more of the family, Carlo (1630–1704) and Francesco the Younger (1662–1738) also became cardinals. BIBLIOGRAPHY: P. Pecchiai, *I Barberini* (1959); G. Gragli, EncCatt 2:825–827; M. T. Disdier and F. Bonnard, DHGE 6:640–645.

[H. JACK]

BARBERINI IVORY, Byzantine work (*c*.500 A.D.) in the Louvre, showing purely Hellenistic style indicative of Alexandrian-trained artists working in Constantinople.

[M. J. DALY]

BARBEY D'AUREVILLY, JULES AMÉDÉE (1808–89), French writer and forerunner of the Catholic Revival, whose major figures, notably Léon Bloy, he influenced. Of aristocratic lineage, B. adopted the surname d'Aurevilly in 1837. After studying law, he began writing melodramatic novels, perspicacious if tendentious literary criticism (e.g., *Les prophètes du passé; Les oeuvres et les hommes),* and polemical journalism. B. returned to Catholicism in 1841, and, as an apologist of ultramontanism, social conservatism, and monarchy, propagated the religious and political philosophy of de Maistre, Bonald, and Blanc de Saint-Bonnet. The chief traits of romantic Catholicism —aloofness, cult of tradition, spiritual dandyism, a dilettantish blend of eroticism, blasphemy, occultism, satanism, and suffering—characterize his work, particularly the consciously Catholic fiction like *L'Ensorcelée* (1854), *Un Prêtre marié* (1865), and *Les Diaboliques* (1874). BIBLIOGRAPHY: R. Besus, *Barbey d'Aurevilly* (1958); P. J. Yarrow, *La Pensée politique et religieuse de Barbey d'Aurevilly* (1961).

[G. E. GINGRAS]

BARBIERI, GIOVIANNI FRANCESCO, see GUERCINO (GIOVANNI FRANCESCO BARBIERI).

BARBIZON SCHOOL, name given to a group of romantic-realist, landscape, and genre painters active around the Forest of Fontainebleau between *c*.1830 and 1870. Associated with the group are Camille Corot, Théodore Rousseau, Diaz de la Peña, Charles Daubigny, and Jean-François Millet. BIBLIOGRAPHY: R. L. Herbert, *Barbizon Revisited* (1962).

[L. A. LEITE]

BARBO, PAOLO (Soncinas; d. 1494), Italian Dominican theologian. His principal work *Divinarum epitoma quaestionum in IV libros sententiarum a principe thomistarum Joanne Capreolo Tolosano disputatarum,* an abridgement of John *Capreolus's work, contributed to the spread of Thomism. BIBLIOGRAPHY: U. Degl'Innocenti, EncCatt 2:832.

[T. C. O'BRIEN]

BARBOSA, AGOSTINO (1589–1649), Portuguese canonist and bishop. After training in canon law at Coimbra, B. continued his studies at Rome where his affability and sanctity gained him entrance to the libraries of that city. About 1632 he went to Madrid to continue his writing, along with other duties assigned him. In all, his works on canon law fill more than 30 volumes and demonstrate B.'s erudition and his familiarity with authors, sources, and controverted questions. He was nominated as bp. of Ugento, in Otranto, Italy (1648) by Philip IV of Spain. BIBLIOGRAPHY: J. Raffalli, DDC 2:203; F. de Almeida, DHGE 6:664–665.

BARBOSA, JANUÁRIO DA CUNHA (1780–1846), Brazilian journalist, politician. He was ordained in 1803 and began parish work in Rio de Janeiro in 1805. He soon gained a reputation as a preacher that grew with the years. In 1814, he became a seminary professor, the last of his ecclesiastical appointments. Journalist and politician, brilliant and clever writer, a Mason, beneficiary of court favors, he was on the government side of any Church-State conflict or controversy. He maintained his political influence to the end by his satirical and vitriolic pen.

[H. JACK]

BARBOSA, RUI (1849–1923), Brazilian statesman, jurist. As minister of finance and justice (1889), B. was responsible for many of the basic laws and the constitutional organization of the republic of Brazil. He served on the Permanent Court of Arbitration, and was elected to (but declined) a position as judge on the Permanent Court of International Justice. As a liberal, B. stood for democratic values; in crucial religious issues, he was on the side of church rights.

[H. JACK]

BARCABBAS AND BARCOPH, Gnostic prophets whose names Basilides invented to bolster the authority of his teaching. Some have identified Barcoph with the prophet Parchor, named in the title of a work attributed to Isidore, son of Basilides, *Exegesis of the Prophet Parchor*. BIBLIOGRAPHY: G. Bardy, DHGE 6:670, 755.

[F. H. BRIGHAM]

BARCHESTER CHRONICLES, THE, a series of novels by Anthony Trollope (1815–82), in fact a classical documentary of the religious establishment in rural Wessex in the mid-19th cent. The first, *The Warden* (1855), was prompted by a visit to the close at Salisbury, and the series continues with *Barchester Towers, Doctor Thorne, Framley Parsonage, The Small House at Allingham,* and ends with *The Last Chronicle of Barset* (1867). Memorable characters abound, esp. from clerical life—the gentle Caroline divine, the high and dry Tory archdeacon, the gaunt and tragic evangelical perpetual curate, the hunting parson and his admirable wife, the bishop and his unctuous secretary, above all the immortal bishopess, Mrs. Proudie, the archetype of female interference in ecclesiastical affairs. Altogether a picture of a society—still happily by no means extinct—that held to the decencies rather than to the ardors of Christianity, though threatened by the railways, the Whigs, and the Puseyites who prowl in the wings.

[T. GILBY]

BARCLAY, JOHN (1582–1621), Scottish satirist and Latin poet. He was the author of various anti-Jesuitical writings and of a celebrated *roman-à-clef, Argenis* (1621), in which he satirized the perils of political intrigue. He defended his father, William Barclay, a distinguished jurist, against the criticisms of Bellarmine. BIBLIOGRAPHY: H. S. Reinmuth, Jr., NCE 2:95.

[F. D. LAZENBY]

BARCLAY, JOHN (1734–98), minister of the Church of Scotland and founder of the Bereans, or Barclayites. The son of a Perthshire farmer, B. was educated at St. Andrews

Univ., where he was strongly influenced by Archibald Campbell (1691–1756), professor of church history. Subsequently B. became assistant minister, first at Errol (1759–63) and later at Fettercairn (1763–72) under Antony Dow. Censured by his presbytery for his work *Rejoice Evermore, or Christ All in All* (1766) in which he taught that every believer receives direct revelation, he was denied the vacant charge on Dow's death in 1772. B. became minister to a small congregation of followers in Edinburgh; having obtained ordination in Newcastle (1773), he returned to form his Church in Edinburgh, the Berean Assembly, which took its name from Acts 17.10–14. He later (1776) established the Bereans in Fettercairn, London, and Bristol. He published several works on the Bible.

[J. A. R. MACKENZIE]

BARCLAY, ROBERT (1648–90), theologian of the Religious Society of Friends. Born in Morayshire, Scotland, and educated at the Scottish Catholic College in Paris, B. followed his father in becoming a Quaker (1667). B.'s reputation as a foremost theologian of the movement was established by a work first published in Latin, *Theologiae verae Christianae apologia* (1676), and later in English, *Apology of the True Christian Divinity as the Same is Set Forth and Preached by the People Called in Scorn "Quakers"* (1678). The work is a corpus of 15 propositions, developed in scholastic style, with arguments drawn from Scripture and the Fathers. Largely a polemic against Calvinist theology, the *Apology* stands as a Quaker classic, esp. for its second proposition, "Concerning immediate revelation," on the doctrine of the *Inner Light. The work is still highly, but not uncritically, esteemed by modern Quakers. While, like his co-religionists, often imprisoned, eventually B., through the favor of the Duke of York (later James II) was able to assist William *Penn in establishing the Quakers in Pennsylvania. B. never came to America. His other writings include a *Catechism and Confession of Faith* (1673), *The Anarchy of Ranters* (1676), and *The Possibility and Necessity of Inward and Immediate Revelation* (1686). BIBLIOGRAPHY: L. Eeg-Olofsson, *Conception of the Inner Light in Robert Barclay's Theology* (1954); D. Freiday, *Barclay's Apology in Modern English* (1967); Mayer RB 415–421, with bibliog.; E. Russell, *History of Quakerism* (1942); E. Trueblood, *Robert Barclay* (1968). *APOLOGY OF THE TRUE CHRISTIAN DIVINITY.

[T. C. O'BRIEN]

BARCLAY, ROBERT (1833–76), sometimes "Junior" to distinguish him from the preceding, English Quaker, historian. B.'s *Inner Life of Religious Societies of the Commonwealth* (1876) is rich in information on the array of religious sects arising during that period of religious ferment. BIBLIOGRAPHY: Knox Enth 169–175; DNB Conc 1:59.

[T. C. O'BRIEN]

BARCO CENTENERA, MARTÍN DEL (1535–1605), politician and poet. Born, educated, and ordained in Spain, B. spent 24 years in Latin America, serving in political and ecclesiastical offices in various parts of the empire, and involving himself in reputable and disreputable affairs. His historical poem *Argentina* (1602) is valuable as a chronicle of the conquest and colonization of Río de la Plata.

[H. JACK]

BARCOCHEBAS, SIMON, see BAR KOKHBA, SIMON.

BARCOS, MARTIN DE (1600–78), Jansenist author. B. studied under Jansen and succeeded his uncle, Jean Duvergier de Hauranne, as reform abbot of St. Cyran in 1643. The same year he provided the foreword to A. Arnaud's *Fréquente communion* with its censured thesis that Peter and Paul were the two heads of the Church. B.'s posthumous *Exposition de la foi catholique touchant la grâce et la prédestination* (1696) was condemned by the Holy Office. BIBLIOGRAPHY: V. Zollini, EncCatt 838–839; Bremond Index 21.

[M. J. SUELZER]

BARDENHEWER, OTTO (1851–1935), exegete and patristic scholar. After earning two doctorates, one in classical philology at Bonn the other in theology at Würzburg, he taught exegesis at the Universities of Münster and Munich. He founded *Biblische Studien* (1896–1928), served as joint editor of patristic translations in the *Bibliothek der Kirchenväter* (1911–35), and wrote valuable exegetical works. Bardenhewer is best known for his *Geschichte der altkirchlichen Literatur* (5 v. 1913–32), a standard reference work in patristics, noted for its completeness and clear presentation. BIBLIOGRAPHY: J. Quasten, NCE 2:97

[H. DRESSLER]

BARDESANES (Bar Daisan; 154–222 or 223), Syrian poet, astrologer and philosopher, who, according to Eusebius, (*Hist. eccl.* 4.30) was first a member of the Oriental school of Valentinus and then an orthodox Christian. After his conversion, he challenged the teaching of the Marcionites and the Valentinians in written dialogue. His teaching, best known by the treatise *Concerning Fate or Book of the Laws of the Countries,* extant in the original Syriac, has B. as the leader of the dialogue. However this work was actually written by his disciple Philip to recount B.'s astrological explanation of man's destiny and freedom. He is acknowledged as the father of Syrian hymnography; his 150 metrical hymns used by his followers to continue his teaching occasioned St. Ephrem's hymns in support of orthodoxy. BIBLIOGRAPHY: Quasten 1:263–264; Altaner 143.

[F. H. BRIGHAM]

BARDI, ANTONIO DI GIOVANNI MINELLO DE' (b. 1480), Italian sculptor in Padua, worked with his father Giovanni Bardi (1460–1527) on marble reliefs for the Chapel of S. Antonio (1500), on Pesaro tomb, Venice (1503–06), in Bologna (1510), and in Padua (1512); executed tomb of Giovanni Calfiernio, professor of Greek at the Univ. of Padua. In 1520 B. finished work in the Chapel of S. Antonio, Padua, finally returning to Venice (1524).

[M. J. DALY]

BARDO OF OPPERSHOFEN, ST. (*c.*980–1051), archbishop. Educated at Fulda and renowned for his eloquence, B. became abbot of Werden in 1029, of Hersfeld in 1031, and in the same year, abp. of Mainz. During his episcopate Pope Leo IX presided at the council of Mainz. BIBLIOGRAPHY: Butler 2:549; A. M. Zimmermann, Bibl-Sanct 2:780–782.

[H. DRESSLER]

BARDSEY ISLAND, CELTIC MONASTERY OF, in Caernarvonshire, Wales, founded before 516 by St. Cadfan, and originally a settlement of hermits. With it are associated the names of many Welsh saints. It became Augustinian, probably in the 13th cent., and was dissolved *c.*1537. BIBLIOGRAPHY: J. E. Lloyd, *History of Wales* (2 v., 1948); Knowles-Hadcock; A. W. Wade-Evans, *Welsh Christian Origins* (1934).

[C. MCGRATH]

BARDY, GUSTAVE (1881–1955), French patrologist. Ordained in 1906, B. taught at Besançon and Lille until 1927 when he joined the faculty of the Major Seminary of Dijon where he spent the rest of his life. While at Dijon, he was also editor of the diocesan paper. B.'s knowledge was encyclopedic and his scholarly production prodigious. He edited patristic texts, wrote articles for learned journals and encyclopedias, and published more than 30 books among which are *Paul de Samosate* (1923), *St. Augustin* (1940), and *La Théologie de l'Église de Clément de Rome au Concile de Nicée* (2 v., 1945–47). BIBLIOGRAPHY: G. Jacquemet, *Catholicisme* 1:1247; F. X. Murphy, NCE 2:97–98.

[R. B. ENO]

BARI (Barensis), ancient Roman town of Barium founded by Illyrians. Relics of St. Nicolas of Myra were brought from Lycia (1087) and housed in the Basilica (1108), the foremost monument in Apulia. The Cathedral of Bari (S. Sabino), built *c.*1050 was rebuilt 1170–78 and restored in 1920. Bari was the medieval point of departure for pilgrims and crusaders and is today the most important port of S Italy after Naples. BIBLIOGRAPHY: S. A. Papa, NCE 2:98.

[M. J. DALY]

BARING, MAURICE (1874–1945), literary craftsman, the son of a famous family of bankers (his father became Lord Revelstoke); educated at Eton; down for Trinity, Cambridge, but confessed with good-humored modesty that he was not found good enough to start or still less to stay the course; accepted for the diplomatic service, fell in love with Russia, and greatly contributed to recommend its literature in the West. He became a RC (1909)—"the only action of my life of which I am quite certain I have never regretted"—and was an intimate friend of H. Belloc, G. K. Chesterton, and R. A. Knox. A man of wide culture and delicate sensitivity, he had the charism of friendship, both fine-spun and robust. He was much loved in the Royal Flying Corps, in which he served in World War I, and of which he wrote a classical account, and in the Royal Navy, where he was often a welcome and memorable guest, not least in the wardroom when the fleet was lit up. A polyglot and wit, an essayist, poet, and novelist, his works at present are not to the general taste, though appreciated by the discerning. BIBLIOGRAPHY: E. Smyth, *Maurice Baring* (1938); L. Lovat, *Maurice Baring, a Postscript* (1948).

[T. GILBY]

BARING-GOULD, SABINE (1834–1924), Anglican clergyman and writer. Educated at Clare College, Cambridge, he was ordained in 1865. Although a clergyman and father of a large family, he achieved prominence as a hagiographer, novelist, antiquarian, and hymn writer. Among his more important writings are: *Lives of the Saints* (15 v., 1872–77); *Lives of British Saints* (1907); *The Origin and Development of Religious Belief* (2 v., 1869–70); and *The Evangelical Revival* (1920). Two of his most famous hymns are "Onward Christian Soldiers" and "Now the Day Is Over." BIBLIOGRAPHY: S. Monk, *Lew Trenchard* (1961); W. Purcell, *Onward Christian Soldier* (1957); S. Baring-Gould, *Historical Sketch of English National Song (1963)*.

[V. SAMPSON]

BARKING ABBEY, Benedictine nunnery in Essex, England. Barking was founded *c*.677; its recruitment was almost entirely from the upper classes, and it numbered among its abbesses three queens and two princesses. It was wealthy and possessed the largest nuns' church in England. Barking was dissolved in 1539. BIBLIOGRAPHY: *Ordinale and Customary of the Benedictine Nuns of Barking Abbey* (ed. J. B. L. Tolhurst, 2 v. 1927–28); F. Corrigan, NCE 2:99.

[J. R. SOMMERFELDT]

BARLAAM OF CALABRIA (d. *c*.1350), Italo-Greek monk, theologian, noted for his hostility to *hesychasm. Born and educated in S Italy, B. taught at Constantinople and Thessalonica. In 1334 he disputed with the papal legates on the Roman primacy and the procession of the Holy Spirit. He incurred the criticism of Gregory Palamas and became engaged in a bitter controversy with the hesychast monks of Mt. Athos. Condemned by a synod in 1341, he was forced to retract. The next year he traveled to the papal court at Avignon, became a RC, and was made bp. of Gerace in Calabria. BIBLIOGRAPHY: J. Meyendorff, *A Study of Gregory Palamas* (tr. G. Lawrence, 1964).

[G. T. DENNIS]

BARLAAM AND JOASAPH, a religious novel in which the monk Barlaam converts the Indian prince Joasaph, who on becoming king converts his subjects and dies a hermit. Adapted from a Buddhist morality story, it was translated into Syrian, Arabic, and Georgian, while St. John Damascene compiled a Greek version. This proved so popular among the Byzantines that Barlaam and Joasaph were regarded as actual persons and venerated as saints. BIBLIOGRAPHY: *Barlaam and Joasaph* (ed. and tr. G. R. Woodward and H. Mattingly, Loeb, 1914); F. Dölger, *Der griechische Barlaam-Roman* (1953).

[G. T. DENNIS]

BARLACH, ERNST (1870–1938), German expressionist sculptor, graphic artist, dramatist. After study in Hamburg and Dresden and travels to Paris, Russia (which inspired his early peasant figures), and Florence, B. settled in Güstrow (1908). Most important are his war memorials in Kiel (1921), Magdeburg (1930), and his most famous bronze, *The Hovering One* (powerful, floating angel)—the Güstrow memorial (1927). The Nazis destroyed several memorials, removed 381 works, and burned a book of his drawings (1936). (A replica of the Güstrow memorial is in Antoniterkirche, Cologne, and the *Head*, in the Museum of Modern Art, N.Y.). With other German expressionists B., influenced by late medieval works, revived serious wood carving in his image of man suffering, forlorn, yet ennobled in misery. The magnificence of his sculpture is rooted in its monumental simplicity, religious feeling, and compassion. His graphic works illustrate his own plays, the works of Schiller, Goethe, and Von Kleist. B.'s social realism influenced American sculptors of the 1930s. BIBLIOGRAPHY: E. Barlach, *Ein selbsterzähltes Leben* (1948); *Das plastische Werk* (ed. F. Schult, 1960).

[M. J. DALY]

BARLETTA, GABRIEL (d. *c*.1480), Dominican preacher, who joined the Dominicans at Florence under S. Antoninus. He is chiefly famous for *Sermones quadragesimales et de sanctis*, which, first printed at Brescia (1499), reached 20 editions. He is an obscure figure and the authenticity as well as the quality of his sermons is much debated. The most recent account is A. Alecci in *Dizionario biografico degli Italiani* (1964) 6:399–400.

[L. E. BOYLE]

BARLINGS, ABBEY OF, Premonstratensian monastery in Lincolnshire, England. Barlings was founded in 1154 by the duke of Lincolnshire. In 1500, a visitor reported that its virtues and religious observance had been rewarded by an abundance of possessions. The last abbot and four canons were executed by Henry VIII after having been unwilling participants in the peasant uprising of 1536. BIBLIOGRAPHY: *Collectanea Anglo-Premonstratensia* (ed. F. A. Gasquet, *Camden Series,* 3d series, V, X, XII; 1904–1906).

[J. R. SOMMERFELDT]

BARLOW, AMBROSE, ST (1585–1641), English martyr. B. was educated at Douai, first at the English Seminary and later at the Benedictine monastery of St. Gregory. Ordained a Benedictine priest (1617), he was sent on the mission to England where he labored for 20 years. Imprisoned and released several times, he was finally arrested, convicted of being a priest, and executed at Lancaster. He was beatified in 1929, and canonized in 1970. BIBLIOGRAPHY: "Apostolical Life of Ambrose Barlow, OSB," DownRev 44 (1926) 235–251; C. Testore, BiblSanct 2:797–798.

[V. SAMPSON]

BARLOW, WILLIAM (d. 1568), Augustinian canon, bishop. He attacked Wolsey for suppressing Bromehill (1528), was condemned for his pamphlets (1529), apologized to Henry VIII (1530), and was rewarded by diplomatic appointments. He was given successively several bishoprics after he joined the Reformers (1535), the last, Chichester, by Elizabeth in 1559. He was morally weak, explosively zealous for whatever he stood for, but readily changed loyalties. BIBLIOGRAPHY: T. F. Tout, DNB 1:1149–51; C. Jenkins, "Bishop Barlow's Consecration and Archbishop Parker's Register," *Church Historical Society Publication* (1935) NS 17.

[H. JACK]

BARLOW, WILLIAM RUDESIND (*c*.1584–1656), theologian. Born in England, B. joined the Benedictines in Spain (1605) and studied at Salamanca and Douai. He was twice prior of the monastery in Douai where he taught theology, and was general of the English Benedictines (1621–29). Both canonist and theologian, he figured conspicuously in controversies with Bp. Richard Smith over a jurisdictional claim and with Augustine Baker over an interpretation of the Benedictine rule. BIBLIOGRAPHY: Gillow BDEC 1:136.

[H. JACK]

BARMEN DECLARATION (1934), a German Protestant manifesto. The so-called *German Christians came to power with Hitler in 1933, and were helped by Nazi power in electing Ludwig Müller imperial bp. of the newly combined German Evangelical Church. Increasingly this Church was used politically. Church youth were lured into the Hitler youth movement; faithful pastors were intimidated. Martin *Niemöller formed an antiestablishment Pastors' Union. He was also influential in calling the first Synod of the *Confessing Church, at Barmen in May, 1934. Karl *Barth was the leader in the formulation of the starkly worded Declaration; it spoke more clearly than any previous Christian formulation in asserting independence of the Church from state authority—a position strange to many European Lutherans, Calvinists, and Roman Catholics. It firmly upheld Jesus Christ as the one Word of God that men are to hear, trust, and obey; no other source of revelation is valid. Six "evangelical truths" are lifted up, each as a sharp annotation of a verse of Scripture: Jn 14.16; 1 Cor 1.30; Eph 4.15–16; Mt 20.25–26; 1 Pet 2.17; and Mt 28.20. Introductory passages of the Declaration are directly circumstantial, and yet, as theologian Emil *Brunner noted, and as has been shown by later "adoption" of the Declaration by at least one communion (United Presbyterian Church in the U.S.A., 1966), this is a historic pronouncement on Christian authority, with importance far beyond the 1934 German crisis. It is a classic refusal of "false doctrine, as though the Church in human arrogance could place the Word and work of the Lord in the service of any arbitrarily chosen desires, purposes, and plans." For text, see *Book of Confessions* (United Presbyterian Church in the U.S.A., 1967). BIBLIOGRAPHY: M. Honecker, "Weltliches Handeln unter der Herrschaft Christi; Zur Interpretation von Barmen II," *Zeitschrift für Theologie und Kirche* 69, No. 1 (1972) 72–99.

[J. O. NELSON]

BARNA DA SIENA (fl. 1330–60), Italian painter whose earlier work shows the delicacy of Duccio and of his teacher Simone Martini. Frescoes of the *Life of Christ* (S. Gimignano) in dense, angular, tragic patterns were influenced by the Black Death. The exquisite small panel, *Christ Carrying the Cross,* is in the Frick collection, N.Y. and a large, impressive *Mystic Marriage of St. Catherine,* in the Boston Museum of Fine Arts.

[M. J. DALY]

BARNABAS ST., surname given to Joseph, a Levite from Cyprus. One of the first Christians, B. brought Paul to Antioch. Both preached the Gospel in Cyprus and in the S of Asia Minor. Acknowledged by the Church of Jerusalem as an apostle of the Gentiles with Paul (Gal 2), he went back to Cyprus alone where he is said to have been martyred. (Acts 4.11–15) BIBLIOGRAPHY: B. M. Ahern, NCE 2:102–103.

[A. VIARD]

BARNABAS, ACTS OF, see APOCRYPHA (NEW TESTAMENT), 12.

BARNABAS, EPISTLE OF, a letter ranked among the works of the Apostolic Fathers. It was not written by Barnabas, as Clement of Alexandria thought, but by an unknown author, probably an Alexandrian, of the late 1st or early 2d century. The work contains a strong attack upon Judaism and attributes the practices of the Mosaic law to the blindness of the Jews. Instead of being interpreted literally, they should be understood, according to the anonymous author, in an allegorical sense and seen as pointing to Christianity. A section on the doctrine of the two ways (ch. 18–20) is very similar to the *Didache. Text and tr. K. Lake, *Apostolic Fathers* 1; J. Kleist, ACW 6, BIBLIOGRAPHY: Quasten 1:85–92.

[R. B. ENO]

BARNABITES, Congregation of Clerics Regular of St. Paul or the Congregation of Barnabites founded by St.

Anthony Marie Zaccaria (1530) to carry out parish ministry, education of the young, preaching, and missions to the unbaptized. BIBLIOGRAPHY: A. Odil, *Catholicisme* 1:1258.

[F. H. BRIGHAM]

BARNARD OF VIENNE, ST. (*c*.778–842), archbishop. Educated at Charlemagne's court as a soldier, married for 7 years, professed at Ambronay (803),abbot in 807, abp. of Vienne (810), confidant of *Agobard, B. joined the revolt against Louis I and was obliged to flee to Italy. Forgiven and restored, he founded the abbey of Romans (*c*.837) where he died. BIBLIOGRAPHY: P. Villete, BiblSanct 3:68–69.

[A. CABANISS]

BARNARD, GEORGE GRAY (1863–1938), American sculptor who worked in the heroic style of Rodin and Michelangelo. B. acquired the collection of medieval art of the Cloisters, Metropolitan Museum of Art, N. Y. BIBLIOGRAPHY: W. H. Gerdts, *Survey of American Sculpture* (1962).

[M. J. DALY]

BARNARD, HENRY (1811–1900), educator, editor. Admitted to the bar in 1835, B. was active in the Connecticut legislature (1837–39), esp. in furthering the reform and supervision of the common school. An advocate of state-controlled education, as secretary of the Connecticut Board of Commissioners of Common Schools, and founder and editor of the *Connecticut Common School Journal,* he was influential in promoting legislative measures that greatly improved educational standards and led to the establishment of teacher training institutions. After introducing his program into the Rhode Island school system (1843–49), he returned to Connecticut and became superintendent of common schools and principal of the state normal school (1850–54). He subsequently served as chancellor of the Univ. of Wisconsin (1858–60), president of St. John's College, Annapolis (1866–67), and first U.S. Commissioner of Education (1867–70), in which capacity he prepared the terrain for the creation of the U.S. Bureau of Education. B. was founder and editor of the *American Journal of Education.* BIBLIOGRAPHY: *Henry Barnard on Education* (ed. J. S. Brubacher, 1931); *Papers on Froebel's Kindergarten* (ed. H. Barnard, republished from *American Journal of Ed.,* 1970).

[M. B. MURPHY]

BARNETT, SAMUEL AUGUSTUS (1844–1913), Anglican cleric, social reformer. He studied law and modern history at Oxford and was ordained deacon in 1867. He was vicar of St. Jude's, Whitechapel, a parish in the London slums (1873–94). He pioneered the social settlement movement in London, starting a university extension program in his parish. His wife, Henrietta Octavia (married in 1873), aided him in his work and collaborated on his important book *Practicable Socialism* (1888). Other works include *Religion and Politics* (1911) and *Service of God* (1897). BIBLIOGRA-PHY: life in two volumes by Henrietta Octavia Barnett (1919).

[P. K. MEAGHER]

BAROCCI, FEDERIGO (1528–1615), Italian painter. After visiting Rome, B. remained in Urbino becoming the greatest painter of his time in central Italy. Eclectic in form, Venetian in color, his baroque works anticipate Rubens and Bernini. BIBLIOGRAPHY: H. Olsen, *Federico Barocci* (1962).

[M. J. DALY]

BARON, VINCENT (1604–74), French Dominican theologian, controversialist. Much of his life was spent as a professor of philosophy and theology at the Dominican studium in Toulouse. Two of his polemical works against *probabilism were placed on the Index for their rigorism. A prolific writer, he addressed himself to the issue of grace and free will, disputed points in moral theology, as well as to apologetics, in refutation of Protestant teaching. He was also a renowned preacher. BIBLIOGRAPHY: P. Mandonnet, DTC 2.1:425–426.

[T. C. O'BRIEN]

BARONIUS, CAESAR, VEN. (1538–1607), Italian Oratorian, cardinal, and church historian. B. was the disciple of St. Philip Neri, whom he succeeded (1593) as superior of the Oratory. Under Philip's direction he undertook a reply to the *Magdeburg Centuries,* a Lutheran ecclesiastical history and apology for the Reformation. B.'s monumental, 12-volume *Annales ecclesiastici,* published in Rome, 1598–1607, is a work of a lifetime of research in the Vatican Archives and other rich Italian libraries. B. began the research when he was 20; 30 years passed before the appearance of the first volume. He attempted a point-by-point refutation of the Lutheran historians, his main thesis being that the Church remained fundamentally uncorrupted through the Middle Ages. He had completed the work only as far as 1198 at the time of his death; it was brought forward to the 16th cent. by Odorico Rinaldi (1594–1671). Like the *Magdeburg Centuries,* the *Annales* was partisan and contained many errors even though B. was meticulous in his research. The manuscript and its revisions were done in his own hand. The work is valuable today principally as a compilation of documentary sources. B. was also Vatican librarian, reviser of the Roman Martyrology, and in 1605 was nearly elected pope. He was declared venerable by Benedict XIV in 1745. BIBLIOGRAPHY: J. Wahl, NCE 2:105–106, bibliog.

[D. NUGENT]

BARONTUS, ST. (d. *c*.720), monk of Lonray. During a severe illness he experienced a series of extraordinary visions of the afterlife, including the torments of hell. The account, found in *Visio Baronti monachi Longoretensis* (MGH *Scriptores rerum Merovingicarum* 5:368–394), is an interesting example of the eschatological preoccupation of the time. BIBLIOGRAPHY: G. Raspini, BiblSanct 2:828–829; J. E. Lynch, NCE 2:106.

[J. E. LYNCH]

BAROQUE MUSIC. Between approximately 1600 and 1750, music, as did other European art, broke away from the restraint of the Renaissance and became characterized by a growing spirit of theatricalism and virtuosity. Used at first in a derogatory sense to describe an art which could be bombastic, overlavish, and filled with cheap sentimentality, baroque, as applied to music, came to denote a vigorous, exuberant, intense, and dramatic style which developed esp. in Italy, Germany, France, and England, and which was distinguished by fullness of sound, use of contrasts, heavy elaboration, and overall grandeur. Influenced as it was by nonecclesiastical bodies—the nobility and upper classes —baroque music saw a consequent "coming of age" of secular music, as well as numerous other developments. Chief among these were the evolution of an independent instrumental style and a continued development of musical instruments, a gradual demarcation of national schools, and advancements in tonality, harmony, texture, and form. The church modes gave way to major and minor tonalities. Greater importance became attached to homophonic texture, although polyphonic music continued and reached even greater heights under Johann Sebastian Bach. Harmony saw more attention given to chord structure and chord progression and the development of a kind of musical shorthand called the "figured bass." The dramatic element became manifest in a number of new vocal forms—the opera, oratorio, cantata, aria, and recitative, and the interest in instrumental music gave rise to new forms such as the fugue, concerto, sonata, suite, etc.

The outstanding composers of the period were: in Italy, Monteverdi, Alessandro and Domenico Scarlatti, Corelli and Vivaldi; in France, Lully, Couperin and Rameau; in England, Purcell and Handel (a naturalized German); and in Germany, Schein, Scheidt, Schütz, Praetorius, Buxtehude, and Bach. Of these, Bach and Handel represent the culmination of the period.

Church music reflected the general developments of the time. Except in the Roman school, *a cappella* choral style was forsaken. Instruments became important. New forms, such as the church sonata, chorale prelude, and the German church cantata evolved. Use was made of soloists and of a *basso continuo* accompaniment. Latin gave way to the vernacular and the church modes to major and minor tonalities. Notable among the church music composers of the period were Viadana, Carissimi, F. Durante, Pergolesi, Monteverdi and A. Scarlatti, in Italy; Schütz, Tunder, Buxtehude, Telemann, and Bach, in Germany; and John Blow and Henry Purcell, in England. BIBLIOGRAPHY: Buk MusB.

[M. T. LEGGE]

BAROQUE THEOLOGY, RC and Protestant scholasticism that emerged from the Reformation period and shared in the exuberant humanism characteristic of art and thought until the *Enlightenment of the 18th century. Mirroring the experience of the freedom of faith in a loving God, it was progressive in its openness to new opinion. Rejecting the divisive and debasing elements of a humanism separated from the Christian gospel, it also emphasized continuity with the early Church. This traditionalist concern spurred the production of patristic and biblical studies and brought a revival of scholastic theology. As a theological methodology it often reduced itself to historicism. The theological enterprise became interpretation of the evidence of the past. Since the new science rejected this limited methodology, theology resisted its discoveries and was unable to incorporate them into any contemporary synthesis. The rise of empirical science and its resultant secularization prepared the demise of baroque theology. BIBLIOGRAPHY: Y. Congar, *History of Theology* (tr. H. Guthrie, 1968) 144–179.

[E. F. MALONE]

BAROZZI, GIACOMO, see VIGNOLA, GIACOMO DA BAROZZI.

BARRÉ, NICOLAS (1621–86), educator, founder. B. joined the Order of Minims (1639) and taught theology in Paris for 20 years. His major interests were pastoral: preaching, spiritual direction, and the promotion of free education. He founded the Schools of Charity of the Holy Infant Jesus for which he developed a curriculum, devised methods, and trained teachers. He also established the Institute of the Sisters of the Holy Infant Jesus *(Dames de Saint-Maur)*. His spiritual doctrine emphasized devotion to the Eucharist and frequent communion. BIBLIOGRAPHY: J. de Guibert, DSAM 1:1252; R. Chalumeau, *Catholicisme* 1:1263; Bremond, Index 21.

[H. JACK]

BARRÈS, MAURICE (1862–1923), French Academician, prominent both in literature and politics. He began as an ardent individualist, then evolved toward the Right, rallying to Boulangism, championing order and patriotism, defending the role of army and Church in the Dreyfus case. He joined the *Ligue de la patrie française* to channel his nationalism into a militant anti-German policy, which he pursued steadily thereafter. As a deputy representing his native Lorraine, he was a leading conservative spokesman in the National Assembly and a zealous patriot during World War I. He championed a nationalism based on traditional institutions, the Catholic Church and the army, on regional, cultural autonomy, and on race pride. He never formally adhered to Catholicism though his *Cahiers* testify that he was personally preoccupied by questions of religious belief. BIBLIOGRAPHY: P. de Boisdeffre, *Maurice Barrès* (1962); J. Godfrin, *Barrès mystique* (1962); R. Griffiths, *Reactionary Revolution* (1965).

[G. E. GINGRAS]

BARRETO, PASCUAL DÍAZ Y, see DÍAZ Y BARRETO, PASCUAL.

BARRIENTOS, PEDRO NOLASCO (1734–1810), Argentinian educator, Franciscan friar. As rector (1768–77) of the Univ. of Córdoba, second oldest American university, B. reorganized its program of studies and introduced changes in its constitution that greatly enhanced that institution's academic prestige.

[H. JACK]

BARRIÈRE, JEAN DE LA, see LA BARRIÈRE, JEAN DE.

BARRON, EDWARD (1801–54), Irish missionary to the U.S., bp., and leader of the first RC mission from the U.S. to Africa. B. studied law at Trinity College, Dublin, entered the seminary in 1825, and finished his studies at the College of Propaganda at Rome. He came to the U.S. (1837) as rector of St. Charles Borromeo Seminary in the Diocese of Philadelphia and became pastor of St. Mary's Church and later vicar general. In response to the call of U.S. bps. for priests to serve in Liberia among newly freed slaves from America, B. volunteered, along with J. Kelly (1802–66), a priest of Albany, N.Y., and a Baltimore lay catechist, D. Pindar (1823–44). When they reached Cape Palmas they found only 18 Catholics among the 3,000 natives and 500 émigrés. Apprised by papal letter (1842) of his appointment as vicar apostolic of Upper Guinea, B. went to Rome to seek help for his vicariate. Pope Gregory XVI designated him prefect apostolic not only of Liberia but of Sierra Leone and the whole W coast of Africa not under another's jurisdiction. At Paris, while seeking missionaries, he obtained the assistance of seven priests of the Holy Heart of Mary mission society (founded by F. M. P. *Libermann). B. also recruited helpers in Ireland, where several young men were preparing for the Liberian apostolate. He returned to Africa in April 1844 but by the end of that year saw most of his missionaries succumb to illness. Ill and discouraged B. resigned (1845) and the mission was entrusted to the Holy Heart of Mary Congregation. The last years of his life were spent as missionary among the Indians of the Diocese of St. Louis and assisting F. X. Gartland, first bp. of that part of Florida from which was formed the Diocese of Savannah. B. died of yellow fever while ministering to other victims of the epidemic in Savannah. BIBLIOGRAPHY: E. Flick, RACHS 34:99–112; H. P. Fisher, *ibid.* 40:249–310; F. Salvatore, *ibid.* 53:65–85; M. Bane, *Catholic Story of Liberia* (1950); R. M. Wiltgen, *Gold Coast Mission History* (1956).

[M. R. BROWN]

BARROW, HENRY (Borrowe; *c*.1550–93), English Congregationalist. Educated at Cambridge, he was converted *c*.1580 from a libertine life to Puritanism. He was arrested by order of Abp. Whitgift in 1586, and while in prison wrote in defense of separatism and congregational independence: *A True Description of Visible Congregation of the Saints . . .* (1589) and *A Brief Discovery of the False Church* (1590). In 1590 he was charged with circulating seditious books and in 1593 was hanged at Tyburn. B. has been mentioned in connection with the *Marprelate Tracts, but there is little evidence to support their attribution to him. BIBLIOGRAPHY: F. J. Powicke, *H. Barrowe, Separatist, and the Exiled Church in Amsterdam* (1900). *CONGREGATIONALISM.

[T. C. O'BRIEN]

BARROW, ISAAC (1630–77), Anglican theologian, scholar, and mathematician. B. came of a family of Royalist sympathies, was educated at Cambridge (Trinity College), traveled in France, Italy, and the Near East (1655–59) and upon his return to England was ordained. Charles II made him his chaplain and later Master of Trinity. During his lifetime he was best known as a preacher, but in later times he has been held in greater esteem for the able and acute theological mind revealed in his writings. BIBLIOGRAPHY: P. H. Osmond, *Isaac Barrow, His Life and Times* (1944).

[V. SAMPSON]

BARROW, term for earth-covered burial site, particularly in the British Isles, where a chamber formed by dolmens was covered by a mound of earth. At *Sutton Hoo (discovered 1935) the burial chamber was a ship. Similar ship burials are found in Scandinavia. BIBLIOGRAPHY: M. P. Charlesworth, *Heritage of Early Britain* (1952).

[M. J. DALY]

BARRUEL, AUGUSTIN DE (1741–1820), French Jesuit writer. When the Jesuits were suppressed, he traveled to Bohemia and Austria until 1774. The French Revolution caused him to remain in England from 1792 to 1802, and difficulties with Napoleon prolonged his stay abroad until 1815. He undertook the defense of the Church against the *philosophes* and the *Encyclopédistes* in journals and books, esp. *Les Helviennes, ou Lettres provinciales philosophiques* (1781). He is known esp. for the *Histoire du clergé pendant la Révolution française* (1794) and *Histoire du jacobinisme* (1797–99). The latter gives a rather one-sided interpretation of the role of Freemasons and secret societies during the Revolution; however, it contains much valuable information. BIBLIOGRAPHY: R. Daeschler, DHGE 6:937; J. Morienval, *Catholicisme* 1:1265.

[I. M. KASHUBA]

BARRY, GERALD, MOTHER (1881–1961), educator and administrator. Leaving Ireland for America as a young girl, B. entered the Dominican Sisters of Adrian, Mich. (1913). She taught in the schools operated by the congregation, became principal (1914–21), novice mistress (1921–33), and prioress general (1933–61). While she was in office, the community tripled in size and the sisters opened two colleges, four high schools, a sisters' house of studies in Washington, D. C., and 70 parochial schools. They also established missions in the Bahamas and Santo Domingo.

B. served as the first chairman of the Sisters Committee for the National Congress in the U.S. In 1956 she was appointed to preside at a meeting of superiors in Chicago. This led to the formation of the Conference of Major Superiors of Women's Religious Institutes. BIBLIOGRAPHY: M. P. McKeough, NCE 2:127.

[J. HILL]

BARSANIANS (c.6th–9th cent.), Egyptian Monophysites, also called *barsanuphiens* or *semidalites,* located on the Nile bank. According to Timothy of Constantinople, Barsanuphius was chosen bp. by them—contrary to the official canons. John Damascene recorded their practice of using their finger dipped in flour as a mysterious symbol for communion. BIBLIOGRAPHY: G. Bardy, DHGE 6:944–945.

[M. H. BEIRNE]

BARSANUPHIUS (fl. 540) hermit of Palestine, a native of Egypt who lived a solitary life in his cell at Gaza for over 50 years. A fragment of his treatise against Origenists and 396 of his letters in reply to questions of people of various ranks on the spiritual life survive in an edition which includes the letters of his friend, John the Prophet (PG 86.891–902). BIBLIOGRAPHY: R. Janin, DHGE 6:946.

[F. H. BRIGHAM]

BARSUMAS, the name of several Eastern bishops and clerics of whom the more significant are: (1) B. (d.458), Monophysite archimandrite of a Syrian monastery who led the monastic party in its defense of Eutyches. The Emperor Theodosius granted him a seat and vote together with the bps. at the Robber Council (449). He and his company of 1000 monks assisted the soldiers in physically coercing the bps. to acquit Eutyches. Charged by the Council of Chalcedon (451) with the assault which resulted in the death of Flavian, Patriarch of Constantinople, and ordered to confess the teaching of the Council, he refused to reject Monophysitism and actively preached it in Syria until his death. (2) B. (c.415–496), Nestorian bp. of Nisibis (457–496) who persuaded the Persian king Pherozes to make Nestorian Christianity the only form allowed in Persia and established a school at Nisibis under Narses which was responsible for the effective propagation of Nestorian teaching throughout Persia and Eastern Asia. BIBLIOGRAPHY: G. Bardy, DHGE 6:946–950.

[F. H. BRIGHAM]

BARTH, KARL (1886–1968), the foremost Protestant theologian of modern times. Born at Basel, Switzerland, he was the son of a *Reformed Church pastor. After his education at Berlin, Tübingen, and Marburg, he was ordained by his father at Bern (1908). B. began his career as a pastor, and became prominent for his socialist political views. In 1919 he published his *Römerbriefe (Epistle to the Romans,* Eng. tr. E. C. Hoskyns, 1933), which revolutionized theological thinking. The publication led to his appointment (1921) as professor of Reformed theology at the Univ. of Göttingen in Germany. He was subsequently professor at the Univ. of Münster (1925–30) and of Bonn (1930–33). In 1932 he published the first part of volume one of his masterwork, *Church Dogmatics,* which by 1962, when he discontinued the work, had become a 6-million-word work in 12 volumes. In 1933, when the Nazis established the puppet *German Christian churches, B. began his opposition to the Third Reich. In 1934 he was the chief author of a resounding protest, the *Barmen Declaration. He was expelled from Germany in 1935, and became professor at the University of Basel. He continued his resistance to Nazism, which he regarded as essentially an anti-Christian heresy. Besides his theological labors, he took an active part in the postwar world's efforts to assist Churches living under Communist regimes. He retired from teaching in 1962.

In his theology Barth spoke from the Calvinist tradition; consequently the themes "Word of God" and "Predestination" are dominant in his thought. His approach, however, was prompted by a strong reaction against Protestant liberalism, esp. as represented by F. *Schleiermacher. B. found fault with this 19th-cent. theologian's analysis of man's religious motivation, the actualizing of which leads to some sort of established union between man and God. The *Kirchliche Dogmatik (Church Dogmatics,* G. W. Bromiley, T. F. Torrance, eds., 1936–62) is based on certain principles that reveal the viewpoint of the system and trend. One key principle may be expressed as the futility of religion, i.e., of any attempt on the part of man to reach or "attain" God, who is, according to B., "altogether other" *(totaliter aliter).* The position includes the rejection on B.'s part of the analogy of being, i.e., the use of man's own ideas and own language to think and speak of God. A famous passage in the introduction to the *Dogmatics* designates such use of analogy as the anti-Christ, and as sufficient motive to reject Roman Catholicism out of hand. The principal correlative to this negation is B.'s affirmation of the possibility of God's reaching man through his Word. For theological discourse, this implies the use of the "analogy of faith," i.e., man's employing the knowledge communicated in God's Word to understand reality (himself included), which remains quite opaque in itself. Thus, for example, B. stated outright that any valid knowledge or understanding we have of man as such is attained through our knowing the Man, Jesus Christ, who is God's Word about man—a word both of judgment and of justification. B.'s system of theological discourse, moreover, is committed to "consequent Christology" (discourse centered on Jesus Christ), which reduces all the particulars of theology to the Christological mystery. Perhaps the best example of this is B.'s reinterpretation of Calvin's doctrine of *double predestination. He professes to accept this doctrine as part of the Reformed tradition. For him, however, the first instance of double predestination is the simultaneous rejection and acceptance of the justification of Jesus Christ on the part of God the Father. This is the paradigm of the human situation and the sole means through which man can really understand his own situation. The example serves to bring out another characteristic, B.'s use of the dialectical method. For him this means that the simultaneous affirmation and negation of a given theological point is necessary on account of the inherent ambiguity of all these matters as far as the human mind is concerned (see DIALECTICAL THEOLOGY). ''Consequent Christology'' is employed in the organization of the *Dogmatics* to the effect that, although the work appears to be organized on trinitarian lines (Doctrine of Creation—the Father; Doctrine of Reconciliation—the Son; and Doctrine of Redemption—the Spirit), in reality each section emphasizes the role of Christ—in creation, as the work of the word of God; in reconciliation, as the work quite proper to Jesus; and in redemption, as the work accomplished by the Spirit of Jesus. B.'s teaching is opposed to the position and style of the *Bultmann school. The debate as it centers on the mystery of the resurrection reveals that B. held that the resurrection of Jesus is a historical event upon which Christian faith and Christian theology are founded. This event is, in fact, the ultimate break-through on God's part into the domain of man, i.e., the world, which man quite wrongly considers to be his own. It might be inferred that Barth's position is fundamentally antihumanist. This is quite true, insofar as humanism means either an implicit form of ''religion'' understood in the liberal sense of man's initiating a relationship with God, or the construction of an idol to human excellence and perfection.

B.'s influence on Protestantism (and mediately on RC thought, too) seems to have been a strong affirmation of divine transcendence set forth at the onset of the technological revolution. Whether or not the affirmation has been (or will be) given the hearing it deserves is a moot question.

Before B. mellowed in attitude toward Rome, he declared, ''My whole work is concerned with the desperate question of achieving an evangelical theology which can stand worthily in opposition to Roman Catholicism, which I hold to be the great heresy.'' A gradual change in B.'s attitude toward the Catholic Church may have been caused by inner transformation of Catholic theology in the 1940s and 1950s, partly under the influence of Protestantism, for many Catholic theologians took B.'s critique of Catholicism quite seriously. Vatican Council II's *Constitution on Divine Revelation* esp. appealed to Barth. As there gradually developed within the Catholic tradition a theology that sought to be authentically evangelical, kerygmatic, and Christocentric, B., with his great evangelical intentions, made Protestant theology itself an earnest evangelical discussion partner. Catholic renewal permitted B. to ask with mixed feelings of sadness and joy whether the Spirit of God was not as much alive in the Catholic Church as in his own.

B.'s ''faith'' was constantly seeking knowledge. His architectonic approach to theology and incredible capacity for system-building, admirable in themselves, opposed the new theological tendencies current in the latter part of his career, esp. the emerging theology of the secular and the new

humanism. BIBLIOGRAPHY: J. Hamer, *Karl Barth* (tr. D. M. Maruca, 1962); H. Hartwell, *Theology of Karl Barth: An Introduction* (1965); K. Barth, *Revolutionary Theology in the Making* (1964); H. Küng, *Justification, the Doctrine of Karl Barth and a Catholic Reflection* (1964); C. O'Grady, *Church in Catholic Theology: Dialogue with Karl Barth* (1969); T. H. D. Parker, *Karl Barth* (1970).

[T. M. MCFADDEN]

BARTHOLDI, FREDERIC AUGUSTE (1834–1904), French sculptor who studied in Colmar and Paris and traveled to Egypt, acquiring a taste for large-scale sculpture. B. visited the U.S. in 1871 and 1876, executing the colossal Statue of Liberty in New York Bay (1886).

[M. J. DALY]

BARTHOLOMAEUS ANGLICUS, (fl. 1230–50), English Franciscan encyclopedist. He studied at Oxford and Paris and lectured at the Franciscan house of studies at Magdeburg. His *De proprietatibus rerum* (On the Properties of Things), completed c. 1240–50, widely used in the Middle Ages, was concerned with the natural sciences and designed for theologians and preachers. It was based largely on the *Etymologies* of others, such as Isidore of Seville and Robert Grosseteste. BIBLIOGRAPHY: Emden OX 2:771–772.

[F. D. BLACKLEY]

BARTHOLOMEW, ST., APOSTLE, one of the Twelve. His name being a patronymic (son of Tolmaï), he is often identified with Nathanael. BIBLIOGRAPHY: A. Le Houllier, NCE 2:131–132.

[A. VIARD]

BARTHOLOMEW OF BRAGA, VEN. (1514–90), Dominican theologian and abp. B. joined the Dominicans in Lisbon (1528) and taught philosophy and theology for 20 years. After becoming abp. of Braga, he was influential at the Council of Trent and labored zealously to put the Tridentine reforms into effect in his diocese. He wrote extensively on catechetics, spiritual doctrine, and the Council. BIBLIOGRAPHY: P. Damino, *Il contributo teologico di Bartolomeo dei Martiri al Concilio di Trento* (1962); F. de Almeida, DHGE 6:983–984.

[H. JACK]

BARTHOLOMEW OF BRESCIA (d. 1258), canonist who studied Roman law under Hugo de Presbyteris and canon law under Tancred at Bologna, where he later distinguished himself as a teacher of law. His most significant contribution to the history of canon law was *Glossa ordinaria decreti*, in which he amended the *Apparatus ad Decretum* of Joannes Teutonicus. BIBLIOGRAPHY: G. Le Bras, DDC 2:216–217; J. Wenner, DHGE 6:984–985; A. M. Stickler, NCE 2:132–133.

[F. H. BRIGHAM]

BARTHOLOMEW OF EXETER (*c*.1100–84), bp. and canonist. After achieving distinction as a master at Paris (1140–42), B. migrated to England and joined the *familia* of Abp. Theobald of Canterbury; he was archdeacon of Exeter by 1155 and bp. there from 1161. A firm but moderate supporter of Thomas Becket in his quarrel with Henry II, he played an important part in the settlement after Becket's death (1170). B. promoted the codification of decretal law, was a renowned scholar and a respected bishop. BIBLIOGRAPHY: A. Morey, *Bartholomew of Exeter* (1937); D. Knowles, *Episcopal Colleagues of Abp. Thomas Becket* (1951) 27–28, 102–104; T. A. Archer, DNB 1:1250–51; C. Duggan, NCE 2:133.

[J. L. GRASSI]

BARTHOLOMEW OF LUCCA (Ptolemy, *c*.1236–1327), Dominican historian. He was a student and companion of St. Thomas Aquinas; books 22–23 of his *Historia ecclesiastica* are primary sources on the life of St. Thomas; and for a long time B. was credited with completion of Aquinas's *De regimine principum*. B. also wrote *Annales*, a chronicle of events from 1061–1303, as well as treatises on the relation of imperial and papal jurisdiction. In his 80s he was appointed bp. of Torcello near Venice. BIBLIOGRAPHY: K. Foster, *Life of St. Thomas Aquinas: Biographical Documents* (1959).

[T. C. O'BRIEN]

BARTHOLOMEW OF MARMOUTIER, ST. (d. 1084), Benedictine abbot of Marmoutier (1064), bp. of Tours. He reformed ecclesiastical discipline, contributed monks to the founding of William I, the Conqueror's Battle Abbey, defended Catholic doctrine on the Holy Eucharist against Berengar (Berengarius) of Tours. BIBLIOGRAPHY: P. Calendini, DHGE 6:1014–15.

[M. H. BEIRNE]

BARTHOLOMEW OF PISA, see BARTHOLOMEW OF SAN CONCORDIO.

BARTHOLOMEW OF ROME (d. 1430), preacher and reformer. He served for short periods as prior of the canons at Santa Maria di Frigionaia near Lucca, whom he helped to reform. The Canons Regular of St. John Lateran developed out of his reformed community in Lucca. He acquired a reputation for great sanctity. BIBLIOGRAPHY: R. H. Trame, NCE 2:134.

[N. G. WOLF]

BARTHOLOMEW OF SAN CONCORDIO (of Pisa; 1262–1347), Dominican theologian. A humanist and renowned preacher, B. wrote extensively on classical antiquity and composed a widely used compendium of moral theology, a series of Lenten sermons, treatises on Latin pronunciation and orthography, and commentaries on Virgil and Seneca. His most influential work is *Summa de casibus conscientiae* (1338), better known as *Summa Pisana* or *Pisanella*. He wrote also *De documentis antiquorum*, his own translation of which, *Amnaestramenti degli antichi*, is a Tuscan classic. BIBLIOGRAPHY: A. Stefanucci Ala, *Sulla vita e sulle opere di frate Bartolomeo de San Concordio* (1838); Quétif-Échard 1:623–625; J. R. Cooney, NCE 2:134; P. Mandonnet, DTC 2:435–436.

[L. E. BOYLE; J. A. WEISHEIPL]

BARTHOLOMEW OF SIMERI, ST. (mid-11th cent.–1130), abbot and promoter of Basilian monasticism in S Italy. B. learned penance from his life with a hermit, Cyril. He built a monastery, Santa Maria Odigitria (she who shows the way), in the mountains near Rossano, helped by Christodoulos, probably a converted Saracen, and by Count Roger of Sicily, brother of Robert Guiscard. This monastery became a center of Basilian monasticism for S Italy and Sicily. Ordained *c*.1104, B. visited Rome and then Constantinople where Basil Kalimeris asked him to reform the Basilian monastery on Mt. Athos. B. also founded the monastery of San Salvatore de Messina. BIBLIOGRAPHY: P. L. Hug, NCE 2:134; G. Giovanelli, BiblSanct 2:893–895.

[G. E. CONWAY]

BARTHOLOMEW OF TRENT (d.*c*.1251), Dominican hagiographer, traveler, papal envoy. His chief work, *Liber epilogorum* (1245–51), initiated a new genre of nonliturgical hagiographic literature, which is seen at its best in the *Golden Legend* of his fellow-Dominican, James of Voragine, some 10 or 15 years later. BIBLIOGRAPHY: G. Abate, "Il *liber epilogorum* di fra Bartolomeo da Trento, O.P.", in *Miscellanea Pio Paschini* (2 v., 1949) 1:269–292.

[L. E. BOYLE]

BARTHOLOMEW OF URBINO (d.1350), Augustinian bp. and theologian. B. continued the theocratic tradition of his order on papal authority and defended the doctrine of Giles, Augustine of Ancona, and Alexander of St. Elpidio against the attacks of Ockham and Marsilius of Padua. He was the first to produce a concordance of the writings of St. Augustine, a project earlier conceived and left in outline by his teacher, Augustine of Ancona. Entitled *Milleloquium S. Augustini,* the concordance comprises some 15,000 excerpts from Augustine's works that Bartholomew appears to have read directly and arranged alphabetically according to leading topics, about 1000 in number. The *Milleloquium,* to which Petrarch contributed an elegant preface, was widely diffused and occasioned a new and important orientation within the Augustinian school toward a more positive theology based mainly upon the teachings of St. Augustine. BIBLIOGRAPHY: D. Perini, *Bibliographia Augustiniana* (1929–38) 1:203–205; R. Arbesmann, "Der Augustiner-Eremitenorden und der Beginn der humanistischen Bewegung," *Cassiciacum* 19 (1965) 36–54.

[R. P. RUSSELL]

BARTHOLOMEW OF VICENZA BL. (*c.*1200–1270), Dominican preacher, spiritual writer, bishop. The author of some spiritual works, he was head of the school of theology of the papal curia for some years. In 1233 he founded the Militia of Jesus Christ for knights. Made bp. of Limassol, Cyprus, in 1252, he was transferred to Vicenza in 1256, dying there in 1270. His cult was approved in 1793. BIBLIOGRAPHY: T. Kaeppeli, *Mélanges Auguste Pelzer* (1947) 275–301; Butler 4:186–187.

[L. E. BOYLE]

BARTHOLOMEW, GOSPEL OF, see APOCRYPHA (NEW TESTAMENT), 13.

BARTHOLOMEW THE APOSTLE, BOOK OF THE RESURRECTION OF CHRIST BY, see APOCRYPHA (NEW TESTAMENT), 14.

BARTHOLOMITES, the name of two religious congregations. (1) *Armenian,* a monastic congregation of Armenian origin which took up residence in Genoa (1307) when their land was attacked by the sultan of Egypt (1296). Initially following the Rule of St. Basil and the Armenian liturgy, they took their name from the Church of St. Bartholomew which was built for them in Genoa. Several more monks of the same congregation soon moved on to Pisa, Siena, Florence, and Rome. Their original autonomous foundations were united into one congregation by Pope Innocent VI and accepted the Rule of St. Augustine and the Dominican habit (1356). They were formally suppressed by Innocent X (1650). (2) *German,* the congregation of priests founded by Bartholomew Holzhauser to improve the training of priests. Named after their founder, they had no relationship with the Armenian congregation. BIBLIOGRAPHY: C. Korolevski and J. Wenner, DHGE 6:1038–41.

[F. H. BRIGHAM]

BARTMANN, BERNHARD (1860–1938), theologian. Born and educated in Germany, B. was ordained in 1888 and became professor at Paderborn in 1898. His widely used dogma text, *Lehrbuch der Dogmatik* (1905, 9th enl. ed. 1939), incorporated Thomistic teaching with a biblical and historical approach. BIBLIOGRAPHY: R. Baumer, LTK 2:16.

[H. JACK]

BARTOLI, DANIELLO (1608–85), Jesuit historian and man of letters. Despite his desire to work in the missionary field, his superiors kept him in Italy where he achieved distinction as a sacred orator and later as a writer. He was commissioned by Carafa, general of the Jesuits, to write a history of the Jesuits in Italian, and was engaged in this and in other literary activities for the remainder of his life. He has an acknowledged place among the classical authors of Italian literature. BIBLIOGRAPHY: E. D. McShane, NCE 2:136.

[P. K. MEAGHER]

BARTOLO DI FREDI (*c.*1335–1410), Sienese painter of the Renaissance, in a cycle of Job (S. Gemignano, 1367) and *Adoration of the Magi* (1375?–1380?). *Deposition* (1382) and *Coronation of the Virgin* (1388) show abstract, expressive style rejecting realistic detail and spatial depth. BIBLIOGRAPHY: L. Rigatusa, "Bartolo di Fredi," *Diana* 9 (1934) 214–267; M. Meiss, *Painting in Florence and Siena after the Black Death* (1951).

[M. J. DALY]

BARTOLOCCI, GIULIO (1613–87), Hebrew scholar. B. was a Cistercian monk and *scriptor hebraicus* of the Vatican Library. His most important work was the *Bibliotheca magna rabbinica de scriptoribus et scriptis hebraicis* (4 v., 1675–94), an alphabetical listing of Jewish writers and literature. Although considered the best compilation at that time, the work has been criticized for poor judgment in the choice of material and an uncritical acceptance of rabbinical statements concerning the origins of their books. BIBLIOGRAPHY: J. Olivieri, DB 1.2:1474–75; C. Bernas, NCE 2:137.

[T. M. MCFADDEN]

BARTOLOMEO DELLA GATTA, see GATTA, BARTOLOMEO DELLA.

BARTOLOMMEO, FRA (Baccio della Porta; 1475–1517), Florentine painter. Pupil of Cosimo Rosselli, fellow student and partner of Mariotto Albertinelli, and teacher of Fra Paolino da Pistoia and Giovanni Antonio Sogliani, B. came under the influence of Savonarola and renounced all works of a profane nature after 1496. When Savonarola was executed, B. put aside his brush entirely and entered the Dominicans (1500). In 1504, at the command of his prior at San Marco, he resumed his painting, producing his *Vision of St. Bernard.* In 1508 he studied the methods of Giovanni Bellini in Venice, and in 1514, those of Michaelangelo and Raphael in Rome. On returning to Florence, he painted his *St. Mark,* considered his masterpiece, and his *St. Sebastian.* Most of his works are altarpieces. He was among the first to make skillful use of three-dimensional movement in the human figure. BIBLIOGRAPHY: H. von der Gabelentz, *Fra Bartolommeo and the Florentine Renaissance* (1922); R. E. Fry, *Transformations* (1926) 82–94.

[W. A. HINNEBUSCH]

BARTON, ELIZABETH (*c.*1506–34), the "Holy Maid of Kent." In 1525, E., a servant girl, began experiencing ecstasies during a serious illness, her recovery from which she attributed to the Virgin's intercession. While in trances she sometimes spoke of things that took place in distant places or foretold future events; she was also credited with performing miracles. Many prominent persons at the time were convinced that she was an authentic visionary, despite the skepticism of others. She gained some stature when in 1526 she became a Benedictine nun after a careful study was made of her case. She might have continued, as others have done in like circumstances, an object of warm but inconclusive debate between those who believed in her and those who did not, had she not ventured to attack King Henry VIII and to predict disaster to him if he continued in his purpose to divorce Queen Catherine. That made her an imposing obstacle to the divorce because of the veneration in which she was held by many. In 1533 Apb. T. Cranmer obtained a confession of fraud from her. In January 1534 she was condemned by attainder along with six of her sympathizers and on April 20 was hanged at Tyburn. She was stated to have reaffirmed her confession of guilt at the gallows. Both her earlier and later confessions have been questioned by some scholars. BIBLIOGRAPHY: J. R. McKee, *Dame Elizabeth Barton* (1925); P. S. McGarry, NCE 2:137–138.

[M. SAGUÉS]

BARUCH, (Heb. blessed), companion and scribe of Jeremiah, who copied down Jeremiah's oracles of doom directed against Jerusalem and Judah and read them publicly in the temple area and other holy places, from which Jeremiah had been excluded, and then privately for the royal scribes and officials. However, when the oracles were read to King Jehoiakim, he scoffed at their message of doom and burned the scroll piece by piece after every three or four columns were read. He then ordered the arrest of Baruch and Jeremiah, who had gone into hiding. The Lord ordered the rewriting of the scroll and revealed to Jeremiah that Jehoiakim's arson was another symbolic prophecy of Judah's doom. Baruch rewrote the scroll at Jeremiah's dictation and had other threats added (Jer 36.1–32). These oracles are probably substantially the same as those contained in Jer 1–25. Baruch continued to serve Jeremiah by officially witnessing his purchase of land at Anathoth, a hopeful sign, (32.12–15), by accompanying him into Egyptian exile (43.5–7), and by preserving his oracles and arranging the memoirs of the great prophet (ch. 33–35; 36–45). Baruch's importance in subsequent Judaism is indicated by the attribution to him of the book of Baruch and the Apocalypse of Baruch.

[J. F. FALLON]

BARUCH APOCALYPSE OF. Two completely different works bear this title, the Syriac Apocalypse, composed shortly before 100 A.D., and the Greek Apocalypse, which belongs to the 2d cent. A.D. They are often referred to as 2 and 3 Baruch (see BARUCH, BOOK OF).

(1) Syriac Apocalypse of Baruch. This work, probably by many authors, represents a series of revelations as having been made to Baruch, the disciple of Jeremiah, on the history of the Jews from Jeconiah (*c*.591 B.C.) to the advent of the Messiah. It purports to explain why the expected judgment of the nations and the advent of the Messiah should be delayed, and more particularly why Jerusalem should have to be destroyed and restored twice over before the Messiah comes to inaugurate a final age of bliss for the Jews alone, prior to the final consummation of the whole world. The authors' evident purpose is to avert the despair occasioned by the destruction of Jerusalem in 70 A.D.; and they seek to do this by pointing back to the earlier destruction of 587, of both city and temple. Before a new and vaster restoration four successive world-empires must rise and fall, the final one being overthrown by the Messiah himself. Again 12 periods of distress and destruction have to intervene in order that the Jews, while remaining faithful to the law, may be purified and tested, and atone for their sins. An allegorical interpretation of history is presented under the image of 14 floods, and the mixture of good and evil in humanity is represented by a cloud pouring out alternate streams of bright and dark water. A further revelation describes the corporeal state of the righteous after the resurrection, and the ultimate fate of the blessed and the damned.

(2) Greek Apocalypse of Baruch. This is a Jewish composition of the 2d cent. A.D. revised and adapted at various points by Christian glossators. Most of the book is concerned with a journey through five different heavens, which Baruch is privileged to make, and with his return. It shows a strong resemblance to the Slavonic Book of *Enoch and, unlike the Syriac Apocalypse, displays strong Gnostic tendencies. BIBLIOGRAPHY: A. M. Ceriani, *Monumenta Sacra et Profana* (1871) 2:113–180 (Syriac); Charles APOT 2:470–526 (Syria), 527–541 (Greek); L. Gry, "La Date de la fin des temps selon les révélations ou les calculs du Pseudo-Philon et de Baruch (Apocalypse syriaque)," RevBibl 48 (1939) 337–356.

[D. J. BOURKE]

BARUCH, BOOK OF, a small collection of disparate writings attributed to the disciple and scribe of Jeremiah, but dating from later than 150 B.C. It makes use of previous Hebrew literature esp. Jeremiah, Job, and Daniel. The first section (1.15–3.8) is a prose prayer inspired by Daniel ch. 9. A hymn to wisdom (identified with the Mosaic Law) follows (3.9–4.4), which is clearly patterned after Job (ch. 28–29). The final section is a song of encouragement for Israel sung by Jerusalem personified and predicting a new salvation for the chosen people of God after they have been punished (4.5–5.9). A further sixth chapter, added in some MSS, contains a polemic against idolatry and purports to be a letter sent by Jeremiah to refugees on their way to Babylon. It is really a pastiche of anti-idolatry texts gleaned from Jer ch. 10 and Ps 115 and is similar in outlook to Is 40.18–20; 41.6–7. The book was used for synagogical worship among Jewish enclaves in Syria and thus was originally written in Hebrew. Its Greek translator may have been the same person who translated the second half of Jeremiah for the LXX. This indicates the probable late-2d cent. B.C. origin of the Greek version and its connection with the books of Jeremiah in the LXX. It is listed among the canonical works by the Council of Trent but is considered by many Protestants not to belong to the authoritative books of the Bible.

[J. F. FALLON]

BARZEO, GASPAR, see BERSE, GASPAR.

BARZYŃSKI, VINCENT (1838–99), Polish missionary. He was born in Russian-held Poland and was ordained there in 1861. He fled Poland and joined the Congregation of the Resurrection in Paris. Sent first to work among Polish Catholics in Galveston, Tex., he was later assigned to Chicago as pastor of St. Stanislaus Kostka, the largest Polish parish in America. Here he worked the rest of his life. He founded a publishing house which began (1890) a Polish Catholic daily, *Dziennik Chicagoski,* that is still being published. B. was an able administrator and served as the first provincial of his congregation's American province. More than anyone else, he was responsible for nurturing the faith of Polish Catholic immigrants at a time when that faith was most severely threatened. BIBLIOGRAPHY: F. T. Serocyznski, CE 16:7–8; L. M. Long, *Resurrectionists* (1947).

[J. HILL]

BASALENQUE, DIEGO (1577–1651), Augustinian chronicler, linguist, and teacher in colonial Mexico. He emigrated to New Spain as a child, later entered the Augustinians, and was professed in 1594. B. held the offices of prior and provincial, was skilled in law and languages, and authored several works. He is best known for his history of the Augustinians in Michoacan, *Historia de la provincia de San Nicolás de Tolentino de Michoacán,* published in three books in 1673. B. was looked upon as a man of holiness as well as of learning; his biography was published in Mexico City in 1644. BIBLIOGRAPHY: A. J. Ennis, NCE 2:139; C. Wilgus, *Library of Latin-American History and Culture* (1965) 24.

[D. M. HUGHES]

BASAN, see BASHAN.

BASCIO, MATTEO DA, see MATTEO DA BASCIO.

BASEDOW, JOHANN BERNARD (1723–90), German educational reformer. After studying theology and philosophy at Leipzig, he taught moral philosophy in Sorö, Denmark (1753–61), and Altona, Germany (1761–68), but was obliged in both cases to withdraw because of unorthodox religious views. From then on he devoted himself to education. Strongly influenced by the naturalistic ideals of Comenius, Rousseau, and Bacon, he published in his *Elementarwerk* (1774) a system of primary education for children emphasizing practical instruction through play, direct experience, and self-expression rather than theoretical instruction. The same year he opened in Dessau the first nonsectarian school in Germany, the so-called Philanthropinum, in which he sought to implement his educational theories. A poor administrator, he had to resign from the school in 1778 and spent the rest of his life tutoring and writing. His ideas influenced other educators such as J. *Pestalozzi, F. *Fröbel

and J. *Dewey. BIBLIOGRAPHY: C. A. Smith, NCE 2:140–141.

[M. B. MURPHY]

BASEL, CONFESSIONS OF, two Reformation *confessions of faith. (1) The first Confession of Basel (*Confessio fidei Basileensis prior*) was written in first draft in 1531 by J. *Oecolampadius, and in final form by O. *Myconius in 1532; it was adopted officially by Basel in 1534. Accepted as well by the city of Mülhausen in Alsace, it is also called the Mülhausen Confession (*Confessio Mulhusana*). The 12 articles of the document express teachings of both *Luther and *Zwingli. (2) The Second Confession of Basel (. . . *posterior*) is a title sometimes given to the First *Helvetic Confession. BIBLIOGRAPHY: Schaff Creeds 1:385–388.

[N. MARING]

BASEL, COUNCIL OF, council summoned by Pope Martin V (1417–31) to meet in Basel in 1431 in compliance with the decree *Frequens* issued (1417) by the Council of Constance. Martin died before the Council convened, and it was left to his successor, Eugene IV (1431–47), to deal with it. The Council of Basel developed in two stages, both dominated by antipapal sentiment. In the years 1431–37 Eugene IV grudgingly extended his approbation. When Eugene transferred the Council to Ferrara in Sept. 1437 (and later to Florence), the most adamant conciliarists refused to move. During the period 1437–49 Basel continued in open defiance of the Pope, even electing a pope of its own, Felix V (1439–49). Attendance at Basel was never very large, and bishops were in a minority throughout. The Council's most notable achievement was negative: it illustrated the failure of extreme conciliarism. The Council's negotiations (1433) with the Hussites led eventually to the agreement known as the *Compactata. BIBLIOGRAPHY: J. Gill, *Constance et Bâle-Florence* (1965); idem, *Eugenius IV: Pope of Christian Union* (1961); idem, NCE 2:141–142. *CONCILIARISM.

[B. L. MARTHALER]

BASHAN, the plateau area S and E of Mt. Hermon in the Transjordan region of Palestine. It was famous among the Israelites for its healthy cattle and grain and oak forests. The bulls of Bashan were proverbial figures of fierce strength (Ps 22.12) and its cows typified the fat, opulent, and lazy women of Samaria (Amos 4.1). During the Israelite-Aramaic wars of the 9th and 8th cent. B.C., it was repeatedly the source and prize of contention.

[J. F. FALLON]

BASHĪR II AL-SHIHĀBI (d. 1850), later known as Bashīr al Kabīr (the Great), the last and most successful of the feudal lords of Lebanon. Under his leadership, the territory of Greater Lebanon was regained and a new network of roads and bridges enhanced government and commerce. Though he professed the Muslim religion, he encouraged RC and

Protestant missionary activity. Together with Mohammed 'Alī, he conquered Palestine and Syria (1831). Unable to sustain his advances against the Ottoman Kingdom of Turkey because of civil disorders and British and French opposition, he sought refuge in Constantinople, where he died. BIBLIOGRAPHY: P. K. Hitti, *History of Lebanon, Including Lebanon and Palestine* (2d ed. 1957).

[F. H. BRIGHAM]

BASIL I (812–886), **BYZANTINE EMPEROR** from 867, founder of the Macedonian Dynasty (867–1056) who became coemperor (866) and then emperor after murdering Emperor Michael III. When he deposed Photius and restored Ignatius as Patriarch of Constantinople, he gained the support of Rome. At the Council of Constantinople (869–870), B. approved the decision of the Eastern patriarchs to make Bulgaria subject to the jurisdiction of Constantinople. After the death of Ignatius, he reinstated Photius with the blessing of Pope John VII. A strong military leader, he strengthened and extended the frontiers of Byzantium among the Slavs and toward the East. Under his leadership a significant revision of Justinian law, the basis for the *Basilika* of Leo VI, was issued. BIBLIOGRAPHY: A. A. Vasiliev, *History of the Byzantine Empire* (2d Eng. ed. 1952); L. Brehier, DHGE 6:1082–89.

[F. H. BRIGHAM]

BASIL II (958–1025), **BYZANTINE EMPEROR** from 976, also called Bulgaroctonus (Slayer of Bulgars) who usurped the throne from his great uncle, the eunuch Basil (985), after the revolt of Bardas Sclerus had been quelled (976–979). His convincing defeat, effected with the aid of Prince Vladamir of Kiev, of the revolt of Bardas Phocas and the Anatolian Guard at Chrysopolis (987–989) made him sole master of the Empire.

A rigid disciplinarian, he maintained civil balance of power by restricting the landholdings of the aristocracy and limiting their judicial privileges. His dealings in matters ecclesiastical revealed the same control. His ruling on illicit marriages resolving the controversy occasioned by the fourth marriage of Leo VI, and his encyclical on the procession of the Holy Spirit addressed to the bps. of Asia Minor, a restatement of the treatise of Photius (996–998), indicated his desire that Constantinople be ecclesiastically autonomous. But the break with Rome became explicit when Patriarch Sergius removed the name of the Pope from the dyptichs (1001–1018). Yet, during the Patriarchate of Eustathius, B. considered it politically expedient to achieve diplomatic and ecclesiastical harmony with the see of Rome. His most significant military and diplomatic success was his complete domination of Bulgaria and the Balkans (991–1018). Here too, he made ecclesiastical jurisdiction autonomous and directed all episcopal appointments.

Through his alliance with Vladimir of Kiev, B. extended the influence of Byzantine Church and Christianity to all of Russia. His rule was highlighted by his diplomatic success with the Arabs in Syria and Palestine, the strengthening of military outposts in the Caucasus and Armenia, and the achieving of mutual respect with the kingdoms of France and Germany, thereby balancing his losses to the Saracens in Italy. BIBLIOGRAPHY: L. Brehier, DHGE 6:1090–1100; A. A. Vasiliev, *History of the Byzantine Empire* (2d Eng. ed. 1952) 302, 311–315, *passim*.

[F. H. BRIGHAM]

BASIL OF ANCYRA (fl. mid-4th cent.), Arian bp. and writer. Elected as bp. of Ancyra, to succeed Marcellus, c.336, B. was deposed in 343 and then reinstated by Constantius about 5 years later. He was sympathetic to the moderate Arians; but, increasingly alienated by the growing radicalism of the extremists, he was banished by the emperor to Illyria in 360, where he died. BIBLIOGRAPHY: PG 42:425–444; 30:669–810; Quasten 3:201–203.

[R. B. ENO]

BASIL OF CILICIA (d. after 527), bp., Monophysite, and writer. A priest of Antioch, he became the bp. of Irenopolis in Cilicia. Through Photius's use he is known as the author of a 3-volume church history which included precise documentation and espicopal letters on the period 450–527.

[M. H. BEIRNE]

BASIL THE GREAT, ST. (329?–379), Father of the Church, one of the "three great Cappadocians" (the others being his younger brother St. *Gregory of Nyssa and their friend St. *Gregory of Nazianzus). After a career in the world he founded various monastic communities, for whom he wrote his *Rule,* which directed the monastic mentality definitively away from the eremitical ideal toward life in common, and which was to become normative in both East and West. (St. Benedict of Nursia intended his own *Rule* for beginners; he sent his "proficient" back to the *Rule of St. Basil*). Later B. enjoyed great success as bp. of his native Caesarea and metropolitan of Cappadocia, and became the leader of the theologians who gradually attracted the adherents of *Semi-Arianism towards orthodoxy. It was he who added "in all things" to the Semi-Arians' "the Son is like the Father," then negotiated with St. *Athanasius of Alexandria and Pope Damasus the rapprochement with the Semi-Arians at Antioch (379), which was to be confirmed by the Council of Constantinople I in 381. BIBLIOGRAPHY: Quasten 3:204–236.

[R. R. BARR]

BASIL OF SELEUCIA (d. after 468), metropolitan of Seleucia from 431, vacillating bp. in the Monophysite controversies; preacher. B. joined in the condemnation of *Eutyches under *Flavian at Constantinople in 448. He reversed himself, however, participating in the Latrocinium at Ephesus (449); then changed again, signing the *Tome of Leo* at the Council of *Chalcedon (451). He was the author of a curious life of St. Thecla. His sermons (two of which are definitely spurious), along with other work dubiously ascribed to him, can be found in PG 88:1–618. BIBLIOGRAPHY: Quasten 3:526–528.

BASIL OF SOISSONS

BASIL OF SOISSONS (d. 1698), French Capuchin theologian. Once confessor to Henrietta Maria of England, he wrote extensively in defense of the faith. His major work, *Fondement inébranable* (4 v., 1680–82), is based on scriptural argument. BIBLIOGRAPHY: É. d' Alencon, DTC 2.1:464–465.

[H. JACK]

BASIL (Gr., *basilikon,* the royal herb), a plant of the same family as mint, thyme, sage, and lavender, which produces a strong, sweet aroma and is used in certain ecclesiastical ceremonies in the East. On the third Sunday of Lent and on the feast of the Exaltation of the Precious Cross (Sept. 14), the holy cross is placed on a tray of basil leaves which are distributed to the faithful after the service.

[A. J. JACOPIN]

BASIL, LITURGY OF ST., a Syro-Cappadocian Greek liturgy existing in two Greek recensions, a shorter Egyptian and a longer Byzantine form, the latter being fairly closely paralleled by a Syriac version, somewhat less so by the oldest Armenian version. The shorter recension is demonstrably the more primitive.

That at least part of the liturgy comes from St. Basil the Great is generally accepted by critical scholars, but opinions differ in attributing to him the formation of the primitive text, or of the secondary, longer redaction, or of both. The two oldest MSS (8th and 10th cent.), containing both the Liturgy of St. Basil and that of St. *John Chrysostom, suggest by their arrangement that the Liturgy of St. Basil was the one more normally used at that time. Today it is used in the Byzantine liturgy only ten times a year: Jan. 1 (the feast of St. Basil), the vigils of Christmas and Epiphany, the first five Sundays of Lent, Holy Thursday, and Holy Saturday. It is united with Vespers on the vigils of Christmas and Epiphany and with Vespers of Holy Thursday, and Holy Saturday in such a way that the *prothesis* is done during None preceding Vespers, while the hour of Vespers itself serves as that part of the liturgy preceding the *Trisagion and readings. Today, the differences between the Liturgy of St. Basil and that of St. John Chrysostom are hardly noticeable. They are concerned with the prayers said by the celebrant in a low voice (except for the *ekphonesis* of the final words), with minor changes affecting the deacon and choir. A form of the anaphora in the liturgy's Egyptian recension, translated into Coptic and Arabic, is the usual one celebrated in the *Coptic liturgy today. The anaphora used in the *Armenian liturgy is a modified form of that of St. Basil. BIBLIOGRAPHY: P. de Meester DACL 6:1599–1604; F. E. Brightman, *Liturgies Eastern and Western* (1896) 1:309–344, 400–411.

[A. CODY]

BASIL, RULE OF ST., a monastic rule written by St. Basil which developed in two forms: one, known as the "Great Asceticon," is made up of 35 questions and answers dealing with basic concepts of spiritual and monastic asceticism, and the second, the "Small Asceticon," which goes into more detail about the monastic life. The latter is a systematic exposition of monastic regulation based on St. Basil's own experience and comprises 313 items in the same question and answer form. It rejects the concept of the solitary seeking his own way to salvation, and insists that while peace of soul is the primary objective of the monastic life, this can only be effectively achieved by living in a monastic community. Love of neighbor is to be a concrete expression of man's love for God. St. Basil was esp. concerned with the necessity of helping people in the world, and he specifically mentions the duty of monks to feed the poor and to establish schools and orphanages. Text: PG 31:889–1428. BIBLIOGRAPHY: E. F. Morison, *St. Basil and His Rule. A Study in Early Monasticism* (1912); M. G. Murphy, *St. Basil and Monasticism* (1930); G. Bardy, DSAM 1:1279–81.

[S. SURRENCY]

BASILI, father and son, Italian church musicians. Andrea (1720–77) was active at Tivoli and Loreto. Many of his sacred works are preserved in MSS at Loreto and Bologna. Francesco (1767–1850), son of Andrea, held posts at Loreto, Milan (director of the Conservatory), and, from 1837, St. Peter's, Rome, as *maestro di cappella*. Besides quantities of church music, he wrote a number of operas that were successful in their day.

[A. DOHERTY]

BASILIAN MONASTICISM, the form of monasticism practiced in the Eastern Church which takes its spirit from St. Basil the Great. Among the Orthodox there are no religious orders or societies, but all Orthodox monks acknowledge their debt to St. Basil for his rule. No monk, whether living in a community or not, feels bound to observe the letter nor, in many respects, the spirit of St. Basil's rule. Orthodox monasticism owes nearly as much to the tradition of the great ascetics and solitaries of the earliest days of Christian monasticism in Egypt. However, when instructing novices and monks, abbots of Orthodox monasteries refer to the Asceticons of St. Basil as a basic consideration for the monastic life. Elementary manuals designed for the use of monks, while not reproducing all or even most of the rules, quote liberally and often verbatim certain of St. Basil's questions and answers. *BASIL, RULE OF ST.

[S. SURRENCY]

BASILIAN NUNS, the name commonly applied to the Order of Basilians of St. Macrina, an Eastern Catholic order. They originated in Caesarea of Cappadocia in the 4th century. At that time St. *Basil the Great, founder of Eastern monasticism, dissatisfied with the eremitical type of life then in favor among ascetics, attempted to restore true observance of the gospel to the monastic life through the rule he began writing in 358 (see BASIL, RULE OF ST.). He introduced *cenobitic monasticism, which was social and evangelical in character. His mother Emelia and sister St. Macrina established a community for women at the same time and used his rule and ascetical writings as guidelines. The order spread from Asia Minor to Greece, Crete, Sicily, Italy, and the Ukraine. At the present time the Basilian Nuns have monasteries in Czechoslovakia, Poland, Australia, Argentina, Yugoslavia, and the largest, in the U.S. The order's chief apostolate is the education of children and young women, in schools, orphanages, and like institutions; the care of the sick and the aged; and the promotion of ecclesiastical arts, particularly of the Byzantine rite, religious publications, and other activities required by particular needs. BIBLIOGRAPHY: OrientCatt 736–743.

[S. BERDAR]

BASILIAN ORDER OF ST. JOSAPHAT, official designation of a Ruthenian Congregation with roots in a monastery in Kiev where St. Theodosius introduced the rule of St. Basil in 1072. Various monasteries followed the model and in 1617 were incorporated in the Lithuanian Congregation of the Holy Trinity initiated by St. Josephat Kuncevyč. Independent monasteries were ordered by the Synod of Zamosc to form the Ruthenian Congregation of the Protection of the Holy Virgin in 1739. Benedict XIV fused the two orders and the resultant Order of St. Basil founded in 1742 had two provinces, one Ruthenian and the other Lithuanian. The latter was suppressed and subsequently disbanded with the political strife in Europe. A reorganization of the order was effected in 1882 under Jesuit auspices. Headquarters were situated in Rome by 1931, and the Holy See officially accepted the new name of Basilian Order of St. Josaphat as well as the extension of the apostolate of teaching and publishing to embrace emigrants of the Eastern rite in the U.S., Latin America, and Canada. BIBLIOGRAPHY: A. Odil, *Catholicisme* 1:1289–90.

[M. E. FORD]

BASILIAN ORDERS OF THE MELKITE RITE, the three religious orders of the Melkite rite which follow the Rule of St. Basil the Great.

The Basilian Order of St. Saviour, founded by Euthymiossaifi, abp. of Tyre and Sidon (1684) and approved under the Rule of St. Basil by Pope Benedict XIV (1743). After several revisions, the constitution and government of the order were approved by the Holy See (1956). Its members are presently exercising parochial ministry in Tyre, Sidon, Acre, Banigas, Tripoli, Damascus, and in seven parishes in the United States.

The Basilian Order of St. John the Baptist, also called the Order of Suwayr or the Baladites, was founded by Gerasim and Solomon, two Syrian monks of the Church of St. John the Baptist in the vicinity of the village of Suwayr,

Lebanon (1712). Pope Benedict XIV placed them under the Rule of St. Basil (1743) and approved their constitutions which had been taken from the Maronite Monks of St. Anthony (1757). From their motherhouse in Kloncara, Lebanon, they administer six parishes in the United States.

The Basilian Order of Aleppo separated from the Baladites (1829) and received approval for their constitutions (1832). The motherhouse is in the monastery of St. Saviour in Sarba, Djunieh, Lebanon. BIBLIOGRAPHY: M. M. Wojnar, NCE 2:153–154; *De Protoarchimandrita Basilianorum* (1958); C. Pujol, *De religiosis orientalibus ad normam vigentis iuris* (1957).

[F. H. BRIGHAM]

BASILIANS, a religious congregation of priests of the Roman rite founded by Abp. Charles d'Aviau of Vienne (1736–1826). Its first rule was prepared by Léorat Picansel, vicar-general of the Diocese of Viviers. Nine priest-teachers joined Fr. Joseph La Pierre forming a community of diocesan priests. Elevated to pontifical rank by Pope Gregory XVI (1837) it has been granted papal approbation by Popes Pius IX (1863), Pius X (1913), and Pius XI (1938). Brought to Canada by Bp. Armand François of Toronto (1850), its growth there and in the U.S. was marked by the foundation of several houses of study, colleges, and universities. Its collaboration with state colleges set a precedent for other Catholic colleges in Canada. In 1922, the French province and the American province (Canada, U.S., and Mexico) were erected as separate communities by the Holy See. A new papal decree united them in 1955. BIBLIOGRAPHY: R. Scollard, NCE 2:149–151.

[F. H. BRIGHAM]

BASILIANS (BYZANTINE RITE), the name given to five branches of the Order of St. Basil the Great in several Oriental rites all of which follow the rule of St. Basil:

Grottoferrata (Italo-Albanian Rite), from the name of the Greek monastery founded by St. Nilus of Rossano in the 10th century. Similar foundations were erected in the 11th cent. in Italy and 16th cent. in Spain. United into one congregation by Pope Gregory XIII (1579) both groups were nonexistent in 1866. Restored as a Greek monastery by Giuseppi Cozza-Luzi (1880), Grottoferrata now has several dependent houses in S Italy and Sicily.

Basilian Order of St. Josaphat (Ukrainian and Romanian rites). The beginnings of this order can be traced to the introduction of the Rule of St. Basil at the monastery of Pecherska Lavra in Kiev by St. Theodosius (1072). A Lithuanian province called the Basilian Congregation of the Holy Trinity (1617) was established by St. Josaphat and the abp. of Kiev, Velamin Rutski and the Ruthenian congregation (1739). Both groups were joined into one order by decree of Pope Benedict XIV (1742). Its present name was approved by Pope Pius XI (1932). They have been hampered by the Soviet occupation of Eastern Europe, but have expanded their apostolate to Eastern people who have emigrated to North and South America. BIBLIOGRAPHY: M. Wojnar, NCE 2:152–153; C. Korolevskij, DHGE 6:1180–1236.

[F. H. BRIGHAM]

BASILICA (Gr. royal [building]), a Roman type of building consisting of a rectangular roofed hall used as a social, commercial, and public meeting place. This style of building was adapted by the early Christians for liturgical use. The earliest Roman basilicas were of a post and lintel construction (Basilica Julia in the Roman forum) but later basilicas were also covered with barrel vaults (Basilica of Maxentius, also in the Roman forum). Both types of construction were employed by the early Christians, but the former is by far the more common. The early Christian basilica was approached through an atrium, a colonnaded outer court, or through a simple portico extending across the front of the church. Within the basilica there was a vestibule or narthex, opening up to the church proper. This consisted of a wide central nave with a raised clerestory and two, four, or even more, narrower aisles along the sides. The timbered roof was supported by columns, and the light coming through the windows in the clerestory and the rows of columns leading toward the rear of the church focused the attention of the faithful upon the altar placed in front of the apse. Behind the altar were the episcopal throne and rows of benches for the clergy, and in front of it on one or both sides was the ambo or pulpit. Larger basilicas had transepts, and were beautifully adorned with mosaics and colored marble. The early Christian basilica developed into a distinctive architectural form of rare beauty as can be appreciated even today in such old churches as Santa Sabina and Santa Maria Maggiore in Rome, San Apollinare Nuovo in Ravenna, and the Basilica of the Nativity in Bethlehem. BIBLIOGRAPHY: R. Krautheimer, *Early Christian and Byzantine Architecture* (1965).

[M. J. COSTELLOE]

BASILIDES, ST. (d.*c.*202), martyr, a soldier at Alexandria during the reign of Septimius Severus and a catechumen of Origen. According to Eusebius (*Hist. eccl.* 6.5) B. had befriended a certain Potamiaena on her walk to martyrdom by shielding her from a hostile crowd. Before her death she assured him that she would reward him for his selfless concern. When B. was imprisoned for not taking an oath, she came to him there, crowned him with a wreath, and promised him final victory. On the next day B. was baptized and martyred. BIBLIOGRAPHY: G. Bardy, DHGE 6:1175; B. Cignetti and F. Caraffa, BiblSanct 2:904–906; Butler, 2:525–526.

[F. H. BRIGHAM]

BASILIDES (fl. 120–140 A.D.), Gnostic teacher in Alexandria. B. claimed a secret revelation from Peter through Glaucias, Peter's translator. He wrote a gospel with a commentary in 24 books. Like other Gnostics, he taught the existence of a Supreme God who is in contact with men only through a long series of mediators, the God of the Jews belonging to the lowest ranks of these spiritual beings. The *Nous* of the Supreme God dwelt in Jesus, and those who follow him will be freed from matter. BIBLIOGRAPHY: Quasten 1:257–259; LexAW 438, bibliog.

[R. B. ENO]

BASILIDES, GOSPEL OF, see APOCRYPHA (NEW TESTAMENT), 15.

BASILIDES AND MARTIAL, Spanish bps. known from Letter 67 (CSEL 3:735–743) of Cyprian of Carthage (254). If Martial's association with a *procurator ducenarius* makes him bishop of Mérida in Lusitania, then Basilides would be bp. of León-Astorga. A council in Carthage supported an appeal from Bps. Felix and Sabinus (and the faithful of León-Astorga and Mérida) against the reinstatement of B. and M., who had been regularly deposed as unworthy prelates and *libellatici* in the persecution. B. had repudiated the resignations and obtained reinstatement from Pope Stephen I (who Cyprian says was ignorant of the facts). The outcome of the dispute is unknown.

[E. P. COLBERT]

BASILISCUS, BYZANTINE EMPEROR (d. 477), brother of Empress Verina. B. usurped the throne from Emperor Zeno at the instigation of Verina (475), and his short rule created bitter enemies as he granted special preference to Arians and Monophysites, repudiated the Council of Chalcedon and the Tome of Leo, harassed the Orthodox clergy of Constantinople and alienated his chief protector, Theodoric the Goth. Political and religious opposition mounted under the leadership of Daniel the Studite and Acacius, patriarch of Constantinople, to such an extent that Verina successfully plotted the deposition of B. and reinstated Zeno (477). BIBLIOGRAPHY: J. B. Bury, *History of the Later Roman Empire* 1:335–403; Fliche-Martin 4:284–285; L. Brehier, DHGE 6:1237–39.

[F. H. BRIGHAM]

BASILISK, legendary king of serpents in medieval bestiaries, causing death by hiss, look, or aura of intense heat (itself destroyed by weasel or mongoose), appearing in Romanesque relief carvings with birdlike, winged body and snake's tail. BIBLIOGRAPHY: T. H. White, *Book of Beasts* (1954).

[M. J. DALY]

BASIN, THOMAS, (1412–91), canonist, historian, bp. of Lisieux. After law studies at Paris, Louvain, and Pavia, he was the first occupant of the chair of canon law in the university founded by Henry VI of England at Caen, and was present at the Council of Florence in 1439. As bp. of Lisieux he worked for the rehabilitation of Joan of Arc. His relations with Louis IX of France were very difficult, and he went into exile twice. The second occasion he resigned his bishopric, taught canon law at Louvain, and died as coadjutor bp. of Utrecht. He is best known for his histories (in Latin) of Charles VII and Louis XI. A useful account of him is in his *Histoire de Charles VII* (tr. C. Samaran, 1933).

[L. E. BOYLE]

BASKIN, LEONARD (1922–   ), American sculptor and printmaker whose impressive, humanistic concepts in unique, monumental, anonymous shapes attain universal significance *(Man of Peace, Old Man, Hanged Man, Dead Men)*. One of the very finest designers and wood engravers, B.'s books printed on his private Gehenna Press are contemporary treasures.

[M. J. DALY]

BASS (It. *basso,* low), one of the four major subdivisions of the human singing voice, the lower range of the adult male voice, with a characteristic range of E to e. The singing range is subdivided into baritone and bass proper (the middle and low male ranges respectively), both of which belong to the bass section in a choir. The term also refers to the part in the music itself, the lowest sounding part, and to instruments employing the bass range and quality, usually the largest of their family.

[J. J. WALSH]

BASSA, FERRER (1290–1348), 14th-cent. Spanish Catalan painter whose forms in Giottesque style evidence an appealing primitive humanism. B. painted the mural of the *Joys of Mary and the Passion of Christ* in the Chapel of S. Miguel, Pedralbes monastery (1345–46). BIBLIOGRAPHY: F. Jiménez-Placer, *Historia del arte español* (2 v., 1955).

[M. J. DALY]

BASSI, MATTEO DA, see MATTEO DA BASCIO.

BATAILLE, NICOLAS (betw. 1330 and 1340–*c*.1405), master weaver of tapestry in the unsurpassed Parisian workshops of the 14th century. By appointment *valet de chambre* to his patron, Duke Louis I of Anjou, B. executed the high warp *Story of Hercules.* From cartoons of Hennequin de Bruges, painter at the court of Charles V, B. completed (1375) the world famous **Apocalypse of Angers*—a series of seven remarkable hangings of which 71 scenes remain only partly intact because of abuses following the French Revolution. Charles VI as well as Philip the Bold (brother of the Dukes of Anjou and Berry), ordered from Bataille. In 1387 upon inheriting Artois, Philip commissioned and made prosperous the workshops of Arras.

[M. J. DALY]

BATAILLON, PIERRE MARIE (1810–77), French born Marist missionary. He was sent first to Wallis Island, and later extended his efforts to New Caledonia, New Hebrides, the Fiji Islands, Tonga, Tokelau, the Futuna Islands, and Samoa. This area was embraced by the vicariate apostolic of Central Oceania. He was consecrated bp. in 1843. He is remembered as a most zealous missionary and an able and far-sighted organizer. BIBLIOGRAPHY: N. Weber, *Brief Biographical Dictionary of the Marist Hierarchy* (1953); A. M. Mangeret, *Mgr. Bataillon et les missiones de l'Océanie Central* (2 v, 1895).

[P. K. MEAGHER]

BATALHA, Dominican church and cloister of Santa Maria da Victoria at Batalha, a town in the vicinity of Leiria, Portugal built by King John I of Portugal to honor and thank the Virgin for his victory over the Castilian Spaniards and to herald Portuguese freedom. The work of two architects, Alfonso Dominques and Master Huguet, the abbey is a model of both Iberian art and Gothic architecture. A Dominican cloister from 1388, it became a national monument in 1840. BIBLIOGRAPHY: V. De Wilde, DHGE 6:1310–11; P. Dony, *Batalha: Un Problème d'influences* (1957).

[F. H. BRIGHAM]

BATE, HENRY, see HENRY BATE OF MECHLIN.

BATH, ABBEY OF, Benedictine monastery in Bath, England. There were various religious communities at Bath from the 7th cent., but the abbey's prominence dates from the reform of St. Dunstan in the 10th century. In 1090, the bishopric of Wells was transferred to Bath and the monastery became a cathedral priory. The bishops allowed the monks insufficient funds and the monastery developed slowly. The abbey church was rebuilt in the early 16th cent., shortly before its dissolution in 1539. BIBLIOGRAPHY: John Britton, *History and Antiquities of Bath Abbey* (1887); E. John, NCE 2:163–164; C. Duggan, *ibid.,* 164.

[J. R. SOMMERFELDT]

BATH AND WELLS, ANCIENT SEE OF, a medieval diocese formed by the union of the Abbey of Bath with the church of the canons regular at Wells, Somerset, England. The monks of Bath and the canons of Wells disputed much on episcopal elections and jurisdiction. With Bp. Jocelin's death (1242), papal authorities imposed the principle of joint election and established the title of Bath and Wells. After the Reformation, Wells functioned as an Anglican episcopal seat. BIBLIOGRAPHY: *Councils and Synods* (ed. F. M. Powicke and C. R. Cheney, 1964).

[M. H. BEIRNE]

BATHILDIS, ST., (d.*c*.680), queen of France, Benedictine nun. She married Clovis II, King of Neustria and Burgundy (649) and was the mother of Chlotan III, Childeric II, and Theodoric. B. ruled as French regent (656–664) and was honored for her struggle against slavery, simony, and abusive taxation. She founded the abbeys of Corbie and Chelles where she was forcibly retired before 673. BIBLIOGRAPHY: É. Brouette, NCE 2:164; J. Marilier, BiblSanct 2:971–972.

[M. H. BEIRNE]

BÁTHORY, Hungarian princely family. (1) Andrew (d. 1345), bp. of Grosswarden and Erbauer from 1329, built the cathedral at Nagyváred. (2) Ladislaus, Bl. (early 1400s), a Hermit of St. Paul who translated the Bible into Hungarian. (3) Stephen (1533–86), who was elected prince of Transylvania (1571) and king of Poland (1575). He made his brother Christopher (1530–81) nominal ruler of Transylvania, but kept actual control himself. He made a truce with the Turks (1573), defeated the Muscovites, and brought the Jesuits to both Transylvania and Poland. (4) Sigismund (1572–1613), son and successor of Christopher in Transylvania. He took over the government from the regent in 1588 and joined the Christian princes against the Turks, precipitating a national disturbance of several years. He was temporarily victorious in 1595. He abdicated the throne in favor of Emperor Rudolph II in 1598; this was not acceptable, so in 1599 he offered his brother, the cardinal, the throne. Michael, his favorite vassal, defeated Andrew, the cardinal, in battle. After three attempts to get back his sovereignty, Sigismund retired to Prague (1601). (5) Andrew (1566–99), who was made bp. and cardinal in 1584. He gave up his diocese to succeed Sigismund, but died in battle. BIBLIOGRAPHY: T. von Bogyay, LTK 2:50–51; Pastor 22, 23, 24 *passim*.

[H. JACK]

BATHSHEBA, the wife of one of King David's military captains, Uriah the Hittite. She committed adultery with David and saw the death of the son of this union. After David had Uriah killed, he made her his wife and eventually she became the mother of David's successor, Solomon. She is mentioned in the genealogy of Jesus of Nazareth in St. Matthew's Gospel.

[J. F. FALLON]

BATIFFOL, PIERRE (1861–1929), French ecclesiastical scholar. After ordination (1884) he continued his studies at Paris under L. Duchesne and at Rome under G. B. de Rossi. Except for the period of his rectorship at the Institut Catholique de Toulouse (1898–1907), he was chaplain at the school of Ste. Barbe in Paris where he dedicated himself to scholarship. In the crosscurrents of the *Modernist crisis, he resigned his rectorship at Toulouse, one of his works having been condemned at Rome (1907). His submission during these difficulties was admirable; but he became the target of much bitterness, e.g., from A. *Loisy. While at Toulouse, B. founded the *Bulletin de littérature écclesiastique*. He was a continuous contributor to journals of Christian scholarship, participated in the *Malines Conversations, and was delegate of the Holy See at the Congress of Historical Sciences in Oslo (1928). Among his numerous books, ranging over the history of Christian literature, liturgy, and dogma, was a *History of the Roman Breviary* (1893; Eng. tr. 1898 and 1913), rev. and improved in 1911; a study of church origins comprised *L' Église naissante et le Catholicisme* (1909; Eng. tr. *Primitive Catholicism,* 1912), *La Paix constantinienne* (1914), *Le Catholicisme de saint Augustin* (1920), *Le Siège apostolique* (1924; *Léon Ier* in DTC, 1926), and *Saint Grégoire* (1928, Eng. tr. 1929). It was the 2d volume, on the Holy Eucharist, of his *Études d'histoire et de théologie positive* (1902) that was placed on the Index (decree July 26, 1907, promulgated Jan. 2, 1911); a rev. and corrected ed. of the volume appeared in 1913. B.'s dedicated scholarship gave impetus to the whole field of liturgical and historical studies. BIBLIOGRAPHY: G. Bardy, *Catholicisme* 1:1306–08 with bibliog.; J. Rivière, *Mgr. Batiffol* (1929); *idem, Le Modernisme dans l' Église* (1929); *idem,* DHGE 6:1327–30.

[R. B. ENO]

BATISTA, CÍCERO ROMÃO (1844–1934), reputed miracle worker. As pastor in Juazeiro, in a poor and isolated region of Brazil, he stirred up a religious ferment that attracted many people from the surrounding areas and gave rise to supposed miracles. The local bp. condemned the miracles (1891) and deprived B. of his pastoral faculties. B. left the area, but religious and political ferment continued for many years. BIBLIOGRAPHY: J. A. Gonsalves de Mello, NCE 2:166–167.

[H. JACK]

BATTHYÁNY, Hungarian noble family. (1) Joseph (1727–99), abp. of Gran, primate of Hungary, and cardinal. Statesman as well as prelate, Joseph played an important part in Church-Empire relations and negotiations. (2) Ignatius (1741–98), bp. of Weissenburg, Transylvania (1780), where he was distinguished as a preacher and administrator. He published several works and erected an observatory in Carlsburg. (3) Louis (1806–49), prime minister of the first modern Hungarian government (1848). He tried to maintain peace when opposition rose against the new constitution, could not control the revolutionists, resigned, and joined the national guard. He was captured by the royal army and shot as a traitor. (4) Casimir (1807–54) was foreign secretary during the brief ministry of Kossuth after Louis's resignation, and with him was exiled to Turkey when the revolution failed (1849). In 1851, he went to Paris and died there.

[H. JACK]

BATTISTA DA CREMA (c.1460–1534), religious name of the Italian Dominican and ascetical writer, Giovanni Battista Carioni. He was the spiritual director of the religious founders SS. Cajetan and Anthony Maria Zaccaria. As director of the Countess Ludovica Torelli, he lived outside the convents of his order at Guastalla, then at Milan (1529), and came under the criticism of his confreres. In his direction and writings, the most important of which is *Della cognitione et vittoria di se stesso* (1531), he taught a rigid asceticism as the way to self-knowledge and self-conquest. His expressions concerning the spiritual combat as well as the exaggerations of some interpreters led to suspicions of *Semi-Pelagianism. His works were placed on the Index by Paul IV in 1559 and on the Tridentine Index; in 1900 they were removed. Modern scholars defend his orthodoxy and emphasize his contribution to Counter-Reformation spirituality. M. *Cano translated the *Vittoria di se stesso* into Spanish. BIBLIOGRAPHY: L. Colosio, DSAM 2:153–154.

[T. C. O'BRIEN]

BATTLE, ABBEY OF, Benedictine monastery near Hastings, England. William the Conqueror founded the abbey in 1067 on the site of his victory over Harold. Battle possessed wide, but ill-defined, civil and ecclesiastical immunities. The abbey was little involved in feudalism and it retained the simplicity and regularity of its original observance well into the 13th century. It was well known for its generosity to the poor and sick. The abbey was suppressed in 1539. BIBLIOGRAPHY: R. Graham, "Monastery of Battle," *English Ecclesiastical Studies,* 29 (1929); J. Brückmann, NCE 2:167–168.

[J. R. SOMMERFELDT]

BATTLE STANDARDS CULT, the divine or quasi-divine honors accorded the emblem of the silver eagle, the official standard of the Roman legion. A symbol of the unity and strength of each legion, the standard of the eagle was entitled to offerings, anointed and garlanded on feast days, had an altar dedicated to it on the anniversary of the legion's commission, and sacrifice offered in celebration of victory. In peace time, the standards were stored at Rome in the *Aerarium* (treasury); in camp they were kept in small shrines (Cicero *Cat.* 1.9.24; Dio Cassius 40.18,1); Pliny mentions their sacred character (*Historia naturalis* 13.23) and Tacitus describes the shrine of the battle standard as an asylum (*Annals* 1.39). BIBLIOGRAPHY: H. J. Rose, OCD 875; W. Heitland, *Roman Republic* (1923) 2:366–367; A. von Domazewski, *Die Fahnen im römischen Heere* (1885).

[F. H. BRIGHAM]

BAUCH, BRUNO (1877–1942), philosopher. A professor at the Univ. of Jena (1911), he was originally interested in mathematics and science, but turned to practical ethics, the philosophy of religion, and epistemology. As a leading neo-Kantian, he sought to adjust Kant's moral and ethical theory to meet the immediate value problems of human culture. His philosophical works include *Immanuel Kant* (1917) and *Grundzüge der Ethik* (1935).

[H. JACK]

BAUDELAIRE, CHARLES PIERRE (1821–67), French poet. B. was the unwittingly spoiled son of opulent parents. Uncertainty and a pathetic possessive love in his early childhood no doubt disturbed the psychological equilibrium of his world. A devotée of the cult of art for art's sake, an aesthetic living a bohemian existence, withal an idealist, plagued by the eternal vision of the struggle between good and evil, B. spoke and sometimes sang of the unity underlying Christian literature. This sketch of B. as a potential Catholic poet is at variance with usual negative interpretations of *Les Fleurs du mal.* In 1857, the government (Second Empire) labeled the collection immoral and ordered six of its poems suppressed. The outcry against *Les Fleurs du mal* is now a muted memory. Fair critics accept the volume as an allegory of man's quest for the absolute. Experimental techniques (imagery and symbol) mingle with traditional versification. Historical setting, personal insecurity, the influence of three women in his life: these served as leaven to the basic genius of the man. B. remains a significant figure in the rise of 19th-cent. symbolistic poetry, not a mere aesthete or poseur. BIBLIOGRAPHY: J. A. Beery, "Relevance of Baudelaire to T. S. Eliot's *Waste Land,*" *Susquehanna Univ. Studies* 7, no. 5 (1966); L. P. Shanks, *Baudelaire: Flesh and Spirit* (1974).

[R. M. FUNCHION]

BAUDISSIN, WOLF WILHELM (1847–1926), scholar of Semitic religions and the OT. After obtaining a degree in theology and Oriental studies, B. taught at the universities of Marburg (1881–1900) and Berlin (1900–26). He is noted for his work in the history of Semitic religions, in which he demonstrated the close relationship between them and the OT. B. saw the Christian expectation of God's coming kingdom as the connecting point and legitimate expansion of the common Semitic view of God as the leader of his people. BIBLIOGRAPHY: O. Kaiser, NCE 2:170.

[T. M. MCFADDEN]

BAUDOUIN, FRANÇOIS (BALDWIN), (1520–c.1573), jurist and humanist. He taught law at the leading universities of Bourges (1549–55), Strasbourg (1566), Heidelberg (1556–62), Angers (1562–73). Among his friends were the humanists Budé, Charles Dumoulin, and the Genevan reformer, John Calvin, to whom B. was secretary for 3 years. Because of his vacillation between the Catholic and Reformed faiths, he was ultimately not well-received either by Protestant or by Catholic intellectuals. He must be understood as a Catholic humanist interested in the reconciliation of both faiths. BIBLIOGRAPHY: D. R. Kelley, "*Historia integra:* François Baudouin and His Conception of History," JHI 25 (1964) 35–37; J. Dedieu, DHGE 6:1426–28; E. G. Gleason, NCE 2:170.

[J. J. SMITH]

BAUDOUIN, LOUIS MARIE, VEN. (1765–1835), religious founder. Ordained in 1789, he was a curate at Luçon when he fled to Spain after refusing to sign the oath demanded by the Civil Constitution of the Clergy. In 1796, he returned to France and conducted an underground apostolate. As parish priest at Chavagnes (1802), he founded the Sons of Mary Immaculate, a congregation of priests, and later, with Gabrielle Charlotte Ranfray de la Rochette, the

Ursulines of Jesus. BIBLIOGRAPHY: P. Michaud, *Life of the Ven. Louis Marie Baudouin* (tr. W. A. Phillipson, 1914).

[H. JACK]

BAUDOUIN, MARIE JEANNE ÈVE (1889–1945), French Catholic writer, a leader in the movement to return working mothers to their families and to prepare women for civic life by a healthy feminism. She produced novels, plays, and essays, and for more than 20 years collaborated in editing *Les Amitiés françaises*. For her courageous work during the German occupation (1940–44) she was posthumously awarded the Resistance medal. BIBLIOGRAPHY: J. Morienval, *Catholicisme* 2:1313.

[M. J. SUELZER]

BAUDRAND, BARTHÉLEMY (1701–87), Jesuit spiritual writer. After the dissolution of the Society in France (1764), he devoted himself to writing and produced numerous works, which went through many editions and translations. His *L'Âme élevée à Dieu* (1765; 20 eds.) established his reputation as a spiritual writer, and his *L'Âme pénitente ou le nouveau Pensez-y bien* (1776; 30 eds.) was still being published in 1876. BIBLIOGRAPHY: H. Monier-Vinard, DSAM 1:1287–90.

[J. C. WILLKE]

BAUDRILLART, HENRI MARIE ALFRED (1859–1942), cardinal, scholar, educator, diplomat. B. was one of the leading Catholic intellectuals of 20th-cent France. As a diplomat he was instrumental in the resumption of French diplomatic relations with the Vatican in 1921; as an educator he transformed the Institut Catholique into a first class institution during his rectorship; as a scholar his most important contribution was the initiation and publication of *the Dictionnaire d'histoire et de géographie ecclésiastiques*, an important French Catholic encyclopedia in progress since 1912. Among his books should be listed *L'Église catholique, la Renaissance, le Protestantisme* which was translated into English by Mrs. Philip Gibbs as *Catholic Church, the Renaissance and Protestantism* (1908). BIBLIOGRAPHY: V. L. Bullough, NCE 2:170–171.

[V. L. BULLOUGH]

BAUDRY OF BOURGUEIL (1046–*c*.1130), poet and bp. A student of Angers he later became a Benedictine and was made abbot of Bourgueil in Vallée (1089); he was consecrated abp. of Dol (1107). B. wrote poetry—often imitating Ovid—epitaphs or metrical letters of friendship, esp. of Godfrey of Reims, and a detailed history of the First Crusade based on the *Gesta Francorum*. BIBLIOGRAPHY: Manitius 3:883–898.

[M. H. BEIRNE]

BAUER, BRUNO (1809–82), Protestant theologian and historian. Born at Eisenberg, Germany, he studied theology and philosophy at Berlin and secured a teaching post there in 1834. He was then identified with the conservative Hegelians and in 1835 and 1836 unfavorably reviewed D. F. *Strauss's *Leben Jesu*. He moved to Bonn in 1839, and his views became increasingly radical. In a work on the Gospel of John, *Kritik der evangelischen Geschichte des Johannes* (1840), he contended that John was not a work of history but of art written under the influence of Philo. Then in a study of the *Synoptics, *Kritik der evangelischen Geschichte der Synoptiker* (2 v., 1841–42), he declared that Mark also was a literary and not a historical work, with Matthew and Luke dependent on Mark. He lost his chair in 1842 and retired to Rixdorf, near Berlin, where he continued to write on historical and theological subjects. His most important historical work was *Geschichte der Politik, Kultur und Aufklärung des 18ten Jahrhunderts* (4 v., 1843–45). In 1850–51 he published a two-volume work in which he denied the historical existence of Jesus and dated the Gospels in the 2d century. He died at Rixdorf. BIBLIOGRAPHY: A. Schweitzer, *Quest for the Historical Jesus* (tr. W. Montgomery, 1961).

[T. EARLY]

BAUER, WALTER (1877–1960), NT-Greek lexicographer. B. taught NT at Göttingen (1916–45), and is best noted for his expansion and thorough revision of E. Preuschen's Greek lexicon. B. published five editions of this work, the last in 1957–58, indicating the relationship between NT-Greek words and their parallels from pre-Christian to Byzantine Greek literature. An English translation and adaptation, *Greek-English Lexicon of the NT and other Early Christian Literature* (1957), was made from B.'s fourth edition by W. F. Arndt and F. W. Gingrich. BIBLIOGRAPHY: L. F. Hartman, NCE 2:171.

[T. M. MCFADDEN]

BAUHAUS (*Das Staatliche Bauhaus*), a school of art founded (1919) at Weimar, Germany by the architect Walter Gropius to deliver art from the aestheticism and historicism of the academies. It sought to integrate art and industry, stressing craftsmanship, replacing romantic individualism by logic and efficiency. The enormous influence of the school which moved to Dessau (1925) was due to the genius of its faculty. Suppressed by the Nazis (1933), a New Bauhaus was founded in Chicago, with important members teaching at Yale and Harvard. A notable example of church architecture by a Bauhaus artist is the abbey church and monastery of St. John's, Collegeville, Minn. by Marcel Breuer. BIBLIOGRAPHY: M. Bill, "Bauhaus Idea from Weimar to Ulm," *Architectural Yearbook* 5 (1953); G. M. McClancy, NCE 2:172.

[M. J. DALY]

BÄUMER, SUITBERT (1845–94), German liturgist whose greatest influence was as liturgical consultant to Desclée, publisher in Tournai, when they published editions of the Missal, monastic Breviary and the Vulgate. Among his works of liturgical, patristic, and monastic history, the most influential was *Geschichte des Breviers* (1895) rev. and enl. in the French ed. by R. Biron (2v., 1905). BIBLIOGRAPHY: S. Mayer, *Beuroner Bibliographie, 1863–1963* (1963) 38–49.

[N. KOLLAR]

BAUMGARTNER, ALEXANDER (1841–1910), Swiss Jesuit literary critic who served on the staff of *Stimmen aus Maria-Laach* (later *Stimmen der Zeit*). He contributed extensively to this periodical and produced a 6-volume study of world literature, *Geschichte der Weltliteratur* (1897–1911). Uncompleted because of B.'s death, it treats the literature of Asia, India, and Egypt (v. 1–2), classical and Christian Greece and Rome (v. 3–4), France (v. 5), and Italy (v. 6, published posthumously). BIBLIOGRAPHY: R. J. Sealy, NCE 2:172; F. Braig, LTK 2:70.

BAUMSTARK, ANTON (1872–1948), liturgist and Orientalist of the first rank whose knowledge of literature, philology, and religious art enabled him to synthesize large areas of liturgical development. He founded the journal *Oriens Christianus* with Anton de Waal, and *Jahrbuch für Liturgiewissenschaft* with Odo Casel. In his *Liturgie Comparée* (1940) he developed a method of comparative liturgy and in *Vom geschichtlichen Werden der Liturgie* (1923) he worked out laws of liturgical evolution. His works are listed in EphemLiturg 63 (1949) 185–207. He was a married layman. BIBLIOGRAPHY: B. Neunheuser, NCE 2:172–173.

[N. KOLLAR]

BAUNARD, LOUIS PIERRE (1828–1919), French writer and hagiographer. After his ordination in 1852, he continued his studies at Rome, Lille, and the Sorbonne, and taught at Orléans. His well-researched biographies include SS. Ambrose, Madeleine-Sophie Barat, and Louise de Marillac. His most important work is *Un siècle de l'Église, 1800–1900* (1902). Other devotional works are included among his many published volumes. BIBLIOGRAPHY: C. E. Maguire, NCE 2:173; G. Marsot, *Catholicisme* 1:1319–20.

[I. M. KASHUBA]

BAUNY, ÉTIENNE (1575–1649), French Jesuit moral theologian. Two of his volumes of casuistry, written in French to assist parish priests, were placed on the Index in 1640. Propositions from one of these, the *Somme des péchés,* were singled out the following year by the Sorbonne and the Jansenists as evidence of the Jesuits' moral laxism. However Pascal's derision of B. in the *Provincial Letters* is somewhat extravagant. BIBLIOGRAPHY: Bremond Index 23.

[T. C. O'BRIEN]

BAUTAIN, LOUIS EUGÈNE MARIE (1796–1867), French philosopher and theologian. A disciple of Cousin, B.

lost his faith at an early age, but recovered it while teaching philosophy at Strasbourg (1816–28). He was ordained in 1828 and became preacher at the cathedral. Throughout his career he was involved successively in a variety of academic and ecclesiastical responsibilities. He was seminary rector, vicar general of the abp. of Paris, professor of moral theology at the Sorbonne, lecturer, preacher, founder of the Sisters of St. Louis, and author of a number of philosophical and theological works. He exerted a strong influence on French philosophy in the 19th century. Involved in philosophical controversy, B. adopted a fideistic position that brought him into conflict with ecclesiastical authority. He was required to retract six statements in 1835 and again, in modified form, in 1838. BIBLIOGRAPHY: W. M. Horton, *Philosophy of Abbé Bautain* (1926); P. Archambault, *Un essai de philosophie chrétienne aux XIXᵉ siècle: l'Abbé Louis Bautain* (1962).

BAVO, ST. (600–660), monastic founder, missionary, hermit. Member of a noble Belgian family, after his wife's death B. founded and endowed the abbey of St. Peter (St. Bavon) in Ghent of which he is a patron saint. He became a disciple of St. *Amandus with whom he traveled as a missionary in Flanders. Returning later to his abbey, he retired to a nearby hermitage where he passed the rest of his life. BIBLIOGRAPHY: H. Roeder, *Saints and Their Attributes* (1955); Butler 4:5–6; A. D'Haenens, BiblSanct 2:982–985.

[M. E. DUFFY]

BAWDEN, WILLIAM, see BALDWIN, WILLIAM.

BAXTER, RICHARD (1615–91), Puritan writer. B. was self-educated in theology, devoting special attention to scholastic theology and the teachings of *Nonconformists. He was ordained in 1638 in the C of E, but within two years had rejected *episcopacy. In parochial work at Kidderminster (1641) and in the Parliamentary army he strove for moderation of religious differences. In keeping with his convictions he rejected the bishopric of Hereford (1660) and was henceforth barred from ecclesiastical preferment. His revisions of the *Book of Common Prayer to make it more acceptable to Puritans were rejected at the Savoy Conference (1661). After the Act of Uniformity of 1662, he left the C of E and suffered harassment until the *Declaration of Indulgence in 1687. His more than 200 writings express his piety, pastoral concern, and desire for religious tolerance; *The Saints' Everlasting Rest* (1650) is a classic of devotional literature. B. also composed several well-known hymns. BIBLIOGRAPHY: H. Martin, *Puritanism and Richard Baxter* (1954); G. Nuttal, *Richard Baxter* (1965); *Practical Works of . . . Richard Baxter* (ed. W. Orme, 23 v., 1830).

[T. C. O'BRIEN]

BAY PSALM BOOK (THE WHOLE BOOKE OF PSALMS FAITHFULLY TRANSLATED INTO ENGLISH METRE), a translation of Psalms fitted to the rhythm of familiar Puritan hymns. Printed at Cambridge in the Mass. Bay Colony in 1640, it was the first book issued in English North America. As explained in the preface to the first edition, the translators, Richard Mather, John Eliot, and Thomas Welde, were attempting to bring the Psalms into increased popular use through song. There were nine editions of the Bay Psalm Book; the ninth, called the New England Book of Psalms (1698), contained annotated music. In over 100 years of use, the book was widely distributed through Puritan congregations in the New World and England. BIBLIOGRAPHY: A. M. Garrett, NCE 2:180.

[B. BLACKLAW]

BAYEUX TAPESTRY, a strip of coarse linen measuring 19 inches by 231 feet, embroidered in woolen threads of eight colors depicting 72 scenes of the Norman Conquest. Its unique survival provides a major South English work of art in an important medium. It shows the earliest representations of St. Edward the Confessor and William I, Duke of Normandy and is an extraordinary, authentic record of arms, architecture, costume, and folklore of its time. The tapestry is now in the Musée de Tapisserie, Bayeux. BIBLIOGRAPHY: J. Gourhand, NCE 2:181; F. Stenton, *Bayeux Tapestry* (1965).

[R. L. S. BRUCE- MITFORD]

BĀYEZĪD I (reigned 1389–1409), Ottoman Sultan. He beseiged Constantinople (1391–98) and laid a heavy tribute on the declining Byzantine Empire. In 1396, he was completely victorious over the Crusade of Nicopolis led by Sigismund of Hungary, and the next year he invaded Greece as far as Corinth. In 1402, however, he suffered a disastrous defeat at the hands of the Mongols under Timur (Tamerlane), was captured, and is said to have been exhibited in a cage like an animal. BIBLIOGRAPHY: Ostrogorsky 486–491, 494; CMedH² 4:765–767.

[M. R. P. McGUIRE]

BAYLE, PIERRE (1647–1706), French philosopher. Though a Protestant, he studied at the Jesuit University of Toulouse, was converted to Catholicism, then reconverted to Protestantism. After taking refuge in Geneva because of his liberal views, he taught philosophy, first at the Calvinist Academy of Sedan, then at the Univ. of Rotterdam. His first work, *Pensées sur la comète* (1682), besides ridiculing the superstition that comets presage evil, treats many themes to which he returned in later works (particularly the *Dictionnaire historique et critique,* e.g.,): condemnation of superstition, belief in a morality independent of religion, mistrust of tradition and authority, and religious tolerance. BIBLIOGRAPHY: H. Robinson, *Bayle the Sceptic* (1931); J. Delvolve, *Religion, critique et philosophique positive chez Pierre Bayle* (repr. 1971).

[A. S. CRISAFULLI]

BAYLEY, JAMES ROOSEVELT (1814–77), eighth abp. of Baltimore. Of a prominent N.Y. family and nephew of Mother Seton, the first American saint, B. studied for the ministry in the Episcopal Church and after ordination served as rector of St. Andrew's Church in Harlem. He resigned this post and went to Europe where he was received into the RC Church (1842). Ordained to the priesthood (1844), he served in administrative positions and as secretary to Abp. Hughes. Appointed first bp. of Newark, he brought in religious communities of men and women to serve the needs of the new diocese. B. attended Vatican Council I, traveled extensively, and became a well-known lecturer and writer; among his writings is a history of the Church in New York. He also showed a great interest in missions to the Indians. In 1872 he was appointed abp. of Baltimore. He is buried at St. Joseph's Convent, Emmitsburg, Maryland. BIBLIOGRAPHY: M. H. Yeager, NCE 2:182–183.

[J. HILL]

BAYLY, LEWIS (1565?–1631). Anglican bishop of Bangor, Wales. B. was chaplain to Henry, Prince of Wales, and later to James I. His chief work, *Practice of Piety,* attained 74 editions by 1821 and was translated into most European languages. Its extreme other-worldliness influenced Puritanism and Pietism. BIBLIOGRAPHY: W. Maurer, RGG 1:947–948.

[M. J. SUELZER]

BAZ, JUAN JOSÉ (1820–87), Mexican politician. Valiant soldier, effective writer, zealous liberal, and virulent anticlerical, he held various positions in the Mexican government and used his power to promote the nationalization of ecclesiastical property, the suppression of religious orders, and the secularization of priests. His long career was a sustained attack upon the Church. BIBLIOGRAPHY: L. González, NCE 2:183.

[H. JACK]

BAZAAR OF HERACLEIDES, or the Book of Heracleides, the Syriac version of the original Greek treatise of Nestorius written as a reply to Cyril of Alexandria. The original Greek was lost when the works of Nestorius were proscribed by decree of Emperor Theodosius II (435), but the entire Syriac version was preserved by a Nestorian community. The book is divided into three sections: (1) a philosophical-theological introduction and commentary on various heresies; (2) a detailed commentary on the acts of the Council of Ephesus (431); and (3) an analysis of the letter of Cyril to Acacius of Melitene. BIBLIOGRAPHY: G. R. Driver and L. Hodgson, *Bazaar of Heracleides Newly Translated from the Syriac* (1925); E. Amann, DTC 11.1.80–84. *NESTORIUS.

[F. H. BRIGHAM]

BAZAINE, JEAN (1904–), French abstract painter. His forms while nonobjective show relation to nature, revealing the essences of natural movements rather than outer appearances. Among his most notable works are the mosaics at Sacré Coeur d'Audincourt, which with Matisse's decorations at *Vence, evidence the midcentury revival of 20th-cent. church architecture enhanced by the creative discoveries of modern painting.

[T. FEIDT]

BEA, AUGUSTIN (1881–1968), Jesuit priest, later cardinal; biblicist and ecumenist. Born in Riedböhringen, Germany, near the Black Forest, he entered the Society of Jesus, 1902; did seminary studies at Valkenburg, Holland, and was ordained in 1912; and pursued higher studies in Oriental philology at the Univ. of Berlin. He was named provincial of German Jesuits, 1921, and subsequently professor at the Pontifical Gregorian University, Rome. From 1928 he was professor for OT at the Pontifical Biblical Institute, Rome; during his tenure there B. was rector 1930–49 and editor of the scholarly journal *Biblica,* 1931–51, to which he contributed numerous studies. In 1959 John XXIII appointed B. to the college of cardinals to head the *Secretariat for Promoting Christian Unity. B's success in organizing the Secretariat and making it a focal point for Christian unity won him international esteem. BIBLIOGRAPHY: R. A. F. MacKenzie, "Augustin Bea (1881–1968)," *Biblica* 49 (1968) 453–456.

[C. P. CEROKE]

BEAD, a small, perforated globule of wood, metal, glass, or other hard material, which when strung together with others is used to count prayers, as in the recitation of the rosary. In its earlier form the word was spelled "bede" which meant prayer. From this it was transferred to the counters used to number the prayers said. BIBLIOGRAPHY: OED 1:724.

[J. C. WILLKE]

BEADLE, an official whose duty in former times was to go before a bishop or other dignitary. He bore a mace or wand to clear the way and to preserve order. The term was also applied to a parish functionary charged with the suppression of disorder at church services and the execution of orders given at vestry meetings.

[J. C. WILLKE]

BEARD. Ancient tradition requires that all Orthodox and Eastern Catholic clergy wear beards. Till the 16th cent. shaving was condemned by the Orthodox Church as effeminate and contradicting the Mosaic law. This is no longer enforced among Eastern clergy living in Western countries.

[F. WILCOCK]

BEARDSLEY, AUBREY VINCENT (1872–98), masterly draftsman, illustrator, and writer whose exotic, sensual, morbidly beautiful images rooted in Art Nouveau, Japanese, and Greek styles express his cynical rebellion against the middle-class values of English society. His 20 illustrations for *Morte d'Arthur* (1893) in an early pre-Raphaelite style brought him immediate fame. Illustrating Pope, Wagner, and Oscar Wilde's *Salomé* (1894), his output—phenomenal

for so short a life—was continuously published from his death until 1925 and today enjoys a fresh revival. BIBLIOGRAPHY: A. E. Gallatin, *Aubrey Beardsley: Catalogue of Drawings* (1945).

[M. J. DALY]

BEATIANS (Ger. *Beatianer*), the followers of a Lutheran preacher, Johann Saliger (Seliger, Ger. for *beatus*). The founder taught that bread and wine were really changed into the body and blood of Christ in the Holy Eucharist and that original sin is identical with human nature and therefore Christ did not have a human nature specifically like that of other men. Congregations of Beatians existed at Lübeck and Rostock only from 1569 to *c*.1600. BIBLIOGRAPHY: K. Algermissen, LTK 2:84.

[T. C. O'BRIEN]

BEATIFIC VISION, the heavenly face-to-face seeing of God "as he really is" (1 Jn 3.2). A Greek patristic tradition represents it as a glorious theophany; to Latin theology, however, it is a direct and immediate insight into the divine essence with no mediating image or concept, enjoyed by the mind strengthened by the light of glory *(lumen gloriae).* Less specifically considered, it includes all the elements of man's final happiness: his beholding the blessed Trinity; his love in an eternal response to God's eternal love for him; the torrent of delight which follows; the praise and thanksgiving which well up; and the sharing of all this in the company of the blessed. The key to this bliss, on the part of the one who partakes of it, is an act of mind, not of will, as it is in every joy: such is the view of St. Thomas Aquinas. A man is happy when he has what he wants, but he "has" it through some kind of knowing. Love is necessary for happiness, but it is the presence of what is loved that makes us happy. Delight follows but the possession or "holding" is ensured only in cognition. "And eternal life is this: to know you, the only true God, and Jesus Christ whom you have sent." (Jn 17.3).

No created intellect can understand God in the way God understands himself, and so the vision is not comprehensive. Why, then, should one think of paradise as an instant and ultimate stop? Wonder will go on forever. God's perfections will be seen, now in this way, now in that, his goodness appreciated ever anew and always more profoundly and deliciously, but never completely. "We teach what Scripture calls: the things that no eye has seen and no ear has heard, things beyond the mind of man, all that God has prepared for those who love him." (1 Cor 2.9). BIBLIOGRAPHY: J. Pieper, *Happiness and Contemplation* (1966); M. J. Redle, NCE 2:186–193; ThAq ST la, 12, 1–11 (esp. in ed. Lat-Eng v.3, ed. H. McCabe); *ibid.* v.1 *Introduction* (ed. T. Gilby, 1964).

[T. R. HEATH]

BEATIFICATION, see CANONIZATION AND BEATIFICATION.

BEATIFICATION (CANONIZATION), EQUIPOLLENT OR EQUIVALENT, a procedure in which some steps of the beatification or canonization processes now normally used in the RC Church are bypassed. This procedure has been most frequently used in cases in which there has been a continuous cult of individuals as saints or blessed, but who lived in such remote times in the past that the normal investigative steps cannot be undertaken with any reasonable hope of discovering new evidence of their holiness of life. In this situation the Holy See may elect simply to confirm the cult and leave the venerated persons in possession of the title they have so long enjoyed in fact. This confirmation is known as an equipollent beatification or canonization, but it is not entirely equivalent to normal beatification or canonization because it lacks the Church's guarantee that the person so canonized or beatified was as holy as he is reputed to have been. *CANONIZATION AND BEATIFICATION.

[P. K. MEAGHER]

BEATING OF THE BOUNDS, a ceremony practiced in medieval England in connection with Rogationtide processions. Beginning c.900 when maps were rare, parishioners were reminded of the location of parish bounds by the practice in which the bounds were beaten with willow rods. The custom has died out in modern times.

[T. EARLY]

BEATITUDE, see HAPPINESS.

BEATITUDES (IN THE BIBLE), a form found frequently to express God's favor upon a person for a specific virtue or for faithfulness in general. Beatitudes usually have three parts: the proclamation of blessedness, the reason for it, and the consequent reward. In the OT, beatitudes are found mainly in the Psalms and Wisdom literature, where they are usually connected with the nearness of Yahweh granted to one who is faithful to the law. In the NT, the Apocalypse begins and ends (1.3; 22.7) with a statement of blessedness for those who keep its prophecies, but the most important NT example of this literary form is Mt 5.3–12 and Lk 6.20–26. The eight beatitudes found in Mt are joined to particular moral virtues such as poverty, meekness, or mercifulness; they stress an interior disposition and the reward mentioned is eschatological—the full realization of the kingdom of heaven. The first of these proclamations reveals the scope of the other seven: the person who is poor in spirit, i.e., the 'ānāwîm Yahweh of the OT—those who are materially destitute and who thereby acknowledge their radical dependence upon God—shall receive the kingdom. To each of the other beatitudes a reward, in fact equivalent to possession of the kingdom but corresponding to the particular virtue, is attached. Thus Mt's listing stressing moral virtues and an eschatological perspective, must be seen as an exhortation to perfection and a preface to the Sermon on the Mount.

The form is changed in Lk who lists only four beatitudes but adds four maledictions. His emphasis is less eschatological and more social: those who are unhappy in this life will obtain an eternal reward; the scandal of the rich man's prosperity will be overturned. Nevertheless, the conclusion of both accounts is the messianic message of Jesus—the salvation of the afflicted foretold by Isaiah is at hand. Thus, within their paradoxical form, the beatitudes espouse a revolution whereby the conventional values of wealth and power are replaced by dependence upon God, poverty, and loving service. BIBLIOGRAPHY: W. D. Davies, *Setting for the Sermon on the Mount* (1964; abridged ed. 1966); J. Dupont, *Les Béatitudes* (1958); JBC 2:69–70, 135–136; J. A. Grassi, NCE 2:193–195.

[T. M. MCFADDEN]

BEATITUDES, Jesus' pronouncements (Mt 5.3–12; Lk 6.20–26) interpreted in theology to mean qualities of the Christian that bear special promise of blessedness *(beatitudo);* more restrictively, the more excellent actions of Christian life that fulfill Evangelical *Counsels. Classical theological sources on the beatitudes are St. Augustine's *De sermone Domini in monte* (PL 34, 1229–1308) and St. Thomas Aquinas's systematic correlation of them with the *virtues and the gifts of the *Holy Spirit (ST 1a2ae.69). Blessedness, the share in God's own life (ST 1a2ae.110,1), is the consummation and reward of living in grace; the beatitudes are qualities of the Christian life of singular merit relative to the many facets of the divine reward. The promises receive fulfillment fully in eternal life but partially even in the present. As lived expressions of the orientations of grace, the beatitudes consist in virtuous actions, but esp. in actions corresponding to the gifts of the Holy Spirit. Directly prompted by the Holy Spirit, such actions in their sure direction and intensity excel the exercise of the virtues; they have as well the experiential quality associated with blessedness (ST 1a.26,1). A pattern of correspondence can be drawn between the specific beatitudes and the gifts: between the peacemakers and wisdom; the pure of heart and understanding; those who mourn and knowledge; the poor in spirit and fear of the Lord; the merciful and counsel; the meek and piety; those who hunger and thirst for justice and courage. But the number both of the beatitudes and the gifts is symbolic; in meaning they apply to the many and rich complexities found in Christian living. The schematization has also served in theology to trace the marks of a life bent upon a more intense striving for evangelical perfection. That does not restrict the applicability of the beatitudes; even as the gifts of the Holy Spirit are necessary for salvation (ST 1a2ae.68,2), so also survival in grace for every Christian from time to time depends on fulfilling the gospel ideal expressed in one or other of the beatitudes. BIBLIOGRAPHY:

L. M. Martinez, *Sanctifier* (tr. M. Aquinas, 1957); A. Royo and J. Aumann, *Theology of Christian Perfection* (1962).

[T. C. O'BRIEN]

BEATON (BETHUNE), name of a Scottish family, three representatives of which had prominent parts in religious and political events at the close of the pre-Reformation era in Scotland.

James (1473–1539), abp. of Glasgow (1509–22), primate and abp. of St. Andrews (1522–39). He was educated at St. Andrews, was made abbot of Dunfermline in 1504, and was one of the regents (1513–26) during the minority of James V. He opposed the spread of the new religious doctrines that were gaining strength throughout the nation and a number of the reformers (among them Patrick *Hamilton) were put to death for heresy. Beaton was much embroiled in politics and appears to have been somewhat insensitive to the abuses existing in the Church in Scotland.

David (c.1494–1546), nephew of James (above), who succeeded his uncle as abp. of St. Andrews in 1539. He also was implicated in political affairs and made a strong but unsuccessful bid for the regency upon the death of James V (1542). His influence was important in the frustration of Henry VIII's hope of subjugating Scotland. Much of the intermittent persecution of heretics was attributed to him and he became esp. unpopular because of the condemnation and execution of G. Wishart (1546), and he was assassinated not long afterwards. He had been made the first Scottish cardinal in 1538.

James (1517–1603), nephew of Card. David Beaton and last RC abp. of Glasgow (from 1552). He was an adviser to Queen Mother Mary of Guise and an opponent to the new religious teachings. He saw more clearly than David or the earlier James the need for reform in the Scottish Church, issuing decrees that called for better preaching and the repair of churches and condemned pluralism and concubinage among the clergy, but it was already too late. He fled to France a few months before the new reformed religious settlement (1560), taking with him valuable records and treasures of his diocese. The rest of his life was spent in France where he served as ambassador for Mary Queen of Scots and James VI. BIBLIOGRAPHY: G. Donaldson, *Scottish Reformation* (1960); F. W. Maitland, "Anglican Settlement and the Scottish Reformation," *Selected Historical Essays* (1967).

[V. SAMPSON]

BEATRICE d'ESTE, BL. Two women bearing this name have received veneration for their sanctity. (1) Beatrice, daughter of Azzo VI d'Este and Leonara of Savoy (1191–1226), but orphaned at 6, she entered the convent St. Margaret at Solarola at 14 and later with some companions established a Benedictine foundation in a deserted monastery near Gemolo. (2) Beatrice, daughter of Azzo VII d'Este and Joan of Apulia (1230–62) entered the convent at St. Lazarus shortly after Galeazzo Manfredi, Duke of Vicenza, chosen by her family to be her husband, died of wounds. She was the niece of the older Beatrice and followed her into the Benedictines. BIBLIOGRAPHY: D. Balboni, Bibl-Sanct 2:995–997.

[N. G. WOLF]

BEATRICE OF NAZARETH (c.1200–68), Flemish Cistercian and spiritual writer. B. entered religious life at 17 and eventually became prioress. From her earliest days she kept a diary that contained her ascetical and mystical experiences, and short essays on spiritual topics. She had special devotion to the Sacred Heart, esp. associated with the idea of reparation. Given to excessive penances, often ill, her writings show touches of morbidity, yet they are important as sources of information on the speculative mysticism practiced by the Beguines at the beginning of the flowering of Flemish spirituality. BIBLIOGRAPHY: J. Verbillon, NCE 2:197; J. Van Mierlo, DSAM 1:1310–14.

[M. E. ALLWEIN]

BEATRICE OF TUSCANY (c.1015–76), noblewoman. As the ruler of strategically located lands in northern Italy with a strong anti-imperial tradition, she and her family supported Gregory VII in his conflict with Emperor Henry IV. BIBLIOGRAPHY: Mann 6:189–190 and *passim;* C. E. Boyd, NCE 2:198.

[J. MULDOON]

BEATUS, ST., a name under which two persons have been honored: (1) Beatus of Switzerland, claimed by a late legend to have been a Gallic disciple of St. Peter. He settled in the Lake Thun region and has been called the Apostle of Switzerland, although no evidence suggests that Christianity penetrated into that region in the 1st century. Opinion differs as to whether such a person really existed. Some think his *vita* is simply a variant of that of Beatus of Vendôme; others, that it is legendary embroidery that accumulated about the name of a real person, possibly a British or Irish missionary of the 6th century. See Butler 2:259; G. B. Villiger, Bibl-Sanct 2:988–989. (2) Beatus of Vendôme, a somewhat better authenticated personage, supposedly an Italian by birth, who settled either at Laon or at Vendôme, lived in a cave, and died at an advanced age in the 3d or 4th century. BIBLIOGRAPHY: Butler 2:259; G. Bataille, BiblSanct 2:989.

[J. L. GRASSI]

BEATUS OF LIÉBANA (fl. 8th cent.), Spanish monk who, with the young Bp. Eterius of Osma, composed (785) a lengthy apologia of his faith and culture against the declining primacy of the adoptionist Bp. Elipandus of Toledo. The work, which displays a knowledge of philosophy and theology, was known in Mozarab Córdoba in 850. B.'s long 12-book *Commentary on the Apocalypse,* taken from earlier authors, was copied in many MSS famous for colorful illustrations. Thirty extant MSS (9th-13th cent.) showing Celtic, Coptic, and Mozarabic influences greatly determined

Romanesque sculpture at *Vezelay, *Saint-Benoît-sur-Loire, and *Moissac. Noteworthy are the Beatus *Apocalypse of Saint-Sever, Paris, and that in the Morgan Library, New York City. BIBLIOGRAPHY: É. Mâle, *L'Art religieux du XIIᵉ siècle en France* (1947); M. R. James, *Apocalypse in Art* (1951); J. Pérez de Urbel, DHGE 7:89–90; M. J. Daly, NCE 2:198.

[E. P. COLBERT; M. J. DALY]

BEATUS OF TRIER, ST. (fl. 7th cent.), hermit and priest. According to local tradition B. and his brother Bantus—also a priest—were renowned for holiness and lived and died near Trier. The earliest reference to B. as a saint is found in a 10th-cent. psalter. BIBLIOGRAPHY: G. M. Fusconi, BiblSanct 2:747–748.

[H. DRESSLER]

BEAUCHAMP, RICHARD (d. 1481), bp. of Salisbury, England. Doctor of canon law at Oxford by 1442, he served as lawyer, chancery clerk, and royal chaplain, becoming bp. of Hereford (1448–50) and then of Salisbury (1450–81). As bp. he successfully reasserted episcopal jurisdiction over the city of Salisbury (1465–74), built a chantry chapel, and was instrumental in procuring the canonization of Osmund, the founder of Old Sarum. As Dean of Windsor (1478), he was also master and surveyor of St. George's chapel there. BIBLIOGRAPHY: Emden Ox 1:137–138.

[L. E. BOYLE]

BEAUDENOM, LÉOPOLD (c. 1840–1916), ascetical writer and spiritual director. Poor health kept B. from fulfilling his desire to be a missionary, so he spent most of his priestly life as chaplain to the Ursulines at Beaulieu and other communities, and in writing. His works, which appeared anonymously, fall into two groups and contain his plan for a life of intimacy with Christ; the first group contains works on the very foundation of sanctity and the second centers on the person of Christ. B. acknowledged the basics of his plan derived from his former exposure to Ignatian and Salesian spirituality. BIBLIOGRAPHY: A. Boucher, DSAM 1:1315–19.

[M. E. ALLWEIN]

BEAUDUIN, LAMBERT (1873–1960), Belgian liturgist and ecumenist. Ordained in 1897, B. joined (1899) the Aumôniers du Travail, a priests' society for the care of workmen, and in 1906 became a Benedictine. His address, "The liturgy should be democratized," at the Malines National Congress of Catholic Action (1909) marked the beginning of the modern liturgical movement. In the same year, he began *La Vie liturgique* (since 1911 *Les Questions liturgiques*). Five years later, he wrote the manifesto of the liturgical movement: *La piété de l'Église* (1914). In 1925 his ecumenical interest led him to found the monastery "de l'Union" in Amay (Liège) and the review *Irénikon*. He came under a cloud in consequence of his condemnation by a Roman tribunal in 1931 and was sent to the Abbey of En-Calcat. But his activities continued; a retreat preached to the French clergy (1942) resulted in the formation of the Centre de Pastorale Liturgique in Paris. In 1950 he returned to Amay, and under Pope John XXIII, who held him in great esteem, his ecumenical methods and ideas found favor. BIBLIOGRAPHY: A. G. Martimort, "Dom Lambert Beauduin et le Centre de Pastorale Liturgique," *Maison-Dieu* 62 (1960) 10–17; S. A. Quitslund, *Beauduin, a Prophet Vindicated* (1973).

[N. KOLLAR]

BEAUFORT, HENRY (c. 1374–1447), English cardinal, half-brother of Henry IV, who dominated politics for 40 years. He opposed Lollards at home, Hussites abroad. Bp. of Lincoln (1398), of Winchester (1404), cardinal (1417), papal legate (1418), H. was three times chancellor of England. BIBLIOGRAPHY: L. B. Radford, *Henry Beaufort, Bishop, Chancellor, Cardinal* (1908); Emden Camb 46–49; Emden Ox 1:139–142.

[F. D. BLACKLEY]

BEAUFORT, MARGARET (1443–1509), countess of Richmond, and mother of King Henry VII. Noted for her piety, she became a munificent patron of education. She established professorships in theology at Oxford and Cambridge, completed Henry VI's foundation of God's House, Cambridge, and founded St. John's College. BIBLIOGRAPHY: C. D. Ross, NCE 2:200–201; E. M. G. Routh, *Lady Margaret* (1924).

[C. D. ROSS]

BEAULIEU, ABBEY OF, Cistercian monastery founded by King John in 1203 near Southampton, England. Beaulieu was richly endowed and built. Its abbots were commissioned with royal and important missions. It was suppressed in 1538. The refectory of the abbey is now the village church, and many other buildings are still in existence. BIBLIOGRAPHY: S. F. Hockey, NCE 2:201; J.-M. Canivez, DHGE 7:181–183.

[S. A. HEENEY]

BEAULIEU-SUR-DORDOGNE, CHURCH OF, French Romanesque church. The unusual, dynamic S portal (1120–30) in Languedoc style with Burgundian influence inspired by Moissac shows in the tympanum a gigantic, powerful Christ as Judge of the World. Below are unsophisticated, apocalyptic images of the damned disappearing into the maw of hell, while the saved are engagingly clasped to Abraham's bosom. BIBLIOGRAPHY: P. Deschamps, *French Sculpture of the Romanesque Period* (1930).

[M. J. DALY]

BEAUMARCHAIS, PIERRE-AUGUSTIN CARON DE (1732–1799), French dramatist, polemicist, and man of many talents. B. is best known for two plays, *Le Barbier de*

Séville (1775) and *Le Mariage de Figaro* (1778, produced in 1784). Both are comedies of intrigue, featuring a type of resourceful, intelligent, and witty servant and satirizing existing social abuses. In the *Barbier,* Figaro helps his master, Count Almaviva, win the hand of Rosine; in the *Mariage,* he defends himself successfully against Almaviva's efforts to seduce Suzanne, his fiancée. Figaro represents B. in his experiences and his attacks against the aristocracy. The *Mariage* is considered a presage of the French Revolution. BIBLIOGRAPHY: R. Thomasset, *Beaumarchais écrivain et aventurier* (1966); P. Frischauer, *Beaumarchais* (1935, repr. 1970); J. Sungolowsky, *Beaumarchais* (1974).

[A. S. CRISAFULLI]

BEAUNE, RENAUD DE (1527–1606), French archbishop. B. became bp. of Mende (1568), abp. of Bourges (1581), and held political posts in Paris 1555–73. He was one of the first bps. to support Henry IV, who showed his gratitude by making B. court chaplain and commander of the Order of the Holy Spirit. B. pronounced the absolution when Henry abjured heresy (1593) but on terms that were less than satisfactory to Rome. As a reward for standing by Henry in his subsequent difficulties with the pope, B. was appointed abp. of Sens (1594), but despite his attempts to occupy the see, the appointment was not confirmed by Rome until 1602. BIBLIOGRAPHY: E. Chartraire, DHGE 7:223–225.

[H. JACK]

BEAUNEVEA, ANDRÉ, (fl. 1360–1403), French sculptor and painter. His fame arises not only from *Froissart's reference to him as the greatest sculptor of his time, but also from such surviving works as the St. Denis tombs (Kings Philip VI, John the Good, and Charles VI) and miniatures executed for the Duc de Berry. BIBLIOGRAPHY: J. Porcher, *French Miniatures from Illuminated Manuscripts* (1960); P. Vitry and G. Brière. *L'église abbatiale de S. Denis et ses tombeaux* (1948).

[S. D. MURRAY]

BEAUVAIS, CATHEDRAL OF, famous Cathedral of St.-Pierre, begun *c.*1247, constructed in French Gothic rayonnant style of great refinement and elegance, with emphasis on extreme slenderness and linearity, the "disappearance" of walls and supports in a skeletal architecture effected by a system *(en délit)* in which stones placed vertically are used with horizontal courses for tension, and with subtlety and elegance thrusts become, in paradox, members in balance. Beauvais—colossal in scale, magnificent, with vast aisles, great height, stone tracery open as lace giving abundant light—through excessive frailty collapsed several times.

Milon de Nanteuil raised at Beauvais the highest Gothic vaults (158 feet) in 1272, but all collapsed except the apse in 1284. Rebuilt with new support were the choir, the transept which Martin Chambige completed *c.*1530, seven chapels, and Jean Vaast's openwork spire (500 feet high) which collapsed in 1573. The 13th- to 16th-cent. stained glass of the windows is famous, as are tapestries depicting the lives of SS. Peter and Paul. The Beauvais tapestry industry was stimulated by royal establishment there under Louis XIV (1664). BIBLIOGRAPHY: H. Focillon, *Art of the West* (1963) v. 2.

[M. J. DALY]

BEAUVILLIER, MARIE DE (1574–1657), reform abbess. At an early age she became a Benedictine at Beaumont. Her brother-in-law obtained for her the abbey of Montmartre, but she arrived (1598) to find spiritual and material chaos. Hers was the first reform of Benedictine nuns. Montmartre became a model community and the reform spread to other abbeys. BIBLIOGRAPHY: G. Marsot, *Catholicisme* 1:1364–65.

[H. JACK]

BEBEL, HEINRICH (1472–1518), German humanist. For over 20 years he taught rhetoric and poetry at Tübingen where Altenstaig, Melanchthon, and John Eck were among his pupils. His *Oratio de laudibus Germaniae* (1504) on the *Germania* of Tacitus gave expression to the national consciousness of the German people. An accomplished Latinist, he wrote *Ars versificandi* (1506); he also published satires on clerical life and the moral decadence of his day.

[J. E. LYNCH]

BEC, ABBEY OF *(Le Bec-Hellouin),* Benedictine monastery originally situated on the banks of the Bec Brook and founded by a Norman knight, Herluin (1040). Lanfranc, who had become a famous lecturer, went to Bec (*c.*1042); he attracted many scholars who were intrigued by his learning as well as by the zeal of Herluin. Lanfranc and Anselm (future Doctor of the Church) served terms as prior of Bec and exerted a profound influence on church history and the progress of theological learning. In 1077 Lanfranc (abp. of Canterbury) consecrated a new abbey church; in 1078 following the death of Herluin, Anselm was named abbot. After the devastation of Bec during The Hundred Years' War with England, the abbey was restored by the Congregation of St. Maur. However it subsequently suffered destruction at the hands of revolutionaries. The most recent reconstruction was effected under the Olivetan Benedictines who restored Benedictine life at Bec in 1948. BIBLIOGRAPHY: A. Porée, *Histoire de l'abbaye du Bec* (1901); D. Knowles, "Bec and Its Great Men," DownRev (1934) 567–585; B. Heurtebize, DHGE 7:325–335.

[C. KEENAN]

BECANUS, MARTIN (1563–1624), Jesuit theologian and controversialist. Born in Holland, he taught successively at Cologne, Würzburg, Mainz, and Vienna and was a leading theologian of his time. A prolific writer, he opposed Protestant teachings with a calm and clear exposition of Catholic doctrine. His works include *controversia anglicana de potes-*

tate regis et pontificis (1612) and *Manuale controversiarum* (1623). In 1620 he became confessor to Emperor Ferdinand II. BIBLIOGRAPHY: E. Lamalle, DHGE 7:341–344; J. Brucker, DTC 2.1:521–523.

[H. JACK]

BECCARIA, CESARE BONESANA, Marquis of (1738–94), criminologist and economist. He was educated by the Jesuits at Parma and at the Univ. of Padua, lived in the full stream of the Enlightenment, and when only 26 years of age published *Tratto dei delitti e delle pene* (1764), which anticipated the reforms of utilitarianism, attacked savage procedures and penalties, and was translated into 22 languages, It was praised by Voltaire, Bentham, and Romilly, and is one of the most influential volumes on criminal procedure ever produced. BIBLIOGRAPHY: C. Phillipson, *Three Criminal Law Reformers* (1923); M. T. Maestro, *Voltaire and Beccaria as Reformers of Criminal Law* (1942).

BECERRA TANCO, LUIS (1602–72), Mexican scholar and historian of the Church of Mexico. B. was distinguished in the fields of mathematics, physics, chemistry, and linguistics. He was also a noted poet, preacher, and philosopher at the Univ. of Mexico. He was ordained in 1631 and labored in the Archdiocese of Mexico. His writings are an important source of information about the apparitions of Our Lady of Guadalupe. *Origen milagroso del Santuario de Nuestra Sēnora de Guadalupe,* published in 1666, was reissued in an enlarged edition in 1675 and has been reprinted many times. As a Christian historian, B. is noted primarily for his research on these apparitions of Mary. BIBLIOGRAPHY: J. A. Magner, NCE 2:211; *Diccionario Porrúa (Historia, biografía y geografía de Mexico,* 1970) 243.

[D. M. HUGHES]

BECHE, JOHN, BL. (Thomas Marshall; d. 1539), Benedictine abbot. Educated at Oxford, he became abbot at Chester and then at Colchester. In 1534 he signed the Act of Supremacy but, when Henry ordered the suppression of the monastery in 1538, he refused to submit and was accused of denying royal supremacy. Imprisoned in the Tower, he retracted this denial and begged for his life. Sent back to Colchester for trial, he apparently repented his retraction, was condemned and executed. BIBLIOGRAPHY: C. Testore, BiblSanct 2:1004–05.

[H. JACK]

BECKER, CHRISTOPHER (1875–1937), German Salvatorian missionary. He served as prefect apostolic in Assam, India, from 1905 until he was expelled from India during World War I. In 1922, B. founded the Medical Mission Institute of Würzburg. He taught missiology at the Univ. of Würzburg and made important contributions to the study of missions in his writings.

[H. JACK]

BECKER, THOMAS ANDREW (1832–99), writer, theologian, first bp. of Wilmington, Del., sixth bp. of Savannah, Ga. He was born in Pittsburgh, Pa., of Protestant parents, but came to be interested in Catholicism while attending the Univ. of Virginia. Becoming a RC in 1853, he began his studies for the priesthood at the College of the Propaganda in Rome. Ordained at St. John Lateran, he was assigned to St. Peter's, Richmond, Va. He was arrested for failing to say prayers for the Union cause. Upon his release he was appointed to teach dogma at Mt. St. Mary's College, Emmitsburg, Md. When the See of Wilmington was erected in 1868 B. was appointed first bishop. As ordinary of the diocese he became discouraged with lack of progress but remained in this post until 1886 when he was transferred to the Diocese of Savannah, where he served until his death. Among his writings are *Catholic Miscellany* and a prayerbook *Vade mecum.* He worked with other theologians to prepare for the second Council of Baltimore (1866) and assisted Card. Gibbons in preparing for the Third Plenary Council (1884). He was among the first to support the creation of a national Catholic university and he advocated the formation of labor unions among workers. BIBLIOGRAPHY: E. B. Carley, NCE 2:212; T. J. Peterman, *Thomas A. Becker, D. D. First Bishop of Wilmington* (The Catholic Univ. of America, 1976).

[J. HILL]

BECKET, THOMAS, ST., (*c.*1118–70), abp., martyr. London-born, B. was a protegé of Abp. Theobald of Canterbury, who made him archdeacon and recommended him to Henry II as chancellor (1154). A staunch servant of the crown and comrade of the King, he was unwillingly elected abp. of Canterbury at Henry's instigation (1162). Changing his life, B. resigned the chancellorship and clashed with the king over ecclesiastical rights, esp. the answerability of "criminous clerks" to secular courts. His opposition to the Constitutions of Clarendon (1164) forced his exile to France. He excommunicated royal supporters, but Pope Alexander II refused the ban against Henry. A tentative reconciliation collapsed, and Henry's denunciation of the "turbulent priest" caused the abp.'s murder in Canterbury Cathedral (Dec. 29, 1170). B. was canonized in 1173, his cult spread throughout Europe, and hundreds of miracles were soon reported at his tomb. BIBLIOGRAPHY: R. Winston, *Thomas Becket* (1967); M. D. Knowles, NCE 2:212–214.

[W. A. CHANEY]

BECKETT, SAMUEL (1906–   ), Irish-born writer who has become a major author of the French New Novel and Theatre of the Absurd. Of Protestant background and educated in modern languages at Trinity College, Dublin, B. held academic posts in Paris and Ireland before settling permanently in France. He wrote his early works like *Murphy* (1938) and *Watt* (1958), in English, but since World War II his novels (*Molloy,* 1951; *Malone Dies,* 1951; *Unnamable,* 1953; *How It Is,* 1961), the 13 *Nouvelles et Textes pour* *rien* (1955) and his major plays (*Waiting for Godot,* 1952; *Endgame,* and *Act without Words,* 1957; and *Krapp's Last Tape,* 1959) were first composed in French and afterwards translated by B. himself into English. Often cast in allegorical forms, anti-realistic in plot and mood, with characters akin to clown types, and ranging in style from farce to lyricism, these works abound in philosophical questions, theological themes, and religious motifs. B. depicts the plight of post-existentialist man; he is alienated in a universe from which God is absent, wrestling to grasp the transcendentals of Self, Time, and Space through the medium of language, which itself is disintegrating; he ultimately finds himself, immobilized and destitute, in a barren limbo where symbols of hope may exist amid general despair.

[G. E. GINGRAS]

BECKINGTON, THOMAS, see BEKYNTON, THOMAS.

BECKMANN, MAX (1884–1950), German painter, pupil at the Art School of Weimar (1899), teacher at the Frankfurter Art School (1925), B. visited Paris frequently, was in Holland during World War II, came to America (1947), where he taught at Washington Univ., St. Louis, Mo., and the Brooklyn Museum Art School, New York. Until 1915 B. painted in an Impressionistic style, but changed to an Expressionistic deformation, intensified by a veristic realism, under the influence of the group *Der Sturm*. After 1930 B.'s paintings attain monumental forms. As with many German artists in the chaotic years between the World Wars I and II, B.'s subjects interpret the situation of man and his state of mind. B. related the space problems of his compositions to man's struggle for existence. He considered painting an existential action through which life and art are related. BIBLIOGRAPHY: L. G. Buchheim, *Max Beckmann* (1959).

[P. H. HEFTING]

BECOMING, in the literal sense of coming into being, a generic term for any process towards existence or a new mode of existence. In classic Greek philosophy the various ways of becoming or change came to be classified (substantial, quantitative, qualitative etc.), but in a sense the rudimentary difference between "becoming" and "being" was central to the development of Greek philosophy. Earlier responses were extremes. The first is *Parmenides' denial of becoming: coming to be implies prior non-being; since from nothing comes nothing, the idea of becoming is contradictory. *Heraclitus, at least as he is known through Plato and Aristotle, denied stable reality, being; all is in flux, always coming to be and passing away. Plato separated sense and mind, becoming and being. The senses perceive only becoming, only continuously changing appearances and can bring only error-prone knowledge; mind, rising above and turning away from sense knownedge, reaches certain truth by sharing in the archetypal, stable being of the Ideas. Aristotle gave to the problem of being and becoming the solution of his distinction between poten-

tial being and actual being. Thus becoming does not imply an antecedent absolute nothingness, but an actual being in which there is a potentiality to another actualization or mode of actualization. What comes into being thus passes from potentiality to actuality; becoming is that process; it requires a constant potential subject and has its term in a new actualization. A further dimension of the distinction between being and becoming is evidenced in Plato's theory of Ideas and the supreme Idea, the Good; in Aristotle's postulating a system of gradually less changeable movers and finally a first unmoved mover; in the emanationism deriving from *Plotinus (see NEOPLATONISM). These positions imply that the world of becoming is a world of multiplicity, of descending concretion in materialization; and that the world of becoming presupposes a world of perfection, unity, simple and unlimited perfection.

In the history of Christian thought early patristic writings took as a major task the exclusion from the godhead of any form of becoming; this was primarily an asertion that God is not caused and that in him there is no imperfection (see also AGENNĒTOS). In classic Catholic systematic theology Aristotle's explanation of becoming as the actualization of a prior potentiality served to articulate key theological themes. The divine transcendence over any form of becoming, whether in the divine attributes or the divine knowledge and causality, is expressed in the *via negativa* that disciplines theological statements. The distinctiveness of the divine act of creation is expressed by contrast with the meaning of becoming: creation does not involve a prior potentiality to existence, but the divine power to bring a total being into existence *ex nihilo*. For created being becoming is a condition of creatureliness, and implies constant dependence on the divine causality. Such classic theological positions have been put aside by *process theology. The question of divine transcendence and causal immanence is given a new solution: the distinction between the antecedent, absolute divine nature and the consequent, processual divine nature. The first seems in fact to be a mental matrix for the logic of the process system. The second is process, and process is the constitutive of the real. Process thought maintains that it surmounts the distinction between potentiality and actuality as well as the stricturer of the principle of contradiction.

[T. C. O'BRIEN]

BECON, THOMAS (*c.* 1513–67), Protestant divine, who wrote also under the name of Thomas Basille. A Norfolk man, educated at St. John's College, Cambridge, and a "diligent hearer" of Hugh Latimer, he was in trouble as a Protestant under Henry VIII. With the accession of Edward VI he enjoyed the favor of Cranmer and the Protector Somerset. On the accession of Mary he was imprisoned and ejected from his living; he repaired to Strassburg and Frankfurt. On that of Elizabeth he was installed as canon of Canterbury. A Lutheran, moderate in tone to begin with, he became more of a Zwinglian and, it is said, rather coarser.

BIBLIOGRAPHY: D. S. Bailey, *Thomas Becon and the Reformation of the Church of England* (1952).

[T. GILBY]

BEDA, THE (Collegio Beda; The College of St. Bede at Rome). At one time in the mid-19th cent. a part of the English College at Rome, it was gradually separated from that institution and in 1917 became independent. The Beda has a special mission for ex-Anglican ministers and late vocations.

BEDDGELERT MONASTERY, a Celtic foundation in Caernarvonshire, Wales, established in the 6th century. It later became Augustinian, possibly at the end of the 12th cent., and after a time was granted to the Benedictine Abbey of Bisham. It was dissolved in 1536. BIBLIOGRAPHY: J. E. Lloyd, *History of Wales* (2 v., 1948).

[C. M. MCGRATH]

BEDE, ST. (672 or 673–735), monk, priest, historian, commentator on the Scriptures, Doctor of the Church. At the age of 7 B. entered the monastery of Wearmouth and was educated under St. *Benedict Biscop; c.681 he transferred to Jarrow and was ordained priest at about the age of 30. He left his monastery only for short journeys; his whole life was devoted to monastic observance, study, teaching, and writing. His biblical commentaries, much esteemed by his contemporaries and widely used throughout the Middle Ages, drew upon the writings of SS. Augustine, Jerome, Ambrose, Gregory, and others, but contained much original material. His *Historia abbatum* traces the history of his own monastery from its foundation to 716. The *Historia ecclesiastica gentis Anglorum* was more than a history of the English Church; it is the principal source for all early English history. Its historical value is great because of the care B. took with his sources and the clear distinction he drew between established fact and what was based on less satisfactory evidence. This work, written in a lively style and in lucid Latin, displays a remarkable perception of events in their relative historical importance. B.'s *De temporibus,* written probably for the clergy to clarify the principles adopted by the Synod of *Whitby (664) for the calculation of Easter, together with his *De temporum ratione* and his historical works did much to establish the dating of events from the Incarnation. The title "Venerable" was given to B. within two generations of his death. The title, being singularly appropriate, has been retained ever since. B. was named a Doctor of the Church by Leo XIII in 1899. Works: *Complete Works* (ed. J. A. Giles, 12 v., 1843–44); repr. PL 90–95; incomplete crit. ed. D. Hurst and J. Fraipont, CCL v. 119, 120, 122; *Hist. Eccl.* (ed. J. Plummer, 2 v., 1896; repr. 1956); *Hist. Eccl.* (Eng. tr. J. E. King, 2 v.) Loeb 246, 248, BIBLIOGRAPHY: A. H. Thompson, *Bede* (1935); T. A. Carroll, *Venerable Bede: His Spiritual Teachings* (1946); C. J. Donahue, NCE 2:217.

[M. S. TANEY]

BEDE, see BEAD.

BEDFORD MASTER (fl. 1405–30), French illuminator who with the *Ronan Master worked in Paris and Angers during the English occupation. Employed by John of Lancaster, Duke of Bedford and regent of France (1423–35), he executed the *Bedford Book of Hours* (British Museum, London) and the *Breviary of the Duke of Bedford* (Bibliothèque Nationale, Paris). His work, though showing the naturalism of the Boucicaut Master, is distinguished by elaborate floral border designs and medallion scenes. BIBLIOGRAPHY: E. Panofsky, *Early Netherlandish Painting* (2 v., 1953).

[M. J. DALY]

BEDINGFELD, FRANCES (1616–1704), English nun and educator. She was a native of Norfolk who joined the Institute of Mary in Munich, a congregation devoted to the education of girls from England, was professed (1633), and became superior general (1666). She opened a school in London (1669) and later another in Yorkshire (1676). She and her religious suffered considerable harassment under the penal laws. She returned to Munich in 1699. BIBLIOGRAPHY: Gillow BDEC 1:166–168.

[H. JACK]

BEDINI, GAETANO (1806–64), cardinal, diplomat. Ordained priest at Sinigaglia, Italy (1828) B. was appointed to several diplomatic posts including that of nuncio to Brazil. On his way there in 1853 he visited the U.S. and saw the problems plaguing the missionary Church because of an ever-growing Catholic population with an insufficient number of priests, bishops, parishes, dioceses, and charitable organizations. Added to these problems was B.'s own experience of the anti-Catholic sentiment prevailing in the U.S. B. never went to Brazil but returned to Rome and was responsible for the foundation of the North American College. In a report to the Vatican he outlined the condition of the Church in the U.S. and the necessity of establishing an apostolic nunciature in Washington. He was unable to convince Rome of this need and it was not until 1893 that an apostolic delegate was assigned to the U.S. BIBLIOGRAPHY: J. F. Connelly, NCE 2:219.

[J. HILL]

BEDJAN, PAUL (1838–1920), missionary and Oriental scholar. A native of Iran, B. entered the Vincentian novitiate at Paris in 1856 and was ordained priest in 1861. That same year he returned to Iran where he worked as a missionary till 1880. He is widely known for composing and translating into Neo-Syriac a considerable number of popular religious works. His most noteworthy works are *Acts of Martyrs and Saints of the East* (7 v., 1890–97), *Sermons of Jacob of Sarug* (5 v., 1905–10), the *Book of Heraclides of Damascus* (1910), an authentic work of Nestorius. BIBLIOGRAPHY: F. Combaluzier, DHGE 7:410–413.

[H. DRESSLER]

BEDLAM, a ME rendering of Bethlehem. Its use as an equivalent for "madhouse" dates from the 16th cent., when the priory and hospital of St. Mary of Bethlehem, then in Bishopsgate, London, was dissolved, becoming in 1547 an asylum for the reception and cure of mentally deranged persons. Originally the priory was founded in 1247 for the sisters and brothers of the Order of the Star of Bethlehem, an order dedicated to the service of pilgrims to the Holy Land. The priory is recorded as a hospital in 1330, and some lunatics were listed among its patients in 1403. The best treatment is in OED 1:754.

[L. E. BOYLE]

BEDNY, DEMIAN (Yefim Alexandrovich Pridvorov; 1883–1945), Russian writer. After 1917 his propagandistic fables, satires, and poems, and his antireligious sentiments faithfully reflected official Soviet policy. He failed, however, to take cognizance of an official shift in policy and was censured for criticizing older Russian culture (i.e., Christianity) and literature (i.e., the *byliny*) in the comic opera *Bogatyrs* (1936). BIBLIOGRAPHY: M. Slonim, *Soviet Russian Literature* (1964) 37–39; A. Kaun, *Soviet Poets and Poetry* (1943) 143–147.

[M. F. MCCARTHY]

BEDÓN, PEDRO (1555–1621), Ecuadorian Dominican painter and social worker. B. studied philosophy in Quito and theology and painting under the Jesuit brother, Bernard *Bitti in Lima. Returning to Quito, B., active in social service among Spanish, Indian, and Negro peoples, founded a school of painting for the Indians. Protesting the sales taxes, B. was forced to leave Quito. Eventually he was elected provincial of his order. A most important representative of Ecuadorian culture and the social apostolate, B. was called the "father of painting" in Quito. BIBLIOGRAPHY: J. M. Vargas, "El venerable maestro fray Pedro Bedón, O.P.," *El Oriente Dominicano* 8 (1935).

[M. J. DALY]

BÉDOS DE CELLES, FRANÇOIS (1709–79), French Benedictine monk and authority on organs. He wrote a comprehensive study of the instrument, *L'Art du facteur d'orgues* (3 v., 1766–78, repr. 1935–36), which remains a standard source on 18th-cent. organ-building principles. BIBLIOGRAPHY: W. L. Sumner, *Organ* (3d ed. 1962).

[A. DOHERTY]

BEDSĀ (SW of Bombay), site of a chaitya hall—a rock-cut Buddhist temple—contemporary with Cave X at *Ajantā (175 B.C.?), having a nave separated from the aisles by great pillars perhaps originally painted, later whitewashed (19th century). BIBLIOGRAPHY: B. Rowland, *Art and Architecture of India* (2d ed. 1959).

[M. J. DALY]

BEDYLL, THOMAS (d. 1537), a man of legal training, secretary to the abp. of Canterbury (1520–32), then court chaplain and clerk of the Privy Council; he was active in promoting the divorce of Henry VIII, the enforcement of the oath of supremacy, and the suppression and despoliation of the monasteries. BIBLIOGRAPHY: C. T. Martin, DNB 2:120–121.

[H. JACK]

BEE, ST., see BEGA, ST.

BEECHER, HENRY WARD (1813–87), editor, social reformer, and preacher. After graduation from Amherst (1834) and Lane Theological Seminary (1837), where his father, Lyman *Beecher, was president, he held small pastorates until being called (1847) to Plymouth Church in Brooklyn. His eloquence made him the most celebrated preacher of his era; he abandoned Calvinistic orthodoxy for a warm, humane, and liberalist presentation of Christianity, and for the cause of liberalism withdrew from the Congregational Church. He supported and dramatically crusaded for the abolition of slavery and later for woman's suffrage. He won early literary fame by his *Seven Lectures to Young Men* (1844), was a constant contributor to periodicals, founding editor (1870) of the non-denominational *Christian Union* (afterwards called the *Outlook); he also wrote a *Life of Jesus Christ* (1871) and, in support of Darwinism, *Evolution and Religion* (1885). During the difficult days of an unsuccessful lawsuit for adultery brought against him, he inaugurated the Lyman Beecher Lectures on preaching at the Yale school of divinity, which had vast influence on American preaching. Biographies were written by Lyman *Abbott (1903) and P. Hibben (1927).

[T. C. O'BRIEN]

BEECHER, LYMAN (1775–1863), American Congregationalist minister. He was the son of a minister and studied at Yale, where he was greatly influenced by Timothy *Dwight. In 1799 he was ordained as pastor of a church at Easthampton, Long Island, remaining there until 1810, when he was called to Litchfield, Connecticut. B. was active in promoting *revivalism and home missions. He was a founder of the *American Bible Society and is credited with beginning the temperance movement in New England with the foundation in 1825 of the American Temperance Society. His theological views were akin to those of his friend Nathaniel W. *Taylor, who taught a moderate Calvinism that permitted man to open himself to divine grace by choosing to accept Christ. This revitalized Congregationalism gave to Conn. a *Second Great Awakening and regained ground lost to the Unitarians. In 1826 B. accepted a call to found a new Congregational Church in Boston, and there opposed the Unitarian W. E. *Channing. B. was active in promoting Lane Theological Seminary in Cincinnati as a center of home missionary effort on the frontier and became its first president in 1832. He was simultaneously called to the Second Presbyterian Church in Cincinnati under the *Plan of Union, but his liberal views led to his presentment in 1835 before the *presbytery. The charges were dismissed but the incident contributed to the détente in 1837 between Presbyterians and Congregationalists. B.'s appeals for home missions included warnings that Roman Catholics were prepared to fill any vacuum left by Protestants in the West and may have fed the anti-Catholicism of the period. He left Cincinnati in 1850 and spent his last years in the Brooklyn home of his famous son, Henry Ward *Beecher, His best-known work is *Plea for the West* (1835). BIBLIOGRAPHY: W. Sweet, *Religion on the American Frontier: The Congregationalists* (1939).

[R. K. MACMASTER]

BEELEN, JAN THEODOOR (1807–84), scriptural exegete, translator, and Orientalist. B. was professor of Scripture and Oriental languages at the Catholic Univ. of Louvain (1836–76), where he established a noted printing plant for Oriental languages. He published commentaries on several NT books, and translated much of the Bible from the Vulgate into Flemish. He also published a three-volume *Chrestomathia rabbinica et chaldaica*. BIBLIOGRAPHY: O. Rey, DB 1.2: 1542–43; F. Bechtel, CE 2:388; M. C. McGarraghy, NCE 2:221.

[T. M. MCFADDEN]

BEELZEBUB, in the OT, name of the god of Accaron or Ekron (2 Kg 1,2–3, 6, 16). Hebrew *ba'al zebub* usually understood as ''lord of flies''; the name may mean ''lord of rulers.'' In the NT versions the name is the ''prince of devils,'' but in the Gr. MSS the name is Beelzebul, from the Aramaic ''lord of dung'' *be'elzebul*. Jesus' enemies call him Beelzebub (Mt 10.25) or attribute the power of B. to him (Mt 12.24, 27; Mk 3.22; Lk 11.15, 18–19). BIBLIOGRAPHY: M. R. Ryan, NCE 2:221.

[J. J. O'ROURKE]

BEERSHEBA (BERSABEE), city marking the southern limit of Israel. The site is probably the modern Tell es Seba. The phrase ''from Dan to Beersheba'' (Jg 20.1) indicated the entire nation. ''From Geba to Beersheba'' (2 Kg 23.8) was used for Judah. The only source of water in the area, Beersheba was an important city and sanctuary from early times. Abraham worshiped El Olam (God Everlasting) there, and the city's name, perhaps meaning well of seven or well of the oath, was attributed to the fact that Abraham there made a covenant with Abimelech (Gen 21.25–34). Beersheba also comes into the history of Isaac (Gen 26.32–33), Jacob (Gen 28.10; 46.1–5), and Elijah (1 Kg 19.3).

[T. EARLY]

BEETHOVEN, LUDWIG VON (1770–1827), German composer. Born into a poor but musical family, B. studied under Christian Gottlob Neefe, composer and organist at the electoral court, where at the age of 14, B. became assistant organist. In 1792 he settled in Vienna as a pupil of Haydn. He there soon won recognition, first as a pianist and, later, as a composer of acknowledged genius. Among his works are 9 symphonies, various concertos, 11 overtures, 16 string quartets and other chamber music, 30 piano sonatas, and the opera *Fidelio*. Of sacred music, Beethoven composed comparatively little. The oratorio *Christus am Ölberg* was an early work which, though musically inappropriate, is of high interest and value. The *Mass in C* is, despite some fine moments, on the whole dry and uninspired. In the *Missa Solemnis* in D Major, however, B. achieved a depth of musical expression, born of a serious and highly personal reflection on the words, capable of profoundly affecting the listener. BIBLIOGRAPHY: W. McNaught, Grove DMM 1:530–595; P.A. Scholes, *Oxford Companion to Music*, (1969) 92–94.

[M. T. LEGGE]

BEGA, ST. (Bee; d. *c*.660), Irish abbess. According to legend she fled Ireland to avoid marriage. She was received as a nun by St. Aidan in Scotland and ultimately founded a cell in Cumberland, at a place now called St. Bee's. She is sometimes confused with a contemporary Anglo-Saxon, Begu, England's first abbess, at Hackness. BIBLIOGRAPHY: G. M. Fusconi, BiblSanct 2:1075–76; Butler 3:498.

[J. DRUSE]

BEGGA, ST. (d. 693), widow, abbess, patroness of the Beguines. Daughter of Bl. Pepin and St. Ida of Landen, sister of two saints, she married Ansegis, son of St. Arnulf of Metz; they were the parents of Pepin of Heristal, father of Charles Martel, and thus were ancestors of the Carolingian dynasty. Begga was buried and honored at Andenne, a convent she had founded on the Meuse; it had seven chapels to represent the seven pilgrim churches of Rome. Her vita did not appear until the 11th cent. BIBLIOGRAPHY: H. Roeder, *Saints and their Attributes* (1955); E. Brouette, ''Le Plus ancien MS de la *Vita Beggae*,'' *Scriptorium* 16 (1962) 81–84; *id.*, NCE 2:224. Benedictine Monks of St. Augustine's Abbey, *Book of Saints* (1966); H. Platelle, BiblSanct 2:1077–78.

[M. E. DUFFY]

BEGGING, the active solicitation of alms to relieve one's real or pretended financial needs. Beggars are distinguished from those who, although poor or destitute, otherwise receive assistance from private or public sources. A not unesteemed profession in religious cultures more favorable to personal beneficence than to social welfare through state subsidy, begging has been increasingly discountenanced with the growth of nationalization and the assumption by the State of functions of responsibilities previously left to individual initiative. Something has been lost; probably more has been gained: almsgiving becomes impersonal and bureaucratized;

but on the other hand fewer languish and die of hunger and cold. The change has been translated into legislation and governmental action prohibiting the practice of begging; the laws vary from jurisdiction to jurisdiction, and so does their enforcement, often left to the discretion of the local police.

From the point of view of morals the question arises whether it is right for a person, or a group of persons, to live by begging. Is not this a form of social parasitism, at least when other productive and gainful occupations are open? Much will depend on how far we think a pluralist society should cherish its misfits, hermits, eccentrics, vagabonds, and to some extent on how far we equate social value with economic productivity. Much, too, will depend on the contemporary social structure and climate. Of course there is nothing in favor of sheer laziness or cadging, or simulating needs to provoke pity. For the rest, it may be noted that the Church has taken no stand to discourage private beggars, so long as they are not breaking or evading social obligations on other counts. Indeed it has elevated mendicants to a position of honor or privilege when they are banded together for the promotion through almsgathering of some good cause, social service, charity, learning, or the life of prayer (cf. CIC c. 1503).

[C. NEELY]

BEGHARDS, an association of laymen that arose in the Low Countries at the end of the 12th cent. as a companion organization to the female *Beguines. Beghards lived a common life, renounced private property, and practiced continence, but they did not take vows. Most of them were employed in the textile industry and exercised considerable influence in forming the religious opinions of the lower classes. They were repeatedly reprimanded by church authorities during the 13th and 14th cents. for their involvement in heresy (D 891–899). They disappeared at the time of the French Revolution. See bibliog. for Beguines.

[C. J. LYNCH]

BÉGIN, LOUIS NAZAIRE, (1840–1925), archbishop. B. studied at Quebec, and at Rome, where he was ordained (1865). Returning to Canada, he taught at the Quebec Seminary until his consecration (1888) as bp. of Chicoutimi. Subsequently, he was named coadjutor bp. of Quebec (1891), abp. (1898), and cardinal (1914). He was a strong advocate of the Catholic position in the controversy over the Manitoba School Law and a sharp critic of the Canadian Liberals.

[R. K. MacMASTER]

BEGUINAGE, see BEGUINES.

BEGUINES, properly a designation for several lay sisterhoods originating in the Low Countries in the 12th cent. as expressions of the contemporary religious fervor of lay urban society. In medieval documents, however, the term was frequently used of the Apostolici, Brothers and Sisters of the Free Spirit, Spirituals, Fraticelli, or of heretics of every sort. The etymology of the term is the subject of considerable debate. Some suggest that it derives from the name of the Belgian priest Lambert le Bégue, who around 1170 contributed his considerable fortune for the construction at Liège of a center for the care of crusaders' widows. Similar but independent foundations were made in Belgium before the end of the century by Bl. Yvette of Huy and Bl. Mary Oignies. The movement spread quickly from the Low Countries to Switzerland, Germany, and France. Members of the Beguines were virgins and widows who agreed to observe continence and obedience, engage in works of charity, and live a semiconventual life. They were not religious in the traditional canonical sense and were free to leave the community at will. They did not take vows and retained ownership of their own property. They observed no common rule, had no motherhouse, and were subject to no superior general. They were not affiliated with any of the established religious orders and were not under the direction of any special ecclesiastical official. Since each foundation was completely autonomous, there was wide divergence in their religious practices and observances. Most of the Beguines, however, wore a gray habit and a distinctive Flemish headdress.

A beguinage was a city within a city. Surrounded by a wall and sometimes by a moat, it contained a church, hospital, perhaps a school, a guesthouse, and several separate cottages in which the pious ladies lived either singly or in two's or three's. They maintained their own households and might have servants. Those who had no income supported themselves, usually as weavers or lace-makers. All devoted part of their time to charitable activities, esp. teaching, nursing, and caring for the poor. The services they rendered earned them the esteem of all classes in society. By the end of the 13th cent. there was scarcely a city in the Low Countries that did not have at least one beguinage. At one time the foundation at Ghent had more than 1,000 members. The use of the name Beguines for heretics came about because the beguinages became influential centers for the propagation of a type of popular mysticism that clearly tended toward illuminism. This tendency was held in check during their early history, when most of the Beguines came from upper-class families and possessed some degree of education. But with the passage of time needy unmarried women seeking security became the majority. Other factors that rendered the Beguines vulnerable to heresy were their loose organizational structure and their almost total lack of hierarchical supervision. Not all the charges of heresy and immorality that were lodged against the Beguines can be taken at face value. Many of their foundations certainly were infected with the antinomianism of the Brothers and Sisters of the Free Spirit and the Joachimism of the Spirituals and the Fraticelli; but others, esp. those in the Low Countries, never strayed far from orthodoxy and were stoutly defended against accusations of heresy by bishops, princes, and the people. When Lateran Council IV (1215) ordered independent religious houses to affiliate with one of the established religious orders, Bp. Jacques de Vitry induced Honorius III to exempt several beguinages from the decree. When the Council of Lyons II (1274) reenacted this law, many groups of Beguines associated themselves with the Franciscan, Dominican, or Augustinian Third Orders. The Council of Vienne (1311–12; D 891–899) accused the Beguines of actively propagating a number of errors on the nature of Christian living, and ordered their suppression. But in 1321 John XXII allowed those beguinages that accepted reform to continue in existence.

In the course of the Reformation beguinages located in areas of Europe where Protestantism became the official religion were suppressed. During the course of the Napoleonic Wars most of the Beguines' foundations in France disappeared. Today there are 13 beguinages still in existence, 11 in Belgium and 2 in Holland. BIBLIOGRAPHY: E. W. McDonnell, *Beguines and Beghards in Medieval Culture* (1954, repr. 1969); D. Philips, *Beguines in Medieval Strasbourg. A Study of the Social Aspects of Beguine Life* (1941); J. Van Mierlo, DHGE 7:426–441 s.v. *"Bégardisme."*

[C. J. LYNCH]

BEHAIM, MARTIN (1459–1507), cartographer and constructor of the earliest extant globe. Born in Nuremberg, he traveled to Portugal in connection with the Flemish trade and was appointed to the king's council on navigation. Beyond that the claims made for him are questionable.

BEHAN, BRENDAN (1923–64), author and playwright. Born in Dublin into a poor, rebel family, B. at 9 joined the Fianna (junior movement of the Irish Republican Army), and in 1937 became a messenger for the Chief of Staff of the IRA. In England he was arrested (1939) for carrying explosives and sent to Borstal. From this experience later came the autobiographical *Borstal Boy* (1958). In Ireland he was for the next few years frequently imprisoned for IRA activities. In 1954 B. began to write a column for the Irish Press, and late in the year *The Quare Fella* (condemned man) was produced in the Pike Theater. It was an immediate success. The following year he married Beatrice ffrench Salkeld, an artist whose gentleness sustained him for the rest of his nomadic life. *The Hostage* (1958) was an adaptation of a work commissioned in Gaelic, *An Giall* (1957). He also wrote one novel, *The Scarperer* (1964). The alcoholic excesses and triumphal clowning of B.'s last years made him a legendary figure in Dublin but he was known also for his gentleness with children, and in their presence he refrained from the vulgarity in speech which was so much a part of all his public conversations. His artistic sensitivity recreated the anguish of the life and death which so often faces modern man and gave his works a universal appeal. BIBLIOGRAPHY: R. Porter, *Brendan Behan* (pa. 1973); U. O'Connor, *Brendan Behan* (pa. 1973); *World of Brendan Behan* (ed. S. McCann, 1965).

[A. WARDLE]

BEHAVIORISM, a school of psychology that confines itself to study of man's externally observable behavior. It seeks to make psychology strictly scientific in the sense of the physical sciences, and makes use of objective methods that can be statistically measured. It was introduced c.1912 by J. B. Watson in revolt against psychological schools that sought to study consciousness and used introspection as a method, both considered unscientific by Watson. Behaviorism has been influential in the U.S. but not in Europe. Though few American psychologists accept the total philosophy of behaviorism, its emphasis on making psychology scientific has had a strong impact. It emphasizes the work of Pavlov on conditioned reflexes, and is sometimes called the S-R psychology (stimulus-response). Denying any essential difference between man and animals, it makes extensive use of laboratory experiments with animals to gain understanding of human behavior.

Students of Christian ethics consider behaviorism unsatisfactory because it ignores the moral personality, human freedom, and the objective basis for holding man morally responsible for his acts. By showing that man's behavior is to some extent conditioned by the stimuli to which he responds, however, it provides a broader context for judging the morality of specific acts. BIBLIOGRAPHY: J. B. Watson, *Psychology from the Standpoint of a Behaviorist* (3d ed., 1929); *id., Behaviorism* (pa. 1970); *Behaviorism and Phenomenology* (ed. T. W. Wann, 1964).

[T. EARLY]

BEHEIM, LORENZ (c.1455–1521), German humanist and canonist. B. studied theology at Ingolstadt and Leipzig, then went to Italy where he received a doctorate in canon law. He entered the service of Card. Rodrigo Borgia who later became Pope Alexander VI. His contemporaries considered him one of the most learned men of the time. His collection of Roman inscriptions is significant for the student of antiquity. BIBLIOGRAPHY: M. Monaco, NCE 2:229.

[J. E. LYNCH]

BEHEMOTH, the powerful marsh animal described in Job 40.15–24, anciently identified as an elephant, but now commonly as a hippopotamus (water buffalo?). The passage's point is that man, so feeble next to this monstrous animal made by God, cannot contend in wisdom and strength with God. Later apocalyptic Jewish literature identifies Behemoth as a monstrous beast warring against God who will destroy it at the Judgment.

[J. F. FALLON]

BEHISTUN INSCRIPTION, the series of reliefs and inscriptions of Darius I set on the precipitous rock face of the Behistun (Bisitun, ancient Baghistan), a 1700-foot mountain overlooking the Kermanshah-Hamadan road in Persia. The monument proclaims the hereditary right of Darius to the throne of Persia by listing his genealogies through eight generations to Achaemenes; lists the provinces of his empire and his victories over various rebels. Darius is portrayed holding his foot on the body of Gaumata with the remaining rebels before him in chains and the symbol of the god Ahura Mazda above his head. It was written in the official languages of the Persian Empire, Old Persian, Babylonian, and Elamite; its translation by H. C. Rawlinson (1846–49) and others was an important link in the decipherment of cuneiform. BIBLIOGRAPHY: L. W. King and R. C. Thompson, *Sculpture and Inscription of Darius the Great on the Rock of Behistun in Persia* (1907); L. L. Orlin, *Ancient Near Eastern Literature* (pa. 1969).

[F. H. BRIGHAM]

BEHRENS, PETER (1868–1940), German industrial designer and architect connected with *Art Nouveau movement in Munich, later in Darmstadt. B. worked in the severe style of cubical masses and free-flowing interior spaces and was influenced by Olbrich and Macintosh. Director of Düsseldorf school (1903) B. established a new concept of industrial complexes in elegant steel framing, poured concrete, and glass-curtain walls. Introducing art into industry, B.'s designs determined trademark, product, and building. His assistants included the geniuses W. Gropius, Mies van der Rohe, and Le Corbusier. BIBLIOGRAPHY: F. Hoeber, *Peter Behrens* (1913).

[M. J. DALY]

BEISSEL, JOHANN CONRAD (1690–1766), German-born mystic, sabbatarian, celibate; founder of the *Ephrata Community. Orphaned at 8, apprenticed to a baker-musician, he became a master baker and an expert creative musician. At Heidelberg, he was converted from a dissolute life to pietistic fervor. Fleeing persecution, he migrated to Pennsylvania, where, lacking opportunity to ply his trade, he apprenticed to learn weaving from Peter Becker, minister of the *German Baptists of Germantown. Before joining this group, he retired to the wilderness and lived as a hermit. In 1724, he affiliated with the Brethren and served as minister. Controversy over his mysticism and sabbatarianism resulted in his withdrawal; he founded the Ephrata Society in 1728. B.'s musical pieces were in a seven-part harmony, written to imitate the music of heaven. BIBLIOGRAPHY: J. C. Klein, *Johann Conrad Beissel, Mystic and Martinet* (1942, repr. 1972).

[A. T. RONK]

BEIT GAZZŌ (Syriac, treasury.) In W Syrian usage it may mean: a liturgical book containing the poetic compositions to be sung by the choirs in the ferial office; or an indicator of melodies for the canonical hours; or a cupboard in the wall behind the altar for storing valuable objects; or, in Jacobite churches, in the wall of the *qestrômō* for keeping liturgical manuscripts. In Nestorian usage it signifies a niche in the north wall of the sanctuary where the paten is kept until it is brought to the altar in the Eucharistic rite. *GAZZĀ.

[A. CODY]

BEIT QADDÎSHĒ, in older West Syrian cathedrals, a mortuary chamber for the burial of bishops. It opens into the church itself.

[A. CODY]

BEIT SHAMMĀSHĀ (house of the deacon), in Nestorian churches, the south sacristy, where vestments and sacred instruments are kept. It is the Byzantine *diakonikon;* and is called by Chaldeans the *beit diyaqûn* (Arabic).

[A. CODY]

BEKENNENDE KIRCHE, see CONFESSING CHURCH.

BEKTASHIS, an order of dervishes supposedly founded by Hájjī Bęktâsh Wālî in the 13th cent. in Anatolia. The doctrine of the Bektashis, which shows some clear *Shiite tendencies, is fundamentally a syncretistic mixture of various elements, Christian and Islamic. They unite *'Ali, *Mohammed, and Allâh into a kind of trinity and, at the initiation of new members, celebrate a kind of eucharistic meal of wine, bread, and cheese. The sect was extremely popular in S Anatolia and Albania and held exclusive spiritual direction of the *Janissary corps. Along with all other dervish orders, the Bektashis were officially suppressed by the Turkish government in 1925, but the order continues to count numerous adherents in both the Balkans and Turkey. BIBLIOGRAPHY: J. K. Birge, *Bektashi Order of Dervishes* (1937).

[R. M. FRANK]

BEKYNTON, THOMAS (Beckington; d. 1465), English bishop, royal official, humanist. Admitted to Oxford (1406), B. became a doctor of civil law in 1418. A protégé and official of Humphrey, Duke of Gloucester, from 1420–38, he was secretary to Henry VI (1438–42). When keeper of the privy seal (1443–44), he became bp. of Bath and Wells (1443–65), where he proved himself a good administrator and builder. A friend of such humanists as Flavio Biondo, he abandoned the profuse style of Latin hitherto in use in the royal and episcopal chancery for the more direct and refined Latin of the humanists, as may be seen in *Memorials of the Reign of Henry VI: Official Correspondence of Thomas Bekynton* (ed. G. Williams, 2 v., 1872). BIBLIOGRAPHY: Emden Ox 1:157–159; A. Judd, *Life of Thomas Bekynton* (1961).

[L. E. BOYLE]

BEL, an ancient Akkadian god, comparable in status and function to the Sumerian Enlil; the god who governed the earth's surface and therefore living men. When Marduk became Babylon's chief god, he was given the title Bel. Thus the Bel and Merodach (Marduk) of Jer 50.2 are the same god.

[J. F. FALLON]

BEL, TEMPLE OF, PALMYRA (A.D. 32), main sanctuary of ancient Palmyra dedicated to the deities Bel (sky), Iarhibol (sun), and Aglibol (moon), built on a great terrace enclosed by a double row of Corinthian columns, with a monumental propylaeum and an additional underground entrance passage for sacrificial animals. The unconventional roof, both flat and sloping, was reached by four stairways and flanked by pediments. The Greco-Roman elements were strongly modified by Oriental inspiration. BIBLIOGRAPHY: R. Amy, "Temples à escaliers," *Syria* 27 (1950); H. Seyrig, "La Parèdre de Bel à Palmyre," *ibid.* 37 (1960).

[M. J. DALY]

BEL AND THE DRAGON, two stories found affixed to the Greek version of Daniel, which are not included in most Protestant Bibles but which are considered canonical by Catholics. Their intent is to criticize by humorous sarcasm the practice of idolatry and to extol the power of the true God and the wisdom and confidence of his faithful servant Daniel.

[J. F. FALLON]

BELASYSE, JOHN (1614–89), English royalist general. He commanded the forces of King Charles I and served as governor of York. After the Restoration, he became governor of Tangier (1664–66). Although he was obliged to resign because of his Catholic faith, he remained in political and military good standing until he became a victim of Titus Oates's accusations and spent 7 years in the Tower without trial. After his release, James II made him lord commissioner of the treasury, an appointment that provoked public censure and religious disturbance.

[H. JACK]

BELAUNZARÁN, JOSÉ MARÍA DE JESÚS (1772–1857), Mexican bishop. A Franciscan ordained in 1796, B. was known as the apostle of Mexico City for his preaching and zeal. As bp. of Linares (1831), he fought for the freedom of the Church from persecution. Worn out by the failure of his efforts and by ill health, he resigned his see in 1839. BIBLIOGRAPHY: L. Medina-Ascensio, NCE 2:236.

[H. JACK]

BELBELLO DA PAVIA (c. 1430–62), Italian miniaturist whose style ranges from early, delicate Gothic (*Estense Bible,* Vatican) to the dramatic *Missal of Barbara of Brandenburg* (Ducal Palace, Mantua). Later works, agitated and often grotesque, show large areas of gold. BIBLIOGRAPHY: S. Samek-Ludovici, *Miniaturi di Belbello da Pavia* (1954).

[M. J. DALY]

BELCOURT, GEORGE ANTHONY (1830–74), Canadian missionary. Ordained in 1827, B. labored for 17 years in Winnipeg among the Chippewa Indians. An outstanding missionary, he learned their language and wrote an Indian dictionary and grammar, still standard works. He also tried to persuade the Indians to become farmers instead of nomadic hunters, but met with disapproval from both his bp. and the Hudson's Bay Company. In 1849 he was sent to North Dakota where he is said to have evangelized the entire Turtle Mountains Chippewa tribe, a fact that kept that tribe at peace with the government during the Sioux troubles following the Minnesota massacre in 1862. However, he met with problems working with other priests, left the diocese (1859), and spent his last years in parishes on Prince Edward Island and the Magdalen Islands. BIBLIOGRAPHY: J. M. Reardon, *George Anthony Belcourt: Pioneer Catholic Missionary of the Northwest* (1955).

[J. HILL]

BELFRY (from ME *berfray,* movable tower used in sieges), a tower for a bell, usually attached to a church or other building; that part of a steeple in which a bell is hung; a room, turret, or cupola in which a bell may be hung.

BELGIC CONFESSION, the *Reformed *confession of faith, first published in 1561 by Guy de *Brès. The document was written in French, then translated into Dutch, German, and Latin. The synod at Antwerp that organized the Reformed Church in the Low Countries in 1566 adopted this confessional standard in a revised form, approved by Geneva, and this text was accepted at the Synod of *Dort (1619). A clear statement of *Calvinism, the Confession ranks next to the *Gallican Confession of 1559, which it closely resembles, as a doctrinal standard for Reformed Churches. The contents are divided into 37 articles; art. 36, on the relations of civil powers to the Church, has presented a continuing problem of interpretation. BIBLIOGRAPHY: L. Verduin, EncRelKnowSuppl 1:121–122; Schaff Creeds 1:502–508 and 3:383–436.

[T. C. O'BRIEN]

BELGIUM, constitutional monarchy in northwestern Europe. Though not independent until the 19th cent., the Belgians have a long and distinguished history of faithfulness to Catholicism. Perhaps the fact of a cycle of suppression and persecution lasting almost 100 years created a people who esteemed their religion highly. Long a part of the Holy Roman and Austrian empires, the Belgians were wrested from Austrian rule by the French Revolutionary Republic, only to find the new tyranny more oppressive than the former, esp. in the suppression of religion. Under Napoleon and his Empire what promised to be a new era for Catholicism became a revival of Gallicanism with the State attempting to regulate the Church. The Concordat of 1801 brought temporary truce, but Napoleon's insistence on making fidelity to the Empire a religious duty lost him ultimately the favor of the Belgian bishops and people. In the last days of the Empire the tyrannical persecution of the Church turned Belgians into enemies of Napoleon.

After Waterloo the victorious Allied Powers imposed on the Belgians the Kingdom of the Netherlands, ruled by the Protestant William I of Orange-Nassau. Dutch dominance was as inimical to the interests of the Church as the French Republic had been. The stupidity of William played the major role in alienating the Belgians. The imposition of an oath of fidelity to the Fundamental Law with its anti-Catholic provisions, the suppression of Catholic education and seminaries, and persecution of various bishops and priests aroused Catholic fury. A persistent source of conflict was the attempt to remove the Belgian Church from the influence of the pope. The Liberals who were anticlerical, if not anti-religious, found themselves targets of the government, joined forces with the Catholics, and forced a revolution in 1830 that freed Belgium from the Dutch.

The Constitution of the new Belgian kingdom assured freedom of religion to all, freedom of the press, freedom of education and association. It was the work of the Catholic majority. The more extreme wing of the Liberal party gradually came to dominate Belgium while the Catholics grew indifferent to public affairs. From 1847 to 1884 with two interruptions, the Liberal party used its power as the government to impose destructive laws on the Catholic majority, centering on the notorious School Law. Finally Catholics took vigorous political action and resumed dominance from 1887 to 1919. The vicious seesaw of Belgian political life has been since then solved by coalition government.

Despite political misfortunes and two devastating World Wars, the Church in Belgium has been a vigorous and generous part of the Catholic world. Its unwavering loyalty to the Holy See, its resistance to German occupation, its highly developed programs of social action, and above all the incredible missionary efforts of this small kingdom make an outstanding record. Numerically the Belgians have given the second highest number of priests and religious to the foreign missions. Since Pope Leo XIII the Church in Belgium has been sensitive in its defense of labor. The organization by Cardinal Cardijn of workers has had worldwide influence. The Univ. of Louvain continues to be the outstanding Catholic university of the world. Charitable organizations are grouped in *Caritas Catholica,* which operates hospitals, specialized institutions, and renders home services. Education in Belgium on all levels is strongly a Catholic tradition and from 50 to 65 percent of all students attend Catholic schools. BIBLIOGRAPHY: É. de Moreau, DHGE 7:520–756.

[J. R. AHERNE]

BELGRADE, PATRIARCHATE OF, see SERBIA, PATRIARCHATE OF.

BELIAL, a noun used in the genitive in the OT as an attributive adjective meaning worthless, of no account, or wicked, e.g., 2 Sam 20.1, "a worthless fellow." In the NT period through the influence of apocalyptic literature the term became in its Aramaic form Belial, a title of the prince of demons, Satan (2 Cor 6.15).

[J. F. FALLON]

BELIEF, a free act of a person in which he assents with his mind under the impulsion of his will to a truth on the word of another. As an act it differs from *doubt, whether negative or positive, which is a suspension of assent; as being quite certain, it differs from *opinion, which admits of fear of error; as directed to an object which is self-evident, it differs from intuition or understanding; and as directed to an object which cannot be demonstrated, it differs from strictly scientific knowledge. Such evidence as is present accordingly is extrinsic, not intrinsic; but in the total situation it gathers to itself the force of both affective and cognitive elements so that an object is held to be not merely reasonably believable *(credibile)* but imperatively to be believed *(credendum).* So far the scholastic grammar, which elaborates on St. Augustine's phrase *(cum assensione cogitare)* to the effect that believing is committing oneself to something but with some lack of purely mental tranquillity, as happens whenever the mind is working in the dark. For a specific consideration of religious assent, see *FAITH.

Kant's distinction between the practical and theoretical reasons marked a turning point in the psychology and epistemology of belief. No objective validity could be claimed for its affirmation; the only verification that might be allowed was that it answered to certain subjective attitudes, mainly those of the will. RC theologians have sought to conciliate this voluntarism with intellectualism and to relate religious sentiment with more hard-headed science. Newman brought out the role of conscience; Blondel, the culmination of the immanent drives implicit in human acting (see IMMANENCE APOLOGETICS). Contemporary psychology, which has moved from the old rationalism that we are constrained only by mathematical and empirical evidences, shows that the will renders a person open or closed to a reality involved, directs his attention, and charges his assent. To speak generally, a balanced account of belief will avoid some prevalent dichotomies, thus mind and will, subjective and objective, judgment of fact and judgment of value, religious experience and credal assent. BIBLIOGRAPHY: J. H. Newman, *Grammar of Assent* (1870); M. C. D'Arcy, *Nature of Belief* (2d ed. 1958).

BELIEVER'S BAPTISM, the practice of administering baptism only to persons old enough to make responsible decisions and personally profess faith in Jesus Christ. Conflicting convictions as to the proper subjects of baptism constitute a major barrier among Christians. The fact that most Christian Churches administer baptism to infants raises the question as to when and why this practice became so prevalent and why so many Christians object to it. Scholars have combed the documents of the early Church, but there is no indisputable reference to *infant baptism prior to Tertullian early in the 3d century. Many interpreters, however, have inferred such a practice from incidents in which Jesus blessed children (Mk 10.13–16 and parallels); from the statements regarding Lydia, who "was baptized and her household" (Acts 16.15); and from presumptive evidence growing out of the strong corporate sense of the Jewish family. The NT and other early documents indicate a close connection of repentance, faith, and instruction with the rite of baptism. Moreover, as late as the 4th cent. Gregory of Nazianzus, Gregory of Nyssa, and Basil of Caesarea were not baptized until adulthood. By the 5th cent. infant baptism had become almost universal, and not until the 16th cent. did the issue again become controversial. In contrast to the other main Reformation traditions, the *Anabaptists rejected infant baptism and administered the rite only to those who made a conscious profession of faith. The practice provoked hostile reactions, and many Anabaptists were martyred. In the 17th cent. the Baptists emerged from the *Independent wing of Puritanism specifically over this issue, for Baptists repudiated infant baptism as both unscriptural and inconsistent with the concept of the *gathered church. A vigorous polemic between Baptists and other Protestants in England and the U.S. continued into the 19th century. A lecture (1943) of Karl *Barth denying any NT basis for infant baptism (see Teaching of the Church Regarding Baptism [tr. E. A. Payne, 1959]; Church Dogmatics [v.4, 1961]) and the fact that a large number of baptized persons never become confirmed or attend church services, have provoked debate about baptism by Protestant and RC theologians. Although some see in believer's baptism too much emphasis upon the element of human decision, others see it as uniting the objective redemptive activity of God in Christ with the personal response of the individual believer. Coming in faith and repentance, he acknowledges the initiative of God's gracious forgiveness, accepts the Lordship of Christ over his life, and by the power of the Holy Spirit is regenerated and incorporated into the Church of Jesus Christ. BIBLIOGRAPHY: D. Moody, Baptism: Foundation for Christian Unity (1967); Christian Baptism (ed. A. Gilmore, 1959) R. S. Armour, Anabaptist Baptism (1967).

[N. H. MARING]

BELINSKI, VISSARION GRIGOREVICH (1811–48), Russian literary critic and political philosopher of the 1830s and 1840s. Under the influence, successively, of Schelling, Fichte, Hegel, and Feuerbach, Belinski developed from a romantic idealist into a materialist and utopian socialist. In his later years, as witness the famous letter to Gogol (1847), he rejected the Russian Orthodox Church and claimed that atheism is inherent in the Russian character. In literature, he praised naturalism (i.e., realism). His literary criticism, which had a strong influence on the so-called "civic critics," Chernyshevski, Dobrolyubov, and Pisarev, revealed both his keen insight and good literary judgment (e.g., his evaluations of Pushkin, Lermontov, and Gogol) and his stress on moral, political, and social, rather than aesthetic, values in literature. BIBLIOGRAPHY: R. Hare, Pioneers of Russian Social Thought (1951); Russian Philosophy (1965) 1:280–312; V. Terras, Belinski and Russian Literary Criticism (1973).

[M. F. MCCARTHY]

BELISARIUS (500–565), Byzantine general who was the official envoy of Justinian in conferences with Pope Vigilius prior to and throughout the Council of Constantinople III (553). His distinguished military and political career included his loyal defense of Justinian during the Nika Revolt (532), military and political victory over the Goths in Italy (536–538), the extension of the empire in Persia (541), and the conquest of Africa. Unjustly accused of complicity in the abortive attempt to assassinate Justinian (562), he was held in disgrace until his return to favor in 563. This disgrace late in life was the subject of a well-known medieval legend depicting his final days in the streets of Constantinople as a blind beggar. BIBLIOGRAPHY: L. Brehier, DHGE 7:776–787; J. Bury, History of the Later Roman Empire (1958) 2:42–69.

[F. H. BRIGHAM]

BELL, CLIVE (1881–1964), English critic of art and letters. A follower of Roger Fry, B. organized the English section of the Second Postimpressionist Exhibition, London (1912). His thesis re "significant form" in Cézanne, Gauguin, etc., is that emotion is conveyed in the same direct manner as in primitive painting, as opposed to the descriptive intentions of impressionism. As art critic B. supported the Bloomsbury group of which his wife Vanessa and Duncan Grant were members. BIBLIOGRAPHY: J. Rothenstein, Modern English Painters: Sickert to Smith (1952).

[M. J. DALY]

BELL, BOOK, AND CANDLE, a literary allusion to excommunication or other ecclesiastical penalties, or to the punitive power of the hierarchy, or sometimes simply a humorously intended reference to the accessories of religious ceremony. The expression owes its origin to the antiquated medieval rite of public and solemn excommunication. Twelve priests with candles assisted the bishop, and when the sentence was read the candles were thrown down and a bell was tolled.

[P. K. MEAGHER]

BELLAMY, JEAN JULIEN (1857–1903), theologian. B. taught philosophy, Scripture, and church history at the seminary in Vannes, France. During his professorship, he contributed to the Dictionnaire de théologie catholique and produced, among other works, a history of Catholic theology in the 19th century.

[H. JACK]

BELLARMINE, ROBERT, ST. (1542–1621), theologian and Doctor of the Church. B. began his teaching career at the Univ. of Louvain, where he sought to restore biblical and patristic studies and was a firm proponent of Thomistic theology. From 1576–88, he taught at the Roman College and published his lectures there under the title Disputationes de controversiis christianae fidei adversus hujus temporis haereticos (3 v.). The Controversies were a major theological contribution to the RC arguments against the Protestant Reformers, and exercised a considerable influence on the training of seminarians. B.'s distinction between the purely spiritual power of the Church and the temporal power of the State was crucial to his time. He insisted that the pope exercises only spiritual power directly but, since spiritual authority is superior to secular authority, that the pope possesses indirect power over those temporal affairs that bear upon the spiritual. But B. too was a man of his times, and his practical application of these principles confuses the Church's obligation to apply this indirect power with the contingent forms of such application that had evolved in the West. B. also composed catechisms in Italian for children and teachers which were used even into the 19th century.

Various ecclesiastical appointments forced B. to give up his teaching: he was rector of the Roman College, provincial of the Jesuit Neapolitan province, theologian to Clement VIII who made him a cardinal (1599), and abp. of Capua. In addition to the various controversies over papal power, B. argued against D. *Báñez on efficacious grace, and handed down the Holy Office's admonition against the heliocentric theories of *Galileo. BIBLIOGRAPHY: R. Bellarmine, *Opera Omnia* (12 v., ed. J. Fèvre, 1870–74); J. C. Murray, "St. Robert Bellarmine on the Indirect Power," ThSt 9 (1948) 491–535; J. Friske, NCE 2:250–252.

[T. M. MCFADDEN]

BELLATOR (fl. 6th cent.), ecclesiastical writer who according to Cassiodorus wrote several commentaries on OT books, e.g., Wisdom, Tobias, Esther, Judith, Machabees, Esdras; and translated all the homilies of Origen from Greek into Latin. Several authors claim that Origen's homilies on St. Matthew's Gospel were translated by a certain Origenist named Huetius. BIBLIOGRAPHY: R. Ruiz, DHGE, 7:828.

[F. H. BRIGHAM]

BELLECHOSE, HENRI (fl. 1415–40), Franco-Flemish painter who succeeded Jean Malouel as official painter to the court of Burgundy (1415), completing Malouel's unfinished *Martyrdom of St. Denis* (Louvre), in which Malouel's style of linear delicacy is easily differentiated from B.'s "plastic" naturalism. Though associated by some authorities with the *Limbourg brothers in the *Très riches heures du Duc de Berry*, B.'s style relates rather to the *Master of Flémalle and to Jan Van Eyck. BIBLIOGRAPHY: G. Bazin, *L'École franco-flamande, XIVe-XVe siècles* (1941).

[M. J. DALY]

BELLESHEIM, ALFONS (1839–1912), ecclesiastical historian. B. studied theology at Cologne and then at Tübingen. After ordination (1862) he studied further at Rome and wrote many articles in German periodicals on history, theology, and current controversy. His most important writings were *Geschichte der katholischen Kirche in Schottland* (2 v., 1883; Eng. tr. 4 v., 1887–90) and *Ge-schichte der katholischen Kirsche in Irland* (3 v., 1890–91). These works are based on considerable research in the archives of Rome, Paris, and London, but they give the impression that B. was not able to master and utilize fully this material. They are important nonetheless because they are the first comprehensive works on the subject. BIBLIOGRAPHY: J. Grisar, DHGE 7:877.

[P. COOPER]

BELLESINI, STEFANO, BL. (1774–1840), a native of Trent who became an Augustinian. Political disorders connected with the French Revolution forced him to return to Trent after his ordination as a deacon, and he was not ordained priest until 1797. With the suppression of the religious orders, he worked as a secular priest, busying himself esp. with the establishment of Christian schools. His success came to the attention of the government and he was appointed inspector of all the schools of Trent. When the Augustinians were reestablished in the Papal States, he returned to his order and served successively in various houses as novice master. He distinguished himself in caring for the sick in a typhoid epidemic, but caught the disease and died. He was beatified in 1904. BIBLIOGRAPHY: P. Billeri, *Vita del Beato Stefano Bellesini* (1904); I. Rogger, BiblSanct 2:1082–83.

[P. K. MEAGHER]

BELLINGS, RICHARD (*c.* 1600–77), Irish historian who was active in the effort to unify conflicting factions among Irish Catholics. In the years 1645–49 he supported the cause of Charles I, after whose execution he fled to France where he remained for 11 or 12 years, but returned to Ireland when Charles II came into power. BIBLIOGRAPHY: F. S. McGarry, NCE 2:254.

[P. K. MEAGHER]

BELLINI, GENTILE (1429–1507), son of Jacopo Bellini, renowned in his day as a great artist (knighted 1469 by Emperor Frederick III; 1479 sent on a mission to Sultan Mahomet II by the city of Venice). His reputation rests today on four canvases depicting the *Miracles of the Reliquary of the Holy Cross* (1496–*c.*1501) and the *Preaching of St. Mark in Alexandria* (1504–07). BIBLIOGRAPHY: S. Bottari, EncWA 2:447–449.

[L. A. LEITE]

BELLINI, GIOVANNI (*c.*1430–1516), the most brilliant and iconographically inventive member of the family and probably the greatest Venetian painter of the Quattrocento, influencing directly or indirectly all the painters of his own and the next generation, among them Giorgione, Titian, and Palma Vecchio. In his early works he was influenced by his brother-in-law, Mantegna (*Agony in the Garden*, 1470s), and by Antonello da Messina (S. Giobbe altarpiece, *c.*1483). However, his style shows a gradual evolution from the stiff Quattrocento manner to the monumentality and poetry of the High Renaissance (*Madonna Enthroned with SS. Peter,*

Catherine, Lucy, and Jerome; Venice, S. Zaccaria, 1505). Although the bulk of his work was religious, he was also a noted portraitist (*Doge Loredano, c.* 1501). BIBLIOGRAPHY: R. Pallucchini, *Giovanni Bellini* (1962).

[L. A. LEITE]

BELLINI, JACOPO (*c.*1400–*c.*1470), founder of an important family of artists in Venice. Aside from four signed pictures (a Crucifixion and three half-length Madonnas), he is remembered for two sketchbooks (Louvre and British Museum) of drawings in pen and ink and silverpoint, comprising a variety of subjects and motifs (architecture, perspective, foreshortenings, etc.) utilized by his sons, Gentile and Giovanni, and by Mantegna in their paintings. BIBLIOGRAPHY: S. Bottari, EncWA 2:444–447.

[L. A. LEITE]

BELLINTANI, MATTIA DA SALÒ (1534–1611), Capuchin preacher, spiritual writer, historian, propagator of the devotion of the Forty Hours. He was held in considerable esteem by SS. Charles Borromeo and Francis de Sales. His most important work was his *Practica dell'orazione mentale,* a treatise many times reprinted and translated into other languages. It is valuable both for its history and theory of methodical prayer. BIBLIOGRAPHY: P. Umile da Genova, DSAM 1:1355–57.

[P. K. MEAGHER]

BELLINZAGA LOMAZZI, ISABELLA CRISTINA (1552–1624), a Milanese woman who advanced to mystical heights under the direction of A. *Gagliardi. She was held in esteem by St. Charles Borromeo, took active part in charitable work, but came under criticism for her revelations, her eagerness for reform, and her association with Gagliardi. The latter was withdrawn from Milan, largely on her account, in 1594. The important and influential *Breve compendio intorno alla perfezione cristiana (Brief Compendium of Christian Perfection)* was published anonymously in 1611. The work was later attributed to her, although scholars agree that Gagliardi's collaboration in its composition was substantial. BIBLIOGRAPHY: M. Viller, DSAM 1:1940–42; M. S. Conlan, NCE 2:255–256.

[P. K. MEAGHER]

BELLO, ANDRÉS (1781–1865), Latin-American author, educator, and diplomat. Born in Caracas, B. is claimed by Venezuela, Chile, and Colombia, although he spoke of himself as Colombian. Trained in the classics by the Jesuits, B. made many translations from Latin and Greek. In 1847 he published his famous *Gramática de la lengua castellana* and in 1850 his *Historia de la literatura.* B. lived for years as Chilean consul in London. The latter part of his life was spent in Santiago as secretary to the Ministry of Foreign Affairs, mediating in the international conflicts between the U.S. and Ecuador and between Colombia and Peru. The Chilean government edited his complete works. The new

Catholic Univ. of Caracas bears his name. BIBLIOGRAPHY: M. L. Amunátegui Aldunate, *Vida de don Andrés Bello,* (2d ed., 1962); A. Caro, *Estudio biográfico y bibliográfico de A. Bello* (1882).

[P. DAMBORIENA]

BELLOC, JOSEPH HILAIRE PIERRE (1870–1953), essayist, historian, novelist, poet; son of a French barrister and his English wife. Educated under Newman (later Cardinal) at the Oratory School, then Balliol College, Oxford, B. served in the French army, and was naturalized as a British citizen in 1902. He married an American, Elodie Hogan, was a member of Parliament, first as a Liberal and then as an Independent, and wrote forceful political essays (*The Party System* [1911] and *The Servile State* [1912]). He had a lively historical sense and a compelling prose style, but as an historian and biographer he is unconvincing and undocumented. His travel and critical essays, *The Path to Rome* and *Averil,* best show his literary ability, as do his nonsense rhymes, his songs and ballads. He produced, in all, more than 150 volumes. BIBLIOGRAPHY: R. Speaight, *Life of Hilaire Belloc* (1957); P. Braybrook, *Some Thoughts on Hilaire Belloc* (1973); J. B. Morton, *Hilaire Belloc* (1955, repr. 1973).

[M. M. BARRY]

BELLOT, PAUL (1876–1944), Benedictine architect active in the modern renewal of church architecture. Educated at L'École des Beaux Arts in Paris, B. entered the novitiate at Solesmes, going into exile to the Isle of Wight (1903). There he built the church of Quarr Abbey. After World War I he designed churches in brick, cement, and stone. Important buildings are Notre-Dame des Trevoix, Troyes (1933), Saint-Joseph at Annecy (1936), and Saint-Benoît-du-Lac, Quebec (1939). Though it is medieval in form, a sensitivity to material, rhythms, and careful proportions makes his architecture superior to popular work of his time. BIBLIOGRAPHY: J. Pichard, NCE 2:258.

[T. FEIDT]

BELLOY, JEAN BAPTISTE DE (1709–1808), French cardinal. He was made bp. of Glandènes in 1752, and in 1755 was named bp. of Marseilles, where he succeeded in preventing a schism. When this see was suppressed by the National Assembly (1790), he protested officially, then retired to Chambly. He resigned as bp. when Pius VII made this request of the French hierarchy in 1801, and became abp. of Paris the next year by Napoleon's appointment. His ministry as abp. was pastoral, not political, and was honored by the cardinalate in 1805. BIBLIOGRAPHY: A. Lesort, DHGE 7:929–931.

[H. JACK]

BELLS. The religious use of bells goes back to antiquity in the Christian Church. Legend, without probable foundation in fact, attributes their introduction to St. *Paulinus of Nola.

By the 6th cent. at the latest they were in common use in some places, for Gregory of Tours (d. 594) makes frequent mention of them, and there are indications that among the Irish, who attached great importance to bells down through medieval times, they were used for religious purposes as early as the 5th century. The first religious bells were small, but from the 8th cent. onward larger bells, often requiring special housing in belfries and campaniles, were common. According to the *Liber pontificalis* Pope *Stephen II (d. 757) built a belfry for St. Peter's. In Carlovingian times the use of bells was so general that every parish church in the Frankish dominion was expected to have at least one bell. As the art of bell-making progressed, the best bell metal was discovered along with improved methods of casting. It became possible to produce a bell precisely tuned in its tone and overtones so that when struck it would give forth the exact quality of sound that was desired. Many churches had several bells, each with a different sound; they could be struck alone or pealed in harmony so as to produce sounds or melodies of varied significance. Along with bell-making, the art of bell-ringing grew up in the service of religion.

The primary purpose of the bell was to invite the faithful to worship, a function of importance before small clocks and watches came into common use. Bells were also rung to remind the faithful of certain practices of devotion to be performed at set times (the *Angelus* and the *De Profundis* bells), to ask prayers for a departing soul (the passing bell), to announce a death or call attention to a burial, to honor a visiting dignitary, or to celebrate a joyful or solemn occasion. In some places it was the custom to ring the church bell at the consecration of the Mass to invite those not in church to join momentarily in the worship. The ringing of the bells was also a sacramental through which the people sought God's protection from evil spirits and the violence of storms, as is indicated in the ritual of consecration. From early times there was legislation against the use of church bells for profane purposes, although certain emergencies justifying such use were traditionally recognized.

Special forms of blessing and consecration for church bells have been in use in the Western Church since early medieval times. The solemn consecration of a bell bears some superficial resemblance to the baptismal ritual and in popular, but quite unofficial metaphor, the rite is sometimes spoken of as a baptism. There are exorcisms; salt and water are used; the bell is anointed with the holy oils; it is washed and given a name, and sometimes, at least in former times, a place was found for "godparents" in the rite. Since the introduction of the elevation at Mass in the 13th cent. small handbells have been used in church to call the attention of the faithful to the consecrated bread and also to certain other esp. significant moments of the Mass such as the Sanctus and the Communion.

Canonical legislation in the RC Church with regard to the large church bells is contained in the Code of Canon Law (c. 1169). The law declares it fitting that every church should be equipped with bells. Their use is subject to ecclesiastical authority; they should be blessed or consecrated according to the rites contained in approved liturgical books; they should not be used for profane purposes except in case of necessity, or with the permission of the ordinary, or when such use is sanctioned by legitimate custom. The substitution of electronic for true bronze bells has not met with favor. Pius XII in his encyclical *Musicae sacrae disciplina* (1955) declared that only the true bell should be considered acceptable. BIBLIOGRAPHY: *Cymbala: Bells in the Middle Ages* (ed. J. S. Waesberghe, 1951); A. L. Bigelow, NCE 2:259–263; H. Hurston, CE 2:418–423.

[P. K. MEAGHER]

BELMONT, FRANÇOIS VACHON DE (1645–1732), Sulpician missionary. B. left France for Canada (1680) and labored as an Indian missionary near Montreal; he devoted his personal wealth to the mission. After 1701 as superior of the Sulpicians in Canada, he played an important part in the spiritual and temporal development of Montreal. B. was also the author of a MS *History of Canada,* first printed in 1840. BIBLIOGRAPHY: H. Gauthier, *Sulpitiana* (1926).

[R. K. MacMASTER]

BELMONT, ABBEY OF, Benedictine monastery in Hereford, England. Belmont was founded in 1859 and until 1920 was a cathedral priory, the monks comprising the chapter for the bp. of Newport and Menevia. The monks operate a boys' school and serve surrounding parishes. BIBLIOGRAPHY: B. Whelan, *History of Belmont Abbey, England* (1959); idem, NCE 2:264.

[J. R. SOMMERFELDT]

BELMONT ABBEY, Benedictine foundation in Gaston County, N.C. Founded in 1876 by Benedictines of St. Vincent Abbey, Latrobe, Pa., the priory was raised to an abbey in 1884, and Leo Haid, OSB, was elected first abbot (1885). In 1910 Belmont Abbey was designated *abbatia nullius diocesis,* and Bp.-Abbot Haid was named first *abbas ordinarius Belmontanus.* Its territory then included eight counties in North Carolina; in 1945 the number was reduced to one (Gaston County), and in 1960 the territory was limited to the geographic confines of the abbey property. Particularly active in education, the abbey conducted the St. Joseph Industrial School for poor boys in Bristow, Va. (1893–1927), and in 1878 opened St. Mary's College for boys, renamed Belmont Abbey College in 1913. The abbey is also active in parish work in the dioceses of Raleigh and Richmond, Virginia. BIBLIOGRAPHY: R. J. Brennan, "Benedictines in Virginia," *American Benedictine Review* 13 (1962) 32, 33; A. G. Biggs, NCE 2:263–264.

[M. S. TANEY]

BELORUSSKAYA S.S.R. (Byelorussia, Belorussian S.S.R., "White Russia"), Soviet republic established Jan. 1, 1919, with its capital in the industrial city of Minsk. The state covers an area of 80,200 square miles along the Polish boundary in Western Russia and includes a population of more than 9 million. White Russia, along with other eastern Slavic areas, was originally Christianized by St. Vladimir (975–1015) and further evangelized by Bulgarian missionaries and Byzantine monastic establishments. Until 1569 Belorusskaya was under the influence of Lithuania, and its dominant religious group was of the Latin rite. However, it was included in Poland's domain at this time, and with the religious crisis of the 16th cent. it fell heir to numerous schismatic and even heretical tendencies. By 1685 the See of Moscow had absorbed much of the White Russian region and this was finalized after the division of Poland at the end of the 18th century. The political turbulence of this period is reflected in the stormy conflicts of the Churches. It culminated in the proclamation of a dissident Ruthenian hierarchy, which disavowed the Union of Brest in 1596 (ending the Eastern Schism) and which ordered Eastern-rite Catholics to follow the schismatic Holy Synod. This dualism of Christian Churches, along with a number of Protestant sects, was brought to an abrupt climax with the death of the Czar in 1917. The subsequent Communist regime systematically destroyed any power or influence of the Churches (esp. the RC Church, a major obstacle), allowing only a "Living Synod" which was an empty mouthpiece for Communist propaganda. Suppression was stepped up in the 1950s; not even the papal apostolic administrator was permitted to function in the joint See of Minsk-Mogiler. The Church of Belorusskaya, although it sustained some underground monastic religious activity, was effectively silenced. BIBLIOGRAPHY: C. Sipovič, NCE 1:36–37 s.v. "Abrantovič, Fabijan."

[M. E. FORD]

BELOVED DISCIPLE. The phrase "the disciple whom Jesus loved" or its near equivalent is found in Jn 13.23; 19.26; 20.2; 21.7, 20. In all of these passages the context is that of the betrayal, Passion, and Resurrection of Jesus, and his post-Resurrection appearance to the disciples in Galilee. In all but one of the passages Peter is a close associate of this disciple. The exception is 19.26, in which the dying Jesus commits his mother to this disciple's care. No serious grounds have been adduced for denying the tradition that this disciple is in fact John the Apostle himself.

[D. J. BOURKE]

BELSHAZZAR, crown prince, son of King Nabonidus of Babylon. B. ruled over his father's kingdom during the latter's long sojourn in Arabia and was coregent when Babylon was conquered by Cyrus the Great. That the Book of Daniel identifies him (Dan 5.2) as the son of Nebuchadnezzar indicates how far removed are Daniel's historical allusions from the true facts of 6th-cent. B.C. history.

[J. F. FALLON]

BELSUNCE DE CASTELMORAN, HENRI FRANÇOIS XAVIER DE (1671–1755), bishop. After attending the Collège de Clermont, B. joined the Jesuits, but left to become vicar-general of Agen (1699). He became bp. of Marseilles (1709), but refused the sees of Laon and Bordeaux offered him by Louis XV in recognition of his heroic service to plague victims (1720–21). He was known for his stringent opposition to Jansenism. BIBLIOGRAPHY: P. Calendini, DHGE 7:951–953.

[H. JACK]

BELTRÁN, LUIS, ST., see BERTRAND, LOUIS, ST.

BELY, ANDREY (Boris Nikolayevich Bugayev; 1880–1934), leading author of novels, poems, and literary criticism in the symbolist tradition; outstanding representative of Russian Ornamentalism. His conscious exploitation of the richness of sound and rhythm inherent in the Russian language is evident in the rhythmic cadences, the musical intertwining of motifs, and the syntactic and verbal experimentation that characterize his works. But B. is more than a stylist. He intended his works to be read on three levels: as pure music, as satire, and as symbolic expressions of reality. Under the influence of Vladimir Solovyov, Kant, Nietzsche, and the anthroposophist Rudolf Steiner, he developed a religious and mystical philosophy that regarded man's reason as too weak to bring permanent order into a basically chaotic world. The poet, however, by the use of symbols that he knows from mystic revelation, can give expression to a new mythic reality. Under the influence of the Scythians, B. hailed the Revolution of 1917 as the beginning of Russia's spiritual mission to the world (cf. the poem *Christ Is Risen* [1918]). Though he soon rejected Bolshevism, he continued to express his belief in Russia's mystical mission. Besides some volumes of poems and four volumes of lyrical prose, which he called *Symphonies* (1902–08), B. produced three volumes of memoirs (1929–1933), which provide an important literary documentation of his era; several novels, of which the best is *Kotik Letayev* (1918); and a number of literary essays, including one on the theory of symbolism (1910). BIBLIOGRAPHY: O. A. Maslenikov, *Frenzied Poets: Andrey Bely and the Russian Symbolists,* (1952, repr. 1968); R. Poggioli, *Poets of Russia: 1890–1930* (1960) 105–111.

[M. F. MCCARTHY]

BEMA (Gr., raised platform; Syr. *vima*), a judge's tribunal in ancient Greece. In Christian architecture a term having several meanings: (1) in Byzantine and Greek-Antiochene usage, the sanctuary or an elevated ambo for liturgical reading or singing by a soloist; (2) in Syrian usage (Mesopotamia and N Syria), a slightly raised area in the middle of the nave, surrounded by a low wall, curved on the west end, entered from the east, with benches for the clergy along the inside of the wall, where the canonical hours and the readings at the beginning of the Eucharistic celebration were carried out; derived probably from Jewish synagogical arrangements. BIBLIOGRAPHY: J. Lassus and G. Tchalenko, *Cahiers archéologiques* 5 (1951) 75–122; R.-G. Coquin, *L'Orient syrien* 10 (1965) 443–474.

[A. CODY]

BEMBO, PIETRO (1470–1547), humanist, cardinal. In his earlier years as a layman he kept a mistress who bore him several children. After the death of his mistress (1535), he underwent a spiritual conversion, adopted an austere way of life, and turned from his interest in the classics to the study of patristic literature and the Scriptures. Paul III made him a cardinal (1538); he received major orders and was appointed successively bp. of Gubbio (1541) and Bergamo (1544). BIBLIOGRAPHY: E. D. McShane, NCE 2:266–267.

[P. K. MEAGHER]

BEN ASHER, Palestinian Masorete family for whom the Ben Asher textual tradition of the Hebrew Bible is named. Moses and Aaron edited the most important texts (9th-10th cent.) The oldest extant MS of the Hebrew Bible, A.D. 895, is that named the Codex of the Cairo Prophets, the work of Moses Ben Asher. Other Ben Asher MSS are the Aleppo Codex, and the Leningrad Codex. BIBLIOGRAPHY: P. Skehan et al., JBC 2:567–568. *MASORA.

[T. C. O'BRIEN]

BEN-HÂDAD OF DAMASCUS, the name of three Damascene kings. (1) B.-H. I broke his peace treaty with King Baasha of Israel (909–866 B.C.) when bribed by King Asa of Judah whose land was being invaded by Baasha. B.-H. conquered many towns and trade routes in N Israel and thus strengthened Damascus' lucrative trade with Phoenicia and Egypt. His control of N Israel continued during the reign of the great king of Israel, Omri (885–874).

(2) Ben-Hadad II, whose real name was Hadadezer, very likely should not be identified with B.-H.I. He was defeated by Ahab of Israel in two battles, Samaria and Aphek, at which he was captured, but Ahab released him in return for the northern cities taken by his father (1 Kg 20.34). The two kings later were allied at the battle of Qarqar against the Assyrians (853), but resumed their war at Ramoth-gilead where Ahab was killed. B. was suffocated by his servant Hazael who became king as Elisha had prophesied (2 Kg 8.7–15).

(3) Ben-Hadad III followed his father, Hazael, on the Damascene throne (805) but because of pressure from Assyria on the N and from Israel in the S, lost most of the territory his father had controlled. Many scholars identify B.-H. I and B.-H. II.

[J. F. FALLON]

BEN NEFTALI (Nephtali), 9th-10th cent. Palestinian Masoretes for whom the Ben Neftali textual tradition of the Hebrew Bible is named. Like the Ben Asher family, they strove to preserve and standardize the biblical text. BIBLIOGRAPHY: P Skehan et al., JBC 2:568. *MASORA.

[T. C. O'BRIEN]

BENARD, EDMOND DARVIL (1914–61), theologian, author, preacher. He was ordained in 1941 and served in the Diocese of Springfield, Mass. In 1943 he joined the faculty of the School of Sacred Theology at The Catholic Univ. of America. His field of competence was apologetics. He was elected president of the Catholic Theological Society in 1951 and received many awards for his excellent work in theology. His writings include: *A Preface to Newman's Theology; The Appeal to the Emotions in Preaching.* In 1959 he was appointed field editor for *The New Catholic Encyclopedia.* He wrote many articles in the CUA *Bulletin* and the *American Ecclesiastical Review.* He died in a fire at the university. BIBLIOGRAPHY: J. P. Whalen, NCE 2:268.

[J. HILL]

BÉNARD, LAURENT (1573–1620), Benedictine reformer, founder. He joined the order at Nevers, became a doctor of the Sorbonne, and after his ordination, a preacher in Paris. He was a reform prior at the College of Cluny and was influential in the reform of other monasteries. By delegation of the chapter of reformed Benedictines (1618), he founded the independent Congregation of St. Maur at the monastery of Blancs-Manteaux. BIBLIOGRAPHY: B. Heurtebize, DHGE 7:1028–30.

[H. JACK]

BENAVIDES, ALONSO DE (*c.* 1580–1636), Franciscan missionary. After working in various parts of Mexico, B. became superior of the Franciscan missions in New Mexico (1623–29). His report to the King and the Pope on conditions in New Mexico served to publicize the work of the Franciscans. He was made auxiliary bp. of Goa (1636), but died before reaching India. BIBLIOGRAPHY: F. B. Warren, NCE 2:269.

[H. JACK]

BENAVIDES, MIGUEL DE (1552–1605 or 07), Dominican missionary, a founder of the Province of the Most Holy Rosary of the Philippines, abp. of Manila from 1597. With a legacy left by him the Univ. of Santo Tomás was established (1611).

[T. C. O'BRIEN]

BENCH RENT, a small monetary offering made by an individual member of the congregation for a reserved seat in a church.

BENDA, JIŘÍ ANTONÍN (1722–95), Bohemian composer of highly esteemed singspiels (comic operas) frequently performed in Vienna and Berlin during the 18th century. He was a member of a talented musical family, many of whom were composers. He is generally considered the virtual introducer of the melodrama, originally a device in which the spoken voice is used against a musical background. In addition to his stage works, he wrote large quantities of Masses and other church music, as well as instrumental pieces. BIBLIOGRAPHY: A. Loewenberg, Grove DMM 1:614–615.

[J. J. WALSH]

BENEDETTI, PIETRO, see AMBARACH, PETER.

BENEDICAMUS DOMINO (Let us bless the Lord), a formula which, together with its response, *Deo gratias* (thanks be to God), is employed in the Latin liturgy and has also been in wide extraliturgical and customary use among Christians of all times. In the liturgy it has been used in place of the dismissal *(Ite missa est)* since the 11th cent. on nonfestal occasions. The substitution is commonly explained as an invitation to the people to remain after Mass and assist at the prayers that would follow on those occasions. The substitution is no longer made in Masses simply because they are nonfestal, but in those Masses only in which the people are not to be dismissed because of functions that are to follow immediately. The *Benedicamus Domino* is also used as a concluding formula in the Latin Divine Office. BIBLIOGRAPHY: J. Jungman, *Mass of the Roman Rite* (1951) 2:434–437.

[N. KOLLAR]

BENEDICITE DOMINUM, Lat. for "Bless the Lord." The canticle is part of an antiphonal hymn (3.57–90a) added to the Aramaic part of Daniel, probably, by Greek-speaking Jews of Alexandria, Egypt, found in all MSS of the Greek Bible and, therefore, accepted by the Early Christian Church as a canonical part of the OT. St. Jerome did not find it in the Hebrew Bible of his day and, thus, considered it doubtfully canonical. Originally composed in Aramaic or Hebrew, it is put on the lips of the three Israelites cast into a fiery furnace by Nebuchadnezzar for refusing to commit idolatry. It calls upon all God's creatures in heaven and earth to "praise and exalt him above all forever" (the antiphon) and resembles Ps 148. Christians have used it for liturgical praise from early times and only recently has the reform of the liturgy in the RC Church drastically reduced its frequency in the Liturgy of the Hours. Verse 88, which is an invitation to the men, Hananiah, Azariah, Mishael, (their Hebrew names), who are supposed to be singing the hymn up to that point, indicates that the final verses are a later addition. The doxology that precedes the hymn (52–56) has also been used in Christian liturgy from early times.

[J. F. FALLON]

BENEDICT, ST. (480–546), founder of Western monasticism, was born in Norcia (Nursia), Italy, of well-to-do parents, was educated in literary studies in Rome, and undertook an eremitic monastic life under the influence of the Eastern Fathers. Since numerous disciples came to his grotto

near Subiaco for guidance, B. responded to them by adopting a cenobitic way of life and setting up numerous monastic groups under his direction. Because of conflict with the local clergy and the development of more mature ideas of monastic life, B. founded a "Grand Monastery" at Monte Cassino. This fortified hill with its surrounding groves sustained the life to which he called monks by his Rule: a moderately ascetical life of self-discipline, prayer, and work. Although influential in the Church at this time, B. remained at Monte Cassino where he died in 546 and was buried near his sister, St. Scholastica, whose life as a contemplative nun was also lived according to the Benedictine Rule. The best source for B.'s biographical data is St. Gregory the Great's *Dialogues* (593–594), which also mention numerous miracles attributed to B.'s intercession and various occasions when B. encountered famous personages including Totila, the Gothic leader who sacked Rome shortly after B.'s death. The barbarian invasions brought about the destruction of Monte Cassino in 577 and subsequent violations of the remains, including the tombs. B.'s relics were believed to have been translated to Fleury shortly before the restoration of the monastery in 720. Paul VI, in a brief dated October 24, 1964, declared B. to be the patron saint of Europe.

B. was responsible for the construction of several other monasteries and his rule has become the guide for all Western monks. His followers reorganized several times and are found today all over the world in Benedictine, Cistercian, and Trappist Orders. In art B. is shown in the earlier black or later white habit of the order with attributes of a raven with a loaf, and a broken wine cup with a serpent. BIBLIOGRAPHY: J. Mallet, NCE 2:271–273; A. Davril, *ibid.* 12:868; Butler 1:650–655; A. Lentini, BiblSanct 2:1104–71.

[M. E. FORD]

BENEDICT I (d. 578), **POPE** from 575. A Roman elected on the death of John III, B. waited 11 months before being consecrated, a delay probably due to the necessity of imperial confirmation. The disorders attendant on the Lombard invasions are responsible for the loss of all contemporary records. Nothing has survived beyond a few statistics about ordinations performed by B. and the information that he died attempting to cope with a famine while Rome was under siege by the Lombards. He was buried in St. Peter's. BIBLIOGRAPHY: J. Chapin, NCE 2:273; H. K. Mann, CE 2:427.

[P. F. MULHERN]

BENEDICT II, ST. (d. 685), elected **POPE** in 683 upon the death of Leo II, but not consecrated for nearly a year because of a delay in securing imperial approval. He was a presbyter of the Roman *schola cantorum* before his election. Relations between the papal and imperial courts were friendly during B.'s pontificate, and to obviate future delay in the consecration of a pope the Emperor Constantine IV voluntarily yielded his right, by that time customary, to confirm a papal election, asking only that the Exarch of Ravenna be notified. This meant a relaxation of imperial control of papal elections, but at the same time it opened the way for a greater intervention by powerful Roman families and factions. As with many 7th-cent. popes, B. was much engaged in the struggle against Monothelite influences in East and West, and he pressed for acceptance of the decrees of the Third Council of Constantinople in Spain and in Constantinople itself. He has been credited with achieving the restoration of Wilfrid of York to his see, but B.'s letters on Wilfrid's behalf were ignored by the King of Northumbria, who kept the exiled bishop out of his see until after B.'s death. BIBLIOGRAPHY: Mann 1.2:54–63; Hughes HC 2:106; Butler 2:252; H. G. J. Beck, NCE 2:273.

[P. F. MULHERN]

BENEDICT III (d. 858), **POPE** from 855. From its beginning his reign was complicated by the attempt of the Emperor Louis II to impose Anastasius (excommunicated by Leo IV) upon the Church as pope. B. had the support of the clergy and people of Rome who refused to accept the imperial antipope. He ruled with firmness, boldly protesting clerical abuses in the Frankish Church and reproving the licentiousness of the Frankish nobles. He espoused the cause of bps. both in England and in France who had been deposed without a proper trial, as when he approved the acts of the Council of Soissons that upheld the right of Hincmar to the See of Reims. BIBLIOGRAPHY: Mann 2:308–329; S. McKenna, NCE 2:273.

[P. F. MULHERN]

BENEDICT IV (d. 903), **POPE** from 900, a Roman who had been ordained priest by Pope *Formosus. Like his predecessor, John IX, B. sought to undo the scandal wrought by *Stephen VI's annulment of the acts and ordinations of Formosus. The Magyar invasion of northern Italy, against which King Berengar could provide no adequate defense, caused B. to look to Louis III of Burgundy for help. Louis was crowned emperor in 902, but was driven from Italy by Berengar, leaving the Holy See without an effective protector. BIBLIOGRAPHY: Mann 4:103–110; S. McKenna, NCE 2:273.

[P. F. MULHERN]

BENEDICT V (d. c.966), **POPE** for one month in 964. B., known as Grammaticus, apparently a learned man, was a Roman and cardinal-deacon of St. Marcellus. He took part in the Roman Synod of 963 that deposed *John XII and put *Leo VIII in his place. Within a few months, however, on John's death, B. accepted election as pope, thus repudiating Leo VIII who had been forced on the Romans while John XII still lived. The Emperor thereupon descended upon Rome with an army to put Leo VIII back on the papal throne. In a synod held at the Lateran, B. was deposed and degraded to a deacon; he lived out his days in custody of the abp. of Hamburg. *Liutprand, not always a trustworthy witness, reports that B. admitted the charges against him and accepted his deposition. BIBLIOGRAPHY: Mann 4:272–281; A. Mer-

cati, "New List of the Popes," MedSt 9 (1947) 71–80; S. McKenna, NCE 2:273–274.

[P. F. MULHERN]

BENEDICT VI (d. 974), **POPE** from 973. Through the influence of the Emperor Otto I, B. was chosen to succeed John XIII. Taking advantage of the death of Otto I and the accession of the youthful Otto II, a certain Crescentius led a revolt of the Roman nobility. B. was put in prison (where he was later strangled), and an antipope under the name of Boniface VII was put in his place. BIBLIOGRAPHY: Mann 4:305–314; S. McKenna, NCE 2:274.

[P. F. MULHERN]

BENEDICT VII (d. 983), **POPE** from 974. B. was bp. of Sutri when he was chosen by the Emperor Otto II to succeed the murdered Benedict VI as pope. His reign was relatively peaceful, in spite of intrigues in Rome stirred up by the party of the antipope Boniface VII, who had fled to Constantinople upon B.'s accession. In the presence of Otto II, B. presided over a synod (981) that gave evidence of a trend toward reform by taking a strong stand against simony. B. was personally interested in the conversion of the Slavs, but his suppression, for political reasons, of the German diocese of Merseburg was hurtful to the cause. He favored with privileges many monasteries in Germany and France that were to be the core of church reform in the next century. BIBLIOGRAPHY: Mann 4:315–329; S. McKenna, NCE 2:274.

[P. F. MULHERN]

BENEDICT VIII (Theophylactus; d. 1024), **POPE** from 1012. Approved by Emperor Henry II, he crowned Henry and the Empress Kunigunde at Rome in 1014. The most significant pope reigning between Sylvester II and Leo IX, B. was both statesman and reformer, following the lead of the Franconian house of Germany. After visiting Bamberg (1020), B. accompanied Henry on his southern Italian campaign (1021–22). His reform efforts against simony and clerogamy culminated in the synod of Pavia, Aug. 1022, whose decrees were enacted as imperial law. BIBLIOGRAPHY: W. Kölmel, *Rom und der Kirchenstaat im 10. and 11. Jahrhundert* (1935); J. Haller, *Das Papsttum* (1951) 2:229–234, 562–564; F. X. Seppelt, *Geschichte der Päpste* (1955) 2:402–408.

[O. J. BLUM]

BENEDICT IX (Theophylactus; d. 1055?), **POPE** (1032 or 33–1045). The son of Alberic III, leader of the Tusculan nobility that dominated Rome, he simoniacally succeeded his uncle John XIX. He was perhaps 30 at his accession, and not 10 or 12 as reported by Rodulphus Glaber. Vague and unspecific charges brought against him by later chroniclers seem to reflect the attitude of Gregorian reformers, influenced by his resignation and his political struggles with both Crescentian and imperial opponents. The early years of his pontificate were normal: he collaborated with Emperor Conrad II and at Christmas 1035 canonized St. Simeon of Syracuse. In 1044 a Crescentian revolt drove B. from Rome, where he was replaced by Bp. John of Sabina, the antipope Sylvester III. The following March B. overcame Sylvester, but wearied by the effort, sold his office to the arch-priest John Gratiano, his god-father, who took the name *Gregory VI. At Sutri in 1046, Gregory was deposed by Emperor Henry III and was replaced by Clement II. At the latter's sudden death (by poison) in 1047, B. again controlled Rome from Nov. 1047 to July 1048, when the forces of Boniface of Tuscany, acting for the Emperor, expelled him from the city. BIBLIOGRAPHY: R. L. Poole, "Benedict IX and Gregory VI," *Proceedings of the British Academy* 8 (1917–18) 199–235; G. B. Borino "Invitus ultra montes . . . ," StGreg 1 (1947) 3–46; V. Gellhaus, NCE 2:274–275 (excellent bibliog.).

[O. J. BLUM]

BENEDICT XI, BL. (Niccolò Boccasini; 1240–1304), **POPE** from 1303. A Dominican scholar, teacher, commentator on the Scriptures, and administrator, B. was elected master general of the order in 1296 and used his influence to keep the Dominicans loyal to Boniface VIII in 1297, and thereafter served the Holy See in various diplomatic capacities. The respect in which he was generally held led to his election as pope on the first ballot in 1303. In the interests of peace he modified somewhat the *Clericis laicos* of Urban VIII, and this led to the reconciliation of Philip IV of France. He was beatified by Clement XII in 1736. BIBLIOGRAPHY: L. Jadin, DHGE 8:106–116; L. Berra, BiblSanct 2:1194–1201.

[P. K. MEAGHER]

BENEDICT XII (Jacques Fournier; d. 1342), **POPE** from 1334. A Cistercian of Boulbonne, B. studied theology at Paris, becoming abbot of Fontfroide (1311), bp. of Pamiers (1317) and of Mirepoix (1326), cardinal (1327), and pope (1334). An austere man, his first act as pope was to send home all clergy who could not show a reason for remaining in the curia. He also attempted to reform the curia and to soften the bureaucracy of his predecessor, John XXII; he was unfavorable to nepotism, but was an indifferent administrator. An able theologian, he terminated the controversy, begun in the pontificate of John XXII, over the Beatific Vision. In 1336 he published a notable constitution for the reform of the Benedictines. He failed to settle the question of Louis of Bavaria, mainly because of pressure from France and Naples. To B. the idea of returning to Rome was not as attractive as it had been to John XXII; and it is to him we owe the construction of the great papal fortress at Avignon. BIBLIOGRAPHY: S. Baluze, *Vitae paparum avenionensium* (ed. G. Mollat, 1914) 1:195–240; G. Mollat, *Popes at Avignon, 1305–1378* (tr. J. Love, 1963); Y. Renouard, *Avignon Papacy* (tr. D. Bethel, 1970).

[L. E. BOYLE]

BENEDICT XIII, ANTIPOPE, (Pedro de Luna; *c.* 1328–1422 or 1423), Spanish cleric. A distinguished canonist and professor, he became cardinal in 1375 and supported the election of Clement VII, antipope. Favoring the reunion of Rome with Avignon, B. was elected pope at Clement's death. As pope, B. hedged on specific steps to end the Western Schism and refused his own resignation as a means to this end. After he lost the support of France (1408), the Councils of Pisa (1409) and of Constance (1417) deposed him. Martin V's papal election healed the schism though B. refused to accept his deposition. Banished from Avignon, he retired alone to Valencia. BIBLIOGRAPHY: G. Pou y Marti, EncCatt 2:1277–79; L. Jadin, DHGE 8:135–163.

[M. H. BEIRNE]

BENEDICT XIII (Pietro Francesco Orsini; 1649–1730), **POPE** from 1724. B. was the third member of the Orsini family to attain the papacy. At an early age he defied his family and became a Dominican. As a friar he proved himself an excellent religious and a good student. He was named cardinal at the age of 23, but tried to resist the honor, knowing that it came through family influence. He became successively abp. of Manfredonia (Siponto) in 1675, of Cesena (1680), and of Benevento (1686), in the last of which posts he served for 38 years, living the life of a simple friar and giving his energies to the performance of his pastoral duties. Though an eminently devout pope and a vigorous opponent of Jansenism, his unworldliness made him too ready a victim of unworthy and venal advisers. BIBLIOGRAPHY: J. S. Brusher, NCE 2:276–277; C. Castiglione, EncCatt 2:1279–81.

[J. C. WILLKE]

BENEDICT XIV (Prospero Lorenzo Lambertini; 1675–1758), **POPE** from 1740. Of Bolognese origin, B. studied at the Clementinum in Rome and at the Univ. of Rome, taking doctorates in theology and law. He held a number of important offices under Popes Innocent XII, Clement XI, Innocent XIII, and Benedict XIII, who raised him to the cardinalate in 1728. As abp. of Ancona (1727) he showed himself a zealous pastor and devoted himself energetically to the spiritual welfare of his flock. As pope he found broader scope for his wide range of interests and abilities. B. was a first-rate scholar, promoted historical studies and research, worked for the conservation and restoration of historical monuments, founded learned academies, enlarged the Vatican Library, and established new chairs at the Univ. of Rome. He administered the Papal States with energy and imaginative foresight, accomplishing much to improve the living conditions of his subjects. His negotiations with secular powers were deft and wise and enabled him to work his way through difficult situations to achieve peace and understanding without weakening the Church. He was well liked and held in great respect by Protestant as well as Catholic monarchs and by scholars far and wide, even some who were otherwise inimical to the Church. He brought to satisfactory solution many serious problems confronting the Church, e.g., the *Unigenitus* issue, the Chinese and Malabar rites controversy. He found means to improve the selection of bishops and settled vexing questions concerning usury and mixed marriages. One of his books, *On the Beatification and Canonization of Servants of God,* remains even now the classical and authoritative work on the subject; another, *On the Diocesan Synod* was one of the most important works on canon law before the Code. Other influential works include the legislation during his pontificate, a collection of pastoral letters and scientific treatises, and private letters, of which 760 have survived. These last reveal his affable, warm, lively personality, his sense of humor, and capacity for gentle sarcasm, along with the amazing breadth of his interests and scholarship. BIBLIOGRAPHY: *Opera* (ed. J. Silvester, 17 v., 1839–47); M. J. Shay, NCE 2:278; Pastor 35–36.

[J. C. WILLKE]

BENEDICT XV (Giacomo Della Chiesa; 1854–1922), **POPE** from 1914. Ordained priest in 1878, B. did graduate work leading to doctorates in theology (1879) and canon law (1880) at the Gregorian Univ. in Rome. He became attached to the papal secretariate of state through the influence of Abp. Rampolla, whose secretary he became when the abp. was made apostolic nuncio to Spain (1882). In 1887 Rampolla was made papal secretary of state by Leo XIII; B. continued to serve him as secretary and in 1901 was appointed undersecretary *(sostituto)* of state. He continued in that office under Card. Merry del Val, who was appointed secretary of state upon the accession of Pius X to the papal throne (1903), but Merry del Val was something less than enthusiastic in his admiration of his undersecretary and at length persuaded Pius to detach B. from the diplomatic service and appoint him abp. of Bologna. In Bologna he distinguished himself by his zealous pastoral solicitude. Pius X, shortly before his death, elevated B. to the cardinalate (1914). He was elected pope in the conclave that followed the death of Pius. A factor influencing his election appears to have been the high esteem in which his diplomatic abilities were held by many who did not share Merry del Val's dim view of them. The outbreak of World War I seemed to require the choice of a pontiff of proven capacity in diplomacy. The war made B.'s reign difficult; he was filled with grief at the suffering of so many and it put a heavy strain upon the Vatican treasury to carry out the works of mercy he initiated and encouraged. He suffered criticism from both sides; his peace proposals were bluntly spurned by Central and Allied Powers alike. Under B. the initial steps were taken that ultimately culminated in the resolution of the *Roman question (1929) and the Code of Canon Law, in the drawing up of which B. took a keen interest, was published in 1917. Steps were taken to better relations between Latin and Oriental Churches. BIBLIOGRAPHY: W. H. Peters, *Life of Benedict XV* (1959); *idem,* NCE 2:279–280.

[P. K. MEAGHER]

BENEDICT OF ANIANE, ST. (*c*.750–821), monk. A noble Aquitanian Visigoth in the service of Pepin III, B. was professed as a Benedictine monk in 773; he founded on his property (779) the monastery of Aniane and became its first abbot. Adviser of Louis I on monastic affairs and superior of all communities in Frankland, he was brought by Louis to Aix-la-Chapelle, and the King erected for him nearby the monastery of Inde. B. became restorer of Western monasticism with new interpretations of the Benedictine Rule, striving for centralization and uniformity. With imperial aid he achieved the first code for all monasteries in one area. Not a spiritual guide, he nonetheless instituted daily recitation of the Office of the Dead. Stressing contemplation, he discouraged outsiders in monastic schools. BIBLIOGRAPHY: S. Hilpisch, NCE 2:280–281; I. Mannocci, BiblSanct 2:1093–96.

[A. CABANISS]

BENEDICT OF BENEVENTO, ST. (d. 1003), missionary and martyr. He was murdered in Poland with the rest of a missionary band called the Five Brothers, of which he was the leader. His cult was early and popular and was confirmed by Julius II in 1508. BIBLIOGRAPHY: J. David, DHGE 8:3–5; Zimmermann 3:291–294; Butler 4:324–325; P. Naruszewicz, BiblSanct 2:1216–18.

[J. L. GRASSI]

BENEDICT BISCOP, ST. (d. 690), Anglo-Saxon abbot. A Northumbrian noble, B. became a religious and made at least five journeys to Rome, returning with materials, workers, and styles with which to build and decorate Anglo-Saxon churches. He founded the monasteries of Wearmouth and Jarrow, amassed an important library, was a teacher of Bede, and helped transmit European religious and cultural influences to Anglo-Saxon England. BIBLIOGRAPHY: G. Mongelli, 2:1212–16; Butler 1:72–74.

[J. DRUSE]

BENEDICT OF CANFIELD (William Fitch; 1563–1610), a native of England, brought up as a Protestant, but was converted to the Catholic faith (1585) while studying law in London. He became a Capuchin friar in Paris (1587) and achieved a considerable reputation as a director of souls and a spiritual writer. B. spent the years 1599–1601 in prison in England where he had been sent to work as a missionary; after his release he returned to France. Two of his works, *Rule of Perfection* (1609) and *Christian Knight* (1609), contributed to shaping the thought of Card. Bérulle and St. Vincent de Paul, and were among the notable contributions to the spiritual doctrine of the 17th century. His teaching, which was most fully expressed in his *Rule of Perfection,* centers the spiritual life about the will of God and correlates the different stages of spiritual development and the different types of prayer that characterize them. In the latter part of the century this work came under suspicion during the Quietist controversy and was for a time on the

Index. BIBLIOGRAPHY: O. Van Veghel, *Benoît de Canfield: Sa vie, sa doctrine et son influence* (1949); C. de Nant, DSAM 1:446–51.

[J. C. WILLKE]

BENEDICT II OF CLUSE, VEN . (1033–91); abbot. Educated from early childhood in a Benedictine abbey in France, B. entered the Abbey of St. Michael in northern Italy and was ordained a priest. He was elected at the age of 33 abbot of St. Michael. The bp. of Turin refused to confirm him and B. appealed to Pope Alexander II, who consecrated him abbot. B. was an ascetic and reformer who brought his monastery back to strict Benedictine observance. He was a friend and advocate of Gregory VII and stood with the Pope in his strenuous efforts to reform the Church of the 11th century. As a result, he earned the enmity of Emperor Henry and many of the bishops and clergy of northern Italy. Cunibert, bp. of Turin, persecuted B. and robbed the abbey time and time again in spite of the protection of Pope Gregory. The saintly abbot died after having headed St. Michael for 25 years. BIBLIOGRAPHY: F. Baix, DHGE 8:200–203.

[J. R. AHERNE]

BENEDICT THE LEVITE or Benedict the Deacon, the name given to the mysterious author of a compilation of pseudocapitularies in the style of the *False Decretals, including 1,319 chapters as books 5, 6 and 7, additions to the 4 books of the authentic collection of Ansegis. In the preface the author claims that he is a deacon of the Diocese of Mainz and that he is writing this book under the commission of Abp. Autgar (d. 847). Yet, the author is probably from Le Mans. The work as a whole is quite different from the collection of Ansegis. Three-fourths of the chapters are apocryphal with quotations from divergent sources, and certain texts are repeated three or four times. The resemblance between this work and the False Decretals suggests that the author was using a pseudonym and that he was trying to remedy the abuses of the metropolitan and provincial councils of the Frankish Church by reiterating the independent prerogatives of ecclesiastical jurisdiction during the crumbling of the Carolingian Empire. BIBLIOGRAPHY: F. Baix, DHGE 8:214–218; S. Williams, "Pseudo-Isidorian Problem Today," *Speculum* 29 (1954) 702–707.

[F. H. BRIGHAM]

BENEDICT THE MOOR, ST. (1526–89), patron of the Negroes of North America, Franciscan lay brother. Born in Sicily, a slave until 18, and then a day laborer, B. devoted himself and his meager earnings to the poor and the sick. On an occasion when he was being taunted about his color, he met Jerome Lanza, a hermit. B. later joined him and his group of solitaries, becoming their leader when Lanza died. When the group was disbanded at the order of Pius IV (1562), B. became a Franciscan lay brother. He was cook at the Palermo friary, was chosen guardian in 1578, and then named master of novices. Finally, he was cook again at his own request. His sanctity became widely known, and people of every class pursued "il moro santo" for spiritual counsel. BIBLIOGRAPHY: G. Morabito, BiblSanct 2:1103–04; Butler 2:30–31.

[H. JACK]

BENEDICT OF NURSIA, ST., see BENEDICT, ST.

BENEDICT OF PETERBOROUGH (d. 1193), abbot and chronicler whose life of Thomas Becket was probably that of an eyewitness. He was a friend of Richard I and a leading historian of his day, the *Gesta Henrici II* being long ascribed to him. BIBLIOGRAPHY: D. M. Stenton, "Roger of Howden" and "Benedict", EHR 68 (1953) 574–582; E. M. Thompson, DNB 2:213–214; M. J. Hamilton, NCE 2:283.

[J. L. GRASSI]

BENEDICT THE POLE (fl. 1245–47), Franciscan missionary. In 1245, as interpreter and companion to the envoy (John da Pian del Carpine) of Pope Innocent IV to the Great Khan of the Mongols, B. reached the camp of Batu Khan and of Kuyuk (Great Khan) in 1246. After returning to Europe late in 1246, he produced an account of his travels with the help of a prelate and a scholastic at Cologne. BIBLIOGRAPHY: A. van den Wyngaert, DHGE 8:250; J. Campbell, NCE 2:283.

[M. E. DUFFY]

BENEDICT, RULE OF ST., a monastic rule of life, probably written in part at Monte Cassino by St. Benedict during the latter part of his life (530). It reveals a maturity in spiritual wisdom and experience in government. The Bible was the principal source of the rule; however, it reflects the philosophies of SS. Leo, Cyprian, and Augustine, and earlier monastic rules. St. Benedict moderated the severity of older rules and offered instead a common-sense way of life more useful to ordinary men attracted to prayer and labor in God's service through entire obedience to the abbot and the rule. It has maintained abbatial authority and autonomy of the individual monastery for more than 14 centuries. One feature of the rule, its remarkable adaptability to a wide variety of cultural and social circumstances, no doubt accounts in large part for the durability of the Benedictine way of life. The rule provides guiding principles for formation, government, and administration of the monastery. It devotes 11 of 73 chapters to the spiritual direction of its monks. The prologue and chapters on obedience and humility are skillful works of wisdom. In comprising his system of daily prayer and general regulations, Benedict exercises a wise moderation and gentleness. Commentaries on the rule are numerous, among which are those written by Paul the Deacon (778–780) and Abbot P. Delatte (1950). The objective of Benedict's rule was to help his monks attain the degree of perfection proper to their state as cenobites. BIBLIOGRAPHY: D. R. Sorg, *Towards a Benedictine Theology of Manual Labor* (1951); C. Butler, *Benedictine Monachism* (1919);

Rule of St. Benedict (tr. A. C. Meisel and M. L. Del Mastro, pa. 1975).

[C. KEENAN]

BENEDICTINE FEDERATION OF THE AMERICAS, see BENEDICTINES.

BENEDICTINE OBLATES, see OBLATES OF ST. BENEDICT.

BENEDICTINE SPIRITUALITY, the monastic way of Christian perfection originating with St. Benedict of Norcia. Monastic, it is a contemplative life, a journey toward perfect union in charity with the Father. Specifics are broad and varied: in origin they have links with the most ancient monasticism of both East and West; in historical spread they include the eremitic life of the *Camaldolese and the multiform Benedictine and *Cistercian foundations. Benedictine spirituality is a pattern not only for vowed, religious life, but for the life of *oblates and other layfolk associated with monasteries. In some eras alien elements have intruded, e.g., the spirit of the 14th- and 15th-cent. *Devotio moderna;* certain non-authentic influences in 19th-cent. forms of restoration; but more recently there has been a marked return to ancient and simpler Benedictine ideals. These have their original formulation in the Benedictine Rule, and their exemplification in St. Benedict's vita as drawn by St. *Gregory the Great, *Dialogues,* Book Two. The rule and its author's life evince a spirit of serenity, moderateness, flexibility towards differing needs. With varying emphases and modes the monastic program consists in observances, labor—both manual and intellectual—ascetic practices, seclusion from the world. All, however, are subordinate to prayer: personal prayer issuing from scriptural and patristic reading and meditation; communitary prayer, the *opus Dei,* which has come to be so identified with Benedictines. The distinctive, vivifying force is the guidance of simple, yet profoundly theological principles. Fundamental is a constant attentiveness to God's fatherly, provident presence. Stress on humility is but the inculcation of an attitude of total reliance on God's nearness and of complete dependence on the workings of his grace. A deep, personal love for Christ, in whom the Father's care and grace are most manifest, motivates as well obedience to the abbot as Christ's representative, and the love of even the least of Christ's brethren. Zeal for living the monastic life is itself an acknowledgment in praise of God's grace as source of every good action. Devotion to the Liturgy of the Hours is above all an eagerness to offer praise due to the Father, and at the same time to enter into the most favorable setting for his presence. It is the supreme source of prayer and the disposition for the Holy Spirit's quickening of charity and the experience of the divine. Benedictine spirituality has formed lives enriching the Church, serving mankind's needs and cultural progress. Because of its antiquity and its closeness to gospel teaching, this way of perfection is at the origin of all others in the Western Church; it remains in itself an abiding witness to the power, profundity, and hardiness of a scripturally and patristically guided evangelical life. BIBLIOGRAPHY: E. C. Butler, *Benedictine Monachism* (1919, repr. 1961); C. Delatte, *Rule of St. Benedict* (tr. J. McCann, repr. 1950); D. Knowles, *Christian Monasticism* (1969); C. Marmion, *Christ the Ideal of the Monk* (repr. 1948); M. Wolter, *Principles of Monasticism* (tr. A. Sause, 1962).

[T. C. O'BRIEN]

BENEDICTINES, monks who follow the Rule of St. Benedict. These do not make up a single order, as later the term was applied to the friars, who were unified in their constitutions and government under single masters-general. St. Benedict apparently did not envisage the spread of his monks beyond the monasteries he himself founded, and these were independent, autonomous communities, each with its abbot or prior when the monastery did not enjoy abbatial status. Thus the bond linking Benedictine monks has been in the main a spiritual rather than an organizational one, viz., their acceptance of a common rule of life.

The nature of Benedictine life. As conceived by the Rule of St. Benedict, Benedictine life was designed to provide a communal mode of living for men who wished to withdraw from the world and dedicate themselves to manual labor and prayer, esp. liturgical prayer, for the celebration of the Eucharist and the chanting of the Divine Office were their most important duties. Originally most of the monks had only lay status, with only one or a few priests in a monastery as these were needed for carrying out the liturgy. But reading, encouraged by the rule, and the work of education gradually led to the development of scholarship and a large increase in the number of monks in a monastery dedicated to its pursuit. Such monks came to be less occupied with manual work than with teaching, writing, the copying of MSS, and other scholarly activities. By the beginning of the 11th cent., most of the monks with sufficient literary capacity were separated from the others; these were called choir monks and their chief occupation became the celebration of the liturgy and scholarly pursuits. Most of the choir monks in due course were ordained priests. As distinguished from the choir monks, the other monks, commonly unqualified by their lack of education, were exempted from the duties of the choir, and became known as lay brothers, i.e., nonclerical brothers or monks. A simpler form of prayer was prescribed for them, and they were exempted from the duties of the choir. They were mainly occupied in agriculture, construction, the arts and crafts, and in the maintenance of the monastery.

The contribution of Benedictine monks to the Western Church was enormous. Their missionary work was (and still is) extensive. To them must be credited, more than to any other single agency, the establishment and consolidation of

Christianity in northern and central Europe. Their pastoral work, esp. among those living within the vicinities of the monasteries, bore great fruit. Their cultural and civilizing influence through their preservation of the learning of the past during the Dark Ages and through the monastic schools they established is acknowledged by all. They provided a source from which the Church drew many of its most distinguished curial and diplomatic officials, bishops, cardinals, and popes for a span of centuries. Their leadership in liturgical worship made itself felt throughout the world. Benedictine scholars have enriched Christian literature, esp. in the fields of history, theology, Scripture, canon law, and in ascetico-mystical writing.

Declines and reforms. Most Benedictine monasteries of early, and some of later foundation, underwent periods of decline which brought some to extinction, but in many cases the declines were matched by periods of reform and renewed vitality. A variety of factors contributed to these periods of decline, some of which sprang from a weakness contained in the Benedictine monastic system itself—the independence of each monastery, which made it difficult for the strong to come to the support of the weak, and the concentration of effective authority in the hands of abbots. This worked well when abbots were able leaders and deeply dedicated to the ideas of the monastic life, but it also opened the way to abuses when circumstances were less favorable. Other factors contributing to decline arose from the monasteries' involvement in the general social structure in feudal times. Their very success during periods of prosperity and good discipline opened the way to deterioration. The power and wealth under monastic control made the office of abbot an enviable prize for worldly men, and in the conferral of it wealthy patrons, nobles, kings, or other feudal overlords often played a decisive role. In later times it became a common practice to make commendatory abbots of ecclesiastics or even laymen who were not members of the order. In the place of such abbots, acting superiors were appointed to see to the administration of the communities. These were commonly less worthy of the office than properly chosen abbots would have been. To the commendatory abbots went a large part of the communities' revenues, and this often left the monks without sufficient means for their support or for the maintenance of the monasteries and the furtherance of their works.

However, despite these difficulties, there never appears to have been a universal decline in Benedictine monasticism throughout the whole of Europe. Individual monasteries waxed and waned, and where there had been decline, it was not infrequently overcome by reform movements, which restored discipline and order and reestablished the type of life St. Benedict had contemplated in his rule. Much was accomplished through the consolidation of monasteries into congregations, through which the influence of the stronger upon the weaker houses was increased.

Nevertheless, with the Reformation came the suppression of many monasteries in countries under Protestant control, and later in Catholic countries under the influence of the Enlightenment. In the British Isles there was a general dissolution of monasteries. In France many monastic and religious establishments were suppressed in the century following the French Revolution, as happened also in Belgium. Under Joseph II, Holy Roman Emperor (r. 1765–90), and for some years thereafter, the monasteries suffered harassment and suppression, and by 1807 none were left in Baden, Bavaria, nor Würtemberg. Elsewhere—in Switzerland, the Rhineland, Spain, Portugal, central Italy, and Brazil—monasteries suffered a similar fate.

Modern period. But even before the tide of confiscation and suppression had run its course, the remarkable recuperative capacity of the Benedictine ideal asserted itself again, and a new resurgence of Benedictine life began. In Austria, Hungary, Spain, and Italy the monks succeeded in founding new houses and recovering some that had been lost. English Benedictines welcomed French refugee monks. The Abbey of Ampleforth was founded in 1802 and that of Downside in 1814, and these became thriving centers from which other foundations were made. A monastic house called Fort Augustus was established in 1876 in Scotland and was raised to abbatial status in 1888; it is now aggregated to the English Benedictine Congregation. Forming the English province of the Cassinese Congregation of Primitive Observance, other monasteries were established: Buckfast (1882), Ramsgate (1856), Prinknash (1914), and Farnborough (1895). Since 1947 this last named establishment has been a house dependent on Prinknash.

In the U.S. the largest Benedictine congregation is known as the American Cassinese Federation (formerly the American Cassinese Congregation). It was founded by a group of Benedictine monks headed by Boniface Wimmer, who came from the Bavarian monastery of Metten in 1846. They settled at Latrobe, Pa., where their house became a priory in 1852 and was raised to abbatial status in 1855. This federation is now represented by one archabbey (St. Vincent's in Latrobe), fourteen abbeys, and four houses of prioral status in the U.S. and one abbey in Canada. The second largest federation is known as the Benedictine Federation of the Americas (formerly the Swiss-American Congregation). The charter members of this federation were two foundations made by Swiss abbeys, one at St. Meinrad in Indiana, and the other, Conception Abbey, at Conception, Mo. This federation is now represented by one archabbey (St. Meinrad's) and ten abbeys and one priory in the U.S. and by one abbey in Canada. Besides these two federations, there are monasteries belonging to other congregations. The English Benedictine tradition is represented in the U.S. by two abbeys and one priory; the Sylvestrine Benedictines by one priory; the Congregation of St. Ottilien for Foreign Missions by one abbey and a mission house; the Hungarian Congregation and the Congregation of the Annunciation each have a priory in California; and there are two priories unaffiliated with any congregation or federation. BIBLIOGRAPHY: D. Knowles and D. Obolensky, *Christian Centuries* (1968), 2:184–197;

E. C. Butler, *Benedictine Monachism* (repr. 1961); H. Van Zeller, *Benedictine Idea* (1960). *MONASTICISM.

[J. C. WILLKE]

BENEDICTINES (SISTERS), a congregation of women who follow the Rule of St. Benedict, originally founded by St. Scholastica in the 6th cent. near Monte Cassino, Italy. Before the end of the 10th cent. they had spread throughout Europe; they experienced remarkable growth in England from Saxon times until the Reformation. Their congregations have survived a history of suppression, reformation, and restoration. In Europe, the majority of the Benedictine nuns are subject to the local ordinary; they are cloistered and lead a contemplative life. In the U.S. they have flourished: of pontifical jurisdiction are the Benedictine Nuns of the Primitive Observance; the congregations of St. Scholastica, (22 motherhouses), of St. Gertrude the Great (15 motherhouses), of St. Benedict (1 motherhouse); the Benedictine Sisters of Perpetual Adoration (1 motherhouse); and the Missionary Benedictine Sisters (1 motherhouse). Of diocesan jurisdiction are the Benedictine Sisters of Westmoreland County, Pa., and of Boulder, Colo.; the Olivetan Benedictine Sisters of Little Rock, Ark.; and the Benedictine Sisters Regina Pacis of New Bedford, N.H. BIBLIOGRAPHY: L. Daly, *Benedictine Monasticism* (1970); J. Oetgen, "Boniface Wimmer and the American Benedictines," ABR (1974) 1–32; T. P. McCarthy, *Challenge for Now* (1974).

[C. KEENAN]

BENEDICTINES, AMERICAN CASSINESE, see BENEDICTINES.

BENEDICTINES, ENGLISH see BENEDICTINES.

BENEDICTINES, OLIVETAN (*Congregatio S. Mariae Montis Oliveti, O.S.B..*), monastic order established (1313) by Bl. Bernard Tolomei at Ancona, near Siena. In 1319 Bp. Guido of Arezzo gave Bernard and his companions the white habit and the Benedictine Rule. The institute flourished initially, but during the next 2 cent. experienced periods of decline and subsequent reform, until the 17th cent. when the order flourished with nearly 2,000 monks in 100 houses. Italian political disturbances and suppressions of the 18th and 19th cent. again reduced their numbers. Exceptional monks helped once more to restore the congregation in Italy, and during the latter 19th cent. and early 20th, houses were established elsewhere in Europe and in South America and the U.S.

[A. A. O'NEILL]

BENEDICTINES, SYLVESTRINE, a religious order founded (1231) by St. Silvester Guzzolini (1177–1267). The monks lived an eremitical life in caves and huts and were engaged in prayer and apostolic work among the neighboring peasants. In 1247 they won the approval of Pope Innocent IV and their number grew until it reached 1,000 monks in the 14th century. In spite of drastic poverty and suppression, the community eventually spread to India, Australia, and North America. Noted for their sanctity, Sylvestrines count several *beati* among their members. Varino Favorine, Bp. of Nocera, composed (1514) the first printed Greek lexicon *Magnum et perutile dictionarium*. In the 1970s the Sylvestrines had 225 religious, of whom 138 were priests, and 21 houses.

[A. A. O'NEILL]

BENEDICTIO THALAMI, a special blessing of the marriage bed, contained in the old Roman Ritual. It consists of several versicles and responses and a prayer, during which the priest makes a sign of the cross and ends by sprinkling the bed with holy water. This blessing appears to be in less frequent use than in former times, although a formula for it is included in P.T. Weller's *Roman Ritual* (1964) under the title "Blessing of the Bridal Chamber" (p. 462).

[R. A. TODD]

BENEDICTION OF THE BLESSED SACRAMENT, a devotion in which the Sacred Host is exposed either in its place of reservation or upon the altar and then held aloft and moved in a sign of the cross to signify the blessing of the people. In its public or solemn form the Sacrament is exposed in a monstrance. It is censed; hymns are sung; a versicle, response, and prayer are chanted; the blessing is imparted, and the *divine praises are recited. In the private or simple form a veiled ciborium is exposed either in the tabernacle or on the altar and is used in the blessing. The practice arose to meet the great desire to look upon the Sacred Host that resulted from the centering of much eucharistic devotion upon Christ's presence in the Sacrament. The elevation was introduced in the Mass in the 13th cent. and by the 14th was generally observed throughout Europe. The exposition of the Host at the various stations of the Corpus Christi procession was common in the 14th century. Benediction, as it is known today, was probably a development of this custom; mention of it occurs from the 15th cent. onward. The Church's approval of the practice has been somewhat guarded. Canon law permits it in its simple form for a reasonable cause, but in its solemn form, except for the Feast of Corpus Christi, only for a serious reason and with the consent of the local ordinary. This caution appears to stem from concern that the practice of looking upon the Blessed Sacrament as an object of worship should not displace or overshadow the view of it as a means of worship, i.e,, as a means of going to God through Christ in the Sacrifice of the Mass and in communion. Benediction, however, was declared to be a true liturgical action in the *Instruction on Sacred Music and Liturgy* (1958). Its use is sanctioned in the *Instruction on Eucharistic Worship* (1967); the Congregation for Divine Worship issued a new instruction and rite in 1973. Nevertheless, the frequency with which Benediction is given has declined in recent years, probably in part because of a reaction against the extremely liberal practice of some bishops in the granting of permission for it, and in part because of removal of restrictions regarding the hours at which Mass may be celebrated and the mitigation of regulations concerning the Eucharistic Fast. These changes have made it possible to center afternoon or evening devotions around the Mass. *Désir de voir l' hostie* (1928); *Rites of the Catholic Church* (1976) 484–492.

[P. K. MEAGHER]

BENEDICTIONAL, a liturgical book containing a collection of blessings. The term is used chiefly in connection with the collections of blessings used by bishops in France, Spain, and England during the early Middle Ages and inserted into the Mass after the Pater Noster. The interpolation of such blessings was regarded with disfavor by Rome.

[N. KOLLAR]

BENEDICTIONAL OF ST. ETHELWOLD, illuminated MS, masterpiece of the *Winchester School and of medieval art, containing 28 full-page miniatures showing scenes and figures in delicate colors within lush foliage borders in heavy gold frames. It was written in gold, red, and black, for Ethelwold, bp. of Winchester (963–984).

[R. L. S. BRUCE-MITFORD]

BENEDICTUS, see CANTICLE OF ZECHARIAH.

BENEDICTUS DEUS, the first words of the apostolic constitution of Benedict XII published Jan. 29, 1336. Before his accession to the papal throne the Pope had participated in theological discussions about the state of the soul after death and the time at which it enters into its final destiny. Some of the disputed points Benedict resolved by an *ex cathedra* definition in the *Benedictus Deus*. Concerning the souls of all the just he defined: (1) after the death and Ascension of Our Lord and before the resurrection of their bodies and the general judgment, these souls, if perfectly pure, are admitted to the intuitive vision of God's essence, face to face, without any intermediary; (2) this vision and its enjoyment constitute true beatitude, eternal life and rest; and (3) this vision will not terminate so as to be superseded by another vision of a higher order. This constitution also defined that acts of faith and hope will cease insofar as they are acts of theological virtues. As for the souls of those dying in mortal sin, Benedict defined that they descend into hell before the general judgment, there to suffer excruciating pains. They will, nevertheless, appear in their bodies before the tribunal of Christ the Judge on the last day. BIBLIOGRAPHY: D 1000–02; X. Le Bachelet, DTC 2.1:657–696.

[T. J. MOTHERWAY]

BENEDICTUS QUI VENIT, a phrase from the Sanctus of the Mass, meaning "Blessed is he who comes in the name of the Lord", a text that has been set to music by composers of all schools.

[A. H. CRANE]

BENEDIKTBEUERN, ABBEY OF. Founded in the Bavarian Alps (739), pillaged, restored, the abbey despite successive fires and other reverses prospered and became a center of learning and of pilgrimage (it possessed a relic of St. Benedict from Charlemagne and a relic of St. Anastasia). The abbey was famous for its library numbering 338 MSS and 40,000 volumes at the time of its suppression. The Benedictine scholar, C. Meichelbeck, worked here. The church is an example of Bavarian high baroque with paintings by H. G. Asams (1646–1711). Suppressed again (1803), it served as a barracks and military hospital, later becoming a theological seminary for Salesian students. BIBLIOGRAPHY: E. D. McShane, NCE 2:305; P. Volk, DHGE 7:1235–36.

[M. J. DALY]

BENEFICE, an ecclesiastical office that carries the right to an income from the endowment attached to the office. The term is from the Lat., *beneficium,* originally used for land given by an emperor to his soldiers. It is sometimes used to refer to the income itself. The appointee is said to receive the temporalities (the income) in return for performing the spiritualities (duties of the office). The system arose in the Middle Ages as a means of supporting the clergy through the gifts of land often presented to the Church by wealthy laymen. It led to such problems and abuses as *simony, one individual holding a number of benefices, nonresident benefices, and conflict with lay authorities over the temporal power involved in heavily endowed benefices.

[T. EARLY]

BENEFICENCE, the active exercise of charity which is not content merely to wish a neighbor well but, when need or occasion arises, actually does or produces the good that is needed.

[P. K. MEAGHER]

BENEFICIARY, as understood in canon law, is a person who holds a benefice or office to which the Church has attached the right to draw a certain income from monies or other properties held by the Church for that purpose.

[P. K. MEAGHER]

BENEFIT OF CLERGY, the exemption of the clergy from prosecution in secular courts, a privilege established in Europe in the 12th century. In RC canon law it is known as *privilegium fori* (privilege of the forum). It is claimed for clerics in the Code (CIC c. 120.1), but since it is no longer recognized in civil law, the canonical provision no longer has any practical effect, except to dissuade Catholics from bringing civil suit against clerics without first obtaining permission from ecclesiastical authority, a permission that should not be denied without grave reason (cf. CIC c. 120.1,2).

The expression "benefit of clergy" is also used sometimes in reference to marriage, as in the phrase, married without benefit of clergy, i.e., without an officiating clergyman.

[T. EARLY]

BENEMERENTI MEDAL, a decoration instituted (1832) by Pope Gregory XVI and awarded to men and women for outstanding performance in military or civil affairs. BIBLIOGRAPHY: D. Dunford, CE 4:670.

BENEVENTAN CHANT, the liturgical chant of the ancient *Beneventan rite. Only a relatively few pieces survive, chiefly Mass propers for some 20 feasts and Holy Week, in MSS in the cathedral library at Benevento and the Vatican Library, but they suffice to show that Beneventan chant was a separate repertory of Latin chant, sharing a common origin with *Gregorian, *Milanese, and other Western chants, but developing independently. Stylistically it tends to be at once excessively florid and repetitious. Its frequent melismas are often mere formulas, while many chants, notably tracts but others as well, consist of a single musical phrase repeated for most, if not all, verses or lines of text. Since the Beneventan repertory was no longer in use c.800 its composition must date back considerably before then. Hesbert attributes the rapid adoption of the Gregorian repertory (upon its introduction to the region) in part to its evident musical superiority to the local product. Interestingly, the S Italian "dialect" of Gregorian chant seen in pieces composed for new local feasts introduced after c.800 shows no stylistic similarity at all to Beneventan chant. Several pieces of Beneventan chant are transcribed by Hesbert in *Paléographie musicale,* v. 15. BIBLIOGRAPHY: B. Baroffio, MGG Supplementband, with bibliog.

[A. DOHERTY]

BENEVENTAN RITE, the extinct liturgical rite of the S Italian city of Benevento and the region of its medieval duchy, from the Abbey of Montecassino to Bari on the Adriatic coast. Benevento's political and geographical partial independence from the rest of Europe is reflected in its liturgical tradition. No liturgical books for the old rite survive, but a few texts and chants are preserved in later Roman rite MSS, notably the Mass Propers for some 20 feasts and the major ceremonies of Holy Week. Although the Beneventan rite shows certain striking affinities with the *Milanese rite, such as the *Ingressa* without psalm-verse in place of the *Introit* and a predilection for newly composed rather than scriptural texts, this connection has been overrated: the term "Ambrosian" as applied in Beneventan sources to local practices only means non-Roman and is never applied to items common to both rites. Hesbert's researches have shown the Beneventan rite to have been an independent tradition with certain ties to the Roman and Milanese rites,

just as the latter two have to each other. Similarly, Beneventan chant differs strikingly from the other Latin chant repertoires. The relationships of South Italy with Byzantium, which included Benevento's political affiliation to Constantinople at various times, are reflected by a group of Beneventan Holy Week antiphons with both Greek and Latin texts, which were probably taken over from the *Byzantine rite. Although the few preserved Beneventan rite texts and chants are in 11th-13th-cent. MSS, the Roman rite must have been firmly established before the beginning of the 9th cent., since Masses for new local feasts composed after that time (such as for St. Bartholomew, whose relics were brought to Benevento and a church built to house them in 808) are purely Roman rite formularies. BIBLIOGRAPHY: B. Baroffio, MGG Supplementband, with extensive bibliog.

[A. DOHERTY]

BENEVOLI, ORAZIO (1605–72), composer of the *Roman school. He held posts at various Roman churches, including St. Mary Major and St. Peter's, and also spent 2 years in the service of the Austrian court. He is best known for his *polychoral Masses and motets for as many as 12 choirs, including a famous Mass in 52 parts for the consecration of Salzburg Cathedral (1628), but his attempts at a fusion of the techniques of the Roman and *Venetian schools are little more than a technical *tour de force* applied to essentially simple musical materials. BIBLIOGRAPHY: H. F. Redlich, MGG 1:1658–61; BukMusB.

[A. DOHERTY]

BÉNÉZET, ST. (1165–84), patron of bridge builders. The name Bénézet is a derivative of his family name Benoît. His life is somewhat obscured by legend; even the papal bull of canonization by Innocent IV (1274) is lost; the documents naming him blessed (1212) and saint (1237) are extant. BIBLIOGRAPHY: M. N. Boyer, NCE 2:310; J. Garin, DHGE 7:1292–93; H. Platelle, BiblSanct 2:1099–1100; AS April 2:254–263.

[J. R. RIVELLO]

BENGAL, ART OF, a major Buddhist school of art that reached its zenith in the Pala (c. 730–1150) and Sena (1150–1280) dynasties, influencing the style of Nepal, Tibet, Burma, and Java. Carved deities, in the ubiquitous hard, black slate, point to an esoteric and syncretic Buddhism with strong Hindu modifications. Superb portable bronzes from Bihar, showing remarkable technical finesse, account for widespread influences. A few paintings in colorful palm leaf miniatures remain. Large monastic centers terraced and decorated in relief were enclosed by great walls containing hundreds of monks' cells. The 13th-cent. Muslim conquest ended the Buddhist art of Bengal. BIBLIOGRAPHY: K. N. Dikshit, *Excavations at Pāhārpur, Bengal* (1938).

[M. J. DALY]

BENIGNI, UMBERTO (1862–1934), professor of ecclesiastical history, journalist, integralist, who took a strong interest in social problems. He founded and edited *La Rassegna sociale,* the first Italian periodical dealing with social problems. His most important work was his *Storia sociale della Chiesa* (5v., 1906–33), which contains a wealth of original material of a heterogeneous type, but shows some lack of a constructive critical sense and a defective notion of the breadth of his subject. He was a strong opponent of Modernism; he established the *Correspondance de Rome* which served as a clearing house for information about Modernism. Much of his anti-Modernist activity was shrouded in the veil of mystery that characterized the integralist movement, and this has left him a controversial figure. BIBLIOGRAPHY: EncCatt 2:1347.

[C. BUCKLEY]

BENIGNUS OF DIJON, ST. (3d? cent.), martyr. Incorrectly listed as disciple of St. Polycarp of Smyrna and missionary of Burgundy, he suffered martyrdom during the reign of Marcus Aurelius. At Dijon, the basilica and Abbey of Saint-Bénigne are built over his tomb. BIBLIOGRAPHY: G. Bardy, DHGE 7:1314–15; A. Amore, BiblSanct 2:1231–32.

[M. H. BEIRNE]

BÉNILDE, ST. (1805–62), confessor and educator. Born Pierre Ramançon, he joined the Christian Brothers at Riom, France (1819). He was assigned head of the Saugues school and superior of the religious community in 1842. His sanctity emphasized a balance between devotion to the education apostolate and to the religious rule. B. was canonized in 1967. BIBLIOGRAPHY: G. B. Proja, BiblSanct 2:1237–38; W. J. Battersby, NCE 2:311.

[M. H. BEIRNE]

BENIN (BINI), 15-cent. Yoruba kingdom, center of impressive, powerful bronze and brass ritual objects, esp. heads of kings *(obas)* placed on eleborate altars in the royal city. In addition to bronze narrative plaques which sheathed palace pillars, the Bini shaped girdles and body masks of complex symbolism. Benin "royal" or "court" style in metal later extended to wood and ivory forms. Benin drew its artistic inspiration from the ancient, sophisticated city-state, *Ife, famed for a classical naturalism in sculpting perhaps unequalled in the continent. BIBLIOGRAPHY: E. Elisofon and W. Fagg, *Sculpture of Africa* (1958).

[M. J. DALY]

BENINCASA, URSULA, VEN. (1547–1618), foundress. When B. was refused admission to the Capuchinesses in 1579, she spent 3 years in a hermitage; then, directed by a vision, went to Rome with a plan for church reform. Returning to Naples, she founded the Oblates of the Immaculate Conception, a teaching order (1583), and the Contemplative Hermit Sisters of strict enclosure (1617). After her death,

Gregory XV put both congregations under the Theatines (1623). B. is credited with the origination of the blue scapular. BIBLIOGRAPHY: N. Del Re, EncCatt 2:1349.

[H. JACK]

BENJAMIN, a name that by popular interpretation has been taken to mean "son of my good fortune" but which actually means "southerner," i.e., someone who comes from the right as one faces eastward toward the sun. From ancient texts found at Mari it appears that the name was given to Bedouins who swarmed northward into the fertile area of the upper reaches of the Euphrates river from the Arabian desert. The traditional violence and valor attributed to the Israelite tribe of Benjamin corresponds to the warlike characteristics of such sons of the desert (Gen 49.27). In the Israelite tradition Benjamin was Jacob's youngest and favorite son, esp. cherished after Jacob thought he had lost Rachel's other son, Joseph. The tribe of Benjamin occupied a small area just N of Jerusalem. It gave to Israel its first king, Saul, but was forced to accept Davidic rule after David's conquest of Jerusalem; it was eventually annexed to the kingdom of Judah and thus some of its tribal strains perdured through the Exile and continued to exist in Judaism.

[J. F. FALLON]

BENJAMIN BEN JONAH OF TUDELA (d. 1173), Jewish rabbi and Spanish traveler whose chronicle *Massa'oth shel Rabbi Benjamin* provides a foremost source for study of Jewish life in Europe, Asia, and North Africa in the 12th century. From 1159 to 1173 he journeyed through France, Italy, Greece, Palestine, Iran and into China, and returned crossing Arabia, Egypt, and Sicily, The first European to penetrate so far east, B. meticulously accounted observations of Jewish life styles, educational institutions, principal vocations, and population figures. Marked with sobriety, B.'s chronicle includes error, fable, and significant, substantiated details of the countries' internal developments and geographical locations. BIBLIOGRAPHY: N. C. Cohen, NCE 2:312.

[M. H. BEIRNE]

BENJAMIN, ASHER (1773–1845), American architect, chief proponent of the delicate, attenuated Federal style. His distinctive elegance is seen in the famous Charles St. Church in Boston (1807).

[M. J. DALY]

BENN, GOTTFRIED (1886–1958), Austrian poet, novelist, and one of the most significant lyrical talents of German literary expressionism. He was born in Mansfeld (Westpriegnitz), Germany, the son of a Protestant minister. His mother was of Franco-Swiss origin. He first studied theology and philology in Marburg and Berlin, then medicine (M.D. 1912). During World War I he was an army physician, stationed in Belgium, and remained there after the War. BIBLIOGRAPHY: *Gesammelte Werke,* (ed. D. Weller-shoff, 4 v. 1958–61).

[B. STEINBRUCKNER]

BENNO OF MEISSEN, ST. (1010–*c.*1106), bishop. Appointed to the See of Meissen in 1066, B. was deposed in 1085, probably for participating in the election of Rudolph of Swabia to supplant Emperor Henry IV, who had been excommunicated in 1077. He was restored in 1088. B. has been called the ''Apostle of the Wends'' for his missionary zeal toward the Slavonic tribes in his diocese. His cult was established at Meissen in 1285, though he was not canonized until 1523. In 1524, Martin Luther protested against the exposition of Benno's relics in Meissen. They were subsequently (1576) removed to Bavaria and are now in the cathedral of Munich. In iconography B. is represented with a fish holding in its mouth the keys of the Cathedral of Meissen. B. is the patron of fisherman and of drapers and is invoked for rain. BIBLIOGRAPHY: M. F. McCarthy, NCE 2:313; A. Zimmerman and A. M. Raggi, BiblSanct 2:1243–47; Butler 2:555–556.

[M. F. MCCARTHY]

BENNO OF METZ, BL. (d. 940), bishop. In 906 B. rebuilt the hermitage and chapel of St. Meinrad and lived there with his companions until 927 when he was named bp. of Metz by King Henry I of Germany. Blinded by his enemies, B. returned to his hermitage in 929 and died there. Under Eberhard, who had joined B. in 934, the hermitage became the well-known monastery of Einsiedeln. BIBLIOGRAPHY: A. Bigelmair, DHGE 7:1361–62; C. Sisto, BiblSanct 2:1247.

[M. F. MCCARTHY]

BENNO II OF OSNABRÜCK, BL. (*c.*1020–88), bp. and architect. From 1068, when he became Henry IV's candidate for bp. of Osnabrück, B. managed to retain the confidence of both Pope and Emperor during the investiture struggle; he acted as a mediator at Canossa in 1078 and at Rome in 1080. He was an able administrator, and as architect of Goslar, Speyer, and Hildesheim cathedrals and of the Abbey of Iburg, he was a major figure in Romanesque architecture. Whether he ever enjoyed a formal cult is open to dispute. BIBLIOGRAPHY: A. D'Haenens, BiblSanct 2:1247–48; E. N. Johnson, ''Bishop Benno II of Osnabrück,'' *Speculum* 16 (1941) 389–403.

[S. WILLIAMS]

BENOIT, PIERRE MAURICE (1906–), Dominican Scripture scholar whose contributions to biblical theology helped lay the groundwork for Vatican Council II. Since 1954 editor of *Revue biblique,* and director of the École Biblique

in Jerusalem (1964–73), he is currently vice-rector of the Ecumenical Institute for Advanced Theological Study at Tantur near Bethlehem. His publications include numerous books and articles on the Synoptics, Paul, the Dead Sea Scrolls, and biblical tradition.

[T. LIDDY]

BENOIT, PIERRE (1834–1901), Belgian composer and initiator of the Flemish school of music composition. While a student of Fétis at the Brussels Conservatory, B. wrote music for plays and an opera. He continued to compose during travels in Germany and as a conductor in Paris. He founded (1867), with government support, the Flemish School of Music (later, the Royal Flemish Conservatory) in Antwerp and remained as its director until his death. In addition to cantatas and other choral works on national subjects, he composed sacred music, of which the chief example is his *Quadrilogie religieuse* consisting of *Messe solennelle, Cantata de Noël,* a *Te Deum* and a *Requiem,* In these, B. proved to be a gifted modern composer. Later, however, in his efforts to reach the people at large , his technique became simpler and more conventional. BIBLIOGRAPHY: A . Corbet, Grove DMM 1:629–630; P. A. Scholes, *Oxford Companion to Music* (10th ed., 1970) 104.

[M. T. LEGGE]

BENSON, EDWARD WHITE (1828–96), abp. of Canterbury from 1883. He was headmaster of Wellington College (1858–68), chancellor of the diocese of Lincoln (1872–77), and first bp. of Truro (1877–83). B. revived the court of the abp. of Canterbury that handed down the Lincoln judgment remarkable for ignoring decisions of the secular courts. His major study, *Cyprian, His Life, His Times, His Works,* was published posthumously. BIBLIOGRAPHY: A. C. Benson, *Life of Archbishop Benson* (1899).

[M. J. SUELZER]

BENSON, ROBERT HUGH (1871–1914), English writer and apologist. Fourth son of Edward, Anglican abp. of Canterbury, B. was educated at Eton and Trinity College, Cambridge, and ordained an Anglican priest in 1894. He converted to Catholicism in 1903 and was ordained in Rome the following year. Until 1908 he served at Cambridge as assistant chaplain, then retired to write, also preaching occasional missions. His works included: *By What Authority?* (1904), *The Queen's Tragedy* (1905), *Confessions of a Convert* (1915). His best writing is found in his historical novels. BIBLIOGRAPHY: biog. by A. C. Benson (1915), and C. C. Martindale (2 v., 1916); J. G. Lawlor, ''Garry Wills' Sour Birds,'' *Journal, American Academy of Religion,* 41 (1973) 122–134.

[P. K. MEAGHER]

BENTHAM, JEREMY (1748–1832), English utilitarian philosopher. B. was born in London and studied at Queen's College, Oxford. By profession a lawyer, his main preoccupation was with philosophy. In his attempt to create what for him was a more humane administration of justice, he conceived a method of decision making in moral matters that is utilitarian and, ultimately, egoistic. The overriding principle to be adopted in all matters is that X ought to be done if and only if it maximizes the pleasure of those affected by the action. And in a further refinement of it, X ought to be done if and only if it maximizes the total amount of pleasure of those affected by the action—each person counting for one. This principle, alleged to be an ethical standard by B., ought then to have consequences that are themselves moral and ethical. The trouble with it is simply that it does not do so. The weighting of hedonic claims is not enough to provide man with guides for legislative and social reform. And more importantly, it fails to provide man with a system of personal moral development. B. rejects any notion of authority in morality such as natural law, yet he replaces it with the authority of "two sovereign masters, pain and pleasure." That rejection along with his denial of a moral ought (other than his own derivation of it from the principle of utility) reduces his theory to ethical hedonism. Any design or reformation of social arrangements ought to consider the schemes and possibilities it permits and the behavior it encourages. One is inclined to reject such reformation if its content is derived purely from metaethical concerns. Besides his political and legal theory B. produced a work on meaning, *Essay on Logic*. He is best known, however, for his influence on utilitarianism and that influence is not to be underestimated. Utilitarianism dominated moral philosophy for almost 2 cent. but that influence is waning somewhat now, esp. with the growth of deontological theories—both rule and act deontology. Representative of the former are such philosophers as W. D. Ross and, more recently, John Rawls. At any rate, B.'s theory, even aesthetically, leaves a great deal to be desired, for *ceteris paribus,* does one really prefer pushpin to poetry? See *Works of Jeremy Bentham* (collected by J. Bowring, 11 v., 1838–43); this includes the *Introduction to the Principles of Morals and Legislation* (1789). BIBLIOGRAPHY: D. H. Monro, EncPhil 1:280–285; J. Rawls, *Theory of Justice* (1972) 198, 325, 455; U. Viglino, EncCatt 2:1355–59; B. C. Parekh, *Jeremy Bentham: Ten Critical Essays* (1974).

[J. R. RIVELLO]

BENTIVOGLIO, Bolognese family risen from a workman's guild to ecclesiastical and political prominence. (1) Guido (1579–1644). Paul V sent him as nuncio to Brussels (1607) and France (1616) and made him a cardinal (1621). After 1625 he served in the curia and exercised powerful influence in Vatican affairs the rest of his life. He represented French interests in Rome for Louis XIII, and was named to his third bishopric, Palestrina, in 1641. (2) Annibale (d. 1663), poet and titular archbishop. (3) Marco Cornelio (1688–1732), held curial offices until he was sent to France as nuncio in 1611. He became cardinal in 1619, and Spanish minister in Rome in 1626. (4) Domenico

(1781–1851), a soldier who served with Napoleon's forces (1800) then entered papal military service.

[H. JACK]

BENTLEY, RICHARD (1662–1742), English classical scholar and Christian apologist. B. was educated at St. John's College, Cambridge. He served as tutor to James Stillingfleet, the son of the dean of St. Paul's, during which time he began to interest himself in textual criticism, a field in which he did much distinguished work. B. was ordained (1690) and appointed chaplain to Stillingfleet, then bp. of Worcester. In 1692 he delivered the Boyle Lectures taking for his subject the confutation of atheism. In his last three lectures B. used Newton's discovery to prove the existence of an intelligent and omnipotent Creator. His arguments are leveled against Hobbes in particular. BIBLIOGRAPHY: R. C. Jebb, DNB 2:306–314.

[V. SAMPSON]

BENVENUTO DI GIOVANNI (1438–1518?), Sienese painter with great decorative skill. B.'s early work in Arezzo shows a predominantly flat pattern. The National Gallery, London, owns a beautiful *Madonna and Child with SS. Peter and Nicholas* (1479). An *Assumption of the Virgin* (1498) is in the Metropolitan Museum of Art, New York City. The *Adoration of the Magi* in the National Gallery, Washington, D.C., shows well how the International Gothic style came to a close in Siena. BIBLIOGRAPHY: C. Brandi, *Quattrocentisti senesi* (1949).

[M. J. DALY]

BENVENUTUS SCOTIVOLI, ST. (d. 1283), bishop of Osimo. After studying law at Bologna, he was ordained in his diocese of Ancona and functioned there as archdeacon. He became bp. of Osimo in 1264. Clement IV made him governor of the Marches of Ancona. On the occasion of the translation of his relics in 1755 he was named protector of the city of Osimo. There is question about the tradition that would make him a Franciscan. He was never canonized, though his cult seems to have been approved by Eugene IV. BIBLIOGRAPHY: G. Odoardi, BiblSanct 2:1252–53.

[J. M. O'DONNELL]

BENZIGER, AUGUST (1867–1955), portrait painter. B., a member of well-known Catholic publishing family, studied in Vienna and Paris. His works evidence great technical finish and idealization of subjects, among whom were Presidents McKinley and Roosevelt, Charles Schwab and J. Pierpont Morgan, Cardinals Gibbons, O'Connell, and Farley, Popes Leo XIII, Benedict XV, and Pius XI. Most works appear stiff and pompous by later standards. BIBLIOGRAPHY: M. G. and R. Benziger, *August Benziger: Portrait Painter* (1958).

[M. J. DALY]

BENZO OF ALBA (*c*.1000–89), bishop. B. appears first as a bp. of Alba at the Roman council of 1059. He was a devoted partisan of the Emperor and supported the antipope Honorius (Cadalus) against Alexander II. Driven from his see by the *Patarines in 1076, he put his writings together in a volume entitled *Libri VII ad Henricum IV*.

[S. WILLIAMS]

BENZONI, GIROLAMO DE (1517–70), Italian chronicler of the New World. He went to America in 1541, stayed 14 years collecting material for a book, took part in Spanish slave raids, and later described the horrors of the slave trade. Upon his return to Italy in 1556, B. published his experiences in *La historia del mondo nuovo* (1565), which was eventually translated into several languages with the exception of Spanish. His work is somewhat prejudicial to the Spaniards and full of atrocity stories. B. is considered a contributor to the development of the Black Legend. BIBLIOGRAPHY: J. Herrick, NCE 2:317; F. A. Kirkpatrick, *Spanish Conquistadores* (1934) 298; S. Madariage, *Fall of the Spanish-American Empire* (1948) 317; C. Wilgus, *Library of Latin-American History and Culture* (1965) 3–4.

[D. M. HUGHES]

BEOWULF, sole surviving 8th-cent. Anglo-Saxon epic, describing the deeds of Beowulf, a legendary hero. It is generally agreed to be the work of a single Christian author, possibly a court chaplain. The theme of *Beowulf* is the conflict of good and evil. Three layers appear to be fused in the poem: the original pre-Christian Germanic story involving the fate of two dynasties; Christian elements found in oral songs about Beowulf during the period of religious conversion; and the Christian ethos directly supplied by the poet. Contrasts and parallels of structure, of character presentations, of theme and style allow Christian and pagan elements to relate meaningfully within the poem. Characteristics of Teutonic culture, such as loyalty to lord, gift giving, blood feuds, burial customs, and the Wyrd-fate concept are all to be found but with a hero distinctively Christian in his features. It is possible to see the epic either as a Germanic tale adapted to Christian taste, or as an allegorical expression in Germanic form of the Christian story of salvation. The author keeps Beowulf poised between the pagan hero and the Christian king; he is "the gentlest and most gracious of men, the kindest to his people, and the most desirous of renown." Text: *Beowulf: With the Finnesburg Fragment* (ed. C. L. Wrenn, 1953). BIBLIOGRAPHY: S. B. Greenfield, *Critical History of Old English Literature* (1965); W. F. Bolton, *Beowulf* (1973).

[M. SAQUÉS]

BERAKHOT, the first division or tractate of 64 in the Mishnah, a written collection of ancient Rabbinical oral rules and regulations governing and guiding moral and doctrinal life. It contains blessings for foods and examines various confessions of Jewish faith (*Shema) and various prayers and rules for saying them. It may thus be considered Judaism's guideline for much of its prayer life. It is a large collection of nine chapters: the first three treat of faith confessions taken from the Bible (e.g., Dt 6.4–9), when they should be recited, and other regulations; ch. 4 and 5 give rules for prayers (the Tephillah); the last 4 chapters list and discuss blessings for all occasions. The proportion of *Haggadah (doctrinal stories) to *Halakah (rules and regulations) is much greater than in the rest of the Mishnah.

[J. E. FALLON]

BERAN, JOSEF (1888–1969), abp. of Prague. After theological studies and ordination (1911) at Rome, B. returned to his native Bohemia to engage in parish work. From 1917 until 1929 he was director of the Teachers Institute of St. Ann, conducted by the Congregation of School Sisters, and taught pastoral theology (1928–32) at the Theological Faculty of The Charles Univ., Prague. In addition, his pastoral interests encompassed that of adviser, retreat master, organizer and leader in all aspects of Catholic Action. In 1936 he was made a papal prelate. The German Gestapo imprisoned him at Dachau, Germany from 1942 until 1945. He was under house arrest and a virtual prisoner from 1949–65 because of his opposition to the Communist regime. In 1965 he was raised to the cardinalate and allowed to go to Rome to receive his red hat, but was forced to remain in exile in Rome. B. became a champion of religious freedom at Vatican Council II and was acclaimed there for his views on the independence of the Church. On a visit to the U.S. (1966) B. was received with great honor by both the hierarchy and the laity. BIBLIOGRAPHY: L. Nemec, *Church and State in Czechoslovakia* (1955); *id.*, NCE 16:25–26.

[P. COOPER]

BERARD AND COMPANIONS, SS., protomartyrs of the Franciscan Order. Berard, a subdeacon who knew Arabic; Odo, a priest; and three lay brothers, Peter, Accursio and Adjutus, were commissioned by St. Francis himself at the Franciscan General Chapter of 1219 to preach the gospel among the Saracens in North Africa. They met their deaths in Morocco at the hands of the Sultan in 1220 and were canonized in 1481. BIBLIOGRAPHY: J. Campbell, NCE 2:319; G. Odoardi, BiblSanct 2:1271–72.

[B. L. MARTHALER]

BERAT (Turk., warrant, privilege), a royal diploma or privilege. After the Byzantine Empire fell to the Turks (1453), *berat* came to mean the document granted by the Ottoman sultan recognizing a newly elected patriarch of Constantinople and other Christian bps. under Turkish rule, confirming them in their ecclesiastical position and, in the case of the ecumenical patriarch designating him as ethnarch or civil head of the Orthodox "nation" *(millet),* an arrangement lasting until 1923. For the *berat* a fee had to be paid, which resulted in corruption and bribery among churchmen. *CONSTANTINOPLE, PATRIARCHATE OF.

[G. T. DENNIS]

BÉRAULT-BERCASTEL, ANTOINE HENRI JEAN FRANÇOIS DE (1720–94), French church historian. Originally a Jesuit, he left the Society to become a parish priest at Omerville and later canon of Noyon. After writing minor poetry and fiction, he achieved fame through his 24-volume *Histoire de l'église* (1778–90), which was geared for the general, educated public. BIBLIOGRAPHY: Sommervogel 1:1322; R. Metz, LTK 2:211.

[M. H. BEIRNE]

BERCHARIUS, ST. (*c*.620–685 or 696), Benedictine abbot, martyr. Educated at Reims, he entered the Abbey of Luxueil, possibly under Waldebert (629–670). He became first abbot of Hautvilliers, founded by St. Nivard, bp. of Reims. Building churches in honor of St. Peter and the Virgin Mary, B. established the monastery of Montier-en-Der and convent of Puelle-Montier. His vita records Bercharius as a martyr since he died of stab wounds inflicted by a monk, Daguinus, whom he had corrected. BIBLIOGRAPHY: J. C. Didier, BiblSanct 2:1278–79; Butler 4:128–129.

[M. H. BEIRNE]

BERDYAEV, NICHOLAS (1874–1948), one of the leading 20th-cent. Russian philosophers and religious thinkers. A prolific writer, he was largely responsible for introducing the West to the major trends of Russian thought. Renouncing the privileges of nobility, B. joined the revolutionary movement and was consequently exiled in 1899 for criticizing the Orthodox Church's subservience to the Czarist regime, and in 1922 was expelled from Russia along with many other intellectuals, for his attacks on Marxism. He founded a religious and philosophical academy in Paris where he wrote most of his works. Called the philosopher of freedom, B. stressed the value and dignity of the individual person. In asserting that freedom begins with the love of God while salvation is communal and universal, B. reflected the influence of Dostoevsky and other Russians before him. His important works include *Beginning and the End, Dostoevsky: an Interpretation, Meaning of History, Origin of Russian Communism,* and *Russian Idea.* BIBLIOGRAPHY: D. A. Lowrie, *Rebellious Prophet: A Life of Nicolai Berdyaev* (1960, repr. 1974).

[D. DIRSCHERL]

BERENGAR I (d. 924), King of the Lombards from 898. B. was crowned Holy Roman Emperor after repulsing the Saracens in southern Italy. A mild and gullible king, he was acceptable to the common people but not to the wealthy magnates, who twice called in rival claimants for the throne. He was defeated by Rudolf II in 923 and assassinated in 924. BIBLIOGRAPHY: B. J. Comaskey, NCE 2:320; *Gesta Berengarii imperatoris* (ed. E. L. Dümmler, 1871).

[M. A. WINKELMANN]

BERENGAR OF POITIERS (fl. mid-12th cent.), a theologian and a disciple of Abelard, of whom little is known except what can be gleaned from his writings, three of which are extant (PL 178). The first of these, his *Apologeticus,* was composed in defense of Abelard and amounts to a bitter invective against St. Bernard of Clairvaux; the second was an attack upon the Carthusians; the third a retractation of his abusive writings. This last work was addressed to the bp. of Mende in the hope of obtaining his protection. As an apology for himself, this letter was inadequate atonement for the offense he had given. BIBLIOGRAPHY: E. Vacandard, DTC 2.1:720–722.

[R. A. TODD]

BERENGAR OF TOURS (*c*.1000–88), Berengarius; author of eucharistic heresy. A student of Fulbert, head of St. Martin's school, and archdeacon of Angers, B. taught that the Eucharist is only the figure of Christ. Condemned at the Councils of Rome (1050, 1059, 1079), Vercelli (1050), Paris (1051), and Bordeaux (1080), he died at peace with the Church. B.'s heresy caused the treatises of his opponents and the council decrees to give new clarity to eucharistic theology. The Eucharist was defined as both the reality and symbol of Christ's presence.

[M. H. BEIRNE]

BERENGARIUS FREDOLI, see FRÉDOL, BÉRENGER.

BERENSON, BERNARD (1865–1959), art connoisseur and "Dean of Florentine Painters." B. was a child immigrant from Lithuania to Boston, graduating from Harvard (1887) in Near Eastern languages. Through European travel financed by friends (notably Isabelle Steward Gardner), B., commanding a sensitive and authoritative power of visual identification, became deeply interested in the attribution of Italian Renaissance paintings. He married Mary Costelloe (1899) and settling in his famous Villa I Tatti near Settignano, published *Venetian Painters of the Renaissance* (1894) creating a stir among collectors, *Florentine Painters* (1896), *Central Italian Painters* (1897), and *North Italian Painters* (1907). B. revised and published all as *Italian Painters of the Renaissance* (1932), a classic in Renaissance studies. Works on aesthetics, criticism, with monographs on Piero della Francesca, Sassetta, Caravaggio, and Lotto followed. Assisted by Kenneth Clark, B. compiled *Drawings of the Florentine Masters*. His 50,000 volume library of art history and the humanities was bequeathed with his estate to Harvard. B. also determined the flow of Renaissance works into U.S. collections. BIBLIOGRAPHY: B. Berenson, *Sunset and Twilight: From the Diaries of 1947–1958* (1963); *Bernard Berenson Treasury* (ed. H. Kiel, 1962).

[M. J. DALY]

BERGENGRUEN, WERNER (1892–1964), German novelist and storyteller. B., a convert to Catholicism in 1936, was an accomplished writer of highly stylized stories that combine romantic imagination with realism and deep psychological insight. Against backgrounds of the Italian Renaissance or the earlier history of the Baltic states, he preferred to trace out eternal order as it was manifest less in ordinary than in great and unusual events. He was strongly opposed to all totalitarian concepts, as appears in his novel *Der Grosstyrann und das Gericht* (1935) in which an Italian prince, who has committed a murder, allures his subjects into accusing their fellow citizens of the crime. B. shows the temptation of the mighty, and the proneness of the weak and insecure to seduction. BIBLIOGRAPHY: T. A. Riley, NCE 2:322–323.

[S. A. SCHULZ]

BERGER, SAMUEL (1843–1900), biblical scholar and historian. B. was instrumental in the founding and development of the faculty of Protestant theology at the Univ. of Paris, and later served as its librarian and secretary. The major part of his scholarly work dealt with the history of biblical exegesis, the Vulgate, and the various Bible translations into European languages. BIBLIOGRAPHY: A. Lambert, DHGE 8:451; J. Schmid, NCE 2:323.

[T. M. MCFADDEN]

BERGERAC, CYRANO DE, see CYRANO DE BERGERAC.

BERGGRAV, EIVIND (1884–1959), Norwegian Lutheran bishop. After being ordained (1908) and teaching for a decade, B. became a country pastor and later a prison chaplain. He also edited (1909–59) the theological review, *Kirke og Kultur,* and wrote more than 30 books. He became bp. of Oslo in 1937 and led a united Christian front against the Nazis. For this he suffered imprisonment (1942–45). He was president of the World Council of Churches (1950–54) and prominent in the Lutheran World Federation. BIBLIOGRAPHY: E. Molland, EncLuthCh 1:208; OCD 159.

[M. J. SUELZER]

BERGIER, NICOLAS-SYLVESTRE (1718–90), French theologian and man of letters. The most able and popular defender of Christian doctrines and Catholic traditions against the *philosophes* particularly Rousseau, Holbach, and Voltaire. His apologetic works are synthesized in his *Traité historique et dogmatique de la vraie religion avec la*

réfutation des erreurs qui lui ont été opposées dans les différents siècles (1780, 1820). BIBLIOGRAPHY: A. J. Bingham, "Abbé de Bergier: An Eighteenth Century Catholic Apologist," *Modern Language Review* (1959).

[A. S. CRISAFULLI]

BERGSON, HENRI-LOUIS (1859–1941), French philosopher of evolution and process, academician, and Nobel Laureate (1927, Literature). Educated first in the sciences, B. enjoyed a brilliant and influential teaching career as professor of philosophy at the École Normale Supérieure and the Collège de France. He came of Jewish parentage but was reared without formal religious belief, and in late life inclined to the RC Church, although he refrained from formal conversion in solidarity with the Jews suffering from Nazi persecution and the rising tide of anti-Semitism in France. B. brought to philosophy a broad acquaintance with and sound knowledge of the sciences, but was constantly opposed to the materialism and scientism that marked late 19th-cent. thought. Spencer was an early influence; Darwin *(The Origin of Species* had appeared in the year of his birth), a constant one. B. accepts evolution as an historical reality, but finds Darwin's explanation too materialistic. He leans in some measure to Lamarck. B.'s key notions are those of pure duration and becoming as the hallmarks of the extramental world; the *élan vital* or vital impetus—a current of consciousness that penetrates matter and gives rise to living bodies and their evolutionary development; and the superiority of intuition to intellect in reaching knowledge of reality. He would build a metaphysics on intuition.

In his earlier works, B. opposed finalism or teleology as operative in the evolutionary process, but later shifted toward it, and in *The Creative Mind* (tr. M. L. Andison 1946 from *La Pensée et le mouvant,* 1934) declared that the appearance of man is the *raison d'être* of life on earth. The creative evolution produced by the *élan vital* is, for him, a cosmic and not merely a terrestrial process. In his *Two Sources of Morality and Religion* (1932, tr. R. A. Audra and C. Brereton, 1935) he saw the closed type of society—static, authoritarian, demanding conformity of its members, and in conflict with other closed societies—as the product of conceptualization and an obstacle to further development and progress. He would have such societies replaced by an "open society," which would not only tolerate but also encourage diversity. In religion, too, the better approach to God is not through the stereotyped dogmas that the intellect has built up, but through the intuitive illuminations that characterize the mystics. Man's intellectual knowledge, though valuable and necessary, unfortunately fragments reality and makes it static.

Although there is no Bergsonian school, B.'s influence in 20th-cent. literature, science, and philosophy is great. Among philosophers it is apparent in J. Maritain, É. Gilson, Lecomte de Noüy, Whitehead, Teilhard de Chardin, and G. Marcel, to name but a few. B.'s style is brilliant, rich in metaphor and analogy. He has been sharply criticized for the anti-intellectual bent that appears in his works and among some of his followers, and for a vagueness and confusion in the identification of God and the *élan vital*. BIBLIOGRAPHY: É. Gilson, *Philosopher and Theology* (1962); J. Hanna, ed. (1962) *Bergsonian Heritage;* J. Maritain, *La Philosophie bergsonienne* (1930); T. A. Goudge, EncPhil 1:287–295.

[W. B. MAHONEY]

BERINGTON, CHARLES (1748–98), English vicar apostolic. He served on the English mission in Essex; became (1776) coadjutor to Bp. Talbot, vicar apostolic; joined (1788) the Catholic Committee, a group anti-Roman in its sympathies that was organized to protest the Penal Laws; signed the oath contained in the proposed Relief Bill and the "Blue Books," both of which were condemned by Rome. When Bp. Douglass was appointed vicar apostolic in London, the Catholic Committee rebelled in favor of B., who publicly disavowed connection with their action. He succeeded to the vicariate of the Midland District when Bp. Talbot died (1795), but confirmation was held up until he had reluctantly renounced his stand on the oath and Blue Books in 1797. He died before notice of the confirmation had reached him. BIBLIOGRAPHY: Gillow BDEC 1:186–189.

[H. JACK]

BERINZAGA, ISABELLA CRISTINA, see BELLIN-ZAGA, LOMAZZI ISABELLA CRISTINA.

BERISFORD, HUMPHREY (d. *c*.1588), English recusant. Son of a Derbyshire esquire, he studied at Douai for 2 years. Tried as a recusant in Elizabeth's reign, he refused to renounce his Catholic faith. He was committed to prison and apparently died in confinement, perhaps in Derby goal, *c*.1588. BIBLIOGRAPHY: J. G. Dwyer, NCE 2:326.

[C. D. ROSS]

BERISTÁIN Y SOUZA, JOSÉ MARIANO (1756–1817), Mexican bibliographer. His monumental work, *Biblioteca Hispano-Americana Setentrional,* was the result of 20 years' research in the libraries of Mexico City and the surrounding area. It includes biographical sketches and lists the works of over 3,600 writers who were born or flourished in Spanish North America. BIBLIOGRAPHY: E. Gómez Tagle, NCE 2:326.

[H. JACK]

BERKELEY, GEORGE (1685–1753), Irish-born Anglican bp. of Cloyne, theologian, philosopher. An earnest pastor, B. strove to understand the people, predominantly RC, of his region and to bring relief to their poverty. His philosophy aimed at revivifying Christian theism in the face of the deism and skepticism of his time. He was an empiricist in the English tradition, but only to a point. His writings show elements of subjective idealism, but he was not a solipsist. His informed critique of 18th-cent. science attacked the materialism, the abstractionism, the distinction of primary and secondary qualities that philosophers and physicists of his day had elaborated from Newton's work. This critique led him to "immaterialism" and to his *omne esse est percipi vel percipere,* the insistence that being lies in knowing or being known. He affirmed the place of spirit (man and God). *Siris,* his last work, moves from an exposition of the medicinal virtues of tar-water to lofty considerations on the human soul that reflect Plato and Plotinus. His analysis of science anticipates E. Mach and his successors. Scorned by the 19th cent., B. is read with respect by more contemporary philosophers of mathematics and physics. BIBLIOGRAPHY: *Works of George Berkeley, Bishop of Cloyne* (ed. A. A. Luce and T. E. Jessop, 9 v., 1948–57); A. A. Luce, *Life of George Berkeley, Bishop of Cloyne* (1949); H. B. Acton, EncPhil 1:295–304.

[W. B. MAHONEY]

BERLAGE, ANTON (1805–81), theologian. B. studied in Bonn and Tübingen, received his doctorate from Munich, and was ordained in 1832 without formal seminary training. He taught in Münster and in 1849 became dean of faculty there. His chief work was *Katholische Dogmatik* (7. v., 1839–94). BIBLIOGRAPHY: R. Bäumer, LTK 2:231.

[H. JACK]

BERLIÈRE, URSMER (1861–1932), Benedictine medievalist and editor. B., a monk of Maredsous Abbey in Belgium, wrote the monumental *Monasticon belga* (1890–1929), which treated the history of monasticism in the Low Countries. In 1906, he undertook the editing of the Belgian-Vatican correspondence, later published as *Analecta vaticano-belgica.* BIBLIOGRAPHY: P. H. Pirenne et al., *L'Hommage à dom Ursmer Berlière* (1931).

[B. F. SCHERER]

BERLINGHIERI BERLINGHIERO (1200?–1243?), earliest known Italian panel painter whose signed, painted *Crucifix* for the Church of S. Maria degli Angeli, Lucca, is one of the most important images of the 13th cent., combining the formal design of Tuscan Romanesque with a Byzantine stylized torso and drapery. B.'s art was perpetuated by his son Bonaventura. BIBLIOGRAPHY: E. B. Garrison, "Early Italian Paintings," *Burlington Magazine* 89 (1947).

[M. J. DALY]

BERLIOZ, LOUIS HECTOR (1803–69), French Romantic composer, one of the most colorful personalities and influential artists of the 19th century. In defiance of his parents, he abandoned medical school and enrolled, first, at the Paris Conservatory to study with Le Sueur and, later, at the Opéra. In time, he became a revolutionary force in the field of orchestration, on which he wrote an authoritative book. He was also a compelling conductor and an excellent critic. Recognized by such established composers as Liszt and Paganini, he lived to find his music appreciated in and beyond France. Chief among his works are *Symphonie fan-*

tastique, L'Enfance du Christ (oratorio), *Les Troyens* (opera) and *La damnation de Faust (opéra de concert).* Although not a church composer as such, B. often used religious themes, and his intimate knowledge of the religious experience is reflected in many pasages of his music. BIBLIOGRAPHY: H. G. Daniels and K. W. Bartlett, Grove DMM 1:653–673. [M. T. LEGGE]

BERMONDSEY, MONASTERY OF, Cluniac priory near London. Bermondsey was founded in 1089. It passed out of the Cluniac family and became an autonomous abbey in 1381. Bermondsey was noted for a miraculous cross which attracted many pilgrims. It was suppressed in 1538. BIBLIOGRAPHY: R. Graham, *English Ecclesiastical Studies* (1929) 188–208.

[J. R. SOMMERFELDT]

BERMUDEZ, JOÃO (d. 1570), adventurer. B. was attached through the Portuguese embassy to Negus David II of Ethiopia (1520). He remained behind when the embassy withdrew. In 1535 he went to Portugal on behalf of the Ethiopians. He claimed to have received ordination as an Ethiopian patriarch, and he returned to Ethiopia with the story that the pope had confirmed him in that office. He appears to have functioned as patriarch—until he was expelled from Ethopia. After his return to Portugal he wrote an account of his ambassadorial experiences. BIBLIOGRAPHY: I. Ortiz de Urbana, DHGE 8:542–543.

[H. JACK]

BERN (BERNO), abbot of Reichenau from 1008 to his death in 1048; liturgist, musician, hymn writer. B. was a strong adherent of the Cluniac reform, a faithful supporter of several emperors, and the author of many liturgical and musical treatises, which are preserved, though not without interpolations, in PL 142:1055–1210. BIBLIOGRAPHY: Stammler 1:204–208; H. Oesch, *Berno und Hermann von Reichenau als Musiktheoretiker* (1961).

[M. F. MCCARTHY]

BERNADETTE, ST., see SOUBIROUS, BERNADETTE, ST.

BERNADOT, VINCENT (1883–1941), Dominican spiritual writer, founder of two monthlies, *La Vie spirituelle* (1919)—which still flourishes—and *La Vie intellectuelle* (1928), of the publishing house, *Le Cerf* (1928), and of the weekly *Sept* (1934), which proved too open to the winds which were to blow through Vatican II and was literally shut up by the Roman authorities. He was the center of a circle that included many of the gifted Catholic writers of the day. [T. GILBY]

BERNANOS, GEORGES (1888–1948), French novelist, essayist, playwright. Brought up at Fressin, in the province of Artois, he met many priests, this being the meeting place of the clergy of the deanery. He later made this region the setting of all his novels, and priests his most prominent characters. As a journalist with a large family, he sought material security in various parts of France, then went to Majorca, which he left in 1938, settling in Brazil. Recalled in 1945 by General de Gaulle, he next left for Tunisia, where he planned to write nothing more except a life of Jesus. But becoming ill, he made a final return to France. B. was an insurance inspector when *Sous le soleil de Satan* (1925) brought him immediate fame. He revitalized the novel of Catholic inspiration in France. Usually his hero is a priest, engaged in a profound spiritual drama. The Abbé Donissan struggles with Satan to ransom souls. The Abbé Cénabre (*L'Imposture*) has lost his faith but is saved by the Abbé Chevance and Chantal de Clergerie, a young girl mystic in *La Joie. Le Journal d'un curé de campagne* (1938) won the Grand Prix of the French Academy. Here the Abbé d'Ambricourt, dying of cancer, is, like Donissan, little gifted naturally; but he conveys that impelling sense of the supernatural that B. saw as an integral part of the wholly engaged life. Yet even skeptical readers are gripped by the profundity of the struggle seen at a purely psychological or social level. B. scorned all mediocrity, seeking the Absolute in a confrontation of good and evil. But love prevails; the stronger support the weak (the play *Dialogue des Carmélites,* 1948); the communion of saints is a basic theme. The same uncompromising spirit informs the author's religious and political essays. BIBLIOGRAPHY: H. U. von Balthasar, *Le Chrétien Bernanos* (tr. M. de Gandillac, 1956); P. Speight, *Georges Bernanos: a Biography* (1974).

[L. TINSLEY]

BERNARD OF AOSTA, ST. (Bernard of Menthon; of Mont-Joux; d. 1081), preacher. In the St. Bernard Pass (named for him) he restored two famous hospices, which he placed under clerics who later became Canons Regular of St. Augustine. He was venerated for his holiness and his devotion as an itinerant preacher in Piedmont; he was proclaimed patron of mountain climbers by Pope Pius XI. BIBLIOGRAPHY: Butler 2:411–412; J.B. Villiger, BiblSanct 2:1325–32.

[M. DUFFY]

BERNARD OF AUVERGNE (d. *c.*1307), Dominican theologian, important to the origins of the Thomist school by his defense of St. Thomas Aquinas's teaching, esp. against *Henry of Ghent. He is known to have taught at Paris 1294–97, and was prior of Saint-Jacques in 1303. An edition of his commentary on the *Sentences* of Peter Lombard was published at Lyons in 1515. BIBLIOGRAPHY: P. Glorieux, NCE 2:334–335.

[T. C. O'BRIEN]

BERNARD OF BESSE (fl. 13th cent.), Franciscan chronicler. Companion and secretary of St. Bonaventure, B. belonged to the custody of Cahors of the province of Aquitaine. The prologue to his *De laudibus b. Francisci* contains the oldest list of Franciscan hagiographers. BIBLI-

OGRAPHY: J.R. H. Moorman, *Sources for the Life of St. Francis of Assisi* (1940) 156–158.

[H. DRESSLER]

BERNARD DE BOTONE, see BERNARD OF PARMA.

BERNARD OF CASTELVETERE (1708–56), Capuchin preacher and ascetical writer. Born Luciano Ferraro in what is now called Cauloni, Reggio-Calabria, B. is chiefly known for his *Direttorio mistico per li confessori* (1750). This work, which had 18 editions up to 1846, was valued highly by St. Alphonsus Liguori. BIBLIOGRAPHY: E. d'Ascoti, DSAM 1:1505–06; F. da Mareto, *Il "Direttorio mistico" del P. B. da Castelvetere* (1950).

[T. C. O'BRIEN]

BERNARD OF CHARTRES (d. *c*.1230), chancellor of the cathedral schools at Chartres. He is regarded as a humanist because of his own love for and promotion of the study of the classical literature of antiquity. Through John of Salisbury it is known that B. was a Platonist whose lectures in logic strongly influenced Gilbert de la Porrée's realistic teaching on the problem of universals. BIBLIOGRAPHY: Gilson HCP 619–620.

[T. C. O'BRIEN]

BERNARD OF CLAIRVAUX, ST. (1090–1153), monastic theologian, Doctor of the Church, and virtual founder of the *Cistercians, so called from Cîteaux, an abbey which the young Burgundian nobleman joined, together with 30 companions, and from which he founded, at the bidding of his abbot, St. *Stephen Harding, a new home in the Vallée d'Absinthe, which was renamed the Claire Vallée. The change symbolized a clear, sweet, and affectionate side to this somewhat thunderous, and certainly austere and forceful man: his lyrical style, notably in praise of our Lady, is an admirable expression of the 12th-cent. Renaissance, when theology still sang and had not been chopped by logic into scientific pieces. Though the most exemplary monk of his period, he threw himself, sometimes precipitantly, into its administrative and theological problems. He answered the papal snub that he was among the noisy frogs coming out of their marshes to trouble the cardinals and the Holy See with less asperity than he showed toward *Abelard and the "Black Monks" of Cluny who he thought threatened his own "White Monks": in both cases a reconciliation was effected, not least because of his fundamental friendliness. He composed political disputes, preached the Second Crusade, and reached the height of his influence when a Cistercian pupil was elected pope as Eugenius III (1145). His theological authority derives less from his intellectual force than from the permeation of well-ordered expositions of the Scriptures and the Fathers by a rich spiritual devotion. BIBLIOGRAPHY: P. Zerbi, BiblSanct 3:1–37, with excellent bibliog.; *idem*, NCE 2:335–339; B. Scott-James,

St. Bernard of Clairvaux (1957); É. Gilson, *Mystical Theology of St. Bernard*, (2d Eng. ed., 1955).

[T. GILBY]

BERNARD OF CLUNY (fl. 12th cent.), Benedictine monk and poet. Also known as Bernard of Morlas, he entered the foundation at Cluny *c*.1126 and dedicated his major work, *De contemptu mundi*, a satiric poem on the moral disorders of his time, to the abbot Peter the Venerable. BIBLIOGRAPHY: B. J. Comaskey, NCE 2:338–339.

[V. L. BULLOUGH]

BERNARD OF COMPOSTELLA, THE ELDER (13th-cent.), Spanish canonist of Bologna, glossator. Archdeacon of Compostella, he put together the *Compilatio Romana*, a compilation of decretals of the first 10 years of Innocent III (1208). BIBLIOGRAPHY: S. Kuttner, NCE 2:339; A. M. Stickler, LTK 2:242.

[M. H. BEIRNE]

BERNARD OF COMPOSTELLA THE YOUNGER (d. 1267), bp., canonist. Chaplain to Pope Innocent IV, he wrote several commentaries on the papal decretals of both Innocent IV and Gregory IX. BIBLIOGRAPHY: A. M. Stickler, LTK 2:242; L. E. Boyle, NCE 2:339.

[M. H. BEIRNE]

BERNARD OF CONSTANCE (d. *c*.1088), Benedictine scholar. Educated by Adalbert of Constance and Meinhard of Bamberg, B. taught at Constance and later at Hildesheim. His letters and ecclesiastical documents give evidence of his competence in the classics and canon law, and reflect as well the influence of the Ottonian Renaissance scholars. Of special historical significance are his *Liber canonum contra Henricum IV* and the *De damnatione schismaticorum*, written in support of Gregory VII. BIBLIOGRAPHY: V. H. Redlich, NCE 2:339–340.

[M. S. TANEY]

BERNARD OF CORLEONE, BL. (1605–67), Capuchin lay brother. B. received no formal education, but while he supported his mother as a cobbler, he learned swordsmanship from the Spaniards in the Corleone (Sicily) garrison. He used his skill in good causes only, but when he seriously wounded an adversary, he joined the Capuchins as a lay brother (1632). He became widely known for his life of penance and prayer and the gift of miracles. BIBLIOGRAPHY: G. Morabito, BiblSanct 3:42–43; Butler 1:124.

[H. JACK]

BERNARD OF FONTCAUDE (d. *c*.1192), Premonstratensian monk and probably first abbot of Fontcaude; in 1184 Lucius III gave jurisdiction over the abbey to the abp. of Narbonne. B.'s polemical works against the Waldenses include *Tria scriptorum adversus Valdensium sectam: Ebruardus Bethunensis, Bernardus abbas Fontis Calidi,*

Ermengaudus. (PL 204:793–840). BIBLIOGRAPHY: J. Daoust, NCE 2:340; A. Borst, LTK 2:243.

[J. R. RIVELLO]

BERNARD GUI (*c.* 1261–1331), French Dominican, inquisitor, bp. (Túy, 1323; Lodève, 1324), historian. His manual for inquisitors and a chronicle, *Flores chronicorum,* both written with great care and detail, are valuable sources on medieval religious protesters (Waldenses, Apostolics, Cathari, etc.), and also on the whole panorama of medieval religious and civil life.

[T. C. O'BRIEN]

BERNARD OF KRAIBURG (1415–77), bp. and humanist. After serving as professor of canon law, chancellor at the Univ. of Vienna, and ambassador to Rome, B. became bp. of Chiemsee and auxiliary and vicar-general of Salzburg. His letters and sermons are of historical and cultural importance. BIBLIOGRAPHY: V. H. Redlich, NCE 2:340–341.

[M. J. FINNEGAN]

BERNARD OF MENTHON, see BERNARD OF AOSTA, ST.

BERNARD OF MORLAIX, see BERNARD OF CLUNY.

BERNARD OF OFFIDA, BL. (1604–94), Capuchin lay brother. Of peasant stock, he entered the order in 1626. At Fermo, he was cook and infirmarian; at Offida, porter and questor. He was known for his service to the poor and for the miracles that attended his life. BIBLIOGRAPHY: B. d'Arenzano, BiblSanct 3:49, Butler 3:410.

[H. JACK]

BERNARD OLIVER (late 13th cent.–1348), Augustinian, Catalan bishop, theologian, diplomat. Among the most learned of his time, he lectured at the Univ. of Valencia and preached at the papal court (1334). As bp. he reformed cathedral chapters and ecclesiastics' lives. He served as ambassador for Peter IV of Aragon and companion to the papal envoy, Bernard of Albi. BIBLIOGRAPHY: D. W. Lomax, NCE 2:341; A. Zumkeller, LTK 2:246.

[M. H. BEIRNE]

BERNARD OF PARMA, ST. (*c.* 1055–1133), abbot, bishop. B. entered the Vallambrosan Order (*c.* 1075), was made abbot (*c.* 1093), and abbot general (1098). He was created cardinal by Urban II and later served Pascal II in the investiture struggle with Henry IV. A friend of Matilda of Tuscany, he was at Canossa in 1102. As bp. of Parma, he fought schism and heresy. BIBLIOGRAPHY: R. Volpini, BiblSanct 3:49–60; Butler, 4:493–494.

[M. A. WINKELMANN]

BERNARD OF PARMA (1710?–66), canonist. Canon of Bologna and a chaplain to the Pope, B., a teacher and commentator on Roman and canon law, wrote widely in explanation of the Decretals (series of papal decrees and promulgations by the popes which formed part of canon law.) His writings are notable for their precision and profound knowledge. BIBLIOGRAPHY: P. Ourliac, DDC 7:781; A. Amore, EncCatt 2:1438–39.

[J. R. AHERNE]

BERNARD OF PISA, see EUGENE III, BL., POPE.

BERNARD OF ST. THERESA, see DUVAL, JEAN.

BERNARD OF SAISSET (1232–1311), bp., abbot. His friend, Boniface VIII, created the diocese of Pamiers and made B. its first bishop. Philip IV the Fair of France accused B. of abetting the cause of Aragon against the King of France. In defiance of canon law B. was arrested, accused of heresy and simony (1301), and dispossessed of his patrimony. Boniface VIII rebuked Philip sharply in his bull, *Ausculta fili* (1301). B. was ultimately (1308) pardoned by the King. He is important for his role in the struggle between royal and papal jurisdictions in France. BIBLIOGRAPHY: J. M. Vidal, *Histoire des évêques de Pamiers. Bernard Saisset 1232–1311* (1926); H. Tüchle, LTK 2:248; É. Brouette, NCE 2:342–343.

[J. SMITH]

BERNARD SILVESTRIS (Bernard of Tours; fl. mid-12th cent.), author of *De universitate mundi,* an obscure cosmological commentary on Genesis employing imagery from classical antiquity; and of an allegorical commentary on the *Aeneid.*

[T. C. O'BRIEN]

BERNARD OF TIRON, ST. (*c.* 1046–1117) Benedictine abbot who was successively a monk at Abbey Saint-Cyprien, Poitiers, abbot of St. Cyprien (1100), and founder of the Abbey of Tiron (1114). Known as the reformer of the Benedictine Order, he restored monastic discipline at Saint-Cyprien after settling at Rome a jurisdictional dispute with Cluny. Later, B. established a monastery of strict observance at Tiron with the encouragement of Ivo of Chartres and King Louis VI. The reformed congregation's success may be measured by the rapid growth of its 10 abbeys and 40 priories in France. BIBLIOGRAPHY: P. Calendini, DHGE 8:754–755; R. Aigrain, *Catholicisme* 1:1482–83; Butler 2:92; I. Mannoci, BiblSanct 3:67.

[F. H. BRIGHAM]

BERNARD TOLOMEI, BL. (1272–1348), founder of Olivetan Benedictines. Born in Siena and educated by the Dominicans, B. left a successful career in law to retire with two companions into solitude in nearby Accona, beginning therefrom (1319) the Benedictine community of Our Lady of Oliveto, renowned for its austerity. Clement VI approved the flourishing community in 1344. B. died while nursing the sick in the "Black Death." BIBLIOGRAPHY: A. G. Biggs, NCE 2:343; Butler 3:379–380.

[G. E. CONWAY]

BERNARD, ÉMILE (1868–1941), Postimpressionist artist and critic. B. was a precocious painter and master of philosophy and aesthetics. Friend of Van *Gogh, *Redon, *Cézanne, and also *Gauguin (with whom he worked closely at Pont-Aven), B. produced paintings, woodcuts, sculpture, and some furniture, traveled to Italy and lived for a time in Egypt. Returning to Paris, he edited the review *La Rénovation Esthétique.* BIBLIOGRAPHY: V. Van Gogh, *Letters to Émile Bernard* (tr. D. Lord, 1938).

[M. J. DALY]

BERNARDES, MANOEL (1644–1710), scholar and writer. He entered the Oratorians at Lisbon, and devoted himself to preaching and study. His numerous spiritual writings rank him a master of Portuguese literary style and an outstanding representative of Oratorian mysticism. BIBLIOGRAPHY: J. S. Ruggieri, EncCatt 2:1403–04; P. Auvray, DSAM 1:1514.

[H. JACK]

BERNARDI, STEFANO (d. *c.*1635), priest and composer of the early Baroque whose most solid contribution to music was his help in importing the Italian musical style to the southern Germanic area while in charge of the music at the Cathedral in Salzburg, for whose dedication he conducted *Benevoli's 52-part Mass. His Mass on *Arcadelt's madrigal *Il bianco e dolce cigno* was one of the few parody Masses (a Renaissance form) written in the Baroque era; otherwise his music is largely in the style of his day without being notably progressive. BIBLIOGRAPHY: T. W. Werner, MGG 1:1775–78.

[P. DOHERTY]

BERNARDINE OF ASTI (1484–1554), Capuchin vicar-general. He joined the Franciscan Observants (1499) and, as provincial, fostered the reform movement within the order. Internal opposition caused him to transfer to the Capuchins (1534). He was elected vicar-general in 1535 and again in 1546, presided over the revision of the constitutions, and gave prudent guidance to the progress and solidification of the Capuchin reform. BIBLIOGRAPHY: A. Teetaert, DHGE 8:783–785.

[H. JACK]

BERNARDINE OF FELTRE, BL. (1439–94), Italian Franciscan Observant, preacher. Struck by the preaching of St. *James of the Marches, B. entered the Franciscans while a student at the Univ. of Padua. He was appointed to preach by the provincial chapter of his order (1469), an office for which he at first thought himself unsuited because of the smallness of his stature and the frailty of his health. Nevertheless he threw himself earnestly into the work and for nearly 35 years fulfilled his mission throughout Northern and Central Italy. His success was astonishing. Everywhere large crowds gathered to hear him and were deeply moved by the power of his words. He courageously denounced wickedness in high places, thereby winning enemies for himself as well as admirers. His influence in many cases was used effectively to bring about desirable changes in legislation. He had great concern for the poor and in their interest took a leading part in the establishment of *montes pietatis* where those in need could get money without paying the ruinous interest demanded by usurers. This brought him under attack by Jewish and Lombard money-lenders, and he also had to face opposition from friars of his own order, many of whom believed that the small interest rates exacted by the *montes pietatis* were in violation of canon law, a point that was not beyond dispute until the Council of the Lateran in 1515 gave its approval to the *montes.* His position with regard to the Jews has been unfavorably criticized, not undeservedly, for he advocated repressive measures against the people as a whole and not simply the abolition of the practices of some money-lenders. He also appears to have been involved in the agitation that followed upon the alleged ritual murder of the infant known as *Simon of Trent. BIBLIOGRAPHY: F. Casolini, *Bernardino da Feltre, il martello degli usuria* (1939); *idem,* EncCatt 2:1406–08; L. De Besse, *Le Bx. Bernadin de Feltre et son oeuvre* 2v., (1902); Butler 3:672–676; G. V. Sabatelli, BiblSanct 2:1289–93.

[P. K. MEAGHER]

BERNARDINE OF SIENA, ST. (1380–1444), Italian Franciscan preacher, reformer, and promoter of devotion to the Holy Name. After completing his studies in philosophy, law, and theology, he became a Franciscan, was ordained a priest, and was commissioned to preach. After preparing himself for this apostolate by several additional years of study and prayer, B. traveled throughout Italy, evangelizing and preaching moral reformation and penance. Everywhere his efforts met with success. His sermons, often 3 or 4 hours long and addressed to as many as 30,000 persons crowded into the open public squares, attacked the vices prevalent at the time so powerfully that a great moral reform was effected. Cities and factions forgot old quarrels and hatreds and made peace; bonfires consumed the objects of sin and superstition. As a means of extirpating vice, he preached devotion to the Holy Name of Jesus and designed a monogram in which the first three letters of the name of Jesus in Greek were set against a blue background in the midst of a blazing sun with bursting rays. Wherever he went, he would display this monogram on his banner and when preaching in the pulpit would hold the emblem before him, blessing the congregation with it as he finished. Artisans copied his design, which soon appeared not only in churches everywhere but also above the gates and on the walls of cities and towns, where it replaced the old emblems of power, superstition, and strife. His enemies made several attempts to have him condemned for heresy and for fostering idolatry, but after an examination of his teachings and a defense by his friend and companion, St. John Capistran, he was vindicated and even offered the miter on three occasions. His popularity and the esteem in which he was held also aroused a new interest in the Franciscan reform movement of which he became chief promoter. Elected vicar-general of the Observants in Italy, by his prudence and moderation he brought about a return to the spirit and ideals of the seraphic founder. His works have survived both in the vernacular sermons copied by scribes exactly as he delivered them and in the polished Latin theological sermons and treatises he wrote for the instruction and edification of the clergy. Franciscan scholars have recently published a new complete critical edition of his works (8 v. 1950–63). He was canonized in 1540. BIBLIOGRAPHY: I. Origo, *World of San Bernardino* (1962); A. G. Ferrers Howell, *S. Bernardino of Siena* (1913).

[D. A. MCGUCKIN]

BERNARDINES, English adaptation of the Italian name of the reformed Cistercians of Les-Feuillans (Fulium) in the vicinity of Toulouse from which the original French foundation took the name Feuillants. Founded in 1577 by Abbot J. de la Barrière (1544–1600) who drew up a strict version of the rule with the approval of Pope Gregory XIII (1581), the order was granted its autonomy by Sixtus V (1589) and numbered several outstanding men among the members of both its French and Italian houses, e.g., Cardinal Bona (d. 1674). It was dissolved in the first half of the 19th century. BIBLIOGRAPHY: J. Besse, DTC 5:2265–68; E. Obrecht, CE 6:64.

[F. H. BRIGHAM]

BERNARDINO OF LAREDO (1482–1540), Spanish Franciscan Observant lay brother, physician, mystical writer. He gave up a promising medical career to live a life of austerity and prayer as a lay brother. Book 3 of his work *Subida del Monte Sion (Ascent of Mount Sion)*, which was greatly admired by St. Teresa of Avila, has been translated into English (tr. and ed. E. A. Peers, 1952).

[P. K. MEAGHER]

BERNARDO BOTTONI, see BERNARD OF PARMA.

BERNAY, ABBEY OF, Benedictine monastery in Lower Normandy (now in the Diocese of Évreux), founded (between 1013 and 1015) by Judith, wife of Duke Richard II of Normandy. The abbey church, built in three stages (1020–55), was characterized by its capitals, which were designed upon those of Burgundian Saint-Bénigne in Dijon. Many famous abbots ruled Bernay. It suffered greatly in the Wars of Religion and was left in ruins (1562–63). The church was rebuilt and improved at various times and was later secularized. BIBLIOGRAPHY: P. Calendini, DHGE 8:812–815; P. Cousin, NCE 2:348.

[S. A. HEENEY]

BERNETTI, TOMMASO (1779–1852), cardinal, papal secretary of state. He accompanied the papal court to France (1808), but was exiled by Napoleon after a short time (1810) and served the Church by acting as an intermediary between the captive pope and the Belgian Catholics. Though elevated to the cardinalate in 1827, he was not ordained priest till 1832. B. displayed considerable diplomatic skill in the troubled times following the Napoleonic disorders and the outbreak of revolutionary activity in Italy and the States of the Church. He acted vigorously to repress the revolution and for that reason was severely criticized by those favorable to the revolutionary cause. BIBLIOGRAPHY: A. M. Ghisalberti, EncCatt 2:1443–44.

[C. BUCKLEY]

BERNGER, (BERENGAR), BL. (d. 1108), Benedictine abbot. At the request of Bishop Ulric of Passau he became the first abbot (1094) of Formbach (founded 1040) near Passau in Bavaria. He was responsible for the first collection of customs of Formbach, and was known for his personal integrity, administrative ability, and generosity to the needy. BIBLIOGRAPHY: J. C. Moore, NCE 2:348; C. Cisto, Bibl-Sanct 2:1281–82.

[M. S. TANEY]

BERNIER, ÉTIENNE ALEXANDRE (1762–1806), prominent ecclesiastical statesman. He was a professor at the Univ. of Angers and pastor of St. Laud's church, when he drew the unfavorable attention of the government by refusing in 1790 to take the oath in support of the Civil Constitution of the Clergy. He was replaced in his pastorate, but his influence made the position of his successor untenable. He took an active role with the army in the insurrection until 1799. Offering his services to Napoleon, he was chosen to represent Napoleon in the negotiations with Spino, who represented the Holy See. For this service he was promised the cardinal's hat, but after the Concordat of 1801, B. encountered trouble because of his attitude to the dubious retractation of some former constitutional bps. who obtained new sees, and this led to his appointment as bp. of Orléans rather than of Paris. He took a prominent part in the negotiations that led to Pius VII's coming to Paris for the coronation of Napoleon and arranged the ceremonial for the event. BIBLIOGRAPHY: J. Leflon, *Étienne-Alexandre Bernier, évêque d'Orléans* (1938); idem, NCE 2:348–349.

[P. K. MEAGHER]

BERNIER, NICHOLAS (1664–1734), French composer. After studying in Rome he served as organist at Chartres cathedral, then went to Paris where he held posts at St.-Germain-l'Auxerrois, Sainte-Chapelle, and Versailles. His sacred works include a *Te Deum* (considered his masterpiece), motets, and other church music. He is also noted for his secular cantatas. BIBLIOGRAPHY: A. Cellier, MGG 1:1742–95.

[A. DOHERTY]

BERNIÈRES-LOUVIGNY, JEAN DE (1602–59), French layman and mystic. He interested himself in charitable works, assisted Mère Marie de l'Incarnation in the foundation of the Ursulines in Quebec, and corresponded with many outstanding ascetics of his time. His notes, not written for publication, were assembled and published after his death—*Le Chrétien intérieure* and *Les Oeuvres spirituelles de M. de Bernières-Louvigny*. These were put on the Index because certain passages were thought to savor of quietism. They have since been corrected. It is not known whether these objectionable passages were the work of B. or of the editors who prepared the MSS for publication. BIBLIOGRAPHY: R. Heurtevent, DSAM 1:1522–27.

[P. K. MEAGHER]

BERNINI, GIOVANNI LORENZO (1598–1680), the greatest sculptor and architect of the Italian Baroque. A child prodigy, B. studied with his father in Naples, coming to Rome in 1605, where he remained except for 6 months at the court of Louis XIV in Paris (1665). For more than 50 years architect to St. Peter's Basilica, B. conceived and executed the *Baldacchino* (1624–33), *Scala Regia* (1663–66), the *Cathedra Petri* in the apse (1657–66), and the impressive double colonnade of St. Peter's Square (1656–67), unifying architecture, sculpture, and ornamentation in overwhelming, dramatic effects expressing the spirit of 17th-cent. Catholicism. B. designed churches, squares, tombs, palaces, and fountains, officiated in civic illuminations and displays, and created costumes and stage machinery for operas. For his *St. Teresa in Ecstasy* (S. Maria della Vittoria) B. further extended his theatrical effects in architectural lighting to transport to exultant mystical reality. One of the last of the "universal men" of the Renaissance, B. gave Rome its baroque character and determined Europe's sculptural style for centuries. BIBLIOGRAPHY: R. Wittkower, *Gian Lorenzo Bernini* (1955); id., *Art and Architecture in Italy 1600–1750* (1958).

[M. J. DALY]

BERNIS, FRANÇOIS JOACHIM DE PIERRE DE (1715–94), cardinal and statesman. Born of a family of noble rank but slender means, B. gained court favor by his charm and literary talents. He became ambassador to Venice (1751), envoy to Vienna to secure the Austrian alliance (1756), and minister of foreign affairs (1757). French vicissitudes in the Seven Years' War brought his political eclipse, but he was recalled, made apb. of Albi (1764), and ambassador to Rome (1769). His influence there protected French interests in two papal elections. He also negotiated for the suppression of the Jesuits. He refused to accept the Civil Constitution of the Clergy (1790), lost his position and fortune, and died in Rome. BIBLIOGRAPHY: M. Cheke, *Cardinal de Bernis* (1959); P. Calendini, DHGE 8:847–849.

[H. JACK]

BERNO, BL. (d. 927), founder and first abbot of Cluny. His date of birth and place of origin are unknown. He obtained from Pope Formosus in 894 the exemption of his monastery from local episcopal jurisdiction and had it placed immediately under the jurisdiction of the Holy See. Other monasteries interested in reform began to be associated with Cluny under his leadership. BIBLIOGRAPHY: G. Bataille, BiblSanct 3:81–82.

[P. K. MEAGHER]

BERNO OF REICHENAU (d. 1048), Benedictine abbot, orator, composer, musician, and liturgist. As abbot of Reichenau, he gave unswerving loyalty to the German throne whether occupied by Henry II, Conrad the Younger, Conrad III, or Henry III. He introduced monastic reforms, had an active role in the Synod of Constance, and wrote on liturgical music, giving insight into the early Gregorian chant. BIBLIOGRAPHY: F.-J. Schamale, LTK 2:258–259; M.F. McCarthy, NCE 2:353.

[M. H. BEIRNE]

BERNOLD OF CONSTANCE (*c*. 1050–1100), chronicler. Educated in the cathedral school of Constance and ordained there in 1084, B. opposed Henry IV in the investiture struggle. Besides his well-known chronicle covering the period from 1075 to 1100, B. wrote on the liturgy, on the Eucharist, and in defense of the authority of papal decrees. BIBLIOGRAPHY: L. Kurras, NCE 2:353.

[M. A. WINKELMANN]

BERNOLD OF OTTOBEUREN, BL. (fl. probably 11th cent.), Benedictine monk of the abbey of Ottobeuren, noted for his mortification and for miracles after his death. Twice translated (1189 and 1553), his remains have rested in the abbey basilica since 1772. BIBLIOGRAPHY: V. Faroni, BiblSanct 3:78–79.

[O. J. BLUM]

BERNOLD OF ST. BLAISE (or Bernold of Constance; *c*. 1054–1100), chronicler and defender of the papacy. His chronicle (see MGH Scrip 5:385–467), esp. for the years 1075–1100, contains valuable information about the investiture struggle and the reigns of Popes Gregory VII, Victor III, Urban II. His numerous polemical treatises are to be found in MGH Lib. Lit. 2:1–168; PL 148. BIBLIOGRAPHY: L. Bréhier, DHGE 8:853–856; L. Kurras, NCE 2:353.

[M. F. MCCARTHY]

BERNULF, ST. (Bernold, Benno; d. 1054), bp. of Utrecht from 1027. The sources for his life contain some obviously legendary material. He had increased the temporalities of his diocese very largely by imperial benefaction, and when certain lay nobles of Lorraine leagued themselves against Henry III, B. rallied to the Emperor's support. B. promoted reform and built many churches. BIBLIOGRAPHY: W. Lampen, Bibl-Sanct 3:79–80.

[S. WILLIAMS]

BERNWARD OF HILDESHEIM, ST. (c.960–1022), bishop. Born of an important Saxon family, B. was educated in the Hildesheim cathedral school. In 978 he became chaplain to Empress Theophano and tutor of Otto III, who later named him bp. of Hildesheim (993). Until his death he worked strenuously to strengthen Hildesheim politically, culturally, and spiritually. He built a system of fortifications to protect the people from Slavic and Norman invasions, founded the famous Abbey of Sankt-Michael in Hildesheim, and encouraged every sort of cultural activity—literature, architecture, painting, sculpture—making his episcopal city and its abbey an outstanding center of art. Before his death he was clothed in the Benedictine habit, and he was buried in a crypt of the abbey church. BIBLIOGRAPHY: G. M. Fusconi, BiblSanct 3:82–85; F. J. Tschan, *St. Bernward of Hildesheim* (3 v., 1942–52). *HILDESHEIM, ART OF.

BEROSSUS (c.340B.C.–c.270B.C.), historian and priest of the god Bel (Marduk) in Babylon who wrote a three-volume history of Babylonia in Greek called *Babyloniaca* in honor of the Seleucid king, Antiochus Soter I, to celebrate the achievements of the Seleucid dynasty. The original work is lost but several fragments quoted by Alexander Polyhistor (1st cent. B.C.) have been preserved in the writings of Josephus Flavius, Eusebius of Caesarea, George Syncellus, and Clement of Alexandria. His work is significant for his account of Babylonian chronology and ancient cosmogonic myths. For the most part, his details are in accord with the information preserved on Babylonian cuneiform tablets, e.g., the story of Xisuthos and the Deluge as found in the cuneiform record of the Gilgamesh Epic. BIBLIOGRAPHY: R. Caplice, NCE 2:354–355; J. Baikie, Hastings ERE 2:533–534.

[F. H. BRIGHAM]

BERQUIN, LOUIS DE (1490–1529), humanist, a member of the circle of Meaux known particularly for his translations of the writings of Erasmus, Luther, Hutten, and Melanchthon. He was arrested several times after 1520, but released by the intervention of King Francis I. The last time, he was condemned as a heretic and burned. BIBLIOGRAPHY: G. Loirette, DHGE 8:882–884.

[H. JACK]

BERRUGUETE, ALONSO (1486?–1561), Spanish Renaissance sculptor and architect. B. probably studied with Pedro, court painter to Ferdinand and Isabella, before working with Michelangelo and others in Italy (1504–17). Commissioned in Zaragoza, Valladolid, Toledo, B. became court painter and sculptor to Charles V. His work in stone and wood (often polychromed) evidences an intensive, mannerist restlessness and distortion, often attaining to frenetic

mysticism. BIBLIOGRAPHY: M. Bartolomé Cossio, *Alonso Berruguete* (1948); F. Jímenez Placer, *Historia del arte español* (1955).

[M. J. DALY]

BERRUYER, ISAAC JOSEPH (1681–1758), French Jesuit, biblical scholar. His monumental *History of the People of God,* published in three parts from 1728 to 1757, caused widespread opposition in orthodox Catholic circles, each section, as it appeared, being put on the Index. A revised and approved edition of the first part, a history of Israel until Christ, appeared (1828) long after his death. The main objections to his works focused on Nestorian tendencies, an irreverent, whimsical attitude toward Sacred Scripture, and a sympathetic acceptance of the strange theories of his fellow Jesuit, Jean Hardouin. BIBLIOGRAPHY: L. Bopp, LTK 2:262.

[J. F. FALLON]

BERRY, JEAN DE FRANCE, DUC DE (1340–1416), a prince distinguished for his political role during The Hundred Years' War. B. held extensive territorial power and is particularly renowned as patron of the arts. During the vicissitudes of the reigns of Charles V and Charles VI, B. negotiated many reconciliations, foreign and domestic. Living sumptuously, he built palaces in Bourges, Poitiers, Paris, and elsewhere, but he is esp. renowned for the very famous illuminated MS, the *Très Riches Heures* (Chantilly Museum) by the *Limbourg brothers, which provides an exact pictorial record of his magnificent residences. Living in a period of great public misfortunes, B., though sensuous and thirsty for power, is to be remembered as an enlightened protector of the arts. He died in poverty in Paris, having spent all on treasures of painting, jewelry, and illuminated MSS, which remain his monument. BIBLIOGRAPHY: F. Lehoux, *Jean de France, Duc de Berri* (2 v., 1966).

[M. J. DALY]

BERSABEE, see BEERSHEBA.

BERSE, GASPAR (Barzeo; 1515–53), Jesuit missionary. He was born in the Netherlands, ordained in Coimbra, and was sent to Goa (1548) where he had Francis Xavier as mentor and associate. For several years B. labored along the Persian Gulf; he was placed in charge of Goa when Xavier went to China (1552). BIBLIOGRAPHY: E. Lamalle, DHGE 6:1059–61.

[H. JACK]

BERSIER, EUGÈNE (1831–89), French Reformed pastor. At 17 B. traveled to America, where an encounter with a pious laborer and the reading of Vinet's essay on joy determined his vocation. He studied theology in Geneva and then went to Paris in 1855 to begin his ministry. He strove for social justice and freedom of conscience and was active in liturgical reform. In 1874 he founded the Church of the Star, separating from the

Free Churches to adhere to the Reformed. He published a history of the Huguenots and seven books of sermons. BIBLIOGRAPHY: R. Voeltzel, RGG 1:1070.

[M. J. SUELZER]

BERTALI, ANTONIO, (1605–69), Italian composer. At an early age B. served the imperial court in Vienna as a violinist and later as a conductor. Besides operas, he composed two oratorios, *Maria Magdalena* and *La strage degli innocenti,* and some Masses and motets. BIBLIOGRAPHY: A. Loewenberg, Grove DMM 1:685.

[H. H. CRANE]

BERTAUT, JEAN (1552–1611), French bp. and poet. B. held various positions, including those of councilor of the *parlement* of Grenoble, lector to Henry III, almoner to Queen Marie de Médicis, abbot of Aunay, and bp. of Séez (1606). Influenced by *Ronsard and *Desportes, he wrote love poetry, poems commemorating court events, and religious poetry, including his *Cantiques,* inspired by the Bible. All of these are collected in his *Oeuvres poétiques* (1601, 1605) and in his *Recueil de quelques vers amoureux* (1602). He also wrote sermons and a funeral oration for Henry IV, in whose conversion he is said to have played a role. BIBLIOGRAPHY: G. Grente, *Jean Bertaut* (1903).

[R. N. NICOLICH]

BERTHA OF BLANGY, ST. (d. *c.*725), Benedictine abbess. A somewhat unreliable 10th-cent. biography states that B. was married and had five daughters. After her husband's death, she founded the monastery of Blangy (*c.*686), which she and her daughters Deotila and Gertrude entered. After organizing the monastic life there, she placed Deotila in charge and retired to live as a solitary. BIBLIOGRAPHY: P. Blecker, NCE 2:257; Butler 3:14–15; G. Bataille, BiblSanct 3:90.

[G. M. COOK]

BERTHA OF VAL D'OR, ST. (d. *c.*690), foundress and abbess. By mutual agreement she lived in a state of virginity with her husband, the saintly Gombert, founder of the convent of St. Peter at Reims. On the murder of Gombert while on a missionary journey, she founded a convent at Avenay at a place once called Val d'Or and was its first abbess. She is said to have been murdered by two nephews of her husband. B. and Gombert are honored as saints and martyrs. BIBLIOGRAPHY: Zimmermann 2:132–133; F. Baix, DHGE 8:943–944.

[M. R. P. MCGUIRE]

BERTHARIUS, ST. (d. 884), abbot and martyr. As abbot of Monte Cassino, B. obtained many privileges for that great monastery, including exemption from episcopal jurisdiction. Poet, homilist, and writer on medical subjects, B. was also interested in theological studies and encouraged learning. He was martyred by invading Saracens at Teano in Campania.

His writings can be found in PL 126. BIBLIOGRAPHY: B. D. Hill, NCE 2:357; B. Cignilti, BiblSanct 3:92–96.

[M. A. WINKELMANN]

BERTHELOT, PIERRE, see DIONYSIUS OF THE NATIVITY, BL.

BERTHIER, GUILLAUME-FRANÇOIS (1704–84), French Jesuit and editor. He engaged in many battles with Voltaire and the Encyclopedists while editing the *Journal de Trévoux* (1745–63). He wrote spiritual works and several volumes of the *Histoire de l' Église Gallicane.* He was wittily and maliciously satirized by Voltaire in his *Relation de la maladie, de la confession, de la mort du jésuite Berthier* (1759). BIBLIOGRAPHY: J. N. Pappas, *Berthier's Journal de Trévoux and the Philosophes* (1957).

[A. S. CRISAFULLI]

BERTHIER, JEAN BAPTISTE (1840–1908), a missionary of Our Lady of La Salette who in 1895 founded the Institute of the Holy Family, a missionary congregation for late vocations to the priesthood. His numerous ascetical writings were widely read and stressed devotion to the Holy Family and fidelity to the duties of one's state in life. BIBLIOGRAPHY: P. Ramers, DSAM 1:1530–32.

[H. JACK]

BERTHIER, JOACHIM JOSEPH (1847–1924), Dominican theologian and savant. A native of Annecy, France, B. studied at Fribourg, and joined the Order of Preachers in 1872. In his rich career B. collaborated (1880) with Card. *Zigliara on the Leonine edition of St. Thomas, and was a cofounder of the Catholic Univ. of Fribourg (1906–19). Besides editing several works, among them Thomas Valgornera's *Theologia mystica* (1890), B. was the author of many original studies, including *Tabulae synopticae totius Summae Theologiae S. Thomae Aquinatis* (1892); *De locis theologicis* (1900); *La Divina Commedia di Dante con commenti secondo la scolastica* (1897). BIBLIOGRAPHY: A. Walz, LTK 2:264–265 with a complete list of B.'s works; AnalOP 33 (1925) 92–96.

BERTHOLD OF CARMES, ST. (d. *c.*1195), considered founder of Carmelite order. As a theological student at Paris, he joined the Crusades. Retiring to Mt. Carmel, he collected the Latin lay hermits of the Holy Mountain into a religious community dedicated to the Mother of God. Aymerius, Latin patriarch of Antioch, appointed him first superior general. BIBLIOGRAPHY: A. de Saint-Paul, DHGE 8:960–963; A. Staring, BiblSanct 3:106–108.

[M. H. BEIRNE]

BERTHOLD OF CHIEMSEE (Pürstinger; 1465–1543). As bp. of Chiemsee (1508–26), he attended the Councils of Salzburg (1512) and Mühldorf (1522), mediated between the burghers of Salzburg and the abp. (1511), and defended the rebellious peasants against prosecution for treason (1526). He wrote a theological treatise in German and a defense of the Mass and the Eucharist.

[H. JACK]

BERTHOLD OF GARSTEN, ST. (d. 1142), Benedictine monk. B. entered the monastery of Saint Blasien and was eventually made superior. In 1107 he was prior at Gottweig and from 1111 to his death, first abbot of Garsten, which became a flourishing center of reform. Noted for fidelity, humility, and charity, he was canonized by the bp. of Passau in 1236. BIBLIOGRAPHY: D. Andreini, NCE 2:358; B. Cignitti, BiblSanct 3:109–110; AnalBoll 77(1959) 488–489.

[M. J. FINNEGAN]

BERTHOLD OF MOOSBURG, Dominican philosopher, theologian. He taught at *studia* of the Dominicans at Regensburg and Cologne (1335–61). His chief work is an exposition of the *Elements of Theology* by Proclus. His thought has been studied briefly by authors such as Grabmann and Klibansky, and in particular by W. Eckert in *Philosophisches Jahrbuch* 65 (1957) 120–133.

[L. E. BOYLE]

BERTHOLD OF REGENSBURG (*c.*1210–72), Franciscan monk, renowned popular preacher in medieval Germany, Switzerland, Czechoslovakia, and Hungary. Though he is known to have preached in German, the only extant sermons positively ascribed to him are in Latin. BIBLIOGRAPHY: For a comprehensive study of his life and work, see A. E. Schönbach, "Studien zur Geschichte der altdeutschen Predigt," *K. Akademie der Wissenschaften, Vienna: Philosophisch-historische Klasse, Sitzungsberichte* (1900–07) 142:7, 147:5, 151:2, 152:7, 153:4, 154:1, 155:5.

[M. F. MCCARTHY]

BERTHOLD OF REICHENAU (*c.*1030–88), chronicler. Pupil of Hermannus Contractus, he continued the Chronicle of Hermannus. Of the two extant versions, B. was probably the author of the simpler, briefer, and pro-imperial version, *Chronici Hermanni continuatio auctore ut dicitur Bertholdo.* The pro-Gregorian and anti-Henry IV version was apparently done by an anonymous Swabian annalist. BIBLIOGRAPHY: A. Fliche, DHGE 8:987; T. Schieffer, LTK 2:268.

[M. H. BEIRNE]

BERTHOLET, ALFRED (1868–1951), Protestant biblical scholar. B. taught OT at the Universities of Basel, Tübingen, Göttingen, and Berlin; wrote commentaries on some of the OT books; contributed articles on the Bible to several German reference works; and helped to edit, among other works, the second edition of *Die Religion in Geschichte und Gegenwart* (1927–33). He belonged to the history of religions school which was so influential in early 20th-cent. biblical criticism. BIBLIOGRAPHY: *Festschrift für Alfred Bertholet* (ed. O. Eissfeldt et al., 1950) 564–578; T. W. Buckley, NCE 2:359.

[T. M. MCFADDEN]

BERTI, GIOVANNI LORENZO (1696–1766), Augustinian friar and theologian. After H. *Noris, B. is the most important representative of Augustinian theologians of the 17th and 18th cent., sometimes called *Augustinenses,* who elaborated a theology of grace based upon the teachings of St. Augustine. Together with other Augustinians of the period, he endeavored to divorce the authority of Augustine from the doctrines of Luther, Calvin, and the Jansenists and to present a new and authentic statement of Augustine's teaching on grace accommodated to the doctrinal demands of the time. At the direction of the prior general of his order, B. undertook a systematic presentation of Augustine's entire theology, with special reference to the problem of grace and free will. The result was a vast and erudite work entitled *De theologicis disciplinis,* of which a compendium was produced by Girolamo Buzio in 1767. B. is also the author of a compendium of church history, *Historiae ecclesiasticae breviarium.* A papal commission appointed by Benedict XIV to investigate charges of Jansenism declared in favor of B.'s writings. BIBLIOGRAPHY: D. Perini, *Bibliographia Augustiniana* (1929–38) 1:120–123; H. de Lubac, *Augustinisme et théologie moderne* (1965).

[R. P. RUSSELL]

BERTIERI, GIUSEPPE (1734–1806), theologian and bishop. He taught theology at the Univ. of Vienna and wrote several theological treatises. He became bp. of Como (1789), where his tendencies toward Josephinism were apparent, and bp. of Pavia (1792–1804). BIBLIOGRAPHY: L. Jadin, DHGE 8:1003–04.

[H. JACK]

BERTILLA OF CHELLES, ST. (d. 705?), Benedictine abbess who entered the monastery of Jouarre-en-Brie *c.*659, where she was noted esp. for her obedience. Queen Bathildis, wife of Clovis II, made her first abbess of Chelles, a monastery that the queen founded and to which she retired. Hereswitha, widow of an East Anglian king, also retired to Chelles. BIBLIOGRAPHY: É. Brouette, NCE 2:359; Butler 4:268–269.

[G. M. COOK]

BERTINUS, ST. (*c.*615–709), Benedictine abbot. Trained first at Luxeuil under St. Walbert, B. became a protégé of St. Audomarus at Thérouanne. He succeeded Mommolinus *c.*660 as abbot of Sithiu, which was afterwards renamed Saint-Bertin, a place noted for preparation of a collection of annals important for Frankish history. BIBLIOGRAPHY: A. Amore, BiblSanct 3:101–102.

[A. CABANISS]

BERTONIO, LUDOVICO (1555–1625), Jesuit missionary and linguist. He became a Jesuit in Rome (1575), was sent to Peru (1581), and for 40 years labored at the mission of Juli in Upper Peru. He followed the principle of adaptation and became skilled in the Aymara language. His dictionaries and other writings in Aymara were a valuable linguistic contribution. BIBLIOGRAPHY: A. de Egaña, NCE 2:360.

[H. JACK]

BERTRAM OF LE MANS, ST. (c.550–c.626), bishop. Ordained priest by St. Germain, bp. of Paris, B. was named Germain's archdeacon. In 586 B. became bp. of Le Mans where he distinguished himself by his care of the poor and afflicted. BIBLIOGRAPHY: Butler 2:676–677; J. Vandamme, BiblSanct 3:136–138.

[H. DRESSLER]

BERTRAND IF AQUILEIA, BL. (c. 1260–1350), patriarch of Aquileia. B. studied canon and civil law at Toulouse, served under Pope John XXII on various diplomatic missions, and became patriarch of Aquileia in 1334. He fought to regain lost possessions of his see and began an initially successful military campaign against Venice, but the ultimate outcome is indicated by the fact that the patriarchate was transferred to Venice in 1450. BIBLIOGRAPHY: P. Paschini, BiblSanct 3:122–128.

[V. L. BULLOUGH]

BERTRAND OF COMMINGES, ST. (c.1050–1123), bishop. Canon and archdeacon of Toulouse, he was elected bp. of Comminges, a see he reorganized and served for 50 years. He participated in the Synod of Poitiers which excommunicated Philip (1100). The story "Great Pardon of Comminges" tells of his success in reforming. BIBLIOGRAPHY: U. Turck, LTK 2:271–272; J. C. Didier, BiblSanct 3:129–132.

[M. H. BEIRNE]

BERTRAND DE GARRIGA, BL. (c.1172–c.1230), early follower and friend of St. Dominic. In 1215 with five other preachers, he joined Dominic in the founding of his order. Appointed provincial of Provence (1221), he was described as humble, austere, and prayerful. BIBLIOGRAPHY: S. M. Bertucci, BiblSanct 1:133–134; Butler 3:498–500.

[M. H. BEIRNE]

BERTRAND, LOUIS, ST. (1526–81), Dominican preacher and missionary. He was ordained in 1547 and became a distinguished preacher in Valencia. During his career he was several times novice master and prior. As a missionary in New Granada (1562–69), he converted extraordinary numbers, and is since known as the patron of Colombia. Along with the sanctity of his life and his remarkable talents as a preacher, he was reputed to have the gift of tongues, of prophecy, and of miracles. He was canonized in 1671. BIBLIOGRAPHY: R. R. Lluch and A. Cardinali, BiblSanct 8:342–348; Butler 4:72–74.

[H. JACK]

BERTRAND, LOUIS (1866–1941), French writer. A doctor in classics from the Sorbonne, B. taught in France and Algeria (1888–1900), then authored works of history, fiction, and general culture about the peoples and countries of the Mediterranean basin. He returned to Catholicism in Jerusalem (1906). Thereafter, his faith and patriotism led him to emphasize North Africa's Latin Christian past and to defend French colonialism as renewing that tradition after centuries of Islamic dominance. To this end he published works of hagiography: *Saint-Augustin* (1913), *Les Màrtyrs africains* (1930), a novel about St. Cyprian, *Sanguis martyrum* (1918), and popularizations of the Christian archeology of North Africa, *Les Villes d'or, Algérie et Tunisie antiques* (1921). B. was chief speaker at the Eucharistic congresses at Carthage (1930) and Algiers (1939). The Christian-Islamic tradition of Spain prompted him to write *L'Histoire d'Espagne* (1932) and novels and biographies like *L'Infante* (1920), *Philippe II* (1929), and *Sainte Thérèse d'Avila* (1927, Eng. tr., 1929). With *Font-Romeu* (1931) he pleaded for the restoration and preservation of historical churches of the Roussillon district of SW France. A work of spiritual readings, *Le Livre de consolation*, was translated as *Art of Suffering* (1936). BIBLIOGRAPHY: M. Ricord, *Louis Bertrand: L'Africain* (1947).

[G. E. GINGRAS]

BERTRAND, PIERRE (1280–1349), French canonist. He was a professor of canon law at several French university centers, including Paris (c.1312); later was engaged in royal and ecclesiastical diplomatic affairs. He was made bp. of Autun (1320), then of Bourges (1330), and a cardinal (1331). In his works he defended the temporal jurisdiction of the Church, esp. in the *Super jurisdictione ecclesiastica et temporali*, a work printed in 1495. BIBLIOGRAPHY: P. Legendre, NCE 2:361–362.

[T. C. O'BRIEN]

BERTULF OF BOBBIO, ST. (d. 640), Benedictine abbot. Convert and later monk of Luxeuil under Eustace (620), he accompanied St. Attala to Bobbio. Elected successor to Attala, he insisted on strict observance and preached against Arianism. From Honorius I, he obtained exemption of the abbey from episcopal jurisdiction—the first recorded case of its kind in history. BIBLIOGRAPHY: E. de Moreau, DHGE 8:1111; Butler 3:356–357; C. Poggi, BiblSanct 3:115–116.

[M. H. BEIRNE]

BERTULF OF RENTY, ST. (d. c.705), almost certainly the founder and later the abbot of the monastery of Renty near Saint-Omer. Since the earliest biography of Bertulf is an 11th-cent. vita drawn from 10th-cent. sources, little can be said with certainty about the saint's life. His relics disappeared during the 16th century. BIBLIOGRAPHY: M. Zimmermann, BiblSanct 3:116–117.

[M. F. MCCARTHY]

BÉRULLE, PIERRE DE (1575–1620), cardinal, diplomat, theologian, and mystic. Born into a distinguished and deeply religious family B. was educated by the Jesuits and at the Univ. of Paris. A leading figure in the French school of spirituality, B. remained essentially a contemplative. He devoted himself mainly to spiritual direction and promoting reform among the Augustinians, Benedictines, and Feuillants. He introduced the Carmelite nuns into France and founded the Congregation of the French Oratory in Paris. B. exerted a powerful influence for good at court, as confidant and counselor to Queen Marie de Médicis and King Louis XIII and carried out a number of successful diplomatic missions for the King. He was forced to resign his position as counselor of state when he refused to sign the Treaty of Alliance between England and the Low Countries, for he saw this as arraigning France against Catholic Spain. BIBLIOGRAPHY: ODCC 162; A. Molien, DSAM 1:1539–81; A. Liuima, NCE 2:362–363.

[M. E. ALLWEIN]

BERYLLUS OF BOSTRA (3d cent.), a heretic who, acc. to Eusebius, taught a form of *Monarchianism. *Origen, summoned in defense of orthodoxy by the neighboring bishops of Arabia, was able to convince B. of his error. BIBLIOGRAPHY: G. Bardy, DHGE 8:1136–37.

[R. B. ENO]

BERZI, ANGELO (1815–84), Italian theologian. As a seminary professor at Bergamo, B. formulated his own theological synthesis. In 1855 his teaching was condemned as a mixture of mysticism and a monistic interpretation of revelation, completely personal and at variance with traditional teaching. B. thereafter lived in solitude, devoted to prayer and writing. Some 80 of his written works went unpublished. BIBLIOGRAPHY: L. Fossati, *Don Angelo Berzi, vita e pensiero* (1942); A. Piolanti, EncCatt 2:1487–88.

[T. C. O'BRIEN]

BESANT, ANNIE (b. Wood; 1847–1933), Anglo-Irish theosophist and political and social reformer. She married an Anglican clergyman, F. Besant, but they were later legally separated (1873). She lost custody of her children in 1879 because she was an atheist. She promoted such causes as free thought, birth control (she was tried for promoting immorality but acquitted), Fabian socialism, workers' strikes, and free education. Converted (1889) to *theosophy by Mme. H. P. Blavatsky (1851–91), B. became the most influential theosophist, heading the Theosophical Society, 1907–33. Settling in India, she founded Central Hindu College, organized the India Home Rule League, and was elected (1917) president of the India National Congress. Of her numerous theosophical writings, *Esoteric Christianity* (1901) esp. helped to inspire the foundation of the Liberal Catholic Church. BIBLIOGRAPHY: A. H. Nethercot, *First Five Lives of Annie Besant* (1960); idem, *Last Four Lives of Annie Besant* (1963).

[E. E. BEAUREGARD]

BESCHI, CONSTANZO GIUSEPPE (1680–1747), Jesuit missionary to South India. Educated at Rome he was a phenomenal linguist, mastering Greek, Latin, French, Portuguese, and other languages. He left for India (1698) where like Robert de Nobili he embraced and adapted himself to the culture of the Tamils. Learning Sanskrit and many other South Indian languages, he produced numerous works. His *Tēmbāvani* (of Mary and Joseph) is his greatest achievement. BIBLIOGRAPHY: K. R. Srinivasa Iyengar, NCE 2:364.

[T. FEIDT]

BESKOW, F. NATHANIEL (1865–1953), Swedish theologian. B. was never ordained but gave sermons in a chapel near Stockholm built esp. for him. He preached and exemplified a social gospel that he felt would be understood by doubting intellectuals and the estranged laboring class. In 1912 he founded along English lines a settlement in the workers' quarter of Stockholm. He was also an active pacifist. Seven of his hymns are included in the official songbook (1937) of the Swedish Church. BIBLIOGRAPHY: S. Rodhe, RGG 1:1094.

[M. J. SUELZER]

BESSARION (d. 1472), Metropolitan of Nicaea, humanist, theologian, diplomat. Born in Trebizond, educated in Constantinople and Mistra, B. became a monk and abbot. Esteemed for his learning he was named metropolitan of Nicaea (1437) and formed part of the Byzantine delegation to the Council of *Florence (1439–45), where he and *Mark Eugenicus served as the spokesmen for the Greeks. He was instrumental in working out a compromise between the Greek and Latin positions on the *Procession of the Holy Spirit and in winning over many of his compatriots. After the council he returned to Constantinople but not long after settled in Rome where Pope *Eugene IV gave him the title of cardinal. Entrusted with several papal missions, he was a prominent member of the Roman curia. He wrote extensively and acquired a large collection of Greek MSS which he bequeathed to Venice; they are now in the Marciana Library there. BIBLIOGRAPHY: J. Gill, *Personalities of the Council of Florence* (1964); Beck 767–769.

[G. T. DENNIS]

BESSARION OF EGYPT, ST. (Passarion; 4th cent.), monk of the desert. Although later tradition has made B. a disciple of SS. Anthony of Egypt and Macarius the Egyptian, and tales have located him in various of the better known Egyptian monasteries, from what can be gathered from the more reliable sources, he was a vagabond and wanderer, free of any ties, seeking food and shelter wherever he could find them. Some of his sayings are recorded in the *Lausiac

History and the **Apophthegmata Patrum*. BIBLIOGRAPHY: Butler 2:563; J. David, DHGE 8:1180–81; F. X. Murphy, NCE 2:366.

[R. B. ENO]

BESSE, JEAN-MARTIAL (1861–1920), French Benedictine, author of many volumes on the nature and history of Benedictine monasticism.

[T. C. O'BRIEN]

BESSEL, GOTTFRIED VON (1672–1749), Benedictine statesman and historian. Vicar-general and supreme judge of the Archdiocese of Mainz, he was employed on several diplomatic missions, including settlement of the differences between the Pope and the Emperor. As abbot of Göttweig (from 1714) he made the abbey a center of art and learning, and encouraged his monks in the pursuit of science and of art. His *Chronicon Gottwicense* (1732) is a comprehensive work in German diplomatics. BIBLIOGRAPHY: P. Schlager, CE 2:528–529; P. Volk, DHGE 8:1207–08; A. Pratesi, EncCatt 2:1499.

[L. MITCHELL]

BESSON, MARIUS (1876–1945), bp. of Lausanne, Geneva, and Fribourg, historian, journalist, ecumenist. B. was born in Turin and after ordination (1899) pursued historical studies there, at Rome, and at Fribourg. He became professor of medieval history at the Univ. of Fribourg; then bp. of Lausanne (1920). B. promoted the Catholic press, and wrote many works of *apologetics. One esp., *L'Église et le royaume de Dieu* (1941), shows his ecumenical spirit. BIBLIOGRAPHY: F. Charrière, *Marius Besson* (1945); E. Schwarz, *Marius Besson* (1946).

[P. K. MEAGHER]

BESTIARY, short pseudo-scientific descriptions of animals and birds of didactic import in verse or prose, traced to the *Physiologus (4th century). Medieval bestiaries fusing myth, legend, and religious symbols with practical problems of training, breeding, and medical care of animals, varied in given periods, flowering in the 13th and 14th centuries. Pliny's natural history, Solinus's exotic accounts, and Isidore's *Etymologiae* mingled in compilations of Bartholomeus Anglicus *(De proprietatibus rerum),* and Vincent of Beauvais *(Speculum naturale).* Bird and beast forms symbolic of intervals appear in medieval choir books. Of Persian origin are the books on falconry following Frederick II's visit to the East (1230). In Latini's works (1260) marked by selectivity and rational didacticism, fabulous creatures and moralizations disappear. Intriguing and exotic creatures of medieval Semitic lore derived from classical, Hebrew, and Arabian sources, fill Bochart's *Hierozoicon* (1660). Bestiaries continue to our day rather as whimsical conceptions of wit and imagination. Probably the most recent is the bestiary of the 20th-cent. American, Alexander Calder. BIBLIOGRAPHY: F. T. McCulloch, *Mediaeval Latin and French Bestiaries*

(1960); F. Carmody, *"De bestiis et aliis rebus* and the Latin Physiologus," *Speculum* 13 (1938) 153–159; B. Latini, *Li livres dou Tresor* (ed. F. J. Carmody, 1948).

[M. J. DALY]

BETANCUR, PEDRO DE SAN JOSÉ, VEN. (Béthencourt; 1619–67) Franciscan tertiary. He left the Canary Islands for Guatemala in 1649, and the hardships he suffered on the journey for lack of money inspired his apostolate. He became a tertiary (1655) and devoted his life to serving the poor and the sick. He founded a hospital, a school for poor children, and a hospice for the homeless. BIBLIOGRAPHY: L. Lamadrid, NCE 2:369–370.

[H. JACK]

BETANZOS, DOMINGO DE (c.1480–1549), Spanish Dominican missionary. B. left Spain (c.1514) and labored in Española, Mexico, and Guatemala. Through his efforts, the new Dominican province of Santiago de Mexico was established (1532), with B. becoming its first provincial.

[H. JACK]

BETANZOS, JEAN DE (1510–76), chronicler and linguist of Peru. Because of his knowledge of the Quichua language, B. became official interpreter and intermediary for the viceroys of Peru and the Inca Indians. Ordered to compile a history of the Incas, B. completed *Suma y narración de los Incas* in 1551. This chronicle, written from a native standpoint, encompasses Inca legends of origin to the reign of Pachacutec; it significantly presented for the first time the idea that the Inca empire was late in being established. B.'s complete MS seems never to have appeared in print. Because of its mediocre style, the work is difficult to read; nevertheless, it is an important source of information on Inca ceremonies and architecture. BIBLIOGRAPHY: J. Herrick, NCE 2:370–371; C. Wilgus, *Library of Latin-American History and Culture* (1965) 13.

[D. M. HUGHES]

BETANZOS, PEDRO DE (d. c.1570), Franciscan missionary. He arrived in Mexico in 1542, learned the language, and after a year, went to Guatemala. There he quickly and thoroughly mastered various Indian languages, translated prayers for the Indians, and cooperated in preparing a catechism. He later moved to Honduras-Costa Rica and is said to have been the first missionary in Nicaragua.

[H. JACK]

BETH SHAN, a city of Palestine in the valley of Jezreel where it joins the Jordan Valley, now proved through archeology to be the same as the present imposing ruin Tell el-

Husm. At the crossing of many roads it was an important commercial and military center until it was captured and destroyed, very likely, by David. Under Greek hegemony it became the main city of the Decapolis with a new name, Scythopolis.

[J.F. FALLON]

BETH-SHEMESH, an important fortified town in the Shephelah of Palestine, which served as a frontier garrison between Judah and the Philistine cities along the coast. It was one of the first ancient ruins to be investigated by modern archeological techniques in Palestine.

[J. F. FALLON]

BETHANY, a village about two miles (Jn 11.18) from Jerusalem on the SE slopes of the Mount of Olives (Mk 11.1) on the road to Jericho. It was the home of Martha and Mary and Lazarus (Jn 11.1). The traditional tomb of Lazarus was mentioned in A.D. 333 by the Bordeaux Pilgrim. Jesus supped at Bethany with Simon (Mk 14.3) and spent the nights there during the week before his Passion (Mt 21.17). Bethany beyond the Jordan (Jn 1.28) is a different place. BIBLIOGRAPHY: S. J. Saller, *Excavations at Bethany 1949–1953* (1957).

[E. LUSSIER]

BETHARRAM FATHERS, a title frequently applied to the Priests of the Sacred Heart of Jesus, a congregation founded by St. Michael Garicoïts at Betharram in S France. Although they follow the Rule of St. Augustine, they composed their own constitutions. They are engaged in preaching, missionary, and educational works. The congregation is governed by a superior general and four counselors. The general motherhouse is located in Rome, Italy. Its members, situated in 14 countries, number over 400 (1974) including 125 priests and 69 brothers living in America (1973). It is the aim of the congregation to develop the virtues of the Sacred Heart, for the salvation of the world. BIBLIOGRAPHY: F. Veuillot, *Les Prêtres du Sacré-Coeur de Bétharram* (1942).

[C. KEENAN]

BETHEL, a town where Abraham worshiped God on coming into Palestine, but more closely related to the Hebrew traditions about Jacob (Gen. 28.10–17). Its site is *c.* 14 miles N of Jerusalem. It has been very extensively excavated in modern times by W. F. Albright.

[J. F. FALLON]

BETHESDA, a pool at Jerusalem where Jesus cured a man infirm for 38 years (Jn 5.2–9). Contemporary scholarship generally accepts the identification of the excavated pools of the Church of St. Ann as the correct site. It is a large oblong pool provided with five porches, four lateral and a fifth central that divides the pool into two parts. The passage (5.3b–4) dealing with the angel stirring the water is probably an interpolation explaining the movement of the water (5.7) apparently caused by an intermittent underground stream.

BIBLIOGRAPHY: C. F. Pfeiffer, *Biblical World* (1966) 141–142.

[E. LUSSIER]

BETHLÉEM, LOUIS (1869–1940), literary critic and moralist. B. was born in the Netherlands, ordained a priest, and devoted his life to promoting morality in books, plays, and operas. His *Romans à lire et Romans à proscrire* (1st ed., 1904) is a moral evaluation of several thousand novels published after 1800. The work is not one of erudite literary criticism, but of simple classification. In spite of the objections raised by the intellectual community, it received wide popular acclaim and sold over 120,000 copies in its 2d edition. But the work, even in its subsequent editions, has serious deficiencies: it often lacks esthetic discrimination, dignity of expression, and exact information. B. also founded three monthly periodicals devoted to the classification of novels, drama, opera, and the press. BIBLIOGRAPHY: J. Morienval, *Catholicisme* 2:3–4.

[H. JACK]

BETHLEHEM, a small town (pop. *c.* 15,000) 6 miles S of Jerusalem, today in the state of Israel. It is situated on a limestone ridge of the Judean highland and overlooks to the W the main highway from Jerusalem to Hebron. Several Canaanite cities bore the name Bethlehem which seems to have meant "Sanctuary of Lahm" (god of grain). The modern Arab name is Beit Lahm, "house of meat." Ephrata, another name of the place, means fruitful. These names are apparently a reflection on the natural fertility of the environs. Bethlehem, already named in the Amarna letters (14th cent. B.C.), is frequently mentioned in biblical history esp. as the city of David (2 Sam 5.7) and the birthplace of our Lord (Mt 2.1, 5–8, 16; Lk 2.4, 15; Jn 7.42). BIBLIOGRAPHY: R. W. Hamilton, *Church of the Nativity, Bethlehem* (1943); C. Kopp, *Holy Places of the Gospels* (1963) 1–48.

[E. LUSSIER]

BETHLEHEM FATHERS, a missionary congregation (Foreign Mission Society of Bethlehem) named for the Bethlehem School in Immensee, Switzerland, site of their foundation in 1921 by P. Bondolfi (1872–1943). The first missioners were sent to China in 1924; missions are maintained in Rhodesia, Japan, and Taiwan. Refugees from Communist China established the congregation in the archdiocese of Denver, Col. in 1955.

[T. C. O'BRIEN]

BETHLEHEMITES, the name of (1) a former religious order of men and women, also known as the Order of the Star of Bethlehem. Their priory in London (*c.* 1247) became the hospital of St. Mary of Bethlehem for mental patients, the second such institution in Europe. After the *Dissolution under Henry VIII it was a royal hospital. In time the ill-treatment of the inmates there gave rise to the word "bedlam." (2) Bethlehemite Order of Guatemala, the only religious order of men founded in colonial South America, a community dedicated to the care of the convalescent poor and to the education of poor children. Confirmed by Clement X (1672) the order spread to Mexico, South America, and the Canary Islands. During the wars for independence the male branch of the order was gradually destroyed. The female branch founded by two women Franciscan tertiaries of Guatemala survived and is known as the Congregation of Bethlehemite Religious Women, Daughters of the Sacred Heart (SCIF).

BETHPHAGE, a village mentioned in Mt 21.1, Mk 11.1, and Lk 19.29 as the start of our Lord's triumphal entry into Jerusalem on Palm Sunday. Its exact site is uncertain, but like Bethany with which it is always associated, it must have been on the E slope of Mt. Olivet. The name is now attached to the church and monastery of the Franciscans between Bethany and the summit of the Mt. of Olives. But this identification cannot be traced further than to the medieval pilgrims, and no evidence of an earlier village has been found in the area.

[E. LUSSIER]

BETHSABEE, see BATHSHEBA.

BETHSAIDA, a city mentioned in the NT as the home of Peter, Andrew, and Philip (Jn 1.44). There Jesus cured the blind man by spitting and touching him (Mk 8.22). In Mk 6.45 and Lk 9.10 mention is made of Bethsaida in relation to the multiplication of loaves, and Jesus claimed Tyre and Sidon would have repented in sackcloth and ashes at his mighty works there (Mt 11.21 and Lk 10.13). The generally accepted location is on the N shore of the Sea of Galilee, E of the point where the Jordan flows into the sea. As the name indicates, it was originally a fishing village, but Herod Philip enlarged it into a city, which he named Julias after the daughter of Caesar Augustus. The remains today are probably at el-Tell. BIBLI-OGRAPHY: C. Kopp, *Holy Places of the Gospels* (1963) 180–186.

[S. MUSHOLT]

BETHULIA, very likely a fictitious city. It is mentioned in Jdt ch. 6-15 as the home of Judith and the site of God's great victory over the enemy hordes through the weak hands of a devoted widow. No identity has ever been seriously advanced for it. It could very well be a symbol of all Israel.

[J. F. FALLON]

BETHUNE, see BEATON.

BETROTHAL, as understood in RC canon law (*sponsalitia*), the agreement to marry, entered into by a man and a woman, when this is done in the manner prescribed by law. It is not simply a matter of becoming engaged; the agreement must be made in writing and signed by the agreeing parties, and also by the pastor of the parish, or the ordinary of the

diocese, or by two witnesses. This procedure is no longer in common use among Catholics, at least in the U.S. It appears to have served a useful purpose only when custom required certain prenuptial arrangements between the espoused couple and/or their respective families be made concerning such matters as dowry and the like. It constitutes no right in either party to go through with the marriage, but a canonical claim to damages (e.g., for expenses incurred with a view to marriage) can be based upon it in the event one of the parties refuses to marry. BIBLIOGRAPHY: CIC c. 1017.

[P. K. MEAGHER]

BETTER GOOD, a term used in theological discussion, designates a good act or deed in the option of a person to whom another or other courses of action, good in themselves but of lesser spiritual value, are also open to choice. Some more rigoristic moralists have held that a lesser good, in comparison with a better one, is relatively evil in that its choice involves the deliberate rejection of some measure of spiritual good. More commonly moral theologians deny this and hold that it is sufficient for a morally good act that an agent's object and intention be good. To some extent the dispute involves less real divergence of opinion than may appear, because even those who hold that the better good should always be chosen in preference to the lesser, admit that very often what is objectively a better good, may not in fact be a better good with respect to an individual because of a variety of subjective considerations.

[P. K. MEAGHER]

BETTI, UGO (1892–1953), Italian poet, lawyer, and dramatist. A soldier in World War I, B. wrote poetry while in prison. After the war, he studied law and became a magistrate, first in Parma and later in Rome. This experience provided abundant material for many of his plays. B. developed with an intensity of religious conviction the motif of the conflict between goodness and evil and the mysterious and ubiquitous presence of iniquity in the world. As a consequence, his characters are formed within the Judaeo-Christian framework. His works overtly reveal not only his strong belief in the innate goodness of man but also a love of God and an acknowledgment of his power and benevolence. Of his 25 plays among the best are *Corruption in the Palace of Justice* (1944) and *Queen and the Rebels* (1949). BIBLIOGRAPHY: J. A. Scott, "Message of Ugo Betti," *Italica* 37 (1960) 44–57.

[S. A. HEENEY]

BETTING, see GAMBLING.

BEUCKLESZOON, JAN, see JOHN OF LEIDEN.

BEUNO, ST. (d. *c.*640), abbot of Clynnog, Wales. B. is reported to have founded monasteries in Hertfordshire but he was active mostly in N Wales, where his burial place was long venerated in Carnarvonshire. He is said to have brought back to life his niece, St. Winifred. BIBLIOGRAPHY: G. M. Fusconi, BiblSanct 3:148–153; Butler 2:142–143.

[M. J. SUELZER]

BEURON, ABBEY OF, Benedictine archabbey near Sigmaringen, Germany, the most important abbey of the Beuronese Congregation. The claim that it was founded in the 8th or 9th cent. is false. It was established in 1077 as a monastery for Canons Regular of St. Augustine and became an abbey in 1687. Suppressed in 1803, it was given (1863) by Princess Kathleen of Hohenzollern to Maurus and Placidus Wolter as a means of restoring the Benedictine Order in Germany. Maurus became the first abbot in 1868. The community was expelled during the Kulturkampf troubles and did not return until 1887. The abbey became a vigorous center of monastic life, liturgical renewal, science, and art. Foundations made from Beuron during the 19th cent. were Maredsous, Mont César, Erdington, Maria Laach, Emaus, and Seckau. The Beuronese Congregation, which now includes 10 abbeys and 6 convents, was responsible for the revival of the order in Brazil and Portugal. BIBLIOGRAPHY: U. Engelmann, NCE 2:377–378; *idem,* LTK 2:268–270.

[N. BACKMUND]

BEURONESE ART, late 19th-cent. religious style begun at Beuron Abbey in SW Germany. The Benedictine monk and architect, Desiderius Lenz, developed his theories and practice at Beuron (1864) in an effort to create a liturgically inspired church art. Egyptian, early Greek, and primitive Christian and Nazarene art were sources of an aesthetic geometric order rejecting naturalism. Beuronese art is static and hieratic in conception. The principal monument is the St. Maur Chapel (1868–71) near Beuron; after decoration of the Monte Cassino crypt (1913) the style declined. Good examples of the Beuronese style are preserved on the walls of the monastic refectory at St. John's Abbey, Collegeville, Minnesota. BIBLIOGRAPHY: O. L. Kapsner, *Benedictine Bibliography* (1962); G. Mercier, *L'Art abstrait dans l'art sacré* (1964).

[R. J. VEROSTKO]

BEVERIDGE, WILLIAM (1638–1708), Anglican bp. of St. Asaph in Wales; theologian. B. was born in Barrow, Leicester, and studied at St. John's College, Cambridge. His ecclesiastical career seems to have suffered from his sympathetic attitude toward the *nonjurors, and he was not made a bp. until 1704. B.'s works include a collection of Greek canons, the *Eunodikón* (1672), and his masterwork, *Exposition of the Thirty-Nine Articles* (1710). His writings evidence a partiality toward Calvinist predestinationism. Several collections, all incomplete, of B's works have appeared: T. Gregory (2v., 1720); T. H. Horne (9v., 1824); J. Bliss (LACT 12v., 1843–48). BIBLIOGRAPHY: DNB (1885)4:447.

[T. C. O'BRIEN]

BEYERLINCK, LAURENT (1578–1627), Belgian theologian and ecclesiastical writer. Ordained (1602), he taught at the seminary of Antwerp and was later superior. Canon, censor, and theologian of the church in Antwerp (1608), he was made protonotary in 1614. B. collected an impressive library which he left to the Univ. of Louvain, and edited numerous historical and theological books. Among his works are *Apophthegmata christianorum* (1608) and *Responsa catholica ad quaesta religionis reformatae* (1612). BIBLIOGRAPHY: F. Stegmuller, LTK 2:330–331.

[L. MITCHELL]

BEZA, THEODORE (De Besze; 1519–1605), Genevan Reformer. Born at Vézelay in Burgundy, France, and educated a humanist, he wished to become a classical scholar, but at his father's insistence he studied law for a time at Orléans (1535–39). He abandoned this career, however, and went to Paris, where he composed in Latin his *Poemata Juvenilia.* The poetry reflected his dissolute way of life. During an illness in 1548 he abandoned Catholicism and was converted to the teachings of Calvin. He was appointed professor of Greek at Lausanne, and in 1558 moved to Geneva to teach Greek. When Calvin died (1564), Beza succeeded him, combining the office of Moderator of the Company of Pastors with work as preacher and teacher. While at Lausanne, he tried to win toleration for the *Waldenses of Piedmont and the *Huguenots of France. In Geneva, he continued his efforts on behalf of French Protestants, attending two futile conferences (Poissy and St. Germain), and then helping to raise men and money to support Condé in the French *Wars of Religion. Through correspondence and personal contacts, he influenced Reformed Protestants in various countries, arguing their right to revolt against a ruler who denies religious liberty. Among his polemical works, one of the most notable was his defense (1554) of the burning of M. *Servetus against the criticisms of S. *Castellio. He arranged several Psalms in French verse, publishing them with others written by Marot. He also published a celebrated Greek text of the NT along with an annotated Latin translation (1565); in 1582 a second edition, which included the codex of the Gospels he had discovered in 1562, the *Codex Bezae,* was published. Several theological treatises also came from his pen *(Tractationes theologicae,* 1570–82); he gave *double predestination great emphasis. BIBLIOGRAPHY: P. F. Geisendorf, *Théodore de Bèze* (1949).

[N. H. MARING]

BÈZE, ABBEY OF, a Benedictine monastery situated at the source of the Bèze, France, founded before 650 by St. Vandelin, a monk of Luxeuil and son of Count Amalgaire. In the 8th cent. the Rule of St. Benedict gradually replaced St. Columban's. Royal protection notwithstanding, the abbey was plundered by Vandals, Saracens, and others and was ruined by the wars. Reconstruction followed most of the destruction. The number of monks gradually declined and the abbey was suppressed during the Revolution. BIBLIOGRAPHY: R. Gazeau, *Catholicisme* 2:8–9.

[S. A. HEENEY]

BEZPOPOVTSY (Russ., without priests), those Old Believers who rejected the priesthood together with the reforms introduced by Patriarch *Nikon in the 17th cent. and who separated from the Russian Orthodox Church.

[F. WILCOCK]

BHAGAVAD GĪTĀ, celebrated episode of the Indian epic Mahābhārata (*c*.5th cent. B.C.). In the *Bhagavad Gītā* (Song of the Celestial One) Krishna, an avatar of Viṣṇu, expounds to Arjuna in two broad streams of thought a philosophy of God and a religious system by which man reaches God. A theistic work, it often describes the ultimate reality as a personal god (Krishna), a supreme transcendent absolute, and finally as the individual awakened soul. Realization comes through works (Karma), love (Bhakti), and knowledge (Jnana), the threefold Hindu path to mystic union. There are numberless commentaries and glossaries from ancient and modern times, and translations into many languages. BIBLIOGRAPHY: S. Radhakrishnan, *Bhagavadgita* (1948); *Bhagavad-Gita* (ed. R. C. Zaehner, 1969); *Gita with Text, Translation and Sri Aurobindo's Comments* (tr. S. S. Jhunjhunwala, rev. ed., 1974).

[M. J. DALY]

BHAJA, in the W Ghats S of Bombay, site of early Buddhist rockcut *caitya* hall and vihāra (monastery) from the Suṅga period. The vihāra walls are decorated in low relief with the Vedic sun-god Sūrya and Indra, god of sky and storm, flanking the E doorway. BIBLIOGRAPHY: B. Rowland, *Art and Architecture of India* (1959).

[M. J. DALY]

BHAKTI, path of devotion. This direction within Hindu thought is oriented toward love of a Supreme Person. It is much less abstract than the theological systems of the Upanishads or the Vedanta. One school of bhakti began in the S of India from the 13th to the 17th century. Some even posit that bhakti's origin in the S goes back to pre-Vedic times, which remains unproven. In N India is another strain of bhakti which depends more on the Gita and the Bhagavata Purana. This bhakti is even more simplified, avoiding much of the complexity of Hindu mythology. Things considered important by many religious persons were discarded by the bhaktas, such as creeds, dogmas, or sacred books. Even fasting, alms, and the practice of Yoga were for nought in bhakti, unless accompanied by a deep love of God and repetition of his name. Bhakti excluded any consideration of caste by rejecting all the outward signs, e.g., ablutions, circumcision, the holy thread. Bhakti or devotion alone and not social status could give an individual any worth. From this popular mysticism grew a school of mystics who explored the spirituality of love and the transformation and deification of human love. They held it to be more important than any other form of worship. BIBLIOGRAPHY: S. N. Dasgupta, *Hindu Mysticism* (1971); K. M. Sen, *Hinduism* (1969); *Sources of Indian Tradition* (ed. W. T. de Bary, 1958).

[M. T. HANSBURY]

BHARHUT, ancient city in the Deccan of India known for its many examples of Suṅga period architecture, and esp. for the great stūpa (Buddhist temple) of Bharhut. One of the earliest (*c*.2d cent. B.C.) elaborately carved stūpas, its brown sandstone remains are now in the Indian Museum, Calcutta. The railing and torana (gateway) show great variation in the quality of carving, which imitates prototypes in wood and depicts narrative scenes of the Buddha that are aniconic (tree, footprints, throne). BIBLIOGRAPHY: A. Cunningham, *Stūpa of Bharhut* (1879); A. K. Coomaraswamy and B. Rowland, Jr., EB (1961) 12:228.

[M. J. DALY]

BHUMISPARSA, the mudra (symbolic gesture) in Buddhist art meaning ''earth-touching,'' used by the Buddha under the Bodhi Tree during the assault of Māra when calling upon the earth to witness his virtue was confirmed. The Buddha in padmāsana (meditation), his right wrist on his right leg, with extended middle finger touches the ground.

[M. J. DALY]

BHUTAN, a semi-independent territory on the NE border of India (18,147 sq mi; pop. 1,100,000). Racially the people are close to the Tibetans whose language they speak. For more than three cent., power in the country was divided between the Deb Raja as civil ruler and the Dharma Raja, the reincarnation of Buddha, as spiritual leader. In 1907 the two authorities were absorbed by the Maharaja who made them hereditary. Foreign affairs were formerly controlled by the British and after 1949 passed to the Indian government. Later Bhutan became the object of discord between India and Communist China. The majority of the people are Mahayana Buddhists, and monks are in virtual control of the land. In 1969 the absolute monarchy was replaced by a form of democratic monarchy. A vote of confidence is required every 3 years. Christianity has never gained a foothold. BIBLIOGRAPHY: N. Singh, *Bhutan: A Kingdom in the Himalayas* (1972).

[P. DAMBORIENA]

BHUVANESVAR, the site of important temples (8th–12th cent.), near the coast of Orissa State, India. The earliest temple, Paraśurāneśvara (40 feet long) has a śikhara 44 feet high, which proliferated in the Rājarāni temple (1100) into a cascade of repetitive śikharas following one upon the other. Other important temples are Mukteśvara (10th cent.) magnificent in carving and structure, Lingarāja, an enormous enclosure 520 feet by 465 feet with three assembly halls of exceedingly delicate carving, and 15 other temples vying in importance. BIBLIOGRAPHY: J. Burgess, *Indian Architecture* (1910).

[M. J. DALY]

BIALIK, CHAIM NACHMAN (1873–1934), modern Hebrew poet, novelist, teacher, translator, and publisher. A highly gifted and versatile writer, B. was esteemed as the poet laureate of the Jewish renaissance. His poetry was charged with bitter absorption in the plight of his people, past and present, reflecting his personal sense of sorrow. His poetic style has been described as "biblical, prophetic, and majestic," and, in his simple poems, lyrical. In contrast to his poems of protest and revolt are his folk songs and children's tales. B. became the center of Jewish culture in Tel Aviv where he settled in 1934. BIBLIOGRAPHY: M. Waxam, *History of Jewish Literature* (1960); *Standard Jewish Encyclopedia* (ed. C. Roth, 1966).

[S. A. HEENEY]

BIANCHI, FRANCESCO SAVERIO MARIA, ST. (1743–1815), Barnabite confessor. He was directed to the Barnabites by *Alphonsus Liguori (1762), was ordained in 1767, and taught for 15 years in Naples, gaining a reputation for his knowledge of literature and science. His zeal turned him from teaching to contemplation and to the apostolate of the confessional where he continued to serve even after stricken by disease. When religious were expelled from Naples, he was permitted to stay on alone and keep up his ministry. BIBLIOGRAPHY: U. Fasola, BiblSanct 5:1238–41; Butler 1:217–218.

[H. JACK]

BIANCHI, IGNAZIO LUDOVICO (fl. 18th cent.), Theatine theologian. B. is noteworthy for his *De remedio aeternae salutis pro parvulis in utero clausis sine baptismate morentibus* (1768), which revives an older opinion that infants could be cleaned from *original sin in virtue of the will and baptism of their parents. BIBLIOGRAPHY: ThAq ST 1a2ae, 81.3 obj. 2.

[T. C. O'BRIEN]

BIANCHINI, FRANCESCO (1662–1729), historian, astronomer, authority on calendar reform. B. was ordained a deacon, but never advanced to the priesthood. A student of both theology and science, he served as librarian to Card. Pietro Ottoboni, was named secretary for the papal commission on calendar reform, and wrote the history of a council held in Rome in 1725.

[M. H. BEIRNE]

BIANCHINI, GIUSEPPE (1704–64), nephew of Francesco Bianchini; Oratorian, Biblist, historian, patrologist. B. was from Verona, where, before joining the Oratory (1732), he was rector of the cathedral and in charge of the chapter library. He was continuator of the *Annales* of *Baronius; also completed Francesco's *Liber pontificalis*.

His personal works include *Vindiciae Vulgatae latinae editionis* (1740), containing a hitherto unknown Greek-Latin text of the Psalms and a critical Latin text of the Gospels, *Evangeliarium quadruplex versionis antiquae* (1749). Liturgical and patristic studies owe to B. what he called the Leonine *Sacramentary and *Liturgia antiqua, hispanica, gothica, isidoriana, mozarabica, toletana, mixta quam . . . digessit J. Pinius SJ* (1741). BIBLIOGRAPHY: C. Gasparri, EncCatt 2:1543 and bibliog. of SACRAMENTARY.

[T. C. O'BRIEN]

BIBER, HEINRICH JOHANN FRANZ VON (1644–1704), Bohemian violinist, church composer, and a conductor of music in the court of the prince abp. of Salzburg. He composed Masses, requiems, litanies, and Vespers in the late baroque concertato style. BIBLIOGRAPHY: *Larousse Encyclopedia of Music* (1974) 184, 330.

[A. H. CRANE]

BIBIANA, ST. (Vivian; 4th cent.?), virgin and martyr. The late and unreliable legend that provides the details of her martyrdom makes her the daughter of Flavian, prefect of Rome. She, her father, her mother (Dafrosa), and her sister (Demetria) were subjected to imprisonment and torture for the faith and all died as martyrs. This is supposed to have occurred in the persecution under Julian the Apostate. She is sometimes honored as the patron of epileptics and the demented because she was held among prisoners of that kind during her ordeal. The legend seems to derive from the *passio* of SS. John and Paul. A church was built over her grave toward the end of the 5th cent. by Pope Simplicius. BIBLIOGRAPHY: Butler 4:470–471; C. van Hulst, EncCatt 2:1587; A. Frutaz, LTK 2:416.

[R. B. ENO]

BIBLE, the collection of books (Gr. *biblia,* books) considered by Christians and Jews to be sacred and authoritative by reason of their origin and contents. They are believed to have been written by men inspired by God and hence are "holy" Scriptures; cf. Ex 17.14; Dt 31.24; Is 30.8; 2 Pet 1.21; 3.15–16, etc.

Division. Through artificial combinations, the number of individual books in the *Hebrew Bible, to which the *Old Testament (i.e., Covenant) of the Christian Bible corresponds, was at one time made to equal the 22 (or 24) letters of the Hebrew alphabet. Today, however, 39 books are customarily listed: the *Law* (Gen, Ex, Lev, Num, Dt); the *Prophets,* divided into Earlier (Jos, Jg, 1–2 Sam, 1–2 Kg) and Later (Is, Jer, Ezek, The Twelve minor prophets—Hos, Jl, Am, Ob, Jon, Mic, Nah, Hab, Zeph, Hag, Zech, Mal); the *Writings* (Ps, Job, Pr, Ru, S of S, Ec, Lam, Est, Dan, Ezra-Neh, 1–2 Chr). A somewhat different arrangement ordinarily occurs in Christian editions: Pentateuch, Historical books; Wisdom (or Didactic) books; Prophets. Catholics furthermore accept the following deuterocanonical writings contained in the *Septuagint Greek version: Tob, Jdt, Wis, Sir, Bar, 1–2 Macc and some additional parts in Dan and Esther. These are listed among the *Apocrypha by Protestants. Catholics and Protestants are agreed in counting 27 books in the NT canon: the 4 Gospels; Acts; 21 Epistles; Rev (see CANON, BIBLICAL). Division of the Bible by chapters has been attributed to Stephen Langton (d. 1228), while the division into verses received its final arrangement from Robert Estienne in 1551.

Language and Manuscripts. The OT is written for the most part in Hebrew; Aramaic sections are confined to Ezra 4.8–6.18; 7.12–26; Jer 10.11; Dan 2.4b–7.28. The uniformity of the Hebrew MSS is due to the strict preservation of a Jewish textual tradition (that of the Masoretes—hence "Masoretic" text) dating from the early Christian centuries. The study of cognate languages, such as that recently discovered at *Ugarit, and the *Qumran writings, has helped to cast new light on this Masoretic text. Of the deuterocanonical books, only Wis and 2 Macc were originally written in Greek; the others have come down to us for the most part only in translation. The NT, which is by far the best attested piece of literature to come from the ancient world, is written in the simplified and popular form of Greek known as *koinē*, often impregnated with a Semitic flavor. It is the task of *textual criticism to attempt the reconstruction of the lost autographs of both Testaments, though the discrepancies in MSS are for the most part minor and do not affect the basic dogmatic content of the Bible. (BIBLE TEXTS).

Versions. The ancient versions—the Greek, Old Latin and Vulgate, Coptic, Ethiopic, Syriac, Arabic, Armenian, Georgian, Slavic, Gothic—aid not only in the reconstruction of the text, but furnish clues to the interpretations of earlier ages. (BIBLIOGRAPHY: BIBLE VERSIONS). BIBLIOGRAPHY: Vat II DivRev; O. Eissfeldt, *Old Testament, an Introduction* (1965); L. Alonso Schökel, *Inspired Word* (1965); *Peake's Commentary on the Bible* (ed. M. Black and H. Rowley, 1962). *EXEGESIS, BIBLICAL; *HERMENEUTICS, BIBLICAL.

[C. BERNAS]

BIBLE, AUTHORITATIVE INTERPRETATION OF THE.

This has varied throughout the ages according to the religious stance of the interpreting person or group. Catholics believe that the Church alone has received the power to interpret authoritatively the Bible in the light of its living tradition. In this way the Church is at the service of the word of God (*Dei Verbum*, 10); the NT writers had already seen the Christ-event as a fulfillment "according to the Scriptures" (1 Cor 15.3–4). In reality, the Church has rarely determined the exact sense of any particular passage, and today the scripture scholar is encouraged to use all the scientific means at his disposal—philology, history, archeology, literary criticism, etc.—to ascertain more clearly the thoughts and intentions of the sacred writers and thus to understand more fully the meaning, as intended by God, of a given passage, individual book, or the Bible as a whole; all this is to be done for the upbuilding of the people of God (2 Tim 3.16–17). "It is

through such preparatory study that the judgment of the Church matures" (*Dei Verbum,* 12), and when the "condescension" of God toward man is properly understood, the Bible can indeed be said to teach "without error that truth which God wanted put into the sacred writings for the sake of our salvation" (*ibid.*). BIBLIOGRAPHY: Vatican Council II, *Dei Verbum* (Dogmatic Constitution of Divine Revelation).

[C. BERNAS]

BIBLE, AUTHORITY OF,

the quality, conceded to be inherent in Sacred Scripture as the word of God that makes it a secure norm of religious faith and practice. For centuries before the time of Christ, but at a period difficult to fix precisely, the books of the OT were accepted by the Jews as authored by the spirit of God. Jesus and the Apostles conformed to this Jewish viewpoint on Israel's sacred books (see Mk 12.36; Jn 10.35), and the early Christian Church conceived of its own sacred literature in the same manner. Because it was believed that the human authors of this religious literature, produced within and for the Jewish and Christian communities, were in a special sense divinely illumined for this purpose, this literature was accepted as the norm of faith. Thus the binding authority of Scripture derived from its divine authorship.

The unique authority of the Bible was taken for granted until the 19th cent., when it was placed in question by the discoveries of various modern sciences, such as astronomy, biology, and ancient history. Some Christians, however, undeterred by the impact of scientific knowledge upon the understanding of the Bible, continue to remain fundamentalist, i.e., they accept biblical statements, independently of their cultural and historical contexts, as formulations of literal truth. The scientific viewpoints on the origin and age of the earth, the universe, and man, as well as discrepancies between archeological findings and biblical data, have required a revision of the traditional concept of the authority of the Bible. Although the principle of the authoritative character of Scripture for faith remains intact, the understanding of the meaning of this principle as underlying truth in the Bible has undergone a considerable evolution. It is now recognized that prior to the 19th cent. sufficient attention was not paid to the role and limitations of the spirit-inspired human authors of the biblical books. Their points of view and modes of expressing their ideas were necessarily limited by the culture and audiences of their own time. Consequently, modern biblical scholarship recognizes the presence even of "myth" in Scripture, i.e., a nonscientific way of perceiving and expressing reality universal in antiquity, and no longer expects of Scripture the kind of accuracy in the understanding of material reality, including history, demanded by modern man. Indeed, to expect this level of truth in Scripture would require a divine illumination that would be an undesirable paternalism derogating from human intellectual striving to discover the meaning of the universe for man's natural life (see Gen 1.26).

The modern discovery of the limitation on the authority of Scripture that restricts its message to man's understanding of his relationship to God and to his neighbor under God brings into full and clear focus the profoundly religious nature of Scripture. In a way that will forever escape complete scientific analysis, the Bible records the privileged moments in human history, initiated by God himself, when man has most directly confronted his creator. Man learns from the Bible to comprehend himself as alienated from God through his own willful caprices, but as yet pursued by the divine love, inviting, guiding, and directing him to overcome this alienation through faith in the divine power, goodness, and mercy, so as to take his place in a renewed community of mankind in the house of his Father (see Hos 11.1–4; Jn 14.2–3).

The Protestant Reformers of the 16th cent. made the authority of Scripture the supreme norm for the life and faith of the Church. Roman Catholicism has consistently maintained that Scripture is not its own interpreter: since the Bible, as the literature of an ancient time, is subject to misunderstanding and misrepresentation, the Church has the role of safeguarding and teaching the authentic biblical meaning. Each of these positions possesses its own elements of truth. Modern critical scholarship into the origin and meaning of the Bible has resulted in considerable unanimity of interpretation between Protestant and Catholic biblical scholars. But the relationship between the authority of the Church and the authority of Scripture continues to be a point of divergence. BIBLIOGRAPHY: J. Levie, *Bible, Word of God in Words of Men* (tr. S. H. Treman, 1961); C. H. Dodd, *Authority of the Bible* (1928). *ANABAPTISTS; *INNER LIGHT; *INFALLIBILITY; *TRADITION; *FUNDAMENTALISM.

[C. P. CEROKE]

BIBLE, CANON OF. The word *canon,* signifying a reed used for measuring, was used figuratively by 2d-cent. Christians to mean a rule of faith, then, a guiding moral principle, then, something unchangeable (the Canon of the Mass), and, finally, by the 4th cent. (St. Athanasius, c. 350 A.D.) the official list of holy writings commonly accepted by the Church as sacred and of divine authorship. The last sense is its meaning here.

Canon of the Old Testament. That Judaism accepted a variety of writings as sacred and divinely inspired is clear from the careful way it preserved them in the Masoretic Text of the Hebrew Bible; from the translations made for Greek-speaking Jews of the last 2 cent. B.C. (LXX and others); from recent discoveries of caches of sacred writings belonging to a Jewish sect that lived along the NW shore of the Dead Sea near Qumran (see DEAD SEA SCROLLS) whose library contained some of the deuterocanonical books (called apocrypha by non-Catholics) and a few examples of apocryphal works (also known, incorrectly, as pseudepigrapha) as well as all the protocanonical works except Esther (canonical in Protestant terminology) and their own sectarian compositions inspired mainly by biblical themes, facts that indicate that they had a wider collection of sacred books than the Rabbinic Judaism of the latter part of the 2d cent. A.D.; and from the foreword of Sirach, the reverence shown the OT by NT writers, by Philo,

Flavius Josephus, and by the Mishnah. Late in the 1st Christian cent. Josephus calls attention to a sacred collection of Jewish writings of 22 or 24 books divided into the Law, the Prophets, and the Writings, but only at the end of the next cent. is it certainly witnessed that official Rabbinic Judaism had excluded many books that had been revered by their ancestors. This shorter list prevailed in the transmission of the Hebrew Bible.

Wider collections came down through Greek-speaking Jews of the Diaspora, from whom the Church received its Bible. These translations were the Bible of Paul, the Evangelists, and other authors of the NT, and through the Apostles they became the Bible of the Christian Church, the heir of the instruction and wisdom of Israel. Only in the late 2d cent. did Christian writers hold back from quoting from the wider collections (the Apologists and Melito of Sardis c. 170 A.D.). Origen in the 3d cent. expressed doubts about the fuller list, and eventually as part of the reaction of the Fathers against a multiplication of apocryphal works and as the shorter canon of Talmudic Jewry became more known, more Church teachers began to agree with him, but the common usage of Christian communities forced them to deal with the disputed books in sermons and lectures with reverence.

The facts indicate that there was never any really definitive Jewish canon until near the end of the 2d cent. and that Christians kept on using the extra books they had inherited from earlier Judaism despite the doubts that arose among some scholars. And so, when St. Jerome in the late 4th cent. was revising the Latin translations of the Greek Bible, he was compelled to include the added books in his revision, although he personally had a very low opinion of them because of the influence of his Rabbinical friends who had coached him in his Hebrew studies. Doubts about their canonicity continued to be voiced by various theologians until the eve of the decision of the Council of Trent, definitively including them in the list of inspired works that have God for their author. Although this decision was based on continuous usage in the Church rather than on intense historical investigation, we now know it correctly represented the common thinking and practise of the Christian Church of the first 3½ centuries. The extra books are: Tobit, Judith, Wisdom, Sirach, Baruch, 1-2 Macchabees and parts of Esther and Daniel.

Christians who separated from Rome in the 16th cent. generally downgraded the extra books, considering them to be edifying at most but not on the same level as the undisputed ones. Thus, they were first relegated to an appendix to the OT and eventually excluded completely from Protestant bibles. Greater awareness of their value and of how they came to be excluded via Rabbinic exclusiveness has led Protestant leaders to include them again, still as an appendix, in modern Bibles. Among Catholics Trent appears vindicated; and, since its decree did not positively exclude apocryphal works as unsacred, a greater reverence and importance is being afforded the other religious writings that the primitive Church received from the synagogues of the Diaspora and laboriously preserved in the codices of the LXX.

Canon of the New Testament The NT Canon grew gradually as a collection with Hebrews, 2 Peter, James, Jude, 3 John, and Revelation being the last to be accepted by both the Eastern and the Western Churches (the Syrian Church remained doubtful of some for centuries, whereas the Coptic and Ethiopian Churches accepted some books rejected by the Church as a whole).

The first two groups of Christian religious writings to be acknowledged as canonical were occasional letters of St. Paul to Churches he established (excepting Romans) and the four versions of the Gospel, preserved by the communities for which they were written. In time other writings from 1st-cent. Christian circles were added to the list of the venerated books, because they were linked by oral or written tradition to some Apostle, or simply because they were used and honored in Christian worship in the 2d and 3d centuries. It is impossible to give satisfying reasons why or how the NT became equal to the Word of God of the OT, but, in fact, by the middle of the 3d cent., it was essentially accepted as inspired by the majority of the Churches and, after the 4th cent., no serious objections were raised against any book now found in it until M. Luther relegated Heb, Jas, Jude, and Rev to an inferiority that the other Reformers found unacceptable. Even that degradation was reversed by the Lutherans of the next century.

Rather than one uniform outlook and formulation of the Christian mystery the NT writers offer facets of varying reflection (Pauline, Lucan, Johannine, Matthean, etc.). And so, the question of a canon within a canon has been raised by some with the intention of having certain parts of the NT appear corruptive or at least not fully in accord with the ideal of Christianity as one sees it depicted in, say, Galatians and Romans. In reaction to this tendency others stress the variegated complexity of the NT and its ultimate harmony that conserves the different viewpoints and evolution of apostolic and subapostolic schools and trends. The books and all their parts are canonical and inspired, but much gratitude is due the inspiring Spirit who did not force the plurality and diversity of his many instruments to fit the pattern of idealistic men who like to look in only one direction. If anything, the accepted NT canon may be too exclusive, as with the OT; some Early Christian writings of the subapostolic age, e.g., Didache, 1 Clement, Barnabas, Ignatius' letters, etc., have been overly neglected by those who limit themselves strictly to canonical works to hear the voice of God.

[J. F. FALLON]

BIBLE CYCLES IN ART, a complex of visual representations illustrating various phases of one subject or many subjects of a single "thematic" idea. First examples found in the catacombs and on Early Christian tombs (2d and 3d cent.) are of a narrative and symbolic nature in the "impressionistic" style of late Roman Imperial painting. Mosaics in St. Mary Major (432–440), evidencing a previously unknown understanding of religious truths, determined Western neo-Latin art of dramatic and solid forms. At Ravenna a highly refined culture is evident in subtle colors, atmospheric effects, and serene balance. The golden period of Byzantine civilization presents the triumph of cycles in masterpieces of illumination (Vienna Genesis, Paris Gospel of St. Matthew, Purple Codex of Rossano). Following the iconoclastic crisis a Greek stylistic manner determined 8th-cent. Roman frescoes (S. Maria Antiqua) and 9th-cent. Byzantine work. During the Carolingian Renaissance at Castelseprio frescoes by Greek artists in Oriental style were followed by a flowering of illuminated Gospels and Psalters (Paris *Psalter, Joshua Roll*). German MSS from the school of Ada (9th cent.) introduced small scenes influencing a close series of squares surrounding the crucified Christ in ivories, at Munich and Narbonne. In the 10th and 11th cent. Ottonian influence determined a narrative form in complete stylistic freedom in the school of Reichenau (*Codex Egberti*, Trier). Related to Reichenau are English illumination at Winchester and Canterbury (*Benedictional of Ethelwold by Godeman), cycles of *Bernward's doors at Hildesheim, and Spanish ivories. Increased complexity in arrangement marks Romanesque sculpture with leading French schools at Aquitaine, Burgundy, Provence, and Auvergne. At the Cathedral of Modena, *Wiligelmo created one of the noblest biblical reliefs of Genesis. *Antelami at Parma (c.1196–1225) displays a dynamism of Gothic inspiration with parallels in French *Bible moralisée* and German *Biblia pauperum*. Gothic cycles are seen in important portal reliefs at Chartres, Paris, and Nuremberg, in stained glass of extraordinary mastery at Chartres and Reims, and in MS illuminations of France and Bohemia. Niccolo Pisano carved cycles upon pulpits at Pisa and Siena, unifying classical form with lively action in a powerful Gothic style. The Florentine Renaissance expresses with epic power the new humanistic relation of man and nature which dominated Europe from the 15th to the 17th century. Michelangelo's supreme cycle of *Genesis* on the ceiling of the Sistine Chapel was followed by colossal, intense, and imaginative paintings in Venice. The 17th and 18th cent. produced sumptuous superficial renderings of biblical themes in which episodic genre effects, pure decoration, or tormented subjectivity eclipsed the sacred character. Generalized spiritual values mark the tortuous social interpretations of the 19th and 20th cent. in works of Van Gogh, Gauguin, Matisse, the German Expressionists, and in Rouault's powerfully moving *Passion* cycle. After World War II Chagall's biblical illustrations (1956) and Manzù's *Door of Death* for St. Peter's, Rome (1964), related the Bible to present events.

BIBLIOGRAPHY: A. Grabar, "Les Sujets bibliques au service de l'iconographie chrétienne," *Nel Bibbia nell' Alto Medioevo* (1963) 384—411; K. Holter, "Das Alte und Neue Testament in der Buchmalerei," *ibid.* 413–471; A. M. Romanini, NCE 2:524–532.

[M. J. DALY]

BIBLE HISTORY, a prophetic interpretation of events in the life of the people of Israel, recorded in the canonical Scriptures. For the biblical authors, history is primarily the activity of God, choosing a people for himself and directing them toward a goal. For example, the earliest extended historical writing in Israel was apparently a presentation of the ancient traditions as fulfilled in the newly founded Davidic dynasty, itself the object of God's choice for establishing his future rule on earth. This doctrine of election, when challenged by the destruction of the monarchy, issued in the teaching of the chosen "remnant" and thus supported Israel's faith during the reconstruction after the Exile (cf. Is 11.11, 16; Jer 23.3; Ezra 9.8, 13, 15). Repeated disappointments, rather than destroying Israelite faith, led to the development of apocalyptic dimension, whereby Israel hoped for God's kingdom beyond the process of human history; this direction toward the future affected even the relatively nonhistorical Wisdom literature, which eventually spoke of an afterlife (Wis 5).

Apocalyptic expectation contributed greatly to the early Church's understanding of the risen Jesus, who was seen as bringing history to a close. The lack of his visible second coming led the Church to interpret in various ways its own continuation in history (contrast I Th 1.10 and Lk 19.11). Some parables of Jesus became allegories for the stages of history (Lk 14.15–24; Mt 22.1–14). The Church developed its theology of a mission to the world (compare Acts 11.18–20 and 1.8) and recognized that the gift of the Holy Spirit was both a fulfillment of the past and a pledge of God's future giving (Rom 8.14–17, 26, 27; 2 Cor 1.21–22; cf. also Acts 1.6–8). This interplay of promise and fulfillment, with each fulfillment becoming a new promise, has been widely proposed as the unifying thread of all Bible history. This theme appears supple enough to account for the unsuspected element in each fulfillment, as well as for the tension between continuity and discontinuity, which characterizes the relationship of the two testaments (cf. Gal 4.4, 21–31; Rom 11.17–24). Nonetheless, some authors caution against overstressing any unifying scheme and urge that the ultimate unity of the Bible lies in God himself (cf. Am 3.4–8; Mk 4.26–29; Jn 6.44–46). This ultimate mystery of the meaning of history perhaps renders more intelligible the coexistence of discordant interpretations within the Scriptures themselves (e.g., promonarchic and antimonarchic sentiments in the prophets; divine action seen as intervention in the patriarchal narratives, but as hiddenness in Wisdom literature). The awareness that any statement about God acting in history is limited by the symbolic nature of human language, by the varying horizon of human culture, as well as by man's inability to grasp more than the partial context of any historical event can aid in the acceptance of the necessary gap between faith and fact. BIBLIOGRAPHY: G. E. Mendenhall, "Biblical History in Transition," *Bible and the Ancient Near East* (ed. G. E. Wright, 1961) 27–58; C. R. North, InterDB 2:607–612.

[P. KEARNEY]

BIBLE MORALISÉE, the most complete visual and literary commentary of the Bible (13th cent.), believed dedicated to King Louis IX (1226–70), now scattered in libraries at Oxford and Paris, and in the British Museum with copies in

Vienna and Toledo. There are French translations of the original Latin. The disposition of 5,000 scenes in roundels reminiscent of stained glass at Ste. Chapelle, Paris (1248) was used also in the *Psalter of St. Louis* and in the Souvigny Bible. A similar layout in a Psalter from Artois suggests an artist from N France. Iconographical texts stress parallelism between "figures" of the OT and "mysteries" of the NT. Using "symbolic imagery" as the basis of meaning, the *Bible Moralisée* comments on the moral and disciplinary implications of the biblical verses. BIBLIOGRAPHY: P. Verdier, NCE 2:535–536; A. de Laborde, *La Bible Moralisée* (4 v., 1911–21).

[M. J. DALY]

BIBLE REGAL, a small *regal or reed organ which could be closed like a book by folding the bellows over so as to resemble a closed Bible.

[A. DOHERTY]

BIBLE SCHOOLS, schools originating in the late 19th-cent. movement to equip laymen to serve better as Sunday school teachers and in personal evangelism. D. L. *Moody founded the Moody Bible Institute at Chicago in 1886, and the Nyack Missionary Training Institute grew out of classes begun in 1882 by A. B. Simpson. The original purpose was supplemented soon by an aim to provide a short course of preparation for pastors and missionaries. As *liberal theology spread, Bible schools and institutes sprang up in many larger cities, intent upon counteracting *modernism. Many of these schools adopted the *Scofield Reference Bible with its *dispensationalism, emphasizing biblical prophecies and the expectation of the imminent second coming of Christ. Conditioned to be suspicious of the major denominations, their graduates tended to be separatistic, serving *independent Churches and mission boards or loosely organized denominations like the Baptists. Since World War II there has been expansion of such schools, but desire for recognition by accrediting bodies has led to changes in curriculum to make more room for liberal arts. In 1947 the Accrediting Association of Bible Colleges was organized to set standards for this type of school. Several schools changed their names from Bible Institute or Bible School to Bible College, and some of them have raised standards sufficiently to be recognized by the regular regional accrediting associations. For example, Barrington College (R.I.), Philadelphia College of the Bible, and Nyack Missionary College (N.Y.) have made such transitions and received regular accreditation.

[N. H. MARING]

BIBLE SOCIETIES, nonprofit organizations for printing and distributing copies of the Bible. The *Society for the Promotion of Christian Knowledge, founded in London (1698), included among its objects the provision of Bibles for poor people. The *British and Foreign Bible Society was established in 1804, with members of the C of E and *Nonconformists cooperating. Its sole purpose was printing and distributing Bibles, and membership was open to all who paid the necessary fee; local societies were started throughout the British Isles. Auxiliary societies were also organized in British colonies, and agencies were developed to reach eastern Europe and Asia. The Canstein Bible Institute was founded at Halle, Germany (1710), to make the Scriptures available to the poor, and during the 19th cent. numerous Bible societies were constituted in Germany, the Netherlands, France, Russia, and Switzerland, most of them formed by Protestants. In the U.S. the first Bible society began in Philadelphia in 1808. In 1816 many local groups consolidated to organize the *American Bible Society, an interdenominational organization. In 1932 the British and Foreign Bible Society and the American Bible Society began to integrate their work in various lands. In 1946 the United Bible Societies was established, bringing together many of the larger national societies. The Bible today is translated into more than one thousand languages and dialects, and inexpensive editions of the Bible, or portions of it, are available in most parts of the world.

[N. H. MARING]

BIBLE TEXTS, MSS of the biblical books either in the language of the original or in ancient *Bible versions that closely reflect the original; there are no extant autograph MSS by the author of any book of the Bible.

OT TEXTS. The earliest, and in the present state of textual criticism, the most significant MSS in this field are the following:

The *Nash Papyrus, a MS fragment of c. 150 B.C. containing the ten commandments and Dt 6.4.–5.

The *Qumran biblical MSS. The remains of over 190 OT MSS have been discovered, dating from c. 250 B.C. to 68 A.D. (See DEAD SEA SCROLLS).

The Masada MSS. Of special importance here is the discovery of substantial portions of Sirach dating from c. 100 B.C. The latest of these MSS must be earlier than A.D. 135.

The Samaritan Pentateuch (see BIBLE VERSIONS), a medieval MS deriving from an original in a peculiar and archaic Hebrew script dating from the 1st cent. A.D.

The vocalized medieval Hebrew MSS. The most important of these, and the one on which the present critical edition of the Hebrew Bible is largely based, is the Leningrad MS of 1009 A.D. A substantial part of the Aleppo MS (c. 930 A.D.) has also survived, and is being studied at the Hebrew Univ. of Jerusalem.

Other Masoretic texts. In some cases these are the product of rival schools to that of Ben Asher, from which the Leningrad MS is derived. The earliest of these other MSS appears to go back to the 12th century.

NT TEXTS. The MSS in this field have been classified by *Westcott and *Hort into the following four main families:

The Neutral Text, held by Westcott and Hort to represent the purest form of the text, and the one least interfered with by revisers.

The Alexandrian Text which is the Neutral Text as revised and polished at the early Christian center of learning of Alexandria.

The Western Text—a misnomer, since several MSS subsequently found to be of Eastern provenance have been included in this group. It is characterized by heavy revisions and the inclusion of explanatory glosses.

The Syrian Text, a tradition appearing in the late 4th cent. at Antioch and characterized by conflate readings, i.e., attempts at producing a compromise between conflicting readings in MSS of other families. This was regarded by Westcott and Hort as the poorest and least reliable of the four families.

In his monumental study, The Four Gospels: A Study of Origins (1924), B. H. Streeter revised these classifications by combining the Neutral and Alexandrian families in the Alexandrian; by including a new family known as the Caesarean (mainly of 2d-cent. Egyptian provenance); by renaming the Syrian group as the Byzantine. All the groups have been subject to revision and corruption, and each of them has important readings to offer. For bibliog. see TEXTUAL CRITICISM.

[D. J. BOURKE]

BIBLE VERSIONS, translations of the Bible, or of any part of it, into a vernacular tongue; a version is distinguished from the text of the *Bible, i.e., the written word in MSS either in the original languages or in ancient versions made from these languages. With regard to the OT, four direct versions (i.e., from the original languages) stand out immediately as the most ancient and important: the Aramaic *targums of Onkelos and Jonathan (pre-3d cent. A.D.), the Greek *Septuagint, the Syriac *Peshitta and the Latin *Vulgate. (The two last named, having been composed by and for Christians, also include the NT). These direct versions derive their special critical value from the fact that they were written considerably before the existing Hebrew text was fixed, and consequently bear witness to earlier variants of it that would otherwise be unknown to us. Substantial parts of certain other versions have also survived, and bear some degree of independent witness to the original text. Among these, the *Samaritan Pentateuch is not strictly a version at all, since it constitutes a dialectical variant of the original Hebrew that, in certain respects, may represent a tradition going back to the 4th cent. B.C.; the earliest extant MSS for this text are medieval. Also important are the Aramaic Targum Yerushalmi I (also known as the Targum of Pseudo-Jonathan) and Targum Yerushalmi II, and numerous fragments of further early targums that have come to light among the writings of Qumran. (See DEAD SEA SCROLLS). The remaining versions are all indirect, i.e., translations of translations deriving mainly from the Septuagint. This applies to the *Old Latin versions prior to the Vulgate, and also to certain Coptic, Sahidic, Ethiopic, and Armenian versions. A version of great importance for the NT is the *Diatessaron of Tatian (c. 150 A.D.). Portions of a number of other Old Syriac versions, some of them deriving from 4th to 6th cent. A.D., have also been preserved.

Of the English versions the most important are: *Tyndale's

NT (1523–26), Erasmus' translation of the Greek NT (1516–35), the *Coverdale Bible, the *Great Bible, the *Geneva or Breeches Bible, the *Bishop's Bible, and the *King James or Authorized Version, the Catholic *Douay-Rheims version and *Challoner's revision of this, the Revised Authorised Version of 1811–15, the American Standard Version, the *Revised Standard Version, which also exists in a separate edition prepared for Catholics, the Westminster Version, the *Confraternity Bible, the *New English Bible, and the Moffat Bible, the Bible in Basic English, the *Chicago Bible, the *Jerusalem Bible, and the *New American Bible. BIBLIOGRAPHY: B. Roberts, *Old Testament Text and Versions* (1951); P. Kahle, *Cairo Geniza* (2d ed., 1959); F. Kenyon, *Our Bible and the Ancient Manuscripts* (rev. ed., 1958); S. Jellicoe, *Septuagint and Modern Study* (1968); H. B. Swete, *Introduction to the Old Testament in Greek* (ed. by H. St. J. Thackeray, repr. 1968); Le Déaut, *Introduction à la littérature targumique* I (1966); H. W. Robinson, *Bible in its Ancient and English Versions* (1940); H. Pope, *English Versions of the Bible* (rev. ed., 1952). For a detailed critical survey of modern English translations of the Old Testament see E. Arbey, "Modern Translations of the Old Testament V. English Language Translations," CBQ 17 (1955) 456–485; P. Skehan et al., JBC 2:561–589.

[D. J. BOURKE]

BIBLE VIGIL, a prayer service based on the reading of the Bible as God's word and structured according to the traditional principles of worship. Generally it consists of an entrance rite, readings, prayers, and a closing rite, but its format is elastic and adaptable to a variety of circumstances of time, place, and participants. The theology and form of the service is not new. It is analogous to the synagogue service, and much like the assemblies for reading and prayer out of which the Divine Office developed. Such services have grown in popularity since World War II as a substitute for repetitious devotions, and growing interest in the Bible has taught people to value the opportunity they provide for a broader exploration of God's word. Vatican Council II has given encouragement to these services in its *Constitution on the Sacred Liturgy* (35.4), declaring them esp. appropriate on the vigils of the greater feasts, on weekdays in Advent and Lent, and in places where no priest is available. The name Bible Vigil came into use because it originated as a substitute for evening devotions, but Bible Devotions would perhaps be a better name. BIBLIOGRAPHY: "Vigil as an Evening Service for the Parish," *Unto the Altar* (ed. A. Kirchgaessner, 1963) 107–118; J. Kemerer, "Celebration of the Word of God without a Priest," *Liturgy of Vatican II* (ed. W. Barauna, 1966) 1:286–293; J. Connolly, "Bible Devotions: Principles and Sample," *Worship* 36 (1962) 115–120.

[N. KOLLAR]

BIBLIA PAUPERUM (Lat. for "Poor Man's Bible"). The name came to be applied to small MSS of biblical scenes that

began appearing in Bavaria and Austria at the beginning of the 14th century. The scenes, depicted in ink drawings of no artistic worth, usually linked types taken from the OT with their fulfillment in the NT and had short relevant biblical quotations ordered to applying catechetical lessons for illiterate or semi–literate Christians. They seem to have been easily transportable visual aids used by traveling catechists. With the advent of printing such illustrated Bibles began to be reproduced through wood-block prints, but, apparently, they soon gave way to Bibles that reproduced the complete text in the vernacular.

[J. F. FALLON]

BIBLICAL COMMISSION, a pontifical agency of the Roman Catholic Church set up by Pope Leo XIII in the early 20th cent. for the advancement of biblical studies and the guarding of the basic validity and worth of the Bible from attacks by rationalism and modernism. Consisting of a nucleus of cardinals, advised and informed by international experts in biblical sciences, in its early stages, the Commission gave officially sanctioned formal responses to certain questions challenging the traditional authorship of some biblical books; the replies aimed at dampening the enthusiastic and unwarranted acceptance of hypotheses not definitively established by a consensus of believing interpreters and experts. When the decisions seemed to have corrected tendencies toward rash conclusions, the Commission lapsed into silence for many years. When it resumed public statements, it was much more positive and even supportive of Catholic scholars' investigations of the Bible. Thus, its members have been presumed in large measure responsible for the papal encyclical on Sacred Scripture of 1943, which encouraged Catholic scholars to carry on courageously in their Bible study despite criticism. This led to a revival of interest in the Word of God among ordinary Catholics who had so long been deprived of much of their biblical heritage. The Commission is empowered to grant higher degrees in Sacred Scripture after an extensive examination of the candidates.

[J. F. FALLON]

BIBLICAL FORM CRITICISM, see FORM CRITICISM, BIBLICAL.

BIBLICAL FUNDAMENTALISM, see FUNDAMENTALISM, BIBLICAL.

BIBLICAL INERRANCY, see INERRANCY.

BIBLICAL INSTITUTE, PONTIFICAL an advanced school for Bible studies established in Rome by Pope St. Pius X in 1909 to fulfill a proposal by Leo XIII for training scholars in the use of specialized skills and methods of linguistic and historical research. A faculty for Ancient Near East studies was added in 1932. The gradated aims were (1) to train instructors to teach seminarians biblical courses, (2) to develop professors to train the instructors, and (3) to promote advanced biblical research for the apologetical needs of the Church and for a greater knowledge of the written Word of God entrusted to the Church's care. To matriculate one must have finished one's theological training by gaining an advanced degree (an amazing reversal of the medieval sequence that required biblical degrees to precede theological). One may gain baccalaureate in 1 year, licentiate, in 2, and be approved as a candidate for doctorate in 3, which cannot be received until 2 more years' productive accomplishment has been approved and defended formally. The Oriental faculty demands even more specialization. The Institute's libraries are exceptionally exhaustive in their fields. Three publications, *Biblica,* a quarterly offering scientific biblical articles, book reviews, and bibliographies, *Verbum Domini,* a monthly for seminarians now defunct because they do not read Latin anymore, and the quarterly *Orientalia* for Ancient Near East Studies have received worldwide acclaim. An annex in Jerusalem concentrates on topographical and archeological interests. The Institute is governed and staffed by scholars of the Society of Jesus and visiting professors at its invitation.

[J. F. FALLON]

BIBLICAL THEOLOGY, a branch of theological study, distinct from both exegesis and speculative theology, in which scriptural revelation is understood and ordered according to the categories, historical circumstances, and themes proper to the Bible. The task of biblical theology is to examine the revelatory events in their temporal character and within the mental perspectives of those who witness to them in the Scriptures in order to identify those events and perspectives within an intelligible pattern of God's self-revelation. All Christian theology is biblical insofar as it is a deliberate attention to the revealed Word, and subsequent speculation and church tradition must always refer back to and be formed by the Bible. Biblical theology is, therefore, an intermediary between exegesis and dogmatic theology. Thus Vat II Div-Rev 10 speaks of the magisterium as serving the word of God, listening to it, guarding it, and explaining it faithfully. BIBLIOGRAPHY: T. Maertens, *Biblical Themes* (2 v., 1964); *Dogmatic vs. Biblical Theology* (ed. H. Vorgrimler, 1964); K. Rahner, SacMund 1:176–177.

[T. M. MCFADDEN]

BIBLICISM, the approach to the understanding of the Bible that combines *fundamentalism and *literalism and insists that the very thought and language of biblical times are the normative source for Christian faith and for its expression. To some extent, traces of biblicism are found in all eras when the Bible enjoys a special vogue in Christian thought and life. The most persistent feature of biblicism is *millenarianism, an interpretation that accepts biblical reflections on the end-time (e.g., Rev; Mk 13.24–27) as literal historical descriptions of events to come, especially the second coming of Jesus. The high-water mark of biblicism in theological circles was reached in the works of Cocceius (1603–69), a Dutch scholar, and of J. A. Bengel (1687–1752), a German scholar. Al-

though modern biblical scholarship has abandoned the approach of biblicism, popular understanding of the Bible remains noticeably affected by it. BIBLIOGRAPHY: G. E. Ladd, *Crucial Questions about the Kingdom of God* (1952).

[C. P. CEROKE]

BIBLIOTHERAPY, healing through books, the developing art and science of effecting salutary change in man by serving the intellect, the will, the emotions in suggesting healthful attitudes and conduct in the face of deteriorating situations, whether physical, psychological, or socioeconomic. Likewise the preventive value of bibliotherapy is adverted to, esp. through schools and in adult education. A. R. Favazza describes it as "the conscious and deliberate use of reading materials and guidance of the patient's use of reading matter for the purpose of furthering or supporting the therapeutic program as a whole, as it relates to a particular patient or in some cases to a more or less homogeneous group of patients."

Pioneer in initiating bibliotherapy as an academic discipline, L. A. Rongione describes it as "selection, evaluation, and acquisition of book and nonbook materials as therapeutic adjuvants in medicine and psychiatry and guidance in the solution of personal problems through directed reading." Bibliotherapy is a cross discipline integrating the fields of librarian, teacher, sociologist with the medical discipline of nurse, physician, physiotherapist, psychiatrist, as well as those of spiritual adviser and guidance counselor. Particular dangers are faced and cautions indicated, and the interdependence of the various contributing agencies is stressed.

The history of bibliotherapy, the "pharmacy of the soul," has yet to be written; that it is ageless is beyond argument, attested by classic reference. Bibliotherapy has witness also in modern times in T. V. *Moore who advanced notably the understanding and use of bibliotherapy; it was at his behest that C. Kircher of the Newark Public Library assembled and catalogued for Moore's clinic at The Catholic Univ. of America a bibliotherapeutic collection.

The guidance technique of bibliocounseling is a derivative of bibliotherapy; films such as those of C. Rogers, F. Pearlman, and A. Ellis on the various approaches of psychiatrists speak to this dimension. (See A. Lucili, "Bibliotherapy: A Counseling Technique," CLW 18 [1947] 147–149.)

That bibliotherapy is of practical interest to society at large is seen in the program for the blind and deaf and otherwise physically handicapped, administered from the Library of Congress (LC) and from its network of regional libraries established under federal law. The Xavier Society for the Blind (XSB) founded in 1900, anticipated the LC in serving the visually handicapped.

Indicative of the growing awareness of need for interdisciplinary action are the writings in library journals, e.g., K. Menninger, "Reading as Therapy," *American Library Association Bulletin* 55 (1961) 316–319; doctors express their views likewise in their own journals, e.g., W. E. Menninger, "Bibliotherapy," *Menninger Clinic Bulletin* 1 (1936) 263–276, and for the neurologist K. Teller, "Bibliotherapy and the Treatment of Emotional Disturbances,'' *Catholic Library World* (CLW) 45 (1974) 428–431. The U.S. Veterans Bureau, early aware of bibliotherapy's value, has offered material in their *Medical Bulletin,* e.g., 5:440. F. R. Hartz calls attention to aid for the imprisoned in ''The Librarian in the Correctional Setting: A Selected Bibliography 1964–1973,'' CLW 46 (1974) 218–224. Responding to the demand for literature on bibliotherapy, a physician, A. Allston, published in *Library Trends* 11 (1962) 159–176, ''Bibliotherapy and Psychotherapy,'' based on a questionnaire sent to general practitioners, psychiatrists, and librarians.

To be noted in assessing the profession of bibliotherapy is the fact that to be effective one must have qualities closely akin to those required in other professions of healing. In the 20th cent. it is apparent that bibliotherapy must develop its own specific aims and techniques, tests and measurements to rank beside, and in cooperation with, other professions of the healing art-and-science. BIBLIOGRAPHY: L. A. Rongione, ''Bibliotherapy: Its Nature and Uses,'' *Catholic Library World* 43 (1972) 494–500; C. Tsempoukis, *Bibliocounseling: Theory and Research Implications* (Univ. of Wisconsin, 1968); P. M. Wiemerskirch, ''Benjamin Rush and John Minson Galt II: Pioneers of Bibliotherapy in America,'' *Medical Library Association Bulletin* 53 (1965) 510–526; A. R. Favazza, ''Bibliotherapy: A Critique of the Literature,'' *ibid.* 54 (1966) 138–141.

[M. R. BROWN]

BICHIER DES AGES, JEANNE ÉLISABETH, ST. (1773–1838), foundress. In 1797, she met Abbé Fournet whom she helped by teaching and charity work, and who proposed the foundation of a congregation for this type of service. She made a brief novitiate with the Carmelites and Sisters of Providence, and in 1805, established with four companions the first community of the Daughters of the Holy Cross of St. Andrew. The bp. of Poitiers approved the order (1816), and by 1830, there were 60 convents of the congregation. BIBLIOGRAPHY: G. Mathon, Bibl Sanct 6:581; Butler 3:410–413.

[H. JACK]

BICINIUM, an instrumental or vocal composition in two *parts without other accompaniment. Many examples exist from the 16th and early 17th centuries, including settings of sacred texts, by such composers as *Lasso, *Senfl, and *Praetorius. The best bicinia are examples of the purest *counterpoint, worthy of comparison with larger works of the period. Most of the later bicinia are without text and are presumably for instruments.

[A. DOHERTY]

BICKELL, GUSTAV (1838–1906), Orientalist. Son of the German Protestant canonist Johann Wilhelm Bickell, B. studied at Marburg and Halle and became professor of Semitics and Indo-European philology at Marburg and later at Giessen. He was converted to Catholicism (1865) and or-dained priest in 1867. His teaching career also included a professorship of Semitics at Münster (1871) and of Christian archeology at Innsbruck and Vienna (1891). As a result of his extensive study of Syriac poetry, he suggested a theory that Hebrew poetry could be scanned like Syriac poetry. Among his many scholarly writings, the most notable is *Grundriss der hebräischen Grammatik (1869–70),* which was later translated into English and French. He also translated the poetry of St. Ephrem, the story of Kalilag and Damna, and other Syriac works. BIBLIOGRAPHY: A. De Meyer, DHGE 8:1419–20.

[T. C. STAHL]

BICKELL, JOHANN WILHELM (1799–1848), authority on civil and canon law. He taught canon law at Marburg from 1820. Sixteen years after entering legal practice he was named a legal consultant to the Ministry of Justice. But his chief interest remained in canon law, upon the sources of which he wrote a number of authoritative works. BIBLIOGRAPHY: R. Naz, DDC 2:825–826.

[P. K. MEAGHER]

BICKERING, see QUARREL.

BIDDING-PRAYER (BIDDING THE BEDES), a series of intercessory prayers read out after the Gospel at Mass in pre-Reformation times in England. Practices similar to the bidding of the bedes (praying the prayers) were observed also in other countries and foreshadowed the Prayer of the Faithful in the new liturgy of the Roman Mass.*BEAD.

[J. C. WILLKE]

BIDDLE, JOHN (1615–62). English religious polemicist. He began as a schoolmaster in Gloucestershire, but was repeatedly arrested and imprisoned for writing and teaching heretical doctrine. He attacked the doctrine of the Trinity, published his own catechisms, and with his followers organized his own worship service. B. is sometimes called the founder of the Unitarians in England, although the sect was not organized until the next century. BIBLIOGRAPHY: A. B. Grossart, DNB 2:475–478.

[H. JACK]

BIDERMANN, JAKOB (1578–1639), most important of the Jesuit school dramatists; theologian. B. was born in Swabia and studied under the Jesuits at Augsburg. His dramas, published in 1666, reflect a typically Baroque preoccupation with the theme of *Vanitas vanitatum.* His master-piece, *Cenodoxus, oder der Parisienische Doktor* (performed in Augsburg in 1602), relates how the scholar Cenodoxus lost his soul by preferring earthly knowledge to heavenly. BIBLIOGRAPHY: W. Grenzmann, NCE 7:895–897 s.v. ''Jesuit Drama'' esp. bibliog.; W. Kosch, *Deutsches Literatur-Lexikon* (1963) 36.

[M. F. MCCARTHY]

BIEDERMEIER, originally (with the spelling Biedermaier) a character invented by Ludwig Eichrodt (1827–92) for the *Fliegende Blätter* (1850–57) and intended as a parody of the unpretentious middle-class citizen of the *Vormärzzeit* (period before 1848). The term was gradually extended to include a whole style of living and its representation in literature (e.g., Mörike, Grillparzer) and art (e.g., Spitzweg). It connotes a Philistine emphasis on duty and family life, a glorification of the past, and political passivity in the present. BIBLIOGRAPHY: J. Hermand, *Die literarische Formenwelt des Biedermeiers* (1958).

[M. F. McCARTHY]

BIEL, GABRIEL (*c.*1410–95), nominalist theologian. Sometimes called the last of the scholastics, B. was sometimes known as *doctor profundissimus.* Born at Speyer, Germany, he studied at Heidelberg (B.A. 1435; M.A. 1438), then at Erfurt, which favored Occamism, and Cologne, which favored *Thomism. He was also an instructor for a time at Heidelberg. He had been ordained *c.*1432 and became the principal preacher and vicar at Mainz *c.*1460. Associating himself with the Brothers of the Common Life, he became provost of the brotherhouse at Butzbach in 1468, and in 1477 established the first chapter of the group at Urach (Württemberg).

In 1484 B. became professor of theology at Tübingen and was invested as rector there in 1485 and 1489. A follower of Occam, he taught the *via moderna,* though he also drew on St. *Thomas Aquinas, *Duns Scotus, *Gerson, and others. His commentary on the Sentences of Peter *Lombard was a classic exposition of nominalism. He was also important for his treatment of social and economic questions, in which he was sympathetic to the rising commercialism of the period. His *Treatise on the Power and Utility of Money* was influential. Both M. *Luther and J. *Eck were influenced by Biel.

Biel and his period have sometimes been portrayed as scholasticism in disintegration and decay. A more positive evaluation has recently been given by H. A. Oberman in his *Harvest of Medieval Theology* (rev. ed. 1967). BIBLIOGRAPHY: F. C. Copleston *History of Medieval Philosophy* (pa. 1973).

[T. EARLY]

BIENVILLE, JEAN BAPTISTE LE MOYNE DE (1680–1768), founder of Mobile and New Orleans in colonial America. Eighth son of Charles Le Moyne, Sieur de Longueuil, and brother of Pierre Le Moyne d'Iberville, he sailed with the expedition to find the mouth of the Mississippi (1698) and reestablish the claim of France. He helped establish Biloxi in 1699, explored the Red River to Natchitoches in 1700, and in 1701 took command of the colony, moving it in 1710 to Mobile. He was replaced by Cadillac in 1712, but remained in Louisiana, laying out New Orleans in 1718 and again governing the colony until 1740, excepting the years 1726–34. A strong supporter of the Jesuit missionaries, he

took a leading role in furthering Catholicism on the Gulf Coast. BIBLIOGRAPHY: G. E. King, *Jean Baptiste le Moyne: Sieur de Bienville* (1892). E. P. Spillane, CE 2:560–61.

[R. K. MacMASTER]

BIFFI, EUGENIO (1829–96), bp. Educated and trained in Milan for mission work, B. was sent (1856) to Cartagena, but worked with the Jesuits in Belize, British Honduras, during Masquera's persecution in Cartagena. He was made apostolic prefect of Eastern Birmania (1867), and bp. of Cartagena (1882), where he served as a vigorous and effective administrator. BIBLIOGRAPHY: E. Van Cauwenbergh, DHGE 8:1448.

[H. JACK]

BIGAMY, in canon law, the act of marrying two or more times. Two forms of bigamy are distinguished. Successive bigamy occurs when a person marries a second time after the death of his first spouse. But if a person marries a second time while still bound by his previous marriage valid in the eyes of the Church, the bigamy is said to be simultaneous.

[P. K. MEAGHER]

BIGARD, JEANNE (1859–1934), cofoundress of the Work of St. Peter the Apostle to aid native missionaries. In 1903 she relinquished direction of the society of the Franciscan Missionaries of Mary and accepted with resignation the approach of mental illness. She lived almost 30 years as a complete invalid. BIBLIOGRAPHY: P. Lesourd, *L'Holocauste de Jeanne Bigard* (1938); S. Béreaux, *Catholicisme* 2:58–59.

[M. J. SUELZER]

BIGG, CHARLES (1840–1908), one of a group of modern British Platonists who subscribed to Platonic philosophy while adopting what can only be described as Plato's "theology" as well. Works: *Christian Platonism of Alexandria* (1866, repr. 1968).

[J. R. RIVELLO]

BIGOTRY, the fanatical attachment to a cause, coupled with intolerance and contempt of those who oppose it and a blind unwillingness to consider evidence contrary to one's own views. It is often accompanied by paranoid suspicions of one's opponents. It is commonly less an aberration of judgment than of the will and the emotions. The bigot feels the triumph of his cause and the defeat of his adversaries as necessary to his own security, and the strength of this feeling is too great to permit dispassionate appraisal of evidence. Although an individual can be bigoted about any subject, religion, race, nationality, politics, or class distinction are among the commoner objects, religion and race being the spheres in which bigotry has wrought its greatest havoc. It is possible for a person to be bigoted in one or several areas and yet be open-minded in others, esp. in cases in which educational or environmental circumstances have kept him from ready access to facts. Bigotry of this kind usually diminishes or clears up altogether upon exposure to broader experience. When bigotry is peculiarly intense, or when it extends over a wide range of matters, it is likely to be rooted in emotional or neurotic disorder and is, accordingly, more difficult to deal with. BIBLIOGRAPHY: G. Allport, *Nature of Prejudice* (1954); G. Meyers, *History of Bigotry in the United States* (1943)

[P. K. MEAGHER]

BIHL, MICHAEL (1878–1950), historian of the Franciscan Order. Born in Alsace, B. was ordained in 1902. In 1907 he assisted in founding the *Archivum Franciscanum historicum* and in 1908 became its director. He edited the *Analecta Franciscana* and wrote many monographs, articles, and essays which clarified Franciscan history. BIBLIOGRAPHY: DE 1:386–387.

[F. D. LAZENBY]

BIHLMEYER, KARL (1874–1942), German church historian. After studying at the Univ. of Tübingen, B. succeeded his teacher, F.X.*Funk, as professor of church history on the faculty of Catholic theology (1907–40). He assumed the task of revising the sixth ed. of Funk's *Kirchengeschichte* and brought it through five new editions (1911–40). The latest revised edition of this was prepared by H. Tüchle (1951–64) and has appeared in English translation as *Church History* (3 v., 1958–65). In addition to contributing articles on early church history to learned journals, B. also brought out a German edition of the works of Bl. Henry Suso (1907). BIBLIOGRAPHY: I. Danielle, EncCatt 2:1635.

[R. B. ENO]

BILBAO, FRANCISCO (1823–65), Chilean liberal. He began his career as a "radical rationalist" among a group of Chilean liberal intellectuals. At 21 he was excommunicated and exiled for a virulent anti-Catholic, anti-Spanish publication. Allowed back in Chile, he founded a Society of Equality (1850), but shortly sought a more favorable climate in Peru. When exiled from there also, he went to Buenos Aires (1857) where he was an active Mason and continued his attacks upon the Church in Latin America. Works: *Obras completas* (2 v., 1866).

[H. JACK]

BILHILD, ST. (d. *c*.734), Benedictine abbess. After the death of her husband, Duke Hetan I of Thuringia, she became foundress (650) and later abbess (660) of Altmunster monastery at Mayence. BIBLIOGRAPHY: A. Bigelmair, DHGE 8:1471–72; T. Freudenberger, BiblSanct 3:188–189.

[M. H. BEIRNE]

BILIO, LUIGI (1826–84), a Barnabite who after some years of teaching in Barnabite houses was made consultor of the Holy Office (1864) and of the Congregation of the Index (1865), bp. of the suburbicarian diocese of Sabina and cardinal (1866). He was made prefect of the Congregation of Rites and head of the Sacred Penitentiary. He played an important

part in the drafting of the Syllabus of Errors. He is also remembered for his role in Vatican Council I. BIBLIOGRAPHY: C. Butler, *Vatican Council* (2v., 1930); Fliche-Martin 21:311–368.

[P. K. MEAGHER]

BILLERBECK, PAUL (1853–1932), NT scholar and Judaic expert. A minister of the Evangelical Church in Germany, B. retired in 1914 to compose his *Kommentar zum NT aus Talmud und Midrasch* (4 v., 1922–28; 2d ed. with 2-v. index by K. Adolph, 1956–61). The work is an expert commentary on the NT in the light of Jewish thought and literature.

[T. M. MCFADDEN]

BILLIART, JULIE, ST. (1751–1816), Born in Cuvilly, Picardy, she manifested unusual spiritual gifts from her childhood. While at the height of her good works she was stricken with a form of paralysis which gradually reduced her to complete invalidism, even impairing her power of speech. During the French Revolution, her religious activities endangered her life and she was forced to leave her home and take refuge at Amiens where she met the woman who was to assist her in her life work, Françoise Blin de Bourdon. Cured through a miracle, Julie successfully established the congregation that developed into the Notre Dame de Namur Sisters. Eminently successful, their schools and catechetical groups spread throughout France. Misunderstanding with members of the hierarchy forced them to leave Amiens and establish the center of the institute at Namur. By 1816 Julie's health was seriously impaired and the care of the congregation was entrusted to her companion. Mother Julie was canonized by Pope Paul VI in 1969. BIBLIOGRAPHY: R. Desreumaux, BiblSanct 3:189–190; M. G. Carroll, *Charred Wood* (1952).

[I. MAHONEY]

BILLICK, EBERHARD (*c*.1499–1557), Carmelite theologian. He was professor of theology at Cologne (1540–52), served as prior at Cassel and Cologne, and was provincial of lower Germany. He worked for the internal reform of the Church and the monasteries, and was equally zealous in his opposition to heresy. B. revealed the defection of Hermann von Wied, abp. of Cologne, and ultimately saved Cologne for Catholicism. He attended the Council of Trent as theologian to Abp. Adolf von Schaumberg of Cologne and took part in negotiations at Regensburg and Augsburg as the Emperor's representative. BIBLIOGRAPHY: A. Postina, *Der Karmelit Eberhard Billick* (1901); P. Ferdinand, DHGE 8:1480–82.

[H. JACK]

BILLINGER, RICHARD (1893–1965), Austrian dramatist and lyricist, whose works deal with the world of the peasant. They express his Catholic faith but with a strange mixture of mythos, the power of demons, "blood," and peasant traditions. The son of a farmer, B. studied German literature at the Univ. of Vienna, where his lyrical talent was discovered (*Über den Äckern*, 1923). Worthy of mention among his numerous plays and dramas are: *Das Perchtenspiel* (1928), a confusing blend of Christian and mythical beliefs; *Rauhnacht* (1931).

[B. STEINBRUCKNER]

BILLINGS, WILLIAM (1746–1800), American sacred music composer. A tanner by trade, B. compensated for his lack of education by his originality and determination. He published six collections of hymn-tunes, the first of which, *The New England Psalm Singer* (1770) is a collection of "fuguing pieces." Several of his hymns, such as "Chester" and "The Rose of Sharon," became popular and were sung by the American troops in the Revolutionary War. He is important as the first native American to make a profession of composing music. BIBLIOGRAPHY: R. Aldrich, Grove DMM 1:707; Baker 151–152; *International Cyclopedia of Music and Musicians* (ed. O. Thompson, 9th ed., 1964) 221.

[M. T. LEGGE]

BILLOT, LOUIS (1846–1931), Jesuit theologian important for his understanding of Thomistic theology. Born in Sierck, Moselle, France, he was ordained in 1869. Because of eminent preaching, Leo XIII in 1887 summoned him to teach at the Gregorian. Created cardinal in 1911, he opposed Liberalism and Modernism, but due to his sympathies for the royalist movement, Action Française, he was forced to resign the cardinalate in 1927. In obedience, he retired to the Jesuit novitiate in Gallero. His principal works include *De Verbo Incarnato* (1892), *De Deo uno et trino* (1895), and *De Ecclesiae sacramentis* which treats of the Mass as mystical immolation. BIBLIOGRAPHY: J. Lebreton, *Catholicisme* 2:61–63.

[T. LIDDY]

BILLUART, CHARLES RENÉ (1685–1757), Dominican theologian, a Walloon who presented the *Summa* of St. Thomas Aquinas in a style adapted to the academies of his period. The work, which is well-rounded and polished, is a clear and dependable presentation of the central Thomist theological tradition at the end of the age of great commentators. It has gone through 15 editions. BIBLIOGRAPHY: L. Flynn, *Billuart and his Summa S. Thomae* (1938).

[T. GILBY]

BILLY, JACQUES DE (1535–81), French Benedictine patrologist, abbot of Saint-Michel-en-l'Herm in the Vendée. Unable to remain in his monastery during the turmoil of the wars of religion, B. lived in Paris and other French cities, publishing translations of, and commentaries on, the works of various Greek Fathers, notably Gregory of Nazianzus, John Damascene, and Epiphanius. He also produced a popular Greek dictionary. BIBLIOGRAPHY: P. Schmitz, DHGE 8:1488–90; R. Metz, LTK 2:478.

[R. B. ENO]

BILOCATION, the state of being observedly present in at least two places at the same moment of time. Physical bilocation would mean that the same atomic body would be simultaneously both here and there, and would seem to be impossible as a contradiction of the principle of identity, that no being can be and not be at once. Therefore reports of bilocation are usually interpreted to mean incidents of apparent bilocation: i.e., that bilocated beings are "seen" in one place while they are known to be "present" in another. For this reason it is difficult to distinguish bilocation from related appearances or visions. It is regarded as a display of miraculous power, of which a saint may be the instrument, providentially ordered to bring us to God. How it works is uncertain. Some think of it as a property of the glorified body after the Resurrection. Serious reports of bilocation are rare. BIBLIOGRAPHY: A. Wiesinger, *Occult Phenomena in the Light of Theology* (tr. B. Battershaw, 1957).

[C. P. SVOBODA]

BINATION, or in its ternary form trination, signifies the act of the priest offering Mass twice or three times on the same day. According to the general law, a priest is not permitted to offer Mass more than once a day, except on Christmas and on All Souls Day when he may do so three times (CIC c. 806.1). To this might be added the general permission for priests who celebrate the Mass of the Easter Vigil at midnight to offer Mass also on Easter day. The bp. may permit priests to offer more than one Mass daily, however, for pastoral reasons, e.g., on Sundays and holydays of obligation when a number of people might otherwise miss Mass. Trination, in fact, is becoming common. BIBLIOGRAPHY: J. H. Miller, *Fundamentals of the Liturgy* (1959).

[N. R. KRAMER]

BINCHOIS, GILLES (Gilles de Binche) (c. 1400–60), priest and composer, one of the great masters of the Burgundian School. B. was a chaplain at Philip the Good's Court of Burgundy, for which he composed not only liturgical works but a large number of secular polyphonic chansons, a form for which he is particularly noted. He rearranged some of the latter with more appropriate texts as motets for use in church services. Highly regarded by his contemporaries, he was called by Ockeghem "le père de fogeusité," a reference to the grace and charm that characterize his work. BIBLIOGRAPHY: Grove DMM 709–710.

[J. J. WALSH]

BINDING AND LOOSING, an expression found frequently in Jewish rabbinic literature. It is of Christian concern only insofar as it is used twice in the NT, both times in passages of considerable theological importance. In the Petrine text (Mt 16.17-19) the function of binding and loosing is the third form of the promise made to Simon Peter, and in Mt 18.18 the same function is committed to the Twelve. The sense in which these words are to be understood has been the subject of much learned discussion. In the rabbinic usage the expression describes the actions of one who in some authoritative way declares that by the Law something is forbidden (in which case he "binds") or that something is allowed (in which case he "looses"). Rarely the expression describes the action of one who excludes from or readmits to the community. The contexts of the two passages in Matthew suggest that what is there intended and conferred is the right to impose and remove penalties and sanctions including that of exclusion from the community or readmission into it (cf. F. Büchsel, Kittel TD 2:60–61). In line with this interpretation one may find a parallel in the promise to the Apostles (Jn 20.23) of the power to retain or remit sins. BIBLIOGRAPHY: F. A. Sullivan, NCE 2:559–560; A. Vögtle, LTK 2:480–482; C. H. Dodd, NTS 2:85 ff.

[S. E. DONLON]

BINET, ÉTIENNE (1569–1639), Jesuit preacher and spiritual writer. He joined the Jesuits in Italy and returned to France when the Society was reestablished there after a period of banishment. A friend of SS. Francis de Sales and Jane Frances de Chantal, B. was one of the most prominent representatives of devout humanism. He published 40 volumes during the years 1614–39. By his writing and preaching he contributed substantially to the awakening of interest in the spiritual life after the Wars of Religion. BIBLIOGRAPHY: Bremond, v. 1; M. Olphe-Galliard, DSAM 1:1620–23; J. De Guibert, *Jesuits: Their Spiritual Doctrine and Practice* (tr. W. J. Young, 1964) 349–350.

[H. JACK]

BINGHAM, JOSEPH (1668–1723), English clergyman and antiquarian. During a current Trinitarian controversy, B. preached a sermon at Oxford that caused him to be unjustly accused of tritheism. Resigning his fellowship at the university, he was given a rectorship near Winchester and devoted himself to historical research. His *Antiquities of the Christian Church* (10 v., 1708–22) is a classical collection of information regarding the organization, rites, and discipline of the Early Church. BIBLIOGRAPHY: DNB 5:48.

[V. SAMPSON]

BINITARIANISM, a classification used esp. in England for the belief or doctrine that the Godhead exists in two persons only, the Father and the Son. Thus the Pneumatomachi (Macedonians), who rejected the divinity of the Holy Spirit, were teaching a form of Binitarianism.

[T. C. O'BRIEN]

BINIUS, SEVERIN (Bini; 1573–1641), canonist. Ordained priest, B. taught at the Univ. of Cologne, served as its rector (1627–29), and was vicar-general of the diocese from 1631 to 1641. He published a new edition of the ecclesiastical histories of Socrates, Theodoret, Sozomen, and Evagrius (1612). However, he is best known for his edition of the councils of the Church, *Concilia generalia et provincialia* (4 v., 1606) which gives only the Latin texts of the acts of the councils, decretal letters, and lives of the popes. To these B. added many explanatory notes. A second edition, including Greek texts, appeared in 1618 and a third, nine-volume edition, in 1636. BIBLIOGRAPHY: J. B. Martin, DTC 2.1:900–901; G. C. Jaroš, EncCatt 2:1644–45.

[L. MITCHELL]

BINSWANGER, LUDWIG (1881–1966), Swiss psychiatrist, founder of existential analysis in psychiatry. Such analysis is an attempt to synthesize E. Husserl's and M. Heidegger's phenomenology with psychiatry *(Daseinsanalyse)*. Its aim is to present a counter theory to the view that man is solely a natural being. Such a view reduces any study of man, whether done in psychology or philosophy, to a one-dimensional object for investigation and inquiry. On the other hand, what B. seeks is the supportive evidence of various disciplines which eventually assist the psychologist in doing two things: first, in seeing the patient in the subjective world of reality in which he lives; secondly, in providing the criterial evidence needed to analyse the patient's referents, esp. those which are the causal conditions for the patient's particular neurosis. Thus, for B., *Daseinsanalyse* is as much a part of *Geisteswissenschaften* as he believes phenomenology is. BIBLIOGRAPHY: J. Needleman, EncPhil 1:309–310; L. Oeing-Hanhoff, LTK 3:168–169 s.v. "Dasein."

[J. R. RIVELLO]

BINTERIM, ANTON JOSEF (1779–1855), German writer whose ardent preaching against Prussian laws on mixed marriage caused him to be imprisoned in 1836 for 6 months. Ordained a Franciscan, he became pastor at Bilk in 1805, when the order was suppressed, and remained there till his death. He wrote extensively on Christian archeology, the Jesuits, and the German councils. BIBLIOGRAPHY: H. Dansend, DHGE 8:1510–11; G. C. Jaroš, EncCatt 2:1645.

[T. LIDDY]

BIOGENESIS, the process whereby living things arise from preexisting living organisms. It is often expressed in the aphorism *omne vivum e vivo* (every living thing from a living thing). The term was used in the 19th cent. by T. H. Huxley to refute the then-prevalent theory of abiogenesis or spontaneous generation. General acceptance of biogenesis today does not, however, preclude the possibility that life began spontaneously in the remote past (theory of biopoesis). Experiments by A. I. Oparin, H. Grey, M. Calvin, S. Miller, N. H. Horowitz, and others lend support to the theory that life might have arisen from nonliving materials present in the primordial seas. For a detailed account of other theories on the possible origin of living things with their theological and philosophic aspects, see A. M. Hofstetter, NCE 2:563–566; S. Beer, EncCatt 2:1649–53.

[P. D. OESTERLE]

BIOMORPHIC ART, the term for modern abstract art in which the created forms suggest living organisms as opposed to geometric abstractions. Exponents are the artists Arp, Miró, Gorky, and others.

[M. J. DALY]

BION OF BORYSTHENES (c.325–c.255 B.C.), eclectic popular philosopher and writer. Of lowly origin, a point which he perhaps overemphasizes through self-depreciation, he followed lectures at the Academy and the Lyceum at Athens, but was influenced more by the Cynics and Cyrenaics. Hence he may be classified as an eclectic, with pronounced Cynic leanings. He traveled extensively as a lecturer on ethical themes, and he did not hesitate to demand fees. In his diatribes he made use of a *spoudaiogeloion* style, that is, he "blended jest and earnest," stated the truth with a laugh. He exercised a definite influence on Horace. BIBLIOGRAPHY: K. von Fritz, OCD 137; LexAW 476–477; D. R. Dudley, *History of Cynicism* (1937) 62–69.

[M. R. P. MCGUIRE]

BIONDO, FLAVIO (1392–1463) historian. He was a humanist scribe and secretary in N Italy before he entered the papal service (1433–63). Gaspar, one of his 10 children, succeeded him as scriptor of apostolic letters. B., who lived and died poor, was a better historian than his humanist colleagues. Two archeological works and a study of old Roman institutions became basic works for the study of antiquity. The *Decades*, originally a contemporary history (1401–41) to which he added an introduction (410–1400), does not pretend to be a history of the Middle Ages; but B. felt that the barbarian invasions ushered in a new age. In his eyes the papacy did more for Rome than did the Roman empire. Other works include a number of letters, some of which are lost. BIBLIOGRAPHY: E. P. Colbert, NCE 2:574. F. Baix, DHGE 8:1513–19.

[E. P. COLBERT]

BIR ES SAB (ISRAEL), see BERSABEE (BEERSHEBA).

BIRAGO, GIOVANNI PIETRO (fl. 1460), Italian miniaturist whose name is linked with the Sforza Book of Hours (betw. 1480 and 1490) by a signed, undated document concerning the theft of a payment from Bona of Savoy, wife of Galeazzo Sforza, Duke of Milan. BIBLIOGRAPHY: G. Warner, *Miniatures and Borders from the Book of Hours of Bona Sforza . . . in the British Museum* (1894).

[M. J. DALY]

BIRETTA, a stiff, brimless form of headgear with three or four ridges or peaks on its upper surface; it is worn by the secular and some of the religious clergy on certain ceremonial occasions. It developed from the soft cap worn by a cleric in the Middle Ages. In earlier times its use appears to have been limited to the clergy of higher rank but from the 16th cent. was extended to all clerics. About the same time it began to be ornamented with a tassel or pompon and fitted with an inner stiff lining to give it a neat appearance. Its color is red for

cardinals, purple for bishops, black with a purple pompon for monsignori, and black for the ordinary clergy. Its use before, after, and during Mass is no longer obligatory. BIBLIOGRAPHY: H. Norris, *Church Vestments: Their Origin and Development* (1950); H. Thurston, CE 2:577–578.

[N. KOLLAR]

BIRGER, GREGERSSON (d. 1383), theologian, canonist, hymnodist, abp. of Uppsala. B. supported St. Bridget as she founded the Bridgettines at Vadstena about 1344. He wrote a Latin life of St. Bridget, and his hymns contributed an early basis for the development of Scandinavian liturgical music. BIBLIOGRAPHY: J. Metzler, LTK 2:485–486; F. Kupferle, DHGE 8:1528.

[M. H. BEIRNE]

BIRINUS, ST. (d.c.649), missionary, bp. of Dorchester. Possibly a Roman, B. was sent by Pope Honorius as a missionary bp. to England. He went to Wessex in 634 and the next year converted the West Saxon king, Cynegils. His relics were later translated to Winchester. BIBLIOGRAPHY: P. Burchi, BiblSanct 3:193–194; Butler 4:500–501.

[J. DRUSE]

BIRITUALISM, a system in which a priest of the Latin rite uses the Liturgy and Offices of the Eastern rites on the occasion of his work or missionary activities among Catholics or dissidents of the Eastern Church. However, the system of "adaptation," an exclusive use of an Eastern rite, is now preferred.

[R. A. TODD]

BIRD, FRANCIS (1667–1731), English sculptor best known for his work in St. Paul's Cathedral, London. B. executed numerous tombs and monuments, the largest, that of the Duke of Newcastle in Westminster Abbey.

[M. J. DALY]

BIRÓ, MÁTYÁS DÉVAI (c.1500–c.1545), Hungarian Reformer. He has sometimes been referred to as Dévai, from his birthplace, Déva in Transylvania. He was a Franciscan chaplain to a Hungarian noble when he became attracted to Reformation teaching. B. became a student at Wittenberg, 1529–30, esteemed by Luther, in whose home he lived. Returning to Hungary, he preached Luther's doctrines in several Magyar regions, and was called the "Hungarian Luther." After 1541 he apparently changed from Lutheranism to Calvinism, esp. in Eucharistic teaching; Luther attacked him as a *sacramentarian in a letter of 1544. B. published (1537) one treatise attacking the doctrine of purgatory; his *Orthographia Ungarica* was published posthumously (1549).

[M. J. SUELZER]

BIRTH, ACCELERATION OF, see ACCELERATION OF BIRTH.

BIRTH CONTROL, a term chosen in 1914 by Margaret Sanger to identify the movement she organized to promote the limitation of the size of families. "Planned parenthood" was later (1942) substituted for the term to give the objectives of the movement a more positive aspect. Literally, "birth control" could be applied to a variety of practices which tend to reduce the number of births. In the official moral doctrine of the RC Church some of these practices are regarded as legitimate, at least in some circumstances—e.g., the observance of continence, permanent or periodic; others, such as contraception which is effected by the use of devices designed to prevent the male sperm from coming into contact with the female ovum or the fertilized ovum from becoming implanted in the uterus, sterilization undergone with contraceptive intent, the withdrawal of the male from the female before semination occurs, the use of the "pill" for its contraceptive purpose, and the direct abortion of a living fetus are judged to be morally objectionable. The RC moral position taken on these various forms of birth control is discussed under other headings (see CONTRACEPTION, STERILIZATION, ABORTION). For a comprehensive treatment of the birth control movement, a topic beyond the scope of this dictionary, see M. J. Huth, NCE 2:576–583; and for a treatment of the civil law and birth control, see R. J. Regan, *ibid.* 2:575–576.

[P. K. MEAGHER]

BĪRŪNĪ, ABŪ-AL-RAYHĀN MUHAMMAD, AL- (973–c.1050), Persian intellectual and writer. Prolific scholar, Al-Bīrūnī's works are characterized by perspective, honesty, and critical clarity; he is considered the major thinker of medieval Islam. B. traveled to India where he taught Greek sciences and studied Sanskrit and Hindu philosophy. Of his some 180 works, his major writings are *Al-Āthār al Bāqiya 'an al-Qurūm al-Khāliyah (Chronology of Ancient Nations)* and *Tahqīq Mā li-al-Hind (History of India),* both translated by C. E. Sachao. B.'s other works include studies on geodetic measurement, Hindu mathematics, latitude and longitude, specific gravity, and the speed of light versus the speed of sound. BIBLIOGRAPHY: D. T. Boilot, EncIslam² 1:1236–38.

[M. H. BEIRNE]

BISHAPUR (3d cent. A.D.), town in SW Iran built by Sassanian King Shapur I and boasting imposing temples and elaborate palaces with historical reliefs. BIBLIOGRAPHY: R. Girshman, *Iran: From the Earliest Times to the Islamic Conquest* (1954).

[M. J. DALY]

BISHOP, EDMUND (1846–1917), the foremost English liturgical scholar of the late 19th and early 20th centuries. He spent most of his life as a civil servant in the British Education Department. In 1867 B. became a Roman Catholic and throughout his life was associated with the Benedictine monastery of Downside, in particular with *Gasquet with whom he wrote many polemical works. His spare time was spent in historical research, the results of which can be seen in

his highly original works on the Missal and Breviary. His more significant contributions can be found collected in *Liturgica Historica* (1918), which was published posthumously. His encouragement and vast knowledge of Western European libraries continually supplied the scholars of Britain and Europe with materials for their work. BIBLIOGRAPHY: N. Abercrombie, *Life and Work of Edmund Bishop* (1959).

[N. KOLLAR]

BISHOP, WILLIAM (1554–1624), English bp. and administrator. Ordained after studies in Reims and Rome, B. returned to England. In the dispute between the seculars and the regulars he was a prominent member of the *Appellant party. He drew up (1603) his *Protestation of Allegiance* to Queen Elizabeth, which was signed by 12 other priests. After 1606, however, he refused to sign an oath of allegiance that Paul V had condemned. After undergoing periods of imprisonment and banishment, B. was appointed (1623) bp. for England and titular bp. of Chalcedon by Gregory XV. In the belief that he had the rights of an ordinary he organized a system of church government made up of five vicars-general, assisted by archdeacons and rural deans; he also established a chapter of 24 canons. BIBLIOGRAPHY: Gillow BDEC 1:218–223; P. Hughes, *Rome and the Counter-Reformation in England* (1942).

[L. MITCHELL]

BISHOP, WILLIAM HOWARD (1885–1953), founder of the Glenmary Home Missioners. Ordained in 1915, B. became pastor of St. Louis Parish, Clarksville, Md., in 1917. He organized a Rural Life Conference in his diocese and became president of the National Rural Life Conference in 1928. He was concerned not only with the economic problems of farmers during the Depression but even more with the lack of priests in nearly half the country. He compiled the "No-Priest Land" map and published a plan for home missions in rural sections of the U.S. In 1939 at the invitation of Abp. J. McNicholas, B. founded the Home Missioners of America, popularly known as the Glenmary Home Missioners. The Glenmary Lay Brothers Society and Glenmary Mission Sisters were also organized by Bishop. BIBLIOGRAPHY: H. W. Santen, *Father Bishop, Founder of the Glenmary Home Missioners* (1961).

[J. HILL]

BISHOP, an ecclesiastical title and office, the meaning of which varies among Christian confessions. This difference of understanding constitutes one of the major obstacles to ecumenical progress. Neither the Lutheran nor the *Reformed traditions acknowledge the office of bishop as the term is understood in the RC, Orthodox, and Anglican Churches. They have only ministers (of the word, of baptism, and of the Lord's Supper). In some confessions in certain countries the title "bishop" has survived in consequence of special historical circumstances, but the meaning attached to the office is without hieratic significance. Thus in northern Lutheran countries—Sweden, Norway, Denmark, and Finland—the Churches have bishops. In Sweden they are officers of the official state Church who are nominated by the king from three candidates elected by the pastors. Their function is to serve as presidents of cathedral chapters and as administrators of the Churches. They ordain and visit. Lutheran bishops in Iceland and Lithuania have a similar role. The Reformed Church in Hungary has bishops at the head of ecclesiastical districts, but their rank is not higher than that of pastors. The Czechoslovak National Church and the Evangelical Lutheran Church of Slovakia also have bishops. In the U.S. several Evangelical Churches have bishops, in imitation perhaps of the Episcopal Church. The Evangelical Church of Germany had no bishops, apart from a short-lived (1524–87) episcopacy in East Prussia, which succeeded formerly RC sees, and with the exception also of certain court clergymen or general superintendents who were granted the title by king or emperor. After 1918, discussions of restoration of the title to leaders of ecclesiastical provinces led to the appointment of territorial superintendents with the title "bishop" in some places, e.g., Bavaria, Hannover, Hamburg. The Anglican Communion holds the order of bishop as the highest of the three orders of the ministry. Ordination by a bishop is essential to all who enter the ministry, although this raises the thorny question of apostolic succession, about which some are disposed to take a broader view.

The Methodist Churches in the U.S. in their concept of the bishop are nearer to the evangelical than to the Anglican position; the order of bishop is not considered to be a sacrament any more than that of deacon or of elder. Bishops are superintendents of districts and form the Council of Bishops. More traditional in its concept is the small Old Catholic Communion formed after Vatican Council I. It has branches in Holland, Germany, Switzerland, Austria, the Philippines, and the U.S., all members of the *Union of Utrecht. These consider themselves national Churches under validly ordained bishops.

In the RC Church, bishops are considered to be, by divine institution, the successors of the Apostles. They hold the place of the Twelve, not, of course, as founders of the Church and witnesses of the resurrection, but as heads of local Churches and jointly responsible for the Church's mission as the universal sacrament of salvation (Vat II ConstCh). Their function is threefold: prophetic (or teaching); sanctifying, through sacrifice and sacraments; and pastoral, as leaders of the people. A priest is joined to the college of bishops by episcopal ordination, the sacramental nature of which was definitely stated by Vatican Council II, although this had previously been subject to some doubt. All bishops, whether residential and in charge of a local church or diocese, or not (as in the cases of titular, auxiliary, coadjutor, or retired bishops), are thus members of the college of bishops jointly responsible for the world mission of the Church. The college of bishops, gathered in ecumenical council with and under the pope (or in communion with him in their dispersion throughout the world) constitutes the supreme doctrinal and jurisdictional authority in the Church, authority being understood, in the mind of Vatican Council II, as service to the people of God. BIBLIOGRAPHY: S. E. Donlon and A. Rock, NCE 2:588–591; A. Adam et al., RGG 1:1300–11; G. Weigel, *Churches in North America* (1961); K. Rahner, *Bishops: Their Status and Function* (tr. E. Quinn, 1964). *APOSTOLIC SUCCESSION.

[P. DE LETTER]

BISHOP, AUXILIARY, see AUXILIARY BISHOP.

BISHOP, COADJUTOR, a bp. who assists the principal bp. or ordinary of a diocese. The CIC (cc. 350-355) lists three types: a coadjutor without the right of succession to the diocese, also called an auxiliary bp.; a coadjutor with the right of succession; and a coadjutor "given to the see," i.e., those traditionally assigned by the pope to certain large European dioceses because of their size and significance. Coadjutors with the right of succession are often appointed when the ill health or old age of the ordinary renders his administration of the diocese difficult. Vat II ConstChurch 21 implied that coadjutor bps. are full members of the apostolic college. BIBLIOGRAPHY: G. E. Lynch and S. E. Donlon, NCE 2:592–593; F. Prat, DTC 5.2:1656–1701.

[T. M. MCFADDEN]

BISHOP, MONASTIC, a title for significant ecclesiastical authorities in the early Irish church. Some historians have interpreted this to mean that all jurisdiction in Ireland was exercised by monastic abbots, but this is an oversimplification. Instead, it appears that the authority of abbots naturally spread from the monastery to the surrounding areas which were dependent upon the monks for their spiritual ministrations. But even in these areas, the abbot was always subject to the local bp. even in those cases in which the bp. lived within the monastic foundation. BIBLIOGRAPHY: J. Ryan, *Irish Monasticism: Original and Early Development* (1972).

[T. M. MCFADDEN]

BISHOP, ORDINATION OF. Vatican Council II called for a revision of the ceremonies and texts of the ordination rites (SacLit, par. 76). Pope Paul VI's apostolic constitution *Pontificalis Romani recognitio* gave approval to the new rites that had been drawn up in accordance with the mandate of the Council. These include new rites for the ordination of bishops, priests, and deacons. So far as the ritual for the ordination (which was formerly more commonly known as the consecration) of bishops is concerned, this ceremony takes place after the Gospel in the liturgy, and it includes an exhortation, ritual questions, invitation to prayers, a shortened Litany of the Saints, and the imposition of hands. The principal minister of ordination is then joined by the other ordaining bps in the 3d-cent. ordination prayer of Hippolytus. This is followed by the anointing of the new bp. and his enthronement, if he is the local ordinary, in his own cathedral.

BIBLIOGRAPHY: H. B. Porter, *Ordination Prayers of the Ancient Western Churches* (1967).

[T. LIDDY]

BISHOPS, APPOINTMENT OF. The method of appointing bps. varies significantly within the RC Church. In the West, the pope appoints bps. at his own discretion, although candidates for the office are designated in a number of ways. In the U.S., a biannual meeting of bps. should be called by the *metropolitan, at which meeting a list of episcopal candidates is sent to Rome. In a few dioceses, a cathedral chapter has the right of designation. In the East, patriarchs are chosen by a synod of bps. and confirmed by the pope. Some rites choose all their bps. in this way. Melkite bps. are chosen by the clergy from among three names submitted by the patriarch of Antioch. But regardless of the manner of election or designation, the actual conferral of the office is reserved to the Holy See. There are several qualifications for the office: a bp. must be an ordained priest for at least 5 years, of legitimate birth, 30 years of age, zealous, unmarried, and skilled in theology or canon law. BIBLIOGRAPHY: T. A. Faulkner, NCE 2:586–588; A. Dumas, *Catholicisme* 4:804–814.

[T. M. MCFADDEN]

BISHOPS, CONGREGATION FOR, the congregation (department, agency) in the reorganized Roman *Curia which replaces the older Consistorial Congregation. It is charged with the erection and suppression of dioceses and the appointment of bishops. It also has jurisdiction over people whose mode of living is such that they are not stably located within established ecclesiastical boundaries—e.g., seamen, emigrés, airline personnel, and nomadic peoples.

BISHOPS' BIBLE, a revision of the *Great Bible sponsored by Matthew Parker, abp. of Canterbury, and published in 1568. The task of revision was assigned to several English bps., who were instructed to follow the Great Bible unless it clearly differed from the Hebrew or Greek original. It is a scholarly work which toned down the Calvinist bias of the *Geneva Bible, but the lack of consultation among the authors makes it uneven. The Convocation of 1571 ordered a copy to be used in all the churches of England, and it remained the official English version until the publication of the Authorized Version in 1611. BIBLIOGRAPHY: ODCC 175; JBC 587.

[T. M. MCFADDEN]

BISHOPS' BOOK, a work of the English Reformation, entitled the *Institution of a Christian Man* (1537), prepared by a commission of English bps. and scholars. Based on the *Ten Articles of 1536, it was a series of popular instructions to be read in churches on the Apostles' Creed, the seven sacraments, the Ten Commandments, the Lord's Prayer, and Ave Maria, with two supplementary statements on justification and purgatory. King Henry VIII gave it no official approval but allowed its publication and use for 3 years. It probably represents the best statement of the "reformed Catholicism"

of the C of E following the break with the papacy and King Henry's openness to alliance with the Lutheran princes of Germany. BIBLIOGRAPHY: C. Loyd, *Formularies of Faith Put Forth by Authority during the Reign of Henry VIII* (1856 ed.); for King Henry's corrections and Abp. Cranmer's comments, see *Works of Thomas Cranmer* (1846) 2:83–114.

[M. H. SHEPHERD]

BISHOP'S PALACE, WÜRZBURG, see NEUMANN, BALTHASAR.

BISITŪN INSCRIPTION, see BEHISTUN INSCRIPTION.

BISMARCK, OTTO VON (1815–98), German statesman and founder of the German Reich of the period 1871–1918. B. was descended from families which had provided Junker army officers and bourgeois civil servants to the Prussian monarchical state. The mature B. had a personal religion with possible Christian elements, but his moral personality found its strongest expression in his deep sense of duty to the state represented by the Hohenzollern monarchy. He was successful as a Prussian diplomat (1852–62), but first achieved national reputation as the Prussian minister-president who carried through the reorganization of the army against prolonged liberal opposition (1862–66). Basically a diplomat who preferred negotiation to war, B. nevertheless willingly accepted armed conflict to achieve German unification under Prussia in wars with Denmark (1864), Austria (1866), and France (1870–71). That aim realized, he then used his great skill to maintain peacefully Germany's leadership in Europe until his fall from power in 1890. He was less successful in domestic affairs in the same period since his view of the State and of his own role permitted no other institution or person to express principled opposition. This basic attitude led him to cause a split in the liberal political movement and to fight unsuccessfully against the Catholic Church (see KULTUR-KAMPF), the Center, and Socialist parties. BIBLIOGRAPHY: E. Eyck, *Bismarck after Fifty Years* (1950); V. Conzemius, NCE 2:594–595.

[J. K. ZEENDER]

BISSETTE, ALFRED, see ANDRÉ, BROTHER.

BISTICCI, VESPASIANO DA (1421–98), author and most famous Renaissance bookseller, whose shop in Florence supplied well-known works, primary sources, and classical authors for famous humanists. His patrons included Cosimo de'Medici, Duke Federico Montefeltre of Urbino, Popes Eugene IV and Nicholas V, the Este, and Matthias Corvinus, King of Hungary. On his retirement, B. composed *Vite di Uomini Illustri del secolo XV (Lives of Illustrious Men)*, vivid descriptions of his Renaissance contemporaries. BIBLIOGRAPHY: G. Toffanin, EncCatt 2:1679–80.

[M. H. BEIRNE]

BISTRE, brown watercolor pigment made from burned wood, used in the 17th cent. as a wash. Most of Rembrandt's drawings are in bistre.

BISTRITA, the name of two abbeys in Romania: (1) founded in 1420 by Prince Alexander the Good and rebuilt in 1554 by Venetian architects and painters. Within its small chapel, 16th-cent. frescoes are still visible. (2) An abbey of Serbo-Byzantine style restored in 1600. Its church, already in ruins, was razed and rebuilt by German architects in 1856. BIBLIOGRAPHY: *Enciclopedia româniei* (4 v., 1936–43) 2:305–306, 506.

[S. A. HEENEY]

BISTROPHA, in *Gregorian chant notation, a neum consisting of two *apostrophae* together on the same pitch, indicating a repeated note.

[A. DOHERTY]

BITRASHÎL (*bitrashîn*), Arabic term, derived from Greek *epitrachilion*, used by Copts, Maronites, and Arabic-speaking Byzantines for their respective forms of the sacerdotal stole, and by W Syrians for the episcopal *ûrōrō rabbō*.

[A. CODY]

BITTI, BERNARDO (1548–1610), Jesuit missionary painter working in Lima (1568), Cuzco, and La Paz, doing most of his painting at Juli where the Jesuits worked among the Aymara Indians. B. painted with tempera in a delicate, Italian mannerist style of fine line and cool colors and influenced the Quito School through the Dominican painter Pedro *Bedón. B.'s works can be seen today in many churches of South America. BIBLIOGRAPHY: J. de Mesa and T. Gisbert, *Bernardo Bitti* (1961); M. S. Soria, *La pintura del siglo XVI en Sudamérica* (1956).

[M. J. DALY]

BIVIRGA, in *Gregorian chant notation, a neum consisting of two *virgae* together on the same pitch, indicating a held or repeated note.

[A. DOHERTY]

BLACHERNIOTISSA MADONNA, the image of the Virgin Mary, frontal and in *orans* posture, first used in the apse mosaic in the Byzantine Church of the Blachernae, Constantinople, showing medallion portrait of Christ Emmanuel on the Virgin's breast. The image is most frequently encountered in Byzantine and Russian art.

[M. J. DALY]

BLACK, WILLIAM (1760–1834), a native of England who moved with his family to Nova Scotia (1775) and became a Methodist (1779). As a lay preacher he worked throughout Nova Scotia and founded the Wesleyan Methodist Church there. After being ordained deacon and elder (1789) he was appointed superintendent of the Wesleyan Missions in British North America. By 1791 he was successfully recruiting lay preachers from England. BIBLIOGRAPHY: J. E. Sanderson, *First Century of Methodism in Canada* (1908).

BLACK CANONS (CANONS REGULAR), congregations of men, following the Rule and spirit of St. Augustine. Of ancient origin, they seem to have been introduced into North Africa by Augustine. There were Austin Canons in Ireland in early days as well as in England from the time of St. Augustine of Canterbury. A celebrated branch is known as the Norbertines or Premonstratensians. The primary congregation is that of St. John Lateran in Rome.

[J. R. AHERNE]

BLACK CARDINALS, a name given to several cardinals punished by Napoleon I following his marriage to Marie Louise of Austria. Cardinal Ercole Consalvi (1757–1824), a leading figure in the negotiations between France and the papacy culminating in the Concordat of 1801, refused to participate in the religious and civil marriage ceremonies of Napoleon and Marie Louise in 1810. Since Pius VII had not ruled on the validity of Napoleon's earlier marriage to Josephine Beauharnais, Consalvi, with 12 other cardinals, in deference to the Pope, resolved not to attend the ceremonies. Furious at the slight, Napoleon at first ordered them executed, but soon relented. Several months later, in January 1811, they were deprived of their property, ordered to wear black garments, and banished from Paris to remote areas of France. Consalvi was ordered to Reims where he wrote his memoirs. The period of banishment lasted 3 years. BIBLIOGRAPHY: J. Crétineau-Joly, *Mémoires du cardinal Consalvi* (2 v., 1866); E. L. Fisher, *Cardinal Consalvi* (1899); Fliche-Martin 20:161–241.

[D. R. PENN]

BLACK CHRISTIANITY, a mid-20th-cent. movement among black Christians, esp. those in predominantly white Churches of the U.S., to develop a form of Christianity expressive of black thought and responsive to the special needs of the black community. It has developed as a conscious reaction to patterns of life in white Churches that are considered racist and harmful to Negro life. In some ways, black Christianity has existed since the days of slavery, when Negro preachers often addressed congregations of converted slaves in a distinctive style of oratory and the congregations sang spirituals. Following the Civil War, Negroes generally separated from white congregations to form their own churches, which were organized into separate denominations, mostly Baptist and Methodist. Those denominations have continued to exist, under black leadership and often related to schools and other institutions. The predominantly white RC and Protestant Churches have had some Negro membership, and, with growing emphasis on integration, the number of blacks has increased. Negroes in integrated denominations increasingly have felt, however, that whites have structured church institutions and developed theological teaching in ways that have maintained white dominance and black subordination. Negro churchmen, furthermore, have participated in the growing emphasis on black self-consciousness in the Negro community and the increasing determination to protest all-white domination or inferences of white superiority. As a part of this black self-consciousness, some Negroes have come to speak of a black Christ, black theology, and black ethics. They refer to Jesus as a "revolutionary black leader" and condemn white Churches for trying to make him white. The proponents of black Christianity charge that white Christians have perverted the Christian message of brotherhood, and that white Churches therefore do not represent true Christianity. Consequently, not only must black Christianity speak to the special needs and experiences of the Negro community, but it also has a mission to renew the white Churches. Black caucuses have been organized in Protestant and RC Churches to promote such goals.

Black Christianity is in some ways akin to what happened throughout history in all cultures as Christianity became indigenous. It portrays Jesus and his mother as black, just as artists in many countries and centuries have drawn biblical characters to resemble people of their own community. Black Christianity in the U.S. follows this pattern, but with more assertiveness and self-conscious opposition to the pattern of the dominant elements of American Churches. Major features of black Christianity have been its positive evaluation of the distinctive features of the Negro Churches and its assertion that traditional white standards in homiletics, music, liturgy, and other elements of church life cannot be used to judge Negro Christians. As in the Negro community at large, some advocates of black Christianity favor withdrawal from the white community into all-black institutions, whereas others favor integration and a struggle for greater black influence within the predominantly white Churches. Some favor temporary separation to build Negro strength so that integration can be accomplished on a more equal basis in the future. Participants generally feel that the movement is essential if the Church is to be of service to the black community in its current efforts to change the structures of American society, and they identify strongly with what is called the black revolution.. They see a need for increasing the Negro's pride in his distinctive appearance, way of life, African ancestry, and inherent worth. Apart from such a movement, they feel, blacks will abandon the Church as irrelevant.

Black Christianity has been strongly ecumenical, emphasizing the common interests of Negro members of all Churches. The National Committee of Black Churchmen (originally named "of Negro Churchmen") was organized in 1967 to promote the movement. Critics point out the danger of perverting the biblical message by interpreting it so largely in the light of the interests of one ethnic group. But there has been general recognition that the failure of white Churches to give full acceptance to Negro Christians has made necessary some movement for change.

Some black Catholics have called for a black rite, but this has not been granted, though in many places aspects of black culture have been incorporated into Catholic worship. James Cone, a Methodist teaching at Union Theological Seminary in New York, has become particularly prominent as an exponent of black theology, finding the essence of the gospel in the liberation of the oppressed and on that basis relating Christianity to the political liberation of black people. Developments in black Christianity of the U.S. and Africa have influenced each other, and with the growing political independence of Africa and increasing self-government of African Churches, some African Christians have made a more favorable assessment of the continent's pre-Christian religious heritage. BIBLIOGRAPHY: J. Cone, *Black Theology and Black Power* (1969); *Black Experience in Religion* (ed. C. E. Lincoln, 1974).

[T. EARLY]

BLACK CLERGY, Russian monastic or unmarried clergy, who wore black robes and on their heads a klobuk with a long black veil. *WHITE CLERGY.

[F. WILCOCK]

BLACK DEATH, a term applied to the second greatest epidemic (1346–50) in recorded history. It was a bubonic plague caused by the germ *Pasteurella pestis*. Accompanied by pneumonic outbreaks, it was characterized by swollen lymph nodes or buboes and usually caused spots of blackened blood under the skin. It was probably brought to Europe from China on ships by infected rats from which fleas transmitted the disease to human beings. It raged in Sicily in 1346 and by 1348 had reached France, Spain, England, and Germany. Contemporary records attribute to it the destruction of from 35 to 65% of the urban, and somewhat less of the rural, population. There were later outbreaks through 1383. Though most contemporary accounts of the plague were exaggerated, it was unquestionably a contributing factor to depopulation, economic depression, a prevalent mood of pessimism, and social unrest (cf. the French and English Peasant Revolts) in Europe in the late 14th century. It also contributed to a widespread decline in the sphere of religion during that period. BIBLIOGRAPHY: D. Cohen, *Black Death* (1974); A. M. Campbell, *Black Death and Men of Learning* (1973).

[M. H. BEIRNE]

BLACK FAST, a strict fast, formerly observed on certain days in some religious communities, or undertaken voluntarily as an act of penance. In some cases the one who observes the fast permits himself, or is permitted, only the use of bread and water; in other cases it involves foregoing wine, flesh meat, fish, eggs, cheese, milk, and butter. One rarely hears of the observance of this fast in modern times.

[P. K. MEAGHER]

BLACK FRIARS, see BLACKFRIARS.

BLACK LEGEND, designation by Spanish apologists for assertions that Spanish treatment of American Indians was cruel and oppressive. The attacks were made notably by the Spanish Dominican missionary B. de *Las Casas (1474–1566) and the Englishman T. Gage (1602–56). BIBLIOGRAPHY: L. Hanke, *Bartolome de Las Casas* (1951).

[T. EARLY]

BLACK MADONNA, the name given popularly to certain dark representations of Mary, Mother of God, esp. honored for their role in intercession; of two types, the first are statuary of black or dark substances—stone, wood, or pigmented metal—and painted images on canvas or other flat surfaces; the other, the more obvious, depict Mary as relevant to the Negro. Perhaps the earliest representation of Mary is that found in the Catacomb of St. Priscilla (*c.*175) scratched in stone and dark from age (see P. D'Elia, "*La prima diffusione nel mondo della immagine de Maria Salus Popali Romani,*" *Fede e Arte* II [1954] 301–311).

At Chartres, claimed to be the oldest Marian shrine in Christendom, in the cathedral crypt is Our Lady Underground, both Mother and Child of shining black, placed there by the earliest of Gallic evangelists at the spot where they found an altar erected by the Druids to *Virgo Partitura* (the virgin who would conceive). More easy of access, in the cathedral above is another, Our Lady of the Pillar, which was burned in the Revolution and not until 1857 replaced by another, with black face and golden hair. No longer in Paris is *La Vièrge Noire* of St.-Étienne-du-Grès; with the church it had disappeared, but the travels of the statue have been traced to the Chapelle de la Rue de Sèvres with the Sisters of St. Thomas of Villanova. It later accompanied them to Neuilly-sur-Seine. In the SW of France also, in the Cathedral of Le Puy with its African decor, is the Madonna "of irresistible charm." The original was destroyed but replaced by an Islamic image made of cedar from Lebanon, given by Louis IX, a gift to him in 1284 from the Sultan; this again suffered vandalism and was replaced by the present one. The Spanish name her who is honored at Montserrat *La Morenata* (the little black one; 9th cent.). Since 1382 the Black Madonna of Częstochowa, Poland, has been revered. It is also known to Americans through the dark, painted Our Lady of Czestochowa near Doylestown, Pennsylvania. The Black Madonna at the Abbey of Einsiedeln (*c.* 1400) and another at Vilna near Schwyz welcome pilgrims to Switzerland. Of special interest is the dark, cedarwood statue (before 1291) in the Santa Casa at Loreto, Italy, which John XXIII visited in prayer for the success of Vatican Council II just prior to its convening. The original statue, destroyed in an accident in 1921, was replaced by Pius XI with one carved from a cedar from the Vatican Gardens.

With the evangelization of Africa, awareness of local and racial needs has grown and the doctrine of the unity of the mystical body more deeply appreciated, as depicted in native art. Mary with negroid features and of ebony hue, in accord with the findings of missiology, is one with the African race. BIBLIOGRAPHY: H. Gillet, *Sanctuaries of Our Lady* (2 v., 1949, 1952); D. M. Madden, *Religious Guide to Europe* (1975); C. Balić et al., BiblSanct 8:814–962; J. Duhr, "*Le Visage de Marie à travers les siècles de l'art chrétien,*" NRT 68 (1946) 282–304.

[M. R. BROWN]

BLACK MARKET, the buying and selling of goods at prices higher (or sometimes lower) than those permitted by civil law. Sometimes the fixing of prices by civil law may be necessary for the economic security or stability of some country or area, and the defiance of these laws would involve an offense against the common good on the part of the seller at least. But even the buyer, encouraging the marketeer by his patronage, could, except in cases of grave need, be morally culpable. It may happen, however, that such economic disorder may exist in an area that the fixed prices are unenforceable and the laws unreasonable. In such a case resort to the black market could be excused on grounds of necessity.

[P. K. MEAGHER]

BLACK MASS, a term used in two senses: (1) a popular term for the *Requiem Mass, used because of the liturgical color for the rite. (2) a pseudo-Mass celebrated in honor of the devil. It is also known as the Satanic mass, since it expresses a worship of Satan. Various elements of the Mass are parodied in the attempt to express a religious attitude opposite to that of the Church. A validly consecrated host is sometimes obtained and desecrated in the rite, and apostate priests are sometimes employed. Some interpreters see it as an underground expression of pre-Christian paganism, seeking in this way to oppose the Christian faith that has conquered the old gods. BIBLIOGRAPHY: A. S. LaVey *Satanic Rituals* (1972).

[T. EARLY]

BLACK MONKS, a name sometimes applied to the Benedictines because of their totally black habit. The designation originated in the Middle Ages and was used in contrast to the White Monks or Cistercians.

[T. M. MCFADDEN]

BLACK MUSLIMS, a movement that stresses black economic and political power, black culture, and black unity as Mohammed appealed strongly for black men to be united. In black communities, the movement has exhibited a taste for publicity. Founded in Detroit (1930) by a man of obscure background known variously as W. D. Fard, Wali Farrad, and Farrad Mohammed, who began to preach to the black community that Islam and not Christianity, was the true religion for black people. He became known as "the Prophet" and founded organizations for the training of his disciples. In 1934 Fard disappeared, and Elijah

Mohammed (Elijah Poole) became the leader of the Muslims. He moved the temple to Chicago which is now the center. Under Mohammed, the movement grew and gained basic political and theological standing while advocating an extremist approach to black power and an unorthodox form of Islam. A new leader arose within the movement, Malcolm X (Malcolm Little) who, in urging a moderate approach to the religious and political goals of the Black Muslims, became a focal point of passionate dissension and was assassinated in Chicago in 1965. Leadership has passed to Walter D. Mohammed, son of Elijah, who seems to be moving closer to orthodox Islam while peaceably strengthening his father's socioeconomic aims for the movement. Black Muslims are noted for their strict discipline, an emphasis on family unity and personal morality, and a conservative style of dress. BIBLIOGRAPHY: M. Little, *Autobiography of Malcolm X* (pa. 1973); R. Golston, *Negro Revolution* (1969).

[C. CARROLL]

BLACK POPE, a term sometimes applied to the general of the Society of Jesus (Jesuits). "Black" is in allusion to the color of his dress, and "pope" refers to a high degree of power, both over his order and by virtue of the order's strength, within the Church as a whole.

[T. EARLY]

BLACK RUBRIC, a name used since the 19th cent. for a "Declaration on Kneeling" in the *Book of Common Prayer (BCP) of the Church of England. Inserted without authorization into the 1552 BCP, it stated that kneeling for holy communion did not imply any "real or essential presence of Christ's natural body and blood" in the Holy Eucharist. Dropped from the 1559 BCP of Elizabeth I, the declaration was resumed in the 1662 revision with the significant alteration of "real and essential" to "corporal presence." The declaration was printed not in red but in black to indicate that it was not properly a rubric but an explanation. The convention is not retained in current two-colored editions of the BCP. The Black Rubric has never appeared in the *American Prayer Book. (See bibliog. for Book of Common Prayer.)

[T. C. O'BRIEN]

BLACKÈRE, GILLES LE, Flemish sculptor of alabaster (fl. Bruges 1450?), who carved sepulchral portrait of Michelle de France, daughter of Charles VI, with four mourners in typical Burgundian style. Sixteen additional mourners were added by Tiedeman Maes (1442–43).

[M. J. DALY]

BLACKFRIARS, written either as one or two words, a name given to Dominicans in late medieval times in England. In the plural the term was also used for a convent in which they lived, or for the district in which such a convent stood. Dominicans were so called, in spite of their white habits, because of the black cloaks (cappas) they wear at some choral services and when they are outside their convents.

[J. C. WILLKE]

BLACKLOE, THOMAS, see WHITE, THOMAS.

BLACKMAN, JOHN (*c.*1407–85), biographer, fellow of Merton College, Oxford, and later of Eton and King's College, Cambridge. B. served Henry VI, of whom he wrote a memoir. In 1457 he retired to the Charterhouse at Witham, and is said to have become a Carthusian. BIBLIOGRAPHY: Emden Camb 670–671.

[T. GILBY]

BLACKWELL, GEORGE (*c.*1545–1613), first archpriest of England. He was educated at Oxford, ordained at Douai, and served on the English mission (1576–98). The lack of leadership after Card. Allen's death led Pope Clement VIII in 1598 to appoint B. archpriest over the English secular clergy. His tenure was troubled by insubordination from a minority of seculars, resentment against Jesuit influence, and controversy over the legitimacy of the oath of civil allegiance. The dissenters twice appealed to Rome, and B. was three times confirmed in his office, although after 1602 his powers were reduced and the Jesuit alliance ended. After B. took the oath of allegiance, which was twice condemned by the Pope, he was deposed (1608). BIBLIOGRAPHY: T. Cooper, DNB 2:606–608; Gillow BDEC 1:225–231.

[H. JACK]

BLAINE AMENDMENT, or more precisely, Art. II, sec. 3 of the New York State Constitution of 1894, which declares that "neither the state nor any subdivision thereof shall use its property or credit for any school or institution of learning wholly or in part under control of any religious denomination." It owes its name to Congressman James Gillespie Blaine of Maine who in 1875 had unsuccessfully attempted to have a similar amendment incorporated into the Federal Constitution. Blaine's proposal was revived and adopted during the New York State 1894 Constitutional Convention. It had been supported by the Know-Nothings and others who were overtly antagonistic to Catholics, Jews, and Negroes, and who held that any aid to denominational schools was a violation of the principle of separation of Church and State, according to the Constitution: "Congress shall make no laws concerning the establishment of religion. . . ." The repeal of the Blaine Amendment was favored by 76% of the delegates at the 1967 Constitutional Convention, but was rejected at the polls, and the amendment remains a part of the N.Y. State Constitution. BIBLIOGRAPHY: A. P. Stokes, *Church and State in the United States* (3 v., 1950)

[M. B. MURPHY]

BLAIR, JAMES (1655–1743), first commissary for the C of E in Virginia; founding president of William and Mary College. B.was a Scotsman and an Anglican priest who went (1685) as rector to Henrico Co. in the Virginia colony at the request of Bp. Compton of London. Four years later he was appointed commissary for Virginia, i.e., Compton's delegate over the Church for all nonepiscopal functions. The office was designed to reform the deplorable condition of the colonial Church, esp. the standard of living, discipline, and training of the clergy. Through B.'s able efforts a measure of success was achieved, and most of the vacant parishes were supplied with rectors. William and Mary College was chartered in 1693. BIBLIOGRAPHY: Olmstead 51–52.

[M. A. GARDNER]

BLAISE OF SEBASTE, ST. (Lat. Blasius; d. *c*.316), Armenian bp., martyr. Legend credits B. with curing the beasts of the forest while he was in hiding in the time of persecution. The custom of blessing throats on his feast day comes from the story that he once miraculously cured a child choking on a fishbone. B. is one of the *Fourteen Holy Helpers, and is invoked against ills of the throat and for sick animals. BIBLIOGRAPHY: Butler 1:239; R. Janin, DHGE 9:60

[R. B. ENO]

BLAKE, WILLIAM (1757–1827), English genius of uniquely personal and original vision.

Poet. All his life B. was a visionary, interpreting experience as material manifestation of spiritual reality. Swedenborg and Boehme taught him that material things are in a fallen state and will return to divine unity. In poetry he was influenced by the Bible, Spenser, Chatterton, Macpherson, and nursery tales and verse. *Poetical Sketches* (1783), *Songs of Innocence* (1789), *Songs of Experience* (1794) were followed by the prophetic books begun *c*.1797, baffling and obscure in symbolism. In politics he favored the French Revolution. He opposed always matter, reason, and law; and exalted spirit, imagination, and satisfaction of desire as necessary for regeneration.

Painter and Engraver. Drawing at 10, apprenticed to an engraver at 14, B. studied Gothic monuments in Westminster Abbey, admired the fantastic forms of Fuseli and J. Barry, but opposed Reynolds' theory of "beauty from nature," holding that ideal forms are compounded of imagination. B.'s Michelangelesque figures, visionary and fantastic, are mannered in line, creating dynamically rhythmic contours and elaborate patterns. He began to illustrate his own and others' books, developing an original printing technique of relief-etching which superimposed text over illustration and could then be colored by hand if he chose. Copies are valued not only for their rarity (often less than 20 per plate) but also for their intensity of mood and symbolic imagery. B.'s illustrations of Milton and Dante were executed in watercolor for himself or private patrons—of whom

John Linnell was responsible for B.'s greatest achievement, *The Book of Job* (1825). Books by B. are in public and private collections in England and in the U.S. BIBLIOGRAPHY: A. Gilchrist, *Life of William Blake* (1942, repr. 1973); H. Bloom, *Blake's Apocalypse* (1963, pa. 1970); T. J. Altizer, *New Apocalypse: The Radical Christian Vision of William Blake* (1967); A. Blunt, *Art of William Blake* (1959, pa. 1974).

[M. M. BARRY; M. J. DALY]

BLANC, ANTHONY (1792–1860), first abp of New Orleans. He was ordained in France by Bp. Dubourg of La. and came to the U.S. in 1817. He labored in La. as a parish priest, vicar-general, administrator of the diocese, and in 1850 was appointed archbishop. As bp. he established parishes for Creole, Irish, German, and English-speaking Catholics. His jurisdiction extended to both La. and Miss. Some of his most serious problems were lay trusteeism, Know-Nothingism, the difficulty of secession by the South, and the challenge of a bishop's right to appoint pastors. During his bishopric, the number of churches increased from 26 to 73, of priests from 27 to 92, and New Orleans became an archdiocese. Until his death he labored actively among the people of his diocese.

[J. HILL]

BLANCHARD, JACQUES (1600–38), French painter who revitalized the Fontainebleau mannerist style through a synthesis of Italian decorative and Northern realistic modes in a new "Venetian" idiom. Though called the "French Titian," B. derived his style rather from Veronese. He earned a reputation as decorator through his series from Ovid, *The 12 Months* (1630). B. painted religious works and many other commissions in his distinctive, delicate colors and produced about 70 engravings. BIBLIOGRAPHY: A. Blunt, *Art and Architecture in France, 1500–1700* (1954).

[M. J. DALY]

BLANCHE OF CASTILE (1188–1252), Queen of France, mother of St. Louis IX. B. was the daughter of Alfonso IX, King of Castile, and Eleanor, daughter of Henry I of England, and the wife of Louis VIII, by whom she had 12 children. When Louis died in 1226 Blanche became regent for her son Louis, and was the dominant political figure in France until 1235 when Louis achieved his majority. She served again as regent during Louis' First Crusade (1248–50). BIBLIOGRAPHY: M. Brion, *Blanche de Castille* (1939); N. Del Re, BiblSanct 3:173–174.

[V. L. BULLOUGH]

BLANCHET, FRANCIS NORBERT (1795–1883), missioner, first abp. in the Oregon country. B. belonged to a Canadian family from which came a number of leaders prominent in Church and State. Ordained in Quebec (1819), he worked among Acadians and Indians in New Brunswick. In 1838 Bp. Signay appointed him vicar general for the Oregon country. He was welcomed by Indians and whites when he arrived at Vancouver, western headquarters of Hudson's Bay Company. With the help of Pierre de Smet, and Modeste Demers, a Quebec missionary, he set up plans for the ecclesiastical organization of Oregon country. He was consecrated first bp. (1845) and went to Europe to obtain money and missionaries. He also appealed to the Congregation for the Propagation of the Faith to subdivide his vicariate into provinces in Walla Walla, Wash., Oregon City, and Vancouver Island. He returned to the U.S. with 21 missionaries. His territory was plagued with Indian massacres and the hatred of Indians by white men; the discovery of gold caused many to leave Oregon and go to California. He had to struggle to meet the debts of his diocese by collecting funds in South America and Canada. He also recruited priests and nuns to staff his missions. This contributed to the continuous growth of the diocese. B. attended the First (1852) and Second (1866) Plenary Councils of Baltimore, and Vatican Council I. He is author of *Historical Sketches of the Catholic Church in Oregon*.

[J. HILL]

BLANDINA, ST. (d. 177), martyr. B., a slave, was among the Christians seized at Lyons in the persecution under Marcus Aurelius. Her mistress, a leading figure among the captives, feared that B. had not the bodily strength to confess her faith boldly, but the event proved her wrong. B. amazed her torturers with her endurance, and, outlasting many of her fellow sufferers, she died only after being cruelly torn and broken in body. BIBLIOGRAPHY: Butler 2:254–258. *LYONS AND VIENNE, MARTYRS OF.

[P. K. MEAGHER]

BLANDRATA, GIORGIO (Biandrata; 1515–c.1590), Italian Unitarian. Because of anti-trinitarian views, B., a physician, had to flee from the Inquisition in Italy in 1556. In Geneva he came into conflict with Calvin over the Trinity, and went to Poland. There he became a leader in the Minor Church. As court physician in Transylvania, he won over Franz *Dávid to Unitarianism. He was a friend and correspondent of Faustus Sozzini (see SOCINUS). BIBLIOGRAPHY: E. M. Wilbur, *History of Unitarianism* (2v., repr., 1965). *SOCINIANISM.

[T. C. O'BRIEN]

BLANLO, JEAN (1617–57), French Sulpician, disciple of M. Olier. His posthumous work on Christian imitation of the infancy of Jesus, *L'Enfance chrétienne* (1665), has been reprinted even in the 20th century. Out of humility B. did not advance in holy orders beyond the subdiaconate. BIBLIOGRAPHY: E. LeVesque, DSAM 1:1722–23.

[T. C. O'BRIEN]

BLANQUI (BIANCHI), ANDRÉS (1677–1740), architect who, with fellow Jesuit, Juan B. Primoli, engaged in construction of the cathedrals of Buenos Aires and Córdoba. In convents and churches as well as in the historic *cabildo* of the capital of Argentina, B. evidenced a style eminently functional with discreet ornamentation. BIBLIOGRAPHY: G. Furlong, *Arquitectos argentinos durante la dominación hispánica* (1946).

[M. J. DALY]

BLARER, a family conspicuous for its part in the Counter Reformation. (1) Ludwig (c.1480–1544), a monk at St. Gall, who became administrator of the abbey at Einsiedeln in 1528, and abbot in 1534. Clement VII granted him the right to confirm and to consecrate churches. (2) Ambrosius (1492–1564), a Benedictine monk who was influenced by Melanchthon and Luther, left the monastery in 1522 and undertook to spread the Protestant reform. He was active in Constance, Württemberg, and parts of Switzerland. (3) Gerwig (1495–1567), abbot of Weingarten (1520) and of Ochsenhausen (1527), an active promoter of the Counter Reformation in Swabia. (4) Thomas (c.1492–1567), a humanist who became a follower of Luther. He was mayor of Constance (1537–47) and a member of the Reichstag. He was active in discussions among the Reformers aimed at reaching an agreement on the Eucharist. (5) Diethelm (1503–64), abbot of Sankt Gallen (1530), who persuaded the civil authorities to restore the abbey. Both there and at Mehrerau, he stimulated a renewal of the spiritual life. He also promoted the reform of the secular clergy and restored religious life for women in Switzerland. (6) Jacob Christoph (1542–1603), bp. of Basel (1575), where he worked to implement the decrees of the Council of Trent. He established a seminary, brought the Jesuits to Prunktrut to open a college, called a synod, united the Catholic cantons in a common effort to evangelize without the use of force, and made regular visitations of his diocese. BIBLIOGRAPHY: P. Polman et al., DHGE 9:148–153.

[H. JACK]

BLASIMON, SAINT-MAURICE, small 12th-cent. French Romanesque church (1150?), aisleless and with a flat *chevet*. Its west portal boasts the most important 12th-cent. sculpture in the Gironde, showing six ranks of angels and virtues, and a vigorous hunting scene interspersed with floral motifs. BIBLIOGRAPHY: F. Salet. "Blasimon," *Congrès archéologique de France* (1939, 1941).

[M. J. DALY]

BLASPHEMY, speech or action that is derogatory to God. It includes words, gestures, and actions directed particularly to the name, work, or being of God. In RC canon law it is called a sin against religion (CIC c. 2323), though it is sometimes defined as a sin against faith or in other terms. It has traditionally been regarded as an esp. serious sin. In the Mosaic law it was a capital offense: "He who blasphemes the name of the Lord shall be put to death; all the congregation shall stone him" (Lev 24.16a). To claim the status or power of God is considered blasphemy, and Jesus was accused of blasphemy for claiming to be the Son of God: "And the high priest tore his mantle, and said, 'Why do we still need witnesses? You have heard his blasphemy. What is your decision?' And they all condemned him as deserving death" (Mk 14.63–64). Stephen was stoned on a charge of blasphemy (Acts 6.11). Jesus said blasphemy against the Holy Spirit was the one sin that would not be forgiven (Mk 4.28–30).

The Code of *Justinian (6th cent.) made blasphemy a capital offense, and it remained so in much of Europe till the modern period. Since the *Enlightenment, secular authorities have come to regard it less severely. They have not generally considered criminal punishment appropriate for an offense against God, and its offensiveness to other people has come to appear less serious. Increasing respect for freedom of religion and of speech has also lessened the inclination to make blasphemy the subject for legal action. BIBLIOGRAPHY: B. Häring, *Law of Christ* (tr. E. G. Kaiser, 1961) 1:205–207; EDB 251–253.

[T. EARLY]

BLASSEL, NICOLAS, THE YOUNGER (1600–59), best known of his family, B. was a most famous sculptor of Amiens of his day, executing many tombs in the Amiens Cathedral and an altar for Notre-Dame-du-Puy.

[M. J. DALY]

BLASTARES, MATTHEW, Byzantine canonist of the 14th cent., monk of Mt. Athos and later of the monastery of St. Isaac in Thessalonica. There he composed (1335) his principal work, the so-called *Syntagma*, a juridical manual containing a prologue on the orthodox faith and 24 sections, following the 24 letters of the Greek alphabet. Each ch. contains a study of the sources, a summary of the legal texts followed by his commentaries, which rely on those of Zonaras and Balsamon. BIBLIOGRAPHY: E. Herman, DDC 6:920–925.

[E. EL-HAYEK]

BLASTUS, 2d-cent. Roman presbyter and schismatic, whom historians list as either a Marcionite, a Montanist, or a "Quartodeciman," the latter probably being the most accurate. According to a pseudo-Tertullian account, B. was considered a sly partisan of Judaism, who supported the idea that the feast of Easter should be celebrated on the 14th day of the month of Nisan, in keeping with the law of Moses. It was during the pontificate of St. Victor (188–189) when the Pope ordered all bps. of the Church to celebrate the feast of Easter on Sunday, that B. decided to separate from the Church. BIBLIOGRAPHY: G. Bardy, DHGE 9:162–163; H. Rahner, LTK 2:526.

[R. A. TODD]

BLASUCCI, DOMENICO, VEN. (1732–1752), clerical student. Born in Italy, B. was received into the Redemptorists by Alphonsus Liguori in 1750, was professed in 1751, and died in 1752. His perfection knew no limits concerning observance of the vows and virtues and in devotion to the Blessed Sacrament and the Blessed Virgin. BIBLIOGRAPHY: O. Gregorio, EncCatt 2:1717–18.

[H. JACK]

BLAUBEUREN, ABBEY OF, former Benedictine abbey in Württemberg, Germany, founded *c*.1085 by the counts of Tübingen. Until 1348 it was a double monastery. The reform of Melk was adopted in 1451 and the monastery flourished to the end of the Middle Ages. In 1535 it came under Protestant control and in 1556 was converted into a school. Since 1818 it has been a Protestant theological seminary. BIBLIOGRAPHY: E. Gonner, LTK 2:527.

[N. BACKMUND]

BLAUE REITER, DER (The Blue Rider), a group of early 20th-cent. Expressionist painters in Munich, Germany, named from a painting of W. *Kandinsky whose statement *Concerning the Spiritual in Art* (1910) was followed by a secession of artists (1911) from the Munich NKV (*Neue Künstler Vereinigung*, New Artist Association). Associated with Kandinsky were Franz *Marc, August *Macke, A. V. *Jawlensky, and Paul Klee. Their work, emphasizing bold, vivid color and simplified forms, contained a contemplative spiritual aspect, distinct from the determined primitivism of other Expressionist groups. BIBLIOGRAPHY: B. S. Myers, *German Expressionists* (1957). *BRÜCKE, DIE.

[T. FEIDT]

BLAURER, see BLARER.

BLAUROCK, GEORG (Görg; fl. 16th cent.), Swiss Anabaptist, former monk, and for a time a follower of *Zwingli at Zurich. He joined with C. *Grebel and others, however, to form the Swiss Brethren. In token of their insistence upon a free and inner belief, he had Grebel rebaptize him; then he did the same for the rest of those present at a meeting of the brethren in Jan. 1525. B. was a powerful preacher and a leader of the Anabaptists in Switzerland and southern Germany after Grebel's early death. BIBLIOGRAPHY: R. M. Jones, *Studies in Mystical Religion* (1923) 374, 378; bibliog. for Anabaptists.

[T. C. O'BRIEN]

BLAVATSKY, HELENA PETROVNA (1831–91), founder of modern *theosophy B. was born in Russia of a German family named Hahn. She married (1848) the elderly Gen. N. P. Blavatsky, but they soon separated. She traveled widely, spending, she claimed, several years in Tibet, where she received the occult tradition. H. P. B. (as theosophists call her) and H. S. Olcott founded the Theosophical Society (1875) in New York City. In *Isis Unveiled* (1877) and *The Secret Doctrine* (1888), B. asserted she had brought together and restated for the West some of the ancient teachings that had appeared through the centuries at different times and places. B. and Olcott went to India (1879), where they reorganized the Theosophical Society, with headquarters in Adyar. She gained a large following, among others, Annie *Besant. While theosophists revere her, honoring her death date (May 8) as White Lotus Day, others have looked on many of her claims as fraudulent. B.'s written works are quite extensive. BIBLIOGRAPHY: A. L. Cleather, *Helena Petrovna Blavatsky* (1922); J. Symonds, *Madame Blavatsky* (1959).

[E. E. BEAUREGARD]

BLENKINSOP. An Irish-American family that made contributions to the development of the Church in the U.S. (1) Peter came to America in 1826 and settled in Baltimore. He opened a publishing house and in 1830 he issued the *Metropolitan,* the first Catholic monthly in the United States. His three children, Peter J., William A., and Catherine entered religious life. (2) Peter J. (1818–96), educator. He entered the Jesuits at Frederick, Md. (1834) and taught at Georgetown University. After ordination he went to Holy Cross College, Mass. where he served as teacher, treasurer, and in 1854, as president. He did missionary work in New England and from 1882 until his death was stationed at the Church of the Gesu, Philadelphia. (3) William A. (1819–92), a missionary, was ordained (1843) for the Diocese of Natchez, Miss. and served there for 7 years. After that, he continued his missionary activities in Boston where, despite the problems of Know-Nothingism, he tried to create an ecumenical spirit between Catholics and Protestants. In 1864 he was appointed pastor of SS. Peter and Paul in South Boston. (4) Catherine (1816–87), educator; entered the Daughters of Charity of Emmitsburg (1831) and took the name of Euphemia. She labored in schools of New York and Baltimore. Appointed assistant at the motherhouse in Emmitsburg in 1855, she directed the houses of her community in the Southern states during the Civil War. In 1866, she became superior of the Daughters of Charity in the U.S. and opened schools and charitable institutions in many cities.

[J. HILL]

BLESILA, ST. (363–383), widow. The eldest daughter of St. Paula and sister of Eustochium, B. was a young bride of 7 months when her husband died. Skilled in languages, she spoke Greek fluently and had a practical knowledge of Hebrew. She was urged to become a recluse by St. Jerome, whom she influenced and encouraged to begin a translation of Holy Scripture. B. led a holy and austere life and died at Rome in her early youth. BIBLIOGRAPHY: G. B. Proja, BiblSanct 3:207–208; Butler 1:144.

[R. A. TODD]

BLESSED, the title of a servant of God to whom public cult is rendered in a particular place or in a religious order or congregation, but only exceptionally in the universal Church. This public cult, growing up spontaneously among the people, was in earlier times confirmed by local bishops; abuses, however, forced the Holy See to intervene, and Alexander III in 1181 demanded previous papal sanction. But bishops continued to permit public cult, and so the difference was soon established between episcopal processes (concerned with the title blessed) and papal processes (concerned with the title saint). In 1634 Urban VIII reserved to the pope the authorization of public cult for both blessed and saints. The process of beatification is first undertaken by the local ordinary (writings, reputation of sanctity, and absence of public cult are examined) and then by the Congregation for the Causes of Saints which, after minute scrutiny, issues the decree of heroicity of virtues or martyrdom (CIC cc. 2065–2124). Then the pope proceeds to the decree and the ceremony of beatification. Blessed is also a title given to the saints in heaven generally; it is as well the initial word of the great blessings pronounced by Our Lord (Mt 5.1–12) and referred to as the Eight Beatitudes. *CANONIZATION AND BEATIFICATION.

[A. M. BERMEJO]

BLESSED SACRAMENT, a title of the Holy Eucharist that designates the paramount position of that sacrament among the seven sacraments. It is also used frequently to designate the Real Presence of Christ in the reservation of the Holy Eucharist.

BLESSED SACRAMENT, BENEDICTION OF THE, see BENEDICTION OF THE BLESSED SACRAMENT.

BLESSED SACRAMENT, SERVANTS OF THE, a cloistered and contemplative congregation of women founded in 1858 by Pierre Julien *Eymard with the assistance of Marguerite Guillot. The mission of these religious was to be perpetual adoration of the Blessed Sacrament and the spreading of this devotion among the laity by means of assistance to poor churches and by catechetical instruction of children and uninformed adults. The congregation spread to Belgium, Canada, and in 1947 to the U.S. at Waterville, Maine. Later houses were established at Pueblo, Colorado, and Melbourne, Australia. In 1975 they conducted houses in the U.S. in the Dioceses of Portland and Pueblo.

BLESSED SACRAMENT, VISIT TO THE. After the consecration, under both species (bread and wine), Christ, in his divinity and humanity, is in RC belief really and substantially present in a sacramental manner. This presence is primarily for the sake of communion, but remains as long as the species retain their natural properties. As a sacrament thus persisting, the Eucharist is also called the

Blessed Sacrament, and is worthy of adoration. Since the 11th cent. this fact has been clearly recognized and resulted in veneration of the Blessed Sacrament. BIBLIOGRAPHY: H. Thurston, CE 15:483–484.

[C. POWERS]

BLESSED SACRAMENT CONFRATERNITY, an association of laymen established to foster public worship of the Eucharist and care for the decor of churches and altars. The name is frequently applied to the Archconfraternity of the Blessed Sacrament founded by Thomas Stella, OP, in the church of Sta. Maria sopra Minerva in Rome and approved by Paul III in 1539. This organization was endowed with many indulgences and the Pope decreed that all confraternities in existence with the same aim or name, and all those to be created in the future, would be automatically affiliated with it. This archconfraternity has enjoyed much favor in Church law. CIC c. 711.2 states that local ordinaries are to establish it in every parish. However, in 1927 the Code Commission issued a new decision regarding CIC c. 711.2, declaring that instead of the archconfraternity, a pious union or sodality of the Blessed Sacrament may be established, and such a union or sodality would not automatically be affiliated with the archconfraternity that has its headquarters at the Minerva in Rome.

A number of such pious unions of the Blessed Sacrament exist in the Church, the most widely known of which is the Confraternity of the Blessed Sacrament that has its headquarters at the church of SS. Andrew and Claude in Rome. This association was founded by St. Pierre Julien *Eymard at Marseilles in 1859. In the U.S. this union is called the People's Eucharistic League, and its national headquarters are located in New York. The similarity in purpose, organization, customs, regulations, etc., with the confraternity of the Minerva are striking, and it is on that account sometimes mistaken for the archconfraternity spoken of in the Code of Canon Law. On the other hand, in accordance with the reply of the Code Commission mentioned above, this confraternity is frequently substituted by local ordinaries for the confraternity of the Minerva. BIBLIOGRAPHY: G. Barbiero, *Le Confraternite del Santissimo Sacramento primo del 1539* (1944); H. Durand, DDC 4:128–176.

[E. R. FALARDEAU]

BLESSED SACRAMENT FATHERS AND BROTHERS, a congregation of religious priests and brothers founded at Paris, France, in 1856 by St. Pierre Julien *Eymard for promoting devotion to the Eucharist. The congregation received papal approval in 1863 by Pius IX. The Blessed Sacrament Fathers are located in predominantly large metropolitan centers and capital cities where they maintain shrines of perpetual adoration and promote devotion to the Eucharist. The priests of the society engage in priestly ministry in parishes and hospitals, conduct eucharistic devotions (especially Forty Hours), preach retreats and days of recollection stressing the Eucharist. In

mission countries the congregation pursues the same goals. In addition to priests, the congregation includes religious brothers. They share in the hours of adoration before the Blessed Sacrament and in the promotion of devotion to the Eucharist. The brothers also cooperate in the task of the congregation through the exercise of skills both professional and nonprofessional. The congregation also maintains its own seminaries and training schools. Those engaged in this work frequently teach in other institutions of learning.

The congregation promotes associations of priests and laymen which seek to orientate the devotional life of their members toward the Eucharist and the spirituality Eymard developed in his ascetical writings. In the U.S.A. these associations include the Priests' Eucharistic League, the People's Eucharistic League, and the Eucharistic Fraternity. The national office of the Nocturnal Adoration Society is also in the hands of the congregation. Publications to foster devotion to the Eucharist are edited by the society: *Emmanuel* (for priests) and *Eucharist* (for the laity) are edited by the New York house.

As a result of Vatican Council II, the goals of the congregation have been extended and updated. Promotion of the liturgy and integration of Eucharistic devotions with liturgical piety will receive greater importance. It is anticipated that work in smaller parishes and for the materially deprived will figure prominently in the congregation's future apostolate.

The American Province of the Blessed Sacrament Fathers and Brothers also includes overseas houses in Manila, Philippines; Leicester, England; and Masaka, Uganda. BIBLIOGRAPHY: F. Trochu, *Le Bienheureux Pierre-Julien Eymard* (1949); E. Nunez, *Commentaire des constitutions de la Congrégation du Très Saint Sacrement (1958).*

[E. R. FALARDEAU]

BLESSED SACRAMENT SISTERS FOR INDIANS AND COLORED PEOPLE (SBS), a congregation founded (1891) for adoration of the Blessed Sacrament and for teaching and social service among Indians and blacks, by Katharine M. *Drexel of Philadelphia at the invitation of Pope Leo XIII. The first aspirants with her made a novitiate (1889–91) at Pittsburgh with the Sisters of Mercy. At their profession Katharine was named foundress and first superior of the new community, which took up residence in the old Drexel home and established nearby at Cornwells Heights the motherhouse. Mother Katharine began a program of education, of care for orphans, of forming centers for youth, and for retreat work. With the great Drexel wealth available to her, the community established schools and convents for other religious as their own membership grew. Providing boarding facilities as well, they built and staffed elementary, secondary, and industrial schools. In 1925 they founded at New Orleans Xavier Univ., the first U.S. Catholic college or university for blacks. SBS also fostered an Indian order, the Oblate SBS, Marty, South Dakota, as well as entrance of black women into their own congregation. In 1975 they had 54 houses throughout the

U.S. BIBLIOGRAPHY: E. Dehey, *Religious Orders of Women in the U.S.* (rev. ed. 1930) 692–697; *Guide to the Catholic Sisterhoods in the U.S.* (comp. T. P. McCarthy, 1964) 15.

[M. R. BROWN]

BLESSIG, JEAN LAURENT (1747–1816), French Protestant theologian whose religious activities during the Revolution caused him to be imprisoned for 11 months. After the fall of Robespierre, he taught theology at Strasbourg and devoted himself to the reorganization of *le grand service* in the Protestant Church. He published numerous theological dissertations along with sermons and ascetical works.

[T. LIDDY]

BLESSING, originally a word or action thought to be productive of good, in contrast to a curse, which was thought to be productive of evil. The word admits of some variety of meaning even in its scriptural uses, and it is differently ascribed to God and man. (1) In the strictest sense it is only God who blesses. He is the source from which all blessings come, and a blessing is indeed nothing other than God's bestowal of his favor upon persons or things. Thus God blessed birds, fish, and men with the gift of fertility (Gen 1.22,28; 5.2); he blessed the seventh day for man's rest and enjoyment (Gen 2.3); he blessed Abraham and through him all nations (Gen 12.3; 18.18; cf. Rom ch. 4). (2) Man is said to bless when he invokes God's blessing upon himself or others. He is also said to bless God, but with an obvious difference of meaning, for to God no good is wanting. Yet even in this case something akin to a bestowal of good is possible. Man can add to God's external glory, and though he add nothing to the infinite completeness of the deity, he can express in praise, thanksgiving, worship, and service, his approval of, and the delight he takes in, the divine goodness. Man's blessing of things (e.g., his food) is in part an invocation of God's favor upon himself and others through the use of what is so blessed, but it is also a blessing of God by praising and thanking him for his gifts. Thus Jesus blessed bread and fish by praising God for them (Mt 14.19); he blessed his disciples by thanking God for them, and they in turn stay in God's holy place praising and thanking God by their own blessing (Lk 24.50–53). (3) In the OT the blessing which a man had from God was regarded as having a force that was transmissible to his son and once given was irrevocable (Gen 27.33–35). (4) Blessing sometimes means to make holy or sacred, or to dedicate to sacred use. Thus in the OT sacrifices were blessed (1 Sam 9.13), i.e., the victims were consecrated with a formula of blessing. Similarly in Christian usage a blessing may be a word or rite used to sanctify or hallow something. In this sense the word often suggests a lesser degree of formality or solemnity than consecration—thus, e.g., the blessing of a church is something less than its consecration. Any words or actions, esp. the sign of the cross, intended to sanctify or hallow a person, activity, or thing, can be referred to as a blessing. BIBLIOGRAPHY: L. DeBruyhe, EncCatt 2:1303–04; EDB 253–254. *BLESSINGS, LITURGICAL.

[P. K. MEAGHER]

BLESSING, APOSTOLIC, see APOSTOLIC BLESSING.

BLESSINGS, LITURGICAL, in present usage a term with various meanings: (1) a thankful and joyous recognition of God's working in history, e.g., the eucharistic anaphora; (2) the calling down of God's favor upon men, e.g., the blessing at the end of the Roman Rite Mass; (3) a verbal formula for the sanctification of objects, e.g., the blessing of a car. Canon law recognizes two principal types of liturgical blessings: constitutive, those which dedicate a person or object to the service of the Church, thus effecting their permanent deputation to worship; and invocatory, those which call upon God to help those in need or those who use certain blessed objects. An example of the former is the solemn consecration of an altar; of the latter, the blessing of a house. Vatican Council II in the *Constitution on the Liturgy* (79–80) asks for a revision of the present blessings. BIBLIOGRAPHY: F. McManus, *Sacramental Liturgy* (1967) 150–153.

[N. KOLLAR]

BLINDNESS, SPIRITUAL, the incapacity, due to faulty education, to prejudice, to habituation to vice of one kind or another (esp. pride), or to native dullness of mind, to grasp some spiritual truth. Like bodily blindness it may exist in varying degrees. Also it may in some cases be a selective blindness, corruptive of spiritual vision in one or some matters, but not in others. When it is concerned with discernment in matters of small importance only, it is not per se destructive of an individual's spiritual life.

[P. K. MEAGHER]

BLOCH, ERNEST (1880–1959). Born in Switzerland, B. studied music in Brussels, Frankfurt, and Munich. From 1911 until 1915 he taught composition at the Geneva Conservatory. In 1916 he came to America where he spent most of his remaining years. B.'s most inspired works were those written with a deep penetration into the Jewish character and with a poignant racial accent. He captured, as no other composer before him, the spirit of a sorrowing people. "Racial consciousness is absolutely necessary in music, even though nationalism is not." Among his numerous compositions are *Macbeth* (opera), *Israel* (symphony), *Shelomoh* (rhapsody for cello and orchestra), string quartets, and concertos. BIBLIOGRAPHY: Grove DMM 1:763–766.

[A. H. CRANE]

BLOIS, LOUIS DE, see BLOSIUS, FRANCIS LOUIS.

BLOK, ALEXANDER ALEXANDROVICH (1880–1921), greatest of the Russian symbolist poets. His poetry is remarkable for spontaneity, brilliant imagery, rhythmic innovations, polyphonic effects, and, above all, musicality. Under the influence of Solovyov, his earlier poems express his mystic but erotic love of Sophia, the eternally feminine incarnation of Divine Wisdom (cf. *Verses about the Beautiful Lady* [1904]). The symbol of the prostitute, the "Unknown Woman" of the poem of that name published in 1906, dominates the poems of his middle period, but is replaced in his later works by the feminine figure of Russia (cf. *Poems about Russia* [1906–1914]). Though its meaning is ambiguous, his masterpiece, *The Twelve* (1918), seems to depict Christ leading twelve revolutionary guardsmen through a blinding snowstorm and thus to reflect Blok's eschatological interpretation of the Revolution of 1917 as the beginning of a wholesome new order. BIBLIOGRAPHY: F. D. Reeve, *Alexander Blok: Between Image and Idea* (1962); C. Kisch, *Alexander Blok, Prophet of Revolution* (1960).

[M. F. MCCARTHY]

BLOMMAERDINNE (Heilwijch Blomart; d. before 1287), pseudomystic, writer, and apparently leader of a group of women of considerable social standing associated with the Brethren of the Free Spirit. Not much is known of her life, but through her writings she exerted influence in the Brabant. She insisted strongly on the spirit of liberty. In her accounts of her visions and mystical experiences, her letters, and her poetry, she described the ideal relation between God and man in terms of courtly love; she called it "seraphic love" and gave it more or less overtly sexual overtones. She seems to have taught that man can in this life achieve a state of perfection in which sin becomes impossible—he becomes free in his spirit, his body is left to do as it pleases, and law exists only for the imperfect. Her influence was still felt in the following century, when *Ruysbroeck was called upon to preach against it. The effort by some to identify her with Hadewijch has been thoroughly discredited. BIBLIOGRAPHY: J. Van Mierlo, DHGE 9:207–212; *idem,* DSAM 1:1730.

[J. C. WILLKE]

BLONDEEL, LANCELOT (*c*.1496–1561), Flemish painter, master of Bruges (1519). It is not known if B. journeyed to Italy, or was earlier a mason. (A trowel appears in his signature.) The *Legend of SS. Cosmas and Damian* (1523) shows B.'s usual proficiency in architectonic conceptions in the Flemish Flamboyant Gothic style. Figures are again secondary to abundant gilded decorations in *St. Luke Painting the Virgin* (1545). B.'s design for the marvelous *Cheminée du Franc* in the Palace of Justice, Bruges, his cartoons for tapestries, engravings, his restoration of the Ghent altarpiece by Van Eyck mark him a typically versatile Renaissance artist. BIBLIOGRAPHY: L. van Puyvelde, *La Peinture flamande au siècle de Bosch et Breughel* (1962).

[M. J. DALY]

BLONDEL, DAVID (1591–1655), Protestant historian. Educated at Geneva, B. was pastor at Houdan near Paris from 1614 until 1650, when he accepted the chair of history at l'École Illustre in Amsterdam. At Paris he was influential in protecting the rights of French Protestants. An erudite and thorough historian, he published many works. His *Pseudo Isidorus et Turcianus vapulantes* (1628; against a book by the Spanish Jesuit Francisco Torres) disproved the authenticity of the False Decretals. This was put on the Index in 1661 for its antipapal slant, and in 1759 for the same reason, as were all of B.'s other historico-theological writings. Among these, to the displeasure of some Protestants, were two exploding the myth of Pope Joan, *Familier éclaircissement de la question si une femme a été assise au siège papal* (1647) and *De Joanna Papissa* (1657). BIBLIOGRAPHY: A. Lambert, DDC 2:936.

[T. C. O'BRIEN]

BLONDEL, MAURICE (1861–1949), French Catholic philosopher of action, disciple of Ollé-Laprune, professor at Aix-en-Provence from 1896 until his death, despite his 20 years of blindness. Attacked during the Modernist hysteria, he was defended by Leo XIII and Pius X. His work was praised by Pius XII and the then Card. G. B. Montini (Paul VI). For B., philosophy must begin from action, not from pure thought. "Action" as he used the term meant the whole of life: thinking, feeling, willing, including even the divine action in man. We have not chosen to live; we know not whence we come nor who we are; but we do take action and engage ourselves. B.'s is a metaphysic of the whole man in his concreteness. Man must act and is driven to question the meaning of his action. Truth in the full sense demands perfect adequation of the known and the knower so that the known is grasped in its fullness and the knowledge is immediate and intuitive. Beyond the senses, there are two sorts of knowledge: *notional* knowledge, which proceeds through abstract concepts, and has its truth; and *real* knowledge which, with the aid of action, attains its object intuitively. Man in his action cannot equal what he himself demands—and tries to close the gap. Truth, then, can be defined as the adequation of our interior tendencies with life. (In the moral order, action looking to self is widened to embrace the social order.)

The demands of action lead from the immanent to the supraphenomenal, the transcendent, to God. God moves us by grace from the inevitable limitations of human actions. For B. the Catholic faith and God's immanence to us are among the truths of life, but he does not found his philosophy on them. Philosophy and reason show that it cannot be proved that God's gift of grace to man is impossible. Man is thus presented with an "option": to seek God without God, or to wait humbly for his intervention. B.'s own position is clear: man must choose positively to seek God, thus opening himself to the divine.

Fully articulated in its own right and highly personal, B.'s thought reflects the method and spirit of Augustine and, among modern Catholic thinkers, of Newman. He knew and appreciated the thought of the Middle Ages, especially that of Aquinas. He anticipates many of the insights of the existentialists, and argues that even the nihilist and pessimist philosopher must affirm a meaning for action. There is a certain anti-intellectualism evident in his earlier years (and in the writing of some of his followers) but this is modified in his later works. Thought and action are never in opposition for B., but philosophical thought is adequate only in conjunction with action. The rational proofs of theism, whose value he admits, are possible only because we first affirm God by reason of our action.

The works and commentaries on B. are to be found mainly in French. BIBLIOGRAPHY: J. M. Sommerville, *Total Commitment, Blondel's l'Action* (1966).

[W. B. MAHONEY]

BLOOD (IN THE BIBLE), regarded by the ancient Israelites as the seat of life or even as life itself. Since God is the author of life, blood belongs to him. Therefore man was forbidden to consume the blood of animals or to shed the blood of men. Blood, as a sign of a flow of life between God and man, held the central place in a sacrifice, as manifested in the covenant sacrifice of Sinai. Here God set up a special bond with his people; Moses sprinkled blood partly on the altar (the symbol of God) and partly on the people saying, "This is the blood, the convenant" (Ex 24.8); the blood ratified the covenant. The slaying of the Passover lamb became an annual reminder that the first-born of the Israelites had been redeemed by the blood of the lamb. Blood became a symbol of freedom and close association with God. BIBLIOGRAPHY: E. O. James, *Origins of Sacrifice* (1933, repr. 1971); H. W. Robinson, Hastings ERE 2:714–719.

[T. C. STAHL]

BLOOD, BAPTISM OF, see BAPTISM OF BLOOD.

BLOOD ATONEMENT, the ancient Israelites' use of the blood of animals to obtain God's forgiveness. "The life of a living body is in the blood" (Lev 17.11). The blood rite was specially celebrated on the Day of Atonement. The high priest entered the Holy of Holies and sprinkled various objects with blood. This ceremony defined the special power of blood in the expiation of sin. "It is the blood, as the seat of life, that makes atonement" (Lev 17.11). The rite effected forgiveness because it liberated life; this life snuffed out in the act was accepted by God who returned it to the repentant sinner in the form of divine life and restored his friendship. BIBLIOGRAPHY: T. C. Vriezen, *Outline of Old Testament Theology* (1974).

[T. C. STAHL]

BLOOD RELATIONSHIP, see CONSANGUINITY.

BLOOD TRANSFUSION, a medical procedure regarded by some, e.g., the Jehovah's Witnesses, as a grave transgression of God's law, and they will sometimes permit themselves, or those under their control, to die rather than permit the procedure to be used. The great majority of Christian moralists, however, disagree with the alleged scriptural basis for this prohibition, and regard the procedure as licit when performed for sufficient reason.

[P. K. MEAGHER]

BLOOD VENGEANCE. In nomadic Israel the clan avenged a member's murder according to the ancient law of talion or retaliation (Ex 21.23–35; Lev 24.20). Self-preservation necessitated this practice as a deterrent to attack, but forbade it within the clan (2 Sam 14.5–12). Further refinements permitted this vengeance to be taken upon the killer alone, precluding punishment of his family (Dt 24.16; 2 Kg 14.6). Israel eventually designated certain cities of refuge, to which a killer could flee. The populace undertook judgment, deciding whether to grant him asylum or to surrender him to vengeance at the hands of the victim's next of kin (Num 35.9–29; Dt 19.1–13; Jos 20.1–9). BIBLIOGRAPHY: De Vaux AncIsr 10–12; EDB 258–259.

[T. CRANE]

BLOODY SWEAT, the more obvious understanding of Lk 22.44 "his sweat became as drops of blood running onto the ground." The verse and the following one are of doubtful authenticity, not being found in a number of important MSS. Modern text critics are not in accord [cf. R. V. G. Tasker, *The Greek New Testament* (1964) and K. Aland et al., *The Greek New Testament* (1966)] in accepting the verses. However the phenomenon, of blood being mixed with the perspiration of a person under great stress, is not unknown.

[J. J. O'ROURKE]

BLOSIUS, FRANCIS LOUIS (1506–66), spiritual writer and Benedictine Abbot of Liessies where he had entered at the age of fourteen. As a novice he was sent to study at Louvain where his complete spiritual works were published in 1568. In his personal character he was distinguished for his devotion to the Mother of God, gentleness, love of chastity, and generosity to the poor. His monastic reform at Liessies was accepted in 1554 and confirmed by a Bull of Pope Paul III. BIBLIOGRAPHY: A. Mancone, EncCatt 2:1721–23.

[C. CARROLL]

BLOUET, JULES ARMAND (1863–1941), French Sulpician who was renowned for his many works on priestly formation and pastoral theology. BIBLIOGRAPHY: P. Pourrat, *Catholicisme* 2:96–97.

[T. C. O'BRIEN]

BLOUNT, CHARLES (1654–93), English deist who sought to establish a purely rational basis for religion, and whose *Anima mundi* (1679) questioned the immortality of the soul. BIBLIOGRAPHY: U. Viglino, EncCatt 2:1723.

[T. C. O'BRIEN]

BLOW, JOHN (1649–1708), English composer and organist of the Middle Baroque. B. was organist to Westminster Abbey (1668–79) and held an appointment to the court of Charles II as organist and composer succeeding *Humfrey as Master of the Children of the Chapel Royal (1674). B., the teacher of Henry Purcell, displays a goodly melodic gift in his works which, though influenced by French and Italian trends, are unmistakably in the English tradition. His works include one opera, *Venus and Adonis* (*c*.1682), the last section of which is esp. fine, and a collection of songs, *Amphion Anglicus* (1700). B. wrote a vast amount of music for the post-Restoration Anglican church, *services, *anthems, and motets. He also delighted in writing music for "special days" both sacred and profane. As is often the case with a prolific composer, the quality of B.'s output is uneven, but esp. in his church music he excels in a solemn, dignified style. BIBLIOGRAPHY: H. W. Shaw, Grove DMM 1:768–775, with list of works.

[P. DOHERTY]

BLOY, LÉON (1846–1917), novelist and pamphleteer. Brought up in an atmosphere of anticlericalism, he early lost his Catholic faith but regained it as a young disciple of the novelist Barbey d'Aurevilly. An obscure mystical experience made him thenceforth an ardent defender of this faith. After a stormy drama in his personal life, he married a Danish convert. Seeing himself as prophet, "pilgrim of the absolute," and "thankless beggar," he accepted poverty for Christ's sake, yet reacted bitterly against what he considered the injustices that kept him poor. An adamant intolerance of mediocrity and a contentious style alienated editors. He made some staunch friends, but also numerous enemies. There have always been admirers of his vigor and sincerity who have nevertheless rejected undeniable extremist tendencies. At once humble and arrogant, he quarreled with those of different views, especially the wealthy, fellow writers, and priests. Concerned with misfortune in every guise, he fought injustice wherever he saw it and took the part of the oppressed. Art, B. considered, should serve only social or religious ends. Yet he was interested in neither social organization nor politics. Conscious of a double mission of denunciation and praise, he found his strength in a paradoxical—sometimes contradictory—expression of loves and hatreds. Although estranged from many of its exponents, he belongs to the Catholic literary renewal of the late 19th and early 20th centuries. His work includes the novels *Le Désespéré* (1887) and *La Femme pauvre* (1890), which are largely autobiographical, his *Journal* (1892–1917), *Le Pèlerin de l'absolu* (1914), and expository, polemical, or historical works, in which are often voiced insistent per-

sonal interpretations. His readers, few until after his death, increased somewhat in numbers later. BIBLIOGRAPHY: J. Bollery, *Léon Bloy* (3 v. 1953); R. Maritain, *Adventures in Grace* (tr. J. Kernan, 1945); J. Morienval, *Catholicisme* 2:96–98.

[L. TINSLEY]

BLUE LAWS, laws such as those regulating observance of the Sabbath, the sale of alcoholic beverages, and censorship of the arts. The term was originally applied to the 17th-cent. laws of the New Haven Colony, which were printed on blue paper. Legislative control of such matters has been relaxed in succeeding centuries, though occasional efforts are made to strengthen it, as in the prohibition movement, and vestiges of the Sabbath legislation remain.

[T. EARLY]

BLUME, CLEMENS (1862–1932), German Jesuit, historian of hymnology, liturgist. B. collected and published the texts of Latin hymns and sequences as collaborator in the series *Analecta Hymnica* and as author of *Ein Jahrtausend lateinisches Hymnendichtung* (1910). He also was a substantial contributor to the *Catholic Encyclopedia*. B. is considered to have been a major influence on modern liturgical studies. BIBLIOGRAPHY: F. Brunhölzl, LTK 2:536.

[T. C. O'BRIEN]

BLUMHARDT, JOHANN CHRISTOPH (1805–80), Lutheran pastor at Möttlingen in Germany, where through faith healing and a deep spirituality he led many to a deeper biblical faith and hope in a rationalistic era. BIBLIOGRAPHY: EncLuthCh 1:313–314.

[T. C. O'BRIEN]

B'NAI B'RITH (Heb. for Sons of the Covenant), Jewish service organization founded in New York (1843), whose aims are moral, social, educational, and philanthropic. Another of its objectives is to guard Jewish political rights and for this purpose its Anti-Defamation League was formed in 1913. During the period of mass migration of Jews to the U.S. (1880–1920), B'nai B'rith was an important factor in the acclimatization of the immigrants. In addition to approximately 2000 lodges in the U.S., B'nai B'rith has lodges in Latin America, Europe, Australia, Africa, and Israel. BIBLIOGRAPHY: M. Ellinger, *Jewish Encyclopedia* 3:275–277.

[C. CARROLL]

BOANERGES, a Greek transliteration, seemingly corrupt, of a Hebrew or Aramaic name that according to Mk 3.17 designated James and John "sons of thunder." The Semitic linguistic background of the Greek transliteration is uncertain. Possibly these disciples of Jesus were so called because of their suggestion that lightning be sent down upon the Samaritans (Lk 9.54).

[J. J. O'ROURKE]

BOAST, JOHN, ST., see BOSTE, JOHN, ST.

BOASTING, the taking of pride in making known to others one's accomplishments, abilities, and performances. It is an act of vainglory and is not per se seriously sinful unless the object about which one boasts is itself seriously evil, for in that case it amounts to an affirmation, or perhaps a reaffirmation, of one's will to offend God. In some cases, indeed, what may give the appearance of boasting without being sinful in any way, may be done for a good purpose rather than for vainglory, e.g., as when St. Paul recounted his sufferings for the Lord. His purpose was not to bring honor upon himself but guidance to others. But a truly humble man, like St. Paul, will generally tend to great reticence where his own good deeds are concerned.

[P. K. MEAGHER]

BOAT, a small receptacle, usually in the shape of an ancient boat, which contains grains of incense for use in the *censer.

[N. KOLLAR]

BOAZ, biblical name, the etymology of which is uncertain, (1) the wealthy farmer of Bethlehem who is the kinsman of Naomi and who married his widowed daughter-in-law Ruth according to the laws of levirate marriage (Ru, ch. 2); (2) one of the two free-standing pillars erected before the Temple of Solomon, the exact function and significance of which is uncertain (1 Kg 7.21).

[D. J. BOURKE]

BOBADILLA, NICOLÁS ALFONSO DE (c.1509–90), Jesuit preacher. He was born in Spain, joined Ignatius of Loyola in Paris, and worked as a missionary and preacher in Italy, Germany, the Valtelline, and Dalmatia. His zeal was frequently imprudent; Charles V expelled him from Germany; the Pope excluded him from Jesuit meetings in Rome. Only one of his theological treatises was published. He also wrote an autobiography important to the history of the Society. BIBLIOGRAPHY: E. Lamalle, DHGE 9:270–272.

[H. JACK]

BOBBIO, ABBEY OF, a famous Benedictine monastery in N Italy, founded (c.612) by St. Columban. From Bobbio Columban and his companions began a monastic and lay spiritual revival the influence of which spread through Europe. Under Columban, a man of considerable learning, and his successors Bobbio became also a center of scholarship, with an outstanding scriptorium and library, containing Dungal's 8th-cent. collection with his *Antiphonary of Bangor,* a 10th-cent. catalogue, and a Bobbio Missal of the same period from its scriptorium. Some of the Bobbio's volumes are in the Ambrosian Library, the Vatican Library, and the National Library, Turin. Governed at first by the Rule of St. Columban, the community adopted part of the Benedictine observance in 643, but the complete Ben-

edictine Rule did not replace St. Columban's until the 10th century. Bobbio was the first monastery to be granted papal exemption (628), and in 643 abbots were given pontifical rights. Emperors from Charlemagne to Frederick I Barbarossa gave substantial grants of land and revenues to the community. The abbey was suppressed in 1803 at the time of the French conquest. The abbey church, having become the parish church, was restored in 1910. BIBLIOGRAPHY:R. Gazeau, *Catholicisme* 2:100–101; F. Bonnard, DHGE 9:275–284; C. Catiglione and T. Leccisotti, EncCatt 2:1726–30.

[S. A. HEENEY]

BOBILLET, ÉTIENNE, (15 cent.), French sculptor who carved forms (1453) for the tomb of Jean de *Berry in Ste. Chapelle, *Bourges (now in Bourges Museum). B. was one of the more refined *imagiers* of his day.

[M. J. DALY]

BOBLINGER, MATTHIAS (c.1450–1505), German architect and sculptor trained in Cologne. B. worked on the Cologne Cathedral and St. Catherine Church, Esslingen. His design for the upper story of the W tower of Ulm Cathedral (1474–92) established his fame.

[M. J. DALY]

BOBOLA, ANDREW, ST. (1591–1657), Jesuit apostle of Lithuania, martyr. He was of aristocratic Polish family and became a Jesuit at Vilna. There and in the surrounding area he carried on a highly successful missionary and pastoral apostolate, sometimes bringing whole communities of Orthodox Christians back into union with Rome. He established a center at Pinsk with other Jesuits, and when Cossacks attacked the city, B. was captured and tortured to death. His remains, which were later discovered incorrupt, were translated various times–to Rome in 1924, and finally to Warsaw. BIBLIOGRAPHY: C. Testore, BiblSanct 1:1153–55; Butler 2:363–364.

[H. JACK]

BOCCACCIO, GIOVANNI (1313–75), Italian poet and prose writer. In Naples where his father had sent him on a commercial venture, B. came under the influence of the learned men of the court and thereafter dedicated himself to the arts. His first works are dominated by the figure of Fiammetta, the name by which he immortalized his idol, Maria d'Aquino, daughter of King Robert. His *Filocolo* and *Fiammetta* give insight into the nature and intensity of his love. His most famous work is the vernacular *Decameron* (1348–51?), a collection of stories recounted by ten people secluded in the country to escape the plague. The *Decameron* presents 14th-cent. Italy in full life. In his later years B. was greatly influenced by Petrarch, who helped him resolve his passionate and unstable nature into a firmly religious one, witnessed by his reception of minor orders at the end of his life. BIBLIOGRAPHY: C. Carswell,

Tranquil Heart: Portrait of Giovanni Boccaccio (1937, repr. 1973); H. G. Wright, *Boccaccio in England: From Chaucer to Tennyson* (1957).

[D. NUGENT]

BOCKING, EDWARD (c. 1490–1534), English Benedictine. Educated at Oxford, he was prior of Canterbury College and then an official at Christ Church, Canterbury. He headed a commission (1525) to investigate the revelations of Elizabeth *Barton, the Nun of Kent. He pronounced them valid and became her spiritual advisor. When her prophecies took on a political tone at the time of Henry's divorce, the government took action (1533) and B. was implicated. Accused of treason, he was executed at Tyburn. BIBLIOGRAPHY: Knowles ROE 3; DNB 2:749–750.

[V. SAMPSON]

BÖCKLIN, ARNOLD (1827–1901), Swiss painter, studied at the Academy of Düsseldorf, taught at the Art School in Weimar (1845–47), and visited in Italy where he died at Fiesole. Classical frescoes of Pompeii and Naples and Raphael's work determined B.'s artistic development (c.1860). His mythological subjects combined vague symbolism with literary elements. His works, distinguished for magic realism and imagination, strongly influenced Giorgio de Chirico (b.1888). BIBLIOGRAPHY: H. A. Schmidt, *Arnold Böcklin*, (4 v., 1922).

[P. H. HEFTING]

BODELSCHWINGH, FRIEDRICH VON, the name of two German Evangelical clergymen, father and son. (1) F.B. (1831–1910) pastor of the Evangelical Church, commonly known as "Father Bodelschwingh." He served the German Church of Paris (1858–64) and the Ruhr area (1864–72). A man of action in his concern for theological problems of his day, he founded the first German work colony. While serving in the Prussian Provincial Diet he introduced the Itinerant Worker's Housing Law (1907). As director of the Bethel Initute in Bielefeld, B. made it the most outstanding institute of charity in his Church. He founded several other charitable institutions and actively supported missionary work in East Africa. (2) F. B. (1877–1946) youngest son of foregoing. A successor to his father as director of Bethel, he broadened the work of this institute. He also continued and expanded many of his father's charitable and social works. He opposed the Nazi policy of euthanasia. Although the people chose B. as State bishop, Nazi propaganda and intimidation forced him to withdraw his candidacy to allow the election of the Hitler candidate, Müller. B. however remained "secret bp." of the Evangelical Church and died shortly after World War II. BIBLIOGRAPHY: M. Gerhardt, *Friedrich von Bodelschwingh* (1952); R. Burkhardt, *Vater Bodelschwingh* (1926); EncLuthCh 1:314–315; M. Bradfield, *Good Samaritan* (1961).

[F. H. BRIGHAM]

BODEY, JOHN, BL. (1550–1583), layman, martyr. He received his M.A. in 1576 at Oxford and was later deprived of his fellowship by Bp. Horne of Winchester because of his religion. After studying civil law at Douai, B. returned to England seemingly as a schoolmaster until 1580. He was imprisoned with John Slade at Winchester. For some reason, not clear, Slade and Bodey were tried twice. In August 1583 they were sentenced to death for denying that the Queen had any supremacy over the Church in England, yet they publicly acknowledged the Queen as their lawful sovereign. BIBLIOGRAPHY: R. Challoner, *Memoirs of Missionary Priests* (ed. J. H. Pollen, 1924).

[L. MITCHELL]

BODHGAYĀ, village in Bihar State, NE India. At Gayā, Prince Siddhārtha Gautama of the Sākya tribe sat in meditation under the Bodhi Tree (the Tree of Wisdom) and attained enlightenment, becoming the Buddha. The tree was enclosed in a shrine by Aşoka (c.273–236 B.C.). The present Mahābodhi temple houses a statue of the Buddha (100–50 B.C., Sunga period). There were numerous additions (7–10 cent.), and restoration (19th century). BIBLIOGRAPHY: B. Rowland, *Art and Architecture of India* (1959).

[M. J. DALY]

BODHI, Sanskrit term meaning "Enlightenment," which refers to that state of wisdom or truth attained first by the Buddha and later by all Bodhisatvas, after extended practices of perfection.

[M. J. DALY]

BODHI TREE, "Tree of Wisdom" under which Prince Siddhārtha, seated in meditation, received final enlightenment (Bodhi), becoming the Buddha. The heart-shaped leaf of this fig, banyan, bo, or pīpal tree is a motif in ancient square Harappan seals from prehistoric Indus Valley culture, is used in teachings of the Upanishads, and shapes the halo and aureole of the holy one in Buddhist iconography.

[M. J. DALY]

BODHISATTVA (Chin., P'u-t'i-sa-t'o; Jap., Bosatsu; in Pali, a bodhisatta or "Wisdom [Enlightened] Being"). In Hīnayanā Buddhism it refers to the Maitreya alone; in Mahāyāna (the Great Vehicle), a Bodhisattva is one who, having reached Buddhahood through practices of perfection, has postponed nirvana that as a compassionate saviour (who may or may not manifest himself) he may devote himself to those in this world of suffering who call on him in faith. Among the most popular celestial Bodhisattvas, wearing crowns, jewels, and scarves, are Avalokiteśvara (Goddess of Mercy—the Kuan-yin of China; Kwannon of Japan), Manjusri (Wisdom), and Maitreya (the Saviour to come.) BIBLIOGRAPHY: N. Thera, *Bodhisattva Ideal* (1944).

[M. J. DALY]

BODILY DEFECT (physical defect), a physical disability or deformity constituting an irregularity that bars admission to holy orders or the exercise of those orders if they have already been received. see CIC, c. 984 n 2.

BODIN, JEAN (1530–96), French jurist and political philosopher. His principal work, *Les six livres de la République* (1577; Lat. tr. by the author, 1584), presents his idea of the well–ordered republic. While using themes from Roman law and Aristotle, B. also incorporates his own interpretations of the socio-political situation of his time. The work, the argument of which is sometimes confused and illogical, stresses human dignity and freedom, the relationship of economics and morality, the effect of climate on character and morals. B. gives a naturalistic interpretation to religion, and regards it as a function of the social order, to be controlled or allowed freedom according to the needs of society. He also wrote a pioneer work in economics, *Réponse aux paradoxes de M. Malestroit* (1568).

[T. C. O'BRIEN]

BODLEY, GEORGE FREDERICK (1827–1907), one of the principal English church architects, a "Puginist" in work marked by sensitive design and refined ornament as seen in St. Mary's, Eccleston, Cheshire.

[M. J. DALY]

BODY. The Hebrew of the OT has no special word for body, but some of the attributes associated with body in the NT, esp. those of weakness, passivity, liability to death etc., can be expressed by the OT term *basar*, "flesh". It is in the gospels that the now familiar distinction between body and soul emerges, as for instance when it is stated that the death of the body alone is less to be feared than the destruction of both soul and body alike forever (Mt 10.28; Lk 12.4). But it is in the Pauline writings that the concept of body acquires a distinctive theological significance in its own right. Very broadly it may be defined as the concrete totality of the individual as existing in this physical and earthly sphere, and as subject to its natural conditions. But Paul's conception of the individual body of man is radically conditioned by the fact that he regards it as destined to rise again (1 Cor 15.35–44), to be transformed and "conformed," *summorphos,* to the already risen and glorified body of Christ. (Phil 3.21). It is to be raised from its present transient state of misery and bondage, the conditions of the *flesh to which it is subject, to a glorified state. Already by anticipation it is consecrated for this end, and must not be desecrated, esp. by sexual sins. (Rom 1.24; 1 Cor 6.18–20). For it is to be presented to God as a living and acceptable sacrifice (Rom 12.1). The effects of faith and baptism upon it are such that already it is organically united to the risen Lord so as to constitute one body with him and with all believers. Thus the concept of the Church as "Body of Christ" is far more than mere metaphor. J. A. T.

Robinson states that the body that Paul has in mind is as concrete and as singular as the body of the Incarnation; that Christians are, in literal fact, the risen organism of Christ's Person in all its concrete reality. BIBLIOGRAPHY: J. A. T. Robinson, *Body, a Study in Pauline Theology* (1955); P. Benoit, *Exégèse et Théologie* II (1961) 107–171.

[D. J. BOURKE]

BODY, GLORIFIED, the condition of the body transformed at the resurrection of the flesh by sharing in the glorious state of the risen body of Christ (1 Cor 15; Phil 3.21). Implied is the union of the body of the Christian with that of Christ whose own glorification is the cause and the pledge of the believer's glorification. Life received through union with Christ affects a person integrally and as such is to be expressed in the body. Life in Christ which makes one's body a temple of the Spirit in this world is directed toward fulfillment. Having shared bodily in this life in the death and resurrection of Christ, the Christian is to share bodily in the fullness of his glory. This sharing, according to St. Thomas, is a participation by the body in the glory of the soul (ThAq ST 3a, 49.3 ad 3). Basing conclusions on 1 Cor 15 theologians have named characteristics of the glorified body, notably impassibility, the freedom of the body from suffering pain or inconvenience. Recent writing tends rather to be concerned with the meaning of the glorification event for the person. The body implies presence and relation to other persons. This reality of life on earth is transformed and perfected in the resurrection so that personal communion with God and other human beings is seen as an essential aspect of the life of man in his glorified body. BIBLIOGRAPHY: A. Winklhofer, *Coming of His Kingdom* (tr. A. V. Littledale, 1963); F. C. Durrwell, *Resurrection: A Biblical Study* (tr. R. Sheed, 1960). *HEAVEN.

[J. CORDOUE]

BODY-PRISON (Tomb). In Greek philosophy and religio-philosophical thought, beginning with Orphism and Pythagoreanism, there is a long tradition of a concept of the body as the prison or tomb of the soul, which finds expression in the formula *sōma sēma*. This notion arose undoubtedly out of the Orphic myth connected with the Titans and the origin of man. Plato incorporates the notion into his dialogues, although in the *Timaeus* he tends to give more favorable recognition to the body and to stress the harmony that should exist between body and soul. However, the more pessimistic view of the body prevails in general in the Pythagorean tradition, in the later Stoicism, in Middle Platonism, and in Neoplatonism. The prison of the soul is regarded as the body itself, sensual pleasures or passions, the material world, the goods of fortune, or hell. It was only natural that Christianity, through its own doctrine of the fall of man, and under the influence of its pagan environment, should find a place for the body-prison concept. It is mentioned repeatedly in Christian writings down to the time of SS. Ambrose and Prudentius. The allusions in St. Ambrose in particular are interesting and revealing. The Origenist controversy, however, led to a more critical examination of the marked difference between the Orphic myth and the Christian doctrine on Adam's fall. Hence we find Epiphanius of Salamis and Theophilus of Alexandria in the East, and St. Jerome and St. Augustine in the West, opposing the concept of body-prison, maintaining that the body itself is good, and that it is only as a result of original sin that a conflict has arisen between body and soul. Among the Gnostics and Manichaeans and related groups the pessimistic view of the body was stressed to a fantastic degree. Despite the teachings of SS. Jerome and Augustine, among others, the pessimistic view of the body in relation to the soul occurs repeatedly in medieval spiritual literature in both East and West, and finds expression in the old image of body-prison. BIBLIOGRAPHY: D. Gorce, DSAM 2.2:2338–78; P. Courcelle, "Tradition Platonicienne et traditions chrétiennes du Corps-prison," *Revue des études latines* 43 (1965) 406–443.

[M. R. P. MCGUIRE]

BOECE, HECTOR (Boyce, Boethius; *c*.1465–1536), Scottish chronicler and humanist. A friend of Erasmus and first principal of Aberdeen Univ., he is known for his *Scotorum Historiae* (1527), a widely read but uncritical work that was used by Holinshed and thence gave Shakespeare his *Macbeth* plot. It also gave George Buchanan material (spurious) for his attack on Mary Queen of Scots. BIBLIOGRAPHY: A. J. G. Mackray, DNB 2:759–762; J. B. Black and W. D. Simpson, *Quatercentenary of the Death of Hector Boece* (1937).

[V. SAMPSON]

BOECKHORST, JOHANN (Lange Jan; 1605–68), Flemish painter, pupil of Jacob Jordaens, excelling in religious, mythological, and allegorical compositions in a manner related, though inferior, to that of Rubens.

[M. J. DALY]

BOEGNER, MARC (1881–1970), Protestant leader. B. was for several decades the leader of the French Protestants. A minister of the French Reformed Church, he wrote extensively on Christian unity and ecumenism. In 1938 he was elected first president of the National Council of Reformed Churches. From 1948 to 1954 he was president of the World Council of Churches, and in 1962 was elected to the French Academy. BIBLIOGRAPHY: *New York Times*, Dec. 20, 1970.

[J. R. AHERNE]

BOEHM, JOHN PHILIP (1683–1749), minister and guiding spirit of the Reformed Church in America. B. was a schoolteacher in Germany, emigrated to Pennsylvania (1720), conducted informal religious services, and began to serve as a minister for several pastorless Reformed Church congregations in Montgomery County (1725), even though he was not ordained. Upon complaints about his status, B.

appealed to the Amsterdam Classis which upheld his previous ministry but required that he then be ordained (1729). B. collaborated in forming the first American Synod (Coetus) of the Reformed Church (1747), agreeing that it should subordinate itself to the Amsterdam Classis, render annual reports, and accept only those ministers endorsed by Amsterdam. BIBLIOGRAPHY: J. P. Boehm, *Life and Letters* (ed. W. J. Hinke, 1916); Olmstead 141–143.

[T. M. MC FADDEN]

BOEHME, JAKOB (1575–1624), German mystic and speculative thinker. A shoemaker and a prosperous merchant, although having only an elementary education, B. dealt with profound questions in original ways. The archaic language of his works, much of it derived from Paracelsus, and their unsystematic form have received varied reactions: W. *Law called him "the blessed Jacob"; John *Wesley characterized his work as "sublime nonsense, inimitable bombast." Nevertheless, B.'s ideas were to influence such philosophers as Schelling, Kierkegaard, Nietzsche, Bergson, and some modern existentialists. B. sought to resolve the problem of God's connection with the disunity apparent in nature and human life. Influenced esp. by a pastor at Görlitz in Silesia, he had a mystical experience in 1600, which was the source of his subsequent views. He always maintained that he wrote of what had been inwardly revealed to him. B.'s teaching, esp. his concern for the reality and value of nature, differed strikingly from the medieval mystical tradition. His first book, *Aurora* (1612), dealt with God in nature and the mystery of God's relationship to evil in the world and in men. Opposed by a local clergyman, he ceased publishing, 1612–19, but thereafter produced numerous works. His mature views were articulated *c*.1622–23 in *The Way to Christ, On the Election of Grace, On the Great Mystery,* and *On Christ's Testaments*. All his works dealt with the basic problem of the unity of the Yes and No, of good and evil. To the theogonic, metaphysical, and cosmological aspects of the problem, he proposed as the answer the indwelling Logos by which man was regenerated and the cosmos was to be made new. BIBLIOGRAPHY: R. M. Jones, *Spiritual Reformers in the 16th and 17th Centuries* (pa., 1959) 151–234; J. J. Stoudt, *Sunrise to Eternity: A Study of Jacob Boehme's Life* (1957); F. Hartman, *Jacob Boehme Life and Doctrines*. (1976).

[N. H. MARING]

BOEHNER, PHILOTHEUS HEINRICH (1901–55), Franciscan medievalist. As a member of the Order of Friars Minor in Germany, he was translator and collaborator of E. Gilson, and in 1939 joined the Pontifical Institute of Medieval Studies in Toronto. From 1941 he was director of the Franciscan Institute for research at St. Bonaventure Univ. in Olean, N.Y. His major contributions were in textual studies of the works of *William of Ockham. BIBLIOGRAPHY: P. Borgmann, LTK 2:565–566.

[T. C. O'BRIEN]

BOETHIUS, Anicius Manlius Torquatus Severinus (480–c.524), philosopher, theologian, and statesman. A member of the celebrated and Christian family of the Anicii, B. himself held high political offices in Italy under the Ostrogothic king, Theodoric. Consul in 510, perhaps head of the senate at one point, he served as *magister officiorum* (chief of civil and other court services) c.520–522. In 522 his two sons were raised to the rank of joint consuls, but shortly thereafter his fortunes changed. Accused of treason and suspected, perhaps, of supporting the Eastern Emperor, B. was imprisoned for some time and then executed, apparently near Pavia. While in prison he composed a work destined to become a classic, *The Consolation of Philosophy*.

His knowledge of both Greek and Latin prepared him well for his declared intention to translate into Latin the writings of Plato and Aristotle and to establish their basic agreement in philosophy. Not surprisingly in the light of his other literary activities, demanding political responsibilities and untimely death, he failed to complete these projects. Among his writings in addition to *The Consolation* were works on logic, the quadrivium, and theology. His logical works include: translations of the *Isagoge* of Porphyry and of Aristotle's *Categories, Perihermeneias, Prior* and *Posterior Analytics, Topics*, and *Sophistic Refutations;* two commentaries on Porphyry's *Isagoge* (one based on a translation by Marius Victorinus, the other on B.'s own translation), a commentary on Aristotle's *Categories,* two on his *Periher-meneias,* commentaries on the *Prior* and *Posterior Analytics,* and a commentary on Cicero's *Topics*; a treatise on categorical syllogism in two redactions known today, perhaps incorrectly, by the titles *Introductio ad syllogismos categoricos* and *De syllogismo categorico; De syllogismo hypothetico; De divisione;* and *De differentiis topicis.* His writings on the quadrivium include treatises on arithmetic, geometry, music, and astronomy. His five theological treatises are entitled: *De Trinitate, Utrum Pater et Filius et Spiritus Sanctus de divinitate substantialiter praedicentur, Quomodo substantiae in eo quod sint bonae sint cum non sint substantialia bona* (usually known as the *De heb-domadibus*), *De fide catholica* (of disputed authenticity), and *Contra Eutychen et Nestorium.* A remark in the third theological treatise suggests that he composed another work, now lost, under the title *Hebdomades.*

In a well-known discussion found in his second commentary on Porphyry's *Isagoge,* B. passed on to subsequent medieval philosophy the problem of universals. As regards genera and species (universals) Porphyry had raised three questions: (1) Do they subsist, or are they found in the understanding alone? (2) If they do subsist, are they corporeal? (3) If they are incorporeal, do they subsist in sensible things apart from them? B. did not follow Porphyry's example in refusing to answer these questions but, under the explicitly acknowledged influence of the commentator Alexander of Aphrodisias, developed an Aristotelian solution. But then, after contrasting this view with that of Plato, he refused to decide between them. If he had presented the Aristotelian position it was not because he necessarily favored that view but because Porphyry's *Isagoge* was an introduction to an Aristotelian treatise. Many recent commentators have concluded that B.'s personal views were closer to the Platonic position in the light of his general theory of knowledge as found in *The Consolation*.

According to B., philosophy is either speculative or practical. In his first commentary on the *Isagoge* he proposes a threefold division of speculative philosophy corresponding to three different levels of being. Theology deals with intellectibles, i.e., those entities that exist outside of matter. A second kind of speculative philosophy, left unnamed by B., studies intelligibles, i.e., intellectibles that have descended into bodies. A third part, physiology (physics), studies natural bodies. But in *De Trinitate* speculative philosophy is divided into natural philosophy, mathematics, and theology, insofar as it studies forms found in matter and subject to motion (natural philosophy), or forms without matter and motion even though they do not exist apart from them (mathematics), or forms that do exist apart from matter and motion (theology). Practical philosophy is divided into ethics, politics, and economics. Logic may be regarded both as a part of philosophy and as an instrument at its service.

Even without his logical works *The Consolation of Philosophy* would have sufficed to establish B.'s fame as a writer and philosopher. In Book I he depicts himself as almost driven to despair by his misfortunes. A majestic woman, representing philosophy, appears to comfort him in his grief. She is unimpressed by his self-pity, however, and notes that his present failure to understand man's true nature and purpose accounts for his weakness in the face of adversity. His belief that God rules the world, however, will aid in the subsequent discussion. In Book II the changeable character of fortune is considered. Philosophy reminds B. that it is foolish to think that happiness depends on good fortune. In Book III philosophy shows that riches, popular acclaim, political power, fame, and bodily pleasure all fail to provide true happiness. The highest good and true happiness are one and the same, are to be found only in God, and are God. In Book IV further discussion leads to the view that evil does not go unpunished, since the wickedness of the evil man is its own punishment. Fate and providence are also considered. Book V raises the question of human freedom and divine foreknowledge. A distinction is made between our human way of knowing things as future and God's knowledge, by which all things are seen as eternally present.

Before the authenticity of the theological treatises had been clearly established, some held that Boethius was not really a Christian at the time of writing *The Consolation*. Although the precise reasons for the absence of distinctively Christian positions in this work are still debated, it seems clear that there is nothing therein to indicate that its author was not a Christian. But it is a philosophical treatise rather than theological.

In the first theological tractate there is an interesting discussion of the categories and the observation that their meaning changes when they are applied to God. Appeal is then made to the distinction between substance and relation in order to safeguard both unity (of substance) and plurality (of persons) in the Trinity. This distinction is also found in the second treatise. The fifth treatise makes important precisions concerning the relationship between nature and person in the context of the theology of the hypostatic union. There B. proposes his well-known definition of person as "an individual substance of a rational nature."

In the *De hebdomadibus* a more philosophical discussion is found wherein the goodness of existing things is grounded in the fact that God, who gave them being, is good. A series of axioms near the beginning of this work would occasion considerable discussion and a variety of interpretations in the 12th and 13th centuries.

In addition to the acknowledged importance of his logical works, translations, and commentaries for subsequent medieval philosophy, B.'s theological treatises were to become highly influential in the 12th century. Gilbert of Poitiers wrote commentaries on the four accepted today as authentic. Thierry of Chartres and Clarembald of Arras commented on the first and third treatises, as did Thomas Aquinas in the 13th century. The far-reaching impact of *The Consolation* is evidenced by its various medieval translations into other languages such as Anglo-Saxon, German, Greek, French, and Italian. Finally, his role in preserving and transmitting a part of classical learning joins with his more original contributions to justify regarding B. as one of the "Founders of the Middle Ages." For a list of editions of his works see: E. Dekkers and A. Gaar, *Sacris erudiri* 3 (1951), 153–156; Dekkers CPL; ODCC 181–182; F. Stegmüller, LTK 2:555; W. Totok, *Handbuch der Geschichte der Philosophie* I (1964), 350–353. For extensive bibliography on Boethius cf. Totok, *ibid.*, 351–353. BIBLIOGRAPHY: H. M. Barrett, *Boethius: Some Aspects of His Times and Work* (1940); H. Brosch, *Der Seinsbegriff bei Boethius* (1931); P. Courcelle, *La Consolation de philosophie dans la tradition littéraire* (1967); V. Schurr, *Die Trinitätslehre des Boethius im Lichte der "skythischen Kontroversen"* (1935); H. R. Patch, *Tradition of Boethius. A Study of his Importance in Medieval Culture* (1935).

[J. WIPPEL]

BOETHIUS OF SWEDEN (fl. 1270), Aristotelian philosopher who lectured on philosophy in the faculty of arts of the Univ. of Paris and along with his colleague Siger of Brabant was condemned by the Synod of Paris (1277) as a leader of the Averroist movement. Later he may have become a Dominican in the province of Dacia. B. taught that philosophical inquiry should not be restricted by the contrary claims of religion. Thus he rejected creation and resurrection on philosophical grounds. At the same time, he acknowledged that the truths of faith are of a higher order and must be accepted. Of his many commentaries on the works of Aristotle, only *De summo bono*, *De somniis* and *De aeternitate* have been published. BIBLIOGRAPHY: A. Maurer, EncPhil.

1:330–331; F. Van Steenberghen, DHGE 9:381–382; Gilson HCP 399, 402, 725.

[F. H. BRIGHAM]

BOETHIUS, HECTOR, see BOECE, HECTOR.

BOÉTIE, ÉTIENNE, see LA BOÉTIE, ÉTIENNE DE.

BOFFRAND, GABRIEL GERMAIN (1667–1754), French architect who, after studying sculpture with Girardon, later rose from pupil to collaborator in the architectural workshop of Jules Hardouin Mansart. B. commanded Gothic, Muslim, and classical styles in buildings of exterior simplicity but luxurious interiors adapted to the royal taste. A creator of exquisite rococo forms, he stated his theories in his *Livre d'architecture* (1745). BIBLIOGRAPHY: L. Hautecoeur, *Histoire de l'architecture classique en France* (1950).

[M. J. DALY]

BOGARÍN, JUAN SINFORIANO (1863–1949), Paraguayan archbishop. Made bp. of Paraguay at age 32, he had a long and constructive career as the only bp. of the country for many years and then as its first archbishop. With incessant travel, largely on horseback, through his large territory, he organized his diocese, established parishes, and formed a curia. He erected a seminary, brought in religious orders, mobilized lay leaders, and began a Catholic press and radio. He participated in the Plenary Council on Latin America (Rome, 1899), and was first president of the council of state created by the 1940 constitution.

[H. JACK]

BOGOMILS (Slavic *Bogomili*), a movement and sect that originated in medieval Bulgaria on dualistic Manichaean foundations and later spread under different names and forms throughout the Balkans, Asia Minor, Russia, and western Europe. The earliest evidence of the movement appears in the second half of the 9th century. Its founder is said to have been an Orthodox priest from Macedonia by the name of Bogomil, a Slavic translation of the Greek *theophilos*, beloved of God. The theological tenets of the movement are known only from indirect sources, the apologetical writings and official documents emanating from the Orthodox and Catholic Churches (late 10th cent., e.g., *Treatise on the Bogomils* by the Bulgarian priest Cosmas; early 12th cent., Euthymios Zygabenos, *Panoplia dogmatica*). Its theological outlook appears to have been dualistic, admitting the existence and eternal conflict of God and Satan, a conflict affecting the whole universe and manifest in it, with spiritual things, such as the soul of man, expressing and fostering the power of God and material things building up the kingdom of Satan. From this follows the rejection by the Bogomils of church ritual and organization. They manifested the same attitude toward organized feudal society, arms, wars, married life, property, and material work. This points to the influence of known heretical movements of the Christian East, such as Messalianism (rejection of work for prayer),

Manichaeism, and Paulicianism. There is definite historical evidence of contacts with and influence from the last of these; a large number of Paulicians were deported in the 10th cent. by the Byzantines from Armenia to eastern Bulgaria, an area which soon became one of the most active centers of Bogomilism. In partial disagreement with the Paulician interpretation of the conflict between God and Satan as a sort of eternal balance of power, the Bogomils generally stressed hope in the final victory of God and the deliverance of the spiritual world from the servitude of the material world through Christ.

The Bogomil movement soon spread in every direction from the two major Bulgarian centers of Thrace and Macedonia. The first to be affected was the Byzantine Empire, which occupied all of Bulgaria at the beginning of the 11th century. The Bogomils seem to have been well established in the major centers of the Empire, where they were known also as "Phoundaites" (scrip bearers). In 1111 one of their leaders, Basil, was tried and burnt at the stake in Constantinople. By the end of the 12th cent. they had appeared in Serbia, Bosnia, and Dalmatia. Bogomilism also spread to Russia, where adherents were known as *strigolnitzi,* to northern Italy and southern France, where they were known by such names as *Cathari, *Patrines, *Albigenses, Bulgarians, or Buggars. These manifested not only a definite theological, ecclesiastical, and social resemblance to the older Bulgarian sect, but there is also evidence of a missionary and organizational dependence of these Western groups on Bogomil centers in Bulgaria. Some Western sources even mention a common head of the dualist sects of Europe, a sort of Bogomil pope, residing in Bulgaria. Bogomilism encountered not only the expected opposition of the established Churches of East and West but also the full might of the secular power, which saw in Bogomilism a disruptive influence on society. Crusades and pogroms, together with the unrelenting missionary work of the Church as well as of Islam, finally brought the movement to an end. The sect did, however, find refuge in Bosnia, where it flourished as the national religion from the early 13th to the mid-15th century. There under Turkish rule the Bogomils became Muslims, and in the 17th cent. the last remnants of the group in Bulgaria were converted to Roman Catholicism. BIBLIOGRAPHY: D. Obolensky, *Bogomils: A Study in Balken Neo-Manichaeism* (1948); A. Borst, *Die Katharer* (1953), D. Angelov, *Le Bogomilisme en Bulgarie* (1972).

[G. ELDAROV]

BOGUMIŁ, ST. (d. *c.*1180?), a saint whose cult in Poland goes back at least to the mid-14th century. According to a 16th-cent. biography he was abp. of Gniezno 1170–82; he disposed of his possessions, making a substantial gift to the Cistercians, resigned his position, and ended his days as a hermit. Attempts by scholars to reconcile what is recorded in his biography with historical data known from other sources have located B. variously in time from the 11th to the 13th

centuries. One hypothesis, more plausible than others, identifies him not as abp. of Gniezno, but as a Benedictine abbot (d. 1179) who gave up his abbatial dignity and spent the rest of his life as a hermit. His cult was approved in 1925. BIBLIOGRAPHY: P. Naruszewicz, BiblSanct 3:227–229; P. David, DHGE 9:415–417.

[P. K. MEAGHER]

BOHEMIA MANOR, a Catholic school founded by the Jesuits some time between 1742 and 1745 in Cecil Co., Md. One distinguished alumnus of the school was John Carroll, who was later to become abp. of Baltimore. Surviving records of the school are few and not much is known of its enrollment and academic program. It appears to have been closed *c.*1749, but it served an important role in its brief existence by preparing boys for admission to European colleges and universities who were later to become leaders in the American Church.

[P. K. MEAGHER]

BOHEMIAN BRETHREN, the common name for the Unitas Fratrum (Unity of Brethren), which was organized in 1457 and flourished in Bohemia, Moravia, and Poland until the Thirty Years' War. Of the factions arising after the death of Jan *Hus (1415), only the *Utraquists, founders of a national Church, survived the civil wars ending in 1434 (see TABORITES). Finally, Hussites of a later generation, inspired by *Peter of Chelcić toward more thoroughgoing reform, left the Utraquists to form a new body. The Bohemian King himself allowed them to settle on crown lands in the village of Kunwald, though later he tried to suppress them. They stressed the Bible as the only source of doctrine, simplicity in worship, commuunion in both kinds and avoidance of human explanation of the sacrament, and godly living as evidence of saving faith. Having among them former Utraquist priests, they delayed establishing their own ministry until 1467, when one of their leaders was ordained at the hands of the Waldenses. Subsequently, they adopted the three orders: bishop, presbyter, and deacon. Though persecuted as an illegal sect, they grew to number 400 churches and 200,000 members by the time of Luther. First-generation austerity gave way to liberalization by the early 16th century. They were renowned for piety, use of Scripture, hymn singing, and their schools. Their first hymnal appeared in 1501. After the Thirty Years' War the Brethren became an underground Church in Bohemia and Moravia. In Poland they kept identity within the Reformed Church. J. *Comenius, one of their bishops, was their leader during this trying period. Surviving Brethren were incorporated into the Renewed Moravian Church, beginning in 1722. BIBLIOGRAPHY: E. de Schweinitz, *History of the Unitas Fratrum* (1885); P. Brock, *Unity of Czech Brethren* (1957); A. W. Schattschneider, *Through Five Hundred Years* (1956).

[J. R. WEINLICK]

BOHEMIAN CONFESSIONS, doctrinal statements of the *Bohemian Brethren issued in 1535 and 1573. (1) The Confession of 1535 was, among a series of Bohemian statements of faith dating from 1467, the first fully Protestant doctrinal expression by the Brethren. It was written in Latin, signed by Brethren noblemen, and presented as a proof of orthodoxy to King Ferdinand in 1535. The document has a long, apologetic preface and 20 articles of faith closely resembling the *Augsburg Confession. It states that formerly the Brethren had rebaptized converts, but that they had dropped the practice; they feared being confused with Anabaptists. Their doctrine of the Lord's Supper, though stated vaguely, shows accommodation to the Lutheran view. At their request and expense, Luther published a slightly amended version with a favorable preface in 1538. (2) The second Bohemian Confession, printed by the Brethren in Wittenberg in March 1573, was, with some variations, essentially the document presented jointly by Protestants in Bohemia to Emperor Maximilian in 1575. It sought to reconcile the positions of Utraquists, Lutherans, Calvinists, and Bohemian Brethren. Substantially conformed to the 1535 Confession, it showed the influence of Melanchthon's views on the Eucharist. It served as the doctrinal statement of the charter granted to Protestants by King Rudolph in 1608, recognizing them as having equal rights with Roman Catholics. BIBLIOGRAPHY: Schaff Creeds 1:576–580; E. de Schweinitz, *History of the Unitas Fratrum* (1885).

[J. R. WEINLICK]

BOHEMIAN SCHOOL. Artists from Germany, Italy, and France gathered at Prague and Karlstein under the patronage of Emperor Charles IV (r. 1346–78), exerting major force in the development of the *International Gothic style in late 14th cent. under the master of Hohenfurth, Theodoric of Prague, and the master of Wittingau. Upon extinction of the House of Luxemburg (early 15th cent.), the Bohemian school declined. BIBLIOGRAPHY: A. Matejcek, *Czech Gothic Painting* (1950).

[M. J. DALY]

BOHEMUND I (*c.* 1052–1111), Norman prince of Tarentum who played a significant role in the wars of the Normans of Italy with the Byzantine Empire (1081–85), led Norman soldiers in the First Crusade, and became the first Latin prince of Antioch (1098). Taken prisoner by the Muslims in battle (1100), he was ransomed but was unsuccessful in his bid to take over the Euphrates Valley and maintain control in a troubled Antioch (1104). He returned to Europe where he fielded an army against the Byzantine Emperor, Alexius I Comnenus who defeated him at Durazzo (1107). BIBLIOGRAPHY: L. Bréhier, DHGE 9:484–498, R. Yewdale, *Bohemund I, Prince of Antioch* (1924).

[F. H. BRIGHAM]

BÖHM, DOMINIKUS (1880–1955), a pioneer of modern church architecture in Germany. His Christ the King Church (Mainz-Bischofsheim, 1926) was the first to employ a poured concrete nave construction. Progress was interrupted by the Nazis from 1933 through World War II, but he contributed to the postwar renewal, building the Church of Maria Königin with stained glass wall extending the length of the nave. BIBLIOGRAPHY: A. Hoff et al., *Dominikus Böhm* (1962).

[R. J. VEROSTKO]

BÖHM, HANS, (*c.* 1450–76), shepherd, religious enthusiast. On Laetare Sunday, 1476, he announced that Mary had appeared to him. Initially B. preached a simple penance but soon turned to more radical fulminations and belligerent encounters. He was arrested; attempts to free him failed. Böhm was burned as a heretic in 1476. BIBLIOGRAPHY: A. Bigelmair, LTK 2:559.

[B. F. SCHERER]

BOILEAU-DESPRÉAUX, NICOLAS (1636–1711), French poet and literary critic, royal historiographer (1677) and member of the French Academy (1684). After beginning a career in the Church and then in law, B. turned to literature, gaining fame with the publication of his *Satires* (1–6, 1666; 8–9, 1668; 10, 1694; 11, 1701), *Epîtres* (1–4, 1674; 5, 1675, 6–9, 1675–77; 10–12, 1698), and his *Art Poétique* (1674), a verse treatise on classical French literature which extolls the role of reason and also advises against the writing of Christian epic. His burlesque epic, *Le Lutrin* (1674 and 1683), based on a real quarrel among the canons of the Paris Sainte-Chapelle (1667) was a satire on the clergy. Involved in the literary "Quarrel of the Ancients against the Moderns," he contributed to the religious disputes of later years with his *Epître 12: Sur l'amour de Dieu* (1698), in which he sides with the Jansenists, and his *Satire 12: Sur l'Equivoque,* attacking Jesuit casuistry along the lines of Pascal's tenth *Provincial Letter.* This *Satire,* opposed by Le Tellier, Louis XIV's Jesuit confessor, was never published in B.'s lifetime (1716). B. is also known for his translation of Longinus' *On the Sublime* (1674). BIBLIOGRAPHY: R. Bray, *Boileau, l'homme et l'oeuvre* (1942). *PASCAL, BLAISE.

[R. N. NICOLICH]

BOISGELIN DE CUCÉ, JEAN DE DIEU RAYMOND DE (1732–1804), cardinal. Bp. of Aix in Provence, B. was an enlightened and effective administrator, concerned for the material and spiritual well-being of his flock. He was elected to the French Academy and served as president for a two-week term. As deputy to the Estates-General he demonstrated his ability as a leader and joined the opposition when the majority voted for the confiscation of church property and passed the civil constitution of the clergy. After 10 years in England he returned to France having signed the Concordat of 1801. Pope Pius VII named him cardinal. His many contributions to literature have not had enduring influence. BIBLIOGRAPHY: C. Testore, EncCatt 2:1768; C. Constantin, DTC 2:942–944; P. Calendini, DHGE 9:575–576.

[L. MITCHELL]

BOISROBERT, FRANÇOIS LE MÉTEL DE (1589–1662), French man of letters, poet, priest. Born of French Protestant parents, B. was converted to Catholicism (1621), was tonsured (1623), and received from Urban VIII, whom he had charmed with his wit and personality, a priory in Brittany (1630), before being named canon of Rouen. A favorite of Richelieu, he used his influence to patronize numerous writers, and played an important role in the literary history of the 17th cent., esp. in the foundation and organization of the French Academy (1635), which he first suggested to Richelieu. A cleric of dubious reputation, he wrote numerous plays (18) and novels of little lasting value, as well as poetry, including his *Paraphrases, in Verse, of the Seven Penitential Psalms* (1627), *Stances* dedicated to the Virgin (1642), and *Epistles in Verse* (1647–59) considered his best work. He held the titles of adviser, preacher, and almoner to the king. BIBLIOGRAPHY: E. Magne, *Le Plaisant abbé de Boisrobert, fondateur de l' Académie Française* (1909).

[R. N. NICOLICH]

BOISSARD, ADÉODAT (1870–1937), jurist, economist, sociologist. He was general secretary of the Association Internationale and the Association Française pour Progrès Social, a founder and secretary of the Semaines Sociales de France. BIBLIOGRAPHY: G. Marsol, *Catholicisme* 2:114.

[H. JACK]

BOLAND, JOHN PETER (1888–1958). Ordained in Rome in 1911, B. became well-known in the field of labor relations. He was chairman of the New York State Labor Relations Board from 1937 to 1942, a director of the National Labor Relations Board from 1934 to 1937, and a member of the New York State Board of Mediation from 1947. B. contributed numerous articles on labor to a variety of periodicals.

[J. R. AHERNE]

BOLAÑOS, JUAN DE HEVIA, see HEVIA BOLAÑOS, JUAN DE.

BOLAÑOS, LUIS DE (c. 1550–1629), founder of the first reductions in Paraguay. A Spanish Franciscan, he went to the Paraguay missions in 1574 where he labored the next 50 years. In 1580 he and his companions began to assemble the converted Indians in villages, or reductions, where their instruction could be continued and they could learn trades. During B.'s time the Franciscans built 15 churches and spread reductions from Guayrá to Barader near Buenos Aires. Many were turned over to the Jesuits when they adopted this method of evangelization in 1609. B.'s catech-

ism, grammar, dictionary, hymns, and poems in the Guarani language became the common property of all the missions in that area. BIBLIOGRAPHY: A. Van den Wyngeart, DHGE 9:599.

[H. JACK]

BOLDNESS (rashness, foolhardiness), a term used by some moralists to designate the vice opposed by excess to the virtue of courage or fortitude. No commonly accepted name for this vice is found in English.

[P. K. MEAGHER]

BOLÍVAR, SIMÓN, (1783–1830), soldier statesman, under whose leadership Spanish control was broken in six countries of South America during the years 1810–1824. His plan for a great federation of South American states however, was unsuccessful. B., unlike many liberal leaders who followed him, was not hostile to religion. BIBLIOGRAPHY: G. Masur, *Simón Bolívar* (1948, repr. 1969)

[H. JACK]

BOLIVIA, predominantly (93.8%) Catholic country of central South America, surrounded by Brazil, Paraguay, Argentina, Chile, and Peru. A center of Indian civilization in pre-Columbian times, it attracted the Spaniards, who exploited its silver mines. Missionaries, mostly Jesuits and Franciscans, converted the Indians to Christianity, though elements of Indian religion have survived. Julius III established La Plata (modern Sucre) as the first bishopric of the area in 1552. The country has many impressive cathedrals and other churches dating from the colonial period. Bolivia proclaimed its independence from Spain in 1825, took its name from Simón Bolívar, and gave the presidency of the republic to his deputy, José de Sucre. Internal opposition led to Sucre's resignation in 1828, and the subsequent political history of Bolivia has been marked by extraordinary instability. About the time of independence, the silver mines went into decline, to be revived toward the end of the century and then supplanted by tin mining. But poverty has remained acute. Bolivia's access to the sea was lost to Chile in the War of the Pacific (1879–84), and it later had to give up a rubber area to Brazil and the Chaco region to Paraguay. The MNR *(Movimiento Nacionalista Revolutionario)*, which held power 1952–64, brought important social changes, including nationalization of mining, universal suffrage, and land reform. "Che" Guevara, the guerrilla leader, sought to lead a liberation movement in Bolivia, but was captured and executed in 1967. BIBLIOGRAPHY: G. Rommerskirchen, EncCatt 2:1774–77; P. C. Wagner, *Protestant Movement in Bolivia* (pa.1969); J. M. Malloy, *Uncompleted Revolution* (1970).

[T. EARLY]

BOLLAND, JAN VAN (1596–1665), Belgian Jesuit from whom the Bollandists took their name. A native of Limburg, B. was commissioned by the Belgian Jesuit provincial to continue the work of the *Acta Sanctorum* begun by H.

*Rosweyde, who had died after gathering much material but before publishing anything. B. modified Rosweyde's plan, conceiving a work of far greater proportion and scholarship. Discovering that his own efforts were insufficient for the task, he sought help; in 1635 G. Henschen, and in 1659, D. von *Papebroch, were assigned to aid him. BIBLIOGRAPHY: C. De Smedt, CE 2:630–639, esp. 631–635; H. Delehaye, *À travers trois siècles, l'oeuvre des Bollandistes de 1615–1915* (1920).

[R. B. ENO]

BOLLANDISTS, the Belgian Jesuit editors charged with the publication of the *Acta Sanctorum*. The project began with the effort of H. *Rosweyde (1569–1629) to prepare a work in 16 v., covering the life of Christ and the saints of the liturgical calendar. He gathered MSS for his task but died before anything was ready for publication. J. van *Bolland (1596–1665) was entrusted with the completion of the undertaking. With the help of G. *Henschen and C. *Papebroch he began at Antwerp the publication of the first volumes, which met with scholarly acclaim. These men and their successors gathered MSS from all over Europe and the publication of new volumes continued. The critical judgment of the editors gave offense to the Spanish Inquisition, which in 1695 condemned the 14 v. published by that time, but the condemnation was partially revoked in 1715. The suppression of the Jesuits in Belgium in 1773 threatened the work. In 1778 the research center was moved to Brussels and the work continued for another 15 years under government subsidy. After 1794 (by which time the 6th v. of Oct. had been published) the work was in abeyance until 1837, when, with the support of the Belgian government and learned societies in many countries, a new group of Bollandists was formed and work resumed. A group of 6 editors carries on the project which has progressed to the month of November. The best known of modern Bollandists was H. *Delehaye. BIBLIOGRAPHY: H. Delehaye, *À travers trois siècles: l'oeuvre Bollandiste 1615–1915* (1920); D. Knowles, *Great Historical Enterprises* (1963).

[R. B. ENO]

BOLLIG, JOHANN (1821–95), Jesuit Orientalist and theologian. In 1855 he became professor of Oriental languages in the Roman College and the Gregorian University. Later at Ghazer, Lebanon, he taught dogmatic theology. He was appointed a consultor of the Congregation of Propaganda and served as prefect of the Vatican Library. During Vatican Council I he acted as a papal theologian. Among his published works are *Brevis Arabica Christomatia* (1882) and *Gregor v. Nyssa: Gedichte* (1895). BIBLIOGRAPHY: Sommervogel 8:1860–61

[T. C. STAHL]

BOLOGNA, GIOVANNI (Giambologna; Jean Boulogne; 1529–1608), Flemish Italian mannerist sculptor, taught by Jacques Dubroeucq of Mons. B. traveled to Rome (1550) and Florence (1556) where B. Vecchietti and the Medici sponsored him. The *Neptune Fountain* in Bologna (1563–66), his

first major work, established his reputation and his name. B. developed his well-known Mercury figures (Medici *Mercury,* 1580) and dynamic, unified conceptions of multi-figured groups which reached a climax in the *Rape of the Sabines* (1579–83). Many voids and projections offered an infinity of views in his dramatic fountains. Whereas Flemish realism determined his equestrian monument to Cosimo I, *Hercules and the Centaur* (1594–99) is a masterpiece of stress. B. established a fashion for garden sculpture perpetuated well into the 17th century. BIBLIOGRAPHY: J. Pope-Hennessy, *Italian High Renaissance and Baroque Sculpture* (1963).

[M. J. DALY]

BOLOGNA, UNIVERSITY OF, an autonomous coeducational state university in Italy. The precise date of its foundation is unknown, although a tradition associates this with the establishment *c.* 1080 of a school in Bologna by a certain Pepo, predecessor of the jurist Irnerius who headed the school of jurisprudence at Bologna in the early 12th century. The school flourished with the revival of interest in the study of law. Under Irnerius the study of law was separated from that of the arts. This proved to be a decisive step and brought widespread fame to its law faculty; Frederick I, the Emperor, further enhanced the school's reputation by consulting its doctors. In 1158 the Emperor granted the Bolognese students the right to be judged by their own masters rather than by the civil authorities, a scholastic privilege later inserted in the code of Roman laws and known as the *Habita.* Following an attempt by the city to interfere in education, the students, theretofore loosely grouped around a master, formed *c.* 1180 two strong organizations, each under a student rector—the cismontanes (native Italians) and the ultramontanes (foreigners—which later subdivided into various national groups represented by each organization. By 1432 these national groups numbered 16. In time, cultural differences and strife between students and masters and civil authorities led to the establishment of new university centers in France, Spain, and Italy. As Irnerius had separated law from the arts, Gratian, a 12th-cent. Bolognese monk, separated the study of canon law from theology. Gratian's *Decretum* became the 13th cent. basis of church legislation. The restoration in the same cent. of Aristotelian philosophy sparked a new interest in the mathematical, liberal, and mechanical arts, which led to the establishment of a third college for instruction in philosophical and technical subjects. The three colleges offered courses leading to a doctorate conferred by the archdeacon in the cathedral of Bologna. The archdeacon acted as papal delegate in conferring degrees, a circumstance that assured their recognition throughout Europe. The university organization, based on the three colleges of students, continued until the late 18th century. It was transformed during the time of the French Revolution and the Napoleonic era from which it emerged as a state university. The university now comprises faculties of jurisprudence; economics and commerce; arts and philosophy; education; medicine and surgery; mathematics, physics, and natural sciences; industrial chemistry; pharmacy; engineering; agriculture; and veterinary medicine. The governing body is composed of an administrative board and an academic senate. The library houses over 600,000 volumes, 7,500 MSS, and 1,000 incunabula. Enrollment averages about 35,000. BIBLIOGRAPHY: H. Rashdall, *Universities in the Middle Ages* (ed. F. M. Powicke and A. B. Emden, 3 v., 1936).

[M. B. MURPHY]

BOLOGNESE SCHOOL, the name given to the Carracci (Annibale, Agostino, and Ludovico) and their followers native to Bologna or trained there according to the principles taught by the Carracci in their private art school (Accademia degli Incamminati) founded *c.*1585. The school reacted against mannerism by stressing the study of models and prototypes. BIBLIOGRAPHY: R. Wittkower, *Art and Architecture in Italy: 1600–1750* (1958).

[L. A. LEITE]

BOLSEC, JÉRÔME HERMÈS (d. *c.*1584), writer and controversialist. He left the Carmelites and Catholicism, studied medicine, was attracted by Calvin, but publicly challenged his doctrine on predestination, and was expelled from Geneva. Later he was rejected by Beza because he would not sign the Confession of Bern. He finally returned to France, to the Church, and to the practice of medicine in Lyons. His biographies of Calvin and Beza recount unsubstantiated scandals about both. BIBLIOGRAPHY: J. Dedieu, DHGE 9:676–679.

[H. JACK]

BOLSHEVISM (from Russian *bolshoy,* majority), the doctrines and practices of the extreme and more violent wing (the Maximalists) of the Russian Social-Democratic Party, which began to split off from the Mensheviks or moderates (the Minimalists) after 1903 and after the Revolution of March, 1917, seized supreme power by Lenin's *coup d'état,* and have held it ever since. "Bolshevik" was maintained as part of the official title of the U.S.S.R. Communists in 1918 in order to preserve continuity, but was dropped in 1952, by which time many of the old Bolsheviks had been "purged." It is little used now, though the jocular and contemptuous "bolshie" still survives. The doctrine of the party was *Marxist Communism; its methods were ruthless and strictly disciplined, and showed how effective a minority faction can be when it exploits a temporary majority in governing counsels. BIBLIOGRAPHY: E. H. Carr, *Bolshevik Revolution, 1917–1923* (3 v., 1951–53).

[T. GILBY]

BOLTRAFFIO, GIOVANNI ANTONIO (1466–1516), pupil of Leonardo at Milan, B. painted forms with brilliant skill in enamel-like finish. His works include the *Casio Altarpiece* (Louvre), *St. Barbara* (Berlin), many small Madonnas (London, Bergamo, and Milan), as well as urbane portraits in many collections. BIBLIOGRAPHY: W. Suida, *Leonardo und sein Kreis* (1929).

[M. J. DALY]

BOLTZIUS, JOHANN MARTIN (1703–65), American Lutheran pastor. B. accompanied emigrants from Salzburg to Oglethorpe's Georgia settlement in 1734. At Ebenezer, Georgia, he served as pastor, teacher, and colony administrator.

[M. J. SUELZER]

BOLZANO, BERNHARD (1781–1848), mathematician, philosopher, and theologian. Ordained priest in 1805, he became professor of the philosophy of religion at the Univ. of Prague. Some years later (1819) he was removed from his position by the emperor of Austria who objected to certain of B.'s views on the social order, though he taught nothing heretical. He went into studious retirement in 1820. He made significant contributions to the development of mathematical theory. BIBLIOGRAPHY: *Bernard Bolzano: Theory of Science* (ed. J. Berg, tr. B. Terrell, 1973).

[P. K. MEAGHER]

BOMB, ATOMIC. The primary ethico-religious problem posed by the atomic bomb concerns the morality of its use in warfare. The doctrine commonly held by RC moral theologians is that even defensive warfare is justifiable only as a last resort, and then only under certain limiting conditions. Prominent among these is the observance of due proportion between the injustice suffered by unjust aggression and the evils to be expected in consequence of violent resistance or defensive war. Resort to thermonuclear bombs, esp. in these days when the possession of weapons of this kind has become widespread, and the evil consequences of their employment, would create, in the judgment of RC moralists, such havoc and destruction of innocent and guilty alike, that no circumstance or injustice could conceivably justify it. The idea of a limited use of thermonuclear weapons, once proposed as legitimate by some moralists, has few if any defenders today among responsible moralists. BIBLIOGRAPHY: R. W. Gardiner, *Cool Arm of Destruction: Modern Weapons and Moral Insensitivity* (1974); *Moral Dilemma of Nuclear Weapons: Essays from Worldview* (ed. W. Clancy, pa. 1961).

[P. K. MEAGHER]

BOMBERG, DANIEL (*c.*1470–1549), Dutch Christian printer of the Hebrew Bible, the *Targums, the Babylonian Talmud. B.'s 2d. edition of the Hebrew Bible (1524–25), edited by Jacob ben Hayyim, remained the accepted Hebrew text until R. *Kittels edition, *Biblica Hebraica* (1930–37).

[T. C. O'BRIEN]

BOMBING. The morality of the bombing of legitimate military targets in the waging of a just war has generally been admitted by RC moralists. But in modern warfare, which so readily escalates into total warfare, the difference between legitimate and illegitimate targets becomes obscure and bombing tends to become directed against a people as a whole without distinguishing between aggressors and noncombatants, with a view to breaking a nation's will to fight. Bombing thus tends to become obliterative, and when this happens, however just the ultimate purpose of such bombing may be, moralists almost universally consider it to be unjustifiable. BIBLIOGRAPHY: R. W. Gardiner, *Cool Arm of Destruction: Modern Weapons and Moral Insensitivity* (1974); *Moral Dilemma of Nuclear Weapons: Essays from Worldview* (ed. W. Clancy, pa. 1961).

[P. K. MEAGHER]

BOMBOLOGNUS OF BOLOGNA (fl. 1265–70). Italian Dominican theologian who taught the *Sentences* at the priory of San Domenico in Bologna and was the first Dominican known to have written a commentary on the *Sentences*. Reflecting for the most part Italian tradition, he defends universal hylomorphism as a valid philosophical explanation of the difference between creatures and God in accord with the teaching of Ibn Gabirol, Solomon ben Judah (Avicebron). BIBLIOGRAPHY:A. Walz LTK 2:578.

[F. H. BRIGHAM]

BON (Boa Ho), a native Tibetan cult that emphasized magic and divination. When fused with Buddhism, Bon resulted in Lamaism. This was an amalgamation of demonistic animism. BIBLIOGRAPHY: L. Govinda, *Foundations of Tibetan Mysticism* (1974).

[C. CARROLL]

BON SECOURS, SISTERS OF (CBS), a religious congregation founded (1824) at Paris by Abp. H. I. de Quélen. The 12 original members made their vows at Saint-Sulpice. Pope Pius IX approved them in 1884; their general motherhouse is in Rome. With Josephine Potel as first superior, their original work was to nurse the ill in their own homes. Engaged eventually in hospital work and clinics, they set up a training school for their sisters. Their apostolate grew to include care of the chronically ill, for whom they conduct homes, as well as an orthopedic one for crippled children, care of aged priests and of orphans. They were also involved apostolically in the Franco-Prussian War. From France the sisters went to Ireland, England, Scotland, and the U.S. Their U.S. motherhouse is in Marriottsville, Md. Bon Secours Sisters formed also in 1840 at Arcis-sur-Aube, with a general motherhouse at Troyes, France; from them stemmed in 1882

the Bon Secours Sisters of N.Y. BIBLIOGRAPHY: M. Badiou, *Les Soeurs du Bon Secours de Paris* (1958).

[M. R. BROWN]

BONA, ST. (*c.*1156–1207), virgin and pilgrim. She was born and spent life, except for her pilgrimages, in Pisa. She reportedly enjoyed the gifts of prophecy, of the reading of hearts, and of miracles. Though her cult did not extend much beyond Italy, it was widespread there, and she was frequently represented by Italian artists from the 13th cent. on. In 1962 Pope John XXIII named her patroness of travel hostesses. BIBLIOGRAPHY: AS May 7:141–161, 858; F. Bartorelli, *Santa Bona da Pisa* (1960); B. Matteucci, BiblSanct 3:234–236.

[W. A. JURGENS]

BONA, GIOVANNI (1609–74), Italian Cistercian, liturgical and ascetical writer; cardinal from 1669. Of his liturgical works, written because of his conviction that the spiritual life is essentially linked to liturgy, the *Rerum liturgicarum libri duo* (1671) and the *De sacrificio missae tractatus asceticus* (1658) are principal. The most frequently reedited of his ascetical works is *Manuductio ad caelum* (1658), a treatise on progress toward union with God. The *De discretione spirituum* (1671) is a guide for discerning the various affects of the soul and their origin. In his numerous works B. presented traditional spiritual theology gathered from a rich knowledge of the Fathers, St. Bernard, the medievals, combined with the more recent ideas of SS. Francis de Sales and Ignatius Loyola. B. advocated the use of ejaculatory prayers (e.g., in *Via compendia ad Deum*, 1657) as an aid to recollection, the orderly practice of the virtues and austerity of life, reliance on a spiritual director, renewal through annual retreats. Possibility of his canonization has frequently been discussed. BIBLIOGRAPHY: J.-M. Canivez, DSAM 1:1762–66.

[T. C. O'BRIEN]

BONA MORS CONFRATERNITY, a spiritual association founded in Rome in 1648. Its founder was Vincent Carafa, general of the Society of Jesus, who was esp. moved by compassion for the suffering and death of many victims of a plague. It is also known as the Confraternity of Our Lord Jesus Christ, Dying on the Cross, and of the Most Blessed Virgin Mary, his Sorrowful Mother. The confraternity was approved by Popes Innocent X and Alexander VII; Benedict XIII elevated it to the status of an archconfraternity. The Jesuit general was first given authority to establish chapters of the confraternity in churches under the jurisdiction of the Jesuits, and this was later extended to churches other than those of the Jesuits. The purpose of the confraternity is to prepare its members for a good death, and to this end chapters hold meetings at which instructions are given accompanied by various acts of devotion. To become a member, one presents himself to a chapter director and makes his desire known. In testimony of his acceptance he is given a certificate or whatever other sign of acceptance is used in his chapter. Only in extraordinary circumstances can one become a member through application made by another on his behalf.

[P. K. MEAGHER]

BONACINA, MARTINO (*c*.1585–1631), Italian theologian, who after teaching at the Swiss College in Milan, went to Rome as theologian of Cardinal Aldobrandini and became a titular bishop. He was chiefly distinguished as a moralist of the probabilist persuasion. His *Theologia moralis,* admired for its clarity and erudition, was frequently reprinted. BIBLIOGRAPHY: C. Testore, EncCatt 2:1827.

[T. C. O'BRIEN]

BONAL, FRANÇOIS DE (1734–1800), Carmelite, bp. of Clermont. As deputy to the Estates-General of 1789, he was named president of the ecclesiastical committee of the assembly and fought anticlerical measures until forced to resign. B's letter advising Louis XVI not to receive the sacraments from the civil clergy was introduced in the trial of the king. Condemned to deportation, he settled in Munich. In 1798 he signed the *Instruction sur les atteintes partées à la religion,* published by French refugee bps. in Germany. Before his death he dictated a spiritual testament giving his last instructions to his diocese. BIBLIOGRAPHY: G. Wagner, *Catholicisme* 2:120.

[L. MITCHELL]

BONAL, RAYMOND (1600–53), French moral theologian and religious founder. His *Cours de théologie morale* (2 v. 1649; Lat. tr. P. Laur, 1674) was used in many French seminaries. B. founded at Villefranche in 1637 the congregation of Prêtres de Ste.-Marie, also called Bonalists. The rule was inspired by the spirituality of St. Francis de Sales; the congregation was devoted to seminary work and to preaching missions and retreats. Papal approval came in 1665, but recruitment dwindled; by the mid-18th cent. the congregation was absorbed into the Vincentians. BIBLIOGRAPHY: E. Levesque, DHGE 9:725–727.

[T. C. O'BRIEN]

BONALD, LOUIS GABRIEL AMBROISE DE (1754–1840), French statesman, social philosopher, exponent of *traditionalism. Beginning with language, which he maintained man could not have invented, B. maintained that all principles of human thought and morality, as well as social structures, came not from the power of reason, but from tradition passing on an original divine revelation. The recipient is society, not the individual; the person depends on and develops completely from society. Recourse to the societal tradition is the sole way to truth, morality, and social stability. Seeking to combat the Enlightenment, B. expounded his system of social theories in *La théorie de pouvoir politique et religieux* (1796) and other works. His ideas had a marked influence on French political and social

thought, esp. on *positivism. BIBLIOGRAPHY: M. H. Quinlan, *Historical Thought of the Vicomte de Bonald* (1953).

[T. C. O'BRIEN]

BONNANUS DA PISA (fl. 1174–86), Italian architect and sculptor recorded as having worked on the Leaning Tower of the Cathedral of Pisa with Master *Guglielmo de Modena. Major works of the Italian School are B.'s magnificent bronze doors for the Cathedrals of Pisa (1180) in Lombard Romanesque style and Monreale (1186), Byzantine in style, important links in the long tradition embracing the Ottonian bronze doors at Hildesheim (1015) by Bp. Bernward, the magnificent baptismal font of St. Barthélemy in Liège (1107–1118) by the Mosan master Renier de Huy, and the later bronze font at Hildesheim (*c*.1200), where figures will break their classical boundaries in the new emotional ecstasy of Gothic. BIBLIOGRAPHY: P. Toesca, *Storia dell 'arte italiana* (1927).

[M. J. DALY]

BONAPARTE, CHARLES JOSEPH (1851–1921), U.S. Secretary of Navy, Attorney-General. His grandfather was King Jerome, the brother of Napoleon I. Educated by tutors and in private schools near Baltimore, he graduated from Harvard law school in 1874. B. was a Republican who often acted independently of party considerations. His early career was devoted to municipal and civil service reform. When appointed legal advisor to the board of Indian commissioners by Theodore Roosevelt, he worked to end corruption among field agents. Serving under Roosevelt as Secretary of the Navy (1905) and Attorney General (1906) B. was often employed as an intermediary between government leaders and the Church. BIBLIOGRAPHY: E. F. Goldman, *Charles J. Bonaparte, Patrician Reformer: His Early Career* (1943).

[J. HILL]

BONAPARTE, JOSEPH (1768–1844), eldest brother of Napoleon I. B. began his diplomatic and political career under the Directory by serving as ambassador to Rome. He negotiated the treaties of Lunéville (1801) and Amiens (1802), and played a minor role in the Concordat of 1801. Under the First Empire he served as grand elector, King of Naples (1806–08), King of Spain (1808–13), and Lieutenant General in 1814. After Waterloo he escaped to the U.S. where he lived as a gentleman farmer under the name of Count de Survilliers near Bordentown, N.J. until 1832. He later went to England and finally to Florence where he rejoined his wife shortly before his death. BIBLIOGRAPHY: T. Aronson, *Golden Bees: The Story of the Bonapartes* (1964).

[I. M. KASHUBA]

BONAPARTE, NAPOLEON, see NAPOLEON BONAPARTE.

BONAVENTURA (Pontificia Facoltà Teologica "San Bonaventura"), institute of higher studies in Rome. The

Pontifical Theological Faculty of the Friars Minor Conventual continues the tradition of the ancient universities that flourished in the order from the 13th century. Founded at Rome as the Collegium Sancti Bonaventurae by Pope Sixtus V (1587), the college prospered until suppressed by law. Reopened (1905) by the Sacred Congregation of Bishops and Religious, the theological faculty was reconstituted in the Collegio Internazionale dei Frati Minori Conventuali, confirmed (1935) as a papal institution, and given its present name in 1955.

BONAVENTURE, ST. (c.1217–74), Doctor of the Church. Born Giovanni Fidanza in Tuscany, he entered the Franciscans about 1240. He studied theology at Paris under Alexander of Hales and John of La Rochelle, becoming a master in 1257. Elected minister general in 1257, made cardinal in 1273, he served order and Church in writing, preaching, and administration. He died at the Council of Lyons. A hallmark of B.'s theological synthesis is its adherence to tradition. He is a scholastic but uses the Scriptures in his writing more than any other master. He knew Aristotle (whose metaphysics he chose not to follow), but his philosophical bent is Augustinian. He is no polemicist and interprets benignly contradictions and differences in the Fathers and other authorities. B., like Augustine, makes no sharp distinction between theology and philosophy. Faith and reason meet. His metaphysics is built around the notions of creation, exemplarism, and illumination. The world, made from nothing by God, must return to him as to its final cause. It reflects God, as a model reflects its exemplar. The human creature rises to God by contemplation of created truth, in which he is assisted by a divine light beyond intellect. B.'s theology is Christocentric: all things are created through the Word of God; Christ is our exemplar; by contemplation of Christ we are led to the height of the mystical union and to the beatific vision.

Even in his own time, B. was recognized as a master of the spiritual life. A mystic himself, a devoted son of St. Francis, he writes from experience and learning. He has no separate treatise on mystical theology, his doctrine is developed throughout his formal tractates, his commentaries, his sermons and his two *Lives* of St. Francis. The passion of Christ is central. For B., Christ is *medium omnium scientiarum* —the means through which all knowledge comes. Two threads run through his teaching, that of Augustine and of Pseudo-Denis: of intellect and will; of knowledge and love. In his synthesis the two become one. Man rises to God through loving contemplation under the divine light, and through the purgative, illuminative, and unitive ways. Not all, perhaps only a few, achieve the ecstatic union in this life, but it is the flowering of the seed. B. places (in contrast to Aquinas) the formal note of union and of eternal beatitude in the act of the will.

The influence of B. in mystical theology has been continuous, esp. in N. Europe, not only among Franciscans, but Dominicans, Carthusians, and the Brothers of the Common

Life. *The Imitation of Christ* bears his stamp. Leo XIII called him *facile princeps*—easily first in the field. Works: *Opera omnia*, 10 v., Quaracchi 1882–1902. BIBLIOGRAPHY: É. Gilson, *Philosophy of St. Bonaventure* (tr. I. Trethowan 1965); E. Bettoni, *Saint Bonaventure* (tr. A. Gambatese, pa. 1964).

[W. B. MAHONEY]

BONAVENTURE OF PERAGA, BL. (1332–88), Augustinian Hermit who studied at Paris, taught theology at Bologna, wrote a number of treatises and commentaries, became prior general of his order (1377), and was made cardinal (1378). He died from an arrow wound inflicted upon him as he was crossing the Tiber. In the defense of the rights of the Church he had infuriated his kinsman, Prince of Carrara, who was suspected of being the instigator of his murder. His claim to be classified as a martyr, or indeed to the title of blessed, has never, apparently, been officially recognized by the Church, though within his own order he was venerated as such soon after his death. BIBLIOGRAPHY: A. M. Giacomini, BiblSanct 3:293–294; Butler 2:251.

[M. H. BEIRNE]

BONDOLFI, PIETRO (1872–1943), Roman-born founder and first superior general (1921) of the Bethlehem Fathers, a missionary congregation, at Immensee in the diocese of Chur, Switzerland. BIBLIOGRAPHY: G. B. Tragella, EncCatt 2:1851–52.

[T. C. O'BRIEN]

BONET, JUAN PABLO (c.1560–c.1620), Spanish priest, pioneer in the education of deaf-mutes. He established a school for them in Barcelona. He was one of the first to instruct in lip-reading. His volume on teaching deaf-mutes, translated into many languages, became a standard. BIBLIOGRAPHY: S. Ruiz, DHGE 9:848–849.

[T. C. O'BRIEN]

BONET, NICHOLAS (c.1280–c.1343), Franciscan theologian, who taught theology in Paris. B. was also a papal legate (1338) to the Tartars, and bp. of Malta (1342). His writings were favored by the Scotists, *Formalitates in vita Scoti* (1489), *Theologia naturalis* (1505). BIBLIOGRAPHY: F. O'Briain, DHGE 9:849–852.

[T. C. O'BRIEN]

BONFRÈRE, JACQUES (1573–1642), Bible commentator. B. taught Scripture and Hebrew at Douai, and was superior of the Scots College there. His commentary on Joshua, Judges, and Ruth has been highly regarded, and the introduction to his commentary on the Pentateuch was chosen by J. P. *Migne to introduce his *Scripturae sacrae cursus* (1839). He also edited Jerome's translation of Eusebius' *Onomasticon urbium et locorum S. Scripturae*. BIBLIOGRAPHY: C. Sommervogel, DB 1.2:1845.

[T. M. MCFADDEN]

BONHOEFFER, DIETRICH (1906–45), German theologian, executed by Nazi captors April 8, 1945, at Flossenbürg. A Lutheran, he began his university study at Tübingen, then traveled; at Rome the rich Roman liturgy and its monastic setting inspired a lifelong fascination. At 19 he studied theology in Berlin with Adolf *Harnack, though his first thesis, *Sanctorum communio*, strongly reflected the thought of Karl *Barth. After teaching briefly in Berlin, he spent the 1930–31 academic year at Union Theological Seminary in New York, wondering at American church life as "Protestantism without Reformation." Back in Germany, his resistance to Nazi power led him to broadcast in 1933 a direct attack on the *führer*-principle and, later, Nazi anti-Semitism. An 18-month London pastorate allowed him to arouse international sympathy for the resistance Church and to visit Anglican monastic communities, which inspired his later work, *Life Together* (Eng. tr., 1954). He took a leading part in framing the 1934 *Barmen Declaration, which became the banner of the *Confessing Church. He taught (1935–37) at the Confessing Church seminary at Finkenwalde on the Baltic, a center of resistance until the Nazis closed it, arresting 27 students. Weeks later *The Cost of Discipleship* (2d rev. ed., Eng. tr., 1960; pa., 1963), the most widely read of his books, appeared. He held secret meetings and, after a brief American visit, began a perilous double life as a privileged Army Intelligence courier and a theological insurgent. In 1942 he offered to an Anglican bp. in Sweden a peace plan involving Hitler's arrest; it was refused.

Imprisoned in 1943, he kept writing, and came to accept the plan to assassinate Hitler that failed in 1944. His self-questioning *Letters and Papers from Prison* (Eng. tr., *Prisoner for God*, 1954; pa., 1962) and some work on his *Ethics* (ed. E. Bethge, Eng. tr., 1955) are from this period. Then he was moved to concentration camps, Buchenwald, Schoenberg, finally Flossenbürg, where he was executed just as the liberating Allies approached. His last act was to lead a worship service with men of many nations. His thinking and example have stirred large currents of commitment and Christian political witness. He saw the Church limiting itself to certain segments of life and demanded that it lay claim to the whole of things and summon men not to be religious but to be fully human. In theology he shared Barth's rejection of *liberal theology, yet from Harnack he developed the idea of a theology for "a world come of age." In ethics he stressed a disciplined obedience to Christ, but in "holy worldliness." B.'s idea of the world, however, is expressed in his *Ethics*: "In Jesus Christ the reality of God entered the reality of this world. . . . God and the world are comprised in this name

[Jesus Christ]. In Him all things consist (Col 1.17). Henceforward one can speak neither of God nor of the world without speaking of Jesus Christ." Hotly condemning "cheap grace," his Christology used existentialist philosophy to restate traditional doctrine. The 1,128-page work *Dietrich Bonhoeffer: Theologie, Christ, Zeitgenosse* (1967), by his close friend Eberhard Bethge, is the largest resource (Eng. tr., E. Mosbacher, *Dietrich Bonhoeffer*, 1970). BIBLIOGRAPHY: M. Bosanquet, *Life and Death of Dietrich Bonhoeffer* (1969); R. Marle, *Bonhoeffer: The Man and His Work* (1968).

[J. O. NELSON]

BONI HOMINES, a name popularly given to the *Perfecti among the *Albigenses, Brothers and Sisters of the Free Spirit, and other medieval sects. The term was also employed to designate members of four religious orders: Order of Grandmont (12th cent.), Canons of Villar de Frades (13th cent.), Friars of the Sack (13th cent.), and Minims (15th cent.).

[C. Y. LYNCH]

BONIFACE, ST. (*c*.675–*c*.754), English missionary to the Continent, martyr. He is known as the apostle of Germany. According to tradition he was born at Crediton in Devonshire. Reared by Benedictine monks, he absorbed the Anglo-Saxon monastic ideals of love for learning, Rome, and missions. He was ordained at the monastery of Nursling and became director of its school. He first visited Frisia in 716 but returned to become abbot of Nursling the following year. In 718 he went to Rome, where Gregory II changed his English name Winfrid to Boniface and gave him broad missionary jurisdiction in pagan areas. He achieved success working in Frisia, Thuringia, Hesse, Franconia, and Bavaria. On a second trip to Rome in 722 he was consecrated bp. by Gregory and received letters to all civil and religious rulers in Germany, including Charles Martel whose support greatly facilitated his work. Gregory III made him abp. with authority over all Germany east of the Rhine in 732. In the 740s he carried out a major reform of the Frankish Church, founded *Fulda monastery, and was appointed abp. of Mainz. He later resigned from Mainz and was massacred with 53 companions on a final mission to the Frisians. He was buried at Fulda. BIBLIOGRAPHY: G. Greenaway, *Saint Boniface* (1955); F. Caraffa, BiblSanct 3:308–318; A. M. Raggi, BiblSanct 3:318–320 for iconography; Butler 2:477–481.

[T. EARLY]

BONIFACE I, ST. (d. 422), **POPE** from 418. As part of an embassy B. was sent to the imperial court in Constantinople during the pontificate of Innocent I. His election as successor to *Zosimus followed an attempt of a faction to win the office for the archdeacon Eulalius by the strategem of a sudden acclamation at the Lateran while the deceased pope was being buried. Symmachus, prefect of the city, favored

Eulalius, but the Emperor Honorius ordered both contenders out of the city until the matter could be adjudicated. When Eulalius returned without permission to preside at the Easter rites, imperial support turned to B. on the ground that Eulalius had forfeited his claim, and B. was accepted as true Pope. B. persuaded St. Augustine to refute Pelagian doctrine but left it to the Emperor to condemn Pelagius and Caelestius. B. took action in several matters affecting his jurisdiction: he deprived *Patroclus of Arles of the legatine authority given him by Zosimus; he heard the appeal of an unworthy priest, Apiarius, against his condemnation by African bishops; he asserted his authority in Illyricum against the patriarch of Constantinople. He was buried in a chapel that he had constructed in the cemetery of St. Felicitas, but his tomb has not been discovered. BIBLIOGRAPHY: G. Bardy, DHGE 9:895–897.

[P. F. MULHERN]

BONIFACE II (d. 532), **POPE** from 530. B. was an Ostrogoth, a Roman archdeacon whom Felix IV named as his successor, bestowing his own pallium upon him. The Roman clergy, however, fearing B.'s Ostrogothic bias, elected Dioscorus of Alexandria after the death of Felix. Both claimants were consecrated the same day but Dioscorus died after 22 days. The opponents of B. then submitted and a united Roman synod accepted him as Pope, Dec. 27, 530. In 531 another synod under B. decreed the Pope's right to designate his own successor. B. then named *Vigilius to succeed him and prevailed upon the Roman clergy to accept his choice. But because of public anger B., in the presence of the Roman senate, revoked the decree and annulled the designation of Vigilius. As Pope, B. confirmed the acts of the second Council of Orange, thus terminating the semi-Pelagian controversies. He won the personal affection of the Roman people by his great charity in time of famine. He was interred in the Vatican. BIBLIOGRAPHY: G. Bardy, DHGE 9:897–898.

[P. F. MULHERN]

BONIFACE III (d. 607), **POPE** for 9 months in 607. A Roman, B. was appointed in 603 papal *apocrisiarius at the court of Constantinople by Pope *Gregory I (590–604). In this position he obtained from the Emperor Phocas a reaffirmation of Justinian's recognition of the Pope as head of all the Churches. Neither Sabinian, B.'s predecessor as apocrisiarius, nor Gregory himself had been able to obtain this action, which was needed to nullify the pretensions of the patriarchs of Constantinople to a dignity that challenged the unique position of the Roman pontiff in the Church. B. held a council in Rome which forbade the discussion of a successor to a deceased pope or bishop before 3 days had elapsed after his death. BIBLIOGRAPHY: Mann 1.1:259–267; G. Bardy, DHGE 9:898.

[P. F. MULHERN]

BONIFACE IV, ST. (d. 615), **POPE** from 608. The Monophysite heresy caused much ecclesiastical and civil turmoil in B.'s reign, but the Pope himself is not mentioned in the controversies, except as a target of abuse from St. Columban for supporting condemnation of the *Three Chapters by the Second Council of Constantinople. With the permission of the Emperor Phocas, B. erected a church on the site of the pagan Pantheon (609). There he enshrined relics from the catacombs, and called the church the Basilica of St. Mary of the Martyrs. A Roman synod of 610 enacted legislation aimed at the restoration of monastic discipline. BIBLIOGRAPHY: Mann 1.1:268–279; T. Oestreich, CE 2:660–661; Butler 2:252.

[P. F. MULHERN]

BONIFACE V (d. *c.*625), **POPE** from 619. B. is noted for achieving order in Rome after the war-filled reign of his predecessor, *Deusdedit I. B. sought to conform Church law to the civil code in the matter of bequests. B. is also credited with establishing the law of sanctuary and issuing regulations on the conduct of the liturgy. To Justin, abp. of Canterbury, he sent the pallium with a letter encouraging him in his apostolic labors. During his reign the ancient patriarchates, Jerusalem, Antioch, and Alexandria, fell into Islamic hands. BIBLIOGRAPHY: Mann 1:294–303; G. Bardy, DHGE 9:899.

[P. F. MULHERN]

BONIFACE VI (d. 896), **POPE** for 15 days in 896. B. was a Roman and the son of a bishop. As subdeacon he had been suspended from his sacred functions for misconduct, and at the time he was chosen to succeed *Formosus as pope he was under a like penalty incurred as a priest. Rome was in a state of tumult, torn between the forces of Arnulf of Germany and Lambert of Spoleto, both claimants of the imperial crown. The withdrawal of Arnulf because of illness enabled Lambert to gain the upper hand and to secure B.'s election, but within a few days the new pontiff died from an attack of gout. In 898 a synod under John IX condemned B. as an intruder. BIBLIOGRAPHY: F. Baix, DHGE 9:899–900.

[P. F. MULHERN]

BONIFACE VIII (Benedict Caetani; 1234–1303), **POPE** from 1294. After studies in Roman and canon law at Bologna, he entered the papal service *c.*1264, and was employed on missions to France (1264) and England (1265). Created a cardinal in 1281, he was at Paris in 1290, where he negotiated a peace between France and Aragon and defended the mendicant orders against the University. Elected pope at Naples in 1294, on the abdication of Celestine V, he immediately moved the curia back to Rome out of the reach of Charles II of Naples. A man of keen practical talents, his finest achievement is the promulgation of a *Liber Sextus* to bring the law of the Church up to date; among the many personal decrees in that volume, the most attractive is that on the education of the parochial clergy *(Cum ex eo)*. In 1300 he proclaimed a remarkably successful Jubilee or Holy Year, the first ever. Most of his pontificate, however, is overshadowed by his celebrated struggle with Philip the Fair of France. Finding that Edward I of England and Philip of France had placed heavy taxes on the clergy in order to support their war with one another, Boniface decreed (*Clericis laicos;* 1296) that any lay ruler imposing taxes without papal permission was *ipso facto* excommunicated. Although an amicable settlement with Philip was reached in 1297, Boniface soon found himself at variance with Philip once more when Philip supported the claims of the two cardinals of the Colonna family, and of the Franciscan Spirituals, claiming that Boniface had really usurped the place of Celestine V. When the papal armies razed the Colonna castles to the ground, and the Colonna cardinals and supporters fled to France, Philip openly sided with them. In 1301 Philip asserted that he had total sovereignty over the persons as well as the property of the French episcopate. Boniface denounced this attitude in *Ausculta fili* and called a council for Rome in 1302 for the reform of the French church. The council proved abortive, but in 1303 Boniface issued the bull *Unam Sanctam* in which he claimed, among other things, that all things were subject to the pope, and that it was in his power to set up, judge, and depose temporal kings. Following a large-scale series of accusations from France, Boniface was preparing in the summer of 1303 at Anagni to proclaim Philip excommunicated, when mercenaries led by Nogaret, the minister of Philip, and by Sciarra Colonna, occupied Anagni and confronted Boniface. Although the attackers were soon driven off, Boniface's health declined as a result, and he died at Rome a month later. BIBLIOGRAPHY: *Les Registres de Boniface VIII* (ed. G. A. Digard, et al., 4 v. 1884–1939); T. S. R. Boase, *Boniface VIII* (1933); H.-X. Arquillière, DHGE 9:904–909.

[L. E. BOYLE]

BONIFACE IX (Pietro Tomacelli; *c.*1355–1404), **POPE** from 1389. Succeeding Urban VI, B. excommunicated the antipope Clement VII. Negotiations to terminate the Western Schism ended in a failure. Though ill-educated, Boniface was prudent and moral; yet he was guilty of nepotism and of selling offices and using indulgences for financial gain. BIBLIOGRAPHY: H. Hemmer, DTC 2.1:1003–05; E. Vansteenberghe, DHGE 9:909–922.

[F. D. LAZENBY]

BONIFACE OF MONTFERRAT (1155–1207), crusader. Elected leader of the Fourth Crusade (1202–04) which ended with the capture of Constantinople, B. aspired to become emperor, but was obliged to accede to Baldwin IX of Flanders. He became king of Thessalonika, but despite his control of Greece as far as Athens, he could not withstand the growth of the Vlacho-Bulgarian state. He was killed in battle with the Bulgarians. BIBLIOGRAPHY: L. Bréhier, DHGE 9:958–966.

[V. BULLOUGH]

BONIFACE OF SAVOY, BL. (*c.*1207–1270), Carthusian monk, abp. of Canterbury from 1241. An aggressive foreigner, uncle of Henry III's queen, B. was initially unpopular but he united the English clergy against royal demands (1256–59) although he supported Henry against the barons (1258–65). BIBLIOGRAPHY: Butler 3:102–103; M. A. Calabrese, BiblSanct 3:321–323.

[F. D. BLACKLEY]

BONIFACIUS, see BONIFACE.

BONITUS, ST. (also, Bonet; *c.*623–706), b. Auvergne, France, government official, bishop, ascetic. He served as chancellor (634–656) for Sigebert III of Austrasia and as prefect of Marseilles (677) under Pepin of Heristal. About 690, he succeeded his brother, St. Avitus, as bp. of Clermont. On his resignation in 700, he became a monk of Manlieu and died after a pilgrimage to Rome. BIBLIOGRAPHY: G. Bataille, BiblSanct 3:337–338; L. Bréhier, DHGE 9:843–847; Butler 1:97–98.

[M. H. BEIRNE]

BONIZO OF SUTRI (*c.*1045–99), historian, bp. of Sutri (*c.*1075), papal legate (1078), and bp. of Piacenza (1086). His *Liber ad amicum* provides a highly favorable life of Gregory VII and a pro-Gregorian history of the contemporary Church. BIBLIOGRAPHY: W. Ullmann, *Growth of Papal Government in the Middle Ages* (2d ed., 1962); L. Jadin, DHGE 9:994–998.

BONN, capital of West Germany since establishment of the Federal Republic in 1949. Located some 15 miles up the Rhine from Cologne, Bonn traces its history to the 1st-cent. establishment of a Roman camp at a river crossing there. Christians were at Bonn from 260, and the medieval city grew up around St. Cassius monastery, whose church dates from *c.*400. When Cologne gained independent status in the 13th cent. its archbishop-electors made Bonn their residence remaining there until the French occupation of 1794. For a time during the Reformation, the abps. supported the Protestant cause, but the area was regained for Catholicism. Religious houses were secularized under French rule (1794–1814), and B. was given to Prussia in 1815. In the 17th cent. B. gained importance as a cultural center, and in contrast to the more orthodox atmosphere of Cologne, the Univ. of Bonn, founded by the abps. in 1786 (refounded 1818), helped spread Enlightenment thought and served as a rallying center for *Febronianism. Following Vatican I, Bonn became a center of Old Catholic influence. With the incorporation of surrounding villages in 1969, its population reached some 300,000.

[T. EARLY]

BONN AGREEMENT, a document issued at a formal Anglican–Old Catholic meeting held at Bonn, July 3, 1931, and chaired by A. C. Headlam, Bp. of Gloucester. The

Agreement was based on dogmatic unity, mutual recognition, and independent cooperation. It was accepted by all Anglican, European Old Catholic, and Polish National Catholic Churches.

[E. E. BEAUREGARD]

BONN REUNION CONFERENCES, meetings to effect Christian reunion. Presided over by I. von *Döllinger, the first two were private meetings of Orthodox, Anglican, and Protestant theologians invited by Old Catholic leaders; these gatherings constituted an important ecumenical dialogue of the 19th century. The first conference (1874) witnessed harmony on several points. The larger, second conference (1875) discussed only the *filioque* question, accepting St. John Damascene's formula. Although Döllinger's hope for more conferences was not realized, the way was paved for later ecumenical initiatives. BIBLIOGRAPHY: C. B. Moss, *Old Catholic Movement* (1966).

[E. E. BEAUREGARD]

BONNANUS (BONINO) DA CAMPIONE (1357–88), one of an Italian Lombard family of sculptors called Campionesi. B. carved the Bernabo Visconti tomb with an equestrian figure (*c*.1363) in Gothic style, thought by Pope-Hennessy to derive from the German Bamberg *Horseman.* BIBLIOGRAPHY: J. Pope-Hennessy, *Italian Gothic Sculpture* (1955).

[M. J. DALY]

BONNARD, PIERRE (1867–1947), French painter earlier associated with the Nabis (1889), later termed an "intimist" with E. Vuillard because of gracious domestic scenes. Sponsored by A. Vollard, B. published lithographs (1894) and illustrations (1904) while consistently showing his paintings. Influenced by *Gauguin, *Sérusier, and the color of the Fauves, B. painted with a glowing palette landscapes and interiors in luminous, sensuously textured panels of saturated oranges, yellows, and pinks. (*The Checkered Tablecloth,* 1911; *Luncheon,* 1927; *Corner of the Dining Room at Le Cannet,* 1932). Upon the deaths of Madame B. and Vuillard (1940), B. retired to LeCannet (1944). Among his last paintings was *St. Francis Healing* in the church of Notre-Dame-de-Toute-Grâce, *Assy. B.'s handsome palette created a French vogue among collectors of modern art. BIBLIOGRAPHY: J. T. Soby et al., *Bonnard and His Environment* (1964).

[M. J. DALY]

BONNE-ESPÉRANCE, MONASTERY OF (*Bona Spes*), former Premonstratensian monastery, dedicated to Our Lady, founded *c*.1125 by Rainaud de la Croix in the diocese of Cambrai (now Tournai), Belgium. Thrice devastated during the religious wars, the abbey was rebuilt in the 17th cent. by Archduke Albert, but was suppressed in 1794. Its buildings were later acquired by the diocese of Tournai to house a minor seminary. BIBLIOGRAPHY: Cottineau 1:424.

[J. DAOUST]

BONNECHOSE, HENRI MARIE GASTON DE (1800–83), French prelate and statesman. After beginning a career in law, B. became a priest and was associated with Abbé Louis *Bautain. He was made bp. of Carcassone (1847), then of Évreux (1854), abp. of Rouen (1858), and cardinal (1863). He became a member of the French Senate in 1863 and actively defended the rights of the Church. He was noted for his relief work in the Franco-Prussian War. In his early career he had inclined toward Gallicanism, but at Vatican Council I he was an infallibilist, favoring, however, a formulation more moderate than the one that prevailed. He was one of the founders of the *Institut Catholique* at Paris. BIBLIOGRAPHY: C. Laplatte, DHGE 9:1027–28.

[T. C. O'BRIEN]

BONNEFOY, JEAN FRANÇOIS (1897–1958), Franciscan theologian born in Laussone, France, whose writings in speculative theology were largely devoted to the teachings of John Duns Scotus. In addition, he compiled scriptural, patristic, and speculative data to support his view that the Incarnation was not conditioned by Adam's sin. Along with numerous writings on the Immaculate Conception and the spirituality of St. Bonaventure (*Le Saint-Esprit et ses dons selon s. Bonaventure*), his principal works are *Christ and the Cosmos* (tr. of *La Primauté du Christ*), and *La Nature de la théologie selon s. Thomas d'Aquin.*

[T. LIDDY]

BONNER, EDMUND (*c*.1500–69), bp. of London and lawyer. He served as chaplain to Card. Wolsey, to whom he remained faithful, and was sent by Henry VIII on missions to Rome and elsewhere. He argued in behalf of the annulment of the King's marriage and the lawfulness of the subsequent marriage with Anne Boleyn, and he also accepted the royal supremacy. However, he was opposed to Protestant doctrines and during the reign of Edward VI was deposed from his see (1549). Reinstated on the accession of Mary, he took part in the prosecution of those charged with heresy, though his role was a less savage one than that attributed to him by John Foxe. He refused to admit Elizabeth's claim to supremacy, was deprived of his see and committed to Marshalsea (1559) where he died. BIBLIOGRAPHY: G. E. Phillips, *Truth about Bishop Bonner* (1910); L. B. Smith, *Tudor Prelates and Politics* (1953); Hughes RE, v. 2 and 3.

[V. SAMPSON]

BONNET, CHARLES (1720–93), Swiss psychologist and naturalist. After his eyesight became weakened, B. turned to botany and philosophy. In the latter field he made his most significant contributions, esp. to the literature dealing with mind–body relation. Bonnet believed that the freedom of the soul resides in its power to follow necessary motives, yet, he denied determinism. A fuller understanding of his philosophy may yield a system of belief similar to process philosophy because of its apparent reliance on the evolving nature of man. An essential difference between Bonnet's thesis and the theory of organic evolution is that the former holds that at the moment of creation the ''germ'' (though in evolutionary process) is fully endowed with its specific history and that specificity bears within it all that it will ever be. The implications of that theory for theology and for philosophy are manifest in Bonnet's argument against atheism and in his development of the traditional theory of the chain of being. The latter theory led A. O. Lovejoy to acclaim Bonnet as one of the most original and speculative philosophers of his age. His works include: *Traité d'insectologie* (1745); *Considérations sur les corps organisés* (1762); *Contemplation de la nature* (1764–65); and *Palingénésie philosophique, ou idées sur l' état passé et sur l'état futur des êtres vivants* (1770). BIBLIOGRAPHY: L. G. Crocker, EncPhil 1:345–346; F. Tinivella, EncCatt 2:1886.

[J. R. RIVELLO]

BONNET, JOSEPH (1884–1944), French organist. A pupil of *Guilmant at the Paris Conservatoire, B. was organist of St.-Eustache, Paris for many years. While his own compositions are concert rather than liturgical pieces, he featured previously little-known organ works in his ''Historical Organ Recitals'' both in Paris and on his American concert tours, and published a collection of these in five volumes under that title. Through these, as well as through his pupils, such as Conrad *Bernier, he was responsible for the enlargement of the standard organ repertory to include many neglected masterpieces, esp. from the period before *Bach. BIBLIOGRAPHY: H. Grace, Grove DMM 1:805.

[A. DOHERTY]

BONNETTY, AUGUSTIN (1798–1879), French publicist and historian, defender of *traditionalism and *fideism. After 4 years of seminary studies, he decided to remain a layman. In the *Annales de philosophie chrétienne,* which he founded in 1830, he sought to serve the Church and combat the liberalism and rationalism of the day by what he called Christian philosophy. He adopted the extreme view that all speculative and moral truths were attainable only on the basis of revelation from God. In consequence he condemned scholasticism as a form of rationalism. He was required to renounce these views by the Congregation of the Index in 1855 (D 2811–14). He published several important collections in ecclesiastical history. BIBLIOGRAPHY: J. Dopp, DHGE 9:1058–60.

[T. C. O'BRIEN]

BONNEUIL, ÉTIENNE DE (fl. *c*.1280–1310), one of many ''travelling'' French master architects. B. directed works at the Cathedral of the Trinity, Uppsala, Scandinavia (1287), witnessing to the spread of French cultural influence throughout all Europe in modes of adaptation, complete copy, or new creation as Gothic genius encountered native Islamic, Romanesque and Byzantine traditions. With B. are numbered *William of Sens at Canterbury, Master Matteo at *Santiago de Compostela, Villard de *Honnecourt in Hungary, Eudes de Montreuil in Palestine, Pierre d'Agincourt in Cyprus, *Matthew of Arras in Bohemia. During the 14th cent. the French style was replaced by Gothic German influences in the Baltic region. BIBLIOGRAPHY: R. Huyghe, *Larousse Byzantine and Mediaeval Art* (1958).

[M. J. DALY]

BONO DA FERRARA (fl. *c*.1449–61), Italian painter of works (now lost) for the Marquis of Ferrara, known for *St. Jerome* (London) probably painted in the workshop of Pisanello, and the *St. Christopher* fresco in the Church of the Eremitani, Padua (destroyed in 1944), showing vigorous forms in Renaissance space. Though Piero della Francesca's influence is often stated the figures rather suggest the style of Andrea del Castagno. BIBLIOGRAPHY: R. Longhi, *Officina Ferrarese* (1956).

[M. J. DALY]

BONOMELLI, GEREMIA (1831–1914), abp. of Cremona in Italy from 1871. Before his episcopate, he was first a professor of theology at Brescia, then parish priest at Lovere. B. distinguished himself for the position, unpopular in ecclesiastical circles at the time, he took on the Church-State situation in Italy. He held that instead of resisting, the Church should adjust realistically to the national aspirations of Italy and champion the social betterment of the workers who were being attracted to an anarchic socialism. He is credited with anticipating the ideas and terms of the *Lateran Pact of 1929 that settled the *Roman Question. When, however, he proposed in a booklet, *Roma e l'Italia e la realtà delle cose* in 1889, that the papacy renounce its claims to the Papal States, he was forced to make a public submission in his cathedral to the condemnation of his views. He published several works on social questions and founded an association for the spiritual and material assistance of emigrants, popularly named the *Opera Bonomelli.* He was also the author of works of Christian instruction. BIBLIOGRAPHY: S. Furlani, EncCatt 2:1887–90.

[T. C. O'BRIEN]

BONONIUS, ST. (mid 10th cent.–1026), abbot. A Benedictine monk first in San Stefano in Bologna, B. later went to Egypt as a hermit. In 990 Bp. Peter of Vercelli (d.997) named him abbot of Lucedio. A Camaldolese tradition, however, makes him a student of St. Romuald. For the variant versions of his life see AnalBoll 48(1930). BIBLIOGRAPHY: E. Crovella, BiblSanct 3:348–349.

[G. E. CONWAY]

BONOSUS OF NAÏSSUS (d. *c*.400), bp. of Naïssus in Illyricum. According to a letter attributed to Pope Siricius but belonging to St. Ambrose, B. denied the perpetual virginity of Mary and maintained that after bearing Jesus she had other children. Condemned by Anysius and the bps. of Illyricum, who had been directed by the Council of Capua (391) to investigate his orthodoxy, B. continued to exercise his episcopal office. Later a question was raised about the validity of the orders he had conferred. Pope Innocent I settled the matter by declaring that new ordinations were not necessary for those whom Bonosus had ordained before his condemnation but that those ordained after were to be deposed from their office. Followers of B., called Bonosians, survived as a sect in Spain and Gaul until the 7th century. BIBLIOGRAPHY: A. Amore, EncCatt 2:1891.

[R. B. ENO]

BONSI, GIOVANNI (fl. Florence 14th cent.), Italian painter who worked with Taddeo Gaddi and Orcagna in the Florence Cathedral (1366). A polyptych signed by B. and dated 1371, depicting the Virgin enthroned with four saints (Vatican Museum), shows the influence of Orcagna. Figures of SS. Bartholomew and Anthony of Padua in the Bandini Museum, Fiesole, may be earlier works by Bonsi. BIBLIOGRAPHY: R. van Marle, *Italian Schools of Painting* (1924).

[M. J. DALY]

BONSIRVEN, JOSEPH (1880–1958), NT scholar. B. studied at Paris and the École Biblique in Jerusalem, but his doctoral dissertation on rabbinic eschatology was rejected by the Pontifical Biblical Commission and he was forbidden to teach Scripture. Reinstated in 1919, B. entered the Jesuits, taught exegesis in France (1928–47), and at the Pontifical Biblical Institute in Rome (1948–53). He is noted for his NT commentaries and studies on Judaism at the time of Christ.

[T. M. MCFADDEN]

BONTEMPS, PIERRE (fl. Fontainebleau 1536–61), French sculptor who carved reliefs for the tomb of Francis I, and the urn holding the heart of Francis I, (both *c*.1550; now at St. Denis, Paris), and the tomb of Charles de Maigny (1557, Louvre). BIBLIOGRAPHY: A. Blunt, *Art and Architecture in France, 1500–1700* (1954).

[M. J. DALY]

BONZEL, MARIA THERESIA, MOTHER (1830–1905), foundress in 1863 of the Congregation of Poor Sisters of St. Francis Seraph of Perpetual Adoration, a community dedicated to the nursing of the sick and aged and to the education and care of children. During her lifelong tenure as superior general her congregation spread from Germany to Austria and in 1875 to the U.S. where it had a membership in 1975 of 287 professed sisters. In the U.S. the congregation staffs schools, colleges, hospitals, and orphanages. In Germany the community numbered 1,831 sisters in 1971. B.'s cause for beatification has been introduced in Rome.

BIBLIOGRAPHY: S. Elsner, *From the Wounds of St. Francis* (tr. M. F. Peters, 1955).

[R. C. TOLLARICO]

BOOK OF ADVERTISEMENTS, instructions for the C of E on the order of services and the apparel of officiants, issued in 1566 by Abp. M. *Parker, under order of Elizabeth I. Intended to achieve uniformity, the regulations, esp. those regarding ceremonial and the use of the surplice in celebrating holy communion, were defied by Puritans intent on ridding the Church of all traces of Roman Catholicism. BIBLIOGRAPHY: V. J. K. Brook, *Life of Archbishop Parker* (1962).

BOOK OF COMMON ORDER (Church of Scotland), title of three official books of worship. (1) The first, by John *Knox, called also Knox's Liturgy, was one of the major documents of the Scottish Reformation. In Frankfurt Knox had prepared a first draft, which expressed the simplified form of service he favored. When he moved to Geneva, he drew up the Order of Geneva, which he brought to Scotland in 1559, and which, as the Book of Common Order, received official sanction in 1564. Intended to be a guide for ministers, the Book, though rugged and sometimes verbose, strongly expresses the biblical character of Scottish worship. It remained in general use until 1637, when the unsuccessful attempt to introduce the liturgy of W. *Laud occurred; part of the resistance of the Church of Scotland included adoption of the Puritan *Westminster Directory for Public Worship in 1643 in place of Knox's book. (2) The "Euchologion or a Book of Common Order" (1867) was published, after a period of liturgical aridity, by the Church Service Society to replace the Westminster Directory. The work helped to restore form and dignity to worship in the national Church. (3) The Book of Common Order (1940) was issued by the *General Assembly of the Church, and remains to the present the accepted and authoritative standard of worship in Scotland. These books have had an influence evident in the various editions of the Book of Common Worship prepared for Presbyterian Churches in the United States. BIBLIOGRAPHY: *John Knox's Liturgy* (eds. S. N. Sprott and T. Leishman, 1868); W. D. Maxwell, *History of Worship in the Church of Scotland* (1955); J. Melton, *Presbyterian Worship in America* (1967).

[J. R. MacKENZIE]

BOOK OF COMMON ORDER (United Church of Canada), a book of worship officially accepted in 1932. A replacement for an older, provisional work, which simply combined the best material from the service books of the three communions joined in the United Church of Canada, the Book of Common Order (BCO) contains distinctive modifications in keeping with the liturgical movements of the time of its adoption. In 1968 the General Council replaced it with the Service Book (SB), which reflects yet further liturgical studies emphasizing the unity of word and sacrament, and the actional and corporate character of public worship. The BCO's content is that found in most service books of the *Reformed tradition. Orders for the Lord's Supper, baptism, and the general conduct of public worship are accompanied by a wide selection of prayers and Scripture lessons appropriate for the various seasons of the liturgical year. Other special services practiced in congregational life are given as well, including confirmation, marriage, and burial of the dead, together with those found in an Ordinal, such as ordination and induction.

The SB, being intended more specifically for regular worship, does not contain the services from the Ordinal but has a greatly expanded selection of materials for public worship and a more comprehensive lectionary, which provides prophecy, epistle, and gospel for each Sunday of a 3-year cycle. An abbreviated, companion "service book for the use of the people" is also planned, containing the basic services, prayers, and readings from the SB, to enable a greater congregational participation in the act of worship. In accepting the Book of Common Order, the intention of the United Church of Canada is to provide a resource for the enrichment of public worship but not to inhibit the leading of the Spirit or the minister's need to respond to specific situations. In actuality, the BCO has been widely used, esp. in the conduct of the sacraments and special services.

[J. C. HOFFMAN]

BOOK OF COMMON PRAYER (BCP), the authorized liturigical book of the C of E, used also by other Churches of the Anglican Communion. The full title is *Book of Common Prayer and Administration of the Sacraments and Other Rites and Ceremonies of the Church*—"common prayer" signifying public divine service (see OED 2:694). The First Prayer Book of Edward VI, which had been preceded by earlier vernacular texts, was imposed by Parliament in the Act of Uniformity of 1549. T. *Cranmer's supervision of this edition gave the BCP its beauty and aptness of language. A first revision (The Second Prayer Book of Edward VI) issued under the Act of Uniformity of 1552 was suppressed by Mary Tudor's Act of Repeal (1553) reinstating the Latin liturgy; but the Act of Uniformity of 1559 under Elizabeth I brought back the BCP of 1552 slightly modified. This was proscribed and supplanted by the *Westminster Directory for Public Worship, 1645–60. After the Savoy Conference (1661) on Puritan objections, another Act of Uniformity (1662) by Parliament prescribed the revision prepared by *Convocations; except for optional shortened services allowed in 1872 and new lectionaries of 1871 and 1922, this remains the current BCP. In 1928 the House of Commons rejected a revision that had been in process since 1904 (see REVISED PRAYER BOOK). Among the non-English adaptations of the BCP, that in use by the Protestant Episcopal Church in the U.S. was established by a general convention in 1789 and modified in 1892 and 1928. (see AMERICAN PRAYER BOOK).

In content (morning and evening prayer services, Psalter, communion service, rites for the sacraments and Ordinal) the BCP derives from the Breviary, Missal, ritual, and pontifical. Cranmer's main sources were the Sarum liturgical tests and the Quignon Breviary for the 30-day distribution of the Psalter. The BCP of 1662 employed the Authorized or King James Version, except for Psalms. Parts of the revision rejected in 1928 are incorporated by some editions and designated "Alternative Orders"; these as well as the supplements used by other Anglican Churches supply rites and ceremonies not in the basic BCP.

Doctrine, of course, had dictated the origins and revisions of the BCP. The 1549 version already obscured the sacrificial aspect of the Holy Eucharist. The 1552 revision, influenced especially by *Peter Martyr Vermigli and M. *Bucer, removed any reference to sacrifice and rejected the "real and essential presence . . . of Christ's natural flesh and blood" (see BLACK RUBRIC) in its order for communion. Some slight concessions to Puritan belief (see MILLENARY PETITION) were reflected in the 1662 revision, but the Black Rubric was so modified as to reject only a "corporal presence of Christ's natural flesh and blood." The 20th-cent. revision was rejected because, while it did not satisfy Anglo-Catholics, it still ran counter to Protestant attitudes toward the Real Presence, the sacraments, and ritual. Modern adaptation of the BCP is an issue beset with a diversity of views, literary, liturgical, and doctrinal.

In the C of E experimental alternative services have been in use since 1967. There have been separate services for Holy Communion, Morning and Evening Prayer, Baptism, Matrimony, Burial, and each of these services has three optional forms. The experiment will run until 1979. In 1980 a complete book will be available, incorporating the most widely favored of the separate services. It is not yet officially named, but is referred to simply as *The Alternative Service Book*. All along the way it has been accepted that the new book will not replace the BCP of 1662, but will have offical standing as an alternative. The 1964 general convention of the U.S. Episcopal Church instructed its Standing Liturgical Commission to prepare a revision of the BCP. Under the chairmanship of Bp. Chilton Powell of Oklahoma, the Commission began by issuing revised liturgies for trial use. After considering responses to these services, it prepared a Draft Proposed Book of Common Prayer, published Feb. 2, 1976, which was favorably received by the Sept. 1976 general convention. Opponents of the revision had meanwhile organized a Society for Preservation of the Book of Common Prayer. Final approval can only be given by vote of the next convention in 1979. The Draft constituted the most extensive change in the U.S. BCP since the Episcopal Church was formed after the American Revolution and issued an American version of the British book. The new revision involved both the use of more contemporary English and the incorporation of concepts from recent liturgical thinking, though some traditional material was retained. For the Eucharist and some other services, the Draft offered three choices: a slightly revised service (called rite 1), a more extensive revision (rite 2) and an outline service that left clergy and congregations free to supply much of the wording. The Draft included a new translation of the Psalms, by a committee under C. M. Guilbert, and a revised lectionary. In some respects it represented a more "high church" approach to worship, but drafters stressed its pastoral orientation. BIBLIOGRAPHY: F. E. Brightman, *English Rite* (2. v., 1915); P. Brooks, *Thomas Cranmer's Doctrine of the Eucharist* (1965); on the 1662 BCP, G.J. Cuming, ed., *BCP: Durham Book, C of E* (1961); C. W. Dugmore, *Mass and the English Reformers* (1958); Hughes RE 2:105–113; F. Proctor and W. H. Frere, *New History of the BCP* (1951); E. C. Ratcliff, *Book of Common Prayer of the Churche of England* (1549 and 1552 texts, 1949); *idem, BCP 1549–1661* (1949); M. H. Shepherd, *Reform of Liturgical Worship* (1961); J. W. Suter and G. J. Cleaveland, *American BCP* (1949); *Liturgy in English* (ed. B. Wigan, 1962); W. K. Lowther Clarke, *Prayer Book of 1928 Reconsidered* (1943). *ANGLICANISM.

[T. C. O'BRIEN]

BOOK OF COMMON WORSHIP (Church of South India), the book of worship containing approved orders for use in the Church of South India (CSI). It contains orders for baptism, confirmation, communion, marriage, burial, and ordination, together with lectionaries and other worship materials. The service for ordination was used at the inauguration of CSI in 1947, but other parts of the book were prepared from time to time subsequently and published separately, first in English and later in Indian languages. After a revision of all materials in 1961 by the Synod Liturgy Committee, the book was authorized by the Synod in 1962 and published in 1963. It is considered a notable product of the ecumenical movement, prepared by a Church composed of varied traditions and making use of material from a wide range of sources, ancient and modern. It reflects much of the work of the liturgical renewal movement. Scripture passages are taken mostly from the RSV. Although the book is officially authorized, used for disocesan and synodical occasions, and generally accepted, its use is not mandatory for local congregations. The Constitution of the CSI states: "No forms of worship which before the Union have been in use in any of the uniting churches shall be forbidden in the Church of South India, nor shall any wonted forms be changed or new forms introduced into the worship of any congregation without the agreement of the pastor and the congregation." BIBLIOGRAPHY: T. Garrett, *Worship in the Church of South India* (1958).

[T. EARLY]

BOOK OF COMMON WORSHIP (PROVISIONAL SERVICES), see WORSHIPBOOK.

BOOK OF CONCORD (*Konkordienbuch; Liber Concordiae*), the assembled confessions of the Lutheran Church,

published in 1580 at Dresden; first authentic Latin ed., Leipzig, 1584. The confessions are the Catholic creeds (Apostles', Nicene, and Athanasian); the *Augsburg Confession; the Apology of the Augsburg Confession; the *Schmalkaldic Articles; the *Treatise Concerning the Power and Primacy of the Pope; the Small Catechism and the Large Catechism of Luther; the *Formula of Concord. Taken together, the confessions in the Book of Concord constitute the doctrinal standard by which Lutheranism defines itself, the norm to which Lutheran Churches and clergymen are pledged, and the official interpretation of the Lutheran relation both to the RC tradition and to other Churches. There has never been, however, unanimous acceptance by all the Lutheran bodies of the complete content of the Book of Concord. BIBLIOGRAPHY: *Confessions of the Evangelical Lutheran Church* (ed. T. G. Tappert, 1959); F. Bente, *Historical Introduction to the Book of Concord* (1965).

[J. PELIKAN]

BOOK OF CONFESSIONS (United Presbyterian Church in the U.S.A.), the volume of *confessions of faith adopted in 1967. The confessions included are the Nicene and the Apostles' Creed, Scots Confession, Heidelberg Catechism, Second Helvetic Confession, Westminster Confession and Shorter Catechism, Barmen Declaration, and the new *Confession of 1967. Officers of the Church promise to perform their duties under the instruction and guidance of this volume of confessions.

[T. C. O'BRIEN]

BOOK OF CONGREGATIONAL WORSHIP, a guide for worship. A feature of early Congregationalism was its dislike of fixed liturgy as denying the freedom both of the worshiper and the Holy Spirit. In the second half of the 19th and into the 20th cent., however, a movement for the better ordering of worship was made by Thomas Binney, John Hunter, W. E. Orchard, and others. It led to the publication by the Congregational Union of England and Wales in 1916 of the *Congregational Hymnary* and in 1920 of *A Book of Congregational Worship*. The latter was designed for use by minister and congregation and consisted of 10 orders of service and suggestions for the sacraments and other occasions. Apart from some infelicities, its weakness was that it sought to combine conflicting theories of worship and was not animated by any clear principles. The Book was not very widely used, but was the first of its kind, and it was followed by better and more popular productions. *BOOK OF SERVICES AND PRAYERS.

BOOK OF DISCIPLINE, see DISCIPLINE; DISCIPLINE (METHODIST); DISCIPLINE, BOOK OF (PRESBYTERIAN).

BOOK OF DOCTRINE AND COVENANTS, collections of revelations, most of them received by the Mormon founder, Joseph *Smith. Along with the Bible, the Book of Mormon, and the Pearl of Great Price, it is a doctrinal authority of the Mormon Church. First printed in 1835, it was an expanded version of an earlier Book of Commandments. A later revelation on plural marriages was subsequently added, as was an 1890 Manifesto renouncing the practice.

[T. EARLY]

BOOK OF DURROW (c.675), a vellum codex of the four Gospels in Latin, with prefatory matter, written probably in Northumbria. It is the first Gospel-book to show the remarkable decorative structure characteristic of later insular Gospel-books such as those of Kells and Lindisfarne. Now in Trinity College, Dublin, this MS is important for the study of the origins of Hiberno-Saxon art. BIBLIOGRAPHY: R. L. S. Bruce-Mitford, NCE 4:1123.

[R. L. S. BRUCE-MITFORD]

BOOK OF GUIDANCE (Kitāb-al-Hudā), an 11th cent. nomocanon containing the canon law of the medieval Maronite Church. It exists only in the Karshuni script, i.e., Arabic written in Syriac characters. The first 13 ch. treat of doctrinal, moral and liturgical matters; the more strictly juridical sections follow. Daily communion is encouraged and the fasting laws are given in detail. A citation from a Nestorian bp. to the effect that the Maronites profess only one will in Christ has occasioned some controversy, but it seems clear from the context that they merely refuse to admit two conflicting wills in him. The book includes the so-called canons of St. Clement and the apocryphal Arabic canons of Nicaea. Legislation about divorce is followed by a statement about Christ addressed to a Moslem. Some 20 ch. contain selected conciliar and patristic canons. The work concludes with excerpts from Roman civil law regarding persons, which were adopted by the Antiochene patriarchate since the 4th century. BIBLIOGRAPHY: Kitāb-al-Hudā (ed. P. Fahed, 1935).

[E. EL-HAYEK]

BOOK OF HOURS (Lat. *Horae;* Fr. *Heures*), a term sometimes used for the liturgical book containing the portions of (now Liturgy of the Hours) the Divine Office to be recited at the daytime hours (*horae diurnae*), i.e., at all the canonical hours with the exception of Matins (see DIURNAL), but more commonly it is applied to nonliturgical devotional books of the late Middle Ages containing offices, Psalms, prayers, etc., supplementary to the Divine Office and intended chiefly for use by the devout laity. In England it was known as the *Primer. Many Books of Hours are art treasures, richly gilded, decorated with miniatures, drolleries, and intricate marginal designs. One of the most famous is the *Très riches heures du Duc de *Berry,* painted by the *Limbourg brothers (Condé Museum, Chantilly).

BIBLIOGRAPHY: H. Thurston, CE 12:351–352; V. Leroquais, *Les Livres d'heures, manuscrits de la Bibliothèque Nationale* (1927). *BREVIARY, BELLEVILLE.

[P. K. MEAGHER]

BOOK OF KELLS, Latin MS of the Gospels, in the library of Trinity College, Dublin, since 1661. Though associated by tradition with St. Columba (591–597), it is dated by scholars c.800. The name derives from the Abbey of Kells in Co. Meath, eastern Ireland, to which the MS belonged prior to the Reformation. Considered the finest example of Celtic illumination, the MS has ornate monogram pages, illustration pages, and initial letters in brilliant color. The text itself is inaccurate, but is copied in a beautiful uncial script. BIBLIOGRAPHY: E. Sullivan, *Book of Kells* (5th ed., 1952). *ANIMAL STYLE.

[T. EARLY]

BOOK OF LIFE, a figurative expression found in both OT and NT to signify the record or listing in the mind of God of the names of those destined to be saved.

[P. K. MEAGHER]

BOOK OF MORMON, one of the sources of divine revelation for Mormons. The book was first published in 1830 by Joseph *Smith, Jr. In 1823 he claimed that a heavenly personage, the Angel Moroni, son of Mormon, led him to the discovery of a set of golden plates on Mount Cumorah, near Palmyra, N.Y., where Moroni had buried them more than 1,000 years before; with the plates were a set of spectacles, the Urim and Thummim, to be used for deciphering the Reformed Egyptian characters inscribed upon the plates. The Book of Mormon is Smith's translation of Moroni's history of the series of extinct races that had inhabited America from 600 B.C. to A.D. 400. To one of these races, the Nephites, Jesus appeared after the Ascension and established his Church. The Mormon Church was founded as the restoration of the Church Jesus had established according to this record, and for Mormons the Book has always been accepted as containing sacred revelation from God. Non-Mormon critics have questioned both the existence of the original golden plates and the veracity of the Book of Mormon. The many anachronisms it contains point to a discrepancy of 12 to 15 hundred years from its alleged time of composition. BIBLIOGRAPHY: F. M. Brodie, *No Man Knows My History: The Life Story of Joseph Smith* (1945); Mayer RB 456–457; E. C. McGavin, *How We Got the Book of Mormon* (1961); T. F. O'Dea, *Mormons* (1957). *LATTER-DAY SAINTS, CHURCH OF JESUS CHRIST OF.

[T. C. O'BRIEN]

BOOK OF RITUAL (Evangelical United Brethren Church), authorized by the General Conference of 1954 and first published the following year, an attempt to enhance the corporate worship of the denomination, which had emerged from revivalistic, *free-church American Protestantism.

Many of the rituals included in this Book had previously been a part of the denomination's *Discipline*. Both the longer and shorter services of holy communion are adaptations of the holy communion service used by the Methodist Church, and were a tie with historic Protestant worship forms through the Anglican Book of Common Prayer. A major departure is the change of the words of administration of the bread (and cup) from reading, "The body (blood) of our Lord Jesus Christ," to "The Lord Jesus Christ, who gave his body (blood) for thee, preserve thy soul unto everlasting life." In addition to a ritual for infant baptism there also appears one entitled "The Dedication of Infants."

[K. J. STEIN]

BOOK OF SERVICES AND PRAYERS, a manual of worship for the Congregational Union of England and Wales. This book, compiled by a committee appointed by the Church, was published in 1959. Its use by ministers was not required, but it came into wider general usage than any previous publication. It was designed and intended not as a book of common prayer but as a guide for ministers and lay preachers in the ordering and conduct of worship. The first part consists of orders of service for public worship, for the sacraments, and for a variety of special occasions. The second part consists of a wide selection of prayers, many specially composed. The third part consists of scripture sentences and a lectionary. A useful book, it represents a contribution to the better ordering of Congregational services. No original understanding of the nature of worship by modern man, however, nor any attempt to move beyond the religiously conventional is evidenced by the Book.

[R. F. G. CALDER]

BOOK OF SPORTS, popular name for a declaration (1618) on Sunday recreation by James I of England. It stated that after divine service on Sundays, "no lawful recreation should be barred to his good people, which should not tend to breach the laws of his kingdom and the canons of his church." Dancing, archery, vaulting, and May-day games were among the sports permitted, contrary to Puritan sabbatarianism. Ordered to be read in the churches, the declaration was, nevertheless, largely disregarded. It was republished by Charles I in 1633, and its reading was staunchly enforced by Abp. W. *Laud to the great dismay and indignation of the Puritans. Parliament in 1643 ordered that all copies of the declaration be gathered up and burned. BIBLIOGRAPHY: C. Hill, *Society and Puritanism in Pre-Revolutionary England* (1964); L. A. Govett, *King's Book of Sports* (1890). *SABBATARIANS.

[F. E. MASER]

BOOK OF THE COVENANT, a title in Ex 24.7 referring to that part of the Sinai legislation given to the people by God through Moses (Ex 20.22, 23.33). Scholars agree that its contents date from various periods, but that its basic structure represents a blending of typically Israelite law (such

as the direct commands in 21.12–17 and 22.17–19) together with the more elaborate case-law tradition (such as 21.1–11) of some older settled population. This latter group has been identified as Canaanite, but is more probably a primitive settlement not fully assimilated to Canaanite culture and tracing its origins to the period of the patriarchs. The composite nature of the book has led some to question whether its unity is purely artificial, but others point to the combination of case laws and direct commands in Mesopotamian and Assyrian codes, as well as to the composite nature of the Deuteronomic Code (Dt 12–26) and the Holiness Code (Lev 17–26).

The book as a whole dates from some period previous to Deuteronomy (about 700 B.C.), which seeks to supplant it by the law of the single sanctuary (contrast Ex 20.24 and Dt 12.5). It reflects the early settlement period, perhaps in Transjordan, or, more likely, in the area of Shechem, where the Exodus tribes probably entered a covenant with older settled tribes. In the latter case, the book would contain the legal material of the covenant renewal in Jos 24, from which context it was detached at some time after the Exile in order to be inserted in its present position as part of the Sinai covenant. BIBLIOGRAPHY: O. Eissfeldt, *Old Testament, an Introduction* (tr. P. R. Ackroyd, 1965) 212–219.

[P. KEARNEY]

BOOK OF THE DEAD, title given by Egyptologists to a collection of texts consisting mainly of spells or magical formulas, written on papyrus rolls and placed in coffins, or in mummies themselves, from the middle of the 2d millennium B.C. down into the Greco-Roman period. The texts, which exist in recensions varying in content and not collected in book form until after 700 B.C., aim at providing the dead person with all the formulas and other information he will need to move past the obstacles to be encountered in his passage through the region of the dead. Ancient elements, esp. from the Middle Kingdom Coffin Texts, recur in the collection, profoundly modified, however, by changes in Egyptian thought and often by misunderstanding by later Egyptians themselves. Despite serious problems of textual criticism and interpretation, the collection is of great value as a source of information on Egyptian mythology, ritual practice, and views on morality and afterlife. BIBLIOGRAPHY: J Vandier, *La religion égyptienne* (2d ed., 1949) 102–107; H. Bonnet, *Reallexikon der ägyptischen Religionsgeschichte* (1952) 824–828; text (from an 18th Dynasty papyrus) with Eng. tr. in E. A. W. Budge, *Egyptian Book of the Dead* (1895).

[A. CODY]

BOOK OF WORSHIP (Methodist), a liturgical manual of the Methodist Church. The history of the Methodist Hymnal reveals a growing interest in liturgy that culminated in the adoption of *The Book of Worship for Church and Home* by the *General Conference of 1944. It won wide acceptance, and in order to meet a still growing need the

General Conference of 1956 ordered a revision that was published in 1960. The book is divided into five parts: (1) general services of the Church (orders of worship, orders for baptism, holy communion, marriage, ordinations, and other services); (2) aids for the Ordering of Worship (the Christian year, prayers, and other aids); (3) the Acts of Praise (Psalter, canticles, and other acts of praise); (4) the Occasional Offices of the Church (consecrating a church, licensing persons to preach, and similar offices); (5) services in the Methodist tradition (morning prayer from John Wesley's Sunday service, Love Feast, Aldersgate Sunday, and other services). BIBLIOGRAPHY:HistAmMeth 3:562; N. B. Harmon, *Understanding the Methodist Church* (1955).

[F. E. MASER]

BOOK OF WORSHIP (Swedenborgian), properly the *Liturgy or Book of Worship for the Use of the New Church Signified by the New Jerusalem,* was adopted by the *General Convention of the New Jerusalem in the U.S.A. in 1834, revised somewhat in 1854, and again revised by a committee appointed in 1911 to prepare a liturgy that would be acceptable to all Swedenborgian groups. The Book of Worship provides for a worship service similar to Morning Prayer and Sermon in an Episcopal Church, with scriptural selections chosen to stress that the Lord in his divine humanity is to be worshiped. There are liturgical services for the celebration of baptism, the holy supper, marriage, and funerals, as well as the Articles of Faith adopted by the New Church General Conference in England, and a hymnal.

BOOKS, LITURGICAL, see LITURGICAL BOOKS.

BOOKS, PROHIBITION OF, in a religious context a ban or proscription against certain pieces of literature. Rabbinic law and Christian theology generally recognize that no one should read books that would seriously jeopardize his faith or moral integrity. Accordingly, the Church's practice of explicitly proscribing heretical works began in the early Christian centuries. The prohibition of books, however, also has a specific canonical meaning in the RC church. As distinct from *precensorship, prohibition refers to books already in print. The pope personally or the Congregation for the Doctrine of the Faith, may proscribe books for the whole Church; a bishop may do the same for his diocese, and a major religious superior for his community (CIC c. 1395). The proscription bars Catholics, unless special permission is given, from publishing, reading, keeping, selling, translating, or circulating the forbidden work (*c.* 1398.1). Permission to read or retain forbidden books is granted for educational or other professional reasons (c. 1402). Specific books condemned by Rome were listed in the *Index of Forbidden Books; the power to condemn remains, although the Index since 1966 has not had the force of law. In addition to books banned by name, there are twelve categories of books that are prohibited in principle by the Code of Canon Law (c. 1399). In Vatican Council II, the Decree on Revelation (n. 22) mitigates this prohibition by approving in principle the use of a common Bible by all Christians. The whole issue of censorship is under discussion in the RC Church; the interpretation of the prohibition of books has broadened considerably; revision of the legislation is expected. BIBLIOGRAPHY: Bouscaren-Ellis-Korth 784–797.

[T. C. O'BRIEN]

BOOTH FAMILY, a 19th-cent. family, of partly Jewish origin; some of its members were the founders of the Salvation Army; later, others established the Volunteers of America.

William (1829–1912). Born in poverty at Nottingham, Eng., and receiving little formal education, B. experienced a conversion at 15 and in 1846 was licensed as a street preacher by the New Wesleyan Connexion, a Methodist body. His thought was greatly influenced by Charles G. *Finney's *Lectures on Revivals.* Public preaching by B.'s wife led to his expulsion by the Methodists in 1861, and he founded the Christian Revival Association in London in 1865 as a non-denominational Bible Christian Church, later called the Christian Mission. In 1878 he adopted the name Salvation Army and wrote *Articles of War* based on the British Army *Field Pocket Book* for his evangelists. In his lifetime he held title to all Salvation Army property and had full authority over all its members; he held the title General of the World Wide Salvation Army (1934–39). His evangelism was directed to the need of repentance for sin and the experience of *sanctification. He launched a successful crusade against white slavery in 1885 with journalist W. T. Stead and in 1890 startled British readers with his appeal for slum dwellers, *In Darkest England,* also written with W. T. Stead. He pioneered in social work for alcoholics and the unemployed. BIBLIOGRAPHY: R. Collier, *General Next to God* (1965).

Catherine (Mumford; 1829–90). Wife of William and "Mother of the Salvation Army," she married William in 1855 and shared in his evangelical preaching and in the formation of the Salvation Army. She devoted herself not only to preaching but also to alleviating the sufferings of destitute women and children.

Evangeline Corry (1865–1950). Daughter of William, under her command from 1904, the Salvation Army made great progress in the United States. She wrote many Salvationist hymns.

Ballington (1857–1940). Son of William and Catherine, with his wife he commanded the Salvation Army in the U.S. (1887–96) but separated to form the Volunteers of America, of which he was general-in-chief and president.

Maud Ballington (Charlesworth; 1865–1948). Wife of Ballington, with her husband she was first a Salvation Army leader. After his death (1940) she commanded the Volunteers of America. She was deeply dedicated to the rehabilitation of prisoners and was one of the founders of the Parent-Teachers Association.

[R. K. MACMASTER]

BOOTH, LAWRENCE (d. 1480), English political prelate, who was bp. of Durham 1457–76 and abp. of York 1476–80. As chancellor to Queen Margaret, and keeper of the privy seal (1456–60), he was closely associated with court politics, and his temporalities were confiscated by Edward IV (1462–64); but he was later chancellor of England (1473). BIBLIOGRAPHY: Emden Camb 78–79; C. D. Ross, NCE 2:702.

[C. D. ROSS]

BOOTH WILLIAM, (d. 1464), bp. of Coventry and Lichfield (1447–52) and abp. of York (1452–64). As chancellor to Queen Margaret (1445), court influence insured his rise in the Church, and he was an active politician. Thomas Gascoigne called him *indignus episcopus Cestriae* and criticized his lack of learning, his avarice, and nepotism. BIBLIOGRAPHY: C. D. Ross, NCE 2:702.

[C. D. ROSS]

BOOTHS, FEAST OF, see TABERNACLES, FEAST OF.

BOOTLEGGING, originally, the selling of contraband liquor to American Indians by smuggling flat bottles to them in one's boots. It was later used for any kind of smuggling of illegal alcoholic beverages during the Prohibition Era in the U.S. Many fortunes were amassed by such traffic, much of which was in the control of organized crime. The paramount moral objection to bootlegging was the harmful manipulation of addicts by unscrupulous elements of society for the furtherance of other criminal activities.

[J. F. FALLON]

BORBORIANS (Borborites; from the Gr., *borboros,* mire), a group of Gnostics of the 2nd to 5th cent., similar to the *Ophites. St. Augustine (Haer. 6) attributes their name to the obscenities practiced in their rites. BIBLIOGRAPHY: G. Bareille, DTC 2:1032–33.

[T. C. O'BRIEN]

BORDA, ANDRÉS DE (d. 1723), Mexican theologian. Trained originally in the Franciscan houses of study in Mexico City, B. was the first Franciscan to receive a doctor's degree from the Univ. of Mexico (1697). He was given the Scotist chair in 1688 and in 1708 helped to draw up an official response to the doubts and pretensions submitted by the Bethlehemites against the university. After his retirement, he became the theological consultant to the Inquisition of Mexico City. B. wrote a series of philosophical treatises (never published); his *Práctica de confesores de monjas* is a highly valued spiritual work. He was an author of his times, despite the fact that the problems and solutions he suggested do not seem to be of much interest today. BIBLIOGRAPHY: S. M. Beristain de Souza, *Biblioteca hispano americana septentrional* (5v., 3d ed., 1947).

[D. M. HUGHES]

BORGESS, CASPAR HENRY (1826–90), bishop. Born in Germany, B. immigrated to the U.S. at the age of 12 with his parents. He entered St. Mary's Seminary, Cincinnati, Ohio and was ordained (1845). After 12 years as pastor of parishes in Columbus and Cincinnati, he was appointed chancellor of the archdiocese. In 1870 Pope Pius IX named him coadjutor and administrator of Detroit, Mich., a diocese left vacant by the departure for Germany of Frederic Rese, its first bishop; B. succeeded to the see at Rese's death (1871). During his administration he worked to establish an indigenous clergy, to reduce nationalistic tensions among immigrant groups, to extend Catholic education, and to improve the administrative structure of his diocese. In 1881 he petitioned Rome for a division of his see; a year later the Diocese of Grand Rapids was established. Ill health and problems with priests caused him to resign in 1887.

[S. J. HILL]

BORGHESE, an Italian noble family, originating in Siena, which rose to great prominence in Rome during the 16th century. With the election of Camillo Borghese to the papacy as Paul V (1605–21), the family fortunes increased considerably. Paul's nephew, Marcantonio (d. 1658), added to the Borghese distinction and secured its position as one of the leading Italian families. He was created Prince of Vivaro by the Pope, and Prince of Sulmona by Philip III of Spain. His marriage to Princess Camilla Orsini in 1619 was a brilliant match; and he arranged an equally brilliant alliance for his son Paolo with Olimpia, heiress of the Aldobrandini. The Borghese continued to be important in Italian affairs until the late 19th century. Camillo Ludovico Borghese (d. 1832) married Marie Pauline, sister of Napoleon, and became influential in the French-dominated provinces of Italy. The splendor of the Borghese came to an end with the great crisis of landed fortunes in the 1890s. Their art collection and library were then sold; and the Villa Borghese was purchased by the State and turned into a park. BIBLIOGRAPHY: P. Dalla Torre and E. Gerlini, EncCatt 2:1903–1906.

[D. NUGENT]

BORGIA, the Italianized name of the great Catalan clan of the Borjas, prominent in the politics of the Western Mediterranean during the late 15th and early 16th centuries. In popular imagination they conjure up a picture of cloak and dagger, poison and plot, all set against a sumptuous background, but though their allegiance often came a bad second to their own aggrandizement, in the main they stood for the established pieties in religion and deserve to be included in a list of RC worthies. Their history was scarcely more treacherous and bloodstained than that of many other late Renaissance families; they compare rather favorably with the first Tudors. Their vices were rarely dull and they had a gift for good government. St. Francis Borgia displays their traits at their best. Twenty or more representatives of the family at this period could be selected for special mention, but besides St. Francis and Pope *Alexander VI, who are treated in separate articles, two must suffice, Alexander's children, Cesare and Lucrezia.

Cesare Borgia (1476–1507). Though his father's favorite, C. appears to have been the most unlikeable of the lot, being crafty, surly, and unsympathetic. After a profligate life at the Vatican, he entered on his career among other princely gangsters, and proved more than a match for most of them. He was not without ability as a soldier, and though his methods of conquest were ferocious, his subjects came to prefer the ordered justice of his rule to the previous anarchy and despotism. He married the sister of the King of Navarre, was created Duke of Valentinois by the King of France, and Duke of Romagna by his father. With the latter's death, however, his dominion fell to bits; he sought refuge with the Spaniards in Naples, and had later to escape from Spain and flee to his brother-in-law, in whose service he was killed in battle.

Lucrezia Borgia (1480–1519), full sister of Cesare. Recent historical research has cleared her name of many of the evil deeds earlier writers had ascribed to her. Her earlier matrimonial career was checkered; one betrothal was broken off and a proxy marriage was annulled by her father when they no longer suited his plans. Another marriage, this time to a Sforza, was also annulled on the ground of impotence. The girl was then married to Alphonso of Aragon, by whom she had a child. Alphonso seems to have loved her, but there was another shift of politics, and Cesare Borgia had him assassinated. After serving her father as regent in Rome, she was now, still only 22, about to enter the most peaceful period of her life. Her marriage with Alfonso d'Este, son and heir to Ercole, Duke of Ferrara, was arranged. She became duchess in 1505 and then, gathering poets and artists at her court, and happily married, she devoted herself to the education of her children and works of charity. BIBLIOGRAPHY: G. Portigliotti, *Borgias* (tr. B. Miall, 1928).

[T. GILBY]

BORGIA, FRANCIS, ST. (1510–72), third general of the Society of Jesus. Francis held important posts in the service of the emperor at the court of Spain. He married Leonor de Castro and became the father of eight sons. After the sudden death of his wife he took his first vows in the newly formed Society of Jesus and secretly made his final profession in 1548. He went to Rome to arrange with St. Ignatius for his official entrance into the society. After ordination he preached and taught catechism to children. Later he was sent to assist Queen Johanna in her last illness. In 1559 a book entitled *Las Obras del Duque de Gandia* was placed on the list of forbidden books for Spain. It contained some treatises of his but also writings not of his authorship. To avoid embarrassment he retired to Portugal until called to Rome by Pope Pius IV. Three years later he was appointed assistant general for Spain and Portugal. After the death of the General Diego Lainez, Francis was nominated vicar-general and then elected general of the society. His seven years of office were noted for activity and the expansion of the Society of Jesus. He started new missions in the Americas, strengthened those in the East Indies and Far East, erected the province of Poland, and planned others. He is noted also for his interior mystical life which throve amid the surroundings of business. He was canonized in 1671 by Clement X. BIBLIOGRAPHY: O. Karrer, *Der Heilige Franz von Borga 1510–1572* (1921). H. Dennis, *St. Francis Borgia* (1956); Sommervogel 1:1808–17, 8:1875–76.

[L. MITCHELL]

BORGIA, RODRIGO DE, see ALEXANDER VI, POPE.

BORGINO DAL POSSO (BORGINO DE PUTEO; fl. Milan 1350?), Italian goldsmith. B. made the enameled and jeweled silver-gilt frontal for the high altar of the Cathedral of Monza, Lombardy (1350–57), showing in *repoussé* scenes of the life of St. John the Baptist within a Gothic framework. BIBLIOGRAPHY: X. B. de Montault, *Le Trésor de la basilique royale de Monza,* (1883).

[M. J. DALY]

BORGO SAN DONNINO (FIDENZA), small Italian town S of Milan with 12th cent. cathedral having noted sculptured facade (*c.* 1175–1200). The main portal with a frieze of the legend of S. Donnino, and Lombard porch columns with lion caryatids, as well as the impressive niche-statues of David and Ezekiel, are works of the master sculptor Benedetto *Antelami. BIBLIOGRAPHY: A. K. Porter, *Lombard Architecture* (1915–17).

[M. J. DALY]

BORGUND: STAVE CHURCH (*c.* 1150), the oldest extant example of the Norse timber church, small in structure with square central nave rising to a graceful pinnacle supported by wooden columns. Steeply pitched roofs with great overhanging eaves give this building the typical pyramidal shape of the stave church. BIBLIOGRAPHY: A. Bugge, *Norwegian Stave Churches* (1953).

[M. J. DALY]

BORIS I (d. 907), **BULGARIAN KHAN** (852–89), one of the most able medieval Bulgarian rulers who is credited with establishing Christianity in that country. Baptized in 864 he also forced his subjects to be baptized. After fluctuating between Rome and Constantinople, he placed the Bulgarian Church under the jurisdiction of the latter.

[G. T. DENNIS]

BORIS AND GLEB, SS. (d. 1015), passion-bearers or sufferers for the sake of Christ and patron saints of Russia. On the death of his father Vladimir in 1015, Prince Svyatopolk of Kiev tried to consolidate his position by eliminating his two half-brothers, Boris and Gleb. Both refused to put up any resistance at all and were murdered. Their attitude of resignation following the example of Christ and their unwillingness to use force to defend their own lives made them immediately the objects of a popular cult that became deeply rooted among the Russians. They are sometimes known by their baptismal names of Romanus and David. BIBLIOGRAPHY: G. Fedotov, *Russian Religious Mind,* (1946) 1:94–110.

[G. T. DENNIS]

BOROBUDUR, see BARABUDUR.

BORRASSÀ, LLUIS (fl.*c*.1400–25), Spanish artist, perhaps apprenticed to Pedro Serra. B. painted glittering ensembles of movement breaking with the 14th-cent. Sienese tradition of his day and introducing the new International Gothic of the 15th cent. in four great retables: St. Peter, Santa Clara, Guardiola, and Seva. BIBLIOGRAPHY: F. Jiménez-Placer, *Historia del arte español* (1955).

[M. J. DALY]

BORROMEO, CHARLES, ST. (1518–84), Italian cardinal prominent in the Counter Reformation. Destined for the Church by his father, C. was invited to Rome in 1559 when his uncle was elected to the papacy as Pius IV. He was soon made cardinal-prefect of the secretariat of state and governor of the new papal states of Romagna and the Marches. He was influential in the third period of the Council of Trent (1562–63) and played a large role in drawing up the Tridentine Catechism. Upon his uncle's death in 1565 C. evaded election as his successor and retired to his see in Milan, which a vicar-general had been governing in his stead. C.'s pastoral activities (1566–84) raised the standard of diocesan administration throughout the Catholic world. He systematically visited all parts of his diocese; established seminaries and colleges; promoted the Confraternity of Christian Doctrine; and used religious orders creatively to implement his reforms. The records of his 6 provincial councils and 11 diocesan synods, along with his pastoral letters, edicts, and the constitutions of a score of organizations he established or encouraged, were published in 1582. They became a model for other bishops and were frequently reprinted. C. favored strict punishment of heretics and paved the way for the Golden League (1586) formed by the Swiss Catholic cantons to expel heretics. During the plague he cared for the sick and the dead with no thought of his own safety. Canonized, 1610. BIBLIOGRAPHY: A. S.-A. Rimoldi, BiblSanct 3:812–846, with extensive bibliog.; for iconography, A. M. Raggi, *op. cit.* 3:846–850; Butler 4:255–262; C. Orsenigo, *St. Charles Borromeo,* (tr. R. Kraus, 1943).

[D. NUGENT]

BORROMEO, FEDERIGO (1564–1631), cardinal archbishop of Milan. Born at Milan, B. was orphaned early in life and guided toward an ecclesiastical career by his cousin St. Charles *Borromeo (1538–84). He studied at Bologna and Pavia, receiving his doctorate in theology in 1585. He served in Rome under Sixtus V, who made him a cardinal in 1587. He was appointed to the see of Milan in 1601, a position earlier held by his cousin, and remained there until his death. A supporter of reform efforts and learning, he is noted for founding the Ambrosian Library. He was a candidate for the papacy in 1623 when Urban VIII was elected. BIBLIOGRAPHY: M. Pettrochi, *Omaggio a Fredrigo Borromeo: L'uomo a la storia* (1940).

[T. EARLY]

BORROMINI, FRANCESCO (1599–1667), most original architect of the Roman high baroque school. B. came to Rome in 1616 and after studying with Maderno became chief assistant to Bernini, whose work may be said to have been carried to its logical extreme by Borromini. B.'s spiritual torment is reflected in the startling originality of designs for S. Carlo alle Quattro Fontane, S. Ivo alla Sapienza, S. Agnese a Piazza Navona, and S. Philip Neri are distinguished by ingenious spatial composition, restless rhythms of concave and convex counter-movement, honeycomb domes, and towers bizarre and fantastic. B.'s work was the basis of northern Italian and central European extravagant, late baroque art. In 1652 he was made a knight of the Order of Christ. BIBLIOGRAPHY: G. C. Argan, *Borromini* (1962); P. Portoghesi, EncWA 2:547–570.

[L. P. SIGER]

BORROW, GEORGE HENRY (1803–81), English linguist, traveler, and author. B. was for some years a tinker. Later he traveled as an agent for the British and Foreign Bible Society. In the interests of a Manchu translation of the NT he went to Russia (1833–35). In 1843 his three volumes *The Bible in Spain,* brought him unexpected fame. He also prepared a Spanish translation of the NT. BIBLIOGRAPHY: M. Adams, *In the Footsteps of Borrow and Fitzgerald* (1973); W. I. Knapp, *Life, Writings, and Correspondence of George Borrow* (1899, repr. 1967).

[M. J. SUELZER]

BOSCARDIN, MARIA BERTILLA, ST. (1888–1921), nursing sister. Born of poor parents at Brendola near Vicenza, Italy, B. was christened Anna Francesca. After intermittent schooling she entered the community of the Sisters of St. Dorothy at Vicenza and was given the religious name Maria Bertilla. B. sought perfection by following the "little way" of St. Thérèse of Lisieux, and although she herself suffered physically the last 12 years of her life, she was untiring in her care of sick children in the hospital at Treviso and of the wounded soldiers removed there during the bombardment of that city (1917). She was canonized in 1961. BIBLIOGRAPHY: Butler 4:161–162; G. B. Proja, BiblSanct 8:1041–42.

[R. C. TOLLARICO]

BOSCH, HIERONYMUS (VAN AEKEN; 1453–1516), the most enigmatic Netherlandish painter between the Middle Ages and the Renaissance. B. lived at 's Hertogenbosch in the Brabant. His works, esp. the three great triptychs (*The

Haywain, Madrid; *The Temptation of St. Anthony*, Lisbon; *The Garden of Delights*, Madrid) rendered in an archaic, flat style, are teeming with monsters and hybrid creatures, sometimes interpreted to reflect occult, alchemistic theories. But intrinsically B.'s message is a moral one. He depicts human folly and sin, their subsequent punishment in fantastic variations, warning that man's salvation can only be achieved through compassion with Christ's Passion (*The Carrying of the Cross*, Ghent). BIBLIOGRAPHY: C. de Tolnay, *Hieronymus Bosch* (1966); L. Baldass, *Hieronymus Bosch* (1960).

[R. BERGMANN]

BOSCO, JOHN, ST. (1815–88), educator, founder of the Salesians. As a priest in Turin he became interested in the plight of country boys who came to the city in search of work, and saw the need of providing them with both housing and education. Eventually he opened a hospice which grew into the Oratory of St. Francis de Sales. This establishment included workshops to train poor boys in manual skills. Count Camillo di Cavour was among his patrons. By the time of B.'s death, his Society of St. Francis de Sales (Salesians) had 57 houses in Italy, France, Spain, England, Argentina, Brazil, and Uruguay. His cheerful disposition and engaging personality contributed to the success of his endeavors. He was canonized in 1934. BIBLIOGRAPHY: E. B. Phelan, *Don Bosco, A Spiritual Portrait* (1963); E. Valentini, BiblSanct 6:968–985; L. C. Sheppard, *Don Bosco* (1957).

[E. A. CARRILLO]

BOSCOVICH, RUGGIERO GIUSEPPE (1711–87), a Jesuit astronomer of great reputation in the 18th cent., much admired by Dr. Johnson, and a member of the Royal Society. A Dalmatian by birth, he was professor of mathematics at the Roman College. He wrote poetry and published more than 70 scientific papers of original research which developed the theories of Newton. He rendered practical service in the draining of the Pontine marshes. The British proposal to send him to California to observe the transit of Venus fell through because of the opposition of Catholic governments to the Jesuits. On the suppression of the Society he was appointed director of optics to the French Navy, an office he held for 9 years. Streets in various European towns are named after him, also a crater on the moon. BIBLIOGRAPHY: A. Muller, CE 2:691.

[H. JACK]

BOSIO, ANTONIO (*c*.1575–1629), Roman archeologist called the "Columbus of the Catacombs" by G. B. de Rossi. From Malta, Bosio came to Rome to study philosophy and law, but at the age of 18 turned to his lifework, archeology. He recognized as a catacomb an underground burial place accidentally discovered in the Via Salaria (1578). In 1593 he made his first descent into one subsequently identified as the Catacomb of Domitilla. His long and painstaking explora-

tions appeared in his *Roma Sotterranea*, completed in 1620 but not published until 1634. This work included rather inept engravings made by artists B. brought into the catacombs. B.'s work stood until supplanted by de Rossi's in the 19th century. BIBLIOGRAPHY: A. Valeri, *Cenni biografici di Antonio Bosio con documenti inediti* (1900); G. Ferretto, *Note storico-biografiche di archeologia cristiana* (1942) 132–162; DACL 2:1084–93.

[T. C. O'BRIEN]

BOSNIA-HERZEGOVINA, part of the federal republic of Yugoslavia. The territory was originally settled by Croats and christianized by the Western Church. From 1150 Bosnia was an independent principality. In the Middle Ages a large part of the pop., esp. the nobility with the ruler (*ban*, king), had become *Bogomils, a dualistic sect, through which they were a link in the chain of heresy that extended from Bulgaria, through N Italy (Patarines, Cathari), to S France (Albigenses). Because of evidence conflicting with the scant, biased contemporary information, it has been suggested that the Manichaean Bogomils merged with the remnants of a first christianization, which had become isolated from Latin and Byzantine ecclesiastical influences. Crusades were preached against them, but Bogomilism endured till the coming of the Turks (1463) when many of them embraced Islam, and their descendants, together with those of Catholic and Orthodox converts to Islam number today some 900,000 Muslims. Serbs settled in Bosnia-Herzegovina after the Turkish victory at Kosovo Polje (1389). Because of the difficulties with the Bogomils and the Turks, there were no Catholic bps. in the region for centuries, although the Franciscans ministered to the faithful from 1340. Leo XIII restored the Catholic hierarchy (1881) with four dioceses; Catholics now number about 600,000. The Serbian Orthodox Church was organized during the Austrian occupation (1878–1918) in four eparchies under the Ecumenical Patriarchate and in 1920 joined the Serbian Orthodox Patriarchate. Today the 1,100,000 Orthodox belong to four dioceses: Sarajevo, Banja Luka, Mostar, Tuzla. Byzantine rite Catholics settled around 1900 in Bosnia from the Ukraine (Galicia), and are under the jurisdiction of the bp. of Križevci. BIBLIOGRAPHY: J. V. Fine, *Bosnian Church: A Study of the Bosnian Church and Its Place in State and Society from the 13th to the 15th Centuries* (1975).

[V. J. POSPISHIL]

BOSO, CARDINAL (d. 1178), possibly a Benedictine monk of St. Albans, who came to Rome (*c*.1149) and was appointed by Adrian IV (his uncle?) papal chamberlain and then cardinal (1156). While in charge of papal finances B. revised the *Liber censuum*. On the death of Adrian, B. presided at the election of Alexander III, whose powerful defender he remained during the strife with antipope Victor IV. BIBLIOGRAPHY: B. C. Skottowe, DNB 2:883.

[G. E. CONWAY]

BOSSI, MARCO ENRICO (1861–1925), Italian organist, teacher, and composer. B. not only maintained the finest traditions of the Italian school but laid the foundations of reform of organ technique, design, and performance in his work, *Mètodo di studio per l'organo moderno* (1893). He composed motets, cantatas, Masses, sonatas, organ concerti, orchestral suites, choral works, and oratorios. BIBLIOGRAPHY: J. A. Fuller-Maitland, Grove DMM 1:831.

[M. T. LEGGE]

BOSSUET, JACQUES BÉNIGNE (1627–1704), French bishop, historian, orator. Destined from boyhood for the Church, B. received a sound training in the classics from the Jesuits, acquired an early and enduring interest in the Bible, studied philosophy and theology at the Collège de Navarre, prepared for the priesthood under St. Vincent de Paul, and was ordained in 1652. For 7 years he lived at Metz and occupied himself with preaching, study, and discussion with Protestants. He then returned to Paris, where he soon gained fame as a preacher. In 1670 he was consecrated bp. of Condom, but he resigned his see after a year because his engagements in Paris made it impossible for him to reside at Condom. B. was made tutor to the Dauphin in 1670, and in that capacity wrote books, notably the *Discourse on Universal History*. This, in B.'s own judgment, was his greatest work. The philosophy of history it propounded is based entirely on Providence. After the Dauphin's marriage (1681), B. was made bp. of Meaux. He attempted as best he could to administer his see in residence, but his presence was frequently required at the French court. His devotion to unity caused him to espouse an absolutism involving both Church and State, but he saw himself as having a role of importance in the unified hierarchy of the two powers, and he played his part with courage and determination. Although he admired Louis XIV as a strong ruler, he did not hesitate to advise the King and even to preach against the King's marital infidelity and plead the cause of the poor in the face of court extravagance. He approved the revocation of the Edict of Nantes but opposed persecution of the Protestants. His early writings include panegyrics on saints and spiritual and polemical treatises. The *Funeral Orations* (e.g., for Henrietta of England and the Prince de Condé), collected later, represent his chief title to literary celebrity. His classical oratory has been called the voice of France in the age of Louis XIV. Bérullian in spirituality, he was nevertheless sympathetic toward early Jansenism and favored its austere morality, yet he complied with both conviction and docility when the doctrine of Port-Royal was finally condemned. By patriotism and family tradition he was inclined to the Gallican point of view, yet he had no thought of renouncing submission to Rome. Indeed his moderation settled the problem and averted schism (*Four Articles,* 1682). In his later years he was disappointed at the incomplete accomplishment of his plans for unity and morality, and for this failure he blamed the theater especially (*Maxims and Reflections on the Comedy,* 1694). His bitterest quarrel was concerned with *Quietism.

Examining Mme. Guyon, whom Fénelon defended, B. found her unbalanced and her mysticism false. He helped to prepare the official condemnation. His action launched the real quarrel, during which B. wrote his *Relation on Quietism* (1698). B.'s last years were marked by a return to the serenity and majesty of his earlier works. Works: *Oeuvres complètes,* (ed. E. N. Guillaume, 10 v., 1877). BIBLIOGRAPHY: J. Calvet, *Bossuet: l'homme et l'oeuvre* (1941); W. J. Simpson, *Study of Bossuet* (1937); G. Terstegge, *Providence as Idée-Maîtresse in the Works of Bossuet* (repr. 1970).

[L. TINSLEY]

BOSTE, JOHN, ST. (1543–94), an English martyr. B. was converted to Catholicism and later ordained at Reims. Returning to England he spent most of his missionary years in the northern counties. He was betrayed by a Catholic apostate, arrested, and confined to the Tower of London. He was tortured several times to force him to reveal his associates. B. was placed on trial in Durham, together with Father John Ingram and George Swallowell, condemned for high treason, and sentenced to be hanged, drawn, and quartered. He endured his martyrdom with great fortitude and joy. He was canonized in October, 1970. BIBLIOGRAPHY: R. Challoner, *Memoirs of Missionary Priests* (ed. J. H. Pollen, new ed. 1924); C. Testore, BiblSanct 3:367–368.

[L. MITCHELL]

BOSTIUS, ARNOLD (1445–99), Belgian Carmelite theologian and humanist. He devoted his life to encouraging classical studies within his order and to promoting devotion to the Blessed Virgin. BIBLIOGRAPHY: E. R. Carroll, *Marian Theology of Arnold Bostius, O. Carm., 1445–99* (1962).

BOSWELL, JAMES (1740–95), literary figure. Son of a Lowland laird, B. studied law at Edinburgh, Glasgow, and Utrecht. In 1760 he ran away and became a Catholic. He always kept a sympathy, shared by his patron, Dr. Johnson, for the RC Church. As a man about London town his performance was assiduous, even superb. His *Life of Johnson* (1791) is an immortal classic. Once overshadowed by the Great Cham, he is now increasingly regarded as a character and literary personage in his own right. His temperance was easygoing, his penitence acute and candid. He was "Dear Bozzy" to Dr. Johnson, whose own standards were very high. BIBLIOGRAPHY: P. Fitzgerald, *Boswell's Autobiography* (1912, repr. 1973); C. B. Tinker, *Young Boswell* (1922, repr. 1973).

BOTTICELLI, SANDRO (1445–1510), Florentine painter much admired for his archaic realism in the manner of Verrocchio and the Pollaiuoli (*St. Sebastian,* 1474), and for his chaste and melancholic female types in elaborately designed and expressive panels (*The Magnificat* and *Madonna of the Pomegranate,* both in Uffizi). In a mature style, classic and intellectual, B. painted *St. Augustine* (1480), frescoes in the Sistine Chapel (1481–82), and the impressive works of

Neoplatonic inference—*Primavera* and *Birth of Venus*. Near the end of his career, when he came under the influence of Savonarola's preaching, he abandoned the lyrical style best seen in his mythological compositions (*Birth of Venus*, c.1478) and changed to a mystical and highly emotional manner (*Pietà*, 1496–98; *Nativity*, 1500). Among B.'s many portraits those of the Medici family with a self-portrait—all in the *Adoration of the Magi* (Uffizi)—and a splendid *Giuliano de' Medici* (National Gallery, Wash., D.C.) are renowned. BIBLIOGRAPHY: R. Salvini, EncWA (1960) 2:580–590; E. Wind, *Pagan Mysteries in the Renaissance* (1958); L. Venturi, *Botticelli* (1961).

[L. A. LEITE]

BOTTICINI, FRANCESCO (Francesco di Giovanni; 1446–97), Italian eclectic painter of Florentine school whose works are imitations of Verrocchio, Botticelli and Ghirlandaio. B. painted *Madonna and Child with Saints* (1471, Paris), *Crucifixion with Saints* (1475, Berlin), and an *Assumption* (1474–76, London).

[M. J. DALY]

BOTULPH, ST. (d. c.680), Anglo-Saxon abbot. Born of English parents, he became a monk (in Germany?). He returned to England and built a monastery at Icanhoe (654). All the vitae are late and their data unreliable. Boston (i.e., Botulphstown) may be on the site of Icanhoe. BIBLIOGRAPHY: P. Burchi, BiblSanct 3:370–371; Butler 2:567–568.

[J. DRUSE]

BOTURINI BENEDUCI, LORENZO (1702–55), historian and collector of Mexican antiquities. While searching for documentary evidence of the miracles of Guadalupe, B. engaged in an intense study of ancient codices and archeological objects relating to the Maya and Aztec Indians; he succeeded in making the best collection of Mexican documents known today. In 1774, however, these papers were confiscated after B. had been indicted, imprisoned, and later exiled to Spain because he solicited funds for a coronation of the Virgin of Guadalupe. Subsequently exonerated, he was named historiographer of the Indies, but never returned to Mexico to reclaim his papers. His *Idea de una historia general de la América septentrional* (1746) deals with the natives of Mexico and the history of New Spain. It can be seen from this literary endeavor that B. was more important as a collector of documents pertaining to Mexican history than as an historian. Others, esp. the historian, Don Veytia, in his *Ancient History of Mexico* (1836), were able to use B.'s information more advantageously. BIBLIOGRAPHY: G. C. Pena, *History of Mexican Literature*, (tr. G. Nance and F. Dunstan, 1943) 139–141: M. Picon-Salas, *Cultural History of Spanish America* (1962) 127.

[D. M. HUGHES]

BOTVID, ST. (d. c.1120), lay apostle of the Swedish province of Södermanland. A native of Sweden, B. was converted to Christianity in England while stopping there on a trading mission. After returning to Sweden he engaged in good works and in evangelizing his fellow countrymen. He is venerated as a martyr because he was treacherously slain by a Finnish slave he had baptized and set free and was taking back to his native land. B. is mentioned in the revelations of St. Bridget of Sweden, who had a special devotion to him. Botkyrka, the church where he was buried, was a center of pilgrimage in the Middle Ages. BIBLIOGRAPHY: A. L. Sibilia, BiblSanct 3:372–373; Butler 3:204.

[F. G. O'BRIEN]

BOUCHARD, JAMES (1823–89), Jesuit missionary. Born of a French-Canadian mother and an Indian father, B. spent his early years with the Delaware tribe in Kansas, where he attended Protestant mission schools. On a visit to St. Louis, Mo. (1847), he became a Catholic, entered the Jesuit novitiate at Florissant, Mo. (1848), and was ordained (1855). Arriving in San Francisco (1861), he devoted his remaining years to Calif., where he became well known as a preacher and lecturer. BIBLIOGRAPHY: J. B. McGloin, *Eloquent Indian: Life of James Bouchard, California Jesuit* (1949).

[R. K. MacMASTER]

BOUCICAUT MASTER, probably identifiable as Jacques Coene, a painter active in Paris c.1405–20. His greatest masterpiece is the *Book of Hours* for the Maréchal de Boucicaut. The Boucicaut Master's rendering of light, natural landscapes and interiors, and attention to aerial perspective make him a key figure in the history of painting in N Europe. The MS is now in the Jacquemart-André Museum, Paris. BIBLIOGRAPHY: M. Miess, *French Painting in the Time of Jean de Berry* (3 v., 1968).

[R. C. MARKS]

BOUDIN, THOMAS (d. 1637), French sculptor of a *Resurrection, Supper at Emmaus, Three Marys* (Chartres) and the tomb of Diane de France (St. Denis) all in his mannerist, theatrical style. His family determined the mode of 17th-cent. French funerary sculpture. BIBLIOGRAPHY: P. Vitry, "Deux familles de sculpteurs: Les Boudin et les Boudin," *Gazette des Beaux-Arts XVII* (1897).

[M. J. DALY]

BOUDON, HENRI-MARIE (1624–1702), French spiritual writer, author of numerous spiritual works which were translated into several languages. His spiritual doctrine embodied pure love of God alone and devotion to Our Lady. BIBLIOGRAPHY: Bremond 6:489; R. Heurtevent, DSAM 1:1887–93.

[D. CARROLL]

BOUGAUD, LOUIS VICTOR ÉMILE (1824–88), French writer. After his ordination he taught dogma, was chaplain for the Visitation nuns, vicar-general of Orléans, and finally bp. of Laval. His somewhat controversial hagiographic works include the lives of SS. Bénigne, Monica, and Margaret Mary. Besides devotional literature, he is known esp. for his 5-volume masterpiece, *Les Christianisme et les temps présents* (1872–74). BIBLIOGRAPHY: L. Calendini, DHGE 9:1494–95; G. Jacquemet, *Catholicisme* 2:194.

[I. M. KASHUBA]

BOUGUEREAU, GUILLAUME ADOLPHE (1825–1905), French painter and exponent of the ''academic'' style with its recipes for the acceptable ''formula'' picture, through majestic devices manufacturing not the ideal but the popular. B. made his debut in the Salon (1853) with a pastiche of Raphael and his continued success there is a judgment of his values. He painted mythological scenes, then works of religious subjects (Cathedral of La Rochelle, 1883). B.'s style is extremely eclectic, photographically real and sentimental. BIBLIOGRAPHY: M. Vachon, *W. Bouguereau* (1900).

[M. J. DALY]

BOUHOURS, DOMINIQUE, (1628–1702), French Jesuit writer, critic, and grammarian. Tutor to the sons of the Duc de Longueville, and to the son of Colbert (1665–66), B. gained entry into high society and admiration for a natural wit and worldliness. A friend of Racine and Boileau, he participated in the literary quarrels of the epoch and expressed his literary and grammatical opinions, considered authoritative, in his *Entretiens d'Ariste et d'Eugène* (1671), *Doutes sur la langue française proposés à MM. de l'Académie* (1674), *Nouvelles remarques sur la langue française* (1675), *La Manière de bien penser dans les ouvrages d'esprit* (1687), and *Pensées ingénieuses des anciens et des modernes* (1691). Author of *Life of Saint Ignatius Loyola* (1675), *St. Francis Xavier* (1682), and *Pensées ingénieuses des Pères de l'Église* (1700), he made a French translation of the Vulgate NT (1697). BIBLIOGRAPHY: G. Doncieux, *Un Jésuite homme de lettres au dix-septième siècle, le Père Bouhours* (1886).

[R. N. NICOLICH]

BOUILLARD, HENRI (1908–), French Jesuit theologian and philosopher. His doctoral thesis on conversion and grace in St. Thomas Aquinas appeared in 1944, followed in 1957 by his most important work, a three-volume analysis and critique of Karl Barth. Later until 1971 four short but important works were published: on Blondel and Christianity, on the logic of faith (dialogues with Protestant thought), on Barth and the capability of knowing God through natural theology apart from revelation (these have been translated into English), and an essay on the intelligibility of what one believes by divine faith. B. presently divides his teaching efforts between the Institut Catholique of Paris and the Gregorian University in Rome.

[J. F. FALLON]

BOULAINVILLIERS, HENRI DE (1658–1722), French political writer. An ultra-aristocrat who inveighed equally against absolute monarchy and popular government, B. was among the first French historians of the institutions and laws of that nation. Among his works are *Histoire de l'ancien gouvernement de la France* (1727) and *Lettres sur les parlements de France que l' on nomme États généraux* (1753). BIBLIOGRAPHY: C. Laplatte, DHGE 10:50–53.

[J. R. RIVELLO]

BOUQUILLON, THOMAS JOSEPH (1842–1902), educator, moral theologian. He studied at the major seminary at Bruges, Belgium and entered the Capranica in Rome. He was ordained in 1865 and in 1867 received his doctorate from the Gregorian University. He taught theology in Belgium and France and joined the original faculty of The Catholic Univ. of America. His theological knowledge was extensive and his expertise was of 16th- and 17th-cent Spanish and Dutch theologians. He influenced the selection of the basic theological volumes in the university library. B. published a pamphlet on education that caused controversy over the question of establishing a Catholic school system. His numerous writings include: *Theologia moralis fundamentalis* (1903); *De virtutibus theologicis* (1890), and *De virtute religionis* (1880). BIBLIOGRAPHY: J. T. Ellis, *Formative years of the Catholic University of America* (1946).

[J. HILL]

BOUQUILLON CONTROVERSY, an educational controversy in the U.S. that arose from an attempt to satisfy Catholic educational ideals within the framework of the public schools by adopting the *Faribault Plan, approved by Abp. J. *Ireland in 1891 in agreement with the public school board of Faribault and Stillwater, Minn. It takes its name from the moral theologian, T. J. Bouquillon, professor at The Catholic University of America, whose pamphlet, *Education: To Whom Does It Belong?*, which appeared (1891) during the parochial school debate, affirmed the right of individuals, parents, Church, and State in education and seemingly championed Ireland's cause. The pamphlet evoked a sharp reaction from René Holaind SJ, professor of ethics at Woodstock, Md., who limited the right to educate to parents and Church alone. To settle the heated and widely publicized discussion, in answer to an appeal to Rome, Abp. F. Satolli came as a representative of the Holy See, and presented (1892) to the assembled hierarchy, as a settlement of the debate, 14 practical propositions, which, however, failed in their purpose. In 1893 Rome issued a statement approving the propositions of the Third Plenary Council in Baltimore, and a pontifical *tolerari potest,* indicating that, although not ideal, the Faribault-Stillwater Plan could be tolerated. BIBLIOGRAPHY: D. F. Reilly, *School Controversy, 1891–93* (1943).

[M. B. MURPHY]

BOURBON, the family name of a great house, taken from

the chief town of the French province called the Bourbonnais, west of Burgundy and north of the Auvergne, which on the extinction of the Valois dynasty succeeded by devious inheritance to the throne of France (1583) in the person of the King of Navarre who became Henry IV: he reckoned that Paris "was well worth a Mass," and accordingly embraced Catholicism. It also succeeded to the throne of Spain (1700) in the person of the Duke of Anjou, who became Philip V, through his Spanish Habsburg grandmother, wife of Louis XIV. The Constable de Bourbon was in command of the imperialist troops which assaulted Rome, 1527; he was killed scaling the walls, by a shot which Benvenuto Cellini claims to have fired; thereafter followed the famous sack of Rome. The rivalry of the two great Catholic houses of the Habsburg and Bourbon dominated European politics for the 2 centuries after the Reformation and did much to hamper the limited reestablishment of Catholicism.

[T. GILBY]

BOURCHIER, THOMAS (c.1410–86), chancellor of Oxford Univ. (1435–37), bp. of Worcester (1435–43), bp. of Ely (1443–54), abp. of Canterbury (1454–86), and cardinal from 1467. Closely involved in politics, B. acted as a peacemaker in the 1450s and later became prominent in the council of Edward IV. BIBLIOGRAPHY: Emden Ox 1:230–232.

BOURDALOUE, LOUIS, (1632–1704), French Jesuit preacher. Entering the Society of Jesus (1648), B. taught philosophy and moral theology before showing an amazing talent for oratory when he began to preach in Amiens (1665). After the success of this beginning, he was sent to Paris (1669), where, as Bossuet's career was ending, he was to become the most popular preacher of the epoch and the orator to preach most frequently before the court of Louis XIV. There he delivered seven series of Advent sermons (1670, 1684, 1686, 1689, 1691, 1693, 1697) and six series of Lenten sermons, among which those *On Almsgiving, On the Last Judgment, On Death, On the Passion* have been considered his best, winning him acclaim as "the king of orators and the orator of kings." In addition, among the 133 sermons that remain of over 450 he delivered, there are sermons for every Sunday of the year, for religious professions, and for special feasts. Of his funeral orations, the one for Louis de Bourbon, Prince de Condé, is frequently contrasted with Bossuet's Condé oration. The success of his sermons is attributed to a simplicity of style, each of his arguments being developed with the same rigorous, almost mechanical logic that his audience found easy to follow, and which facilitated, according to tradition, his own astonishing recitation of the sermons from memory, with eyes closed. His further appeal lay in the moral portraits he included, with contemporary allusions, and comprehensible everyday language. Unlike *Bossuet, he preached constantly, which explains his greater popularity, and devoted himself to the direction of souls, to the confessional, and to the poor, thereby setting an example

by his saintly life. In the dispute over the Gallican Articles he tended to favor the crown. BIBLIOGRAPHY: *Great French Preachers* (ed. and tr. C. H. Brooke, 2 v., 1904); R. Daeschler, *Bourdaloue: Doctrine spirituelle* (1932).

[R. N. NICOLICH]

BOURDEILLE, ELIAS OF, BL. (1413–84), Franciscan prelate. He taught and preached at Mirepoix, was named bp. of Périgueux, promoted to the archbishopric of Tours, and created a cardinal. He attended the Council of *Florence, supported the beatification of Joan of Arc, and opposed the *Pragmatic Sanction of Bourges. BIBLIOGRAPHY: G. Bataille, BiblSanct 3:374–375.

[H. DRESSLER]

BOURDICHON, JEAN (c.1457–1521), French painter in Touraine, noted for MS. illuminations, most important of which is the *Hours of Anne of Brittany* (1508, Paris) showing late Gothic style with the influence of Italian Renaissance in architectural details. BIBLIOGRAPHY: D. MacGibbon, *Jean Bourdichon, Court Painter of 15th Cent.* (1933).

[M. J. DALY]

BOURDOISE, ADRIEN (1584–1655), French priest and educator who worked for the improvement of clerical education in many dioceses of France, founded a school for the children of the poor, and attempted to establish a religious congregation. His faults of character prevented his efforts from bearing much fruit. BIBLIOGRAPHY: P. Pourrat, *Catholicisme* 2:209: H. Daniel-Rops, *Church in the 17th Century* (tr. J. J. Cunningham, 2 v., 1963) *passim*.

[M. J. SUELZER]

BOURGEOYS, MARGUERITE, BL. (1620–1700), foundress of the Sisters of the Congregation de Notre Dame. The daughter of a French merchant, B. joined a pious association in Champagne (1640), and devoted herself to educating children of poor families. With *Maisonneuve she went to Canada (1653) and founded schools for Indians and the poor, as well as for the children of merchants. Others joined the work and the group formed the Congregation de Notre Dame, which she served as superior until 1693. The congregation received canonical approval in 1698. B. was beatified (1950) by Pius XII. BIBLIOGRAPHY: M. Bourgeoys, *Les Écrits de Mère Bourgeoys, autobiographie et testament spirituel* (1964); K. Burton, *Valiant Voyager* (1964).

[R. K. MacMASTER]

BOURGES, CATHEDRAL OF (1172–1500), one of the most important French Gothic cathedrals, having a crypt and two lateral portals (1172) from the Romanesque period. Initiated by the abp.-brother of Eudes of Sully, Bourges derives from Paris and in turn determined forms at Toledo and Burgos. Longitudinal in type, without transepts, its nave (1270) 390 feet long—having pillars with colonnettes (as at Notre Dame)—and double side-aisles, Bourges attains remarkable height through many-storied elevations cresting over the central nave. The pointed radiating chapels are of modest size. Dominating the five sculptured portals of its façade is the vast three-tiered *Last Judgment* tympanum of grandeur and elegance. Most magnificent 13th-cent. stained glass fills the many-storied windows of the aisles, the great west window by Guy de Dammartin (*c*.1390) and the ambulatory by the Poitiers master. The chapel of Jacques *Coeur (1445–50) and the tomb of the Duc de Berry by Jean de Cambrai (d. 1438), pupil of André *Beaunevue are noteworthy. BIBLIOGRAPHY: H. Focillon, *Art of the West* (1963) v. 2.

[M. J. DALY]

BOURGET, IGNACE (1799–1885), Canadian RC churchman. He was consecrated coadjutor bp. of Montreal in 1837 and 3 years later succeeded to the see. He fostered education, undertook programs for immigrants from Ireland who arrived sick and penniless, invited numerous religious orders to his diocese, and was founder of a number of other institutes. He was chief spokesman for ultramontanism in the Canada of his day, advocated traditional rural French-Canadian values, and was often in conflict with the liberal party. He gave a conservative élan to French–Canadian Catholicism and French–Canadian nationalism. BIBLIOGRAPHY: L. Pouliot, *Monseigneur Bourget et son temps* (1955–56).

[R. K. MacMASTER]

BOURGET, PAUL (1852–1935), French writer. Trained in science and philosophy, B. achieved early success in poetry, the psychological novel, and esp. literary criticism (e.g., *Essais de psychologie contemporaine; Nouveaux essais*). Until then a positivist, B. published in 1889 *Le Disciple,* a thesis novel critical of Taine's determinism; thereafter he figured in the ranks of the Catholic Revival, although his formal conversion occurred only in 1901. In politics he defended monarchy and espoused an anti-*Dreyfusard* position, while his later novels, which he called *romans à idées,* reflected an increasingly moralistic attitude and pronounced conservative Catholic social and religious views. They include *L'Étape* (1902), *Un Divorce* (1904), *L'Émigré* (1907), *Le Sens de la mort* (1915) and especially *Le Démon de midi* (1914), critical of Modernism, liberal Catholics, democratic-minded priests, and Christian social action. Interestingly, his travels to America resulted in his *Outre-mer* (2 v., 1895), which interpreted perceptively and sympathetically the experiment of American Catholicism and its leading churchmen, Abp. Ireland and Card. Gibbons. Plays like *La Barricade* (1910) and *Le Tribun* (1911) also deal with socio-economic themes, but his short stories, novelettes, and criticism (e.g., *Au service de l'ordre,* 1928) constitute the best of his later writings. B. differed from the Catholic Revival's mainstream by adopting the methods of positivism for Christian apologetical ends, by emphasizing religion's intellectual content and reason's role in the spiritual de-

velopment of his characters, and by shunning invective. His insistence on the Church's role in stabilizing the social order led some critics (e.g., P. de Rivasso) to regard his adherence to Catholicism as pragmatically motivated. Most critics, e.g., J. Sageret, *Les Grands convertis* (1906); J. Calvet, *Le Renouveau catholique* (1931); and A. Feuillerat, *Paul Bourget* (1937) accept his commitment as sincere. BIBLIOGRAPHY: L. J. Austin, *Paul Bourget* (1951); M. Mansuy, *Un Moderne: Paul Bourget* (1961).

[G. E. GINGRAS]

BOURGOING, FRANÇOIS (1585–1662), one of the ten early Oratorians. He wrote many treatises on asceticism, became assistant to Charles de Condren, Superior General of the Oratorians and succeeded him in that office in 1641. BIBLIOGRAPHY: A. Molien, DSAM 1:1910–15.

[C. CARROLL]

BOURGUEIL-EN-VALLÉE, ABBEY OF (*Burguliense*), former Benedictine monastery, dedicated to St. Peter. B., founded in 989 by the wife of Duke William IV of Poitiers, was situated in the diocese of Angers (now Tours) in France. During its most flourishing days, the abbey directed 42 priories and 64 parish churches. It was placed under commendatory abbots after 1475 but was reformed by the Maurists in 1630. Suppressed in 1791, its buildings were for the most part destroyed. BIBLIOGRAPHY: Cottineau 1:464–465.

[J. DAOUST]

BOURIGNON, ANTOINETTE (1616–80), self-styled visionary and prophetess. A. was born at Lille, France. From youth she claimed to be guided by visions and inner inspiration to a mission of religious reform. She was frequently suspect to the authorities and spent many hours in law courts. While she had collected circles of followers at Lille, Ghent, and Malines, she enjoyed her finest successes at Amsterdam from 1667 to her death. Although she denied the divinity of Jesus Christ, B. always counted herself a Catholic, bent on reforming the whole Church. Some have labelled her a quietist, but her writings, edited by P. *Poiret (19 v., 1679–84), are a mélange drawn from many, often contradictory, religious traditions. They are distinctive chiefly as evidence of her utter reliance on her own inner experience. Decrees of the Holy Office proscribing B.'s writings were issued in 1669, 1687, and 1757. "Bourignonism" had a surprisingly strong impact in Scotland. BIBLIOGRAPHY: Knox Enth 352–355; A. MacEwen, *Antoinette Bourignon, Quietist* (1910); P. Pourrat, DSAM 1:1915–17.

[T. C. O'BRIEN]

BOURNE, FRANCIS (1861–1935), abp. of Westminster and cardinal. He studied at St. Cuthbert's and St. Edmund's, and after that entered the seminary at Hammersmith and later completed his studies at St. Sulpice in Paris and Louvain. After serving in several parishes he was put in charge of a minor seminary in Sussex (1895), was made coadjutor at Southwark (1896), and succeeded to that see upon the resignation of his predecessor. In 1903 he succeeded Cardinal Vaughan as abp. of Westminster and was made a cardinal in 1910. He is remembered for his consecration of the Westminster Cathedral and his efforts toward educational reform as well as for his defense of Catholic schools against governmental restriction. BIBLIOGRAPHY: E. Oldmeadow, *Francis Cardinal Bourne* (2 v., 1940–44).

[P. K. MEAGHER]

BOURNE, GILBERT (d. 1569), distinguished preacher, bp. of Bath and Wells (from 1554), the last Catholic to hold that office. Educated at Oxford, B. became chaplain to Bp. E. Bonner, to whom he remained faithful during the latter's troubles under Edward VI. He himself may have conformed to the religious changes during Edward's reign; at least he held offices, though not of conspicuous importance, at that time. If he had defected, with Mary's accession he returned to the old religion and became royal preacher. As bp. he worked zealously to restore the old order of the Church. His refusal to take the oaths of supremacy and allegiance under Elizabeth led to his imprisonment in the Tower (1559). Later he was released, though kept under house arrest. BIBLIOGRAPHY: Hughes RE; W. Hunt, DNB 2:936–937.

[V. SAMPSON]

BOURNE, HUGH (1772–1852), founder of the Camp-Meeting Methodists in England, who in 1811 joined the Clowesites, forming the Primitive Methodist Church. Converted by reading Methodist literature, he joined a Methodist *society, began preaching in 1801, and in 1808 was expelled for supporting camp-meetings, which were forbidden by Wesleyan Methodists. In 1810 B. formed the Camp-Meeting Methodists. He was general superintendent of the Primitive Methodist Church, 1814–19, and visited the Primitive Methodists in the U.S. and Canada. BIBLIOGRAPHY: J. Ritson, *Romance of Primitive Methodism* (1909); *New History of Methodism* (eds., W. J. Townsend, et al., 2 v., 1909) 1:561ff.

[F. E. MASER]

BOUSSET, WILHELM (1865–1920), Protestant NT exegete who cofounded the school of comparative religions at Göttingen, Germany. B.'s ideas showing the influence of Hellenism on Judaism and Christianity have influenced NT scholars even to the present day. BIBLIOGRAPHY: H. Schlier, LTK 2:632.

[R. C. TOLLARICO]

BOUTRAIS, CYPRIEN MARIE (1837–1900), French Carthusian writer. He was a Redemptorist before entering the Grande Chartreuse in 1870. His published works included Carthusian history and biography, and studies on the

Carthusian devotion to the Sacred Heart. BIBLIOGRAPHY:L. Ray, DSAM 1:1918–19.

[T. C. O'BRIEN]

BOUTROUX, ÉTIENNE ÉMILE MARIE (1849–1921), French philosopher of science, Academician (1914). A relentless critic of 19th-cent. mechanism and determinism, B. holds that reality is contingent, not necessary, and that scientific "laws," even mathematical ones, are but compromises imposed by our reason on shifting reality. B. insists on teleology, not blind mechanism, as the ultimate explanation of nature. Mind is primary and reality stretches hierarchically from God as spiritual perfection to inanimate matter. From B.'s concepts of contingency and finality comes the emphasis he places on religious experience as enriching the life of man. Religion brings together the life of pure instinct and the life of abstract intelligence that produces science, thus ennobling and completing both. Chief works: *The Contingency of the Laws of Nature* (Fr. 1874; tr. F. Rothwell, 1916); *Science and Religion in Contemporary Philosophy* (Fr. 1908; tr. J. Nield, 1909). BIBLIOGRAPHY: M. Schyns, *La Philosophie d'Émile Boutroux* (1924).

[W. B. MAHONEY]

BOUTS, DIRK (1415–75), Netherlandish artist, official city painter of Louvain (1468). A link between the early and later masters, B. introduced a psychological intensity and a new recession of landscape isolating his noble though stiff figures and establishing through the low horizon a direct line between northern Netherlandish landscape and the "Little Dutch Masters" of the late 17th century. Attributed to B. is *Life of the Virgin* (Prado) and probably the *Pearl of Brabant* (Munich), a triptych of the *Adoration of the Magi with the Baptist and St. Christopher*. His last and greatest work is the *Altarpiece of the Blessed Sacrament* (1464–67) in the Church of St.–Pierre, Louvain. BIBLIOGRAPHY: W. Schöne, *Dieric Bouts und seine Schule* (1938).

[M. J. DALY]

BOUVET, JOACHIM (1656–1732), French Jesuit missionary in China, where he was sent at the request of Louis XIV, to conduct astronomical investigations and extend French influence. He became court mathematician to the Emperor K'ang-Hsi, from whom he was instrumental in obtaining a declaration that certain Chinese rites were nonreligious. He prepared a geographical survey of China, compiled a Chinese dictionary, and was a correspondent of Leibniz, who translated his *Portrait historique de l'Empereur de Chine* into Latin. It was also translated into English, Dutch, German, and Italian. BIBLIOGRAPHY:C. Cary-Elwes, *China and the Cross* (1957).

[H. JACK]

BOUVIER, JEAN BAPTISTE (1783–1854), reformer of moral theology who opposed Jansenism and enforced the doctrine of St. Alphonsus as a reaction against rigorism. His manuals were used in most of the seminaries of France, the U.S., and Canada. BIBLIOGRAPHY: L. Calendini, DHGE 10:276–277.

[C. CARROLL]

BOVA, ST. (d. *c*.680), putative daughter of Austrasian King Sigebert (I or III?); sister of Baldericus of Montfaucon, who founded abbey of St. Peter at Reims where B. took the veil and became first abbess. Her niece Doda succeeded her. BIBLIOGRAPHY: AS April 3:285–293; BiblSanct 3:377.

[A. CABANISS]

BOVILLUS, CAROLUS (Charles de Bouvelles; *c*.1470–*c*.1553), humanist philosopher and theologian whose *De sapiente* is a typical Renaissance document placing man at the center of reality. Other works include seven books on the creation of the angels, the pleasures of paradise, the Deluge, the Gospel of John, and the Lord's Prayer, as well as treatises on geometry, physics, and linguistics. He is indebted to Nicholas of Cusa for the synthesis of his theology with that of the Aristotelian tradition. BIBLIOGRAPHY: A. Van Steenberghe, DSAM 1:1894–95.

[T. LIDDY]

BOWET, HENRY (*c*.1350–1423), English canon and civil lawyer, bp. of Bath and Wells (1401–07), abp. of York (1407–23), supporter of Henry IV. He held posts at the papal curia and at home, including the English treasurership (1402). BIBLIOGRAPHY: Emden Camb, 83–84; T. F. Tout, DNB 2:971–973.

[F. D. BLACKLEY]

BOWING, the inclining of the head, or of the head and the upper part of the body, used in the liturgy as an expression of greeting, or a mark of reverence, or as a gesture denoting supplication and adoration. Scriptural precedent for giving bodily expression to reverence for the name of Jesus can be found in Phil. 2.10. From an early date it has been customary in the West to bow toward the altar. Over the centuries the uses of the bow were considerably extended, but there has been some curtailment of its use in the modern revision of the rubrics. Three types of bow are prescribed by the rubrics: an inclination of the head, and an inclination involving the upper part of the body which bends forward moderately (medium bow) or deeply (profound bow). For the practice of the East, see METANY.

[N. KOLLAR]

BOWNE, BORDEN PARKER (1847–1910), Methodist philosopher of "personalistic-idealism." His career was spent as professor of philosophy and theology at Boston Univ. (1876–1910). Relying on reason as the sole criterion of truth, B. sought to develop a system free of theological, philosophical, or scientific dogmatism. In his system, also called "personalism," person, thinking-self, is the ultimate reality. Person is either the creator, God, or the created person, man. Nature has its reality in relation to man's knowing and willing, and as the expression of God's rational willing. Man relates himself to God through his ethical response to the world as manifestation of God's will. B.'s philosophic system influenced Methodist theology esp. through the liberal theologians E. S. *Brightman and A. C. *Knudson. His works include *Metaphysics* (1898) and *Personalism* (1908). BIBLIOGRAPHY: F. J. McConnell, *Borden Parker Bowne* (1929) bibliog.; P. A. Bertocci, EncPhil 1:356–357.

[T. C. O'BRIEN]

BOXING, see PRIZE FIGHTING.

BOY BISHOP, the title given to the boy chosen from a cathedral choir or a monastery school to dress in miter and cope and preside at the Holy Innocents' Day festivities (Dec. 28). The custom began in the 10th cent. as a playful exaltation of the innocent and lowly, considered appropriate to the occasion. As it developed it was marked by a more general inversion of the order of precedence, other choirboys on the same occasion being advanced to the positions of greater dignity, except, of course, in the celebration of the Mass itself. The custom spread over Europe and continued in one form or another until the 19th century. BIBLIOGRAPHY: K. Young, *Drama of the Medieval Church* (2 v. 1933) 1:106–111, 552.

[N. KOLLAR]

BOYCE, HECTOR, see BOECE, HECTOR.

BOYCOTT, a form of coercion in which a group conspires to abstain, and to induce others to abstain, from social, commercial, and/or other relationships with a person, corporation, trade union, or political organization, for the purpose of compelling submission to its will. The name was taken from Charles Boycott, whose evictions of many tenants in County Mayo, Ireland, caused the Land League to organize a campaign of this kind against him in 1880. The tactic has since been used in a wide variety of local, regional, national, and even international conflicts. In the U.S. boycotts have most often been employed as a means of bringing pressure to bear on industry or trade in labor disputes. Any effective boycott does some injury, not only to the persons or organizations against which they are launched, but also to the public at large. From the moral point of view, therefore, a boycott is not a thing to be undertaken lightly, and it seems unethical to engage in them without grave reason, e.g., the rectification of serious and certain injustice that cannot be remedied by less drastic means. Moreover, the harm expected to be suffered, esp. by innocent parties, should be weighed against the good the boycott is expected to accomplish.

[J. C. WILLKE]

BOYLE, ROBERT (1627–91), physical scientist and chemist. Son of the first Lord Cork ("the great earl"), B. was one of a family prominent in the scientific, literary, religious, and political affairs of his century. He is famous as the author of Boyle's Law, on the proportional relation between elasticity and pressure. His physical researches were wide-ranging and important. He studied Hebrew, Greek, Chaldaic , and Syriac for better understanding of the Scriptures. He supported missionary work in the East and America, and was at once a director of the East India Company and governor of the Corporation for the Spread of the Gospel in New England. BIBLIOGRAPHY: J. F. Fulton, *Bibliography of the Honourable Robert Boyle, Fellow of the Royal Society* (2d ed., 1961).

[T. GILBY]

BOYLE, ABBEY OF, originally the Celtic foundation Áth Da Loarg of Bp. Mac Cainne. It became Cistercian in 1161. Many of its abbots became bishops, and four of its monks died for the faith (1580–85). From it were founded Assaroe (1178) and Knockmoy (1190). It was suppressed before 1569. BIBLIOGRAPHY: J. -M. Canivez, DHGE 10:315–316.

[C. MCGRATH]

BRACCIOLINI, POGGIO, see POGGIO BRACCIOLINI, GIOVANNI FRANCESCO.

BRACKLEY, JOHN (Friar Brackley; d. 1467), Conventual Franciscan. A Grey Friar of Norwich, Brackley was admitted to Cambridge *c.*1418 and received a doctorate in theology there. He was a friend and confessor of Sir John Fastolf, (a possible prototype of Shakespeare's Falstaff), and of John Paston. Paston inherited the great wealth of Fastolf, a relative of his wife. He was the principal administrator and legatee of Fastolf's estate in 1459. Paston's claims were challenged and Friar Brackley was involved because he "proved" Sir John's will. Paston's claims were eventually upheld. Some of Brackley's letters are included among the Paston Letters, which also mention several sermons. BIBLIOGRAPHY: *The Paston Letters,* (ed. J. Gairdner, 1904); Emden Camb 87.

[N. F. GAUGHAN]

BRADFORD, WILLIAM (*c.*1590–1657), Pilgrim father and governor of Plymouth Colony. At the age of 16 he joined the Church formed by Puritan *Separatists at Scrooby, England. After a brief imprisonment, he went into exile with the group in Leiden, where he became learned in Calvinist theology. He came with the Pilgrims to Plymouth, and was a signer of the *Mayflower Compact; he was chosen governor (1621), and held the office for 30 years. His *History of Plymouth Plantation* (not published in full until 1856) is the primary source for all knowledge of the Plymouth Colony (modern ed. S. E. Morrison, 1952). B. showed some degree of religious toleration, a rare quality among the Puritans of New England. BIBLIOGRAPHY: B. Smith, *Bradford of Plymouth* (1951).

BRADLEY, DENIS MARY (1816–1903), bishop. A native of Ireland, B. came to the U.S. in 1854, studied at Holy Cross College, Georgetown Univ., and St. Joseph Seminary in Troy. After his ordination (1871) he served at Portland, Maine, as curate of the cathedral and later as rector and chancellor of the diocese. He was transferred to Manchester, N.H. and in 1884 became the first bp. of the Manchester diocese. There he organized the scattered Catholics, developed a Catholic school system, took an active interest in labor problems, and strove to ease tensions created by Nativist agitation. BIBLIOGRAPHY: T. F. Meehan, CE 2:727; M. H. Down, *Life of Denis M. Bradley* (1905).

[H. JACK]

BRADLEY, FRANCIS HERBERT (1846–1924), English philosopher. A graduate of Oxford, B. held an exclusively research fellowship at Merton College throughout his life. Opposed to the empiricism of Locke, Berkeley, Hume, and Mill, his first book, *Ethical Studies* (1876), is an attack on utilitarianism and hedonism. B. defined morality as self-realization, in which self-assertion must work with self-sacrifice so that man may bring himself into harmony with the reality of the world. He refused to identify his belief in a higher divine will with a personal God but speaks of the Absolute as the reality beyond nature. His book *Appearance and Reality* (1893) stirred the whole philosophical world, and his constant efforts to re-state idealism made a real contribution to philosophical thought. T. S. Eliot considered B. one of the most nearly perfect stylists in the English language. BIBLIOGRAPHY: Copleston 8:187–218.

[M. J. BARRY]

BRADWARDINE, THOMAS, see THOMAS BRADWARDINE.

BRADY, MATTHEW FRANCIS (1893–1959), bp., educator. After attending St. Thomas Seminary, Bloomfield, Conn., the American College, Louvain, and St. Bernard Seminary, Rochester, N.Y., he was ordained in Hartford, Conn. (1916). He served in parishes in New Haven, taught Scripture at St. Thomas Seminary, Bloomfield, and was responsible for organizing the Fourth National Catechetical Congress held in Hartford in 1938. Appointed bp. of Burlington in 1938, he established CCD and a diocesan school department. During World War II he set up centers for servicemen. In 1944 he was transferred to Manchester, New Hampshire. He served as president-general of the National Catholic Educational Association in 1957–58.

[J. HILL]

BRADY, NICHOLAS FREDERIC (1878–1930), financier, philanthropist. After attending school at Albany

Academy and at Yale Univ. he entered his father's public utilities business. He was converted to Catholicism in 1906. Left in control of the family business, B. doubled his fortune and showed great skill in managing public utilities corporations. Aware also of the needs of his employees, he significantly increased their benefits. In 1929 he received papal recognition for his many contributions to charity, for which he was the first U. S. citizen to receive the *Ordine Supremo del Christo*. He provided funds for the construction of a Jesuit novitiate in Wernersville, Pa. BIBLIOGRAPHY: J. J. Daly, *Nicholas Frederic Brady* (1935).

[J. HILL]

BRADY, WILLIAM MAZIERE (1825–94), Irish church historian. Born in Dublin, B. studied at Trinity College there, and after ordination in 1848 in the (Anglican) Church of Ireland, he held various parishes and served as chaplain to lords lieutenant of Ireland. In the process of historical research he came to views expressed in the title of his book, *The Irish Reformation, or, The Alleged Conversion of the Irish Bishops to the Reformed Religion at the Accession of Queen Elizabeth and the Assumed Descent of the Present Established Hierarchy in Ireland from the Ancient Irish Church Disproved* (1866). He continued his studies in the Vatican archives and published additional works. With his wife, whom he married in 1851, he was received into the Catholic Church in 1873. He died in Rome.

[T. EARLY]

BRAGA, RITE OF, an ancient rite of the Western Church observed in the cathedral at Braga in Portugal. In the absence of sufficient sources it is impossible to describe the earliest forms of the rite or to determine its origin. It is commonly regarded as a special form of the Roman rite, but it shows the influence of Gallican customs. The extant sources are a Pontifical from the 12th cent. and a Missal from the 10th or 11th cent. that was still in use as late as the 15th cent. The calendar is close to the Roman. It evinces a strong Marian devotion, esp. in the prayers before and after Mass. There are three elevations at Mass: after the consecration, at the beginning of the Our Father, and before the communion of the celebrant. BIBLIOGRAPHY: A. A. King, *Liturgies of the Primatial Sees* (1957) 155–185.

[N. KOLLAR]

BRAHMAN (Hindu, supreme Reality, the Godhead; from the root *brih* meaning "to be great"). Brahman is being, awareness, and bliss. The basic Hindu view of God is absolute reality, absolute consciousness, and utterly beyond all possibility of frustration. Brahman cannot be described, defined, or properly conceived by man's mind because human minds deal only with finite objects. The Hindu Supreme Reality is not a mass of nothing. Although Brahman cannot be described by man, this does not mean that God is nothing. Hindus encourage believers to conceive of Brahman in a way that is best for the individual. Brahman is

personal for some; impersonal for others. BIBLIOGRAPHY: T. Berry, *Religions of India* (1971); S. Dasgupta, *History of Indian Philosophy* (5v., 1932–55).

[C. CARROLL]

BRAHMS, JOHANNES (1833–97), German composer, pianist, and conductor. B. was the son and student of a humble musician; his association, early in his career, with Schumann brought him into wide notice. After holding positions for a few years in Germany, he settled in Vienna where, though rejected for a time by partisans of Wagner, he finally came to be recognized as the logical successor of Beethoven and continuer of the symphonic form. B.'s works, while romantic in temper, are classical in form. He is regarded as one of the great purists—a creator of works chaste, noble, and intellectually and emotionally profound. His compositions include four symphonies, concertos, chamber music, piano and choral music, songs, and duets. B. produced comparatively little sacred music: the *Marienlieder;* some motets; a *Benedictus;* settings of *O bone Jesu, Adoramus te,* and *Regina Coeli;* 11 choral preludes and, best known, his *Requiem,* a deeply personal expression of a text which, though biblical, is almost wholly nonliturgical. BIBLIOGRAPHY: P. F. Radcliffe, Grove DMM 1:870–903; W. J. Henderson, *International Cyclopedia of Music and Musicians* (ed. O. Thompson, 9th ed., 1964) 268–275.

[M. T. LEGGE]

BRAINERD, DAVID (1718–1747), American Protestant missionary. B. was licensed as a Presbyterian preacher in 1742, worked among the Indians in New York, and was ordained in Newark in 1744. After his engagement as a missionary by the Society for the Propagation of Christian Knowledge, B. rode horseback along the Delaware and Susquehanna rivers, preaching to the Indians through an interpreter. He reached the Delawares, Seven Nations, Senecas, and Tutelas, recording his experiences in a diary and a journal. He contracted tuberculosis during his travels and died at 29. BIBLIOGRAPHY: J. Edwards, *Life and Diary of David Brainerd* (ed. P. Howard, 1955); Moyer WWW 55.

[H. JACK]

BRAINWASHING, the use of torture, drugs, or psychological stress to change a person's attitudes and beliefs. It is a procedure known to have been employed by totalitarian regimes. The use of means of this kind is obviously a serious violation of an individual's right to the independence and integrity of his own personality, and it cannot be ethically condoned for any reason. The application of the term to indoctrination by repetition, confusion, falsehoods or plausible half truths, as, e.g., in TV advertising, is repugnant to most moralists, but is excused by some as "fluff" which the general populace should be able to detect and reject.

[J. C. WILLKE]

BRAMANTE, DONATO (1444–1514), greatest Italian architect of his generation, engineer of domes, trained earlier as painter by Piero della Francesca and Mantegna from whom no doubt he assimilated the spirit of classical simplicity and harmony furthered by his study of Roman ruins. He domed the E end of Sta. Maria presso S. Satiro (Milan, 1482). In Rome (1499) B. built the first, and to this day most nearly perfect High Renaissance building—the small, circular, colonnaded Tempietto of S. Pietro in Montorio (1502) of such wonderful harmony of dome, drum, and base, Palladio called it the "ideal church" demonstrating the unity and perfection of God. From 1505 Pope Julius II engaged B. on monumental projects. Most famous was B.'s plan for St. Peter's, a gigantic domed Greek cross plan—a favorite with B., to whom mathematical perfection was a symbol of the Godhead. Plans for the Belvedere Courtyard of the Vatican (1505) were not fully realized. The play of light and shade, void and solid gave to B.'s architecture a sculptural effect relating it to that of Michelangelo. BIBLIOGRAPHY: O. H. Forster, *Bramante* (1956).

[L. A. LEITE]

BRAMHALL, JOHN (1594–1663), Anglican abp. of Armagh in Ireland, controversialist. A Yorkshire man, educated at Cambridge, ordained in 1616, B. became bp. of Derry in Ireland in 1634. He was named abp. of Armagh in 1661, after an absence from Ireland during the period of the Civil War and the Puritan ascendancy. In his polemical writing he attacked the Presbyterianism of the Puritans, the materialism of T. Hobbes, and the RC doctrines on the Eucharist and the papal primacy. His best known work was *A Just Vindication of the Church of England from the Unjust Aspersion of Criminal Schism* (1654). He was desirous of the reunion of the Churches.

[T. C. O'BRIEN]

BRAMMART, JOHANNES (*c.* 1340–1407), German Carmelite theologian, a founder of the Univ. of Cologne.

[T. C. O'BRIEN]

BRANCACCI CHAPEL, see Masaccio, Tomasso di Giovanni di Simone Guidi.

BRANCATI, LORENZO (1612–93), Conventual Franciscan theologian, cardinal from 1681. After teaching in various studia of his order, B. became professor at the Sapienza in Rome in 1593. In Rome he served the Holy See on the Congregation of the Index, and as prefect of the Vatican Library. As theologian he is renowned for his commentaries on Duns Scotus, his pioneer work in missiology, his contribution to the norms for the canonization of saints, and his refutation of Quietistic theories of mental prayer. BIBLIOGRAPHY: J. Heerinckx DSAM 1:1921–23.

[T. C. O'BRIEN]

BRANCH THEORY, the view that although the Church is in internal *schism, with its main segments not in communion with one another, nevertheless those segments, retaining the historic *apostolic succession and holding to the faith of the undivided Church continue as living branches of the Church. In this form, the theory became popular in 19th-cent. England, following the *Oxford movement. Three branches were usually identified, Roman, Orthodox, and Anglican. In some broader usages of the theory, particularly in the U.S., the *historic episcopate disappeared as a criterion, and the number of branches was multiplied to include most or all of the major Christian divisions. The theory commands little contemporary respect save, perhaps, as a simple historical diagram of the successive divisions in the Church's life. With ecumenical attention increasingly focused on the given unity of Christians in baptism and in the saving acts of God, and with the development of common ecumenical action and even united Churches, the theory seems to explain little and justify even less. It may be said, however, that the idea served, at a critical time, to remind Christians both of the continuing, organic nature of the Church's life manifested in its historic institutions and also of the very givenness itself of unity in Christ as a reality which in some way overcomes the breaches in the visible Church.

[S. F. BAYNE]

BRANCUSI, CONSTANTIN (1876–1957), Romanian, undoubtedly one of the greatest sculptors of the 20th century. Graduating in Bucharest (1902), B. traveled across Europe, arriving in Paris in 1904. He became a French citizen 1957. Though A. *Rodin admired and influenced him, B. was an innovator of unique expression. Widely acclaimed throughout the world for purity of form and meticulous skill, he couched simplest shapes—human, bird, animal—in varied materials seeking always the perfect solutions to formal problems. B. was influenced by a study of the 11th-cent. Tibetan monk, Milarepa, and by the Gregorian chants he sang in the Romanian Orthodox Church in Paris. His works are profoundly philosophic in a search for the shape of absolute truth. BIBLIOGRAPHY: I. Jianoa, *Brancusi* (1963); S. Geist, *Brancusi: the Sculpture and Drawings* (1975); D. Lewis, *Constantin Brancusi* (1975).

[M. J. DALY]

BRANDSMA, TITUS (1881–1942), Dutch Carmelite, executed by the Nazis at Dachau for his defense of religious schools and of the Jews. B. had been a leader in Catholic education and journalism, rector of the Catholic Univ. of Nijmegen (1932), an historian of medieval mysticism, and a specialist in Frisian culture. His cause of beatification is under consideration. BIBLIOGRAPHY: E. Rhodes, *His Memory Shall Not Pass* (1958).

[T. C. O'BRIEN]

BRANGWYN, FRANK (1867–1956), painter, muralist, and printmaker. Son of a Catholic ecclesiastical architect, B. first designed textiles under William *Morris. Traveling extensively, he captured in his paintings exotic colors of the Orient, but in his prints he depicted in dark tones poor and tattered workers. B. received a gold medal from the Emperor of Austria and was knighted in 1941. His decorative works can be seen in London, Ottawa, and Radio City, New York. BIBLIOGRAPHY: V. Galloway, *Oils and Murals of Sir Frank Brangwyn (1867–1956)* (1962).

[M. J. DALY]

BRANN, HENRY ATHANASIUS (1837–1921), writer. In 1849 his family left Ireland and came to Jersey City, N. J. Ordained (1862) for the Diocese of Newark, he became professor of metaphysics and vice president at Seton Hall College, and for a time director of the seminary in Wheeling, West Virginia. From 1870 he labored as pastor in N. Y. where he built churches and schools. He wrote many articles for Catholic periodicals and among his published books are: *Age of Unreason* (1880), *Life of Abp. Hughes* (1892), and *History of the American College, Rome* (1912). BIBLIOGRAPHY: F. D. Cohalan, NCE 2:755–756.

[J. HILL]

BRANT, SEBASTIAN (1457–1521), German humanist, author, and satirist. He studied and later (1498–99) taught Roman and canon law at Basel, then became imperial councilor under Maximilian I. B. took no interest in the Reformation movement. He wrote on legal, religious, political, and moral topics and produced translations of Vergil and Petrarch. His best known work was *Das Narrenschiff* (1494), which was often imitated and translated (first Eng. tr. by Alexander Barclay, *The Ship of Fools,* 1509; modern Eng. tr. by E. H. Zeydel, 1944). Embarking on a ship, fools of 112 categories set off for Narragonien, the land of fools. They all perish in a shipwreck. B.'s friend Geiler von Kaisersberg (1445–1510) based more than 100 sermons on B.'s categories; T. *Murner followed B.'s satirical style; and in the following century *Abraham of Sancta Clara was marked by the same influence. BIBLIOGRAPHY: W. Kosch, *Deutsches Literature-Lexicon* (2d ed., 4v., 1947–58) 1:210, with bibliog.

[S. A. SCHULZ]

BRAQUE, GEORGES (1882–1963), a major French cubist painter. Schooled at Le Havre and Paris, B. painted landscapes (1905–06) in *Fauvist style. Moving toward *cubism, B. developed with *Picasso (1908–12) most important theories in the history of 20th-cent. art. Analytical cubist works (1910–11) with simultaneity of views and fractured images in a severe, subdued palette were followed by large forms in the bright colors of synthetic cubism, and *papiers collés* (collages, 1912–14) of letters, numerals, and textured effects of marble and wood (B.'s father was a decorator). After service in World War I, B. applied his sophisticated palette (always more refined than Picasso's) in distinctive brown, green, and gold in most ingenious spatial designs with a mastery of drawing, tone, shape, and texture.

B. worked extensively in lithograph and did some sculpture. He won the first prize in the International Venice Biennale (1948). His specific religious works include devotional cards for the Club des Nouvelles Images (1961), stained glass for his parish church at Varengeville and for the chapel of the Maeght Foundation at St.-Paul-de-Vence (1962). BIBLIOGRAPHY: J. Richardson, *Georges Braque* (1961); E. Mullens, *Braque* (1974).

[M. J. DALY]

BRASÍLIA, new capital of Brazil (1960) on a plateau 600 miles NW of Rio de Janeiro, planned in three zones, monumental, commercial, and residential. Oscar Niemeyer, head of the Dept. of Architecture, designed the imposing presidential palace with chapel, the cathedral, and parliament buildings, all impressive, imaginative shapes conceived to exploit the cantilever construction of huge forms that stand on delicate pins of support in vast open spaces accenting contours and confirming lines in reflecting pools, where dramatic sculptured forms extend a visual impact of supreme imaginative magnificence. BIBLIOGRAPHY: O. Niemeyer Soares, *Minho Experiencia em Brasília* (1961).

[M. J. DALY]

BRASK, HANS (1464–c. 1538), bp. of Linköping in Sweden, a Swedish patriot who supported the revolt against Denmark, but vigorously opposed the introduction of Lutheranism into Sweden. When King Gustavus sought to take over church property and was supported in this by the diet, B. refused to submit and went to Danzig in exile. BIBLIOGRAPHY: H. Jägerstad, LTK 2:653.

[J. C. WILLKE]

BRASSEUR DE BOURBOURG, CHARLES ÉTIENNE (1814–74), French clergyman, missionary, ethnographer, and expert in the prehistory of Central America. Becoming interested in the pre-Hispanic cultures of the Americas in 1846, B. did extensive research and study on this topic. In 1848 he traveled to Central America where he served as pastor in several locales while perfecting his knowledge of Cacchiquel and Quiché. His publication of *Popol-Vuh* (1861), the French translation of the sacred book of the Quiché Indians, and of Diego de Landa's *Relación de las cosas de Yucatán,* a condensation of the early history of Yucatan, helped to arouse interest in the scientific study of Central American prehistory. Later scholars, however, have disputed many of his findings. BIBLIOGRAPHY: A. F. Bandelier, CE 2:743–744.

[D. M. HUGHES]

BRATISLAVA, a Czechoslovakian town, the capital of Slovakia, S central Czechoslovakia on the left bank of the Danube about 34 miles E by S of Vienna near the Austrian and Hungarian frontiers. Until 1918 its German name was Pressburg; its Hungarian name is Pozong.

Settled by Slavs and Avars between the 6th and 8th cent.,

it was the military center for the princes of Great Moravia when it was evangelized by SS Cyril and Methodius (840–894). A prominent town in the 11th and 12th cent., it was a frequent meeting place for the rulers of Austria and Hungary. After the Turks captured Budapest, it became the capital of Hungary (1541–1784). Its chief buildings include its Gothic cathedral where the Hapsburgs were crowned kings of Hungary (1536–1791), the parliament house in which the Hungarian Diet met until 1848, a Franciscan church (1290–1297), and the town house with its natural history collection (1288). Formerly under the See of Esztergom (Hungary), it has been subject to the apostolic administrator of Trnava since 1922. It is the chief port of Czechoslovakia on the Danube linking the republic with the Black Sea. BIBLIOGRAPHY: M. Lacko, LTK 10:369–370.

[F. H. BRIGHAM]

BRAUER, THEODOR (1880–1942), labor leader and influential writer of the Catholic social movement. Born in Germany, B., as a member of a union for salaried employees, was interested in the Catholic social movement. He became assistant director of the Catholic People's Union (1907) and staff assistant of the German Federation of Christian Trade Unions at Cologne (1908). Editor of the latter's "Central Organ" (1914–19) and then of the monthly *Deutsche Arbeit,* he attained the doctorate in economics at the Univ. of Bonn (1919) and afterwards taught at the Baden Institute of Technology, Karlsruhe. In 1928 he was made director of the Institute for Social Research. Professor of labor economics and social legislation at the Univ. of Cologne and (after 1930) director of the Labor School of the Christian Trade Unions in Königswinter, he was arrested by the Nazis and jailed for a time. His last years were spent in the U.S. BIBLIOGRAPHY: F. H. Mueller, NCE 2:760.

BRAULIO, ST. (*c.*590–*c.*651), bp. of Saragossa, Spain. Born of a family of high rank, B. became a protégé of St. *Isidore of Seville, in whose school he made his later studies, and whom he helped in the revision of his writings. In 631 B. was chosen to succeed his brother John as bp. of Saragossa. In this office he carried out his pastoral duties with zeal, seeking to restore discipline and order and to complete the overthrow of Arianism. B. participated in the 4th, 5th, and 6th Councils of Toledo. Even during his lifetime he had a widespread reputation for sanctity. BIBLIOGRAPHY: Butler 1:685–686; N. Scipioni, EncCatt 3:47.

[R. B. ENO]

BRAUN, JOSEPH (1857–1947), German Jesuit, distinguished for his work in the fields of archeology and liturgy. A Jesuit from 1881, he taught at the theologates of Valkenburg, Frankfurt, and Pullach. His works are basic to any knowledge of Christian archeology, iconography, and liturgy because of the mass of material he assembled and because of his description and evaluation of the literary sources. His most significant contribution was his *Der christliche Altar in seiner geschichtlichen Entwicklung* (1924). BIBLIOGRAPHY: E. Kirschbaum, EncCatt 3:47–48.

[N. KOLLAR]

BRAUN, PLACIDUS (1756–1829), German Benedictine scholar. Born at Peiting, near Schongau, Bavaria, he entered the Benedictine Abbey of SS. Ulrich and Afra, Augsburg, and was ordained in 1779. B. served the abbey as librarian and published catalogues of its books (3 v., 1787) and MSS (6 v., 1791–96). After it was dissolved in 1806, he served Augsburg parishes and wrote historical works on the Augsburg diocese and its suppressed religious houses.

[T. EARLY]

BRAUNAU (BROUMOV), ABBEY OF, a former monastery converted from a castle which the Czech King Atakar I gave to the Benedictine monks in 1322. Its church is dedicated to SS. Wenceslaus and Adalbert, and its library was constructed between 1683 and 1733. Because of the size of the religious community, its abbots exerted considerable influence in national affairs. Here a Protestant attempt in 1618 to build a church met with the forcible resistance of Abbot Wolfgang Solander. The resulting protest from Czech estates and the defenestration of the ministers in Prague was a major cause of the Thirty Years' War (1618–48). After the Battle of White Mountain near Prague (1620), the abbey was deprived of many privileges. It survived, nevertheless, and saw the restoration of many of them during the ensuing years. In 1945, German monks were expelled by the Czech government and in 1947, the abbey was placed under the administration of the Czech Benedictines from St. Procopius, Lisle, Illinois. In 1950, it was closed by the Communists and since that time has served as a government-controlled dwelling for religious women of the many disbanded orders and congregations whose members are employed in neighboring factories. BIBLIOGRAPHY: L. Nemec, *Church and State in Czechoslovakia* (1955) *passim.*

[L. NEMEC]

BRAUNS, HEINRICH (1868–1939), RC priest of Cologne, social and political leader. In 1900 he became head of the Volksverein für das katholische Deutschland, was minister of labor (1920–28), and Center Party representative in the Reichstag (1920–33). He helped prevent civil war in Germany in 1918 and used his position and influence afterwards to promote legislation in behalf of the workers. His works include: *Christian Labor Unions* (1908); *Truth about the German Catholics and the Trade Unions* (1908); *The Center Party and the Protestant Population.* BIBLIOGRAPHY: O. Deuerlein, LTK 2:656.

BRAUWEILER, ABBEY OF, former Benedictine monastery near Cologne, Germany, founded (1024) by Count Palatine Erenfrid of Lorraine and his consort Matilda. In 1469 Brauweiler was affiliated with the Congregation of Bursfeld. Since the end of the 15th cent., Brauweiler acquired renown for the scientific works of the monks; for the achievements of individual monks such as Dom Franz Kramer who, in 1783, was named professor of history at the academy of Bonn. The abbatial church was under construction from 1408 to 1629. Secularized in 1802, the monastery was transformed into a hospice (1810), then into a house of correction (1815). In 1806 the church became the property of the parish. BIBLIOGRAPHY: P. Volk, DHGE 10:457–458.

[S. A. HEENEY]

BRAY, THOMAS (1656–1730), Anglican priest, founder of the *Society for Promoting Christian Knowledge (SPCK) and the *Society for the Propagation of the Gospel (SPG). While rector of Sheldon in Warwickshire, B. was made commissary of the bp. of London for the American colonies to develop support for the C of E there. The experience of planning this work prompted him to establish the SPCK (1698); he went to Md. in 1699, but decided he could contribute most to his mission by working in England. He established the SPG in 1701. His efforts to have a bp. appointed for the Church in New England were unsuccessful. Many free parochial libraries in England were part of the legacy of his labors. See life by E. L. Pennington (1934). *PROTESTANT EPISCOPAL CHURCH.

BRAZIL, largest country of South America and largest predominantly Catholic country in the world. Under the Treaty of Tordesillas, Brazil (though not all its present area) came into the Portuguese sphere, and it was claimed for Portugal by Cabral in 1500. Priests accompanied him, and numerous clergy, particularly Franciscans and Jesuits, came later. In 1551 the first diocese was established at Salvador (Bahia), the Brazilian capital until it was moved in 1763 to Rio de Janeiro. José de *Anchieta, leader of the Jesuits who came with a new governor in 1553, became the Apostle of Brazil. A recurrent feature of colonial Brazil was conflict between clergy seeking to Christianize Indians and colonists, particularly Paulistas of Sao Paulo, wishing to enslave them. Converted Indians were commonly settled in villages *(aldeias),* and a 1574 royal decree gave Jesuits control of these Indians while allowing colonists to enslave those captured in war. Jesuits became the principal educators of Brazil, and their expulsion in 1759 by Portuguese Prime Minister Pombal severely damaged the schools and church life generally. When Napoleon attacked Portugal, the Prince Regent, later John VI, went to Brazil. After his return in 1821, his son became Pedro I of an independent Brazil. The 1823 Constitution affirmed Catholicism as the state religion, but Church-State conflict continued. A new constitution in 1891 brought separation of Church and State. Today Catholicism remains dominant, but the population includes numerous Protestants and Spiritualists.

[T. EARLY]

BREACH OF PROMISE, as understood here, the viola-

tion of the promise to marry a specific person. In the U.S. in a growing number of states, courts no longer attempt to enforce the promise to marry or to assess damage for the violation of such a promise. It seems that this change has come about by the recognition of the fact that suits for breach of promise are commonly not in the public interest because of the opportunity they provide for blackmail or coercion. In ecclesiastical law in the RC Church no action of this kind is permitted, even when the promise to marry has been made in a formal *betrothal. However, in conscience a person may well be bound to compensate the injured party for damages incurred by expenditures made with a view to the promised marriage.

[P. K. MEAGHER]

BREAD, one of the elements used in the Eucharist. The kind of bread varies in different Churches. In the 11th cent. the use of unleavened bread was general in the Western Church, whereas the East retained the leavened. Protestant denominations for the most part adopted leavened bread. Symbolic significance can be advanced in support of both practices. Despite the trouble the divergence of use has occasioned between East and West, no doctrinal issue was involved in the controversy. In the RC Church only bread (leavened or unleavened) made from wheaten flour is held to be valid matter for eucharistic consecration (D 1320; CIC c. 815.1). Bread is also employed in the liturgy for cleansing the fingers of blessed oil, for the offering of a newly consecrated bishop, for an offering to the pope at a solemn canonization, and for distribution to the faithful in the form of *eulogiae.* Several blessings for bread are to be found in the Roman Ritual, including those in honor of certain saints for protection against various hazards to health. BIBLIOGRAPHY: J. A. Jungmann, *Mass of the Roman Rite* (tr. F. Brunner, 2 v. 1951–55) 1:78–80; R. M. Wooley, *Bread of the Eucharist* (1913).

[N. KOLLAR]

BREAD, EUCHARISTIC (IN THE EAST). This is a bread specially prepared and baked, but its basic composition is that of a bread traditionally used in the region. The use of unleavened bread among the Armenians is attested before the first clear evidence of its use in the West. The other Eastern Churches which use it, the Maronites and the Malabar Syrians in union with Rome, may have learned it from the Latins, but the use of unleavened bread in some places in Syria is probably older than the influences that came in with the Crusaders. Elsewhere leaven is used. The designs on the breads vary in character not only between but within the rites. These however are always related to the arrangement of the breads at the preliminary *prothesis where one or more are set apart for consecration, while others provide the blessed bread distributed at the end of the liturgy. The shape of the bread and its patterning are also related to the fraction, where Jacobites have an elaborate arrangement of figures, differing according to the season. Other rules are concerned with the ministers, generally clergy or nuns, involved in the preparation and baking.

[G. EVERY]

BREAD OF LIFE, a term used in Jn 6 to indicate the person of Jesus (v. 35) and also the eucharistic bread (v. 51). It occurs in the Offertory in the new liturgy, and, in equivalent form (life-giving bread), in the *anamnesis of Eucharistic Prayer II.

[P. K. MEAGHER]

BREAKING OF BREAD, in itself a phrase describing the opening act of a communal meal. In the Ancient Near East, as in archaic societies generally, a meal always has a ritual connotation, symbolizing fraternity and social unity. Usually it was in a context at least implicitly religious (e.g., Ex 24.3–8; Dt 26.1–11). Isaiah 58.7; Jer 16.7; and Lam 4.4 mention the breaking of bread as a religious act of compassion toward the needy. According to OT (Jewish) practice, the head of the family or group presided at the meal. After reciting the opening blessing (prayer of thanks to God), he broke and distributed the bread first, then the other foods. The gospels show Jesus doing this, both in the multiplication of the loaves (Mt 14.19; 15.36; Mk 6.41; Lk 9.16; Jn 6.11–14), and at the Last Supper (Mt 26.26; Mk 14.22; Lk 22.19; 1 Cor 11.23). The breaking of bread occurs also, after Jesus' resurrection, at Emmaus (Lk 24.30–35). Along with community of goods and common prayer, the breaking of bread was a characteristic sign of the fraternity of the primitive apostolic church (Acts 2.42–46; 20.7,11; 27.35) after the ascension of Jesus. However, scholars dispute as to how explicitly each NT occurrence of the phrase describes a deliberate eucharistic (sacramental) rite. Form criticism has led to the supposition that the NT authors retroject, at least implicitly, into the Gospels and Acts the more developed eucharistic understanding of their own day. In the post-apostolic era the breaking of bread is more and more clearly synonymous with the Sacrament of the Eucharist and with the sacrifice of the Mass (Didache 14.1; St. Ignatius *Ad Ephes.* 20.2). BIBLIOGRAPHY: EDB 276–277; A. Piolanti, EncCatt 5:1564–65; J. Dupont, ''Le Repas d'Emmaüs'' *Lumière et vie* 6 (1957) 77–92.

[T. CRANE]

BREAST, STRIKING OF, a gesture in religious use among the Hebrews and pagans which was adopted by the early Christians as an expression of sorrow for sin. It has this meaning in the two places for which it is prescribed at Mass, viz, the *Confiteor and *Nobis quoque peccatoribus* in the Eucharistic Prayer I (old Roman Canon). Later piety has also used the gesture to express adoration, as at Benediction or at the elevation at Mass.

[N. KOLLAR]

BREASTPLATE, armor piece protecting the chest. Often the front part of a cuirass or corselet. Consisting of scales,

chains, or solid metal, it was worn over a leather jerkin or tunic and was supplemented by protection for the back and other areas (see 1 Kgs 22.34). The Bible also uses the term symbolically. The breastplate is included in the imagery of Revelation (9.9, 17). Righteousness is called a breastplate (Is 59.17; Eph 6.14), as are faith and love (1 Th 5.8). In the KJV the term is used for the breastpiece that the high priest wore when performing his official functions (Ex 28.4).

[T. EARLY]

BREASTPLATE OF ST. PATRICK (Lorica), an ancient Irish morning prayer invoking the Holy Trinity, Christ, and the powers of heaven for protection against various evils that threaten body and soul. The earliest known copy is from the 9th cent., but its thought and syntax and meter suggest that it was composed in the 6th cent. at the latest. Scholars do not commonly attribute it to St. Patrick, although the possibility that he wrote it cannot be definitely excluded. Text in translation: J. Stokes and J. Strachan, *Thesaurus Palaeohibernicus* (1903) 2:354–358; an emended version of the same translation can be found in L. Bieler, *Works of St. Patrick,* ACW 17 (1953) 69–73.

[P. K. MEAGHER]

BREATHING, a liturgical action that, understood as an insufflation, signifies the communication of life or power (see Jn 20.12), or as an exsufflation, the expulsion of an evil spirit. Examples of both insufflation and exsufflation occur in the rite of baptism. Breathing is also used in the rite of consecrating the oil of chrism and the oil of catechumens, and in the blessing of baptismal water.

[N. KOLLAR]

BRÉBEUF, GEORGES (GUILLAUME) DE (1617–61), French poet. Nephew of St. John de Brébeuf, B. is author of French Counter Reformation religious poetry, *Entretiens solitaires ou prières et méditations pieuses en vers français* (1660), and a *Traité de la défense de l'Église romaine* (1664). He is, however, more generally known for his French translation of Lucan's *Pharsalia* (1658), as well as for his satirical *Lucain travesti* (1656), and *Parodie du VIIe livre de l'Énéide* (1650). BIBLIOGRAPHY: R. Harmand, *Essai sur la vie et les oeuvres de Georges de Brébeuf* (1897); Bremond Index 45.

[R. N. NICOLICH]

BRÉBEUF, JOHN DE, ST. (1593–1649), Jesuit missionary martyr. Born in Normandy, he entered the Jesuits at Rouen (1617), and was first sent to Canada in 1625. When expelled with other Jesuits in 1629, he returned to France but was sent back to Canada in 1633 to work among the Hurons. B. composed a Huron dictionary and catechism, and saw 7000 Indians converted and baptized through the efforts of the missionaries. In 1649, he was captured by a band of marauding Iroquois who destroyed the mission of St. Ignace. He died after four hours of excruciating torture, March 16, at

Sainte-Marie near Georgian Bay, Ontario. His journal gives evidence of his remarkable sanctity and courage. For bibliog. see NORTH AMERICAN MARTYRS.

[P. K. MEAGHER]

BRECHT, BERTOLT (1898–1956), German dramatist and poet. An avowed but heterodox Marxist, B. left Germany in 1933 and later moved to Hollywood. After World War II he lived from 1948 in East Berlin where he founded and directed the Berliner Ensemble, a theatrical group devoted exclusively to the staging of his plays. Using new dramatic techniques, B. produced plays that range in theme from bald communist propaganda to the poetic examination of subtle moral problems. Despite the propaganda, some see in his writings an antidote to Christian indifference and institutional self-righteousness. BIBLIOGRAPHY: F. Ewen, *Bertolt Brecht: His Life, His Art, and His Times* (1967).

[S. A. SCHULZ]

BREDA, DECLARATION OF, see DECLARATION OF BREDA.

BREECHES BIBLE, popular name for the Geneva Bible of 1560, derived from its use of "breeches" in Gen 3.7 where the King James Version used "aprons."

[T. EARLY]

BRÉHIER, LOUIS (1868–1951), Byzantine scholar. B. served as professor of ancient and medieval history of the Univ. of Clermont-Ferrand from 1898 to his retirement in 1938. He was primarily concerned with Greek and Latin relations in the Middle Ages. He was also a specialist in the history of Byzantine art. His last and most important work is his three-volume survey of Byzantine civilization in its various aspects under the title *Le Monde byzantin* (1947–50). BIBLIOGRAPHY: J. A. Brundage, NCE 2:782; P. Lemerle, *Revue historique* 208 (1952) 380–382.

[M. R. P. McGUIRE]

BREMER BEITRÄGER, disciples of J. C. Gottsched (1700–60); founders of the journal *Neue Beiträge zum Vergnügen des Verstandes und Witzes* (Bremen 1744–48). Unlike Gottsched, they published only literature, not polemical or critical articles. Most talented of the group were Johann Elias Schlegel (1719–49), Gottlieb Wilhelm Rabener (1714–71), and Christian Fürchtegott Gellert (1715–69). BIBLIOGRAPHY: J. G. Robertson, *History of German Literature* (4th ed., 1962) 215–219.

[M. F. McCARTHY]

BREMOND, HENRI (1865–1933), French spiritual writer. Born at Aix-en-Provence, France, B. studied there and in England where he was influenced by Card. Newman. Ordained a Jesuit in 1892, he returned to France (1899) and taught philosophy and the classics. When he met Abbé Ernest Dimnet while writing for *Études religieuses* he began to publish a great deal of literary criticism. His most significant work is a six-volume work, *L'Histoire littéraire du sentiment religieux en France,* which was translated into many languages. His life of Ste. Jeanne de Chantal was placed on the Index. In 1904 he left the Jesuits and lived as a secular priest in many places in France. Also among his works: *Newman: Essai de bibliographie psychologique* (1904); *Prière et poésie* (1926). BIBLIOGRAPHY: P. Debongnie and J. DeBrandt, DHGE 10:518–529; G. Jacquemet, *Catholicisme* 2:239–242; ODCC 194; J. DeGuibert, DSAM 1:1928–38.

[C. CARROLL]

BRENDAN, ST. (*c.*486–578), abbot, navigator, and patron of the diocese of Kerry. Born at Tralee, Co. Kerry, he was tutored by St. Ita, Bp. Erc of St. Finian's Clonard, and St. Jarlath of Tuam. B. founded several monasteries in Ireland and Scotland including Clonfert, Co. Galway. St. Adamnan's *Life of Columba* indicates he sailed to Iona, and other sources suggest that he visited Wales and Brittany. His notable reputation as a traveler and discoverer of America is based on the fictitious 10th-cent. voyage romance *Navigatio Sancti Brendani Abbatis* (The Voyage of St. Brendan the Abbot). This had considerable influence on medieval geography, and the mythical islands of B. were included in atlases up to the 18th cent. His cult spread throughout Europe and resulted in many places in the British Isles and on the Continent being named after him. BIBLIOGRAPHY: Butler 2:328–329; F. O'Briain, DHGE 10:533–534; C. McGrath, BiblSanct 2:404–409.

[R. T. MEYER]

BRENNAN, FRANCIS (1894–1968), cardinal. After ordination at Rome in 1920, B. taught moral theology and canon law. The "quiet" cardinal was little known in the U.S., but no other American rose higher than he in the Roman Curia. His career was a series of "firsts": he was the first American named to the Sacred Roman Rota; the first American dean or chief judge of the tribunal; the first American to become head of a curial department, the Congregation of the Sacraments.

[A. H. CRANE]

BRENNAN, PATRICK THOMAS (1901–1950?) Columban missioner, prefect apostolic. B. was ordained for the Chicago Archdiocese (1928), and did parish work before joining St. Columban's Foreign Mission Society (1936). He was then assigned to Kwangju, Korea, was interned by the Japanese after Pearl Harbor, but was repatriated in 1942. He then served 3 years in Europe as an army chaplain, and was awarded a medal for heroism in the Battle of the Bulge. In 1948 B. returned to Kwangju as prefect apostolic. When the North Koreans captured the city of Mokpo (1950), he and two other Columban priests were arrested and imprisoned. Nothing has been heard from them since, but it seems certain that they were massacred with other prisoners in Taejon.

[H. JACK]

BRENT, CHARLES HENRY (1862–1929), Protestant Episcopal bishop, leader in the *ecumenical movement. Born in Newcastle, Ont., and graduated (1884) from Trinity College in Toronto, he was ordained in 1886 and served in parishes in Buffalo, N.Y., and Boston, Massachusetts. He was bp. of the Philippines (1901–18) and served on many local and international commissions to end the opium traffic. He was elected bp. of western New York in 1918. As a missionary bp. he attended the *Edinburgh Conference of 1910. Impressed with its promise for Christian unity, he influenced the *General Convention of the Protestant Episcopal Church to set in motion the program that led to the *Lausanne Conference (1927). This first world conference of *Faith and Order met under his presidency. It was B.'s hope that the Churches could find areas of basic doctrinal unity, while maintaining the variety of their own proper traditions. BIBLIOGRAPHY: A. C. Zabriskie, *Bishop Brent, Crusader for Christian Unity* (1948); F. W. Kates, *Charles Henry Brent* (1948).

[M. A. GARDNER]

BRENTANO, CLEMENS MARIA (1778–1842), poet and novelist; member of the younger (Heidelberg) group of German romanticists. His best known works include *Des Knaben Wunderhorn* (3 v., 1806–08), a collection of German folksongs which he edited with Achim von Arnim (1781–1831); *Die Geschichte vom braven Kasperl und dem schönen Annerl* (1816; published 1838); and the unfinished *Romanzen vom Rosenkranz* (1852). From 1819 to 1824, he recorded the revelations of the stigmatized nun, Anne Catherine *Emmerich. His later works are almost entirely of a religious nature. BIBLIOGRAPHY: W. Kosch, *Deutsches Literatur-Lexikon* (1963) 50–52.

[M. F. McCARTHY]

BRENTANO, FRANZ (1838–1917), Austrian philosopher. B. was born at Marienberg to RC parents. He was ordained a priest in 1864 and soon began lecturing at Würzburg, becoming a full professor there in 1872. Because of his views on the Trinity and the then recently proclaimed doctrine of papal infallibility, he left the Church in 1873. He was a professor at Vienna (1874–80), but gave up his post when he married. He remained in Vienna as an unsalaried lecturer until 1895 when approaching blindness forced his retirement. He traveled in Italy and Switzerland until his death in Zurich. A critic of idealism, B. was influential in the development of *phenomenology. He sought to establish psychology as an independent science on an empirical basis. His most important work was *Psychologie vom empirischen Standpunkt* (1874). BIBLIOGRAPHY: H. Spiegelberg, *Phenomenological Movement* (2 v., 1960).

[T. EARLY]

BRENZ, JOHANN (1499–1570), Lutheran reformer. After seeing Luther at Heidelberg, B. became his follower. In the Sacramentarian controversy with the Swiss Reformed Churches, he held to the doctrine of the Real Presence of Christ. His *Syngramma suevicum* is considered one of the best statements of the Lutheran doctrine. During the Schmalkaldic War B. fled to Switzerland. He established schools, orphanages, homes for the poor and proseminaries in Württemberg. B. helped reform Tübingen Univ. and developed a church order in 1559 which was used as a model in other parts of the empire. The "Swabian Confession" which he composed for the Council of Trent was rejected. BIBLIOGRAPHY: J. Hartmann and K. Jäger, *Johann Brenz* (2 v., 1840–42); W. Köhler, *Bibliographia Brentiana* (1904, repr. 1963); H. Fausel, RGG 1:1400–01.

[L. MITCHELL]

BRÈS, GUY DE (Guido de Bray; 1522–67), Calvinist preacher in the Low Countries. A Belgian artisan born at Mons, B. first embraced Lutheranism c. 1548. He became an itinerant student and preacher and, after a stay at Geneva and Lausanne, changed over to Calvinism. He had a prominent role in the establishment of the *Reformed Church in the Low Countries, as pastor and preacher at Sedan, Antwerp, and Valenciennes. The last was then under Spanish rule, and B. was accused of conspiracy and hanged. He was the author of the *Belgic Confession (1561), and of two polemical works, one against Catholics and the other against Anabaptists. BIBLIOGRAPHY: W. F. Dankbaar, RGG 1:1401–02; J. Dedieu, DHGE 10:545–546; Schaff Creeds 1:504.

[T. C. O'BRIEN]

BRESDIN, RODOLPHE (1822–85), French printmaker whose 12 etchings in *La Revue fantaisiste* (c. 1850) and later fantastic and grotesquely Gothic designs (*The Good Samaritan*, 1861) influenced *Redon. BIBLIOGRAPHY: N.Y. Museum of Modern Art, *Odilon Redon, Gustave Moreau, Rodolphe Bresdin* (1961).

[M. J. DALY]

BREST, UNION OF, the reunion in 1596 of a segment of the Ruthenian Orthodox Church with the Roman Catholic Church. Eastern and Western Christians had settled their differences at the Council of *Florence in 1439, but the union failed to last because of a lack of psychological and spiritual preparation and also because reconciliation for many was based on political considerations. A more permanent settlement was actually achieved at Brest-Litovsk, Lithuania, in June 1595. The Florentine solutions served as the pattern for doctrinal matters. The basic issues included recognition of the pope, the *Filioque* and purgatory controversies, and the right of Eastern clergy to marry. Upon reaching agreement, Michael Ragoza, Metropolitan of Kiev, and the bps. of Kholm, Lutsk, Pinsk, Polotsk, and Vladimir petitioned Rome for reunion. On Dec. 23 the union was solemnly proclaimed at the Vatican. At the Pope's request a synod was held in Brest in Oct. 1596 for a more popular ratification of the reunion. From these conferences the designation Uniates or Catholics of the Eastern Rite came into being. Hopes that the spirit of union would spread into the heart of Russia and the Balkans never materialized. Even during the ceremony of union in Oct. an anti-synod was in process to thwart the drive for Orthodox-Catholic unity, largely under the leadership of Orthodox Prince Ostrogski. As at Florence, the masses and lower clergy were not won over. BIBLIOGRAPHY: O. Halecki *From Florence to Brest, 1439-1596* (1958); J. Ostrowsky, DHGE 10:615–618.

[D. DIRSCHERL]

BRETHREN CHURCHES, those bodies springing from the German Baptist Brethren movement originating in the Rhenish Palatinate of Germany in 1708. The founding group, separatists from the state Churches (principally *Reformed), were Pietists and Anabaptists. Persecution drove them from their homes to the lower Rhine and Low-lands, and thence to Pennsylvania. The migration was complete by 1735. They referred to themselves as Baptist Brethren but in Germany were dubbed Dompelaars, and in America Tunkers, Dunkers, and Dunkards. They adopted the legal name Fraternity of German Baptists in 1836. Distinguishing features in doctrine and practice are: baptism by *trine immersion; a threefold holy communion of *footwashing, Lord's Supper, and Eucharist (love feast); anointing the sick with oil; *nonconformity to the world; *nonresistance; and refusal to swear an oath. This last conflicted with the Pennsylvania oath of allegiance during the Revolutionary War and scattered many of them westward to the wilderness; they became the backbone of many new settlements. A schism arose among the Baptist Brethren in Pa. as early as 1728, led by Johann Conrad *Beissel, advocating extreme mysticism, celibacy, and sabbatarianism. The schismatic group divided the Church, and set up the *Ephrata Community. The Baptist Brethren grew in numbers rapidly after the Revolution. Controversy as to methods of witness and *church order (1850–80) divided the membership into three discordant elements—ultra-conservative, progressive, and middle-ground conservative. The matters in dispute included evangelistic meetings, Sunday schools, prayer-meetings, paid ministry, high schools, personal dress, and ecclesiastical authority. In 1881, an estimated 4,500 ultra-conservatives seceded and organized as Old German Baptist Brethren because the Church would not disown the progressive element. In 1882, reacting, the main body expelled the progressive leader, Henry R. Holsinger, and his sympathizers; these progressives—4,000–6,000 strong—formed the Brethren Church. No dissent concerned theology, rites, or biblical doctrine; all elements in the new relationships held to the basic doctrine. All three Brethren groups continued: the Old Order Brethren, ultra-conservative; the Fraternity of German Baptists (name changed to The Church of the Brethren in 1908), becoming

more progressive; and the Brethren Church, theologically conservative. Theological disagreement in the Brethren Church during the 1930s about *Arminianism, and a clash of leadership, divided the Church into the Ashland, Ohio, group and the National Fellowship of Brethren Churches, or Grace group. BIBLIOGRAPHY: F. Mallot, *Studies in Brethren History* (1954).

[A. T. RONK]

BRETHREN IN CHRIST, a denomination, formerly known as River Brethren, that developed as a distinct Church in Lancaster Co., Pa., about 1778, among German-speaking settlers of Anabaptist and Pietist background. They were originally known as River Brethren (or Brotherhood by the River) because they were groups of fervent Christians living in communities near the Susquehanna River. Jacob Engle (1753–1832) was recognized as the first overseer of the Brethren in their organization into districts in the 1780s; he visited congregations in Ontario, Canada, in 1789. The Brethren refused to take oaths or bear arms and were strict pacifists. They adopted a distinctive garb and frowned on anything that would detract from a religious simplicity. Until late in 19th cent., Brethren worshiped in barns and private homes. Doctrines include fundamental articles of Christian belief, with emphasis on justification from past sins and sanctification as purifying the heart. They baptize by immersion and combine an agape meal with the service of the Lord's Supper. The Brethren divided in 1843 and again in 1855 over the issue of building churches and otherwise departing from traditional ways. These divisions led to the formation of the Old Order, or Yorker, Brethren and the United Zion Church. Brethren congregations became numerous in south-central Pa. and were transplanted to the Midwest U.S. by settlers from that section. In 1968 there were 159 congregations of the Brethren in Christ, with a combined membership of about 8,600, chiefly in Pa. but also in Ohio, Ind., Ill., Iowa, and Kansas. The Brethren were not legally incorporated as a Church until 1904, but from the first they have been organized into districts, which usually correspond to civil counties, under an elected overseer. Local congregations retain much autonomy under their own elders. The Brethren in Christ support foreign missions in Africa and Asia. The Foreign Mission Board and publishing activities have been centralized at Harrisburg, Pennsylvania. BIBLIOGRAPHY: A. W. Climenhaga, *History of the Brethren in Christ Church* (1942).

[R. K. MacMASTER]

BRETHREN OF CHRIST, see CHRISTADELPHIANS.

BRETHREN OF THE COMMON LIFE, an association of men intent upon a more perfect interior life, which was organized among the disciples of Gerard Groote (1340–84) at Deventer in the Netherlands. Its members, clerical and lay, took no vows but lived in common; instead of seeking alms, they supported themselves largely by their work as copyists. From Deventer, houses of the Brethren spread to other cities in the Netherlands and in Germany, and everywhere they exerted an important influence by their promotion of the *Devotio Moderna—the new approach to spirituality that had its beginning in the teaching of Groote—of which the Deventer house was a leading center. In some places they established schools, a few of which flourished remarkably and contributed much to the improvement of education in the Low Countries and, through eminent pupils, to the rise of the *New Learning. The Brethren encountered opposition, some of it resulting from the attacks leveled by Groote and his disciples against ecclesiastical abuses, and some from the mendicant orders, which looked with disfavor upon the ''uncanonical'' type of organization the Brethren had adopted. The opposition impeded the growth of the society, and in many cases the Brethren or those imbued with their spirit sought surer canonical status by becoming canons regular. The religious upheaval of the 16th cent., the rise of new teaching orders, the establishment of diocesan seminaries, and the growth and development of the universities led to the extinction of the Brethren by the end of the 17th century. BIBLIOGRAPHY: W. J. Alberts, NCE 2:788–790; A. Hyma, *Brethren of Common Life* (1950); T. P. Van Zijl, *Gerard Groote, Ascetic and Reformer, 1340–1384* (1963).

[P. K. MEAGHER]

BRETHREN OF THE CROSS, name designating several religious communities founded during the Crusades. The chief order was the *Ordo sanctae Crucis*, the Canons Regular of St. Augustine or the Crosier Fathers, established by Theodore of Celles (1166–1236) in 1211 in Liège. Peter of Walcourt, second superior general, adopted much of the Dominican constitutions and the Crosiers spread rapidly throughout Europe. Despite much suffering during the Reformation and the French Revolution, the Crosiers experienced a 19th-cent. revival and today have provinces in Indonesia, the Congo, and New Guinea. Other orders known by a similar name were: the Italian Cruciata (1169), Portuguese Canons Regular of the Holy Cross of Coimbra (1131); the Bohemian Military Order of the Cross with a Red Star (1233), and the Order of the Holy Cross with the Red Heart (1250). Both the Italian and Portuguese communities have been suppressed. BIBLIOGRAPHY: A. van de Pasch, LTK 6:619–621; M. Vinken, DSAM 2.2:2561–76.

[M. H. BEIRNE]

BRETHREN OF THE LAW OF CHRIST (Fratres Legis Christi), one of the names for the 15th-cent. *Bohemian Brethren or *Unitas Fratrum. The name connotes their emphasis on practical Christian life (see Gal 6.2).

[T. C. O'BRIEN]

BRETON, ANDRÉ (1896–1966), poet, novelist, and esp. theorist of surrealism and its artistic progeny. After medical and psychiatric studies, B. began to reassess Valéry, Apollinaire, Jarry, Rimbaud and others; his *Manifesto of Sur-*realism* (1924) proclaimed an art of automatic, associative texture, influenced by Freudianism. The surrealism of Breton, Dali, Eluard and Magritte differs sharply from iconoclastic Dadaism. Though a significant novelist (*Nadja*, 1928) and poet (*Magnetic Fields*, 1924), B. was influential primarily as spokesman, and after 1940 almost exclusively so. BIBLIOGRAPHY: A. Balakian, *André Breton: Magus of Surrealism* (1971).

[J. P. WILLIMAN]

BRETON, JUAN (1560–1627), Spanish *Minim, theologian. B.'s work *Mística teología y doctrina de la perfección evangélica* (1614) makes use, in part, of the MSS of St. John of the Cross. In its original sections the treatise describes the ascent through contemplation to union. The work, widely diffused, was tr. into French by Claude Burens (1626). *Molinos made use of it to his own purposes. BIBLIOGRAPHY: J. Duhr, DSAM 1:1938–40.

[T. C. O'BRIEN]

BRETON, VALENTIN MARIE (baptismal name, Henri; 1877–1957), French Franciscan spiritual writer, preacher, spiritual director, who worked in both France and Canada. Some of his works on Franciscan spirituality were translated into English, *Community of Saints* (tr. R. E. Scantlebury, 1934); *Franciscan Spirituality* (tr. F. Frey, 1957); *Lady Poverty* (tr. P. J. Oligny, 1963).

[T. C. O'BRIEN]

BRETSCHNEIDER, KARL GOTTLIEB (1776–1848), German Protestant theologian. B. was general superintendent of Gotha from 1816. The foremost proponent of rational supernaturalism, he was a critic of F. *Schleiermacher and P. K. *Marheineke. He founded (1834) the *Corpus Reformatorum,* a series of reprints of the writings of the 16th-cent. reformers, and he himself edited the works of P. Melanchthon as the first 15 volumes of the series. BIBLIOGRAPHY: H. R. Guggisberg, RGG 1:1409.

[M. J. SUELZER]

BREU, JORG THE ELDER (1475–1537), German painter influenced by Hans Burgkmair the Elder. B.'s scenes from the *Life of St. Bernard* (c.1500, Monastery of Zwettl) and the *Passion Altarpiece* (1502, Monastery of Melk) show a talent for landscape and dramatic style. After travels to Italy (c.1514–15) B. borrowed from Fra Filippo Lippi and Dürer (*St. Ursula Altarpiece*, Dresden).

[M. J. DALY]

BREUER, MARCEL LAJOS (1902–), Hungarian–American master architect of the 20th century. Educated at the *Bauhaus (1920), B. traveled in Europe and N Africa, came to the U.S. (1937), joining W. *Gropius as architectural partner and instructor at Harvard Univ., where B.'s design program influenced the quality of contemporary form in every architectural school in the U.S. In New York

(1946) B. began his international practice. Innovator in modular units, B. designed the first metal-tube furnishings (1925), a noted house at Wiesbaden (1932), and apartments in the Dolderthal, near Zurich, in new forms of enduring materials. With Pier Luigi *Nervi and B. Zehrfuss he planned UNESCO headquarters, Paris (1958), the Benedictine *St. John's Abbey and Univ. at Collegeville, Minn. (1953–63), showing early the new *brutalism in uncompromising truth to materials and pure structure, and the Whitney Museum of American Art, N.Y. (1966). B. won the gold medal of the American Institute of Architects in 1968. BIBLIOGRAPHY: G. C. Argan, *Marcel Breuer, disegno industriale e architettura* (1957); Metropolitan Museum of Art, *Marcel Breuer* (pa. 1973).

[M. J. DALY]

BREUIL, HENRI ÉDOUARD PROSPER (1877–1961), French scholar of prehistory and international expert on paleolithic art. B. published his first paper in 1899 and after ordination (1900) gave full time to prehistoric scholarship. He established a cultural sequence of dating as opposed to the earlier epoch system, and made spectacular contributions to the art of Stone Age man, copying with his fine draftsmanship pictures from cave walls. His studies of French and Spanish examples at Combarelles (*Font-de-Gaume) and *Altamira culminating in the great caves at *Lascaux were recorded in many splendidly colored monographs made possible through Prince Albert of Monaco. B. visited sites in England, Portugal, Italy (excavating Neanderthal skulls at Saccopastore), China, and N and S Africa. Professor in Switzerland, the Sorbonne, Collège and Institut de France, and honored member of many learned societies, B. published 27 monumental books and 878 articles. BIBLIOGRAPHY: A. H. Brodrick, *Fathers of Prehistory: the Abbé Breuil* (1963, repr. 1973).

[M. J. DALY]

BREVIARIUM ALARICI, the name given in the 16th cent. to an ancient collection of laws, the *Lex Romana Visigothorum*. It was compiled by a commission of jurisconsults appointed by Alaric II, king of the Visigoths, ''to correct what could seem unjust or ambiguous in ancient laws.'' The work was completed in 506, submitted to a council of bishops and nobles at Aire in Gascony and approved by them. Alaric caused a certified copy to be forwarded to each *comes* with the injunction that the collection was to be the only law used for Roman subjects of the Gothic kingdom. Mildest of the barbaric laws, its text and the accompanying commentary became widely diffused and influenced Visigothic law. BIBLIOGRAPHY: M. Conrat, *Breviarium Alarici* (1903).

[M. J. SUELZER]

BREVIARY, ROMAN, liturgical book of the Roman rite that contains the complete text of the Divine Office. It is the result of the compilation of many liturgical books used in the divine services, e.g., the *collectarium, hymnarium, psal-*terium, and *responsoriale*. The earliest MS of the Breviary is dated 1099; this is a large choir book. The portable Breviary, the type most commonly used in modern times, appeared in the 13th century. The modern Roman Breviary originated in the curia of Innocent III, was adopted and revised by the Franciscans in 1240, and the friars made it popular throughout Europe. Subsequent accretions called for reform, and the revision demanded by the Council of Trent was published by Pius V in 1568. There have been later revisions, esp. in the 20th century. Vatican Council II declared its desire to carry through the restoration already begun by the Apostolic See and laid down general norms that were to be followed (see Vat II SacLit 83–101). Such a revision was set forth by Paul VI in the apostolic constitution *Canticum laudis*, dated Nov. 1, 1970. Now referred to as the *Liturgy of the Hours,* its four complete volumes in authorized English translation have been published since May 1975. BIBLIOGRAPHY: P. Salmon, *Breviary through the Centuries* (tr. D. Mary, 1962); *Divine Office: The Renewed Liturgy of the Hours according to the Roman Rite* (eds. Collins, Dwyer and Talbot, 3 v., 1974).

[N. KOLLAR]

BREVIARY, SHORT, an abbr. form of the Divine Office in the vernacular. A number of different short breviaries have been published in English—e.g. ed. W. G. Heidt, *A Short Breviary* (3d ed. 1962); T. Stallaert, *The Little Breviary* (tr. Benedictine nuns of Stanbrook Abbey, 1957). The use of breviaries of this kind, when it is in accord with the constitutions of a religious institute, was approved by Vatican Council II (Vat II SacLit 98). Among the common features of such breviaries are an emphasis on the temporal cycle of the liturgical year, an inclusion of only a few of the major feasts, and provision for the recitation of fewer psalms in the course of a week, but the general structure of the Divine Office is retained.

[N. KOLLAR]

BREVIARY OF BELLEVILLE (*c.* 1325), illuminated MS by Master Jean Pucelle (active *c.* 1320–70) in which the Paris school was revitalized by expansion of the pictorial area within the text, the entire page becoming the province of the illuminator. Tendrils, ivy and floral designs, myriads of insects, animals, and grotesques fill the margins. Rich colors, graceful postures, and flowing drapery reflect the Sienese influence of the International style. The gorgeously illustrated *Très riches heures du duc de Berry* (1416) is an extension and perfection of the Belleville Breviary. Pucelle's witty signature (the ''Bagpiper,'' translating his name) graces his margins. The Books of Hours were most precious treasures of the N aristocracy in the 14th and 15th centuries.

[M. J. DALY]

BREVNOV, ABBEY OF, see BRAUNAU, ABBEY OF.

BRIAN BORU (941–1014), king of Ireland from 1002. Son of Kennedy or *mac Cennédigh* and leader of the Dál Cais, B. became king of Munster (978) and high king of Ireland (*c*.1002). With his exceptional abilities as soldier, statesman, and promoter of learning and the arts, he consolidated his universal control of Ireland with the title *Imperator Scotorum* at Armagh in 1005. He was killed by the fleeing Brooir during the Irish victory at Clontarf. BIBLIOGRAPHY: J. Ryan, "Battle of Clontarf," *Journal of the Royal Society of Antiquaries of Ireland* 68 (1938) 1–50.

[M. H. BEIRNE]

BRIAND, ARISTIDE (1862–1932), French statesman. An early leader and organizer of the Parti Socialiste Français, B., with Jean Jaurès founded the socialist newspaper *L'Humanité*. Elected to the Chamber of Deputies in 1902, he soon devoted his energies to working out the separation of Church and State, serving as *rapporteur* in drafting the necessary legislation. As minister of public instruction in the Sarrien and Clemenceau ministries, he used a diplomatic and moderate approach in the application of the separation laws. In 1906 Briand became minister of religion. After World War I he successfully promoted the exemption of Alsace-Lorraine from the application of these laws. He was responsible for the resumption of French diplomatic relations with the Holy See (1921). In the years 1909–29 he was premier of France 11 times and foreign minister 1925–32. Noted for world peace efforts, he was awarded the Nobel Peace Prize in 1926. He negotiated the Kellogg-Briand anti-war pact of 1928 and in 1929 proposed a European Federation. BIBLIOGRAPHY: A. Leger, *Briand* (1943); G. Suarez, *Briand, sa vie, son oeuvre* (6 v., 1938–52).

[D. R. PENN]

BRIAND, JEAN OLIVIER (1715–94), RC churchman in Canada. A native of France, B. was made vicar-general of Quebec in 1741. He was permitted to remain as "superintendent" of the Catholic Church in Canada after the British victory of 1758 and was consecrated bp. of Quebec in 1766. His conciliatory attitude gained concessions for the Canadian Church and his loyalty to the British at the time of the American invasion (1775–76) helped to secure the French-Canadian allegiance to the British crown. He resigned his see in 1784. BIBLIOGRAPHY: H. Têtu, *Les Évêques de Québec* (1889).

[R. K. MacMASTER]

BRIANT, ALEXANDER, ST. (1553–81), English Jesuit martyr. He studied at Oxford and was there reconciled to Catholicism (1574). B. then continued his studies at Douai, where he was ordained (1578). After returning to his native Somerset (1579), he labored to reconcile people to the Church. He was arrested, tortured in an effort to make him reveal the whereabouts of R. *Persons, and executed at Tyburn with Edmund *Campion. He was beatified in 1886 and canonized in 1970. BIBLIOGRAPHY: C. Testore, BiblSanct 3:413–414; Butler 4:469–470.

[V. SAMPSON]

BRIBERY, the giving of something of value to a person in a position of trust to influence him to make a decision in the briber's favor. It is always morally wrong if the purpose is to obtain a decision that is itself immoral, a violation of a legitimate trust. It may be tolerated under the conditions of material cooperation if it is the only practicable way to obtain a decision that should be made. Even in the latter case, efforts should be made to change the system which permits such actions. The person in the position of trust is guilty of graft if he accepts such payments; of extortion if he demands them. Bribery may be civil, economic, or ecclesiastical according to the kind of position of trust involved. BIBLIOGRAPHY: T. Cranny, NCE 2:796.

[J. P. FARRAHER]

BRICE OF TOURS, ST. (*c*.370–444), monk, and bishop. B.'s biography by Gregory of Tours is intertwined with legend. B. was a disciple of St. Martin of Tours whom he succeeded as bishop of that city. Tried for alleged misconduct by several local synods, B. was exonerated by Pope Zosimus in 417. He was later removed from office on a morals charge but pleaded his case successfully and was restored to his see in 437. His cult became widespread in the West during the Middle Ages. BIBLIOGRAPHY: G. Bataille, BiblSanct 3:542–545; S. Hanssens, DHGE 10:670–671; Butler 4:328–329.

[H. DRESSLER]

BRICEÑO, ALONSO (1587–1668), Chilean philosopher and prominent theologian. Receiving the Franciscan habit in 1605, B. held various positions of authority in his community and eventually became vicar-general. During the period following 1636, he published two large volumes on the doctrines of Duns Scotus which have been highly praised for their scholarship. In 1639 he took part in the general chapter in Rome and was active in the beatification proceedings of Francis Solano. Upon his return to the New World, B. served as bp. of Nicaragua (1646) and later of Caracas (1649) until his death at Trujillo.

[D. M. HUGHES]

BRIÇONNET, family name of a group of French ecclesiastics, three of whom are esp. noteworthy. (1) Robert (d. 1497), abp. of Reims (1493), chancellor of France under Charles VIII from 1495. (2) Guillaume (d. 1514), brother of Robert, financial minister under Louis XI and Charles VIII, then cardinal of Saint-Malo. His ecclesiastical career began after the death of his wife; he was successful in obtaining a number of lucrative benefices, among them Saint-Germain-des-Prés at Paris. By political intrigue he had himself created cardinal (1494–95). For participation in the conciliarist Council of Pisa-Milan, as part of his support of King Louis XII against the Holy See, he was stripped of his prerogatives by Pope Julius II, but was reinstated by Leo X. (3) Guillaume (1472–1534), son of the preceding; reform-minded bishop. Although he participated in the schemes of his father, he is chiefly renowned for his later efforts to revitalize church life. As abbot of Saint-Germain-des-Prés (1507) he restored a religious and intellectual spirit. Bishop of Meaux from 1516, he was an exemplary pastor of his see. The "Cenacle of Meaux" was a group of humanists, spiritually minded men, whom he attracted to his diocese. Among them were G. *Farel and J. *Lefèvre d'Étaples. A shadow was cast on the genuine evangelical spirit and accomplishments of this circle by accusations of Protestant sympathies, and it was disbanded in 1535. But the bishop's own motives and the measures he took to defend Catholic teaching are unquestionable. BIBLIOGRAPHY: A. Duval, *Catholicisme* 2:263–265.

[T. C. O'BRIEN]

BRICOUT, JOSEPH (1867–1930), French parish priest, author of many popular works of devotion and instruction. He was also editor of the *Revue de clergé français* and of the *Dictionnaire pratique des connaissances religieuses* (3 v., 1924–28).

[T. C. O'BRIEN]

BRICTINIANS, Congregation of hermits (1200–15), so named from their first monastery, S. Blasius de Brettino in Fano, Italy. Subsisting on alms alone, they lived austere lives of poverty and mortification with the sanction of Gregory IX. Under the Fourth Lateran Council (1228) they adopted the Rule of St. Augustine. The Great Federation (of hermits) in 1256 in the reign of Innocent IV found the Brictinians and other existing hermit groups joined in one Order of Hermit Friars of St. Augustine. This formation lasted but 4 years when a bull of Pope Alexander IV (1260) assured the Augustinian hermits the right of independent existence. BIBLIOGRAPHY: O. Zockler, EncRelKnow 2:265.

[A. A. O'NEILL]

BRIDEGROOM, THE, a term used in the NT to indicate Christ (Mt 9.15; 25.1, 5–10; Mk 2.19–20; Lk 5.34–35; Jn 3.29) who stands related to his Church as bridegroom to bride, a figure comparable to the OT concept of Yahweh, whose bride was Israel.

[P. K. MEAGHER]

BRIDEL, PHILIPPE SIRICE (1757–1845), Swiss Protestant pastor and writer, known as Dean Bridel, who inspired the French-Swiss literary awakening of the 18th and 19th centuries. He revived interest in Swiss history, literature, topography, mores, and folklore, thereby instilling in French-speaking Switzerland a sense of national consciousness that led to emancipation from foreign cultural dominance and to closer union with other parts of the Swiss Federation. In theology he was a latitudinarian equally unsympathetic to the Pietist revival and the emerging liberal Protestantism. In his attitude toward Catholicism he moved from a position of respectful tolerance to a sympathetic appreciation of its role in Swiss history. BIBLIOGRAPHY: G.

de Reynold, *Le Doyen Bridel et les origines de la littérature suisse romande* (1909).

[G. E. GINGRAS]

BRIDGEBUILDERS, BROTHERHOOD OF, see BROTHERHOOD OF BRIDGEBUILDERS.

BRIDGET OF SWEDEN, ST. (*c.* 1303–73), patron saint of Sweden, mystic, foundress of the Bridgettines (Order of the Most Holy Savior). Born of a wealthy aristocratic family, B. was married at the age of 14 to Ulf Gudmarrson; she bore eight children, one of whom was St. Catherine of Sweden. In 1335 she became principal lady-in-waiting at the court of King Magnus II and his bride, Queen Blanche. In this position she strove to develop in the royal couple a more serious recognition of their responsibilities, but, though she was well-respected, her words produced little effect. In 1341 or 1342 she went with her husband on pilgrimage to Compostela, and they were determined on their return to enter the religious life. Ulf died as a *familiaris* in the Cistercian monastery of Alvastra in 1344. B. remained for some time in Alvastra, quartered in a small house adjoining the monastery. There she developed her plan to found a religious order to counterbalance the worldliness of her country, to expiate its sins, and to promote the cult of Christ's Passion and the compassion of his Blessed Mother. The King gave her a castle at Vadstena and funds for the construction of the monastery (1346–47). In 1349 B. left Sweden and went to Rome to gain the jubilee indulgence of 1350, to secure papal approval for her order, and to work for the return of the Pope from Avignon. In Italy she was joined by her daughter Catherine, who remained with her for the rest of her life. In Rome she lived a life of prayer and good works, esp. on behalf of the poor and pilgrims. In 1371–73 B. went on a pilgrimage to the Holy Land and died two months after her return to Rome. From childhood B. had visions, and much of her activity was inspired by what was revealed to her in these experiences. Many of her revelations concerned the sufferings of the Savior, but many also involved events of her own time, some of greater, some of lesser, historical importance. She made use of her revelations to admonish, scold, exhort, implore, and threaten others concerning a great variety of matters. The extensive literature that has grown up about B. and her revelations is evidence of the interest that not only Catholics but Protestants as well have taken in the subject. BIBLIOGRAPHY: J. Jörgensen, *St. Bridget of Sweden*, (tr. I. Lund, 2 v., 1954); H. Redpath, *God's Ambassadress: St. Bridget of Sweden* (1947); Butler 4:54–59; F. Vernet, DSAM 1:1943–58, bibliog.; I. Cecchetti, BiblSanct 3:439–530, bibliog.

[P. K. MEAGHER]

BRIDGETT, THOMAS EDWARD (1829–99), priest and author. Converted to Catholicism (1850), successively rector of Limerick, where he founded the Confraternity of the Holy Family (1868), and of Clapham, he is best known for his lives of Blessed John Fisher (1888) and St. Thomas More (1891). BIBLIOGRAPHY: L. C. Sheppard, NCE 2:799–800.

[C. D. ROSS]

BRIDGETTINE OFFICE, an expanded form of the Little Office of the Blessed Virgin, which is proper to the Bridgettine nuns. All of the Psalms are recited in the course of one week, the antiphons are proper to each day, the three lessons at Matins are from the *Sermo Angelicus* of St. Bridget. And at the start of daily Vespers the two sides of the choir ask each other's pardon for offenses.

[N. KOLLAR]

BRIDGETTINES, the Order of the Most Holy Saviour *(Ordo Sanctissimi Salvatoris)* established by St. Bridget of Sweden at Vadstena, Sweden (1346). Their initial formation of joint communities of men and women who occupied different sections of the same monastery but prayed in the same chapel was discontinued in the 16th century. Their remaining houses today are in England, Holland, Germany, and Spain where they are called Bridgettines of the Recollection. BIBLIOGRAPHY: B. Williamson, *Bridgettine Order* (1922); P. Debongnie, DHGE 10:728–731.

[F. H. BRIGHAM]

BRIDGIT, ABBEY OF, Swed. monastery founded *c.* 1365 by St. Bridgit (usu. Bridget) on the estate at Vadstena given her by King Magnus Erikson, the abbey plans called for a monastery and convent under the general superiorship of an abbess assisted by a general confessor, with visitation rights granted the bishop of Linköping in whose diocese the abbey was located. Bridget's daughter, St. Catherine of Sweden, reestablished the community known as the Bridgettine Order in 1374 and became its first abbess. Comprising more than 900 estates, Vadstena became the richest abbey in Scandinavia with one of the largest libraries in the country. Most of this collection is to be found at the Univ. of Uppsala and the royal library at Stockholm. Many literary and artistic works had their inception at Vadstena, and the abbey dedicated to the Blessed Mother became a center of Marian devotion in Sweden esp. under the direction of Magister Petrus Olavi (d. 1378). The Abbey's influence diminished with the spread of Protestantism into this country and in 1595, it was formally dissolved, being preserved only as an historical monument. BIBLIOGRAPHY: H. Cnattingius, *Studies in the Order of St. Bridget of Sweden* (1963); T. Nyberg, *Birgittinische Klostergründungen des mittelalters* (1965).

[L. NEMEC]

BRIDLINGTON, JOHN OF, ST., see JOHN OF BRIDLINGTON, ST.

BRIEF, PAPAL, a term in use from the time of Pope Martin V (1417–31) to designate a papal letter written on parchment in relatively simple style and dealing with a matter of lesser importance. Briefs are signed by the secretary of briefs or by the cardinal secretary of state and sealed with the seal of the fisherman, i.e., the papal ring bearing the image of St. Peter in a boat pulling in a net from the sea.

[J. C. WILLKE]

BRIEUC, ST., (*c.*410–*c.*502). According to a late (11th cent.?) biography of dubious value, B., born of supposedly pagan parents became a convert and disciple of St. Germanus of Auxerre whom he accompanied to Gaul where he was ordained a priest. He returned and worked among his countrymen till forced to flee during an invasion of the Picts and Saxons. Subsequently B. founded a monastery near Tréguier. A town named after the saint grew up around the monastery and *c.*848 became the see city of a diocese. BIBLIOGRAPHY: H. Waquet, DHGE 10:712–713; Butler 2:208–209; G. Bataille, BiblSanct 3:534–536, s.v. Brioco.

[H. DRESSLER]

BRIGGS, CHARLES AUGUSTUS (1841–1913), American biblical scholar. After graduating from the Univ. of Virginia, B. for 2 years attended Union Theological Seminary, New York City, then the Univ. of Berlin (1865–70). There he was trained in the methods of higher criticism in biblical studies. Upon his return to the U.S., he was pastor of a Presbyterian church in Roselle, N.J., until his appointment (1874) as professor of Hebrew at Union. In his lectures and writings he opposed the *Princeton theology, and proposed a study of the Bible that was critical but not rationalistic. His inaugural lecture (1890) as professor of biblical theology, however, in which he warned against a literalist view of the Bible, brought a demand for his dismissal by the *General Assembly of the Presbyterian Church. The seminary refused to accede; a few years later it became non-denominational. B. was tried and acquitted of heresy, but the General Assembly withdrew his credentials as a minister in 1893. He received Episcopalian ordination in 1899. As general editor of the *International Critical Commentary on the Holy Scriptures,* he contributed his major work, *Commentary on the Book of Psalms* (1906). He was also active in seeking RC and Protestant reunion. BIBLIOGRAPHY: L. A. Loetsche, *Broadening Church* (1957); B.'s defense against heresy charges was published by Scribner's in 1892.

[M. A. GARDNER]

BRIGHTMAN, EDGAR SHEFFIELD (1884–1953), Methodist philosopher-theologian. He was professor of philosophy at Boston Univ. (1919–53), where he kept prominent the personalist-idealism of B. P. *Bowne. Much of B.'s interest was in religion, esp. in grounding all religious truth in reason. He stressed the revelation of God through the evidence of divine reasonableness and proposed that experience finds God to be finite, because of limits within the divine nature, from the cosmos, and from human freedom.

His works include *The Problem of God* (1930), *The Finding of God* (1931), *Is God a Person* (1930) BIBLIOGRAPHY: D. W. Soper, *Major Voices in American Theology* (1954) 194–218; *Person and Reality* (ed. P. A. Bertocci, 1958), with bibliog.

[F. E. MASER]

BRIGID OF IRELAND, ST. (*c*.456–*c*.524), virgin and monastic foundress who together with St. Patrick and St. Columbkille is one of the three patron saints of Ireland. Her life has been the subject of innumerable hagiographical legends and her cult has been extensive throughout the British Isles and Europe. More reliable sources suggest that she was born in Fotharta in ancient Leinster. According to Cogitosus, a 7th-cent. monk, she founded a monastery called *Cill Dara* (Kildare, Church of the Oak) where she died and was buried. His description of her monastery as a prosperous *double monastery appears to be a picture of the monastic life of his own time. It is more likely that B. had a small group of virgins and pious women who assisted missionaries in their work with the poor. The abiding Gaelic devotion to her cult is reflected in the songs of the *Book of Lismore:* "It is she that helpeth everyone who is in straits and danger; it is she that abateth the pestilence, she is the prophetess of Christ, she is the Queen of the South, she is the Mary of the Gael." BIBLIOGRAPHY: F. O'Briain, *St. Brigid of Ireland: her Legend, History and Cult* (1938); *id.*, DHGE 10:716–719, C. McGrath, BiblSanct 3:430–437; Butler 1:225–229.

[F. H. BRIGHAM]

BRIGIDINES (Sisters of St. Brigid; CSB), a congregation founded (1807) in Ireland by D. Delaney, bp. of Kildare and Leighlin, for education. It was one of the first of its kind established since the Reformation in Ireland; its constitutions are based on the Augustinian Rule, with particular devotion to St. Brigid of Ireland (Kildare). Papal approval was given by Pius X in 1907. The congregation in the early 1970s numbered 726 and had 53 houses. A group of the sisters came to the U.S. in 1953, where they had (1975) seven houses in the Archdiocese of San Antonio, Texas, and the Diocese of Madison, Wisconsin. Their general motherhouse is at Tullow, County Carlow, Ireland. Their apostolate in grade and high school teaching and in teacher training is exercised in provinces, one for Ireland and Great Britain (for members in Australia and New Zealand); another in the U.S. (1960) at San Antonio.

[M. R. BROWN]

BRIHADEŚVARA TEMPLE (*c*. A.D. 1000), at Thanjavur, S India, a beautiful example of Chola dynasty (846–1173) temple architecture, which is notable for its architectonic order, sensitive detail, and sculpture. Expressing the imperial grandeur of the Cholas, the temple, 160 feet high and replete with many deities in niches at ordered intervals, further evidences the aesthetic achievement of the

10th and 11th cent. by which the *mandapa, through a pyramidal superstructure is brought into harmony with the tall sikhara and its cascade of forms.

[M. J. DALY]

BRINDISI, SAN BIAGIO, a small Byzantine rock-cut chapel attached to a monastery of Greek and Syrian monks, noted for its Byzantine frescoes (*c*. 1200). BIBLIOGRAPHY: J. A. Hamilton, *Byzantine Architecture and Decoration* (1956).

[M. J. DALY]

BRINKLEY, STEPHEN (fl. 1580), printer, translator, who collaborated with the English Jesuits during the reign of Elizabeth I. Educated at Cambridge, B. organized and operated a secret press for Edmund *Campion and Robert *Persons. He was arrested and imprisoned in the Tower in 1581, but was released in 1583. He later worked at the secret press in Rouen. BIBLIOGRAPHY: W. R. Trimble, *Catholic Laity in Elizabethan England* 1558–1603 (1964).

[V. SAMPSON]

BRIOSCO, ANDREA (Riccio; 1470–1532), Italian architect, sculptor, master metalworker in gold and bronze. B. executed for S. Antonio, Padua, two bronze reliefs for the choir screen (1506–07) and a bronze paschal candlestick (1515), considered his masterpiece, combining a wealth of Christian allegorical and narrative reliefs in a classical style tempered by humanism. BIBLIOGRAPHY: F. Cessi, *Andrea Briosco detto il Riccio* (1965).

[M. J. DALY]

BRIOUDE, BASILICA OF ST.-JULIEN, largest of the Auvergnat churches in France (234.8 feet in length) with narthex (11th cent.), apse (12th cent.), vaults (*c*.1254), and a tribune noted for important Romanesque frescoes. The beautiful *chevet* of red sandstone, with mosaic in colored lavas and five radiating chapels, has impressive animal corbels and figural metopes. BIBLIOGRAPHY: A. Gybal, *L Auvergne berceau de l'art roman* (1957).

[M. J. DALY]

BRISACIER, JACQUES CHARLES DE (1642–1736), director of the seminary of the Paris Foreign Missionary Society. He was also chaplain to Queen Marie Thérèse. As superior of the seminary he sent 49 missionaries to the Far East. In the controversy over the Chinese rites he sided with the Dominicans and Franciscans against the Jesuits and the Sorbonne. Through his association with Mme. de Maintenon he became involved in the dispute over quietism. He was esteemed by his contemporaries for his intelligence, piety, and skill in spiritual guidance. BIBLIOGRAPHY: A. Launay, *Mémorial de la Société des missions-étrangères, 1658–1913* (2 v., 1912–16) 2:95–98; H. Sy, DHGE 10:758–759; R. Chalumeau, *Catholicisme* 2:275–276.

[L. MITCHELL]

BRISACIER, JEAN DE (1603–68), French Jesuit who held various administrative positions in the Society and distinguished himself by his attacks upon Jansenism. BIBLIOGRAPHY: P. Delattre, *Catholicisme* 2:76–77.

[M. J. SUELZER]

BRISSON, LOUIS ALEXANDRE (1817–1908), religious founder. While chaplain at the Visitation Convent of Troyes, he founded the Oblate Sisters of St. Francis de Sales in 1866 and the Oblates of St. Francis de Sales *c.* 1871. He directed them and composed devotional literature for them in the spirit of St. Francis de Sales. The cause for his beatification was introduced in 1955. BIBLIOGRAPHY: P. Dufour, DSAM 1:1962–66; K. Burton, *So Much, So Soon: Father Brisson, Founder of the Oblates of St. Francis de Sales* (1953).

[I. M. KASHUBA]

BRISTOW, RICHARD (1538–81), Catholic apologist during the English Reformation. He had a brilliant career at Oxford and with Edmund *Campion debated before Elizabeth I in 1566. Because of his Catholicism he left England, and was the first student to be ordained at the English College at Douai (1573). The associate of William *Allen, he became pro-rector and lecturer in NT studies. He died in England, at Harrow. He published several works in defense of RC teaching. BIBLIOGRAPHY: Gillow BDEC 1:300–303.

[T. C. O'BRIEN]

BRITHWALD OF CANTERBURY, ST. (Berthwald; d. 731), abp. of Canterbury. He was born of noble parents, entered religious life, and became abbot of Reculver in Kent (670). Elected abp., he was consecrated in Gaul to avoid irritating Abp. Wilfrid of York. He was a friend of Aldhelm and presided over several church councils in his long tenure of office (692–731). BIBLIOGRAPHY: P. Burchi, BiblSanct 3:540; Butler, 1:59.

[J. DRUSE]

BRITHWALD OF WILTON, ST. (Berhtwald; d. 1045), abbot and bp. B. was a monk and then abbot of Glastonbury, elected bp. of Ramsbury (or Wiltshire) in 995. Little is known of his life, and he is remembered only for his reputed prophecy of the accession of King Edward the Confessor. BIBLIOGRAPHY: Butler 1:147; S. Mottironi, BiblSanct 3:540.

[J. L. GRASSI]

BRITISH AND FOREIGN BIBLE SOCIETY, largest of all *Bible societies; established in London, 1804, with Anglicans and members of other communions cooperating. Local societies were started throughout the British Isles, and later in the British colonies. The Society has remained strictly interdenominational in organization and policy and has restricted its activities to the printing and distribution of Bibles.

[T. C. O'BRIEN]

BRITISH COUNCIL OF CHURCHES an amalgamation into one organization, 1942–43, of those British agencies that had carried on the work of interdenominational cooperation begun largely by the *Oxford and *Edinburgh Conferences in 1937. The theological basis for the Council is the same as that of the *World Council of Churches, except that it qualifies itself as "a fellowship of churches which accept our Lord Jesus Christ as God and Saviour" in these words: "with the understanding that any body which has hitherto been represented on the Commission [for union] shall continue in membership of the Council, if so willing, even though it does not itself accept this basis." Included, therefore, are 118 members representing the Church of England, of Scotland, of Wales and of Ireland as well as the Salvation Army, the Society of Friends, the Unitarian and Free Churches, five interdenominational organizations, and 20 other agencies. Besides carrying on the work of the amalgamated agencies, the Council has a fourfold purpose: (1) "to facilitate common action by the churches in evangelistic enterprize, in stimulating a sense of social responsibility, and in guiding the activities of the churches for the welfare of youth; (2) to facilitate such other common action as may later be determined; (3) to promote cooperation in study and . . . in the studies promoted by the World Council of Churches; (4) to assist the growth of ecumenical consciousness. . . ." BIBLIOGRAPHY: *Documents of Christian Unity* (ed. G. K. A. Bell, Third Series, 1948) 142–145.

[F. E. MASER]

BRITISH ISRAEL THEORY (Anglo-Israelism), theory that the British people are descended from the Israelites taken into captivity by Sargon after the fall of the northern kingdom in 721 B.C., the so-called ten lost tribes. Proposed as early as 1649, the idea gained some popular interest, particularly in the heyday of British imperialism. The English naval officer R. Brothers (1757–1824) was a strong advocate of this theory, which lacks any scientific support.

[T. EARLY]

BRITISH MORALISTS, a classification that includes a considerable number of British philosophers and religious writers who dealt with ethical theory and practice from the 17th into the 19th century. They are usually associated with reaction against empiricism in philosophy that developed as an outgrowth of natural science, or with certain attitudes having roots in the Renaissance and Protestant Reformation, or with an effort to ameliorate social and economic conditions.

Typical of this broad range of moral theorists were the *Cambridge Platonists of the 17th cent. headed by Benjamin Whichcote (1609–83)—religious thinkers who strove to harmonize the ethics of Christianity with the humanism of the Renaissance, and to reconcile faith with science. At Cambridge, Whichcote's principal disciples were R. *Cudworth, John Smith (1616?–52), and H. *More, and at Oxford, Joseph Glanvill (1636–80). Among them, Cudworth is outstanding for his systematic opposition to the atheistic and materialistic doctrines of Thomas Hobbes (1588–1679), and also notable are Richard Cumberland (1631–1718) and John Norris (1657–1711), neither of whom, however, fully subscribed to the moral ideals embodied in the Christian humanism that characterized the movement. Emphasizing the rational character of morality, the Platonists viewed the love of goodness as based upon its understanding. In this they stood in strong opposition to both Hobbes and the Calvinists who claimed assent to an arbitrary divine will to be the core of morality. Their Puritan background, on the other hand, put them out of sympathy with the Anglicanism represented by W. *Laud, and they held that ritual, dogma, and ecclesiastical government are not fundamental to Christianity. Their tolerance and liberality won them the name "the latitude men," and they were often denounced as atheists or free-thinkers. Nevertheless they feared the growing influence of science and strove to bolster traditional religious attitudes.

From the time of *Roger Bacon and *William of Ockham, an empiricist tendency had been discernible in British thought. In J. *Locke and D. *Hume, whose epistemology reduced all human knowledge to sense knowledge, this tendency received definitive formulation. Like Hobbes, Locke saw man as essentially egoistic and presented an ethical view consistent with his epistemological empiricism. It was an egoistic hedonism that rejected all innate moral truths and admitted only those acquired by human experience. Pleasure and pain were held to be the arbiters of morality, which in fact became identified with the pursuit of self-interest. The idea of universal and necessary moral truths was kept alive in the 18th cent. by men such as Samuel Clarke (1675–1729), William Wollaston (1659–1724), and Richard Price (1723–91). This view also received support in the Scottish philosophy of Thomas Reid (1710–96), James Beattie (1735–1803), and Dugald Steward (1753–1828). Others such as Richard Cumberland in his *De Iegibus naturae* (1672) repudiated the selfish portrayal of man in favor of a being affected by sympathy and benevolence and capable therefore of promoting the general welfare as well as his own individual interests. Many came to emphasize feelings rather than reason as the source of ethical knowledge, distinguishing between egocentric and social affections dictated by a moral sense, as did F. Hutcheson in his *System of Moral Philosophy* (1755). D. Hume in his *Inquiry Concerning the Principles of Morals* (1751) and Adam *Smith in *Theory of the Moral Sentiment* (1759) reinforced the emotive or appetitive role in moral behavior to the exclusion of reason.

In the 19th cent. J. *Bentham and J. S. *Mill advanced the doctrine of *utilitarianism, which evaluated human action according to its utility in promoting the general happiness

within the frame of which each man would realize his own. BIBLIOGRAPHY: E. Cassirer, *Platonic Renaissance in England* (tr. J. P. Pettegrove, 1954, repr. 1970); F. J. Powicke, *Cambridge Platonists* (1926, repr. 1971); W. R. Sorley, *History of English Philosophy* (1965); L. Stephen, *History of English Thought in the Eighteenth Century* (rev. ed., 1963).

[J. T. HICKEY]

BRIXI, FRANTIŠEK XAVER (1732–71), prolific Bohemian composer of church music who held posts at various churches in Prague. His works include 105 Masses and over 300 motets and other sacred compositions. BIBLIOGRAPHY: G. Černušák, Grove DMM 1:957.

[A. DOHERTY]

BRNO (BRÜNN), capital of S Moravian region, Czechoslovakia, which boasts Gothic, Renaissance, and Baroque monuments: cathedral SS. Peter and Paul (15th cent.), church of St. Jacob (1314–1480), the Königinkloster (14th cent.), and the Parnassus Fountain by Master Johann Bernhard *Fischer von Erlach. BIBLIOGRAPHY: B. Bretholz, *Brünn, Geschichte und Kultur* (1938).

[M. J. DALY]

BROAD CHURCH, a 19th-cent. phrase now little used, inspired by the older *high-church and *low-church categories, describing a temper of mind within Anglicanism generally opposed to doctrinal definition and sympathetic to the most liberal interpretation of Scripture, creed, rubric, etc. The sense of it might be found in "liberal" or (a generation ago) "modernist." In some ways, broad church corresponds in meaning to *latitudinarianism, but the two should not be confused.

BROAD STOLE, a vestment once worn by the deacon from the epistle to the communion at high Mass on certain days during penitential seasons. Although not properly a *stole, it was so called because it was worn in the manner of a stole, i.e., over the left shoulder and under the right arm. It was used for the sake of convenience in place of the folded chasuble prescribed by the rubrics.

[N. KOLLAR]

BROCH, HERMANN (1886–1951), Austrian novelist and philosopher whose works reflect the ambivalent situation of modern man and his perishing values. The son of a Jewish textile manufacturer, B. studied philosophy, mathematics, and psychology at Vienna besides preparing to take over his father's factory. He began to write in his 40s and was able to escape to the U.S. from the Nazis in 1938, where he wrote and taught at Yale University. His best-known work is *Der Tod des Vergil (The Death of Vergil,* 1945), originally a radio play; a mystical search for salvation as portrayed in the last 18 hours of a dying man. *Die Schlafwandler (The Sleep-*

walkers, 1932) is an earlier novel trilogy on the destruction of ethical values. BIBLIOGRAPHY: W. F. Somm, NCE 2:810.

[B. F. STEINBRUCKNER]

BROCKELMANN, CARL (1868–1956), German scholar who made a major contribution to Semitic studies through his many volumes on philology, grammar, and literature. BIBLIOGRAPHY: T. W. Buckley, NCE 2:810–811.

[T. C. O'BRIEN]

BROGLIE, ALBERT DE (1821–1901), French statesman, writer. B. supported Catholic education, religious liberty, and ultramontanism. He served in various government positions and became a prominent member of the Orleanists. He wrote many books, the most famous of which is *L'Église et l'empire romain au IVe siècle.* BIBLIOGRAPHY: J. Dedieu, DHGE 10:808–813.

[R. C. TOLLARICO]

BROGLIE, MAURICE JEAN DE (1766–1821), bp. of Ghent. B. served as almoner in the court of Napoleon I. Because of his later opposition to Napoleon during the French National Synod (1811) he was imprisoned and exiled. Reinstated as bp. of Ghent after Napoleon's death, he again fled to France because of his opposition to the Fundamental Law of the Low Countries. BIBLIOGRAPHY: F. Claeys-Bouuaert, DHGE 10:813–818.

[R. C. TOLLARICO]

BROGNE, ABBEY OF (Bronium), former Benedictine monastery founded in the Diocese of Liège, Namur, Belgium by St. Gerard of Brogne (d. 959). A nobleman of the region, Gerard was probably initiated into the monastic life at Saint-Denis in France. The founder gave his name to the monastery and to the region, reestablishing the regular observance in many abbeys of Lorraine and Flanders. His reform extended as far as Normandy (Saint-Wandrille, Mont-Saint-Michel, Saint-Ouen of Rouen). The bp. of Liège, Nithard, consecrated the second church of the monastery in 1038. From the 11th to the 14th cent., numerous liturgical MSS were transcribed in its scriptorium. These are at present preserved in the seminary of Namur. Brogne suffered in the wars of the 15th and 16th centuries. After it had adopted the reform of Louis of Blois in 1645 and the statutes of Bursfeld in the same year, it was incorporated into the episcopal property of Namur and governed by priors elected for 3 years. Its history from that time on was nothing more than a series of disputes between the monks and the bishop. Today there are remaining only a few farms and the 18th-cent. palace of the abbey, which was suppressed in 1792. BIBLIOGRAPHY: Cottineau 1:510–511; J. Daoust, NCE 2:812.

[J. DAOUST]

BROLLO, BASILIO (1648–1704), vicar-apostolic to China. B. became a Franciscan friar and went to the Orient in 1680, assuming the name Yeh Tsun-hsiao. He was the main instrument in establishing vicariates apostolic to rid the missions of the obsolescent Portuguese and Spanish patronage. Noted for great learning, wisdom, zeal, and supreme charity, B. left numerous mission letters, reports, and essays, as well as five Chinese works, including two Chinese-Latin dictionaries, one of which was much followed and plagiarized. BIBLIOGRAPHY: *Sinica Franciscana* (ed. G. Mensaert, 1961) v. 6; B. Willeke, LTK 2:702–703.

[L. MITCHELL]

BROMPTON ORATORY, house and church of the Oratorians in Brompton Road, London. The Oratorians first settled in King William Street (1849), mainly through the efforts of Card. Newman. In 1854 the Oratory was moved to its Brompton Road location, and the present church, modelled on S. Andrea della Valle in Rome, was consecrated in 1884.

[P. K. MEAGHER]

BROMYARD, JOHN OF, 14th-cent. Dominican friar, scholar of Oxford, famous preacher and author of *Summa Praedicantium* (*c.* 1360). The *Summa* contains 189 topics arranged alphabetically, with a thousand or more stories or exempla (see EXEMPLUM) for use of medieval preachers. It explains the art of preaching, gives vignettes of everyday life (many taken from earlier sources), attacks the ignorance of the parish clergy, denounces the bishops for their selfish interest in ecclesiastical dignities and their failure to instruct the people, accuses merchants of trickery and profiteering, the common people of looking for entertainment in sermons and for chattering and joking when they should be attentive, and condemns fellow friars who fawn on the rich. The *Summa* is important as a source work on 14th-cent. England. BIBLIOGRAPHY: G. R. Owst, *Preaching in Medieval England* (1926).

[M. M. BARRY]

BRONDEL, JOHN BAPTIST (1842–1904), first bp. of the Helena, (Mont.) Diocese. B. was taught by Xaverian Brothers, at the Episcopal Institute, Brussels, and in the American College in Louvain, Belgium. After ordination in 1864 he joined Bp. Augustin Blanchet in Seattle, Wash., and did missionary work in Walla Walla until he was appointed bp. of Vancouver Island in 1879. When the Diocese of Helena was created (1884) B. became the first bp. He changed his territory from missionary status to diocesan, built hospitals, schools, and orphan asylums, and made fund-raising tours to aid the Indians. His diocese was split and the Diocese of Great Falls was created in 1904. BIBLIOGRAPHY: DAB 3:67–68.

[J. HILL]

BRONISŁAWA, BL. (1203–59), recluse, contemplative. According to a late tradition B. came of noble Polish family and was related to St. Hyacinth and Bl. Ceslaus of Silesia. At an early age, she entered a convent of Premonstratensian nuns near Kraków. She was a contemplative and a recluse: a hill near her convent is venerated as her place of prayer. Popular devotion to her in Kraków and throughout Poland was approved in 1839. BIBLIOGRAPHY: Butler 3:449; P. Naruszewicz, BiblSanct 3:554.

[M. E. DUFFY]

BRONOWSKI, JACOB (1908–74), humanist. A mathematician by training and well known for his work in literature, intellectual history, and philosophy of science, B. was born in Poland. When he was 3 years old his family moved to Germany and 9 years later to England where he received his doctorate at the Univ. of Cambridge in 1933. Though his career began in the academic world at the Univ. of Hull, he soon veered into government service during World War II, supervising studies in the physical and economic effects of bombing. At the same time, he wrote a book focusing on the mystic poems of William Blake. The combination of literary and scientific interests established him as a leader in the modern movement of scientific humanism. For him, the understanding of nature had to have as its goal the understanding of human nature and of the human condition within nature. He was invited by the Massachusetts Institute of Technology to initiate a pioneer study of the ethics of science as Carnegie visiting professor. His book, *Science and Human Values,* was the product of his famous series of lectures. In 1964 he became a fellow at the Salk Institute for Biological Studies where he was able to do work of a more speculative and evolutionary nature than that done in most biology departments. Among other things, he researched human language and concluded that language was "not tied to lips but much more to mental processes." In 1969 his first outline for "The Ascent of Man" was written for the British Broadcasting Co. After more than a year of preparation, he and a film crew traveled around the world producing a 13-part film-study. Treating a broad range of topics in science and history, it focuses on the innovative ideas that had shaped different cultures. The man behind "The Ascent of Man"—mathematician, poet, literary critic, historian, administrator, statistician, philosopher, and biologist—effectively spread secular humanism.

[E. L. HENNESSEY]

BRONZE SERPENT, see SERPENT, BRONZE.

BRONZINO, ANGELO (1503–72), Florentine *Mannerist painter and decorator (sometime poet), assistant to *Pontormo, whose chief claim to fame rests on his elegant, aristocratic portraiture, emphasizing in true mannerist style through hauteur and sophistication the station rather than the personality of his subjects. B. is also noted for religious works of the same mannered elegance, allegorical paintings, and cartoons for tapestries. His style is cold tending toward relief with a simplification of planes, occasionally almost abstract, in a color which though often frigid was at times rich in the black and bronze greens of an age of "Spanish etiquette." B.'s style, through the dry academism of his followers, led to the final dissolution of mannerism. BIBLIOGRAPHY: A. McComb, *Agnolo Bronzino: His Life and Works* (1928); A. Emiliani, *Il Bronzino* (1960).

[L. A. LEITE]

BROOK FARM, the best known of the early 19th-cent. U.S. *communal movements inspired by the *perfectionism and *millenarianism of the time. Among the prominent New England writers who participated, many of them *transcendentalists, were George Ripley (1802–80) and William E. Channing (1810–84), founders; Theodore Parker (1810–60), George W. Curtis (1824–92), Nathaniel Hawthorne (1804–64), Charles A. Dana (1819–97), and Margaret Fuller (1810–50), close associates; Orestes Brownson (1803–76) and Isaac Hecker (1819–88), visitors. Brook Farm, near West Roxbury, Mass., was founded in the belief that it was the business of Christianity to overthrow social evils. The community was structured to unite intellectual and manual work in a noncompetitive society. When efforts at farming were unsuccessful in supporting cultural and creative pursuits, the members became dependent upon outside help to supplement the income from their excellent school. In 1844, influenced by the socialism of Charles Fourier (1772–1837), the members converted Brook Farm into a Fourierist phalanx. Thereafter, the school was neglected, and a fire (1846) left the community insolvent; it was disbanded in 1847. The literary organs of the Brook Farm experiment were, successively, the *Dial* (1840–44), the *Phalanx* (1843–45), and the *Harbinger* (1845–49). BIBLIOGRAPHY: L. Swift, *Brook Farm: Its Members, Scholars, and Visitors* (1900); E. R. Curtis, *Season in Utopia* (1961); K. Burton, *Paradise Planters: The Story of Brook Farm* (1939).

[M. CARTHY]

BROOKS, JAMES (1512–60), first and last RC bp. of Gloucester. Scholar of Corpus Christi College, Oxford, B. became master of Balliol College (1547), vice-chancellor of Oxford University (1552), and bp. of Gloucester (1554). He was delegated by the Pope to examine and try Cranmer, Ridley, and Latimer. After Elizabeth's accession he was deprived of his see for refusing to take the oath of supremacy and was committed to prison where he died. BIBLIOGRAPHY: T. Cooper, DNB 2:1346–47.

[V. SAMPSON]

BROOKS, JAMES (1825–1901), English architect whose simple brick churches (London's East End) are models of English Victorian Gothic. Best known is the Church of the Ascension, Lavender Hill, but St. Savior's (1865) and St. Chad's (1867) are noteworthy.

[M. J. DALY]

BROOKS, PHILLIPS (1835–93), Episcopal bp. of Massachusetts, celebrated preacher. A graduate of Harvard

(1855) and Virginia Theological Seminary (1859), B., then rector in Philadelphia, first came to national attention by his eulogy of President Lincoln when the latter's body lay in state. He added to his renown by distinguished service as rector of Trinity Church in Boston from 1869 until his consecration as bp. in 1891. The influence of the Anglican F. D. *Maurice is seen in B.'s positive view of tolerance; believing that denominations should receive those whom Christ does, he showed a *comprehensiveness that found agreement even with the conservative Presbyterian C. *Hodge. B. pursued interest in German theology in a year abroad (1882), and shared Lotze's conviction that truth was not gained solely by the intellectual powers. He searched constantly for ways to bring the power of ideas to bear on the human will to change human behavior. Integrity, personal conviction, and imaginative powers of inspiration through a poetic use of words were among his special gifts. In his theology he was Christocentric and liberal incarnationalist without forensic or penal views of the atonement. He preached about sin, yet proclaimed: "You can never make men see all their sins aright except by seeing rightly the very highest idea and possibility of their existence. Man has been preached to too much on the bad side. . . . the Fall has in it the capacity of Man." He shared the limitations of the optimistic age of *liberal theology. To this he added a humanistic heritage derived from 17th-cent. Anglicans and the idealism of the *Cambridge Platonists. H. *Bushnell's theory of language and the interrelatedness of reality influenced him. The controversy over his election to the episcopate epitomized the historic tension between *high-church and *broad-church parties that polarized within Anglicanism at the time in consequence of the *Oxford movement, and it points out B.'s own representative role. Among his published lectures were *Lectures on Preaching* (1877), *Influence of Jesus* (1878), and *Lectures on Tolerance* (1887). In 1865–66 he wrote the carol "O Little Town of Bethlehem." BIBLIOGRAPHY: B. S. Clark, "Phillips Brooks in Biography," *Historical Magazine of the Protestant Episcopal Church* 31 (1962) 54–57, which compares the biography by R. W. Albright *(Focus on Infinity,* 1961) esp. with that by A. V. G. Allen (3v., 1900).

[B. S. CLARK]

BROTHER, a term that from NT times has been used to indicate a fellow member of the Christian Church as a whole, Christ being "the first-born of many brethren" (Rom 18.29). More specifically, it has also been applied to members of particular Christian sects, societies, or fellowships. The most pointed example of this has been the use of the term from the earliest days of monasticism in both East and West in reference to members of religious communities of men. After the distinction between clerical and non-clerical religious became more prominent, popular usage often restricted the term to members of non-clerical orders of men (e.g., Christian Brothers), or to members of essentially clerical orders who happen not to be priests (e.g., novices, clerical students, lay brothers).

[P. K. MEAGHER]

BROTHER IN CHRIST, a term that refers to the uniquely Christian concept of love and fellowship in Jesus. "By this shall all men know that you are my disciples if you have love, one for another" (Jn 13.35). By obeying this precept one becomes a brother of Jesus who by his death and Resurrection became the "firstborn among many brethren, reconciling divided humanity." To live as a brother in Christ, one must share in the common life of the Church, the community of faith, but more esp. help to create a community of sacrificial love with one's brethren with the love of Jesus as its binding force.

[T. LIDDY]

BROTHERHOOD OF BRIDGEBUILDERS, medieval society of laymen organized to complete and maintain bridges. In the 12th-cent. religious fervor regarded bridgebuilding as a charitable work. Only three mutually independent societies could with certainty be termed bridgebuilder brotherhoods: one at Avignon (*c.*1181); at Lyons (*c.*1184); and at Pont Saint-Esprit (*c.*1277). No evidence indicates that the brothers were artisans. By the early 14th cent., the societies had either disappeared or had become a hospital order of oblates. BIBLIOGRAPHY: M. N. Boyer, "The Bridgebuilding Brotherhoods," *Speculum* 39 (1964) 635–650.

[M. H. BEIRNE]

BROTHERHOOD OF MAN. Correlative to the way God, the Father, grants his creational benefits to all men, whether they acknowledge him or not, Jesus demands his disciples to love and do good to men who are not connected with them through kinship or friendship (Mt 5.44–48; Lk 6.27–36). This idea, coupled with biblical statements about salvation's being offered to all men (1 Tim 2.5,6; 2 Pet 3.9; Rom 3.29,30) and others that indicate that Jesus, in his resurrected human reality at God's right hand, is the cosmic Son of God and the Lord of all creation, who offers all humanity fellowship with him in his eternal life (1 Cor 15.22; Rom 5.15–18; Eph 1.10; Col 1.14–23; 2 Cor 5.14–21; Jn 3.16,17; Heb 2.5–18), is the Christian basis for believing in the brotherhood of all men under God and in Christ.

Other religions base varying notions of universal brotherhood on God's providential care for the most noble part of his creation (Judaism and, to some degree, Islam), on pantheistic notions of the oneness of all in God (Hinduism, Buddhism), while natural mystics and humanistic rationalists base their notions on the biological and evolutionary unity of the human race and its common lot and habitat on the earth.

[J. F. FALLON]

BROTHERS AND SISTERS OF THE FREE SPIRIT, designation for lay sects arising in the 13th cent. in parts of

Germany, the Low Countries, Switzerland, and Italy. Their teaching stemmed from a crude pantheism; their oneness with God meant freedom from all moral restraint (see ANTINOMIANISM) and the rejection of Church and sacraments. The teachings of certain *Beghards and *Beguines that were condemned by the Council of Vienne (1312; D 891–899) were derived from the Brothers and Sisters of the Free Spirit. In spite of the Inquisition, they survived down to the Reformation; some historians attribute to them an influence on the Anabaptists. BIBLIOGRAPHY: Bihlmeyer-Tüchle 2:307–308; R. Knox, *Enthusiasm* (1950), 86–87, 100, 103, 173; R. M. Jones, *Studies in Mystical Religion* (1923) 203–216; R. E. Lerner, *Heresy of the Free Spirit in the Later Middle Ages* (1972).

[T. C. O'BRIEN]

BROTHERS OF CHRISTIAN INSTRUCTION OF PLOËRMEL (FICP: La Mennais Brothers), a French religious institute formed (1820) from the union of (1) the community founded (1819) by Jean-Marie Robert de La Mennais (1780–1860) at St. Brieuc and (2) the Auray foundation of Gabriel Deshayes (1767–1841). Papal approbation, given in 1891, was renewed in 1910. The work of the brothers in elementary education grew to include secondary schooling, with commercial, agricultural, and nautical training. FICP, entering the mission field in 1837, went to Tahiti (1859), Haiti (1864), and Canada (1886). They were in Spain, England, and the U.S. in 1903 when the lay laws had dispersed their forces in France. Twenty of the brothers assisted (from 1903 to 1910) the Jesuits at the Indian reservations in Idaho, Montana, and Alaska. Their first U.S. school was at Plattsburgh, N.Y. (1903). The community spread to Italy by 1921; Africa, 1926; S America, 1933; and Japan, 1951. Their generalate is in Rome. In 1975 they had 240 houses, including 6 in the United States. BIBLIOGRAPHY: I. Vittoria, EncCatt 5:1712–13.

[M. R. BROWN]

BROTHERS OF CHRISTIAN INSTRUCTION OF ST. GABRIEL (FSG), known until the mid-19th cent. as Brothers of the Holy Ghost, an institute founded (1821) by Gabriel *Deshayes for teaching in country schools. The beatification of Louis-Marie Grignon de Montfort in 1888 raised the question whether the FSG was a restoration of his community begun in 1705 and not a new institute; the Sacred Congregation of Rites affirmed that the FSG was indeed a new body (AAS 39 [1947] 240–241). Established in the Vendée at Saint-Laurent-sur-Sèvre, they spread from France to Canada (1888), Belgium and Gabon (1900), and Thailand (1901). When the legislation of J. É. Combes closed all French schools operated by religious, the institute, until then a diocesan congregation, was suppressed by the Bp. of Luçon in 1903. Reorganized, it received papal approbation in 1910. Events of 1901–03 served to propagate their work abroad. In 1903 the brothers were located in England, Spain,

Madagascar, and India. They spread (1904) to Italy and the African mainland and later to North and South America (the U.S. in 1950; Colombia, 1961; Peru, 1962). In 1975 they conducted 285 houses. BIBLIOGRAPHY: G. Löw, EncCatt 5:1706–07.

[M. R. BROWN]

BROTHERS OF JESUS, relatives of Jesus who were reluctant to accept him during his lifetime (Mk 3.21,31; Jn 7.5) and therefore probably were not among the Twelve. However, they were important figures in the early Church (Acts 1.14; 1 Cor 15.7), when "brother of the Lord" was probably a title of honor (Gal 1.19; 1 Cor 9.5). The NT names four of them: James, Joses (or Joseph), Jude, and Simon (Mk 6.3; Mt 13.55). With some exceptions, Catholic tradition has denied that they were the sons of Mary and Joseph, and has expressed this conviction in the dogma of the perpetual virginity of Mary, defined at a council held at the Lateran in 649. Other explanations for the meaning of "brother" have varied. Some ancient authorities regarded them as stepbrothers of Jesus, sons of Joseph from an earlier marriage, despite their hesitation to accept the historical value of the apocryphal Protoevangelium of James (2d cent.), the earliest witness to this theory. On the other hand, Jerome (4th cent.) made a questionable identification of James the Less, son of Alpheus, with James the brother of the Lord. His conclusion that the brothers were cousins of Jesus gained acceptance in the Western Church and is widely known as "the Catholic position."

Many Protestant exegetes have opposed such theories as contrary to the "natural" sense of the Scriptures and dependent on too little early evidence. Catholic tradition, however, can point to the Semitic usage of "brother" for a variety of blood relationships, as well as to a deeper modern understanding of the theological purpose in some pertinent scriptural statements. Thus Mt 1.18 probably owes its formulation to Is 7.14 rather than to an implication that Mary bore children after Jesus; similarly, Lk 2.7 should be understood as a preparation for Lk 2.23. The argument for a wider meaning of "brother" draws strength from a comparison of Mk 6.3 and 15.40, since Mark's general usage would not favor identifying the mother of Jesus with the mother of James and Joses.

The biblical texts themselves, however, have not been clear enough to establish consensus between Catholics and many Protestants. The road to further progress seems to lie in more theological study of the various Christian traditions, with Catholic emphasis placed on understanding the development of dogma. BIBLIOGRAPHY: J. Blinzler, "Die Brüder Jesu," *Theologie der Gegenwart* 10 (1967) 8–15; H. von Campenhausen, *Virgin Birth in the Theology of the Ancient Church* (tr. F. Clarke, 1964).

[P. J. KEARNEY]

BROTHERS OF ST. PATRICK, see PATRICIAN BROTHERS.

BROTHERS OF THE CHRISTIAN SCHOOLS, see CHRISTIAN BROTHERS.

BROTTIER, DANIEL (1876–1936), French priest of the Congregation of the Holy Spirit. B. served as a missionary in Africa (1903–11) until poor health forced his return to France. After serving as a chaplain in World War I, he devoted himself to the care of orphans. At his death his young charges numbered 1,500. BIBLIOGRAPHY: E. Lecocq. *Catholicisme* 2:284–285.

[M. J. SUELZER]

BROU, ALEXANDRE (1862–1947), French Jesuit hagiographer and spiritual writer. Some of his life was spent teaching in England. He was interested in the history of the missions and wrote a notable biography of St. Francis Xavier (2 v., 1914). His historical learning enabled him to give more accurate perspective to the controversies of the Jansenists with the Jesuits in his *Les Jésuites de la légende* (1906–07). His name is particularly associated with the exposition and diffusion of Ignatian spirituality, e.g., *The Ignatian Way to God* (tr. W. Young, 1952) and *Ignatian Methods of Prayer* (tr. W. Young, 1949). BIBLIOGRAPHY: E. Lamalle, AHSJ 16 (1947) 223–225; *idem*, EncCatt 3:125–126; Bremond Index 47.

[T. C. O'BRIEN]

BROUILLET, JOHN (1813–84), leader in Catholic mission work with U.S. Indians. Born near Montreal, he was ordained in 1837 and 10 years later accompanied Bp. A. M. Blanchet, who went to establish Walla Walla diocese in Oregon territory. B. founded the Umatilla mission at Nesqually, and became the center of a national controversy when he was accused of inciting an Indian massacre of Presbyterian missionary Marcus Whitman and family. In 1872 B. went to Washington, D.C., to represent Catholic Indian missions to the government. He served (1874–83) as the first director of the Bureau of Catholic Indian Missions.

[T. EARLY]

BROUWER, CHRISTOPH (1559–1617), Jesuit historian. His major work was a history of the archdiocese of Trier to the year 1600 (26 v.). Because of his historical objectivity he included details unflattering to the bps. and was accused of presenting a partisan view. Publication was stopped, and an altered version prepared (1626), but the Jesuits at Trier obtained a copy of the first printing and the remaining MSS and sent them to France where they were enlarged by Jacob Masenius, to include events up to 1652. B. also published an edition of the poems of Fortunatus and Rabanus Maurus and an account of the lives of some German saints. BIBLIOGRAPHY: Sommervogel 2:218–222; A. De Bil, DHGE 10:865–866.

[V. SAMPSON]

BROWE, PETER (1876–1949), German Jesuit theologian and historian whose special interest lay in the field of medieval moral and pastoral theology. He produced valuable studies on the development of Eucharistic devotion in the West, on frequent and obligatory Communion in the Middle Ages, on ordeals, and a work on medieval thought on the subject of sexual morality. BIBLIOGRAPHY: B. Neunheuser, NCE 2:824; A. Stenzel, LTK 2:710 (for a list of B.'s works).

[N. KOLLAR]

BROWN, FORD MADOX (1821–93), English painter and designer who after years on the Continent settled in England (1846), becoming the pupil and friend of Dante Gabriel Rossetti though not a member of the Pre-Raphaelite Brotherhood. Through pride and his hatred of the Royal Academy of Arts, B. suffered serious poverty (1850s). He did stained glass designs for William Morris (1861), held a successful show (1865), and began (1878) his last major undertaking—12 large paintings for the Manchester Town Hall (completed 1892), in which B. modified influences of the Pre-Raphaelites with a pronounced individuality. Ever revolting against Victorian inequities, B. finally expressed his dedication to Socialism (and Carlyle) in his composition *Work.* BIBLIOGRAPHY: F. M. Ford, *Ford Madox Brown* (1896).

[M. J. DALY]

BROWN, GEORGE (*c.* 1500–1559) first Protestant abp. of Dublin and chief instrument for Henry VIII's reformation policies in Ireland. Provincial of the Austin Friars in England, he administered to them the oath of royal supremacy. He was consecrated abp. of Dublin by Thomas Cranmer after the murder of Abp. Allen (1536) and was active in suppressing the monasteries and in pushing the English Prayer Book of 1544. On the translation of the primatial see from Armagh he was made primate of Ireland by patent. He was cordially disliked for his harshness and arrogance. Deprived of his see as a married man by Queen Mary, he received a benefice through the kindness of Cardinal Pole after his marriage had been declared invalid and his opposition to extreme Protestant eucharistic teaching had been confirmed. BIBLIOGRAPHY: R. D. Edwards, *Church and State in Tudor Ireland* (1935).

[V. SAMPSON]

BROWN WILLIAM ADAMS (1865–1943), Presbyterian clergyman and professor of theology. Educated at Yale, Union Theological Seminary, N.Y., and the Univ. of Berlin, B. taught at Union after his ordination (1893) until his retirement. Under the influence of German liberals and American pragmatists, he became an evangelical-liberal and a mediating voice in the theological debates of the period (see LIBERAL THEOLOGY). In 1913 he was severaly criticized by the *General Assembly of the Presbyterian Church because some of his writings were regarded as too liberal. He was deeply involved in ministerial education, the work of the Board of Home Missions of the Presbyterian Church in the U.S.A., the development of the Federal Council of Churches, and in early conferences that led to the formation of the World Council of Churches. He was the author of *Essence of Christianity* (1902), the widely used textbook *Christian Theology in Outline* (1906), and the autobiographical *A Teacher and His Times* (1940).

[J. H. SMYLIE]

BROWNE, MICHAEL (1887–1971), renowned Irish Dominican prelate who served the Church in Rome for more than 60 years. Born at Grangemockler, Diocese of Waterford, B. entered the Order of Preachers at Tallaght (1903), completed his studies in Rome, and was ordained (1910). After graduate studies at the Univ. of Fribourg, he taught at Tallaght and served a term as master of novices. B. returned to Rome (1919) as professor of philosophy at the Collegio Angelico. He became Rector Magnificus (1932–41) at the Pontifical Univ. of St. Thomas and during the papacy of Pius XII was master of the Sacred Apostolic Palace (1951). In addition to his teaching both at the Angelicum and at the Lateran Univ. and his great doctrinal activity in the Roman Curia (Congregation for the Doctrine of Faith, Congregation for the Causes of Saints), he ministered for many years as confessor to American students in Rome. B. was master general of the Dominicans from 1955 to 1962, when he was made cardinal and called by Pope John XXIII to the central pontifical preparatory commission of Vatican Council II.

During the council he was vice president of the doctrinal commission and vice president of the commission for the revision of the schema on the fonts of divine revelation. He also made significant contributions to the schemas on the Church and on religious liberty. In 1967 he took part in the commission for the revision of the Code of Canon Law. Among advanced liberals he was labeled, somewhat unjustly, as an arch-conservative. BIBLIOGRAPHY: Anal OP 32:107–109; 40:80, 160–163, 164–166, 173–174, 320–324.

[A. WARDLE]

BROWNE, ROBERT (c. 1550–1633), "father of the Congregationalists." As a student at Cambridge, B. was influenced by T. *Cartwright's presbyterian theories on the Church. Without license or ordination B. formed his own *Nonconformist congregation at Norwich; after a prison term for this, he took his followers to Middelburg in Holland. There he published (1582) *A Book which showeth the Life and Manner of True Christians*, and *A Treatise of Reformation without Tarrying for Any*. Eventually he returned to England, submitted to the C of E, and was ordained. He was put in prison for a civil altercation, and died there. His idea that the local congregation is independent of superior civil or ecclesiastical authority was the inspiration of the Congregationalists (see INDEPENDENTS), who in their early days were often called Brownists. BIBLIOGRAPHY: C. Burrage, *True Story of Robert Browne* (1906); *Writings of*

Robert Harrison and Robert Browne (eds. A. Peel and L. H. Carlson, Elizabethan Non-Conformist Texts 2; 1953).

[R. B. ENO]

BROWNE, THOMAS (1605–82), English writer and physician. *Religio Medici*, his private journal, was published in 1642 without his consent and he revised it for the authorized edition (1643). It presents religious attitudes hard to reconcile. In dogma Browne professes to follow the teachings of Scripture and Church, but he shows great skepticism in some matters and great credulity in others. *Pseudodoxia Epidemica* (1646) displays wide reading in quasi-scientific works but also accurate observation in areas of botany and medicine. *Urne Burial* (1658), best reveals his fully developed Latinate style, rich in imagery, whimsical, majestic, and over-literary. BIBLIOGRAPHY: E. Gosse, *Sir Thomas Browne* (1905); A. H. Bullen, DNB 7:64–72.

[M. M. BARRY]

BROWNING, ELIZABETH BARRETT (1806–61), English poet, wife of Robert Browning. She was well read in Greek and Latin, had many literary friends, published some early poetry, but was generally unrecognized as a poet until *Poems by Elizabeth Barrett* (2 v. 1844) won attention, Browning's among others. *Sonnets from the Portuguese* (1847), contains thinly disguised the story of Browning's love and her hesitation to marry because of ill health and parental opposition. *Casa Guidi Windows* (1851), shows her sympathy for the Florentines. *Aurora Leigh* (1856), a novel in verse, achieved popularity. She is not a great poet but shows strong spirituality and a sense of righteousness. She wrote some essays and some translations from the Greek. BIBLIOGRAPHY: V. Woolf, *Flush* (1933); J. Marks, *Family of the Barretts* (1938); R. Besler, *Barretts of Wimpole Street* (1930), a dramatized version of the Brownings' love story.

[M. M. BARRY]

BROWNING, ROBERT (1812–89), English poet. He married Elizabeth Barrett secretly in 1846 and lived with her in Italy until her death in 1861. His early work was generally ignored, but he secured admiring recognition with *The Ring and the Book* (1868–69), a series of 12 dramatic monologues presenting different points of view of an old Roman murder case. His early dramas are studies in psychology, and are somewhat vague and obscure in action. His lyric poetry is rarely subjective but gives the feeling of some character in a dramatic situation in conversational style and often ironically. In this genre of dramatic monologue B. is forceful and vivid in characterization, showing strong ethical interests and keen analysis of motives of action. *Men and Women* (1855) and *Dramatis Personae* (1864) present his best shorter poems. After he had dabbled briefly in atheism in his youth, his religious convictions evolved through a period of theism to a full acceptance of Christianity and its basic doctrine, but he remained uncommitted to any particular Church. BIBLIOGRAPHY: W. H. Griffin, *Life of Robert*

Browning, (ed. H. C. Minchin, 3d ed., 1938); W. Whitla, *Central Truth: the Incarnation in Robert Browning* (1964); R. M. Schell, *Critical Study of the Plays of Browning* (Villanova Univ., 1938).

[M. M. BARRY]

BROWNSON, JOSEPHINE VAN DYKE (1880–1942), author, teacher. B. received her early education in a school conducted by the Religious of the Sacred Heart and later attended Detroit Normal School and the Univ. of Michigan. She taught at Barstow School, Detroit and Cass Technical High. In 1930 she formed the Catholic Instruction League for children attending public school. She was the author of: *Stopping the Leak* (1926); *Catholic Bible Stories* (1919); *Living Forever* (1928). She was honored by receiving *Pro Ecclesia et Pontifice,* a papal decoration, and the Laetare medal from the Univ. of Notre Dame. BIBLIOGRAPHY: W. Romig, *Josephine van Dyke Brownson* (1955).

[J. HILL]

BROWNSON, ORESTES AUGUSTUS (1803–76), American clergyman journalist, philosopher, author. A convert to Catholicism in 1844, B. published *Brownson's Quarterly Review,* by means of which he exercised a wide influence. As a journalist, he was noted for his vigorous position on social and religious questions. Before his conversion B. was also a leader: in movements for social reform; in criticism of the transcendental movement; in discussions on the foundations of authority; and on problems of an industrial society. He was a prolific writer—and at times a controversial one—in such diverse fields as religion, philosophy, literature, and politics. Sacrificing his own inclination to discontinue the publication of his *Review* and to study law, and honoring the suggestion of Bp. John B. Fitzgerald of Boston that as a Catholic journalist he would be a power in publicizing the Church's position on the great issues of the times, he agreed and did become highly influential. He was among the earliest critics who hailed the advent of French and German literatures into America, thus lessening the dependence of American authors on British writers. Probably his best work was *American Republic* (1867). BIBLIOGRAPHY: A. M. Schlesinger, Jr., *Orestes A. Brownson* (1939); T. Maynard, *Orestes Brownson: Yankee, Radical, Catholic* (1943, repr. 1971).

[S. A. HEENEY]

BRU, ANYE (Luricus Brun; fl. 16th cent.), German artist living in Barcelona. B. painted the retable for the high altar at San Cugat del Vallés and two oil panels, *Martyrdom of St. Cucufas* and *St. George* (both in the Museum of Catalonian Art), Barcelona, evidencing German, N Italian, and Flemish influences. BIBLIOGRAPHY: J. Ainaud and F. P. Verrié, "El retablo . . . del Monasterio de San Cugat del Vallés . . ." *Anales y Boletín de los Museos de Arte de Barcelona* (1941) v. 1.

[M. J. DALY]

BRUCE OF TOURS, ST. see BRICE OF TOURS, ST.

BRUCHÉSI, LOUIS JOSEPH PAUL NAPOLÉON (1855–1939), Canadian RC churchman. B. studied at the Seminary of Issy in France and was ordained at Rome (1878). Returning to parochial work in his native diocese of Montreal, he became its abp. in 1897. Closely identified with French-Canadian interests, he was a close friend of Sir Wilfrid *Laurier and helped reduce tensions between the Canadian hierarchy and the Liberal Party. BIBLIOGRAPHY: J. Bruchési, *Témoinages d'hier* (1961) 225–301.

[R. K. MacMASTER]

BRÜCK, HEINRICH (1831–1903), ecclesiastical historian. Ordained in 1855, B. taught church history and canon law at the seminary in Mainz until 1899 when he was consecrated bishop. He is best remembered for his literary achievements, esp. his studies on church history: *Lehrbuch der Kirchengeschichte* (1874, 9th ed. 1906) and *Geschichte der katholischen Kirche in Deutschland in 19. Jh.* (5 v., 1887–1905). BIBLIOGRAPHY: V. Conzemius, NCE 2:830.

[R. C. TOLLARICO]

BRÜCKE, DIE ("The Bridge") a group of painters who founded the German Expressionist movement in the first decade of the 20th century. Influenced by the ideas of Nietzsche, rejecting the delicacies of French Impressionism and the niceties of a "decadent contemporary culture," these artists painted nature with a primitive directnesss, employing intense color, often adding sardonic psychological overtones. Principal members of *Die Brücke* were E. L. *Kirchner, Otto *Müller, Erich *Heckel, and Max *Pechstein. BIBLIOGRAPHY: P. Selz, *German Expressionist Painting* (1957); Tate Gallery, *Painters of the Brücke* (1964); W. Grohmann, *E. L. Kirchner* (1961). *BLAUE REITER.

[T. FEIDT]

BRUCKNER, ANTON (1824–96), Austrian symphonist, composer, and organist. Like all the members of his family, B. was a teacher and musician, a devout Catholic whose music grew out of a fervent religious conviction. His attachment to Wagner impeded but did not prevent his recognition in his own country. His influence extended into the 20th cent. through his disciple Mahler and thence through Schoenberg. Aside from his symphonies, B. wrote mainly sacred music: three Masses, of which the E Minor is considered a masterpiece, a *Requiem,* a splendid *Te Deum,* and a memorable *Psalm 150.* BIBLIOGRAPHY: H. F. Redlich, Grove DMM 1:969–976; G. Engel, *International Cyclopedia of Music and Musicians* (ed. O. Thompson, 9th ed., 1964) 294–296.

[M. T. LEGGE]

BRUDERHOF, the German designation for the unique and efficient settlements established by Hutterites to carry out their principle of community of goods. In the 1600s in

Moravia and Slovakia, the population of a Bruderhof was about 300; but in 1951 the 96 Bruderhofs of several denominations existing in various parts of the world averaged about 100 persons each. Each Bruderhof consists of a number of houses around a common square, together with farmland, pond, mill, woods, and workshops. The ground floor of a house contains common workrooms, a kitchen, and a dining room, which also serves for the celebration of the Lord's Supper. High, steep roofs allow for two levels of small upper rooms for married couples and their young children. Each household elects a brother to act as steward to make purchases and to organize and direct work on farm and shop. BIBLIOGRAPHY: J. C. Wenger, MennEnc 1:445–448; E. Arnold, *Torches Together* (1964); B. Zablocki, *Joyful Community* (pa. 1972). *SOCIETY OF BROTHERS.

[M. J. SUELZER]

BRUEGHEL. Family of Flemish painters of whom the oldest and most famous was (1) **Pieter Brueghel the Elder** (*c.* 1525–69), called Peasant Brueghel, equal in importance to Jan Van Eyck and Rembrandt in the history of Netherlandish painting. B. painted in a satirical vein biblical subjects, genre and fantastic allegories. First apprenticed to Pieter *Coecke van Aelst, then to the engraver Hieronymous *Cock, B. was influenced by the moralistic works of *Bosch. His early landscapes are background, moving to high foreground, middle and distant views (*The Fall of Icarus*—a satire on the Italian Renaissance), and in mature works marked by a low horizon with vistas. Peasant figures generalized to abstract patterns, at first small, crowded, and linear, move to groups in depth. B. extols the simple life in the pure genre ''Calendar'' landscapes (1565) of which *Hunters in the Snow* and *Harvesters* are famous. His biblical works, moralistic and often satiric, through contemporary dress and Flemish landscape render more caustic his condemnation of 16th-cent. hypocrisy (*Christ Carrying the Cross*). B.'s older son, (2) **Pieter Brueghel II, the Younger** (1564–1638), called Hell Brueghel because of the hells and underworld subjects he painted, taught his son Pieter III, a lesser artist, and Frans Snyders (later assistant to Rubens). Younger son of Peasant B., (3) **Jan Brueghel I** (1568–1625), called Velvet, was the versatile, successful friend and collaborator with *Rubens. His son Jan B. II (1601–78) copied his father exactly. BIBLIOGRAPHY: C. de Tolnay, *Pierre Bruegel l'Ancien* (1935); M. J. Friedländer, *Die altniederländische Malerei* (1937); C. G. Stridbeck, *Bruegelstudien* (tr. Horb and Elmer, 1956); M. Vaes, ''Le Journal de Jean Brueghel II,'' *Bulletin de l'institut historique belge de Rome* (1926); M. Eemans, *Brueghel de velours* (1964); G. Glück, *Brueghels Gemälde* (5th ed., 1951); idem, *Large Bruegel Book* (1953).

[M. J. DALY]

BRUGES, JEAN DE, see HENNEQUIN, JAN.

BRUGES (BRUGGE), predominantly Catholic city of NW Belgium; a Flemish city serving as capital of West Flanders province. The first recorded preaching of Christianity in the area was *c.* 650 by St. Eligius (Eloi) of Noyon-Tournai, and Bruges remained part of Tournai diocese until Paul IV made it a bishopric in 1559. A center of the wool trade and member of the Hanseatic League, Bruges reached a peak in the 14th–15th centuries and was then superseded by Antwerp as the Bruges way to the sea silted up. From the 9th cent. Flanders was nominally a fief of France but enjoyed virtual independence, and Bruges enjoyed many liberties under the counts of Flanders. The county came under the dukes of Burgundy from 1384 to 1477, a period when Bruges enjoyed artistic as well as economic eminence. Subsequently it came into the hands of the Spanish Hapsburgs, who ruled, except for a period when Calvinists held the city (1578–84), until the Peace of Utrecht (1714) gave Flanders to Austria. During a period of French rule (1797–1815), Bruges was suppressed as a see (Concordat of 1801), but restored in 1834. In addition to the Cathedral of St. Salvator (12th–16th cent.) and other churches, Bruges has notable secular buildings from the medieval period and art treasures produced by the Flemish school there. BIBLIOGRAPHY: E. de Moreau, DHGE 10:895–906.

[T. EARLY]

BRUGES, HOLY BLOOD OF, a relic, supposedly a portion of the blood shed by Christ on the Cross, in the Basilica of the Precious Blood in Bruges, Belgium. It was brought by Count Diederik (Thierry) of Alsace from Palestine following a crusade, and has been venerated at Bruges, one of several places that have claimed to possess particles of Christ's blood, since 1158. It is kept in a shrine, and its annual procession has attracted crowds since 1303.

[T. EARLY]

BRÜGGEMANN, HANS (1480–1540), German woodcarver with affinities to the Netherlandish style. B.'s masterpiece, the *Bordesholmer Altar* (1514–21) is the last of the great carved altars in medieval style. BIBLIOGRAPHY: F. H. Hamkens, *Der bordesholmer Altar Meister Brüggemanns* (1952).

[M. J. DALY]

BRUMEL, ANTOINE (*c.* 1460–1525), Flemish composer. The pupil of Okeghem, he endeavored along with Josquin and his contemporaries to achieve a combination of structural clarity and verbal expression in music composition. Many of his Masses were published and a large number of his MS works, including Masses, Magnificats, and chansons, are preserved in libraries throughout Europe. BIBLIOGRAPHY: J. F. R. Stainer, Grove DMM 1:978–9; K. G. Fellerer, *History of Catholic Church Music* (tr. F. A. Brunner, 1961) 210.

[M. T. LEGGE]

BRUNEAU, JOSEPH (1866–1933), Sulpician educator. He studied in France and after ordination was sent to the U.S. to teach at St. Mary's Seminary, Baltimore, Md. His next assignment was professor of philosophy at St. Joseph's Seminary, Dunwoodie, N. Y., (1904–1906). He returned to Baltimore in 1909 and taught philosophy, dogmatic theology, and Scripture. His writings include: *Harmony of the Gospels* (1898), *Priesthood* (1911), *Our Priestly Life* (1928).

[J. HILL]

BRUNELLESCHI, FILIPPO (1377–1446), Italian architect and sculptor. Member of the silk guild (1398), engaged on the silver altar, Pistoia (1399), in 1401 B. lost to *Ghiberti the historic competition for the bronze doors of the Baptistery, Florence. Through a complete grasp of Roman construction, B.'s brilliantly inventive mind determined plans (1417) for the innovative Renaissance dome of the Cathedral of *Florence (1420–36), an engineering feat winning *Alberti's praise for this first dome of exterior impact in powerful, visual effect. The Hospital of the Innocents (1419) whose Piazza porticoes mark an early planned city space, the Church of San Lorenzo (1420) and Pazzi Chapel at Sta. Croce (1429–43) represent B.'s early "wall emphasis" and loss of fluid interplay. His mature style of "plastic architecture" with its apogee in S. Spirito (1436) set the norm of deeply carved planes for the Renaissance "sculptural architecture" of Tuscany. BIBLIOGRAPHY: P. Sanpaolesi, *Brunellesco e Donatello nella Sacristia Vecchia di San Lorenzo* (1948); A. Manetti, *Life of Brunellesco* (1970).

[M. J. DALY]

BRUNETIÈRE, FERDINAND (1849–1906), French literary critic, apologist. A professor of language and letters, B. also headed (from 1894) the influential *Revue des deux mondes*. B.'s gradual return to Catholicism, beginning after an audience with Leo XIII (1894), issued rather in intellectual adherence than in religious practice; before death he asked for and received the last Sacraments. B. expressed his religious ideas in such works as *La Science et la religion* (1895) and *Discours de combat* (3 v., 1900–07); and in his lectures he gave forceful and frequent evidence of his Catholic convictions. BIBLIOGRAPHY: E. Hocking, *Ferdinand Brunetière* (1936); J. van der Lugt, *L'Action religieuse de Ferdinand Brunetière* (1936); J. Morienval, *Catholicisme* 2:289–290, gives complete list of B.'s works.

[T. C. O'BRIEN]

BRUNHILDE, QUEEN OF AUSTRASIA (c.534–613). As wife of Sigebert I, King of Austrasia, and regent for her son, grandsons, and great-grandsons, she reigned c.566–613. Feuds among the Merovingian royalty resulted in the murder of her sister Galswintha and her husband, and ultimately in her own death. She used her political power to assist the Church, and is generally lauded by Gregory of Tours (*History of the Franks*, books 4–10). Some later historians regard her as evil and unscrupulous. BIBLIOGRAPHY: J. M. Wallace-Hadrill, *Long-Haired Kings and Other Studies in Frankish History* (1962) 203–206.

[M. S. TANEY]

BRUNI, LEONARDO ARETINO (c. 1369–1444), humanist and historian. Student of the classics and law, B. served as papal secretary to Innocent VII, Gregory XII, Alexander V, and the antipope John XXIII. After John's deposition, he returned to Florence (1415) and wrote a *History of Florence*. Though criticized by scholars for its excessive rhetoric, prejudicial viewpoint, and rejection of the Middle Ages, the *History* contributed to the development of historiography through its evaluation of Florentine culture and its theme of liberty seen in a human and psychological perspective. As chancellor of Florence from 1427 until his death, Bruni made Latin translations of Aeschines, Aristotle, Demosthenes, Plato, St. Basil, and Xenophon. He also wrote historical commentaries and biographies. BIBLIOGRAPHY: A. DeMeyer, DHGE 10:944–946; G. Fallani, EncCatt 3:146–147.

[M. H. BEIRNE]

BRÜNING, HEINRICH (1885–1970), German statesman and professor. Born in Münster, B. gave many years to the service of his country. He was an officer in World War I, secretary of the German League of Trade Unions, Prussian minister of welfare, leader of the Center Party, and chancellor of the Reich (1930–32). During his term of office the economic crisis reached its peak in Germany, an important factor in the undermining of his cabinet and ultimately, of the Weimar Republic. B. was a capable man, but his coalition was assailed by both Communists and National Socialists. With the approval of President von Hindenburg, he ruled until 1932 by emergency decree permitted under Article 48 of the Constitution. Seven weeks after the re-election of von Hindenburg to the presidency in 1932, for which he had campaigned untiringly, B. was forced out of office. He emigrated to England and later went to the U.S. where he was on the faculty of Harvard Univ. (1937–52). He returned to Germany and taught at the Univ. of Cologne and was professor emeritus there. BIBLIOGRAPHY: K. S. Pinson, *Modern Germany* (rev. ed. 1966) 469–474; W. L. Shirer, *Rise and Fall of the Third Reich* (1960) 221–230; *Heinrich Brüning: Reden und Aufsatze eines Deutschen Staatsmanns* (ed. W. Vernekohl, 1968).

[M. A. WATHEN]

BRUNNER, EMIL (1889–1962), Swiss theologian, linked with Karl *Barth as pioneer proponent of *crisis theology. B. taught systematic theology at Zurich from 1924 to 1953. Through his lectures and the rapid translation of his works into English, his influence in the U.S. has been considerable. His extensive involvement in the ecumenical movement proceeded according to his concept of the Church as a noncultic fellowship of believers. B. gave early direction to the Oxford

Group movement as a voluntary association based on this concept but abandoned it in 1938, when it changed into *Moral Re-Armament and lost its Christological basis.

B. manifests his debt to S. Kierkegaard and M. *Buber in his attempt to synthesize the biblical message with an existentialist emphasis on personalism and the impossibility of a merely rational approach to God. Unlike Barth, he admitted a *natural theology, but not as a saving knowledge of God. The notion of revelation is pivotal in his theology: since saving human knowledge of God exists only insofar as God has disclosed himself, the criterion for doctrine is its correspondence to revelation, not any coherence within a theological system. Revelation is a person (Christ) and an event (the incarnation and resurrection); it transcends both dogma and the biblical "cradle" in which Christ is to be found. The word of God in the Bible is only an indirect revelation, not to be identified (as in the theory of verbal inspiration or the notion of revealed doctrine) with the word of God properly speaking. Christ is God's revelation in his continual manifestation to the man of faith. B. stresses that man can be understood only as a being-in-response. Man, as the image of God, is personally related and totally responsible to the holy, loving God. But man is also in revolt against God: he is sinfully irresponsible and must be saved by the effective action of Christ enabling man to achieve integrity through personal communion with God and his fellow men. Works in Eng. tr.: *Divine Imperative* (1937); *Man in Revolt* (1939); *Dogmatics* (3v., 1950–62); *Letter to the Romans* (1959). BIBLIOGRAPHY: *Theology of Emil Brunner* (ed. C. Kegly, 1962).

[T. M. MCFADDEN]

BRUNNER, FRANCIS DE SALES (1795–1859), founder of the American province of the Society of the Precious Blood. B. entered the Benedictines and was ordained in 1819. He did missionary work in Switzerland, but in 1829 B. left the Benedictines and joined the Trappists in Alsace. In 1838 he joined the newly formed Society of the Precious Blood in Italy and was sent back to Switzerland to make a foundation. In 1843 B. and some companions immigrated to work in north central Ohio. He worked to develop his society in the New World and succeeded in the establishment of nine religious houses. B. also established the Precious Blood Sisters in America. B. was a prolific writer on religious subjects, however, few of his works have been published and none translated from the German.

[J. HILL]

BRUNO THE CARTHUSIAN, ST. (d. 1101), founder of the Carthusian order. Born in Cologne before 1030; believed to be of a noble family, B.'s education was completed at Reims where he later became a canon; there he engaged in teaching theology, among other things. In 1056 he was master of the schools and later chancellor of the diocese in 1075. Among his students was the future pope, Urban II. Along with his intellectual interests he exercised a rigorous

interest in ecclesiastical reform, esp. among the clergy. Ultimately his energies were directed toward the life of the spirit; in response to that call he first settled at Sèche-Fontaine under the direction of Robert of Molesme, future founder of the Cistercians, but he left Reims with two friends in 1082; eventually (1084) he settled in Chartreuse and established, with the help of Hugh of Grenoble (bp.), a kind of eremetic house. He was reunited with Urban II in 1090 and both fled Rome in the summer of that year. He is credited with the composition of ascetic treatises, letters, and commentaries on the epistles of Paul. He was canonized (*viva voce*) by Leo X in 1514. BIBLIOGRAPHY: L. Oliger, EncCatt 3:148–150; H. Wolter, LTK 2:730–731; Y. Gourdel, DSAM 2.1:705–776.

[J. R. RIVELLO]

BRUNO OF COLOGNE, ST. (925–965), abp. of Cologne from 953. In 940, he became chancellor for his brother, Emperor Otto I, whom he accompanied to Italy in 951. From 961 to 965, during Otto's second trip to Italy, Bruno and his half-brother William, abp. of Mainz, were coregents of the kingdom. As abp., B. was remarkable for his personal sanctity and his ceaseless efforts to ensure the strict observance of monastic rule in the monasteries of his archdiocese. As statesman, he provided the Emperor with loyal administrators and worked uninterruptedly to establish peace in the Duchy of Lorraine and in France. BIBLIOGRAPHY: G. Allemang, DHGE 10:956–957; N. Del Re, BiblSanct 3:581–583.

[M. F. MCCARTHY]

BRUNO DE JÉSUS-MARIE (1892–1962), French Discalced Carmelite, psychologist and writer. Born Jacques Froissart, he entered the Discalced Carmelites in 1917 and was ordained in 1924. He was a specialist in the history and spirituality of his Order; from 1930 until his death he edited *Études Carmélitaines*. He was also instrumental in launching in 1933 the first Congress of Religious Psychology and pioneered in investigating psychic phenomena connected with religion. BIBLIOGRAPHY: A. Plé, "Le Père Bruno Jésus-Marie," VieS Suppl 63 (1962) 523.

[M. J. SUELZER]

BRUNO OF MAGDEBURG (d. after 1084) chronicler. In 1082, he dedicated his *Liber de bello Saxonico* for the years 1073–81 to Bp. Werner of Merseburg. Little else is known about him except that he favored the Saxons against Henry IV. His chronicle, though inaccurate, is vividly told and contains valuable, because unaltered, letters and documents of the Merseburg and Magdeburg bishoprics. BIBLIOGRAPHY: G. Allemang, DHGE 10:966–967.

[M. F. MCCARTHY]

BRUNO OF QUERFURT, ST. (Boniface; *c.*974–1009), bishop, monk, missionary, martyr. Educated at Magdeburg under St. Adalbert, B. was the friend and companion of Otto

III on a journey to Italy (996). Joining the Camaldolese and taking the name Boniface, he formulated missionary plans and was consecrated *archiepiscopus gentium* (1004). His evangelization took him to Hungary, Kievan Russia, and the Polish border (1008), where he was martyred with 18 companions. As a hagiographer, B. wrote the life of Adalbert of Prague and the martyrdom of the Polish Brothers. BIBLIOGRAPHY: J. Ostrowski, DHGE 10:963–966; C. Somigli, BiblSanct 3:583–584.

[M. H. BEIRNE]

BRUNO OF SEGNI, ST. (1049–1123), bp., abbot, hagiographer, polemicist, liturgist, exegete, papal legate. He was appointed bp. of Segni *c.* 1080 by Gregory VII. He was a firm supporter of the Holy See in the investiture struggle and was for a time imprisoned by partisans of the Emperor. He entered the monastery of Monte Cassino and became abbot in 1107 but did not resign his episcopal responsibility. His writings can be found in PL 144–145. BIBLIOGRAPHY: R. Grégoire, *Bruno de Segni, exégète médiéval et théologien monastique* (1965); Butler 3:140–141; F. Caraffa, BiblSanct 3:578–580.

BRUNO OF WÜRZBURG, ST. (*c.*1005–45), bishop and imperial counselor. Son of Conrad I of Carintha and cousin of Emperor Conrad II, B. was both chancellor of Italy and special adviser of Conrad II and Emperor Henry III. Elected bishop of Würzburg (1034), he fostered church building and education, and composed an exegesis on the Psalms. B. was killed accidentally, while traveling with Henry III to Hungary. BIBLIOGRAPHY: C. Testore, BiblSanct 3:580–581; G. Allemang, DHGE 10:972.

[M. H. BEIRNE]

BRUNO, GIORDANO (1548–1600), Neapolitan occultist philosopher-poet, burned at the stake by the Inquisition in the Campo dei Fiori, Rome. Modern interest in the man and in Brunoniana is explained less by intrinsic merit than by 19th-cent. romanticism toward all "free thinkers" and Italian nationalism (the anticlericalism and Freemasonry of which are represented by the statue of B. erected on the site of his execution). Brutal as the Inquisition was, its sentence against B. was based on his proposal of a magico-religious system (in which Christ was the great magician) to replace Christianity, and on his refusal to recant. He was neither a defender of Copernicus's proper methods, since he despised them, nor a martyr to science, since he developed his own syncretistic thought on the basis of occultism. If it is possible to isolate the philosophical elements in B.'s thought from the esoteric and Hermesian (SEE HERMES TRISMEGISTUS) he is to be classified as a pantheist, or panpsychist, and an atomist; whatever philosophic principle of organization is present in his cosmological view must be designated as Neoplatonic (he was a bitter anti-Aristotelian). But the substance of his thought on both the physical universe and on moral and religious reform derives directly from the Renaissance vogue interest in magic

and the occult. The greatest single influences on B. are the favorite Renaissance text, *De occulta philosophia* of Henricus Cornelius Agrippa and Marsiglio Ficino's *De vita caelitus comparanda.*

B. began his career as a Dominican at Naples, came under suspicion of heresy there, and apostatized from his order in 1576. From that time he began an itinerant life, lecturing in various Protestant centers before being received in France in 1581 by King Henry III. With Henry's patronage B. was received at the French embassy in London in 1583. During his stay in England he aroused an outcry against his secretly printed books and his lectures at Oxford. He also published: *La cena delle ceneri* (1584); *De l'infinito, universo e mondi* (1584); two works dedicated to Sir Philip Sydney, *Spaccio della bestia trionfante* (1584) and *De gli heroici furori* (1585). He returned to Paris in 1586 and during this next period published a series of Latin poems, also marked by occultism. Soon after returning to Italy in 1591 he was imprisoned in Venice for 8 years, then transferred to Rome where his trial by the Inquisition led to his final fate. Works: *Opere di Girodano Bruno e di Tommaso Campanella* (ed. A. Guzzo and R. Amerio, 1956). BIBLIOGRAPHY: F. A. Yates, EncPhil 1:405–408.

[J. R. RIVELLO]

BRUNSCHVICG, LÉON (1869–1944), French idealist philosopher, and historian. B. taught philosophy at various French lycées and at the Sorbonne. He also served as adviser to the government on educational reform and in the armed forces. While his philosophy is mainly concerned with mathematics and science, he devotes much time as well to the development of a process of philosophical reflection which, while it yields intellectual activity, moves toward the subject's rational self-appropriation. The process makes a progress of conscience and consciousness imperative for the subject; in the wake of such a progression, the subject then confronts the necessity for intellectual and moral conversion. For B. the primacy of intelligence is bound up with the primacy of moral development. Some have seen strands of Bergson's philosophy in B.'s thought. There is evidence also of similarity between B. and other continental philosophers. Among the influences on B. one must make mention of Kant and Descartes. Works: *La Modalité du jugement* (1897); *Les Étapes de la philosophie mathématique* (1912). *L'Expérience humaine et la causalité physique* (1922), among others. BIBLIOGRAPHY: B. Elevitch, EncPhil 1:408–409; A. R. Caponigra, NCE 2:840–841; E. Behler, LTK 2:735.

[J. R. RIVELLO]

BRUNSWICK (BRAUNSCHWEIG), important artistic center (12th cent.) under Henry the Lion. The cathedral, begun 1176, contains the tomb of Henry and Mathilda, a most important German sculpture of the 1st half of the 13th century. Brunswick housed in the past most precious collections of religious reliquaries.

[M. J. DALY]

BRUSSA (BURSA) ARCHITECTURE (1299–1501), period of Turkish architecture deriving from variety of forms erected in Brussa, the first capital of the Ottoman Empire. Important are the Mosque of Orhan Bay (1334), with roofed court; Ulu Cami (1394–99), a rectangular plan with rows of pillars, each bay crowned by a small dome; the Alauddin Mosque (1326), a single large dome over a square chamber; and the noted Green Mosque (1421), its many domed chambers flanked by smaller domed halls. BIBLIOGRAPHY: B. Unsal, *Turkish Islamic Architecture* (1959).

[M. J. DALY]

BRUSSELS, capital of Belgium and Brabant province. A predominantly Catholic city, it became in 1961 an archdiocese with Mechelen (Malines), primatial see of Belgium since 1559. St. Gery or Gaugerius (d. *c.*625) of Cambrai is credited with founding Brussels by building a chapel on an island in the Senne. A village grew up, in part because an economically important road from Flanders crossed the river at that point. In the 10th cent. the relics of St. Gudula (d. *c.*712) were taken to Brussels, and in 1047 placed in the Church of St. Michael. She became patroness of the city. Part of the diocese of Cambrai till 1559, it then was incorporated in the diocese of Mechelen, though it was held by the Calvinists from 1578 to 1585. The dukes of Brabant, who ruled the city until 1430, were succeeded by the dukes of Burgundy and then the governors of the Spanish Netherlands. The Duke of Alba (Alva), notorious for his ruthlessness, ruled the Netherlands from Brussels (1567–73), unsuccessfully seeking to root out the Protestantism of the northern provinces. Though Brussels lies slightly inside Belgium's Flemish area, most of its citizens are French-speaking. Several international bodies maintain headquarters at Brussels. BIBLIOGRAPHY: É. de Moreau, *Histoire de l'Église en Belgique* (5v., 1945–52).

[T. EARLY]

BRUT, the first English account of the Arthurian stories, translated and expanded from the Norman French poetry of Wace by the English poet Layamon (fl.1189–1207). Wace followed the story as given by Geoffrey of Monmouth in his *History of the Kings of Britain* (1137), a Latin prose account. The title comes from Brutus, the mythical founder of the British nation and the great-grandson of Aeneas. *Brut* covers a long span of British history and legend. Layamon is essentially an English poet, who loved the old stories and pictured them in a world of human action. The author is not specifically religious, but the poem is lofty, chivalrous, and noble in tone.

[M. M. BARRY]

BRUTALISM (ART BRUT), from the French *brut* (uncut, rough, raw) a 20th-cent. style ruthlessly dedicated to the blunt, frank statement of materials in their essences (undressed concrete—textured by the mold), contributing a massive, forceful sculptural quality to architecture. Brutalism was influenced by the pure structural forms in the architecture of *Mies van der Rohe. *Le Corbusier had inaugurated and dramatized brutalism in ferro-concrete structures at Unité d'Habitation, Marseilles (1947–52), Notre-Dame du Haut, *Ronchamp (1950–54), one of the great religious structures of the 20th cent., the Monastery of *La Tourette at Évreux near Lyons (1957–60) and in the awesome Assembly Building at *Chandigarh, India (1959–62). Marcel *Breuer showed an early brutalism in the Abbey Church of *St. John's, Benedictine College, Collegeville, Minnesota (1953–63), its concrete-slab bell-tower a monumental abstract sculpture in one of the most compelling religious structures in the U.S. The term "New Brutalism," coined by the English architects A. and P. Smithson (1954) extends in painting to the frank and sometimes inelegant revelation of materials by Dubuffet and the liberated media of the American abstract expressionists. BIBLIOGRAPHY: R. Banham, *New Brutalism: Ethic or Aesthetic?* (1966); A. J. Speyer, *Mies van der Rohe* (1968); S. Papadaki, *Le Corbusier: Architect, Painter, Writer* (1948).

[M. J. DALY]

BRUTALITY, acting in a cruel, insensitive, and extremely harsh way against others, usually with the connotation of physical violence. *CRUELTY; *TORTURE; *VIOLENCE.

[J. F. FALLON]

BRUTÉ DE REMUR, SIMON WILLIAM GABRIEL (1779–1839), first bp. of Vincennes, Indiana (now Archdiocese of Indianapolis); member of a wealthy French family. Ordained a Sulpician in 1808, B. came to the U.S. in 1810 and taught at St. Mary's Seminary, Baltimore and at Mt. St. Mary's College, Emmitsburg where he became Mother Seton's spiritual director. His brilliant mind and strong character were soon recognized by the American hierarchy and B. was made bp. of the frontier Diocese of Indiana and E Illinois in 1834. The subsequent 5 years were difficult ones of constant journeying, preaching, and teaching. Although he did not publish any works, his letters and diaries are valuable historically as they involve prominent Frenchmen and Americans of this era. BIBLIOGRAPHY: J. R. Bayley, *Frontier Bishop: Life of Bishop Simon Bruté* (pa. 1971); M. S. Godecker, *Simon Bruté de Remur* (1931).

[D. M. HUGHES]

BRUYÈRE, JEANNE HENRIETTE CÉCILE (1845–1909), French Benedictine abbess. Spiritual daughter of P. *Guéranger, B. collaborated with him in establishing the Abbey of St. Cecilia for Benedictine nuns at *Solesmes. She was the first abbess and provided for several daughter foundations. B. wrote *La vie spirituelle et l'oraison d'après la Sainte Écriture et la tradition monastique*, which was first circulated privately, then published in 1899, corrected in 1909, and was tr. into many languages, including English. Prayer based on Scripture and liturgy is presented as the center and the source of the spiritual life. Some have questioned B.'s slighting of systematic methods of meditation, BIBLIOGRAPHY: J. de Puniet, DSAM 1:1972–74.

[T. C. O'BRIEN]

BRUYNE, DONATIEN DE, see DE BRUYNE, DONATIEN.

BRYENNIOS, JOSEPH (1350–1432), Byzantine monk and theologian, one of the last great theologians before the fall of Constantinople. Following the hesychastic movement he defended the dogmas of the Orthodox Church, esp. the dogma of the Trinity. He was sent to Crete in 1381 to defend the Orthodox position against Roman propaganda on the part of the Venetians. Twenty years later he was forced to leave the island because of his strong criticism of the local clergy. In 1405 he went to Cyprus to recall the Catholic Uniates to Orthodoxy and presided over a local synod, denouncing the public life of the clergy. He wanted union with Rome but not submission. The work of B. is principally theological but also social. His writings consist mainly of homilies and controversial tracts. BIBLIOGRAPHY: Beck 749–750.

[P. FOSCOLOS]

BRYENNIOS, PHILOTHEUS (1833–1914), Orthodox scholar and metropolitan. He attended the universities of Leipzig, Berlin, and Munich (1856–61), was ordained priest (1863), and held many important teaching and administrative positions. He was named metropolitan of Serrai in 1875 and 2 years later became metropolitan of Nicomedia, a post he held until his retirement (1912). He is best known for the discovery, in the hospice of the Church of the Holy Sepulcher in Constantinople, of an 11th cent. Greek MS containing the *Didache*. This he published at Constantinople in 1883. BIBLIOGRAPHY: EncCatt 3:163.

[H. DRESSLER]

BRYUSOV, VALERI YAKOVLEVICH (1873–1924), Russian symbolist writer; founder of the symbolist journal *The Scales* (1904). After 1917, he joined the Communist Party and held an official position in the commissariat for education. The metrical experiments, exotic language and imagery, and *fin de siècle* decadence of his earlier collections of poems (*Chefs d'oeuvres* [1895]; *Me eum esse* [1897]) found ready acceptance among the Moscow symbolists. Later collections (*Tertia Vigilia* [1900], *Urbi et Orbi* [1903], *Stephanos* [1905]) treat themes of erotic love and "urbanism," not, however, without eschatological undertones of destruction and dread. Bryusov is also the author of plays (e.g., *The Earth* [1905]); short stories on fantastic themes, which reveal the influence of Poe; novels (e.g., *The Fire Angel* [1907]); and translations from French, Armenian, and

English. BIBLIOGRAPHY: R. Poggioli, *Poets of Russia: 1890–1930* (1960) 96–105, passim; Georgette Donchin, *Influence of French Symbolism on Russian Poetry* (1958).

[M. F. MCCARTHY]

BUBASTIS, in Lower Egypt on the E Nile, site of the ruins of a temple to the goddess Bast begun by Cheops and Chephren and remodeled by Rameses II, showing the earliest examples of the Hathoric capital, a cubic block having two sides carved with the face of Hathor. BIBLIOGRAPHY: E. Naville, *Bubastis and the Festival Hall of Osorkon II* (1891–92).

[M. J. DALY]

BUBER, MARTIN (1878–1965), Jewish religious and social philosopher. B. was born in Vienna and received his doctorate there in 1904. Following this he made an intensive study of Hasidism, which became an important influence in his life. He early became a Zionist, emphasizing, however, its cultural rather than its political aspects. After some years of editorial work in Vienna and Berlin he moved to Frankfurt (1923), where he taught in the Free Jewish Academy founded by F. Rosenzweig (1886–1929) and at the Univ. of Frankfurt. Forced from the latter position in 1933, he remained active in the German Jewish community until 1938, when he became professor of social philosophy at Hebrew Univ., Jerusalem, a post he held until 1951. Author of many scholarly works and, with Rosenzweig, translator of the Bible into German, he was best known for *I and Thou* (1923), a short book in a poetic, allusive style influenced by Nietzsche. He emphasized the difference between the I-thou relationship and the I-it. His view of personal relationship has influenced numerous Christian theologians, including E. *Brunner and F. *Gogarten, particularly in their views of revelation. BIBLIOGRAPHY: M. Diamond, *Martin Buber* (1960); R. C. Zaehner, *Christianity and Other Religions* (1964).

[T. EARLY]

BUCCERONI, GENNARO (1841–1918), Italian Jesuit theologian. During political crises of 1860 he left Italy and studied philosophy and theology in Belgium. In 1884 he returned to Rome to teach moral theology at the Gregorian Univ. and became a member of the commission to write the Code of Canon Law. BIBLIOGRAPHY: E. Lamalle, EncCatt 3:165.

[C. CARROLL]

BUCELIN, GABRIEL (Buzlin) (1599–1681), Benedictine church historian. When war threatened, B. fled from Weingarten to Switzerland and to Admont, where he could resume his writing. He returned to Weingarten 3 months before he died. Among his monastic, profane, and church history writings are *Historiae universalis nucleus* (1658) and *Germania topo-chrono-stemmatographica sacra et profana*

(4 v., 1655–78). He wrote more than 50 studies of phases of German history. BIBLIOGRAPHY: T. Stump, "Gabriel Bucelin" in *Festschrift zur 900-Jahr-Feier des Klosters, 1056–1956* (ed. G. Spahr, 1956) 370–395; *idem*, LTK 2:737–738.

[L. MITCHELL]

BUCER, MARTIN (Butzer; 1491–1551), leading figure in both the continental and English Reformation. He was born in Alsace, at Schlettstadt, where in 1506 he entered the Dominican Order. At Heidelberg, through Luther's disputation there in 1518, he became convinced of Reformation teaching; in 1521 he received papal dispensation from his religious vows; in Landstuhl he was excommunicated in 1523 for his Lutheran preaching. He became a pastor at Strassburg and worked with W. *Capito to implement the reform in the city. He also promoted the Reformation in Hesse, Ulm, Augsburg, and elsewhere. He was one of the first priests to marry (1522); after his first wife's death (1541) he married the widow of Capito. In 1548 at the invitation of T. *Cranmer he went to England and became regius professor of divinity at Cambridge until his death. His bones were disinterred and burned during Mary Tudor's reign, but the dust from the execution site was reburied at Great St. Mary's Church when Elizabeth I came to the throne.

B.'s attempts to conciliate in the disputes between the Lutheran and the Swiss segments of the Reformation brought him into disrepute with both sides. His church order at Strassburg formed the basis for the one developed at Geneva by John Calvin, who worked with B. at Strassburg, 1538–41. He also contributed to Calvin's theology of predestination. In the disputes over the Real Presence, B. was largely responsible for the conference at Marburg between Luther and Zwingli in 1527 (see MARBURG ARTICLES); he collaborated in the formulation of the *Tetrapolitan Confession (1530); and the *Wittenberg Concord (1536). His own *receptionism concerning the Real Presence attempted to mediate between the Lutheran and Zwinglian interpretations. B. participated as well in several efforts at conciliation between Protestants and Catholics both in Germany and in France. He developed a theory of the Church as an extension of the incarnation and as the true communion of saints, transforming the whole social and political sphere with works of charity and mercy. These views were contained in his chief work, *De regno Christi* (posthumous, 1557). His departure from Germany was based on the conviction that the Augsburg Interim was an interference of the State with the realm of conscience. In England B. was largely responsible both for the ordinal of 1550, which rephrased the ordination formula (see ORDINALS, ANGLICAN), and for the 1552 revision of the *Book of Common Prayer. BIBLIOGRAPHY: H. Eels, *Martin Bucer* (1931); C. Hopf, *Martin Bucer and the English Reformation* (1946); *Common Places of Martin Bucer* (tr. and ed. D. F. Wright, 1972).

[T. C. O'BRIEN]

BUCH, MICHEL HENRI (1598–1666), Belgian shoemaker. B. strove to turn the workmen of Paris away from secret societies because of the immorality of some of their practices. His community of Worker Brothers, men who followed a religious life but without vows, spread quickly through France and the neighboring countries and lasted until the French Revolution. BIBLIOGRAPHY: A. Bessières, *Deux grands inconnus: G. de Renty et Henri Buch* (1931); A. Van den Wyngaert, DHGE 10:1021.

[M. J. SUELZER]

BUCHANAN, GEORGE (1506–82), Scottish humanist and historian. B. studied at Paris and Scotland and taught humanities in France, Scotland, and Portugal. He attacked the Franciscans in *Somnium* and *Franciscanus*. He returned to Scotland in 1561 and was an acknowledged Calvinist. At Bordeaux, where Montaigne was one of his pupils, he wrote two original dramas: *Jephthes* and *Baptistes*. B. was an instructor to Mary Queen of Scots, and also to James VI, her son. His two works, *De jure regni apud Scotos* and *Rerum Scoticarum historia* reflected his political theories concerning the revolution of 1567 which deposed Mary. He gained a wide reputation in Europe until the time when Fr. Thomas Innes's *Critical Essay* revealed that B. was not true to history, esp. in the matter of the Casket Letters which were first made known in B.'s *Detectio Mariae reginae scotorum*. His reputation as one of the greatest postclassical Latin writers of his time is less valid as more Scottish humanists are discovered. BIBLIOGRAPHY: V. Gabrieli, EncCatt 3:168; P. H. Brown, *G. Buchanan, Humanist and Reformer* (1890).

[L. MITCHELL]

BUCHAREST, PATRIARCH OF, the head of the autocephalous Orthodox Church in Romania. More properly his title is abp. of Bucharest, metropolitan of Ungrovalachia, and patriarch of Romania. In 1865, the Orthodox Church in Romania announced its independence from the patriarchate of Constantinople, after Colonel Alexander Ion Cuza (1859–1866) became prince of the principalities of Walachia and Moldavia, and ordered compulsory civil marriage, secularized monasteries, and made the Church autocephalous, answerable only to the State. When Constantinople finally recognized its autocephalous status, its metropolitan was declared primate of Romania (1885) and included Romanian Churches in Transylvania and Bukovina (Austria-Hungary). With the formation of the kingdom of Romania after World War I, the Romanian patriarchate was erected and the abp. of Bucharest designated as patriarch by the Holy Synod (1925). Before World War II his patriarchate numbered 5 metropolitanates with 18 dioceses. After 1948, the Communist government reduced the number of dioceses to 12. The five archiepiscopal sees include (1) Ungrovalachia of which the abp. of Bucharest and patriarch is chief with its two suffragan eparchies Buzau and Galatzi; (2) Moldavia-Succava with a see at Jassy and one suffragan eparchy of Roman-Husi; (3) Oltenia with a see at Craiova and one suffragan eparchy, Rimnic-Arges; (4) Transylvania with the see at Sibiu and two suffragan eparchies, Cluj and Oradea; and (5) Banat with a see at Timisoara and one suffragan eparchy, Arad. BIBLIOGRAPHY: M. Lacko, NCE 12:714–716; R. W. Seton-Watson, *History of the Roumanians* (1934); J. Georgesco, DTC 14.1:17–101.

[F. H. BRIGHAM]

BUCHEZ, PHILIPPE JOSEPH BENJAMIN (1796–1865), French social theorist. Although B. was trained as a physician, he was primarily interested in promoting social change. With A. Bazard he founded *La charbonnerie française* (1821), which aimed at the overthrow of the Bourbons and the convocation of a national assembly. He became a convert to Catholicism in 1829 but was dissatisfied with the social thinking accepted among his coreligionists and founded what was called the Neo-Catholic school of social theory (Buchezism). Originally a follower of Saint-Simon, he adopted a position that foreshadowed Christian socialism. He was a strong proponent of associations of workers and credit unions. BIBLIOGRAPHY: E. T. Gargan, NCE 2:845.

[M. J. SUELZER]

BUCHMAN, FRANK NATHAN DANIEL (1878–1961), founder of *Moral Re-Armament (MRA). Born at Pennsburg, Pa., B. was an ordained Lutheran minister when he experienced a religious conversion at Keswick, Eng., in 1908. This led him to develop new evangelistic methods aimed at changing the world by changing men. He continued his religious work and study in the U.S. until 1921, when he returned to England. With university members of both Oxford and Cambridge, he formed an organization for personal and world betterment called the First Century Christian Fellowship, later (1929) the Oxford Group, and finally (1938) Moral Re-Armament. B.'s evangelical program had great success, especially among students and members of the upper classes, primarily as a way of personal holiness; at the outbreak of World War II many dissociated themselves from the MRA because of disappointment with it as a way to world peace; after the war it enjoyed some resurgence, esp. as an anticommunist crusade. Throughout its history the movement has been guided fundamentally by B.'s principles: adherence to the Four Absolutes—purity, unselfishness, honesty and love; public confession of sins as a step toward conversion; surrender to the will of Christ and to divine guidance. B. traveled widely promoting his ideas and experienced some opposition from churchmen and university authorities. His views are contained in his work *Remaking the World* (1947). BIBLIOGRAPHY: bibliog. for Moral Re-Armament.

[W. WHALEN]

BUCHMANISM, a name, sometimes used disparagingly, for *Moral Re-armament (MRA), after the founder Frank *Buchman.

[T. C. O'BRIEN]

BUCHNER, ALOIS (1783–1869), theologian. B. taught dogma at Dillingen, Würzburg, and Munich. From 1840 to 1857 he was rector of the theological faculty of the Lyceum at Passau. His chief works are a *summa* of dogmatic theology (4 v. 1838–39) and a theological encyclopedia (1837). BIBLIOGRAPHY: M. Schmaus, NCE 2:846.

BÜCHNER, GEORG (1813–37), German writer. In a short lifetime, B. produced four memorable works: *Dantons Tod* (1835), a psychological drama; *Woyzek* (1836), a powerfully realistic drama about a life without meaning; *Leonce und Lena* (1836), a romantic comedy; and *Lenz,* an unfinished novella. His themes and his treatment of them anticipate those of naturalism and expressionism at the end of the 19th century. BIBLIOGRAPHY: H. Lindenberger, *Georg Büchner* (1964).

[M. F. MCCARTHY]

BUCK, PEARL (1892–1973), American novelist. Daughter of American missionaries, apologist for China whose topology and culture she knew minutely, B. experienced the ferment wrought by modern ideas on traditional Chinese custom and culture. She merits attention not because of her religious preferences but because of her optimistic universality. Man's spiritual quest, as well as his terrestrial struggles, is her focus. Her regard for the Chinese peasant forces a comparison with Tolstoy. Unfortunately, her literary artistry suffers because of her polemical and social bent. She won the Pulitzer Prize (1932) for *The Good Earth,* which later supported her claim to the Nobel Prize (1938), along with *This Proud Heart* and others. BIBLIOGRAPHY: P. A. Doyle, *Pearl S. Buck* (1965); T. F. Harris, *Pearl S. Buck: A Biography* (2v., 1969).

[R. M. FUNCHION]

BÜCKERS, HERMANN JOSEPH (1900–64), Redemptorist biblical scholar. Ordained in 1926, B. completed his doctoral studies at the Pontifical Biblical Institute in 1937. Most of his teaching career was spent at the seminary at Hennef near Cologne, where he lectured on OT topics and collaborated on a new German translation of the OT. In his doctoral dissertation B. advanced the view that the doctrine of immortality in the Book of Wisdom was attributable to the author's rational speculation and the influence of Hellenism. BIBLIOGRAPHY: W. Pesch, NCE 2:846.

[M. J. SUELZER]

BUCKFAST, ABBEY OF, Benedictine monastery in Devonshire, England. Buckfast was founded in 1018, became a part of the Savigny Congregation in 1136, then Cistercian in 1147 when a new church was built. Buckfast was suppressed in 1538; but in 1882 was reestablished by monks from La-Pierre-qui-Vire, France, and from Germany. Under the second abbot, Anscar *Vonier, the church was rebuilt (1906-22) on the old foundations. The monks are well-known for their scientific work in bee-keeping. BIBLIOGRAPHY: J. Stéphan, *Buckfast Abbey* (1923); idem, NCE 2:846.

[J. R. SOMMERFELDT]

BUCKLAND, ABBEY OF, Cistercian monastery in Devonshire, England. Amicia, countess of Devon, founded Buckland in 1278 on Dartmoor. Buckland was a daughterhouse of Quarr and was of moderate size and wealth. The last abbot, John Tucker, secured his position through the pressure of the Marquis of Exeter, patron by grant of Henry VIII. Tucker surrendered the abbey to the crown in 1538 after having made ample provision for himself and his relatives. BIBLIOGRAPHY: C. Gill, *Buckland Abbey* (rev. ed., 1956); C. H. Talbot, NCE 2:846.

[J. R. SOMMERFELDT]

BUCKLER, REGINALD (1840–1927), English Dominican spiritual writer. A Catholic from 1855, a Dominican from 1856, a priest from 1863, B. completed his long and varied ministry by serving as a missionary in the West Indies (1911–27). His spiritual classic, *The Perfection of Man,* was first published in 1889. He also wrote several other treatises on the religious life. BIBLIOGRAPHY: S. Bullough, NCE 2:847.

[M. J. SUELZER]

BUCKLEY, JOHN, see JONES, JOHN, ST.

BUCOLICS, pastoral poems pertaining to shepherd life in rustic settings, esp. Sicilian in its origin. Nymphs, satyrs, and love of nature are also conventions. Theocritus, a Greek poet of the 3d cent. B.C., is credited with writing the earliest recorded pastoral poetry, a type notable in general for simplicity of thought and action. It is not confined to poetry but embraces drama and fiction as well. Theocritus was followed by a giant figure in Roman and world literature, *Virgil, whose *Bucolics (Eclogues)* appeared in 37 B.C. From the idyls of Theocritus come the well-known pastoral characters called Daphnis, Amaryllis, Lycidas, Corydon, and others. The pastoral eclogue enjoyed a revival during the Renaissance. English literature provides familiar examples. Sir Philip Sydney's *Arcadia* (1590) is a prose romance in pastoral garb. Spenser's *Shepherds' Calendar* (1579) uses the pastoral as a vehicle for political and religious discussion. Many of the love lyrics of Shakespeare, Marlowe, and others have a pastoral setting. In drama, a well-known example is Shakespeare's *As You Like It.* Milton's *Lycidas* and his companion poems *L'Allegro* and *Il Penseroso* utilize the conventions. *Lycidas,* a great elegy, introduces a new note. In connection with Edward King's death, this poem touches on immortality, Milton's career, and on corruption in the Church—all within the pastoral framework. Shelley's

Adonais and Matthew Arnold's *Thyrsis* are also considered great pastoral elegies. The tradition still lives in modern culture in such areas as art, music, and the ballet. BIBLIOGRAPHY: G. Highet, *Classical Tradition* (1949); T. G. Rosenmeyer, *Green Cabinet: Theocritus and the European Pastoral Lyric* (1969).

[S. A. HEENEY]

BUCOVINA, a region of east central Europe N and E of the Carpathians, S of Galicia, W of the Prut River, and bounded on the S by the Romanian province of Moldavia. The metropolis is Chernovtsy (Russian) or Cernauti (Romanian), a city of about 100,000 inhabitants. The population numbered 500,000 in the old Romanian province with about 200,500 of Romanian nationality, and about an equal number of Ukrainians. The whole population is Orthodox, depending upon the abp. of Chernovtsy. The post-World War II arrangements in Bucovina divided the province with the Ukrainians of the North becoming a part of the Ukrainian Soviet Socialist Republic and thus a part of the Moscow patriarchate, while the Romanians of the South, including the capital city, remained under the patriarch of Bucharest. However, there still remain about 2,500,000 Orthodox Romanians both in northern Bucovina and in Bessarabia under the Moscow patriarchate. There is an Orthodox faculty of theology at the Univ. of Chernovtsy where the clergy can receive their theological formation. Some of its professors are contributing solid work to one or more of the four theological publications allowed in Romania at present by the Communist regime.

[A. WALKER]

BUDAPEST, capital of Hungary formerly of the Hungarian moiety of the Dual Monarchy, a single municipality since 1872 combining the united towns of Buda and Obuda on the right bank of the Danube and Pest on the left. Obuda, a well-known military colony of the Roman Empire for over 400 years was the residence of Hungarian kings for a short time. Buda, the century-old Hungarian capital was the seat of the Holy Roman Empire under Emperor Sigismund (1368-1437), and Pest was a trade center for over 1,000 years. After the destruction (1241) of Obuda (then a flourishing German town) by the Mongols, Buda became capital until the conquest of the Turks (1527) who held it from 1541 until 1686 while Pest was utterly destroyed and did not recover until the 1st half of the 18th century. Established as a Renaissance center of Western Christendom with its famous library by Matthew Corvinus (1458–1490), it was changed to a city of Oriental character during the domination of the Ottoman Turks. Now under Communist rule, its economic and cultural recovery from the destruction of World War II and the abortive resistance of Freedom Fighters in 1956 has been slow. BIBLIOGRAPHY: W. Juhász, NCE 7:255–266; F. Dvornik, *Making of Central and Eastern Europe* (1949).

[F. H. BRIGHAM]

BUDDE, KARL FERDINAND REINHARDT (1850–1933), German biblical scholar, who made major contributions to modern OT studies, esp. in his analysis of the sources of the *Pentateuch and his investigation into Israelite religion. BIBLIOGRAPHY: E. Würthwein, NDB 2:714–716; E. Kutsch, RGG 1:1468–69.

[T. C. O'BRIEN]

BUDDHA (enlightened), a title particularly applied to Siddhārtha Gautama of the Sakyas (*c.*560 B.C.–*c.*480 B.C.). His life is wrapped in many legends. He was born in N India where his father was a feudal lord. According to the standards of his day, his upbringing was luxurious, and at 16, he married a neighboring princess. Despite all this, during his 20s he experienced a discontent that led him to break completely with his worldly estate. This discontent was embedded in the legend of the Four Passing Sights—old age, disease, death, and the possibility of withdrawal from the world. To answer the question, "Where is the realm of life in which there is neither age nor death?" he determined to follow the call of a truth-seeker. When he was 29, he made his "Great Going Forth." He bade his wife and their son a silent good-bye as they slept, and left to seek enlightenment, asceticism, and mystic concentration. One night he sat beneath a fig tree (Bo tree, short for Bodhi [enlightenment] tree). Here he was tempted but persevered in meditation until Gautama's being was transformed and came forth the Buddha (the Enlightened One). After 45 years of arduous and loving ministry to all in need in N India, he died at the age of 80. B. is considered one of the greatest personalities of all times. BIBLIOGRAPHY: *Teachings of the Compassionate Buddha* (ed. E. A. B., 1955); T. Berry, *Religions of India* (1971); *Buddhist Tradition: In India, China and Japan* (ed. W. T. de Bary, pa. 1972). *BUDDHISM.

[C. CARROLL]

BUDDHISM, the religion of the followers of Gautama Buddha, originated in India in the 6th cent. B.C. and remained one of that country's predominant religions until 1000 A.D. Based on the Buddha's teachings—mostly in sermons and discourses—of his unique doctrine, Buddhism was its founder's means of protest against the rigidly ritualized Vedic religion that predominated in India at the time.

The Buddhist, according to the Buddha's Wheel of Doctrine, finds true happiness in life by rejecting worldly values and gaining a complete knowledge of his inner self. By following the paths defined in the Four Noble Truths, he achieves a complete cessation of pain—the state known as *nirvana*. The Buddha held that life's suffering had its roots in spiritual and physical craving, and that pain ceases only when the individual controls his craving through "rightness" in thought and deed.

The principles and precepts of Buddhism are diametrically opposed to those of other religions of Asia. Unlike Hindus, Buddhists do not believe that man's soul transmigrates, a complete and unchanging unit, from one life to the next; they believe that each deed, good or bad, brings like consequences. The Buddhist's objective is to live "rightly," bringing therefore only good in return for good. (The Eightfold Path, defining right view, right thought, right action, right livelihood, right effort, right mindfulness, right concentration, and right speech, provides a general guideline for Buddhist life.) The law of causality figures so prominently in Buddhism that it is used to explain cycles of life as the Buddhist transmigrates toward *nirvana*. There are 12 states of being in the individual, each of which supposedly determines the occurrence of another. Sensations, activities, mental impressions, and life's stages of physical development are included in the 12, and each functions as a means of passing cyclically from birth to death to birth again, and, eventually, to *nirvana*–the result of right living and complete enlightenment.

Gautama Buddha organized his movement's disciples into a religious order known as the Sangha. The monks of the Sangha were not separated by rank or privilege; they lived an extremely austere life which consisted mainly of alms-begging, prayer, meditation, and the teaching of Buddhist doctrines to the laity. About 100 years after Gautama's death, this large monastic community split into two schools—the School of Elders (Theravada) and the School of the Great Assembly (Mahasanghika). The School of Elders favored a more orthodox perpetuation of old Buddhist doctrine than did the School of the Great Assembly. Further fragmentation of the Buddhist clergy resulted in formation of about 20 new monastic sects, and missionaries were sent by these groups throughout Asia. Through efforts made by the School of the Great Assembly, many changes in Buddhist doctrine were effected. The crystallization of this movement toward more liberal interpretation of Buddhist precepts resulted in a new kind of Buddhism—Mahayana. Claiming to be a deeper, more significant examination of the Buddha's thoughts and teachings, the Mahayana differed from the Theravada in that it held that the followers of Buddha were capable of *becoming* a Buddha by becoming a Bodhisattva—one who has vowed to become a Buddha, rather than attempting, as a Theravadin would attempt, to become, through adherence to the Buddha's teachings, as much like him as he is able. Faith, in Theraviadin Buddhism, is belief in the truth as taught by Buddha; in Mahayanist Buddhism, faith is belief in worthiness granted the faithful worshiper of a Bodhisattva.

In China and Japan, where Buddhist missionary influence left indelible marks on Oriental culture, another major type of Buddhism arose. The Zen (Meditation) movement, dating from the 7th cent. A.D., itself split into two sects—Rinzai and Sōtō (both Japanese spellings). A special practice of Rinzai is meditation upon paradoxes in order to discover new truths beyond mere logic; in Sōtō, silent meditation while in a sitting position is a means of preparing for moments of spiritual illumination. (Sōtō Zen is more widely practiced among the Orient's working classes than is Rinzai, primarily because Rinzai has had, from its beginnings, affiliations with the established aristocracy.)

In modern times, Buddhism—both Theravada and Mahayana—has maintained the bond between the Sangha and the laity, though there are differences in this relationship on both sides. While the Theravadin monks (orange-robed, tonsured, and called, in Indian Pali dialect, *bhikkus*) do not permit much participation by the laity in religious practice (though it is not unusual for a young man to join the Sangha temporarily in order to benefit from the teaching of senior monks), there is much more variety and participation in Mahayanist religious practice on the layman's part. While the Theravadin clergy serves the lay community in a direct manner, with sermons and ritual participation in burials, monastic ordinations, and festivals such as the Wesak (celebration of Buddha's birth, enlightenment, and death), social services in the Mahayana are somewhat more institutionalized.

The basic doctrinal differences between the Theravada and the Mahasanghika also serve to divide the body of Buddhist religious-philosophical literature. The literature of the Theravada is in Pali dialect, the language in which Gautama Buddha first presented it; it consists of the Tipitaka (three collections) of Buddha's sermons and discourses, transcribed directly from their oral presentations of Buddha and his followers. The literature of the Mahayana is much more expansive, and is grouped in three subdivisions: treatises (*sastras*), discourses (*sutras*), and monastic rules (*vinaya*). Though the Mahayana retains the orthodox doctrines of Theravadin Buddhism, interpretation of them is considerably more liberal. The *sastras* deal with the question of what constitutes Ultimate Reality; *sutras* are many and varied, but perhaps the one that is most prominent in the Mahayana's literary tradition is the Maharatnakuta (Heap of Jewels) which combines 49 discourses on a number of topics; *sastras* deal with problems of thought, consciousness, and enlightenment.

In 1974 Buddhists accounted for more than half the populations of Japan, Thailand, Burma, Cambodia, Laos, and Tibet. The number of Buddhists in the entire world was estimated to be more than 223,000,000. BIBLIOGRAPHY: *Buddhism* (ed. R. A. Gard, 1961); E. Conze, *Buddhism: Its Essence and Development* (1951); H. de Lubac, *La Rencontre du Bouddhisme et de l'occident* (1952); M. Spiro, *Buddhism and Society* (pa. 1972); J. Blofeld, *Beyond the Gods: Buddhist and Taoist Mysticism* (pa. 1974). *ZEN BUDDHISM.

[D. H. BRUNAUER]

BUDDHIST CHURCHES OF AMERICA (BCA), association formed in 1942 and comprising 60 U.S. Buddhist churches at the time of its 1974 report. Buddhism was established in the U.S. by Japanese-Americans in 1899, after its establishment earlier in the century by Chinese and Japanese immigrants. The Buddhist Mission of North America was organized in 1914. In the U.S., Buddhism has taken on many of the organizational patterns of American Christian Churches, and has established youth associations, periodicals, Sunday Schools, and social service agencies. BCA is headed by a president and executive secretary, and its religious life directed by a bishop. It maintains an Institute of Buddhist Studies at Berkeley, Calif., for the training of ministers. Headquarters are in San Francisco.

[T. EARLY]

BUDDHIST MISSION OF NORTH AMERICA, see BUDDHIST CHURCHES OF AMERICA.

BUDDHIST MONASTICISM, a movement of Buddhist groups pledged to poverty and chastity and historically forming the organizational center of Buddhism, though lay Buddhist associations have emerged in recent years. Buddha is said to have outlined monastic rules for the men who followed him as disciples, and at the request of his foster mother to have founded an order for nuns. The community of Buddhist monks is known as the Sangha, with the Buddha and the Dharma (Buddha's teaching) one of the three valued components of Buddhism. For those who joined Buddha's monastic order the traditional caste distinctions were eliminated. Any male might join, provided he was not sick, disabled, a criminal, a soldier, a debtor, or a minor lacking parental consent. Monks were required to wear the yellow robe, shave their heads, carry the begging bowl, meditate daily, make an initiate's confession, and obey certain precepts. The monasteries came to be the center of Buddhist life and esp. important for Hinayana Buddhism, the prevailing form in Ceylon, Burma, Thailand, Laos, Vietnam, and Cambodia. They have been the intellectual centers of Buddhism, and taking a strong role in society they have sometimes been important political centers. Prior to the 1950 takeover by China the monks of Tibet held total political power. Generally Buddhist laymen support the monks in return for religious instruction, with laymen commonly spending some months at a monastery. BIBLIOGRAPHY: *Buddhism* (ed. R. A. Gard, 1961); S. Dutt, *Early Monastic Buddhism* (1941).

[T. EARLY]

BUDÉ, GUILLAUME (1467–1540), French humanist who played an important role in the revival and progress of Greek studies. Proficient in theology, philosophy, mathematics, law, and medicine, he studied Greek under John Lascaris, noted Byzantine émigré humanist, and became one of the world's foremost authorities in the field. Sent by Louis XII as ambassador to Rome for the coronation of Julius II (1502) and again on a mission to Leo X (1515), he directed the Fontainebleau Library, origin of the Bibliothèque Nationale, and obtained from Francis I permission to found the Collège des lecteurs royaux (1530), which later became the Collège de France, for the study of Latin, Greek, and Hebrew. In his *Commentarii linguae graecae* (1529) he urged the study of Greek letters and departed from the scholastic spirit; however, desiring to reconcile the Renaissance spirit with Christianity, he demonstrated this possibility in his *De transitu hellenismi ad christianismum libri III* (1535). He is also author of *Annotationes in XXIV libros Pandectarum* (1508), on Roman law; *De asse et partibus eius* (1514), on Roman money, displaying his ability as philologist, archeologist, and numismatist; and *L'Institution du prince* (1547). Among his correspondents were Thomas More and Erasmus. Although B. had been one of the judges who condemned the humanist Louis de Berquin to be burned as a heretic (1529), he was for a while considered to have Calvinist leanings. After his death, his wife and two sons, Jean and Louis, converted to Calvinism and as professor of Oriental languages at Geneva, Louis translated into French the Hebrew Psalter (1551). BIBLIOGRAPHY: J. Plattard, *Guillaume Budé et les origines de l'humanisme français* (1923); A. Roersch, DHGE 10:1040–41.

[R. N. NICOLICH]

BUDOC, ST. (*c.* 6th cent.), name applied to several saints. Possibly son of King Goello of Brittany and Azenor, daughter of the king of Brest, B. entered the monastery near Waterford, Ireland, became abbot, and later succeeded St. Maglorious at Dol. Other traditions call him the founder of the settlements at Beuzec-Cap-Caval and Beuzec-Cap-Sizun, and the teacher of St. Winwaloe. He may also have been an Irish hermit who settled at Budock near Falmouth. BIBLIOGRAPHY: F. O'Briain and A. M. Raggi, BiblSanct 3:586–587; Butler 4:525–526.

[M. H. BEIRNE]

BUENHOMBRE, ALFONSUS DE, see ALFONSUS BONIHOMINIS.

BUFALO, GASPARE DEL, ST. (1786–1837), founder of the Society of the Precious Blood. Ordained in 1808 B. was appointed canon of San Nicola in Carcere. Because he refused to swear allegiance to Napoleon I, he was exiled for 4 years. Upon his return to Rome he founded (1815) his society and thereafter worked particularly in the Papal States and the Kingdom of Naples. He was canonized in 1954. BIBLIOGRAPHY: G. Cepites, BiblSanct 6:40–43.

[R. C. TOLLARICO]

BUFFET, BERNARD (1928–), French painter developing a highly personal style. A social realist, B. expressed with broken black lines and sombre palette the pathos, anguish, and anger of a tragic postwar world; his angular, elongated forms caught in a contemporary Gothic silence and immobility. Bottles and plates attain a like monumentality on B.'s plateau of transcendence. His intense *misérablisme* informs the *Descent from the Cross* (1948), *La Passion* (1952), panels on the life and death of Joan of Arc, illustrations for J. *Cocteau's La Voix humaine*, and his series on the *Passion of Christ* (1962) in the chapel of Chateau d'Arc.

B's figural works are a reaction to *tachism and geometric abstraction. BIBLIOGRAPHY: D. Fabre, *Bernard Buffet: Exposition rétrospective* (1959). *ABSTRACT ART.

[M. J. DALY]

BUFFIER, CLAUDE (1661–1737), French philosopher and author. B. entered the Jesuits (1679) and later taught literature and the humanities in Paris and theology at Rouen. He published works on history, asceticism, biography, education, and esp. philosophy. His *Traité des vérités premières,* in which he attempts to discover the ultimate principle of knowledge, established his reputation as a philosopher. He also wrote *Grammaire française sur un plan nouveau* (1701), often reprinted, and *Eléments de métaphysique* (1724) which was translated into several languages. BIBLIOGRAPHY: A. De Bil, DHGE 10:1083–87; Bréhier HistPhil 2:331–334.

[L. MITCHELL]

BUGENHAGEN, JOHANN (1485–1558), a close associate of Martin Luther in the early years of the Reformation. Born at Wollim, Pomerania—thus called Pomeranus or Dr. Pomer—he was a Premonstratensian Canon, who became a well-known humanist, and was attracted to biblical studies by Erasmus. By 1521 he had embraced Lutheranism, taught at the Univ. of Wittenberg, exercised pastoral duties there, and was Luther's confidant and confessor. He was the first Reformation priest to marry (1522) and he officiated at Luther's own marriage (1525). B. remained an enthusiastic defender of the Lutheran system, encouraged the British to join in the Reformation, and wrote strongly against Zwinglian eucharistic teaching. He helped Luther translate the Bible into German, and was commissioned to organize the Lutheran Church in the N German provinces and in Denmark. His *church orders helped shape the Reformation in those places. In 1537 he crowned King Christian III and his consort as monarchs of Denmark and consecrated seven men as superintendents (i.e., bishops) of the Lutheran Church, disregarding *apostolic succession. At Luther's funeral, he was chosen to preach the eulogy of his master, the man "through whom has Christ now conquered for nearly thirty years." BIBLIOGRAPHY: W. Tillmanns, *World and the Men around Luther* (1954) 90–94; E. W. Zeeden, *Legacy of Luther* (tr. R. M. Bethell, 1954).

[P . DAMBORIENA]

BUGGING, see WIRETAPPING.

BUGIA, a small candlestick with a short handle. It is held near the Missal at the Mass of a bishop or of certain other church dignitaries. It came into use at a time when additional candlelight for reading from the book was helpful; its use was abolished from the liturgy in 1968. The name is derived from Bougie in NE Algeria, which was a source of wax.

[N. KOLLAR]

BUGLIO, LUDOVICO (1606–82), Jesuit missionary and theologian. Born in Mineo, Sicily, of a noble family, B. was sent to China in 1637 where he suffered great persecution for his faith. He was taken prisoner but was later freed to exercise his ministry. He spoke and wrote Chinese fluently, collaborated with Fr. Magalhaens and others in the reform of the Chinese calendar, and produced more than 80 volumes in Chinese, for the most part to relate and to defend the Christian religion. He translated into Chinese Parts I and III of the *Summa* of St. Thomas, the Roman Missal, the Breviary, and the Ritual. B. also taught the technique of perspective to Chinese artists. BIBLIOGRAPHY: A. De Bil, DHGE 10:1090–93; E. Lamalle, Enc Catt 3:189–190; G. H. Dunne, *Generation of Giants* (1962).

[L. MITCHELL]

BUKOFZER, MANFRED (1910–55), musicologist. A native of Germany, he studied there and in Basel, Switzerland, where he completed his doctorate. He then came to the U.S. via England, and taught at the Univ. of California, Berkeley, until his death. One of the most brilliant of modern musicologists, he specialized in medieval English music and published a number of important studies on it and related topics, often solving unusually difficult historical questions. He also edited the complete works of *Dunstable (1953). B.'s *Music in the Baroque Era* (1947) is the standard history of that period. BIBLIOGRAPHY: D. D. Boyden, MQ 42(1956) 291–301.

[A. DOHERTY]

BÛKRĀ (Syr., first-born), the ordinary word for the E Syrian eucharistic bread, a cake about two inches in diameter and a half inch thick, stamped with a large central cross and four small crosses, leavened, with a little salt and oil added. Nestorians leaven with *malkā* and add a little dough from the preceding baking. Also called *perîstā, qeṣātā, pûrshānā*. In W Syrian usage it is called *bûkrō* or *tab'ō*.

[A. CODY]

BULGAKOV, MAKARII (1816–82), a foremost 19th-cent. Russian theologian. After a career as teacher and rector of the theological academy at St. Petersburg (1850), he was made a bp. in 1854 and ruled several sees before being elected Metropolitan of Moscow in 1879. An assiduous if unoriginal scholar, he published a *History of the Russian Church* (12 v., 1857–83). His theological works were used by Slavic, Greek, and Romanian Orthodox, and were translated into many languages, including French. These works included an *Introduction to Orthodox Theology* (1847), and *Orthodox Dogmatic Theology* (5 v., 1845–53; 5th ed. 2 v., 1895). A compendium of the *Introduction* called *Study Manual of Orthodox Dogmatic Theology* (1868) was widely used by seminarians. B. belonged to a transitional period of Russian theology, the reaction, inaugurated *c.* 1836 by N. A. Protasov (1798–1855), against Protestant influences. B.'s method and content were criticized by other Orthodox theologians for their reliance on RC theological manuals. BIBLIOGRAPHY: M. Jugie, *Catholicisme* 2:306–307. DTC 9.2:1443–44.

[T. E. BIRD]

BULGAKOV, SERGEĬ NIKOLAEVICH (1871–1944), Russian religious philosopher. After undergoing a spiritual crisis in 1901, Bulgakov abandoned Marxism, was converted to Orthodoxy, and became a priest in 1918 (see his *From Marxism to Idealism,* 1904; *The Unfading Light,* 1917). Expelled from the Soviet Union in 1922 with other leading intellectuals for attitudes irreconcilable with the Soviet regime, he went first to Prague then to Paris where he became a professor at the Russian Orthodox Institute (1925–44). Under the influence of Solovyev (1853–1900), whose concept of Divine Wisdom as Sophia, the Eternal Feminine, had a profound influence on him, he developed his own religious philosophy, esp. in *Agnus Dei* (1933), *Comforter* (1936), and *Bride of the Lamb* (1945). Other important works are *Die Tragödie der Philosophie* (1927) and *Philosophy of Language* (1948). BIBLIOGRAPHY: N. O. Lossky, *History of Russian Philosophy* (1951) 192–232.

[M. F. MCCARTHY]

BULGARIA, People's Republic of Bulgaria located in SE Europe, 42,830 sq mi on the E part of the Balkan peninsula facing the Black Sea and bordered by Romania, Turkey, Greece, and Yugoslavia. The population averages 8,620,000 (U.N. est. 1973). As an ethnic group, the Bulgarians may be traced back to the 7th cent. when the Bulgars, who were originally from Central Asia and possibly related to the Huns, migrated into the Balkans from a region N of the Black Sea. Christianity began in this area as early as the 4th cent., when in 343 a famous council met at Sardica, now Sofia; but the faith almost disappeared when the Slavs migrated into the peninsula during the 6th century. Later a Slav-Bulgarian state was formed and in 679, the first Bulgarian Kingdom came into existence. More than a cent. later the Byzantine Empire was influential in spreading Christianity among them and in 863 sent Cyril and Methodius to convert the Slavs. The two brothers devised a new alphabet known as the Cyrillic, which soon replaced Latin and Greek as the only form of writing among the people. This language later became the basis for a new Slavic literature. Cyril and Methodius also introduced a new liturgical form out of which grew the present Bulgarian rite. In 864 Boris I accepted Christianity and was baptized by clergy from Constantinople. By 870 Orthodox Christianity became the official religion of Bulgaria. The kingdom was also influenced by territorial ambitions and in 1018 fell into the hands of Byzantium. A second kingdom was established in 1186 and lasted until 1396, at which time the Ottoman Turks, a powerful enemy and neighbor, conquered the country. After 5 cent. of Turkish domination, Bulgaria was liberated by Russia and became a principality in 1878. It was not until 1908 that it became an independent kingdom again, but when World War

II ended for Bulgaria in 1944, the country fell under Soviet control where it remains. The 1947 constitution of "satellized" Bulgaria resulted in the separation of Church and State, prohibited religious instruction in schools, arrested clergy, and secularized monasteries. Though the Bulgarian Orthodox Church was later restored to the rank of state Church, the education of youth and sharing in social services was forbidden. The patriarchical seat is at Sofia, where Metropolitan Maksim of Lovech was enthroned as the new patriarch in 1971. About this time the patriarchate had 3,200 churches, 11 dioceses, each under a metropolitan, 12 bps., and 2,000 priests. Most of the country's believers belong to the Orthodox Church, but total membership is not available. Freedom of conscience and belief is said to be "guaranteed" and the state provides 17% of church funds. In 1971 there were 50 RC churches, 60 priests, and a Catholic population of 50,000 representing the Bulgarian and Latin rites. There were also 20,000 Protestants and between 3,000 and 7,000 Jews. In 1975 the Catholic Church had 1 diocese, 1 vicar apostolic, 1 apostolic exarchate, and 2 bishops; also about this time, statistics show 750,000 Muslims, including mostly Turks of whom some 50,000 are Pomaks (Bulgarians converted to Islam during Turkish rule). BIBLIOGRAPHY: F. Dvornik, *Slavs in European History and Civilization* (1962); I. Sofranov, *Histoire du mouvement bulgare vers l'Église catholique au XIX siècle* (1960); M. MacDermott, *History of Bulgaria 1393 to 1885* (1962); H. Daniel-Rops, *Our Brothers in Christ* (tr. J. M. Orpen and J. Warrington, 1967); E. K. Keefe et al., *Area Handbook of Bulgaria* (1974).

[R. A. TODD]

BULGARIA, CHURCH OF. The territory which was to become Bulgaria was widely Christianized during the early cent. of the Church. It embraced numerous episcopal sees, was distinguished by many martyrs, and a famous council was held during the Arian controversy at Sardica (now Sofia) in 343. But successive waves of invaders from the 5th to the 7th cent. practically destroyed Christian life and church organization in the land. A new start was therefore necessary when the territory was settled by Slavic tribes and was consolidated politically by the Proto-Bulgarians (late 7th cent.), a warrior race of Central Asian origin, akin to the Huns.

Although there was constant contact with Christianity, the formal conversion of the Bulgarian State did not occur until 864 when Khan Boris accepted baptism from Constantinople. There ensued a lengthy struggle between Rome and Constantinople for jurisdiction over the young Church, which, for its part, was intent on obtaining as much autonomy as possible. Such was the historical setting of the famous *Responsa ad quaesita Bulgarorum* of Pope Nicholas I, an interesting and at times candid picture of the simple religious problems of the Bulgarians. The Council of Constantinople in 870 determined that the Bulgarian Church belonged under the jurisdiction of the Byzantine patriarch.

The question of its independence arose again about 15 years later, when the rearguard of the Moravian mission of SS. Cyril and Methodius, Clement, Naum, and Angelari arrived in Bulgaria and were given shelter and protection by Prince Boris (885). Soon they were at work on a vast plan of Slavicization of the Bulgarian Church, which in a few years produced both the personnel and the necessary Slavic books. By 893 Christianity had become solidly established, the Slavic liturgy was officially accepted, and St. Clement was appointed first bp. of "the Bulgarian language." During the reign of Czar Simeon I (893–927) the country developed remarkably in power and culture. The Church was reorganized with native Bulgarians replacing Byzantine prelates and with the establishment of a patriarch at Preslav. But political instability caused the patriarchate to be moved to Dorostol and to other cities further to the W until it finally settled in Ohrid. When this too fell to the Byzantines (1018), the see was reduced to the rank of an archbishopric with a Greek incumbent. Two of these, Leo of Ohrid and Theophylact of Bulgaria, both of the 12th cent., strenuously supported Constantinople in its confrontation with Rome that culminated in the schism of 1054. The Bulgarian Church recovered its autonomy when the State regained its political independence in 1186; Rome granted Kaloian the title of king and recognized Basil, the abp. of Trnovo, as primate with the title of abp. of Bulgaria and Valachia. The hostility of the Balkan states against Latin conquest and occupation of Constantinople (1204) led to a separation from Rome and a rapprochement to the Byzantine patriarchate then in Nicaea. In 1235 the abp. of Trnovo was recognized as patriarch and the union with Rome was terminated. This second period in the life of the Bulgarian Church was marked by activity in the spheres of letters, liturgy, and spirituality that spread throughout the Slavic world. Of fundamental significance was the literary reform made under the last patriarch of Trnovo, Eutimi (1375–94).

When the Second Bulgarian Empire fell to the Turks (1396), the Bulgarian Church lost its independence and its patriarchal rank and came under the jurisdiction of the patriarch of Constantinople. The See of Ohrid was allowed to retain its jurisdiction over the W part of the Bulgarian lands (Macedonia), but it too was suppressed in 1766–67. To political and social oppression under the Turks was added religious oppression under the Patriarchate of Constantinople, which sought to exploit and Hellenize the Bulgarian people. Greek bps. replaced Bulgarians and the Greek language displaced the Bulgarian in the liturgy. The spark that kindled a national awakening is generally believed to have been the *Slavo-Bulgarian History* of the Athonite monk, Paissi of Chilandar, with its moving exhortation to the Bulgarian people to be proud of their past and their language (1762). After a long struggle (1856–70) that led to formal schism from the See of Constantinople (1872), the Bulgarian Church again proclaimed its autonomy in March 1870. The Turkish government recognized the Bulgarian exarch residing in Constantinople with jurisdiction over most of the

Bulgarian Orthodox in the Turkish Empire, an area covering present day Bulgaria, Greek and Yugoslavian Macedonia, and parts of Greek and Turkish Thrace.

As a result of the Balkan Wars and World War I, the Bulgarian Church became confined to the diminished borders of the Bulgarian State. From 1915 to 1945 it remained without an exarch. In 1945 the excommunication of Constantinople was lifted and the Bulgarian Church entered again into full communion with all the Orthodox Churches. In 1953 the patriarchate was restored, Maksim of Lovech ruling since 1971. The Bulgarian Church is guided by a Holy Synod under the presidency of the patriarch and is divided into 11 dioceses within the country itself and 1 for the Bulgarians of America and Australia. It has about 2,000 priests, 3,200 churches, 120 monasteries, a seminary, and a theological academy, the faithful est. at c.7 million. The Bulgarian Church has been a member of the World Council of Churches since 1961 and has been particularly active in peace movements. Although greatly handicapped by the Communist regime since 1944, the Bulgarian Church enjoys state support for its personnel and some of its activities.

The Bulgarian Orthodox communities in Europe, chiefly in Hungary, Romania, and Austria, are under the jurisdiction of the Holy Synod. The Bulgarian monastery on Mt. Athos, Zographou, and two churches in Istanbul are under the nominal jurisdiction of the patriarch of Constantinople. In 1937 an eparchy was created for the approximately 100,000 Bulgarian Orthodox (chiefly from Greek and Yugoslavian Macedonia) of N and S America and Australia with its center in New York; its first incumbent, Bp. Andrej, was made a metropolitan in 1963. But the majority of the clergy and faithful later sided with the new bp. Kiril (Yonchev), who resided in Toledo, Ohio. BIBLIOGRAPHY: S. Runciman, *History of the First Bulgarian Empire* (1930); M. Spinka, *History of Christianity in the Balkans* (1933); R. Janin, DHGE 10:1120–94; *People's Republic of Bulgaria and the Religious Denominations in It* (1966).

[G. ELDAROV]

BULGARIAN CATHOLICS.

BULGARIAN CATHOLICS. The Catholic Church is represented in Bulgaria by two communities of widely different origins. The Latin rite community of some 50,000 faithful derives mainly from the missionary work of Franciscans from Croatia and Bosnia in the 16th and 17th cent. among the Bulgarian Bogomils around Sofia, along the Danube, and in the Plovdiv area in the South. These Catholics played a remarkable role in the struggle for freedom of the Bulgarian nation; the Chiprovzi uprising of the Bulgarian Catholics in 1688 is one of the major events of the dark age of Bulgarian history under the Turks (1393–1878). In more recent times they have been under the spiritual care of the Passionist Fathers in the north and of the Capuchins in the south. They are organized in the Diocese of Nikopol and the Vicariate Apostolic of Sofia-Plovdiv with 49 priests and 32 churches. The Oriental rite community, now about 15,000 strong, was started in 1860 in Istanbul when several thousand Orthodox Bulgarians in conflict with the Greek Patriarch of Constantinople entered into communion with Rome and were soon followed by others, particularly in Macedonia. Pope Pius IX gave the Bulgarian Uniates an abp., Josif Sokolski (1861), but he was soon kidnapped by Russian agents and held a virtual prisoner in an Orthodox monastery near Kiev. Notwithstanding this heavy blow, the community was able to recover and in the final decades of the 19th cent. expand in Macedonia. At that time the Church was organized in two apostolic vicariates of Salonika for Macedonia and of Adrianople for Thrace, with an apostolic administrator with the rank of abp. in Constantinople. The community suffered much during the Balkan Wars (1912–13) and World War I (1914–18), which were fought largely in territories inhabited by Bulgarian Uniates. Through the exchange of populations following World War I the surviving members were resettled within the diminished boundaries of Bulgaria proper. After a visitation made by the special envoy of the Holy See, Bp. Angelo Roncalli, later Pope John XXIII, the Church was reorganized. At present there is an apostolic exarch residing in Sofia and some 19 priests serving 17 churches throughout the country. The Bulgarian Catholics of both rites have suffered much under the Communist regime, which took control of the country in 1944. In 1952 several Catholic priests, including one bp., were condemned to death. All church property has been confiscated by the State, all Catholic schools, hospitals, convents, even some rectories, have been closed down; it is a serious offense to teach religion to children and youngsters under 18, and there have been no seminaries or seminarians for over 20 years. About 5- or 6,000 Bulgarian Catholics live in neighboring Yugoslavia, Greece, and Turkey, while others have settled in Europe and America, and are served by a number of exiled Bulgarian priests and religious. In 1966 the Holy See appointed a visitator delegate for the Bulgarian Catholics outside Bulgaria. BIBLIOGRAPHY: *OrientCatt* 191–198; I. Sofranov, *Histoire du mouvement bulgare vers L'Église catholique au XIX siècle* (1960); M. Lacko, NCE 2:863–865.

[G. ELDAROV]

BULGARIAN CHURCH OUTSIDE BULGARIA.

BULGARIAN CHURCH OUTSIDE BULGARIA. The Bulgarians immigrated to Canada and the U.S. near the turn of the century. By 1940 there were 9,000 Bulgarians in residence in the U.S. where the Bulgarian Church began as a mission when the first church was built c.1907 in Madison, Illinois. Later a diocese was established; in 1938, the Holy Synod of Bulgaria sent Bp. Andrej to fill the episcopate in New York, which became the official see in 1947, when the same Bp. was elected its first metropolitan. Following a decision of the Holy Synod in 1972, the Church was divided into two dioceses: New York and Akron, Ohio. The Bulgarian Eastern Orthodox Church outside Bulgaria probably includes members belonging to what is called the Diocese of

N and S America and Australia. The most recent statistics (1971) report 13 churches with an inclusive membership of 86,000. BIBLIOGRAPHY: F. S. Mead, *Handbooks of Denominations in the U.S.* (1970); YBACC (1974).

[R. A. TODD]

BULGARIAN HERETICS, also known as *Bogomils, a dualist sect that began in Bulgaria and spread throughout the Balkans between the 10th and 14th centuries. They took their name from the Bulgarian translation of the Gr. *Theophile* (pleasing to God) and their founder, a certain Jeremiah who called himself Pope Bogomil. Tracing their origin through a group of 8th-cent. Paulicians back to Manichaeism, they were initially located in the city of Phillippopolis (Plovdiv) in Thrace but spread to Constantinople by the 11th cent. and thence to Asia Minor. In France and Italy they were called *Patarines or *Cathari.

Thwarted by Emperor John II Comnenus at Constantinople (1110) with the execution of its leader Basil and later in Serbia and Bulgaria, the sect spread to Dalmatia and Bosnia. Despite repeated intervention of the Popes, e.g., Innocent III (1203), Honorius III (1221), Gregory IX (1234), and the Hungarian Crusade (1237), Bogomilism was dominant in Bosnia for two centuries. When King Thomas demanded a return to Catholicism (1450), 40,000 Bogomils relocated in Herzegovina until the Turks conquered both Bosnia (1463) and Herzegovina, and the majority accepted Islamic teaching. BIBLIOGRAPHY: G. Bardy, DHGE 9:408–410; S. Runciman, *Medieval Manichee: a Study of the Christian Dualist Heresy* (1947, repr. 1955); M. Jugie, DSAM 1:1751–54.

[F. H. BRIGHAM]

BULGARIAN RITE, one of 18 canonical rites of the RC Church, which probably had its beginning in Bulgaria in 863 when Photius, patriarch of Constantinople, introduced Christianity to Boris I. Soon Boris was intent on establishing a Bulgarian hierarchy, and his allegiance alternated between Constantinople and Rome whenever his requests for a national bishopric were rejected. As a result, neither the Byzantine rite nor the Latin rite could assert itself, and from 863 to 870 Bulgaria was isolated from ecclesiastical ties. At this critical time Constantinople sent two missionaries, St. Cyril and his brother St. Methodius, who while in Moravia within the limits of the Roman liturgical tradition first began to use Slavonic for liturgical and scriptural purposes. This was the first time the Slavonic language was written down (863–866). When SS. Cyril and Methodius were called to evangelize the Slavs in Bulgaria, they returned to the Byzantine rite. The real conversion of the people began with the new Byzantine-Slav liturgy, which had been approved by Pope Adrian II. In the reign of Simeon the Great (893–927) the national assembly proclaimed Christianity the state religion, officially adopted the Slavonic language, and decreed that Byzantine books be replaced by those of the new Slavic rite. Simeon reorganized the hierarchy and replaced Greek bps. with those of Slavic origin. The new Bulgarian rite was approved definitively, and finally Bulgaria could boast of a national hierarchy and clergy, as well as a liturgy and religious practices of its own. BIBLIOGRAPHY: N. Liesel, *Eucharistic Liturgies of the Eastern Churches* (tr. D. Heimann, 1963); P. De Meester, DACL 6.2:1607–10 s.v. "Grecques (Liturgies)"; I. H. Dalmais, *Eastern Liturgies* (tr. D. Attwater, 1960).

[R. A. TODD]

BULGARIS, EUGENIUS (1716–1806), an important Greek theologian of the 18th cent. Born in Corfu, B. studied philosophy and theology in Padua, then taught in Janina, Greece, where he was ordained deacon and changed his name from Eleutherius to Eugenius. He entered the monastery of Vatopedi on Mt. Athos (1749) and also taught at the patriarchal School of Constantinople. Dismissed because of his liberal methods of teaching, he migrated to Leipzig. Later the Czarina Catherine II brought him to St. Petersburg. Ordained priest in 1775, B. became abp. of Kherson in 1776, but soon resigned his bishopric, returned to St. Petersburg, and composed a series of exegetical and polemical works, as well as works on philosophy, philology, history, physics, and mathematics. BIBLIOGRAPHY: A. Palmieri, DTC 2:1,1236–41; R. Janin, DHGE 10:1195–98.

[P. FOSCOLOS]

BULGARS. The history of the inhabitants of what is modern Bulgaria goes back hundreds of years before Christ and predates by 15 cent. or more the arrival of the Bulgars, after whom the country was named. The earliest people in the area were Thracians who had control of much of the Balkan peninsula. In the course of time, the Thracians were conquered by the Macedonians and then by the Romans, who completely dominated the area by the first cent. A.D. A number of mass migrations into the Balkans began in the 3d cent. and concluded in the 6th cent. with the Slavs who crossed the Danube and occupied much of the Balkan area. The Slavs overthrew the social order and replaced it with their own, and before long all the Thracians had become Slavicized. In the 7th cent., the Bulgars, who had lived N of the Black Sea, overran what is now the NE part of Bulgaria. This tribe of people originally came from Central Asia and may have been related to the Huns. In stock, they were the same as the Turks and their language was similar to Turkish. Their social system was quite different from the Slavs. The Bulgars were ruled autocratically by Khans, whereas the Slavs rejected the idea of kingship. They were Asiatic in dress and custom and as warriors fought on horseback. Since the Slavs were far greater in number, the Bulgars soon became part of their culture and within 2 cent. were totally Slavicized. They adopted the Slavic language but retained the Bulgarian political structure, upon which a Slav-Bulgarian state was formed with the capital at Pliska. BIBLIOGRAPHY: R. Janin, DHGE 10:1116–20; E. K. Keefe et al., *Area Handbook for Bulgaria* (1974).

[R. A. TODD]

BULL, JOHN (*c.*1562–1628), organist, virginalist, and composer. B. was a noted figure in early English music. He sang in Queen Elizabeth's Chapel Royal; became organist at Hereford Cathedral at 20, subsequently holding the positions of Gentleman of the Chapel Royal, doctor of music in the Univ. of Oxford and Cambridge, and professor of music at Gresham College, London. He traveled in France, Germany, and Belgium and in 1617 became organist at the Cathedral in Antwerp. Though sometimes lacking in imagination, his music is admirable for its contrapuntal mastery. He was a brilliant keyboard artist and contributed much to the development of both harpsichord and organ music. He is represented in the *Fitzwilliam Virginal Book* and by many MSS in the British Museum, Berlin Library, etc. BIBLIOGRAPHY: E. F. Rimbault et al., Grove DMM 1:1008–10; *Oxford Companion to Music* (ed. P. Scholes, 1963) 139–140.

[M. T. LEGGE]

BULL, PAPAL, the most solemn form of papal document. It is written on parchment, and to it is attached by cords of silk a leaden seal *(bulla),* which bears on one side the image of the reigning pontiff, and on the other a representation of SS. Peter and Paul. Papal bulls deal with matters of the greatest importance.

[J. C. WILLKE]

BULLA CRUCIATA, a papal document granting various privileges and indults to those who took part in the wars against the Muslims. Many bulls and apostolic letters are grouped under this general title, and their provisions and reasons for concession vary significantly. The expulsion of the Muslims from Spain occasioned the first such bull which Alexander II addressed to Ramiro I of Aragon in 1063. Succeeding popes renewed the privileges for Spain and in 1095 Urban II granted a plenary indulgence for the First Crusade to the Holy Land. *Quantum praedecessores* (1145), issued for the Second Crusade by Eugene III and considered to be the first formal crusade bull, lists such privileges as a plenary indulgence, protection of family and property, and an exemption from interest on debts. In the course of time, these pontifical concessions became more and more frequent, and were offered to participants or financial supporters of numerous European conflicts. After the crusades the *bulla cruciata* was applied exclusively to Spain, Spanish territories, and resident foreigners in those countries, and was extended to cover any work that propagated religion. Instead of the original plenary indulgence, the privileges came to include various dispensations, notably from fast and abstinence. Benedict XV (1915) and Pius XI (1928) renewed the bull, but sought to make the privileges and obligations much more precise. BIBLIOGRAPHY: E. De Hinojosa CE, 4:543; G. Constable, "Second Crusade as Seen by Contemporaries," *Traditio* 9 (1953) 213–279; J. Brundage, *Crusades: A Documentary Survey* (1962).

[J. MCGLYNN]

BULLARIUM, the name given to any private collection of papal bulls and official papers such as that of the canonist Laertius Cherubini (d. 1626), whose own collection (1586) together with the Luxembourg Bullarium (1727–30), the Roman Bullarium of Mairnardi (1737–62), and the Bullarium of Turin (1857–85) are significant. Their authority attaches to the documents themselves rather than their private compilers. BIBLIOGRAPHY: T. Ortolan, DTC 2:1243–55; H. Leclercq, DACL 8.2:2977–82.

[F. H. BRIGHAM]

BULLFIGHTING, the national sport of Spain in which men bait and fight bulls for the entertainment of the public. Brought to Spain by the Moors, combats with bulls were common in ancient Crete, Thessaly, and in the contests of the amphitheatres of the Roman Empire. Up to the 18th cent. it was the custom to fight the bull on horseback with a lance. At that time the practice of fighting the bull on foot with a short sword and a small red cloth wound around a stick to entice the bull was initiated.

Pope Pius V assigned excommunication to all participants and spectators of bullfights (1567), but Gregory XIII maintained such penalties only for those in major orders. Theologians regard bullfighting as morally wrong when there is extreme cruelty to animals, risk of serious injury, and unwarranted savage reaction of spectators and participants. As justification for their position they cite the fact that hunting and fishing are permissible for purposes of recreation and that animals may be used for man's amusement and sport. BIBLIOGRAPHY: J. Pereda, "La iglesia y los toros," *Razon y Fe* 130 (1944) 505–524; J. Fulton, *Bullfighting* (1971).

[F. H. BRIGHAM]

BULLINGER, HEINRICH (1504–75), Swiss reformer. His early education with the *Brethren of the Common Life and his association with the humanists at the Univ. of Cologne led to a distaste for scholasticism, a cultivation of the Fathers of the Church, esp. Augustine, and an interest in the thought of Erasmus and the theological innovations of the Reformers. While pastor of Bremgarten (1529–31) he married a former nun, Anna Adlischwiler, by whom he had 11 children. He was won to Zwinglianism through a sermon by *Zwingli at the Great Minster of Zurich and succeeded him as pastor there in 1531. B. strove particularly to achieve doctrinal concord among the Reformers. He collaborated with Calvin on the *Zurich Consensus (1549). He assisted in the formulation of the First *Helvetic Confession (1536); the Second, adopted in 1566, was his personal testimony of faith, written in 1562. The First was accepted by the Protestant cantons (excepting Strassburg and Constance); the Second won not only the approval of all the Protestant cantons but also acceptance throughout Europe and Great Britain. B. offered generous hospitality to those fleeing from the Huguenot wars in France and from the persecution of Mary Tudor. He had strong links with England; he supported the coup to seat Lady Jane Grey on the throne (1553) and later counseled Elizabeth in her dealings with the Puritans. He is the author of 12,000 letters and more than 150 works, among which are a biography of Zwingli, the *Diarium*, the *Zürcher Chronik*, and the *Decadi*. BIBLIOGRAPHY: *Zwingli and Bullinger* (ed. and tr. G. W. Bromiley, Lib CC 24, 1953); O. E. Strasser, RGG 1:1510–11, bibliog.

[E. D. McSHANE]

BULLOUGH, SEBASTIAN (1910–67), Dominican scripture scholar, lecturer, and writer. B.'s father was Edward Bullough, Dante scholar and professor of Italian at Cambridge, and his maternal grandmother Eleanora Duse, the actress. He was brought up trilingually. In 1931, after graduating from Cambridge with an honors degree in Hebrew and Aramaic, he became a Dominican. He studied two years in Rome (1937–39), where he took his licentiate in theology. The outbreak of World War II prevented his going on to the École Biblique in Jerusalem, as had been planned. Instead he became a schoolmaster at Blackfriars School, Laxton, then prior of the novitiate house in Woodchester, and after that lecturer in theology at Blackfriars, Oxford. In 1960 again at Cambridge, he was ecumenical preacher and lecturer in Hebrew until his death. He did much periodical writing, esp. on scriptural topics. He contributed to the *Catholic Commentary on the Scriptures* and to its revision and also a number of articles to the *New Catholic Encyclopedia*. He was a man of great energy and the range of his interests and enthusiasms was almost too broad.

[P. K. MEAGHER]

BULTMANN SCHOOL, the theological movement of the 20th cent. that has its origin in the thought of Rudolf Bultmann, German Protestant exegete of the Univ. of Marburg. The immediate context of Bultmann's work is twofold: (1) the continued search for the "historical Jesus" on the part of Protestant biblical scholars, according to the methods of the 19th-cent. school of higher criticism (with 20th-cent. improvements or modifications); (2) the existentialist philosophy of Martin Heidegger, once a colleague of Bultmann at Marburg, whose system Bultmann has employed in his program of demythologizing the Scriptures, especially the NT. The immediate impetus for Bultmann, however, was the rethinking of Protestant positions just after World War I, which he undertook together with Karl *Barth, from whom he rather quickly dissociated himself.

The program of demythologizing takes as its point of departure the acceptance of modern man's supposed incapacity either to comprehend or to accept the "mythical" categories in which most of the NT is expressed: the cosmogony of a "three-layered" universe (the world, the underworld, and the world of heavenly beings), with man caught in the middle and acted upon or manipulated by demons from the one side and angels (and even God) from the other. Once this sort of cosmogony is put aside, a serious question arises for Bultmann as to the meaning of the Gospels, which witness to the role of Christ in history.

Bultmann's exegesis is a rather devastating attack on the Gospels' historicity in the ordinary sense of the word, while he makes use of Heidegger's distinction between what is *historisch* and what is *geschichtlich*. The former term qualifies a reality that takes place objectively in the physical world. The term *geschichtlich* stands for reality that has meaning for man, without regard for whether or not it occurred or exists as a physical entity. For Bultmann the word of the Gospel is *geschichtlich;* and this is verified eminently as regards the event of Jesus' Resurrection. This event speaks to man in his peculiar situation in the world, a world in which he has the choice of living either inauthentically, i.e., by lending himself as an instrument of all those brute forces that determine his existence; or authentically, i.e., by faith. Thus the Heideggerian categories of authentic and inauthentic existence for man are transposed into Christian terms. Man may either live by faith or cede to the fear of death and thus deliver himself up to some form of escape. The physically historical event of Jesus' Crucifixion is the paradigm of living by faith (authentic existence); and the resurrection-event (Bultmann makes no positive statements as regards its being physically historical) is the sign of the reality of the life into which man passes by facing death with Jesus. Thus it appears that, according to Bultmann, the preaching of the word in the Church is, in substance, a challenge offered to man to take Jesus as a model—but in the context of the modern world.

The influence of Bultmann (so as to constitute a school) upon theologians and Christians at large (German Lutherans in the first instance, but also Protestants and Catholics throughout the world) would be difficult to overestimate, esp. with regard to his perfecting of the "history of traditions" method of exegesis. BIBLIOGRAPHY: J. Macquarrie, *Scope of Demythologizing* (1960); J. Beckmann, "Rudolph Bultmann: the man and the method," HPR 73 (1972) 9–16. J. M. Robinson et al., "Bultmann School of Biblical Interpretation," *Journal for Theology and the Church* 1 (1970).

[M. B. SCHEPERS]

BULTO, 18th-and 19th-cent. carved wood religious statue, the work of native New Mexican artisans. Derived from the Spanish *bulto redondo* (bulk or form, in the round), the figures are also termed *Santos*, holy figures. Bultos are covered with gesso, polychromed, often costumed in stiffened cloth with iconographical accessories. While related to traditional Spanish carvings, bultos are characterized by naïve vigor through their highly expressive crudity. BIBLIOGRAPHY: W. Hougland, *Santos, a Primitive American Art* (1946).

[M. J. DALY]

BŪNDAHISHN, *Original Creation or Cosmology,* a religio-philosophical work written in Pahlavi or Middle Persian dealing with Persian cosmogony and cosmology. It covers the creation of man, animals, and plants, and the long struggle and the stages of the struggle between *Ahura Mazda* and *Ahriman*. It includes the destruction of the world, its renewal, and the sole rule of *Ahura Mazda*. The work is based not only on later speculation but on earlier parts of the Avesta no longer extant. BIBLIOGRAPHY: J. Duchesne-Guillemin, *La Religion de l'Iran ancien* 52–56; R. C. Zaehner, *Dawn and Twilight of Zoroastrianism* (1961).

[M. R. P. MCGUIRE]

BUNDERIUS, JAN (van den Bundere; 1481–1557), Flemish Dominican and opponent of the Reformers, who was *prédicateur* and inquisitor general of the Diocese of Tournai. A philosopher and theologian who taught for many years at Ghent and authored collections on Ambrose, Jerome, Augustine, and Gregory, he is esp. known for his controversial volumes on Luther and Calvin. BIBLIOGRAPHY: P. Mandonnet, DTC 2.1:1263–64; M. H. Laurent, DHGE 10:1215.

[T. LIDDY]

BUNIN, IVAN ALEXEYEVICH (1870–1953), author of poems and short stories; first Russian to receive the Nobel prize for literature (1933). In his works, themes of love and death are presented now with terse realism, now with exotic romanticism, but always with conscious attention to style. His best-known work is the title story of the collection *The Gentleman from San Francisco* (1915). His *Reminiscences* (1950) suffers from a lack of objectivity in treating Soviet writers. BIBLIOGRAPHY: R. Poggioli, *Poets of Russia: 1890–1930* (1960) 113–115; M.J. Olgin, *Guide to Russian Literature* (1920) 251–256.

[M. F. MCCARTHY]

BUNSEN, CHRISTIAN KARL JOSIAS VON (1791–1860), Prussian diplomat and scholar. After studies at Göttingen followed by research in the libraries of Florence and Paris, B. served as secretary to B. G. Niebuhr, Prussian envoy to the papal court. He succeeded Niebuhr in that post from 1823 until 1839, proving himself a skilled diplomat. William Frederick IV, whose enthusiasm for evangelicalism he shared, appointed B. minister to London (1841–54). In this position he tried to effect some sort of union between German Protestantism and the Anglican Church and played a major role in the establishment of the controversial joint bishopric of Jerusalem, which was designed to be filled alternately by a Lutheran and by an Anglican bishop. His numerous theological and historical writings are no longer deemed valuable.

BUNTING, JABEZ (1779–1858), dominant leader of the Wesleyan Methodist Church during the first half of the 19th century. He was born in Manchester, educated at Manchester Grammar School, and became a Methodist minister in 1803. Appointed to London, he won acclaim as a preacher and founded the *Eclectic Review*. Elected president of the *conference four times, he greatly strengthened Methodist organization, promoted missionary work as secretary of the Wesleyan Missionary Society 18 years, and supported higher education, becoming first president of Wesleyan Theological Institution, Hoxton, in 1834. A rebellion c.1848 against his dominance eventually cost the Church 100,000 members. BIBLIOGRAPHY: T. B. Bunting, *Life of Jabez Bunting* (1859); M. Edwards, *After Wesley* (1935); *New History of Methodism* (eds. W. J. Townsend et al., 2 v., 1909).

[F. E. MASER]

BUNYAN, JOHN (1628–98), author of the *Pilgrim's Progress*. B. was born at Elstow near Bedford at a time when Puritanism was at its height. As a child his imagination was affected by sermons. At 16, when about to follow his father in the tinker's trade, he was called up on the Parliamentary side of the Civil War. He married and after an agonizing religious conversion joined a *Nonconformist group. For defying the law against lay preaching he was imprisoned for 12 years. He wrote 60 books, of which five have survived, the most famous being *Grace Abounding to the Chief of Sinners* (1666) and *Pilgrim's Progress* (1678). BIBLIOGRAPHY: J. Brown, *John Bunyan, His Life, Times and Work* (1883; rev. F. M. Harrison, 1928); O. E. Winslow, *John Bunyan* (1961); H. Talon, *John Bunyan: The Man and His Works* (tr. B. Wall, 1951).

[M. O'CONNOR]

BUON (BON; BONO), family of 15th-cent. Venetian sculptors and architects. Giovanni and his son Bartolommeo executed the façade figures for S. Maria dell' Orto, the Ca' d'Oro, and a tympanum at Scuola di S. Marco. After the death of Giovanni, Bartolommeo worked in Verona and Venice. BIBLIOGRAPHY: J. Pope-Hennessy, *Italian Gothic Sculpture* (1955).

[M. J. DALY]

BUONAIUTI, ERNESTO (1881–1946), noted Italian Modernist. Ordained in Rome in 1903, B. taught at the Urbanian Univ. and the Apollinaris in Rome. He espoused Modernism, which was condemned by Pius X, and his many books and periodicals defending Modernism were placed on the Index. He was excommunicated in 1925. BIBLIOGRAPHY: V. Ceresi, EncCatt 3:218–219.

[R. C. TALLARICO]

BUONINSEGNA, DUCCIO DI, see DUCCIO DI BUONINSEGNA.

[M. J. DALY]

BUONPENSIERE, ENRICO (1853–1929), Italian Dominican theologian, the author of respected commentaries on the dogmatic parts of Aquinas's *Summa theologiae*. He was a professor at College of St. Thomas and at the

Lateran Univ. in Rome. BIBLIOGRAPHY: A. D'Amato, EncCatt 3:222.

[T. C. O'BRIEN]

BURCHARD OF WORMS (965–1025), bp. and canonist who was educated at the Benedictine abbey of Lobbes and ordained deacon by Abp. Willigis of Mainz (975–1011) where he served as first chamberlain and judge. Appointed bp. of Worms by Emperor Otto III, B. was ordained priest and consecrated bp. by Abp. Willigis at Seligenstadt (1000). A leader in both civil and ecclesiastical affairs, he helped to rebuild the city of Worms, e.g., the walls, the cathedral, the schools, etc. and to restore the spirit of its people after the many attacks of the Hungarians. His concern for a balanced pastoral guide for the clergy and religious of his diocese led him to collaborate with Walter, bp. of Spire, Baudrio, bp. of Liège, and Olbert, monk of the Abbey of Lobbes in preparing a summary of canon law and directives in 20 books, based on several earlier collections, notably that of Regino of Prüm. The work is known as the *Decretum collectorium* (PL 140.491–1090) or simply *Brocardus (Brocardica)* after its author. B. also published *Leges et statuta familiae S. Petri Wormatiensis* (Laws and Statutes for the Family of St. Peter of Worms), a code of laws for the feudal subjects of the abp. of Worms (MGH 1.639). B. was a participant in the provincial councils of Thoinville (1003), Frankfurt (1007) which erected the See of Bamberg, and Seligenstadt (1023), which proclaimed significant decrees of reform. At his death, he was interred in the Cathedral of Worms. His life (*Vita Burchardi*, PL 140.507) written a few years after his death by Ebbo, a cleric of the Cathedral of Worms, is a valuable record of his times. BIBLIOGRAPHY: G. Allemang, DHGE 10:1245–47; J. Pétrau-Gay, DDC 2:1141–57.

[F. H. BRIGHAM]

BURCHARD OF WÜRZBURG, ST. (d. 753 or 754), bishop. B. was born in England and after entering the Benedictines there, he joined St. Boniface in Germany (*c.*735) and became first bp. of Würzburg in 741 or 742. In 748, he brought the report of the general synod of Franconia (747) to Rome. In 750–751, he went to Rome to secure the support of Pope Zacharias for the dynastic change proposed by Pepin III. Two medieval lives of the saint (neither is wholly reliable) are contained in O. Holder–Egger, MGHS 15.1:47–62. BIBLIOGRAPHY: I. Mannocci and A. M. Raggi, Bibl Sanct 3:608–610.

[M. F. MCCARTHY]

BURCHARD, DECRETUM OF, a collection of canon law in 20 books with 1,758 chapters. Written by Burchard, bp. of Worms, in collaboration with Olbert, monk of the Abbey of Lobbe, it is one of the most significant canonical collections of medieval times. Books 1–18 list the canonical directives that are to be followed in the Diocese of Worms; book 19 (*Corrector sive Medicus*) is a penitential guide for confessors; and book 20 is a doctrinal explanation of es-chatology. In the first 18 books Burchard defends the basic prerogatives of the papacy as the final authority in approving the decrees of councils and ordering ecclesiastical discipline. At the same time, he upholds the authority of local bps. as judges and legislators for their own subjects, allowing no interference from secular authority. Appeals are to be made to the provincial councils and then to the pope (1.42, 179; 2.80). He defends celibacy for the clergy but encourages the faithful to continue to accept the ministry of priests who have married (2.108). Realistic in his regard for the indissolubility of marriage, he makes some allowance for remarriage after divorce (17.10,11; 19.5). Book 19 is an important historical source for the popular beliefs and superstitions of the 10th and 11th cent., and for its encouragement of the confessor's respect for the needs of the individual penitent. Its most influential source was the collection of Regino of Prüm. Other sources include the *Anselmo-dedicata*, the *Dionysius-Hadriana*, the *False Decretals, the councils of the 9th cent., the Collectio Hibernensis,* Carolingian capitularies, and *Benedict the Levite. In several items, Burchard supplements the decrees cited with his own contemporaneous application. This collection came to the *Decretum* of Gratian through the collections of Ivo of Chartres. BIBLIOGRAPHY: J. Petrau-Gay, DDC 2:1142–57.

[F. H. BRIGHAM]

BURCKHARDT, JAKOB (1818–97), Swiss historian, born in Basel and later lecturer in the Univ. of Basel and Zurich; known esp. for his work, *The Civilization of the Renaissance in Italy* (1860) because of its influence on future studies of both Renaissance and medieval history. B. laid emphasis on the role of the individual who was "typical"; hence, he underestimated the Middle Ages and its greater concern with the community. B. is one of the first "cultural" historians, seeking to establish contact with the human mind in various periods of history so as to understand better the development of society. His other works include: *The Age of Constantine the Great* (1852), *Lectures on Force and Freedom* (1869–71). The latter contains his philosophy of history and has contributed to his reputation as an original thinker as well as a careful historian. BIBLIOGRAPHY: P. Gardner, EncPhil 1:426–427.

[M. A. GALLIN]

BUREAU OF CATHOLIC INDIAN MISSIONS, official Church agency authorized to represent its interests to the U.S. government in matters pertaining to work among the Indians and to aid this apostolate in other respects. Established in 1874 at the instance of western U.S. bps., it was made a permanent institution by the Third Plenary Council of Baltimore (1884) and has its headquarters in Washington, D.C. It has secured from the federal government fair and equal treatment for Catholic Indians, missionaries, and reservation schools; stimulated and participated in a vast increase in mission centers and schools by obtaining substantial financial aid from Catholics; and induced religious orders of men and women to lend their services to the Indian apostolate. BIBLIOGRAPHY: J. B. Tennelly, NCE 2:889–990. *INDIAN MISSIONS (U.S.).

[J. B. TENNELLY]

BURGES, WILLIAM (1827–81), English architect who expressed the early Gothic of N France in a warm, personal idiom as seen in Cork Cathedral (1863), a major 19th-cent. monument. BIBLIOGRAPHY: H. R. Hitchcock, *Architecture, 19th & 20th Century* (1958).

[M. J. DALY]

BURGFELDEN, CHURCH OF (11th–12th cent.), German Romanesque church in Baden-Württemberg, noted for its fresco which is one of the oldest extant northern depictions of the *Last Judgment,* and an important example of early Romanesque painting. BIBLIOGRAPHY: P. Clemen, *Romanische Monumentalmaler ei . . . Rheinlanden* (1916).

[M. J. DALY]

BURGHOA, FRANCISCO DE (c. 1600–81), Mexican chronicler, descendant of the conquistadores of Oaxaca and related to families of prominence. Professed in 1620 and ordained a Dominican in 1625, B. later held positions of authority in his community (provincial, procurator, vicar-general). After his term as vicar-general (1662), he wrote two of his best literary works. *Palestra historial* (1674), largely biographical in content, tells of the work of the Dominicans in Mexico City and Oaxaca. *Geográfica Descripción* (1670) deals chiefly with Oaxaca and is mainly a history of the city's monasteries. B.'s works are irreplaceable sources of Oaxaca's history, even though his prose is somewhat extravagant and hard to read. BIBLIOGRAPHY: G. C. Pena, *History of Mexican Literature* (tr. G. Nance and F. Dunstan, 1943) 145; C. Wilgus, *Library of Latin-American History and Culture* (1965) 24.

[D. M. HUGHES]

BURGKMAIR, HANS (1473–1531), German painter and designer of woodcuts. Associated with and influenced by M. *Schongauer in Colmar (1490), B. finally worked independently in Augsburg (1498). After an Italian visit, B. was associated with German humanists and artists, and, commissioned by Maximilian I, great patron of the graphic arts, designed dramatic chiaroscuro woodcuts (1508–18). Returning to painting (*St. John Altarpiece,* 1518 and *Esther before Ahasuerus,* 1528), B. blends Italian humanist ideals with northern naturalism in a manner that marks him one of the leaders of German Renaissance style. BIBLIOGRAPHY: A. C. Burkhard, *Hans Burgkmair d. A.* (1934).

[M. J. DALY]

BURGUNDIAN ROMANESQUE SCHOOL, with Languedoc, one of two major schools of French Romanesque sculpture embracing the 11th-cent. St. Bénigne, Dijon, the Cathedral of Autun (1120) with its magnificent carvings by Master *Gislebertus, La Madeleine, *Vézelay (1120–50), *Cluny (1090–1130), and Charlieu (1094–1140). In Burgundian sculpture, naturalistic vegetative motifs and dynamic, moving figures proliferate in a highly intellectualized iconographic scheme at once decorative, pseudo-scientific, humanistic, and whimsical. BIBLIOGRAPHY: K. J. Conant, *Carolingian and Romanesque Architecture (800–1200)* (1959).

[M. J. DALY]

BURGUNDIAN SCHOOL, leading school of composers of the early 15th cent., represented chiefly by Dufay and Binchois. At the time, the duchy of Burgundy included E France, Belgium, and the Netherlands. Its court at Dijon was the center of culture for Western Europe and the cathedral at Cambrai was a center of musical composition and performance. The musical style of the Burgundian School, influenced by the English school of Dunstable and possibly also by Italian models, stands in marked contrast to the complexity of the late 14th cent. and the severe rigidity of the "early Parisians." Important contributions of this school are the establishment of the third as a principal melodic interval, the Burgundian cadence, and the use of fauxbourdon. Burgundian composers, with the exception of Dufay, concentrated on secular forms. Dufay aimed at making polyphonic music an essential part of the liturgy and is regarded as the originator of the Ordinary of the Mass compositions. Under his influence, church music was fused with the older techniques into a new integrated style: melody often in the top voice, use of four-part writing, use of major and minor tonalities, and a certain rhythmic vitality. From the Burgundians the development of church music passed on to the Flemish school. BIBLIOGRAPHY: M. Velimirovic, Apel HDMUS 114–115; A. Robertson, *Christian Music* (1961) 82–84; E. Dannemann, Grove DMM 1:1019–24.

[M. T. LEGGE]

BURGUNDIANS, a Germanic people whose powerful kingdom in SE Gaul was brought under Frankish control in 534. Under Gundahar they established (409–412) a kingdom on the Rhine, with a capital at Worms. They accepted Arian Christianity. Recognized by the Romans as *foederati,* they attempted further expansion in 435, and the Roman general Aëtius, aided by the Huns, destroyed them—a story immortalized in the *Nibelungenlied.* Surviving Burgundians transferred to Savoy (443), where incessant conflict with the Franks resulted in their complete conquest by Clovis' sons (534). King Gundobad (474–516) promulgated the *Lex Gundobada* for his Germanic subjects and the *Lex Romana Burgundionum* for his Roman subjects; he practiced tolerance toward Catholic Christianity. His son Sigismund (516–523) officially adopted Catholicism. BIBLIOGRAPHY: R. H. Schmandt, NCE 2:893; *Burgundian Code* (tr. K. Fischer, 1949).

[G. M. COOK]

BURIAL. The disposal of the dead has always had religious significance in all cultures. This article limits its description to the burial practices of the Western world as exemplified by the Greco-Roman and Judaeo-Christian traditions.

Greco-Roman. Disposal of the dead included both inhumation and cremation but the use of either, varying from age to age, does not seem to have been the result of different eschatalogical beliefs as much as the prevalence of local custom or simply practicality. What was most important was that the remains of the person, whether cremated or not, had to be covered with earth. The Greek symbolic burial required three handfuls of earth sprinkled on the body; the Roman law stipulated that burial was not official until no bone was showing above the earth or until the body was enclosed in some vault that kept it out of sight. This practice was thought to assure the passage of the departed to the underworld and prevent the displeasure of the celestial gods whose responsibility for them ceased at the moment of death. The burial rite for the average Greek or Roman had few variations. Immediately after death, the corpse was cleansed, dressed in everyday attire, placed on a bed, and formally mourned. Then came the funeral procession to some location outside the city designated for burial, e.g., along the side of the road. In early Rome, the burial place was sometimes on the land worked by the deceased. The deceased was then buried in the ground or in a vault in a coffin or, if cremated, his ashes were interred in a burial urn. After the funeral, a meal was held together with a rite of purification. In Greece, offerings at the grave were made on the 3d and 9th days after burial. In Rome, the period of strict mourning was concluded after the 9th day's offering (*novendiale sacrificium*). In many locales, there was an annual family reunion and meal at the grave to renew by a symbolic, common meal the bond of brotherhood that had existed while the deceased was alive. More elaborate ceremonies attended the burial of distinguished citizens with differences characteristic of each nation and epoch. Taking part in the funerals of important Roman officials were the general public, invited guests, a long masked retinue representing the ancestors of the deceased, professional women mourners, and musicians. But the laws of classical Greece and republican Rome forbade excess in such rites. Possessions found in tombs are also an indication of the importance of the deceased in the community. It was the classical belief that for survival in the underworld the deceased have the same material needs as they had while still alive. Hosever Mycenaean nobles were interred with expensive treasures but men of later ages were buried with relatively few possessions. In Greece, some were given cheese cake to appease the vicious hound Cerberus at the entrance to the underworld; in later times, a coin was placed in the mouth of the departed as fare to be paid to Charon, the grim ferryman of the river Styx. Sepulchers in Greece and Rome were marked by posts (*stelae*), columns (*kiones*), small shrines (*naidia*), ortable-like pieces of stone (*trapezai*) with

appropriate inscriptions. BIBLIOGRAPHY: G. Sergi, Hastings ERE 4:472–475; G. Showerman, *ibid*. 4.505–507.

Biblical. The Bible records different methods of burial but in Syria and Palestine inhumation was preferred to cremation. The corpse was washed, anointed, dressed in the clothes of everyday life until a later period when the death shroud or linen wrappings became common. The burial took place within 24 hours because of the danger of rapid decomposition in the warm climate. The corpse was carried by friends amid their lamentations and those of hired mourners. There was no set ritual at the grave with the exception of an occasional eulogy. The mourning period differed depending upon the rank of the deceased and his relationship with the mourners, but it was usually 7 days. Mourners rent their garments and wore the outer garment cut and unbound for 30 days, fasted, beat their breasts, sprinkled ashes on their heads, went barefoot and bareheaded. The fast on the day of burial concluded with a meal called *funeral baked meats* and in the OT *lehem 'ohnim* (bread of mourners). It was also customary to visit the grave and eat a meal there on the Sabbath after the burial.

Though there is some evidence of burial in towns and on the property of the deceased, early burial chambers were in natural caves; later there were burial ledges, and in Greco-Roman times, chambers with several niches and a vestibule. Sarcophagi were used only for prominent citizens. For the most part the place of burial was concealed underground with no monument post (*stele*) to mark its location. BIBLIOGRAPHY: W. H. Bennett, Hastings ERE 4:497–500.

Ancient Christian. Contrary to the pagan conviction that proper burial was essential for an individual's happiness in the afterlife, the Early Christians insisted that this was not so (see St. Augustine, *De civ. Dei* 1.12). Nevertheless, out of reverence for the body as the temple of the Holy Spirit and in view of the future resurrection, they were zealous in their care for the dead. The first Christians naturally followed Jewish burial customs, but these were later modified under the influence of local practices and Christian hope. When a person died, his eyes and mouth were closed, his body washed, anointed, and wrapped in linen as a sign of immortality. It could then be dressed in the clothes worn during life. For pagans and Jews death was the occasion for loud and even violent cries of grief. Christians were accustomed to obviate such outbursts by the recitation of Psalms. Burial could take place on the day of death or the following day. A wake could be held at the home, church, or graveside before or after burial. When the time came for interment, the body was placed on a bier and carried in a kind of triumphal procession to the place of burial, which could be a grave dug in the ground or in a natural or artificial crypt. A eulogy was pronounced either in the church or at the side of the grave by a relative, friend, or cleric. In many places a Mass was celebrated at the grave, as happened at the funeral of St. Monica in Ostia (St. Augustine, *Confess.* 9.23). Like the Jews before them, the Early Christians never cremated but always buried their dead. BIBLIOG-RAPHY: A. C. Rush, *Death and Burial in Christian Antiquity* (1941); J. Kollwitz, RAC 2:208–219.

Modern Practice. At present, Jewish burial rites have substantially retained ancient practice. The deceased is symbolically washed and then dressed in a shroud. In the West, it is customary to use a coffin for interment, but in the East and the state of Israel, the corpse is transferred to the grave on a bier. After a brief prayer ceremony, those present assist in filling the grave. Before departure from the grave, an appropriate version of the doxology known as the *Kaddish* is recited and the mourners form two lines through which the next of kin pass to receive words of consolation. This marks the beginning of official mourning. Cremation, though forbidden by rabbinic tradition, is at times preferred by Reformed Jews. In Protestant denominations, variations follow local customs and denominational practices but the central theme of the burial rite is proclamation of belief in the Resurrection of the Lord and the resurrection of the dead. The service may include prayers at the home, scripture readings, Psalms, hymns, and a sermon for the consolation of the bereaved at the church followed by prayers and blessing at the grave. Cremation is optional. Some Protestants prefer a simple graveside ceremony. For the recently revised burial rite now in use in the RC church, see *FUNERAL RITE. BIBLIOGRAPHY: Bouscaren-Ellis-Korth 673–697; B. Jordahn, EncLuthCh 1:341–345; W. H. Bennet, *Hastings* ERE 4:497–500.

[F. BRIGHAM]

BURIAL WITH CHRIST, a scriptural metaphor. In the Gospel narratives of Christ's Passion and Resurrection, his burial is accorded a prominent place, and this is reflected in the early creeds and in such creedal formulas as 1 Cor 15.3–4. Christ rose living from the tomb (see Acts 2.29–36). "The thing which is sown is perishable, but what is raised is imperishable" (1 Cor 15.42; cf. 15.43–44); the grain of wheat falls to the ground and dies in order to yield a rich harvest (Jn 12.24); the new Adam, like the first, is taken from the earth (1 Cor 15.45–49). Salvation comes to the Christian by his sacramental union with Christ in his whole paschal mystery, in each of the various moments that go to constitute that mystery. Just as he dies and rises with Christ, so "when we were baptized we went into the tomb with him" (Rom 6.4; Col 2.12). This is a clear reference to the burial symbolism (and efficacy) of baptism, esp. when administered by immersion. Just as Christ's burial showed the reality of his death and the newness of his risen life, so the Christian's baptismal burial expresses and effects his total death to sin, that death which is part and parcel of his birth to new life. Some commentators also see in this baptismal symbolism a reference to Christ's descent into hell, for this too was a soteriological mystery by which the just members of the old Israel were aggregated to the new people of God, the redeemed community. BIBLIOGRAPHY: J. Daniélou,

Bible and the Liturgy (1960) 43–47; W. F. Flemington, *New Testament Doctrine of Baptism* (1957); O. Rousseau, "La Descente aux enfers, fondement soteriologique du baptême chrétien", Rech SR 40 (1952) 273–297.

[R. L. STEWART]

BURKE, EDMUND (1729–97), British statesman and political philosopher. B. was born in Dublin of a Protestant father and Catholic mother, and reared an Anglican. He attended Trinity College, Dublin, and then studied law for a time in London, but abandoned this to embark on a literary career. He became private secretary to the Marquis of Rockingham, the Whig prime minister at the time (1765), and the same year entered the House of Commons, where he sat until his retirement in 1794. He was the philosopher and spokesman for the Whig aristocracy, and following his writings against the French Revolution became a leader of European conservatism. Yet he favored political and social reform to be effected by gradual adaptation to changing times and circumstances. He was opposed to the penal laws against Catholics, the inequities of the criminal law, and the slave trade. B. did much to arouse the conscience of the nation to a sense of its responsibilities toward colonial peoples. He scorned the "natural rights" proclaimed by doctrinaire revolutionaries in France, but in his own thinking he embraced the doctrine of a natural law that had come down from medieval times. BIBLIOGRAPHY: F. P. Canavan, *Political Reason of Edmund Burke* (1960); idem, NCE 2:898–899.

[T. EARLY]

BURKE, THOMAS (1830–82), Irish Dominican, a preacher renowned in Ireland, England, and the U.S., associated with the reform of his order by A. Jandel. In 1871 he was visitator to the American Dominican Province of St. Joseph, and sought to curtail pastoral activities in favor of a more conventual life. BIBLIOGRAPHY: W. J. Fitzpatrick, *Life of the Very Rev. Thomas N. Burke, O.P.* (2 v., 1886).

[T. C. O'BRIEN]

BURKITT, FRANCIS CRAWFORD (1864–1935), British Scripture scholar, Orientalist, and historian. B. was an expert in Oriental languages, esp. Syriac; he applied this knowledge to the textual criticism of the Gospels and transcribed the Syriac palimpsest of the Gospels found on Mount Sinai. The apocalyptic interpretation of Jesus' teaching was championed by B., who maintained that later Christianity distorted the eschatological mentality of the historical Jesus. He also devoted himself to studies of Early Christian history, Manichaeism, and *Gnosticism. BIBLIOGRAPHY: J. F. Bethune-Baker, DNB 1931–40) 124–125; JTS 36 (1935) 337–346, extensive bibliography.

[T. M. MCFADDEN]

BÜRKTŌ, W. Syrian blessed bread, distributed after the Eucharistic Liturgy. It is comparable to the Byzantine *antidoron*.

[A. CODY]

BURMA, the most westerly country in SE Asia (261,789 sq mi; pop. [est. 1971] 28.2 million. The people are of Mongoloid stock of varying tribal affiliations. Burma was annexed to the British Empire through a series of wars (1824–85) and until 1937 was administered as a part of India. In 1937 it achieved dominion status; from early 1942 until 1945 it was occupied by the Japanese; in 1948 it became completely independent. Buddhism, the religion of about 90% of the people has been the most cohesive element of national life. Isolated attempts by RC missionaries were made to evangelize the country in the 16th and 17th cent., but Buddhist opposition prevented the establishment of any foothold of importance. Systematic effort began with P. Bigandet, vicar apostolic of Rangoon (1865–93), with the help of French missionaries. These were aided later by the Columbans, the Christian Brothers, Italian missionaries from Milan, and the Jesuits. Progress was made and the outlook was fairly bright from 1914 until 1939. The missions, however, were ravaged during World War II, and since that time the responsibilities for the development of the Church in Burma have been turned over, as far as possible, to the Burmese clergy. A Burmese priest was consecrated bishop in 1954 and a second in 1961. In 1955 the territory was divided into two ecclesiastical provinces, Rangoon and Mandalay, and there are suffragans in Kengtung, Myitkyina, Bassein, Prome, Taunggyi, and Toungoo.* There are some 189 priests and 600 religious men and women to minister to the needs of the 285,000 Catholics of the country and to carry on the evangelical effort. Among the obstacles that impede the work are the lack of transportation, the multiplicity of dialects, and Buddhist opposition. In 1961 Buddhism was declared the state religion. Communist propaganda causes much trouble. There was a wholesale expulsion of missionaries in 1966. Protestantism was brought to Burma by Adoniram Judson in 1815 and has been vigorously promoted by the American Baptist Convention. Extensive and effective work has been done among the Karens, who make up 60% of the whole Protestant body with a total community of c.700,000. Anglicans, Methodists, Pentecostals, and Adventists have also contributed to the gains made by Protestantism. The high percentage of native leadership used by these bodies illustrates the importance of that method in missionary work.

[P. DAMBORIENA]

BURMA, ART OF. Earliest Buddhist art (6th–8th cent.) in late Gupta style determined stupas and temples in a classical period (10th–13th cent.) terminated by the Mongol invasion (1287). First stupas are massive cylindrical forms of Orissa (NE India) type. Their masterpiece is the great Ananda temple (1084–c.1112) in a Greek cross plan, rising in a pyramidal mass to the crowning stupa with a vertical emphasis distinctive of Burmese forms. Later temples opened a sanctuary within, creating a second story uniquely Burmese (Thalbyinnyu, 1144; Tilominlo, 1218). Wall reliefs illustrate lively Jataka tales. Following the Mongol conquest colossal size and lavish ornamentation in gilt and jewels mark a decline culminating in the sentimental alabaster Buddhas of the 19th century. There was great destruction by bombings in World War II. BIBLIOGRAPHY: T. G. M. Louis-Frédéric, *Art of Southeast Asia* (1965).

[M. J. DALY]

BURNE-JONES, EDWARD COLEY (1833–98), English painter and designer, friend of William Morris. A pupil of Dante Gabriel Rossetti, B. assisted in decorating the Oxford Union. After travels in Italy (1859–73), he created a sensation with his paintings. Prolific designer of stained-glass windows and tapestries, B. also illustrated *Chaucer* (1896). Replacing the early sensuous medievalism of Rossetti by the mysticism of a sad, languid dream world in decorative line, B. is rather Byzantine than Gothic, as evident in mosaics for the American Episcopal Church, Rome. BIBLIOGRAPHY: A. L. Baldry, *Burne-Jones* (1909), G. Burne-Jones, *Memorials of Edward Burne-Jones* (2 v., 1904, repr. AMS).

[M. J. DALY]

BURNET, GILBERT (1643–1715), English bp. and historian. Prepared for the Scottish ministry, he refused a position because of the unsettled state of church affairs, but worked to effect a compromise between episcopacy and presbyterianism. Failing in this, he left Scotland and settled in London. There he proved very helpful to William of Orange and Mary in their occupation of the English throne, for which service he was appointed bp. of Salisbury. His writings include *History of the Reformation in England* (3 v., 1679–1714), *History of My Own Time* (2 v., 1723–34), and many pamphlets defending the *Broad Church. The best part of his historical work is that based on personal knowledge: the history of the Church of Scotland and the events leading up to the revolution in England. BIBLIOGRAPHY: O. Airy, DNB 7:394–405.

[M. J. BARRY]

BURNING BUSH, an unknown species of desert shrub at the site of God's first revelation to Moses (Ex 3.2–4). Its location on a "mountain of God" (Ex 3.1) most likely marked a revered shrine, one perhaps already known to the Midianites before Moses' arrival; the "fire" may have been caused by electrical activity. The association of this holy place with Sinai may be a relatively late development in the tradition, prompted in part by the similar sound of "Sinai" and "seneh," the Hebrew name of the bush. In any case, the episode now seems an introduction for the fiery theophany of Ex 19. BIBLIOGRAPHY: M. Noth, *Exodus* (tr. J. S. Bowden, 1962) 38–40.

[P. J. KEARNEY]

BURNS, JAMES ALOYSIUS (1867–1940), educator. Ordained a priest of the Congregation of the Holy Cross (1893) he taught chemistry at the Univ. of Notre Dame, where he urged that college instructors should become involved in advanced studies before starting to teach. In 1900 he was appointed superior of Holy Cross College, Washington, D. C., the house of studies for the congregation. He helped start the National Catholic Educational Association (1904) and wrote books on education including: *Principles, Origin and Establishment of the Catholic School System* (1908) and *Growth and Development of the Catholic School System* (1912). In 1919 B. was elected president of the Univ. of Notre Dame which he reorganized into four distinct colleges of arts and letters, science, engineering, and law. He also began a campaign for funds from the Rockefeller and Carnegie Foundations. In 1926 he again became superior of Holy Cross, and in 1927 was appointed provincial of the Indiana Province of his congregation, becoming first assistant superior general in 1938.

[J. HILL]

BURNT OFFERING, a type of sacrifice offered the Deity in OT Times. Animals and agricultural produce were burned on the altar during the daily temple worship and on special occasions (Num 28–29; Ex 29). This form of sacrifice was already familiar in Canaan before the arrival of the Israelites, who apparently adopted the practice during the settlement period. The notion of the sacrifice as "food" for God seems to be a pre-Israelite expression retained in the liturgical vocabulary of Israel (Num 28.2; Lev 21.6, 8, 17; 22.25), but the offering was reinterpreted to mean probably a total gift of oneself, symbolized by imposing hands on the animal victim (Lev 1.4). BIBLIOGRAPHY: De Vaux AncIsr, 415–456.

[P. J. KEARNEY]

BURROWS, ERIC NORMAN BROMLY (1882–1938), Jesuit Orientalist. After studies in Beirut and Rome, B. did biblical research in Rome and the Holy Land, and served as the cuneiform expert for archeological expeditions to Kish and Ur in modern Iraq. He published a study of the oldest written documents found at Ur and contributed much new information about the time of Abraham. BIBLIOGRAPHY: J. A. Brinkman, NCE 2:905.

[T. M. MCFADDEN]

BURRUS, PETRUS (1430-1507), poet, theologian, educator. An author whose works reflect the revival of interest in classical literature, he was employed as a teacher of young men until his appointment as a canon of Amiens (1495). BIBLIOGRAPHY: *Biographie nationale de Belgique* 4:851–852; M. Monaco, NCE 2:905.

[J. MULDOON]

BURSE, a square, stiff container for the folded corporal in carrying it to and from the altar. Though becoming optional, when used for Mass it is placed on top of the veiled chalice, with its upper surface of the same colored material as the vestments of the day. Otherwise, it is usually white or gold. The word also designates the small purselike container for the pyx in taking communion to the sick.

[N. R. KRAMER]

BURSFELD, ABBEY OF, former Benedictine abbey near Münden (Hanover), founded (1093) by Count Henry the Fat of Northeim, daughter monastery of Corvey. In 1430 Abbot John Dederoth started a reform congregation, which comprised under the title "Bursfeld Union," almost all Benedictine abbeys of N and W Germany, Denmark, Holland, Belgium, and Luxemburg. This Union, one of the most vigorous movements of reform, perdured until the 19th century. Bursfeld itself became a Protestant titular abbey in 1543; its baroque church still stands. BIBLIOGRAPHY: Cottineau 1:534–535; P. Volk, LTK 2:796–798.

[F. N. BACKMUND]

BURSFELD UNION, Benedictine reform congregation which originated with amalgamation of several monasteries with the Bursfeld Abbey on the Weser River about 8 miles from Hanover in the Diocese of Mainz, Germany. Johann Dederoth, Abbot of Clus, renewed the Bursfeld Abbey (1433) and united it with Clus. The Abbeys of Reinhausen, Huysburg, and Cismar joined the movement and held the first chapter of the Bursfeld Congregation (May, 1446). Approved by Pope Pius II (1459) the congregation grew rapidly, though the abbey itself became Protestant. The Bursfeld Union ended with the secularization of 1802–03. BIBLIOGRAPHY: P. Volk, LTK 2:796–798; *idem,* DHGE 10:1389–93.

[M. H. BEIRNE]

BURSHÂNAH, an Arabic word, used: (1) as the normal name for the Maronite unleavened host; also called (Arabic) *qurbân,* (Syriac) *qûrbōnō*; and (2) occasionally for the W Syrian leavened bread (*tab'ō*).

[A. CODY]

BURTON, KATHERINE (1884–1969), writer. A convert to Catholicism, B. is best known for a series of biographies of outstanding American Catholics. Associate editor of *McCall's* magazine and later of *Redbook,* for 20 years she contributed a lively column to *Sign* magazine. Among her biographies the most widely read are *Sorrow Built a Bridge* (1937) on Rose Hawthorne and her community, *His Dear*

Persuasion (1940) about St. Elizabeth Seton, and *Celestial Homespun,* (1943) the life of Isaac Hecker.

[J. R. AHERNE]

BURTON, ROBERT (1577–1640), English clergyman and author of *The Anatomy of Melancholy,* published (1621), republished and revised in six editions by 1651. It is a serious medical treatise but in addition contains much information on the life and thought of the period. B. is particularly interested in melancholy, its causes and possible cures, and in the degree of difference between melancholy and madness. His *Anatomy* is the culmination of Elizabethan handbooks on psychology, which are particularly absorbed in problems of abnormal personalities. These psychologists saw man as a little state wherein unruly passions, unless governed by the faculties of the soul, would result in abnormal behavior. They treated the topic as a sub-department of theology. BIBLIOGRAPHY: B. Evans and G. J. Mohr, *Psychology of Robert Burton* (1944).

[M. M. BARRY]

BURTSELL, RICHARD LALOR (1840–1912), civic leader, canonist. After studies in the Sulpician seminary in Montreal, Canada, B. went (1857) to Rome, obtained a doctorate in philosophy and theology, and was ordained (1862). He founded the Epiphany parish (1867) and established St. Benedict the Moor, the first parish in the New York archdiocese for Negroes. In 1890 he was appointed pastor of St. Mary's in Kingston and was an excellent administrator. He wrote for many scholarly journals and contributed articles to the *Catholic Encyclopedia.* More civic-minded than most priests of his day, he was a highly regarded citizen and served on the boards of trustees for the City Hospital and Library. He was named a papal chamberlain (1905) and a domestic prelate (1911). BIBLIOGRAPHY: E. H. Smith, NCE 2:906.

[J. HILL]

BURY, JOHN BAGNELL (1861–1927), Irish historian. Born in the county of Monaghan and educated at Trinity College, Dublin, B. became a fellow of Trinity and professor of modern history at both Dublin and Cambridge Universities. He was the recipient of numerous honorary degrees from the univ. of England, Scotland, and Ireland. Among his best known works are: *History of the Later Roman Empire from Arcadius to Irene* (1889), *Life of St. Patrick and His Place in History* (1905), and *Idea of Progress* (1920). Though B. was a profound scholar of Byzantine history, critics recognize his failure to understand the dynamic and leading part that religion played in Byzantine civilization. BIBLIOGRAPHY: N. H. Baynes, *Bibliography of the Works of J. B. Bury . . . with a Memoir* (1929); idem, EncRelKnow(Suppl)1:192.

[R. A. TODD]

BURY ST. EDMUNDS, ABBEY OF, originally Edmundsbury, in Co. Suffolk, one of the great Benedictine abbeys in medieval England. To the original foundation by Sigebert, King of the East Angles (630), the body of St. Edmund, king and martyr (869), was transferred so that it became an important pilgrimage shrine. Destroyed by the Danes and refounded by King Canute (1020), it was splendidly enlarged by a succession of abbots, among whom Samson (1182–1211) was conspicuous as a patron of learning (see Jocelyn of Brakeland's *Chronicle*). It contained a rich library and became a center for monastic history and music: the poet John Lydgate was an alumnus. There was no sign of decay when Henry VIII dissolved the monastery (1539).

[T. GILBY]

BURY ST. EDMUNDS BIBLE (1121–48), a masterpiece of Romanesque art. The work of Master Hugo, a versatile craftsman in the Benedictine scriptorium of one of England's wealthiest, most influential, and most scholarly monasteries (a chief center of pilgrimage), the MS is characterised by firm draftsmanship, notably in schematized draperies, deep rich colors, and noble foliate initials. It is now in Corpus Christi College, Cambridge. With the *Life of St. Edmund* (Pierpont Morgan Library, N.Y.) it is an outstanding production of the above scriptorium. See R. W. Hays, NCE 2:908.

[R. L. S. BRUCE-MITFORD]

BUS, CÉSAR DE, BL. (1544–1607), French catechist, founder of the Fathers of Christian Doctrine (Doctrinaires). After a career as captain of the guard of Charles IX, during which period he also wrote poetry and dramas, B. became a priest (1582) and devoted himself to teaching catechism at Cavaillon. His cousin, J. B. Romaillon, a convert from Calvinism, was also ordained and worked with him. Additional followers joined them and the company received papal approval (1598). B. was distinguished for his works of charity, and for his zeal in preaching, and esp. for his catechizing in an age when it was sorely needed. He was declared venerable by Pius VII (1821) and blessed by Paul VI (1975). BIBLIOGRAPHY: P. Giloteaux, *Le Vénérable César de Bus: Fondateur de la Congrégation des Prêtres de la Doctrine Chrétienne, 1544–1607* (1961); G. Bataille, BiblSanct 3:613–614.

[L. MITCHELL]

BUSAEUS (BUYS), family name of two brothers prominent in the Counter-Reformation.
Petrus (1540–87), Jesuit theologian. Encouraged by Peter Canisius, he added to the catechism of Canisius (1st ed., 1569–70) the best available texts of the scriptural and patristic authorities cited in it. The author's purpose was to establish the agreement of the catechism with the teaching of the primitive Church. A revised edition appeared in 1577. In 1571 he was teaching Scripture at the Univ. of Vienna. He

was called to Rome (1584) and appointed to the commission charged with drawing up the Jesuit *Ratio studiorum*. On his return he was appointed rector of the college of nobles in Vienna.

Johannes (1514–1611), Jesuit theologian. After studying theology at Rome, he taught for 22 years at Mainz. His first written works attacked Protestant doctrines, esp. ubiquitarianism regarding the person of Christ. There is a mildness in these writings, polemical as they are, remarkable for that time. After 1595, he devoted himself to editing and translating ascetical works, the most important of which were his *Enchiridion piarum meditationum* and *Viridarium christianarum virtutum*. BIBLIOGRAPHY: A. Rayez, LTK 2:799; J. Brucker, DTC 2.1:1265–66; A. de Bil, DHGE 10:1414–15.

[J. M. O'DONNELL]

BUSENBAUM, HERMANN (1600–68), Jesuit moral theologian. A Westphalian, B. was adviser to Christof Bernhard von Galen, prince-bishop of Münster, and was esteemed as a spiritual director. His most celebrated work, *Medulla theologiae moralis (The Marrow of Moral Theology, Solving Cases of Conscience by a Clear and Easy Method Gathered from Various Approved Authors, Equally Serviceable for Penitents and Confessors*, 1650) went through 40 editions in his lifetime, and 2 cent. later the number neared 200. The method is strictly casuistic and analytical; it concentrates on the notion of legal obligation and, as the title indicates, is not a treatise on moral perfection. A few of B.'s opinions were considered overindulgent by Alexander VII and Innocent XI, and he was unfairly made a scapegoat by those who wished to father on the Jesuits the doctrines of tyrannicide and of the end's justifying the means. BIBLIOGRAPHY: Sommervogel 2:444–455; J. Brucker, DTC 2.1:1266–68; L. Vereecke, NCE 2:909–910.

[T. GILBY]

BUSH, (JOHN NASH) DOUGLAS (1896–   ) critic, teacher, Christian humanist. The long and distinguished career of B. has given literary criticism and teaching in the U.S. one of its great traditions. Thirty-three of his 42 years as an English professor were spent at Harvard where he gained the Ph.D., and for his last 9 years was Gurney Professor of English. His voluminous critical writing embraces the Renaissance, and the 17th and 19th centuries. He is the definitive editor of Milton, having written or edited five works on that poet. He has written extensively on the 19th-cent. poets Keats and Tennyson. B. is essentially a Christian humanist and has returned to that tradition many times in books and critical essays in scholarly publications.

[J. R. AHERNE]

BUSHNELL, HORACE (1802–76), American Congregationalist theologian, "father of *liberal theology" in the United States. Graduated from Yale in 1827, he studied law until he was moved at a revival meeting in 1831 to enter Yale Divinity School. Ordained in 1833 as pastor of the North Congregational Church, Hartford, Conn., B. remained there until 1859, when he resigned to devote all his time to writing. As a preacher, he was Christocentric, and Christ as the vitalizing principle was the keynote of his preaching. He drew on Jonathan *Edwards and on German idealists, esp. F. *Schleiermacher for his theological insights. On the basis of his theory that language is symbolic and imperfect, deriving full meaning from social use, he acknowledged that dogmatic and theological language is inadequate and, in the spirit of charity, hoped that different insights might be combined in comprehensive truth, so as to elevate what was science and opinion to the level of spirit and life. B. stressed the interrelatedness of human beings, esp. in the Church, and the immanence of the supernatural in the natural. His *Discourses on Christian Nurture* (1847) defended the claim of the children of Christian parents to a share in Christian fellowship, against those who relied on revivals to bring regenerate adults into the Christian family (see CHRISTIAN NURTURE). His *God in Christ* (1849) raised a storm of controversy by acknowledging that the Trinity signified God not in his ultimate being but only in the modes by which he reveals himself as Father, Son, and Holy Spirit; B. clarified his concepts in *Christ in Theology* (1851). In *The Vicarious Sacrifice* (1866) and *Forgiveness and Law* (1874), he gave his mature views on the atonement, not as vicarious expiation but as a moral example. B. was the key figure who eased the transition for evangelical Christians from the old to the new theology, by presenting them with a Christocentric theology that relied less on external proofs and rationalizations than on inward testimony and Christian experience. His *Christian Nurture* and other writings helped break down extreme individualism and directly influenced the *Social Gospel of Washington Gladden and others. BIBLIOGRAPHY: B. M. Cross, *Horace Bushnell, Minister to a Changing America* (1958).

[R. K. MACMASTER]

BUSINESS, a broad term here understood to embrace activities concerned with the production, distribution, and sale of goods or services when these are undertaken with a view to profit. It is a field in which injustice in one or another of its varied forms is frequently practiced. More blatant offenses against justice are generally prohibited by civil law, but it is quite beyond the power of civil law to provide ample protection against every injustice. In the interests of the common good it is therefore necessary that the law be supplemented by the observance of ethical standards reaching beyond the limits of effective legislation. In many trades and professions codes have been adopted to define ethical behavior, and these codes, derived from religious and ethical principles, are generally considered to bind in conscience.

[J. C. WILLKE]

BUSKINS, a bishop's ceremonial stockings worn at a pontifical Mass. They are made of silk or elastic material corresponding in color to the other vestments and are worn over the bishop's ordinary purple stockings; their use is now optional.

[N. KOLLAR]

BUSNOIS, ANTOINE (family name de Busne; d. 1492), contrapuntist and musician in the Burgundian court, and a contemporary of Okeghem. His works, which include Magnificats, Masses, chansons, and motets are preserved in various libraries of Europe. BIBLIOGRAPHY: J. F. R. Stainer, Grove DMM 1:1040-41.

[M. T. LEGGE]

BUSTAMANTE, CARLOS MARIA (1774-1848), Mexican historian, editor, politician, and liberal statesman in the era of independence (1805-48). In 1812, serving in Mexico's first war of independence, B. endured imprisonment and many hardships; his later opposition to the new government of Iturbide (1821) again brought imprisonment. From 1824 until his death, however, he served as a member of Congress. B. was also instrumental in the fight for the return of the Jesuits to Mexico. His writings, which have often been described as confusing and inaccurate, can be divided into two classes: original works and those he edited. *Cuadro histórico de la revolución mexicana (1843-46)*, written in the form of letters and published in six volumes, is perhaps the most important of this prolific historian's writings. Although his 107 works of various kinds show a general lack of plan and development, Mexican history is indebted to him for preserving abundant material on Mexico's revolutionary period and its era of independence. BIBLIOGRAPHY: C. G. Peña, *History of Mexican Literature* (tr. G. Nance and F. Dunstan, 1943, 3d ed. 1968) 243-245.

[D. M. HUGHES]

BUTIN, ROMANUS (1871-1937), Marist Orientalist. After early studies in his native France, B. came to America and completed his preparation for the priesthood in Maryland where he was ordained in 1897. He later received a doctorate in philosophy at The Catholic Univ. of America and there maintained a teaching post for the remainder of his life. Proficient in Semitic languages, B. was appointed Director of the American School of Oriental Research in 1926, and was influential in the founding of the Catholic Biblical Association of America. BIBLIOGRAPHY: J. A. Grispino and R. T. Cochran, "Rev. Romain François Butin, S. M.," CBQ 24 (1962) 383-393.

[R. C. TOLLARICO]

BUTLER, ALBAN (1710-73), English priest, author of the *Lives of the Saints* (4 v., 1756-59), a work later critically revised by H. Thurston (1926-38) and D. Attwater (1956). The work of 30 years, his biographies of about 1600 saints provided the most comprehensive collection of hagiographical information available to English-speaking Catholics.

Ordained at Douai in 1735, B. was a professor there until 1749, when he returned to do pastoral work in England. After the expulsion of the Jesuits from France, he held the office of the president of the English College at Saint-Omer from 1766 until his death. BIBLIOGRAPHY: H. Thurston, "A Memoir of Alban Butler," Butler 4:651-666.

[T. C. O'BRIEN]

BUTLER, CHARLES (1750-1832), English Catholic lay leader. Nephew of Alban *Butler, the hagiographer, he studied at Douai and Lincoln's Inn and practiced law as a conveyancer until the Catholic Relief Act (1791) enabled him to become the first Catholic to be called to the bar since 1688. Secretary to the Committee of Catholic Laymen and a leading figure in the *Cisalpine Club, both of which worked for the repeal of the penal laws, he advocated making concessions, for instance, the acceptance of a governmental veto in the appointment of bishops, but met stiff opposition from Bp. John Milner and Daniel O'Connell. His many writings on law, history, music, Scripture, and social questions are indicative of his versatile scholarship; he is best known for his *Historical Memoirs of English, Scottish and Irish Catholics since the Reformation.* BIBLIOGRAPHY: B. N. Ward, *Dawn of the Catholic Revival in England, 1781-1803* (2 v., 1909); idem, *Eve of Catholic Emancipation* (3 v., 1911-12).

[V. SAMPSON]

BUTLER, EDWARD CUTHBERT (1858-1934), Benedictine abbot and scholar. After studying at Downside, B. entered the Benedictine novitiate there (1876) where he made his theological studies and later taught. He was a leader in making his society's abbeys autonomous. He was the first head of the Downside house of studies at Cambridge (1896). From 1906 until 1922 he served as abbot at Downside. He strengthened the community's liturgical life and stressed mental prayer. His inability to reduce Downside's parochial commitments, which he conceived as an obstacle to its proper function, led to his resignation in 1922. He then moved to Ealing Priory where he remained until his death. Among his works were a study and text of the *Lausiac History of Palladius* (1898, 1904); *Benedictine Monachism* (1919); *Western Mysticism* (1922); *Life and Times of Bishop Ullathorne* (1926); *History of the Vatican Council* (1930). BIBLIOGRAPHY: M. D. Knowles, "Abbot Butler: A Memoir," DownRev 52 (1934), 347-440; idem, NCE 2:915.

[G. J. RUPPEL]

BUTLER, JOSEPH (1692-1752), English theologian, bp. of Durham. Ordained in the C of E, B. preached in 1726 his famous "Fifteen Sermons" and in a time of general skepticism urged the maintenance of churches and the holding of regular services. His outstanding literary work, *Analogy of Religion, Natural and Revealed, to the Constitutions and Course of Nature* (1736), is the most solid defense in the 18th cent. of revealed religion against the theories of the deists. B. argues that religion cannot lie wholly within the sphere of reason, that the evidences of revelation, while they cannot be strictly proved, are very probable and are not unreasonable. Offered the See of Canterbury in 1747 he was reported to have declined, saying that it was too late for him to try to support a falling Church. BIBLIOGRAPHY: W. A. Spooner, *Bishop Butler* (1901); E. C. Mossner, *Bishop Butler and the Age of Reason* (1936); W. J. Norton, *Bishop Butler, Moralist and Divine* (1940).

[M. J. BARRY]

BUTLER, JOSEPHINE ELIZABETH (1828–1906), English social reformer. She strove many years to reclaim prostitutes and to suppress enforced prostitution. She was instrumental in establishing at Geneva an international federation for abolishing state regulation of vice. Her life was one of almost uninterrupted prayer modeled on St. Catherine of Siena's. BIBLIOGRAPHY: L. Hay-Cooper, *Josephine Butler* (1922).

[M. J. SUELZER]

BUTLER, MARIE JOSEPH, MOTHER (1860–1940), religious superior, educator. Born in Ireland, B. entered the Congregation of the Sacred Heart of Mary at Béziers, France, at the age of 16, and before taking first vows, was sent to Portugal. She was appointed in 1903 to head the congregation's second American foundation in Long Island City, New York, where she inaugurated a program that produced during her lifetime a chain of educational institutions across the U.S. Her cause for beatification was officially opened in 1948. BIBLIOGRAPHY: K. Burton, *Mother Butler of Marymount* (1944).

[J. HILL]

BUTLER, SAMUEL (1835–1902), English author, Anglican bp. of Lichfield. A man of varied accomplishment, he is best known for his books on evolution, in which he opposed his friend Darwin's theory of natural selection because it seemed to contradict all ideas of purpose in the universe. B. maintained that heredity and evolution are due to a striving or cunning in the individual by which it adapts to its environment and hands this adaptation on by unconscious memory or habit. This theory which, as B. saw it, reintroduced teleology into organic life, made little impression on his contemporaries but was favorably considered by some later scientists. Among B.'s works are *Life and Habit* (1878), *Evolution Old and New* (1879), *Unconscious Memory* (1880), *Luck or Cunning. . . ?* (1887), and the novel, *The Way of All Flesh* (1903), which satirizes English family life. His theological views, published in his posthumous *God the Known and God the Unknown* (1909) included the view that God is not pure spirit, and his explanation of this led him through panzoism to a kind of pantheism. He also thought it conceivable that behind the God known to man there may be a yet higher God, behind whom was possibly a yet more eminent deity, and so on. BIBLIOGRAPHY: T. A. Goudge,

EncPhil 1:434–436; P. N. Furbank, *Samuel Butler* (1948); B. Willey, *Darwin and Butler, Two Versions of Evolution* (1960).

[M. J. BARRY]

BUTLER, WILLIAM JOHN (1818–94), Anglican dean of Lincoln. Ordained in 1841, B. served most of his life as High Church vicar at Wantage. In 1850 he founded in his parish a sisterhood which is now one of the most active Anglican religious groups: the Community of St. Mary the Virgin. He continued as its warden until his death. BIBLIOGRAPHY: A. L. Hoare, *Butler of Wantage: His Inheritance and His Legacy* (1948).

[M. J. SUELZER]

BUTTERFIELD, WILLIAM (1814–1900), English architect noted for harmony and fine proportion with excellence of detail, as seen in All Saints, Margaret St., London (1849–55), which became a model for the Ecclesiological Society. Distinctive are B.'s ''polychromatic'' glass and tile decorations. At St. Alban's, Holborn (1859–63) fine proportions are more evident in restrained detail. The chapel (1873) at Keble College, Oxford, shows excessive ornamentation. BIBLIOGRAPHY: H. R. Hitchcock, *Architecture, Nineteenth and Twentieth Centuries* (1958).

[M. J. DALY]

BUTZBACH, JOHANNES (Piemontanus; 1477–1526), wandering scholar, tailor, student at Deventer (1498), a Benedictine from 1500 and later prior of Maria-Laach. B. was a deeply religious humanist. He wrote, apart from Latin poems, the first German books on painting (*Libellus de praeclaris picturae professoribus*, 1505). His *Auctarium* contains 1155 biographies of famous personalities. In *Hodoporicon* (1505), he describes in cheerful and simple style his youth and journeyman's years (German pub. D. J. Becker, *Chronika eines fahrenden Schülers* (1896). BIBLIOGRAPHY: S. Hilpisch, LTK 2:844–845.

[S. A. SCHULZ]

BUTZER, MARTIN, see BUCER, MARTIN.

BUXHEIM ORGAN BOOK, an extremely valuable source for 15th-cent. organ music. This MS, now in Munich (Staatsbibliothek Cim. 352b), originated *c.* 1460 in the Buxheim monastery. *Dunstable, Dufay, and *Binchois as well as some of their German and French contemporaries are represented among the more than 250 pieces, most of which are keyboard transcriptions of originally vocal works. The pieces are notated in German keyboard *tablature, which combined the French and Italian system with the Spanish. The MS's repertory presents an interesting contrast between the Franco-Flemish and the German styles of composition. Facs. ed. of MS, B. A. Wallner (*Documenta musicologica*, 1955); modern ed. of pieces, B. A. Wallner (*Das Erbe deutscher Musik,* 1958, 37–38). BIBLIOGRAPHY: Reese, MusR.

[P. DOHERTY]

BUXHOVEDEN, ALBERT, see ALBERT I OF RIGA.

BUYING AND SELLING, a contract transferring title or ownership of a commodity or service from seller to buyer for a determined price. If goods or services are exchanged without the medium of money, the transaction is called barter, but this does not differ essentially from purchase or sale in which money serves as the medium of exchange. From the moral point of view, it is a form of contract governed by what RC moral theologians call commutative justice, though under some circumstances general or social justice may impose obligations apart from those which derive simply from commutative justice's principle of fair exchange (e.g., the sale of narcotics). The purchase or sale contract, as this falls under commutative justice, should, if it is to be fair and just, be mutually advantageous, and thus there should be a reasonable equality between the value of the thing sold and the money or goods paid in exchange for it (*JUST PRICE). Derived from the obligation of the just price are other more specific obligations, some of which fall upon the seller and others upon the buyer. Thus the seller must be the owner of what he sells; he must reveal hidden substantial defects of the product he sells if these make it notably inferior in quality or useless to the purchaser for the purpose for which he buys it. Lesser or accidental defects, if they are hidden, need not be revealed, but in justice the price should be lowered to make allowance for the lesser value of what is sold. The seller must also turn over or deliver to the buyer the commodity sold according to the terms agreed upon or understood in coming to the sale agreement. For his part, the buyer is obligated to accept the goods he has purchased and to pay for them according to the terms of the contract or as determined by custom or law. Where the violation of one of these obligations on the part of either the seller or the buyer involves loss to the other party, an injustice has been committed and restitution should be made to the extent of the damages.

[P. K. MEAGHER]

BUYL, BERNAL (Boyl; d. 1520), first vicar apostolic of the Americas. The place and date of his birth are unknown. He rose to the rank of captain of a galley crossing between Spain and Sardinia and then became secretary to Philip V. After his seminary studies and ordination he lived as a hermit on Montserrat. In 1493 B. accompanied Columbus on his second voyage. Alexander VI named him vicar apostolic of the newly discovered lands of Hispaniola (Santo Domingo), but his acquaintance with the Amerindians remained superficial. His return to Spain was prompted by misunderstanding with Columbus; in fact, he has been accused of being one of the discoverer's detractors. He died as abbot of Cuxa. BIBLIOGRAPHY: F. Fita, *Fray Boyl y Cristobal* (1891); E. W.

Loughran, "The First Vicar-Apostolic of the New World," AER 82(1930) 1–14.

[P. DAMBORIENA]

BUYS, see BUSAEUS.

BYBLOS, a Phoenician seaport city, the ancient Gebal, the inhabitants of which are mentioned in Scripture as skilled in hewing stones (1 Kg 5.18) and in ship building (Ezek 27.9). The Greeks changed the name to Byblos, from which the word Bible derives. Byblos was engaged at the time in the import of papyrus from Egypt. Byblos was always an important religious center. The Egyptians called it the land of the gods. The Roman colonnade led to the ancient city from the sanctuary of the acropolis. The most important monument of the ancient city is a small temple to Baal with several votive obelisks. BIBLIOGRAPHY: N. Jidejian, *Byblos Through the Ages* (1973); M. Dunand, *Fouilles de Byblos* (atlas 1937; text 1939).

[J. E. LUSSIER]

BYRD, WILLIAM (1543–1623), Elizabethan composer. Although B.'s parentage and early years are obscure, it is certain that he was appointed organist at Lincoln Cathedral in 1569. Along with Thomas Tallis, he was granted (1575) by Queen Elizabeth what amounted to an exclusive license for printing and selling music. Despite the fact that duties at Lincoln and at the Court required him to serve and write for the Anglican Church, B. remained a staunch RC throughout his life.

Early called by his countrymen the "Father of Musick," B. excelled in all branches of music composition. In the field of secular music he produced three large collections of excellent madrigals; he ranked with John Dowland in the evolution of the English solo song; he established the character of instrumental writing in England through his chamber music for strings; he set a new standard in keyboard composition, in which genre he held first place in all of Europe. B.'s church music is divided into that which he composed for the RC Church and that which he wrote for the Anglican Church. Belonging to his Latin church music are three great Masses, the *Cantiones sacrae* (v. 1 with Tallis), two books of *Gradualia,* and vocal and instrumental motets. His compositions of English liturgical music comprise four Services (of which his Great Service is a masterpiece), anthems, Psalms, and sacred songs. B. proved to be an innovator in the field of English church music, but he is considered to be the finest composer of Latin church music of the Elizabethan period. BIBLIOGRAPHY: E. H. Fellowes, *William Byrd* (2d ed., 1948); I. Holst, *Byrd* (1972).

[M. T. LEGGE]

BYRNE, ANDREW (1802–62), bishop. A seminarian from Ireland, B. came to the U.S. as a volunteer to work in the new Diocese of Charleston, S.C. After finishing

BYZANTINE ART 567

studies under Bp. John England, he was ordained in 1827. An active missionary for several years in S.C. and N.C., B. became vicar-general of the diocese. At the Second Baltimore Council he acted as Bp. England's theologian. In 1836 he went to New York and served in parishes there until he was named the first bp. of the new Diocese of Little Rock, which comprised all of Arkansas and part of the Indian Territory. He became active in promoting migration to the Southwest, built churches, stations, and schools, and saw the Catholic population (5,000 in 1844) increase tenfold during his lifetime. BIBLIOGRAPHY: T. Meehan, CE 3:93; J. D. Hackett, *Bishops of the United States of Irish Birth or Descent* (1936).

[J. M. HILL]

BYRNE, EDMUND (*c.*1656–*c.*1724), abp. of Dublin (from 1707) in the difficult times of persecution. He was the first resident abp. to bear the title after the death of Russell (1692). Compelled to live in hiding much of the time, he managed nevertheless to hold a diocesan synod (1712), founded three new parishes, and wrote on controversial matters. BIBLIOGRAPHY: J. J. Meagher, NCE 2:920–921.

[P. K. MEAGHER]

BYRNE, PATRICK JAMES (1888–1950), Maryknoll missioner. Ordained for Baltimore, B. became the first priest to join the Catholic Foreign Missionary Society (1915). He founded the Maryknoll mission in North Korea (1923), where he was named prefect apostolic (1927); returned to Maryknoll as vicar-general and seminary rector (1929); and was appointed to pioneer the Japanese mission (1935), where he was again named prefect apostolic. He spent the years of World War II under house arrest; worked with Japanese and American officials on post-war adjustments; but returned to Korea as visitator apostolic (1947). Two years later, he was made the first apostolic delegate to Korea and titular bishop. When the Communists captured Seoul (1950), B. was taken prisoner and died in the "death march" to the Manchurian border. BIBLIOGRAPHY: R. A. Lane, *Ambassador in Chains* (1955).

[H. JACK]

BYRNE, WILLIAM (1833–1912), educator and author. Born in Ireland, B. attended Mt. St. Mary's College, Emmitsburg, Md., where he taught mathematics and Greek. Ordained (1864) for the Diocese of Boston, he was named diocesan chancellor (1866) and rector (1874) of St. Mary's Church, Charlestown, Massachusetts. During this period he worked vigorously for penal reform, founded the Boston Temperance Missions, and edited the *Young Crusader*. He became (1881) the 12th president of Mt. St. Mary's College, and pulled it out of financial difficulties. He wrote several religious manuals in addition to a *History of the Catholic*

Church in the New England States (1899). BIBLIOGRAPHY: M. M. Meline and E. F. X. McSweeney, *Story of the Mountain: Mount St. Mary's College and Seminary* (2v., 1911).

[J. M. HILL]

BYZANTINE ART, an amalgam of styles, Christian, Roman, and Greek with strong Eastern modification, developed under royal patronage at Constantinople, new capital of the Roman Empire (A.D. 330), and distinguished for magnificence of material and excellence of craftsmanship. The Constantinian Period (330–378) is a synthesis of Hellenism, Christianity, and the Orient with new perforated surface decoration in lacelike designs (Church of St. John the Baptist in Studion, Constantinople). In the Justinian Period, "First Golden Age" (518–610), painting, mosaic, and sculpture having been destroyed by the iconoclasts, evidences are chiefly architectural in the grandiose, domed *Hagia Sophia—greatest of Byzantine achievements; Church of SS. Sergius and Bacchus; and in Ravenna, the world's greatest mosaics at S. Vitale in court panels of Justinian and Theodora (*c.*547), in the jewelled "mausoleum" of Galla Placidia and the churches of Sant'Apollinare Nuovo and Sant'Apollinare in Classe. From the 6th-cent. Alexandrian ivory carvers' workshops are the Throne of Bishop Maxentius (546–556) and the Barberini Diptych (Louvre). Manuscripts of importance show classical naturalism in the Vienna Genesis (5th cent.), and the 7th-cent. Joshua Roll (Vatican). The Rossano and Rabula Gospels (6th cent.) show strong Eastern influence. The Hellenistic figures of the Cyprus silver treasure (610–641, Metropolitan Museum, N.Y.) and the Antioch Chalice (The Cloisters, N.Y.) in sumptuous Oriental decorative design evidence again the dual strains of Byzantine expression. The Oriental style reached its apogee in silks with a strong Persian influence (Cluny Museum, Paris). The Macedonian Renaissance (867–1056), a "Second Golden Age," shows Justinian types in the Nea Ecclesia, Basil I's court church (881), with central dome and domed cross-arm bays in a synthesis of provincial types smaller, more slender with decorative brick masonry (St. Mark's, Venice; Mt. Athos; St. Sophia, Kiev). Mosaics of the 10th cent. are hierarchical and dogmatic in scheme expressing the Church as cosmos. Two important ivory workshops—Romanos and Nicephorus—with magnificent enamels and metal work seen in the Reliquary of the True Cross (*c.*960), at Limburg an der Lahn, and finest 10th- and 11th-cent. chalices of onyx, silver-gilt, pearls, and enamels, exemplify Byzantine love of sumptuousness and beauty of materials. Manuscripts show two styles—classical naturalism in the 12th-cent. *Octateuch* (Istanbul) and an admixture of Oriental formalism in the *Homilies of St. John Chrysostom* (*c.*1075, Paris). Similar styles influence the Menologion of Basil II (antique) and 12th-cent. mosaics of Hagia Sophia (Oriental). The Paleologan dynasty (1258–1453) built slender, provincial forms with domes and strange drums (14th-cent. Church of the Holy Apostles, Salonika) and intermixed East and West at

Mistra. Most important Paleologan masterworks are frescoes from two major schools in Salonika and Constantinople. At Kariye-Djami (Church of the Chora) is the exciting fresco, *The Anastasis* (1310–20), in a new Byzantine renaissance. The Byzantine achievement, other worldly and humanist, was a formative influence in many lands from Greece to Russia. BIBLIOGRAPHY: R. Krautheimer, *Early Christian and Byzantine Architecture* (1965); G. Matthew, *Byzantine Aesthetics* (1964); W. C. Loerke, NCE 2:921–936, with excellent bibliography.

[M. J. DALY]

BYZANTINE CHANT, a form of chant which, like that of the Western Church, was based on Hebrew and Syrian, rather than on Greek models. Like Gregorian chant, it is monophonic, unaccompanied, chiefly diatonic and devoid of strict meter. Unlike Gregorian chant, its texts are mostly nonscriptural. The notation of Byzantine chant involves a distinction between ekphonetic signs, which represent certain stereotyped formulas, and neumes which are an intervallic notation. Byzantine notation developed in several stages: (1) the ekphonetic (9th cent.), a system of recitation marks; (2) the early Byzantine (10th–12th cent.), a system of neumes giving only a general direction to the singer; (3) the middle Byzantine or Round System (13th–14th cent.), which gave both intervals and values; (4) the late Byzantine or Cucuzelian System (15th cent.), an amplification of the Round System; (5) the modern or Chrysanthine notation. The modern notation of Chrysantos of Madytos, which has been used since 1821, is a practical simplification of Byzantine notation. As in Gregorian chant, distinction is made among eight modes, four authentic and four plagal. The origin and significance of these modes, as well as other aspects of this chant, however, need further investigation. In 1935 C. Hoeg, H. J. W. Tillyard, and E. Wellesz began a scholarly edition of medieval Byzantine musical MSS entitled *Monumenta Musicae Byzantinae*. Theirs and other studies will show how profoundly the Byzantine melodies reflect the spirit of Eastern piety and that the music of the Byzantine Church is no less great than that of the Western Church. BIBLIOGRAPHY: C. Sachs, *Our Musical Heritage* (2d ed., 1948) 52–53; G. Reese, MusMA 75–91; K. H. Wörner, *History of Music* (5th ed., 1973) 69–72; *BYZANTINE MUSIC.

[M. T. LEGGE]

BYZANTINE CHURCH, a term often used for the Churches, singly or collectively, which derive from the Church of the Byzantine Empire. In current usage it could refer to the Orthodox Churches united to Constantinople, or incorrectly to the Eastern Catholics of the *Byzantine rite, but more precisely, it applies to the Church that existed in the Byzantine Empire from the 4th cent. to 1453.

The acceptance of Christianity by Constantine and his establishment of the imperial capital at Constantinople, the ''New Rome'' (330), mark the beginnings of the Byzantine Church. In the East Roman or Byzantine view, when the Roman Empire became Christian the perfect world order willed by God had been achieved: one universal empire was sovereign, and coterminus with it was the one universal Church. In spite of historical events, this ideology remained and must be taken into account to understand the Byzantine Church. The emperor was God's vicar on earth, whose task it was to care for both the temporal and spiritual welfare of his subjects. It is in these terms that the Byzantine State and Church must be understood and not in the sense conveyed by the superficial term *caesaropapism. The emperor was obliged to defend and expand the orthodox faith and to refrain from interfering in dogmatic questions, although the latter was not always observed. Yet he governed the Church by enforcing its laws, punishing heretics, arranging diocesan boundaries, convoking councils and observing due formality, naming and deposing patriarchs and bishops.

The patriarch of the imperial capital gradually and by a natural process became the leading bp. in the empire, prescinding from the special position of Rome. (See CONSTANTINOPLE, PATRIARCHATE OF). Elected by a synod of bps., he was then officially promoted by the emperor, who had usually already suggested his name. Often the second personage in the State, the patriarch of Constantinople headed a vast curia and other bps. who resided in Constantinople constituted a *permanent synod, which became the real governing body of the Church. Ecclesiastical administration and celebration of the sacraments were carried out by the married secular clergy, but in many respects the backbone of the Church was the monks, whose ascetical life inspired and encouraged the faithful. They were the spiritual counselors of the people and at times aroused them against emperors whose orthodoxy was suspect.

The Byzantine Church was profoundly affected by the theological conflicts of the early centuries. *Arianism was important not so much as a dogmatic deviation but as the precedent it set for constant imperial interference in ecclesiastical matters, most of it occasioned by intriguing bishops. The controversies caused by *Nestorianism, *Monophysitism, and *Monothelitism produced more serious and long-lasting results. While primarily doctrinal, they were complicated by imperial attempts to dictate dogma, rivalry among prominent bps., political intrigue, and regional hatred. The Churches of Syria, Egypt, and Armenia became separated from the Byzantine, which then tended to turn in on itself. (See EASTERN CHURCHES). The condemnation of *Iconoclasm in 843 marked the origin of what became known as the Holy Orthodox Church or the *Church of Seven Councils. The latter title indicates that the Orthodox accept as dogma only what was defined by the first seven ecumenical councils, thus limiting theological speculation. Gradually the Byzantine Church split into two factions, generally referred to as the moderate and the extremist, a division that plagued the Church's history and sometimes led to actual schisms.

In accord with Byzantine ideology, the Christian emperor was obliged to extend Roman law and order to the barbarians and also to bring them Christianity. The emperor sent missionaries to such peoples as the Slavs, Bulgarians, and Russians, among whom they planted Byzantine Christianity and vastly extended the influence of the Church of Constantinople. But most of these newly converted peoples developed *autocephalous or *autonomous Churches which often came into conflict with Constantinople. Byzantine relations with Rome were marred by disputes often occasioned by external factors, but basic religious unity lasted for centuries.

Arguments arose over divergent customs and discipline, e.g., the use of leavened bread, clerical marriage, but neither these nor even the doctrinal problem of the *filioque caused the schism. Political complications, esp. in S Italy, led to a series of mutual condemnations by the papal legates and Patriarch Michael Cerularius, but it was only after the Crusaders' conquest of Constantinople (1204) that one can truly speak of separation. (See SCHISM, EAST-WEST). Popular animosity, variant traditions—all played a role. The basic problem, however, not really discussed by contemporaries, was that of a different concept of the nature and structure of the Church. Byzantine ecclesiology was influenced by the Church's union with the empire, and such matters as relations among bps. were regarded as mere administrative problems. The *pentarchy theory, stressing the collegiality of the five patriarchs, developed into a practical denial of papal primacy. As the Western concept of primacy became more definite, universal, and absolute, the Byzantine Church still dwelt on its position within the imperial framework. The resulting schism was inevitable in spite of possible solutions.

After the death of Michael Cerularius (1059) attempts at reunion were made at the Councils of *Lyons II (1274) and *Florence (1439), but these had merely temporary or superficial results. The Byzantine Church itself suffered further theological upheavals with the controversies over Hesychasm and *Palamism. Although accused of liturgical and theological stagnation, it was the Byzantine Church which had to a large extent created and clarified the Christian tradition shared also by the West, and which made it a daily, living reality to millions within the empire and ultimately in foreign lands. The real tragedy of the Byzantine Church seems to be that it became merely the Byzantine Church; it merged itself with the empire not only administratively but also psychologically. Its bps. found it difficult to think in terms of a Christianity without an emperor. In December, 1452, with the threat of Turkish invasion, one final effort at union was made by the Catholic Emperor *Constantine XII and Card. Isidore, the papal legate. Despite all opposition they solemnly proclaimed reunion, but 6 months later the Byzantine Empire fell to the Turks, and Muslim domination divided East from West in a way that fostered the development of two separate Churches. BIBLIOGRAPHY: Beck 27–232; M. J. Higgins, NCE 2:936–950; CMedH² (1967) 4.2:104–133; L. Bréhier, *Les Institutions de l'empire byzantin* (1949) 430–586; F. Dvornik, *Byzantium and the Roman Primacy* (1966); G. Every, *Byzantine Patriarchate* (2d ed., 1962);

[G. T. DENNIS]

BYZANTINE CIVILIZATION, the imperial administrative tradition, the social and economic character, the ecclesiastical and monastic influence, and the educational and artistic contributions that accompanied the rise and fall of Constantinople (527–1453).

The policy of Byzantium was marked by a close working interdependence of Church and State which is quite evident in its imperial administrative tradition. When crowned by the patriarch of Constantinople, the emperor declared his adherence to orthodox teaching and promised to safeguard the tradition of the Church. The empire was always ruled by a monarch whose authority was a temporal expression of divine power. He was therefore autonomous as lawgiver, judge, administrator, and commander-in-chief. Though originally elected by the people, the army was most often the key to his election. He chose his successor from his own family and could only be removed by rebellion or abdication. His responsibility to expand the well-being of the Church is reflected in the daily court ceremonial. Byzantine law was very much influenced by Roman law, the 6th-cent. collection of Justinian and the 9th-cent. Greek compilation, the *Basilica*. The by the development of nomocanons, i.e., secular law (Gr., *nomoi*) and ecclesiastical rulings (Gr., *canones*). Civil laws were promulgated by an edict of the emperor, church laws by the patriarch.

Having survived the difficult theological controversies of the 4th, 5th, and 6th cent., the patriarch of Constantinople began a very successful missionary program in the 9th cent. in Central Europe and the Balkans. While Rome was evangelizing the lands of Moravia, Constantinople established the Church in Serbia, Bulgaria, and Russia, and had a profound cultural influence on Slavonic peoples. Slav rulers imitated the administrative procedures of Byzantium and sent their children to Constantinople to be educated. After the long struggle between Rome and Constantinople with its continuing schisms (see PHOTIUS; MICHAEL CERULARIUS) the Orthodox Church became autonomous and was the mainstay of Byzantine culture after the empire had succumbed to Turkey. One of the reasons for this was the impact of monastic life throughout the Orthodox Church. Monks were detached from the temporal order, but their houses gave hospitality to the stranger, cared for the sick, sheltered political outcasts, were schools for future bishops and ecclesiastics, provided special advice and ideals for the whole empire. This was their greatest strength in resisting invaders from the East.

It was in Byzantine education that continuity with Greco-Roman tradition was most evident. Byzantium did not look to the Church in matters educational even though many ecclesiastics and monks were excellent scholars. There were schools in the provinces and a state-financed university at Constantinople. This continuing interest in education produced a massive literature. Most noteworthy were the contemporaneous histories of Michael Psellus, Anna Comnena, Nicephorus Gregoras, and the Emperor John VI Cantacuzenus. Theological writing included many distinguished works on spirituality, e.g., *The Ladder of Heavenly Ascent* of St. John Climacus and voluminous lives of the saints. Poetry both secular and religious was outstanding. Medieval church poetry and music in their finest artistic tradition have survived and are consistently used by the Eastern Churches. Their greatest artistic expression whether in jewelry, silks, architecture, or painting manifests an abiding sensitivity to Christian culture. The best of this is seen in the Hagia Sophia of Constantinople. Byzantium illumined the Slavic world with the positive, living interpretation of Christian and Greco-Roman culture. Preserving the best of classical literature of the past for East and West, its own vitality was a major factor in the development of European and Islamic culture. BIBLIOGRAPHY: S. Runciman, *Byzantine Style and Civilization* (1975); A. Vasiliev, *History of the Byzantine Empire* (1952, pa. 1968).

[F. H. BRIGHAM]

BYZANTINE EMPIRE, the continuation of the later Roman Empire in the East lasting until 1453, centered around *Constantinople and consisting essentially of Asia Minor, the Balkans, Greece, and parts of S Italy. The adoption of Christianity and the establishment of the capital at Constantinople by Constantine the Great (330) began a transitional period lasting until the end of the 7th century. Despite the Western reconquests of *Justinian I (527–565), the empire became more oriented toward the East and less Roman in its outlook and institutions. It evolved into a highly centralized, bureaucratic state, Greek in language and culture, and Orthodox Christian in religion. Owing to religious and ethnic strife and to the Muslim conquests, Syria, Palestine, and Egypt were definitively lost to the empire by the mid-7th cent., but its reduced boundaries actually made the empire more manageable and cohesive. Beginning about the end of the 7th cent. a long struggle drove out the Arabs and paved the way for the most flourishing period of the empire, lasting from about the mid-8th cent. to the mid-11th century. Although disturbed from within by the iconoclastic conflict (see ICONOCLASM) and threatened from without by Arabs and Bulgarians, the empire prospered and developed its specifically Byzantine characteristics in administration, religion, art, literature, etc. The Macedonian dynasty (867–1081) produced a remarkable series of emperors, including several usurpers, who were statesmen of outstanding ability. Byzantine influence spread far and wide, esp. throughout the Slavic world. After the death of Basil II (1025) the empire fell into weaker hands, and the civil aristocracy and the landed nobility contended for power. At the same time it was faced by nomadic tribes to the N, Seljuk Turks to the E, and Normans to the West. The statesmanship of *Alexius I Comnenus saved the empire for a time, but the Italian maritime republics were sapping its economic strength, internal strife was endemic, and finally (1204) French and Venetian Crusaders captured and pillaged Constantinople. Byzantium never recovered from this blow, even though its capital was regained in 1261, and further threats were staved off by the brilliant

diplomacy of *Michael VIII Palaeologus. During the 14th cent. the empire was torn by civil wars and invaded by Serbs, Catalans, and Ottoman Turks. The last crossed into Europe (1354) and gradually occupied what was left of the empire, finally capturing Constantinople (1453). BIBLIOGRAPHY: G. Ostrogorsky, *History of the Byzantine State* (3d ed., 1969); A. A. Vasiliev, *History of the Byzantine Empire* (1952); N. H. Baynes and H. S. L. B. Moss, *Byzantium. An Introduction to East Roman Civilization* (1948); L. Bréhier, *Le Monde byzantin* (3 v., 1947–50); C. Diehl, *Byzantium: Greatness and Decline* (1957).

[G. T. DENNIS]

BYZANTINE LAW, the legal system of the Roman Empire as codified and modified during the Byzantine period (330–1453). The first major codification of Roman law, which had become obsolescent, contradictory, and obscure, was made in the 6th cent. at the order of Emperor *Justinian I (see CORPUS IURIS CIVILIS). This codification had a tremendous influence on the later development of civil and canon law in the Byzantine Empire and in Western Europe in the late Middle Ages. The law schools were reorganized, the law itself was made more humane and practical, and Greek replaced Latin as the legal language. While the codification of Justinian remained fundamental, legal activity did not cease. In 739 Leo III promulgated the *Ecloga* with the intention of introducing Christian principles into the law. Several unofficial legal handbooks were also published. In the 9th cent. Basil I had a revised handbook, the *Epanagoge*, prepared, and his son Leo VI issued the *Basilika*, which became the authoritative legal work. BIBLIOGRAPHY: CMedH² 4.2:55–77.

[G. T. DENNIS]

BYZANTINE LITERATURE, the writings in Greek in the Byzantine Empire from c.300 to 1453. Byzantine authors generally tried to employ classical Attic Greek, but were often incapable of doing so, and the language underwent a number of changes. At the same time some made use of the spoken (demotic) tongue. As a whole, Byzantine literature is characterized by a love for classical antiquity, and much of it consists of compilations, philological studies, and commentaries on classical texts. The writers were strongly addicted to rhetoric, and many of their phrases are so strained and contrived as to be often unintelligible. They were also so overawed by the faultless authority of antiquity that they tended to limit themselves to imitating classical models. The general result is that Byzantine literature is remarkably lacking in originality. A major amount of Byzantine literary output was concerned with theology, including ascetical and dogmatic treatises, exegesis, polemics, and sermons, none of which display any real creativity.

In history the Byzantines continued the ancient Greek tradition with notable success and produced a large and varied historical literature, of which two principal types survive, the history and the chronicle. The chroniclers were often monks or clerics who set out to edify their readers with a record of the divine interventions in history from creation to their own day. They wrote in the vernacular for the ordinary people and covered some important events passed over by the more sophisticated historians. The historians, on the other hand, were usually well-educated laymen connected with the imperial court, and often eyewitnesses of, or participants in, the events they describe. They aimed at objectivity, but their writings are often obscure and ambiguous.

Although secular poetry was composed, most Byzantine poetry was of a liturgical nature, in which some ingenuity and creativity appear. Somewhat similar to the Western romances were the verse epic of *Digenes Akritas* and the Greek romances of the later period. BIBLIOGRAPHY: M. V. Anastos, NCE 2:977–1000; K. Krumbacher, *Geschichte der byzantinischen Literatur* (1897; repr. 1958); CMedH² 4.2:207–263; S. Impellezzeri, *La letteratura bizantina da Costantino agli iconoclasti* (1965).

[G. T. DENNIS]

BYZANTINE LITURGY, the liturgy of the patriarchate of *Constantinople (ancient Byzantium), adopted by the 12th cent. in the other ancient Eastern patriarchates in communion with Constantinople and used today in all Churches of the Orthodox communion, as well as in the former Orthodox groups now united with Rome and the Italo-Greek communities of Sicily and S Italy. The early history of the liturgy used in Constantinople itself is obscure, since no records earlier than the 8th or 9th cent. are extant. In the Eucharistic Liturgy Antiochene influence can be detected esp. from the Cappadocian area of Antioch. The composition of the Divine Office, with its hymnody and strophic pieces found now also in the Eucharistic Liturgy, is essentially that which the monks of Constantinople gradually adopted from Palestinian monasteries, in which the poetic activity of Antiochene monks like St. Andrew of Crete and St. John Damascene was considerable. The ritual for the administration of the sacraments, for monastic rites, funerals, blessings, and other ceremonies owes much to the usages of Antioch, but the nuptial rites are essentially Constantinopolitan. The liturgical texts were gradually translated into the local languages, but the liturgical languages of the Greek and Slavic Churches and of the Catholicate of Georgia are now archaic, though not unfamiliar to the people. Much Greek is used by the Catholic Byzantine communities of Sicily and Calabria, although the spoken language of their members is Italian or Albanian. The liturgical texts are fairly uniform in all Churches of the rite, the Russian books having been brought into line with developed Greek usage in 1666; the western Ukrainian dioceses, which had already united with Rome in 1595 to form the nucleus of the Catholic Ruthenian rite, were not affected by this Russian reform, and the Slavonic liturgical books still exist in two recensions, one Russian and the other Ruthenian. Latinizing influence on the Catholic Byzantine rites, though not absent, has been less strong than in many other Eastern Catholic rites and is almost totally absent from the practice of the Byzantine Catholics in Greece.

The Eucharistic Liturgies used today are three: that of St. *John Chrysostom (the one usually celebrated), that of St. *Basil (celebrated 10 times a year), and that of the *Presanctified (the only liturgy permitted on fast days of Lent). While the Byzantine priest is behind the iconostasis, he recites most of the liturgical prayers in a low voice, singing only the final words *(ekphōnēsis),* and outside the screen, the liturgical action continues with the cantors' singing and with diaconal invocations to which the people respond. The liturgies of St. John Chrysostom and of St. Basil are identical today except for four preanaphoric prayers said entirely in a low voice and the prayers of the anaphora of which only the *ekphōnēseis* are heard, along with a few changes affecting the deacon and the cantors. The Liturgy proper begins with the *prothesis,* or preparation of the gifts, done quietly behind the iconostasis at a table to the left of the sanctuary, before the curtain of the central door is opened for the beginning of the Liturgy of the Catechumens. The latter consists of a preparatory synaxis (including incensation, diaconal litany, Little Entrance, and Trisagion) and of readings (one from the Epistles or Acts, another from the Gospels) concluded by a diaconal litany and dismissal of the catechumens. In the Liturgy of the Faithful, a series of prayers and ceremonies, including the Great Entrance, the kiss of peace, and the recitation of the Creed, leads to the anaphora itself, introduced by a dialogue between priest and people and comprising a series of prayers with a strong Trinitarian note; the words of institution, the anamnesis of acts of divine favor in the world, and the epiclesis asking for the coming of the Spirit to transform the gifts into the Son's body and blood are all integrated with the prayer of thanksgiving addressed to the Father. The prayers of intercession for the living and the dead all follow the epiclesis. After the anaphora proper and the Lord's Prayer, the rite of communion begins with the elevation of the Holy Bread, the fraction, and the intinction, and concludes with a thanksgiving after the communicants, standing, have received the species of bread taken from the chalice, along with a little of the species of wine from a spoon. The people, dismissed by a blessing with the cross, approach to receive an unconsecrated piece of bread *(antidōron)* before leaving the church.

The seven Byzantine sacramental mysteries *(mystēria)* correspond to the seven Roman sacraments, although the ceremonies are often quite different. Baptism is conferred by a triple total immersion and a declarative Trinitarian formula, and is immediately followed by *myrōma* (the rough equivalent of confirmation), the ceremony being concluded by communion, under the species of wine alone if the neophyte is an infant. BIBLIOGRAPHY: P. de Meester, DACL 6:1591–1662; L. Gillet, "Le Génie du rit byzantin," *Questions liturgiques et paroissiales* 9 (1924) 81–90; R. Janin, *Les Églises orientales et les rites orientaux* (4th ed., 1955) 24–74; I.-H. Dalmais, *Eastern Liturgies* (tr. D. Attwater, 1960) 47–52, 62–141.

[A. CODY]

BYZANTINE MONASTICISM, an institution of Eastern Christian communal living introduced into Byzantium by St. Basil (c. 330–379) on the basis of his Pachomian apprenticeship. The Fathers of the Church from various parts of the world flocked to certain religious houses for an apprenticeship in the art of monasticism. St. Pachomius (c. 290–346) whose "heart was moved toward the humanization of monasticism" felt that a greater number of pious men would be called to the monastic life if a combination of asceticism and cenobitic life was inaugurated. St. John Chrysostom (c. 347–407), bp. of Constantinople, lived under the Pachomian rule in the Thebaïd from 373 to 381. The Eastern Christian monastic movement was greatly influenced by Theodore the Studite (759–826), abbot of the monastery of Studios. Under his leadership the community grew rapidly and became the main monastic center of Constantinople. The application of the principles of the monastic life as drawn up by Theodore soon became the pattern for the large cenobitic communities in the Byzantine and Slavic worlds. Throughout the entire history of the Orthodox Church, Mount Athos has been the chief center and stronghold of monasticism for the past 10 centuries. It has been said that the monastic community has taught the Byzantines how to pray and that prayer was understood as a way to reach the goal of Christian life by participation in God through communion with the deified humanity of Christ in the Holy Spirit.

BIBLIOGRAPHY: A. S. Atiya, *History of Eastern Christianity* (1967); S. Painter, *History of the Middle Ages 284–1500* (repr. 1964); E. Amand De Mendieta, *Mount Athos* (tr. M. R. Bruce, 1972); P. Bratsiotis, *Greek Orthodox Church* (tr. J. Blenkinsopp, 1968); S. Runciman, *Great Church in Captivity* (1968); T. Ware, *Orthodox Church* (1963); S. Kostof, *Caves of God: The Monastic Environment of Byzantine Cappadocia* (1972); J. Meyendorff, *Byzantine Theology* (1974).

[R. A. TODD]

BYZANTINE MUSIC, music of the Byzantine cultural circle, thus the music not only of the Greek Orthodox Church but also the secular music of the imperial court in Byzantium up to the fall of the Empire in 1453. Of this body of music the only secular compositions extant are songs of greeting and congratulation, referred to as acclamations and polychronia, music found in ceremonial books, particularly those of the Emperor Constantine VII. Thus music was sung antiphonally, with instrumental accompaniment and interludes supplied principally on the organ.

The hymns of the Byzantine Church are Eastern Christianity's most distinctive contribution to music and poetry. In the 4th cent., when St. Basil the Great and St. John Chrysostom fixed the order of the liturgy, the hymn, sung without accompaniment, began its development under poet-composers such as Sophronios of Jerusalem, Sergios of Constantinople, Romanos, Anastasios, Andreas, and John of Damascus. This period (up to the 8th cent.) saw the evolution of the *troparia*, short passages inserted in the psalmody; the *kontakia*, long hymn-poems of from 20 to 30 stanzas; and the *kanons*, compositions consisting of nine odes. The 9th cent. brought a decline in the separation of poet and composer, but in the 13th and 14th cent., there came a new flourishing of hymn composition with enriched melody by composers such as John Kukuzelas. The majority of Byzantine hymns are contained in three collections: the *hermologion*, comprising the melodies of the odes of the *kanons*; the *sticherarion*, the collection of one-stanza hymns; the *kontakarion*, which contains the melismatic songs. Treatises called "Hagiopolitis" and "Papadikai" tell how the music of these songs was performed.

Byzantine music remained monophonic and, though it never developed into polyphony, it is the common ancestor of all of the Orthodox East European Churches. BIBLIOGRAPHY: C. Sachs, *Our Musical Heritage* (2d ed., 1948) 52–53; Reese MusMA 75–91; K. H. Wörner, *History of Music* (5th ed., 1973) 69–72.

[M. T. LEGGE]

BYZANTINE PHILOSOPHY, the philosophy that flourished in the Byzantine Empire. It was characterized by the study of Plato, Aristotle, and the Neoplatonists in the schools and by its application to theology. The 4th-cent. Fathers—Basil, Gregory of Nazianzus, and Gregory of Nyssa—set the pattern for the future by expressing Christian doctrine in philosophical terms, not as apologetic, but to instruct those within the Church and to elucidate Trinitarian theology. Thus the Church countered heresies such as Arianism and later monophysitism and monothelitism which were influenced by Neoplatonic concepts of a celestial hierarchy.

The Neoplatonic school established by Plotinus, Porphyry, and Iamblichus was for the pagan circle of the Emperor Julian a religion rivaling Christianity. In the 5th and 6th cent. at Athens and Alexandria the Neoplatonist teachers produced commentaries on Plato, Aristotle, and Porphyry. They debated with the Christians questions of the immortality of the soul and of the eternity of the world. At Athens, Plutarchus, Syrianus, Proclus, and Damascius directed the privately endowed Academy. It is said that Justinian, in legislating against paganism, closed this overtly pagan school in 529 A.D., but countenanced the Alexandrian school where pagan teachers, Hierocles, Ammonius, and Olympiodorus were succeeded by Christians or men who were not aggressively pagan, such as John Philoponus, David, Elias, and Stephen. The theology of Pseudo-Dionysius the Areopagite reflects Neoplatonism. His identity and orthodoxy were much debated then and are still controversial.

There is little evidence concerning the intellectual life in the next cent. when the empire was reduced by the Arab conquests. However, Maximus the Confessor who wrote mystical theology and John Damascene who successfully justified the veneration of icons at the Council of Nicaea II (787 A.D.) were both educated in the seven liberal arts and in philosophy. In the mid-9th cent. Leo the Philosopher was in charge of the univ. at Constantinople. He and Photius and Arethas contributed to the study and preservation of mathematical and philosophical texts, but the revival of Neoplatonic and Aristotelian studies in the 11th cent. was more spectacular in the history of philosophy. Michael Psellus (1018–96) headed the school. He was a Platonist of great learning and his writings are extensive. His successor, John Italus, who brought from Calabria a knowledge of Italian scholasticism, taught Aristotelian philosophy and was condemned as unorthodox.

In the 12th cent. the patriarchal school was the chief center for all the liberal studies as well as for theology. Michael Italicus and Theodore Prodromus taught the quadrivium, physics, medicine, philosophy, literature, and theology. Byzantine philosophers were rarely concerned only with philosophy. The four mathematical subjects forming the liberal arts quadrivium, arithmetic, geometry, astronomy, and music (harmony), were always within the province of philosophers. If not totally involved in teaching the whole range of the liberal arts, philosophers might be active churchmen or politicians, historians or poets. Under the Latin domination (1204–61) Nicephorus Blemmydes taught Aristotle, medicine, and geography at the philosophy school established at Nicaea. His student George Acropolites, historian and poet, restored the univ. at Constantinople at the end of the Latin rule, and lectured on mathematics and philosophy. Theodore Metochites (1260–1332) was a politician and Platonist with a special interest in mathematics and astronomy. His contemporary Maximum Planudes translated Augustine, Boethius, and Thomas Aquinas into Greek and introduced Arabic arithmetic. He and George of Cyprus, who was later the patriarch Gregory II, taught Aristotelian philosophy at the school associated with the Church of St. Savior in Chora in Constantinople. George Pachymeres taught Aristotelian philosophy and the new arithmetic at Trebizond. Gregory Chionides and Theodore Meliteniotis investigated Persian astronomy, John Pediasimos was interested in Neopythagorism, and Joseph the Philosopher wrote an encyclopedia. In the early 15th cent. Joseph Bryennius wrote on the quadrivium and taught rhetoric, philosophy, and theology in the patriarchal school, attracting students from Italy.

This period was remarkable for the Hesychast controversy. The monks of Mount Athos had the support of the mystic and theologian Gregory Palamas (1296–1359) in their stress on prayer and contemplation as a means of direct union with God achieved through a state of induced ecstasy. Both the Western Greek Barlaam, an Aristotelian, and Nicephorus Gregoras, a Platonist, attacked this extreme mysticism and anti-intellectualism. The conflict was linked with efforts to reunite the Churches, most anti-Palamites being in favor of union with the Latins. George Gemistus Pletho, who taught Platonic philosophy at Mistra, was an opponent of union in contrast to his pupil Bessarion. George Scholarius, a great admirer of Aquinas and commentator on Aristotle, subsequently became a Hesychast and changed his position regarding union, thus opposing both Pletho and Bessarion. All three

attended the Council of Florence in 1438–39. There Pletho persuaded Cosimo de' Medici to found a Platonist Academy. Bessarion became a Latin cardinal and his house in Rome, a salon for Greek scholars. George Scholarius, after the fall of Constantinople, became the patriarch Gennadius II of the conquered city. Byzantine philosophy had nourished Greek philosophy in a continuous tradition, had contributed to Christian theology, and had stimulated the Italian Renaissance. BIBLIOGRAPHY: CHGMP; J. M. Hussey, *Church and Learning in the Byzantine Empire 867–1185* (1937); K. M. Setton, "Byzantine Background to the Italian Renaissance," *Proceedings of the American Philosophical Society* 100, 1 (1956) 1–76; B. Tatakis, *La Philosophie byzantine,* supplementary volume to E. Bréhier, *Histoire de la philosophie* (1947).

[M. A. MOFFATT]

BYZANTINE RITE, one of the five principal rites in use today by the majority of Eastern Catholics and by the Eastern Orthodox Church throughout the world. In the U.S. alone, recent statistics show that there are more than 598,722 Catholics of the Byzantine Rite. The faithful of this rite include: Albanians, Bulgarians, Byelorussians, Georgians, Greeks, Hungarians, Italo-Albanians, Melkites, Romanians, Russians, Ruthenians, Slovaks, Ukrainians, Yugoslavs, Serbs, and Croatians. Historically, it was the rite of the ancient Byzantine Empire, and its rich heritage goes back to early Christianity to the two great Syrian centers of Antioch and Jerusalem. The most important and lasting of early liturgical work was done in Palestinian monasteries, esp. in the laura of Mar Saba (478). It was here that the *kanon* form of hymnody originated during the 8th century. Gradually this liturgical form became known at Constantinople and was used along with Mar Saba service books. The books now in use for the Divine Office of the Byzantine rite may be attributed to the work of the Studite monks. After the long struggle against iconoclasm, the sacred images were finally restored in the spring of 842 and the occasion was celebrated by the institution of the feast of Orthodoxy (1st Sunday in Lent). This date marked the beginning of the unification and regulation of liturgies throughout the empire. When the bishops of Constantinople, who were practically all from Caesarea and Antioch, kept the Antiochene and Basilian liturgy and adapted it, esp. by shortening it, they gave to all posterity the Byzantine rite or the "Divine Liturgy of our father amongst the Saints, John Chrysostom." By the 12th cent., the Byzantine liturgy had replaced the liturgy of St. James in Syria and Palestine, and by the 13th cent., it had pushed the liturgy of St. Mark out of existence. As late as the 15th cent., the Byzantine rite acquired the form in which it is celebrated today. The deep unity of the Byzantine rite is manifested in all its grandeur at a concelebration, when the various celebrants officiate, each in his own language, and this commingling of chant gives witness to the diversity of peoples that are there, united in one and the same faith. BIBLIOGRAPHY: N. Liesel, *Eucharistic Liturgies of the Eastern Churches* (tr. D. Heimann, 1963); Attwater CCE

I-H. Dalmais, *Eastern Liturgies* (tr. D. Attwater, 1960); DACL 6.2:1591–1662.

[R. A. TODD]

BYZANTINE TEXT, see BIBLE TEXTS.

BYZANTINE THEOLOGY, the theology developed in the Byzantine Empire from the Council of *Chalcedon (451) to the empire's fall in 1453. The older Syrian and Egyptian theological centers became separated from Byzantium as a result of Chalcedon and, later, because of the Muslim conquests. The Latin West also gradually lost contact with the empire. Basing itself, then, on its patristic and conciliar heritage, the Byzantine mind created a theology that can be called specifically Byzantine, and which is still viewed as normative for the Orthodox Church.

The Byzantine theological tradition does not express itself in a formal authority, pattern, or *summa,* but in a consistent way of understanding man's destiny in relation to God and the world. Its essential note was formulated by St. Athanasius: "God became man so that man may become God." This concept of *theosis,* or *deification, esp. as elaborated by St. *Maximus the Confessor (d. 662) placed positive stress on man's nature, not as autonomous, but as destined to share the divine life made attainable in Christ. Fundamental to this is the doctrine of the full humanity of Christ; *theosis* then enables man to recover his own pristine image and become fully human.

Byzantine theology tends to regard the visible world as a manifestation, an icon, of the invisible world, which alone can satisfy man. This supernatural reality is a mystery and thus incomprehensible to the soul still imprisoned in matter. There is no place for the rational investigation of the mysteries of revelation. The Byzantines were not interested in speculation nor in positive theological systems, but generally limited themselves to correcting doctrinal distortions. They were reluctant to define dogma unless necessary, but they did hold *theologoumena,* truths generally accepted without being imposed as articles of faith on all.

The sources of Byzantine theology are Scripture and tradition. Scriptural exegesis is that of the *Fathers of the Church, usually preserved in *catenae, and is largely typological or allegorical, focusing on the hidden or spiritual meaning of a text. Tradition comprises the creeds, conciliar definitions, certain synods, and the Fathers, to which may be added the liturgy and ascetical works.

The intense Christological debates of the 5th to the 7th cent. gave final form to Byzantine theology. Its real father was St. Maximus the Confessor, whose writings present a coherent view of the Christian faith as a whole. St. *John Damascene (d. 749) was more complete in his presentation of doctrine, but his work was not meant to be creative, but to serve as a manual of theology. Subsequent Byzantine theology displayed little or no development, but was generally content with assembling patristic citations, and largely confined itself to ascetical,

exegetical, and polemical writings. Innumerable treatises were composed against heretics, Jews, Manichaeans, Muslims, and particularly against Latin teachings and usages. In the 11th cent. speculative theology was definitively ruled out by the condemnation of John Italus and others, who had tried to apply philosophical reasoning to dogma. The controversy over Hesychasm in the 14th cent. resulted in the condemnation of scholastic trends and the official adoption of the theology of *Gregory of Palamas by the Byzantine Church. The writings of Aquinas, translated into Greek by Cydones, had some influence in intellectual circles. Still, to the end of the empire, Byzantine theologians continued to compile their traditional exegetical catenae and uninspired polemics. BIBLIOGRAPHY: Beck; Jugie; M. Gordillo, *Theologia orientalium cum latinorum comparata* (1960); CMedH², 4.2:185–206; J. Meyendorff, *Christ in Eastern Christian Thought* (1969); *idem, Byzantine Theology* (1974).

[G. T. DENNIS]

BYZANTIUM, a city founded by colonists from Megara *c.*607 B.C. on the Bosporus, now the site of Istanbul. After a history of commercial prosperity and decline, it was officially refounded in 330 by Constantine the Great and renamed New Rome as the imperial capital. It was soon called *Constantinople, but its older name is used to designate the Byzantine Empire, Church, liturgy, etc.

[G. T. DENNIS]

BZOMMAR, MONASTERY OF, a famous Catholic monastery in Lebanon established (1707) to shelter Armenian refugees from Turkish persecution. At the foundation of a Catholic Armenian patriarchate (1741), it was located first at Kraim. It was then moved to Bzommar (1749), where it became the center of the missionary apostolate, esp. with the establishment of the Patriarchal Institute. The missionaries carried on their work in secret, disguised as tradesmen, and received numerous converts into the Church. Pius IX afterwards transferred the patriarchal seat to Constantinople, but the community of Bzommar did not cease to operate. They highly esteemed the many martyrs at the time of the Turkish massacre of Armenians (1915–24). BIBLIOGRAPHY: DE 1:455; M. Kurkjian, *History of Armenia* (1959).

[S. A. HEENEY]

BZOVIUS, ABRAHAM (BZOWSKI), 1567–1637, Polish theologian, preacher, and historian. After his ordination as a Dominican priest, B. was sent to Italy for further study and became professor of theology at Ferrara and of philosophy at Milan. He distinguished himself as a church historian in his work on the *Annales.* With Odoricus Raynaldus, his contribution remained the standard church history until the 19th century. BIBLIOGRAPHY: M. H. Laurent, DHGE 10:1518–20; B. Stasiewski, LTK 2:864.

[M. H. BEIRNE]

C

CABALA (Heb., tradition), a name given to a Jewish, medieval theology that emphasized the mystical interpretation of the Bible to gain a more intimate knowledge of God. Its doctrine explains God's creation as resulting from emanations of the created order itself, which thereby preserve his transcendence, attempts to solve the problem of good and evil through speculation about these emanations, and offers mystical methods for attaining to divine intimacy. Although similar to Neoplatonic and Gnostic thought of the 2d cent. A.D., cabala remains essentially Jewish. After a development and dissemination in the Near Eastern Judaism of the 10th cent. it spread to Europe through Italy, Germany, and Provence, thence to Spain where it attained its most famous codification in the *Zohar,* the *Book of Splendors* (13th cent.), attributed to Moses de Leon. Most later cabala derives from this work. Despite strong opposition from within Judaism, cabala remained popular among the Sephardic Jews who settled in Palestine after their expulsion from Spain in 1492. It has profoundly influenced Hasidism of the 18th cent. and continues to be an important element in Jewish heritage. BIBLIOGRAPHY: EDB 294–295.

[A. P. HANLON]

CABALLERO, ANTONIO (*c.* 1602–69), founder of Franciscan missions in China. C. was ordained in 1626, entered China in 1633, left under duress but returned as prefect apostolic in 1649. He baptized about 3,000 converts, established churches throughout Chi-nan, Shan-tung, and was banished in 1665. C's published books include *Wan Wee Pen Mo Yo Yen* (published before 1667) and *T'ien Ju Yen* (1664).

[A. P. HANLON]

CABALLERO Y GÓNGORA, ANTONIO (1723–96), archbishop. He was born and educated in Spain, made bp. of Mérida in Mexico (1775), and abp. of Bogotá (1778). During the Comuneros revolt, he negotiated an agreement between the insurgents and the government (1781), but, as a royalist, failed to protest when the viceroy violated its terms and seized Comunero leaders. C. himself was later appointed viceroy. In 1787 he resigned his offices and returned to Spain as bp. of Córdoba. BIBLIOGRAPHY: J. Restrepo Posada, NCE 2:1035.

[H. JACK]

CABASILAS, NICOLAS (*c.* 1320–91), noted theologian, liturgist, and spiritual writer of Thessalonica. C. studied under his uncle, Nil Cabasilas with whom he is often confused owing to a preface that C. wrote in a posthumous work of his uncle, *La Procession du Saint-Esprit*. C. served in the court of the emperor, John VI Cantacuzenus, and as a layman was recommended for the patriarchate of Constantinople in 1354, but was not chosen for this office. One of his best known works is a thorough theological commentary on the various rites and ritual formulas of the Byzantine Eucharistic Liturgies. The work was published in French translation as *L'Explication de la divine liturgie* (1624). From his study of the work the great Bossuet concluded that C. was to be classified as "one of the most solid theologians of the Greek Church." Some question of orthodoxy arose in regard to C.'s interpretation, in an anti-Roman section of the work (cc. 29-30), of the words of consecration in the Eucharist; nevertheless the commentary is regarded as an important source on the history and tradition of Eucharistic theology. It was consulted during the Council of Trent in the discussions preparatory to formulation of the conciliar decree on the Mass as truly Christ's own sacrifice (promulgated Sept. 17, 1562). On the meaning and development of doctrine regarding the sacrificial character of the Mass, C.'s work remains a valued resource for theologians. His life of Christ, consisting of seven books, is a remarkable treatise in ascetical and mystical theology. In it C. develops the elements and dynamic of the spiritual life, treats of the meaning of human cooperation under divine grace, and of the divine causality in the effectiveness of the sacraments. C. is also known to have engaged in the Hesychast disputes of the time (see HESYCHASM) and to have written religious poetry. BIBLIOGRAPHY: M. Jugie, ÉO 18:383–388; S. Salaville, *Catholicisme* 2:339–340.

[A. P. HANLON]

CABASILAS, NILUS (1298–1363), Byzantine theologian and apologist. He succeeded Gregory Palamas as metropolitan of Thessalonica, although he never took possession of the see. C. became involved in the Hesychast controversy, sustaining Palamas against Barlaam and Acindynus. His anti-Latin writings include tracts on the procession of the Holy Spirit, the primacy of the pope, and the causes of the Eastern schism. He has always been held in great esteem by the Greek Church. BIBLIOGRAPHY: F. Vernet, DTC 2.1:1295–97.

[P. FOSCOLOS]

CABASSUT, JEAN (1604–85), French Oratorian, a moral theologian much esteemed by St. Alphonsus, canonist, and historian of the councils (*Notitia ecclesiastica historiarum, conciliorum,* 1680). BIBLIOGRAPHY: J. Raffalli, DDC 2:1185.

[T. C. O'BRIEN]

CABEZÓN, ANTONIO DE (1510–66), Spanish organist and composer. Although blind, he was accomplished enough to become court organist to the courts of Charles V (1526) and Philip II (1548). His travels in the latter's service brought him into contact with musicians throughout Europe, whose influence helped perfect his own compositional style. His works, published posthumously by his son Hernando as *Obras de música para tecla, arpa y vihuela* (1578), consist of keyboard variations, verses for *alternation with sung verses of psalms, and *tientos*. These compositions combine technical perfection in *counterpoint with an austere beauty proving C. to be a neglected master. *Obras de música . . .* ed. H. *Anglès, 3 v. (*Monumentos de la música española* 27–29, 1966). BIBLIOGRAPHY: Reese MusR; G. B. Sharp, *Musical Times* 107 (1966) 955–56, 1053–55.

[A. DOHERTY]

CABLE, GEORGE WASHINGTON (1844–1925), regional American writer. A veteran of the Confederate Army, C. worked for a time as a reporter on the New Orleans *Picayune.* He read widely in old issues of New Orleans newspapers until he had a keen sense of the life of that city, publishing (1879) a collection of short stories, *Old Creole Days.* His first novel and best work, *The Grandissimes* (1880), like the short stories, is a rich tapestry of all segments in New Orleans—Creole and Frenchman, Irish, Negro and octoroon, Dutch, and a motley group of seamen from all over the world. C. wrote with poetic power, realism, and quiet humor. He did not hesitate to poke gentle fun at his characters, but his love for the Creole shines through. *Madame Delphine* appeared in 1881 and *Dr. Sevie,* in 1885. The entire body of creative writing by C. constitutes a unique contribution to American literature. BIBLIOGRAPHY: L. L. Bikle, *George W. Cable, His Life and Letters, by His Daughter* (1928, repr. 1967); K. Ekstrom, *George Washington Cable: A Study of His Early Life and Works* (1950, repr. 1969).

[J. R. AHERNE]

CABRERA, JUAN BAPTISTA (1837–1916), a leader of the evangelical movement in Spain. C. entered the Clerks Regular at Valencia in 1852 and was ordained in 1862. After teaching for a time he retired to Gibraltar, where he became a Protestant. He returned to Spain to minister after the revolution of 1868 and was consecrated bp. of the Spanish Reformed Church in 1894. BIBLIOGRAPHY: H. Priebe, RGG 1:1577.

[M. J. SUELZER]

CABRERA, MIGUEL (1695–1768), Mexican painter. Establishing a successful workshop in Mexico City (1719), C. painted in provincial, two-dimensional form and rich color excellent portraits and religious panels of rococo delicacy. Called the "Mexican Murillo," he painted a series on the lives of St. Dominic and St. Ignatius in characteristic, soft coloring and beauty of physiognomy. His work may be seen in the Museo de Historia at Chapultepec. BIBLIOGRAPHY: M. Toussaint, *Arte colonial en México* (2d ed., 1962).

[M. J. DALY]

CABRERA, PABLO (1857–1936), Argentine priest, historian. His knowledge of scholarly material gained through fine historical research made his contributions invaluable. He was a self-taught scholar, considered a genius. C. published 450 books, monographs and articles. He corrected many errors in the fields of ethnography and archeology, as well as ecclesiastical history. Some of his important works are: *Ensayos de etnografía argentina* (1910), *Tesoros del pasado argentino* (1911), *Universitarios de Córdoba* (1916), *Córdoba de la Nueva Andalucía* (1917), *Los aborígenes del país de Cuyo* (1929), *La segunda imprenta de Córdoba* (1930). P. was loved by all for his just treatment of rich and poor.

[A. P. HANLON]

CABRIÈRES, FRANÇOIS MARIE ANATOLE DE ROVÉRIÉ DE (1830–1921), bp. of Montpellier from 1873, cardinal from 1911, a leading figure among the French hierarchy of his time, who enjoyed wide popularity because of his concern for the vineyard workers of his diocese during labor trouble in 1907. In addition to his pastoral activities he wrote numerous biographies of saints. BIBLIOGRAPHY: G. de Bertier, *Catholicisme* 2:343–344.

[M. J. SUELZER]

CABRINI, FRANCES XAVIER, ST. (1850–1917), foundress of the Missionary Sisters of the Sacred Heart whose special work was the care of Italian immigrants and their children. Born in Italy, she established approximately 70 foundations, including schools, orphanages, and hospitals, which were scattered over eight countries in North and South America, Italy, Spain, and England. Her earliest missionary dream was of saving souls in China, but she was sidetracked to the U.S. by her local bp. and the abp. of N.Y., who were aware of the desperate needs of Italian emigrants. Pope Leo XIII blessed her and her missionary activities in 1887.

In disposition C. had Italian drive, energy, and business acumen, but also great faith and trust in God. Her journeys across the Atlantic were numerous. To reach Argentina she traveled the W coast of South America to Chile, from which she made a perilous journey across the Andes. She returned to Italy many times to oversee the training of novices and to select the nuns best qualified for foreign missions.

C. became an American citizen in 1909. At her canonization in 1946 she was hailed as America's first citizen-saint. BIBLIOGRAPHY: P. DiDonato. *Immigrant Saint, the Life of Mother Cabrini* (1960); T. Maynard, *Too Small a World: the Life of Frances Cabrini* (1945); G. Pelliccia, BiblSanct 5:1028–45.

[C. KEENAN]

CABROL, FERNAND (1855–1937), Benedictine scholar and liturgist. He made his monastic profession in 1877, was ordained in 1882, served as claustral prior of Solesmes (1890–96), and became prior (1896) and first abbot (1903) of St. Michael's at Farnborough, England. He relinquished the administration of his abbey to a coadjutor in 1924. In 1903 C., together with the monks of Farnborough, undertook the *Dictionnaire d'archéologie chrétienne et de liturgie* (DACL) to provide definitive studies on archeology to *c.* 800 and on the liturgy down to modern times. The *Dictionnaire* (continued by H. Leclercq [1913–45] and completed by H. Marrou in 1953), the *Monumenta ecclesiae liturgica,* and a study of the liturgy of Jerusalem as described in the *Itinerarium Aetheriae* (see ETHERIA) are C.'s best known works. BIBLIOGRAPHY: A. des Mazis, DHGE 11:45–46; R. Gazeau, *Catholicisme* 2:344–345.

[H. DRESSLER]

CACCIAGUERRA, BONSIGNORE (1494–1566), Italian spiritual writer. After a worldly life as a successful merchant in Palermo, he experienced a conversion and was ordained at Rome (1547). He became a friend and disciple of St. Philip Neri and devoted himself to spreading the practice of frequent communion. His *Trattato della communione* (1557) and other devotional writings were widely read. BIBLIOGRAPHY: P. Auvray, DSAM 2:10–14.

[T. C. O'BRIEN]

CADAVERIC COUNCIL, a name sometimes given to the synod convoked at Rome in 897 at the insistence of *Lambert of Spoleto who was infuriated by the coronation of King Arnulf as emperor, which Formosus had performed in 896. Having reestablished his political power over Rome, Lambert sought to invalidate what the Pope had done. The subservient council did as Lambert demanded. It declared the acts of Formosus null and void; it had the body of Formosus, then 9 months dead, exhumed, outraged with a mock trial, and then thrown into the Tiber.

[J. C. WILLKE]

CADILLAC, ANTOINE DE LA MOTHE (*c.* 1660–1730), founder of Detroit. A French soldier who first settled at Port Royal (later Annapolis Royal), Nova Scotia (1684), C. established a trading post at Mount Desert Island off the shore of what is now Maine (1687). With governmental approval he founded a post at Detroit (1701) which he hoped would serve as a center of Catholic influence in the Great Lakes region, provide a strategic outpost against the English, and secure for himself a personal monopoly of trade. His efforts involved him in controversy until he left Detroit (1711). He succeeded Bienville as governor of Louisiana (1713), but was recalled to France under a cloud (1716) and died in obscurity.

[R. K. MacMASTER]

CADOC, ST. (d. *c.* 570), Welsh bishop venerated as a martyr. C. is traditionally recognized as the founder of monasteries in Wales and Scotland, the most famous being Llancarfan in Wales. Accounts of miracles and strange happenings abound in the stories told of him. Because of conflicting and frequently unrealistic accounts it is impossible to verify historically anything except some basic facts of C.'s life. He died at the hands of the Saxons. BIBLIOGRAPHY: Butler 3:633–634; F. Mostardi, BiblSanct 3:632–634.

[M. S. J. McCAREY]

CADOUIN, ABBEY OF, French Cistercian abbey in Périgord, founded (1115) by followers of Robert d'Arbrissel. It was taken over by Cistercians from Pontigny (1119). The abbey, destroyed during the 15th cent., was rebuilt by Louis XI, but languished under commendatory abbots after 1516. Although reformed in 1643, Cadouin numbered only 4 monks when it was suppressed in 1790. Its church has served the local parish. BIBLIOGRAPHY: J. Sigala, *Cadouin en Périgord* (1950); L. J. Lekai, NCE 2:1041.

[L. J. LEKAI]

CAECILIA, see CECILIA.

CAECILIAN (d. after 340), bp. of Carthage whose consecration was repudiated by the Donatists. Archdeacon of Carthage and successor to Mensurius as bp. after the cessation of the persecution under Diocletian (311), C. met opposition for two reasons: the Numidian bps., led by *Donatus, were delayed and thus not able to give their assent to his election, as custom demanded, and his consecrators, esp. Felix of Aptunga, were allegedly *traditores* (see TRADITOR). C. had also incurred the wrath of *Lucilla, a devout widow in the Church, by publicly rebuking her for her practice of giving excessive honor to the confessors and martyrs. The indignation of this woman, whose means were considerable, made her willing to support the cause of the disaffected Numidians. Holding a synod at Carthage they elected the lector Majorinus as a rival bp. to Caecilian. Thus began the long *Donatist Schism. The Synods of Rome (313) and Arles (314), as well as the imperial government, confirmed C. in his post. C. was the one African bp. present at the Council of Nicaea in 325. BIBLIOGRAPHY: Bihlmeyer-Tüchle 1:52.1; L. Cristiani, *Heresies and Heretics* (tr. R. Bright, 1959) 31–33.

[R. B. ENO]

CAECILIAN MOVEMENT, a 19th-cent. reform of RC church music that originated in Germany. Rejecting the more elaborate symphonic and orchestral approaches to composing, this reform found its inspiration in the music of the Italian Renaissance composers, esp. Palestrina. A key leader, K. *Proske, did original research in the MSS of the Renaissance masters and his library at Regensburg became an influential center. Unaccompanied vocal music with a polyphonic texture became the ideal of composition, although the reform did involve some monophonic chant and occasionally included instrumental accompaniment. The reform took its name from the patron saint of music, St. Cecilia, and later achieved a complex organizational structure. Most of Europe and the U.S. felt its influence. Pius IX gave official sanction to the organization on Dec. 16, 1870 in the brief *Multum ad novendos animos*.

[D. J. SMUCKER]

CAEDMON (fl. *c*.670), first English Christian poet. His story is told by Bede (*Hist. eccl.* 4:24). A cowherd of Streanes Healh (probably Whitby), C. received one night a miraculous gift of song. Brought to the attention of Abbess Hilda, he was instructed, and what he learned he turned into verse. Most critics today feel that the miracle in the story is the expression of Christian concepts in Anglo-Saxon vocabulary and meter. Caedmon's 9-line *Hymn* is found in 17 MSS from the 8th to the 15th century. Poems formerly called Caedmonian are no longer accepted as Caedmon's. BIBLIOGRAPHY: E. V. K. Dobbie, *Manuscripts of Caedmon's Hymn and Bede's Death Song* (1937); *Caedmon Poems* (tr. C. W. Kennedy, 1916); C. L. Wrenn, *Poetry of Caedmon* (1947); S. H. Gurteen, *Epic of the Fall of Man: A Comparative Study of Caedmon, Dante and Milton* (1896, repr. 1969).

[M. M. BARRY]

CAEDWALLA (*c*.659–689), king of Wessex from 685 or 686. His successful guerrilla warfare brought him the kingdoms of Wessex, Sussex, and the Isle of Wight. C. was a friend of St. Wilfrid and became a Christian in 688, resigned his crown, and was baptized in Rome. BIBLIOGRAPHY: W. R. W. Stephens, DNB 8:201–202; F. M. Stenton, *Anglo-Saxon England* (2d ed., 1947) 68–70.

[J. DRUSE]

CAELESTIUS, see CELESTIUS.

CAELICOLAE (Lat., heaven-worshipers), the members of a late 4th- and early 5th- cent. cult in N Africa. St. Augustine in 397 or 398 mentions (Ep. 44, PL 33:180) encountering them at Tubursicum, and that they had an elder *(maior)* and a new kind of baptism. In 409 the Emperor Honorius passed a law against them. Whether they were Christians, Jews, or did in fact worship the heavens, is unknown. They did not long survive. BIBLIOGRAPHY: G. Bareille, DTC 2.2088–89.

[T. C. O'BRIEN]

CAEN (CHURCH ARCHITECTURE). In Normandy, France, Caen, prominent under William the Conqueror, was the site of numerous and most important architectural monuments. The Abbaye-aux-Hommes (St. Étienne, 11th cent.) is a prime example of Norman Romanesque—a bold transition to Gothic. The sister-church, Abbaye-aux-Dames (La Trinité, 1062–1140) founded by Queen Mathilde, with its early use of the flying buttress (concealed), and the Church of St. Nicolas (1084–93), its strange roof rising from vaults, witness to the daring experimentation in Norman architecture of the 11th century. Later churches of note are St.-Jean (15th-cent. flamboyant) and the 17th-cent. Jesuit chapel, Notre Dame de la Gloriette.

[M. J. DALY]

CAERE (Cerveteri), Etruscan city NW of Rome, famous for its 140-acre necropolis (8th-6th cent. B.C.), showing huge circular mounds (tumuli) or rectangular chambers carved from solid tufa with reserved columns in Ionic (Aeolic) design, slanted ceilings, shelves in walls for bodies, and lively decorative wall painting. Tombs yield rich jewelry and furniture. Sarcophagi in clay (*c*.520 B.C.) carry figures of the dead (man and wife) reclining as at banquet in the gay mode of Etrurian life. Important is the Regolini-Galassi tomb (7th cent. B.C.). After 400 B.C. terrifying demons key a pervasive melancholy air in Etruscan funerary expression. BIBLIOGRAPHY: R. Bloch, *Etruscans* (1958).

[M. J. DALY]

CAERWENT MONASTERY, a monastery founded by St. Tathan (or Tatheus) on the site of the Romano-British town of Venta Silurum in Gwent, Monmouthshire, Wales, mainly under the patronage of Caradog, king of Upper and Lower Gwent (between the reaches of the Wye, Monnow, and Usk). It became the ecclesiastical center of the kingdom of Gwent, an important monastic school. Its later history is unknown. BIBLIOGRAPHY: J. E. Lloyd, *History of Wales* (2 v., 1948); A. W. Wade-Evans, *Welsh Christian Origins* (1934).

[C. MCGRATH]

CAESAR, GAIUS JULIUS (*c*.100–44 B.C.), Roman general and statesman. C. attained the consulate in 59 B.C. Disregarding the veto of his colleague, he raised troops to use later in the conquest of Gaul, his allotted province. In 50 B.C. he defied the senate's order that he lay down his command before returning to Italy, and in 3 months of civil war he mastered the peninsula. The senate conferred on him extraordinary powers and honors after his final victories in 45 B.C.; but senators who feared his ambition struck him down within a year. As general, Caesar had no superior; in oratory he ranked second to Cicero. He wrote masterly descriptions

of warfare in *De bello Gallico* and *De bello civili* (his other writings have not survived). Caesar introduced the Julian calendar and promoted economic development and greater social equality. BIBLIOGRAPHY: R. Syme, *Roman Revolution* (1939); M. Gelzer, *Caesar: Politician and Statesman* (6th ed. 1968); M. W. Fanning, *Attitude of Julius Caesar to Roman Religion* (Univ. of Pa., 1927); S. Weinstock, *Divus Julius* (1971).

[M. J. SUELZER]

CAESAREA, SCHOOL OF, center of Christian teaching located in Caesarea, Palestine. Its importance derives particularly from Origen, who settled there *c*. 230 and taught until his death *c*. 250. Caesarea also had the most important library of Christian antiquity, containing many of Origen's works, including his *Hexapla. The library was destroyed in the 7th century. Other notable figures associated with the school included Pamphilus, who went there *c*. 290 and continued the method of Origen; Eusebius, who became bp. at Caesarea *c*. 315; and Jerome, who studied there. The school was heavily influenced by Hellenistic philosophy and used the allegorical method for Scripture interpretation, in contrast with the school of Antioch, which followed the grammatical and historical method. BIBLIOGRAPHY: R. Cadiou, "La Bibliothèque de Césarée," RevScRel 16 (1936) 474–483.

[T. EARLY]

CAESAREA IN CAPPADOCIA, originally a Persian city, Hellenized in the 2d cent. B.C. under the name of Eusebia and later Caesarea (12–9 B.C.), and finally annexed to the Roman Empire. A Christian community existed there in apostolic times (1 Pet 1.1), and in subsequent centuries its bp. became a prominent figure and exercised authority over much of Asia Minor. The prestige of Caesarea reached its highest point during the pontificate of St. Basil (370–379), but it was soon overshadowed by the See of Constantinople and lost its importance. The city was taken by the Turks in 1064 and is now called Keyseri. BIBLIOGRAPHY: R. Janin, DHGE 12:199–203; A. H. M. Jones, *Cities of the Eastern Roman Provinces* (2d. ed., 1971).

[P. FOSCOLOS]

CAESAREA IN PALESTINE, a city, probably founded by Straton, King of Sidon, that came under Roman rule and, with its name changed to Caesarea, was entrusted to Herod the Great, who rebuilt it in magnificent fashion. It became the principal port and the Roman administrative center of Palestine. The Apostle Philip seems to have first established the Church there. Peter baptized the centurion Cornelius in the city (Acts 10), and Paul was later imprisoned there (Acts 23–26). The first known bp. is Theophilus (*c*. 195). Origen (*c*. 230) founded a famous theological school there and began a large library, which was destroyed by the Arabs in 638. Caesarea was the highest ranking see in Palestine until Jerusalem was made a patriarchate in 451. It was also the site of

several councils held against Arianism. BIBLIOGRAPHY: R. Janin, DHGE 12:209–211.

[P. FOSCOLOS]

CAESAREA PHILIPPI, a city built in Roman times by Philip the Tetrarch, son of Herod the Great, as his capital. It was built on the site of the ancient Paneas, now Banja Luka at the foot of Mt. Hermon. It was called Philip's Caesarea to distinguish it from several other Caesareas, or cities built in honor of Caesar. Peter's confession of faith in Christ (Mt 16.13; Mk 8.27) occurred in the vicinity of this gentile city. BIBLIOGRAPHY: D. Baly, *Geography of the Bible* (1957) 194–196.

[J. E. LUSSIER]

CAESAREAN TEXT, see BIBLE TEXTS.

CAESARIA, SS., the name of the first two abbesses of the monastery for women established at Arles by St. Caesarius. (1) The first, C. the Elder (d. a little after 524), sister of St. Caesarius. She illuminated and commented upon MSS useful in the spiritual direction of her sisters. (2) The second, C. the Younger (d. *c*. 559), is memorable for having induced St. Cyprian, bp. of Toulon, to write a biography of St. Caesarius. Two of her letters, one to a nun called Rachilde and the other to Queen *Radegunda, have survived.

CAESARIUS OF ARLES, ST. (*c*. 470–*c*. 542), abbot, abp., theologian. A monk of Lérins, C. succeeded to the See of Arles (*c*. 502) his kinsman Eonus who had ordained him. Briefly C. had been abbot (probably at Trinquelaille). As vicar for Gaul and Spain, he had proved benevolent and prudent. First Western prelate to receive the pallium (513), in his 40-year episcopate he convoked numerous synods and councils, for which he composed most of their decrees. He introduced the hours of Terce, Sext and None, and encouraged the insertion of hymns in the Office. His sister Caesaria was eventually abbess near Arles. C.'s numerous *Sermons* are well regarded by modern scholars esp. for their pastoral concern. BIBLIOGRAPHY: J. C. Didier, BiblSanct 3:1148–50; Butler 3:418–421.

[M. R. BROWN]

CAESARIUS OF HEISTERBACH (d. 1240), Cistercian author. Educated at the Cologne cathedral school, C. joined the Cistercians at Heisterbach (1198), where later he was master of novices and prior. Besides sermons, theological, hagiographic, and historical works, he wrote *Dialogus miraculorum,* a collection of stories and legends concerned with monastic virtues. BIBLIOGRAPHY: A. Hilka, *Die Wundergeschichte des Caesarius von Heisterbach* (3 v., 1933); *Dialogue on Miracles, 1220–1235* (tr. C. S. Bland, 2 v., 1929); G. Baader, LTK 2:965.

[L. J. LEKAI]

CAESARIUS OF NAZIANZUS, ST. (d. 369), physician, younger brother of St. *Gregory of Nazianzus. After studying medicine in Alexandria and Constantinople, C. became the court physician of the Emperors Constantius, Julian, and Jovian. When he narrowly escaped death in an earthquake at Nicaea in Bithynia in 368, he renounced the world and was baptized. He died shortly after; his brother preached the funeral oration over his body. BIBLIOGRAPHY: Butler 1:413–414; F. Pericoli-Ridolfin, EncCatt 3:1354.

[R. B. ENO]

CAESARIUS OF SPEYER (d. c. 1239), Franciscan provincial. After theological studies in Paris and a career as a preacher in Speyer, C. became a Franciscan. He collaborated with St. Francis in redacting the Rule of 1221. Sent as provincial to Germany, he established the order there but relinquished his office in 1223. Reports about his imprisonment and the manner of his death are not fully reliable. BIBLIOGRAPHY: A. Van den Nyngaert, DHGE 12:197–198.

[H. DRESSLER]

CAESAROPAPISM, the concept of government in which the supreme lay ruler (Caesar) also exercises supreme authority over the Church. The term is often, although erroneously, applied to the form of government in the Byzantine Empire. It is true that the Christian emperor was regarded as God's vicar on earth, whose duty it was to care for his subjects' temporal and spiritual welfare, which meant that he had to oversee the proper functioning of the Church. He made and enforced ecclesiastical regulations, convoked synods, appointed and deposed bps., but was not supposed to intervene in doctrinal or liturgical matters. Several emperors, however, actually did intrude in doctrinal questions, of which the best and most frequently cited example is *Justinian I (527–565). But esp. after the iconoclastic controversy of the 8th cent., the emperors did not so intervene. Caesaropapism, in one form or another, prevailed in the empire of Charlemagne, in Czarist Russia, and in many Protestant principalities where it was based on the phrase, *cuius regio eius religio. It was very much a part of later European forms of government, such as *Josephinism in Austria and *Gallicanism in France. BIBLIOGRAPHY: J. R. Palanque, *Dawn of the Middle Ages* (tr. F. Murphy, 1960) 13–21; H. Raab, LTK 6:289–295.

[G. T. DENNIS]

CAFASSO, JOSEPH, ST. (1811–60), moral theologian. He studied at the Institute of St. Francis in Turin. Later he lectured there in moral theology and in 1848 was named rector. It was at this institute that St. John Bosco met C., who was to become spiritual director for Bosco. Besides his work at the institute he was also preacher, confessor, and retreat master. C. was canonized in 1947. BIBLIOGRAPHY: J. Cottino, BiblSanct 6:1317–21.

[J. R. RIVELLO]

CAFFÀ, MELCHIORRE (1635–67), Italian baroque sculptor, the most important of Bernini's followers. In an intensely spiritualized relief of *St. Catherine in Ecstasy* (Rome, 1667), C. uses a varicolored marble background and a "mystic" light-source in the manner of Bernini. Noteworthy works are *St. Thomas of Villanova* and *St. Eustace in the Lion's Den* (both finished by others) and a sensitive portrait of Pope Alexander VII (Metropolitan Museum of Art, New York). BIBLIOGRAPHY: R. Wittkower, *Art and Architecture of Italy, 1600–1750* (1958).

[M. J. DALY]

CAGLIARI, PAOLO, see VERONESE.

CAGLIERO, JUAN (1838–1926), missionary, cardinal. A favorite pupil of St. *John Bosco, C. joined the Salesians, was ordained (1862), and led the first group of Salesians to South America (1875), founding five houses in Argentina and Uruguay. After serving as spiritual director for the Salesians in Italy (1877–85), C. was named vicar apostolic of Patagonia and titular bp. of Magida. He became apostolic delegate to Central America (1908), cardinal (1915), and bp. of Frascati, Italy (1921). BIBLIOGRAPHY: M. de Camillis, EncCatt 3:294.

[H. JACK]

CAGOTS (also known in med. France by other names, e.g., Gahets, Capots, Crestias, Chrestians, Agots), an outcast people or class in S France who from the 13th cent. until the French Revolution were obliged to live in isolation and were denied ordinary political and social rights. They dwelt chiefly in the countryside; in towns, they were grouped together in ghetto-like areas. The reason for their segregation is unknown. It has been suggested that they were the remains of an unassimilable foreign stock, or that they were the descendants of excommunicated heretics (*Albigenses or perhaps *Beghards); however there is little evidence to support either view. More likely they were the descendants of people isolated because of contagious disease, esp. leprosy. BIBLIOGRAPHY: G. Marsot, *Catholicisme* 2:351–352.

[P. K. MEAGHER]

CAHENSLY, PETER PAUL (1838–1923), a successful German merchant who helped establish the St. Raphael Society for the purpose of preserving the Catholic faith among European emigrants to the U.S. and other countries. This movement, often referred to as Cahenslyism, was judged, mistakenly, to have as its objective the buttressing of Germanic culture and rule and not the preservation of the faith. As a result, there was a period of dissension and distrust among Catholic clergy and hierarchy, esp. those of Irish and German origin, in the U.S. during the 1891–1910 era. BIBLIOGRAPHY: *Roman Catholicism and the American Way of Life* (ed. T. T. McAvoy, 1960); J. T. Ellis, *Life of James Cardinal Gibbons* (1952).

[C. KEENAN]

CAHIER, CHARLES (1807–82), French Jesuit archeologist, specializing in research on medieval cathedrals, stained glass, and iconography; author of many learned volumes on these subjects. BIBLIOGRAPHY: P. Bailly, *Catholicisme* 2:352–353.

[T. C. O'BRIEN]

CAHORS CATHEDRAL (St.-Étienne Cathedral), simple Aquitanian, domed structure dedicated in 1119. It has a 65-foot span covered by two enormous rubble domes on pendentives, a choir (13th cent.), chapels (14th and 15th cent.), a N portal with a notable sculptured tympanum in Burgundian style, and 15th-cent. Gothic cloisters (now in ruins). Cahors exerted a wide influence, esp. in the beautifully proportioned church at Souillac (*c.* 1130). BIBLIOGRAPHY: K. Conant, *Carolingian and Romanesque Architecture, 800–1200* (1959).

[M. J. DALY]

CAIAPHAS (CAIPHAS), Jewish high priest from A.D. 18 to 36, thus during the entire period of Jesus' public activity. By appointment of Valerius Gratus, C. became high priest and was deposed by Vitellius, legate in Syria. According to Jn 18.13 the real religious power was his father-in-law Annas, who had been high priest between 6 and 15, a view supported by Acts 4.6 which speaks of Annas, "the high priest," Caiaphas, John, and Alexander as presiding at the trial of Peter and John. BIBLIOGRAPHY: H. Holzmeister, *Historia Aetatis Novi Testamenti* (2d ed., 1938).

[J. J. O'ROURKE]

CAIN AND ABEL, the first two children of Adam and Eve, whose original sin (Gen 3.6) began the disintegration of human nature symbolized in Cain's murder of his brother (Gen 4.1–16). The earlier forms of this latter episode have an obscure history, but certain inconsistencies show that it was an independent story not associated with human origins (note the social organization assumed in vv. 2–4 and the presence of avengers in v. 14). Some hold that the earliest form of the story was a myth based upon ritual slaughter; thus v. 7 would refer to the shedding of blood in a field, performed to appease a demon for the purpose of assuring an abundant harvest. Babylonian magic texts tell of such rites performed by a priest who, symbolizing the guilt of the community, would then undergo a ritual flight into the wilderness, where he could rely on the sacred tattoo of his priesthood to be a warning against attack or harm (cf. v. 15). Others see the story as originally folklore explaining the origins of the Kenite tribe, nomadic metal-workers who worshiped Yahweh but did not share in the blessings of the Promised Land (cf. Jg 1.16 and Num 10.29–32). The crime of their ancestor Cain (cf. Num 24.21; his name means "metalworker") would explain their continued wandering, and the mark on Cain (Gen 4.15) would account for the origin of the clan tattoo, which was a sign that the clan would exact blood vengeance if the person were attacked.

Somewhat later in the history of this tradition, the figure of Cain probably expressed an opposition both to the Chanaanites, who were settled farmers, and to the nomadic tribes that harassed the Israelites (e.g., Jg 6). When the tradition was finally incorporated into the history of human origins sometime early in the monarchical period, earlier meanings faded before the theological concerns of the narrator (the "Yahwist"), for whom the story now alluded to God's free choice of Israel, man's responsibility to avoid sin, God's love for sinful man and esp. the spreading decay of society caused by man's original sin against God. BIBLIOGRAPHY: S. H. Hooke, "Genesis," *Peake's Commentary on the Bible* (1962); G. von Rad, *Genesis, a Commentary* (rev. ed., 1973).

[P. J. KEARNEY]

CAINITES, a Gnostic sect, possibly of pre-Christian origin, mentioned by Irenaeus, Hippolytus, and Tertullian. According to their bizarre teaching, the God of the OT was the source of evil in the world, and hence those who resisted God—Cain, Esau, and Korah—were looked upon as heroes. BIBLIOGRAPHY: ODCC 215.

CAIRD, the name of two brothers. (1) Edward (1835–1908), philosopher and theologian, born in Greenock, Scotland, was educated at Glasgow Univ. where he was appointed professor of moral philosophy in 1866. From 1893 until 1907, he was master of Balliol College. A chief exponent of neo-Hegelianism in British philosophy, he wrote works on Kant (1877), Hegel (1883), and Comte (1885). His Glasgow Gifford lectures are entitled, *The Evolution of Theology in the Greek Philosophers* (2 v., 1904).

(2) John (1820–98), preacher and theologian, was born in Greenock, Scotland. Educated at Glasgow Univ. and ordained in 1845, he was elected professor of divinity at the Univ. in 1862, becoming its Principal in 1873. He was renowned for his sermons, esp. *Religion in Common Life,* preached in 1855. His neo-Hegelian interpretations are stated in *Introduction to the Philosophy of Religion* (1880), and *Fundamental Ideas of Christianity* (1899). BIBLIOGRAPHY: ODCC 215–216.

[J. A. ROCHE]

CAIRO (Arab. *El Qâhira*), capital of Egypt and spiritual center of the Coptic Church. The city fans out from the Roman Fortress of Babylon N along the Nile. A series of Muslim cities have occupied the vicinity beginning with Fostat which the Arab invaders made their military headquarters. In the 10th cent., the Fatimid general, Jauhar al-Rumi, built his capital just to the N of Babylon and called it al-Kahira (the Victorious), from which the name Cairo is derived. Christians inhabited the area at least by the 4th century. The oldest church in Cairo is Abû Saragh (St. Sergius), located in the Fortress. The crypt contains a 6th-cent. chapel that replaces a 4th-cent. shrine commemorating a traditional resting place of the Holy Family. The other churches in the Fortress date from after the 7th century. The most interesting is Al Mu'allaqah (the Suspended) which forms a bridge between two sections of the Roman wall. The patriarchal cathedral of St. Mark is in the Christian quarter of the new city. The Coptic patriarch has resided in Cairo since the 11th century. There are also Armenian, Syrian, Maronite, Greek, and Roman Catholic churches in the Christian quarter. BIBLIOGRAPHY: E. R. Hardy, *Christian Egypt: Church and People* (1952); J. Abu-Lughod, *One Thousand One Years of the City Victorious* (Princeton Studies, 1971).

[D. W. JOHNSON]

CAIRO GENIZA, a fund of biblical MSS recovered 1890–98 from an ancient synagogue in Cairo, Egypt. The thousands of MS pages that had accumulated through many centuries in the *geniza (storage place for worn out sacred MSS or scrolls) of this synagogue, permitted scholars to trace the Babylonian and Palestinian development of the Masoretic system of vowel points (*see* MASORA). The original Hebrew text of Sir was also found, and fresh evidence on the OT canon and on the *Targums came to light. BIBLIOGRAPHY: P. E. Kahle, *Cairo Geniza* (2d ed., 1959); S. D. Goitein, *Mediterranean Society: the Jewish Communities of the Arab World as Portrayed in the Documents of the Cairo Geniza* (v. 1, 1968; v. 2, 1971).

[T. C. O'BRIEN]

CAITYA, (Sanskrit for chaitya), in India a sacred spot—a single tree, often small groves of trees, or tumuli where earth-spirits (yakshas, Nagas) dwelt accessible to simple folk. Buddha and his followers revered the cult of the *caitya* near to which lived holy men and later, Buddhist monks built monasteries. Stupas or tumuli were built over the ashes of the Buddha; and the *Bodhi Tree at Gayā, the Lumbinī; grove of Buddha's birth, the grove near Kuśinagara where he died, and the Deer Park at Benāres became holy places *(caityas)*. The great *caitya* hall at *Kārlī, Bombay (1st cent. B.C.–1st cent. A.D.) is the finest example of rock-cut cave temples with splendid reserved columns and a *caitya* or shrine at the end of an apsidal hall. Associated with these *caitya* halls are rock-cut monasteries or *sanghārāmas*, the most famous at *Ajanta, proliferating (2d cent. B.C. to 7th cent. A.D.) into 27 caves, where paintings and sculpture are the glory of India.

[M. J. DALY]

CAIUS, see GAIUS.

CAJETAN, ST. (Gaetano da Thiene; 1480–1547), lawyer, religious reformer, cofounder of the Theatines. Educated at the Univ. of Padua, C. distinguished himself in theology and in 1504 received a doctorate in civil and canon law. In 1506 he went to Rome, where soon he became engaged as a jurist in several diplomatic missions for Pope Julius II. Following his ordination in 1516, he founded the Oratory of Divine Love and devoted himself to charitable works and religious reform in Rome. The following year he returned to Rome and with three associates founded (1524) the *Clerici regulares*, better known as the Theatines, from the name Teate (Chieti), town of Gianpietro Caraffa, the first superior. When Rome was sacked in 1527, the Theatines took refuge in Venice. C. was superior of a new foundation at Naples from 1533 until his death except for a term as superior at Venice (1540–43). His example, preaching, and labor brought success and improvement to the institute. During his last years he helped to establish "benevolent pawnshops" (see MONTES PIETATIS), which later became the Bank of Naples. He was canonized by Pope Clement X in 1671. BIBLIOGRAPHY: G. Llompart, *Gaetano da Thiene* (1969); F. Andreu, BiblSanct 5:1346–49; Butler 3:272–274.

[R. A. TODD]

CAJETAN (1468–1534), Dominican philosopher, theologian, master general, cardinal legate in the Germanies and Hungary, but indeed, much more than the original recipient deserving Dryden's tribute, "A man so various, that he seem'd to be/Not one, but all Mankind's Epitome." Born at Gaëta—hence his sobriquet—Jacopo (afterwards called Thomas in religion) de Vio studied in Naples, and as a young lecturer in metaphysics at Padua and Milan was befriended by the Gonzaga and Sforza. There he debated with Pico della Mirandola and stood against the returning tide of Latin Averroism. Called to Rome in 1507, he was a professor at the Sapienza, and elected master general of his order (1508–17). Thenceforth he was to be centered at the papal court, a respected and influential adviser, but a powerful agent for reform and a lean and leathery contrast with the colorful opulence of the last two Medici pontiffs. Still he had style himself and moved with dignity as legate to the Empire, where two tasks faced him, both beyond the powers of any man. The first was the two-pronged thrust through Rhodes and Belgrade of Ottoman power, then rising to its height under Suleyman the Magnificent; it was Cajetan's work to promote the crusade, the success of which did not show until Lepanto and Vienna many decades after his death. More sapping to the life of Europe was the religious revolt which was to split it in two. He viewed Lutheranism with understanding and the resulting prospects for religion without illusion; at Augsburg he would strike no compromise with Luther but treated him with gentleness, and, indeed, exceeded his instructions and helped him to escape prison, and worse. In practice, as well as in thought, he was ever able to take an original line. He was a prime mover in the election of the Cardinal of Utrecht as Adrian VI, the last non-Italian pope, and the first reforming pope of the 16th cent. One of his last acts was to protest to Henry VIII about his marriage to Anne Boleyn. He died a simple religious disdaining all pomp, and was buried, according to his own instruction, under the flagstones at the door of the Dominican church of the Minerva.

Throughout all his public occupations he continued to study and write; indeed the chief stamp he left on his order was the obligation to pursue the scientific contemplation of divine truth. As an analytical thinker he was superb, "more acute than felicitous," as Melchior *Cano remarked of him. Yet from time to time the flagging student of his semantics is brought up short by the pleasant reassurance that all this is as nothing compared with simple loving faith in God. His style was sharp, but never sour; he was courteous in controversy, even with that stormy petrel of the Dominicans, Ambrogio Catarino. His original development of the philosophy of analogy was criticized by the alternative theory of Francesco Sylvester *Ferrariensis, himself also to become master general of the Dominicans: the two men remained great friends. After his first-hand contact with Lutheranism, he grew convinced of the need for getting at the literal sense of Scripture; he entered into friendly exchanges with *Erasmus, criticized the sufficiency of the Vulgate, and wrote exegetical works his contemporaries considered too daring. He came to doubt whether the immortality of the soul could be demonstrated by reason: he is accused of being more Aristotelian than his master Aquinas was. His theological classic is his commentary on the *Summa theologiae* of St. Thomas Aquinas, his patron saint and fellow countryman, which is incorporated in the folio Leonine edition. Even there, his original view on the salvation of infants in the faith of their parents, as well as other points we now take in our stride, were too much for another Dominican of narrower views, St. *Pius V, who ordered them to be deleted in the folio Pianan edition. Later Thomists put him in the first rank and sometimes pay him the compliment of well-considered disagreement. One may well wonder whether some are not venturing out of their class. Among C.'s perceptive points in his *Summa* commentary are his interpretation: of the nature of the science of theology in ST 1a,1; of the "five ways" for proving God's existence, esp. as to the unity of their conclusions (*ibid.* 2.3); of the natural desire to see God (*ibid.* 12.1); of the divine knowledge of the future (*ibid.* 14.8.9.13). He is also one of the few commentators who does not perfunctorily pass over but follows carefully through the detailed consideration of the virtues in the *Secunda secundae* part of the *Summa*. Among the important modern editions of his philosophical commentaries may be noted: M. H. Laurent, ed., *In De ente et essentia D. Thomae Aquinatis commentaria* (1934); P. N. Zammit, ed., *De nominum analogia; De conceptu entis* (1934); J. Coquelle, ed, *In De anima Aristotelis commentaria* (1938). BIBLIOGRAPHY: M. J. Congar, "Bio-bibliographie de Cajétan," *Revue thomiste* 39 (1934–35, centenary edition) 3-49; S. Ramirez, *De analogia* (1970)—the most profound study of C.'s teaching on analogy; J. P. Reilly, *Cajetan's Notion of Existence* (1971); T. C. O'Brien, *Metaphysics and the Existence of God* (1960) 38–40; 235.

[T. GILBY]

CALANCHA, ANTONIO DE LA (1584–1654), Augustinian historian. Of Spanish parentage, C. entered the Order of St. Augustine (1598) and after studies at the Univ. of San Marcos, Lima, attained the doctorate in theology. He became successively definitor, secretary of the province, rector of the Colegio San Ildefonso, Lima, and prior of his convent. Gathering information about the natives of the Peruvian coast and the Lake Titicaca region of Bolivia, he wrote his best-known work, *Crónica moralizada del orden de San Augustín en el Perú, con sucesos egemplares en esta monarquia* (1638, 1653), which is valuable not only as a history of

contemporary Augustinians but also of the Indians of Peru and Bolivia.

[A. P. HANLON]

CALAS, JEAN (1698–1762), French Calvinist and successful cloth merchant of Toulouse. C. reared all his seven children in the Calvinist faith. In 1760 his second son Louis became a Catholic and left home because of his father's hostile attitude to his conversion. When his eldest son Marc Antoine, 28, declared his proposed conversion, his father's rage was felt in and out of the house. Shortly after, in 1761, Marc Antoine was found hanged, and his father was charged with the murder. Unfortunately, his vacillating testimony helped to incriminate him, although he protested his innocence up to his execution. The whole affair was the occasion for anti-Calvinist manifestations. The intervention of Voltaire secured a reversal of the verdict and the reinstatement of the family in 1765. Voltaire waged an intense campaign through personal influence and his famous pamphlet *Sur la tolérance à cause de la mort de Jean Calas* (1763). Although the clergy and the system of justice were greatly discredited, and anti-Protestantism was lessened, current historical research is unable to prove the case decisively either way. BIBLIOGRAPHY: G. Jacquemet, *Catholicisme* 2:370–372.

[I. M. KASHUBA]

CALCED, an adjective derived from the Lat. *calceus,* meaning shoe. This word is used to distinguish the branches of some religious orders. The calced are those that wear shoes or boots as opposed to the discalced, that branch that wears sandals or goes barefoot.

[M. S. J. MCCAREY]

CALCIDIUS (4th cent. A.D.), a Christian Neoplatonist, translator of Plato's *Timaeus*. His Latin translation of the *Timaeus* is partial only, terminating at 53C. He compiled a commentary on the *Timaeus* also, covering 31C to 53C. It is based in part on the commentary of Posidonius through the medium of Adrastus of Aphrodisias (early 2d cent. A.D.) and Numenius of Apamea (*c.* 150–200 A.D.). His translation and commentary were the chief sources for the knowledge of Plato's cosmology in the West to the late Middle Ages. BIBLIOGRAPHY: Ueberweg 1:649–650; J. H. Waszink and P. J. Jensen, *Timaeus a Calcidio translatus commentarioque instructus* (1962); J. K. Feibleman, *Religious Platonism* (repr. 1971) 173.

[M. R. P. MCGUIRE]

CALDARA, ANTONIO (1670–1736), Italian composer of the baroque style, and primarily of compositions for voice. He spent the most productive years of his life in Vienna, where he held the post of assistant *Kapellmeister* at the imperial court of the Habsburg King, Charles VI. Though he composed string quartets, operas, and oratorios, C. is known best for his vocal works in sacred settings. An excellent example of his finest contrapuntal writing is the 16-part *Crucifixus*.

[D. J. SMUCKER]

CALDEY, ABBEY OF, ancient monastery founded in the 5th cent. on Caldy Island in Carmarthen Bay, Wales. The monastery, Benedictine in the Middle Ages, was dissolved in 1534. In 1906 the Island was purchased by Anglican monks who in 1913 were converted to Roman Catholicism. In 1928 the abbey was purchased by Cistercians of the Strict Observance (Trappists). BIBLIOGRAPHY: P. F. Anson, *Benedictines of Caldey* (1940); J. E. H. Nolan, "Caldy, the Monks' Island," *National Geographic Magazine,* 108 (1955) 564–578.

[L. J. LEKAI]

CALDWELL, MARY GWENDOLINE (1863–1909), a woman who through her friendship with Bp. John Lancaster Spalding became interested in the establishment of The Catholic Univ. of America, to which she donated $300,000 or one-third of her patrimony. In recognition of her gift she was awarded Notre Dame Univ.'s Laetare Medal in 1899. In 1904 she announced her renunciation of Catholicism. BIBLIOGRAPHY: J. T. Ellis, *Formative Years of the Catholic Univ. of America* (1946).

[C. KEENAN]

CALEB, eponymous ancestor of the Calebites, who captured and settled Hebron during the Israelite occupation of Palestine (*c*. 1250 B.C.). Analysis of the biblical references indicates the following reconstruction: C., son of Jephonne, was a member of the Edomite tribe of Cenez (pre-Israelite inhabitants of S Palestine); he allied himself with the invading Israelites, probably with the tribe of Juda (Num 13.6), and received title to the city of Hebron (Jos 14.6–15). The tradition seems to have crystallized by the time of David (*c*. 1000 B.C.), when the area around Hebron became known as the Negev (Southland) of C. (1 Sam 30.14). In Sir 46.7–10 the same narrative is recalled. This C. seems identical with the Chelubai or Caleb who appears in slightly variant traditions recorded in 1 Chr 2.19, 24.50; 4.4. BIBLIOGRAPHY: InterDB 1:482–483; EDB 299.

[T. CRANE]

CALEFACTORY: (1) the room in a monastery that is kept heated; here the monks warm themselves. This room might also be used as the common room in the monastery. (2) A device used in the middle ages to warm the hands and fingers.

[M. S. J. MCCAREY]

CALENDAR, a system of dividing the solar or lunar year (or both) into an orderly succession of days, weeks, months, etc., so that civil, agricultural, and religious events can be recorded and observed at the proper times. We are concerned here with the fixing of dates significant in religious history and observance.

Jewish Calendars. Adequate and readable expositions of the calendars in use in early times in Palestine and among the Jewish people can be found in EDB 299–303 and in the article by G. W. MacRae in NCE 2:1068–69. The detailed explana-

tion of the complexities of these calendars lies somewhat beyond the scope of this article.

The Julian Calendar. This was the calendar system established by Julius Caesar in 46–45 B.C. It remained the generally followed calendar of the West until it was replaced by the Gregorian Calendar in 1582. The Julian Calendar replaced an older Roman system of 4-year cycles. Soon after 200 B.C. the pontifex maximus gained control of the calendar and sometimes used it for political ends, so that by Caesar's time the seasons were months off their original cycle. On the advice of his astronomer Sosigenes, Caesar added 90 days to 46 B.C., bringing the spring of 45 to begin in March. The Julian year, based on an Egyptian system, was 365 days and six hours. Because it was slightly too long, it was to require adjustment in the future.

The Gregorian Calendar. This was the name given to the calendar that replaced the Julian Calendar after the calendar reform proposed by Pope Gregory XIII in 1582.

Calendar Reform. The basic defect in the Julian Calendar was that it exceeded the tropical or solar year by 11 minutes and 15 seconds. The Middle Ages recognized that the calendar was getting out of accord with the season dates, e.g., the Easter date; by the 13th cent., the discrepancy had grown to just over 7 days; by the 15th, to 9 days. In the 16th cent. Gregory XIII appointed a commission to study the problem. Ten extra days which had accrued over the centuries were canceled by making the day after Oct. 4, 1582, Oct. 15. To prevent such excess time in the future, leap years were admitted every fourth year, but not in century years unless these were divisible by 400. Thus 1600 was a leap year, but not 1700. The resulting average length of the year was 365.2425 days as compared with 365.2422 of the tropical year, a variation of only 25 seconds. More accurate methods for predicting full moons resolved problems connected with the Easter cycle. Catholic countries were quick to adopt the new calendar. In other countries, its adoption lagged: England and Germany accepted it in the 18th century; Russia, in 1918; Romania and Greece, in 1924; Turkey, in 1927.

Today proposals are being made to give the Gregorian Calendar greater regularity: e.g., a definite Sunday for Easter. To this Vatican Council II offered no opposition provided the Protestant Churches would agree. Similarly, Vatican II did not oppose in principle the perpetual calendar (each date falls on the same day of the week in each year). This is known as the World Calendar. BIBLIOGRAPHY: D. J. K. O'Connell, NCE 2:1067; E. Achelis, *Calendar for the Modern Age* (1959).

The Calendar Problem in Eastern Churches. Eastern Christianity, as it developed within the late Roman Empire, followed the time computation of the Julian Calendar. This had established the year as equivalent to 365 days and six hours. These six hours were taken care of by assigning to every fourth (or leap) year 366 days, but this resulted in an excess of 10 days by the time of Gregory XIII, as explained above. The mean Gregorian year is still too long by 26 seconds, and this will need correction *c*. 2500 A.D. By the 18th cent. all Christian countries had introduced the Gregorian calendar with the exception of the Eastern Orthodox nations, the Russian Empire, Greece, Romania, Serbia, and Bulgaria. After World War I these countries accepted the Gregorian Calendar for civil use. As the initial resistance to the new calendar by non-Catholic countries was prompted largely by religious motives, so also was its propagation by the Roman curia among Eastern Catholic communities. However, the possible damage was soon realized, and further suppression of the Julian Calendar was dependent on the initiative of Eastern bishops. Among the Melkites, Patriarch Clement Bahuth caused upheavals in his church when he introduced the Gregorian Calendar in 1857.

Some Eastern Orthodox Churches began to adopt the Gregorian Calendar for immovable feasts, e.g., Christmas. This was done by the patriarchate of Constantinople, the Churches of Greece and of Cyprus (1924); the Orthodox Church of Poland (1924), the Orthodox and the Catholic Byzantine Churches of Romania (1924), the Catholicate of Georgia (U.S.S.R.) in 1927, the patriarchate of Alexandria (1928). They preserved the Julian Calendar for the movable feasts based on Easter because of the decree of the Council of Nicaea (325) to the effect that Easter was to be celebrated on the first Sunday after the first full moon that follows the vernal equinox. Since this was computed on the basis of the Julian Calendar, the Eastern Orthodox Churches consider any change impossible. Thus, Easter, according to the Julian Calendar, may fall, in its Gregorian computation, any time from April 4th to May 8th. Between 1938 and 1970 Easter occurred on the same day in both calendars 11 times; the Julian Easter occurred later by one week 11 times; by four weeks four times; by five weeks, seven times.

The opposition to a change of calendar in general, even in respect to the immovable feasts, which always fall on the same day of the month, has several motives: a genuine persuasion of the value of adhering to ancient traditions, nationalistic considerations (e.g., Ukrainians and Poles), psychological causes in countries where the population did not become accustomed to using the civilian Gregorian Calendar.

In Greek-speaking countries, adherents of the old calendar (palaioimerologites), organized themselves, established their own hierarchy, and some still exist despite coercive measures of the Greek government. Similarly, attempts at changing the calendar among the Catholic Ukrainians and Ruthenians in North America resulted in apostasies and schismatic movements. The Gregorian Calendar is preferred by the clergy and the majority of the faithful in order to prevent the desertion of members to the Latin rite because of the inconvenience caused by the difference between the everyday calendar and the calendar of the Church. Today all Ruthenian Catholics and most Ukrainians in the U.S. follow the Gregorian Calendar, although in Canada the Julian is still prevalent.

Vatican Council II has permitted Catholics of all rites living in the Near East to follow the Julian calendar and celebrate Easter together with the Orthodox, thereby giving a better example of basic Christian unity (Vat II EastCath, 20). The same council declared its readiness to accept an immovable Easter date, recurring every year on the same Sunday, provided other Christians concurred (Vat II, SacLit, Appendix).

[P. K. MEAGHER]

Calendar, Armenian. The old Armenian calendar contained 12 months of 30 days, plus 5 epagomenal days at the end of the year. The "Era of the Armenians" was reckoned from the calendar reform of the catholicos Moses II in 551 (July 11, 552 A.D. was the beginning of year 1, Era of the Armenians). Since there was no bissextile, it was impossible to coordinate this calendar with the Julian, which began to replace the national calendar in Armenia after 1084. In 1912 the Catholic Armenians adopted the Gregorian calendar, used now by the Gregorian Armenians also in many places.

The greater part of the liturgical year is contained in four blocks of Sundays, each block governed by the day on which a particular feast falls, and each containing a fixed number of Sundays (with the week following), viz.: (1) 8 Sundays governed by Theophany (Jan. 6)—7 Sundays before Theophany and 1 of the Octave; (2) 25 Sundays governed by Easter—9 Sundays before Easter (including 6 of Lent plus Palm Sunday), Easter and the other 6 Sundays of the Paschal Fifty-Days, Pentecost and its following 6 Sundays, Transfiguration Sunday and its Sunday following, (3) Assumption (the Sunday nearest Aug. 15) and its following 3 Sundays, (4) Exaltation of the Cross (the Sunday nearest Sept. 14) and its following 9 Sundays. These four blocks comprise 47 Sundays in all. The remaining Sundays of the year fit into any periods remaining between the end of a given block and the beginning of the following one. The number of feasts assigned to a fixed calendar date is very small, most feasts being assigned to a given day of a given week (including some Sundays) in the system described above. While the Catholic Armenians celebrate both Christmas and the Epiphany on the dates traditional in the Roman Church, the Gregorians celebrate the single feast of Our Lord's Theophany, Jan. 6.

[A. CODY]

Calendar, Chaldean. In the temporal cycle of the East Syrian liturgical year, Sundays are ordered around the feasts of Easter and, secondarily, of the Nativity and Epiphany. The year is divided into nine liturgical periods: Annunciation, Epiphany, Lent, Resurrection, Apostles, Summer, Elias, Moses, Dedication. The division of the year into periods is attributed to Patriarch Išoʻyahb III (c. 660). These periods are called šaboʻe, from the root ŠBʻ (sevenfold), since ideally there are seven Sundays in all periods except the first and last, which have four. Additional offices provided for the two Sundays between Christmas and Epiphany and for an eighth Sunday after Epiphany bring the number of Sunday offices to sixty. But in fact the number of Sundays varies, esp. in the periods of Epiphany and Moses, because of the mobility of Easter. The Chaldean sanctoral cycle is largely undeveloped, and commemorations of saints usually fall on Friday. For among the East Syrians and Maronites, Friday and Sunday, not Saturday and Sunday as among Byzantines and others, are the two most important days in the liturgical week. BIBLIOGRAPHY: J. Mateos, *Lelya-Ṣapra, Essai d'interprétation des matines chaldéenes* (1959) esp. 14–16.

[R. F. TAFT]

Calendar, Coptic. The method of reckoning the yearly cycle used by the Coptic Christians of Egypt. Three different eras are used by the Copts, those of the Messiah, of the Hegira (from A.D. 622), and of the martyrs. The last is peculiarly Coptic and begins in August, A.D. 284, the beginning of Diocletian's persecution, particularly severe in Egypt. The Coptic year is divided into three parts: innundation, sowing, and harvest, reflecting an agricultural society dependent on the Nile River. The year has 12 months of 30 days each. A little month of 5 days (6 in leap year) fills out the year. The names of the months are ancient Egyptian, slightly modified. The ecclesiastical year begins with the month *Tout* (*c.* Sept. 10). The ecclesiastical year is marked by rigorous fasts, the 52 days before Easter (Lent), 13 days before the feast of SS. Peter and Paul (the Lent of the Apostles, 5 *Ahib* or June 29), and the 43 days before Christmas (Advent). The saints are given a simple commemoration on their feast days. There are 7 greater and 7 lesser feasts of Our Lord and approximately 30 feasts of Our Lady. Easter is determined either according to the Gregorian calendar or by the reckoning of the patriarch, as local custom dictates. BIBLIOGRAPHY: A. King, *Rites of Eastern Christendom* (2 v., 1947) 1:396–404.

[D. W. JOHNSON]

CALENDAR, FRENCH REVOLUTIONARY, a calendar in use in France from Sept. 22, 1792 (1 *vendémiaire, an* I) to Dec. 31, 1805 (10 *nivôse, an* XIV), i.e., from the beginning of the first French Republic to the early days of Napoleon I's empire. The decree of the National Convention of Oct. 5, 1793, instituted the calendar based on the decimal system. It numbered 360 days per year, 12 months (30 days per month), 36 weeks (10 days per week), and 5 complementary days; in leap year one day was added as "the day of the Revolution." Each day contained 10 equal parts of "hours" with the 10th day in the long "week" a legal holiday. Each month received a name based on phenomena appropriate to the season, e.g., *thermidor* 1–30 ("hot weather" month), *an* II, corresponded to July 19–Aug. 18, 1794, in the Gregorian calendar. Each of the 360 days in the year received a name representing either flora, fauna, or some agricultural tool. At a time of intense de-Christianization the inventors alienated both calendar and daily reflection from traditional religious associations, e.g., Dec. 25 (Christmas Day) was 5 *nivôse*, the "snow-month." Because it clashed with market or fair days and customary Christian days of rest and worship, and it lacked universal validity, the Senate reestablished the Gregorian calendar effective Jan. 1, 1806. BIBLIOGRAPHY: P. Caron, *Manuel pratique pour l'étude de la Révolution Française* (1912; new ed., 1947); F. A. Gevaert, *Le Calendrier républicain avec les tables de concordance du calendrier grégorien* (1965); N. M.

Denis-Boulet, *Christian Calendar* (tr. P. Hepburne-Scott, 1960) 100–102.

[R. J. MARAS]

CALENDAR, ISLAMIC, the method in use among Islamic peoples of computing the year and its divisions. In the Near East a lunisolar system was in common use before the death of the Prophet, but after his death Mohammedan Arabs began to number the years of the Muslim era from the date of the Hegira (June, 622), and proceeded from that date on a purely lunar basis. It is the only lunar calendar in wide use. Each year has 354 or 355 days. In 33 years it gains one full year on the year-date as computed according to the Gregorian calendar. Its months bear no fixed relationship to the season of the year.

CALENDAR, SYRIAN, a calendar that follows the Gregorian calendar and in which the ecclesiastical year begins on the Sunday nearest to October 31. It is substantially the ancient calendar of the Church of Antioch. The seasons of the year are Advent, Christmas, preparation for Lent, Lent, Paschaltime, time after Pentecost, time after the feast of the Holy Cross. Some of the feasts such as Corpus Christi, the feast of the Sacred Heart, and Trinity Sunday have been adopted from the West. The Eastern Church calendar has a feast relating to Mary for every day throughout the year.

[C. R. CAWLEY]

CALENDAR OF THE EARLY SAINTS, a list of feasts celebrated in the Church during the first centuries arranged in chronological order. From earlier pagan calendars upon which they imposed the Jewish 7-day week, the Christians derived their system for determining the movable feasts of the year such as Easter and Pentecost and the anniversaries of the deaths of the martyrs. The dispute that Polycarp had with Pope Anicetus *c.* 155 A.D. over the date of Easter and the care that the Church of Smyrna had to celebrate the anniversary of the former's martyrdom (*Martyrium Polycarpi* 18.2) indicate the importance of such calendars for the liturgy. The earliest calendars contained dates, names, and places of burial, and to these were later added further details such as the manner of a martyr's death. The oldest extant ecclesiastical calendar is found in the Chronographer of 354 and is divided into a *Depositio episcoporum* and a *Depositio martyrum*. The former gives the dates of burial of 12 popes of the 3d and 4th centuries. The latter gives the anniversaries of Roman martyrs of this same period and those of 3 martyrs of Carthage, SS. Cyprian, Perpetua, and Felicitas. In addition to these it includes the feasts of St. Peter's Chair, of SS. Peter and Paul *in Catacumbas,* and of the Nativity of Christ. Other calendars or "martyrologies" are the Syriac Martyrology of 411, a fragment of a 5th-cent. Gothic calendar, a 5th-cent. calendar of Tours, a 5th- or 6th-cent. calendar of Carmona in Andalusia, 6th-cent. calendars from Carthage and Oxyrhynchus in Egypt, and a 7th- or 8th-cent. calendar from Naples. BIBLIOGRAPHY: H. Leclercq, DACL 8.1:624–667; R. Aigrain, *L'Hagiographie* (1953) 11–31; M. J. Costelloe,

NCE 2:1064–65.

[M. J. COSTELLOE]

CALEPINO, AMBROGIO (*c.*1440–*c.*1510), Italian Augustinian, author of an influential Renaissance dictionary. In Latin, the work was titled *Cornucopia* (1502: rev. 1505 and 1509). Other humanists continued to revise and amplify his work, and by the Basel edition of 1590 had introduced 10 more languages to the work. BIBLIOGRAPHY: C. A. Dubray, CE 3:169; D. Francazi, EncCatt 3:372.

[M. R. BROWN]

CALÈS, JEAN (1865–1947), scriptural scholar. C. taught OT exegesis at the Jesuit seminary in Vals, France, for almost 40 years. He is best known for his translation and commentary on the Psalms, *Le Livre des Psalms traduit et commenté* (2 v. 1936). BIBLIOGRAPHY: B. F. Sargent, NCE 2:1070.

[T. M. MCFADDEN]

CALIFORNIA, a Pacific coastal state, admitted to the Union (1850) as the 31st state. Sailing under the orders of Viceroy Antonio de Mendoza, a Portuguese navigator named Juan Rodríguez Cabrillo discovered California in 1542. During the next 2 cent. numerous expeditions from New Spain and the Philippines visited the area, as did such English raiders as Francis Drake in 1579. The first Spanish settlement (1769) was prompted by such factors as the need for a supply port in the Philippine trade, the menace of Russia and England, and the missionary zeal of the Franciscans. Most prominent of these Franciscan priests was Junípero *Serra, who had been chosen president of the Lower California missions following the expulsion of the Jesuits from New Spain. After founding his first mission at San Diego, Serra established (1770) permanent headquarters at San Carlos Mission, Monterey-Carmel. During the next 12 years he founded additional missions at San Antonio (1771), San Gabriel (1771), San Luis Obispo (1772), San Francisco (1776), San Juan Capistrano (1776), Santa Clara (1777), and San Buenaventura (1782). Other Franciscans carried on after Serra's death, establishing more than a dozen missions in the next half century. In 1833 the N California missions were placed under the administration of the Franciscan Fathers of the Apostolic College of Our Lady of Guadalupe, Zacatecas. Francisco García Diego of Moreno became the first commissary-prefect of the Zacatecan missionaries, and from 1840 until his death in 1846 he served as the first bp. of California. Meanwhile, the S California missions were placed under the control of San Fernando College.

When California attained statehood, the area had 24 churches, 22 priests, and about 50,000 Catholics. In 1853 Joseph Sadoc *Alemany, OP, was named abp. of the newly created Archdiocese of San Francisco. Under Abp. Alemany, the Dominicans, the Brothers of Mary, and the brotherhood of St. John Baptist de la Salle were established in California. Missions, schools, and hospitals were staffed by the Sisters of Charity from Emmitsburg, Md., and by Presentation Nuns, Sisters of Mercy, Holy Name Sisters, Holy Cross Sisters, Ursulines, and Sisters of St. Joseph of Carondelet.

By the time of Alemany's resignation (1884), the archdiocese contained 120,000 Catholics served by 156 priests in 133 churches. Alemany's successor, Patrick W. Riordan, brought in additional religious communities, multiplied the number of parish schools, began publications of the *Monitor*, and supported the first Newman Club at the Univ. of California at Berkeley in 1909. Abp. Riordan also dedicated St. Mary's Cathedral (1891) and opened St. Patrick's Seminary (1898). Many of these new facilities were destroyed in the great earthquake of 1906, but the next abp., Edward J. Hanna, after his consecration (1915) continued archdiocesan development by building numerous schools and by establishing a teachers' institute and the Catholic Youth Organization.

By 1960 the archdiocese had a Catholic population of 1,093,595, with 256 parishes and 88,200 elementary and secondary school students. The present abp., Joseph T. McGucken, was consecrated in 1962. He has engaged in a disputed drive to replace the cathedral, a school construction program, and an effort to create social action committees in every parish. His suffragan sees now include the Dioceses of Sacramento, Calif., (established 1886), Salt Lake City, Utah (1891), Reno, Nev. (1931), Honolulu, Hawaii (1941), Oakland Calif. (1962), Santa Rosa, Calif. (1962), Stockton, Calif. (1962), and Agana, Guam Island (1965).

The Archdiocese of Los Angeles was established in 1936, making California the first and only state which has two metropolitan sees. John Joseph *Cantwell, who had been bishop of Monterey-Los Angeles since 1917, became the first abp. and served until his death (1947). His successor, Cardinal Apb. James Francis A. McIntyre, had a controversial episcopacy but he promoted institutional growth and improved administrative procedures. In 1970, Timothy Manning was appointed abp. and made cardinal in 1973.

California's population of 20,933,371, which is more than 80% urban, makes it the most populous state in the Union. In 1975 Catholics numbered 4,604,296, or 22% of the total state population. The major Protestant sects are the Methodist Church, with 1.8% of the population (1971), and the Presbyterian Church, with 1.6%. The Jewish population (1968) was 693,085, or 3.37%.

There are more than 35 major church-related colleges in California, 13 of which are Catholic. The Archdiocese of San Francisco contains 5 Catholic colleges with a total enrollment of about 15, 129, while Los Angeles has 5 with an enrollment of 7,171. More than 70,000 students are attending California's 139 Catholic high schools, 69 of which are in the Archdiocese of Los Angeles. Almost 200,000 students are enrolled in 615 Catholic elementary schools, 272 of which are in the Archdiocese of Los Angeles and 109 in the Archdiocese of San Francisco. BIBLIOGRAPHY: A. F. Rolle, *California: A History* (1963); J. W. Caughey, *California* (2d ed., 1953); M. J. Geiger, *Life and Times of Fray Junípero Serra* (2 v., 1959).

[J. L. MORRISON; R. M. PRESTON]

CALIPH, the chief of the Muslim community (from Arab. ḫalîfa, pl. ḫulafâ', successor, vice-regent, i.e., the successor of the Prophet). As religious head of all Muslims, the caliph was also called *Imam and as chief of the armies of Islam, amîr al-mu'minîn, Commander of the Faithful. The first four caliphs, abû Bakr (d. 634), 'Umar (d. 644), 'Uthmân (d. 655) and *'Alî (d. 661) are commonly called the "rightly guided caliphs" of what is considered traditionally as the golden age of faith, although the *Shiites generally reject the validity of the first three (see RÂFIḌITES). When the Umayyads came into power in 661 the center of government moved to Damascus from *Medina, where it remained until the establishment of the 'Abbâsid caliphate in 750, when the new capital city of Baghdad was founded. The real authority of the caliph progressively declined from the 9th cent. on and the institution came to a complete end with the death of al-Musta'sim in 1258. The title has been taken by other Islamic rulers, e.g., the *Fatimids and the Umayyads of Spain and by others to lend prestige to their claims. Some modern writers, most importantly Rashîd Riḍâ, have urged the reestablishment of the caliphate as a purely religious authority. BIBLIOGRAPHY: T. W. Arnold, *Caliphate* (1924, 1967); E. Tyan, *Institutions de droit public musulman* I; id., *Le Califat* (1954); A. A. Dixon, *Umayyad Caliphate: A Political Study* (1971).

[R. M. FRANK]

CALIX, SOCIETY OF, a society organized in 1947 to assist Catholic alcoholics. It advocates total abstinence and the spiritual development of its members through Mass and the sacraments. It encourages members to practice the spiritual and corporal works of mercy. The society is divided into units, each having its own spiritual director. Units are found in the U.S., Canada, India, and Scotland. International headquarters is in Minneapolis, Minnesota. The society publishes the newspaper *Chalice*.

[M. S. J. MCCAREY]

CALIXT, GEORGE (Calixtus, Kallisen; 1586–1655), German Lutheran theologian; professor at the Univ. of Helmstedt, 1614–55. Moved by the horrors resulting from religious division in the Thirty Years' War and by contacts established with Catholics and Reformed Churches, C. devoted his life to the cause of church reunion. To achieve this purpose he proposed that differences between denominations be settled by a minimum of *credenda* (fundamental articles of faith), which would be determined according to the *consensus quinquesaecularis, i.e., the teachings agreed on during the first 5 Christian centuries. He participated in ecumenical dialogues, notably, the Colloquy of *Thorn (1645). C.'s efforts are now often praised by ecumenists, although with reservations; Lutherans, both in his time (see CALOV, A.) and since, have charged him with a *syncretism ultimately harmful to ecumenism. In his works (e.g., *Epitome theologiae*, 1619; *Apparatus theologicus*, 1698; *Epitome theologiae moralis*, 1634) C. set out as the aim of theology not pure doctrine but Christian living, based on a message more ethical than dogmatic. BIBLIOGRAPHY: J. T. McNeill, *Unitive Protestantism* (rev. ed., 1964); R. Rouse and S. Neill, *History of the Ecumenical Movement* (2d ed., 1967).

[P. DAMBORIENA]

CALIXTINES, another name for the 15th-cent. *Utraquists of Bohemia, because of their insistence that at holy communion the chalice (Lat. *calix*) be given to the laity.

CALL, God's gracious relationship toward man by which he summons man to a share in his kingdom and a participation in the redemptive graces of Christ. In Scripture, call generally refers to the summons to a particular task, e.g., the call of Matthew (Mt. 9.9); but in its dogmatic use, call is the divine invitation to election and salvation (Rom 8.30). Hence, call is related to predestination in its strict and proper meaning of election to glory. In this sense it is always effectual, so that the "called" and the "elect" are co-extensive. Since the time of Augustine, ecclesiastical writers and theologians refer to a general and external call, which is the divine invitation to the privileges of the kingdom, and which men are free to accept or reject, and a special and internal call, which is the free act of the grace of God in which the divine election is revealed and realized in man. This special call has its origin in God, and Scripture refers to it as a "holy" (2 Tim 1.9) or "heavenly calling" (Heb. 3.1). The term is prominent in Protestant dogmatics. It is explained as occurring when an individual, hearing or reading the word, becomes aware that God, through the illumination of the Holy Spirit, efficaciously offers him salvation. Hence, it is a divine pledge of salvation and is dependent upon *election, since God calls to salvation those whom he has elected.

Reformed theologians distinguish two calls: an external call offered by the preaching of the word and directed to all men, and the internal or special call, the truly proper efficacious call, which, through the activity of the Spirit infallibly inculcates faith in the heart of the elect. This efficaciousness proceeds from the Spirit's power to bring about man's conversion. Lutheran theologians reject this double call as weakening the universality of God's salvific will and appearing to make his external call to the nonelect a nonserious invitation. These theologians hold that the call is given through the gospel, as mediated through word and sacrament. It expresses the earnest will of God to save all, it is adequate and sufficient for conversion if man offers no resistance to the Spirit, and it is universally offered to man. The reason why it may remain ineffectual in certain cases is rooted not in the divine will in denying the Spirit but in the fact that God recognizes man's potentiality to so actuate his selfhood that he may choose to rebuff the gospel. Though the call is at times described as the initial step in the process of salvation, it is not a once-for-all event for the Christian. It may come at any moment in life, but when it does come and gains a response, it never departs; it remains as a continuously present active power so that the Christian is "called" every day of his life. The call does not excuse the recipient from certain conditions;

he must respond in faith, embrace the offering of new life, live in repentance unto regeneration, until he matures in sanctity. These conditions do not nullify the basic truth that the call is a purely gratuitous grace of God.

Call may also designate a "call to the ministry," as that movement of God inspiring an individual to the service of the word; or it may designate the "ministerial call," i.e., the invitation on the part of a congregation to a minister to become their resident pastor. In RC terminology a vocation means a call to the religious or priestly life. The call is considered to come from God, not as a direct inspiration, but through the inclinations of grace. A canonical call refers to approval of a candidate for orders by church authorities.

[J. TYLENDA]

CALLAN, CHARLES JEROME (1877–1962), American Dominican theologian, collaborator with J. A. McHugh on many volumes of scriptural, theological, and liturgical works. Both were for many years professors at the Maryknoll Seminary, Maryknoll, N.Y., and were coeditors of the *Homiletic and Pastoral Review*.

[T. C. O'BRIEN]

CALLES, PLUTARCO ELÍAS (1877–1945), Mexican revolutionary and opponent of the Catholic Church. As commissioner of Agua Prieta, he joined the Carranza revolution that deposed Huerta and became a high official in Carranza's government. In 1920 C. joined Obregón against Carranza. After Carranza's assassination, Obregón became president with C. in his cabinet; C. succeeded Obregón in 1924. C.'s animosity towards the Church had long been apparent, but now he attempted to establish a separate national Church. Failing this, he used the antireligious articles of the constitution of 1917 to effect a severe religious persecution. Public worship was suspended, and resistance met with bloody suppression. Even after his term of office he remained a power until one of his protégés exiled him to the U.S.

[H. JACK]

CALLEWAERT, CAMILLE (1866–1943), Belgian liturgical scholar known both for his scholarly and practical contributions to the field of liturgical research. His *Liturgicae institutiones* (3v, 1919–37) is his most important work. The liturgical study group he began at Bruges (1907) led to the formation of many similar groups elsewhere in Belgium. He was also the organizer of the Dutch liturgical weeks. BIBLIOGRAPHY: C. van Hulst, EphemLiturg 58 (1944) 319–326.

[N. KOLLAR]

CALLICRATES (fl. 450 B.C.), Greek architect who worked with Ictinus on the supreme Doric Parthenon. C. designed several Ionic works: Temple of Athena Nike on the Acropolis and the Athenian temple on Delos (417 B.C.). BIBLIOGRAPHY: W. B. Dinsmoor, *Architecture of Ancient Greece* (3d ed., 1950, repr. 1975).

[M. J. DALY]

CALLIERGIS, ZACHARIAS, Byzantine humanist (c. 1473–c. 1524). He came from Crete to Venice, where he established the first Greek press. Later he set up the first Greek press in Rome. He is esp. important as a copyist, printer, and editor of Greek texts, and was on close terms with Manutius, Bembo, and Erasmus. He published, among other works, the 1st ed. of the *Etymologicum Magnum*, the 1st ed. of Simplicius' *Commentary on the Categories of Aristotle,* and an edition of Pindar that remained the standard text before the early 19th century. BIBLIOGRAPHY: D. J. Geanakoplos, NCE 2:1079–80; idem, *Greek Scholars in Venice: Studies in the Dissemination of Greek Learning from Byzantium to Western Europe* (1962) 201–222.

[M. R. P. MCGUIRE]

CALLIMACHUS (fl. c. 425–400 B.C.), Greek sculptor whose work is characterized by overelaboration of drapery effected by a running drill seen in relief figures of dancing maenads. It is said C. made the first of elaborately styled Corinthian capitals (Bassae, c. 425 B.C.). BIBLIOGRAPHY: G. Richter, *Sculpture and Sculptors of the Greeks* (rev. ed., 1950).

[M. J. DALY]

CALLINICUS, PATRIARCH OF CONSTANTINOPLE (693–705). Honored as a saint in the Eastern Church, C. had resisted the brutal Byzantine Emperor Justinian II and supported his successor Leontius in sending him into exile (695). When in 705 Justinian laid siege to Constantinople, C. was apprehended, blinded, and exiled to Rome. BIBLIOGRAPHY: I. A. de Urbina, EncCatt 3:385; M. V. Brandi, BiblSanct 3:673–675.

[M. R. BROWN]

CALLISTUS I, ST. (d. 222), **POPE** from 217. The chief source of information about C.'s life is *Hippolytus, a disappointed rival for the papacy and a bitter critic of C.'s theology and of the relaxation of discipline that marked his pontificate. According to Hippolytus, C. had been a slave condemned to the mines in Sardinia because of his mishandling of a banking operation entrusted to him by his Christian master. Freed with the help of a Christian concubine of the Emperor Commodus, he was made superintendent of the Christian cemetery on the Via Appia by Pope *Zephyrinus, to whom he became counselor, deacon, and finally (c. 217) successor. Hippolytus, refusing to accept Callistus as pope, appears to have been elected pope by his own followers, thus becoming the first antipope. Although C. condemned Sabellius for heresy (see SABELLIANISTS), Hippolytus accused him of being virtually guilty of the same error. Among the points of relaxation in discipline for which Hippolytus reproached him were his permitting the ordination of men who had been married twice or even three times, his recognition of the validity of marriages between free women and slaves, his assertion of the Church's authority to absolve from all sins, and his attitude of mercy toward the *lapsi. Despite the conformity of its doctrine to what is known of the mind of C., the so-called Edict of *Callistus probably did not emanate from this pontiff. The fact of C.'s martyrdom, though called into question because he did not die in a time of general persecution, appears well attested. He is the first pope after Peter to be named as a martyr in the oldest Roman martyrology (c.354), and his tomb on the Via Aurelia—discovered in 1960 in a crypt built during the reign of Pope Julius I (337–353)—contains pictures of his martyrdom. He was probably slain in a popular uprising. The catacomb of Callistus bears his name, not because he is buried there, but rather because of his superintendency of the cemetery. The *Liber pontificalis* attributes to C. establishment of the *Ember Days. BIBLIOGRAPHY: Quasten 2:204–207, 233–235; E. Weltin, *Ancient Popes* (1964) 98–107; G. Ferretto, BiblSanct 3:680–689.

[R. B. ENO]

CALLISTUS II, (Guido of Burgundy), **POPE** (1119–24). He was the son of a Burgundian count related to influential Salian and other royal houses. Named abp. of Vienne in 1088, he directed his see with vigor and sought (at times with questionable means) primatial dignity for Vienne. Pope Paschal II appointed him legate in France, in which capacity Guido presided at a synod in Vienne which condemned lay investiture and excommunicated Henry V who had extorted the investiture ''privilege'' from the Pope. After the death of Gelasius II at Cluny, the cardinals who were present elected Guido pope. Before departing for Rome, C. tried unsuccessfully to settle difficulties with the Emperor who was excommunicated again at the council of Reims in 1119. After an enthusiastic welcome the new Pope restored order to Rome and dislodged antipope Gregory VIII at Sutri. He then turned his attention to the investiture struggle. His efforts culminated in the Concordat of Worms, September 23, 1122, by which the Church in return for the guarantee of free episcopal elections and consecrations permitted the Emperor to confer the temporalities by bestowing a scepter on the electee. This solution was a compromise. The first Lateran Council (1123) ratified the Concordat. BIBLIOGRAPHY: E. Jordan, DHGE 11:424–438; H. Jedin, *Handbuch der Kirchengeschichte* 3.1 *Die Mittelalterliche Kirche* (1966) 456–461; D. McGarry, NCE 2:1081.

[H. DRESSLER]

CALLISTUS III, ANTIPOPE who reigned 1168–78. He was the third of a series of four antipopes elected by a faction of ecclesiastics favorable to the cause of Frederick Barbarossa in his struggle against Pope Alexander III. His name was John and he had been abbot of Struma. He submitted to Alexander and was forgiven.

[J. C. WILLKE]

CALLISTUS III (Alfonso de Borgia; 1378–1458), **POPE** from 1455. He was made bp. of Valencia by Martin V and cardinal in 1444 by Eugene IV. In 1455 he succeeded Nicolas V, choosing the name Callistus III. His outstanding achievement was a crusade against the Turks who had seized Constantinople in 1453. Luckily, Sultan Mahomet II, wounded at Belgrade, had to flee. In commemoration of this event, Callistus instituted the Feast of the Transfiguration. His reign was troubled by opposition from Germany, Burgundy, France, Castile, and Portugal. He was guilty of nepotism. However, he favored religious mendicants and strengthened their privileges. BIBLIOGRAPHY: L. Choupin, DTC 2:1345–62.

[F. D. LAZENBY]

CALLISTUS I, PATRIARCH OF CONSTANTINOPLE (d. 1363). Monk of Mt. Athos, C. became patriarch in 1350. Deposed (1353–54) because of his opposition to the crowning of Matthew Cantacuzenas as emperor, he was reinstated until his death. Convinced of the doctrine of Gregory *Palamas, C. in his homilies (some discovered but recently) and his writing, particularly biographic, defended the Palamite teaching. BIBLIOGRAPHY: M. Jugie, *Catholicisme* 2:391–392; idem, EncCatt 3:386.

[M. R. BROWN]

CALLISTUS II XANTHOPULUS, PATRIARCH OF CONSTANTINOPLE (fl. 1397). Of the monastery of Xanthopulos, using as base the work of Callistus Angelicudes, C. composed the influential tract on the asceticism of the Hesychastic monks, called *Century* because of its 100 parts. The compilation was incorporated into the *Philokalia* of Nicodemus. Borrowing from Evagrius, John Climacus, Maximus the Confessor, and other Greek Fathers, the work contained many practical guides. BIBLIOGRAPHY: E. Jordon, DHGE 11:424–438; T. Schieffer, LTK 5:1263.

[M. R. BROWN]

CALLISTUS ANGELICUDES, a 14th-cent. Palamite and mystical writer. In Byzantine literature C. is known as Callistus Meliteniotes or Callistus Telicudes. Credited to him is a work on Hesychastic doctrine, which expounds a theory of mysticism and a system of contemplation first practiced by Athonite monks. C. was apparently involved in the Hesychast movement, which emerged in the last days of the Byzantine Empire and was chiefly defended by Gregory Palamas (1296–1359).

[R. A. TODD]

CALLISTUS, EDICT OF, a decree or statement on penance attributed by many scholars to Pope *Callistus I. The existence and tenor of this decree is known from a sarcastic reference made to it by *Tertullian in his *De pudicitia.* He states that he had heard of an edict published by the bp. of bishops, the *pontifex maximus,* declaring that he remits the sins of adultery and fornication for those who have done penance. Other modern scholars think that Tertullian did not have Callistus I in mind but rather a certain bp. of Carthage. BIBLIOGRAPHY: E. Josi, EncCatt 3:386–391.

[P. K. MEAGHER]

CALLOT, JACQUES (1592–1635), French printmaker. First apprenticed as goldsmith in Nancy (1607–11), then working with the engraver Philippe Thomassin in Rome, C. achieved success at the Medici court of Cosimo II (d. 1621), in Brussels (1625), and in Paris under Richelieu (1629). C.'s innovation of a hard varnish ground made possible his notable skill in organizing numerous figures in vivid action on small surface areas. In prolific etchings and engravings embracing themes light *(Balli di Sfessania)*, tragic *(Miseries of War)*, and grotesque *(The Hunchbacks)*, C. foreshadowed 18th-cent. masters *Watteau and *Goya. A rare wash drawing *(Agony in the Garden,* 1625) combines C.'s skill and dramatic imagination. BIBLIOGRAPHY: E. de Bechtel, *Jacques Callot* (1955).

[M. J. DALY]

CALLUS, DANIEL ANGELO PHILIP (1888–1965), Dominican priest and medievalist. He studied in his native Malta and in Fiesole-Florence, and later did postgraduate work at the Angelicum in Rome. C. taught in Dominican schools in Malta (1914–21) and England (1921–23), at the Univ. of Malta (1924), and served as regent of studies at Viterbo and Malta (1923–31), and at Oxford (1942–54). In 1931 he took up permanent residence in England (at Oxford from 1932). He published extensively, lectured in the U.S., Canada, England, and at international congresses. Toward the end of his life he was visiting professor at the Angelicum. From 1938 he lectured, supervised, and examined at the Univ. of Oxford, where he was recognized as an authority on the early history of the Oxford schools, esp. of Aristotelian studies and Thomism there; he became the center of a group of scholars and pupils interested in medieval thought and learning. A bibliography of his works to 1963, with an appreciation of his life and writings is to be found in *Oxford Studies Presented to Daniel Callus* (Oxford Historical Society, n.s. 16, 1964); BIBLIOGRAPHY: A. Vella, ''Tribute to Professor Daniel Callus,'' *Journal of the Faculty of Arts* 3 (Univ. of Malta, 1965) 66–72.

[W. A. HINNEBUSCH]

CALLY, PIERRE (d. 1709), French priest, Cartesian. He was a professor (1660), then parish priest at Caen. With his *Universae philosophiae institutiones* (1695), the revision of an earlier work in French, he became one of the first exponents of Descartes' philosophy. A work, *Durand commenté* (1700), which sought to apply a Cartesian notion of matter to the Eucharist, effectively denied *transubstantiation, and incurred episcopal condemnation after it was circulated against C.'s intention. He publicly recanted.

[T. C. O'BRIEN]

CALMET, AUGUSTIN (1672–1757), eminent French Benedictine biblical commentator. C. is best known for his *Commentaire littéral sur tous les livres de l'Ancient et du Nouveau Testament* (26 v., 1707–16), a highly regarded commentary that went through three editions and several

Latin translations. The work, in spite of many limitations, is a careful compilation of expert opinion, which avoided contemporary allegorical interpretations and concentrated on the literal sense. C. also wrote a commentary on the Rule of St. Benedict and an important history of Lorraine. He served as abbot of Saint-Léopold in Nancy and Senones, and twice as superior general of the Benedictines. BIBLIOGRAPHY: P. Schmitz, DHGE 11:450–453; M. Strange, NCE 2:1084.

[T. M. MCFADDEN]

CALMETTE, JEAN (1693–1740), missionary to India and Oriental scholar. He strove to find the resemblances between the Veda and Christianity in order to facilitate the conversion of the Indian people. He is believed to have transcribed, edited, and adapted the text of the *Ezour-Vedam* which was brought to Paris. Believing this text to be the original, Voltaire tried to use it in opposing the originality of Christianity.

[I. M. KASHUBA]

CALOEN, GERARD VAN (1853–1932), Benedictine liturgist, missionary, and bishop. After serving for a year as rector of the abbey school at Maredsous, C. was removed from that office because some of his ideas (including the dialogue Mass) were considered too advanced. In 1884 he began the *Messager des Fidèles* (later, the *Revue Bénédictine*), which he conceived as a means of promoting the liturgical movement. The years 1895–1919 C. spent in Brazil where he helped to reorganize and infuse new life into the Brazilian Benedictine congregation. There he also engaged in missionary work, for he was a stout proponent of the monastic apostolate. From 1907 until his resignation in 1915 he was bp. of Rio Branco. BIBLIOGRAPHY: N. Huyghebaert, NCE 14:532–533.

[N. KOLLAR]

CALOV, ABRAHAM (Calovius, Kalau; 1612–86), German Lutheran polemical theologian. After receiving his doctorate at Rostock (1637), he was a pastor at Danzig; then from 1650 he held various scholastic and ecclesiastical offices while living at Wittenberg. At the Colloquy of *Thorn (1645) he first came in contact with G. *Calixt and thereafter made what he called the *syncretism of Calixt the target of many of his writings. His works, rigorously logical and almost always polemical, assailed not only Calixt but RC, *Reformed, Socinian, and mystical teachings as well. The *Systema locorum theologicorum* (12 v., 1655–77) is a monument of orthodox Lutheran scholasticism. BIBLIOGRAPHY: A. C. Piepkorn, EncLuthCh 1:352–353.

[T. C. O'BRIEN]

CALUMNY, see DETRACTION.

CALVAERT, DENIS (1540–1619), Flemish artist in Rome (c. 1572). Opening an academy in Bologna (c. 1575), C. painted *Vision of St. Francis, Paradise,* and *St. Michael,* exerting a strong mannerist influence on students Reni,

Domenichino, and Agostino Caracci. BIBLIOGRAPHY: S. Bergmans, *Denis Calvart* (1934).

[M. J. DALY]

CALVARY (Lat. *calvaria*; Gr. *kranion*; Heb. *golgotha*, all meaning skull), the place just outside Jerusalem where, according to the NT, Jesus was crucified (Mt 27.32–33; Mk 15.22; Jn 19.17). A legend already in existence at the time of Origen explained the name by supposing that Adam was buried in that place by Noah after the Flood. Scholars generally believe that the place was named because of its configuration. Even today in the East the word *ras* (head) applies to any natural hill or rock mound even when its resemblance to a skull is slight. Today Calvary is located within the compound of the Church of the Holy Sepulcher. BIBLIOGRAPHY: A. Parrot, *Golgotha and the Church of the Holy Sepulcher* (1957); C. Kopp, *Holy Places of the Gospels* (tr. R. Walls, 1963).

[J. E. LUSSIER]

CALVERT FAMILY: (1) *George Calvert, first Lord Baltimore* (1580–1632), founder of Maryland. He was a member of a Catholic family forced to conform to the Church of England. In 1606 he became private secretary to Sir Robert Cecil where he came to enjoy the favor of James I. In 1609 he became a member of Parliament and in 1613 a clerk of the Privy Council. Knighted (1617), he was appointed one of two secretaries of state and a member of the Privy Council. With considerable courage he announced his conversion to Catholicism, in spite of which the King retained him on the Council and made him a peer with the title Baron of Baltimore. Long interested in the colonization of America, C. received from the King a grant to the peninsula of Avalon in Newfoundland. A tentative effort to colonize this area did not succeed. From Charles I he received a grant of the province of Maryland. Lord Baltimore died before the transaction was completed. The Charter he had fashioned for Avalon became that of Maryland and laid the foundation for a successful colonial government in that colony. (2) *Cecil Calvert, second Lord Baltimore* (1606–75), proprietor of Maryland. He commissioned his brother Leonard as governor of the province and issued a pamphlet defending religious toleration for the new colony, making the principles contained therein the law of the province. However, the Assembly of Maryland adopted the Toleration Act of 1639, which eliminated the controversial aspects of Baltimore's statutes. It did emphasize the rights of all citizens to religious freedom. (3) *Leonard Calvert* (1610–47), son of the first Lord Baltimore. He sailed with the *Ark* and the *Dove* carrying 300 colonists and took possession as governor of the province of Maryland in the name of the King of England. He cultivated trade with the Indians and called the first assembly of freemen to meet in 1634. Through a series of negotiations with his elder brother he secured for the assembly the right to initiate legislation, an early effort at popular government in the colonies. (4) *Charles Calvert, third Lord Baltimore* (1629–1715), last Catholic proprietor. He

served as governor of Maryland for 23 years and proprietor for 13. The revolution of 1688 spelled the end of the Catholic Calvert influence and the tolerance that the family had protected. BIBLIOGRAPHY: "Calvert Family," *Maryland Historical Magazine* 16 (1921).

[J. R. AHERNE]

CALVERT, EDWARD (1799–1883), English painter and graphic artist. C. met in London (1824–25) S. Palmer, J. Linnell, H. Fuseli, and W. *Blake, the last influencing him profoundly. In wood blocks and lithographs C. expressed his early vision of idyllic magic with great mastery. In the painting *A Primitive City* C.'s style is medieval while in *The Morning of the World* he echoes Blake and Palmer. C. developed an analogy of color with music in later paintings, larger and more classic in style. BIBLIOGRAPHY: R. H. Wilenski, *English Painting* (4th ed., 1964).

[M. J. DALY]

CALVET, JEAN (1874–1965), literary critic and historian. C. was educated at the Cahors seminary, the Institut Catholique in Toulouse, and after ordination (1896) at the Sorbonne and Institut Catholique in Paris. He taught for 17 years, first in Toulouse, then in Paris, obtaining a professorship in literature at the Institut Catholique. He was named acting rector there in 1942, but resigned before his nomination as rector (1945) had been confirmed by Rome. His major works represent the best in French literary history and criticism, but he also published biography, literary sketches, stories, and two collections of meditations. He directed and contributed to the *Histoire de la littérature française*, a 10-volume history of French literature written by professors from the Sorbonne and the Catholic Institutes. BIBLIOGRAPHY: L. Chaigne, *Catholicisme* 2:404–405.

[H. JACK]

CALVIN, JOHN (1509–64), Reformer and theologian, one of the major figures of the Reformation. From him came the most incisive and systematic doctrinal formulation in early Protestantism, and his *Institutes of the Christian Religion*, which first appeared in 1536, is the major Reformation theological work. C.'s activity centered in Geneva, but his influence dominated Reformed Protestantism in France, the Netherlands, and Scotland and was very strong in England and in parts of Germany and central Europe. Léonard says that he organized and consolidated Protestantism, and created the "Reformed" man and the modern world.

He was born in France, at Noyon in Picardy, where his father, Gérard Cauvin, or Chauvin (Calvin is a latinized form), was a functionary in the service of the bp. and cathedral chapter. Destined by his father for a career in the Church, he was tonsured (he never received any kind of ordination throughout his life), endowed with ecclesiastical benefices, and sent to Paris at the age of 14 to study at the university. He attended the Collège de la Marche, then the Collège de Montaigu, where he received a Master of Arts degree in 1528.

Undoubtedly many of his ideas were formed by his close association with Mathurin Cordier, a humanist scholar, with a cousin Pierre Robert *Olivétan, already attracted by Lutheran teaching, with the family of Guillaume Cop, the physician of the French King. About the time that C. finished at Montaigu his father directed him to study for the more lucrative profession of law. Accordingly the young scholar went to the Univ. of Orléans (1528–29) and then to the Univ. of Bourges (1529–31), studying with some of the most eminent jurists of his day. In these years he also pursued humanist and literary interests and learned Greek from the scholar Melchior Wolmar, a Lutheran. In 1531 his father died (excommunicated because of a quarrel with the cathedral chapter over the closing of an estate), and C. terminated his studies in law to devote himself wholly to literary scholarship. He returned to Paris, attended the new trilingual college—later called the Collège de France—which Francis I founded, and in 1532 published his first work, a commentary in the humanist tradition on Seneca's *De clementia*.

Classical humanism, however, was not long to remain his chief preoccupation. Sometime in late 1533 or early 1534—the exact time and circumstance are not clear—there occurred what he once referred to as a *conversio subita*; it was not, however, a sudden conversion in a revivalistic sense. This great turning point in his life has been linked with an address his friend Nicholas Cop, rector of the Univ. of Paris, delivered on All Saints' Day, 1533. The address, containing passages from Erasmus and Luther, provoked speedy action by the authorities against Cop and others believed to be implicated. C. (who for a long time was thought to have been the real author of the discourse) fled Paris for a time, returned briefly, then left again. At Angoulême, it appears, he gathered his thoughts and arrived at his decision to break with the old Church and devote himself to the cause of Protestant reform. The Reformation had won its most formidable exponent after Luther. In May 1534 he renounced his benefices at Noyon; he left France late in 1534 or early in 1535, because of the stringent measures against Protestants, and found haven in Protestant Basel. There he entered into contact with other Swiss and Strassburg Reformers, and in March 1536, published the first draft of the *Institutes of the Christian Religion*. Prefaced by a letter to the King of France, Francis I, the *Institutes* was intended as a statement and defense of the beliefs of the persecuted French Protestants. Subsequent editions and enlargements of this magisterial work were published throughout his lifetime, the most important being those of 1539 and 1559. He returned briefly to France in 1536 to settle some family business, and in June set out once again, intending to go to Strassburg, but war between Francis I and Emperor Charles V obliged him to take a long detour, during which he stopped for the night at Geneva. There G. *Farel pleaded with him to remain and help spread the new gospel. C. reluctantly gave in, and Geneva henceforth became the center of his ministry and of his dynamic reform.

When he began this new phase in his own life and in the course of the Reformation, this city of some 13,000 inhabi-

tants was engaged in a struggle to maintain its municipal independence against the efforts of the Duke of Savoy to reestablish control. In the course of that struggle, Protestantism, backed by neighboring Bern, had made its appearance in the city, and Farel and other preachers had won acceptance of their reforms by the municipal authorities. By Nov. 1535 the Mass had been finally suppressed. Geneva had turned from Catholicism largely for political and anticlerical reasons; the task of organizing and establishing the new *church order remained, and it was this task that C. now made his own. He soon rose to a position of leadership alongside the elder Farel. In Jan. 1537 they submitted to the city council for approval a set of articles on church government reflecting C.'s ideas and style. In Feb. they added an *Instruction and Confession of Faith according to the use of the Church of Geneva*, based on the *Institutes*; a short time later a confession of faith obligatory for all Genevans was appended (see GENEVAN CATECHISMS). C. planned a strict unity of belief and practice and the close supervision of conduct; he insisted that the ministers of the Church have the right to excommunicate the wayward. In early 1538 the Genevan government came under the control of men hostile to the Calvin-Farel uniformity and discipline, and in April the city council ordered the two to leave Geneva. C.'s banishment was temporary; it lasted from April 1538 to Sept. 1541, during which time C. settled in Strassburg at the invitation of M. *Bucer and took charge of a church for French Protestant refugees. His activities as pastor and theological lecturer kept him very busy. Bucer's influence on his ideas of predestination, the Church, and the ministry was very strong; and C. adapted Bucer's liturgy for use by his own congregation. In 1540 he married Idelette de Bure (d. 1549).

As division and contention continued among the rival factions at Geneva, C.'s supporters urged his recall from Strassburg. This sentiment gained ground, and in 1540, with the city government now controlled by the pro-Calvin faction, or *Guillermins*, he was officially invited to return. Resisting at first, he finally accepted and in Sept. 1541 reentered the turbulent city that had once cast him out. He remained there the rest of his life, and in this great period of his dominance Geneva became an austere stronghold of Protestant orthodoxy, the model city of a vibrant and aggressive Protestant faith. His new constitution for the Genevan Church, the *Ecclesiastical Ordinances (Ordonnances ecclésiastiques)*, was approved by the city fathers on Nov. 20, 1541, with modifications restricting the autonomy of the Church. The *Ordinances* structured the so-called theocracy in Geneva and became the basic charter of Calvinist or Presbyterian *polity. They provided for four ministries or offices—pastors, teachers, elders, and deacons—and for a council, or consistory, of pastors and elders to maintain moral discipline and good behavior in the community. Not until 1555 did the consistory, however, gain the long-disputed right to excommunicate. To implement the *Ordinances* C. published a form for worship services, and the second of the Genevan Catechisms. A struggle to achieve conformity and rigid ecclesiastical discipline in the city ensured after 1541, and the conflicts occupied C. till the last years of his life. When Sebastian *Castellio, the college rector, quarreled with C. over certain minor doctrinal points, Castellio was banished (1545). In a more serious encounter, C.'s vehement critic, Jacques Gruet, was beheaded (1547). In flight from France, the antitrinitarian Michael *Servetus stopped at Geneva in Aug. 1553, was arrested on C.'s demand, tried for heresy, and burned alive. During these years C. also faced the opposition of a faction known as Spiritual *Libertines, headed by Aimé Perrin. These opponents of C.'s theocratic system were finally suppressed in 1555, and thereafter his dominance was unchallenged. In the later years refugees from abroad flocked to Geneva as to the fountainhead of reform, and a more concerted effort to evangelize distant lands, particularly C.'s native France, was begun. Calvinism became a revolutionary movement of international scope toward the close of its founder's life. In spite of the sufferings of illness in his final years, he continued tirelessly to direct his Church and proclaim the scriptural word as he so sternly and dogmatically conceived it.

In addition to the *Institutes* C. continuously published theological treatises on main points of his system, and polemical works to meet challenges to his doctrine. He also wrote commentaries on most of the books of the Bible. (Key works, including the 1559 definitive edition of the *Institutes* are in LibCC 20–23.) Both in Latin and French his style was superb, his expressions precise, and his logic formidable. He displayed in his works a vast knowledge of the Fathers. For Protestantism in its second generation he deepened the reliance on the word of God (although his own exegesis was by no means always restrained by the letter of the sacred text); he also created a practical sense of cohesiveness and solid strength. To the Reformed tradition he left its distinguishing themes, the sovereignty of God, predestination, the disciplined Church, the fourfold order of ministry. His was the ideal of Church and State working together to establish God's kingdom on earth; but while he extolled obedience to a godly civil power, he established also the power of the Church and freed it from strictly national limitations. C.'s Reformed man was the active Christian, whom stern Christian virtue fitted for the modern world, the world of business. Much of Western history, esp. in the English-speaking world, from C.'s time to the 20th cent. was shaped by his theology, his political and ecclesiastical theory, and his practical administration. BIBLIOGRAPHY: F. Wendel, *Calvin* (tr. P. Mairet, 1963); J. T. McNeill, *History and Character of Calvinism* (repr., 1968); E. Doumergue, *Jean Calvin* (7v., 1899–1927); J. Calvin and J. Sadoleto, *Reformation Debate* (ed. J. C. Olin, 1966) containing C.'s important and autobiographical "Reply to Sadoleto"; Léonard HistProt 1:292–351, 411–428, bibliog. *Heritage of John Calvin,* (ed. J. H. Bratt, 1973); L. J. Richard, *Spirituality of John Calvin* (pa. 1974). *CALVINISM; *PRESBYTERIANISM.

[J. C. OLIN]

CALVINISM, the theological teaching of John *Calvin or, more broadly, the doctrine and way of life of the Reformed and Presbyterian Churches. Even before Calvin's death the influence of his teachings reached beyond Switzerland. In the Palatinate the Elector Frederick III was so firmly persuaded of the virtues of Calvinism that he adopted and promoted its doctrines in his territories. In France the first national synod (1559) adopted a solidly Calvinist form of discipline and the *Gallican Confession. In the Netherlands the organization of the Reformed Church had increased particularly between 1562, when the *Belgic Confession was published, and 1574, when the first provincial synod was held. Dutch Calvinism was constantly divided from this time, partly over the Church-State issue, but particularly over *Arminianism. The Synod of *Dort (1618–19) rejected this modification of Calvinism on the doctrine of election and approved a rationalistic expression of Calvinism in the so-called *Five Points of Calvinism. In England Calvinist ideas found acceptance among some leaders of the English Church, and during the reign of Edward VI, M. *Bucer (1491–1551) proposed a system of church discipline based on Scripture. From 1570 Thomas *Cartwright (c.1535–1603) advocated Calvinist views at Cambridge with some effect; in 1572 the *Admonition to Parliament* set forth the views of English Presbyterians on the ministry, worship, and polity. In 1643 commissioners from the General Assembly of the Church of Scotland attended the *Westminster Assembly of English divines summoned to advise the Long Parliament on the form of government for a Church united on a Presbyterian basis. The *Westminster Confession follows Calvin's stress on the sovereignty of God and the authority of the Holy Spirit speaking in Scripture, and expressly teaches *double predestination. It also adds to Calvin, however, by its doctrine of two covenants, i.e., of works and of grace (see WESTMINSTER CATECHISMS). Calvinism has persisted in England in the evangelical tradition, though it never took root as strongly as it did in Scotland and later in North America (see CHURCH OF SCOTLAND; UNITED PRESBYTERIAN CHURCH IN THE U.S.A.).

The Theology of Calvinism. Classic Calvinism is marked by certain main themes.

The Sovereign Regulating Will of God. The peculiar dynamism of the Calvinist Reformation came from the dominant stress it laid upon the idea that all things are governed by God's providence. "Not only heaven and earth and the inanimate creatures, but also the plans and intentions of men, are so governed by his providence that they are borne by it straight to their appointed end" (*Institutes of the Christian Religion* 1.6.18). Fundamental to all of Calvin's thought was the conviction that his whole life was mastered by God and that no real freedom was possible until his own will was gathered up into the sovereign will of God. From this conviction Calvin derived his doctrine of election and *predestination, i.e., God's eternal decree "by which he determined with himself what he willed to become of each man. For all are not created in equal condition; rather, eternal life is decreed for some, eternal damnation for others" (*Inst.* 3.21.5). We may not question this ineluctable will of God: "God has sufficiently just cause for election and reprobation in his own will'' (*Comm. on Rom* 9.11). Merits are of no avail, worthiness is disregarded—the goodness of God reigns alone. While it seems evident that Calvin here goes beyond Scripture—despite his stated aim: ''Let this be our sacred rule, . . . not to seek to know anything about it except what Scripture teaches us'' (*Comm. on Rom* 9.14)—and while it is notorious that this is the doctrinal core against which all opposition to Calvinism has been directed, it must also be borne in mind, first, that Calvin (in common with all the Reformers) based his doctrine of predestination on Augustine and earlier scholasticism; second, that his doctrine of predestination cannot be isolated from his doctrine of the Church, and both must be understood in their relation to Christ; third, that Calvin intended his teaching to be a consolation for the persecuted of France, a discipline for the undisciplined of Geneva, and also the source of his own encouragement in his ''extraordinary battles.'' What Calvin found in the doctrine of election, in Karl *Barth's words, was ''a final word on the whole reality of the Christian life, a word which tells us that the existence and the continuance and the future of that life are wholly and utterly of the free grace of God'' (*Church Dogmatics,* 2.2, 86).

If Calvin's doctrine has a weakness, it is that in explaining predestination he points to God rather than to Christ. Election is a secret and absolute decree, independent of and antecedent to the person and work of Christ. Calvin can even say that election precedes grace (*Inst.* 3.22.2, 9). The darker side of the *decretum horribile,* however, came to dominate in much of later Calvinism. The Westminster Confession is typical: ''By the decree of God, for the manifestation of his glory, some men and angels are predestinated unto everlasting life, and others foreordained to everlasting death'' (ch. 3). Thomas Boston of Ettrick (1676–1732) could even write: ''The godly husband shall say *Amen* to the condemnation of her who lay in his bosom; the godly parents shall say *Hallelujah,* at the passing of the sentence against their ungodly child.'' (*Man's Fourfold State,* 4.4). Modern Calvinism has moved almost completely away from such expressions and has sought to give the work of Christ a more central place. Barth, for example, has criticized Calvin for failing to understand that the subject of the decision reached at the beginning of all things is the triune God, the Son of God no less than the Father and the Spirit, and therefore he feels it necessary to part with Calvin at this point (*Church Dogmatics,* 2.2, 60 ff., 106 ff.).

Christocentricism. Nevertheless, in common with nearly all early Protestant thought, Calvinism does have a strongly Christocentric character. ''We cannot move the smallest distance from Jesus Christ without our salvation's vanishing away, since it resides entirely in him'' (*Inst.* 2.16.1). In all his teaching Calvin sought to bring the person and work of Christ into the center. The older confessions and catechisms of the Reformation, e.g., the Second *Helvetic Confession and the *Heidelberg Catechism, are markedly more Christological in both content and attitude than, e.g., the later Westminster Confession and Catechisms. The fundamental contention of

the earlier documents is that there is one absolute authority for Church and man alike, Jesus Christ, and one covenant of grace that is completely fulfilled in Christ, who is its whole substance. The characteristic emphases of Calvinism—*solus Christus, sola gratia, sola fide,* and *sola scriptura*—are primarily Christological affirmations that the life and faith of the Church have their sole source in the person and work of Christ, and that the doctrine and practice of the Church must be subjected constantly and critically to a radical Christological correction.

Scripture As the Supreme Rule of Faith and Life. In his *Reply* to J. Sadoleto (1477–1547), who raised with Calvin the question of authority, Calvin answered: ''There is no other light of truth which could direct our souls into the way of life [than Scripture].'' Scripture is the only source of our knowledge of Christ, and we are not to look beyond it for guidance in faith or conduct. As the *Scots Confession (1560) states, Scripture is ''sufficient to instruct and make the man of God perfite'' (Art. 19). In its essential meaning, i.e., in all things necessary to be believed for salvation, Scripture is clear and certain, but it ''seriously affects us,'' Calvin writes, ''only when it is sealed upon our hearts through the Spirit'' (*Inst.* 1.8.5). When he speaks of the inward testimony of the Holy Spirit, Calvin means that the Bible is authoritative because it is authenticated by the witness of the Spirit. Though he appears at times to hold a narrow doctrine of verbal inspiration and even speaks of Scripture as ''produced by the dictation of the Holy Spirit'' (*Inst.* 4.8.6), it is more accurate to say that Calvin related the function of the Holy Spirit in God's ''authorship'' of Scripture to the Spirit's function in interpreting Scripture to us. The Spirit is bound to Scripture as the medium of his revelation; Scripture and Spirit are two aspects of the same testimony (*Inst.* 1.9.3).

All ecclesiastical traditions must therefore be subservient to Scripture; indeed, on the principle of *quid non iubet, vetat* (i.e., what God does not expressly command in Scripture he forbids), Calvin and many later Calvinists insisted that the only doctrine, worship, and polity allowable are those explicitly laid out in Scripture. Doctrinally, this meant for Calvinism that theology must be grounded on the biblical revelation alone; liturgically, that the use of hymns, responses, and instrumental music is to be excluded from worship, and the Christian Year abandoned; and in polity, that the practice of the ancient Church (which for Calvin meant something like Presbyterianism) was alone permitted. In most Reformed Churches today some of these interpretations have been substantially modified, though the idea that the Church must always listen to the living word of the Spirit in the written words of Scripture has made Calvinism typically critical of any unalterable or irreformable structures of church life, formulations of faith, or forms of worship.

The Church. Following the teaching of the early Fathers, notably Cyprian and Augustine, Calvin did not hesitate to speak of the Church as essential for salvation. ''Let us learn even from the simple title 'mother' how useful indeed how necessary it is that we should know her'' (*Inst.* 4.1.4). To abandon the Church is to revolt from Christ also. God's covenant of grace has been since the beginning, and there has never been a time when there was not a true Church of God in the world. There has been a "Kirk in all ages fra Adam" (Scots Confession, Art. 5; cf. Second Helvetic Confession, ch. 17). This Church is invisible, in a sense, since only God knows his own. "The Church may be called invisible," as the Second Helvetic Confession states, "not that the men composing it are invisible, but because they are known only to God" (ch. 17). The Church, however, is also visible and discernible, not by what the Scots Confession calls "Antiquitie, Title usurpit, lineal Descence, Place appointed, nor multitude of men approving ane error" (Art. 18), but by "the Word of God purely preached and heard, and the Sacraments administered according to Christ's institution" (*Inst.* 4.1.9). To these "certain marks and tokens" of the Church the Scots Confession added "Ecclesiastical discipline, uprightlie ministred . . . whereby vice is repressed and vertew nurished" (Art. 18). Continuity in the Church is therefore understood within Calvinism not in a static but in a dynamic and Christological way. It is constituted not by *apostolic succession or even by the ministry, but by Jesus Christ himself who calls his Church into being through the ministry, without which the Church cannot exist (cf. Second Helvetic Confession, ch. 25). Christ is the Word which he himself proclaims—in the daring phrase of the Reformers, *praedicatio verbi divini est verbum divinum*—and the minister of his own sacraments of baptism and the Supper. The means by which Christ calls his Church into being and sustains it is the ministry of word and sacraments. This ministry, however, is distinguished from the *priesthood of all believers. The real continuity of the Church is guaranteed, therefore, only if the ministerial continuity corresponds to doctrinal continuity, and apostolic continuity without reference to doctrine is a "vain pretense." Above all the Church is a community—"the society of all the saints which, spread over the whole world, and existing in all ages, yet bound together by one doctrine, and the one Spirit of Christ, cultivates and observes unity of faith and brotherly concord" *(Reply to Sadoleto)*. If, then, as Calvin affirms, the Church is one, holy, catholic, and apostolic, on what grounds did he justify the Reformation? He answered the question by calling the Romanists to contemplate the ruins of the Church surviving among themselves. They were the schismatics; for among them, he observes to Sadoleto, "the light of divine truth had been extinguished, the Word of God buried, the virtue of Christ left in profound oblivion, and the pastoral office subverted." Calvin's view of the Church is marked by what would today be called a strong and comprehensive ecumenism. Because the Church lives in Christ, its unity is not only commanded by him but also given by him, and through the Lord's Supper we are "forged into one body with Christ" (*Inst.* 4.17.2). Though it must be conceded that later Calvinism is notoriously divisive, an ecumenical openness has nevertheless been typical of Calvinism at its best. As J. T. McNeill says, "the idea of catholic unity dominated the church theory of Calvin" (*Uni-*

tive Protestantism [1964], 217). His was an ecumenism not simply of space (i.e., of those Churches now found throughout the world) but also of time. The Church is one with what the Scots Confession calls "the Elect of all ages, of all realmes, nations and tongues," but it also includes "the Elect that be departed, commonlie called the Kirk Triumphant" (Art. 16).

Obedience to God in the Political Order. Church and State, to use the definition of Marc-Édouard Chenevière (*La Pensée politique de Calvin,* 1937), are two complementary institutions, aiding but distinct from one another, each with its own sphere of work and its proper mission. In general, it may be said that Calvinism has exhibited a firm respect for law and order, a deep antipathy toward any kind of political authoritarianism, and a resolute commitment to religious freedom. In particular, the following characteristics may be noted: (1) The duty of the State is to preserve order and promote piety. The magistrate as much as the minister has been called by God to his office, and Christians may therefore legitimately seek political office and express their faith in civil responsibilities. (2) Though Calvin himself favored as the ideal form of government a combination of aristocracy and democracy, one of the distinctive strengths of Calvinism has been its resilience under varying political forms. The democratic and representative character of the Reformed Church in France probably enabled it to survive the early persecutions up to the *Edict of Nantes (1598). (3) Calvin allowed the possibility of passive resistance to tyranny, though only cautiously and as a last resort. In more recent years the role and resistance of the *Confessing Church in Germany under Hitler testify to the vigor of the Calvinist commitment to religious freedom. The *Barmen Declaration (1934), which climaxed the church struggle in Germany, was a notable modern attempt by Lutheran and Reformed Christians to take their stand in the word of God against a hostile ideology. (4) Calvinism has attempted, though with obvious failures, to seek to obey the will of God within the political order. The *theocracy of Geneva and the Puritanism of New England both demonstrate the Calvinist axiom that the life of faith and the political sphere alike are to be regulated by the word of God. At a time when the pulpit still molded public opinion and clergymen were often presidents and leading professors in colleges, John Witherspoon (1723?–94), a Presbyterian minister, president of the College of New Jersey (now Princeton), and the only clerical signer of the Declaration of Independence, taught moral philosophy to numbers of future American statesmen, among them James Madison (1751–1836). Witherspoon's political teaching was based upon the Calvinist emphasis on God's sovereign rule over the whole of life, his confidence in human ability under God, and a suspicion of man's sinfulness that led him to favor a government of checks and balances and a separation of powers. This kind of approach to government has been aptly summarized by a contemporary theologian, Reinhold *Niebuhr, who draws on the broad Calvinist tradition when he says: "Man's capacity for justice makes democracy possible; but man's inclination to injustice makes democracy necessary'' (*The Children of Light and the Children of Darkness* [1960] xi).

Modern Theological Developments. In *The Nature of the Atonement* (1855), John McLeod Campbell attacked, on the one hand, the hyper-Calvinism that subordinated everything to the arbitrary act of God in election and substituted a legal for a filial relationship to God, and, on the other hand, the religious subjectivism that failed to take seriously the saving significance of the human obedience of Christ. The logical determinism that Campbell opposed persisted in the 19th and 20th cent. in the extreme evangelical form of fundamentalism and the radical secular form of positivism (Hegel, Marx, et al.), while subjectivism persisted in the influence of F. *Schleiermacher's pietism and the liberal quest for the historical Jesus. In the 20th cent. three major theologians in the general Reformed tradition have helped to turn Protestant theology in a different direction. In Zurich, where he was professor of systematic theology from 1924, Emil *Brunner opposed the Calvinist orthodoxy and idealistic liberalism of the 19th cent. in his *dialectical theology and contributed major works to the new debate—*The Mediator* (Eng. tr., 1934), and *Man in Revolt* (Eng. tr., 1939). Karl Barth, in his *Church Dogmatics,* opposed both hyper-Calvinism and the older liberalism with a Christological concentration of breadth, scope, and balance. Barth forced theologians to contemplate anew the full humanity of Jesus Christ—what Calvin expressively called ''the vivifying flesh of Christ''—and insisted that dogmatic theology must be grounded on the reality and norm of the incarnate Word of God; he was also a truly ecumenical theologian who spoke a theological language increasingly understood by Catholic and Protestant alike. In the U.S. the publication of *The Nature and Destiny of Man* (2v., 1941–43) by Niebuhr was an attempt to relate Reformation theology to the problems of human existence, and in Niebuhr's works the impact of *neo-orthodoxy has been brought to bear in a distinctive way on U.S. theology and political life. BIBLIOGRAPHY: F. Wendel, *Calvin* (1963); W. Niesel, *Theology of Calvin* (1956); E. A. Dowey, *Knowledge of God in Calvin's Theology* (1952); J. T. McNeill, *History and Character of Calvinism* (repr., 1968); Léonard HistProt 1:420–428, bibliog.; E. H. Palmer, *Person and Ministry of the Holy Spirit: the Traditional Calvinist Perspective* (1974).

[J. A. R. MacKENZIE]

CALVINISM, THE FIVE POINTS OF, see FIVE POINTS OF CALVINISM, THE.

CALVINISTIC METHODIST CHURCH (Presbyterian Church of Wales), a Church that originated through the revivalistic preaching of certain men, who, though associated with John *Wesley, rejected his *Arminianism. H. *Harris, G. *Jones, and others were successful in their preaching in Wales and established many *societies of the Methodist type; in 1743 these were organized as the Welsh Calvinistic Methodists, with George *Whitefield as first (and nominal)

moderator. The initial success was followed first by decline, then by a new growth *c*. 1790. Until that time the societies remained within the C of E, but persecution led in 1795 to the first steps toward separation. The Church first ordained its own ministers in 1811; in 1823 a confession of faith, patterned on the *Westminster Confession, was adopted; in 1864 the first general assembly of the Church was held. Total autonomy was formally guaranteed by the Calvinistic Methodist or Presbyterian Church of Wales Act (1933). The polity of the Church is through associations, similar to Methodist *conferences. Membership in 1974 was 104,000. BIBLIOGRAPHY: W. Williams, *Welsh Calvinistic Methodism* (1872); M. W. Williams, *Creative Fellowship* (1935).

CAMAIANI, PIETRO (1519–79), bp. of Fiesole (1552) and of Ascoli Piceno (1566). Papal nuncio (to Charles V, to Philip II, and at Naples), C. exhibited in his negotiations the transition from Renaissance diplomacy to the pastoral approach of the Tridentine reform. As bp. of Fiesole he had attended the Council of Trent and tried upon his return to introduce into his diocese its spirit and the fulfillment of its decrees. BIBLIOGRAPHY: M. Morseletto, EncCatt 3:420; C. Tihon, DHGE 11:508–509.

[M. R. BROWN]

CAMALDOLESE, a Benedictine congregation founded by Romuald, a Benedictine monk, as part of the monastic reform movement of the 11th and 12th centuries. Camaldoli became an independent offshoot of the Benedictines (*c*. 1012) with its foundation at Camaldoli near Arezzo, Italy. St. Romuald intended to combine the eremitic, or hermitlike life with the cenobitic or communal life of Western monasteries, notably the Benedictines. The monastery and the hermitage formed one unit known as the Congregation of Monk Hermits of Camoldoli. Beginners resided in the monastery; the proficient and more perfect, in the judgment of the abbot or prior, lived in the hermitage. This mode of union lasted for 6 cent., both categories united under the rule of one superior until 1534 when they separated, and independent foundations of both monks and hermits were founded. The two branches were reunited in 1935. A reform group known as the Congregation of Monte Corona was founded in 1523 and still exists, although it numbered fewer than 100 members in the early 1970s.

Scholarship and evangelization has long been the hallmark of the Camaldolites. They founded hermitages and monasteries outside Italy in France, Poland, Germany, Austria, and Hungary. In the 17th and 18th cent. there were five autonomous congregations with a membership of about 2,000. Of these, two continued to flourish in 1975, Camaldoli, the original house with 108 members, and Monte Corona with 75 members. A house was founded in Brazil in 1899, and a foundation of the Camaldoli Congregation was established at Big Sur, California, in 1958. This U.S. foundation known as the Immaculate Heart Hermitage consists of 10 priests and 9 brothers. The latest American foundation is a branch of the

Monte Corona Congregation founded at McConnelsville, Ohio, in 1959. The Camaldolese habit is white, thus the title "White Benedictines." The monks fast and observe periods of silence although the practice and extent of this has varied considerably with different congregations. There are also a few convents of Camaldolese nuns.

[M.. FENNINGHAM]

CAMALDOLI, ABBEY OF, the name of two Camaldolese monasteries. The first of these was built by St. Romuald himself c. 1015; it was originally intended to serve as a hospice and guest house, and was later converted into a cenobitical monastery. It is located in the Appenines in the commune of Poppi in the diocese of Arezzo. The other, also erected by St. Romuald, is located 2 miles farther up the mountains. This is an eremitical monastery in which the monks live in small separate buildings. Together the two monasteries exemplify the cenobitical-eremitical modes of life characteristic of the Camaldolese.

CAMARA, JAIME DE BARROS, (1894–1971), Brazilian cardinal. C. was ordained in 1920, became bp. of Mossoro in 1936, and served as abp. of Rio de Janeiro from 1943 until his retirement. In 1946 the Pope conferred on him the title of cardinal. As a church official and mediator between the Church and the Brazilian government, C. was active in efforts to alleviate the growing tensions over civil rights, esp. the torture of political prisoners.

[C. KEENAN]

CAMBIASO, LUCA (1527–85), greatest Genoese Renaissance artist. Using the mannerist proportions of Correggio in altarpieces and mythologies, C., in his mature work (*Madonna of the Candle, Christ before Caiphas*), shows a nocturnal light and peasant realism that presages Georges de la Tour and Zurbarán. BIBLIOGRAPHY: P. Zambetti, EncCatt 3:422–423.

[M. J. DALY]

CAMBODIA, see KHMER REPUBLIC.

CAMBRAI, PEACE OF, a treaty signed August 3, 1529, by Francis I of France and Charles V of Spain through the efforts of Louise de Savoie and Margaret of Austria; hence it is sometimes called the "Ladies' Peace." It attempted to end the Wars of Italy which under Francis I had expanded into a fierce rivalry between the two monarchs. In addition, Pope Clement VII supported Charles V, hoping to have the Papal States restored through him. After the Peace of Cambrai was signed, reapportioning French territory, abrogating French claims in Italy, and restoring Francis' two sons from their captivity in Spain, Francis immediately made plans to resume the war. BIBLIOGRAPHY: L. Batiffol, *Century of the Renaissance* (1929).

[I. M. KASHUBA]

CAMBRIDGE, UNIVERSITY OF, a center of higher learning in England since the early 13th century. The date of its foundation is unknown. There may have been schools there before the year 1200, whose development was possibly stimulated by an exodus of scholars from Oxford c. 1209. John XXII in 1318 recognized the university as a *studium generale.* Although the students and masters were drawn mainly from the secular clergy, monks and friars were also prominent until the Reformation. Like Oxford, Cambridge came to be organized into residential colleges, the first of which, Peterhouse (St. Peter's), was a Benedictine establishment founded (1284) by Hugh de Balsam, Bp. of Ely. By the 16th cent. all the students and masters belonged to one or another of the 16 colleges then in existence, among which King's (1441), St. John's (1511), and Trinity (1546) were the most prominent. The university did not achieve great distinction during the 13th and 14th cent., but it gained some recognition in the 15th when John *Wycliffe, the Oxford Reformer and professor, aroused suspicion of Oxford's orthodoxy.

It was John *Fisher, later cardinal and martyr, who brought Cambridge to prominence. He was the university's first professor of divinity, and as chancellor he did much to promote the "new learning," among other things by conferring the professorship of Greek and theology upon *Erasmus. In the reign of Elizabeth I (1558–1603) the university, which had become Protestant during the chancellorship of T. *Cromwell, became a center of Reformation theology. As a Puritan stronghold in the 17th cent. Cambridge exerted a considerable influence on the colonization of New England and the foundation of Harvard College. Interest in scientific and mathematical studies gradually overtook and surpassed the preoccupation with Aristotelian and scholastic philosophy. Isaac Newton was appointed Lucasian professor in 1669, and early in the 18th cent. the mathematic tripos replaced the traditional disputation as a final degree requirement.

The mid-19th cent. brought some radical changes. A royal commission, abetted by Parliament, initiated a new era of expansion. The curriculum was revised, a new emphasis was laid upon the natural sciences, university and college statutes were revised and women's colleges were established: Girton (1869), Newnham (1873), and Hughes (1885). In these colleges women could prepare for university examinations, but not until 1921 could they qualify for degrees, nor until 1948 did they enjoy full university status. A second royal commission of inquiry led to a new revision of university and college statutes (1926–28) that is still in force. The withdrawal of religious tests (1871) opened the way for the establishment of Catholic residences: Fisher House, named for St. John Fisher; St. Edmund's, for secular priests, seminarians, and laymen; and Bênet House for Benedictine students. Other religious orders also maintain residences for their members. The university has faculties of classics, divinity, English, fine arts, modern and medieval languages, oriental studies, economics and politics, history, law, moral science, engineering, geography and geology, mathematics, physics and chemistry, agriculture, archeology and anthropology, biology, medicine, and education. There are now 21 colleges for men and 5 for women. The ultimate governing body is the senate, which is composed of doctors and masters in all the faculties and bachelors of divinity. Professors and lecturers share the responsibility of teaching and research, and tutors, who are college officials, are responsible for student welfare and discipline. The university library contains more than 3,000,000 printed books and more than 12,000 MSS. Enrollment averages about 11,000. BIBLIOGRAPHY: R. Tibbs, *University and Colleges of Cambridge* (1974).

[M. B. MURPHY]

CAMBRIDGE-CAMDEN SOCIETY, an association formally organized in 1839 by J. M. Neale and B. Webb for the study of ecclesiastical art. Thomas Thorpe was the first president (a post he retained for 20 years). The group committed itself to the study of the Middle Ages and most esp. to church architecture, Gothic, they felt, being the true Christian style. The restoration and building of churches in this style with concentration on detail was advocated somewhat dogmatically by the society. In the 1840s the society came under the attack of members of the Anglican Church (though the society and its members remained faithful Anglicans). The publication of the society, *Ecclesiologist,* first appeared in 1841. The society collapsed soon after the final issue of the *Ecclesiologist* in 1868. In 1879 it was revived and published *Transaction.* In 1937 the society was reorganized as the Ecclesiological Society.

[M. S. J. MCCAREY]

CAMBRIDGE PLATFORM, a 1648 statement of organization for Congregational Churches. In 1646 the General Court of the Massachusetts Colony called a synod of representatives of the Churches of the four confederated New England colonies—Massachusetts Bay, Hartford, New Haven, and Plymouth. Three sessions were held in Cambridge in that year and the next 2 years. At the last session there was adopted *A Platform of Church Discipline,* known historically as the Cambridge Platform. ''The Cambridge Platform is the most important monument of New England Congregationalism, because it is the clearest reflection of the system as it lay in the minds of the first generation on our soil after twenty years of practical experience'' (W. Walker, *The Creeds and Platforms of Congregationalism,* 1893). It was not a doctrinal confession but a practical plan based on four principles: the autonomy of the *local church; the representative character of the ministry; the covenant relationship of church membership; and the obligation of fellowship and friendly counsel with other churches. *CONGREGATIONALISM; *COVENANT THEOLOGY.

[R. F. G. CALDER]

CAMBRIDGE PLATONISTS, a group of philosophical divines, mostly from Emmanuel, a distinctly Protestant college by foundation and tradition. Under the *Commonwealth

and the *Restoration they stood rather aloof from the warring ecclesiologies of Puritans and high Anglicans; they advocated policies of tolerance and *comprehensiveness and taught a rational illuminism deriving from neoplatonism, early and medieval, and influenced by Descartes. The judgment of reason, the arbiter of both natural and revealed religion, depended on a man's being *dikaios* and *agathos,* upright and good at heart; it was the light in our world by virtue of God's indwelling in the mind. The group, which seems to have originated with N. Culverwel, included B. *Whichcote, R. *Cudworth, and H. *More. They breathed a spirit of piety and charity, at once gentle and confident, in an atmosphere of general *odium theologicum,* and this spirit is still alive among Anglicans with scientific interests who would set themselves down neither as strong sacramentalists nor as muscular Christians. BIBLIOGRAPHY: J. Tulloch, *Rational Theology and Christian Philosophy in the Seventeenth Century* (2 v., 1872, repr. 1972); F. J. Powicke, *Cambridge Platonists* (1926, repr. 1971).

[T. GILBY]

CAMBUSKENNETH ABBEY, an Augustinian abbey in Stirlingshire, Scotland, founded by David I *c.* 1140. The ill-fated King James III (d. 1488) and his Danish Queen Margaret (d. 1486) were both buried before its high altar. All that remains of the abbey today is its splendid 13th-cent. bell tower. BIBLIOGRAPHY: S. Cruden, *Scottish Abbeys* (1960) 78–79; *Registrum monasterii S. Marie de Cambuskenneth* (Grampian Club, 1872).

[L. J. MacFARLANE]

CAMERA, APOSTOLIC, an office that traces its roots to the Middle Ages. It began as the administrator of properties and revenues collected on behalf of the Holy See. The Camera soon took on judicial duties and became a very influential tribunal. The power of the Camera declined until now the posts are of an honorary nature. Today, it is only during the vacancy of the Holy See that the Apostolic Camera assumes the temporal administration. In the person of the chief officer or camerlengo and his assistants the Camera performs its duties. The personnel who compose this Camera are: cardinal chamberlain, vice chamberlain, auditor, treasurer, five *chierici di Camera,* and two other officials.

[M. S. J. MCCAREY]

CAMERA SECRETA, personal secretaries of the Roman Court first organized by Martin V to handle official correspondence. The Apostolic Camera and the Secretariat of State are outgrowths of this chamber.

[M. S. J. MCCAREY]

CAMERARIUS, GULIELMUS, see CHALMERS, WILLIAM.

CAMERARIUS, JOACHIM (Kammermeister; 1500–74), German Lutheran humanist and biographer. C. joined the

Erfurt circle of humanists in 1518. In 1521 he went to Wittenberg and became in time *Melanchthon's favorite pupil. After teaching in Nuremberg and Tübingen (1526–41), C. moved to Leipzig, where he reorganized the university. Striving for Lutheran unity, he endeavored to gain acceptance for the *Augsburg Confession and to mediate in the controversies aroused by A. *Osiander's theory on justification. He was the earliest biographer of Melanchthon and the author of many philological, historical, pedagogical, and biographical works. Ludwig Camerarius (1573–1651), a statesman prominent in the Thirty Years' War, was his grandson. BIBLIOGRAPHY: R. H. Fischer, NCE 2:1105; F. Lau, RGG 1:1602.

[M. J. SUELZER]

CAMERLENGO, the head of the Apostolic Camera. It is the camerlengo, assisted by the other members of the Camera, who takes charge of the property of the Holy See during its vacancy. He verifies the death of the pope, takes immediate possession of the Vatican, Castel Gondolfo and the Lateran, affixes seals to the papal apartments, and makes arrangements for the conclave.

[M. S. J. MCCAREY]

CAMERON, JOHN (*c.*1579–1625), Scottish Protestant theologian. Educated at Glasgow, C. migrated to Bordeaux where he taught classical languages at the new college of Bergerac. He later served as professor of philosophy at Sedan. Endowed with a scholarship to study Protestant theology, he was named (1618) professor of divinity at the Univ. of Saumur. Civil unrest in France in 1620 forced his return to England. In 1622 he was appointed principal of the Univ. of Glasgow. His slavish advocacy of the divine right of kings endeared him to James I but aroused opposition in Glasgow. Removing again to France he was appointed professor of divinity at Montauban where his doctrine on civl obedience caused him to be physically assaulted, an act resulting in his death in 1625. Much admired by certain English contemporaries, including John Milton, he wrote a number of theological works including *De triplici Dei cum homine foedere* (1608) and *Theses de gratia et libero arbitrio* (1618). A Calvinist, C. held that believers had infused knowledge of good and evil which exerted moral influence on choice but left man physically able to do evil, a capacity that absolved God from responsibility for evil. BIBLIOGRAPHY: T. F. Henderson, DNB 3:747–748.

[J. M. BRADY]

CAMERON, JOHN, (1826–1910), Canadian educator and bishop. Of Scottish ancestry, C. studied at the Urban College, Rome, and was ordained (1853). He was returned to his native Canada and was instrumental in the foundation of St. Francis Xavier College (later University), Antigonish (1855), where he taught and served as rector. He was made coadjutor bp. of Arichat (1869) and became its ordinary (1887). The see was transferred to Antigonish, where C. made St. Francis Xavier a center of Catholic education in the provinces. BIBLIOGRAPHY: D. J. Rankin, *History of the County of Antigonish* (1929).

[R. K. MACMASTER]

CAMERONIANS, those Presbyterians in Scotland named for Robert Cameron (1648–80), who resisted when Charles II began after the Restoration (1660) to impose his authority on the Church and restore *episcopacy. In the Southwest Cameron and others who disassociated themselves from "the unfaithful, silent complying ministers of the times," made public both their *covenanting loyalty and their opposition to royal tyranny, in the Sanquhar Declaration of 1680. Cameron himself was slain by dragoons in that same year, when the "killing times" began. The Cameronians, calling themselves the "Witnessing Remnant of the True Presbyterian Church in Scotland," are best known from 1712 as the Reformed Presbyterian Church. This body was united with the Free Church in 1876. Strongly nationalistic, holding to the divine right of Presbyterianism, and embracing a narrow evangelical faith, the Cameronians left a distinctive mark on later Presbyterianism. BIBLIOGRAPHY: P. Walker, *Six Saints of the Covenant* (repr., 1901) 1:218–365.

[J. A. R. MacKENZIE]

CAMILLIANS, i.e., the Order of Clerics Regular, Servants of the Sick, founded by St. Camillus de Lellis in Rome (1582). Members take a fourth vow, to serve the sick. Originally the Camillians concentrated their efforts on hospital visits and care but later nursed the sick in their own homes. The 18th cent. saw the community established in Italy, Hungary, and Latin America. After a disastrous series of setbacks in the 19th cent., the order enjoyed a new growth. In the mid-1970s Camillians numbered more than 1,000 members in 130 houses located in 11 European countries, the U.S., Canada, and Latin America.

[A. P. HANLON]

CAMILLUS DE LELLIS, ST. (1550–1614), founder. A soldier of Venice, a gambler who turned to service of the sick and dying out of remorse, C. suffered all his life from an incurable disease. He studied for the priesthood at the Jesuit College in Rome and was ordained in 1584. With a handful of companions he founded a group that ultimately carried his name but was originally known as Ministers of the Sick. He and his fellow religious served in hospitals and homes, on galleys and battlefields. C. was canonized in 1746; Leo XIII named him protector of the sick and Pius XI, patron of nurses. BIBLIOGRAPHY: C. C. Martindale, *Life of St. Camillus* (1946).

[A. P. HANLON]

CAMISARDS, French Calvinist extremists who revolted against the attempt of Louis XIV to suppress the *Reformed faith. The curtailment of Huguenot worship that followed the revocation of the *Edict of Nantes in 1685 and the growth of *apocalypticism, inspired largely by the writings of Pierre Jurieu, gave rise to a resistance movement in southern France. In the Cévennes and neighboring areas *c.*1700 a variety of prophets were claiming direct divine inspiration, and their predictions of doom were accompanied by ecstasies, trances, and convulsions. The Camisards broke into open revolt in 1702, assassinating a priest who had imprisoned some Huguenots and fighting with a fanatical ferocity against the RC Church and its priests. Government forces retaliated with similar cruelty until the revolt was suppressed in 1704. A subsequent outbreak in 1709 was quickly put down. Some Camisards fled to England, where they were known as "French prophets," and to Germany. The movement was disavowed and its religious pretensions condemned by many leading French Huguenots, but the spectacle of revolt was used by the government to justify the reinforcement of its severe policy in regard to the Huguenots. Because of the occurrence of *glossolalia and ecstatic experiences among the Camisards, they are sometimes considered among the antecedents of modern Pentecostals. BIBLIOGRAPHY: H. Baird, *Huguenots and the Revocation of the Edict of Nantes* (2 v., 1879, repr. 1970); A. Ducasse, *La Guerre des Camisards* (1946); Knox Enth 357–370.

[J. C. WILLKE]

CAMÕES, LUÍS VAZ DE (1524?–80), Portuguese poet. He served as a soldier in Africa (1546–49), losing an eye in battle, and later (1553) was sent to India on military duty. He spent 14 years in the Orient, and upon his return published his best known work, *Os Lusíadas,* an epic whose hero was Vasco da Gama. The poem celebrates Portugal's greatness, the excellence of its people, and Da Gama's voyage to India and return. Intertwined with the chronicle is a complicated mythological framework, depicting pagan gods as friends or enemies of Portuguese achievements. C. also wrote shorter lyric poetry and three comedies in verse. BIBLIOGRAPHY: *Lusiads* (tr. L. Bacon, 1950); *Rimas* (ed. A. J. Da Costa Pimpao, 1953).

[T. M. MCFADDEN]

CAMP MEETING, a frontier revivalistic method originating in Logan County, Ky., *c.* 1800, during the *Second Great Awakening, when Presbyterian and Methodist ministers organized a 4-day sacramental meeting. To accommodate the throngs of people, meetings were held outdoors. Each minister preached, and many people were visibly affected and converted. Soon similar meetings became common. Preachers of every denomination exhorted crowds simultaneously, and conversions were accompanied by emotional stress expressed in shouting, weeping, and various other physical manifestations. The Methodists institutionalized the camp meeting, changing it eventually to an annual inspirational summer conference. BIBLIOGRAPHY: C. A. Johnson, *Frontier Camp Meeting: Religion's Harvest Time* (1955). *REVIVALISM.

[N. H. MARING]

CAMP MEETING HYMN (also known as the revival spiritual), the religious song that first appeared during the second *Great Awakening in Kentucky in the first decade of the 19th century. Generated by the highly spontaneous and emotional setting of frontier revivals, these hymns are a blend of religious folk poetry and the secular tunes of the time. The unique verse-chorus pattern of these hymns testifies to the communal setting, in that short, repetitive, and easily memorized phrases often made up these choruses. The verses often express a tortured conviction of sin and an equally ecstatic experience of the Holy Spirit.

[D. J. SMUCKER]

CAMPAGNOLA, Italian artists. (1) **Giulio** (1482–1515), engraver and precocious genius from Padua, who discarded his earlier style upon exposure to Venetian shadow, effecting by "clouds" of dots dissolving edges and merging forms (*Christ and the Woman of Samaria*) in a unique technique revived in the 18th century. (2) **Domenico** (1500–*c.*1581), brother of Giulio, engraver and painter. C.'s numerous impressive prints (1517–18) were followed by paintings of the prophets (Venice, 1531), *Madonna with the Protectors of Padua* (1537), and *Christ with the Protectors* (1562), smaller altarpieces (one in the Philadelphia Museum of Art) and frescoes of the Carmine and S. Rocco, all echoing the form and color of Titian and Pordenone.

[M. J. DALY]

CAMPANA, EMILIO (1874–1939), Italian theologian and Mariologist. A pupil of Alexis Lépicier, C. is principally known for his two works on Mary: *Maria nel dogma cattolico* (1923) and *Maria nel culto cattolico* (2 v., 1933). BIBLIOGRAPHY: A. Piolanti, EncCatt 3:449.

[T. LIDDY]

CAMPAÑA, PEDRO (1503–*c.*1580), Flemish painter, architect, sculptor, astronomer, and mathematician. After traveling from Brussels to Bologna and Venice, C. finally painted in Seville (1537), influencing later Spanish masters. The fluttering drapery in *Descent from the Cross* (1547) relates to 15th-cent. Gothic Flanders. Spiraling movement (*Presentation in the Temple,* 1555), dark forms against light, and certain figures suggest Tintoretto. BIBLIOGRAPHY: D. A. Iñiguez, *Pedro de Campaña* (1951).

[M. J. DALY]

CAMPANELLA, TOMMASO, (1568–1639), poet, scientist and one of the major representatives of Renaissance philosophy. He joined the Dominican Order, but soon found himself at odds with his superiors and confreres because of his heterodox positions. From 1592 C. was subjected to various trials on account of his heresies. Basically, C., in the works of his youth, pleaded for a reform of religion by a return to nature (he had a great interest in natural science and an aversion to Aristotelian philosophy) and for the abolition of all that is supernatural in Christianity. In 1599 C. became involved in a plot to overthrow the Spanish government in Naples, was caught and imprisoned until 1626. In this period C. underwent a philosophico-religious conversion (the sincerity of which is disputed). The empiricism of his youth is now taken up in a metaphysics, according to which knowledge is not merely an expression of the object, but the act of the self-conscious subject specified by the object. Its certainty is guaranteed by the subject's participation in absolute spirit (pantheistic tendencies). Christ is no longer considered as merely human, but as the Logos who unveils himself in nature as creator and in revelation as savior. In prison C. also wrote his most famous work *Città del Sole* (1602): the city of the sun is a Utopian island in the Indian Ocean where men live according to pure nature, expecting the Christian revelation and a better life to come from it. Freed by the Spaniards in 1626, C. was put under arrest in a convent in Rome until 1629. In 1633 he intervened on behalf of Galileo in the famous trial. He left Rome in 1634 for Paris, where he was honored by Louis XIII and acted as advisor to Richelieu. A new edition of the works was begun by L. Firpo, Milan 1954– . An English translation of his *Città del Sole* (tr. W. J. Gilstrap) is available in *The Quest for Utopia*, eds. G. Negley and J. M. Patrick (1952). BIBLIOGRAPHY: B. M. Bonansea, *Tomasso Campanella: Renaissance Pioneer of Modern Thought* (1969); L. Blanchet, *Campanella, 1568–1639* (1920, repr. 1964).

[B. A. NACHBAHR]

CAMPBELL, THOMAS and ALEXANDER, father and son, leaders of an American reform movement that issued in the Christian Churches (Disciples of Christ).

Thomas (1763–1854), father of Alexander, was reared in Co. Down, northern Ireland, as an Anglican. He was converted to Seceder Presbyterianism and educated for its ministry at the Univ. of Glasgow and the Seceder Seminary at Whitburn, Scotland (see SECEDER TRADITION). He established an academy and served a pastorate in Co. Armagh until emigration to western Pa. in 1807. Disciplined by his *synod for anti-Calvinist teachings and for "unfencing" the communion table, he renounced its authority and organized the Christian Association for promoting church unity, writing his now classic ecumenical document *Declaration and Address* (1809), which proclaimed that the Church is "essentially, intentionally, and constitutionally one." He relinquished leadership of the new movement to his son, but continued his ministry, established academies in Pa. and Ky., and assisted his son in editing religious publications. See biographies by his son (1861); W. H. Hanna (1935); L. G. McAllister (1954).

Alexander (1788–1866), son of Thomas, born in Co. Antrim. He renounced communion with Seceder Presbyterians while a student at the Univ. of Glasgow. Joining his father in Pa. in 1809, he became part of the Christian unity movement. He settled on his farm, later called Bethany, in what is now W. Va.; ordained in 1812, he soon assumed leadership in the movement begun by his father. After several years' connection with the Baptist Association, the adherents by 1830 were forced into separate communion. He propagated the principles of the Disciples in lecture tours; in notable debates with the Socialist Robert Owens (1829) and RC Bp. John Purcell (1837); and in 55 volumes published by his Bethany Press, as well as in two monthlies, the *Christian Baptist* (1823–30) and the *Millennial Harbinger* (1830–64). From 1840 he was founder, president, and professor of Bethany College, which provided free education to ministerial students. Inspired by the *Enlightenment and John Locke, the American system and Thomas Jefferson, he advocated a system of church government embracing both local autonomy and organic unity, freedom and order, through democratically delegated authority and elective assemblies. His theology combined high, or Catholic, doctrines of the Church and sacraments with Protestant emphasis on the *priesthood of all believers and acceptance of St. Peter's confession of faith in Mt 16.16 as the only prerequisite for Christian communion. Although he opposed slavery, his stand for tolerance and reason prevented schism among the Disciples on this issue. He fostered advance of the ecumenical movement, from new Bible translations to evangelical alliances, favoring organic rather than federal plans of union and forecasting eventual cooperation between American Protestants and Roman Catholics. BIBLIOGRAPHY: *Sage of Bethany: A Pioneer in Broadcloth* (ed. P. Gresham, 1960); E. J. Wrather, *Creative Freedom in Action: Alexander Campbell on the Structure of the Church* (1968).

[E. J. WRATHER]

CAMPEGGI, CAMILLO (d. 1589), a Dominican, born in Pavia, who served as general inquisitor in Ferrara and Mantua and as the pope's theologian at the Council of Trent. Pope Paul IV named him bp. of Sutri and Nepi, but he died before his installation. Though he left some polemical treatises and commentaries, he is best known for a sermon delivered to the Council of Trent; this was inserted in the Council's proceedings.

CAMPEGGIO, LORENZO (1472–1539), cardinal, diplomat. A widower with five children, C. chose the priesthood and embarked on a distinguished career as church diplomat. Made a cardinal in 1517, he was sent by Leo X to England to secure the aid of Henry VIII in a crusade against the Turks. C. earned the respect of Henry who nominated him as bp. of Salisbury and entrusted English affairs at the papal court to him. C. was papal representative at the Diets of Nuremberg (1524) and Augsburg (1530). A reform proponent, he was opposed to a council that included Lutherans and other dissidents but served as legate of Paul III who convened a council at Vicenza in 1538. C. played a leading role in the crisis over Henry VIII's attempt to divorce Catherine of Aragon. Named to preside over the proceedings in England, C., through delays and persuasion, attempted to avoid a decision by the Church. In the reaction by Henry both Wolsey and C. fell from favor at the court of Henry. An able diplomat and sincere advocate of reform, C. stood out among churchmen of the early 16th century. BIBLIOGRAPHY: E. V. Cardinal, *Cardinal*

Lorenzo Campeggio: Legate to the Courts of Henry VIII and Charles V (1935).

[J. M. BRADY]

CAMPENDONK, HEINRICH (1889–1957), German painter, assistant on murals in the Cathedral of Osnabrück. In 1911 C. is identified with the *Blaue Reiter group, embracing the color theories of Kandinsky and Delauney, the animal mysticism of Marc, primitive forms of Rousseau, and Chagall's fantastic images. C.'s long career as teacher continued even after his dismissal by the Nazi government (1933). BIBLIOGRAPHY: P. Wember, *Heinrich Campendonk* (1960).

[M. J. DALY]

CAMPIN, ROBERT (*c.*1378–1444), probably the Master of Flémalle, teacher of Jacques Daret and supposedly Roger van der Weyden, dean of the painters' guild in Tournai in 1423. Founder of early Netherlandish painting with the Van Eyck brothers, C. endowed the new realistic religious painting with a disguise and extended symbolism as seen in his Mérode *Annunciation* altarpiece (New York), *Marriage of the Virgin* (Prado), and *Nativity* (Dijon). Through the influence of the Master of Flémalle (Campin?) and van der Weyden, the International Style of sculpture in N Europe entered a Late Gothic phase of "pictorial carving" rooted in "sculptural painting." BIBLIOGRAPHY: M. J. Friedländer, *Rogier van der Weyden and the Master of Flémalle* (*Early Netherlandish Painting*, v. 2, tr. H. Norden, 1967); *idem, Altniederländische Malerei* (14 v., 1924–37); E. Panofsky, *Early Netherlandish Painting* (2 v., 1953).

[S. N. BLUM]

CAMPION, EDMUND, ST. (*c.*1540–81). A scholar and junior fellow of St. John's College, Oxford, a brilliant and popular leader, C. was chosen to give the address honoring Queen Elizabeth when she visited the university in 1566. He took the Oath of Supremacy and was ordained deacon in the Church of England but returned to the Catholic Church at Douai, Belgium, *c.*1571. He became a Jesuit, was ordained at Prague in 1578, and returned to England the following year. Almost immediately upon arriving he wrote his "Challenge to the Privy Council," often called "Campion's Brag," openly proclaiming his mission "to preach the gospel . . . to confute the errors . . . wherewith many (of) my dear countrymen are abused. . . ." Often changing his dress and name he traveled about England giving new courage to Catholics and attracting all by his personality, saintliness, and eloquence. Betrayed, imprisoned in the Tower and several times racked, he was condemned and hanged, drawn, and quartered in 1581. His chief written work is *Decem rationes,* a challenge to the Protestant clergy to debate Catholicism with him. He was beatified by Leo XIII in 1886 and canonized by Paul VI in 1970. BIBLIOGRAPHY: E. Waugh, *Edmund Campion* (1935) with bibliog.; C. C. Martindale, *Edmund Campion* (1933); C. Testore, BiblSanct 3:723–727; Butler 4:466–469.

[M. J. BARRY]

CAMPO SANTO, (It. *camposanto,* holy field), a cemetery or graveyard. The most celebrated camposanto, known as the *Campo Santo de' Tedeschi* or *Camposanto Tedesco* (holy field of the Germans) embraces a cemetery, church, a hospice, and now a college located on the S side of St. Peter's in Rome. After the erection of the basilica over the graves of SS. Peter and Paul by Constantine, this area became a popular place for burial for Christians desiring to be buried near the tombs of the Apostles. According to legend soil brought from Mount Calvary by St. Helena and spread over the area may account for its being called *campus sanctus;* but it was also holy ground because of its association in place with the Circus Vaticanus in which so many Christians died during the persecution under Nero. With the approval of Pope Leo III, Charlemagne established in 796 a hospice for pilgrims on adjoining ground with a graveyard to be used for the burial of his Frankish subjects. Following its restoration after the return of the popes to Rome and the Western Schism, it was enlarged and encircled by a wall. It was given over to the use of the then large and influential German colony in Rome. A brotherhood was established there during the pestilence of 1448 to provide a burial place for poor Germans dying in Rome. This brotherhood, which since 1519 has enjoyed the status of an archconfraternity, built a church and a new hospice on adjacent land, thus making the Campo Santo a German national institution. Under Pius IX it became also the site of a college for priests working in the fields of church history and archeology, an enterprise furthered by the generous donations of German Catholics. This institution has served the Church well in its training of scholars and in its publication of learned works. BIBLIOGRAPHY: J. E. Gugumus, NCE 2:1116; A. De Waal, CE 3:224–225.

[J. C. WILLKE]

CAMPOSANTO, PISA, cathedral cemetery, part of complex including cathedral, baptistry, and campanile (Leaning Tower), that became a "holy field" when Bp. Ubaldo in the 12th cent. brought earth from Calvary in ships returning from the Holy Land. Framed architecturally by Giovanni de Simone in slender Gothic style, the Camposanto boasts frescoes by F. da Volterra, A. da Firenze, T. Gaddi, and Benozzo Gozzoli with the renowned *Triumph of Death* in 14th-cent. Sienese style ascribed to F. Traini. A museum partially destroyed in World War II has been restored. BIBLIOGRAPHY: M. Salmi, *L'arte italiana* (2 v., 1953).

[M. J. DALY]

CAMPRA, ANDRÉ, (1660–1744), French composer of opera and church music during the Baroque era. His work spans the period between Lully and Rameau of the French Baroque.

[P. MURPHY]

CAMPUS MINISTRY, the active presence and witness of the Church on the college and university campus. Formerly known as the *Newman Apostolate, it received official recognition during Vatican II (see Vat II ChrEduc 10) and is considered one of the principal areas of pastoral concern in the Church today. While the Newman Apostolate, founded in 1893 at the Univ. of Pennsylvania, sought to preserve a Catholic identity amid what was considered the alien and hostile climate of the secular university, campus ministry considers the university, both Catholic and nonsectarian, as the creative center of society and seeks to involve itself at every level. Thus, it projects the pastoral ministry of service not only to students but to administration, faculty and staff through a concern and care for persons, by the proclamation of the Gospel and through the celebration of the liturgy. Catholic campus ministry, like its counterparts in the Protestant and Jewish community, sees its goals classified within the biblical categories of the pastoral, prophetic, priestly and kingly modes of service. Pastoral duties include concern for individuals and their needs at all levels; the prophetic role urges a ministerial concern for social justice; the priestly role emphasizes worship, community, and tradition; and the kingly mode calls for responsible governance on the part of the academic institution in maintaining high standards and values. While many campus ministers today are priests, the numbers of religious women, lay men and women are increasing. Many see the need for team ministry, several men and women, each with special areas of concern and interest, working together to build a community of faith on the college campus.

[T. LIDDY]

CAMUS, ALBERT (1913–60), French writer. Born in Algiers, of poor, illiterate parents, C.'s frequent references to poverty, to his mother, to Mediterranean warmth are the consequence of his background. He was educated in schools in Belcourt, distinguishing himself there and at the Univ. of Algiers by his philosophical and political, as well as critical, acumen. A confrontation with serious illness, tuberculosis, added a new and deep dimension to his view of life. To work assiduously, to live intensely in every direction, to develop artistically what knowledge was constantly unfolding in and around him became his cause, his aim. After working with theater groups and dramatizations in Algiers, he wrote his essay *Christian Metaphysics and Neoplatonism* (1936), a compendium of his reading on Christian thought and a preview of his thinking on the absurd. Several works were published, e.g., *Caligula*, a drama, between 1936 and 1940 in which year he went to Paris to work in the editorial offices of *Paris-Soir*. In 1942, with the publication of *Le Mythe de Sisyphe*, came the C. manifesto, henceforward to be labeled the absurd. *The Stranger* (1942), *The Plague* (1945), and *The Fall* (1956), treat in some way C.'s nonreligious transcendental quest for truth and man's ultimate conquest in an unequal struggle. He was awarded the Nobel Prize for literature in 1957. He was killed in an automobile accident as he was returning to Paris. BIBLIOGRAPHY: J. Onimus, *Albert Camus and Christianity* (tr. E. Parker, 1970); R. Quilliot, *Sea and Prisons: A Commentary on the Life and Thought of Albert Camus* (tr. E. Parker, 1970); L. Braun, *Witness of Decline—Albert Camus: Moralist of the Absurd* (1974).

[R. M. FUNCHION]

CAMUS, JEAN PIERRE (1584–1652), bp. of Belley, friend of St. Francis de Sales, for a study of whose life in 6 volumes—or rather for its abridgment in the following century—he is chiefly remembered. He published more than 200 books: romances, controversial articles, sermons, panegyrics, and works of hagiography, spiritual direction, theology, and catechetics. His intemperate attacks on the religious orders, thus *The Anti-Monk Well Prepared,* drew forth replies in kind, such as *Lucian of Samosata Risen Again in the Person of J. P. Camus*. A work of his on the love of God found its way into the Spanish Index of prohibited works (1747). BIBLIOGRAPHY: R. Heurtevent, DSAM 2:62–73; J. Calvet, *Catholicisme* 2:249–250; J. F. Sollier, CE 3:225–226.

[H. JACK]

CANA CONFERENCES, a movement that traces its origins to Family Renewal Day begun in 1943, in New York. The name was then changed to the Cana Conference and endorsed by the bps. of the U.S. Each diocese organizes its own conferences. The Family Life Division of the USCC coordinates the programs. The relationships between husband and wife, parents and children, God and family, society and family are the interests of this organization. Marriage experts, priests, and doctors give the conferences. The Cana Club and Pre-Cana Conference have grown from this movement.

[M. S. J. MCCAREY]

CANA OF GALILEE, the town where Jesus changed water into wine at a wedding feast (Jn 2.2) and later met the official whose son he cured (4.46). Cana was also the town from which Nathaniel came (21.6). Khirbet Qana 10 miles N of Nazareth is identified by many as the biblical site. The modern village of Kefr Kenna on the road from Nazareth to Tiberias attracts most of the modern pilgrims. BIBLIOGRAPHY: C. Kopp, *Holy Places of the Gospels* (tr. R. Walls, 1963) 143–154.

[J. E. LUSSIER]

CANAAN AND CANAANITES, the biblical name for an area of Palestine and its people before its conquest by the Israelites. The land was bounded by the Taurus Mountains on the N, extended below the Gaza in the S, the Mediterranean on the W, and the Jordan-Orontes Rivers in the east. Canaan was situated between Egypt and Mesopotamia and gleaned much from those civilizations. The Israelites, in turn, assimilated much of their culture from the Canaanites, whom they never completely conquered and frequently married. With such close contact the Israelite leaders feared contamination, esp. of their religious practices, and they frequently persecuted the Canaanites. The OT contains references to their possible annihilation, and mention of the Canaanites is also found in the NT when Jesus cured the daughter of a woman of Canaan. In time, the Canaanites settled on the N coast of Palestine. They were known as Phoenicians to the Romans. BIBLIOGRAPHY: EDB 343–345.

[M. S. J. MCCAREY]

CANAANITE RELIGION, the religion of the NW Semitic peoples of Syria and Palestine, and of the Phoenician colonies spread around the Mediterranean in the 1st millennium B.C. Even the official and legitimate religion of the settled Hebrews, Canaanite in language and largely so in culture, certainly absorbed many Canaanite religious practices and much Canaanite mythological imagery, when such elements were compatible with the transcendent and austere worship of Yahweh. Our knowledge of Canaanite religion is not full. Phoenician and Punic inscriptions are too limited in scope to establish an extensive interpretive context, and archeological finds are difficult to interpret for want of adequate written sources. The OT is an important source, but specifically Canaanite elements absorbed by the Hebrews are not easy to isolate, except in instances where there is comparative material elsewhere, while elements consciously rejected are deformed by bias in presentation. Very valuable sources are the abundant texts and material objects brought to light by French archeologists since 1929 in the upper strata (c. 1550–1200 B.C.) of Ugarit (modern Ras Shamra) near Latakia on the N Syrian coast. They confirm admirably the information found in Philo of Byblos (64–161 A.D.).

The sense of numinous powers in natural phenomena remained stronger in Canaanite notions of divinity than it did in most contemporary Near Eastern cultures. El, the head of the pantheon in Ugarit, was a remote high god, but he dwelt in a vague place having a cosmic, and indirectly earthly, reference, the "Sources of the Two Deeps" (in certain texts, "the Two Rivers"). The dominant active god of the pantheon, Baal, identified by the mid-2d millennium B.C. with the storm god Hadad, was known to the Phoenicians as Baal (or Bel) Shamen, "Lord of the skies"; he was the "Rider of the Clouds," thunder was his voice, and his power was felt behind other manifestations of the vital power in nature—in moving streams, and in trees blown by the wind. He had daughters whose names are formed from the Canaanite nouns meaning "earth" and "dew." The forces of the world's seas and floodwaters were abstracted to form the god Sea (Yamm), while desert places (including the world of the dead) were the domain of personified Death (Mot). Dagon, of enduring popularity throughout the NW Semitic area, was essentially a grain god. Thus, the most important and the most popular of the Canaanite gods were gods of nature and its forces, a position of little importance being held by the numerous other divinities, including those divinized heavenly bodies like the Sun who elsewhere, esp. in Egypt, held a primary role in the pantheon. The personalities of the principal feminine divinities, Ashirat, Astarte, Anat, are somewhat blurred by the fluctuation of their attributes. Ashirat, the consort of El in the Ugaritic mythological texts, shows the qualities of wife and mother. Both Astarte and Anat appear sometimes with the traits of a fertility goddess, sometimes with those of a goddess of combat.

El, whose very name is the generic Semitic word for "god" and whose mythological actions were less reenacted, it seems, in cultic rites, was sufficiently transcendent in character to allow his attributes as supreme god of all, kingly, wise, father of mankind, and creator, to influence the Hebrew concepts of Yahweh, whom the earliest Yahwistic Hebrews surrounded rather with the imagery of a storm or mountain god. Baal, too was a storm god; but, less remote than El, Baal was the focal god of Canaanite worship; his mythological actions were reenacted in a type of cultic drama that often had immoral adjuncts, and the Hebrew attitude toward him was entirely negative. Nevertheless, certain elements of mythology associated with Baal do appear, transferred to Yahweh, in the OT. The victory of Baal over the forces of the sea and the floods (the god Yamm) can be found, with Yahweh the victor, in Ps 74(73). 13–14 and Job 7.12 (in which *yamm*, "sea," can be read as a proper name). Perhaps Hos 6.1–2, which speaks of Yahweh's raising people up to new life after striking them to lead them to repentance, is rooted in the myth of Baal's victory over death and withering summer heat personified as the god Mot, now with Yahweh the sole divine actor, the whole being infused with an ethical content.

It is still very difficult to reconstruct the details of cultic practice in Canaan. As elsewhere in antiquity, ultimate responsibility for the good order of cultic arrangements lay with the king, who is often called a priest in Phoenician royal inscriptions. Attached to the actual service of sanctuaries were several types of officials, including those called *khnm,* an appellative cognate to the Hebrew *Kōhanîm* translated into English as "priests," but we have almost no indications of what the duties of these various officials were. Phoenician temple tariffs do show the *khnm* to have been the administrators of a temple, and the colophon of a Ugaritic mythological text shows the priesthood to have been concerned with the literary preservation of such texts. The available evidence does not indicate whether divination was done by priests or by other types of temple personnel. Hebrew sacrificial vocabulary recurs in Ugaritic texts, but no contexts show whether the corresponding rites and practices were the same or not. Phoenician temple tariffs reveal a certain correspondence with OT provisions for the distribution of sacrificial animals, but the sacrificial vocabulary is largely different. Human sacrifice, an abomination in Israel, was practiced in Canaan. Canaanite temples, like the Temple in Jerusalem, show a division of the building itself into a series of two or three rooms succeeding one another between the entrance and the rear wall, with the sacrificial altar standing in the open air before the building. Altars of incense have been found, along with other objects whose possible correspondence with those of the Hebrews is often difficult to establish because of obscurity in the Hebrew terminology. Cultic meals in Ugarit show traits of a kind of banquet, prepared by the king, shared by gods and by the people, accompanied with music, and marked by considerable drinking. Cultic drama, the ritual miming of mythological exploits in various types of cultic action, was certainly an important element of Canaanite worship. The mythological texts from Ugarit most probably had some relation to ritual, but it is hazardous to say what that relation might be in a given case. Two extremes to be avoided in this regard are that of seeing all the mythological texts as scripts for cultic drama, and that of applying uncritically to Canaan a whole pattern of cultic drama constructed from elements found in other ancient Near Eastern civilizations. There are divinities like Dagon who, while figuring largely in properly cultic lists and enjoying much popularity, have a minimal role in the mythological texts. Conversely, there are divinities like Anat who play a leading role in the myths but who receive little or no mention in the cultic lists found so far. Unfortunately the extant material on Canaanite religion, because of its fragmentary and laconic character and the often uncertain meaning of Ugaritic and Phoenician words, lends itself readily to speculation or hypothesis, and, apart from studies in mythology, which have a fairly adequate textual basis, much that has been written on Canaanite religious ideas and practice goes beyond the evidence. BIBLIOGRAPHY: R. de Langhe, *Myth, Ritual, and Kingship* (ed. S. H. Hooke, 2d ed., 1958) 122–148; T. H. Gaster, *Thespis* (2d ed., 1961); J. Gray, *Legacy of Canaan* (VT Suppl. 5, 2d ed., 1964); translations of selected texts by H. L. Ginsberg and F. Rosenthal in J. B. Pritchard ed., *Ancient Near Eastern Texts Relating to the Old Testament* (2d ed., 1955) 129–155, 499–505; a larger selection, but from Ugaritic alone in C. H. Gordon, *Ugaritic Literature* (1949).

[A. CODY]

CANADA. Perhaps the principal motivating force in French exploration and settlement policy in the 16th cent. was the spread of the faith. The first missionaries at Quebec, the Franciscan Récollets (1615), were followed by the Jesuits (1625), who became the nucleus of missionary efforts in Canada. Acadia was an idyllic Catholic settlement even before the founding of Quebec by Champlain in 1608. While the Church provided for the spiritual welfare of the French settlers, the main thrust was conversion of Algonquin and Huron-Iroquois tribes in the interior. In the 1640s most of the Huron nation in the Georgian Bay region, with their missions, were destroyed by the Iroquois. This was the time of the death of the North American Martyrs. Missionaries preceded and accompanied explorers and fur traders. Although they made few converts, their heroic work won them a place in Canada's history. By the end of the 17th cent. much of the zeal created by the Catholic reformation in Europe had cooled, but the population of New France was growing and demands for new services by the Church were made. The Jesuits opened a college in Quebec in 1635, the first N of the Spanish settlements. In 1639 the Ursulines opened a school for Indian girls, and the Hôtel Dieu (hospital) was opened the same year by the hospitallers. In 1641 a mission was founded at what is now Montreal, with the establishment of a school and a hospital. The Sulpicians, arriving in 1657, became the dominant order

in Montreal and contributed to missionary and educational work. The increasing population and call for expanded services by the Church were met by the foundation of elementary, secondary, and technical schools, charity for the needy, and loans to start local industries. Tithes and large land grants enabled the Church to carry on this work.

In 1666, the first census numbered 3215 inhabitants, 49 priests, and 46 women religious. Canonesses of St. Augustine, Sisters of the Congregation of Notre Dame, and Hospitallers of St. Joseph were also among the pioneer religious women.

Laval arrived in 1659 as the first bishop. He was a dynamic leader who vitalized the Church, centralized control of the clergy, and opened seminaries. Although there was usually cooperation between Church and State officials, friction developed occasionally, esp. regarding the sale of liquor to the Indians. The economic factors won out over moral considerations. Since the Huguenots were excluded from the colony, there was unanimity in religious profession. A long period of peace and growth ended with the onset of the French and Indian War. In 1755 French settlers were expelled from Acadia and priests were excluded. By the Treaty of Paris in 1763, control of New France passed to England. While the treaty guaranteed freedom of religion, under British law Catholics were granted little liberty. Since English Protestants did not flock to the colony as expected, Britain permitted Bp. Jean-Olivier Briand (1715–94) to fill the vacant see in 1766. Emigrés fleeing anticlerical excesses of the French Revolution were allowed to come to Canada. The Quebec Act of 1774 extending to French Catholics rights enjoyed under the French regime was an expression of British gratitude for acceptance by the RC Church of the new regime and the preaching of loyalty to it. Objection of New England colonists to the Quebec Act, which they numbered among the "Intolerable Acts" that precipitated the American Revolution, ensured the loyalty of the French in Canada to the British crown. The influx of Catholic Scots, the Irish, and returning Acadians to the Maritime Provinces made it necessary to establish two vicariates apostolic; in 1818 Edmund Burke (1753–1820) became their first bp. in Halifax. In 1820 Joseph Norbert Provencher (1787–1853) was consecrated bp. of the new suffragan see of the Northwest, St. Boniface, Manitoba. An episcopal see was erected at Kingston (1826) with Alexander Macdonell (1762–1840) as first bp. of Upper Canada to minister to Irish and Scottish Catholics. Transportation in the 1830s of immigrants on overcrowded ships where sanitation was minimal caused epidemics and political discontent. Many priests and sisters gave their lives in caring for cholera victims. When rebellion broke in Upper and Lower Canada, the Church for a time worked for reform but withdrew support when violence threatened. In 1871 Upper and Lower Canada were united, and separate schools for minorities were provided by law. In 1851 "free exercise and enjoyment of religious worship" was guaranteed; in that same year assembled the First Council of Quebec. By 1860 fear of repression was diminishing, and the Church exerted a strong influence on society. New dioceses were created and religious communities increased in size and number. Oblates of Mary Immaculate and Grey Nuns were doing great work in the Northwest. Jesuits, Sulpicians, Franciscans, Fathers of the Holy Cross, Clerics of St. Viateur, and Christian Brothers all made their contributions. By the early 1900s there were 8 archdioceses, 23 dioceses, and 3 vicariates-apostolic served by 3500 priests, 30 communities of men and 70 of women religious. Canada by 1975 had 18 archdioceses and 52 dioceses, served by 8,015 diocesan and 5,820 religious clergy, and by 10,867 men religious and 41,789 women religious. Approximately 9½ million RCs formed 43.8% of the total population. Priests, sisters, and brothers engage in parish activities, in educational work, and serve in hospitals and orphanages. Canada sends overseas more missionaries per capita than any other country, except possibly Ireland. BIBLIOGRAPHY: C. A. Liederbach, *Canada's Bishops from 1120 to 1975 . . . from Allen to Yelle* (pa. 1975); S. D. Clark, *Church and Sect in Canada* (1948).

[S. F. JOHNSON]

CANADA, EASTERN CHURCHES IN. Although Chaldeans, Armenians, and Croatians indicate a growing membership, the Ukrainian Catholic Church is the major Eastern rite Church of Canada. The growth of the Church began in 1918, when the Ukrainian people began to leave their homeland and migrate to Canada. According to the 1970 census the Ukrainian rite comprises 228 churches with a membership of over 140,000. Pope Paul VI created a new eparchy for Ukrainian rite Catholics at New Westminster, Canada in 1974. Father Jerome Chimy, rector of the Ukrainian College in Rome and member of the Order of St. Josaphat, was appointed to head the eparchy. BIBLIOGRAPHY: M. H. Marunchak, *Ukrainian Canadians* (1970).

[C. KEENAN]

CANADA, UNITED CHURCH OF, see UNITED CHURCH OF CANADA.

CANADIAN CATHOLIC CONFERENCE (CCC), an association of the Canadian bps., established (1943) as a voluntary and permanent body; approved (1948) by the Holy See, it acquired after Vatican Council II the status of episcopal conference. The function of CCC is twofold: it serves as an ecclesiastical body with pastoral authority and has an operational secretariat through which the bps. of Canada act for the good of Church and society. All of its six departments are bilingual, and there is both a French- and an English-speaking general secretary. Headquarters is in Ottawa.

[M. R. BROWN]

CANADIAN COLLEGE (*Pontificio Collegio Canadese*), pontifical seminary for Canadian students in Rome. It was established by Leo XIII in 1888 and raised to the status of a pontifical institute by Pius XI in 1932. It is used only as a residential college for priests engaged in graduate work and is directed by the Sulpician Fathers.

[M. S. J. MCCAREY]

CANADIAN COUNCIL OF CHURCHES, an organization formed in 1944 as an agency for cooperation among member Churches. It is the authorized counterpart in Canada of the *World Council of Churches, and has the same basis for membership, acceptance of "Our Lord Jesus Christ as God and Saviour." Member bodies are the Baptist Federation of Canada, Evangelical United Brethren, Presbyterian Church in Canada, Reformed Episcopal Church, United Church of Canada, Salvation Army, and Society of Friends. The Council has no legislative authority over participating bodies but serves as an instrument for their common interests and concern. Biennial meetings are held; an executive council carries on interim administration of the departments of Christian Education, Ecumenical Affairs, Evangelism, Overseas Missions, and Social Relations. Headquarters are in Toronto, Ontario.

[F. E. MASER]

CANADIAN LUTHERAN COUNCIL, a cooperative agency of Lutherans in Canada. It was organized in 1952 at Winnipeg, when representatives of Canadian Lutheran Churches adopted a constitution modeled on the National Lutheran Council (U.S.A.). The council grew out of the need for cooperation in ministering to military personnel in World War II. The members of the Canadian Council are the American Lutheran Church, the Augustana Lutheran Church, the Evangelical Lutheran Church, the Lutheran Free Church, the United Evangelical Lutheran Church, and the United Lutheran Church in America. The council has five divisions: Canadian Missions, Public Relations, Welfare, Student Service, and War Service. BIBLIOGRAPHY: W. A. Mehlenbacher, EncLuthCh 1:361–362.

[M. J. SUELZER]

CANAL, JOSÉ DE LA (1768–1845), Augustinian historian. After teaching philosophy at Salamanca, Burgos, Toledo, and Madrid, C. collaborated with Antolín Merino, a fellow Augustinian, on volumes 43 and 44 of *España Sagrada,* a collection of documents and researches concerning Spanish ecclesiastical history. Using the archives of Barcelona and Gerona, C. was sole author of volumes 45 and 46, which contained hitherto unpublished documents of the Diocese of Gerona. A noted scholar, C. became director of the Royal Academy of History and was a member of many other scholarly institutions of Spain. BIBLIOGRAPHY: E. de Hinojosa, CE 3:242–243; A. Ortiz, DHGE 11:698–700.

[A. P. HANLON]

CAÑAS Y CALVO, BLAS (1827–86), Chilean priest noted for his love of the poor. Ordained (1849) in Santiago, C. taught at the seminary there. An eloquent preacher, he was also admired for his piety and humility. In 1856 he opened La Casa de Maria, a home for the protection and education of poor girls, and he founded a congregation of nuns to staff it. Later these sisters established other such homes in Santiago and also in Valparaiso and Mendoza (Argentina). Patrocinio de San José, a home for boys, was started by C. in 1872. BIBLIOGRAPHY: C. Fernández Freite, *Don Blas Cañas el Vincente de Paul chileno* (1936).

[A. P. HANLON]

CANDELA, FELIX (1910–), Spanish Mexican creative engineer-architect, esp. noted for daring reinforced concrete shell forms: Cosmic Ray Laboratory, Mexico City (1952) and the Coyoacán Market (1956). C. is comparable in genius to Pier Luigi Nervi.

[M. J. DALY]

CANDIA (CRETE), Mediterranean island and one of the five governments general constituting the nation of Greece. Christianity was introduced to Crete at the time of the Apostles. St. Paul described his voyage along the coast of Crete (Acts 27.7–21) and preached there in 62 or 63 A.D. Titus, his disciple, was the first bp. of the island. Christianity spread rapidly: 8 Cretan bps. participated at the Council of Chalcedon (451) and 11 at the Council of Nicaea II (787). Crete belonged to Illyricum and depended directly on Rome, until 750 when it was annexed to the patriarchate of *Constantinople with Gortyn as the metropolitan see. Crete was occupied by the Mohammedans in 824. Little is known about the period of occupation, and it was not until Nicephore Phocas reconquered the island in 961–962 that details of its history reappear. In 1210 after the Fourth Crusade Crete passed into the hands of the Venetians; its capital became Candia. The Greek bps. were removed and a Latin hierarchy of 11 bps. established. Convents of Fransciscans, Dominicans, and Augustinians were also founded at Candia but the Latin Church in Crete never prospered. The Turks came during the period 1645–69, and they were welcomed first as liberators, but soon manifested themselves as tyrants. The Greek hierarchy was reestablished but without real power; ecclesiastical property was confiscated and churches transformed into mosques.

Crete participated in the Greek insurrection of 1821 which, however, brought massacres and greater restrictions. In the last insurrection (1898) the great European powers forced Turkey to grant autonomy to Crete. The island was united with Greece in 1913. The Orthodox Church of Crete became virtually autonomous in 1900, and the metropolitan see was established at Herakleion (Candia) with seven bishoprics. The bps. are elected by the Synod of Crete which is composed of all the bps. of the island, whose president is the metropolitan. The metropolitan himself is chosen by the patriarch of Constantinople from a list of three names presented to him by the Synod of Crete; this choice must be accepted by the Greek government. In 1970 the adherents of the Orthodox Church numbered about 430,000. There were fewer than 425 RCs, organized into two parishes and served by two priests. BIB-

LIOGRAPHY: H. Leclercq, DACL 3.2:3030–36; M. R. P. McGuire, NCE 4:444–446.

[P. FOSCOLOS]

CANDIDUS, Arian writer of the latter half of the 4th century. C. is the author of a work addressed to Marius Victorinus, *De generatione Verbi* (364) which, together with the reply of Victorinus, can be found in Zeigler's Commentary on Genesis (1548). Another letter to Victorinus is preserved in *Vetera analecta* (4 v., 1675–85) by the Benedictine scholar, Jean Mabillon.

[T. LIDDY]

CANDIDUS (BRUUN) OF FULDA (d. 845), monk, painter, writer. Educated in the school of Alcuin under Einhard, C. wrote a life of St. Eigil in two books, one in prose and the other in verse (PL 105:381–418), important as a source for the history of Fulda. He also composed a work on the passion of Christ (PL 106:57–105). The *Dicta Candidi de imagine Dei,* sometimes attributed to him, may have been the work of Wizo (i.e., Candidus), the Anglo-Saxon friend of Alcuin, with whom Bruun has been confused. BIBLIOGRAPHY: Manitius 1:660–663; Gilson HCP 608; M. Mähler, DSAM 1:1971–72.

CANDLEMAS, the feast celebrated Feb. 2 commemorating the meeting of Simeon and Christ, the presentation of Christ in the temple, and the legal purification of Mary. The feast, mentioned by *Etheria, was observed in Jerusalem in the 4th cent. where it was called *Hypapante, i.e., the feast of the meeting, and was celebrated on Feb. 14, the 40th day of the Epiphany. It was a Christological feast, as it still is in the Byzantine liturgy. Justinian (d. 565) ordered the observance of the feast throughout the empire. It was adopted at Rome perhaps as early as the 6th cent. and it was kept on Feb. 2 because of the acceptance by that time of Dec. 25 as the date of Christmas. Even before the adoption of the feast at Rome a procession of penitential character appears to have been held on Feb. 2; this was probably a Christian replacement for the pagan *amburbale* or *amburbium,* an expiatory procession around the city. The two observances seem to have fused into one, although the procession retained its penitential character as a vestigial remnant of its origin. With Candlemas the Christmas cycle is concluded, the candles of the day symbolizing Christ the light of the world. Before A.D. 700 it was customary for the pope to distribute candles to participants in the Mass and procession. The special blessing of the candles, from which the feast takes its name, was introduced before the 12th century. In Rome and in the W generally the feast took on a Marian character, but its originally Christological nature is apparent in the theme of the present Mass, although the Office and the processional antiphons are Marian. The changes in the rubrics introduced in 1961 suppressed the penitential character of the procession. BIBLIOGRAPHY: Podhradsky 47.

[N. KOLLAR]

CANDLES have various uses in religious services, but because pagans used them in their cult of the dead, the earliest Christians in Rome hesitated to employ them except for the practical purpose of illumination. When it became less urgent to avoid practices with pagan associations, they began to be used for religious purposes. In the 4th cent. they were carried in funeral processions and were burned at martyrs' graves and later before relics and sacred images. Their use at Mass appears to have developed out of the practice of carrying them before church dignitaries, just as torches and fire were carried before persons of high civil rank in their official appearances. Thus about the 7th cent. it was customary to conduct the celebrant to the altar in a procession with candles, and, upon arrival at the altar, the candles were placed around it, and later upon it (although this practice was not universal before the 13th cent.). Not until the 17th cent. was there any general legislation about the number or quality of the candles on the altar at Mass (see CANDLES AT MASS). The candles carried at the Gospel at Mass were intended, like the processional candle, to do honor, in this case to the word of God. The candle is symbolic of Christ the light of the world, as in the Easter Vigil. In other circumstances it has other meanings, not all of which are clearly identifiable. Sometimes it is a sign of joy, at other times a way of showing honor. They are used at baptism, at the anointing of the sick, the Liturgy of the Hours, the churching of women, in certain blessings. Since the later Middle Ages candles have been used as offerings in the ordination rite.

Candles are used in all Eastern liturgies at the altar during divine service and for many sacraments, processions, and other ecclesiastical celebrations. In present Byzantine usage there are no specific rubrics concerning the number of candles to be used during divine services. Invariably Russian churches place a large seven-branched candlestick, reminiscent of the great temple *menorah* and symbolic of the gifts of the Holy Spirit, behind the altar. Often these are the only candles or lamps used, but in some places two additional candles are placed on the altar itself. Among the Greeks, although the seven-branched candlestick is occasionally seen, four or six candles are usually placed on the altar in two double or triple candlesticks. Most Eastern Catholics follow this Greek practice, although the candles are often seen placed in four or six separate candlesticks placed in a row in obvious imitation of the Roman usage. Candles are carried by servers to accompany the Gospel Book at the little entrance of the liturgy and during the singing of the Gospel. During the anaphora a single large candle is placed before the royal doors by the Russians. One or two candles are also placed on the *prothesis table. Congregational candles are carried by the people at baptisms, funerals, on Good Friday and during the Easter service, and for certain other ceremonies. Bishops bless the faithful with candles during the liturgy (see DIKERION and TRIKERION), and votive candles are often obtained by the people at the doors of the church to be lighted and placed before venerated icons.

Candles are used in the C of E, esp. after the Oxford Movement. Lutherans often use them, but other Protestant Churches less frequently. BIBLIOGRAPHY: Podhradsky 47;

J. B. O'Connell, *Church Building and Furnishing* (1955) 208–210; F. Cabrol, DACL 3.2:1613–22.

[N. KOLLAR]

CANDLES, BLESSING OF. A blessing of candles used in the liturgy is obligatory for the Paschal candle and the candles used in the liturgy of Candlemas. There is also a special blessing for candles associated with the feast of St. Blaise. A blessing for candles used in the liturgy has been in the Roman ritual since the 15th century.

[N. KOLLAR]

CANDLES, VOTIVE, candles burned by the faithful before relics, shrines, or images of Christ or of the saints. The practice had an ancient counterpart in (and perhaps developed from) the custom of putting lamps and candles at the graves of the Christian martyrs. The candle in this case is intended as a manifestation of honor which the one who offers it thinks fitting by way of thanksgiving or as an adjunct to petition.

[N. KOLLAR]

CANDLES AT MASS appear to have been originally the candles carried to the altar before the celebrant. Their use at Mass was not obligatory until the 17th century. Since that time two burning candles are required at low Mass, six at a solemn festal Mass, and seven at a festal pontifical Mass when celebrated by the ordinary. The candles used at Mass, like the paschal candle, must be made entirely or at least in major part of beeswax, major part being interpreted to mean 65%. In regions where beeswax is hard to come by, episcopal conferences are empowered to determine what proportion of beeswax is necessary for altar candles.

[N. KOLLAR]

CANFIELD, BENET, see BENEDICT OF CANFIELD.

CANISIUS, HEINRICH (1548–1610), canonist and historian. Born in Nijmegen, C. was a nephew of St. Peter Canisius. He held doctorates in canon and in civil law, taught canon law at Ingolstadt from 1590, and was engaged in research in church history. The published results (1601–08) in the latter field were not systematically arranged and contained many useless documents. Basnage later critically edited the work and published (1725) a revision entitled *Thesaurus monumentorum ecclesiasticorum.* BIBLIOGRAPHY: C. M. Rosen, NCE 3:24; T. Oestrich, CE 3:250.

[J. P. COOKE]

CANISIUS, PETER, ST. (1521–97), Jesuit theologian, writer, educator, pioneer of the Catholic press, Doctor of the Church. A native of Nijmegen, C. entered the Society of Jesus (1543) after making a retreat under Bl. Peter Faber. In 1545, C. was spokesman for the Catholic clergy and citizens of Cologne before Emperor Charles V in their controversy with Abp. Hermann von Wied. Card. Otto Truchsess, Bp. of Augsburg, chose him as his theological consultant at the

Council of Trent. He was summoned to Rome by Ignatius Loyola in 1547 and the following year proceeded to Messina where he taught in the first Jesuit school until 1549, when he made his solemn profession. C. spent the great part of his religious life traveling through Germany, teaching, preaching, writing, and reviving the faith shaken by the German Reformation, esp. in S and W Germany. He was the first superior of the Jesuit German province (1556–62) and continued as provincial of the S German province when that became a separate entity (1562). He promoted the development of colleges at Vienna, Prague, and Ingolstadt, and was influential in establishing other colleges in Munich, Innsbruck, Dillingen, Tyrnau (Trnava), and Hall (Tyrol), as well as other colleges in the N German province. Among his outstanding contributions to Christian doctrine for children and adults are his catechisms which went through innumerable editions down to the 19th century. Following some misunderstanding with his successor in the provincialate, Paul Hoffaeus, regarding his writings against the *Centuriators of Magdeburg, and the then controversial question of moneylending with interest, C. was transferred to Fribourg where he was active in the development of the newly founded college, and there ended his days. He was beatified in 1864, canonized and declared a Doctor of the Church in 1925. BIBLIOGRAPHY: J. Brodrick, *St. Peter Canisius, 1521–97* (1950); Sommervogel 2:617–688.

[M. B. MURPHY]

CANNIBALISM, the practice of eating human flesh. It is derived from the Spanish *canibal*, an altered form of carib, a West Indies tribe. Apart from cases of cannibalism because of hunger, cannibalism or anthropophagy belongs to the phenomenal complex of human sacrifice. However, while human sacrifice points primarily to the act of taking and/or offering life and power, anthropophagy emphasizes the incorporation of life and power. Like human sacrifice the custom has been widespread, and if the interpretation of certain skull findings is correct, already existed in paleolithic times. Cannibalism was often connected with the institutionalization of social tensions between neighboring tribes. Usually the victims were prisoners of war whose bodies or parts of them (organs of power) were eaten within the framework of rituals, often very elaborate and occasionally spread over long periods of time. Apart from assimilating the power of life—the Aztecs spoke of "eating God"—such incorporation might also be interpreted as a protective device against an enemy, since it makes the latter's annihilation final. A special, though less frequent form of anthropophagy is known as endocannibalism, i.e., the consumption of the deceased by his relatives in order to incorporate him into the stream of life. BIBLIOGRAPHY: J. A. MacCulloch, Hastings ERE 3:194–209; G. Hogg, *Cannibalism and Human Sacrifice* (1958); Tannahill, R. *Flesh and Blood: A History of the Cannibal Complex* (1975).

[W. DUPRÉ]

CANNON, JAMES (1864–1944), Methodist bp., pro-

hibitionist. C. was editor of the *Christian Advocate* (1904–18), general superintendent and bp. (1918) of the Methodist Episcopal Church South (1911–19), and supervisor of mission work. He was an important leader in the Anti-Saloon League and head of the World League Against Alcoholism. Prohibitionism and distrust of Roman Catholicism led him to organize the 1928 political campaign in the South against Alfred E. Smith. C.'s latter years were spent in libel suits against newspapers, and in refuting charges of financial mismanagement. BIBLIOGRAPHY: Autobiography, *Bishop Cannon's Own Story* (ed. R. L. Watson, Jr., 1955); *HistAmMeth* III, passim; V. Dabney, *Dry Messiah* (1949).

[H. JACK]

CANO, ALONSO (1601–67), Spanish architect, sculptor, and painter. Influenced by Montañés and with Velasquez trained in painting by Pacheco, C. carved figures for the façade of Granada Cathedral. Though his sculptures have convincing integrity, his paintings are rather sentimental. *The Angel and St. John the Evangelist* (London, 1635) and *Christ Supported by an Angel* (Prado, 1638) are affected though technically excellent. *The Maternity of Mary* and other studies of the Virgin are more satisfying. His polychromed wood sculptures are delicately graceful expressions of holiness (S. Diego de Alcalá, Granada, 1653). Despite his weaknesses C. is an important artist of 17th-cent. Spain. BIBLIOGRAPHY: H. E. Wethey, *Alonso Cano* (1955).

[M. J. DALY]

CANO, MELCHIOR (c. 1505–60), Spanish Dominican theologian whose *De locis theologicis* established the methodological principles of subsequent RC theology, and who is a controversial figure in the history of spirituality. His teaching career began in 1533 at the College of San Gregorio, Valladolid, under Bartolomé de *Carranza; the two became bitter rivals. C. occupied the principal theological chair at Alcalá (1542–46), then as the successor of his master F. de*Vitoria, at Salamanca (1546–52). He was Charles V's theologian at the Council of Trent (1551–52). Nominated as bp. of the Canary Islands in 1552, he resigned the appointment, became rector of San Gregorio in 1553, prior at San Esteban in Salamanca in 1557. He died as provincial of Spain, a post in which he was confirmed only after the death of Pope Paul IV, who had opposed C.'s election for political reasons.

C.'s published academic works include *Relectio de poenitentia,* and *Relectio de sacramentis in genere* (both 1550); in the second he explained the causality of the sacraments by a theory of moral, rather than instrumental causality. The *De locis theologicis* (posthumous, 1563), inspired by de Vitoria, establishes the sources of theological argumentation: its proper sources, Scripture, tradition, authorities—the whole Church, the Councils, the Church at Rome, the Fathers, theologians and jurists; its adapted sources—human reasoning, philosophies, and history (cf. ThAq ST 1a, 1.8 ad 1). In an elegant style, C. discusses each; the plan was proposed for 14 books, but the last two were not completed.

In regard to Christian spirituality, C. considered as unsound emphasis on a universal call to mental prayer or contemplation and deemphasis of asceticism and self-denial. On these grounds he sternly censured Carranza's *Comentarios sobre el catecismo cristiano* (1558), and criticized Louis of Granada, and the *Spiritual Exercises* of St. Ignatius Loyola, esp. in his *La victoria de si mismo* (1550), a translation from Italian of a work on self-conquest through the practice of the virtues, by G. B. *Carioni. C.'s stance was based in part on the Spanish experience of the illuminism of the *Alumbrados, and by fear of the incursion of Lutheranism. BIBLIOGRAPHY: V. Beltrán de Heredia, DSAM 2:73–76; E. Marcotte, *La Nature de la théologie d'après M. Cano* (1945); E. Schillebeeckx, *Revelation and Theology* (tr. N. D. Smith, 1967) 1:223–225.

[T. C. O'BRIEN]

CANON (Gr. *Kanon,* a measuring rod or rule), the term used to designate the core of the Liturgy of the Eucharist, the basic outline of which does not vary. The Roman Canon dates from the end of the 4th cent. but is only one of many Canons found in different rites of Christianity (often under the name anaphora). Among other forms are the anaphora of Hippolytus, the Palaeo-Hispanic anaphora, and the Greek Alexandrine anaphora of St. Basil, as well as the Greek Alexandrine anaphora of St. Mark, and the many Syriac versions. The Roman Canon today reflects those elements common to each anaphora or Canon historically. There are essentially 8 elements: (1) thanksgiving (particularly in the Preface); (2) acclamation (the Sanctus); (3) epiclesis (petition that the gifts be made the body and blood of Christ in consecration); (4) the narrative of the institution by Christ of the Eucharist and the actual repetition in the liturgy; (5) anamnesis (the memorial of Christ's Passion, Resurrection, and Ascension as mandated by Christ; (6) offering (the congregation offers Christ the victim to the Father in the Holy Spirit and through this act offers itself); (7) intercessions (the offering is made in the name of the whole Church, the living and the dead); (8) great doxology (praise to the Trinity, echoed by the "amen" of the faithful). BIBLIOGRAPHY: *Selected Documentation from the New Sacramentary* (U. S. Catholic Conference, 1974); C. Vagaginni, *Canon of the Mass and Liturgical Reform* (1967).

[J. R. AHERNE]

CANON (ART), a basic principle or standard referring to the total aesthetic concept, esp. a law governing the proportions of the human form. In the famous Doryphorus (Spear Bearer (*c.*450–440 B.C.), Polycleitus established a canon (rule, measure) of ideal proportion for the classical human form.

[M. J. DALY]

CANON (ECCL.). (1) a member of a cathedral chapter appointed by the bishop. He has a stall in the cathedral sanctuary and sings the Liturgy of the Hours with the other canons. He has a voice in the cathedral chapter. Residing in the cathedral city, he assists the bp. in the administration of the diocese. Cathedral canons are not found in the U.S. but exist in European countries. (2) A member of a collegiate chapter who assists in the administration of the college. His duties are similar to those of a cathedral canon.

[M. S. J. MC CAREY]

CANON (MUSIC), a compositional device whereby a melody stated in one part is imitated fully in one or more other parts. Most often this imitation occurs within a measure or two of the original statement. Thus in addition to the melodic and harmonic elements, there exist diagonal or canonic relationships between the various parts. Canons are classified, e.g., according to the harmonic intervals between parts, the distance between imitative figures, or the melodic similarities between parts. More particularly, a canon of augmentation or diminution means that the tempo of the original melody is either doubled or halved when it appears in another part. In a canon of inversion, the melody line is turned in the opposite direction. First used in the 13th cent., this style achieved its zenith in the works of Johann Sebastian Bach.

[D. J. SMUCKER]

CANON, BIBLICAL, see BIBLE, CANON OF.

CANON, COADJUTOR, a priest appointed to take over the choir duties of a canon who, because of official business is unable to carry out those duties. The canon coadjutor may succeed to a canonry.

[M. S. J. MC CAREY]

CANON, HONORARY, one who bears the title of a canon. He may wear the dress of a canon, but does not have the rights or duties of a canon; he is a canon in name only.

[M. S. J. MC CAREY]

CANON, LAY, a layman on whom an honorary canonry is conferred by a chapter.

CANON, PONTIFICAL, a liturgical book containing the Ordinary and Canon of the Mass. It is used by bishops, abbots, and protonotaries apostolic.

CANON, PRIVILEGE OF THE, a regulation going back to Lateran Council II in 1139 which prohibits the malicious infliction of real injury upon persons recognized as clerics. Those who perpetrate such injury are declared to be guilty of sacrilege (CIC c. 119). Real injury here is understood as opposed to verbal. It supposes an act or deed issuing in an offense against the body, or liberty, or dignity of the cleric. The law extends this privilege also to religious of either sex, including novices and members of societies without vows (CIC cc. 614 and 680). When the injury involves the malicious use of physical violence, canon law punishes the crime with *ipso facto* excommunication, absolution from which is reserved to the proper ordinary (CIC c. 2345.6).

[J. R. AHERNE]

CANON, TITULAR, a priest who has the honor of a canonry but not necessarily the duties or responsibilities. He is appointed by the bishop. He is a member of the chapter and has a voice in its proceedings.

[M. S. J. MC CAREY]

CANON LAW (EASTERN) The Eastern Churches, Catholic and non-Catholic, do not differ from the Western Church in regarding the Church as a divinely established visible society with legislative authority exercised by the hierarchy. The Churches of the East have given close attention from their beginnings to the enactment and systematic collection of the rules and regulations that compose canon law. During the first millennium of the Christian era, the Byzantine Church evolved necessary legislation; systematic collections of laws were compiled; and commentaries for their explanation were prepared. The great jurists John Zonaras in the 11th cent., Alexis Aristenes in the 12th, and Theodore Balsamon in the 13th, surpassed the contemporary canonists of the W in their scientific method.

The fountainhead of all rules and laws is held to be the divine revelation contained in Sacred Scripture, understood in accordance with the tradition of the Church. The function of interpretation is exercised by the various constitutive sources of canon law: (1) The Roman pontiff, who is recognized as such only by the Catholic Eastern Churches, and whose legislative role has been much reduced by the declaration of Vatican Council II (Vat II EastCath, 5): "that the Churches of the East as much as those of the West fully enjoy the right, and are in duty bound, to rule themselves . . ."; (2) ecumenical synods; (3) ancient local or topical synods; (4) patriarchs, some of whose opinions have been incorporated into canon law; (5) patriarchal and other synods, such as the *synodos endemousa* in Constantinople, composed of the bishops residing in or visiting the city, which greatly influenced Byzantine canon law; (6) liturgical and penitential books, which contain rules regarding worship, fast and abstinence, holy days, sin and penance, external transgressions and punishments; (7) Fathers of the Church, some of whose writings have been accorded legislative authority; (8) custom or unwritten laws, as mentioned at Nicea I (325); (9) canonists, some of whose opinions are regarded as having quasi-legal force; (10) civil law, because of the close relationship of Church and State in Christian countries such as the Byzantine Empire, pre-Soviet Russia, and modern Greece, in which the rules of the Church have often been enforced by civil statutes; (11) the particular legislation that is continually enacted by synods of various Eastern Churches.

Collections of canon law began being made at an early date. These became increasingly systematic, as can be seen in the *Nomocanons. Only in the present century have attempts been made to codify canon law in the East. Instances of such

codification are the Patriarchal Statute of the Russian Church (1918); the codifications of the Serbian Orthodox Patriarchate in Yugoslavia—marriage law (1933), procedural law (1933), and constitution (1931–47). For the Eastern Catholic Churches a complete codification has been prepared, paralleling that of the Latin Code of Canon Law, and four parts of this were promulgated: marriage law (*Crebrae allatae*, 1949); procedural law (*Sollicitudinem nostram*, 1950); law of religious and temporal property (*Postquam apostolicis*, 1952); principles concerning rites, and the law with regard to persons or the Constitution of the Church (*Cleri Sanctitati*, 1957). In the wake of Vatican Council II, however, this codification has been discontinued and one based on the new principles enunciated in the documents of the council, esp. in *Orientalium Ecclesiarum* (1964), is in the making, but without dependence upon the Latin code.

[V. J. POSPISHIL]

CANON LAW, (WESTERN), the norms or rules that are applied to govern the Church as a temporal institution. Its goal is to work with the Holy Spirit to construct and maintain a Christian Church and society which will be conducive to growth in grace and faith, and ultimately, to salvation. Canon law is often called "applied theology," because the implications of belief for life in the Church are explicitly worked out there. Thus specific instructions for the government of the Church, for the proper administration of the sacraments, and for teaching and preaching are provided in canon law.

The sources of ecclesiastical law are diverse. Ideally all law derives from general principles established by God which are accessible through the use of reason or through revelation from God. Once these general principles are known, specific regulations are instituted for particular societies, times, or situations. The law of the Church has been compounded from various traditions, both Christian and non-Christian; it is acceptance by the Roman Church and its bishop that has been decisive in determining which laws and legal principles should be accepted into the body of ecclesiastical law. Holy Scripture is a principal source for canonical precepts. The New Testament provides specific instructions for Christian life and for ordering the Christian community which are of special importance because of their dominical or apostolic origin. The OT also has provided important models for Christian life, although the Christian has been released from the full rigor of the Mosaic law. The great councils of the Church, both ecumenical and provincial, have specifically promulgated canons regulating the life of the Church. Many of these conciliar decrees have been honored by long observance and by papal approbation, and form an important source of canon law. The opinions of the Fathers of the Church have been cited, on account of the great personal authority of their authors, as contributions to the law of the Church. Decretal letters, dispatched by popes to settle specific legal controversies, have been incorporated into canon law because they contain decisions that can be generally applied in similar cases. Finally, the ancient Roman law has been mined by

Christian jurists, and its insights appropriated for Christian use. Today, canon law can be made only by papal decree or by an ecumenical council.

Until the 20th cent., canon law was practiced as a law of precedents (like American law); when a problem arose, lawyers would search the sources for similar problems and their solutions. This soon became an unwieldy task; the sources were often repetitive and sometimes contradictory. Around the year 1140 a monk of the monastery of Camaldoli in Italy, Gratian, helped to correct the situation by compiling in one book the most important texts and precedents for judging every type of canonical case. He called his collection the *Concord of Discordant Canons,* but it is most often referred to simply as Gratian's *Decretum.* Although it was never officially promulgated, the *Decretum* became the accepted source for decision-making in church courts and for legal study at the universities. It was periodically supplemented and brought up to date by official collections of papal decretal letters and conciliar decrees which were called *Libri extravagantium,* because they presented in one place decretals that had previously been in circulation outside Gratian's work. The entire body of canon law or *Corpus iuris canonici,* consisting of the *Decretum* and the decretal collections, was revised in the 16th cent. by a group of legal scholars known as the *Correctores romani,* at the order of the Council of Trent.

At the beginning of this cent., Pope Pius X called for a complete reappraisal of the canon law which would replace the precedent law of the *Corpus iuris canonici* with a new codified law, a *Codex iuris canonici.* The purpose of codification was to clarify the law by unifying the diverse, repetitive, and complex sources into a general statement based on a thorough consideration of the traditions. The code is divided into five books which treat (I) General Norms; (II) Persons (clerics, religious, laity); (III) Things (sacraments; places, forms, and obligations of worship; the teaching office of the Church; ecclesiastical property); (IV) Procedure; (V) Crimes and Penalties. The Code was promulgated in 1917, has been in effect since 1918, and replaces all previous ecclesiastical law. The interpretation of the Code has been entrusted to the Commission for the Authentic Interpretation of the Code of Canon Law.

The Code of Canon Law is binding on all Christians in the Western world over the age of six (There is a separate Code for the Oriental Church). Since it is baptism that incorporates one into the Church, non-Catholic Christians are obligated by the Code, although because of their ignorance of the law they may often be excused from its observance. Individual Christians are also bound by other forms of church law, either territorial or personal. Various territories, dioceses, and religious orders may bind their members to particular laws.

Canon law has as its purpose the good of society as a whole, the good of the entire Church rather than the good of its individual members. For this reason, a Christian may consider that the obligation of positive law does not apply if the law no longer works for the service of the community, or if,

in certain circumstances, the law has become dangerous or unreasonable. BIBLIOGRAPHY: C. H. Lefebvre, NCE 3:29–53; T. L. Bouscaren, *ibid.* 3:973–975; A. Van Hove, *Prolegomena ad codicem iuris canonici* (2d ed., 1945); A. Stickler, *Historia iuris canonici latini* (1950).

[R. A. ARONSTAM]

CANON LAW (REVISION OF) The revision of the CIC was part of the plan of renewal in the Church announced in 1959 by John XXIII when he convoked Vatican Council II. One consequence of the new and optimistic view of the Christian community that issued from the Council was the establishment, March 1963, of a Pontifical Commission for the Revision of the Code of Canon Law (Pontificia Commissio Codicis Iuris Canonici Recognoscendo). The Commission did not begin its work until the beginning of 1966, but since that time has in its regular publication, *Communicationes,* issued its proposals for the future promulgation of a revised Code.

The first phase of the work was completed in 1974. The need for revision is contested by no one. The present Code has been in force since 1918, and reflects concerns and assumptions about the very nature of the Christian community, which need to be modified in the light of post-Vatican II perceptions. Although comprehensive, the Code overemphasizes the hierarchical and juridical nature of the Church to the extent that the dignity and liberty of the individual Christian are placed in jeopardy. Lay people, esp., are viewed as requiring specific instruction in every sphere, since they are seen to lack the capacity for making responsible judgments; on the other hand the legislation gives the impression that the majority in the Church consists of clergy and religious. The tendency of the Code to centralize the administration of the Church has proved unwieldy, often causing delay in the pursuit of justice and unnecessary hardship in the lives of the faithful; it has also made difficult the adaptation of the law to the particular customs or conditions prevailing in any given region of the Church.

In the years immediately following the Council, suggestions for extreme changes in the canon law were frequent. Some experts favored the total abandonment of a codified law, in favor of a law that would be based (like English and American common law) on a system of precedents. Others, while favoring the retention of a revised Code, thought that this Code ought to be viewed as serious advice to the conscience, rather than as law with the authority to compel obedience. These suggestions have been set aside, however, and the Commission has proceeded to a reconsideration of the law that is based on the form of the present Code.

The commission has prepared a *Lex fundamentalis,* a kind of constitutional law of the Church and schemata on the various Books of the existing CIC with revisions proposed for consultation. The revision includes removal of purely dogmatic statements and exclusion of liturgical laws. The new Code will nevertheless be far more flexible than that which it will replace. Consciousness of the need for continuing revision has altered the concept of the law as absolutely fixed (although the principles behind the law remain constant). The need for allowance or regional differences has been fully recognized, and the practice of consultation in making law has been established.

Perhaps the most significant changes that have been proposed and set forth in the *Communicationes* are those that deal with the position of the laity within the Church, a subject on which the Code is virtually silent. In keeping with the Constitution on the Church of Vatican II, all the People of God are seen as full, equal, and responsible members of Christ's body; their baptism calls them to lead a perfect Christian life (although clergy and religious are still reminded of a particular form of duty to pursue Christian perfection). Within the established doctrine of the Church and the guidance of their pastors, lay people are encouraged even to study, to teach, and to write in the sacred sciences. The general tenor of the proposed revisions is to preserve the spirit of the Code, but to allow the greatest possible latitude in practices that honor that spirit (e.g., the principle of penitential fasting is approved, but the way in which it is to be observed is not prescribed). Greater emphasis will be placed on local authorities within the Church, and the reservation of cases to Rome will become less common. The draft of a new penal law corresponding to Book V of the CIC indicates a more pastoral and merciful trend in the conception of remedial and punitive measures in the Church (see PENAL POWER OF THE CHURCH).

The revised Code of Canon Law has not yet been completed or promulgated, and until this is done, the present period of experimentation and consultation in the Church's law will continue. BIBLIOGRAPHY: T. J. Green, "Revision of the Code: The First Decade," *Jurist* 36 (1976) 353–441.

CANON PENITENTIARY, a member of a cathedral chapter who is appointed and acts as a confessor for the diocese. He has the power to absolve the sins and censures reserved to the bishop. He may even absolve members of his diocese when out of the diocese. There should be a confessional reserved for his use in the cathedral church.

[M. S. J. MCCAREY]

CANON TABLES, a design developed in the 4th cent. by Eusebius of Caesarea, correlating the Four Gospels in parallel form. In medieval times illuminators set these columns in ornamented architectural frames. BIBLIOGRAPHY: C. R. Morey, *Medieval Art* (1942).

[M. J. DALY]

CANON 28 OF CHALCEDON, the most controversial disciplinary Canon of the Council. With the Emperor and Senate in residence, Constantinople was the new Rome of the East in civil matters. Therefore the Council thought it should equal the old Rome in matters ecclesiastical. Canon 28 declared Constantinople a patriarchate equal to Rome in jurisdiction of the East, e.g., consecration of the metropoli-

tans of the civil dioceses of Pontus, Asia Minor, and Thrace, and reaffirmed its primacy of honor second only to Rome which had been granted by Canon 3, Council of *Constantinople I (381). The Roman legates objected on the grounds that it violated Canons 6 and 7 of the Council of *Nicaea (325) which determined the jurisdiction of the patriarchates of Rome, Alexandria, and Antioch, and was at variance with the prerogatives of the bp. of Rome as outlined in their instructions from Leo. Despite these objections of the papal legates, the canon was included in the acts of the Council. In 453, Leo declared it null and void for the same reasons. However, the patriarchs of Constantinople and the emperors continued to regard it as valid. From this time on, the primacy of Constantinople became the symbol and the actual center for jurisdiction in the Eastern Church. BIBLIOGRAPHY: Bihlmeyer-Tüchle 1:111–117; 308–311; R. Sellars, *Council of Chalcedon* (1953). *CONSTANTINOPLE, PATRIARCHATE OF.

[F. H. BRIGHAM]

CANONESSES (1) the name given to those women, widows and virgins, who desired religious life but for some reason were unable to follow the rules of the established communities. They followed a milder rule and were allowed to keep property. These communities were not sanctioned by Rome but received wholehearted support from many rulers whose relatives were or might some day seek sanctuary there. During the Reformation many canonesses followed the lead of their relatives and became members of Protestant sects. (2) Those women who in the Middle Ages adopted the dress and rule of monasteries of canons. *CANONESSES REGULAR.

[M. S. J. MC CAREY]

CANONESSES REGULAR, communities of nuns associated historically with *canons regular. Of diverse origin, the typical beginnings were rooted in double monasteries, one for men, the other for women, which arose in the 11th and 12th centuries. They followed the same rule as the canons and wore a similar habit, usually white. Contemplatives like the Carmelites, the canonesses were attached to independent houses rather than congregations. Most famous in the Middle Ages were those of St.-Victor and Ste.-Geneviève in Paris and Windesheim in the Netherlands. Today the canonesses are organized in these congregations: Canonesses of Windesheim, Canonesses of the Congregation of Notre Dame, Missionary Canonesses of St. Augustine, and a number of independent houses. Most of the groups are engaged in active apostolates. BIBLIOGRAPHY: T. Torquebiau, DDC 3:448–500.

[J. R. AHERNE]

CANONICAL HOURS, ROMAN, times set for the recitation of common liturgical prayer, formerly called the Divine Office, now designated as the Liturgy of the Hours. The custom of allocating prayer to fixed times, an inheritance from Judaism, became widely practiced in the 4th cent. in larger churches. The monastic tradition gave the Hours the form they were to retain until Vatican Council II. Matins were recited in the monasteries at 2 A.M., Lauds at 6 A.M., Prime and Terce before the community Mass, Sext and None were midday prayers, Vespers the evening Hour, Compline night prayer. Psalms formed the bulk of the prayer, with readings, responses, and a prayer of the day. In private recitation, some distribution according to the time of day was recommended but not mandatory. The new liturgy provides a different scheme: Lauds to be recited in the morning and Vespers in the evening. The Office of Readings (formerly called Matins) is properly nocturnal but may be recited at any hour. The Middle Readings (prayer at mid-day) are preserved in the monastic tradition, one Hour being prescribed for those outside that tradition. BIBLIOGRAPHY: A. Bugnini, *General Instruction on the Liturgy of the Hours* (1971).

[J. R. AHERNE]

CANONICALS (1) those vestments prescribed by law or canon to be worn at Mass or other religious functions. (2) An examination prescribed by canon law for the clergy.

[M. S. J. MC CAREY]

CANONICITY, the status attributed to all the sacred writings contained within the authorized collection or *canon of Holy Scripture. Jewish and Christian tradition agree that canonicity presupposes the divine inspiration of the canonical book. The canon of the Hebrew Bible became fixed on the basis of long-standing use and tradition. The Christian canon also was based on acceptance in the Church. Canonicity in RC teaching, however, rests on the authoritative recognition by the Church that a book is inspired and part of the canon (D 1501–04; 3006). For Protestants and other Christians canonicity is determined by Jewish and Christian tradition, apostolic authorship, the power of the book to communicate religious experience. BIBLIOGRAPHY: R. Murphy et al., "Symposium on the Canon of Scripture," CBQ 28 (1966) 189–207; J. C. Turro and R. Brown, JBC 2:515–534.

[T. C. O'BRIEN]

CANONIZATION (EASTERN CHURCHES). Churches of the East have evolved the same theological premises as the West concerning the veneration of saints, the value of their intercession with God, and have therefore also adopted procedures to ascertain which former members of the Church on earth deserve such a cult, although the pertinent regulations are much less elaborate than those of the Roman Church. In the medieval Byzantine and Russian Churches the veneration of saints was accorded by the spontaneous decision of the faithful or by the decree of any bishop. After the 14th cent. the right of declaring somebody a saint was reserved to the metropolitan of Moscow. After the abolition of the patriarchate under Peter the Great (1714), a canonization decided by the Holy Synod had to be confirmed by the tsar. A similar procedure is followed by other Orthodox Churches, esp. the Patriarchate of Constantinople. A conspicuous feature of the solemn rite of canonization is the last memorial service celebrated for the repose of the soul of the respective saint,

which is then followed at once by a service in his honor. There are no classes of persons in these categories recognized in the Latin Church: servant of God, venerable, and blessed. Saints may be canonized because of such social virtues as martyrdom in order to avoid civil strife (e.g., SS Boris and Hlib-Gleb), distinguished performance as rulers, etc. BIBLIOGRAPHY: N. Golubinski, *History of the Canonization of Saints in the Russian Church* (2d ed., 1903); J. Bois, *Canonisation dans l'Église Russe,"* DTC 2.1:1659–72.

[V. J. POSPISHIL]

CANONIZATION AND BEATIFICATION, (WESTERN CHURCH), the processes by which the RC Church publicly honors and upholds for veneration a person who has lived an extraordinarily holy life and/or has been martyred for the faith. A papal decree of beatification simply permits public veneration of that person for a specified territorial region or religious order, and allows for a Mass and Office in his honor although a blessed may not be the titular patron of a church. Canonization mandates public veneration throughout the universal Church, and is a definitive, irrevocable judgment that an individual is among the saints of God. The procedures for canonization and beatification have changed significantly in the Church's history. In the first centuries of the Christian era, the martyrs were regarded as having attained the height of Christian virtue and, through their martyrdom, to be indubitably united with Christ. Under the constant threat of similar persecution, the Christian community felt a strong communion with these martyrs, exalted them as models of dedicated Christianity, perceived the value of their intercession, and commemorated them in the Mass. With the end of the Roman persecutions, different norms for Christian sanctity naturally emerged and, since canonization can be demonstrably linked with the virtues held in highest regard by the believing community at any particular time, different classes of saints come to be venerated. Thus those who had strongly and perceptively defended the faith (confessors and doctors), or who had lived highly ascetical lives (monks and hermits), or who had been great bishops or missionaries came to be regarded as saints. From the 6th to the 10th cent., the number of saints so venerated increased significantly. The connection between sanctity and the performance of miracles became strong, the liturgical calendar became crowded with saints' commemorations, and some abuses regarding the number of saints, the norms for judging miracles, and the quality of heroic virtue became evident. Intervention by the local bishop became necessary, and a fairly uniform procedure was adopted: a biography and description of the miracles attributed to a person who had come to be venerated by the faithful were presented to the bishop for his judgment. After the 10th cent. these episcopal judgments were submitted to the pope for his approval, solemn declaration of canonization, and extension of veneration to the universal Church. The first record of such a papal declaration was in 973, but by 1234 Pope Gregory IX made the practice of papal investigation and certification the only legitimate procedure. As a consequence of this centralization, canonization enjoyed a greater juridical value and the processes whereby it was decided upon became much more specific and precise. Thus Pope Sixtus V in 1588 established the Congregation of Rites and assigned it a twofold function: the regulation of the Latin liturgy and the evaluation of causes submitted for canonization. In his still significant *De servorum Dei beatificatione et beatorum canonizatione,* Benedict XIV (pontificate 1740–1758) explicited the procedures and norms necessary for a papal decree of canonization. In 1914 Pius X divided the Congregation of Rites into two distinct sections corresponding to its two responsibilities, and a further reorganization was effected by Paul VI in 1969 when he established two separate congregations: the Congregation for Divine Worship and the Sacred Congregation for the Causes of Saints.

The procedure leading to beatification and canonization is complex and lengthy, although it has been somewhat simplified by Paul VI in his motu proprio *Sanctitas clarior* (AAS 61 [1969] 149–53). Previously the procedure began when a local bishop gathered information about the individual in question, collecting evidence of his reputation for sanctity and the facts upon which that reputation was based. This evidence was sent to the Congregation of Rites which conducted its own investigation that was then defended by a postulator from the congregation and an advocate of the cause. The promoter-general of the faith questioned the cause, and these deliberations were submitted to the members of the congregation. If the case was deemed worthy of further inquiry, the pope decreed the introduction of the cause. The postulator, advocate and promoter of the faith further examined the cause before three separate groups: theological advisers, prelates, and the cardinals of the Congregation of Rites. If the cause successfully passed these discussions, the pope decreed that the servant of God is blessed (in the case of a martyr) or venerable (in the case of a nonmartyr). The beatification of a nonmartyr requires the authentication of at least two miracles performed upon the invocation of his name. This authentication of miracles requires strict scientific and medical evidence in addition to the evidence of heroic sanctity previously demanded. After beatification, evidence of new miracles—seen as divine confirmation of sanctity—is required before a person is canonized as a model of Christian virtue for the whole Church.

The 1969 reforms of Paul VI give greater responsibility and power to the local ordinary and/or the territorial conference of bishops. Whereas previously there were two processes to gather evidence—one by the local bishop and the other by the Congregation of Rites—a concerted procedure is now followed. After consulting with the Holy See, the local bishop within his jurisdiction may introduce a cause for canonization. After the evidence has been submitted to the Sacred Congregation for the Causes of Saints, any further clarifications may be effected either by the congregation or the local bishop. In order to discharge its new responsibilities more competently, the national episcopal conference has the right to erect a special territorial tribunal to examine cases that might lead to canonization. BIBLIOGRAPHY: Pope Paul's Apostolic Constitution *Sacra Rituum Congregatio,* in *The Pope Speaks* 14 (1969) 174–180; A. E. Green, NCE 3:55–61; P. Hebblethwaite, "The Meanings of Canonization," *Month* 2(1970) 101–105.

[T. M. MCFADDEN]

CANONS OF DORT, the five "heads of doctrine" issued by the Synod of Dort (1619) against *Arminianism. A technical and scholastic presentation of Calvinist doctrine on predestination and grace, they became normative for many *Reformed Churches. *DORT, SYNOD OF.

[T. C. O'BRIEN]

CANONS REGULAR, priests who live in a community under rules, bound by vows. They sing the Liturgy of the Hours and live a life similar to that of monks; however, unlike the monk, holy orders is essential to their institutes. Their origin is uncertain, although some authorities (Pope St. Pius V) have traced them to the common life of the Apostles. It was not until the 11th cent. that their gradual development reached its full strength. Examples of canons regular are *Canons Regular of St. Augustine, and the Crosier Fathers. BIBLIOGRAPHY: J. C. Dickinson, *Origin of the Austin Canons and their Introduction into England* (1950).

[C. KEENAN]

CANONS REGULAR OF PRÉMONTRÉ, see PREMONSTRATENSIANS.

CANONS REGULAR OF ST. AUGUSTINE, or Austin Canons, a religious family, dedicated to church worship and consequently to pastoral service, in which the full common life is led and which is essentially clerical rather than monastic by profession. The recommendations of St. Augustine provide the model, his brief Rule, the practical injunctions that could be adapted to a variety of customs in different periods and regions. A continuous history can be traced from Italy and S France in the 11th century. The movement was approved, 1059, and promoted by Hildebrand, as part of his policy of clerical reform; it spread N and came to England and Ireland in the 12th century. The houses followed a wide range of observances, drawn from Carolingian canonical institutions, as well as from Benedictine, Camaldolese, Vallambrosan, and Cistercian customs. They tended to be unified with the formation of provincial congregations, and in 1339 Benedict XII promulgated a common code for the order in the bull *Ad decorem.*

In the Middle Ages their importance was second to that of the monks, and later to that of the friars. But the abbey of St. Victor, founded by Abelard's teacher, *William of Champeaux, rose together with the Univ. of Paris, and was illustrious for its theological writers. A notable feature was the connection of houses with hospitals, those of the Great St. Bernard, and St. Bartholomew's and St. Thomas's in London. The *Premonstratensian Canons showed great vitality from the first. The Congregation of Windesheim founded under the influence of Gerard Groote in 1386 numbered Thomas à Kempis among its members. The Canons Regular of the Lateran, confirmed 1421, are active in Cornwall, England, while the most recent congregation, the Canons Regular of the Immaculate Conception, founded in 1871, represent an adaptation of the clerical common life to modern conditions.

[T. GILBY]

CANONS REGULAR OF THE IMMACULATE CONCEPTION, see CANONS REGULAR OF ST. AUGUSTINE.

CANONS REGULAR OF THE LATERAN, see CANONS REGULAR OF ST. AUGUSTINE.

CANOPIC JAR, one of four vases named from the site Canopus in ancient Egypt, used for entrails of the deceased, having lids in the forms of heads (hawk, dog, ape, man) of the four sons of the god Horus. These jars are differentiated from the terra cotta "canopic" cinerary urns of the Etruscans containing remains of the dead—earlier placed in a simple pit. Later Etruscan urns (c. 700 B.C.) made in human shapes, with body markings and with portrait heads of the deceased as lids, were raised on a seat or thronelike shape.

[M. J. DALY]

CANOPY, see BALDACHINO.

CANOSA CATHEDRAL, 12th-cent. Italian church dedicated to St. Sabinus, in the Latin cross plan, having an Eastern note in five large domes (26 feet in diameter) over bays of the nave and transept. BIBLIOGRAPHY: A. Petrucci, *Cattedrali di Puglia* (1960).

[M. J. DALY]

CANOSSA, a village in the Emilia Province of N Italy which contains the ruins of the castle where Emperor *Henry IV in 1077 made his humiliating submission to Pope *Gregory VII and performed public penance. Bismarck in 1871 used the phrase "going to Canossa" as a contemptuous expression for humble submission.

[S. F. JOHNSON]

CANOSSA, MADDALENA GABRIELLA BL. (1774–1835) foundress. A descendant of the celebrated Matilda, Countess of Tuscany and friend of Pope Gregory VII, the future marchioness had an unhappy childhood and a sickly adolescence. She entered the Carmelite convent but soon left. On a visit to Verona Napoleon Bonaparte acceded to her request to take over the empty convent of St. Joseph in Verona with the purpose of aiding the poor and taking care of neglected children. In 1808 C. and a few companions opened a house for poor girls in the slums of Verona. The community which she founded under the title of Sisters of Charity (Canossians) grew, and new foundations were established all over N Italy. Her own interior life was intense but never interfered

with her apostolic work among children. She was beatified in 1941. BIBLIOGRAPHY: Butler 2:309–311; N. Del Re, Bibl-Sanct 3:751–753; P. Pieri, DSAM 2.1:85–86.

[J. R. AHERNE]

CANOVA, ANTONIO (1757–1822), Italian sculptor. Traveling from Venice to Rome, C. executed the tomb for Clement XIII (1787–95) followed by the "Roman" portraits of Napoleon (1810) and George Washington (1820, later destroyed). Foremost of neoclassical sculptors, C. in his sensuous Venus (Pauline Borghese) relates to David and Ingres, and further, influenced the Danish master, A. B. Thorvaldsen. BIBLIOGRAPHY: A. Chastel, *Italian Art* (1963).

[M. J. DALY]

CANTARINI, SIMONE (1612–48), Italian painter and engraver. C. painted at Pesaro (1639) the *Virgin, Child and Saints* and *St. Peter Healing the Cripple,* with the realism of Caravaggio, and *Rest on Flight into Egypt* in an early eclectic style anticipating late 17th-cent. Bolognese painting.

[M. J. DALY]

CANTERBURY, ANCIENT SEE OF, the primary see of England. In 597 Pope Gregory the Great sent a group of Benedictine monks, headed by Augustine, to convert the Anglo-Saxons. Ethelbert, King of Kent, gave them a place to live in Canterbury and permission to preach. Augustine founded a Benedictine monastery and later set up Christchurch Cathedral of which he became the first archbishop. From this beginning Christianity spread throughout England.

[M. T. GRIFFIN]

CANTERBURY PSALTER, early 8th-cent. MS combining classical figurative scenes (modified by Byzantine Oriental style) with interlaced patterns, whirling triskeles, and confronted monsters (derivatives of Celtic and Germanic *bestiaries) and of Mesopotamian-Persian *animal style. Succeeding the Irish missionaries, Anglo-Saxon Benedictine monks (particularly *Alcuin) as the 8th-cent. nucleus of the Carolingian elite, effected a wide diffusion of Celtic-Germanic interlace, which later influenced Romanesque and Gothic decorative motifs.

[M. J. DALY]

CANTERBURY TALES, THE, one of the great poems of the English language. In its way a flowering of the late Middle Ages and early Renaissance, the Canterbury Tales is a rich and varied picture of English life in the 14th century. Geoffrey Chaucer used the popular pilgrimage to the tomb of St. Thomas à Becket as the framework of his long poem. His original design would have had each pilgrim tell two stories on the way to Canterbury and two on the return to London. Actually only 22 of a possible 120 stories were completed. The poem is notable for its penetrating psychology, its rich characterization, and its blending of story and storyteller. The tales illuminate our understanding of the narrator. The work is distinguished by poetic power, humor, compassion, and above all a realism that accepts good and bad for what they are. BIBLIOGRAPHY: D. R. Howard, *Idea of the Canterbury Tales* (1975); G. K. Chesterton, *Chaucer* (1973).

[J. R. AHERNE]

CANTICLE, hymns in the RC and Anglican liturgies, comprising a scriptural text found elsewhere than in the Psalms. Canticles fall into two categories: *cantica majora* come from the NT, *cantica minora* from the OT. According to the Roman rite three major canticles are used each day: the Benedictus or Canticle of Zachary (Lk 1.68–79) used at Lauds; the Magnificat or Canticle of the Blessed Virgin Mary (Lk 1.46–55) used at Vespers; the Nunc Dimittis or Canticle of Simeon (Lk 2.29–32), used at Compline. The Roman rite uses numerous minor canticles as the fourth of the psalm-elements of Lauds. They include texts, slightly altered, from Ex 15, 1–18; Dt 32.1–43; 1 Sam 2.1–10; 1 Chr 29.10–13; Tob 13.1–8; Jdt 16.13–17; Sir 1.1–13; Is 20.1–6; Is 45.15–25; Is 38.10–20; Jer 31.1–14; Dan 3.52–88; Hab 2–19.

[D. J. SMUCKER]

CANTICLE OF ANNA, song of Hannah (Anna) expressing her reaction to God's gift of the child Samuel (1 Sam 2.1–10). Though set in a prose book, it is in poetic form and generally considered by scholars to be later than the material of its context. A song of thanksgiving, it became the model for the *Magnificat. It has been used as a hymn in Christian worship, in the RC liturgy appearing in the second Lauds of Wednesday. OT scholars suggest that the song was probably an expression of national thanksgiving, with the "I" referring to the nation personified, as well as to the individual worshiper.

[T. EARLY]

CANTICLE OF CANTICLES (Lat. *Canticum canticorum*), the OT book called also the *Song of Solomon or Song of Songs. The title reflects the Hebrew superlative, i.e., that this is the greatest of all songs.

[T. C. O'BRIEN]

CANTICLE OF MIRIAM, probably identical with the ancient Canticle of *Moses (Ex 15:1–21), though some authorities would confine this to verses 1–18, the Canticle of Miriam proper being comprised by verses 19–21.

[D. J. BOURKE]

CANTICLE OF OUR LADY, the song found in Lk 1.46–55 and popularly known as the Magnificat after the first word in the Vulgate translation. Several Old Latin MSS attribute it to Elizabeth, and some modern scholars have adopted this view. The majority of ancient witnesses, however, as well as the majority of modern critics, ascribe it to Mary. In structure, theme, and phrasing the song relies heavily on the Song of Hannah in 1 Sam 2.1–10, with many reminiscences of the Psalms and other OT poetry. The themes

they express in common are the manifestation of God's power, holiness, and goodness; his predilection for the poor and his judgment of the rich; and hope in his redemption of his people. It is unlikely, though not impossible, that the hymn represents Mary's own words. There is no specific reference to the birth of the Messiah, the angel's message, or the words of Elizabeth. If it is detached from its context, verse 56 follows logically on verse 45. It is more probably a composition of early Palestinian Christianity used by Luke because it was a suitable expression of the sentiments of Mary. Some modern scholars believe that it arose in a circle associated with John the Baptist where it conveyed a future hope of redemption. Luke's understanding would be that of the fulfillment of this hope in the coming of Christ. BIBLIOGRAPHY: J. T. Forestell, "Old Testament Background of the Magnificat," *Marian Studies* 12 (1961) 205–244.

[M. A. MC NAMARA]

CANTICLE OF SIMEON, poetic statement of Simeon upon seeing the infant Jesus in the temple (Lk 2.25–32; the canticle comprises verses 29–32). Simeon is not otherwise known, and scholars suggest Luke has placed in his mouth a liturgical hymn of the early Church. The canticle has been in daily use at least since the 4th cent. as a part of Christian worship. It is used in the RC liturgy each day at Compline and in the Orthodox Church at Vespers. The Anglican Book of Common Prayer includes it in the Evensong liturgy. It is also known as the Nunc Dimittis from its opening words in the Latin version.

[T. EARLY]

CANTICLE OF THE SUN, a hymn of joy and praise to God for the glories of creation. It was composed by St. Francis of Assisi, supposedly in 1225 in the garden of San Damiano in Assisi. The hymn contains the quintessence of Francis' message: that the love of God flows into all creatures, filling them with divine goodness. Its title is derived from the second stanza: "Be thou praised, my Lord, with all thy creatures, above all Brother Sun."

[T. M. MC FADDEN]

CANTICLE OF THE THREE CHILDREN (Song of the Three Young Men), song of Shadrach, Meshach, and Abednego in the fiery furnace. Dating from *c.*150–50 B.C., the passage is not included in the MT, but in the LXX and Vulg is placed along with the Prayer of Azariah (Abednego) after Dan 3.23, forming verses 24–90. The canticle proper consists of 3.52–88, divided into two hymns: 3.52–57 and 3.57–88. Also known as Benedicite Dominum, from the opening words of the Latin version, it is accepted as canonical by the RC Church, which uses it at Lauds on Sunday, but it is relegated to the Apocrypha by Protestants.

[T. EARLY]

CANTICLE OF ZECHARIAH, poetic passage attributed to Zechariah upon the birth of his son John the Baptist (Lk

1.68–79). It is also known as the Benedictus from the opening word of the Latin version. According to Luke, Zechariah was ''filled with the Holy Spirit and prophesied'' when he uttered the song (1.67). He had been unable to speak after he had questioned the angel's announcement that his wife Elizabeth would have a son (1.18–20). Verses 68–75 praise God for fulfilling the messianic hope in the birth of the forerunner; the concluding verses are addressed to the child. The canticle is included in numerous Church liturgies.

[T. EARLY]

CANTICLES, BIBLICAL, liturgical hymns, other than Psalms, taken from the Bible. Possibly borrowed from Jewish worship, they have had a place in Christian worship since the early centuries of the Church. The RC Church uses several OT canticles, such as the *Canticle of Anna (1 Sam 2.1–10) and the Canticle of Jeremiah (31.10–14) at Lauds, varying from day to day. And it uses three NT canticles in the Liturgy of the Hours each day; those of Zechariah (Lk 1. 68–79; *Benedictus*), Mary (Lk 1.46–55; *Magnificat*), and Simeon (Lk 2.29–32; *Nunc Dimittis*). Biblical canticles are also widely used in the liturgies of other churches.

[T. EARLY]

CANTILENA, often used as a substitute for *cantabile,* a musical term with three meanings: (1) In general, it refers to a vocal or instrumental line of a lyrical nature. (2) In medieval writings it refers to secular vocal compositions. (3) It refers to a composition style developed in 14th- and 15th-cent. Europe. This style, found in some of the sacred motets and Masses of G. de *Machaut, was characterized by an upper vocal part and two lower instrumental parts.

[D. J. SMUCKER]

CANTOR, a leader in the choir at liturgical services whose duty is to intone hymns, Psalms, antiphons, etc. Originally this function was performed by the presiding minister, the deacon, or the lector, but in the 4th cent., as the music became more complex and difficult and as the desire grew for more splendor in the liturgy, this role began to be entrusted to specially trained individuals distinct from the celebrating officials. Until the clef came into use in the 11th cent., the cantor was expected to have his repertory by heart. In the East the cantor and the deacon were usually the same person. BIBLIOGRAPHY: S. Corbin, NCE 3:71.

CANTOR IN SYNAGOGUE SERVICE, the official of a Jewish synagogue whose function is to lead the congregation in prayer and singing. Formerly the cantor was the chief agent of the synagogue congregation. His duties included supervising the maintenance of the synagogue facilities. In the liturgy he was charged with taking the scrolls of the Scriptures from the Ark, pointing out to the readers the passages to be recited, and returning the texts to their place. Gradually the cantor's function became more associated with music, even the composing of melodies for the various feasts. This is his chief role

now: to lead the musical portion of the synagogal liturgy, in cooperation with the rabbi whose role includes reading the Scripture, preaching, and giving religious instructions. BIBLIOGRAPHY: I. Elbogen, UnivJewishEnc 3:17–18.

[T. CRANE]

CANTU, CAESARE (1804–95), historian. When his father died, leaving a large family, C. gave up teaching to become a professional writer. As a writer he displayed unbelievable energy. The bulk of his work is historical, starting with works on his own area, N Italy, and culminating in his most famous work, *Storia universale,* a 35-volume history, which went through 40 editions. As a historian he is not totally objective but the monumental universal history is clear and generally balanced. C. was a friend and advocate of Manzoni, the novelist and patriot. In 1833 as a result of his book on Manzoni he was imprisoned by the Austrians for a year in Milan. During that time and in spite of overwhelming difficulties he wrote the novel *Margherita Pusteria,* a historical narrative of religious persecution. It went through 36 editions.

[J. R. AHERNE]

CANTWELL, JOHN JOSEPH (1874–1947), first abp. of Los Angeles, California. Born in Ireland, he studied for the priesthood there and was ordained in 1899. He came to the U.S. and labored in the San Francisco area until 1917 when he was appointed bp. of Monterey-Los Angeles, a diocese that stretched from the Monterey area to the Mexican border. In 1936 he became the first metropolitan of the new Province of Los Angeles. He administered an archdiocese undergoing spectacular growth, founding parishes, building elementary and secondary schools, bringing into the area 56 religious communities, and showing special concern for minority groups. Two outstanding achievements of C.'s were the securing of released time for Catholic children in public schools and the establishment of the Legion of Decency. BIBLIOGRAPHY: J. B. Code, *Dictionary of American Hierarchy* (1940).

[J. R. AHERNE]

CANUTE (Cnute; *c.* 995–1035), **KING OF ENGLAND** from 1016 **AND DENMARK** from 1018. Son of Sweyn Forkbeard, C. warred against Ethelred II and Edmund Ironside, becoming king of all England after Edmund's death (1016). Sole king of Denmark after 1018, C. gained Norway through war and intrigue. He was a munificent benefactor of the Church. BIBLIOGRAPHY: L. M. Larson, *Canute the Great, 995–1035* (1912, repr. AMS).

[W. A. CHANEY]

CANUTE IV, ST., KING OF DENMARK (*c.* 1043–86), grandnephew of Canute the Great, natural son of Sweyn II Estrithson, who had founded a Scandinavian kingdom on feudal and European lines following the dissolution of Canute the Great's empire after his death. Canute IV was an energetic ruler who continued the reorganization of his father's kingdom according to Hildebrandine models. He was slain before the altar in a church in which he had taken refuge during a revolt of the independent aristocracy. Because of his reputation for sanctity and miracles at his tomb at Odense—a monastery of English Benedictines he had founded—he was canonized in 1099 by Paschal II. He was the father, by his marriage with Adela (a Flemish princess) of Bl. Charles the Good, Count of Flanders. BIBLIOGRAPHY: A. L. Sibilia, BiblSanct 3:755–757; Butler 1:121.

CANUTE LAVARD, ST. (*c*. 1096–1131), son of King Erik Evergood of Denmark. Having learned the arts of war and government in Germany, C. distinguished himself in battle, was made duke of Schleswig and later prince of the Wends, in which position he was a vassal of the Emperor, who conferred on him the title of king. The justice and effectiveness of his rule made him popular with the people, but his German manners and ideas gave offense to some of the nobles. In particular, Magnus, son of King Niels, hated him as a probable obstacle to his own succession to his father's crown. With the help of his brother, Magnus slew C. in the forest of Haraldsted, near Ringsted. Waldemar I, C.'s son, secured his father's canonization from Alexander III (1170). Butler thinks "dynastic hero" describes him better than "martyr," as he is officially classified. BIBLIOGRAPHY: A. L. Sibilia, BiblSanct 3:753–755; Butler 1:49.

CAODAISM, a politico-religious movement developed by Le Van Trung in South Vietnam about 1920 and officially declared a formal religion in 1926. At that time Caodaism had 28 leaders and 247 adherents. The sect believes and preaches the principal founders of all religions as incarnations of the one Supreme God (Cao-Dai). It is primarily a syncretic movement and claims to sum up and surpass all the local religions as well as to draw on all the major religions, Islam excepted. From Catholicism it has adopted not only the ideal of universal love but also hierarchical organization, with the addition of female cardinals. It venerates as saints such personages as Sun-yatsen, Churchill, the Vietnamese prophet Trang-Trinh, St. Joan of Arc; Victor Hugo, Buddha, Christ, and Confucius. As a political group, the Caodaists favored the Progressive Forces Alliance, an opposition party, but under the Diem government it lost interest in politics and progressed only as a religion. In 1969 Caodaism claimed nearly 3 million adherents, and in the mid-1970s, about 2 million. The principal Cao-Dai shrine is located 60 miles NW of Saigon at Tay-Ninh, the seat of its cathedral and administration. BIBLIOGRAPHY: E. Thiel et al., StL 8:266–275; P. Gheddo, *Cross and the Bo-Tree* (tr. C. U. Quinn, 1970) 174–175.

[R. A. TODD]

CAOINE, (pronounced keen), an ancient Irish dirge sung by the village bard. Similar to the coronach, the Scottish counterpart, it was sung when a chief or prominent person died. The bard would intone the *caoine,* recounting the virtues and heroic deeds of the deceased. It was performed in a highly emotional setting, women often interrupting the *caoine* with loud ritual wailing. A biblical example of a similar ritual can be found in Jer 9.17.

[D. J. SMUCKER]

CAPPACCINI, FRANCESCO (1784–1845), cardinal, papal diplomat. Ordained in 1807, he was secretary to Card. Consalvi, papal secretary of state, then engaged successively in other areas of Vatican affairs, particularly those questions pertaining to the Low Countries. He was one of the signers of the Concordat of 1827 made with the Kingdom of the Netherlands. From Brussels he exercised wide influence on matters affecting the Catholic Church. His activity made enemies who falsely accused him of immorality, but King William defended him and exiled his accuser. Despite this vindication C.'s value as diplomat was somewhat lessened. He continued, however, to be a strong voice in support of the Belgian bishops in their running battle with King William. Lord Palmerston, British prime minister, and Talleyrand admired his diplomatic competence. It was C. who arranged for the restoration of the Catholic hierarchy to Holland in 1841. He was named a cardinal in 1844. BIBLIOGRAPHY: L. Jadin, DHGE 11:821–823.

[J. R. AHERNE]

CAPANNA, PUCCIO (fl. mid-14th cent.), Italian painter with prominent workshop in Florence (1350). Vasari's claims to C.'s working with Giotto on frescoes in the Lower Church of S. Francesco, Assisi, in Florence and Pistoria are highly improbable. BIBLIOGRAPHY: F. Barroni, EncCatt 3:658–659.

[M. J. DALY]

CAPECELATRO, ALFONSO (1824–1912), cardinal, author. Ordained in 1847 as a member of the Congregation of the Oratory he became superior general of his society. Pope Leo XIII appointed him assistant librarian of the Vatican Library. Named abp. of Capua (1880) and cardinal (1885), he became prefect of the Vatican Library. In political matters he attempted to mediate between the royal house of Italy and the Holy See, an effort that was not regarded favorably by the Vatican. C. conducted voluminous correspondence with such notables as Montalembert, Manzoni, and Mercier. His scholarship was deep and is apparent in a substantial output of published writings, the most impressive of which was his *Storia di S. Caterina da Siena* (1856). BIBLIOGRAPHY: G. Fallani, EncCatt 3:659–660.

[J. R. AHERNE]

CAPELLA PALATINA, Latin term for a royal private chapel within a palace complex: at Aachen (*c*.786) for Charlemagne; at Palermo (1132–40) for Roger II, Norman king of Sicily; at Paris (Ste. Chapelle, 1243–48) for Louis IX; at Versailles (1689–1710) for Louis XIV—all of diverse architectural plans.

[M. J. DALY]

CAPELLE, BERNARD (1884–1961), Benedictine monk of Abbey Mont-César, Louvain. He contributed greatly to Belgium's leadership in the liturgical movement both as editor of *Revue Bénédictine* (1919–1922) and as teacher of liturgy at the Univ. of Louvain, the Institut Supérieur de Liturgie at Paris, and numerous liturgical seminars. In addition, C. was a consultor for the Congregation of Rites, a member of the preparatory liturgical commission of Vatican Council II, and the author of *Travaux liturgiques de doctrine et d'histoire* (1955, 1962).

[K. O'NEILL]

CAPELLMEISTER, see KAPELLMEISTER.

CAPÉRAN, LOUIS (1884–1962), theologian and writer who published many works on matters of contemporary interest and evangelization, among them *Histoire contemporaine de la laïcité française* and *France nouvelle et Action Catholique*. He died at Toulouse where he had been canon of the cathedral. BIBLIOGRAPHY: R. Brouillard, *Catholicisme* 2:498.

[T. LIDDY]

CAPERNAUM (CAPHARNAUM), a town of Galilee identified with the modern Tell Hum. It is located about 3 miles SW of the Jordan's entrance into the Sea of Galilee. The place is frequently mentioned in the Gospels because Jesus used it as the center for much of his ministry (Mt 9.1). Matthew was a publican there before his call (Mt. 9.9). The impressive ruins of the excavated synagogue date back to the end of the 2d cent. A.D. This building probably replaced the synagogue in which Jesus preached (Mk 1.21; Mt 4.13; Jn 6.59). BIBLIOGRAPHY: C. F. Pfeiffer, *Biblical World* (1966) 162–164.

[J. E. LUSSIER]

CAPETIANS, the line of French kings which began when the protracted death-throes of the Carolingian line ended with the election and coronation of Hugh Capet at Reims, (987). It lasted in direct succession from father to son until 1328, and included such great rulers as Louis the Fat (d.1137), whose principal minister was Abbot *Suger, Philip Augustus (d. 1223), St. Louis of France (d. 1270), and Philip the Fair (d. 1314). After 1328 it was continued through cousins in the three branches of the *Valois until 1589, and the *Bourbon 1589–1792, 1815–1830, and Bourbon-Orléans 1830–48.

[T. GILBY]

CAPGRAVE, JOHN (1393–1464), English Augustinian historian and theologian. Augustinian provincial (1453–57), he wrote the first vernacular chronicle of England to 1417. He also wrote Latin commentaries on almost all books of the Bible. His most famous work, *Nova legenda Angliae* (published 1901) is a rearrangement of the *Sanctilogium* of John of

Tynemouth, OSB. BIBLIOGRAPHY: Emden Camb 121–122; E. M. Thompson, DNB 3:929–931.

[J. A. WEISHEIPL]

CAPILLAS, FRANCIS DE, BL. (1607–48), Dominican protomartyr of China. Born in Spain, he volunteered for the mission in the Philippines, where he was ordained (1631) and labored for 10 years. Sent to China (1642), he joined Francisco Diaz in missionary activities in Fukien. After mastering the language C. is said to have made many converts. Caught in the political upheaval following the end of the Ming dynasty, he was arrested, tortured, and decapitated. He was beatified in 1902. BIBLIOGRAPHY: Butler 1:98–99; C. Testore, BiblSanct 3:762–763.

[E. T. MCGOVERN]

CAPITAL PUNISHMENT, a term now generally restricted to the penalty of death inflicted by civil authority in punishment for certain grave crimes. Under Roman law the term was applied not only to the death penalty but also to the penal deprivation of liberty or of civil and political rights. On the basis of God's revealed law as contained in the Bible no certain argument can be drawn to prove the legitimacy of the penalty under any or all circumstances. It was practiced by the Jewish people under the Mosaic Law and presumably enjoyed divine sanction. In the NT no question was raised about the penalty when it was justly imposed by competent authority. St. Paul appears to have approved its administration in some cases at least (cf. Rom 13.1–5). In the underlying thought of St. Paul and the Mosaic Law, the penalty seems to have been valued as a deterrent to serious crime and also for its retributive character, an idea not acceptable to many contemporary abolitionists. But this does not require one to think that the penalty is necessarily just and reasonable when social conditions are such that the intended purpose of its application can be secured by other and less violent means. Relatively primitive societies offered no satisfactory alternatives to the State in its promotion of order and the security of the community. In modern times penal institutions have been developed to cope with serious criminal offenders more humanely. Although in the early Christian centuries and in the Middle Ages a few scattered voices were raised in protest against the death penalty, the great majority of Christian authors accepted it as a practical necessity. St. Thomas Aquinas justified it by drawing an analogy between the relation of a member of the human body to the body as a whole and the relation of an individual man to the community of which he forms a part (ST 2a2ae 64.2). The analogy, however is not entirely satisfactory, because the parts of a human body have no other purpose than to serve the interests of the body as a whole, while the human individual as a person has a destiny transcending the welfare of the community. In modern times strong opposition to capital punishment began with Cesare Beccaria who in 1764 published his classic treatise *Dei delitti e delle pene* in which he condemned capital punishment as cruel, unreasonable, and ineffective. Beginning with the Enlightenment the movement toward penal reform gained momentum and this led ultimately to the abolition of capital punishment in many countries and to the notable curtailment of its use in countries in which it was not abolished. In the U.S. the efforts of abolitionists culminated in 1972 in the decision of the Supreme Court which outlawed capital punishment as opposed to the Eighth Amendment to the Constitution which prohibits cruel and unusual punishment. The Court appeared to be motivated by the inequity of the penalty as it was actually applied under prevailing law and therefore left the way open to its reestablishment under laws framed to make its application more equitable. Since that time a number of states have reenacted the penalty for a variety of crimes in a form designed to make it acceptable to the Supreme Court. Much of the haste with which these new laws have been enacted is attributable to the outrage with which the public has reacted to the growing crime rate and the relative impunity enjoyed by many guilty of serious crime who are freed after short periods of imprisonment to return to their violent way of life. The diversity of opinion that exists on this matter shows a lack of compelling evidence in support of the basic suppositions underlying the conflicting opinions, e.g., does imprisonment effectively rehabilitate the hardened criminal? Is capital punishment a real deterrent? Has the idea of retribution no reasonable role in the punishment of the criminal? Many Christian moralists have taken a somewhat intermediate position, holding that the power of imposing and inflicting the death penalty is within the radical competence of the State, but that the State ought not to use this power except when in the prudent judgment of lawmakers it is deemed necessary for the protection of the common good. BIBLIOGRAPHY: D. R. Campion, NCE 3:79–81; *op. cit.*, J. J. Farraher, 16:48–49; S. Adamo, "Capital Punishment, Yes or No?" HPR 65 (1965) 300–306; G. Grisez, "Toward a Consistent Natural Law Ethics of Killing," *American Journal of Jurisprudence* 15 (1970) 64–96.

[P. K. MEAGHER]

CAPITAL SINS. These are sins, or more accurately, *vices, which, esp. as *final causes, lead to other sins. In English they are usually, if imprecisely, called the seven *deadly sins, or even *cardinal sins (OED 2:113; 3:62). The modern listing is *pride, *covetousness (avarice), *lust, *anger, *gluttony, *envy, and *acedia (sloth). While the Bible has lists of sins and mentions all the sins in this list, it does not present any one precisely as capital, i.e., as giving rise to a different kind of sin; this notion had its traceable origins in the desert fathers of Egypt. *Evagrius of Pontus is the first one known to have written of these eight vicious thoughts (PG 40:1271 ff), but the general allegorizing tendency of the Alexandrians using Dt 7.1–2, and Lk 11.24–26, together with the ascetic experience of the hermits established a fairly widespread tradition. John *Cassian reported this tradition to the West in his *Institutes of Cenobites* and *Conferences of the Fathers* (PL 49:359–611). St. Gregory the Great in his *Moralia* (PL 76:620) slightly rearranged the list, reduced the number to seven, and in this form it prevailed in the Latin Church. The theme enjoyed enormous popularity in the Middle Ages; with Creed and Commandments it was one of the chief homiletic topics and often seemed to crowd out the virtues. The sermons were reflected in artistic forms. Capital sins were personified in drama, and pictured in gargoyles; they serve as the structure for Dante's *Purgatorio* and conclude Chaucer's *The Parson's Tale*. With the Renaissance and Reformation, emphasis on them diminished. In his theological system, notwithstanding popular medieval interest in them, St. Thomas relegated the capital sins to a subordinate place (ThAq ST 1a2ae, 84.3 ad 4). He relates the term capital to *caput* as meaning source, not as connoting the kind of punishment these sins deserve. The term deadly should be understood in the same way, i.e., as suggesting that they endanger spiritual life, not that they are the worst sins or even always *mortal sins. BIBLIOGRAPHY: U. Voll, NCE 13:253–254; R. J. Ianucci, *Treatment of the Capital Sins* (1942, repr. 1970).

[U. VOLL]

CAPITAL VIRTUES, see CARDINAL VIRTUES.

CAPITALISM, the system where wealth used to produce more wealth is privately owned and directly operated for private profit, by contrast with *socialism where it comes under public ownership. Note first, that the term came into general currency only about the beginning of the 20th century; second, that there is no general unanimity among economists about what capital really is; and third, that the pure extremes of the antithesis, capitalism-socialism, have been historically realized only in small and rudimentary self-sufficient communities.

Judged merely in an economic frame of reference, Christianity has nothing to say for or against capitalism; accordingly the advantages and disadvantages of running the telephone service as a government department can be debated without introducing moral judgments. Thus Pius XI in *Quadragesimo anno* recalled that Leo XIII, though a severe critic of its abuses, had not in *Rerum novarum* considered capitalism to be inherently vicious and irreformable. Its psychological, moral, and social effects may be profound and widespread, as indeed they have been by reason of its association with *laissez-faire* economics and *industrialism. Here Christianity has had much to say, and that in no uncertain terms; the abuses have called, not for whimpers, but for the energetic promotion of remedies.

It spread from Great Britain after the Industrial Revolution; the introduction of machinery brought about large units of production, and in consequence the abnormal concentration of power in the hands of the few. The predominance of the profit-motive often dictated producing as cheaply as possible and selling as dearly; the promotion of a sectional advantage went with an exploitation of the workers and the provision of inferior goods to the consumer, this last fault being aggravated when they were made to wear out quickly in order to support increased production and its subsidiary, the advertising industry. This last was but one example of other fringe interests, notably the purely financial, which intervened in the just producer-consumer relationship and, together with destructive wars, were responsible for the ramshackle socioeconomics from which, it is hoped, we are emerging.

Still we must not accept too credulously the caricatures according to which all capitalists are bloated and their victims lean and hungry. As a historical phenomenon, capitalism opened up the riches of the world and made them more generally accessible than its opponents allow. Moreover, a system of free-enterprise, properly controlled, as by legislation against monopolies, provides built-in regulators for the benefit of producer and consumer alike by encouraging competition, incentives, profit-sharing, and a diligence that is less noticeable in the administration of public property.

However the old antithesis is now dead, for all Western countries favor a mixed-economy and in various degrees control the working of capital; some matters, e.g., atomic power, are obviously too big for private ownership: the social problem now concerns the managers rather than the owners. Where to draw the line is a question of pure *politics so long as the decencies essential to the Christian social gospel are not infringed.

[T. GILBY]

CAPITANIO, BARTOLOMEA, ST. (1807–33), foundress. In her short span of 26 years, C. produced an astounding volume of work. Refused permission by her parents to become a nun, she took private vows and devoted herself to the apostolate of educating the young. With St. Vincentia Gerosa she founded an institute known as Sisters of Charity of Milan, which combined hospital work and educating the poor. C. wrote hundreds of letters and voluminous notes on spirituality, both later published in book form. She was canonized in 1950. BIBLIOGRAPHY: Butler 3:191; G. Drago, BiblSanct 2:849–852; J. DeGuibert, DSAM 2.1:119.

[J. R. AHERNE]

CAPITO, WOLFGANG FABRICIUS (1478–1541), Reformation theologian. Capito is the Latinized form of the family name, Köpfel. When still a Catholic priest, C. was a preacher at Basel and Mainz, where he also became chancellor of the archbishop. He was a friend of Erasmus and entered into correspondence with Luther and Zwingli. C. obtained an ecclesiastical appointment at Strassburg in 1523, but soon became a Reformer. His chief service to the Reformation was the effort to moderate theological differences between Lutherans and Zwinglians, esp. in regard to the Holy Eucharist. Thus he collaborated with M. *Bucer on the *Tetrapolitan Confession (1530) and the Concord of *Wittenberg (1536). He published a *Responsio de Missa* (1537) and *Hexaemeron Dei* (1539). BIBLIOGRAPHY: O. E. Strasser, *La Pensée théologique de Wolfgang Capito* (1938); R. Stupperich, RGG 1:1613.

[T. C. O'BRIEN]

CAPITOLINE HILL, Rome, symbolic hill of importance from ancient Roman times, the site of numerous temples to Jupiter's many powers, crowned by the monumental, magnificent design (1537–39) of Michelangelo (finished according to his plans after his death.) The Piazza del Campidoglio rises in energetic progression by way of the monumental stairway Cordonata, which supports at the top statues of the Dioscuri, to the bronze equestrian statue of Marcus Aurelius at the apex of a gently rising oval mound of dynamic elliptical pattern in the center of a trapezoidal piazza. This huge "outdoor room" is flanked on two sides by the Palazzo del Museo Capitolino and Palazzo dei Conservatori, both diverging at 80° angles and oriented to the dramatic climax of the massive Senator's Palace—its colossal orders distinctive of Michelangelo's genius—the whole conception a most imposing civic center, establishing a repertory for monumental structures of all times. BIBLIOGRAPHY: J. S. Ackerman, *Architecture of Michelangelo* (2 v., 1961); C. De Tolnay, *Michelangelo* (5 v., 1943–60).

[M. J. DALY]

CAPITULANT, a member of an ecclesiastical voting unit, e.g., a cathedral chapter. The orders, properly so defined, provide for a chapter (voting body) in each religious house. Where there is provincial organization, the province convenes a chapter at stated periods. Where the order is governed by a superior general, there is a worldwide or general chapter every 6 years. The term capitular is also used.

[J. M. BRADY]

CAPITULARIES, IMPERIAL AND ECCLESIASTICAL, enactments promulgated by the Carolingian rulers. Their contents were divided into *capitula* or chapters and dealt with administrative regulations, the royal domains, public order, or ecclesiastical problems. According to the Germanic concept, laws were a tribal heritage and passed down unchanged. The 65 that remain of Charlemagne's legislation were considered an extension and application of the earlier barbarian codes to new needs. Charlemagne formulated them from suggestions made by smaller groups of nobles or bps. at semiannual assemblies and then submitted them to the multitude for their shouted approval. BIBLIOGRAPHY: R. Hoyt, *Europe in the Middle Ages* (1966).

[M. T. GRIFFIN]

CAPITULATIONS (EPISCOPAL AND PAPAL), prearranged agreements by electors which outlined the limits of the power of the one to be elected. These were of frequent occurrence in medieval episcopal elections, though they were repeatedly forbidden and pronounced null and void by the Holy See. But after the election of popes became reserved to the college of cardinals (11th and 12th cent.) the Holy See was confronted with the same disorder in its own elections. The cardinals made use of capitulations with a view to the establishment of what amounted to an oligarchical form of government on the Church in place of the papal monarchy. The cardinals sought to enhance their own status and power, and to do so they made the effort to put limits on the power and authority of the popes they elected. Such restrictions were again and again declared null and void from the mid-14th to the early 17th cent., when the *Aeterni Patris* of Gregory XV finally succeeded in putting an end to the practice.

[M. H. BEIRNE]

CAPITULUM, the Latin term for what is known in English as a *chapter in the sense of an official assembly of religious or *canons. It is also used to designate a corporate group or college of canons charged with certain elective, liturgical, and administrative responsibilities in a cathedral or collegiate church. Such a group was called a *capitulum* from the fact that it was accustomed to meet in chapter. The term is also applied to what is known in English as a "little chapter," i.e., a short reading consisting of one or two verses from Scripture recited at certain places in the liturgy (e.g., after the Psalms of the canonical hours) or upon certain occasions. Originally such readings were longer but in the course of time they were considerably abbreviated. This was the basic meaning of the term, chapter in the sense of an assembly being so called because the meeting customarily opened with the reading of a little chapter.

[N. KOLLAR]

CAPPA Y MANESCAU, RICARDO (1839–97), Spanish Jesuit historian. C. became a Jesuit in Cádiz (1866) and taught in Quito and Lima. He began in Peru a series of historical publications which he carried to completion in Spain: *Estudios críticos acerca de la dominación española en América* (20 v., 1889–97), covering every aspect of Spanish America.

[H. JACK]

CAPPA MAGNA, a large cloak worn on ceremonial occasions by bishops, cardinals, and certain other prelates. It has a long train and a large hood lined with scarlet silk for cardinals and scarlet wool for bishops.

[N. KOLLAR]

CAPPADOCIA, region in central Anatolia, Turkey, site of numerous rock-carved churches of Middle Byzantine period (9th–12th cent.) with historical, monumental fresco cycles important to the documentation of provincial Byzantine painting, an evolution not Cappadocian but the result of the penetration of models from Constantinople. Whereas Cappadocian painters represented the life of Christ, Byzantine artists engaged in commentaries on the liturgy and the symbolism of architectural form. BIBLIOGRAPHY: N. and M. Thierry, *Nouvelles églises rupestres de Cappadoce* (1964).

[M. J. DALY]

CAPPADOCIANS, THE, SS. *Basil the Great, *Gregory of Nazianzus, and *Gregory of Nyssa, all three natives of the Province of Cappadocia. Basil and Gregory of Nyssa were

brothers. Gregory of Nazianzus was their personal friend. They expanded the theological insights of Athanasius in the dispute with Arianism and prepared the way for the definitions of Nicaea. Their witness to the Christian faith made use of the significant achievements of classical thought and culture. Thus they were able to speak with authority in balancing political order and in the development of monasticism. Despite their close relationship, each made his distinct contribution: Basil as a leader in political and ecclesiastical decision making; Gregory of Nazianzus as an accomplished orator; Gregory of Nyssa as a profound intellectual in matters theological and philosophical. BIBLIOGRAPHY: Quasten 3:203–204.

[F. H. BRIGHAM]

CAPPELLA, any large group of musicians. During the medieval period it more narrowly meant the clerical or church choir that sang in the chapel.

[D. J. SMUCKER]

CAPRANICA, brothers prominent in ecclesiastical affairs in the 15th century. **Domenico** (1400–58), humanist and cardinal. Educated at Padua and Bologna, he entered the papal service and was made bp. of Fermo (1425) and cardinal (1426, publicly recognized as such 1430). Nicholas V appointed him grand penitentiary. A critic of Callistus III's nepotism, he founded the Collegio Capranicense (1458) for poor scholars in theology and canon law. **Angelo** (c. 1400–78), bp. and cardinal. As abp. of Siponto-Manfredonia (1438) and later, Ascoli (1447), he was influential in securing the canonization of John Capistran. Appointed governor at Bologna (1458), he showed ability in administration and diplomacy. He spent his life working for improvement in seminary training and revival of religious life. BIBLIOGRAPHY: J. G. Rowe, NCE 3:90–91.

[E. T. MCGOVERN]

CAPRARA, GIOVANNI BATTISTA (1733–1810), papal diplomat. The troubled path of a diplomat, esp. in the 18th cent., is nowhere more evident than in C.'s career. As nuncio to the leading courts of his day, he was called upon to exercise a difficult prudence as a representative of the Holy See who was also sensitive to the problems of the secular powers, and as one who had to exercise the authority of Rome among the local dioceses of his jurisdiction. As nuncio to Cologne he faced the heresy of *Febronianism, at Vienna he had to contend with the interference in the Church by Emperor Joseph II, and finally as extraordinary legate of Pius VII to France he dealt with Napoleon and the aftermath of the French Revolution. Throughout the many crises that drew him into delicate negotiations with the heads of state, C. demonstrated a spirit of conciliation which earned him frequently the hostility of the Roman Curia. And yet he was greatly effective in representing the Holy See. His years as legate to France (1801–10) accomplished three major effects: the Concordat of 1802, the reconciliation of the constitutional clergy, the restoration of an established order for the Church in France. The Concordat was disappointing to Pius VI, and C. has been criticized for not insuring more vigorously the rights of the Church. The truth is that the Concordat was the best compromise possible with Napoleon. C. brought back large numbers of bishops and clergy who were called "constitutional" and had accepted the Revolution contrary to decrees by the Holy See. In spite of disappointing limits, it must be said that the Church had a new life in France because of C.'s work. When Napoleon extended his realm into Italy, it was again C. who concluded the Italian Concordat in 1802. In that same year he was named abp. of Milan. In his remaining years C., who enjoyed the friendship of Napoleon, strove to prevent the inevitable rift between emperor and Pope, but without success. Upon his death C. was buried by imperial decree in the Patheon of Paris. R. Molls, DHGE 11:944–957.

[J. R. AHERNE]

CAPREOLUS, JOHN (c. 1380–1444), Dominican theologian, entitled "the Prince of Thomists," and probably the most celebrated of the late Middle Ages. Born in Guienne when it was being contested between the English and French, he died there, at Rodez, before the Valois had finally expelled the Lancastrians. He was professor at the Univ. of Paris between 1408 and 1426. One might hazard a guess from his movements that he was not of the party championed by St. Joan of Arc. The work for which he is famous is his commentary on the four books of the Sentences, which in effect systematically takes up a position against the Avicennist Augustinianism of *Duns Scotus, the semi-Platonism of *Henry of Ghent, and the nominalism of *Ockham (which labels are to be taken for no more than they deserve), and is called *Defensiones theologiae divi doctoris Thomae de Aquino* (last edition 1900–07).

[T. GILBY]

CAPRICHOS, LOS, see GOYA Y LUCIENTES, FRANCISCO JOSÉ DE.

CAPSULA, short-stemmed, round, metal vessel used to reserve the large host for Benediction and exposition of the Blessed Sacrament. The capsula is placed in the tabernacle until it is used.

[N. KOLLAR]

CAPTIVITY EPISTLES, the name commonly used to designate four Epistles in the NT, Eph, Phil, Col, Philem. Each of these Epistles claims St. Paul for its author and depicts him as imprisoned (Eph 3.1; 4.1; Phil 1.7, 13–14; Col 4.3, 18; Philem 1.9–10, 13); hence, the name, "Captivity Epistles." The Epistle 2 Tim is not included in this group, even though its author is likewise imprisoned, because this Epistle presents itself as written during Paul's final imprisonment before his martyrdom. The NT records only two other imprisonments of Paul: at Caesarea (Acts 23.31–26.32) and at Rome (Acts 28.16), the latter being a house arrest. The Captivity Epistles have been commonly assigned to the period of this first Roman imprisonment of the Apostle, 61–62 A.D.; but some modern scholars have advanced the hypothesis that they were written during an unrecorded imprisonment of Paul at Ephesus (cf. Acts 19.1–20.1), 55–56 A.D. This Ephesian hypothesis is plausible in the case of Phil, esp. since this Epistle speaks of the Phillippians' care of Paul during his imprisonment. The several journeys that would have been involved make a Roman imprisonment improbable because of the distance (4 or 5 weeks' travel) between Philippi and Rome. Colossians, Philem, and perhaps Eph are better placed during the Apostle's first Roman imprisonment. BIBLIOGRAPHY: D. Guthrie, *New Testament Introduction* (1961) 92–98; A. T. Robinson, *Epochs in the Life of Paul* (1974).

[C. P. CEROKE]

CAPUCHINESSES, see FRANCISCANS (SISTERS).

CAPUCHINS, see FRANCISCANS, CAPUCHIN.

CAPUTIATI, a name applied to several groups because of some special association with the cowl or hood (Lat. *caputium*). Among these were: (1) A lay confraternity, founded c. 1182 by the carpenter Durando Chaduiz at Le Puy in the Auvergne. He claimed that in a vision the Blessed Virgin commissioned him to promote peace; thus his followers were also called *Paciferi* (Lat., peace-bearers). They wore a white habit and a hood with an image of the Virgin attached. The confraternity attracted many members to a life of poverty and simplicity. These Caputiati played an important part in overcoming the marauding bands of mercenaries called *routiers* (see COTEREAUX), but their history was brief because they fell out of favor with the nobility. There is no evidence that they held doctrines contrary to the teaching of the Church. (2) A violent, iconoclastic faction of *Lollards, led by an ex-Augustinian, Peter Pateshull, in 1387. They kept their heads covered with the cowl in the presence of the Blessed Sacrament. (3) A group of Spanish Franciscan Observants, led by Juan de Guadalupe and approved by Alexander VI in 1496. They lived an eremitic life and wore a distinctive cowl as part of their habit. BIBLIOGRAPHY: F. Courtney, NCE 3:94; L. Spatling, EncCatt 3:715; F. Vernet, DTC 2:1695–96.

[C. J. LYNCH]

CARA, Center for Applied Research in the Apostolate, a research and development agency concerned about the RC Church's worldwide religious and social mission. CARA's purpose is to gather information, evaluate it, then promote and apply modern techniques and scientific information for practical use in an effective and coordinated approach to the social and religious mission of the Church in today's world. Reports have been made on procedures for assessing candidates for the religious life, studies on the training of the clergy in the U.S., and on other aspects of the ministry. Concentration on Church personnel began in 1967. CARA is a member of the International Federation of Institutes for Social and Socio-Religious Research.

[N. M. ABBOTT]

CARABANTES, JOSÉ DE (1628–94), Spanish Capuchin missionary. Ordained in 1652, he was sent to the Venezuelan missions in 1657 where he labored for 9 years. He returned to Spain and devoted himself to preaching and writing. His publications include *Práctica de las misiones* (2 v., 1674–78), still of use to modern missiologists. His cause for beatification was introduced in 1910. BIBLIOGRAPHY: I. de Villapadierna, NCE 3:94.

[H. JACK]

CARACALLA, ROMAN EMPEROR (188–217 A.D.), elder son of Septimius Severus and Roman Emperor after his father's death at York in 211. He had his brother Geta assassinated and a great many others, including the jurist Papinian. After campaigning in Germany and along the Danube, he set out to conquer the East, but was slain by order of Macrinus, his praetorian prefect, near Carrhae. C., who derived his name from the Celtic cloak that he wore in Rome, was cowardly and cruel but not without military talent. His erection of huge buildings, including the famous Baths of Caracalla at Rome, his granting of citizenship to all free inhabitants of the empire in 212, and his attempt to imitate the deeds of Alexander the Great all manifest his extravagant nature. BIBLIOGRAPHY: J. Straub, RAC 2:893–901.

[M. J. COSTELLOE]

CARACCIOLO, FRANCIS, ST. (1563–1608), cofounder of the Congregation of Clerks Regular Minor. Miraculously cured of a virulent skin disease at the age of 22, C. vowed to devote his life to God. He studied for the priesthood at Naples and was ordained there (1587). The following year he became associated with John Augustine Adorno, who was intent on founding a congregation of priests who would combine the active with the contemplative life. The two drew up the rules for the new society, which was solemnly ratified by Sixtus V (1588), and opened its first house outside Naples. Adorno died in 1591 and C. succeeded him as rector general, serving until 1598 and establishing during this period other houses in Italy and in Spain. He was local superior and novice master until 1607 when he resigned to spend his time in contemplation and prayer. A man of great piety, mortification, and apostolic zeal, C. was canonized in 1807 by Pius VII. BIBLIOGRAPHY: Butler 2:470–472; G. Coniglio, BiblSanct 5:1197–1201.

[E. T. MCGOVERN]

CARACCIOLO, GIOVANNI BATTISTO (1570–1637), Italian painter. Influenced by Caravaggio, C. in his *Liberation of St. Peter* (1608–09) shows sharp contrasts of light and dark and dramatic intensity of gesture. In later frescoes he emphasized volume and form, stressing light over color.

[M. J. DALY]

CARACCIOLO, LANDOLF (1287–1351), Franciscan theologian, *Doctor collectivus*. He studied at the Univ. of Naples and the Univ. of Paris. He was consecrated bp. of Castellammare and later was transferred to the Diocese of Amalfi. Among his works are MSS dealing with commentaries on biblical morality, on the Immaculate Conception, and a tract on the art of sermonizing. He is probably noted for his adherence to the theology of Duns Scotus more than for the specific content of any of these tracts or MSS. He influenced later theologians, among them, Bernardine of Siena and Alphonsus of Toledo. BIBLIOGRAPHY: A. Emmen, NCE, 3:96–97; E. Caggiano, EncCatt 3:739.

[J. R. RIVELLO]

CARACCIOLO, ROBERTO (1425–95), Franciscan preacher acclaimed by common folk and church prelates alike. Among the latter were *Callistus III and *Paul II. C. was made bp. and served in that capacity in Aquila and Aquino. His preaching was renowned enough to gain him the recognition of Ferdinand I, King of Naples, and the title of preacher for a crusade against the Turks. BIBLIOGRAPHY: J. C. Willke, NCE 3:97; W. Forster, LTK, 2:933; F. Diotallevi, EncCatt 3:740–741.

[J. R. RIVELLO]

CARADOSSO, CHRISTOFORO FOPPA (c. 1452–1526 or 1527), Italian master medalist and goldsmith who worked for Popes Julius II, Leo X, Hadrian VI, and Clement VII, executing medals and coins with superb skill. BIBLIOGRAPHY: G. F. Hill, *Corpus of Italian Medals of the Renaissance before Cellini* (2 v., 1930).

[M. J. DALY]

CARAFA (CARAFFA), a Neopolitan noble family whose members included many of the prelates of Naples and Avesa. Its peak of influence came when Gian Pietro Carafa became Paul IV (1555–59) and its low point was reached when his nephews Card. Carlo and the Duke of Paliano were executed for crimes including treason. BIBLIOGRAPHY: H. H. Davis, NCE 3:97–99.

[E. T. MC GOVERN]

CARAMUEL Y LOBKOVITZ, JUAN (1606–82), Cistercian theologian and savant. Born of a noble Spanish and princely German family, this many-sided man was trained in astronomy by his father and in Oriental languages by a Syrian tutor; he studied philosophy at Alcalá, entered the Cistercians, gained his doctorate of theology at Louvain, and took a gallant part in the Thirty Years' War. He was grand prior of the Knights of Calatrava, titular abbot of Melrose, suffragan bp. at Mainz, minister of state in Hungary, preacher to the imperial court, member of the Aulic Council, commendatory abbot of Vienna and Montserrat, bp. of Campagna in the kingdom of Naples: these titles reflect only part of his interests and pursuits. He died as bp. of Vigevano in Lombardy; there he had proved an energetic reformer, and the façade of the

Bramante cathedral and the grand staircase of the ducal palace remain as monuments to his architectural skill. He spoke 24 languages, and wrote 70 considerable works on grammar, poetry, mathematics, astronomy, physics, canon law, politics, logic, metaphysics, asceticism, theology, and military fortification. His cavalier dash drove him to untenable dogmatic positions, and in moral theology earned for him, from St. Alphonsus Liguori, the title "the prince of laxists." BIBLIOGRAPHY: V. Oblet, DTC 2.2:1709–12; L. F. O'Neil, CE 3:329–330.

[T. GILBY]

CARAVAGGIO, MICHELANGELO MERISI DA (1573–1610), Italian painter and genius of violent nature and chequered fortune. Under the patronage of Card. del Monte, he executed in a series (1598) the monumental *Calling of St. Matthew,* an extraordinary work in a new realism of sacred subject in contemporary scenes of low life, with chiaroscuro lighting and emotional intensity. C.'s light, defining form and binding the composition, is imaginary and symbolic—an exposition in the Counter-Reformation of the new spontaneity of inward religious experience rather than faith through theological speculation. C.'s work was acclaimed by artists, but simple people, who preferred the idealized, found it lacking in reverence. Many followers spread C.'s baroque style throughout Europe. BIBLIOGRAPHY: W. F. Friedlaender, *Caravaggio Studies* (1955).

[M. J. DALY]

CARAVANTES, JOSÉ DE, see CARABANTES, JOSÉ DE.

CARAYON, AUGUSTE (1813–1874), bibliographer. A member of the Society of Jesus, C. spent his life as editor and bibliographer. Much of his editing was in the field of asceticism. His most important contribution to scholarship was a bibliography of writings on the Jesuits both favorable and unfavorable. It contains more than 4,500 titles of writings concerning the society. BIBLIOGRAPHY: Sommervogel 2:714–718.

[J. R. AHERNE]

CARBONARI (It. "charcoal burners"), members of a secret revolutionary society in Italy in the early 19th century. Organized in lodges with a ritual that combined Freemasonry with Christianity, the Carbonari made their first appearance in S Italy about 1806 and then spread to the North. Anti-Napoleonic before 1814, they became anti-Hapsburg, anti-papal, and anti-Bourbon after 1815. Ideologically heterogeneous, they were united by a common hatred of reaction and of clericalism. They played a major role in the Neapolitan Revolution of 1820, when King Ferdinand was temporarily forced to grant a constitution. Their last notable revolutionary efforts were expended in 1830–31 in the uprisings in the States of the Church, Parma and Modena. After that date their idea of an elite uprising without reference to the general political and social environment was discredited, and a former Carbonaro, Giuseppe Mazzini, formed the Young Italy movement for the purpose of creating an open and general revolutionary movement. BIBLIOGRAPHY: R. J. Rath, "Carbonari: Their Origins, Initiation Rites and Aims," *American Historical Review* 69 (1964) 353–370.

[E. A. CARRILLO]

CARCHEMISH (CHARCHAMIS), for more than 1,000 years the dominant city of the upper Euphrates. Its strategic and commercial importance was due to the fact that it commanded one of the best fords on the road linking E and W at the N end of the Syrian plain. In the 9th cent. B.C., Carchemish was the Syro-Hittite capital. In 717 B.C. the Assyrians captured it and laid it waste (Is 10.9). In 605 it was the site of the defeat of Neco of Egypt by Nebuchadnezzar of Babylon (2 Chr 35.20) in a decisive battle described in Jer 46.2–12.

Distinctive are sculptured friezes on city walls, earliest Hittite sculpture-in-the-round (Ankara Museum), and exquisitely carved figures of stealite and lapis lazuli. The Yumus cemetery (1200–600 B.C.) yielded cinerary urns, craters, jugs, and skilled metalwork in bowls of bronze and gold. The manna of Carchemish was a standard weight of exchange in the ancient world. BIBLIOGRAPHY: C. F. Pfeiffer, *Biblical World* (1966) 165–168; L. Wooley, *Art of the Middle East* (1961).

[J. E. LUSSIER]

CÁRDENAS, JUAN DE (1613–84), Jesuit moral theologian. Besides works of an ascetical nature, his most important writings lay in the field of moral theology. Among the latter, *Crisis theologica bipartita* (1670) is the most famous; it is a work that records and evaluates many of the moral theses prevalent at the time.

[J. R. RIVELLO]

CARDIEL, JOSÉ (1704–81), a Spanish Jesuit missionary in S America. He was working with the Indians on the Paraguay Reductions when the Jesuits were expelled. He spent the rest of his life in Italy. C. left three reports which include maps, an account of events in the clash between the government and the Jesuits, and many interesting observations concerning the people and the natural environment of the mission posts.

CARDINAL, a prince of the Church who is a member of the Sacred College of Cardinals and who serves as an adviser to the pope. A cardinal receives his appointment from the pope and is given his red hat at a consistory. According to current canon law, a cardinal must be at least a priest before receiving the cardinalate. He is also a member of the conclave that elects the pope if one dies during his incumbency. There are six cardinal bishops who reside in Rome. They possess the titles to the seven suburbicarian dioceses but the actual administration is in the hands of others. The majority of the members of the College of Cardinals are cardinal priests. These are the ordinaries of a diocese. Cardinal deacons hold administrative offices at the Vatican.

[M. S. J. MCCAREY]

CARDINAL BISHOP, the highest of the three ranks within the *College of Cardinals. The office is held by those cardinals who are the ordinaries or bps. of the neighboring dioceses of Rome: Frascati, Velletri, Palestrina, Ostia, Porto-Santa Rufina, Albano, and Sabina-Poggio Mirteto; two Eastern patriarchs also hold the rank. These bps. sat in synod with the bp. of Rome from early times and gradually came to assist him in arriving at significant decisions. The designation seems to have arisen in the 6th century.

[T. M. MCFADDEN]

CARDINAL CANONS, priests who hold the seven canonries at the shrine of St. James of Compostela in Spain. They are the only priests permitted to offer Mass at the shrine and may wear the mitre and cassock of a cardinal.

[M. S. J. MC CAREY]

CARDINAL DEACON, the lowest of the three ranks within the *College of Cardinals. The office was originally held by seven deacons in the Roman Church, each of whom was closely associated with the bp. of Rome. They were originally in charge of the care of the poor in the seven regions into which Rome was divided. When this division was abandoned, the title was extended to other ecclesiastics and the number extended to 14. Today, the cardinal deacons are all priests and are usually associated with various administrative offices within the Vatican. Recent popes have created cardinal deacons who were not bps., but have immediately consecrated them bishops. BIBLIOGRAPHY: K. F. Morrison and H. G. Hynes, NCE 3:104–106.

[T. M. MCFADDEN]

CARDINAL DEAN, president of the *College of Cardinals. Formerly the *cardinal bishop who had been cardinal longest but since 1965 chosen by election, he becomes, *ipso facto,* the bp. of Ostia but also retains his previous see. He presides over the college when it meets as a body, announces the election of a new pope, and presides at his coronation.

[T. M. MCFADDEN]

CARDINAL PRIEST, the middle of the three ranks within the *College of Cardinals. The designation is an ancient one, although its meaning has undergone considerable change. Cardinal priests were originally the parish priests of the more important Roman churches; they assisted the pope in liturgical functions and came to exercise a consultative function as well. When, in the 11th cent., the practice began of naming non-Roman prelates to the cardinalate, the role of a cardinal as personal advisor to the pope became dominant. Most members of the College of Cardinals today are cardinal priests who also function as ordinaries of dioceses throughout the world.

BIBLIOGRAPHY: K. F. Morrison and H. G. Hynes, NCE 3:104–106.

[T. M. MCFADDEN]

CARDINAL PROTECTOR, a member of the *College of Cardinals to whose care are entrusted the interests of a particular religious order, educational institution, pious association, etc. His role is solely advisory, and he does not exercise any jurisdictional control. The pope himself is the protector of the Benedictine, Dominican, and Franciscan Orders. The title originally arose in connection with those cardinals who would represent the interests of one of the more important Catholic nations in any ecclesiastical disputes with Rome or surrounding nations.

[T. M. MCFADDEN]

CARDINAL (CARDINALATIAL) SEES, see SUBURBICARIAN DIOCESES.

CARDINAL SINS, a designation sometimes used for the *capital sins (see OED 2:113). A parallel with the *cardinal virtues is implied with some justification. The cardinal virtues are concerned with the principal areas of virtuous living; the capital sins are bent upon the principal sinful enticements to human appetite. BIBLIOGRAPHY: ThAq ST 1a2ae, 84.3.

[T. C. O'BRIEN]

CARDINAL VICAR, a popular designation for the vicar general of Rome. His formal title is Vicar of the City *(Vicarius Urbis).* He is always a cardinal; is in charge of administering the spiritual affairs of Rome; and is assisted by a vicegerent or permanent auxiliary bishop. His office does not cease with the death of the pope.

[T. M. MCFADDEN]

CARDINAL VIRTUES, so named from the Lat. *cardo* (hinge), the four chief moral virtues on which Christian living is traditionally considered to revolve. Called "cardinal" first by St. Ambrose, they are prudence, justice, fortitude, and temperance. Pagan moralists wrote of them; as charged with grace they are called infused virtues and in this light have been dealt with by Christian moralists. They are moral virtues, that is they make for balanced living within a human frame of reference, and do not go out of it directly to God, as do the theological virtues of faith, hope, and charity. Greek and Latin thought within the Church particularized the more diffused Hebraic conception of righteousness and attended to distinct emphases in Christian activity, and these later were seen as distinct types. At first the fourfold enumeration of moral virtue represented the four general conditions that should always be present; a deed should be practically wise, fair to others, high- and fine-spirited, and many other qualities from the Stoic grammar were clustered around these four. This conception was retained even when the more exact Aristotelian typifications were covered and Thomas Aquinas treated each as a specific kind of virtue. As such they form the four main headings for his detailed study of the moral life. Though all are closely interdependent, each can be taken according to its component elements *(partes integrales)*, subspecies *(partes subjectivae)*, and allied virtues *(partes potentiales)*. Thus between 50 and 60 virtues are systematically presented, and more than twice that number of contrary vices. BIBLIOGRAPHY: ThAq ST 1a2ae, 61, esp. in ed. Lat-Eng (v. 23, ed. D. Hughes, 1969).

[T. GILBY]

CARDINALS, COLLEGE OF, see COLLEGE OF CARDINALS.

CAREY, WILLIAM (1761–1834), a Baptist missionary, born in Northamptonshire, England. After serving an apprenticeship, he became a shoemaker. Converted at 17, he joined the Baptists at 22 and was ordained 4 years later. Through reading *Captain Cook's Voyages,* geography books, and biographies of John Eliot and David Brainerd, he became concerned about the unsaved millions around the world and helped found the *Baptist Missionary Society (1792). Sent to India by that organization, he became a pioneer missionary who has been called "the father of modern missions." After 6 years, he and several associates founded a missionary colony at Serampore. Here they became self-supporting through operating schools, printing for the government, and Carey's work as professor of Bengali at Fort William College. Having a gift for languages, Carey had learned Greek, Hebrew, Latin, Dutch, and French before leaving England. In India he mastered Bengali, Sanskrit, and Hindustani, as well as a number of dialects. Besides his services in spreading Christianity, his chief contributions were the establishment of Serampore College, translation of the Bible into numerous Indian tongues, publication of grammars and dictionaries in six Indian languages, establishment of the first Indian newspaper, helping to abolish infanticide and suttee (the custom prescribing that a widow must die at the time of her husband's funeral), and encouragement of agricultural improvements through his Horticultural Society. BIBLIOGRAPHY: S. P. Carey, *William Carey, D.D., Fellow of Linnaean Society* (1923).

[N. H. MARING]

CARGO CULT, millenarian movement in New Guinea and Melanesia. The name derives from the idea that after the final cataclysm bringing the present order of things to an end, ancestors of the people will return with a cargo of goods and will institute an age of bliss. Originating in the late 19th cent., cargo cults spread in the 1930s, and again after World War II. The cult combines elements of Christian missionary teaching with the reaction of island natives to their position relative to white colonials. Natives saw that desired material goods arrived on ships or later on planes, that the goods came to the whites without their personal labor, but to natives only for work under white domination. The idea arose that ancestors were sending these goods to the natives with the whites

intercepting them, but that soon the ancestors would come to rectify the situation. The cargo cults were opposed by missionaries for religious reasons, and by the white colonial governments because of political considerations. BIBLIOGRAPHY: P. Worsley, *Trumpet Shall Sound* (2d ed., 1968); G. Cochrane, *Big Men and Cargo Cults* (1970); P. Lawrence, *Road Being Cargo: A Study of the Cargo Movement in the Southern Madang District, New Guinea* (1968).

[T. EARLY]

CARILLON, a set of bells hung fixed so as not to swing and tuned chromatically with a compass of three octaves or more. A carillon is distinguished from a chime in that the latter has a diatonic tuning and tends to involve about 8 to 12 bells. The diatonic chime tuning is a definite scalar order of full tones and half tones, of a more restricted flexibility in comparison to the chromatic carillon. A modern carillon has 30 to 50 bells, which range in weight from 1 lb. to as heavy as 4,700 lbs. They operate by either the manual keyboard method, in which the player strikes the keys with his gloved, closed hand, or by an automatic clockwork mechanism. Carillon making, composing, and performing achieved their peak from the 15th through the 18th cent. in the Low Countries and N France. Originally they were the bells of municipal clock towers, announcing the passing of the hours. But they were also installed in other municipal buildings and became the pride of the townspeople. Bells were regarded as spoils of war, ransom materials, and objects for elaborate municipal rituals. Pieter and Frans Hemony were master craftsmen in producing and tuning bells in 17th cent. Belgium. In the U.S. most carillons are in church towers.

[D. J. SMUCKER]

CARIONI GIOVANNI BATTISTA, see BATTISTA DA CREMA.

CARISSIMI, GIACOMO (1605–74), Italian composer, primarily of oratorios and chamber cantatas. His chamber cantatas achieved widespread recognition during his lifetime for their incorporation of operatic elements. Dramatization through excellent lyrical writing for the solo voice characterized the works.

Even more significant was his contribution to the oratorio. He excelled in vocally dramatizing various biblical episodes, using a narrator, solo voice, duet, and chorus; *Jephthah* is considered to be his finest oratorio. In addition to composing, G. taught many students, including Alessandro Scarlatti and Marc-Antoine Charpentier.

[D. J. SMUCKER]

CARITAS CHRISTI, an institute of pontifical right, established for lay women at Marseilles, France, in 1937. Its members are dedicated to a rule that includes the vow of chastity and promises of poverty and obedience, and they perform apostolic tasks in the environment of their secular professions. Its international membership numbered approximately 1700 in 1970. BIBLIOGRAPHY: J. M. Perrin, *Caritas Christi* (1961); J. McCarthy, *Total Dedication for the Laity* (1964).

[C. KEENAN]

CARLETON, WILLIAM (1794–1869), Irish author. Although he was reared a Catholic and was intended for the priesthood, C., under the influence of C. Otway, a scholar antipathetic to the RC Church, began his literary career by publishing sketches and stories critical of Catholicism, which he represented as encouraging superstition among the poor. His anti-Catholic preoccupation lessened in later years. The literary merit of his work is generally acknowledged. No other writer was his equal in the skill with which he discerned and put in words the traits and foibles of the Irish in pre-famine days. BIBLIOGRAPHY: *Autobiography* (rev. ed., 1968); B. Kiley, *Poor Scholar* (1947).

[V. SAMPSON]

CAROLMAN (d. 754), Merovingian mayor of the palace, elder son of *Charles Martel. Together with his brother, Pepin the Short, he administered the Frankish kingdom to the great benefit of Church reform. In 757 he retired to Rome and became a monk near Subiaco. He is remembered as a saint in the Benedictine calendar. He is to be distinguished from three other men of the same name: his nephew, the brother of Charlemagne and King of the Franks (d. 777); the King of France (*c*. 884), the son of Louis II, "the Stammerer"; and the King of Bavaria and of the Lombards (d. 880) who negotiated unsuccessfully with the papacy for the imperial title. BIBLIOGRAPHY: A. Mancone, BiblSanct 3:872–874; C. M. Aherne, NCE 3:111–112.

[T. GILBY]

CARLOS, FREI (fl. 1517–40), Portuguese painter of Flemish origin, through his works of tenderness and grace called the "Portuguese Fra Angelico." *The Good Shepherd* (Lisbon) by C. shows the influence of Memling and Gerard David. C. entered the monastery at Evora and worked with F. Henriques on the altar panels of S. Francisco (Lisbon). BIBLIOGRAPHY: R. Reis Santos, *Frei Carlos* (1940).

[M. J. DALY]

CARLSTADT, ANDREAS RUDOLF, see KARLSTADT, ANDREAS RUDOLF BODENSTEIN VON.

CARLYLE, AELRED (1874–1955), English Benedictine abbot. C. became an Anglican Benedictine oblate in 1893. In 1902 he was named abbot of his monastery and undertook to move his community to Caldey Island. Seven years after the move he and 22 of his monks became Roman Catholic. He made his novitiate and solemn profession at the Abbey of Mardesous and was ordained and blessed as abbot of Caldey. In 1921 he resigned and engaged in pastoral work in Canada. Upon his return to England he renewed his vows (1953) and was appointed abbot of Prinknash. A colorful figure, C.

encountered many difficulties in carrying out his ambitious plans for Caldey. BIBLIOGRAPHY: P. Anson, *Abbot Extraordinary* (1958).

[M. J. SUELZER]

CARLYLE, THOMAS (1795–1881), Scottish essayist and historian, the "Sage of Chelsea." Unsuccessful in teaching and in law, he gained a reputation with his *Life of Schiller* (1823) and a translation of Goethe's *Wilhelm Meister*. Married to Jane Welsh he lived for 6 years at lonely Craigenputtock, writing essays and his first original book *Sartor Resartus* (1833), partly autobiographical, partly transcendental speculation depicting all material things as *clothes,* symbols of eternal realities. At Chelsea, London, he published *The French Revolution* (1837). He vehemently opposed in speech and writing utilitarianism, democracy, and ideas of progress; he saw England in a crisis to be saved only through a wise governing class. His style is idiosyncratic and obscure, his historical portraiture vivid; he saw history as a revelation of eternal justice delivered to leaders for the guidance of mankind. BIBLIOGRAPHY: J. Symons, *Thomas Carlyle: The Life and Ideas of a Prophet* (1952, repr. 1973); C. Moore, NCE 3:112–113.; G. K. Chesterton, *Thomas Carlyle* (1973 repr.); J. Wilson, *Thomas Carlyle: The Iconoclast of Modern Shams* (1973).

[M. M. BARRY]

CARMEL, MOUNT (from the Heb., orchard or garden land), a mountain and mountain ridge on the NW coast of Palestine nine miles SW of Acre. It is mentioned in the OT in various places, esp. in connection with Elijah and Elisha, and was the mountainous site where Elijah contended with the priests of Baal (1 Kg 18.21–46). Traditionally the mountain is believed to have been, at least at some periods, a favored location of schools of prophets. Some Carmelites have attempted to trace their order's beginnings back through such schools to Elijah himself. The word Carmel is also used sometimes to designate a monastery of Carmelite nuns.

[M. S. J. MCCAREY]

CARMELITANUM, first international college of the Discalced Carmelites. This foundation opened in 1620. It was closed in 1873 when religious orders were suppressed in Italy. The present foundation, which is known as Teresianum, opened in 1926. Its theological facilities were canonically erected for members of the order in 1935. The title "pontifical" was conferred in 1963. The institution grants Th. L. and Th. D. degrees. In 1957 the Institutum Spiritualitatis was established, and in 1959 this faculty was made available to men and women who are not Carmelites.

[M. S. J. MCCAREY]

CARMELITE MARTYRS, a group of 16 Carmelite nuns executed during the French Revolution (July 17, 1794). The antireligious fury of the revolutionary government of France was nowhere more evident in its senselessness than in the guillotining of the community of Carmelite nuns from Compiègne. Led by a dynamic and dedicated superior, 15 ordinary women became selfless martyrs in a 4-year period. Thérèse of St. Augustine was an extraordinary religious of deep spirituality. In 1790 the nuns were offered their freedom if they would accept the new French constitution. They refused. Two years later they were expelled from the convent but went into hiding in Compiègne. In June 1794, they were discovered, arrested, and conveyed for trial to Paris in open carts. In the Hall of Liberty the court held them guilty of practicing the religious life contrary to the constitution, of being religious fanatics and sympathizers with the king. When sentence of execution was passed, they received it with joyous expression. In prison they fashioned themselves approximations of the Carmelite habit and dressed thus were transported to the scaffold, chanting hymns. Eyewitness accounts give a feeling of the drama of this episode in the Reign of Terror. There was a great hush over the crowd throughout the event. Mother Thérèse asked that she be the last to be executed so as to be a source of encouragement to the others. Beginning with the novice in her 20s and going to the two octogenarians, the slaughter finally engulfed all. There were no customary cheers nor the usual drum rolls at such executions. The horror of such scenes brought an end to the Reign of Terror and within 10 days Robespierre, its originator, was himself guillotined on the same spot. The Carmelite martyrs were beatified in 1906.

BIBLIOGRAPHY: P. T. Rohrback, *Journey to Carith* (1966); V. di S. Maria, BiblSanct 4:135–138; Butler 3:132–134.

[J. R. AHERNE]

CARMELITE SPIRITUALITY.

There is no question that the 800-year history of the Carmelites has greatly enriched the Western Church. The depth and variety of its teaching constitutes a phenomenon of Christianity. The essential elements of Carmelite doctrine are bound up with the origins of the order and center on imitation of the Prophet Elijah and devotion to the Blessed Virgin. The Teresian reform of the 16th cent. and the writings of St. John of the Cross did nothing more than sound a call to revive the spirit and life of the original Carmelites. Other elements of Carmelite spirituality will be described: vocation to the mystical life and to contemplation; love of solitude; the sensory, intellectual, and affective combination of elements in the contemplative life; primacy of the contemplative vocation; devotion to the Blessed Sacrament. Shining through all of these elements, however, is the ancient dual dedication to Elijah and the Blessed Virgin.

The original foundation of the Carmelites was a small band of men living the life of hermits on Mount Carmel in the Holy Land to which the Prophet Elijah had retired when his mission to Israel was completed. There is abundant witness by contemporary writers that by the mid-11th cent. "brothers of Carmel" were living in the place and under the influence of the spirit of Elijah.

It is a matter of prime importance that the chapel built for the first hermits of Mount Carmel was dedicated to the Blessed Virgin under the title St. Mary of Mount Carmel. The second superior, St. Brocard, spoke of the brethren as Brothers of Our Lady. The Prior General Pierre Enullien in 1282, writing to Edward I of England, refers to the order as having been founded for the honor and glory of the Blessed Virgin. The well-known Carmelite writer, John Baconthorp, cites the special attachment of the Carmelites to Mary. She is viewed as the "owner" of the order and therefore one to whom Carmelites can turn for special protection. The widespread use by the laity of the scapular of Mt. Carmel, representing the religious habit of Carmelites throughout the world, and the favor shown the practice by many popes are evidence of this current in the life of the order.

From early days writers in the Carmelite tradition have stressed the formal vocation to the mystical life as an integral part of the order's spirituality. The doctrine affirmed that a Carmelite by living the life of the rule prepared himself to receive graces of mystical awareness which were a free gift of God.

Even when conditions of 13th-cent. Europe required Carmel to undertake more active work and to go into the cities, the ancient tradition of contemplation and solitude persisted in varying degrees. Houses of solitude which allowed for the eremitic life were established. The contemplative ideal was expressed in the adage "to leave God (i.e., contemplation) because of God" (i.e., to do apostolic work). The advocates of the contemplative tradition were present even in a period of decline. St. Peter Thomas, St. Andrew Corsini, John of Hildesheim, the English Carmelites who translated the works of Richard Rolle, all reiterated the traditional preoccupation with contemplation and solitude.

Among the characteristics of Carmel from early days was devotion to the Blessed Sacrament. Even in the heyday of hermit-style living, a chapel for the Eucharist was the focal point. Among many who were exemplars of extraordinary devotion were St. Peter Thomas, Blessed John Soreth, and St. Mary Magdalene de' Pazzi.

In the mid-15th cent. the teaching of the Prior General Bl. John Soreth had profound influence. Soreth emphasized systematic meditation centering on contemplation of nature as reflecting the law of God, Holy Scripture, and our own lives as they reveal the presence of God.

A remarkable man, the lay brother John of Saint-Samson, was the heart of the reform of Touraine in the 17th century. His doctrine emphasized again that the essential vocation of Carmelites was a mystical union by contemplation, which was itself a free gift of God, for which they prepare themselves by a life of virtue. Perfection consists in the union of the soul with God who dwells within it.

The 16th cent. saw the advent of the most celebrated spiritual writers of Carmel: the reformists St. Teresa of Avila and St. John of the Cross. It is important to realize that these powerful figures regarded their work as a restoration of the ancient spirit of the order. Their reflections on the spiritual life are consonant. The Teresian doctrine was addressed to those committed to the contemplative life. The contemplative approach is a gift of God. Other approaches are valid but this approach is the highest. The contemplative ideal calls for a passage through the "dark night" of the purifying way before one reaches the illuminative way. Every posture of the soul is intended to place one in the hands of God; it is an active, not passive, state. Not all are called to the highest levels of contemplation, but all can achieve some progress to that ideal.

A second consideration of Teresian spirituality is the need for purity of heart as a prerequisite to contemplation. Fraternal charity, humility, self-denial are the antecedents. A third characteristic of the Teresian spirituality is the concept of totality. However limited the strength of a soul, it is required to attempt a total giving of self to God. Short of that giving, one cannot expect the returning gift of himself to the soul. A final trait of Teresian spirituality is its developmental aspect. The doctrine of Teresa and John is not to be regarded as closed. Theological speculation and reasoning on the contemplative life will always enlarge and enrich the doctrine of the 16th-cent. mystics. A prime example of such reflection is Thomas of Jesus in the 17th cent. who applied in a remarkable way the theological examination of Teresa and John. The literature of commentary and enlargement of the Teresian doctrine has developed in late centuries a vast number of interpreters. The Teresian tradition today is perhaps more lively than it was in the 16th century. BIBLIOGRAPHY: P. T. Rohrback, *Journey to Carith* (1966); R. Pierret, DSAM 2.1:136–140; E. Flicoteaux, *ibid.*, 2.1:140–151; T. Brandsma, *ibid.*, 2.1:156–171; Gabriel de Saint-Marie-Madaleine, *ibid.*, 2.1:171–209.

[J. R. AHERNE]

CARMELITES. Whether one looks at the legendary or historical version of the story of the founding of the Carmelites, the account stands unique among narratives of the beginnings of a religious community. The legend that traced the order back to the Prophet Elijah in OT times was long defended as authentic by Carmelite writers. When more demanding historical tests were made of the authenticity of the Elijahan legend, however, it gave way to a realistic dating of the founding in mid-12th cent. A.D. In spite of this correction, there is no doubt of the persistent and effective Elijahan tradition as one of the chief influences on Carmelite life and spirituality. Mount Carmel in Palestine, associated with the Prophet and with the Blessed Virgin, brings together two dominant currents of Carmelite life. The order has always been devoted to exercising the prophetic function, i.e., witnessing the presence of God in the world, and has acknowledged the Blessed Virgin as not only patron but owner of the order with special protection for its members. Through all its vicissitudes over 8 cent., this dual orientation never ceased.

The first historically demonstrable foundation of the order was on Mount Carmel about 1155. The Crusades had established the Latin Kingdom of Jerusalem and it was in this milieu that Carmel was born. A small group of Europeans led a semi-eremitic life, but from the beginning went out from their monastery to preach and do works of charity. The second superior, Brocard, built the chapel and dedicated it to the Blessed Virgin. He also appealed to the Latin Patriarch of Jerusalem for a rule that was composed by the Patriarch Albert, drawing considerably on the Eastern monastic tradition of St. Basil and Cassian. It gave an essentially contemplative character to the order. New foundations sprang up but the superior of Mount Carmel retained the primacy.

Turkish oppression eventually drove most of the Carmelite communities to Europe. In 1291 the final attack resulted in the destruction of the monastery of Mount Carmel and the murder of all its monks. The history of the order would henceforth be European. From the European beginnings, the order fell on troubled times. Their way of life as hermits seemed to have little service to the Church and their location perforce in rural areas did not help. Under the vigorous leadership of St. Simon Stock, an Englishman who can be termed the second founder of the Carmelites, an appeal was made to Rome that resulted in two major changes in the rule: the eremitic mode of living in separate huts was abolished and the order was permitted to establish itself in urban areas. Under Simon the friars moved into pastoral work and the universities. It was Simon whose vision of the Blessed Mother brought the Carmelite scapular into Catholic life because of its wide adoption by lay people who thus associated themselves with the Carmelites.

The flowering of the order in the Middle Ages saw the Carmelites accepted as one of the great mendicant (as contrasted with monastic) orders: Augustinians, Carmelites, Dominicans, and Franciscans. The work of the order at the Univ. of Paris and at other flourishing medieval universities was outstanding. Two illustrious saints graced its medieval period: St. Andrew Corsini and St. Peter Thomas. The latter became a hero of the order, seeking in his career to epitomize the Elijahan concept of a man of prayer, solitude, and action for God.

Europe in the 14th and 15th cent.—and the Church —suffered serious setbacks and decline largely because of the devastation of the Black Plague and the incessant wars between the English and the French. Religious orders declined and the general state of religion and morality declined with them. The Carmelites were no exception. Scandals and abuses riddled the order. The Great Western Schism with its confusion of jurisdictions contributed to its decline. An extreme example of the decadent period of the Carmelites is the renowned painter Fra Filippo Lippi, immortalized by the poet Robert Browning. The Protestant Reformation created havoc with the Carmelites as with all other orders of the time and by the end of the 16th cent., the order had lost half its membership and was in a state of serious decline.

In the 13th cent. the Franciscans and Dominicans founded communities of women who constituted the Second Order, the communities of men being regarded as the First Order. The Carmelites for a long time had no formally organized nuns though groups of women living an informal religious life were often affiliated with the order. John Soreth, the Carmelite general, established the first group in the mid-15th century. From the beginning there were diverse practices in such groups, some adhering more strictly to the Carmelite tradition, others to a more relaxed regimen. Among the latter was the Convent of the Incarnation in Avila, Spain, where the most influential and remarkable of all Carmelites was to begin her career, St. Teresa of Avila.

Beautiful, charming, on a conversational basis with God as a mystic, but convincingly human, Teresa joined one of the relaxed communities of the 16th cent. and was not unhappy about her life until she was 38 years old. She underwent a conversion that made her dissatisfied with the good but unexacting life of Carmel in that time. Determined to found a convent that would restore the strict observance of the first Carmelites, and enjoined by God to pursue the project, Teresa encountered some support but much more opposition, both within and outside the order. Appealing directly to Rome, Teresa received approval to establish one convent in Avila in 1562. Her next move was to appeal to the Carmelite general to establish monasteries for men who wished to follow the ancient observance. The request was granted and Teresa found an ally in the great Carmelite mystic and poet St. John of the Cross. It was, however, Teresa the builder and administrator who vigorously pursued foundations for men.

There ensued a violent contest between the nonreformed (Calced, literally "shod") and the reformed Carmelites (Discalced, i.e., wearing sandals), a struggle marked by intrigue and counterintrigue, involving religious, prelates, and finally Phillip II himself. The upshot of the agitation was a papal decree in 1580 separating the Discalced as a distinct province. By 1588 they were constituted a separate order.

No one suffered more than John of the Cross from the intrigues of the Calced. He spent time in prison under horrible conditions. Yet John became one of the most notable writers of Spanish literature. *The Spiritual Canticle, Ascent of Mount Carmel,* and *Dark Night of the Soul* constitute an unrivaled body of spiritual writing that is of the highest literary quality.

It is difficult to trace separately the development of the two distinct orders that emerged at the end of the 16th cent. and yet they have distinct histories. For 200 years, by decree of the general superiors of the Discalced friars and nuns, the order was confined to the Iberian peninsula and the Spanish and Portuguese missions in Latin America. In spite of this and through papal action, foundations were established in Italy but were not affiliated with the Spanish Discalced. Through the persistence of Madame Acare, Spanish nuns established a foundation in Paris, and shortly numerous convents opened throughout France.

Reform among the Carmelites was not limited to the Discalced. In pre-Tridentine times as well as later, the older group instituted a number of reforms. Because they followed the mitigated rule of St. Simon Stock, the Calced were engaged much more in apostolic activities. In the 17th cent. the Calced friars established missions in Persia, India, China, and the West Indies. In 1631 a group of Discalced reestablished the order on Mount Carmel in Palestine. The English mission was supplied with a number of Carmelites, as were Ireland and Scotland. The Discalced Carmelite Thomas of Jesus wrote the first important work on missiology in 1610.

This remarkable man was instrumental in the establishment of the Society for the Propagation of the Faith in Rome. As a writer on mystical theology he invites comparison with Teresa and John of the Cross. Among both groups there was a persistent flow of mystical and devotional writings in the 17th and 18th cent., with special emphasis on the Blessed Virgin.

As with all religious orders, the years from the last quarter of the 18th cent. to the first quarter of the 19th were a time of persecution and decline in Europe. The French Revolution and the succeeding pattern of repression and revolution wrought havoc on the Carmelites. A recovery began in the late 19th cent. and is evident today. The first permanent foundation of the order in the U.S. was the Discalced Carmelite convent in Baltimore in 1790. The growth of the Carmelite nuns in the U.S. has been phenomenal, 68 convents having been established by 1966.

Discalced Carmelite friars came later to America but now have foundations in seven states.

The older order, the Calced, suffered similar decline and recovery. Today they are represented in 17 provinces and 5 vice-provinces in Italy, Spain, Portugal, Germany, Austria, Poland, Czechoslovakia, the Netherlands, England, Ireland, Australia, Brazil, and the U.S. In America they are laboring in 19 dioceses and administer 11 secondary schools and 30 parishes. BIBLIOGRAPHY: P. T. Rohrback, *Journey to Carith* (1966).

[J. R. AHERNE]

CARMELITES (DISCALCED)

CARMELITES (DISCALCED), an order of cloistered women who follow the primitive Carmelite Rule and follow the contemplative way of life. After a period of decline St. Theresa of Avila initiated a reform in 1562, a reform that spread throughout the world. In 1790 John Carroll, first bp. of Baltimore, invited the Carmelites into his vast diocese "to pray for the American missions." From this foundation many Carmels sprang up in all parts of the U.S. In 1975 Carmelite nuns numbered 11,075 worldwide and conducted 727 monasteries. *CARMELITES.

[R. C. CLIGGETT]

CARMELITES (SISTERS)

CARMELITES (SISTERS), congregations of women who from the 13th cent. on followed a modified Carmelite Rule but led an active as opposed to a strictly contemplative life. Their works include teaching, caring for the aged, hospitals, missions, catechetical work, retreats and other charitable works. These sisters are found throughout the world and number at least 12 active sisterhoods. Some of the congregations are: Carmelite Sisters for the Aged and Infirm, Carmelite Sisters of Charity, Carmelite Sisters of Corpus Christi, Carmelite Sisters of St. Therese of the Infant Jesus, Carmelite Sisters of the Divine Heart of Jesus, Carmelite Sisters of the Third Order, and the Congregation of Our Lady of Mt. Carmel. *CARMELITES.

[R. C. CLIGGETT]

CARMELITES OF MARY IMMACULATE, a religious congregation of priests and brothers founded in India in 1831. Their first constitutions were approved in 1855 and 1906. It was the first religious institute among Catholics of Syro-Malabar rite. Its members follow a modified version of the Discalced Carmelites' rule and conduct schools from primary to college level, maintain mission stations, catechetical centers, hospitals, and orphanages. In 1975 the congregation numbered 1,192 members.

[R. C. CLIGGETT]

CARMEN ADVERSUS MARCIONEM (MARCIONITAS), longest work of Tertullian, which is the principal source of information about the Gnostic ascetic movement initiated by Marcion and active from the 2d to the 7th centuries, which rejected the OT and belief in Christ as God incarnate.

[S. F. JOHNSON]

CARMICHAEL, MONTGOMERY (1857–1936), novelist, essayist, officer of the British consular service, and an authority on Franciscana. Two of his works of fiction merit to be still in print: *The Life of John William Walshe* (1902), a delicate study of a devout layman, and the *Solitaries of the Sambuca* (1914), which evokes the peace of a religious community clustered round a hermitage in Tuscany.

[T. GILBY]

CARMINA BURANA (Lat., songs of Beuren), the famous collection of medieval Latin songs and poems in the 13th-cent. MS (Munich, Staatsbibliothek Lat. 4660) formerly belonging to the Abbey of Benediktbeuern. It contains 190 Latin, High German, and macaronic (mixed languages) poems plus a few prose works and *liturgical dramas. The poems are usually ascribed to the goliards (wandering students and clerics) and include religious and moralistic texts, satire about corrupt ecclesiastics, and love lyrics, some quite lascivious. They all show highly developed poetical talent and a variety of meters. Illumination of the MS is notable for a landscape (breaking with the Carolingian style of landscape as symbol or as background to the figure) that displays an anthology of Romanesque plant ornament with birds and animals. Trees, though abstract, have vitality in a compressed, dynamic space suggesting energy, release, and exuberance, and, though wholly imaginative, evoke the essential reality of nature. Carl Orff's *Carmina burana* (1935–36), a setting of a selection of the poems for soloists, chorus, and orchestra has achieved considerable popularity. Facs. ed. of Munich StBibl, 4660, B. Bischoff (1967); crit. ed. of texts, A. Hilka and O. Schumann (1930–41). BIBLIOGRAPHY: H. J. Waddell, *Wandering Scholars* (1932, repr. 1955); Reese MusMA.

[P. MURPHY]

CARNAC, on the S coast of Brittany, France, site of 3000 table stones (dolmens) 16 feet tall in three parallel rows, over 3 miles in length. The stones were erected for ritual purposes at the end of the Neolithic Age. BIBLIOGRAPHY: F. Hibben, *Prehistoric Man in Europe* (1958).

[M. J. DALY]

CARNEADES OF CYRENE (213–128 B.C.), founder of the New Academy and of modified skepticism through his theory of probability. After heading the academy for many years, C. resigned in 136. In 156–155, he was one of the Athenian delegation, (the other members being the Stoic Diogenes of Babylon and the Peripatetic Critolaus) that visited Rome and had such an intellectual impact on the Romans. In his famous *disputatio in utramque partem,* he shocked Cato the Elder by defending justice in one speech and by demolishing all his arguments in its favor in a second. He left no writings, but as a teacher and thinker he exercised a great influence on contemporary and later Greek and Roman philosophy. In some respects he exhibited eclectic tendencies, esp. in ethics. He continued the polemic of *Arcesilaus against the Stoics, attacking their theory of sense-presentation, their theology including their doctrine of Divine Providence, and all forms of divination and fatalism. He modified the doctrine of strict supervision of judgment (Gr., *epoche*) as formulated by Arcesilaus and developed a theory of probability *(pithanotes)*, in which various grades of probability are recognized and serve as the basis for decision and action. C. was the most systematic and influential representative of ancient Skepticism. His doctrine of probabilism became a permanent feature of the epistemology of the New Academy and constituted a new philosophical method. BIBLIOGRAPHY: Copleston 1:414–417; OCD s.v.; Lex AW s.v. "Karneades von Kyrene"; A. Schutz, *Reflections on the Problem of Relevance* (ed. R. M. Zaner, 1970).

[M. R. P. MCGUIRE]

CARNESECCHI, PIETRO (1508–67), beheaded and burned as a traitor. The well-educated son of a Florentine merchant, he was secretary to Clement VII. Among his friends were Ochino and Vermigli, whose apostasy made C. suspect. Lack of evidence favored him (1546) but in 1552, he again was supporting the Lutheran view of Reformation. Condemned by Paul IV for contumacy, he appealed the decision after the death of Paul. The appeal was granted but Pius V reopened the case. C. was found guilty and on Oct. 1, 1567, he was decapitated. BIBLIOGRAPHY: E. A. Carrillo, NCE 3:127–128.

[E. T. MCGOVERN]

CARNIVAL, season (generally 3 days) preceding Lent observed in some places with merrymaking, usually public. It ends with Mardi Gras celebrated in Paris and New Orleans with parades and special festivities. It is also a traveling show with amusements and rides to celebrate special feasts.

[S. F. JOHNSON]

CARNUS, CHARLES BL., martyr of Paris. During the French Revolution in 1792 a group of priests and religious who had refused to take the oath of the Civil Constitution of the Clergy were imprisoned in Paris. The revolutionary forces were under pressure from invading armies and panic ensued. This gave the anti-religious elements of the Revolution an excuse to massacre great numbers who were opposed to the atheistic drive in the Revolution. Among those who were martyred was C., who was executed at the age of 43.

[J. R. AHERNE]

CARO, JOSEPH BEN EPHRAIM (1488–1575), outstanding codifier of Jewish law. Exiled from Spain during the expulsion (1492), C. and his family, after much wandering, went to Constantinople. In 1535 he settled at Safed, Palestine, where he wrote *Beth Yoseph* (House of Joseph; 1550–59) and its abridged version, *Shulhan Arukh* (The Prepared Table; 1564–65). A scholar of Jewish law second only to Maimonides, C. included in his works not only the collections of previous codifiers but also his own opinions on disputed points. Some of his decisions were strongly opposed by Ashkenazi scholars, esp. Moses Isserles in his *Darkhe Mosheh* and *Ha-Mappah* (Tablecloth). However, *Shulhan Arukh*, combined with Isserles's additions, became and remains the authoritative code of Orthodox Jews throughout the world. BIBLIOGRAPHY: R. Werblowsky, *Joseph Karo: Lawyer and Mystic* (1962); H. Graetz, *History of the Jews* (1927) 4:537–539.

[A. P. HANLON]

CARO, MIGUEL ANTONIO (1843–1909), Colombian writer, poet, and politician. C. received an excellent education in the classics from the Jesuits and became an outstanding translator of Virgil and Horace. With Rufino Cuervo he wrote a Latin grammar that is still used in parts of Latin America. In 1873 he established the Colombian Academy of Languages. Politically, he was one of the founders of the conservative party and an architect of the constitution of 1886. He held various important posts and as vice-president governed Colombia from 1892 to 1896 in the voluntary absence of its president. His messages to the congress made a great impact on the country. C. remained to the end a faithful son of the Church and its staunch defender. BIBLIOGRAPHY: M. A. Bonilla, *Caro y su obra* (1947); L. López de Mesa, *Miguel Antonio Caro y Rufino José Cuervo* (1944).

[P. DAMBORIENA]

CAROL, a popular form of religious song in England in the late Middle Ages. Although generally thought of as Christmas songs, carols were written for all important holidays and festivals. R. I. Greene has defined the carol as a poem ''intended, or at least suitable for singing, made up of uniform stanzas and provided with a burden (refrain) which begins the piece and is to be repeated after each stanza.'' The texts were English, Latin, or *macaronic, and according to tradition originated in the French ring-dance in which participants clapped their hands or inserted a vocal refrain at intervals. Manuscript evidence shows that the earliest Middle English carols were often for church processions, or were used for didactic purposes in the same way as the Italian *lauda*. Carols were preserved through a written tradition as opposed to the oral transmission of the ballads and folk songs. Of the existing 500 medieval carols more than 100 have musical settings that range from simple melodies to the elaborate polyphonic arrangements of the Tudor period. The carol fell into disuse during the Reformation but continued to exist in the guise of popular song. A revival occurred in the early 19th cent., and many of the most popular Christmas carols date from this period; but because it was a pietistic, sentimental development, a reaction followed. The texts of medieval carols have been used in numerous modern musical settings, esp. for Christmas, though the original 15th-cent. music is almost unknown. The medieval carol has become a favorite of 20th cent. English composers such as Peter Warlock, Ralph *Vaughn-Williams, and Benjamin Britten. BIBLIOGRAPHY: R. L. Greene, *Selection of English Carols* (1962); J. Stevens, NCE 3:130–132; Reese MusR; D. Gilbert, *Some Ancient Christmas Carols with the Tunes to Which They Were Formally Sung in the West of England* (1972); E. Routley, *The English Carol* (1959, repr. 1973).

[P. MURPHY]

CAROLINE BOOKS, see LIBRI CAROLINI.

CAROLINE DIVINES, Anglican theological writers who, esp. in the 17th cent., stressed RC elements in Anglicanism as essentials. They defended episcopacy, ritual, and the doctrine of the Real Presence. Among those so classified were Richard *Hooker, Lancelot Andrewes, William *Laud, and Jeremy *Taylor, but there were many others. The classification, despite the name, is not restricted to theologians who wrote during the reign of Charles I (1625–49) or of Charles II (1660–85). BIBLIOGRAPHY: G. Albion, NCE 3:133–134, for complete list and for bibliog.

[R. B. ENO]

CAROLINGIAN ART (later 8th and early 9th cent.). Under the impetus of Charlemagne whose alliance with Adrian I (772) implemented the Germanic North's critical interest in the culture of ancient Rome, an art of royal patronage on a scale hitherto unknown in N Europe, is attested by architecture, metalwork (with Einhard as director), ivories, and illuminated manuscripts. Different styles are distinguished, notably the schools of Metz and Reims. The Gospels of Godescalc (781-783), first book from the palace in Aachen; the Gospels of St. Médard-de-Soissons; the Vivian Bible (mid-9th cent.) from school at Tours; the most creative MS, the Utrecht psalter from Hautvillers near Reims (*c.*832); and the *Codex aureus* from St. Emmeram of Regensburg are treasures of Carolingian scholarship and magnificence. Carolingian architecture (Palatine Chapel, Aachen, 792) shows Roman and Byzantine—even Visigothic—emulations, but few buildings survive. Great abbeys over the world (e.g., Sankt Gallen in Switzerland) are a final flowering of the great monastic centers of Carolingian culture. BIBLIOGRAPHY: J. G. Beckwith, *Early Medieval Art* (1964); R. P. Hinks, *Carolingian Art* (1935); K. J. Conant, *Carolingian and Romanesque Architecture* (1959).

[R. C. MARKS]

CAROLINGIAN DYNASTY, the great dynasty of Western Europe (754–987). The family rose to power as mayors of the palace under the Merovingian kings. In 751 Charles Martel's son, Pepin the Short, deposed the puppet ruler and made himself king with the pope's approval. Strong administration, military and cultural expansion to the east, and alliance with the popes characterized the early history of this dynasty that transformed Gaul into France. Government was personal and primitive and reflected the policy and will of the monarch himself. The unity of Charlemagne's empire was shattered by civil wars and new barbarian invasions. BIBLIOGRAPHY: R. Hoyt, *Europe in the Middle Ages* (1966).

[M. T. GRIFFIN]

CAROLINGIAN LEGENDS, epic poems chiefly from the 12th and 13th cent. expressing the idealized life and deeds of Emperor *Charlemagne (742?–814). These legends began as early as Charlemagne's own lifetime and were largely fostered in religious houses having or claiming Carolingian foundation. With the *Chanson de Roland* (1100), one of more than 100 French *chansons de geste* relating exploits of well-known heroes and kings of history and legend, Charles entered vernacular literature and became an embodiment of an ideal of religious kingship. The epic inflates Charles' abortive Spanish campaign of 778 into a long, bitter war against the Saracens by recounting the culminating episode, the destruction of the young hero Roland at Roncesvaux, the defeat of the victorious Saracens by Charles, and his vengeance on their accomplice Ganelon. Roland emerges as an ideal hero who dies serving God through pledging allegiance to Charlemagne, lord of Christendom and champion of Christ on earth. Many later Carolingian epics further develop the crusading theme of the defense and extension of Christendom, and show the Emperor fighting in Italy against immense Saracen hosts or they serve as introductions or epilogues to the Roncesvaux story. Works set in Spain (e.g., *Gui de Bourgogne, Anseïs de Carthage*) reflect the influence of the Pseudo-Turpin chronicle (*c.*1150), a Latin prose work embodying the theme of Charlemagne's campaigns to free the shrine of St. James of Compostela. The Italian group (e.g., *Fierabras, La destruction de Rome*) relate legends of Italian pilgrimages. *Le pèlerinage de Charlemagne* tells of Charlemagne's journey to Jerusalem and his return to Europe with relics. Another group of epics (e.g., *Berte aus Grans Pies*) is built around the folkloric theme of the persecuted child. In many Carolingian legends, Charlemagne's life and exploits are contaminated with pre-existing tales. In these *chansons de geste* Charlemagne's twelve peers are usually

more prominent than he and highlight the Emperor's legendary old age more than his prowess. A certain burlesque quality characterizing some of the chansons may owe its origin partly to the looseness of Charlemagne's actual life, but as a king in an age when genius and kingship were both attributed to divinity, Charlemagne generally appears the ideal king-hero. BIBLIOGRAPHY: H. Newstead, NCE 1:920–922; J. Misrahi, NCE 6:150–157.

[M. SAGUÉS]

CAROLINGIAN MINUSCULE, style of handwriting established during the educational reforms of Charlemagne. The beautiful and clear script developed by Alcuin's school of calligraphy at Tours spread rapidly throughout western Europe. It combined majuscules, or capital letters, and minuscules, or small letters, and was more easily legible than other forms in use at that time. In the 15th cent. the early printers, using this script as a model, designed the common roman type in use today. BIBLIOGRAPHY: R. Hoyt, *Europe in the Middle Ages* (1966).

[M. T. GRIFFIN]

CAROLINGIAN REFORM, a century-long reform movement (*c.*740–840) in the Frankish realm. It aimed at correcting clerical corruption, ignorance, immortality, pagan survivals, the great diversity in religious observances, and widespread seizure of Church property in the Frankish kingdom. The impetus derived from the influence of St. Boniface and the other Anglo-Saxon missionaries established in the N and E fringes of the kingdom. These reforms conformed closely to the papal policy in the early 8th cent. and succeeded in creating a solid ecclesiastical organization with a disciplined clergy.

Pepin III, Charlemagne, and Louis I the Pious intensified the reform with their political power. They worked for a deeper spiritual life among their subjects and for an effective political regime through a strengthened Church. The royal court issued ecclesiastical legislation on the prevalent problems and introduced clergy zealous for reform such as Alcuin, Paul the Deacon, and Benedict of Aniane, in crucial court offices. Each ruler supervised clerical positions closely; Charlemagne patronized a revival of learning with much papal support. The Carolingian reform originated the norms for future reform efforts. It redefined the heritage of the early Church within the context of the Germanic society.

[M. H. BEIRNE]

CAROLINGIAN RENAISSANCE, an aesthetic and intellectual revival of Latin classicism emphasizing education and church reform, which was initiated by Charlemagne and carried through the 9th century. The fall of the Roman Empire and the barbarian invasions that accompanied it left a critical hiatus in the cultural development of Europe. With a few notable exceptions the centers of learning disappeared and with them the groups of scholars who had clustered around them. There could be no development of intellectual and cultural life until the tribal and fragmented rule of the Franks and other groups gave way to a unified kingdom. It was Charlemagne who set to work on this endeavor in the last quarter of the 8th century. This wise and far-seeing creator of the new Roman Empire saw that education alone could raise the level of his people. Because the Church and its continued vigor were very much entwined with any attempt to bring a revival of learning to the new era in the West, the Emperor gave every encouragement to its educational efforts.

The unity of Christian faith became the fostering spirit of the Carolingian renaissance. Though its purpose and early direction were religious, the whole field of learning was developed. Because the West had lost touch with the Hellenic East, the sources were Latin, with almost no influence of Greek except insofar as the former rested on the latter. Through vigorous legislation and personal influence, Charlemagne encouraged the monasteries to cultivate scholarship, saw to the founding of cathedral schools and schools associated with the royal palace. The collecting of MSS and copying of important works developed a whole new network of libraries and scriptoria in the monasteries and episcopal houses. While the principal beneficiaries of the new learning were clergy and religious, laymen and laywomen were encouraged to take advantage of educational opportunities. The scope of education included elementary training for children and liberal arts education for adults. The program devised by Charlemagne and his scholars was to be the pattern of education for 400 years.

The aesthetic and literary influence of Isidore of Seville (d. 636) and Ven. Bede (d. 735) on the Carolingian renaissance were incalculable: they pursued the classics not only for their cultural interest but also for the practical use that contemporary society could draw from them in learning to read and write Latin. Charlemagne brought to his kingdom two Italian scholars, Peter of Pisa and Paul the Deacon, eminent Latinists. Paulinus of Aquileia, a theologian, held a position at the court. Most famous of all invited to share in the cultural revival was the English monk *Alcuin, who became abbot of St. Martin of Tours and acted as chief educational adviser to Charlemagne. It was Alcuin above all who created a new interest in theological research and discussion that tended to bring the Frankish Church into the mainstream of Rome and Constantinople. Another feature of the Carolingian renaissance was the study of law, both canon and civil. The movement to substitute the universality of Roman law for the fragmentary and often absurd Germanic tribal laws began under the great Emperor. Many of the developments in theology and law continued under Charlemagne's successors, esp. Louis the Pious.

The intellectual rebirth in Carolingian times embraced grammar, literature, law, history, music, science, philosophy, and theology. It was the gateway to the new high point in intellectual history which occurred in the 13th century.

Corresponding in its manifestation of the civilized spirit to the intellectual revival was the development of the visual arts in the Carolingian renaissance. The early wooden structure of Frankish origin gave way to stone buildings that showed dependence on both the Latin and Byzantine tradition. The Royal Chapel at Aix is the crowning church of the period. It was begun in 792 and consecrated in 805. In 806 the small church of Germigny-des-Prés showed original artistic design. Carolingian architecture was an original revival of Roman classicism. The decoration of churches in the period made much use of mosaic, fresco, and work in gold and silver. Liturgical furnishings provided the medium for some extraordinary artistic creation: altars, chalices, patens, reliquaries, and crosses. The glory of the artistic productivity of the Carolingian period, however, was the illuminated manuscripts. The art of illumination was learned from the Irish and Anglo-Saxon monks, but in the Carolingian era it took on new dimensions. Partly influenced by Byzantine painting, the new illuminating technique produced effects unknown before. Drogo's Sacramentary and the work of the school of the Abbey of St. Martin of Tours are magnificent examples of Carolingian illumination. The Grandval Bible of Tours is a masterpiece of this school. BIBLIOGRAPHY: J. Broussard, *Civilization of Charlemagne* (1968).

[J. R. AHERNE]

CARON, REDMOND (*c.* 1605–66), Irish theologian who made significant contributions in the methodology of missiology. He was born in Westmeath and did his priestly studies (as a Franciscan) in several places, most notable among them, Louvain. After ordination he taught philosophy and theology and apparently was successful. Less successful was his service as canonical visitor within the order. Besides fulfilling that post he spent time writing. Among his works are his manual of apologetics (1653) and a manual of missiology (1659). BIBLIOGRAPHY: B. Millett NCE 4:143–144.

[J. R. RIVELLO]

CAROSSA, HANS (1878–1956), Catholic novelist and poet. He began publishing in 1913 and in the 1930s gave up his medical practice to devote himself exclusively to literary work. He was rooted in the classical tradition. Like Goethe, to whom he bears some resemblance in outlook and approach, he transforms events of personal experience into universal symbols reflecting a higher world. All of his works are in some sense autobiographical. BIBLIOGRAPHY: J. Bithell, *Modern German Literature: 1880–1950* (1959); R. Hofrichter, *Three Poets and Reality* (1942, repr. 1969).

[I. MERKEL]

CARPACCIO, VITTORE (*c.* 1465–1525), Venetian painter assisting (1507) Giovanni Bellini in the Ducal Palace. C. was chiefly inspired by the panoramic, narrative style of the lesser great Gentile Bellini, but differs in the quality of light on geometric architectural forms. For lay confraternities, C. painted many series on the life of St. Ursula (1490–95); the life of Mary (*The Virgin Reading*, National Gallery, Washington, D.C.); and many altarpieces in later years for small towns outside Venice; a *Meditation* on the Passion (Metropolitan Museum, N.Y.); and a *Dead Christ* attributed earlier to Mantegna (brother-in-law of the Bellini brothers) with details and style in landscape showing close affinity to patterns of the Mantua master, Mantegna. BIBLIOGRAPHY: J. Lauts, *Carpaccio, Paintings and Drawings* (1962).

[M. J. DALY]

CARPANI, MELCHIORRE (1726–97), missionary. C. entered the Barnabites at 18 and was assigned to Burma in 1764. After studying the Burmese language, he tried to set it into print. Recalled to Rome (1774), he published the *Alphabetum Burmanum* and the *Memorie sopra la vita di Hyder Ali Kan.* BIBLIOGRAPHY: V. M. Colciago, EncCatt 3:926–927.

[E. T. MCGOVERN]

CARPOCRATES, Gnostic of the 2d cent. who taught in Alexandria. Some modern authorities deny his existence and claim that people of the sect were followers of the Egyptian god Horus-Horpacrates. Nevertheless, he is said to have taught a Platonic philosophy which was also influenced by Oriental thought whereby all things emanated in an unbroken chain from the first principle of existence, unknown and ineffable. Creation was necessarily evil, and to arrive at salvation one must despise all laws. Jesus was a great man because he so despised Jewish law. When a person died in the state of perfect hatred, his soul was reincarnated in a special way in another human form. The most celebrated of the disciples of Carpocrates was said to be his son Epiphanes, whose work, *On Justice,* is the most famous treatise of this sect. BIBLIOGRAPHY: G. W. MacRae, NCE 3:145.

[T. LIDDY]

CARPZOV, surname of a German family of theologians and lawyers who served the cause of Lutheranism in the 17th and 18th centuries. (1) Benedikt (1595–1666), professor of law at Leipzig from 1645 until his death. B. was the first to give methodical arrangement to German criminal law and to prepare a complete system of Protestant church law. He was an implacable opponent of G. *Calixt. (2) Johann Benedikt I (1607–57), theologian, brother of the preceding. He served as archdeacon at St. Thomas, Leipzig, and as professor of theology at the university there. His elucidation of the Lutheran confessions gained him the title of father of symbolics. (3) Johann Benedikt II (1639–99), theologian, son of the preceding. Professor of ethics and later of theology at Leipzig, he also worked as pastor and editor. His revision of his father's homiletic manual led him to oppose *Pietism. The bitter enmity in which he held Philipp *Spener was rooted partly in the latter's criticism of the theological training imparted at Leipzig. (4) Samuel Benedikt (1647–1707), court chaplain at Dresden, brother of the preceding. He became court preacher at Dresden as early as 1674. Called to the Kreuzkirche and later made superintendent, he was well disposed toward the Pietists until his brother became leader of the opposition and

persuaded him to change his attitude. (5) Johann Gottlob (1679–1767), theologian, son of Johann Benedikt II. Most learned of the Carpzovs, he was pastor at Dresden and professor of Hebrew at Leipzig. He wrote a valuable introduction to OT studies (1714–20), which maintained the verbal inspiration of the Scriptures and opposed the rising rationalist biblical studies. (6) Johann Benedikt V (1720–1803), classical scholar and theologian, grandson of Johann Benedikt II. Professor of Greek at Helmstedt and editor of classical texts, he wrote *Liber doctrinalis theologiae purioris* (1768) to oppose the rationalism of Albrecht Teller. BIBLIOGRAPHY: I. Ludolphy, EncLuthCh 1:370–371; F. Schühlein et al., LTK 2:955–956.

[M. J. SUELZER]

CARR, THOMAS MATTHEW (1755–1820), Augustinian friar, founder of the Augustinian Order in the U.S. A well-known priest in the Dublin of penal days, he was sent to America when Bp. John Carroll of Baltimore requested help from the Irish Augustinians in 1796. C. was assigned to St. Mary's Church in Philadelphia at a time when the neighboring parish, Holy Trinity, was embroiled in the lay trustee conflict that resulted in schism. Bp. Carroll appointed C. vicar-general for Pa. east of the Susquehanna River (1799), and much of his labor for the ensuing 8 years was occasioned by that assignment. His work entailed much travel in a diocese that was as large as the nation. In his capacity of vicar-general he was able to end the schism at Holy Trinity (1801), a tribute to his combination of firmness and diplomacy. Meanwhile, with the approval of Bp. Carroll, C. carried out the cherished ambition of establishing his order in the young republic. The first step was to build a new church and religious house in the area of Philadelphia near the Delaware River. Public subscription raised the money needed to begin. The list of subscribers carried the names of many prominent Philadelphians including that of George Washington. St. Augustine's Church was dedicated in 1801. It is of some interest that part of the cost was realized through a state-approved lottery, perhaps portent of things to come in the American Church. In 1804 C. obtained from the Pa. legislature an act establishing the Corporation of the Brothers of the Hermits of St. Augustine, a corporation that is operative today. Two pioneering works remained for him, St. Augustine's Academy, a preparatory school for boys, opened (1811) but forced to close (1815) because of the War of 1812. In 1814 St. Elizabeth Seton sent the first group of her Sisters of Charity to leave Emmitsburg as staff for St. Joseph's Asylum for Catholic Orphans, which C. had founded in 1797. Aspects of his pastoral dedication are noted in contemporary documents: his selfless devotion to his people suffering in the recurrent plagues of yellow fever drew the praise of civic and medical authorities. The second area is C.'s preaching and public addresses, which made a lasting impression on Philadelphians. He introduced to the city a solemnity of liturgy not seen there before and maintained a choir directed by the leading musician of the day. BIBLIOGRAPHY: F. E. Tourscher, *Old Saint Augustine's in Philadelphia,* with Some Records of the Work of the Austin Friars in the United States (1937).

[J. R. AHERNE]

CARRÀ, CARLO (1881–1966), Italian painter, who signed *futurist sacred art manifesto (1909) and advocated (1915) "total painting" using color, sound, and smell. Meeting Giorgio de Chirico, C. became active (1915) in the "metaphysical school," ranking second only to the master De Chirico in panels, working nostalgia and apprehension through imagery and eerie light. C. developed a personal style, joining the Valori Plastici movement (1920) and the Novecento group of figurative artists (1924). As teacher at the Brera Academy, Milan, C. had profound influence on Italian art. BIBLIOGRAPHY: G. Pacchioni, *Carlo Carrà* (1959).

[M. J. DALY]

CARRACCI, family of Italian artists. (1) **Agostino** (1557–1602), painter and printmaker. After studying in Bologna with his cousin Lodovico, C. assisted his brother Annibale with frescoes in the Farnese Palace, Rome (1597–99), and in 1600 began frescoes in Parma. Influenced by Denis Calvaert, the Flemish Bolognese Mannerist, the Venetian masters, and Correggio, he moved toward classicism, influencing the Carracci Academy and the Bolognese reform leading to the classicistic trend of 17th-cent. painting in Rome. (2) **Annibale** (1560–1609), painter. Studying under his cousin Lodovico in Bologna, C. traveled to Parma and Venice, then to Rome (1595) to paint famous frescoes in the Farnese palace. Breaking from the academic Bolognese tradition, C. in his painterly, emotional expression through dramatic light, genre, realism, and exuberance, prepared the way for the baroque painting of Domenichino, Reni, Rubens, and Caravaggio. Based on nature, antiquity, and the High Renaissance masters, C.'s grand classical style was the outstanding contribution to baroque painting in Rome. (3) **Lodovico** (1555–1619), painter, head of Carracci Academy, Bologna. Less classicistic than cousins Agostino and Annibale, he emphasized through movement and light an emotional quality, training artists for Annibale's "Bolognese circle" in Rome, influencing directly Domenichino, Guido, Reni, and finally the baroque style.

[M. J. DALY]

CARRANZA, BARTOLOMÉ DE (sometimes called de Miranda from his birthplace in Navarre; c. 1503–76), Dominican theologian, abp., the most eminent of the victims of the Spanish Inquisition. He served as imperial theologian at the Council of Trent, was provincial of his order in Castille, spent 3 years in England under Queen Mary Tudor, and in 1557 was made abp. of Toledo. Suspected of heresy because his criticism of Lutheranism was more sympathetic than the stiffer party-line enforced by the authorities largely for reasons of state, he was imprisoned by the Inquisition at the instance of the hostile Grand Inquisitor, Ferdinando de Valdés, who had the support of Paul IV. This reaching out of

the politico-ecclesiastical police to a respected member of a powerful order and a primate of Spain was a glaring manifestation of their great power. However, a fellow Dominican, *Pius V, was not disposed to truckle to them; he had C. released after 7 years confinement and brought to Rome, but unfortunately Pius died before he could pronounce an acquittal. His successor, *Gregory XIII, was more sinuous; to placate the dominant Spanish party, he ordered the retraction of 16 propositions open to misunderstanding and a suspension of 2 years from episcopal functions. The old man submitted but was broken and soon, forgiving his enemies, died. The Pope ordered a laudatory inscription on his tomb in the Minerva. BIBLIOGRAPHY: J. I. Tellechea, LTK 2:957; A. D'Amato, EncCatt 3:932.

[T. GILBY]

CARREL, ALEXIS (1873–1944), French surgeon and biologist, Nobel laureate (physiology and medicine, 1912). C.'s career in research, principally in the U.S., led him to important discoveries in the preservation of living tissue *in vitro*. The wider public knows him chiefly for his book *Man, the Unknown*. C. points out that science, in serving man's material needs, has been of disservice to him in that it knows nothing of man himself. All of C.'s own research sought to know man in all his aspects, including the mental and the religious. C. had published early in his career a scientific study of the miracles at Lourdes, a subject of abiding interest to him, for in his later writing he emphasized the factors of faith and prayer in those cures. A life-long believing, if not practicing, Christian, he was reconciled to the Church a few weeks before his death. BIBLIOGRAPHY: R. Soupault, *Alexis Carrel, 1873–1944* (1951); W. S. and P. D. Edwards, *Alexis Carrel, Visionary Surgeon* (1974).

[W. B. MAHONEY]

CARRIÈRE, JOSEPH (1795–1864), Sulpician moral theologian. His major work was published in three sections: *De matrimonio* (1837), *De justitia et jure* (1839), and *De contractibus* (1844–47). His work is important because of the special attention he gave to the Napoleonic Code and its relations to moral theology. He served as 13th Superior General of the Sulpicians. BIBLIOGRAPHY: E. Levesque, DHGE 11:1131–32; *idem*, DTC 2.2:1804–05.

[J. R. RIVELLO]

CARRIÈRE, VICTOR (1872–1946), French priest (from 1908) and church historian. Long attached to the church of St. Roch in Paris, C. did his earliest research in the regional history of the town of Provins. After 1912 his attention centered more and more upon the Reformation. He wrote numerous articles for the *Revue d'histoire de l'Église de France,* of which he became co-editor in 1912 and sole editor in 1914. To strengthen the review and assure its continuation, he founded (1914) the Société d'histoire ecclésiastique de la France and served as its general secretary until his death. In 1930 he became professor at the Institut catholique de Paris.

His principal work was his *Épreuves de l' Église de France au XVIe siècle* (1936). BIBLIOGRAPHY: G. Bardy, *Catholicisme* 2:597–598.

[M. J. SUELZER]

CARRILLO DE ALBORNOZ, GIL ÁLVAREZ, see ALBORNOZ, GIL ÁLVAREZ CARRILLO DE.

CARROLL, CHARLES (1737–1832), signer of the Declaration of Independence, statesman. Educated in a clandestine academy of the Jesuits in the Maryland countryside and in France, C. studied law, even though by statute he was deprived as a Catholic from practice in Maryland. Inheritor of a great landed family, he first came to public notice, though anonymously, in a controversy over stipends to be paid the clergy of the Established Church. In the *Maryland Gazette* an unsigned article by "First Citizen" opposing the official position was answered by "Second Citizen," both being compositions of Daniel Dulany, secretary of the province. In opposition C. assumed the position of "First Citizen" and the exchange finally brought him the sympathy of the province both from the cogency of his argumentation and also because of his opponent's referring slightingly to C. as a disenfranchised Catholic. An unofficial consultant to the first Continental Congress, he became a figure of importance when appointed to the diplomatic mission to win the approval of Canada, accompanying Benjamin Franklin and Samuel Chase in a vain effort to form a union with that province. A delegate to the Maryland convention of 1776, he helped secure the passage of the resolution on separation from England. He was then elected to Congress and became one of the signers of the Declaration of Independence. He continued to hold office in the Assembly of Maryland at the same time and helped write the state constitution. Though elected to the Constitutional Convention in 1787, he did not accept, but nevertheless fought for adoption of the Constitution before the Maryland senate. From 1789 to 1792 he served as a U.S. Senator, leaving the Senate when a law was passed prohibiting state legislators from serving in Congress. In 1800 his active political career in Maryland ended with the defeat of the Federalist party. C. spent his remaining years in study and charitable and business pursuits. He headed the American Colonization Society which founded Liberia. C. lived to be the sole surviving signer of the Declaration of Independence, a revered elder statesman. BIBLIOGRAPHY: E. H. Smith, *Charles Carroll of Carrollton* (1942).

[J. R. AHERNE]

CARROLL, DANIEL (1730–96), Maryland delegate to the Continental Congress and the Constitutional Convention, and a signer of the U.S. Constitution. C. was the brother of John Carroll, Abp. of Baltimore. His wealth and position as merchant and landowner gave him the prominence and independence to play a significant role in politics. He participated in the Maryland Senate and Council (1777–80), in the Conti-

nental Congress from 1780 to 1784, and in the Constitutional Convention (1787–1788). He wanted a strong central government, free from financial dependency of the states, one which could unite both states and new lands to the west. He was an advocate of independence who came from a state (Maryland) most opposed to independence. He trod the middle road between proprietary central government and independent states, envisioning a nation sustained by a strong, centralized federal government. He was a believer in the reservation of certain rights to the individual. C.'s political philosophy embraced belief in the dignity of man, and the right to religious freedom.

[J. M. BRADY]

CARROLL, JOHN (1735–1815), first RC bishop of the U.S. It would be impossible to overstate the influence C. exerted on the character of American Catholicism. The fact that he was prevented by historical circumstance from showing the vigorous leadership of which he was capable until he was over 40 years of age makes his achievements even more remarkable. Descendant of two distinguished Maryland families, C. was educated at St. Omer's in France because the penal laws of Maryland prohibited Catholics from receiving higher education in the province. He entered the Society of Jesus and was ordained, probably in 1767. The ensuing years both in Europe and on his return to Maryland were years of obscurity made more bitter by the suppression of the Jesuits by Pope Clement XIV. C. was drawn from seclusion by invitation of the Congress in 1776 to accompany Benjamin Franklin and the commission to Canada to seek support for the American Revolution. The chaotic conditions of the Catholic Church in the new republic, separated from regulation by the vicar apostolic of London, prompted him to write a "Plan of Reorganization" in which he chastised his ex-Jesuit confrères. By 1783, a committee, including C., petitioned the Holy See to appoint a superior with quasi-episcopal powers to govern American Catholics. In 1785, in answer to an attack on the Church by an apostate Jesuit, C. wrote an essay, "Address to the Roman Catholics of the United States of America." Shortly thereafter he was named prefect apostolic by Pope Pius VI.

The obstacles to establishing an orderly regimen for the American Church were manifold. C. had to contend with ecclesiastics in France who schemed to bring the Church in America under a French vicar apostolic. Acceding to the request of a convocation of clergy at Whitemarsh, the Holy See appointed C. bp. of Baltimore (1789), and a new life began for the Church in the U.S. The territory covered by the new diocese was of staggering proportions, comprising the entire Eastern seaboard (except for Florida) and vast undefined areas of the South and Midwest. A group of Jesuits, embittered by the suppression of the Society, caused trouble. More came in consequence of the character of many of the priests who came to the U.S. and offered their help—too many of them were trouble-makers. Then there was the vexing problem of lay trustees who, in the absence of strong ecclesiastical authority, created difficulties, esp. in Philadelphia and New York. The loose arrangement by which missionaries could come and go in the new republic made orderly regulation impossible. C. suffered many an ignominious charge from itinerant clerics who were at best of dubious standing. Composing differences among the ethnic groups who made up his scattered flock, esp. the Irish and German, constituted a primary task for him. The mere physical exertion involved in the thousands of miles he had to travel was itself an obstacle to success.

Two documents, one of which he issued alone, the other in conjunction with four prominent Catholic laymen, made a lasting impression. An attack on Catholicism by "Liberal" in the *Gazette of the United States* he answered with a lucid defense of the American Catholic. The "Address of the Roman Catholics" to George Washington represented the view of the Church in America and elicited the celebrated response by the new president. Nothing epitomized the greatness of C. more than the first synod he convoked in 1791. It demonstrates the rare tact and leadership that the Bishop brought to his task. The synod did much to establish discipline among the clergy. It also promulgated wise legislation for the administration of the sacraments and divine worship. Notable is the prudent handling of mixed marriages, which were seen to be inevitable in the American milieu. Another achievement was provision for creating new dioceses. The Holy See was wise in allowing the American clergy to nominate candidates in deference to possible feeling on the part of the American government. Altogether the synod was impressive and far-reaching in its effects.

Because he understood the need for a native clergy, C. established (1789) a college at Georgetown, later confided to the Jesuits. He brought the Sulpicians to Baltimore, opened St. Mary's Seminary, and later approved their foundation of St. Mary's College (now Loyola) in Baltimore and Mt. St. Mary's in Emmitsburg. C. understood the need for religious to work in the newly created diocese. Carmelite and Visitation nuns and Trappist monks were added so that the contemplative life might nourish American Catholicism. He supported the Augustinians in Philadelphia, the Dominicans in Kentucky, and Elizabeth Seton's new community in Emmitsburg. In 1808 C. was named archbishop with suffragan sees in Boston, New York, Philadelphia, and Bardstown, Kentucky. By the time of his death, C. had achieved his objective of an American Church free from foreign domination but loyal to the Holy See, an accepted influence in the life of the republic, and a Church ready to assimilate the great waves of immigrants about to engulf American Catholicism in the mid-century. BIBLIOGRAPHY: P. J. Guilday, *Life and Times of John Carroll* (1922); J. G. Shea, *Life and Times of the Most Rev. John Carroll* (1888); A. M. Melville, *John Carroll of Baltimore* (1955); T. O. Hanley, *John Carroll Papers* (3 v., 1976).

[J. R. AHERNE]

CARROLL, JOHN PATRICK (1864–1925), educator, bishop. Ordained in 1889, C. was professor at St. Joseph's College (later Loras) in Dubuque and president of the institution from 1894 to 1904 when he was named bp. of Helena, Montana. There he founded Mt. St. Charles College (now Carroll College) in 1909. C. was a celebrated orator appearing in many areas in the Pacific Northwest. He was one of the vigorous opponents of the Oregon School Bill, which was finally declared unconstitutional.

[J. R. AHERNE]

CARROLL, WALTER SHARP (1908–50), papal diplomat. From 1944 to 1950, C. served as attaché to the Vatican Secretariat of State, embarking on a mission to North Africa (1943) to establish regular communication with the Holy See and to help war prisoners. A like mission took him to Austria and Germany in 1944. C. represented the Vatican at the 1947 meeting of the International Refugee Organization.

[J. R. AHERNE]

CARRON, GUY-TOUSSAINT-JULIEN (1760–1821), French priest, writer, and social worker. After his ordination in 1782, he not only established centers to aid the laboring class but also began an immense literary work that was to number over 60 volumes. In 1792 the Revolution forced him to live abroad, finally in London, where he continued his charitable works. He returned to Paris in 1815, where he established l'Institut Marie-Thérèse for orphans. At this time he became friendly with Lamennais and supported his ideals. C.'s most important work is *Les confesseurs de la Foi dans l'Église gallicane à la fin du XVIIIᵉ siècle* (4 v., 1820), an important source on the émigrés of the period. BIBLIOGRAPHY: C. Lemarié, *Catholicisme* 2:600–601.

[I. M. KASHUBA]

CARTER, JAMES GORDON (1792–1849), American educational reformer and advocate of public education. As a young Harvard graduate and teacher, he published a series of pamphlets, *Letters . . . on the Free Schools of New England,* in which he decried the defects of the district school system, and the small importance attached to the common school, which was generally outranked by private schools and academies. The articles were instrumental in promoting the much opposed law of 1826, which obliged each township to set up an advisory school board. His pamphlet, *Essays upon Popular Education with an Outline of an Institution for the Education of Teachers* (1826), helped forward the establishment of teacher training institutes. As co-founder of the American Institute of Instruction (1830) and member of the state legislature (1835), he devoted his time to fostering public education. His crowning achievement was the passage of the bill creating the first state board of education in the U.S. (1837). BIBLIOGRAPHY: *Educational Biography: Memoirs of Teachers, Educators, and Promoters and Benefactors of Education, Literature, and Science* (ed. H. Barnard, 1859).

[M. B. MURPHY]

CARTER, WILLIAM, VEN. (d. 1584), English printer and martyr. He suffered imprisonment several times for printing attacks upon the Protestant religion. Incarcerated finally in the Tower in 1582, he was tortured and brought to trial for printing Gregory Martin's *Treatise of Schisme,* a passage of which, it was claimed, advocated the assassination of Elizabeth. He was executed at Tyburn. BIBLIOGRAPHY: Niccolò Del Re, BiblSanct 7:810.

[V. SAMPSON]

CARTESIANISM, a philosophic term referring either to the system of thought advanced by the French philosopher, René Descartes (1596–1650), or to any of a number of attitudes developed by thinkers influenced by his doctrines.

In Western civilization, Descartes is usually termed the father of modern philosophy because he posed the problems that have provided the chief content for elaboration in the philosophic discourse from his time to the present. These are largely of an epistemological character, i.e., they have to do with the theory of knowledge, but at the same time they involve certain metaphysical commitments as to the nature of reality as known. Like Francis Bacon (1561–1626), Descartes rejected all accepted authorities of the past, thus giving his philosophy a highly skeptical orientation in its effort to achieve the precision, clarity, and certainty of mathematics. Viewing philosophy as essentially practical, he sought through it to reconcile and harmonize the growing mechanism of the new science with time-honored demonstrations concerning God, man, and the relation between them; and though he claimed to be starting afresh, by implication he accepted a great body of scholastic tradition in which he earlier had been trained. The results of his efforts offered an extreme dualism of matter and mind which he hoped would leave nature free for mechanistic explanations, reserving to the mind a special realm guaranteeing human freedom and moral responsibility.

Insisting upon the importance of method in speculation and adopting skepticism as its point of departure, the Cartesian view posed a universal and systematic doubt of everything not yet established as true beyond doubt—this in the hope of arriving ultimately at certainty in knowledge rather than mere conjecture. He aspired to end much controversy by proving on solid grounds the existence of God, the reality of the external world, the immortality of the human soul, etc., at the same time to provide a firm foundation for the natural sciences. To do this, he saw it was necessary to start from absolutely certain first principles, perfectly clear and self-evident, and through these to reach conclusions that could be accepted with equal certitude. His universal doubt required him to distrust even the testimony of the senses, for they often deceive and we have no assurance that what they report is truly real. Hence, we cannot be certain that our own bodies, our actions, and the entire external world beyond personal consciousness truly exist. There was, however, one apprehension he found to be impervious to doubt, namely, his own existence as apprehended even in the act of doubting it. This provided Descartes with an uncontestable datum that he could use as the basis for his entire system of thought, *Dubito ergo sum.* He could take the fact of his doubting as absolutely certain, true, and clearly and distinctly apprehended, and this established a criterion for the evaluation of other truths, i.e., all other data clearly and distinctly grasped by the mind may be taken likewise as certain and true.

Descartes then proceeds to prove the existence of God, advancing at least two demonstrations, one of which is very akin to the *ontological argument of St. *Anselm (1033–1109)—a deduction of God's existence from the very concept of God, or showing that the idea of God implies his existence. The other is a causal proof also dealing with our idea of God and arguing that from our idea of such a being, man necessarily infers the being's existence as the cause of the idea. Finally, from God's existence, Descartes concludes to that of the external world of reality predicated upon the logic that it must exist—for otherwise, God would be a deceiver in endowing us with the conviction of a reality which has no existence. But since deceit is incompatible with the nature of a perfect being, our sensations must be caused by real bodies, and hence, the external world truly exists.

By this route, Descartes concludes to the existence of three substances: God—an independent and transcendent substance responsible for the existence of all else; and mind and matter, two relative substances dependent upon the Absolute. *Res cogitans* or mind is immaterial and unextended but has the attribute of thought or consciousness, whereas *res extensa* or matter is material and unconscious with the attribute of extension. This famous division is referred to as Descartes' bifurcation of Nature, or simply Cartesian dualism, giving rise to a great variation of thinking either founded upon it, or in reaction against it, in the centuries following. It stands at the root of the so-called "mind-body problem," or the enigma of two fundamentally disparate realities interacting as they do in the life of man.

Cartesian philosophy provoked myriad problems, esp. centering around the dualism of mind and matter, some thinkers being well disposed toward Cartesian doctrine and striving to work out solutions within its framework; others being hostile and so seeking answers elsewhere. Thomas Hobbes (1588–1679) avoided the difficulties of dualism by advocating a complete materialism, eliminating mind as a reality in its own right, while Benedict Spinoza (1632–77) asserted that both mind and matter are but manifestations of a single reality variously termed God, Substance, or Nature. Gottfried Leibnitz (1648–1716) offers a parallelism in his doctrine of "pre-established harmony" which sees no interaction or causal relation between mind and body, but rather a perfect and simultaneous co-operation in natural concert. On the other hand, Nicholas de Malebranche (1638–1715) denies nature as an independent entity and sets forth an absolute idealism in which man sees all things in God, the things being ideas rather than the material objects themselves which constitute a *terra incognita,* since the idea of matter, and not matter itself is known by the human mind.

Finally, Blaise *Pascal (1623–62) manages to accept Descartes' dualism by introducing a mystic skepticism in which a knowledge of ultimate realities is beyond human capability, so that we cannot demonstrate such truths as the existence of God and the immortality of the soul. However, while reason thus leaves us unsatisfied, our religious feelings give us a profound experience of God and we come to know peace, for "the heart has its reasons which reason does not know." BIBLIOGRAPHY: A. B. Gibson, *Philosophy of Descartes* (1932); K. Fischer, *Descartes and His School* (tr. J. P. Gordy, 1887); L. J. Beck, *Method of Descartes* (1952); J. Maritain, *Dream of Descartes* (tr. M. L. Andison, 1944); W. Doney, EncPhil 2:37–42.

[J. T. HICKEY]

CARTHAGE, city founded by the Phoenicians in the 9th cent. B.C. on the coast of N Africa 12 mi NE of the modern city of Tunis. Because of its favorable position, it soon dominated the W Mediterranean. After centuries of conflict with the Greeks in Sicily and S Italy, Carthage became involved in three prolonged wars with Rome and was finally destroyed in 146 B.C. Though the Carthaginians engaged in trade and manufacture, they produced no true native art of their own. Their ultimate defeat by the Romans was not due to a lack of military talent but to their oligarchic form of government and too great a reliance upon mercenary troops. A Roman colony was founded at Carthage by Augustus, and under the Roman Empire it became a great center of culture and education. The grandeur of the city can be appreciated even today from its imposing ruins—baths, cisterns, theaters, and amphitheater. As a Christian city it was second only to Rome in the West. Among the Christian writers who labored there were Minucius Felix, Tertullian, St. Cyprian, Arnobius, Lactantius, Commodian, Marius Victorinus, Dracontius, and St. Augustine. Many important councils were held there, the first recorded in 220 under Bp. Agrippinus. It resisted the early onslaughts of the Moslems but finally fell to them in 698. BIBLIOGRAPHY: B. H. Warmington, *Carthage* (1960); J. Ferron and G. Lapeyre, DHGE 11:1149–1253; G. C. and C. Picard, *Life and Death of Carthage: A Survey . . . .* (1969).

[M. J. COSTELLOE]

CARTHAGE, COUNCILS OF, synods held in the city of Carthage, in North Africa. Christian Carthage from the 3d until the 6th cent. held ecclesiastical primacy in North Africa. From the time of the episcopate (248–258) of St. Cyprian, a number of provincial councils were held in Carthage, some of them of more than local importance. Several of the councils convoked by Cyprian dealt with the reconciliation of the *lapsi;* the practice of granting sacramental reconciliation to repentant apostates became universal, but not the view that baptism administered by heretics was invalid. The most important councils of Carthage were those held under Bp. Aurelius (391–429) with the active participation of St. Augustine. Some of them dealt with the *Donatists, esp. on the rebaptism of those who had been baptized by heretics. By far

the most important teaching condemned at these councils was *Pelagianism, which denied the Fall, original sin, and the need of grace and therefore called into question a basic Christian truth, men's need of Christ the Redeemer. The 15th (or 16th) Council of Carthage (May 418), at which 214 African bps. met, promulgated 8 (or 9) canons on original sin and grace (D 222–230). Pope Zosimus's encyclical letter to the East (D 231) may not have had the force, generally attributed to it, of raising these canons to the status of infallible decisions; nor perhaps did their approval at the subsequent council of Carthage (418) in the presence of papal delegates. But in actual fact they have had a decisive influence on the theology of grace. They were resumed and sanctioned at the Second Council of Orange (529) and again, 10 centuries later, at the Council of Trent (D 1511–12, 1551–53). With the Vandal conquest of North Africa (429), the era of the great African councils came to an end. BIBLIOGRAPHY: C. M. Aherne, NCE 3:160–161; P. Fransen, LTK 6:3–4.

[P. De LETTER]

CARTHAGE, SYNOD OF (419), the most celebrated of the several councils of Carthage under Bp. Aurelius (391–424) in which canons were approved limiting the jurisdiction of the bp. of Rome in Carthage. The collection of canons included in the decrees of this council were from earlier councils and are known as the *Codex canonum Ecclesiae africanae;* they were influential in later medieval canonical definitions of the jurisdiction of the bp. of Rome and local sees. BIBLIOGRAPHY: A. Audollent, DHGE 1:805–822; *CARTHAGE, COUNCILS OF; *APIARIUS; *AFRICA, EARLY CHURCH IN ROMAN.

[F. H. BRIGHAM]

CARTHUSIAN SPIRITUALITY. Because the Carthusian Order is eremetical and contemplative, its spiritual doctrine rests on the necessity of silence and solitude as paths to mystical union with God. Though a few Carthusians in history have entered upon apostolic work as spiritual directors, the paramount influence of the monks has been through writing. In fact, the principal commitment to apostolic activity, as enjoined by early writers, was to preach by multiplying books. The rule, summarized in the *Consuetudines* of Guigo I, lays down the requirements of a life of prayer. The well-known English work *Ancren Riwle* shows the influence of Guigo's document. Following the direction of *Consuetudines,* Carthusians were among the first to establish printing presses in the 15th century. St. Barbara's in Cologne established a press in 1465, the monastery at Strasbourg in 1474, Parma in 1477, and Grispsholm in 1498.

The Carthusians Lanspergius in Cologne and Beaucousin in Paris were celebrated directors, the former influencing the early Jesuits; the latter influencing among others François du Tremblay (the Grey Eminence of France.) This time of spiritual direction was limited, however, because it did not accord with Carthusian solitude. Such Carthusian writers as Hugh of Balma, Denis the Carthusian, and Lanspergius were published as well as other mystic writers. The list of Carthusian writers includes Guigo I, Guigo II, Denis of Ryckel, and Guigo de Ponte, all of whom made major contributions to Carthusian spirituality. In later centuries the work of translating and editing mystical writing was carried on voluminously by the order. Ludolph of Saxony in patristic literature and Surius on the lives of the saints produced notable volumes. Carthusian writers promoted in an important way the rosary and devotion to the Sacred Heart. Innocent Le Masson wrote ascetical works in opposition to Jansenism and quietism. In the 20th cent. the writings of François de Sales Pollien, Augustine Guillerand, and Thomas Verner Moore made important contributions to Catholic spirituality. BIBLIOGRAPHY: Y. Gourdel, DSAM 2.1:705–776.

[J. R. AHERNE]

CARTHUSIANS, members of a strictly contemplative order founded in 1084 by St. Bruno, who with a few companions sought the solitude of La Chartreuse near Grenoble in France. They wore rough garments, partook of vegetables and bread, and slept on straw in crude hermitages. The early Carthusians "occupied themselves continually with reading, prayer, and the labor of their hands, especially the writing of books." Members of the community include choir monks and brothers, and since the 12th cent. nuns have been associated with the order. Though each monastery has a prior, the government of the order is very centralized. A general chapter meets every 2 years at the Grande Chartreuse. Since Bruno had no intention of founding a monastic order, no rules were drawn up, but in 1127 Guigo, the fifth prior, compiled a code of customs, which were supplemented by the ordinances of the chapters. In 1581 the first edition of the ordinances, *Nova collectio,* was published and a revision of it received approval in 1924. After receiving papal approbation in the late 12th cent., the order began to expand rapidly. By 1521, there were 195 houses, and never before nor since has the community been so flourishing. Decline set in during the time of the Reformation and also the French Revolution; houses were suppressed, monasteries confiscated, and monks were imprisoned and put to death. In the early 19th cent., a period of restoration resulted in the reacquiring of charterhouses and monasteries, esp. in France and Italy. About the same time, the order was divided into three provinces with a total membership of about 700 monks and brothers and 100 nuns. Twentieth-cent. anticlerical laws caused the Carthusians to leave France and seek refuge in Farneta in Italy where they remained until 1929, when the first French house was reopened at Montrieux. In 1970, the order had houses in Spain, France, and Italy, with charterhouses in Portugal, Yugoslavia, Germany, Switzerland, and England. They established a house in the U.S. in 1951 in Vermont. Today vocations to the solitary life of the Carthusians are comparatively rare. BIBLIOGRAPHY: H. Sommer, LTK 5:1381–84; Y. Gourdel, DSAM 2.1:705–776; C. M. Boutrais, *La Grande Chartreuse* (rev. 1964).

[R. A. TODD]

CARTIER, JACQUES (1491–1557), explorer. A Breton shipmaster, C. had visited Newfoundland on fishing trips before his first voyage under French governmental auspices (1534). He then sailed the Strait of Belle Isle and discovered Prince Edward Island, the Gaspé Peninsula, and the Gulf of St. Lawrence. On his second expedition (1535), he ascended the St. Lawrence River as far as Montreal and spent the winter in Canada. When France determined to follow up his discoveries (1541), command was divided between C. and Jean de Roberval. C.'s third expedition wintered in Canada (1541–42), but returned home before Roberval's colonists arrived. By misinterpreting an Algonquin term, C. gave the name Canada to the lands he discovered. BIBLIOGRAPHY: *Voyages of Jacques Cartier* (ed. and tr. H. P. Biggar, 1924); G. Vattier, *Jacques Cartier et la découverte du Canada* (1937); J. F. Pendergast and B. G. Trigger, *Cartier's Hochelaga and the Dawson Site* (1972).

[R. K. MacMASTER]

CARTULARY, see CHARTULARY.

CARTWRIGHT, PETER (1785–1872), pioneer Methodist evangelist on the American frontier. His family moved in his childhood to Ky., where he was converted at a Methodist *camp meeting in 1802. He was licensed to preach soon afterward and was commissioned to organize a new circuit in W Kentucky. He was ordained a deacon in 1806 and an elder in 1808. C. was one of the Methodist circuit riders of the frontier country, tirelessly traveling over Ky., Ind., and Ill., holding meetings and establishing new churches; he received over 12,000 into the Methodist Church. A lifelong foe of slavery, he moved in 1824 to Sangamon County, Ill., and served in the state legislature in 1828 and again in 1832. He was influential in the movement to establish public school systems in the young state and was a founder of Illinois Wesleyan University. In his old age he traveled as far as Boston on evangelistic tours. His *Autobiography* (new ed., 1956) inspired Methodists of later generations. BIBLIOGRAPHY: H. H. Grant, *Peter Cartwright, Pioneer* (1931); W. W. Sweet, *Religion on the American Frontier* (1946) v. 4.

[R. K. MacMASTER]

CARTWRIGHT, THOMAS (*c.* 1535–1604), leader of the Elizabethan Puritans and the chief exponent of Presbyterianism in England. C. was educated at Cambridge. There in 1567–68 he "preached vehemently against the surplice," and from 1569, when elected Lady Margaret professor of divinity, he sought to reform the existing ecclesiastical *polity of the C of E according to the Geneva model of discipline and government. Should the Church fail to reform itself, he taught, the magistrate must assume the enforcement of godly discipline. The *Admonition to Parliament* (1572), which he supported, and his translation of Walter Travers's *Disciplina ecclesiastica* are important statements of English Puritanism. Despite opposition, exile, and imprisonment, C.'s influence was strong. BIBLIOG-

RAPHY: A. S. Pearson, *Thomas Cartwright and Elizabethan Puritanism, 1535–1603* (1966).

[R. K. MacMASTER]

CARUSI, BARTHOLOMMEO, see BARTHOLOMEW OF URBINO (DE CARUSIIS).

CARVAJAL. (1) **Juan de** (*c*. 1400–69), cardinal bishop and papal legate. In 1440, he traveled to Germany in an attempt to persuade the German princes to support Eugene IV in his struggle with the Council of Basil. He worked with Tommaso Parentucelli (later Nicholas V) and both were named cardinals upon successfully completing their assignment. Later he was involved in the negotiations for the Concordat of Vienna and served on missions to Bohemia, Hungary, and Venice.

(2) **Bernardino Lopez de** (1456–1523), cardinal bishop, nephew of Juan, member of the uncanonical Council of Pisa-Milan. Named cardinal in 1493, he went as legate to Germany (1496). Favored by Alexander VI, he was not trusted by Julius II. Charged with the custody of Cesare Borgia, he let him escape. Later, he joined a group of dissident cardinals who proclaimed a council. They were excommunicated by Julius II who called the Fifth Lateran Council. After Julius II died, C. accepted the Fifth Lateran Council and Leo X absolved him and restored his honors. BIBLIOGRAPHY: D. R. Campbell, NCE 3:172.

[E. T. McGOVERN]

CARVAJAL, LUISA DE (1568–1614), Spanish ascetic and missionary in England. Of noble birth, C. exhibited sanctity at an early age. As a young woman, she and a group of other women began a life of poverty and prayer. Upon learning of the execution of Henry Walpole (1596), she resolved to serve the faith in England. There she gathered helpers to assist persecuted Catholics in their homes and in prison and won many converts to Catholicism. The English government arrested her twice, finally releasing her to the custody of the Spanish ambassador in whose home she died soon thereafter.

[E. T. McGOVERN]

CARVE, THOMAS (Carew; 1590–1672), Irish historian. Before 1620 C. was ordained priest for the Diocese of Leighlin. He then became chaplain of the Irish regiment of Walter Butler (colonel in the army of Ferdinand II of Austria) and later of Butler's successor, Walter Devereux. Chaplain of all the English, Scotch, and Irish forces from 1640 until 1643, C. spent the rest of his years as prothonotary apostolic and choral vicar at St. Stephen's, Vienna. C.'s participation in several campaigns of the Thirty Years' War provided him with much valuable material for his work, *Itinerarium R. D. Thomae Carve* . . . (parts 1 and 2, 1639–41; part 3, 1646). He provided in the *Itinerary* not only an important contemporary account of the Thirty Years' War but also firsthand information concerning the conspiracy that resulted in *Wallenstein's

death. BIBLIOGRAPHY: T. Cooper, DNB 3:1143–44; P. S. McGarry, NCE 3:173; J. McCaffrey, CE 3:395.

[A. P. HANLON]

CASALE, GIACINTO DA (1525–1627) Capuchin preacher, diplomat. Student of letters, science and law, C., formerly Count of Alfiano, was at the court of Mantua, played a role in the Catholic reformation, and became a Capuchin in Venice. He reconciled Emperor Rudolph II with his brother Matthias and was chosen by Gregory XV to accompany Card. Carlo Gaudenzio Madruzzo to the Diet of Regensburg in 1613. He refused to accept the rank of cardinal. C. is the author of 10 volumes of sermons and 3 of ascetical conferences. BIBLIOGRAPHY: G. A. Cittadella, EncCatt 6:308 s.v. "Giacinto da Casale."

[A. P. HANLON]

CASANATE, GIROLAMO (1620–1700), cardinal, librarian. A Neapolitan, C. had a long and distinguished career in the service of the papacy. Named a cardinal as a layman, he was ordained in 1686 and in 1693 was appointed by Innocent XII as Librarian of the Holy Church. A scholar of great breadth, C. was qualified to deal with the controversies of his time. As a librarian he built up one of the most impressive collections in Europe, purchasing many of its volumes himself. He endowed the Casanate Library and assigned it to the Dominicans who were charged with using it as a Thomistic center for the defense of Catholic doctrine. The library at his death contained over 25,000 volumes and became one of the first libraries to serve the public. In the 19th cent. the Casanate Library was expropriated by Italy. BIBLIOGRAPHY: M. D'Angelo, *Il Cardinale Girolamo Casanate, 1620–1700* (1923).

[A. P. HANLON]

CASANI, PIETRO, VEN. (1570–1647), educator and preacher. Ordained priest (1600) in the Congregation of the Mother of God at Lucca, Italy, C. became a Piarist when the Luccan congregation joined the Clerks Regular of the Pious Schools. Serving as novice master, later assistant general and visitator of schools, C. was *Joseph Calasanctius' principal associate in the spreading of the congregation throughout Germany and Italy. BIBLIOGRAPHY: C. Petini, BiblSanct 3:892; M. O. Callaghan, NCE 3:175.

[A. P. HANLON]

CASAS MARTÍNEZ, FELIPE DE JESÚS, ST. (1572–97), Mexican protomartyr of Japan. Not yet ordained, C. was one of 3 Franciscans, 3 Jesuits, and 17 other Japanese Franciscan tertiaries including several catechists and interpreters who were crucified on a hill near Nagasaki by Hideyoshi, not the emperor but in practice ruler of the country. C. was bound to his cross by cords and chains with an iron collar round his neck; the pedestal was too low for his feet so the neck ring quickly choked him. He was the first of the group to die. C. was beatified in 1627, declared the patron of Mexico

(1629), and canonized in 1862. BIBLIOGRAPHY: Butler 1:259–260; M. Steichen, *Christian Daimyos* (1903); F. Caraffa, BiblSanct 5:727–728.

[J. P. COOKE]

CASAS Y NOVOA, FERNANDO DE (d. 1751), Spanish supervising architect at Santiago de Compostela, who designed the principal façade, the Obradoiro (1738–50), a masterpiece of Churrigueresque style.

[M. J. DALY]

CASAUBON, ISAAC (1559–1614), Huguenot classical scholar and teacher. A man of profound classical learning, C. was the lifelong victim of poverty and intrusive friends. Born of French refugee parents in Geneva, he took poorly paying positions as a teacher in Geneva, Montpellier, and Paris. A firm Calvinist, he resisted all efforts to bring him into Catholicism, though he was shaken by the arguments of Card. du Perron in a public disputation at which C. was one of the judges. Henry IV made him royal librarian, against the protests of the Jesuits. Unhappy and threatened in France, he migrated to England where he found a friend and patron in King James I and a living at Canterbury Cathedral. C. found his way to accept Anglicanism and was much admired by the Anglican bps., esp. by his friend Lancelot Andrewes, Bp. of Ely. Deeply religious and often involved with theology, C. is memorable as one of the great classical scholars of his time. Among his principal works are *Ephemerides* (1850), a diary of his study each day interspersed with prayers. His classical works, all written in Latin, treat of Strabo, Athenaeus, Suetonius, and Polybius. BIBLIOGRAPHY: M. Pattison, EB (1961) 4:955–956; *idem, Life of Isaac Causabon* (1892).

[J. R. AHERNE]

CASE (Lat. *casus*), a term used in RC moral theology and canon law to indicate a particular and concrete situation of some perplexity that is to be resolved by the application of appropriate general principles of law or morality. The case method of teaching has been useful up to a point and indeed necessary sometimes in matters in which the applicability of general principles to particular instances is likely to be obscured by the variety and complexity of the circumstances that mark individual human acts. Overuse of the method, however, tends to induce an undesirably legalistic habit of mind, and this, together with the exaggerated subtlety indulged in by some casuists and a tendency on the part of some to reduce moral obligation to a minimum, has caused *casuistry to be commonly understood in a pejorative sense.

CASEL, ODO (1886–1948), Benedictine theologian of the liturgy who exerted a strong influence through his editorship of the *Jahrbuch für Liturgiewissenschaft* (1921–41), and esp. through his "mystery" theory by which he succeeded in bringing to the fore the meaning of the liturgy as a celebration of the deeds of Christ and the Church. His thought represents a reaction against theological rationalism. More than anything else theology was for him the adoration of the mystery of God which man knows not because he grasps it for himself, but because God gives it to those who approach him in a spirit of adoration. C. collapsed while intoning the *Exsultet* at the Easter Vigil of 1948 and died a few hours later. BIBLIOGRAPHY: O. Casel, *Mystery of Christian Worship and Other Writings* (ed. B. Neunheuser, tr. I. T. Hale, 1962); *Maison-Dieu* 14 (1948), 1–106.

[N. KOLLAR]

CASELIUS, JOHANNES (1533–1613), German humanist who studied under Melanchthon and Camerarius. He was professor of eloquence at Rostock (1563–89) and in close touch with many scholars. In 1589 C. accepted a call to Helmstedt, where his last years were embittered by the attacks of the followers of Peter *Ramus and intransigent Lutherans. BIBLIOGRAPHY: K. Kayser, RGG 1:1625.

[M. J. SUELZER]

CASHEL, stone wall surrounding fortifications and ecclesiastical buildings, particularly in ancient Ireland.

CASIMIR, ST. (1458–84), prince, patron of Poland and Lithuania. Third of 13 children of King Casimir IV, he governed Poland successfully in his father's absence (1481–83), and was grand duke of Lithuania where he died and was buried (Vilna). C. is venerated for his love of celibacy, his piety, his special devotion to Mary; by the Poles he is called "The Peacemaker." BIBLIOGRAPHY: P. Rabikauskas, BiblSanct 3:895–906; Butler 1:478–479.

[M. E. DUFFY]

CASONI, FILIPPO (1733–1811), cardinal, papal secretary of state. A governor of Narni and Loreto in the Papal States, C. was also vice-legate to Avignon where he vainly tried through a policy of moderation and concession to head off the move to bring the region into the French revolutionary orbit. His efforts to share power with the local municipalities were repudiated by Pius VI, and in the ensuing upheaval C. had to flee Avignon. Sent to Spain as nuncio, he found himself in opposition to the prime minister who was attempting to create a Spanish Church with fewer ties to Rome. C. appealed to King Charles IV and forced the dismissal of the prime minister. Created cardinal in 1801 C. became papal secretary of state in 1806, but the insistence of Pius VII on conducting relations with Napoleon made the role of the secretary ineffectual. BIBLIOGRAPHY: S. Furlani, EncCatt 3:987.

[J. R. AHERNE]

CASPAR, ERICH (1879–1935), German Protestant historian of the papacy. C. began his scholarly career by collaborating in the editing of papal documents for the *Monumenta Germaniae historica* (the letters of John VIII and Gregory VII). As a professor, he taught history at the Universities of Königsberg (1920–28), Freiburg (1928–30), and Berlin (1930–35). From 1931, C. was co-editor of the

Zeitschrift für Kirchengeschichte. During the last decade of his life he devoted himself to the writing of a history of the papacy based on the documents with which he was very familiar from his earlier studies. C. originally projected a work in four volumes, but the two volumes that appeared before his death reached only to the mid-8th cent. This work is commonly considered to rank among the best histories of the papacy. BIBLIOGRAPHY: M. Scaduto, EncCatt 3:990–991; W. Ullmann, NCE 3:179–180.

[R. B. ENO]

CASPAR, KARL (1879–1956), German painter. Professor at Munich Academy (1922–37), C. is best known for religious subjects, esp. of the Passion of Christ. Influenced by Gauguin and Cézanne, C. moved toward an emotional expressionism of free brushstrokes and vivid color. BIBLIOGRAPHY: K. Weiss, *Karl Caspar* (1929).

[M. J. DALY]

CASPICARA (nickname for Manuel Chili), Ecuadorian Indian sculptor and painter. C.'s works were produced in the years 1790–1810, but there is no record of the years of his birth and death. He was a master of detail and made much use of polychrome. Among his works are pictorial rendering of the theological virtues called *Sábana Santa, Coronation of the Virgin,* and *Assumption with the Twelve Apostles.* C. was the last Indian artist of colonial Ecuador.

[J. R. AHERNE]

CASSANDER, GEORG (c. 1513–66), Flemish lay theologian, liturgist, and humanist. After becoming a master of arts at Louvain, C. began teaching antiquities at Bruges in 1532. Later he lectured at Ghent. In 1544 he transferred to Cologne for study, but at the request of the Duke of Cleves he went to Duisburg to work toward reconciling the Anabaptists. There he became the first director of the academy founded in 1549. Confident of restoring Christian unity, he labored from 1561 until his death to unite Catholics and Protestants in Ferdinand I's territories, but his efforts pleased neither side. His first anonymous treatise, *De officio pii ac publicae tranquillitatis vere amantis viri in hoc religionis dissidio* (1561), was attacked by Calvin and by both Catholics and Protestants at the Conference of *Poissy (1561). His writings, accepting clerical marriage and communion under both kinds, were placed on the Lisbon Index in 1581. Another collection of his works, when published posthumously at Paris (1616), were likewise opposed by Rome. C. minimized creedal differences, particularly in the doctrines of original sin, the Lord's Supper, and justification. His hope was to achieve consensus on the doctrines contained in the Apostles' Creed. It is recorded that he retracted his teachings on his deathbed and forbade publication of his last writings; but his friends did not honor his wishes. C. contributed to the primitive science of liturgics by his essay on the liturgy for the celebration of the Lord's Supper (1556) and his *Ordo romanus de officio Missae* (1558). BIBLIOGRAPHY: J. Lecler, *Toleration and the Refor-*

mation (tr. T. L. Westow 2v., 1960); J. Baudot, DACL 2.2:2333–40; R. Koper, LTK 2:968–969.

[M. J. SUELZER]

CASSANT, MARIE JOSEPH (1879–1903), Cistercian. C. entered the Trappists in 1894. Because he lacked the necessary intellectual gifts for ordination, he was precluded from ordination at first. He was solemnly professed in 1900. Besides his apparent intellectual shortcomings, he was afflicted with weak health. Neither prevented him from leading a heroically virtuous life. Owing to the intensity of his spiritual life and the guidance of his director, C. was ordained in 1902, several months piror to his death.

[J. R. RIVELLO]

CASSATION, the exercise of a power vested in certain higher superiors to annul, quash, cancel, or veto elections or legislative acts of chapters, etc., that require their approval or validation before being put into effect.

CASSIAN OF NANTES, BL. (1607–38), Capuchin missionary and martyr. Most of his missionary activity was centered in Cairo where he worked with Agathage of Vendôme. Despite his dedication to the afflicted during the plague of 1631–32, his mission was not successful, mainly because of the scandalous lives of Catholics in the area. In 1637 he and his companions went to Ethiopa in the habit of dissident Coptic monks, for he worked to reunite the Coptic Church with Rome. When his disguise was discovered, he refused to accept the dissident doctrines and was martyred. C. was beatified in 1904. BIBLIOGRAPHY: B. d'Arenzano, BiblSanct 3:912–913; Butler 3:277–280.

[I. M. KASHUBA]

CASSIAN, JOHN (c. 360–c. 435), monk, priest, spiritual writer. After some years in a monastery at Bethlehem, C. studied the monastic life in Egypt, was ordained deacon at Constantinople by John Chrysostom (c. 400), and some 4 years later went to Rome to enlist the aid of Pope Innocent I for the exiled Chrysostom. Probably in 414 or 415, after ordination to the priesthood, C. went to Marseilles, where he founded two monasteries, one for men and the other for women. The rules of these monasteries are not extant, but their tenor may be deduced from the founder's ascetical writings. The *Institutes* in 12 books set forth external observances (Bks. 1–4) and discuss the eight principal vices opposed to religious perfection and the remedies to overcome them (Bks. 5–12). The *Conferences,* tripartite and consisting of 24 conferences in all, were greatly admired for their edifying content. They were recommended by authorities on the monastic life and enjoyed great popularity as spiritual reading throughout the Middle Ages, despite the fact that C.'s doctrine, esp. in Conferences 3, 5, and 13, was patently Semipelagian (see SEMIPELAGIANISM). C.'s third work, *Against Nestorius on the Incarnation of the Lord,* was written at the request of a Roman archdeacon, later Pope Leo I; C. contended that Nestorianism was derived from Pelagianism. BIBLIOGRAPHY: O. Chadwick, *John Cassian: A Study in Primitive Monasticism* (2d ed. 1968); P. Godet, DTC 2.2:1823–29; M. Olphe-Galliarde, DSAM 2:214–276.

[H. DRESSLER]

CASSIANO DE MACERATA (Beligatti; 1708–91), Capuchin priest, missionary, scholar. C. went to Tibet (1738) with 12 companions, but after a short time they were opposed by the lamas and ordered by the king to leave. C. then went to Nepal with three Capuchins and was joined there by other missionaries in 1745. He was successful in evangelizing much of that region and Bengal until illness forced him to return to Rome. There he taught young missionaries about the regions of Tibet and Mongolia and wrote detailed accounts of his experiences in those countries. His works also include Brahmanic and Hindustani alphabets, and he assisted in the work on the *Alphabetum thibetanum* (1773). BIBLIOGRAPHY: A. Teetaert, DHGE 7:769–770; I. de Milano, EncCatt 2:1179.

[P. HIGGINS]

CASSINESE CONGREGATION, a Benedictine reform inaugurated in 1408 under the leadership of Luigi Barbo (d. 1443) when he became abbot of Santa Justina in Padua. When discipline had been restored at Santa Justina, new recruits came in large numbers, and new monasteries were founded and other existing monasteries associated themselves with the movement, eventually including all the monasteries of Italy and Sicily. As a stratagem to avoid the appointment of commendatory abbots, abbots of this federation were chosen for a limited term of office. Authority was concentrated in an annual general chapter. When Monte Cassino entered the federation, the association became known as the Cassinese Congregation. The congregation was plundered by the Italian government in the 19th cent., and the number of monks included in it was greatly reduced. However, the Cassinese Congregation of Primitive Observance was formed in 1872 at Subiaco. This is divided into five provinces under the jurisdiction of an abbot general whose headquarters are at Subiaco.

[J. C. WILLKE]

CASSIODORUS SENATOR, FLAVIUS MAGNUS AURELIUS (*c*.490–*c*.583), Roman statesman, writer, monk. Of a distinguished family which, under Emperor Theodoric, was granted patrician status, C. succeeded his grandfather and father in high offices in Bruttium (S Italy). C. had two very different careers, each occupying half his life. His first career was political. Quaestor and governor of Lucania and Bruttium, he was consul in 514 and minister to Theodoric in 526. As a public official C. was a noted orator, more intent on flattering princes than writing the history of his era. He was a prolific writer, and his work had wide influence for centuries, though it is at best faulty his-

tory. His history of the Goths (*Chronica*, *c*.530) shows his prejudice in favor of the Goths. In 537 C. published his *Variae* in 12 books, correspondence and panegyrics of little worth as history. In the turbulent atmosphere of 540 C. decided to leave public life. His new career was that of a monk and founder of a form of monasticism. Probably influenced by St. Benedict and his monastery at Monte Cassino, C. established on his estate the monastery of Vivarium. Much influenced by St. Augustine, he wrote a *Commentary on the Psalms* for his monks. His *Historia ecclesiastica tripartita* drew on Theodoret, Sozomen, and Socrates, ecclesiastical historians, and though it contains many errors the work had a profound influence for centuries. By far his most important work, written between 543 and 555 was *Institutiones divinarum et saecularium literarum,* a plan of study for his monks (ed. R. A. B. Mynors, 1937; Eng. tr. with introd. and notes by L. W. Jones, 1946). He made intellectual labor part of the work of the monks, an area neglected by St. Benedict. Following St. Jerome and St. Augustine, he expatiates on the liberal arts and sciences: grammar and rhetoric, the arts, geometry, arithmetic, music and astronomy, and the sciences. C. gives invaluable information on early Church music, information often used in the revival of the chant of the Church. With St. Benedict, C. constitutes the most powerful influence on Western monasticism. BIBLIOGRAPHY: D. M. Cappuyns, DHGE 11:1350–1408; Manitius 1:36–52; A. Momigliano, "Cassiodorus and Italian Culture of His Time," *Proceedings of the British Academy* 41 (1955) 207–245.

[J. R. AHERNE]

CASSIRER, ERNST, (1874–1945), philosopher and historian of philosophy. C. studied law, philosophy, and mathematics, and obtained a doctorate in philosophy in 1899. He taught philosophy and history of philosophy in Berlin (from 1906) and Hamburg (1919). C. left Germany in 1933 because of his Jewish origin and taught at Oxford, Göteborg (Sweden), and, from 1940, at Yale and Columbia. He is a representative of Neo-Kantianism (Marburg) as interpreted by his teacher Hermann Cohen, but he broadened its outlook considerably. From a study of the history of science as increasingly mathematical and of man's scientific activity as a progressively symbolic transformation of "data," he developed a theory of all human activity as creation of symbols that give form to the otherwise chaotic world of the senses. This creative activity constitutes the objects of science, art, law, religion, and in general produces human culture. The unity and coherence of his forms of symbolic activity make man into a person. In this context C. studied, during the last 30 years of his life, especially myth, art, historiography, and language. Myth is constituted by an artistic element (mythical images) and a theoretical element (belief in those images). Religion, which is based on this mythical activity, adds an awareness of human finitude. Artistic activity intensifies reality in an emotional relationship to it (functional aesthetics), whereas historiography orders and (re) interprets past symbols. Language introduces certain conceptual distinctions in reality and expresses these concepts in symbols. C. was a prolific writer. Important among his works are *Philosophy of Symbolic Forms*. (tr. R. Manheim, 3 v., 1954–57); *An Essay on Man: An Introduction to a Philosophy of Human Culture* (1944). BIBLIOGRAPHY: S. W. Itzkoff, *Ernst Cassirer: Scientific Knowledge of the Concept of Man* (1971); *The Philosophy of Ernst Cassirer* (ed. P. A. Schilpp, 1949) with complete bibliography; S. Körner, EncPhil 2:44–46.

[B. A. NACHBAHR]

CASSIUS, DIO, see DIO CASSIUS COCCEIANUS.

CASSOCK, a close fitting, long sleeved garment of ankle length, the ordinary dress of the clergy in the RC Church for indoor and (in Catholic countries) outdoor wear. It is sometimes fitted with a cape. It is analogous to the official dress of lawyers, judges, and academic persons where such is required by custom. The cassock is the development of a garment once worn by all that became distinctively clerical when a change in fashion made it obsolete for secular wear, and the clergy, with some legislative encouragement, continued in the older style. In color the cassock varies with a cleric's rank: for diocesan priests, it is black, though white is often permitted in the tropics; for bishops and other prelates on ceremonial occasions it is purple; for cardinals, red; and the pope's cassock is white. Distinctive colors are also worn by some religious orders and by members of certain colleges. Boys serving at the altar and, commonly, men and boys of the choir, wear the cassock in the performance of their duties. BIBLIOGRAPHY: Podhradsky, 50; H. Norris, *Church Vestments: Their Origin and Development* (1950).

[P. K. MEAGHER]

CASTAGNO, ANDREA DEL (1421–57), Italian painter. Recent 20th-cent. study has been complicated by problems of biography, false attributions, and loss of works. C.'s sculptured form may point to Donatello or Ghiberti. Four major fresco cycles, five major frescoes, and a large number of panels (many lost) reveal C.'s stylistic evolution: frescoes in S. Zaccaria in Venice, showing six male saints in the apse; in Florence, the austere *Crucifixion* for the monks of Sta. Maria degli Angeli (1443?); a series of emotional power on frescoes of the Passion of Christ for the Convent of S. Apollonio (1445–50), with vigorous underdrawing revealed in 1953; the famous leather shield of David with a strong male portrait (both in the National Gallery, Washington, D.C.); the lyrical *Assumption of the Virgin* (1449), a key piece lost in Berlin during World War II; from 1451–53 important but almost wholly destroyed frescoes in S. Egidio, Florence; the emotional fresco of Niccolò da Tolentino (1457, Cathedral of Florence); and 15 other works, lost. C. influenced Baldovinetti, A. del Pollaiuolo, Verrocchio, Botticelli, Mantegna, and many others. BIBLIOGRAPHY: A. M. Fortuna,

"Earliest Works of Andrea del Castagno," *Art Bulletin* 41 (1959); *idem, Andrea del Castagno* (1957).

[M. J. DALY]

CASTAÑEDA, FRANCISCO DE PAULA (1776–1832), Franciscan journalist, polemicist, and patriot in Argentina. Through six newspapers published by him, C. defended religious orders in a time of persecution. He pioneered in education, esp. by establishing art schools in many places. BIBLIOGRAPHY: A. Capdevila, *La santa furia del padre Castañeda* (1933).

[J. R. AHERNE]

CASTE, INDIAN, the rigid hierarchical groups in which Hindu society is divided. In theory, there are four castes: Brahmana or the priests and teachers; Kshatriya or the kings and warriors; Vaiśya or the merchants and traders; Śūdra or servants. There is no evidence that at any time Hindu society was divided into four castes only. There are references to many more castes that are sometimes regarded as subcastes under the four major castes. However, the subcastes are as exclusive as the castes. Not only were intercaste marriages forbidden, but people differing in caste were expected also not to eat or sit together. Besides the castes, there is the group of outcast or untouchables outside the main body of Hindu society, who live in subhuman conditions. Gandhi, in order to change their status, named them *Harijana* or people of God. The Hindu term for caste is *jati* or *varna*. *Jati* means birth or descent and class. *Varna* means color. The history of the Christian era shows that caste is determined by heredity. However, some old literatures (e.g., *Chandogya Upanishad* 4:4; *Mahabharata: Vana parva* 180) indicate that caste is more of a matter of character than of birth. The term *varna* is responsible for the theory of racial origin of caste. However, the differences of color mentioned about the different castes (Brahmana—fair, Kshatriya—red, Vaiśya—yellow, and Śūdra—black) need not mean differences of skin color. It may indicate the difference of *guna* (aptitude), as the three *guna*—*sattva* (intelligence), *rajas* (activity), *tamas* (indolence)—are represented by white, red, and black respectively. Lord Krishna said in the Bhagavadgita (4:13) that he created the four castes according to the differences of aptitude and consequent differences of duty. Hence, the close relationship of caste and occupation. However, at the present time this relationship is not strictly maintained. Caste system has been the source of strength as well as weakness for Hindu society. Its rigidity helped Hinduism to maintain its solidarity under the adverse conditions of foreign domination. The tyranny of determination of caste by birth caused frustrations among people of lower castes, and a large body of them embraced Islam and Christianity.

[K. MITRA]

CASTEL GANDOLFO, a town on Lake Albano about 15 mi SE of Rome, site of the summer residence of the popes. The Law of Guarantees allowed popes the use of their residence in 1871, and in 1929 the Lateran Treaty assigned to the Holy See extraterritorial rights to Castel Gandolfo and the nearby villas which cover about 100 acres. BIBLIO-GRAPHY: E. Bonomelli, EncCatt 3:1018; ODCC 244.

[A. P. HANLON]

CASTEL NUOVO, Naples, Italian castle built (1282) by Pierre d'Agincourt, architect of Charles I of Anjou, and altered by Aragonese monarchs, with triumphal arch by Francesco Laurana (1467) and bronze door by Guglielmo (1468). At end of the courtyard is the 14th-cent. Church of St. Barbara.

[M. J. DALY]

CASTEL SANT' ANGELO (Hadrian's Tomb), an imposing Roman mausoleum, variously used through the centuries as fortress, prison, papal refuge and residence, foundry, and barracks. Today it is a national monument and houses a military museum. Emperor Hadrian (d. 138) began its construction as a tomb for himself and his family; Antoninus Pius completed it in 139. Emperor Aurelian (d. 275) converted it into a fortress, and Theodoric (d. 526) used it as a prison. In the 10th cent. it was the stronghold of the Theophylacti and the Crescentii, and there Popes John X (982), Benedict VI (974), and John XIV (984) were imprisoned and murdered. Lorenzo Ricci, general of the Society of Jesus at the time of its suppression, died there in 1775 after a 2-year imprisonment. During the struggle between Church and State, Pope Gregory VII took refuge from Emperor Henry IV within its walls, until he was delivered by Robert Guiscard (1084). In 1527 Clement VII likewise sought safety there from the armies of Charles V. Today, though stripped of its earlier marble surface and statues, it is decorated with an 18th-cent. bronze statue of St. Michael commemorating Pope Gregory I's vision of the archangel during a penitential procession to implore the cessation of a plague. BIBLIOGRAPHY: E. D. McShane, NCE 3:187–188; H. V. Morton, *Traveller in Rome* (1957); E. Gerlini, EncCatt 3:1025–30.

[G. M. COOK]

CASTELLINO DA CASTELLI (1476–1566), an Italian priest of Milan remembered for his pioneering efforts in the field of religious education for children. He founded (1536) the first school for the religious instruction of children in Milan. The novelty of this undertaking aroused some suspicion at first, but the Council of Trent approved the work. Many new foundations were made. With the establishment of the Confraternity of Christian Doctrine in the archdiocese, however, these schools were superseded by it. They deserve due credit, nevertheless, for having prepared the way. BIBLIOGRAPHY: M. S. Conlan, NCE 3:189.

CASTELLIO, SEBASTIAN (1515–63), a French Reformer. Educated in the humanist tradition, he was a noted classical scholar and champion of religious toleration. Be-

coming acquainted with Calvin at Strassburg in 1540, he was persuaded the following year to move to Geneva, where he headed the academy there. In 1544, he became alienated from Calvin, who refused his request to be ordained a minister. Although Castellio had volunteered to minister to plague victims when other ministers feared to do so, his ordination was denied because he questioned the inspiration of the Song of Solomon and disagreed with Calvin's interpretation of the phrase "descended into hell" in the Apostles' Creed. Moving to Basel in 1545, he lived in dire poverty until his appointment in 1553 as professor of Greek. Among his works were a collection of Bible stories in classical Latin and both a Latin and a French translation of the Bible, the Latin in classical, the French in popular style. Advocating toleration of diverse religious opinions, he criticized Calvin's part in the burning of Servetus (1553) in a pseudonymous work, *Concerning Heretics*. This book, one of the earliest and most articulate defenses of religious liberty, evoked rejoinders from Calvin and T. *Beza. BIBLIOGRAPHY: F. Buisson, *Sebastien Castellion, sa vie et son oeuvre* (2 v., 1892); R. Bainton, *Studies on the Reformation* (1963), Léonard HistProt 1:430–431, bibliog.

[N. H. MARING]

CASTELLVÍ, MARCELINO DE (1908–51), linguist and anthropologist. Born in Spain, C. joined the Capuchins in 1924. After ordination he was assigned to Sibundoy, S Colombia. His knowledge of languages led him to further ethnologic and linguistic studies of Colombia, and he founded the Linguistic and Ethnological Research Center of Colombia Amazonia (CILEAC). He published its journal, *Amazonia Colombia,* and wrote several important works, among them *Manual de investigaciones lingüísticas* (1934). Outstanding as a priest as well as a scholar, C. taught in schools and universities, was a noted preacher, and acted as rector of the seminary for secular clergy.

[A. P. HANLON]

CASTELSEPRIO, ancient seat of the abp. of Milan (12 mi from that city), where was discovered accidentally during World War II a significant fresco series of the Virgin and Christ, classical in form, color, and landscape renderings, with original iconographic variants and a heightened spirituality that distinguish them from other contemporary works. Stylistically Byzantine through Italo-Byzantine or Ottonian Byzantine relationships, they are the subject of controversy as pre-Carolingian (8th cent.) or Macedonian (10-11th cent.), the former affinity based on 7th- or 8th-cent. frescoes in Rome, coinciding with the iconoclastic controversy and the consequent influx of Byzantine artists into Italy in the 8th century. (John III being Greek, there were probably Byzantine workshops in S Italy.) Yet the refined and illusionistic technique relates also to the Paris Psalter (9th cent.) and the Homilies of Gregory of Nazianzus (9th cent.). Accurate dating of frescoes at Sta. Maria del Castelseprio would clarify issues of frescoes in Capua. BIBLIOGRAPHY: A. Grabor and C. Nordenfalk, *Byzantine Painting* (1953).

[M. J. DALY]

CASTI CONNUBII, the official Latin title for Pius XI's encyclical on Christian marriage. Promulgated in 1930 as a clarification of Catholic teaching on marriage, the encyclical was also seen as a response to the report on marriage issued by the Anglican bps. at the 1930 Lambeth Conference that justified contraceptive practices under certain conditions for married couples. The Pope's position on contraception is clear, "Any use whatever of marriage, in the exercise of which the act by human effort is deprived of its natural power of procreating life, violates the law of God and nature. . . ." Thus the encyclical represents the most forceful RC opposition to artificial contraception. *Casti connubii* also considers other areas of morality relating to marriage and family life. It defends the perpetuity of marriage, proscribes abortion and sterilization, reiterates the Church's attitude toward mixed marriages, exhorts bishops to establish programs of Christian education for marriage, and reminds governments of their obligation to provide a socio-economic milieu in which a married man can earn a family income. BIBLIOGRAPHY: Pius XI, "Casti connubii," AAS 22 (1930) 539–592, Eng. tr. *Catholic Mind* 29 (1931) 21–64; J. Ford and G. Kelly, *Contemporary Moral Theology* (2 v., 1964); J. T. Noonan, *Contraception: A History of its Treatment by the Catholic Theologians and Canonists* (1965). *CONTRACEPTION.

[J. J. FLOOD]

CASTIGLIONE, GIUSEPPE (1688–1766), Jesuit missionary and artist, who became a principal member of the Imperial Painting Bureau at Peking. C. painted in Genoa and Portugal before going to Peking (1715), where he became known as Lang Shih-ning, favorite painter and architect of the emperors K'ang Hsi (d. 1722), Yung Cheng (d. 1735), and Ch'ien Lung (d. 1795). C.'s style fused Western and Oriental elements in interesting but not noteworthy paintings, as seen in his 30-foot scroll of 100 horses. (National Palace Museum, Formosa). BIBLIOGRAPHY: G. R. Loehr, *Giuseppe Castiglione* (1940); R. J. Verostko, NCE 3:192.

[R. J. VEROSTKO]

CASTILHO. (1) **João de** (fl. 1515–52), Portuguese Plateresque architect, one of the founders of the Manueline style. C. built the nave and vaults of the Hieronymite church in Belém near Lisbon, the most important Portuguese building of the period, and was active also at Tomar, Batalha, and Alcobaça. (2) **Diego de** (fl. 1517–75), Portuguese architect. He assisted his brother João on the Hieronymite Church in Belém and directed work on the Manueline cloister of Sta. Cruz in Coimbra.

[M. J. DALY]

CASTILLO Y GUEVARA, FRANCISCA JOSEFA DEL (1671–1742), Poor Clare mystic, nun, and author. C. wrote as directed by her confessors, *Autobiografía,* (1817), and *Sentimientos espirituales* (v. 1, 1843), (v. 2, 1942), and was considered one of the best writers of 18th-cent. Colombia.

[A. P. HANLON]

CASTLE OF PERSEVERANCE, one of the English morality plays. Its hero, *Humanum Genus,* appears in all the phases of his life, from infancy to death. He succumbs to the various personified deadly sins, but about halfway through the play he repents and enters into a stronghold of the virtues, which are represented as holy women guarding this Castle of Perseverance. The vices long besiege the dwelling unsuccessfully, until, in his old age, *Humanum Genus* departs from it at the urging of Covetousness. Struck down by Death, he dies with a cry for mercy and is rescued from the devils at the plea of Mercy and Peace, who debate against Justice and Truth before God's throne. BIBLIOGRAPHY: *Macro Plays: The Castle of Perseverance, Wisdom, Mankind* (ed. M. Eccles, 1969).

[E. C. DUNN]

CASTNER, GASPAR (1665–1709), missionary, scholar. A German Jesuit, he went to China as a missionary in 1697. After 5 years there, he accompanied Father Francis Nöel to Rome representing the bps. of Nanking and Macao in the controversy over Chinese rites. Returning to Peking, he served at the court of the Emperor as mathematician and tutor to the crown prince. C. achieved celebrity as a mapmaker.

[A. P. HANLON]

CASTOR, ST. (d. *c*. 305 ?), a stonemason or carver who was martyred with four fellow workers at the stone quarries of Pannonia. Confusion of name, deed, and date of these Pannonian martyrs with the Four Crowned Martyrs arose because the remains of the Pannonian group were at some later and indeterminate date brought to Rome and buried in the Coelian Hill basilica where the Four Crowned Martyrs were also buried. The latter were martyred at Rome perhaps a year after the Pannonian group had been slain. But this explanation has not satisfied all who have investigated the matter, despite having behind it the weighty authority of H. *Delahaye. In medieval times, when the Pannonian martyrs were commonly identified with the Four Crowned Martyrs, they were held in great veneration by the guild of stonemasons. BIBLIOGRAPHY: H. Delehaye, *Legends of the Saints* (1962); C. D. Gordini and F. S. P. Ridolfini, Bibl Sanct 3:941–943; Butler 4:293–294.

[M. R. BROWN]

CASTRATION, here understood as the surgical excision of the male testicles. There is some evidence of its use among the Chinese as far back as 1100 B.C. for the purpose of punishment. It was not practiced in ancient Egypt, Greece, or among the Hebrews. The OT forbade the castration of either man or beast (so far as suitability for sacrifice is concerned). The practice was introduced by some religious cults in Asia Minor, apparently through Eastern influence, and it figures prominently in the Cybele-Attis myth. Castration was later adopted for the more practical purpose of providing servants and custodians for harems. Some early fanatical Christian sects undertook castration for ascetical purposes, perhaps misled by too literal an interpretation of Mt 18.18–19 and Mk 9.43–48, and revivals of this practice have recurred in later times. During the 16th and 17th cent. castration was employed as a means of preserving the soprano or contralto voices of boys. Because such *castrati* were employed in church choirs, it has been erroneously inferred that moralists of the time considered the practice legitimate. Some have advocated castration for eugenical purposes, a practice condemned by the RC Church. Castration has been proposed as a suitable punishment for certain crimes, a proposal that has had the hesitating approval of some moralists. Castration for contraceptive purposes need not be discussed, for surgical procedures of a less drastic kind are readily available. In general it can be said that castration is a serious *mutilation of the human organism; not only does it involve the suppression of a major human function, but it is also likely to result in a hormonal imbalance seriously detrimental to the welfare of the patient. RC moralists in general hold that castration can only be justified in cases in which the total physical well-being of the patient makes it necessary, e.g., when the testicles are seriously diseased or the activity of the gonads is likely to aggravate a cancerous condition elsewhere in the body. The justification is then based on the principle of *totality.

[P. K. MEAGHER]

CASTRATO, a male singer combining the chest and lungs of an adult with the larynx of a boy. The practice of castration to achieve this purpose reached its peak in the 16th to the 18th centuries in Italy. The first documentation of the practice dates from 1562, in the papal chapel, though most theologians did not approve the practice.

[D. J. SMUCKER]

CASTRIOTA, GEORGE, see SCANDERBEG.

CASTRO, AGUSTÍN PABLO (1732–90), Mexican Jesuit humanist. He taught, did pastoral work, served as administrator in houses of the Society, and wrote extensively: poetry, literary commentary, a three-volume philosophy text, and articles on economics. At various times, C. held professorships in literature, philosophy, moral theology, civil and canon law, and jurisprudence, in the major Jesuit colleges and universities in Mexico. His contemporaries recognized him as a keen and versatile, if somewhat less than profound, intellectual. BIBLIOGRAPHY: M. Valle Pimentel, *Augustín Pablo de Castro, 1728–1790* (1962).

[H. JACK]

CASTRO, ALFONSO DE, see ALFONSO DE CASTRO.

CASTRO, MATEO DE (*c.* 1594–*c.* 1668), Brahman convert and first native bp. of India of the Latin rite. After his conversion by the Theatines, C. studied with the Franciscans in India, then at the Propaganda in Rome where he was ordained. He was sent by the Congregation to India as apostle of the Brahmans, but opposition by the Portuguese royal patronage and the bp. of Goa forced him to return to Rome. He was named the first vicar apostolic of his race and sent to Idalkan, adjacent to Portuguese Goa. He trained and created a native Brahman clergy. The conflict of the Portuguese royal patronage grew bitter, and C. was often imprudent in his response. His last years were spent in Rome. Two cousins also failed to be acceptable as vicars apostolic, and as a result the Holy See no longer chose natives as vicars apostolic. It remained for Pius XI in the 20th cent. to reverse this policy. BIBLIOGRAPHY: A. M. Christensen, NCE 3:195.

[A. P. HANLON]

CASTRO-PALAO, FERDINAND DE (1581–1653), Spanish theologian. C. entered the Society of Jesus in 1596. He achieved a considerable reputation as a moralist and was held in high esteem by St. Alphonsus Liguori. He taught at the Universities of Compostela, Salamanca, and Valladolid, and was rector of the College of Medina. He also held the office of consultor and qualificator of the Holy Inquisition. C. was distinguished for his learning and sanctity. His works include *Opus Morale* 7 v. (1631–51), and a posthumous work, a prayer manual in Spanish, (1633). BIBLIOGRAPHY: A. J. Maas, CE 3:415; R. Brouillard, *Catholicisme* 2:268.

[A. P. HANLON]

CASUISTRY (from Lat. *casus,* case), the art and practical science of resolving issues of conscience when there is a question of doubt, the bringing to bear of the principles and conclusions of moral theology on particular instances where it appears that there is a conflict of duties or that circumstances alter cases. From the start the term has often had sinister implications, like Jesuitry, named from the men who were its chief practitioners; a more respectful term would have been casuism. In fact it must remain a perennial and indispensable occupation as long as we are in a world where general moral precepts never quite meet the individual situation and these sometimes clash.

It was practiced by Jews, Stoics, and Christians at the time of Cassian. The growth of private confession produced the later medieval *summae* of penance, legal digests which had succeeded the early medieval Penitentials, and which anticipated the classical period of casuistry, the 2 centuries closing with St. Alphonsus Liguori, not only in the Roman but in the Anglican Church (e.g., Jeremy Taylor and Robert Sanderson) and among the Puritans (William Ames and Richard Baxter). Much ingenuity was deployed to defend the systems, probabilism, probabiliorism, equiprobabilism, and the rest, but usually the issues were so strongly inflected with matters of canon law that the critical acumen displayed was often more legal than properly theological. Sometimes the more genial practitioners give the impression of rescuing human freedom from the mesh of regulations their own juridico-morals had helped to create. Recent moral theologians have tended to side-step the system, and going back to the Aristotelian and Thomist notion of equity, the rectification of law because of its generality, have stressed the confident yet flexible role of Christian *prudence instead of the mechanism, fine-spun yet rigid, of *reflex principles. BIBLIOGRAPHY: T. Wood, *English Casuistical Divinity during the Seventeenth Century* (1952); J. C. Ford and G. Kelly, *Contemporary Moral Theology* (v. 1, 1960); J. Pieper, *Prudence* (1959).

[T. GILBY]

CATACOMB PAINTING, decorations of Christian burial chambers (catacombs) mostly in Rome (though similar Jewish painting is extant) in fresco technique of limited palette (with occasional underpainting) on walls and ceilings, as testimony to Christian belief and hope of salvation. Chronology, determined not by style but by dates of areas and burials, with a study of epigraphy and iconography, establishes finds from the 1st cent. to the 9th cent., with the greatest period from the 2d to the 5th century. They embrace both crude and sophisticated examples of salvation themes from the OT and the NT, significantly Christian, with landscapes similar to Roman pagan works. Catacombs are also found in Sicily, Sardinia, and N Africa. BIBLIOGRAPHY: O. Marucchi, *Le Catacombe romane* (3d ed., 1932).

[M. J. DALY]

CATACOMBS, complex of underground rooms and tunnels used for burials. Though they were used in many parts of the Roman Empire, the term usually refers to those around the city of Rome. By the 1st cent., pagan Romans generally practiced cremation, but Jews did not and Christians followed the Jewish tradition. As ground level space for graves became inadequate, underground burial rooms were dug, and then tunnels leading off from these rooms. In time, some of the catacombs became very extensive, containing miles of intricate tunnel works and descending to several levels. After barbarian invasions brought a decline in the Roman population, Christians buried their dead in city churches and no longer needed catacombs. But because many early martyrs, including popes, were buried in the catacombs, they became places of pilgrimage, and relics were taken to many parts of Europe. Later, many of the entrances were caved in, and knowledge of the catacombs virtually disappeared in the 9th century. Chance discovery of a catacomb in 1578 led to renewed interest and exploration.

Several Jewish catacombs have been found, including one dating to the first cent. and identified by a drawing of a seven-branched candlestick. A total of some 40 Christian catacombs are known around Rome, the first dated *c.* 150.

All were outside the city walls because Roman law forbade burial inside the city, and usually they were alongside the roads.

Some catacombs suffered damage when basilicas were built over them in the early medieval period. Then immediately after their rediscovery, they were subjected to considerable looting. Numerous artifacts, inscriptions, etc., were removed. But a more scientific approach was undertaken in the 19th cent., with investigation led by G. Marchi and G. B. de Rossi. At the suggestion of the latter, Pius IX founded the Pontifical Commission of Sacred Archaeology to take responsibility for studying the catacombs. The 1919 Concordat with Italy left them in the hands of the Church.

The catacombs were dug in volcanic strata of granular tufa, which is easy to cut and porous for good drainage. Bodies were usually buried in niches dug into the walls, several at the same place with niches at different heights from the floor. The openings were then covered by slate, marble, or other materials. Frescoes were often painted on catacomb walls and the occasional sarcophagi, and the catacombs now provide the chief resource for study of early Christian art. The oldest Christian paintings date to the 3rd century.

Religious services were sometimes held at the graves of those buried in the catacombs, particularly at the tombs of the martyrs. But evidence appears to be lacking for the widespread belief that Christians found refuge in the catacombs during times of persecution. BIBLIOGRAPHY: L. Hertling and E. Kirschbaum, *Roman Catacombs* (tr. M. J. Costelloe, rev. ed. 1960).

[T. EARLY]

CATAFALQUE, a temporary structure set up in church to hold the coffin of a deceased person or, in the commoner use of the term, to take the place of the coffin when the body of the deceased is not present. The catafalque simulating the presence of the deceased is placed outside the sanctuary and is covered with a pall. The catafalque is obsolescent, since the simulation according the respect due the corpse itself, with candles and use of holy water and incense at the absolution, is thought to be inappropriate by many contemporary liturgists.

[P. K. MEAGHER]

CATALDINO, JOSÉ (1571–1653), Jesuit missionary who founded the Reductions of San Ignacio Mini and Loreto in Paraguay. At Vallarica he labored for the conversion of the Indians of Uruguay.

[J. P. COOKE]

CATALDO, JOSEPH MARY (1837–1928), Jesuit missionary to the Indians of the Pacific Northwest. Frail in health, he was to live to the age of 91 and devote over 60 years to the demanding life of a missionary. Ordained in 1862, he left his native Italy and went to California. He created in the Rocky Mountain area a network of Indian missions, directing the Jesuit mission field of the Pacific

Northwest for 16 years. C. established the first Catholic church in Spokane and founded Gonzaga University. A master of many Indian languages he wrote a life of Christ in the language of the Nez Percés. Typically, on his deathbed he heard the confessions of a group of Indians who had come to visit him. BIBLIOGRAPHY: J. J. Walsh, *American Jesuits* (1934).

[J. R. AHERNE]

CATALDUS OF TARANTO, ST. (Cathal; d. *c.*671), Irish monk of Lismore who became abbot there and later bp. of Ratham (near Lismore; the designation of his see as Rachau—he is often called Cataldus of Rachau—appears to stem from a misreading of the "Cathaldus Racham" inscribed on his tomb). He died in Taranto while on pilgrimage to the Holy Land and was buried in the cathedral there. C. was rescued from oblivion by the discovery of his tomb when the church was being rebuilt in 1094 after its destruction by the Saracens. The people of Taranto straightway began to claim him as their own, and fantastic legends grew up accounting for his identity and claim to greatness. It was said he was an early bp. of Taranto, perhaps even the city's proto-bishop, appointed by St. Peter himself. Even when his Irish origin was established, some stubbornly insisted that he had become bp. of Taranto after suffering shipwreck near the city, and in that office had distinguished himself greatly. His cult flourished in southern Italy and Sicily and he is patron of Taranto. BIBLIOGRAPHY: F. O'Briain, DHGE 11:1490–91; C. Carata, BiblSanct 3:950–952.

[P. K. MEAGHER]

CATALONIAN ART, a wealth of art produced in Catalonia, the region of Spain NE of the Ebro. Renowned Romanesque frescoes of great originality from S. Clemente de Tahull, Sta. Maria de Tahull, and S. Juan de Bohí have survived together with beautiful sculptured capitals at Barcelona, Tarragona, Ripoll, and Estany. San Pedro de Roda (Gerona) is the principal monument of Catalonian Romanesque architecture, with other notable examples at Seo de Urgel (Lérida), the cathedral of Gerona, the abbey church of S. Cugat del Vallés (Barcelona), the monastery of S. Maria of Ripoll (Gerona), and Sta. Maria del Estany. Oriental designs of Arab Spain dominate hangings of silk tissue from local workshops at the Cathedral of Gerona. Mozarabic ivories carry Christian subjects with Moorish ornament.

[M. J. DALY]

CATAPHRYGIANS (Phrygians), a title used by a number of early ecclesiastical writers, e.g., Eusebius and St. Epiphanius, to designate the *Montanists, a prophetic and chiliastic movement founded by *Montanus in Phrygia in the latter part of the 2d cent. and persisting into the ninth. BIBLIOGRAPHY: G. Zannoni, EncCatt 3:1062.

[M. J. COSTELLOE]

CATECHESIS, a term rooted in the NT that emphasizes oral teaching and the handing on of what had been received. In the 3rd cent. it took the precise sense of the teaching given to one preparing for baptism. As the catechumenate developed, the word catechesis took on the meaning of instructions given either preparatory to baptism or subsequent to it. Catechesis and catechumenate are so intimately linked that the term catechesis disappeared when the catechumenate vanished in the 8th and 9th centuries. With it passed away an early form of Christian teaching. Other forms succeeded it with a new terminology to express the elementary teaching given by parents or sponsors to the baptized child. Later ages identified the need for some institution specifically designed for basic instruction in the faith, particularly for baptized children and only occasionally for adults. The institution that emerged was not called catechesis but catechism, the name given to the book which was the prime source of that form of teaching. This marked the complete transition from an oral to a visual form of teaching. Despite the intent of its pioneers for an approach that was Christological and based on the living word of God, the trend of catechisms was away from these. As book and institution, catechism proved inadequate to maintain the living word in the Christian community. The emergence of the word catechesis in recent years indicates another change in form of religious teaching. According to students of the media, such as Marshall McLuhan, the visual, compartmentalized culture of the book is giving way to an oral, retribalized culture of computer and television. Education thereby is becoming total and modern man's main concern. Accordingly, all institutions of society are being reshaped. The vocabulary switch from catechism back to catechesis indicates that religious teaching cannot be reduced to class for children. Adolescent and adult needs require fulfillment as well. The whole contemporary effort is toward restoration of the living word, catechesis, to its due place in the life of the Church. In recent times catechesis is taken to mean all activity that resounds the word of God. The real task of catechesis is to communicate the word of God with a view to spreading faith. By catechesis one means enlightening human existence as God's saving activity by giving witness to Christ's mystery in the form of the proclamation of the word to foster faith and to stimulate men to live a real life of faith. Catechesis is the proclamation of the word of God as giving meaning to the whole of human existence as it is concretely lived.

Proclamation is supported by another element of the catechetical task, namely, that of disposing people for a right listening to and understanding of the word of God. Hence it is a question of calling forth fundamental questions regarding man's life in general. It is concerned with the existential elements of the formation of personality and human existence that consciously or unconsciously influence the growth to maturity in surrender to God's love. These are essential aspects of the human situation which spontaneously lead to questions that catechesis can answer on the basis of revelation.

At the center of catechesis is the mystery of the Incarnation in which the whole experience of being human is radically changed in this man, Jesus, because of an absolutely unprecedented exposure to divine presence. Yet the finality of the Incarnation is directed toward the transformation of the whole human race. One can point to the experience of Christ as the criterion of what human experience is meant to become. Thus catechesis is to be incarnate. For this reason the creation of a proper disposition is a permanent substratum of the whole catechesis from early childhood to maturity. Themes developed as well as methods vary according to psychological development and the social situation of those who are to be catechized.

Catechetical development of the past 35 years has rediscovered catechesis as based in the living word and the oral character of the teaching of the early Church. This development has stressed as its strategy proclamation based on concrete psychological and sociological conditions of the learner. How the meaning of catechesis will be shaped by modern theorists whose basic strategy is the learning situation structured to produce a behavioral outcome remains to be seen. Indeed the connection of catechesis and catechumenate in ancient times suggests such a possibility, for the catechumenate was a kind of structured learning environment meant to produce a determined outcome: a mature Christian faith. BIBLIOGRAPHY: J. Audinet, SacMund 1:263–267; National Conference of Catholic Bishops, *To Teach as Jesus Did* (1973); *Shaping the Christian Message* (ed. G. Sloyan, 1958); C. H. Dodd, *Apostolic Preaching and Its Developments* (1936, repr. 1963); J. A. Jungmann, *Handing on the Faith* (tr. and rev. A. N. Fuerst, 1959).

[C. C. MCDONALD]

CATECHESIS, MISSIONARY, the prebaptismal process involved in introducing the nonbeliever to the Christian message, and in guiding him to a proper understanding and full acceptance of it. Missiologists describe the process in three phases: pre-evangelization, *evangelization, and catechesis proper. Pre-evangelization consists in a variety of preparatory steps that aim to dispose the individual or a particular society to listen to the Christian message. Entry into the society must be achieved, friendships cultivated, and trust engendered. Prejudices must be tactfully encountered and fears allayed, while moral patterns and religious beliefs and practices incompatible with Christianity must be carefully studied and patiently approached with a sincere desire to assist the person to make a decision in favor of Christian ways and values. Finally, an interest in Christian beliefs and attitudes must be aroused. During this preparatory period basic elements of religion, such as the existence of God, the immortality of the soul, and the Christian concern for human needs are discussed and compared with those of the local community. Pre-evangelization is carried out through Christian witness and charity, various forms of educational and health services, community development, liturgical and paraliturgical ceremonies, and through the missionary's in-

terest and involvement in local customs, esp. in his attempt to master the local language and to adjust to the local culture (see ADAPTATION, MISSIONARY).

Evangelization is the proclamation of the core of the Gospel (kerygma), the basic teaching regarding man's salvation, God's goodness and love for man manifested esp. in Christ. It is at this point that the first response of faith is expected from the non-Christian. Once the individual has accepted Christ through his initial response of faith, he is now ready for catechesis, a more systematic and complete presentation of Christian doctrine. Inasmuch as he is now a *catechumen, he must learn to live Christianity. Depending on the statutes of the particular mission diocese or vicariate and on the background of the individual, the catechumenate may last from 6 months to as long as 5 years. This triple process of communicating the Christian message to non-Christian peoples has made rapid progress in recent years, esp. because of developments in religious education and the growing missionary appreciation of cultural anthropology. BIBLIOGRAPHY: E. A. Nida, *Message and Mission: The Communication of the Christian Faith* (1960); M. Ramsauer, *Qualities and Achievement of a Good Mission Catechism* (1960); A. M. Nebreda, *Kerygma in Crisis* (1965); L. J. Luzbetak, *Church and Cultures: An Applied Anthropology for the Religious Worker* (2d ed., 1970). *CATECHETICS.

[L. J. LUZBETAK]

CATECHETICAL CENTERS, places that serve as a focus of research for and foster creativity in the area of catechetics. While the centers are often affiliated with universities, they serve specifically as places where professional catechists are trained and degreed or certified. While initiated in Europe as a response to the new thrust in catechetics, these centers have developed in the U.S. (St. Pius XII Center, Detroit) and Canada (Divine Word, London) in recent years. Other centers, on the national or area basis, promote excellence in religious education by serving as coordinators, gatherers and distributors of new ideas and materials. The Division of Religious Education/CCD (formerly the National Center of the Confraternity of Christian Doctrine) has exerted an impact upon local religious education programs, most recently through its publication, *The Living Light*. BIBLIOGRAPHY: V. M. Novak, NCE 3:218–219.

[C. C. MCDONALD]

CATECHETICAL SCHOOL, a term referring to the organization of religious instruction as the official form of religious teaching for all the children of a determined ecclesiastical territory. This development occurred particularly during the 15th century. Throughout the entire Middle Ages the catechesis of children was done substantially within the Christian family. However, in the 15th cent. a change took place in that schools were founded to collaborate with the family. This movement seems to have been part of an interest aroused by the Renaissance in the need for education of youth. These schools of Christian doctrine were to care for the regular teaching of doctrine, the sacramental and spiritual life, the initiation to prayer and liturgy, and the Christian attitude toward daily life. At this time the Confraternity of Christian Doctrine was founded which continues to the present. BIBLIOGRAPHY: *Shaping the Christian Message* (ed. G. S. Sloyan, rev. ed., 1963).

[C. C. MCDONALD]

CATECHETICS, the science or art devoted to structuring the principles of religious teaching. Its concern is the engagement of the whole person with all his faculties; it views Christian education as a progressive teaching or initiation into a new life; it seeks an integration of the individual's personality with those types of behavior identified as Christian.

There are two main theories of catechetics in the United States. The first and more traditional approach, progressively refined since the days of Clement of Alexandria and Augustine, is espoused by European and most American catechists. This approach views catechetics as a branch of pastoral theology and as allied to homiletics and pastoral liturgy. While catechetics is concerned with all the faculties of a person, it has a special concern for knowledge as leading to love. Catechetics is geared toward faith. A living faith is seen as the general objective of the whole Christian life; the particular aim of catechetics is faith as a kind of knowledge. Faith is personal commitment to God by way of knowledge, not mere theoretical knowledge, but knowledge that involves conversion. A supreme value is placed on the witness to Christ provided by the community and by individuals, for, as a branch of pastoral theology, catechetics is an aspect of that endeavor of the people of God to confront men in their concrete situation with God's offer of salvation in Christ in order to awaken and foster faith. This witness and enlightenment are achieved by the announcement of the glad tidings as giving meaning to the whole of human existence. This is that proclamation of the word that gives concrete expression to the abstract pastoral mission of the Church. Finally, this approach stresses the cognitive or intellectual domain as primary. Catechetics is a thoroughly intellectual endeavor to work with the intelligence of the one catechized according to the concrete structures of his understanding; for faith–knowledge is only effectively communicated when the laws of human psychology and physical and emotional maturity are taken into account. The teaching places emphasis upon content; while careful to point out that there is no dichotomy between doctrine and life, the transferal from the cognitive to affective zones of personality is left to the student.

A second theory of catechetics sees it as a genre of teaching that stresses the process whereby the student can be most fruitfully taught to become a worthy son of God. It holds for a fundamental distinction between theology and religious education. Theology is a speculative intellectual inquiry, an intellectual discipline concerned with truth about God, and his revelational activities with men. Religious education, on the other hand, is a practical human endeavor whereby the religious educator utilizes the data supplied by speculative and empirical research to facilitate acquiring the specific forms of behavior involved in Christian living. Religious education is thus taken to be a type of social science, in that the starting point is the actual, existential, internal and external behavior of persons and groups of persons. Religious education as social science is rooted in the actual dynamics of the teaching-learning process, as this aims to inculcate a way of life in the student. Such religious instruction pertains primarily to the affective domain. Since religion is more an affective affair, catechetics should stress the affective, with the cognitive and theological exerting a supportive role. The ideal is that the cognitive elements will flow into, enrich, and reinforce the student's affective life. Similarly, religious instruction is primarily process-oriented and emphasizes the way in which the object of religious education is acquired. Teaching means a structuring of the learning situation within a living process; content is so fashioned and presented that it is learned in an actual living experience. In such a learning situation the student does not learn about faith or love, but learns faith and love by doing faith acts and love acts in a concrete process of life situation. Finally, religious instruction and religious counseling are seen as sharing a number of features in common, both stimulating the student to self-activity rather than simply imparting information. Both, have distinct functions that make them complementary elements in every effective religious education program. Instruction assists the student to achieve both cognitive and affective results and is concerned with the self-actualization of the person only in so far as it furthers specified instructional goals. Counseling assists the student as a person towards self-actualization. This second theory of catechetics, because of its emphasis on the affective, on results attained by a lived process, and on the structured learning situation is geared toward charity, rather than faith, as the key learning aim and anticipated conclusion of the pedagogical situation.

At university level, catechetical programs, such as those at The Catholic Univ. of America and Manhattan College, that stress a training totally theological, exemplify the first theory. The second theory, most prominently proposed by James Michael Lee, is followed at the Univ. of Notre Dame, where the program of religious instruction operates within the department of education. BIBLIOGRAPHY: G. S. Sloyan, NCE 3:220–225; *Toward a Future for Religious Education* (ed. J. M. Lee and P. C. Rooney, 1970); National Conference of Catholic Bishops, *To Teach as Jesus Did* (1973); L. McKenzie, *Process Catechetics* (pa. 1970); M. Van Caster, *Values Catechetics* (1970); CCD of U.S. Catholic Conference, *Study Aid for Basic Teachings for Catholic Religious Education* (1973); J. T. McGinn, *Doctrines Do Grow* (1972).

[C. C. MCDONALD]

CATECHISM (Gr. *katechein,* cause to be heard; hence, instruct orally), the act of instructing in Christian doctrine, but esp. a book presenting such instruction, usually in question-and-answer form. The first use of the term to mean a book was probably by Lutheran authors *c.*1528, but instruction given in the early Church to catechumens in preparation for baptism is reflected in many writings (e.g., the *Didache,* Irenaeus' *Epideixis,* Tertullian's exposition of the Lord's Prayer). St. Augustine's *De catechezandis rudibus* and *Enchiridion* shaped catechetical instruction in the West, esp. as to the organization of material under the headings of the Creed, the Our Father, and the Commandments; by the 13th cent. sections on the sacraments and the Hail Mary were added. The *Disputatio puerorum per interrogationes et responsiones,* attributed to Alcuin, and the *Catechesis Weissenbergensis* were 9th-cent. catechisms for the clergy and literate laity. Throughout the Middle Ages there were manuals for parish priests to use in imparting instruction to the illiterate by oral repetition. St. Thomas Aquinas's *Compendium theologiae* (1272–73) and his instructions on the Creed, the Our Father, the Hail Mary, and the Commandments may be regarded as adult catechisms. John *Wycliffe prepared expositions of the Creed, the Commandments, and the Lord's Prayer for use in the family. In 1420 J. Gerson wrote *L'ABC des simples gens;* the *Cathecyzon* (*c.*1510) by J. *Colet was the attempt of a humanist at a more Bible-centered catechism in contrast to medieval compilations on Christian conduct and sins.

The era of the Reformation formed the catechetical tradition that prevailed until recent times. On the Protestant side, the catechisms of the Hussites (1426–36) and of the Moravian Brethren (*c.*1502) influenced Martin Luther. In 1529 he published his *Smaller Catechism,* a classical text in Lutheranism, and a *Larger Catechism,* for the clergy, (see CATECHISMS, LUTHER'S). John Calvin's first catechism (1536) was too ponderous for children, and 5 years later he prepared a second (see GENEVAN CATECHISMS). But in the *Reformed tradition, the *Heidelberg Catechism (1562) is preeminent. In Presbyterianism the *Westminster Catechisms (1648), esp. the Shorter Catechism, famous for its beauty and preciseness, had lasting and widespread influence. These catechisms not only were works of instruction, they also became accepted as official *confessions of faith (see RACOVIAN CATECHISM). The Anglican *Book of Common Prayer has always included a catechism, which originally was printed in the section on confirmation. Methodist catechisms grew out of a 39-page pamphlet by John *Wesley, *Instructions for the Young.* Baptist catechisms date from as early as 1653. In all languages and in most Protestant traditions there appeared not only the classic catechisms but also adaptations reflecting theological currents, thus the catechisms of *Pietism and the 19th-cent. rationalist catechisms. Those Churches which were anticreedal resisted the use of catechisms.

In the RC post-Reformation period the work of St. Peter Canisius became classic. He published a catechism, *Summa*

doctrinae christianae, in three forms (1555; 1556; 1558 or 1559); the third, of intermediate length and level, was translated into German and other languages and was widely accepted. The *Catechism of the Council of Trent, or Roman Catechism (1566), was more a theological guide for pastors, and was considered to have special authority. From the Tridentine era into the 20th cent. catechisms usually followed the traditional order of Creed, Lord's Prayer, Commandments, and sacraments. Contents were capsulized theological formularies and were strongly apologetic. Esp. in the 19th cent. a quasi-authoritative status was achieved in England by the "Penny Catechism" (*Catechism of Christian Doctrine,* 1898) and in the U.S. by the Baltimore Catechism (*Catechism of the Third Plenary Council of Baltimore,* 1885).

Contemporary conception and use of the catechism in RC and Protestant Churches is a radical departure from the past. This is very evident in comparing RC education texts before and after Vatican Council II. A realization of the need for a formational approach has led many Christian educators to question the suitability of a formal catechism for classroom use. They see a need for Christian nurture to be expressed in terms of the personal love of Christ for every man and for this nurture to be conveyed in a person-oriented methodology. They are wary of a verbal indoctrination that would disregard the element of mystery in faith. Examples of this approach may be seen in the Protestant works of Randolf Crump Miller and Wesner Fallaw and in the RC *New Catechism* and *Fundamentals and Programs of a New Catechesis* issued by the Higher Institute of Catechetics in Nijmegen, Holland. Current emphasis on the development of ecumenically directed formats has resulted in the *Common Catechism* (1974), compiled by a joint group of Catholic and Protestant theologians. Other recent catechisms are the *Catholic Catechism* (ed. J. A. Hardon, 1975) and the *American Catholic Catechism* (ed. G. D. Dyer, 1975).

[F. E. MASER]

CATECHISM, IMPERIAL (*Catéchisme à l'usage de toutes les Églises de l'Empire français*), a catechism for the French Empire issued by Napoleon I, May 1, 1806. A uniform catechism was desired for two reasons: (1) there were often several different catechisms being used in the same diocese, since the dioceses set up by the Concordat of 1801 often included several pre-Revolutionary dioceses; (2) Napoleon wished to inculcate submission to his regime and person through catechetical instruction. Pius VII refused ecclesiastical approval for the catechism, and the bishops gave it only token acceptance. After Napoleon's downfall it was suppressed (1814). BIBLIOGRAPHY: A. Labreille, *Le Catéchisme impérial de 1806* (1935).

[T. C. O'BRIEN]

CATECHISM OF FILARET, a symbolic book in the Slavic Churches. The first edition (1823) of this work by *Filaret (Philaret), metropolitan of Moscow, was published as the Christian Catechism of the Orthodox Catholic Oriental Greco-Russian Church (*Christianaki Katichisis pravoslavniva Katholicheskiva vostochniva greko-rossikiva Tserkvi*). The title of the 2d ed. (1827) was prefixed with the word Expanded (*Prostranii*), which remains in the final, 3d ed. (1839). Commissioned in 1822 by the Holy Synod, the first edition was withdrawn from circulation because the Lord's Prayer and the Creed had not been left in liturgical, Old Slavonic, but translated into Russian. The 2d edition, commissioned by Nicholas I, restored all prayers and Scripture to the old language. The 3d edition entailed revisions dictated by a campaign against the Protestantization of Russian theology. Filaret included emendations on the place of tradition alongside Scripture, on predestination and on the eucharistic change. The 3d edition, official for the whole Russian Church, also was translated into other Slavic languages. Many 19th-cent. Orthodox theologians wrote commentaries on it. The Catechism, however, was never universally recognized as authoritative throughout Orthodoxy, a point emphasized by Greek representatives at the Lambeth Conference of 1930 and at the Orthodox Congress of Athens in 1936. The body of the Catechism in question and answer form follows the same division as that of Peter *Mogila, namely under the three headings, faith, hope, and charity. The first treats of the Creed, the second of prayer and the Beatitudes, the third of good works and the Decalogue. BIBLIOGRAPHY: Schaff Creeds 2:445–542 for Eng. translation.

[T. C. O'BRIEN]

CATECHISM OF THE COUNCIL OF TRENT, a summary statement of doctrinal matters concerned principally with the Creed, the sacraments, the Commandments, and the Lord's Prayer. It is also called the Roman Catechism in view of the fact that it was issued at Rome in 1566 by the order of Pope Pius V. It is designed for the use of parish priests and teachers and not specifically for the laity or for catechetical instruction to the young. It was projected early in the Council of Trent (1546) but was not completed until 1564, after the close of the council. It was published originally in Latin and since has been translated into many languages. It was used widely in seminaries and had a semiauthoritative standing because of its auspices and connection with the Council of Trent. The theological reasoning involved in the doctrinal expositions contained in the Catechism is based largely on Thomistic theology, and its contents are expositional and pedagogic rather than polemic. BIBLIOGRAPHY: J. A. McHugh and C. J. Callan, *Catechism of the Council of Trent* (1923, repr. 1947); E. Mangenot, DTC 2.2:1917–18.

[J. P. WHALEN]

CATECHISMS, CALVIN'S, see GENEVAN CATECHISMS.

CATECHISMS, LUTHER'S, the chief statements of the Lutheran doctrine for laymen and part of the *Book of Concord (the collection of Lutheran confessions). During the autumn of 1528 Luther had participated in a visitation of the parishes of Saxony. He found there a shocking ignorance of the fundamentals of Christian teaching, not only among the common people, but even among the clergy. To remedy this condition, he wrote two catechisms, both in 1529. They were written in German, then translated into Latin. The *Small Catechism (Kleine Catechismus)*, or *Enchiridion*, is intended for use by the laity as an introduction to the essentials of Christianity; there is probably no summary of Christian doctrine more representative of Luther and Lutheranism than this. The *German Catechism*, or *Large Catechism (Grosser Catechismus)*, was addressed to the clergy, as a kind of epitome of doctrinal and moral theology. It was based on several series of sermons delivered by Luther during 1528 and 1529. The plan of both Catechisms follows three points: the Ten Commandments, the Creed, and the Lord's Prayer. Taken together, the two works show the concern of the Lutheran Reformation for an authentic renewal of the teaching of the Church in accord with the meaning of Scripture and in response to the need of the laity for the "doctrine of the gospel." BIBLIOGRAPHY: *Book of Concord* (ed. T. G. Tappert, 1959); *Luther's Large Catechism*, (tr. J. M. Lender, 1967). There are many individual editions of the *Small Catechism* in English and other languages.

[J. PELIKAN]

CATECHIST, in the Christian context, a teacher of doctrine, a believer who gives witness to the mystery of Christ, illuminates men's earthly life, helps them achieve an authentic religious self-commitment. The task of the catechist is the limited but essential human task of freeing men for life in the Spirit by awakening intelligence and freedom. The catechist invites men to respond to God by showing what a Christian life is because he lives it himself. He offers the possibility of a personal relationship which may begin to awaken realization of the deeper, already existing relationship with God. The catechist is the faithful herald of the consciousness of the Church. He addresses himself in this context to the situation in which his students live and to everything that occupies their attention in order to inspire them. The catechist like the apostle shares his experience and vision with others by presenting his life as a testimony to a reality beyond himself. BIBLIOGRAPHY: G. Moran, *Catechesis of Revelation* (1966).

[C. C. MCDONALD]

CATECHISTS, MISSIONARY, local, generally salaried, lay auxiliaries functioning as teachers of religion and general assistants to the missionary. They conduct schools, lead the faithful in paraliturgical prayer, administer private baptism, assist the dying, hold burial services, and perform other functions in the name of the local pastor. They may serve as lay assistant pastors at a remote outpost connected with the main mission station, or may assist the missionary at a central station. The training received by catechists varies greatly. In recent times, standards have risen considerably throughout the mission world because of recent papal encouragement as well as greater appreciation of religious education by the missionaries themselves. Also responsible for the rise in standards are such catechetical centers as Lumen Vitae (Brussels), the East Asian Pastoral Institute (Manila), the Canisius Institute (Nijmegen), the Institut Supérieure Cathéchétique (Paris) and the catechetical center at Munich. These centers have greatly influenced catechetical theology and have provided teachers for the growing number of catechist training centers throughout Asia, Africa, and Latin America. In recent times esp., emphasis has been placed on utilizing native lay catechists or, in the case of foreigners, the cultural conditioning necessary before communicating the Gospel to the native population. Vat II MissAct (41) praises the work of the lay catechists and speaks of their role as entirely necessary in spreading the faith. At present, there are over 40,000 lay catechists in Asia and Africa alone. BIBLIOGRAPHY: *Teaching All Nations* (ed. J. Hofinger, tr. C. Howell, 1961); W. J. Richardson, *Modern Mission Apostolate* (1965). *CATECHESIS, MISSIONARY; *CATECHETICS.

[L. J. LUZBETAK]

CATECHUMEN, someone under immediate preparation for baptism. In the early Church this preparation included a series of exorcisms as well as actual teaching. Catechesis on these lines continued in Nestorian missions into the Middle Ages and in Russian missions in Asia later. But in the East generally the adaptation of baptismal forms to the needs of infants was early, earliest in parts of Syria where most people were Christian. By the 5th cent. the exorcisms were reduced to one, and in the 6th and 7th cent. the first part of the baptismal service, still called "the making of a catechumen," was assimilated into the liturgy of the Word in the Eucharist. Preliminary services were introduced at home 8 days after birth, and when the child was first brought to church. These are no longer in general use. The dismissal of the catechumens is still in the text of Eastern liturgies. Its survival may be explained partly as a signal to penitents and possessed persons *(energumens)* dismissed with the catechumens, but also by the presence of unbaptized babies, who are not old enough to communicate and could be sources of distraction by their crying. *CATECHESIS; *CATECHUMENATE.

[G. EVERY]

CATECHUMENATE, an institution in which adult candidates are prepared for baptism. As it developed in the 3d cent. it was a strict discipline including adequate doctrinal preparation and was probably occasioned by the rise of the Gnostic sects which were a source of confusion to the faithful. It usually lasted 3 years, although it could be shortened with industry and application. When the conversion of the masses began, an adequate preliminary instruction was given after which one could be received into the catechumenate and progress toward baptism. After the 6th cent. adult baptism became a rarity. The traditional rites of the catechumenate

were used for infants with only superficial adjustment. By the time of the Middle Ages the catechumenate had disappeared, even for adults.

Modern times have witnessed a rebirth of the catechumenate. There are a number of factors that have brought this about: historical research on the catechumenate, the rediscovery of adult conversion, missionary concerns, and the desire to place baptism within the communal life of the Church. Today the concern of situating baptismal acceptance in the context of the faith of the Church has led to a new dimension of the catechumenate. The new rite of baptism itself stresses the parental role and responsibility in the growing faith of a child presented for baptism. There is increasing the practice of a "catechumenate" in which the teachers in the Church clarify and constantly update the responsibilities parents and godparents assume in the baptism of an infant. These usually consist of a few meetings to clarify the role of adult faith and responsibility. BIBLIOGRAPHY: J. A. Jungmann, NCE 3:238–240; *Rites of the Catholic Church* (Pueblo ed., 1976) 40–117.

[C. C. MCDONALD]

CATECHUMENS, OIL OF, see OIL OF CATECHUMENS.

CATEGORICAL IMPERATIVE, the unqualified obligation resting on every person, which, according to the German philosopher I. *Kant (1724–1804), is the basis of morality. As formulated by Kant, the categorical imperative is that one should act only according to such principles as could be considered valid for all men. Another formulation, which Kant considered essentially the same, was: treat every rational being, including yourself, always as an end, and never as a mere means. He set the categorical in contrast with the hypothetical imperative, by which an act is required to obtain a certain end. According to Kant, an act is moral without regard to the circumstances in which it is done or the consequences to which it leads. He held, furthermore, that morality could not be based on theology since, in his view, the human mind was not capable of knowing God. Rather, the existence of moral duty was the basis on which the practical reason was led to posit the reality of freedom, immortality, and God, all necessarily existing if there is an imperative that man ought to obey. Kant's ethics, therefore, rested upon a formal principle that he considered universally binding on all rational minds in the same way that science is. Critics have objected that emphasis on form apart from content is unsatisfactory, and that the motives of compassion and love are mistakenly ignored. Christians object, too, that ethics are made autonomous rather than theonomous. BIBLIOGRAPHY: H. J. Paton, *Categorical Imperative* (1948).

[T. EARLY]

CATEGORIES OF BEING, in Aristotle, 10 kinds of logical predicates *(katēgoriai,* Lat. *praedicamenta)* that can be asserted of a subject in a sentence or proposition. Indicating that they are themselves incomplex or simple terms,

Aristotle lists them as follows: "Each unencumbered word or expression means one of the following things: what (or substance), how large (that is, quantity), what sort of things (that is, quality), related to what (or relation), where (that is, place), when (or time), in what attitude (posture, position), how circumstanced (state or condition), how active, what doing (or action), how passive, what suffering (affection)" (*Categories* 4.1b 25). Through this tenfold classification logic characterizes propositions accordingly as they express either the substantial nature (generic or specific) or an accidental attribute (whether it be an essential property or simply a factual condition) of a subject. Real beings are not as such predicates, but have this status only in their logical conception and expression. But real beings are either substances or accidents; of the connection between these real modes of being with the categories, Aristotle remarks: "The senses of essential being are those indicated by the figures of predication [the categories]; for 'being' has as many senses as there are ways of predication. Now since some predicates indicate what a thing is, and others its quality, quantity, relation, activity or passivity, place, time—to each of these corresponds a sense of 'being' " (*Metaphysics* 1017a 19–26). The logical classification, then, reflects one fundamental difference in the meaning of "being," i.e., between that which is a being *(ens),* namely substance; and "beings of a being" *(entia entis),* namely the accidents that affect or belong to a substance. Further, it presupposes the various kinds of accidents, or ways in which substance is affected; but Aristotle's ninefold listing need not be taken as exhaustive. From the metaphysics of St. Thomas Aquinas it may be added that because of the real distinction between essence and *esse* in every being other than God, the full actuality of a being is composed of its substantial being and its accidental being; only God, by being himself substantially, is all of himself. (ThAq ST la.6.3). Ziegler gives a concise account of the place of the categories in philosophical demonstration (see bibliog.). The also celebrated scheme of categories proposed by I. *Kant is not a classification of predicates reflecting modes of real being, but of pure, a priori thought forms. Through them Kant maintains that all judgments are classifiable as they make, in his epistemology, the matter of sensory intuitions conceivable as thought objects. A complex scheme of categories (of the ultimate, of existence, of explanation) is fundamental to the process philosophy of A. N. *Whitehead. BIBLIOGRAPHY: J. A. Oesterle, *Logic, the Art of Defining and Reasoning* (2d ed., 1963); J. J. Ziegler NCE 4:844 s.v. "Dialectics."

[T. C. O'BRIEN]

CATENAE, BIBLICAL (Lat., chains), an early form of scriptural commentary. After the golden age of exegesis in the Greek Church creative work in this field declined, and interpreters came to rely increasingly on the interpretations of the Fathers and other ancient writers. Hence compilations emerged in which brief quotations from one or more of the Fathers were strung together into a continuous scriptural commentary. Greek catenae, notably those of Procopius of Gaza (d. 538) appeared from the 5th cent. onward. Of the Syriac catenae mention may be made of the anonymous *Garden of Delights* (7th cent.), one by Severus of Antioch (9th cent.), and the *Storehouse of Mysteries,* a commentary on both testaments by Bar Hebraeus. Of the Latin catenae the most famous is the *Catena aurea* of St. Thomas Aquinas. He himself called the work simply a running comment on the four Gospels; the 1484 edition gave it the title, and invented this use of the term catena. The Greek catenae are of some importance to biblical exegesis and textual criticism. BIBLIOGRAPHY: C. O'C. Sloane, NCE 3:244–246.

[D. J. BOURKE]

CATESBY, ROBERT (1573–1605), chief architect of the Gunpowder Plot. Member of a zealous Catholic family which refused to accept the C of E, C. was imprisoned under Elizabeth I, and for joining the revolt of the Earl of Essex and again for attempting to persuade the Spanish to invade England. When James I came to the throne, C. determined to blow up King and Parliament. With a group of fellow Catholics, including Guy Fawkes, plans were made but the government discovered the plot the day before the gunpowder was to be laid. C. fled London but was killed by government troops at his hiding place in Staffordshire.

[J. M. BRADY]

CATHACH OF ST. COLUMBA (late 6th cent.), Irish psalter. Ninety enlarged decorative initials with fluid outlines displaying spiral terminations, trumpet-pattern devices, etc., mark the initial application of the dynamic tradition of *Celtic art to the new field of Christian manuscripts. The Cathach is an important document in the post-Roman revival of Celtic art. BIBLIOGRAPHY: R. L. S. Bruce-Mitford, NCE 7:636.

[R. L. S. BRUCE-MITFORD]

CATHARI (Gr. *katharoi,* the pure or perfect ones), a name properly applied to full-fledged members (Perfecti) of several neo-Manichaean sects that appeared in western Europe during the 12th cent. but generally employed as a collective designation for the sects themselves. Catharism, the most widely diffused of all medieval heresies, was not only anticlerical and antisacramental, but also anti-Christian and antisocial. Its creed combined elements of Manichaeism, Docetism, Monarchianism, Gnosticism, and Hinduism. Doctrinal unity was lacking among the various Cathar groups, but all of them professed some form of dualism. They affirmed two mutually opposed principles: one spiritual, which was the plenitude of all goodness; and the other material, which was the source of all wickedness. Some, such as the *Albanenses and *Albigenses, professed absolute dualism, holding that the two principles were equal and coeternal. Others, such as the Concorezzenses, held that the material principle was a lesser being that did not create but only formed the world out of preexisting matter. All the

Cathari, however, affirmed that the two principles were engaged in perpetual warfare, that the earth was their battleground, and that man's primary concern must be to free himself from servitude to matter. Because matter was evil, Christ could not have had a true human body, have died, or have risen from the dead; because human procreation resulted in the union of spirit with matter, marriage was essentially evil; and because sacred suicide, called *endura,* liberated man's spirit from matter, it was the highest act of virtue.

The dualism of the Cathari was derived from the Eastern *Bogomils and Paulicians, and was probably introduced into Western Europe by merchants, pilgrims, and returning crusaders. By the beginning of the 13th cent. numerous Cathar sects were established in S France, N Italy, NE Spain, and the Rhineland. Each was headed by a bishop and included two classes of adherents—Perfecti and believers, or hearers. Initiation of the Perfecti was a ceremony called *consolamentum,* consisting of imposition of hands and the book of the Gospels on the head of the recipient. Thereafter, one so initiated was obliged to a life of poverty, continence, asceticism, and preaching. Believers' only obligations were to tender reverence (the *melioramentum*) to the Perfecti, to support them, to attend their sermons, to refrain from oaths and military service, and to receive the *consolamentum* before death. Beyond this, they were held to no fixed moral code and usually lived accordingly. Suppression of the Cathari proved extremely difficult. Their final extirpation was accomplished by vigorous activity of the *Inquisition and the Albigensian Crusade. By the opening of the 15th cent. all traces of Catharism had almost completely disappeared. BIBLIOGRAPHY: A. Borst, *Die Katharer* (1953); L. Cristiani, *Heresies and Heretics* (tr. R. Bright, 1959) 61–65; H. Daniel-Rops, *Cathedral and Crusade* (1957) 527–552; S. Runciman, *Medieval Manichee* (1961) 116–170; F. Vernet, DTC 2:1987–99.

[C. J. LYNCH]

CATHARINUS, AMBROSIUS, see AMBROSIUS CATHARINUS.

CATHEDRA, the chair or throne of a bp. in his cathedral church; also the see of a bp. enjoying apostolic succession; a symbol of the authority of the pope, where speaking *ex cathedra* signifies a formal pronouncement on doctrine which carries infallibility. The use of a throne to symbolize authority dates from pre-Christian times. It is evident in the catacombs where Christ is depicted seated and instructing the Apostles. In the West the cathedra was usually highly ornamented, in the case of Ravenna the chair carved of ivory with much storied ornamentation. The most famous chair still preserved is that of St. Peter in the Basilica of St. Peter in Rome. Known in the 6th cent., it was encased in bronze in the 17th and was removed from the bronze enclosure by Pius IX in 1867. Parts of the chair date back to the early years of Christianity.

[J. M. BRADY]

CATHEDRAL, the principal church of the diocese where the bp. is accustomed to exercise his liturgical functions. The name is derived from *cathedra,* the seat or throne, from which the bp. used to address the congregation in the early Church. Canon 41 of the Council of Aachen prohibits a bp. from neglecting his cathedral church and residing too frequently elsewhere (Hefle-Leclercq 3.2, 1030). A cathedral is distinguished from an ordinary church solely by its designation as the seat of the bishop. Just as there is only one ordinary, one residential bishop, in a diocese, so there is usually only one cathedral. BIBLIOGRAPHY: B. J. Comaskey, NCE 3:247–248.

[J. E. LYNCH]

CATHEDRAL (ART), the episcopal church in which is located the throne *(cathedra)* of the bishop, first pastor of the diocese.

The Roman basilica, its longer axis reorientated toward the altar, is the earliest type of building specifically constructed for Christian worship, e.g., St. John Lateran (after 313) and St. Peter's (324–44), although traces of earlier ones have been found elsewhere, as in the church of Tebessa (Algeria) and in Bp. Theodore's church in Aquileia (c. 306).

Early Christian Styles

The sites of early cathedrals are historically interesting. In Gaul pagan sanctuaries in wood were replaced by Roman altars in stone placed at the boundaries of Gallo-Roman villas. Upon these sites many of the first Christian shrines were built, frequently orientated toward the E, a custom surviving from primitive times, to which Christians also attached a mystical significance. A 5th-cent. tradition reported by *Gregory of Tours says that in the mid-3d cent., bps. were sent from Rome to cities of the French Midi: St. Saturninus to *Toulouse, St. Trophimus to luxurious *Arles, Paul to the city of *Narbonne. *Martin, Bp. of Tours (371–397), established many churches in his diocese, transforming miraculous wells into baptismal fonts and Druid trees into altars.

Merovingian basilicas were heavy and dark, their exterior walls decorated with gems and metals set in barbaric abstractions, black against white, red against yellow. None of these ancient Merovingian cathedrals survived the invasions, wars, and fires. That of St. Stephen mentioned by Venantius *Fortunatus in the 6th cent. is buried beneath the parvis at Notre Dame, Paris. Under the Paris nave are the ruins of the Carolingian cathedral (857). Further vestiges of the Carolingian era survive in the old nave at Beauvais, the crypt at Clermont-Ferrand, the *martyrium* (chapel of St. Lupin) at Chartres, and the rear crypt of Bourges. Cluny "the great civilizer" arose in 909, and by the year 1000, Glaber writes, the world began to clothe itself in a "white robe of churches." The Romanesque age became the first golden age of sacred architecture.

The Romanesque Style

Romanesque cathedrals are stone constructions; they tend to be heavy and ponderous, but have richly textured surfaces and a great concentration of architectural carving around recessed doorways. Since the best masons came from Lombardy, the Lombard style prevailed everywhere, in France and Germany as well as in Italy. Romanesque builders used a variety of stone, e.g., the white Upper Cretaceous stone in churches as in Périgueux and Angoulême, the hardened lava that blackened in the rain in Clermont-Ferrand, the red sandstone of the Rhineland, the limestone of the Loire Valley so easily cut in friezes. The Romanesque builder used many towers: some for bells, some as abutments to façades, and some over transept crossings.

Romanesque architects preferred vaulting in stone for insurance against fire but particularly for the beauty of the vault itself. A vault is a thing alive, sustaining weight, transferring it, and persistently stabilizing the pressures. Romanesque builders experimented with a variety of vaults. Romanesque was truly Roman in its consistent use of the Roman arch, engaged piers, and arcades, but French Romanesque decoration combines Greco-Roman, Byzantine, Persian, and barbaric motifs. Portals and capitals are derived from Honorius Augustodunensis and from Isidore of Seville whose "science" is responsible for the tympanum at Vézelay with its *cynocephaloi* (dog-headed men) and large-eared *Panotii*. At Moissac the Jewish elders are drawn from the MS of Beatus of Liébana; the portal statue of Isaiah at Souillac is a transcription in stone from the Utrecht Psalter. The devil with his legendary dog-shaped head and the Queen of Sheba with her goose's foot appear together with fantastic beasts, whose interlaced tongues and tails are found as far N as Sutton Hoo, as far E as the Asiatic steppes, and in England's Lindisfarne. Stylized motifs and naive didactic scenes were carved *in situ*. The tympana of cathedrals depicted the Last Judgment, Pentecost, or themes from the Apocalypse.

French Romanesque. Romanesque schools are distinct and scattered. The Poitevin builder emphasized detail, making even each voussoir unique. Burgundian Romanesque produced at Autun the great church of St. Lazare (cathedral from 1195) with its lineal carvings by Giselbertus. In the Périgord region, cathedrals at Cahors, Périgueux, and Angoulême have naves covered with a series of domes (either Byzantine or, as *Leclercq says, "distinctively French"). In Provence cathedrals in towns originally Roman are characteristically classical with draped statues and friezes, with robes aligned along the edges as in the Arch of Constantine. The tympanum at Arles is framed in concentric arches, varied and unadorned as were Roman stringcourses. But the Corinthian supports rest upon fantastic beasts and Persian animals. In the N of France Norman Romanesque churches, austere and unornamented, were achievements in vaulting. Predecessor of Gothic, their prophetic buttressing was often cautiously hidden within the masonry, as at Caen. The oldest Romanesque is found in Auvergne—the masses heavy and solid expanding into graceful absidioles lightened by rhythmic corbels and symmetric windows. At Toulouse, the principal city of Languedoc, they built a replica of *Santiago de Compostela.

Few French cathedrals of the 11th and 12th cent. have remained unaltered. Nevertheless important Romanesque portions remain at Arles, Autun, Bourges (two side portals, an arch, and two capitals in the chapel of St. Solange); Cahors, Poitiers, Chartres (where the Romanesque crypt constructed by Bp. Fulbert [d. 1048], the royal portal with lancets, and areas of the ground stage survive); Le Puy (the cloister is one of the most beautiful known); Nevers (no longer a cathedral) retaining parts of the Carolingian church; Périgueux with the oldest belfry in France, and Strasbourg where the later Gothic is eclipsed by the more impressive Romanesque remains.

Italian Romanesque. Italy provided more than Lombard masons and decoration. At Sant' Ambrogio the Italians advanced "organic structure" in the most important constructional discovery of the Middle Ages; they concentrated support upon ribs, transverse, longitudinal, and diagonal, each of which was supported by individual members of the clustered piers along the nave. In a system of semicircular arches, diagonal ribs thrust higher than longitudinal and transverse ones, leaving a darkened vault. Side-aisle walls at right angles to the clustered piers transferred the weight to the outer walls where a system of pier buttresses secured the structure. Still cautious, the builders at Sant' Ambrogio covered the vault with an unbroken gable roof, eliminating the clerestory and making the interior very dark. Italy produced no further structural development but concentrated on exterior ornamentation.

The Lombardy band confirmed and enhanced structural lines; Lombardy façades were decorated with compound arches and thin pilasters (Modena); the small Lombardy porch consisted of a pediment advanced upon two columns supported on fantastic caryatids (Parma). The elaborate lacework of open arcadings upon slender colonnettes is distinctive of Pisa. The Tuscan wheel window in stone tracery is a vigorous predecessor of the Gothic rose. At San Michele, Lucca, and Florence, Tuscan aniconic inlays of light and dark stone decorate the façades; floors have Eastern lozenged animal patterns. Sicily, at the crossroads of Greek, Lombard, Muslim, and Norman cultures, produced the resplendent cathedral of Monreale, sumptuous in marbles, Byzantine mosaics, Islamic arches, Corinthian columns, storied capitals cut like ivories, and famous bronze doors by Bonnanus of Pisa.

Spanish Romanesque. A remarkable unity in architectural styles that developed along the French pilgrimage roads to Compostela joined Spain to northernmost France, relating Santiago de Compostela (c. 1077–1124), with its magnificent Portico de la Gloria, to Languedoc.

English Romanesque. The Normans brought to England the Romanesque of St. Étienne and La Trinité of Caen (Abbaye aux Hommes and Abbaye aux Dames respectively). The cathedrals at Durham (begun 1093), Ely (begun before 1094), and Canterbury (11th-19th centuries) are massive and sturdy, with heavy rectangular towers at façades and over transept crossings. Pillars and soffits of arches are cut in abstract patterns e.g., zigzags and diamonds.

German Romanesque. Romanesque in the Rhineland was closely related to Lombardy: Worms cathedral (consecrated 1181) has thin pilasters, Lombardy bands, and arcadings. Stonework in Germany shows greater precision than that in France. Distinctive of German Romanesque are double apses which eliminate the central portal, polygonal and rhomboidal towers as at Speyer (12th cent., but rebuilt five times after fires). Cathedrals at Mainz (rebuilt after 1081), Paderborn (built at various times), and Regensburg (c.1240) are remarkable in size. The famous bronze doors at *Hildesheim cathedral are the work of the artist-bishop *Bernward (d. 1022). The sumptuous metalwork of Ottonian artists, e.g., from the school of goldsmiths established at the Abbey of Essen, appeared in splendid jeweled chalices, croziers, and gospel books, maintaining a unity of style between architecture and minor arts in the Romanesque period.

The Gothic Style

Gothic building, the rival rather than the heir of Romanesque, began c.1150 and continued past 1500.

Ogival Construction. The ogive combined ribbed vaulting with the pointed or broken arch and usually (but not invariably, e.g., Ste. Chapelle, Paris) the flying buttress. The introduction of the pointed arch permitted arches of various measurements to rise to a single crown. Interiors were flooded with light. Gothic expresses the logical French mind when it discovered the precise point of strain along the haunch of the arch and placed against it those fingers of stone, the flying buttresses, now out in the open, freeing the areas of wall between for expanses of fragile glass. Gothic is light filtered through colored glass. Gothic is rather space than form. Heaviness is alien to it. Gothic is royal and ideal—*Suger and *Louis VII. It is communal, speaking fully of man in the benign and tender *humanitas* of its saints and shepherds and kings. Whereas Romanesque depicts the God of majesty, Gothic offers the *Beau Dieu* of Amiens and the radiant faces of the dead rising at Bourges (1270). Yet everything takes its place in the medieval dialectic of a preconceived order. Thus the sculpture is architectural, correctly restricted to the pillar shape, more ordered and coherent in earlier façades; later in a new naturalism, it loses a little decorum and some nobility.

French Gothic. France is the homeland of Gothic, and the best of French Gothic was built within a 50-mile radius of Paris at Amiens, Laon, Reims, Sens, Orléans, Chartres, Beauvais, and Rouen. The greatest French Gothic is at Chartres (11th-12th cent.), consecrated 1260 in the presence of King *Louis IX.

Chartres is a miracle of proportion in the rigorous nave where each rib is functionally engaged. The most beautiful piers occur at the transept crossing, rising in a fine unbroken ascent. (Some call them "harp-string" piers and the ribs "nerves".) Chartres's towers are unequal—the older S tower the better in design. The stained glass at Chartres is the most beautiful medieval glass in the world. Irregularities produced by bubbles and blisters in the glass enhance its effect by multiplying and varying refractions. Stained glass

was placed according to theories of color interplay, in an imaginative, highly decorative, and utterly nonrepresentative way. Medieval glass-setting in many small pieces was not a fluid technique; images attained a fixed, linear style proper to the medium. Later as the art declined toward naturalism and the pictorial, glass was cut in large pieces with details and variations of tone painted upon them.

The first ogival churches of the 12th cent. were those of Sens, Noyon, Senlis, Laon, Paris, Lisieux (oldest in Normandy), and Soissons (completely destroyed in World War II). In the 13th cent. Chartres, Reims, and Amiens rose, and Bourges, Beauvais, and Rouen tried to surpass one another. It is the apogee of Gothic. A popular verse extolled "the steeple of Chartres, the nave of Amiens, the choir of Beauvais, the portal of Reims." Reims, the national cathedral, is celebrated for lightness of line—and for its "Smiling Angel"; Amiens with its very high nave (138 feet) has the most perfect proportions. According to Viollet-le-Duc, Amiens is the "ogival church par excellence." In the 14th cent. not many new cathedrals were built for by then nearly every place had its prized example. Ambitious Beauvais' nave (157 feet high) collapsed twice, but its tower rose an amazing 501 feet. The 15th cent. developed Flamboyant Gothic, introducing the ogee arch, its compound curve an example of decoration that denies structure. Façades became cluttered and confused, as in the cathedrals at Rouen and Louviers, where many details are completely unrelated and mutually destructive. After the devastation of the Hundred Years' War (1337–1453), builders engaged in reconstruction or completion rather than in designing. Few new cathedrals (11 in all) were erected in the 17th and 18th centuries. And the 19th cent. established itself as the age of imitations and pastiches.

Italian Gothic. French Gothic is foreign to the classic tradition of Italy. The cathedrals of Siena and Florence pay lip service to the French style. Pointed façades and splayed doors are decorative not structural at Siena and Orvieto. It is only in details of tracery and pinnacles that the Gothic spirit is evident. The cathedral of Milan (begun 1386) is a bizarre French design built in Italy by two German architects, its marble luxury remarkably ornamented by 3,159 statues.

German Gothic. Gothic architecture was introduced into Germany by Abp. Albrecht of Magdeburg (d. 1232), who had studied in Paris. By temperament Germans were not attuned to the lightness of Gothic; they referred to it as the "French style." The cathedral of Cologne (1248) imitated Amiens; Limburg (consecrated 1235), Bamberg (1237) and Naumburg (after 1250) were inspired by the French, while stone tracery at Minden is reminiscent of Tuscan wheel windows. At Freiburg (1122–1252; nave 1513) and in other German cathedrals sculpture (chiefly in the interior) was dramatically exaggerated and starkly realistic (as in the *Foolish Virgins* of Marienkirche, Erfurt). At Ulm the single tower (528 feet) at the center of the façade was the highest in the world (1337). Gothic churches built in red brick were a German innovation, the white plastered vaults often delicately edged with foliate patterns between the red brick ribs.

The outstanding example of German brick Gothic is Lübeck's Marienkirche (1250).

English Gothic. The English cathedral, set in a park, is low with double transepts, square apse, and rectangular towers. The façades present screen-like forms of somewhat unrelated parts. The specific development of English Gothic was an elaboration of the ceiling through a multiplication of decorative, nonfunctional ribs. Accordingly ceilings may be palm, keel, lierne, or fan vaulted. A "Perpendicular Style" (1340–1500) of strong unbroken verticals in reaction against the "Decorated Style" (1250–1340) characterized later additions to cathedrals. The inverted arch is a unique note at Wells (1338); Bristol cathedral is a hall church; Exeter, Winchester, and Gloucester have beautiful windows of Late Gothic style. The Westminster chapel of Henry VII (d. 1509) and the cloisters at Gloucester exploit the intricacies of fan vaulting. Later, English windows are frequently colorless except for heraldic patterns set at intervals. In the lead tracery of windows as in vaulting, the English concentrated on decorative elegance of line. There are great Gothic cathedrals at Salisbury (1220–60)—the finest in England—Lincoln (1220–30), Exeter (1280 ff.), Winchester (14th cent.), and York (13th-15th centuries).

Spanish Gothic. Spain was an artistic province of France, as were most countries with regard to Gothic. The cathedral of Burgos was begun by Bp. Mauritio in 1221; it has a W front that is lavishly ornamented, its spires (1442) designed by Master Hans of Cologne. At Toledo (1227) moldings and piers are very French, while the west façade of León is a weak derivative of Chartres. In the South, roofs are not steeply pitched and clerestories are omitted. Decoration is exuberant in ceilings, choirs, and altars, combining Moorish and Christian motifs. The cathedral of Palma de Mallorca, begun in the 14th cent., is a basilica vaulted on 14 slender octagonal piers; it is related to Albi (1282–1365) in France. The cathedral of Seville (1401), though it has spires and pinnacles, is truly Spanish in its low, solid walls.

Renaissance

Gothic was a name applied with derision by the man of the Renaissance to an art he considered "barbaric" compared to the serene, classical ideal; yet Renaissance architects frequently denied the essence of this ideal in their composite plans. Interest in nature and life in this world culminated in Renaissance individualism and secularization. Flamboyant Gothic gave way before Greek and Roman forms which were noble, reserved, and dignified. The Renaissance built with pomp. Contrary to the Gothic in which form and structure were absolutely functional, the Renaissance architect concealed structure in the interest of an ideal effect.

Florence. The cathedral of Florence, begun (1296) as Tuscan Gothic by Arnolfo di Cambio, is lavishly inlaid with colored marble. Giotto continued the work (1336), erecting the beautiful "Lily Tower" as its campanile. Over the crossing of the heavy and austere nave that is feebly Gothic in its pointed arches, rises Brunelleschi's impressive dome. (The Renaissance dome, unlike the Roman, e.g., that of the Pantheon, is an exterior note of emphasis in the architecture.) The elliptical lines of the dome add grace and lightness; the dome dominates the church as well as the Florentine skyline. Its dimensions are vast: 140 feet in diameter and 180 in height. Its support is concealed within the base of the dome, a second, inner shell serving as ceiling. The famous baptistry has magnificent bronze doors, earlier Gothic ones by Andrea Pisano (1336), and a later pair by Ghiberti, on the N (1402) and on the E (the so-called Gates of Paradise, 1425–52).

Rome. In Rome, St. Peter's old (4th cent.) basilica was demolished in the 16th cent. to make room for a Renaissance basilica of enormous scale. As many as 14 architects were engaged upon the project between 1450 and 1667. Michelangelo, finally put in charge (1546), designed a church on a central Greek cross plan with short, compact arms to serve as a pedestal for the magnificent dome. He died (1564) never dreaming that his plan would be changed. Giacomo della Porta completed the great dome in elliptical lines, probably only slightly modifying Michelangelo's design. The dynamism of the dome derives from its three-dimensional movement in space. Della Porta's lantern is a perfect finial in its carefully harmonized details. Michelangelo's dome is best seen from the rear of St. Peter's, where one's view is not obstructed by the elongated nave and Maderno's façade (1606–12). In the interior the enormous nave, the complicated, overwhelming detail, the statues astride their niches in true Baroque abandon unite to fulfill a gigantic, magnificent purpose. Bernini at 26 comprehending Michelangelo's genius, planned the baldachino on a scale in keeping with the immense dome, using gigantic twisted columns, active angel finials, and swinging volutes—a tribute to tradition and the triumph of the Church. The *cathedra* of Peter is Baroque itself, operatic, luxurious, both inviting and defying inspection. The colonnaded piazza is the greatest monument to the Baroque aesthetic of Bernini's forms.

London. St. Paul's Cathedral in London (1675–1710) has a two-storied pedimental façade similar to Perrault's wing at the Louvre (1665), well chosen by Christopher Wren for strong emphasis in London mists. St. Paul's boasts one of the great Renaissance domes.

Spain. Spanish Renaissance style was severe in the Herreran period under Philip II (1556–98). José Churriguera (1650–1723) gave his name to an ultra-Baroque style more expressive of Spain. At Seville retables of gilded and polychromed wood enshrine statues and oil paintings, giving a luxurious effect in an otherwise unadorned, curiously luminous and airy interior. Toledo boasts intricate iron grilles; simpler in their lower stages but baroquely elaborated above, they frame heraldic ornaments richly gilded and painted.

The Spanish plateresque style (from *platero* meaning silversmith) is an elegant relief carving in stone, delicate as chasing in silver in the lower stages of façades but deepening in the upper zones. Arabesques, medallions, twisted columns, and portrait carvings of kings and saints are concentrated with sumptuous effect around doors and windows.

Latin America

Latin American cathedrals were related to contemporary Spanish and Portuguese styles.

Mexico. The cathedral in Mexico City (17th cent.) has towers and façade in the true Herreran tradition of classical restraint and symmetry, while the sacristy is Baroque, Churrigueresque. In Puebla (1552–1647) the cathedral is even more strictly Herreran than that of Mexico City. Very ornate Spanish plateresque decoration enriches the entire panel of the portal of the cathedral of Taxco (18th century). Elaborate towers, twisted columns, sculpture in the mystical ecstatic style of Spain, and rounded windows framed with rich borders are authentically Churrigueresque. The cathedral at Tepozotlán (18th cent.) is unusual in its single tower to the right of a façade completely ornamented in plateresque style. A magnificent retable, carved probably by Jeronimo de Balvás, frames statues and oil paintings in polychrome and gilt.

Peru. The cathedral of Cuzco, Peru (1564) is severe in towers and walls (of Inca stones in some areas), with an undulating Baroque portal decorated in the heavier Italian style. The pulpits in carved wood in this area rival the rococo of Balthasar Neumann and Fischer von Erlach. Sometimes a flat, linear patterning reminiscent of the ancient Indian culture quiets the Baroque by a sort of native imperturbability.

Ecuador. The lovely façade of the cathedral at Quito, Ecuador, cut in low relief, gives a soft, textural effect. Huge, twisted columns freed from the wall are in dramatic contrast to the delicate stone tracery.

Brazil. The architecture in Portuguese Brazil has a lightness and gaiety similar to French rococo. Churches are tall and slender, with no transepts, vaults or domes; frequently the façade is curved; the ground plan may be an oval (sometimes two) of a studied elegance. Windows in a delightful variety of shapes make strong patterns of dark on walls of light plaster. The cathedral of Salvador (Baía), severely Herreran in its façade, has a richly Baroque interior of gilded carvings broken by Portuguese tiles in brilliant blues, furnished with carved mahogany rails and colored marbles.

United States of America

New Orleans' basilica of St. Louis is Spanish with eventual French modifications. In the Far West are quiet, white façades of Spanish style with gently undulating cornices and belfries. American cathedrals of the 18th and 19th cent. are eclectic and often composite, Neo-Gothic, High Renaissance, and Neo-Byzantine. The Neo-Byzantine cathedral of St. Louis (1907–65) replacing the old cathedral on the riverfront, is lavishly decorated with marbles and mosaics; those of the main dome by J. de Rosen measure 11,000 square feet. The cathedral of the Immaculate Conception of the Blessed Virgin Mary in Philadelphia, Pa., the mother church of the Ukrainian metropolitan province (eparchy) in the U.S., is a contemporary version of the Byzantine domed church, introducing Venetian gold glass in exterior concrete walls and golden domes. The cathedral of St. Patrick, New York City,

the masterpiece of the noted architect James Renwick (1818–95), has a Gothic nave, choir, apsidal chapels, and ambulatories. Completion of Sacred Heart Cathedral in Newark, N.J. (begun 1898; consecrated 1954) was urged by the noted authority on Gothic, Ralph Adams *Cram. Twin Gothic towers are set obliquely to the horizontal axis. The interior is a very authentic imitation of Gothic forms. St. Raphael's Gothic cathedral (1839–57) Dubuque, Iowa is the mother parish of the great Northwest. Samuel Mazzuchelli, OP, who also designed the old State Capitol in Des Moines, Iowa, was architect and builder. The Gothic cathedral of the Assumption in Louisville, Ky. (1849–52) was designed by W. Keely. The cathedral of the Holy Cross, Boston, Mass. (1866–75) in English Gothic style, was designed by Patrick Keeley, the architect of the Chicago cathedral as well as of 600 churches throughout the U.S. Covering an area of 45,000 square feet (its nave is 120 feet high and 320 long), the Boston Cathedral is almost as large as Notre Dame of Paris or St. John Lateran in Rome. The arch over the main entrance is constructed of stone salvaged from the Ursuline Convent in Charlestown, Mass., which had been sacked and burned in 1834 by an anti-Catholic mob. The stained glass is in the French medieval tradition. The protocathedral of the Assumption in Baltimore, Md., primatial see of the Church in the U.S., has a fine low dome in Italian Renaissance style designed by Benjamin Latrobe (d. 1820), one of the architects of the Capitol in Washington, D.C. The cathedral of St. Matthew in Washington, D.C. has an austere Neo-Renaissance façade and dome (1893–1912), but its interior is sheathed with rich marbles in the Italian manner.

The cathedral of St. Vibiana, Los Angeles, Calif. (consecrated 1876) is Herreran Spanish, related in its design to the church of Puerto de San Miguel, Barcelona. The cathedral of SS. Peter and Paul, Philadelphia, Pa., designed by architect Napoleon le Brun, was based on the Lombard church of S. Carlo al Corso in Rome. Begun in 1846, renovated and enlarged in 1950, the cathedral has a High Renaissance portal with Corinthian columns supporting the pediment; the dome was designed by Thomas U. Walter (1802–87), the Philadelphia architect who designed the dome of the Capitol in Washington, D.C. The bronze screen of the baptistry was inspired by that of Coro de Raja in the cathedral of Toledo. The cathedral of St. Cecilia in Omaha, Neb. (1907–59), originally a mission of Santiago de Cuba, is Spanish Renaissance in the restrained, noble Herreran style with towers 198 feet high. It has Baroque ornamentation and magnificent glass by the firm of Connick of Boston. The beautiful campanile of the cathedral of Portland, Ore. (1925) is in 15th-century style.

The cathedral of St. James, Seattle, Wash. (1905–07) is Italian Renaissance with two imposing towers 175 feet high. Originally crowned with a 40-foot dome which collapsed under heavy snow in 1916 ruining the interior, it was rebuilt in 1917 and redecorated in 1950. J. W. Maloney designed St. Paul's Cathedral in the diocese of Yakima, Wash. (1926–27), in Spanish style. Built as a parish church by the

Rev. Robert Armstrong, future bp. of Sacramento, Calif., it was raised to a cathedral church in 1951. The cathedral of the Nativity of the Blessed Virgin Mary (1910) of the Diocese of Juneau, Alaska, is built in the style of early American churches ultimately derived from English designs of Wren and Gibbs, its gabled roof crowned with a small belfry. Seating 125 people, it is probably the smallest cathedral in N America having a nave 24 feet high and 50 feet long. The Romanesque cathedral of Our Lady of Lourdes, Spokane, Wash. (1902–08), designed by H. J. Williams, is 45 feet high and 106 long with stained glass from Munich, Germany.

The new cathedral of Mary Our Queen in Baltimore, Md. (1954–59) is one of the few national examples of "organic structure" in cathedral building. The carving throughout is correctly architectural and noble. (When too strongly geometricized however, it becomes a little mannerist.) Sensitive deviations and inventively patterned masonry make this a great contemporary construction. The windows were designed and made by the best glaziers of the 20th cent., such as Gabriel Loire of Chartres, still famous for its fine glass, and the Americans Connick, Willet, and Pickel. Rambusch's use of blue in the Lady Chapel magnificently demonstrates glass-colored light. The cathedral, the result of the benefaction of one man, Thomas O'Neill of Baltimore, is an example of superior design and craftsmanship.

The cathedral of St. Joseph in Hartford, Conn. (1958–62) by Eggers and Higgins constructed of reinforced concrete has a nave 110 feet high and 26 magnificent windows in slab glass (a significantly new glass technique) designed by Jean Barillet of Paris. A ceramic reredos by Enzo Assenza of Rome exploits tile in a distinctively modern decorative style.

The new cathedral of St. Mary in San Francisco (1965–70) relates appropriately to a complex of modern residences. Its winged concrete tower resembles the beautiful forms of Oscar Niemeyer of Brazil, but it lacks lightness because of its low and squared proportions.

Africa and Asia

From colonial times, African and Asian mission churches have had a composite of European, Neo-Byzantine, Muslim architectural tradition. Since the Church has established the sound mission principle of respect for indigenous cultures, unique African and Asian Christian styles have developed which should affect cathedral architecture.

Current Developments

Contemporary cathedral construction is excellent in the lightly lined and winged concrete forms of Oscar Niemeyer at Brazilia, in which the airy arches standing tip-toe on the plain, far from concealing structural devices exploit them. The cathedral at Brazilia, crowned with points on straddling supports, is an impressive design. Gaudi's cathedral of the Holy Family in Barcelona is the expression of an exuberant, even overwrought aesthetic.

Important trends are manifested in the cathedrals of Tokyo and of New Norcia, Australia, in postwar Germany's new dialectic in the restoration of churches, by the new architects in Mexico as in Candela's open church at Cuernavaca with its nave of trees, and in Le Corbusier's urban renewal at *La Ville radieuse*—the "garden city" into which the new cathedrals must fit. BIBLIOGRAPHY: *Gothic Europe* (ed. H. Busch and B. Lohse, 1958); E. Mâle, *Religious Art from the Twelfth to the Eighteenth Century* (1949); *idem, La Fin de paganisme en Gaule, et les plus anciennes basiliques chrétiennes* (1950); C. R. Morey, *Medieval Art* (1942); D. Robb and J. J. Garrison, *Art in the Western World* (1942); J. I. Sewall, *History of Western Art* (1961); A. Temko, *Notre Dame of Paris* (1955). (For other notable cathedrals, see listing under individual names.)

[M. J. DALY]

CATHEDRAL CHAPTER, see CHAPTER, CATHEDRAL.

CATHEDRAL SCHOOLS, medieval Christian diocesan educational institutions attached to the cathedral and under the control of the bishop. Established in the 4th cent. for the education of the clergy, they gradually developed into centers of learning for both clergy and laymen, and in some instances, became the nucleus of great universities, such as the cathedral school of Notre Dame in Paris, famous as a theological center. The course of studies, ranging from elementary to higher education, included the seven liberal arts—the trivium and quadrivium—Scripture, theology, computus (the science of reckoning time), and later, philosophy and mathematics. In the first 3 cent., the bp. was immediately responsible for the education of the clerics in episcopal schools. From the 4th cent. onward, this task was often entrusted to a cleric called a *scholasticus*. By the 8th cent., canons, so called because they were attached to the cathedral and lived in community under a rule or canon, replaced the bp. in the work of the school, although it remained under his jurisdiction. Important cathedral schools developed in the 6th cent. onward at Paris, Tours, Orléans, Chartres, Reims, Canterbury, York, Le Mans, Poitier, Clermont, and Toledo. Some early episcopal schools were those of Rome, Carthage, and Arles. BIBLIOGRAPHY: W. K. Medlin, *History of Educational Ideas in the West* (1964).

[M. B. MURPHY]

CATHEDRATICUM, a tax paid annually to the bp. of a diocese by churches, benefices, and lay confraternities subject to his jurisdiction in token of their subjection to him. In the U.S. the term is extended to include the tax paid by parishes for the support of the bp. and the maintenance of diocesan activities. The amount paid is proportionate to the income of the parish.

CATHER, WILLA (1873–1947), novelist. A native of Virginia, C. was brought up in Nebraska, whose pioneer immigrants she later celebrated in novels. She developed an interest in ritual and tradition and the efforts of pioneering people to carry these into new surroundings. In *Death Comes for the Archbishop* (1927) and *Shadows on the Rock* (1931) C. dealt with Catholic characters and themes with understanding and sympathy. BIBLIOGRAPHY: J. H. Randall, *Landscape and the Looking Glass: Willa Cather's Search for Value* (1960, repr. 1973); *Five Essays on Willa Cather: The Merrimack Symposium* (ed. J. J. Murphy, 1974); for critical material published in the past 50 years see B. Slote, ''Willa Cather,'' *Fifteen Modern American Authors* (ed. J. R. Bryer, 1969).

CATHERINE II (THE GREAT) (1729–96), **EMPRESS OF RUSSIA** from 1762, German princess of Anhalt-Zerbst. The wife of Peter III, she seized power shortly before her husband's mysterious death. Although she lacked experience in affairs of state, she had been educated in the ideas of the French Enlightenment. Inspired by the philosophes, she undertook the codification of the confused mass of Russian law. The project was never completed, but she is noted for her *Nakaz* (Instruction) regarding the principles of law. She wished to free the serfs, but political reasons prevented her. She did however revise local government, improve education, and foster building and the arts. Her foreign politics included war against Turkey and participation in the partitions of Poland. Later she protected the Jesuits and admitted them into Russia after their suppression in 1773. Her tolerance, however, did not extend to Uniates or Jews. Although she greatly advanced Russian culture and politics, she reigned as absolute monarch and ruthlessly crushed opposition. BIBLIOGRAPHY: J. Clarkson, *History of Russia* (1962); O. Hötzsch, CModH 6:657–701.

[I. M. KASHUBA]

CATHERINE OF ALEXANDRIA, ST., legendary virgin and martyr, one of the most popular saints of the Middle Ages, patroness of young girls and philosophers. Her life and martyrdom are recounted in two late accounts, her *Conversio* and *Passio,* neither of which is supported by any early historical evidence. Devotion to her appears to have begun in the East in the 10th cent. and to have spread to the West with the Crusades. According to the legend, C. was of noble birth, was mystically espoused to Christ after her baptism, converted pagan philosophers at her trial before the Emperor Maxentius in Alexandria, was flogged, imprisoned, tortured on a wheel, and finally beheaded. Her body was later translated by angels to Mt. Sinai. In art C. is protrayed with a book, a crown, and a wheel. BIBLIOGRAPHY: D. Balboni et al. BiblSanct 3:954–978; Butler 4:420–421; A. P. Frutaz, EncCatt 3:1137–39.

[M. J. COSTELLOE]

CATHERINE OF ARAGON (1485–1536), Queen of England. Daughter of Ferdinand of Aragon and Isabella of Castile, C. married Arthur, eldest son of Henry VII in 1501, but Arthur died the following year. The King then betrothed her to his next son, Henry, still a boy, obtaining in 1504 a dispensation from Pope Julius II from the impediment of affinity that stood in the way of the proposed union, but the marriage did not take place till after her betrothed had succeeded to the throne as *Henry VIII. When Henry began to wish to be rid of C. is not known. He wanted a son, and C. had borne him only one daughter, Mary. He claimed to have scruples at having married his brother's widow, and he also wished to marry Anne Boleyn. In 1527 he applied to Clement VII for a declaration of nullity on the ground that the dispensation had been invalid. This appeal failed. For 6 years, advised by T. Wolsey, then by T. *Cromwell, Henry tried to force wife and Pope to yield, only to be frustrated by C.'s stubbornness and Clement's vacillation. By 1533 Anne was pregnant and Henry hurriedly married her, repudiating papal supremacy and creating T. *Cranmer, abp. of Canterbury. Cranmer immediately granted the divorce and pronounced the King's marriage to Anne valid; the ties uniting England with Rome were severed; Parliament pronounced Henry supreme head of the Church of England. Clement responded by excommunicating Henry and declaring C.'s marriage valid. After 3 years, during which she was harassed about her title, fearful for her daughter's safety, and in danger from Henry's spite, C. died in 1536. BIBLIOGRAPHY: G. Mattingly, *Catherine of Aragon* (1941, pa. 1960); M. M. Luke, *Catherine the Queen* (1967, pa. 1971); A. DuBoys, *Catherine of Aragon and the Sources of the English Reformation* (ed. C. M. Yonge, 1881, repr. 1969).

[J. OGDEN]

CATHERINE OF BOLOGNA, ST. (1413–63), native of Bologna, Poor Clare mystic, and influential spiritual writer. At the age of 11 she entered the court of Princess Margaret d'Este of Ferrara where she received an excellent education. In 1427 or 1428 she put herself under the guidance of Lucia Mascaroni, the devout directress of a community of young women. In company with some other members of this community she received the Poor Clare habit in 1432 and became novice mistress in her convent. Seeking a fuller observance of the Poor Clare rule she founded a new monastery in Bologna over which she presided as abbess until her death. Some of her works were written in Latin, e.g., a metrical rosary of the Passion and the life of the Blessed Virgin. Others were written in Italian, in prose and in verse, on a variety of pious topics. Her principal work was *Le armi necessarie alla battaglia spirituale* (The Arms Necessary for the Spiritual Battle) in which she singled out the attitudes and virtues and the practices of prayer and devotion that lead to spiritual perfection. This was composed in 1438 and was republished many times and translated into other tongues. Her body, still incorrupt, is venerated in the chapel of the Poor Clares in Bologna. BIBLIOGRAPHY: J. Heerinckx, DSAM 2.1:288–290; Butler 1:536–539; G. D. Gordini, BiblSanct 3:980–982.

[J. C. WILLKE]

CATHERINE OF CARDONA, VEN. (1519–77). Born of a noble Spanish family, C. was a member of the court of Philip II. She left the court to become a recluse for 20 years, after which she entered a Carmelite convent but still lived as an anchoress. BIBLIOGRAPHY: V. a S. Maria, LTK 6:61–62; J.-M. de L'Enfant-Jésus, DSAM 2.1:135–136.

[J. R. AHERNE]

CATHERINE OF GENOA, ST. (Caterina Fieschi Adorno; 1447–1510), mystic who spent much of her life in the service of the poor and the sick as well as in contemplation, and whose writings, *Dialogues of the Soul and the Body* and *Treatise on Purgatory* have had a great influence on mystical and ascetical literature. At the urging of her father, who was interested in recouping the fortunes of his family, she entered an unhappy marriage at the age of 16. For 10 years she lived in misery but was led out of the lukewarmness induced by her pursuit of pleasure, when in answer to her prayer God gave her a revelation in which she saw her own sinfulness and the greatness of God's love. With this she became a new woman. She never thereafter faltered in the works of penance and of mercy she undertook, nor in her prayer. She had many disciples and spiritual children during her life, and many admirers in the centuries that followed. Card. Newman was much interested in her *Treatise on Purgatory* as appears in his celebrated *Dream of Gerontius*. Baron F. von Hügel became an ardent disciple. Satisfactory evidence that she herself composed these works is lacking; they appear rather to have been gleaned by others from her conversations, and to have gone through some change at the hands of editors. But there is little question that the doctrine was hers. BIBLIOGRAPHY: Butler 3:557–560; F. von Hügel, *Mystical Element in Religion* (2 v., 2d ed., 1923); M. Villier and U. da Genoa, DSAM 2:290–325; *Life and Sayings of St. Catherine of Genoa* (ed. and tr. P. Garvin, 1964); G. D. Gordini, BiblSanct 3:984–989.

[J. C. WILLKE]

CATHERINE OF JESUS (CARMELITE; 1589–1623), French mystic. While quite young, C. was attracted to a life of penance in imitation of St. Catherine of Siena. She entered the Carmel de l'Incarnation at Paris at the age of 19. The prioress, Madeleine of St. Joseph, aware of her virtue, directed her carefully and allowed her to make her final profession at the age of 20. She soon arrived at the mystical stage, dwelling esp. on the Holy Childhood, the humiliation and suffering of Christ's Passion, and eventually on the Blessed Trinity. These special graces were a source of great suffering to her, rather than a holy joy. She was even tormented by the devil. During all her trials, she never succumbed to melancholy but bargained for souls in France and in foreign missions. In 1617 she accompanied Madeleine to the Carmel at Rue Chapon where she died an edifying death. BIBLIOGRAPHY: C. de l'Incarnation, *Catholicisme* 2:693–694; J.-M de L'Enfant-Jésus, DSAM 2.1:351–352.

[M. HIGGINS]

CATHERINE OF JESUS (URSULINE; 1602–51), French mystic. Born Catherine Ranquet, she was educated at an Ursuline boarding school that had been established by Frances Bermond, the first Ursuline, in 1610. Guided by Abp. Marquemont of Lyons, this convent had embraced enclosure in 1619. There Catherine received the religious habit in 1620 and made her profession in 1622, taking the name of Catherine of Jesus. She was entrusted with the mission of establishing Ursuline convents at Grenoble, Chambéry, and Gap. In 1630 she returned to Grenoble and remained there until her death. Her interior life is revealed in her correspondence between 1629 and 1651. Having experienced the dark night of the soul and other trials, C. arrived at the heights of the simple presence of God. Her correspondence relates her previous suffering and the peace she enjoyed by abandoning herself to the love of God. BIBLIOGRAPHY: P. Pourrat, *Catholicisme* 2:694.

[M. HIGGINS]

CATHERINE DE MÉDICIS (1519–89), French regent and queen-mother. An Italian noblewoman of the powerful family of the Medici, niece of Pope Clement VII and wife of King Henry II of France, C. reached the summit of her power during the reign of her sons, Francis II (1559–60) and Charles IX (1560–74). Although still influential under her third son, Henry III (1574–89), her power began to decline. She worked above all to achieve political and religious unity, ignoring the doctrinal disputes of Protestants and Catholics. Her methods, though aimed at tolerance, were frequently unscrupulous, utilitarian, and inconsistent. She ruthlessly suppressed every threat to the monarchy, most notably the Huguenot leader Gaspard de Coligny. Fearing revenge after his assassination, she persuaded the king to eliminate numerous other Huguenots in the famous St. Bartholomew's Night Massacre, August 24, 1572. C. was highly intelligent, endowed with political talent, and a generous promoter of the arts. However, her duplicity and spirit of intrigue prevented her attaining true greatness. BIBLIOGRAPHY: J. Héritier, *Catherine de Médicis* (tr. C. Haldane, 1963).

[I. M. KASHUBA]

CATHERINE OF RACCONIGI, BL. (1486–1547), Dominican mystic. She was born in humble circumstances, took a vow of virginity in her youth, and devoted her life to penance and contemplation. At the age of 28 C. became a Dominican tertiary, continuing to live with her family and work for the poor. Her mystical favors included visions, spiritual espousals, stigmata, prophecies, and bilocation. These special graces brought her both recognition and persecution. She died, abandoned by her friends, in exile at Caramagna. Her cultus is observed principally in parts of Italy and in the Dominican Order. BIBLIOGRAPHY: A. Guarienti, *La Beata Caterina da Racconigi* (1964); idem, BiblSanct 3:992–993 with bibliog.; Butler 3:488–489.

[J. C. WILLKE]

CATHERINE OF RICCI, ST. (1522–90), a contemplative nun whose life was marked by extraordinary mystical phenomena. At the age of 14 she made her profession as a Dominican at the convent at Prato. For 2 years she suffered greatly from a succession of physical disorders, during which trial she learned patient endurance through her contemplation of the Passion of Christ. She was made novice mistress, then subprioress, and finally, at the age of 30 prioress of her community, an office in which she remained for the rest of her life, a fact that suggests she was level-headed and an able administrator. From the time she was 20 for at least 12 years she was favored with weekly experiences of ecstasy lasting from noon on Thursday till midafternoon on Friday. She was a stigmatic and an outstanding example of the phenomenon of mystical espousal, having received from Christ, who appeared to her on Easter of 1542, a ring taken from his own hand and placed on the forefinger of her left hand. A red circle about her finger was generally apparent to all, and some testified that they had seen the ring itself; her stigmata were not always visible to others, and their appearance was diversely described by those who testified they had seen them. She corresponded with St. Philip Neri, who, though something of a skeptic in matters concerning mystical phenomena, gave witness that during her lifetime she had appeared to and conversed with him in Rome. When her cause was introduced in 1614, the office of defender of the faith (the devil's advocate) was exercised by no less an authority on canonization procedure and the type of evidence it requires than Prospero Lambertini (*BENEDICT XIV, POPE). BIBLIOGRAPHY: Butler 1:328–331; A. Walz, EncCatt 3:1157–60; G. Di Agresti, BiblSanct 3:1044–45.

[J. C. WILLKE]

CATHERINE OF SIENA, ST. (Catherine Benincasa; 1347–80), Dominican mystic. After a childhood marked by unusual spiritual gifts, C. became a Dominican tertiary, probably in 1365. The following 3 years were spent in prayer and solitude, a mode of life that provided her with the spiritual strength and conviction to succumb to the guiding Spirit which ultimately brought her into a life of dedicated service to others. Initially, this dedication took form in spiritual direction of her adopted "family," a coterie of like-minded persons deeply interested in spiritual growth who lived with her. Later, her attention was given to such public issues as the Crusade against the Turks. Her concern for such things led to her summons to the Dominican General Chapter held in Florence in June 1374. She properly defended herself against a number of untoward accusations, and for that and other reasons her work was approved by the Chapter and *Raymond of Capua was assigned as her director. This and another event, the war waged by Florence and its Italian allies against the Church, in which C. became involved through her letters, is said to have impressed several popes, notably, Gregory XI and his successor, Urban VI. She is in fact credited with convincing Gregory XI to return the Curia to Rome. From 1378, when the Great Schism

began, and during the remainder of her life she prayed and worked for unity in the Church. She died in 1380 and was canonized in 1461 by Pius II. Along with St. Francis of Assisi she is by Pius XII's proclamation, patron of Italy. C. was declared Doctor of the Church in 1970. BIBLIOGRAPHY: Butler 2:192–198; A. Curtayne, *Saint Catherine of Siena* (1935); M. Gorce, DSAM 2.1:327–348; BiblSanct 3:996–1028.

[J. R. RIVELLO]

CATHERINE OF SWEDEN, ST. (c. 1331–1381), Bridgettine. Fourth child of St. Bridget, C. married Eggard von Kurnen, a lifelong invalid with whom she lived in continence. In 1350 C. joined her mother in Rome in a life of prayer, pilgrimage, and charitable works. After her husband's death in 1351, she continued for 25 years in her mother's work. She accompanied the return of her mother's body to Sweden c. 1373 and supported the growth of the convent founded by Bridget at Vadstena; C. became its first superior. From 1375 to 1380 she promoted the papal approbation of the Brigettine Rule and the canonization of her own mother. C. was never formally canonized though she is listed in the Roman Martyrology.

[M. H. BEIRNE]

CATHERINE THOMAS, ST. (Catherine of Palma; 1533–74) virgin. Born on the Island of Majorca, C. was orphaned at the age of 7 and reared by her maternal uncle. She expressed early a desire for the religious life and after overcoming obstacles imposed by her guardian, she entered the convent of St. Mary Magdalen in Palma as a Canoness Regular of St. Augustine. Her great sanctity and the extraordinary spiritual gifts with which she was endowed were known, even during her lifetime, not only throughout the Balearic Islands but on the Spanish mainland as well. Beatified in 1792, she was canonized by Pope Pius XI in 1930. BIBLIOGRAPHY: Butler 2:6–7; *Book of Saints* (comp. by the Benedictine Monks of Ramsgate, 5th ed., 1966) 154.

[P. HIGGINS]

CATHOLIC, a word derived from the Gr. *catholicos* meaning "general" or "universal." It does not occur in the Scriptures in reference to the mission of the Church, its membership, or its descriptive title. It first occurs in Christian use in the letter of St. Ignatius of Antioch to the Smyrnaens (*Apostolic Fathers* ed. and tr. K. E. Lake, Loeb ed. repr. 1919, v. 1:261), and in the somewhat later document, *Martyrdom of Polycarp* (*op. cit.*, v. 2:321). In Christian terminology the word has been used in different senses: (1) as descriptive of the Church as a whole as distinguished from local Christian churches or communities; (2) in application to the doctrine of the Church as a whole as distinguished from unorthodox dissidents (heretics or schismatics); (3) of the Church before the split between Eastern and Western Christianity in 1045; (4) after the schism, by Latin Christians to distinguish themselves from the Orthodox Church of the

East; (5) by the Anglican Church, Old Catholics, and others who claim to possess a historical and continuous tradition of faith and doctrine; (6) in apologetics to identify a special note or mark by which the true Church of Christ can be recognized. Since Vatican Council II there has been a renewal of dogmatic interest in the concept of catholicity, and this is currently being explored in the bilateral conversations between RCs and Orthodox, Anglicans, and Protestant religious communities.

[T. LIDDY]

CATHOLIC ACTION, a term long-existing in Italy and other parts of the world, commonly used in reference to Catholics who under organized activities bear witness to Christ in their everyday living, and likewise apply the principles of faith and morals in whatever phase of society they become involved. Specifically, the term took universal significance when in 1922, Pope Pius XI, in his first encyclical, *Ubi arcano,* defined Catholic Action as "the participation of the laymen in the hierarchical apostolate." In organization, Catholic Action is as varied as its work. It must be motivated throughout by Christian principles, always under the jurisdiction of the bp. and his clergy, and it ought to avoid involvement in political activities. In Italy Catholic Action was highly organized and became very important at the time of the Fascist regime. BIBLIOGRAPHY: J. Newman, *What is Catholic Action?* (1958); L. Mathias, *Catholic Action, Theory and Practice* (1952); D. J. Geaney, NCE 3:262–263.

[R. A. TODD]

CATHOLIC-ANGLICAN DIALOGUE, see ANGLICAN-ROMAN CATHOLIC INTERNATIONAL COMMISSION.

CATHOLIC APOSTOLIC CHURCH, a body established in England as a mission to announce to all the Churches Christ's second coming and the restoration of the primitive Church. The early members came from a prayer circle at the home of Henry Drummond (1786–1860), banker and member of Parliament. E. *Irving, by his preaching of *premillenarianism and of the renewal of the charismatic gifts of the early Church, exercised great influence, and the members of the Church, against their preference, are often designated Irvingites. The Church acknowledged the rule of the twelve Apostles as the sole authority in the true Church; accordingly, by the "outpouring of the Holy Spirit" twelve apostles (Irving not among them) were chosen by 1835, and the first community was established. Other offices were angel (bishop), prophet, evangelist, pastor, and teacher (see Eph 4.11). Besides premillenarianism and features similar to those of modern *Pentecostalism, the doctrines of the Church included the Apostles', Athanasian, and Nicene Creeds. The Church recognized seven sacraments as signs of interior grace; the Eucharist was celebrated as a sacrifice; and auricular confession was required for mortal sins. Confirmation was known as sealing, the reception of the

fullness of the Holy Spirit by those of mature age. Roman Catholic devotions, esp. to the Blessed Virgin Mary, vestments, and ceremonials were adopted.

The spread of the new Church began with a missionary tour, lasting 1,260 days, by the original twelve apostles to many countries; only in Germany, where some RC priests joined them, did they win many converts. A congregation was formed in the U.S. in 1848. It was the belief of the Church that the apostles would live until the second coming of Christ, and when they began to die, a schism in Germany about appointing successors led in 1863 to the formation of the New Apostolic Church. By 1901 the last apostle had died; there have consequently been no new ordinations or administration of confirmation. Only a few priests survive, the liturgy is much curtailed, and the Church has dwindled in membership. BIBLIOGRAPHY: P. E. Shaw, *Catholic Apostolic Church, Sometimes Called Irvingites* (1946). *PENTECOSTALISM.

[W. J. WHALEN]

CATHOLIC ASSOCIATION FOR INTERNATIONAL PEACE (CAIP), an organization established in 1927 among U.S. Catholics devoted to the promotion of world peace through justice and charity; to further the spread of peace by educating all men of good will on their obligations under Christian peace principles. Membership is open to all interested Catholics. In its first decade it held close contact with international relations clubs at Catholic colleges and universities. An annual awards program in recognition of noteworthy contributions to world peace has been established; the organization has also pioneered in proposing many programs later adopted by government and private agencies.

[N. M. ABBOTT]

CATHOLIC AUDIO-VISUAL EDUCATORS ASSOCIATION (CAVE), a society of educators that has been an active organization since 1953. Its membership is open to administrators and teachers of all levels. It has the broad purpose of promoting improved teaching techniques; of great concern is the evaluation of teaching aids. In addition, the association publishes a directory of audio-visual aids. Its official publication is the *Catholic Educator,* issued monthly.

[N. M. ABBOTT]

CATHOLIC-BAPTIST DIALOGUE, see INTERFAITH DIALOGUE.

CATHOLIC BUSINESS EDUCATION ASSOCIATION (CBEA), an organization founded in 1945 to promote a more effective fusion of business theory and practice with Catholic principles. Membership is open to teachers and administrators of the secondary schools and colleges who have a major interest in economics and other business subjects. Regional meetings are held throughout the year. The *Catholic Business Education Review* is a quarterly publication of the association.

[N. M. ABBOTT]

CATHOLIC CAMPUS MINISTRY ASSOCIATION, see NEWMAN APOSTOLATE.

CATHOLIC CENTRAL UNION, a benevolent organization established (1855) in Baltimore, Md., by Catholics from German parishes throughout the U.S. Modeled after the Piusvereine of Germany, it shared the objective of bringing Catholic principles into personal, social, and civic life. Made up of a variety of societies and called originally the Central Verein, the American organization supported charitable work, cared for immigrants, and took an early interest in social problems. It was the first society ever given (1936) official mandate for Catholic Action by the American bishops. A feature of the state units was consistent lobbying at state legislatures. The union publishes an influential magazine, originally in German and called *Central-Blatt,* later called *Central Blatt and Social Justice.* Since 1946 entirely in English, it is known as *Social Justice Review* and is written for the general Catholic public. The union operates St. Elizabeth Settlement House in St. Louis (location of its headquarters) and for many years supported the Pontifical College Josephinum, Worthington, Ohio, and Holy Family Teachers College near Milwaukee. BIBLIOGRAPHY: C. Barry, *Catholic Church and German America* (1953); M. L. Brophy, NCE 3:264–266.

[J. M. BRADY]

CATHOLIC CHARITIES, an official organization of most Catholic dioceses in the U.S. for the overall planning and financing of social work under Catholic auspices. The first central all-diocesan agency in the U.S. was established in 1903. Coordination by Catholic Charities ensures a balanced program that will meet the needs of the community, including both Catholics and non-Catholics. In turn Catholic Charities are coordinated on a national level by the National Conference of Catholic Charities. The national coordinating body promotes research and provides basic social services. A magazine is published monthly.

[N. M. ABBOTT]

CATHOLIC CHURCH. The Catholic Church in principle extends to all nations, all races, and all ages; it contains all truths necessary to be known, and furnishes humanity with all graces necessary for salvation. The term was first used to distinguish the entire body of believers from local churches. It was later applied to the RC Church at the separation of the Latin and Greek Churches, the latter assuming the name "orthodox". In England the term Anglo-Catholic was adopted by those wishing to emphasize Anglican agreement with the early councils and Fathers.

[T. LIDDY]

CATHOLIC COMMISSION ON INTELLECTUAL AND CULTURAL AFFAIRS, association founded in 1946 to promote intellectual exchange and a sense of solidarity among Catholic scholars. It also seeks to explore contemporary intellectual and cultural problems with particular reference to Catholic involvement and to encourage Catholic international intellectual and cultural co-operation. Members are admitted on the basis of scholarly, creative, or leadership achievements. It sponsors national and regional meetings, conducts seminars for younger scholars, and maintains a professional register of American Catholic scholars.

[J. C. WILLKE]

CATHOLIC COMMITTEE OF THE SOUTH, an organization established at a 2-day regional meeting of bishops, clergy and laity at Atlanta, Ga. in 1940. To implement its objectives, a department of the lay apostolate stressed the apostolic character of the other five departments: education, race, labor relations, rural life, and youth. National publicity was given to the committee for its advocacy of racial integration of the schools. However, the committee held its last convention at Columbia, S. C. in 1951. It has been dormant for some years.

[N. M. ABBOTT]

CATHOLIC CONFERENCE ON INDUSTRIAL PROBLEMS, an association founded upon the initiative of the Department of Social Action of the National Catholic Welfare Conference. Its purpose is to discuss and promote the study and understanding of industrial problems. However, in time its interests were too restricted and it gave way to a successor organization of broader scope, the National Catholic Social Action Conference.

[N. M. ABBOTT]

CATHOLIC COUNCIL ON WORKING LIFE, formerly known as the Catholic Labor Alliance, an organization formed in Chicago for the purpose of establishing labor schools and training Catholic workers to teach the encyclicals on labor, parliamentary law, public speaking, and communistic tactics. These schools contributed significantly to combating communism in the labor movement, esp. in the CIO. With this example Catholic social action has had a notable part in assisting the development of the labor movement in the U.S.

[N. M. ABBOTT]

CATHOLIC DAUGHTERS OF AMERICA, a charitable organization of women founded by the Knights of Columbus in 1903, with membership in the mid-1970s of nearly 200,000. The purpose of this organization is the preservation and propagation of the faith, the spiritual and intellectual development of Catholic womanhood, and the promotion of charitable projects. Of significance is their work with mentally retarded and physically handicapped children, their service in homes for the aged and for orphans, their help with migrants and immigrants, and their participation in overseas programs. In 1974 they pledged the endowment of a chair in American Catholic church history at The Catholic Univ. of America.

[N. M. ABBOTT]

CATHOLIC DOCTRINE, a term commonly understood to include whatever the Catholic Church proposes for acceptance by all the faithful as infallible truth somehow pertaining to revelation. It embraces both teaching that was formally revealed, like Christ's bodily presence in the Eucharist, and teaching only connected with revelation, like the canonization of saints. When the doctrine has been directly—even though implicitly—revealed by God, the Church presents it for belief as an object of both Catholic and divine faith: Catholic because emanating from the Church and universally binding in conscience on all Christians, and divine because revealed by God. On the other hand, a doctrine comes under the scope of Catholic and ecclesiastical faith when the Church presents it for universal acceptance but not as something that was formally (i.e., as such) contained in the revelation to be found in Scripture or sacred tradition. Catholic theology recognizes three forms of Catholic (but not divine) truths, the qualification indicating that their immediate content by which they are believed is Catholic and ecclesiastical. First are rational principles that underlie the truths of revelation, e.g., freedom of the human will. Second are theological conclusions derived from one premise that was revealed and another known only by natural reason. Most theologians dispute this terminology, preferring to call such conclusions implicitly (and formally) revealed. Third are contingent facts pertaining to history and intimately related to revealed truth, e.g., the Roman episcopate of St. Peter. There are several other, less common, uses of the term Catholic doctrine. It sometimes means whatever theologians generally agree is revealed and certainly true, but which the Church has not yet officially proclaimed to be a dogma of faith. It may also mean any doctrine that the Church teaches authoritatively in such writings as papal encyclicals but without expressly saying it is dogma or the revealed word of God. BIBLIOGRAPHY: E. J. Fortman, NCE 10:523–525; I. Salaverri, STS BAC 1.3:884–913; *Teaching of the Catholic Church* (ed. K. Rahner, 1967 pa.).

[J. A. HARDON]

CATHOLIC EDUCATION, CONGREGATION FOR, in the reorganized Roman *Curia the congregation established to replace the older Congregation for Seminaries and Universities. The concern of the new congregation has been expanded; distinct subsections deal with seminaries, universities, and with education at lower levels.

CATHOLIC EMANCIPATION, in 19th-cent. England, the movement, in the words of the culminating Roman Catholic Relief Act of 1829, "for the relief of his majesty's roman catholic subjects" (10 George IV, *c*.7). Catholics looked for support less to the Tories than to the Whigs, who by their history and *hauteur* were more tolerant of nonconformity to the Establishment, as long as it did not menace the security of property or evoke vulgar enthusiasm. The way for emancipation was opened by the Quebec Act, 1774, which, to the anger of Protestants both at home and in the American colonies, accorded the French Canadians nearly all the privileges they had enjoyed under the Bourbons. The clergy and people of French Canada showed their gratitude by the stand they took in the American War of Independence. The lesson did not pass unnoticed. Roman Catholics in Great Britain and Ireland existed under civil disabilities and penalties of the penal laws dating back to the 16th cent., many of them draconian, and indeed savage measures, which, though no longer enforced, still hung over them like a threat. The first concession was the abolition of penalties for religious observance (1778); it was greeted by outbreaks of mob fury in Edinburgh and Glasgow, and by the Gordon Riots in London, the worst disturbance the capital had known for 4 centuries. Further steps followed in Ireland, which then had its own parliament; Catholic ecclesiastics were granted legal protection and security of property rights (1783); successive acts admitted Catholics to the professions (1791) and to the franchise (1793) and established the Royal College of Maynooth (1795). Moves to extend these benefits to England and Scotland were actively promoted, leading to something of a rift between clergy and laity, or at least between those ecclesiastical leaders who were suspicious of state nomination and veto and those of the gentry who were prepared to be statutorily designated as "protesting catholic dissenters."

The atmosphere was eased by the influx of thousands of French priests, *emigrés* from the French Revolution, who received much sympathy and support and who gave much edification (as, later, Pius VII was warmly regarded for his sufferings under Napoleon); the cause was espoused by the eloquence of Edmund Burke and Henry Grattan; and some hopes were cherished because of the Prince of Wales's morganatic marriage to a devout Catholic, Maria Fitzherbert. Further relief, however, was postponed by George III's scruples about his coronation oath to maintain the Anglican Establishment unimpaired. Yet support was growing, even from such Tories as George Canning. Also Jacobitism had been dead for 50 years as a political cause, and the House of Stuart had become extinct with the Cardinal of York early in the 19th century. Thus no difficulty remained about swearing allegiance to the Hanoverian succession. Liberalism was in the air that was breathed on both sides of the House.

But it was because of one man that the windows were flung open. Daniel O'Connell, the newly elected member for Clare (1828), one of the most powerful political influences of the time, and a foremost figure in the Catholic Association, organized to gain civil liberties for Catholics; he faced the Tory government of the Duke of Wellington and Sir Robert Peel with the imminent prospect of a solid bloc of Irish Catholic members of Parliament prepared to disrupt the

Union if necessary. Both men made a clean break with their past commitments—Wellington with characteristic common sense and pragmatism; Peel with a more tortured conscience, the first of the two great switches for which that honorable man was charged with apostasy by supporters; he resigned his seat for Oxford Univ. and was not reelected. In 1829 the bill was passed; oaths to which no Catholic could subscribe were abolished for membership in the legislature and for public offices, though denial of the temporal power of the papacy within the United Kingdom was still required, and some petty restrictions were inserted as a sop to bigotry.

When the shouting was over, men might well wonder what all the fuss had been about. Grievances still remained in Ireland, but they arose chiefly from injustices inevitable when an ascendancy class is largely alien in religion and culture; they were not to be settled until the next century, and then on purely political grounds. For the rest, obsolescent discrimination against Catholics on points of detail was removed by later acts (1844, 1871, and finally in 1926). Now Catholics are restrained only from the Crown, the offices of Lord Chancellor and Keeper of the Seal, and a few university posts. BIBLIOGRAPHY: D. Gwynn, *Struggle for Catholic Emancipation, 1750–1829* (1928); *idem, Hundred Years of Catholic Emancipation* (1929).

[T. GILBY]

CATHOLIC EPISTLES, description traditionally attached to the Epistles of Jas, 1–2 Pet, 1–3 Jn and Jude because they are addressed to the Church in general and not to particular, local Churches. Strictly speaking, however, this does not apply to 1 Pet or 2 and 3 Jn, which, though normally included among the Catholic Epistles, are in fact addressed to individuals. In the West the same Epistles have also been called "canonical Epistles," i.e., accepted by all the Churches. BIBLIOGRAPHY: R. Leconte, *Les Épîtres catholiques,* Bible de Jérusalem (2d ed., 1961); J. Moffatt, *General Epistles* (1945); B. Reike, *Epistles of James, Peter and Jude,* Anchor Bible 37 (1964).

[D. J. BOURKE]

CATHOLIC EVIDENCE GUILD, an organization of apologists for the spread of RC teaching at street corners, in outdoor assemblies as in Hyde Park, London, and Times Square, New York City, chief laboratories of the speakers. Initiated in England (1918), the movement spread to the U.S. (1931), and then to Australia. Heckling is encouraged not only as exercise of fortitude, but that by presenting facts the force of truth may prevail. Speakers must pass stiff tests; such outstanding scholars and theologians as H. Pope, J. P. Arendzen, and V. McNabb have trained members who continue serious reading on problems raised by the crowd. Maisie Ward and her husband Frank Sheed, active in the Guild from the beginning, compiled the *Catholic Evidence Training Outline* (1925, rev. 1948–). Response to the Guild speakers has declined, says Sheed, owing to the flood of unreliable theologians that followed in the wake of Vatican Council II. Present accent of the speakers on the Scriptures is a salutary sign, however, of its survival.

[M. R. BROWN]

CATHOLIC HOSPITAL ASSOCIATION (CHA), an organization founded 1915 to improve hospitals directed by the RC Church in the U.S.; it reaches more than 900 health-care service institutions by its monthly *Hospital Progress* (1920—) and its annual national meeting. Proposed by the Sisters of St. Joseph of Carondelet in cooperation with the Jesuit, C. B. Moulinier, of Marquette Univ. in 1914, and the Medical School of St. Louis Univ., CHA developed into a service organization which through research informs its members on special RC concerns (educational, professional, medical, and moral) regarding health care. Working in harmony with the American Hospital Association, it encourages and aids members to meet standards of the American College of Surgeons. Particularly in regard to federal legislation, CHA has associated itself with the Social Action Department of USCC. BIBLIOGRAPHY: D. M. Dougherty et al., *Sisters of St. Joseph of Carondelet* (1966) 200 and *passim.*

[M. R. BROWN]

CATHOLIC KNIGHTS OF AMERICA, an organization founded (1877) in Nashville, Tenn.; it was the first Catholic fraternal insurance society in the U.S., with present national headquarters in Cincinnati, Ohio. Under the patronage of St. Joseph, it sponsors, along with the insurance plan which is financially strong, monthly publication of the *Catholic Knights of America Journal;* it promotes spiritual and cultural activities, supports foreign missions, and encourages religious vocations.

[M. R. BROWN]

CATHOLIC KOLPING SOCIETY, a fraternal organization having a membership of more than 2,000 with headquarters at Mount Pleasant, Ill.; it is an offshoot of the socio-religious association projected (1849) in Cologne, Germany, by a RC priest, A. *Kolping. The prolific writer in the Catholic social movement, T. Brauer, lent his expertise in the German Federation of Catholic Trade Unionists in Cologne and in other socio-economic pursuits, to the strengthening of the society. A branch of the German Kolping Society was established in St. Louis, Mo. (1856), but the independent American group was formed only in 1923. Toward its end of fellowship among young workmen, the society publishes the monthly *Kolping Banner.* BIBLIOGRAPHY: H. Fischer, NCE 8:247–248.

[M. R. BROWN]

CATHOLIC LABOR ALLIANCE, see CATHOLIC COUNCIL ON WORKING LIFE.

CATHOLIC LAY MISSION CORPS, founded (1958) as Volunteer Teacher Service by the Holy Cross priests, J. E. Haley and F. Underwood. Centered in Austin, Texas, the corps is a missionary society of the lay apostolate in Catholic schools, in the catechetical field, working among youth, fostering vocations and community development, esp. in Texas and Latin America. A group of permanent members undertakes the formation of volunteers who assist in the apostolate; membership includes married couples and single men and women. The corps holds membership in the Committee of International Lay Associations.

[M. R. BROWN]

CATHOLIC LIBRARY ASSOCIATION (CLA), an organization (headquarters, Haverford, Pa.) founded to promote and help in bettering Catholic libraries. Originally it was a section of the National Catholic Education Association, but it became independent in 1931 through the initiative of W. Stinson, SJ. CLA's purpose is to encourage good reading, which it does through the promotion of Catholic Book Week and the distribution of reading lists; to stimulate good writing (it has granted the annual Regina Medal award since 1959 for children's literature); and to strengthen library personnel by an annual scholarship (since 1960) for graduate study in library work; to cooperate on the professional level with standardizing agencies, e.g., the American Library Association; to represent the Catholic library before government agencies; and to assist in perpetuating or developing libraries and library schools in the U.S. and elsewhere. It publishes the monthly *Catholic Library World* and the *Catholic Periodical and Literature Index.* The CLA has a membership of more than 4,000 in 41 local units.

[M. R. BROWN]

CATHOLIC-LUTHERAN DIALOGUE, see INTERFAITH DIALOGUE.

CATHOLIC MAJESTY, a title of the kings of Spain. Usually rendered as "the Catholic Kings" *(los Reyes Catholicos),* it was formally conferred on Ferdinand of Aragon and his wife, Isabella of Castille, by Pope Alexander VI in 1494. The ostensible reason for the grant was their services to Catholicism, particularly the conquest of Granada from the Moors (1492), which represented the climax of the Reconquista. A more likely reason was the need of Alexander for the services of the Spanish monarchs in the expulsion from Italy of Charles VIII of France. The title actually has roots deep in the Middle Ages. The first Catholic king (in contradistinction to Arian) goes back to Visigothic Spain: Recared, who died in 601. The title was assumed from time to time in the Middle Ages, but with Ferdinand and Isabella it became permanent and assumed Erastian connotations.

[D. G. NUGENT]

CATHOLIC MEDICAL MISSION BOARD, INC., group founded in 1928 to coordinate efforts in the promotion and support of medical missions in foreign lands. Offices are in New York City and San Francisco, and publications include the bimonthly *Medical Mission News* and the monthly *Professional Placement News Notes* for those interested in serving in mission fields.

[J. C. WILLKE]

CATHOLIC-METHODIST DIALOGUE, see INTERFAITH DIALOGUE.

CATHOLIC MIGRANT MISSION PROGRAM, an organized effort to serve the needs of farm workers of Latin origin (from the Southwest U.S., Mexico, and Puerto Rico) who follow the harvest across the land, living for the growing season in temporary shelters largely under substandard conditions. Attempts to procure humane working conditions have been constantly stifled by lack of free unions; the majority of the transient workers are RC, and the Church has made repeated efforts to improve their condition. Bishops of the U.S. Catholic Conference supported C. Chavez in his attempt to form a free union (UFW) among the farm workers. The child labor and the health aspect of the migrants is esp. alarming (see D. Janson's special report, *New York Times,* April 26, 1971). An Hispanic society of women religious, Las Hermanas, was formed in 1971 to help their people achieve justice in charity; the sisters are based for periods in different locales where they can aid directly, or by lecturing call attention to the migrants' plight; helping are sister associates and lay affiliates. BIBLIOGRAPHY: D. Day, "On Pilgrimage," *Catholic Worker* (Feb. 1974); UFW of America, AFL-CIO, *Philadelphia Newsletter* (Apr. 1975); C. G. Higgins, " 'La Causa': the Rank and File in Step," *America* 133 (1975) 11–12; R. B. Taylor, *Chavez and the Farm Workers* (1975).

[M. R. BROWN]

CATHOLIC NEAR EAST WELFARE ASSOCIATION, an organization founded (1926) as a papal mission aid in the implementation of the decree of Pope Pius XI for the consolidation of all American organizations working for the Near and the Middle East. It aids missions in 18 countries of Europe, Africa, and Asia under the jurisdiction of the Sacred Congregation of the Oriental Churches. Its aim is to inform the Western world of the needs of the Eastern; besides its weekly column, "Near East Missions," in many diocesan newspapers, with the Pontifical Mission for Palestine it publishes (since 1974) *Catholic Near East Magazine.* Headquarters are in N.Y. City.

[M. R. BROWN]

CATHOLIC PEACE FELLOWSHIP (CPF), an organization founded (1964) for peace education and action with the intent to foster a pacifist tradition in the RC Church, publishing to this end the *CPF Bulletin;* with headquarters at Upper Nyack, N.Y. it has a national secretary with a membership (1975) of 6500. Since 1971 it has held a peace conference annually. BIBLIOGRAPHY: "New England CPF

Conference," *Catholic Worker* (March-April 1975).

[M. R. BROWN]

CATHOLIC RECORD SOCIETY (CRS), an association founded in 1904 for the printing and distribution of original records, both historical and genealogical, pertaining to English RCs from the 16th cent. onward. Its motto is *Colligite fragmenta ne pereant* (Jn 6.12). A similar organization was proposed 50 years earlier by Lord Acton, who wanted it called the Lingard Club, but this came to nothing. The London CRS publishes *Recusant History* triennially. The English CRS inspired the organization of an Irish CRS, which publishes the annual *Archivum Hibernicum*.

[M. R. BROWN]

CATHOLIC RELIEF ACTS, see CATHOLIC EMANCIPATION.

CATHOLIC RELIEF SERVICES (CRS), official overseas aid and development agency of American Catholics, founded (1943) by the bps. of the U.S. to help civilians in war-torn Europe and N Africa. It collected, bought, and shipped huge quantities of food, clothing, medicine, and other relief supplies to hundreds of thousands of people whose lives had been disrupted by World War II. After the war, CRS expanded its operations to Asia, Africa, and Latin America until in 1976 it was serving in 68 countries, maintaining warehouses in strategic locations so that its services to those in need of them could be administered as soon as possible after an emergency arose. In 55 of the poorest countries CRS is also involved in installing nutrition-health programs designed to raise standards of living and to enable the people to become more self sustaining. Revenue for CRS operations is obtained: (1) to a great extent from an annual collection (during Lent) in more than 15,000 churches in the U.S.; (2) by donations from private philanthropic foundations in the U.S., Europe, and Australasia; (3) from the federal government in the forms of: (a) food available under Title II of Public Law 480; (b) defrayment of ocean freight costs; (c) grants for refugee relief and resettlement. The agency, a separately incorporated organization of the U.S. Catholic Conference, estimated (1975) the total value of its services since 1943 to be $2.8 billion. BIBLIOGRAPHY: E. E. Swanstrom, *Pilgrims of the Night: a Study of Expelled Peoples* (1960).

CATHOLIC SOCIAL GUILD, an English organization that owes its inception (1909) and early development to Charles D. Plater, SJ, whose aim was to promote the social teachings of the RC Church; it soon became an adult education movement centered at Oxford where it maintains the Catholic Workers College at Plater Hall; the guild organizes summer schools annually. With a privileged position at Oxford, members may sit for examinations for which a diploma is awarded but no degree. The guild publishes a monthly, the *Christian Democrat*.

[M. R. BROWN]

CATHOLIC STUDENTS MISSION CRUSADE (CSMC), national federation of mission societies organized (1918) at Techny, Ill., with the object of acquainting Catholic students with the needs and the problems of home and foreign missions, esp. through prayer and self-denial, through writings and lectures. From its beginnings the crusade has shown strong interest in black people, awareness of whom was aroused by the writer and missionary priest, J. T. Gillard, SSJ. Now centered in Cincinnati, Ohio, the federation has more than 1 million members. Besides the *Yearbook,* it publishes the magazine *The Shield* and occasional texts and research reports.

[M. R. BROWN]

CATHOLIC THEOLOGICAL SOCIETY OF AMERICA, an organization established in 1946 for the purpose of promoting interest, scholarship, and continuing education in the field of Catholic theology. Membership is open to all who possess a doctoral degree in theology or related studies. The objectives of the society are achieved by regional meetings, an annual national convention, and the publication of its proceedings. Some non-Catholic theologians who take an interest in Catholic theology have become members in recent years. At present the society has more than 1100 members in the U.S., Canada, and in many countries abroad.

[A. R. ZINK]

CATHOLIC TOTAL ABSTINENCE UNION OF AMERICA, an organization founded in Baltimore (1872) by convention delegates representing over 200 total abstinence societies. The union aimed to work by means of moral suasion, because they believed that neither prohibitory nor restrictive laws would be effective unless supported by public opinion. As substitutes for social drinking, member societies provided libraries, bands, and other recreational activities. The union was an effective force until the era of federal Prohibition. Since then several priests have tried to revitalize the organization, which has never ceased to hold conventions.

[A. R. ZINK]

CATHOLIC TRADITIONALIST MOVEMENT, educational organization founded in 1964 by Rev. Gommar A. DePauw, "to provide the Catholic laity with all information necessary for the correct understanding and implementation of the Vatican Council II's decisions in full conformity with the traditional doctrine and practices of the Roman Catholic Church." In 1968 the movement concentrated its efforts on maintaining, completely unchanged, the Latin RC Mass, and the "Tridentine" Mass as it is sometimes called was offered, on questionable authority, at the Ave Maria Chapel in Westbury, New York. Pope Paul VI discountenanced the Catholic Traditionalist Movement in affirming the obligation of RCs to accept the Vatican Council II decree on the Sacred Liturgy.

[A. R. ZINK]

CATHOLIC TRUTH SOCIETIES, organizations with the purpose of disseminating Catholic doctrine in publications of low cost to the buyer. Originating (1869) in England under Herbert Vaughan (later cardinal abp. of Westminster), the Catholic Truth Society was revised by him and James Britten, a layman, in 1884. From the beginning the goal was to spread low-cost publications on Catholic doctrine among Catholics and non-Catholics. Frequently the society had to engage in polemics to defend Catholic positions, but such was not its purpose. In 1888 the society inaugurated annual Catholic Conferences for clergy and laity. Other offshoots were The Apostleship of the Sea, The Catholic Social Guild, The Catholic Guardian's Guild. The society is active also in Scotland, Ireland, Australia, and the U.S.

In the U.S. a separate organization, the *International Catholic Truth Society, was founded (1899) in Brooklyn, N.Y. by Bp. William McGinnis.

The Catholic Truth Society of Ireland was established in 1899 for the same general purpose as the English Society. It publishes historical and biographical works as well as religious. The annual conferences draw a number of outstanding clergy and laymen and result in a publication of the proceedings. BIBLIOGRAPHY: M. McDonnell, NCE 3:331; T. Meehan, CE 15:78.

[J. R. AHERNE]

CATHOLIC TRUTH SOCIETY, INTERNATIONAL, see INTERNATIONAL CATHOLIC TRUTH SOCIETY.

CATHOLIC UNIVERSITIES, INTERNATIONAL FEDERATION OF, a Catholic organization established under canon law by the apostolic letter *Catholicas studiorum universitates,* issued by Pius XII in 1949. Its purpose is to promote union and collaboration among the many Catholic universities throughout the world; to examine and seek solutions for existing problems; to promote the diffusion of truth, and to foster research. The federation, which is administered by a board of directors whose president is elected by the general assembly of rectors, includes universities representing more than 40 nations. The general assembly meets in a different country every 3 years to discuss the most important problems concerning academic excellence, and matters of scientific, religious, social, and international import. Publications include the *Annuarium Foederationis universitatum catholicarum* (1954); *Catalogus catholicorum institutorum de studiis superioribus* (1957); and *Supplementa* (1960). Headquarters is in Vatican City. In the Americas, 14 universities in the U.S., 4 in Canada, and 14 in South America belong to the Federation.

[M. B. MURPHY]

CATHOLIC UNIVERSITY OF AMERICA, THE, a coeducational institution in Washington, D.C., the first pontifical university in the U.S., incorporated by Congress under the laws of the District of Columbia in 1887 and canonically erected by Leo XIII in 1889. Its establishment, initiated in 1884 at the Third Plenary Council of Baltimore by Bp. John L. Spalding of Peoria, Ill., was furthered by a founding endowment of $300,000 from Mary Gwendolyn Caldwell of New York. Originally established as a graduate school of theology, in 1895 the university opened the schools of philosophy and of social sciences for men. In 1905 it admitted qualified undergraduate male applicants and gradually expanded its curriculum to include the liberal arts, natural and social sciences, engineering and architecture, nursing and teacher education, civil and canon law, and speech and drama, leading to baccalaureate, masters', and doctoral degrees. Women were admitted in 1928. In 1911 the university inaugurated the Summer School with branches later established in California, Iowa, Texas, and Ohio; in 1938, the Commission on American Citizenship to further education in the social ideals recommended by Pius XI; in 1946, a child center to treat emotional problems; in 1952, the marriage counseling center, and in 1953, a speech clinic. A Joint Graduate Consortium was formed in 1964 to enable the five participating D.C. universities—American, Catholic, George Washington, Georgetown, and Howard—to coordinate their respective graduate faculties. The university is governed by the bishops of the U.S. who exercise their authority through a board of trustees composed of members of the hierarchy and laymen. The administration and professorial personnel comprise priests, religious, and laymen. The university's Mullen Library houses more than 620,000 catalogued holdings, the Clementine Library, originally part of Pope Clement XI's personal collection (1700–21); the special library of the Institute of Christian Oriental Research, and the Lima Library, with its specialized holdings for research in Brazilian, Portuguese, Spanish, and other Latin American cultures. Student enrollment averages about 7,000. BIBLIOGRAPHY: J. T. Ellis, *Formative Years of the C.U.A.* (1946); R. J. Deferrari, *Memoirs of The Catholic University of America, 1918–1960* (1962).

[M. B. MURPHY]

CATHOLIC WORKER, a monthly newspaper devoted to social justice; also the lay Catholic movement associated with it. The paper was started in N.Y. in 1933 by Dorothy *Day, a Catholic convert from Communism. Searching for a way to apply Catholic teachings to social problems, she met P. *Maurin, a French Catholic radical who inspired her to start a newspaper to bring the Church's message to the worker. The Catholic Worker program was set forth in Maurin's "Easy Essays," calling for round-table discussions, houses of hospitality, and farming communes. The round-table discussions soon grew into a workers' school. The first house of hospitality was a slum tenement flat; in a short time Catholic Worker groups were providing lodgings, distributing clothing, and serving hundreds of meals daily. The Catholic Worker established farms successively in Easton, Pa., on Staten Island, and in Newburgh and Tivoli, N.Y.; others were established by associated groups. Volunteers joined the movement, and soon there were groups throughout the U.S. and in England and Australia. There was no formal affiliation, and the groups varied considerably according to local needs. For a time many young people in the movement constituted a youth auxiliary, which became active in the liturgical movement and in ecumenical work, basing both its social and its liturgical and ecumenical approach on the Catholic Worker belief in the participation of all in the mystical body of Christ. In its early years the Catholic Worker was active in strikes, picketing, and other activities for the cause of organized labor. More recently the emphasis has shifted to campaigning for the rights of such groups as the migrant farm workers. Antiwar principles have become dominant since World War II, and the movement has given rise to groups ranging from outright pacifism to selective conscientious objection and has supported various forms of nonviolent resistance to war and to the draft. BIBLIOGRAPHY: D. Day, *Loaves and Fishes* (1963); W. D. Miller, *Harsh and Dreadful Love: Dorothy Day and the Catholic Worker Movement* (1972).

[D. CODDINGTON]

CATHOLIC YOUTH ORGANIZATION, national youth-serving agency commonly known as the CYO. The CYO traces its origin back to the early 1930s when a number of dioceses experimented with Catholic youth organization. As a national movement, it began in 1951 when the youth department of the NCWC in Washington set up a three-part organization called the National Council of Catholic Youth. One part of this council was the diocesan section which became the National CYO Federation in 1961. The goals of the Catholic Youth Organization are to promote and develop among youth a personal faith in God and to give its members opportunities to respond to that faith, to reach greater maturity in the likeness of Christ, as well as to provide processes for Christian growth. The core of the CYO, the parish unit, seeks to provide young people with active examples of how these goals can be attained. The CYO is primarily a leisure-time program aiming at the development of youth through participation in social, religious, cultural, and athletic activities. The CYO has a recommended organizational structure at the parish, deanery, diocesan, regional, and national levels. BIBLIOGRAPHY: National CYO Federation, *There's a Place for You in CYO* (1974).

[A. R. ZINK]

CATHOLICATE, the territory under the jurisdiction of a catholicos. In some instances the jurisdiction may be autocephalous and extend to an entire country, as in the catholicate of Georgia, or a catholicate may depend on a primatial see, as in the *Armenian Church. *CATHOLICOS.

[F. T. RYAN]

CATHOLICISM, the universal community formed by the teaching, worship, and practice of the Catholic Church, usually understood of the RC Church, which tightens the meaning of the term to intercommunion within a common obedience and discipline. Unlike *catholicity, which refers to a quality, Catholicism refers to a system. After the disruption of East and West, the name *Orthodox was assumed by the Greeks, the name, Catholics by the Latins; after the Reformation those who remained in communion with Rome kept the name, and Catholicism was contrasted with Protestantism, Lutheranism, Calvinism, and so forth. This is also its ordinary, noncontroversial usage in England, though Roman Catholic is the designation known to English law, and the C of E has never renounced the title of Catholic and claims to be a branch of the universal Church. The term is then given the comprehensive sense of transcending diverse communions, hence *Anglo-Catholicism. Good manners and a sense of the occasion and knowing when not to be a stickler for words will dictate whether one centers Catholicism on Rome or leaves it with a more diffuse meaning.

[T. GILBY]

CATHOLICITY (Gr. *katholikos,* the quality or the characteristic of universality). Though not of scriptural origin, the adjective "Catholic" has been considered properly descriptive of the Church as a whole since the time of Ignatius of Antioch (d. *c.*110); by the 3d cent. it was commonly accepted as part of the Church's title; from the 4th cent. it has been incorporated in the principal creeds. In its earliest use it designated the whole Church spread throughout the world as distinguished from the *local Church, and esp. from heretical and (later) schismatic sects. In this sense it meant in effect much the same as orthodox. In controversy with the *Donatists, St. Augustine insisted that the Donatist sect, confined to a small portion of Africa, could not possibly qualify as the true Church. In later theology a wide interpretation was given to the word and numerous ways were pointed out in which universality could be attributed to the Church, which was Catholic, e.g., by geographical diffusion; by the temporal dimension of its mission; by its inclusion of men of all nations, types, and walks of life; by its possession of revelation in its full integrity and of all the means necessary to salvation. At the time of the Reformation, defenders of the Roman faith were quick to point out that the bodies separating themselves from communion with Rome sacrificed the catholicity in which the Church had always set great store. Appropriating to themselves the description of Catholic, they reproached the Protestants, as St. Augustine had the Donatists, for separating themselves from the unity of the Catholic faith. Some Protestant bodies dropped the word Catholic from their versions of the creeds, substituting "Christian" in its place. But the majority claimed a *de iure* catholicity. The *Augsburg Confession (Art. 22) distinguishes between the Catholic Church and the Roman Church. The Second *Helvetic Confession, the *Scots Confession, and the *Westminster Confession make the same distinction implicitly; catholicity refers to the universality of the Church, and its fidelity to the true gospel. The Reformation is understood to be precisely the recovery of orthodoxy from the distortions of Rome. The

Church as Catholic, however, was not emphasized in subsequent Protestant history. Yet the idea perdures in all references to the Church universal, realized in many forms and locations and present wherever the gospel is rightly preached and the sacraments rightly administered.

Anglicans see the note of catholicity verified in their Church by reason of a *comprehensiveness large enough to embrace conflicting interpretations of the faith. In post-Tridentine RC theology the notion of catholicity was stressed and developed for polemical purposes as a note or mark by which the true Church can be recognized. Among modernists there were those who found value in catholicity understood in the Anglican sense of comprehensiveness (see MODERNISM). In more contemporary RC theology there has been a tendency to see catholicity as implying the legitimate and indeed necessary diversity of thought and practice within the latitude permitted by the unity of faith. From this point of view, the idea of catholicity is complementary to that of unity. This notion has been fruitful in the modern development of the theology of the missions, and it underlies the currently popular concept of missionary adaptation. In current ecumenical discussion, e.g., in the Consultation on Church Union, the catholicity of the Church refers to the elements of the ancient Church that survived in the Reformation, esp. the creeds, the historic episcopate, the priesthood, and the sacraments. BIBLIOGRAPHY: H. Thurston, CE 3:449–452; G. Thils, "La Notion de catholicité de l'église à l'époque moderne," EphemThLov 13 (1936) 5–73; idem, NCE 3:339–340; G. H. Tavard, Quest for Catholicity: A Study in Anglicanism (1964); D. T. Jenkins, Nature of Catholicity (1942); J. Pelikan, Riddle of Roman Catholicism (1959). *UNITY OF THE CHURCH.

[P. K. MEAGHER]

CATHOLICON, a musical composition that can be sung in any of the church *modes. Monophonic examples exist from as early as the 10th cent., but use of the technique reached a peak in Renaissance *polyphony. BIBLIOGRAPHY: Reese MusR.

[P. MURPHY]

CATHOLICOS, a title given to the chief bp. of a Church either because he made use of the universal (Gr., katholikos) jurisdiction of a patriarch, or was considered a general delegate of the patriarch. The title of patriarch was not assumed by a catholicos as long as the bond with the Mother Church remained intact. The head of the Nestorian Church in Persia was honored with the title of catholicos-patriarch in 544 when the bond with Antioch was definitely severed. The bp. of the Armenian Church received this title in the 5th century. The Syrian (Monophysite) metropolitan of Mossul, the representative of the Syrian patriarch of Antioch in Persia, was styled catholicos of the East. Today there is no Catholic catholicos who is not also a patriarch, namely, the catholicos-patriarch of Cilicia of the Armenians and the catholicos-patriarch of Babylon of the Chaldeans. Among the Orthodox the title is given to the catholicos-patriarch of Georgia (U.S.S.R.), to the three Armenian catholicoses of Etchmiadzin (Soviet-Armenia), Constantinople, and Jerusalem, to the Nestorian catholicos-patriarch of Babylon, now residing in the U.S., and to the head of the Jacobite Church in India. The office of a catholicos is defined in Catholic canon law: cc. 324–339 of ClerSanc. BIBLIOGRAPHY: V. J. Pospishil, Law on Persons (1960) 155–160.

[V. J. POSPISHIL]

CATHREIN, VIKTOR (1845–1931), moral theologian, philosopher, sociologist, and spiritual writer. Swiss by birth, C. became a Jesuit in 1863. He is esp. remembered for the incisive counter-position he built up in opposition to the positivism that had spread through most European universities, and for his analysis of the effects of that philosophical system upon both ethics and legal philosophy. His major works were: Moralphilosophie (2 v., 1890–91); Der Sozialismus (1890, with 23 later editions and many translations), a major contribution to Catholic thought on the subject of socialism; Grundbegriffe des Strafrechts (1905); Die Einheit des sittlichen Bewusstseins (3 v., 1914); and Die Grundlage des Völkerrechts (1918). Although he was always a remarkably devout man and an excellent religious, his spiritual works were mainly the fruit of his later years. Among these were: Die Verheissungen des göttlichen Herzens Jesu (1919, with many later editions); and Eucharistische Konvertitenbilder (1923). Spiritual theology is indebted to him for the clarity of the distinction he drew between venial sin and moral imperfection. BIBLIOGRAPHY: G. Gundlach, EncCatt 3:1163; E. Raitz von Frentz, DSAM 2:352.

[P. K. MEAGHER]

CATLIN, GEORGE (1796–1872), portrait painter until 1830. C. recorded the American Indian in a missionary endeavor to depict the customs and crafts of a noble people. At St. Louis (1832), up the Missouri in the Rockies (1834), and on the Mississippi River (1835), traveling light with few colors, C. worked in thin paint and though weak in anatomy showed strong composition and vitality. C. assembled his Indian Gallery, crafts, and live Indians (1837) and toured in the U.S. and abroad. His later sad-faced drawings are memorable. C. is an important figure in American painting through authentic and powerful renderings of an heroic people.

[M. J. DALY]

CATO, MARCUS PORCIUS, the name of two men celebrated in Roman history; it is customary to distinguish them by calling one the Elder and the other the Younger.

The Elder (234–149 B.C.), Roman soldier and statesman, consul in 195 and censor in 184. A stern advocate of the old morality, he was strongly opposed to Greek influences in Rome. His severity as censor earned him the surname of "the Censor." Idolized by later conservatives, he was, despite his genuine patriotism, a harsh and narrow-minded reactionary, as is apparent from his one extant work, the *De agricultura,* and from his insistence upon the destruction of Carthage.

The Younger (94–46 B.C.), great-grandson of Cato the Elder, also known as "Uticensis" because of his suicide at Utica. A self-righteous, unamiable Stoic, he stabbed himself to death after the defeat of the Pompeian forces at Thapsus. As a "martyr" of the Republic he was a greater danger to Caesar after his demise than he had been in life. BIBLIOGRAPHY: A. Hermann, PW 2:927–942; N. W. Forde, *Cato the Censor* (1975).

[M. J. COSTELLOE]

CATRIK, JOHN (d. 1419), English royal negotiator. Educated in law at Oxford, C. became bp. of St. David's (1414), of Coventry and Lichfield (1415), and of Exeter (1419). At the Council of Constance he had part in the deposition of John XXIII and election of Martin V. BIBLIOGRAPHY: C. L. Kingsford, DNB 11:78–79; Emden Ox 1:371–373.

[A. WARDLE]

CATROU, FRANÇOIS (1659–1737), French preacher, littérateur, and historian. Having entered the Jesuits at the age of 18, he manifested during his student days an inclination and remarkable talent for writing and speaking. In his early ministry he was chiefly occupied in preaching, establishing for himself a distinguished reputation for pulpit oratory throughout France. But his career took a different turn in 1701 when he founded a review called officially *Mémoires de Trévoux pour servir à l'histoire des sciences et des beaux-arts,* more commonly known as *Journal de Trévoux.* He stayed on the staff of this journal for 12 years, during which time he engaged in the research that prepared him for his chief historical works: a history of the Mogul Empire, studies on the Anabaptists and Quakers, and a history of Rome (21 v. 1725–37). Earlier he had written a life of Virgil and produced an influential though somewhat inaccurate translation of Virgil's works.

[J. C. WILLKE]

CATTANEO, LAZZARO (1560–1640), Jesuit missionary. His work among the Chinese brought him to such remote places as Peking, Nanking, and Shanghai. After 29 years of missionary labor among the Chinese, C. retired to Hangchow where he wrote treatises on spirituality in the Chinese language.

[J. R. RIVELLO]

CAUCHIE, ALFRED HENRI JOSEPH (1860–1922), Belgian church historian. Ordained a priest in 1885, C. studied at Louvain, receiving the doctorate (1890). C. held the chair of history there until his death. In 1900 he with P. Ladenze founded the *Revue d'histoire écclésiastique.* He also founded the *Institut historique Belge* at Rome, becoming its third director (1919–22). BIBLIOGRAPHY: L. Van

der Essen, RHE 18 (1922) 213–239; L. Mohlberg, LTK 2:981.

[N. F. GAUGHAN]

CAUCHON, PIERRE (1371–1442), bp. of Beauvais (1420) and then of Lisieux (1432). He is known esp. for his diplomatic service for the Duke of Burgundy and Kings Henry V and VI of England, and for his part in the trial of Joan of Arc. Historians are generally critical of the part C. played in this trial. Attempts to rehabilitate his name have met with no success. The best that can be said of him is that he was a "collaborator" in circumstances that may have attenuated his guilt. BIBLIOGRAPHY: J. E. J. Quicherat, *Aperçus nouveaux sur l'histoire de Jeanne d'Arc* (1850); G. Mollat, *Catholicisme* 2:728.

[J. J. SMITH]

CAUDA, Lat., tail, the vertical dash attached to notes in the mensural system of musical notation prevailing in Western Europe from the 14th to the 17th centuries. The presence or absence of the cauda determined the time value of the note. In the 13th century it referred to musical passages without texts, i.e. extended vocal passages sung on the first or last vowel of the textual line.

[D. J. SMUCKER]

CAUDEBEC-EN-CAUX, Church of Our Lady (1426–1520), one of finest Flamboyant Gothic churches in Normandy, designed by Guillaume Le Tellier, having a nave with circular pillars, blind triforium, and a clerestory with 15th- and 16th-cent. stained glass. Without transept the interior flows uninterruptedly from portal to altar behind which is an unusual hexagonal chapel. BIBLIOGRAPHY: R. de Lasteyrie, *L'Architecture religieuse en France* (2 v., 1926–27).

[M. J. DALY]

CAULET, FRANÇOIS ÉTIENNE (1610–80), bp. of Pamiers. Having aided M. Olier in the founding of the Sulpicians, C. succeeded Olier as rector of Saint-Sulpice (1642). Two years later he was made bp. of Pamiers. As bp., C. busied himself in developing schools and reforming the chapters of Foix and Pamiers, in which effort he stirred up much hostility against himself. He was among the few French bps. who refused to sign the formulary of Alexander VII, not so much, it seems, because he favored Jansenism, but because he objected on principle to the way the formulary was put together. Later, when he encountered difficulty with certain Jesuits, he was accused of Jansenism, a charge that was unjust or at least unproven. Among the French bps. he stood out as an unyielding foe of Louis XIV's plan to extend the *régale.* This opposition aroused against him the anger of the King and of parliament as well as that of his own metropolitan. In consequence he suffered the loss of his temporalities.

[J. C. WILLKE]

CAULITES, an extinct monastic order named after the motherhouse, Val-des-Choux (Vallis Calium), founded in France in 1193 by Ven. Viard, a Carthusian brother, who adhered to a Cistercian-interpreted Benedictine rule. The order prospered during the 13th cent. but by the mid-18th cent. the numbers had decreased so greatly that the monks were forced to merge with the Cistercians at Sept-Fons, where within another quarter of a cent., that monastery was suppressed by French revolutionaries.

[R. A. TODD]

CAUSALITY, DIVINE, From the beginning of the history of philosophy, man has sought an ultimate explanation of the world: Anaxagoras's nous, Socrates' demiurge, Plato's exemplar, Aristotle's pure act. Studies of causality led some philosophers to posit the existence of a first uncaused cause whose proper effect is finite being. If cause is that which positively influences the being or becoming of another, it is seen operative in a metaphysical analysis of the structure of finite being. Finite beings change; change indicates the presence of act and potency. Nothing can be reduced from potency to act except by a being in act; i.e., the nature of change requires an agent or cause of change. An infinite series of *per se* efficient causes is not possible: because any actual series of *per se* causes is real, it cannot be actually infinite; or, if it be thought infinite, the infinite series, not having in itself any reason for existence, demands a cause of the series of causes. Regardless of the number of intermediate causes, a first cause is needed to explain the reality of the others. Likewise, a first cause is needed not only for the composition of finite beings (essence and existence) but also to effect the substantial unity of the principles of essence and existence found in every finite existent.

The exercise of divine causality must be an eternally free act of creation, producing finite existents from nothing but the infinite power of a divine *fiat* exercised in the creatural duration of time. Creation explains both the limitation and multiplicity of finite being. God is neither so immanent that physical effects are properly identified with him, nor so transcendent that there is no continuing relationship with any of his effects. In terms of human effects, divine causality and the free will of man pose a perplexing problem. St. Thomas poses guidelines for harmonizing the facts of divine causality and human freedom by noting that there is nothing repugnant in saying that God creates some things to act in a determined manner and some to act freely. His immutable will causes changing beings to operate according to their several changing natures. While divine causality is constantly operative as continuing creation, man also operates truly, although with secondary causality, according to his free nature. Descartes, as well as Anselm, tended toward emphasizing an *a priori* consideration of God. Descartes made possible the occasionalism of Malebranche and the pantheism of Spinoza. Kant said that God is knowable by practical reason only. Evolutionary theories of the post-Darwinian era, particularly when coupled with process philosophy, affect man's consid-eration both of the nature of God and divine causality. When admissible considerations must be empirically verifiable, causality in general and divine causality in particular are eliminated from consideration. Such mechanistic and evolutionary theories logically lead to agnosticism or to varied forms of current atheism. In modern philosophy, with its shift in the notion of causality from analogical explanation to phenomenological description or analysis of language, and its tendency to eliminate finality and to focus on efficient causality in terms of physical laws mathematically expressed and correlated, the existence and nature of divine causality often are not considered. BIBLIOGRAPHY: ThAq St 1, 2.3; T. C. O'Brien, NCE 3:347–351, with bibliog.

[M. HALPIN]

CAUSALITY, PRINCIPLE OF, the philosophical axiom that every effect depends upon its cause. The axiom is called "principle," not because it is an immediately given law of thought, but because it functions in reasoning from effect to cause. That any reality is an effect, however, is not immediately evident, but the yield of an inquiry into the reality actually given; should its actuality not be self-explanatory, then the question of causality arises. (Such a process of inquiry is illustrated in St. Thomas Aquinas's celebrated five ways, ST 1a.2,3.) Further, the dependence of any effect is of many kinds and of many degrees. The kinds may be generalized according to the basic division of causes into dependence on: internal causes, material and formal (the from what and the what); external causes, agent, or efficient and final (the by what and the for what). As to degree, dependence means that an effect derives its existence from its causes; in some cases that extends only to its coming into being; in others, to its continuing in existence. Thus a composite being depends for its continuation on the conjunction of its material and formal principles. An action in pursuit of an end depends for its sustained continuation on the attraction exercised by that end. The fire, however, depends on its ignition for its beginning, but not for its continuation. The principle of causality has most often been discussed, and denied, with respect to agent or efficient causality. Its basic meaning here is that whatever is in potentiality cannot bring itself to actualization, but for that depends on another, actual existent. The denial of the objective validity of the principle by the *Nominalists, by D. *Hume, I. *Kant, and many contemporary philosophers rests on epistemological presuppositions that limit the real content of thought to the pure sum of sensory experiences.

[T. C. O'BRIEN]

CAUSE. The notion of causality is understood, taken for granted, and acted upon by people in the ordinary living of their lives; by it they understand the influence or sum of influences that bring an effect about. Thus, in the case of an artist who provides for his livelihood by his painting, people agree—at the popular level—that his need to live is the cause of this action (his purpose in acting: the final cause), that he is the agent responsible (he does the brushwork: the efficient cause), that certain materials are necessary if the painting is to be made (material cause), and that the materials must be put into a particular form if the painting is to have meaning (formal cause). Any action that results in the production of something requires that these four influences exist together. Thus in scholastic philosophy (following Aristotle) a full analysis of the influences that combine in the production of any human artifact necessarily includes, in addition to its efficient cause, its final, formal, and material causes. Furthermore, the efficient cause, as in the example given, may use an instrument (the brush), in which case the agent is the principal cause and the brush the instrumental cause. The terms material cause and formal cause are not used in modern philosophy; efficient causality alone is understood as the strictly correct use of this notion.

If the term is taken in this restricted sense, the real influence of the cause in the production of the effect is popularly recognized. Thus the striking of a ball is the reason why the ball moves, and why the harder it is struck the farther it travels (provided no special circumstances prevent the action from having its normal effect). But this real influence of the cause on its effect had been variously denied on philosophical grounds. The Occasionalists (Nicholas of Autrecourt, Malebranche) regard the cause as nothing more than the necessary occasion for the production of the effect, which is in fact produced directly by God. In this view there is no created causality. God as first cause alone exercises causality; nothing created ever acts as a secondary cause in dependence on God. However, Occasionalism accepts the legitimacy of seeking a metaphysical explanation of change. D. Hume and J. S. Mill, on the contrary, do not allow any metaphysical explanation of change; for them there is no provable influence that passes from the cause to the effect; the cause is merely the antecedent to which the effect is invariably and unconditionally consequent. I. Kant stated that there is no more to causality than invariable succession of effect to cause, but denied that it applies outside the world of phenomena, thus denying the metaphysical reality of causality. These views have led many to deny a metaphysical proof of God's existence. BIBLIOGRAPHY: J. F. Anderson, *Cause of Being* (1952); G. B. Klubertanz and M. R. Holloway, *Being and God* (1963); R. Taylor, EncPhil 2:56–66; D. R. Heise, *Causal Analysis* (1975).

[B. FORSHAW]

CAUSE, FIRST, a term that is applied to God insofar as he is considered as the ultimate explanation of all created reality; it is analogous to the designation of God as the maker of everything in Scripture (Wis ch. 13; Rom, ch. 1). The usual philosophical demonstration of God's existence is that of St. Thomas Aquinas given in the first three of the five ways, which may be summarized as the application of the principle of causality to observed reality and its processes of being and becoming, so that change, causality, and contingency are seen to involve an unchanging changer, a first cause, and a

necessary being on which all created things depend for their activity and being. The second way is concerned precisely with causality as such; causality is an observed phenomenon and nothing is the cause of itself; therefore ultimately every series of essentially subordinated causes must find its explanation in an uncaused first cause. This valid argument does not prove more than it explicitly states; it does not therefore *by itself* exclude the possibility of there being more than one such uncaused cause or prove the existence of the God in whom Christians believe. However in fact God is the one first cause on which all series of causality depend so that ultimately it is on it that all things depend for their being and activity. BIBLIOGRAPHY: M. R. E. Masterman, NCE 3:352; R. C. Smith, NCE 6:563–568; T. C. O'Brien, *Metaphysics and the Existence of God* (1960).

[B. FORSHAW]

CAUSES OF THE SAINTS, CONGREGATION FOR, the congregation or department of government in the reorganized Roman Curia responsible for procedures and decisions in matters pertaining to the beatification and canonization of servants of God. The work of this newly established congregation was previously performed by the Congregation of Rites, which has now been abolished, its work being divided between this new congregation and the Congregation for Divine Worship.

CAUSSADE, JEAN PIERRE DE (1675–1751), Jesuit spiritual writer and director. A native of Cahors, C. studied at the Jesuit school in that city and entered the Society in 1693. He was ordained priest in 1704 and after his profession in 1708 spent six years as a professor at Aurillac and Toulouse. In 1715 he began to work as an itinerant preacher. During the course of his travels he became acquainted with the Visitation nuns at Nancy who came to hold him in high esteem and who preserved his correspondence and letters of spiritual direction with great care. These letters contained much of the best of his thought. In his interpretation of the spiritual life he shows the influence of Fénelon, St. Francis de Sales, and Bossuet. He published in 1741 a work containing spiritual instructions in dialogue form on the different states of prayer according to the teaching of Bossuet. But his best known and most influential work, generally known as *Abandonment to Divine Providence,* was not composed by C. for publication. It was constructed by the Visitation nuns from letters of spiritual direction he had written them. Their MS was later reworked and reorganized by H. Ramière and was first published in 1861. BIBLIOGRAPHY: M. Olphe-Galliard, DSAM 2.1:354–370.

[J. C. WILLKE]

CAUSSIN, NICOLAS (1583–1651), Jesuit preacher noted for his work as confessor to nobility, particularly to Louis XIII and the Prince of Condé. Once exiled by Card. Richelieu, he later returned to Paris where he continued his work as confessor and spiritual writer. One important work,

Cour Sainte, was published in 1624. BIBLIOGRAPHY: M. Olphe-Galliard, DSAM 2.1:371–374.

[J. R. RIVELLO]

CAUWE, FRANÇOIS (d. 1679), a Flemish Franciscan mystical writer. A member of the province of St. Joseph in Belgium, he is noted for his spirituality in the tradition of 15th- and 16th-cent. Franciscan mysticism. His principal works are the *Pèlerinage de l'Enfant Jésus* (1673) a life of Christ and *La Vie et les enseignements divins de Claire de S.-Lieven* (1677). BIBLIOGRAPHY: M. Verians, DSAM 2.1:373.

[I. M. KASHUBA]

CAVA, see LA CAVA, ABBEY OF.

CAVALCANTI, JOAQUIM ARCOVERDE DE ALBUQUERQUE, see ARCOVERDE DE ALBUQUERQUE CAVALCANTI, JOAQUIM.

CAVALLERA, FERDINAND (1875–1954), French theologian and patrologist. He entered the Society of Jesus in 1892, was ordained in 1906, and later served as ordinary professor of positive theology at the Institut Catholique of Toulouse and as director of the *Bulletin de littérature ecclésiastique, Revue d'Ascétique et de Mystique,* and the *Dictionnaire de spiritualité ascétique et mystique.* Though a frequent contributor to learned and influential periodicals, he is perhaps best known for his *S. Jérôme, sa vie et son oeuvre* (1922). DTC, Tables generales, 1:560–561.

[H. DRESSLER]

CAVALLI, FRANCESCO (1602–76), Italian composer. He held various positions at San Marco, Venice, beginning as a choirboy under Monteverdi (1617) and finally becoming *maestro di cappella* (1668). One of the leading exponents of early popular Venetian opera, he also composed a number of Masses and motets in various forms from solo monody to polychoral works. The Masses were dramatic but not operatic; C. was able to cross-fertilize but not confuse his church and stage music. BIBLIOGRAPHY: A. A. Abert, MGG 2:926–932.

[P. MURPHY]

CAVALLINI, FRANCESCO (fl. 17th cent.), Italian sculptor who collaborated on decorations of Church of Gesù e Maria, Rome (1670s) and executed huge stucco saints in Church of S. Carlo al Corso, Rome (1678–82). BIBLIOGRAPHY: R. Wittkower, *Art and Architecture in Italy, 1600–1750* (1958).

[M. J. DALY]

CAVALLINI, PIETRO (*c.* 1250–1330), most influential artist of his day except for Giotto. C. turned from Byzantine models to classical, in monumental decorative works (mosaics, S. Maria in Trastevere, 1291; frescoes, 1293). Painter to King Charles of Anjou (1308) C. reportedly did interior and exterior frescoes (later destroyed) at St. Paul-outside-the-Walls. His Roman school helped free Italian painting from Byzantine forms. BIBLIOGRAPHY: J. White, *Art and Architecture in Italy 1250–1400* (1966).

[M. J. DALY]

CAVALLINO, BERNARDO (1616–56), Italian painter, supreme in Neapolitan baroque style. C. studied with G. Reni and was indirectly influenced by the Caravaggesque *sfumato* qualities of J. de Ribera and the delicacies of Gentileschi. Rich color, extraordinary textures, and sophisticated gesture of supreme grace and dignity mark C.'s work as a perfection of Caravaggio's style in Naples of the 17th century. BIBLIOGRAPHY: R. Wittkower, *Art and Architecture in Italy, 1600–1750* (1965).

[M. J. DALY]

CAVAZZONI, GIROLAMO (1520–60), Italian organist and composer. He lived in Venice and initiated the organ canzona. In 1542 he composed organ music under the title, *Intavolatura cioè Ricercari, Canzoni, Hinni, Magnificati.* In 1543 he wrote three organ masses: *Missa Apostolorum, Missa Dominicalis* and *Missa de Beata Virgine.*

[D. J. SMUCKER]

CAVE, WILLIAM (1637–1713) Anglican clergyman and scholar. C. studied at St. John's College, Cambridge (1653–60), and subsequently served as vicar at Islington and All Hallows the Great and as rector of Isleworth (1690–1713). His chief works are *Apostolici,* a history of the principal persons in the Church of the first 3 cent., and *Scriptorum ecclesiasticorum historia literaria,* a history of eccl. writers down to the 14th century. Though impressively learned, C. is criticized by scholars for lack of critical acumen and his attempt to identify the Anglican Church with primitive Christianity. BIBLIOGRAPHY: C. Constantin, DTC 2.2:2044–45.

[H. DRESSLER]

CAVE (ASSOC.), see CATHOLIC AUDIO-VISUAL EDUCATORS ASSOCIATION.

CAVE TEMPLE, shrine or place of worship excavated into rock, specifically Indian forms in the Barābar and Nāgārjunī Hills with the most famous in the W Deccan at Bhājā, Karlī Ajantā (27 caves) and Ellorā (34 caves), the latest at Elephanta, famous for the great sculptured Trimūrti figure of Śiva.

[M. J. DALY]

CAVELL, EDITH LOUISA (1865–1915), "Nurse Cavell." She was a Norfolk woman who trained at the London Hospital and became matron of the Berkendael Medical Institute in Brussels. There C. sheltered British and French wounded and stragglers from the early battles of

World War I, and aided them to escape to neutral Holland. C. also tended German wounded with devoted care. Arrested by the Germans, she was tried by court-martial and condemned. She faced the firing-squad with dignity. Her simple words to the chaplain who brought her viaticum rang through the world: "Patriotism is not enough." BIBLIOGRAPHY: R. Ryder, *Edith Cavell: A Biography* (1975).

[T. GILBY]

CAVES, MONASTERY OF THE (KIEV), a monastic foundation established by SS. Anthony and Theodosius Pechersky in 1051. It was a product of Byzantine-Slav Christianity. The monks dwelt in caves along the Dnieper near Kiev and followed the rule of the Studion monastery in Constantinople. The *Pechersky Paterik* gives a documented account of the lives of the monks. BIBLIOGRAPHY: G. P. Fedotov, *Russian Religious Mind: Kievan Christianity* (1960); Butler 3:65–68, s.v. "SS. Antony and Theodosius Pechersky"; I. Sofranov, BiblSanct 2:221–223, s.v. "Antonio Pecierskij"; I. Dujčev, *ibid.*, 12:292–295, s.v. "Teodosio di Pečersk."

[R. A. TODD]

CAVOUR, CAMILLO BENSO DI (1810–61), Piedmontese statesman responsible for the unification of Italy under House of Savoy. Member of an aristocratic family, his political career began in 1848 when Charles Albert granted Piedmont a constitution. As a leading figure of the Risorgimento and as the editor of a newspaper by that name, Cavour had repeatedly urged liberal reforms. In 1852 Cavour was appointed premier by Victor Emmanuel II. With the aid of Napoleon III of France, Cavour brought Piedmont into war against Austria and gained Lombardy (1859). In the years 1859–61 his opportunistic diplomacy enabled his country to absorb the Kingdom of the Two Sicilies and the greater part of the States of the Church. Because of his support for the Rattazzi bill in 1855, by which the property of religious orders was to be confiscated and sold so as to increase the salaries of the lower clergy, Cavour was excommunicated from the Church. By the time of his premature death in 1861, the expanded Piedmontese kingdom had become the Kingdom of Italy. BIBLIOGRAPHY: W. R. Thayer, *Life and Times of Cavour* (2 v., 1911); M. L. Shay, NCE 3:358; F. J. Coppa, *Camillo di Cavour* (1973); A. J. Whyte, *The Political Life and Letters of Cavour, 1848–1861,* (1930, Repr. 1975).

[E. A. CARRILLO]

CAXTON, WILLIAM (*c.* 1422–91), first English printer. Apprenticed in London to a mercer, he finished his apprenticeship in Bruges. There C. became governor of the English Association of Merchant Adventurers. He learned printing to meet the demand for copies of his translation from French, *The Recuyell of the Historyes of Troye,* the first book printed in English (1475). In 1476 he set up his press at Westminster. Best known works of his press are Chaucer's *Canterbury Tales* (before 1480) and Malory's *Morte d'Arthur* (1485). BIBLIOGRAPHY: N. S. Aurner, *William Caxton* (1926, repr. 1965); *Prefaces and Epilogues* (ed. W. J. B. Crotch, EETS, 1928); H. S. Bennett, *English Books and Readers, 1475–1557* (1952); E. G. Duff, *William Caxton 1422–1491* (1905, repr. 1970).

[M. M. BARRY]

CAYET, PIERRE VICTOR PALMA (1525–1610), historian and controversial theologian born at Montrichard, (Loire) France. After early studies under the Calvinist Ramus C. became a Protestant and served as a pastor. He became an official at the court of the future Henry IV, and an advisor to Catherine de Bourbon. In 1595, he returned to the Catholic Church and subsequently became embroiled in religious controversy over works published in defense of the Catholic Church. Ordained in 1600, he continued to publish till his death at Paris. Among his works are the histories of religious wars in France from 1589 to 1604 in two series. His *Chronologie septennaire* was placed on the Index because it denied the authority of the pope. At his death his loyalties were still in question.

[T. LIDDY]

CAZZATI, MAURIZIO (1620–77), Italian composer. His sacred works include Masses, psalms, litanies, antiphons, hymns and motets. His secular works include madrigals, instrumental sonatas, oratorios and cantatas.

[D. J. SMUCKER]

CCD, see CONFRATERNITY OF CHRISTIAN DOCTRINE.

CEADDA, ST., see CHAD, ST.

CECILIA OF THE NATIVITY (Cecilia Morillas; 1570–1646), discalced Carmelite. Tutored by her mother in Scripture, painting, and philosophy, she became a Carmelite at 19. She served as prioress in her order twice and was instrumental in getting the discalced Carmelite friars to come to the city. Two of her works were published in the early 20th century: *Transformación del alma en Dios* and *Unión del alma con Dios.* Manuscripts of her spiritual canticles survive in the Carmel of Burgos. BIBLIOGRAPHY: Crisogono, DSAM 11:374–375.

[J. R. RIVELLO]

CECILIA, ST. (fl. 3d or 4th cent.), one of the most celebrated of Roman virgins and martyrs, but who is not mentioned by the Chronographer of 354, or by Ambrose, Damasus, Jerome, or Prudentius. A fragmentary inscription of the late 4th or early 5th cent. refers to a church of her name, and her feast was celebrated in her basilica in the Trastevere on Nov. 22, 545. According to a 6th-cent. legend, C. was a young Christian of high rank who told her husband Valerian on the night of their marriage that her virginity was protected by an angel. In order to see the angel,

Valerian accepted baptism from Pope Urban. He saw the angel standing by C.'s side with a crown of roses in one hand for C. and in the other, of lilies for himself. After further adventures, first Valerian and his brother Tiburtius, then C. were executed. The time of their martyrdoms is variously given as early as the reign of Marcus Aurelius and as late as that of Diocletian. The lack of an early cult to C. makes her martyrdom somewhat doubtful. In April, 821, her body was removed from its crypt in the catacomb of Callistus and placed beneath the altar in her basilica. From the time of the Renaissance she has been a patroness of musicians and is represented with an organ or viola. BIBLIOGRAPHY: E. Josi, BiblSanct 3:1064–81; Butler 4:402–405.

[M. J. COSTELLOE]

CECILIA ROMANA, BL. (*c.*1200–90) In 1221 C. joined the convent of S. Sisto, founded by St. Dominic; in 1225 she and three other sisters were sent by Honorius III to Bologna to establish Dominican life in S. Agnese. Her reminiscences from Bologna (*c.*1280) include the only eyewitness description of St. Dominic's features. BIBLIOGRAPHY: A. Redigonda, BiblSanct 4:595.

[L. E. BOYLE]

CEDD (CEDDA) ST. (d. 664), English Benedictine bishop. Brother of St. Chad, C. was born in Northumbria and educated by St. Aidan and the Irish monks of Lindisfarne. He assisted in missionary work in Mercia and in Essex. He was consecrated bp. of the East Saxons by St. Finan at London in 654. C. established monasteries at Bradwell-on-Sea, Tilbury, and Lastingham. In 664 C. participated in the Whitby conference to settle the Easter controversy. The conference ultimately decided whether the Church of England should remain linked with the Celtic Church or with Rome. C. acted as the interpreter for the Irish party, yet at the synod he accepted the council's Roman decision. C. died of the plague at Lastingham.

[M. H. BEIRNE]

CEDRON, see KIDRON.

CEFALÙ, THE MOSAICS OF (1131–48), executed near Palermo for the Norman King Roger II (d. 1154). These mosaics seem to have been the work of Byzantine artists who adapted the traditional centralized scheme of decoration to fit the Western longitudinal building (basilica). In the conch of the apse is depicted the Pantocrator; immediately underneath are the Virgin and archangels, while rows of Apostles occupy the two lowest registers. Mosaics on the side walls and in the choir (including deacons and saints, with celestial orders) seem slightly later in style. BIBLIOGRAPHY: O. Demus, *Mosaics of Norman Sicily* (1950); G. di Stefano, *Il Duomo di Cefalù* (1960).

[S. MURRAY]

CEILLIER, REMI (1688–1763), French Benedictine scholar. C. entered the monastery of Moyen-Moutier in the Vosges in 1704, was ordained in 1710, and in 1718 became prior of St. Jacques de Neufchateau. In 1733 C. was appointed prior of Flavigny-sur-Moselle, a post he filled until his death. His most important work is the *Histoire générale des auteurs sacrés et ecclésiastiques* (23 v., 1729–63). The work begins with the writers of the OT and continues down through the middle of the 13th century. A two-volume index appeared in 1782. There are evidences of Jansenistic tendencies in his works. BIBLIOGRAPHY: A. Beugnet, DTC 2.2:2049–51.

[H. DRESSLER]

CELEBRANT, the bp., priest, or deacon who officiates at a liturgical ceremony. Because liturgical services are not private functions, but a celebration of the Church in which all actively participate, each in his own capacity (see Vat II SacLit 26), all can in a sense be said to celebrate them together. In order to highlight the communal character of such celebrations, many have come to prefer the term president in place of celebrant.

[N. KOLLAR]

CELEBRATIONS IN CATECHETICS. The celebration in catechetics has become an organic part of the catechesis of children since the 1950's. It was initiated by French catechists and perfected by the Higher Institute of Catechetics in Paris. The catechetical celebration has three essential parts: the recalling of a historical event by means of the solemn reading of a biblical passage and by means of gestures meaningful to the children, the turning to the mystery being explored by placing the children before the mystery itself and by leading them to a sincere religious attitude before God, and the communal profession of faith by means of procession, song, gestures, prayers, and silence enacted together. Usually the catechetical celebration follows this theme: an entrance procession accompanied by song, reading of Sacred Scripture, communal prayer related to the reading, a brief homily on the reading which exhorts toward a better life, a hymn of thanksgiving for the light received from the reading and explanation of the word of God, a recessional, and the blessing of the priest. The setting is normally the classroom. Adaptations are made when a priest does not preside.

The celebration in catechetics is not limited to the catechesis of children. It is part of that development called paraliturgy, which while not the official sacramental worship of the Church is nevertheless deeply inspired by liturgical and scriptural sources. Such celebrations have become a part of the religious educational efforts directed toward persons of all ages. These celebrations indicate the interrelatedness of the liturgical and catechetical renewals. BIBLIOGRAPHY: L. Csonka and G. C. Negri. *Educare: sommario di scienze pedagogiche* (ed. P. Braido, 3d ed., 3 v., 1964) 3:293–553; "Catechetics for the Future," *New Concilium: Religion in the Seventies* (ed. A. Müller, 1970).

[C. C. MCDONALD]

CELEBRET (Lat., let him celebrate), an official commendatory letter or document testifying to a priest's sacerdotal status and good standing. A priest who is traveling or visiting a place in which he is unknown may be required to show such a document before being permitted to celebrate Mass in a church. For a diocesan priest letters of this kind are issued by his ordinary; for religious priests, by the superior of the order or congregation or by a provincial superior. See CIC c. 804.

CELESTIAL HIERARCHY, see HIERARCHY, CELESTIAL.

CELESTINE I, ST. (d. 432), **POPE** from 422 in succession to St. Boniface I. After having approved the elevation of *Nestorius to the See of Constantinople (428), C. was disturbed by reports of the doctrine the patriarch was preaching. When the council C. held in Rome (430) condemned Nestorius, C. wrote to him demanding a retraction under penalty of excommunication. Unfortunately C. selected *Cyril of Alexandria to execute the sentence. When Nestorius refused to subscribe to Cyril's list of 12 propositions, a council was convoked by the Emperor at Ephesus (431), which, under the presidency of Cyril, hastened to condemn Nestorius and his doctrine before the Antiochene bishops and the papal legates arrived. These had been instructed not to condemn Nestorius but to execute the papal condemnation already formulated. Finding themselves presented with a *fait accompli,* however, they approved what had been done. C. inherited from his predecessors two conflicts with the North African Church. Zosimus had unwisely espoused the cause of Apiarius, a priest put under censure by African ecclesiastical authority, and Boniface had restored Anthony, bp. of Fussala to his see after he had been deposed by African bishops. St. Augustine made a vigorous but respectful protest about the Holy See's wishes in the matter of Anthony and even threatened to resign if C. persisted in seeking to restore him. In the case of Apiarius a council of African bishops (c.425) declared that the African Church's autonomy in such matters was guaranteed by ancient precedent, and when the accused broke down and confessed to the charges against him, the papal legate was obliged to withdraw his support. C. sent *Germain of Auxerre to Britain to combat Pelagianism and dispatched Palladius to missionary work among the Irish. He wrote a letter to the bishops of Gaul recommending the teaching of St. Augustine on the subject of grace as opposed to the Semipelagian ideas that were then finding some favor. The so-called *Capitula Caelestini,* which are appended to this letter in many MSS and which summarize decisions of the Holy See regarding grace, are now acknowledged to be the work of another hand, probably that of *Prosper of Aquitaine (see E. Portalie, DTC 2:2052–61). In C.'s pontificate the church of Santa Maria in Trastevere was renovated and the construction of Santa Sabina on the Aventine was begun. C. was buried in the cemetery of Priscilla. Works: *Epistolae et Decreta* PL 50. BIBLIOGRAPHY: J. Chapin, NCE 3:363–364; Butler 2:40–41.

[P. F. MULHERN]

CELESTINE II (Guido of Città di Castello, birth date unknown), **POPE,** 1143–44. He studied under Abelard and became a cardinal priest and staunch supporter of Innocent II. As Pope he reappraised the treaty of Innocent II with Roger II of Sicily. The so-called prophecy of Malachy designates by epithets the 111 Popes to follow Celestine II. BIBLIOGRAPHY: H. Wolter, LTK 2:1254; R. Mols, DHGE 12:59–62.

[H. DRESSLER]

CELESTINE III (Giacinto Bobo; c.1106–98), **POPE** from 1191. Already 85 at the time of his election, C. was a man whose energies and diplomatic skills were well past their prime. He sought peace but was willing to achieve it at the cost of temporizing and of granting discreditable concessions such as those he made to the Romans and to Henry VI, whom he crowned emperor. BIBLIOGRAPHY: Mann 10:383–441.

[J. C. WILLKE]

CELESTINE IV (Goffredo Castiglioni; d. 1241), **POPE** for less than a month. Cardinal bp. of St. Sabina, C. was elected pope Oct. 25, 1241, by a divided conclave that lasted 11 weeks, as the Emperor Frederick II waited outside Rome. He had served as a canon and chancellor of Milan before entering the Cistercian house of Hautecombe (Altacomba); in 1227 he went to Rome as cardinal priest of St. Mark's. Without ever assuming the insignia of office, he died Nov. 11, 1241. BIBLIOGRAPHY: E. Kantorowicz, *Frederick the Second, 1194–1250* (tr. E. O. Lorimer, 1957); Potthast Reg 1:940–941; Mann 13:440–450.

[S. WILLIAMS]

CELESTINE V, ST. (Pietro de Morrone; c.1215–96), **POPE** in 1294. In 1231 he entered the monastery of S. Maria di Faifoli, then left it after a few years to become an anchorite. After some wandering about, he was ordained priest in Rome in 1238. He then established himself in 1241 on Mount Morrone in the Abruzzi, and in 1246 founded a colony of hermits nearby on Mount Maiella. The new society of the Brothers of the Holy Spirit (later called Celestines) was approved by Urban IV (1263) and confirmed by Gregory X (1275). Peter resigned the headship of the society in 1286, building an oratory (S. Onofrio) for himself on Mount Morrone. It was there that he reluctantly heard of his election in July, 1294, to the Chair of Peter. The story of his election is celebrated and is not devoid of mysterious angles. That of his 6-month episcopate is full of shadows. Consecrated at Aquila in August, C. was totally out of his element as pope and was no match for the intrigues of various cardinals, of the Franciscan Spirituals (for whom he became a rallying-point), and of his "protector" Charles of Anjou, king of Naples. Possibly his renunciation of the papacy on Dec. 13, 1294, was made under extreme pressure. Placed in protective custody by his successor Boniface VIII, C. escaped briefly, then died, after recapture, on May 19, 1296 in the castle of Fumone. He was canonized by Clement V in 1313. BIBLIOG-

RAPHY: G. L. Longhi, BiblSanct 3:1100–09; R. Mois, DHGE 12:79–101; Butler 2:345–347.

[L. E. BOYLE]

CELESTINES, a congregation within the Benedictine Order founded by Peter of Morrone (Celestine V) about 1240. He became a monk in 1235 and soon after retired into the wilderness around Monte Morrone in Abruzzi, where he lived a very austere life in imitation of St. John the Baptist. He was soon joined by a number of companions and in 1263 Urban IV approved their way of life, which incorporated Cistercian severity, Franciscan poverty, and some of the organizational features of the mendicant orders. In the 15th cent. the order had about 150 houses, mostly in Italy and France. The Celestines ceased to exist as an order under the suppressions of anticlerical governments in the late 18th and early 19th centuries. The *Clareni, a group of Franciscan *Spirituals authorized as a separate community by Celestine V, are also referred to as Poor Hermits of the Lord Celestine, as Celestines, or as Franciscan Celestines. BIBLIOGRAPHY: J. Duhr, DSAM 2:377–385.

[C. J. LYNCH]

CELESTIUS (Caelestius; d. 429), a principal exponent of *Pelagianism. C. probably was born in Italy; after being educated as a lawyer, he became a monk. He first met Pelagius c. 405 during the latter's sojourn in Rome. When the city fell (410), the two went to Africa, where C. propagated Pelagius's doctrine with intemperate zeal, and was condemned in 411 for denying original sin and criticizing *infant baptism. Later he was ordained at Ephesus. In 416 he transferred to Constantinople; but the local bp. had him removed almost at once, and Pope Innocent I excommunicated him along with Pelagius in 417. The following year C. turned up in Rome, presented the new pope, Zosimus, with a complete account of his beliefs, and succeeded in gaining his favor. Renewed investigation, however, and the condemnations of the Council of *Carthage XVI (418; see D 222–230) made Zosimus confirm Innocent's excommunications (see D 231). C. thereupon went into hiding for several years and then proceeded to Rome once more. The Council of Ephesus (431) condemned him along with Pelagius, but by that time C. had probably died. In propagating Pelagianism C. played a larger role than Pelagius himself; and the judgments against the teaching were in the first place directed against him. BIBLIOGRAPHY: G. Bardy, *Catholicisme* 2:753.

[T. C. O'BRIEN]

CÉLI DÉ, see CULDEES.

CELIBACY, the condition of life without marriage that is undertaken by clerics upon the reception of major orders in accordance with the discipline of the Church. Scriptural basis for the practice is claimed in the example and teaching of Christ, who spoke of leaving one's wife for his sake (Mk 10.29) or for the kingdom of God (Lk 18.29), thus indicating a special value to be found in virginity, as can be seen also in eschatological perspective in the statement that in the resurrection there will be no marriage (Mt 22.30). The calling to this state, however, was a special grace and vocation (Mt 19.11–12). Paul, although he wished all men to be in the same state as himself, also presented this as an individual charism (1 Cor 7.7).

Development of the Law of Celibacy. From the early days of the Church the inner affinity of religious celibacy and evangelical office made itself manifest. Many clerics chose to be unmarried or discontinued marital relationships after ordination. The earliest statutes, like that of Elvira (306), were not universal. The attempt to prescribe clerical celibacy as a law for the universal Church at Council of Nicaea I (325) did not succeed, but the council did forbid marriage after receiving higher orders according to what it described as the "ancient tradition of the Church." The situation in patristic times was complicated by the currency of a dualistic trend of thought, such as was manifest, e.g., in Encratism, which attacked the goodness of the married state and hence threatened to distort the authentic NT ideal of celibacy. In the East, the Trullan synod (691) enforced the rule that still prevails in principle in the Eastern Churches: married bishops had to separate from their wives; priests and deacons could marry only before ordination. In the West, the Church moved gradually toward the canonical obligation of clerical celibacy through the combined efforts of popes and regional councils. In practice, much of the legislation centered about the enforcement of continence for the married clergy. The rule of celibacy was a main point of the reform of Gregory VII (d. 1085), which was carried out without benefit of new legislation. The notion that the obligation to celibacy arises from a vow implicit in the reception of orders seems to have originated with this pontiff. A decisive step was taken when Lateran Council II (1139) declared that marriages of subdeacons, deacons, and priests after ordination were not only unlawful but invalid. Thenceforth, for the Latin Church, only those who freely accepted strict celibacy "for the sake of the kingdom of God" were to be admitted to higher office in the Church, and celibacy was established substantially unchanged in the Roman Catholic Church down to the present time.

Notwithstanding the fact that clerical celibacy was clearly a canonical obligation after Lateran II, the general observance of the law throughout the West was neither easily nor speedily secured. But consistent pressure and the application of severe penalties against priests practicing concubinage —after Lateran II all married priests could be so classified—brought about a fairly high level of compliance by the mid-13th century. There were scandalous exceptions, chiefly among the unbeneficed clergy, yet they were recognized almost everywhere as scandalous and exceptional.

From the Reformation to Vatican Council II. In the 2 centuries that preceded the Reformation an accumulation of troubles and disasters—among which were the Great Western Schism, the Black Death, the Hundred Years' War—led to a great decline in the morality of the clergy. In the face of this situation either of two courses could appeal to men seriously intent upon reform: mandatory celibacy could be abolished entirely, or a mighty effort could be made to bring about its general observance. The Protestant Reformers chose the first course; the Counter-Reformation the latter. Luther at first made no quarrel with priestly celibacy, but in 1523 he condemned the practice as a human institution. In this he was followed by the other Reformers. Thus obligatory celibacy was repudiated by the Augsburg Confession, the First and the Second Helvetic Confession, the Thirty-Nine Articles, and other confessional formulas. This decision was in part at least a consequence of the rejection of the Mass and much of the sacramental system of the old Church, a position that required them to take a new and largely desacralized view of the priestly office. The Council of Trent voiced the Counter-Reformation's insistence on the observance of celibacy. It reaffirmed the stand taken by Lateran II, but in so doing rejected the opinion of some extremists that marriage and the priestly office were incompatible by divine law. The council declared that the invalidating prohibition of marriage for clerics in major orders was based either on ecclesiastical law or on the vow implicit in the reception of orders, thus leaving open to dispute the question of the ultimate source of the obligation (see D 1809). More important perhaps in the long run for the future of celibacy in the RC Church than the council's reaffirmation of the position of Lateran II was its insistence upon the establishment of seminaries wherein candidates for the priesthood could receive proper training for their priestly work and an effective spiritual formation to prepare them for the obligations they would undertake. Gradually the seminaries did their work, and little by little the scandal of incontinence was overcome until at length it could be said that the clergy as a whole throughout the world were observing the law of celibacy with substantial fidelity.

Nevertheless, it cannot be reasonably claimed that RC priests have all been of one mind about the value and reasonableness of the obligation under which they live. No doubt some have accepted, or have continued in its observance, with some degree of unwillingness, but the actual prevalence of such sentiment down to recent times is difficult to estimate. That some disaffection existed is clear enough. Groups withdrawing from communion with Rome (e.g., the Old Catholics, the national Czechoslovak Church) have invariably repudiated celibacy as a requirement for their clergy. Individual priests defecting from clerical ranks quite commonly have done so with a view to marriage. But until recently defection statistics have been closely guarded secrets, and open discussion and writing in favor of the abrogation of celibacy were discouraged by ecclesiastical authority. Still there is evidence of recurrent agitation against celibacy to be gathered from official documents in which church authority has sought to quell opposition to the law. In the early 19th cent. an association was formed in Germany to advocate a change in the law, and Gregory XVI denounced

the move in his encyclical *Mirari vos* (1832); 14 years later Pius IX defended the law in his *Qui pluribus;* Pius X in *Pascendi* (1907) noted with disfavor the attempt of modernists to question the right of the Church to impose the obligation; Benedict XV in a consistorial allocution (1920) declared that the Church would not mitigate its discipline on this point. Under Pius XI a decree of the Congregation of the Sacraments required that every candidate for the priesthood take an oath in writing to attest that he was assuming the obligation freely and with full knowledge of what he was doing, and the same Pope made a point of celibacy in his *Ad catholici sacerdotii* (1935). Despite the efforts of the Holy See, agitation continued. It was apparent in the German reform program *Der Katholizismus der Zukunft* published anonymously in 1940, and it has gained force and come much more into the open since that time.

Current Discussions. No discussion of the problem of celibacy as a whole was permitted at Vatican Council II. After the council, however, those eager to press forward with the work of reform have included celibacy among the established institutions and practices they think should be questioned. In the new climate of dialogue, ecclesiastical authority, esp. at local and regional levels, has been hesitant—or perhaps unable—to stifle discussion. In any case, the pastoral problems raised by the scarcity of vocations, coupled with an unprecedented increase in the number of priests giving up their ministry, has caused the celibacy issue to clamor for attention. Other factors contributing to the increasing criticism of celibacy include: the attention concentrated by the debate about contraception on the excellence of the married state and the highlighting of values realized in sexual activity; the readiness of many contemporary personalists to see marriage as necessary to an individual's fulfillment; and the veering of certain theologians toward a less sacralized view of the priestly ministry and a new definition of the role and function of the priest in contemporary society. Moreover, some have probably been encouraged by recent apparent mitigations in the Church's discipline in this matter to think that an ultimate modification of the law is possible. For example, Vatican Council II approved of a restoration of the permanent diaconate, and the norms of its restoration, as published by Pope Paul VI (1967), permit in certain circumstances the reception of married men to that order. Popes Pius XII, John XXIII, and Paul VI have granted dispensations to married ministers converted to Catholicism permitting them to receive Catholic orders without separating from their wives. The Church has also shown greater indulgence in recent times in granting laicized priests permission to marry.

In the face of the widespread and sometimes obstreperous criticism of the law, Paul VI in 1967 published his encyclical *Sacerdotalis celibatus,* in which he reaffirmed the position taken by Lateran II and Trent, pointed to the values of celibacy raised against it, and denied that the exceptions admitted in the contemporary practice of the Church represent a weakening of the ideal or a true mitigation of the law itself. The encyclical, however, far from quieting the debate, served rather to intensify it. There was protest and denunciation from those already firm in their opposition. In the U.S. an organization was formed to promote the cause of optional rather than mandatory celibacy for priests. This organization, which took the name National Association for Pastoral Renewal (NAPR), at first operated with some degree of secrecy but later came out into the open, and its membership, advisory board, and activities are now known to the public. Among other things, it conducted a survey of opinion among RC priests regarding their views on celibacy; it arranged a National Symposium on Clerical Celibacy (Sept. 6–8, 1967), and it has been urging the National Conference of Bishops to make a study of the problem. Organizations of the same type in other countries, notably in Holland, have been engaging in similar activity. Latterly there has been a notable decline in the attacks on celibacy on the part of RC priests, which may be due in part at least to the numerous defections from the priesthood among those who were most antagonistic to celibacy and most vocal in their opposition. BIBLIOGRAPHY: Pope Paul VI, *Encyclical Letter on Priestly Celibacy* (USCC, 1967); for canon law of, J. W. Rehage, NCE 3:481–488; for history of, P. Delehaye, NCE 369–374; E. Vacandard, DTC 2.2:2068–88; H. Thurston, CE 3:481–488; G. H. Frein, *Celibacy: The Necessary Option* (1968); J. Blenkinsopp, *Celibacy, Ministry, Church* (1968); *Celibacy in the Church* (*Concilium* 78, ed. W. W. Bassett and P. J. Huizing, pa. 1972).

[J. B. MORRIS]

CELIBACY, CLERICAL (IN THE EASTERN CHURCHES).

The praise of virginity in the NT led to the practice of voluntary clerical celibacy in the Christian East. It became obligatory first for married bishops (5th cent.), who were required to separate from their wives. It was decreed that deacons and priests could continue a marriage contracted before ordination but they were not to be permitted to marry after ordination, even if they should become widowers (Council *In Trullo*, 691). This rule is still observed in all Eastern Orthodox Churches. Celibate candidates are not ordained unless they profess monastic vows. Only the Nestorians permit widowed priests and deacons to marry after laicization. The demands of widowed priests in various Orthodox Churches to remarry and remain in the clergy were successfully repelled by the hierarchy. So far as priests and deacons are concerned, the rule regarding clerical celibacy may be stated thus: with the exception of priests who have become widowers after ordination, there is no obligation to celibacy apart from that connected with monastic vows.

The canonical discipline among the Eastern Catholic Churches is identical with that of their Orthodox counterparts, with these exceptions: (1) Celibate candidates can become secular priests without entering the monastic state. (2) The Chaldeans have not followed the Nestorians in

permitting widowed priests to remarry. (3) All groups favor celibacy in various degrees. Celibacy is the rule for all candidates among the Malabars. Married men may be admitted to orders with a dispensation from the bp. or patriarch among the Ethiopians, Syrians, and Copts. Although there is no law enjoining celibacy, all candidates are unmarried among the Greeks, Italo-Albanians, Ruthenians, and Ukrainians of North America. The majority are celibates and religious among the Melkites and Maronites. Among the Rumanians, Croats, and others in Yugoslavia, the Slovaks and Ruthenians in Europe, the Armenians, Chaldeans, and Magyars (Hungary), the majority are married. Most of the married Byzantine Catholic clergy in North America were ordained in Europe. Only recently have there been ordinations of married men in Canada who had done their theological studies in the Western Ukraine. BIBLIOGRAPHY: J. W. Rehage, NCE 3:368–369 s.v. "Oriental Churches."

[V. J. POSPISHIL]

CELL (MONASTIC), the monk's private place, where he prays, reads, meditates, studies, and sleeps. At certain periods cenobites, living a more common life, did without cells properly so called. When their common dormitory was partitioned to give some privacy during sleep, these divisions were called cells. For *hermits the cell is something set apart from a monastery, and is also used for eating and working. For the semieremitical groups (e.g., the Carthusians, Camaldolese), cells are usually little cottages of several rooms, gathered within the monastery enclosure, where the monks spend most of their time in seclusion. But for most cenobites the cell is a small room, simply furnished; the monks still share with their brothers the common refectory, library, etc., and go regularly to the monastic church for liturgical prayer. BIBLIOGRAPHY: A. de Vogüé, "Comment les moines dormiront," *Studia Monastica* 7 (1965) 38–62; J. Leclercq, "Pour une spiritualité de la cellule," *Collectanea Cisterciensia* 31 (1969) 74–82.

[M. B. PENNINGTON]

CELLARER, an official in a monastery, originally in charge of wine and spirits, who came in later times to be assigned the duties of procurator or bursar in many monasteries.

[S. F. JOHNSON]

CELLES-SUR-BELLE, MONASTERY OF, a monastic institution founded in the early 11th cent. by Augustinian Canons and raised to abbatial rank in 1140. Located near Melle in the diocese of Poitiers in France, it was a center for pilgrimages, esp. in the 14th and 15th cent., because of the fame of its miracles. The chief pilgrimage, the *Septembresch*, honored annually the Nativity of the Virgin Mother, and this celebration was revived in 1926. The monastery suffered greatly in attacks made upon it by Huguenots and by powerful families struggling to acquire its income. It became a Benedictine house, a member of the Congregation of

France (1651), and its church and cloisters were restored. It was suppressed in 1791. Its buildings now serve as a novitiate for the Montfort Fathers who are charged with the care of the local parish.

CELLINI, BENVENUTO (1500–71), greatest of the Italian Renaissance goldsmiths and sculptor of somewhat lesser distinction. C. worked throughout Italy, executed the Rospigliosi Cup of gold and enamel, and the famous salt-cellar of extreme grace and virtuosity for Francis I at Fontainebleau. It was here, with Primaticcio, that C. established Mannerism as the dominant style of 16th-cent. France. C. achieved amazing skill in bronze casting, and though his *Perseus* is inferior to work of G. *Bologna, he influenced the French sculptor J. Goujon. BIBLIOGRAPHY: J. Pope-Hennessy, *Italian High Renaissance and Baroque Sculpture* (3 v., 1963).

[M. J. DALY]

CELLITES, see ALEXIAN BROTHERS.

CELSUS (2d half of 2d cent. A.D.), Middle Platonist and the most important pagan intellectual opponent of Christianity before Porphyry. His Middle Platonism is similar to that of *Albinus. He stressed the utter transcendence of God, and to bridge the gulf between God and the world he admitted demons, angels, and heroes as intermediaries. His attack upon Christianity in his *True Discourse* (c.178) can be largely reconstructed from the extracts and arguments found in Origen's *Contra Celsum*. He showed a marked familiarity with the OT and NT and with Christian doctrines in general—but without distinguishing carefully between Jewish, Christian, heretical, and Gnostic teachings. He ridiculed the Christian concept of God as an absolute Creator, and he ridiculed the Incarnation and Crucifixion. He regarded the Christians as unpatriotic and a threat to the venerable tradition of Hellenism. Origen regarded Celsus' attack so important that he wrote his own answer to it nearly 70 years later (246). Celsus' arguments against Christianity were resumed by Porphyry and the Emperor Julian. BIBLIOGRAPHY: M. R. P. McGuire, NCE 3:382; C. Andresen, *Logos und Nomos: Die Polemik des Celsus wider das Christentum* (1955); P. de Labriolle, *La Réaction païenne* (6th ed., 1942) 109–169.

[M. R. P. MCGUIRE]

CELSUS AND NAZARIUS, SS., according to tradition, companions martyred in Milan in the 1st cent. A.D. Nazarius was the son of a Christian mother and pagan father. He left Rome to preach as a disciple of the Apostles and took with him the youthful Celsus. Their bodies were discovered in Rome by St. Ambrose c.395 and buried in his church, the Church of the Apostles. BIBLIOGRAPHY: Butler 3:200–201; A. Amore, BiblSanct 9:780–784.

[J. R. AHERNE]

CELTIC ART, distinctive art of the Celtic peoples known chiefly in highly stylized, powerful sculpture, in metalwork (weapons and armor, vessels of all kinds—notably ritual cauldrons, flagons, pails, brooches, mirrors, and horse-trappings), and in pottery. This art evolved in the Alpine homeland of the Celts (6th and 5th cent. B.C.), stimulated by strong influences from Greek, Etruscan, and Oriental art. The early phase (6th–4th cent. B.C.) is known as the Hallstatt period, followed (4th cent. B.C. onwards) by the La Tène period which in Britain attained distinctive expression 150 B.C.–50 A.D. A favorite theme is stylized geometric scrollwork of spirals embossed or engraved, often with foliate or animal elements. The revival of Celtic Christian art (A.D. 450) reached a peak in the metalwork and glorious gospel books of *Irish art (A.D. 700). BIBLIOGRAPHY: R. L. S. Bruce-Mitford, NCE 3:382.

[R. L. S. BRUCE-MITFORD]

CELTIC CHURCH, Christianity as it existed among the Celts of Britain in its earliest centuries there, sometimes called the British Church. It is distinguished from the pattern closer to Roman usage brought by St. Augustine of Canterbury and his successors. Christianity was apparently established in England by 200, and the country was represented at the Synod of Arles (314) by three bishops. With the Anglo-Saxon invasions of the 5th cent., the Celts were pushed into Cornwall, Wales, and Ireland. The Scottish Church also, largely converted from Ireland (St. Columba), is considered Celtic up to the reforms of St. Margaret (c.1070). Augustine failed to secure the submission of the Celtic bps. at a meeting in 603, and while he worked for the conversion of Anglo-Saxon England from Canterbury, Celts such as St. Aidan worked in the north. At the Synod of *Whitby (664) Roman usage was victorious, and the authority of Canterbury and Rome increased in the years following. Traces of Celtic independence continued to exist during the period of the *Anglo-Saxon Church, however. BIBLIOGRAPHY: J. Bulloch, *Life of the Celtic Church* (1963); J. T. McNeil, *Celtic Churches: A History, A.D. 200–700* (1974); K. Hughes, *Church of Early Irish Society* (1967).

[T. EARLY]

CELTIC RELIGION, traces of which have been found from Ireland to Asia Minor, was basically a form of nature worship. Dominated by anthropomorphic chief deities, it abounded in cults of minor divinities also. Greek and Roman authorities, from the 3d cent. B.C. on, including Julius Caesar, clouded the picture by providing the names of their own deities in substitution for those of Celtic gods. Thus, we know that Celts worshiped gods resembling Apollo, Mars, Jupiter, Mercury, and Minerva, but we are not always sure which Celtic epithet refers to which. The sun-god Apollo, usually called Belenus, is identified with Abellio in S France and with Grannus in the valleys of the Rhine and the Danube. He is the god of healing and of springs. Jupiter is known as

Taranis, Esus (possibly derived from Sanskrit *Asu*, chief god). Both Jupiter and Mars are referred to as Teutates. Ogma corresponds to Heracles, also god of eloquence; images of the horse-goddess Epona are numerous in W Hungary. Modern Lyons derives its name from the phrase, "town of Lug," Lugdunum. Suleviae, mountain nymphs, were frequent in the Roman provinces of Pannonia and Dacia, which abound in place-names of Celtic origin. Budapest was originally settled by Celts; the Latin name of Budapest, Aquincum, derives from the Celtic *Akh-Inkh*, meaning "abundant waters" and referring to the many healing springs to be found there. Mother goddesses (*matronae*, or *matres*), the French *vierges noires*, represent mothers with children on their knees; they are the genii, defenders of families, districts, and castles. There is a British Mars, Beletucadrus, with a consort called Nemetona or Nemon. In Ireland, where Celtic religion was preserved from admixture of Roman elements, recent research unearthed many previously unknown myths and legends. The father and mother of all gods, Addai and Anna, founded the divine dynasties. Ogma, whose name means "of the shining face" and "of the honeyed lips", is noteworthy as the ancestor of Prydain, first legendary king of Britain. Heroic myths center around Cuchulainn and his circle, Fionn and Feinn, and Arthur. Cuchulainn is of the "branch" of Dana, the great mother, goddess of life and death; through her one-legged horse, she may be connected with moon-cults and horse-cults as distant in space and time as India and the ancient Scythians of the Black Sea region. Celts venerated mistletoe, certain trees, trolls, mountains, rivers, springs and remote open spaces. Cultic traces survive to show a veneration of bulls, horses, boars, and bears. Celtic religion was rich in tales of the *Sid*-folk, or fairies, dwelling under hills. In addition to such magic practices as spells, curses, and taboos, there is evidence of a belief in life beyond the grave and possibly even in the transmigration of the soul. Some of the tenets of the Celtic religion have survived to this day in neo-Druidic cults—esp. in the U.S. BIBLIOGRAPHY: J. Rhys, *Celtic Britain* (1904); A. Machain, *Celtic Mythology and Religion* (1917); J. G. Frazer, *Golden Bough*, part 7 (1935–36); J. A. MacCulloch, Hastings ERE 3:277–304.

[D. H. BRUNAUER]

CELTIC RITE, a name given not so much to a single uniform rite as to a variety of rites or eclectic collections of liturgical practices used in the ancient churches of Ireland, England, and Wales, and by the Celtic missionary monks elsewhere. The rite was Gallican in its main characteristics but was much modified by local and, increasingly as time went on, by Roman influences. The principal sources of information about it are the Bangor Antiphonary (7th cent.), the Bobbio Missal (7th cent.), and the Stowe Missal (8th or 9th cent.). The rite was marked by its difference in determining the date of Easter and the manner of administering baptism. The chalice was prepared before Mass, a litany and other prayers were inserted between the reading of the epistle and gospel, and there was a commemoration of the dead and a reading of the diptychs before the preface. BIBLIOGRAPHY: A. A. King, *Liturgies of the Past* (1959); L. C. Sheppard, NCE 3:384–385.

[N. KOLLAR]

CELTIS, CONRAD (Bickel; 1459–1508), the "archhumanist" of Germany. After studies at Cologne, Heidelberg, and in Italy, C. was crowned poet laureate by Emperor Frederick III in 1487. He founded various literary sodalities (*Sodalitas Vistulana, Sodalitas literaria Hungarorum, Sodalitas Danubiana, Sodalitas Rhenana*) and gave impetus to humanism in Germany. He discovered and published (1501) the writings of Roswitha of Gandersheim. BIBLIOGRAPHY: L. W. Spitz, *Conrad Celtis, the German Arch-Humanist* (1957).

[S. A. SCHULZ]

CEMETERY, a word deriving from the Gr. *koimeterion* (a sleeping place or chamber, a burial ground for the dead). From earliest Christian times Christians have favored burial in the ground or entombment of the body, sometimes in a church itself or in a burial ground used by other Christians. In present-day practice in the RC Church, where Catholics are sufficiently numerous to have a cemetery of their own in any locality, they do so; such a burial ground may be consecrated, except for portions of it set aside for the burial of non-Catholics and of Catholics who for specific offenses committed during their lifetime and for which they manifested no repentance before death are denied the right of Christian burial. When Catholics have no cemetery of their own, they may be buried in general cemeteries but it is usual to bless the individual grave into which the body is lowered. Often, because of the complications arising from mixed marriages and other causes, Catholic cemeteries are not consecrated in the strict sense of the term, but the individual gravesites are simply blessed as in the case of the burial of Catholics in general cemeteries.

CENACLE, a second-story room of a building built on a site in Jerusalem venerated as the place of the Last Supper (Lk 22.12). An Israeli shrine of King David's tomb (based on a late tradition) occupies the first floor. It is located on the Hill of Sion to the SW of the present walls of Old Jerusalem. The most ancient traditions of the place associate it with the descent of the Spirit at Pentecost; *Epiphanius preserves information about a small church located there in the 2d cent., built on the spot of the upper room mentioned in Acts 1.13. The first association of the place with the Last Supper occurs in a Syriac text of the 4th cent.; after some hesitation, this tradition became firmly established in the 7th century. Around this time there also appears the first evidence of an actual "upper room" constructed on the site (apart from the original room of Acts 1.13, if it was located here). After several reconstructions, the Cenacle was given over to the perpetual care of the Franciscans in the 14th cent.; they then gave the building its present form as primarily a shrine of the Last Supper, with a smaller adjoining room which commemorates the events of Pentecost. BIBLIOGRAPHY: C. Kopp, *Holy Places of the Gospels* (1963).

[P. J. KEARNEY]

CENACLE, RELIGIOUS OF THE, a congregation of women religious founded in France in 1826 by Fr. Etienne Terme and Bl. Marie Victoire Thérèse Couderc. Its formation was in imitation of the first retreat in the supper room (*coenaculum*) where Our Lady and the Apostles met in prayer before Pentecost. The community is both contemplative and active, and its constitutions are based on the Rule of St. Ignatius of Loyola. In 1892 it was established in the U.S., and by 1964 the congregation had spread throughout the world with a membership of 1,500 sisters who administered 71 retreat houses for women. BIBLIOGRAPHY: H. M. Lynch, *In the Shadow of Our Lady of the Cenacle* (1941); L. Le Moine, *Catholicisme* 2:789–790.

[R. A. TODD]

CENCI, a notorious Roman family of the Renaissance, chiefly remembered because of a famous instance of patricide. The persons involved in the case were Francesco Cenci (1549–98) and his daughter Beatrice (1577–99). Francesco, a dissolute and violent man, not only alienated his other children but even imprisoned and maltreated Beatrice and his second wife, Lucrezia Petroni. The consequence was a family plot to murder the father. Though his death was designed to appear accidental, the truth was soon discovered. Clement VIII refused clemency. Beatrice, Lucrezia, and Francesco's eldest son, Giacomo, were executed and the family property confiscated. Beatrice's death excited the compassion of her fellow citizens, who were ignorant of the facts and considered her a martyr. BIBLIOGRAPHY: H. Lutz, LTK 2:991–992; R. O. Ausenda, EncCatt 3:1289–90.

[D. G. NUGENT]

CENNINI, CENNINO (c. 1370–1440), Florentine painter, important as author of *Il libro dell'arte* (The Craftsman's Handbook), stating the aims, methods, and technical aspects of Florentine painting. Thoroughly medieval in attitude, C. holds that the painter makes religious images in piety for his own delight, in a manner traditionally and conventionally prescribed, and more important for craft than for originality. He is the first to explain the tempera technique and discusses mosaic, fresco, stained glass, and the making of casts. BIBLIOGRAPHY: D. V. Thompson, *Practice of Tempera Painting* (1936).

[M. J. DALY]

CENOBITE, a word derived from two Greek words meaning common life. It designates a monk, or one who lives in community, as contrasted with a hermit living separately from others. The cenobitic model originated in the Eastern Church under regulations composed by St. Pachomius in the 4th century. St. Basil the Great gave Eastern monasticism its complete form. In the Western Church St. Augustine, among others, lived in a community, but it was St. Benedict in the 6th century whose rule became the predominant one for Western monks.

[J. R. AHERNE]

CENOBITIC MONASTICISM (Gr. *koinos bios,* common life), the form of monasticism in which the monks lead a community life. It began in Egypt under St. *Pachomius in the early 4th century. The self-sacrifice involved in obedience to the religious superior assumed a primary role among the ascetical practices of the monk. Cenobitism, with its common prayer and service, became the model followed by most monks down to the present time. St. Basil the Great, whose *Asceticons* contributed substantially to monastic legislation, insisted that for most monks the path to salvation and union with God could better be followed by leading a life of asceticism in a community and under the direction of a superior than by living in a state of solitude. In the early 9th cent. St. Theodore the Studite reaffirmed the value of the monastic community, stressing the responsibilities of the monks in matters of personal and liturgical prayer, manual labor, and poverty. In this St. Theodore was not an innovator, but a reformer striving to get rid of the laxity that characterized much monastic practice at the time. St. Simeon, the New Theologian, continued the Studite tradition. The monasticism exemplified on Mt. Athos and in Slavic monasteries illustrates cenobitism, and it is also practiced in Cistercian monasteries and many Benedictine monasteries in Western Christianity. BIBLIOGRAPHY: H. Leclercq, DACL 2.2:3047–3248.

[S. SURRENCY]

CENSER, container used for burning incense over hot coals, used in rituals since ancient times. It is mentioned frequently in the Bible (e.g., Ex 27.3; 1 Kg 7.50; Rev 8.3, 5). It was introduced into the Christian liturgy about the 4th century. In its present form it is usually covered and suspended from one or more chains.

[T. CRANE]

CENSOR OF BOOKS (*censor librorum*), ecclesiastical official appointed to judge the soundness of a book dealing with faith or morals before publication. The Roman censors, charged initially with the census, became also guardians of public morality. RC canon law (CIC c. 1393) requires appointment from among the clergy, secular and religious, of competent official censors. The censor of any work must base his judgment on objective norms of Catholic teaching, not on his private preferences; he may also judge on the timeliness of any work. The censor's evaluation is submitted to the bishop in writing; a favorable decision, the *nihil obstat,* is sent to the author with the *imprimatur* and the name of the censor. Before the *nihil obstat* is granted, the censor's name may not be divulged. In religious communities censors for works by members of the community are also appointed. *PRECENSORSHIP.

CENSORSHIP, the process by which public authority, civil or ecclesiastical, restricts the dissemination of printed material and the activities of the media of communication (radio, TV, the motion pictures). This is not to be confused with criticism, even highly organized criticism, for the essence of censorship lies in the power of the authority to enforce its controls. In the RC Church the competence, and sometimes the duty, of civil authority to impose controls whenever the common good demands them has always been recognized. For its own members the Church exercises such control by demanding that books that deal explicitly with faith or morals be submitted to ecclesiastical preview (*PRECENSORSHIP) before publication, and although the Roman *Index of Forbidden Books was abolished in 1966, individual bishops can forbid the reading of individual books. It is to be noted that any such curtailment, civil or ecclesiastical, is to be exercised to the minimum extent necessary to the protection of the common good. The presumption is always in favor of freedom, which is to be restricted only in order to safeguard a great good. BIBLIOGRAPHY: H. C. Gardiner, *Catholic Viewpoint on Censorship* (1958), esp. app. 2, "Statement of the U.S. Bishops on Censorship."

[H. C. GARDINER]

CENSURE, ECCLESIASTICAL, a penalty inflicted by ecclesiastical law on a person for the commission of a crime or delict to which a specific punishment is attached.

Censures fall into two general classes. Those called *latae sententiae* censures are incurred *ipso facto* by the commission of the act to which the penalty is attached. Others, known as *ferendae sententiae* censures, are incurred if competent ecclesiastical authority inflicts them when the violation of the law or precept becomes known. After their infliction censures of this latter kind are said to be *ab homine,* because their incurrence has come not directly and immediately from the law, but from an ecclesiastical superior who has used the authority conferred upon him by the law to inflict them.

A censure supposes the penalized individual to have been delinquent and contumacious in his violation of the law, and it is not incurred when certain extenuating circumstances, such as the force of passion or ignorance of the penalty attached to the law, diminish his responsibility or the contumacy of his transgression.

Censures *ab homine* may be absolved only by the ecclesiastical superior who inflicted them, or by his superior or successor, or by one specially delegated to absolve from them. *Latae sententiae* censures, if their absolution is not reserved to any particular ecclesiastical superior, may be absolved by any confessor when the penitent expresses sorrow for them. But in the case of some *latae sententiae* censures the law reserves the right to grant absolution to certain designated superiors, e.g., to the local ordinary, or to

the Holy See. In cases of emergency, as when one is in danger of death, or when absolution is urgently needed and the delay involved in appealing to the proper superior would be difficult to bear, absolution may be granted by a simple confessor, but in this case the confessor enjoins the penitent to submit the case to the Sacred Penitentiary, or to someone having the power to absolve; usually the confessor undertakes to do this for the penitent. Absolution granted in danger of death does not require submission of the case to higher authority in the event of the penitent's recovery except in cases of censures *ab homine* and censures reserved in a most special way to the Holy See.

A censure penalizes the contumacious transgressor of the law by depriving him of certain spiritual goods—e.g., the right to share in the public prayers of the Church; the right to assist at divine worship; the right to perform certain ecclesiastical functions or to exercise acts of orders or of jurisdiction. It may also deprive him of certain temporal goods connected with spiritual privileges, e.g., revenues attached to ecclesiastical offices and benefices.

Censures may be either excommunications, suspensions, or personal interdicts. But suspensions and interdicts are only properly classified as censures when they are medicinal rather than vindictive penalties. BIBLIOGRAPHY: CIC cc. 2241–90.

[P. K. MEAGHER]

CENSURE, THEOLOGICAL, an unfavorable judgment made by ecclesiastical authority upon propositions or statements held to be detrimental in some way to faith or morals. Since medieval times these condemnations have been expressed in terms that indicate the degree or measure in which the proscribed doctrine stands, or appears to stand, opposed to Catholic teaching. Thus, a theological censure may fall into one of three main categories: heretical, erroneous, or rash (temerarious). A heretical proposition is one that manifestly contradicts a defined dogma of faith. Annexed to this classification, but lacking its full force, is the qualification of a proposition as close to heresy *(haeresi proxima),* or as savoring of heresy *(haeresim sapiens),* or as suspect of heresy *(suspecta de haeresi).* The categorization of a doctrine as erroneous means that it stands opposed to common Catholic doctrine or the common teaching of theologians. Subspecies of this classification may be made which are analogous to those attached to the category of heresy. Rash propositions are those not necessarily opposed either to faith or the common teaching of the Church, but which are nevertheless regarded as objectionable for any of a number of reasons, e.g., because they are ambiguous and hence subject to false interpretation, or because they are false-sounding or offensive to pious ears *(male sonans* or *piarum aurium offensiva),* or derisive of religion or civil society, or because they pose a threat to Church unity, or the general social good, or to sound moral practice in general. A censure has weight and authority depending on the source from which it originates.

[P. K. MEAGHER]

CENSUS (IN THE BIBLE), the enrollment of the Israelites according to tribe, family, and lineage. The first recorded census in Israel, that of David (2 Sam 24.1–9; 1 Chr 21.1–5), was carried out for purposes of military organization, taxation, and probably also the recruitment of forced labor (cf. 1 Sam 8.10–18; 2 Sam 20.24; 24.9). The abandonment of the older military system, relying on volunteer forces in time of emergency (e.g., Jg 5), was for a time understood as an insult to God's protective power and hence a sin punishable even by plague (2 Sam 24.10–17; cf. also Ex 30.12). Shortly after the Babylonian exile, new purposes for a census emerged. The numbering of those newly returned from captivity (Ezra 2 and Neh 7) was apparently carried out to establish legal authorization for the resettlement of Israel and for the work of reconstruction (Ezra 5.3–4; Neh 7.61–65); the subsequent census of Nehemiah was most likely directed to an efficient distribution of the population (Neh 7.4–5; 11). In the late writings of the priesthood tradition, the old attitude is so changed that God himself is said to command a census (Num 1.2), even after a plague (Num 26.2); these two lists, although linked with Moses (Num 1 and 26), are probably based on the document of the census conducted under David; the numerical variations between them express the changing historical importance of the tribes. The highly inflated numbers are probably due to a post-exilic confusion about the Hebrew word meaning both "thousand" and a tribal "subsection" from which soldiers were recruited. An appended census of the Levites (Num 3–4) seems to be largely artificial, based on the genealogy of Ex 6 (cf. also Num 1.49).

The census of the "whole world" at the time of Christ's birth (Lk 2.1–2) remains an unsolved historical problem, since it seems to conflict with nonbiblical records. It is possible that a certain freedom with history, characteristic of Lk 1–2, has permitted the author to transform a later census conducted by Quirinius into an earlier universal census, thus highlighting the importance of the birth of Christ for world history. BIBLIOGRAPHY: S. C. Doyle, NCE 3:396–397; A. N. Sherwin-White, *Roman Society and Roman Law in the N.T.* (1963) 162–171.

[P. J. KEARNEY]

CENTENERA, MARTÍN DEL BARCO, see BARCO CENTENERA, MARTÍN DEL.

CENTER PARTY (*die Zentrumspartei*), a political party established in Germany in 1870 by Catholics fighting Bismarck's *Kulturkampf*. It played an important role in Germany continuously until the rise of Hitler.

CENTONIZATION, a process whereby musical works are derived from selections of other works. Gregory I compiled an *antiphonarius cento,* i.e., a combination and revision of earlier texts for the sung parts of the Mass.

[D. J. SMUCKER]

CENTRAL CONFERENCE (Methodist), a *jurisdictional conference outside the territory of the U.S. *CONFERENCE (METHODIST).

CENTURIATORS OF MAGDEBURG, the authors of *Historia Ecclesiae Christi* (1559–74), which is also called the *Magdeburg Centuries, a Lutheran, apologetical church history divided by centuries. The principal "centuriator" was M. *Flacius Illyricus, who conceived the plan for the work.

[T. C. O'BRIEN]

CENTURION, the commander of a *centuria,* the smallest unit of the Roman army generally consisting of 100 men. In the NT, centurions are mentioned in Mt 8.5–13; 27.54; Mk 15.39, 44–45; Lk 7.2–10; 23.47; Acts 10.1–48 (Cornelius); 22.25–26; 24.23; 27.1–44 (Julius).

[J. J. O'ROURKE]

CEOLFRID OF WEARMOUTH, ST. (642–716) abbot. A Benedictine monk of the dual foundation which included the later monastery at Jarrow, C. was a member of the Saxon nobility. After serving as prior and deputy to the abbot St. Benedict Biscop he succeeded the latter as abbot in 690. C. did much to enlarge the monastic libraries of both houses. After resigning as abbot he went to Rome to present the pope with the *Codex Amiatinus* written in his monastery and containing the oldest text of the Vulgate of St. Jerome.

[J. R. AHERNE]

CEPEDA, FRANCISCO (1532–1602), Spanish Dominican missionary. Sent to Chiapas in Guatemala before 1560, he became prior at Zacapula, provincial (1593), definitor at four provincial chapters, and commissary of the Holy Office. He compiled a simplified grammar of local Indian languages. BIBLIOGRAPHY: F. Ximénez, *Historia de la provincia de San Vicente de Chiapa y Guatemala de la Orden de predicadores (3 v., 1929–31).*

[R. I. BURNS]

CEPEDA ÁLVAREZ, FÉLIX ALEJANDRO (1854–1930), Claretian missionary, theologian. A native of Chile, C. was ordained a diocesan priest (1876) but 12 years later entered the Sons of the Immaculate Heart of Mary (Claretians) in Santiago. He first worked in Spain where he became provincial superior of Catalonia (1895–1902) and was later sent to head the vice-province of Mexico (1902–18). Though his writings include 20 volumes, he was still an active administrator and was responsible for the founding of a number of new houses for his congregation. His last years were spent in Madrid where he served the congregation as general consultor. BIBLIOGRAPHY: R. A. Squadrilli, EncCatt 3:1307–08.

[J. J. SMITH]

CEPHALICUS, a particular notational sign used in the

medieval period for writing down plainsong. It is a special *neume that indicates both the tone and the manner of singing it. The *cephalicus* occurs where the text has two consonants in succession and indicates that a smooth vocal transition should be made by interpolating an *e* vocal. For example, "Christus" would be sung as "Chris (e) tus".

[D. J. SMUCKER]

CERBONIUS, ST. (d. *c.*574), bp. of Populonia. According to two accounts, neither dating from before the 7th cent., C., a companion of St. Regulus, fled from Vandal persecution in Africa, settled on the Tuscan coast, and was chosen bp. of Populonia. The Vandal persecution in question cannot be identified, and it may be that C. was a native of Populonia and not a refugee from Africa. Better attested is the earlier account given by Gregory the Great in his *Dialogues* (PL 77:237–240)—he claimed that eyewitnesses were still alive when he wrote who would vouch for the story—that when Totila the Ostrogoth ordered C. exposed to hungry bears in punishment for harboring Roman soldiers, the beasts became gentle and would do him no harm. C. died on the island of Elba, where he had taken refuge from the Lombards. BIBLIOGRAPHY: S. De Paoli, BiblSanct 3:1130–31; Butler 4:80.

[P. K. MEAGHER]

CERDO (2d cent.), Gnostic teacher who taught in Rome (*c.*140) and is known only through the writings of SS. Irenaeus, Epiphanius and Hippolytus. From these sources it seems that C.'s teachings are reflected in those of *Marcion, his disciple. C. did not found a sect. BIBLIOGRAPHY: G. Bareille, DTC 2:2138–39, with patristic texts.

[T. C. O'BRIEN]

CEREAL OFFERING, a Hebrew grain offering to God made up of fried or baked grits, flour, cake, or bread (Lev 2.1–16). Frankincense and olive oil were poured over these offerings; part was burned as a token to God, and the remainder was eaten by the priests. Salt was used for seasoning; the use of fermented foods such as honey or leaven was forbidden. BIBLIOGRAPHY: De Vaux AncIsr 421–422.

[F. J. MONTALBANO]

CERECLOTH or chrismale, a cloth waxed on one side, formerly placed beneath the three altar cloths. If accidentally the Precious Blood was spilled, it was absorbed by the three cloths and wax prevented its seeping into the altar stone.

[S. F. JOHNSON]

CEREMONIES, CONGREGATION OF, former congregation of the *Curia Romana, in charge of papal and cardinalatial ceremonies and also of matters of diplomatic protocol. The congregation dated from the 16th century. The apostolic constitution *Regimini ecclesiae universae* reorganizing the Roman Curia in 1967 abolished this congregation; some of its functions were assumed by the papal Secretariat of State; there is also an office of the curia in its new form called the Office for Papal Ceremonies

CEREMONY (CEREMONIAL), the English word derived from the Latin *caeremonia,* a word of uncertain but probably Etruscan provenance. In its original Latin use it had both an objective and a subjective meaning: objectively it signified the sacredness of the divinity or what pertains to the divinity; subjectively (and more commonly) it signified the feeling of awe and holy fear experienced by the worshiper in his approach to the deity. Thence by metonymy it was applied to the sacred rites associated with the worship. In English usage the term is also applied to the formal acts expressive of respect or honor to persons of high rank or to others as required by social custom. But in its strictly religious sense it signifies the formal outward expression of the worship of God or of reverence to things that pertain to God. It is realized esp. in liturgical prayer (the Mass, the administration of the sacraments, the Liturgy of the Hours) but it also extends to other set forms of external acts that are not properly speaking liturgical. If we wish to distinguish ceremony (and ceremonial) from rite (and ritual), we might say that ceremony puts more stress on external acts (e.g., gesture and the like), while rite spells out in more specific detail the formulas of prayer that are to be employed, as, e.g., in the *Roman Ritual.* But the difference is at best an overlapping one, for in practice rituals concern themselves with external acts of worship, and ceremonials rarely omit reference to specific formulas of prayer.

[P. K. MEAGHER]

CEREZO, MATEO (*c.*1626–66), Spanish painter. Influenced by Murillo, Velasquez, Titian, and Rubens, C. painted ecstasies and passions with a pathos often vapid (*Ecce Homo,* Budapest; *The Assumption,* Madrid). A promising talent who died young, he marked the late flourishing of Spain's Baroque Golden Age. BIBLIOGRAPHY: G. Kubler and M. Soria, *Art and Architecture in Spain and Portugal (1500–1800)* (1959).

[M. J. DALY]

CERINTHUS, (fl. *c.* A.D. 100), an early Gnostic of W Asia Minor. Irenaeus (*Heresies* 1.26) said he taught the world was not made by the primary God but by a certain power far separated from him, that Jesus was the merely human son of Mary and Joseph upon whom at his baptism the Christ descended, but left him before the crucifixion, so that the Christ, a spiritual being, remained impassible. Epiphanius (*Heresies* 38) makes him a Jewish Christian heretic, the great opponent first of Paul, then of John, and adds that he wrote a gospel (not extant). The statements of Epiphanius are quite dubious. The *Epistle of the Apostles* lists him with Simon Magus as one of two false apostles. BIBLIOGRAPHY: G. Bardy, RevBibl 30 (1921) 344–373; E. Peterson, EncCatt 3:1319–20.

[W. G. MOST]

CERIOLI, COSTANZA, BL. (1816–65), religious foundress. C. belonged to the petty nobility of Bergamo. In 1835 she married a wealthy widower; they had three children, all of whom died in their youth. In 1854, after the death of her husband, C. gave her wealth and vitality to the service of the less fortunate, esp. to the care of orphaned peasant children, opening her own home to the girls among them. In order to continue her work, she founded the Sisters of the Holy Family of Bergamo and took the name Paola Elisabetta. Soon after, in cooperation with Giovanni Capponi, she founded the Brothers of the Holy Family for the care of orphaned boys. The rules for both congregations, which she wrote, received papal approbation. C. was beatified in 1950. BIBLIOGRAPHY: Butler 4:606–607; S. Mattei, BiblSanct 3:1138–39.

[C. KEENAN]

CERONE, DOMENICO PIETRO. (1560–1625), Italian priest, singer, and musical theorist. He sang for a time in the chapel of Philip II and Philip III, Spanish kings. Later he held that position under the Spanish viceroy of Naples. In 1613 he published an extensive theoretical treatise on 16th-cent. counterpoint and musical practices. His information on such items as vocal ornamentation and the tuning of instruments has proven useful to historians of music.

[D. J. SMUCKER]

CERQUEIRA, LUÍS DE (1551 or 1552–1614), Portuguese Jesuit, bp. of Japan in 1598. C. taught philosophy at Coimbra and later theology at Evora. Manuscript copies of his treatises as professor are preserved in the public libraries of Lisbon, Evora, and Braga. As bp., C. contributed numerous writings regarding the status of the Japanese Church, and a report on the martyrs of Higo (1603). During C.'s episcopate the young Japanese Church flourished, and many of noble rank were converted. In 1612 the Church of Japan suffered persecution that led to its downfall. C. did not live to see the missionaries expelled in 1614. BIBLIOGRAPHY: J. F. Schütte, NCE 3:407; E. Lamalle, EncCatt 3:1324–25.

[M. C. BRADLEY]

CERTAINTY (CERTITUDE), MORAL. The terms certainty and certitude are often used loosely and indistinguishably, despite the effort of some writers careful in their speech to differentiate between them. For the purpose of this entry we accept J. H. Newman's distinction: certainty is an objective thing, a quality of propositions which are supported by such evidence that the mind cannot reject them, while certitude is an attitude of mind in assenting to a proposition which appears to be beyond doubt and to exclude all fear of error. Different kinds of either certainty or certitude are distinguishable on the basis of the type of evidence seen as supporting the truth of a proposition. Thus we distinguish metaphysical, mathematical, physical, and moral certainty. The term moral certainty is often used loosely to mean virtual or practical certainty, a type of certainty that exists when the truth of a proposition cannot be strictly demonstrated beyond all possibility of doubt. Moral theologians use the term to indicate the highest type of certainty attainable in moral judgments, esp. when these concern propositions dealing with variable and contingent matters, such as, e.g., propositions deriving more or less remotely from the first principles of morality, and almost all propositions concerned with the application of moral law to concrete and particular cases. In this case it indicates a certainty something less than absolute or strictly demonstrable. It does not exclude all fear of error, but only all reasonable fear of error. If there is ponderable evidence both for and against the truth of a proposition, it cannot be regarded as morally certain. In such a case full moral certainty may possibly be established by further analysis of the evidence, or when that is not possible, by the application of reflex principles. *REFLEX PRINCIPLES; *SYSTEMS OF MORALITY.

[P. K. MEAGHER]

CERTAINTY, THEOLOGICAL, a qualifying note applied to a proposition deduced from a formally revealed truth and a second premise naturally known and held to be certain. For instance, Cyril of Alexandria concluded from a revealed truth (Jesus shared our humanity) and a reasoned truth (ignorance is basic to humanity), that Jesus was ignorant of some things (PG 75.369). Thus a proposition which contradicts a theological certainty may be erroneous (*ERROR, THEOLOGICAL), but it is not on that account necessarily heretical. A theologian may rightly declare his conclusions clear and certain although others disagree. The reasoning involved need not be strictly syllogistic, but must accord with the deposit of faith. In this way theology contributes not to the multiplication of dogmas, but to the progressively clearer understanding of the unique mystery of God's saving relationship with man. Sometimes the designation, theologically certain, is less properly applied to propositions commonly held by theologians as certain. But the technical designation for these propositions would be "common and certain teaching." BIBLIOGRAPHY: S. Cartechini, *De valore notarum theologicarum et de criteriis ad eas dignoscendas* (1951); K. Rahner, *Theological Investigations* 5 (tr. C. Ernst, 1965) 3–93. *THEOLOGICAL CONCLUSION.

[W. DAVISH]

CERTITUDE OF FAITH, firmness of mind in assenting to the truth of what is believed by theological faith; different from *assurance of salvation. Faith's certitude, i.e., adherence without fear of being wrong, rests on two supports. The first is proper to the mind itself, as the virtue empowers it to give cognitive assent; faith gives the power to accept God as he "speaks," i.e., guarantees the truth of matters of belief. Faith gives the assurance that it cannot assent to the false (ThAq ST 2a2ae, 1.3). Faith, however, does not make evident the intrinsic meaning of what is believed. Thus faith is imperfect as a way of knowing; in the face of the unseen the mind remains in a state of "pondering with assent" (*ibid.*,

2.1). A second sort of certitude is derived from the will: what faith assents to means eternal life. The will's firm cleaving to God as loved above all redounds upon the mind's act of faith and gives it a subjective certitude that quietens its restless pondering. Thus faith is made perfect by loving; the affectivity of *charity brings secure affinity or connaturality toward the divine realities faith accepts. BIBLIOGRAPHY: ThAq ST (Lat-Eng) v. 31, ed. T. C. O'Brien, App. 4; v. 33, ed. W. J. Hill, App. 7.

[T. C. O'BRIEN]

CERTON, PIERRE (1510–72), Renaissance composer. A pupil of Josquin *Desprez, he was engaged for much of his life at the Sainte-Chapelle, Paris. His works include Masses, motets, and chansons, and exhibit a pleasant and direct quality. His *parody Masses are interesting examples of that form. BIBLIOGRAPHY: F. Lesure, MGG 2:976–981; Reese MusR.

[P. MURPHY]

CERTOSA, THE, Pavia (1396–1450), Carthusian monastery. Begun in Gothic style and called the "most magnificent in the world," it was founded as a mausoleum for the Visconti of Milan (completed by the Sforzas). It is notable for two cloisters with rich terra-cotta decorations, the Italian Lombardic Romanesque open arcaded galleries of its façade, and a low, arcaded lantern over the crossing. The elaborate Renaissance marble W façade by G. A. Amadeo, with a fantasy of decoration, is its glory. BIBLIOGRAPHY: W. Anderson, *Architecture of the Renaissance in Italy* (5th rev. ed., 1927).

[M. J. DALY]

CERULARIUS, see MICHAEL CERULARIUS.

CERVANTES SAAVEDRA, MIGUEL DE (1547–1616), Spanish novelist, dramatist, and poet. Little is known of his early life and education, and it is doubtful that he ever obtained a university degree. He left Spain for Italy in 1569 where he became an attendant of Card. Giulio Acquaviva. C. was wounded in the Battle of Lepanto (1571), and on his way home to Spain he was captured and held prisoner in Algiers until ransomed by Trinitarian friars. On his return to Spain, in 1580, he held modest positions. Throughout his life he was constantly worried by financial matters and was once imprisoned for debt. C.'s crowning achievement is his novels: *La Galatea* (1585), *Don Quixote* (1605 and 1615), *Novelas ejemplares* (1613), and *Los Trabajos de Persiles y Sigismunda* (1617). His satirical masterpiece, *Don Quixote,* is the story of a country gentleman who sets out to right wrongs. Through the adventures of the hero and his squire, Sancho Panza, the author presents universal themes: the meaning of existence, the nature of man, the significance of values and morality, the essence of truth and reality. Although he has been accused of atheism and hypocrisy, C. was profoundly religious and joined the Franciscan Third Order before his death. His view of man was pessimistic, yet he firmly believed that God is ready to help sinners. BIBLIOGRAPHY: A. Bell, *Cervantes* (1947); J. Casalduero, NCE 3:414–417; H. Hatzfeld, "Thirty Years of Cervantes Criticism," *Hispania* 30 (1947) 321–328; J. Fitzmaurice-Kelly, *Life of Miguel de Cervantes Saavedra: A Biographical, Literary . . . . (1973).*

[D. G. NUGENT]

CESARINI, family notable for four cardinals between 1400 and the late 1600s. It produced **Card. Giuliano** who taught at the Univ. of Padua and was nuncio to France and England, legate to the Council of Basel, and a participant in the Council of Florence (1437). He was influential in promoting against the Turks (1442) the Hunyadi crusade in which he was killed (1444). **Card. Alessandro** Cesarini (d. 1542) was legate of Pope Paul III to Emperor Charles V, legate to France, and one of the commission which prepared for the Council of Trent.

[J. R. AHERNE]

CESBRON, GILBERT (1913–   ), French writer. C. prepared for a government career at l'École des sciences politiques, turned to the communicating arts and served as program director for a private radio network. Primarily a novelist, C. has used several media to depict contemporary social problems from a Christian point of view impregnated with personalism. His chief works are *Les Saints vont en enfer* (1952), which grasped the anguished dilemma of the worker-priest movement, foreshadowing its eventual suppression by Rome; *Vous verrez le ciel ouvert* (1956), which introduces the miraculous into the cadre of industrial proletarian tragedy, and the play *Il est minuit Docteur Schweitzer* (1952). Other novels treat the mystery of God's love for man in the context of education (*Notre prison est un royaume,* 1948), juvenile delinquency (*Chiens perdus sans collier,* 1954), euthanasia (*Il est plus tard que tu ne penses,* 1958) and civil disobedience and nonviolence (*Entre chiens et loups,* 1962). The play, *Briser la statue* (1952), and the film, *Il suffit d'aimer* (1957), seek the authentic spirituality behind the façade of religiosity surrounding devotions to Theresa of Lisieux and Bernadette of Lourdes. His essays, like the *Introduction à la méthode de Ponce Pilate* in the collection *Libérez Barabbas* (1957), focus on attitudes of the Catholic bourgeoisie confronting new ethical situations. BIBLIOGRAPHY: M. Barlow, *Gilbert Cesbron, témoin de la tendresse de Dieu* (1965).

[G. E. GINGRAS]

CESLAUS OF SILESIA, BL. (1184–1242), Dominican missionary. A brother of St. Hyacinth and canon of the cathedral of Cracow, he joined the Dominicans with Hyacinth in 1218, established the first Dominican house in Prague, and became a famous preacher. He also founded the first Dominican house in Poland c.1224. BIBLIOGRAPHY: J. Gottschalk, LTK 2:997–998.

[J. R. AHERNE]

CÉSPEDES, PABLO DE (Paolo Cedaspe; 1538–1608), Spanish humanist, painter, sculptor, and architect, influenced by Michelangelo, Raphael, and the mannerism of the Zuccaris while painting frescoes in Italy. In Córdoba (1576–77) C. painted a Last Supper and the dome of the Cathedral in Seville (1585) in strong chiaroscuro and intensive foreshortening, owing much to Correggio. C. wrote discourses on painting and perspective (now lost). BIBLIOGRAPHY: F. M. Túbino, *Pablo de Céspedes* (1868).

[M. J. DALY]

CESSATIO A DIVINIS, a kind of interdict in which the bp. forbids the holding of divine service in a certain church or chapel for a time. It is imposed because of some profanation to which the building has been subjected.

[S. F. JOHNSON]

CESSATION OF LAW, concept in canon law, used regarding circumstances under which a law ceases to bind. This may occur through repeal (called extrinsic cessation) or by a change of conditions making the law harmful or devoid of purpose (intrinsic cessation). A law which through changing circumstances has become unreasonable is assumed to have lapsed, even if not repealed.

[T. EARLY]

CESTI, MARC ANTONIO (1623–69), Italian composer who wrote both secular operas and sacred cantatas. In 1637 he joined the Minorites, but later, after achieving operatic fame and experiencing difficulties with chastity, he obtained release from his vows. His successful operas include *Orontea, Serenata,* and *Filiae Jerusalem.* A sacred cantata setting of the Song of Songs reveals that little difference existed in musical content between his sacred and secular compositions.

[D. J. SMUCKER]

CEUPPENS, FRANCIS (1888–1957), Belgian Dominican biblical scholar. C. taught Scripture at the Dominican theologate in Louvain, in Ghent, and at the Angelicum in Rome (1927–54). His principal works are precise, conservative studies in biblical theology, intended to complement the typical seminary course of study in dogmatic theology. BIBLIOGRAPHY: P. G. Duncker, NCE 3:418, with listing of works.

[T. M. MCFADDEN]

CEYLON, see SRI LANKA.

CEYLON, ART OF, see SRI LANKA, ART OF.

CÉZANNE, PAUL (1839–1906), French artist, termed by Matisse "father of all modern painters." Self-taught, C. abandoned an early somber palette for intense, lighter colors. Averse to impressionist theories, he advised a return to the solid forms of the "cube, cylinder and cone," the permanent

substance of objects in an innovative compositional structure—a new aesthetic syntax. From 1889–90 C. achieved a "realization" in the greatest works of the 19th century. Architectonic form and radiant color based on invention rather than visual reality distinguish his landscapes, still lifes, and figures (1890–1906). From 1895 his work was exhibited, admired, and widely acquired. A retrospective show (1907) had a profound effect on leading artists, e.g., Matisse, Picasso, and Braque. C.'s works are treasured in public and private collections throughout the world. BIBLIOGRAPHY: J. Rewald, *Ordeal of Paul Cézanne* (1950).

[M. J. DALY]

CHAADAYEV, PYOTR YAKOVLEVICH (c.1793–1856), Russian philosopher and essayist, predecessor of the Westerners. In their entirety, his *Lettres philosophiques* (written 1829–1831) combined elements of Neoplatonism, German idealism, and Christianity into a philosophy of cosmic unity under the guidance of divine Providence. The "First Letter," published in Russian in 1836, brought reprisals from the government for its attack on Orthodoxy and serfdom and its pro-Catholic leanings. BIBLIOGRAPHY: *Russian Philosophy* (ed. J. M. Edie et al., 1965) 1:101–154; M.-B. Zeldin, EncPhil 71–72.

[M. F. MCCARTHY]

CHABENEL, NOËL, ST. (1613–49), Jesuit missionary, martyr. He entered the Jesuits in 1630 and was sent to Canada in 1643 to work with the Hurons. In 1649, he was assisting Charles *Garnier at the mission of Etarita. Returning from the nearby mission of Sainte-Marie, he was murdered by an apostate Indian on Dec. 8. For bibliog. see *NORTH AMERICAN MARTYRS.

[P. K. MEAGHER]

CHABOT, JEAN BAPTISTE (1860–1948), French Orientalist. After studies in Louvain and Paris, C. succeeded his former teacher, R. Duval, as professor of Syriac at the Collège de France. In 1903, he was one of the founders of *Corpus scriptorum christianorum orientalium* and later became its director, a position he held until shortly before his death. In this *Corpus* and in other series, he published a steady stream of editions and translations of Syriac texts as well as studies of patristic theology. C. was also active in the study and publication of Semitic inscriptions. BIBLIOGRAPHY: G. Bardy, *Catholicisme* 2:255; G. Ryckmans, "Jean-Baptiste Chabot," *Muséon* 61 (1948) 141–152.

[R. B. ENO]

CHAD, ST. (Ceadda; d. 672), Northumbrian-born monk, brother of St. Cedd, trained at Lindisfarne under St. Aidan. After spending some years in Ireland C. was recalled to England and made abbot of Lastingham in Yorkshire. King Oswy had him consecrated bp. of York by a Celtic bp., despite the fact that St. Wilfrid had already been named to that see and was in France to be consecrated. St. Theodore, abp. of Canterbury, ruled in favor of Wilfrid and C. humbly stepped down. Impressed by C.'s holiness, Theodore soon had him made bp. of Mercia, though he insisted upon reordination and reconsecration because he considered C.'s orders had been irregularly conferred. C. moved the seat of his diocese from Repton to Lichfield. After his death, his cult quickly spread with the report of many cures and miracles at his tomb. BIBLIOGRAPHY: H. Inskip, BiblSanct 3:1058–59; Butler 1:457–459.

[P. K. MEAGHER]

CHAGALL, MARC (1889–), Russian Jewish painter of uniquely personal style, born in Vitebsk, moving to Paris in 1910. Assimilating cubist, surrealist, and expressionist styles, C.'s fantastic subjects in original color embrace poignant folk fantasies of his Russian Jewish heritage (1920s). Internationally famous by 1933 and deeply disquieted by European persecution and war, C. produced darkly exciting religious works during the 1930s. Settling in the U.S. in 1941 (having won first prize in the Carnegie International Show in 1939), C. was saddened by the death of his wife in 1944. Returning to Europe for many shows, C. did ceramic work in Vence (1949), and designed (1950s) for the Hadassah-Hebrew Univ. Medical Center in Israel 12 famous stained-glass windows, which were exhibited in Paris and New York before going to Israel (1962). C. designed also (1967–68) a triptych of tapestries, *The Creation, Exodus,* and *Entry into Jerusalem,* ordered by A. *Malraux, renowned French Minister of Cultural Affairs, for the Israeli parliament. C. further decorated the ceilings of the Paris Opéra and engraved illustrations for Gogol, La Fontaine, Boccaccio, *The Arabian Nights, Daphnis and Chloe,* and his own *Ma vie.* BIBLIOGRAPHY: U. Apollonio, *Marc Chagall* (1951); M. Chagall, *Biblical Message* (tr. W. Stevenson, 1973).

[M. J. DALY]

CHAIGNON, PIERRE (1791–1883), French Jesuit. C. dedicated his life to the service of priests in the dioceses of France, where he offered spiritual direction and gave hundreds of retreats. He constituted a union of prayer for deceased priests and also wrote several works on the spiritual life, notably *Méditations sacerdotales.* BIBLIOGRAPHY: Sommervogel 9:25; *ibid.* 11:1030; A. Pottier, DSAM 2.1:438–439.

[C. KEENAN]

CHAIN PRAYERS, a name given to anonymous prayers or a system of praying in which directions are given to recite certain prayers a particular number of times and to pass the practice on without fail to a definite number of persons. The origin of chain prayers is uncertain, but their use appears periodically, e.g., in Belgium in 1918 and in France at the battlefront in 1939. This method of praying has probably made its rounds throughout the world, but in 1934 chain prayers were considered "the latest pious fraud" and were classified in the Roman Index at that time as "a novel devotion without ecclesiastical approbation." However, it was thought that good faith and simplicity would exonerate one who made use of chain prayers. In recent years this superstitious practice has declined. BIBLIOGRAPHY: R. Brouillard, *Catholicisme* 2:862–863; "Chain Prayers: a Superstition" *Sign* 13 (1934) 728.

[R. A. TODD]

CHAINE, JOSEPH (1888–1948), biblical scholar. C. studied at the École Biblique in Jerusalem and taught both the OT and NT at the Institut Catholique in Lyons (1927–48). He contributed significantly to the growth of RC biblical scholarship by propagating the methodology of the École Biblique and publishing numerous critical studies and reviews. His commentary on Genesis (1948) was the first work to reflect the freedom afforded RC scholars after the encyclical *Divino afflante Spiritu.* BIBLIOGRAPHY: JBC 2:603; H. Cazelles, *Catholicisme* 2:858–859.

[T. M. MCFADDEN]

CHAIR OF PETER, a theological expression that signifies the authority and doctrinal power that resides in the bp. of Rome, the successor of St. Peter. In early times the bp. presided over his people and instructed his flock on the Word of God from his official chair. Similarly, speaking *ex cathedra* from the Chair of Peter, the pope defines doctrine that is infallibly binding on all the people of God.

[T. LIDDY]

CHAIR OF UNITY OCTAVE, also called the Church Unity Octave, a period of prayer for Christian unity held each year, Jan. 18–25. The Octave, which finds its inspiration in the prayer of Christ for his followers, "That all may be one" (Jn 17.21), was founded (1908) by Lewis Thomas Wattson (1863–1940), an American Episcopalian clergyman. The distinctive purpose of the Octave was the corporate reunion esp. of the Anglican Church with the RC Church, although the intentions for prayer also included other Christians and non-Christians. Originally called the Church Unity Octave, the prayer movement was stimulated by a suggestion in 1907 that a special sermon on Christian unity be preached each year on June 29th, the Feast of SS. Peter and Paul. Wattson replied by launching an 8-day period of prayers for Christian unity from the Feast of St. Peter's Chair in Rome, Jan. 18, to the Conversion of St. Paul, Jan. 25. Among the first results of the Octave was his own reception, together with a small group of Anglican religious (the Franciscan Friars of the Atonement and the Franciscan Sisters of the Atonement), into the RC Church (Oct. 30, 1909). The Church Unity Octave was extended by Benedict XV on Feb. 25, 1916, to the whole Church and enriched with indulgences. At the insistence of Pius XII the name was changed, becoming the Chair of Unity Octave. Born out of a desire for corporate reunion in a period antedating the ecumenical movement, and formed in its most flourishing period by a theology of the Counter-Reformation, the Octave today under the influence of ecumenism has yielded to and combined with the *Week of Prayer for Christian Unity. The contributions of the Octave have been the manifold prayers for unity it stimulated, the view of corporate reunion that it upheld, and the preparation it gave to the RC world for receiving the ecumenical movement. BIBLIOGRAPHY: D. Gannon, *Father Paul of Graymoor* (1959).

[R. MAZERATH]

CHAISE-DIEU, ABBEY OF—former Benedictine Abbey in the Diocese of Le Puy in south central France, founded in 1046. After a period of initial fervor it reached the height of its influence during the 2d half of the 13th century. The congregation began to decline in the 14th century. A new church was built by a former monk, Pope Clement VI. It is a Gothic structure with three naves of equal height. Completed in 1352, it still serves as a parish church. A notable part of the archives is preserved at Le Puy.

CHAKRA (*cakra,* Sanskrit, wheel), wheel or disc, referring esp. to Buddha's Wheel of the Law *(dharmacakra),* its eight spokes symbolizing the Eightfold Path by which man, extinguishing desire, attains to liberation and eternal bliss (nirvana). *BUDDHISM.

[M. J. DALY]

CHALCEDON, COUNCIL OF (451), the fourth *ecumenical council, convoked by Emperor *Marcian with the assent of Pope *Leo I to settle the continuing dispute about the natures of Christ. Over 500 Eastern bps. including two from Africa and three legates of Pope Leo I were in session from Oct. 8 to Nov. 1. In the initial sessions, the decrees of the *Robber Council of Ephesus were nullified and *Eutyches and *Dioscorus were condemned. The two synodical letters of St. *Cyril and the *Tome of Leo were formally accepted. The fifth session dealt with the formula of faith (at the insistence of Marcian). The first draft was unacceptable to Paschasinus, the papal legate, because it did not reflect the teaching of Leo. A new commission of six bps. appointed by the 19 imperial commissioners revised the formula to agree with Leo's definition of the natures of Christ. This formula was formally ratified by the bps. in the presence of the Emperor Marcian on Oct. 25. It confirms the creeds of Nicaea and Constantinople I and supports the two synodical letters of Cyril and the *Tome of Leo.* It affirms that Christ is one person, recognizable *(gnōrizomenon)* in two distinct natures, without confusion, change, division, or separation, with the respective properties of each nature intact, coming together in one *prosōpon* (person) and one *hypostasis* (subsistence). In the 10 or 11 remaining sessions the bps. reinstated *Theodoret of Cyr and *Ibas of Edessa and formally approved 27 canons clarifying the jurisdiction of bps. and the obligations of monks and priests. However, *Canon 28, which equalized the patriarchal privileges and jurisdiction of Constantinople in the East with Rome in the

West, brought vigorous protest from the papal legates. Finally the bps. sent a detailed report of their activities to Leo and requested his confirmation of their decrees. On March 21, 453, he ratified all decrees pertaining to faith and vetoed any change in the order of patriarchal sees approved by the canons of Nicaea. BIBLIOGRAPHY: R. Sellers, *Council of Chalcedon* (1953).

[F. H. BRIGHAM]

CHALCONDYLES, DEMETRIUS (1423–1511), leader in the revival of Western Greek studies and brother of the historian Laonicus Chalcondyles. Born in Athens, he went to Rome *c.*1447. Later he taught at Perugia, Padua, Florence, and, from 1492, Milan. He edited a number of Greek texts, and his Greek grammar became a standard work.

[T. EARLY]

CHALDEAN ART (612 B.C.-539 B.C.), art of the Chaldean or neo-Babylonian Kingdom, of Babylonian or Kassita style not in Assyrian angularized fierceness but in soft, rounded forms of gentle elegance. The "ceramic" architecture is dazzling with glazed tiles, the Ishtar Gate carrying in relief decorative fantastic bulls and lions with yellow bodies and blue manes. The walls of the Processional Way flash with 60 life-size, brightly colored lions on a blue ground studded with rosettes. Marduk's ziggurat (temple) of three stages (in ruins) and that at Ur (the best preserved) featured, Herodotus states, stages of different colors ascending to an uppermost shrine area in blue glazed brick. From ancient Chaldea come our zodiacal signs and winged guardians called cherubim. BIBLIOGRAPHY: H. Frankfort, *Art and Architecture of the Ancient Orient* (1954).

[M. J. DALY]

CHALDEAN CHURCH, the East Syrian Rite or Church composed of former Nestorians united with Rome. The scene of the first union of Nestorians with Rome was Cyprus, where from the 13th cent. on attempts were made to convert all non-Latins to Catholicism. The earlier attempts had been foiled largely by the opposition of the laity. The Cypriot Nestorians were at last united with Rome in 1445, and it was to them that the name Chaldean was first given. The Cypriot Chaldeans were totally Latinized when the Venetians took over Cyprus in 1489. In Mesopotamia itself Nestorian union with Rome began in 1552 when a Nestorian faction objecting to the patriarchal succession from uncle to nephew elected as patriarch (Simon VIII or John VIII) Sulaqa, superior of the monastery of Rabban Hormizd near Alqosh, and sent him to Rome for confirmation, which he received as Patriarch of the East Assyrians in 1553. The patriarchs of this line lived first in Diarbekir (the center of unionistic sentiment), then in Seert, before moving to Salmas in NW Persia. The ancient Nestorian patriarchate remained at Rabban Hormizd. Sometime after 1670 the Chaldean patriarch Simon XIII returned to Nestorianism and moved the patriarchal residence to

Kotchannes in Kurdistan. There were thus two Nestorian patriarchates.

A second movement of Roman union began around 1670 with the conversion of the Nestorian bp. of Diarbekir. In 1681 Rome named the converted bp., Joseph I, Patriarch of the Chaldean nation, with the result that there were now three East Syrian patriarchates: the new Chaldean one at Diarbekir, the ancient Nestorian one at Rabban Hormizd, and the newer Nestorian, formerly Catholic, one at Kotchannes. In the 18th cent. sentiment favorable to union began to grow among many Nestorians of the ancient patriarchate, the Nestorian patriarch Elias XII himself making unsuccessful overtures toward union c. 1750. Upon Elias XII's death in 1783, some of his people remained Nestorian with his nephew and successor, Elias XIII, and some became Catholic with his other nephew, John Hormizd. Rome, in the hope of peacefully uniting the two Catholic parties (those of Diarbekir and the newly converted of the Mossul area), ceased giving the title of patriarch to the metropolitans of Diarbekir. A period of struggle and rivalry ensued, the two principal protagonists being Augustine Hindi, metropolitan of Diarbekir, and John Hormizd, now administrator of Mossul, his cousin Elias XIII soon passing from the scene. The rivalry between the Diarbekir faction and the Mossul faction continued even after the death of Augustine Hindi in 1827, until finally, in 1834, John Hormizd was enthroned as Chaldean Patriarch of Babylon, thus inaugurating the patriarchal succession which continues to the present day. As it has turned out, the modern Nestorian patriarchs are of the originally Catholic lineage established by John Sulaqa in 1552, which returned to Nestorianism at the end of the 17th cent., while the modern Chaldean Catholic patriarchs are of the ancient lineage which in 1552 had remained Nestorian. The Chaldean patriarch Joseph Audo was one of the most frankly independent of all Oriental prelates in dealing with Rome during and after Vatican Council I, but his fundamental loyalty to the union led him regularly to submission when the only alternative would be schism. Today the Chaldeans number some 200,000 despite the Turkish and Kurdish massacres after World War I. They are to be found mostly in Iraq and Iran, with organized groups also in Syria, Lebanon, and the U.S. The patriarch resides in Baghdad. BIBLIOGRAPHY: E. Tisserant, DTC 11:225–249; W. de Vries, LTK 2:1004–05. *EAST SYRIAN CHURCH.

[A. CODY]

CHALDEAN LITURGY, as here understood, the liturgy used by Catholics of the Chaldean Rite, chiefly in Iraq. It begins like other Eastern liturgies with an *enarxis* after the model of an office, abbreviated somewhat at the low Masses which Catholics have introduced with the custom of daily Mass. The elements are prepared during the *lakhumira* ("To thee, O Lord . . ."), a chant at the end of this with prayers corresponding to the Byzantine *prothesis,* and (at solemn Masses) a blessing of incense. The Liturgy of the Word follows. This always includes the *Trisagion* and four if not

five lessons. The prophecy is read only on Sundays and feasts and in some penitential seasons, but there is always an OT lesson and two from the NT before the Gospel. A litany follows this in solemn liturgies. At all, some intercessions are said before and after the old place of the dismissals of catechumens and others. This is now omitted, but the celebrant still washes his hands at this point. The Creed is recited at the end of these intercessions in a form derived from the baptismal rite and used in the liturgy since the 6th century. The Chaldeans have made some changes in the older form still used by Nestorians, but apart from the *filioque* these are not significant theologically and could depend on another MS tradition. In view of the Nestorian controversy it is significant that the Catholic Chaldeans continue to call Christ "the firstborn of every creature . . . who for us men and our salvation came down from heaven and was incarnate of the Holy Spirit and was made man, and was conceived and born of the Virgin Mary, and was crucified in the days of Pontius Pilate." The Catholics add that he died, but this may have been inserted more against Islam than against Nestorianism.

In addition to the Anaphora of the Apostles, both communities use the hallowings ascribed to Theodore of Mopsuestia and to Nestorius, but the Catholics do not use these names, calling them instead the second and third hallowings. The Anaphora of the Apostles is based on a very early original, which does not seem to have contained an explicit account of the institution of the Eucharist. This is inserted in the prayer of the fraction in Chaldean liturgies printed for Catholics in 1697 and 1767. On the other hand some of the evidence from Malabar suggests that the addition of the narrative of the institution in this place was done before the Portuguese arrived by those who felt that something was missing, but still regarded the invocation of the Spirit as the climax of the consecration. In all three hallowings the intercession precedes this.

In the Anaphora of the Apostles, the invocation is immediately preceded by an *anamnesis* including a reference to "the example from thee delivered to us." This may at one time have been considered as equivalent to the narrative of the institution, which is now inserted in the Catholic rite not at the fraction, as in the earlier Missals, but before the *anamnesis* and the intercessions, as in the other hallowings. This Liturgy of the Apostles is prescribed from Holy Saturday until Advent, in Masses for the dead, memorials of the saints, and at all low Masses. The second hallowing is used from Advent to Palm Sunday; the third, only on a few special occasions, including the Epiphany and Maundy Thursday. BIBLIOGRAPHY: A. A. King, *Rites of Eastern Christendom* (2 v., 1950) v. 2; C. K. Von Euw, NCE 3:430–432.

[G. EVERY]

CHALDEAN ORACLES, (*oracula chaldaica*) a collection of oracles in Greek hexameters made most probably by a certain Julianus, a theurgist, in the age of Marcus Aurelius. The collection itself is no longer extant, but it has been reconstructed by modern scholars from the numerous citations found in Neoplatonic writers from the 3d to the 6th century. The oracles contain Pythagorean, Platonic, Stoic, and Oriental elements and are presented as having been divinely revealed. They gave a powerful impulse to theurgy in theory and practice and exercised a great influence on Late Greek philosophical thought in general. *Iamblichus of Chalcis may be mentioned as one of the ardent devotees of the *Chaldean Oracles* and one of the chief disseminators of their teachings. BIBLIOGRAPHY: W. Kroll, *De oraculis Chaldaicis* (1894); H. Lewy, *Chaldean Oracles and Theurgy* (1956); E. R. Dodds, "New Light on the Chaldean Oracles," HTR 54 (1961) 263–273.

[M. R. P. MCGUIRE]

CHALDEANS, former Nestorians now reunited with the Roman Catholic Church. *CHALDEAN CHURCH.

CHALDEANS (IN THE BIBLE), an Aramaic-speaking people whose origins are traceable to the end of the 2d and the beginning of the 1st millennium B.C., who settled in the semi-swamp region of the Persian Gulf. In the Bible they are also referred to as Babylonians. From the 7th cent. B.C. on, many OT references, e.g., in Kg, Is, and Ezek, demonstrate this. They are mentioned, too, as magicians and astrologers (Dn 1.20; 2.2). BIBLIOGRAPHY: EDB 341–342.

[E. C. HUBBERT]

CHALGRIN, JEAN FRANÇOIS THÉRÈSE (1739–1811), French classical architect in Paris, associated with Soufflot. C. designed the Church of St. Philippe du Roule, Paris, but is best known for his masterpiece, the monumental Arc de Triomphe de l'Étoile completed after his death. BIBLIOGRAPHY: L. Hautecoeur, *Histoire de l'architecture classique en France* (1952) v. 4.

[M. J. DALY]

CHALICE, the cup or vessel used to hold the wine consecrated in the Eucharistic Liturgy. The first chalices were undistinguished from the drinking cups in common use. They were usually made of glass, but bronze and other metals were used even in the early centuries. By the 9th cent. almost all chalices in the West were made of precious metals. The chalice has three parts: a cup *(cuppa),* a base, and a knob *(nodus)* between cup and base. When, as is generally but not necessarily the case, a stem separates cup and base, the *nodus* is located on the stem. Before the faithful in the Western Church ceased to communicate under both species, two kinds of chalice were in common use, the smaller holy or sacrificial chalice *(calyx sancta)* from which the celebrant drank, and the larger ministerial chalice *(calyx ministerialis)* from which the wine was given to the faithful. The *cuppa* of the latter was generally fitted with two handles. The materials and the styles of cup, knob, and base used in different periods reflect current art forms and the greater or lesser affluence of the institutions or persons for whom they were

made. Sometimes they were elaborately ornamented with inlaid precious stones, enamel medallions, and intricate filigree work. The modern trend is toward functionalism and simplicity of line. According to the rubrics of the Missal, the cup should be of gold or silver or of solid and noble material not easily breakable or corruptible, a nonabsorbent material; if made of a metal subject to rust the inside surface should be plated with gold. Before a chalice is used it should be consecrated by a cardinal, or a bishop, a prefect or vicar apostolic, an abbot or prelate *nullius* (see Abbo 2:545–546). BIBLIOGRAPHY: CIC c. 1306.1; H. Leclercq, DACL 2.2:1595–1645; C. W. Howell, NCE 3:432–437.

[N. KOLLAR]

CHALICE (IN ORIENTAL RITES; Gr., *poterion,* cup, goblet; Sl., *potir),* the cup used to contain the wine which is consecrated at the Divine Liturgy. Formerly made of crystal, semi-precious stone, or other material, it now is universally made of silver, gold, or gilded metal of other kinds. Because of the practice of distributing communion in both species the Byzantine chalice usually has a rather large cup. The influence of the 17th- and 18th-cent. European baroque and rococo styles of chalice design is still seen in the rather high, broad-based chalices found in most Orthodox churches. It is unfortunate that the more aesthetically pleasing earlier Byzantine models such as those seen in the treasury of the Cathedral of St. Mark in Venice have not had a similar influence. There does not have to be a formal blessing or consecration of the chalice in the Byzantine rite; it is considered hallowed by use and contact with the Holy Gifts.

The cup full of unconsecrated wine is used at the Byzantine wedding service and presented successively to both bride and groom after the crowning ceremony. Its origin is seen in the Jewish marriage ritual, although it may have had eucharistic overtones, and it symbolizes the common life and love now mutually shared by the spouses.

[A. J. JACOPIN]

CHALK, BLESSING OF, a blessing given after the Epiphany Mass over the chalk to be used in the blessing of the homes on this day. After blessing the home the initials of the legendary kings, Gaspar, Melchior, Balthasar, are written with white chalk on the inside of the door together with the year. The initial letters are written between the first two and the last two digits of the year and separated from each other and from the numerals by crosses, e.g., 19+G+M+B+77. BIBLIOGRAPHY: F. X. Weiser, *Handbook of Christian Feasts and Customs* (1958) 149.

[N. KOLLAR]

CHALLONER, RICHARD (1691–1781), English RC bishop, vicar apostolic, and author. Born at Lewes, Sussex, of Presbyterian parents, C. was early converted to Catholicism and in 1705 was admitted to the English College at Douai, where he later taught. He returned to England in 1730 and served as a priest despite legal restrictions on Catholics.

In 1758 he succeeded Bp. B. Petre as vicar apostolic, administering the London district comprising 10 counties, the Channel Island, and British N America. Of his writings *The Garden of the Soul* (1740), a devotional book, was esp. popular. His revision of the Douay Bible (1749–52) was the standard Catholic version in English until recently. BIBLIOGRAPHY: M. Trappes-Lomax, *Bishop Challoner* (1936); T. Cooper, DNB 3:1349–52.

[T. EARLY]

CHALLONER'S BIBLE, a revision of the *Douay Bible and until recently the standard Catholic version in English. The revision was carried out by R. *Challoner with the NT published in 1749 and the OT in 1750. It was the basis for the classical American Baltimore Bible of Gibbons (1899).

[T. EARLY]

CHALMERS, WILLIAM (d. 1678), known also as Camerarius, the name he used in his Latin writings. Born in Aberdeen, Scotland, he was briefly with the Jesuits and then became an Oratorian. C. edited some of the writings of Augustine, Anselm, and Fulgentius, published selected philosophical studies, a theological treatise on mortal and venial sin, and a short ecclesiastical history of Scotland. But he is chiefly remembered for his spirited attack upon Molinism published in 1641. BIBLIOGRAPHY: A. Ingold, DTC 2.2:2211.

[T. LIDDY]

CHALON-SUR-SAÔNE, COUNCILS OF. Chalon-sur-Saône in the province of Lyons was the site of several national councils in Merovingian times. One held *c.*650 promulgated 20 disciplinary canons, which, among other things, forbade the selling of slaves outside the realm and farm labor on Sunday; it prescribed private sacramental confession. It was also the site of a great reforming council under Charlemagne in 813 which recommended the establishment of cathedral schools, the restoration of public penance, and the reception of communion on Holy Thursday; it also forbade masters to dissolve the marriages of their slaves. One of the many provincial councils in Chalon-sur-Saône was presided over by St. Peter Damian in 1064. BIBLIOGRAPHY: A. Condit, NCE 3:439, C. Laplatte, DHGE 12:302–329.

[B. L. MARTHALER]

CHÂLONS-SUR-MARNE, NÔTRE DAME EN VAUX, French Romanesque cathedral with two towers (12th-13th cent.) flanking the choir, and two (*c.*1250), the nave and transepts. The main portal, W front, and first two bays of the nave are dated 1628–34. A fine 12th-cent. Passion window and excellent N rose window (13th cent.), with a 16th-cent. series in the S aisle, are notable. BIBLIOGRAPHY: M. Aubert and S. Goubet, *Gothic Cathedrals of France and Their Treasures* (1959).

[M. J. DALY]

CHAMBERLAIN, see PAPAL CHAMBERLAIN.

CHAMBERLAIN, HOUSTON STEWART (1855–1927), English Germanophile, a student of Wagner, who became a naturalized German (1916), and whose *Die Grundlagen des neunzehnten Jahrhunderts* (1899), translated into English by J. Lees under the title *The Foundations of the Nineteenth Century* (1912), influenced Hitler in the development of his notion of Aryan superiority and destiny and his detestation of the Jewish people.

[G. J. RUPPEL]

CHAMBERS, JOHN CHARLES (1817–74), Anglican priest. After some years in Sedbergh and Perth, he became pastor in Soho and warden of the house of charity there. Among other religious writings, he published the anonymous *Priest in Absolution* (1866, 1870), that produced an outbreak of anti-High Church sentiment in the House of Lords after his death. BIBLIOGRAPHY: W. Wroth, DNB 10:19.

[M. J. SUELZER]

CHAMINADE, GUILLAUME JOSEPH (1761–1850), founder of Marianist Sisters (1816) and Marianists (1817). After ecclesiastical studies at Périgueux, Bordeaux, and Paris, he was ordained (1784) and received his S.T.D. (1785). He taught at the seminary at Mussidan until forced into exile in Saragossa, Spain (1797–1800) because he was a nonjuring priest. There, at the shrine of Our Lady of the Pillar, he was inspired to found the sodalities and their outgrowth, the religious societies. He was administrator of the Diocese of Bazas (1800–02), made canon of the Bordeaux cathedral (1803), and credited by Abp. d' Aviou with responsibility for most of the religious activity in Bordeaux. His chief work, published in his lifetime, is the *Manuel du serviteur de Marie* (1801). Six volumes of his letters and sermons have been printed since his death. BIBLIOGRAPHY: K. Burton, *Chaminade: Apostle of Mary,* (1949); M. Darbon, *Guillaume Joseph Chaminade, 1761–1850* (1946); J. Verrier, *Mélanges Chaminade* (1961); G. J. Ruppel, NCE 3:440–441.

[G. J. RUPPEL]

CHAMOND, ST., see AUNEMUND, ST.

CHAMOS, see CHEMOSH.

CHAMPAGNAT, MARCELLIN JOSEPH BENÔIT, BL. (1789–1840), French founder. After ordination to the priesthood, C.'s interest in the Catholic education of boys led to the founding of the Marist Brothers (1817), an institute that received approbation from Rome in 1836. C.'s vision for the future included a congregation of teaching brothers and priests. After the institute of brothers was established and norms for growth were initiated, as evidenced in his publication, *Guide des Écoles,* he directed his energies toward the founding of the Marist Fathers. He was beatified in 1955. BIBLIOGRAPHY: Brother John Baptiste, *Life and Spirit of J. B. M. Champagnat* (1947); *Origines maristes* (ed. J. Coste and G. Lessard, 1960–66).

[C. KEENAN]

CHAMPAIGNE, PHILIPPE DE (1602–74), painter of the French school who was trained in his native Brussels. In Paris C. modified his Flemish style to suit the taste of his French patrons, among whom were Marie de Médicis, Louis XIII, and Card. Richelieu. The increasing sobriety of his art after 1643 reflects the influence of Jansenism. BIBLIOGRAPHY: A. Blunt, *Art and Architecture in France, 1500–1700* (1953) 173–176.

[R. E. FLEISCHER]

CHAMPLAIN, SAMUEL DE (*c.* 1567–1635), founder of New France. C. was the son of a French naval officer and served in the religious wars. In 1603 he first visited Canada with the Pontgravé expedition, trading at Tadoussac and the St. Lawrence. As a member of Sieur de Monts' expedition to plant a colony in Acadia, first near the mouth of the St. Croix River in Passamaquoddy Bay, later at the site of Annapolis, Nova Scotia, C. mapped the coast of New England south to Cape Cod. Because of difficulties in France, the colony was temporarily abandoned and he returned to France (1607). Under a new charter, he led colonists to establish a permanent settlement in Quebec (1608), descended the Richelieu River to discover Lake Champlain (1609), and defeated a party of Iroquois near Ticonderoga. Unfortunately, the skirmish resulted in almost constant harassment of New France by the savage Iroquois for the next 5 decades. A royal charter (1614) granted a monopoly to a company of merchants under the patronage of the Prince de Condé to develop Canada for 11 years and named C. as their governor in New France. In an effort to develop the infant colony, he divided his time between Quebec and France. He surrendered Quebec to the British (1629) and then spent 3 years in Europe negotiating for its restitution, returning again (1632) as its governor. BIBLIOGRAPHY: *Works,* ed. and tr. by H. P. Biggar (1922–36); M. G. Bishop, *Champlain: The Life of Fortitude* (pa. 1963).

[R. K. MacMASTER]

CHAMPOLLION, JEAN FRANÇOIS (1790–1832), Egyptologist who discovered the key for understanding hieroglyphic and demotic scripts. C. published a two-volume geography of Egypt (1814), and in 1822 announced in his *Lettre à M. Dacier* that his extensive study of the *Rosetta Stone had enabled him to decipher hieroglyphics. His conclusions were published in the *Précis du système hiéroglyphique* (1824). C. also catalogued the Egyptian holdings of several Italian museums, led an Egyptian expedition with Rosellini, and prepared an Egyptian grammar and dictionary. BIBLIOGRAPHY: H. Hartleben, *Champollion:*

Sein Leben und sein Werk (2 v., 1906); B. Marczuk, NCE 3:443.

[T. M. MCFADDEN]

CHAMTIGES, MARTIN DE (d. 1532), Parisian architect, flamboyant in style, who executed transept façades of Sens Cathedral (1490–1512), Beauvais (1500), and Senlis (1504).

[M. J. DALY]

CHANCE, a philosophic and popular term from the Latin verb *cadere,* "to fall," as in the fall of dice, used in various meanings to account for the happening of human and nonhuman events. With Democritus, Epicurus, and Lucretius, it refers to that which has no cause, and with Laplace and Bertrand Russell it designates that of which the cause is unknown. Aristotle and John Stuart Mill view it as the intersection of two independent causal series, whereas Spinoza and Leibnitz deny the existence of chance. Certain modern scientific minds hold it to be the cause of all events, and others, while naming it a cause, insist upon its indeterminacy.

The Scholastic teaching on chance, based largely on Aristotle's analysis, is noteworthy for its simplicity and clarity: in an absolute sense, chance does not exist in the universe because it is governed by an omniscient and omnipotent God who literally intends its every activity. Hence, he is author of all events, knowing and willing them, without exception. In a relative sense, however, meaning so far as man's knowledge and will are concerned, chance may be said to exist with respect to human acts and acts of nature. Strictly, chance refers to the latter only, whereas "fortune" is the proper term for the former. With reference to chance happenings in nature, man has neither foreknowledge nor control of independent lines of causal activity, so that when these intersect while moving toward their respective, different goals, man speaks of chance as the cause of the unseemly event, as when the scampering squirrel is crushed beneath the rolling stone. What happened was inevitable, but man calls it chance. Similarly, in his own activities, man intends a certain effect as the goal of his actions, but despite his intention quite unexpectedly achieves instead an unintended effect —as in the instance of the well-digger discovering treasure. Again, chance is adduced as the cause, amounting to a confession of ignorance as to the real causal series at work. BIBLIOGRAPHY: J. Venn, *Logic of Chance* (1888); R. Proctor, *Chance and Luck* (1887); E. Nagel, *Structure of Science* (1961); M. Born, *Natural Philosophy of Cause and Chance* (1949).

[J. T. HICKEY]

CHANCEL, that part of the church designated for the clergy. The term is from the Lat., *cancellus* (lattice), and arose from the custom in the early centuries of the Church of separating the area by a low lattice-work or railing. In the Middle Ages the chancel came to be separated from the *nave by a choir screen or rood screen. Orthodox churches continue to use screens separating the two areas, but most Western churches now use no more than a low railing; some relinquished even this separation. Originally comprising just the space around the altar, the area now known as the sanctuary, the chancel was enlarged to include the choir when it became a standard feature of church design. Non-liturgical churches that do not have an altar normally do not have a chancel.

[T. EARLY]

CHANCELLOR, an official whose title is derived from that of the gatekeeper who stood *ad cancellos*—at the bars or grating that separated the public from the magistrate in a court of law in the Roman Empire—and whose duty it was to see that only those entitled to enter were admitted. In its principal religious and religion-related uses, chancellor is the title of: (1) the cardinal heading the Apostolic *Chancery, formerly charged with expediting certain documents issued by the Consistorial Congregation and by the pope; (2) the diocesan official who under present law in the RC Church is responsible for the preservation in archives of the acts of the diocesan curia; (3) the official who in the C of E represents the bishop of a diocese in the administration of temporal affairs and who commonly exercises many of the functions of the bishop's official principal and vicar-general. Unlike his Roman counterpart, the diocesan chancellor in the C of E is not ordinarily a priest; (4) the honorary head of some universities. When an institution is headed by a titular chancellor, the actual administration of the office is generally committed to a vice-chancellor.

[P. K. MEAGHER]

CHANCERY, APOSTOLIC, former office of the Roman *Curia, charged with issuing papal documents, e.g., apostolic letters or papal bulls, and acts of the former *Consistorial Congregation. By the *motu proprio* of Feb. 27, 1973, *Quo aptius,* these functions were transferred to the papal *Secretariat of State.

[S. F. HIGGINS]

CHANCERY, DIOCESAN, governing office of the diocese that includes persons who assist the bp. in the administration and discipline of the diocese and the execution of justice. For ordinary administration the vicar-general is in charge. The chancellor keeps the archives of the diocese. The officialis heads the diocesan tribunal. Defender of the bond deals with cases concerning marriage and holy orders.

[S. F. JOHNSON]

CHANEL, PETER, ST. (1803–41), French missionary and martyr. As a member of the Marist Fathers, C. was assigned to Futuna Islands, Oceania, where he lived among a group of primitive and savage peoples. Although circumstances prolonged his stay, his missionary work among the people seemed fruitless. Baptism was administered to only a

few, but his faith and strong character supported him as he suffered persecution and finally a martyr's death. Not many years after his death, the entire island converted to Catholicism. C. was canonized in 1954. BIBLIOGRAPHY: W. Symes, *Life of St. Peter Chanel* (1963); Butler 2:186; C. Rozier, BiblSanct 10:814–818.

[C. KEENAN]

CHANGE RINGING, the ringing of church bells in methodical order, according to mathematical permutations. For example, with three bells numbered 1, 2, and 3, the first change may be ringing them in the order of 2, 1, 3; the second, 3, 2, 1, etc. Change ringing is widely practiced in England, and certain standard permutations have acquired names, e.g., Grandshire Triple and Treble Bob.

[D. J. SMUCKER]

CHANNING, WILLIAM ELLERY (1780–1842), American Unitarian minister. Born in Newport, R.I., of a distinguished family, C. graduated from Harvard in 1798. He was elected regent at Harvard in 1801. After receiving approval to preach, he began his ministry at the Federal Street Congregational Church in Boston in 1803. When Jebidiah Morse attacked the liberal Congregationalists in 1815, accusing them of covertly agreeing with the strictly humanitiarian Christology of the English Unitarian Thomas Belsham, C. defended them as "liberal Christians." He emerged into clear leadership of the liberals with his famous sermon, "Unitarian Christianity," which he preached at Baltimore in 1819 for the ordination of Jared Sparks. When younger Unitarian ministers pressed for the organization of a separate denomination, however, C. expressed his disapproval of Unitarianism as a sect. He declined the offer of the presidency of the American Unitarian Association when it was organized in 1825. In later years, he became increasingly an advocate of social reform, with particular opposition to slavery. He and Theodore *Parker are recognized as the two greatest leaders in the development of American Unitarianism.

Basic intellectual influences on his theological development were derived from Francis Hutcheson, Adam Ferguson, Richard Price, and Samuel Hopkins. The influence of John Locke is seen in C.'s emphasis on the rational character of revealed religion. He was convinced of the unique authority of Jesus and of the validity of miracles as "Christian evidences." He distrusted a transcendentalist reliance upon immediate intuition. The concepts of the unipersonality and the moral character of God were crucial in his theology. In Christology, he was an "Arian." He rejected the Chalcedonian interpretation of the Incarnation on scriptural and rational grounds. His optimistic evaluation of human nature is shown in his belief that Christ's life demonstrated that the achievement of moral perfection is possible for other men. There were several editions of his writings, the latest of which was *Works of William Ellery Channing* (6 v., 1903). BIBLIOGRAPHY: J. W. Chadwick, *William Ellery Channing*

(1903); R. L. Patterson, *Philosophy of William Ellery Channing* (1952); D. P. Edgell, *William Ellery Channing* (1955); A. W. Brown, *Always Young for Liberty* (1956); *Theology in America* (ed. S. E. Ahlstrom, 1967) 193–210.

[J. C. GODBEY]

CHA-NO-YU, tea ceremony introduced by Zen (Chinese, Ch'an) monks, during which one engaged in contemplation of the refined, eternal aspects of life. As it became a cult, under the Japanese tea master, Sen-No-Rikyu (1520–91), architecture, painting, and pottery were modified by the Zen tenet of beauty in simplicity.

[M. J. DALY]

CHANSONS DE GESTE, the Old French epics comprising three major groups: (1) The King's Cycle, concerning Charlemagne, his vassals and lineage; this group includes the *Song of Roland, Fierabras,* and the satirical Parisian *Pilgrimage of Charlemagne;* (2) The Cycle of Doon de Mayence, or the ''Rebellious Vassal'' Cycle, focusing on the relentless vanquishing of some outlaw baron by his overlord, usually Charlemagne; the most famous are *The Four Sons of Aymon, Gormont and Isembart, Girart de Roussillon,* and *Raoul de Cambrai;* (3) The Cycle of Garin de Monglane, or the ''William'' Cycle; the exploits of Count William of Toulouse (d. after 806) against the Saracens, expanded to include deeds of his father Aymeri, his great-grandfather Garin de Monglane, and his own feats after entering a monastery to end his days. The *Song of William,* the *Crowning of Louis,* the *Capture of Orange,* and the *Death of Aymeri of Narbonne* belong to this cycle. The common origins of these epics are influenced by saints' lives, Germanic epics, prose sagas, popular chanted *cantilenae.* Pilgrimage routes to Spain, Rome, and Jerusalem probably used the *chansons* as advertisement. BIBLIOGRAPHY: M. Gildea, *Expressions of Religious Thought and Feeling in the Chansons de Geste* (1943, repr. 1969).

[J. P. WILLIMAN]

CHANT, music to be sung, esp. a repertory or style for the musical declamation of liturgical texts in the course of a service. Liturgical chants range from simple recitations on a single pitch of scriptural texts and orations by officiating clergy to fully developed musical compositions to be performed by a trained choir or soloist. Relatively few liturgical chant melodies are exclusively associated with but one text, and many are mere formulas to which any text of a given type can be sung. Liturgical chant was and is a traditional part of *Jewish religious music, and Christian chant evolved from the Palestinian synagogue service at the beginning of the Christian era. The various rites developed their own repertories, which have often had an official status. The principal Latin chant repertory is known as *Gregorian chant; related chant repertories are the *Milanese (Ambrosian), *Old Roman, *Beneventan, *Mozarabic, and *Gallican. The principal chants of the Eastern Christian rites include

*Byzantine, *Armenian, and *Syrian chants. Only in the case of Byzantine chant is a substantial medieval repertory preserved in a decipherable notation, although it is not performed in Greek Orthodox or Greek Catholic Churches today, as Gregorian chant has been in the Latin Church. Liturgical chanting has been employed in Protestant worship chiefly by the Anglican and Lutheran Churches whose service remained close to Catholic forms. *Anglican chant was an extension of the *falso bordone* style for the choral singing of psalmodic texts, while Lutheran composers made frequent use of Gregorian melodies and forms. Certain Lutheran chorales preserve both the texts (in German translation) and melodies of Latin hymns. Chants for the clergy, when used at all in Protestant services, were based on Latin models. The rise of vernacular worship from the 16th cent. in Protestant churches and since Vatican Council II in the case of the Catholic Church has resulted in a lessened use of liturgical chant in services, particularly for scripture lessons, reflecting a shift in emphasis from the reading of Scripture as a ritual act to the meaning of the text being read. *MUSIC, CHRISTIAN RELIGIOUS.

[A. DOHERTY]

CHANTAL, JANE FRANCES DE, ST. (1572–1641), foundress of the Order of the Visitation of Holy Mary. Born Jeanne Françoise Frémiot, at Dijon, France, she was married to Baron Christophe de Raboutin-Chantal in 1592 and was left a widow with four children in 1601. Her efforts to live an intense spiritual life were made difficult by a complex regime imposed by an unyielding spiritual director. In 1601, however, St. Francis de Sales became her director and introduced her to a more joyous and simple understanding of the way of perfection. At Annecy in 1610 with two companions she received from him a rule of life for a community dedicated to the Visitation of Mary. Members were to include both young girls and widows striving to imitate the contemplative spirit of the Magnificat by their prayer and the active mercy of the Visitation by their visits to the sick. Through the intervention of the abp. of Lyons, however, the group had to adopt the status of a religious order, solemn vows, and the cloistered life. C. personally established many new houses of the order, and there were 85 at the time of her death. Her intense, mystical prayer life inspired and is reflected in St. Francis de Sales' *Treatise on the Love of God.* After his death, she was under the direction of St. Vincent de Paul; she was also a close friend of Mère Angélique Arnauld. C. was beatified in 1751 and canonized in 1767. BIBLIOGRAPHY: E. Stopp, *Madame de Chantal* (1963); H. Bremond, *Sainte Chantal* (1912); L. Chierotti, BiblSanct 6:581–586.

[T. C. O'BRIEN]

CHANTEPIE DE LA SAUSSAYE, PIER DANIËL (1848–1920), Dutch Protestant historian of religions. C. taught at Amsterdam (1878–99) and at Leyden (1899–1916). He was interested in the ethical content of all religions. His somewhat rationalistic handbook of the history of religions has frequently been reedited. BIBLIOGRAPHY: S. Furlani, EnccCatt 3:1386.

[M. J. SUELZER]

CHANTRY, a *benefice maintained to celebrate Mass for the founder or others designated by him. By extension the term also refers to the chapel where the Masses are said, either an area within the main church or a separate structure, attached or detached. Formerly priests appointed to chantries often conducted schools.

[T. EARLY]

CHAOS (BIBLICAL) Gr., for primeval, disordered matter that preceded the ordered cosmos. The Heb. phrase, *tōhū wābōhū*, of Gen 1.2, "a formless wasteland," when linked with "darkness," the "abyss" of "waters," and the "mighty wind," expressed for the priestly authors of the first creation account a notion comparable to the Greek chaos. To describe God's effortless creation of the visible universe by spoken commands, they used this ancient belief that the world was originally a watery mass of confusion and darkness in which the earth was engulfed, a concept that appeared to them to be a concrete expression of what more abstract thinkers would later call nothingness. An important problem of Gen 1.1 is whether the text affirms that God created chaos first and then proceeded to put order into it by further creations. Since the account describes God's creative activity as a command, the authors could hardly have conceived that the first act of creation, without a word being spoken, resulted in such disorder. For them a dark abyss of waters hiding a desolate earth and churned up by a violent wind could not have been an apt product of God's purpose to make what was good. Indicative of this conclusion are the widely accepted translation of verse 1 as a temporal clause: "In the beginning, when God created the heavens and the earth, ..." and/or the acceptance of it as a summation of the whole account, which would then not affirm anything about the creation of the chaos of verse 2. Later biblical theology used a less concrete expression of the nothingness "out of which" God created (2 Mac 7.28; Heb 11.3). However, it is apparent from Rev 21 that certain Jewish Christians still held that some observable elements of the original creation were not fit to be retained in God's ultimate re-creation, such as darkness and the sea. BIBLIOGRAPHY: L. F. Hartman, NCE 3:452; EDB 449–458.

[A. P. HANLON]

CHAPEL, a word derived from the diminutive of *cappa*, "cloak" or "cape." Upon the legendary cape of St. Martin of Tours, preserved as a precious relic by the Frankish kings, important oaths were sworn. The place where the cape was kept came to be called a chapel *(capella)*, and its custodian a chaplain *(capellanus)*. In the early Church there were a number of informal places of worship including the *martyrium* where relics of martyrs were enshrined. Kings and nobles also built oratories on their estates where the liturgy

might be celebrated, except on principal feasts (council of Agde [506 A.D.], c. 21). Charlemagne constructed a magnificent house of worship at his palace in Aachen. Gradually the term *capella* supplanted *martyrium* and *oratorium*. Today chapels include subsidiary areas within a larger church, as well as oratories in institutions, cemeteries, and private residences. BIBLIOGRAPHY: P. J. Mullins, NCE 3:452–453.

[J. E. LYNCH]

CHAPEL OF EASE, a small place of worship within the boundaries of a large parish. It is usually established to offer the faithful a more accessible place to attend Mass. It is under the charge of the local pastor but often becomes the site of a new parish.

CHAPELAIN, JEAN (1595–1674), French writer and literary critic of enormous influence, one of the first members of the French Academy and author of the *Sentiments de l'Académie sur le Cid*. An opponent of Descartes and follower of Gassendi, C. tried to apply empirical philosophy to literary criticism. Hailed for his outline of a heroic poem on Joan of Arc, *La Pucelle,* he lost much respect as a poet 25 years later (1656) when the 12 first *chants* finally appeared. Along with his critical writings, his correspondence, and his remarkable preface to Marino's *Adone,* he also wrote a *Paraphrase sur le Miserere* (1636). BIBLIOGRAPHY: G. Collas, *Un Poète protecteur des lettres au 17ᵉ siècle: Jean Chapelain* (1912).

[R. N. NICOLICH]

CHAPELLE, PLACIDE LOUIS (1842–1905), diplomat and archbishop. In 1898 C. was appointed apostolic delegate to Puerto Rico and Cuba, and was also chargé d'affaires of the Philippine Islands. There he secured the release of clergy taken prisoner by Aquinaldo and helped solve problems pertaining to church property and rights of Spanish clergy in the islands. In New Orleans he succeeded in liquidating the diocesan debt. His love for his people forced him to return to New Orleans during the yellow fever epidemic, and he succumbed to the disease. BIBLIOGRAPHY: H. C. Bezou NCE 3:453; T. Roemer, *Catholic Church in United States* (1950) 323.

[J. L. HALPIN]

CHAPLAINS, originally clerics in charge of a *chapel; in later usage, priests or clergymen appointed to conduct religious services for a particular group, association, confraternity, or institution, Because of historical and jurisdictional considerations, the following different ecclesiastical uses to which the term has been put are identified separately. Military chaplains, since their office implies some civil as well as ecclesiastical status, are treated in a distinct article (see below).

(1) *Court chaplains,* clerics attached to royal or imperial courts, with the original function of serving special chapels

of the palace. The practice began under the early Frankish kings; the chaplains often taught in palace schools, served as confessors for the royal or imperial household, gave advice and assistance in the administration of alms (cf. almoner; Fr. *aumônier*). A chaplaincy was frequently a position of power and influence and carried with it considerable dignity of rank. In later times the chaplains at royal and imperial courts in Germany formed a body of canons and the palace chapel had the status of a collegiate church.

(2) *Episcopal chaplains*, priests who were members of the bp.'s household and assigned to private oratories in the episcopal palace. They often served the bp. in special capacities, e.g., as secretaries, librarians, archivists, and as assistants in liturgical services. A vestige of this office exists in the honorary chaplains who assist the bp. at pontifical functions.

(3) *Papal chaplains*, members of the clergy attached to the pope's chapel. Their duty is to assist the pope at the altar, and they differ in rank according to their special responsibilities. The title is now often given as an honorary one to clerics in the different dioceses throughout the world, despite the fact that they are rarely if ever able to perform the function of their office.

(4) *Cathedral chaplains*, clerics employed by cathedral canons to perform choral duties required by their office. The custom of fulfilling these duties vicariously arose when it became common for cathedral canons to live at a distance from their cathedral or collegiate churches.

(5) *Parochial or auxiliary chaplains*, a term used in some European countries in former times for clerics appointed to assist parish priests who were unable personally to care for all the faithful of their parishes. Today priests serving in this capacity are generally called assistants, assistant pastors, or curates.

(6) *Domestic chaplains*, priests appointed to celebrate Mass in the homes of families having the privilege of a private chapel and the means to support a private chaplain. Such chaplains often served also as tutors for the children of the household.

(7) *Beneficed chaplains*, priests having the duty to celebrate, or to procure the celebration of, certain Masses, and/or to take part in designated liturgical services (e.g., choral services). In consideration of this, they receive support from a pious foundation established for that purpose.

(8) *Lay chaplains*, the name given to persons in charge of foundation funds intended for the support of beneficed chaplains performing the services designated in the foundation, when they are also entitled by the terms of the foundation to nominate and present to the bp. the clerics by whom the services are to be performed. It is the bp., however, who actually confers the chaplaincy on the nominee.

(9) *Chantry chaplains*, beneficed chaplains in charge of a *chantry established for the celebration of Masses for the benefit of particular persons or in honor of some saint or mystery of faith.

(10) *Chaplains of religious communities*. In the RC Church nonexempt lay religious communities depend for their pastoral care upon the local parish priest; he is the official immediately in charge of liturgical services held within nonexempt religious houses situated in his parish. The bp., however, may withdraw a particular religious community of this kind from the pastoral care of the local pastor and entrust it to a special chaplain (see CIC c. 464.2). The rights and duties of the chaplain appointed by the bp. in such circumstances are defined in making the appointment, and they may vary according to circumstances in different cases. In exempt religious communities, the regular superior designates the chaplain.

(11) *Institutional chaplains*. According to RC canon law, the pastoral care of institutions (schools, hospitals, prisons, etc.) are the responsibility of the parish priest of the territory in which they are located. As in the case of nonexempt lay religious communities, the bp. may see fit to withdraw such an institution from the care of the local pastor and confide it to a specially appointed chaplain. The chaplain in this case will have those powers and responsibilities indicated by the bp. in making the appointment. Usually they include the hearing of confessions, the distribution of holy communion, and the administration of the last rites in the institution. If the institution has an oratory, the chaplain offers Mass. The chaplain does not administer solemn baptism, unless the oratory is privileged to have a baptismal font, nor does the chaplain, as such, have jurisdiction to officiate at marriages.

(12) *Confraternity chaplains*, priests appointed with the authority, during their tenure of office, to conduct certain services according to the authorized ritual of the confraternity, to bless the habit, scapular, medal, and other insignia used by the members, and to invest candidates with the habit or scapular. They are not, as chaplains, entitled to preach or give conferences to the members, although they are generally empowered to do this in virtue of the local diocesan faculties granted to them by the local ordinary. BIBLIOGRAPHY: R. J. Murphy, NCE 3:453–454; W. H. W. Fanning, CE 3:579–591.

[P. K. MEAGHER]

CHAPLAINS, MILITARY, clergymen attached to the armed forces, a service provided for military personnel by almost all Christian nations. In the U.S. military services, chaplains are under the dual authority of the military and of the Church. Churches are allotted a number of places in proportion to their numerical strength in the nation as a whole, and each chaplain must have the approval of his Church to fill one of its places. The chaplain is given rank as an officer and is under the command authority of his military superiors.

Special regulations outline the rights and responsibilities of chaplains. They vary to some degree in different branches of the service, but all branches respect the doctrinal position of each chaplain, who cannot be required to do anything contrary to the teaching of his Church.

Chaplains regularly conduct worship services according to

the rites of their Church, perform baptisms, officiate at weddings and funerals, and give religious counsel to individuals. Though the religious ministry is acknowledged to be their primary responsibility, they are often asked to perform additional duties relating to the general welfare of the servicemen, e.g., give talks on general morality, assist individuals in various kinds of personal difficulty, and advise commanders on matters of morale.

At permanent bases, chaplains generally have chapel facilities and carry out programs similar to those in civilian parishes, with regular programs of Sunday schools, sodalities, and other organizational activities. In combat areas, of course, the chaplain may only be able to hold brief services in the open air, give occasional pastoral support to individuals, and render spiritual assistance to the wounded and dying.

Most American Churches have established some means of relating to the chaplaincy and military life in general. Since 1917 the RC Church has placed all Catholics in the military services under the *military ordinariate.

The chaplaincy system has given rise to some controversy. On the one hand, some of the more dedicated proponents of complete separation of Church and State have objected to it as an instance of unwarranted interaction of Church and State. But the question is perhaps more theoretical than practical, because few separationists would press the issue so rigorously because of the manifest inhumanity of forcing men into the danger of death without the support of the religious practices they feel to be necessary. Moreover, enforced military service without chaplains would have the practical effect of depriving people of the opportunity of worshiping according to the dictates of their consciences, a step repugnant to separationist principles. From the standpoint of the military, access to religious ministry is considered both a right of the serviceman and a contribution to his general welfare that will make him a better serviceman.

On the other hand, question about the desirability of the system has been raised by some on religious grounds. Some are offended because they are pacifists, others because they think that chaplains, by accepting their salaries from the military services and becoming an integral part of the military, are in danger of compromising their ultimate loyalty and of uncritically giving divine blessing to limited nationalistic goals. Some also think chaplains ought not to take officer rank; defenders of the practice reply that the rank enables the chaplain to serve more effectively.

[T. EARLY]

CHAPLET, from a French word meaning wreath or crown, a set of beads strung together and used for counting prayers. By extension the word is also applied to the devotion whose prayer parts are counted on such beads. Most commonly the term is used in connection with the *rosary, esp. the more familiar five-decade rosary. But it is also applied to other devotions in which prayers or aspirations are counted, e.g., the chaplet of St. Bridget, or the devotion introduced in the C

of E by M. W. T. Conran, with prayers that differ from those of the rosary.

[T. EARLY]

CHAPMAN, JOHN (baptized Henry Palmer; 1865–1933), English Benedictine biblical scholar, patrologist, church historian, spiritual writer, abbot of Downside from 1929. In 1890 C., then an Anglican deacon, entered the Catholic Church and 2 years later became a Benedictine at *Maredsous. He served in various capacities at the Abbey of Erdington near Birmingham from his ordination (1895) until 1912 when he returned to Maredsous, but later his monastic stability was transferred to *Downside (1919). His scholarly activity in the various fields in which he took an interest was enormous, and his writings (books, articles in learned journals and encyclopedias) won him a distinguished reputation, esp. for his patristic studies that centered about the early papacy. His views on contemplative prayer are an interesting contribution to the literature of spirituality, as is also his doctrine regarding a "mystical faculty," which is not a gift of the Holy Spirit, but a vestige of man's primordial and quasi-angelic approach to the unseen and incommunicable, a faculty damaged but not obliterated by the fall. This was propounded in Hastings ERE 9:90–101. BIBLIOGRAPHY: F. X. Murphy, NCE 3:545; G. R. Hudleston, DSAM 2.1:488–492; R. Gazeau, DTC Tables Générales 1:580–581.

[R. B. ENO]

CHAPPOTIN DE NEUVILLE, HÉLÈNE DE (1839–1904), French missionary. As a member of the Society of Mary Reparatrix, she was known as Mother Mary of the Passion. During her 10 years of missionary work in India, she became the provincial superior, and by 1896 had founded the Missionaries of Mary and had merged her institute with the Franciscans. The order became known as the Franciscan Missionaries of Mary, and the constitutions were approved by Rome in 1896. Her writings have been the means of spiritual growth to her congregation. BIBLIOGRAPHY: T. F. Cullen, *Mother Mary of the Passion* (abr. ed., 1942).

[C. KEENAN]

CHAPPUIS, MARIA SALESIA, VEN. (1793–1875), French religious. With Louis Brisson, C. was instrumental in founding the Oblate Sisters of St. Francis and the Oblates of St. Francis de Sales. As a Visitandine nun, C. spent many years as superior and mistress of novices at Troyes and Paris. BIBLIOGRAPHY: L. Brisson, *Vie de la vénérée Mère de Sales Chappuis* (1891); P. Dufour, DSAM 2:496–498.

[C. KEENAN]

CHAPTAL, EMMANUEL ANATOLE (1861–1947), bp. After some years in the foreign service of France, C. entered St. Sulpice and was ordained in 1897. Made a titular bishop in 1922, he served as assistant to the abp. of Paris.

During the German occupation of France in World War II, C., as archbishop wore a Star of David to indicate his rejection of German persecution of the Jews. BIBLIOGRAPHY: J. Rupp, *Catholicisme* 2:949.

[J. R. AHERNE]

CHAPTER, the English translation of the Lat. *capitulum*. In liturgical use the term refers to a brief scriptural passage for reading after the psalms of one of the liturgical hours. In reference to an institutional practice among canons and some religious communities, it designates an official assembly of canons, monks, friars, or members of a religious community held for elective, administrative, consultative, or legislative purposes. Various kinds of chapters are distinguished according to the nature of the community and the scope of the authority of a particular assemblage. Thus, in religious orders or congregations there are house (conventual), provincial, and general chapters, depending on whether the assembly is composed of qualified religious of a single house, or of a province, or of the order or congregation as a whole. A chapter of canons is a college of canons instituted to carry out the liturgical functions of a cathedral (cathedral chapter) and to serve as a kind of council or senate for the bishop; if the church to which the canons are attached is not a cathedral, the college is referred to as a collegiate chapter. In some religious orders in older times the house (or conventual) chapter met daily to hear announcements, admonitions, or exhortations of the abbot or superior, to pray for the living and the dead, and to hear the confession of the faults of its individual members; thus it was often called the chapter of faults. In later times chapters of this kind have more commonly been held periodically than daily.

[P. K. MEAGHER]

CHAPTER, CATHEDRAL, an organized group of clergy attached to a cathedral. The institution reached its peak of influence in the High Middle Ages. In the early centuries of the Church, all clergy generally lived with the bp. and served the cathedral church. In the Middle Ages the cathedral clergy acquired personal property and separate houses. The cathedral chapter therefore became an entity separate in some ways from the bp., and at times was in contest with him. In some cases monks were introduced to serve the cathedrals as a result of the conflict (canons regular as distinguished from canons secular), but they also sought to extend their rights at the expense of the bishop. Cathedral chapters became recognized in canon law, and chapter officers—dean, precentor, treasurer, chancellor—became powerful figures. In some cases the chapter elected the bp., a development encouraged by some popes to offset lay influence. The loss of that power began in 1305 when Clement V reserved to himself power to name bps. in the diocese of Rome. His successors gradually extended the practice to cover all dioceses. From the 13th to the 16th cent., the chapter governed the diocese during a vacancy. The Council of *Trent directed that the chapter appoint a vicar capitular to administer the diocese within a week of the bp.'s death.

At the Reformation chapters were abolished in the Lutheran and Calvinistic Churches and modified in the C of E. Today Anglican cathedrals are generally governed by a small group of residentiary canons. RC canon law (CIC c. 391–444) provides for cathedral chapters, which now generally assist with services and act as the bishop's council. But in some areas, such as the U.S., they do not exist.

[T. EARLY]

CHAPTER, COLLEGIATE, the clergy attached to a collegiate church. Such a church, often supported by endowments, is one served by a group of clergy who share responsibility. It differs from the cathedral in having no bishop. Examples in the C of E include Westminster Abbey and St. George's Chapel, Windsor.

In the RC Church collegiate chapters are regulated by CIC cc. 391–422. Though they may be founded by the gift of a benefactor, they can be established, suppressed, or recreated only by act of the Apostolic See. They comprise canons, among whom the offices of the chapter are distributed, and dignities conferred by the Holy See. Holders of lesser benefices, who assist the canons, do not belong to the chapter. Bishops may appoint honorary canons after consulting the chapter, but the honorary canons have no vote in the chapter. Among the offices the chapter may have are canon theologian and canon penitentiary, but it must have no more canons than its income will support. If the collegiate church has pastoral responsibility, it must elect a parochial vicar. Except for dignities, the bishop normally appoints each holder of a benefice or canonry after seeking the advice of the chapter. Each chapter operates under its own statutes, but these laws must be approved by the bp. and be in accord with general regulations of the Church. Chapters meet regularly to care for the affairs of their churches, and they may also have special meetings as occasion demands. When asked, canons of collegiate churches must assist their bp. in services at other churches. In their own church the chapter must perform the Divine Office daily in choir and such other services as may have been specified in the founding of the church. BIBLIOGRAPHY: Woywod-Smith.

[T. EARLY]

CHAPTER, CONVENTUAL, a meeting held periodically or upon special occasions in some religious orders or congregations at which the professed members of a monastery, convent, or house are in attendance. At such meetings important announcements are made, prayers are offered for benefactors and the deceased, votes are taken regarding matters concerning which superiors are obliged to hear the views of their subjects before making decisions. Sometimes the individual members of the community make public confession of their faults against the rule, for which penances are imposed. In many early monasteries the conventual chapter met daily. When the confession of faults constitutes the major concern of the meeting, the assembly of the religious is generally referred to as a chapter of faults.

[P. K. MEAGHER]

CHAPTER, GENERAL, a canonical assembly of provincials and other delegated members of a religious order or congregation, who meet at regular intervals to discuss and legislate on matters of general importance to the institute and of specific concern to the individual members. The business of amending the constitution and electing officers is also a part of the chapter. Aside from the pope, the general chapter represents the highest authority for religious in their respective communities.

[R. A. TODD]

CHAPTER, PROVINCIAL, a conference of superiors and other members delegated to represent the religious in a certain territory or province. They assemble to discuss, improve, or change the rules pertaining to their local province, and to elect provincial officials.

[R. A. TODD]

CHAPTER, RURAL, meeting of the clergy in the rural deanery of the Church of England. Also known as a ruridecanal chapter, it is composed of all incumbents and clergy licensed under seal in the deanery, a subdivision of the diocese.

From at least as early as the 6th cent., the Church has had archpriests exercising supervisory functions over other clergy. Of special importance for later historical development were the archpriests appointed to supervise other priests of a cathedral and the archpriests with responsibility for priests of other churches in a section of the diocese. The former developed into the office of dean (Lat., *decanus,* one over ten), and the latter developed into the office of rural dean, sometimes called an archpresbyter.

The office of rural dean is said to have been brought to England from Rouen, probably by Lanfranc. The rural dean held the lowest court of jurisdiction, visiting churches, installing clergy, punishing moral offenders, dealing with marital cases, and performing certain other duties. In the 13th cent., archdeacons took over the functions of rural deans, and the office remained generally dormant until the 19th cent., when it was revived.

The rural dean now presides over the rural chapter, an administrative level under the diocese. The chapter sometimes chooses one of its members for the office of rural dean, but the appointment is made by the bishop.

The RC Church has the rural dean (vicar forane), who gathers the clergy of his deanery for conferences and handles other responsibilities for the area, but the term chapter is not generally used in connection with that work.

[T. EARLY]

CHAPTER OF FAULTS, see CHAPTER, CONVENTUAL.

CHAPU, HENRI MICHEL ANTOINE (1833–91), French sculptor who after studying in Paris spent 5 years in Rome. A pleasing naturalism qualified his academic classicism, visible in his *Jeanne d'Arc* (1870, Paris). BIBLIOGRA-

PHY: O. Fidière, *Chapu: Sa vie et son oeuvre* (1894).

[M. J. DALY]

CHARACTER, SACRAMENTAL, see SACRAMENTAL CHARACTER.

CHARACTER PROBLEMS, a classification not sharply distinguished from other categories of mental, emotional, or behavioral problems. Generally speaking, what are called character problems do not involve the emotional distress of *neuroses or the cognitive distortions of *psychoses or the severe alienation from social rapport characteristic of *psychopathic behavior. Since the word "character" tends to be used for a person and his behavior as morally praiseworthy or blameworthy, the label "character problem" is likely to refer to a type of problem that elicits social or personal disapproval and condemnation. Thus a personality problem, e.g., how to overcome timidity, would not be a character problem unless timidity were considered morally reprehensible. However, the line between character problems and personality problems is thin; the terms are frequently used interchangeably. Character problems generally handicap a person less than psychiatric disorders, although they tend to make interpersonal relations more difficult and to limit a person's effectiveness. Typical character problems, rooted generally in an exaggerated rigidity in the interpretation of moral and social norms, include excessive captiousness, uncontrollable temper, overdefensiveness in personal relations, hypersensitivity, habitual self-aggrandizement, boasting, sarcasm, teasing, overdependence on others, insatiable ambition, overaggressiveness, inability to work perseveringly, excessive indulgence in food and drink, prejudices and bigotry, emotional instability, and tendencies to lie, cheat, and steal. These are commonly indicative of deeper personality disorders, and while general experience in life, along with friendly counseling, advice and support, divine grace and personal effort, overcome them to some extent, they are difficult to eradicate entirely.

[M. E. STOCK]

CHARACTER, STRUCTURE OF, a distinctive sign of something used in psychology to designate particular dispositions of an individual or a group of individuals, which might account for their specific behavior. Structure of character is described in its psychological sense. In a descriptive sense character is treated as a consideration in the fields of psychopedagogy, psychomedicine, and psychophilosophy. When one speaks of character in psychopedagogical terms, one generally is speaking of the ethical dimensions of character. In the psychomedical conception of character, one is inclined to see character as a set of impulses and drives. Dominant in this field are the names of C. G. *Jung and H. Rorschach. In any case, in psychomedical considerations character is studied in a mind/body context. When one speaks of the psychophilosophical understanding of character, one is identifying the personality. For some scientists in this field character is seen as a set of personal values from which issue the various acts one associates with particular types of persons, e.g., the theoretical, the economic-minded, the aesthetic, the political. Each designation has an antecedent of specific values that contributes toward the designation of the person as aesthetic, political, etc. P. Lersch subscribes to the layer theory in his explanation of character. Each individual according to him, emerges in a self unit from layers of nature. The dispositions of the character are always interrelating and moving the individual toward awareness. It is these interrelations that constitute the structure of character. And, it is from the structure of character that there emerges the particular modality of being in the individual. BIBLIOGRAPHY: E. Martinez, NCE 3:457.

[J. R. RIVELLO]

CHARBONNEAU, JOSEPH (1892–1959), Canadian churchman. C. studied at the seminary in Montreal, was ordained in 1916, and was consecrated bp. of Hearst, Ont., in 1939. He was transferred to Montreal as coadjutor abp. in 1940 and shortly succeeded to the see. A supporter of social justice, he did much to reconcile the Church and the trade unions in Canada. After siding with workers in a strike and so opposing the Quebec premier, Maurice Du Plessis, he retired from his see in 1950 and spent his last years in Victoria, British Columbia.

[R. K. MacMASTER]

CHARBONNEL, ARMAND FRANÇOIS DE (1802–91), Sulpician, later a Capuchin, missionary and bishop. Ordained in his native France, he volunteered for missionary work and was sent to Montreal, Canada (1840). He was chosen the first bp. of Toronto (1850) and did much to develop the Catholic school system of his diocese. He was a vigorous proponent of public aid to religious schools. He resigned his see in 1860 and entered the Capuchin novitiate at Rieti, Italy. His last years were spent in France promoting foreign missions. BIBLIOGRAPHY: C. Causse, *Vie de Monseigneur de Charbonnel: Évêque de Toronto* (1931).

[R. K. MacMASTER]

CHARDIN, JEAN BAPTISTE SIMÉON (1699–1779), French painter. Son of a master cabinetmaker, trained academically and working under N. N. Coypel, C. developed a direct painting of careful, visual analysis. He gained recognition (1728), became a member of the Royal Academy, attaining to quarters in the Louvre (1757). A laborious perfectionist, his scenes of simple, sober bourgeois life (*Grace after Meals*) recall Vermeer and the Le Nain brothers. From 1751–71, C.'s commonplace objects, discreetly composed and flawlessly rendered in rich impasto and glowing tones, elicit eternal qualities in modest things, which become monumental and sanctified in a spiritual solitude fusing classicism and naturalism. In the mid-19th cent. there was a revival of interest in C.'s engagement with

formal abstract problems, tensions of surface and space, and minimal means to an expressive end. BIBLIOGRAPHY: J. Seznec and J. Adhémar, *Diderot Salons* (1957) v. 1.

[M. J. DALY]

CHARDON, LOUIS (1595–1651), Dominican theologian and spiritual writer. C. pursued higher studies in Paris, where he entered the Order of Preachers. After ordination he preached for a time but spent most of his life in writing and spiritual direction. His most popular work is *Meditations on the Passion of Our Lord Jesus Christ*. His principal work, *The Cross of Jesus*, presents a theology of Christian suffering. BIBLIOGRAPHY: F. Florand, DSAM 2.1:498–503.

[M. E. ALLWEIN]

CHARDON, MATHIAS CHARLES (1695–1771), Benedictine. Born at Yvois-Carignan, France, C. served as novice master and later as teacher of philosophy and theology at the Abbey of St. Arnold de Metz. Because of his severity, his Jansenistic ideas (he saw Jesuits as the enemy of the Church), and his refusal to submit to the papal bull *Unigenitus*, he was forced by his general chapter to resign. He died at St. Arnold, but his great work, *Histoire des sacrements et de la manière dont ils ont été célébrés et administré dans l'Église* (6 v., 1745) is still of value today.

[T. LIDDY]

CHARENTON (QUARTON), ENGUERRAND (c.1420–c.1470), French painter, schooled in Franco-Flemish Gothic linearism, who blended the Sienese 14th-cent. style at Avignon with a Provençal three-dimensional form in major altarpieces of his period. C. was commissioned (1452) to paint a *Virgin of Mercy* (showing posthumous portraits of Jean Cadart and his wife) and SS. John the Baptist and John the Evangelist (Condé Museum). His *Coronation of the Virgin* (1453, Villeneuve-les-Avignon) revealing details dictated by the donor, presents a whole Christian cosmos—the Virgin and the Holy Trinity, paradise (reduced in scale) and earth beneath (showing the landscape of Avignon, with the holy cities of Rome and Jerusalem separated by the Crucifixion), and below, purgatory and hell. The famous *Avignon Pietà* (before 1457, Louvre), sharing certain characteristics with the above, has recently been attributed to him. BIBLIOGRAPHY: M. Laclotte, *L'École d'Avignon: La Peinture en Provence aux XIVe et XVe siècles* (1960).

[M. J. DALY]

CHARGE, in Methodism, the local church (station charge) or a group of local churches (circuit charge). It is the basic unit of Methodist organization. *CONFERENCE; *DISTRICT SUPERINTENDENT.

[T. C. O'BRIEN]

CHARISM, from the Gr., *charisma,* a gift of grace, a favor graciously given. In its technical scriptural and theological meaning, it is a supernatural, transitory gift from God, given to the recipient primarily for the benefit of others. St. Paul defines it as a "manifestation of the Spirit . . . for profit" of the Church (1 Cor 12.7). It is on this account that charism retains in its definition the merely generic term of grace (gratia gratis data). It differs specifically from the other type of grace, the primary purpose of which is to render the individual holy in God's sight (gratia gratum faciens). At times, however, there might exist some correlation between the two types. Charisms reflect a special intervention of God in man's powers by which these are elevated to behavior beyond their natural capacity. They consist in different kinds of intellectual illuminations, in facility to communicate divine things to others, in ability to perform extraordinary or miraculous deeds, etc. There are some eight different lists of charisms in the NT: Mk 16.17–18; 1 Cor 12.4–10; 12.28–31; 14.6–13; 14.26; Rom 12.6–8; Eph 4.11; 1 Pet 4.10–11. From these lists three groups could be formed according to function and purpose, namely, teaching charisms, service charisms, and miraculous charisms. Other arrangements and classifications made by theologians are arbitrary. St. Thomas Aquinas visualized the role of these gifts in the Church in their doctrinal and apologetic functions (ThAq ST 3a, 7.7). Charisms play a special role in the corporate Church. As signs of God's presence in the Church they perform the vital function of making the Church visible and credible to the world. Although they can exist outside the Church, they find their natural habitat in the Church where the Spirit, their author, dwells. In fact, some of these charisms are given precisely to provide the Church with its very ministerial and hierarchical structure. These are holy orders, authority, etc. Others, the more extraordinary ones such as prophecy, glossolalia, etc., are given indiscriminately to clergy or laity for the purpose of enriching the life in the same Church. BIBLIOGRAPHY: F. Prat, *Theology of St. Paul* (tr. J. Stoddard, 2 v., 1926) 1:127–133, 423–428; K. Rahner, "Charismatic Element in the Church," *Dynamic Element in the Church* (tr. W. J. O'Hara, *Questiones Disputatae* 12, 1964).

[R. J. TAPIA]

CHARISMATIC GIFTS, spiritual, preternatural gifts given for the work of ministry in the Church (Eph 4.12). The NT gives various lists (e.g., Rom 12.6–8; 1 Cor 12.4–10; Eph 4.11, etc.). The charisms serve the activities of teaching, governing, and sanctifying in the Church. Medieval theology referred to them as *gratiae gratis datae,* i.e., given for the good of others and not, per se, as is *gratia gratum faciens,* for the recipient's own sanctification. Working with the text of 1 Cor 12.8–10, St. Thomas Aquinas (ST 1a2ae, 111.4) classifies them on the basis of assistance needed by one engaged in leading others to divine realities: a need for fuller knowledge (thus the charisms of *faith, the utterances of wisdom* and *of knowledge*); a need for divine confirmation of his teaching (thus the *graces of healing,* the *working of miracles,* the gifts of *prophecy* and the *discernment of*

spirits); the need to teach persuasively (thus the gift of *tongues* and of the *interpretation of tongues*). In view of Christ's promises of the Holy Spirit, the charismatic is to be expected as essential in the life of the Church. The phenomena of Pentecost have in fact been repeated; one obvious way is in the preaching and the miracles of the saints who have brought renewal to the life of the Church throughout the ages. The continued exercise of teaching, sanctifying, and serving ministries in the Church attests to the charismatic assistance of graces given to the faithful for the building up of the body of Christ. An essential separation, then, between the hierarchic and the charismatic in the life of the Church cannot be defended on sound theological grounds. Vatican Council II has in fact clearly affirmed that the Holy Spirit endows the Church with both hierarchical and charismatic gifts (Vat II ConstCh n.4), i.e., its sacraments and ministries and special graces given to the faithful at all levels for the good of the Church (see also *ibid.* n.12; Vat II ApostLaity n.3). Among charisms the Council makes a division between ordinary gifts for service and *dona extraordinaria,* giving recognition to such extraordinary gifts as are those cultivated in the *Neo-Pentecostal movement. (Vat II ConstCh *ibid.*). Historically, however, there has been an official conservatism towards private revelations, claims of miracles, or other special gifts; and, esp. in the era of opposition to *Modernism, there has been a negative attitude toward experiential or charismatic expressions, and an emphasis on objective, doctrinal teaching, and sacramental life. The charismatic renewal, so widespread in the Church, seems to indicate a more balanced acceptance of the experiential in the Christian life. The movement has received both papal and episcopal encouragement; in turn, one of the distinctive effects on its adherents is a deepening fidelity and attachment to the doctrinal and sacramental traditions of the Church.

[T. C. O'BRIEN]

CHARISMATIC PRAYER, the nonliturgical, but communitary prayer characteristic of the charismatic renewal (see NEO-PENTECOSTALISM IN THE RC CHURCH). Among the widespread prayer groups in the contemporary Church, charismatic expression sets apart the Neo-Pentecostal from others. But while essential and distinctive, the charismatic event should be seen within the whole setting of the prayer meeting. In intent and in fact the meeting of any charismatic group is kept spontaneous and free. One universal mark, however, is that the group prays as a community, constituted not by the use of common, set formulas for praying, but by a shared sense of Christ's promise to be present wherever two or three are gathered in his name (Mt 18.20). Within that atmosphere the meeting—which may last 1 to 3 or 4 hours, depending on how it develops—proceeds in confidence of being led by the Spirit. The group may dwell on scriptural passages; some may give testimony to their own experiences; frequently the Our Father is recited with great devotion; someone may call for a "word of prayer," and all pray aloud in whatever form or tongue they choose. Then or at another point in the meeting, the charismatic moment comes with the exercise of the gift of tongues. This charism is regarded to be essentially a gift of prayer (see 1 Cor 14.2), the external manifestation of the Holy Spirit's power inspiring prayer. The language is not important as a vehicle of communication (although several recognizable languages have been spoken in such meetings); rather its effect on the hearers is the heightening of their confidence in the Spirit's power, the experience of being in touch with the divine, and of praising the Father. The charismatic expression does intensify the community's unity in prayer, the individual's own prayer life, and awareness of the divine presence. A final, fairly frequent occurrence in the prayer meeting is the communitary laying on of hands upon one in special need, or praying for baptism in the Spirit.

[T. C. O'BRIEN]

CHARITÉ-SUR-LOIRE, ABBEY OF, a Benedictine monastery founded in 706 near Nevers, France. Destroyed in 771, it was restored in 1056 by monks of Cluny. It was a strong and important house in the Cluniac reform but fell into serious decline in the mid-15th and 16th centuries. In 1634 it was taken over by the Cluniacs of the Strict Observance. It was suppressed in 1790, but many of the buildings and the church remain.

[J. C. WILLKE]

CHARITY, from the Vulg *charitas,* translating the Gr. NT *agapē*. This term, which has no parallel use in classical Gr., expresses the revelation of the Father as love (1 Jn 4.16; Rom 13.9–10) and as embracing man by that love; it expresses as well the state and act of one in God's grace responding with wholehearted love for God, and in its continuance in the love for neighbor (Mt 22.37, 39) that Christ enjoins as his own, new commandment (Jn 13.34–35). In charity consists the bond of perfection (Rom 12.10; Eph 4.15; Col 1.4; 3.14); it is supreme among all gifts of grace and will endure in eternity (1 Cor 13.1–13). The noun *agapē* and the verb *agapaō,* then bear the burden of conveying the intimacy and immediacy of loving union between man and God fully revealed by and in Christ. "Charity" dulls the force of that revealed signification in its secular use, meaning philanthropy or even a faint tolerance towards the failings of others. The substitution of "love" for "charity" in recent translations of scriptural and liturgical texts does not seem to set apart the special force of the NT term that the use of *charitas* instead of *amor* intends.

Because of its prominence in the NT, early Christian pastoral and homiletic writings centered, not on analyzing it, but on instilling its meaning as the way of Christian living. Before the formal theological formulations of the 13th cent., the writings of Augustine (he addresses his congregations in sermons as *charitas vestra*), the *Rule of St. Benedict, the preaching of St. *Bernard of Clairvaux, the theology of the *Victorines are evidence of the understanding of the primacy of charity. An early indicator of the theologians' adherence to this is the position of *Peter Lombard (I *Sent.*17,1, Quaracchi ed., I,p. 106) that, unlike other good acts that have as inner source a virtue in the doer, the act of love for God and neighbor has as its inner source the Holy Spirit immediately present and prompting such an act. St. Thomas Aquinas, in developing the meaning of the life of grace and the theological virtues, appreciated this attempt at expressing the sublimity of charity, but showed that just because of its preeminence loving God presupposes an inner, connatural responsiveness to the prompting of the Holy Spirit; this is the theological virtue of charity (ThAq ST 2a2ae,24.1). To describe its distinctive meaning he chooses the idea of friendship (see Jn 15.15); it falls short of the reality, but does convey the idea of a "mutual loving between persons who are sharers" (Gilby, NCE 3:465); "Charity signifies not only the love of God, but also a certain friendship with him, which implies besides love, a certain mutual return of love, together with mutual communion" (ST 1a2ae,65.5). The union and communion with God rest on God's self-communication, drawing man into a share in the divine good that God himself is, and into the vitality of the divine love itself (*ibid*. 110,1 & 4). The communication is not simply God's beneficence bestowing a thing, as in creation, but the loving of another person, taking another into a love relationship with himself. The place and primacy of charity in the grace life, then, rests on its being the response to God's own love, making the recipient his friend, his son by adoption (Rom 8.15). Charity's act is the living expression of one's being as God's child; it is a rest in the Father because he is Father. The superiority of charity over faith and hope is its immediacy: they both rest on God as their motive, but as moving towards attainment; charity is motivated by God and also is immediate union with him. It is a tending toward, it needs growth, but in what it is, it will never pass away, because it is what grace is given for. As an immediate love for God, charity is at once a love for neighbor. For the union of love is with, so to speak, all that God is, and he is our Father, who loves each with the one love; to love him is to love with him, to love all. Because the union of charity is first between God and each person, the order of preference charity observes is first God above all, then self, then neighbor. Where other priorities enter, the measure of charity's preference is determined by the relationship each person and each reality has to the divine good on which charity is bent (ThAq ST 2a2ae,26).

In the living of Christian life that charity is the bond of perfection comes out first negatively from the Christian meaning of sin. A sin is mortal, fatal to spiritual life, because it breaks off from and blocks the divine communication of life in love; without that there is no longer a communion, a living love that rests in the Father as he is and in what he commands (*ibid*. 1a2ae,108.2). A sin is mortal not because of its ethical aberration, but because it cuts off the loving communion (*ibid*. 2a2ae,24.12) with God. Positively, charity is the essence of the Christian life because it is what gives both the meaning and the experience proper to what grace is revealed to be. The meaning because the "preeminence of the New Law is the grace of the Holy Spirit made manifest in us in a faith that works through love" (*ibid*. 1a2ae,10.8). The law of the gospel is the law of love, and no moral virtue nor moral precept as an expression of or a safeguarding of charity (*ibid*. ad 2; 107,1 & ad 2); it is the directive and the mother of all the virtues (*ibid*. 2a2ae, 23.6–8). Charity brings with it the experience of grace, first because the living of the Gospel is a burden lightened and a yoke sweetened by its love: "to one who loves the commandments are not heavy" (Augustine, *De natura et gratia* 69, PL44.289; cf. 1 Jn 5.3). It brings experience as well because the promise of the Divine Persons' dwelling in the soul is conditioned on the presence of charity (Jn 14.23); that bond of love, of connaturality and transformation into the divine (1a2ae,62.3) is the basis for a quasi-experimental knowledge of the divine that sustains in crisis and deepens the loving response to Father, Son, and Holy Spirit. BIBLIOGRAPHY: T. Gilby, NCE 3:464–470.

[T. C. O'BRIEN]

CHARITY, BROTHERS OF, a religious community of brothers founded at Ghent, Belgium, in 1807 by Canon Peter Joseph Triest. The apostolate comprises primarily charitable and educational works. Since papal recognition in 1899, the congregation has established five provinces: Belgium, Netherlands-Indonesia, England-Ireland, Africa, and Canada-Peru, with a U.S. district house in Philadelphia. Statistics in 1976 indicate 1,068 professed members in 94 houses. The general motherhouse is in Rome, Italy. BIBLIOGRAPHY: C. Reichgelt, *Les Frères de la Charité* (1957); S. Mattei, EncCatt 5:1706.

[R. A. TODD]

CHARITY, DAUGHTERS OF, a religious order of sisters, which includes numerous individual congregations in Europe and the U.S. Probably the earliest of these was founded in France in 1633 by SS. Vincent de Paul and Louise de Marillac. Some of the congregations are branches of the Sisters of Charity founded by St. Elizabeth Ann Seton at Emmitsburg, Md., in 1809. The institutes as a whole have adopted the rule of St. Vincent with some modifications suitable to the constitutions of each. Provinces have been founded throughout the world, and their apostolate encompasses primarily education, hospital services, and social work. In 1976, over 2,000 sisters in Mother Seton's congregations worked in five provinces in the U.S. alone. BIBLIOGRAPHY: P. Coste et al. *Les Filles de la Charité* (1933); A. Bugnini, EncCatt 5:1262–64; J. I. Dirvin, *Mrs. Seton* (1962).

[R. A. TODD]

CHARITY, WORKS OF. The first, inner effect of charity as the love of God includes as well the love of neighbor in mercy, an attitude that reaches out to and is not repelled by another's wretchedness. Traditionally the exterior works prompted by this merciful love are *almsgiving, in its various forms, and fraternal correction, when a neighbor is in need spiritually. To these may be annexed the spiritual and corporal works of mercy. In their distinctive meaning all these effects of charity are more than humanitarianism or the "social gospel." They are a love of neighbor that he will share in the divine good that God in his love wishes all to share, the divine life itself. BIBLIOGRAPHY: ThAq ST 2a2ae, 25:30–33. *BENEFICENCE.

[T. C. O'BRIEN]

CHARLEMAGNE, (742–814), king, emperor. Son of Pepin III and Bertha, he succeeded his father in 768 with his brother Carloman. Carloman's death in 771 left him sole ruler of Frankland. Most of his reign was consumed by warfare in Spain, Lombardy, Saxony, Slavic lands, and against the Avars. At his death the realm extended from the Ebro in Spain to the Elbe in Germany, from below Rome to the North Sea and Atlantic Ocean, with a capital at Aachen. It was governed simply, but quite effectively, by royal envoys *(missi dominici)* who traveled two by two, a lay magnate and an ecclesiastic, throughout the area. They conveyed C.'s will and heard complaints, settling them if possible, otherwise reporting them to him for decision.

C. was deeply interested in cultural development. He created a palace school for his own children and those of his retainers. He ordered schools established by bishops and abbots throughout his empire, open to all children. His scholars devised the form of letters called Caroline minuscule, still in use today as the basis of our book and cursive hands. He spent much time in study, becoming facile in Greek and Latin as well as in his own Germanic tongue. Importing intellectuals from Italy, Spain, and England to consort with his native scholars, he sowed the seeds for a renaissance of learning which came to fruition under his son. Part of the cultural achievement was an intimate alignment with the bishop of Rome. C., concerned for spread of the Roman rite and Gregorian chant, took himself seriously as eldest son and protector of the Church.

In recognition of his extensive domain as well as of his special relation to the Church he was crowned as emperor by Pope Leo III in Rome on Christmas Day, 800—an event that provoked the Byzantine emperor, who, however, finally recognized the *fait accompli*. Harun al Rashid of Baghdad entered into relations with C. as did some of the kings of the British Isles and some of the Christian and Muslim rulers of Spain.

Einhard, C.'s friend, left an inimitable biography of the hero, describing not only his military and political career, but also his personality and family life. According to Einhard, C. was unusually tall (seven times the length of his own foot), garrulous, loving the society of his family, friends, and retainers, a student of St. Augustine's *City of God*, devout in his attendance at religious services, aware of his place in the life of his day, admiring the old songs of his Germanic forebears, cruel and merciless against foes when occasion seemed to demand. He had four known wives (Sullivan says five) and six known concubines, who bore him 18 children. He was devoted to his mother Bertha who lived to a ripe old age at court and to his sister Gisela who succeeded Bertha as abbess of Chelles.

In the sober prose of Einhard it is obvious that C. was a legend during his life. The passage of time lent increasing stature to his fame. In Slavic lands the word for *king* was derived from the first half of *Charlemagne,* and in Scandinavian lands a common name for noblemen developed from the second half. The Emperor became a heroic figure in European saga and legend, a progenitor of most of the royal families of the West, the saint of an antipope who favored imperial as opposed to papal claims. His empire was the "first Europe," combining the Graeco-Roman, Judaic-Christian, and Teutonic barbarian heritages into a viable entity. It became a dream of those who have striven—still strive—for a common government of Europe. BIBLIOGRAPHY: Einhard, *Vita Karoli* (tr. S. E. Turner (repr. 1960); W. Braunfels, ed., *Karl der Grosse: Lebenswerk und Nachleben* (4v., 1966–68); R. E. Sullivan, NCE 3:497–500 (excellent bibliog.).

[A. CABANISS]

CHARLES I (1600–49), **KING OF ENGLAND** from 1625, of the royal family of Stuart, second son of James I. After an unsuccessful attempt to negotiate a marriage with the Infanta Maria of Spain, in the interests of which he had promised to repeal the penal laws against RCs in England, he then sought a French bride, Princess Henrietta Maria, daughter of Henry IV, promising freedom to RCs in the practice of their religion and guaranteeing that her own liberty of faith would not be interfered with. C. was himself a supporter of the C of E and thought that the English had grown weary of the Calvinism that had been dominant in the preceding century. He appointed W. Laud abp. of Canterbury, whose vigorous stand against Calvinism and Puritanist dissenters reactivated old antagonisms; disorders increased which led in 1642 to the Civil War in which C. suffered defeat (1645–46), and on Jan. 30, 1649, died on the scaffold as a tyrant and an enemy of the people. The trial and execution, instigated by fanatical army leaders, were quite illegal, and among Anglicans he was accounted a martyr. Among his contributions to religious tolerance was the favor with which he looked upon the desire of George Calvert (Lord Baltimore) to establish a colony free of religious oppression. BIBLIOGRAPHY: E. C. Wingfield-Stratford, *Charles King of England 1600–1637* (1949, repr. 1975); *idem, King Charles the Martyr, 1643–1649* (1950, repr. 1975).

[J. C. WILLKE]

CHARLES II (1630–85), **KING OF ENGLAND** from 1649, son of Charles I of the royal house of Stuart. After the execution of his father (1649), C. fled into exile which lasted until the restoration of the monarchy (1660). His inclination to the RC faith was probably lifelong, for his mother, Henrietta Maria, daughter of Henry IV, King of France, was Catholic; but his desire to restore and strengthen the British monarchy was the dominant influence in his life and this prevented him from openly professing Catholicism until his deathbed. He adopted Presbyterianism in 1650 to win Scottish support for his cause, though he abandoned it the next year when the attempt at restoration proved abortive. When he was restored to the throne he went as far as he dared in the face of a hostile Parliament to put an end to the persecution of RCs; but Parliament kept his revenues far short of what he needed not only for the maintenance of his court but also for the upkeep of the army, navy, and diplomatic service, which, at that time, were all supported by the crown. His desire to mitigate the lot of RCs was countered at every turn by a tightening of the purse strings or by the threat to tighten them, and by legislation to forestall the different measures of indulgence favored by Charles. Thus C. was obliged to assent to the legislation and to stand idly by while the persecution continued, including the execution of 35 innocent RCs (1678–81) condemned in consequence of the denunciations made by Titus Oates. On one point, however, he would not yield. In 1680–81 Parliament pressed for the exclusion of the Duke of York from succession to the throne because he was a Catholic. C. evaded this demand by ruling during the years 1681–85 without convoking Parliament. BIBLIOGRAPHY: D. Ogg, *England in the Reign of Charles II* (2 v., 1935); H. Belloc, *Charles II: The Last Rally* (1939); M. D. R. Leyes, *Catholics in England 1559–1829, A Social History* (1961) 93–104.

[J. C. WILLKE]

CHARLES VII (1403–61), **KING OF FRANCE** from 1422. Valois king, and "the Dauphin" of St. *Joan of Arc. Through her intervention he was crowned at Reims in 1429 and proved a more effective sovereign than might have been expected. In church matters, while protesting against the renewal of the Great Schism, healed at the Council of *Constance, he supported antipapal influences at the Council of *Basel and sought to support the liberties of the Gallican Church. In 1438 he promulgated the Pragmatic Sanction of *Bourges, which maintained certain ecclesiastical prerogatives of the crown.

[T. GILBY]

CHARLES VIII (1470–98), **KING OF FRANCE** from 1483. Valois king whose marriage with Anne of Britanny joined her duchy to the realm of France. His dreams of glory revived the claims of Anjou to the throne of Naples, and he looked beyond to the conquest of Constantinople. His Italian campaign (1494–95) was at first a glittering success; he was hailed by *Savonarola as the sword of the Lord and a new Cyrus, and was crowned at Naples with great display. By the craft of Pope *Alexander VI a concert of powers was formed against him, and he was forced to retire. His troops brought back with them syphilis, then, according to well-founded judgment, a disease newly arrived in the Mediterranean from America.

[T. GILBY]

CHARLES X (1757–1836), **KING OF FRANCE** (1824–30). Charles Philippe, grandson of Louis XV, an archconservative opposing the French Revolution, lived in exile until 1814. While his brother Louis XVIII ruled, C. became the spokesman of the ultraroyalists who opposed even moderate reforms. Though in earlier years he had been anything but pious, when he came to the throne in 1824 he was a person of great religious feeling. C. was highly favorable to the Church and particularly supportive of Catholic education. His refusal to entertain any moderation of strictly authoritarian rule eventually proved his downfall. The Revolution of 1830 forced him to abdicate and spend his remaining years in exile. BIBLIOGRAPHY: J. Vincent, *Charles X* (1958).

[J. R. AHERNE]

CHARLES II THE BALD (823–877), **KING AND GERMAN EMPEROR.** Son of Louis I, C. received the western third of the state at Louis's death. He acquired Aquitaine from Pepin II, a portion of Lotharingia from Lothair II, and, in 875 on the death of Louis II, the imperial title. Prominent scholars made his court more brilliant than Charlemagne's. BIBLIOGRAPHY: E. S. Duckett, *Carolingian Portraits* (1962); A. Cabaniss, NCE 3:502.

[A. CABANISS]

CHARLES III, FRANKISH KING AND GERMAN EMPEROR (Charles the Fat; 839–888), the youngest son of Louis the German and the great-grandson of Charlemagne. At the death of his brothers in 880 and 882, he inherited the entire East Frankish kingdom. The West Franks elected him king in 884. His incompetence and the ambitions of his nephew Arnulf caused an uprising of the East Frankish nobles. The Diet of Trebur deposed him in 887 and he died the following year in prison. His downfall marked the final disintegration of Charlemagne's empire.

[M. T. GRIFFIN]

CHARLES IV (1316–78), **HOLY ROMAN EMPEROR** from 1355. Brought up at the French court and well educated and religious for the times, he became a diplomat in Italy and a popular administrator for his father in Bohemia. Through papal influence C. was elected to the German throne (King of Romans) as antiking to Louis IV of Bavaria (Wittelsbach family). After his father was killed in the battle of Crécy (1346), C. succeeded as King of Bohemia. Though derisively called *Pfaffenkönig* (Priest-king) at his crowning in Bonn, he managed to secure his hold on Germany after the death of Louis IV in 1347. He went briefly to Italy at Easter 1355 for his imperial crowning. In Dec. 1356 he published at Metz the *Golden Bull, later regarded as the fundamental law of the empire, which sought to stabilize Germany with a weak centralized monarchy. Most of his efforts, largely successful, were spent strengthening his family holdings in Bohemia. BIBLIOGRAPHY: B. B. Szczesniak, NCE 3:503; F. Dvornik, *Slavs in European History and Civilization* (1962).

[J. E. LYNCH]

CHARLES V (1500–58), **HOLY ROMAN EMPEROR** from 1519 to 1556. Through his parents Philip of Burgundy and Joanna, third daughter of Ferdinand and Isabella, he became a ruler of envied political strength. At the death of his father (1506) he inherited the Netherlands and claims to the Burgundian Circle; at the death of his grandfather Ferdinand (1516) he became Charles I of Spain with title not only to Castile, Aragon, Navarre, the conquered territory of Granada, but also to Naples, Sicily, and the colonial settlements on the coast of Africa and in the New World. The Habsburg duchy of Austria, rights over Bohemia and Hungary came to him at the death of his paternal grandfather, Emperor Maximilian I (1519), as well as certain candidacy for the imperial crown. Such a concentration of power alarmed Pope Leo X, Henry VIII of England, Frederick the Wise of Saxony, and Francis I of France. Against their opposition, particularly Francis I's own aspirations for imperial honors, C. won the votes of the seven electors, not without bribery and intrigue, and was crowned at Aachen on Jan. 23, 1520. In spite of his youth he showed astuteness in consolidating his far-flung domains. Defiance from Spain, which had looked upon him as an alien, was countered by the dispersal of the *comuneros* (1521), the arrest of the captain general of the *Germanía* (1522), and the defeat of the *Moriscos* of Valencia (1525). He defended his interests in the Italian peninsula and in Burgundy against Francis I through four wars and as many quickly dishonored treaties. The first war resulted in the capture of the French King and the favorable terms of the Treaty of Madrid (1525); during the second war Pope Clement VII, an ally of Francis, was besieged in the Castel Sant' Angelo while imperial troops sacked Rome (1527). C. made peace with the Pope (Treaty of Barcelona, 1529) and with Francis (Peace of Cambrai, 1529), and was crowned by Clement in 1530. In the third war, which ended with the Treaty of Nice (1538), Francis allied with Suleiman I, Ottoman Emperor (r. 1520–66). The Treaty of Crépy (1544) concluded the fourth war, and by its terms C. relinquished his claims to Burgundy, while Francis ceded his in Italy, Flanders, and Artois.

C.'s reign was above all a struggle to defend the Catholic faith and maintain his power as universal Emperor in an era disturbed by the religious and political force of the Reformation. He strongly insisted on a general council to deal with the issues raised by the Reformation, but was in continuous conflict with the popes over the progress and program of the Council of *Trent. His condemnation of Martin Luther at the Diet of Worms (1521) led to the Knights' Revolt (1522–23), where ecclesiastical lords clashed with the armies of Franz von Sickingen and Ulrich von Hutten; the Peasants' War (1525–25), where sympathy for the peasants was first avowed by Luther and then rejected; the Diet of Speyer II (1529) in which princes partisan to the Reformation rejected the terms of the Diet of Worms, the unsuccessful series of *interims; the Schmalkaldic Wars (1546–47); and the fateful Treaty of Augsburg (1555), which assured protection both to Catholics and Protestants within the empire, as long as they followed the religion of their prince (*cuius regio, eius religio*). To these troubles within the empire were added growing threats from the Ottoman Empire. After the capture of Constantinople by Mohammed II (1453), Eastern Europe became the field for conquest. Belgrade fell (1521), and King Louis of Hungary was overcome in the battle of Mohacs (1526), an encounter that encouraged the Turks to besiege Vienna (1529). C. organized a counteroffensive, which had but little success, and Suleiman I was stopped only by a truce in 1547 that did not diminish Turkish power. C. saw the opportunities of exploration in the New World. Thus he encouraged the great explorers and *conquistadores*. Their efforts brought fiscal vitality to his empire, as Spanish galleons returned laden with gold and silver bullion from the Americas. It also brought jurisdictional conflict with the Church in policies of colonialization, particularly in the reign of his son, Philip II (see PATRONATO REAL). Frustration of his religious and political objectives led him to abdicate. He handed over the Netherlands (1555), Spain and Sicily (1556) to Philip, and the empire to his brother Ferdinand (1556), and then retired to a house near the Hieronymite monastery of San Yuste, where he lived in the practice of piety and continued to advise in affairs of state. BIBLIOGRAPHY: K. Brandi, *Emperor Charles V: The Growth and Destiny of a Man and a World-Empire* (tr. C. V. Wedgewood, 1939); E. D. McShane, NCE 3:503–506, bibliog.

[E. D. MCSHANE]

CHARLES OF THE ASSUMPTION (Charles de Bryas; 1625–86), theologian, born at Ghislain, Belgium. After an early military career which ended in capture and imprisonment, he entered the Discalced Carmelites at Douai. Following his appointment as prior he began to write under the pseudonym of Germanus Philalethes Eupistinus and became embroiled in controversy over predestination and grace. In 1678 he published without permission *Pentalogus diaphoricus,* which later was publicly burned by his superiors because it did not stress full contrition and firm purpose of amendment as necessary for the remission of mortal sins. He died at Douai still seeking approval for his works from the bp. of Arras and the King of France.

[T. LIDDY]

CHARLES OF BLOIS, BL. (1319–64), nephew of Philip VI of France, Franciscan tertiary. He married (1337) Joan of Penthièvre, heiress presumptive of John III, duke of Brittany, and through this acquired a claim to succession to the duchy. At the duke's death, C., with the support of France, engaged in war (1341–47) to secure his succession. The De Montforts, backed by Edward III of England, supported the claim of John de Montfort, half-brother of the deceased duke. In 1347 C. was wounded and taken prisoner at La Roche-Derrien; after his liberation in 1356 he resumed his fight. He was slain in battle in 1364. C. was esteemed as a saint and was credited with miracles; the Franciscans enthusiastically promoted his cause. John de Montfort, then in possession of the duchy, prevailed upon Urban V in 1368 to put a temporary stop to the process. It was later delayed by other causes, and C.'s cult was not confirmed until 1904. BIBLIOGRAPHY: H. Claude, BiblSanct 3:793–794, bibliog.; Butler 3:685–686.

[P. K. MEAGHER]

CHARLES BORROMEO, ST., see BORROMEO, CHARLES, ST.

CHARLES MARTEL (*c.*688–741), Frankish ruler and establisher of unity in Gaul. He was mayor of the palace in the Merovingian kingdom, the effective head when the kings were puppets; he extended his power from Austrasia, the eastern part, to Neustria, the western part. At the battle of Tours (732), he beat back the invasion of the Arabs and earned his title, ''the Hammer'' (*Martellus*). They never came so far north again, and before the end of the cent. had been driven back beyond the Pyrenees. Though his sequestration of church lands for the benefit of his officers—the *precarium* which helped to found the later feudal fiefs—was resented by churchmen, he was the protector of St. Boniface and supported missionary expansion. Pope Gregory II used him to counterbalance the Lombards. The project of offering him the Roman consulate, to offset the power of the Eastern emperor, marked the beginning of papal policies that culminated when his grandson, Charlemagne, whom he so far resembled that *chansons de geste* sometimes confuse them, was acclaimed Patrician of the Romans and was crowned Emperor of the West, 800. BIBLIOGRAPHY: C. M. Aherne NCE 3:507.

[T. GILBY]

CHARLES OF ORLÉANS, see ORLÉANS, CHARLES D'.

CHARLES OF SEZZE, ST. (1613–70), Franciscan lay brother and spiritual writer. After a simple home life with little education, C. joined the Franciscans in Rome in 1635. His intense prayer life was marked by passage through the stages of contemplation to ecstatic union. In a simple style he wrote five treatises on the spiritual life. His autobiography, like that of St. Teresa of Avila, analyzed the phases leading to mystical union. All his writings are marked by distinctly Franciscan ascetical and mystical theology. C. was canonized by Pope John XXIII in 1959. BIBLIOGRAPHY: Butler 1:125; S. Gori, BiblSanct 3:801–810; J. Heerinckz, DSAM 2.1:701–703.

[V. GILLIGAN]

CHARLES OF VILLERS, BL. (d. *c.*1215), convert from a worldly life who became a Cistercian at Himmerod *c.*1185.

In 1197 he was made abbot of Villers-en-Brabant, and under his rule the monastery prospered materially and spiritually. Resigning in 1209, he returned to the life of a simple monk at Himmerod, but was shortly afterward obliged to resume abbatial responsibility at the Abbey of St. Agatha, which was desperately in need of reorganization. BIBLIOGRAPHY: A. D'Haenens, BiblSanct 3:810–812; Zimmermann 1:141.

[B. F. SCHERER]

CHARLEVOIX, PIERRE FRANÇOIS XAVIER DE (1682–1761), French Jesuit historian. C. entered the Society of Jesus in 1698. He taught in a Jesuit college in Canada (1705–09) and in France until 1719. Commissioned by the French government to seek a new route from Acadia to the Western Sea, he traveled (1720–22) up the St. Lawrence River, through the Great Lakes, and down the Mississippi River to the Gulf of Mexico. Failing in his mission, he returned to France where he spent the remainder of his life teaching and writing. His most outstanding work is *Histoire et description générale de la Nouvelle France* (1744; Eng. tr. J. G. Shea, 6 v., 1866–72), the first general history of Canada. BIBLIOGRAPHY: E. P. Spillane, CE 3:631–632.

[J. L. HALPIN]

CHARLIEU, ABBEY CHURCH OF SS. PETER AND PAUL, French Benedictine church founded in the 9th cent., rebuilt in the grand manner of Cluny (11th–12th cent.). Remaining is the fine two-storied narthex profusely carved in late Burgundian Romanesque, the tympanum being especially noteworthy. BIBLIOGRAPHY: J. Evans, *Romanesque Architecture of the Order of Cluny* (1938).

[M. J. DALY]

CHARLOT, JEAN (1898–   ), Mexican painter. Born and schooled in Paris, C. came to Mexico as pioneer of the mural movement (1921), painted the *Fall of Tenochtitlán* (1922), and assisted D. Rivera both at the Preparatory School, Mexico City, and on frescoes of the Ministry of Education (1923). On a Carnegie expedition, after studying Mayan art at Chichén Itzá, C. became instructor of mural painting at the Art Students League, N. Y., taught in many U.S. colleges and universities, received a Guggenheim Fellowship, and after 1951 was a professor in the Univ. of Hawaii. In 1955 he executed frescoes on Psalm 22 for the Church of the Good Shepherd, Lincoln Park, Michigan. C. investigated and published aesthetic and technical theses and in achieving a blend of primitive and modern styles has sought solutions to problems of modern religious art. BIBLIOGRAPHY: J. Charlot, *Mexican Mural Renaissance, 1920–25* (1963).

[M. J. DALY]

CHARM, an object, formula, gesture, or potion believed to have the capacity to insure against the undesirable. Charms are thought by some of superstitious bent to have some magical efficacy by drawing on supernatural power. Use of charms is the result of primitive, illogical reasoning in an attempt to control the forces of nature. *SUPERSTITION.

[V. GILLIGAN]

CHARNEL HOUSE *(carnarium, oss[u]arium)*, a structure during the Middle Ages at times separate from, at times attached to a church or churchyard wall, used as a depository for bones, esp. painted or inscribed skulls. BIBLIOGRAPHY: *Handwörterbuch des deutschen Aberglaubens* (ed. H. Bächtold—Stäubli, 10 v., 1927–42) 5:1427.

[J. BLAIR]

CHARPENTIER, MARC-ANTOINE (c. 1634–1704), French Baroque composer. In his youth he studied with Carissimi in Rome and collaborated with Molière in Paris at the French Theater. He wrote numerous secular and sacred works, including 17 operas and several oratorios based on biblical episodes known as *histoires sacrées*. *Medée* is his most widely recognized opera and *La reniement de St. Pierre* is his best known oratorio.

[D. SMUCKER]

CHARRON, PIERRE (1541–1603), French philosopher and theologian. After studying law, C. turned to theology, took orders, and became a celebrated preacher and theologian in S France, serving as preacher in ordinary to *Marguerite of Navarre. His request to withdraw to a monastic order (1589) was denied because of his age. Meeting *Montaigne in Bordeaux (c. 1589), C. became his disciple; his works reflect M.'s influence. In his *Trois vérités* (1593), refuting Duplessis-Mornay's Calvinistic *Traité de l'Église* (1578), C. attempted to show that (1) God exists; (2) Christianity alone is true; and (3) Catholicism alone is true Christianity. The work combines skepticism about the reliability of human knowledge with fideism. In his popular *De la sagesse* (1601), a mixture of borrowed doctrines but essentially Montaigne's skepticism, C. asserts that the wise man in complete doubt is better prepared to receive religious truth through revelation, until which moment he should observe natural morality. Important for its separation of ethics from religion, this work blends neo-Stoic natural virtue with an Augustinian emphasis on human weakness. Thus it paradoxically influenced both the 17th-cent. *libertins* and the Jansenists, was attacked as irreligious for undermining religious belief, and was placed on the Index (1606); and yet it was defended in varying degrees by prominent churchmen including *Saint-Cyran, who saw C. as a prominent Counter-Reformer who attacked Calvinism with skepticism. C.'s ambivalence still remains unsolved. His other works include *Octave du Saint-Sacrement* (1600) and *Discours chrétiens* (1601), of Augustinian tendencies, attesting as does his upright life, his Christian sincerity. BIBLIOGRAPHY: J. D. Charron, *"Wisdom" of Pierre Charron, an Original and Orthodox Code of Morality* (1961).

[R. N. NICOLICH]

CHARTER OF CHARITY (*Carta Caritatis*), early constitution of the Cistercian Order, attributed to the Englishman *Stephen Harding, third abbot of Cîteaux (1109–33). The initial version, modified and added to, was completed in the late 12th century. It granted legislative and judicial powers to the annual general chapter at Cîteaux attended by all the abbots of the order. Each abbey was visited annually by the abbot of the founding house to check on the implementation of chapter decrees, Cîteaux itself being visited by the four "protoabbots" of La Ferté, Pontigny, Clairvaux, and Morimond. Within this framework each abbey remained autonomous. The same document also regulated abbatial elections, ranks and precedence, hospitality and mutual material assistance. It called for emergency measures against unworthy abbots and emphasized uniform observance of the Benedictine Rule. Though not entirely original, the Charter of Charity proved highly successful and served as model for subsequent religious constitutions. The concepts of corporate responsibility, mutual dependence, and a graduated hierarchical structure were borrowed from feudalism. BIBLIOGRAPHY: "Cistercii statuta antiquissima," (ed. J. Turk) AnalOCist 4 (1948) 109–159; L. J. Lekai, *White Monks* (Eng. tr. 1953) 267–273; D. Knowles, *Great Historical Enterprises* (1963), 199–222.

[L. J. LEKAI]

CHARTERHOUSE, English name for a *Carthusian religious house. The order took its name from the Chartreuse Mountains, locale of its first house, and charterhouse is from the French *maison chartreuse*.

[T. EARLY]

CHARTIER, ÉMILE AUGUSTE, see ALAIN.

CHARTOPHYLAX (Gr., guardian of documents, archivist), in many eparchies of the Byzantine Church a position equivalent to the Western chancellor. Since the small size of many dioceses did not warrant the appointment of a syncellus (vicar-general), the chartophylax was in charge of the executive office of the bp., including the care of the archives. He was a general delegate and permanent official representative of the bp., granting in his name dispensations, etc. The chartophylax of a patriarch is sometimes an important dignitary, and the grand chartophylax of the patriarch of Constantinople was one of the leading ecclesiastical dignitaries in the Byzantine Empire.

[V. J. POSPISHIL]

CHARTRES CATHEDRAL (NÔTRE-DAME DE CHARTRES), great French High Gothic cathedral unsurpassed in sculpture and glass, setting the standard for Gothic architecture of Europe. Following a fire (1134) the face (1150), brought flush with the towers, was enriched by the sculptured Royal Portal (1145–70), one of the greatest achievements of the 13th cent. in calm and monumental grandeur. The magnificently modeled and restrained figures preserve a perfect relationship with the architectural whole. The entire complex of figures of Old and New Testament reference, together with martyrs, princes of the Church, and calendar designs, confirm the lofty Scholasticism of the school of Chartres, which stressed humanism under Bps. Fulbert and John of Salisbury with Bernard de Chartres. Exquisitely sensitive and mystical interpretations in finest carving enrich the interior also. Greatest of all French cathedrals in the riches of its stained glass, Chartres's oldest windows in the W front and, most venerated, the *NôtreDame de la Belle Verrière* in the S choir are glorious in the beauty of a special 12th-cent. flax blue, unfaded through the centuries. Chartres became a center of colored glass, producing 173 windows within a few years. The more elaborate N tower (1507–13) and ambulatory screen (1520–29) were added by Jean Texier (known as Jean de Beauce). Incomparable in architectural sculpture and stained glass, Chartres realizes a final organic "flowing" High Gothic. BIBLIOGRAPHY: M. Aubert and S. Doubet, *Gothic Cathedrals of France and Their Treasures* (1959); R. Branner, *Chartres Cathedral* (1969).

[M. J. DALY]

CHARTREUSE, LA GRANDE-, see GRANDE-CHARTREUSE, LA.

CHARTREUSE DE CHAMPMOL, church (Dijon, France), the largest single artistic enterprise of that great sponsor of the arts, Philip the Bold of Burgundy (1364–1404). He intended Chartreuse to receive the tombs of his family and gave it an endowment which attracted artists from all parts of N Europe. Executed by Jean de Marville (1381–89), the church boasts Claus Sluter's sculptured symbolic "Well of Moses," showing the majestic figure of Moses with five other prophets (6 feet high), surrounding a base in a group intensely realistic in texture and detail. Sluter's characteristically heavy, voluminous drapery over swelling forms exemplifies the 15th-cent. Flemish fascination with the tangible, while lacking *Donatello's weight-shift. Sluter did the portal (1385–93) where expansive figures overpowering the architectural framework include splendid portrait carvings of Philip and his wife with patron saints. Only one of the many altarpieces survives, the carved *Adoration of the Magi*. Its wings, painted by the Flemish master M. Broederlam (fl. 1385–1409), present an *Annunciation, Visitation, Presentation* and *Flight into Egypt* (Dijon Museum) in the International Style, the elegant silhouettes freed in the Sienese manner, and the small intricate shapes in rich color reflecting the older style of MSS and stained glass. BIBLIOGRAPHY: J. Huizinga, *Waning of the Middle Ages* (1956); O. Benesch, *Art of the Renaissance in Northern Europe* (1967).

[M. J. DALY]

CHARTREUX, see CARTHUSIANS.

CHARTULARY, during the Middle Ages a MS record containing copies of original title deeds and other documents. Contents relate to foundation property privileges, legal rights of church establishments, city and other corporations, colleges, universities, or private parties. BIBLIOGRAPHY: H. Bresslau, *Handbuch der Urkundenlehre für Deutschland und Italien* (2 v., 2d ed., 1912–31).

[J. BLAIR]

CHASIDISM, see HASIDISM.

CHASSE, a container, usually portable, in the shape of an ark or coffin, which contains a number of the relics of a saint.

[N. KOLLAR]

CHASTITY, a virtue that regulates the sexuality of persons. Natural chastity is the self-moderation of one's sexuality because of the nature of personal and social human life. The biblical notion of chastity regards sexuality as sacred and purposeful, capable of integration with the life of the spirit. Chastity in modern Christian teaching is seen as an integration of sexuality with the whole life of persons, depending on their state in life. As a vow of religion, chastity is meant to aid the singleness of charity's love of God and the diffusiveness of its love of neighbor.

[V. GILLIGAN]

CHASUBLE (Lat. *casula, paenula, planeta;* Gr. *phelones*), the outer liturgical vestment worn by the priest when he celebrates Mass. It is the development of a garment in common use in the later Greco-Roman world. The French and English "chasuble" and the German *Kasel* are derived from *casula,* the popular name given to the garment because it covered the entire body like a conical or bell-shaped tent. It had an opening at the top through which the wearer's head would fit. It was not at first distinctive of priestly rank and came to be peculiar to clerics as it passed out of fashion for secular wear. According to an 8th-cent. Roman ordinal it was presented to acolytes in their ordination. In the 12th cent. the chasuble began to be shortened at the sides to facilitate the movement of the wearer's arms. The oval-shaped vestment that resulted from this change is known as the Gothic chasuble. Various forms of ornamentation began to be used, esp. a border down the seams of front and back, often joined together with an ornamented strip across the shoulders so as to form Y-shaped crosses. In the 17th cent. the curtailment at the sides increased until the chasuble no longer covered any part of the wearer's arms. It thus became in effect two panels of cloth, joined end-to-end where they fitted over the shoulders. Both these panels, and esp. that worn in front, were much reduced in length. The shortening of the chasuble, its frequently excessive ornamentation, and the absurd shape in which the panels were sometimes cut (one variety of which is described as fiddle-backed) led many to desire a restoration of the more dignified Gothic or even the original bell shape.

The Congregation of Rites, after twice (1863 and 1925) discouraging this departure from accepted practice, by a decree of 1957 permitted ordinaries to allow the introduction of new forms or the reintroduction of old forms. The chasuble should be made of silk and it should be of a color suited to the liturgical occasion for which it is intended. The 1970 *Missale Romanum* allows Episcopal Conferences to admit to use vestments that in design and material conform to the culture of their regions, provided they are appropriate to the dignity of the liturgy. In common use recently is a chasuble that in design is a combination chasuble-alb. The oldest and best attested explanation of the chasuble's symbolism sees it as a sign of charity and the yoke of Christ. BIBLIOGRAPHY: H. Norris, *Church Vestments: Their Origin and Development* (1950); for illustrations, NCE 3:518.

[P. K. MEAGHER]

CHATARD, FRANCIS SILAS (1834–1918), American bishop. C. was appointed rector of the North American College, Rome, in 1871, papal chamberlain in 1875. In 1878 he became bp. of the See of Vincennes (now Indianapolis); he greatly reorganized his diocese with zeal and ability. The controversy of secret societies was of special interest to him. C. attended the preliminary sessions of the Third Plenary Council of Baltimore. He wrote numerous articles for American magazines esp. the *Catholic World,* a Paulist publication. His formal lectures were published in 1881, *Occasional Essays,* and *Christian Truths.* BIBLIOGRAPHY: R. Gorman, NCE 3:519.

[J. L. HALPIN]

CHATEAUBRIAND, FRANÇOIS RENÉ DE (1768–1848), French writer. C. endured a depressing childhood at St. Malo and Comburg. He later attended classes at the Collège de Dol where he revealed competency in Latin and mathematics. Congenitally a romantic, he was further nourished by readings in the classics and in biblical literature. His father destined him for the navy and sent him to the Jesuits at Rennes for training toward this end. Uncertain what course to follow and torn by the political and philosophical currents of the time, he sailed on the *St. Pierre* to the U.S. (1791). C. returned to France but in further quest for the right direction soon went to England, where he lived until 1800. His writings at this time (1802), *The Genius of Christianity* esp., made him one of the foremost writers in France. His disillusionment with Napoleon led him to support the Bourbons, who honored him several times; he was ambassador to London (1822). By 1830 he had withdrawn actively from political life, though his temperament kept him academically attuned to it (*Le Congrès de Vérone,* 1838). C.'s personal life was inextricably bound with love affairs and romantic relationships. Though deeply in love with his wife, his interest in such women as Madame Récamier never diminished. His last years were devoted to completing his *Mémoires d'Outre-tombe* (1803–50). Like his *Génie du Christianisme,* it enunciates his adherence to Christian perspective and to the influence of Christianity on poetry and music. His *Génie* contains several novels of love showing the power of Christianity on the human heart. *Atala, René,* and *Les Natchez* reflect this attitude. Other works are *Itinéraire de Paris à Jérusalem* (1811), *Études historiques* (1831), and the *Vie de Rancé* (1844). BIBLIOGRAPHY: P. Moreau, NCE 3:519–521; C. B. Bell, *Chateaubriand et la tasse* (repr. 1973); C. Lynes, *Chateaubriand as a Critic of French Literature* (repr. 1973).

[R. M. FUNCHION]

CHATILLON, ODET DE, see COLIGNY, ODET DE.

CHATZINARIANS, an Armenian sect of the 7th cent. who were essentially iconoclasts, venerating only the cross. They claimed falsely the authority of St. Gregory the Illuminator for a doctrine on the dual nature of Christ which seemed to postulate two persons: one suffering on the cross and the other separately contemplating the suffering Christ. They were accused by the orthodox Greeks of unorthodox liturgical practice in the Mass and of observing a week-long fast before the beginning of Lent. Since information on the sect depends on the writing of an avowed Greek enemy, Nicephorus Callistus, one may question its authenticity. BIBLIOGRAPHY: S. Vailhé, DTC 2340.

[J. R. AHERNE]

CHAUCER, GEOFFREY (c. 1340–1400), greatest English poet of the Middle Ages, diplomat, and civil servant. Son of John Chaucer, vintner, C. became a page in the household of the Earl of Ulster, served in French wars, was taken prisoner, and was ransomed by Edward III. He married Philippa Roet, then lady-in-waiting to the queen and later sister-in-law to the powerful John of Gaunt. Frequently sent on diplomatic missions, C. was in Italy in 1372 and 1378, and in France in 1376 and 1377. From 1374 to 1378, he enjoyed a prosperous career as comptroller of customs; he was clerk of the King's works in 1389. In 1394, he received additional pensions from Richard II, was sued for debts in 1398, and received additional pension from Henry IV in 1399. His major works are *Book of the Duchess, House of Fame, Parlement of Foules, Troilus and Criseyde,* and *The *Canterbury Tales.*

Chaucer has been accused of lacking high seriousness, of being indifferent or noncommittal as to moral, social, and religious issues. It has been noted that he received pensions from three different kings; that his patron was the Lollard-Wyclif sympathizer, John of Gaunt; that his one good churchman is accused of Lollardry; that he wrote racy fabliaux; that the worst of his rogues are churchmen; and that if he showed any animosity, it was against the friars. Early scholars who accepted *The Retraction* as authentic dismissed it as mere convention. Recent criticism takes more seriously the religious current in Chaucer. It argues that his satire is against churchmen rather than the Church, against abuses rather than against doctrines or beliefs; that in Chaucer's charges against the friars he is merely giving artistic form to the most important accusations made against the friars by William of St. Amour (1256) and repeated in every generation up to his time. Today, the majority of scholars see no reason to question the authenticity of the *Retraction* or to regard it as empty convention; and, indeed, much recent criticism interprets not only the frame but many of the individual *Canterbury Tales* in the light of medieval scriptural exegesis. BIBLIOGRAPHY: J. Gordon, "Chaucer's Retraction: A Review of Opinion," *Studies in Medieval Literature* (ed. MacEdward Leach, 1961) 81–96; R. Loomis, "Was Chaucer a Laodicean?" *Essays and Studies in Honor of Carleton Brown* (1940) 128–148; D. W. Robertson, *Preface to Chaucer* (1963); A. Williams, "Chaucer and the Friars," *Speculum* 28 (1953) 499–513.

[N. MALTMAN]

CHAUMONT, HENRI (1838–96), French priest; spiritual director who propagated the spirituality of St. Francis de Sales among the laity and clergy by his personal counsel, by the written word (*Directions spirituelles de Saint François de Sales,* 1870–79), by the establishment of societies for the study and practice of Salesian principles of the spiritual life. BIBLIOGRAPHY: H. Debout, DSAM 2.1:813–818.

[T. C. O'BRIEN]

CHAUNCY, surname of two New England clergymen. (1) Charles (1592–1672), Puritan minister, second president of Harvard. After a brief imprisonment (1634) in England for his hard Puritan line on church order, he migrated to the Plymouth Colony (1637). After a parish ministry until 1654, he was chosen to be president of Harvard. He was a staunchly conservative theologian, a scholar, and a respected preacher.

(2) Charles (1705–87), great-grandson of the preceding, spokesman of a rationalist enlightenment in New England. From 1721 until his death he served the First Church of Boston. He strongly opposed the emotionalism in the *Great Awakening, and the ideas of Jonathan *Edwards, e.g., in his *Enthusiasm Describ'd and Caution'd Against* (1742) and *Seasonable Thoughts on the Present State of Religion in New England* (1743). His *Arminianism, *universalism, and rationalist views on the Trinity began the departure from Calvinist doctrine among New England Congregationalists that culminated in the emergence by 1825 of *Unitarianism as a distinct denomination. He also strongly opposed *episcopacy in the American colonies.

[T. C. O'BRIEN]

CHAUTARD, JEAN BAPTISTE (1858–1935), Trappist abbot and spiritual writer. He was abbot of Chambarand (1897–99), then of Sept-Fons until his death; he also was active in the restoration and care of other Cistercian houses, and by his eloquence before the Senate helped prevent expulsion of the Trappists from France. By his conferences and correspondence he became renowned as a spiritual director. His enduring influence was through his *L'Âme de tout apostolat* (1910; Eng. tr. *Soul of the Apostolate*), a short treatise insisting on the need of an intense interior life as the basis for apostolic activity. BIBLIOGRAPHY: M. Godefroy, DSAM 2.1:818–820.

[T. C. O'BRIEN]

CHAUTAUQUA MOVEMENT, a lecture, discussion, and entertainment enterprise popular in the U.S. in the late 19th and early 20th cent., of particular service to communities in which cultural and educational opportunities were limited. The movement, forerunner of later adult education programs, began in 1873 when Methodist minister, and later bp., John H. Vincent (1832–1920) proposed that the Methodist *camp meeting association include a training course for Sunday school teachers in its summer institute at Chautauqua Lake, New York. Subsequent changes broadened offerings to include courses in the arts, sciences, and humanities, and lengthened the term of the institute. The Chautauqua Literary and Scientific Circle was organized to sponsor local programs to accommodate those who wished to read and study under guidance but who could not attend the institute. Some 80,000 members were enrolled by 1887, and the total increased to more than 100,000 by 1891. For a time (1885–98) the operation was given formal status as Chautauqua University under a charter from the State of New York. However, the more popular programs were the reading circles and the summer assemblies, which after 1880 featured preachers and speakers of national reputation. Until World War I, the circles and assemblies were widely imitated, and spread across the country in various forms. A decline set in and the movement practically disappeared in the postwar years. BIBLIOGRAPHY: J. E. Gould, *Chautauqua Movement* (1961); H. P. Harrison, *Culture under Canvas* (1958); J. H. Vincent, *Chautauqua Movement* (1886).

[M. CARTHY]

CHAUVINISM, named from Nicolas Chauvin of Rochefort, a Napoleonic veteran whose demonstrative loyalty to the Empire was both celebrated and ridiculed and who became a legend for a stock character in vaudeville, an extravagant and bellicose *patriotism, a French quality which found a parallel in British jingoism, and is still expressed in excessive nationalism and racialism. Sexist connotations have accrued in recent history, thus also male and female chauvinism.

[T. GILBY]

CHAVES DE LA ROSA, PEDRO JOSÉ (1740–1821), Spanish bp. and reformer. His major reforms were some of the most successful in Peruvian history. He restored and modernized the seminary. Because of opposition he resigned in 1805. BIBLIOGRAPHY: E. T. Bartra, NCE 3:531.

[J. P. COOKE]

CHEATING, a form of dishonesty in which by deception or trickery one gains something above his due, whether money, goods, the honor of winning, or a better grade in school. It is a sin against justice if it deprives another of what is due him in distributive or commutative justice. Even if it does no harm to anyone else, it is a form of dishonesty and has often been called a lie in action. Cheating can take many forms: using forbidden means to win a game, or to charge more than is fair in a sale or other contract, or to use forbidden means to get a better grade in a school examination. Even when it seems that no one is hurt but the cheater, cheating may still deprive others of winning a prize or the higher position that they deserve.

[J. J. FARRAHER]

CHECA Y BARBA, JOSÉ IGNACIO (1829–1887), archbishop. C. convoked the Second and Third Councils of Quito and brought the Daughters of Charity and the Vincentians to Ecuador. He held steadfast in quarrels between Church and State. He died a martyr by poisoned wine used to purify the chalice at the Mass of the Presanctified on Good Friday. BIBLIOGRAPHY: W. Loor, NCE 3:532.

[J. P. COOKE]

CHEESEFARE SUNDAY, term used among Eastern Christians for Quinquagesima. For those keeping the strict Lenten fast, cheese but no meat may be eaten from the Monday preceding Quinquagesima until the Monday following, after which even cheese is excluded.

[T. EARLY]

CHEFFONTAINES, CRISTOPHE DE (1532–95), Franciscan theologian and controversialist born at Saint-Pol-de-Léon in Brittany of a noble family known in Breton as de Penfentenyou, a word that C. translated into French as Cheffontaines and into Latin as *a Capite Fontium*. Still in his youth he became a Franciscan Observant and soon after his ordination began to establish for himself a reputation as a preacher. Preaching at that time inevitably involved him in controversy with Huguenots and other Protestants. He was chosen minister general of his order in 1571. At the end of his term of office he was made titular abp. of Caesarea (1578) and sent as auxiliary to the cardinal abp. of Sens in Flanders. Indefatigable in his writing on polemical matters, he sometimes, in the heat of controversy, came forth with novel and rash ideas. His works were investigated by the Holy Office. Three of them were condemned outright and were put on the Index; the others were banned from publication until they were corrected (*donec expurgentur*). Much later the works were withdrawn from the Index. After the censure of his works C. lived at Rome in the Convent of S. Pietro. BIBLIOGRAPHY: E. d'Alençon, DTC 2.2:2352–53.

[T. LIDDY]

CHEKHOV, ANTON PAVLOVICH (1860–1904), influential Russian playwright and author of short stories. Until c.1886, when he began to contribute regularly to the conservative journal *New Times,* C.'s short, usually humorous, stories and anecdotes were written from financial necessity and without much attention to form. Thereafter, under the influence of Grigorovich (1822–99), his works reveal more careful craftsmanship; under the influence of Tolstoy's ethical teachings, they came to manifest a new sensitivity to social problems. By the beginning of 1890, however, C. was convinced that science would eventually reform human society; he rejected Tolstoyanism and began to regard himself, not as an ideologist, but as a "free artist." The prevailing mood of his works is one of gentle melancholy. In a realistic style, chiefly characterized by a constant use of understatement and often combined with lyricism and symbolism, he portrays in masterful short stories and dramas the intellectual pessimism of the *fin de siècle*. His greatest short stories include "Vanka" (1886), "A Dreary Story" (1889), "Ward No. 6" (1892), "The House with the Attic" (1896), "Gooseberries" (1898), "The Betrothed" (1903). His dramatic masterpieces are *Ivanov* (1887), *The Sea Gull* (1896), *Uncle Vanya* (1897), *Three Sisters* (1901), and *The Cherry Orchard* (1903). BIBLIOGRAPHY: E. J. Simmons, *Chekhov: a Biography* (1962); *Chekhov, a Collection of Critical Essays* (ed. R. L. Jackson, 1967).

[M. F. McCARTHY]

CHELCIC, PETER OF, see PETER OF CHELCIC.

CHELIDONIA, ST. (d. 1152), virgin and anchoress. She is known exclusively through the vita composed by the 16th cent. monk of Subiaco, Guglielmo Capisacchi, who claimed that he used an earlier anonymous vita. According to his account she was a virgin who took the veil in the Church of St. Scholastica at Subiaco, but subsequently returned to her life as an anchoress. In 1578 her remains were placed in a shrine beneath the altar of the Blessed Virgin in the abbey church of Subiaco. BIBLIOGRAPHY: M. R. P. McGuire, NCE 3:533; Zimmermann 3:177; B. Cignitti, BiblSanct 3:1179–81.

[M. R. P. McGUIRE]

CHELLES, CONVENT OF, an abbey in the area of Seine-et-Marne, France, founded in 656 by Queen Bathildis. It was staffed by nuns from Jovarre-en-Brie (658–659) and followed the Rule of St. Columban. It became a *double monastery and housed a notable scriptorium. After suffering pillage at the hands of the Normans, it was restored. It underwent several forms and in time adopted the Benedictine Rule. It was finally suppressed in 1792. Now only some ruins of its ancient cloister, a few tombs, and several buildings long since converted to secular use remain. BIBLIOGRAPHY: H. Tardif, NCE 3:533.

[P. K. MEAGHER]

CHEMNITZ, MARTIN (1522–88), German Lutheran theologian, a co-author of the *Formula of Concord. After studies at several Lutheran centers in Germany, he was librarian for Albert of Prussia (1550); he entered the ministry at Wittenberg (1533), where he also lectured briefly. Throughout the rest of his life he maintained the post of pastor in Braunschweig. His first major contribution to theology was a reply to the teachings of the Council of Trent (*Examen Concilii Tridentini*, 4 v., 1565–73). He was called upon to resolve doctrinal disputes besetting the Lutheran churches, and prepared *corpora doctrinae* for several of them. In the Lutheran controversies on ubiquity (see UBIQUITARIANISM) and the person of Christ he contributed ideas reflected in Article 8 of the Formula of Concord. Together with J. *Andreä he was largely responsible for the draft of the whole Formula. In addition C. also was engaged by the authorities in the establishment of church polity and practice. His influence has been recognized as one of standardization of Lutheran doctrinal formulas and church organization. BIBLIOGRAPHY: A. C. Piepkorn, EncLuthCh 1:390–391; E. G. Schwiebert, NCE 3:548–549.

[M. J. SUELZER]

CHEMOSH (*Chamos*), god of the Moabites (Num 21.29; Jer 48.46; in Jg 11.24 the word is perhaps a scribal error for *Milcom, god of the Ammonites). In providing sanctuaries for his foreign wives, Solomon built a *high place for C. east of Jerusalem (1 Kg 11.1–8) and it was destroyed in Josiah's reform (2 Kg 23.13). Some scholars deduce from references in the *Moabite Stone that C. was a local manifestation of Athtar, the Venus Star. The Moabite Stone states that the Israelites prevailed against Moab because of C.'s anger. It was perhaps at that time that the Moabite king sacrificed his eldest son (2 Kg 3.27).

[T. EARLY]

CHENCHI, see CENCI.

CHÉNIER, ANDRÉ (1762–94), French poet. After receiving an excellent classical education together with a broad exposure to culture in his mother's *salon*, he traveled abroad on political posts. At first enthusiastic towards the Revolution, he later condemned its excesses and was guillotined. Relatively unknown during his lifetime, C. is now famous for his poetry, which manifests a harmonious classical style and inspiration, together with political and personal passion that make him a precursor of Romanticism. Among his best works are *La Jeune Tarentine* and a political satire, *Iambes*. BIBLIOGRAPHY: G. Walter, *André Chénier, son milieu et son temps* (1947).

[I. M. KASHUBA]

CHENOBOSKION (also Shenesit-Chenoboskion), ancient city of Upper Egypt, site of the discovery of a Coptic Gnostic library. These MSS known as the Chenoboskion (also called the Nag Hammâdi MSS from a nearby modern village), were found by local fellahin in a cemetery in 1945. The collection comprises 13 Coptic MSS mostly in the Sahidic dialect dating from the 3d and 4th centuries. The works appear to be translated from Greek, which may indicate earlier authorship. There are 51 works, some represented more than once, and they draw on diverse Gnostic traditions. With the exception of the *Jung Codex in Zurich, all are now in the Coptic Museum in Cairo. Only some of the codices have been published. Two important works now available are the *Gospel of Truth,* probably by Valentinus, and the *Gospel of Thomas,* containing 114 sayings of Jesus. The collection contains a wide variety of literary types and adds substantially to the heretofore meager collection of Gnostic primary sources. Chenoboskion MSS rank among the greatest Christian finds of the century. BIBLIOGRAPHY: J. Doresse, *Secret Books of the Egyptian Gnostics* (1960, repr. 1972); H. Jonas, *Gnostic Religion* (2d ed., 1963).

[D. W. JOHNSON]

CHERNYI, DANIIL (Tschorny; fl. 15th cent.), Russian painter, monk, and friend of Andreǐ Rublëv. C. assisted Rublëv on frescoes and icons for the Cathedral of the Dormition, Vladimir (1408–09), and at Trinity-St. Sergius Monastery near Moscow (1425–27; later destroyed).

[M. J. DALY]

CHERNYSHEVSKI, NIKOLAY GAVRILOVICH (1828–89), Russian journalist, radical political philosopher, and literary critic. His novel *Shto Delat'?* ("What Is to Be Done?"), published in 1863 while he was in prison on charges of fostering radicalism, and his essays on literary, economic, and social themes, reveal him as a materialist and positivist, a utopian socialist, atheist, and utilitarian. He exercised a strong influence on the Russian intelligentsia of the 1860s and is rightfully regarded as a forerunner of Populism. BIBLIOGRAPHY: W. F. Woehrlin, *Chernyshevski: The Man and the Journalist* (1971); F. B. Randall, *N. G. Chernyshevski* (1967).

[M. F. MCCARTHY]

CHERUBIC HYMN: (1) from Is 6.3, the biblical source for the Sanctus part of the Roman rite. Isaiah envisions the angels crying to one another, "Holy, holy, holy is the Lord of Hosts"; (2) in the Byzantine rite, the portion sung by the choir in the liturgy at the symbolic entrance of Christ and the cherubim. *CHERUBIKON.

[D. J. SMUCKER]

CHERUBIKON, Hymn of the Cherubim. This Eastern hymn is sung prior to the Great Entrance during which the hymn is interrupted and continued only after the Great Entrance is completed. It reminds the faithful to put aside earthly cares and prepare themselves to receive the heavenly King worthily. While the first part of this hymn is being sung, the priest prays for purity of mind that he may consecrate the gifts of bread and wine worthily.

[P. A. MORLINO]

CHERUBIM, celestial beings of the OT symbolizing man's awareness of the divine presence as specially sacred. They serve as a chariot (2 Sam 22.11; Ps 18.10) or a throne (1 Sam 4.4; Ps 99.1; Ex 25.22) for God himself and also act as guardian spirits for sacred places such as Eden or the Holy of Holies in the Temple (Ezek 28.14, 16; Gen 3.24; 1 Kg 6.23–28). Apparently a development of this latter function is their use as a decorative motif within the Temple (1 Kg 6.29, 32, 35; 7.29, 36). Their parallel ornamental function for the Tent of Meeting (Ex 26.1, 31) is probably a projection of the Temple design into the past; also, it is possible that the two cherubim serving as God's throne on the ark (Ex 25.18–20) do not date back to the desert period, if the notion of God's kingship arose during the settlement in Chanaan.

The outward appearance of the cherubim remains somewhat obscure to us; the biblical texts themselves do not offer a fully consistent picture. Perhaps the affirmations of Ezek 10.15, 21 are an attempt to bring the cherubim of Ezek 10 into line with Ezek 1, which does not know the creatures of the vision to be cherubim; Ezek 41.18, 20, 25 yields a different description, probably from a different author. Rev 4.6–8 varies Ezekiel's imagery in part by means of Is 6.2. In general, the cherubim follow the description of a winged sphinx, known esp. in Syria and Palestine.

In Christian angelology, cherubim rank after the seraphim and constitute the second highest of the heavenly choirs. BIBLIOGRAPHY: W. F. Albright, "What Were the Cherubim?" *Biblical Archeologist* 1 (1938) 1–3; reprinted in *Biblical Archeologist Reader* (1961).

[P. J. KEARNEY]

CHERUBIM (IN ART), an order of winged celestial beings, part man, part beast, probably derived from Mesopotamian winged lions and bulls, associated in OT art with the representation of God's glory and power. Guardians of temples and palaces, cherubim (*krb* or *kāribu*) are often depicted as composite beasts on ivory furniture fragments also. Cherubim were used to decorate the doors and walls of Solomon's Temple and to guard the Ark in the Inner Sanctuary. BIBLIOGRAPHY: J. Finegan, *Light from the Ancient Past* (1959).

[S. D. MURRAY]

CHERUBIN OF AVIGLIANA, BL. (1451–79), Augustinian friar. From his entrance into the Augustinian community, his life was marked by a deep piety that was built on devotion to the crucified Christ and was manifested by his obedience and purity. The wonders attributed to him in the typical medieval accounts helped to spread devotion to him. He was beatified in 1865. BIBLIOGRAPHY: D. A. Perini, *Bibliographia Augustiniana* (4 v., 1929–38) 1:71; N. Del Re, BiblSanct 3:1192–93.

[J. M. O'DONNELL]

CHERUBINI, LUIGI (1760–1842), Italian-born composer of opera and sacred music in France during the difficult time after the French Revolution. Well-versed in the traditions and components of German, Italian, and French music,

C. wrote in a pure, classical style, both following and enriching the legacy of Gluck in the musical lyric-drama. A marked conservative, disliking Bach's music and often locking horns with Hector Berlioz, C. served as director of the Paris Conservatoire, of which he was cofounder, until Napoleon I, out of imperial pique, replaced him by Gasparo Spontini. C., bitter but unbending, devoted his later years to the composition of church music, writing his *Missa Solemnis* in D minor in 1811, his *Requiem* and a Mass in C in 1816. Along with Franz Schubert, C. wrote some of the finest Catholic church music of the early 19th century. BIBLIOGRAPHY: E. Bellasis, *Cherubini: Memorials Illustrative of His Life and Work* (1912, repr. 1971).

[P. DOHERTY]

CHESTER BEATTY PAPYRI, a group of MSS, eight of the OT, three of the NT, portions of the apocryphal Book of Enoch, and a homily on Christ's Passion by Melita of Sardis. The collection is named for Sir (Alfred) Chester Beatty (1875–1968), who purchased them in Egypt in 1930. They are older by more than a century than the earliest known vellum MS. Chester Beatty I (P 45) dates from just after 250 A.D. The 30 badly mutilated leaves include 2 pages of Mt, 6 of Mk, 7 of Lk, 2 of Jn, and 13 of Acts. The Caesarean readings of the text were important to NT textual criticism. Chester Beatty II (P 46) dates from perhaps as early as 200 A.D. From an original 104 leaves, 46 survive in the Chester Beatty Library in Dublin, Eire; 30 others are at the Univ. of Michigan. The contents are the Pauline epistles arranged in unusual order: Rom, Heb, Cor, Eph, Gal, Phil, Col, 1 Thess; the pastoral epistles are lacking as are 2 Thess and Philem (perhaps by design). This papyrus is a significant example of the Alexandrian textual tradition. Chester Beatty III (P 47) dating from *c*. 265–300 A.D., has 10 leaves from an original 32 (certain other fragments also survive). This is the earliest MS for Rev, containing substantial portions of ch. 9–17. BIBLIOGRAPHY: F. G. Kenyon, *Chester Beatty Biblical Papyri I–III* (1933–36) with Supplement (1936–37); H. A. Sanders, *Third Century Papyrus Codex of the Epistles of Paul* (1935).

[D. J. BOURKE]

CHESTERTON, GILBERT KEITH (1874–1936), essayist, poet, philosopher, and wit. Educated at St. Paul's and the Slade School, the influence of the latter appearing in the undisciplined but striking book illustrations done in later life, as a student C. displayed a curious mixture of indolence and brilliance. He began his career in a London publishing house. Passionately dedicated to ideas and their articulation, he drifted into journalism, and that is a key to all his subsequent writing. C. gloried in the title journalist. The incredible outpouring of 40 years can be attributed to his single-minded determination to be heard. John Sullivan's two-volume bibliography of the writings of C. is incomplete, though it records well over 100 volumes in addition to innumerable shorter pieces. In the *Illustrated London News*

and the *Daily Mail* appeared over 2,000 essays. He wrote poetry, criticism, polemics, novels, biographies, detective stories. His two plays prompted his friend George Bernard Shaw to urge him to give up journalism and write for the theater. C.'s style relied heavily on paradox and did grow a bit tiresome. Yet his writing is a series of lightning flashes illuminating the familiar but unnoticed. He was essentially a poet, whatever the form his writing took. Central to his thought was an overwhelming sense of wonder combined with a surging optimism. No one in modern times has fought the battle of the common man more brilliantly and more consistently. A man of many causes, he fought big business, imperialism, and called for a revolution against industrial capitalism. His most profound book, *Orthodoxy,* was written 14 years before he entered the Catholic Church in 1922, but it was a complete statement of his beliefs before and after conversion. Friendship with Bernard Shaw, H. G. Wells, Hilaire Belloc, and Maurice Baring demonstrated C.'s ability to disagree without rancor. With Belloc he espoused an economic system called Distributism, idealistic and impractical, but providing him a platform from which to formulate some keen insights into the problems of the century. Meanwhile he published a series of detective stories centering in an eccentric cleric, Father Brown, which were and are enormously popular. *The Man Who Was Thursday* is an intellectual thriller unique of its kind. No one has written more competent studies of Dickens, Shaw, Browning, and Stevenson. They are not always accurate in biographical detail but shed intuitive light that makes that fact unimportant. *The Victorian Age in Literature* proved that even a handbook of literature could be filled with insight. Of C.'s *St. Thomas Aquinas* the great Thomist, Étienne Gilson, said, ''I consider it . . . the best book ever written on St. Thomas.'' C. has not been treated seriously by some critics since his death in 1936, but discerning writers like W. H. Auden, Lionel Trilling, and Christopher Isherwood have paid him high tribute. It is significant that 40 years after his death and in spite of radical changes in literary tastes there are 60 of his books in hardcover editions still in print and a dozen in paperback. C. wrote more than one wishes he had attempted, but in that mass of published work there lies the unmistakable track of a man of genius. BIBLIOGRAPHY: M. Ward, *Gilbert Keith Chesterton* (1943); J. Sullivan, *G. K. Chesterton: a Centenary Appraisal* (1974).

[J. R. AHERNE]

CHEVALIER, JULES (1824–1907), religious founder. After ordination (1851), he served as vicar in several parishes in Bourges and became pastor and archpriest at Issoudun (1872). In 1854 C. founded the Sacred Heart Missionaries and served as their superior general until 1901. With the collaboration of Marie Hartzer, C. also founded the Daughters of Our Lady of the Sacred Heart in 1882. All of C.'s writings center around devotion to the Sacred Heart. BIBLIOGRAPHY: A. Bundervoet, DHGE 12:647–648; L. Despresse, DSAM 2.1.829–831.

[H. DRESSLER]

CHEVALIER, ULYSSE (1841–1923), French bibliographer and historian. Serving as professor of church history at the Institut Catholique of Lyon after 1887, he was honored for his scholarship by several French academies. His most noteworthy works, controversial but still significant, include the *Répertoire des sources historiques du moyen âge: Bio-bibliographie* (2d ed. 1905–07) and *Topo-bibliographie* (repr. 1962); *Repertorium hymnologicum* (6 v., 1892–1921). BIBLIOGRAPHY: H. Leclercq, DACL 9:1743–44.

[O. J. BLUM]

CHEVERUS, JEAN LOUIS LEFEBVRE DE (1768–1836), first bp. of Boston, Mass., abp. of Bordeaux, cardinal. Born and ordained (1790) in France, C. refused to take the Constitutional oath and fled to England (1792). In 1810 he became the first bp. of Boston. C. founded an Ursuline convent in that city. His eloquent preaching attracted many Protestants to Catholicism, esp. Mother Elizabeth Bayley *Seton. His greatest contribution was to cement a friendly spirit between Catholics and Protestants. He was named bp. of Montauban in 1823, abp. of Bordeaux in 1826. Member of the French legislature, 1827–30, and councillor of state for Charles X, C. was created card. in 1836. BIBLIOGRAPHY: A. M. Melville, NCE 3:555–556.

[J. L. HALPIN]

CHEVET, the apse or termination of the apse of a church, esp. the end consisting of a main apse and secondary (usually five) apses or chapels radiating from it.

[S. F. JOHNSON]

CHEVETOGNE, MONASTERY OF, in Belgium, a Catholic center of ecumenism founded by Dom Lambert Beauduin, OSB (1873–1960). It was originally established in Amay-sur-Meuse, Belgium, in 1925, as an attempt at a new approach to the problem of reunion between East and West with a spirit of true respect for the East and a deep involvement in its spiritual life. The prevalent fear of Modernism made it difficult to promote such an approach, and the monastery suffered crisis after crisis. As a consequence, Dom Beauduin had to leave his community and spent almost 20 years in virtual exile in France. In the meantime, the monastic community moved to its present location, an old manor near the little village of Chevetogne in S Belgium (1939). The monastery is composed of two groups of monks, one of Latin and one of Byzantine rite, has a rich ecumenical library, and a remarkably authentic Novgorod style Oriental church. It is a favored site for ecumenical meetings and has had a wide influence through its periodical, *Irénikon*. BIBLIOGRAPHY: L. Bouyer, *Dom Lambert Beauduin; un homme de l'Église* (1964); S. A. Quitslund, *Beauduin: A Prophet Vindicated* (1973).

[G. ELDAROV]

CHEVRIER, JEAN (fl. *c.*1300–50), French MSS illuminator in the workshop of the master Jean Pucelle. C.'s name appears on folios 268 and 300 of the Belleville Breviary (before 1343). He probably executed borders and terminal figures in this and other works of the master.

[M. J. DALY]

CHEYNE, THOMAS KELLY (1841–1915), OT critic and scholar. Educated at Worcester College, Oxford, and at Göttingen, C. adopted H. von Ewald's method of biblical criticism and was instrumental in initiating the scholarly trend in English biblical criticism. However, his methods, esp. in his later work, resulted in some extravagance of opinion. BIBLIOGRAPHY: DNB (1912–21) 119.

[T. C. O'BRIEN]

CHEZAL-BENOÎT, ABBEY OF (St. Pierre de Chezal-Benoît), Benedictine abbey founded in 1093 by Andrew of Vallombrosa and located in the Diocese of Bourges, France. Nothing certain is known of his history before 1479 when Peter of Mas became abbot and introduced reforms in the length of Offices, in mortifications, and in the rigor of its penitential practices. He legislated a term of 3 years for abbots, who were elected by a general chapter. The abbey later merged with the Congregation of St. Maur. Since the dissolution of the abbey in 1790, the abbey church alone remains. BIBLIOGRAPHY: J. Laporte, NCE 3:557–558.

[A. P. DEEGAN]

CHÉZARD DE MATEL, JEANNE MARIE (1596–1670), foundress of the Sisters of the Incarnate Word and the Blessed Sacrament, mystic and writer. Almost illiterate herself, she wrote letters, spiritual journals, an autobiography and spiritual history, all containing technical theological terms, a lofty mysticism, and a purity of style. Her Institute was approved in 1644 and spread in France, but it was not until she was nearing death that she received its habit and made her profession. BIBLIOGRAPHY: L. Cristiani, DSAM 2.1:837–840.

[I. M. KASHUBA]

CHIAVETTA, GIOVANNI BATTISTA (d. 1664), Sicilian priest, historian, and theologian. C. wrote a critique, *Enigma dissolutum de modo existendi Christi Domini sub speciebus panis et vini in augustissimo eucharistiae sacramento,* on the Eucharistic theory of G. *Balli. BIBLIOGRAPHY: C. Morin, EncCatt 3:1432–33.

[T. C. O'BRIEN]

CHIBCHAS (MUYSCAS), the native inhabitants of the Bogotá plateau in central Colombia at the time of the coming of the Spaniards. They were an agricultural people, lived in cities (some of considerable size), and possessed an advanced culture comparable in many ways to that of the Aztecs, Incas, and Mayans. They had a knowledge of astronomy and craftsmanship, wove cotton cloth for clothing, and made jewelry of gold and precious stones. Their religion, well organized and ideologically supported by an extensive mythology, was polytheistic. Among their gods were a number of nature deities, the Sun being one of the more important. The worship of the gods abounded in elaborate and colorful ceremonies and processions. The worshipers practiced fasting and ritual bathing and made generous offerings to the deities, which included not only gold and jewelry and other prized materials, but also human sacrifice. The priests, who were expected to be celibate, constituted a separate caste. By the 18th cent. the Chibchas had been merged into the general Hispano-American culture and their language was forgotten. BIBLIOGRAPHY: A. L. Kroeber, "The Chibchas," *Handbook of South American Indians,* Bureau of American Ethnology Bulletin 143, v. 2:887–909 (1946).

[P. K. MEAGHER]

CHICAGO BIBLE, popular title for the independent translation by U.S. scholars, the proper title of which is *The Complete Bible. An American Translation,* published by the Univ. of Chicago. The revised edition was published in 1939. The history of this Bible begins with the translation of the NT, based on the text of B. F. *Westcott and F. *Hort, by E. J. *Goodspeed in 1923. Goodspeed has been hailed as the first scholar to break, and indeed to shatter, the "chains of Bible English" and to produce a version that is uncompromisingly modern and totally devoid of archaisms and mannered turns of phrase. The translation of the OT in 1927 was the work of a group of scholars headed by J. M. Powis Smith and was slightly less startling in the modernity of its language. This 1927 edition contained nearly 100 pages of textual notes to justify the readings adopted in all cases of doubt or ambiguity, and it is regrettable that these have been omitted in subsequent editions. A revised edition of the whole translation was produced in 1935 by T. J. Meek with the assistance of L. Waterman. In 1938 *The Apocrypha. An American Translation* appeared, and the complete Bible was produced in one volume in 1939. Finally an edition of the NT in the Greek text of Westcott-Hort with the English of this translation on facing pages was produced in 1954 with the title *The Student's New Testament. The Greek Text and the American Translation.* In spite of its general excellence the Chicago Bible must be treated with a certain caution, since the findings of modern scholarship have at times been accepted too uncritically.

[D. J. BOURKE]

CHICAGO-LAMBETH QUADRILATERAL, a more precise title for the *Lambeth Quadrilateral. The four-point basis for church reunion was approved by the *General Convention of the Protestant Episcopal Church at Chicago in 1886; then by the *Lambeth Conference of 1888.

[T. C. O'BRIEN]

CHICHELE, HENRY (1362?–1443), lawyer, diplomat, and ecclesiastical statesman; bp. of St. David's (1408–14); abp. of Canterbury (1414–43). As primate he protested Martin V's grant of a cardinal's hat and a legateship to Bp. Henry Beaufort of Winchester (1417). His large loans supported English pretensions in France, while his Oxford foundation, All Souls College (1443), offered prayers for the English war dead. He was an enemy of Lollardry and a conscientious administrator. BIBLIOGRAPHY: E. F. Jacob, *Henry Chichele and the Ecclesiastical Politics of His Age* (1952, repr. 1971).

[F. D. BLACKLEY]

CHICHÉN ITZÁ, village in Yucatán state, Mexico, site of the ancient Mayan city of that name. From the 12th to the 15th cent. it was the Mayan ceremonial center and its architecture rose to new heights, including the largest pre-Columbian Ball Court, the imposing pyramid of Kukalcán, the Temple of Warriors and the Temple of the Jaguars with important murals, the Astronomical Observatory (El Caracol), and the principal temple, the so-called Castillo, covering an acre of ground and rising 100 feet above the plain. Though its ruins are extensive, some of the temples, pyramids, towers, etc., are still well preserved. BIBLIOGRAPHY: I. Marquino, *Arquitectura prehispánica* (1964).

[M. J. DALY]

CHIEF PRIESTS, translation of Gr. *archiereis,* the plural of the word meaning high priest. There was at a given time only one high priest. Many consider them as the priestly members of the Sanhedrin; others, the heads of the families from which high priests were chosen, former high priests, and the then high priest. A third opinion is that the heads of the courses and certain administrative officers of the priesthood formed the group.

[J. J. O'ROURKE]

CHIEREGATO, FRANCESCO (1478–1539), bp. of Teramo, who served as nuncio for Pope Leo X in England, Spain, and Portugal. He was sent by Adrian VI to the Diet of Nuremberg, where he succeeded in inducing Archduke Ferdinand to oppose Lutheranism. At the Diet he read a letter from the Pope, who recognized that many failures on the part of the Curia and clergy were in part responsible for current problems, and he declared it his intention to correct them; but he also expressed a firm opposition to Lutheranism which aroused the fury of the Lutheran princes. These succeeded with the approval of the emperor in convoking a council to act in disregard of the papal directives. C. withdrew from Nuremberg in 1523, and with the death of Adrian VI, C.'s diplomatic career came to an end. BIBLIOGRAPHY: V. H. Ponko, Jr., NCE 3:567; E. Santovito, EncCatt 3:1434–35.

[R. C. EGAN]

CHIESA, BERNARDINO DELLA, see DELLA CHIESA, BERNARDINO.

CHIGI, a distinguished family of Sienese origin. The Chigi began as bankers, were ennobled in 1377, and later became prominent in Rome. Probably the two best known are Agostino the Magnificent (1464–1520), a highly successful merchant prince and confidant of popes; and Fabio, who became Pope Alexander VII in 1655. The Chigi Pope was not only a great nepotist in the usual sense, making three of his nephews cardinals, but he even beatified three of his ancestors: Bl. Giovanni Da Lecceto (d. 1313), Bl. Angela (d. 1400), and Bl. Giuliana (d. 1400). The great Chigi library begun by Fabio is now integrated with that of the Vatican. BIBLIOGRAPHY: L. Ceyssens, NCE 3:567–568.

[D. G. NUGENT]

CHIGI, FABIO, see ALEXANDER VII, POPE.

CHILD BUREAU, INTERNATIONAL CATHOLIC, see INTERNATIONAL CATHOLIC CHILD BUREAU.

CHILDERIC III, KING OF THE FRANKS (743–751), last of the Merovingian dynasty. The throne had been vacant from 737 to 743. Pepin and Carloman, mayors of the palace, to secure stability, elevated him to it, although his precise origin was unknown. In 751 he was set aside by order of the usurper Pepin. He died obscurely in monastic confinement. BIBLIOGRAPHY: J. M. Wallace-Hadrill, *Long-Haired Kings and Other Studies in Frankish History* (1962).

[A. CABANISS]

CHILDERMAS, Old English term for the Feast of the *Holy Innocents (Dec. 28); it has also been used for the day of the week throughout the year on which the feast occurred, considered by some a day of bad fortune.

[T. EARLY]

CHILDHOOD SPIRITUAL, see SPIRITUAL CHILDHOOD.

CHILDREN, RIGHTS AND DUTIES OF, see PIETY, FAMILIAL.

CHILDREN OF GOD, the children of Adam and Eve who participate in the nature of God, who adopts them as his own. This NT teaching is found most explicitly in the Johannine and Pauline writings. Even in the Synoptics Jesus refers to the peacemakers, the charitable, and the (risen) just as children of God. In Paul's letters adoption as sons, already one of the privileges of Israel, is a present reality through the gift of the Spirit which allows those who have thus become coheirs with Christ to call upon God as Jesus did by the title of familiarity and trust not used before, *Abba*. Those thus renewed in spirit are called to reproduce in themselves the image of the only Son. According to the Johannine writings, God gives to those who believe in the true Light that comes into the world the power of becoming children of God. Such believers, born again of water and the Holy Spirit, are indeed born of God. This divine life is a present reality of which the world is now ignorant. One day it will be manifest, when God's children will be like God and shall see him as he is. This teaching is in basic harmony with the doctrine of the intertestamental Wisdom of Solomon, according to which the risen just will forever be associated with the angels of God and be called by the same name, sons of God.

[E. J. DILLON]

CHILDREN OF MARY, a title used by many confraternities and sodalities established to promote devotion to Mary and the ardent desire to live a good Christian life. Commonly such sodalities restrict their membership to girls and young women, but some have been open to persons of either sex. Many such sodalities are affiliated with the archsodality (or the *prima primaria* sodality) established in Rome in 1584, but others are not.

CHILDREN'S CRUSADE (*c.* 1212), a movement originating in France and Germany between the fourth and fifth Crusades. Young French pilgrims, led by Stephen, a shepherd boy of Cloyes, set out unarmed for Provence and Italy. It is estimated that several thousand children, ranging from 10 to 16 years of age, died of hunger, cold, and hardship on their long march S to the Mediterranean Sea. The German counterpart, led by Nicholas of Cologne and composed of older children, shared the same fate. The expeditions were opposed by Pope Innocent III, rulers, parents, and priests. BIBLIOGRAPHY: S. Runciman, *History of the Crusades* (3 v., 1951–54).

[J. BLAIR]

CHILE, a South American republic situated to the W of the continental divide of the Andes and extending from the border of Peru in the N to the tip of Tierra del Fuego in the S (286,397 sq mi; pop. [est. 1975] *c.* 10,410,000). Sixty-five per cent of its population is of mixed European and Indian descent, 30% of unmixed European (mainly Spanish) ancestry, and 5% is pure Indian. It is a country of great mineral resources, esp. nitrates; the illiteracy rate is low (20%); it has a slowly developing but influential middle class, conscious of socio-political problems. It was discovered by Almagro in 1535 and its conquest was completed *c.* 1557. The city of Santiago was founded in 1541, La Serena in 1544, and Concepción in 1550. In 1776 Chile became a captaincy general under a governor of its own. Independence was won (1810–18) esp. through the efforts of José de San Martín and Bernardo O'Higgins. During the 19th cent. there was continuing conflict and even civil war between conservatives and liberals. Somewhat greater political stability prevailed from 1900 to 1970 except for a military coup in 1925 and a government of the Popular Front in 1938.

Priests accompanied the conquistadors; these were followed by the regular clergy, the Mercedarians in 1548, the Franciscans and Dominicans in 1553, the Jesuits in 1593, the Augustinians in 1595, and the Hospitalers in 1617. The first monastery of nuns was established in 1574. The See of Santiago was erected in 1561 and that of La Imperial, in 1563. A century of missionary effort resulted in the conversion of all the peaceful Indians. The creation of lay catechists (doctrineros) compensated for the shortage of priests. Schools and colegios, and even the beginning of a university at Santiago (1623), were undertaken. When Chile became independent, Catholicism was recognized by the new regime as the state religion; but in the years that followed there was conflict between Church and State regarding the rights of *patronage, and at times the State resorted to expropriation and other measures offensive to the Church. The separation of Church and State was incorporated into the Constitution of 1925. For about 30 years relations between the Church and State were cordial, but during the regime of Marxist president Salvator Allende Gossens (1970–73) relations were strained. He was overthrown in a bloody coup and was reported to have committed suicide Sept. 11, 1973. According to a report of the ecumenical Committee on Cooperation for Peace in Chile, more than 35,000 persons were aided since the overthrow of the Allende government, 15,500 of them political prisoners. The Chilean hierarchy is composed of 1 cardinal, 4 abps., and 24 bishops. There are 2,174 priests (of whom 1,354 are religious), who care for the c. 8,950,000 Catholics. This means there is 1 priest for about every 4,100 Catholics. There are about 4,745 nuns. Catholic education has made some progress in the last 100 years, and there are now three universities conducted by the Church. Progress has also been made in the matter of social reform (e.g., the Centro Belarmino) and of liturgy. But the general level of Catholic practice is low. Vocations to the priesthood are scarce, and the masses, among whom Marxist influence is widespread, need to be re-Christianized. Chile has a higher proportion of Protestants in its population than any other country of Latin America—some estimates, probably exaggerated, setting their total number at one million. Among the Protestants there are as many as 700,000 Pentecostals. Other bodies represented are the Methodists, Presbyterians, Southern Baptists, and Lutherans. Adventists and Jehovah's Witnesses are quite active. Some fruitful dialogue is going on between Catholics and Protestants, including the Pentecostals. BIBLIOGRAPHY: L. Galdames, History of Chile (ed. and tr. I. J. Cox, 1964); J. A. De Ramón, NCE 3:583–587.

[P. DAMBORIENA]

CHILIASM (Gr. chilias, a thousand), the belief, based chiefly on the literal interpretation of Rev ch. 20, that Christ will come to rule visibly upon earth for 1,000 years before the end of the world. It is used as a synonym for *millenarianism, but it is less proper to identify it with any but the premillenarian variety of millenarian thought since chiliasm, insofar as it has a distinctive meaning, expects the personal corporeal reign of Christ upon earth for 1,000 years.

[P. K. MEAGHER]

CHILLINGWORTH, WILLIAM (1602–44), British theologian. C. was born at Oxford and reared an Anglican.

Following a controversy with the Jesuit John *Fisher (Percy), he became a Catholic (1630), but after studying at Douai, returned to England and recanted (1634). His best-known work is The Religion of Protestants, a Safe Way to Salvation (1638), a defense of the individual's right to free inquiry into doctrine and a denial of the infallibility of any one Church. BIBLIOGRAPHY: R. R. Orr, Reason and Authority: the Thought of William Chillingworth (1967).

CHILPERIC I, KING OF THE FRANKS (561–584), son of Clotaire and grandson of Clovis, who reigned in the Kingdom of Neustria (Kingdom of the West). On the death of Clotaire the monarchy was divided among his four sons, Gontran, Charebert, Sigebert, and Chilperic. When Charebert died in 567 there was rivalry between C. and his brothers over the division of his estate. To complicate matters further, Sigebert's wife determined to avenge the death of her sister, the first wife of C. who had been assassinated by him. C., whose reign was marked by savagery, died at the hands of an assassin. Continued chaos contributed to the steady weakening of royal authority and eventually resulted in the extinction of the Merovingian dynasty.

[J. BLAIR]

CHINA, People's Republic of, Communist state in E Asia (3,704,400 sq mi; pop. [1974 government est.] 800,000,000). From the time of the Hsia dynasty (c. 2000 B.C.) to the establishment of the republic in 1911 A.D., China was a land of rich culture and deep learning, but in recent years it has been in turmoil in consequence of social, economic, and political developments. Large areas of the country were occupied by the Japanese in the years 1937–45, and the state was taken over by the Communists in 1949. The official language is Mandarin; the dominant religion, a blend of Confucianism, Taoism, and Buddhism, but Marxist atheism is now systematically taught. Christianity was first introduced to parts of China by Nestorian Christians in the 7th century. After the decline of this missionary endeavor in the mid-9th cent., Nestorianism, brought by monks from Central Asia, was active in China down to the end of the Mongol dynasty (1368). In the 13th cent. Western Christianity was introduced by Franciscan missionaries under the protection of Mongol emperors, but what gains were made were swept away when the Mongols fell from power. In the 16th and 17th cent. missionary effort was revived. The Jesuits found favor in the imperial court by bringing in men of science and culture who adapted themselves to the Chinese way of life. Dominicans, Franciscans, Augustinians, and priests of the Paris Foreign Mission Society moved into the field. But in the struggle between the Ming and Manchu dynasties there was a reaction against the missionaries. Some were put to death and many were deported. Matters became even worse after the condemnation by the Holy Office of the Chinese rites (1704) and the publication (1715) of Clement XI's apostolic constitution sanctioning the decree of the Holy Office. Missionary work was forbidden by imperial decree, and missionaries were made subject to deportation. From that time till the mid-19th cent., the Church suffered intermittent persecution, sometimes of great severity, in which many lost their lives. Under the protection of concessions granted to Western powers after 1842, the missionary effort in China was resumed on a gradually increasing scale. By 1949 the Catholic Church in China was divided into 20 provinces, 79 dioceses, and 38 prefectures. There were 5,449 missionaries, 2,800 native priests, 900 religious brothers (the majority native), 6,227 sisters (4,832 native). The Catholic population numbered between 3½ and 4 million. (There is no way of obtaining up-to-date statistics.)

The coming of the Communists to power put an end to this progress. Some missionaries were slain, others imprisoned, but most were expelled. There were martyrs among the native bishops, priests, sisters, and laity, and many were jailed. An organization fostered by the Communists, the Chinese Catholic Patriotic Association, is ruled by bishops illicitly consecrated.

Robert Morrison of the London Mission Society brought Protestantism to China in 1807, and many other denominations entered into the work after that time. Protestant effort, like that of the Catholics, was cut short by the Communists. Perhaps the greatest Protestant contributions have been in the fields of medicine and education. There were 13 denominational universities, 300 high schools, and 322 hospitals. In 1949 Protestants numbered about a million and a half. It was estimated (1968) that the whole Protestant community was then scarcely half that figure. BIBLIOGRAPHY: C. Carey-Elwes, *China and the Cross: A Survey of Missionary History* (1957); R. S. Latourette, *History of Christian Missions in China* (1929); *Bilan du Monde* 2:225–240.

[P. DAMBORIENA]

CHINA, MARTYRS OF, the 119 persons who died in China for their Christian faith and were beatified between 1889 and 1956. The group includes 61 Chinese lay persons, 26 European priests, 8 Chinese catechists, 7 Chinese seminarians, 7 European nuns, 5 European bps., 4 Chinese priests, and a European lay brother. The protomartyr of the Chinese Church is Francisco de *Capillas, OP, who was beheaded in 1648 and beatified in 1909. Persecution of Christians in China was prevalent from the 17th through the 19th cent., largely because of the Chinese opposition to foreigners and the fear that their traditional religion would be undermined. European governments forced a denunciation of persecution by the Treaty of Nanking (1842), but it emerged with great violence during the Boxer Rebellion when an estimated 30,000 Catholics were killed. Pius XII beatified 86 of these martyrs in 1946, 1951, and 1956. BIBLIOGRAPHY: J. Krahl, NCE 3:602–603; E. H. Edwards, *Fire and Sword in Shansi: Story of the Martyrdom of Foreigners and Chinese Christians* (repr. 1970).

[T. M. MCFADDEN]

CHINA, NESTORIAN CHURCH IN. China received its first knowledge of Christianity in the 7th cent. during the Tang Dynasty, when a Nestorian monk from Syria or Palestine settled near modern Siam. An important source of knowledge comes from the uncovering in 1625 of the famous marble monument of Sianfu. The inscription gives the main points of Christian doctrine of the Nestorian Church in China from 635 until 781 and the names and titles of about 70 Western missionaries. The Nestorian missionaries worked hard in translating into Chinese the Christian books that they had brought with them. The destruction of Buddhist monasteries in 845 dealt a serious blow to Nestorianism. It revived again during the 11th and 13th cent. when Nestorian leaders had success in converting many Chinese tribes. Marco Polo found Nestorian influence in northern, central, and southern China. The sect grew until the beginning of the Chinese Ming Dynasty when the destruction of its influence was complete.

[E. C. HUBBERT]

CHINA, ORTHODOX CHURCH IN. The first Orthodox church was built in Peking in 1685 for Russian prisoners. Bp. Innocent Figurovsky was responsible for translating the liturgical books into Chinese at the turn of the 20th cent., the period of the greatest evangelizing effort and most rapid growth. The Chinese mission established in the 18th cent. was replaced by the East Asian Exarchate in 1945. The first Chinese bp., Simeon Du, was consecrated in Moscow in 1950. When a second Chinese, Basil Yo Fuan, was named for Peiping in 1957, the Chinese Orthodox Church was given its autonomy by the Russian Church. No reliable information on the existing situation of this Church is currently available. BIBLIOGRAPHY: R. Stephanopoulos, EncModChrMiss 236.

[T. BIRD]

CHINESE PHILOSOPHY. The development of Chinese philosophy is marked by four distinct phases: the ancient, which lasted until 221 B.C.; the middle (221 B.C.–960 A.D.); the modern (960–1900 A.D.); and the contemporary. The so-called Hundred Schools, among which are the Confucianists, the Taoists, Moists, the Logicians, the Yin Yang school, and the Legalists, all held that man is of primary concern and central to their philosophy. For all, man was important as an individual and as a member of society. For this reason one finds that Chinese philosophy is marked by the humanistic, moral, and legal considerations upon which it is grounded. Search into the earliest Chinese philosophy shows a preoccupation with fear of spiritual beings. It further shows the Chinese reliance on the approval of such beings. This is esp. true of the period of the Shang dynasty (1751–1112 B.C.). After that time and after the Chou overcame the Shang, there occurred a development toward reliance on human initiative at least to solve human questions. Gradually, the dependency of the Chinese on the human Lord (*ti*) was replaced with a belief in an impartial Heaven

(T'ien). In that system of belief the right to rule was grounded in the moral worth of the ruler. In other words, even at such an early stage of Chinese philosophy the concept of "divine right" was not confused with despotism. For the Chinese, right living (morally) was essential to right ruling. It was not, however, until Confucius (551–479 B.C.) that humanism in Chinese philosophy reached its highest peak. Confucius preached "Man-at-his-Best" i.e., the "superior man" and a well-ordered society—both rationally achieving their plans in equilibrium. Man in such a society pursued, through study and practice, the Way (Tao). It was by two followers of Confucius, Mencius (*c*.372–*c*.298 B.C.) and Hsün Tzu (*c*.313–*c*.238 B.C.) that the need for clarification of this ideal was felt. Mencius built his theory on the belief that all men are essentially good and that the "four beginnings," humanity *(jen)*, righteousness *(i)*, propriety *(li)*, and wisdom are possessed by all men. Poor environment and lack of education accounted for the presence of evil in the world as Mencius saw it. He further saw it as the result of something similar to the Judaeo-Christian concept of man's free will, which he called, "casting oneself away." The other, Hsün Tzu, held that man, although capable of achieving this superior state, has a nature which is evil. For him, the existence of moral prescriptions prove that man is evil since such rules and prescriptions are the result, not of man's benevolent right action, but of his deviations from such behavior; prescriptions are thus set up to restrain these deviations. It is the superior man who proves the rightness of the theory. The ideal of the individual harmoniously reconciled to himself and his society is seen in *The Great Learning*, a work ascribed to Tseng Tzu (505–436 B.C.). In that work eight successive steps are described: investigation of things, extension of knowledge, sincerity of the will, rectification of the mind, cultivation of the personal life, regulation of the family, maintenance of national order, and world peace. The integration of all steps is achieved by the harmonious individual who, by practice of acts under these eight stages, implements harmony in himself and in the society of which he is a part. Such harmony is particularly connected with kindness, benevolence, and affection. The true man of *jen* (humanity) establishes his own character and that of others. Thus, it is correct to speak of the aspects of *jen* —conscientiousness *(chung)* and altruism *(shen)*. In another sense, one might want to designate another distinction in the way Mencius and Hsün Tzu achieved the Confucian ideal. For the former, the mode was moral and naturalistic, and for the latter, it was legal and positivistic, if modern terms may be ascribed to ancient beliefs. The concept of rectification was seen by Mencius as a rectification of one's heart—in the sense of a change of heart's issuing in a change (for the better) of one's habits. For Hsün Tzu such rectification was a process of logicality—one, perhaps, involving consistent, logical interpretation of one's behavior. The concept of moderation *(chung-yung)* which was advocated by Confucius was described by his grandson Tzu-ssu (492–431 B.C.). The mean (point of moderation) is seen as

twofold: centrality *(chung)* and harmony *(yung)*. When both the individual and society are harmoniously reconciled, a state of equilibrium ensues and the Way (Tao) prevails. In other words, man makes the Way (Tao) a reality. He endows it with meaning and not vice versa. Thus to the Confucian school Tao is a system of moral truth and Tao is Heaven. The development of the Taoist school dates from the *Lao Tzu* also called *Tao-te Ching* attributed to Lao Tzu (*c*.6th cent. B.C.). Diametrically opposed to Confucianism, Taoism teaches naturalism in the social and political orders: simplicity, spontaneity, tranquility, weakness, and most important of all, nonaction *(wu-wei)*. One of the most influential of the Taoists was Chuang Tzu (b. *c*.369 B.C.), who viewed the Way as an opportunity for unceasing transformation. This dynamism endows Taoism with characteristics of universality and particularity—a combination that affected later Taoist developments. Like Confucianism, Taoism was humanistic—its fullest development entails man's spiritual freedom and peace. The Moist school, founded by Mo Tzu (*c*.468 B.C.–?), was prior to the Taoist and, like it, opposed to Confucianism. The Confucian concept of love with distinctions (one shows special love toward one's parents) was at variance with the Moist conception of absolutely universal love. The Moist placed ethics on a religious plane. The Logicians, a minor school, were the only metaphysicians of ancient China. Simultaneous to all these was the development of the Yin Yang school. The two main forces it distinguished are *yin*, negative, passive, weak, feminine; and *yang*, positive, active, strong, masculine. It is generally associated with Tsou Yen (305–249 B.C.) whose thinking integrated the elements of both with the five agents of metal, wood, water, fire, and earth. There are two important implications of this theory: first, that both man and nature are governed by the same process; and second, that the universe is a systematic, structural one, determinate and predictable. Since the effect of such a school is visible in every aspect of life, it is perhaps the first to reach cosmological proportions. The Legalist school was realistic and totalitarian, marked by concentration on the practical implementation of law in the Ch'in state. It helped establish the Ch'in dynasty as the first united empire in China. The overthrow of the dynasty by the Han (206 B.C.) marked the beginning of the middle period (221 B.C.–960 A.D.). It was during this period that Confucianism became the state ideology (136 B.C.). It was not a period that was free from other influences; in fact the concepts of Yin and Yang were very influential. This is reported in the *Book of Changes (I Ching)*. It was also during this period that Tung Chung-shu (176–104 B.C) combined the Confucian doctrine of ethics and history with the ideas of Yin and Yang. A subsequent revision of Taoism occurred during this period. Its importance lay not so much in its contributions to the period but in its position as bridge between Chinese and Buddhist philosophies. At first a popular religion, Buddhism moved eventually into a dialectic with Neo-Taoism. It is that dialectic, esp. the concepts of being and nonbeing, that grounded the beginning of Buddhism. This period of Buddhism is, in turn, marked by the emergence of two systems of thought: the Middle Doctrine (Chung-lun) or Three Treatise school and the Dharma Character or Consciousness Only school. The Middle Doctrine, essentially nihilistic, was based on three Indian scriptures, and it regarded the synthesis of being and nonbeing as syncretized in the Truth Middle, the empty set, so to speak. The Consciousness Only school regarded the phenomenal world as real as any one could hope for. In a sense, the Middle Doctrine rejects phenomena since it rejects their existences, but it likewise rejects the noumenal since it refuses to deal with any being—spiritual, intellectual, or physical. But in this rejection it holds on to the designation of, at least, the need for a middle ground, if only for the sake of reconciling the fact that neither exists, with the fact that one must account for those nonexistences in some way—this, for them, was emptiness. It was through the later of the Hua-yen and the T'ien-t'ai schools in the 6th and 7th cent. that the Buddhist school came to be more Chinese. The development in the 8th and 9th cent. of Ch'an or the meditation school (Zen) aimed at meditation to reach ultimate reality. Its dualism (true mind as opposed to false mind in terms of detachment) was rejected by Hui-neng (d. 713) who believed in basic goodness of nature. Buddhism, increasingly modified by Chinese philosophers, all but supplanted Confucianism until Han Yü (d. 824) prepared for a Confucian renaissance, demanding the burning of Buddhist and Taoist texts. The modern period (960–1912 A.D.) is marked by a gradual revision of Confucianism. It was Chou-Tun-i (1017–73) who inaugurated the Neo-Confucianism which dominated Chinese thought for four centuries. The new Confucianism developed in two strands; the rationalist School of Principle and the idealistic School of Mind. The extreme idealism of Wang Yang-ming (d. 1529) dominated Chinese philosophy for 150 years, to be modified by Confucianists of a more practical bent, e.g., Wang Fu-chih (d. 1692) and Tai Chen (d. 1777). The last great Confucianist was K'ang Yu-wei (d. 1927) who emphasized the need for unity and compassion. The Contemporary Period began in 1912 and is marked by influences on the traditional Chinese philosophy—influences that give rise to confusion and obfuscation at times. Notable among such influences are those of Darwin, Nietzsche, Schopenhauer, Kant, Bergson, Dewey, James, and Marx. The pragmatism of both James and Dewey, as well as the Logical Positivism of Russell, have all left their influence on Chinese philosophy. Maoism is the state philosophy, but both Confucianism and Buddhism were revitalized during this period. Three contemporary figures stand out in that development: Fung Yu-lan, Hsiung Shih-li, and Chang Tung-sun. The first developed a philosophy based on rationalistic Neo-Confucianism; Hsiung Shih-li developed a new concept of the "Consciousness-only" theory that marked the Dharma Character school some 15 cent. before. Chang Tung-sun is predominantly Kantian, yet he rejects Kant's theory of

knowledge, and, of course, the a posteriori and a priori. Notwithstanding the influence of these three, Marxism has become the way of life as well as the method of thinking for the Chinese today. Yet, one needs only to read what can here be only superficially outlined to discern in this historical review the logical framework, as well as the psychological one, for the seeds of Marxism. The previous 35 cent. of Chinese philosophy are periods of dialectic marked both in content and direction by humanistic concerns. It is a history dominated as well by the desire for harmonious reconciliation of man with his world and the entire universe. BIBLIOGRAPHY: Wing-Tsit Chan, EncPhil 2:87–96; A. Tzen, NCE 3:608–610.

[J. R. RIVELLO]

CHINESE RELIGION, the basic spiritual foundation, established upon several philosophical and mystical movements, which forms the Chinese conception of a Supreme Being, man, the world, and ethics. Throughout their history, there has been a strong syncretism among the Chinese so that they could retain a tendency toward animism and ancestor worship while accepting Confucianism, Taoism, and Buddhism. The idea of God and man's search for him has not occupied Chinese art and literature as it has so often in the West. To the Chinese, God is not a clearly defined personality. They acknowledge a Supreme Power (T'ien or heaven) over the world, and even a Supreme Ruler (Shang-ti), who is the lord of heaven. The interpretation of these terms has caused considerable difficulty (see CHINESE RITES CONTROVERSY), with some scholars maintaining the monotheism of the ancient Chinese religion and others regarding this belief in a supreme power as the personification of the cosmic world-order and spiritual force that directs man's fate. The emperor was regarded as the representative on earth of this supreme power; the emperor alone offered sacrifice, and it was by Heaven's allowance that he ruled. Since both emperor and people were eager to know the will of Heaven, many forms of *divination were practiced. No feast was celebrated or project begun without the advice of experts well versed in the laws of feng-shui (literally, wind and water). Sacrificial offerings of rice, cakes, and wine were often made.

From classical antiquity, the Chinese have inherited a belief in the spirits of nature (see ANIMISM) and the cult of ancestral souls (see ANCESTOR WORSHIP). For millions of Chinese, the most vital component of religion lies in the recognition of the powerful forces that abide on land, in the sea, and in the air. These spirits, whether they be beneficent or malevolent, must be propitiated and thanked since they too govern the fortunes of men. In Chinese mythology the dragon personifies the benign powers of nature. Dragon worship is associated with several festivals, esp. their most important feast of the New Year, when the dragon's image is carried throughout the streets. Where it passes, evil spirits and misfortune are exterminated. The spirits of ancestors play an important role also; they are the protectors of the living and enter into every aspect of daily life. They must be reverenced, sustained by food offerings, and invoked for assistance.

There have been three major influences upon this pattern of Chinese religious belief: *Confucianism, *Taoism, and *Buddhism. Confucius made no attempt to modify China's basic religion; he was uninterested in metaphysics and sought to evoke the human element, the relationship between one man and another. He taught that man is good by nature, although this nature must be developed by moral education. Filial piety is the basis of his ethical code, which was more a philosophy than a religion. Taoism, at least insofar as it follows the teaching of *Lao Tsu, condemns self-seeking, ambition, and worldly involvements; humility and kindness are the key virtues, and both government and people must identify their actions with cosmic movements. As a religion, Taoism has incorporated a great deal of superstition and magic. Buddhism entered China from India c.70 A.D. and was quickly adopted by the people. Several different schools of Buddhism developed, incorporating both pantheism and polytheism.

Chinese religious life, therefore, is singularly free of strong doctrinal tensions and sectarian conflict. There would be nothing strange in being Confucianist, Taoist, and Buddhist at the same time, and for the past 1500 years these three systems have been mutually penetrated and interrelated. But Confucianism's basic rationalistic humanism has been universally accepted: man is the center of the universe and the end of all knowledge is to serve human happiness. BIBLIOGRAPHY: K. S. Latourette, *Chinese: Their History and Culture* (2d ed. rev.; 1946); W. G. Walshe and J. J. De Groot, ERE 3:549–556; J. A. Hardon, *Religions of the World* (1963) 142–187; L. G. Thompson, *Chinese Religion: An Introduction* (1975); M. Weber, *Religion of China* (1951).

[V. T. JOHNSON]

CHINESE RITES CONTROVERSY, dispute within the RC Church over retention by Chinese converts of such customs as honoring Confucius and family ancestors, and the use of certain terms of Chinese thought for Christian concepts such as *T'ien* for heaven and *Shang-ti* God. The controversy developed from a decision in 1603 by the Jesuit missionary M. *Ricci (1552–1610) to allow the usages. That position was subsequently followed by the Jesuits, who conducted most of the mission work in China during that period. In 1693 Bp. C. Maigrot, vicar apostolic of Fukien, initiated an attack on the rites, and they were forbidden by Clement XI in 1704. They were again condemned, more strictly, by Benedict XIV in 1742, with an antirites oath required. Advocates of the rites contended they were civil ceremonies that did not necessarily express superstitious beliefs, particularly among the scholar class dominant in the state, and that evangelization of the Chinese would be severely handicapped if converts could not continue customs so central to

national life. Opponents argued that the Church must not compromise and that the rites were inextricably bound up with superstitious ideas.

The papacy has taken an increasingly tolerant position in the 20th cent., holding that rites formerly associated with heathen practices now signify no more than respect for ancestors and patriotic regard for the nation. Pius XII approved a 1939 instruction of the Congregation for the Propagation of the Faith to that effect. The realization of the need to evangelize in a manner that avoids syncretism but is genuinely suited to the socio-cultural pattern of each nation is evidenced in Vatican Council II's Decree on the Missionary Activity of the Church. BIBLIOGRAPHY: F. A. Rouleau, NCE 3:611–617. *ADAPTATION, MISSIONARY.

[T. EARLY]

CHIROMANCY, or palmistry, a mode of *divination that claims to discover personal characteristics and future prospects from an examination of the palm of the hand. The lines and seven "mounts" or small protuberances at the base of the fingers and thumb and along the perimeter of the palm are scrutinized. Parts of the palm may be linked to astrological influences, though not in all forms of chiromancy. As one form of physiognomy, the art of discovering mental and moral characteristics from physical appearances, chiromancy has flourished in China and the West for thousands of years, although its claims have not always been widely accepted. Allusions to chiromancy occur in Aristotle, *Hist. anim.* 1.15 and Pliny, *H.N.* 11.114; and Ex 13.9, "You shall have the record of it as a sign upon your hand," has been used to support chiromantic practices. Serious resort to palmistry is a sin against the virtue of *religion. BIBLIOGRAPHY: W. A. Lessa and E. Z. Vogt, *Reader in Comparative Religion* (2d ed., 1965) 352–363.

[E. V. GALLAGHER]

CHIRONOMY, the art of indicating a melody to a choir by motions of the hand. Various systems of hand and arm motions have been used in directing Gregorian chant.

[S. F. JOHNSON]

CHIROTHESIA (Gr. *cheiros,* hand, and *teinein* to stretch), in the administration of the sacraments of confirmation and holy orders, the imposition of hands by the bishop.

[S. F. JOHNSON]

CHIROTONIA (chirotony), the act of extending the hands in bestowing a blessing or praying in a person's behalf.

[S. F. JOHNSON]

CHIVALRY, term designating standards and habits considered appropriate to the life of a medieval noble. The characteristic noble of this era was a knight usually committed to his feudal lord by a special bond. The true knight was expected to be courageous in battle, loyal to his lord, generous toward his fellow knights, a protector of the poor and weak, and a defender of the faith against heresy and schism. He was expected to battle only in the cause of right and justice. BIBLIOGRAPHY: S. Painter, *French Chivalry* (1940); M. Bloch, *Feudal Society* (tr. L. A. Manyon, 1961).

[J. BLAIR]

CHIVASSO, ANGELO CARLETTI DI, see ANGELO CARLETTI DI CHIVASSO.

CHLODULF OF METZ, ST., see CLODULF OF METZ, ST.

CHOICE (from Fr. *choisir,* the equivalent of Lat. *electio,* Gr. *proairesis*), a preferential determination among objects proposed; more precisely, a component activity within a full *human act, which follows the resolve to obtain a certain end and the deliberation about how to do so, and includes a decision of mind about, and an impulse of will toward, the course to be adopted, and precedes its effective prosecution and terminal achievement. This note attempts to make clearer this somewhat technical definition.

Human activity moves at two levels, known as the order of *intention and the order of *execution; they correspond to the field of thoughts and intentions and the field of deeds, whether they be successes or failures. Roughly, though not exactly, the distinction is that between ideals and facts, or even between theory and practice. At each level a succession of phases can be observed; in an incomplete human act the series is unfinished, either because it peters out or because it is arrested. Here we are concerned only with the order of intention, for that is where the act of choice takes place, namely somewhere in the series of alternating cognitive and affective activities that make up the interior attitude a person adopts toward his environment. He may not go on actually to do anything about it, for as we know from experience, sometimes unfortunate yet not always, our choices are not inevitably translated into deeds, because we may change our mind, or may lack the follow-through, or may be stopped by outside forces.

Choice, then, is anterior to, though implicit in, human execution and behavior, and belongs to the category of immanent activity. Now this, which comprises both knowing and loving, can be a response either to first principles and ends or to derivative conclusions and means to ends: hence the distinction in the intentional order between the primary postulates of an act which as such are willed, but not chosen, and the secondary corollaries which are chosen. This calls for amplification. We begin with an object that strikes us as good and desirable; accordingly we wish to have it, go on to judge that it is attainable, and then resolve to have it. Stripped down to the bare bones of the scheme, no manifestation of choice has so far appeared. Our responses are to an aim or end, which precisely as such, like an axiom which is accepted and not proved, is taken as the basis of the subsequent activity which involves choice or choices: within the frame of reference thereby constituted, it is an object of *volition, not election, of simple *will, not *free will. In the widest terms, we may choose how to be happy but we cannot choose not to

be happy; in the narrow terms of medical practice a doctor may choose to restore health, but leaves unquestioned the value of restoring health, happily for his patient. In other words choosing works within the bounds of a willing which though enforced and voluntary is not free in respect to the system adopted to define the freedom in question.

Accordingly choice belongs to that part of intentional activity concerned with objects subordinate to an end that has been already resolved on. Here we are offered some latitude together with various alternatives of acting or not acting, of acting so or otherwise. From the ensuing deliberation of the mind and consent of will to the appreciation of ways and means, one course emerges as the most advantageous of all. On the part of mind it appears as a decision or selective judgment, on that of will, as a choice or preferential approbation—the two so interpenetrate in a vital and dynamic unity as to be scarcely distinguishable.

This is not the place to pursue the analysis. It may be remarked, however, that in a bad choice one side will emphasize the cognitive element of *error, thus Socrates and many psychological penologists; whereas another side will emphasize the affective element of *fault, thus Aristotle and most moral theologians. Moreover, will-activity itself will be differently nuanced by the intellectualist and voluntarist schools of moral theology. Furthermore, the part of the will is more predominant in Kantian, deontological, and existentialist than in empirical, naturalistic, *utilitarian, and *eudemonian theories of morality.

Nor need we pursue the dissection and inquire into where precisely our choice starts. During our deliberation? At the moment of coming to a judgment as to what we should do? Or of adopting that judgment as the course we actually mean to pursue? Or even in making an effective beginning by commanding the deed through our mind and applying ourself to its actual performance through our will? What is certain is that a human act does not originate from a choice, nor does it end with one, for once we have started a train of events they soon escape our mastery. It is well to reflect, not least when we are imposing a useful scholastic grid on the questions raised, that the structure of a human act is not a geometrical composition in which each part has an exclusive location.

In moral theology the decision in choice is the judgment of *conscience and is governed by those parts of the cardinal virtue of prudence that are named *synēsis and *gnomē; good counsel, *euboulia,* is the part governing deliberation. Its own special function is to govern the executive and effective self-command *(imperium),* which issues from choice. BIBLIOGRAPHY: ThAqST (Lat-Eng) 1a2ae, 13 (v. 17, *Human Acts,* ed. T. Gilby, 1970).

[T. GILBY]

CHOIR (Lat. *chorus*), a group of singers with more than one voice to a part, today generally concerned with performances of sacred music or secular music of a serious order. The cognate term chorus is usually reserved for singers more completely concerned with secular music, as in opera. Originally, in the Christian Church the choir was generally monastic (men or women), was devoted to the singing of the Divine Office in plainsong, and was composed of the literate members of the community, hence the term choir monk as opposed to lay brother. The section of the monastic church reserved for the choir monks, usually between the high altar and the communion rail, was also called the choir. Thus the term passed into the nomenclature of church architecture, and thus also it acquired the liturgical meaning: ''in choir'' refers to members of a monastic community, then clergy generally, taking part in a service, not as vested ministers, but seated in the choir area and (in principle) joining in the singing or reciting of the service.

While monastic choirs were frequently small, the appearance of additional singers, usually boy sopranos from monastic schools, in late medieval times led to the formation of more professional groups chosen for their vocal ability without reference to their clerical status, witness the appearance of the great cathedral choirs in the 15th and 16th centuries. By that time music was being written for divided choirs placed strategically around the church, notably in St. Mark's, Venice, where the practice reached its apogee in the works of G. Gabrieli.

With the Reformation the choir followed divergent paths in various countries, with the Lutheran and Anglican choirs generally retaining a more closely involved place in the service, as evidenced in the works of W. Byrd and J. S. Bach. With the appearance of the Oratory in Rome during the Counter Reformation and the resultant development of the oratorio, Catholic choirs lost their liturgical character to some degree and followed secular trends. The eventual employment of women to sing the soprano and alto parts in Catholic choirs led to an almost complete separation of the liturgical and the musical choir in many European countries and the U.S., a development that did not take place in most Protestant churches.

While the 19th cent. was generally a period of decline in the quality of music written for church choirs, it also saw the appearance of great choral festivals devoted to the works of Bach, Handel, and Berlioz. The participating choirs sometimes had more than 1,000 singers, a phenomenon that has practically disappeared in the present day, because of the current emphasis on historically authentic performance. The 20th cent. has seen a marked revival in sacred choral music, with notable contributions from such composers as Britten, Bernstein, Roger Sessions, Igor Stravinsky, Lou Harrison, and Messiaen, as well as many others associated more exclusively with religious music. Although the choir underwent a period of neglect in some countries, particularly the U.S. immediately following the introduction of liturgical changes after Vatican Council II (this was in large part due to a lack of repertory for the new rites in the vernacular), the beginnings of a renaissance soon became apparent as new choral music of high quality began to appear, and the opportunity was taken of using the great church music of the Protestant tradition, esp. Anglican church music.

The term choir is used in music to refer to instrumental ensembles of a particular family of instruments, e.g., brass choir, and is also the name of one of the divisions of the organ.

[J. J. WALSH]

CHOIR DRESS, the clerical apparel worn at all liturgical functions aside from the Mass. The secular priest wears the cassock and surplice; the religious, the special robes designated for special occasions. A cope is worn at some liturgical functions, e.g., Benediction. At Mass the clerics, servers, and noncelebrating priests wear choir dress, while the president wears his robes of office.

[N. KOLLAR]

CHOIR MONK, a member of a religious institute or order of men with solemn vows, obliged to recite the Liturgy of the Hours (Divine Office) daily in common, i.e., in choir. In the beginnings of *monasticism, these monks were solemnly professed but did not necessarily proceed to holy orders. Later in the Western Church, all choir monks had to intend to continue toward ordination. Since Vatican Council II, all monasteries and communities of men that are not exclusively lay in their character, can admit both clergy and laity on the same basis and with equal rights and duties, excepting those that result from ordination. It was the intention of the council to strengthen the bond of brotherhood among members of the community by bringing them into the heart of its life and activities.

CHOIR NUN, a member of a religious institute or order of women obliged to recite the Liturgy of the Hours (Divine Office) daily in common. She generally took solemn vows and was thus distinguished from a lay sister. Since Vatican Council II, women's communities were advised to produce a single category of sister, so that there may be no distinctions between persons, except those demanded by the diversity of works.

CHOIR ORGAN, also chair organ, originally a small organ used in cathedral churches to accompany voices. Its tone contrasted with the might of the great organ and so provided variety and color to the music. Today choir organ refers to the third manual of normal organs, which has stops useful for accompaniment.

[S. MURPHY]

CHOIR PITCH, standard musical pitch of 440 cycles per second for treble A. This standard was accepted by the International Standards Association at a conference held in London in 1939. It replaced the old standard of 435 cycles per second. The absolute pitch of one specific note is established to obtain identical pitches on all instruments and is to be maintained by soloists, orchestras, and choirs.

[S. MURPHY]

CHOIR SCREEN (rood screen), usually an elaborately decorated stone screen used to isolate the altar. It served for the convenience of monks, who gathered in churches without heat and sometimes without windows, to sing long Offices. Eventually it was used as a space set apart for the clergy; separated by the screen from the rest of the church, the space became known also as the chancel.

[S. F. JOHNSON]

CHOIR STALLS, see STALLS.

CHOIRS OF ANGELS, the orders or groupings of the angelic spirits based upon Judaic and Christian literature and tradition. Thus Tob 12.15 reads: "For I am the angel Raphael, one of the seven. . . ." St. Paul mentions different kinds (Col 1.16). From the 4th cent. nine of these orders, or choirs, have been customarily recognized in both East and West. Pseudo-Dionysius provided a Neoplatonic elaboration of their hierarchical structure. BIBLIOGRAPHY: J. Michl, RAC 5:115–258; ThAq ST (Eng-Lat) v. 14, *Divine Government,* ed. T. C. O'Brien (1974).

CHOISEUL, ÉTIENNE FRANÇOIS DE (1719–85), French statesman. He began his political career in 1754 through the protection of Mme. de Pompadour, and his first success was the peaceful solution of the controversy with Benedict XIV over the papal bull *Unigenitus*. From 1758–70, he directed French politics with the virtual authority of a prime minister. He made significant political contributions, esp. military reforms. He supported the nobles, the Encyclopedists and was instrumental in the suppression of the Jesuits. Haughty, extravagant, and irreligious, he failed to survive the intrigues of the new court favorite, Mme. du Barry, who caused his exile to his estate at Chanteloupe in 1770. Though in political disgrace, he was still considered a leader by those in opposition to Louis XV. The excesses of his style of life caught up with him eventually, and he died practically a pauper. BIBLIOGRAPHY: G. Goyau, CE 3:694.

[I. M. KASHUBA]

CHOISEUL DU PLESSIS PRASLIN, GILBERT DE (1613–89), French bp. and writer. As bp. of Commingues and Tournai, he showed great concern for his people, reformed the clergy, established schools and seminaries, and helped the poor. A staunch defender of the Jansenists, he gave them an important foothold in Tournai and became himself a belligerent upholder of Gallicanism. His writings include *Mémoires touchant la religion* and *Lettre pastorale sur le culte de la Vierge*.

[I. M. KASHUBA]

CHOLMOGORY, ABBEY OF, a former Russian monastery situated on one of the islands in the Northern Dvina River 50 miles SE of Archangel (Arkhangelsk) in Russia. The monks maintained themselves by establishing trade in fish and salt. In the 14th cent. the area became a thriving mercantile outpost of Novgorod. Later a town, known today as Kholmogory, developed in the vicinity of the monastery. The monastery was dedicated to the Assumption of the Blessed Mother and was for long a center of religious piety. In 1691, the Transfiguration Cathedral was erected, and the pastoral efforts of the abbey were combined with those of the diocese. The present condition of this ancient abbey is unknown to the outside world.

CHOLULA, a holy city of pre-Hispanic Mexico, associated with the worship of Quetzalcoatl. The earliest pyramid (its base 44 acres) with four superimposed temple platforms relates to Teotihuacán style. Numberless churches and colonial structures rise from the ruins of the Indian temples. The "mosque" Royal Chapel and the "fortress" church of S. Gabriel (both 16th cent.) are noteworthy. BIBLIOGRAPHY: F. de la Maza, *La ciudad de Cholula y sus iglesias* (1959).

[M. J. DALY]

CHOMONIE, a 16th- and 17th-cent. development in Russian chant. Longer coloraturas were sung to meaningless syllables such as "chom" or "chomo", hence the name. It is also known as *anenaiki,* again referring to meaningless syllables. Historians consider this development an abuse that contributed to the decline of Russian chant.

[D. J. SMUCKER]

CHOPIN, KATE O'FLAHERTY (1851–1904), short-story writer and novelist. Born to a St. Louis family prominent in society, she was at 17 one of the belles of St. Louis. Marriage to Oscar Chopin brought her to Louisiana, which was to provide the background of her writing. Here she learned the ways of blacks and Creoles whom she was later to make the subjects of her stories. The death of her husband and the difficulties of managing a large plantation made her decide to return to St. Louis. A disciple of the French masters of the short story, De Maupassant and Daudet, she wrote polished and deeply touching tales of the bayou country. It was the age of the local-color story, and C. stood in the front rank of its practitioners. The two collections, *Bayou Folk* (1894) and *A Night in Acadie* (1897), established her as an American master of the short story. Her novel *The Awakening* (1899) is an amazing portrait of the inner life of a woman completely unique in her day. As a consequence it shocked the critics whose attacks on a work far beyond their understanding hurt her so deeply that she wrote no more. The novel was reissued recently and won the praise of all critics; it was unhappily published 30 years before its time.

[J. R. AHERNE]

CHORA, MONASTERY OF, in Constantinople a monastery of which the church, noted for its striking mosaics and frescoes, near the gate to Adrianople (modern Edirne), is all that remains. Dedicated to Christ the Savior, it was referred to as Chora, the Greek word for country, since it was constructed (probably in the 5th or 6th cent.) in the countryside, that is, outside the Constantinian walls. Later the word, which also means a place, acquired a mystical signification. Fourteenth-cent. inscriptions on the mosaics refer to Christ as the place (*chōra*) of living, that is, the true life of man is found in Christ; Mary is referred to as "the place (*chōra*) of him who has no place (*achōrētou*)," stressing the idea that Christ, who had no place to lay his head (Mt 8.20), did find a place in Mary; or it may allude to Christ as being every where because of divine infinity but consenting to be limited to a place in Mary's womb. After periods of decline the monastery and church were renovated by Theodore Metochites, grand logothete of the Byzantine Empire, who is depicted in an oft-reproduced mosaic located over the entrance to the church. After the Turkish conquest it was transformed into a mosque and known as Kahrie Djami (the mosque of Kahrie, a corruption for Chora), and is now a museum. The mosaics (mostly from the 14th cent.) in the main church and the frescoes in the side chapel plastered over by the Turks have now been cleaned and restored. BIBLIOGRAPHY: R. Janin, *La Géographie écclesiastique de l'empire byzantin* (v. 3 *Les Églises et les monastères*, 1953) 545–553.

[G. T. DENNIS]

CHORAL, used as an adjective (choŕ al) means pertaining to a chorus or choir; as a noun (chor aĺ), originally the word indicated the plainsong of the RC Church—later the hymn tunes of the German Protestant Church. In the latter case, in order to avoid confusion, the spelling *chorale* is preferred. *CHORALE.

[S. MURPHY]

CHORAL CANTATA, a cantata that makes use of a chorus as opposed to one using soloists only. Most Bach cantatas are of the choral type.

[S. MURPHY]

CHORAL MUSIC, vocal music written for more than one singer to each part. The music may be monophonic or polyphonic, accompanied or not. Choral music has been part of music literature since biblical times. Early choral music was monophonic. Polyphonic music appeared in written form around 1425. Distinguished composers of every century since have contributed to the vast supply of secular and sacred choral music. BIBLIOGRAPHY: D. J. Grout, *History of Western Music* (1960) 506–510.

[S. MURPHY]

CHORALBEARBEITUNG, a term used to include all compositions based on the German Protestant Chorale. These compositions of the 17th and 18th cent. include the chorale cantata, chorale fantasia, chorale partita, chorale fugue, chorale prelude, and chorale motet.

[S. MURPHY]

CHORALE, the hymn tunes of the German Protestant Church. These tunes were derived from the plainsong of the RC Church and the folk songs of the German people. In time these rhythmically free and relatively simple melodies became the foundation and backbone of much German Baroque music. BIBLIOGRAPHY: D. J. Grout, *History of Western Music* (1960) 229–234; 332–340.

[S. MURPHY]

CHORALE CANTATA, a German church cantata that utilized the chorale. Text and frequently melodies of chorales were incorporated into the cantatas. Since no specific form dictated the method of including the chorale, a variety of forms existed. Such works were cultivated by Bach and his forerunners.

[S. MURPHY]

CHORALE FANTASIA, an organ composition in which a chorale melody is treated as a fantasia. In a chorale fantasia the music is free, filled with ornamentation and designed to produce brilliant virtuoso effects. Such works were cultivated by the German precursors of Bach. BIBLIOGRAPHY: H. Ulrich and P. A. Pisk, *History of Music and Musical Style* (1963) 283.

[S. MURPHY]

CHORALE FUGUE, an organ chorale that utilizes the initial line of a chorale as the theme of a fugue. Though similar to the chorale motet, the chorale fugue is a shorter and simpler form.

[S. MURPHY]

CHORALE MOTET, a musical form in which a chorale melody is used as a *cantus firmus*. Since no specific standard for the development of the work existed, the composer displayed his creative genius. There are numerous examples of chorale motets in the vocal and organ music of the 16th and 17th centuries.

[S. MURPHY]

CHORALE PARTITA, a musical composition consisting of a set of variations based on a chorale tune. First introduced in the time of Sweelinck, chorale partitas continued to be written during and after the time of Bach. The freedom of form allowed the skill and individuality of the composer to be shown.

[S. MURPHY]

CHORALE PRELUDE, an organ composition based on a chorale and by custom played before it. Some chorale preludes merely suggested the chorale by elaborating a few notes of the theme. Others treat each line of the chorale surrounding the melody with decorative counterpoint. BIBLIOGRAPHY: M. Bauer and E. Peyser, *Music through the Ages* (1967) 283–285.

[S. MURPHY]

CHORALE VARIATION, a musical form in which each stanza of a chorale is the basis for elaboration by voices and instruments. The many techniques used result in free polyphonic variations. This form was important throughout the entire middle Baroque period.

[S. MURPHY]

CHORALIS CONSTANTINUS, a cycle of motets based on liturgical texts and melodies of the Proper of the Mass. The three-volume work, commissioned by the Cathedral of Constance in 1508, was begun by Heinrich Isaac and completed by his pupil Ludwig Senfl. Musically, the work is representative of the era. It is polyphonic, dramatic, and involved. BIBLIOGRAPHY: H. Ulrich and P. A. Pisk, *History of Music and Musical Style* (1963) 129.

[S. MURPHY]

CHORAZIN (COROZAIN), a city in Galilee whose ruins still remain. It was located 2 miles N of Capernaum. Jesus cursed Chorazin along with Bethsaida and Capernaum for lack of belief (Mt 11.21 and Lk 10.13). It lay in a desert region. The remains of a 3d- or 4th-cent. black basalt synagogue have been found there. BIBLIOGRAPHY: C. Kopp, *Holy Places of the Gospels* (1963) 187–189.

[S. MUSHOLT]

CHORBISHOP, a title given in the East to a bp. caring for people in villages and rural areas (Gr., *chōra*, country). They seem to have been numerous in Asia Minor and Syria esp. during the 2d and 3d centuries. After the persecutions they came more and more under the authority of the bp. of the city, and their power was more limited. By the 12th cent., if not earlier, the institution died out. Today the name is given to auxiliary bps. among the Maronites, and among the Melkites it is purely honorary. BIBLIOGRAPHY: P. Joannou, NCE 3:625.

[G. T. DENNIS]

CHOREPISCOPUS (Gr., *Chorepiskopos*), a title used in the Western Church in the 10th century. At first a person so designated received episcopal ordination, and his function was to serve as an archdeacon, a title that came to displace that of *chorepiscopus*. Among Catholics of the Syrian, Chaldean, and Maronite Rites, the title is honorific, and those who possess it generally perform the functions of vicars general. In the Greek Orthodox Church a *chorepiskopos* was an ordained bishop whose duty it was to serve as auxiliary bishop in charge of a district or city.

[E. C. HUBBERT]

CHORISTER, singer in a choir; at present, choristers are members of the choir of a church or cathedral. Among the Anglicans they are boy singers attached to cathedrals. The position of chorister has assumed importance in Catholic churches since the promulgation of liturgical reforms in the 20th cent.—Pius X's revival of Gregorian chant and the decrees of Vatican II. Many composers gained their initial knowledge of music as choir singers; among them, Palestrina, Frescobaldi, di Lasso, Johann Sebastian Bach, Haydn, and Purcell. BIBLIOGRAPHY: W. L. Woodfill, *Musicians in English Society from Elizabeth to Charles I* (1969) 144–146.

[J. S. PALLOZZA]

CHORON, ALEXANDRE (1771–1834), French theorist, pedagogue, and composer. He was chiefly self-taught in music, but was a scholar in mathematics and languages. Having become a partner in a music publishing firm in 1805, C. devoted his life to editing and publishing theoretical works as well as music by great Italian and German masters. Under Louis XVIII he was entrusted with the reorganization of the training schools for cathedral choirs. He was appointed director of the Paris Opera in 1816, but the post was taken away from him in 1817 because he favored new music written by unknown composers. In 1817 he established his own school for the study of music, for which he was granted a government subsidy. C. composed a number of hymns and psalms for the Church as well as a Mass and "Stabat Mater" for three voices. He wrote "La Sentinelle," a song that later became popular on the French stage. His fame, however, lies in his treatises, translations, and editions of other composers' works. His treatises *Méthode de plain-chant* (1818), and *Manuel complet de musique vocale et instrumentale, ou Encyclopédie musicale*, (6v., 1836–38) as well as his 1803 and 1804 works, in which he introduced his own system of harmony, contributed greatly to the improvement of musical pedagogy in France.

[J. S. PALLOZZA]

CHOSEN PEOPLE, a concept of divine election rooted in the origins of Israel. It persists through both the OT and NT with modifications that reflect the limited attempts of man to understand the divine purpose. Thus God's choice could be seen as supporting the ancient holy wars (Jg 1.2), the political structure of the monarchy (2 Sam 23.5), defensive isolation from other peoples (Ezra 9–10), and also national pride (Jer 7.4). Nonetheless, the history of revelation witnesses to divine purposes that transcend political interest and even human understanding. The people were chosen, for no merit of their own (Dt 7.7–8; cf. 1 Cor 1.27), for the salvation of all men (Gen 12.3; Ezek 20.9; Is 49.6; Eph 1.10). Since the benefits of God's choice could only be shared by those who accept its moral demands (Am 3.2; 1 Kg 8.33–34; 1 Pet 2.9–12; 2 Pet 1.10), the chosen people could not be simply identified with the visible community (Is 10.22; Mt 3.9; Jn 8.39). Despite man's failings, God's choice is everlasting (Jer 31.35–37); it precedes all human action (Is 49.1; Eph 1.4); the chosen cannot fall away (Mk 13.22). Yet man can only discern God's choice after seeing his work in the lives of man (1 Th 1.4–5) or even in part through experiencing the failure of some to accept God (Mt 22.14; Lk 12.32; 1 Jn 2.19). Faith can demand a trust that God's love continues even when the bond with him appears broken (1 Kg 8.49–50; 2 Kg 22.15–23.3; Joel 2.12–17; Rom 11).

Jesus showed his acceptance of the tensions within the concept "chosen people" by extending his mission only to the Jews (Mt 10.6; 15.24), for whom the 12 disciples were to be symbols of the renewed 12 tribes of Israel. The Church saw itself as heir to God's election (Acts 2.17–18; 1 Pet 2.9–10). Even though it became separate from Judaism (Gal 4.21–31; Mt 10.17; Jn 16.2) and the OT period was fulfilled (Heb 7.18–19), God's choice of the Jewish people remains faithful and summons the Church to further understanding and praise of his mysterious plan (Rom 11). BIBLIOGRAPHY: G. E. Mendenhall, InterDB 2:76–82; H. Küng, *Church,* (tr. R. and R. Ockenden, 1967) 107–150.

[P. J. KEARNEY]

CHOTKI, a Russian name given to prayer beads. Commonly made of wool, they consist of 100 knots with a large knot at each tenth. Their use is customarily associated with the Jesus Prayer: "Lord Jesus Christ, Son of God, have mercy upon me a sinner." In the past they were used mostly by monks, but some lay émigrés have adopted the practice of using them. The Old Believers use a *chokti* in the form of a triangle.

[T. BIRD]

CHRÉTIEN DE TROYES (c.1130–c.1185), the first known French lyricist, better known for his romances (*Yvain, Lancelot, Cligés, Eric and Enid,* and *Perceval*). His earliest writings were adaptations of Ovid made under Celtic influences and a lost *Tristan.* He later turned from *courtly love themes, written for Marie de Champagne, to religious allegory (*Perceval*). His *William of England* is a romance in the Byzantine manner. BIBLIOGRAPHY: U. T. Holmes, Jr. and M. A. Klenke, *Chrétien, Troyes, and the Grail* (1959) for research into Chrétien's background and his allegory on the *synagoga-ecclesia* motif; K. D. Uitti, *Story, Myth, and Celebration in Old French Narrative Poetry* (1973).

[J. P. WILLIMAN]

CHRISM, HOLY, a mixture of olive oil and balsam used in liturgical anointings, *viz,* the blessing of baptismal fonts, at baptism, confirmation, and the consecration of bps., and in consecrating churches, altars, chalices, patens, and church bells. Anointing with chrism signifies dedication to God's service and a fullness of grace. Since Pius XII's Ordinal for Holy Week, chrism is blessed by a bp. at a Mass of the Chrism, celebrated in cathedral churches on Holy Thursday morning. *ANOINTING: *OIL OF CATECHUMENS: *OIL OF THE SICK.

[T. M. MCFADDEN]

CHRISM MASS (*missa chrismalis*), the Mass on Holy Thursday at which the *holy oils are blessed. According to *Hippolytus, the blessing of the oils in the early Church took place just before the baptism of catechumens, therefore as part of the Easter Vigil, but by the 6th cent. at the latest it was transferred, probably to reduce the accumulation of liturgical events on that occasion. Pius XII's Ordinal for Holy Week (1955) required that a Mass be celebrated in cathedrals on the morning of Holy Thursday at which the oils are blessed for use in the diocese. This Mass is distinct from the solemn evening liturgy of that day. The rites of the blessing of the oils and of consecrating the chrism were revised (1970) by the Sacred Congregation for Divine Worship. BIBLIOGRAPHY: *Rites of the Catholic Church* (Eng. tr. International Commission on English in the Liturgy, 1976).

[P. K. MEAGHER]

CHRISMATION (Gr., *chrisma,* anointing), in the Eastern Church the name for the sacrament which in the West is called confirmation. Unlike Western confirmation, however, chrismation is always administered immediately after baptism in the same liturgical celebration even to infants. It is administered by priests and not necessarily by bishops. It is performed by anointing with a special episcopally consecrated oil called chrism, whence its name. The purpose of the visible intervention of God into time and history in his own humanity. In his person, Christ combined the divine reality of God's chrism, whence its name. The purpose of chrismation and the reason for its essential connnection with baptism in the East is to give "the seal of the gift of the Holy Spirit" to the newly baptized, thus fulfilling the baptismal passover from death to life in Christ by the pentecostal outpouring of the gift of the Spirit in chrismation.

[T. HOPKO]

CHRISMON, Greek monogram or symbol for the name of Christ (first dated use 269) and having many forms: ✳ (Chi and Iota), ☧ (Chi and Rho), ✝ (Tau surmounted by Rho). A Latinized version adding a tail to the Rho ☧ appeared in Spain, Gaul, Italy, Africa, and Greece. First and abbreviation, the chrismon was later used by Constantine I as a symbol on the *labarum, at the Battle of the Milvian Bridge (312), and subsequently on coins. Decorative forms appear in mosaics and on sarcophagi, lamps, rings, and seals. *John Chrysostom mentions its use in epistles (PG 62:364). Merovingian scribes developed an ornate form in the early Middle Ages. The imperial chancery used it until *c.*1200, and the papal officials on documents until the time of Leo IX (d. 1054). BIBLIOGRAPHY: H. Leclercq, DACL 3.1481–1534; K. Honselmann, LTK 2:1095; C. M. Aherne, NCE 3:627.

CHRIST, THE, *christos,* the verbal adjective used by the Septuagint to translate the Hebrew *mashiah,* "anointed." The term, under various forms, was used in the OT of kings (1 Sam 24.6, 10; Ps 18.50), priests (Ex 28.41), patriarchs (Ps 105.15), and even the nation (Hab 3.13). Eventually the designation was reserved especially for the expected descendant of David, the Messiah or Christ of Jewish hope. As the primary messianic title, its roots run deep in Judaism and the Old Testament. Of particular importance is the oracle of Nathan promising David an eternal dynasty (2 Sam 7.5–16; 1 Chr 17.4–14; Ps 89.20-38). The sufferings of Jewish national life from the exile on through the Seleucid domination made of this promise the bedrock of national hope. Yet Messianism was not all of one piece, and the expected Christ was conceived of in different ways.

There were, however, certain basic thrusts to the idea. First of all, the hope was very much for an earthly Messiah, a political leader and restorer of the nation. He was to be the forerunner of God and introduce an interim period prior to the final reign of God. (cf. 1 Cor 15.24). Later Psalm 72, attributed to Solomon, pictured the Messiah himself as the one who inaugurates the end-time. Finally, as a fulfillment of the Davidic promise, the Messiah would be of the royal line, a Son of David, though there were also isolated hopes, as at Qumran, for a priestly Messiah of Levi or Aaron as well. These disparate ideas of the Christ, current at the time of Jesus, perhaps best explain his hesitancy to claim the title for himself. The evidence of the Synoptic Gospels shows that, except for two post-Resurrection sayings (Lk 24.26, 46), "the Christ" is instanced only as a title applied to Jesus and not one claimed by him. In Mark, where it is found seven times, the pattern is typical. In the first occurrence (1.1) it is used as a personal name (cf. Mt 1.1). Sayings of Jesus twice speak of "the Christ" in neutral fashion (Mk 12.35; 13.21). A fourth and similar usage (9.41) is possibly an example of textual corruption (cf. Mt 10.42). The name is confessed of Jesus by Peter (8.29); it is the object of Caiaphas' question (14.61); and it is made a matter for mockery by the chief priests and scribes (15.32). John follows the same basic scheme (cf. 10.24). The title is found only once in a saying of Jesus (17.3) but as a personal name, the definite touch of the Evangelist.

This apparent silence of Jesus does not reflect a lack of belief in his own Messiahship but rather fear of misinterpretation. He preferred the less narrow and nationalistic descriptions "Son" and "Son of Man." The primitive Church, however, did not hesitate to confess Jesus as "the Christ" (Acts 2.36; 3.20; 4.26; 8.5; 9.22; 17.3; 18.5,28; 26.23). But expansion of the Gospel to peoples unaware of Jewish traditions behind the title inevitably meant that it would lose its messianic force and gradually take on the properties of a personal name: Jesus Christ, Christ Jesus, or simply Christ. St. Paul uses it predominantly in this sense (e.g., 1 Cor 1.13, 17; Rom 1.1, 6, 8; but cf. Rom 9.5) as does the rest of the New Testament. Liturgical usage is also reflected in such combinations of names as Christ Jesus, the Lord Jesus Christ, Our Savior, Christ Jesus (2 Tim 1.10; Titus 1.4). Thus the word evolved in the early Church from simply a messianic title to a personal and even cultic name for Jesus. BIBLIOGRAPHY: O. Cullmann, *Christology of the New Testament* (tr. S. Guthrie and C. Hall, 1963); L. Sabourin, *Names and Titles of Jesus* (tr. M. Carroll, 1967); V. Taylor, *Names of Jesus* (1962).

[J. J. CUNNINGHAM]

CHRIST, FREEDOM OF, see FREEDOM OF CHRIST.

CHRIST, KINGSHIP OF, see KINGSHIP OF CHRIST.

CHRIST, PRIMACY OF, see PRIMACY OF CHRIST.

CHRIST, THE GREAT SACRAMENT, a theological view of Christ as the personal embodiment of God's desire to save all men. The mystery *(mysterion)* of God is his plan of salvation in which he communicates himself to men in a sacramental way, that is, in a way consonant with the nature of men by means of a visible intervention. Christ is the realization of God's mystery, the visible intervention of God into time and history in his own humanity. In his person, Christ combined the divine reality of God's love and grace and the fullness of humanity. In this way he is a visible manifestation of the divine reality or truly the first and great sacrament of God's saving mercy. The Church as sacrament and the seven sacraments are extensions of the primordial sacrament that is Christ. Man, by responding to the Church and the sacraments, responds to Christ and realizes his saving encounter with God. Thus the mystery of God is realized in and by means of Christ.

This view of Christ as the great sacrament of God underlies and gives depth to the whole of sacramental theology and provides a valuable synthesis for an understanding of the Christian faith. It concentrates attention on Christ's human nature, his role as mediator between God and man, the personal nature of the encounter with God, and the homogeneity of the Christian mystery of salvation. It is a notion sanctioned both by Scripture and the Fathers. The attention given to the seven sacraments individually in the Middle Ages and after resulted in a certain disregard for this broader sacramental approach, but in modern times, under the leadership esp. of E. Schillebeeckx, the concept has been thoroughly reinstated in Christian theology, and the deep implications it contains searched out. BIBLIOGRAPHY: C. Regan, NCE 7:955–956; E. Schillebeeckx, *Christ, the Sacrament of the Encounter with God* (tr. P. Barrett, 1963).

[B. ROSENDALL]

CHRIST HEALING THE SICK (Hundred Guilders Print), famous etching (1646) by *Rembrandt van Rijn, executed at the height of his powers, in the drypoint technique he himself developed. The subtitle derives from his own modest pricing of the work.

CHRIST IN MAJESTY *(Majestas Domini),* representation of Christ enthroned within an aureole or *mandorla*-shaped glory, accompanied by the four evangelical symbols from the Apocalypse (man, lion, ox, eagle). It became an important tympanum theme during the Romanesque and Gothic periods.

[M. J. DALY]

CHRIST THE KING, FEAST OF, a feast celebrated on the last Sunday of the liturgical year, i.e. preceding the First

Sunday of Advent, to encourage the recognition of Christ's universal rule over mankind and the establishment of universal peace through such recognition. Pius XI (1925) placed the feast in the universal calendar. It reduplicates to some extent the feast of the Ascension, which celebrates Christ's role as ruler and judge at the Father's right hand.

[N. KOLLAR]

CHRISTADELPHIANS, a sect founded in 1848 by J. Thomas (1805–71), an English physician who settled in the U.S. in 1832. Thomas joined the *Disciples of Christ but severed his connection with that body in 1834 for doctrinal reasons and developed a theology of his own. He refused to describe himself and his followers as Christian because that term had become corrupted by the connotation of apostasy; in its place he chose the name "Christadelphians," i.e., brethren of Christ. The brethren reject the doctrine of the Trinity and the existence of hell; call for a revival of primitive Christianity; look to the second coming of Jesus Christ to reign for 1,000 years; claim that only baptism by immersion is effective; and teach *conditional immortality, that only those who hold the divine truth as recognized by the Christadelphians will be saved. Like *Jehovah's Witnesses they are opposed to war and military service and indeed seek to dissociate themselves from the activities of the civil community in general; they forbid marriage with nonmembers. Church *polity is congregational; the separate societies (called ecclesias) are only loosely bound together. There are no salaried clergy, but the liturgical and administrative functions usually exercised by ministers are committed to "serving brethren" elected to that office by congregations for a term of 3 years. In 1974 overall membership was estimated to be about 20,000 in Britain and probably a similar number in the U.S. BIBLIOGRAPHY: R. Roberts, *Dr. Thomas, his Life and Work* (1884); B. R. Wilson, *Sects and Society* (1961).

[P. K. MEAGHER]

CHRISTEN, an old English word meaning to make Christian and hence esp. to baptize. Since children were given their names at baptism, the word also came to signify their naming. The names given on this occasion were called christening or Christian names. A christening as a liturgical service includes the act of baptizing, together with the conferring of the name and all the accompanying ceremonies.

[N. KOLLAR]

CHRISTENDOM ("Christian" plus the "dom" suffix that signifies dignity or domain), in general the condition or state of being Christian; Christianity; Christians collectively. In its early use it was contrasted with "heathenness" and it came to have a geopolitical meaning, in which sense it means the Christian domain, or the countries professing Christianity. By the late Middle Ages Christendom included the territory of the old Roman Empire with the addition of Ireland, Scandinavia, the new German lands, the Slav countries, and, in popular feeling, the African regions of Prester John. It was enlarged by later colonialism but diminished in the East by the inroads of Islam. The term has contemporary relevance, it would seem, only in its early and general sense.

[T. GILBY]

CHRISTENING, a term in use for centuries to signify the baptism and naming of a child. By extension it was sometimes applied to the consecration and naming of church bells.

CHRISTIAN OF PRUSSIA (d. 1245), Cistercian missionary, first bp. of Prussia. He preached successfully among the Prussians and was consecrated bp. in 1215. He founded the Knights of Dobrin and also called upon the Teutonic Knights for help. While C. spent 5 years as a captive of the Prussians, the Teutonic Knights gained control of Prussia and replaced the Cistercian missionaries with Dominicans. C., who never regained his bishopric, died in a Polish Cistercian abbey. BIBLIOGRAPHY: M. Tumler, *Der Deutsche Orden* (1955) 224–232; F. Winter, *Die Zisterzienser des nordöstlichen Deutschlands* (1868) 1:266–294; C. Spahr, NCE 3:629.

[L. J. LEKAI]

CHRISTIAN OF STABLO (d. after 880), Benedictine exegete. Scholar of the Carolingian Renaissance, he had a fine knowledge of Greek and is best known for his commentary on St. Matthew which demonstrates 9th-cent. methods of compiling scriptural expositions and monastic teaching. In his biblical interpretations he presented the historical or literal rather than the allegorical meaning. The commentary shows C.'s excellence as a teacher as well as his profound biblical knowledge. BIBLIOGRAPHY: F. Dressler, LTK 2:1124.

[A. P. HANLON]

CHRISTIAN, JOHANN JOSEPH (1706–77), collaborator with the Swabian architect Johann Michael Fischer in extensive sculptures at the churches of Zweifalten (1744–56), Ottobeuren (1757–66), and many others. Though rococo in the profuse decoration of altars, choir stalls, and statues, C.'s ecstatic figures attain a monumentality and dignity through a certain classical restraint. BIBLIOGRAPHY: R. Huber, *Joseph Christian, der Bildhauer des Schwäbischen Rokoko* (1960).

CHRISTIAN, a term that as a noun means one who believes in Christ and as an adjective means that which pertains to the historical movement stemming from Christ. According to Acts 11.26 the term was first used at Antioch by outsiders to describe the followers of Christ. It is not the usual designation of the NT, which more commonly uses such terms as brethren (Acts 1.16), believers (Acts 2.44), saints (Acts 9.32), and disciples (Acts 11.26). It appears to have been more widely used by pagans, and according to Tacitus it was in common use by the time of the Neronian persecution (*Annals*, 15.44). In times of persecution the acknowledgment or denial of the name was often crucial. Pagans sometimes confused Christus with *chrēstos,* meaning good or kind, and used the term *chrestiani.* The apologists answered that although this was a misunderstanding, it was a true indication of the character of Christians (Tertullian, *Apol.* 3 and 5). The term Christian also came early to describe the type of character appropriate to a disciple of Christ. Approaching his martyrdom, Ignatius wrote, "Let me not merely be called Christian but be found one" *(Ad Romanos* 3.2). Thus Christian came to be used as an adjective to describe not only those persons and institutions that claimed a relationship to Christ but more properly those who showed the character considered proper to this relationship, as in references to Christian character, Christian acts, and the like.

In the modern period, with the many divisions of Christianity and the varying attitudes toward Christian doctrine, there has been discussion as to which persons, groups, and movements are properly designated Christian. Some have held that good character is more important than right belief and that a Christian is one who has such traits as humility and kindness, whether or not he accepts Christian doctrine. Unitarians have been divided between those who wish to consider Unitarianism a Christian body, though departing from many points of orthodox doctrine, and those who wish to consider it a body transcending the differences of the various world religions. In the doctrinal conflicts among other Churches the question has been discussed whether their opponents could properly be reckoned Christian, and what were the basic points that were essential to merit that designation. The followers of Alexander *Campbell wished to eliminate denominational differences and be called simply "Christians." In the modern movement toward Christian unity, the determination of what constitutes a Christian Church has been a question of considerable importance. The constitution of the *World Council of Churches has determined a definition in these words: "churches which confess the Lord Jesus Christ as God and Savior according to the Scriptures and therefore seek to fulfill together their common calling to the glory of the one God, Father, Son, and Holy Spirit."

[T. EARLY]

CHRISTIAN AND MISSIONARY ALLIANCE, a missionary association that has taken on the characteristics of a Protestant Church in the Holiness tradition. Dr. A. B. Simpson (1843–1919), a Canadian-born Presbyterian clergyman, held several pastorates before embarking on an independent evangelistic career in New York City in 1881. At a convention in 1887 his followers organized twin societies: the Christian Alliance, which concentrated on home missions, and the Evangelical Missionary Alliance, which sent missionaries overseas. In 1897 the two bodies were combined as the Christian and Missionary Alliance. In 1974 membership in the 1,200 congregations in the U.S. and Canada totaled 170,000. There are almost twice as many members in foreign

mission fields. The Alliance supports close to 900 active foreign missionaries and 1355 pastors, evangelists, and other licensed ministers in North America. This small denomination had a 1977 budget of $10.5 million for missions. Major mission fields served include India, Guinea, the Ivory Coast, Mali–Upper Volta, Gabon, Thailand, Colombia, Ecuador, Peru, Chile, Argentina, Guatemala, Dominican Republic, much of the West Indies, Hong Kong, Israel, Japan, the Philippines, Indonesia, New Guinea, and several Arab countries. In the U.S., missionaries work among Mexicans, Indians, Negroes, Jews, and mountain people. The Alliance seeks to establish native Churches as soon as possible and to move on to new areas. Missionaries and native workers preach in 180 languages and dialects. The Christian and Missionary Alliance is strongly fundamentalist and evangelical. It teaches the *foursquare gospel (that Jesus Christ is Savior, Sanctifier, Healer, and Coming Lord), the second coming, *baptism with the Holy Spirit, and *divine healing. Local churches are known as "Alliance" churches but are sometimes called Alliance Gospel Tabernacles. Congregations are relatively autonomous but they must adhere to the General Constitution of the Church. There is no creedal statement. The Alliance operates three Bible colleges in the U.S. (Nyack, N.Y.; St. Paul, Minn.; San Francisco, Calif.) and one in Canada (Regina, Sask.) to prepare missionaries. BIBLIOGRAPHY: L. L. King, EncModChrMiss 133–137; YBACC 1976; A. B. Simpson, *Fourfold Gospel* (1925); *idem, Wholly Sanctified* (1925).

[W. J. WHALEN]

CHRISTIAN ATHEISM, a concept associated with the *death-of-God thinking of some American Protestants and, more specifically, with the writing of Thomas J. Altizer. The concept has emerged from a disturbing encounter of this thinking and events and forces of contemporary culture. The dissolution of the Christian era is proclaimed, together with a dawning awareness that the totality of human experience points to the death of God. Those who share this conviction are advised to find some meaning in affirming and discerning a profane form of Christ's presence to the world. The Christian atheist, holding fast to Christ even without God, feels cut off from all previous forms of faith. Elements allegedly drawn from Christian tradition include eschatology as orientation of life to an absolute future and devotion to Christ as the Incarnate Word. In the absence of a viable theism, it is difficult to maintain a Christology without radically revising the concepts and propositions of orthodoxy. Altizer makes considerable use of two kinds of material, the history of religions and the insights of visionaries of recent times, and his concern presupposes that the arguments and conclusions of Christian theism are presently bankrupt. The role of negation in speaking of God provided a clue for the extreme pronouncement of God's death. In Christ God empties himself, alienating himself from transcendence and absoluteness. God is dead as the alien other in heavenly isolation, as an enemy to the fullness of man. Man goes forward, with

Christ, without God. The theme of Christian atheism has proved to be ephemeral. BIBLIOGRAPHY: T. J. Altizer, *Gospel of Christian Atheism* (1966); T. W. Ogletree, *Death of God Controversy* (1966); *Meaning of the Death of God* (ed. B. Murchland, 1966).

[J. P. REID]

CHRISTIAN BROTHERS, a congregation of laymen founded about 1680 at Rheims, France, by St. John Baptist de La Salle for the purpose of teaching Christian doctrine to the poor and working classes. The brothers take the three vows to which they added a vow to persevere and another to teach gratuitously. Later a rule was written by De La Salle. In 1685, he established a teacher training college, the first of its kind in the world. Soon other houses were founded throughout Europe, North and South America, Africa, and Australia. The brothers came to the U.S. in 1819, and in 1976 there were about 1,800 members of the U.S. Conference, while world membership totaled 12,641 brothers. The general motherhouse is in Rome, Italy. BIBLIOGRAPHY: W. J. Battersby, *History of the Institute of the Brothers of the Christian Schools in the Eighteenth Century, 1719–1798* (1960); . . . *in the Nineteenth Century, 1800–1900* (1961–1963); A. Gabriel, *Christian Brothers in the U.S., 1848–1948* (1948).

[R. A. TODD]

CHRISTIAN CATHOLIC CHURCH, a denomination organized in Chicago (1896), then transplanted to Zion City, Ill., in 1901 by John Alexander Dowie, evangelist and faith healer. Zion City became the center of the Church; the community successfully operated business enterprises and was organized theocratically under Dowie, until his deposition and replacement by Wilbur G. Voliva in 1906. From Dowie the Church has retained *faith healing, *universalism (the belief that punishment for sin is temporary), baptism by *trine immersion, tithing, and a strong opposition to tobacco, liquor, and medical doctors. Since Voliva *millenarianism and biblical fundamentalism, as well as general conformity to other conservative Protestant bodies, have characterized the Church. Zion City has ceased to be exclusively a church community. The Church has congregations in only four other cities but conducts extensive foreign missions.

[R. K. MacMASTER]

CHRISTIAN CHARITY, SISTERS OF, a congregation of religious founded (1849) at Paderborn, Germany, by Pauline von Mallinckrodt. The members follow the Rule of St. Augustine and, after the example of their foundress, observe Christian charity as a particular rule and spirit of the community. In less than 20 years after its founding, the institute established many houses throughout Europe. In 1873 the sisters came to the U.S. where their work was primarily catechetical. In the following year others went to South America where they engaged in teaching and nursing.

Today the sisters concern themselves with every type of charitable work, but teaching is their chief apostolate. The general motherhouse is in Rome. In 1975 world membership totaled 1812 religious. In 1976 the two provinces in the U.S. had 820 professed sisters. BIBLIOGRAPHY: J. Wenner, LTK 6:1333; C. Testore, EncCatt 7:1922–23.

[R. A. TODD]

CHRISTIAN CHURCH OF NORTH AMERICA, GENERAL COUNCIL, Pentecostal body incorporated under its present name at Pittsburgh, Pa., in 1948. The history of this Church goes back to the Pentecostal movement among Italian immigrants in Chicago, beginning in 1907. Autonomous Pentecostal assemblies were established in Calif. and throughout the East and Midwest. Their decentralized association was known as the Unorganized Italian Church of North America. In 1939 "Unorganized" was dropped from the title; in 1942, because the English language was increasingly used in services, the word "Italian" was replaced by "Christian." The autonomy of local churches is stressed. Membership in 1968 was about 8,000; mission activity is conducted in Belgium, Italy, the Philippines, Puerto Rico, Mexico, and Canada. BIBLIOGRAPHY: J. T. Nichol, *Pentecostalism* (1966) 132–133.

[T. C. O'BRIEN]

CHRISTIAN CHURCHES, a title adopted in the name of Christian unity and anticreedalism. Besides the Christian Churches (Disciples of Christ), the name has been used by another group of Churches, the first of which was originally the Republican Methodist Church, established (1793) in Va. under the leadership of James *O'Kelly in protest against *episcopacy in the Methodist Church. The name was changed to Christian Church a year later, when the Church adopted the Bible as the only creed, Christian living as the only basis for membership, and congregationalism as the form of polity. In 1801 the Baptist minister Abner Jones established in Vt. a Christian Church along the same lines. During the *Great Awakening in Ky., Barton W. *Stone led a group of followers out of the Presbyterian Synod, and soon they also took (1804) the name Christian Church, for the same basic reasons. Stone himself united with the Disciples of Christ, but most of his Christian Churches remained apart. The three lines in this "Christian movement" came to be united on principles representing their original inspiration. Because of their rejection of creeds, they avoided even Trinitarian formulas and doctrines. Most of the Christian Churches joined in the 1931 merger that formed the General Council of Congregational and Christian Churches and later (1957) became part of the *United Church of Christ. Whether in or outside of the mergers, the local congregation remains absolutely autonomous and continues the heritage and name of the Christian Church.

[F. E. MASER]

CHRISTIAN CHURCHES, INTERNATIONAL COUNCIL OF, see INTERNATIONAL COUNCIL OF CHRISTIAN CHURCHES.

CHRISTIAN CHURCHES (DISCIPLES OF CHRIST), INTERNATIONAL CONVENTION OF, a Protestant body originating in the ministry of Barton W. *Stone and of Thomas and Alexander *Campbell on the American frontier. In 1804 Stone, a Presbyterian minister, and a group of colleagues in Ky. dissolved the Springfield *presbytery, calling their congregations ''Christian Churches,'' and their members, ''Christians.'' They sought freedom and union for all believers on the basis of the Bible alone. In 1809 Thomas Campbell, a Presbyterian of the Seceder tradition from Ireland, formed the Christian Association of Washington (Pa.). Decrying *sectarianism, he called for biblical ''unity, peace and purity'' in the Church. His son, Alexander, soon assumed the greater prominence. From 1813 to 1830 they worked within Baptist *associations, promoting a ''new Reformation'' on the basis of the NT alone and calling themselves Disciples of Christ; they designated their congregations biblically as Churches of Christ. They opposed as unscriptural human creeds and *confessions of faith, authoritarian ecclesiastical government, and sectarian names. Led by Walter *Scott to model their evangelism on Acts, they won thousands of converts. Under A. Campbell's leadership as editor *(The Millennial Harbinger),* debater (against the agnostic Robert D. Owen, the RC Abp. John B. Purcell, and others), and preacher, they presented a rational, biblical, practical interpretation of Christianity, free of theological subtlety and of revivalist emotion. In 1832 a number of Disciples and Christians in Ky. joined hands to signify their union as one people. By the 1840s Campbell was urging cooperation and church organization. In 1849 the first general convention formed the American Christian Missionary Society. In due course other national agencies also came into being (for foreign missions, benevolence, church extension, ministerial relief, temperance). In 1917 the International Convention of Disciples of Christ was formed to review the work of all reporting agencies, to advise them and the congregations on policy, and to provide a means of fellowship and inspiration. In 1934 the agencies formed Unified Promotion, voluntarily accepting a procedure for the allocation of contributed funds. In 1956 the convention changed its name to International Convention of Christian Churches (Disciples of Christ) and in 1967 constituted a delegate assembly elected by the congregations.

Meanwhile the practical problems of coordinating the work of scores of agencies (state and national) led to demands for ''restructure.'' These demands coincided with a growing uneasiness over the concept of agencies as ''societies of individuals'' and the inherited doctrine that located the Church only in local congregations. *A Provisional Design for the Christian Church (Disciples of Christ),* adopted in 1968, provides for the Christian Church in the U.S. and Canada with a general assembly composed of voting representatives from congregations and from regions, an interim general board, and an administrative committee; for the Christian Church in regions; and for the Christian Church in autonomous congregations. Power of decision on policy resides in the General Assembly; its chief officer is the General Minister and President. The course just sketched, as well as other sociological and theological factors, resulted in divisions within the movement. Before 1900 resistance grew against ''innovations'' that some accounted unscriptural —missionary societies, the use of musical instruments in worship, the one-man pastoral system that began to replace the collegial pastorate of the nonsalaried elders. In 1904 the dissidents issued a separate preacher list and the Federal Religious Census of 1906 named *Churches of Christ as a body distinct from Disciples of Christ. After 1900 some Disciples took offense at other tendencies: *open communion (reception of persons from other Churches without requiring immersion), the inroads of *liberal theology, and participation in councils of Churches and other ecumenical enterprises (interpreted by the opponents as an acceptance of *denominationalism). ''Independent'' or ''direct support'' missions developed, along with Bible colleges and seminaries ''loyal to the plea,'' separate conventions, and rival publishing enterprises. In 1955 a *Directory of the Ministry of the Undenominational Fellowship of Christian Churches and Churches of Christ* appeared as a listing distinct both from that of the Churches of Christ mentioned above and from the *Year Book of Christian Churches (Disciples of Christ).* Some congregations and ministers, however, continue to let their names appear both in the *Directory* and the *Year Book.* In 1967 the former recorded 1,086,000 members for the ''undenominational fellowship''; the latter indicated 1,875,400 Disciples in the U.S. and Canada.

The early Disciples undertook to set forth a simple biblical theology. Distinctive elements centered chiefly in the doctrine of conversion and in ecclesiology. As to conversion, the emphasis fell on a rational response in faith to the message of the gospel, with the baptism of the obedient believer by immersion signifying his acceptance of the lordship of Christ. In ecclesiology, Disciples sought to return to the faith and order of the apostolic Church as they found it in the NT, repudiating creeds as tests of faith and fellowship and seeking the union of Christians on the basis of the revealed essentials of the Church. Campbell outlined his views in the *Christian System* (2d ed., 1839), the arguments of which were restated and expanded by lesser authors for three generations. At the beginning of the 20th cent., new approaches in biblical criticism undercut the absolutism that had characterized the mind of Disciples, but a liberal reformulation of their theology emerged, later somewhat tempered under the influence of *neo-orthodoxy. A major reassessment was undertaken by the Panel of Scholars appointed in 1956; their work appeared in three volumes, W. B. Blakemore, ed., *The Renewal of Church: The Panel Reports* (1963).

The worship of Disciples has followed the practices of the liturgically free Churches in America, except for the observance of holy communion each Lord's Day. Traditionally the elders presided, with the words of institution and prayers of thanksgiving, but now the minister commonly officiates. The original ministry of the Disciples included elders and deacons ordained to care for the congregations and a general order of evangelists, under no authority and exercising none except that of influence. Elders and deacons generally earned their living at secular callings. The evangelists who planted and guided the congregations gained a meager living from their ministry. With urbanization, congregations began to engage full-time pastors. Under the *Provisional Design* congregations call their ministers with the counsel of the regional minister. Policies as to ordination and ministerial standing are set by the General Assembly and administered by the regions. The polity of the Church remains congregational insofar as internal congregational life is concerned but recognizes the Church as existing also in regions and in nations. General offices are in Indianapolis, Indiana. The Disciples of Christ Historical Society maintains an important library and archival collection in Nashville. The Christian Church, by changing its corporate name from "The Christian Churches," reluctantly but unequivocally accepted status as a denomination. The commitment to the unity of Christians continues unabated. The Church holds membership in the National Council of Churches, the World Council, and the Consultation on Church Union. BIBLIOGRAPHY: W. E. Garrison and A. T. DeGrott, *Disciples of Christ: A History* (2d ed., 1958).

[R. E. OSBORN]

CHRISTIAN DEMOCRACY, a term that has had different meanings at different times and places. Generally speaking, it refers to those movements that are inspired by Christian principles and organized by laymen in the pursuit of political and socio-economic objectives. Historically, the most important Christian Democratic movement developed in Italy as an immediate consequence of the Church-State quarrel that accompanied political unification in the 19th century. As the movement developed, socio-economic issues were of major interest to its proponents, as is clear from the program adopted by Christian Democrats in 1899. Inspiration for the program came from Pope Leo XIII's *Rerum novarum* (1891) and the writings of Giuseppe Toniolo, professor of political economy at the Univ. of Pisa, who was also responsible for coining the term "Christian Democracy." As employed by Leo XIII in *Graves de communi* (1901), the term had a social, not a political connotation. By 1919 changed political and social conditions necessitated a removal of the previous papal ban on direct Italian Catholic participation in national politics, and the first political party of Christian Democratic inspiration was Luigi Sturzo's *Partito Popolare*. Destroyed during the Mussolini era, it was revived by Alcide de Gasperi and other former popularists during World War II under the name of the Christian Democratic Party. After World War II similar parties have been organized and have made their strength evident in Holland, Belgium, Luxembourg, Germany, and Austria, and they have been active in France, Switzerland, and Norway also. BIBLIOGRAPHY: R. A. Webster, *Cross and the Fasces* (1960); M. P. Fogarty, *Christian Democracy in Western Europe 1820–1953* (1957) with a full bibliography.

[E. A. CARRILLO]

CHRISTIAN DOCTRINE, SISTERS OF OUR LADY OF, a community of sisters founded about 1910 in New York by Marian Gurney (Mother Marianne of Jesus), a pioneer social service worker, a cofounder of a catechetical training school, and in 1902 a secretary of New York City's first *CCD. The congregation was established for the purpose of supporting pastors in the teaching of religion to public school students and adults. With the aid of volunteer and paid workers, the sisters engage in a wide program of social services, as well as serve as catechists, in New York, New Hampshire, South Carolina, and Florida. In 1976 the membership totaled 53 professed sisters. The motherhouse is located in Suffern, N.Y.

[R. A. TODD]

CHRISTIAN DOCTRINE (NANCY), SISTERS OF, a congregation founded in France *c.* 1700 for the education of girls. They are sometimes called Vatelottes after their founder, Abbé Jean Baptiste Vatelot, who, with three of his own sisters, opened a school for girls in his family home at Bruley near Toul. From this humble beginning the congregation spread into E France and from there into Belgium, Luxembourg, Algeria, Italy, Morocco, and the Belgian Congo; their work expanded to include nursing. They received papal approbation in 1886 and in 1929. By 1975 they numbered 1,386 sisters in 216 houses. Their motherhouse is in Nancy, France.

[R. C. CLIGGETT]

CHRISTIAN EDUCATION, RELIGIOUS OF, a congregation of women religious dedicated to restoring the Catholic faith in a small parish in Échauffour, Normandy. It was founded under the Rule of St. Augustine in 1817 by Louis François Martin La Fosse. As their apostolate of Christian education grew, they soon established 25 houses in 5 different countries. In 1964 the total membership was about 500, and 12 years later the U.S. province had 78 sisters in Massachusetts and North Carolina, where they conduct 3 parochial schools and 4 religious education centers. The general motherhouse is in Paris, France. BIBLIOGRAPHY: G. Allemang, LTK 6:730.

[R. A. TODD]

CHRISTIAN ENDEAVOR, INTERNATIONAL SOCIETY OF, interdenominational youth movement founded in 1881 by Francis E. Clark, a Congregationalist pastor in Portland, Maine. Clark organized a group of young people in order to involve them in the work of the Church and to strengthen their religious commitment. The idea spread rapidly, esp. among the evangelical Churches, and in 1885 the United Society of Christian Endeavor was formed. In 1927 the present name was adopted; it designates the union of local societies in the U.S., Canada, and Mexico. Growth outside the U.S. was similarly rapid, and in 1895 national unions of local societies were brought together in the World's Christian Endeavor Union. The movement has been expanded to include all age groups, and presently numbers millions of adherents in thousands of local societies representing 80 denominations in 50 countries. Essential requirements for membership are the confession of Christ, service for Christ, loyalty to the Church, and Christian fellowship. Local societies offer courses in religious training and leadership, sponsor devotional and recreational activities, and provide opportunities for participation in social welfare projects.

[J. C. WILLKE]

CHRISTIAN FAMILY MOVEMENT (CFM), an apostolic organization founded in 1943 to promote the Christian way of life in the family, in the families of the community, and in institutions that affect the family by servicing, educating, and representing the family. Originally started as a Catholic Action group, the CFM has been opened to all Christians since becoming a national movement in 1949. Its basic unit is a small group of married couples who meet in their homes. They follow a program of discussion and action to educate and activate themselves as family units of the lay apostolate. The national headquarters in Chicago prepares annual programs and various publications, including the monthly bulletin *Act*. BIBLIOGRAPHY: Peter and Mary Goulding, "A CFM History," *This Is CFM* (1952).

[A. R. ZINK]

CHRISTIAN FELLOWSHIP, a unity of persons that results from the shared life of the Spirit. St. Paul used the Gr. term *koinonia* to express this unity. Those who believed in Jesus, as Lord, became one with each other because of their oneness in him. Today this term describes the experience of those who pray together in the Spirit, help each other, and enjoy each other's company for the sake of Jesus Christ, and who share the Eucharist as the best expression and source of their oneness. BIBLIOGRAPHY: R. Kugelman, JBC 51:10.

[V. GILLIGAN]

CHRISTIAN KING, MOST, title that came into use during the reign of Charles V and was considered a special prerogative of the kings of France. Philippe de Mézières, a contemporary of Charles VI, wrote: "Because of the vigor with which Charlemagne, St. Louis, and other brave French kings, more than any other kings of Christendom, have upheld the Catholic faith, the kings of France are known among the kings of Christendom as Most Christian." From 1464 papal bulls addressed to the kings of France bore the title *Rex Christianissimus*.

[J. BLAIR]

CHRISTIAN LAW, the law of Christ, which is a law of love. Christ made love the central precept of the dispensation of salvation that he brought to the world. Love sums up the Christian existence. Christian love has a double dimension: love of God and of neighbor (Mk 12.28–34). The two cannot be separated (Mt 22.39), for love of neighbor is the practical test and the concrete expression of one's love for God (1 Jn 4.20). Christ's precept of charity is not entirely new; the old law and the teaching of the prophets already hung on the same twofold commandment (Mt 22.40). With Christ, however, the law of love takes on a new breadth and a new depth: love for men gains in universality and self-forgetfulness (Mt 5.43–47); love for God receives a new foundation. Christian charity is man's response to the love that God has first shown man in Jesus Christ (1 Jn 4.10–11). The incarnation of God's Son is the supreme proof and the perfect expression of his love for men (Jn 3.16); it is also the foundation of the Christian law of love. Its model and exemplar is the human love of Jesus Christ for his Father and for all men. Christian charity attempts to reproduce, however imperfectly, the perfect love of the Son of God made man. BIBLIOGRAPHY: G. A. Gilleman, NCE 3:639–640; *idem, Primacy of Charity in Moral Theology* (1959); T. Barrosse and G. A. Gilleman, NCE 8:1043–45; C. Wiéner, DBT 283–288.

[J. DUPUIS]

CHRISTIAN METHODIST EPISCOPAL CHURCH, a denomination that had its roots in a proposal made in 1866 by the *General Conference of the Methodist Episcopal Church, South, when faced with desertion of its Negro members. The Conference voted to organize black members into "separate missions, churches, charges, districts, and Annual Conferences of their own." It also legislated that, whenever an entire congregation with sole use of a building joined either of the two African Methodist Episcopal Churches then in existence, the congregation be allowed to keep the edifice. When differences arose between the two African Churches, the bps. recommended that a new Negro Church be established. In 1870 delegates met in Jackson, Tenn., to organize a denomination, which they named the Colored Methodist Episcopal Church (changed in 1954 to Christian Methodist Episcopal Church). They adopted the doctrine and discipline of the Methodist Episcopal Church, South, "after taking out and putting in such things as would be for the highest interest of the Church." Until 1880 the Church received only token support from its parent body, but after that date support increased; and in the 1939 union that formed the *Methodist Church, a recommendation was made that in the South the Methodist Church should continue its historical support of the Negro body. From the first, the Christian Methodist Episcopal Church made the establishment of schools of higher education one of its major objectives. It conducts schools in five states and publishes several periodicals. It is a member of the World Council of Churches and of the Consultation on Christian Union. In 1965 membership of the Church totaled 446,718, in 2,598 churches.

Plans for union with the African Methodist Episcopal Church and the African Methodist Episcopal Church Zion were progressing in 1974. BIBLIOGRAPHY: HistAmMeth 3:385–386.

[J. H. SATTERWHITE]

CHRISTIAN MOTHERS, ARCHCONFRATERNITY OF, a society of Catholic women that originated in France in 1850 when mothers met to pray with and for one another and their children, to discuss their problems, and to advise one another regarding the Christian rearing of their children. The confraternity has as its goal the home education and character building of children by Christian mothers. Its members try to achieve this goal by daily recitation of prescribed prayers, by attending monthly conferences, and by performing good works. The society was introduced into the U.S. by the Capuchin friars in 1881. Its headquarters are located in Pittsburgh. BIBLIOGRAPHY: *Conference Booklet: Confraternity of Christian Mothers* (1973).

[A. R. ZINK]

CHRISTIAN NURTURE, as a technical term, a theory of religious education. Although owing something to the contributions of such Unitarians as W. E. *Channing and T. *Parker, the origin of the concept is found in H. *Bushnell's *Christian Nurture* (1847). Reacting against the revivalism of his day, which assumed a dramatic conversion in adulthood to be necessary, he declared that "the child is to grow up a Christian, and never know himself as being otherwise." He believed it wrong to expect a child to grow up as a sinner on the assumption that he could not become converted until he reached maturity. Such a presupposition ignored the family, the Church, and other organic means of God's bestowal of grace. In Bushnell's thought there were, at least implicitly, certain tendencies that became prominent in the latter half of the century: (1) divine immanence; (2) organic development in religion and morals; (3) an emphasis upon the human element in Jesus Christ; and (4) recognition that children have potentialities for good as well as for evil. Under the influence of such Europeans as A. *Ritschl and A. *Harnack, as well as of American educators, these concepts were developed in the 20th cent. into an extremely anthropocentric type of religious education, optimistically seeking to establish a perfect democratic society that was equated with the kingdom of God, leaving little place for divine transcendence. Some reactions against these trends came in the 1940s. BIBLIOGRAPHY: H. S. Smith, *Faith and Nurture* (1941).

[N. H. MARING]

CHRISTIAN PHILOSOPHY. In a loose sense an individual's philosophy is understood as the sum total of his convictions, thoughts, or attitudes with respect to realities of experience, regardless of the source of these convictions, etc., or the ground in which they are rooted. A Christian's philosophy in this sense would not be, strictly speaking, a

philosophy at all, but a complexus of his ideas, views, convictions, etc., many of the most important of which are derived from what he takes to be divine revelation. But if philosophy is taken in its narrower sense as the science which examines the most general facts and principles of reality, of human nature, of ethics, aesthetics, and politics as these are knowable in the unaided light of human reason, then it can be qualified as Christian only to the extent that it is not contradictory to the truths known by faith. The Fathers of the Church began the elaboration of a philosophy of this kind for the purpose of defending the faith, drawing upon the great Greek philosophers of antiquity for their basic concepts and principles. In doing so they began the production of the synthesis of Hebraic-Christian thought that contributed so greatly to the cultural formation of Western civilization. The work of synthesizing and systematizing reached its highest point of development in the 12th and 13th cent. and appeared in several different and to some extent conflicting traditions. The expression "Christian philosophy" is used sometimes to indicate one or another or all of these systems. *FAITH AND REASON.

[P. K. MEAGHER]

CHRISTIAN PREACHING CONFERENCE, an organization of priests and ministers dedicated to a more effective proclamation of the Word. The conference's charter convention was held in New York in 1958. Its original proponents were mainly RC seminary professors who desired to improve the practical techniques of verbal communication and to encourage research on the theory of homiletic methods. Formerly known as the Catholic Homiletic Society, it was renamed in 1967 to enhance the ecumenical nature of the organization. The central office is in St. Louis where the bimonthly journal *Preaching* and a newsletter are published. Assistance has been given to its members through regional and national workshops, sermon outlines *(Novalis)*, multi-media presentations, research studies, and book recommendations. An ecumenical sharing with Protestant clergymen has been typical of recent conventions. BIBLIOGRAPHY: D. Morrisey, "Catholic Preaching in the United States, England and the English-speaking World," *Renewal of Preaching: Theory and Practice (Concilium* 33, 1968) 151–156.

[W. J. TOBIN]

CHRISTIAN SCHOOLS OF MERCY, SISTERS OF THE, see ST. MARIE MADELEINE POSTEL, SISTERS OF.

CHRISTIAN SCIENCE, the doctrines of the *Church of Christ Scientist, received from Mary Baker *Eddy, esp. those on the power of spiritual mind to dominate material forces.

[T. C. O'BRIEN]

CHRISTIAN SOCIAL EDUCATION, a constructive study and training in a program of social action based largely on papal encyclicals, mainly Leo XIII's *Rerum novarum;* Pius XI's *Quadragesimo anno;* Pius XII's *Summi pontificatus,* and John XXIII's *Mater et Magistra* and *Pacem in terris.* It is designed to inculcate in youth a better understanding of contemporary society; to awaken them to their responsibilities to their fellowmen and society at large; and to help them acquire a grasp of Christian doctrine relative to social problems emerging from social evolution and an understanding of their role in the solution of such problems. Starting from the truth that every human being is a person endowed with an inherent dignity, redeemed by Christ's blood, his nature gifted with intellect and will, and with consequent rights and duties, the program seeks to instill universal respect for all, an enlightened appreciation of work as a noble, human function, an awareness of remunerative and distributive justice; and an understanding of the natural right to private ownership with its concomitant individual, familial, and social functions. It emphasizes a Christian concept of authority and respect for the principle of subsidiarity and an honest and knowledgeable concern for the common good, which, as *Mater et Magistra* expresses it, "embraces the sum total of those conditions of social living whereby men are enabled more fully and more readily to achieve their own perfection." BIBLIOGRAPHY: M. J. Smith and M. N. McGreal, *Guiding Growth in Christian Social Living* (1952–59).

[M. B. MURPHY]

CHRISTIAN SOCIALISM, a term that, taken narrowly, refers to the short-lived movement (1848–54) that rose from within the C of E against the *laissez-faire* doctrine of Bentham and James and J. S. Mill, which combined with capitalism to dispossess the people and produce the squalor of early industrialism. The movement advocated the reform of society by the application of Christian principles. Its effective founder and organizer was J. M. F. Ludlow, a barrister well versed in law, politics, and economics; his fame is overshadowed by F. D. *Maurice and C. *Kingsley. A vigorous campaign was launched, by meetings and periodical publications, and after the scares of Chartism and the revolutions of 1848 encountered great hostility. This did not kill it, however; rather it died from the indifference of the workers themselves, from the counterinterest of the Great Exhibition and the Crimean War, and from the spreading bourgeois mid-Victorian confidence in inevitable material progress. Its monument is the Working Men's College, its legacy the growth of the Cooperative and the Trade Union movements.

The *Tracts on Christian Socialism* (1850), like the *Tracts for the Times,* belong to the confines of a period, but the Christian Socialist movement, like the *Oxford movement, opened out into wider power. The early Tractarians were pre-Disraeli Tories without much concern for social problems as such, but those of the next generation were very alive to them: a comparison between J. H. Newman and H. E. Manning will suggest the difference. One feature of

*Anglo-Catholicism has been an involvement with the cause of social reform, which can be traced from the Guild of St. Matthew to the Christian Social Union, and which culminates in the Malvern Declaration (1951). The encyclicals of Leo XIII promoted a like RC concern, of which one expression was the Catholic Social Guild. The movement was even more influential on the Continent; Bishop Ketteler of Mainz and the Comte de Mun, to mention but two names, grounded their policies on well-articulated and classical RC moral doctrines, and were the harbingers of the days when the RC electorate in democratic countries often voted well to the left; in the Austria of Ignaz Seipel it called itself Christian Socialism. In the U.S. the movement was later in starting, and for various reaons has not made a political impact under that name. To go no farther back than Washington Gladden and W. D. P. Bliss, the evils of economic individualism have been diagnosed and the remedies, the social responsibility of ownership and a more equitable distribution of wealth, have been applied, ever more and more comprehensively.

The movement has differed from the socialism of the first and second International by its stress on the right to private property, and from communism by its order of priorities; the first has tended to scorn it as offering mere palliatives, the second to suppress it or give it the kiss of death. In the 2d half of the 20th cent., however, the dimensions of the debate have changed, religious men of different obediences have converged, and there are not a few who proclaim themselves both Christian and Marxist. BIBLIOGRAPHY: C. Raven, *Christian Socialism* (1921); G. C. Binyon, *Christian Socialist Movement in England* (1931); J. Dombrowski, *Early Days of Christian Socialism in America* (1936).

[T. GILBY]

CHRISTIAN UNITY, SECRETARIAT FOR PROMOTING (SPCU), a Vatican office created by Pope John XXIII with the immediate aim of facilitating fruitful participation of the Orthodox and other Christian Churches in Vatican Council II, and with the broader aim of working with those Churches toward unity. Under Cardinal Augustine *Bea as president, the SPCU arranged for participation of representatives of the Churches in the council as observers and supplied guidance to the council on matters bearing on Christian unity. In 1967 the SPCU issued a *Directory on Ecumenism* for implementation of the council's decisions on ecumenical matters. Since the conclusion of the council the SPCU has been the official voice of the Vatican in the growing ecumenical dialogue. Its new approach to the Churches, not as adversaries but as separated brethren seeking unity in Christ, has resulted in a broad range of active consultations, joint sponsorship of programs and conferences, joint publishing ventures, and collaboration in service programs. A Joint Working Group has been established with the World Council of Churches to consider subjects of mutual concern in the quest for unity; and specialized agencies, such as the Joint Theological Commission on Catholicity and Apostolicity, the Pontifical Council on the Laity, and the Pontifical Commission on Justice and Peace, have been set up to channel joint action in various areas. The SPCU issues a quarterly information bulletin in French and English.

[D. CODDINGTON]

CHRISTIANA OF LUCCA, BL. (Christiana of Santa Croce; 1240–1310), virgin. She was christened Oringa, but was later popularly called Christiana because of the example she gave of Christian charity. As a young girl she fled from home and became a servant to avoid being forced into marriage by her brothers. Notable for her devotion to the Blessed Virgin and the Eucharist, she founded an Augustinian convent in Santa Croce, Italy. BIBLIOGRAPHY: N. Del Re, BiblSanct 4:324–325; M. Baciocchi de Péon, *La vergine Oringa* (1926).

[J. L. GRASSI]

CHRISTIANITY, the historical movement stemming from Jesus Christ and based upon commitment to him. A distinction is sometimes drawn between the historical movement that has existed under the name of Christianity and the ideal that would exist if those who call themselves followers of Christ were true to his spirit and teachings. Thus, on the one hand, much that has gone under the name of Christianity is said not to be true Christianity, whatever the church affiliation of those who have been unfaithful to Christ's teaching may have been. On the other hand, Christians and Christian bodies that have no visible communion with others because of disagreement on points of doctrine tend to look upon one another as heretical or at least as guilty of departing in some respect from Christ's teaching. Yet the persistence even in opposing bodies of a strong commitment to the person of Christ, fidelity in worship, devotion to the Scriptures, and Christian service is evidence of a rightful sense of the term that transcends many specific differences of belief. Christianity in the ideal sense can be further subdivided, understanding it from the doctrinal standpoint or from the ethical. Although some have placed greater emphasis upon the distinctive Christian teachings and others upon the Christian ideal of ethical behavior, most Christians have held that to some degree the two are properly indivisible. In general usage everyone who affirms a commitment to Christ is considered in some sense a part of historical Christianity.

[T. EARLY]

CHRISTIANS, the name used after 1830 by the followers of Alexander and Thomas *Campbell to indicate opposition to *denominationalism; they also called themselves Disciples of Christ. *CHRISTIAN CHURCHES (DISCIPLES OF CHRIST), INTERNATIONAL CONVENTION OF.

[T. C. O'BRIEN]

CHRISTINA, ST. (of Bolsena), martyr. Daughter of a noble pagan, C. was converted to Christianity. Zeal prodded her to break up the priceless idols of her father's house,

distributing the valuable fragments as alms to the poor and needy. She suffered a martyr's death under Diocletian and has been venerated since the 4th century. She has been long considered the patroness of millers and archers. BIBLIOGRAPHY: A. Amore, BiblSanct 4:330–332, Butler 3:173–174.

[E. C. HUBBERT]

CHRISTINA, QUEEN OF SWEDEN (1626–89), the only child of Gustavus Adolphus II and Maria Eleanora of Brandenburg. When she was orphaned at the age of six, Sweden was ruled by a regent until C. reached her 18th birthday when she was crowned queen. Her father had left orders that she be soundly educated in a manner suited to the upbringing of a male heir, and she became well versed in matters of scholarly and artistic interest. But she lacked prudence and shrewdness in financial dealings. She reduced the crown's resources by her lavish benefactions to artists, scholars, and those whose favor she sought among the nobility. In 1654 she resigned her crown in favor of her cousin, Charles Augustus, went to Brussels, and entered the RC Church. Most of her remaining life was spent in Rome where she became noted for her eccentric and unconventional behavior and was constantly plagued with a shortage of funds.

[J. C. WILLKE]

CHRISTINA OF HAMM, BL. (b. 1464), stigmatic of the Westphalian town of Hamm. According to W. Rolevinck in the *Fasciculus temporum* (1482), she experienced the stigmata in her hands, feet, and side. Twelve witnesses bore testimony to this phenomenon. Her cult became widespread enough to warrant a feast day, which was probably derived from that of Christina of Stommeln. BIBLIOGRAPHY: K. Honselmann, LTK 2:1129; A. Schütte, *Handbuch der deutschen Heiligen* (1941) 88.

[J. M. O'DONNELL]

CHRISTINA OF MARKYATE (d. *c.*1155), recluse. She was the daughter of Auti and Beatrix of Huntingdon, England, who strongly opposed her determination to observe a vow of virginity. She was finally established in a convent at Markyate built for her by Abbot Geoffrey of St. Albans. C. was famous for the gift of prophecy and miracles. BIBLIOGRAPHY: C. H. Talbot, *Life of Christina of Markyate, a Twelfth Century Recluse* (1959).

[H. DRESSLER]

CHRISTINA OF SPOLETO, BL. (baptismal name, Agostina Camozzi; *c.*1435–56), Italian Third Order Augustinian, penitent. Legendary accretion long confused her identity and life story; the facts were brought to light by E. Motta in 1893 *(Bolletino storico della Svizzera italiana* 15 [1893] 84–93). Born in Porlezza (Como)—she is called "of Spoleto" (Perugia) because she died there—C. was married at an early age, quickly widowed, married a second time, and for a period lived a sinful life. Converted, she entered the Third Order Regular of St. Augustine and thereafter her life was remarkable for its penitential austerity and her works of charity. She moved from place to place to maintain her privacy and to avoid interference with her penitential observances. Her cult was approved by Gregory XVI in 1834. BIBLIOGRAPHY: Butler 1:324–325, which gives the legendary story of her earlier years; N. Del Re, BiblSanct 4:341.

[P. K. MEAGHER]

CHRISTINA OF STOMMELN, BL. (1242–1312), Beguine. At 13 she became a *Beguine in Cologne. Her singular devotions and austerities having disquieted her companions, she returned to Stommeln. Because of her sensational experiences, which were recorded by her Dominican director, Peter of Dacia, some scholars surmise hallucinations or hysteria without, however, questioning her faith and purity. She was beatified in 1908. BIBLIOGRAPHY: Butler 4:277–279; M. J. Finnegan, NCE 3:655; A. Codaghengo, BiblSanct 4:342.

[M. J. FINNEGAN]

CHRISTINE DE PISAN (c.1364–c.1430), French poet, translator, historian, and polemicist. Of Italian origin, C. lived at the court of King Charles V of France whom her father served as astrologer and physician. Excellently educated and widely read in the literature of her time, she turned to writing to support herself and her children after the death of her husband. She wrote a biography of Charles V, a work in praise of Joan of Arc, and attacked the erotic cynicism of Jean de Meung. Her lyric verse, varied in genre, recalls the earlier *cours d'amour,* though a gentle, philosophical vein prevails. Her adaptations of Boccaccio, Vegetius, and her *Vision of Christine* are models of prose style. BIBLIOGRAPHY: M. J. Pinet, *Christine de Pisan* (1927); M. J. Hamilton, NCE 3:655.

[J. P. WILLIMAN]

CHRISTMAS CAROL, traditional song in the vernacular for the celebration of the feast of Christmas. The term may refer to the fixed song-form of the 15th-cent. English carol. The French *virelai* and the Italian *ballata* closely resemble the English song-form. The carol in its polyphonic setting was an important vehicle of musical thought in late 15th-cent. England. The time of the year esp. favored by carol composers was Christmas, although Easter carols and other joyful carols existed at that time. The refrain that begins each carol and recurs between stanzas shows this song-form to be related to the medieval French *carole,* a round-dance, from which the name is derived. BIBLIOGRAPHY: W. J. Phillips, *Carols: Their Origin, Music, and Connection with Mystery Plays* (1970) 1–15.

[J. S. PALLOZZA]

CHRISTMAS CONFERENCE, meeting of Methodist preachers in Baltimore, Md., in 1784, which organized the Methodist Episcopal Church. The conference was called by F. *Asbury and T. *Coke, who had been ordained by John *Wesley as a general superintendent (bishop) of the Methodist work in America. At the Conference, Asbury was ordained a general superintendent, after being elected to the office by the preachers. A *ritual, a *Book of Discipline, and standards of doctrine were also adopted. BIBLIOGRAPHY: HistAmMeth 1:197–240; F. E. Maser, *Dramatic Story of Early American Methodism* (1965) 84–97.

[F. E. MASER]

CHRISTMAS CYCLE. Christmas is the feast celebrated on Dec. 25 in commemoration of the redemptive mystery of Christ's entrance into this world. The cycle of this feast extends from the first Sunday of Advent through the Advent season to Christmas Eve, through Christmastide and the feasts associated with the Epiphany, down to the Sunday after the Epiphany when the last echoes of the Christmas mystery are heard in the liturgy.

The origin of the Christmas feast and the determination of Dec. 25 as the day for its celebration have been variously accounted for. Two theories are favored today. One, that of B. Botte, holds that the feast was established to replace the Mithraic festival honoring the "birthday" of *Sol Invictus,* which came at the solstice when the sun began its return, with the celebration of the birth of Christ, the Sun of Justice. The pagan festival was kept at Rome on Dec. 25 according to the Julian calendar, and in Egypt, on Jan. 6. The other theory, that of A. Baumstark, holds that the feast originated from the Arian controversy over the nature of Christ. Both opinions have their merits. The earliest clear reference to the feast in Rome is dated c.354. Between 378 and 530 the feast of Christmas was gradually accepted in the East. The basic content of the feast has evolved from Augustine, who saw it as a remembrance of an historical event; to Leo, who saw it as a mystery feast, to the Middle Ages, which emphasized the historical humanity of Christ's birth.

The three Masses for Christmas, celebrated at midnight, dawn, and midday, are all proper to the feast. The midnight Mass probably began during the reign of Pope Sixtus III (432–440), who converted the basilica of Santa Maria Maggiore, as it is now known, into a Marian shrine. Here a Mass was celebrated over the crypt containing a replica of the crib. *Etheria mentions c.400 a celebration held at Bethlehem at midnight on Jan. 6. The Romans may have imitated this practice. The second Mass, at dawn, may also have been imitative of the practice observed at Jerusalem of having a synaxis at the Holy Sepulcher at dawn as the pilgrims made their way back from Bethlehem. However, it is certain that in Rome the original Mass at dawn was not a Christmas Mass but one in honor of the martyr *Anastasia who was held in high esteem by the Greeks. The basilica of St. Anastasia was the church frequented by Greeks residing in Rome, and her feast was celebrated on Dec. 25. The popes said Mass in that church on that day from the 6th century. The third Mass of Christmas is the oldest and the principal Mass of Christmas. During the reign of Leo I (440–461), this Mass began to be said at St. Peter's. Gregory the Great (590–604) is the first to refer to these three Masses as Christmas Masses. Their celebration was proper to Rome until the Roman liturgy spread throughout Europe. In other places in Western Europe there was originally only one Mass, that of Christmas day.

The core of the Christmas cycle is Christmas Eve, Christmas, its octave, and the Epiphany. The vigil of Christmas was introduced into the liturgy in the 6th century. The octave of Christmas, probably introduced in imitation of that of Easter, is unusual in that the feasts of certain saints are celebrated within it, although the number of these has been reduced by the elimination of the feasts of SS. Thomas Becket and Sylvester, Dec. 29 and 31 respectively. Still, the feasts of SS. Stephen, and John the Evangelist, and that of the Holy Innocents remain. The octave of Christmas has been concluded at different periods with celebrations of different character. The earliest practice of which there is record was the dedication of this day to prayer against pagan observances. But at an early date this was superseded by a feast in honor of Mary. In the Gelasian and Gregorian sacramentaries, the occasion was designated simply as the Octave of the Lord. Because of the Gospel read on this occasion (Lk 2.21), the day began to be called the Feast of the Circumcision, a title it bore in Roman liturgical books from the 15th cent. until 1961, when the title Octave of the Nativity was revived. With the new Missal and calendar of 1969 the still earlier Marian character of the celebration was restored and the day is now called the Feast of the Solemnity of Mary, Mother of God. Although this day concludes the octave, the spirit of the season continues for a time, esp. in the celebration of Epiphany. BIBLIOGRAPHY: C. Smith, NCE 3:655–660; A. Strittmatter, "Christmas and the Epiphany: Origins and Antecedents," *Thought* 17 (1942) 600–626; B. Botte, "La Première fête mariale de la liturgie romaine," EphemLiturg 47 (1933) 425–430.

[N. KOLLAR]

CHRISTMAS EVE, the day before Christmas, celebrated as the vigil of the feast. In popular usage the term applies particularly to the late evening hours of the day. Until 1966 it was observed in the RC Church as a day of fast and abstinence. Associated with the evening hours of the day are many customs, such as the coming of St. Nicholas (Santa Claus), the decoration of the *Christmas tree, a celebration around the crib with the reading of the Christmas Gospel, the singing of hymns, a prayer, the singing of carols, etc. The evening culminates in the Midnight Mass of Christmas, an observance introduced during the pontificate of Sixtus III (432–440). BIBLIOGRAPHY: F. X. Weiser, *Handbook of Christian Feasts and Customs* (1958) 77–120.

[N. KOLLAR]

CHRISTMAS PLAYS, a genre of medieval liturgical drama flourishing in the 11th and 12th cent., consisting at first only of the shepherds' visit to the manger but gradually acquiring other related incidents like the offering of the Magi and the slaughter of the Holy Innocents. Christmas plays do not compare in frequency with the hundreds of surviving Easter dramas, perhaps because they tended to be still-life tableaus rather than genuine plays and often made use of statues instead of actors for the figures of the Holy Family. The shepherds of the Latin plays were formal, almost stately characters, but in the vernacular versions of the late Middle Ages, they became homely and even comic peasants, best known in the immortal role of Mak from the English *Second Shepherds' Play*. BIBLIOGRAPHY: E. C. Dunn, NCE 4:1041–42.

[E. C. DUNN]

CHRISTMAS TREE, an evergreen tree decorated with lights, ornaments, etc. For Christians the tree and decorations are reminders of Christ, who is the tree of life and the light of the world. The Christmas tree was first used by the people of Western Germany. It was a combination of two earlier customs: the paradise tree (11th cent.) and the Christmas light. The paradise tree was a fir tree hung with red apples reminiscent of the apple eaten by Eve. The Christmas light was a large candle lit on Christmas eve and kept burning throughout the night. In Germany the larger candle and many smaller candles were arranged in the shape of a pyramid, and it was a short step from this to combining both customs. The Christmas tree spread from Germany to France (1837), then to England (mid-19th century). It came to the U.S. much earlier (early 18th cent.) brought over by German immigrants. BIBLIOGRAPHY: F. X. Weiser, *Handbook of Christian Feasts and Customs* (1958) 98–103.

[N. KOLLAR]

CHRISTOCENTRISM (Gr., *Christos,* Christ + *kentron,* center), a characteristic of any approach to theology, spirituality, or history by virtue of which such an approach accords a central role to Jesus Christ in his human nature—or to God precisely as incarnate. Etymologically the term might apply to a view that accords a special prominence to Christ as God, but this usage is ruled out, theologically, by two factors. First, the traditional dictum that the Divine Persons act as one principle in relation to the created world has precluded the attribution of a centrality to the Word that would not apply equally to the Father and the Spirit. And, second, the term *theocentrism has customarily been used to characterize a view which accords a central role to the Divinity as such. Christocentrism has been a major influence recently in both doctrinal and moral theology. É. Mersch, e.g., sought to replace the earlier, theocentric approach with one that presented every revealed doctrine in relation to that of Christ's Mystical Body. In moral theology, B. Häring and G. Gilleman are the most prominent in a group of theologians attempting to replace the commandment-centered approach with an emphasis on Christ's new law of love.

Unlike theology, Christian spirituality has always been Christocentric in response to Christ's admonition, "No one can come to the Father except through me" (Jn 14.6). The

Jesuit ideal, e.g., has been to follow Christ's leadership; the Salesian, to reproduce Christ's traits in one's life; and the Franciscan, to imitate Christ literally. New emphasis is given to Christocentric spirituality by E. Schillebeeckx's teaching on Christ as primordial Sacrament.

The Christocentric approach to history is evident in recent Christian literature, both Catholic (J. Daniélou, H. von Balthasar) and Protestant (O. Cullmann, H. Berkhof), as well as in the evolutionary hyper-physics of Teilhard de Chardin. Despite differences in emphasis and terminology, the point emerges clearly in all these authors that as man, God works in history. The whole of human history is viewed as the paschal mystery writ large, and cosmic history is the story of Christ drawing all things to unity in himself. BIBLIOGRAPHY: É. Mersch, *Theology of the Mystical Body* (1951); B. Häring, *Law of Christ* (1964); E. Schillebeeckx, *Christ the Sacrament of the Encounter with God* (1963); H. von Balthasar, *Theology of History* (1963); S. Wroblewski, *Christ-centered Spirituality* (1967); P. Teilhard de Chardin, *Hymn of the Universe* (1965).

[M. D. MEILACH]

CHRISTOLOGICAL CONTROVERSIES, conflicts in the Early Christian cent. between orthodox and heterodox explanations of how Jesus Christ is true God and true man. *Ignatius of Antioch in the 1st cent. condemned *Docetism, the denial that Christ has a genuine, physical body; *Irenaeus combated the same error against various uses in *Gnosticism. Pope Callistus I (d. 217) condemned a form of *Adoptionism, as well as *Patripassianism. The Council of Nicaea I condemned *Arianism and sanctioned the term *homoousion* (consubstantial) to describe Christ's oneness in nature with the Father. The Council of Constantinople I (381) censured the teaching of *Apollinaris of Laodicea that the Word took the place of a human soul in Christ. Under *Cyril of Alexandria's leadership, the Council of Ephesus (431) condemned the teaching of *Nestorius because it made the union of divine and human nature in Christ merely operational, not substantial in the person of the Word. The definitions of the Council of *Chalcedon (451), together with the *Tome* of Pope *Leo I, gave final form to orthodox terminology, rejecting *Monophysitism and affirming in Christ two natures, unmixed and distinct, in the one person, the Son and Word, Jesus Christ (see D 301–302). The Council of Constantinople III (681) rejected *Monothelitism, the attempt to explain Christ's oneness by denying two wills, divine and human, in Christ and affirming but one. The work of *John of Damascus, *De fide orthodoxa,* is an important synthesis, bringing together orthodox Christological teaching and terminology developed out of the controversies of the first 6 centuries. *MODALISM; *SABELLIANISTS.

[T. C. O'BRIEN]

CHRISTOLOGY, theology as it concentrates on the mystery of Christ and esp. on the union in him of the human and the divine ("soteriology" concentrates on his saving acts).

For classic theology the terms of discussion were set by the early ecumenical councils, particularly Chalcedon (see CHRISTOLOGICAL CONTROVERSIES); thus a traditional Christology is a Chalcedonian Christology. Its principal theme is the *hypostatic union: that in the one person, the Word, and the Lord Jesus Christ, human and divine nature are united, each retaining its distinctiveness. The terms of discourse are: union, substance, accident, nature, person, personality or subsistence. The most precise, metaphysical exploration of these terms emerged in medieval theology, particularly in the *Summa theologiae* of Thomas Aquinas. On the basis of the determinations expressing the hypostatic union, the subsidiary issues are faced, among them: the attributes of nature and grace belonging to Christ's human nature; the rules for statements having a divine or human name for Christ as subject (*communication of idioms); the unity of his activity, and the effectiveness of his saving acts. With some variations most manuals of RC theology presented Christology along these lines, until very recent times. The classic Anglican, Calvinist, and Lutheran *confessions of faith profess a Chalcedonian Christology; Reformation theologians, however, concentrated more on soteriological issues. One issue controverted between Lutherans and Calvinists was the communication of idioms or attributes, esp. whether omnipresence is an intrinsic attribute given to Christ's human nature.

In modern times new interpretations of Christ's humanity and divinity have developed in both RC and Protestant theology. To the degree that *rationalism has prevailed, the essential Christological issue—how Christ is the incarnate Word—vanishes: Jesus is simply a man, different from others merely by the preeminence of his holiness and example. Many forms of *liberal theology take this simply for granted. Even where traditional orthodoxy is maintained, there has been a developing dissatisfaction with a Chalcedonian Christology. Two attempts at reformulation are noteworthy. The one, marked by the wish to separate the Christ of faith from the Jesus of history, perceives a discrepancy between the static Christ of scholastic theology and the Gospel portrait of Jesus, growing in grace as well as in consciousness of self and of mission. The Christology inspired by this view is one more biblically based, shaped primarily by the consideration of Jesus' saving work. A second major interpretation involves use of the categories of process thought. P. Teilhard de Chardin's theory of Christogenesis rests on a theory of the processual development of the universe towards a final convergence in the Omega Point. More formally systematic process theologians variously offer a Christology in which Christ is the primary illustration or occurrence of God's immanent, caring relationship and involved presence in the world. The compatibility of process categories with traditional dogma, however, is not altogether obvious.

[T. C. O'BRIEN]

CHRISTOLYTES (Gr., *Christo* and *lytos,* dissolved, separated), heretics existing probably between 650 and 750.

Only St. John Damascene (PG 94:757) and Constantine Capronimus, cited by Nicopherus of Constantinople (PG 100:288), name the Christolytes, and this suggests the time of their existence. The name comes from the doctrine that Christ set aside human nature with the Ascension. If the Christolytes were the same group as the early *Eutychians, who taught something similar, their date would be mid-5th century. BIBLIOGRAPHY: G. Bareille, DTC 2:2417–18.

[T. C. O'BRIEN]

CHRISTOPHER, ST., possibly a martyr in Lycia, whose cult was widely spread in the East and West. As early as 452 a church in Bithynia was dedicated in his honor. According to the early martyrology, C. was martyred under Decius. Many legends have risen up about him, the most popular, his bearing the Christ child while fording a river, becoming the source of his name, Christbearer. Another legend deals with a cure effected by a drop of his blood; this gave rise to the popular medieval belief that anyone looking upon his picture would be free from harm. He is the patron of travelers. The 1969 revised calendar for the whole Church dropped his feast.

[E. C. HUBBERT]

CHRISTOPHER (d. 904), POPE (or antipope?) from 903. C., cardinal-priest of San Damaso, seized the person of *Leo V, then pope for 3 months, and assumed the papal office for himself. He imprisoned Leo and may have had him murdered. C. is excluded from many lists of the popes because he seized the papacy by force. Nevertheless some have thought that he was truly pope because he was recognized and accepted by the Church for the few months after Leo V had been killed (precise date unknown). This view is based on the mention of C. in the *Liber Pontificalis,* and on a reference made to him as a predecessor by St. *Leo IX, and on C.'s inclusion in a series of portraits of the popes in Rome and in S. Pier-in-Grado, near Pisa. The manner of C.'s death is disputed. After being driven from the papacy by *Sergius III in 904, he either passed his remaining days as a monk or was strangled in prison. BIBLIOGRAPHY: Mann 4:111–118; H. Mann, CE 3:729.

[P. F. MULHERN]

CHRISTOPHER MACASSOLI, BL. (*c.*1415–85), Franciscan. He became a Franciscan Observant in 1435, guardian of the Abbiategrasso friary in 1477, and spent his last years in the friary of Vigevano. His sanctity was recognized by his contemporaries, Aloysius Gonzaga among others. In 1890 Leo XIII permitted an Office and Mass to be celebrated in his honor in the diocese of Vigevano and among the Franciscans. BIBLIOGRAPHY: P. M. Sevesi, *B. Cristoforo Macassoli* (1941); G. Lucchesi, BiblSanct 8:434.

[J. J. SMITH]

CHRISTOPHER MOVEMENT, a challenge "in line with Christian principles" to raise standards of human en-

deavor. Inaugurated (1945) by Maryknoll priest, J. Keller, it evokes individual responsibility and motivates human initiative by directing attention to communications and societal engagements at all levels, esp. in five vital fields: government, education, entertainment, industrial relations and labor management, and the arts, particularly literature in print and in other media. The planned approach is positive, constructive, optimistic, and elevating. The Christophers' motto is: "Better to light one candle than to curse the darkness." The group issues its *Christopher News Notes* seven times yearly, free to any who request them.

[M. R. BROWN]

CHRISTOPHER OF ROMANDIOLA, BL. (C. of Romagna, or of Cahors; d. 1272), disciple of St. Francis of Assisi. Giving up his post as parish priest in Romandiola, C. joined the Franciscans (1215) and was sent (1219) to Aquitaine where he established a house of his order at Cahors, preached against the Albigensians, and distinguished himself for his austerity of life and his care of the lepers. BIBLIOGRAPHY: Butler 4:200; P. Burchi, BiblSanct 4:366–367.

[G. E. CONWAY]

CHRISTUS, PETRUS (*c.*1410–1472 or 1473), Netherlandish painter, most important follower, perhaps pupil, of Jan Van Eyck at Bruges. By simplifying complex Eyckian compositions, he creates more unified spaces for homelier religious scenes (*St. Eloy,* Metropolitan Museum, N.Y.; *Lamentation,* Brussels). His portraits no longer appear before neutral backgrounds, but, consistently lighted, in an interior opened-up space within a broadened stage. (*Sir Edward Grymstone,* National Gallery, London). He transmits Eyck's heritage to Bouts, Ouwater, and Geertgen. BIBLIOGRAPHY: M. J. Friedländer, *Early Netherlandish Painting* (1967) 1:81–90.

[R. BERGMANN]

CHRODEGANG OF METZ, ST. (712–766), abp., liturgist. Chancellor of Charles Martel, nominated bp. of Metz (742) while still a layman, C. continued to fulfill his civil function. Devoted to Bonifacian reform, he founded the abbeys of Gorze and Lorsch. Pope Stephen II made him papal legate to Frankland and granted him the personal title of archbishop. As such he convoked and presided over many councils. It was he who introduced the Roman rite and Gregorian chant into the Frankish Church. He was successful also in organizing his cathedral clergy under an original rule of common life, thereby inaugurating the institution of canons regular. BIBLIOGRAPHY: Hauck 2:54–70; I. Daniele, BiblSanct 4:370–372; M. Viller, DSAM 2:877–878.

[A. CABANISS]

CHROMATIUS OF AQUILEIA, ST. (d. 407), bp. of Aquileia. His name is associated with Rufinus of Aquileia and St. Jerome, both of whom dedicated works to him. He sought to mediate the quarrel over Origen. He knew St. John Chrysostom, whose deposition he tried to have reversed through Honorius's intercession. St. Ambrose consecrated C. bishop in 387 or 388. Of his writings, 17 commentaries on Matthew's Gospel and a homily on the beatitudes are important. BIBLIOGRAPHY: G. Orlandi, NCE 3:665; CCL 9:371–447.

[G. M. COOK]

CHRONICLER, BIBLICAL, the name given to the author of 1–2 Chronicles (1 and 2 Paralipomenon in the Septuagint and Vulgate) and Ezra-Nehemiah. These books (originally one work) are uniform in style, vocabulary, spirit and doctrine, and record religious history from the beginnings of the world to the reforms of Ezra and Nehemiah in post-Exilic Judaism. The priestly and liturgical interests of the chronicler suggest that he was connected with the temple as a Levite or a singer. For him the ideal Israel is a worshiping community, a holy people under a messianic ruler. Emphasis is put on the temple of Zion as the center of the community and on the messianic hopes of Israel which originate from Nathan's prophecy to David (2 Sam 7). Recent research places the lifetime of the Chronicler c.400 B.C., and favors the Jewish tradition that identifies the Chronicler with Ezra. BIBLIOGRAPHY: J. M. Myers, *I and II Chronicles* (1965) 18–40.

[F. J. MONTALBANO]

CHRONICLES, recordings of historical events in the order of their occurrence. Chronicles may be distinguished from annals, a simpler form at times amounting to no more than single-line notations, and from fully developed works of modern history, though the boundaries are not clearly defined. Chronicles have been written from ancient times, but carry particular importance for medieval history. They commonly represent "official" history that is intended to preserve knowledge of the deeds of kings and other important persons, or notable occurrences at monasteries, episcopal sees, etc. Since the clergy were the educated class of the medieval period, they were the authors of virtually all chronicles, whether of the secular or the ecclesiastical sphere. Early in the Christian era, church writers began producing chronicles that combined biblical and classical sources to trace world history from the creation of Adam. Later, chronicles sometimes began with Christ, and years came to be numbered from his (incorrectly calculated) birth. Medieval chronicles generally had little capacity for critical assessment of sources, and their reliability is therefore limited except for their own period. But within those limits they have considerable value. Especially influential with later writers was the *Chronicle* of Eusebius, written in 303 and later expanded by him and then by Jerome. Also well known are such chronicles as the *Ecclesiastical History* (731) *of Bede* and the *Anglo-Saxon Chronicle* (c.890).

[T. EARLY]

CHRONICLES, BOOKS OF. These books, together with Ezra-Nehemiah, originally formed a single compilation. Chronicles in particular consists of a presentation of sacred history beginning with Adam and ending with the decree of Cyrus directing that the Jewish people shall repossess their land and city (2 Chr 36.22–23). In this presentation of sacred history, the following four main parts are to be distinguished: (1) genealogies from Adam to David concentrating primarily on Judah, the house of David, the Levites and the inhabitants of Jerusalem (1 Chr ch. 1–9); (2) an idealized history of David in which his persecution by Saul, his adultery, and the rebellion of his sons are omitted, and in which David is presented primarily as the guardian of the ark, founder of the cult at Jerusalem, and organizer of the cultic personnel. Special prominence is given to the oracle of Nathan (1 Chr ch. 10–29); (3) The history of Solomon, in which the building of the temple and its dedication, the prayer of Solomon and the promises he receives from Yahweh are emphasized (2 Chr ch. 1–9); (4) The history of Judah from the schism to the Exile, in which successive kings are judged by the standard of the ideal set by David. All disasters, including the final defeat, are interpreted as acts of divine retribution, while all successes are viewed as rewards. The sinfulness of the kings (even of Manasseh 2 Chr 33.11–20) is minimized.

The author of this compilation clearly drew freely upon the canonical books from Genesis to Judges, and also upon the earlier complex of Samuel to Kings. Apart from these unacknowledged sources he also refers explicitly to the "Book of the Kings of Israel and Judah" (1 Chr 9.1, etc.), and the "Annals," etc., of Samuel, Nathan, Gad (1 Chr 29.29) as also the "Words" of other prophets. Some at least of the sources he used were of considerable historical value and supply information not available elsewhere. He himself may have been a Levite of the second temple closely identified in outlook with Ezra, and perhaps nearly if not quite contemporaneous with him (c.400). It is noticeable that Judah's glories and victories are ascribed entirely to the force of prayer and devoted observance of the official cult, which secures Yahweh's direct intervention on her behalf. BIBLIOGRAPHY: E. L. Curtis and A. A. Madsen, *Chronicles I-II*, (rev. ed., 1952); H. Cazelles, *Les Livres des Chroniques* (2d ed., 1961); W. A. L. Elmslie, *Chronicles* (1954); M. Noth, *Überlieferungsgeschichtliche Studien I* (1943) 110–180; G. von Rad, *Das Geschichtsbild des chronistischen Werkes* (1930).

[D. J. BOURKE]

CHRONICON EDESSENUM, see EDESSA, CHRONICLE OF.

CHRONICON PASCHALE (*Chronicum Alexandrinum* or *Constantinopolitanum*), name given to a valuable Byzantine chronicle written in the 7th cent. with notes of historical and theological worth. It gave an outline of events from creation to 628 A.D., but not all of the work is extant. The name derives from the Easter reckoning. The author was a Byzantine cleric in the circle of the patriarch Sergius. BIBLIOGRAPHY: H. Leclercq, DACL 3:1554–55; J. M. Hussey, EB 17:353.

[M. C. BRADLEY]

CHRONISTA, liturgical term designating the person (properly a deacon) who chants the narrative portions of the four gospel accounts of the Passion when they are sung solemnly during Holy Week.

[T. M. MCFADDEN]

CHRONOGRAPHER OF 354, THE, the name given to the compiler of a 4th cent. reference work of the almanac type. Only fragmentary MSS are extant, but from them scholars have been able to reconstruct the work almost entirely. It contains the oldest extant martyrology—that of Roman martyrs and other martyrs venerated at Rome. The almanac portion, which gives astronomical and astrological information, is the only extant example of Roman MS miniatures. Other items in the work include a list of the bps. of Rome; a list of the consuls from A.U.C. 245 to A.D. 354; an Easter table from 312 to 411; a list of the urban prefects of Rome from 254 to 354; a world chronicle to 354, and a chronicle of the city of Rome to 324, including a description of the 14 regions. BIBLIOGRAPHY: MGH Auct. ant. 9.1 (1892); H. Stern, *Le Calendrier de 354* (1953).

[M. J. SUELZER]

CHRONOLOGY (OT). Ancient Orientals had no universal chronology; peoples had autonomous chronologies based usually on pivotal events of their own history, e.g., accession years of kings. Israel followed this pattern, dating events by distance in years from Abraham, the Exodus, the building of Solomon's Temple, accession years of kings, from the Babylonian exile, and later, from regnal years of Persian and Syrian kings.

Complications arise from variant readings. Furthermore, some dates given in the OT appear to have symbolic intent more than historical precision, e.g., the ages of the early Patriarchs (Gen 5–12). Uniformly reliable chronology requires comparison of the various systems used, and reconciliation of all of them with the present universal chronology determined from A.D. 1.

Patriarchs. The biblical traditions assign no chronology for the Patriarchs; dating them is possible only by comparison of the contents of the patriarchal narratives with the general cultural history of the ancient Orient. Scholarly opinion now tends to date the patriarchs in the first half of the Middle Bronze Age, i.e., c.2000–1750 B.C., and the descent of the Hebrews into Egypt with the ascendancy there of the Hyksos kings (c.1710–1550 B.C.).

Exodus. The chronology of the Exodus results from relating biblical and extrabiblical data regarding the Pharaoh of the Exodus. The greatest probability is that this Pharaoh was Rameses II (1290–1224 B.C.), and that the Exodus

event itself took place early in his reign (c.1270 B.C.). The 40 years' wandering can be taken as a protracted period embracing two generations (Num 14.26–35).

Conquest of Canaan; Judges; Monarchy. The incidents described in Jos and Jg are more probably contemporaneous than successive. Israelites were present in Canaan in the 5th year of Egypt's Pharaoh Merneptah (c.1220 B.C.). Israel's victory at Megiddo-Taanach (Jg 4–5) occurred c.1125 B.C. Establishment of the monarchy under Saul (c.1020 B.C.) marks Israel's transition to nationhood. The reigns of David and Solomon (1 Kg 2.10–11; 11.42) can be placed respectively from 1000–960–922 B.C.

Divided Monarchy. OT authors use varying systems to date events between Solomon's death and the Babylonian exile. However, abundant archeological data from Assyrian and Babylonian archives offer comparisons ensuring considerable accuracy. Shalmaneser V (727–722 B.C.) and Sargon II (722–705 B.C.) sacked Samaria and destroyed the northern kingdom (Israel), deporting the survivors, in 721 B.C. Nebuchadnezzar twice sacked Jerusalem and exiled the Jews to Babylon, in 598 and 587 B.C.

Exile; Post-Exilic Period. Cyrus of Persia took Babylon in 539 B.C. and allowed the exiles to return to Judah in 538 B.C. Zerubbabel led reconstruction of the Temple 520–515 B.C. Nehemiah's civil governorship began in the 20th year of King Artaxerxes of Persia (i.e., 445 B.C.). Ezra's chronology is uncertain; alternative possibilities are 458, 432, 428, and 398 B.C.

The interval from Ezra to the Maccabees is obscure. Antiochus IV Epiphanes, Seleucid king of Syria, pillaged Jerusalem in 167 B.C.; the Maccabean revolt occurred 166–134 B.C. The last event mentioned in the OT is the accession of John Hyrcanus as ethnarch of Judah, 134–104 B.C. (1 Mac 16). The last book of the OT written is the apocryphal (deuterocanonical) Wisdom of Solomon, c.50 B.C. BIBLIOGRAPHY: J. Finegan, *Handbook of Biblical Chronology,* (1964); F. Schmidtke, NCE 3:672–673.

[T. E. CRANE]

CHRYSANTHUS AND DARIA, SS. (d. late 3d cent.?), martyrs. These saints were venerated in Rome from the 4th cent., and some basis in fact probably underlies their cult, but the details of their romantic *passio* (of late origin) are evidently legendary. Chrysanthus, a wealthy youth of Alexandria, is supposed to have been converted in Rome. His pagan father, seeking to turn him away from his new faith, proposed that he should marry Daria, a priestess of Minerva. But instead of inducing him to give up his faith, Daria herself became a Christian. The two married, agreeing to live in continence. Many pagans were converted by their efforts. They were martyred together in a sandpit on the Via Salaria where they were stoned and buried alive. BIBLIOGRAPHY: Butler 4:196–197; P. Allard, DACL 3.1:1560–68.

[R. B. ENO]

CHRYSELEPHANTINE, colossal, sumptuous wooden statues covered with plates of ivory and sheets of gold in Greek temples of the 5th and early 4th cent. B.C. Outstanding were the Athena Parthenos and Olympian Zeus by Phidias and the Hera of Argos by Polycleitus. BIBLIOGRAPHY: G. M. A. Richter, *Sculpture and Sculptors of the Greeks* (1957).

[M. J. DALY]

CHYRSIPPUS OF JERUSALEM, (d.479), ecclesiastical writer and preacher who was born in Cappadocia and educated in Syria, perhaps in Antioch. He went with his two brothers to Jerusalem and became a monk under the direction of St. Euthymius the Great (428). At the behest of the Empress Eudoxia, who had resided in Jerusalem since 440, C. was ordained a priest (*c.*456) and for 12 years was guardian of the relics of the True Cross. Of his many sermons and panegyrics, four have survived. BIBLIOGRAPHY: G. Bardy, DHGE 12:784–785.

[F. J. MURPHY]

CHRYSOBERGES, ANDREW (d. 1451), Greek Dominican scholar, abp. of Rhodes. One of three brothers who became Catholics and Dominicans under the influence of Demetrius *Cydones C. taught philosophy in Padua and took part in several papal missions concerned with the Byzantine Church. In 1432 he was named abp. of Rhodes and participated in the debates at the Council of *Florence.

[G. T. DENNIS]

CHRYSOBULL (Gr. *chrysoboullos logos,* a declaration bearing a gold seal), the most solemn, official document issued by Byzantine emperors. Sometimes they were written in gold ink on purple-dyed parchment, and the emperor always signed in red. The attached gold seal bore on one side an image of the reigning temporal emperor and on the other, one of Christ, the eternal emperor.

[G. T. DENNIS]

CHRYSOGONUS, ST. (d. *c.*304?), martyr named in the Canon of the Mass. Little is known of him; he was probably martyred in Aquileia, and in the 5th cent. his cult was introduced at Rome where a church in Trastevere bears his name. According to a legend dating from the 6th cent. he was a Roman official and the Christian teacher of St. Anastasia. BIBLIOGRAPHY: Butler 4:418–419; E. Josi, BiblSanct 4:306–308.

[R. B. ENO]

CHRYSOLORAS, MANUEL (d. 1415), Byzantine humanist. A close friend of Emperor *Manuel II, C. served on several diplomatic missions to Europe. In 1396 he began teaching Greek in Florence, where he attracted the leading Italian humanists. His translations into Latin and particularly his Greek grammar (*Erotemata*) were very instrumental in the dissemination of Greek learning in the West. He also served on a number of diplomatic missions for the popes. BIBLIOGRAPHY: G. Cammelli, *Manuele Crisolora* (1941).

[G. T. DENNIS]

CHRYSOSTOM, JOHN, ST., see JOHN CHRYSOSTOM, ST.

CHRYSOSTOM OF SAINT-LO, JOHN (1594–1646), Franciscan, spiritual director. He entered the Third Order Regular of St. Francis at the age of 16. After holding various administrative positions he became provincial. He was respected as a spiritual director and was confessor to several members of the nobility. Three short works of his writings on the spiritual life remain, including *Divers traités spirituels et méditatifs.* He is regarded as a leader in the area of French spirituality in the 17th cent., esp. in connection with the school of Norman mystics. BIBLIOGRAPHY: J. C. Willke, NCE 3:676–677; R. Heurtevent, DSAM 2.1:881–885.

[V. GILLIGAN]

CHTHONIC DIVINITIES, deities of the earth or underworld. The term is from the Greek *chthōn,* earth. In addition to the Olympian gods and sea gods, ancient Greece had gods of the earth, often associated particularly with fertility. Gaea (or Ge), daughter of Chaos, was the Greek goddess of earth, identified by the Romans with Tellus, and was honored as the mother and nourisher of all things. Another chthonic divinity was Demeter, the goddess of fertility and harvest, who was honored in the Eleusinian Mysteries. Latins identified her with Ceres, goddess of the growth of food plants. In the Eleusinian Mysteries, Persephone, the daughter of Demeter by Zeus, appeared as Kore. She was said to have been seized by Pluto and held captive in the underworld. Demeter's grief led her to neglect the earth and vegetation died. Pluto eventually allowed the return of Persephone, but she had to go back to the underworld for four months each year, a myth symbolizing an agricultural cycle. The Greeks knew various other earth deities, such as Hades, god of the lower world who was married to Persephone. At Athens, Zeus was associated with a god Chthonios in certain sacrifices. In worship, sacrifices to earth deities were commonly made by burial, as sacrifices to gods of the air were made by burning or to sea gods by casting into the water.

Religions of other ancient cultures had earth deities comparable to those of Greece, related both to fertility (surface) and the dead (lower earth).

[T. EARLY]

CHUR, MONASTERY OF, abbey in the Diocese of Chur, Switzerland. Before 1149 Conrad, bp. of Chur, gave possession of the monastery to the Premonstratensians from Roggenburg and relocated the nuns of the original double monastery at St. Hilary, not far from the abbey. The monastery was suppressed in 1538 and the community found refuge in Liechtenstein. In 1624 Chur was restored. The last abbot gave the monastery back to the bp. of Chur. It is now used as the diocesan seminary. BIBLIOGRAPHY: Cottineau 1:831; N. Backmund, DHGE 13:213–221.

[A. P. DEEGAN]

CHURCH, etymologically, house of the Lord (from Middle Eng. *chirice,* Old Eng. *cirice,* and ultimately from late Gr. *kyriakon,* of the Lord). Apart from designating a building for worship, usually Christian, the term is variously applied to religious associations. (1) In legal or political usage the Church may refer to the established Church, e.g., in England. In discussion of the relations of Church and State both terms have an abstract meaning, Church referring to religious association and interests of citizens in contrast to State, their civil association and interests. Any specific religious body may be referred to as a Church in the same legal context. (2) The sociology of religion uses various classifications for religious associations. Church is contrasted with sect or mysticism, e.g., by E. *Troeltsch. The bodies classified as Churches are more institutionalized and stress historical origins, confessions of faith, form of government, and use of sacraments and liturgy (see SECT). (3) Christian ecclesiastical use of the term varies with theological presuppositions. There are two main contrasting uses. In RC terms the Church is the Roman Catholic Church, which believes itself to be the one true Church in historical and doctrinal continuity with the Church as Christ founded it. In this identification the visible institutional Church and the Church of the NT are regarded as one. The language and viewpoint of Vatican Council II, however, opened the way to a less rigid acceptance in recognizing the authentic ecclesial elements in other Christian bodies. While there have been and are minor Protestant groups that have identified themselves as the only true Church, the general Protestant use of the term is more comprehensive. Both historically and doctrinally Protestants refuse to identify the one true Church with any institutional body. The Church is the Church of the gospel; it is the community of believers; it exists wherever the true gospel is preached. Visible forms and institutions, always reformable, vary. The Church is the Church universal and includes the various Churches or denominations. Each specific Christian body may be called a Church, in the sense and to the degree that it is an authentic expression of the Church that Christ intended.

[T. C. O'BRIEN]

CHURCH (GENERAL HISTORY). The historical outline presented here concentrates on church history in Western Christendom. The persons, events, and themes indicated are a record of the past and an explanation of what there is both of unity and of diversity in church life in the present. (See EASTERN CHURCHES.)

THE CHURCH TO THE REFORMATION

The history of the Church in the West for 16 centuries is the history of one historical reality. By the 13th cent. that Church had become finally separated from the Church in the East. With the Reformation the external unity of the Church in the West also was shattered, so that the Reformation is the central dividing mark in Western Church history.

Pentecost to the Edict of Milan. The only actual annals or chronicles in this period, until Eusebius of Caesarea (260–340), the father of church history, are the NT Acts of the Apostles. Together with some pastoral and polemical writings, Acts show that Pentecost began a period of phenomenal expansion. The Church became a recognizable entity in the Roman world: early there were *local Churches, not only those addressed by Paul, but others in Italy, Gaul, Spain, Germany, the Danubian provinces, North Africa, and Egypt. They were organized either monarchically under the bishop or under a college of presbyters presided over by the bishop. From Clement of Rome, Ignatius, Irenaeus, Tertullian, and in the *rebaptism controversy of Cyprian of Carthage with Pope Stephen I, there is evidence of the See of Rome consciously exercising her primacy as teacher and center of unity. The doctrinal life of the Church manifested itself in the composition of the Gospels and the other NT books. Internally the Judaizing Christians were put down; the need to face the pagan world motivated the apologists, esp. Justin Martyr and Irenaeus. A further test was the first of the perennial appearances of dualism, in the form of Manichaeism. *Tertullian opposed Marcion, who separated the God of law in the OT from the God of love in the NT; but Tertullian embraced the apocalyptic doctrines of the *Montanists. The first efforts at positive theological elaborations came from Clement of Alexandria and his disciple Origen. The Church, regarded as a force inimical to the interests of Rome, lived in the catacombs as imperial persecutions made this the age of martyrs, who were revered as living with Christ, and whose intercession was sought. With the conversion of Constantine and the Edict of Milan (313) the persecutions ceased and, save for the brief interlude under Julian the Apostate, the Church came into a favored position in the Empire and manifested its presence by the splendid edifices that were built for the worship of God.

The 4th to the 7th Century. Benevolent as it was in fact, Constantine's attitude toward the Church marked the beginning of a caesaropapism, stifling to the Byzantine Church—e.g., in the laws and conduct of Justinian and in the beginnings of the schism between East and West—but also foreshadowing the conflicts between medieval popes and emperors. Nevertheless, from Constantine on the Church flourished. Monasticism was born, first in the East through Anthony, Athanasius, and Basil, in Ireland through Patrick, and on the Continent through Martin of Tours, Benedict, and Gregory the Great. The monks contributed mightily to the missionary activities which would lead to the conversion of all of Western Europe. With the baptism of Clovis (496), Gaul was brought into the Church; the evangelization of England was resumed in 596 by Augustine of Canterbury; gradually the barbarians, some Arian, some pagan, who invaded the empire, became Catholics. The doctrinal life of the Church was no less intense; there was a continuous defense of orthodoxy and a growth in theological thought. In Africa the struggle with the *Donatists, which dragged on for centuries, was complicated by political issues, as were the Christological controversies that led to the first great *ecumenical councils: Nicaea (325) and Constantinople I (381), against Arianism; Ephesus (431), against Nestorianism; Chalcedon (451), against Monophysitism; Constantinople III (680), against Monothelitism. These centuries are also the era of the Fathers. In the East there were Athanasius, Basil, Gregory of Nazianzus, Gregory of Nyssa, John Chrysostom. In the West Jerome labored to provide a sound text of the Scriptures; Augustine's writings against Manichaeism and Pelagianism set the tone of theological thought in Europe for centuries; Gregory the Great's moral writings had lasting influence on the practice of the Christian life.

Medieval Period (600–1500). In these centuries, the Church passed through cycles of reverses and reform in all phases of its life.

Church Expansion. At the outset expansion met serious setbacks. Beginning about 600 Islam tore away North Africa and most of Asia from the Church and even extended itself into Spain. The Iconoclast emperors in the East beginning with Leo III (717–741) began a process of alienation between the Byzantine patriarchates and Rome, which by the early 13th cent. had become complete schism (see SCHISM, EAST-WEST). Missionary activity continued to effect the conversion of all of Europe: begun earlier by St. Boniface (d. 442) and St. Columba (d. 597), it spread to the Slavs with SS. Cyril (d. 869) and Methodius (d. 885); the Magyars and Poles were converted by the 10th cent.; the Scandinavian countries by the 11th; and those east of the Baltic by the 12th or 13th.

Papal Rule. Because of the prestige of Gregory the Great and the absence of civil authority, a process begun in his reign (590–604) led to the formation of the States of the Church. The pope became a secular ruler, and a problem new in the West, the conflict between pope and princes, had its beginnings. The alliance of the papacy with the Frankish monarchy in the person of Pepin III culminated in the coronation by Pope Leo III of Charlemagne (800) as the first Holy Roman Emperor. Although during the reign of the Carolingians there was notable progress, with their collapse the papacy became a chattel within the feudal scheme, first of the Roman princes, then of the German monarchy. This situation was arrested beginning with the pontificate of Leo IX (1048–54), during which a reforming decree on papal elections was enacted. Church reform, which owed much to the monastic foundation of Cluny (910), reached its peak in the work of the great Hildebrand, Gregory VII (1073–85),

and extended not only to the opposition to Emperor Henry IV over lay investiture, but also to all levels of ecclesiastical life. Urban II (1088–99) continued it and gained new moral prestige for the papacy by inaugurating the Crusades (1095).

By the second half of the 12th cent. the Gregorian reform had begun to lose impetus and the papacy became involved in resisting the absolutism of Frederick Barbarossa (1152–90). A new vigor emerged with the election of Innocent III, whose reign (1198–1216) marked the summit of papal sovereignty, and whose reform was crowned by the work of Lateran Council IV (1215). Under Innocent the Church was institutionalized by the canonists. His policies of centralization and control were not wisely carried out by his successors. The papal right to nominate all bishops, the right of provision, was exploited for financial gain; under Innocent IV (1243–54) heavy papal taxation began. At the Council of Lyons I (1245) he also successfully excommunicated Frederick II, thus achieving a kind of victory of pope over emperor. The extreme expression of papal claims to supremacy came with Boniface VIII's bull *Unam sanctam* (1302) in the disputes with Philip IV of France. There followed immediately, however, the election of the Frenchman Clement V (1305–14) and the beginnings of the *Babylonian captivity of the papacy at Avignon (1309–77). Much antipapal sentiment resulted; it was articulated by *Marsilius of Padua and *William of Ockam and put into practice with England's statutes of *Praemunire and Provisors. No sooner had the Pope returned to Rome than the *Great Western Schism (1378–1417) erupted with the scandal of rival claimants to the papacy. Among the attempts to heal it was the theory of *conciliarism that dominated the Councils of *Pisa (1409), *Constance (1414), and *Basel (1431–49). A degree of reform was achieved under Martin V (1417–31) and Eugene IV (1431–47), who also fashioned a brief reunion with the Greeks at the Council of Florence (1438–40), but *Gallicanism was born in France and everywhere the prestige of the papacy dimmed. In the period of the Renaissance, the popes presented themselves to the world as unabashedly secular potentates. This had its benefits in the form of papal patronage of the arts, but the worldliness and corruption surrounding the papacy under Innocent VIII (1484–92), Alexander VI (1492–1503), and Julius II (1503–13) cried out for reform.

Christian Life. The 7th through the 12th cent. were a monastic era. Early fervor gave way to a period of decadence, but in 910 Cluny emerged. The strong federation of Cluniac houses had parallels elsewhere (see MONASTICISM). In the 11th cent. the renewal was centered in Cîteaux, whose greatest representative, Bernard of Clairvaux (1090–1153), by his writing and preaching powerfully affected Christian devotion, esp. to Mary and to the Passion of Christ. A reform movement of clerics, the Order of Prémontré was founded in 1120. When the older orders failed to meet the needs of the times, in the 13th cent. the two great mendicant orders, the Dominicans and the Franciscans (soon to be followed by others of their type —Carmelites, Augustinians, and Servites), came into being. St. Dominic's ideal was to fulfill the need for doctrinal preaching; St. Francis of Assisi gave the noblest expression to the lay evangelical movements of the time. The bitter years of Avignon and the Western Schism saw also factious rivalries among the mendicants and a decline in their ideals, a decline hastened by the general havoc worked by the Black Death.

Christian life was also deeply affected by *apocalypticism and by the spiritual renewal fostered by groups of laity. The Franciscan *Spirituals, the *Fraticelli (see JOACHIMISM), and the *Flagellants often assailed the institutional Church and its sacraments. Some of the lay movements, e.g., the Humiliati and the Waldenses, stressed reform through evangelical poverty; they met with ecclesiastical resistance for their preaching. A more theologically guided poverty movement was inspired by John Wycliffe (see LOLLARDS), whose ideas were followed by Jan Hus (see HUSSITES) in Bohemia. The Brothers and Sisters of the Free Spirit, as well as the *Beghards and Beguines, concentrated on a spiritual renewal through a more intense, personal, devotional life. At the end of the 14th cent. the *Devotio moderna fostered by the *Brethren of the Common Life was a religious revival in the same spirit of personal prayer and sanctification.

Christian Thought. Such learning as survived in the early centuries of this era was due to the monk-missionaries. Under Charlemagne, however, Alcuin, himself from the cathedral school of York, presided over the Carolingian renaissance. His pupil Rabanus Maurus made Fulda a source of ecclesiastical learning in Germany. Rabanus also was involved in doctrinal disputes with *Gottschalk on predestination and with Paschasius Radbertus on the Eucharist. In the period of the Gregorian reform the cathedral schools, like that at Chartres, flourished. By the end of the 12th cent. these schools had begun to decline, but the seeds of future glory had been planted. St. Anselm (c. 1033–1109) had given strong impetus to the intellectualizing of theology; Gratian had composed his Decretals; Peter Lombard (c. 1100–60), his *Sentences;* and Peter Abelard (1079–1142), his *Sic et non.* The 13th cent. saw the full flower of scholasticism, through the translation of the complete text of Aristotle's works, and the emergence of such great universities as Paris, Oxford, and Bologna. This was the environment of William of Auvergne (c. 1180–1249), Alexander of Hales (c. 1170–1245), Bonaventure (1221–74), Albert the Great (c. 1200–80), Robert Kilwardby (d. 1279), John Peckham (c. 1225–92). Thomas Aquinas (c. 1225–74) was able to give to the Church his monumental synthesis of Christian thought. There followed, however, the parceling of theology into schools and the gradual ascendancy of *nominalism, with an adulteration of the understanding of the Christian message. The rationale of the Devotio moderna was a kind of anti-intellectual reaction to the empty rationalism of nominalism. The Renaissance itself paralleled the secularization of the papacy in the tendency to divorce learning and life from the influence of the Church.

PROTESTANTISM

The abuses in doctrine and in life that had festered and spread in the Renaissance Church demanded remedy and reform. The Reformation by its *formal principle, the sole authority of Scripture, and by its *material principle, justification by grace through faith alone, revolutionized Christian history in the West. The external unity of the Church was shattered. Roman Catholicism and Protestantism became two divergent views on man's relationship to God, the sacraments and esp. the Eucharist, the ministry, and the Church, as well as two opposed practices of the Christian life, in devotion, liturgy, and discipline. Both Protestants and Catholics profess the "one, holy, catholic, and apostolic Church"; that profession has a dimension of historical continuity with the Church established by Christ. But with the Reformation, church history becomes an account of historically different Churches. The term Protestant originated from the *protestatio* at the Diet of Speyer (1529) of Lutheran princes against the policies of Charles V. It came to be accepted as a designation for the Churches that had their immediate or remote origins in the Reformation inaugurated by Martin Luther. Protestantism is here used to group such Churches. (See PROTESTANTISM for the presentation of doctrinal themes of agreement and diversity.)

The Various Protestant Traditions. The Reformation, inaugurated by Martin Luther, immediately gave rise on the Continent to three main traditions. Luther's own doctrines were most faithfully followed by Lutheran or Evangelical Churches, mainly in Germany and in Scandinavia. The reform teachings first of Zwingli, then of John Calvin, became the doctrines of the *Reformed Church, mainly in Switzerland, the Rhine Valley, the Netherlands, and among the Huguenots of France. The radical or left wing of the Reformation was represented by the various groups, often of differing beliefs, in Germany and Switzerland, called Anabaptists. Their heritage was perpetuated by the Mennonites and similar groups (see REFORMATION). In the British Isles the Church of England, first under Henry VIII, then finally under Elizabeth I, became a national Church. Within Anglicanism some defend its Protestant character, i.e., adherence to Reformation ideas and to Calvinist influences; others stress its Catholic continuity. Under John Knox, the Church of Scotland became a model of Presbyterianism (see REFORMATION). Removed from the mainstream, yet often classified as Protestant, was the small rationalistic and Unitarian movement called *Socinianism.

During the reign of Elizabeth I (1558–1603) the Puritan party arose in the Church of England, protesting against ritual and episcopacy. Puritans who separated from the C of E gave rise to Congregationalism. Also Congregational in their concept of the Church, were the Baptists, named for their practice of *believer's baptism, and originating c.1608. To the Nonconformist or *free Churches in the 17th cent. were joined the Society of Friends (Quakers) founded by George Fox, whose ideas reflected many of the spiritualizing and experiential emphases of the left-wing Reformation. In the 18th cent. on the Continent the Moravians were a renewal of the pre-Reformation *Unitas Fratrum. In England John Wesley formed the first Methodist societies, at first as circles for a more personalized spiritual life within the C of E (see METHODISM). The Methodist revival became a powerful factor in the development of American Protestantism. Other groups arose in the Protestant background, e.g., the Catholic Apostolic Church, Swedenborgians, Mormons, Adventists, and Jehovah's Witnesses, that do not have an obvious connection with the mainstream of Protestantism (see CHURCH, U.S. HISTORY). Pentecostalism had its remote origins in the Holiness interpretation of Wesley's doctrine (see HOLINESS MOVEMENT). While adhering to many common Protestant teachings, the Pentecostal movement is sometimes classified as a "third force" (i.e., distinct from Catholicism and Protestantism) because of its own specific doctrines.

Doctrinal and Theological Trends. The need to enunciate the essentials of Reformation teaching and the exigencies of controversy arose in the Reformation era itself. The 16th and 17th cents. were an era of *confessions of faith. The Anglican Thirty-Nine Articles reflected both the Lutheran *Augsburg Confession and the theology of the Reformed tradition. The principal Lutheran confessions were gathered in the Book of Concord (1580). In theology, Lutheran orthodoxy was marked by a highly scholastic method and form; Johann *Gerhard was its greatest exponent. The Reformed confessions of faith relied on Calvin's *Institutes of the Christian Religion (see GALLICAN CONFESSIONS; SCOTS CONFESSION; BELGIC CONFESSION; SECOND HELVETIC CONFESSION; HEIDELBERG CATECHISM). Calvinist theological orthodoxy was marked by the development of *covenant theology. The Synod of Dort reflected this scholastic Calvinism in the canons directed against Arminianism. The *Westminster Standards were patterned on the mode and content of the canons of Dort. The *Caroline Divines in the C of E emphasized ancient Catholic elements as essentials of Anglicanism.

In reaction to the speculative concern for orthodoxy, Pietism arose in the 18th cent., with the theologizing of A. *Franck, the devotional writing of P. *Spener, and by its spread affected most of the Protestant Churches. The Pietist influence first on Methodism, then on the revival movement in all the Churches, remained a formative influence on Protestantism; it also largely inspired the missionary expansion. The effect of the Enlightenment and deism was to dilute the faith of many church members, even clergy, into a mere nominal adherence to Christian belief. After the cold rationalism of the Enlightenment came the subjectivism or romanticism of F. Schleiermacher, the development of emphasis on the socio-historical interpretation of Christianity, and the growth of biblical criticism. These were prominent features of *liberal theology, with its stress on the historical, ethical, and subjective interpretation of the gospel. The work of E. Troeltsch, A. Ritschl, and A. Harnack were particularly formative of the liberal spirit. The liberalism of the 19th cent. was not universally accepted. The strength of conservative, evangelical Protestantism manifested its resistance to liberal theology and led to the fundamentalist-modernist controversies that continue in the 20th century. Both the Oxford movement and the evangelical reaction to it may be viewed as a conservative concern for the true essentials of the Christian Church. In the post–World War I era, with the confidence of liberal theology shattered, the theological movement called *neo-orthodoxy arose, led by Karl Barth. It was a reassertion of the doctrines of Reformation teaching and above all of the primacy of the transcendent word of God. The impetus to regain the Christian gospel as a unique divine revelation affected all the major 20th-cent. theologians (see TILLICH, P.; NYGREN, A.; AULÉN, G.; CULLMANN, O.; BULTMANN SCHOOL).

Ecumenical Protestantism. A desire for church unity was a part of the Reformation. Politics and polemics, however, built walls of separation both between Protestants and Catholics and between Protestants and Protestants. The Reformation principle *cuius regio, eius religio, and the assumption of the need for unity of religion in the State, also served to harden division and to promote persecution of dissidents. The missionary expansion of Protestantism at first reflected divisions and rivalries. Begun under the Pietist impulse, esp. by the Moravians, the Protestant missionary endeavor widened until nearly all denominations became involved (see MISSIONS). The missionary experience itself was the source of the modern ecumenical movement. By the late 19th cent. Protestant missionaries had extended their work throughout the world, and new Churches had been formed in many countries. The mission societies were often experiments in cooperation, and the realization of missionaries of the need to present Christianity as united led to the Edinburgh meeting in 1910 of the *International Missionary Council. A missionary bishop of the Episcopal Church, Charles *Brent, was its inspirer. Out of this beginning grew *Life and Work, *Faith and Order, and eventually (1948) the *World Council of Churches. Besides the denominational mergers, actual and planned, that have resulted from the ecumenical movement, it has had other broad effects. Among them has been the liturgical movement within Protestantism, a deeper examination of central ecclesiological questions, the Church and its mission, Scripture and tradition, the ministry. These inquiries have not been conducted in denominational isolation or in a polemical spirit. They have profited the Protestant Churches themselves; they have opened the way to Roman Catholic self-evaluation and broadened its Catholic theological perspective. They have created a better appreciation of the dimensions of Christian disunity and a sense of urgency for Christian unity. (The specific Protestant bodies are the subject of special articles.)

ROMAN CATHOLICISM

The term *Roman Catholic was first used disparagingly by the Reformers, but then came to be accepted as an official title. The Roman Catholic Church is the continuing institution and the body of believers who, despite the Reformation, remained in communion with the Pope.

Roman Catholic Reform. What has been ineptly called a "Counter-Reformation" was an inner reform seeking to remedy the same ills that created receptivity to the Reformation. This inner revival had begun first as a renewal of Christian life before the Reformation, and it continued. In Spain there were reforming bishops, Fernando de Talavera y Mendoza and Francisco Ximenez de Cesneros; and at Salamanca a vigorous resurgence of theology, esp. of *Thomism. In Italy there were St. Philip Neri and the Oratory of Divine Love; the Theatines of St. Cajetan; the Barnabites of Antonio Maria Zaccaria; the Somaschi of St. Jerome Aemiliani; Ursuline nuns were founded by Angela Merici. In 1540 the Jesuits, with their Ignatian spirituality, their complete availability to the Holy See, and their educational system, came into existence. A strict congregation of Benedictines (the Camaldolese) and an austere branch of Franciscans (the Capuchins) were founded and the Augustinians were reformed, esp. under Girolamo *Seripando; Teresa of Avila and John of the Cross established the Discalced Carmelites. When the Church addressed itself to the issues of doctrine and practice raised by the Reformation, the inspiration behind the reform movement within the Church made itself felt. The Council of Trent (1545–63) succeeded against all odds in enunciating the Church's teaching and in fashioning instruments of practical reform because of the great popes of the period, Paul III (1534–49), Julius III (1550–55), Paul IV (1555–59), Pius IV (1559–65), and the devotion of learned and loyal conciliar fathers. In the same era the sustained purposefulness brought success to new missionary efforts; side by side with Spanish and Portuguese colonizers went the friars of the mendicant orders as well as the Jesuits, to evangelize the New World and the Far East. Here unfortunately persecution and the Chinese Rites controversy, which led to the imposition of European ways on the missionary activity, did much harm to the effort.

After Trent the effort at inner reform continued, esp. under Pius V (1566–72), Gregory XIII (1572–85), and Sixtus V (1585–90). In Germany Catholic recovery was aided enormously by St. Peter Canisius (1521–97) and his catechisms. St. Charles Borromeo (1538–84) in Italy was the personification of Tridentine reform decrees. St. Robert Bellarmine (1542–1621) led RC apologetics against Reformation thinking. In France there were St. Francis de Sales (1567–1622), De Bérulle (1575–1629), De Condren (1588–1641), Olier (1608–57), St. John Eudes (1601–80),

and St. Vincent de Paul (1580–1660). Cardinal Hosius (1504–79) and the Jesuits saved Poland for the Church; in Hungary the leader was Cardinal Pazmany (1570–1637). The ultimately vain disputes of the *Congregatio de auxiliis (1597–1607) were a setback to theological progress. The political upheavals that were part of the Reformation brought on the Thirty Years' War (1618–48), which intensified Catholic-Protestant bitterness and losses to Catholic political power and property.

The Thirty Years' War to the French Revolution: 1648–1709. Two different sets of crises, internal theological quarrels and the attempts of kings to enslave the Church, left it weakened at the eve of the French Revolution. The philosophical developments of the Enlightenment and the revolutions in scientific thought existed apart from any ecclesiastical auspices. The case of Galileo evidenced the suspicion and hostility of churchmen toward science. The deists and Encyclopedists successfully discredited the Church in the minds of the educated. Meanwhile the intellectual energies of churchmen were expended in controversies occasioned by Jansenism and Quietism. The moral rigorism of Jansenism left its influence, perhaps into the 20th century. These movements were also rallying points for Gallicanism and had political consequences. Roman authority was openly challenged at this time by the Bourbon Kings in France. Gallicanism dated back to the days of Avignon; Louis XIV made it a political doctrine amounting to the headship of the monarch over the Church. A German rebellion against Rome received its rationale from Johann Nikolaus von Hontheim (1701–90), under the name Febronius, whose teachings were in fact put into practice by Joseph II under the influence of the Enlightenment. Both Febronianism and Josephinism were resisted by the popes. The same sort of interference, along with the hatred of deists and Jansenists, underlay the outlawing of the Jesuits in Portugal, France, and Spain. To this the Holy See acceded, with Clement XIV (1769–74) officially suppressing them in 1773.

In these years too, however, the Passionists were founded by St. Paul of the Cross (1694–1775), the Redemptorists by St. Alphonsus Liguori (1696–1787), the Brothers of the Christian Schools by St. John Baptist de la Salle (1651–1719); there were also St. Benedict Joseph Labre, St. Leonard of Port-Maurice, and St. Louis Grignon de Monfort. It was also the era of the popularization of the devotion to the Sacred Heart after the apparitions to St. Margaret Mary Alacoque (1647–90), which did much to counteract the teachings of the Jansenists in the devotional life of the Church.

Century of Liberalism: 1789–1870. From the time of the French Revolution the forces of liberalism were most often openly and violently hostile to the Church, the response of the churchmen was usually, but perhaps inevitably, defensive and reactionary.

Assaults on the Church. Through the Revolution the Church lost all its properties in France; the *Civil Constitution of the Clergy stripped the Church of its rights; there were bloody persecutions, a *Constitutional Church, and finally the replacement of Catholicism by the cult of reason. With Napoleon Bonaparte the damage was legally undone through the Concordat published in 1802; but, by the subsequent attachment of the Organic Articles and Napoleon's personal interference, papal power in France was thwarted. In 1809 the Papal States were annexed to the Empire and Pius VII made prisoner. When he was released upon Napoleon's exile in 1814, not only had the Church lost much property, but the universities (Salamanca, Sorbonne, Alcalá, Coimbra, Bologna, Louvain) had been secularized, the faculties of theology abolished, monasteries destroyed or emptied, and many religious orders decimated or weakened.

The so-called restoration of the Church was a struggle against liberalism by popes who could not but identify with the absolutist, monarchist ideas of the *ancien régime*. Not only were they temporal rulers, who had suffered at the hands of the revolutionaries, but the forces of liberalism were anti-clerical and predominantly devoted to destroying the Church as an influence in human affairs. Unfortunately, papal resistance put the Church out of touch with the movement of history and the sentiments of mankind, for the liberals alone seemed intent on facing the real political and social ills. Papal opposition to liberalism showed itself in the condemnation of F. Lamennais (1782–1854) by Gregory XVI (1831–46). Pius IX (1846–78) condemned the teachings of rationalism, liberalism, and indifferentism in his *Syllabus of Errors* (1864). He became a victim of some of the forces he sought to oppose in the Risorgimento, and saw Rome itself captured (1870) and papal temporal sovereignty lost by the Law of Guarantees (1871). An exception to the damaging effect on the Church was in Germany. There the prince-bishops finally disappeared from ecclesiastical life. Concordats in Bavaria, Prussia, Hannover, and the Rhineland led, because of papal firmness, to a clear establishment of the papal primacy over the German Church. In 1848 the Congress of Mainz made a move toward promoting Catholic ideas in social-political life, which had its bearing on the foundation of Centrum, a Catholic political party, in 1859. Catholic life and learning flourished with leaders like F. Stolberg (1750–1819), F. Schlegel (1772–1829), J. von Görres (1776–1848), and J. *Möhler (1796–1838).

Inner Life of the Church. Politically perplexed and harassed as the Church was throughout this era, the Church's own life was strengthened. Catholics reacted to the continued mistreatment of the popes with a devotion to the person of the Holy Father that became a characteristic of Catholicism for the next century. In 1814 the Jesuits were restored; during the 19th cent. many new religious orders were founded, e.g., the Salesians; of the older orders, the Dominicans were reformed by H. Lacordaire and A. Jandel and the Benedictines revitalized by Dom Guéranger. The ministry of the Church was enriched by the holiness of St.

John Vianney, the Curé d'Ars (1786–1859) and St. John Bosco (1815–88). The Society for the Propagation of the Faith was established by Pauline Marie Jaricot (1799–1862). The expansion of the Church took on a new aspect in the great century of immigration to the U.S., Canada, and Australia. The sons and daughters of the immigrants became the source of a new vitality for the Church. Mission activity was increased, often with great suffering, in the Orient and in Africa, notably by the Holy Ghost Fathers, White Fathers, Society for the African Missions, and Scheut Fathers. Finally, on the initiative of Pius IX, two dogmatic pronouncements were made. In 1854 Pius personally proclaimed as dogma the Immaculate Conception of Mary (4 years afterward the apparitions at Lourdes occurred). He also convoked Vatican Council I (1869). It was attended by a larger body of bishops than had attended any previous council. Before it was suspended (1870), its work included proclamation of papal infallibility as a dogma and a series of pronouncements on the soundness of reason, the transcendence of faith, and the relationship between the two.

Between the Two Vatican Councils: 1870–1963. The century between the two Vatican Councils was an age of papal leadership. The popes directed the Church in the spheres of politics, social and doctrinal teaching, and practice in an effort to reach where possible, or to confront where necessary an alienated world.

Social Teaching. Leo XIII ended the reactionary attitude toward liberalism by teaching Catholics, e.g., in the encyclical *Immortale Dei* (1885), to exercise their rights and powers as citizens in the secularist states. In the encyclical *Rerum novarum* (1891) he condemned atheistic communism. He dealt with the *Kulturkampf of Bismarck; faced anti-Catholic policies of the Third Republic in France; and refused to submit papal sovereignty to the Italian monarchy. The firmness of Pius X against the government of Combes and the *Associations Cultuelles* in France meant material loss to the Church but established freedom from state interference. Benedict XV staunchly refused to take sides during World War I; he strove rather for peace and the alleviation of suffering. Pius XI reestablished the relations of the Holy See with many governments by a series of concordats and solved the Roman Question on papal territorial sovereignty through the Lateran Treaty (1929). He condemned the persecution of the Church in Spain and Mexico; denounced the excesses of state absolutism in Benito Mussolini's Fascist Italy in the encyclical *Non abbiamo bisogno* (1931); and took a stand against the antihuman, anti-Christian ideology and practice of Adolf Hitler's Nazi Germany in *Mit brennender Sorge* (1937). He condemned atheistic communism and the persecution of the Church in Russia in the encyclical *Divini Redemptoris* (1937). To the Catholic faithful he expressed the sacred meaning of their political life with the encyclical establishing the feast of Christ the King *(Quas primas,* 1925). Pius XII had the heartbreaking task of being peacemaker to a world at war. His *Summi pontificatus*

(1939) set out a program for peace and for rule by law that he repeated over and over. In his reign he was the implacable enemy of atheistic communism.

The social problems caused by the industrial revolution, urbanization, and the exploitation of the worker by unrestrained capitalism for a century were addressed in the encyclicals *Rerum novarum* (1891) and *Quadragesimo anno* (1931). These were supplemented by the teaching of Pius X and Pius XI on Catholic Action and the encyclicals of Pius XI on Christian marriage *(Casti connubii,* 1930) and education *(Divini illius Magistri,* 1930), in which the rights of the person and the family were defended against the encroachments of the State. A whole Catholic social program of teaching and action was inspired and flourished. Pius XII's addresses on problems of marriage and family life opened the way to investigations of the urgent questions of the population explosion and birth control.

Doctrinal Life. Leo XIII's *Aeterni Patris* (1879) was more than a revival of Thomistic studies; it was a call to Catholic intellectuals to reenter the world of learning, to follow the example of St. Thomas Aquinas by respect for the autonomy of human intelligence whereby a better service can be rendered also to faith. A great resurgence began in Catholic universities and among Catholic scholars. Pius X defended the same soundness of reason against the religious subjectivism of *Modernism. The *Deus scientiarum Dominus* (1931) of Pius XI reorganized seminary studies. Pius XII's *Humani generis* (1950) was more than a restraint on theological extremism; together with the astonishing range of the Pope's addresses over every field of knowledge, it opened up and encouraged Catholic theology and thought. Biblical studies received a strong impetus from the *Providentissimus Deus* (1893) of Leo XIII, which was renewed and extended by the *Spiritus Paraclitus* (1920) of Benedict XV and the *Divino afflante Spiritu* (1943) of Pius XII. Not only was Catholic biblical scholarship encouraged to meet the new rationalist criticism on its own grounds, but a more profound appreciation of the Bible in Catholic theology and life was fostered.

Christian Life. This period was marked also by a deepening of the spiritual life and devotion of the faithful. Leo XIII issued his encyclicals on the rosary and on the Holy Spirit *(Divinum illud munus,* 1897); Pius X by his decrees (1905, 1910) on frequent communion fostered a practice that transformed the spiritual life of Catholics. His reforms of church music, the breviary, and the calendar in a sense initiated the liturgical movement. He also had canon law codified. The jubilees (1933) proclaimed by Pius XI were marked by numerous canonizations; he also zealously promoted the retreat movement and devotion to the Sacred Heart. In the reign of Pius XII the Holy Year 1950 was climaxed by the proclamation of the dogma of the Assumption; a Marian Year was observed in 1954. Pius XII's encyclicals, *Mystici corporis Christi* (1943) and *Mediator Dei* (1947), intensified the study and appreciation of the structure of the Church and the meaning of the liturgy in its

life. In its worldwide status the Church in the 20th cent. lost free external communication with her members in many countries of Eastern Europe, China, and Cuba. The progress of the missions in Africa was disturbed by the political turmoil in the emerging nations. Latin America suffered a dire shortage of clergy. Neopaganism and atheism created an atmosphere that made for leakage in membership and a dearth of vocations to the priesthood and religious life. But the Church in North America also came of age in the 20th century. Missionary activity expanded, and new stress was laid on the development of a native clergy. In Latin America the Church began to fulfill its responsibilities in the movement for social reform. Catholic scholarship matured and progressed.

Age of Vatican Council II. In the person and pontificate of John XXIII the efforts of his predecessors were in one sense fulfilled, in another transformed. He renewed and adapted the Church's social teaching in *Mater et magistra* (1961) and *Pacem in terris* (1963), later supplemented by Paul VI's *Populorum progressio* (1967). On the political level a modus vivendi was achieved with many of the Communist regimes. The moral prestige of the papacy in the cause of world peace grew; Paul VI addressed the United Nations (1965). But John's *aggiornamento most of all transformed the doctrinal and practical life of the Church itself. The Church became and will remain for some time a changing Church. In its preparations, deliberations, and aftermath Vatican Council II brought to the whole Church the full impact of the energies that had built up in theological, biblical, and liturgical studies since Leo XIII. The documents of the Council spread a new consciousness of the nature and internal life of the Church as the People of God. The collegiality of the bishops and the positive development of the place in the Church of the laity diminished in the minds of Catholics the monolithic, centralized image of Church government and communicated a sense of a broader active participation in the life of the Church. A full and responsible engagement in the ecumenical movement was fostered. Practical Christian life was most directly affected by the reformed liturgy, permeated with scriptural readings, and integrated with the preached word of God.

The state of the Church after Vatican II remains one of fluidity. The rethinking of the structure of the Church has brought a desire in many to rid it of all its institutional structures. An *underground Church movement that treats the parochial system as obsolete has developed. The encyclical *Humanae vitae* (1968), reaffirming conservative RC teaching on birth control, provoked many manifestations of an authority crisis that exists on all levels in the Church. The personal cult of the Holy Father that had characterized Catholic life no longer flourishes. Popular devotions, such as the rosary and novenas, long typical of Catholic piety, are not widely cultivated. The priest's obligation of celibacy and the nature of his ministry are debated. The main thrust of theological study has been dominated by the pursuit of biblical themes and by kerygmatic motivation; the scholastic instruments of theology have been abandoned; yet theologians have experienced the need of new philosophical methods, new language, and a new world view for theological development. BIBLIOGRAPHY: E. Sauras et al., SacMund 1:313–337.

[T. C. O'BRIEN]

CHURCH (NT), the community of believers in Jesus of Nazareth as the risen, ascended Messiah and Lord (Acts 2.36), who are baptized in his name (Acts 2.38), receive the teaching of the Twelve about him (Acts 2.42), and as members of the community of believers share in the Eucharistic table (Acts 2.42). The community of believers was early designated as the *ekklēsia* in Christian preaching to Greek audiences. *Ekklēsia,* meaning an assembly, was used in the LXX translation of the Hebrew Bible to translate the Hebrew *qahal,* also meaning a meeting, gathering, or assembly. The actual assembly, where the baptized and instructed believers in Jesus came together, occurred at the Eucharistic liturgy (Acts 2.42). Since the assembly was unified in its religious ideas and aspirations ("one Lord, one faith, one baptism," Eph 4.5.), the term *ekklēsia,* "church," acquired the meaning in the NT of all those who, whether actually physically gathered together for worship or not, held to the same faith in Christ. They were expected to express this faith on the first day of the week in actual physical assembly to worship through the Eucharistic rite (Acts 20.7). Thus the term *ekklēsia* carries in the NT its own specific connotations with reference to Jesus of Nazareth, to other believers with whom one is in the community of faith, and to a formed sociological reality, an actual grouping of people who share the same concerns over the purpose and shape of life.

The first epistles of St. Paul, 1 and 2 Th (A.D. 50–52), use *ekklēsia* in this sense. Paul writes to "the church of the Thessalonians in God the Father and the Lord Jesus Christ" 1 Th 1.1; 2 Th 1.1), i.e., to those in Thessalonica who profess faith in Jesus as Savior and Lord. He envisions them as listening to the reading of his letters on the occasion of the Eucharistic gathering. In 1 Th 2.14 he uses the plural *ekklēsiai* to refer to the members of the Christian communities scattered throughout Palestine who were persecuted for their faith: "For you, brethren, have become imitators of the churches of God in Christ Jesus which are in Judea; for you suffered the same things from your own countrymen as they did from the Jews . . . . ." The *ekklēsia* is thus a community of believers, who, as individuals, carry their faith with them as persons, and who, whether in actual physical assembly for the Eucharist or not, are viewed as forming a unity through the identity of their religious beliefs and aspirations of conduct. The *ekklēsia* is not a mere aggregate of believers in Jesus of Nazareth. Its determinative element is prophecy, the divine call, entering into history first through Jesus himself (see Mk 1.14–15) and then through the proclamation by the Twelve of his Resurrection (Acts 2.14–36). The acceptance of this proclamation and its

implications is an act of faith in the word of God (1 Th 1.5–8;2.13), which carries with it the continuing presence of God in Christ bestowing the gift of salvation (Phil 2.12–13), i.e., the liberation of man from sin and its effects (1 Cor. 6.11). From the standpoint of this sanctifying divine presence acting upon believers, the Church is viewed by Paul as destined for a holy and sinless existence, toward which it takes its first faltering steps within the reality of history (Eph 5.25–27).

In NT times local Churches lay under two sources of leadership. The first was an administrative function, held by the *presbyter* (literally, elder) or *episkopos* (literally, overseer; in English, bishop), terms undifferentiated in meaning in the early decades of the history of the NT Church (Acts 14.23; 20.28). One of the primary responsibilities was to conserve the teaching of the Twelve and St. Paul in its authentic meaning (Acts 20.17–35). The second source of leadership was a charismatic endowment, shared by other members of the Church besides the administrative leaders. Charism in this sense was a manifestation of the presence of the Holy Spirit, esp. through prophecy (Acts 11.27–28), teaching (Acts 13.1–2), and preaching (Acts 6.8–10). The NT employs various images to sound the depths of theological meaning in its concept of the Church, e.g., the people of God (its own self-understanding as called to faith), the new creation (the renewal of humanity through the Church), and the body of Christ (the Church's transcendental relationship to God through Christ). BIBLIOGRAPHY: R. Schnackenburg, *Church in the New Testament* (1965); Paul S. Minear, *Images of the Church in the New Testament* (1960).

[C. P. CEROKE]

CHURCH (PLACE OF WORSHIP). Basically, the term Church refers to the community of faith, the body of believers. It is also used derivatively to name the building or hall in which that community celebrates its liturgy. What was called the house of the church in early Christian times is now termed simply church. Usually it means that the building or hall is used exclusively or primarily for liturgical celebrations.

Christian public worship first developed quite independently of any special edifice. Early Christian communities gathered for prayer and "the breaking of bread" in homes. As the Church grew, however, this custom presented obvious difficulties, and relief from persecution permitted the erection of church buildings to accommodate larger gatherings. Theoretically, original priorities retained their place. The essentials of Christian public worship were the community, its liturgical action, and its bishop or his vicar. But the Jewish temple tradition and pagan emphasis on sacred places profoundly influenced the course of Christian history in regard to church buildings.

It is also natural for the human community to give architectural expression to any important common and social activity. The centuries of Christendom saw church building gain in attention, respect, even dominance, until cathedrals and parish or monastic churches were frequently the center of a town and the landmark of an area. The church then was not merely a shelter for the Eucharistic assembly, but a monument erected to illustrate the power and dominance of God. Church architecture became one of the more important indices of culture, of the total life of the community.

Secularization, pluralism, and theological-liturgical renewal have returned the late 20th cent. to earlier concepts and criteria of church building. The structure designed to impress and dominate is regarded by increasing numbers of church leaders as unsuitable sociologically, theologically, and liturgically. Stress on simplicity, poverty, the witness of Christian lives rather than of pretentious buildings —these aspects of conciliar renewal are beginning to affect the planning and architecture of churches. Modest structures designed to be homes for Christian assembly are today's trend. The preoccupation of the contemporary church architect is with the liturgical action, not with the external boldness or monumentality of the edifice.

Churches of a sacramental-liturgical tradition face problems in architecture different from those presented by churches whose emphasis in worship is less sacramental. Liturgical renewal in Catholic churches requires a basic concern for creating an environment favorable to common action, prayer and song—favorable to the interaction of a community of actors (not an audience). It requires a central altar, with adequate provision for congregation, presider, other ministers, commentator, cantor, and musicians (both instrumental and vocal). The architect aims at a living room, not an auditorium or spectator-arena.

Other aspects of contemporary renewal may also affect the future of church building. In a few places can be seen the beginnings of shared or common facilities, where churches of different confessional traditions build together. Experimental parishes (nonterritorial groups of common interest or vocation) exist in several Catholic dioceses and may be much more common in the future. These groups will vary in size and function and will present requirements for facilities different from those of territorial parishes. Some multipurpose church buildings have been erected, enabling part of the space used for Sunday's liturgical gathering to be employed as a social hall or other facility at other times. The comparatively new emphasis on the congregation as an assembly marked by commitment to social mission may make the multipurpose structure more desirable in certain areas. BIBLIOGRAPHY: F. Hahn, *Worship of the Early Church* (ed. J. Reumann, tr. D. Green, 1973). *PARISH.

[R. W. HOVDA]

CHURCH (THEOLOGICAL INTERPRETATIONS). Throughout the entire history of Western Christianity notions of the Church are proposed as reconstructions or developments of one or another aspect of NT teaching. In the NT documents, moreover, various points of view may be discerned: the Pauline emphasis upon the Church as the body of Christ; Luke's description of the Church as the historical fulfillment of God's plan; the Johannine reflection on the Church as life in Christ; and Matthew's thought concerning the Church as the community of the New Law.

Patristic Era. In the patristic period, several heterodox currents of thought stand as prototypes of later ecclesiological theories. The earliest is the 2d-cent. Marcionite concept of the Church as altogether cut off from the people of God of the Old Covenant. This concept is rooted in the radical opposition alleged by Marcion between the God of the OT and the God of the New. In the second half of the 2d cent. Montanist doctrine was exclusivist in another direction, namely that the Church subsists only in a community of holy ones, the elect, who look to the Holy Spirit, rather than to the Lord Jesus, as the principle of their cohesion and activity. Tertullian professed (c. 200) this type of "pneumatic ecclesiology." A modification of this position is present in the 4th-cent. Donatist view, according to which ecclesial ministry is invalid unless the minister is holy. St. Augustine concerned himself esp. with the Donatist contention; and from the polemic he instituted against it comes the strong Catholic tradition concerning the objective value of the exercise of the ministry in the Church, without immediate regard for the minister's holiness. Perhaps more important, however, is Augustine's synthetic development of various NT themes concerning the Church, e.g., in the *City of God*. While not an ecclesiological treatise, this work is an idealistic description of the Church, with special emphasis upon the idea that the Church is the locus wherein the New Law bears fruit in the obedience of faith.

Medieval Period. The medieval period produces no explicit treatises in ecclesiology. This does not mean, however, that views concerning the Church were not developing. The various spiritualist movements were recrudescences, in one form or another of the Montanist movement. Abbot *Joachim of Fiore (c. 1132–1202) set forth a more elaborate theory of the historical transition from the age of the Father (the OT), through that of the Son (the NT up to the time of Joachim), to that of the Holy Spirit (which was then to be inaugurated). Mainly, however, medieval thought on the Church was concerned with an interpretation of its relationship to the civilization engendered by the spread of Christianity. The close association of Church and State occasioned the theories of the canonists concerning the precedence of the pope over all other powers in the world, and the exercise of the "two swords." A step toward a comprehensive description of the mystery of the Church was made in the period during which the various forms of *conciliarism were put forth. Yet Juan de Torquemada's treatise, *De Ecclesia* (1489), was more an attempt to put to rights the claims of the conciliarists in favor of papal prerogatives than a broad ecclesiology. In the same age, Jan Hus and his disciples were professing a theory of the Church close to that of the Montanists, though the emphasis was not so much on holiness as on *election as constitutive of the true Church. Thus, for the patristic and medieval descriptive formulas *communio sanctorum* and *communio fidelium,* Hus substituted *communio electorum.*

Reformation. Each wing of the Reformation adopted an ecclesiology peculiar to itself. Luther and his disciples saw the Church as the congregation of saints or believers, among whom the Gospel is purely preached and the sacraments are rightly administered (cf. Augsburg Confession, Art. 7). Implicit in this description is a further distinction, namely between the external and the internal Church, the latter of which is the "true" Church. The true Church does not come into being, however, except through the external preaching of the gospel, which may either bear fruit (thus the internal Church) or for practical purposes, i.e., for the Christian life, remain unheeded (external Church). In the *Reformed tradition a broader definition, akin to that of Hus, is given. The Church is comprised of all those who are predestined. The preaching of the gospel and the administration of the sacraments are the normal (though not indispensable) ways in which predestination is realized (cf. Second Helvetic Confession, Ch. 17). Nevertheless, the later notion of the invisible Church really has its origin here (cf. Westminster Confession, Ch. 25). The Anglican tradition influenced very deeply in the beginning by Reformed preachers from the Continent, developed according to its own style. The episcopal structure of the Church was maintained (as in the Swedish branch of Lutheranism), though without reference to the primacy of the pope. Finally, in Reformation times the so-called left-wing movements emerged, with quite spiritualized ideas about the Church, reminiscent of Montanism and the more recent theories of Hus. In their ideas of the Church, groups like the Anabaptists were forerunners of the Nonconformists in Great Britain (Baptists, Methodists, Quakers). RC theologians of the Reformation era, esp. Robert Bellarmine, composed their theology particularly in reaction to theories of the Reformers. Thus they put heavy emphasis on the external aspects of the Church, the Church as a visible, juridic society. Once these lines had been drawn, the only thing that could apparently change the situation would be the introduction of an entirely new way of thinking, which would challenge both Protestant and Catholic.

18th–19th Centuries. In fact, the Enlightenment was such a challenge. The rationalist movement, insofar as it affected Western Christianity, produced the so-called liberal interpretation of the nature of the Church. In its most extreme form, e.g., in the thought of J. S. Semler (1725–91), the Church was viewed as a free society wherein the values of freedom of conscience and fraternity are realized—and nothing more. The romantic reaction to such a radical view of the Church is exemplified in the thought of F. Schleiermacher, the father of *liberal theology. Given his interpretation of the nature of the Christian life, i.e., as consisting in the development of "religious feeling," the Church could be nothing more than the association of men who experience this feeling of dependence

upon God, after the pattern set by the religious experience of Jesus himself. More orthodox views of the Church prevailed during the post-Reformation period where Protestantism more or less maintained its original thrust. In the U.S., among Baptists, Methodists, and Presbyterians, the idea of the free covenanting of believing Christians was much in evidence (see COVENANT THEOLOGY). Modern RC ecclesiology also was affected by the rationalist movement, but in a different way. Especially under the influence of the Roman theological school, a negative reaction to the rationalist movement caused an even greater emphasis to be placed upon the role of the magisterial authority in the life of the Church than had previously been the case. This culminated in the definition, at Vatican Council I, of the dogma of papal infallibility.

20th Century. With the beginning of the 20th cent. a new era of ecclesiology seems to have been begun, ushered in by the movement of modern critical biblical research. The liberal view of the Church has been challenged from within Protestantism, with a consequent return to a concern for the structural aspects of the Church, e.g., the authenticity of a duly constituted ministry—though interpretations vary widely, as became evident in the early days of the ecumenical movement (e.g., the first meeting of *Faith and Order in Lausanne, Switzerland, in 1925). Many Protestants, however, have come to recognize the necessity of abandoning the idea of a separation between visible and invisible Church. Thus they maintain, in common with Roman Catholics, the integrity of the body of Christ as a mystery that has both visible and invisible aspects. Similarly, RC reassessments took place and culminated in the deliberations of Vatican Council II. One of the major documents of the Council had to do directly with the mystery of the Church. The dogmatic constitution, *Lumen gentium,* presents a view of the Church that is quite comprehensive and takes into account the ecumenical dialogue. Thus a broader theory of membership in the Church than has hitherto been developed is presented, with a view toward putting the entire ecumenical movement in the perspective of the mystery of the Church as the people of God, which exists in the form of the mystical body of Christ.

Vatican Council II. The Dogmatic Constitution on the Church (*Lumen gentium,* Nov. 21, 1964) describes the Church as the "new *People of God." (Vat II ConstCh 17). This scriptural theme (cf. 1 Pet 2.9–10) brings out the nature of the Church as the sign of union with God and the unity of all mankind and as the instrument for achieving both (n. 1).

The Church is the community of salvation. As the People of God, the Church exists because God has freely called and chosen men to be saved from sin and to share in his own life. The divine plan embraces men, not just as individuals but as a "people," as a community. This plan first unfolds under the Old Covenant in the chosen people of Israel, with whom the new People of God now in the New Covenant are in continuity. But as the community of salvation, the

Church is an eschatological reality, i.e., pointed towards the purpose of salvation, when the just men of all time will be gathered into God's glorious universal Church in heaven (n. 8). On earth the Church is a "pilgrim Church" experiencing persecution from without, and the need of salvation within, in the continuing struggle of flesh against spirit (nn. 48–49).

The Church is the community of Christ. God saves and makes mankind his people only in and through the Lord Jesus, who by his life, death, and resurrection established and now sustains the community of salvation. The People of God exists, therefore, in the form of the Mystical Body of Christ; from Christ the Head comes the saving grace, the inner life by which this People are united to God and to one another in a community of faith, hope, and love. Thus the Church is a holy people, i.e., called to holiness, to living the evangelical life which Christ teaches, and for which the Holy Spirit, the Spirit of Christ, sanctifies and vivifies the Church (nn. 39–42). The People of God and of Christ are also a priestly people. Baptism brings about incorporation into Christ and so participation in his priesthood. The common priesthood of all the baptized and the ministerial priesthood are joined together in offering both the spiritual sacrifices of the Christian life and the Eucharistic Sacrifice. The People of God exercise their priesthood in worship and sacraments, esp. in the Eucharist, the sign and source of the unity of God's people (nn. 10–11). They also share in Christ's prophetic office, by the communion of a shared sense of the faith, and by the charismatic gifts through which special tasks and offices are fulfilled for the building up of the Church (n. 12).

The organic structure of the People of God includes invisible and visible elements as two aspects of the one reality; the visible structure fosters the community of faith, hope, and charity (n. 8). The fullness of the priesthood is conferred on the bishops. In them the apostolic college continues, with the successor of St. Peter, the Roman Pontiff, as head. With him they serve the People of God by their office of sanctifying, teaching, and ruling. The infallible teaching authority in the Church resides in the pope and in the college of bishops teaching with him. Thus the Church is preserved faithfully apostolic in doctrine, sacraments, and life (nn. 18–29).

The Church is one and Catholic. The Church is one and unique because there is one divine plan of salvation, one mystical body under one head, Christ, and one Spirit, the Lord and Giver of life, who on behalf of the whole Church and each and everyone of those who believe, is the principle of their coming together, and remaining together in the teaching of the Apostles and in fellowship in the breaking of the bread and in prayers (n. 13). "This Church, constituted and organized in the world as a society, subsists in the Catholic Church" (n. 8). All men are called to belong to the new People of God, but they belong completely who are "fully incorporated" into the society of the Catholic Church. Nevertheless, there are elements of sanctification

and truth in all Christians, in individuals and in "ecclesial communities" outside her visible structure, which point toward Catholic unity. In non-Christians too there can be certain relations to the new People of God (nn. 14–16; see MEMBERSHIP IN THE CHURCH). The Church carries on the mandate given by Christ to the Apostles to proclaim the Gospel so that the whole world may be the People of God (n. 17). BIBLIOGRAPHY: F. X. Lawlor, NCE 3:683–693 for bibliog.; G. Florovsky, *Bible, Church, Tradition: An Eastern Orthodox View* (1972); F. H. Littell, *Origins of Sectarian Protestantism* (pa. 1964); *VISIBLE CHURCH.

[M. B. SCHEPERS; T. C. O'BRIEN]

CHURCH (U.S. HISTORY). This article is limited to the Western Christian tradition. Church history in the U.S. is the history of two separate, and until the mid-20th cent. usually antagonistic, forms of Christianity, Protestantism and Roman Catholicism.

PROTESTANTISM IN THE U.S.

While the uniqueness of American Protestantism often has been exaggerated, it remains true that religious patterns imported from Great Britain and the Continent have been adapted in the New World through the interaction of its diverse peoples to produce the peculiar ethos of American Protestant Christianity. By the end of the Revolutionary era characteristic traits had begun to develop: *denominationalism, *revivalism, religious *freedom in the setting of *Church-State separation, *voluntaryism.

Colonial Period. Determinationalism was not planned; with varying degrees of success, establishment in the European pattern was attempted in most of the colonies: of the C of E throughout the South; of the Reformed Church, by the Dutch in New York; of Congregationalism in New England, except for Rhode Island. There, and in Pa., N.J., and early Md., diversity of belief was accepted. Enforcement of uniformity in all the colonies, however, gave way to the need for settlers; toleration had to be granted. Gradually the denominational system, not E. Troeltsch's church-sect pattern, emerged, with each group accepting others as genuine expressions of Christianity. Revivalism appeared in the *Great Awakening, which began about 1726 in N.J. with T. J. Frelinghuysen, a Dutch Reformed pastor, and which through G. Tennent, J. Edwards, and G. Whitefield spread throughout the colonies. One important reason was that, in sharp contrast with the European situation, only about a tenth of the colonials were church members. Revivalism became a continuing means of evangelism and fostered both division and cooperation. Tensions developed over the place of emotions in genuine religious experience (thus C. Chauncy's *Enthusiasm Described and Cautioned Against,* 1742, and J. Edwards' *Treatise Concerning Religious Affections,* 1746). Disagreement also arose over whether education or vital Christian experience was the primary qualification for ministry (thus G. Tennent's *Danger of an Unconverted Ministry,* 1740). Stress on religious experience tended to overshadow doctrinal distinctions, and denominational differences often gave way to a spiritual unity of shared religious feeling. John Wesley's words were often quoted: "Is thy heart right, as my heart is with thine? . . . . If it be, give me thy hand."

With the winning of independence, most of the state constitutions abolished existing forms of establishment (although vestiges remained in Mass. until 1833) and granted a measure of religious freedom. Religious tests for voting or office holding, retained against Roman Catholics, antitrinitarians, and atheists in some places, were ended by the First Amendment of the U.S. Constitution. Thus, because of the *de facto* existence of diverse denominations, the cooperation fostered by revivalism, the activities of Baptists and Quakers, and the rationalism of the Enlightenment, the U.S. embarked on the "great experiment," religious freedom. Separation from the State gave to the Churches in the U.S. a fourth, and in some senses their most distinctive, characteristic: voluntaryism. Separating civil and religious functions did not prevent religion from exerting a marked influence on social and political life, even from Revolutionary days. A religious survey made *c.* 1780 shows the following numbers of Protestant Churches: Congregational, 749; Presbyterian, 495; Baptist, 457; Anglican, 406; Lutheran, 240; German Reformed, 201; Quaker, 200; Dutch Reformed, 127. (There were also 56 RC churches.)

From the Revolution to the Civil War. The postwar movement westward beyond the Appalachians challenged the Churches to provide a ministry and church buildings in the West. A new wave of revivalism to reach the unchurched and to combat *deism began in the 1790s and led to new conversions and the establishment of new Churches. Beginning in the East, this *Second Great Awakening motivated college students to become missionaries, pastors to move westward, and laymen to propagate their faith as they joined the westward trek. In the West the revivals were inaugurated with interdenominational sacramental gatherings, which developed into the *camp meeting, esp. among Methodists. A new phase of revivalism began *c.* 1825 with Charles G. Finney. Instead of the strict Calvinism of the Westminster Confession, he emphasized individual freedom and responsibility in conversion and developed new measures to elicit decision, e.g., protracted meetings, the *anxious bench, public prayers naming individuals, public prayer by women, emotional music, and moving illustrations in sermons (see OBERLIN THEOLOGY). These means subtly contributed to a change in theology as emphasis shifted from the workings of God's Spirit to human influences. Evangelism and church extension were carried on not only by the new revivalist methods but also by formal organizations for home missions. By the *Plan of Union of 1802 Congregationalists and Presbyterians collaborated to open churches in the western states. Most denominations organized home mission societies, or cooper-

ated in the American Home Mission Society (1826). Baptist preachers and Methodist circuit riders, both drawn from the ranks of the common man, greatly appealed to the American spirit, and by 1860 these two denominations comprised nearly four-fifths of American Protestants. The first half of the 19th cent. was an era of Protestant optimism, in which the further characteristic of activism emerged. Foreign and home mission agencies, both denominational and interdenominational, were formed, e.g., *American Board of Commissioners for Foreign Missions, 1810; American Bible Society, 1816; American Sunday School Union, 1824 (see SUNDAY SCHOOLS); *American Tract Society, 1825. Under church auspices hundreds of academies and colleges were established, many of which survive. Protestant agencies for social and humanitarian causes multiplied, e.g., American Education Society, 1816; American Colonization Society, 1817; American Temperance Society, 1826; American Anti-Slavery Society, 1833. Religious optimism was also reflected in the numerous utopian communities that sprang up.

Voluntaryism was a source of vitality, yet it also fostered individualism and a proliferation of denominations, strengthened lay control sometimes to the point of anticlericalism, and eroded *confessionalism. Revivalism was criticized by H. Bushnell in his *Christian Nurture* (1842) and by J. W. Nevin in *The Anxious Bench* (1843; see MERCERSBURG THEOLOGY). Both deplored the once-for-all dramatic conversion. Many among the newer Lutheran and Reformed immigrants feared an exaggeration of subjective experience as detrimental to the objective elements of salvation, Church, ministry, and the sacraments. The phenomenon of denominationalism became intensified. In New England a rationalistic Unitarianism led by W. E. Channing drew many away from Congregationalism. *Universalism appealed chiefly to the rural and less-educated classes. Under the impact of the revivalistic accent on freedom and the *New England theology represented by N. Taylor and L. Beecher, Arminianism undermined rigid Calvinism. Over this issue Old School and New School Presbyterians divided (*c.* 1837). Among the Baptists, Old School or Primitive Baptists (*c.* 1830) and Landmarkists (1850) split off (see LANDMARKISM), claiming to preserve the true Baptist heritage. A *high-church movement led first by J. H. Hobart appeared within the Protestant Episcopal Church. Divisions over theology, evangelistic methods, standards for membership, and ministry splintered other denominations; new groups appeared, e.g., Christian Churches, Disciples of Christ, and Latter-day Saints (Mormons). Differences over slavery also moved the major denominations into sectional divisions, many of which remain. At a time when Christian unity had an opportunity to transcend differences, the major bodies failed as a reconciling force to prevent a fratricidal war. Another unfortunate aspect of the era was Protestant support of *nativism.

From the Civil War to World War I. In the postbellum period the Churches sought to help the freedmen establish their own Churches, mission and education societies, and national organizations. The majority of black Americans found special affinity for the Baptists and Methodists, and many black Churches date from this time. Economic changes spurred by the Civil War created the industrial society of the North, and with it the religious and social problems of an urban population, often exploited by capital and victimized by fluctuations of the economy. To reach the masses in the big cities, the methods of revivalism were again employed; D. L. Moody was the outstanding revivalist of the period, adapting and refining older methods. Home and foreign missions were accelerated, notably by the Student Volunteer movement (1888). The larger denominations organized special ministries to the various ethnic groups among the immigrants. Early social reform movements relied on individual persuasion and charitable organizations; by 1880 a few pioneers (e.g., Washington Gladden) were becoming aware of the changing nature of ethical problems and the new social mission of the Church. The *Social Gospel movement did not fully penetrate the Christian conscience until the early 20th century. A tract for the times was W. Rauschenbusch's *Christianity and the Social Crisis* (1907); his *Theology of the Social Gospel* (1917) was a statement of the theological basis for individual and social salvation. Denominations formed departments to educate their membership in social concern and methods of service and established Christian centers, settlement houses, and *institutional churches. The YMCA and YWCA also were founded. The Churches faced a new problem occasioned by liberal theology. The truth of the Genesis account of creation was challenged by Darwin's *Origin of Species* (1859). Higher criticism of the Bible began to find its way into the seminaries soon after the Civil War and was generally accepted by 1914. The developments in psychology, sociology, and comparative religion offered naturalistic explanations of the origin of religion, without any supernatural reference. Exponents of the adaptation of Christianity to new learning were called progressives or modernists. Evolutionary theory became the source of great Protestant optimism for the continual betterment of the world. World War I came as a blow to the Social Gospel movement; conferences and conventions still talked of social reform but the drive was gone. Revivalism lost its effectiveness in the North, and many Churches reacted against the theatrics of Billy Sunday and his imitators. Unrest over the Social Gospel and biblical criticism became fixed in an organized fundamentalism; while exhibiting various forms, it was essentially a protest against a surrender of what were regarded as essentials of the gospel. The denominations hardest hit by the fundamentalist-modernist controversy of the 1920s were the Northern Baptists and the Presbyterians. Theological factors were added to cultural ones to bring about secessions and new denominations, with liberal or conservative polarizations. The pattern of denominationalism had become more complex with the appearance of the Church of Christ, Scientist (c. 1875) and the

Ethical Culture Movement (c. 1876); in the 20th cent. Pentecostalism emerged and spread among those who regarded the older Churches as cold and impersonal.

Since 1920. The 1929 economic depression seemed to deepen a religious depression that had already begun. Theological changes introduced in the 1930s, however, were to pave the way for the progress of the ecumenical movement and the post-World War II religious renewal. *Neo-orthodoxy, a name disavowed by many classified as its spokesmen, was a reaction to liberal theology (see BARTH, K.; TILLICH, P.). R. Niebuhr's *Moral Man and Immoral Society* (1932), E. Lewis's *A Christian Manifesto* (1934), and the series "How My Mind Has Changed" in the *Christian Century, c.* 1940, reflected the departure from liberal theology in the United States. The new mood was marked by recognition of man's capacity for evil and inability to save himself and of salvation history as the core of the Bible; new appreciation developed for a high Christology, the transcendence of God, and the place of the Church. Greater unity and cooperation of the Churches was fostered; it was both evidenced and assisted by the formation of the National Council of Churches of Christ in the U.S.A. (1950) and the World Council of Churches (1948). In 1962 a *Consultation on Church Union began, with the goal of forming a united Church comprising the majority of American Protestants. With Vatican Council II a great change in Protestant-Catholic communication took place on the theological and practical levels. The quickening of interest in religion during the 1950s was regarded by some as ephemeral, by others as a genuine religious renaissance. Involvement of laymen in Christian witness through their work, sociopolitical activity, and participation in public worship increased. Renewal was sought through the mass evangelistic methods of Billy Graham and through small fellowship groups and programs of Christian social action.

By the 1960s the revival of religion seemed to wane; statistics of church membership evidenced a leveling off or a decline. Confusion and division beset theology, as radical theologians proclaimed the *death of God, critics advocated abandonment of the institutional Church, ethicians proclaimed the new morality. Earlier accent on human sinfulness gave way to stress on man's ability to revitalize the secular city and to transform the changing social environment. The immanence of God and his action in the world independently of the Church became primary themes. At the same time the new evangelicals appeared, seeking to reassert the essentials of fundamentalism without its anti-intellectualism, quarrelsomeness, and narrow base of fellowship. Opposed to the National and World Council of Churches, they formed organizations such as the *National Association of Evangelicals and the Evangelical Theological Society. More rigidly doctrinaire and separated individuals organized the *American Council of Christian Churches.

Thus at the end of the 1960s considerable confusion was apparent in Protestantism, as the theologies of Barth, Bultmann, and Tillich seemed to have lost their appeal, and no clear new direction was in sight. New bases of assurance regarding the reality of the triune God, new means of winning men to Christian discipleship, new approaches to Christian unity, new styles of personal and social ethics, new methods of Christian instruction and nurture, new forms of apologetics to confront a technological society and the world's religions, and new ways of expressing concern for the totality of human life were being sought. It was clearly a period of transition from old and accustomed ways to the development of other forms of structure and belief whereby the Church could fulfill its mission in a pluralistic society. BIBLIOGRAPHY: E. S. Gaustad, *Historical Atlas of Religion in America* (1962); W. S. Hudson, *Religion in America* (1965); H. S. Smith, R. T. Handy, and L. A. Loetscher, *American Christianity: An Historical Interpretation with Representative Documents* (2 v., 1960, 1963); S. Ahlstrom, *Theology in America* (1967); Smith-Jamison v. 1; S. E. Mead, *Lively Experiment* (1963); S. E. Ahlstrom, *Religious History of the American People* (2 v., pa. 1975).

ROMAN CATHOLICISM IN THE U.S.

The history of Catholicism has been a process of gradual, often painful maturing, self-realization, and Americanization.

Early Missionary Efforts. Starting with Juan Ponce de León's Florida expedition, the Spanish attempted a program of acculturation centered around the mission system. Although criticized by historians under the spell of the "Black Legend," or by those who regretted the destruction of Indian culture, the Spanish missionary effort was basically successful. In California, Junípero Serra founded nine missions (1770–82), including Monterey-Carmel, San Gabriel, San Francisco, Santa Clara, and San Buenaventura. Before that time, 17th-cent. Franciscans had converted some 35,000 Indians in New Mexico and established numerous missions in Florida. In Texas and throughout the Southwest, Spanish clergy developed missions for the Indians, introduced new forms of architecture, and acquired cartographical knowledge of the area. French missionaries worked among the Indians of the Great Lakes and Mississippi Valley. While several Jesuits, including Jean de Brébeuf and Isaac Jogues, suffered death at the hands of the Indians, the general peace that prevailed after 1649 permitted Jesuits, Recollects, Capuchins, and diocesan priests from New France to extend French influence into the future states of Ill., Mich., and Wis., and down the Mississippi River. Despite the expulsion of the Jesuits (1763), Catholicism had become the dominant religion in the Mississippi basin by the time of the American Revolution.

Catholics in the Colonies. English settlers along the East Coast of the future U.S. were steeped in an anti-Catholic tradition. Legal and social restrictions against the very small Catholic minority therefore abounded through-

out the British colonies, with some exceptions in Md., N.Y., and Pennsylvania. Under the first proprietors of Md., the Catholic Lords Baltimore, Catholics controlled the colony and used their power to adopt (1649) an Act Concerning Religion, which guaranteed religious toleration to all but non-Trinitarians. However, the defeat of the Catholics (1654) by Protestant forces resulted in the repeal of the Toleration Act and subjection to Puritan rule. After the Revolution of 1688 in England the Anglican Church became the established Church, and Catholics in Md. experienced disabilities comparable to those in other colonies. The Revolution of 1688 also ended a period of religious liberty for Catholics in New York. Some Catholics had migrated there after the English acquired the colony from the Dutch (1644). The new proprietor, James, Duke of York, appointed (1682) a Catholic governor, Col. Thomas Dongan, whose act of religious toleration lasted only until his overthrow (1688) by the Calvinist Jacob Leister. Five years later, the C of E became the established Church in the colony. Pennsylvania, founded as a "Holy Experiment" in political and religious pluralism, afforded Catholics a unique opportunity to establish churches and other institutions. In 1734, Joseph Greaton, S.J., opened a chapel in Philadelphia, and other Jesuits ministered to Palatinate Catholics in the Conestoga and Lancaster region. Even in areas like Pa., with 1,300 Catholics in a population of 200,000 (1756), the number of Catholics in British America remained small throughout the colonial period. By 1785 there were but 25,000 Catholics among the American population of 4 million. Nevertheless, as the colonial era ended with the Revolution, the condition of American Catholics markedly improved.

Problems, Conflicts, and Growth. The French Alliance of 1778 brought French clergy and an unofficial moratorium on anti-Catholic propaganda. Catholics outstanding in the service of the new nation included Charles Carroll, delegate from Md. to the Philadelphia Congress; Daniel Carroll and Thomas FitzSimons, members of Congress; Stephen Moylan, Washington's mustermaster general; and John Barry, one of the founders of the American navy. Many states abolished legal restrictions, providing a more tolerant milieu for Catholics. John Carroll, who had been named superior of the American Catholic missions (1784), was consecrated (1790) first bp. of the American Church. In Carroll's diocese of Baltimore, coextensive with the national boundaries, the lack of clergy was critical. In 1785 there were but 24 priests to serve 25,000 Catholics scattered throughout the United States. Some relief was afforded by the arrival of priest-refugees from the French Revolution; among them were Sulpicians who established St. Mary's Seminary in Baltimore (1791). Carroll also encouraged the creation of other educational facilities. Georgetown Academy and Georgetown Visitation Convent were founded in Washington, D.C., in the 1790s. In 1808 and 1809 Mount St. Mary's Seminary and St. Joseph's School were begun in the town of Emmitsburg, Md.; St. Joseph's was established by St. Elizabeth Seton, foundress of the Sisters of Charity, the first native sisterhood.

As Carroll recruited additional clergy from Spain, Ireland, and Germany, priests were often assigned to congregations with a language and culture different from their own. Conflicts developed between pulpit and pew and between clergy and episcopal authority. The focus of the problem was lay trusteeism. In the presence of foreign and refugee clergy, lay trustees began to assume not only control of the purse and of church property, but power over the pastor as well. In Philadelphia, German members of St. Mary's Church established a separate church, Holy Trinity, which remained in schism until 1802. Other lay trustee conflicts erupted in St. Louis, Mo., Baltimore, Md., Norfolk, Va., and Charleston, South Carolina. To the bishops, lay trusteeism was a usurpation of episcopal prerogative and a violation of canonical provisions for episcopal appointment and dismissal of pastors. After the famous Hogan schism in Philadelphia, the issue was presented to the Vatican. Pius VII in *Non sine magna* (1822) upheld the principle of lay trusteeism in temporal matters but condemned the excesses that had occurred in the American system. In the 50 years following *Non sine magna,* the American Catholic population increased from 195,000 to 4,504,000. Natural reproduction and territorial acquisitions in the Mexican War accounted for part of this growth, but immigration was the principal factor. About 2,700,000 Catholic immigrants, more than half of them from Ireland, came to the U.S. at this time, and ecclesiastical jurisdictions multiplied. Beginning in 1808, when Baltimore was made a metropolitan see with suffragan dioceses at Bardstown (later Louisville), Boston, Philadelphia, and New York, some 43 dioceses and 7 archdioceses were created by the time of the Civil War.

Early Parochialism. The presence of enormous numbers of immigrants in the cities, where they chiefly settled, raised questions of urbanology that a century later remained partly unanswered. Poor and socially alienated, the Catholic immigrants had common bonds only with one another and their clergy. As a result, they flocked to ghettos, welcomed clerical dominance, and displayed generally parochial and passive characteristics. Their defensive posture was hardened by outbreaks of anti-Catholic *nativism after the 1820s. At times sophisticated, as in the John Breckinridge-John Hughes debates, and at times biased, as in the case of Samuel F. B. Morse's *Foreign Conspiracy against the Liberties of the U.S.* (1834) and Maria Monk's *The Awful Disclosures of the Hotel Dieu Nunnery of Montreal* (1836), the anti-Catholic movement occasionally assumed violent form, as in the burning (1834) of the Ursuline Convent at Charlestown, Mass., and the riots (1844) in the Kensington section of Philadelphia, where 13 were killed and 50 injured. Nativist attacks strengthened Catholic parochialism, which found expression in the development of a separate school system, unsurpassed in size by any other private school system in the world. With foun-

dations of the system laid by the First Provincial Council (1829), the establishment of parochial schools was made virtually mandatory by the Third Plenary Council of Baltimore (1884). The cost of the system led Bps. J. Hughes and J. Ireland, as well as Catholic groups in Savannah, Ga., and Poughkeepsie, N.Y., to make unsuccessful bids for state aid. As a result, parochial schools have since been maintained without significant assistance from public funds.

Attitudes toward Social Problems. Although the school question set Catholics somewhat apart in society, they displayed considerable conformity to the mainstream of American thought and mores. Catholics tended to shun reform movements, although some Catholic support was given esp. in the 1830s, to such peripheral concerns as temperance and prison reform. Catholics tended to identify with the Democratic Party and to adopt the most conservative Democratic position on the central issue of the day, Negro slavery. While many Protestant Churches were splitting over slavery, the Catholic Church in the U.S. continued to be united and in general harmony. Abolitionists and antislavery Quakers obtained little if any support for their cause among American Catholics. However, Catholics did respond to the Civil War itself, supplying chaplains, nurses, and soldiers to both the Union and Confederate armies. Like other institutions, the Church suffered heavy physical losses in the wartime devastation of the South. After the war, the Second Plenary Council of Baltimore (1866) addressed itself to the problem of the emancipated Negro, decreeing that every means be taken for the religious care and instruction of the freedman. Through a combination of racial prejudice, timidity, and inadequacy of resources, the conciliar aims were not enforced, although a few indications of concern for the Negro can be noted—e.g., Bp. John Mary Odin's support for St. Joseph's School in Louisiana; Mother Katharine Drexel's founding of the Sisters of the Blessed Sacrament (1891); and the establishment in the U.S. (1871) of the Josephite Fathers for the Negro apostolate. The number of Catholics continued to increase in the postwar era, trebling between 1870 and 1900. Many Catholics joined the new labor organizations then being formed, forcing the controversial union question upon church leadership. In general the Church supported labor's efforts to improve wages and working conditions through unionization. However, several U.S. and Canadian bps. feared the Knights of Labor and opposed its policy of secrecy, but Card. Gibbons, along with Abp. J. Ireland of St. Paul, Minn., Bp. J. J. Keane of Richmond, Va., and Rector Denis J. O'Connell of the North American College in Rome, acted to block any Roman condemnation. They argued, successfully, that any censure of the Knights would be regarded as a rejection of labor's legitimate rights. These same prelates were among those in the vanguard of the movement to relate Catholicism more effectively to the American way of life. Their efforts were frequently opposed by the more conservative bps. led by Abp. Michael Corrigan of New York. The two groups held differing views over such questions as the censoring of the teachings of Henry George, parochial schools, and the assimilation of large numbers of immigrants.

From Americanism to Vatican II. Aided by the Paulist journal, *Catholic World,* which urged greater lay concern with the liturgy and activity of the Church, laymen were becoming more involved in church affairs, notably in diocesan newspaper work. Their resurgence was symbolized by a lay congress, held in Baltimore (1889) and organized by three dynamic lay leaders: Peter L. Foy, William J. Onahan, and Henry F. Brownson. Participants read papers on major issues, chiefly Church-State relations. As the bps. were guiding the lay renaissance, they themselves began to feel the restraining hand of Rome. Despite widespread American opposition, the office of apostolic delegate to the U.S. was established by Leo XIII, and F. Satolli was named to the post (1893). Of even greater moment was Leo XIII's letter *Testem benevolentiae* (1899). The errors condemned in the letter stemmed from a faulty understanding of *Americanism propagated initially by the French edition of W. Elliott's *Life of Father Hecker.* Although the condemned views were never held in the U.S., the effect of the papal letter was to strengthen the hand of the conservative bps. and to dampen enthusiasm for reform among the hierarchy. Thereafter the bishops' efforts were diverted from adjustment to democratic society toward development of the physical plant of the Church and pastoral care of its flock.

One late 19th cent. effort to raise the intellectual tone of American Catholic life was the founding of The Catholic University of America in Washington, D.C.; first proposed at the Second Plenary Council (1866) by Abp. Martin J. Spalding of Baltimore, the idea was not accepted until the eloquent plea of John Lancaster Spalding was delivered at the Third Plenary Council (1884). It gained strong support from Gibbons, Ireland, and Keane, and 5 years later became a reality. Out of the Catholic University came the Catholic equivalent of the Social Gospel movement, formulated by such professors as W. J. Kerby, John A. Ryan, and John O'Grady. But as Catholic efforts concentrated on the amelioration rather than the solution of problems of social injustice, agitation for change continued. A liturgical reform movement began in the 1920s, led by such pioneers as V. Michel, W. Busch, and G. Ellard. A kind of intellectual revolution, reflected in various periodicals and reviews, in the organized striving of a number of different movements, in the foundation and activities of learned societies, was already astir in the 1920s; it expanded during the 1930s, and gained great momentum after World War II. The brick-and-mortar preoccupations of earlier times began to be superseded by a conception of new goals and new standards of excellence and achievement. The role of the laity in the activity of the Church, fostered by Catholic Action and emphasized in different ways by such groups as the Catholic Worker Movement and the Grail, began to grow in importance. All this helped to prepare the Church in the

U.S. for Vatican Council II's decrees adapting the Church to the modern world. In post-Vatican II years "new nuns," "new laymen," a vernacular and adapted liturgy, a new ecumenical spirit to replace its antiquated separatism, and a new sense of social responsibility began to find their place within the traditions of the American Catholic Church. This has not taken place without some disturbance and turmoil as Catholics felt their way toward a more common understanding of what was and what was not conformable to their traditions.

The Catholic Church in the U.S. by 1976 had grown to a total of 48,881,872, nearly 23% of the total national population. Catholic strength is greatest in the northeastern U.S., where 38% of the nation's Catholics reside, and in the north-central states, with 28%. BIBLIOGRAPHY: J. T. Ellis, *Guide to American Catholic History* (1959); *idem, Catholics in Colonial America* (1964); M. H. Rice, *American Catholic Opinion in the Slavery Controversy* (1944); J. T. Ellis, *Life of James Cardinal Gibbons, Archbishop of Baltimore* (2 v., 1952); T. T. McAvoy, *Great Crisis in American Catholic History 1895–1900* (1957); H. T. Browne, *Catholic Church and the Knights of Labor* (1940); R. Trisco, NCE 14:563–572 s.v. "Vatican Council II"; A. Greeley, *Catholic Experience: A Sociological Interpretation of the History of American Catholicism* (1967).

[N. H. MARING]

CHURCH, HOLY MOTHER, see MATER ECCLESIA.

CHURCH, INVISIBLE AND VISIBLE, see INVISIBLE CHURCH.

CHURCH, NATIONAL, see NATIONAL CHURCH.

CHURCH AND STATE, a problem of relationships varying with different concepts of State and of Church, and with the relative power of each institution to support its claims. Although potential conflicts of interest and loyalty existed from the outset, no formal theory of relations between Church and government was sought until Christianity became the state religion. Even then, theories developed slowly, and not until the later Middle Ages were precise definitions of State and Church (and their relations) formulated. No final solution has been discovered, and probably no model would be universally applicable. Progress has been made toward attaining *religious freedom, while still allowing opportunity for religion to influence values and structures of society. The varied typologies proposed for analyzing Church-State relations (H. Stroup, *Church and State in Confrontation,* 1967) testify to the difficulty of developing an adequate theory. It should be noted that similar problems have arisen relative to older religions and emerging modern governments (see, e.g., D. E. Smith,

India As a Secular State, 1963; *idem, Religion and Politics in Burma,* 1965).

NT Indications. In reply to a question, Jesus said: "render to Caesar the things that are Caesar's, and to God the things that are God's" (Mk 12.17). This command recognizes that a distinction exists between the two realms, but it does not explain just where the dividing line lies. Paul's admonition to "be subject to the governing authorities" (Rom 13.1–7) acknowledges the Christian's duty to obey political powers on the grounds that God has appointed civil governments to keep evildoers in check. Therefore, he explains, payment of taxes and respect are due them. Elsewhere Christians are urged to pray "for kings and all who are in high positions" (1 Tim 2.2). Peter wrote, "Fear God. Honor the emperor." (1 Pet 2.17), but he implied that deference to rulers had limits when he declared: "We must obey God rather than men" (Acts 5.29). In the Apocalypse, however, the Roman Empire is symbolized as a beast who is opposed to Christ and his disciples (ch. 13), and some think that this represents a position contradictory to that of Paul. The two passages are not necessarily inconsistent, however, since the underlying presupposition carried over from the OT is that human governments are all in God's hands and are his instruments in fulfilling his redemptive purpose. The duty of obedience to civil rulers therefore, is always qualified by the condition that they are doing their work of restraining evil and seeking peace and safety. When they, like Roman emperors, claim divine prerogatives and demand worship that belongs only to God, they are to be resisted. In such situations, Caesar is claiming what belongs to God.

The Church and the Roman Empire. In spite of these indications regarding Church-State relations, the NT does not formulate a clear theory on the subject. From Nero to Constantine, the Church had no legal right to exist, and there was no need to frame a Church-State theory. Persecution was frequently the lot of Christians, beginning at least as early as the reign of Nero. The final effort to eradicate Christians from the Roman world came under Diocletian and began in 303, but with the Edict of Milan (313), issued by Constantine and Licinius, Christianity became a *religio licita* and was tolerated. Whatever his motives may have been, Constantine progressively offered assistance to Christianity, ordering Sunday observance, giving privileges to the clergy, calling councils, and helping to suppress schisms and heresies. By the late 4th cent. (380), Gratian and Theodosius the Great ordered that Christianity be recognized as the sole religion of the Empire. This new situation created a need for closer definition of the relationships between Church and State, but such theory developed only gradually. Constantine, in accord with previous custom, regarded himself as the religious leader *(pontifex maximus)* and assumed the power of intervening in church affairs. Gratian gave up that title, but he and his successors continued to regard themselves as responsible for directing church affairs. The establishment of the capital at Constan-tinople (Byzantium), as well as other factors, led to a different conception of Church-State relations in the East than that which developed in the West. In the Byzantine Empire, caesaropapism became the prevailing theory, but in the West the Church had more freedom from direct control by the civil governments, and the Middle Ages witnessed the tendency for the Church to gain superiority over civil government.

Medieval Ascendancy of the Church. Partly because of the ineffective leadership in the western part of the Empire, the bishops of Rome had to take responsibility for judicial affairs, military defense, and other secular interests. When Ambrose of Milan warned Theodosius that even emperors are subject to the Church, he took a step that signaled the direction to be taken in Western Europe. It was Pope Gelasius I, however, who first clearly stated the doctrine of the two realms (494), as it was generally conceived in medieval Western Europe: "There are . . . two powers by which this world is chiefly ruled: the sacred authority [*auctoritas*] of the Popes and the royal power [*potestas*]. Of these the priestly power is much more important, because it has to render account for the kings of men themselves at the divine tribunal. . . . You know that it behoves you, in matters concerning the reception and reverent administration of the sacraments, to be obedient to the ecclesiastical authority rather than to control it." This text was the subject of endless debate as later canonists analyzed the etymological significance of his use of *auctoritas* and *potestas,* trying to deduce the implications of spiritual supremacy for temporal affairs. Long, involved struggles ensued as the concept of a single society with two aspects, each with its own responsibilities, was worked out. In the West, the Empire existed only in theory after the deposition of Romulus Augustus (476), except for a brief revival under Justinian I. The Teutonic invasions resulted in a series of Germanic kingdoms over which the Byzantine rulers lacked effective control. Freed from direct control of Byzantium, popes increased in prestige and power; the baptism of Clovis, missions to frontier peoples, alliance with Frankish kings, the spurious Donation of Constantine, the genuine Donation of Pepin, and other influences contributed to winning the Germanic tribes to orthodoxy and fellowship with Rome and to establishing the temporal power of the papacy. Having been crowned by Pope Leo III as emperor of the Romans, Charlemagne sought to revive the Empire in the West. He held views tending toward caesaropapism and would have liked to limit the role of the pope to spiritual affairs, but he had no competent heirs to continue his policies. Later popes used the precedent of Charlemagne's coronation to show that emperors received their crowns from the papal office; emperors claimed the right to approve those elected to the papal office. Hence by the 11th cent. the elements of an inevitable struggle were present.

The death of Charlemagne had been followed by decentralized government and the feudal system, which tended to subordinate the Church to secular authorities. Since bishops and abbots were often also vassals of a temporal lord, kings and noblemen often appointed bishops as well as lower clergy, investing them with the insignia of their offices simultaneously with the reception of their homage as vassals. Popes might protest this situation, but not until the 11th cent. was secular control checked and the freedom of the Church ensured. When Gregory VII (Hildebrand), an advocate of reform, challenged the right of Henry IV to appoint a bishop of Milan, the issue was joined in the investiture struggle. In 1075, he issued a decree forbidding lay investiture, following it with the *Dictatus papae,* which asserted the powers of a pope, including the explicit claim "that he may depose emperors." Although Gregory won a victory at Canossa, the struggle was resumed after Henry returned home, and Gregory died in exile from Rome. The question was tentatively settled by the Concordat of Worms in 1122, which represented a compromise between the proponents of royal theocracy and those of papal theocracy. Bishops in Germany were to be chosen according to canon law and invested with their insignia by an ecclesiastical officer. The king or emperor could be present at the election, and he could accept the homage from the appointee. Since, however, he could refuse to make the chosen person his vassal, he had a virtual veto power over clerical appointments. Similar agreements were made elsewhere, and tensions were somewhat eased; but the theory of papal right to depose kings remained unsettled.

By the reign of Innocent III (1196–1216), the question of relationships between temporal and spiritual authorities appeared to be solved, with the latter being dominant and granting rights to the former. The papal claims were stated in an analogy: "The moon derives her light from the sun, and is in truth inferior to the sun in both size and quality, in position as well as in effect. In the same way the royal power derives its dignity from the pontifical authority." Innocent successfully challenged kings and lesser nobility on numerous occasions, using his power of interdict and the right to absolve citizens of allegiance to a disobedient sovereign as proof of his contention that the royal power is subordinate to pontifical authority. His success in forcing John of England to accept a papal appointment to the See of Canterbury was one of the most striking manifestations of his power. The period of Innocent III, however, was the zenith of papal power, and the aspirations of kings to consolidate their powers to form strong national states led to the curtailment of papal influence and prestige. When a century later Boniface VIII ventured to force Philip IV of France and Edward I of England to cease taxing the clergy, he had to compromise with them. When he clashed with Philip over the trial of a clergyman by a civil court, his bull *Unam sanctam* (1302) proclaimed that both temporal and spiritual swords "are in the power of the Church" and "the temporal authority subject to the spiritual power." Moreover, the spiritual power can sit in judgment on earthly powers, but the spiritual power can be judged "only by God not by man." These assertions no longer carried the weight of authority with kings that Innocent III's words had had, and Boniface came to an ignominious end as the prisoner of Philip's soldiers.

Emergence of the Secular State. The Avignon residence of the popes (1309–77) and the *Great Western Schism (1378–1417) further weakened the authority of the papal office, and the decision to vote by nations at the Council of *Constance indicated the growing self-consciousness of national states. Simultaneous with these developments canonists and theologians were proposing theories that challenged the whole concept of the pope's temporal power. *Marsilius of Padua in *Defensor pacis* (1324) argued that power resided with the people and the princes who represented them, and he denied all clerical authority over temporal affairs. Conciliar theorists such as Conrad of Gelnhausen, Henry of Langenstein, John Gerson, and Nicholas of Cusa sought to make popes subject to the corporate community. John *Wycliffe in his *De civili dominio* (1376) stated that ecclesiastical power is rightly held only by those who are in a state of grace, and therefore unworthy clergy (even the popes) may be deposed by temporal rulers. With these trends, the balance of power seemed to be swinging more toward the State.

With the upheaval of the Reformation, the concept of a single society with temporal and religious aspects continued, and a close relationship between Church and State was almost everywhere assumed. Luther sharply distinguished the temporal from the spiritual but considered many ecclesiastical matters (such as administration) nonessentials. So long as they did not interfere with the gospel itself, he permitted princes to exercise episcopal supervision of church affairs. Thus developed the Erastian territorial system that characterized most of the Lutheran states (see ERASTIANISM). Calvin sought to make clear distinctions between the spheres of Church and civil government, believing that it was the duty of the latter to maintain peace and to protect the Church and to get its instruction from the Scriptures through the pastors. He was not entirely successful in making this system work in Geneva, but the *Reformed Churches generally tended to accept such views and to avoid civil domination. The Church of England began by substituting the king for the pope as the head of the Church, and king and Parliament took responsibility for regulating ecclesiastical government, worship, and discipline. The Catholic theologian Card. Bellarmine sought to clarify the position of the national State by denying the "direct power" of the Church over temporal authorities. Since he held that it had an "indirect power," however, his position still allowed for clerical intervention in civil affairs. Only the left-wing of the Reformation, the Anabaptists, insisted that the spheres of Church and State were completely separate; their views seemed so anarchical that they were persecuted by all of the other parties. In England in the 17th cent. left-wing Puritanism (Baptists, some Independents, Quakers) contended for religious liberty, supported by a separation of Church and State; Richard *Hooker was strongly

Erastian. With the emergence of a theory of natural rights (e.g., Hobbes, Grotius, Locke), a new view arose that rooted civil government in a social contract rather than in God's appointment (see COLLEGIALISM; TERRITORIALISM), and the secular State tended to make the Church subservient to the common good of society, but eventually where it took democratic form it fostered tolerance and expected religion to steer clear of political issues. In various forms, however, attempts at state control of the Church have recurred: in *Gallicanism; the *Civil Constitution of the Clergy; *Febronianism; *Josephinism; and the *Kulturkampf and 20th cent. totalitarianism, both fascist and communist.

The U.S.: Separation of Church and State. The U.S. was the pioneer in a new system that sought to guarantee religious freedom through separation of Church and State. Although the proprietors who founded colonies usually expected to reproduce institutions with which they were familiar in Europe, including an *established Church, conditions in America were not favorable to this arrangement. During the colonial period there were established Churches in most colonies. In the South (Md., Va., N.C., S.C., and Ga.), as well as in four counties of N.Y., the C of E was established by law, although with varying effectiveness. In New England (Mass., Conn., and N.H.), Congregationalism represented the "Standing Order." In R.I., N.J., Pa., and Del. there was no state Church; Md. had begun without one, but before the end of the century had established the Anglican. In spite of laws regarding church attendance, tithes, etc., it was difficult to enforce provisions for establishment, because the need to attract settlers led to the offer of religious toleration for dissenting groups. By the time of the Revolution, when the new states wrote their constitutions, most of them disestablished their Churches. In Va. establishment was abolished only after a 10-year struggle (1786), and Mass. maintained the vestiges of its establishment until 1833.

First Amendment. The U.S. Constitution forbade religious tests for public office, and its First Amendment provided that "Congress shall make no law respecting an establishment of religion, or prohibiting the free exercise thereof." Hence, an experiment began in the U.S. that was regarded as hopelessly utopian by most Europeans. Debates have long been carried on as to the reason for this decision, but the outcome was the result of a number of influences. Baptists such as Isaac *Backus favored separating Church and State in order to protect the freedom of the Church and the individual conscience from the State; the rationalistic deists were more concerned to protect the State from clerical domination; and from a practical standpoint, the pluralistic nature of the population would have made it impossible for all to agree on which Church to establish. The lack of a religious establishment in a state did not keep constitution writers from incorporating clauses that denied the right of atheists to hold office, kept Catholics from voting or holding office, or otherwise required conformity to some religious belief for full citizenship. Nevertheless,

for all practical purposes a new experiment in Church-State relationships had been inaugurated.

Throughout much of the 19th cent., it was assumed that the American doctrine of separation of Church and State was perfectly clear, but the 20th cent. has revealed inconsistencies and problems that show that it was never clearly defined. Much debate has centered on the question of the intention of the Founding Fathers in framing the First Amendment. The question is not easily answered, for they did not all mean the same thing. Taken at face value, the Amendment says simply that the federal government cannot establish a religion or deny religious liberty to anyone. The intention of men like Thomas Jefferson is obvious. They considered that government best that governs least, regarded religion as primarily a private affair between an individual and God, and so saw no reason for conflict between government and religion. Others clearly had as their primary concern to keep the federal government from interfering with religious matters in order that each state could handle such questions. Some interpreters contend that the intent was to make a secular nation of the U.S.: others hold that the aim was to make the U.S. a Christian nation, but neutral with respect to particular denominations. If a secular nation had been desired, chaplains would not have been appointed for the Senate and the House of Representatives, as well as for the military services. If the Founding Fathers had wanted to establish Christianity without favoring a denomination, they could have assessed taxes for religion and allowed everyone to designate where he wanted his money to go. Such a proposal was seriously considered in Va. and elsewhere. There was actually no unanimity among those who wrote and voted for the First Amendment, and the quest for the "original intention" is seeking a will-o'-the-wisp.

Supreme Court Decisions. Religious issues of a controversial nature arose in the 19th cent., but they were settled in state courts, since the First Amendment left such matters to the states. Today, however, religious disputes have come under the umbrella of federal law. Only since c. 1940 has this been true, for in that year the Supreme Court decided that the religious liberty clause of the First Amendment applied to the states because it was guaranteed by the Fourteenth Amendment (*Cantwell et al. v. State of Conn.*). Since that time the Supreme Court has dealt with a number of critical religious issues, and has gradually been seeking a working definition of the religious clause of the First Amendment. Whatever the original intention may have been, conditions have changed and have altered the way in which the Amendment must be understood today. The Supreme Court has often been criticized for its decisions, but it has a difficult task to decide what is, or is not, equivalent to "an establishment of religion" in the 20th cent. and to determine where the freedom of an individual (or group) conflicts with the freedom of others or with obligations to the larger good of the community. The role of government has changed, so that the welfare state has taken over functions that once were primarily in the hands of the Churches. The care of the poor, hospitals, homes for the aged, and children's homes involve expense that goes beyond church capabilities; but there is still need for such church institutions, and they can be operated only with government aid. Private colleges render aid through research and other means to their communities as well as to the state and federal governments, and questions of aid are put into a new light. Questions of individual conscience, laws governing business on Sundays, taxation of church property, religious tests for office-holding, religion in the public schools, and public support for parochial schools have all come before the Supreme Court in recent years for adjudication.

With the rising tide of secularism, no Church-State issues have been of greater importance or evoked more heated arguments than the questions of religion in the public schools and the public support of private schools. Certain decisions have become landmarks, laying down guidelines for the development of a more consistent constitutional approach to the problems. In 1947 (*Everson v. Bd. of Ed.*, N. J.), the bussing of Catholic school children was approved on grounds of the child-benefit theory. The first significant decision regarding religious exercises in the public schools was that of *McCollum v. Bd. of Education* (Ill., 1948). Releasing children from classes during regular hours and using the school building for religious instruction was declared unconstitutional. In *Zorach v. Clauson* (N.Y., 1952), however, it was declared constitutional to release children from school to attend religious classes in a church. The Supreme Court in *Engel v. Vitale* (N.Y., 1962) ruled that a prayer provided by the Board of Regents could not be required of pupils. Furthermore, in the following year a decision on two cases (*Abingdon School District v. Schempp* and *Murray v. Curlett*) concluded that any prayer, Bible reading, or other religious exercise required by public officials was a violation of the freedom of children who did not wish to participate. In 1966 the refusal of the Supreme Court to review a decision of the Maryland high court seemed to sanction the use of public funds for private colleges, but the basis of such support was to be determined by the extent to which such a college could be considered secular or sectarian. Two further significant decisions were handed down in 1968. By a 6–3 vote (*Bd. of Ed. v. Allen*) the Supreme Court upheld a New York law that provided for the loan of textbooks to parochial schools. At the same session it opened the way for citizens to challenge congressional acts (*Flast v. Gardner*), where questions of "standing" had closed this avenue before. A 1969 decision (*Presbyterian Church, U.S.A. et al. v. Mary Elizabeth Blue Hull Memorial Church et al.*) ruled that civil courts could not intervene in legal disputes that arise from the withdrawal on doctrinal grounds of a local church from a denomination. The court decision both indirectly favored one side in a controversy over church doctrine and directly affected denominational structures.

The years 1970–76 were marked by several significant cases which had their philosophical and legal bases grounded in the interpretation of the First Amendment. Several of these are worth mentioning. In 1970 in *Walz v. Tax Commission of New York,* the Supreme Court affirmed the exemption of Church-owned property from taxation by upholding the constitutionality of a New York statute. In 1971 the court in *Earle v. DiCenso* and several similar cases ruled unconstitutional a 1969 Rhode Island statute providing salary supplements to teachers of secular subjects in parochial schools. In the same decision it ruled (*Lemon v. Kurtzman*) that a Pennsylvania statute authorizing the state to purchase service for the teaching of secular subjects in nonpublic schools was unconstitutional. In both cases the court argued that there was evidence of excessive entanglement. A landmark decision was that of the Amish Decision (1972). The court ruled that Amish parents were exempt from a Wisconsin statute requiring them to send their children to public school until age 16. Other subsequent cases that involve the nonestablishment clause are: *Committee for Public Education and Religious Liberty, et al. v. Nyquist, et al.* No. 72–694 (1973); *Sloan, Treasurer of Pennsylvania, et al. v. Lemon, et al.,* No. 72–459 (1973); *Levitt, et al. v. Committee for Public Education and Religious Liberty, et al.* No. 72–269 (1973); *Wheeler v. Berrera* (1974); *Norwood v. Harrison* (93 S. Ct. 2804); *Wiest v. Mt. Lebanon School District* (1974); and *Meek v. Pittenger* (1975). A more recent case was *Roemer v. Board of Public Works of Maryland* 96 S. Ct. 2337 (1976). This case was decided by the Supreme Court of the U.S. in a 5–4 decision upholding the constitutionality of a Maryland statute. The statute allocated funds to private institutions of higher education but forbade the use of those funds in religious programs. The majority upheld the statute in the face of an attack that it violated the separation of Church and State under the Establishment Clause of the First Amendment. The court adhered to its precedents and stated that, "the religious programs at each school are separable from the secular programs and the latter are the only beneficiaries of state aid." The Supreme Court agreed with the District Court that there was "no excessive entanglement from the federal government at the private institutions and that the dominant purpose of the program was to further secular education."

These are all crucial decisions, and they illustrate the democratic process at work seeking a viable solution to a vexing and ambiguous constitutional amendment; it is clear that the phrase separation of Church and State is not so precise as it once seemed. Many, following a statement of Jefferson in a letter to a Baptist association, have spoken of a "wall of separation" between Church and State. Such absolute separation is almost an impossibility in our complex society, and in a pluralistic society some workable solution must be found. It appears that instead of a single wall, there are two parallel walls between Church and State. On one side of the two are matters that are clearly religious and not subject to civil interference; on the other side are political questions that are not in the province of the Churches. Between the walls, however, is a middle gray area, which the Supreme Court and continuing dialogue between contesting parties must work out in the interests of justice. BIBLIOGRAPHY: C. A. Antieau, et al., *Religion under the State Constitutions* (1965); *idem, Journal of Church and State* (1959–); O. Cullmann, *State in the New Testament* (1956); S. Z. Ehler and J. B. Morrall, *Church and State through the Centuries: A Collection of Historic Documents with Commentaries* (1967); N. Q. King, *Emperor Theodosius and the Establishment of Christianity* (1960); J. J. McGrath, *Church and State in American Law* (1962); M. R. P. McGuire et al., NCE 3:726–758; K. F. Morrison, *Two Kingdoms: Ecclesiology in Carolingian Political Thought* (1964); A. P. Stokes and L. Pfeffer, *Church and State in the United States* (rev. ed., 1 v., 1964); B. Tierney, *Foundations of the Conciliar Theory: Contributions of the Medieval Canonists from Gratian to the Great Schism* (1955); P. R. Coleman-Norton, *Roman State and Christian Church* (3 v., 1966); W. G. McLoughlin, *New England Dissent 1630–1833* (2 v., 1971); F. J. Sorauf, *Wall of Separation* (1976).

[N. H. MARING]

CHURCH AND SYNAGOGUE (ART), two female figures, *Ecclesia exaltatur* and *Synagoga deponitur,* expressing in allegory the Old and New Law of the Jewish and Christian religions, the Church erect and crowned, often holding a chalice and banner, the Synagogue blindfolded and dejected. Seen in early Christian mosaics and in 10th-cent. French ivories, the finest Gothic examples in sculpture are at Bamberg and Reims. BIBLIOGRAPHY: C. R. Morey, *Medieval Art* (1942).

[M. J. DALY]

CHURCH ARCHITECTURE, see CATHEDRALS.

CHURCH AS SACRAMENT, the quality of the Church by which it is the visible expression of Christ's salvation made present as a sign in the form of the believing community. This understanding of the Church is based upon a fundamental religious concept lying at the heart of Christianity, i.e., that the material world and humanity itself can be signs of the presence of God who transcends both material world and humanity. In post-Tridentine RC thought, the concept of a material sign as sacrament was limited to the seven liturgical rites or traditional sacraments. More recently, renewed study of Scripture and of patristic writings have led to an understanding of Christian sacrament which is more ancient and more extensive in application than that of the post-Tridentine period. The OT roots of the Christian concept of sacrament are found in the Sapiential literature (Wis 2.22–23) and in Dan 2.18–19, 27–30, 44–47, where sacrament is understood as an obscure revelation of God's

mysterious plan for the salvation of mankind, which will be completely revealed at Christ's second coming. The NT understanding of sacrament is developed in the Pauline literature where sacrament appears as the person of Jesus Christ revealing the divine plan for the salvation of the human race. Christ as God-man reveals the Father and the Father's salvific will for mankind by using his human nature, a material, created entity, as a sacramental sign to make the Father's redemptive salvation present in this world. Christ is the primordial sacrament of God the Father because through his death, resurrection, ascension, and sending of the Spirit, Christ wins salvation for humanity.

Proceeding from the saving events of Christ's life are both the salvation he brings in the Father's name and the Church as sacrament or instrumental sign whereby this salvation is continuously made present to the world. That the Church is born from Christ's death and resurrection is the constant teaching of Christian tradition. Augustine witnessed to this truth when he wrote: "Christ dies that the Church might be born" (*In evan. Ioan.* 9.10). Vat II Const-Church 2–7 places the beginnings of the Church in Christ's paschal mystery. The Church is the sacrament of Christ because it visibly expresses Christ's salvation made operative among men. The Church as sacramental prolongation of Christ continues to mediate to this world the Father's salvation for all mankind, which was revealed in its fullness in Christ. This mediating activity is most obviously expressed when the Church as sacrament of Christ offers to men one of the seven basic bestowals of grace. These seven rites are called sacraments because under the veil of material elements, the Church as sacrament communicates to the recipients of these rites a sharing in what she herself is: the sign, of the Father's salvation revealed in Jesus Christ. BIBLIOGRAPHY: E. Schillebeeckx, *Christ: The Sacrament of the Encounter with God* (1963); K. Rahner, *Church and the Sacraments* (1963); M.-J. le Guillou, SacMund 1:318–321; M. Schmaus, *Dogma Five: Church as Sacrament* (ed. T. P. Burke, tr. W. McKenna and M. Lederer, pa. 1975).

[J. J. FLOOD]

CHURCH ASSEMBLY, formal title, The National Assembly of the C of E; established by the Enabling Act of Parliament in 1919, and composed of three divisions—the House of Bishops, including all the members of the Upper Houses of the two *Convocations; the House of Clergy, including all the members of the Lower Houses of the Convocations; and the House of Laity, consisting of laymen and women elected by the dioceses of both Convocations for 5-year terms. The Church Assembly is primarily responsible for preparing ecclesiastical measures for consideration by Parliament; it also prepares and administers the central financial budgets of the C of E, and establishes and oversees the Church's main national administrative agencies. It is not authorized to make decisions on theological matters. Meetings are usually held three times a year, in London, under the presidency of the abp. of Canterbury. Annually an official yearbook is published, which is a useful guide to the organizations and agencies of the Church of England. BIBLIOGRAPHY: G. Mayfield, *Church of England, Its Members and Its Business* (1958).

[S. F. BAYNE]

CHURCH ATTENDANCE, presence at church services. Among RCs the expression, as commonly used, generally refers to presence at Mass; among Protestants, to presence at Sunday morning worship and communion services; in neither case, to participation in other services held for purposes of worship, study, or church-related activity. Among Catholics church attendance on Sundays (and holy days of obligation) is obligatory under church law; the relevance of this law and its binding force have been questioned since Vatican Council II. Among Protestants it is encouraged, but as a privilege one ought to delight in using rather than as an obligation. Some Protestant denominations require candidates for church membership to make a promise of attendance, but one who neglects to attend incurs no specific penalty. Consistent failure, however, might lead to one's being dropped from the church rolls. The sense of obligation commonly felt by Catholics makes attendance and nonattendance a rough basis for the distinction sometimes drawn between practicing and nonpracticing Catholics. The absence of a sense of obligation among Protestants makes nonattendance less significant in the interpretation of the statistics of church membership. The statistics of the *World Christian Handbook* (1968) distinguish between "Communicants or Full Members," and "Total Christian Community." Actual church attendance is a factor in determining each. BIBLIOGRAPHY: *World Christian Handbook 1968* (eds. H. W. Coxill et al., 1967) 57–58. *SUNDAY OBSERVANCE; *STATISTICS OF RELIGIOUS BODIES.

CHURCH COMMANDMENTS, see COMMANDMENTS OF THE CHURCH.

CHURCH DOORS, see DOORS, CHURCH.

CHURCH IN WALES, title of the autocephalous Church of the *Anglican Communion, since 1920, when the four dioceses of the C of E in Wales were disestablished and disendowed; two additional dioceses have subsequently been created. The Church is organized as a single province, but with no fixed metropolitan see, the bishops electing one of their number to serve as metropolitan. Membership of the Church is estimated at 1,300,000. In general the Welsh people accepted the principles of the English Reformation. This was supported by a policy, begun by Elizabeth I, of appointing Welsh bishops and encouraging the use of the Welsh language. The NT was translated into Welsh in 1567 as was the BCP of 1559, and the entire Bible in 1588.

Following the Restoration, however, the Crown began generally to appoint Englishmen, often nonresidents and in plurality, to major Welsh ecclesiastical posts. By the end of the 18th cent. the position of the established Church had been drastically eroded among the Welsh; and the 19th cent. saw a rapid growth in the dissenting bodies, notably Calvinistic Methodists, which ultimately made the disestablishment of the Church inescapable. Since 1920 the Church in Wales has gained markedly both in numbers and in its indigenous character, with wide use of Welsh and a vigorous independence from the C of E in both direction and policies. BIBLIOGRAPHY: S. Neill, *Anglicanism* (pa., 1958).

[S. F. BAYNE]

CHURCH MEETING, a distinctive element of the congregational polity of Congregationalists and Baptists, the gathering of the entire congregation to consider material or spiritual concerns of the local church. Acknowledging that Christ alone is head of the Church, they seek through prayer and discussion to ascertain the mind of Christ. Unanimity is sought, but when decisions must be reached before all are in agreement, a majority vote may be accepted BIBLIOGRAPHY: D. Jenkins, *Congregationalism: A Restatement* (1954). *GATHERED CHURCH.

[N. H. MARING]

CHURCH MERGER, see MERGER.

CHURCH MILITANT, a term characterizing the Church's stance as it lives in the world, as distinguished from its situation in heaven spoken of as the Church Triumphant. The Church as it exists in the world is considered to be in a state of conflict with the forces of evil, a conflict that calls for aggressive action in conquering the world for Christ. The motif of Christian warfare is prominent both in the NT and in church history.

[T. EARLY]

CHURCH MODES (Ecclesiastical or Medieval Modes), medieval system of eight scales used in Gregorian chant. Each scale consists of the tones of the C-major scale (white keys on the piano), but starts and closes on d, e, f, or g, and is limited to the range of an octave. For each of these four notes, called a *finalis,* there exist two modes, authentic and plagal (borrowed), distinguished by the arrangement of the five whole tones and two semitones within the octave range. In the authentic modes the *finalis* is always the lowest tone of the scale which ascends to the octave above its final. A plagal mode is one whose scale ascends a fifth above and descends a fourth below its final. The *finalis* is the note on which melodies in a particular mode usually end. In each mode a different note called the *tenor* or reciting tone is favored as the one on and around which most of the chant is centered. Names of the Church Modes were borrowed from terms the Greeks applied to octave species; musically the Greek modes are not the same as the medieval modes.

AUTHENTIC MODES		RANGE	FINALIS	TENOR
I	Dorian	d-d'	d	a
III	Phrygian	e-e'	e	c
V	Lydian	f-f'	f	c
VII	Mixolydian	g-g'	g	d

PLAGAL MODES

II	Hypodorian	A-a	d	f
IV	Hypophrygian	B-b	e	a
VI	Hypolydian	c-c'	f	a
VIII	Hypomixolydian	d-d'	g	c'

BIBLIOGRAPHY: C. Sachs, *Our Musical Heritage* (1955) 46–49; J. C. Thomson, *Music through the Renaissance* (1968) 29–30; J. Schrembs, *Gregorian Chant Manual* (1935) 8–12.

[J. S. PALLOZZA]

CHURCH MUSIC, music which is an integral part of divine worship. The limits of its expression and its form are clearly defined by the shape of the liturgy. In the historical course of church music there are four large periods of development. (1) All ancient Christian music was vocal. Psalmody, the oldest type of music for worship, was adopted by the Roman Church from Eastern Christians, who in turn adopted it from Oriental song. Hymns, which differ from psalms in their metrical text and syllabic style, were introduced around the 3d century. From the 6th to 11th cent. Gregorian plainsong became the universal musical language of the Church. (2) Early in the 14th cent. polyphony had conquered all domains of music, secular as well as sacred. Gregorian chant was no longer used as the *cantus firmus* in polyphonic settings of the Mass; instead, secular melodies, as well as newly composed material, became the fixed voice. (3) In the 16th cent. music was considered an ornament of worship and a means of providing artistic display; no longer was it an integral part of the liturgy. Music was conceived of in terms of man and his search for personal religious expression. By 1700 the unity between church music and liturgy as it existed in the Middle Ages was no longer a reality. By the 18th cent. the rationalists' "art for art's sake," which penetrated every aspect of musical life, embraced church music also. However, the liturgical reformers of the 19th cent. found a model in the simplicity and clarity of the ancient classics. They were led back to the liturgical song of the Middle Ages, making Gregorian chant and ancient classical polyphony the church music of the 19th century. (4) Pius X's *Motu proprio* of 1903 became the basic document of church-music legislation, evaluating the liturgical music of the 19th century. According to the document, Gregorian chant occupies first place in church music. In the second place stands ancient classical polyphony, esp. of the Roman School of Palestrina, and in the third is modern music with its many stylistic forms insofar as they are appropriate to liturgical texts and avoid the theatrical.

After World War I liturgical reform spread from Belgium, where it began under the direction of Card. Mercier, into Germany, Austria, and Italy. The restoration of Gregorian chant by the Benedictine monks of Solesmes in France gave impetus to the reform movement, which endeavored to bring church music back to the liturgical and artistic ideals of medieval worship, thereby giving the congregation an active role in liturgical services. Liturgists attempted to combine the 16th-cent. Palestrinan style with Gregorian chant, and detach church music from 19th-cent. Romantic sentimentalism. The combination of congregation, choir, soloists, and orchestral instruments opened new possibilities of liturgical composition.

Further aspects of church music were dealt with in Pius XI's *Constitutio apostolica* of 1928 and Pius XII's *Musicae sacrae disciplina* of 1955. Catholic church music today is characterized by the popular choral movement, which encourages active participation of the congregation in liturgical worship, and by newly created works in the spirit of contemporary music, with the emphasis on the art of vocal composition.

Many organizations have been formed in the 20th cent. to promote good liturgical music: the Pontifical Institute of Sacred Music, founded in Rome in 1911; the International Society for the Renewal of Church Music, founded in Germany in 1927; and the world-wide Organization of Catholic Church Musicians, founded in 1961 as a result of the International Congresses of Church Music at Rome, Vienna, Paris, and Cologne. BIBLIOGRAPHY: *History of Catholic Church Music* (tr. F. A. Brunner, (1961) 9–45; H. Leichtentritt, *Music History and Ideas* (1973) 22–50; *Guide to Music for the Church Year* (4th ed., 1974); K. Wörner, *History of Music* (tr. W. Wager, 1973). *MUSIC, LITURGICAL.

[J. S. PALLOZZA]

CHURCH OF CHRIST (Temple Lot), a small Mormon Church at Independence, Missouri. Although most of the followers of the Mormon prophet Joseph Smith, Jr., accompanied Brigham Young from Nauvoo, Ill., to Utah, some stayed in the Midwest. Several congregations around Bloomington, Ill., rejected what they believed to be false teachings in Utah Mormonism, such as polygamy. An early leader of this splinter group was Granville Hedrick, and the dissidents were known as Hedrickites. These people returned to Independence, Mo., in 1867 and began purchase of the "temple lots," real estate parcels that had been dedicated by Smith in 1831 as the site of the greatest Mormon temple. Although both the Utah Church of Latter-day Saints and the Reorganized Church of Latter Day Saints have tried to obtain possession of this land, it remains the property of the Church of Christ (Temple Lot). This Church accepts the *Book of Mormon and all revelations given to Smith up to Feb. 1834. A general bishopric directs the activities of the Church under supervision of a general conference and a council of apostles. About one-third of the members and their leader, Apostle Otto Fetting, were disfellowshipped in 1930. In the 1970s the Temple Lot Church reported 2,800 members, in 24 congregations.

CHURCH OF CHRIST, SCIENTIST, a religious body founded by Mary Baker Eddy in 1875 as the Christian Science Association and chartered in 1879 as the Church of Christ, Scientist. In the first edition of *Science and Health* (1875), Mrs. Eddy laid down the fundamental truths that were to guide her followers. There is no such thing as matter. Eternal Mind is the source of all being. The apparent dualism of mind and matter is an error. Our senses are fallible and sense-impression does not convey true knowledge. Disease is caused by mind alone, and the appearance of disease conveyed by the senses is an error of incorrect thinking. The new discovery by the Christian Scientist is of the real meaning of the gospel message that had been obscured by centuries of misunderstanding. Christian Science is the wisdom of the Eternal Mind revealed through Jesus Christ, who taught the power of Mind (i.e., Truth, God) to overcome the illusions of sin, sickness, and death. What is the key to an understanding of God? It is that God, infinite Love, is Mind. He is not material, and his creation, man, is spiritual, governed by Mind, not matter. Every individual has the inherent power from God to think and act rightly. He can love instead of hate, be confident instead of fearful. Hate, fear, prejudice, and sensuality stem from the erring material concept of existence. God did not create these evil characteristics, therefore they can be dispelled through a correct understanding of him. The role of Christ is to make this understanding possible. He is the divine manifestation of God, which comes to the flesh to destroy incarnate error. Since sin is an example of incorrect thinking, Christ's atonement is simply an invitation to correct the erroneous thought. He released men from sickness, sin, and death, and exhorted them not to be afraid, to love one another, to sin no more. When erring human beliefs were routed, God's law was expressed in healthy bodies, love, purity, and justice.

In its earliest form, the Church of Christ, Scientist, was composed of healers who sought to end the illusory conflict of mind and body by dispelling belief in disease and thus to bring health to the sick. The success of these early practitioners, all trained by Mrs. Eddy in her Massachusetts Metaphysical College, brought large numbers of converts to Christian Science, and by 1886 the movement was widespread enough to need a National Christian Science Association with annual conventions. In addition to providing her followers with the doctrinal work *Science and Health*, Mrs. Eddy drew up a legal code to direct and preserve her movement. The *Manual of the Mother Church,* first published in 1875, provided for every detail of church government, worship, and permissible activities. In polity, the Church of Christ, Scientist, is totally centralized. Branch churches depend directly on the Mother Church in Boston, and no local or regional organization is permitted. In turn, the board of directors, who succeeded Mrs. Eddy, have no authority beyond what is already set down in the *Manual of the Mother Church,* so that they merely administer Mrs. Eddy's decisions and may not innovate. Services for worship are centrally prescribed and consist of selections chosen from the Bible and from *Science and Health* and a lesson-sermon prepared for all Christian Science churches by a committee at the Mother Church in Boston. There are no clergy in the usual sense, but each branch church has two readers to perform the service. Only specially trained practitioners take part in the healing ministry. In the U.S. in 1965 there were some 3,300 branch churches. The directors are forbidden to publish membership figures. BIBLIOGRAPHY: G. Atkins, *Modern Religions, Cults and Movements* (1923, repr. 1971); C. S. Braden, *Christian Science Today: Power, Policy, Practice* (1958); G. Wilmine, *Life of Mary Baker G. Eddy and the History of Christian Science* (repr. 1971).

[R. K. MacMASTER]

CHURCH OF DIVINE SCIENCE, a religious denomination with many similarities to Christian Science, developed from the *New Thought movement. In 1887 Malinda E. Cramer founded the San Francisco Home College of Divine Science, while Nona L. Brooks, Fannie Brooks James, and Emma Curtis Hopkins began a New Thought study group in Pueblo, Col., in the same year. Both groups united in 1889 as an association of kindred spirits. In 1898 they determined to organize churches and ordain ministers and established the Divine Science College at Denver, Colo., for this purpose. In 1899 Nona Brooks was settled as pastor of the First Church of Divine Science in Denver, the mother church of the denomination. The master ideas of the Church of Divine Science can be found in *Truth and Health* by Fannie James and *Divine Science and Healing* by Malinda Cramer, which are the twin founts of its doctrine. They hold that God is everywhere, that God and man are one, that creation is self-manifestation or the emanation of the life and substance of God. Creation, then, is spirit and both spirit and substance are aspects of God. From this starting point, they argue the unreality of disease and the ability of mind to cure the body by bringing it to a harmony with the universe of Spirit. The Church of Divine Science has been associated with the International New Thought Alliance since its formation in 1914.

[R. K. MacMASTER]

CHURCH OF ENGLAND, the Church established by law as the national Church of the kingdom (not of Northern Ireland, Scotland, or Wales). The C of E included in 1974 some 27½ million baptized members in 43 dioceses, grouped in the two provinces of Canterbury and York. The abp. of Canterbury is primate of all England. Apart from legendary fragments, the earliest witnesses to Christianity in the British Isles are probably references in Tertullian and Origen, which suggests that a permanent Christian presence can be identified by the beginning of the 3d century. The first Christians may well have been soldiers and merchants, and perhaps also slaves brought to work in Britain's tin and lead mines. The attendance of British bps. at the Council of Arles (314) bespeaks a Church already settled and organized, a process in which the Roman garrisons probably played a significant part. But with the withdrawal of the imperial forces and the coming of the Anglo-Saxons, the Church entered a period of confusion and disorder. Much of the Christian community seems to have retreated into Wales and the W and N of England. Tribal life revived, in a renewed isolation from the Continent, and monastic and eremitical communities appeared; with these, Celtic church life developed its unique characteristics that were to play a significant part in later English church history.

A second period of church life began with the Roman mission under Augustine, in 597. This tradition soon began to govern the renewed church life in S England, while in the N, as at Iona and Lindisfarne, Celtic influences were strong. This resulted in a nourishing cross fertilization of the medieval Church in England, in constitution and polity as well as arts and liturgy. Still sharply isolated from the Continent, pre-Conquest England was a singular laboratory for the development of national unity and characteristics. The coming of the Normans in 1066 added yet another rich element to the amalgam already present, but even this powerful continental impulse did not displace the strongly independent spirit within the Church and among the people of the islands. Never a part of the Holy Roman Empire and always far from the centers of ecclesiastical power, England and its Church notably reflected the growing national spirit that was to find classic expression in the Tudors. Yet the Church remained stanchly loyal to the Roman See, despite the increasing restlessness at papal control of English affairs.

The Reformation in England strongly reflected the kingdom's peculiar tradition and situation (see REFORMATION). All the diverse elements that entered into the explosive continental scene were felt and echoed in England. The essentially conservative Luther and the more radical and intellectual Calvin were heard and studied; and the renewal movement within the RC Church, the so-called Counter-Reformation, made its mark. The extremist teaching of the Anabaptists was as much part of the English scene as was the humanist tradition identified with Erasmus. Yet, while each of those elements was reflected in aspects of the English Reformation, that movement of renewal still followed its own course and came to its own solution in the reformed Church of England. In coming to that solution, certain forces had major effect: the personal power and ability of both Henry VIII and Elizabeth I; the growing significance of kingship; the ferment of the Renaissance; the influence of printing and the control of it; the new vigor of nationalism; anticlericalism; the New World; a growing sense of lay responsibility; changes in economic power. The solution was more than a cent. in its formulation—from the first

Book of Common Prayer (1549) to the Act of Uniformity (1662)—and reflected the agony of those turbulent years. But the Church that emerged understood itself as in no way a "new" Church but only the reformed and renewed Church which had been part of English life from the first—which, indeed, had played a determining role in the creation of the nation.

The reformed Church exhibited certain particular characteristics. One was an emphasis on continuity (as in the determination to maintain the historic episcopal succession). Another was nationalism; it was a national Church established by law of which the Crown is the supreme governor. The supremacy of Holy Scripture as the test and proof of doctrine was reemphasized. Still another characteristic is sometimes called "inclusiveness" but is perhaps more clearly described as a "nonconfessional" attitude, a will to establish only the most central Christian statements and creeds as essential to the Church's life, and to leave as "opinion" much that in other traditions finds confessional expression (see COMPREHENSIVENESS). During the centuries of separation that followed the Reformation, the C of E has been both strengthened and weakened by those characteristics. The national principle can help the Church serve as the nation's conscience; it can also degenerate into mere privilege and *Erastianism. "Inclusiveness" can become a cloak for formalism and indifference as well as serve the Christian faith well in helping to meet the challenge of scientific discovery and theological restatement. The instruments of continuity can defend the faith; they can also breed indifference to new movements of the spirit. The history of the C of E illustrates both such strengths and weaknesses.

An unexpectedly powerful influence within the history of the Church has been the birth and growth of autocephalous Anglican Churches outside of England. The oldest of these, the Protestant Episcopal Church in the U.S., was only the first of the now 21 gathered in the Anglican Communion. Whether originally planted in empire or Commonwealth soil or by missionary expansion elsewhere, each of the young Churches brought to its own people the inheritance of faith and order, of tradition and temperament, found in the mother Church. Each has adapted those gifts to its own setting; each in turn has illuminated in a new way the insights and agreements characteristic of the English Church. Thus, while the C of E retains its strongly national character, it has been able to make a vivid contribution to world Christianity and to the ecumenical dialogue. Perhaps the most marked characteristic of the C of E in its post-Reformation history has been its capacity to retain within its life many of the theological and social tensions that elsewhere often have been destructive to church unity and vitality. In part, this reflects its tradition of "inclusiveness"; in part, it reflects a peculiar strength of national establishment. Perhaps most significantly, it reflects the strong sense of historical continuity that in turn tends to foster a patient temper of mind able to hold in tension forces and ideas often violently at odds with one another. Puritanism, evangelicalism, the Catholic revival (see OXFORD MOVEMENT), the controversy about evolution or the fundamentalist problem all have illustrated critical issues that have threatened to divide Christians yet have been contained within the life of the Church of England. BIBLIOGRAPHY: J. W. C. Wand, *Anglicanism in History and Today* (1962); id. *What the Church of England Stands for* (1972) H.G.G. Herklots, *Church of England and the American Episcopal Church* (1966); *Doctrine in the Church of England: The Report of the Commission on Christian Doctrine Appointed by the Archbisops of Canterbury and York in 1922* (SPCK, 1938) *ANGLICANISM.

[S. F. BAYNE]

CHURCH OF GOD, a designation used by more than 200 separate religious denominations in the U.S., many of them numerically very small, and by many similar religious bodies in other countries. Fundamentally the name Church of God has been used to stress the fact that all of these Churches are gathered by the power of God and claim no historic continuity with the historic Reformation Churches. With a few possible exceptions, these Churches share the view that the Church is an assembly of the regenerate, who are summoned by the Holy Spirit out of every nation and tribe and out of the existing religious denominations as well. Because of this basic view of the Church as the visible form of the invisible community of the elect, these Churches have all relied on the experience of religious conversion, repentance, acceptance of Jesus Christ, and subsequent baptism as the only means of adding new members to their congregations. The revival service and the evangelist are of great importance as a consequence. A firm literal belief in the Bible as the only rule of faith is also a marked characteristic. Emphasis on particular biblical texts may vary, but all denominations agree that the organization and practices of the Church described in the NT provide an adequate picture of the Christian life; therefore, they practice baptism by immersion and footwashing, recognize the several orders of ministers, apostles, deacons, exhorters, evangelists, bishops, and teachers, and frequently accept the speaking with tongues that follows upon *baptism by the Holy Spirit (see GLOSSOLALIA). Strongly committed to the religious revival, these Churches teach that salvation is freely given to those willing to accept it. Signs of a true conversion are essential for membership and for ordination, and a converted ministry is more highly valued than an educated one.

Denominations that call themselves the Church of God arose in three distinct circumstances; the religious revival among German-speaking Pennsylvanians in the 1820s, the Holiness movement after the American Civil War, and the Pentecostal movement in the early years of the 20th century. John Winebrenner was closely associated with the revival in south-central Pa. in 1823–25. His converts agreed to form themselves "into a church on the New Testament plan called the Church of God" ... and "to take the Scriptures of the Old and New Testaments as the only authoritative rule of [their] Christian life and practice." The Winebrenner movement by 1830 was formally organized as the Churches of God in North America (General Eldership). A similar movement toward nondenominational Christianity among the Pennsylvania German Brethren in Christ led to the establishment of the Church of God As Organized by Christ under the leadership of P. J. Kaufman in 1886. The Holiness movement had a marked influence on the Churches of God (General Eldership), as well as on other denominations. Daniel S. Warner, one of its ministers, became convinced of the importance of the second work of grace, or the experience after initial conversion of the cleansing from inner sin by the Holy Spirit. He found many of his colleagues were likewise preaching Holiness. They gathered together in the Holy Alliance Band and later left the Churches of God (General Eldership) to form the Church of God (Anderson, Indiana). Except for its emphasis on Holiness, it holds the same doctrinal position as the older denomination. The Holiness movement inspired the preaching of Richard J. Spurling, Sr., in Monroe Co., Tenn., in 1886. He gathered a small number of followers into a Holiness Church that developed into the Church of God, formed in 1906 at Cleveland, Tennessee. Speaking with tongues as a sign of baptism with the Holy Spirit was recognized in the Church of God at Cleveland, Tenn., and it was a major factor in the Pentecostal movement. Several divisions have split the Cleveland group into the Church of God (Cleveland, Tenn.), the Church of God of Prophecy, the Church of God (Queens Village, N.Y.) and the (Original) Church of God. These divisions have been primarily concerned with the attitude of their members toward Ambrose J. Tomlinson, the first general overseer of the Church of God, and do not reflect real differences on doctrine or polity. Nearly all of the other denominations that use the designation Church of God are also a part of the Pentecostal movement. BIBLIOGRAPHY: W. W. Sweet, *Revivalism in America* (1944); B. Warfield, *Perfectionism* (1958); J. T. Nichol, *Pentecostalism* (1966); H. Tomlinson, *Diary of A. J. Tomlinson* (3 v., 1953).

[R. K. MacMASTER]

CHURCH OF IRELAND, official title of the autocephalous Church in both Eire and Northern Ireland that is in full communion with the See of Canterbury and the other Churches of the Anglican Communion. It is organized in 14 dioceses in two provinces, Armagh and Dublin (not corresponding to the political divisions of the island). Its membership of about 500,000 is heavily concentrated in the N, where 27% of the population is estimated to be Anglican, as against 3% in the Republic. Except for the years 1800–69, when it was united with the C of E, it has been autocephalous. Its origin as a separate body is to be found in the Reformation in Ireland. The ecclesiastical policies of Henry VIII and his successors in England were also generally pursued in Ireland, but were not acceptable to the great majority of the people. The situation was complicated by the fact that the established Church of Ireland was under powerful English influence, extending even to the refusal to permit the translation of the BCP into Irish, and to the encouragement given by the Crown to Scottish and English Protestants to settle in Ireland, early in the 17th century. A new RC hierarchy was established in 1614, around which the bulk of the Irish people gathered. However, the Church of Ireland continued to be the established Church of the nation until 1869. Anglican life in Ireland is characterized by extreme simplicity in ceremony and liturgy, coupled with a theological tradition strongly orthodox and deeply rooted in the classical sources of Christian doctrine. As in the case of the RC Church in Ireland, the Church of Ireland has played a major role in overseas missionary effort. BIBLIOGRAPHY: *History of the Church of Ireland from the Earliest Times to the Present Day* (ed. W. A. Phillips, 3 v., 1933, 1939); T. J. Johnston et al., *History of the Church of Ireland* (1953); R. B. McDowell, *Church of Ireland* (1975).

[S. F. BAYNE]

CHURCH OF JESUS CHRIST OF LATTER-DAY SAINTS, see LATTER-DAY SAINTS, CHURCH OF JESUS CHRIST OF.

CHURCH OF ROME. Very little is known about the origins of the Church in Rome. It may well have been founded by the "visitors from Rome" (Acts 2.11) who were among those baptized by the Apostles on the first Pentecost. A rather late tradition places the arrival of St. Peter in Rome *c*.42 A.D. (Eusebius, *Hist. Eccl.*, 2.13.3–14.6), though this is probably too early. Some years later, *c*.49, the Emperor Claudius expelled the Jews from Rome for disturbances which seem to have been occasioned by the presence of Christians in their midst (Suetonius, *Claudius* 25). Among those forced to leave the city at this time were Aquila and Priscilla, who during their exile became acquainted with St. Paul in Corinth (Acts 18.2). By the winter of 57–58, the Church must have been well established in Rome since, according to St. Paul in his greeting to them, their faith was "proclaimed all over the world" (Rom. 1.8). In July, 64, a fire destroyed over half of the city, and in order to turn the blame for the disaster away from himself, the Emperor blamed it upon the Christians. In the persecution that followed a "huge multitude" *(multitudo ingens)* were put to death (Tacitus, *Annales* 15.44). Though the number should not be exaggerated, the sufferings of the Christians were undoubtedly great (cf. Clement, *I Corinth.* 5.1–6.4). Despite occasional attempts by Roman authorities to check the spread of Christianity, the Church prospered at Rome. At the time of Pope Cornelius (251–253), it included "46 presbyters, 7 deacons, 7 subdeacons, 42 acolytes, 52 exorcists, readers, and doorkeepers, and more than 1500 widows and persons in distress, all supported by the grace and kindness of the Master"

(Eusebius, *Hist. eccl.* 6.43.11). But the interests of the Church were not confined to the poor. There is literary and archeological evidence for the presence of members of the Roman nobility within it. Among those thought to have embraced the faith are Pomponia Graecina, Flavius Clemens, Flavia Domitilla, Acilius Glabrio, and Marcus Aurelius Prosenes.

Various ancient papal lists trace the succession of the popes from the time of St. Peter, one of the most important being that of St. Irenaeus, bp. of Lyons, drawn up *c*.180 (*Adv. Haereses* 3.3.3). As the see of Peter and his successors, to whom Christ promised, and upon whom he later conferred, a primacy of jurisdiction (Mt 16.16–19; Jn 21.15–17), the Church at Rome held a dominant position within the early Church. This may be seen in the intervention of Pope Clement I *c*.96 in the affairs of the Church of Corinth and of Pope Stephen I *c*.257 in the question of rebaptizing heretics as practiced by the Churches in North Africa. With the passage of time the supreme authority of the bishops of Rome came to occupy a central position in the official teaching of the Church, as may be seen in the teaching of Vatican Council I: "If anyone shall say that it is not according to the institution of Christ our Lord or to divine law that blessed Peter has successors in the primacy over the whole Church, or that the Roman pontiff is not the successor of blessed Peter in this same primacy, let him be anathema" (D1825). BIBLIOGRAPHY: E. Dublanchy, DTC 4.2:2108–2224; M.-J. Le Guillou, K. Rahner, E. Sauras, SacMund 1:313–337; D. W. O'Connor, *Peter in Rome* (1969). *PAPACY; *ROME

[M. J. COSTELLOE]

CHURCH OF SCOTLAND, before the Reformation, the Scottish Church, now the national Church, adhering to Presbyterianism. The true founder of the Scottish Church was St. Ninian (360?–432), a shadowy figure who came to Britain from Rome as a missionary bp. and at Candida Casa (Whithorn) built a church of stone, dedicated to St. Martin of Tours. Ninian was active 397–431 in the area of Galloway, Dumfriesshire, and Cumberland, and there is some archeological evidence of a successful mission among the southern Picts. The best-known figure in the early Scottish Church, however, is St. Columba, an Irish abbot, born in Donegal in 521. The Irish Church differed in certain ways from the Roman, and when Columba came to Scotland in 563 with 12 monks to establish a monastery on Iona, the island became the center from which Celtic Christianity spread to Scotland. In a later period the influence of Iona was extended into Northumbria by Aidan, who founded a settlement on the island of Lindisfarne, but at the Synod of Whitby, 664, the usage of Northumbria was conformed to that of Rome. The Synod marks the beginning of the decline of the Celtic influence, though until the time of Margaret (1070–93) clergy known as Célidé, or Culdees, who represented the Celtic tradition, were active from Iona to St. Andrews. Repeated Norse attacks on Christian centers in the 9th cent. made it impossible for Iona to remain a center of leadership, and increasingly royal and ecclesiastical power gravitated toward the East, where from c.900 St. Andrews became the chief seat of ecclesiastical power. In the reign of Malcolm Canmore (1058–93) Scotland began to emerge from its political and cultural isolation, largely through Margaret, his devout Saxon wife, who exerted a civilizing influence on her husband and helped to introduce the customs of the Catholic Church in which she had been reared, e.g., the date for the beginning of Lent and the abolition of certain "barbarous rites" (the vernacular?) in the Mass. Margaret's reforms represent the final overthrow of Celtic Christianity in Scotland. Her son David became king in 1124, and David's reign must be reckoned the most important of any before the Reformation. He continued Margaret's policies of conforming the Church in Scotland to the Churches of England and the Continent. He also encouraged the introduction of new monastic orders, esp. Canons Regular, Benedictines, and Cistercians. The medieval period gave Scotland the splendor and vitality of its monastic institutions, its universities, its vernacular Scriptures, and its sacramental life; yet the defects of the medieval period are also obvious: a general relaxation of discipline, impoverishment of the parish churches, pluralism, the intellectual and moral decline of the clergy, and a decline in church attendance and religious devotion. Many of the abbeys and priories had fallen into the hands of royal bastards or the nobility, and anticlericalism was widespread. Moneys paid in taxation to Rome diminished the authority of the king and the resources of the country.

The Reformation was first introduced to Scotland through Lutheran teachings brought in by merchants trading from the Low Countries; but an act of Parliament prohibited such teachings, and in 1528 Patrick Hamilton was burned at the stake in St. Andrews for advocating Lutheran views. By 1530 copies of Tyndale's New Testament were being distributed, and a new faith and hope began to stir. The Reformation came to Scotland in 1559–60 with the return of John Knox from Geneva. By June 1559 the Army of the Congregation (i.e., the Reformers) seized Edinburgh, Mary of Guise was deposed, and with English help, the French were expelled. The Estates of Scotland, meeting in the "Reformation Parliament," in Aug. 1560, abolished the jurisdiction of the pope, forbade the celebration of Mass, and approved the Scots Confession. The exiled Mary, Queen of Scots, returned in 1561 and for the next 6 years sought to restore her kingdom to its Roman allegiance in face of the outspoken criticisms of Knox. In Dec. 1560 the first General Assembly met and began to appoint ministers and readers to various parishes. In Jan. 1561 the first Book of Discipline was submitted to Parliament and in 1564 the Book of Common Order was confirmed by the General Assembly as the standard of worship in the Reformed Kirk. The Scottish Reformation is characterized by its stress on the primacy of the word of God, the development of popular education and the independence of the

Church. The presbyterian polity that emerged from 1575, however, was the creation not of Knox, but of A. Melville and his followers. Melville's Book of Discipline (1581) asserts against episcopacy the absolute parity of ministers and against the supremacy of crown or parliament the absolute freedom of the Church. From Melville's time the balance of power shifted constantly between the presbyterian and episcopal parties in the Church of Scotland until 1690, when Presbyterianism was finally established and the Westminster Confession officially approved.

From 1680 to 1843 the history of the Church of Scotland is one of constant division and secession, largely over the question of patronage or state intrusion (see CAMERONIANS; SECEDER TRADITION; FREE CHURCH OF SCOTLAND). In the latter half of the 19th cent., however, despite the doctrinal and biblical controversies occasioned by the intellectual ferment of the age and symbolized by the heresy trial of W. R. Smith (1846–94), movements toward reconciliation and reunion began to be seen, and in the reunion of the United Free Church with the established Church in 1929 the last major division in Scottish Presbyterianism was healed. The concise statement of the Articles Declaratory appended to the uniting act of 1929 well expresses the character and enshrines much of the history of the Church of Scotland: "The Church of Scotland is part of the Holy Catholic or Universal Church . . . adheres to the Scottish Reformation; receives the Word of God which is contained in the Scriptures of the Old and New Testaments as its supreme rule of faith and life; and avows the fundamental doctrines of the Catholic faith founded thereupon. The principal subordinate standard of the Church of Scotland is the Westminster Confession of Faith approved by the General Assembly of 1647, containing the sum and substance of the Faith of the Reformed Church. Its government is Presbyterian, and is exercised through Kirk Sessions, Presbyteries, Provincial Synods, and General Assemblies. . . . The Church is in historical continuity with the Church of Scotland which was reformed in 1560. . . . As a national Church it acknowledges its distinctive call and duty to bring the ordinances of religion to the people in every parish of Scotland through a territorial ministry. . . . This Church . . . receives from . . . its Divine King and Head, and from Him alone, the right and power subject to no civil authority to legislate, and to adjudicate finally, in all matters of doctrine, worship, government and discipline in the Church." BIBLIOGRAPHY: J. H. S. Burleigh, *Church History of Scotland* (1960); W. D. Simpson, *St. Ninian and the Origins of the Christian Church in Scotland* (1940); A. B. Scott, *Pictish Nation, Its People and Its Church* (1918); J. Knox, *History of the Reformation in Scotland* (ed. W. C. Dickinson, 1949); J. R. Fleming, *History of the Church in Scotland, 1843–1929* (2 v., 1927, 1933). *CALVINISM; *PRESBYTERIANISM.

[J. A. R. MacKENZIE]

CHURCH OF SOUTH INDIA, a Church formed Sept. 27, 1947, at St. George's Cathedral, Madras, through the union of about one million members of the South India United Church (Congregational and Presbyterian); the South India Province of the Methodist Church; and the S Indian dioceses of the Church of India, Burma, and Ceylon (Anglican). Bp. M. Hollis was elected first moderator of the Synod, the chief governing body. The Church of South India (CSI) is significant for the ecumenical movement as the first union of nonepiscopal Churches with a Church holding to the historic episcopate. It attempts to maintain the contributions of the congregational, presbyterian, and episcopal traditions that it incorporates, though it is not itself the continuation of any one of them. Since its formation the CSI has negotiated with Baptists and Lutherans, but has so far not achieved union with them. Discussions leading to the formation of the CSI began at a conference in May 1919 at Tranquebar, site of the landing of the first Protestant missionaries to India in 1706. An official joint committee began work in 1920 and issued the Basis of Union and the Constitution in 1941. Unity was achieved basically along the lines of the 1888 Lambeth Quadrilateral. No difficulty arose over the first three points, but the fourth, historic episcopate, led to extended discussion. It was agreed to accept episcopate, with bishops to be ordained by bishops, but to affirm no theory of its meaning. The five existing Anglican bps. were accepted, and nine additional bishops were ordained, including representatives of each of the uniting Churches. Of the fourteen, six were Indian and eight British.

At the time of union all communicant members of the uniting Churches were accepted as full members of the CSI, and all ministers of the uniting Churches were given full standing without further ordination. A local congregation, however, is not compelled to accept a pastor lacking episcopal ordination, and all ministers entering the CSI after the union are episcopally ordained. The 1955 Lambeth Conference expressed reservations about the union because of the acceptance of ministers not episcopally ordained but approved a limited form of intercommunion. CSI developments have occasioned extensive discussion in other parts of the world, both among the parent bodies of the Churches involved and among others who see in the CSI plan possibilities for union elsewhere. The CSI has served as an example particularly to other younger Churches seeking unity under somewhat similar circumstances. The drive toward unity in S India was motivated in large measure by the desire to achieve greater missionary effectiveness. Also, with growing nationalism, Indian Christians began to assert greater independence from Churches and mission societies of the West and to seek a form of church life suited to their own needs. BIBLIOGRAPHY: M. Hollis, *Significance of South India* (1966); B. Sundkler, *Church of South India* (1954).

[T. EARLY]

CHURCH OF THE AGAPEMONE, a 19th-cent. English revivalist body founded by Henry James Prince with

the help of Samuel Starky. Both were C of E clergymen who together began a revivalist movement in Somerset in the 1840s. Because of their bizarre doctrine they were forbidden to preach. Leaving the C of E, they established their own ministry, claiming to be personifications of the Holy Spirit. In the village of Spaxton, *c.*1850, they founded "Agapemone" (Gr., abode of love), a religious community of men and women holding property in common. Charges brought against them led to a trial that revealed licentious practices. Briefly the sect gained new members when J. H. Smyth-Pigott became its head and opened (*c.*1890) a branch establishment in London called the Ark of the Covenant. The sect disappeared in the early 20th century.

CHURCH OF THE NAZARENE, a Protestant denomination, specifically committed to the propagation of the doctrine of *entire sanctification as espoused by John Wesley, the founder of Methodism. It traces its beginning to a meeting at Pilot Point, Tex., in 1908, when sectional Holiness Churches, namely, the Church of the Nazarene, chiefly centered in Calif., the Association of Pentecostal Churches, chiefly in New England, and the Holiness Church of Christ, chiefly in Okla., Tex. and Ark., met and formed a single organization under the name Pentecostal Church of the Nazarene ("Pentecostal" was dropped in 1919, in repudiation of Pentecostalism, esp. glossolalia). The Nazarene belief stated briefly is: "That there is one God, the Father, Son and Holy Spirit. That the Old Testament scriptures given by plenary inspiration contain all truth necessary to faith and Christian living. That man is born with a fallen nature and therefore is inclined to evil and that continually. That the atonement through Jesus Christ is for the whole human race, and that whosoever repents and believes on the Lord Jesus Christ is justified and regenerated and saved from the condemnation of sin. That the finally impenitent are hopelessly and eternally lost. That believers are to be sanctified wholly, subsequent to regeneration, by the incoming of the Holy Spirit through faith in the Lord Jesus Christ. That the Holy Spirit bears witness to the new birth and to entire sanctification in the heart of believers. That our Lord will return, the dead will be raised, and the final judgment will take place" (*Nazarene Manual*).

Nazarene services are open to demonstrations of praise, but modern trends are toward more formality. The Church forbids use of liquor and tobacco, as well as worldly amusements. The government of the Church is representative. Local churches are grouped to form districts. Each district is under the jurisdiction of a superintendent elected by the district at its annual assembly, which is composed of lay representatives and ministers from each congregation. Every 4 years the various districts send representatives, in proportion to membership and equally divided between ministers and laymen, to a general assembly, which in turn elects general superintendents and a general board of approximately 40 persons, made up equally of lay and ministerial members, to direct the work of the denomination through its several departments. Each local church elects its own pastor, provides its own facilities, and is free to carry on its particular program of worship and evangelism. However, each congregation supports the broader interests of the Church through annual budgets and operates under the jurisdiction of the district and general superintendency. The Church in 1974 was composed of approximately 5,000 congregations, with a world membership of nearly 500,000 in 50 countries. The Sunday schools enroll in excess of 1 million. The Church maintains eight liberal arts colleges, a central Bible College, a graduate school of theology in the U.S., and Bible colleges in Canada, the British Isles, and other areas. The Lillenas Publishing Company, music division of the Nazarene Publishing House, is the largest denominational publisher of gospel music in the world. BIBLIOGRAPHY: C. T. Corbett, *Our Pioneer Nazarenes* (1958); T. C. Smith, *Called unto Holiness* (1962).

CHURCH OF THE SEVEN COUNCILS, a term sometimes applied to the Orthodox Church, signifying the Church at the stage of doctrinal development it had reached after the seventh *ecumenical council, the Council of Nicaea II (787). Because of the later split between E and W, that is the last council accepted as ecumenical by the East. Some ecumenists have seen the early councils as the basis on which Christian unity might be established.

[T. EARLY]

CHURCH OF THE UNITED BRETHREN IN CHRIST, see EVANGELICAL UNITED BRETHREN CHURCH.

CHURCH ORDER, norms for church life. In this broad sense the term is virtually interchangeable with "church polity." Some writers (e.g., D. Stevick, *Canon Law: A Handbook,* 1965) distinguish the concepts by defining polity strictly in political terms, as the "arrangement of authority whereby power is distributed and the work of the group is carried out." "Order" is then made to refer to something more basic, inhering in the essential constitution of the Church (74–76). It is difficult, however, to find such a consistent distinction in the general use of these terms. "Church order" was an early term applied to manuals setting forth norms for church life in particular localities. J. Quasten, e.g., refers to the *Didache,* the *Didascalia,* and the *Apostolic Tradition* as church orders (see Quasten 1 and 2), and these documents cover a wide range of subjects, including government, liturgy, and discipline. R. Hooker chose the term polity because it "containeth both government and also whatsoever besides belongeth to the ordering of the Church in public" (*Of the Laws of Ecclesiastical Polity,* 3.1.14). Today each denomination has its own books describing or stating, in normative regulations, its polity.

Church order also has a specific reference, namely, to Reformation Churches, esp. in Germany. The church order (Ger. *Kirchenordnung*) comprised the regulations in each territory, promulgated usually by the secular ruler, regarding worship, sacraments, discipline, and polity. Church orders implemented Reformation theology in practical church life; they remain an important source for Reformation history. BIBLIOGRAPHY: N. Brox, SacMund 1:373–375.

[N. H. MARING]

CHURCH POLITY, see POLITY.

CHURCH PROPERTY, canon 1498 of the CIC in the section *de bonis ecclesiae temporalibus* (church property) gives a special meaning to *church: not only the universal Church or the Apostolic See are intended but every moral person (a person in law: a diocese, parish church, approved religious order; but not fraternal or pious societies; c. 1495, §2). By church property the law intends: all temporal goods belonging to the church as defined above: material possessions and the legal rights to them, fixed and movable goods; sacred, i.e., consecrated, and precious, i.e., of special historical or artistic value. The law asserts that church property is rightfully acquired in any of the just means of acquisition commonly recognized (e.g., labor, bequest, contract, etc.; *ibid.,* c. 1499, §1); in addition there are ways of acquisition proper to the Church as a religious society, e.g., tithes, first fruits, begging (*ibid.,* c. 1502). The ownership of property belongs to the ecclesiastical moral person that rightfully acquired it, but that ownership stands subject to the supreme authority of the Holy See (*ibid.,* c. 1499, 2). The law means, first of all, that ownership is vested in the canonically constituted moral person, not in any individual or group of individuals; their control is administration, not ownership; practically speaking, therefore, neither a pastor nor the parishioners for example, own the parish property. (This understanding was one of the issues in the 19th-cent. *trusteeism controversy in the U.S.). In fact the canonical law of ownership does not coincide with U.S. civil law of corporate ownership; a church as such cannot have legal standing, but corporations are formed in a diocese or parish that meet the laws of the various states, but that also adhere to canonical norms. In civil law the principle has also been established that in disputes over ecclesiastical property the litigant favored by ecclesiastical laws is favored by the courts.

The subjection of all ownership to the authority of the pope, or in a diocese to that of a bp., does not mean that either is the owner; it does mean that papal or episcopal jurisdiction does include a kind of eminent domain that can be exercised where a notable need or advantage is clearly present. The universal administrative power of the Holy See is exercised through the *Curia Romana (*ibid.,* c. 1518); one notable function is that a transfer ("alienation") of church property of major monetary value or of esp. precious objects requires papal authorization. In a diocese the local bp. is the supreme administrator (*ibid.,* c. 1519); he is to have an administrative council capable of advising him in financial and legal matters (*ibid,* c. 1520, §1); the council, however, makes recommendations, not decisions. Episcopal administration extends to parish churches, other parochial properties, the houses of diocesan religious communities; diocesan funds, the seminary; the *mensa episcopalis;* the cathedral church (*ibid.,* c. 1357–59; 1472–83). The bp. can demand the parish accounts on his official parish visit every 5 years (*ibid.,* c. 343). In a parish the pastor, usually with the aid of two lay trustees, exercises administration, in subordination to the bishop. As to details of administration, the CIC gives specific guidelines on: the acquisition of property (c. 1472–83); tithes and first fruits (c. 1502; begging and alms gathering (c. 1503); the *cathedraticum,* a tax for the bp.'s support and a token of subordination to his administrative power (c. 1504); stole fees (c. 1507); *prescription (c. 1508–12). It also deals with contracts (involving alienation of property, gifts, loans, mortgages, sales, leases, etc. (c. 1529–43). Obviously most of these matters come under civil law as well and the CIC enjoins conformity to this law in each locale, unless the law is prejudicial to the autonomous rights of the Church (c. 1529).

The meaning of the details about church property derives ultimately from the rights of ownership and administration belonging to the Church. Thus the CIC states as a principle: the Catholic Church and the Apostolic See have the innate right freely and in independence from the secular power to acquire, possess, and administer property *(bona temporalia)* for the purpose of pursuing the ends proper to the Church (c. 1495). This statement of principle reflects a long history: the struggles, both ancient and modern, between Church and State; the challenges from reformers assailing church possession of property (see POVERTY CONTROVERSY: J. *HUS; J. WYCLIFFE); abuses within the Church, e.g., nepotism, simony, the cupidity of popes, esp. during the Avignon papacy. There must always be a tension between the spiritual identity, the mission, the true goals of the Church, all of which are inspired by the Gospel that extols poverty as an ideal, and the need for temporalities with the concomitant danger of abuses (see POVERTY AND REFORM). Such abuses in the past with regard to ecclesiastical finances are part of the history of the Church, in part because the Church became a land owner, the papacy a temporal power through sociological and cultural influences (see STATES OF THE CHURCH). Vatican Council II reasserted both the theological principle of the Church's right of ownership (VatII RelFreed n. 4) and the evangelical ideal that the exercise of the right be marked by the Church's identifying itself with the poor (*ibid.,* BpPastOff n. 6; MinLifePriests, n. 17). The council also proclaimed that the spirit of poverty and charity is the glory and the authentication of the Church of Christ (*ibid.,* ChModWorld, n. 88). These teachings have already had their effect in such post-conciliar phenomena as a greater openness about church finances; clearer identification, esp. in Latin America, of clergy with the causes of the poor; distribution of wealth; the discarding of pomp and splendor (*ibid.,* n. 71).

[T. C. O'BRIEN]

CHURCH SESSION (in Scotland, Kirk Session), the lowest court in Presbyterianism. The session consists of the pastor or minister and the ruling *elders (who in most Presbyterian Churches may be women) of a particular church or congregation. The minister is usually the moderator or chairman of the session. The session is charged generally with maintaining the spiritual government of the church, and for this purpose its powers include the reception, dismissal, and pastoral overseeing of members (discipline over members is a constitutional function now rarely exercised); the instruction, examination, and ordination of ruling elders; the development and supervision of the educational work of the Church; and the regulation of times and places of worship (though the conduct of worship is a ministerial not a sessional act). Meetings are held at times approved by the session, usually at least quarterly. Ministers are subject not to the session but to the *presbytery, in which the session is represented by the minister and a representative elder.

[J. A. R. MacKENZIE]

CHURCH STATE, see STATE CHURCH.

CHURCH SUFFERING, the souls in *purgatory. According to RC theology, the souls that must be cleansed of sin prior to their admittance into heaven are purged by suffering in the intermediate state. In the past the suffering has often been portrayed as physical, but it is now more generally interpreted as spiritual. Christians also speak of the Church Suffering on earth as it imitates Christ in accepting opposition and persecution (Mk 8.31).

[T. EARLY]

CHURCH UNITY OCTAVE, the name from 1908 to 1949 of the annual period of prayer for Christian unity, Jan. 18–25, begun by Lewis Thomas Wattson. In 1949 the name *Chair of Unity Octave was adopted. *WEEK OF PRAYER FOR CHRISTIAN UNITY.

[T. C. O'BRIEN]

CHURCH WORLD SERVICE (CWS), an organization founded (1946) to integrate the refugee and other overseas relief programs of U.S. Protestant and Orthodox Churches. In 1950 CWS became a department of the National Council of the Churches of Christ in the U.S.A. and in 1964 combined with the Division of Foreign Missions to form the Division of Overseas Ministries. The work of CWS in over 40 countries is channeled mainly through local or regional churches and missions, often in cooperation with other agencies, such as Catholic Relief Services and international and government organizations. Direct aid is supplemented by technical and economic assistance aimed at long-range self-help. BIBLIOGRAPHY: H. E. Fey, *Cooperation in Compassion: The Story of Church World Service* (1966).

[D. CODDINGTON]

CHURCH YEAR, the annual cycle of liturgical seasons and occasions celebrating the redemptive mysteries of Christ and the fruit they have borne in Mary and the saints. It begins with the first Sunday of *Advent and concludes with the last Saturday of the week following the last Sunday of Ordinary Time, feast of Christ the King. The temporal and the sanctoral cycles unfold concurrently. The temporal cycle is the ordered program according to which the redemptive events of Christ's life are commemorated or given liturgical *anamnesis; it has two great parts, the Christmas and the Easter cycles, each with its proper period of preparation, celebration, and prolongation. The sanctoral cycle is the annual sequence of the celebration of the feasts commemorating the saints. The evolution of the church year was a gradual process. At an early date Sunday became the day of assembly and *Eucharistic celebration commemorating the paschal mystery. What Sunday was to the week, Easter became to the year as a whole. There is evidence of an Easter celebration from the mid-2d cent., and out of it there developed in time the Easter and Pentecost cycles. In the 4th cent. Christmas was observed in the West and Epiphany in the East, and in the following cent. the desire to prepare for Christmas as Lent prepared for Easter gave rise to Advent. The beginnings of the sanctoral cycle appeared before the celebrations of Christmas and the Epiphany were established. It grew out of annual commemorations of the martyrdom of local heroes of the faith. Later this cycle expanded with the inclusion of confessors and virgins. From the early Middle Ages a proper balance between sanctoral and temporal cycles has been difficult to maintain because of pressures arising from the piety of the faithful. Implementing Vatican II's directives, Paul VI's *motu proprio* in 1969, *Paschalis mysterii,* reformed the church year; the new calendar was adopted in the U.S. in 1972. BIBLIOGRAPHY: Vat II SacLit, ch. 5, 102–111; N. Denis-Boulet, *Christian Calendar* (tr. P. Hepburne-Scott, 1960); T. Maertens, *Feast in Honor of Yahweh* (tr. K. Sullivan, 1965); A. A. McArthur, *Evolution of the Christian Year* (1953); T. Maertens and J. Frisque, *Guide for the Christian Assembly* (4 v., 1965).

[N. KOLLAR]

CHURCHES, sacred edifices dedicated to divine worship and established by law for the services of all the faithful (CIC, c. 1161). As intended for all, churches are distinct from *oratories, places of worship that serve a specified group or even an individual. The church has always been understood to mean basically a parish church, i.e., as a center of pastoral ministry; included is the cathedral church, seat of the bp., and also the collegiate church staffed by a group (college) of secular priests who are canons (there are no such churches in the U.S.). A house of clerical religious may sometimes have a church attached (called a conventual church), which is not a parish church but has been granted status as a church, i.e., for the pastoral care of all the faithful. "Basilica" is an honorary title, granted now only

by the Holy See, and based on a church's antiquity, magnificence, or importance in history and Christian devotion (*ibid.,* c. 1180). One reason for the juridic restrictions on which places of worship have status as churches is the need to protect the rights and income of the parish church, e.g., in feudal times when the local lords often built their own private churches and in the high Middle Ages when the popularity of the mendicant orders drew the faithful to their churches. One of the conditions in law, therefore, for the local bp.'s granting status to a church is consultation with the pastors of existing churches on the possibility of damage to their rights, and on the issue of genuine need for another church (*ibid.,* c. 1162). The local bp. must also have assurance that a new church will have the means necessary for its upkeep and the fitting conduct of the liturgy. The church building must have a design that conforms to Christian history and the norms of sacred art (*ibid.,* c. 1164, § 1); Vatican Council II in this regard called for an early revision of laws on the church building and its embellishments, and for laws suited to the proper performance of the revised liturgy; it also emphasized the adaptation of church architecture and ornamentation to the culture and customs of the region (Vat II SacLit, n. 128). Canon law also requires that a church be free-standing, i.e., with no secular building beneath or above it (CIC, c. 1164, §2). Before it can be used for worship, the church must be dedicated by a solemn consecration or at least by a simple blessing (*ibid.,* c. 1165, §1). *CHURCHES, DEDICATION OF.

[T. C. O'BRIEN]

CHURCHES, DEDICATION OF. According to RC canon law, divine services should not be held in a church before it has been dedicated for worship either by solemn consecration or at least by a simple blessing. In popular usage the term dedication is often applied indifferently either to a solemn blessing (consecration) or to the simple blessing, but sometimes the term is restricted to the solemn blessing only. The Church desires that cathedral, collegiate, conventual, and parish churches should be solemnly blessed or consecrated, provided their structure and other circumstances make that possible (CIC c. 1165.3). This article is concerned with the solemn blessing only.

The earliest places of worship in the Christian Church were dedicated by no special rite, but during the 3d and 4th cent. the erection of special and more splendid places for worship made the dedication, or first use, of a church a particularly significant and memorable occasion. But until the 6th cent. in Rome places of worship were dedicated simply by the celebration of the Eucharist. However, by the 8th cent. a fairly elaborate dedicatory ceremonial was in use. This was possibly the result of a renewed interest in the OT (cf. Ex ch. 40; 2 Chr ch. 5–6); possibly also the memory of ancient Roman practices of consecrating temples by processions, the sprinkling of lustral water, prayer, and sacrifice exerted some influence. Later fusion of the Roman ceremony with that of the Gallican liturgy resulted in a very elaborate ritual in which the themes of the two rites are distinctly discernible. The central idea of the Roman rite was the burying of the relics of the martyr(s); it was a joyous funeral. That of the Gallican rite was washing and anointing of the church corresponding to the initiatory rites of baptism and confirmation. The rite in use in the RC Church since 1961 is that contained in the revision of part 2 of the *Pontifical*. The elaborateness of the ancient amalgam has been considerably simplified. It consists of four parts: (1) ceremonies of cleansing and expulsion of evil powers conducted both outside and inside the church, and the taking possession of the church; (2) the entombment of the relics; (3) the consecration of the church and altar; and (4) the celebration of the Mass of dedication. An annual feast is celebrated to commemorate the event, either on its anniversary day, or upon the feast of the saint to whom the church is dedicated, or, very commonly, on a day chosen for the common celebration of the occasion by many churches.

Every church that is consecrated or even simply blessed must have its own title (CIC c. 1168), and after the dedication this cannot be changed. The title is the name under which the church is known. It is the person or thing (religious mystery or sacred object) to which the church is dedicated. By certain crimes (CIC c. 1172) a church is violated or desecrated, i.e., in effect it becomes unconsecrated in a sense, and it must be reconciled by the bishop or his representative before it may be used again for worship. BIBLIOGRAPHY: J. Loew, "New Rite of Consecration," *Worship* 35 (1961) 527–536; R. W. L. Muncey, *History of the Consecration of Churches and Churchyards* (1930); Podhradsky 68–69.

[N. KOLLAR]

CHURCHES OF CHRIST, a group of autonomous local churches, originating in the Restoration movement. With a membership in 1974 of 2,400,000 in the U.S., they are particularly strong in the South, esp. in Tenn. and Tex., but are rapidly spreading throughout the N and abroad. The early history of this group is the same as that of the Disciples of Christ, or Christian Churches. Within the Disciples of Christ a conflict in the late 19th cent. between progressives and conservatives led to gradual separation, the conservative group calling themselves Churches of Christ. The separation was officially recognized in 1906, when the U.S. census of religious bodies for the first time listed the Churches of Christ as distinct from the Disciples of Christ. Participants in the Restoration movement of the early 19th cent., calling themselves Disciples or Christians, had the dual goals of Christian unity and the restoration of simple NT Christianity. Congregational in church polity, anticreedal in outlook, they affirmed no creed but Christ and no authority but the Bible. They observed adult baptism by immersion, and the Lord's Supper each Sunday. Essentially the conflict between conservatives and progressives centered on whether changes being made in the movement were compatible with the NT. Conservatives opposed the estab-

lishment of a missionary society, believing that no intercongregational organization existed in the 1st cent. (see ANTIMISSIONARY MOVEMENT). They opposed the addition of instrumental music in worship as lacking any NT basis. They also opposed the assumption of pastoral powers by some preachers on the grounds that the early Church was ruled by elders and that preachers were simply preaching elders. They also opposed the practice of *open communion. Some objected to Sunday schools and to individual communion cups. As Disciples moved into the mainstream of Protestantism, they were influenced by *liberal theology, biblical criticism, the *social gospel, and the ecumenical movement. All these the conservatives rejected. In general the Churches of Christ believe that the Disciples have accepted many "innovations," whereas they have maintained the original approach of the leaders of the Restoration movement.

Churches of Christ have *a cappella* singing in their services. Local churches are autonomous; they are governed by elders and deacons appointed under NT qualifications. Biblical doctrines stressed include the view that the Father, the Son, and the Holy Ghost are members of the one Godhead; the Incarnation, virgin birth, and bodily resurrection of Christ; the universality of sin after the age of accountability, the only remedy being the vicarious atonement of Christ; the Church as the body and bride of Christ. A vigorous program of evangelism has led to rapid growth in membership. A "Herald of Truth" radio and television program sponsored by a church in Abilene, Tex., is nationwide. A large number of publications are issued. There are 21 colleges, 41 secondary and elementary schools, and 20 homes for the aged sponsored by these churches. Under a planned exodus movement, groups of member families have moved from regions in which the churches were well established to other sections of the U.S. in order to found new churches. The group of families from Midland, Tex., which moved to Somerset Co., N.J., made the move, they said, in order to establish there "a strong nondenominational church patterned after the doctrine of the New Testament." In recent years efforts have been made to expand inner-city missions and to make the church colleges racially inclusive. Missionary expansion has been most extensive since World War II in Europe, Asia, and Africa, where there are more than 450 full-time workers. All of this has been done without benefit of a missionary society or a national headquarters. Unlike the Disciples of Christ, the Churches of Christ are not members of the National or World Council of Churches. They maintain that this form of ecumenicity is a departure from the Restoration movement, which called for unity through return to the faith and practices of the early Church. Participation in the ecumenical movement means acting as a denomination among other denominations and accepting post-NT ecclesiastical developments; Churches of Christ disclaim being a denomination. BIBLIOGRAPHY: E. West, *Search for the Ancient Order* (2 v., 1951).

[P. J. BOCK]

CHURCHES OF THE NEW JERUSALEM, also called the Swedenborgian or the New Church, religious bodies relying on the writings of Emanuel Swedenborg for much of their distinctive beliefs and forms of worship. Swedenborg himself had nothing to do with the foundation of a distinct denomination; he conceived of a spiritual association of devotees from all the Churches. The movement toward a distinct New Church began with a group gathered by Robert Hindmarsh in London in 1783 to discuss the thought of Swedenborg; formal organization was in 1815. Swedenborgianism spread rapidly to the U.S., where the first congregation was formed at Baltimore in 1792. The ideas expressed by Swedenborg in his voluminous writings on theological subjects were in sharp contrast to the Lutheranism he professed in his life. He wrote of his visions of heaven and hell and of the things revealed to him by spirit messengers. His unique communications with the other world made him, in the eyes of those who chose him as the prophet of their New Church, the privileged channel of revelation, the "new Jerusalem" of Rev 3.12; 21.2. His writings on theological subjects and his interpretations of the Bible are held to be directly inspired and inerrant revelation. It was revealed to Swedenborg that his writings would be the basis for the teachings of a new Christian Church. The fundamental doctrine of the Churches of the New Jerusalem is the correspondence of the natural world to spiritual reality. The movement had a significant influence in preparing American and British Christians for acceptance of spiritualism and psychic phenomena.

Through the "science of correspondence" Swedenborg developed a personal interpretation of the Scriptures and traditional Christian teaching. Thus the Trinity is understood as a trinity of attributes of the one divine Person; the Incarnation, as God becoming the Lord Jesus, identifying himself with humanity; the Atonement, as putting man right with the spiritual world. At death man is liberated from the body forever, then as free spirit he makes his choice of living in the heaven of good or the hell of evil. Thus, while Swedenborgians profess Christian truths, observe infant baptism and the Lord's Supper, and have a quasi-episcopal polity, judgment of their Christian orthodoxy depends on how closely any group follows Swedenborg's interpretations. The Churches place great emphasis on spiritual self-realization, leading to philanthropic service. In the U.S. there are two Swedenborgian bodies: the General Convention of the New Jerusalem in the U.S.A. and the General Church of the New Jerusalem. BIBLIOGRAPHY: E. Swedenborg, *Four Leading Doctrines of the New Church* (1882, repr. 1972); M. B. Block, *New Church in the New World* (1968).

[R. K. MacMASTER]

CHURCHING OF WOMEN, the name given to the rite which the Roman ritual calls the blessing of a mother after childbirth. The rite is of ancient origin; the earliest mention of it occurs in an Arabic collection of canons attributed to the Council of Nicaea I. The service was probably suggested in the beginning by the Jewish rite of purification (Lev 12.1–8; Lk 2.22), an association that is more apparent in the ancient Eastern practice of observing the rite on the 40th day after childbirth. Gregory the Great (d. 604) protested against the notion that any kind of defilement is incurred by childbirth, and all suggestion of purification is carefully avoided in Western ritual in which it is essentially a thanksgiving service. Some Protestant Churches retain the practice, although they do not term it a blessing but a thanksgiving, e.g., "Thanksgiving of Mothers," or "Thanksgiving after Childbirth."

[P. K. MEAGHER]

CHURCHWARDEN, a lay officer in the Churches of the Anglican Communion. Since early medieval times in England, churchwardens (usually two) have been appointed in every parish to take care of the temporalities. Though the rector has control of the church edifice and its appurtenances, the wardens are responsible for its repair and for providing the furnishings necessary for the performance of divine service. They are also required to maintain order in the church and churchyard, and have the power to arrest offenders. Shortly before the Reformation, and continuing after, they assimilated the originally distinct office of sidesmen (synods men) or questmen, who represented the parish in diocesan synods or visitations and were responsible for presenting offenders against ecclesiastical law to the ordinary. The office, which is elective, exists with some modifications of function in all branches of the Anglican Communion. BIBLIOGRAPHY: R. Burn, *Ecclesiastical Law* (8th ed., 1824), 1:396 and 397–415; J. H. Blund, *Book of Church Law* (1873) 248–278.

[W. W. MANROSS]

CHURCHYARD, the plot of ground in which the church building is set. Since churchyards, or an area within them, have often been set apart as a place for burials, the term has sometimes been considered almost equivalent to cemetery. The churchyard was also sometimes known as God's acre or God's field. Churchyards have also been important as the frequent location of general gatherings, including such secular affairs as markets and trials. *CEMETERIES.

[T. EARLY]

CHURRIGUERA, JOSÉ (1665?–1723 or 1725), Spanish architect, painter, sculptor, of a family famous in the 17th and 18th centuries. In Madrid in the 1690s, C. executed large retables for altars, was court painter to Philip V, and as *maestro mayor* of the cathedral turned Salamanca into a Churrigueresque showplace. Exuberant in detail of Spanish baroque fantasy, C.'s decoration was always subordinated to structure. Excesses of the Churrigueresque style should be attributed to other members of his family. BIBLIOGRAPHY: J. Lees-Milne, *Baroque in Spain and Portugal and Its Antecedents* (1960).

[M. J. DALY]

CIASCA, AGOSTINO (1835–1902) Orientalist, ecclesiastical diplomat, and cardinal. C. mastered several Oriental languages, held the chair of Hebrew at the Propaganda College in Rome, and served as a *peritus* at Vatican Council I. He often acted as an advisor to Leo XIII and to the Holy Office, and in 1891 was appointed titular abp. of Larissa and prefect of the Vatican archives. As papal envoy, C. presided over the Ruthenian synod at Lemberg (1891), was named secretary of the Congregation of the Propaganda (1893), and elevated to the cardinalate (1899). As a scholar, C. edited fragments of an ancient Coptic OT MS and an Arabic version of a gospel harmony by *Tatian. BIBLIOGRAPHY: A. Palmieri, DTC 2.2:2472–73; B. A. Lazor, NCE 3:869–870.

[T. M. MCFADDEN]

CIBORION (Gr. *kibōrion,* a seed pod; in Sl. *sien nad prestolom*); in Eastern Church architecture, a canopy of wood, stone, or other material supported on four or more columns and placed over the altar table. It is the equivalent of the Western baldacchino or ciborium. If a eucharistic dove is used as an *artophorion,* it is usually suspended by a chain from the interior of the ciborion dome. The canopy came into use as a special sign of reverence for the altar beneath and as an architectural device to concentrate attention upon it.

[A. J. JACOPIN]

CIBORIUM, a term that in its earliest ecclesiastical use was applied to the dome or canopy supported by pillars that began in the 6th cent. to be placed above the altar; its purpose was to accent the altar. From the late Middle Ages onward it was also used in reference to a rectangular box enshrining the pyx with the reserved eucharistic bread. With the increase of devotion to the Eucharist there was a corresponding development in the vessels used in connection with the sacrament. A base was added to the pyx to make it easier to handle and perhaps also to give prominence to the pyx for purpose of exposition. The cup of the pyx retained the form of a bowl with a flat bottom; it had vertical sides and a pointed lid. This vessel came to be called a ciborium. Originally only a few hosts, to be used for the sick, were kept in such ciboria. With the increase in the frequency of communion after the Council of Trent and the growth of the custom of distributing communion outside of Mass, there was a need for larger ciboria, which often took a form not much different from that of the chalice, and the lid was commonly rounded. Today, when the practice of giving communion with hosts consecrated at the Mass attended by the communicants is spreading, smaller ciboria are more appropriate when the number of communicants is not large. Some object to the use of ciboria because their cup-shape suggests drink rather than food. The ciborium can be made of solid and noble metal or of other durable material regarded locally as noble and suited to sacred use. It must have a close-fitting, detachable lid.

[P. K. MEAGHER]

CIBOT, PIERRE MARTIAL (1727–80), French Jesuit missionary to China, who collected and edited valuable historical, cultural, and scientific information on that country. BIBLIOGRAPHY: H. M. Brock, CE 3:767–768.

[T. C. O'BRIEN]

CICERO, MARCUS TULLIUS (106–43 B.C.), Roman lawyer, statesman, orator, and litterateur. Born in Arpinum, C. was early taken to Rome where he received an excellent education. Assuming the *toga virilis* in 91, he served briefly during the Social War under Pompeius Strabo in 89. His first appearance in the courts was in a civil case, *Pro Quinctio,* in 81. The following year, risking the wrath of Sulla, he successfully defended Sextus Roscius charged with parricide. In 79 he sailed to Greece and Rhodes to regain his health and to continue his studies in oratory and philosophy. Upon his return to Rome, he married Terentia, who bore him a daughter and a son. In 75 he was a quaestor in Sicily, and in 70 he successfully prosecuted Gaius Verres, a former governor there, for extortion. He was elected aedile in 69. In 66, as a praetor, he delivered his first important political speech, supporting Pompey for the command of the Mithridatic War in the *Pro lege Manilia*. Consul in 63, he crushed the Catilinarian conspiracy, but his execution of the participants left him vulnerable to the political assaults of Clodius and he was forced to retire into exile in 58. Returning the following year, he took up his legal practice again and devoted much time to writing. Against his wishes he was sent out as proconsul to Cilicia in 51. Joining Pompey in the Civil War, he became reconciled with Caesar after Pharsalus. Because of his attacks on Antony after Caesar's assassination, he was proscribed, executed, and had his hands and head displayed in the rostra in Rome.

C.'s translations of Greek poems, like his own original verse, are technically competent but without much inspiration. His 58 extant orations (some incomplete) rightly rank him among the world's greatest orators. His seven rhetorical treatises are valuable for the history of Roman oratory and for an understanding of his own methods and ideals. They also show him to have been an acute literary critic. Twelve philosophical essays, ranging from a discussion on the nature of the gods to reflections on friendship and old age, though largely derivative, are important for the history of philosophy, for having created an interest in the science in Rome, and for having provided a vocabulary to be used by later authors. Some 864 letters, 98 of which were written to Cicero, have been preserved from his correspondence. These were not written for publication and are as a consequence all the more interesting and valuable as a mirror of the man and his age.

Though inclined to vanity, C. was essentially a good and noble person. His political outlook was too narrow to grasp the realities of the time. His seeming lack of decision came from a fear of mistakes. A warm friend and devoted father, he had on occasion to suffer from a somewhat shrewish wife, whom he ultimately divorced. Subject to fits of depression and elation, he became, despite his faults or perhaps even because of them, the supreme architect of the Latin tongue, molding it to become the vehicle of every sentiment and emotion. In later times his name became synonymous with eloquence (Quintilian 10.1.112). St. Ambrose modeled his *De officiis,* a series of instructions for his clerics, on a work of the same name by Cicero. As a young man in the desert of Chalcis, St. Jerome was accused in a vision of being more of a Ciceronian than a Christian (Ep. 22.30). But it was still a lost work of C., his *Hortensius,* that first turned the mind of St. Augustine to a love of wisdom and of God (Confess. 3.4.7). BIBLIOGRAPHY: J. W. Duff, *Literary History of Rome: Golden Age* (3d ed., 1953) 255–290; M. R. P. McGuire, NCE 3:870–871.

[M. J. COSTELLOE]

CICOGNANI, AMLETO (1883–1973), apostolic delegate to the U.S., cardinal, Vatican secretary of state. A canonist and official of several Sacred Congregations in Rome, he was esp. active in work with the Congregation for the Oriental Churches. In 1933 he was consecrated abp. and named as apostolic delegate to the U.S. where he exercised considerable influence on the American Church for 25 years. Pope John XXIII named him a cardinal and Vatican secretary of state, a position he kept also under Pope Paul VI. Two of his published works have attained wide circulation: *Jus canonicum* (1925) and *Sanctity in America* (1939).

[J. R. AHERNE]

CICONIA, JOHANNES (c.1340–1411), Belgian composer and theorist. He ranks as the most important composer in the period between Landini and Dufay. At least 37 of his works survive. Seven settings of the ordinary of the Mass, 10 motets, and 6 *chansons* are preserved at Bologna. Some of his motet texts, referring to specific persons and events, show him to have been a canon at both Padua and Venice. Though traditional in technique, he achieved freshness and clarity of style, using both the French isorhythmic system and the Italian imitative style. BIBLIOGRAPHY: D. G. Hughes, *History of European Music* (1974) 109–110.

[J. S. PALLOZZA]

CID, LE, see CORNEILLE, PIERRE.

CIENFUEGOS, ÁLVARO (1657–1739), Spanish Jesuit, theologian, cardinal, abp. of Monreale in Sicily from 1724. He is noted for a singular doctrine on the nature of the eucharistic sacrifice in his *Vita abscondita* (1728). He had to give up his see in 1735 after the Bourbons took over Sicily and spent the rest of his life in Rome. BIBLIOGRAPHY: H. Dutouquet, DTC 2.2:2511–13.

[T. C. O'BRIEN]

CIENFUEGOS, JOSÉ GNACIO (d. 1845), Chilean bp. and reformer. C. published a *Catechism of Christian Doctrine* (1829) and was the chief representative among the Chilean clergy of the so-called Catholic Enlightenment. BIBLIOGRAPHY: M. Góngora, NCE 3:872.

[J. P. COOKE]

CIEPLAK, JAN (1857–1926), bishop. Born in Poland, C. was ordained in 1881. He taught at the Catholic academy in St. Petersburg and in 1908 was named auxiliary to the bp. of Mogilev, whom he succeeded as administrator when the Russian Revolution imprisoned the ordinary. In 1923 C. was accused of antirevolutionary conspiracy and sentenced to death, a sentence changed to imprisonment through the efforts of the Vatican, the U.S. and British governments, and Edmund Walsh, SJ. Exiled in 1924, C. came to the U.S. in 1925 where he embarked on a tour of 25 dioceses. In 1926 he was appointed abp. of Vilna in Poland but died before he could assume his see. His cause for beatification is under consideration. BIBLIOGRAPHY: J. Ledit, *Archbishop Jan Baptist Cieplak* (1963).

[J. R. AHERNE]

CIGOLI, LUDOVICO CARDI DA (1559–1613), Italian painter and architect in Florence and Rome whose early style of Florentine mannerism (*Noli me tangere,* Florence, 1585) was later modified by Correggio and the Venetians. A certain mysticism and emotion (*Stigmatization of St. Francis*) presage the Baroque. After 1595 his painting reflected the new realism (*Martyrdom of St. Stephen,* 1595; *Ecce Homo* c.1607).

[M. J. DALY]

CILICIA, ARMENIAN KINGDOM OF, also known as Lesser Armenia. From 1089 to 1375, the Armenian kingdom of Cilicia perdured, largely through alliance with the Crusaders. Cilicia was fearful of both the Turks and the Greeks and depended upon Latins for support against these enemies. Through the friendly relations with the Crusaders, Roman influence was strengthened. King Leo II held his title from Emperor Henry VI and was crowned by a representative of Pope Celestine II in 1199. In this period of Roman influence the catholicos moved to the capital, Sis. While the catholicoi worked with Rome, the majority of bishops and clergy clung to the earlier anti-Roman traditions of Cilicia. Ultimately there were two dominant prelates, the catholicos of Sis and a rival in Agthamar who represented the anti-Roman group. In 1441, after the collapse of the dynasties friendly to the West, the dissident catholicos resided at Echmiadzin (now in Soviet Russia). BIBLIOGRAPHY: A. Atiya, *History of Eastern Christianity* (1968).

[J. R. AHERNE]

CILICIA OF THE ARMENIANS, PATRIARCHATE OF, a see in Lesser Armenia, which includes Tarsus, the birthplace of St. Paul. The patriarchate traces its origin to St. Gregory the Illuminator in the 4th century. The tangled and complex history of the patriarchate shows centuries of conflict with the Western Church and a series of devastating conquests by Arabs and Turks. The Monophysite struggles divided the adherents into two factions: Melchites and Jacobites, the latter representing the Monophysite tradition. During the Crusades the alliance of the Armenian kingdom of Cilicia with the Crusaders created a line of catholicoi-patriarchs in harmony with Rome. Several attempts were made to reunite formally the patriarchate and Rome, but none was of long duration. After the fall of the dynasty in late 15th cent., the Armenian Church, long ruled by patriarchs friendly to Rome, established a national Church with a patriarchate at Echmiadzin (now in Soviet Russia). In 1746 the Catholic bp. of Aleppo became patriarch at Sis, the Cilician capital, but the see was moved successively to Beirut, to Istanbul, and finally again to Beirut which is still the Melchite center. In the 20th cent. the most celebrated catholicos-patriarch was Card. Gregory Peter XV *Agagianian (1937–1962). BIBLIOGRAPHY: F. Tournebize, DHGE 4:290–391.

[J. R. AHERNE]

CILICIUM, see HAIR SHIRT.

CIMA, GIOVANNI BATTISTA (Cima da Conegliano; *c.*1460–1517 or 1518), Venetian painter whose half-length Madonnas suggest Giovanni Bellini's composition. C.'s significant lighting and modeling are evidenced in *A Madonna with SS. John and Jerome* (Vicenza). In *The Baptism* and *Madonna with the Orange Tree* (both in Venice) architectonic forms are softened by delicate light and romantic detail. In interiors, figures relate to cubic furniture (*Annunciation,* Leningrad). After 1500 C.'s softer forms show influences of Leonardo and Giorgione. BIBLIOGRAPHY: L. Coletti, *Cima da Conegliano* (1960).

[M. J. DALY]

CIMABUE, GIOVANNI (*c.*1240–after 1302), Florentine painter assumed to be Giotto's teacher, mentioned by Dante as an example of the transiency of earthly glory (*Purgatory* 11.94–96). C. is credited with only one authenticated work, the figure of St. John in the mosaic of the Deësis (Pisa Cathedral, 1302). Among attributed works are the damaged frescoes in the upper and lower churches of S. Francesco, Assisi (*c.*1288–96), two *Crucifixions,* and scenes from the Apocalypse, the life of the Virgin, and the Acts of the Apostles. C.'s importance may be gauged by the number of artists who worked under him as the "School of Cimabue" (*Christ between St. Peter and St. James Major,* National Gallery, Washington, D.C.). Though rooted in Byzantine style, C.'s innovation is seen in a vital, dynamic energy of angular and curved forms actually observed. BIBLIOGRAPHY: A. Nicholson, *Cimabue: A Critical Study* (1932, repr. 1971); E. Battisti, *Cimabue* (1966).

[L. A. LEITE]

CINCTURE, a long cord of linen or hemp used to gather and hold the *alb at the waist. It is usually white but it may be the color of the other vestments.

[N. KOLLAR]

CINGRIA, ALEXANDRE (1879–1945), Swiss artist active in the modern renewal of religious art. He founded the Society of St. Luke (1920), *avant-garde* sculptors and painters dedicated to a renewed religious art. Supported by Bp. Bresson and Abbé Dusiller (Fribourg), C. audaciously emphasized a rational approach in the early modern renewal. He designed stained glass (Notre Dame, Fribourg), mosaics, paintings, and costumes for theater (Henri Gheon's *Pendu dépendu,* René Morax's *Le Roi David*). BIBLIOGRAPHY: J. B. Bouvier, *Alexandre Cingria* (1944).

[R. J. VEROSTKO]

CINITES (KENITES), a non-Israelite seminomadic group, considered one of the indigenous tribes of Palestine (Gen 15.19) and living in the Wadi 'Arabah region (Num 24.21–22) and as far south as Midian. Israelite ideas of Kenite antiquity may be indicated in Gen 4.2–24 and possibly 5.9–14. Their name means "smith," and copper is found in many regions where the Kenites lived (see also Gen 4.22). Moses married a Kenite (Jg 4.11); in Ex 2.16–21; 18.1, she is said to be Midianite, perhaps because the Kenites were in Midian. Other traditions have Kenites accompanying Israel in the Exodus (Jg 1.16; perhaps Num 10.20–32) and settling among the Amalekites (1 Sam 15.6) and even in Galilee (Jg 4.11; 5.24). Chronicles connects the Kenites and Rechabites (1 Chr 2.55). These wandering smiths probably influenced Israel (perhaps Num 21.8–9), but the hypothesis that Israel borrowed the worship of Yahweh from the Kenites is unproved. BIBLIOGRAPHY: G. Cornfeld et al., *Pictorial Biblical Encyclopedia* (1964) 480–481.

[E. J. CROWLEY]

CIONE, DI, artist brothers of Florence: (1) **Nardo** (fl. 1343–56), brother of Jacopo and Andrea (called *Orcagna). A member of the Florentine painters' guild (1343), he executed the frescoes *Paradise* and *Inferno* according to Dante, and a *Last Judgment* in the Strozzi chapel (by *Ghiberti's attribution). Nardo's most valued pictures are small portable altars. He was one of the most important Florentine painters of his time. (2) **Jacopo** (fl. 1365–98), who completed an altarpiece of St. Matthew (1368, Uffizi, Florence) in 13th-cent. style, the saint figure in center flanked by smaller scenes in vertical strips on either side; a *Coronation of the Virgin* in collaboration with two other painters (1373, National Gallery, London); and a *Madonna of Humility with Angels* (New York). BIBLIOGRAPHY: M. Meiss, *Painting in Florence and Siena after the Black Death* (1951).

[M. J. DALY]

CIRCUIT, a term used more often in early Methodism than today, signifying a group of churches served by one minister, sometimes with the help of one or two associates, who traveled among the churches. Geographically a circuit was quite large in early Methodism, sometimes comprising 10 or more churches. The preachers often used horses to travel their circuits and thus were called "circuit riders." With the growth of the churches, single church stations with settled pastors supplanted the circuit stations, although in rural areas and the South and West there still are circuits, not, however, with the large number of churches that characterized early Methodism. BIBLIOGRAPHY: N. B. Harmon, *Understanding the Methodist Church* (1955) 102; *Cyclopaedia of Methodism* (ed. M. Simpson, 1880) 219; *Doctrines and Discipline of the Methodist Church* (1964).

[F. E. MASER]

CIRCUMCELLIONS, bands of *Donatist peasants who terrorized Upper Numidia and Mauretania in the 4th and 5th centuries. Their name was derived from the attacks they made upon the settlements about which they roamed *(circum cellas vagantur;* Augustine, *In Psalm.* 132.3). The movement began as a protest against Roman landlords and an attempt to secure the abolition of debts and the liberation of slaves, but it later took on the character of a religious war. The Circumcellions, who looked upon themselves as *Agonistici* (Gr., champions) or *Milites Christi* (Lat., soldiers of Christ), waylaid travelers, sacked towns, burned churches, and committed every kind of excess to shouts of *Deo laudes* ("Praise to God"; Augustine, *Ep.* 108.14). Despite the numerous attempts of Roman authorities to suppress them, they succeeded in gaining new recruits because of their easy code of morality, religious fanaticism, and conviction that one who fell in battle with either pagans or Catholics received a martyr's reward. BIBLIOGRAPHY: Optatus, *De schism. Donat.* 3.4; G. Bareille, DTC 2:2513; W. H. C. Frend, *Donatist Church* (1952).

[M. J. COSTELLOE]

CIRCUMCISION, the cutting off of the foreskin of the male genital organ. It was a pre-Israelite practice and may have reached the Hebrews through the Egyptians or Canaanites. Originally it may have been a puberty rite and a preparation for marriage, but among the Hebrews it was first a sign of membership in the community (Gen 34.14–16) and later a sign of the covenant between God and Abraham and his seed (Gen 17.9–14). During the Israelite settlement under Joshua (*c.* 1220–1200) it was generally practiced, but only during the Exile (587–538 B.C.) was its religious meaning stressed. The Christian Church did not attribute any religious significance to the rite (Acts 15); in fact St. Paul bitterly opposed those who tried to impose circumcision on Gentile converts (Gal 5.6; 6.15; Phil 3.2–3). BIBLIOGRAPHY: J. P. Hyatt, InterDB 1:629–631; P. C. Remondino, *History of Circumcision from the Earliest Times to the Present* (1891, repr. 1975).

[F. J. MONTALBANO]

CIRCUMCISION OF OUR LORD (Lk 2.21), an observance of Jewish law that took place at home 8 days after birth. In the case of Jesus, the act was presumably performed by St. Joseph. The rite incorporated Our Lord in the Jewish community and was the occasion for the bestowal of the sacred name Jesus ("Yahweh saves") who as Savior of the world belongs to the race of Abraham.

[F. J. MONTALBANO]

CIRCUMINCESSION (circuminsession), the technical theological term for the interpenetration of the three Persons of the *Trinity. The scriptural basis for the doctrine appears in Christ's words, ". . . believe that the Father is in me and I am in the Father" (Jn 10.38; also 14.11; 17.21). St. *John Damascene was the first to use the term (Gk. *perichorēsis*) in its Trinitarian context, and it was subsequently translated into Latin as *circumincessio* (literally, a proceeding around) by Burgundio of Pisa (d. 1194); *circuminsessio* also was used. The doctrine was stated at the Council of Florence (1442): "Because of this unity [of the Godhead] the Father is totally in the Son, and totally in the Holy Spirit; the Holy Spirit is totally in the Father, and totally in the Son" (D 1331). Circumincession elucidates two fundamental aspects of the Trinity: first, that the activities of each Person, except for the *processions themselves, issue from a single source, the divine nature. There is a fusion of personal activities of the Father, Son, and Holy Spirit within the Godhead. Secondly, the very basis of each Person's dynamic life is to be related to the other Persons of the Trinity, e.g., the Father knows the Son and so loves the Son that the Spirit proceeds as the expression of that love. This eternal circulation of life is the core of any Trinitarian explanation, and the reality expressed by circumincession. BIBLIOGRAPHY: A. Chollet, DTC 2.2:2527–32; A. M. Bermejo, NCE 3:880.

[T. M. MCFADDEN]

CIRCUMSTANCES, MORAL, the variable situational factors affecting the moral goodness or evil of a concrete human act. Examples of such factors would be the agent's motive, his condition or state in life, the time, place, or manner in which he acts, the means he employs, and the effects of his action. Thus, among other ways, circumstances may bear on morality: by adding a radically new moral character to an act, as when a cup of cold water is given to a little one because he is a disciple (motive; cf. Mt 10.42); or when murder is committed in a cathedral (place); by increasing the degree of goodness or evil—it is better to give larger alms, worse to steal greater sums (effect); by giving goodness or evil to an act morally indifferent in itself, as when a gun is shot in a careful or careless way (manner); or when one walks to obtain needed exercise (good motive); or to avoid obligatory work (bad motive); by depriving an act of the goodness it would otherwise have, as when one prays at a time he should be studying (wrong time) or out of vainglory (wrong motive).

As these illustrations suggest, an action must be considered according to its essential moral character before the influence of circumstantial variables can be evaluated. On this point the proponents of "situation ethics" take issue with traditional morality, contending that each moral situation is so entirely unique as to preclude any action (even murder, adultery, etc.) from being classed as intrinsically good or evil apart from circumstances. However, the traditional view appears no less situational, and considerably more profound, in recognizing that a morally good act must be justified by all its situational elements beginning with those which define the action itself, not just by the elements which are circumstantial. "Murder is always wrong" means that whenever an innocent life is deliberately taken, that very situational fact will render the action irreparably evil notwithstanding whatever goodness may be present among the surrounding situational elements or circumstances. BIBLIOGRAPHY: ThAq, ST 1a2ae.7 and 18; J. Fletcher, *Situation Ethics* (1966); J. Burtchaell, "Conservatism of Situation Ethics," *New Blackfriars* 48 (1966) 7–14.

[B. A. WILLIAMS]

CISALPINE CLUB, a group organized in 1792 under the leadership of the English RC layman, C. *Butler (1750–1832). The term is from the Lat., meaning on this side of *(cis)* the Alps, as opposed to *ultramontane. It aimed to advance Catholic emancipation in England by rejecting ultramontane ideas.

[T. EARLY]

CISNEROS, GARCÍA DE (1455–1510). Benedictine ascetical writer, a cousin of the famous Card. Ximenes. Renouncing his nobility, C. entered the austere priory of St. Benedict in Valladolid in 1470. He worked to reform monastic life and was later abbot for life in the Catalan monastery, shrine of Our Lady of Montserrat. His writings on the spiritual life drew on Devotio Moderna sources and influenced later Spanish schools of spirituality. BIBLIOGRAPHY: M. Alamo, DSAM 2.1:910–921.

[V. GILLIGAN]

CISON (KISHON), see KISHON (CISON).

CISTERCIAN ART, primarily a noble and austere architecture rooted in the rules and *Apologia* of St. Bernard. The earliest churches were distinguished by structural simplicity and lack of ornamentation because of St. Bernard's reforms. Following several oldest ornamented MSS directed by Stephen Harding (*c.*1109–1111), there was decreed *c.*1150 that one color be used for initial letters. Care was then given to parchment, arrangement of text, and calligraphy. Stained glass was prohibited and windows of clear glass were enhanced by intricate interlacing arabesques of lead. But in all these fields Cistercian austerity ultimately relaxed, and immense baroque churches, rich illumination, and representational window glass expressed the styles of successive ages. BIBLIOGRAPHY: J. Bilson, "Architecture of the Cistercians," *Archaeological Journal* 66 (1909) 185–280; C. Oursel, *Miniatures cisterciennes* (1960).

[R. C. MARKS]

CISTERCIAN NUNS, a general title for several groups of cloistered nuns traditionally associated with the Cistercian Order. Their first foundation was at Tart, probably between 1120 and 1125, as a filiation of *Cîteaux. It is uncertain when the nuns were first fully incorporated into the Cistercian Order, but they originally enjoyed a much greater autonomy than in the following centuries. The Cistercian reform spread rapidly among previously established convents, and new foundations were numerous. Many were not directly attached to the male order and independent congregations arose, notably a group of 18 convents formed from Tart and a Spanish group controlled by the Las Huelgas Abbey. But the burden of caring for and directing nuns began to press heavily on the abbots, so that the general chapter decided (1228) that it would not accept the responsibility for the spiritual direction and canonical visitation of any further communities of women. In the following centuries, the vicissitudes of the nuns followed those of the monks in regard to decline, division, exile, and active apostolic involvement. The convent at Port-Royal, which figured prominently in *Jansenism, was a Cistercian foundation. Today the Cistercian nuns, who for the most part live an integrally contemplative life, are divided into two orders: the Common Observance (Bernardines) and the Strict Observance (Trappistines). They have various types of juridicial and/or spiritual bonds with the male branches. In the U.S. there are three monasteries of the Strict Observance and one of the Common Observance. BIBLIOGRAPHY: A. J. Luddy, *Cistercian Nuns* (1931); Religious of Holy Cross Abbey, *Cistercian Nuns of Today* (1962); L. J. Lekai, NCE 3:885. *TRAPPISTS.

[M. B. PENNINGTON]

CISTERCIANS, a reformed branch of the Benedictine monastic family inaugurated in 1098 when *Robert, abbot of Molesme, with his prior (*Alberic), subprior (*Stephen Harding), and 18 other monks founded the New Monastery (later called *Cîteaux) in the marshes not far from Dijon (Burgundy). They sought to live the Benedictine Rule more integrally, with emphasis on solitude and poverty, manual labor, and simplicity of life and liturgy. The renewal received great impetus in 1113 when *Bernard of Clairvaux joined the community along with 30 relatives and friends. As the number of foundations increased, a constitution (the Charter of Charity) was formulated, approved by Callistus II (1119), and ratified by a general chapter (1123), thus establishing the new order. It gradually won independence from the local ordinary, beginning with the papal privilege of Paschal II (1100) until full exemption was obtained (1181) from Lucius III. The Cistercian reform adopted many of the new ideas developing within the monastic revival of the 11th cent. and brought them to perfection: lay brotherhood (which always enjoyed solemn vows among the Cistercians), general chapters, and regular visitations. Their fervor and purity of life won them many benefactions, leading to great material prosperity. The order saw rapid expansion throughout Europe and beyond; as many as 51 houses were incorporated in 1147. The order reached a peak in the 17th cent. with more than 1,500 monasteries. Its social influence was felt in the area of agrarian reform and in the opening of full religious status to the simple and poor. Its leadership, esp. in the 11th cent. through *Bernard of Clairvaux and *Aelred of Rievaulx, exercised extensive political influence and promoted the Crusade movement. The Cistercian Fathers, including Bernard of Clairvaux, Aelred of Rievaulx, *William of St. Thierry, *Isaac of Stella, *Guerric of Igny, and others produced an articulate school of spirituality. In the course of succeeding centuries, the order divided into congregations, often along national lines, into diverse observances, and finally (1892) into two separate orders (the Sacred Order of Cistercians [Common Observance] and the Order of Cistercians of the Strict Observance [*Trappists]). Historical accidents forced some of the congregations to adopt certain active apostolic labors, but the more contemplative monastic observance has flourished most in modern times. In response to the democratization of the mid-20th cent., the Strict Observance has recently (1967) set aside class distinctions (choir monk and lay brother) and established simplified unified observance within their communities. More recent foundations are experimenting with new structures and forms, retaining always the essentials of an integrally contemplative life. In the U.S. there are 2 abbeys and a number of filial houses of the Common Observance and 12 abbeys of the Strict Observance with various foundations, including three outside the U.S. (Argentina, Chile, and Hong Kong). BIBLIOGRAPHY: L. J. Lekai, *White Monks* (1953); *Cistercian Spirit: A Symposium* (ed. M. B. Pennington, 1969); J. B. Van Damme, *Three Founders of Cîteaux* (tr. M. Connor, 1970); L. Bouyer, *Cistercian Heritage* (tr. E. A. Livingston, 1958).

[M. B. PENNINGTON]

CÎTEAUX, ABBEY OF (Cistercium), chief abbey of the Cistercian Order, situated in the present diocese of Dijon, France. It was founded in 1098 by St. Robert, abbot of the Cluniac monastery of Molesme, who with the monks accompanying him wished to live the Benedictine rule in its primitive simplicity. Raynard, Viscount of Beaune, donated the land and Odon I, Duke of Burgundy, provided the buildings. Under the third abbot, Stephen Harding, the four principal daughters of Cîteaux were founded: Clairvaux, La Ferté, Pontigny, and Morimond. In 1119 the pope approved the *Charta caritatis,* the basic document of the Cistercian Order, long ascribed to Stephen Harding. It imposed absolute poverty, forbade secular studies, and provided for the autonomy of each monastery, for annual canonical vis-

itation, and for an annual general chapter at Cîteaux. By 1153 the monasteries affiliated with Cîteaux numbered 343. Many of them became very rich through the sale of wool in Flanders and fell into a relaxation that necessitated drastic reform. During the wars of religion the abbey was twice pillaged and burned; and in 1636 imperial troops plundered it. In 1772 the first of a planned series of new buildings was erected. In 1791 the abbey was secularized, the property sold, and the 12th-cent. buildings still extant torn down. A school for young delinquents was established at Cîteaux in 1846; but the reformed Cistercians repurchased the building in 1898, and the abbey received confirmation from the Holy See as titular abbey of the abbot general and site of the annual general chapter. BIBLIOGRAPHY: Cottineau 1:787–790; A. A. King, *Cîteaux and Her Elder Daughters* (1954).

[J. DAOUST]

CITIZENS FOR EDUCATIONAL FREEDOM (CEF), a nonsectarian, nonprofit, nonpartisan organization sponsoring equal government financial support for students, whether in independent, church-related, or public schools. Founded in St. Louis, Mo., in 1958 and legally incorporated in 1961, CEF's slogan is "A fair share for every child." The society's basic operating principle is that the parents' right to educate their children where they choose is primary and inalienable. The national office is in Washington, D.C.

[M. B. MURPHY]

CITIZENSHIP, the state of being a member of a city, state *(civitas, polis),* and esp. of being, whether native or naturalized, entitled to participate in the business of government and to be protected by the laws. Whereas to one's kin-group one owes the service of loyalty and respect, to one's political "national state," there is the duty of juridical obedience. Grace confirms man's nature as a social and political animal, and the condition of being a homeless, displaced, or stateless person is a tragic consequence of wickedness in high places. For a person to opt out of the obligations while claiming the privileges of citizenship is indefensible. BIBLIOGRAPHY: T. Gilby, *Between Community and Society. A Philosophy and Theology of the State* (1958).

[T. GILBY]

CITY OF GOD, title of a book by St. *Augustine in which he uses the phrase to signify human society controlled by the love of God. It is set in contrast to the city of man or of earth: "Accordingly, two cities have been formed by two loves: the earthly by the love of self, even to the contempt of God; the heavenly by the love of God, even to the contempt of self" (14.28). The sack of Rome by Alaric (410) was the immediate occasion for the writing of the book, which Augustine carried out over a lengthy period (413–427). That such an event should befall Rome was a deep shock to civilized men of the empire, and some of them asserted that it was due to the acceptance of Christianity and the forsaking of the old gods. Augustine wrote to answer that contention, and the first 10 of the work's 22 "books" are devoted to answering the charge. He says that rather than attribute their misfortune to Christianity, the Romans should give thanks to God that their lives were spared because of Christ—by their taking refuge in Christian churches spared by Alaric. After making his arguments against the pagan religion, Augustine turns in book 11 to the more general questions of society, developing what is generally considered one of the most important expressions of the Christian view of history. It ranges over the history of God's dealings with men recorded in the Old and New Testaments and discusses a wide variety of theological and philosophical issues. BIBLIOGRAPHY: J. H. Burleigh, *City of God* (1949); P. Brown, *Religion and Society in the Age of Saint Augustine* (1972).

[T. EARLY]

CIVEZZA, MARCELLINO DA (d. 1906), Franciscan missiologist and historian. He wrote the history of the Franciscan missions called *Storia universale delle missioni francescane,* complete in nine volumes. This is considered his most important work. His writings exceed 100 works. His studies on the sources of St. Francis' life are of outstanding importance. BIBLIOGRAPHY: L. G. Canedo, NCE 3:894.

[J. P. COOKE]

CIVIL ALLEGIANCE, the obedience citizens are conscience-bound to give to political authority when it is legally exercised within the limits of morality and on behalf of the common good. The general principle that civil law obliges in conscience is found in Rom 13 and 1 Pet 2. The Fathers of the Church and the social encyclicals have called for civil allegiance. Some notable examples of occasions when civil allegiance could not be rendered because the authority ordered actions opposed to Christian morality are the conflict between Christianity and the Roman state and in France during the Civil Constitution of the Clergy. Civil allegiance was an issue in the U.S. in the 1970s because of forced participation in wars considered by some to be unjust. BIBLIOGRAPHY: C. E. Curran, NCE 3:896–897.

[V. GILLIGAN]

CIVIL AUTHORITY, the power of commanding or forbidding types of action, that is, of making laws and of enforcing them, vested in the ruler or rulers representative and guardian of the common good of a state (Gr. *polis,* Lat. *civitas*), whether this be predominantly monarchic, aristocratic, or democratic, or—preferably in the classical view—a balanced blend of all three. Civil authority supposes a civilization, that is a people in agreement about the laws, and strictly speaking, is not possessed by the head of a kin-group, the chief of a clan, the leader of a horde, or the power-boss of an agglomeration however large. Civil au-

thority as a "rightful" power is a legal and moral value, entitled to the loyalty, respect, and obedience of citizens, and this in the name of God, though the common theory of Christian political thinkers is that government rests in some manner on popular consent. On civil disobedience, therefore, lies the onus of justifying itself because of exceptional and passing circumstances.

[T. GILBY]

CIVIL CONSTITUTION OF THE CLERGY, the law of July 12, 1790, restructuring the Church in France, making it virtually a department of state effectively severed from Rome. Although matters of dogma were left to Rome, the revolutionary decree, an achievement of the National Constituent Assembly, inspired by *Gallicanism, revoked the privileged status the clergy had enjoyed for centuries and subordinated them to the State. The legal document, which King Louis XVI signed (Aug. 24) unwillingly, together with the clerical loyalty oath decreed on Nov. 27, created a schism and turned a sizable force of nonjuring clergy and faithful against the Revolution.

The new French Church was given the following organization: each of the 83 *départements* (largest political subdivisions in the nation) constituted one religious diocese, all in turn being consolidated regionally into 10 metropolitan sees; only one parish was allotted to towns with a population of less than 6,000; the law abolished benefices, titles, offices, and privileges except those specifically retained in the new Constitution. Bishops were to be elected by majority vote in each departmental assembly; eligibility to bishoprics required 15 years of service in the particular diocese. The newly elected bishop was not to apply to the pope for confirmation; rather, he would be canonically instituted by his senior bishop and take a solemn oath in public to uphold the Constitution of the Clergy, and his episcopal responsibilities to the nation. Curés, usually rectors, eligible after 10 years of service, were elected by majority vote in the district assemblies; an oath was obligatory. Each bishop received the right to choose assistants *(vicaires),* but only from his diocese. In all these elections any tax-paying citizen, Catholic or not, had suffrage. The State fixed and paid the salaries of the clergy, ranging from 50,000 livres for the bp. of Paris to 1,200 livres for the curé, and 700 livres for vicars in the smallest towns. Laws regarding clerical residence were quite strict, and infractions were penalized. Pius VI in one brief suspended or excommunicated clergy submitting to the revolutionary regime. Then in the bull *Charitas* (April 13, 1791) he rejected clerical elections and termed the oath sacrilegious and the Constitution heretical and schismatical. The schism in the French Church lasted until the Concordat of 1801. BIBLIOGRAPHY: J. H. Stewart, *Documentary Survey of the French Revolution* (1951); F. Mourret, *History of the Catholic Church* (tr. N. Thompson, 1955) v. 7; Fliche-Martin 20:57–87.

[R. J. MARAS]

CIVIL DISOBEDIENCE, the violation of the laws or ordinances enacted by legitimate governmental authority. In modern usage it usually connotes an act done by way of demonstration for a cause, esp. in defense of one form or another of civil rights. The State certainly has the authority to make laws that oblige in conscience (Rom 13.1-7). Most theologians hold that many civil laws do not bind directly in conscience to the matter prescribed (are "purely penal"). Nevertheless the State has the right to enforce just laws, and presumption favors laws made by legitimate authorities; that is, a citizen should presume that the law is just unless he has clear evidence to the contrary. Unjust laws certainly do not bind in conscience of themselves. If they command unjust acts (like imposing direct abortion), they must be disobeyed by good Christians. If they do not command an immoral act, but are truly unjust (e.g., segregation laws), they may be disobeyed.

In addition to the obligation imposed by the law itself, there is another laid upon us by justice and charity, which always oblige us to avoid unnecessary harm to life, limb, or property. Unnecessary blocking of business, or even causing trouble and inconvenience by blocking traffic, can easily be violations of justice and/or charity. If a cause is just, one may try to use persuasion by picketing, displaying placards or distributing leaflets, but not by doing physical damage or injury, nor by physically preventing the carrying on of business simply as a means of persuasion. If the "sit-in" or such is in protest against not being served by a business where the demonstrators have a right to service and are able and willing to pay for it, then the "sit-in" would seem to be justified. Whether the more objectionable forms of civil disobedience are ever truly necessary is debated by some, but most theologians would agree that they are rarely justified except possibly under conditions in which general rebellion against a government would be justified; i.e., almost never. BIBLIOGRAPHY: J. J. Farraher, "Natural Law and Conscience-based Claims in Relation to Legitimate State Expectations," *Hastings Law Journal* 17 (1966) 439-451; R. T. Hall, *Morality of Civil Disobedience* (1971).

[J. J. FARRAHER]

CIVIL DIVORCE, the legal separation of husband and wife by a judicial verdict which dissolves the marriage relation. It is also called divorce *a vinculo matrimonii,* or absolute divorce. A decree of separate maintenance suspends the marital relation as far as cohabitation is concerned without dissolving the marriage bond. It is also called separation *a mensa et thoro,* or limited divorce. Divorce and separation present canonical and moral problems. The Church reserves to herself to hear and judge the matrimonial causes of Christians (CIC c. 1016; 1960), and the verdict of divorce is the exercise of a power that Catholic opinion denies the State has been given by God (CIC c. 1013.2). The moral problems are more acute. The possibility of escaping from an unfortunate marriage by divorce weakens the motivation to be more careful in the selection of a marriage partner and in the timing of the marriage. The ease with which divorce is obtained and accepted by society removes a powerful incentive for the spouses to strive harder to solve their difficulties. Divorced spouses are lonely, exposed to temptations, and often feel increasing bitterness towards each other. Children are hurt, bewildered, and deprived of the day to day guidance of the absent parent. Often the entire responsibility for the home falls upon the mother who finds herself overburdened by her dual role of being substitute father as well as mother. Nevertheless, divorce and separation sometimes have good effects, which can only be achieved by means of these legal institutions. The verdict of divorce makes the separation of invalidly married persons possible; civil sanction is given to those persons who have the right to use the *privilege of the faith; divorce and separation lends state protection to a spouse who has the right to separate permanently or for a time from an erring partner.

While the personal dimensions of marriage are the concern chiefly of the spouses themselves, still the Christian community has an interest in the stability of the individual marriage and the family. Therefore canon law requires spouses to share a common life together (CIC c. 1128), and allows canonical separation only for very serious causes, and divorce, if the marriage is valid, only for the sake of the civil effects. The attorney's role belongs to the moral category of cooperation with the contending spouses and the state. He must judge whether there are sufficient reasons to permit his material cooperation. The general moral principle is that an attorney may represent a client in a divorce action whenever it is morally lawful for the client to sue in the courts. When the marriage has been celebrated according to the canonical form, the attorney ordinarily should not take the case until the bishop's permission for the divorce has been obtained by the client or the attorney. In cases where the spouses are non-Catholics, charity should urge him honestly to attempt a reconciliation. Ordinarily he should not represent a client whose manifest purpose is to seek a divorce from a valid marriage in order to remarry. He may represent other non-Catholic clients who have serious and provable causes for divorce. He may represent the respondent in order to safeguard his rights. While attorneys can usually refuse a case, the judge, unless he can legitimately disqualify himself, must hear and decide according to law any case brought before him. There is solidly probable opinion that the verdict of divorce and separation is not intrinsically evil because it can be understood as withdrawal of state support of the marriage and as affecting the purely civil effects of marriage. Judges and attorneys should cooperate with those who are trying to reform divorce laws and procedures.

[R. H. DAILEY]

CIVIL LAW, see LAW, CIVIL.

CIVIL MARRIAGE, a marriage witnessed by an authorized representative of the State. (1) The marriage entered in this way by two nonbaptized persons is a true marriage contract; it is classified as civil in the sense that it is nonsacramental and the partners are not subject to the jurisdiction of the Church, which extends only to the baptized. In this meaning, even a marriage contracted at a non-Christian religious ceremony could be termed "civil" as far as its canonical evaluation is concerned. The Church recognizes civil marriages so understood as true and lawful marriages, and the legitimate jurisdiction of the State over them. Such marriages, however, come within the terms of the *Pauline and *Petrine privileges. (2) The appearance before a civil magistrate required by some governments, e.g., those following the Napoleonic Code, over and above a religious ceremony, is tolerated by the Church in the case of baptized Catholics, but simply as an exercise of the State's jurisdiction over civil factors in the marriage contract. (3) In the case of baptized Catholics who are bound to the canonical form of the sacrament or who are not free to marry, a civil marriage is merely an attempted marriage; the marriage is invalid; the parties are not married at all. Canon law attaches penalties to attempted marriages. Lay persons thus attempting marriage (i.e., those bound by a valid marriage bond, even if they are civilly divorced) automatically incur *infamy, and may be excommunicated by their bp. (CIC, c. 2356; the Third Plenary Council of Baltimore also attached the penalty of excommunication to attempted marriages by Catholics after a civil divorce, whether it was the Catholic who obtained the divorce or not; this excommunication was abrogated by the National Conference of Catholic Bishops in 1977). Clerics in major orders or religious of solemn vows, as well as their partners, incur excommunication reserved to the Holy See (c. 2399, §1); clerics lose all ecclesiastical offices (c. 188, n.5) and are subject to being degraded canonically (2388, §1); religious *ipso facto* incur dismissal from their institute (c. 646, §1, n.3).

[T. C. O'BRIEN]

CIVIL RELIGION, the acceptance and, to varying degrees, the institutionalization, of a set of values, symbols and rituals, based upon universal and transcendent truths, which serve as the cohesive force and center of meaning for a nation. Although the truths of a civil religion have a transcendental value, their transmission and symbolic expression are through the history of a particular people. The term is found in J. J. Rousseau's *Social Contract* (bk. 4, ch. 8), and designates the external rites or dogmas centering on a nation's god(s). Several recent studies have applied the term to the U.S. as a genuine apprehension of religious realities revealed through the experience of the American people. American civil religion would maintain belief in a creating and provident God, the reward of virtue and the punishment of vice either now or in an afterlife, and that the most acceptable service of God is the assistance given to others. Civil Religion can be promoted to the exclusion of the essentials of Christian revelation; in the U.S. it has in periods of national crisis reduced the Christian message, to the divine concern for the nation's destiny. BIBLIOGRAPHY: R. Bellah, *Beyond Belief* (1970); *America in Theological Perspective* (ed. T. M. McFadden, 1976); S. Ahlstrom, *Theology in America* (1967); *American Civil Religion* (ed. R. Richey and D. Jones, 1974).

[T. M. MCFADDEN]

CIVIL RIGHTS, those that a person possesses in virtue of civil law. In this most general sense this is the equivalent of a term that Aristotle used in his *Ethics* and *Politics* to classify rights due to the citizen on the basis of the written law. The term currently, however, has many more concrete connotations; it stands even as a slogan or rallying cry, and calls for some clarification. Taken to mean rights belonging to a person in virtue of civil law the term may cover rights that coincide with *human rights, endowed upon or at least commonly attributed to people simply because they are human beings, independently of any positive law (see RIGHT AND RIGHTS). But the claim to civil rights strictly speaking rests on and must be vindicated by the law of the land. In the U.S. legal system the distinction also is made between civil rights and civil liberties: the first provide protection from infringement of freedom by other individuals; the second, from infringement by government. Civil rights concretely in the U.S. are stated in the U.S. Constitution: the Bill of Rights, the first 10 amendments added at the time of the original ratification, effective in 1791; the 14th, 15th, and 19th amendments; the various Civil Rights laws passed, esp. in the last 20 years; the interpretations and decisions of the U.S. Supreme Court. The purpose of American law and its enforcement is the safeguarding of equal status for all citizens in their enjoyment of the benefits of citizenship. That equality, however, until recent times was not protected or promoted uniformly. The history of the nation includes not only the denial of fundamental human rights and citizenship to blacks by the institution of slavery, but the failure to respect the principle of equal treatment after abolition. That history also includes a de facto denial by the majority of equal treatment to minorities, ethnic, religious, or economic; to women; to the poor. The Civil Rights Movement began slowly in the 1940s to seek to alleviate inequities. Pres. F. D. Roosevelt acted towards this end; the Supreme Court began to outlaw segregation. Segregation in public schools was forbidden, and the "separate but equal" doctrine rejected by the famous decision of 1954, *Brown v. Board of Education,* Topeka, Kansas, 347 U.S. 483. The activity of the National Association for the Advancement of Colored People and of Martin Luther King's Southern Christian Leadership Conference and Congress of Racial Equality enlisted blacks to promote their own cause of equality and also attracted white support, some of it from religious bodies. The strong civil rights bill passed under Pres. L. B. Johnson in 1964 created agencies to attack discrimination in public facilities, housing, employment opportunity. The desegregation of schools has been accelerated by the device of court-ordered busing—not without resistance. Thus civil rights legislation, and to a degree its enforcement, are achieved in the case of the blacks; yet their full enjoyment of citizenship is by no means achieved; that requires an assent to the demands of justice by individuals.

The atmosphere of the civil rights movement on behalf of the blacks, however, has furthered the cause of equality for other minorities. In the late 70s long delayed attention has been directed to the injustices suffered by native Americans, the Indians. The cause of Hispanic Americans, migrant workers, and ethnic minorities has also received attention. Among the most prominent campaigns is that of the Women's Liberation Movement and the attempt to have the states ratify an equal rights amendment to the Constitution. There are efforts as well to protect the elderly, the handicapped, the unemployed, homosexuals, even prostitutes. Claims to civil rights are claims to the power of civil law; they may or may not coincide with what is right and just morally; they may or may not coincide with the competency of civil law itself, which cannot create equality in fact but only endeavor to safeguard equal opportunity and equal treatment before the law. Further, it is odd to defend as a civil right a minor's right to an abortion without parental consent, when the same law does not allow a tonsilectomy without such consent.

[T. C. O'BRIEN]

CIVITALI, MATTEO (1436–1501), Tuscan sculptor and architect, perhaps in Florence in 1460 as evidenced in ateliers of Rossellino and Desiderio da Settignano. C. completed for the Lucca cathedral a tomb and chapel, and the Altar of St. Regulus, the last perhaps his greatest work.
BIBLIOGRAPHY: E. Carli, EncCatt 3:1763–64.

[M. J. DALY]

CIXILA, bp. of Toledo (745–754), predecessor of *Elipandus. His vita of Ildefonsus (EspSagr 5:485–490), based on the report of two learned clerics of Toledo who died in 742, recounts miraculous appearances of the Blessed Virgin and several items of ecclesiastical interest. If, on the evidence of style, a detailed chronicle completed in 754 is also ascribed to C., then he compiled the most precious historical source on early Muslim rule in Spain. León had two bps. of this name about the time it was becoming the capital of the Reconquest; the second, a Mozarab refugee monk from Córdoba, founded (904–905) and probably died at (938–940) the monastery of Abellar.

[E. P. COLBERT]

CLAIRVAUX, ABBEY OF (*Clara Vallis, Vallis Absinthialis*), former Cistercian abbey, founded in 1115 by St. Stephen Harding, abbot of *Cîteaux. It was located in a valley called "Val d'Absinthe" in the present diocese of Troyes, France. St. Bernard, its first abbot, brought it to so flourishing a state that at his death the community numbered 700, and almost 80 houses had been founded from it. Most prolific of all monastic establishments, its offshoots eventually totaled 356; but a needed reform closed the branches in England, Scotland, and the Scandinavian countries. Clairvaux had greatly declined by the time of its suppression in 1792. The buildings were made into a prison in 1808, and the church was destroyed in 1819. During the French Revolution the books of the abbey library, founded by St. Bernard himself, were transferred to Troyes. They are now widely scattered in France and Italy.
BIBLIOGRAPHY: Cottineau 1:799–800; A. A. King, *Cîteaux and Her Elder Daughters* (1954), J. M. Canivez, DHGE 12:1050–61.

[J. DAOUST]

CLAIRVOYANCE, a type of *ESP phenomena, the ability to perceive facts or events that are not and have not been present to the senses. Clairvoyance differs from telepathy, which is the communication from one mind to another otherwise than through sense-channels, and from premonition, which is knowledge of future events. Various types have been recognized, and for more than a century many occult phenomena have been put under its heading. Societies for psychical research have been formed to identify it and define its character. Today clairvoyance is studied under strict scientific controls in a number of universities and parapsychological laboratories. The clairvoyant is given the task of determining the sequence of ESP cards already shuffled but unknown to anyone: the presupposition is that clairvoyance has a natural explanation, though its connection with magic still lingers in the popular mind. *TELEPATHY.

[C. P. SVOBODA]

CLAIRVOYANCE, SPIRITUAL, the phenomenon by which a person is able to know what is taking place within another or at some distance in time and place by means other than the ordinary use of his intellectual faculties. This need not always be a supernatural or preternatural prodigy, at least in some of its manifestations. The fact that spiritual clairvoyance has been experienced by those in pathological states as well as by saints argues for a natural as well as a supernatural explanation. Although science has not yet given any adequate theory, a phenomenon such as *extrasensory perception or the existence of a spiritual force that emanates from one person to another cannot be excluded. Modern studies tend to emphasize the yet unknown potentialities of human psychology and nervous forces. Christian theology does not rule out the intervention of angels, good and bad, but reserves certain forms, such as a certain as opposed to a conjectural insight into the soul of another, exclusively to divine intervention operating directly on the clairvoyant's intellect. When the phenomenon occurs in the lives of the saints (*e.g.*, the Curé of Ars, St. Catherine of Siena, Pope Pius V), it is accepted as a supernatural phenomenon and taken as a sign of holiness. BIB-

LIOGRAPHY: H. Thurston, *Physical Phenomena of Mysticism* (ed. J. H. Crehan, 1952); J. G. Arintero, *Mystical Evolution in the Development and Vitality of the Church* (tr. J. Aumann, 2 v., 1949–51). *TELEPATHY.

[M. B. PENNINGTON]

CLANDESTINE MARRIAGES,

marriages contracted secretly in the sense they are not witnessed officially in the manner prescribed in RC canon law. Such marriages were forbidden in the decree *Tametsi* issued by the Council of Trent (D 1813–16), which also declared that thenceforth secret marriages of this kind were to be considered null and void. The aim of this legislation was to prevent the injustice and domestic chaos that followed in the wake of secret marriages when parties to them chose later to repudiate their obligations to their secret spouses and enter upon other marriages. Their freedom to enter upon second marriages could often not be successfully contested because of the clandestine character of their earlier marriages. *Tametsi* required that thenceforth a certain "form" must be observed. A marriage could only be entered upon in the presence of the local parish priest, or the ordinary of the diocese, or a priest delegated by one or the other, and in the presence also of at least two witnesses. However, the decree was not universally effective because it was not officially published in many regions and in those places it was not binding. Moreover, it failed to deal explicitly with the marriages of baptized non-Catholics, or with those who, though baptized Catholics, were alienated from the Church, or with certain rare emergency situations in which access to a qualified priest was impossible. In time, the inadequacies and uncertainties of *Tametsi* were remedied. In 1741 Benedict XIV exempted baptized non-Catholics, when marrying among themselves, from the observance of the form. A decree of Pope Pius X, *Ne temere,* which went into effect on Easter Sunday, 1908, extended to all Latin-rite Catholics the form prescribed by *Tametsi,* thus eliminating the exemption from its requirements of those living in areas in which *Tametsi* had not been officially promulgated. *Ne temere* also confirmed the exemption granted by Benedict XIV to baptized non-Catholics when marrying among themselves. Furthermore it declared that in imminent danger of death, when access to the local pastor or ordinary was impossible, a marriage could be legitimately contracted in the presence of a priest, even though he lacked proper delegation, and of two other witnesses. It also provided that in situations in which it was foreseen that access to the proper pastor or ordinary, or indeed to any priest, would be impossible for at least a month, marriage could be contracted simply in the presence of at least two witnesses. The Code of Canon Law, which went into effect in 1918, adopted substantially the legislative modifications contained in *Ne temere,* but to them it added a further modification by exempting the children of non-Catholic parents (or of at least one non-Catholic parent), who, though baptized as Catholics, had been reared from infancy in heresy, schism, infidelity, or without any religion at all, in cases in which they were contracting marriage with other non-Catholics (CIC c. 1099.2). However, this last mentioned exemption was later withdrawn by a *motu proprio* of Pius XII, which went into effect Jan. 1, 1949.

[P. K. MEAGHER]

CLAPHAM SECT,

an appellation by Sydney Smith (1764–1840) that stuck to an informal group of Anglican evangelicals, who in the late 18th cent. worshiped at Clapham parish church and shared a sense of social responsibility and the conviction that religion should be manifested in good works. They were people of substance and were conservative-minded; many were interrelated through marriage, and they formed a pressure group with an influence out of proportion to its size. The best-known members are Zachary Macaulay and William Wilberforce. It promoted the abolition of Negro slavery and the increase of missionary work and Sunday schools, and founded the *British and Foreign Bible Society and the Society for Bettering the Condition and Increasing the Comfort of the Poor (1794).

CLAPPER,

an instrument devised to produce a sharp carrying noise by bringing two flat surfaces of wood together, repeatedly if so desired, by shaking it like a handbell. It is used to replace the ringing of bells in church or in religious houses from Maundy Thursday until the Easter Vigil.

[N. KOLLAR]

CLARE OF ASSISI, ST.

(1194–1253), foundress of the Second Order of St. Francis, known as "*Poor Clares." At the age of 18, moved by the preaching of St. Francis, she fled from the home of her wealthy father and dedicated herself to a life of poverty under the direction of St. Francis. When she was joined by other companions, including her mother and two sisters, Francis gave them a simple rule of life and appointed her abbess. For 40 years Clare held fast to her ideals of poverty, resisting all papal efforts to relax the rule. Her rule, written in 1247, received papal approval 2 days before her death. She was canonized in 1255 and in 1958 was declared the patron saint of television. BIBLIOGRAPHY: H. Daniel-Rops, *Call of St. Clare* (tr. S. Attanasio, 1963); N. De Robeck, *St. Clare of Assisi* (1951).

[D. A. MCGUCKIN]

CLARE GAMBACORTA, BL.

(1362–1419), widow, Dominican reformer, daughter of the ruler of Pisa (1369–93), sister of Bl. Peter of Pisa. C. accepted a political marriage at the age of 12 but was a widow 3 years later. At the age of 16, upon joining the Poor Clares, she was pursued and imprisoned by her family. After 5 months her father released her and permitted her to join the Dominicans. In 1382 she and five companions founded a community of strict observance. When her body was exhumed 13 years after death, her tongue was found incorrupt. BIBLIOG-

RAPHY: T. McGlynn, *This Is Clare of Pisa* (1962); Butler 2:117–119.

[J. BLAIR]

CLARE OF MONTEFALCO, ST. (*c.*1275–1308), abbess, a woman remarkable from early childhood for her austerity of life and dedication to prayer. For some years she lived as a Franciscan tertiary in a hermitage, but in 1290 she joined with her sister and certain other companions in the establishment of a convent under the Rule of St. Augustine, and upon the death of her sister she became the abbess. To her were due the discovery and suppression of a quietistic group known as the Sect of the Spirit of Liberty. Her incorrupt body is preserved at Montefalco. BIBLIOGRAPHY: E. A. Foran, *Life of St. Clare of the Cross* (1954); N. Del Re, BiblSanct 3:1217–22; Butler 3:341; L. Oliger, *De secta spiritus libertatis in Umbria saec. XIV* (1943).

CLARE OF RIMINI, BL. (Clare Agolanti; 1280–1326), foundress of a Poor Clare convent. Converted from a worldly life at the age of 34, C. gave herself to penance and works of charity in reparation for her sins. She gathered a group of young women, built a convent where they could live under the rule of St. Clare of Assisi, and spent the last 10 years of her life there doing penance, contemplating the passion of Christ, and attending to the formation of the nuns. BIBLIOGRAPHY: G. B. Proja, BiblSanct 1:422–423.

[J. J. SMITH]

CLARENDON, CONSTITUTIONS OF, 16 regulations set forth by Henry II of England in 1164 at a council held at Clarendon Park, Wiltshire. They were designed to assert the authority of the royal over the ecclesiastical courts and to forbid appeals to Rome without the king's consent. St. Thomas *Becket, abp. of Canterbury, opposed some of them as contrary to canon law. He was upheld by Alexander III, and after Becket's murder Henry gave up the claims in order to secure absolution. For the text of the constitutions see *Documents of the Christian Church* (ed. H. Bettenson, 2d ed., 1970).

[T. EARLY]

CLARENI, a group of Franciscan *Spirituals founded by Liberatus of Macerata and later given brief legal existence by Celestine V. This pope granted them immunity from the authority of the minister general of the Friars Minor in 1294; they are therefore referred to as Poor Hermits of the Lord Celestine, or simply as Celestines. Their autonomy was revoked by Boniface VIII, but they refused to disband. In 1307 *Angelus Clarenus assumed leadership, and it is from him that the group is called Clareni. Even before his death in 1337 they became suspect of *Joachimism and identified with the *Fraticelli. In 1473 several groups of friars known as Clareni were reunited to the Franciscan Order; it is not clear whether the remnant of Angelus's group was among them. BIBLIOGRAPHY: L. Bernardini,

Frate Angelo a Chiarino alla luce della storia (1964); D. Douie, *Nature and Effects of the Heresy of the Fraticelli* (1932); L. Oliger, DHGE 3:17–19 s.v. "Ange de Cingoli."

[C. J. LYNCH]

CLARET, ANTHONY MARY, ST. (1807–70), Spanish abp., founder of the Claretians. A weaver's son, C. worked for several years in the mills of Barcelona before entering the seminary at Vich where he was ordained (1835). He tried his vocation in the Jesuit novitiate at Rome but was advised, because of his health, to return to Spain and an apostolic ministry. In 1849 he founded the congregation of the Missionary Sons of the Immaculate Heart of Mary, afterwards known as Claretians. The following year he was appointed bp. to the see of Santiago de Cuba. There amid hostility and suspicion he labored to improve not only the spiritual condition of his flock but also to alleviate their economic and social miseries. In 1857 he returned to Spain as confessor to Queen Isabella II. Again he devoted himself to the problems of social reform, preaching vast numbers of sermons and writing dozens of pamphlets. When the Queen was exiled (1868), he accompanied her to Italy and to Rome (1870) where he participated in the debate on papal infallibility, which he strongly supported. That same year he died in the Cistercian monastery of Fontfroid near Narbonne, where he was buried. He was beatified in 1934 and canonized in 1950. An autobiographical account of his life was published in Madrid in 1959, *Escritos autobiográficos y espirituales*; several biographies exist in Spanish, French, and English. BIBLIOGRAPHY: F. Royer, *St. Anthony Claret* (1957); D. Sargent, *Assignments of Antonio Claret* (1948); Butler 4:195–196; G. M. Viñas, BiblSanct 2:205–210.

[I. MAHONEY]

CLARET DE LA TOUCHE, LOUISE (1868–1915), Visitandine nun and mystic. At 22 Louise entered the Visitation of Holy Mary convent at Romans where she daily recorded the mystical graces she received. She wrote that Christ said to her, "Margaret Mary showed my heart to the world, you will show it to priests." After having been separated from her community because of opposition to her message, she made a new foundation at Vische. This community encourages devotion to the Sacred Heart among priests. BIBLIOGRAPHY: J. Verbillion, NCE 3:916.

[V. GILLIGAN]

CLARETIANS, Missionary Sons of the Immaculate Heart of Mary (CMF), community of priests and brothers organized in Spain in 1849. St. Anthony Mary Claret founded this congregation of simple vows for the purpose of preaching centered on devotion to the Holy Eucharist and to the Immaculate Heart of Mary. The Claretians have since extended their apostolate to include teaching and parish work. They came to the U.S. in 1902 to preach to the Spanish-speaking people of Texas. The Claretians edit and publish magazines and booklets dealing with religious education and problems of modern society. There are more than 3,000 Claretian priests, brothers, and scholastics in the U.S., Canada, Central and South America, Africa, Europe, Japan, and the Philippines.

[A. R. ZINK]

CLARITUS, BL. (*c.*1280–1346), Florentine monastic founder. Of the distinguished Del Voglia family, C. delighted in divine services at the cathedral of Florence, but instead of taking orders himself, he married, took part in public affairs, engaged in much charitable activity, and in particular interested himself in helping young women who wanted to enter the religious life. With the approval of the abp. of Florence he founded a monastery for women under the Rule of St. Augustine and dedicated it to Mary Queen of Heaven, but it was popularly known as Chiarito after him. His wife and daughter joined the community, the former becoming the first abbess. C. busied himself providing for the establishment until his death. BIBLIOGRAPHY: S. de Paoli, BiblSanct 3:1229–30.

[P. K. MEAGHER]

CLARKE, ADAM (1760 or 1762–1832), Wesleyan preacher, antiquarian, and Oriental and biblical scholar. Born at Moybeg, Londonderry Co., Ireland, he joined a Methodist *society in 1778 and began preaching at once. John *Wesley invited him to Kingswood School in 1782, later using him as a preacher. As a scholar, C. aided the Bible Society in editing Oriental versions of the Scriptures and was recognized by many learned societies. He was three times president of the Wesleyan Methodist Conference. In 1808 the British government employed him in editing historic state papers. His many writings include *Memorials of the Wesley Family* and his chief work, a labor of 30 years, *Commentary and Critical Notes* on the Bible. BIBLIOGRAPHY: J. W. Etheridge, *Life of the Rev. Adam Clarke, LL.D.* (1858); J. Everett, *Life of Adam Clarke* (1849).

[F. E. MASER]

CLARKE, MARY FRANCES, MOTHER (1803–87), foundress in 1833 of the Sisters of Charity of the Blessed Virgin Mary, with the help of Father Terence J. Donaghoe. The sisters labored in Philadelphia until 1843 when C. responded to request of Bp. Mathias Loras and Pierre De Smet, SJ, to serve in Dubuque. They were the first sisters in Iowa. In 1896 C. applied for pontifical status for her community. Final approbation was given by Pope Leo XIII in 1885. C. governed for 54 years, leaving schools that pioneered the 19th cent. movement for women's colleges. BIBLIOGRAPHY: M. St. V. Berry, NCE 3:917; *Dictionary of American Biography* 4:159–160.

[J. L. HALPIN]

CLARKE, SAMUEL (1675–1729), English philosopher and divine. After earning the doctor of divinity degree, he received from Queen Anne the rectorship of St. James, Westminster, where he delivered two impressive series of sermons (1704, 1705), later published (1705–06) with the joint title (from 1716) of *A Discourse concerning the Being and Attributes of God, the Obligations of Natural Religion, and the Truth and Certainty of the Christian Revelation.* In 1712 he published his celebrated treatise *Scripture Doctrine of the Trinity,* which, betraying Unitarian and latitudinarian ideas, brought him for a time into conflict with Convocations. An ardent disciple of Isaac Newton, he tried to use in natural theology a method as nearly mathematical as possible. He ranks among the foremost rationalist theologians of his time. BIBLIOGRAPHY: E. Sprague, EncPhil 2:118–120.

[M. J. BARRY]

CLARKE, WILLIAM NEWTON (1841–1912), Baptist clergyman and theologian. C., a professor of theology at Colgate from 1890, presented his own theological system in his *Outline of Christian Theology* (1890), which went through many editions and did much to diffuse *liberal theology. He sought to incorporate evolutionary theory and the new biblical criticism. Departing from the rationalistic theologizing of the 19th cent., C. tried to formulate theological concepts on historical and experiential grounds. He explained the authority of the Bible by the universality of its moral teachings; the Church meant simply a collective name for those living practical Christian truths. His other writings include: *What Shall We Think of Christianity?* (1899) and *The Use of Scripture in Theology* (1905). BIBLIOGRAPHY: C. L. Howe, Jr., ''William Newton Clarke: Systematic Theologian of Theological Liberalism,'' *Foundations* 6 (1963) 123–135; Smith-Jamison 1:290–294.

[N. H. MARING]

CLARUS, ST. (d. *c.*660), abbot of Saint-Marcel of Vienne from *c.*625. His cult goes back at least to the 8th cent. in the province of Vienne, where many parishes, communes, and villages were named after him. Official confirmation of the cult did not come, however, until 1905. He is regarded as the patron saint of tailors. BIBLIOGRAPHY: L. Gaillard, BiblSanct 3:1232.

[B. F. SCHERER]

CLASS (Methodist), a small subdivision (at first about 12 persons and a leader) within an early Methodist *society. Each member of the society was placed in a class; leaders supervised the lives of the class members, who met each week for prayer and spiritual exhortation. A few Methodist bodies still have class meetings. BIBLIOGRAPHY: HistAmMeth v. 1; F. E. Maser, *Dramatic Story of Early American Methodism* (1965) 52–55.

[F. E. MASER]

CLASS DISTINCTION, preferential status of one group over another in a society on the grounds of race, lineage, wealth, or some other real or claimed privilege. Diversity of gifts or advantages is a fact of human society. Class distinction is a threat to justice when it leads to discrimination and denial of equality before the law. *EQUALITY; *EQUALITY IN THE CHURCH; *SOCIAL JUSTICE; *CIVIL RIGHTS.

[T. C. O'BRIEN]

CLASS-STRUGGLE, a term too comprehensive to permit of a simple definition, for struggle may mean anything from a healthy tension in a pluralistic State, which neither should nor can form a classless society, to a civil war which may be its death. Class, which is an aggregate of persons of approximately the same status representing a stratification within the whole, can be variously determined. Thus first, economically, by reference to the possession of property; second, politically, according to the power exercised, governmentally and legislatively; third, vocationally, according to the occupation followed; fourth, sociopsychologically, according to the deference accorded or at least expected, which may arise from the inequalities of the dignities awarded according to *distributive justice (cf ThAq ST 2a2ae, 61.2) or from considerations arising from rank or birth; fifth, ethnically, according to racial strains; and sixth, religiously, according to a caste-system. All these, which may overlap, go to form a non-egalitarian social group.

The fourth, which according to some sociologists is the differential constitutive of class, may produce envy and resentment, but it is the first and the fifth that are the most potent causes of contention, war, riot, and sedition. Cases in point are the class wars of Marxist programs in the past and our racial conflicts in the present. When the proper equilibrium between classes was lost because the few had grown richer and the many poorer to the extent of forming a proletariat possessing little property but the wages earned that day, it was not surprising that extreme violence was advocated as indispensable for a social revolution. So also when a numerous racial group feels itself affronted. We may remind ourselves that derision, actual and virtual, is a special and grave injustice (op. cit., 2a2ae, 75); nevertheless fundamentally, the problem is one of Christian friendship or charity, and the fact that St. Thomas Aquinas regards the sins mentioned above as being directly contrary to its joy and peace (op. cit., 2a2ae, 36–42) is in line with modern findings that class-conflicts are best remedied by the growth of man-to-man dealings.

[T. GILBY]

CLASSICAL MUSIC, term applied to the music composed during the period, 1770–1830, of the Viennese classicists Haydn, Mozart, Beethoven, and to a limited extent, Schubert. Eighteenth-cent. Vienna is regarded as the background of the musical Classical Era, in which the instrumental sonata was the dominating form. The four sons of Bach, particularly C.P.E. Bach, an innovator in employing sonata-allegro form, were partially responsible for ushering in the new era, as was the German Mannheim School of the mid-18th cent. which gave direction to the symphonic style of the Viennese composers. Features of the new style were a definite attempt to perfect the melodic line; an essentially homophonic, transparent, noncontrapuntal style; contrasting tonality between themes in sonata-allegro form; enlarged scope of orchestral tone color through use of new dynamic devices; replacement of the Baroque thoroughbass with written-out orchestral parts. The Classical Period saw the perfection of the larger instrumental forms—the symphony, sonata, string quartet, and solo concerto as we know them today. BIBLIOGRAPHY: *New Music Lover's Handbook* (ed. E. Siegmeister, 1973) 141–189.

[J. S. PALLOZZA]

CLASSIS, an ecclesiastical governing body for a particular geographical district in *Reformed Churches; Presbyterian denominations employ the term *presbytery for the same body. Classis membership consists of the clergymen and representative *elders of the district. The classis ranks in authority above that of the Reformed consistory (Presbyterian church session) and below that of the particular or regional synod and the general synod (Presbyterian general assembly). The classis serves a judicial function by acting as a court of appeal from the consistory of the local congregation. The classis oversees its congregations and the personal conduct and ministerial labors of each clergyman. It grants licenses to preach, ordains clergymen, and can admonish, suspend, and depose them.

[E. M. EENIGENBURG]

CLAUDEL, PAUL LOUIS CHARLES MARIE (1868–1955), French poet and dramatist. Of an indifferently Catholic family, C. received little religious education and soon lost his faith under the influence of the prevailing scientism. Yet C. continued to yearn for an understanding of the meaning of life. Reading the works of Rimbaud in 1886, he discovered under the poet's symbolism the existence of a boundless spiritual domain; he attended Mass at Christmas, and later Vespers, in Notre Dame Cathedral, and in the story of his conversion he says: "In one instant my heart was touched and I believed." An intellectual struggle followed before his return to the sacraments in 1890, but thereafter his immense literary production was marked by faith and continuing spiritual development. *Tête d'Or*, a drama composed in the 4-year interval, presents a conflict between hunger for power and the mystery of death; *L'Annonce faite à Marie* (1912) treats of sacrifice; *Partage de midi* (1905) reflects a personal crisis in the author's life; *Soulier de satin* (1921) is a vast culmination of C.'s concept of reaching divine through human love. Regarding the use of his gifts as an apostolate, he drew upon the universe for a panoramic poetic reflection of God and the supernatural. His idea of the cofruition of art and faith is expressed in *L'art poétique* (1907). C. married and became the father of five children; he was also a career diplomat and served in consular posts in the U.S., Brazil, the Orient, and European countries. He published quietly at fir, but his genius was immediately recognized by a limed circle. Widespread acclaim came only in the 1940s. BIBLIOGRAPHY: L. Estang, NCE 3:919–921; M. Ryan, *Introduction to Paul Claudel* (1951); *Claudel: A Reapprisal* (ed. R. Griffiths, 1969).

[L. TINSLEY]

CLAUDIANISTS, a turbulent sect of *Donatists founded by Claudianus, a Donatist bp. of Rome who was banished because of the riots occasioned by his disputes with Pope Damasus. He went to Carthage, where he soon quarreled with the Donatists there. He broke with Parmenian, the Donatist bp., and set up his own rival community. He was later readmitted to the Donatist communion by Primian over the opposition of the church elders. BIBLIOGRAPHY: P. Monceaux, *Histoire littéraire de l'Afrique chrétienne* (1922) 6:112–113.

[M. J. COSTELLOE]

CLAUDIANUS MAMERTUS, Gallo-Roman theologian, brother of St. Mamertus, bp. of Vienna about 473. He relinquished his worldly goods and embraced the monastic life. C.'s chief importance is the contribution he made to liturgical chant.

[E. C. HUBBERT]

CLAUDIUS CLAUDIANUS (second half of the 4th and first part of the 5th cent. A.D.), last of the classical Latin poets. C. was probably born in Alexandria and wrote his first poems in Greek, but he possessed a perfect knowledge of Latin and, though remaining a pagan, became the court poet of Stilicho and Honorius. His work includes occasional verse, panegyrics, invectives, and developments of mythological themes. The most famous of the latter is his unfinished *Rape of Proserpine.* Claudian was a true poet and a master of allegory and mythological allusion. His verse is firm and harmonious and his poems well constructed, though occasionally marred by excessive declamation. BIBLIOGRAPHY: H. J. Rose, *Handbook of Latin Literature* (1936) 529–533.

[M. J. COSTELLOE]

CLAUDIUS OF CONDAT, ST. (d. 696), Benedictine abbot. Born of a senatorial family in the Frankish kingdom, C. was trained originally as a soldier. He turned to the priesthood and monasticism and as abbot introduced the Benedictine Rule at Condat. About 685, at an advanced age, he was made bp. of Besançon, but he soon resigned, retiring to Condat. BIBLIOGRAPHY: C. Boillon, BiblSanct 4:13–17.

[A. CABANISS]

CLAUDIUS OF TURIN (d. *c*.830), bp. from *c*.817, Iconoclast. Of Spanish origin, C. studied in Lyons, concentrating mainly on the Scriptures. Between 811 and 826 he

wrote commentaries on a number of books of the Bible. After becoming a bp. he embarked on a violent campaign of iconoclasm, going so far as to order the removal of all images and pictures, even the crucifix, from the churches of his diocese. His attack was answered by *Jonas of Orleans and the Irish monk, Dungal, theologians to Louis the Pious. He wrote an *Apologeticum* (*c*.825) of which only fragments have survived. BIBLIOGRAPHY: PL 104:615–928; E. Martin, *History of the Iconoclastic Controversy* (1930).

[R. B. ENO]

CLAUDIUS AND COMPANIONS, SS. Claudius, Asterius, Neon, Domnina, and Theonilla were martyred in the reign of Diocletian and were commemorated in the Western martyrologies. Details of their lives are vague, though their deaths at the hands of the proconsul of Cilicia, Lysias, is recorded to have been extremely cruel. BIBLIOGRAPHY: Butler 3:388–390; A. Moreschini, BiblSanct 4:18.

[E. C. HUBBERT]

CLAUDIUS, MATTHIAS (1740–1815), German writer. Under the pseudonym "Asmus," C. edited the literary section of *Der Wandsbecker Bothe* (1771–75), contributing to it the prose pieces, short stories, critical writings, reviews, letters, and poems which he later collected under the title *Asmus, omnia sua secum portans, oder sämtliche Werke des Wandsbecker Bothen* (1812). His lyric poems, though not inspired, are beloved for the simple piety, joy in nature, and depth of feeling that inspire them (e.g., "Abendlied"). BIBLIOGRAPHY: J. Julian, *Dictionary of Hymnology* (1957) 1:236–237.

[M. F. MCCARTHY]

CLAUSURA, see CLOISTER.

CLAVER, PETER, ST. (1580–1654), Spanish Jesuit, the great protector of the Negro slaves shipped from Africa to America. C. entered the Society of Jesus in 1602 and on the advice of the saintly Alfonso Rodríguez volunteered for the American mission. After his ordination in Bogotá, he was assigned to Cartagena, a port of passage for hundreds of thousands of Negro slaves. In the infested holds of the ships C. became doctor and friend to those who suffered from ill-treatment and epidemics. Moved by his compassion, many Negroes embraced the faith and were baptized. C. was canonized in 1888. His shrine in Cartagena is a center of pilgrimages from Colombia and neighboring countries. BIBLIOGRAPHY: A. Astrain, *Historia de la Compañía de Jesús en la Asistencia de España*; A. Valtierra, *Peter Claver: Saint of the Slaves* (1960); A Lunn, *Saint in the Slave Trade: Peter Claver* (1935); A. Rayez, BiblSanct 10:818–821.

[P. DAMBORIENA]

CLAVUS, CLAUDIUS (Nicholas Niger; d. after 1424), cartographer. Known chiefly for the first scientific extension of Ptolemy, he prepared two charts with lines of latitude and longitude that were the earliest maps to include Northern Europe, Greenland, and Iceland in their correct geographical positions. A descriptive text which accompanied one of his maps indicates he may have witnessed the destruction by the Eskimos of the eastern settlement of Greenland. BIBLIOGRAPHY: L. Bagrow, *History of Cartography* (ed. R. E. Skelton, tr. D. L. Paisey, 1964).

[F. G. O'BRIEN]

CLEAR VISION, DOCTRINE OF, the theory, originally proposed by *Uthred of Boldon, that the soul at the moment of death has a clear vision or full realization of divine truth and the nature of sin, and thus illumined makes a final acceptance or rejection of God. Uthred's theory was censured in 1368. A similar opinion was revived in the 19th cent. (SEE DEATH, THEOLOGY OF). BIBLIOGRAPHY: D. Knowles, "Censured Opinions of Uthred of Bolden," *Proceedings of the British Academy* 37 (1951) 305–342.

[T. M. MCFADDEN]

CLEMENCEAU, GEORGES BENJAMIN (1841–1929), French statesman. C. received a degree in medicine from the Univ. of Paris in 1865 and then traveled extensively in the U.S. (1865–69). Mayor of the Montmartre section of Paris in 1870, deputy to the National Assembly in 1871, president of the Paris municipal council (1871–76), senator, cabinet minister, twice premier of France (1906–09, 1917–20), he had a long and stormy public career. He opposed Boulanger, supported Zola in the Dreyfus case, and backed the anticlerical legislation of the Combes ministry. A strong advocate of the separation of Church and State, he favored the separations bill of 1905, promoted laicism, and opposed all attempts to reopen diplomatic relations with the Holy See following World War I. A strong war leader, he succeeded in unifying the Allied high command, thus helping immeasurably to bring the war to a speedy conclusion. He fell from power shortly after the Versailles peace treaty. After a brief visit to the U.S. in 1922, he returned to France. He devoted the last years of his life to his memoirs. BIBLIOGRAPHY: G. Bruun, *Clemenceau* (1943); J. H. Jackson, *Clemenceau and the Third Republic* (1948, repr. pa., 1962).

[D. R. PENN]

CLEMENCY, a virtue disposing a person in authority to temper justice with mercy when imposing punishment upon violators of the law. As a virtue, this disposition stands between two extremes. It is equally removed from an unreasonable leniency that will allow the common good to suffer by failure to use adequate severity in dealing with offenders, and from a cruelty too ready to insist upon exacting the last farthing of retribution from a wrongdoer. The discovery of the proper middle course between these extremes requires a delicate and enlightened *prudence. BIBLIOGRAPHY: T. Aq ST 2a2ae, 157.4; W. Herbst, NCE 3:925.

[P. K. MEAGHER]

CLEMENS WENZESLAUS (1739–1812), duke of Saxony, youngest son of Friedrich August II, King of Poland and Elector of Saxony. Deciding upon an ecclesiastical career, C., thanks to his distinguished birth, was rapidly promoted to churchly eminence and became elector-archbishop of Trier. *Febronian in his sympathies, C. was represented at the Congress of Ems which drew up a list of articles, most of which were directed against the Roman Curia. The reforms he instituted in his diocese were largely inspired by the Enlightenment. BIBLIOGRAPHY: H. Raab, *Clemens Wenzeslaus von Sachsen und seine Zeit 1739–1812* (1962); L. Just, NDB 3:282–283.

CLEMENS NON PAPA JACOBUS (Jacques Clement or Jacob Clemens; c.1510–c.1555), Flemish composer of sacred music in the generation between Josquin and Palestrina. The exact meaning of *non Papa* is not clear. A recent interpretation is that he took this name to distinguish himself from the priest-poet Jacobus Papa, also of Ypres. C. lived in France for a time, then returned to the Netherlands in 1540, settling in Bruges as priest and *succentor* at the church of Saint-Sauveur. As *succentor* he acted as deputy to the *precentor,* the supreme authority in all matters concerning music in the church. Like his contemporaries C. achieved a clearly personal style of counterpoint; he favored variation technique, imitative style, *basso ostinato* structure, and the parody-Mass type. There exist 16 Masses by C., all but one of the parody type, 15 settings of the Magnificat, and 230 motets, set for the most part to biblical texts. A *Missa pro defunctis,* based on Gregorian melodies, was thought partially lost, but was reprinted as recently as 1959. BIBLIOGRAPHY: D. G. Hughes, *History of European Music* (1974) 109–110; R. L. Crocker, *History of Musical Style* (1966) 194–198.

[J. S. PALLOZZA]

CLEMENT I, ST. (d. 101?), **POPE** from 92?, third successor to St. Peter as bp. of Rome, first of the Apostolic Fathers. According to Origen and others he was the Clement of Phil 4.3, but this is doubtful. Almost certainly incorrect is his identification made in the Clementine *pseudepigrapha with the T. Flavius Clemens of the imperial Flavian family who was executed for treason in A.D. 95, according to Dio Cassius because of his Jewish proclivities; but C. may possibly have been connected with that family either as a relative or freedman. It is unknown whether before his conversion he was a Jew or a pagan. The apocryphal *Martyrium Clementis* (PG 2:617–632), dating from the 4th cent., tells of his martyrdom in the Crimea, but the want of early evidence makes this incredible; and it is uncertain where or how he died. The relics preserved in the Basilica of S. Clemente in Rome are of doubtful authenticity, esp. if they were, as tradition relates, found by St. Cyril in the Crimea and brought to Rome. But the present basilica is built upon a 4th-cent. church underneath which are the remains of a building of imperial time. Very probably this was the house of a Clement, believed by G. *De Rossi to have been Pope Clement, from whom the basilica took its name *(titulus Clementis)*. C.'s fame in the Church has rested upon a literature attributed to him in antiquity, but of this only one work, his *First Epistle to the Corinthians,* is authentic. A dispute arose among the Christians at Corinth (*c.*96) and several presbyters were deposed. C. wrote in the name of the Church of Rome to urge repentance and reconciliation. He pointed out the necessity of good order in the Church and due succession from the Apostles in the ministry. The presbyters received the care of the community from God and could not, therefore, be deposed by the people. This letter was prized by its recipients and was still read in Corinth in the time of Bp. Dionysius (*c.*170); it is important for the early view it provides of the ministry and for its testimony to Peter's sojourn in Rome. The so-called *Second Epistle* is actually a homily, the earliest surviving Christian sermon. It is the work of an unknown author of the 2d century. The Epistles: PG 1:199–326; text and tr. ed. K. Lake, Loeb, *Apostolic Fathers* 1:8–163; tr. ed. J. Kleist, ACW 1 (1946); a new tr. and comment., ed. R. Grant and H. Graham, AF 2 (1965). See J. B. Lightfoot, *Clement of Rome* (enl. and rev. ed. 1890); Quasten 1:42–63; J. Chapman CE 4:12–17.

Various writings in addition to the *Second Epistle* have been wrongly ascribed to Clement, among which are the *Apostolic Constitutions,* two letters to virgins, the *Apocalypse of Peter,* and the *Clementine Liturgy.* Certain other works to which convention has restricted the term Clementines make up a single religious romance, which expounds Christian doctrine against a legendary setting. These are the *Homilies,* the *Recognitions,* and the *Epitomes.* The *Homilies* (PG 2:25–467) are a narrative telling of Clement's travels and conversion by St. Peter. The *Recognitions* (PG 2:1157–1474) cover much the same ground but with additional details. The *Epitomes* are abridgments of the *Homilies* and *Recognitions* (PG 2:469–603). In their doctrine the Clementines emphasize the unity of God, oppose pagan polytheism and magic, propose an exaggerated asceticism, and contain discernible evidences of Judaism, Gnosticism, and Arianism. They were probably used for the instruction of catechumens. Nothing is known of their authorship. At least in their common source they appear to have been written in the 3d century. Much controversy centered about them in the 19th cent., the Tübingen School contending that they are evidence of the strong opposition between the original Petrine, Jewish section of the Church and the Pauline section before their reconciliation in the 2d half of the 2d cent., a contention no longer taken seriously. BIBLIOGRAPHY: J. Chapman, CE 4:39–44; G. Zannoni, BiblSanct 4:38–47.

[R. B. ENO]

CLEMENT II, (Suidger) **POPE** (1046–47). Suidger had been bp. of Bamberg. After the removal of the antipope Sylvester III and the verdict of the synod of Sutri against Gregory VI, Suidger was named pope with the acclamation of clergy and people. C. crowned Henry III emperor, introduced reforms at Rome, and legislated against simoniacal clerics. BIBLIOGRAPHY: F. Dressler, NCE 3:928; Jedin-Baus 3.1:290–293.

[H. DRESSLER]

CLEMENT III, ANTIPOPE, see GUIBERT OF RAVENNA.

CLEMENT III (Paolo Scolari, d. 1191), **POPE** from 1187. He was a Roman by birth and related to several influential families in that city. Before his election he was cardinal bishop of Palestrina. The Third Crusade, already projected by his predecessor, with the new Pope's financial aid and the Saladin tithe got underway in the spring of 1189. C. settled his difficulties with the Romans and ended the struggle of rival claimants at Trier by appointing the imperial chancellor to that bishopric. The Pope aimed to carry on the reform movement by establishing ecclesiastical hierarchies and strengthening monastic observance. BIBLIOGRAPHY: R. Foreville, DHGE 12:1096–1109; G. Schwaiger, LTK 2:1224; Jedin-Baus 3.2:98–99; 109–110.

[H. DRESSLER]

CLEMENT IV (Guy Fulcodi; *c.*1199–1268), **POPE** from 1265. Born at Saint-Gilles (Rhône), Guy Fulcodi surpassed his father to become a famous lawyer and counselor of St. Louis. The successful jurist and father of two daughters abandoned the world in 1256 on the death of his wife. Seven years after his ordination, he had served as bp. of LePuy, abp. of Narbonne, cardinal bishop of Sabina, and papal legate. He strongly supported Henry III against Simon de Montfort and played an active role in destroying the last of the Hohenstaufens in Italy. To assure the preponderance of French influence and to further a crusade, he invested Charles of Anjou, St. Louis's brother, king of Sicily, June 1265. BIBLIOGRAPHY: Potthast Reg. 2:1542–1650; J. J. Smith, NCE 3:928–929; Mann 15:207–343; F. M. Powicke, *Thirteenth Century, 1216–1307* (2d ed. 1962) *passim.*

[S. WILLIAMS]

CLEMENT V (Bertrand de Got; 1264–1314), **POPE** from 1305. After law studies at Toulouse, Orléans, and Bologna, he became bp. of Comminges (1295) and abp. of Bordeaux (1299). He was elected pope when, on the death of Benedict XI, the cardinals went outside their own circle. Although a subject of the king of England, C. soon found himself in dependence upon Philip the Fair of France, who, in a clear effort at intimidation, occupied Poitiers while C. was staying there en route for Italy. Thereafter he lived either in the papal territory of Venaissin or at Avignon in the territory of the king of Naples, where, from 1309, he settled the curia. The first of the Avignonese popes, C. was well-meaning but weak and was too much inclined to rely upon his near relatives, mainly because he was an outsider who had never been part of the curia before his election. Under pressure from Philip he agreed to an inquiry into the conduct of Boniface VIII, but by procrastination thwarted the king's desire to have Boniface declared a heretic. When the king turned his attention to the Templars and their riches, C. was less resourceful. Although the Council of Vienne, convoked in 1311, was not at all inclined to suppress the Templars on the basis of the evidence that had been gathered by very dubious means all over Europe, C. forced the council by a threat of excommunication to agree to the suppression, possibly because Philip had occupied Vienne with French troops when it seemed that the Council was not going to cooperate. Part of C.'s difficulty was that he was cut off from the income of his Italian dominions. To remedy this, he resorted to increased taxation, introducing a scheme whereby each recipient of a benefice from the pope had to donate the revenue of the first year *(annate)* to the papacy. Among the achievements of his pontificate were the Council of Vienne, the preparation of a book of constitutions (later published in 1317 as the *Clementinae* or Seventh Book of the Decretals), the foundation of universities at Orléans and Perugia, and the decree that chairs of Hebrew, Syriac, and Arabic should be set up at Paris, Bologna, Oxford, and Salamanca, with a view to furthering missionary work. BIBLIOGRAPHY: *Regestum Clementis Papae V* (9 v., 1885–92); G. Mollat, *Popes at Avignon, 1305–1378* (tr. J. Love, 1963); Y. Renouard, *Avignon Papacy* (tr. D. Bethell, 1970).

[L. E. BOYLE]

CLEMENT VI (Pierre Roger; 1291–1352), **POPE** from 1342. Having entered the Benedictine abbey of La-Chaise-Dieu (Haute-Loire), he studied theology at Paris, later becoming abbot of Fécamp (1328), bp. of Arras (1328), abp. of Sens (1329) and of Rouen (1330), and cardinal (1338). Since he had risen in ecclesiastical ranks not by service to the Church but to the King of France, his political allegiance was always that of France. Possibly it was under French influence that he finally succeeded (1343) in depriving the recalcitrant Louis of Bavaria of the empire, causing a new election to be held. Certainly his subservience to French interests created a wide impression that the Avignon papacy was nothing more than a French instrument. He ruled as a great prince, spending money so lavishly that the treasury was soon in difficulties from which it never fully recovered. His blatant traffic in benefices caused both Edward III of England (1345) and Philip VI of France (1347) to sequestrate all benefices held by foreigners in their countries. His most lasting achievement, perhaps, was the purchase of the sovereignty of Avignon from Queen Joan of Naples in 1348. BIBLIOGRAPHY: G. Mollat, *Popes at Avignon, 1305–1378* (tr. J. Love, 1963); Y. Renouard, *Avignon Papacy* (tr. D. Bethell, 1970).

[L. E. BOYLE]

CLEMENT VII (Giulio de' Medici; 1478–1534), **POPE** from 1523. The illegitimate son of Giuliano de' Medici, born after his father's death, C. was reared by his grandfather, Lorenzo de' Medici. Having received a dispensation from the impediment to holy orders because of his illegitimacy, he was made bp. of Florence in 1513 and was named cardinal the same year by his cousin, Pope Leo X. In 1521 there were many who favored his election to the papacy, but the conclave finally chose *Adrian VI instead. However, in the conclave that followed the brief reign of Adrian, C. was chosen his successor. During his reign he faced four major problems: the growing Lutheran movement; involvement in the struggle between Francis I of France and Charles I for the domination of Europe; the marriage of Henry VIII of England; and the urgent need of a council to reform the Church. With none of these did C. deal successfully. He was weak and indecisive in times when a strong and able pope was greatly needed. BIBLIOGRAPHY: Pastor v. 9–10.

[J. C. WILLKE]

CLEMENT VII, ANTIPOPE (Robert of Geneva; 1342–94), the first antipope (r. 1378–94) of the *Western Schism. When the cardinals assembled in Rome in 1378 to elect a successor to *Gregory XI, their choice fell upon Bartolomeo Prignano, who became *Urban VI. By his bad temper and incivility Urban alienated many of his supporters. The cardinals withdrew to Fondi. Italian cardinals were present but took no active part in the proceedings; the remaining cardinals, mainly French, repudiated the election of Urban, claiming they had acted in fear of the Roman populace; they then proceeded to elect Robert of Geneva in his place. C. was unable to occupy Rome by force of arms; he eventually returned to Avignon and the loyalty of Europe became divided until the end of the schism. BIBLIOGRAPHY: Pastor 1:134–174.

[J. C. WILLKE]

CLEMENT VIII (Ippolyto Aldobrandini; 1536–1605), **POPE** from 1592. A distinguished jurist of a prominent Italian family, C. first served in the Roman Rota where he was rapidly promoted and made cardinal in 1585. His election as pope marked the weakening of Spanish influence in papal policy. C. absolved Henry IV and recognized him as legitimate king of France. The implementation of Tridentine reforms in the French Church followed, as well as further political settlements between France and Spain and also France and Savoy. These developments on the Continent facilitated a new effort to reconcile the English Church. C. was disappointed in his dealings with James I, but the plight of English Catholics was improved and English colleges on the Continent were strengthened. C. supported reform and missionary efforts in Poland and Germany where large areas were reclaimed for Catholicism. He received the reunion of the metropolitan of Kiev and a number of Ruthenian bishops with the conclusion of the

Union of *Brest. Clement promoted ecclesiastical reform in a series of decrees and ordered a new and important edition of the *Vulgate as well as new editions of the Breviary and the Missal. When the Molinist controversy between the Dominicans and the Jesuits was referred to Rome, C. established a commission (*Congregatio de Auxiliis) to investigate the matter and personally presided over its meetings. He was a devout and upright man whose pontificate was marked by pastoral concern and whose achievements as pope were considerable. BIBLIOGRAPHY: Pastor v. 23 and 24; R. Mols, DHGE 12:149–97; J. de la Servière, DTC 3.1:76–86; J. C. Willke NCE 3:934.

[J. C. WILLKE]

CLEMENT VIII, ANTIPOPE (Gil Sánchez Muñoz; r. 1425–29), elected by three schismatic cardinals with the support of Alfonso of Aragon. When he failed to achieve recognition by any other nation, he made his submission to Pope *Martin V.

[J. C. WILLKE]

CLEMENT IX (Giulio Rospigliosi; 1600–69), **POPE** from 1667. Of an old Lombard family, C. rose in papal service and was nuncio to Spain before he was made cardinal and secretary of state by Alexander VII. Politically, he worked to bring about peace between France and Spain (Aix-la-Chapelle, 1668) and assisted the Venetians in their long defense of the Christian stronghold in Crete against the Ottoman Turks. He failed to obtain the help of Louis XIV in this effort, and C.'s sorrow at the fall of the island is said to have hastened his death. A major difficulty of his reign was the Jansenist heresy and the recalcitrance of certain French bishops. C. obtained a measure of submission from these bishops and thereby secured a temporary respite (Pax Clementina) in the Jansenist struggle. C. was an able administrator of papal finances and promoted missionary organizations in Asia and America. While a man of erudition and considerable literary talent, he was loved by the Romans as a simple and devout pastor of great affability and many charitable works. BIBLIOGRAPHY: Pastor 31:314–430; R. Mols, DHGE 12:1297–1313; J. de la Servière, DTC 3:86–94.

[J. C. WILLKE]

CLEMENT X (Emiliero Altieri; 1590–1676), **POPE** from 1670. After a long career distinguished by diplomatic and curial service, he was the oldest member of the college of cardinals when he was elected a caretaker pope after a conclave of more than 4 months in which the French and Spanish cardinals were deadlocked. C. was confronted by difficulties with Louis XIV over the right of *regalia and certain matters involving religious orders. His resistance to the French King was to be continued by his successor when the crisis over Gallicanism heightened. By various decrees C. promoted missionary activity. In 1674 he erected the See of Quebec, the first in Canada. He also gave large financial aid to Poland, which, under John Sobieski, was leading the Christian forces against the Turks. C. confined himself for the most part to religious affairs, which he handled well, and committed the civil administration of the Papal States to his adopted nephew, Card. Paoluzzi-Altieri—an arrangement resented by the Romans. BIBLIOGRAPHY: Pastor 31:431–508; R. Mols, DHGE 12:1313–26; J. de la Servière, DTC, 3.1:94–98.

[J. C. WILLKE]

CLEMENT XI (Giovanni Francesco Albani; 1649–1721), **POPE** from 1700. He was of a noble Umbrian family and became an accomplished scholar in the classics, law, and theology. After a career of administrative posts in the Papal States, he was made cardinal deacon in 1690 and became a trusted advisor of Innocent XII. He was ordained shortly before the opening of the conclave in which he was elected pope. A charitable man, austere and virtuous in his personal life, he devoted himself as pope to the best interests of the Church and Christendom, but his pontificate was marked by political difficulties and religious problems. The war of Spanish Succession broke out and involved all the major powers of Europe. Unable to maintain neutrality, he first recognized the title of Philip V to the Spanish throne and suffered the wrath of Austria in the invasion of the Papal States. Forced to acknowledge Archduke Charles, the Austrian claimant, he incurred the antagonism of Louis XIV and Philip V. In the peace of Utrecht (1713) the papacy lost Sicily, Parma and Piacenza, and, over the protests of the Pope, the Elector of Brandenburg was recognized as King of Prussia and the cause of the pretender to the English throne, James III, was abandoned. While these events evidence the shortcomings of Clement XI, they also reflect the general decline of the papacy as a power in European political affairs. Continuing difficulties with France, Spain, and Sicily marked his later reign, but C. was successful in persuading Spain and Austria to join Venice against the Turks.

The Jansenist controversy raged in France, and C. was an implacable, if patient, opponent. His condemnations of the heresy came in the bulls Vineam Domini (1705) and Unigenitus (1713), a detailed analysis of P. *Quesnel's doctrine. The recalcitrant abp. of Paris, Card. Louis de Noallis, and his followers were condemned and excommunicated in Pastoralis officii (1718). C. also had to deal with the culmination of the Chinese rites controversy, which had already involved the Jesuits and the Dominicans in a long and heated dispute over the adaptation of certain local Chinese customs and Confucian practices on the Christian missions. After lengthy investigations and deep personal study, C. decreed against the Jesuits, but this failed to terminate the dispute. BIBLIOGRAPHY: R. Mols, DHGE 12:1326–61; J. de la Servière, DTC 3.1:98–111; Pastor v. 33.

[J. C. WILLKE]

CLEMENT XII (Lorenzo Corsini; 1652–1740), **POPE** from 1730. Of an influential Florentine family, he became an experienced diplomat and administrator. Although not a scholar, he was nevertheless a patron of learning and the arts. He came to his pontificate in failing health and after the 2d year was completely blind. Yet he was a vigorous leader and maintained his mental alertness to the end. He acted immediately to restore order and financial regularity in the chaos of public administration left by the subordinates of his predecessor. In foreign affairs he experienced severe difficulties arising from the War of Polish Election, and in the treaty of Vienna (1738) the balance of power settlement among the European monarchs ignored the Pope and his interests. Worse were the difficulties in Church-State relations in the Kingdom of the Two Sicilies. In this and other political affairs C. was obliged to make frequent concessions to the absolute monarchs. He stood firmly on the policy of his predecessors in the battle against Jansenism. With the cooperation of Card. Fleury the heresy was finally suppressed in France, although its effects in religious attitudes and practice were to linger long. A new threat to the faith, Freemasonry (at that time a manifestation of Deism and naturalism) was spreading rapidly in Europe and lodges were founded in Italy. In *In eminenti* (1738) C. condemned Freemasonry and forbade Catholics to join the lodges under pain of excommunication. He sponsored various projects for the interest of Eastern Christians (Maronites, Coptics, and Greek Catholics) and fostered missions in Asia and S America. BIBLIOGRAPHY: BullRom v. 23 and 24; Pastor 34:301–510; R. Mols, DHGE 12:1361–81, bibliog.; J. de la Servière, DTC 3.1:111–115.

[J. C. WILLKE]

CLEMENT XIII (Carlo della Torre Rezzonico; 1693–1769), **POPE** from 1758. Of a noble Venetian family, he was educated by the Jesuits in Bologna and studied theology and canon law at Padua. During his career he was governor of Rieti and then of Fano, auditor of the Rota for Venice, and was made cardinal in 1737. In 1743 he became bp. of Padua where he served with charity and zeal. Regarded by the Paduans as a saint and by others as a scholar, he was industrious and genial but inclined to timidity and indecision. He relied heavily on his advisors, some of whom did not share his admiration for the Jesuits. The chief preoccupation of his pontificate was the suppression of the Jesuits in the Catholic countries of Western Europe. This problem itself was symptomatic of the fundamental antagonism between papal authority and the principle of Enlightened Despotism, particularly in the Bourbon courts of Europe then bound together in a kind of family alliance. It also revealed the force of antireligious sentiment cultivated by the "enlightened" writers of the time. The movement to suppress the Jesuits, staunch defenders of papal prerogative, began in Portugal when Pompal, under pretext of Jesuit conspiracy in an attempted attack on the life of King Joseph I, ordered the imprisonment or deportation of all Jesuits within the realm and the confiscation of all Jesuit property. All attempts by the Pope to negotiate were re-

ceived with blank refusal and relationships between Rome and Portugal were severed in 1760. In France, where Gallicanism and Jansenism had made many enemies for the Jesuits, the failure of a commercial venture involving the Jesuits of Paris brought the Society and its constitutions under the scrutiny of Parliament. When Louis XV requested that the French Jesuits be subject to a special vicar general, who would be appointed by the crown and independent of the generalate in Rome, the Pope refused. The Society was then suppressed in France by royal decree in 1764. Clement responded in *Apostolicum pascendi munus* (1765) in which he strongly defended the Jesuits and praised their work. Charles III, enlightened despot of Spain, by royal decree and for reasons unstated, banished the Jesuits from Spain and her colonies in 1767. Clement's plea for justice and clemency went unheeded. Ferdinand IV, King of the Two Sicilies and son of Charles III, through regent Bernardo Tanucci, followed with a decree of expulsion in 1768; and the Duke of Parma, also a Bourbon, did likewise—the latter also renouncing the pope's traditional suzerainty over Parma. C.'s stern censure of the Duke of Parma brought reprisals from the Bourbon courts as France occupied the papal territories of Avignon and Venaissin and Ferdinand took Pontecorvo and Benevento. In early 1769 the ambassadors of France, Spain, and Naples presented identical demands for the worldwide suppression of the Jesuits, an event believed to have hastened the Pope's death. He died a few days afterward, the night before a scheduled meeting of a special consistory which he had called to decide on the problem. BIBLIOGRAPHY: *Bullarii romani continuatio* (9 v. 1840–56) v. 3; Pastor v. 36 and 37; J. Mols, DHGE 12:1381–1410, bibliog.; J. McShane, NCE 3:937–940.

[J. C. WILLKE]

CLEMENT XIV (Giovanni Vincenzo Antonio Ganganelli; 1705–74), **POPE** from 1769. After early schooling under the Jesuits and the Piarists, he entered the Conventual Franciscans, taking the name of Lorenzo. He studied and later taught theology and philosophy, was advanced to high positions in the order and in the curia, and was made cardinal in 1759. The conclave following the death of *Clement XIII was long and troubled since the fate of the Jesuits was at issue. The French and Spanish cardinals were instructed to support only a candidate likely to take the action against the Society demanded by their monarchs. The pro-Jesuit faction was equally determined to elect a man likely to protect the Society. Ganganelli received every vote except his own, showing the conflict between opinions held of him by his own contemporaries and by later historians. While he probably had no animosity toward the Jesuits (there is argument to substantiate his esteem, affection, and indebtedness to the Society) C. was convinced that peace for the Church and cooperation from the monarchs in dealing with other pressing problems could be achieved only by appeasement. The threats of full schism in France, Spain,

Portugal, and the Two Sicilies, where the society was already suppressed by royal decree, reinforced this belief. Although the charge that he was elected as a consequence of a bargain with the Bourbon courts seems unfounded, he moved immediately to assure Charles III of Spain and Louis XV of France of his conciliary intentions. He negotiated a settlement with Portugal, which had been estranged from the Holy See since 1760, and awarded the red hat to the brother of Pompal. He dropped the annual promulgation of reserved censures used by Clement XIII in excommunicating the Duke of Parma and further placated that ruler by granting him a dispensation to marry his cousin, the daughter of Maria Theresa. These efforts of his first year brought improved relations, but the monarchs were adamant in demanding the full and final suppression of the Jesuits. C. at best delayed action for several years, but by 1772 the pressure of the Spanish ambassador in Rome, José Moniño, and the threat of schism could no longer be resisted. C. ordered Moniño to collaborate with the papal representative, Bp. Francisco Zelado, in preparing the brief of suppression, *Dominus ac Redemptor* (1773).

In suppressing the order, Clement relied on ample precedent for his disciplinary action. He gave as the only reason the peace of the Church and the Jesuits' affinity for trouble—an observation not unfounded since the Jesuits were at the height of their power and frequently in the vanguard of the defense of the Church and its interests. The Pope did not condemn the morals or the orthodoxy of either individual Jesuits or of the Society as a whole. Since Catherine II of Russia refused to promulgate the papal brief, the order survived in the Polish provinces of Russia.

C.'s appeasement was rewarded by the return of Avignon and Benevento, which had been taken by the Bourbon monarchs from Clement XIII, but many problems, some involving other religious orders in France and Portugal, continued to develop. The people of Rome were hopelessly alienated, and the last year of C.'s life was one of deteriorating health and continuing psychological depression. The report that he retracted his order of suppression in a letter entrusted to his confessor and addressed to the next pope is still in dispute. BIBLIOGRAPHY: *Bullarii romani continuatio* v. 4 *Clementis XIV . . . epistolae et brevia selectiora . . .* (ed. A. Theiner, 1852); E. McShane, NCE 3:940–942; E. Préclin, DHGE 12:1411–23, bibliog.; Pastor v. 38.

[J. C. WILLKE]

CLEMENT OF ALEXANDRIA (Titus Flavius Clemens; *c.*150–*c.*215), philosopher and theologian. Probably a native Athenian, C. was converted to Christianity in his early youth and traveled widely in search of Christian instruction. Settling finally in Alexandria, he studied under *Pantaenus, whom he succeeded as head of the catechetical school near the close of the 2d cent., when *Origen was a student there. Driven from the city by persecution in 202, C. sought refuge in Cappadocia where he spent his last years. He seems to have planned a trilogy of works. The first was the *Protrepticus* (PG 8:49–246), an exhortation to the Greeks to examine the claims of Christianity. Like the usual apology, this showed the errors and evils of pagan religion and the superiority of the Hebrew revelation; pagan philosophy admittedly contained some truth, which in its totality is to be found only in Christ. The second work was his *Pedagogus* (PG 8:247–684), the first book of which shows Christ to be the educator and master and contains a refutation of Gnosticism; the remaining two books are a treatise on practical morality. The third work of the trilogy was not written, but C.'s *Stromata* (anthology; PG 8:685–1381; 9:9–602), a diffuse and somewhat disorganized work, contain materials gathered for it. In the *Stromata*, C. goes further than any other early Christian author in his appreciation and praise of pagan learning and philosophy. He would want to effect a synthesis of Greek, esp. Platonic thought, and Christian teaching. He has been called the first of the Christian Platonists. But he shows the influence of Stoicism also in making Christian perfection a thing to be achieved in a life of unalterable calm. He is conspicuous for his tendency to understand the OT in allegory. He took a broad and optimistic view of the ultimate salvation even of sinners. His *Hypotyposes* (outlines), preserved in the Greek only in fragments, was a commentary on the whole of the Scriptures. *Photius, who had read it, declared it unorthodox on a number of points. Down to the 17th cent. he was venerated as a saint, but Clement VIII had his name dropped from the calendar because so little was known of his life and cult and because of suspicion concerning some of his doctrines. Some works include crit. ed. GCS 1–4; text and tr. of *Protrepticus* and *Quis dives salvetur?*, ed. G. W. Butterworth, Loeb (1919). BIBLIOGRAPHY: Quasten 2:5–36; F. P. Havey, CE 4:45–47; E. F. Osborn, *Philosophy of Clement of Alexandria* (1957); G. Floyd, *Clement of Alexandria's Treatment of the Problem of Evil* (1971).

[R. B. ENO]

CLEMENT HOFBAUER, ST., see HOFBAUER, CLEMENT, ST.

CLEMENT OF IRELAND, ST. (Clemens Scotus; d. after 818), Irish born successor of Alcuin as head of Charlemagne's palace school. He wrote a grammar which for long was credited to his student, Lothair. BIBLIOGRAPHY: W. H. Grattan-Flood, CE 4:47–48; R. L. Poole, DNB 4:487–488.

[R. T. MEYER]

CLEMENT OF SLOVENSKY, ST. (Clement of Ochrida; *c.*840–916), missionary, bp., one of the fathers of Slavonic literature. Probably of Slavic rather than Greek origin, a disciple of SS. Cyril and Methodius, C. worked on the missions in Moravia. He took a strong pro-Slavic position in the struggle with the German bps. concerning the use of

Slavic in the liturgy and in consequence was driven from the country in 885. Taking refuge in Bulgaria, where he was received with honor, he went about teaching Christian doctrine and Slavic letters in what is now central Albania. In 893 he was made bp. of Velitsa, a see whose territory cannot now be precisely identified. However, it is known that Ochrida (Ohrid, Okhrida) in what is now SE Yugoslavia was a favored center of his activity. His writings include translations of liturgical texts, homilies, and lives of the saints. BIBLIOGRAPHY: G. Eldarov, BiblSanct 4:29–35.

CLEMENT, CAESAR (d. 1626), Catholic missionary in England. Ordained (1585) at the English College, Rome, C. was sent to England (1587), but nothing is known of the nature or locale of his missionary activities there. Later he served as dean of St. Guddule's, Brussels, and vicar-general of the Spanish army in Flanders. He assisted his aunt, Margaret Clement, in the foundation of St. Monica's Convent, Louvain (1609), and by appointment from Rome was associated with R. Chambers in investigating the troubled situation at Douai College (1612). BIBLIOGRAPHY: Gillow BDEC 1:496.

[V. SAMPSON]

CLÉMENT, JACQUES, a Dominican who poignarded and killed Henry III of Valois (1589), in revenge for his murders of the Guises and because of his ambiguity in defense of the Catholic cause. It was regarded by the French clergy as a fanatical application of the doctrine of tyrannicide, but the act took the French Dominicans many years to live down, even in the eyes of Henry IV who benefited.

[T. GILBY]

CLEMENT, JACQUES, see CLEMENS NON PAPA, JACOBUS.

CLEMENT, JOHN (d. 1572), physician, protégé of Thomas *More, whose foster daughter he married. His wife attracted the unfavorable attention of authorities by helping the starving Carthusians in Newgate (1537) and was ordered to desist. During the reign of Edward VI, the Clements were in exile in Louvain and again were obliged to flee to Belgium because of the religious policy of Elizabeth. C. then practiced medicine in Mechlin until his death. He was a man of scholarly interests and translated from Greek into Latin the letters of St. Gregory Nazianzus and the homilies of Nicephorus. BIBLIOGRAPHY: DNB 4:489; Gillow BDEC 1:498–500.

[V. SAMPSON]

CLEMENT AND ALDEBERT, see ALDEBERT AND CLEMENT.

CLEMENTINAE, a collection of the legislation of Clement V and of the Council of Vienne (1311–12), important to the history of canon law. The collection was completed for Clement V in 1314, but only promulgated in 1317 by John XXII. It was sometimes referred to as *Liber septimus,* i.e., following on the *Liber sextus* of Boniface VIII. It was printed with the *Corpus juris canonici* of 1582.

[T. C. O'BRIEN]

CLEMENTINE EPISTLE, see CLEMENT I, ST., POPE.

CLEMENTINE INSTRUCTION, an instruction issued by Pope Clement XII in 1731 regulating the *Forty Hours Devotion, setting down in minute detail the rubrics for the services. The present rubrics for *Benediction and exposition of the Blessed Sacrament (1973) considerably modify former observance of this instruction.

[R. B. ENO]

CLEMENTINE LITURGY, a manner of celebrating the Eucharist as found in Book 8 of the *Apostolic Constitution.* It is called "Clementine" because it purports to give the decrees of Pope Clement of Rome. The work is apocryphal. Book 8 is derived from the *Apostolic Tradition* of Hippolytus of Rome. The Clementine liturgy is Syrian and was written c.380. It was never the liturgy of a particular congregation, but it did have a considerable influence on the majority of later Eastern rites.

[N. KOLLAR]

CLENOCK (CLYNNOG), MAURICE (c.1525–80), Welshman, first rector of the English College in Rome. Chaplain and secretary to Card. Pole, C. was obliged to retire to the Continent in exile after the death of Mary Tudor. In 1567 he was camerarius and in 1578 warden of a hospice for exiled English scholars. He was active in the negotiations that converted the hospice into a seminary and was appointed the seminary's first rector. Upon the complaint of English students, who wanted the college to be administered by the Jesuits, that he was unreasonably partial to Welshmen, he was removed from his office. BIBLIOGRAPHY: DNB 11:37; BDEC 1:501–505.

CLEOPAS (CLEOPHAS), one of the disciples who spoke with Jesus on the road to Emmaus (Lk 24.18). It is disputed whether his name is the same as that of Clopas (or Cleophas; Jn 19.25), who was in some way related to a Mary who stood near the cross (her husband?). There have been attempts to identify this Clopas as the stepfather or brother-in-law of the Virgin Mary, or as the Alpheus of Mk 3.18. His name recurs in discussions of the perpetual virginity of Mary; his identity in all the above cases remains doubtful, but it is in no case a crucial argument for the Catholic tradition concerning Mary.

[P. J. KEARNEY]

CLERGY (Gr. *klēros,* lot; see Acts 1.17), those persons who have been set apart from the general body of church members, the laity, by ordination as leader of the Church. The term traditionally embraces bishops, priests (presbyters, elders), and deacons, though in some Churches, such as those in the *Reformed tradition, the deacons are lay persons. The concept of special persons within the Church who exercise a distinctive function is generally traced to the NT and Jesus' setting apart the 12 Apostles, together with the action of the apostolic Church as recorded in Acts and the outline of requirements for bishops and deacons in 1 Tim ch. 5 and Tit ch. 1. In the Eastern and the RC Churches, ordination is considered a sacrament (holy orders), which gives an indelible character to the one ordained. Protestant Churches recognize only baptism and communion as sacraments, though they generally have special rites of ordination. Congregationalists, Baptists, and Quakers, as well as some groups within other Churches, minimize or deny outright the distinction between clergy and laity. The authority and power of the clergy are variously conceived. Administering the sacraments, preaching, and leading in worship are generally considered their responsibilities. The RC clergy govern the Church, but in the Protestant Churches governing power is normally shared by the laity. BIBLIOGRAPHY: *Ministry and the Sacraments* (ed. R. Dunkerley, 1937). *ORDINATION; *LAITY.

[T. EARLY]

CLERGY, BENEFIT OF, see BENEFIT OF CLERGY.

CLERGY, CONGREGATION OF THE, the congregation or department of Church government in the reorganized Roman *Curia that replaces the older Congregation of the Council. It exists to deal with matters concerning the pastoral ministry of priests and deacons throughout the world.

CLERGY, INDIGENOUS, priests who fulfill their sacerdotal apostolate in their native land. Vat II MissAct 16 states that the Church's work is more effectively carried out when the orders of bp., priest, and deacon are assumed by an indigenous clergy. From apostolic times to the 16th cent. it was church practice to ordain indigenous priests for new Christian communities whenever possible. With the establishment of missions among non-Western peoples and continuing until relatively recent times, however, this practice was often reduced to a mere aspiration, an ultimate but unattained goal. But a new vision of modern missionary action and the insistence of Leo XIII and his successors caused a renewed thrust toward the actual nativization of the clergy in mission areas. A turning point was reached with the promulgation of Pius XI's *Rerum ecclesiae* and his consecration of six Chinese bps. in 1926, one of whom, Thomas Cardinal Tien, became the first non-Western cardinal. This policy was further strengthened by Vatican Council II. The advantages of an indigenous clergy are numerous and proceed mainly from the fact that they have been conditioned for the socio-cultural environment in which they operate. They have an inborn empathy for their

people's way of life and share in the local value system, thus making effective communication and meaningful cultural accommodations possible. BIBLIOGRAPHY: J. Beckmann, *Der einheimische und Gegenwart* (1950); A. Lee, *De formatione cleri localis in missionibus* (1958); L. J. Luzbetak, *Church and Cultures: An Applied Anthropology for the Religious Worker* (1963).

[L. J. LUZBETAK]

CLERGY, MARRIAGE OF. The Eastern Orthodox Churches know only a celibate religious clergy or a married secular clergy. Unmarried candidates before receiving ordination must either enter the religious state by monastic profession or be married. Once ordained, deacons, priests, and bishops are prevented from marrying by the diriment impediment of sacred orders, which continues to bind them even if they have become widowers (Trullo, 692). Only the Nestorians permit widowed priests to remarry. Secular and regular priests and deacons may be laicized and thereby reacquire the legal capacity to marry.

[V. J. POSPISHIL]

CLERI SANCTITATI, a *motu proprio of* Pius XII on the Eastern Churches (June 2, 1957). It deals with physical and moral persons (cc. 1–37), with the laws on clerics in general and particular (cc. 38–526), and with those on the laity (cc. 527–558). The authority of patriarchs, major archbishops, and their synods is considered in some detail. BIBLIOGRAPHY: V. Pospishil, NCE 10:763–766.

[E. EL-HAYEK]

CLERIC, designation of one who has been accepted to the diaconate. The Ceremony of Admission to the diaconate and the presbyterate admits candidates to the clerical state. Diocesan candidates also participate in a prior ceremony marking them for the clerical state. These ceremonies replace the former practice in which tonsure constituted entrance to the clerical state.

[J. R. AHERNE]

CLERICAL DRESS, see DRESS, CLERICAL.

CLERICAL HABIT, see HABIT, RELIGIOUS.

CLERICAL STATE, the set manner of life in the Church proper to those ordained for the hierarchic ministries. By Paul VI's *motu proprio, Ministeria quaedam* (Aug. 15, 1972), implementing the directive of VatII SacLit 62, entrance into the clerical state comes by ordination to the diaconate (tonsure and minor orders as well as subdiaconate are suppressed in the Latin Church). Clerics, then, are deacons, priests, and bishops; they have a hierarchic or ministerial share in the one priesthood of Christ, distinct from the universal priesthood of the faithful (VatII ConstChurch 10). By entry into the clerical state through holy orders clerics receive the radical power to share in the ministries of teaching, sanctifying, governing in the Church. By traditional enumeration the states of perfection in a canonical sense always included episcopacy; it is debated whether priesthood or diaconate is a state of perfection. But Vatican Council II clearly set forth norms that give clerics a way of heeding the universal call to Christian holiness in specific ways appropriate to their place in the Church. In general it is through a charity or love that is truly pastoral that they achieve their own sanctification. Their prayer and sacrifice are for the People of God, the perils and hardships of the apostolate are their asceticism. All their work is to be nourished by their contemplation. Cooperation of deacons and priests with their bishop is a special form of their fraternal love (VatII ConstChurch 39). The Council develops these basic themes in VatII MinLifePriests, esp. in ch. 3 on the priest's call to perfection ("Priests will acquire holiness on their own distinctive way by exercising their functions sincerely and truthfully in the spirit of Christ") and in the Decree on Priestly Formation. The clerical state in the still operative Code of Canon Law entails certain obligations that are meant to safeguard the cleric's pursuit of holiness and fulfilment of ministry. They include obedience to the bp., avoidance of worldliness, unseemly business or conduct, the regular reception of the sacrament of penance, annual retreat, continued sacred study. The obligation to *clerical dress also applies, but the meaning of clerical dress has received a broad interpretation recently, esp. in view of Vatican II's encouragement of the priest's being close to his people in the manner of his life (VatII MinLifePriests 3).

[T. C. O'BRIEN]

CLERICALISM, a term originating in the latter half of the 19th cent., and generally used in a pejorative sense, signifying domination of civil government and temporal affairs by the Church. It emerged from opposition to RC influence in France during the Second Empire, being popularized by Gambetta's slogan, "*Le cléricalisme, voilà l'ennemi!*" Although the word was new, the condition it represented had existed during certain periods of history, as from the time of Gregory VII through the papacy of Innocent III. Similar domination by the Church also resulted from some of the concordats arranged between popes and the rulers of national states. Its meaning has been broadened by some to apply to all attempts of Churches to influence social and economic aspects of life. BIBLIOGRAPHY: J. Lecler, *Two Sovereignties: A Study of the Relationship between Church and State* (1952).

[N. H. MARING]

CLERICIS LAICOS, bull issued by Boniface VIII in 1296 in reaction to increasing exactions from Philip IV of France and Edward I of England. It forbade secular authorities to tax the clergy without papal permission. "If the clergy do pay, or the laymen receive, let them fall under sentence of excommunication by the very deed," the bull

decreed. However, in 1297 Boniface was forced to concede in his bull *Etsi de statu* that the French king could tax the clergy in time of necessity. The original prohibition was further modified by Benedict XI and revoked by Clement V. BIBLIOGRAPHY: T. Boase, *Boniface VIII* (1933).

[T. EARLY]

CLÉRISSAC, HUMBERT (1864–1914), French Dominican contemplative, spiritual director, and retreat master. He was trained in the classics at a Jesuit college in Avignon and entered the Dominican province of Lyons in 1880. Because of the antireligious laws prevailing at the time, he spent most of his active ministry in England and Italy. He acquired a broad English culture and a facility in the language that enabled him to preach effectively in it. He preached innumerable retreats, not only to French religious in exile, but to other religious as well in England and in Italy. His best known work was put together from his notes by J. *Maritain and published under the title, *The Mystery of the Church* (1919). Among Dominicans his *Spirit of St. Dominic* (1924) is much esteemed as one of the finest expositions in modern times of the Dominican ideal. BIBLIOGRAPHY: P. Deploye, DSAM 2.1:793–794.

[C. R. CAWLEY]

CLERK, JOHN (d. 1541), bp. of Bath and Wells from 1523. He held degrees in arts from Cambridge and in law from Bologna, became T. Wolsey's chaplain and dean of the King's chapel, served as ambassador to Rome (1521) where he presented to the Pope Henry VIII's *Defense of the Seven Sacraments,* and twice sought to secure Wolsey's election to the papacy. In 1526 he attempted to arrange a marriage between Francis I and Princess Mary Tudor. Though he acted as counselor to Queen Catherine in the divorce proceedings of 1529, he joined in pronouncing the King's divorce. He is believed to have helped Cranmer to write certain works on the King's supremacy and divorce. BIBLIOGRAPHY: W. Hunt, DNB 4:495–496.

[V. SAMPSON]

CLERKS REGULAR, communities of priests bound by the vows of the religious life and living a common life under a rule. They differ from canons regular by the fact that they are dedicated primarily to the active ministry and are excused from choral obligations. In most such communities the priests are expected to cultivate the sacred sciences in addition to their priestly ministry. They generally observe a uniformity of clerical dress.

[R. C. EGAN]

CLERKS REGULAR OF THE MOTHER OF GOD (CRMD), a religious order of priests, also known as Leonardini, founded at Lucca, Italy, by St. John Leonardi (1574) to promote the Counter Reformation and to combat Protestantism. They became active in various pastoral works and in literary movements, producing many scholars.

The order flourished in Italy until a decline during the 19th cent. when it was almost destroyed. Revived in the 20th cent., the order opened new foundations in France and Chile. The members conduct parishes, preach, direct Catholic organizations, and promote devotion to the Eucharist and to the Blessed Virgin. In 1976 they maintained 14 houses and numbered 49 religious of whom 42 were priests.

[A. R. ZINK]

CLERKS OF ST. VIATOR, see VIATORIANS.

CLERMONT-TONNERRE, ANNE ANTOINE JULES DE (1749–1830), bp., later abp. and cardinal. After his studies C.-T. was ordained priest in 1774 and the same year was made vicar-general of the archdiocese of Besançon. In 1881 he was promoted to the bishopric of Châlons-sur-Marne. In 1789 he was elected a deputy to the Estates General, but when in 1791 he refused to take the oath of submission to the Civil Constitution of the Clergy, he was obliged to go into exile in Belgium and Germany. Returning to France after 1801, he resigned his see and continued for a time his life of retirement. But in 1820 he was named abp. of Toulouse and in 1822 a cardinal. He worked zealously for the restoration of discipline in his archdiocese. BIBLIOGRAPHY: C. Laplatte, DHGE 12:319–322.

[C. R. CAWLEY]

CLERMONT, COUNCILS OF. Two councils bear the name, one held in that city in 535 and the other in 1095. The latter is the more important. There Pope Urban delivered an address that inspired the First Crusade (1096–99). Urban pleaded for help for the Eastern Christians and for the recovery of Jerusalem from non-Christian hands. He denounced the sins of the nobles and called them to penance, thus combining the idea of a pilgrimage to Jerusalem with that of a holy war. He so stirred his listeners that they rallied with the battle cry, "God wills it!" In addition to issuing regulations governing the proposed crusade, the council also addressed itself to the problems of the Church in France. It passed laws regulating the government of the French dioceses. It also decreed that a king should not invest bps. and abbots with crosier and ring, symbols of their spiritual authority, and that no fees should be asked for burials. Regulations concerning the fast of Lent and the times when holy orders should be conferred were also promulgated. An attempt was made by the council to curb the barbarity of war. Although local, the council aroused much interest throughout Christendom. It was attended by approximately 200 bishops, 400 abbots, and thousands of other clergy, as well as by many knights and nobles. BIBLIOGRAPHY: Fliche-Martin 8:279–288.

[J. BLAIR]

CLEROMANCY, divination by casting dice or lots. Cleromancy was practiced in medieval times by throwing black and white beans, little bones, or dice. If the casting of lots is used by general agreement to settle a disputed decision involving no moral issue, it is not properly a form of divination and so is without taint of superstition. But when the element of magic enters into the picture and certain reliance is put on God's intervention (except in special circumstances, as when one acts under the inspiration of the Holy Spirit as in Acts 1:23–24), or puts reliance upon the intervention of spirits, the act is in some degree superstitious and blameworthy.

[T. LIDDY]

CLERVAUX, ABBEY OF, monastery founded in Luxembourg (1909–10) by monks of St. Maur-sur-Loire, who left France during anticlerical rule. Pope Pius XI invited monks of Clervaux to accept the foundation of St. Jerome in Rome in 1933 for the revision of the Vulgate Bible. Expelled by the Nazis in 1941, the monks returned to their ruined abbey in 1947. They brought distinction to their community by ecumenical work, esp. in Scandinavia. BIBLIOGRAPHY: R. Gazeau, *Catholicisme* 2:1247.

[S. A. HEENEY]

CLETUS (ANACLETUS), ST. (also sometimes Anencletus; d. *c.*90), **POPE** from *c.*79. According to Irenaeus, C. was the second successor to St. Peter. Some early listings (e.g., the *Liber pontificalis* and the *Roman Martyrology*) made two distinct popes from the confusion caused by the variants of his name. Nothing of historical value is known of his life or the manner of his death. The *Liber pontificalis* confuses him with Anicetus who built the burial monument for St. Peter. Modern excavations do not show that he was interred near St. Peter as was once believed. BIBLIOGRAPHY: E. G. Weltin, NCE 1:460; J. P. Kirsch, CE 4:54–55; T. J. Campbell, CE 1:446–447; J. S. Brusher, *Popes through the Ages* (1959).

[P. F. MULHERN]

CLEVE (CLEEF), JOOS VAN (*c.*1485–1540), Master of Antwerp. C. did portraits of Francis I in Paris (Phila. Museum of Art), of Maximilian I and Eleanor (Vienna), a small triptych of the *Death of the Virgin* (1515, Cologne), and a large version of the same (Munich), an altarpiece, *Lamentation over Christ,* with predella of Last Supper influenced by Leonardo (1524), and an Adoration of the Kings and copies after Rogier, Gerard David, Van Eyck, Dürer, and Leonardo. C.'s conservative works though lacking profundity are graceful with a high level of traditional Flemish craftsmanship. BIBLIOGRAPHY: M. J. Friedländer, *Die altniederländische Malerei* (1931).

[M. J. DALY]

CLICHTOVE, JOSSE (*c.*1472–1543), Flemish humanist and theologian. A doctor at the Sorbonne from 1506, he became associated with Jacques *Lefèvre d'Étaples and Abp. G. *Briçonnet in humanist studies and their spirit of ecclesiastical reform. To the period before 1520 belong his works on literary style and editions of several Greek Fathers. From that year, however, alarmed by Lutheranism, he separated himself from the humanist circle and devoted himself to theological polemics against the ideas of the Reformers. His last years were spent at Chartres as personal theologian of Bp. Louis Gillard, a former student. BIBLIOGRAPHY: H. M. Féret, *Catholicisme* 2:1248–49; C. A. Dubray, CE 4:58.

[T. C. O'BRIEN]

CLIFFORD, RICHARD (d. 1421), bp. of Worcester (1401), translated to London (1407). He enjoyed royal favor under Richard II and was on that account imprisoned for a short time by the lords appellant (1388). After the accession of Henry IV and his own consecration as bp., he was little involved in secular matters. He presided at the heresy trials of John Oldcastle (1413) and John Clayton (1415) and as spokesman for the English delegation to the Council of Constance played an important part in the election of Pope Martin V. BIBLIOGRAPHY: T. A. Archer, DNB 4:525–526; Emden Ox 1:440–441.

[P. K. MEAGHER]

CLIFTON, VIOLET (1883–1961), playwright, biographer, travel writer. Daughter of a British diplomat, C. traveled with him and spent several years in South America. A visit to India aroused her interest in Oriental religion. Marriage to Hugh Clifton, a traveler and explorer, took her to many parts of the world. Partly through her study of St. Elizabeth of Hungary in preparation for the play *Sanctity* (1934) and partly through her husband who had been converted to Catholicism 10 years earlier, she became a Roman Catholic in 1917. Her principal work is a biography of her husband, *The Book of Talbot* (1933), which won the coveted Tait-Black Memorial Prize in 1934. Admired by Lord Dunsany and Oliver St. John Gogarty, she preferred husband and family to a literary career.

[J. R. AHERNE]

CLIMACUS, a *neume in *Gregorian chant notation signifying a succession of three or more notes descending in pitch.

[A. DOHERTY]

CLIMENT, JOSÉ (1706–81), Spanish bishop. C. studied at the Univ. of Valencia where he earned his doctorate and later taught philosophy. After laboring several years as a parish priest, he was consecrated bp. of Barcelona (1766). He devoted his income as well as his energies to building primary schools, to establishing a Chair *De locis theologicis* at the Univ. of Valencia, and to helping the poor. Distinguished for his charitable work, C. was also an outstanding preacher. He resigned his see in 1775 and, for conscientious reasons refusing appointment to the wealthy See of Málaga, he retired to Valencia. C.'s writings are found in *Coleción de las obras del ilustrísimo Señor D. José Climent* (1788).

[S. A. HEENEY]

CLINICAL PSYCHOLOGY, a branch of psychology that deals with the abnormal. It is not the whole of psychology, yet it is often taken for its main branch. In another sense, it is often confused with psychiatry. Since the clinical psychologist is not a medical doctor, the use of medicine is not part of diagnosis or treatment for abnormal behavior manifestations. Applied methodology is an important part of the clinical psychologist's work. Yet, it is also true that research and development are pursued by some clinical psychologists. At any rate, the human person is the primary concern of the clinical psycholgist, and experimental research and methodology which is not directed toward improved understanding of the person fails to fulfill an essential component of its meaning. BIBLIOGRAPHY: R. J. McCall, NCE, 3:956–958.

[J. R. PIVELLO]

CLITHEROW, MARGARET, ST. (1553?–1586), English martyr. She was a woman of firm but lively character who married a rich butcher of York, John Clitherow, in 1571. He called her "the best wife in all England." Converted to the Catholic faith (1574), she was imprisoned several times under edicts against practicing Catholics. Charity to other, poorer, prisoners became one of her chief works of mercy. Mass was said constantly in her house, and she was eventually charged with the capital crime of harboring priests. She refused to plead guilty and be tried by a jury because, she said, she did not wish her children or her servants to be obliged to give evidence against her, nor a jury to be guilty of her death. She was accordingly condemned to death by pressing *(peine forte et dure)*, the ancient penalty devised to persuade accused persons to plead, and died at York in 1586. She was declared venerable in 1906, beatified in 1929, and canonized in 1970. BIBLIOGRAPHY: M. T. Munro, *Blessed Margaret Clitherow* (1947); Butler 1:679–682; C. Testore, BiblSanct 4:61–63.

[J. OGDEN]

CLIVIS, a *neume in *Gregorian chant notation signifying a succession of two notes, the second lower in pitch than the first.

[A. DOHERTY]

CLODULF OF METZ, ST. (Cloud; *c.*600–betw. 663–667), bp., son of Arnulf of Metz. C. became bp. of Metz in 652. In a 9th- and 10th-cent. record, his episcopacy is reported to have been 40 years in length. Two other documents offer evidence to the contrary, thus creating the discrepancy regarding the year of his death. His relics are in the Benedictine church, Lay-Saint-Christophe, near Nancy, and in St. Arnulf's, Metz. BIBLIOGRAPHY: J. Depoin, "Grandes figures monacales des temps mérovingiens,"

Revue Mabillon 11 (1921) 245–258; Beler 2:503; G. Mathon, BiblSanct 4:63.

[J. BLAIR]

CLOISTER. (1) The covered passage surrounding a quadrangle (the *garth) around which the buildings of a monastery are grouped. (2) That part of a religious house reserved for the exclusive use of the religious. In its strict sense, the cloister is the enclosure of a convent or monastery, which members may not leave or outsiders enter without due permission. Vatican Council 1 decreed that cloister should be maintained by those in the contemplative life but adjusted to conditions of time and place by those engaged in the active apostolate.

[A. R. ZINK]

CLONING, see Genetics.

CLONMACNOIS, MONASTERY OF, in County Offaly, Ireland, founded by St. Ciarán in 545. It became the most influential monastery in Ireland with a parish extending over about half of the country; and, in a period of general decline, it was a reforming influence. It had also a famous school, and from its scriptorium came many valuable manuscripts. It was razed by the English in 1552. BIBLIOGRAPHY: Kenney 1:376–383; C. McGrath, NCE 3:961, excellent bibliog.

[C. MCGRATH]

CLORIVIÈRE, PIERRE JOSEPH PICOT DE (1735–1820), French mystic. C. began his studies in an English Benedictine college and continued them in Louis-le-Grand College, Paris. In 1756, he entered the Jesuit novitiate in Paris, but at the suppression of the Jesuits by the Royalists, he went to the English province in Belgium. Ordained in Cologne, C. became assistant master of novices in England and made his solemn profession in 1773, the year Clement XIV dissolved the society. C. was named rector of the College of Dinan but was obliged to resign because of the revolutionary spirit of the students. He established two similar secret congregations, Société des Prêtres du Coeur de Jésus and La Société des Filles du Coeur Immaculé de Marie with the help of Mlle. Champion de Cicé. C. was arrested as a religious fanatic in 1804, his papers concerning his double organization were seized, and he was retained without trial. After 1814, he obtained the restoration of the Jesuits and became the first provincial in France. A profound mystic, he wrote several treatises on the spiritual life, which remain unedited. BIBLIOGRAPHY: A. Rayez, LTK 2:1237; H. Monier-Vinard, DSAM 1:1039; 2:974–979; E. Lamalle, EncCatt 3:1878–79.

[M. HIGGINS]

CLOSED COMMUNION (Close Communion), restriction by a Church of participation in the Lord's Supper to its own members; the opposite of open communion, the more general practice among Protestant Churches. While the term is not used, closed communion is in fact the law in the RC Church. Closed communion has been particularly associated with Baptist history. Until the 20th cent., most Baptists practiced closed communion, i.e., refused to share in the Lord's Supper with pedobaptists. Their argument was: Nearly all Christians consider baptism a prerequisite to communion; *infant baptism is not true baptism; therefore, pedobaptists are not baptized and should not partake of the bread and the cup. From the beginning there were some open-communion Baptists, such as John *Bunyan, who defended his practice in *Differences in Judgment about Baptism No Bar to Communion*. The adherents of closed communion, however, constituted the great majority in Great Britain, North America, and elsewhere. Since Baptists acknowledged others to be Christians, and had close relations with Congregationalists and Presbyterians in England, they sometimes felt embarrassed by their positions; it was awkward to refuse to share in the Lord's Supper with people with whom they worshiped and sometimes exchanged pulpits. In England, Robert Hall advocated open communion in *The Terms of Communion* (1815). During the ensuing century, British Baptists retreated from their closed-communion practice. In the U.S., progress toward open communion was slower, but it had clearly begun by 1914. Today most Baptists in the North practice open communion, a minister usually announcing that all Christians are welcome to the Lord's Table. In the *Southern Baptist Convention there is a diversity of practice; the tendency in the SW is strongly toward closed communion, but in the SE many churches practice open communion. Many smaller fundamentalist Baptist bodies retain closed communion. *Landmarkism interpreted closed communion even more narrowly, restricting participation in the Lord's Supper to members of a particular congregation; but this view has had limited influence outside its ranks. BIBLIOGRAPHY: D. M. Himbury, "Baptist Controversies, 1640–1900," *Christian Baptism* (ed. A. Gilmore, 1959).

[N. H. MARING]

CLOSED SHOP, provision for union security requiring that only union members be hired. Until it was outlawed by the Taft-Hartley Act in 1947, closed shop was a part of most labor contracts in collective bargaining agreements. In practice it persisted in certain industries that had special skill requirements, e.g., construction, printing, entertainment. Since the Landrum-Griffin Act in 1959, closed shop continued only in the construction industry. Individual states passed laws against both closed shop and the similar union shop, both of which raise some ethical questions. One is political freedom when union dues might be spent for ideological purposes opposed to the desires of an individual member. While Catholic Church pronouncements defend the right of workers to unionize and recognize the benefits of labor unions, they also require that union activity be always responsible and ordered to the common good.

[V. GILLIGAN]

CLOTH-OF-GOLD, a color of liturgical vestments used sometimes on major feasts as a substitute for other colors except purple and black.

CLOTHING, see MODESTY.

CLOTHING (IN THE BIBLE). It is virtually impossible to determine with any precision the shape and size of the individual garments mentioned in the Bible. Thus the *'ezor* (Jer 13.1–7; Is 5.27; Ezek 23.15; 2 Kg 1.8) may have been a short knee-length kilt or alternatively simply a broad waistband. The *kuttonet* seems to have been a tunic reaching to the ankles and made with or without sleeves. For greater freedom of movement the skirts could be tucked into the waistband (Ex 12.11; 2 Kg 4.29; 9.1). A long-sleeved (not "many colored") tunic such as that worn by Joseph (Gen 37.3) could be a sign of high or even royal rank. The *simlah* seems to have been a mantle worn over the tunic, and there were several different shapes and styles of this. It seems to have been used as a covering at night (Ex 22.25–26; Dt 24.13), and was ample enough to be used for carrying various objects (Ex 12.34; 2 Kg 4.39; Hag 2.12). The *me'il* was a more costly kind of outer garment worn by kings (1 Sam 18.4; 24.5, 11) and by the high priest (Ex 28.31–35; Lev 8.7), and there seems to have been yet another type of cloak known as the *'adderet* woven of camel's hair and worn esp., though not exclusively, by prophets. This was the type of mantle bequeathed by Elijah to Elisha (2 Kg 2.13–14). In addition to the tunic and cloak of everyday wear (e.g., Mt 5.40; Lk 6.2), there seem to have been special garments (presumably brightly colored) for festive occasions and weddings (Gen 27.15; Jg 14.12; Mt 22.11; Lk 15.22, etc.). Though the basic tunic and cloak as worn by women must have differed markedly from those worn by men, the Bible offers no clues as to what the differences were. It was customary for women to wear a veil also.

[D. J. BOURKE]

CLOTILDE, ST. (Clothilde, Clotilda; *c.*474–545), queen of the Franks. Although she was the daughter of the Arian Burgundian King Chilperic, C. was reared a Catholic by her mother. She was married *c.*492 to *Clovis, King of the Franks, who, largely through her influence, was converted to the Catholic faith (496). Her husband died in 511, and C.'s widowhood was saddened by the fratricidal strife in which her sons engaged in their pursuit of power and by the mistreatment of her daughter at the hands of her Visigothic husband Almaric. The charge that to avenge the death of her parents C. goaded her husband and sons to war upon St. Sigismund, King of Burgundy, has been shown to be without historical foundation, although the story was long credited by chroniclers on the authority of the uncritical and credulous Gregory of Tours. C. withdrew from Paris to

Tours and spent her last years near the shrine of St. Martin in prayer and good works. BIBLIOGRAPHY: G. Kurth, *Saint Clotilda* (tr. from the German by V. M. Crawford, 1898); Butler 2:462–463; A. Codaghengo and E. Croce, BiblSanct 4:64–67; A. Dumas, DHGE 13:20–22.

[H. DRESSLER]

CLOUD, ST. (Chlodoald, *c.*524–560), grandson of Clovis and youngest son of Chlodomer, King of Orléans. After the death of his father, C. escaped attempted murder by his uncles and voluntarily gave up the throne. Having entered religion, he led an exemplary life founded a monastery at Novigentum near Paris, and died a priest. By 811 his foundation was known as Saint-Cloud. BIBLIOGRAPHY: *History of the Franks by Gregory of Tours* (2 v., ed. and tr. O. M. Dalton, 1927) 1:98–100; G. Mathon, BiblSanct 4:63–64; Butler 3:503–504.

[J. BLAIR]

CLOUD (IN THE BIBLE), in the OT sometimes a symbol of the presence of God. God rides the clouds (Ps 68.4); they are his chariot (Ps 104.3) and his tent (Ps 18.11). A column of cloud led Israel to the promised land as a sign of God's protection (Ex 13.21–22). The NT mentions clouds at the transfiguration (Mt 17.5) and ascension (Acts 1.9). At the second coming, the faithful will be carried to Christ upon clouds (1 Th 4.17).

[F. J. MONTALBANO]

CLOUD OF UNKNOWING, a 14th-cent. English masterpiece of the spiritual life, distinguished by beauty of phrasing, skillful use of scriptural language and imagery, profound thought and simplicity of style. The unknown author, writing with force and originality, gives direct, practical instruction on the life of mystical prayer to a disciple who finds himself "between a cloud of forgetting (of creatures) and a cloud of unknowing (of God)." This work, the first of its type in English, was highly prized, as the number of extant manuscripts indicates. BIBLIOGRAPHY: D. Knowles, *English Mystical Tradition* (1961); W. Johnston, *Mysticism of the Cloud of Unknowing* (1967); S. R. Bradley, "Present Day Themes in the 14th-Century English Mystics," *Spiritual Life* 20 (1974) 260–267.

[M. J. BARRY]

CLOUET, court painters. (1) **Jean** (*c.*1480–1540), probably the son of a Flemish artist. He became court painter in France, executing the famous *Portrait of Francis I* (*c.*1525, Louvre). He represents, with his son François, the French element of Renaissance art at court. With no religious paintings extant now, his fame rests on portraits, particularly a corpus of drawings (*Guillaume Budé*, Chantilly), which excel in their northern plasticity and luminosity. (2) **François** (*c.*1510–72), who succeeded his father as court painter in 1541, executing decorative, conventional yet personalized portraits in the Florentine mannerist style of mid-16th-cent. France. His *Diane de Poitiers* (*c*.1571, National Gallery, Washington, D.C.) evidences the Italian manner of the Fontainebleau school. BIBLIOGRAPHY: P. du Colombier, *L'Art renaissance en France* (rev. ed., 1950); A. Chatelet and J. Thuillier, *French Painting from Fouquet to Poussin* (tr. S. Gilbert, 1963) 121–136, *passim*.

[R. BERGMANN]

CLOVIO, GIULIO (1488–1578), Italian painter and miniaturist. A Croatian by birth, he was influenced by Michelangelo. C. worked for Louis II of Hungary and the Cardinals Grimani and Allesandro Farnese, executing for the latter his masterpiece, the Farnese Book of Hours (Pierpont Morgan Library, New York) in skillfully imitative mannerist style. C. appears in El Greco's *Cleansing of the Temple* in lower right corner with portraits of Michelangelo and Raphael. BIBLIOGRAPHY: M. Harrsen and G. K. Boyce, *Italian Manuscripts in Pierpont Morgan Library* (1953).

[M. J. DALY]

CLOVIS I (*c*.466–511), **KING OF THE FRANKS** from 481, founder of the Merovingian dynasty. Coming to the throne of the Salian Franks at the age of 15, C. first moved against the last post of Roman authority in Gaul and defeated his enemy. Ruthlessly C. soon dominated all the Frankish territory. Married to the devout Catholic Clotilda, he ultimately accepted baptism after a signal victory over the Alamanni, which he attributed to the Christian God. Next the Burgundians and Visigoths were conquered, leaving C. master of almost all of modern France. He made Paris his capital. More than a conqueror, C. issued the *Lex Salica*, the penal code of the Franks. He also called a national council of the Church in Gaul at Orléans in 511. He is buried in what is now the Church of St. Genevieve, which he had built on the bank of the Seine. BIBLIOGRAPHY: G. Kurth, *Clovis* (1923).

[J. R. AHERNE]

CLUGNY, FRANÇOIS DE (1637–94), French Oratorian. Ordained in 1662, C. passed most of his life in Dijon, where despite almost total blindness he spent himself in preaching and counseling. He wrote three works "for a sinner by a sinner," two of which were placed on the Index (1714), a censure probably attributable to their exaggerated language and imprecision. BIBLIOGRAPHY: A. Guny, *Catholicisme* 2:1266–67.

[M. J. SUELZER]

CLUNIAC ART reached its zenith *c*.1090–*c*.1150 under Abbots Hugh of Cluny and Peter the Venerable, when the third abbey church of Cluny, the greatest of Romanesque churches, was built. Although Paray-le-Monial, La-Charité-sur-Loire, and St. Sernin, Toulouse, reflect Cluny III, there was never a Cluniac school of architecture. Nor was there a Cluniac sculptural style, although Cluniac monasteries contain some of the best Romanesque sculpture

(e.g., Moissac, Beaulieu, and Vézelay), and the ambulatory capitals of Cluny III are of vital importance for the origins of Romanesque architectural sculpture. BIBLIOGRAPHY: K. J. Conant, *Cluny* (1969); J. Evans, *Romanesque Architecture of the Order of Cluny* (1938); idem, *Cluniac Art of the Romanesque Period* (1950).

[R. C. MARKS]

CLUNIAC REFORM, an important monastic movement from the 10th–12th cent. which had significant temporal and spiritual effects upon the Church. The reform was centered at the Abbey of *Cluny, whose foundation charter (909) placed it under the immediate protection of the Holy See, thus freeing it from the interference of secular lords. This autonomy, made possible by significant changes in the feudal system itself, was a key factor in the reform since the Church at that time was largely dominated by laymen. Under the successive guidance of several great and holy abbots, and often with the actual cooperation of monks from Cluny, the reform spread through France, Italy, Spain, England, and even to Palestine. The reform monasteries established variant bonds with Cluny; some became completely dependent, governed by a prior named by the abbot of Cluny, while others adopted the observance but retained their autonomy. The reform, drawing upon the Rule of St. *Benedict and the heritage of *Benedict of Aniane, sought to renew all the monastic virtues: silence, manual labor, stability, enclosure, but was esp. concerned with the liturgy. After the death of Peter the Venerable (1157), the reform began to decline, largely because of its temporal involvements, overly rapid expansion, and lack of centralized authority. Thus the 11th-cent. *Cistercian reforms became necessary to effect a return to Cluny's original monastic ideal. In the 14th cent., the Cluniac Order itself began to disintegrate, gradually to be replaced by different observances and new congregations. BIBLIOGRAPHY: J. Evans, *Monastic Life at Cluny* (1968); P. Cousin, *Précis d'histoire monastique* (1956) 224–254, 360–385; R. Grégoire, NCE 3:966–967.

[T. M. MCFADDEN]

CLUNY, ABBEY OF, a Benedictine abbey in the Rhone Valley near Mâcon, and an important center of ecclesiastical reform in the 10th–12th cent. (see CLUNIAC REFORM). It was founded with the aid of William of Aquitaine (909), who donated the monastery to the Holy See, thus freeing it from the secular control typical of the time. Three successive churches were built; the last (completed *c*.1113) became the largest church in Christendom when the narthex was added in *c*.1225. Both the church and monastery were monumental examples of Romanesque architecture and elaborate sculpture. Only the S arm of the W transept remains today; the rest of the church was destroyed between 1798 and 1823. Cluny benefitted from a succession of great abbots (e.g., *Odilo; *Hugh of Cluny; *Peter the Venerable), who spread the Cluniac reform throughout Europe.

At the beginning of the 12th cent., there were *c*.400 monks at Cluny and 1,184 monastic foundations within the Cluniac Order. They lived according to the *Benedictine Rule, with various statutes and *consuetudines* (liturgical directories) enacted as the need arose. Cluny's decline, which began in the 13th cent., was caused by economic difficulties and the papal practice of appointing *commendatory abbots. Despite various reform efforts, the monks were dispersed in 1791, and after the abbey was auctioned (1798) the church was dismantled and the conventual buildings put to other uses. BIBLIOGRAPHY: J. Evans, *Monastic Life at Cluny* (1968); N. Hunt, *Cluny under St. Hugh* (1967); K. J. Conant, "Mediaeval Academy Excavations at Cluny, VIII; Final Stages of the Project," *Speculum* 29 (1954) 1–43; "Mediaeval Academy Excavations at Cluny, IX: Systematic Dimensions in the Buildings," *ibid*. 38 (1963) 1–45; R. Grégoire, NCE 3:967–970.

[T. M. MCFADDEN]

CLYNNOG, MAURICE, see CLENOCK, MAURICE.

CLYNNOG FAWR, MONASTERY in Caernarvonshire, Wales, which was founded by St. Beuno (d. *c*.630). It seems to have had an extensive monastic parish, with foundations in Herefordshire, Gloucestershire, Merionethshire, Flintshire, and Anglesey. Clynnog Fawr was abandoned in the 13th century. BIBLIOGRAPHY: J. E. Lloyd, *History of Wales* (2 v., 1948); A. W. Wade-Evans, *Welsh Christian Origins* (1934).

[C. MCGRATH]

CNUTE, see CANUTE, KING OF ENGLAND AND DENMARK.

COADJUTOR, a bp. who assists a diocesan bp. in the rule of his diocese and in the exercise of the episcopal power of orders. Until Vatican Council II, Western canon law distinguished between coadjutors attached to the person of the bp., either with or without the right of succession, and coadjutors given to the diocese (CIC c. 350). Vat II BpPastOff 25–26 modified this terminology so that today a coadjutor *(episcopus coadjutor)* always has the right of succession while an auxiliary *(episcopus auxiliaris)* never does. This new terminology brings Western law into harmony with Oriental and Anglican canon law. The coadjutor bp. must also be appointed vicar general (Vat II BpPastOff 26). BIBLIOGRAPHY: G. E. Lynch, *Coadjutors and Auxiliaries of Bishops* (1947); Vorgrimler 2:176–179, 242–249.

[L. M. KNOX]

COADY, MOSES MICHAEL (1882–1959), crusader for social justice. C. graduated from St. Francis Xavier College, Antigonish, Nova Scotia (1905), was ordained at Rome (1910), and returned to teach at his alma mater (1910–28). There he developed the program of credit unions and marketing cooperatives for fish and farm pro-

duce that characterized the Antigonish Movement. He described his efforts in *Masters of Their Own Destiny* (1939), giving a blueprint for cooperative enterprise widely copied in Canada and in many emerging nations.

[R. K. MACMASTER]

COALESCENCE, the cumulative growth of amounts stolen so that in their ensemble petty thefts become gravely sinful. In general, theft is a grave sin when the amount stolen either absolutely or in reference to the victim constitutes a serious loss. A petty theft in itself is a light sin, not doing a grave injury. But a series of petty thefts may coalesce in several ways: (1) where the direct intent of the thief is to steal a large amount little by little; each single theft is the execution of the gravely sinful intent; (2) where the thefts will cause foreseeable, grave harm; (3) where many persons conspire together, so that the petty thefts of each add up to a sizable amount; (4) where, without explicit planning, the thefts do in fact lead up to a considerable sum. The last instance of coalescence is qualified by several conditions: the petty thefts must be less than two months apart; must be continuous, i.e., not interrupted by *restitution; do in fact accumulate into a large sum. With reference to the last condition, because the acts are spread out, the amount counted as grave is half again as great as for a single theft, when the petty thefts are from one victim; twice again as great, when the thefts are from several persons.

[T. C. O'BRIEN]

COAT-OF-ARMS, a design, originally of secular heraldry, that came to be adopted as representative of ecclesiastical persons, such as the pope, cardinals, bishops, archbishops, as well as ecclesiastical foundations, colleges, universities, etc. Such designs are displayed on thrones, seals, and architecture.

COBO, BERNABÉ (1582–1657), a native of Spain who became a Jesuit in the New World in 1601, worked in Peru and Mexico, and engaged in extensive missionary and scientific expeditions through large areas of Peru, Bolivia, Central America, and Mexico, recording many things of interest concerning the natural features of the land as well as his observations of the inhabitants. His writings are an important source of ethnological and other scientific information. BIBLIOGRAPHY: A. F. Bandelies, CE 4:74.

COBRA, 1948 group of artists and critics, named for cities of Copenhagen, Brussels, and Amsterdam, interested in direct expression of creative energy and establishing the art work as a reality, an entity per se. Though disbanded in 1951, CoBrA exerted a great influence on the art of N Europe. Important members were Corneille, Alechinsky, Dubuffet.

[M. J. DALY]

COCCEIUS, JOHANNES (Coch, Koch; 1603–69), pioneer in biblical theology. Of German birth, he spent the major portion of his professional career in the Netherlands at the Univ. of Leiden. He was an expert in Hebrew and in rabbinic literature. In his masterwork, *Summa doctrinae de foedere et testamento Dei* (1648), he systematized *federal theology. This and some of his other writings are important because they sought to develop theology not on the basis of scholastic Calvinist orthodoxy but on biblical concepts, esp. that of God's covenant. His thought had a marked influence on *Pietism. After his death there was a protracted controversy between his followers and the orthodox *Reformed theologians of Leiden. His collected works were published in 8 volumes at Amsterdam (1673–75). BIBLIOGRAPHY: R. Koper, LTK 2:1242.

[T. C. O'BRIEN]

COCHEM, MARTIN VON (1634–1712), Capuchin preacher and administrator of the archbishoprics of Mainz and Trier. His pious books enjoyed great popularity in his time and had a great impact on the subsequent religious literature of Catholic Germany, even on secular poets like Clemens von Brentano and Franz Grillparzer. Among his writings are: *Leben und Leiden Jesu Christi* (1677); *Lehrreiches History- und Exempel-Buch* (4 v., 1696–99); *Legenden der Heiligen* (1705). BIBLIOGRAPHY: W. Kosch, *Martin von Kochem* (1915); Bernardus a Bononia, *Bibliotheca scriptorum Ordinis Minorum S. Francisci Capuccinorum* (1747).

[S. A. SCHULZ]

COCHLAEUS, JOHANNES (Johann Dubeneck; 1479–1552), German humanist, theologian, and polemicist. His first interests were in humanism, both in his studies at Cologne (1504–07) under Ulrich von Hutten, and as rector of a Latin school in Nuremberg (1510–17). He also studied law at Bologna (1515–17), and theology at Ferrara (1517) and Rome (1517–19), where he was ordained. He was sympathetic with the desire for reform, but Luther refused (1520) to engage in debate with him, and C. launched his series of nearly 200 polemical writings. They are strong in rhetoric, weak in theology; Luther replied to only one of them. With J. Eck and J. Faber, C. prepared the *Confutatio* in response to the *Augsburg Confession (1530). He also attended most of the other conferences of the period that sought to reunite Protestants and Catholics. His polemical temper prevented him from being effective. C.'s *Historia Hussitarum Libri* XII (1549) is a source work on the Hussites. For 4 cent. his *Commentaria de actis et scriptis Martini Lutheri* (1549) shaped RC Reformation studies, until abandoned as distorted and naïve. BIBLIOGRAPHY: J. P. Dolan, *History of the Reformation* (pa., 1965) 24–25; R. Baümer, LTK 2:1243–44.

[M. J. SUELZER]

COCK (KOCK), HIERONYMUS (*c.* 1510–70), Flemish painter and publisher of prints after Raphael, G. Romano, Brueghel, and others. C. contributed significantly to Netherlandish art through views of Roman ruins and masters' compositions.

[M. J. DALY]

COCK, JAN DE (fl. early 16th cent.), Flemish painter of religious scenes in extensive landscape settings. C. worked in Notre Dame church in Antwerp *c.* 1507. Though there are many attributions, only a *Landscape with St. Christopher* is documented.

[M. J. DALY]

COCTEAU, JEAN (1889–1963), French poet, playwright, essayist, film director, designer, illustrator. Extremely versatile and cultivated, C. considered himself above all else a poet. He participated in many movements of his day, but belonged officially to none. Among the currents that attracted him most were Fauvism, Cubism, the *Ballets russes* of Diaghilev, the music of Stravinsky, Dada, and Surrealism. He collaborated with Picasso, Eric Satie, Darius Milhaud, and the other musicians of the "Group of Six." His best-known plays are *Orphée* (1923), *Les Enfants terribles* (1950), and *La Machine infernale* (1955). Some of his plays were made into films; other works were created exclusively for the cinema, a medium that he preferred and that suited his style admirably. Most of his illustrations were for his own works, but before his death, in a resurgence of religious fervor, he redecorated three chapels, the most famous being Saint-Pierre at Villefranche-sur-mer in 1957. In 1955 he was elected to the French Academy. His baroque spirit was as versatile as his work, from classical myth to modern idiom. Most of all he explored themes of transformation and disguise through limitless poetic and artistic images. BIBLIOGRAPHY: F. Steegmiller, *Cocteau* (1970).

[I. M. KASHUBA]

CODDE, PIETER (CODDAEUS; 1648–1710), titular abp. of Sebaste, vicar of Holland. Born in Amsterdam, C. went to Paris where he joined the Congregation of the Oratory before being ordained in 1672. His appointment as abp. came in 1681. Under suspicion of Jansenism he was suspended in 1702 and deposed two years later. He was implicated in the Schism of Utrecht.

[P. HIGGINS]

CODE OF CANON LAW (*Codex iuris canonici*), the official systematized collection of the universal legislation by which the Latin Church is governed. The preparation of such a code was sorely needed because of the multiplication of new laws and the confused state of previously existing legislation. The Code was completed while Benedict XV was pope. He officially promulgated it on May 27, 1917, and it went into effect on May 19th of the following year. Several matters of law are excluded: those affecting the Oriental Churches in union with Rome (excepting such laws as those which by their very nature are applicable to

Orientals as well as Latins); strictly liturgical regulations; and the legislation enacted by the Holy See in entering into concordats. The Code contains canons numbered successively from 1 to 2414 and six documents that are incorporated by reference to certain canons and are printed in the Code itself. These canons are divided into five books, each with its individual parts, sections, titles, and chapters. Book I (cc. 1–86) deals with general norms; Book II (cc. 87–725) with persons in the Church—clerics, religious, and laity; Book III (cc. 726–1551), with things, including such topics as sacred times and places, divine worship, the teaching authority of the Church, benefices, and ecclesiastical property; Book IV (cc. 1552–2194), with procedures, comprising such materials as trials, cases of beatification and canonization, and with procedures in certain matters or in the application of penalties; Book V (cc. 2195–2414), with crimes and penalties in church law. A thorough revision of the Code is now in progress. It was called for by Pope John XXIII in 1959, and in 1963 the work was assigned to a commission of cardinals. It has moved forward considerably since that time. BIBLIOGRAPHY: CIC.

[P. K. MEAGHER]

CODE OF CANON LAW, COMMISSION FOR THE AUTHENTIC INTERPRETATION OF, a commission of cardinals established by Pope Benedict XV with the power to give authentic interpretations of the Code. This power includes the issuance of instructions that both throw light on the provisions of the Code of Canon Law and provide efficaciously for their observance. It is drawn up, first, by the proper Roman Congregation; then, if it is in accord with the Code, the Congregation informs the pontiff of that fact. After the decree has been approved by the Holy Father, it is presented to the Commission whose office it is to draw up a new canon or canons to be inserted in the Code. The new canons are designated by the number of the preceding canon and the addition, *bis* or *ter,* "so that no canon of the Code shall ever lose its place, nor the series of numbered canons be in any way confused." BIBLIOGRAPHY: L. T. Bouscaren, NCE 3:975.

[M. RILEY]

CODEX, (pl. codices), in biblical studies, a MS of the Bible or part of the Bible, the leaves of which are assembled in book form, not rolled together in a scroll. The codex supplanted the scroll or roll early in the Christian era. In the classification of biblical MSS, the term Codex with an identifying letter refers to MSS written on vellum or parchment. These are subdivided into uncials (majuscules) or cursives (minuscules) according to the script style. Biblical MSS written on papyrus are classified as papyri, and are designated by the letter P with a number corresponding to their time of discovery (see NASH PAPYRUS; CHESTER BEATTY PAPYRI). BIBLIOGRAPHY: F. G. Kenyon, *Our Bible and the Ancient Manuscripts* (5th ed., 1958).

[D. J. BOURKE]

CODEX ALEXANDRINUS, a Greek MS, thought to have been compiled *c.*400–450, containing the LXX, the NT, and 1 and 2 Clement. In scholarly works on the biblical text it is designated by the letter A or the numerals 02, and is regarded as one of the most important of the biblical manuscripts.

It was apparently brought from Alexandria, where it perhaps had been from *c.*1300, by Cyril Lucar (1572–1638) when he became patriarch of Constantinople in 1612. He wished to present it to James I of England, patron of the 1611 English translation of the Bible, but James died before the presentation was made. It was given to Charles I in 1627 and was put in the Royal Library, which in 1757 became part of the British Museum, where the codex is today. At the time it was given to Charles and became known to Western scholars, it was 1000 years older than the MSS on which current texts were based. It stimulated enormously scholarly thought in regard to the problems of establishing the authentic text of the Bible. It remained the most important single text until the 19th cent. when *Codex Vaticanus and *Codex Sinaiticus became known, both probably dating about a cent. earlier.

Codex Alexandrinus contains 773 vellum leaves (630 OT, 143 NT), each about 12¾ by 10¼ inches. It is fairly complete, though a few chapters are missing. An uncial, it has two columns per page with 46–52 lines per column. Its inclusion of 1 and 2 Clement indicates the canon was not yet set in its present form. The British Museum published a full-sized facsimile (1879–83). BIBLIOGRAPHY: W. H. P. Hatch, *Principal Uncial Manuscripts of the New Testament* (1939).

[T. EARLY]

CODEX AMIATINUS, a MS of the Vulgate. Generally considered the best witness to the Vulg text, it was produced *c.*700 and contains the whole Bible, including the Apocrypha. Amiatinus was produced for Ceolfrid, abbot of Wearmouth and Jarrow, Northumbria, England. According to the Ven. Bede, who received his monastic training and education at Wearmouth and Jarrow, Ceolfrid set out in 716 to take the MS to Gregory II. However he died at Langres on the way. From *c.*900 to 1786 the codex was in the monastery of Monte Amiata, Tuscany, from which it gets its name. It is now in the Laurentian Library at Florence. It was brought to Rome for use by scholars preparing Sixtus V's edition of the Vulgate.

The text of Amiatinus was based on a variety of Vulg sources. Ceolfrid and his predecessor, Benedict Biscop, had brought Italian MSS of the Vulg back to Northumbria from their travels. The external layout and the first eight leaves were based on a codex produced by Cassiodorus in S Italy *c.*550. The Gospels of Amiatinus are based on a 6th cent. MS that was also used to produce the volume at Fulda, made under the direction of Bp. Victor of Capua (d. 554). The editions of Bp. Victor, Cassiodorus (d. *c.*580), and Amiatinus are known as the South Italian group of Vulg texts, with the Milan and St. Gall MSS constituting the North Italian group. The *Lindisfarne Gospels are thought to belong to the same family of texts as Amiatinus.

The codex is written two columns to the page, in uncial script. The text of the NT was published by K. von Tischendorf in 1850. He and T. Hevse published part of the OT in 1873.

[T. EARLY]

CODEX AUREUS, luxurious MS gospel books in gold or silver ink on purple vellum, made for royal Carolingian and Ottoman patrons (8th–11th century). Famous are the Codex Aureus of Canterbury, that of Sankt Emmeran, and the Codex Aureus Eptanercensis (or Golden Gospels of Echternach, Nürnberg). The Sankt Emmeran Codex is noted for its jewelled cover (c.850) from St. Denis or the Reims court of Charles the Bald. It shows in relief Christ with the four Evangelists and four scenes from the life of Christ, and demonstrates the classicizing style of Italy in accord with Charlemagne's desire for Roman culture. BIBLIOGRAPHY: A. Grabar and C. Nordenfalk, *Early Medieval Painting from Fourth to Eleventh Century* (1957).

[M. J. DALY]

CODEX BEZAE, a MS dating from the 5th or 6th cent. that contains the Gospels (in the order traditional for Latin MSS—Mt, Jn, Lk, and Mk), Acts, and a small fragment of 3 John. It is named for T. *Beza (1519–1605) who made some use of it in his annotated editions of the NT. It was in the monastery of St. Irenaeus in Lyons, France, and came into Beza's possession after Lyons was sacked by Huguenots in 1562. It is the earliest MS containing both Greek and Latin. They face each other on opposite pages, Greek on the left. Each page contains one column of 33 lines, the lines of varying length and divided according to sense. In textual criticism the codex is designated by the letter D (Gk.; Lat., d) or the numbering 05. An uncial, it is the most important witness of what is called the Western text and contains several variations from the received text and the *Codex Vaticanus, *Codex Sinaiticus, and *Codex Alexandrinus. Beza gave it to Cambridge Univ. (1581) and it is sometimes called the Codex Cantabrigiensis. The 3 Jn fragment indicates it may have originally contained the Catholic epistles. It now contains 406 vellum leaves, 10 by 8 inches, plus 9 leaves added by a later hand. The place of origin is unknown, but the inclusion of the Latin suggests that it was made in the West. Westcott and Hort held that it gives a truer picture of the Gospels and Acts as they were known c.200 than any other known manuscript. It is the oldest MS containing the story of Jesus and the woman taken in adultery (Jn 7.53–8.11). An annotated edition was published by F. N. Scrivener in 1864, and a facsimile by Cambridge Press in 1899. BIBLIOGRAPHY: W. H. P. Hatch, *Principal Uncial Manuscripts of the New Testament* (1939).

[T. EARLY]

CODEX CALIXTINUS, mid-12th-cent. pilgrim's guide to the roads leading to Santiago de Compostela, Spain, with reference to accommodations, shrines along the way, and description of the cathedral.

[M. J. DALY]

CODEX EPHRAEMI RESCRIPTUS, 5th-cent. Greek MS of the Bible, regarded as among the most important for establishing the biblical text; siglum C or 04. The name derives from the fact that the leaves were erased and a 12th-cent. Greek translation of sermons by St. Ephraem the Syrian written over *(rescriptus)* them. Codex C was published in 1845 by K. von Tischendorf who was able to retrieve the original text with the use of chemicals. A compound of various text types, it is considered primarily of the neutral or Alexandrian family. Two correctors made changes in the MS, one probably working in Palestine in the 6th cent., and the other perhaps in Constantinople in the 9th century. An uncial, it originally contained the complete Bible, but now has only parts of Job, Pr, Wis, Ec, and S of S, as well as parts of all NT books except 2 Th and 2 John. It now contains 209 vellum leaves (64 OT, 145 NT) which are thought to constitute perhaps ⅝ of the number it originally contained. Each leaf is about 12¼ by 9½ inches, and it has one column of 40–46 lines per page.

The codex is thought to have been brought to Florence from the East by John Lascaris (c.1445–1534). At one time it belonged to Card. Niccolò Ridolfi of Florence, and later came into the possession of Catherine de Médicis, who took it to France when she became the wife of Henry II. It became a part of the Royal Library and then a part of the Bibliothèque Nationale in Paris, where it remains today. BIBLIOGRAPHY: W. H. P. Hatch, *Principal Uncial Manuscripts of the New Testament* (1939).

[T. EARLY]

CODEX SINAITICUS, a 4th-cent. Greek MS of the Bible; siglum S or Hebrew aleph, or 01. The only uncial containing all the NT, it is considered one of the most important of existing MSS for establishing the original NT text. It also includes the Epistle of Barnabas and part of the Shepherd of Hermas, but much of the OT has been lost.

Perhaps originating in Caesarea, it was discovered by K. von Tischendorf (1815–74) at the Monastery of St. Catherine at Mt. Sinai where monks were using its leaves to light the monastery oven. He secured 43 sheets on his first visit in 1844 and discovered the remainder in 1859. After some delays he was allowed to have the codex copied in Cairo, and he persuaded the monks to present it to Czar Alexander II of Russia, under whose patronage Tischendorf was working. It remained at St. Petersburg (Leningrad) until 1933 when the British Museum purchased it for 100,000 pounds. The Museum had it bound in 1935 to facilitate handling by scholars. The sheets secured in 1844 are now in the University Library at Leipzig. A fragment is in the Library of the Society of Ancient Literature, Leningrad.

Textual critics assign it to the family of early texts known as Alexandrian, along with *Codex Vaticanus. Out of an estimated original 730 or more sheets, it contains 346½ (OT 199, NT 147½), each about 15 by 13½ inches, with four columns of 48 lines per page, except the poetical books, which have two columns.

Tischendorf told the story of the finding in *When Were Our Gospels Written?* (1866). H. and K. *Lake edited a photographic facsimile (NT 1911, OT 1922). BIBLIOGRAPHY: H. J. M. Milne and T. C. Skeat, *Scribes and Correctors of the Codex Sinaiticus* (1938).

[T. EARLY]

CODEX VATICANUS, 4th-cent. Greek MS of the Bible, usually designated by the siglum B or 03. Scholars rank it as one of the most important sources for reconstructing the original text of the LXX and the NT. When integral, Codex B contained the entire Bible except for the Prayer of Manasses and the books of Macc, but it has suffered considerable mutilation, including the loss of almost 46 chapters of Gen, some 30 Ps, as well as the pastoral letters and Revelation. Like all MSS up to *c.*800 it is an uncial. It comprises 759 folios of fine vellum (617 OT, 142 NT), each about 10½ by 10 inches. The unornamented pages are in three columns of 40–44 lines per page, except for the two-column pages for the poetical books. The work of one or two scribes, it was corrected by two other hands, one nearly contemporary and one *c.*1000.

The Vatican Library has possessed the MS since before the first cataloguing of the library (1475). One conjecture on its presence in the Vatican Library is that it was brought to Italy from Alexandria following the Arab conquest and later came into the possession of Card. Bessarion, who obtained many Greek MSS from the Greek monasteries in Italy.

New Testament scholars place Codex B in the neutral or Alexandrian family of texts that also includes *Codex Sinaiticus and is thought to represent a text current in Egypt in the 3d century. Codex B is the basic text used for the Westcott and Hort NT (1881). A photographic edition was published by the Vatican Library (7 v., 1889–90). BIBLIOGRAPHY: W. H. P. Hatch, *Principal Uncial Manuscripts of the New Testament* (1939).

[T. EARLY]

CODRINGTON, THOMAS (d. *c.*1691), English secular priest who, after serving as chaplain and secretary to Card. Howard in Rome, went to England (1684) and was appointed chaplain and preacher to James, then Duke of York and later King. While in Rome C. had associated himself with a German institute of secular priests, which he attempted unsuccessfully to introduce into England. C. accompanied the King into exile at Saint-Germain and continued to serve as his chaplain. BIBLIOGRAPHY: T. Cooper, DNB 4:666.

[V. SAMPSON]

CODUCCI, MAURO DI MARTINO (*c.*1440–1504), major Renaissance architect in Venice. C. built the Churches of S. Michele and S. Zaccaria, developing the curvilinear façade characteristic of Venice in the late 15th and 16th centuries.

[M. J. DALY]

COECKE (KOECK) VAN AELST, PETER (1502–50), master of the Antwerp guild (1527). C., who taught Pieter Brueghel the Elder (1529), was in Constantinople in 1533 designing tapestries. Extant are drawings for the weavings *History of David* and the *Seven Capital Sins,* an engraving by Goltzius of a *Last Supper* by C., and an attributed *Descent from the Cross.* In 1553 C.'s wife published *Les Moeurs et fachons de faire des Turcz* with his engravings. BIBLIOGRAPHY: G. Marlier, *La Renaissance flamande: Pierre Coeck d'Alost* (1966).

[M. J. DALY]

COEDUCATION, an educational policy that permits both sexes to follow courses together in the same school. It began in Protestant countries during the Reformation at the elementary level to promote universal education. It was adopted on the secondary level in Europe and the U.S. in the 19th cent. as a practical socio-economic expedient, although sternly opposed by religious leaders. With the large-scale development of education for women in the late 19th and 20th cent., it was gradually extended to colleges and universities. Catholic parochial schools have been almost entirely coeducational. Diocesan secondary schools are generally coinstitutional; Catholic colleges are largely restricted on the undergraduate level to men or women, but are becoming more frequently coeducational. Papal documents (Pius IX, Leo XIII, Pius XI) issued stern warnings against the naturalistic foundations of coeducation. The recent Vatican Council II document, *Decree on Christian Education,* makes no reference to the subject. BIBLIOGRAPHY: D. F. Kenny, NCE 3:977–980.

[M. B. MURPHY]

COEFFETAU, NICOLAS (1574–1623), Dominican theologian, spiritual writer, and litterateur. He had a brilliant youthful career as a professor, regent, and prior at Saint-Jacques in Paris, and was also court preacher of Henry IV. In 1617 he became suffragan bp. of Metz; in 1621 he was named by the King, bp. of Marseilles, and approved by the Pope in 1623, but ill health kept him from assuming residence. His theological works included RC defenses against Calvinist eucharistic teaching, and one of the earliest vernacular paraphrases of the *Summa theologiae* of St. Thomas Aquinas. His spiritual writings were widely read for their warmth of devotion. His pure and clear French literary style is regarded as one of the formative influences on French prose. BIBLIOGRAPHY: H. Féret, *Catholicisme* 2:1278–79; M. H. Laurent, DSAM 2:1022–23.

[T. C. O'BRIEN]

COELESTINUS, see CELESTINE.

COELLO, CLAUDIO (1642–93), Spanish painter whose style is a distillation of the masters Raphael, Titian, Rubens, and others, in an easy virtuosity. A Baroque dynamism characterizes the *Annunciation* and *Holy Family with Angels and Saints* (both in Madrid). C.'s *Adoration of the Holy Eucharist,* a last expression of the great Spanish Baroque golden age, combines architectural grandeur and buoyant figures in an intense, theatrical spectacle. BIBLIOGRAPHY: J. A. Gaya Nuño, *Claudio Coello* (1957).

[M. J. DALY]

COERCION, in moral theology, force applied to someone to make him do what he does not want to do, a matter of interest to moralists because of its bearing upon the voluntariness and moral imputability of what is done under its influence. The force may be either physical or moral: physical, when it is bodily irresistible (as when a person is moved along by captors stronger than himself); moral, when one is prevailed upon to act by threats. Physical coercion has the effect of making an act involuntary; what is done under its influence is not imputable to the agent but only to those who apply the force. What is done under moral coercion is voluntary, simply speaking, because a person under such compulsion chooses to do what he does rather than to suffer the consequences of refusing, but it is also involuntary *secundum quid,* i.e., in the sense that he would not do it except under pressure of fear. However, though the act remains essentially voluntary, its imputability may be considerably diminished in particular cases or even totally ruled out, depending on the degree to which *fear lessens the agent's capacity for responsible human action. BIBLIOGRAPHY: J. A. Oesterle, NCE 5:1004–05, s.v. "Force and Moral Responsibility; ThAq ST 1a2ae, 6.4–5.

[P. K. MEAGHER]

COERCIVE POWER, a form of administrative or executive power by which a superior who is vested with it is entitled to enforce his will on a person subject to his authority. According to the type of authority in question, the superior may exercise this power directly upon the will of his subject who is then required to conform his will to that of his superior, or it may extend only to demanding that certain external actions be performed or others avoided in accordance with the superior's commands.

[P. K. MEAGHER]

COFFIN, EDWARD (al. Hatton; 1570–1626), English Jesuit polemicist. Having studied at the English College in Rome, C. was ordained (1593) and sent to the English mission. In 1598 he entered the Jesuits, but en route to Flanders for his novitiate, he was captured by the Dutch and returned to England where he was imprisoned until his release and exile after the accession of James I (1603). He died at Saint-Omer on his way back to the English mission

after 20 years spent in Rome. He was the author of several controversial works against the English Protestants and *A Treatise in Defense of the Celibacy of Priests* (1620). BIBLIOGRAPHY: T. Cooper, DNB 4:671–672.

[V. SAMPSON]

COGITATIVE POWER, in scholastic philosophical psychology a sensory power of comparative perception of the concrete objects of experience. This "inner sense" has its proper characteristic in man because of the essential union of soul and body, by reason of which there is a higher form of sense perception: the inner senses dispose, as it were, the objects of experience for the judgment of intelligence. Human judgment of the singular is a combined knowledge of mind and sense. The function of the cogitative power is particularly important to the exercise of the mind in its practical decisions in the moral order, since moral actions deal with concrete situations of human living. The same power is also referred to as "particular reason." BIBLIOGRAPHY: ThAq ST 1a, 78.4; 2a2ae, 47.3.

COGLEY, JOHN (1916–76), editor and journalist. Executive editor of *The Commonweal* and onetime religious news editor of the *New York Times.* C. had been associated with the Center for the Study of Democratic Institutions in Santa Barbara, California. Critical of Catholic church pronouncements, he joined the Episcopal Church in 1973 and was ordained a deacon.

[M. A. MCFADDEN]

COHEN, HERMANN (Augustin Marie de S. Sacrement; 1820–70), German Jewish convert, Carmelite priest. A concert pianist in Paris, he lived a free artist's life until a spiritual experience in 1847 led him to embrace Catholicism and then to become a Discalced Carmelite. He became a celebrated preacher, helped restore his order in England, and died ministering to prisoners of war in Berlin during the Franco-Prussian War. BIBLIOGRAPHY: life by C. Sylvain (tr. F. Raymond-Barker, 1925).

[T. C. O'BRIEN]

COHEN, HERMANN (1842–1918), Jewish philosopher. Born at Coswig, Germany, and educated at Breslau and Berlin, in 1876 he became professor of philosophy at the Univ. of Marburg and influenced many of the leading professors and theologians in Germany before 1933. His philosophy, never losing touch with biblical ideas, restored the sovereignty of "pure" thought: existence is rooted in reason. After retiring from Marburg in 1912, he lectured at the Institute for the Science of Judaism in Berlin. During his retirement, he wrote *Die Religion der Vernunft aus den Quellen des Judentums,* a systematic presentation of Judaism. BIBLIOGRAPHY: *Reason and Hope: Selections from the Jewish Writings of Hermann Cohen* (tr. and ed. E. Jospe, 1973).

[J. A. ROCHE]

COIMBRA, OLD CATHEDRAL, Portuguese Romanesque structure (1162) influenced by Santiago de Compostela, having transept with projecting bays, and three E apses, its façade distinctive in Moorish crenelations and corner turrets. Sixteenth-cent. additions by Jean de Rouen, the flamboyant retable of the high altar by the Flemings Olivier de Gand and Jean d'Ypres, and many important medieval tombs are notable. BIBLIOGRAPHY: K. J. Conant, *Carolingian and Romanesque Architecture 800–1200* (1959).

[M. J. DALY]

COIMBRA, UNIVERSITY OF, a national coeducational university of medieval origin in Portugal. Founded originally in Lisbon by King Diniz in 1290, and confirmed by Nicholas IV, the university shifted between Lisbon and Coimbra until it permanently settled in Coimbra in 1537. King John II, the reigning Portuguese sovereign, spared no effort to make the university worthy of high place among Renaissance institutions, inviting to it the most outstanding national and foreign scholars: the Portuguese mathematician, Pedro Nunes; the Spanish canonist, Martín Azpilcueta; the learned anatomist, Guevara. Among distinguished alumni was Luiz Camões, author of the Portuguese national epic, the *Lusíadas*. John II also sponsored the foundation of univ. colleges, the majority of which belonged to religious orders until their suppression in 1834. The university comprised the faculties of medicine, civil and canon law, and arts, to which theology was added in the 15th century. The introduction of astronomy in the 14th cent. paved the way for the 15th cent. geographical discoveries under Prince Henry the Navigator. From 1555 until their suppression in 1773, the Jesuits directed the university education. Political disturbances in the 16th cent. resulted in a period of decline, although the university roster still counted outstanding professors, among them the Spanish Jesuit theologian, Francisco Suárez (1540–1617). A far-reaching reform under Marquis de Pombal in 1772, which among other advances established the faculties of mathematics and philosophy, restored the university's academic standing. In the early 20th cent. the faculty of letters replaced the faculty of theology. In its contemporary organization, Coimbra comprises faculties of letters, law, medicine, sciences, and a school of pharmacy which grant the licentiate and doctorate. The faculty of letters sponsors a summer session in Portuguese language, literature, and culture for foreigners. In addition to specialized libraries with holdings totaling 435,000, the main library houses approximately 1,200,000 bound volumes and 5,000 manuscripts. Enrollment averages about 7,000. BIBLIOGRAPHY: H. Rashdall, *Universities of Europe in the Middle Ages* (ed. F. M. Powicke and A. B. Emden, 3 v., 1936); M. Brandão and M. Lopes D'Almeida, *A Universidade de Coimbra: Esbôço da sua história* (1937).

[M. B. MURPHY]

COINAGE, ANCIENT JEWISH. The oldest coin found so far in Palestine was dug up at Shechem and belongs either to Thasos or N Macedonia and was struck *c*.500 B.C. Jewish coinage began with the bronze coins of John Hyrcanus I (135–104 B.C.); only bronze coins were minted by the Hasmoneans. The first revolt (66–70 A.D.) was marked by the issue of the famous silver shekels. The Roman victory over the Jews was celebrated by a series of so-called *Judea Capta* coins. The second revolt (132–135) brought the greatest development of autonomous Jewish coinage. These coins were generally overstruck on Roman imperial or provincial silver and local bronze coins, so that the date of issuance is absolutely certain. A great variety of coins, especially Roman, Herodian, and Procuratorial, were in circulation in Palestine at the time of our Lord. In the OT specific references to coined money are very scarce. The shekel is often mentioned, but the reference is not to a coin but to a weight. In the NT silver coins are often mentioned: the denarius, drachma, didrachma, stater, and shekel. BIBLIOGRAPHY: B. Kanael, "Ancient Jewish Coins and Their Historical Importance," *Biblical Archaeologist* 26 (1963) 37–62.

[J. E. LUSSIER]

COINCIDENCE OF FEASTS, the occurrence of two or more feasts on the same day. When this happens the feast of higher rank takes precedence and the lesser feast is commemorated, transferred to another day, or is not observed. Since Sunday is the Church's celebration of the paschal mystery and thus the nucleus of the liturgical year, it takes precedence over all feasts except those of truly overriding importance. The feasts of Our Lord in which the mysteries of salvation are celebrated also have precedence over the feasts of the saints. Proper procedure is given in the current Ordo. BIBLIOGRAPHY: Vat II, SacLit 106–111.

[T. M. MCFADDEN]

COINSTITUTIONAL SCHOOLS, a mid-20th cent. development in Catholic education, inspired largely by economic expediency. Coinstitutional schools, mainly diocesan or central high schools, are organized to offer ample classroom space in separate wings for boys and girls, but make joint use of the more costly facilities such as gymnasiums, cafeterias, laboratories, auditoriums, and chapels. The administration may be confined to one principal, usually a diocesan priest, assisted by a vice principal for each wing; or it may include two principals, one for each wing, with a coordinator to facilitate intercommunication. In either case, sisters and laywomen staff the girls' department; diocesan or religious priests or brothers and laymen, the boys' department. BIBLIOGRAPHY: R. F. McCoy, *American School Administration: Public and Catholic* (1961).

[M. B. MURPHY]

COKE, THOMAS (1747–1814), first bp. of the Methodist Episcopal Church in the United States. C. was born of wealthy parents at Brecon, Wales; educated at Oxford, he was ordained in the C of E and given a parish in Somersetshire. He traveled 20 miles expressly to meet John Wesley. When he later preached Methodism in his own church, he was dismissed, and he joined Wesley, helping him supervise the Methodist *societies and write the *Deed of Declaration. In 1784 Wesley ordained C. as general superintendent (bishop) of Methodist work in America, sending him with two other preachers to ordain F. *Asbury. C. met Asbury at Barratt's Chapel, Del.; they arranged that all Methodist preachers should meet in Baltimore in Dec. 1784, when the Methodist Episcopal Church in America was organized and Asbury ordained. C. crossed the Atlantic 18 times, at his own expense, to assist both British and American Methodism. He frequently presided at the Irish Conference as well as at the British Conference and with Asbury in the United States. He encouraged Methodist work in Nova Scotia, and esp. in the West Indies. He died on a missionary journey to India and was buried in the Indian Ocean. BIBLIOGRAPHY: J. W. Etheridge, *Life of the Rev. Thomas Coke, D.C.L.* (1860); HistAmMeth 1; J. A. Vickers, *Thomas Coke: Apostle of Methodism* (1969). *CHRISTMAS CONFERENCE.

[F. E. MASER]

COLA DI RIENZI (1313 or 1314–54), Roman politician and revolutionary. Though of humble birth, C. succeeded by devoting himself to the study of antiquity and law in securing an important position as delegate to the Avignon court of Pope Clement VI (1343). Due to his personality and eloquence, he was able to rise in Roman politics and in 1347, supported by the lower classes as well as the gentry and merchants, led a successful *coup d'état*. As tribune he initiated some new reform policies, but his sumptuous and costly way of life began to stir the wrath of the people. He was forced to resign and then, arriving at the court of Emperor Charles IV, was imprisoned and excommunicated. A trial in 1352 at Avignon acquitted him, however, and he returned to Rome and again to power. The violence and cruelty of this new rule, combined with many unpopular acts, led to his death at the hands of the populace in 1354. BIBLIOGRAPHY: M. Monaco, NCE 3:986–987; M. Petrocchi, EncCatt 3:1941–43.

[D. G. NUGENT]

COLBERT, JEAN-BAPTISTE (1619–83), French statesman and minister. Trained under Mazarin from 1651, he entered the direct service of Louis XIV in 1661. Noted esp. for his economic policies, he also helped to codify French law and patronized artistic and literary productions. He was particularly interested in commerce and to this end he strengthened the navy. Though unable to ruin Dutch domination in trade and make France a great maritime power, he built up an economic system within the country that encouraged state-directed industry. A firm believer in productivity, he resolutely placed political and economic interests above religion. His principal rival was Louvois, minister of war, but C., although not generally popular, retained royal favor and almost exclusive administrative power until his death. BIBLIOGRAPHY: C. W. Cole, *Colbert and a Century of French Mercantilism* (2 v., 1939).

[I. M. KASHUBA]

COLDINGHAM PRIORY, a Benedictine monastery in Berwickshire, Scotland, which first emerged about 1139 on lands that had been given by earlier Scottish kings to the monks of Durham Cathedral. Because of its nearness to the Border and its English connections, it had a turbulent history throughout the Anglo-Scottish wars of the Middle Ages, being finally annexed by the Scottish crown in 1509. Although badly damaged by the 16th-cent. English Reformers and again by Oliver Cromwell in 1648, its church is still in use today. BIBLIOGRAPHY: D. E. Easson, *Medieval Religious Houses: Scotland* (1957), 49–50; G. W. S. Barrow, "Scottish Rulers and the Religious Orders," *Transactions of the Royal Historical Society* (1953).

[L. J. MACFARLANE]

COLE, HENRY (*c.* 1500–80), last RC dean of St. Paul's. C. acknowledged Henry VIII as head of the Church in England and during the early part of the reign of Edward VI became known as an ardent reformer, but he gradually (1548–51) dissociated himself from the Reform movement; at the accession of Queen Mary he made public profession of Roman Catholicism and received preferments, including the deanship of St. Paul's. He was one of the disputants against Cranmer, Ridley, and Latimer at Oxford and preached the sermon before the execution of Cranmer (1556). Under Elizabeth he was one of the eight leading Catholics appointed to take part in the disputation at Westminster Abbey in 1559. He was fined for his defense of the faith, deprived of his preferments, and spent the last years of his life in prison. BIBLIOGRAPHY: DNB 11:266; Hughes RE.

[V. SAMPSON]

COLEMAN, EDWARD (d. 1678), English martyr. C., a Cambridge graduate, was converted from Puritanism to Catholicism in 1670, and was appointed secretary to Mary, wife of James, the King's brother and successor. He engaged in correspondence with civil and ecclesiastical authorities at the French court in the hope of finding aid for a Catholic revival in England under the leadership of the newly converted James. Titus *Oates implicated him in the "popish plot," and he was arrested and interrogated. No evidence linked him with the alleged conspiracy apart from the dubious accusation of Oates, but the fanatical William Scroggs, president of the tribunal, declared that the peaceful missionary effort he proposed would surely have turned to violence if it had been unsuccessful. Found guilty of treason and executed at Tyburn, he was beatified in 1929. BIBLIOGRAPHY: M. V. Hay, *Jesuits and the Popish Plot* (1934); C. Testore, BiblSanct 4:75–76.

[V. SAMPSON]

COLEMAN, WALTER (d. 1645), a native of England who was educated in France where he became a Franciscan of the Strict Observance. He worked on the English mission and died in prison 3 years after Charles I had granted him a reprieve from a death sentence. BIBLIOGRAPHY: Gillow BDEC 1:536–537; DNB 11:396.

COLERIDGE, SAMUEL TAYLOR (1772–1834), English poet, critic, and philosopher. C. left Cambridge without a degree, was a close friend of William and Dorothy Wordsworth, wrote and talked incessantly about religion, politics, language and literature, and tried out many Utopian schemes. With Wordsworth he produced *Lyrical Ballads* (1798). *Biographia Literaria* (1817) contains his greatest criticism, chiefly concerned with Wordsworth. His reaction to the mechanistic psychology of the 18th cent., his revival of Platonism, and his introduction into England of German idealism made him the intellectual center of the Romantic Movement. He produced the revolution in literary thought that regards the imagination as the sovereign creative power. His literary work is largely fragmentary as he was unable to achieve the wholeness which he taught was the great poetic possession. BIBLIOGRAPHY: J. D. Campbell, *Samuel Taylor Coleridge* (1894); J. D. Boulger, *Coleridge as a Religious Thinker* (1961).

[M. M. BARRY]

COLET, JOHN (1467–1519), dean of St. Paul's, humanist. Of a wealthy family (his father was twice lord mayor of London), C. studied at Oxford and on the Continent, where he acquired a love for the New Learning. After his return to England he was ordained (1498) and began lecturing on the Epistles of St. Paul at Oxford, using the findings and the method of humanistic scholarship in his critical study of the text. At the same time he undertook a campaign of criticism against the ecclesiastical abuses of the time. In 1504 he was named dean of St. Paul's, in which office he proved himself an able and vigorous administrator. He used a considerable portion of the large fortune inherited from his father in the foundation of St. Paul's School. His outspoken attacks upon the scandals in the Church led to some questioning of his orthodoxy; he was brought up once for trial, but the charges against him were dismissed as frivolous. At Oxford he had become a close friend of Erasmus, and in London he was the intimate friend and spiritual adviser of Thomas More. He represents the calmer, humanistic, Erasmian stream of Catholic reform that was soon to be overwhelmed by the swifter onrush of the Reformation. The basic account of Colet's life was given by

Erasmus (*Epistolae* 3.335). BIBLIOGRAPHY: E. Hunt, *Dean Colet and his Theology* (1956).

[R. B. ENO]

COLETTE, ST. (1381–1447), religious reformer, foundress of the Colletine Poor Clares. Admitted to profession as a Poor Clare by antipope Benedict XIII, C. worked courageously to restore observance of the primitive rule of St. Clare. She reformed many houses and founded 20 new monasteries. BIBLIOGRAPHY: Butler 1:506–507; M. da Alatrie, BiblSanct 4:76–81.

[H. DRESSLER]

COLETTE, SIDONIE GABRIELLE (1873–1954), French novelist and essayist. Colette, as she signed herself, was the author of the *Claudine* series and other novels. She was the writer also of what may best be classified as sketches, classic in expression and sometimes romantic in mood. Sensitive to sights and sounds, her prose was enriched by her minute observations of trees and flowers and animals. Her prose might be said to be her poetry. Although she never spoke of God, she was in a sense a moralist immersed in compassion for sinners and respect and admiration for man and nature. Her sensitivity to sight and sound led to interest in dramatic criticism and to dramatic process in her own works (*Dialogues de bêtes,* and *Chéri*). C. was married three times. Her first husband, Henry Gauthier-Villars (Willy), wrote in collaboration with her the early *Claudine* novels. This marriage as well as her second to Henry de Jouvenel ended in divorce. It was her third marriage to Maurice Goudeket, many years her junior, that enriched her life and brought further maturity to her judgment. *Julie de Carneilhan* (1941) represents her best work of this period and is a prime example of C.'s genius for characterization of woman. C. was the first woman president of the Goncourt Academy. Some of her works are *Le Pur et l'impure* (1932), *Paris de ma fenêtre* (1942), *Gigi* (1943). BIBLIOGRAPHY: *Colette, par elle-même* (ed. G. Beaumont and A. Parinaud, 1951); R. D. Cottrell, *Colette* (1974); M. Crosland, *Colette: The Difficulty of Loving* (1973).

[R. M. FUNCHION]

COLGAN, JOHN (1592–1658), Irish Franciscan hagiographer. Ordained in 1618, C. entered the Franciscans at Louvain in 1620. While at Louvain he began his lifelong work on the lives of Irish saints. Before his death he published two hagiographical works: *Acta Sanctorum* and *Triadis Thaumaturgae Acta*. BIBLIOGRAPHY: F. O'Briain, DHGE 13:247.

[P. HIGGINS]

COLIDAEI, see CULDEES.

COLIGNY, GASPARD DE (1519–72), French Huguenot leader. A member of the French nobility, he was appointed by Henry II colonel general of infantry, admiral of France, and governor of Paris and Isle-de-France. He was converted to Protestantism in 1560, and after the death of the Prince of Condé in 1569 became the Huguenot leader. C.'s influence with Charles IX led the queen mother, *Catherine de Médicis to attempt having him assassinated Aug. 22, 1572. Two days later she instigated the Massacre of *St. Bartholomew in which he was the first victim. BIBLIOGRAPHY: A. W. Whitehead, *Gaspard de Coligny* (1904).

[T. EARLY]

COLIGNY, ODET DE (1523–71), French nobleman. At 10 he was named cardinal deacon; at 11, bp. of Toulouse and later bp. of Beauvais. When he became a Calvinist, he was deprived of his rank and benefices (1563) but insisted on calling himself the "cardinal of Châtillon." During the civil war of 1567 he represented the Huguenots but then retired to England, where he was poisoned by a servant. BIBLIOGRAPHY: J. Jordan, LTK 3:2.

[M. J. SUELZER]

COLIN, FRÉDÉRIC LOUIS (1835–1902), superior of Canadian Sulpicians. A native of France, C. studied at Issy, France, became a Sulpician, was ordained (1862) and sent to Canada as a seminary professor. C. served as superior of the Sulpicians in Canada from 1881 until his death. He was instrumental in the development of the University of Montreal and the Seminary of Montreal and he founded the Canadian College at Rome for theological studies. BIBLIOGRAPHY: H. Gauthier, *Sulpitiana* (1926).

[R. K. MacMASTER]

COLIN, JEAN CLAUDE MARIE, VEN. (1790–1875), founder of the Marist Fathers and Sisters, religious societies dedicated to Mary. Born in Bonnet le Troncy, France, C. was ordained in Lyons (1816). With a group of his associates from the seminary he drew up the rule for the Marists. Despite opposition the congregation was approved by Pope Gregory XVI. C. was superior of the Marists from 1836 to 1854. Houses were established in France and missionaries were sent to Oceania.

[C. R. CAWLEY]

COLLATERAL RELATIONSHIP, see CONSANGUINITY.

COLLATION, light meal in place of lunch or supper, which was permitted on fast days in addition to the full meal. It was originally confined to the light evening meal of monks.

[A. R. ZINK]

COLLECT, a short prayer which usually concludes the entrance rite at Mass. It is generally addressed to God the Father through Christ, and embraces the petitions of the congregation. The term is derived from the Latin *oratio ad collectam* (prayer at the assembly) and is of very early liturgical use. The revised *Missale Romanum* uses the term *collecta*, but the preferred term, as in the *Sacramentary*, is "opening prayer." Only one is permitted now in the Mass.

[N. KOLLAR]

COLLECTARIUM, a medieval liturgical book containing collects and capitula. *LITURGICAL BOOKS.

[N. KOLLAR]

COLLECTIO PALATINA, a valuable gift of the Palatine Library, Heidelberg, made in 1622 to the Vatican Library by Maximilian I, Palatine elector and duke of Bavaria. The collection contains 432 Greek and 2,128 Latin MSS as well as 4,945 printed books. BIBLIOGRAPHY: L. Hammermayer, *Zur Geschichte der Bibliothek Palatina in der Vatikan* (1959); E. Jammers, LTK 5:67 (pt. 2, "Universitätsbibliothek Heidelberg").

[M. R. BROWN]

COLLECTION AT MASS, the gathering of gifts, now esp. in the form of money, during the eucharistic celebration. These gift-offerings are an expression of the congregation's right and duty to participate fully in the Eucharist. In origin the collection was primarily utilitarian; the offerings necessary for the Eucharist had to be brought to the altar. St. Justin (c.150) stated that wine, water, and bread were brought to the altar, but he made no mention of their being collected from the people. But there is evidence to show that by the 4th cent. there was a collection in which either the gifts were gathered upon tables before the Mass, of which some would be brought up to the altar at the offertory, or the gifts would be placed upon or around the altar at the offertory by the faithful. At the same time items other than bread, wine, and water began to be included among the gift-offerings, e.g., candles, gold, oil, fruits and other things useful for the support of the church and the promotion of its activities. The presentation of these gifts was made just after the homily and before the prayer over the gifts. An ancient Roman ordinal (c.695) gives an indication of how the gifts were collected. The pope went from the sanctuary to the nave where the gifts were gathered first from the men's and then from the women's side of the church. The procession of gifts at the offertory died out in the 10th century. From the 11th cent. onward the offering of money gradually replaced the offering of gifts in kind. The celebrant no longer took up the collection. In later times in a number of dioceses in the U.S. it was forbidden, in some cases under ecclesiastical penalty, for the priest, clothed in vestments, to take up the collection personally. According to the existing custom the collection is taken up after the creed and before the prayer over the gifts, but in many places, the practice of having the faithful, or certain of their representatives, bring bread, wine, and water to the altar has been adopted. The ceremony associated with this bears some resemblance to the Great Entry in the Gallican and Eastern rites. The money taken up in the collection is often brought forward at the same time; it helps provide for the requirements of public worship, the upkeep of the church, the maintenance of a school, the provision of pastoral care, and the help of the poor. BIBLIOGRAPHY: A. Clark, "Function of the Offertory Rite in the Mass," EphemLiturg 64 (1950) 309–344; J. A. Jungmann, *Mass of the Roman Rite* (1959) 315–326.

[N. KOLLAR]

COLLECTIVE RESPONSIBILITY, a term whose meaning hangs on the double hinge of the meanings assigned to both responsibility and collectivity. By responsibility most understand answerability. But answerability looks to both the past and the future, implying either accountability for past activity or free and careful future activity. The retrospective connotation of responsibility is primarily legal in usage, employed in the determination of guilt for crimes committed. The prospective connotation is the one with which ethics is mainly concerned, as a tool in the preparation of moral conscience for a greater degree of answerability in future actions. The first connotation has always been popular, but has been examined carefully of late in the light of knowledge from the behavioral sciences related to culpability. The second connotation has enjoyed a new popularity in this century. It has not only increased in common usage, but has also been extensively employed in moral and ethical studies. Still, the modifying of responsibility with the adjective collective raises problems if historical factors are ignored. It is worth noting that preliterate peoples have abundant symbols for corporate guilt and obligation. This is found in all the cultures from which our Western understanding of crimes and duties arises. Early Judaism as well as early Grecian civilization manifests a strong awareness of kinship ties and common answerability in both praiseworthy and blameworthy behavior. But literacy, education, and their accompanying self-awareness bring with them more individualized interpretations of responsibility. In Western civilization, responsibility has more frequently been cast in individual rather than collective symbols. With few exceptions, both legal action and moral education have focused on the particular person rather than the group. This was encouraged by postenlightenment social and political theory which placed the individual higher than the aggregate of people contracting with each other. Responsibility theory based on this understanding promoted the notions of personal accountability in both the retrospective and prospective senses. However, in the course of this century, sociological studies have raised some questions about this tradition, and have brought some clarity to the discussion of responsibility as applied to groups of people.

The most generic term for a group of people is *collectivity,* connoting a simple gathering of individuals. A *communion* is the most intimate type of collectivity, based on devotion to each other, typified by friendship, and noted for its nonroutinized interaction. A *community* rests on custom and obedience with sentiments of duty; it is typified by the

family, and its interaction is purposeful and moderately routinized. The *society* is by far the most businesslike collectivity. Its bases are contractual, sustained by good faith, with interactions that are primarily economic and juridical. *Communions* seem to exhibit the highest degree of "wefeeling," and would be the most likely kinds of collectivities to be corporately answerable. The extent and depth of mutual influence is greatest in such collectivities. Hence, the members usually have something of a common conscience. They would not only agree to be accountable for each other, but also for the behavior of one another in both the retrospective and prospective senses. *Communities* also demonstrate a willingness to be accountable for each others' behavior. But some limits are generally set to the extent of community responsibility. Lines of demarcation are established between prospective and retrospective responsibility. Taking considerable care in mutual provision for the future, members show a reluctance to be accountable for each other's past. Praiseworthy actions of the members' past activities are frequently flown with the community's colors, while blameworthy behavior is usually the sole burden of the individual. *Societies* show the least amount of willingness to be held accountable for the behavior of those belonging to them. The national reaction to accusations that the U.S. as a whole was to blame for the events of the sixties is strident evidence that collective responsibility means little if anything to a society. The nature of the problems facing us in the near future stirs awareness of responsibility held in common for the sustenance and quality of life on the whole planet. But the very nature of the ties and interactions in societies seems to rule out any genuine possibility of retrospective responsibility in either our awareness or treatment of past mistakes.

[J. F. SMURL]

COLLECTIVE RESPONSIBILITY (IN THE BIBLE). The notion of corporate personality was characteristic of archaic societies including those of the ancient Orient. Hammurabi's law code (1728–1686 B.C.) prescribes instances in which an offender's children must bear the punishment (including death) for their father's crime. The classic OT example of collective responsibility is that of Adam and Eve, whose sin is imputed to all their descendants, as also the promise of eventual victory (Gen 3.15) extends beyond Eve to her seed (i.e., all humanity).

Early Israel followed this principle from its nomadic days, in which clan solidarity was a necessity of desert life and in which whole clans were traditionally either friend or foe to each other. The sins of Cain (Gen 4.13–14); of Ham/Canaan (Gen 9.18–27); of the Pharaoh (Gen 12.15–20); of Dathan and Abiram (Num 16.27) and of Achan (Jos 22.20) exemplify this principle, which becomes canonized in the Decalogue (Ex 20.5–6; Dt 5.9). Deuteronomic theology applies this responsibility to Israel's history up to the exile (Jg 2.2–15; 2 Kg 17.7). The kindred notion of collective reward for justice is also an aspect of corporate personality; see, e.g., Noah (Gen 7.1); Lot (Gen 19.12–13); Caleb (Dt 1.36). Postexilic OT theology retains the insistence of collective responsibility, but shows an increasing tendency to emphasize individual retribution. This is adumbrated briefly in Dt 24.16, but became more frequent beginning with Ezek (14.20; 18.2; see also Pr 24.12; Sir 16.14). NT theology, esp. that of St. Paul, retained collective responsibility as basic to Christianity, deriving from the doctrine that Jesus is the second Adam (Rom 5.12–19; 1 Cor 15.20–28). Thus, just as Adam's descendants receive both his sin and his promise, so also those whose head is Jesus are one with him in receiving the heavenly reward (Eph 4.25; 1 Cor 12.26). However, the NT also insists strongly on individual faith as a condition for salvation (Mk 16.16). BIBLIOGRAPHY: EDB 2032–36 s.v. "Retribution"; M. Rodríguez, NCE 3:1002–03.

[T. CRANE]

COLLECTIVE UNCONSCIOUS, a concept associated with the *analytical psychology of C. G. Jung, although Freud also employs it, esp. to explain concepts of God and religion. For Jung, the collective unconscious is the most fundamental structure of the human psyche. The conscious ego and the personal unconscious are built upon it, for the contents of the collective unconscious profoundly influence the manner in which the individual responds at all other levels of personality. These contents are the *archetypes, which are latent memory traces of typical universal and striking events in human life, repeated over and over again through countless generations so that the evolving brain has become conditioned or predisposed to recognize and respond to expectable events in the individual's life in terms of racial experience. Since all men have a common, ancient ancestry, the racial unconscious is the same in all, just as the brain structure with which it is connected is common to all. As the contents of the collective unconscious emerge and fuse with personal experience, the wisdom and experience of forgotten ancestry is brought to bear in the individual's life. If, however, the unconscious is repressed or ignored by the *ego, it may disrupt and distort conscious rational processes, producing the symptoms of psychic disorder. The concept of collective unconscious has been severely criticized because it presupposes the possibility of the heritability of characteristics acquired by individual experience and not gene-connected, a possibility completely unproven. Many critics also believe that the so-called universality of the archetypes can be explained by the fundamental similarities in all human experience. BIBLIOGRAPHY: V. White, *Soul and Psyche* (1960); *idem, God and the Unconscious* (1961); P. Homans, *Theology after Freud: An Interpretive Inquiry* (1970).

[M. E. STOCK]

COLLECTIVISM, a term generally understood as the opposite of individualism. In France, England, and America it is often used in specific reference to a form of ownership and economic system, e.g., that espoused by communism. But in addition to economic collectivism, though often associated with it, there is a philosophical, social, or political collectivism which seeks to emphasize and increase the power and effectiveness of the State at the expense of the rights and responsibilities of its individual members. Man is not an individual standing alone and responsible only to himself. By his very nature he is a part of the community in which he lives. Being essentially related to the collectivity of which he forms a part and from which he derives immense benefit necessary to his full human and personal development, he has responsibilities toward the community and these must at times transcend what may appear to be his own personal interests. The tension that often results from the conflicting claims of the individual and those of the community has been noted by philosophers from antiquity onward. The extremities of both individualism and collectivism must be avoided at all costs if we are to avoid the jungle to which uncontrolled individualism leads, or, on the other hand, the brutalizing enslavement of the masses in which pure collectivism debouches. The Christian will try to strike a balance between the extremes, seeing the community as necessary to the complete realization of the human potential, but denying that man is only a part of the State and has no destiny or fulfillment apart from the State. BIBLIOGRAPHY: J. Maritain, *Person and the Common Good* (1947); N. A. Berdyaev, *Slavery and Freedom* (tr., R. M. French, 1944); J. C. Bennett, *Christians and the State* (1958).

[P. K. MEAGHER]

COLLEGE, in its broadest and most general sense, any organized group of individuals exercising certain specific activities and possessed of certain rights and privileges. More specifically the term is used of: (1) an institution of higher learning; (2) a major division of a university; (3) the corporate entity made up of the cardinals of the RC Church; (4) an electoral body; (5) a body of secular priests known as canons who form a chapter and may live together. Hence the church of such a group is known as a collegiate church.

[P. K. MEAGHER]

COLLÈGE DE FRANCE, a public institution of higher learning and research. Founded in Paris in 1530 when Francis I, influenced by the Greek scholar and humanist, Guillaume Budé (Budaeus), signed a decree establishing the three chairs of Hebrew, Greek, and Latin for royal lecturers, the *Collegium Trilingue,* as it was originally called, becamed a distinguished center of European humanism and scholarship. In 1539, the Collège added mathematics to its curriculum, and in 1542, medicine. It has jealously preserved its independence from the Sorbonne, which in the 17th cent. sought its control. At present, the Collège comprises faculties of letters and science, which offer a wide field of studies, including oriental languages. The contribution to oriental studies made by the Collège is of special value to Scripture scholars and those interested in Eastern Christianity. The Collège, which requires no examinations, awards neither diplomas nor degrees. It is under the direct supervision of the Ministry of Public Instruction and is financed by the government, with supplementary revenues from French and foreign foundations. BIBLIOGRAPHY: S. D'Irsay, *Histoire des universités* (2 v., 1933–35); *World of Learning* (1972).

[M. B. MURPHY]

COLLEGE OF CARDINALS, that body of ecclesiastics who assist the pope in governing the RC Church, act as his principal advisors, head the various curial offices and Roman Congregations, administer the Holy See during a vacancy, and elect a new pope in conclave. It is divided into three ranks: *cardinal bishops, *cardinal priests, and cardinal deacons. The origin of the term is obscure, but it seems to have designated those clerics who were serving in churches other than those for whose service they had been ordained. In Rome, the title came to be applied to members of the local clergy who assisted the pope in a particular way. Thus the ordinaries of the seven sees adjacent to Rome who performed certain liturgical functions at the *Lateran basilica were called cardinal bishops since they performed these functions outside of their own diocese; cardinal priests were the pastors of the titular churches of Rome who also assisted the pope liturgically; and cardinal deacons administered for the poor in the seven Roman districts. Gradually wider administrative duties were added to these liturgical functions, and in 1059 the cardinals became papal electors. At the same time, the practice of designating prelates from distant sees arose and emphasis was increasingly placed upon their advisory rather than their liturgical role. Today, the great majority of the college of cardinals are ordinaries of their own sees, although several others serve within the Vatican itself. They have no legislative authority; are appointed directly by the pope; and are now officially invested at a public consistory. From 1586, the number of cardinals was fixed at 70 but this tradition was broken by John XXIII and there is no limit to the number who could be appointed. Recent papal practice has inclined toward appointing a greater percentage of non-Italians to the cardinalate. BIBLIOGRAPHY: K. F. Morrison and H. G. Hynes, NCE 3:104–106.

[T. M. MCFADDEN]

COLLEGES AND SEMINARIES, ROMAN, institutions, many of pontifical status, in Rome designed to bring seminarians from all over the world to study at the seat of Christianity. The majority of them were founded by popes and share the special interest of the Holy See. The most venerable is Capranica, founded in 1457 by Card. Domenico Capranica. The colleges are generally residences for students attending one of the large Roman universities. Some are organized along national lines, others are for seminarians of a particular rite. The following will give an idea of the wide representation: Armenian, English, Belgian, Canadian, American, Ethiopian, Philippine, German, Russian, Greek, Irish, Lithuanian, Polish, Maronite, Bohemian, Dutch, Brazilian, Spanish, Portuguese, Latin American, Romanian, Ruthenian, Croatian, Scottish, Slovenian, Hungarian and the Urban College of the Propagation of the Faith (for mission lands). The North American College was established in 1859 by Pius IX for seminarians from the U.S.

[J. R. AHERNE]

COLLEGIALISM, a concept of Church-State relations, derived from the natural-right theories of H. Grotius (1583–1645) and S. Pufendorf (1632–94). The term itself is attributed to J. Boehmer (d. 1745) of the Univ. of Halle. Both Church and State are *collegia,* voluntary associations created by the members' will to unite; both societies are independent of each other in aim and purpose. Thus the State has no inherent right over ecclesiastical matters (see IUS CIRCA SACRA). Collegialism goes further in separating Church and State than does *territorialism. The concept of the Church that collegialism implies is opposed to *episcopalism; authority in the Church resides equally in "teacher and hearers," not in the body of bishops. BIBLIOGRAPHY: EncRelKnow 3:159–160.

[T. C. O'BRIEN]

COLLEGIALITY, as used in reference to RC bishops (collegiality of bishops, episcopal collegiality), a term indicating that the episcopal office or function is of its nature corporate, that episcopal consecration aggregates a bishop per se to a body bearing corporate responsibility for the whole Church, although for actual membership in the episcopal college it is necessary that the one so consecrated be "in hierarchical communion with the head of the college [the Roman pontiff] and the members" (Vat II ConstCh 22). In past centuries the emphasis has been strongly placed on the individual role of the bishop as pastor of a single diocese and also upon his subordination to the pope as pastor of the whole Church. In more recent times and during Vatican Council II that emphasis has been balanced by insistence on the bishop's inclusion within the college that succeeds the apostolic college, and consequently on the fact that joined with the pope and the rest of the episcopate each bishop shares in the pastoral direction of the whole Church.

Ultimately this collegial arrangement rests on Christ's free determination in founding and organizing the Church as he saw fit. But in keeping with the teaching of Vatican II (*ibid*. 22–23) it is possible to discern the fitness of such an arrangement. It manifests the catholicity of the Church; it reflects the variety of individual communities within the Church; it ensures that the pastors of individual, local communities cultivate, as members of the college, a concern for the whole Church; it brings out more clearly the virtuality (potentiality, capacity) of each local Church so to represent the totality that the whole may realize itself as event (in the eucharistic celebration) in it as a part. If the vitality of each part is such that it could become the whole, it would seem more fitting that its head and center of life should share collegiately in the direction of the whole. BIBLIOGRAPHY: J. Colson, *L'Épiscopat catholique: Collégialité et primauté dans les trois premiers siècles* (Unam Sanctam 43, 1963); C. Journet, *Church of the Word Incarnate* (tr. A.H.C. Downes, v. 1, 1955) 1:98–120; K. Rahner, *Bishops: Their Status and Function* (tr. E. Quinn, 1964); K. Rahner and J. Ratzinger, *Episcopate and the Primacy* (tr. K. Barker et al., 1962).

[S. E. DONLON]

COLLEGIATE CHURCH, see COLLEGE.

COLLEONI, IL, see VERROCCHIO, ANDREA DEL.

COLLOQUY OF THORN, see THORN, COLLOQUY OF.

COLLUTHIANS, a sect that arose in Alexandria during the Arian disturbances. Colluthus was one of the first to agree with Bp. Alexander in condemning Arius (320–321). But when Athanasius became bp. (328) Colluthus withdrew from his jurisdiction and formed his own party. Epiphanius (*Panar.* 69.2) mentions only that he taught false and perverted doctrines. Filaster (*Haer.* 79) implies that these heretics favored dualism, ascribing to an evil principle the many evils and trials to which men are subject.

[L. G. MÜLLER]

COLLYRIDIANS, a 4th-cent. Thracian sect, composed principally of women, who were so named for their offering cakes (Gr. *kollyris*) to the Blessed Virgin Mary. It was an idolatrous cult of the Virgin and could have had its origin in the pagan worship of Ceres. BIBLIOGRAPHY: G. Bareille, DTC 3:369–370.

[L. G. MÜLLER]

COLMAN, SS., five 6th–7th-cent. Irish saints. (1) **Colman of Cloyne** (6th cent.), first bp., a poet of great skill who became royal bard at Cashel. He was almost 50 years old when he was converted and baptized by St. Brendan. Later C. was ordained priest and consecrated bp., preaching at Limerick and the E parts of Cork. (2) **Colman** (6th cent.), bp., patron of the diocese of Dromore. C. founded a monastery there, probably *c.*514. Nothing is known of his parentage and career, later MSS purporting to give his biography being anachronistic and extravagant in details. His achievements include erecting the monastery and establishing his community there. (3) **Colman of Lann Elo** (*c.*555–611), founder in 590 of a famous monastery now called Lynally, in County Offaly. It is said that near the end of his life he made a pilgrimage to Clonard where he had a vision of St. Finnian. Attributed to him is the authorship of *Aibgitir in Chrabaid (Alphabet of Devotion).* (4) **Colman**

of **Kilmacduagh,** (*c.*632) who lived as a hermit in the Burren district of Co. Clare and is said to have hidden himself because he had been unwillingly made a bishop. He founded a monastery at Kilmacduagh. Colorful legends about him abound. (5) **Colman of Lindisfarne** (d. 676), third bishop. His three years' rule was significant chiefly for his part in the Synod of Whitby (664), convened to settle the disputed date of Easter. C. refused to accept the Roman date and adhered to Celtic tradition. He resigned his bishopric and established a new monastery off the coast of Connacht for all the Irish monks at Lindisfarne and 30 Englishmen. Eventually he transferred the latter to a monastery in Mayo. He remained abbot of both until his death. BIBLIOGRAPHY: F. O'Briain, DHGE 13:256; D. D. C. Pochin Mould, *Irish Saints* (1964) 89–90; N. del Re, BiblSanct 4:89–96; Butler, 4:686.

[S. A. HEENEY]

COLMAR, JOSEPH LUDWIG (1760–1818), German bishop. Ordained in 1783, C. taught history and Greek and also served as curate in Strasbourg during the French Reign of Terror. He was appointed bp. of Mainz in 1802. Through his influence the cathedrals of Mainz and Speyer were restored to the Church, and through his work and personal fervor religious life was renewed. He edited a collection of old church hymns and published several volumes of sermons and various spiritual works. BIBLIOGRAPHY: L. Lenhart, LTK 3:7.

[C. R. CAWLEY]

COLOGNE, SCHOOL OF, a name commonly given to the group of theologians who developed the theory of double justice. Four names esp. are associated with this group: J. Gropper (d. 1559), A. Pigge (d. 1542), G. Contarini (d. 1542), and G. *Seripando (d. 1563). Contarini worked out a formula which was proposed to and accepted by both Protestants and Catholics at the conference of Regensburg of 1541, but it was rejected by Luther. Seripando included his own view in his proposal for the Tridentine decree on justification, admitting an inherent justice but requiring a further extrinsic application of the merits of Christ. His view was not accepted by the Council. BIBLIOGRAPHY: J. Mercier, DTC 14.2:1923–40; R. W. Gleason, *Grace* (1962) 94–95, 213–218.

[P. DeLETTER]

COLOGNE, UNIVERSITY OF, an autonomous institution of medieval origin, under the jurisdiction of the Ministry of Education of W Germany. The university traces its origin to an early Dominican *studium generale,* which had established a reputation as a center of learning, and to the concerted efforts of the Dominicans and the Franciscans, Carmelites, and Augustinians, who together with the town council persuaded Urban VI to establish a *studium generale.* Chartered in 1388, and organized on the model of the Univ. of Paris, with faculties of theology, canon law, and civil law, to which arts and medicine were later added, the university was administered by a rector who was elected by the professors. Like other medieval German universities, Cologne was under pontifical rather than imperial patronage. Various popes—Boniface IX, Eugene IV, Paul IV—reserved certain church benefices to provide endowments for professors and grants for needy students. The university's reputation for academic excellence attracted numerous national and foreign students and inspired the foundation of other universities in Belgium, Germany, and Denmark. It was represented at the Councils of Basel and Constance; remained a stronghold of the Catholic faith during the Reformation, the Counter-Reformation, and the Enlightenment; but, gradually weakened by its rival, the University of Bonn (1786), it was suppressed during the French occupation in 1798.

In 1919 after World War I the University of Cologne was reconstituted through the influence of Konrad Adenauer and by popular appeal, with faculties of economics and social sciences, law, medicine (including dentistry), philosophy (including liberal arts, education, and musicology), mathematics and natural sciences, the Institute of Physical Education, and about 120 institutes, seminars, and clinics attached to the faculties. It is governed by a board of trustees and the senate. The library contains approximately 1,000,000 v., enrollment averages about 20,000, of whom about 1,500 are foreigners. BIBLIOGRAPHY: H. Rashdall, *Universities of Europe in the Middle Ages* (ed. F. M. Powicke and A. B. Emden, 3 v., 1936).

[M. B. MURPHY]

COLOGNE SCHOOL (1350–1450), painting culminating in the work of Stephen Lockner, marked by gentleness even in its Calvaries. Elegant figures in delicate linear pattern on sumptuous gold grounds are attributed anonymously to the Master of the St. Ursula Legend, Master of the St. Bartholomew Altarpiece, the Veronica Master. Lochner from S Germany (fl. 1430) placed heavier figures within landscapes. The realism of Netherlandish artists destroyed the delicacy of the Cologne School in the 16th century. BIBLIOGRAPHY: F. J. Mather, *Western European Painting of the Renaissance* (1948).

[M. J. DALY]

COLOMAN, ST. (Colman; d. 1012), Irish pilgrim to the Holy Land who in passing through Stockerau near Vienna had the misfortune to be taken for a spy; he was tortured and hanged from a tree. His cult began almost immediately after his death and spread through the south of Germany, Austria, and Hungary. Many shrines and chapels were built in his honor, and his help was invoked by young women looking for a good husband, by farmers for the blessing of their animals, and by all for protection against pestilence. BIBLIOGRAPHY: C. Marcora, BiblSanct 4:96–97; Butler 4:105.

[P. K. MEAGHER]

COLOMBE, JEAN (fl. 1467–1519), French miniaturist. In Bourges (1467), C. worked later for Charlotte and Charles I, both of Savoy. One of the first northern artists to use classical borders and architectural details in Renaissance style, C.'s reputation is proven in the commission to complete the magnificent *Très riches heures* of the Duc de Berry and the *Apocalypse*. His work is a worthy addenda to the masterly designs of Pol de Limbourg. BIBLIOGRAPHY: H. M. R. Martin, *Les Miniaturistes français* (1906).

[M. J. DALY]

COLOMBE, MICHEL (c. 1431–c. 1519), important 16th-cent. French sculptor. C.'s tomb of Francis II, duke of Brittany (Nantes cathedral) shows an Italian late Gothic style in reclining effigies *(gisants)* with Burgundian Virtues at the corners. His *St. George Slaying the Dragon* (1508–09, Louvre) from a château at Gaillon further attests to C.'s assimilation of the Italian Renaissance style into his native tradition. BIBLIOGRAPHY: A. Blunt, *Art and Architecture in France* (1954).

[M. J. DALY]

COLOMBIA, in area third largest of the countries of South America, rich in natural resources, bordered by Brazil, Ecuador, Venezuela, Peru, and Panama. Originally named the New Kingdom of Granada (until 1819), Colombia drew Spanish missionary activity from its earliest colonization in 1509. Though the colonization was the work of the Spanish crown, it was the missionary who became the agent of civilization as well as of Christianization. Natives were gathered into settlements and given churches, schools, and hospitals. The missionary taught them new industries and crafts, opened new roads, and fostered commerce. Above all, it was the missionary who defended the Indians against the cruelty and exploitation of the Spanish encomenderos (holders of land grants). The religious orders played a definitive role in civilizing and evangelizing the natives. Augustinians, Franciscans, Dominicans, Mercedarians, Jesuits, and Capuchins all came to New Granada in the 16th century. Famed missioners were St. Louis Bertrand, St. Peter Claver, the Augustinians Francisco Romero and Agustín de la Coruña, the Jesuits Alonso de Sandoval, José Gumilla and Juan Ribero. The work of the orders and the secular clergy wrought great numbers of converts to Christianity. There were serious obstacles: the doctrine of Catholicism was difficult for natives to understand and the moral code even more painful to a people whose morality was less demanding. The scandal of the Spanish conduct toward the Indians belied the doctrine of the Church. A problem also was the multiplicity of Indian dialects. It should be noted, however, that forced conversion was never approved in Colombia. The early flourishing period for missionary activity was damaged by the increasing interference of the crown, by dissension among religious orders, and rivalry between bishops and the communities of men religious. By mid-18th cent. the orders were completely frustrated by the royal decrees. Ironically, the wealth that the Church had acquired largely by royal patronage became a source of envy to the Spanish government. From then on the government-supported diocesan clergy dominated. This is not to assert that episcopal and diocesan influence was not a substantial contribution in Colombia. The first dioceses were founded in Santa Marta and Cartagena in 1534. A celebrated defender of the Indians was the first bp. of Popayán (established in 1546). Bp. Zapata de Cárdenas of Santafé de Bogotá ordained Creoles and mestizos, much to the chagrin of local authorities, who were reluctant to accept them. In the 19th cent. Colombia became an independent republic and the disestablishment of the Church followed as did a period of conflict and persecution. Concordats were concluded with the Holy See in 1887 and 1892. The Church is recognized as the custodian of the religion of the majority of Colombians and receives subsidization. The latter half of the 20th cent., esp. since Vatican Council II, shows the Church in Colombia, as in other countries of Latin America, facing challenges from communism and Pentecostals. It may be said that these forces and the thrust of Vatican II, as well as major encyclicals of John XXIII and Paul VI, have given new directions in the political and social order to the Church in Colombia. Not as quick to move in other directions as Chile, Colombia has shown distinct progress and greater awareness of the problems of contemporary society. The population numbers more than 23 million, of whom 95% are Catholics. There is a vigorous organization of the Church in Colombia. In 1975 there were in the country 9 archdioceses, 30 dioceses, 9 vicariates and 7 prefectures; with a total of 2,079 parishes. BIBLIOGRAPHY: E. Ryan, *Church in the South American Republics* (1943); *Roman Catholic Church in Colonial Latin America* (ed. R. Greenleaf, 1971); I. Vallier, *Catholicism, Social Control, and Modernization in Latin America* (1970).

[J. R. AHERNE]

COLOMBIÈRE, CLAUDE DE LA, BL., see LA COLOMBIÈRE, CLAUDE DE, BL.

COLONIALISM, ECONOMIC, foreign domination of politically independent countries through control of their economic life; sometimes called neo-colonialism. Until the 1960s struggles against colonialism largely focused on efforts to gain political autonomy for the various countries whose governments remained under the control of European colonial powers. But after large numbers of these countries had secured formal independence, it became apparent that economic considerations still prevented many of them from exercising real self-determination. Attention then shifted to dealing with those factors, and religious leaders concerned with issues of international justice have pressed the affluent countries to accept corrective measures.

Newly independent nations often found substantial portions of their natural resources and basic industries controlled by private corporations owned and based in Europe or North America. Often a country's export earnings came principally from one or two minerals or agricultural commodities, and their production and marketing often lay in foreign hands. With this degree of economic control, foreign interests could often bring political coercion to bear on the national leadership.

Poor countries of Asia, Africa, and Latin America also found themselves subject to economic colonialism because of their shortage of capital. Development of their economies usually required the infusion of outside capital in large quantities. These funds normally had to come from Europe and North America, and the necessity of meeting lender criteria could put a country in a dependency relationship. This could develop whether loans came from private sources or from governments of the richer countries. And when governments of the lending countries worked in concert with private economic interests, officials of a poor country could find their freedom greatly restricted.

As a third factor reinforcing effects of the others, markets where developing countries secured their foreign exchange earnings tended to lie in the same areas from which came loans of capital and the controlling decisions of international corporations.

To counteract these pressures, developing countries have sometimes nationalized foreign-owned industries, or placed restrictions on the degree of control that foreign corporations could exercise over local business. Developing countries have also found strength in unity, and by working together politically through the United Nations and other channels have exerted pressures for a new international economic order. As the major powers have competed for influence in the Third World, the poorer countries have also found themselves at times in a position to play one against another.

In a parallel move, Churches of former colonial areas have sought to reduce the control that foreign mission agencies could exercise through allocation of funds even when mission Churches had gained formal autonomy.

[T. EARLY]

COLONNA, a noble Roman family of which the early history belongs to fable rather than to history. The authentic pedigree begins *c.* 1100 with Pietro, the lord of Columna, the ancestor of three branches, Palestrina, Gallicano, and Gelazzono. Their shield displays a column; part of the reputed pillar at which Christ was scourged was brought back from the Holy Land by Giovanni Colonna (d. 1244), cardinal legate during the Fifth Crusade, and placed in his titular church, St. Praxedes.

The family history falls into two periods, before and after 1562, the date of their final reconciliation with the temporal power of the papacy. Until then the story was one of opposition, often turbulent, at first to *Guelf policies, and afterwards to the extension of papal rule in Central Italy exemplified in the projects of the *Borgia. The Colonna Pope, *Martin V (d. 1431), with whom the Great Schism was healed, marks the dividing line between their *Ghibelline period and afterwards.

Too much should not be made of their political theory of Church and State; it was largely a matter of defending and extending their economic and feudal rights against a centralizing force. It was not that they questioned the spiritual power of the pope, but that they possessed the independent resources, the spirit, and the resilience to maintain their resistance to his civil power and to conduct their hereditary feud with the *Orsini and Gaetani who supported him: in this they could count on the support of the Roman populace, and, when need served, on that of emperor and later, of the *regalist power of France. This phase culminated in the violent scene at Anagni (1303) when Sciarra Colonna insulted Boniface VIII (a Gaetani and no mean antagonist), and would have killed him on the spot.

Frequently defeated and disgraced, the family manifested unusual powers of recovery and would be as often reinstated. Even during their time of bad relations with the papacy, the Colonna contributed cardinals to the Church: of these the most considerable was another Giovanni (d. 1348), learned, public-spirited, and the friend of Petrarch. Pope Martin V did most to enrich the fortunes of his family, which after his time tended more and more to be part of the establishment, though on occasion capable of armed rebellion until close to the end of the 15th cent.; as when Marco Antonio II (d. 1584) successfully asserted his claims against *Paul IV by marching on Rome with the Duke of Alba. Less than 13 years later the breach was permanently closed when *Pius V appointed him to command the papal galleys, and he served as lieutenant to Don John of Austria at the victory of Lepanto, 1571.

The family gradually became domesticated at the papal court; its head, and that of the Orsini, were created hereditary princes in attendance at the throne, and in two centuries there were 12 Colonna cardinals. The official saint in the family is Bl. Margaret, a Poor Clare (d. 1290). The great Augustinian doctor, *Giles of Rome (d. 1316), is sometimes called Colonna; he may have been kin, but his papalism certainly did not accord with the attitudes of the family. BIBLIOGRAPHY: P. D. Torre, EncCatt 4:14–21; NCE 3, 1027–29.

[T. GILBY]

COLORADO, a Rocky Mountain state, admitted to the Union (1876) as the 38th state. Chipped flints found in the area suggest the presence of a culture perhaps 20,000 years old, while artifacts at the Mesa Verde site indicate a highly developed culture in the period 1000 A.D.–1300 A.D. Spaniards were the first Europeans to reach Colorado. Coronado crossed the SE portion of the area in 1541, and by the 18th cent. Spanish Franciscans had established missions in Colorado.

A gold rush in 1859 led to a major increase in population and the creation at Denver of a vicariate apostolic for Colorado and Utah. Joseph Machebeuf, a missionary, was named as the first vicar (1868) and became the first bp. when the Diocese of Denver was created (1887). There were then 40,000 Catholics in Colorado served by 59 priests in 49 churches and 85 missions. Machebeuf's successor was Nicholas Chrysostom Matz, who served from 1889 until his death in 1917. Matz convened the first diocesan synod, erected the Cathedral of the Immaculate Conception, and increased educational facilities. The third bp. John Henry Tihen, expanded St. Thomas Seminary, unified charitable works, and supported the development of the *Register,* a national weekly edited by Matthew Smith. During the 1920's the bp. also concerned himself with the power of the *Ku Klux Klan. Tihen's successor was Urban J. Vehr, who became the first abp. of Denver when it was made a metropolitan see in 1941. Its suffragan sees are the Dioceses of Pueblo, Colorado and Cheyenne, Wyoming. Colorado's population of 2,201,985, more than 60% urban, makes it the 28th most populous state in the Union. In 1975 Catholics numbered 408,678, or 16.3% of the total state population. The main Protestant bodies are the Methodists, with 4.7% of the total population (1971), and the Presbyterians, with 2.7%. The Jewish population (1968) was 25,140, or 1.14%. Of the five church-related colleges in Colorado (1973) two were Catholic institutions located in the archdiocese of Denver. BIBLIOGRAPHY: L. R. R. Hofen, *Colorado Story* (1953); W. H. Jones, *History of Catholic Education in the State of Colorado* (1955); D. W. Johnson et al., *Churches and Church Membership in U.S.* (1974).

[J. L. MORRISON; R. M. PRESTON]

COLORBASOS (Colarbasos; 2d cent.), Gnostic of the school of *Valentinus. Irenaeus (*Adv. haer.* 1.12.3), who also speaks of Colorbasians, is the primary source, but his information is vague. Apparently Pythagorean astrology and numerology figured prominently in C.'s teaching. BIBLIOGRAPHY: G. Bareille, DTC 3:378–380; H. Rahner, LTK 6:399–400.

[L. G. MÜLLER]

COLORS, LITURGICAL, the colors of the vestments worn at the celebration of Mass. The vestments used at Mass give, by their color, some expression to the significance of the mysteries of faith and to the special occasions on which Mass is celebrated. In the new liturgy the wish of the RC Church has been expressed to retain the traditional colors, but some changes have been introduced. White is used in the Easter and Christmas seasons, on feasts and commemorations of the Lord, excepting those of his Passion; on feasts and memorials of Mary, the angels, and the saints who were not martyrs, as well as on All Saints (Nov. 1), John the Baptist (June 24), John the Evangelist (Dec. 27), the Chair of St. Peter (Feb. 22), and the Conversion of Paul (Jan. 25). Red is used on Passion Sunday (or, as it was formerly called, Palm Sunday), Good Friday, on celebrations of the Passion, on the feasts of the Apostles and Evangelists other than John, and on feasts of martyrs.

Green is used in Masses of ordinary time. Violet is used in Lent and Advent, except on Gaudete Sunday in Advent and Laetare Sunday in Lent, when rose-colored vestments may be used instead. For Masses for the dead, white, black, or purple vestments may be used. Less stress is laid upon unvarying conformity to the proper color of the day, and on special occasions, where handsomer vestments are available, they may be used even when they do not conform to the color of the day. (See Sacramentary of 1974, in its General Instructions of the Roman Missal, ch. 6.) In the Eastern Churches a system of prescribed colors for each liturgical day does not exist. The Byzantines have a custom of wearing vestments that are white on feast days, red in Lent and other times of mourning and penance, and black for liturgies of the presanctified. The custom, however, does not have the force of law. The Coptic Church recognizes white as the only liturgical color, but even the Copts sometimes use other colors.

[P. K. MEAGHER]

COLOSSAE, a city in SW Asia Minor. At the time of the Persian Empire, Colossae had been a populous city, but in the 1st cent. A.D. it lost its former splendor. It was situated in the fertile valley of the Lycus river about 10 mi from the sister cities of Laodicea and Hierapolis, and like them was a Phrygian city belonging to the Roman proconsular province of Asia. The great trade route to the E from Ephesus (125 mi from Colossae) to the Euphrates passed at Colossae. The city was abandoned in the 8th cent. and the site has not yet been excavated. BIBLIOGRAPHY: S. E. Johnson, "Laodicea and Its Neighbors," *Biblical Archaeologist* 13 (1950) 1–18.

[J. E. LUSSIER]

COLOSSEUM, see AMPHITHEATER.

COLOSSIANS, EPISTLE TO THE, the 12th book of the NT canon. Pauline authorship of this epistle, first contested in the 19th cent. on literary and theological grounds, is now accepted by the great majority of NT scholars. The epistle's peculiarities of vocabulary and style (e.g., 34 *hapax legomena,* lengthy sentences, frequent use of the participle, synonyms and parallel clauses) are matched in recognized Pauline letters, such as Romans and Philippians. Unusual words, like "philosophy" (2.8), "divinity" (2.9), and "despoiling" (2.15), are easily explained by the religious subject-matter of the letter. The high Christology of Colossians (1.15–20), that expresses the divinity of Christ in ineluctable terms and states Him to be the agent of creation as well as its principle of unity, is an authentic development of earlier Pauline reflection (cf. 1 Cor 8.6; 10.4; 2 Cor 5.19; Rom 8.38–39). The epistle's Christological expression was occasioned by the infiltration into the Colossian community of a concept of angelic spirits whose power over men required neutralization by a cult paid to them (2.9, 15). In this context the epistle articulates the absolute preeminence of Christ, deriving from traditional Christian faith in His divine person and redemptive role, over all creation. It asserts that this preeminence of Christ is unveiled in Christian baptism. Baptism places in the Christian the power of Christ to reconcile man with God (2.11–15). Consequently, liturgical and ascetical practices that do not reflect and draw upon the redemptive power of Christ are to be repudiated (2.16–3.4). In the judgment of NT scholars these data suggest that the religious ideas and practices combatted in Colossians originated in pagan and Jewish influences, introduced into the community probably by gentile converts, that were in process of being synthesized into a kind of Gnosticism. The epistle confronts this incipient intrusion into Christian faith in a calm spirit but with a firm emphasis on the all-sufficiency of Christ. After the customary greeting and thanksgiving (1.1–8), the letter offers a prayer for the spiritual well-being of the community (1.9–14) that stresses the redemptive function of Christ. After its development of the preeminence of Christ, won through the cross (1.15–20), it reminds the Colossians of their reconciliation through Him (1.21–23) and of the author's apostolic responsibility to proclaim this mystery of Christ (1.24–2.5). It develops the theme of life in Christ, rejecting the worship of angelic beings and warning against inappropriate liturgical and ascetical practices (2.6–3.4). It concludes with moral exhortation (3.5–4.1) and with observations and greetings of a personal character (4.2–18). The mention of Aristarchus, Mark, Epaphras, Luke and Demas (4.10–14) links Colossians with the letter of Philemon in which the same group is mentioned (23–24), indicating that these letters were composed by Paul at about the same time. Scholars have debated whether Colossians was written at Rome, Caesarea, or Ephesus; the balance of probability favors Rome during Paul's first imprisonment there, A.D. 59–61. BIBLIOGRAPHY: D. Guthrie, *New Testament Introduction* (1961); Wikenhauser NTI; P. Feine et al., *Einleitung in das Neue Testament* (1964).

[C. P. CEROKE]

COLOSSUS, term referring to any very large statue, but esp. to the bronze Helios (sun god) 105 feet over the harbor of Rhodes, one of the seven wonders of the world, erected 280 B.C. by Chares of Lindos, pupil of Lysippus, and destroyed in 224 B.C. by earthquake. BIBLIOGRAPHY: G. M. A. Richter, *Sculpture and Sculptors of the Greeks* (1957).

[M. J. DALY]

COLUM, PADRAIC (1881–1972), Irish-American poet, playwright, essayist. With Lady Gregory, C. was instrumental in the foundation of the Abbey Theatre in Ireland. He came to the U.S. for the first time in 1914 where, with his wife Mary, he was associated with various literary circles. Mary's *Life and the Dream* (1947) may be considered a source book of that period. C.'s own works include *Wild Earth,* a volume of poems, and *The King of Ireland's*

Son. BIBLIOGRAPHY: Z. Bowen, *Padraic Colum: A Biographical-Critical Introduction* (1970).

[R. M. FUNCHION]

COLUMBA OF IONA, ST. (Colum, Columkille; 521–597), Irish monastic founder and abbot, poet, and hymnodist. Educated at Moville and at Clonard, C. established in the year he was ordained (551) a monastery at Derry, and again in Ireland, one at Durrow. With 12 disciples on the island of Iona, he set up a center for the pacification and conversion of the Picts, the Scots, and the Northumbrians. Called the "Apostle of Caledonia," he is greatly revered by the Scottish people. Reputed author of numerous poems in Gaelic and Latin, he composed also three hymns, one presumably the *Altus Prosator*. His life is well attested by Ven. Bede and by the abbots of Iona, Cuimine Ailbe and Adamnan. Though C. left no rule, Adamnan in his *Vita Columbae* describes well the life of the monks. BIBLIOGRAPHY: P. Corish, BiblSanct 4:126–128; Butler 2:506–509; A. M. Tommasini, EncCatt 3:1995–96.

[M. R. BROWN]

COLUMBA OF RIETI, BL. (1467–1501), Dominican tertiary, patroness of Perugia. Having vowed virginity, C. lived as a recluse and at 19 became a Dominican tertiary. She founded the convent of St. Catherine in Perugia (1490). Civic rulers and members of the hierarchy sought her advice and she gained fame as a peacemaker. BIBLIOGRAPHY: Butler 2:359–361; M. H. Laurent, DHGE 13:322–323; A. Blasucci, BiblSanct 4:101–103.

[M. J. FINNEGAN]

COLUMBA AND POMPOSA, SS. (d. 853), virgin martyrs of Córdoba. Having witnessed to Christ and renounced belief in the prophet Mohammed before Muslim authorities, Columba was martyred. Her body was recovered by Christians from the Guadalquivir River and buried in a basilica outside Córdoba. In imitation of her sister, Pomposa repeated Columba's profession of faith in the presence of a cadi and was also slain. Her body was likewise recovered from the river and buried at the feet of Columba. By 1583 both names were included in the Roman martyrology. BIBLIOGRAPHY: E. P. Colbert, *Martyrs of Córdoba* (1962) 850–859; Butler 3:580.

[J. BLAIR]

COLUMBAN, ST. (*c.* 543–615), Irish monk, also known as Columbanus or Columba the Younger. Born at Leinster, Ireland, he studied at the school of St. Sinell, a disciple of St. Finnian of Clonard, and then entered the monastery and school of St. Comgall at Bangor. After teaching several years he went *c.* 590 with 12 companions to do missionary work on the Continent. At the invitation of the Merovingian King Childebert he settled in Burgundy, establishing monasteries at Annegray, Luxeuil, and Fontaines, for which he composed a rule. Vigorously attacking the moral practices of the local clergy, court, and general populace, he introduced the strict system of Irish penance, and generally supported traditions of the Celtic Church. After censuring King Theuderic for living in concubinage, he was expelled from Burgundy in 610. He settled near Zurich among the Alemanni, but was driven out in 612. He then crossed the Alps and founded a monastery at *Bobbio, which became an important center of learning and from which his influence passed throughout Europe. His writings continued to be influential in the literature of the Middle Ages, though the rigor of his monastic rule was softened by Benedictine influence. Authorship of a penitential rule commonly attributed to him has been questioned by some modern scholars. He died at Bobbio and is buried there at the Church of St. Columbanus. BIBLIOGRAPHY: M. Dubois, *Saint Columban* (1961); Butler 4:409–413; C. Poggi, BiblSanct 4:108–120.

[T. EARLY]

COLUMBAN, RULE OF ST., monastic regulations ascribed to the early 7th-cent. Irish monk St. Columba the Younger; his authorship is questioned. The rule consists of two parts: the first lays down the general principles on which monastic life is based; the second prescribes the penalties for various offenses against the rule. The Columbanian Rule was adopted by about 40 monasteries of the period, both of men and women. However, because of its Celtic austerity, the Rule of St. Columba was supplanted even in his own monasteries by that of St. Benedict.

[A. R. ZINK]

COLUMBAN FATHERS, St. Columban's Foreign Mission Society (SSC) was founded in Ireland in 1917. Bp. Edward Galvin and Father John Blowick organized a committee to get permission to train secular priests as missionaries for China. Late in 1918 an American headquarters was established in Omaha and is now at St. Columbans, Nebraska. In 1920, the Columbans set up a third headquarters in Melbourne, Australia and have since established missions in the Philippines, Korea, Burma, Japan, Fiji, Peru and Chile. They staff mission parishes and schools, operate clinics and hospitals and direct self-help projects of various kinds. Between 1920 and until their expulsion in 1954, more than 200 Columban Fathers served in China. During World War II and the Communist revolution, Columbans endured persecutions and imprisonment. Two lost their lives to Red terrorists. In 1977, the Society numbered 1,075 priests and brothers who care for more than 30 million souls. BIBLIOGRAPHY: R. Reilly, *Christ's Exile: Life of Bishop Edward J. Galvin* (1958).

[A. R. ZINK]

COLUMBUS, CHRISTOPHER (1451–1506), seaman, chartmaker, navigator, discoverer of America. Possessing a rare ability to acquire knowledge through observation and experience, C. demonstrated an eminent degree of competence as a seaman and navigator during his four famous voyages to the New World. His confidence in his own ability as a navigator, combined with ignorance of the enormous distance involved, led him to chart a westward voyage to Asia. With the help of Juan Pérez, a Franciscan priest, he won the support of Queen Isabella of Spain. With three small vessels and a total of 90 men he set out from Palos, Spain, August 3, 1492. Despite the fears and threats of his crew, he continued the journey and eventually sighted the island of San Salvador Oct. 12, 1492. Subsequent voyages brought him to the islands of Dominica, Trinidad, and Martinique. He believed that the islands were part of Japan and died not knowing he had discovered a new world. His discoveries not only gave Spain an empire and extended Christian civilization but opened up the vast reaches of new continents to Western Europe. BIBLIOGRAPHY: F. Colón, *Life of the Admiral Christopher Columbus* (ed. and tr. B. Keen, 1959); S. E. Morison, *Admiral of the Ocean Sea* (1942).

[J. BLAIR]

COMB, LITURGICAL, a hair comb made of ivory, metal, or wood, used extensively in the liturgy of the Middle Ages. Today the comb is used only at the ordination of a bishop to smooth his hair after the chrism has been wiped away.

[K. O'NEILL]

COMBEFIS, FRANÇOIS (1605–79), French Dominican patristic scholar. First a professor at Toulouse and Paris, from 1640 he devoted himself to research into patristic texts. In 1656 he was entrusted with an edition of the Greek Fathers commissioned by the Assembly of the French Clergy. Many excellent volumes, with text and critical notes, appeared in the following years. One, *Historia haeresis monothelitarum* (1648) was placed on the Index (1662), possibly because it was critical of the work of C. *Baronius. BIBLIOGRAPHY: A. Duval *Catholicisme* 2:1333–34.

[T. C. O'BRIEN]

COMBES, JUSTIN LOUIS ÉMILE (1835–1921), French anticlerical statesman. A French former seminarian and philosophy lecturer in several colleges, C. entered politics in 1875 and became a violent foe of the Catholic Church. He was minister of education in 1895–96 and premier combined with minister of cults (1902–05). A vigorous proponent of the Association Law of 1901, designed to suppress the religious orders, C. worked to abrogate the Concordat of 1801, an effort achieving success in 1905 with the law of separation of Church and state. C. was the author of *Une campagne laïque* (1904).

[J. R. AHERNE]

COMBONI, DANIELE (1831–81), Italian missionary, titular bp. of Claudiopolis, founder of two religious societies for the evangelization of Africa. Prepared by study of medicine and language and ordained in 1854, he worked from 1857 in Africa. He founded after 10 years the Verona Fathers (FSCJ) and in 1872 the Verona Sisters. In that same year C. was appointed pro-vicar apostolic of Central Africa. As vicar apostolic (1877) he set up missions from the Nubian desert, down through the Sudan (where he had to combat slave trading), on south to the Lakes of Tanganyika and Uganda. Besides other linguistic studies, C. published a Nubian dictionary; his correspondence and other writings are rich with observations on African civilization. The ordinary process for his beatification has begun. BIBLIOGRAPHY: A. Capovilla, EncCatt 4:40–41; *idem, Il servo di Dio D. Comboni* (1949).

[M. R. BROWN]

COMENIUS, JOHN AMOS (Komenski; 1592–1670), bp. of the *Unitas Fratrum (Unity of the Brethren) and pioneer educational reformer. Born in Moravia of a family belonging to the Unitas Fratrum, he was educated in schools of his Church, and at Herborn and Heidelberg. Returning to Moravia (1614), he combined teaching and writing books on education with pastoral service, having been ordained in 1616. Driven from Moravia by the Thirty Years' War, he headed the Brethren's schools in Lissa, Poland; he brought about pedagogical reforms in Sweden and Hungary. Civil War in England thwarted the plans for universal education he had projected with friends there. As a bp. in exile he helped his Church maintain episcopal succession, which was later transferred by his grandson to the Renewed *Moravian Church. C. spent his last years in Amsterdam, teaching and writing celebrated devotional and pedagogical works. BIBLIOGRAPHY: M. Spinka, *John Amos Comenius* (1940); ODCC 315.

[J. R. WEINLICK]

COMFORTER, THE, a title of the Holy Spirit found in liturgy and tradition. It is used in the sequence for Pentecost Sunday, "Come Holy Spirit." The Spirit is the Comforter because he brings rest, refreshment, relief, ease, and consolation.

[V. GILLIGAN]

COMGALL, ST. (*c*.520–*c*.602), Irish monastic founder. Under the guidance of St. Fintan of Clonenagh, C. was given an excellent training in both secular and religious subjects, which was important to him later as founder of the monastery of Bangor in Belfast. The quality education imparted to monks in Bangor included a life rich in piety and liturgy. As regards the monastic rule given by C. to his monks, it is not certain how far he was influenced by the Rule of St. Benedict. To his credit and that of his monks is due the spread of monasticism in the Irish Church. BIBLIOGRAPHY: A. Rimoldi, BiblSanct 4:131; Butler 2:270–271; Kenney 1:395–397.

[R. C. EGAN]

COMINES, PHILIPPE DE (Commynes; c.1446–c.1510), noble, diplomat, and memorialist. C. served Louis XI and Charles VIII in positions of high trust, thereby enriching himself while acquiring material for his eight books of *Mémoires*. This acute and profound study of kings and kingship anticipates Montaigne with its reflective manner based on personal observation. C.'s privileged access to the throne gives much precious detail to the work, a monument of early French prose. BIBLIOGRAPHY: *Memoirs of P. de Commines* (tr. A. R. Scoble, 2 v., 1855–56); G. Mattingly, *Renaissance Diplomacy* (1955, repr. 1964).

[J. P. WILLIMAN]

COMITOLI, PAOLO (1544–1626), Spanish Jesuit, who helped prepare a new edition of the *Septuagint (1587) commissioned by the Pope, and who as a moral theologian opposed *probabilism.

[T. C. O'BRIEN]

COMMA PIANUM, a phrase referring to a controversial issue connected with the history of *Jansenism; it concerns a comma missing from the censure in Pius V's bull, *Ex omnibus afflictionibus* (D 1980). The controversy centered on the phrase *in rigore et proprio verborum sensu ab assertoribus intento*; taken as preceded by a comma, therefore governing the words following, the phrase makes the censure apply to the propositions listed in the bull (D 1901–79) as heretical; taken as followed by a comma, thus governing the words preceding it, the phrase allows a sense in which the listed propositions are acceptable. C. *Jansen in *Augustinus* defended the second interpretation. The controversy became bitter in 1643 following the renewal of *Ex omnibus afflictionibus* by Urban VIII's *In eminenti,* which inserted the comma preceding the key phrase. Modern scholarship is that the placing of a comma after the disputed phrase is in accord with Pius V's own pastoral intent toward Michael *Baius, the author of the censured writings.

[T. C. O'BRIEN]

COMMANDERY, an individual or group in a position of authority over one or more knights of a military order. A commandery is part of a hierarchical structure and encompasses a certain geographical territory. The highest type of commandery is called a supreme commandery and is the central governing body of the semimilitary fraternal organization. Beneath it are grand commanderies which include local commanderies and district commanderies. BIBLIOGRAPHY: R. C. Noonan, NCE 8:221.

[H. P. ANNAS]

COMMANDMENTS, TEN, in summary form the moral framework for God's chosen people. The Ten Commandments (ten words, *decalogue, cf. Ex 34.28; Dt 4.13; 10.4) are found in Dt 5.6–21 and Ex 20.1–17. Of 20 variations in the two lists the principal difference is the motivation for the Sabbath rest: in imitation of God at creation (priestly tradi-

tion in Ex), or in remembrance of the deliverance from Egypt (deuteronomic tradition).

The decalogue's source has been disputed for a cent. J. Wellhausen's denial of its Mosaic authorship has since given way to the traditional acceptance of its antiquity and association with Moses and Sinai. S. Mowinckel proposed (1927) the cult as the origin for the literary type of the decalogue. The original cultic prescriptions were expanded to include general rules for admittance to God's people. A. Alt (1934) focused on the distinction between apodictic law (absolute, unconditional commands and prohibitions) and casuistic law (situationally oriented directives). The decalogue represented the exclusive claim of the Lord proclaimed to the people at the cultic celebration of the covenant. G. E. Mendenhall (1954) proposed the suzerainty treaties of the Hittite kings as extrabiblical parallels for apodictic law. W. Beyerlin has recently affirmed the connection between the suzerainty treaties and the Sinai and Exodus traditions. Yet the decalogue may be older than its cultic and extrabiblical settings. E. Gerstenberger maintains (1965) that the origins of the decalogue lie in the authoritative commandments of elders in the Semitic clan-association.

The content of the decalogue is limited. The first four commandments (three in the Catholic enumeration, traditional since Augustine and based on Dt) concern man's relationship with God. Monolatry (worship of only one God), not monotheism (there is only one God) is demanded. The last six commandments prescribe honor for one's parents and forbid arbitrary taking of human life, adultery (violation by a man of another man's wife or betrothed), kidnapping of a free Israelite, perjury and theft. Thus, the rights of the free Israelite were protected: his right to life, marriage, freedom, reputation and property.

Theologically, the giving of the decalogue represented another gracious act of God. Covenant and decalogue are so connected as God's gift and man's response that in the Commandments the covenant comes to expression. Their observance represents the obedience implicit in the covenant relationship of fidelity.

The decalogue is the heart of the moral teaching of the Torah. Originally this meant a comprehensive direction for living whose authority rested on its divine origin; only later did postexilic emphasis on law as means of salvation and mediator between man and God and the Septuagint translation of Torah as *nomos* restrict law to a list of prescriptions to be fulfilled. Nowhere in the OT is there any indication that the decalogue is supplanted, even though cultic and social prescriptions change. Jesus' attitude toward the law is one of honor and respect, for he came "not to abolish but to fulfill" the law and the prophets (Mt 5.17). He objected to the limitations men had placed upon God's commands regarding the Sabbath (Mt 5.21–43) and parents (Mk 7.9–13). His affirmation that the law extends also to internal attitudes and desires (Mt 5.17–48) and his prohibition of mere external conformity (Mt 6.1–7; 23.3–36) are explanations of the true meaning and scope of the law.

Paul's respect for the law is coupled with his condemnation of every attempt at self-justification through performance of the works commanded by the law (Rom ch. 4–5), even if it would be possible for any man to keep the whole law (Rom ch. 7). He denies that man is justified by keeping the law while he nowhere exempts the Christian from the demands of the decalogue.

Thomas Aquinas associated the moral precepts of the decalogue with the natural law (ThAq ST 1a2ae, 100.1, 3). The precepts are not always clear to every man (ThAq ST 1a2ae, 94.4,5; 100.8) because of the effects of sin and of man's developing knowledge of himself. The Ten Commandments do not stand alongside the command to love; they point to critical areas where the command to love must be given expression (cf. Mt 22.34–40; Rom 13.8–10; Gal 5.14; ThAq ST 1a2ae, 100.3 ad 1; 4 ad 1; 5 ad 1). Since they antedate the preaching of the prophets, the Ten Commandments do not emphasize social justice. Thus, for the Christian they can provide only a minimum moral guidance that must be augmented by Scripture, theology, and ethics. BIBLIOGRAPHY: J. J. Stamm and M. E. Nadrew, *Ten Commandments in Recent Research* (1967); W. Zimmerli, *Law and the Prophets* (1967); W. Beyerlin, *Origins and History of the Oldest Sinaitic Traditions* (1965); M. Noth, *Exodus—A Commentary* (1962); W. Gutbrod, Kittel TD (1967) s.v. *nomos*; C. H. Dodd, *Gospel and Law—The Relation of Faith and Ethics in Early Christianity* (1951).

[P. STENGER]

COMMANDMENTS OF THE CHURCH, in its widest sense, the laws by which people of God live in a communion of order with one another and with ecclesiastical authority. Thus all the canons of ecclesiastical law, both in and outside the Code or other authorized collection, could be considered the commandments of the Church. However, the expression is customarily taken to mean the precepts used in catechetical instruction and examination of conscience to remind the faithful of those obligations which are refinements and applications of the commandments of God. Thus the early collections, e.g., St. Antoninus' *Summa theologiae moralis* (1439) list ten in obvious imitation of the decalogue. St. Peter Canisius in his catechism a cent. later gave but five, as German catechisms still do. St. Robert Bellarmine's list of six (1589) was followed by the Italians, but the French subtracted the commandment on the payment of tithes. Catechisms in the U.S. by the directive of the Third Council of Baltimore (1886) follow a British enumeration of the 19th cent. thus: (1) to hear Mass on Sundays and holy days of obligation; (2) to fast and abstain on the days appointed; (3) to go to confession at least once a year; (4) to receive communion at Easter-time; (5) to contribute to the support of one's pastor; (6) not to marry within certain degrees of kindred, nor to solemnize marriage at forbidden times. BIBLIOGRAPHY: Davis MorPastTh 2:427–439.

[P. F. MULHERN]

COMMEMORATION, the former practice of adding *Collects to the Collect of the day. The Roman practice until the 10th cent. was one Collect for each Mass. The introduction of many Collects or Commemorations came from Gaul where it was felt that various saints' days or votive Masses should be mentioned in the principal Mass of the day. From about the 11th cent. onward the Roman rite also increased the number of Collects and Commemorations. This practice was retained until recent liturgical reforms. At present, only the Collect for the day is permitted. Feasts of the saints are now classified liturgically as "Memorials" or as "Optional Memorials" in the revised Roman Calendar.

[N. KOLLAR]

COMMENDATION, canonical term for bestowal of a *benefice in trust (thus, *in commendam*). The practice, mentioned from the time of St. Ambrose, was originally intended to provide for the care of a church, monastery, or diocese during the vacancy of its proper head. Soon, however, the emphasis was on the revenues accruing through commendation. Abuses were already rampant in the Carolingian era, and grew worse during the Middle Ages. Originally temporary, commendation became perpetual and even hereditary, contributed to the abuse of one person holding many benefices, to *simony, and to the decline of monastic discipline. In spite of efforts in the Council of Trent, the practice continued through the 18th and 19th centuries. In present RC church law the term *commenda* is described as a temporary granting of the revenues of a church or monastery to some person (CIC, c. 1412.5).

[T. C. O'BRIEN]

COMMENDATION OF A SOUL (COMMENDATIO ANIMAE), the prayers contained in the Roman Ritual for use at the bedside of a dying person. Originally the person whose soul was commended in this service was not dying but already dead, but since the 9th cent. the prayers have been offered for the soul before its departure. The 1972 Rite for the Pastoral Care of the Sick provides readings from the Scriptures that may be added or omitted according to circumstances. There are special prayers as death nears and for the moment after death occurs. BIBLIOGRAPHY: *Rites of the Catholic Church* (1976), 622–628.

[N. KOLLAR]

COMMENDATORY ABBOT, a person, lay or cleric, given a monastic *benefice to receive its revenues without performing its duties, also known as abbot *in commendam*. A common practice of the late Middle Ages, it was forbidden by the Council of *Trent, but continued into the 19th century. It was part of a wider practice of allotting benefices *in commendam* (in trust) during the absence of a titular authority—originally a temporary arrangement but later often a permanent financial expedient. *COMMENDATION.

[T. EARLY]

COMMENDONE, GIOVANNI FRANCESCO

(1524–84), cardinal, papal diplomat. After receiving his education at the Univ. of Padua, C. went to Rome in 1550 and entered the service of Pope Julius III. He was sent to London in 1553 on a secret mission to Queen Mary Tudor to evaluate the religious and political conditions in England, and the possibility of a Catholic restoration. Eight years later he traveled to N and W Germany extending an invitation to the followers of Luther to participate in the conciliar sessions at Trent. This untiring and zealous diplomat made a considerable contribution to the revival of the Catholic Church in central Europe. BIBLIOGRAPHY: A. M. Graziani, *De vita J. F. Commendoni* (1669, Fr. tr. 1694).

[J. BLAIR]

COMMENTATOR, LITURGICAL,

a cleric or layman appointed to explain the rites and prayers of the liturgy to the faithful and to direct and lead them in their participation. The office of commentator was introduced into the liturgy in the 20th cent. when the liturgical movement was directing attention to the need of a more active and intelligent participation on the part of the faithful. Historical precedent for the office was claimed in the directives given to the faithful by the deacon in many rites, and the office has been seen as a practical fulfillment of the Council of Trent's injunction that the faithful be instructed during Mass about what they witness in the liturgy (D 1745). The office of commentator was expressly recognized by Vatican Council II (Vat II SacLit 29; 35.3) and more detailed instructions were given for the proper performance of the functions of the office in the 1964 *Instruction for Implementing the Constitution on the Liturgy*. The commentator's explanations of what is taking place should be brief, prepared in writing, and so delivered that they will not prove to be a distraction. As the faithful become more familiar with the liturgy, less explanation is necessary, but the commentator's responsibility in directing and leading the response of the faithful remains important. BIBLIOGRAPHY: Podhradsky, 60–61; F. R. McManus, NCE 4:10.

[N. KOLLAR]

COMMINATION,

a threatening or menacing; a term for the theological classification of *prophecy. St. Thomas Aquinas speaks of a prophecy of predestination and a prophecy of commination. The first is the foretelling of the blessings to be given in God's dispensation of graces for salvation; the second promises divine punishments for sin. The first expresses the divine, infallible foreknowledge of God's willed plan of salvation and is always fulfilled. The prophecy of commination reflects God's foreknowledge of the systems and relationships of created causes (ThAq ST 1a, 14.7, 13); that knowledge extends to changes dependent on variable conditions among created causes. The prophecy of commination, therefore, is not always fulfilled, esp. because of man's repentance over the actions for which punishment was threatened. BIBLIOGRAPHY: ThAq ST 2a2ae, 171.6 ad 2; 174.1; also 1a, 19.7 ad 2.

[T. C. O'BRIEN]

COMMINGLING

(commixture), the dropping of a piece of the consecrated bread into the consecrated wine in the chalice after the breaking of the bread at Mass, at which time the priest prays (*Haec commixtio . . .*) "May this mingling of the body and blood of Our Lord Jesus Christ bring eternal life to us who receive it." The practice is a remnant of the papal liturgy (8th cent.) when the pope before his communion, broke off a piece of his host and dropped it into the chalice. It is also a continuance of the ancient custom of the *fermentum. The action and accompanying words have no deep symbolic value. Secondarily the term refers to the mixing of the water with wine at the preparation of the gifts at the Offertory, with the priest praying "By the mystery of this water and wine may we come to share in the divinity of Christ, who humbled himself to share in our humanity."

COMMISSARIAT OF THE HOLY LAND,

a Franciscan monastery with special responsibility for the Holy Land. There are commissariats in some 33 countries in the world. Commissariats promote interest in the Holy Land, collect money for support of the holy places, and train missioners to work there. In the U.S. the principal commissariat is the Monastery of the Holy Sepulcher in Washington, D.C. The commissary there is elected by the Franciscan general council in Rome, and the monastery is directly subject to the custodian of the holy places in Jerusalem.

[J. R. AHERNE]

COMMISSARY APOSTOLIC,

delegate commissioned by the pope to take evidence and pass judgment or to administer a special matter in the pope's name. Today he is usually a cardinal living in Rome who judges the appeal of a special case. No appeal of his decision can be made except to the pope.

[J. BLAIR]

COMMISSARY PROVINCIAL,

provincial superior of the Friars Minor and Conventuals when the group of friars he governs is not sufficiently numerous to form a province. He is dependent on an established province. In cases in which he is not dependent upon a province but has his authority immediately from the minister general of the order, he is called a commissary general.

[H. P. ANNAS]

COMMISSION FOR CATHOLIC MISSIONS AMONG THE COLORED PEOPLE AND THE INDIANS.

Authorized by the Third Plenary Council of Baltimore (1884) and formally organized (1886) by Card. Gibbons, the commission aids, through an annual collection in the U.S., Indians in 43, and blacks in 83 dioceses ($2,606,000 provided in 1974). The major Indian population of Catholics is in Arizona, New Mexico, South

Dakota, and Montana, esp. on the reservations; approximately 10,000 live in Alaska. For predominantly black congregations 680 churches are maintained. The abps. of Baltimore, Philadelphia, and New York head the commission, which has headquarters in Washington, D.C.

[M. R. BROWN]

COMMISSION OF REGULARS, a royal commission established in France in 1766 at the suggestion of the Assembly of the Clergy for the purpose of regulating religious orders in France. It was composed of five abps. and five lay councilors. A great mass of information was assembled providing evidence of the decadence of some religious orders and houses in France. In the light of this, regulations of various sorts were issued under royal authority. The commission suppressed some orders and houses in France, and some houses it strengthened by uniting in them members of weaker communities. It went so far as to demand that orders having generalates in Rome revise their constitutions to bring them into accord with the new regulations. In 1780 the commission was replaced by the Commission of Unions, which in turn gave way to the Bureau of Regulars in 1784. This was abolished in 1790. BIBLIOGRAPHY: J. McManners, *French Revolution and the Church* (1969, repr. 1970) 5–18.

[R. A. TODD]

COMMISSIONS, PAPAL, permanent bodies established by papal authority to operate in certain areas of concern to the Church. Among the commissions are several that pertain to Italy (Ecclesiastical Archives, Sacred Archeology, and Sacred Art). Other commissions have a worldwide or continental scope. The Pontifical Commission for Historical Science, established in 1954, promotes international historical scholarship and represents the Vatican on the International Committee of Historical Science. The Pontifical Commission for Latin America was established by Pius XII in 1958, and its work is important to the Church's current ministry of justice and evangelization in Latin America. Several commissions stand as implementations of decrees of Vatican Council II. Dating from 1902 in the pontificate of Leo XIII, the Pontifical Biblical Commission was reorganized in 1971 by Paul VI and its work coordinated with that of the Congregation for the Doctrine of the Faith. The Pontifical Commission for the New Vulgate was organized in 1965 by Paul VI to give the Church a critical text of the Latin Bible based on the fruits of modern scholarship. The Council of the Laity, established in 1967 to implement the decree on the apostolate of the laity, n.26, was given the title "Pontifical" in 1976. Also established in 1967, in response to Vat II ChModWorld n.90, was the Pontifical Commission for Justice and Peace. The work of the Commission for the Revision of the Code of Canon Law, established by John XXIII in 1963, its work has proceeded along the pastoral guidelines laid down in the Council. The Commission for the Revision of the Oriental Code of Canon Law was established by Paul VI in 1972. The Commission for

Social Communications, whose origins go back to the Commission for Educational Cinematography of Pius XII, 1948, is concerned with carrying out the conciliar decree on the media and covers church issues involving all the media. The Commission for the Family was created in 1973 to study social, moral, and spiritual problems of family life.

[J. R. AHERNE]

COMMITMENT, an act of committing oneself to a cause or a course of action. This is a relatively new understanding of the term. From its still common meaning of a legal warrant to place someone in custody, it later entered religious (mainly Protestant) literature as fidelity to Christ. In current usage, it means spiritual dedication on a permanent basis to a way of life that demands above-average generosity and requires more than ordinary grace of God.

The spiritual dedication implies religious motivation or a religious cause. Its permanency is implicit in that to which a person commits himself, e.g., the Christian faith, marriage, celibacy. Since commitment involves the whole person, its proper object is a way of life. In religious language a man commits himself only to what will engage his entire personality, i.e., a way of life, and only by an extension of the term can it be applied to anything less comprehensive.

Theologically, commitment is the human response to a divine vocation. The biblical term call (Lat., *vocare;* Gr. *kaleō*) from God or Christ is correlative with commitment, which in Scripture is most often expressed by "follow" or "go along with" *(sequi* and *akoloutheō).* Thus commitment is man's free acceptance of God's invitation to follow him in generosity of spirit. It suggests a degree of loyalty not expected of everyone, since it presupposes a divine election. God chooses whom he wills, and he assures the one called the graces he will need. Christianity itself requires such commitment of all who would follow Christ, in contrast to those who are either not actually called or are unwilling to respond. Within Christianity are further commitments, e.g., to monogamy in marriage and service in the priesthood. And within these states of life may be other commitments according to the dispositions of Providence and a man's willingness to "go along with" the divine invitation received. BIBLIOGRAPHY: K. Rahner, *Christian Commitment* (tr. C. Hastings, 1963); OED 2:683–684.

[J. A. HARDON]

COMMIXTURE, see COMMINGLING.

COMMODIANUS, (fl. mid-3d cent.?), Christian Latin poet whose dates and places of origin and activity are uncertain. Theological peculiarities in his poems such as *Millenarianism and *Patripassianism, as well as his references to persecution, suggest an early date that would justify the claim sometimes made that he was the earliest Christian Latin poet. But the metrical and stylistic properties of his poetry are characteristic of a much later time. (The rhythm is governed by word accent and number of syllables rather than by quantity.) Two of his works are extant: his *Instructions,* divided into two books, the first of which is a denunciation of Jews and pagans, and the second a series of moral exhortations addressed to different categories of Christians; and his *Carmen apologeticum,* which urges conversion on Jews and pagans and ends with a celebrated description of the end of the world. The reading of the works of C. was proscribed in the *Gelasian Decree (PL 59:163). Works: PL 5:201–262; critical ed. B. Dombart, CSEL 15 (1887). BIBLIOGRAPHY: Altaner 485–486.

[R. B. ENO]

COMMODUS (161–192), ROMAN EMPEROR.

Though aware of his son's cruel and dissolute nature, Commodus' father, Marcus Aurelius, destined him as his successor by conferring highest honors upon him. In 177, e.g., he was named consul, *pontifex maximus,* and Augustus. After the death of Marcus (180) Commodus made peace with the Sarmatians and began to enjoy to the full the pleasures of Rome. An abortive attempt on his life in 182 and the intoxication of power deranged his already unstable mind. Rome was renamed *Colonia Commodiana,* and he himself took the title of *Hercules Romanus* in the belief that he was the reincarnation of that legendary hero. Because of his excesses he was poisoned by his concubine and the prefect of the guard, and when this proved ineffective, strangled by an athlete with whom he used to exercise. In contrast to his personal life the empire during his reign was largely at peace and even the Christians were but little molested. BIBLIOGRAPHY: J. Straub, RAC 3:252–266.

[M. J. COSTELLOE]

COMMON GOOD

(Lat., *bonum commune;* Gr. *koinón agathón),* an ambiguous term in moral and social theory, the meaning of which is not always immediately apparent from the context of an argument. Broadly speaking its meanings fall into three classes; the first and second are variously nuanced, and with some writers shade off into one another: (1) a collective notion signifying the good of a whole to which the parts are subservient; (2) a more distributive notion according to which the good proper to a group is communicated in differing degrees to its members; (3) a causal notion which sees all widespread particular goods as flowing from one single and common principle that comprehends them all. In the following consideration of these notions in turn, it should be understood that the treatment is extremely simplified, and that none of the titles for ideologies is used in a pejorative sense.

The Collective Notion. If the social whole, whether it be a caste, a class, a nation, a people, a State, a religion, or even all of mankind, be considered as constituting one single person or organism, then its good will be so far paramount that the individual parts composing it will be just tools or instruments for bringing it about, and their good, as apart from the common good, will have no standing and will have to be sacrificed at need. How constantly and se-verely this rule is applied will depend on the crisis-mindedness of the author, and also on his social logic, for some are aware they are using metaphor and analogy, whereas others are less critical about their inflation of the biological concept of organism and the psychological concept of person. Briefly, it is the *bloc* or mass notion of the common good put forward by social and political theories of collectivism and totalitarianism, though it is not absent from some religious teachings about corporate state or the Mystical Body of the Church, and the consequent inculcation that personal devotion has to be submerged in manifestations of community solidarity. It is present, too, in the classical surgical argument for *capital punishment: some wrongdoers are so dangerous to the health of the body politic that they have to be cut out like diseased members.

Distributive Notion. The foregoing notion of the common good is, of course, little to the mind of the traditional temper and philosophy of *individualism and *liberalism which, reinforced by *nominalism, stress that values exist only as embodied in particulars, and are critical of attempts to blow out generalizations into entities with a life of their own. Accordingly the common good is first looked for in the lives of individual human beings, and then, esp. by empirical thinkers dubious about metaphysics and more secure in a mathematical reading of reality, is multiplied to produce a sum total, expressed in the *utilitarian formula, the greatest possible happiness of the greatest possible number. A common presumption is that this is best secured by a majority vote according to the methods of modern democracy. Less dominated by this statistical reading, although sometimes using the term "common" to denote what happens in the majority of ordinary cases, classical moral theologians agree with this solicitude for human persons under the threat of the very groups they comprise. Though some are more Aristotelian and others more Platonist, all agree that the common good is a value that each human being should make his own. Thus it is the special interest, *objectum formale,* that engages the virtue of general or legal *justice (roughly approximate to what nowadays is called social justice), and that calls upon the social function of prudence, namely statesmanship in rulers, and political good sense in citizens. These are virtues for everybody, and so, without pursuing the intricacies of the argument, it can be said that the common good is a universal category *(universale in praedicando),* which as such lives in all and each, unlike the common good of the first heading, which is not a universal notion at all, but the particular good of one integral whole, even though this may be as big as the universe itself. Yet under both headings the common good, it should be noted, is a value lying within the world of creatures. It now remains to consider the third and more deeply theological meaning.

The Causal Notion. Aristotle was wiser than he knew when he spoke about a certain godlike quality of the common good, and the theologians, notably St. Thomas Aquinas who developed from him an original and profound doctrine of creation, looked beyond the embodiments or "participations" of good, whether taken singly or lumped together, whether treated in depth or at breadth, to the common good which is the universal cause of all goodness (universale in causando), exemplar, final, and efficient, and which singly and simply holds as its own, while infinitely surpassing them, all the values scattered throughout the universe, even those we misplace. This is not the "all-good" if that means the accumulation of every created good, but pure goodness subsisting in itself and transcending the universe (a bonum separatum), though creating and maintaining and activating all that is attractive there. A sustained effort of metaphysical speculation was combined with the dialectic of Christian *agape, and man was recognized as born in and belonging to the world, but not wholly committed there; for his ultimate end and the full common good is God Himself. This culmination can be properly appreciated only when it is stated in terms of the theology which explains that God is related to us as "object" to our knowing and loving, and not merely as cause to effect, and in terms also of the revelation that all things are recapitulated and restored in Christ.

It may be added by way of postscript that the common good is sometimes spoken of as the public good, and the particular, individual, or personal good as the private good; both terms belong rather to juridical than to philosophical and theological social theory; they witness to Roman rather than Greek preoccupations, and though crucial to the political philosophy, both civil and ecclesiastical, of men living under Western institutions, do not arise from the essential predicament of any person in any community. BIBLIOGRAPHY: ThAq ST 1a, 5–6; 2a2ae 58.5–6; T. Gilby, Between Community and Society (1953).

[T. GILBY]

COMMON LIFE, a manner of living that involves a group of individuals who participate in common activities to attain a common goal. In religious life it is "dwelling together in a canonically erected house and contributing toward and sharing in a common fund," as well as submitting to a rule and a superior and carrying out certain activities together, as prayer and meals. This phase of common life is rightly called community life. BIBLIOGRAPHY: A. Plé, Communal Life (1957); J. Daniélou, Christian Today (tr. K. Sullivan, 1960).

[R. A. TODD]

COMMON LIFE, BRETHREN OF THE, see BRETHREN OF THE COMMON LIFE.

COMMON OF THE SAINTS, the body of texts contained in the Missal and Breviary in which are found the Masses and Offices for those saints who do not have a completely prescribed text of their own. The texts are divided into various classes: pastors, martyrs, virgins, etc.

[T. M. MCFADDEN]

COMMON ORDER, BOOK OF, see BOOK OF COMMON ORDER.

COMMON PRAYER, BOOK OF, see BOOK OF COMMON PRAYER.

COMMON SENSE, a term with two principal uses in scholastic philosophy. (1) Sometimes it translates sensus communis, an internal cognitive power that totalizes the sense impressions proper to the external senses into one image; (2) the intelligence in its pre-philosophical state as the connatural power to apprehend being as objective and as manifesting an intelligible structure expressed in *first principles. This sense of the term is associated with the thought esp. of R. M. Garrigou-Lagrange, but was also treated by J. *Maritain. *SCOTTISH SCHOOL OF COMMON SENSE.

[T. C. O'BRIEN]

COMMON TEACHING OF THEOLOGIANS. A theological note (qualification) used in *systematic (dogmatic) theology to characterize certain theses. The certitude it describes is of a lower grade than that attaching to a *theological conclusion in the strict sense. BIBLIOGRAPHY: STS BAC 1.3:884–913.

[E. A. WEIS]

COMMON WORSHIP, a translation of the Lat. *communicatio in sacris, referring in RC terminology to participation by members of the Church in worship services of other Churches.

COMMON WORSHIP, BOOK OF, see BOOK OF COMMON WORSHIP.

COMMONWEALTH, in English history, the government during the period 1649–60. The victorious parliamentary army, after the beheading of Charles I (1649), proclaimed England a commonwealth. Oliver Cromwell became Lord Protector in 1653, and the subsequent period is also called the Protectorate. The Restoration of the Stuart monarchy terminated the era. These were years of great religious difference among the Puritans, the appearance of many *Nonconformist bodies (Familists, Seekers, Ranters, Diggers, Levelers, Quakers), and the growth of the Baptists. BIBLIOGRAPHY: R. Barclay, Inner Life of the Religious Societies of the Commonwealth (1876); W. C. Braithwaite, Beginnings of Quakerism (ed. H. J. Cadbury, 2d ed., 1955), 1–28; Knox Enth (1950) 139–175.

[R. B. ENO]

COMMUNAL MOVEMENTS, non-monastic communities motivated by religious or ethical ideals, which to some extent own property in common; sometimes called communistic settlements or intentional communities. Although found in several civilizations and religions, the communal movement most typical in Western society has generally originated from a deliberate attempt to revive the structure of the primitive Christian community of Jerusalem, which "held all things in common" (Acts 2.44; 4.32). After this first apparently unsuccessful experiment, Christian communitarian life, with some exceptions, developed within the monastic context. During the Middle Ages a common life was led by several lay religious groups such as the *Beghards and *Beguines and the *Brothers and Sisters of the Free Spirit. In colonial Spanish America paternalistic communal societies were established for the Indians, the Jesuit Reductions in Paraguay being the best-known example.

In the wars and general disorder following the establishment of Lutheranism in Germany many peasants joined Anabaptist and millenarianist groups, some of which, like the *Hutterian Brethren, practiced community ownership of property. To avoid persecution several of these groups immigrated to America, where the idea of communal living developed and expanded. The first significant group was the *Ephrata Community, established in 1732 in Pennsylvania. But the full flowering of communitarian experiments took place in the first half of the 19th cent. with *revivalism and the multiplication of sects. Some secular communities, e.g., New Harmony, Ind. (1825), and Icaria, Ill. (1849), were founded but did not long survive. The religious societies were largely millenarianist in inspiration, and their survival depended mainly on the strength of their leaders. Those still in existence have had to change their way of life significantly. The most important of the 19th-cent. groups were the following: the *Harmony Society, also known as Rappites after their founder Johann Rapp; the Separatist or Zoar Community; the Hopedale Community, or Miniature Christian Republic; the Adonai Shomo; and the *Oneida Community, which was the most prosperous. Of the older groups still in existence the best known are the Hutterites from Germany, the *Doukhobors from Russia, now in Western Canada, and the *Shakers in New England.

Most contemporary communal movements have had a rather ephemeral existence. The Catholic Worker Movement, e.g., gave rise to several short-lived farming communes. But a number, chiefly pacifist in outlook and encouraging marriage, have managed to prosper. Among Catholics the most flourishing are the Nomadelfia Community in southern Italy (1947) and the Laborious Order of the Ark founded by Lanza del Vasto in France (1954). The *Society of Brothers and the Brethren of Early Christianity are fundamentalist in theology, similar to the Hutterites, and engage in profitable farming and manufacture. Most other Protestant communal movements have become more nondenominational. The more significant ones are the Zions Order of the Sons of Levi in Missouri, Koinonia Farm in Georgia, the Holy Apostles Church in Nigeria, and the Riverside Community in New Zealand. The outstanding example of a contemporary secular communal society is furnished by the kibbutzim in Israel, which began in 1909 and have played a major role in the development of that nation.

While religious groups continue to found communal societies, a large number of contemporary communities have been formed without any specifically religious motive in view. They manifest a great variety in their manner of communal life, their organization, and motivation. Some, e.g., the Esalin community in California, regard communal living as a vital aid in attaining emotional or psychological maturity. Others have chosen to drop out of contemporary society, rejecting its values, such as monogamy, as meaningless, and have formed so-called "hippie" communities. Many of these, in contrast to earlier communal societies, have decided to remain in the cities, although such groups as the Diggers in California sometimes engage in farming.
BIBLIOGRAPHY: R. Brown, NCE 4:29–32.

[G. T. DENNIS]

COMMUNAL PENANCE, a term applicable either to an ecclesial community's expressing together their exercise of the virtue of *penance; or to its receiving together the sacrament of *Penance. The theological significance, stressed by the Decree of the Congregation of Divine Worship, Dec. 2, 1973, promulgating the new Rite of Penance, is the ecclesial dimension of sin and repentance. The Church is a union of its members in the bond of charity that unites each to Christ and so to each other; sin is an injury to that bond; penance is a healing of the injury, and the reconciliation of each member with God is also a restoration of the bond of the community itself. Communal repentance within the Church includes the manifestation of its corporate life as a conversion to God (see METANOIA), an imitation of Christ in bearing the sufferings of life, in the expressions of repentance in penitential services, including the Eucharistic liturgy, and in the community reception of the Sacrament of Penance (*Rite of Penance,* n. 4). There is need to distinguish the nonsacramental, but ritual acts of communal penance from the sacrament itself. The introductory, penitential rite at Mass, which has always been part of the liturgy, includes the acknowledgment of sin, contrition, a plea for mercy, and general absolution; further as the Mass is an act of expiation, the penitential sentiments of the worshiping community are expressed throughout. Since Vatican Council II penitential services outside Mass have been developed, and are marked by scriptural readings appropriate to the meaning of penance. But where there is grave sin, "individual and integral confession and absolution [i.e., the sacrament] remain the ordinary way for the faithful to reconcile themselves to God and the Church" (*ibid.,* n.31). Communal reception of this sacrament, in the new *Rite of Penance* is distinguished from the rite of reconciliation of an individual penitent; it is recommended because in it the faithful listen together to the word of God proclaiming his mercy; they examine whether their life in the Church conforms to God's word; they help each other by their prayers (*ibid.,* n.22). The communal rite of reconciliation is of two kinds: that of several penitents who individually confess their sins and receive individual absolution; that of several penitents who together make a general confession and receive general absolution. In both rites the preparatory elements include appropriate prayers, readings of the word of God, a homily. The homily in the case of general confession and general absolution, however, must include the instruction that for valid reception of the sacrament the penitents must have not only the usual dispositions of *contrition, but the resolve to make an individual confession of mortal sins at an opportune time. The opportune time should at least mean fulfilling the paschal precept of annual confession of serious sins (*ibid.*, nn.60, 33, 34). Other restrictive norms, which comply to those of the Congregation of the Doctrine of the Faith, June 16, 1972, (AAS [1972]:513–514), require that the rite of general confession and general absolution be used only where there is serious need (shortage, of time or of confessors); that the existence of such need be determined if possible by the local bp.; where the confessor judges that he must anticipate that judgment, he must inform the bp. afterwards (*Rite of Penance,* nn.31,32). In the U.S. introduction and adaptation of the rite for communal penance are being studied in the various dioceses. BIBLIOGRAPHY: *Rite of Penance.* Study Edition, U.S. Catholic Conference (1974); *New Rite of Penance, Background Catechesis:* Federation of Diocesan Liturgical Commissions (1974).

[T. C. O'BRIEN]

COMMUNE, MARTYRS OF THE. Three groups of Catholics were massacred in or near Paris during the last days of the Prussian siege of Paris (May 24–26, 1871) shortly before the defeat of the revolutionaries. The first group was led by Georges Darboy, abp. of Paris, and included Abbés Deguerry and Allard, Jesuits Ducoudray and Clerc, and a judge, Senator Bonjean, all of whom were imprisoned at La Roquette in Paris. They were put to death by members of the Commune on May 24. The second group consisted of members of the faculty, clerical and lay, of the Collège d'Arcueil near Paris. Eugène Captier, a Dominican and the superior of the college, four religious, and eight laymen were arrested, imprisoned, and shot in the streets by revolutionaries, May 25. Pierre Olivaint, a Jesuit headed the third group, 51 in number, clerics and laymen, who were slaughtered in the streets of Belleville by a mob on May 26. BIBLIOGRAPHY: M. A. Fabre, *Les Drames de la Commune* (1937); *idem, Les Martyrs d'Arcueil* (1938).

COMMUNICANT, strictly, one who "communicates," i.e., partakes of holy communion, is in the habit of doing so, or is eligible to do so. The term may distinguish in some Churches those who have been confirmed from those who have not, or connote one who meets minimum church membership standards (e.g., where a Church requires at least annual communion). In a broader sense, communicant is used as a synonym for church member.

[N. H. MARING]

COMMUNICANTES, the first word and identifying name of the fourth paragraph of the Roman Canon of the Mass (Eucharistic Prayer I in the New Order of the Mass). In the English text the paragraph begins: "In union with the whole Church. . . ." This paragraph is the continuation of the *Memento* (Commemoration of the Living) and expresses the union with the saints in the offering of the Mass. After the mention of Mary and Joseph, whose name was here introduced by Pope John XXIII, the paragraph lists the names of 12 apostles and 12 martyrs specially venerated in Rome in the early centuries of the Church. The name of Paul rather than of Matthias (mentioned later in the *Nobis quoque peccatoribus,* or the "For ourselves, too, we ask . . . ." in the new form of the Roman Canon) is used to complete the number of the apostles. In the English text Thaddeus is called Jude, the name by which that Apostle is generally known in English. The complete enumeration of the names of the Apostles and martyrs is now optional and not obligatory. As indicated in the new form of the Roman Canon, those from the Apostle James to Damian may be omitted if the celebrant so wishes. The introduction of the *Communicantes* is variable. Special forms are provided for Christmas and its octave, for the Epiphany, Holy Thursday, for the Easter Vigil and the following week, for the Ascension, and for Pentecost.

[N. KOLLAR]

COMMUNICATIO IN SACRIS, a Latin expression used in canon law and theology to signify participation with others of another faith in liturgical worship. Should such participation involve a profession of belief in something contrary to faith, or should it be likely to lead to a weakening of faith on the part of the participant or others, it is forbidden by divine law. But these evils are by no means essentially inherent in all communication in worship, and when there is sufficient provision against their occurrence, to join with others in worship may be a commendable thing. In the more ecumenical climate that has prevailed since Vatican Council II, the RC Church has modified its attitude toward communication in some circumstances, esp. with respect to communication in worship with the faithful of the Eastern Orthodox Churches. The Ecumenical Directory of May 14, 1967, implementing Vat II Ecum and Vat II East-Cath declares that Catholics may join Eastern Orthodox in public prayer, esp. in ecumenical services. They can occasionally satisfy the Sunday obligation by assisting at the Divine Liturgy of Eastern Orthodox, and are even encouraged to do so if they are unable to assist at Mass in a RC church. Catholics may act as godparents in an Orthodox church, and Orthodox, at a Catholic baptism. Penance and communion may be received from Orthodox priests by Catholics in case of necessity and also "if special circumstances make it physically or morally impossible over a long period for one of the faithful to receive the sacraments in his own Church." The Orthodox are permitted to make use of Catholic churches, buildings, cemeteries, and "other things necessary for their religious rites" if there is need of such. They may take part in Catholic liturgical acts and can receive sacraments whenever they so desire, but "the greatest possible attention" is to be given to reciprocity. BIBLIOGRAPHY: C. Hollis, *Achievements of Vatican II* (1967) 64–65.

[V. J. POSPISHIL]

COMMUNICATION OF IDIOMS, the theological term for the mutual predication of properties or attributes of the two natures in Christ of the one person. It is not a semantic trick or merely a question of terminology but a mode of expressing the mystery of the Incarnation. Because the Word of God is the one ultimate subject or person of both the divine and human natures, qualities or attributes of both natures may be predicated of this person. Because the two natures remain distinct and unmixed (D 302), the qualities of one nature do not belong to the other nature.

Examples of communication of idioms can be found from the earliest days of Christianity, although the speculative explanations were of somewhat later origin. The *Tome* of Leo I is an early example of papal usage (D 293–295). In the patristic era and more explicitly in the scholastic period rules for the communication of idioms were formulated. The most basic rule asserts that, in general, concrete terms or names may be affirmed of concrete terms; abstract names may not be affirmed of abstract terms. Since a concrete name signifies a form or quality in a subject—man, e.g., signifies a subject or person of human nature—concrete attributes of either nature can be predicated of the one subject or person in Christ. Thus we say "This man is God" or "The Son of God died for us." Abstract names, however, signify a nature or form separated from any subject. Since the natures in Christ are distinct, it is false to say that "Humanity is divinity" or "Humanity is omnipotent."

Since negations are more extensive than affirmations, any proposition is false that denies an attribute of Christ that is his in virtue of either nature. A reduplicative expression, e.g., Christ as man, does not follow the general norm, since it refers to the nature rather than to the subject or person. Special caution should be exercised with regard to derivatives or compounds involving "God" or "man" and to expressions that designate the "becoming" of the hypostatic union. Expressions of heretics, even though they of an orthodox sense, should be used cautiously. Some early Lutherans, affirming the ubiquity of the humanity of Christ in their explanation of the Real Presence, used the communication of idioms in a manner Roman Catholics understood to be heterodox. BIBLIOGRAPHY: J. F. Rigney, NCE 4:35–37; ThAq ST 3a, 16.

[J. HENNESSEY]

COMMUNICATIONS, see MEDIA, MASS.

COMMUNION, a term sometimes used to refer to a Church, denomination, or other religious group, e.g., the Presbyterian communion or the Methodist communion. It is sometimes used in reference to Christian bodies when some question exists concerning whether it is theologically proper to use the term Church. The word recalls the phrase "communion of saints" in the Apostles' Creed. It also suggests a sense of fellowship, particularly as this may center around the service of holy communion, through which Christians are united. The problem of *intercommunion, to bridge the separation of the various Christian communions, has been one of the difficult questions of the ecumenical movement. From one point of view the service of holy communion is the center of the life of the Church, and those who participate in it share a common life. For some, therefore, it would seem to be pretending something that is not yet true if Christians who are not united nonetheless participate in the service together. Others, however, hold that because of a common faith in Christ the members of the various Christian groups already form one communion in the most essential matters, despite their differences, and that this unity is appropriately expressed in common participation in the service of holy communion, even while the doctrinal and organizational differences persist. Some Roman Catholics have acted in accord with this second view, but official approval has been given only in regard to receiving holy communion in the Eastern Churches. BIBLIOGRAPHY: Vat II Ecum 8; EastCath 26–29.

[T. EARLY]

COMMUNION (MUSIC), one of the most ancient chants of the RC liturgy, the last of the five parts of the Proper of the Mass, sung after or during the distribution of communion. The communion antiphon was sung with a psalm, usually the 33d Psalm, and was originally chanted during the distribution of communion. By adding a number of versicles alternating with the antiphon, the time could be extended to that required for the administration of the sacrament. However, these verses disappeared in the 12th cent. and only the antiphon remained. The communion antiphons were melismatic melodies sung chorally with a soloist intoning the initial words of the text. BIBLIOGRAPHY: Apel HDMus (1973) 189; E. E. Nemmers, *Twenty Centuries of Catholic Church Music* (1949) 18–19.

[J. S. PALLOZZA]

COMMUNION, CLOSED, see CLOSED COMMUNION.

COMMUNION, FIRST, see FIRST COMMUNION.

COMMUNION, HOLY, see HOLY COMMUNION.

COMMUNION, OPEN, see OPEN COMMUNION.

COMMUNION, SOLEMN, a practice more common in France and Belgium of children receiving the Eucharist at the age of twelve in a solemn ceremony that includes the recitation of the Creed. Originally a reflection of Jansenist insistence on delaying first communion for children, the custom is looked upon today as a sign of the child's coming of age. Solemn communion terminates the preadolescent years of religious instruction and is usually preceded by a retreat of preparation. BIBLIOGRAPHY: J. Honoré, *Pastoral catéchétique, texte, notes et commentaires* (1964).

[P. F. PALMER]

COMMUNION, SPIRITUAL, see COMMUNION.

COMMUNION ANTIPHON, a verse of the Scriptures which served as the refrain for the psalm originally sung during the distribution of communion. In the early church, the congregation sang psalms during the communion procession. As the melodies of the antiphons became more complex and the number of communicants decreased, these psalms were taken over by the *schola cantorum* and subsequently said privately by the celebrant. Liturgical reform has restored the practice of singing during the communion procession and stipulates that if the liturgical text itself is used, the celebrant should not recite it privately.

[T. M. MCFADDEN]

COMMUNION OF SAINTS, a name applied to the bonds of God's gracious love that links persons who are already with the Lord in heaven, those who have died but have not yet attained the full enjoyment of God, and those who are still pilgrims on earth. The sharing in help, satisfaction, prayer, and good works among the persons flows from their common sharing in Jesus Christ and in his Spirit. The reality itself is central to the life of the Church while its expression has received different emphases through the centuries. BIBLIOGRAPHY: Vat II ConstChurch 51.

[V. GILLIGAN]

COMMUNION OF THE SICK, the distribution of the Eucharist to persons unable to attend church because of illness. In the RC Church it is considered obligatory for a person in danger of death to receive communion if it is morally possible for him to do so. Apart from any imminent danger of death, sick persons (and others impeded from getting to church) are encouraged to seek communion at least occasionally. The custom of distributing communion to such persons has existed in the Church from the earliest times, when deacons and sometimes lay persons were entrusted with carrying the Eucharist. In the present discipline of the RC Church, the public carrying of the Eucharist to the house or room of the sick is accompanied, where this is customary, by the ringing of bells, the carrying of candles by attendants, etc. Where this custom does not exist, or when the Sacrament is taken privately to the sick, the procedure is less ceremonious. Nevertheless, even in this case some preparation should be made in the sickroom. A table covered with clean linen should be prepared; holy water, candles, a glass of water, and a spoon should be available. If Mass is said in the sickroom, communion under both species is permitted. Confession and the anointing of the sick may precede communion. For the rules regulating the communion of the sick and for the rite to be followed, see *The Rites of the Catholic Church* (Eng. tr. the International Commission on English in the Liturgy, 1976) 577–598. *COMMUNION OUTSIDE MASS; *VIATICUM.

COMMUNION OUTSIDE OF MASS, the sharing of the Eucharist in a context other than the Mass itself. This practice was common in the early Church where the faithful would carry the host home after Sunday Mass for daily reception (cf. Cyprian, *De lapsis,* 26). In the medieval Church, however, widespread misunderstanding of the nature of the Mass and communion gave rise to several abuses. The Eucharist was not regarded as food which should be eaten frequently. At those times when communion would be given, the host was often distributed before the Mass which came therefore to be regarded as a period of silent thanksgiving. The contemporary liturgical movement has properly emphasized the Eucharist as meal and thus the reception of communion within Mass. Nevertheless, communion may be distributed outside of Mass when there is sufficient reason. If possible, this should be done within a scriptural service. BIBLIOGRAPHY: J. Jungmann, *Mass of the Roman Rite* (tr. A. Brunner, 2 v., 1951–55) 2:409–411; *Rites of the Catholic Church* (Eng. tr. the International Commission on English in the Liturgy, 1976) 459–474.

[T. M. MCFADDEN]

COMMUNION SERVICE, in some Christian communities the designation for the celebration of the Eucharist. The BCP, for example, contains a Communion Service. Historically the term implied rejection of the RC celebration of Mass as Christ's sacrifice represented sacramentally. *HOLY COMMUNION.

[T. C. O'BRIEN]

COMMUNION TABLE, a place designated for the faithful to receive communion. In early times communion was received at the altar. Gradually a rail, often fairly wide and of stone, separating the sanctuary from the nave, came to symbolize the communion table. In the 16th cent. the communion rail was mandated. For the most part, the communion rail has been a continuous divider running across the sanctuary limit. A variation in medieval times was a cloth held by deacons where the faithful received. Since Vatican Council II the trend has been to eliminate the communion rail altogether. BIBLIOGRAPHY: J. Jungmann, *Mass of the Roman Rite* (tr. F. Brunner, 2 v., 1951–55).

[J. R. AHERNE]

COMMUNION UNDER BOTH KINDS, the form of administration of holy communion whereby the laity receive both the bread and the wine. It is in contrast to the practice of giving only the bread to the laity, with the wine consumed by the priest.

Communion under both kinds, or species, was the normal practice in the Church from the beginning; withdrawal of the cup from the laity began in the 12th century. St. Thomas Aquinas in the 13th cent. supported the new practice, though he allowed communion under both kinds. The older practice continued in Rome as late as the 14th cent., but it was outlawed by the Council of Constance (1415). The change was accompanied by no explicit dogmatic justification, but apparently resulted from a desire for simplified administration. It may also have reflected an increased emphasis on the distinction between clergy and laity. Theologically, however, it was asserted that the laity were not deprived of any spiritual benefit when the cup was withheld from them, since Christ was fully present in any part of either species. The theological defense suggests the emphasis was now on the reception of the physical elements, rather than on the action of participation in a community meal, as had been the case earlier.

In the early 15th cent. the question became a major issue in the Hussite movement, though it was not emphasized by Jan *Hus himself. Those who advocated communion under both kinds (sub utraque specie) became known as *Utraquists or *Calixtines from their demand for the cup (calix). The creed of the Utraquists was contained in the "Four Articles of Prague" (1420) of which article 2 states, "The sacrament of the most Holy Eucharist shall be freely administered in the two kinds, that is bread and wine, to all the faithful in Christ who are not precluded by mortal sin—according to the word and disposition of our Savior." The Articles were incorporated in the *Compactata, approved at the Council of Basel in 1436 for the Church of Bohemia. They remained the creed of that Church until 1620, when all non-Roman rites were prohibited.

Communion under both kinds became a mark of the Churches of the Reformation, and has been the practice of Anglican and Protestant Churches subsequently (see e.g., *Augsburg Confession, Art. 22, Thirty-Nine Articles, art. 30). Restoration of the cup to the laity was a symbol of overcoming the distinction between clergy and laity, and an assertion of the *priesthood of all believers. It also reflected the rejection of *transubstantiation.

In recent years the RC Church has made some moves toward restoring communion under both kinds. Liturgical studies generally have placed emphasis on the practice of the earlier centuries of the Church, and that has led to new interpretations of the meaning of the Eucharist. Out of the liturgical movement has come a renewed understanding of it as a meal in which the community shares, a meal comprising both food and drink. The importance of common participation in the liturgical action of the Church, as contrasted with a passive laity receiving the ministrations of the clergy, has been another theme of liturgical renewal.

The Constitution on the Liturgy approved by Vatican Council II allowed the cup to the laity in certain cases, such as the first communion of newly baptized adults (Vat. II Sac Lit 55), this concession has been further extended since the

Council. Such a development has importance not only for the RC worship, but also for the *ecumenical movement. The difference in practice from Protestantism and Eastern Orthodoxy has been one of the most readily noticed by the average layman. In principle, it is now possible for all Churches to develop a common practice. Inasmuch as the withholding of the cup from the laity was often seen as a mark of their secondary position in the Church, the change is also valuable in restoring the concept of the Church as a community or as a family. BIBLIOGRAPHY: F. Amiot, *History of the Mass* (tr. L. C. Sheppard, 1958); J. A. Jungmann, *Mass of the Roman Rite* (tr. F. A. Brunner, 2 v., 1951–55) 2:382–386. *EUCHARIST.

[T. EARLY]

COMMUNION WITH ROME. Contemporary ecclesiology, drawing on biblical, patristic, and medieval traditions, has restored the notion of communion as a definition of the Church. For those in the Catholic tradition, ecclesiastical communion requires a bond of union between bishops in apostolic succession and the faithful, among the bishops, and among the faithful. This bond of union, according to common Catholic belief, is both effected and made visible in eucharistic communion. For those in the RC tradition, the role of the Roman pontiff, as a foundation and guardian of unity among the bishops and for the faithful, is of paramount importance.

Communion in the NT Church meant a sharing of life in and with Christ, which was life with the Father and the Spirit, and, as a member of the body of Christ, a sharing in the communion of saints and in the many gifts received by the Church. In a classic passage in Acts (2.42–47), the elements binding together the early community were described as the teaching of the apostles, fraternal communion, the breaking of the bread, and prayer. Church traditions and scholars have not been in agreement in interpreting all the details of how the structural organization of this fraternal communion developed. The RC interpretation has been that the Church was and is a hierarchically structured society, and that from the first, by a commission of Jesus himself (cf. Mt 16.18; Jn 21.17), Peter had a special role among the apostles and, consequently, Peter's successor also had a special role among the bishops, the successors of the apostles. Catholic tradition holds that Peter came to Rome and that the Bishop of Rome locates the Petrine succession.

In the early Church, communion and the special importance of communion with Rome was more of a lived reality than an elaborate theory. To be in communion connotated bonds of communication and peace, of fellowship and love. The close relationship between ecclesiastical communion and the Eucharist was evidenced concretely by the practice of carrying from one church to another the *fermentum, letters of communion, and acts of excommunication. When disputes and questions arose about the criteria for such communion, appeal was made to union with a large number of bishops, or communion with the most ancient Churches. Among such criteria, union with the bishop of Rome came to be recognized as decisive. With the growth of the papacy and Church centralization, the theory and norms for this socio-sacramental union were also elaborated in strong juridical terms, culminating in the definition of Vatican Council I on the papal office (Session IV, 1870; D 3050–75).

Vatican Council II revitalized the notion of communion, insisting at the same time that it be understood as an organic and hierarchical reality, animated by charity but demanding a juridic form (cf. Abbott, p. 99). Collegial communion between the bishops was also revitalized and reaffirmed as essential to the Church's hierarchical structure. The third chapter of Vat II ConstCh (no. 18) described the role of the Bishop of Rome among all the bishops as being "a permanent and visible source [*principium*] and foundation of unity of faith and fellowship [*communionis*]." Union with a bishop in hierarchical communion with the Bishop of Rome, consequently, is in the RC view decisive for full union with the Church (*ibid.* 8, 14–15, 18, 20–23).

In reaffirming the institutional fullness of the Catholic Church's visible structure and the sacramental and juridical necessity of union with its hierarchical system as a means of salvation, Vatican Council II went beyond earlier Roman statements in recognizing a certain, although "imperfect," ecclesial communion existing between Roman Catholics and those other Churches and ecclesial communities not in "full" union with the Bishop of Rome. The aim of the ecumenical movement, according to the Vat II Ecum 3–4 is to overcome the obstacles to full ecclesiastical communion. The RC vision of the Church is thus a body united in faith, sacraments, ecclesiastical government, and communion between all the faithful and bishops throughout the world and the Bishop of Rome. BIBLIOGRAPHY: L. Hertling, *Communio: Chiesa e Papato nell'antichità cristiana* (1961); J. Hamer, *Church Is a Communion* (1964); F. X. Lawlor, NCE 3:683–693, s.v. "Church, Theology of."

[L. B. GUILLOT]

COMMUNISM, a form of social organization in which property is held in common. As understood historically since the 19th cent., it is considerably more complicated than the simple forms of common possession and enjoyment of goods often attributed to primitive societies and advocated by Plato for his ruling class of guardians. It differs essentially from these two prototypes of the various historic versions of communism—monasticism, perfectionist colonies, and so forth—in that it demands a high level of production before the experiment can be sanctioned. It refuses to equate leadership with class distinctions, which it is committed to eradicate, and claims in practice a monopoly in explaining the nature and organizing the development of communism for the Communist party of the U.S.S.R. as the authorized interpreter of the "science" of Marxism-Leninism. Soviets, like traditional Communists, foresee a state of society in which goods are produced and distributed in accordance with the rule: "from each according to his abilities; to each according to his need." Soviet communism, however, while retaining this simple aim in principle, adds two pertinent features to the methods of achieving it: (1) it must be based on and pass through a transitional form of socialism and the dictatorship of the proletariat and (2) the transition from socialism to communism depends on production at a level high enough to provide for everyone's needs under conditions of 20th cent. urban-industrial life.

Communism today represents chiefly the condition of men described by Marx in his vision of a mythical future society, brought about through revolution, and the comprehensive movement of which the core is the party founded by Lenin. In both aspects communism has had a close and continuing interest in religion, a concern characterized largely by ideological conflict and persecution varying in intensity. Communism is a complex whole, comprising a doctrine, an organization, and a way of operating, and with each of these aspects religion is found to be, respectively, incompatible.

The heart of Communist doctrine is its eschatology, the assertion of the historical inevitability of a future social order to which all men are naturally supposed to tend. To rationalize this vision communism has constructed an elaborate, fully articulated philosophy and has claimed to have identified the laws governing the development of the world and of human society. No part of this philosophy and none of these postulated laws allow for an interpretation of religion as other than an illusion, a falsehood, and the expression of social and economic alienation. There is a theory, as well, of the intermediary goal to be achieved before the eschatological and absolute end to history is attained. This goal, the establishment and building up of a socialist state, requires that revolutionary forces, led by the party of the working classes, seize and retain power. Communism includes, therefore, a formidable methodological apparatus to be employed in the area of holding and exercising power. This same power is regularly, both in fact and on principle, directed to the effective discrediting and suppressing of religion wherever Communist regimes are installed.

Communism is organized in national units and, less firmly, on an international scale. Power radiates out from a center and is diffused in peripheral groups and cadres, charged with realizing immediately the intermediate goals, allowing for the limitations and imperatives of the concrete situation. Religion has no positive role whatever in Communist schemes and plans, which envisage a social order from which religious teachings and values are to be definitively excluded. The party is supreme, the seat and source of all power, guidance, enlightenment, leadership, and the party, as Stalin said in 1927, cannot be neutral regarding religion; it conducts antireligious propaganda against all and every religious prejudice, because it stands for science, and religious prejudices are opposed to science. The party insists on an antireligious commitment on the part of all its members and supporters and on the promotion, throughout the Communist world and in all party-controlled organizations, of atheistic ideas.

The antireligious operational strategy of communism is complex and shifts in a manner that tends to obscure its underlying singleness of purpose. Communism itself has undergone considerable changes in many spheres but the fundamental hostility toward religion has never been abandoned or seriously modified. In this area the Communist predilection for unity between theory and practice expresses itself in a dialectic of operational, organizational, and eschatological elements. The Communist dealings with religion are determined by a dogmatic attitude and deep moral feeling. The orthodox Communist faith regards the party as sole repository of truth, infallible both in teaching and in action, and working always for the authentic good of mankind. Communism is a monistic doctrine: the only reality is matter in motion, the physical universe, of which man is a part. It is also thoroughly totalitarian; since the party incarnates supreme wisdom and insight, it must be obeyed absolutely and control everything. Even a man's most private sentiments and convictions must be subject to party discipline and available as tools for the promotion of Communist aims.

Communism is presented as the only rational, morally sound, and historically indicated alternative to religion; as such it has been called a pseudo- or ersatz religion, although it may be advisable to avoid speaking of communism in this way. The appeals of communism are many and varied and may or may not succeed in fulfilling the needs to which religion conventionally ministers. Some of these appeals are spurious, in the sense that Communists exploit genuine needs without being able or willing to satisfy them, or deliberately encourage demands which are unrealistic and incapable of being met. The first principle of Communist morality, viz., everything that serves the ends of the party is morally good, means that communism may be constantly presented as the only way to complete fulfillment of desires and needs. Thus, there is an appeal to nationalistic feelings, especially in countries striving for independence from foreign rule. Another is the appeal to the desire of workers for improved conditions, and a third is the appeal to the desire of peasants for more land. In actual fact, Communists predict the eventual amalgamation of nationalities, subordinate workers' claims to party interests, and, as soon as feasible, expropriate all the land the peasant has.

Yet no other movement in history has offered so many and such powerful genuine appeals to such a variety of fundamental human cravings. Man has a profound urge to base his views, beliefs, and actions on an absolute authority, on a dogma. He desires no less deeply to improve human relations at all levels. Among the most cherished convictions of contemporaries are the impetus to transform the world by concerted action, a belief in the unbounded possibilities of science and technology, the prospect of a controlling knowledge of history. The world asks for

heroism and sacrifice, a challenge particularly attractive to the best of men. There are resentments against physical and mental suffering and injustice. To all of these needs and aspirations communism makes a strong appeal.

The need for a secure, trustworthy foundation for one's belief, for something that can attract commitment and give a clear meaning to life and a solid basis for thought, is generally experienced and has traditionally been met by religion. Where religion is attenuated, its inspirational capital spent, and its credibility diminished to the vanishing point, men find themselves in a spiritual void that is hard for them to bear. Into that void, which it has helped to exacerbate but which it did not in the first place simply create, communism enters with an extremely dogmatic and absolute belief-system that purports to explain everything, to reveal the explicit meaning of life, and to overcome an insecurity and uncertainty that some men find intolerable. Many intellectuals become Communists precisely because they have been religious skeptics languishing in an unbearable void.

The resolve to improve human relations, to suppress injustice, to help the poor and the weak is one of the most pressing moral urges. It has been incorporated into the great world religions, including Buddhism, Christianity, and Islam. To this noble desire communism appeals in its eschatology, by proposing an ideal of complete equality, social security, and brotherhood, an end to all injustice and discrimination, and in its revolutionary program, by stirring the downtrodden masses to strike a blow on their own behalf.

Communism exploits man's Promethean impulse; it teaches that social improvement must be accompanied and prepared by a complete restructuring of the world of man and of man himself, and all this to be accomplished by man's own courageous effort. This prospect appeals strongly to youth, for whom communism describes life as a lofty adventure, a monumental struggle against an old world order whose resistance must be overcome, if necessary, by revolutionary violence. Another sort of appeal is to modern man's rationalistic mentality, his temperamental obsession with scientific credentials. The Communist system is described as thoroughly reasonable, carefully planned; in it everything is elaborated and guided by scientific knowledge. All this is flanked on the one side by an appeal to heroic sacrifice and on the other by an appeal to resentments found smoldering in varying degrees in most human beings. Dissatisfaction with one's own situation is thus coupled with noble moral ideals to become an irresistible force in favor of communism.

Communism cannot be properly challenged in many of these areas of appeal by religion, although religious people often mistakenly try to compete by promising, in the name of faith or on God's word, satisfaction, relief, fulfillment comparable to that which Communists claim to deliver. Communist tactics with respect to religious institutions and activities are elastic and may change repeatedly but the governing principle remains intact, which is the eventual total suppression of religion in every form. Persecution is undertaken if indicated, although it may be carefully camouflaged if this is expedient. The propaganda line remains constant: religion, and everything connected with it is bad, but, and this is the dialectical counterpart to the condemnation of religion, Communists declare that they are trying to maintain a tolerant and human attitude toward believers. The Communist arguments against religion denounce it as (1) false, (2) socially harmful, and (3) spiritually destructive. The first line of attack follows the classical Marxist position that religion is opposed to materialism, the only scientific outlook, which is atheistic. Because religion is an anti-scientific ideology, Communists cannot remain indifferent to it. In the second place, religion corrupts social life by furnishing an ideological superstructure to a system of exploitations, comforting the victims of injustice and diverting them from revolution while offering a cheap balm to the consciences of the exploiters. This argument has found a ready response even among Christians, in Europe and Latin America, and partly accounts for huge Communist votes in those countries. The cornerstone of the argument is that religion is the opium of the people, a form of spiritual oppression that counsels patience and humility on earth and holds out hope of a heavenly reward. Lenin called religion a kind of spiritual gin, a type of intellectual bad liquor in which the slaves of capitalism drown their human shape and their claims to a decent life. The third charge is that religion, in its essence and not merely in its corrupt forms, as Lenin insisted, is unutterable vileness. The purer the religion, the more dangerous it is. This explains why, in the Spanish Civil War, Communists fell with such fury on the Carmelites, who were in no way politically active, and murdered large numbers of them.

Antireligious propaganda is never to be relaxed and is to be directed primarily at young people. Policy toward the Churches in Communist lands implements two basic aims: (1) to utilize the Church for the party's purposes and (2) to keep Church influence to an absolute minimum. The State may find it expedient to tolerate religion in some areas, but for the party the battle is unremitting and may be relaxed only if it should interfere with more fundamental goals of the party. BIBLIOGRAPHY: *Handbook on Communism* (ed. J. M. Bochenski and G. Niemeyer, 1962); G. A. Almond, *Appeals of Communism* (1954); R. N. Carew Hunt, *Theory and Practice of Communism* (1950); G. MacEoin, *Communist War on Religion* (1959); *Values in Conflict: Christianity, Marxism, Psychoanalysis and Existentialism* (ed. V. Comerchero, pa. 1970); R. Garaudy, *Alternative Future* (tr. L. Mayhew, 1974).

[J. P. REID]

COMMUNITAS (Community), the main body of *Franciscans in conflict with the *Spirituals. The moderate Franciscans were called *Fratres de communitate*; they favored a more juridical organization of Franciscan life and apostolate, as well as a less literal understanding of Franciscan poverty. *POVERTY CONTROVERSY.

[T. C. O'BRIEN]

COMMUNITY, a collectivity of people united by all or most of the following characteristics: spatial proximity, shared goals and values, an acceptance of significant interdependence, some structure of governance or authority, and a degree of permanence. The term is commonly used analogously insofar as it may be applied to a family, an ethnic group within a neighborhood, a religious association or order, and even to all of humankind (the community of man). Contemporary sociology uses the term for a structured, residency-based, frequently interacting and consciously interdependent societal subdivision distinct from a mere aggregate, or the larger society, or kinship groups such as the family. The communal nature of human existence has consistently been a theme within philosophy: a person can realize his unique individuality only by experiencing existence as shared by other persons. Growth in self-realization is directly proportionate to the recognition of, and commitment to, being-with-others. On one level, this being-with-others extends to the whole of humanity; but human beings also require smaller, affective units with moral bonds of responsibility, values, and objectives. Christian theology also interprets human life communally and extends it to a participation in the divine community of the Father, Son, and Holy Spirit. The bond of that community is the love of charity given by the Spirit that vivifies the mystical Body of Christ. Community is also the ideal of religious life, esp. as this applies to small, local groups of religious who share certain objectives and moral bonds. BIBLIOGRAPHY: the various articles under "Community" in *International Encyclopedia of the Social Sciences* 3:156–180; G. Moran, *Experiences in Community* (1968); R. Roth, *Person and Community* (1975).

[T. M. MCFADDEN]

COMMUNITY CHURCHES, *local churches, independent of denominational connections, that accept members from any Protestant denomination. They vary in patterns of organization, worship, and membership conditions, but usually have a doctrinal basis broad enough to admit Christians of all persuasions, who, as members of these Churches, may still retain their own denominational loyalties. Community churches originated in villages and rural areas that could not support more than one church, but are common today in newer suburban areas where religious pluralism exists along with a minimizing of denominational distinctions. Although these Churches are independent, they sometimes belong to the loose association called the National Council of Community Churches, organized in 1950. This organization has no jurisdiction and serves primarily to provide fellowship and a channel of missionary outreach. In 1974 only about 219 of 3,000 known community Churches were associated with this Council. BIBLIOGRA-PHY: *That They All May Be One* (ed. J. Ruskin Howe, no date); Mayer RB 376–377.

[N. H. MARING]

COMMUNITY LIFE, in general the sharing of mutual interests and needs by members of a group: in canon law and theology, the dwelling together of religious or priests, the sharing a common table, and joining together in worship. Ascetical and mystical writers recommend these means to holiness, which are firmly embedded in the whole tradition of Christian spirituality. BIBLIOGRAPHY: J. Daniélou, *Christian Today* (tr. K. Sullivan, 1960) 127–150. *CENOBITIC MONASTICISM.

[T. GILBY]

COMMUTATION, (1) as a transliteration of *commutatio,* a transaction or exchange to be regulated by *commutative justice; (2) mitigation of a burden or obligation. In the case of obligation to undergo penalty or punishment, canon law provides that a judge in a canonical process or trial may lessen the prescribed penalty in circumstances where culpability is not full, or where the liable person has already been punished by civil law (CIC c. 2223, § 3, n. 3). Canon law also provides for commutation of vows: a private vow, except of perpetual chastity or to enter a religious order of solemn vows, can be commuted by the person who has made it in order to substitute a greater or equal good than that previously vowed. But in the case of commutation pure and simple, the authority of one having power of dispensation is required (*ibid.,* c. 1314). A special case of commutation reserved to the Holy See is the reduction of the obligation to offer *foundation Masses (c. 1551).

[T. C. O'BRIEN]

COMMYNES, PHILIPPE DE, see COMINES, PHILIPPE DE.

COMNENIAN ART, see BYZANTINE ART.

COMO, GUIDO DA (fl. 13th cent.), sculptor from Pisa, active in Tuscany at the cathedral of S. Martino, Lucca. C.'s equestrian figures of *St. Martin with the Beggar* (*c.*1240), octagonal marble font (Baptistery, Pisa), and monumental *Archangel Michael* (S. Guiseppe, Pistoia, 1250), evidence his style of simple sculptural volumes projecting from smooth backgrounds.

[M. J. DALY]

COMPACTATA, a religious agreement between *Hussites and the Council of *Basel. The Compactata were designed to end the Hussite Wars; they evolved from negotiations that were begun (1433) with Hussite representatives invited to Basel by Eugene IV, and continued at Prague. By the time of Hussite acceptance, which was tied to the political aims of the Emperor Sigismund, at the Diet of Iglau (1436), and ratification by Basel (1437), this Council was at odds with Eugene IV; the Compactata never received papal approval and were annulled by Pius II (1462). A drastic curtailment of the *Four Articles of Prague, they provided that: (1) approved preachers were free, but were obligated to respect ecclesiastical authorities; (2) communion under both kinds was permissible as long as faith in communion under one was safeguarded; (3) the clergy had the right to hold property, but those in vows could not hold temporal office; (4) serious public sins should be punished by lawful authority. BIBLIOGRAPHY: Bihlmeyer-Tüchle 2:442–443; Hughes HC 3:322–325.

[T. C. O'BRIEN]

COMPAGNIE DU SAINT-SACREMENT, religious organization influential in France from 1627 to 1665. Founded as a secret society by Henri de Lévis, Duke of Ventadour, it included many illustrious laymen and clerics. The aims of the society were prayer, devotion to the Eucharist, and charitable works such as aid to the poor and to prisoners. The members undertook to preserve public morality and often manifested fierce anti-Protestant rigor. In 1664 they attacked Molière's *Tartuffe* and succeeded in suppressing its performance. Their admonitions to the morally lax Mazarin ultimately caused their breakdown, although by this time they had spread to about 50 centers around France. Some members did become fanatic; however, the *Compagnie* was responsible for much salutary influence on the 17th-cent. French religious revival. BIBLIOGRAPHY: E. Levesque, DSAM 2.2:1301–05. For the Compagnie's spiritual doctrine, see R. Heurtevent, DSAM 2.2:1305–11.

[I. M. KASHUBA]

COMPANATION (Lat. *cum,* with; *panis,* bread), a term that was sometimes used in Eucharistic discussions as a synonym for *consubstantiation. *IMPANATION.

[T. C. O'BRIEN]

COMPANY OF JESUS, a title formerly given the *Jesuits who are now referred to as the Society of Jesus, founded in France (1534) by St. Ignatius Loyola. They take solemn vows to which they add a fourth vow of obedience to the Holy See to go wherever sent on missions. It is the largest of the religious orders and is divided into provinces governed by provincials under a father general in Rome. In 1974 world membership was 30,860 of whom 20,908 were priests. The 10 provinces in the U.S. have a total of 4,844 priests and 543 brothers.

[R. A. TODD]

COMPANY OF MARY, a community of sisters dedicated to the Christian education of youth, founded (1607) at Bordeaux, France, by St. Jeanne de Lestonnac. The work of the congregation extended throughout Western Europe.

Originally their apostolate was meant to parallel that of the Company of Jesus. In 1926 the first house was established in the U.S. at Douglas, Arizona. In 1974 the community had a total of 68 professed sisters conducting 5 kindergartens, 6 catechetical centers, and 3 elementary schools in the archdioceses of Los Angeles and Santa Fe and in the Diocese of Tucson, Arizona. The general motherhouse is in Rome.

[R. A. TODD]

COMPANY OF ST. PAUL, an approved secular institute for lay people and priests organized (1920) in Milan, Italy under the guidance of Card. Andrew Ferrari. The members take simple vows and live as a community to support and strengthen one another that they may become better witnesses to Christ in continuing his work through an apostolate in the world. Their works have included a hospice in Rome, printing-presses and publications in Bologna and Milan, and conducting missions, schools, and technical training centers. The Company is established in Jerusalem, Paris, Buenos Aires, and in the U.S. with headquarters at Washington, D.C. BIBLIOGRAPHY: G. Penco, EncCatt 5:1190–91; G. Galbiati, LTK 4:88.

[R. A. TODD]

COMPARATIVE STUDY OF RELIGION, see RELIGION, COMPARATIVE STUDY OF.

COMPARATIVE SYMBOLICS, the branch of theological studies that treats the various Christian creeds and public confessions of faith (symbols); it investigates the origin, nature, and contents of such statements, in comparison with other confessions or symbols. Most Churches regard the so-called *ecumenical creeds as normative in some sense. But individual Churches have also adopted specific creeds and confessions, e.g., the Lutheran *Augsburg Confession; the Reformed *Heidelberg Catechism or *Westminster Confession; the RC decrees of the Council of *Trent. A number of factors complicate the study of comparative symbolics. Some Churches refrain from drawing up any specific creedal statements, either because they hold to the principle of "deeds, not creeds," or because they feel that each individual Christian has the right to interpret the Scriptures on his own. Other Churches have formulated creeds in the past but view them only as the record of past experience and in no way normative for doctrine or practice in the present.

[R. BEESE]

COMPELLE INTRARE (Compel them to enter), the Vulg text of Lk 14.23, alleged in the Middle Ages as a kind of scriptural charter for the *Inquisition. The authority of St. Augustine was claimed for such an interpretation. But neither Augustine, this text, nor the teaching of the whole NT sanctions the use of force to exact faith from the individual.

[T. C. O'BRIEN]

COMPENSATION, a psychological term covering a broad range of reactive behavior motivated by the need to overcome feelings of inferiority. When an individual is conscious of characteristics or tendencies which are deficient in relation to the prevailing group norms, and he cannot overcome the deficiency directly, he will tend to strive to excel in other areas to regain his sense of personal worth, e.g., the short man will be aggressive, the homely woman, gracious and kind. Compensation, as reaction formation, is behavior of a kind opposite to repressed attitudes, the purpose of which is to disguise the repressed attitude, as when a parent is specially kind to the child he or she dislikes. Compensations can be healthy ways of handling personal defects or unhealthy ways of avoiding their recognition.

[M. E. STOCK]

COMPENSATION, OCCULT, the secret taking from another of what belongs or is due to oneself. It is rarely, if ever, justified; and then only if the other person is able to give what is due without undue loss to himself, is clearly obliged to give it immediately, and if all efforts to obtain it by ordinary means are unavailing. Failure to fulfill these conditions will ordinarily be a violation of justice and always of charity. The obligation of the other party to pay is not to be presumed but must be clear and certain. For example, one who feels he should be receiving a higher salary but cannot prove that his present salary is unjust, would violate justice in taking occult compensation. Even if the matter in question is an object which belongs to the first party but was lent to the other person for a specific use, the loan gives the other person a right to the legitimate use of it. To take it back secretly could offend charity and perhaps even justice by the inconvenience caused as well as by the mental anguish the other would suffer in thinking the object had been stolen. BIBLIOGRAPHY: F. C. O'Hare, NCE 4:89–90.

[J. J. FARRAHER]

COMPENSATIONISM, one of the *moral systems, and consisting in the position that in the case of a doubt whether a law prohibits an action, the action may be pursued if there is a good and sufficient reason. Such a reason "compensates" for the possible violation of law if in truth it does prohibit the action at issue. The casuistic kind of moral theology to which the moral systems belong is now widely deplored for its negative conception of morality and law, and for its neglect of the true meaning of Christian *prudence. Compensationism was developed in the historical context of the systems, and defined itself in their terms, specifically that a doubtful law obliges, but less strictly than a law known with certainty; that for proportionately good reason even a merely probable opinion legitimating an action may be followed in spite of the possibility that the law in doubt may demand the opposite. But what compensationism points to in essence is one function of prudence: to guide a positive choice of the moral good in concrete circumstances. That frequently entails a decision to act in the face of the possibility of a bad but unintended side effect. That is but one of the uncertainties with which true prudence must deal; an honest and appreciative weighing of values is the best that prudence can achieve, and no more is demanded of a right conscience.

[T. C. O'BRIEN]

COMPÈRE, LOYSET (Louis; *c.*1455–1518), Flemish composer. Pupil of Okeghem and fellow-student of Josquin, C. was chorister, canon, and chancellor of the Cathedral of St.-Quentin where he was buried. He belonged, together with Josquin, to the Netherlander School which had formed around Dufay. His known works include 2 complete Masses, 26 motets, 4 Magnificats, and the *chansons* in which he excelled. Among his motets is the famous *Omnium bonorum plena,* often called the "Prayer for the Choirmen," because the second part of the motet contains a prayer imploring the Virgin to intercede for the salvation of singers, whom C. names in the motet, beginning with Dufay and ending with himself.

[J. S. PALLOZZA]

COMPETENCY (CANON LAW), the jurisdictional power of a particular tribunal to apply the law to certain persons in certain types of cases. A competent tribunal is one to whose jurisdiction the defendant is subject, and before which the defendant can be brought by the plaintiff in the particular cause. A tribunal can thus be incompetent for two reasons. It can lack jurisdiction over the person of the defendant (e.g., only the pope has the power to judge cases of cardinals or papal legates, CIC c. 1557.1), or it can lack jurisdiction over the cause of action (e.g., a case concerning a benefice must be tried before the local ordinary of the place where the benefice is situated, CIC c. 1560). Except for cases reserved to the Holy See and cases whose tribunal is determined by law, every person can be sued before the ordinary of the place where he has a domicile or quasi-domicile (CIC c. 1561). There are special norms for determining the competent forum in matrimonial causes (CIC cc. 1960–1965). BIBLIOGRAPHY: T. J. Burke, *Competence in Ecclesiastical Tribunals* (1922).

[L. M. KNOX]

COMPIÈGNE, MARTYRS OF, sixteen Carmelite nuns martyred in 1794. In 1790, France's National Assembly abolished monastic vows and suppressed all religious orders and congregations. These nuns remained in their convent, but after the decree of August 17, 1792, requiring the sale and evacuation of all religious houses, the nuns, after taking the Oath of Liberty and Equality, dispersed into several associations. Subsequent search disclosed compromising materials in their possession, and this led to their imprisonment in June, 1794. They retracted the oaths they had taken and after a trial before Paris' Revolutionary Tribunal they were pronounced guilty and sentenced to death. They were beatified in 1906. BIBLIOGRAPHY: H. LeClercq, *La Révolution, 1794–1798* (1913); M. André, *La Véridique histoire des Carmélites de Compiègne* (1962); M. Lawlor, NCE 4:93–94.

[R. J. MARAS]

COMPLETORIUM, see COMPLINE.

COMPLEXIFICATION, a phenomenon within the process of evolution by which the exterior structures of matter move on an axis from the simple to the more complex. According to Teilhard de Chardin, complexity refers to the measurable "without" of things, the patterns of atomic arrangement from hydrogen to uranium moving up the biological scale to compound bodies increasing their molecular weight. To the extent they increase their molecular weight they complexify. In Teilhard's view the universe rides an axis of complexity ranging from simple subatomic particles of matter to complex mega-molecular structures. The axis is tilted so that downward on the scale is also backward in time to a point when only a simple world-stuff or layers of cosmic dust existed. Moving upward on this axis, increasingly complex forms of matter appear. Along this axis of complexification matter has been continually evolving both exteriorly in regard to measurable complex structure and interiorly in regard to intensity of consciousness. Man stands at the highest point of the axis because of his closely knitted cellular complexity and his self-reflective consciousness. BIBLIOGRAPHY: Teilhard de Chardin, *Phenomenon of Man* (1959); *Future of Man* (1964).

[W. J. DUGGAN]

COMPLINE, the last hour of the Divine Office (now called the *Liturgy of the Hours) in the Roman rite. As a night prayer, it considers the themes of sleep and waking, life and death, sin and grace. Originally, Compline was a private prayer of monastic communities, but, as *Vespers was moved to an earlier time, Compline came to be said in common and gradually assumed a solemnity comparable to Vespers itself. Compline resulted from the union of two distinct religious exercises: the evening spiritual reading of the monastic community which was followed by the abbot's commentary, an examination of conscience, and *Confiteor; and the hour of prayer built around the recitation of Psalms. As revised in 1971, the principal parts of Compline are one or two Psalms, a brief biblical reading, Simeon's Canticle (Nunc Dimittis), a concluding prayer, and an antiphon in honor of Mary.

[T. M. MCFADDEN]

COMPLUTENSES, the Discalced Carmelite editors, at Alcalá (Lat. *Complutum*) of a complete course of Thomistic philosophy, celebrated for its fidelity to St. Thomas Aquinas's thought; the name is also used for the volumes themselves. In its original form this *cursus artium* appeared 1624–28 in 4 v.; the standard edition, through additions and revisions, is in 7 volumes. The work is regarded as a companion piece to the *Salmanticenses, a theological *cursus*. BIBLIOGRAPHY: Elie de Jésus-Marie, *Catholicisme* 2:1426–28.

[T. C. O'BRIEN]

COMPLUTENSIAN POLYGLOT, the polyglot Bible edited at the direction and expense of F. *Ximénez de Cisneros, at Alcalá de Henares (Lat., Complutum in Spain. The work was undertaken in 1502, printed 1514–17, but not circulated until 1522. The OT includes the Septuagint and an Aramaic version of the Pentateuch, with Latin translations. The Greek text of the NT, based on carefully chosen Vatican MSS, was of a critical value superior to that of Erasmus' text of 1516. *TEXTUS RECEPTUS.

[T. C. O'BRIEN]

COMPRECATION, literally a praying together. The term usually refers to the *intercession which the saints make for others. Liturgical prayers, esp. eucharistic prayers frequently allude to this intercession.

[T. M. MCFADDEN]

COMPREHENSION (Lat. *comprehendere*), a theological term with two senses. The first is cognitional; it is the knowing of an object as much as it can be known, and thus God is comprehended by himself alone. The second is appetitional; in this sense it is the relation of will to a good really present and held in the mind and therefore enjoyed. And thus, developing the thought of I Cor 9.24, the theologians write of creatures of intelligence comprehending God in the *beatific vision. BIBLIOGRAPHY: ThAq ST 1a, 12.7; 1a2ae 4.3, with the commentary of Cajetan.

[T. GILBY]

COMPREHENSIVENESS, most often used with respect to the Anglican tradition, a word denoting any of three characteristics: (1) the moderation that characterized much of the Reformation in England, a moderation in large part intended to provide a reformed Church within which it would be possible for the people generally to find their place, without compromising any element of essential individual belief; (2) the necessity, if such inclusiveness is to exist, that the reformed Church conserve every essential element of historic Christian faith and order and require conformity to as little of what is nonessential as possible; (3) the characteristic often held before individual Anglicans as an ideal, that their manner of discipleship be such as to open to them as many diverse understandings of God and of the traditions of Christian life as is possible, for the deepening and enriching of their own ministries. BIBLIOGRAPHY: Mayer RB 274; Schaff Creeds 1:598–600; H. R. McAdoo, *Spirit of Anglicanism* (1965). *ANGLICANISM.

[S. F. BAYNE]

COMPULSION, an emotional, frequently irresistible drive towards an action that neither in itself nor for the compulsive person is reasonable or explainable. In a strictly psychiatric sense it is the urge to act upon an obsession or obsessive neurosis, i.e., an abnormal fantasy or irrational preoccupation rooted in the unconscious as the result of repression. In more general usage a compulsion may describe any uncontrollable urge, no matter what its basis. In either sense, an emotional compulsion includes physiological elements. Some compulsive actions in themselves have no moral quality, e.g., compulsive tidiness or compulsive work habits. Others are actions that considered in isolation are morally wrong: e.g., drunkenness, masturbation, theft. But where such actions are pathologically compulsive they are not morally responsible acts, and so are not culpable. A compulsion in the strict psychiatric sense requires professional diagnosis and therapy. A completely compulsive act even in its broader sense is also outside control, therefore lacks moral imputability; it may, however, be the effect of prior voluntary acts, and may be subject to gradual diminution through prayer and penance.

[T. C. O'BRIEN]

COMPULSORY EDUCATION, the requirement enforced by law that children acquire at home, by tutoring, or at school, certain information and rules of conduct generally recognized by civilized peoples as means of transmitting the cultural tradition. It should be distinguished from compulsory school attendance, a later development. Attendance at school was first legally required in Europe in the 16th cent. but not enforced until the 19th. It first became law in the U.S. in 1852 in Massachusetts; after 1900 it was mandatory in all states.

[M. B. MURPHY]

COMPUNCTION, a word which in common theological use is often employed as more or less synonymous to repentance, sorrow, or contrition for sin. But in its scriptural, patristic, and ascetico-mystical sense, it implies, in addition to sorrow for sin, the anguish of dissatisfaction with the things of this life and a strong yearning for God that is also a painful interior experience. It arises from the active cooperation of a number of different virtues such as faith, hope, love, penitence, and in ascetical and mystical literature it is considered as an essential requirement to spiritual development and advancement in the art of prayer. It precedes spiritual growth and is in turn augmented by that growth. Profound compunction is often accompanied by the gift of tears. BIBLIOGRAPHY: J. Pegon, DSAM 2.2:1312–21; D. Hurst, NCE 4:96.

[P. K. MEAGHER]

COMPURGATION, a judicial proof of innocence permitted in medieval ecclesiastical courts. Deriving from the statement, "An oath for confirmation is the end of all controversy" (Heb 6:16), it allowed a defendant to clear himself (*purgare*) of an accusation by calling on specified "oathhelpers" (*compurgatores*). By the 14th cent. it was almost wholly discredited. BIBLIOGRAPHY: F. Pollock and F. W. Maitland, *History of English Law Before the Time of Edward I* (2d ed. 1898, repr. 1952) 2:633–637.

[L. E. BOYLE]

COMPUTUS, a term covering those rules by which the date of Easter is calculated. After Dionysius Exiguus (*Liber de Paschate,* 526), a 19-year cycle (Golden Number) was the basis of all calculations; e.g., those of Bede (8th cent.), William Duranti the Elder (13th cent.), until the Gregorian Calendar (1582) adopted the Epact (age of the moon on 1 Jan.). BIBLIOGRAPHY: H. Nillis, *De computo ecclesiastico* (2d ed., 1864); M. Noirot, *Catholicisme* 2:1430–31.

[L. E. BOYLE]

COMTAT VENAISSIN, see VENAISSIN.

COMTE, AUGUSTE (1798–1857), French social philosopher, the most original of the Saint-Simonians; his social philosophy and religion of humanity are largely elaborations of *Saint-Simon's ideas. Comte represents the 19th cent. French secular mind in some of its most characteristic attitudes and aims. He distinguishes three successive stages in the cultural history of man: the religious, the metaphysical, and the positive or scientific. In 1848 Comte founded the Positivist Society and published *Discourse on Positivism as a Whole.* He regarded positivist sociology as the supreme science and the religion of humanity as the strongest guarantor of altruistic feeling. Comte's *Catéchisme positiviste* of 1852 (tr. R. Congreve, *Catechism of Positive Religion,* 1855), is the greatest expression in his day of the human value of science. BIBLIOGRAPHY: H. Gouhier, *La Vie d'Auguste Comte* (1931); G. Dumas, *Psychologie de deux Messies positivistes: Saint-Simon et Auguste Comte* (1905); J. Lacroix, *La Sociologie d'Auguste Comte* (1956); B. Mazlish, EncPhil 2:173–177.

[J. P. REID]

CON, GEORGE (Conn, Connaeus; d. 1640), papal agent. A native of Scotland, educated on the Continent, C. was employed by Card. Montalto in Rome and later by Card. Barberini, Urban VIII's secretary of state. He was sent to England by Barberini as papal representative to Queen Henrietta Maria (1636). He made some converts among those he met at court and engaged in conversations with Charles I aimed at improving the situation of English Catholics. Ill health compelled his return to Rome in 1639. BIBLIOGRAPHY: S. R. Gardiner, DNB 4:945–946.

CONATY, THOMAS JAMES (1847–1915), bp. and educator. After having founded the Catholic Summer School of America, he was appointed rector of The Catholic University, named domestic prelate, and consecrated titular bp. of Samos. Under his guidance, The Catholic University became a charter member of the Association of American Universities (1900). Upon termination of his rectorship, he was appointed bp. of Monterey-Los Angeles. He also contributed much to the preservation of the historic Catholic landmarks of California, namely the old missions. BIBLIOGRAPHY: P. E. Hogan, NCE 4:102; *idem, Catholic University of America, 1896–1903: The Rectorship of T. J. Conaty* (1949).

[J. P. COOKE]

CONCEIÇÃO, APOLINÁRIO DA (1692–1759), Franciscan writer. A Portuguese by birth, C. became a Franciscan lay brother in Brazil. He undertook to collect biographies of Franciscan lay brothers of saintly reputation. Much of his life was spent in Lisbon in research which also took him to France, Spain, and Italy. He published in four volumes biographies of 2,350 brothers under the title *Pequenos na terra, grandes na céu* (1735–54). He wrote another and more valuable historical work *Primazia seráfica* (1733), dealing with the Franciscans in Brazil. BIBLIOGRAPHY: D. de Freitas, *Elenco biográfico* (1931).

[J. R. AHERNE]

CONCELEBRATION, the celebration of any liturgical action by several ministers, or the congregational participation in the celebration of the liturgy. In the East the Greek term *sulleitourgein* (to concelebrate) may mean the simultaneous participation of more than one ordained minister in a liturgical function (e.g., the anointing of the sick, and in the Eucharist) and deacons as well as priests may be called concelebrants. But even in the East the term is most commonly understood to mean the participation *as such* of more than one minister of at least presbyterial rank in the celebration of the Eucharist. In the West the word most commonly refers to the celebration of the same Mass by two or more priests.

Concelebration has had different history in different places. Primitively it appears to have been the participation of the presbyterial college in the Eucharist of the bp. as a sign of unity, the key notion in all early eucharistic piety. This participation was expressed in various ways: common presence around the altar (Ignatius of Antioch), hands extended over the oblation (Apostolic tradition), etc.

One cannot say how frequently concelebration was practiced in the early Church, but we do know that visiting bps. were often honored by invitations to concelebrate with the local ordinary, and that the concelebration of priests with their bp. was customary throughout the East. In the ancient manner of concelebration, the principle of the distribution and nonduplication of liturgical roles appears to have been operative. The important thing was that the rite be accomplished and that all participate, but not that each presbyter "confect" the sacrament himself. Since the eucharistic prayer was extemporaneous in the early Church, it is clear that only the principal celebrant could have said it, at least in its entirety. This division of roles is still seen in the Chaldean and Coptic traditions, and partly, at least in the Greek Orthodox. The practice of verbal concelebration, i.e., the simultaneous recitation in common of the eucharistic prayer, developed in the 7th-cent. West and was spread by the Roman Ordinals. By the early Middle Ages there is evidence of a similar practice in various MSS of the Byzantine, Coptic (both Melkite and non-Chalcedonian), and Ethiopian traditions.

In the West concelebration continued to exist, esp. in the common celebration on important feasts of the bp. with his priests, until the 12th century. Thereafter the practice was dropped except at the ordination of priests and bishops. By that time the only form of concelebration regarded as sacramental in the West required all the concelebrants to recite the words of consecration together. It is argued that Western insistence upon verbal concelebration derived from the development in the Latin Church of the idea of the priesthood and what it means to function as such, and from a Latin spirituality.

It is also argued by some that this manner of concelebration is less fortunate liturgically, that it detracts from the eucharistic prayer, and that insistence upon it as sacramentally necessary appears unreasonable in the light of the early history of concelebration. One cannot impose on an already primitively established ecclesial reality a later theology, which, however legitimate, represents the practice and theory of but one tradition.

However, even in the East the practice of concelebration in the Byzantine Church bears some mark of the influences felt in the West. The Latinizing influence of the Kievan school of Peter Moghila (d. 1646) introduced the practice of verbal concelebration into the Russian Činovnik (Pontifical) of 1677, and consequently into the liturgical usage of the Slavic Churches that used the Russian liturgical books. The Latin practice has also been adopted by the Coptic Catholics for great feasts, but the Church of Ethiopia seems to have preserved the older form. Among the Greek Orthodox only the main celebrant consecrates, though the concelebrants recite the other prayers themselves. The West Syrians (except for the Maronites) have no concelebration, but practice a synchronized Mass. Daily concelebration among Catholic Byzantines is a uniate practice, a compromise based on the desire of priests to celebrate daily —itself a fruit of Latin piety—without accepting the full consequences of Western liturgical individualism by multiplying altars and saying private Masses, though even this is found in the more fully Latinized groups. The Byzantine rite is the only Eastern rite in which concelebration is a common practice today, though the influence of Vatican Council II is beginning to be felt among other Eastern Catholic groups.

Vatican Council II's constitution on the liturgy (Vat II SacLit 57) extended significantly the occasions on which Mass may be concelebrated, notably to Holy Thursday, priests' meetings, conventual Masses, and the principal Mass in churches when the needs of the faithful do not require individual celebration. Further extension of the practice is permitted in various places.

The theological arguments for concelebration are the unity of the priesthood and of the ecclesial community, posited as a visible sign in and through the Eucharist. Since Christ's sacrifice on the cross is of infinite value and as such is not increased by the multiplication of Masses, the form of celebrating Mass that allows for the most meaningful participation of priests and laity should be adopted when this can be managed without difficulty. Regardless of the position one may take concerning the theological disagreement on the sacramentality of a nonverbal consecration in which the concelebrants intend to consecrate but do not pronounce the words of consecration, nonverbal consecration is not permitted. BIBLIOGRAPHY: J. McGowan, *Concelebration* (1964); P. Tibon, "Eucharistic Concelebration," YBLS 6 (1965); A. Raes, "La Concélébration eucharistique dans les rites orientaux," *La Maison Dieu* 35 (1953) 24–47; K. Rahner and A. Häussling, *Celebration of the Eucharist* (1968).

[R. TAFT; T. M. MCFADDEN]

CONCENTUS, term used in church music to signify (1) the portions of liturgical chanting performed by the schola or choir rather than by the celebrant or other ministers; (2) the musical style of such chants, i.e., the neumatic and melismatic Gregorian melodies of the Mass chants and antiphons, responsories and hymns of the office as opposed to simple liturgical recitative. *ACCENTUS.

[P. DOHERTY]

CONCEPTION ABBEY, founded in 1873 in NW Missouri by Benedictines of the Swiss abbey of Engelberg, a monastic and educational center established in the 11th century. At that time known as New Engelberg, Conception was raised to abbatial status in 1881 and Frowin Conrad, its founder, became first abbot. Also in 1881 the abbey joined St. Meinrad Abbey, forming the Swiss-American Congregation of Benedictines. The monks of Conception Abbey are noted for missionary activities among Sioux Indians. At present they operate Conception Abbey Press, conduct lay and family retreats, a pastoral institute, and a Latin school in summer. The monks' educational emphasis is centered in Conception Seminary where they prepare candidates for the priesthood.

[A. P. DEEGAN]

CONCEPTUALISM, a broad generic term in philosophy used to indicate a position with respect to the epistemological problem of universals. Although there are variations of its meaning, in general it signifies the view that general ideas or concepts, sometimes called universals, exist only in the mind and not outside the mind in nature. Thus, e.g., man's concept of tree is said to be a universal in the sense that the definition of the essence "tree" as contained in the concept extends to all existing and possible trees, without exception. But as a universal, the concept exists only within the mind where it refers to an entire class of individuals, whereas outside the mind only the individuals exist—the distinct and separate trees. Hence, there is no real extramental class that corresponds to the content of the concept in the mind. In sum, the problem is one basic to reality and man's knowledge of it. Posed first by the Greeks of antiquity and debated throughout the Middle Ages, it seeks the nature of true reality by asking whether the universal in the intellect or the object in nature is the true reality.

As an epistemological view, conceptualism is usually portrayed as poised between two extreme positions—logical realism and *nominalism. Plato typifies the realists in holding for the existence of separated forms or ideas —universals such as ''treeness'' and ''dogness,'' in a real and independent state apart from the mind. William of Ockham represents the nominalists in completely denying the existence of universals. Individual entities found in nature bear in common only a common name, a so-called *flatus vocis,* so that the word tree is a mere sound identifying all individual trees but not signifying anything such as essence discovered as universally the same in every tree. The conceptualist concurs with the realist that universal concepts exist—but in the mind alone; he also agrees with the nominalist regarding the common character of names—but insists that they stand for general concepts in the mind which themselves signify essences found in nature. BIBLIOGRAPHY: G. Berkeley, *Treatise Concerning the Principles of Human Knowledge* (ed. G. Warnock, 1964); R. L. Aaron, *Theory of Universals* (1952); H. Price, *Thinking and Experience* (1953).

[J. T. HICKEY]

CONCERT, a performance of a fixed program by a group of musicians for the entertainment of an audience. Concerts, in the sense of public performances to which an audience is admitted by payment of a fee, originated in London between 1672 and 1678 with those given by John Banister, violinist, composer, and leader of the band of Charles II. Thomas Britton, a coal merchant and self-taught musician, carried on the practice, organizing a series of weekly concerts over the next 36 years. To a series of public concerts, *concerts spirituels,* founded in Paris in 1725 by Anne Dunican-Philidor, the modern concert-goer owes much of the present concert tradition. The *concerts spirituels* served as models for similar institutions on the Continent, and by 1791 the public concert had become commonplace throughout Europe and even to some extent in America. BIBLIOGRAPHY: T. M. Finney, *A History of Music* (1947) 334; P. A. Scholes, *The Oxford Companion to Music* (10th ed., ed. J. O. Ward (1970) 227–229.

[J. S. PALLOZZA]

CONCILIABULA, a term used historically to describe illegitimate councils of the Church. Famous examples are the Councils of Carthage (312), Ephesus (the Latrocinium, 449), Basel (1431, 1438), Pisa (1409, 1511).

[T. C. O'BRIEN]

CONCILIAR CATECHISMS, manuals for instruction containing a summary of doctrine which stems from a church council. The only one from an ecumenical council is the Catechism of the Council of Trent. Some examples of catechisms from plenary or provincial councils are the Baltimore Catechism (1885), the Catechism of Paris (1849), and the Catechism of the Council of Prague (1860). A small catechism was begun after Vatican Council I but never completed. Rather than a catechism, Vatican Council II prescribed that first a general directory concerning the care of souls be drawn up for use of both bishops and pastors and then directories for particular nations or regions. BIBLIOGRAPHY: P. DeLetter, NCE 4:109.

[V. GILLIGAN]

CONCILIARISM, the teaching that an *ecumenical council exercises supreme authority over the whole Church; the term was formerly also often used as a catchword for theories asserting that a council is superior to the pope. Historically conciliarism appeared in a variety of forms, some orthodox, some not. The conciliar movement, which peaked at the Council of *Constance (1414–18) and led to the resolution of the *Great Western Schism (1378–1417), was an outgrowth of conciliarism. Though antipapal conciliarism was later condemned because of the ecclesiology it implied, it reappeared both in *Gallicanism and in *Febronianism. Appeal to a general council was also a recurrent theme in the early days of the Reformation in Germany.

Modern authors trace the roots of the conciliar theory to the canon lawyers of the early 13th century. Although in practice canonists generally supported papal claims to a plenitude of power, in theory they discussed curbs and restraints to forestall the abuse of this power if it were to fall into the hands of a venal or incompetent pope. To safeguard the Church against such an eventuality, they established the norm that even the pontiff is bound by councils in matters touching the faith and the general state of the Church. These canonists commonly taught that conciliar decisions are to be preferred to the word of the pope alone.

By the start of the 14th cent. various conciliar theories were brought from the academic forum into the political arena. Political theorists, retained to defend the prerogatives claimed by emperors and kings from papal encroachment, elaborated antipapal conciliarism. *Marsilius of Padua (c. 1275–1342), in the employ of Louis IV of Bavaria, denied, in his work *Defensor pacis,* the divine origin of the papacy and asserted that supreme authority resides in a council representing laity as well as clergy. During the Western Schism, when the Church was divided by allegiance to rival popes, conciliar theories were put into action. Theologians from all over Europe worked together in the amorphous effort known as the conciliar movement; the leaders were Conrad of Gelnhausen (c. 1320–90), Peter d'Ailly (1350–1420), and Jean Gerson (1363–1429) of the Univ. of Paris; Francesco Zabarella (1360–1417) in Italy; and Dietrich of Niem (1340–1418) in Germany. Their aim was to convoke a council that would heal the schism and reform the Church in head and members. Although canon law legislated that only the pope can convoke a council, the conciliarists agreed that the extraordinary situation created by the schism had to be dealt with by extralegal means. Their first attempt, the Council of *Pisa (1409), compounded the confusion by electing a third claimant to the papacy, but their efforts finally bore fruit at the Council of Constance.

Two decrees illustrating the impact of conciliar theory on Constance are: Sacrosancta (April 6, 1415; sometimes called Haec sancta, from its opening words) and Frequens (Oct. 5, 1417). The first contains the classic statement of conciliarism: that being a general council representing the Catholic and militant Church, Constance held its power directly from Christ, and that even the pope must obey the council in matters pertaining to faith. Modern theologians continue to debate whether the Sacrosancta carries the weight of a dogmatic definition. Modern historians all agree that the decree Frequens was primarily disciplinary. It stipulated that, as councils are an ordinary part of church life, they should be held frequently to ensure continuing reform.

The conciliar movement exhausted itself during the protracted and sterile proceedings of the Council of *Basel (1431–49). Pope Pius II (1458–64) dealt the coup de grâce with the bull Exsecrabilis (D 1375) in 1460. He denounced appeals from papal authority to a general council. Nonetheless the 16th-cent. Reformers called for a council to vindicate their position. Later the Four *Gallican Articles (1682) cited Constance to the effect that general councils are superior to the pope. In the 18th cent., Febronianism held for conciliar rather than papal primacy. It was largely in response to Gallicanism and Febronianism that Vatican Council I defined papal supremacy and denounced those who would appeal to an ecumenical council as being superior to the Roman Pontiff (D 3063). BIBLIOGRAPHY: B. Tierney, Foundations of the Conciliar Theory (1955); E. F. Jacob, Essays in the Conciliar Epoch (rev. ed., 1963); H. Küng, Structures of the Church (1964); B. Tierney and L. M. Örsy, NCE 4:109–113.

[B. L. MARTHALER]

CONCINA, DANIELE (1687–1756), Dominican preacher and moral theologian. Trained by Austrian Jesuits, he joined the Venetian Dominicans, and proved an exemplary religious, devoted to primitive observance. He took a strict position on religious poverty, eating meat on fast days, taking interest on money loans, and going to the theater. His continual polemics against *probabilism made him a controversial figure, but he professed his intention of not attacking persons, only perniciously lax opinions. His 12-volume Dogmatico-Moral Christian Theology may be taken as representing the views of the high ecclesiastical establishment of the day, when Jansenism had been expelled and the influence of the Jesuits was declining, a middle-of-the-road course between too stiff and too indulgent a treatment of human nature. The introduction to his two-volume History of Probabilism and Rigorism opens with a revealing sentence, "Between the two extremes, benignity is a lesser evil than excessive rigor." BIBLIOGRAPHY: R. Coulon, DTC 3.1:676–707.

[T. GILBY]

CONCLAVE, a word used to describe the meeting of cardinals to elect a pope or to the place of election, a sealed-off area in the Vatican. Initiated by Pope Gregory X in 1274, the process of election today is governed by the regulations issued by Popes Pius XII, John XXIII, and Paul VI. Fifteen days after the death of a Pope, an election is held in an area cut off from all outside contacts. The cardinal camerlengo presides, assisted by three senior cardinals. The customary method of election is by secret ballot, a two-thirds majority required for election. Ballots are cast, two in the morning and two in the afternoon, until a majority is achieved. Paul VI in 1973 added several regulations: no cardinal after age 80 may take part in the conclave and the number of cardinals involved may not exceed 120. New instructions were given as to how a deadlock should be resolved: all cardinals in the conclave vote to suspend the two-thirds rule, or to delegate the election to a committee of cardinals, or to reduce the candidates to the two having the highest number of votes.

[J. R. AHERNE]

CONCOMITANCE, in the theology of the *Eucharist, the manner in which under the appearance of the bread, the blood of Christ; under the appearance of wine, the body of Christ; under the appearance of both, the soul of Christ are really present. Concomitance is taken in distinction from real presence "by virtue of the sacrament"; the theological point implied is that each sacrament directly brings about what the sacramental action and words signify. By virtue of the twofold consecration, then, Christ's body and blood are present separately; but because Christ becomes really present, there is concomitance in that in the risen Christ his whole humanity and divinity exist together inseparably. "If two realities are in themselves united, where the one is really present, so too the other" (ThAq ST 3a, 76.1). Thus the Council of Trent teaches that the whole Christ is wholly present under each of the Eucharistic elements; and adds particularly that the divinity of Christ is present in virtue of the *hypostatic union of humanity with divinity in him (D 1640, 1653).

[T. C. O'BRIEN]

CONCORD, BOOK OF, see BOOK OF CONCORD.

CONCORD, FORMULA OF, see FORMULA OF CONCORD.

CONCORDANCE, an alphabetical list of words in the Bible, arranged to show the location and context of each individual occurrence. Works of this kind are called concordances because the first listing of biblical words were made to show the harmony between different occurrences of the same word. The first verbal concordance in the sense in which the term is now understood was that of the Latin Vulgate produced under the direction of *Hugh of St. Cher (1240). The concordances in use in modern times are: for the Vulg, E. Peultier, L. Étienne, and L. Gantois (rev. ed., 1939); for the Hebrew, S. Mandelkern (4th ed., 1959); for the Septuagint, E. Hatch and H. A. Redpath (1892–97; supplement 1906); for the Greek NT, that of F. Moulton and A. S. Geden (1926), and that of A. Schmoller (8th ed., 1949). For English versions there are: for the AV, that of A. Cruden first published in 1737 and still available, and that of R. Young (1873); for the AV and RV, that of J. Strong (1894); for the DV, that of N. W. Thompson and R. Stock (1943); for the RSV, that of J. Ellison (1957). BIBLIOGRAPHY: G. Glanzman and J. Fitzmyer, *Introductory Bibliography for the Study of Scripture* (1961), 49–52; C. O'C. Sloane, NCE 2:537–539; EDB 410–411.

[C. BERNAS]

CONCORDAT, a public treaty between the Holy See and a secular State. The purpose of this agreement is to conserve and promote the interests of religion and esp. to safeguard the spiritual rights of Catholics residing as nationals in the country. Among the 150 concordats negotiated since the Concordat of *Worms (1122) are that of the Lateran (see LATERAN PACTS) and those described in the following entries.

[M. RILEY]

CONCORDAT OF 1801, an agreement between the papacy and France that settled the schism among Catholics which had arisen during the French Revolution, esp. in consequence of the Civil Constitution of the Clergy and the de-Christianization movement. The agreement called for the liquidation of the Constitutional Church established July 12, 1790, the removal of certain bishops invested in the pre-Revolutionary era, and determined the reduction of dioceses from 83 to 60. The preamble recognized Catholicism as "the religion of the majority of Frenchmen." The terms upon which agreement was reached after long and difficult negotiations were contained in 17 articles, whose content was as follows. (1) Catholicism was to be permitted free public exercise. (2) The Holy See would reorganize the dioceses. (3) The Pope expected sacrifices from the French bishops, even their sees. (4) The right of nominating bishops and archbishops under the new reorganization was conceded to the First Consul, although the Pope retained the right of institution. (5) The preceding article was continued in the instance of vacant bishoprics. (6) The bishops were to take an oath of fidelity to the government according to a certain formula. (7) There was to be an oath of fidelity taken by minor clergy. (8) There was to be a prayer in the Divine Office for the Republic and Consuls. (9) There was to be a reorganization of parishes with governmental approval. (10) Bishops were to appoint approved curés. (11) Dioceses were permitted to have cathedral chapters and one seminary each. (12) Bishops were to have disposition of nonalienated church properties. (13) The Revolution's expropriation of church lands was recognized, and their present ownership accepted as indefeasible. (14) The State was to pay clerical salaries. (15) Foundations for churches were declared acceptable. (16) Pope Pius VII fully recognized the First Consul's rights and prerogatives. (17) An elastic clause made provision for a situation in which the First Consul was not a Catholic, in which case a new convention would reinterpret art. 16 and the appointment to bishoprics.

Agreement on the above points was reached July 16, 1801; Pius VII ratified it Aug. 15 and Napoleon on Sept. 8. It was approved by the French legislature April 8, 1802. To the above articles of agreement, Napoleon later appended the 77 Organic Articles by a unilateral action that greatly diminished the advantages the Church might have gained by concordat. These articles regulated the relations of Church and State and, in fact, established the State as the sole judge of measures relating to the exercise of cults and Church life. Although Card. Caprara accepted these articles, the Pope gave them no approval. BIBLIOGRAPHY: H. H. Walsh, *Concordat of 1801: A Study of the Problem of Nationalism in the Relations of Church* (1933); A. Boulay de la Meurthe, *Documents sur la négociation du Concordat et sur les autres rapports de la France avec le Saint-Siège en 1800 et 1801* (1893–97) v. 3–4; Fliche-Martin 20:178–223; S. Delacroix, *La Réorganisation de l'Église de France après la Révolution* (1801–09) v. 1 (1962).

[R. J. MARAS]

CONCORDAT OF 1933, known as the *Reichskonkordat,* an agreement signed by the Holy See and the German government July 20, 1933, and ratified Sept. 10, 1933. It abrogated existing prohibitions against membership in the Nazi Party, agreed to curtail *"Political Catholicism," made no mention of racism, and presumably reached a satisfactory agreement about a number of "rights" of the Church. Laws concerning education were to be uniform, so that the establishment of confessional schools would be possible in all parts of the country. Although the State was accorded a limited privilege of challenging future appointments to episcopal sees, the Vatican secured control of theological professorships. Churchmen were forbidden to speak or act politically and all Catholic organizations having even semi-political programs were to dissolve. Groups serving purely religious or charitable objectives were sanctioned. None were named, but provision was made for reaching agreement between the German bishops and government authorities. This agreement was never satisfactorily concluded. Even before the ink had dried a series of violations was reported.

This concordat is one of the most controversial in history. Pius XI declared that he had assented with profound misgivings. It was supported by Card. Eugenio Pacelli, later Pius XII, largely for canonical reasons and because the German bishops urged it. The principal sponsors were Ludwig Kaas, leader of the Center Party, and Franz von Papen, conservative member of Hitler's Cabinet. BIBLIOGRAPHY: L. Volk, SJ, *Der Bayerische Episkopat und der Nationalsozialismus 1930–1934* (1965); *Documents and Readings in the History of Europe since 1918* (ed. W. C. Langsam, 1951) for text; *Documents on German Foreign Policy 1918–1945* Series D. 1:935–941 for violations of Concordat 1933–1937.

[G. N. SHUSTER]

CONCORDAT OF FONTAINEBLEAU, Jan. 25, 1813, a convention between the Holy See and Napoleon I intended to settle the issue of the institution of bishops in vacant bishoprics. Since 1808 Pius VII had refused canonical institution to "bishops" appointed by Napoleon, so that 27 episcopal sees had became vacant and religious life had regressed. To avoid further complications Napoleon convened an ecclesiastical commission. There Card. Maury suggested that uncanonical bishops might possess their sees as provisional administrators. On meeting again in March 1811, the commission referred the impasse to a national council if the Pope "refused to insert into the concordat [1802] a clause authorizing bishops . . . to confer canonical institution in the case of prolonged refusal." The council met in the summer with Card. Fesch, Napoleon's uncle, presiding and approved canonical institution by the metropolitan if it "had not been conferred on a bishop by the Pope within 6 months of his nomination." Although the Pope, imprisoned in Savona, signed the decree, Napoleon was still dissatisfied with the papal position. In January 1813, 6 months after the Pope arrived in Fontainebleau, Napoleon visited him and discussed the grave matter. The resultant convention of Jan. 25, 1813, pending definitive settlement, provided for papal renunciation of canonical institution of new bishops after 6 months of inaction. On March 24 in a letter to Napoleon the Pope retracted his agreement. Following his defeats in Russia and Germany, Napoleon abdicated and the Pope returned to Rome. Thus, the concordat was never put into effect. BIBLIOGRAPHY: Dansette v. 1; P. Féret, *La France et le Saint-Siège sous le premier empire, la restauration, et la monarchie de juillet* (1911); Fliche-Martin 20:269–274.

[R. J. MARAS]

CONCORDAT OF WORMS, see WORMS, CONCORDAT OF.

CONCRETE ART, term coined by Theo van Doesburg in 1930 as a refinement of "abstract art" with precise reference to the purely geometric works of Van Doesburg, Mondrian, and De Stijl. Emphasis is upon the painting as an entity in itself, as something concrete rather than abstracted or derived from nature. Eliminating all association, concrete art avails itself exclusively of the fundamental elements of visual art. Emancipated from models, it is a pure creation, absolute painting (comparable to absolute music). Important are later extensions into constructivism, color-field painting, systemic painting, optical art.

[M. J. DALY]

CONCUBINAGE (CANON LAW). (1) In general: a settled arrangement wherein a man and woman not married to each other habitually engage in sexual intercourse. The couple need not live together; they may be partners in an attempted marriage (see CIVIL MARRIAGE); or be unable to marry because of legal obstacles or canonical impediment. The concubinage may be secret or notorious. Public concubinage can be grounds for incurring the matrimonial impediment called *public propriety (CIC c. 1078); or the penalties of exclusion from holy communion (*ibid.*, c. 855, §1) or Christian burial (*ibid.*, c. 1240, §1, n. 6). (2) Clerical concubinage. The institution of clerical *celibacy in the Latin Church has required constant legislative discipline and sanctions. Because of that obligation no cleric in major orders can contract a valid marriage. Thus any state of sexual union with a woman is classified as concubinage. The current penalties against clerics in major orders include *suspension and the deprival of all privileges and proceeds from ecclesiastical offices and benefices (*ibid.*, cc. 2177, 2359, §1); the mode of procedure in cases of concubinage is set out in c. 2176–81. Those clerics having continuous contact with women that might give cause for suspicion and scandal are subject to a presumption of concubinage (*ibid.*, c. 133, §4).

[T. C. O'BRIEN]

CONCUBINE (IN THE BIBLE), a genuine wife above the rank of a mere slave but not enjoying all the privileges of the legal wife. Her husband did not have to support her; she could remain in her father's house where her husband went to her for sexual relations (Jg 15.1). Abraham (Gen 25.6), Jacob (35.22), Saul (2 Sam 3.7), David (5.13) and Solomon (1 Kg 11.3) all had concubines.

[F. J. MONTALBANO]

CONCUPISCENCE, a term entering theological discussion from the Vulgate *concupiscentia* found esp. in Rom 7.7–24; Gal 5.24; see also 1 Jn 2.15–17. As reflecting these sources, it came to mean the unruly propensity or tendency to sin existing in man from *original sin. In English, except in technical theology, the word has all but lost this meaning. For both Lutheranism and Calvinism, original sin and concupiscence were identified: the abiding propensity to evil in man was held to be a sinful condition, inherited by every man and imputed to him until he was saved by grace.

John *Wesley's doctrine of *Christian perfection, and the later doctrine of *entire sanctification concerning deliverance from involuntary, inbred sin, presume that evil tendencies remaining after justification are sinful. The Council of Trent affirmed that the RC Church never understood concupiscence to be sin, except in the sense of being the fruit of original sin and the seed of personal sins. Both *Baianism and *Jansenism asserted the sinfulness of concupiscence. St. Augustine's heated emphasis on concupiscence is exaggerated and lent itself to the interpretation that it is identical with original sin and is the direct source of the transmittal of original sin. St. Thomas Aquinas expressed a view equivalent to that adopted by Trent: concupiscence, the lack of an original harmony in man's desires with his true destiny, is part of original sin (the "material" element, he calls it); this ceases to be a sinful condition once the absence of the will's right relationship to God (the "formal" element) is rectified through baptism.

Concupiscence has also had a place in the vocabulary of moral theology as a designation for human emotion in general, and the emotion of desire in particular. As part of man's makeup, it is good, not evil; its relationship to his moral choices can be either beneficial or adverse. Because the desire for temporal ends does frequently subvert right moral decisions, concupiscence is often considered as a cause of personal sin. The narrowest use of the term identifies it with lust, e.g., when one of the benefits of matrimony is said to be "the allaying of concupiscence."

[T. C. O'BRIEN]

CONCURRENCE, DIVINE (Lat. *concursus divinus*), a term used by some theologians for the meeting of divine and creaturely activity. There is general agreement that God's causality is effective not only of the being of creatures by *creation and *conservation, but also of their acting; and it is this which is considered under the present heading. That he is the universal cause and that creatures are true causes are the two principles to be kept in sight if we are to steer clear of the extremes of *deism on the one hand, which holds that God, having wound up the universe, as it were, now leaves it to run under its own mechanism, and of *occasionalism, which teaches that the divine creative activity continues to account for all the causality in the universe.

Difficulty and differences crop up in the explanation of the mode of divine activity in the operation of rational beings through their *free will, and they appear at the levels both of natural and of Christian theology. First, how can the infallible action of the first cause leave intact the indeterminacy of a secondary cause? Second, how can the subjects by actual grace of God's irresistible love be said to choose him? This is a perennial debate, which, conducted with more refinement of logic than of feelings, found its classical baroque expression in the engagement between Dominicans and Jesuits (see CONGREGATIO DE AUXILIIS). Papal action at least stopped the two sides from labeling their opponents with *Calvinism and *Pelagianism; instead they spoke of *Bañezianism and *Molinism, and the attribution, if not comfortable, was not found intolerable by either side. Though the battlefield is somewhat deserted at the present time, what the fight was about remains a matter of interest.

Both sides were aware of the weakness not too well concealed by the term, "concurrence," which suggested that the first cause and the secondary cause was each a partial cause of the effect in which both cooperated. At this the Thomists hammered, with all the force of the truth that in none but a metaphorical sense is man a coordinate cause with God. In defense the Congruists held that he is subordinate to God's universal causality, in that a human act is sustained by a divine motion (*concursus simultaneus*) but not predetermined. They introduced a variety of distinctions, which may be pursued in the authors, *concursus* as God's own immanent activity and as productive of a transitive action, as *oblatus* or offering grace and as *collatus* or granting grace; but while resisting the attempt to reduce their position to the holding that God's influence on the human will was merely moral or persuasive, they would not concede that any preceding divine causality (*concursus praevius* or *praeveniens*) was intrinsically wholly effective. The Thomists do not like the term "concurrence"; for themselves they use the term "premotion," and apply it to divine causality as bearing on the secondary agent, not only on his acting, that is to say, as applied to its initiation, not only to its maintenance.

[T. GILBY]

CONCURRENCE OF FEASTS, the order of precedence in liturgical feasts. Sundays yield only to solemnities and feasts of the Lord. Solemnities occurring on Sundays of Advent, Lent, or Easter are observed on the preceding Saturday. Memorials are so arranged that elements proper to the saints are inserted within the Hours and Mass of the current day. Optional memorials may be observed; obligatory memorials must be celebrated. As for optional memorials: On Advent weekdays from December 17–24, the days within the Octave of Christmas, and Lenten weekdays (except Ash Wednesday and Holy Week), the Mass of the day is celebrated but the celebrant may use the opening Collect of the memorial at Mass. On Advent weekdays before December 17, weekdays of Christmas and Easter seasons, and weekdays in ordinary time, the celebrant may use the Mass of the day, Mass of the saint of the day may be found in the Lectionary. Weekdays yield to solemnities and feasts and are joined in the observance of memorials. If several celebrations occur on the same day, the one observed is that holding higher rank in the Table of Precedence of Liturgical Days. BIBLIOGRAPHY: Sacred Congregation of Rites, *Roman Calendar* (1975).

[K. O'NEILL]

CONDAMIN, ALBERT (1862–1940), French Jesuit biblical scholar. C. taught OT in Toulouse and at the Jesuit scholasticates in Canterbury and Lyons-Fourvière. He published numerous scriptural articles in French periodicals; began the "Bulletin des religions babyloniennes et assyriennes" in the *Recherches de science réligieuse* (1910–31), and edited the "Chronique biblique" in *Revue practique d'apologétique.* His special field of study was the structure of biblical poems and the relationship between Babylonia and the Bible. BIBLIOGRAPHY: F. Spadafora, EncCatt 4:209.

[T. M. MCFADDEN]

CONDÉ, a French family influential in politics for 10 generations, from Louis I (1530–69) to the death of Louis-Henri-Joseph in 1830. The Condé belonged to the Bourbon-Vendôme branch of the Capetians. Among the most famous are Louis I, Henri II, and Louis II, or the Grand Condé. Louis I, the first to receive the title, joined the Huguenots in 1559 and became involved in the religious struggle in which he was killed in 1569. Henri II (1588–1646) fought against the Huguenots in Languedoc in the service of Richelieu and thus acquired political favors. He was also instrumental in the founding of St. Sulpice for the training of priests. Louis II (1621–86), the Grand Condé, took part in the Fronde and thus alienated himself from Mazarin. Later under Louis XIV his successful military strategy won him full restoration of his privileges. Less capable as a statesman, he finally retired to Chantilly, where he patronized the arts and led an edifying life. His funeral oration was pronounced by Bossuet.

[I. M. KASHUBA]

CONDEMNED BOOKS, see BOOKS, PROHIBITION OF.

CONDIGN AND CONGRUOUS MERIT, see MERIT.

CONDILLAC, ÉTIENNE BONNOT DE (1715–80), French philosopher, priest, and commendatory abbot of Mureaux. C.'s life was devoted to speculation rather than to sacerdotal functions. (He is reputed to have celebrated Mass but once.) He is the founder of sensationalism, the philosophical tenet that all our ideas arise uniquely from exterior sensation. His psychology derives from Locke's empiricism, but denies Locke's "reflection" as a source of ideas. Somewhat inconsistently, for his stated position is agnostic, C. held for the demonstrability of God's existence and for the immateriality of the soul. The most influential of the 18th cent. French *philosophes,* C. was nevertheless repelled by the atheistic and materialistic conclusions drawn by others from his works. His major contribution lies in psychology and analysis, not in the synthesis of a coherent system. His best-known and most influential work is *Traité des sensations.* BIBLIOGRAPHY: E. H. Gilson and T. D. Langan, *Modern Philosophy: Descartes to Kant* (1963); Copleston 6:28–35.

[W. B. MAHONEY]

CONDITIONAL IMMORTALITY, the teaching that the human soul is inherently mortal and receives immortality only as a gift of grace or on condition that a person has lived an upright life. The term is often used interchangeably with annihilationism, because the teaching usually concomitant to conditional immortality is that the souls of the wicked are annihilated. Annihilationism strictly speaking, however, presupposes that the soul is immortal; total extinction is a punishment for sin. The doctrine of conditional immortality is ascribed to the 4th-cent. apologist Arnobius the Elder (PL 5:908) and to 16th-cent. *Socinianism. But the idea had its widest circulation in the 19th cent., esp. in the U.S., England, and Germany. In England the chief exponent was E. O. White; in the U.S. Charles F. Hudson's *Debt and Grace* (1857) and *Christ Our Life* (1860) were influential in the adoption of the teaching as a fundamental doctrine of the Advent Christian Church. Some form of conditional immortality is taught by Seventh-Day Adventists and by Jehovah's Witnesses. Lateran Council V (1513) condemned those who taught that the soul was mortal (D 1440).

[T. C. O'BRIEN]

CONDONATION, the giving up of the right to *restitution by one to whom it is owed in justice. Since theft or any other form of unjust injury consists in a person's being unwillingly deprived of what is his by right, the balance or *equality that justice demands can only be achieved by restitution or by the victim's willingly discounting the wrong done him. Such a concession, condonation in its proper sense, altogether remits, not merely delays, the debtor's obligation. A remission extracted by fraud or fear is not genuine condonation and does not excuse from restitution. In some matters, however, condonation may be tacit, namely where the victim can be rightfully presumed not to demand restitution, e.g., in the home where a child might take a trifling sum of money.

[T. C. O'BRIEN]

CONDREN, CHARLES DE (1588–1641), preacher and spiritual director. Though of delicate health C. persisted in his ambition to be a priest and was ordained in 1614. He entered the Congregation of the Oratory, established in France by Card. de Bérulle, and was to be the founder's successor in 1629. His tenure as superior general would last a lifetime in spite of his efforts to shed the responsibility. C. was the prime interpreter of de Bérulle, but enlarged his concepts. His central doctrine was the dependence of man on God the Creator and devotion to the Incarnate Word as the perfect priest and victim who offered the one sacrifice worthy of the Creator. The personal charm of C. made him acceptable to many, and among his admirers were St. Vincent de Paul and St. Jane Frances de Chantal. Posthumously published were his works *Discours et lettres* (1643); *L'Idée du sacerdoce et du sacrifice de Jésus-Christ* (1677); *Considérations sur les mystères de Jésus-Christ* (1899).

BIBLIOGRAPHY: A. Molieu, DSAM 2:1373-88; Bremond 3:284-418.

[J. R. AHERNE]

CONDUCTUS, medieval monophonic church composition with metrical text performed during those parts of the liturgy where the celebrant was conducted in procession from one place to another. By the end of the 12th cent. the term was applied to any nonliturgical Latin song of serious character with metrical text on a secular or sacred subject. In the polyphonic conductus of the 13th cent. the tenor or principal voice was no longer a pre-existing liturgical chant, but a newly composed melody, to which one, two, or rarely, three parts were added in note by note progression, a technique contrasting with the rhythmically differentiated voices of medieval organum or descant. Conductus was the first polyphonic form in church music in which the composer was completely free of chant.

[J. S. PALLOZZA]

CONFERENCE (MENNONITE), meetings of the representatives of Mennonite congregations, which deal with matters of doctrine, discipline, and church activities. In some Mennonite bodies the conference has authoritative power; in others its function is advisory. Use of the conference dates from the earliest days of Mennonite history. Originally members were the ministers, but in modern times lay representatives have been included. Formal organization and a regular schedule of meetings began in the late 18th and early 19th centuries. The district conference represents the congregations in one region; the general conference, the congregations of a whole Church. BIBLIOGRAPHY: MennEnc 1:669–670.

[T. C. O'BRIEN]

CONFERENCE (METHODIST), a term with both a geographical and a jurisdictional sense in Methodist *polity. Originally the Conference designated those ministers called together for consultation by John Wesley; then after his death, the 100 preachers named by him (see DEED OF DECLARATION). In England the Conference is now a body meeting annually in two sessions, one made up of ministers, the other of ministers and lay representatives of the Churches. The conference may not alter doctrinal standards, but it controls other church matters.

In the U.S. the Methodist Church has the following interrelated conferences. (1) Quarterly Conference, the ruling body of the local church. Besides its many obvious functions, it elects the lay representatives to the Annual Conference. (2) Annual Conference, the basic governing unit of the Church. It is composed of ministerial members and lay representatives from each Quarterly Conference; it is presided over by a bishop. Ministerial members vote on ordination of new ministers and their election to the conference; the whole conference votes on constitutional amendments and elects delegates to the Jurisdictional and the General Conferences. Boundaries of an Annual Conference within the U.S. are set by the Jurisdictional Conference; of one outside the U.S., by the Central Conference. (3) Jurisdictional Conference, a regional division of the Church, administering affairs within the United States. It is composed of equal numbers of lay and ministerial delegates elected by the Annual Conferences. The chief work is setting boundaries for Annual Conferences, and electing bishops. Quadrennial meetings, presided over by a bishop, immediately follow the General Conference, which determines the number of members and the boundaries of the Jurisdictional Conference "upon the consent of the majority of the Annual Conferences of each of the Jurisdictional Conferences involved" (Discipline 1964, 23). At the time of the merger of three branches of Methodism into the Methodist Church (1939), six Jurisdictional Conferences (five geographical and one racial), were constituted, all the Negro Annual Conferences being placed in a Central Jurisdiction. The latter is fast disappearing, since later legislation has admitted Negro Conferences to other Annual Conferences within their Jurisdictional Conference. (4) Central Conference, the name given to a Jurisdictional Conference outside the U.S. and its territories. (5) General Conference, the highest legislative body of the Church. Meeting quadrennially, it is made up of equal numbers of lay and ministerial delegates elected by the Annual Conferences. Bishops preside, but are not members. Functions include the revision of the Methodist Ritual, Hymnal, or Discipline, and the establishment of a budget for the whole Church. The General Conference may not alter the *Twenty-Five Articles of Religion, abolish episcopacy, change the General Rules, or appropriate Publishing House funds for any purpose but the support of retired preachers, their widows, and orphans. BIBLIOGRAPHY: N. B. Harmon, *Understanding the Methodist Church* (rev. ed., 1955) 102–114; *Doctrines and Discipline of the Methodist Church* (1964).

[F. E. MASER]

CONFERENCE OF HAGENAU, see HAGENAU, CONFERENCE OF.

CONFERENCE OF RATISBON, see REGENSBURG, CONFERENCE OF.

CONFERENCE ON CHURCH, COMMUNITY AND STATE, see OXFORD CONFERENCE.

CONFESSING CHURCH (Bekennende Kirche, 1934–45), German anti-Nazi evangelical movement. Even before Adolf Hitler's appointment as chancellor (1933), a *German Christian program, starting in Prussia and Thuringia, had begun to combine doctrinal liberalism, extremist nationalism, and anti-Semitism. As he came to power, Hitler encouraged them, bidding his little "brownshirts" go to church, portraying Jesus as hero and *Führer,* seeking a monolithic ecclesiastical structure. A

German Evangelical Church was indeed formed by German Christians who claimed that they represented National Socialism in the Churches. Soon disloyal pastors were suspended and church order disrupted. Martin *Niemöller, an important Berlin pastor, resisted this usurpation by forming an independent Pastor's Emergency Federation. A young theologian, Dietrich *Bonhoeffer, broadcast a stirring refusal to accept the Nazi *Führer-Prinzip* (leader-principle) and anti-Semitism. At Barmen in May 1934, the first synod of the Confessing Church was held, despite threats by political Nazis and the sycophantic German Christians. A resounding Theological *Barmen Declaration rejected the false doctrine that the Church should and could appropriate the characteristics, the tasks, and the dignity of the State, thus itself becoming an organ of the State and claimed that Christian and churchly obedience is owed only to Christ. The national bishop of the German Christians, Ludwig Müller, was rejected.

Redoubled persecution followed. Confessing Church bishops were arrested and variously harassed. But a second synod, at Dahlem in Oct. 1934, again stood firm. Three uncommitted church bodies now joined, though the government refused to recognize the now considerable body. Before the third synod met, in Augsburg in 1935, Nazi pressure was increased; some church finances were taken over, church courts were disallowed, and a Nazi Ministry of Church Affairs was given new powers. Torn between allegiances, Lutherans withdrew from the Confessing Church into their own council, the Lutherrat, weakening the resistance. The Gestapo now prevented notable pastors from preaching. The state forbade ecumenical contacts abroad. Neimöller was placed under house arrest. When World War II came in 1939, Confessing Church emphases were voiced anew by a Confidential Council of Clergy, which spoke out boldly against euthanasia (1940), secularizing of the Church in Poland (1941), Nazi indignity to Christianity (1942), the taking of church funds, and the crushing of the Jews (1943). The Nazis drafted 45% of the clergy, leaving mostly old and weak pastors. State rituals were timed to coincide with church observances. Paper for Bibles was barred (1940), most church publications were throttled (1941), and missions and chaplaincies were downgraded. Finally, when the war ended (1945), Bp. Theophil Wurm summoned leaders to Treysa to dissolve the German Christian state Church and form a new *Evangelical Church of Germany (EKD). Soon these leaders also created Evangelische Hilfswerk for crucial relief work and drew up the Stuttgart Declaration acknowledging war guilt. The Confessing Church demonstrated heroic resistance to state interference, to denaturing theology, to persecution of Jews, to political acts long regarded by many Lutherans and others as exempt from Christian comment. Its Barmen Declaration ranks among classic statements of Christian freedom and obedience under Christ. BIBLIOGRAPHY: S. Herman, *Rebirth of the German Church* (1946).

[J. O. NELSON]

CONFESSIO AUGUSTANA, see AUGSBURG CONFESSION.

CONFESSIO GALLICANA, see GALLICAN CONFESSION.

CONFESSIO TETRAPOLITANA, see TETRAPOLITAN CONFESSION.

CONFESSION, a term with several religious uses: (1) self-accusation of sin, whether public in liturgical prayers, or private to a priest, as in the RC sacrament of penance (see CONFESSION, AURICULAR); (2) a Church or denomination, so designated because a *confession of faith has been regarded by many as essential to church life; (3) the tomb of a martyr, e.g., the Confession of St. Peter, in Rome.

CONFESSION, the act of the penitent in the sacrament of *penance in which he accuses himself of his sins for the purpose of obtaining sacramental absolution. In recent years there has been much discussion of the utility and necessity of the sacrament of penance in general and of the act of confession in particular, and one effect of this has been a notable decline among the faithful in the frequency with which they make use of the sacrament of penance. Some, in urging a relaxation of the Church's policy of requiring the individual's confession of his serious sins before receiving absolution, have been motivated by the desire of some liturgists to see the liturgical character of the sacrament emphasized more clearly by *penitential services in which a group of people participate and receive a general absolution without further obligation of confessing specific mortal sins to a confessor in private. In any fair statement of the situation and the doctrine involved, it is essential to distinguish and discuss separately the role of confession when the penitent is conscious of having committed only venial sins, and when, on the other hand, he is aware that he has cut himself off from friendship with God by grave or mortal sin.

Venial sin. It is not, and never has been, part of Catholic teaching that a person whose habitual union with God and the Church has been unbroken by grave sin must at any time confess his lesser offenses in order to obtain forgiveness from God. There are many ways of obtaining God's pardon for the venial sins that are more or less inseparable from human living—e.g., by participation in the Mass and the reception of communion, by general absolution, by prayer, by almsgiving and other works of love and mercy. That is not to say, however, that the confession of venial sin and sacramental absolution serve no useful purpose in the life of a Christian who manages to avoid serious sin. The confession of venial sin, rightly made, is also a means of obtaining forgiveness. The use of the sacrament for this purpose has in fact been encouraged by the Church (cf. D 1679; D 3818), esp. for those who are striving to achieve an ever closer and more perfect union with Christ (CIC c. 595). Moreover, the explicit confession of venial sin has the added advantage of requiring the penitent, who would articulate his failings intelligibly to his confessor, to focus some attention on his specific failings and to give thought to means of overcoming them. In the experience of many confessors, the infrequent penitent is the one more likely to have difficulty in seeing that there are shortcomings in his life. However, it must be admitted that the purpose of the specific confession of venial sin can be frustrated to some extent by the routine and careless way in which such confessions are sometimes made. Still, the better remedy for such a situation is for the penitent to take the sacrament more seriously instead of abandoning its use entirely.

Mortal sin. The more serious question revolves about the obligation of a person in the state of mortal sin to submit his grievous sins to a confessor according to their specific nature and the number of times he has committed them. This obligation, according to the Council of Trent (D 1667) is one of divine law, as expressed in the communication of the power to bind and loose, a power that cannot reasonably be exercised without the revelation to a qualified minister of the Church of the penitent's misdeeds and of his inner dispositions. In recent years some theologians have suggested that the "divine law" mentioned in the statement of Trent ought to be taken to mean "ecclesiastical law," an interpretation not easily defended unless one is prepared, as some are, to abandon Trent's understanding of the texts concerning the power of binding and loosing. Still, even those theologians who hold to the stricter interpretation grant that in certain exceptional cases penitents may validly receive absolution without the actual confession of their sins. It has been the common doctrine of RC theologians that in urgent cases a priest obliged to celebrate Mass (D 1647), or one in need of receiving communion, who lacks access to a confessor, may do so after a perfect act of contrition; or if he has access to a confessor, but one with whom communication is impossible (e.g., because the confessor is deaf, or does not understand the language of the penitent, or because any form of private communication is impossible, as when an accident victim is receiving emergency treatment), he may receive absolution without prior confession; but it has been the common teaching of theologians that the penitent so absolved, or the perfectly contrite sinner, is obliged when he makes his next confession to make explicit mention of the sins forgiven but unconfessed. This would appear to be an obligation based on ecclesiastical rather than divine law. In view of the admitted exceptions to the obligation to make explicit confession of one's mortal sins, a more complete statement of the "divine law" requiring confession, or the ecclesiastical law (as some contemporary theologians would have it), must be understood to mean that the confession of one's mortal sins is necessary when this is not physically or morally impossible. *CONFESSION, INTEGRITY OF; *FIRST CONFESSION; *PENANCE, NEW RITE OF.

[P. K. MEAGHER]

CONFESSION, AURICULAR, the practice of confessing one's sins specifically and in private to a priest in order to receive absolution or pardon. Auricular, or private, confession in the RC Church is part of the sacrament of penance and is distinguished from public confession, whether specific or generic. According to the Council of Trent, secret confession (the term auricular is not used) has been practiced in the Church "from the beginning." The Council does not deny that the penitent may confess his sins publicly, for his own humiliation and for the edification of the Church, but states that such confession is not necessary by divine law. Nor is it always prudent (D 1683). More recent historians of penance are in general agreement that public confession was never obligatory in the early Church, although penitents may well have confessed publicly the major sins for which they were doing penance. The reason for private rather than public confession is explained by the 5th-cent. Greek historian Sozomen: "Now in seeking pardon it is necessary to confess the sin; and since from the beginning the bishops decided, as is only right, that it was too much of a burden to announce one's sins as in a theater with the congregation of the Church as witness, they appointed for this purpose a presbyter, a man of the best refinement, a man silent and prudent. To him sinners came and confessed their deeds . . ." (*Eccl. Hist.* 7.16; PG 67:1457). Some local churches in the vicinity of Rome had the practice of reading out the sins for which penitents were performing their penance; this was regarded by Leo the Great as a "defiance of Apostolic rule" (*Letters* 168; PL 54:1210).

Intimately bound up with the question of auricular confession is the necessity of confessing one's serious sins according to number, kind, and the circumstances that may change the nature of the sin. According to Trent such sacramental confession is necessary by divine law (*iure divino*). Trent allows, however, that a confession may be incomplete because of forgetfulness (D 1707). RC theologians offer other reasons besides forgetfulness that excuse a person from making an integral confession of sins, e.g., the physical or moral impossibility of making a complete confession. In such cases, the sins that have been indirectly absolved by the grace of the sacrament are to be confessed in a subsequent confession.

Martin Luther, while rejecting RC doctrine and practice on penance as a sacrament, strongly proposed confession and absolution. Article 4 of the *Augsburg Confession and Part IV of the Smaller Catechism extol private confession and absolution but reject the need for detailed enumeration of sins. Early in Lutheran history, however, auricular confession fell into disuse; there have been some modern efforts to restore it. The *Reformed Churches rejected private confession outright (e.g., Second *Helvetic Confession, c. 14). Both traditions retained general, public confession as preparation for the Lord's Supper, which became the practice generally of all Protestant Churches. In the Anglican Communion, the Book of Common Prayer includes a general confession as part of the communion service; some Anglo-Catholics observe auricular confession. Within the

Old Catholic movement, auricular confession is recognized, but its use is not obligatory. BIBLIOGRAPHY: *Sacraments and Forgiveness* (ed. P. F. Palmer: *Sources of Christian Theology* 2, 1960); C. J. Peter, "Auricular Confession and the Council of Trent," CTS 22 (1967) 185–200; B. Poschmann, *Penance and the Anointing of the Sick* (rev. ed., tr. F. Courtney, 1964); O. D. Watkins, *History of Penance* (2 v., 1920); H. Lindroth, EncLuthCh 1:561–565; K. Rahner, LTK 2:805–815.

CONFESSION, FIRST, see FIRST CONFESSION.

CONFESSION, GENERAL, see GENERAL CONFESSION.

CONFESSION, INTEGRITY OF, the quality of completeness that should mark the penitent's revelation of his grave sins to his confessor in the sacrament of penance. A confession is said to be integral when the penitent discloses all his serious sins according to their moral kind and the number of times he has committed them. Because in some circumstances no complete enumeration (and sometimes no enumeration at all) is physically or morally possible, theologians distinguish two forms of integrity. Material integrity occurs where there is exact correspondence between what the penitent accuses himself of having done and the sins he has in fact committed. Formal integrity, on the other hand, is said to exist when the penitent's self-accusation is as complete as is physically or morally possible in the circumstances in which he seeks or is granted absolution. Thus memory failure could make material integrity impossible, but the penitent's confession would nevertheless be formally integral and suffice in the circumstances for the valid reception of the sacrament. In a variety of other circumstances formal without material integrity would be sufficient—e.g., when there is a possibility the penitent (or confessor) could be overheard, when many in an emergency are given general absolution without the possibility of individual access to a confessor, when a language barrier makes communication with the only available confessor impossible, etc. Sins unconfessed in these or similar curcumlaw be mentioned in the penitent's next confession. *CONFESSION.

[P. K. MEAGHER]

CONFESSION OF AUGSBURG, see AUGSBURG CONFESSION.

CONFESSION OF BASEL, see BASEL, CONFESSIONS OF.

CONFESSION OF CRIME. A guilty person charged with a crime may positively deny his guilt. He is not obliged to confess or testify at his own trial. This is a natural right which is also granted by secular and canon law (CIC c. 1743). The denial is not a lie; it is either a mental reservation or equivalent to invoking a privilege. If he testifies he is obliged to tell the truth. The suspect is not obliged to permit tests upon his body, e.g., blood tests. The immunity is a natural right and may be granted by law. It is uncertain that he has the right to refuse a test which does not touch his person, e.g., a breath test. Theologians discuss the obligations of the criminal when he has deliberately cast suspicion upon an innocent person, and when, though he has not deliberately cast suspicion on another, someone else faces punishment for the crime. BIBLIOGRAPHY: R. H. Dailey, NCE 4:135–136.

[R. H. DAILEY]

CONFESSION OF CZENGER, see HUNGARIAN CONFESSION.

CONFESSION OF DORT, see DORDRECHT CONFESSION OF FAITH.

CONFESSION OF FAITH, an external acknowledgment of belief. Because the Christian faith is ecclesial, it calls for a public acknowledgment of Christ (Mt 10.32–33). The Gospels themselves are confessional literature rather than sheerly objective historical sources. The most ancient and most basic confession of the early Christian community was "Jesus is Lord" (1 Cor 12.3; Acts 2.21–36; Rom 10.9; Phil 2.11). As the expression of faith was elaborated upon, esp. in the liturgy, catechetics, and polemics, it crystallized into Christological, Trinitarian, and ecclesial formulas. The confession of faith is often taken synonymously for creeds, symbols, and professions of faith containing specific and principal beliefs. During the Reformation various communions drew up official doctrinal statements, e.g., the *Augsburg Confession of 1530. Since then the term "confessions" has come to designate the Protestant groups that espouse statements of doctrine, sacramental matters, and polity. The trend is to amend such statements into formulations that are briefer and more contemporary, but binding only to the extent that they are consonant with the Scriptures. See particular confessions of faith under proper titles. BIBLIOGRAPHY: W. A. Curtis, Hastings ERE 3:830–901.

[J. FICHTNER]

CONFESSION OF LA ROCHELLE, see LA ROCHELLE, CONFESSION OF.

CONFESSION OF 1967 (UNITED PRESBYTERIAN CHURCH IN THE U.S.A.), part of the revision of the confessional position of this Church, and the most important doctrinal shift in American Presbyterianism since organization in the colonial period. As one of the results of the union of the Presbyterian Church in the U.S.A. and the United Presbyterian Church of North America (1958), a special committee was formed to compose a contemporary statement of faith for the new denomination. The conception of the committee grew. Believing that the living Church of Jesus Christ has the right and duty to restate the faith from time to time, the denomination followed the proper constitutional steps to revise its confessional position. This invoked a Book of Confessions, including the Nicene Creed, the Apostles' Creed, the *Scots Confession (1560), the *Heidelberg Catechism (1563), the Second *Helvetic Confession (1561), the *Westminster Confession and *Shorter Catechism (1647), the Theological Declaration of Barmen (1934), and the Confession of 1967. This new Confession is notably biblical; it is based upon the theme of reconciliation in 2 Cor 5 (God's Work of Reconciliation, the Ministry of Reconciliation, and the Fulfillment of Reconciliation). Trinitarian and ethical in its emphasis, the Confession attempts to suggest what reconciliation means in regard to modern war, poverty, and race and sex relations. The Book of Confessions was adopted overwhelmingly and with a subscription formula; officers of the denomination promise to perform their duties under the "continuing instruction and guidance" of this volume of confessions.

[J. H. SMYLIE]

CONFESSION OF WÜRTTEMBERG see WÜRTTEMBERG CONFESSION

CONFESSIONAL, the place designated for the private celebration of the sacrament of *penance. Canon law provided in the past that women make their confession in the confessional except in case of necessity; men were permitted to confess in other suitable places. Since penance was originally administered before the assembled congregation, the early Church did not have confessionals. When the practice of frequent private penance began to emerge in the 6th cent., it took place in the priest's residence. From the 12th to the 16th cent., confession was made before the priest who sat on a chair between the altar and the communion rail. A subsequent emphasis on secrecy gave rise to a metal grille separating the priest and penitent. In the Baroque period the place for hearing confessions was decorated, and a boxlike structure, usually containing three compartments, developed. The priest sits in the center, separated from the penitent on either side by the grille. Contemporary liturgical reform favors a type of confessional chapel allowing for greater ease of expression and a more personal administration of the sacrament. A new rite of penance offers the penitent the option of receiving the sacrament in the traditional way, i.e., in the confessional or in a more informal situation, face to face with the confessor. *PENITENTIAL SERVICES; *PENANCE, NEW RITE OF.

[T. M. MCFADDEN]

CONFESSIONALISM, the position that adherence to a *confession of faith is necessary for church life. In this literal sense any Church that is confessional, i.e., expresses its faith in a doctrinal standard, accepts confessionalism as a principle; it was operative in the establishment of the Lutheran and Reformed Churches. The opposite is anticreedalism. The pejorative use of confessionalism connotes an exclusive adherence to a confession, implying the superiority of one Church over all others. The RC Church is often singled out as most extremely confessionalist. In theory Protestant ecclesiology is able to justify the coexistence of many confessions of faith thus: even if Christ established one Church, its actual existence will find diverse expressions. Practically, however, an exclusive confessionalism has often manifested itself and caused divisions. The ecumenical movement strives to overcome such confessionalism without advocating *syncretism or indifference to confessions, or desiring their abolition. Protestant thought seeks a solution in reemphasis on the witness of Christ in Scripture as the supreme rule of faith. RC acceptance in Vatican Council II of the ecclesial character of other Christian communions has been regarded as a hopeful ecumenical step. But confessionalism remains one aspect of the problem of church unity.

[T. C. O'BRIEN]

CONFESSOR (Lat., *confiteri,* to declare openly), a title of honor used in sanctoral classification to designate those male saints who do not fall within the category of martyrs but who proclaimed the faith by their way of life. The name has an exceptionally broad extension, including popes, bps., ascetics, monks, priests, religious, and laymen. In early Christianity the only sanctoral designation was that of martyr, and all who had suffered for Christ, even if only by imprisonment, torture, or exile, rather than by the actual loss of life itself, were indiscriminately called martyrs. In the 2d cent., the category of confessor began to be used. According to *Eusebius of Caesarea in his *Ecclesiastical History* (5.2), the martyrs of Lyons disclaimed the title of martyr for themselves because they had not yet proclaimed Christ by dying and therefore deserved no more than to be called confessors of Christ. Further reservation of the term martyr was sought by Tertullian and Origen who wanted to restrict its use to those who were no longer living and had actually shed blood in proving their faith. The distinction between martyr and confessor gained ground in the 3d cent., but the meaning of the latter term still was not that of its present understanding. Confessor was then associated with one who, although he had not given his life for the faith, had still suffered for it. It was not until the cessation of the persecutions in the 4th cent. that the asceticism and holiness of saintly men were recognized in a metaphorical way as a confession of Christ on a level with that of the martyrs, and the cult of these men, as confessors, began to flourish. BIBLIOGRAPHY: E. Day, NCE 4:141–142; J. Miller, *Fundamentals of the Liturgy* (1959) 417–419; H. Leclercq, DACL 3.2:2508–15; A. Bugnini, EncCatt 4:249–252.

[B. ROSENDALL]

CONFESSOR, REGULAR, a priest to whom a penitent with deliberate regularity opens his conscience and makes his confession. In ordinary circumstances the repeated use of a single confessor in preference to a random or perhaps deliberate selection of different confessors for successive confessions is a practice that has been encouraged by theologians and masters of the spiritual life. It is not obligatory, however. A situation in which the same confessor deals with the same penitent is, generally speaking, favorable to greater continuity of spiritual effort and to the channeling of it in directions more suited to the needs of the particular penitent. The regular confessor is more likely, other things being equal, to understand the particular penitent's state of soul, his individual characteristics and capacities, his special problems, difficulties, and graces. He is thus better qualified to correct, offer advice, give consolation and encouragement, impose suitable penances, and indicate objectives toward which the penitent can reasonably strive. The regular confessor in practice often fills the role of spiritual director, although the two offices are not necessarily inseparable. BIBLIOGRAPHY: P. Scharsh, *Confession as a Means of Spiritual Progress* (tr. F. A. Marks, ed. A. Preuss, 1942); J. C. Heenan, *Priest and Penitent: a Discussion of Confession* (1937).

[N. HALLIGAN]

CONFIGURATION WITH CHRIST, a theological metaphor for the likening to Christ brought about by grace, particularly *sacramental grace. Such likeness means that all grace is derived from Christ as exemplar and source; this is an interpretation of Rom 8.29, "to be conformed to the image of his Son" (e.g., by St. *Ambrose, *De Spiritu Sancto* 1.6; PL 16.723). St. Thomas Aquinas comments on these words, "The Son of God willed to communicate a conformity with his own sonship, so that he is not only the Son, but the firstborn of many" (*In Rom.* 8, lect. 6). To be alike in form or in figure are terms related to quantitative shape, but the metaphorical use intends spiritual likeness (ThAq ST 3a, 63.2 ad 1). "Configuration" became a term in the medievals' vocabulary particularly to describe the effects of the sacraments. In general, sacramentally received graces configure the recipient to Christ as he suffered, died, and rose (*ibid.*, 1a2ae, 85.5 ad 2; 3a, 49.3 ad 2; 52.1 ad 2). More particularly, a commonly quoted "school" definition of the *character conferred by baptism, confirmation, and orders termed it a configuring of the recipient to Christ as priest, able to share actively in the worship Christ's sacrifice pays to the Father (*ibid.*, 3a, 63.3; see also Vat II ApostLaity, 2–4; MinLife Priests 2).

[T. C. O'BRIEN]

CONFINALIS *(Affinalis),* in medieval psalmody, the name for the pitches a, b, and c', which occur as the finals of transposed chants. When the dominant or reciting tone becomes so conspicuous that it becomes the *confinalis* or substitute final, instead of one of the four regular finals d, e, f, or g, a change of mode or modulation has taken place to a scale beginning five tones higher or four tones lower. This is done to avoid use of the chromatic Bb-B. The transposed chant makes use of the same scale pattern without requiring the use of Bb. BIBLIOGRAPHY: D. N. Ferguson, *History of Musical Thought* (repr. 1975).

[J. S. PALLOZZA]

CONFIRMATION, or strengthening, a part of the Christian process of initiation, a complement to baptism in which the Holy Spirit is given. It is one of the seven sacraments of the New Covenant. In the East this sacrament is known as anointing or chrism; the popular Western designation, *confirmatio,* did not appear until about the 5th cent. in Gaul.

Because of its close association with baptism, much difficulty surrounds early Christian witness to this sacrament, esp. as a distinct phase of the process of Christian initiation. There is, however, some scriptural testimony, even though it is far from explicit and must be sought in those narratives concerning the outpouring of the Spirit and the laying-on-of-hands. Three passages are relevant: first, the Pentecostal narrative (Acts 2.1–41) which projects a type rather than the reality of confirmation; and second and third, the distinct episodes of Acts 8 and 19 in which baptism is clearly distinguished from a further rite that follows and complements it in which a new gift of the Spirit is realized through the imposition of hands. The further rite is surely that of confirmation.

The distinction between baptism and confirmation attested to by Scripture is not, however, observable in the activity of the community in the immediate postscriptural era. The historical development, esp. of the ritual, of confirmation for this period lies buried in confusion and controversy. The obscurity begins to lift about the 3d cent. in the writings of Hippolytus (*Apostolic Tradition, c.*215) where the rites of baptism and confirmation are again viewed as distinct. Tertullian and St. Cyprian in the same century continue and accentuate this distinction to the extent that the individual sacramentality of confirmation is almost universally acclaimed by Christian writers from the 4th cent. on. The doctrine was made definite in the 13th cent. when confirmation was listed as one of the seven sacraments and affirmed as such by the Council of Lyons (1274). The present era has witnessed a renewal of interest in confirmation, esp. in seeking a theological clarification of its relationship with baptism.

Although confirmation is distinct ritually, as has been shown, from baptism, its theology demands that it be regarded as a complement to baptism. As part of the rite of Christian initiation, confirmation perfects and finishes the work of baptism and orients the confirmed toward the final stage of that initiation, the Eucharist. The work of baptism is completed in the sealing of the Spirit, i.e., in the affirmation afforded by confirmation of the presence of the Holy Spirit in the initial saving event of one's baptism. As a seal of the Holy Spirit's work, confirmation deepens the person's union with Christ and pledges God's commitment toward him. In orienting toward the Eucharist, confirmation appears as an anointing of the Spirit, i.e., a consecration of the Christian to a sacred office. The consecration is twofold: a priestly anointing and a consecration as a prophet or witness of Christ. By the priestly anointing, an individual is drawn more deeply into the mystery of eucharistic worship, entering thereby more intensely into the re-enactment of Christ's paschal mystery. The prophetic consecration strengthens the Christian in his witness to Christ before the world. It is a witness to the type of life one is expected to lead in helping to build the Christian community, which task is also associated with the immediate objective of the Eucharist.

In effect, then, confirmation is the sacrament of mature encounter with Christ, affording an opportunity for an adult adherence to the Christian commitment and community. It binds one closer to the Church by urging a call to community service with resoluteness and dedication and carried out in terms of adult prudence and courage. In a related sense, then, confirmation is the sacrament of social awareness demanding a deeper involvement in Christian witness.

The same theological point is apparent when the sacramental character is considered. Like baptism and holy orders, confirmation imprints a sacramental character or seal which effects a more direct participation in the priesthood of Christ. The character is a spiritual power that orders the recipient to acts of Christian cult; in the case of confirmation, to the propagation and defense of the cult.

As a sacrament, confirmation has a sign-value, varied yet reasonably clear, which has just been described in the discussion of its theology. The sign itself, however, an external and sensible thing observable in its ritual, is far less easy to distinguish. The process of seeking to determine the essential action of the sacrament—imposition of hands or anointing—is greatly complicated by history. Scriptural evidence points to the imposition of hands, but in the East, from which it was gradually introduced into the West, conferral of confirmation was by anointing with chrism, and this was eventually to become the predominant rite. The historical argument, as to which action is essential, continues largely unresolved, but is avoided in practice by church law which determines that both rites be used (CIC c. 780). Paul VI in the apostolic constitution *Divinae consortium naturae*, Aug. 15, 1971, decreed that the anointing is the essential element in Confirmation. The symbolism of the ritual extends back to the religious traditions of the OT people where both the imposition of hands and the anointing with oil were gestures of blessing and consecration. The regular minister of this sacrament is the bishop.

Without harm to the essential matter and form of the sacrament, Vatican Council II called for a revision of the ritual of confirmation in order to bring out its intimate connection with the whole process of Christian initiation (Vat II SacLit 71). The new rite was promulgated in 1971. Debate also presently continues over the desirable age for the reception of this sacrament, whether it ought to be in late adolescence to preserve the character of confirmation as the sacrament of maturity, or at an earlier age to restore the normal order of Christian initiation (baptism—confirmation—Eucharist). The instruction accompanying the new rite leaves the age for children's confirmation to be determined by the Episcopal Conferences. BIBLIOGRAPHY: M. Thurian, *Consecration of the Layman* (tr. W. J. Kerrigan, 1963); M. Bohen, *Mystery of Confirmation* (1963); *Rites of the Catholic Church* (1976), 298–334.

[B. ROSENDALL]

CONFIRMATION IN GRACE, a special supernatural gift whereby a person cannot fall into the state of mortal sin. Sanctifying grace is conceived of by theologians both as life and a relationship established by love. Life and love per se tend to perpetuate themselves. But, replying to the teaching of Calvin that grace once given cannot be lost, the Council of Trent taught that even the graced person can sin and thereby lose divine life and fall out of God's love. Divine life and personal love are, however, bestowed with complete gratuitousness on the part of God. Thus no limit can be set upon them any more than actual graces that precede justification or that are proposed by some theologians to implement it can be qualitatively or quantitatively restricted. It is possible for God to give actual grace of such strength and frequency that man will not resist. Such grace is called efficacious. It would also seem possible for God to bestow his life and love in such abundance that it will not be lost. Whether, as some theologians think, the result is produced through a series of efficacious actual graces, or, as others hold, it comes from sanctifying grace itself, a person who cannot fall into grave sin is said to be confirmed in grace. Although such a person remains free, God's special providence protects him against abandoning his fundamental option by committing sin. Various solutions to the problem of reconciling freedom with confirmation in grace are proposed by different theological schools. Theologians commonly cite as examples of persons confirmed in grace the Virgin Mary and the Apostles. The rare gift of confirmation in grace differs from the great but common one of final perseverance in that the latter takes into account the circumstance of dying in grace. BIBLIOGRAPHY: J. Gummersbach, *Unsündlichkeit und Befestigung in der Gnade* (1933); *idem* and M. Viller, DSAM 2:1422–41.

[C. R. MEYER]

CONFIRMATION NAME, the name chosen by the person to receive the sacrament of confirmation and given by the confirming bishop or priest. The 1971 revised Rite of Confirmation makes no mention of a confirmation name.

[J. R. AHERNE]

CONFIRMATION OF AN ELECTION. Where a superior's confirmation of an election is required by canon law (e.g., of a general religious superior by the Holy See), the one elected, the elective body or other representative in his name must request it within 8 days of the election; otherwise the one elected loses all title to the office. The appropriate superior cannot deny confirmation of one duly elected and competent. Confirmation, which is to be given in writing, brings with it from the moment of its reception full rights to office. (See CIC c. 177).

[T. C. O'BRIEN]

CONFITEOR, (Lat., I confess), a prayer acknowledging sinfulness and petitioning forgiveness. In the 11th cent. the Confiteor was introduced into the Roman rite to occupy a period of silent adoration before the beginning of Mass. Together with its accompanying prayers, it came to be regarded as a sacramental absolution until the rite of penance was more precisely established. Since the Confiteor expressed well the mentality, prevalent in much medieval theology, which stressed man's sinful separation from God, the prayer came to be used within several sacramental rites. Recent liturgical reforms have limited its use, e.g., before the distribution of communion and the beginning of Mass.

[T. M. MCFADDEN]

CONFLICT OF INTEREST, in its technical meaning, the opposition between personal advantage (usually economic) and the proper administration of influence held by reason of official position. The two principal areas of its impact are government and business, and the fundamental problem in both areas is the same—the integrity of officials. Although the details of cases greatly vary, the situations in which conflict of interest arises seem to come to four: (1) personal financial interest in a producer or supplier with which the official's own company or governmental department does business; (2) the acceptance of gratuities, gifts, or entertainment from such producers or suppliers; (3) the holding of an outside job such as agent or consultant in firms which, again, may be suppliers; and (4) the use of "inside" information to buy or sell stock. Obviously if a government official engages in such self-dealing as to cause the public unnecessary expense or to endanger public safety, he is derelict in duty. Likewise an official of a corporation who causes loss to his stockholders by directing company business to his personal outside interests is guilty of injustice.

More subtle and elusive is the question of merely holding an interest in supplier or customer, or doing business on the side with one's own firm or department, where no fraud is involved. These actions cannot be condemned as wrong in themselves. Yet they place the official in an equivocal position and put him in the way of temptation; rather importantly they also give the appearance of wrongdoing which destroys public confidence. For these considerations it is generally agreed that there should be legal control of such action for government officials. This general agreement is due to the fact that these officials are regarded as public servants, elected or appointed to care for the public welfare; their office then is a trust. Consequently complete devotion to the public interest is the integrity required of them. This integrity must be preserved not only in fact but even in appearance, for public confidence is endangered when this devotion appears to falter. And public confidence is the basis of effective government.

The case for business executives, directors, and managers is not quite the same, nor is the same consensus found. An individualistic ethic has made the morals of the market place somewhat looser than those of government. Two considerations of Catholic social teaching make it clear that the business executive, besides his acknowledged trust towards the stockholders of his company, has also a duty of trust to the general public somewhat analogous to that of the government official. These considerations are the social aspect of property and the concept of business as a profession. Given the preponderant place of the corporation in modern economy, the social aspect of property imposes a special obligation on those whose decisions direct it. The concept of business as a profession further accentuates the public trust of the businessman, so that business is to be seen not merely as a means of enriching those who engage in it, but also of having a social function to supply certain goods and services to the community. The good of business as a profession demands that codes of professional ethics be drawn up, defining and delimiting the activities of business officials in the area of conflict of interest. Without such regulation, the service of the common good is impaired. Public confidence in the integrity of the businessman is necessary for the common welfare. If this integrity appears to be lacking, mistrust is inevitable in labor-management relations, and social agitators seeking the destruction of the system of private enterprise can play on the emotions of a suspicious public; the morale of other employees is damaged, and an unhealthy cynicism seeps through the entire social order.

[W. F. DRUMMOND]

CONFORMITY TO GOD'S WILL, the correspondence of a morally good action with the divinely intended good. A moral act is good when it is the choice of a genuinely good object. But the good in every reality chosen is its reflection of the divine good, and its conduciveness to a sharing in that divine good. God's will is in fact the imperative force in the eternal law: it makes that law, and every way of sharing in it, directive towards the final end. Conformity to God's will may be explicitly intended, but it is always implicit in every choice of the true good. The correspondence, however, does not always consist in an agreement between what is chosen and the good that God intends. What it does mean is the reason and motivation for choosing; it is the value intended, implicitly or explicitly. More concretely, conformity to God's will is inherent in the meaning of *charity: a union in will with God is love for God. The term can also be associated with the high spiritual ideal of abandonment to God's will, and with the resolution of the crises of Christian life by resignation to God's will. BIBLIOGRAPHY: ThAq ST 1a2ae, 19.9, 10. *ABANDONMENT, SPIRITUAL; *RESIGNATION.

[T. C. O'BRIEN]

CONFORTI, GUIDO MARIA (1865–1931), bp., founder of Xaverian Missionary Fathers. Ordained in the diocesan seminary in 1888, he was appointed abp. of Ravenna in 1902. Pope Pius X in 1907 requested him to become bp. of Parma where he labored for 24 years. In 1898 he founded a missionary congregation. Thus, while he cared for his diocese, he demonstrated his zeal for the world. In 1960 the process for his beatification was begun in Rome.

[J. A. ROCHE]

CONFRATER, a term that stems from the late medieval period but in its modern use it generally refers to the secular oblates of the Benedictine Order. In both periods the term *confrater* designated one who aids or has aided the monastery in a special way and consequently is given a share in the good works and prayers of the monks. BIBLIOGRAPHY: J. C. Almond, CE 11:188–89.

[H. P. ANNAS]

CONFRATERNITIES AND ARCHCONFRATER-NITIES, sodalities established as moral persons for the purpose of promoting a specific form of public worship, usually suggested by the title. When empowered by the Holy See to affiliate similar confraternities they are called archconfraternities. The confraternity must have a corporate structure with a body of officers who lead and guide its common activities. Constituted ecclesiastically as a moral person, the confraternity may acquire, own, and administer church property and sue or be sued in ecclesiastical courts. Every parish is required to have a Confraternity of the Blessed Sacrament and a Confraternity of Christian Doctrine (CCD). Affiliated confraternities enjoy any communicable privileges and favors of the affiliating confraternity.

[H. P. ANNAS]

CONFRATERNITY OF CHRISTIAN DOCTRINE (CCD), lay organization established in 1571 for the purpose of offering religious education to Catholic children, youth, and adults. In 1905 Pius X began a modern revival and expansion of the program when his directive, that CCD be established in every parish, was incorporated into canon law. A decree of Vatican Council II reaffirmed the directive, and today the CCD in the U.S. has become the "basic cell of catechetical activity"; it includes numerous new developments outside the school system from the parish to national levels. In 1969 CCD became a division of the department of education of the U.S. Catholic Conference. According to recent figures some 5½ million Catholic children participate in its programs.

[C. KEENAN]

CONFRATERNITY VERSION (CCD), an authorized translation of Old and New Testaments undertaken by the Catholic Biblical Association of America at the request of the episcopal committee of the Confraternity of Christian

Doctrine. The NT, published in 1941, was an American revision of the Rheims-Challoner NT, and although the revisers made constant use of the Greek text, it was ultimately based on the Vulgate. Subsequently, and partly as a result of the lead given by the encyclical *Divino afflante Spiritu,* the policy was radically changed, and the translators set themselves the aim of producing a version ". . . from the original languages or from the oldest extant form of the text, and to present the sense of the biblical text in as correct a form as possible . . . combining due reverence for the text with strict observance of the rules of criticism" (Preface to the OT, v. 1, 2d ed., 1953, p. 6). The OT was published in four volumes, and these, combined with the new translation of the NT, were published in 1970 under the title *New American Bible (NAB).

[D. J. BOURKE]

CONFUCIANISM, a philosophy based on the writings of the Chinese philosopher, *Confucius. It was the most important educational force in China until the Communist takeover in 1950. Confucius, who traced his descent back to 2550 B.C., preached no religion but encouraged a system or code of ethics that influenced education, government, and attitudes toward correct personal behavior and one's duty to society. It stressed a system of reciprocity, a negative version of the Golden Rule. "What you do not wish others to do to you, do not do to them," and encouraged the moral and social virtues. Confucius himself was a religious man in the sense that he accepted the main religious beliefs of his people. Yet he was reluctant to speak of a personal God and life after death. He attended the rites connected with propitiatory fasting, war, and sickness, yet for him heaven was an impersonal deity, a moral power of providence on the side of men struggling for righteousness. Society could be saved if it attended to sincerity in personal and public conduct. Hence the virtuous lives of rulers had a greater effect on the governed masses than did harsh laws and punishments. When Confucius died he was unknown but his followers spread his ideas. Among his more famous adherents was Mencius (392–289 B.C.) and Hsun-tzu (fl. mid-3d cent. B.C.). Mencius taught a Confucianism based on the natural goodness of man while Hsun-Tzu stressed a righteousness based on education and law. By 200 B.C., after the unification of the Chinese Empire, the teachings of Confucius became the basis of the educational system and the *Five Classics,* the five books of Confucian thought, were the foundation of the education of all leaders in China. However, with the rise of Buddhism and Taoism the emphasis shifted to more theistic belief. These religions dealt with the problems of human existence, such as the meaning of suffering and death, which Confucianism ignored. Later developments during the Middle Ages saw the establishment of the rational and the intuitional wings of Confucianism which have been called Neo-Confucianism. Their followers sought enlightenment by meditating on the nature of their own minds. Today Confucianism is forbidden in China because it encourages people to revere the past rather than look to the future, but the ideas of Confucius are still held by many in the East. BIBLIOGRAPHY: A. S. Rosso, NCE 4:156–164; H. Fingarette, *Confucius: The Secular as Sacred* (1972).

[T. LIDDY]

CONFUCIUS (*c*.552–*c*.479 B.C.), Chinese teacher. The name is the Western form of K'ung Fu'tzu, Master K'ung. According to the *Analects,* C. was born in Lu (modern Shantung) to a family of modest circumstances. He sought to reform society by his teaching and by training his disciples to take government positions. Though he did not have a government position where he might put his theories into effect, and generally failed to have any effect in his own time, his thought later triumphed. A state cult of Confucius began under the former Han dynasty (202 B.C.–23 A.D.). BIBLIOGRAPHY: H. G. Creel, *Confucius and the Chinese Way* (1949); *idem, Confucius, the Man and the Myth* (1973); H. Fingarette, *Confucius: The Secular As Sacred* (1972).

[T. EARLY]

CONGAR, YVES (1904–   ), French Dominican ecclesiologist. C. was born in Sedan (Ardennes), France, entered the Dominican Order in 1925, was ordained in 1930, taught at the Dominican studium, Le Saulchoir near Paris, and served as director of the Dominican monastery in Strasbourg, France. C.'s principal theological concerns have been ecumenism and the reform and renewal of the Church; he has developed many of his ideas out of the thought of Aquinas. By rethinking and restating the traditional doctrines such as the humanity of Christ, the role of Mary, the mystery of the Church, and the role of the layman, C. has broken new ground for understanding and uniting divided Christendom. He is the founder of the series, *Unam Sanctam,* and served as peritus and member of the Theological Commission at Vatican Council II. Among his principal works are: *Divided Christendom* (1937); *Lay People in the Church* (1952; rev. ed. 1965); *The Mystery of the Temple* (1962); *Catholic Church and the Race Question* (1966); *Ecumenism and the Future of the Church* (1967). BIBLIOGRAPHY: S. P. Schilling, *Contemporary Continental Theologians* (1966).

[S. C. TOTON]

CONGÉ D'ÉLIRE (Fr., leave to elect), in English law, the royal permission to choose a bishop. The congé d'élire before the Reformation was in effect a compromise in the disputes between kings and popes over the right to appoint bishops. From 1214 the crown granted permission to cathedral chapters to elect bishops, reserving the right of confirmation by royal assent. By the Annates Statute (1534) under Henry VIII, renewed in the *Act of Supremacy (1559) under Elizabeth I, the congé d'élire was changed:

cathedral chapters were to elect to vacant sees candidates nominated by the crown in "letters missive."

[T. C. O'BRIEN]

CONGREGATIO DE AUXILIIS (1598–1607), a commission instituted at Rome by Pope Clement VIII and continued by Paul V, because of the bitter dispute between Jesuits and Dominicans "on the helps of divine grace." Clement took the dispute into his own hands (1594) because in Spain and Portugal it had upset the academic world and even had become a scandal to the faithful. The controversy, begun at Salamanca in 1582 and having its counterpart at Louvain in 1587, became violent when the Jesuit L. *Molina published his *Liberi arbitrii cum gratiae donis . . . Concordia* (1588). The Dominicans, led by Domingo *Báñez, denounced him to the Spanish Inquisition; the Jesuits made countercharges. The Dominican position, labeled by the Jesuits as a form of Lutheranism or Calvinism, was this: grace is efficacious in itself, not because man cooperates with it; grace causes man's cooperation since it is a physical premotion and predetermination of his will, consistent with God's gratuitous, infallible predestination. The Jesuit position, branded as a new *Pelagianism by the Dominicans, was this: grace, offered equally and sufficiently to all, becomes efficacious because of man's free acceptance; it does not directly move the will, but cooperates with it; yet God's predestination remains gratuitous and infallible because of *scientia media,* the knowledge by which before offering his grace God foresees man's free acceptance. The main agenda for the 120 sessions *De auxiliis* (after 1602 under the personal presidency of the Pope) was the examination of propositions from Molina's *Concordia.* Beginning in 1602 the position of each side was also debated; the principal spokesmen for the Dominicans were Diego Álvarez and Tomás de Lemos; for the Jesuits, Gregory of Valencia and Ferdinand de la Bastida.

Under Clement in 1598, 1602, and 1605, and under Paul V in 1606, the commission recommended condemnation of Molina's teaching. Neither Pope acted on the recommendation, however; many universities as well as political friends interceded against a step that would have been damaging to the Jesuits. At the meeting, on Aug. 28, 1607, of eight cardinals with Paul there was no clear consensus. He suspended the inquiry, reserving final judgment, and declared each side free to defend its teaching but not to label the other as heretical (see D 1997). In 1611 both were forbidden to publish on the debated issue, a prohibition renewed in 1625, 1641, and 1654, but which later became a dead letter. Never has a doctrinal point been more thoroughly examined. Yet the *De auxiliis* exhausted eminent theologians not in the cause of theological progress but in a controversy that was fruitless and was an influence in the rise and progress of *Jansenism. The classic histories of the *De auxiliis,* both partisan and polemical, are the version by the Jesuit L. de Meyer, *Historiae controversiarum de di-*

vinae gratiae auxiliis (2d ed., 2 v., 1742), and the version by the Dominican J. H. Serry, *Historiae congregationum de auxiliis libri quinque* (2d ed., 1740). BIBLIOGRAPHY: T. Ryan, NCE 4:168–171; L. Bournet, DHGE 5:959–970, with bibliog. *BÁÑEZIANISM; *MOLINISM.

[T. C. O'BRIEN]

CONGREGATION, those gathered together for worship, as distinguished from minister or preacher; also the local church. In English versions of the Bible the word is used for the collective body of Israel or for a public solemn assembly. It may refer to the entire Church, as in the *Thirty-Nine Articles, which define the Church as "a congregation of faithful men." In reaction to the Anglican term "parish," which implied that all residents of a given area were church members, Congregationalists and Baptists held that the true Church was made up only of genuine Christians and that local assemblies, or "congregations," of such persons constituted the visible Church on earth (see GATHERED CHURCH). In the U.S. the tendency toward self-governing local congregations affected nearly all Protestants, and the term is generally synonymous with *local church. In RC usage the administrative departments of the Roman Curia are called Congregations; one type of religious community is called a congregation; the association of several monasteries of one religious order is also called a congregation, e.g., the Benedictine Congregations.

[N. H. MARING]

CONGREGATION DE NOTRE DAME, SISTERS OF THE (CND), the first religious community of women founded in North America. Established in 1658 by Marguerite Bourgeoys at Montreal, Canada, this uncloistered congregation follows St. Augustine's Rule. Education is their primary work. Pope Leo XIII gave final papal recognition in 1892 when their constitutions were revised in accordance with the Code of Canon Law. In the 1970s the sisters conducted 200 schools—elementary, secondary, college, and specialized—with foundations in Canada, the U.S., Guatemala, and Japan.

[H. P. ANNAS]

CONGREGATION OF NOTRE DAME DE SION, a community founded in Paris, France (1843), by the wealthy Ratisbonne brothers, which has as its purpose the promotion of a real understanding between Jews and Christians. The active members fulfill this aim through education while the contemplatives center their life in the Eucharist and Liturgy of the Hours. Approbation of their rules was given on Dec. 14, 1874, by Pope Pius IX. The community numbered 1,475 in 1975 and maintained 148 houses on five continents; the generalate is in Rome.

[H. P. ANNAS]

CONGREGATIONAL, related to the form of church polity in which the *local church, or congregation, is au-tonomous. While Congregationalism is named from this polity, many other Christian bodies, esp. those originating from English *Nonconformists, are congregational. Congregational polity is distinguished from both episcopal and presbyterian forms of government.

[T. C. O'BRIEN]

CONGREGATIONAL AND CHRISTIAN CHURCHES, GENERAL COUNCIL OF, union of local Christian and Congregational Churches (see CONGREGATIONALISM) effected in 1931; most participants became (1957) part of the United Church of Christ (UCC). The General Council was strictly an association of local churches, not a national Church or denomination. The merger was based upon mutually accepted principles of polity, esp. the autonomy of the local congregation. The association fostered fellowship in missionary and educational work; local churches continued their historic traditions. At the time of the formation of the UCC there were about 1,300,000 members of the Congregational and Christian Churches. (On the local congregations that did not enter the UCC, see CONGREGATIONAL CHRISTIAN CHURCHES, NATIONAL ASSOCIATION OF; CONSERVATIVE CONGREGATIONAL CHRISTIAN CONFERENCE.)

[T. C. O'BRIEN]

CONGREGATIONAL SINGING, singing of hymns by assembled worshipers, a feature of most religions, but esp. Christianity. Early Christians, following Jewish tradition, sang Psalms, and there is mention of a hymn sung by Jesus and his disciples in the Upper Room (Mk 14.26). In the early Middle Ages hymn singing underwent considerable development in both the Greek and the Latin Churches. The later Middle Ages saw congregational singing decline, partly because church worship continued to be in Latin and singing was largely restricted to clergy and choirs. Outside the churches folk songs in the vernacular were popular. The Reformation restored congregational singing to a prominent place, making it one of the distinguishing marks of Protestant worship. This development was well under way even before Luther, and much of pre-Reformation change in the Church found its expression in song. Jan *Hus made use of popular song to advance his cause, translating Latin hymns and writing original hymns in Czech. Quick to use the newly invented printing press, the *Bohemian Brethren published a Czech hymnal in 1501. Their first German version appeared in 1531, and their first Polish version, in 1554. With Luther congregational singing came into its own on a national scale. His use of hymns, many of which he wrote himself, along with his translation of the Bible and his catechisms, played an important part in the establishment of the Reformation. Among Calvinists congregational singing was long restricted to metrical versions of the Psalms, esp. in England and Scotland. Anglican hymnody was slow to develop because of the Anglican Church's retention of pre-Reformation patterns of worship. Not until the time of Isaac Watts (1674–1748), first English hymn writer of note, did hymnody in England catch up with its much earlier development in Germany. By then England began to feel the upsurge of song characteristic of the Wesleyan revival. Back of this revival was German *Pietism, brought to England by the Moravians. Their hymns were one of the first items to attract John *Wesley to them, though it was his brother Charles who became the great hymnist of Methodism. Count *Zinzendorf occupied a similar role in the Renewed *Moravian Church. More enduring were the hymns of the English Moravian James Montgomery (1770–1848).

Prominent in German hymnody, both of the Lutherans and the Moravians, is the chorale tune marked by plain melody, strong harmony, and stately rhythm. Both Pietist and English revival hymns tend to be subjective and individualistic. The 19th- and 20th-cent. equivalent are the so-called Gospel songs. Many of these are the product of American frontier *revivalism. The hymnody of every Church is subject to a winnowing process in which hymns of quality, expressive of the best of Christian thought and feeling, become the great hymns of other Churches. Interdenominational exchange of hymns and their translation into many languages has made all church hymnals significant symbols of ecumenicity.

In the RC Church, although the structure of the Roman rite provided for congregational participation in liturgical song, the actual singing was long left to specially trained choirs, except in religious houses in which the whole community was commonly expected to join in. The retention of the Latin liturgy tended to discourage interest on the part of the people at large, and even the attempt of Pius X to improve ecclesiastical music, in the long run retarded the development of any widespread congregational participation in the singing, for efforts were focused on Gregorian chant, which proved too esoteric a medium for general use by ordinary people. Leaders in the liturgical movement continued to call for more active participation on the part of the congregation. Their desire found official voice in Vatican Council II's *Constitution on the Liturgy* (ch. 6) and in the decree *Musicam sacram,* which urged that whenever a sacred action is celebrated with song, the whole body of the faithful should contribute the active participation, which is rightly theirs. The adoption of the vernacular for the liturgy encouraged the hope that these directives could be successfully carried out, but many obstacles remained to be overcome: the traditional reluctance of many Roman Catholics, esp. in the U.S., to sing out in church; the banality of many liturgical songs when translated into the vernacular; the dearth of really good music and suitable hymns; the lack of agreement with regard to standards and taste; and esp. the unwillingness on the part of many to experiment, a reluctance due in some cases to ingrained habit and conservatism but understandable in other cases as a reaction to the extravagance of some experimentation. Against these obstacles some progress has been made, but much remains to

be done. BIBLIOGRAPHY: H. B. Marks, *Rise and Growth of English Hymnody* (1948); J. Gelineau, *Voices and Instruments in Christian Worship* (1964); F. J. Guentner, NCE 4:171–173; *idem, Crisis in Church Music?* (1967).

CONGREGATIONAL WORSHIP, BOOK OF, see BOOK OF CONGREGATIONAL WORSHIP.

CONGREGATIONALISM, that form of church life maintained and expressed in the independence and autonomy of the local church or congregation. The Church is held to consist essentially in a gathering of covenanted believers under the sole headship of Christ and guided by his Spirit. Independence is freedom from binding creedal statements and from any control, ecclesiastical or civil, over the local church. Defending the rights of the believer's private judgment, those adhering to Congregationalism believe that by their association and fellowship the assembly of believers derives an understanding of matters of belief, worship, and *church order suited to actual experience and need. A congregational form of polity is maintained by Baptists and other denominations; the churches called specifically Congregational have their main history in the U.S. and England.

Congregationalists regard themselves as conforming to the order prevailing in the NT Churches. They find their ideal affirmed in the early ecclesiology of both Luther and Calvin and that practiced by the Swiss Anabaptists. In English history, J. *Wycliffe and the *Lollards are regarded as precursors of the ''Congregational Way.'' The first Congregational Church is claimed, with some probability, to have been one pastored by Richard Fytz in London as early as 1567. It was Robert *Browne in his *Reformation without Tarrying for Anie* (1581) who became the explicit advocate of *independency. Congregationalists took their place in the 17th cent. alongside Puritans and Separatists in their opposition to the C of E in theological agreement on the basic tenets of Calvinism and in sustaining persecution. By 1609 many, led by Browne and John *Robinson, took refuge in Holland. Under the *Commonwealth, Congregationalism was able to establish itself in England, although disabilities against all *Nonconformists continued until the 19th cent., and in 1658 the *Savoy Declaration, a modification of the *Westminster Confession, was adopted. Congregational Churches were united in fellowship and formed county associations; and such ties led to the establishment in 1832 of the Congregational Union of England and Wales. Congregationalists led in the formation of the London Missionary Society (1795); the colonial Missionary Society (1836) led to the spread of Congregationalism to Australia, New Zealand, Canada, and South Africa.

Under the inspiration of John Robinson Congregationalists left Holland on the *Mayflower* and in 1620 founded the Plymouth Colony in Mass., basing the settlement on the Mayflower Compact. These Plymouth people with the Bay people in 1648 set forth an agreed program of church government in the *Cambridge Platform. The Congregational Churches in the New England colonies became practically established Churches, and traces of establishment lasted into the 19th century. Congregational Churches were formed in the Northwest Territory from 1796 onward by settlers from New England. A *Plan of Union in effect (1801–52) for cooperation with Presbyterians on the expanding frontier actually worked to the diminution of Congregational influence. In New England itself, doctrinal division (1819–25) led to the loss of a third of the churches there to *Unitarianism. Congregational churches throughout the nation drew together in regional or state associations. A denominational consciousness in keeping with the American pattern increased, and by 1871 the first National Council of Congregational Churches was held in Oberlin, Ohio. The Council continued to function until the merger of Congregational with Christian Churches in 1931 created the General Council of Congregational and Christian Churches. In 1959 a further merger, regarded as a landmark in the ecumenical movement, brought about the *United Church of Christ (see CONGREGATIONAL CHRISTIAN CHURCHES, NATIONAL ASSOCIATION OF; CONSERVATIVE CONGREGATIONAL CHRISTIAN CONFERENCE).

Congregational Churches have been notably active in educational and missionary works. Most of the older colleges in New England, and more than 40 others, as well as 10 theological seminaries, are of Congregational origin. Missionary work began among the Indians from the beginning of the Plymouth Colony. In 1810 the *American Board of Commissioners for Foreign Missions was formed, and 2 years later it sent out the first American foreign missionaries; the Board now forms part of the United Church Board for World Ministries. The American Home Missionary Society, organized in 1862, helped the spread of Congregational churches throughout the West; it still continues as an agency for home missions and other evangelical services. Internationally most Congregational Churches are members of the International Congregational Council, set up in 1948 after a series of occasional meetings dating from 1891. Reckoned as the official confessional agency, it has represented Congregationalism throughout the world in the ecumenical movement. Douglas *Horton was its official observer at Vatican II. In 1966 decisions were taken that led to union with the Alliance of Reformed Churches in 1970. The body thus formed called itself the National Association of Congregationalists.

The history and life of Congregationalism reflect its nature as primarily a form of church polity. There is considerable emphasis on full lay involvement in the life of the local church and in all forms of association; government is normally by meetings of members. While local churches are not constituted as parts of national or regional Churches, they are normally voluntary participants in regional, national, or international associations. The extent of organization and the degree of surrender of autonomy have increased considerably since 1900. Ministry is ordinarily also functional to the local church, though in ordination the wider fellowship is almost invariably associated and recognition given for a general ministry. Women are ordained.

Because of its independency and noncreedalism, Congregationalism is not characterized by fixed tenets of doctrine. English Congregationalism retained the Savoy Declaration. In the U.S. the changing patterns of American theology have been reflected in, and often shaped by, Congregationalists. The Calvinism of the Westminster Confession and Catechism was the background of the *covenant theology of the theocratic New England colonies, and of the *New England theology of Jonathan *Edwards in the *Great Awakening. Reaction to Calvinism, as well as the inroads of rationalism, set off the split of Congregationalists into Trinitarians and Unitarians. Liberalism became a characteristic of Congregationalists in the 19th and into the 20th cent., but some local churches were strongly evangelical and conservative (see LIBERAL THEOLOGY; BUSHNELL, HORACE; SOCIAL GOSPEL; GLADDEN, WASHINGTON). A renewed consciousness of specifically Christian identity and tenets has grown in contemporary Congregationalism. The emphases of private judgment, independency, and Congregational fellowship remain, but are accompanied by aspiration to a unity with the branches of the Universal Church of Christ (see KANSAS CITY STATEMENT). These elements are apparent in Congregationalist participation in the ecumenical movement and esp. in the United Church of Christ. BIBLIOGRAPHY: G. G. Atkins and F. L. Fagley, *History of American Congregationalism* (1942); M. Starkey, *Congregational Way* (1966); H. M. Dexter, *Congregationalism of the Last Three Hundred Years As Seen in Its Literature* (2 v., 1880, repr. 1970).

[R. F. G. CALDER; T. C. O'BRIEN]

CONGREGATIONS, ROMAN, see CURIA ROMANA.

CONGRUISM, in RC theology, a theory attempting to reconcile the efficaciousness of grace and the freedom of the human will. The Jesuits Francisco de Suárez (1548–1617) and Robert Bellarmine (1542–1621) were principal exponents of congruism. The theory rests its reconciliation of the suitableness, or congruity, of an efficacious grace to the state or condition of the will of the recipient. Mere congruity does not explain the efficacy of grace, since a grace must be congruous even to be sufficient (see GRACE, SUFFICIENT). Congruism explains that grace becomes efficacious from three sources: from the consent a person would give, should a particular grace be offered; from the divine foreknowledge anterior to any divine decree *(scientia media)* of the consent that would be given; and from God's benevolent absolute decree to give the grace. Both congruism and *Molinism agree in explaining the efficacy of grace by elements not inherent in the grace itself and in recourse to *scientia media*. They agree as well that there is a divine decree that a person shall perform a good action, a decree that is infallibly effective and anterior to the actual consent of the human will. Congruism differs from Molinism by holding that God first decrees absolutely (not on condition of man's accepting grace) that a man shall perform a good act, and therefore decrees the efficacious grace to perform it.

Congruists also hold that in the divine plan God first intends to give the reward of glory to some adults and consequently intends absolutely that they acquire merit. This is the doctrine of formal predestination prior to foreseen merit that distinguishes congruism from Molinism.

Congruists, with all Catholics, admit reprobation of the lost, but unlike Molinists they hold it to be, in the divine plan, negative and prior to divine prevision of man's final state of soul. Some are antelapsarian (Suárez), others postlapsarian (Bellarmine). All, however, conceive reprobation to be a mere nonpredestination, or nonefficacious election to glory. BIBLIOGRAPHY: H. Quilliet, DTC 3.1:1120–38.

[F. L. SHEERIN]

CONINCK, GILES DE (1571–1633), Flemish Jesuit theologian, professor at Louvain, author of works in moral theology esteemed by St. Alphonsus Ligouri. BIBLIOGRAPHY: *Catholicisme* 3:33–34.

[T. C. O'BRIEN]

CONJUGAL LOVE, true love between husband and wife, which manifests itself in a variety of ways. Conjugal love is eminently human because its object is the good of a whole person and its expression flows from an affection of the will. Both body and mind of married persons are enriched and ennobled through the expression of this love that is distinctive of marriage. Conjugal love finds unique expression and perfection through the marital act which both signifies and promotes spouses' mutual self-giving. Conjugal love is an extension of divine love and is structured on the model of Christ's union with his Church. See Vat II Pastoral Constitution on the Church in the Modern World #49.

[V. GILLIGAN]

CONN, GEORGE, see CON, GEORGE.

CONNATURAL KNOWLEDGE, see KNOWLEDGE, CONNATURAL.

CONNECTICUT, a New England state, the fifth of the original thirteen states admitted to the Union (1788). The area was first explored (1614) by Adriaean Block, a Dutch navigator, who sailed up the Connecticut River. A Dutch settlement was established (1633) at Hartford; Rev. Thomas Hooker and his congregation established the first English community (1636). Connecticut developed around the river towns of Windsor, Wethersfield, and Hartford, which were joined by the colony of New Haven after 1664.

Congregationalism was the established religion until 1818. Congregationalists and Presbyterians were the leading church groups throughout the 17th and 18th centuries. Catholics, however, enjoyed many liberties and profited from immigration in the 19th century. Bp. Benedict *Fenwick of Boston provided for Connecticut Catholics by sending (1828) a resident priest, Robert D. Woodley, and by converting a wooden Episcopal church into the first Catholic church in the state (1830). There were then fewer than 200 Catholics in New Haven and about 70 in Hartford.

The Diocese of Hartford was established in 1843, with William Tyler as its first bishop. His successor in 1849, Bernard *O'Reilly, met the needs of the growing Catholic population by bringing to Connecticut such orders as the Sisters of Mercy from Pittsburgh and by founding schools, two female academies, and an orphan asylum. After O'Reilly was lost at sea in 1858, the new bp., Francis Patrick McFarland, obtained the services of the Sisters of Charity from Mt. St. Vincent, N.Y., and the Order of Friars Minor. In 1868 McFarland also established the first national parish in Connecticut, for Germans, by which time the state had nearly 200,000 Catholics. Following the short episcopate of Thomas *Galberry, first provincial of the Augustinians in the U.S., Lawrence Stephen McMahon was consecrated as the fifth bp. of Hartford. McMahon's efforts were devoted to the welfare of immigrants and the creation of 13 national parishes and chapels. He was succeeded in 1894 by Michael Tierney, the first local priest so honored. Tierney founded some 69 parishes, 32 schools, and other institutions to care for the 150,000 Catholics added during his episcopate. The present incumbent (1976) is John F. Whealon. Henry J. O'Brien became the first abp. of Hartford when the metropolitan see was created in 1953. Its suffragan sees are the Dioceses of Bridgeport and Norwich.

Connecticut's population (1970) of 3,032,217, which is over 75% urban, makes it the 24th most populous state in the Union. In 1976 Catholics numbered 1,353,106, or 43.4% of the total state population. The major Protestant bodies are the United Church of Christ 4.9% of the total population (1971), and the Episcopal Church, with 4.2%. The Jewish population (1968) was 103,730 or 3.4%.

Connecticut is the site of several noted universities, including Yale, Trinity, Wesleyan, and the Univ. of Connecticut. There are (1976) eight Catholic colleges in the state, with a total enrollment of 7,958. Some 19,878 students attend the state's 34 Catholic high schools, while 45,399 pupils are enrolled in 171 Catholic elementary schools. BIBLIOGRAPHY: O. Shepard, *Connecticut, Past and Present* (1939); T. S. Duggan, *Catholic Church in Connecticut* (1930); D. W. Johnson et al., *Churches and Church Membership in U.S.* (1974).

[J. L. MORRISON; R. M. PRESTON]

CONNECTIONAL, referring to a Methodist form of polity, or one similar to it, i.e., one based on a system of *conferences. The term *connexion was used by John *Wesley for the interassociation of Methodist *societies. Conference replaced the term connection as the designation for regional divisions and organizational units in church structure. Connectional polity is more centralized than the *congregational; unlike the *presbyterian it allows for *episcopacy as a function, not a sacred order, in the Church.

[T. C. O'BRIEN]

CONNELL, FRANCIS JEREMIAH (1888–1967), Redemptorist moral theologian. C. was educated at Boston College, St. Alphonsus Seminary in Esopus, N.Y., and the Angelicum in Rome. He taught theology at Esopus until 1940 when he joined the theology faculty at The Catholic University of America. He served as dean of the school of theology (1949–57), was appointed counselor of the Sacred Congregation of Seminaries and Universities (1956), and was a *peritus* at four sessions of Vatican Council II. During his 40 years of teaching, he wrote 10 books on moral theology, contributed innumerable articles, esp. to the *American Ecclesiastical Review,* ran a question and answer column for newspapers, and was a popular retreat master. He was a representative of the more legalistic Redemptorist tradition still in high favor in the earlier part of his career. BIBLIOGRAPHY: P. Granfield AER 157 (1967) 74–82.

[H. JACK]

CONNELLY, CORNELIA, MOTHER (1809–79), foundress of the Society of the Holy Child Jesus (SHCJ), a community dedicated to education. C. married Episcopalian rector Pierce Connelly in 1831. Both later embraced the Catholic faith, and when her husband, desirous of becoming a Catholic priest, received a papal decree of permanent separation, C. informally became a postulant in the Convent of the Sacred Heart in Rome. At Card. Wiseman's invitation she established the SHCJ in Derby, England in 1846, opening schools there and in the U.S. and France. When her husband tired of his priesthood and abandoned the RC faith, she refused his demand that she resume married life with him. Her process of beatification began in England in 1959. BIBLIOGRAPHY: M. T. Bisgood, *Cornelia Connelly* (1963).

[H. P. ANNAS]

CONNEXION (Connection), a term often used by John *Wesley of Methodism itself, or of the interassociation of Methodist *societies. The term is still in use and connotes a form of polity that is not *congregational but connectional, i.e., through the various *conferences. BIBLIOGRAPHY: N. B. Harmon, *Understanding the Methodist Church* (rev. ed., 1961) 14; OED 2:839.

[F. E. MASER]

CONNOLLY, CORNELIUS JOSEPH (1883–1954), anthropologist. C. obtained his bachelor's degree in Antigonish, Nova Scotia; attended the Montreal seminary; was ordained in 1907; received his Ph.D. in biology and anthropology from the Univ. of Munich in 1911. He taught at St. Francis Xavier College in Antigonish (1911–22); did 2 years of research at Harvard; joined the faculty of The Catholic University (1924). He was appointed professor of physical anthropology in 1934 and became chairman of the department in 1949. His publications were based on anatomical laboratory and field research. He is recognized for his *External Morphology of the Primate Brain* (1950).

[H. JACK]

CONNOLLY, HUGH (1873–1948), English Benedictine and authority on Syriac and early Christian liturgy. He greatly influenced the trend of modern liturgical research both by his own articles appearing in the *Journal of Theological Studies* and the *Downside Review* (of which he was editor for a number of years), and also through personal communication with other liturgists. His most important works are *So-called Egyptian Church Order and Derived Documents* (1909 and 1916) and *Didascalia Apostolorum* (1929). BIBLIOGRAPHY: DownRev 66 (1948) 239–245.

[N. KOLLAR]

CONNOLLY, JOHN (1750?–1825), bp. of New York. He was born in Ireland and, after entering the Dominicans and excelling in his studies at Liège and Louvain, was ordained *c.*1774. In Rome (1775–1814), he filled important posts in his order until Pius VII named him second bp. of New York (1814), where he was installed late in 1815. Although hampered by the evils of lay *trusteeism and the lack of adequate personnel and finances, C. provided a rapidly growing Catholic population with additional churches, an orphan asylum and free school, and introduced the Sisters of Charity of St. Vincent de Paul. BIBLIOGRAPHY: M. Carthy, *Old St. Patrick's, New York's First Cathedral* (1947) 19–47; J. B. Code, *Dictionary of American Hierarchy* (1940).

[M. CARTHY]

CONNOLLY, MYLES (1897–1964), novelist, motion picture scriptwriter. A journalist who began his career on the *Boston Post* after World War I, he contributed short stories to national magazines. From 1928 to 1960 he was a motion picture writer and producer, responsible in one or the other capacity for 40 motion pictures. C.'s best-known novel is *Mr. Blue* (1928), a fantasy that combines something of the joyous hope of St. Francis of Assisi and the utopian vision of St. Thomas More. It has been translated into three languages. Other works include *The Bump on Brannigan's Head* (1950) and *Dan England and the Noonday Devil* (1951). C. had a vision of hope and Christian joy. BIBLIOGRAPHY: *New York Times* July 17, 1964.

[J. R. AHERNE]

CONNOLLY, THOMAS LOUIS (1815–76), an Irish-born Capuchin prelate who served (1852–59) as bp. of St. Johns, New Brunswick, where he founded a community of Sisters of Charity and commenced the construction of a cathedral, and then as abp. of Halifax (1859–76). His chief interests were works of charity and education, but he was also influential in curbing activities of the Fenian movement. At Vatican Council I he stood with the minority against the definition of papal infallibility, but upon its definition he made his submission. BIBLIOGRAPHY: N. F. Davis, *Irishman in Canada* (1877).

[J. P. COOKE]

CONON (d. 687), **POPE** from 686. The son of an army officer, he was educated in Sicily and became a priest of the Roman Church. He was old and feeble when, on the death of John V, he was elected pope as the result of a compromise between the clergy and an army faction. Few records of his reign are extant. But it is known that he received a letter from the Emperor Justinian II on the decrees of the Third Council of Constantinople. He appointed a Constantine of Syracuse, who proved unworthy, to administer the papal lands known as the Patrimony of St. Peter in Sicily. He is buried in St. Peter's. BIBLIOGRAPHY: C. M. Aherne, NCE 4:182; J. S. Brusher, *Popes through the Ages* (1959) 166.

[P. F. MULHERN]

CONQUES, ABBEY OF, former Benedictine monastery founded in the Diocese of Rodez, NW France. In 790 the hermit Dadon lived in an abandoned chapel and founded (*c*. 800) the first monastery, which *Louis the Pious called Conques. Pepin II, King of Aquitaine, richly endowed the abbey. The abbey church, Ste. Foy, was completed in 1130, having a famous *Last Judgment* tympanum of the school of Auvergne which showed a superb Christ in Majesty with heaven and hell in the lower registers. Among 10th-cent. treasured reliquaries is the world-famous gold, jeweled statue of Ste. Foy handsomely preserved. The monastery flourished until *commendation was instituted there in 1474. The abbey was secularized (1537), but large holdings by the collegiate church remained under clerical care until suppressed during the Revolution. The abbey church was restored in the 19th cent. and given to the care of Premonstratensians from Frigolet. It presently serves as a parish church. BIBLIOGRAPHY: F. Bosquet, DHGE 13:472–478; R. Gazeau, *Catholicisme* 3:42–44.

[A. P. DEEGAN]

CONQUISTADORES, the name given to men of varying talents, importance, and character who, in the era of Spanish expansion into the New World, acted as agents of the Spanish empire. Their purpose ostensibly was to enlarge and enrich Spain but also to bring Christianity and civilization to the newly discovered territory. With them went the missionary who was called on frequently to investigate the harsh treatment given the Indians by their conquerors. Hernán Cortés stands out as the conquistador par excellence. Not only was his posture essentially one of genius, but he wrote copiously of his expeditions and was the sub-

ject of writing by contemporaries. Cortés was in command of an expedition from Cuba to Yucatán. Founding the city of Vera Cruz and acknowledged as its governor, he marched against the capital city of the Aztecs, Tenochtitlán, with 700 Spaniards and a sizeable force of Indians.

The peaceful entry to the city in 1519 was soon frustrated by the savage massacre of Aztecs by some of Cortés' men. Driven from the city with heavy losses, Cortés returned and in 1520, after destroying the Aztec capital, appropriated its vast treasures. On the site of the ancient Aztec capital he built Mexico City. His ability to win over even hostile Indians of other areas was a matter of genius. Appointed governor of New Spain, he fell victim ultimately to local intrigue and the changeable monarchy and was deposed. Cortés had an unbelievable power of turning the assorted Indian groups opposed to him into allies who fought under his banner.

Francisco Pizarro was destined to find the Incas of Peru as highly civilized and formidable as Cortés found the Aztecs. Pizarro was with Balboa at the discovery of the South Sea. Authorized by the King of Spain to lead an expedition from Panama to the fabled riches rumored to be to the south, he and his associates came upon the Inca empire then engulfed in civil war. This highly developed civilization was easy prey to the Spanish force. Pizarro's men massacred thousands of Incas and killed their emperor, Atahualpa. In 1530 Pizarro took the celebrated city of Cuzco, and left his brothers to rule while he proceeded to found the city of Lima. The savage plundering of the city led to an Inca revolt, and the Indians recaptured Cuzco. Civil war among the Spaniards followed. The followers of Diego de Almagro, associate of Pizarro, took Cuzco; he was ultimately killed by Pizarro's brother. Pizarro himself was assassinated in 1541.

The first attempt to subdue the Indians of Chile, undertaken by Pedro de Valdivia, ended in the commander's execution by the Indians. Colombia was subdued peacefully by the most enlightened of the conquistadores, Jiménez de Quesada. He established control of Chibcha Indian country and founded the city of Santafe de Bogotá in 1539.

In the Caribbean and in Panama the great conquistador was Vasco Nuñez de Balboa who seized the leadership of an expedition led by another and discovered the South Sea. He was originally intended to head the expedition to Peru but was arrested and beheaded. Ponce de León, who is remembered as searcher for the fountain of youth, sought also the same goals as most of his contemporaries. He explored Florida on several expeditions but was wounded by the Indians and died in Havana. Coronado in the U.S. southwest and De Soto in Florida and the Mississippi were also notable explorers.

Each of these extraordinary men and many more engaged in the activity of spreading Spanish influence in South America, Central America, S and SW U.S. Between the beginning of the 16th cent. and the middle of the 17th cent., the conquistadores carved out a massive empire for Spain in the New World. BIBLIOGRAPHY: F. A. Kirkpatrick, *Spanish Conquistadores* (1946).

[J. R. AHERNE]

CONRAD II (*c.*990–1039), **HOLY ROMAN EMPEROR,** elected (1024), crowned in Rome (1027), the founder of the Salian or Franconian imperial dynasty. He was crowned with the Iron Crown of Lombardy in 1026 and did much to establish the imperial authority in Italy. He substituted Justinian's Code for the old Lombard laws. His firm policy of centralization led to property conflicts with civil and ecclesiastical magnates.

[T. GILBY]

CONRAD III (1093–1152), **KING OF GERMANY** from 1138. Though C., a Hohenstaufen, was king, he was never emperor. He was a personable, intelligent, popular monarch, but his reign was a total failure. The Wendish crusade and the Second Crusade accomplished nothing. Church-State relations were never more harmonious as the kingdom disintegrated. BIBLIOGRAPHY: CMedH 5:346–359; J. H. Hill, NCE 4:186–187.

[S. WILLIAMS]

CONRAD IV (1228–54), **KING OF GERMANY** from 1237. He was son of Emperor Frederick II (Hohenstaufen) who induced the German princes to elect C. king at Vienna. Leaving Germany soon after, never to return, Frederick left his son C. as his representative. C. supported his father in the papal-imperialist struggle. After Frederick's death (1250), C. invaded Italy. He was under excommunication and in the process of subduing Apulia when he died of illness, leaving a young son, Conradin, in Germany. BIBLIOGRAPHY: D. Andreini, NCE 4:187.

[C. J. LYNCH]

CONRAD OF BAVARIA, BL. (*c.*1105–54), Cistercian monk. An ardent disciple of St. Bernard, C. spent some years at the Abbey of Clairvaux before going to the Holy Land where he lived as a hermit. In his last days he set out for Clairvaux to die with Bernard at his side. The saint, however, died first, and C. spent his remaining days as an anchorite in Modugno, Italy.

[J. R. AHERNE]

CONRAD BOSINLOTHER, BL. (d. 1145), abbot, reformer. He was chosen to reform the episcopal abbey of Mondsee, Austria, in 1126. His insistence on maintaining the abbey's rights led to his murder by the abbey's tithe payers. His cult, once popular, is almost extinct today. BIBLIOGRAPHY: Zimmermann 1:87, 89–90; J. L. Grassi, NCE 4:188.

[J. L. GRASSI]

CONRAD OF CONSTANCE, ST. (*c.*900–973), monk of the abbey of Sankt Gallen who was sent to the cathedral school at Constance to be educated and was elected bp. of Constance. He was a zealous bp. who provided generously for the building of churches and hospitals. Although he abstained from political activity, he was held in great esteem by the Emperor Otto I. His name is associated with churches in Einsiedeln, Rheingau, and the chapel of St. Maurice in Constance. BIBLIOGRAPHY: L. Falkenstein, BiblSanct 4:202; Zimmermann 3:360–361.

CONRAD OF GELNHAUSEN (*c.*1320–90), theologian. He is most significant for his two tracts, *Epistola brevis* and *Epistola concordiae,* in which he argued for the calling of a general council to end the Great Schism. These writings had little immediate effect, but they did influence later proponents of the conciliar theory. His career was climaxed by his appointment (1386) as first chancellor of the Univ. of Heidelberg. BIBLIOGRAPHY: B. Tierney, *Foundations of the Conciliar Theory* (1955); G. Mollat, NCE 4:188.

[J. MULDOON]

CONRAD OF MARBURG (d. 1233), diocesan priest of Mainz, inquisitor from 1227. C. was intent upon the pursuit of Luciferians, against whom he obtained a bull from *Gregory IX. His intemperate zeal lead to his assassination. *LUCIFERIANS, esp. bibliog.

[T. C. O'BRIEN]

CONRAD OF MAZOVIA (*c.*1190–1247), Polish prince who, together with Christian, first bp. of Prussia, founded the Knights of Dobrin (approved 1228) to safeguard the Christians of Prussia and to promote the Christianization of the remaining pagans. When this step proved ineffective, C. and Christian invited the Teutonic Knights, who, by the exploitation of the concessions made to them, acquired control over Prussia and made it into a Germanic state. BIBLIOGRAPHY: F. Dvornik, *Slavs in European History and Civilization* (1962).

CONRAD OF MEGENBURG (*c.*1309–74), German scholar and writer of prodigious industry. After study at Erfurt, he received at Paris the master's degree. He taught at the Univ. of Paris, serving several terms as procurator, from 1334 to 1342. As canon (1348) and pastor (1359) of the cathedral in Regensburg, he continued his scholarly writing. C. was author of many works in Latin and in his own tongue; very influential was his German translation from the Latin of the first natural history to appear in Germany (1349–50). BIBLIOGRAPHY: R. Baurreiss, LTK 6:469.

[M. R. BROWN]

CONRAD OF OFFIDA, BL. (1237–1306), Franciscan. After entering the order (1251), he spent 10 years in various hermitages. While at La Verna, he came to know St. Margaret of Cortona, Leo of Assisi, and the Franciscan

Spiritual leaders Ubertino of Casale and Peter John Olivi. He favored eremitic separatism, but was dissuaded from this movement by Olivi. C. is one of the heroes of the *Fioretti,* and his *Verba* contains prophecies of Francis about the order's future. BIBLIOGRAPHY: R. Sciamannini, Bibl-Sanct 4:206–207; Butler 4:560–561.

[O. J. BLUM]

CONRAD OF OTTOBEUREN, BL. (d. 1227), Benedictine abbot. Elected abbot of Ottobeuren in 1191, he held the office for the next 34 years. During his tenure he twice rebuilt his monastery, the second time after a fire in 1217. BIBLIOGRAPHY: A. M. Zimmermann, BiblSanct 4:207.

[O. J. BLUM]

CONRAD OF PARZHAM, ST. (1818–94), Capuchin brother of Altötting, Upper Bavaria. Ninth of a family of 10, he was born to a farming couple who died in his youth. He worked on the farm until 30 years of age when he entered the Capuchin order, pronouncing solemn vows in 1852. Devotion to the Mother of God and to the Blessed Sacrament began and ended his days spent as porter at Altötting, where he served a constant stream of pilgrims and esp. the poor. Forty years after his death, C. was canonized, and his relics enshrined in the church of St. Anne close by the monastery. BIBLIOGRAPHY: Butler 2:143–144; B. d'Arenzano, BiblSanct 4:211–212.

[M. R. BROWN]

CONSALVI, ERCOLE (1757–1824), Italian cardinal and diplomat. Born of an aristocratic family, C. entered the papal service in 1783. In 1800 Pius VII, for whose election he had been responsible, made him a cardinal deacon and secretary of state. Although C. negotiated the concordat with Napoleon, the latter came to consider him an enemy, forcing his resignation as secretary of state. He was considered a ringleader of the so-called black cardinals. In 1814 C. was sent as papal plenipotentiary to the Congress of Vienna, where he secured the restoration of the States of the Church (except for Avignon and Comtat-Venaissin). Resuming the secretaryship of state (1814–23), he pursued moderate policies in the Metternichian era, much to the disgust of the ultraconservatives at the papal court. When Leo XII became pope (1823), C. was again dismissed as secretary of state. For his own account of his papal service, see *Memorie . . .,* (ed. M. N. Rocca di Cornelliano, 1950). BIBLIOGRAPHY: M. Petrocchi, EncCatt 4:394–397 (bibliog.)

[E. A. CARRILLO]

CONSANGUINITY, blood relationship, a matter of some importance in canon as well as in civil law because such a tie may be an obstacle to marriage between two people. Two different kinds of blood relationship are distinguished: one is direct or lineal, which exists between a person and his forebears and descendants; the other, called collateral, ex-

ists between two persons who have a common ancestor. Degrees of lineal consanguinity are measured by the number of steps or generations intervening between a person and his ancestor or descendant; thus a father or mother is related to a son or daughter in the first degree of the direct line, and a grandfather or grandmother are related to their grandchildren in the second degree. Collateral relationship is measured by determining the degree in the direct line in which the person more remotely connected with the common ancestor is related to that ancestor when the lines of descent are of unequal length. If they are of the same degree of relationship to the common ancestor, then the determination of the relationship between collaterals is ascertained by counting the number of steps or generations in either line. Thus a brother and sister are related to each other in the first degree of the collateral line; a person is related to his cousins (children of an aunt or uncle) in the second degree of that line; a cousin to the children of his first cousins, in the third degree. Sometimes, however, it is insufficient to simply compute the degree of relationship between blood relatives by counting back the generations between the common ancestor and the one more distantly related to that ancestor, viz., when a question arises concerning the possibility of a marriage between an uncle and niece, or an aunt and a nephew. In the petition for a dispensation from the impediment to marriage, the closeness of the relationship of aunt or uncle to the common ancestor must also be indicated; the relationship would be described as being in the second degree of the collateral line mixed with the first. In RC canon law blood relationship constitutes a diriment impediment to marriage in all degrees in the direct line and to the third degree inclusively in the collateral line (CIC c. 1076). The impediment is never dispensed in the direct line nor in the first degree of the collateral line. In civil law blood relationship is also a bar to marriage, but the degrees of relationship in which marriage is prohibited vary from state to state. For a sketch of the history of this impediment in Latin and Oriental Churches, see C. Henry, NCE 4:192–196. *AFFINITY.

[P. K. MEAGHER]

CONSCIENCE, from Lat. *conscientia,* the equivalent of Gr. *suneidēsis,* both originally meant consciousness or self-awareness, which later, particularly with the Stoics, ran into the sense of some sort of moral awareness, often expressed as an adverse judgment about evil actions, to which modern usage tends to reserve it. The term in Middle English took the place of "inwit" in common speech. So tangled are the meanings in which it is used, such is the mystique which may invest it in religious, ethical, political, and psychological discussion, and so bound up is it with feelings of *guilt, that some effort of teasing out the main strands will be useful.

The word was used neither in the OT nor in the Gospels, but was taken up by St. Paul (for a conspectus of its senses, see Heb 9.9, 14; 10.2, 22; 13.18); it condemns, but also approves, and covers decisions in advance about what should be done, the sense in which, as we shall see, it was later developed by scholastics. Patristic writers associated *suneidēsis* with the Stoic *suntēresis*, a holding safe or watchful guarding, translated by St. Jerome as "the spark of conscience." The terms are not connected, but they look alike, and the confusion of *synderesis*, the grasp of moral principles, and conscience rather tagged discussion for later Latin theology: the tag still persists, though not always for the same reason.

From the generalized conception of a moral sense of our responsibility before God, St. Thomas Aquinas sharpened "conscience" to a technical meaning. It did not constitute the core of the Christian life; it was not a special faculty nor even a frame of mind such as is formed by the virtues, but an act of practical judgment about what should be done here and now in a particular case. It could be right or it could be wrong (cf. Rom 14.14, 23), but as the immediate noetic decision, *proairesis*, it could never be disobeyed without fault. It was always binding, though fault, of course, might have entered into its coming to make a mistake. As an adjustment to an individual issue it was not exactly a norm or rule, which must be looked for in the less intermittent and fallible light of virtue, notably practical wisdom, *prudentia*, *phronēsis*, in its function of forming a sound judgment, *sunesis*. It was not a guarantee of a good action being done; in fact, looked at in this narrow sense, a condition of sinning is that, implicitly at least, one has made a good act of conscience and not followed it. There are moral theologians close to the mind of St. Thomas who would prefer to shift the discussion of many problems back from conscience to *prudence and set the free play of persons against a settled background of Christian virtue rather than of the laws. They are not altogether at ease with the post-Tridentine technicians of the classical period of *casuistry who were out to protect the individual in a legalistic society, and, it may be said, to remedy the conditions they themselves had assisted in creating; these closely examined the varieties of conscience—objective right or wrong, subjectively sincere or not, assured or doubtful, tough or tender, scrupulous or lax—and devised the famous systems—*Probabilism, *Equiprobabilism, *Probabiliorism, and so forth—for resolving a moral doubt.

These preoccupations are not shared by modern RC moral theologians, many of whom tend to neglect the earlier precision and balance of St. Thomas, which was taken into the high theology of Anglicanism, and to go back to more diffuse concepts of conscience according to scriptural and patristic exegesis which have been maintained in the Protestant tradition, sometimes with an admixture of elements from Kantian and Existentialist philosophy. The Hebraic "heart and loins" (*kelâyot waléb*), the Pauline *pistis* come into the response (*Antwort*) of the human creature to the Word (*Wort*) of God. The involvement may be rendered as an experience of the wrath of God, or, without the identification of justifying faith and conscience, as an imperative instinct from a deity in one's bosom, or just from a consciousness of autonomy combined with responsibility. All this contributes to the richness of debate, but is attended by much untidiness. However, the word conscience in these and many other senses has come to stay. To clear up the semantics of dialog, it might be well to talk about conscience *a, b, c,* and so forth, to show whether we intend to treat it as a consciousness of basic value, or a moral conviction, or a moral decision, or a being conscientious, or a psychological power of being free, or a subject of rights, or a feeling that gives one pangs, or a suppression of the libido in the name of the super-ego, or what. Some of the senses are allied, some quite the contrary. BIBLIOGRAPHY: ThAq ST 1a, 79, 12–13, esp. in ed. Lat-Eng (v. 11, ed. T. L. Sutton, 1970); *op. cit.*, 1a2a, 19, 3–6, esp. in ed. Lat-Eng (v. 18, ed. T. Gilby, 1970); E. D'Arcy, *Conscience and the Right to Freedom* (1961); C. A. Pierce, *Conscience in the New Testament* (1955); J. Stelzenberger, *Syneidesis, conscientia, Gewissen* (1963); H. R. McAdoo, *Structure of Caroline Moral Theology* (1949).

[T. GILBY]

CONSCIENCE, EDUCATION OF, training of the person in right moral judgments about his own actions. In this context conscience means the deciding of the morally right way to act in any given situation; any single action is morally good or bad, right or wrong, as it either conforms or conflicts with conscience so taken. That conscience can be trained presupposes a human being to be capable of personally responsible actions; that it needs to be trained presupposes a range in such capability: between immaturity and maturity, between error and truth about moral values, between obtuseness and sensitivity toward them. This moral education, then, purposes to prevent or correct a culpably false conscience, or an erroneous conscience, or a scrupulous conscience, or one callous to the moral good. Since conformity or conflict with conscience determines the rightness or wrongness of an action, the duty to form a right conscience stands in direct proportion to a person's capacity for moral responsibility. For the adult this is an abiding, personal obligation. The right formation of the conscience of the young is primarily incumbent upon parents, then on surrogates—teachers and other counselors—and is part of the specific meaning of Christian education. Instruction in universal, absolute moral values enters in, and in many forms: the liturgical proclamation of gospel teachings, religious education from catechism on up through moral theology, parental or other forms of guidance. But moral instruction cannot achieve its own purpose, right living; for this is a matter, not of having information, but of acting virtuously. What immediately guides concrete action is not a knowledge of generalities, but an evaluative judgment colored by appropriate emotional and volitional elements, in a word, a knowledge through affectivity. The education of conscience is complete and effective only through prudence, the virtue that ensures not only a conscience judgment as to the morally right, but also an affective determination that this evaluation be strong and put into practice. The moral sensitivity in prudence rests upon the affinity of virtues in the affective powers toward the truly good, and their restraint of these powers from the opposite. Virtue cannot be taught, but those charged with the guidance of others can supply the opportunity for growth by environment, example, discipline. The developing responsiveness of virtue can then make moral instruction have its effect in the working of conscience. The subject of the education of conscience is part of the current pastoral question about the appropriate time for first sacramental confession. The instructional and appetitive aspects of conscience formation have bearing on such issues as catechetical technique, counseling and sex education, as well as on the perplexities raised by the "new morality" with respect to the possibility of universal or absolute moral values.

[T. C. O'BRIEN]

CONSCIENCE, EXAMINATION OF, the calling to mind of personal sins for the purpose of repenting. In liturgy its place is in conjunction with the community confession of sins at the beginning of Mass or in communal services of reconciliation, and with the sacrament of penance as a preparation for personal confession. The requirement that confession and contrition be complete obliges the penitent to recall, according to his capabilities at the moment, serious sins of which he deems himself guilty, in their number and kind; the recollection of venial sins has as its purpose the arousal of sorrow for sin, and of a more aware reliance on sacramental grace for spiritual progress. In private devotion the examination of conscience has its place and purpose as preparation for the act of contrition in daily prayer. Used in this context, "conscience" does not have its most proper meaning as the anterior judgment of what is morally right and called for in any concrete action, but as a subsequent consciousness of having acted in accord or at odds with that anterior judgment.

[T. C. O'BRIEN]

CONSCIENCE, FREEDOM OF, see FREEDOM.

CONSCIENCE, MANIFESTATION OF, in canon law for religious, a subject's giving an account of matters of conscience (failing, doubts, temptations, etc.) to a superior. Superiors are strictly enjoined from doing anything, even indirectly, to exact such a manifestation of conscience. At the same time, where a superior is also a priest, the law commends the practice of the subject's freely approaching the superior with filial confidence for guidance on conscience matters (CIC, c. 530, 1 & 2). Since conscience is the proximate rule of morality to which each person must answer, freedom of conscience, so strongly affirmed by Vatican Council II (VatII ChurchModWorld n. 41; Rel-Freed n. 3) as essential to the dignity of the human person, cannot be infringed. At the same time the mutual help that

Christians can give to one another in charity proves the rightness of seeking counsel from those who are competent.

[T. C. O'BRIEN]

CONSCIENCE, MARRIAGE OF, see MARRIAGE OF CONSCIENCE.

CONSCIENTIOUS OBJECTION, the refusal by an individual, because of a sense of duty to his fundamental ethical understanding, to be inducted into the armed forces or to participate in or to support the military activities of his country. Conscientious objection has been part of the history of several Christian Churches (see PACIFISM). Two general types of conscientious objectors exist: the absolute pacifist and the ordinary pacifist, or selective objector. The absolute pacifist maintains that no violence of any type may ever be employed, even if it means that an innocent person may die or suffer untold injuries. The ordinary pacifist distinguishes between international armed conflicts and the suppression of crime and injustice within the framework of an established society. He objects to support of, or participation in, any international conflicts but concedes that a defensive type of violence can be employed to rectify domestic conflicts. In either case, both types of pacifists object to war between nations.

The absolute pacifist may base his objections on religious or nonreligious grounds. The religious pacifist will normally predicate his opposition to warfare on the Sermon on the Mount (Mt 5.3–11) and the Fifth Commandment, "Thou shalt not kill" (Ex 20.13). The nonreligious or ethical pacifist bases his opposition on a personal moral code, derived from an understanding of a fundamental ethical order and, in particular, the meaning of human interrelations. Like the religious pacifist, he would rather suffer even martyrdom than violate the dictates of his conscience.

The selective objector is opposed to a particular military action because he feels it is immoral or unjustified or because the means employed in effecting it are immoral. Included in this category are military personnel who refuse to obey a command that would force them to participate in an immoral war or to commit a crime against humanity. Vatican II defined the moral position of such personnel when it urged military men to follow their consciences in wartime situations and to refuse to carry out any order they consider to be violations of natural law (Vat II ChurchModWorld 79). The principles of the selective objector can be either religious or nonreligious or a combination of both. He often cites the just-war doctrine, the Nuremberg principle, or some basic principles derived from an existential philosophy as his criteria for objection. The just-war doctrine is the norm traditionally used by Christians in justifying a country's resort to war. Unless a Christian's conscience is in some measure and in some way assured that the conditions for the just war are met, he would not be justified in participating in such a war. The Nuremberg principle simply claims that every individual is personally responsible for any act that he may commit, even if he is ordered to commit the act. Finally, numerous selective objectors are opposed to contemporary warfare. They might have been willing to engage in some conventional wars in the past, but they feel that only two patterns of warfare will exist in the future: a nuclear missile war between great powers and a counterrevolutionary or imperialist war. They object to both, either because the means of warfare are intrinsically evil or destructive of humanity, or because the end of the war is immoral and not conducive to the welfare of mankind.

As a general rule, the historic Christian Churches have approved of violence or war whenever all the conditions for a just war are fulfilled. The Churches have condoned the suffering of injustice in silence until the point is reached where the injustice becomes so intolerable that one's conscience dictates some form of corrective action. If the Christian does not then act, he assumes partial guilt for the injustice. The Churches have also taught that the individual cannot participate in any undoubtedly unjust war; further, if the individual is convinced that, because of circumstances peculiar to himself, participation in a military activity would violate his conscience, he should claim conscientious objector status.

Conscientious objection and pacifism were doctrines characteristic of the Swiss Anabaptists and the Mennonites. Frequently they were persecuted and had to migrate because of their refusal to bear arms. From George Fox the Quakers received a similar doctrine and have been leaders in the cause of pacifism. Some of the German Brethren Churches have maintained the same opposition to war. The Jehovah's Witnesses refuse military service, but on the grounds that all political governments are corrupt, and enemies of the kingdom of God. All of these religious strains directly contributed to the U.S. legal recognition of conscientious objection. While in 1968 the World and National Councils of Churches, the American RC bishops, and the major organizations of many denominations have endorsed selective conscientious objection, it is not recognized in law, and many conservative church groups have repudiated it. The RC Church, well aware of the complexities of contemporary societies and international relations and conflicts, has attempted to redefine its moral position on conscientious objection. Vatican II declared: "It seems right that laws make humane provisions for the case of those who for reasons of conscience refuse to bear arms, provided, however, that they accept some other form of service to the human community" (Vat II ChurchModWorld 79). The National Conference of Catholic Bishops emphasized the place of personal responsibility in decisions about war: "No one is free to evade his personal responsibility by leaving it entirely to others to make moral judgments."

The conscientious objector thus faces a moral dilemma, the consequences of which can be deleterious to his future welfare. But the sincere conscientious objector is aware of these consequences and is willing to suffer them, in order to preserve his conviction and integrity. BIBLIOGRAPHY: P. Ramsey, *War and the Christian Conscience* (1961); P. McNeal, "Catholic Conscientious Objection," CHR (April, 1975) 222–242. *AMNESTY.

[J. P. MECK]

CONSCRIPTION, the nonvoluntary induction of men into the armed forces of a country for the purpose of maintaining or enlarging the military forces of that country. Conscription is a rather unique phenomenon of the 20th cent. and almost universal during war. Its origin may possibly be traced to the citizen army of Napoleon and the fact that political thinkers in democratic societies of Western civilization have felt that a citizen rather than a professional army was more in keeping with the principles of democracy. The support of the entire population, not only in electing representatives and supporting national policy but also in providing for programs of national defense, has become an integral characteristic of every democratic society. Therefore the premise seems accepted: the enjoyment of the rights and privileges of citizenship entails the correlative obligation of service to the country, which may include military service.

Conscription, functionally speaking, exists to further the society's national goals and foreign policies and to provide for that nation's security. Conscription laws are devised empirically so that the military forces will possess the manpower capability necessary to attain these goals. These laws are also, in keeping with democratic principles and in drawing upon the concept of civic responsibility, as equitable as possible.

Underlying the phenomenon of compulsory military service is the perennial question of its morality: is government morally justified in forcibly enlisting the services of men in that society? Traditionally, the reply to this question has been affirmative. For the sovereignty of a nation demands that the government take what steps are deemed necessary to preserve the existence and security of that political unit. This can at times require the sacrifice of citizens to realize these goals. The moral dilemma, however, does not arise in sacrificing or risking one's life for country but in the killing of an enemy, the taking of another's life. Christian civilization and culture plus man's basic human instincts condition him against killing others. The average person so conditioned cannot kill except under stress of violent emotion aroused by a great sense of injury. Thus taking another's life in a combat situation is a severe test of civic duty, now become military.

Concurrently, the shift to conscription as a means of maintaining a standing army in democratic societies presents the additional dilemma of providing for those citizens, who, in good conscience, could either not support any military establishment or at least not participate in an unjust war. To protect these individuals against violations of their right of conscience and religious freedom, many democratic societies introduced the principle of *conscientious objection.

Catholic theologians have, from at least the 5th cent., maintained that a Christian can in good conscience serve in the military forces of his country so long as that military force does not contradict man's will to peace. For the man who does so serve and participate in warmaking is conceivably an instrument of peace by contributing to the deterrence of warlike situations or by forcing an aggressor to cease his aggression and accept peaceful coexistence. The conscripted individual faces the choice of either willingly complying with the order of the common good or stating the reasons for his refusal. Whenever an individual after due consideration of objective factors comes to the sincere and certain judgment that his government's policy involving the use of military force is contrary to the moral order and, in turn, the will of God, or that the use of force in this case is a crime against humanity, he should refuse induction and seek other ways to promote the common good. BIBLIOGRAPHY: R. T. Powers, NCE 9:848–849 s.v. "Military Service."

[J. P. MECK]

CONSECRATION, a set of formalized actions or words that set a person or thing aside for religious office or use. The word may refer to the consecration of altars, churches, bishops, virgins, et al., but generally, when used without qualification, it applies to the action by which the eucharistic bread and wine are changed into the body and blood of Christ. Originally the whole of the Preface-Canon was looked upon as the consecratory prayer, but gradually the Consecration of the Mass was seen to consist in the recitation of Christ's words whereby he instituted the *Eucharist at the Last Supper. These words were seen to contain the essence of the eucharistic prayer in such a way that they were instrumental in the *transubstantiation of the bread and wine into the body and blood of Christ. The words of institution gained such importance that many Protestant Churches order their communion service almost exclusively around them and eliminate other elements of the eucharistic prayer found in the Roman rite. BIBLIOGRAPHY: G. Michell, *Eucharistic Consecration in the Primitive Church* (1948).

[T. M. MCFADDEN]

CONSECRATION (IN HOLINESS AND PENTE-COSTAL TEACHING), the act of one who, after justification, dedicates himself to living a perfect Christian life; it is a preparation for *entire sanctification, by which the sinlessness willed in consecration is achieved.

[T. C. O'BRIEN]

CONSECRATION, PERSONAL, an act by which a person is dedicated, or dedicates self, to the service of God. Theologians recognize that every Christian is, in effect, consecrated to the service of God by the reception of baptism and again by confirmation. Priests and bishops in the sacrament of orders are consecrated for the special service of God at the altar. Nuns who are vowed to virginity ac-

cording to the rites of the Church are said to be consecrated. By extension, common speech recognizes a consecration to the service of God in the vows of religious. The foregoing are public acts of consecration performed or, at least, witnessed by an official of the Church. In addition, there are many private acts of consecration as, e.g., the act of consecration to the Sacred Heart, by which one deliberately makes an offering of self to God directly or through an intermediary. Such acts have value in that they reinforce the basic Christian consecration made in baptism. BIBLIOGRAPHY: R. Royo, *Theology of Christian Perfection* (ed. and tr. J. Aumann, 1962); J. de Finance, DSAM 2:1576–83.

[P. F. MULHERN]

CONSECRATION OF A VIRGIN, see VIRGIN, CONSECRATION OF.

CONSEJO EPISCOPAL LATINOAMERICANO (CELAM), an organization formed (1956) by the Latin American prelates who met in general conference at Rio de Janeiro after the Eucharistic Congress celebrated (1955) in that city. Its object is to encourage cooperation and consultation among the dioceses of their continent. The regional approach movement begun at that time initiated further contacts with the U.S. and Canadian hierarchy. With a general secretariat in Bogotá, Colombia, CELAM in their 1964 meeting in Rome set up 10 departments of special interest. The 1968 Medellin Documents of CELAM are of primary importance as statements on church renewal and the ministry for justice and human rights. The 1974 Roman meeting delighted Pope Paul VI who was "greatly impressed and comforted" by results of the survey sponsored by CELAM that revealed the nonviolent theory and attitudes of the Latin-American church. (See H. Camara, "Nous avons présenté un christianisme trop passif," *Documentation Catholique* 72 [1975] 679–681.)

[M. R. BROWN]

CONSENSUS, THEOLOGICAL AUTHORITY OF. Consensus is here understood as a secondary criterion of revelation based upon the unanimous or near unanimous agreement of a particular theological opinion among the Fathers of the Church, competent theologians, or the Christian community. Augustine taught, and early ecumenical councils implied, that a truth is certainly revealed if the Fathers of the Church agree that it is. Vatican Council I forbade interpreting Scripture "contrary to the unanimous consent of the Fathers" (D 3007). Not every Father need profess the doctrine, provided that none contradict those who do. That similar consensus among theologians attests the revealed nature of a doctrine is suggested by theologians' disposition to disagree when permitted; and, on the other hand, their agreement is a clear indication of the mind of the Church. The faithful also, enlightened by the Spirit, clarify tradition when they agree on truths not yet explicitly taught as revealed. BIBLIOGRAPHY: R. A.

McCormick, "Teaching Role of the Magisterium and of Theologians," *Proceedings of the Catholic Theological Society of America* 24 (1969); H. Bacht, LTK 3:43–46.

[W. DAVISH]

CONSENSUS FORMULA, HELVETIC, see HELVETIC CONSENSUS FORMULA.

CONSENSUS OF GENEVA *(Consensus Genevensis),* a polemical treatise written (1552) by John *Calvin in defense of his doctrine of predestination against Albertus Pighius (c.1490–1542) and others. In 1542 Pighius had published a criticism of Luther's and Calvin's doctrine of predestination, maintaining an almost Pelagian view of human freedom. Jerome Bolsec (d. 1584) also declared that Calvin's doctrine of predestination was a denial of God's grace. While alluding to Bolsec, the Consensus was mainly a violent attack on Pighius. Absolute predestination, said Calvin, is the only solid ground for a believer's assurance of salvation. The document was subscribed by the pastors in Geneva; in other cities, however, reaction was largely unfavorable, as many objected to the idea of a divine decree of reprobation. Philipp *Melanchthon, who had changed his views on free will and predestination, was among the critics of the Consensus. Further controversy was stirred by the burning of M. *Servetus (1553) and by Calvin's conflict with Sebastian *Castellio, a former colleague who had become a bitter enemy. While *double predestination came to be accepted by the *Reformed Churches everywhere, the Consensus was not generally used as a doctrinal standard. BIBLIOGRAPHY: Schaff Creeds 1:474–477.

[N. H. MARING]

CONSENSUS OF SANDOMIERZ, a formula agreed on among Lutherans, Calvinists, and Bohemian Brethren at Sandomierz, Poland (1570), as an attempt at unity. Retaining their identities, the three bodies recognized as true expressions of Christian faith the Augsburg, Bohemian, and Helvetic Confessions. For a brief period the Consensus brought about a federated union with pulpit exchange and *intercommunion. Lutheran participation ended with the *Formula of Concord (1580). BIBLIOGRAPHY: Schaff Creeds 1:586–588.

[J. R. WEINLICK]

CONSENSUS QUINQUESAECULARIS (Lat. *quinque,* five, *saeculum,* century; also Quinquecentennial Consensus), a term applied by Georg Doisch (1597–1694) to a conciliatory theory of the Lutheran theologian G. *Calixt. In an attempt to overcome differences among Lutherans, both with each other and with other Churches, Calixt proposed a distinction between fundamental and nonfundamental teachings. The first were those concerning which there was universal agreement during the first 5 cent., and which are necessary for salvation; all other creeds, including those of the Reformation, were to be regarded as interpretations

or extensions of the Apostles' Creed and not necessary for salvation. The theory touched off the Syncretistic Controversy, in which Calixt was attacked, esp. by A. *Calov. Most Lutherans repudiated Calixt's approach to irenics as neither historically nor theologically sound. The *consensus quinquesaecularis* still is discussed in connection with *ecumenism. BIBLIOGRAPHY: J. L. Neve, *Lutherans in the Movement for Church Union* (1921); A. C. Piepkorn, EncLuthCh 1:350.

[N. H. MARING]

CONSENSUS TIGURINUS, see ZURICH CONSENSUS.

CONSENT, MORAL. In RC theology no sin is considered mortal unless it involves grave matter (i.e., is a serious violation of God's law), sufficient reflection (i.e., awareness of and advertence to the moral character of what one proposes to do), and full consent of the will (i.e., the will must fully consent to doing what should not be done or to neglect what ought to be done). Factors that interfere with the mind's apprehension of or advertence to the morality of what it proposes, or with the will's freedom in its consent to what the mind proposes, diminish in some degree the voluntary and human character of an act performed under their influence. Among such factors the following are commonly enumerated: ignorance, passion, violence, and fear. When these forces, aggravated in some cases by psychotic or neurotic conditions, operate in such a way as to obscure the judgment of the mind or to lessen the will's freedom of choice, they diminish responsibility. Even when their influence is minor, they take away some of the malice of a sinful act; if their influence is notable, they may make a sin, which would otherwise be mortal, imputable only as a venial offense; when their influence is overwhelming, they may even excuse from all fault. BIBLIOGRAPHY: ThAq ST 1a2ae q.6; Davis MorPastTh 1:16–33.

[P. K. MEAGHER]

CONSEQUENCES, MORALITY OF, the ethical question of whether something foreseen as likely to follow upon the performance or omission of an action, but not intended by the agent, is morally imputable to that agent. A completely unforeseen result of one's action can in no way be counted either to the agent's credit or discredit, since there is nothing voluntary about it. On the other hand, a foreseen and intended result of one's action is not properly speaking a consequence, for it becomes the object or end (or part of the object or end) for which one acts. Thus the question concerns only the foreseen but unintended results of one's action. When these results are good, they cannot be reckoned to the agent's moral credit because he is uninterested in and has done nothing willingly to promote their occurrence, and they are, so far as he is concerned, nonvoluntary. When it is a question of evil consequences, however, the case is quite different. We are under obligation as responsible moral agents to refrain from avoidable actions when we see there is some probability of their resulting in evil or harmful consequences, e.g., one should refrain from driving when he is under the influence of alcohol. It is not enough to say that, when he does drive under such circumstances, that the consequent accident is not in any positive sense intentional or voluntary; in a negative sense it is both intentional and voluntary. The will fails to act, when it could and should do so, to obviate a possible accident by not driving. BIBLIOGRAPHY: F. D. Nealy, NCE 4:212.

[P. K. MEAGHER]

CONSERVATION, DIVINE, the continuation of the creative act whereby God initially bestowed existence upon creatures (ThAq ST 1a, 104.1 ad 4). It is an essential aspect of divine *providence—a direct, immediate, and positive action in which God sustains his created effects. The notion is seminally present in Scripture which affirms God as consistently operative in the world. Early Christian thought explicitly acknowledged this aspect of providence: *Irenaeus taught that things last as long as God wills them to have existence and duration; St. *John Chrysostom states that a creature deprived of God's efficacious action would perish. Scholastic theology tended to understand conservation in terms of its theory of *participation. Only in God is existence and essence identified; creation entails not only an initial act but a sustenance in being. Although God certainly uses secondary causes in his providential care of the universe, his causality is not simply the first of a series but is unique and transcendent. BIBLIOGRAPHY: A. J. Benedetto, NCE 4:212–214; *idem, Fundamentals in the Philosophy of God* (1963).

[T. M. MCFADDEN]

CONSERVATISM, a spirit, attitude, or tendency rather than a school of thought within the Church. Conservatism is disposed to preserve doctrine, tradition, law, and custom. The fact that the Spirit of truth has been present to the Church throughout history imposes a certain theological conservatism upon all Christians. To maintain that the Church in the past has totally misunderstood or erroneously formulated the Gospel fails to recognize the force of Christ's promise to be with us forever. On the other hand, a triumphal attitude that all truth has already been expressed in the most precise way possible or that the Church does not need reform amounts to the deification of a community of sinful men. Conservatism, as well as its opposite, liberalism, is often used as a term to designate greater or lesser degrees of openness to administrative, canonical, social, or liturgical change, or to the reformulation of doctrine. BIBLIOGRAPHY: L. Dewart, *Future of Belief* (1967). *REFORM AND THE CHURCH; *LIBERALISM.

[T. M. MCFADDEN]

CONSERVATIVE MENNONITE CONFERENCE, a body organized at Pigeon, Mich. (1910), as the Conservative Amish Mennonite Church; the present name was adopted in 1954. The organizing members were Amish Mennonites who favored a greater progressivism than the Old Order Amish, esp. in regard to organized church work. This Church has always subscribed to the *Dordrecht Confession of Faith. It has close ties to the Mennonite Church. There are congregations in Pa., Md., Del., N.Y., Va., Ky., Ohio, Ind., Ill., Kans., and Iowa. BIBLIOGRAPHY: MennEnc 1:700–702.

CONSIGNATION (sealing, marking, branding), an act of marking with the sign of the cross at baptism, confirmation; a confirmatory indication by a sign or token that a person so marked belongs to Christ.

[K. O'NEILL]

CONSISTORIAL CONGREGATION, see BISHOPS, CONGREGATION FOR.

CONSISTORY COURT, in some Presbyterian Churches a church court corresponding to the *session (in Scotland, kirk session) or, as in French Reformed Churches, to the presbytery.

[J. A. R. MACKENZIE]

CONSOBRINO, JOÃO (early 15th cent.–1486), theologian. A Portugese Carmelite, C. taught theology and canon law in Lisbon where he was a noted professor. He was confessor and court preacher to King Alfonso V and author of *De justitia commutativa, arte campsoria ac alearum ludo* (1483), notable for its doctrine on problems of economics. BIBLIOGRAPHY: P. Servais, DTC 3.1:1197.

[J. R. AHERNE]

CONSOLAMENTUM, the Catharist rite of initiation for the *Perfecti. Consolamentum was also received by the ordinary believers at the hour of death. *CATHARI.

CONSOLATA MISSIONARY FATHERS (Institute of the Consolata for Foreign Missions; IMC), a foreign-mission congregation founded at the Church of the Consolata in Turin, Italy in 1901 by Giuseppe Allamano. Its members consist of priests and lay auxiliaries dedicated to propagating and conserving the Christian faith, particularly among pagan peoples. They received final papal approval in 1923. The congregation established its first house in Canada (1947) and in the U.S. (1950). In 1976 they numbered 1,082 and maintained 249 houses throughout the world. Headquarters are in Rome.

[H. P. ANNAS]

CONSOLATION, an important ancient literary genre that became well represented in Christian as well as in pagan writers. *Crantor of Soli (*c*.335–*c*.275 B.C.), in his *On Grief*, a treatise cast in the form of a letter, raised the informal kind of consolation already noted in Democritus of Abdera (*c*.440–370 B.C.) to the status of a literary genre. It subsequently made use of the treatise, letter, diatribe, funeral oration, and sermon as the vehicles for its expression. The consolation could be applied to almost any kind of misfortune, but it was concerned most frequently with the occasion of death. Among the *topoi* or commonplaces formulated by Crantor and others for the genre may be listed: fortune rules all and one must always be ready to meet its blows; all men are mortal; to have lived virtuously, not long, is of prime importance; time cures all ills; death gives freedom from the ravages of disease, the evils of old age, and all other misfortunes; the example of others ought to give one comfort and courage; the dead no longer suffer grief or pain; many think there is a happy life for the soul beyond the grave; reason must temper grief; displays of emotion are unmanly. Apart from Seneca's occasional emphasis on the warmth of family affection as a source of consolation, the commonplaces listed are pretty much impersonal arguments based on reason and have a certain philosophical coldness about them that is peculiarly Stoic. Christianity gave a new life to the traditional commonplaces by adding the incomparably superior consolation based on the fundamental tenets of the Christian faith, in particular, the vivid belief in the future life as the only true life, the resurrection of the body, and eternal happiness with God in heaven. Among the pagan writers of consolations it will suffice to mention, after Crantor, Cicero, Servius Sulpicius Rufus, Seneca, and Plutarch; and among the Christians, St. Ambrose, St. Paulinus of Nola, St. Jerome, and St. Augustine—and the famous *Consolation* of *Boethius. The great funeral orations of St. Gregory Nazianzen and St. Ambrose illustrate the Christian form of the genre esp. well. BIBLIOGRAPHY: OCD 226; LexAW 3135–37; C. Favez, *La Consolation latine chrétienne* (1937); M. Melchior Beyenka, *Consolation in Saint Augustine* (CUA PatrSt 83, 1950).

[M. R. P. MCGUIRE]

CONSOLATIONS, SPIRITUAL, in a wide sense, the relief experienced after a period of spiritual desolation, aridity, or suffering; in a narrower and more exact sense, the delight that accompanies certain exercises and practices of the spiritual life or the joyful feeling God sometimes bestows on faithful souls as an incentive or a reward. The consolations that proceed from the practice of virtue and the exercises of the spiritual life presuppose a certain perfection and facility on the part of the one who engages in them, since delight in operation is one of the effects of a perfected habit. On the other hand, some virtues tend by their very nature to produce consolation, e.g., joy is an effect of charity, spiritual refreshment accompanies the practice of prayer, peace of soul is a consequence of hope, and so forth. Spiritual consolation is also a characteristic of certain types of prayer, and esp. affective prayer, the prayer of simplicity, and the mystical grades of infused contemplation. The spiritual consolations granted as favors from God are not restricted to any particular stage of spiritual development nor to any particular exercise of the spiritual life, since the Spirit moves as he will. Thus, some enjoy interior consolations in the midst of the greatest suffering, as is evident from the testimony of the saints and the history of the martyrs. Sometimes God grants these consolations as an incentive to greater virtue and more intense love; at other times they are given as a reward to faithful Christians. So far as spiritual consolations are dependent upon the dispositions of the recipient, the more common obstacles to the experience of consolation are: difficulty in the exercise of virtue, temperamental indisposition, sadness, scrupulosity, anxiety, excessive attachment to the things of sense, physical illness, and exhaustion. Among the factors that foster spiritual consolation and delight are: facility in the practice of virtue, positive predispositions of temperament (esp. in those of sanguine and choleric temperaments), optimism, generosity, trust in God, detachment from worldly things, physical and mental health. Since spiritual consolations are good in themselves and can become powerful aids to growth in the spiritual life, it is lawful to desire them. Nevertheless, the spiritual writers, and esp. St. John of the Cross, repeatedly warn against the danger of seeking spiritual consolations because of the satisfaction and delight they provide. The one who does this is likely to concentrate on the gift received and to have less interest in growing in love of the God who bestows the gift. This warning is particularly important for those in the ascetical stages who are just beginning to experience the delight of their growing facility in virtue or the consolations of affective prayer. The proper attitude toward spiritual consolations is therefore one of holy indifference, yet thanking God for favors received. BIBLIOGRAPHY: A. Tanquerey, *Spiritual Life* (tr. H. Branderis, repr. 1945); J. G. Arintero, *Mystical Evolution in the Development and Vitality of the Church* (tr. J. Aumann, 2 v., 1949–51); A. Poulain, *Graces of Interior Prayer* (tr. L. L. York Smith, 1950); St. John of the Cross, *Dark Night of the Soul* (tr. E. A. Peers, repr., 1963).

[J. AUMANN]

CONSORTIUM PERFECTAE CARITATIS, a fellowship formed among religious superiors of many of the major women's religious institutes in the U.S. as an initial response to Vatican Council II's request for renewal (Vat II RenRelLife). The experimentation that arose from this document resulted in divergent goals and methods of implementing renewal. Consequently, in Dec. 1970 in Chardon, Ohio, major superiors of those institutes with similar aims formed a separate fellowship (*consortium*) in order to communicate and to share their experiences of renewal. The primary purpose of the fellowship is to bring together those who accept the conciliar documents of Vatican Council II regarding religious life, subsequent papal statements, interpretations, and directives of the Holy See emanating from the Sacred Congregation of Religious. National assemblies have been held yearly since the formal establishment of the Consortium.

[A. WARDLE]

CONSPIRACY, a secret combination of two or more persons in an agreement to foster some specific cause. Generally understood to be aimed at some evil or criminal cause, or to do a lawful act by unlawful means. Each party is bound to make right whatever wrongs are wrought by the entire group; e.g., in a theft each of the conspirators is bound to restitution of the total amount stolen, if the other conspirators refuse to bear their share of the responsibility. A question commonly raised by moral theologians concerns the morality of a conspiracy aimed at unseating a tyrant. While it is agreed that a people have the right to depose an abuser or usurper of civil power, a conspiracy against him must be representative of the community.

[T. GILBY]

CONSTABILIS, ST., (c. 1060–1124), Benedictine abbot. A member of the Gentilcore family, he entered the monastery at La Cava at the age of 7. Two years before his death he became fourth abbot of that house. He was venerated as patron of the town of Castel Abbate; his cult was approved in 1893. BIBLIOGRAPHY: AS Feb. 3:42–46; G. M. Fusconi, BiblSanct 4:157–158.

[W. A. JURGENS]

CONSTABLE, CUTHBERT (d. 1746), English Catholic landowner and antiquarian. Educated at Douai, C. earned a doctorate in medicine at Montpellier. Upon the death of his uncle he came into a substantial fortune that enabled him to spend large sums in the cultivation of his antiquarian, literary, and religious interests. He helped R. *Challoner to compile his *Memoirs of Missionary Priests* and contributed to the publication of C. Dodd's *History of the Church.* BIBLIOGRAPHY: Gillow BDEC 1:548–549.

CONSTABLE, HENRY (1562–1613). Educated at Cambridge, C. spent much of his life in public affairs, not to mention political intrigue. He seems to have embraced Catholicism in 1591. His best known contribution to poetry, *Diana,* a series of sonnets, was published in 1592. In 1593 appeared *Spiritual Sonnets,* a work that clearly shows his Catholic convictions. C. labored hard to improve the position of Catholicism in England, even to the point of planning a way to convert Queen Elizabeth. He had hopes for a Stuart succession but ultimately worked, apparently with approval of the Holy See, for a French succession as a way to restore the old faith in England. C. lived in voluntary exile in France and when he returned to England under James I was committed to the Tower and then sent into exile where he died. L. I. Guiney, *Recusant Poets* (1939).

[J. R. AHERNE]

CONSTANCE, COUNCIL OF, one of the most important councils in the history of the Church and the papacy, held at Constance in S Germany. It surpassed all previous councils in duration (Nov. 5, 1414, to April 22, 1418) and rivaled most in the number, if not in the dignity, of prelates attending. The Council's chief task was to end the *Great Western Schism, which began in 1378 with two rival popes and later, after the Council of *Pisa (1409), a third. The Council of Constance also had to adjudicate the doctrinal issues raised by John *Wycliffe and Jan *Hus and to initiate a program of church reform.

Procedures. From the beginning the Council was plagued by procedural problems. In 1413 the Pisan Pope, John XXIII, under pressure from the Emperor, Sigismund, authorized the Council, but early in 1414 he withdrew from Constance. Encouraged by Sigismund and supported by the argumentation of the conciliarists, the Council continued without papal approbation. In the 5th session (April 6, 1415) it passed the controversial decree *Sacrosancta* (called also *Haec sancta,* from its opening words), constituting itself as a general council representing the Catholic Church and holding authority immediately from Christ. The notorious misconduct of John XXIII caused the Council to depose him (May 29). Gregory XII, the Roman pope, formally abdicated on July 4, 1415, after reconvoking Constance as a general council. Efforts to persuade Benedict XIII at Avignon to resign were fruitless, and he too was finally deposed in July 1417. Another procedural problem was presented by the large Italian majority. It was resolved by a decision to vote in blocs; each of the four "nations," the Italian, German, French, and English, was to have one vote. The Spaniards joined the proceedings at the end of 1415 as a fifth "nation."

Doctrinal Issues. From the writings of Wycliffe 24 propositions already censured at the Synod of London in 1382, together with 21 others, were condemned at the 8th session (D 1151–95). At the 15th session, the Bohemian nationalist and Reformer Jan Hus heard himself condemned for views similar to Wycliffe's (D 1201–30). The safe conduct granted him by Sigismund apparently was not a guarantee of immunity against trial. Hus was handed over to the secular arm and burned at the stake, July 6, 1415. The execution made Hus a national hero in Bohemia, and inspired the *Hussite movement. In the following session, the Council repudiated a proposition justifying tyrannicide (D 1235).

Reform. The Fathers at Constance, esp. the Germans and the English, were insistent on the need for reform "in head and members." They shared a suspicion that the papacy was unable or unwilling to pursue the cause of reform effectively, and therefore, before proceeding to the election of a pope, the Council promulgated several reform measures (Oct. 5, 1417). The most important was the decree *Frequens,* which sought to establish councils as instruments of reform by stipulating that they were to be convoked frequently and at regular intervals. Constance was not successful as a reform council because the Fathers were more concerned about the head than the members; they attacked the symptoms rather than the causes of corruption.

Schism. The Council's main achievement was to heal the schism that had divided Western Christendom for almost 40 years. After receiving the resignation of Gregory XII and deposing John XXIII and Benedict XIII, the way was clear to elect a pope who would be accepted by all. The choice was Oddo Colonna, a cardinal of the Pisan obedience, who took the name Martin V (1417–31). The abnormal circumstances of the Western Schism raised constitutional and ecclesiological issues that have been much discussed ever since Constance. The broad questions revolve around the very nature of an ecumenical council and its authority vis-à-vis the pope. Specifically it is asked what constituted Constance as a legitimate council: the original convocation by John XXIII, the decree *Sacrosancta,* the convocation by Gregory XII immediately before his resignation, or subsequent approval of its proceedings by Pope Martin V? Much of the debate turns on the force of *Sacrosancta*: whether it is a dogmatic decree defining the nature and function of a council or essentially a practical decision justifying Constance in terms of the extraordinary circumstances created by the Western Schism. There is as well the problem of the extent to which *Sacrosancta* and *Frequens* sanction conciliarism. As much for the dogmatic issues it raises as for its procedures, Constance is unique in the history of councils. BIBLIOGRAPHY: B. Tierney, NCE 4:219–223; *Das Konzil von Konstanz: Beiträge zu seiner Geschichte und Theologie* (eds. A. Franzen and W. Müller, 1964); A. Franzen, ''Council of Constance: Present State of the Problem,'' *Concilium,* 7:29–68.

[B. L. MARTHALER]

CONSTANS I, (Flavius Julius; 320 or 323–350 A.D.), **ROMAN EMPEROR.** The youngest son of Constantine and Fausta, C. was appointed Caesar in 333 and became Augustus with his brothers Constantine II and Constantius II on the death of their father in 337. He received as his portion Illyria, Italy, and Africa. In 340, after Constantine II had been slain in an ambush, C. became sole ruler in the West. Victorious over the Franks in 342 and 343, he lost favor with his people because of his oppressive taxation. He was slain attempting to flee to Spain by the followers of Flavius Magnentius, who had himself proclaimed Augustus at Autun. As a baptized Christian, C. richly endowed the Church; passed edicts against pagans, Jews, and heretics, particularly the Arians; and promoted public morality, though his own life was not above reproach. BIBLIOGRAPHY: O. Seeck, RAC 4:948–952; J. Palanque, DHGE 13:583–584.

[M. J. COSTELLOE]

CONSTANS II POGONATUS (630–668), **BYZANTINE EMPEROR** from 641. A member of the Heraclian dynasty, which long dominated the Eastern empire, C.

shared the autocratic and despotic nature of Justinian. When he came to power, the senate in Constantinople had regained much of its former authority but in the reign of C. this was eroded. The ascendancy of the Arabs led to the loss by the empire of its richest province, Egypt. Following this, Muslim seapower challenged the empire throughout the Mediterranean, and C. was defeated in a great naval battle in 655. A compensating victory came to him in a campaign against the Balkan Slavs. Another problem of his reign was the opposition to Constantinople in North Africa where the Orthodox and the Monophysites both opposed the theology espoused by Byzantium. Here Maximus the Confessor, the outstanding theologian of the area, led the opposition, asserting that the empire had no voice in theological matters. In Rome Pope Martin I was elected without imperial approval and at a Lateran synod condemned the views held by Constans. Pope Martin was arrested and tried in a mock miscarriage of justice in Constantinople. Maximus was also subjected to exile and imprisonment. In an effort to win favor in the West, C. made the curious decision to transfer his regime from Constantinople to Rome. On his journey W he was assassinated by a member of his entourage. BIBLIOGRAPHY: Ostrogorsky-Charanis.

[J. R. AHERNE]

CONSTANT, GUSTAVE LÉON MARIE JOSEPH (1869–1940), French priest and church historian. Professor of modern church history at the Institut Catholique de Paris from 1908, C. centered his research on two themes, the Reformation in England and Germany's role in the Council of Trent. In 1910 he published a critical catalogue of documents on the Council. The first volume of his study of the English Reformation—*The English Schism, Henry VIII (1509–47)*—was published in English translation (tr. R. E. Scantlebury) in 1934. In this he refused to see any evidences of Protestantism in the English Church under Henry. The second volume, *Introduction of the Reformation into England, Edward VI (1547–53),* was published in 1941 (tr. E. I. Watkin). BIBLIOGRAPHY: Y. Congar, *Catholicisme* 3:93–94.

[M. J. SUELZER]

CONSTANTINE (d. 715), **POPE** from 708, the fourth Syrian to be elected to the papacy within a brief span of years. At the invitation of the Emperor Justinian II, he visited Constantinople (710–711) where he was received with great acclaim. On the death of Justinian, C. refused to recognize his successor, Phillipicus, a Monothelite. Phillipicus was soon deposed, and C. recognized the new emperor, Anastasius II, who sent a profession of faith to the Pope. BIBLIOGRAPHY: H. K. Mann, CE 4:294–295; Mann 1.2:127; G. Bardy, DHGE 13:589–591.

[P. F. MULHERN]

CONSTANTINE THE GREAT (285–337), Roman emperor who embraced Christianity. Son of Constantius I, C. was proclaimed Caesar by Roman troops in Britain and accepted as Augustus by the Emperor Maximian, but C. later claimed to rule by hereditary right as descendant of Claudius II. Maxentius, his rival for the imperial title, was defeated by him in the battle of the Milvian bridge. The army of C. carried on its shields the Chi-Rho monogram of Christ indicating C.'s intended conversion to Christianity. The victory over Maxentius made C. undisputed ruler of the West. With Licinius who emerged as ruler in the Eastern empire, he drew up in 313 the edict that proclaimed full' toleration for all religions throughout the empire. From this time on C. would be a munificent benefactor of the Church and an active proponent of Christianity. Despite interpretations of his conversion by later historians, the most acceptable view is that he was sincere. He saw himself as entrusted by God (as Christians presented him) to rule the empire. He attributed victory to the favor of Divinity and feared to neglect what God wanted of him and the State. It was with this philosophy that C. felt a responsibility to intervene in ecclesiastical matters, not as a theologian but as an arbiter.

The first major involvement was with the Donatists in N Africa. Through a long series of appeals C. sided consistently with the Church, ultimately granting the Donatists reluctant toleration. Much more serious to the Church and empire was the Arian conflict. The joint rule of Licinius and C. ended in civil war when the Eastern ruler began a persecution of Christians. C. emerged as sole emperor. As a memorial to his victory and an acknowledgement of what he saw as the favor of God, he rebuilt Byzantium and named the new city Constantinople. It was to be a city where Christianity would flourish with no antecedents in paganism and marked the beginning of the Christian empire.

C. soon found vexation in the dispute between Alexander, bp. of Alexandria, and one of his priests, Arius. Throughout years of conflict C.'s aim was to reconcile the two men and their followers. He convoked the great Council of Nicaea and presided over its sessions. From the Council came the Nicene Creed and the prominence of St. Athanasius, who became bp. of Alexandria and the chief foe of Arianism. The intransigent attitude of Athanasius toward the heresiarch Arius angered C. and he banished the bishop. More and more in his later years C. turned his attention to theology under his preceptor, Eusebius of Caesarea, and increasingly he lavished attention and wealth on the Church.

His greatest accomplishment was making Christianity the religion of the empire. At his death the relations of Church and State were set in a pattern that would endure for a thousand years. The new strength of the Church was almost entirely his achievement. At the same time the drawbacks to a system that mingled the secular and the sacral were set in motion. BIBLIOGRAPHY: A. H. M. Jones, *Later Roman Empire* (1964); F. X. Murphy, NCE 4:226–229.

[J. R. AHERNE]

CONSTANTINE IV (*c.*652–685), **BYZANTINE EMPEROR** from 668. During his reign the westward advance of the Arabs was stopped (678), and the *Monothelite controversy was finally settled at the Council of *Constantinople III (680), convened by C. in consultation with Rome. BIBLIOGRAPHY: Ostrogorsky 110–116.

[G. T. DENNIS]

CONSTANTINE V (718–775), **BYZANTINE EMPEROR** from 741, called Copronymos by his enemies. Though he was an efficient ruler and a valiant soldier, his memory has been blackened by his vigorous promotion of *iconoclasm; he was probably a Monophysite himself. He convoked the iconoclastic Council of *Hieria (754) and with great violence persecuted the orthodox, particularly the monks. BIBLIOGRAPHY: Ostrogorsky 147–155.

[G. T. DENNIS]

CONSTANTINE VII PORPHYROGENITUS (before 906–959), **BYZANTINE EMPEROR** from 908, son of Emperor Leo VI. Though he was the legitimate emperor from the age of 6, he was not the real ruler of the empire until 33 years later. Married to the daughter of Romanus Lecapenus, C. was overshadowed by his father-in-law who proclaimed himself senior emperor and later gave precedence to his son Christopher over C. The sons of Romanus plotted to exile their father and were themselves exiled by C. who then assumed at last his rightful position as sole emperor. He was far more an educator and scholar than a political figure. His own writings are invaluable history, and his encouragement of scholarship both by example and by patronage made his an important reign in the Byzantine Empire. C. adopted the agrarian reforms of his predecessor Romanus and carried on the war against the eastern Arabs, ineffective at first but ultimately settled in favor of Byzantium. A distinctive mark of the sole reign of C. was the highly successful diplomatic relationship with other courts, including the Arab states and the newly emerging Russian state. BIBLIOGRAPHY: Ostrogorsky-Charanis 208–213, 224–228; H. Leclercq, DACL 3.2:2695–2713.

[J. R. AHERNE]

CONSTANTINE IX MONOMACHUS (d. 1055), **BYZANTINE EMPEROR** from 1042, last of the Macedonian dynasty. A distinguished senator and member of the rising aristocratic class of Constantinople, C. became emperor through marriage to the Empress Zoë who with the Co-Empress Theodora ruled the empire after the deposition of Michael V. To the incompetence of the Empresses was thus added the incompetence of C. All three were pleasure-seeking and frivolous. Their escapades depleted the treasury. The one redeeming feature of the divided reign was the influence given to scholars like the philosopher Michael Psellus and Constantine Leichudes in public affairs. Psellus in particular was the outstanding philosopher of Byzantium and perhaps the first great humanist of post-Classical times. These men and others restored (1045) the university as a center of classical learning and a training ground for judges and civil servants. At the same time the power of the central administration and the army was deteriorating because of the increased power of the senate and the relative freedom from invasion. Worst of all developments was the final break between the Papacy and the Patriarch of Constantinople, Michael Cerularius, a schism that would have been prevented by a strong emperor. BIBLIOGRAPHY: Ostrogorsky-Charanis 289–298; S. Runciman, *Eastern Schism (1955).*

[J. R. AHERNE]

CONSTANTINE XI (1404–53), **BYZANTINE EMPEROR** from 1449. He was the last emperor of Byzantium, and lost his life in the final defense of Constantinople (May 29, 1453). He tried unsuccessfully to settle the unionistic controversy, although he himself accepted the promulgation of the decree of the Council of *Florence in Dec. 1452. BIBLIOGRAPHY: J. Gill, *Council of Florence* (1959).

[G. T. DENNIS]

CONSTANTINE III LEICHUDES, PATRIARCH OF CONSTANTINOPLE from 1059 to 1063, Byzantine scholar and statesman. With Michael Psellus, C. was a leading influence in Constantinople as a teacher and scholar. He was active in the administration of the empire under Emperor Constantine IX. He was chosen patriarch by Emperor Isaac I on the death of Michael Cerularius. The account written by his contemporary and colleague, Michael Psellus, shows C. to have been an able administrator and admirable churchman as well as a scholar. BIBLIOGRAPHY: Michael Psellus, *Chronographia* (ed. E. R. A. Sewter, 1953).

[J. R. AHERNE]

CONSTANTINE THE AFRICAN, (*c.* 1010–*c.* 1087), Benedictine translator of Arabic medical texts. After spending most of his adult life traveling in the Middle East, C. returned to Tunis, and then to Salerno, Italy, where he entered the service of Robert Guiscard. About 1078 he entered Monte Cassino where, under the tutelage of Alphanus of Salerno, he began his paraphrase-translations of Greco-Arab medical works. He anticipated by several generations the 12th-cent. translations of scientific literature, and he introduced the Latin-speaking world to Hippocrates, pseudo-Galen, Isaac Israeli, and others. Manuscripts of his writings, widely distributed, attest to his fame in the medical schools of the West. BIBLIOGRAPHY: O. J. Blum, NCE 4:230 with bibliog.

[O. J. BLUM]

CONSTANTINE HARMENOPOULUS, see HARMENOPOULOS, CONSTANTINE.

CONSTANTINE MELITENIOTES (d. 1307), Byzantine cleric and friend of *John Beccos. C. favored union with Rome signed at *Lyons in 1274, and wrote on the *procession of the Holy Spirit. When the union ended in 1282 he was excommunicated and imprisoned. BIBLIOGRAPHY: M. Jugie, *Catholicisme* 3:100.

[G. T. DENNIS]

CONSTANTINE AND METHODIUS, SS., see CYRIL.

CONSTANTINE, ARCH OF, ROME, Rome's largest and best preserved triumphal arch in honor of the Emperor Constantine I, commemorating his victory over Maxentius at the Milvian Bridge (A.D. 312). Completed in 315, its triple archway carrying entablature is flanked by detached Corinthian columns on pedestals. The attic carries a dedicatory inscription. The arch is richly carved with reliefs in medallions and friezes which are repeated in the classical Romanesque tympanum carvings in S France (St. Trophime, Arles). BIBLIOGRAPHY: B. Berenson, *Arch of Constantine* (1954).

[M. J. DALY]

CONSTANTINE, DONATION OF, see DONATION OF CONSTANTINE.

CONSTANTINOPLE (modern Istanbul), capital of the Byzantine Empire from 330 to 1453 and residence of the *ecumenical patriarch. To make the administrative and military operations of the late Roman Empire more efficient, several emperors had moved their capital farther east. *Constantine the Great (306–337) transferred it permanently by constructing a new capital on the location of the ancient Greek colony of Byzantion (Byzantium), which had survived as a small commercial city on the Bosporus. The new capital received the same institutions and privileges as Rome, which theoretically still remained an imperial capital. It was solemnly dedicated on May 11, 330, and given the name of New Rome and called Constantinople, the City of Constantine, or often simply The City. It controlled the land routes from Asia to Europe and the sea lanes from the Aegean to the Black Sea. With its excellent harbor in the Golden Horn it occupied a unique strategic position accessible by land on only one side, which was protected by a series of immense walls. It was ideally situated to be the political, economic, and military center of the highly centralized Byzantine Empire and to play a significant role in international affairs. The history of the Empire is largely the history of Constantinople. From the beginning the strongly Christian character of the city was evident. Churches and monasteries were erected on a magnificent scale, and their relics made it a center of pilgrimages. The bishop soon came to be the most important in the East and as patriarch was recognized as second only to the Roman pope. The city was the site of four ecumenical and many local councils. Through most of the Middle Ages Constantinople was the most significant Christian cultural, intellectual, and artistic center and, even in its decline, played a key role in the transmission of classical Greek learning to the West. The city never fully recovered from the wanton destruction by the Latins in 1204. On May 29, 1453, it was taken by the Turks and became the capital of the Ottoman Empire. BIBLIOGRAPHY: G. Downey, NCE 4:231–237; *idem, Constantinople in the Age of Justinian* (1960). *BYZANTINE EMPIRE; *CONSTANTINOPLE, PATRIARCH OF.

[G. T. DENNIS]

CONSTANTINOPLE, COUNCILS OF, four general councils of the Church (three by Eastern Orthodox reckoning) that met in Constantinople to deal with various disciplinary and dogmatic questions.

First. This, the second general or ecumenical council of the Church, assembled at the invitation of Emperors Theodosius I and Gratian in 381. It was attended by 186 bishops, 150 of whom were orthodox and 36 heretical. Though no Western bps. were present, the conciliar fathers regarded the assembly as ecumenical. There is no evidence that the contemporary Pope (Damasus I; d. 384) officially confirmed its acts (which have been lost), and Leo I (d. 461) protested one of its canons; but Chalcedon (451) cited it in terms that imply recognition of its ecumenical character. This was generally accepted in the West as well as in the East by the time of Gregory I (d. 604).

The purpose of this Council was to put an end to the disunity caused, esp. in the East, by the Arian heresy. It confirmed the teaching of Nicaea I, affirmed the consubstantiality and coeternity of the three persons of the Trinity, and gave clearer expression to the perfect humanity of the Son. In its four canons it: (1) condemned Arianism; (2) set limits to the jurisdiction of bishops (this to curb the interference of Alexandria); (3) accorded to Constantinople a dignity second only to the see of Rome; and (4) condemned Maximus, the Arian bp. of Constantinople, whom it deposed and replaced, first with St. Gregory of Nazianzus, and, *upon his resignation, *with Nectarius. Although tradition ascribes the completion of the Nicene (or Niceno-Constantinopolitan) Creed to this council, evidence does not support the claim, although the Creed in this form, already in use in Jerusalem, appears to have been recited by Nectarius upon his appointment. BIBLIOGRAPHY: J. Bois, DTC 3.1:1227–31.

Second. This, the fifth general council of the Church, was convoked by the Emperor Justinian to put an end to the controversy concerning the Three Chapters. In attendance were 165 bishops, 154 of them from the East. Pope Vigilius with an entourage of Western bishops, though in Constantinople at the Emperor's insistence, refused to take part in the deliberations. The Council, in compliance with the Emperor's wish, dutifully condemned the Three Chapters and their authors. When Vigilius refused to accept the Council's decision, the conciliar fathers responded by condemning him. Under pressure from the Emperor, Vigilius eventually stated his adherence to the condemnation of the

Three Chapters, but he appears to have been uninformed of the Council's condemnation of himself. The circumstances in which Vigilius acted and the wording of his statement make the extent of his approbation of the Council's work somewhat ambiguous. The name of Origen, possibly interpolated at a later date, is included in a list of heretics anathematized by the council. *THREE CHAPTERS; *VIGILIUS, POPE; *PELAGIUS I, POPE.

Third. This, also called the First Trullan Council (see TRULLO, COUNCILS IN), is accounted the sixth general council of the Church. Convoked by Emperor Constantine IV, it met 681–682 in a hall of the imperial palace. It was sparsely attended, the only Western bishops present being the three of the Pope's own delegation. The purpose of the assembly was to deal with *Monothelitism, which held that there was only one will and one natural energy or operation in Christ. The Council reaffirmed the doctrine of the two distinct natures in Christ and spelled out from this the conclusion that there must also be in him two wills and two natural energies or operations. Included in the list of those anathematized by the Council for having taught the contrary of this was the name of Pope Honorius I. Pope Leo II in 683 ratified the council and declared it to be ecumenical. For the acts of the Council see Mansi 11:190–192.

Fourth. According to Latin reckoning, this was the eighth ecumenical council of the Church, but it is not held to be so by the Orthodox Churches, for whom Nicaea II is the seventh and last ecumenical council. This Council met to solve the difficulties arising from the affair of Photius and Ignatius and their conflicting claims to the patriarchal throne. Only 18 bishops were present at the opening session, but at the 10th and last session 102 were in attendance. The Council was convoked in 869 by Emperor Basil the Macedonian and Pope Adrian II. Only those bishops who had not had part in the consecration of Photius and who would sign the formula of Pope Hormisdas were permitted to take their seats. During the Council Photius was summoned, tried, and sentenced, and his antipapal writings were consigned to the flames. An attempt of his partisans to defend him was put down by the papal legates. The Council then formulated 27 canons, most of which were concerned with the promotion of men to episcopal, metropolitan, and patriarchal offices. Laymen were not to be chosen and promoted without the required interstices. Priests ordained and bishops consecrated by Ignatius and Methodius, predecessors of Photius in the see of Constantinople, were, if they had been associated with Photius in his antipapal campaign, to be deposed and allowed to receive communion only as laymen. No authority can depose a patriarch and esp. the pope, and all are to be punished who dare to make the attempt, or who put in circulation writings defaming a pope or calling for his deposition, as did Dioscorus and Photius. All those ordained or consecrated by Photius were to be regarded as laymen, since Photius was never validly a bishop. Photius has since been canonized by the Orthodox Church, which honors him as a great champion against

Latin pride and papal domination. *PHOTIAN SYNOD OF 879–880.

[A. WALKER; P. K. MEAGHER]

CONSTANTINOPLE, ICONOCLASTIC SYNOD OF

(815). When Emperor Leo V the Armenian came to the throne of the Eastern Empire, he had two goals: to restore the military power of the empire and to revive the iconoclast movement. He directed John Grammaticus, the leader of the new phase, to gather information in preparation for a synod that would deal with the traditional group (iconodules, literally idol worshipers.) In violation of his pledge to the Patriarch Nicephorus, the emperor showed himself to be a partisan of iconoclasm. The Patriarch wrote in vain many defenses of the use of icons and protested imperial interference with strictly theological matters. It was clearly a matter of the effort of the imperial authority to control the Church. Nicephorus was deposed as patriarch, and a courtier Theodatus was named in his place (815). With Theodatus as presiding officer, a synod was held in the church of St. Sophia which rejected the ecumenical Council of Nicaea II (787) and accepted the decrees of the iconoclast council of 754. Though the synod refrained from calling icons idols, it declared that they should be destroyed. The synod was distinguished for vague, watered-down views, but it reflected the character of Leo V and led to a new and cruel persecution of adherents to the traditional belief. BIBLIOGRAPHY: Ostrogorsky-Charanis.

[J. R. AHERNE]

CONSTANTINOPLE, LATIN PATRIARCHATE OF

(1204–1261). In the stormy relationship between East and West, political and religious, no period is so unfortunate for the universal Church as that during the ill-advised imposition of a Latin empire on Constantinople. Conceived as an extension of the Crusades, it was in reality a raid on the Eastern empire by a coalition of Frankish knights and the republic of Venice. Count Baldwin of Flanders was elected emperor and Thomas Morosini became Latin patriarch of Constantinople. The empire was divided among Baldwin, the knights, and Venice. Even Constantinople was divided. Venice profited most as a maritime republic, controlling the seaways from Italy to the Bosporus. The behavior of the Latin contingent in the capital city was so ruthless that it spelled doom for the new empire from the start. Replacing Greek with Latin clergy only intensified the hatred of the Greeks for the Church of Rome. Much of the theological venom which was to make unity impossible thereafter can be traced to this era of repression and injustice. While the popes hoped for a better atmosphere for reconciliation, their mistaken policies in the Latin empire made any concord impossible. The ill-fated interregnum lasted only 57 years when at last the shaky Latin empire collapsed. BIBLIOGRAPHY: Ostrogorsky-Charanis.

[J. R. AHERNE]

CONSTANTINOPLE, PATRIARCHAL SCHOOL

OF, the higher school of theology under the authority of the patriarch of Constantinople. Sources from the 9th cent. clearly distinguish between the university in Constantinople and the patriarchal school designed to form clerics and theologians. Under the direction of an ecumenical professor (*didaskalos oikoumenikos*) the faculty, composed of deacons of Hagia Sophia, provided a general education and then seemed to concentrate on scriptural exegesis. Under Turkish rule (since 1453) the school continued to exist, but in difficult and rather isolated circumstances. It still survives as the patriarchal seminary on the island of Halki (Heybeli) near Istanbul, although it has been overshadowed by the more important theological academies of Athens and Thessalonica.

[G. T. DENNIS]

CONSTANTINOPLE, PATRIARCHATE OF, one of

the four eminent Eastern patriarchates. Originally called *Byzantium, the city was a suffragan see of Heraclea, capital of Thrace. Its importance developed when Constantine moved his government from Italy to this city on the Bosporus in 324. After the bps. of Byzantium withdrew from the authority of the Arian bps. of Heraclea, Constantinople grew in importance, and imperial influence caused it to be given precedence of honor after Rome by the Council of *Constantinople I (381). With this affirmation of independence Constantinople began to assert its influence on the surrounding Churches of Ephesus and Caesarea in Cappadocia. Because the emperor began to use the patriarch as his representative to the surrounding ecclesiastical jurisdictions, including the patriarchates of *Antioch and *Alexandria, jurisdictional difficulties arose among the three leading Eastern Churches. Unfortunately, the dogmatic quarrels of the 5th cent. were influenced greatly by the ecclesiastical politics that attended this rivalry. *Nestorius, patriarch of Constantinople, was condemned by the Council of *Ephesus (431) because of pressure exerted by St. *Cyril of Alexandria. On the other hand, at the Council of *Chalcedon (451), Constantinople secured the condemnation of *Monophysitism taught by Dioscorus, patriarch of Alexandria, and also acquired the Dioceses of Thrace, Asia, and Pontus. Antioch suffered internal division because of *Nestorianism and Monophysitism, and lost 57 dioceses when the Patriarchate of *Jerusalem was created (451). Alexandria was weakened by the Monophysite controversy and later Muslim persecutions. This deterioration of the other Eastern patriarchates augmented the importance of the patriarch of Constantinople whose ecclesiastical jurisdiction gradually coincided with the emperor's civil power. Thus he came to be called the *ecumenical patriarch, a title that contributed to East-West tensions. Ironically, the Byzantine emperors came to think of themselves as the *basileus* who not only possessed full civil power but also represented God in church affairs. At times, the emperor challenged the popes and patriarchs by promulgating dogmatic decrees, e.g., the *Henoticon of Zeno, and the imperial approval of *Monothelitism and *iconoclasm. The popes reacted by excommunicating the patriarchs of Constantinople for supporting the emperor. Opposition between East and West increased as emerging differences of cultural and religious outlook became more prominent. The actual separation of East and West is traditionally linked with the two Patriarchs *Photius (858–867; 878–886) and Michael Cerularius (1043–59). Photius was chosen by Emperor *Michael III to replace the deposed Patriarch Ignatius. Rome reinstated Ignatius and anathematized Photius. But when Ignatius died 7 years later Photius validly became patriarch of Constantinople. Although this struggle was short-lived it did raise problems over papal authority and the *filioque that were to influence the schism 2 cent. later. After becoming patriarch, Michael Cerularius closed the Latin churches of Constantinople that refused to adopt Greek usages. The legates of Pope Leo IX, failing in their efforts to persuade the Patriarch to change his course, excommunicated him; he, in turn, excommunicated the head legate, Card. Humbert of Silva Candida. It is inaccurate to regard 1054 as the year of final separation, since cordial relations between East and West continued until the Crusades. In 1182 feeling against the Crusaders became so strong that there was a slaughter of Latins in Constantinople. A more violent retaliation took place in 1204 when members of the Fourth Crusade pillaged the city. The Byzantine government went into exile and a Latin patriarchate of *Constantinople with Latin clergy controlled church affairs until the Byzantines recaptured the city in 1261. The attempts at reunion through the Councils of Lyons (1274) and Florence (1439) were ineffective. The Turks sacked Constantinople in 1453, the patriarch's residence was moved to the *Phanar section, and Hagia Sophia became a mosque.

Ironically, under the Muslim sultans the patriarchs were permitted not only ecclesiastical jurisdiction but also acted as civil head for the Greeks, thus becoming *ethnarch (millet-bashi). This fusion of sacred and secular powers turned the patriarchate into a political "plum" with the usual consequences of bribery, graft, and simony. Of the 160 patriarchs who held the see of Constantinople after the Turkish invasions, 105 were forced from their thrones, 27 abdicated, and 6 were murdered. During these years the ecclesiastical jurisdiction of the patriarch diminished with the establishment of new patriarchates: *Moscow and All of Russia in 1589, Serbia in 1830, Romania in 1856, and Bulgaria in 1870. The Church of *Greece became autocephalous in 1833. Today the patriarch of Constantinople is elected by a synod of 12 metropolitans and 70 laymen; but the candidates must be approved by the Turkish government, and upon election the patriarch becomes a Turkish citizen. On the ecclesiastical level his authority is subject to the synod which has become a miniature version of the *Holy Synod which could no longer meet after 1923. On a practical level, the patriarchate is reduced to the five Orthodox dioceses of Turkey, but the ecumenical patriarch enjoys a general jurisdiction over the faithful of Crete and the Dodacanese; he enjoys similar authority over the exarchate for Western Europe and the Russian Exarchate of Western Europe, the Greek Orthodox Archdiocese of North and South America (with Albanian, Carpatho-Ruthenian, and Ukrainian affiliates), and the Archdiocese of Australia and New Zealand. At present, the Patriarchate of Constantinople maintains a general jurisdiction over approximately 1,350,000 communicants. BIBLIOGRAPHY: G. Every, *Byzantine Patriarchate* (2d ed., 1962); S. Vailhé, DTC 3.2:1307–1519.

[F. T. RYAN]

CONSTANTINOPOLITAN CREED, a designation of the Nicene Creed, applied because the acts of the Council of Chalcedon (451) attribute the Nicene Creed to the fathers of the Council of Constantinople I (381). *NICENE CREED.

[T. C. O'BRIEN]

CONSTANTIUS II (317–361), **ROMAN EMPEROR** from 337, son of Constantine the Great. Upon the death of his father the empire was divided between C. and his two brothers, an arrangement that made him ruler of the Eastern Empire. He became continually engaged in defending his realm against the Persians. The next 13 years saw the brothers quarreling over political and religious affairs, with C. being survivor of internecine as well as foreign wars. In 351 he defeated the Western usurper, Magnentius, in a historic battle at Mursa, Pannonia, thereby reuniting the Roman Empire. He did considerable meddling with the Church. An adherent of Arianism, he was an implacable foe of St. Athanasius and the Council of Nicaea. He exiled Pope Liberius and many others. At the same time he enacted numerous laws against paganism.

[J. R. AHERNE]

CONSTANTIUS OF FABRIANO, BL. (1410–81), Italian Dominican. A man of exceptional holiness, he became vicar of the Dominican congregation of strict observance. Having studied under St. *Antoninus of Florence, he became professor of theology at Bologna and Florence. He was also prior of the convent at Fabriano (1440 and 1467), at Perugia (1459), and at Ascoli (1470) where he died. BIBLIOGRAPHY: S. M. Bertucci, BiblSanct 4:266–268; Quétif-Échard 1.2:858–859.

[J. A. WEISHEIPL]

CONSTELLATIONS, see ASTRAL RELIGION.

CONSTITUTION, APOSTOLIC, see APOSTOLIC CONSTITUTION.

CONSTITUTIONAL CHURCH, the Church formed in France by the *Civil Constitution of the Clergy, July 12, 1790. A loyalty oath to this Constitution imposed on all clergy, Nov. 27, 1790, led to a separation of jurors and nonjurors; and a schism into the Constitutional Church and the Refractory Church, continuing faithful to Rome, resulted. The organization of the Constitutional Church was worked out in 1791; the hierarchy was formed, Bps. Talleyrand-Périgord and Gobel instituting and consecrating new bps. without papal sanction. The "old" Church, the nonjuring clergy, and most of the French faithful continued, esp. after papal condemnation of the Civil Constitution (1791), to repudiate the Constitutional Church, in spite of persecution. With the fall of Louis XVI, Aug. 1792, the Constitutional Church itself began to suffer. In Sept. the Assembly took away clerical jurisdiction over the registration of vital statistics and legalized civil marriage and divorce. Under the Convention (1792–95) the cult of reason was decreed and the Constitutional Church was disestablished; many of its priests fled or apostatized. With the Directory (1795–99), the abolition of salaries for the clergy deprived them of practically their sole income. The Constitutional Church continued a feeble existence until the Concordat of 1801, at which time it was abolished by Napoleon Bonaparte. BIBLIOGRAPHY: F. M. Anderson, *Constitutions and Other Select Documents Illustrative of the History of France, 1789–1908* (2d ed., 1908); L. Gershoy, *French Revolution and Napoleon* (1964); J. H. Stewart, *Documentary Survey of the French Revolution* (1951).

[R. J. MARAS]

CONSTITUTIONAL CLERGY, bishops and priests who swore allegiance to the Civil Constitution of the Clergy passed by the Constituent Assembly of the French Revolution in 1790. Only seven bishops, of whom four were titular, accepted, thus leaving 80 out of the 83 newly created sees vacant. Constitutional bishops had little difficulty occupying their posts as many of their predecessors had emigrated. In the parishes, however, about 45% of the clergy took the oath of fidelity; this number was considerably lower in such areas as the N and W and higher in the Haute-Saône and Vosges. For some, the oath was a difficult case of conscience; for others, the result of ignorance and misunderstanding; still others used it for opportunism and gain. The people frequently refused admission to the new curé who could then establish himself by force of arms. Not only the Church, but families were divided, and this religious strife had a great impact on the ensuing events of the Revolution. After 3 years, the Revolution itself became hostile to the Constitutional Church, persecuting both groups of clergy equally, after gradually encroaching on their religious status. A small but powerful minority under Abbé Grégoire continued to press the claims of the Constitutional clergy. The Concordat of 1801 technically ended their power, although a number of them received dioceses and parishes, and echoes of the rift remained apparent until 1840. BIBLIOGRAPHY: J. Leflon, *Catholicisme* 3:118–126; Fliche-Martin 20:115–138.

[I. M. KASHUBA]

CONSTITUTIONS, RELIGIOUS OR MONASTIC, the body of regulations for a particular religious or monastic institute which concretely applies the general provisions of a religious rule if the institute possesses one, or establishes the institute's religious principles and particular applications if the group does not possess a rule. The earliest organizers of cenobitic life, e.g., Pachomius, Basil, and Benedict, formulated rules to govern the daily life of the community. With the monastic renewal of the 11th cent., new institutions arose and their organizers developed various forms of legislation to coordinate their life (e.g., Prior Guigo's *Consuetudines* for the Carthusians). The most famous constitution of this time was that of *Cîteaux, the *Charter of Charity.* Succeeding centuries saw the variety of forms continue until the Lateran Council (1215) forbade the formulation of new rules. (Honorius III, however, approved the last rule properly so called in 1223, the *regula bullata* of the Franciscans.) Constitutions then began to fulfill the important function of applying the principles and spirit of an old approved rule to new institutes (e.g., the Dominican constitutions based on the Rule of St. Augustine). However some, like Ignatius of Loyola, formulated constitutions without any explicit reference to an ancient rule. With Louis Barbo, there arose among the Benedictines the prevailing form of legislation called Declarations on the Holy Rule, which adapted the Rule of St. Benedict to the present-day life of the different congregations. More recent religious institutes have tended to produce increasingly juridical codes in which citations even from Sacred Scripture were forbidden. Vat II RenRelLife (implemented by the *motu proprio, Ecclesiae sanctae*) has called for a return to earlier forms in demanding that the revised constitutions include the evangelical and theological principles of the religious life as well as the necessary juridical norms. Today, changes in constitutions are usually effected by the institute's general chapter or its equivalent. Final approval of the changes by either the Holy See, the proper Oriental patriarch, or the local ordinary is required depending upon the particular juridical status of the religious institute. The constitutions are not of themselves binding under pain of sin, although both the Latin and Oriental code provide that the religious pattern his life according to the rules and constitutions of his institute (CIC c. 593; PostApost. c. 136). BIBLIOGRAPHY: D. Knowles, *From Pachomius to Ignatius: A Study in the Constitutional History of the Religious Orders* (1966); M. B. Pennington, "New Constitutions: A Life Charter," *Studia Canonica* 2 (1968) 77–98,; J. I. O'Connor, NCE 12:276–277.

[M. B. PENNINGTON]

CONSTITUTUM CONSTANTINI, see DONATION OF CONSTANTINE.

CONSTRUCTIVISM, term for a 20th-cent., significant concept in sculpture, which asserts not sculptural mass but sculptural space, no longer creating form as mass but framing voids by planes. Achieved first in Russia (Vladimir Tattin, 1919) then in Holland and Germany, constructivism affirmed a new Platonic reality of form as absolute idea. Later through movement (kinetic form) the idea of time was added to that of space. *CONCRETE ART.

[M. J. DALY]

CONSUBSTANTIALITY, the term used in Christian tradition mainly to express that the three persons of the *Trinity have one and the same divine nature. The term is not found in the Bible, although the basis for its later use is established in the scriptural statements concerning the relationships between Jesus and the Father, e.g., the identification of Jesus as the preexistent Word of God (Jn 1.1), or as the radiant light of God's glory and the perfect copy of his nature (Heb 1.3). Consubstantiality was a key issue in the early Trinitarian controversies, and is generally used as the translation of the Greek *homoousios*. It was employed by the *Alexandrian school of theology in an orthodox sense, interpreted in a Monarchian manner by *Paul of Samosata, but accepted at the Council of *Nicaea I (325) against the Arians to affirm the full divinity of the Son. As used at Nicaea, therefore, consubstantiality denies the Arian teaching that the Son was merely a creature, and affirms that he is from the substance of the Father, true God from true God, born not made, and of one substance with the Father (D 125). Consubstantiality continued in use against other Trinitarian heresies (see SEMI-ARIANISM), and was also applied to the Holy Spirit (D 853). The Council of Chalcedon (451) employed the term in Christology as well, and defined that Christ possesses a true human nature, i.e., that he is consubstantial with other men. The Church continues to use the term in its Trinitarian context to affirm that the absolute simplicity of the Godhead is not contradicted by the trinity of divine persons. Father, Son, and Spirit are distinct, but equally possess the divine nature. BIBLIOGRAPHY: J. N. D. Kelly, *Early Christian Doctrines* (2d ed., 1960) 223–279; J. Lebreton, *Histoire du dogme de la Trinité* (1928); T. E. Clarke, NCE 4:251–253.

[T. M. MCFADDEN]

CONSUBSTANTIATION (Lat. *cum,* with; *substantia,* substance), the teaching that the substance of Christ's body and blood is conjoined to the substance of bread and wine in the *Eucharist; companation occurs, though rarely, as a synonym for consubstantiation. The eucharistic theories of John *Wycliffe included an affirmation of the perdurance of the whole reality of bread and wine. But consubstantiation has been particularly associated with Lutheran eucharistic teaching; the designation, however, has never been regarded as adequate by Lutherans. Lutheranism does reject *transubstantiation, i.e., the change of the substance of the eucharistic elements, and does affirm that the body and blood of Christ are truly distributed and taken with the bread and wine (*Formula of Concord, art. 7). The Lutheran understanding of body "with the bread," however,

is meant simply as a full acceptance of the literal meaning of the words of the sacrament, so strongly affirmed by Luther in his *Confession Concerning the Lord's Supper* (1528) and defended against *Reformed teaching by Lutherans. The mode of Christ's eucharistic presence is simply called a "sacramental union" (*ibid.,* art. 7). The term consubstantiation is less than satisfactory to Lutherans because it represents an attempt to philosophize about the manner of the *Real Presence and implies a union of the body and blood of Christ with the bread and wine other than the union existing in actual sacramental use. BIBLIOGRAPHY: H. Sasse, *This Is My Body* (1959). *IMPANATION.

[T. C. O'BRIEN]

CONSUETUDINARY, see CUSTOMARY.

CONSULAR DIPTYCHS, two-leafed wax writing tablets with elaborately carved ivory covers, given as presents by consuls in the late Roman period (later restricted because of too widespread circulation). The covers carved in relief are of great beauty and importance in late Roman and early Christian art, expressing in stylized decorative relief symmetric compositions of historical personages in significant architectural settings (Diptych of Consul Anastasius, 517; Consul Magnus sseated with Symbolic Figures of Rome and Constantinople, 518, both in the Bibliothèque Nationale).

[M. J. DALY]

CONSULTATION ON CHURCH UNION, discussions concerning merger of several U.S. denominations. Originally proposed by Eugene Carson Blake in a sermon at Grace Cathedral, San Francisco (1960), during the episcopate of Bp. James Pike, the Consultation on Church Union (COCU) is often called the Blake-Pike Proposal. The United Presbyterian and the Protestant Episcopal Churches invited the Methodist Church and the United Church of Christ to an exploratory meeting at Washington, D.C., in April 1962. By the second meeting, at Oberlin, Ohio (1963), the Evangelical United Brethren and the Disciples of Christ had also become participants, and several other denominations sent observer-consultants. Subsequent meetings have been held almost annually: Princeton, N.J., 1964; Lexington, Ky., 1965; Dallas, Tex., 1966; Cambridge, Mass., 1967; Dayton, Ohio, 1968; Atlanta, Ga., 1969; St. Louis, Mo., 1970; Denver, Colo., 1971; Memphis, Tenn., 1973; Cincinnati, Ohio, 1974; and Bergamo (near Dayton), Ohio, 1976. During the 60s enthusiasm was high, and delegates were able to cut through knotty problems, producing *Principles of Church Union,* which were adopted at Dallas in 1966 and sent to member Churches for study. Encouraged by response to this document, the COCU voted in 1968 that a plan of union be presented for consideration not later than 1970. Underlying the impulse to church union were diverse forces, but also some common assumptions. (1) The Church of Jesus Christ is one, and that oneness ought to become visible to the world. (2) Renewal is needed in the Churches, and an emphasis upon mission and servanthood of the Church should be central to union. By clarifying convictions concerning the gospel, by linking public worship more closely to mission, and by involving the entire laity in the ministry of the Church, reform and renewal can be furthered. (3) A complex, urban society calls for new forms and approaches on the part of the Church, and a reconciling Church must itself be reconciled.

At Denver, in 1970, A Plan of Union, was presented, dealing with faith, worship, ministry, and organization. That the new Church was to be confessional, liturgical, sacramental, and episcopal had been previously determined. Also, from the beginning the aim had been to establish a Church which would be "truly catholic, truly reformed, and truly evangelical." By *catholic* is meant continuity in time and doctrine, inclusiveness of all peoples, and comprehensiveness of witness in all areas of life. The term *evangelical* conveys a concern to invite all the world to be reconciled to God and one another, and to live under the Lordship of Jesus Christ. A church *reformed* is one which "subjects all its traditions and practices . . . to the judgment and correction of the Holy Spirit as he works through the Scriptures and in history." Affirming belief in a trinitarian God, the confessional statement acknowledges the unique and normative authority of the Scriptures, recognizes the important relationship between Tradition and the traditions, accepts the sacraments of baptism and the Lord's Supper, approves the Apostles' and Nicene Creeds, and allows wide latitude for the use of other expressions of faith in Jesus Christ. Operating on four levels (parish, district, region, and nation), the chief governing body would be a National Assembly comprising laity, presbyters, deacons, and bishops. Ordained ministries would be open to both men and women, and reordination of existing ministries would not be required. The parish, a distinctive feature, would combine congregations roughly along geographical lines, but would include diverse ethnic, social, and economic groups. Two final chapters express an intention to be continuously open to new relationships with other ecclesiastical bodies and indicate procedures for the transition from being a Consultation to becoming the Church of Christ Uniting. The Plan endeavored to incorporate the essential doctrines of historic Christianity, to delineate clear lines of authority and decision-making, and to achieve a balance between flexibility in worship and organization and enough uniformity to sustain a sense of unity and stability.

By 1970, changes in theological climate and in secular environment had produced attitudes and issues unfavorable to the ecumenical movement. Distrust of bureaucratic organization and centralized authority, apathy at the grassroots level, resistance from middle judicatories, conflict between loyalties to world-wide confessional bodies and to a new united Church, dissension over social involvement of Churches, and divergent views on specific provisions of the Plan constituted formidable obstacles to its coming to fruition. Moreover, the raised consciousness of ethnic minorities, women, and youth were reflected in new criticisms and demands directed to the Consultation. Successive plenary sessions strove to deal with the comments and suggestions elicited from the Churches, as well as to adjust to requests of special-interest groups. Commissions and task forces sought ways to combat institutional racism and sexism, to devise means for allowing maximum local autonomy within the parish concept, to generate new forms of church life, to foster interim eucharistic fellowship, and to make room for greater participation of minorities, women, and youth. In 1974, a change of leadership took place, as Gerald F. Moede and John H. Satterwhite succeeded Paul A. Crow, Jr., as General Secretary and Associate Secretary, respectively.

At Bergamo, in 1976, the main agenda was a document, "In Quest of a Church of Christ Uniting," which was basically a rewriting of the first seven chapters of the Plan of 1970. The revision met with general agreement on the first six chapters and most of the seventh. Nevertheless, serious differences emerged with regard to the roles and authority of bishops and certain other aspects of the ministry. Acceptable modifications were worked out before adjournment, and the document was sent to member Churches. Churches were requested to accept it as "a statement of emerging theological consensus for study, response, and guidance in furthering the mutual recognition of members and working toward mutual recognition of ministries." Responses were to be returned by November 1977, in order that another plenary could be convened to consider a revised statement on ministry. In appendices, the Churches were cautioned against "the church-dividing potential of some persistent issues," such as "racism, sexism, bureaucratic institutions, and congregational exclusiveness." Thus, the 1976 meeting showed that the movement toward union was still alive. A paramount need noted by delegates was that of enlisting younger persons who would become future church leaders, and to that end plans were laid for a national conference of COCU church youth on the life and mission of the Church to be held in 1979. Ten Churches were participants in the COCU by 1976. Three black denominations (African Methodist Episcopal, African Methodist Episcopal Zion, and the Christian Methodist Episcopal) had joined in the 60s, as had the Presbyterian Church of the U.S. Of the other six enumerated above, the Evangelical United Brethren had merged with Methodists to form the United Methodist Church; and in 1976, the National Council of Community Churches became the tenth member. BIBLIOGRAPHY: *COCU: Principles of Church Union* (1967); *Plan of Union* (1970); and *Church Union at Midpoint* (ed. by P. A. Crow, and W. J. Boney, 1972).

[N. H. MARING]

CONSULTORS, advisory members of the Sacred Congregations of the Roman Curia, among whom are represented both secular and religious clergy. In the case of diocesan consultors, they are priests of high character, noted for piety, learning, and prudence, appointed by the bishop in dioceses where there is no cathedral chapter. They act as members of the diocesan *curia.

[M. RILEY]

CONTARINI, GASPARO (1483–1542), lay theologian, cardinal, and diplomat. Born in Venice, educated at the Univ. of Padua, C. was an able scholar and public servant. The high esteem in which he was held derived from his achievement as a statesman and later cardinal. He served under Clement VII as ambassador to the papal court. His diplomatic skill enabled him to serve as an intermediary in a variety of civil and ecclesiastical disputes; notable among these was his handling of the conflict between Venice and the court of Charles V and his participation in the settling of disputes over church abuses (1516). One effort at intermediation ended less felicitously. In the attempt to settle the dispute between Lutherans and Catholics which occurred after Luther's break with the Church, he proposed a compromise which entailed of a double justification; this proved acceptable to neither party.

[P. K. MEAGHER]

CONTARINI, GIOVANNI (d. 1451), Latin patriarch of Constantinople. A Venetian by birth, educated at Oxford and Paris, C. was made patriarch of Constantinople by the Venetian Pope Gregory XII in 1409. He served as Gregory's nuncio in Germany and took active part in negotiating the abdication of Gregory in 1415. Because there were two Latin patriarchs of Constantinople, both appointed during the last confused years of the Western Schism, Pope Martin V made C. Latin patriarch of Alexandria in 1422, but 2 years later he was restored to Constantinople. His letters of 1428–51 contain valuable information on the patriarchate of Constantinople. In 1451 the Latin patriarchate was transferred to the still-living Greek patriarch, Isidore of Kiev. BIBLIOGRAPHY: M. Monaco, NCE 4:258; J. Ruysschaert, DHGE 13:784–785; Emden Ox 1:478.

[M. R. P. MCGUIRE]

CONTEMPLATION, as understood in Catholic theology, a cognitive act by which God and divine things are the object of quasi-intuitive intellectual vision. The act is accompanied with delight both in the object and the act itself. The human faculties brought into play may be on the lowest level—physical sight, imagination, or memory—but more essentially it is the higher powers of the mind that are engaged; on the appetitive side both emotions and will have their proper role. Contemplation is distinguished from other types of knowing because it is not discursive; it does not search for knowledge by processes of reason, but is rather an intuitive viewing of truth already possessed. Since contemplation is experiential knowledge, it has its own delight

which may affect the will and emotions, and at times even overflow to the physical senses.

Various types of contemplation are distinguished according to the human faculties affected, the object contemplated, or the cause of the contemplative activity. The human faculty primarily involved is the intellect, but appetitive activities form part of the total picture, for the contemplation under discussion is the act of a human and not an angelic being. With regard to the involvement of will and emotions, writers distinguish contemplation in which this is antecedent, concomitant, or consequential to the activity of the intellect. The division between natural and supernatural is obvious and refers not only to the object contemplated but also to the origin of the act. Distinctions are made between aesthetic, philosophical or scientific, and theological contemplation, depending upon what is contemplated, and between acquired and infused or mystical contemplation, depending on whether it is achieved by human effort or infused into the soul by God. Infused or mystical contemplation is the most perfect form. It is unattainable by any purely natural effort and is therefore said to be a gift.

The possibility of a purely natural acquired contemplation of divine truth has been debated since the early Fathers saw the Christian tradition of grace confronted with the vision of Plato and Plotinus. Many Fathers and Doctors demanded an experiential love of charity for any contemplation on the theological level. Reasons for doubting the possibility of acquired contemplation include the traditional manner of speaking of contemplation as a gift, as well as modern differences in terminology. More directly, the normal knowledge processes of human beings always start with sense experience and are intimately associated with activity of the imagination. This makes experiential knowledge (such as contemplation, according to all descriptions) of an object that is suprasensual and in a sense even supraconceptual seem impossible.

The contemplation of the theologian, who possesses the habitus of theology, is an acquired contemplation, but it is also supernatural in the sense that it is rooted in the theological virtue of faith. Charity need not intervene, although that was the teaching of St. Augustine, St. Bonaventure, St. Albert the Great, and Alexander of Hales (cf. M. R. Gagnebet, "La Nature de la théologie speculative," RevT 44 (1938) 1–39; 213–255; 645–674.)

As the theology on contemplation was further refined, the question arose concerning the possibility of an ascetical contemplation, i.e., an intuitive and experiential knowledge of God achieved through the operation of the ordinary virtues of faith and charity. The majority of modern theologians (e.g., Thomas of Jesus, Philip of the Holy Trinity, G. B. Scaramelli, St. Alphonsus Liguori) defend the possibility of an acquired supernatural contemplation and refer to St. Teresa of Avila as a justification for this position. As described by St. Teresa, the prayer of acquired recollection is the highest type of prayer in the ascetical state, but St. Teresa never refers to it as a type of contemplation. The

Dominican school in general rejects the term "acquired contemplation," preferring to speak only of the mystical grades of prayer as contemplation. An acquired type of contemplation would involve, in addition to a purely natural contemplative activity which has God as its object, the intervention of actual charity whereby the God known through faith is loved for himself. Some theologians (Garrigou-Lagrange, Royo, de la Taille, Maréchal, Scaramelli, Poulain, De Guibert, Truhlar) tend toward the opinion that acquired supernatural contemplation, through the operation of the virtues of faith and charity, is admissible and perhaps logically required as a transition from the ascetical to the mystical grades of prayer. There seems also to be no great difficulty in admitting St. Teresa of Avila and St. John of the Cross as proponents of acquired contemplation.

As regards truly mystical contemplation, which is infused and supernatural, theologians generally agree that it is an experiential knowledge of God which, as a stage of prayer, is not attained by all fervent Christians. The classification of prayer by St. Teresa of Avila is the basis for all later divisions since her time. The first completely mystical prayer in the Teresian categories is the prayer of quiet, and it is separated from ascetical prayer by the prayer of recollection. The prayer of recollection admits of two types: acquired recollection (called by Bossuet the "prayer of simplicity" and by later writers "affective prayer," or "the prayer of simple gaze," or the "prayer of the presence of God"); and infused recollection, which is variously interpreted by theologians. Thus, for Gabriel of St. Mary Magdalen, infused recollection is the prayer of transition between ascetical and totally mystical prayer. For Garrigou-Lagrange, the prayer of acquired recollection is the prayer of transition and infused recollection then becomes the first stage of mystical prayer. The remaining forms of mystical prayer are the prayer of quiet and the prayer of union. In the prayer of infused recollection the intellect is acted upon by God's grace; in the prayer of quiet the will is captivated, although there may still be some distractions because as yet the intellect is not completely captivated. The prayer of union admits of the following grades or degrees: simple union, ecstatic union (terminating in conforming union or mystical espousal), and transforming union (terminating in mystical marriage). Prior to the prayer of union the soul usually experiences the "sleep of the faculties," which some authors classify as a distinct stage of mystical prayer of quiet (e.g., Gabriel of St. Mary Magdalen) but others consider to be simply a concomitant of the prayer of quiet (e.g., Arintero, Royo, Aumann). In the prayer of quiet the will is captivated; in the sleep of the faculties the intellect is captivated; in the prayer of simple union the imagination and memory are also captivated, so that only the external senses remain free; in the prayer of ecstatic union the external senses are so alienated that ecstasy occurs as a concomitant phenomenon; it will cease to occur in the higher stages of the prayer of union. In the

highest point of the prayer of ecstatic union, the mystical espousal or betrothal often occurs, accompanied sometimes by visions, locutions, or some other epiphenomenon. This is followed by the transforming union or mystical marriage which constitutes the summit of mystical prayer, wherein the soul is totally surrendered to God, confirmed in grace, and enjoys a quasi-permanent union with God in love (cf. Teresa of Avila, *Interior Castle,* "Seventh Mansions," ch. 1–4, and *Way of Perfection,* ch. 10; John of the Cross, *Spiritual Canticle,* st. 22).

Among the Fathers and theologians the outstanding authorities on the theology of contemplation are Gregory of Nyssa, Pseudo-Dionysius, Augustine, Gregory the Great, Richard of St. Victor, Bonaventure, and Thomas Aquinas. The Carmelite, Dominican, and Franciscan schools agree on the role of the gifts of the Holy Spirit in contemplative prayer which is truly mystical; the Jesuits generally deny the necessity of the actuation of the gifts and state that contemplation is the operation of the virtues of faith and charity. The doctrine of SS. Thomas Aquinas, Bonaventure, John of the Cross, and Teresa of Avila readily lends itself to the conclusion that although rare in practice, mystical contemplation is within the normal development and perfection of the life of grace; for the majority of Jesuit theologians, mystical contemplation is an extraordinary grace, although all souls can attain to acquired contemplation. Among the Benedictines perhaps the outstanding authority in the theology of mystical contemplation is C. Butler, who maintains that contemplation is an experiential perception of the presence of God; infused contemplation is passive (all theologians agree on this); it is extraordinary in relation to the development of grace; acquired contemplation is ordinary and is the normal summit of the spiritual life; theoretically no soul is excluded from mystical contemplation and, having reached the prayer of recollection, may humbly aspire to it, but it is excessive to say that every Christian is called to the transforming union (cf. C. Butler, *Western Mysticism*).

A. Saudreau, who has contributed generously to the theology of contemplation, defines infused contemplation as a superior knowledge of God, infused in the soul by God through the gifts of the Holy Spirit, together with an intensification of charity that unites the soul with God experientially. The soul is passive in receiving it, but active in using it. Contemplative knowledge is normally general and indistinct, an "abstraction of inclusion" as is proper to the metaphysical concept of "being." Contemplative love is a filial love of affection and intimacy, thus accounting for the experience of God, even during the passive purgations. All souls are called to infused contemplation although not all are culpable for not experiencing it (cf. A. Saudreau, *Degrees of the Spiritual Life.*) BIBLIOGRAPHY: J. Lebreton et al., DSAM 2:1643–2193; J. G. Arintero, *Mystical Evolution in the Development and Vitality of the Church* (tr. J. Aumann, 2 v., 1949–51); *idem, Stages in Prayer* (tr. K. Pond, 1957); R. Garrigou-Lagrange, *Christian Perfection and Contemplation* (tr. M. T. Doyle, 1937); *idem, Three*

Ages of the Interior Life (tr. M. T. Doyle, 1947–48); J. De Guibert, *Theology of the Spiritual Life* (tr. P. Barrett, 1953); G. Lercaro, *Methods of Mental Prayer* (tr. T. F. Lindsay, 1957); A. Poulain, *Graces of Interior Prayer* (tr. L. L. Yorke Smith, ed. J. F. Bainvel, 1950); F. M. Moschner, *Christian Prayer* (tr. E. Plettenberg, 1962); P. Pourrat, *Christian Spirituality* (tr. W. H. Mitchell et al., 4 v., v. 1–3 repr. 1953, v. 4 1955); A. Royo and J. Aumann, *Theology of Christian Perfection* (1962); A. L. Saudreau, *Degrees of the Spiritual Life* (tr. B. Camm, 2 v., 1907); A. Tanquerey, *Spiritual Life* (tr. H. Brandeiis, 2d ed. 1930, repr. 1945); T. Merton, *New Seeds of Contemplation* (1972).

[J. AUMANN]

CONTEMPLATIVE LIFE. A distinction should be drawn between the psychological and theological sense of the term on the one hand and its ecclesiological or canonical sense on the other; the first calls for unmitigated approval, the second for reverent yet not uncritical appraisal. When the distinction has been obscured, the result has been a confusion of means and ends; people called to *contemplation, that is everybody, and even those who are living it, have been told that it is a professional avocation for dedicated experts, while among those who profess a state of being committed to the appropriate exercises, a certain spiritual snobbishness has not been undetected with regard to the ordinary members of Christ's flock, or to other religious committed to the active works of mercy or to that hybrid known as "the mixed life." Pius XII in 1958 led the way in shaking down some of the plasterwork overlaying authentic apostolic, patristic, and scholastic theology on the subject. It was time.

The truth of the matter, recognized both by pagan and Christian authors, is that contemplation is proper to all human beings. The term has become over-solemn and too mannered in the hands of technical specialists with religious tastes, and to tell the truth, rather off-putting to those children of God who while responsive to the sacred are not ungrateful for the profane. Whereas in order to see what it means you have to confirm your own experience by listening to the teaching of the Greeks on the felicity of the *epiekeis*–the leisured ones who are equitable because they are not immersed in the chores of living—to the command of *Genesis* to keep the day of rest (of profound social importance), to our Lord's commendation to Martha of Mary, and to the consistent teaching of Christianity from the days of the Alexandrian Fathers in the East and of St. Augustine and St. Gregory in the West. Indeed Catholic theology does not restrict the life of contemplation to a privileged class; on the contrary the doctrine of the gifts of the Spirit springing from charity invites all to cease from being busy and fussed and to be at peace, to know the prayer of quiet and a wordless content. Clearly contemplation does not necessarily mean a stylized activity, nor one reserved for set occasions.

We are in the presence of something more formal when we come to the contemplative life according to canon law: it is the juridical establishment of a state vowed, not precisely to contemplation for this falls within the ambit of no human law, but to the works of contemplation, about which ecclesiastical authority is competent to legislate. This state constitutes contemplation no more than it does Christian *perfection, but it deals with certain instruments thereto. Contemplation and perfection can be treated as identical in the present question. Its hallowed form, which dates back into the early Christian centuries, is the eremitical and cenobitical life according to the three vows of poverty, chastity, and obedience. The cloistered life, which was formerly the norm for religious women, still manifests vitality; in the past it possessed such reserves of strength as to throw itself dramatically and lastingly into the course of history. It represents one well-recognized way of doing things, and no more implies either approval or disapproval of a solitary temperament than of seeking to escape from domestic cares. The popular esteem for some forms of religious life because they are "strictly enclosed" is founded on a respectable convention rather than on theology, or on an admiration for heroic abnegation rather than on firsthand information about how it works out in practice. It is a high ideal, and it is accompanied by special dangers, and these less frequently are temptations in the world of the spirit than lower addictions to a routine; less to romantic than to petty attachments to a this-worldliness; less from outside the cloister than from inside. There is no value in enclosure as such; it all depends on what is kept out, and on what is kept in. It is meant for a contemplative leisure that is rich and fruitful, not for repetitions that are poor-spirited and sterile—and fundamentally lazy. BIBLIOGRAPHY: ThAq St 2a2a, 179–182 (esp. in ed. Lat-Eng, v. 46, *Contemplation and Action* ed. J. Aumann, 1966).

[T. GILBY]

CONTEMPLATIVE ORDER, a religious community which engages exclusively, or almost exclusively, in activities directly ordered to contemplation. Such groups, made up of men (e.g., Carthusians, Trappists) or of women, (e.g., Poor Clares, cloistered Carmelites and Dominicans) live in monasteries generally removed from the ordinary activities of life, where they may achieve silence and recollection. Members of these communities, for the most part, do not engage in the external works of the apostolate such as conducting parishes and schools. Ordinarily they perform some type of manual labor by which they support themselves, e.g., farming, the manufacture of ecclesiastical appointments such as vestments, candles, and altar breads. One of the principal functions of a contemplative order is the solemn recitation of the Liturgy of the Hours by which, day and night, they offer worship to God and prayers for the Church and its members. BIBLIOGRAPHY: Vat II RenRelLife 7; J. Leclercq, *Aspects of Monasticism: Yesterday and Today* (1975).

[P. F. MULHERN]

CONTENSON, GUILLAUME VINCENT DE (1641–74), French Dominican theologian. Whereas the *Devotio moderna* of the 14th and 15th cent. had reacted sharply against the intellectualism and speculative energy of 13th-cent. scholasticism, his work, *The Theology of Mind and Heart* (9 v., the last being edited by *Massoulié and published posthumously, 1681) combines a systematic and well-informed study of the *Summa theologiae* of St. Thomas Aquinas with ascetico-mystical reflections from the Fathers and his own holy life. This pioneer work of affective theology is still highly esteemed by students. BIBLIOGRAPHY: Quétif-Échard, 2:656–657; I. Colosio and M.-H. Laurent, DSAM 2.2:2193–96.

[T. GILBY]

CONTEXTUAL ETHICS, a method of analyzing moral content, its directions, structures, and functions, in and through concrete issues. Accordingly it can be contrasted with ethical formalism and with ways of thinking which start from the postulates of a duty or law binding on all. Yet it implies neither ethical relativism, for it does not identify moral values with what in fact moral subjects happen to approve of, nor situationalism, for though it agrees that moral factors are given only in individual situations, it does not hold that they are given by incidents as such. This would in effect substitute a catalogue of case histories for a systematic theory, and reduce moral science to the role of recording or of evaluating acts in merely biographical terms. Contextual ethics offers a fresh and valuable emphasis, a grappling with human acts in the very dimensions of Christian history; and, as not excluding constant moral meanings, which are not circumstances, has been welcomed even by moralists who also envisage the importance of settled personal intentions and objective kinds implied in human acts, which last can be framed according to some sort of law. Contextual ethics, too, is an attempt to narrow the gap, recognized by Aristotle and the classical moral theologians, between moral norms and moral acts, and can therefore be praised as being like casuistry, though without the legalism. That will come. BIBLIOGRAPHY: P. Lehman, *Ethics in a Christian Context* (1963); *idem, Dictionary of Christian Ethics* (ed. J. Macquarrie, 1967) 71–73.

[T. GILBY]

CONTI, ARMAND DE BOURBON DE (1629–66), French nobleman and penitent. Deformed but full of spirit, C. became governor of Languedoc and commander of the armies of Spain and Italy. He began to do penance in 1655 to repair the scandal and injustices of his earlier years. Of his writings the best known is his essay in collaboration with Abbé Voisin against dramatic spectacles (1667). BIBLIOGRAPHY: J. Calvet, *Catholicisme* 3:141.

[M. J. SUELZER]

CONTI, SIGISMONDO DE (1432–1512), diplomat, historian, humanist. A career papal official employed in the government of the States of the Church, he is significant for his memoirs, *Historiae sui temporis libri XVII* (1475–1510), an important source concerning the activities of the Renaissance papacy. BIBLIOGRAPHY: Pastor v. 4 and 6 *passim*; P. Brezzi, EncCatt 4:454.

[J. MULDOON]

CONTINENCE (Lat. *continentia*), a term that can refer both to a virtue and a practice. In the first case it can comprehend all temperance or moderation in our desires for pleasure, and esp. in matters of sex (Acts 24.25; Tit 1.6), is numbered among the fruits of the Spirit (Gal 5.23), and is expressed *par excellence* in *virginity. A more specific usage is found in the moral theology of St. Thomas Aquinas (ThAq ST 1a2ae, 155). Basing himself on Aristotle, Aquinas draws a distinction between the full virtue when the emotions themselves are finely tempered in their desires for pleasure and a lesser condition when their turbulence is held in check by will-power. The first is chastity in a more positive sense, a *sōphrosunē* whereby passion itself is charged with intelligence and affection, whereas with the second the self-control is more a self-restraint, *enkrateia*, and this is continence. An equivalent distinction appears in *Cassian's account of the degrees of chastity. As a practice continence refers to voluntary abstention from conjugal intercourse at times and by agreement (cf. 1 Cor 7.5). Also to the clerical discipline, which differs between the Oriental and Latin Churches, relating to the marriage lives of bishops, priests, and deacons, or to their celibacy.

[T. GILBY]

CONTINGENCY, one of the four classical modes of being, is applied to being which can be or not-be, and can sustain contrary possibles. In contradistinction, necessary being cannot not-be; possible beings can be; impossible beings cannot be. Both the contingent and possible denote a capacity for being; the necessary implies actuality; the impossible excludes both real and potential actuality. Contingent beings, i.e., those capable of generation and corruption, are dependent upon extrinsic cause(s); secondary elements of necessity are found in them once they come to be outside their causes: necessity in essence, and necessity in effect and causal activity.

The deeper question asked of contingency is why any finite existent exists. On the metaphysical level of being and change, contingency is involved with causality. The experienced fact of contingent beings demonstrates the existence of a necessary being as their source. In the moral dimension, considerations of contingency affect theories of freedom of choice. Aquinas denies absolute freedom to the human will in terms of man's ultimate end and necessary means to a predetermined end. Human freedom is both internal and external and concerns choice of contingent ends and appropriate means. The English empiricists limit freedom to lack of external restraint. For Locke, Hobbes and Hume, internal necessity is not incompatible with human freedom. In theological studies, contingency is important in the proofs for the existence of God as well as in the description of his volitional activities. Aquinas asserts that God creates all freely; some beings act of their nature with necessity, some freely. Leibniz maintains that there are an infinite number of possibilities in God, but all is as it must be and is the best possible; Descartes claims that self-caused is identical with uncaused and the power of God's essence effects his existence; Spinoza teaches that both God and all his creation are necessary, and are monistically identified as one substance. BIBLIOGRAPHY: ThAq ST 1a, 2.3; 19.3; 82.1,2; 83.1; L. M. Régis, *Epistemology* (tr. I. C. Byrne, 1959); *Syntopicon* 2:251–269.

[M. HALPIN]

CONTINUING EDUCATION, a term used to designate the extension of educational opportunities for study, reading, and training in work skills to young people and adults whose formal schooling, for various reasons, was interrupted at the elementary, secondary, or college level. The term also applies to education for adults seeking deeper personal enrichment and better understanding of contemporary social, religious, and moral problems through study centers or special courses in colleges and universities offering flexible schedules for credit and noncredit programs. Several Catholic institutions have received government grants for this purpose. Others conduct these programs on their own initiative. BIBLIOGRAPHY: U.S. Department of Health, Education, and Welfare, Office of Education, *First Annual Report of the National Advisory Council on Extension and Continuing Education* (1967); *Yearbook of Continuing Education* (1975).

[M. B. MURPHY]

CONTRABAND, see DUTIES (IMPOSTS); SMUGGLING.

CONTRACEPTION, a word of irregular formation, almost a portmanteau term derived from the Latin *contra* (against) and *conceptio* (conception in the sense of uterine conception). Not rarely it is used as a portmanteau term for birth-control, with which it is not identified, for that is an end which can be secured by other means, such as abstinence from sexual intercourse. The word stands for certain methods of achieving the prevention of conception by means other than abstention from intercourse.

The coincidence of the twin purposes of sexual congress—procreation and pleasurable closeness—presents a perennial problem. This does not arise on the purely animal level, at least for the female, but is peculiarly human because of psychological factors which become moral from the play, generosity, relief, and comfort ideally present in the union. By the demands of a human situation one can be sought without the other, usually the intimacy without the begetting, though the reverse can be the case. The matter has been judged by RC moral theologians according to the

principle that purposes natural to human activity should not be dislocated.

Contraceptive methods are immemorial, but the most primitive and for long the most widespread was *coitus interruptus* in which intercourse is broken off just before semination. Though this kind of act was in former times commonly called *onanism, the condemnation of Onan (Gen 38.8) has in recent times been interpreted by some Scripture scholars as due to his unwillingness to raise up children to his brother as he was required to do by the law of the levirate marriage. Drugs, supposedly either sterility-inducing or abortifacient, have been used from ancient times. In antiquity the effectiveness of these drugs was sometimes thought to be based on medical principles, or what were taken as medical principles, concerning the action of sympathetic or antipathetic forces in nature, though in fact their use was often associated with magic. With the growth of the physiological and biochemical sciences in the last 100 years, new and more effective methods of contraception have been discovered and put on the market to meet the demand for freer and less anxious intercourse and for means of dampening the population explosion or of lessening the burdens of parenthood which lie heavy on some for want of inclination or for reasons of family economy or health. Some of these methods are mechanical and prevent the meeting of semen and ovum; others—surgical, radiological, or pharmaceutical—ensure that either or both spouses are barren; still others arrest the process of fertilization.

Some methods are neater and more effective or revocable than others. These facts should not sway moral judgment within the immediate field of sexuality. If a practice is to be condemned, its awkwardness or chanciness offer no recommendation. Nor should a moralist derive even a melancholy satisfaction from the medical hazards. His specific interest lies in the human act or acts of sexuality, and his science as such, prescinding from individual circumstances and personal intentions, will class them into kinds of acts, some of which he will consider as right in themselves, others as wrong, and others as morally neutral. Taking intercourse as a kind of act in which two people share, a Christian moralist will require it to be a marriage-act. This is different in its moral kind from acts such as fornication, e.g., and adultery, which need not concern us here. Furthermore, he will require it to be what it claims to be, i.e., an unreserved giving and receiving then and there, not just between two bodies, male and female, not just between two individuals, a man and a woman, but between two persons committed to one another and to what they are of their nature. He will then observe that this surrender may be so qualified by contrivances of human art that within the sexual situation either the husband is secured from being a potential father or the wife from being a potential mother, or both from being potential parents. This art is called contraception.

There are some further precisions. If the human act of intercourse is to be isolated and regarded *in atomo* (as it needs to be for scientific discussion), then this can be directly operative before, during, or after it. In the first case it induces sterility, in the second it allows for mutually shared sexual release, in the third it causes an initial sort of abortion. It would be idle to pretend that these distinctions picture complete predicaments in real life of two people together; they are as fragile—and as strong—as spiders' webs and can be as easily meshed. Yet they are essential for exact and profitable examination. For the first and the third raise problems of justice: what sort of dominion do we exercise over the integrity of our bodies and what sort of rights over the life of another that is, or is going to be, a human being? Only the second directly engages the question of what is or is not a sex act. Perhaps it is too much to hope that the term contraception should be limited to this meaning: it would clear the air wonderfully.

In the early centuries of the Church there were Gnostics, both within and outside the Christian community. Their dualistic principle of thought led them to repudiate the idea of the procreation of children and they advocated either total abstinence from sexual activity or the separation of intercourse from procreation. Clement of Alexandria (fl. 3d cent.), attacking Gnosticism, condemned its rejection of material things and in particular of the institution of marriage. In the development of his thought on marriage Clement adopted the Stoic rule that the only legitimate reason for undertaking marital intercourse was the procreation of children. This became the commonly accepted principle among the Fathers and was adopted by St. Augustine in his controversial writing against Manichaean doctrine in the early 5th century. Manichaeism was also dualist and it continued Gnostic teaching concerning procreation, as did later developments of dualism, e.g., the Bogomils, Cathari, and Albigensians. For Augustine, not only must the sole purpose of blameless sexual intercourse be procreation, but the deliberate restriction of marital intercourse to times when procreation was deemed less probable amounted to using one's wife as a harlot. Nevertheless, Augustine considered marital intercourse between sterile spouses legitimate and did in fact admit motivations for acts of intercourse other than the hope of offspring, e.g., the sedation of concupiscence, the fulfillment of the marital obligation. In this he provided the foundation for a distinction between nature's purpose in the marriage act and the psychological intention of the individual in its actual performance. Furthermore, even when the individual was excessive in his pursuit of pleasure in the otherwise natural use of his marital privileges, Augustine considered his sin no more than a pardonable (or venial) offense. Thus theology inherited from St. Augustine a basis not only for a strict but also for a more lenient view of the use of marriage.

Through the era of the *penitentials and down to the 13th cent. greater emphasis was laid upon the stricter view, but among theologians thereafter more consideration was given to values other than procreation that could be legitimately associated with marital intercourse, provided there was no positive interference with the natural finality of the act as directed by nature toward procreation.

In the late 18th cent. contraception began to be more generally practiced, at first presumably by means of *coitus interruptus* and later with the use of condoms and pessaries. Inquiries concerning the practice were put at various times to the Sacred Penitentiary and to the Congregation of the Inquisition in the 19th century. Specifically these inquiries turned upon the question of whether a confessor should interrogate and admonish a penitent if he had prudent or well-grounded suspicion that the penitent was practicing contraception. To the first of these it was declared that only passive cooperation on the part of a wife was permissible and that only if she feared that resistance and refusal would result in harm to herself or to her children. To the second, though the responses generally did not encourage interrogation without well-grounded suspicion, one response given by the Penitentiary did seem to acknowledge the possibility of good faith on the part of penitents in which they might be left if there was no hope of their amendment.

The highpoint of the Church's attack upon contraception came in 1930 with the publication of *Casti connubii*, an encyclical of Pope Pius XI on the subject of Christian marriage. In this the Pope expounded upon the dignity of Christian marriage and condemned without ambiguity the practices of contraception, sterilization (except for therapeutic purpose), and abortion, but he declared that the performance of the marriage act at times when conception was, for natural reasons, impossible did not fall under the heading of contraception. He furthermore admonished confessors that they must not dare to allow their penitents to remain in ignorance about the sinful nature of contraceptive practices.

Protestant theologians were not at that time commonly making an issue of contraception. For Churches of the Anglican Communion, the Lambeth Conference of 1930 gave a guarded approval "where there is a clearly felt moral obligation to limit or avoid parenthood."

In the RC Church, after the publication of *Casti connubii* some theologians continued to teach that the systematic restriction of intercourse to the infertile period of the woman's cycle was immoral. But in 1951 in an address to Italian midwives Pope Pius XII gave approval to the systematic use of the rhythm method when serious reasons—medical, eugenic, economic, or social—made propagation inadvisable. This meant the final abandonment of Augustine's opinion that the restriction of the marriage act to certain days when conception was considered less probable was equivalent to using one's wife as a harlot.

Meanwhile, two developments were being fostered by some RC moralists. In the late 1940s dissatisfaction began to be expressed by some with the concept of natural law, upon which RC moralists appeared to base their repudiation of contraception. The second sprang from a growing discontent some theologians felt with the so-called primary and secondary purposes of marriage, as these had been understood (sometimes vaguely and with a certain ambiguity) in the theology of the past. The importance of the unitive function of marriage, as distinguished from its purely procreative end, was stressed, and the necessity of intercourse for the fostering of mutual love was recognized and often rhapsodically dwelt upon. This approach caught the fancy of many, esp. among the young, who were as time went on feeling the pressures favoring a personalist philosophy of life. A man's chief concern was seen more and more to center about his own fulfillment and the realization of his personal potentialities. This disposed many to look with disfavor on the policies and teachings of the Church that restricted an individual's freedom to achieve his fullest possible stature and accounted for a mounting demand for the revision of the stand the Church had hitherto taken in the matter of contraception as well as of its policy of demanding that candidates for major orders assume the obligation of *celibacy.

With regard to contraception the situation was aggravated by the progesterone pill, perfected in 1953, which, when taken orally by a woman over a number of days, could effectively control her ovulation and render conception impossible for a time. Pills of this kind were approved for sale in the U.S. in 1960. Not all the uses of this type of medication were condemned by RC moralists. Practically all conceded the legitimacy of the use of the pill when it was taken for serious medical reasons other than its contraceptive effect, a position declared acceptable by Pius XII in 1958 (AAS 50:735).

Nevertheless, with the increase in worldwide concern about demographic problems and the so-called population explosion, a number of bishops and theologians favored a rethinking of the Church's traditional stand on contraception in general and in particular on the legitimacy of the anovulant pill for admittedly contraceptive purposes, as these had been hitherto interpreted. Vatican Council II against the wishes of some avoided open debate on the most critical of the issues on grounds that the matter required further study. For the rest the Council was content to assert that the marriage act by which the partners are intimately and chastely united is good and right, and when it is performed in a manner worthy of the dignity of man, expresses and arouses the mutual gift of love. It also declared that marriage and married love are inherently ordained toward the procreation and education of children.

To implement the further study seen to be necessary a commission was appointed by Pope John XXIII in March of 1963 to study the use of anovulant pills as a measure of birth prevention. Twice this commission was reconstituted by Pope Paul VI, who enlarged its membership so that it ultimately included experts from all over the world in the fields of economics, sociology, demography, etc. He also expanded its objective so as to include the reevaluation of the Church's position regarding contraception. The majority report of the commission, issued prematurely in June of 1966, favored a relaxation of the Church's attitude toward contraception. Paul VI rejected this report and undertook an independent study of the problem. On July 25, 1968, he published his encyclical letter *Humanae vitae* in which he upheld substantially the teaching of his predecessors, Pius XI and Pius XII, but in some details there was a notable mitigation of the tone in which he dealt with the problem. He took care to abstain from some of the harsher language of Pope Pius XI in *Casti connubii*—e.g., ". . . the criminal licence some claim for themselves . . ."; ". . . the divine majesty looks upon this nefarious crime with the greatest hatred. . . ." He recognized more clearly and compassionately the sad plight of married couples who for serious reasons such as health or family economy feel unable to face the responsibility of bringing children into the world or of curbing their desire for intimate relationship. He called on medical science to search out more reliable means of ascertaining the "safe period."

In the third and pastoral part of his letter, besides acknowledging these difficulties, he urged married couples to face up to the spiritual effort needed to live in accord with the demands of marital chastity as he had expounded them. Foreseeing that the sin he deplored would continue its hold over many, he urged them not to lose heart but to persevere in their effort to observe the necessary restraint and, where they failed, to have recourse with humble perseverance to the mercy of God, which is poured forth in the sacrament of penance. He admonished priests dealing with those who failed in this matter to imitate the patience and goodness manifested by the Lord himself in his encounter with sinners.

This encyclical letter came as a great disappointment to many of the faithful and to many priests and theologians as well who had been encouraged by the majority report of the commission to expect a change in the Church's stand and who, in anticipation of this, had already begun to counsel others that the practice of contraception was licit. There were widespread statements of dissent, and these have led to considerable confusion among the faithful, in consequence of which it is difficult to sustain in the altered circumstances of the present time the position taken by Pius XI in *Casti connubii* to the effect that priests allowing a penitent to remain in ignorance in this matter are worthy of the severest condemnation, a position that seems to suppose that continuing good faith on the part of a penitent practicing contraception is impossible.

It should be noted that in *Humanae vitae* the problem of contraception is dealt with in an objective and almost abstract manner. This is generally the case in pronouncements of the Holy See and in the writings of moral theologians on specific moral questions, the object of which is to decide whether certain types of act, according to their kind, are or are not morally objectionable. But for these acts in their performance in concrete individual cases to be judged sinful or at least grievously sinful, certain other conditions must be verified. The individual who performs the act must do so deliberately, with full knowledge of its moral character, and with full consent of his will. Now, as is admitted by all theologians, ignorance, fear, and passion may so influence the performance of an act judged from the objective point of view to be a seriously evil kind of act, that in concrete individual cases its malice may be considerably attenuated or even rendered totally unimputable. This was not mentioned in *Humane vitae*, because it is not commonly the practice of the Holy See in making a pronouncement on the objective morality of some type of action to enter into the consideration of the almost infinite variety of subjective circumstances in which the act may be performed. Theologians, confessors, and the faithful are left to apply for themselves to individual cases the general principles governing subjective responsibility, and only when this is done can it be said that an individual act is gravely or venially sinful, or perhaps not sinful at all. The judgment concerning concrete cases of contraceptive activity may be quite complex, because of the undoubted role which fear and the force of passion may play in it. BIBLIOGRAPHY: J. T. Noonan, *Contraception* (1965); J. Sommer, *Catholic Thought on Contraception through the Centuries* (1970); S. Ernst, *Man, Greatest of Miracles* (tr. M. Nathe & M. R. Joyce, 1976); M. R. Joyce, *Meaning of Contraception* (1976).

[T. GILBY; P. K. MEAGHER]

CONTRACT, as understood in RC moral theology and canon law, a mutual and externally manifested agreement made between two or more parties to do or to refrain from doing something. It supposes a seriously intended compact and induces an obligation in one at least of the parties (a unilateral contract), or in all of them (bilateral contract) to abide by its terms. The obligation binds in commutative justice, and in this respect it differs from a mere promise, the violation of which is an offense against fidelity, but not against commutative justice.

Bilateral contracts are mutually advantageous and also mutually onerous, all the contracting parties gaining a benefit from the negotiation and all accepting in return a responsibility to provide a stipulated compensating benefit to the other party (or parties) to the contract, as, e.g., in the contract of sale. Unilateral contracts, on the other hand, are advantageous only to the party or parties in whose interests they are made, and onerous only to the benefactor.

Object. The object (or as some moralists prefer to call it, the matter) of a valid contract must be both physically and morally possible, capable of precise determination, and it must lie within the moral and legal capacity of the contracting parties to offer. Nothing that is morally evil or forbidden by just civil or ecclesiastical law can be validly made an object of contract.

Subject. The subject of a contract (i.e., a contracting party) is any human being who enjoys the use of reason at the time the contract is entered upon. However, law —natural, divine, civil, or ecclesiastical—may prohibit certain persons from making certain contracts except under special circumstances. Thus, an essential condition for the contract of marriage is that the contracting parties be of sufficient maturity in terms of years to bind themselves to the responsibilities of marriage. The age required by canon law is absolutely essential, and if one attempts to enter into marriage before that age, the marriage is invalid. Under civil law, the marriage of underaged persons in some places is not looked upon as per se invalid, but rather as rescindable.

Consent. The mutual consent of the contracting parties is the basis of a contract. This consent must be true, internal, deliberate, free, unvitiated by substantial mistake, misrepresentation, fraud, duress, or undue influence. It must be externally expressed. In some contracts civil or ecclesiastical law may require the observance of certain formalities.

[P. K. MEAGHER]

CONTRADICTION, PRINCIPLE OF, the principle which expresses the metaphysical and logical opposition between being and non-being. In Aristotelian philosophy it is formulated thus: a thing cannot be and not be at the same time and under the same respect (*Metaph.* 996 b 30). Its expression, whether Aristotelian or analytic (a thing cannot be X and not-X at the same time) is common to every school of philosophy. The principle is antecedent to all other predications about being, and as such, is a necessary (but not sufficient) condition to the understanding one has about being. If a philosophical concept is to have any meaning, then that meaning must have linguistic formulation. The principle of contradiction is prior to the principle of identity and part of the logical framework of philosophers. BIBLIOGRAPHY: Copleston 1.2:24; U. Viglino, NCE 3:277–278.

[J. R. RIVELLO]

CONTRITION, a word which in its theological sense is of strictly Christian origin. It is used to signify the change of heart, the interior sorrow and regret of the sinner repenting his transgression of God's law. A man is contrite when he regrets and detests the wrong he has done, when he would that he had not sinned, when he would undo the sinful act so far as that is possible and repair or put right the harm or injury he may have caused, and when he is determined not to repeat his offense in the future. Simple regret does not qualify as contrition unless it springs from a supernatural motive, i.e., from a value apprehended by Christian faith and longed for by Christian hope. Contrition is more or less perfect to the extent that Christian love enters into its motivation. A regret that an individual may have for his sin when this is based on the fear of God's punishment rather than the love of God is called imperfect contrition or *attrition. Perfect contrition brings about the remission of sin, since it implies a love of God above all things, and such a love is per se incompatible with a state of grave sin. Contrition, properly speaking, is regarded as an act of the will which may or may not be accompanied by emotional grief. BIBLIOGRAPHY: D 1676; P. DeLetter, NCE 4:278–283.

[P. K. MEAGHER]

CONTRITION, ACT OF, a prayer in which one formulates his inner change of heart with respect to the sins he has committed. It is the expression of one's *contrition. Most prayer formulas in use for this purpose give explicit expression to the motives upon which the change of heart is grounded, and include as primary the love of God above all things. If one sincerely and truly means what he says in making such an act of contrition, the prayer, being an expression of the perfect love of God, is in itself sufficient for the remission of sin, but, according to the Council of Trent (D 1677), such an act of contrition implicitly contains a desire to receive the sacrament of penance, and the penitent remains obligated in a subsequent confession, if that is possible, to mention the grave sins from which he feels he has been granted forgiveness through an act of perfect contrition. The place of the act of contrition in the rite of penance has been changed, so that the penitential recitation is no longer simultaneous with the priest's pronouncement of absolution. But contrition remains primary in the sacrament. The change intends to emphasize that the penitent's preparation by examination of conscience should lead to his prayer of contrition and that contrition is what prompts his confession.

[P. K. MEAGHER]

CONTRITIONISM, a post-Tridentine movement in theology stressing that for the forgiveness of sins in the sacrament of penance sorrow motivated by the love of God is necessary. Unlike the Jansenists the contritionists admitted that sorrow motivated by fear of God's punishments is both good and salutary. They denied, however, that such sorrow is a sufficient preparation for obtaining pardon in the sacrament of penance. Without going to the extremes of the Jansenists, who demanded perfect love or the "fervor of charity" for sacramental pardon, the contritionists insisted that contrition be motivated by disinterested love or benevolence towards God. By way of reaction to both Jansenists and contritionists, the attritionists taught that attrition from the motive of fear, along with hope of pardon (a love of hope, if you will), is all that the Council of Trent demands as the proximate disposition for obtaining pardon in the sacrament of penance. The controversy between the contritionists and the attritionists waxed so warm that the Holy Office in a decree, May 7, 1667, warned both parties "not to dare to affix a note of theological censure" to either opinion. It noted at the same time that the view of the attritionists "appears to be more common among scholastics" (D 2070). BIBLIOGRAPHY: *Sacraments and Forgiveness (Sources of Christian Theology* 2, ed. P. Palmer, 1960); H. Dondaine, *L'Attrition suffisante* (1943).

[P. F. PALMER]

CONVALIDATION, the juridical process by which an invalid marriage or a religious profession becomes valid. There must be a putative marriage or profession, although some impediment, defect of intention, or failure to observe the prescribed form in fact renders it null. Concubinage, for example, cannot be converted to matrimony by convalidation, since it is not a putative marriage but no marriage at all. In the case of a marriage, invalid because of a diriment impediment (which automatically prevents marriage), convalidation occurs either when the impediment disappears or when a dispensation from the impediment is granted, and when the consent of the parties is renewed. Canon law insists that this renewal of consent is necessary for convalidation of the marriage. When the invalidity of a marriage proceeds from an imperfection in the consent of one or both of the parties, then the partner (or partners) concerned is required to give a full consent in order for the marriage to be convalidated. If the lack or defect of consent is public, then the new consent must be publicly given, but if only the party concerned is aware of this lack or defect of consent, he may privately convalidate the marriage by supplying his consent. If on the other hand, the marriage is invalid because of a defect of form (i.e., was not entered into before an authorized priest and two other witnesses) this must be emended by the performance of a new marriage ritual according to the form prescribed by the Church. In all of these cases, the marriage is considered to be valid from the moment of convalidation. The situation for the convalidation of an invalid religious profession is analogous. Diriment impediments may pass or be dispensed from, provided explicit consent to religious profession is renewed, defects of form may be corrected, lack or defect of consent may be emended. *SANATIO IN RADICE.

[R. A. ARONSTAM]

CONVENIENCE, ARGUMENT FROM (*argumentum convenientiae*), a reasoning process for the plausibility of its conclusion because it fits in or agrees (*convenit*) with accepted premises. Such an argument is distinct from *proof: a reasoning process for a conclusion as necessarily following from its premises. (See ThAq ST 1a, 32.1 ad 2.) Arguing for plausibility also is distinct from showing that a given truth is not contradictory (*ibid.*, 2a2ae, 2.10 ad 2). Theology employs all three kinds of argument (see THEOLOGY AND FAITH; THEOLOGY AND PHILOSOPHY). St. *Anselm of Canterbury strongly influenced the use of the argument from convenience; for the most part his *rationes necessariae* amount to arguments of fittingness. Their theological function is dictated both by the historical contingency of God's plan of salvation, and the incomprehensibility of the divine life, made known by revelation alone. Much of what theology considers transcends, therefore, the level at which the human mind can establish necessary proofs. Yet theology is intent upon more than negative arguments that defend the articles of faith from being contradictory. The argument from convenience fulfills this positive intent. The claim for it is modest: it "saves appearances," i.e., such an argument plausibly squares its conclusion with some given fact—e.g., as in arguments for the fittingness of the Incarnation. Yet the argument from convenience does make a positive claim. On the basis of faith theology accepts what it argues about as true. Plausibility to the human mind is one sort of intelligibility. As such it is not irrelevant to the full, divinely understood truth of what is proposed for belief. This general justification and the overall character of theology as a search for understanding how what is revealed is true "is the context which gives use of the individual arguments of convenience their fruitfulness" (Gilby, p. 51). BIBLIOGRAPHY: ThAq ST (Lat-Eng), v. 1, ed. T. Gilby, App. 2, 5, 6, 10.

[T. C. O'BRIEN]

CONVENT, a term that in its commoner use today refers to a house of religious women. Originally, and still in a quite proper sense it is applied to a dwelling for religious which houses a number sufficient to observe the full monastic rules. From the 14th cent., 12 professed religious were considered necessary for a house to qualify as a convent. Although the term is not used in canon law, a distinction is made regarding number and quality of personnel in canonically established houses.

[H. P. ANNAS]

CONVENTICLE ACT (1664), in English history an act aimed at enforcing religious uniformity by forbidding religious gatherings. The *Act of Uniformity (1662) had affected *Nonconformist ministers, and the Conventicle Act was directed against dissenting laymen. A special incitement to its passage was fear of political insurrection, as Baptists and Independents had been suspected of involvement in Venner's Plot (1661) against Charles II. Rumors were rife that another conspiracy was afoot. The Act prohibited persons 16 years and older from attending private religious meetings held "in other manner than is allowed in the Liturgy" at which more than five persons besides the householders themselves were present. Heavy penalties were provided for offenses. Originally limited to 3 years, it was reenacted with a few modifications in 1670. It was abolished by the *Toleration Act of 1689. BIBLIOGRAPHY: H. Gee and W. J. Hardy, *Documents Illustrative of English Church History* (1921); H. W. Clark, *History of English Nonconformity* (2 v., 1911–13), v. 2.

[N. H. MARING]

CONVENTION (from Lat. *convenire,* to come together), here used for human agreement which by repetition comes after a time to compose a well-established social pattern of codes of conduct, institutions, opinions, tastes, manners of dressing, eating, speaking, playing, building, painting, making music, worshiping and so forth. What is by convention is contrasted with what is by nature, and frequently carries a stronger sense of the arbitrary than does what is by custom. Conventional is used pejoratively of rules felt to be too artificial, formal, and repressive of the natural. Convention can set up rights and duties in morality. As explicitly or implicitly witnessing to *contract, it may engage *commutative justice; as rooted in the history of one's country, the virtues of patriotism and respect; as part of civility, the virtues of modesty and common friendliness or *urbanitas*. Of course it can tax one's patience as well. One title to interest on a money loan is the legal charge for the convenience, called the *poena conventionalis*. Communities where the social unanimity strikes deep and confident can afford to be tolerant of unconventional behavior and even to be gratefully amused by it. Paradoxically it is the highly mannered groups which in fact produce the grand eccentrics.

[T. GILBY]

CONVENTION (BAPTIST), a state and national organization through which local churches cooperate. In 1821 Baptists began to form state organizations. Opinions varied as to a suitable name; most states adopted the term "convention," but a few described themselves as a general, or union, association. In 1845 Southern Baptists organized separately as the *Southern Baptist Convention, and subsequently other national conventions followed. State and national conventions are not considered to have churchly character and authority, but are instruments by which churches work together. Delegates, or "messengers," usually meet annually, and between meetings permanent officers and agencies carry on the work. BIBLIOGRAPHY: P. Harrison, *Authority and Power in the Free Church Tradition* (1959).

[N. H. MARING]

CONVENTUAL, an adjective used in reference to religious or monastic life as opposed to secular life or even the life of a secular or diocesan priest. A conventual church is one attached to a monastery or religious house.

CONVENTUALS, see FRANCISCANS, CONVENTUAL.

CONVERSI, Lat. for those converted to, a term originally applied to a class of monks who were not brought up in a monastery from childhood (*oblati* or *nutriti*), but entered it by a conversion of life after reaching adulthood. In later times the term became restricted to those religious who for lack of education or distaste for clerical occupations, were not suited to an active part in the choral chanting of the Divine Office. Because they could not aspire to clerical orders or status, they were sometimes called *lay brothers (*fratres laici*). Practice in different monastic traditions was not uniform with respect to the kinds of vows the *conversi* were permitted to take or the degree of their incorporation into the life of the monastic community. In modern times the distinction between the profession of the *conversus* and that of the choir monk has generally been abolished. In the mendicant orders such distinction never existed; the *conver-

sus was always accepted as a full-fledged religious no less than the cleric.

[J. C. WILLKE]

CONVERSIO MORUM (Lat., conversion of manners), a phrase generally understood to mean "the rooting out of vices and the planting of virtues." In its original meaning, this was taken to include entering a monastic community. For Benedictine forms of monasticism it is the object of a vow.

[H. P. ANNAS]

CONVERSION, a term with several Christian uses. (1) Conversion is a turning from sin to God in faith and repentance. Whether this is a work totally of God by his grace or a work in which man also cooperates has been a matter of controversy (see PELAGIANISM; SYNERGISTIC CONTROVERSY; ARMINIANISM). The Arminian emphasis on man's cooperation is a decisive principle in revivalism, which has conversion as its objective. (2) Conversion may also mean a drawing closer to God from a routine, insensitive, to a more intense way of living the Christian life. This use of the word enters the *conversio a saeculo* or *morum* (turning from the ways of the world), which is a part of the meaning and history of monasticism. In a similar use the term is applied to turning points in the lives of those who became evangelists or leaders of movements of spiritual renewal in the Churches. John Wesley's own experience of conversion in this sense underlies his doctrine of Christian *perfection, which has given a special nuance to the term conversion. In this reference the term connotes an experiential, often emotional awareness of the saving grace of Christ. The ideal of conversion in this sense is the living of a life free of the domination of inbred sins (see SANCTIFICATION). (3) Conversion also is used to mean change from complete nonbelief in Christ to belief. One may become a Christian from being either an atheist, an agnostic, or an adherent of a non-Christian religion. (4) Conversion in a particular RC usage was used until Vatican Council II to mean change from membership in another Christian Church to membership in the Roman Catholic Church. The *Decree on Ecumenism does not use this terminology but speaks of one who becomes a Catholic as "being reconciled" with the Church, and as one who seeks "full Catholic communion" (Vat II Ecum 4). Such phraseology follows the Council's acknowledgment of other Christian Churches as "ecclesial communities," and of all who share in baptism and trinitarian faith as brothers. Thus joining the RC Church from another Christian body is not to be compared to conversion from being a non-Christian to being a Christian. BIBLIOGRAPHY: P. Aubin, *Le Problème de la "conversion"* (1963); W. Barclay, *Turning to God: A Study of Conversion in the Book of Acts and Today* (1964); C. Williams, NCE 4:287–290; H. Pinard de la Boullaye, DSAM 2:2224–65.

[T. C. O'BRIEN]

CONVERSION TO LIFE OF GRACE, attaining the supernatural life, for a morally adult sinner necessarily involves a *metanoia,* a change of heart, whether through baptism or penance or the desire (*votum*) of either of these sacraments. The state of sin is a willful separation from God consequent on actual sin by which man gives preference to a creaturely good above God. The state, or life, of grace means loving union with God in charity. To pass over from one to the other, a change of mind is necessary. The biblical *metanoia* means conversion to God in faith and repentance (Mk 1.15); it is the core of the Council of Trent's description of the preparation for justification (D 1526), which is the same as conversion to a life of grace. It is not possible without the help of actual grace, both prevenient and assisting. In every case it is God who takes the initiative (Jn 6.44, and Trent, D 1525). Generally this conversion is a gradual process, although a sudden conversion, or what looks like it, is not excluded. It grows from fear through hope to love till it leads up to the last-but-one disposition for sanctifying grace. The infusion of sanctifying grace in justification is the actual inauguration of the life of grace. BIBLIOGRAPHY: G. F. Kirwin, NCE 4:290–292; M. Flick, *De gratia Christi* (1962) 140–176, 239–288.

[P. DELETTER]

CONVERT, in general, one in whom a change has occurred in ideas, convictions, beliefs, values, or allegiance from a prior attitude of positive opposition or at least indifference to acceptance and adoption. Most often the term is used in reference to religious conversion, and when so used may denote: (1) one who turns away from a life of sin to a life of moral goodness and integrity (the NT concept of *metanoia* can be identified with this view; see Mt 3.2; Lk 1.77; 3.8); (2) one who passes from ignorance or indifference to Christ to acceptance and commitment to him and his way of life (some Protestant communions emphasize "acceptance of God's plan of salvation," which includes repentance, faith in Jesus Christ, and regeneration); or (3) one who accepts new denominational adherence with renunciation of former confessional loyalties. In the last sense the RC Church has conducted a vigorous convert apostolate, which has declined after recent ecumenical involvement. Vatican II, however, noted that ecumenism is not opposed to conversions, since "both proceed from the marvelous ways of God" (Vat II Ecum 4).

[R. MAZERATH]

CONVERT APOSTOLATE, efforts to interest persons in full membership in the RC Church. In the U.S. in the 19th cent. there were only meager efforts in this apostolate because of the minority status and defensive attitude among Catholics. In the early 20th cent. the convert apostolate was extended. The renewal called for by Vatican II esp. in the area of ecumenism modified the aims and methods of conversion efforts. The greatest change has been occasioned by the renewed rite for the baptism of adults and the restoration of the liturgical catechumenate. BIBLIOGRAPHY: J. T. McGinn, NCE 4:292–294.

[V. GILLIGAN]

CONVERTS, RECEPTION OF, the liturgical rites by which a non-Catholic adult is received into the Church. The expression generally refers to the whole procedure of instructions and ceremonies for those who have an interest in becoming Catholics. Since Vatican Council II and the promulgation of the new extended rite of adult baptism, such instructions may be given within the intervals of a seven-stage ceremony of receiving baptism. Thus an effort to reestablish the ancient Christian catechumenate is in progress, to impress the convert with the fullness of meaning of personally committing himself to Christ, liturgically and morally as well as doctrinally, within the Christian community of believers. In the case of those who have been previously baptized, the sacrament is not repeated and the ceremonies are centered around a profession of faith. BIBLIOGRAPHY: A. McCormack, *Christian Initiation (1969); Rites of the Catholic Church* (Eng. tr. The International Commission on English in the Liturgy, 1976) 13–181.

[N. R. KRAMER]

CONVOCATIONS OF CANTERBURY AND YORK, provincial gatherings of the clergy of the C of E; often referred to simply as "Convocations." The origin of the Canterbury Convocation is traced to Theodore of Tarsus, Abp. of Canterbury from 668 to 690; York originated in 733. At first they included prelates only; but in 1225 representatives of cathedrals and monastic communities were added, and by the end of the 13th cent. they had reached their present basis of membership. Since the 15th cent. each Convocation has met in two houses—the Upper House of bps. and the Lower House of representatives of the clergy, called "Proctors." In pre-Reformation times Convocations were the bodies through which the clergy taxed themselves and made grants to the Crown. Under Henry VIII their powers were sharply curtailed, but they remained in increasingly stormy existence until 1717, when Whig objection to the independence of the clergy resulted in the royal decision to forbid further meetings of Convocations. In 1851, however, meetings were resumed. Currently they meet two or three times a year, often jointly and, since 1885, in association with a House of Laymen in each province. The Convocations themselves, however, remain clerical in membership. They are concerned mainly with theological and liturgical matters, and increasingly with ecumenical and inter-Church affairs. As the oldest continuing deliberative and legislative religious assemblies in England, they have played a central part in the history of both Church and State. Since the Reformation settlement, their relationship to Parliament has been confused. With the establishment in the C of E of the *Church Assembly, which has many characteristics of a national synod, their situation is still more unclear. They remain, however, the only collective embodiment of

the clergy of the C of E capable of sharing in decisions about such central doctrinal matters as the *Book of Common Prayer.

[S. F. BAYNE]

CONVULSIONARIES, Jansenist zealots who opposed the bull *Unigenitus* and whose behavior was marked by bizarre phenomena. After the death (1727) of François de Pâris, a young clergyman noted for rigorous asceticism and firm adherence to the cause of the *Appellants, his grave in the churchyard of St. Médard became the site of supposedly miraculous cures understood to vindicate Jansenist beliefs. With the cures came large crowds and instances of trances, convulsions, *glossolalia, prophecies, and erratic behavior. After the cemetery was closed (1732) by government order, groups continued to meet in private homes, where emphasis shifted from cures to convulsions to endurance of peculiar tortures without physical harm as proof of divine favor. Despite being suspected of indecencies and of subjection to diabolical influence, sects of convulsionaries survived in diminishing numbers to the 18th century. Although condemned by many responsible Jansenists, the convulsionaries divided the hitherto united Jansenist ranks in France. BIBLIOGRAPHY: Knox Enth ch. 16.

[J. WILLKE]

CONWAY, BERTRAND (1872–1959), Paulist priest, missioner, writer. Born in New York City he was ordained in 1896 and completed his studies at The Catholic Univ. of America in 1902. As a missionary to Catholics and to other religious denominations he founded the Catholic Unity League, was instrumental in the conversion of over 6,000 persons, and wrote many pamphlets and book reviews. His book *The Question Box,* a summary of Catholic apologetics, was translated into several languages and attained great popularity.

[V. GILLIGAN]

CONWELL, HENRY (1745–1842), bishop. Ordained in Ireland, C. served as vicar-general of Armagh for 21 years. Passed over for abp. of Armagh, he was offered the bishopric of Madras, India, or Philadelphia in the U.S. Unhappily he chose Philadelphia, which was riven by trusteeism and the Hogan schism. C. was an old man when consecrated in 1820 and quite incapable of dealing with the vexatious problems of Philadelphia. The Rev. William Hogan who had taken over St. Mary's Cathedral with the aid of its lay trustees was his first problem. After Hogan's cause had been disposed of by the priest's own scandalous conduct, C. made the mistake of writing William Harold, OP, who had been dismissed by C.'s predecessor because of trusteeism, to return to St. Mary's. Shortly thereafter C. had to suspend Harold. A more serious error of C.'s was his signing an agreement with trustees of St. Mary's giving them the right to veto his appointments to that parish. Rome, of course, rescinded the pact. He was ordered to Rome and instructed to remain there permanently, but he returned to the U.S. incurring for that a suspension. When the American bishops pleaded for him C. was permitted to live in Philadelphia, but Bp. Francis Kenrick was named administrator of the diocese. BIBLIOGRAPHY: J. Kirlin, *Catholicity in Philadelphia* (1909).

[J. R. AHERNE]

COOMARASWAMY, ANANDA KENTISH (1877–1947), scholar of Indian, Persian, and Islamic art. Born in Ceylon, educated at Wycliffe College, and Gloucester and University Colleges, London, C. first worked in geology. He helped found the India Society (1910); as research fellow at the Boston Museum of Fine Arts (1917–47) he assembled a most important collection of Far Eastern art. In hundreds of books and articles on aesthetics, religion, symbolism, metaphysics, and democracy, C. sought universal principles of art and life by which one might achieve wholeness for self and others. BIBLIOGRAPHY: *Homage to Ananda Coomaraswamy* (ed. S. Durai Raja Singam, 2 v., 1947–52); L. Coomaraswamy, NCE 4:296–297.

[R. J. VEROSTKO]

COOPER, JOHN MONTGOMERY (1881–1949), anthropologist. A native of Maryland, C. was ordained priest in 1905 and began his teaching career at The Catholic Univ. of America in 1909. Although he did important work in the department of religion and was a leader in the effort to adapt religion courses to the practical needs of the students, he achieved his greatest distinction in the field of anthropology. He founded the Catholic Anthropological Conference, whose periodical *Primitive Man* (called the *Anthropological Quarterly* after 1953) he founded (1928) and edited. He earned an international reputation as an authority on primitive cultures by his studies of North and South American Indians. BIBLIOGRAPHY: R. Flannery, "John Montgomery Cooper," *American Anthropologist* 52 (1950) 64–74; *idem, International Encyclopedia of the Social Sciences* 3:383–384.

COOPERATION IN SIN, see SIN, COOPERATION IN.

COORDINATE COLLEGE, a private, autonomous institution of higher learning for women, of full college caliber, established as an adjunct to and under the same charter as an already existing university originally or generally intended for men. Occupying the same, or separate campuses within geographical proximity, the coordinate college, for the most part, shares with the university facilities and faculties, and in some instances, classroom lectures, seminars, and symposia. Four among the oldest American colonial universities today have coordinate women's colleges established in the late 19th or early 20th cent.: Harvard—Radcliffe; Columbia—Barnard; Rutgers—Douglass; and Brown—Pembroke. Within more recent years Catholic colleges for women, for practical pur-

poses, have become adjuncts of long-established Catholic men's universities, among them, St. Mary's—Notre Dame, Ind.; and Marymount—Loyola, Los Angeles, Calif.

[M. B. MURPHY]

COORNHEERT, DIRCK VOLCKERTSZOON (1522–90), Dutch literateur and engraver, who also held political positions at Haarlem and in the States General. His principal work, *Zedekunst dat is Wellevens Kunste* (Art of Living Well, 1582; modern ed., 1942) was one of the first books of ethics written in a modern language. He was under the influence of the writings of S. *Franck and S. *Castellio and of the *Theologia germanica;* thus his writings stress the religion of inner experience (see INNER LIGHT). He taught that the true Church was invisible, made up of those who believe the simple and clear Scripture teaching; no authoritarian or teaching Church was necessary. Still C. opposed the excessive subjectivism of D. *Joris and H. *Niclaes. His opposition to rigid Calvinism and to religious persecution had a marked influence on J. *Arminius. C. was also one of those whose thought inspired the Seekers. BIBLIOGRAPHY: H. Bonger, *Dirck Volckertszoon Coornheert* (1941); R. M. Jones, *Spiritual Reformers in the Sixteenth and Seventeenth Centuries* (pa. 1959) 104–113; and MennEnc 1:709–710.

[T. C. O'BRIEN]

COPE, a semicircular cloak reaching to the feet and having a hood or a vestigial hood in the form of a shield-shaped piece of material. It evolved during the 10th cent. from the cloak worn by choir monks during the celebration of the Divine Office.

[N. KOLLAR]

COPEAU, JACQUES (1879–1949), French drama critic, director, actor, and playwright whose *Théâtre du Vieux Colombier* became a center for the renaissance of dramatic art in 20th-cent. France. C. edited (1909–14) *La Nouvelle revue française,* of which he was a founder. His influence in the theater has been considerable, and his accomplishments include forming a generation of innovative directors and actors, experimenting with antinaturalistic techniques of staging, and creating imaginative productions of Shakespeare, Molière, Claudel, and Ghéon. C. conceived theater as liturgy and ritual and, after becoming a Catholic (1926), he increasingly developed the stage's potential for religious drama. In order to revive popular religious theater his dramatic school, Les Copiaux (1925–29), produced many of his plays. His theories on dramatic art are summarized in *Le Théâtre populaire* (1941) and numerous articles. BIBLIOGRAPHY: M. Doisy, *Jacques Copeau ou l'absolu dans l'art* (1955); C. Borgal, *Jacques Copeau* (1961).

[G. E. GINGRAS]

COPERNICUS, NICOLAUS (1473–1543), Polish scientist, noted particularly for his theory that the earth revolves around the sun rather than the reverse, which had been the commonly accepted theory to his time. Born at Torún, he died at Frauenberg, Polish Prussia. After studies at Kraków and Bologna he became professor at Rome in 1499. He later received doctorates in medicine at Padua and canon law at Ferrara. Between 1504 and 1506 he went to the province of Ermland, where he remained until his death, serving as physician and secretary to his uncle, who was bishop, as canon of the cathedral, as military leader against the Teutonic Knights, and as administrator. His major work on astronomy, *De revolutionibus orbium coelestium (Revolutions of the Celestial Orbs)*, was published in 1543. BIBLIOGRAPHY: A. Armitage, *Copernicus, the Founder of Modern Astronomy* (1957); *Reception of Copernicus' Heliocentric Theory: Proceedings* (ed. J. Dobrzycki, Symposium of Nicolas Copernicus Committee of International Union of History and Philosophy of Science, 1973); *Copernican Achievement* (ed. R. S. Westman, 1975).

[T. EARLY]

COPPÉE, FRANÇOIS (1842–1908), French writer and representative figure of the Catholic Revival. C. held minor administrative posts and was archivist of the *Comédie-Française* (1872–83). Although he achieved popularity with plays written in a neoromantic style like *Le Passant* (1869) and *Pour la couronne* (1895) and with prose fiction, his literary reputation rests on his poetry. Originally a disciple of the Parnassians, C. evolved a personal poetical style characterized by an intimate, natural, and sentimental treatment of social themes, most evident in the collections *Intimités* (1868), *Les Humbles* (1872), *Le Cahier rouge* (1874), and *Contes en vers* (1881). His return to Catholicism, which he recounted in the preface to *La Bonne souffrance* (1898), accentuated his natural sense of pity, and his depiction of certain themes like vicarious suffering became increasingly sentimental. His religion influenced his politics. He abandoned an anti-Dreyfus position, broke with old radical literary friends, and was honorary president of the conservative, nationalistic *Ligue de la patrie française* (1899–1902). BIBLIOGRAPHY: L. Le Meur, *La Vie et l'oeuvre de François Coppée* (1932).

[G. E. GINGRAS]

COPTIC, a term used to designate the indigenous Christian population of Egypt and its language. The term is probably derived from the Arabic, *Ḳibti,* a shortening of the Greek, *Aigyptos,* used by the Arabs to distinguish Christians from Muslims. By the Roman conquest (30 B.C.), native Egyptians had been reduced to the status of agricultural serfs (*fellahin*). A few Copts regained precarious political power and wealth after the Arab conquest, but today Arab socialism and revived Islamic religious feeling have gone against the Copt. The Coptic language is the final phase in the development of Egyptian, with many Greek loanwords. The script is Greek uncial with several Egyptian symbols added. The two chief dialects are Sahidic or Theban and Bohairic. Sahidic, the dialect of Upper Egypt, flourished in the 4th and 5th centuries. Bohairic, the dialect of Lower Egypt, replaced it from the 5th cent. on. Akhmimic, Sub-Akhmimic and Fayumic are less important local dialects. Coptic died out as a spoken language by the 16th cent. and is now used only in the liturgy. BIBLIOGRAPHY: W. Kammer, *Coptic Bibliography* (1950); E. Wakin, *Lonely Minority: the Modern Story of Egypt's Copts* (1963).

[D. W. JOHNSON]

COPTIC ART, the folk art of the Coptic-speaking Christians of Egypt. Coptic art is distinct from the "official" art of the Roman-Byzantine Empire and from the folk art of the Egyptian hellenistic colonies. Like Coptic literature, Coptic art has its source in the ordinary life of the *fellahin* and of monastic society drawn from the *fellahin*. It flourished from the 4th to the 7th cent., when the Arabs conquered Egypt. Almost all types of art are represented. Wood, stone, and ivory are used in sculpture which, characteristic of folk art, is never massive. Statues, friezes, and capitals tend toward two-level relief with designs giving a cutout appearance. Human figures have outsized heads, simple garments with the few folds merely incised, and unnatural stances. Backgrounds and borders are filled with highly abstract floral and animal designs or frets. Figure and ground display little individuality. Paintings on wood and plaster are similarly composed. They rely on juxtaposed masses of solid color with little delineation to portray the image. The famous Coptic textiles share the characteristics of painting. In church architecture, the Copts used basilican style with trefoil apse, side galleries, and open wooden rafters. After the 7th cent. Coptic art ceased any notable development and gradually merged with Islamic art. BIBLIOGRAPHY: K. Wessel, *Coptic Art in Early Christian Egypt* (1965); *Larousse Encyclopedia of Byzantine and Medieval Art* 66–71.

[D. W. JOHNSON]

COPTIC CALENDAR, see CALENDAR.

COPTIC CHRISTIAN LITERATURE, the literary productions of the Coptic-speaking Christians of Upper and Lower Egypt, or, more broadly, writings both original and translated. Like Coptic painting and sculpture, it is folk art written for the fellahin by people drawn from this class. Nonspeculative and pastorally oriented, it is rich in legends about the saints and apocryphal scripture stories. Coptic literature flourished earliest in the monastic centers located in the *Thebaïd where the Sahidic dialect reached full development in the 4th century. Seven authentic fragments of St. Anthony's letters are extant in Sahidic. St. *Pachomius wrote his rule in Sahidic, and his disciples Theodore and Orsiesi composed works on monastic life. St. *Athanasius knew Coptic and composed letters to the monks of Upper Egypt. The most original Coptic-Sahidic author was Shenoute of Atripe. His sermons and letters served as the model for Sahidic grammar and style, and his sharp, blunt approach reflects the Coptic character. His sermons have a pronounced eschatological tone, a preoccupation the Copts retained from their ancient religion.

By the 6th cent., the Bohairic dialect of Lower Egypt with its monastic center in Wâdi el Natrûn began to supplant Sahidic, and most earlier works were translated into Bohairic. A few Christian works are extant in Akhmimic, Sub-Akhmimic and Fayumic with at least part of the Bible in each. Much of Coptic literature consists of translation from the Greek, beginning c.350 with the Sahidic Bible. Except for Scripture and the Apostolic Fathers, which are carefully and critically rendered, translations into Coptic tend to edit out the speculative and exegetical and to concentrate on exhortation and instruction. The Arab invasion (c.640) and the inroads of Islam on Christianity brought an end to the Coptic literary tradition. By the 9th cent. the spoken language began to give way to Arabic and subsequent Coptic theologians turned more and more to that language. The systematic exploration and editing of Coptic Christian texts is still in its first stages. BIBLIOGRAPHY: W. Kammer, *Coptic Bibliography* (1950); Quasten esp. v. 3; D. L. O'Leary, DACL 9.2:1599–1635.

[D. W. JOHNSON]

COPTIC CHURCH, the Monophysite Church of Egypt. From the latter part of the 3d cent. a large number of *Coptic-speaking Christians existed in Egypt, but as a subculture within the Greek-dominated patriarchate of Alexandria. Egyptian opposition to the definition of the Council of Chalcedon (451) concerning the two natures of Christ, mixed with a revival of Egyptian nationalism, helped to create a national Monophysite Church. By the time Constantinople reluctantly recognized the Monophysite patriarchate in 567, it had become evident that the rejection of Chalcedon was less a rejection of a theological position than the rejection of nearly 8 cent. of Greco-Roman oppression. Today the Coptic Church is still officially Monophysite. It seems, however, that most Copts do not understand the intricacies of Christological speculation and that the assertion of Monophysitism is more a question of custom than of intellectually grounded conviction. To insure against the possible return of Greco-Roman imperial power to Egypt, the Copts (c.640) welcomed the Arab invaders. This proved to have a devastating effect on the Coptic Church. By social pressure and bloody persecution, the Copts were intimidated into deserting Christianity for Islam in great numbers. Churches were destroyed, monasteries abandoned, and those Copts who remained Christians were heavily taxed and finally even made to wear discriminatory garments and headgear. The Latin Crusades of the 13th cent. jeopardized the Copts by angering the Muslims, and affronted the Copts themselves by expelling them from Jerusalem and forbidding them to come to the Holy Land on pilgrimages. Again in the 14th cent., there was destruction of churches, a curtailment of any public services outside of the necessarily inconspicuous church buildings, and martyrdom. In spite of this, a minority of Copts clung to their faith and managed to keep their traditions alive. Several Coptic patriarchs added to canonical literature, produced works of religious instruction, and tried to bring about necessary reforms in Church life. The noted 14th-cent. Coptic theologian, Ibn Kabar, edited an ecclesiastical encyclopedia, *The Lamp in the Darkness,* which is still a guide in canonical and liturgical matters. Copts were represented at the Council of *Florence (1442), but reunion was not accepted in Egypt. Several more attempts at reconciliation with Rome were also unsuccessful. With the accession of Mohammed Ali (1805) the condition of the Copts improved somewhat. But as Christians gained wealth and power, internal dissension grew within the Church between laity and clergy, esp. regarding the distribution of church funds. These quarrels caused scandal and impelled the Egyptian government to intervene in church affairs. Today with the rise of an Arab nationalism linked to Islam, the fortunes of the Copts are again on the decline. The Coptic patriarchate of *Alexandria has been centered in Cairo since the 11th cent. and encompasses approximately one and a half million people in 23 eparchies. BIBLIOGRAPHY: Attwater CCE v. 1; E. R. Hardy, *Christian Egypt: Church and People* (1952).

[D. W. JOHNSON]

COPTIC LITURGY, the liturgical rites of the Church of Egypt after the Council of Chalcedon (451). The early rites of Egypt developed in Alexandria and were in Greek. When the Egyptian Church became Monophysite after Chalcedon, the Coptic-speaking native Egyptians gained control, and Coptic largely supplanted Greek in the liturgy. The rites themselves underwent some modifications. After the Arab invasion (c.640), the Coptic language declined and was gradually replaced by Arabic in the liturgy. The Eucharistic Liturgy is based on the Alexandrian Liturgy of St. Mark in its completed form, which probably dates from the time of St. Cyril (5th cent.). It is often preceded by a service called the rite of morning incense. Following this, the priest, assisted by deacons, begins the rite of preparation, vested in typical Eastern style. The Copts have one special vestment, the *tailasan,* a long piece of cloth with a hood, that is worn throughout the liturgy. The round leavened cakes stamped with squares are baked for each service and, together with the chalice, are covered with veils at the end of the preparation. After the *Enarxis, the Mass of the Catechumens begins, consisting of a censing, three readings, the *Trisagion and the Gospel. The Mass of the Faithful begins with a Litany, followed by the Creed, and the Kiss of Peace. The Copts use three *Anaphoras, the commonest being that of St. Basil. The Anaphora commences with the thanksgiving, interrupted by a lengthy prayer of intercession, then continues the thanksgiving with the institution and the invocation (*epiclesis*). At the consignation, the priest dips his finger into the blood and anoints the body of Christ with it. After the *fraction of the host, the Lord's Prayer is recited.

The priest then takes the center part of the host, elevates it and drops it into the chalice. Communion is distributed under both kinds either separately or by *intinction. The liturgy concludes with prayers of dismissal and a blessing. Blessings during the liturgy are administered with a hand-cross, and incense is used generously throughout the service. The chanting, in which the people take part, is often accompanied by flute, triangle, or cymbals. The Eucharistic Liturgy is celebrated on Sundays and feasts. The Divine Office (al-Agbieh) consists of seven hours of psalms and lessons at 3-hour intervals, except from midnight to dawn. It has been entirely in Arabic since 1906. The Catholic Copts have essentially the same liturgy, although they allow a *low Mass as a form of Eucharistic Liturgy. BIBLIOGRA-PHY: Coptic Morning Service for the Lord's Day (tr. John, Marquis of Bute, 1908); Coptic Offices (tr. R. Woolley, 1930); N. Liesel, Eucharistic Liturgies of the Eastern Church (tr. D. Heimann, 1960).

[D. W. JOHNSON]

COPTIC RITE, one of the 18 Eastern Catholic rites. After *Monophysitism was condemned by the Council of *Chalcedon (451), the majority of the clergy and people of Egypt refused to accept this decision and thus gave rise to an indigenous national Church. An orthodox minority adhering to Chalcedon became known as *Melchites and later followed *Michael Cerularius in separation from Rome (1054). There have been distinct Coptic and Orthodox patriarchates of *Alexandria since 567. Although the Copts signed the act of union at the Council of *Florence, this and other unitive attempts never became effective. In the 17th and 18th cent. Catholic missionary efforts were begun by the Capuchins and Jesuits. Little was achieved until 1741, when Pope Benedict XIV appointed Amba Athanasius, the convert Coptic bp. of Jerusalem, to govern the faithful of his rite, but because of political difficulties he was unable to take up residence in Egypt. No bishop was consecrated for the Catholic Copts until 1824, when Pope Leo XIII reestablished the Coptic Catholic Patriarchate of Alexandria. Further political and ecclesiastical problems prevented this Catholic patriarchate and rite from achieving full realization until 1895. In 1975 there were about 107,500 members of the Coptic Rite in four jurisdictions. BIBLIOGRAPHY: Attwater CCE v. 1. *COPTIC CHURCH; *COPTIC LITURGY.

[F. T. RYAN]

CORBAN, in the priestly tradition of the OT a general term for sacrifice or even nonsacrificial offerings to God (Lev 1.2; 23.14; Num 7.3; 9.7). In NT times it was a dedicatory formula for removing something from profane use and reserving it for sacred purposes. Jesus opposed a tradition (perhaps based on Num 30.3) which apparently considered the oath of dedication indissoluble (Mk 7.11); whether it would have been pronounced as a legal fiction to escape the obligation of parental support or as an impulsive expression of anger remains obscure. Later rabbinic tradition expressed solutions similar to that of Jesus and also broadened the usage of corban to an exclamation implying either strong assertion or even a curse. BIBLIOGRAPHY: K. Rengstorf, in Kittel TD 3:860–866; J. A. Fitzmyer, "Aramaic Qorban Inscription from Jebel Hallet et-Turi and Mark 7:11-Matt 15:5," JBL 78 (1959) 60–65.

[P. J. KEARNEY]

CORBIE, ABBEY OF (Corbeia), former monastery founded c.657 in the Diocese of Amiens (Somme, France) in honor of SS. Peter, Paul, and Stephen by St. Bathilde, wife of Clovis II, for the monks of Luxeuil. They adopted the Benedictine Rule c.700. The monastery reached its height in the beginning of the 9th cent. under the abbot St. Adalhard (d. 826) and his brother Wala (d. 836), both cousins of Charlemagne. In 822 Adalhard reformed Corbie and enacted the Statuta Adelhardi. In 823 he founded Corvey in Saxony, where he left St. Anschaire as director of the school. About 840, a eucharistic controversy caused a conflict between two monks of Corbie, Paschasius Radbertus and Ratramnus. From the 7th to the 9th cent. there was great activity in the scriptorium of the monastery, including a reform in MS writing. The Norman invasions of the 9th cent. ruined the monastery. In 1142 it adopted a rule inspired by the statutes of Peter the Venerable at Cluny. Having become a commendatory abbey in 1523, Corbie was reformed in 1619 by the Maurists, who remained there until the Revolution. The choir of the abbey-church of St. Pierre, begun in 1498 by Abbot Dottrel (d. 1506) and completed in 1709, is still standing, as well as the church of St. Étienne. Here can be seen the "retreat" of St. Colette, reformer of the Franciscan nuns, who from 1402 to 1406 lived near the shrine. BIBLIOGRAPHY: Cottineau 1:868–870; B. L. Ullman, NCE 4:318–319.

[J. DAOUST]

CORBIE SCHOOL, debated abbey school of Carolingian MS illumination sometimes linked to the Franco-Saxon school and at times identified with the school of St. Denis. A Psalter and Coronation Sacramentary of Charles the Bald (both in Paris) are illuminated in an eclectic style of illusionism (Reims) and heroic narrative (Tours) with Franco-Saxon decoration—a diversity suggestive of St. Denis provenance.

[M. J. DALY]

CORBINIAN OF FREISING, ST. (d. c.725), itinerant missionary bp. in Bavaria. The account of his life written by Arbeon (Aribon) of Freising is questioned in many of its details by scholars. He appears to have been Irish-born rather than a native of Castrum (Chartres) in the region of Melun. His journey to Rome and his deputation to missionary work by Gregory II is questionable, and he was not the first bp. of Freising, a see founded by Boniface in 739, although he was active in that area. BIBLIOGRAPHY: R. Aigran, *Catholicisme* 3:179–180; F. Caraffa, BiblSanct 4:169–171.

[R. T. MEYER]

CORCORAN, JAMES ANDREW (1820–89), theologian, editor. A native of South Carolina, C. became in 1842 the first priest ordained from the Carolinas. A linguist with special skill in Semitic languages, he was recalled to Charleston where he taught in the seminary and was cofounder of the *United States Catholic Miscellany*, the pioneer literary periodical of American Catholicism. His ambitious study of Martin Luther was lost in a fire. C. acted as secretary to the Baltimore Provincial Councils of 1855 and 1858 and the Second Plenary Council in 1866. He represented the bishops as theologian at Vatican Council I for which he wrote a compromise draft of a resolution on papal infallibility, which was not adopted by the Council. Offered the chair of theology at St. Charles Seminary in Philadelphia by Bp. Wood, he accepted and remained there until his death. C. was made editor of the *American Catholic Quarterly Review* upon its inception in 1876. In 1884 he was appointed secretary of the Third Plenary Council of Baltimore. Though a prolific writer, C. left less than one would expect in the way of publication, largely because he was an unofficial theologian to the American bishops and spent much of his time in correspondence with them. BIBLIOGRAPHY: J. J. Hennesey, NCE 4:319–320.

[J. R. AHERNE]

CORD, a sash or cincture worn to honor some saint or to serve as a reminder or symbol of some virtue one seeks to practice, e.g., humility, mortification, chastity. The use of such cords by members of devout societies was popular in the Middle Ages, and some examples of confraternities of this kind have continued down to the present time, as for example the Archconfraternities of Our Lady of Consolation, the Cords of St. Francis, of St. Joseph, and the Confraternity of the Cord of St. Thomas Aquinas.

[P. K. MEAGHER]

CORDELL, CHARLES (1720–91), English missionary. Educated at Douai, C. was ordained in 1739 and served in England at Arundel. He worked on the Isle of Man, in Yorkshire, and Newcastle-on-Tyne. Offered the presidency of the English College of St. Omer, he declined. A Jacobite, C. was defender of the Pope's dealings with the Jesuits. BIBLIOGRAPHY: T. Cooper, DNB 4:1138; Gillow BDEC 1:565–568.

[J. R. AHERNE]

CORDI-MARIAN MISSIONARY SISTERS, a diocesan congregation founded (1921) by Julian Collell, a Claretian priest, and Mother Carmen Serrano in Mexico City. In 1926, because of persecution, the sisters moved to Texas, and 6 years later opened a novitiate in San Antonio. Their apostolate includes education, catechesis, and social work.

In 1975 they numbered 172 and conducted 21 houses. The community is esp. dedicated to the Immaculate Heart of Mary. The general motherhouse is in Mexico.

[H. P. ANNAS]

CÓRDOBA, ANTONIO DE (1485–1578), Spanish Franciscan theologian, participant in the Council of Trent, author of several treatises in moral theology. BIBLIOGRAPHY: É. Longpré, *Catholicisme* 1:673.

[T. C. O'BRIEN]

CÓRDOBA, PEDRO DE (1482–1521), Dominican preacher, writer, and catechist. Born in Córdoba, C. desired to Christianize the Indians. This brought him to Santo Domingo in 1510; there he established the first convent and was vice provincial of the Holy Cross province of the Dominican Order. His missions were on Española, Cuba, and at Cumaná on the mainland. His catechetical work was influential: his *Doctrina cristiana,* published first in Mexico in 1544, appeared 4 years later in a bilingual edition of Nahuatl and Spanish. Mention of him by Card. F. Cisneros in a royal decree is extant, but much of C.'s own writing concerning his American apostolate is yet unpublished.

[M. R. BROWN]

CÓRDOBA, MARTYRS OF, some 50 Spanish Christians executed by the Muslim rulers (850–859) in resistance to a determined demonstration of Christian faith and culture against the fairly well-established Muslim Arabic society. Debate continues about the legality and prudence of voluntary professions of faith by certain Christians of Arab or Arab-Spanish birth and of open attacks against the prophet Mohammed by zealous ascetic monks. Arabic sources are silent about the events, which are described in several contemporary Latin accounts, notably those of Eulogius and Albar. The Christian accounts defend the martyrdoms against an uncompromising Muslim position and against Christians who argued that the martyrs were at fault. Justification of the martyrs depends on the seriousness of the scandal involved in Muslim molestation of the Christian religion.

Already *c*.825 the Muslims had executed two Arab nobles, the brothers Adulfus and John, because they were Christians; their vita was written by Esperaindeo, who nurtured a revival of Latin culture in Córdoba. In 850 a group of Muslims baited the bilingual priest Perfectus with questions about their prophet and later made a public sacrifice of him in Ramadan (April 18) for what he said. In 851 the Muslims made a spectacle of the Christian merchant John under similar circumstances, imprisoning him after 400 lashes. A few months later the monk Isaac, expert in Arabic, volunteered before the cadi a denunciation of Mohammed such as the Muslims had tricked out of Perfectus and John; Isaac was executed forthwith (June 3, 851). Isaac's death evoked a long series of martyrdoms, as Christians and Crypto-Christians began to publicly acknowledge their faith. An episcopal council met in Córdoba, probably in late 852, to discourage the martyrdoms without condemning them; but Muslim provocation led to a new outburst within 6 months. By 858 the fame of the martyrs had reached N Spain and drew the Frankish monks Usuard and Odilard to Córdoba in search of relics. After the death of Eulogius in 859 the martyr movement faded. One of its important features was the systematic collection of material against Mohammed and Islam on the part of the Christians of Córdoba; the Muslims who baited Perfectus in 850 probably knew of this effort.

In greater or less detail Eulogius describes the following martyrdoms after Isaac: Sanctius (June 5, 851); Peter, Walabonsus, Sabinianus, Wistremundus, Habentius, and Jeremias (June 7); Sisenandus (July 16); Paul (July 20); Theodemirus (July 26); Nunilo and Alodia (Oct. 22); Flora and Maria (Nov. 24); Gumesindus and Servus Dei (Jan. 13, 852); Aurelius, Felix, George, Sabigotho, and Liliosa (July 27); Christopher and Leovigildus (Aug. 20); Emila and Hieremias (Sept. 15); Rogellus and Servus Dei (Sept. 16); Fandila (June 13, 853); Anastasius, Felix, and Digna (June 14); Benildis (June 15); Columba (Sept. 17); Pomposa (Sept. 19); Abundius (July 11, 854); Amator, Peter, and Louis (Apr. 30, 855); Witesindus (855); Helias, Paul, and Isidore (Apr. 17, 856); Argemirus (June 28); Aurea (July 19); Rudericus and Salomon (March 13, 857). Albar describes the passion of Eulogius (March 11, 859) and Leocritia (March 14); in 884 the relics of these two martyrs were translated to Oviedo in N Spain, but no great cult seems to have developed there. BIBLIOGRAPHY: E. P. Colbert, *Martyrs of Córdoba* (1962); J. F. Alonso, BiblSanct 4:173–176.

[E. P. COLBERT]

CÓRDOVA Y SALINAS, DIEGO DE (1591–1654), historian. A Franciscan of Lima, Peru, C. was appointed historian of the order's provinces of Peru. He visited old Franciscans and took notes on their reminiscences. His great work, *Crónica franciscana de las provincias del Perú* (1651), is a monumental history not only of the Peruvian provinces but of Franciscan work in most of South America in the 1st cent. of Spanish occupation. BIBLIOGRAPHY: L. Canedo, NCE 4:323.

[J. R. AHERNE]

CORE, DATHAN, AND ABIRAM, see KORAH (CORE).

COREDEMPTION, in RC theology, the Blessed Virgin Mary's active share in the redemptive work of her son, Jesus Christ, during his life on earth. This cooperation should be distinguished from her participation in the actual distribution of Christ's redemptive graces to mankind throughout history (see MEDIATRESS OF ALL GRACES). Although the term has been used by theologians since the 14th cent., appears in several recent papal documents, and is susceptible of interpretation in accord with generally accepted RC doctrine, its use was purposely avoided by Vatican Council II to eliminate the possibility of misunderstanding and to avoid setting up a terminological barrier to an ecumenical understanding of Mary's role in the economy of salvation. The reality signified by the term, however, is agreed upon by the great majority of RC theologians: during her life Mary cooperated directly and immediately in the redemptive process insofar as Christ and Mary constitute one single principle of salvation. This does not mean that Christ and Mary are equal causes. Christ is alone the unique, primary, and self-sufficient cause of mankind's redemption, whereas Mary is a secondary cause, freely chosen by God and totally dependent upon the infinite merits of her son. She was herself redeemed by Jesus, but her merits and satisfactions were accepted by God as *de facto* contributing to the objective, historical redemption.

The scriptural roots for the developed doctrine of Mary's share in the objective redemption are Gen 3.15 where the woman who will be at enmity with Satan is, in a prophetic sense, seen to be Mary; the full consent to God's plan expressed by her *fiat* at the Annunciation (Lk 1.38); her compassion at the foot of the cross; and an interpretation of Christ's words, "Woman, behold thy son" (Jn 19.27) as a proclamation of Mary's spiritual motherhood for all men. Church tradition since early medieval times has specifically accepted Mary's soteriological role, and since the 18th cent., this interpretation has received general acceptance. Benedict XV's apostolic letter *Inter sodalicia* (1918) maintains ". . . we may rightly say that she (Mary) redeemed the human race together with Christ." The same doctrine is repeated by Pius XII in the encyclical *Haurietis aquas* (1956) and in Vat II ConstChurch 61 where Mary is said to be our mother in the order of grace because of her singular cooperation in Christ's redemptive act. BIBLIOGRAPHY: Carol Mariol 2:373–425; J. B. Carol, NCE 9:359–362; M. J. Horak, *ibid.* 4:323–324; Vorgrimler 1:285–295.

[T. M. MCFADDEN]

CORELLI, ARCANGELO (1653–1713), Italian composer, violinist. Son of impoverished peasants, C. studied violin with several notable teachers and went to Rome in 1671. He held numerous posts as a violinist and had for his patron Card. Pietro Ottoboni. In 1681 C. published his *12 Trio Sonatas for Two Violins and Cello, with Organ Basso Continuo,* Opus 1, and in 1685, *12 Chamber Trio Sonatas for Two Violins, Violone and Violoncello or Harpsichord,* Opus 2. During these years he published also *12 Church Trio Sonatas for Two Violins and Archlute with Organ Basso Continuo* Opus 3 (1689) as well as three other collections of sonatas. His great work, *Concerti Grossi,* Opus 6, was published after his death. C. was originator of a method of playing the violin that revolutionized violin technique and he established the *concerto grosso,* a mode of composition marked by setting off a small group of strings against a larger group.

[J. R. AHERNE]

CORESSIOS, GEORGIOS (1554–1651?), Greek theologian. A highly controversial figure of the Eastern Church, a practicing physician, and a polemicist, he wrote much against Calvinism and Lutheranism. His principal target, however, seems to have been Roman Christianity. His most fully developed work was on the procession of the Holy Spirit. Of his 63 known works, the majority are anti-Roman tracts. He has been variously described as a man of great wisdom and a rash vulgarian. BIBLIOGRAPHY: A. Audino, EncCatt 4:547–548.

[J. R. AHERNE]

CORINTH, LOVIS (1858–1925), German painter. Influenced by old masters in study at Munich and Paris, C. finally moved toward Expressionism in a rough, spontaneous technique, becoming, as president of the Berlin Secession (1911), a most influential painter in Germany. In his late, colorful *Red Christ* (1923, Munich) and lithographs of dramatic lights and darks (*Apocalypse*, 1921; *Adam and Eve*, 1923), C. demonstrates a forceful Expressionism. BIBLIOGRAPHY: G. von der Osten, *Lovis Corinth*, (1955).

[M. J. DALY]

CORINTH, an ancient city of Greece (Old Corinth), located at the W edge of the Corinth Canal (New Corinth) with an estimated population of about 16,000 (1961). Corinth is a titular archbishopric, whose Catholic members (4% of the population) belong to the archdiocese of Athens. The city has a prehistoric legendary foundation, but its origin is traceable to the Ionic and Doric peoples. It was the wealthiest city in ancient Greece, a result of its favorable situation for trade and the development of its pottery and bronze industries. In the Peloponnesian Wars, Corinth sided with Sparta against Athens, whose rise to power challenged Corinth's commercial supremacy. Later Corinth came under the domination of Macedonia until 394 B.C., when it joined the Achaean League and became the capital city. The city of Corinth, destroyed by the Romans in 146 B.C. was a little more than a century later restored by Julius Caesar. Pausanias visited Corinth in the 2d cent. and left descriptions of the monuments in the restored city. American excavations unearthed the remains of many of the buildings described by Pausanias. The Temple of Apollo, dating from the 6th cent., was the most prominent brought to light. Corinth had a highly mixed population of Romans, Greeks, Orientals, and Jews. About two-thirds of these were slaves, the rest were poor working people and a small number of wealthy merchants. Situated between two great harbors Corinth grew into an international seaport which became notorious for its moral corruption (Rom 1.18–32). The Apostle Paul, unsuccessful in Athens, went to Corinth and made it the center of his missionary work in Greece. He founded a church there in A.D. 50, and wrote letters to its members of which two survive. Because of its immorality and pagan cult, Paul's work in Corinth began "in fear and trepidation." Despite internal difficulties, the Church of Corinth prospered. Its bps. attended the Councils of Ephesus (431) and Chalcedon (451). The Martyrology of St. Jerome records the Corinthian martyrs Leonidas and companions. From the 9th cent. Corinth was a province of the Latin Church, with 8 suffragans, until the Turkish conquest in 1458. From 1100 to 1833, the Eastern Church was also active, Greek Orthodox bps. becoming "Exarchs of the Peloponnesus." BIBLIOGRAPHY: H. Payne, *Microcorinthia, a Study of Corinthian Art* (1971, repr. of 1931); W. Smithals, *Gnosticism in Corinth* (tr. J. Steely, 1971); J. G. O'Neill, *Corinth* (1930); R. L. Scranton, *American School of Classical Studies, Antiquities* (1951); G. Finley, *History of Greece from its Conquest of the Romans to the Present Time* (1877).

[C. KEENAN]

CORINTHIANS, LETTERS TO THE, the 7th and 8th books of the NT canon. Paul evangelized Corinth on his second missionary journey, A.D. 51–52. His effort was rebuffed by the Jews, but was successful enough among the gentiles of the city to result in a lengthy stay of a year and a half (Acts 18.1–18). While at Ephesus on his third journey (1 Cor 16.8), Paul received news from the house of Chloe (1 Cor 1.11) of rivalries among the Corinthian Christians and also a letter concerning religious questions confronting the community (1 Cor 1.7). In response he wrote First Corinthians, about A.D. 55. Prior to this, however, Paul had already written a letter to Corinth (1 Cor 5.9), perhaps delivered by Timothy and Erastus (Acts 19.22). According to 1 Cor 16.5–6 he intended to follow this epistle with a visit of some duration to Corinth, but seemingly was compelled to make an earlier visit to the community: Second Corinthians 12.14 and 13.1–2 speak of Paul's visit to follow Second Corinthians as the "third", therefore implying a visit there between 1 and 2 Cor; this visit is mentioned in 2 Cor 2.1 as an unpleasant experience. Between First and Second Corinthians, despite Paul's visit, the religious situation in Corinth worsened, and Paul sent Titus there with a letter of strong reproof (known as "the sorrowful letter", 2 Cor 2.4; 7.6–7) that received a favorable response from the Corinthians. In this situation Paul sent Second Corinthians to the community to solidify the gains achieved by the mission of Titus. The letters prior to First and Second Corinthians are known as the "lost letters" of Paul to the Corinthians. Some scholars maintain that these lost letters have been incorporated into Second Corinthians. On this hypothesis the material of 2 Cor 6.14–7.1 and 2 Cor 9 is taken from the letter written prior to First Corinthians; and the material of 2 Cor 10–13 is the letter of reproof written prior to Second Corinthians. This hypothesis is plausible, esp. for 2 Cor 10–13, the tone of which contrasts sharply with 2 Cor 1–8, but it is not accepted by all Pauline scholars. Many of them think that it requires a degree of literary unity in these Pauline letters that the Apostle would not have been concerned to achieve.

First Corinthians is a well-constructed epistle treating of a variety of topics, always with some degree of depth: the rivalries within the community (1.10–4.21); its toleration of an incestuous union (5.1–8); its misunderstanding of Paul's previous instruction on relationship to pagans (5.9–13); the question of lawsuits before Roman courts (6.1–11); sexual immorality (6.12–20); a variety of questions on marriage that cover the sexual relationship in marriage, the remarriage of widows and widowers, the status of the Christian party married to a pagan, the relative merits of marriage vs. the celibate state in view of the possible proximity of the parousia (7.1–40); conscience and the eating of meat offered to idols (8.1–13); Paul's defense of his lack of employment of certain apostolic rights (9.1–27); the Christian conscience concerning idol-worship and the eating of idol-meats (10.1–11.1); the headdress of women at the liturgical assembly (11.2–16); correction of abuses at the *agapē* and instructions on the Eucharistic Celebration (11.17–34); instructions on the value of the charismatic gifts, on the primacy of charity, and directions on the use of the charismatic gifts at the liturgical assembly (12.1–14.40); the Christian doctrine of the resurrection of the dead (15.1–58); and the collection for the poor of Jerusalem (16.1–4).

Second Corinthians is concerned chiefly with the Apostle's reflections on the restoration of the relationship between himself and the Corinthian community. He speaks of it as a comfort (1.3–11). He protests his sincerity and his apostolic concern for them throughout the difficult period of misunderstanding (1.12–6.13; 7.2–16). He urges that the collection for the poor Christians of Jerusalem be resumed again and successfully completed as the mark of their love for him and of their concern for Christian unity (8.1–9.15). He reaffirms his apostolic authority, responding in particular to criticisms made against him by itinerant missioners who infiltrated the Corinthian community (10.1–13.10). Second Corinthians is generally considered to have been written about 6 months after First Corinthians. The Pauline authorship of these epistles is not contested. BIBLIOGRAPHY: D. Guthrie, *New Testament Introduction* (1961); Wikenhauser NTI; P. Feine et al., *Einleitung in das Neue Testament* (1964); E. B. Allo, *Saint Paul: Première épître aux Corinthiens* (1935); *idem, Seconde épître aux Corinthiens* (1937).

[C. P. CEROKE]

CORINTHIANS, THIRD EPISTLE TO THE, see APOCRYPHA (NEW TESTAMENT), 16.

CORKER, JAMES MAURUS (1636–1715), Benedictine monk on the English mission. Son of an Anglican vicar who served as a spy for the government of Cromwell, C. became a Catholic. Professed a Benedictine at the Abbey of Lambspring in Germany, he returned to the English mission. He was tried at the time of the Titus Oates plot, released, retried as a priest in 1680, and condemned to death. In prison C. was spiritual director to St. Oliver Plun-

kett. Also in prison he wrote several works, including Stafford's *Memoirs* (1682) which told the story of the trial and execution of Viscount Stafford, and *A Remonstrance of Piety and Innocence* (1683) on other victims of the Titus Oates conspiracy. With the coming of James II to the throne C. was released. Among his converts in London was John Dryden. Leaving England in the Revolution of 1688, C. became abbot of Lambspring but differences with the monks caused him to resign and return to England. BIBLIOGRAPHY: Gillow BDEC 1:568–571.

[J. R. AHERNE]

CORKERY, DANIEL (1878–1964), Irish writer and critic. In earlier years C. used the theater as his medium, several of his plays being produced at the Abbey Theater. Turning to the short story he produced his most notable work. C. is unique among his contemporaries in that he did not find either Gaelic stories or the Anglo-Irish tradition sufficient for what he felt was a true Irish milieu. His work shows the influence of Russian masters such as Chekhov more than Irish. Writing of Cork and its people, his use of setting to convey character and his insight into the reality of character, together with an overriding concern for presenting the isolation of the individual, constitute a singular approach to the short story. C. wrote two studies in literary criticism, *The Hidden Ireland* (1925) and *Synge and Anglo-Irish Literature* (1931). His most enduring work is in the area of fiction with works such as *The Threshold of Quiet* (1917), *The Stony Hills* (1929), and *Earth to Earth* (1939). BIBLIOGRAPHY: B. Kiely, *Modern Irish Fiction* (1950).

[J. R. AHERNE]

CORMIER, HYACINTHE MARIE (1832–1916), French spiritual writer for religious. An Orléanais, C. was formed in the Sulpician school and became a Dominican after his ordination. As secretary and companion to the master general, A. V. *Jandel, who was then insisting on primitive observances, C. received a stamp that was to prove not altogether to the mind of those more inspired by H. D. *Lacordaire. After serving as provincial of Toulouse, he was elected master general, and he died in the odor of sanctity a few months after the expiration of his generalate. His election had been providential for his order, for he was trusted and revered by Pius X, whose suspicions of its temper might otherwise have become more drastic than they proved. As it was, the order grew and flourished, and it was then that the Collegio Angelico in Rome was founded. C. was a prudent, gentle, and revered superior, devoted to Dominican ideals, though more possessed by the order's monastic elements than by profound appreciation of its characteristic theology, or indeed of theology as such. One result is that his numerous spiritual writings now appear, in manner at least, rather like pieces of repository art. Yet there is more to the picture. He was the spiritual father of M. J. *Lagrange and the *Revue biblique,* and of T. Coconnier and the *Revue thomiste.* BIBLIOGRAPHY: M. A. Genevois, DSAM 2.2:2329–36; S. Szabó, *Hyacinth-Marie Cormier* (tr. C. G. Moore, 1938).

[T. GILBY]

CORNARO, ELENA LUCREZIA PISCOPIA

(1646–84), Benedictine oblate (from 1665), mathematician, linguist, writer, and poet. Of the family on which the noble Piscopias had conferred their name for special service rendered by the Cornaro, C. was the daughter of the procurator of St. Mark's, Gianbattista Cornaro, and was early recognized as exceptionally gifted. Her parish priest tutored her from the age of 7. At home she prepared herself for higher learning, and, encouraged by her father and her tutor, in her 26th year applied to the Univ. of Padua. A challenge by a prestigious group of scholars to the entrance of a woman was of no avail, and C. for the next 5 years pursued a rigorous course of study. Naturally gifted in mathematics, she plumbed the profundities of philosophy and theology with like ease. Master of languages (including Arabic, Hebrew, Latin, and Greek), "the Cornaro" in 1678 defended her thesis and, her request for secret ballot ignored, was acclaimed by a resounding shout from ecclesiastic and lay scholars. She was invested with the ermine mozzetta, the ring, the laurel wreath, and enrolled as *magistra et doctrix philosophiae,* the first student for whom the feminine inscription was necessary. The rest of her short life was spent in study and in many good works. Although she had destroyed much of her own work, what remained was published posthumously (1688), including correspondence with Renaissance scholars, with Innocent XI, and King John Sobieski. Hers also were eulogies to political and ecclesiastical personages, an acrostic in French for the King of France, and poems in Greek and Latin, mostly spiritual. C. had requested burial in the Benedictine mortuary of Sta. Giustina at Padua.

Her death was attended by an unusual number of honors from distinguished scholars. The Univ. of Padua had a memorial medal struck for her. With the approach of her tercentenary (1978) a number of women's organizations and other interested groups have formed a committee in the U.S. and procured funds from the Hunt Foundation for the restoration of her grave site, in which the Univ. of Padua is also interested. BIBLIOGRAPHY: G. E. Forbush, "Elena Cornaro: First *Doctrix Philosophiae* Remembered 300 Years Later," *American Association of University Women Journal* 68 (1974) 30–32; F. Noetzel, "Cornaro: Patron Saint of Educated Women," *Kappa Gamma Pi News* 43 (1974) 6; N. Fusco, *Elena Cornaro Piscopia: 1646–1684* (1975).

[M. R. BROWN]

CORNAY, JEAN CHARLES, BL. (d. 1837), martyr.

At the age of 24 C. was ordained priest of the Paris Society of Foreign Missions. After laboring secretly in Ban-no, Annam, Indochina, during the persecution of Minh-Mang,

C. was arrested on trumped-up charges of treason, imprisoned in a series of cages, and finally beheaded at the age of 28. His compelling cheerfulness and steadfastness moved his captors on many occasions and even caused his sentence of gradual dismemberment before beheading to be commuted to the single blow of the sword. BIBLIOGRAPHY: Butler 3:79–80 s.v. "Martyrs of Indo-China."

[J. R. RIVELLO]

CORNEILLE, ANTOINE (1611–57), French clergyman

and poet, brother of Thomas and Pierre Corneille. Augustinian canon regular at Mont-aux-Malades near Rouen, C. became subprior there (1641), was named curé at Fréville (1642), and after a serious illness took the habit of the reformed Congregation of Sainte-Geneviève (1652). Among his poems, which won him several awards from the Académie des Palinods de Rouen, is a *Chant royal sur saint Augustin* (1638). His *Poésies chrétiennes et paraphrases sur les cantiques et hymnes de l' Église, à l'honneur de la Sainte Vierge* . . . include a curious paraphrase of the Stabat Mater imitating Rodrigue's stanzas in Pierre Corneille's *Le Cid.* BIBLIOGRAPHY: *Poésies chrétiennes* . . . . (ed. P. Blanchemain, 1877).

[R. N. NICOLICH]

CORNEILLE, PIERRE (1606–84), French dramatist.

Educated by the Jesuits at the Collège de Maulevrier, Rouen (1615–22), C. studied law and began legal practice (1624–50), but was more attracted to a literary career. His first play, *Mélite,* a comedy, performed in Paris (1628 or 1629), was received with acclaim which, with his next plays, drew the attention of the court so that for a short time he collaborated as one of "The Five Authors," Richelieu's personal group of dramatic ghost-writers. His tragicomedy, *Le Cid* (Dec. 1635 or Jan. 1636), was so well received that it became one of the most famous works of French literature. However, its success sparked a literary dispute, *la querelle du Cid* resulting in the intervention of the Académie Française, which reproached C. for not following the dramatic rules (1638). After a 3-year silence, he returned with his more "regular" tragedies and masterpieces, *Horace* (1640), *Cinna* (1640 or 1641), and *Polyeucte* (1641 or 1642), this last generally considered his best. It is a Christian tragedy, based on the martyrdom of St. Polyeuctus (4th cent.) as reported by Simeon Metaphrastes, recopied by Surius. Its originality lay in the dramatic role given to the workings of divine grace in conjunction with both the love–intrigue popular in secular drama and the secular ethic of "glory" newly emerging in C.'s plays from the religious moralists of the Stoic revival and Christian Neoplatonist tradition. The religious subject-matter, however, surprised Parisian audiences who thought it daring. Another Christian tragedy, *Théodore vierge et martyre* (1645), was C.'s first failure.

Elected to the Académie Française (1647), he was driven into temporary retirement (1652–59) by the failure of

Pertharite (1651 or 1652), during which time, however, he turned to translating and paraphrasing in verse the *Imitation of Christ* (1651–56). His decline is reflected in his last group of plays, which include his *Tite et Bérénice* (1670), compared unfavorably by the public to Racine's *Bérénice*. Besides tragicomedies and the tragedies, among which are also noteworthy his *Rodogune* (1644), and *Nicomède* (1651), C. wrote eight comedies; a tragedy-ballet, *Psyché* (1671), in collaboration with Molière; and works of dramatic criticism. A lifelong pious Catholic, he made a French verse and prose translation of the *Office of the Blessed Virgin* and *The Seven Penitential Psalms, Sunday Vespers and Compline, and all the Hymns of the Roman Breviary* (1670). BIBLIOGRAPHY: H. C. Lancaster, *History of French Dramatic Literature in the Seventeenth Century* (9 v., 1929–42) v. 1–3; P. Bénichou, *Morales du Grand Siècle* (1948).

[R. N. NICOLICH]

CORNELIUS, ST. (d. 253), **POPE** from 251, popularly venerated as a martyr. After the death of Pope St. *Fabian, the Roman See was vacant for more than a year owing to the fury of the Decian persecution, and then C., probably a Roman of the *gens Cornelia,* was elected, a choice that brought dismay to *Novatian, who had expected the office to fall to himself. Novatian, finding some support, set himself up as pope in opposition to Cornelius. He and his followers adopted a rigorous position in regard to penance, insisting that the *lapsi* (those who had apostatized during persecutions) could not be pardoned. C. called a Roman synod of 60 bps. (251) and condemned this teaching. His stand was supported by *Cyprian of Carthage, who came to admire him greatly. C. was sent to Centumcellae (Civitavecchia) in exile (252) and died shortly thereafter. Cyprian called him a martyr, but it is not clear whether he was put to death or died in consequence of the hardships he suffered in exile. BIBLIOGRAPHY: Quasten 2:236–237; E. G. Weltin, *Ancient Popes* (1964) 116–122; Butler 3:560–561.

[P. F. MULHERN]

CORNELIUS, THE CENTURION, according to Acts ch. 10, the first notable gentile convert to Christianity. Underlying this narrative is the problem of the acceptance of converts to Christianity from paganism. C.'s conversion and baptism by Peter had far-reaching consequences, for it meant that one could become a Christian without first becoming a Jew (Acts 10.34–35), and further indicated that contact with the nonbaptized was not something to be avoided. The extent to which gentile Christians were to observe Jewish religious law and custom was settled at the so-called Council of Jerusalem (Acts ch. 15). BIBLIOGRAPHY: M. Dibelius, "Conversion of Cornelius," *Studies in the Acts of the Apostles* (tr. M. Ling, 1956) 109–122.

[R. T. A. MURPHY]

CORNELIUS, PETER (1783–1867), German painter. After study in Düsseldorf, C. went to Rome (1811) joining there the Nazarene group of German artists and working in a grand but highly eclectic style. C. painted the *Last Judgment* and the *Four Horsemen of the Apocalypse* (both in Berlin) with significant grandeur and energy.

[M. J. DALY]

CORNELY, RUDOLPH, (1830–1908), German Jesuit biblical scholar. He was the initiator of the great series *Cursus scripturae sacrae,* a classic of its time, which he completed in collaboration with J. Knabenbauer and F. von Hummelauer. He himself wrote the introductory volumes, *Historica et critica introductio in utriusque testamenti libros sacros* (3 v., 1885–87), as well as the commentaries on 1 Cor (1890), 2 Cor (1892), Gal (1892), Rom (1896) and Wisdom (1910, ed. by J. Zorell). BIBLIOGRAPHY: A. Merk, DB Suppl 2:153–155.

[D. J. BOURKE]

CORNERSTONE, the first stone laid in the construction of a church. It is blessed and set in place according to a ritual that has not changed since the Pontifical of 1572. After it is placed in one of the principal walls of the church, the other foundations of the church are blessed.

[N. KOLLAR]

CORNET, NICOLAS (1592–1663), theologian who, as syndic of the faculty at the Collège de Navarre in Paris, formulated (July 1, 1649) the five propositions that were intended to represent the doctrine of C. *Jansen's *Augustinus and that became a central issue in the Jansenist controversies. *JANSENISM.

[T. C. O'BRIEN]

CORONACH, see CAOINE.

CORONATION GOSPELS (9th cent.), favorite Carolingian illuminated Gospel Book of Charlemagne, according to tradition found on the knees of the dead Emperor when Otto III opened the imperial tomb (1000 A.D.) The illusionistic definition of drapery over the form beneath and the acanthus motif on the "picture" window frame in Pompeian style (St. Matthew page) mark the influence of the late Antique in books imported from Italy and Byzantium under Charlemagne's patronage. The MS is now in the Treasury, Vienna.

[M. J. DALY]

CORONATION OF A KING, the ceremonial crowning and investiture which, in Christian times, has always been invested with religious ritual. Added to the crowning is the anointing with oil, no doubt a transfer from the ordination ceremony of priests and bishops. The sacred character of the coronation reflected the belief that the king was a chosen representative of God as well as ruler of the people. In England the coronation ceremony has four phases: entry with acknowledgement and oath, anointing, investiture and crowning, enthronement and reception of homage. The Holy Roman emperors were crowned by the pope, beginning with Charlemagne in the year 800, until the 16th cent., when Aachen became the place of crowning by bishops. In France from the 11th cent. coronation took place at Reims and was performed by the abp. of Reims. Hungary, Poland, and Russia followed the general custom with a bp. or patriarch bestowing the crown.

[J. R. AHERNE]

CORONATION OF A POPE, the ceremony at which the newly elected pope receives the papal *tiara as a symbol of his jurisdiction. Since Pius X (1903), the rite takes place in St. Peter's Basilica at a solemn pontifical Mass. A cleric precedes the pope to the main altar, sets fire to a ball of flax three times and intones, "Holy Father, thus passes the glory of the world." During the Mass, the pope receives the *pallium. Afterwards the dean of the cardinal deacons places the tiara on the pope's head, saying "Receive the tiara adorned with the three crowns and know that you are the father of princes and kings, ruler of the earth, and earthly vicar of our Savior Jesus Christ, to whom is honor and glory forever. Amen." The ceremony ends with the papal blessing *urbi et orbi. In 1964, Pope Paul VI gave away his own tiara as a gesture toward freeing ecclesiastical ceremonies from elaborate, feudal remnants.

[T. M. MCFADDEN]

CORONEL, GREGORIO NUÑEZ (fl. first half of 17th cent.), Portuguese Augustinian theologian, appointed secretary of the *congregatio de auxiliis, firm opponent of Molinism. BIBLIOGRAPHY: J. A. Knowles, CE 4:386.

[T. C. O'BRIEN]

CORONEL, JUAN (1567–1651), Spanish Franciscan missionary to Yucatán, expert in the Mayan language in which he published a catechism and a series of sermons. BIBLIOGRAPHY: E. Gómez-Tagle, NCE 4:336.

[T. C. O'BRIEN]

COROT, JEAN BAPTISTE CAMILLE (1796–1875), French painter whose early discipline in classical composition assured him distinctive command of landscape organization. Traveling (1825–28), C. painted fresh, spontaneous Italian landscapes of exquisitely simple serene arrangement, radiant in a narrow range of rich color, and landscapes of Normandy and Burgundy. His works, though predominantly landscapes, include such sacred subjects as *Hagar in the Desert* (1835), *St. Jerome* (1836), *The Flight into Egypt* (1840), *Baptism of Jesus* (1840), and *Christ in the Garden of Olives* (1849). While C.'s spontaneous studies of nature in precise nuances of light and atmosphere are masterful, his figure studies of pensive women in colorful, often fantastic costume are today prized as his most powerful and beautiful work. The years 1845–55 marked a high point of C.'s early luminous style and a beginning of the silvery,

poetic, misty landscapes which, though at times facile, were long considered his best works (*Memory of Mortefontaine,* 1864). Successful and wealthy by 1850, C. supported Millet and Daumier. He preserved to the last his refinement of color (*Interior of Cathedral of Sens,* 1874). In the 20th cent. C. is considered a supreme master of 19th-cent. romantic realism. BIBLIOGRAPHY: G. Bazin, *Corot* (1951).

[M. J. DALY]

COROZAIN, a variant spelling for *Chorazin.

CORPORAL, a square linen cloth on which the chalice, paten, and host are placed at Mass. Outside the Mass other vessels containing the Eucharist, e.g., the monstrance, are also placed on the corporal. The corporal originally was the uppermost *altar cloth.

[N. KOLLAR]

CORPORATE STATE, a term not to be confused with the familiar American business corporation, but referring in theory to the idea of national corporations as means of all economic activity. Such corporations are subordinate to the state and, since they cover all economic activity, they eliminate the need for representative political institutions.

Conceived as a device to preserve national solidarity against the divisive individualism of laissez-faire economics and politics, the corporate state has roots that run back to the period when capitalism displaced feudalism as a system for organizing economic activity. Both Puritans and Catholics proposed forms of corporate regulation to gain social control over unfettered business enterprise, and to reconcile opposing class interests in industrial society. Best-known Catholic theorist was Adam Mueller (d. 1829) who entered Austrian government service in 1813 and proposed an idealized feudalism with emphasis on organic unity of economic activity under strong authority from a national state, imbued, however, with Christian principles.

In practice, the notion of the corporate state (sometimes called "corporatism" or "corporativism") is most visible in the period of Italian fascism under Mussolini. Here syndicalism (the idea that unions of workers should be the base for social and industrial organization in a socialist society) and nationalism were merged in corporatism. The fascist corporate state rejected both socialism and capitalism, and substituted associations (syndicates) embodying all employers and workers in a given industry or profession. These associations were instruments of the state.

Twenty-two corporations were established in Italy in 1934. They covered every major category of productive activity. Employers and employees were equally represented on the governing council of each corporation; all such councils were coordinated at the national level. World War II brought an end to the system. Faint echoes of corporatism lived on in Catholic proposals for autonomous industrial councils, but this concept has received little attention since the 1950s. BIBLIOGRAPHY: R. Arès, *What is Cor-*

porative Organization? (ed. and tr. T. P. Fay, 1939); F. Pitigliani, *Italian Corporate State* (1933); J. L. Spring, *Education and the Rise of the Corporate State* (1973).

[W. J. BYRON]

CORPORATION ACT, the first act of the so-called Clarendon Code, designed to secure loyal supporters of Charles II in local governments. During the Interregnum, Baptists and Independents had been active in military service and public offices, and they were suspected of disloyalty to the Restoration. In 1661, Parliament passed an "Act for Regulating Corporations" in order to exclude such persons from municipal governments. All mayors, town clerks, and other magistrates were, by March 25, 1663, to take oaths of allegiance and supremacy. Each such person was also to declare that it was unlawful to take arms against the king for any reason, and to abjure the *Solemn League and Covenant. Moreover, everyone holding such office must have taken the sacrament of the Lord's Supper according to the rites of the C of E within a year previous to election or appointment. In 1828 this act was repealed. BIBLIOGRAPHY: H. Gee and W. J. Hardy, *Documents Illustrative of English Church History* (1921).

[N. H. MARING]

CORPUS CATHOLICORUM, a title with two uses: (1) name of the body of Catholic imperial states of Germany *(Reichsstände)* from *c*.1700 to 1806, founded as the counterpart of the Protestant *corpus Evangelicorum,* but never achieving political significance; (2) a society in Bonn, Germany, founded in 1917 by J. Greving (d. 1919), and the collection of Reformation writing published under the same name, *Corpus Catholicorum.* A Roman Catholic counterpart to the Protestant *Corpus Reformatorum,* the collection contains writings of RC theologians and controversialists of the Reformation (1517–63). The series, however, also incorporated the Reformation studies and texts begun in 1905 by J. Greving; and since 1926 issued more popularized accounts of Catholic life and struggles during the Reformation. BIBLIOGRAPHY: H. Jedin, LTK 3:63.

[J. R. FANG]

CORPUS CHRISTI, a doctrinal feast established in honor of Christ present in the Eucharist. Its purpose is to instruct the people in the mystery, faith, and devotion surrounding the Eucharist. The celebration of the feast evolved during the 13th and 14th centuries. The Berengarian controversy (mid-11th cent.) over the presence of Christ in the Eucharist preceded this evolution. By the 13th cent. reception of communion was less emphasized and was to some extent superseded by seeing the Host. At this time (1209) Juliana of Liège had a vision which demanded a feast for the Eucharist. After much persuasion the feast was celebrated for the first time in 1247, and was extended to the whole Church in 1264. Resistance to the feast was found in Rome

and Liège, but by 1317 its celebration had spread throughout the world.

Although there is trustworthy evidence that St. Thomas Aquinas composed two Offices for the feast, it is by no means clear that the Office now used for the feast is from his pen.

From the late 14th cent. the most conspicuous feature of the feast was the procession. According to the requirements of church law the procession is to follow Mass and the host used at the procession is to be consecrated at the Mass. The procession seems to have originated in the English Palm Sunday Procession (11th cent.) in which the Host was carried. By mid-14th cent. the procession became an integral part of the Corpus Christi celebration. The Eucharist (at first in the veiled chalice and by the 15th cent. in the monstrance) was treated as the triumphant Christ the King. The whole community took part in this procession. In Germany it became associated with the procession for good weather and thus there was benediction of the four corners of the earth at the four stations. BIBLIOGRAPHY: W. J. Shea, NCE 4:345–347; F. Oppenheim and P. Toschi, EncCatt 4:611–614.

[N. KOLLAR]

CORPUS CHRISTI PLAYS, cycles of mystery plays covering the Old and New Testaments, performed at or near the feast of Corpus Christi in the early summer, mainly in France, Germany, and England. The cycle dramatized "salvation history," displaying God's intervention on behalf of his people at crucial moments like the Flood, the Exodus, and the Incarnation. A prophetic principle governed the selection of incidents and characters, so that all elements represented were related to Christ's Redemption of mankind and were arranged in a prefigurative series leading up to this culmination. The plays were distributed among craft guilds like those of the carpenters and the masons, who assumed responsibility for staging and acting, subject to strict supervision by the municipal corporation for standards of excellence in the production. The cycles flourished on the Continent from the late 14th to the 16th cent., and even beyond this time. BIBLIOGRAPHY: E. C. Dunn, NCE 4:1043–44; M. L. Spencer, *Corpus Christi Pageants in England* (1911, repr. 1975).

[E. C. DUNN]

CORPUS DOCTRINAE (pl. *Corpora doctrinae),* name used for a collection of confessions of faith by 16th-cent. German Protestants. In 1560 a private printer in Meissen published the *Corpus doctrinae Philippicum* (or *Misnicum*), a collection of Philipp *Melanchthon's writings. The *territorial Churches published numerous other *corpora doctrinae* containing their confessional statements. They were finally replaced by the *Formula of Concord (1577) and the *Book of Concord (1580), which sought to bring confessional unity among all German Lutherans. BIBLIOGRAPHY:

E. Wolf, RGG 1:1012–13; G. Kaweran, EncRelKnow 3:273–275.

[J. R. FANG]

CORPUS EVANGELICORUM, political union of the Protestant imperial estates *(Reichsstände)* formed under the leadership of the Duke of Saxony after the Peace of Westphalia (1648) to represent Protestant interests in the German Diet *(Reichstag)*. The parallel organ, the *Corpus Catholicorum,* did not achieve the same political importance, since RC interests were furthered by the Emperor and a large part of the nobility. The *Corpus Evangelicorum* played a role in obtaining tolerance for Protestant minorities, and in the Gregorian Calendar Reform (1699). Both the *Corpus Catholicorum* and the *Corpus Evangelicorum* were discontinued after the collapse of the Holy Roman Empire (1806). BIBLIOGRAPHY: J. Heckel, RGG 1:1873–74; K. Repgen, LTK 3:64–65.

[J. R. FANG]

CORPUS HERMETICUM, see HERMETIC LITERATURE.

CORPUS IURIS (JURIS) CANONICI, principal compilation of Western ecclesiastical law prior to the Code of Canon Law of 1917. The Corpus included six earlier collections that were put together 1499–1502 by two lawyers in Paris—Jean Chappuis and Vitalis de Thebes. The title was first used in 1671, but the words had been used by Gregory XIII in a 1580 brief, *Cum pro munere,* in reference to a new edition. Until the Middle Ages, the canons were studied as part of theology, but at Bologna in the 12th cent., Gratian established canon law as a science and paved the way for its development as a separate field of study. Around 1140 he produced a systematized collection of the existing body of canon law, called the Harmony of Contradictory Laws, or, later, the *Decretum.* Included in the Corpus were this work and five subsequent collections: the Decretals of Gregory IX (1234), the *Liber sextus* of Boniface VIII (1298), the *Clementinae* of Clement V (promulgated by John XXII in 1317), the *Extravagantes* of John XXII (1325) and the *Extravagantes communes* (1500). The Corpus included no material later than 1484 and not everything before that. BIBLIOGRAPHY: A. G. Cicognani, *Canon Law* (2d rev., Eng. tr. 1935).

[T. EARLY]

CORPUS IURIS CIVILIS, a name given in the Middle Ages to the body of Roman law codified by Emperor Justinian with some later editions. It is made up of (1) the Institutes, a brief introductory survey in 4 books; (2) the Digest or Pandects, 50 books of excerpts from legal writings ranging from the 1st cent. B.C. to the 4th A.D.; (3) the Justinian Code, 12 books of imperial constitutions; and (4) the Novels, a private collection of imperial legislation promulgated by Justinian after the publication of the code with a few laws of his two immediate successors. Work on the codification of Roman law was inaugurated by Justinian a few months after his accession in 527 and was completed between 530 and 534 under the direction of Tribonian. Earlier attempts had been made to put some order into the chaos of imperial constitutions with the Codex Gregorianus (291) and its supplement the Codex Hermogenianus (295), private compilations for the use of lawyers and scholars, and the official Codex Theodosianus (438). Justinian's aim was more comprehensive. He wished to integrate the old law of the republic with the new of the empire, to preserve the old legal doctrines, concepts, and customs and at the same time to establish a legal system which would answer the needs of the time. Despite defects in plan and execution his new code was a truly remarkable achievement and the most successful of his various attempts to restore the Roman Empire by bringing it under one ruler, one religion, and one law. It has served as the basis for most subsequent European codes and for the Code of Canon Law. BIBLIOGRAPHY: H. J. Wolff, *Roman Law, an Historical Introduction* (1951) 162–174; P. Torquebiau, DDC 4:610–664.

[M. J. COSTELLOE]

CORPUS MYSTICUM (Mystical Body), the term used until the mid-12th cent. to designate the Eucharist. At that time, however, the terms *Corpus Mysticum* and *Corpus Christi* were permuted: the latter came to mean the Eucharist and *Corpus Mysticum* was applied to the Church. BIBLIOGRAPHY: H. de Lubac, *Corpus Mysticum* (1949) 88.

CORPUS REFORMATORUM (CR), the title of a collection of Reformation works written before 1555. Those of Luther were not included because of the existence of the so-called Erlanger edition. The first section of CR began with P. *Melanchthon (ed. K. G. Bretschneider, H. E. Bindseil, v. 1–28, 1834–60), but was incomplete and required some 53 supplements. The 2d section, works of John Calvin, is considered superior and complete (ed. W. Baum et al., v. 29–87, 1863–1900). The 3d section, works of H. Zwingli, is also a complete collection (ed. E. Egli et al., v. 88–98, 1905–41). Reprints of the Melanchthon and Calvin volumes were issued in 1964.

[J. R. FANG]

CORRADO, GIOVANNI BATTISTA (1536–1606), Dominican canonist and moralist, at Perugia, Italy, who wrote frequently republished manuals on casuistry and canonical questions.

[T. C. O'BRIEN]

CORRECTION, FRATERNAL, an act of gracious friendship (charity, *agapē*) which, through an admonition, turns one's neighbor away from some evil. It seeks to lead him to God since it flows from our loving companionship together as children of God, actual or potential. It thus differs in type from admonitions which are the duty of those charged by justice to protect the common good or to ensure fair dealing. Its exercise is difficult, for one must be careful not to be meddlesome or to let one's own feelings of offense obtrude, and it calls for delicacy and tact. It ought to be carried out privately, except in obstinate cases of public scandal. It may be given vocally, or by some other sign, or, perhaps best of all, by the silence that speaks through example. It is not conspicuous in pagan ethical writings, although it was praised by Seneca (*De ira*, 3.36). In the OT, Lev 19.17–18 indicates that it was honored among Jews, and Jesus commanded it (Mt 18.15–17; cf. Gal 6.1–2; Jas 2.1–17). BIBLIOGRAPHY: ThAq ST 2a2ae, 33; M. Nepper, DSAM 2:2404–2414.

CORRECTOR, title of superior of the Minim friars. The responsibility is for him to correct himself and then in paternal charity those in his care.

[M. R. BROWN]

CORRECTORIA. Two kinds of 13th–cent. book are so designated. (1) Biblical Correctoria. By the 13th cent. variant versions of the Latin Vulgate had proliferated to such an extent that the leaders of certain religious orders (notably the Dominicans and Franciscans) sought to produce corrected versions to be held in common by all the members of a given order. Because of a lack of critical method, however, the correctoria they produced were usually grossly inaccurate. The best example is the *Correctio textus biblici* compiled by the English Franciscan *William de la Mare. (2) Scholastic Correctoria are the Franciscan anti-Thomist and the Dominican pro-Thomist works important for the research into the early history of Thomism. The Franciscan William de la Mare in 1278 wrote his *Correctorium Fratris Thomae*; at least five Dominican correctories in rebuttal are known. BIBLIOGRAPHY: C. Spicq, *Esquisse d'une histoire de l'exégèse latine au Moyen Age* (1944) 165–172; D. A. Callus, NCE 4:349–352.

[D. J. BOURKE]

CORREGGIO (ANTONIO ALLEGRI; 1489–1534), Italian Renaissance painter. Born at Correggio, Parma, C. combined the *sfumato* effects of Leonardo and the Venetian style in a proto-Baroque not fully appreciated until the 17th century. Among his many paintings are an altar-piece, *Madonna of St. Francis* of broad forms and intense light; a *Nativity* and *Adoration of the Magi* (both in the Brera); the famous frescoes in the parlour of the Convent of S. Paolo (Parma); *Adoration of the Child* (Uffizi); and *The Marriage of St. Catherine* (Detroit), all filled with figures of smiling charm, luminous, feathery, and supremely elegant. C.'s cupola frescoes in the cathedral of S. Giovanni Evangelista, Parma (1520–30), led to the commission for the famous fresco of the *Assumption of the Virgin* (1524–30) in which C. "painted away" the cathedral dome in a dramatic, acute funneling of extreme illusionistic perspective. Of many nocturnal panels the Adoration of the Shepherds (*The Night*, *c*.1530) is most forceful. After 1530 C. left Parma. Com-

missioned by Federigo Gonzaga, Duke of Mantua, C. painted a mythological series of the loves of Jupiter, where suavely sensual forms (rivalling those of Titian) absorbed in hazy atmosphere, convey in concentrated essence C.'s style. BIBLIOGRAPHY: S. Bottari, *Correggio* (1961).

[M. J. DALY]

CORRIDO, a forceful woodcut in a satirical vein popular in Mexico, gaily colored and cheap, and reaching a climax in the 20th-cent. works of Possa who featured the *calaveras* (skeletons), familiar symbols in Mexican folk art.

[M. J. DALY]

CORRIGAN, MICHAEL AUGUSTINE (1839–1902), abp. of New York. Of Irish immigrant parents, C. was born in Newark, N. J., attended the North American College in Rome where he was ordained (1863), and received a doctorate in theology from the College of Propaganda (1864). He returned to the Newark diocese and served as teacher and administrator at Seton Hall College and Seminary in S. Orange and, after 1868, as vicar-general of the diocese. As bp. of Newark (1873–80), he advanced the spiritual and temporal affairs of his diocese, devoting particular attention to the immigrant problem, the establishment of educational and charitable institutions, and the implementation of the decrees of the Councils of Baltimore. In 1880 he was appointed coadjutor, with right of succession, to Card. John McCloskey of New York and succeeded to the see in 1885. His attempts to restrain the rector of St. Stephen's in New York City, Edward *McGlynn, who opposed parochial schools and actively supported the reformer Henry George, were singularly unsuccessful; and the controversy was settled only by Roman intervention. C.'s position on Catholic membership in secret societies and the issues involved in the so-called heresy of *Americanism put him in opposition to such liberals in the American hierarchy as *Gibbons and *Ireland. However, within his archdiocese, he was successful in reorganizing the various administrative departments, improving seminary education, advancing the construction of St. Patrick's Cathedral, and coping with the problems of the rapidly increasing Italian immigrants. BIBLIOGRAPHY: *Memorial of the Most Rev. M. A. Corrigan,* (comp. J. M. Farley et al. 1902); J. T. Ellis, *Life of James Cardinal Gibbons* (2 v., 1952).

[M. MCCARTHY]

CORSINI, prominent family of Florence, Italy. The family included St. Andrew Corsini (d. 1373) and Pope Clement XII (1730–40). There were many Corsinis prominent in the government of Florence and in the Church. Cardinal Pietro was a bp. and legate to Emperor Charles IV and was named Prince of the Empire in 1371. Cardinal Neri (d. 1678) was nuncio to France. A second Cardinal Neri (d. 1770) was representative of Cosimo III de'Medici at The Hague, London, and Paris. He added to the library begun by the first Cardinal Neri and Clement XII, a library given to the State in 1884. Cardinal Andrea (d. 1795) was an opponent of the Jesuits and sympathetic to the Jansenists. BIBLIOGRAPHY: L. Passerini, *Genealogia e storia della famiglia Corsini* (1858).

[J. R. AHERNE]

CORTESE, GREGORIO (Giovanni Andrea; 1483–1548), lawyer and humanist, abbot and cardinal. Legal adviser to the future Pope Leo X and auditor in the Curia, in 1507 C. became a Benedictine at Polirone. Writing to Leo X on his coronation, he urged him to general reform of the Church; meanwhile he pressed forward reform in his own order. C. fostered learning among the monks at Lérins, whence he had been summoned in 1516 to aid in the Cassinese reform and had been its prior and abbot. He served on the committee to report on abuses in the Church, was made cardinal by Paul III in 1542, and was placed permanently on the committee preparing for the Tridentine Council. C. was distinguished for his Latin writings; Bp. Gradenigo of Ceneda edited his works in two volumes, adding a vita (1774). In the academy C. had instituted at Lérins, students well-educated in the humanities were to form a bridge joining France to Italy in the humanistic revival. BIBLIOGRAPHY: M. Ott, CE 4:400–401.

[M. R. BROWN]

CORTONA, PIETRO DA (1596–1669), Baroque painter and architect, leader of high Baroque painting in Rome. His famous *Triumph of Divine Providence,* a ceiling fresco for the Barberini Palace (begun 1633), is rich in a new splendor and freedom, having particular reference to his patron Urban VIII, a Barberini. From 1637 to 1640 he worked chiefly in Florence, decorating the Sala della Stufa and the rooms of the planets in the Pitti palace. He rivaled Bernini and Borromini as architect of Baroque facades and superb domes. BIBLIOGRAPHY: G. Briganti, *Pietro da Cortona* (1962).

[L. P. SIGER]

CORVEY, ABBEY OF, Benedictine monastery founded in Westphalia (822) by Abbot Adalard and his brother Wala. It came to be an important center for the Christianization of the North and a cultural center of great influence. One of its first monks, Ansgar, set out (826) for Denmark and later Sweden to evangelize those areas, becoming known as the apostle of the North. Many of the monks of Corvey who labored with him later occupied sees in N Germany. Ansgar became the first bp. of Hamburg in 831 and later abp. of the joined Sees of Bremen and Hamburg. The abbey developed though the centuries a great library; the only extant MS of the Roman historian Tacitus was preserved there. The monks wrote a number of historical works, notably *Rerum gestarum Saxonicarum* by *Widukind. Corvey later was famous for its distinctive style of illuminating MSS, a style influencing illumination in N Europe. The abbey was destroyed in the wars following the

Reformation but was given new life by Christopher Bernard de Galen, bp. of Münster. In 1803 it became part of the diocesan organization and was suppressed as an abbey nullius. The territory of the abbey passed to Prussia in 1815. BIBLIOGRAPHY: A. Franzen, DHGE 13:922–925; G. Spahr, NCE 4:358–359.

[J. R. AHERNE]

COSIN, JOHN (1594–1672), Anglican bp. of Durham. A native of Norwich, educated at Caius College, Cambridge, C. aroused the hostility of the Puritans by his friendship with W. *Laud and R. Montagu, whose dedication to High Church principles he shared. Deprived of his benefices in 1640, he fled to Paris (1642), but with the Restoration he returned to England and was made bp. of Durham. C.'s writings were mainly polemical, for the most part directed against Roman Catholicism. His works were published in five volumes in the LACT (1843–45), the first volume containing a sketch of his life. BIBLIOGRAPHY: DNB 12 (1887) 264–271.

[R. B. ENO]

COSMAS AND DAMIAN, SS. (early 4th cent.), martyrs of whom nothing but the fact of their martyrdom is known with certainty. According to the basic legend, they were twin brothers of Arabian origin who practiced medicine in Aegeae in Cilicia. They took no money for their services and were in other respects also shining examples of Christian piety and virtue. During a period of persecution they were tortured and beheaded by Lysias, the governor of Cilicia. The legend is further embellished by other marvels. Their cult was popular in the East by the 5th cent. and became widespread in the West not long after. They are mentioned in the Canon of the Roman Mass among the martyrs esp. venerated at Rome, where a church was dedicated to them as early as 530. While certain elements of their legend can be paralleled by similar details in pagan mythology (the Dioscuri, Aesculapius), it cannot be asserted that the story is therefore without foundation. Cosmas and Damian, with St. *Luke, are the patrons of physicians. BIBLIOGRAPHY: Butler 3:659–661; R. G. Ryan, NCE 4:360–361; G. Schreiber, LTK 6:566–567.

[R. B. ENO]

COSMAS INDICOPLEUSTES (6th cent.), a merchant of Alexandria who traveled to regions far to the S and E of Egypt and gathered information on those lands and their inhabitants. He seems to have visited India or Ceylon. About 550 he wrote his *Christian Topography* in 12 books. In general his astronomical doctrines are bizarre and cut to the measure of his literal understanding of the biblical text. The most valuable of the 12 books is the 11th which describes the flora and fauna of Ceylon or India. He may have been a Nestorian. Toward the end of his life, he retired to the monastery of Raithu on the Sinai peninsula. BIBLIOGRA-

PHY: PG 88:9–476; critical ed. of his works by E. Winstedt (1909); Altaner 624.

[R. B. ENO]

COSMAS THE MELODIAN, ST. (d. *c.*770), hymnographer. According to fairly early but not well authenticated accounts, C. was the adopted brother of St. John Damascene and was educated with him by a Sicilian ascetic, also called Cosmas, who had been rescued from the slave-market in Damascus by St. John's wealthy father. Both brothers eventually withdrew to the laura of St. Sabas near Jerusalem. Whether or not this story is true, C. and John were certainly monks at St. Sabas at the same time. C. composed a number of hymns later included in the Byzantine office, esp. in the *Triodion*, the office for Lent. Some of these are canons (chants) in the style devised by St. Andrew of Crete in the previous century. If John's learning and experience as an administrator and controversialist provided much of the doctrinal substance in the hymns of C. as well as in his own, the style of those ascribed to Cosmas, with very few exceptions, is sufficiently homogeneous to make them recognizable as the work of a single poet. He became bp. of Maiouma in Palestine (743). BIBLIOGRAPHY: G. Caliò, BiblSanct 4:219–221; Beck 515–516; F. De Sa, NCE 4:360.

[G. EVERY]

COSMAS OF PRAGUE (*c.*1045–1125), chronicler. As a cleric and bishop's secretary he had occasion to travel extensively. Ordained in 1099, he became canon and dean of the cathedral chapter in Prague. His fame stems chiefly from his *Chronica Bohemorum,* the earliest extant chronicle of Bohemia, which is a detailed and reliable history to 1125. BIBLIOGRAPHY: L. Nemec, NCE 4:360.

COSMATI FAMILY, the name given to the marble decorators and builders active in Rome and vicinity from about the beginning of the 12th to the end of the 13th centuries. They are remembered chiefly for their polychrome decoration of ecclesiastical objects (ciboria, etc.), and sacred buildings (pavements, columns) inlaid with ornamental mosaic patterns of spirals, interlace, and discs. BIBLIOGRAPHY: E. Hutton, *Cosmati* (1950).

[L. A. LEITE]

COSMETIC SURGERY, i.e., an operation performed for the sole purpose of enhancing physical appearance; it presents a fairly easy moral problem. Its solution depends initially on sound medical prognosis. Theologically, surgery means *mutilation however foreign that may sound to medical ears. Moral justification then is sought in the quality and degree of benefit foreseen accruing to the patient. If that benefit is judged proportionate to the risk involved, no moral objection should be forthcoming on that score. But if risk notably outweighs likely advantages, the procedure is on this count open to criticism. A further factor might be, as

in the case of *cosmetics, a sinful intention, e.g., mastoplasty for sexual seductiveness. Again, operations like buttock-lifting when healthy exercise would serve the same purpose seem callous indifference in a world of want. BIBLIOGRAPHY: J. J. Lynch, NCE 4:361–362.

[J. J. LYNCH]

COSMETICS, preparations designed to conceal defects or enhance physical beauty; today they are generally used in a way which, despite the strictures of prophets (Is 3.16–24) and doctors of the church (ThAq ST 2a2ae, 169.2) do not constitute a serious, if any, violation of moral standards. The violation is more often to the canons of good taste. If—by way of relatively rare exception—these beauty aids are applied with sinful intent, e.g., sexual seduction, their use would have a morality corresponding to the motive. Beyond that, there is the question of the lavish expense employed on physical pulchritude while so many of God's children still need the essentials for decent sustenance. But of those most likely to read this paragraph for practical guidance, few need proceed beyond its initial sentence.

[J. J. LYNCH]

COSMOGENESIS, the process of evolution which accounts for the origin of the universe. The process, according to *Teilhard de Chardin, began with layers of cosmic dust in a state of expansion. The explosive force of the universe expanding placed great pressure on the subatomic particles of cosmic dust causing them to unite and condense, forming more complex structures. Under the cosmic pressure, subatomic particles moved to atoms, atoms to molecules, micra-molecules to mega-molecules, inorganic compounds to organic compounds. Within this process of expansion and condensation, our universe with its suns and planets came forth. BIBLIOGRAPHY: Teilhard de Chardin, *Phenomenon of Man* (1959); *idem, Future of Man* (1964). *NOOSPHERE.

[W. J. DUGGAN]

COSMOGONY (IN THE BIBLE), the biblical view of the universe. The Babylonians, Egyptians, Sumerians, and Phoenicians as well as the Hebrews accepted the same general, popular, and unscientific world picture, based on visual experience. The Hebrews, however, were unique in claiming that the world was the creation of God and as such belonged to him. Hebrew has no special word for universe or world, but uses the expressions "heaven(s) and earth" (Gen 1.1; 2.1,3), or the three-tiered description "heaven above, earth beneath, or water under the earth" (Ex 20.4) to describe the world. In this construct the sky (firmament) was a solid dome (Gen 1.6; Job 37.18) resting on high mountains (Job 26.11). It separated the upper and lower waters (Ex 20.4; Ps 148.4). Through trapdoors or windows in this dome escaped the rain, snow, wind, hail, light, and darkness (Job 37.18; 38.22; Pr 8.27; Gen 7.11). God's abode was in the highest heaven above the upper waters; the sun, moon, and stars moved in the middle heaven, and the birds flew in the lower heaven. The earth, an immense disc, floating on a primitive sea, was anchored by foundations sunk deep in the lower waters of the great abyss (Job 9.6; 38.4–6). This explains how earthquakes shaking the earth made the earth seem like a boat tossed about on turbulent waters (Ps 23.2; Job 38.4.11). Sheol, the land of the dead, was in the darkest region of the universe. BIBLIOGRAPHY: T. H. Gaster, InterDB 1:702–709.

[F. J. MONTALBANO]

COSMOLOGY, literally the study *(logos)* of the universe *(cosmos)*. The term is sometimes used of scientific theories on the origin of the universe. In philosophy the term has been used as a synonym for the *philosophy of nature, the philosophical study of changeable being. The usage derives from C. *Wolff; he divided philosophy, as the study of how beings are possible, into ontology, on general laws, cosmology, on the world, psychology, on man; theology, on God. The terminology, along with Wolff's conception of philosophy, was taken over by some 18th- and 19th-cent. scholastic manuals of philosophy.

[T. C. O'BRIEN]

COSSA, FRANCESCO DEL (*c.*1435–77), Italian artist who painted for the Duke of Ferrara at the Palazzo Schifanoia a cycle of months with imagery of astrology, pagan divinities, and human occupations, a dramatic expression of secular art of the early Italian Renaissance. In Bologna C. painted an Annunciation, and the Griffoni and Mercanzia altarpieces. His earlier linear intricacies are balanced by majestic sculptural mass showing influences of Andrea Mantegna and Piero della Francesca.

[M. J. DALY]

COSTA RICA, a Central American republic (19,653 sq mi; pop. [est. 1976] 1,925,179), bounded by its Pacific and Carib. coastlines, by Nicaragua on the N and by Panama on the E. Its population is 80% white, a little more than 17% mestizo, 2% Negro, and less than 1% pure Indian. Catholics numbered (1976) 1,852,021 (96.2%). It was discovered by Columbus (1502) on his fourth voyage; its conquest was not complete till 1563. Civilly it became part of the captaincy general of Guatemala and ecclesiastically it was under the jurisdiction of the Diocese of León de Nicaragua. Independence from Spain was achieved in 1821, and Costa Rica was part of the Central American Federation until 1839, from which time it has been an independent and sovereign state. In 1871 a concession was granted to the United Fruit Co. (a domestic business largely funded, however, by U.S. investors), for the exploitation of Costa Rica's banana potential. Education was made free and compulsory. The revolution of Otilio Ulate (1948) eliminated the army as a permanent institution. Ulate's presidency was followed by the leftist regime of José Figueres (1953–58), and this by the more moderate governments of M. Jiménez,

F. Orlich, and José Joaquin Trejos. Costa Rica has been known for the stability of its government and its fairly prosperous economy.

In the 16th cent. the country was evangelized mainly by the Franciscans, among whom was Pedro de *Betanzos, noted both for his knowledge of the Indian tongues and his great concern for the welfare of those to whom he brought the faith. By the end of the 18th cent., the Church in Costa Rica showed clear signs of decadence. In the second half of the 19th cent., the Capuchins by their pastoral and catechetical activities did much to improve the situation. In 1850 the bishopric of San José was established, giving Costa Rica for the first time a bp. of its own. The first constitutions of the republic (1844, 1847) were favorable to the Church, and a concordat was concluded in 1852. Other cults were authorized in 1860, and an open attack upon the Church began in 1884: the bishop was exiled; diplomatic relations with Rome were broken; the Jesuits were expelled; cemeteries were nationalized; the clergy was forced to accept secularized education; and monastic orders were excluded from the land. Many of the restrictions were rescinded by the constitution of 1949 through the influence of Martínez Víctor Sanabria, second Abp. of San José (a metropolitan see from 1921). Catholicism is the state religion; religious instruction is compulsory in the schools; the State supports the clergy with 1% of its income. Divorce is permitted and abortion is legalized. Costa Rica has five dioceses: San José, San Isidro de El General, Tilarán, Alajuela, and Limón. There were 381 priests (1976), 262 diocesan. There were 145 (1976) parishes. There is a great need for more priests, for a more thorough religious instruction, and for a healthier Christian atmosphere in the home and in public life. There is some cause for encouragement. More help is coming from religious orders; systematic work is going forward in the social field; and some of the laity are being prepared for a more active role. The main Protestant groups represented in C.R. are the Latin-American Mission, the Central-American Mission, the Methodists, and the Pentecostal sects. These operate a school of languages for missionaries, a publishing house, and a radio station. The total membership of the Protestant community is about 40,000; there are 134 missionaries and 90 national ministers and auxiliaries.

[P. DAMBORIENA]

COTIN, CHARLES (1604–82), French writer and preacher, member of the Académie Française (1655). Counselor first, then almoner to the King, C. frequented the *précieux* society of the Hôtel de Rambouillet. While his verses merited for him ridicule by Boileau as well as Molière, who satirized him as Trissotin in *Les Femmes savantes,* his ability as a preacher seems to have been respected by many of his contemporaries, who attended his 16 series of Lenten sermons delivered in prominent Parisian churches. Well-versed in Latin, Greek, Hebraic, and Syriac literature, he revealed his erudition in such works as *La*

Jérusalem désolée, ou méditation sur les leçons de ténèbres (1634) and *La Pastorale sacrée* (1662, a paraphrase of the Song of Solomon). Some of his other works are: *Recueil des énigmes de ce temps* (1646); *Rondeaux* (1650); *Poésies chrétiennes* (1657); *Oeuvres galantes en prose et en vers* (1663, 1665); and *La Ménagerie* (1666, attacking Gilles Ménage). BIBLIOGRAPHY: E. C. Buisson, *Les Victimes de Boileau: l'abbé Cotin* (1895).

[R. N. NICOLICH]

COTON, PIERRE (1564–1626), French Jesuit, preacher, controversialist. Trained by St. Robert Bellarmine, he became a staunch defender of the Church against the Huguenots in S France and instrumental in the establishment of the Jesuits in France in 1603. He was confessor to Henri IV and the future Louis XIII, but frequent attacks at court caused his disgrace in 1617. His chief works, vigorously contested by his opponents, the Anti-Cotonists, include *L'Institution catholique* (1610) and *Lettre déclaratoire de la doctrine des Pères Jésuites* (1618). He was acquainted with many spiritual writers of the period, esp. *Bérulle. His own spirituality resembles that of St. Francis de Sales.

[I. M. KASHUBA]

COTTA, shortened *surplice, with less ample sleeves.

COTTAM, THOMAS, BL. (1549–82), Jesuit martyr. C. was educated at Brasenose College, Oxford. He was converted to the Catholic faith in London, studied for the priesthood at Douai, France (where he was ordained in 1580), and sought to become a Jesuit but was refused admission because of his frail health. He left for the English mission in 1580, only to be arrested as soon as he landed at Dover. He was imprisoned, subjected to torture, and finally condemned and executed in 1582. While he was awaiting execution, he made his profession as a Jesuit. He was beatified in 1886. BIBLIOGRAPHY: Butler 2:416; C. Testore, BiblSanct 4:273–274.

COTTOLENGO, GIUSEPPE BENEDETTO, ST. (1786–1842), Italian founder of several religious orders, most notably the Piccola Casa della Divina Providenza (Little House of Divine Providence) in 1832. C. earned a doctorate in theology after his ordination (1811). The example of St. Vincent de Paul inspired him both in his personal dedication to the sick and in his foundation of several religious communities. These formed a network of service institutions to the needy, the handicapped, the ill, and the destitute. He joined Marianna Nasi in the foundation of the Sisters of St. Vincent de Paul (1834). This consortium of foundations flourished. C. was beatified in 1917 and canonized in 1934. BIBLIOGRAPHY: J. Cottino, BiblSanct 6:1310–17; Butler 2:191–192.

[J. R. RIVELLO]

COTTON, JOHN (1584–1652), leader in Puritan New England. Born in Derby, Eng., educated at Cambridge, where he was imbued with Puritan ideas, C. early adopted *congregational principles but did not experience conversion until 1612. In that year he was called to St. Botolph's Church, Boston (Eng.), and, despite scruples against the *BCP and certain ceremonies, remained there 20 years. By 1633, finding his position untenable, he resolved to emigrate to the Massachusetts Bay Colony. Already 48 years old, he had won a reputation as a scholar and preacher and had been associated with the leading Puritans of his day. On arrival, he was chosen teacher of the church in new Boston and soon became a popular preacher. In the episodes that led to the expulsion of Roger *Williams and Anne *Hutchinson, he tried to play a mediating role. In politics his theocratic ideas helped to shape New England government. His views on Church and State provided a springboard for Roger Williams's *The Bloudy Tenent of Persecution* (1644), and his rejoinder led to *The Bloody Tenent Yet More Bloody* (1652). During the English Civil Wars, he declined an invitation to the *Westminster Assembly of Divines; and as New England sought to avoid Presbyterian polity, the Synod of 1648 embodied in the *Cambridge Platform ideas from Cotton's *The Keyes of the Kingdom of Heaven* (1644) and *The Way of the Churches of Christ in New England* (1645). BIBLIOGRAPHY: L. Ziff, *Career of John Cotton: Puritanism and the American Experience* (1962); *John Cotton on the Churches of New England* (ed. L. Ziff, 1968).

[N. H. MARING]

COTTON GENESIS, early Christian illuminated MS of the Book of Genesis from Alexandria, now in the British Museum, London.

[M. J. DALY]

COUDERC, MARIE VICTOIRE THÉRÈSE, ST. (1805–85), French foundress of the Religious of Our Lady of the Cenacle. Originally, C. was a member of a teaching congregation. While at La Louvesc where she was assigned, a transformation took place within the congregation, and eventually the new Congregation of the Cenacle was formed. C. served a short time as its superior but she renounced that position in a gesture of humility (1837). The beginning years of the congregation were marked by internal turmoil and financial troubles. It perdured in spite of these conflicts, and its humble foundress was beatified by Pope Pius XII (1951) and canonized by Pope Paul VI (1970). BIBLIOGRAPHY: Butler 3:658–659; A. Combes, BiblSanct 4:275–278.

[J. R. RIVELLO]

COUDRIN, PIERRE MARIE JOSEPH (1768–1837), religious founder. He was ordained secretly (1792) during the French Revolution. The ordination took place in the library of the Irish Seminary in Paris because the revolutionaries had taken over the chapel and were actually holding meeting there. During that same year he worked (still secretly) in the Dioceses of Poitiers and Tours. In 1800 he solemnly took his religious vows, devoting himself entirely to love of the Sacred Hearts of Jesus and Mary and founded the missionary society of men, Fathers of the *Sacred Hearts (Picpus Fathers) and *Picpus Sisters, both papally approved in 1817. C. also served as vicar general for the Dioceses of Rouen, Mende, Séez, and Troyes.

COUGHLIN, MARY SAMUEL, MOTHER (1868–1959), educator and superior. In 1886 she received the Dominican habit of the Congregation of the Most Holy Rosary and in 1910 was elected superior general. Her long direction of the community produced incredible achievement, including the establishment of 63 foundations. In 1918 she founded Rosary College in Illinois and in 1927 Edgemont College of the Sacred Heart in Wisconsin. Other foundations were Villa des Fougères in Fribourg, Switzerland (1917), and the Pius XII Institute in Florence, Italy (1948), a graduate school of fine arts. Among her distinctive works were founding a catechetical center and five schools for blacks, as well as receiving black candidates into the community. BIBLIOGRAPHY: M. McCarty, *Sinsinawa Dominicans: Outlines of Twentieth Century Development* (1952).

[J. R. AHERNE]

COULTON, GEORGE GORDON (1858–1947), scholar and teacher of medieval history. English-born, C. was educated in England and France. Ordained an Anglican deacon in 1883, he later gave up the clerical life to teach, a work he pursued for 30 years in preparatory schools and then at Cambridge. An authority on medieval history, C. wrote many books, esp. on ecclesiastical history, among which are *Five Centuries of Religion* (4 v., 1923–50) and *Inquisition and Liberty* (1938). A critic of medieval monasticism, C. was regarded by Catholic writers of his day as a controversial though scholarly historian. BIBLIOGRAPHY: J. T. Covert, NCE 4:370.

[C. R. CAWLEY]

COUNCIL, CONGREGATION OF THE, see CLERGY, CONGREGATION OF THE.

COUNCIL FOR THE ADVANCEMENT OF SMALL COLLEGES (CASC), an educational organization established in 1956 to advise accredited or nonaccredited, small, non–tax-supported, 4-year liberal arts colleges granting a bachelor's degree. CASC conducts annual summer workshops on curriculum and issues a monthly newsletter. Membership includes many church-related small colleges.

[M. B. MURPHY]

COUNCIL OF BISHOPS (METHODIST), an official body composed of all the bishops of all the Jurisdictional and Central Conferences. The Council of Bishops was not a traditional constitutional body within Methodism, but was instituted at the Uniting Conference of the three major American Methodist bodies, which formed the *Methodist Church in 1939. It meets at least annually, planning "for the . . . oversight and promotion of the temporal and spiritual interests of the entire church and for carrying into effect the rules, regulations, and responsibilities prescribed and enjoined by the General Conference. . . ." *(Discipline).* The Council annually elects a president and chooses the bishop to deliver the episcopal address (state of the Church message) at the General Conference. By a two-thirds vote, it may call a special session of the *General Conference. BIBLIOGRAPHY: *Doctrines and Discipline of the Methodist Church* (1964) index; HistAmMeth 3:463–464.

[F. E. MASER]

COUNCIL OF THE TWELVE APOSTLES, in the Church of Jesus Christ of Latter-day Saints (Mormons), the body that, subordinated to the *First Presidency, oversees the Church and ordains its ministers. Members are chosen by the revelation that Mormons believe continually to be given to the Church, esp. through its president.

[T. C. O'BRIEN]

COUNCILS (ROMAN CATHOLIC), official church meetings convoked to deliberate doctrinal or disciplinary issues of common concern. The Code of Canon Law, reflecting historical precedent, divides councils geographically: diocesan synods and provincial councils deal with local and regional problems; *ecumenical councils, both in representation and in breadth of concern, are worldwide and exercise supreme authority over the whole Church.

[B. L. MARTHALER]

COUNSEL, a gift of the Holy Spirit, a complement to the cardinal virtue of prudence and esp. to that part of it called *euboulia,* i.e., the condition of being well advised. Even the best practical judgment left to its own devices would find itself baffled in the human environment by thronging individual incidents, were it not lifted up and instructed by God who comprehends everything, even the least and most fugitive factors in a situation. This prudential flair, though esp. pronounced as an exceptional prophetic gift, a *gratia gratis data* (cf. 1 Cor ch. 12), is a normal accompaniment of living in God's grace; by it people are helped to come to decisions, as it were, beyond their own psychological resources, and without anxiously looking back for reassurance. It is the remedy for scruples. Theological tradition accepts St. Augustine's apt matching of it with the fifth Beatitude, "Blessed are the merciful, for they will find mercy." For what makes us more like God than this, in a shifting world which cannot be wholly reduced to our reasons and duties and rights? BIBLIOGRAPHY: ThAq ST 2a2ae, 52.

[T. GILBY]

COUNSELING. Ethical considerations about counseling are founded in the counselor–counselee relationship. It is ethically adequate insofar as it truly develops the relationship of persons; inadequate insofar as it is destructive of that. There are three interrelated matters concerning which important ethical questions are most likely to arise for a counselor: professional competence, psychic privacy, confidentiality.

Professional competency involves adequate professional preparation, continuing self-evaluation, appropriate skill in applying tests, a reasonable certainty that he and his organization have the resources for giving the kind of help they claim able to give, an awareness on the part of the counselor of his own personality strengths and limitations.

The counselee's intimate life may not be probed without his free, informed consent, even when it is judged that it would be helpful to the counselee to do so. Withholding information or providing misinformation to a counselee for the purpose of psychic evaluation is morally unjustifiable.

As regards confidential information, the counselor's role is to be helpful to the one who is freely sharing his inner life; his role is not to lead the life of the one who freely shares himself. He is bound not to reveal the confidential material without the free, informed consent of the owner of the secret; this is a requirement postulated for social living. BIBLIOGRAPHY: E. F. Falteisek, "Ethical Considerations for Counselors," *The Catholic High School Quarterly Bulletin* 24 (1966) 37–42; idem, "Moral Adequacy of Present Codes of Ethics for Counselors," *National Catholic Guidance Conference* 9 (1964) 38–39; D. Pond, *Counseling in Religion and Psychiatry* (1973).

[E. F. FALTEISEK]

COUNSELS, EVANGELICAL, advisory directives that enable a person to imitate Jesus Christ; traditionally they include active love of enemies, poverty, chastity, and obedience. These counsels, based on the words and example of Christ, differ from the Commandments or *precepts binding on all for salvation; counsels are embraced freely for a more perfect fulfillment of the comand to love God and neighbor wholeheartedly. The counsels are practiced both privately and in community forms of religious life. They derive from certain passages in the NT. Virginity, in Matthew 19:11–12, indicates a gift from God not granted to all Christians. Poverty finds support in the incident of the rich man in Mark 10:17, and obedience is implicit in the call to service in Mark 9:34. BIBLIOGRAPHY: J. D. Gerken, NCE 4:383–384.

[V. GILLIGAN]

COUNTER REFORMATION, a name for the spiritual revival, administrative renovation, and political confrontation whereby Roman Catholicism responded to the challenge of the Reformation of the 16th century. The name, coined by the 19th-cent. church historian L. von Ranke, is unsatisfactory insofar as RC reform anteceded the Reformation and was partially independent of it. On the strictly spiritual and ecclesiastical side, the groundwork of Catholic reform was laid by Christian humanists, e.g., Erasmus, and by men of a more ecclesiastical type, e.g., Ximénez de Cisneros (1436–1517) and the founders of the Oratory of Divine Love—all prior to the Reformation. The movement effectively entered the service of the papacy under Paul III (1534–49). The papacy would thereafter retain the direction of reform, though it was given a more militant turn under Paul IV (1555–59), who earlier inspired the Roman Inquisition (1542). He instituted the Index of Forbidden Books (1558) and an uncompromising if despotic reform of morals. The reorganization of the Roman Curia under Sixtus V in 1588 created the modern papal bureaucracy. The manpower for reform came particularly from such new or reformed religious orders as the Theatines, Capuchins, Oratorians, and above all the Jesuits, founded by St. Ignatius Loyola in 1540. Other key personalities of reform were SS. Charles Borromeo, Teresa of Avila, John of the Cross, Vincent de Paul, and Francis de Sales. Their characteristic piety was sacramental, dynamic, and often mystical. This spirit dominates the Baroque art of the time. The most conspicuous institutional aspect of reform was the Council of *Trent (1545–63). Trent belatedly clarified doctrine and provided the reform decrees that, along with the resurgent papacy, shaped RC history up to the mid-20th century. Conflicting conceptions of a *general council militated against effective Protestant attendance, and Trent's generally anti-Protestant stance confirmed the religious schism.

The phrase "Counter Reformation" has its most apt application to political history, particularly the Wars of Religion. Here the leading Catholic champion was the Habsburgs. After the failure of his earlier efforts to conciliate the German Lutherans, the Holy Roman Emperor, Charles V (1519–56), resorted to the Schmalkaldic War (1546–55). This ended in stalemate and the Religious Peace of *Augsburg (1555), which allowed toleration for Lutherans. The Counter-Reformation entered its major phase about 1559, when the son of Charles, Philip II (1556–98) of Spain, and Henry II (1547–59) of France terminated the long Italian wars for a concerted effort to eradicate Protestantism. The last chance for religious reunion in France was the Colloquy of *Poissy (1561), followed by 30 years of religious and civil wars, including the infamous *St. Bartholomew's Day Massacre (1572). Philip of Spain's reign was marked by efforts to subdue the rebellious Netherlands, intervene in France, and settle accounts with England, highlighted by the disastrous Armada, 1588. The final phase of the Counter-Reformation was the largely political Thirty Years' War, terminated by the Peace of *Westphalia in 1648. The Counter-Reformation failed to restore religious unity primarily because it became too identified with

Habsburg power. Henceforth, religion was a diminishing feature in politics and the Protestant-Catholic schism a reluctantly accepted fact. BIBLIOGRAPHY: P. Janelle, *Catholic Reformation* (1949); H. O. Evennett, *Spirit of the Counter Reformation* (1968); H. Daniel-Rops, *Catholic Reformation* (tr. J. Warrington, *History of the Church*, v. 5, 1962); E. L. Lampe, NCE 4:384–389; A. G. Dickens, *Counter Reformation* (1969).

[D. G. NUGENT]

COUNTERPOINT (Lat. *punctus contra punctum*, point against point), in music, a type of *polyphony, specifically the art of writing two or more melodic lines to be played together so that the listener's attention is constantly made to shift from one voice to the next without losing awareness either of the harmony of the whole or the individuality of the parts. Originally the term referred to the notation of polyphonic music in which each note appeared as a point (*punctus*). BIBLIOGRAPHY: F. Davis and D. Lybbert, *Essentials of Counterpoint* (1970); K. Kennan, *Counterpoint* (2d ed., 1972).

[J. NEWSOM]

COUNTESS OF HUNTINGDON'S CONNEXION, a federation of chapels, having no central ecclesiastical authority, established in England by the Countess of *Huntingdon in the 18th century. After building a large number of chapels and using C of E clergymen as ministers, she began employing unordained Methodist preachers trained in her college at Trevecca, Wales. Invoking the *Toleration Act, she formally established the Countess of Huntingdon's Connexion, ordaining her first ministers in 1783. Presbyterian in policy, Anglican in liturgy and *Calvinistic Methodist in theology, the chapels were independent of each other, and many joined other denominations. There were (1968) about 3,500 members, with 37 chapels in England. *CONNEXION.

COUPERIN, FRANÇOIS (1668–1733), most illustrious member of a distinguished family of French organists and composers. Son of Charles Couperin, his first teacher, he was later the pupil of J. D. Thomelin, organist of the King's Chapel. C. held the positions of organist at St. Gervais, organist of the Royal Chapel, and clavecinist at Versailles, where he stood in high favor with the king and earned the title "le Grand." C. wrote religious and secular vocal music, organ Masses for the Catholic liturgy, and instrumental chamber music. Influenced by Corelli and the first to introduce into France the trio-sonata for violins and continuo, C. was, however, most important for his works devoted to the harpsichord. His compositions indicate a definite break with the Baroque and inaugurated the period of musical Rococo. His treatise *L'Art de toucher la clavecin* influenced the keyboard style of his great contemporary J. S. Bach.

[M. T. LEGGE]

COUPPÉ, LOUIS (1850–1926), missionary. Born in France and ordained at 24, C. joined the Sacred Heart Missionaries in 1880. Serving in Melanesia he established a headquarters for his community in Australia. During his missionary journeys in the S continent, he made several exploratory voyages in New Guinea. He established a mission headquarters at Rabaul and soon became its first vicar apostolic (1890–1923). He thus opened the way to a developing culture and educational system among the tribes of Guantana, where he established formal schools and workshops in farming and carpentry. At his death, his mission numbered approximately 30,000 Catholics and catechumens, and 150 priests and religious, of whom many were natives. Just before his death he was consecrated titular abp. of Hieropolis. BIBLIOGRAPHY: H. Wiedemann, LTK 3:79.

[R. C. EGAN]

COURAGE, VIRTUE OF, the cardinal *virtue of steadfastness in pursuing the good through control of adverse feelings attendant on the arduousness of the pursuit. Aristotle (*Ethics* III,6–9) takes as the noblest model of moral courage the soldier in battle who neither deserts his post out of fear of mortal danger nor plunges to the attack in foolhardy disregard of danger. He also notes that "the courageous man endures the terrors and dares the deeds that manifest courage for the sake of a noble cause" (*ibid.* III,7.1115b25). St. Thomas Aquinas incorporates Aristotle's model and language into his treatise on courage (ThAq ST 2a2ae. 123–140), but also quotes from the Stoics, Cicero and Seneca esp., and from the Christian writers, esp. St. Ambrose and St. Augustine. As in other theological matters, he transforms almost imperceptibly the meaning of courage in the light of the Gospel. The noblest example of the virtue is *martyrdom; but the most applicable meaning for Christian life is endurance amid the fears and sorrows attendant on hardships and losses sustained for love of God above all. Christian courage, patterned on Christ's own words and example, means above all *patience, which controls fear, grief, even boredom, occasioned by the loss of physical and psychological comforts or even necessities, as taking up the cross of Christ demands. Thus it rests on faith in the supremacy of life with God over all other human values, and is a steadfastness that corresponds to the fixity of *charity and *hope in God as the supreme object of love and of desire. The firm connection of Christian courage with the reality, the true existence of Christian goals and ideals, puts it at a diametrical remove from the atheistic existentialists' "courage to be." For this is the naked will to affirm and accept one's own existence in the face of absurdity and dread, because there is no "essence" and no ideal, but only death and nothingness.

[T. C. O'BRIEN]

COURBET, GUSTAVE (1819–77), French artist, political activist, and a strong revolutionary force in 19th-cent. painting who introduced the school of realism. Rejecting abstract ideals and poetic effects, and contemptuous of academic standards, C. saw all life as the proper subject of art, recording all the world about him, a richly sensuous brush and knife technique concealing occasional crudity in drawing. Of great natural talent and independence, C. painted the dramatically and elegantly designed *Self-portrait with Dog* (1842), *Man with the Pipe* (1846), the *Stonebreakers* and the monumental *Funeral at Ornans*. His socially realistic panels were termed vulgar and trivial. Rejected by the Academy, C. erected his own Pavilion of Realism (1855), hanging among 40 works the now famous *Studio of the Artist* showing himself painting surrounded by complex groups of people both historical and allegorical with characteristic social overtones. By 1867 C. was admired by critics and painters alike. A militant anarchist, C. was imprisoned in 1870 and finally fled into Switzerland (1873) after the fall of the Commune. There he continued to paint through his last years. BIBLIOGRAPHY: G. Mack, *Gustave Courbet* (1951).

[M. J. DALY]

COURCY DE LAROCHE-HÉRON, HENRI DE, see DE COURCY, HENRY.

COURT (PRESBYTERIAN), any of the governing bodies in *Presbyterianism; also called a judicatory. *CHURCH SESSION; *PRESBYTERY; *SYNOD; *GENERAL AS-SEMBLY.

COURT, PAPAL, see CURIA ROMANA.

COURT OF ARCHES, see ARCHES, COURT OF.

COURTENAY, PETER (d. 1492), bp. of Exeter (1478), translated to Winchester (1487). He plotted against both Henry IV and Richard III, was implicated in an unsuccessful insurrection in Cornwall in 1484, and upon its failure fled to Brittany but returned with Henry VII (1485) under whom he became keeper of the privy seal (1485–87). BIBLIOGRAPHY: T. F. Tout, DNB 4:264–265; Emden Ox 1:499–500.

[A. WARDLE]

COURTENAY, RICHARD (*c.*1381–1415), Oxford university chancellor (1406–08, 1411–13), bp. of Norwich (1413–15). For resisting the anti-Lollard visitation of Abp. Arundel, he temporarily lost his position as chancellor (1411). He regulated and enlarged the university library. After an unsuccessful peace mission to France (1414), he died at the Battle of Harfleur. BIBLIOGRAPHY: J. Dahmus, NCE 4:392; T. F. Tout, DNB 4:1265–67.

[F. D. BLACKLEY]

COURTENAY, WILLIAM (*c.*1342–96), bp. of Hereford (1370–75), London (1375–81), abp. of Canterbury (1381–96). Son of the earl of Devon, C. gave firm leadership, condemning Wycliffe's doctrines and purging Oxford of heresy (1382). He resisted parliamentary attempts to curb papal powers (1390, 1391). BIBLIOGRAPHY: J. Dahmus, NCE 3:393; W. Hunt, DNB 4:1267–72.

[F. D. BLACKLEY]

COURTESY (POLITENESS), in common speech, good manners; in moral theology, a part of justice or fairness by which one shows himself kindly and considerate in his social exchanges. Aristotle recognized it as a sort of friendship *(philia),* though there is no proper term for this mean between obsequiousness and flattery on one side and surliness and quarrelsomeness on the other. Roman moralists spoke of it as *urbanitas,* the scholastics as *amicitia,* which can be translated "friendliness," and affability. It is not the same as love or charity, although its exercise may be—and in the case of a person who lives in God's grace normally is—directed to the end of charity. Theologians classified it as a form of justice because it is concerned with something owed to others, yet it falls short of justice in the narrower sense because what is "owed" cannot be demanded as of strict right. The function of courtesy is to reduce to a minimum the friction likely to develop in social relationships by reason of human aggressiveness and self-concern. Although it is not among the highest ranking virtues, it is nevertheless a necessary one, for without the candor and congeniality it affords, Christian men would not be able to live comfortably together. Therefore H. Belloc could say: "Of Courtesy is is much less/ Than courage of heart or holiness/ Yet in my walk it seems to me/ That the grace of God is in Courtesy." BIBLIOGRAPHY: ThAq ST 2a2ae, 114–116; Aristotle, *Nicomachean Ethics* 4.6.

COURTET, GUILLAUME (d. 1637), French Dominican missionary. C. served as novice master and later as professor of theology at Toulouse but was expelled from his order for some serious but unrecorded fault. Repentant, he was permitted to join the Philippine province. He and three companions entered Japan secretly to engage in missionary work but were apprehended and barbarously executed. BIBLIOGRAPHY: A. Duval, *Catholicisme* 3:249–250.

[M. J. SUELZER]

COURTLY LOVE, a powerful and complex cultural current originating in Provence and France in the 12th cent.; it reoriented woman's role to one of dominance and judgment over man's behavior. The "Court of Love" of Marie de Champagne attracted Chrétien de Troyes and Andreas Capellanus; the latter's *Art of Courtly Love* ruled that obstacles purify love, that marriage and love are incompatible, that lovers submit totally to love's dictates. BIBLIOGRAPHY: Valency, *In Praise of Love* (1958); D. de Rougemont: *Love and the Western World* (1956); and A. J. Denomy, *Heresy of Courtly Love* (1947); K. Foster, *Courtly Love and Christianity* (1963).

[J. P. WILLIMAN]

COURTS, ECCLESIASTICAL, see TRIBUNALS, ECCLESIASTICAL

COUSIN, VICTOR (1792–1867), French philosopher and founder of *eclecticism as an explicitly held modern position. He was born in Paris to a working-class family. After studies at the École Normale, he became assistant to P. P. Royer-Collard (1763–1843) there and professor in 1830. C. held that there are four systems—idealism, materialism, scepticism, and mysticism—and that all four must be brought into a higher unity to arrive at the full truth. He became a peer of France, director of the École Normale, and minister of public education. He reorganized and centralized the primary educational system and established philosophical freedom in the universities. He continued to write after his retirement in 1851. He died in Cannes. His influence in philosophy was significant for a time but declined with the rise of *positivism.

[T. EARLY]

COUSINS, MARRIAGE OF, see CONSANGUINITY.

COUSSEMAKER, EDMOND DE (1805–76), French musicologist and jurist. While pursuing his law studies at Paris and later at Douai, C. also studied violin, cello, harmony, and composition. His interest in history and archeology led him to make musical research his avocation. He published a great number of valuable treatises on medieval music: medieval instruments (1845), the rise of polyphony (1852), and medieval drama (1861). He composed a few Masses and other church music and published a volume of songs, besides editing the works of the 13th-cent. trouvère-composer, Adam de la Halle. His series, *Scriptorum de musica medii aevi nova* (4 v., 1864–76), a collection of medieval treatises on music, is a sequel to the *Scriptores ecclesiastici* of the 18th-cent. priest-historian Martin Gerbert, and with it forms one of the most important collections of early sources of music scholarship.

[J. S. PALLOZZA]

COUSTANT, PIERRE (1654–1721), Benedictine scholar and writer. Among his most important literary contributions are the editing of the works of St. Hilary of Poitiers and a general index to the works of St. Augustine. He planned to edit the letters of the popes from St. Clement I to Innocent III, but this work was delayed because of his involvement in controversy. Only one volume, containing letters from 67–440 was published; Jansenist opposition impeded the rest of the work. In addition to his literary talents, C. was known for his deep humility and piety. BIBLIOGRAPHY: Y. Chaussy, *Catholicisme* 3:257; M. Ott, CE 4:454–455.

[I. M. KASHUBA]

COUSTOU, French sculptors, brothers who studied under their father François and their uncle C. A. *Coysevox: (1) Nicolas (1658–1733), member and professor of the Royal Academy of France. Among his many commissions from the crown was sculpture for the royal palaces at Versailles (Trianon) and at Marly. His most important religious work was *Descent from the Cross* (1725) for the high altar at Notre Dame. (2) **Guillaume,** (1677–1746), director of the Royal Academy, who executed the famous Horses of Marly (*Chevaux de Marly,* 1740–45), a Mars and a Minerva for the Invalides, and for the Versailles chapel the Pietà of the High Altar and Jesus in the Temple, among countless other works. Both brothers worked in a reserved classical Baroque.

[M. J. DALY]

COUTANCES, CATHEDRAL OF NOTRE DAME (1218–74), finest extant example of 13th-cent. Norman Gothic, with 14th-cent. additions in name chapels and axial Lady chapel, its chevet with seven radiating chapels recalling Amiens and Beauvais.

[M. J. DALY]

COUTURIER, PAUL (1881–1953), French Trappist, ecumenist. C. was the leading spirit of the Ecumenical Conversations carried on (1937–55) at Les Dombes, the Trappist monastery near Lyons. The publications of the group are a monument to his vision, energy, and dedication. BIBLIOGRAPHY: M. Villain, *Paul Couturier, apôtre de l'unité chrétienne* (1957).

[M. J. SUELZER]

COUTURIER, PIERRE MARIE ALAIN (1897–1954), French Dominican priest and artist, pioneer in modern liturgical art. After WW I C. worked with M. Denis and G. Desvallières in their newly found Ateliers d'Art Sacré. He joined the Dominicans (1925) and was ordained priest (1930). C. executed frescoes and stained glass in houses of his order and became codirector of the review *Art Sacré* (1937 to WW II; 1946–54). In America during WW II (College of Notre Dame, Baltimore), he lectured variously and published *Art et Catholicisme* (1941). In France after 1946 he helped achieve building the controversial churches at Assy, Vence, Audincourt and Renchamp. BIBLIOGRAPHY: *Art Sacré* (May-June 1954).

[R. J. VEROSTKO]

COVARRUBBIAS, ALONSO DE (1488–1570), Spanish sculptor and architect of conservative style, who executed the portal for the Church of La Piedad, Guadalajara (1526) and work in Sigüenza and Toledo. As royal architect (1534–53), C. designed the Alcázar, Toledo (1537) and the archbishop's palace in Alcalá (*c.*1540).

[M. J. DALY]

COVARRUBIAS Y LEYVA, DIEGO DE (1512–77), Spanish bp., jurist, and historian. At Salamanca (to 1534) C. developed an intense interest in the New World Indians;

at the univ. he lectured on the problems they presented, esp. concerning slavery in colonial America. He refuted Aristotle, basing his own teaching on the natural law while appealing to Greek thought and Roman law, to Sacred Scripture and Thomistic theology. A canon lawyer, C. published *Epitome de sponsalibus et matrimoniis* (1545) and other works influenced by the Council of Trent. He was made bp. of Ciudad Rodrigo in 1560, and in 1565, of Segovia. BIBLIOGRAPHY: A. Scola, EncCatt 4:794; J. Malagón-Barceló, NCE 4:401.

[M. R. BROWN]

COVENANT (IN THE BIBLE), in the ancient Near East a widespread convention for establishing social relationships (e.g., Gen 21.32; Jos 9.15; 1 Sam 18.3–4). Depending on the circumstances, it assumed a variety of forms (note four covenants in 2 Kg 11.4, 12, 17), several of which became symbols of the relationship between God and man. The history of that relationship is largely reflected in the development and interaction of these various forms to such an extent that covenant may be called the central concept of the OT.

The major covenant forms are those of Abraham (Gen 15; 17.1–14), Moses (cf. esp. Ex 19–20; 34) and David (2 Sam 7.4–16; Ps 89.19–37). When the ancient tradition of the Abrahamic covenant was incorporated into the history of Israel written during the early monarchic period, it was surely intended as a foreshadowing of the Davidic (note the Davidic themes in Gen 15.5, 18). This latter is in the form of a divine oath without mention of conditions to be fulfilled. It was perhaps derived from a pre-Israelite Jerusalem practice (Ps 110.4) and may have caused an omission of specific commandments from the Abrahamic covenant. The Mosaic covenant tradition, also under the royal tutelage (Ps 132.12; 2 Kg 11.17; 23), contained explicit stipulations and became the focus of the deuteronomic tradition, which placed limitations upon the Davidic promise (Dt 17.18–20; 1 Kg 8.25) and gave only slight emphasis to the patriarchs (e.g., Dt 9.27; 2 Kg 13.23).

The eventual collapse of the monarchy prompted the authors in the priestly tradition to give new importance to the Abrahamic covenant as the basis for renewed hope, since it existed in a form without stipulations and thus symbolized God's self-giving love without reference to Israel's failure to live up to the Mosaic legislation. Of the three principal forms, the Abrahamic alone was now given the name "covenant" (cf. Neh 9–10, esp. 9.8; note the exception in Lev 26.45); such an emphasis on the unconditioned promise, with its implicit affirmation that the covenant survives man's failure to keep the (Mosaic) law, was later expressed analogously by Paul (Rom 4).

The prophets were surely familiar with the covenant traditions, but it is still disputed to what extent they based their moral demands and threats of punishment precisely on the Mosaic covenant traditions. Scholars also do not agree in explaining the limited explicit reference to the covenant in the prophets generally. The hope of a new covenant (Jer 31.31–34; cf. Ezek 36.25–27) stressed God's future gift of man's inner renewal; its achievement through Christ prompted the declaration that the old forms have passed away (Heb 8.6–13; Gal 4.21–28), yielding to a new relationship expressed preeminently in the covenant ritual of the Eucharist (compare Ex 24.8; 1 Cor 11.25; Mt 26.28; Mk 14.24; Lk 22.20). BIBLIOGRAPHY: D. J. McCarthy, "Covenant in the Old Testament: The Present State of Inquiry," CBQ 27 (1965) 217–240; *idem, Old Testament Covenant: A Survey of Current Thought* (pa. 1972); R. E. Clements, *Abraham and David* (1967); L. Christensen, *Covenant* (pa. 1974).

[P. J. KEARNEY]

COVENANT RELATIONSHIPS, in the ecumenical movement a bond between parishes of different Churches that unites them, short of *intercommunion, in prayer, social ministry, study, and dialogue. Synchronization of liturgical prayers and readings (e.g., the use of a common Lectionary) is often another uniting element. Such covenants are meant to affirm at the local level the bilateral and international dialogues going on between the RC and other Churches. They are esp. common between RC and Episcopalian Churches; at present more than one hundred parishes have entered into covenant relationships. An even closer form of such a bond is planned for the Diocese of Richmond, Va. where a coparish and copastorate is planned between a RC and an Episcopalian parish.

[T. C. O'BRIEN]

COVENANT THEOLOGY, not so much a separate system as an idiom used to explain the mystery of the election and perseverance of the saints, within the framework of the Calvinist tradition. While covenant or *federal theology (Lat. *foedus,* covenant) has a wider history in which the writings of H. *Bullinger and J. *Cocceius are particularly prominent, its English and Scottish development are alone considered here. Federalism came into prominence in the era of the Westminster Assembly (1643–49); the *Westminster Confession (c.7) speaks of a covenant of works and a covenant of grace. The covenant idea and covenant thinking greatly influenced theological developments on both sides of the Atlantic among Presbyterians and Congregationalists; the concept of covenant also regulated the interpretation of church order and of the socio-political order, esp. in New England. Prominent in the development of covenant theology were John Preston's *The New Covenant or the Saints Portion* (1629) and James Durham's *Sum of Saving Knowledge* (1650). Covenant terminology was taken from the OT and interpreted through legal and commercial notions of contract. The covenant was a contractual relationship between the Christian and God; at the moment of regeneration the Christian is received into a compact with his creator; the sacraments are given as seals of this covenant. By portraying regeneration as a contract, requiring mutual consent, covenant theology could preserve the doctrine of predestination while urging the unregenerate to accept God's free gift of grace. Because the covenant was binding, it expressed the sureness of salvation. Personal covenanting came to be more strongly emphasized than baptism; the private act of the believer, more than the act of God or Christ. Covenant theology also tended to sharpen the distinction between the *visible Church and the *invisible Church. The true Church was thought to be constituted of those covenanting together to form a congregation, i.e., of those already personally covenanted to God. The *Mayflower Compact and the whole political order in New England were motivated by the covenant idea, and Perry Miller has discussed the influence of covenant thinking on early American history. BIBLIOGRAPHY: P. Miller, *New England Mind* (2 v., pa. 1961); *idem, Errand into the Wilderness* (1956); *idem,* "From the Covenant to the Revival," Smith-Jamison 1:322–368.

[J. A. R. MACKENZIE]

COVENANTERS, name given to those who followed the old Scottish practice of covenanting, i.e., entering into a band to maintain a religious or political cause. The covenants of the 16th cent. were reflected in the *King's Confession of 1586. In the 17th cent., the *Scottish National Covenant (1638) was signed amid scenes of enthusiasm in Greyfriars Kirk by persons of all ranks who repudiated "all kinds of papistry" (meaning in particular the form of Anglicanism proposed in Abp. W. Laud's attempt to impose the Book of Common Prayer on the Scottish Church) as tending to "the subversion and ruin of the true Reformed religion and of our liberties, laws and estates." In 1643, while the *Solemn League and Covenant was being widely signed, the English Parliament summoned the *Westminster Assembly to secure "the nearest conjunction and uniformity in religion" advocated in the Solemn League. The supporters of the Covenants were in turn, however, later crushed by Oliver *Cromwell, and after the Restoration of Charles II a policy of repression was undertaken. The battle of Rullion Green (1666) scattered the Covenanters, whose open-air conventicles were regarded as seedbeds of rebellion; the battle of Bothwell Bridge (1679) was the prelude to fearful persecution, imprisonment, and deportation. The struggle came to an end at the Revolution Settlement (1668). Marked by an evangelical devotion and loyalty to the crown and kingdom of Christ, the Covenanters waged a struggle, fanatical at times, in defense of the spiritual independence that has characterized the history of the Scottish Church. BIBLIOGRAPHY: J. King Hewison, *Covenanters* (2 v., 1908). *GENERAL SYNOD; *CHURCH OF SCOTLAND; *CAMERONIANS.

[J. A. R. MACKENZIE]

COVENANTING, a term with two meanings: (1) the practice begun early in the Scottish Reformation of entering into a band to maintain a religious or political cause (see

COVENANTERS; SCOTTISH NATIONAL COVENANT; SOLEMN LEAGUE AND COVENANT); (2) the believer's act of entering into the special relation with God that is stressed in covenant theology, or *federal theology.

[J. A. R. MACKENZIE]

COVENTRY CATHEDRAL. The first building was erected (1053) by Leofric and Lady Godiva as minster church for the Benedictine monastery, and raised to cathedral status in 1100 in the joint Diocese of Coventry and Lichfield, the bp. residing at Coventry. In the mid-16th cent. Henry VIII dismantled the cathedral and Coventry ceased to be a see for nearly 400 years. In 1918 a new Diocese of Coventry was founded and the central and beautiful St. Michael's Church, built as a parish church in 1326, became the cathedral. In Nov. 1940 German bombing completely gutted and destroyed all but the tower and some outlying walls. In 1956, a contract was signed with Sir John Laing to rebuild Coventry Cathedral according to the new visionary, imaginative, and wildly controversial plans of Sir Basil Spence, conceived in dramatic contemporary style of glass, steel, and concrete and enhanced by work of leading artists and craftsmen of the age. Noteworthy are: the commanding bronze *St. Michael Conquering the Devil* by Sir Jacob Epstein at the entrance stairway; the magnificent 70-foot high tapestry, *Christ in Glory,* by the great painter Graham Sutherland; the huge baptistery window by John Piper "one of greatest works in stained glass since the Reformation"; John Hutton's mystical engraved glass-screen; the mosaic floor of the Chapel of Unity by Swedish artist Elinar Forseth, gift of the Church in Sweden; and numberless examples in metal, wood, and engraved lettering in stone—all works of excellence, poignance, and overwhelming spiritual value. As signified in the Chapel of Unity, Coventry has become a symbol of reconciliation and unity in the world after the division of war. BIBLIOGRAPHY: G. E. Kidder Smith, *New Churches of Europe* (1964).

[M. J. DALY]

COVERDALE, MILES (1488–1569), translator of the Bible. Educated at Cambridge, C. was ordained at Norwich (1514) and entered the Augustinians at Cambridge, among whom he came under the influence of his prior R. Barnes, a man of Puritan views later executed for heresy under Henry VIII. Under the patronage of T. *Cromwell, C. preached against the Mass, images, and other Catholic practices; he was forced into exile on the Continent. At Antwerp he completed an English translation of the whole Bible (1534–35); he also edited the *Great Bible. In England in 1548 he was appointed chaplain to the King and almoner to the Queen (Catherine Parr), whose funeral sermon he preached. He was made bp. of Exeter in 1551, but was obliged to give up that office at the accession of Mary and retire again into exile. After his return to England when Elizabeth came to the throne, he was dissatisfied with the Act of Uniformity of 1559, and the last years of his life were spent fostering Puritan opposition. BIBLIOGRAPHY: J. F. Mozley, *Coverdale and His Bibles* (1953); H. R. Tedder, DNB 4:1289–97; P. Levi, *English Bible 1534–1859* (1974) 51–69.

[V. SAMPSON]

COVERDALE'S BIBLE, translation by M. *Coverdale, the first complete printed Bible in English (1535). It was not made from the Hebrew and Greek texts, but was based principally on the Vulgate, Luther's German translation, and W. *Tyndale's translations of the Pentateuch, Jonah, and the NT. Coverdale's Bible helped form the "biblical English" of the *Authorized Version.

[T. EARLY]

COVETOUSNESS, see GREED

COWARDICE, a vice opposed to *fortitude or courage, the moral virtue that moderates the emotions of fear and boldness. For St. Thomas Aquinas, cowardice (lack of daring) and timidity (excessive fearfulness) are not really distinct but are two aspects of the same weakness, though other theologians draw a distinction between generalized timidity and a cowardice that shirks duties. The moderation or control of fear exercised by courage does not extinguish the passion of fear itself or its activity, for a man insensitive to danger would be ill-equipped to face life. Courage should rather aim to control an excess of fear that would disorganize a man and turn him from the path of duty. The feeling of fear and the impulse not to dare do not constitute cowardice; their presence in a man who does not allow himself to be overwhelmed by them is rather an indication of the greatness of his courage. BIBLIOGRAPHY: ThAq ST (Lat-Eng, v. 42, ed. A. Ross and P. Walsh), 2a2ae, 125–127; J. Pieper, *Fortitude and Temperance* (tr. D. F. Coogan, 1954); R. A. Gautier, "Fortitude," in TL 4:487–531.

[T. GILBY]

COWL, the most characteristic and proper garment of the monk. It is usually a long, flowing garment with ample sleeves and a hood, conferred on a monk when he makes his solemn vows. For many Benedictines it is usually black, while the Cistercians and some groups of Benedictines wear a white cowl. Some mendicants and other religious at times speak of their hooded cloaks or capes as a cowl, and the name is often confused with the hood, which is commonly a part of the monk's religious habit.

[M. B. PENNINGTON]

COWLEY FATHERS, popular name for the Society of St. John the Evangelist (SSJE), an Anglican monastic community established at Cowley, near Oxford, where the founder R. M. Benson (1824–1915) was vicar. Benson and two associates pronounced vows Dec. 27, 1866 (St. John's Day), and the society later spread to the U.S. (1870), India

(1874), South Africa (1883), Canada (1927), and Japan (1933). The oldest Anglican monastic order for men, the society includes both priests and lay brothers and emphasizes missionary work. BIBLIOGRAPHY: A. M. Allchin, *The Silent Rebellion: Anglican Religious Communities 1845–1900* (1958).

[T. EARLY]

COWPER, WILLIAM (1731–1800), English poet and hymnographer. Subject to spells of insanity under emotional stress and of religious obsession, he did not marry. A gentle, quiet man, profoundly religious, he had a playful sense of humor. His poems vary from the sincere *Olney Hymns* (1779), produced in collaboration with John Newton, a Calvinist preacher, to *John Gilpin,* a delight to children, and *On the Loss of the Royal George,* a patriotic ballad. *The Task* (6 v., 1785) shows his love of nature, of quiet scenery, of the seasons, and his careful observation of animals, particularly his own pets. He helped to redeem English verse from artificiality and rhetoric. His reflective verse concerns contemporary abuses, social, political, moral, and religious. His pleasantly gossipy letters describe everyday activities and reveal sympathy with humanity's ills. BIBLIOGRAPHY: M. J. Quinlan, *William Cowper* (1953); G. Thomas, *William Cowper and the Eighteenth Century* (1935).

[M. B. BARRY]

COYSEVOX, ANTOINE (1640–1721), court sculptor. C. worked for the bp. of Strasbourg (1666–71), in Paris at the Grande Galerie, Versailles (1678) executing the famous stucco *tondo* of Louis XIV, and statues for the façade of Church of the Invalides. Most important in a series of tombs are those of Colbert (1685–87) and of Card. Mazarin (1689–93). C. directed the school of Gobelins Tapestries and carved a statue of Louis XIV offering himself to the Virgin (1715) for the choir of Notre-Dame (Paris). C. trained his nephews, the *Coustous and Le Lorraine and is largely responsible for the mythological travesty, the Duchess of Burgundy as Diana, 1710. He worked in a reserved classical style.

[M. J. DALY]

CRACOW, CHURCH OF OUR LADY, 13th-cent. Gothic church renowned for the stupendous altarpiece (1489) by Veit Stoss, a culmination of late Gothic wood-carved altarpieces.

[M. J. DALY]

CRAM, RALPH ADAMS (1863–1942), American architect. He was an exponent of the Gothic revival, in which he was preceded by such architects as R. Upjohn (1802–78) in the U.S. and A. W. Pugin (1812–52) in England. C. was born at Hampton Falls, N.H., the son of a Unitarian minister, and received his training in Boston. In 1888 he became an Anglo-Catholic and came to view the Gothic form of architecture as the ideal for churches. He formed a partnership with F. Ferguson (1889) and B. G. Goodhue (1891); Goodhue left the partnership in 1914.

C. designed numerous buildings in the U.S., Canada, and Cuba. Among his more notable achievements were designs for the West Point Military Academy, St. Thomas Episcopal Church, New York, and the Episcopal Cathedral of St. John the Divine, New York. He also designed the graduate school and chapel at Princeton Univ. and buildings at Rice, Williams, and Phillips Exeter Academy. His RC churches include Sacred Heart, Jersey City, N.J. (1925), St. Mary's, Redford, Detroit, Mich. (1929), and Holy Rosary, Pittsburgh, Pa. (1931).

C. was professor of architecture at the Massachusetts Institute of Technology and was a fellow of the American Institute of Architects. He was one of the early contributors to *Commonweal* magazine. His principles were expressed in *Church Building* (3d ed., 1924) and numerous other works. BIBLIOGRAPHY: R. A. Cram, *My Life in Architecture* (1936).

[T. EARLY]

CRAMPON, JOSEPH THEODORE (1836–94), biblical scholar and translator. C. held various pastoral posts in the Diocese of Amiens, but also devoted himself to scriptural studies. He is best known for his translations of the Bible, first from the *Vulgate but later an OT translation from the original languages, which was published posthumously (6 v., 1894–1904). BIBLIOGRAPHY: F. Vigouroux, DB 2.1:1100–01; A. Cousineau, NCE 4:412.

[T. M. MCFADDEN]

CRANACH, LUCAS, THE ELDER (1472–1553), German painter and engraver, representative artist of the Reformation at Wittenberg, friend of Luther. His early journey to the Danube and Vienna inspired strong feeling for landscape in religious paintings (*Rest on Flight*, Berlin; *Crucifixion*, Munich). Later, portraits and mannerist mythological scenes prevail (*Venus; Judgment of Paris*). C. was frequently assisted by sons and members of his workshop. BIBLIOGRAPHY: W. L. M. Burke, "Lucas Cranach, the Elder," *Art Bulletin* 18 (1936) 25–53. J. Jahn, *Lukas Cranach als Graphiker* (1955).

[R. BERGMANN]

CRANIOTOMY, in general, a surgical procedure on the skull, as in the cutting of the fetal head to facilitate delivery. The interest of moral theologians in the procedure is limited to the case just cited as an example. It involves the opening and evacuation of the fetal skull. The size of the head is then reduced by crushing the skull, so that it can be more easily delivered. Formerly the most common indication for the procedure was hydrocephalus. Today there is no medical need for this type of procedure. In cases of obstructed delivery, it is always possible to effect the delivery of the fetus by some other method. From the standpoint of RC moral theology, craniotomy involves direct killing of the fetus and cannot be justified. The fact that the child will be born an idiot or will soon die anyhow is no justification for direct killing. On May 28, 1884, the Holy Office declared that "it may not be safely taught in Catholic schools that craniotomy is licit" even where without it both mother and child would perish.

[J. R. CONNERY]

CRANMER, THOMAS (1489–1556), Abp. of Canterbury at the beginning of the English Reformation. His character was so composed of light and shade that it can scarcely be suggested in a brief account. Yet through his shifts there runs a consistent *Erastianism, and genuine devotion must have infused his noble liturgical style in the BCP of 1549, the *Homilies,* and the *Litany.* Considering the risks he allowed, he must have been blessed with a high survival value, until his pitiable but finally not inglorious end. A Nottinghamshire man, he lost his fellowship at Jesus College, Cambridge, when it was discovered that he kept a secret wife at the Dolphin Inn; but on her death in childbed he was reinstated. Entering into the household of the Earl of Wiltshire, the father of Anne Boleyn, he was appointed to embassies to Italy and Germany to lobby in favor of Henry VIII's divorce from Catherine of Aragon. Although he had compromised his position by intrigues with the Protestant princes and by marrying the niece of A. *Osiander—he had to keep her well out of sight until the next reign—he was promoted to abp. of Canterbury on the death of Warham and was confirmed by Clement VII (1533). The King knew his man; his marriage to Anne Boleyn was duly pronounced valid, and 3 years later it was duly pronounced invalid. Though active in the desecration of St. Thomas's shrine at Canterbury, C. seems of all the Protestant magnates to have had least to do with the *dissolution of the monasteries. He married Henry to Anne of Cleves, 1540; a few months later he was the chief instrument in procuring the divorce. Selected by the council to convey to the King information about the misconduct of his fifth wife, Catherine Howard, he was commanded to visit her in the Tower, where he held out delusive hopes of mercy. Henry clearly liked "my chaplain," and it cannot have been just for his subservience. He attended the King on his deathbed and celebrated the solemn Requiem Mass (1547).

After the accession of Edward VI he could display a more open Protestantism. Continental Reformers were welcomed, images destroyed, ancient ceremonies abolished. C.'s own theological views, which shifted from Lutheranism towards Zwinglianism, seem to have been both latitudinarian and perplexed, which may help to explain his later recantations; only on the Royal Supremacy was he relatively constant. He was not a persecuting man, by the standards of his times, and was liked by his friends, though he betrayed the Seymours to the Dudleys, and made but a timid gesture to save his colleague Thomas *Cromwell from disgrace. His judgment on whether the Princess Mary should be allowed the practice of the Catholic religion was that "to give license to sin was sin, but to suffer it and wink at it for a time might be borne." Drawn into the rising for Lady Jane Grey (1553), he at first pleaded not guilty but later confessed to the indictment, and was condemned to be executed at Tyburn. Queen Mary's clemency spared his life, but charges of heresy were closing in against him. After long delays, disputations, pleas, and counterpleas, he was publicly degraded at Oxford; despite a series of increasingly submissive recantations, he was sent to the stake two months later. In his final address he repudiated all that he had written out of fear. He put his hand into the flame, and crying out "This hand has offended," very soon was dead. BIBLIOGRAPHY: biographies by A. F. Pollard (1904); F. H. Hutchinson (1951); J. Ridley (1962). *BOOK OF COMMON PRAYER.

[T. GILBY]

CRANMER'S BIBLE, the 1540 edition of the *Great Bible, so called because of the preface by T. *Cranmer.

CRANTOR OF SOLI IN CILICIA (*c*.335–*c*.275 B.C.), a member of the Old Academy, esp. important for his treatise *On Grief.* He was a pupil of *Xenocrates and the teacher of Arcesilaus, the founder of the Middle Academy. He wrote the first commentary on Plato's *Timaeus.* In his interpretation he maintained that the cosmogony of the *Timaeus* should not be understood as referring to a temporal origin of the world. His *On Grief,* a treatise cast in the form of a letter, is distinguished for its comprehensiveness and religious depth. In contrast to the *apatheia* of the Stoics, he emphasized *metriopatheia,* "moderation" or "restraint," in respect to the emotions. He formulated a number of the characteristic *topoi* or commonplaces applicable to consolation. His work became the model for the consolation literature in Latin—beginning with Cicero—as well as in Greek. BIBLIOGRAPHY: OCD 238; LexAW 1609; Copleston 1:265. *CONSOLATION.

[M. R. P. MCGUIRE]

CRASHAW, RICHARD (1612–1649), English poet and convert to Catholicism. Son of a Puritan divine, C. was expelled from Cambridge for his Anglican beliefs. As a poet he belongs to the group called Metaphysical Poets and even more to the moral tradition in English poetry. His principal collection is *Steps to the Temple* (1646, enlarged 1648), which contains two approaches, one secular, the other religious. Shortly before this C. converted to Catholicism, in part through his fervent admiration of the newly canonized St. Teresa of Avila. He journeyed to Italy and became a member of the household of Card. Palotta, but his critical attitude toward the relaxed manners of the Italians made him unwelcome. Through the Cardinal he received a minor benefice at the Shrine of Loreto but died a month later. C. is a poet of high merit in an age that was distinguished for excellence in poetry. He has written some of the

most powerful reflections on religious themes in English literature. A skilled artist, he was a deeply spiritual thinker. Among Catholic poets of the past 300 years he ranks with the best. BIBLIOGRAPHY: *Complete Works of Richard Crashaw* (ed. W. B. Turnbull, 1858, repr. 1974); H. C. White, *Metaphysical Poets* (1936); A. J. Bennis, *Catholicity of Richard Crashaw* (Columbia Univ., 1952).

[J. R. AHERNE]

CRASSET, JEAN (1618–92), Jesuit spiritual writer, director, and preacher, esp. against the Jansenists. He directed a sodality of men known as the *Congrégation des Messieurs* and wrote retreat manuals adapting the *Spiritual Exercises* of St. Ignatius Loyola to laymen. He is also known for his manuals of prayer and Marian devotions, biographies, and religious poetry. BIBLIOGRAPHY: Sommervogel 2:1623–46; M. Olphe-Galliard, DSAM 2.2:2511–20.

[I. M. KASHUBA]

CRATES OF THEBES (*c*.365–285 B.C.), Cynic philosopher. Converted to Cynicism by *Diogenes of Sinope, he bequeathed his fortune to his fellow-citizens, and with his wife Hipparchia, who was equally devoted to the Cynic ideal, he entered upon a wandering life of preaching and of promoting Cynicism by his own writings and by adapting the writings of others to serve the same purpose. Unlike his master, he was kindly in his manner and became a beloved figure. He maintained that he was not bound to any one state, and he may well have been the coiner of the term *kosmopolitēs,* "citizen of the world." BIBLIOGRAPHY: OCD 240; LexAW 1611.

[M. R. P. MCGUIRE]

CRAWFORD, FRANCIS MARION (1854–1909), American romantic novelist, dramatist, critic, and lecturer. Born in Italy, C. studied in the U.S., England, Italy, Germany, and India, where he became a Catholic. His education and extensive travels foreshadowed the diversity of settings in his 44 novels. In addition to these novels, C. wrote many articles, four plays, three volumes of poetry, books of travel, and an important book of criticism, *The Novel: What It Is.* His first novel *Mr. Isaacs* (1882) was an immediate success, and he found a large reading public for this and for subsequent works. A gifted narrator, C. achieved his major success in his novels. His philosophy concerning this literary genre was that novels should be "pocket drama" intended to entertain, primarily love stories combining romance and reality. Most highly praised was his trilogy of a wealthy aristocratic Italian family: *Saracinesca* (1887), *Sant' Ilario* (1889), and *Don Orsino* (1892).

Also of distinguished caliber was his historical romance *Via Crucis* (1898), a story of the Second Crusade. Honored by the French Academy were *Zoroaster* (1885) and *Marzio's Crucifix* (1887). BIBLIOGRAPHY: J. Pilkington,

Francis Marion Crawford (1964) for a critical study of his life and works; J. F. Cooper, *Some American Storytellers* (1911) for criticism and bibliography.

[S. A. HEENEY]

CRAWLEY-BOEVEY, MATEO (1875–1960), proponent of devotion to the Sacred Heart. A Peruvian, he was ordained (1898) a member of the Congregation of the Sacred Heart. In 1903 he founded the Catholic Univ. of Valparaiso; in 1907 he inaugurated a movement to establish enthronement of the Sacred Heart in the home, a work to which Pope Pius X enjoined him to commit all his efforts. C.-B.'s influence on the clergy throughout the world was enormous. Pope Pius XI requested him to preach Catholic Action throughout Italy.

[J. R. AHERNE]

CREATED ACTUATION BY UNCREATED ACT, a theological explanation of certain gifts of grace. The mystery of the supernatural order consists in God's self-gift by which, on his gratuitous initiative, he enters into a personal communion with created spirits and calls them to share in his own life. God's personal communication actuates a created potency, open to his gift, yet naturally unadapted to it. Hence every supernatural elevation has a twofold aspect: it is at once God's immediate communication to a potency and the adaptation of the same to God. Equivalently it is union and transformation. Both aspects are aptly expressed by the phrase "created actuation by uncreated act" (M. de la Taille). The formula applies at three different levels. At the deepest level Christ's humanity is actuated by the divine act of being of the Word of God; by the grace of union, it subsists as God's own human nature. Men's elevation to the supernatural order differs from this insofar as every man's nature subsists by a connatural human act of existence; nevertheless it is raised to personal communion with God by the added actuation of created grace. Lastly, in the beatific vision man's intellect becomes intentionally united with God's essence; the blessed see God immediately in the light of glory. BIBLIOGRAPHY: M. de la Taille, *Hypostatic Union and Created Actuation by Uncreated Act* (1952). P. De Letter, "Theology of God's Self-Gift," ThSt 24 (1963) 402–422.

[J. DUPUIS]

CREATION, as usually understood in philosophy and always in theology, the making of something by bringing it, together with the totality of its constituents, into being. It is said to be the production of a thing out of nothing in the sense that what is created is not produced from any preexisting matter. In Christian theology the universe was brought totally into being by the free act of God alone, who is accordingly termed the Creator. This is a distinctive tenet of the Judeo-Christian tradition, in opposition to alternative explanations in the ancient world such as emanationism or dualism. Today those who reject creation usually deny the

need for an explanation of the existence of the universe and are satisfied to state the eternity of matter. Creation is, however, compatible with the eternity of matter, as St. Thomas Aquinas pointed out in *CG* 2.38, since matter can be dependent on God either eternally or in time, without the fact of its total ontological dependence being affected; this hypothesis does, however, cause difficulty for the imagination. Creation in (or more accurately with) time is therefore not provable by reason; that the universe had a beginning is, according to Lateran IV (1215) and Vatican I (1870), known from revelation (see D 800, 3002), although the purely scriptural grounds for this statement do not seem conclusive. Creation of the world by God does not involve fixism; evolution, in fact, is now admitted to be completely compatible with the Genesis narratives, which are concerned to teach that all things were totally produced by God and were created good, rather than the particular manner of their origin. BIBLIOGRAPHY: DTC Tables générales 1:843–854; M. Flick and Z. Alszeghy, *Il Creatore: L'inizio della salvezza* (2d ed., 1961).

[B. FORSHAW]

CREATION ACCOUNT, a term sometimes used of the theological exposition of creation in Gen 1.1–2.4a. The Bible begins with this composition, one of the last to be written for the Pentateuch. It is the result of a long development from its origins in Mesopotamian myth, from which it borrowed and against which it was directed. For example, traces of ancient mythology remain in the presence of the watery chaos, now depersonalized (1.2), but retained in the narrative in order to symbolize the constant danger of evil, the threat of divine punishment for sin (cf. the return to chaos in Gen 7–9 and Jer 4.23–26). Also, Gen 1.2 may refer to a "mighty wind" as part of the mythological chaotic condition; others translate "Spirit of God," seeing a reference to God's absolute tranquil power over chaos. The structure of the universe in this passage is also a mythological heritage (cf. details in Job 38 and Ps 104), as are the allusions to the creative power of earth (Gen 1.24) and the primordial inviolability of animal life (v. 30). The demythologizing tendency of the whole narrative is unmistakable, however. Unlike the common store of myth, the narrative eliminates the notion of divine combat as the prelude to creation of the world or of man. All is subject to the serene decisions of God's will, whose action by "word" places him outside the creative process itself (cf. Is 44.26–28 as background). Light, the mythological aura of divinity (Ps 104.2), is now a mere creature (1.3–5); the sun and moon are deprived even of their names, with their ancient resonance of divinity, and merely divide day and night (1.16). The mythological court of heaven emerges when God with special solemnity decides to create man (1.26; cf. Job 1.6), but only so that the transcendence of God may be indirectly affirmed through man's creation both in the image of God himself and yet also in the image of a lesser heavenly being (cf. Ps 8.5). In his total human personality, man is to be a visible sign of God's dominion over creation. Further, the timeless existence of myth is broken as creation is brought into God's saving historical plan (cf. Gen 2.4a; 5.1; 10.1), a development heightened by the imposition of a 7-day system on the older tradition. Thus the author seems to point to man's historical goal, the "rest" which is a positive creation of God (2.1). It is made on a day that, perhaps intentionally, is not said to end, a day in which man can share through his Sabbath rest on earth.

The following narrative (Gen 2.4b–24) presents an older account composed during the early monarchical period by the "Yahwist" historian. It is directed toward explaining the origin of human sexual attraction (verse 24) and leads into the narrative explaining the origin of evil (Gen 3). God here creates like a potter (2.7,19), an image known in Egyptian and Mesopotamian literature. The creation of woman from Adam's rib may originate in a Sumerian pun on a single word meaning both "rib" and "bring to life" (cf. Gen 3.20). The two trees (2.9) are a fusing of originally separate traditions; the section on the four rivers (2.10–14) is an addition to the narrative that apparently was intended to bring the above material, mythological in tone, into the dimension of man's historical experience. BIBLIOGRAPHY: G. von Rad, *Genesis* (tr. J. H. Marks, 1961).

[P. J. KEARNEY]

CREATION EPIC. Though several myths of creation are known from antiquity, the most famous is the Babylonian epic known as the *Enuma Elish*. In this, Tiamat, the original female deity who gave birth to all beings, is a chaos monster who seeks to destroy her own offspring, the gods. Marduk, the champion of the gods, succeeds in slaying Tiamat, splitting her body in two and using it to form the cosmos. The lower half of her body constitutes the subterranean deep on which earth, conceived of as a flat disc, rests, with the vault of heaven, complete with the stars and planets, extending over it. Above this again are the storehouses of the rain and the wind. Marduk builds himself a magnificent palace in heaven, the earthly counterpart of which is the *esagil*, the temple of Babylon. Men are created to be the servants of the gods. They are composed of clay mingled with the blood of the god Kingu, an ally of Tiamat. Of supreme significance in all this is the idea of creation as the conquest of chaos and the use of chaos as the basic "stuff" from which to compose an ordered cosmos. The myth reflects the basic cycles of the seasons and the rhythmic processes of nature, in which life must be born anew each year in the spring.

This myth has its counterpart in Canaanite mythology, in which Aleyan Baal, the god of life and the rain giver, conquers the representatives of death and sterile waste, Mot and the "Sea-River" god.

In the OT the polytheistic elements are purged away, but vestigial traces of the language and thought-forms of these and similar myths have survived. For instance the Hebrew *tehom*, the deep, corresponds to the name Tiamat. BIBLIOG-RAPHY: A. Heidel, *Babylonian Genesis* (2d ed., 1954); T. Jacobsen, *Intellectual Adventure of Ancient Man* (ed. H. Frankfort, 1966) ch. 5–7; *Ancient Near Eastern Texts* (ed. J. B. Pritchard, 2d ed., 1955) 60–72. *CREATION ACCOUNT; *GENESIS, BOOK OF.

[D. J. BOURKE]

CREATION OF MAN. The biblical *creation account is a religious teaching that explains the origin of sin and misery; as God created the world and mankind they were good; man was made to the image and likeness of God. This is the main point of Genesis's accounting for man's origin. The phrase "creation of man" also has another, theological connotation: because of the spirituality of the human soul (a truth presupposed to the whole meaning of man's supernatural destiny and of the reality of grace) the physical factors involved in human conception cannot account for the soul's origin. Whatever moderate evolutionary theory may be admissible concerning the origin of mankind, God's immediate causality is required for the production of the soul. Thus Catholic teaching maintains the doctrine of *creationism against any purely materialistic explanation of the origin of each human being.

[T. C. O'BRIEN]

CREATIONISM (from the Lat. *creatio*) is, first, the doctrine that the triune God created the whole extradivine reality out of nothing (dogmatized against pantheism, monism, and materialism; D 125, 150, 800, 3001–03). It is, second, an antiquated theory that all living beings were immediately and directly created by God (i.e., a literal interpretation of Gen ch. 1–2, opposed to transformism, evolutionism, Darwinism). Creationism is, third, the Catholic doctrine (also called consecrationism) that God (primary cause) by his transcendent dynamism creates every individual human soul out of nothing in the moment of its union with the body, i.e., at conception. Thus this normal (not miraculous) intervention of God acts through and in the human parents (secondary causes) and results in procreation of a new whole human being, who is a substantial psychosomatic whole. The ordinary magisterium teaches creationism in this sense (D 190, 360–361, 685, 1007, 1440, 2015, 3896) and rejects traducianism, generationism, preexistentism, emanationism, and metempsychosis (D 403, 456, 360–361, 1007, 3220). BIBLIOGRAPHY: ThAq ST 1a, 118.2 ad 2; *idem*, CG 2.86–89; P. B. T. Bilaniuk, NCE 4:428–429.

[P. B. T. BILANIUK]

CREATURE. (1) In the theology of divine *causality, every being other than God is a being by participation, dependent for its existence upon God who alone is the proper cause of being as such. Thus every being other than God is a creature, whether caused by the act of creation itself, in the origin of all things, or caused by the activity of secondary causes acting in subordination to God's primary causality (see ThAq ST 1a.44,1;104.1). (2) In the context of moral and spiritual theology the "creature" sometimes signifies a temporal or passing good. Such goods are the objectives of human will and desire. When they are sought in their proper relationship to the intent of charity to love God above all, they enhance human life; when they become objectives chosen in disregard of their true limitations and subordination, the choosing can be sinful, out of keeping with the orientation of charity.

[T. C. O'BRIEN]

CREBRAE ALLATAE SUNT, *a motu proprio* of Pope Pius XII promulgated on Feb. 22, 1949. It contains the marriage laws for the Eastern Catholic Churches; 101 of the 131 canons are identical to those of the Latin canon law, differing only in terminology. This served to unify the marriage legislation of the Eastern Catholic Churches and to bring it closer to the Latin discipline. BIBLIOGRAPHY: V. J. Pospishil, NCE 10:763–767.

[E. EL-HAYEK]

CREDENCE TABLE, a side table (cf. credenza, a Renaissance sideboard) on which the chalice, cruets, basin and towel are laid out for use in the Eucharistic Liturgy.

CREDENDITY, a term coined from the Latin gerundive *credendum,* to be believed. The judgment concerning credendity is the practical judgment preparatory to faith which posits the personal obligation of belief. Distinct and even separable from the judgment of *credibility, the judgment of credendity imposes itself upon the freedom of the human will out of a conviction that faith in God gives meaning to human existence. The will is left free to believe, but the authority of God revealing impresses itself in the form of an imperative. The will, prompted by grace, feels it ought to believe (D 3008, 3010, 3031, 3035). This moment marks the beginning of faith.

[J. FICHTNER]

CREDI, LORENZO DI (*c.*1458–1537), Florentine painter, sculptor, and goldsmith. In the studio of Verrocchio until the master's death (1488), C. then completed Verrocchio's renowned equestrian monument of B. Colleoni (Venice) and, according to *Vasari, the tomb of Card. Forteguerri (Pistoia cathedral). In 1493 C. painted an altarpiece of the *Madonna and Child with Two Saints* (Louvre), a *Nativity* and *St. Bartholomew* (*c.*1510, Florence), *Madonna and Child with Four Saints* (Pistoia) and an *Annunciation* (Uffizi), one of his finest works. C.'s work shows the influence of Verrocchio and the young Leonardo da Vinci, with Flemish detail and finish of surfaces. BIBLIOGRAPHY: G. Passavant, *Andrea de Verrocchio als Maler* (1959).

[M. J. DALY]

CREDIBILITY, in theology, the object of a judgment that prepares the way for the act of faith. This is a value judg-

ment in which the human mind estimates the fact and content of divine revelation to be worthy of belief. It is one in a series of steps (preambles, preconditions) logically, if not temporally, preceding the assent of faith. Credibility presents a twofold problem: the one of a witness truly perceiving the objective facts; the other of his veracity in reporting them. Vatican Council I affirmed that the testimony given to revelation is credible because it affords human reason sufficient motive for belief (D 3013, 3033, 3876). The epistemological character of faith is such that it depends upon both the psychology of the believer and the richness of revelation. BIBLIOGRAPHY: J. Mouroux, *I Believe* (tr. M. Turner, 1959); G. de Broglie, *Les Signes de crédibilité de la révélation chrétienne* (1964).

[J. FICHTNER]

CREDIT UNION, an association organized to collect funds from its members which can be lent to fellow members on more favorable terms than are available on the open market. Interest is usually minimal with little or no security required. Credit unions also provide a realistic and systematic savings plan for their members, with built-in incentives. The credit union phenomenon has antecedents in 19th-cent. Germany. Its history in N America began in Canada in 1900. *ANTIGONISH MOVEMENT.

[M. T. HANSBURY]

CREDO, first word of the Nicene Creed, the third part of the Ordinary of the Mass. Although part of the Mozarabic liturgy as early as 589, the Credo was not finally admitted as part of the Ordinary until 1014 at the insistence of Henry II. In plainsong the celebrant intones the initial phrase, "Credo in unum Deum," and the choir enters at "Patrem omnipotentem." There are in the *Liber usualis,* the comprehensive liturgical book of the RC Church, 18 settings of the Credo in Gregorian chant. The music varies in ornateness according to its use on more or less solemn occasions. The Credo is largely syllabic, made up of long successions of short verbal phrases without repetition; however, certain musical strains reappear to give unity to the chant. The Credo has received extensive musical treatment by great composers throughout the centuries. In polyphonic Masses of the 17th and 18th cent., the Credo was usually treated in majestic style with contrasting expressive settings with the sections "Et incarnatus est" and "Crucifixus." BIBLIOGRAPHY: D.N. Ferguson, *History of Musical Thought* (repr. 1975).

[J. S. PALLOZZA]

CREED (Lat. *credo,* I believe), a summary statement of the principal items of Christian belief, sometimes specifying errors to be rejected. The term is also used to include any *confession of faith, declaration of belief, or the body of church teachings. Several of the creeds, including the Apostles' and Nicene, are constructed according to a three-part formula, referring to the three persons of the

Trinity, a pattern thought to have been modeled upon Mt 28.19. The creeds developed from baptismal rituals in the early centuries; the candidate for baptism memorized the basic statement of the Church's belief and declared it at baptism as his own commitment. Official creeds in fixed form began to develop in the 3d and 4th cents., but important affirmations of faith are found earlier, as in the Shema of Dt 6.1–25, as well as in the NT. The most fundamental of the latter is generally held to be "Jesus is Lord" (1 Cor 12.3; Phil 2.11). The creeds are generally regarded as *doctrinal standards in the Churches and as a witness to the world of what Christians stand for. They serve affirmatively as guides to what is basic Christian teaching, and negatively as bulwarks against distortions of the Christian message. Worshiping congregations recite them in unison as an expression of their common faith. Creeds have been opposed by some Christians who regard them as an infringement on individual freedom, and by others who consider the Bible the sole authority for Christian belief. Nonetheless, almost all Christian groups have found it important, even essential, to make some statement expressing their central convictions. BIBLIOGRAPHY: J. Leith, *Creeds of the Churches* (1963); J. N. D. Kelly, *Early Christian Creeds* (3d ed., 1960); Schaff Creeds; F. X. Murphy, NCE 4:432–438. *APOSTLES' CREED; *ATHANASIAN CREED; *NICENE CREED; *CONFESSION OF FAITH; *CONFESSIONALISM; *ANTICREEDALISM.

[T. EARLY]

CREED (IN THE MASS). The introduction of the *Nicene Creed into the Eucharistic Liturgy was begun in the East, at Antioch by the Monophysite Bp. *Peter the Fuller in 476, and thereafter spread throughout the Eastern Churches. The Creed was chanted at the end of the Canon, before the Our Father. The same practice, under Byzantine influence, was decreed for Spain in 589 by the Council of Toledo. In the palace of Charlemagne at Aix-la-Chapelle, the custom of reciting the Creed after the Gospel began *c.*794, and spread throughout the Carolingian Empire. Not until 1014, however, on the occasion of the coronation of the Emperor Henry II was the practice sanctioned for Masses in Rome by Pope Benedict VIII.

In the East the Creed was recited at every Eucharistic Liturgy. In the West practice varied. At first it was recited only on feasts connected directly with one of the creedal articles. In the Middle Ages it became more frequent; Pius V's reform of the liturgy (1570) restricted its use to Sundays and certain other great feasts. In the liturgical reforms after Vatican Council II, frequency of use was further restricted, but the Creed is always recited on Sundays.

[T. C. O'BRIEN]

CREED, ORTHODOX, see ORTHODOX CREED.

CREED OF PIUS IV, a brief summary of RC teaching, stressing the points questioned by the Protestant Reformers,

drawn up by Pius IV at the close of the Council of *Trent in 1563. It became known as the *Professio fidei Tridentina* or the Creed of Pius. All appointees to ecclesiastic office and candidates for advanced degrees were required to read it as a profession of orthodoxy. Later it became part of the ceremony for the reception of adult converts into the RC Church. The Creed, slightly modified by Pius X, continued in use until the end of Vatican Council II. The English text may be found in the 1964 *Collectio Rituum,* 152–154. BIBLIOGRAPHY: Pastor 16:11–12.

[B. L. MARTHALER]

CREEDS, ECUMENICAL, see ECUMENICAL CREEDS.

CREGLINGEN ALTARPIECE (1495–99), carved-wood altarpiece of the *Assumption of the Virgin* in the parish church of Creglingen, the work of Germany's great sculptor, Tilman Riemenschneider (*c.*1460–1531). The canopy is an intricate weaving of Flamboyant Gothic forms echoed in restless draperies not descriptive of figures but in rhythmic transitions tying all together. The spiritual, weightless figures are distinctively Riemenschneider's, their faces strained, melancholy, and anxious—consonant with the troubled age of the *Schmerzensmann* (man of sorrows), weary and unsmiling.

[M. J. DALY]

CREMATION, the reducing of corpses to ashes by fire. Some pagan societies in antiquity, e.g., the Roman Empire, practiced cremation. In apostolic times Christians followed the Jewish practice of burial, often risking their lives to recover the corpses of martyrs before they were cremated. By the 5th cent. cremation was abandoned in the Western world in favor of inhumation. In the last quarter of the 19th cent. several cremation societies were organized in various European countries which were able to have laws passed recognizing cremation as an acceptable funeral custom.

The Catholic Church reacted against this trend, starting in 1886 and culminating in two canons of the Code of Canon Law (CIC cc. 1203, 1240). The proponents of cremation give two main arguments in favor of it: public hygiene and the conservation of land. The Church countered with two arguments: cremation was hardly compatible with the unbroken custom of Christian burial in the liturgy for the dead; and, perhaps more important, the 19th-cent. proponents were motivated by materialistic and anti-Catholic sentiments.

However, by the 1960s, the climate of Christian attitudes toward cremation seemed to be changing. Some non-Catholic Christians in the U.S. urged cremation from different and Christian motives. They proposed it in opposition to what seemed to them an anti-Christian and materialistic denial of death and an overemphasis on the importance of the body implied in some American funeral customs. Today those who advocate cremation apparently do not commonly do so as a sign of contempt for the body and/or person, nor as a denial of the resurrection of the dead. The penalties attached to CIC c. 1240 (deprival of ecclesiastical burial for those who ordered their bodies to be cremated) were withdrawn by a decree of the Holy Office (July 5, 1963), except for those who practice cremation for anti-Catholic purposes. This seemed to indicate a change in the presumption of the law as it was previously understood, namely that a person leaving orders that his body be cremated after his death, was in bad faith. This became clearer with the publication of the *Ordo Exsequiarum* (Aug. 15, 1969). The pastor who considers denying Christian burial because of cremation is required to consult the ordinary, and he should only do so provided he has some evidence of bad faith.

[C. NEELY]

CRESCAS, HASDAI BEN ABRAHAM (1340–1410), Spanish philosopher and rabbi. Born into a distinguished family, C. was influential in the Jewish community; after his son died in the persecution of the Jews in Aragon (1391), he went to Saragossa. It was there that he undertook to protect Jewish theology and philosophy from the subversions he believed Christian theology held for both. One of his major works, *Light of the Lord* (or *Adonai*) was first published at Ferrara (1556). Like other Judaic thinkers, he refused to compromise Judaic thought with Aristotelian theory. In this work, he gives a critical presentation of Maimonides' 26 basic propositions of physics. C. pointed out the inadequacies of the theory by counter-proposing another theory, which held that time is duration independent of motion and that a vacuum exists, which is based on a conception of space independent of body. In this way he was able to account for infinity of time and space without the Aristotelian reliance on the prime mover. Throughout his theological speculations C. retained his belief in God's simplicity while still insisting on his essential attributes which are unified by his divine goodness. Other concepts with which C. took issue were those of divine foreknowledge and man's free will. C. insisted on the dual component of contingency and necessity in man's actions. Man's free will is dependent on his feelings of approval and disapproval of certain acts he does. In some ways, C. influenced such Renaissance thinkers as Giordano *Bruno and Pico della *Mirandola.

[J. R. RIVELLO]

CRESCENTII, a Roman family prominent for 50 years over the turn of the 10th cent. in the tangled, shifting, and rather squalid disputes when the papacy almost became a chaplaincy to the Ottonian Empire or, what was worse, to a Roman faction. In 963 Crescentius de Caballo Marmoreo attempted to depose John XII; in 964 his kinsman Crescentius de Theodora led a revolt against Benedict VI, who was strangled; later he was pardoned by Benedict VII and became a monk. His sons, John and Crescentius II, brought about the return of the antipope Boniface VII who starved

the lawful Pope to death and created John Roman Patrician. Crescentius II took the title of Roman Consul and ruled the city while John XV was kept a virtual prisoner in the Lateran. He rose against the Emperor's nominee, Gregory V, and, possibly in hopes of Byzantine support, set up a Greek-speaking antipope, but was executed on the battlements of Castel Sant'Angelo (998), and his antipope was blinded. His son John, however, continued to control the papacy until the pontificate of Sergius IV (1009–12). On John's death (1012) political power passed to the Tusculani. A cadet branch of the Crescentii supported an antipope in 1045, and, deprived of the countship of Sabina by Nicholas II in 1060, disappeared from history.

[T. GILBY]

CRESPI, ANTONIO MARIA (Il Bustino; fl. 17th cent.), Italian painter from Busto Arsizio near Milan, who with his father painted the series of frescoes of the life and triumph of St. Lawrence in Val d'Intelvi and a portrait of the Dominican Pio Rossi, later engraved by G. B. Coriolano.

[M. J. DALY]

CRESPI, DANIELE (c. 1600–30), Italian artist, who after study in Milan under Il Cerano (see CRESPI, GIOVANNI BATTISTA), painted with the austere religious feeling of St. Charles Borromeo in a direct realism (*St. Charles Borromeo at Supper*, c. 1628). C.'s use of overhead light and popular types recall Zurbarán. BIBLIOGRAPHY: R. Wittkower, *Art and Architecture in Italy, 1600–1750* (1958).

[M. J. DALY]

CRESPI, GIOVANNI BATTISTA (Il Cerano; 1575–1632), Italian painter and sculptor, born in Cerano, finally director of Federico Borromeo's academy (1620). Using Venetian color, Michelangelesque forms, and Mannerist space (*St. Charles Borromeo Blesses the Crosses*, Milan), C. expressed in his works the emotional intensity of the 17th cent. (*Resurrected Christ with Saints*, c. 1625). BIBLIOGRAPHY: M. Valsecchi, "Notizie sul Cerano," *Paragone* 15 (1964).

[M. J. DALY]

CRESPI, GIUSEPPE MARIA (Lo Spagnuolo; 1664–1747), Italian painter from Bologna influenced by Carracci, Correggio, Barocci, and the Venetians. Considered a genius, C. expressed with technical mastery in chiaroscuro a psychological analysis of man (*Massacre of the Innocents; St. John of Nepomuk as Confessor to the Queen of Bohemia*) influencing the 18th-cent. Venetians Longhi and Tiepolo. BIBLIOGRAPHY: R. Wittkower, *Art and Architecture in Italy, 1600–1750* (1958).

[M. J. DALY]

CRESPY, PEACE OF, treaty of 1544 ending the war between the Emperor Charles V and Francis I of France. The treaty was concluded at Crépy-en-Laonnois, formerly spelled Crespy. Charles gave up claims to Burgundy and Francis to Naples, Flanders, and Artois. Francis also agreed to support the Council of Trent, which was thereby enabled to begin the following year. In a secret treaty Francis promised to aid Charles against the Protestants and Henry VIII.

[T. EARLY]

CRETAN-MYCENAEAN RELIGION. Though there are numerous archeological remains that once pertained to Cretan rites and beliefs, they are not easily interpreted. The remains from Mycenae are far fewer and even more ambiguous. The Minoans of Crete built no separate temples but worshiped in caves or in small chapels within their homes or palaces. One of their most popular cult objects was a bare-breasted goddess holding in her hands a pair of snakes. Sir Arthur Evans and others have contended that this represents a chthonic deity, a Great Goddess like the Great Mother of Anatolia, and that the Minoans consequently practiced a kind of primitive monotheism. M. P. Nilsson, on the other hand, has argued that the snakes indicate that the goddess was a household deity and that the Minoans worshiped a multiplicity of gods, even though the majority were female. There is evidence also that they worshiped trees and pillars and believed in demons and monsters. Besides offering sacrifices and libations, they seem to have performed ritualistic dances in honor of their gods. Stepped altars, tables for liquid offerings, horns of consecration, bilobed shields, and double axes were variously used in their cultic practices. In contrast to the Minoans, whose beliefs and civilization were of a Mediterranean origin, the Myceneans were of Indo-European descent and must have worshiped the original sky-gods who became the Olympian deities of Homeric and classical Greece. When they conquered Knossos, they brought with them these deities. The names of Potnia Atana (Athena), Zeus, Hera, and Poseidon are among those that have been deciphered on tablets written in Linear B. Along with Minoan art, the Myceneans must have adopted in turn a number of the beliefs and symbols, e.g., that of the pillar, from the people they conquered. BIBLIOGRAPHY: M. P. Nilsson, OCD 762–763; E. Vermeule, *Greece in the Bronze Age* (1964) 280–297.

[M. J. COSTELLOE]

CRETAN SNAKE GODDESS, Earth deity highly venerated in Minoan Crete. The ivory and gold, or faïence statuettes with typical Cretan tight bodice, exposed breasts, flounced skirt, and tall headgear, having one or more snakes around the body and arms, honored the snake goddess *Okiouros* as guardian spirit of the house. Two faïence statuettes (c. 1600 B.C.) were found at the Palace of Knossos, of which one figurine 35 centimeters high is considered the largest extant example of Minoan sculpture in the round. There are Cretan snake goddesses in the Boston Museum of Fine Arts. BIBLIOGRAPHY: R. W. Hutchinson, *Prehistoric Crete* (1962).

[M. J. DALY]

CRETE, see CANDIA.

CRÉTIN, JOSEPH (1799–1857), first bp. of St. Paul, Minnesota. Born at Montluel, Ain, France, C. studied at Saint-Sulpice, Paris, and was ordained priest in 1823. He served for a time as parish priest at Ferney but wanted to become a missionary. When Bp. Loras, first bp. of Dubuque, Iowa, came to France (1838) to recruit priests for his new diocese, C. volunteered, returning to the U.S. with him. At first vicar-general of Dubuque, he labored for 11 years chiefly at Dubuque, Prairie du Chien, Wis., and among the Winnebago Indians of Winneshiek County, Iowa. In 1850 St. Paul, Minn., became the seat of a new diocese and C. was named its first bishop. Building a church and school, he brought to St. Paul the Sisters of St. Joseph and the Sisters of St. Benedict to instruct the children. He also built a hospital and laid out plans for a seminary. Through letters published in U.S. and German newspapers C., together with F. X. *Pierz, encouraged Catholic immigrants from Europe to settle in Minnesota.

CRÉTINEAU-JOLY, JACQUES AUGUSTIN MARIE (1803–75), French journalist, historian, poet. Though his aggressive temperament embroiled him in recurring controversy, C.-J. was a substantial historian. A royalist, he founded the journal *Le Vendéen* in 1830 as a vehicle for anti-revolutionary and antirepublican ideas. Two volumes of poetry depart from the direction of most of his work, *Les chants romains* (1826) and *Les Trappistes* (1829). Among the many historical works he published in the years 1840–69, the most important was *Histoire religieuse, politique et littéraire de la Compagnie de Jésus* (1844–46), a six-volume work in defense of the Jesuits. Again he returned to the history of the Jesuits in *Clement XIV et les Jésuites* (1847), an illuminating if polemical account of the suppression of the order. BIBLIOGRAPHY: M. U. Maynard, *J. Crétineau-Joly* (1875).

[J. R. AHERNE]

CREUZER, GEORG FRIEDRICH (1771–1858), German philologist and specialist in mythology. C. studied at his native Marburg, where in 1800 he became a professor. In 1804 he was appointed professor of philology at Heidelberg, a position he held for 45 years. His famous work, *Symbolik und Mythologie der alten Volker, besonders der Griechen,* contained his theory of Homeric mythology. His fantastic views became a subject of controversy in his own lifetime and were refuted by C. A. Lobeck, K. O. Müller, and J. H. Voss. C.'s other works included a critical edition of Plotinus and a history of Greek art. BIBLIOGRAPHY: N. Turchi, EncCatt 4:872.

[J. A. ROCHE]

CRIB, the place where Jesus was laid after his birth. More frequently the term refers to the entire Nativity scene. One finds such Nativity scenes on the early Christian sarcophagi (c.343). St. Francis of Assisi (13th cent.) initiated that special devotion to the crib which has become part of the modern celebration of Christmas. The home crib became popular in Europe during the 19th century. BIBLIOGRAPHY: N. De Robeck, *Christmas Crib* (1956).

[N. KOLLAR]

CRICHTON-STUART, JOHN PATRICK (1847–1900), third marquis of Bute, Scottish scholar and philanthropist. After study at Harrow and Oxford, C. was converted to Catholicism. He helped develop Welsh vineyards and the port facilities at Cardiff, where he became mayor and president of University College. He was twice rector of St. Andrews Univ. (1892–98) and gave generously to it as well as to Glasgow University. Among his published writings the best-known is his translation of the Roman Breviary (1879). BIBLIOGRAPHY: J. Quinn, NCE 4:448.

CRIME (CANON LAW), a word preferred by some RC canonists to translate into English the term *delictum* (delict) defined in CIC c. 2195. As there understood, a crime (or delict) is an external and morally imputable violation of law (i.e., divine or ecclesiastical law) to which a canonical penalty, whether determinate or indeterminate, is attached in canon law.

[P. K. MEAGHER]

CRIME (IMPEDIMENT TO MARRIAGE), a diriment impediment of ecclesiastical origin barring marriage between a man and a woman who have violated a legitimate marriage of one or the other in any of the four following ways: (1) by committing adultery together when this is coupled with a promise to enter into a future marriage (e.g., after the death of the legitimate spouse). (2) By committing adultery together and attempting marriage (even civil marriage) while the legitimate spouse is still alive. (3) By committing adultery together and taking the life of the legitimate spouse, the actual homicide being perpetrated by one of the adulterous partners, even without the knowledge or consent of the other. (4) By mutual conspiracy and/or cooperative effort between a man and a woman in bringing about the death of the legitimate spouse of one or the other, even if there has been no adultery between them. In this last case, moral cooperation suffices to give rise to the impediment; actual physical cooperation is not necessary. CIC c. 1075.

[P. K. MEAGHER]

CRIMINALI, ANTONIO (1520–49), Jesuit protomartyr. A native of Parma, C. was a Jesuit from 1542. He was sent to Goa in 1545 and worked as a missionary along the Malabar Coast of India. St. Francis Xavier confirmed him as superior of the mission in that area. He was slain in Vêdâlai (Ramnâd, Madras) while attempting to save Christian women and children during a Muslim attack. BIBLIOGRAPHY: Sommervogel 2:1659.

[P. K. MEAGHER]

CRIOPHORUS, a Greek statue of a man carrying a ram, which with the *Moscophorus* (Calf-bearer) was the prototype of later figures of Christ the Good Shepherd.

[M. J. DALY]

CRISIS THEOLOGY, name given to the earliest phase of the theology of Karl *Barth and those associated with him, esp. Emil *Brunner (see DIALECTICAL THEOLOGY). "Crisis" here may be taken in either of two senses. It may refer to the proximate occasion prompting this theological trend, i.e., the outbreak of World War I and the consequent disillusionment of Barth and his associates with the optimism of *liberal theology, esp. as regards its thought about society and culture. "Crisis" may also refer to the mode in which the Barthians tended to express themselves, i.e., in "critical categories," such as the negation of any power in man to reach God, the absolute necessity of God's grace, and the importance of eschatology.

One of the important features of the theology of crisis was its return to the sources of Reformation thought, bypassing Protestant scholasticism. Barth esp. repudiates, however, the interpretation given the fathers of the Reformation by F. *Schleiermacher and E. *Troeltsch. Barth's commentary (1919) on the Epistle to the Romans was like the charter of crisis theology. He employed the Pauline polemic against justification by works of the Law to upbraid modern theologians for having fallen into the trap of granting to human nature the capacity of attaining to God and of practicing "religion" effectively.

[M. B. SCHEPERS]

CRISÓGONO DE JESÚS SACRAMENTADO (1904–45), writer. A Spaniard, he entered the Discalced Carmelites and was ordained in 1927. In 1941 he founded *Revista de Espiritualidad*. C. wrote a number of works in his brief career, notably *San Juan de la Cruz; Su obra científica y su obra literaria* (2 v., 1929) and *Compendio de ascética y mística* (1933). BIBLIOGRAPHY: E. A. Peers, *St. Teresa of Jesus and Other Addresses* (1953) 198–200.

[J. R. AHERNE]

CRISPIN OF VITERBO, BL. (Pietro Fioretti; 1668–1750), Italian Capuchin brother. Taught by Jesuits in his youth, he was for some years a cobbler. Becoming a Capuchin in the Roman province (1693), he assumed the name Crispin, patron of his trade. For almost a half cent. he served as quaestor, begging for the poor as well as for the needs of the monastery. Notable for miracles that accompanied his apostolate, he attracted many of the laity and of the clergy by his joy and spirit of trust. His devotion to the Mother of God was tender and constant. In 1806 he was beatified. BIBLIOGRAPHY: C. Hammer, "Our Lady's Favorite," *Round Table of Franciscan Research* 23 (1958) 17–21; B. d'Arenzano, BiblSanct 4:312–313; Butler 2:365.

[M. R. BROWN]

CRISPIN AND CRISPINIAN, SS. (3d cent.), martyrs. According to legend, they were highborn Romans who left home to preach the Gospel in Gaul. Settling in Soissons, they supported themselves as shoemakers at night while preaching the Gospel by day. Because of pagan complaints, they were tortured and killed. Their names are also connected by another legend with Faversham, Kent, England. They are thought by some to have been Roman martyrs whose relics were later brought to Soissons. They are esp. remembered in English-speaking countries because of their mention by Shakespeare's Henry V in his speech on the eve of the battle of Agincourt. (*Henry V:* act 4, scene 3). BIBLIOGRAPHY: A. Amore, EncCatt 4:887; Butler 4:197–198.

[R. B. ENO]

CRISPINA, ST. (d. 304), martyr. During the persecution of Diocletian, C., a matron of Thagora in Numidia and the mother of several children, was summoned before the proconsul Anulius at Tebessa and urged to apostatize. When she refused, she was decapitated. Her *passio,* despite some additions, is fairly reliable and contains the court record of her interrogations. The ruins of her shrine have been found at Theveste (Tebessa). BIBLIOGRAPHY: Butler 4:497–499; A. Amore, EncCatt 4:886; St. Augustine, *Sermons* 286 and 354; *idem, Enarrationes in Psalmos* 120 and 137.

[R. B. ENO]

CRISPOLTI, FILIPPO (1857–1942), Italian journalist and senator. C. wrote for newspapers in Turin, Rome, and Genoa before he founded *Avvenire* (later *Avvenire d'Italia*) at Bologna in 1896. He also contributed numerous articles to other Catholic dailies and magazines besides writing volumes in many genres. In 1919 he was elected deputy by the first political party of Italian Catholics. In 1922 he became a senator. When popularism attacked fascism in 1924 C. published a manifesto against the Popularists which was branded as a betrayal of the party. BIBLIOGRAPHY: E. Lucatello, NCE 4:462.

CRITERION, CRITERIOLOGY, terms that refer to the vindication of the truthfulness of human knowledge. G. *Vico used the term "criterion of truth" in his discussion of R. *Descartes' philosophy; criteriology is a name for the philosophical, critical discipline that deals with the possibility and the establishment of a criterion of truth and objectivity. *EPISTEMOLOGY.

[T. C. O'BRIEN]

CRITICAL PHILOSOPHY, historically, the philosophy and its method developed by I. Kant, particularly in his *Critique of Pure Reason* (1781) and *Critique of Practical Reason* (1783). The criticism undertaken is directed toward the very possibility of knowledge and questions the faculty of knowing; the term transcendental also was employed by Kant as equivalent to critical. Critical philosophy may also be taken in a more general sense to describe any philosophy, or phase of it, having a similar intent. *KANT, I.; *NEO-KANTIANISM; *EPISTEMOLOGY.

[J. R. RIVELLO]

CRITICISM, PHILOSOPHICAL: (1) see CRITICAL PHILOSOPHY; (2) in *aesthetics, questioning, as I. *Kant did, the possibility of objectively valid judgments of beauty, particularly necessary because of the clearly subjective elements in aesthetic response.

[T. C. O'BRIEN]

CRIVELLI, CARLO (fl. 1457–93), Italian painter and chief artist of the rural Marches. His earliest signed work (*Madonna and Child,* Verona) of sharp line and polished surface, with C.'s distinctive ornamental garlands of fruits, points to Schiavone of Padua. C.'s early work, delicate, light in tone, and brilliantly graceful in ornamentation, is expressed in a sharp linear style. Many Pietàs are in U.S. museums. His later *Annunciation* (1486) and *Madonna of the Candle* (1493), monumental, dark, and brilliant of execution are less emotional, evidencing the fixed style of provincial isolation. BIBLIOGRAPHY: P. Zambetti, *Carlo Crivelli* (1961).

[M. J. DALY]

CROAGH PATRICK, peak in County Mayo (2,510 feet high), singular for its almost perfect conical formation. It is sometimes referred to as the "Sinai of Ireland," because it is piously believed that Patrick, the Apostle of Ireland, like Moses and Christ, spent 40 days and 40 nights there in contemplative prayer and penance. A place of pilgrimage throughout history, it remains today a focus of Catholic piety.

[R. C. EGAN]

CROATIA, predominantly Catholic region in NW Yugoslavia. The people known as Croatians (*Hrvatska*) are of uncertain origin, but traditionally they have been considered Slavs who migrated from beyond the Carpathians in the 5th-6th cent. to Roman Pannonia and settled there. The first definite reference to them comes from the time of Charlemagne, when they accepted Frankish overlordship. From about the same period they were Christian, and though they gained the right to use Croatian in their liturgy, they adopted the Latin alphabet and became culturally oriented to the West. Croatia became a kingdom under Tomislav, who received the crown in 925 from Pope John X. Following the East-West schism, Petar Kresimir (1058–74) broke relations with Byzantium and allied with Rome. Croatians and their neighbors to the northwest, the Slovenes, subsequently remained Roman Catholic, while Serbs and Macedonians to the East stayed under the influence of Constantinople and developed as Eastern Orthodox peoples. Dimitar Zvonimir, crowned by a legate of Pope Gregory VII, was killed by Croatians who accused him of accepting the role of papal vassal. In the late 11th cent., Ladislaus I of Hungary took sovereignty over Croatia, and it remained under the Hungarian monarchy for 8 cent., though exercising virtual independence part of the time.

Territorial bounds of Croatia have varied considerably. Much of the area came under Turkish rule as a result of the 1526 Battle of Mohacs. In 1527 Croatian feudal lords accepted Habsburg overlordship, and Croatia became a Habsburg outpost against the Turks. Dalmatia, at times part of Croatia, was ruled by Venice for 4 cent. after 1403. Croatia now includes Dalmatia, Slavonia, and most of Istria, as well as Croatia proper.

Through the centuries that Croatia was under the Hungarian crown, Croatians continuously struggled to preserve their national rights and culture. Upon the collapse of the Austro-Hungarian Empire in 1918, the Croatian Diet declared independence and then joined in formation of a union of the Yugoslavs (South Slavs).

In 1941, with Yugoslavia under German and Italian domination, the Fascist Ustachi set up an independent Croatia. But following the war, Tito, whose father was a Croatian peasant, became president of a Communist Yugoslavia, with Croatia one of six constituent republics. A period of intense conflict between the Communist state and the Catholic Church in Croatia ensued as the government abolished many religious institutions. Abp. (later Card.) A. Stepinac (1898–1960) of Zagreb was tried and sentenced to prison in 1946 for having supported establishment of the independent Croatia in 1941, though he had criticized the regime for violation of human rights. But Yugoslavia renewed diplomatic ties with the Holy See in 1970, and in 1971 Tito became the first Communist chief of state to visit a pope. BIBLIOGRAPHY: *Croatia* (ed. F. H. Eterovich and C. Spalatin, 2 v., 1964, 1970).

[T. EARLY]

CROCE, BENEDETTO (1866–1952), Italian philosopher-statesman. C.was the founder of *La Critica,* a cultural journal that influenced much of Europe, and later, of the Institute for Historical Studies (1946). He was made a life member of the Italian Senate (1910). At first he subscribed to the newly formed Fascist party; ultimately he broke with the party (1925) and with his friend, G. Gentile, who had collaborated with him in the reformation of the Italian school system. Influenced by *Hegel and G. *Vico, C.'s most important contributions in philosophy are in the field of aesthetics, but even this was influenced by his absolute adherence to the principle of historicism (which holds that history is human consciousness, self-validating and self-constituting, in a specific generation) as the guide for interpretation of art. There are four phases of his aesthetic

theory; at first that theory was strongly idealist, and metaphysically grounded, but he later moved into a purely idealist position. The phases of aesthetic experience are cognitive and comprise the following: aesthetic intuition, lyrical intuition, cosmic intuition, and the fourth stage, which is a negative response to the intuitive, his theory of literature. Although first influenced by Kant's *Anschauung* in the theory of intuition and by Hegel's dialectic in history, C. later revised his thinking on both issues. His works include some on ethics, politics, economics, and law. Chief among these are: *Aesthetic* (tr. D. Ainslie, 1909); *Logic* (tr. D. Ainslie, 1917); *What Is Living and What Is Dead in the Philosophy of Hegel?* (tr. D. Ainslie, 1915); *Essence of Aesthetic* (tr. D. Ainslie, 1921); *Autobiography* (tr. R. G. Collingwood, 1927). BIBLIOGRAPHY: H. S. Harris, EncPhil 2:263–267; B. Bosanquet, *Croce's Aesthetic* (pa. 1974); G. N. Orsini, *Benedetto Croce, Philosopher of Art and Literary Critic* (1961).

[J. R. RIVELLO]

CROCKAERT, PETER (d. 1524), Dominican pioneer in the "Second Scholasticism." Born in Brussels, he studied at Paris in the nominalist tradition of William Ockham. After entering the Dominicans at the convent of Saint-Jacques in 1503, he became an ardent Thomist. He was one of the first (1509) to use as his lecture text St. Thomas Aquinas's *Summa theologiae* instead of the *Sentences* of *Peter Lombard. Through the enthusiasm for the thought of St. Thomas communicated to his students, notably F. de *Vitoria, C. was directly responsible for the Thomistic renaissance of the 16th century. Besides his logical and physical treatises, with de Vitoria C. wrote a commentary on ThAq ST 2a2ae (1512).

[T. C. O'BRIEN]

CROMWELL, OLIVER (1599–1658), English Puritan, military and political leader. He was born in Huntingdonshire of a landowning family that owed its start to property gained from Henry VIII's *dissolution of the monasteries (see CROMWELL, THOMAS). Influenced by Puritan preachers and teachers, C. experienced a religious conversion *c.*1628. In the Long Parliament, which opened in 1640, he early became identified with the *Independents and took an active part in the steps that led to the Civil Wars. Impelled by a Puritan concscience and a sense of divine calling, he played an important role in decisive victories at Marston Moor (1644) and Naseby (1645) and eventually gained control of the New Model Army, composed of Baptists, Independents, and various sectaries. After the execution of Charles I, C. and his Independents established England as a Commonwealth. Troubles took him to Ireland (1649), where he subdued the populace by drastic measures, including the massacres at Drogheda and Wexford. In 1651–52, at Dunbar and Worcester, the commander-in-chief put down Scottish forces supporting the Pretender, Charles II. Faced with internal and external crises, C. needed greater power. Convinced that providence had destined him to save his country, he became Lord Protector (1653) and exercised power in an arbitrary but benevolent way. He refused the title of king, however, when it was proffered him in 1657. In religious matters, he ended the attempt to establish Presbyterianism and allowed toleration to *Nonconformists who agreed on essential gospel truths. Even Catholics and others were generally tolerated, as long as they did not disturb the peace. Continuing domestic unrest, financial crises, threats from abroad, and his own poor health plagued him all of his days as Lord Protector. When he died, his son, Richard, proved incapable of forwarding his father's policies, and Charles II was invited to return to the throne. BIBLIOGRAPHY: R. S. Paul, *Lord Protector: Religion and Politics in the Life of Oliver Cromwell* (1955); C. H. Firth, *Oliver Cromwell and the Rule of the Puritans in England* (1953); H. Aveling, NCE 4:470–471.

[N. H. MARING]

CROMWELL, THOMAS (*c.*1458–1540), lay political figure prominent in the English Reformation. Born in Putney, he became a mercenary soldier in Italy, an entrepreneur in the Low Countries, moneylender, lawyer, general factotum to Cardinal Wolsey, who employed him as agent in the dissolution of the lesser monasteries and for his foundations at Oxford and Ipswich, and member of Parliament, where he rose steadily as fixer for the King's business. Though included in *Foxe's Book of Martyrs, he was in fact a ruffian whose brutality broke through his smooth and witty address; he was able, unscrupulous, lewd, indifferent to religious values, and looked to the Reformers because they seemed the supporters of absolute power. The only cause to which he was devoted was the single polity under the Royal Supremacy. He arranged for the translation of the *Defensor pacis* of *Marsilius of Padua at his own expense. He belonged to the seamier side of the Renaissance, and was the first English politician to be familiar with Machiavelli; contemptuous of dreamers like Plato, he set himself to consult the inclination of the prince. It was destined to destroy him, but in the meantime he became the second most powerful person in the realm. He was appointed royal secretary in 1534, and under the Act of Supremacy proceeded against Thomas More and John Fisher (whom he succeeded as chancellor of Cambridge University), sent Reynolds and the Charterhouse monks to their death, suppressed the religious houses, persecuted the Princess Mary for her Catholicism, and bullied the clergy. Appointed the king's vice-regent "in spirituals," he exercised a lay tyranny over the Church in England such as had not been seen before and has not been since. His only positive service to the Church for which posterity can be grateful was to order the keeping of parish-registers for every wedding, christening, and burial. He was generally hated, and the chief demand of the Catholic rising in the North was that he should be expelled from the council and condignly punished. His main incursion into foreign policy led to failure and his death. To gain the support of the Protestant party in Germany against a coalition between the Emperor and the King of France, he arranged the marriage of Henry VIII with Anne of Cleves (1540). The threat was never real, and the King, unattracted by the lady, divorced her a few months afterwards. Though C. was created Earl of Essex, the royal rage was smouldering and suddenly burst without warning. Without trial, but by bill of attainder, C. was indicted on charges as devious as his own proceedings and sentenced to the block and a clumsy headsman on Tower Hill. In his final address he repudiated all heresy and declared that he died in the Catholic faith. BIBLIOGRAPHY: A. G. Dickens, *Thomas Cromwell and the English Reformation* (1960); R. B. Merriman, *Life and Letters of Thomas Cromwell* (2 v., 1902). *DISSOLUTION OF THE MONASTERIES.

[T. GILBY]

CRONACA, IL (Simone del Pollaiolo; 1457–1508), Italian architect. In Florence C. worked on the Palazzo Strozzi (1489–1500) and, as *capomaestro* of the cathedral, built the sacristy of Santo Spirito (1495). C.'s most important work is the church of S. Salvatore al Monte (*c.*1504), its spare and sober design admired by Michelangelo.

[M. J. DALY]

CROSIER FATHERS (Canons Regular of the Order of the Holy Cross), an order of religious that began about 1210 at Clairlieu, Belgium, where Theodore of Celles and a few companions chose to live a common life under the rule of St. Augustine. During the long history of the community the members undertook spiritual reform, suffered religious persecution, and were saved from extinction by a revival in 1840. Today the apostolate of the Crosier Fathers includes mission, retreat, and educational work. They have houses in three European countries and missions in Brazil, the Congo, and the Far East. World membership in 1976 was 634 including 456 priests; the U.S. province had 113 priests and 46 brothers. The generalate is at Amersfoort, Netherlands. BIBLIOGRAPHY: A. Van De Pasch, LTK 6:619–621; J. W. Rausch, *Crosier Story* (1960).

[R. A. TODD]

CROSS, THE, the most venerated of all Christian images, because it is the sign and symbol of Christ's Passion. The Lord himself and St. Paul both used the term as a figure of speech: to signify the whole Christian life as it includes suffering in imitation of Christ (cf. Mt 16.24; 1 Cor 1.23; Gal 5.24; 6.14); to signify the redemptive act of Jesus and its power (cf. 1 Cor 1.17; Gal 6.14; Eph 2.16). In the Christian vocabulary, then, "the cross" stands both for the trials of life to be borne by following Christ and for Christ's saving act. Both meanings were given outward expression from the 2d cent. in the sign of the cross, i.e., the tracing of the cross on forehead and breast. This practice, as well as the tracing of the cross in blessings, became part of the liturgy. The large sign of the cross, made by touching in turn forehead, breast, and shoulders dates from the 5th cent., and became accompanied by recitation of the formula, "In the name of the Father, and of the Son, and of the Holy Spirit." Making of the sign of the cross became a profession of faith. The practice of carving or painting the cross as an artifact came late. The cross itself or the crucifix, i.e., the image of Christ on the cross, as any other visible symbol could not be displayed during the age of persecutions; further, it is believed, for those who had witnessed execution by crucifixion it would have been repugnant to depict Christ's cross. Representations of Christ as glorified and ruling from the cross date from the 5th cent.; the more realistic representations date from the later Middle Ages. The theological meaning of veneration of the cross was clarified because of *Iconoclasm in the 8th century. Veneration of the symbol is *latria because of the one symbolized, Christ crucified; veneration of the cross is veneration of the person crucified (Council of Nicaea II, D 600-601; see IMAGES, VENERATION OF). The design of the cross has varied with different artistic traditions; some of the more common forms are: the Latin cross, the Greek cross, the Celtic cross, the Maltese cross; the Russian cross, the cross of St. Andrew (in the form of the letter "X"), the cross of Lorraine.

[T. C. O'BRIEN]

CROSS, ADORATION OF THE, see ADORATION OF THE CROSS

CROSS, ALTAR, see ALTAR CROSS

CROSS, DAUGHTERS OF THE, a religious congregation and a branch of the order founded in 1640 at Paris by Marie l'Huiller de Villeneuve. After the congregation reorganized, it received papal approval (1853). Two years later, the sisters came to the U.S. where they established a house at Shreveport, La., which is now the general motherhouse. In 1902 the community became independent of the original foundation in France. The sisters conduct elementary and secondary schools of Christian doctrine and women's retreat houses in the diocese of Alexandria, La. In 1976 the congregation numbered 42 members in the United States.

[R. A. TODD]

CROSS, EXALTATION OF THE, see TRIUMPH OF THE CROSS.

CROSS, FINDING OF THE HOLY. The story of the finding of the true cross by St. Helena, mother of the Emperor Constantine, about the year 325 has little historical support. It is not mentioned by the most accurate of writers on the Church during the reign of Constantine, Eusebius of Caesaria. And yet there is abundant testimony, esp. that of St. Cyril of Jerusalem, that the cross had been found before the year 350 and that relics of the true cross were already

scattered throughout the world. The pilgrim Aetheria recorded veneration of the true cross in Jerusalem in the second half of the 4th century. Melania the Elder, another pilgrim, refers to the veneration in Jerusalem about the year 400 and Paulinus of Nola also mentions the existence of the true cross in the year 403. There are four distinct accounts of the legend of how the cross was found, three of them naming Helena as the chief agent who led the way to the excavation that uncovered three crosses, the cross of Christ being identified by application to a dead man to whom it brought restoration to life. Whatever the authenticity of the story of the finding, there is no doubt that Christianity accepted the identity of the true cross from the 4th cent. on. BIBLIOGRAPHY: H. Quilliet, DTC 3.2:2342-63; H. Chirat, NCE 4:479-482.

[J. R. AHERNE]

CROSS, HAND, in the Eastern Churches a cross with the lower bar ending in a handle, prescribed by the rubrics at certain times for blessing the people or some object of sacred use. In the East and West Syrian churches it has a thin veil attached, and is used only by a bishop. In the Armenian Rite it is held with a small cloth of silk. In the Coptic liturgy, when the priest incenses the altar on each side, the deacon holds the hand cross aloft and moves from side to side, facing the celebrant.

[A. CODY]

CROSS, PECTORAL, see PECTORAL CROSS.

CROSS, RELICS OF THE TRUE. St. Cyril of Jerusalem in the mid-4th cent. mentions the fact that pilgrims to Jerusalem have taken relics of the cross to all parts of the world. Relics of the cross are mentioned in an inscription at Setif dating from the year 359. The Patriarch of Jerusalem, Juvenal, sent a fragment of the true cross to Pope Leo the Great about the year 455. Emperor Justin II in 569 sent a relic of the cross to Radegunda, Queen of the Franks. Its reception occasioned the hymn of Venantius Fortunatus, the celebrated "Vexilla Regis." Throughout subsequent centuries there are records of many relics of the cross. In the late 19th cent. Rohault de Fleury catalogued all known relics of the cross and estimated that they constituted less than one-third of the size of the cross as estimated to have been used in the crucifixion.

[J. R. AHERNE]

CROSS, WAY OF, see WAY OF THE CROSS.

CROSS PRO ECCLESIA ET PONTIFICE, a papal honor, the Latin portion meaning "For Church and Pope." Pope Leo XIII initiated the decoration as a reward for men and women who rendered important services to the Church.

[H. P. ANNAS]

CROSSED FRIARS, see CRUTCHED FRIARS.

CROSSRAGUEL ABBEY, a Cluniac monastery in Ayrshire, Scotland, founded as an oratory by Duncan, earl of Carrick, a little before 1214, and later erected into an abbey dependent on Paisley. Rebuilt in the early 15th cent., suppressed at the Reformation, it is now a ruin. BIBLIOGRAPHY: *Charters of the Abbey of Crossraguel* (1886); D. E. Easson, *Medieval Religious Houses: Scotland* (1957) 56.

[L. J. MacFARLANE]

CROTUS RUBIANUS (Johannes Jäger; *c.*1480–*c.*1545), German humanist. He studied at Erfurt, where he knew Luther, and in 1510 he became head of the monastery school of Fulda. He initiated production of the *Epistolae Obscurorum Virorum* (*Letters of Obscure Men*, 1515), satirical letters supposedly attacking the humanist J. *Reuchlin but so written as to make Reuchlin's opponents appear ignorant and corrupt. He received a doctorate in theology at Bologna and became rector at Erfurt in 1520. A supporter of Luther for a time, he returned to the Catholic Church in 1531.

[T. EARLY]

CROWLAND, ABBEY OF, former Benedictine monastery dedicated to SS. Mary, Bartholomew, and Guthlac; it was located in Lincolnshire. Following a disastrous fire, Abbot Godfrey rebuilt the church *c.*1110. The best-known work of the monks was the *Abbey Chronicle* compiled *c.*1360. The abbey continued through the 15th century. During the Protestant Reformation it was surrendered by an unpopular and arbitrary abbot, John Bridges, and its monks were pensioned. BIBLIOGRAPHY: Knowles-Hadcock.

CROWN, EPISCOPAL, headgear of Eastern bishops or higher prelates. It is embellished with religious images and mounted by a cross. The origin is obscure, but seems to be a copy of the imperial crown. It resembles the jeweled turban of the Persians from whom the Byzantines probably adopted it. It was only after the 15th cent. that any type of head-covering was worn by prelates. It was first used by the Greeks who began to use it before 1589, for it was at this time that the Patriarch of Moscow was presented a liturgical crown. He was the only prelate who wore the crown at first. In time certain metropolitans began to wear it. By the end of the 18th cent. all Byzantine rite bishops had adopted it as a part of their liturgical dress.

[P. A. MORLINO]

CROWN, FRANCISCAN, a rosary (*corona*) of seven decades, an Our Father and ten Hail Marys in each with two Hail Marys and an Our Father at the end, followed by a Hail Mary for the Holy Father. The mysteries commemorated are the Annunciation, Visitation, Nativity, Adoration of the Magi, Finding of Christ in the Temple, the Resurrection, and the Assumption. In the Middle Ages there were several different forms of chaplets promoted by the Franciscans. The *corona* of St. Joan of France and her associates

was popular in France in the 16th century. The *corona* as later used seems to be a mingling of the two traditions.

[J. R. AHERNE]

CROWN, MARRIAGE. The wearing of a crown by brides and bridegrooms came from pagan antiquity but was also practiced among the Jews. At first Christianity forbade the custom but gradually it came to be accepted by both the Western and Eastern Churches. Though still customary in some parts of the West, it is much more common in the Eastern Church. The usual custom is for the bride to place the crown on the groom, who in turn places a crown on her. The officiating priest says: "O Lord, crown them with glory and honor." The crowning is part of the wedding ceremony in most areas of northern Europe; it is also practiced among Hindus and Arabs.

[J. R. AHERNE]

CROWN OF THORNS, an instrument of torture and mockery, used by Jesus' executioners (Mt 27.29). Most likely taken from the kindling at hand, the exact material is not known; nor whether the crown was a cap or a circlet. Known to have been venerated in Jerusalem in the 5th cent., after the Muslim conquest of Palestine it appeared in Constantinople in the 11th cent. and was given to St. Louis IX, King of France, in the 13th cent., who built a beautiful shrine for it in Paris, the famous Sainte-Chapelle (1248). The authenticity of the relic cannot be established, although its veneration has evoked fervent devotion to Jesus' Passion.

[J. F. FALLON]

CROWNING OF IMAGES, a practice in both East and West of adorning icons, pictures, or statues with a crown of gold or other precious material. It has been much more widely evident in the East (after the Iconoclast conflict ended in the 9th century). In Rome many popes have followed the example of Clement VIII who in the 16th cent. crowned with ceremony a picture of Christ and Mary in the basilica of St. Mary Major. When the crowns were lost, Gregory XVI in 1837 held a solemn rite of restoration. The Chapter of St. Peter's basilica has had the right to crown images of the Blessed Virgin from the 17th century.

[J. R. AHERNE]

CROWNING WITH THORNS, the event described in Mt 27.29 and Mk 15.17 after Jesus' condemnation by Pilate; John places the incident within Jesus' trial before Pilate (19.2), perhaps to heighten the irony in the public rejection of Jesus' kingship (19.5). Luke has a shorter version of the mockery, without the crowning, but performed by Herod and his guards (23.11); Luke's treatment is in line with his tendency to deemphasize reasons for enmity between the Church and Rome. The crown itself, whether intended to cause physical pain or not, was most likely a caricature of the radiate crown worn by Hellenistic "divinized'' rulers and known from coins in the near East for some centuries before this incident. It was probably made from some variety of palm tree possessing thornlike leaflets at the base of its branches. BIBLIOGRAPHY: H. St. John Hart, ''Crown of Thorns in John 19.2–5,'' JTS 3 (1952) 66–75.

[P. J. KEARNEY]

CROZIER (crosier, pastoral staff), a staff conferred on bishops at their consecration and upon abbots at their investiture, and used also by certain prelates not of episcopal rank when performing pontifical functions. According to the present Roman Pontifical it is not conferred upon abbesses, although in some places it was formerly presented to them as well as to abbots. In the Western Church the crozier is curved on top, and this emphasizes the symbolism which sees this staff as the shepherd's crook and hence a mark of the pastoral authority with which the bishop rules his flock. However, it is not clear that the symbolism was not worked out until long after the staff came into use. The actual origin of the staff is not known; it may have been originally an ordinary walking stick. The earliest known reference to its liturgical use dates from the 7th century. Popes, at least since the 12th cent., have not used the crozier, but the reason for this is not known. In time croziers became very ornate, esp. around the curved section. With the liturgical reform the tendency is toward a simpler style. BIBLIOGRAPHY: P. Morrisroe, CE 4:517–518.

[N. KOLLAR]

CRUCIFIX, a *cross to which is affixed an image of Christ. The image may be either painted on the cross, carved, or in bas-relief. The varieties of form are many. The Latin cross, which is the most popular, has a longer vertical or upright bar while the transom or crossbar is shorter. In Slavic countries the more familiar form is that of two transoms and a slanting crossbar at the bottom of the upright bar. In the East the image is almost always painted on the cross. The use of the crucifix was not common before the 6th cent., and the representation of Christ as suffering did not attain general usage until the 13th century. Prior to this time the living, triumphant Christ was portrayed to emphasize his Resurrection and victory over sin and death. BIBLIOGRAPHY: H. Leclercq, DACL 3.2:3045–3141. *ALTAR CROSS.

[P. A. MORLINO]

CRUCIFIXION, a Roman method of execution traceable to a Near Eastern origin, perhaps as a variation on impalement. The cross was a fixed vertical beam and a portable crossbeam which was tied on the shoulders of the scourged prisoner and which he carried naked to the place of execution, a practice modified in the case of Jesus out of concession to Jewish sensibility (Mk 15.20). The victim was fixed to the cross with ropes and sometimes also with four nails (cf. Jn 20.25) and left to a lingering death, caused princi-

pally by asphyxiation, when the exhausted criminal could no longer raise his body from a crouched position to allow his lungs breathing space (hence the breaking of the legs to hasten death, Jn 19.31).

The death of Jesus was clearly a Roman execution, carried out, therefore, because of an alleged offense against Roman law; commentators often note a tendency in the gospel texts to deemphasize, for missionary purposes, the share of Rome in this act. Although it is agreed that developing friction with Judaism in the early Church has to some extent colored the gospel narratives, it should be noted that Luke, varying somewhat from his usual tendency, is more explicit than Matthew and Mark about the threat of Jesus to Roman interests (Lk 23.2,5,14) and that John alone, despite his late composition and strong antipathy to the Jewish leaders (8.44; 10.8), involves the Romans directly in the capture of Jesus (18.3).

The tradition of the crucifixion was esp. important in the formation of the Gospels. It was probably the oldest extended narrative. Mark, most likely the first author of a Gospel, joined the traditions of the earthly life of Jesus to the passion narrative precisely in order to give those traditions an explicit orientation to the death of Christ. John's Gospel, despite its distinctive origins, has a similar orientation to the death of Jesus through numerous symbolic allusions (e.g., 2.4,19; 3.13), possibly intended in opposition to incipient Gnostic movements denying salvific value to Jesus' death.

The affirmation that Jesus' crucifixion was a saving event was expressed very early in the Church (cf. the pre-Pauline formula in 1 Cor 15.3) and was developed through symbols, each conveying partial insights into the mystery; cf., e.g., 1 Cor 5.7 (Passover lamb); 1 Cor 6.20 (paying a price); 1 Cor 11.24–25 (covenant sacrifice); Gal 6.14 (crucifixion of the world); Col 2.15 (victory over angelic spirits); Mt 27.51–52 (new world). Modern study of the words and deeds of Jesus has sought to understand the continuity between the death and resurrection of Jesus on the one hand and his proclamation of total self-giving as preparation for the kingdom of God on the other. The tendency to interpret Christ's death as an act of divine love evoking human love (2 Cor 5.15; Eph 5.2) reaches its sublimest expression in the Gospel of John (e.g., Jn 3.16; 10.14,15,17; 14.31; 15.13,17; 17.23). Christians from NT times on have found special depths of meaning that have evolved into key themes in the theology of Redemption. For example:

The theme of kenosis. The Son of God accepts not only the mission to empty himself by taking on the human condition and death. His self-emptying extends even to accepting death on the Cross, thus identifying himself with the lowliest of human outcasts (Phil 2.8). For the Jew, the man who hung on a tree was cursed (Dt 21.23); Christ redeems man from the Law's curse by accepting this fate for him and transforming its meaning (Gal 3.10–13).

The theme of exaltation. The mystery of Christ's dying is

one in the divine plan with that of his passing over into glory. The two aspects are fused into a single notion, and in St. John's view into a single act (Jn 13.1). His being lifted above the earth on the cross gives visibility to this paschal mystery (Jn 12.32–33).

The theme of healing. Jesus lifted on the cross in death is the source of life and health to those who believe, as was the brazen serpent Moses lifted up in the desert (Jn 3.14–15). St. John Chrysostom finds in Christ's elevation above the earth a sign of the Redemption of the whole cosmos: renewing the air while his blood purifies the earth (PG 49:400–408; cf. ThAq ST 3a, 46.4).

The crucifixion of Christ overturns the values of unredeemed man. Where death came to man by the tree, life comes by the tree in Christ (cf. Preface of the Cross). Henceforth full human life belongs only to him who takes up the cross (Lk 14.27; 9.23) and lives crucified with Christ (Gal 5.24). From being the mark of ignominy, the cross has become the throne from which the Messiah-King reigns (Pius XII, *Myst. Corp.* 35). BIBLIOGRAPHY: J. de Fraine, EDB 462–465; J. P. Schanz, NCE 4:497–498.

[P. J. KEARNEY; C. REGAN]

CRUELTY, the unreasonable infliction of suffering on another. To bring pain upon another is not always unreasonable. One sometimes causes suffering in the effort to alleviate suffering, e.g., as in the pulling of a bad tooth. Reasonable also is the infliction of some suffering in the defense of public order or in the punishment of crime, but in this case the suffering must be imposed according to the balance of justice, and if it is excessive, i.e., more than is necessary, even though cooly and impersonally inflicted, it argues a harshness and severity out of harmony with the justice it is meant to serve. When cruelty springs from a disorder in the human passions of desire and contention, it is to be regarded as unregulated lust or intemperance, counter to the *meekness that should moderate the spleen and to the *clemency that should make gentle the application of discipline. The human maliciousness that goes so far as to seek pleasure in hurting another and in human suffering as such is qualified as a savagery that is truly bestial.

[P. K. MEAGHER]

CRUETS, the containers used to hold the wine and water at the Eucharistic Celebration.

CRUMPE, HENRY (fl. 1376–1401), Irish Cistercian monk of Baltinglass Abbey. As doctor of theology and later professor at Oxford, he was a strenuous opponent of Wycliffe, whose followers he was the first to call "Lollards." He also engaged in controversy with the Dominicans who accused him of heresy. BIBLIOGRAPHY: Dugdale's *Monasticon Anglicanum* (1819), 2:319; DNB (1950) 5:262–263.

[L. J. LEKAI]

CRUSADE BULL, see BULLA CRUCIATA.

CRUSADES, medieval military expeditions organized by the Church for the liberation of the Holy Land and the defense of Christianity. Despite some dispute about its origins, the idea of the crusades had its roots in pilgrimages, esp. to the Holy Land, in the use of military force against excommunicates and heretics, and in the efforts of the Church to put an end to warfare between Christians. The actual crusades, however, were occasioned by the Byzantine need of military assistance against the Seljuk Turks in the late 11th century. Pope Gregory VII had planned to lead the vassals of the Holy See to help Byzantium and then go on pilgrimage to Jerusalem. With Pope Urban II this plan was revived. Although the sources are not clear on all details, it seems certain that Emperor Alexius I requested Western military assistance and that he and the Pope hoped to reestablish formal union between the Greek and the Latin Churches (one cannot rightly speak of schism at this date). At Clermont in France, Nov. 27, 1095, Urban II proclaimed the crusade, appealing to the Western knights to cease fighting one another, to aid their Christian brothers in the East, and also to free Jerusalem. This last element impressed itself most on the simple religious imaginations of the warriors and led to an amazing wave of popular enthusiasm. So successful in fact were the Pope's words that the crusade took on a vastly different form than had been intended. The carefully laid plans of Pope and Emperor called for a highly disciplined military expedition. Instead, unruly mobs wandered and pillaged their way to Constantinople. Eventually, however, the better-organized troops led by Western nobles arrived and, after some diplomatic problems, proceeded on their long and laborious march through Asia Minor to Antioch and finally, July 14, 1099, fought their way into Jerusalem. Subsequent crusades were organized to aid the Latin states of Palestine and Syria, but in 1187 the Turks recaptured Jerusalem. Papal efforts to keep the crusading ideal alive met with more and more criticism and skepticism, and the crusades that did take place either accomplished little or proved disastrous.

It is difficult to evaluate the results of the Crusades. For a time they kept the Turks at bay; they greatly stimulated cultural development and trade; they gave rise to the military and hospital orders. Yet those whom they were designed to help, the Eastern Christians, suffered more as a result, esp. in the so-called Fourth Crusade of 1204. This, perhaps more than anything else, solidified the schism between East and West; it was no longer a dispute between theologians and bishops but a resentment and hatred felt by all classes. Yet, although they went about it poorly, most of the crusaders did make enormous sacrifices for what they felt was a sacred obligation, the defense of Christians and the liberation of the Holy Land. It was an enterprise well in harmony with the medieval mentality. BIBLIOGRAPHY: S. Runciman, *History of the Crusades* (3 v., 1951–54); *History of the Crusades* (ed. K. Setton, 2 v., 1955–62); H. E. Mayer, *Bibliographie zur Geschichte der Kreuzzüge* (1960).

CRUSIUS, CHRISTIAN AUGUST (1715–75), German Lutheran professor. C. taught philosophy and theology at the Univ. of Leipzig. He was the most prominent theological opponent of C. *Wolff's philosophy and exerted influence through his *Opuscula philosophica* (1749). By his attack upon the admissibility of synthetic a priori judgments he won I. *Kant's esteem. C. maintained that the basic subject matter of the entire Bible is salvation history. Some of his interpretations, e.g., of a 2,000-year physical reign of God on earth, dimmed his reputation as a scholar. BIBLIOGRAPHY: I. Ludolphy, EncLuthCh 1:643.

[M. J. SUELZER]

CRUTCHED FRIARS (Crossed Friars), a term used in medieval England for several orders: *Knights of Malta, *Templars, *Trinitarians, perhaps *Bethlehemites and Cruciferi, but esp. the Order of the Holy Cross, known also as the *Crosier Fathers, who had a red and white cross on their scapular.

[T. EARLY]

CRUZ, DIEGO DE LA (fl. *c.* 1486–*c.* 1500), Spanish sculptor and painter. Collaborator with Gil de Siloe, C. polychromed Siloe's altarpiece, *The Tree of Jesse* (1477–88), in the Burgos Cathedral.

[M. J. DALY]

CRUZ, JUANA INÉZ DE LA (Juana Inés de Asbaje y Ramírez; 1651–95), Mexican Discalced Carmelite nun, the first outstanding poet of the New World. Abandoning a life at court, where she was lady-in-waiting to the viceroy's wife and already much esteemed for her wit, knowledge, and charm, J. became a nun before her 16th birthday and from 1669 lived in the Convent of St. Jerome in Mexico City. Until 1693 she devoted much time to literary work. Her many sonnets, ballads, plays, and carols, ranging in subject matter from theological and philosophical topics to the theme of unrequited love, were the first important expressions in poetry of the Mexican spirit. In an autobiographical letter entitled *Reply to Sister Philothea*, she wrote a justification of her life. From 1693 until her death she gave herself entirely to charitable works. She died of the plague contracted while attending the sick. Works: *Obras completas* (ed. A. Méndez Plancarté, 4 v., 1951–57); *Pathless Grove* (tr. P. Cook, 1950). BIBLIOGRAPHY: I. A. Leonard, *Baroque Times in Old Mexico* (1966).

[C. KEYSER]

CRUZADA, see BULLA CRUCIATA.

CRYPTO-CALVINISM, a censorious name for views originating with P. *Melanchthon, esp. in regard to the *Real Presence (see PHILIPPISM). The Gnesiolutherans saw Melanchthon's position as a dangerous compromise with the Calvinist teaching on the Eucharist—hence as a hidden or secret Calvinism. The bitter conflict among second-generation Lutherans is reflected in the *Formula of Concord, Art. VII, strongly reaffirming Luther's doctrine on the Real Presence. *FLACIUS ILLYRICUS, M.; *UBIQUITARIANISM.

[M. B. SCHEPERS]

CRYPTO-JUDAISM, see MARRANOS.

CRYSTAL OF LOTHAIR II, late 9th-cent. engraved rock crystal (with gold frame) of great beauty and uniqueness, showing stylistic affinities with the Reims school, yet in delicacy and beauty of technique transcending all schools (now in the British Museum, London).

[M. J. DALY]

CUBA, island and nation in the Carib. Sea (area, including coastal islands and keys, 44,218 sq mi; pop. [U.N. est. 1971] 8,860,000; ethnic distribution, 75% white, 25% negro, mulatto, and oriental). With 57% of its population living in cities, it is among the most urbanized countries of Latin America; its illiteracy rate is less than 20%. It was discovered by Columbus in 1492; colonization began in 1511 under Diego Velázquez; independence from Spain was achieved in 1898; a socialist republic under Fidel Castro was established in 1959. Cuba was evangelized by Franciscans and Dominicans. B. de *Las Casas worked on the island for 50 years and, together with the Franciscans, rose up against the inhuman treatment of the Indians. Among those engaged in later missionary effort were Piarists, Jesuits, Marists, Christian Brothers, and North American Augustinians. There was a significant religious revival in the 18th cent. marked by notable progress in education. A seminary and a college were established in Havana and, in 1728, a university. Slavery was abolished in 1847. In the years that followed independence, laws were enacted under Masonic influence that restricted the power and influence of the Church, and there were periods when anticlerical feeling was strong. Despite this, the religious orders and sisterhoods increased their work in the fields of education and charity. In 1946 the Augustinians established the Catholic University of St. Thomas of Villanova. Under the Castro regime Cuban Catholics have been sorely tried. In 1959 religious education in public schools was abolished and the Christian Democratic Party was suppressed. There were strong attacks upon the Church in 1960–61. The cardinal archbishop at Havana became a refugee in the Spanish Embassy, the auxiliary Bp. Boza was sent into exile, and 590 priests, 970 brothers, and 2,400 sisters were forced to leave the country. Only 200 priests, many of whom were of advanced age, remained on the island. A few Belgian and Canadian priests have been admitted. There has been some improvement in the relations between the government and the Vatican. A limited freedom is permitted to Catholics to worship in the churches. Many of the better educated Catholics have left the country. Cuba has two ecclesiastical provinces. The archbishopric of Havana has two suffragan sees, Pinar del Rio and Matanzas; that of Santiago also has two suffragan sees, Cienfuegos and Camagüey. In 1962 the Protestant community (Episcopalians, Baptists, Methodists, Presbyterians, and others) numbered about 265,000. It had 900 places of worship, 98 schools, 5 seminaries, and 1 university. The major churches form the Concilio Cubano de Iglesias Evangélicas. BIBLIOGRAPHY: J. M. Pérez Cabrera, NCE 4:514–517.

[P. DAMBORIENA]

CUBISM, movement in art begun by Picasso and Braque between 1907 and 1910, continuing into the 1960s, and exercising a penetrating and far-reaching influence upon modern art, rivaled only by abstract Expressionism. Analytical Cubism (1910–12) rendered landscape, figure, and still life in geometric forms, from simultaneous points of view (simultaneity) in planes overlapping and interpenetrating in shapes decreasingly representative, yet never completely abstract since subject remained important as the substance of things. A neutral palette of subdued browns, tans, grays, confirmed Cubism's intellectual aspect until 1913 (through the 1920s) when in a "synthetic" phase Cubists introduced rich pigmentation subordinating volume to decorative, inventive flat planes. In *papier collé* (collage) Cubists applied cutouts of paper (letters, numerals) to the canvas. Orphist-Cubists (1912) advocated luminous color and abstract form inspiring the *Blaue Reiter and Futurist groups. By 1914 Cubism was known throughout Europe and the U.S., influencing all major artists and determining Rayonist M. Larionov, Suprematist K. Malevich, and Neoplasticist P. Mondrian. Picasso's Cubist bronze *Woman's Head* (1909), rooted in African carving, affected the work of A. Archipenko and J. Lipschitz. His *Glass of Absinthe* (1914) was a first "assemblage." Scattered by the World War I Cubists continued independently, Picasso moving toward Expressionism, Braque attaining the refined grandeur of composition and palette. Purism (architectural and machine forms) followed. Cubists were inventive printmakers, illustrators of books, and designers of theater decor. Widespread public and private collections (Kahnweiler, Gertrude and Leo Stein, Stieglitz) affirm the importance and influence of Cubism in modern art. BIBLIOGRAPHY: A. Gleizes and J. Metzinger, *Du "cubisme"* (1912); M. Raynal, *Modern Painting* (1956); E. Fry, *Cubism* (1967).

[M. J. DALY]

CUBIT, standard linear unit of measurement of the Hebrews. Approximately 18 inches, it was determined by the distance from the elbow to the tip of the middle finger.

[F. J. MONTALBANO]

CUCCHI, MARCO ANTONIO (d. 1565), canonist. As a professor of law at the Univ. of Pavia, C. introduced a new method of systematizing the treatment of canonical questions. BIBLIOGRAPHY: B. R. Piskula, NCE 4:518; J. Raffalli, DDC 4:845.

[M. J. SUELZER]

CUCULLA, see COWL.

CUDWORTH, RALPH (1617–88), a Somerset man, fellow of Emmanuel, afterwards Master of Christ's College, Cambridge, and a familiar of the *Cambridge Platonists. He was on good terms with the government of the Lord Protector, but though he was confirmed in his office after the *Restoration, he soon retired from Cambridge. He was a learned Hebrew scholar and the author of biblical and ethical writings; his great book is *True Intellectual System of the Universe, wherein all the reason and philosophy of Atheism is confuted and its impossibility maintained* (1678). Aimed at Hobbes, the great contemporary advocate of materalist philosophy, it states the arguments of the ancient atheists so fairly that, as Dryden said (dedication to the *Aeneid*), "he raised such strong objections against the being of a God and Providence, that many think he hath not answered." In fact he elaborated, if rather antiquatedly to a generation that read Descartes and Spinoza, strong and balanced Platonic and Aristotelian theism, which in part anticipates later theories of the unconscious. BIBLIOGRAPHY: J. A. Passmore, *Ralph Cudworth* (1951).

[T. GILBY]

CUEVAS, MARIANO (1879–1949), Mexican Jesuit historian. C. entered the Society of Jesus in Spain but completed his ecclesiastical studies in Belgium, Italy, and the U.S. He carried on extensive research in the archives of the Old and New World. Anxious to raise the quality of writing on the history of the Church in Mexico, he published in five volumes his *Historia de la iglesia de México,* which has gone into several editions and remains the outstanding work in its field. Critics, however, have noted C.'s tendency to polemics and his inaccuracy. Much of the material he collected still remains unpublished. BIBLIOGRAPHY: J. Bravo Ugarte, "El P. Mariano Cuevas, 1879–1949," *Revista de historia de América* (1949) 103–107.

[P. DAMBORIENA]

CUIJPERO, PETRUS JOSEPHUS HUBERTUS (1827–1921), Dutch architect working in Amsterdam. C. is known for archeological restorations of Dutch Gothic churches and the building of Neo-Gothic churches using exposed brick. The Rijksmuseum and Central Station are C.'s works.

[M. J. DALY]

CUIUS REGIO, EIUS RELIGIO (a territory's religion [is] that of its prince), the formula approved in the Religious Peace of *Augsburg, whereby princes of the empire were given the right to determine the religion of their subjects. The phrasing is attributed to Joachim Stephani, a canonist of Greifswald. The most important result that flowed from the *ius reformandi,* as the principle came to be called in the 17th cent., was to ensure the permanence of the Reformation. Originally it allowed only the Lutheran and the

Catholic religions. Not until the Peace of *Westphalia (1648) was provision made for the *Reformed Churches and for any minorities that had been tolerated in 1624, the normative year. The efficacy of the *ius reformandi* was limited by the so-called ecclesiastical reservation, which decreed that a bp. or abbot going over to the Reformation must surrender his office and possessions. During the deliberations attendant on the Peace of Augsburg the majority of Protestants favored allowing individuals freedom of choice in religion; but during the *Counter-Reformation whole principalities were kept true to the Reformation by law. Theoretically, the *ius reformandi* is still operative; if a Swiss canton, for instance, would vote to change its religion, the principle could be invoked. BIBLIOGRAPHY: J. Heckel, RGG 1:1888–89; H. Rabe, LTK 5:825.

CULDEES, Irish and Scottish monks of great austerity appearing *c.*800. Originally anchorites, they came to live in community somewhat like canons secular. Though beginning as a reform movement, they were regarded in later centuries as esp. corrupt. Remnants of the order continued at Armagh until 1541. The name is thought to be from the Irish *Celí Dé,* companions or vassals of God. They are regarded by some as the last remnants of the *Celtic Church. BIBLIOGRAPHY: K. Hughes, *Church in Early Irish Society* (1966).

[T. EARLY]

CULLEN, PAUL (1803–78), abp. primate of all Ireland, cardinal, rector in Rome of the Irish College (from 1832). C.'s correspondence and documents of the college indicate his key position in the exchange of thought among churchmen of America, Australia, and Ireland. In a time of political strife, as rector of Propaganda (1849) his appeal to the U.S. minister on behalf of American students saved the Roman college from dissolution. Consecrated abp. of Armagh in 1850, and of Dublin in 1852, C. became in 1866 Ireland's first cardinal. He played a leading role at Vatican Council I, helping to formulate the definition on papal infallibility. BIBLIOGRAPHY: P. MacSuibhne, NCE 4:521–522; R. D. Edwards, *ibid.* 7:624–625, s.v. "Ireland."

[M. R. BROWN]

CULLMANN, OSCAR (1902–), biblical theologian, NT exegete, and patristic scholar. Since 1938, he has been professor of NT and ancient church history at the University of Basel. Committed to the ecumenical movement, he was a Protestant observer at the Vatican Council II. C. insists on a strict philological-historical method of exegesis, i.e., an unprejudiced openness to the terminology and thought patterns of the NT authors. The gospel message is not metaphysical speculation but the proclamation of concrete historical events that occurred at a particular time and place. Although C. acknowledges dependence on Schweitzer for his emphasis on eschatology and on Bult-

mann for form criticism, he rejects the philosophical and theological presuppositions of both Protestant *liberal theology and Heideggerian existentialism. The explanation of salvation history *(Heilsgeschichte)* is pivotal in C.'s thought. In contrast to the Greek understanding of time as cyclical, the Bible presents time as linear and dynamic. The Christian does not escape time or consider it meaningless; time is the arena where God acts to accomplish redemption. The biblical time line can be divided into three sections: the period before creation; the time between creation and the end of the world, during which a succession of redemptively decisive events take place and move toward eventual consummation; and the segment stretching forward eternally from the end of the world. This succession of redemptive acts is called salvation history. Since the Christ event is at the qualitative midpoint of salvation history and is the decisive center of time, the fulfillment of time has already happened, even though this fulfillment is still being accomplished in the present. Salvation has come; only its consummation is awaited.

The study of salvation history enables C. to achieve the main goal of his theological enterprise, the NT idea of Christ. He maintains that the communities responsible for the formation of the NT evolved their Christology primarily in terms of the various Jewish messianic titles. These Christologies must be placed primarily in a Judaic rather than Hellenistic frame of reference. The messianic titles manifest not the nature of Christ but his functions in salvation history. They apply to the earthly work of Jesus (Servant of the Lord), to his future work (Son of Man), to his present work (Lord), or to his preexistence (Word). Moreover, the working out of this Christology is directly traceable from the self-consciousness of Jesus, which can be known from the NT data, to the post-Resurrection faith and theological reflections of the earliest Christian communities. The Gospels give an accurate picture of Jesus's own self-concept as the source from which the Church could establish the connection between Christ and the total expanse of time and eternity.

In his patristic studies, C. wrote extensively on the Pseudo-Clementine literature of the 3d and 4th cents., the meaning of the Eucharist in primitive Christianity, the earliest Christian confessions of faith, and the relationship between Church and State in the first 2 centuries. Both in patristics and in biblical theology, he raised issues of considerable ecumenical importance. He upheld the practice of *infant baptism but denied the RC notion of the relationship between Scripture and tradition. His study of Peter's role in the Church concluded that Peter's special position and power expired with the apostle's death. BIBLIOGRAPHY: Cullmann's works: *Christology of the New Testament* (tr. S. C. Guthrie and C. A. M. Hall, rev. ed., 1964); *Early Church* (tr. A. J. Higgins, 1959); *Vatican Council Two: The New Direction* (ed. and tr. J. D. Hester et al., 1968); *Peter: Disciple, Apostle, Martyr* (tr. F. V. Filson, 2d rev. ed., 1962).

[T. M. MCFADDEN]

CULROSS ABBEY, a Cistercian monastery in Fife, Scotland, founded by Malcolm, earl of Fife, in 1218 and colonized from Kinloss Abbey. It fell into ruin after the Reformation, but the present parish church of Culross is built on the site of its choir. BIBLIOGRAPHY: J.-M. Canivez, DHGE 13:1104–05; D. E. Easson, *Medieval Religious Houses: Scotland* (1957) 63.

[L. J. MACFARLANE]

CULT (Lat. *cultus,* worship), a term denoting either worship or a certain type of religious body. In the first sense cult is the act of worship, a specific set of worship forms, or the veneration of God or the saints under some particular title. As a classification, a cult resembles a *sect. Although these terms are sometimes distinguished, in popular usage and even in the language of many who have a professional interest in the subject, "cult" and "sect" are used interchangeably. For example, E. T. Clark's *The Small Sects in America* (1949) deals with many of the same groups as does Jan K. Van Baalen's *Chaos of the Cults* (1953). Sociologists of religion have tried to arrive at more precise definitions by analysis of belief systems and rituals of such religious groups. J. M. Yinger, e.g., distinguishes the cults by their small size, localization, dependence upon a leader with magnetic personality, and beliefs and rites that deviate widely from the norms of society. Because of its deviant beliefs and the problems of succession following the death of a leader, the cult tends to be of short duration, and unlike the sect it is not apt to become transformed into a *denomination. The focus of a cult, Yinger says, is upon the individual; there is no interest in changing the social order. Pure types of the cult are rare in the U.S., according to Yinger, but examples are some Muslim and spiritualist groups among Negroes. In the 1970s some have classified the various forms of the Jesus movement as cults, particularly where estrangement of children from parents occurs. Satanic cults, devil worshipers, have also sprung up. BIBLIOGRAPHY: J. M. Yinger, *Religion, Society, and the Individual* (1964).

[N. H. MARING]

CULT, DISPARITY OF, see DISPARITY OF CULT.

CULTURE, the sum of customary ideas, images, affections, and physical factors as forming the patterns characteristic of social behavior in a human group and as expressed in its rituals and works of art. The Lat. *cultura* means the cultivation, improvement, or refinement, esp. of individuals, by training and education; this sense remains in English and the humanistic tradition; in German *Kultur* is associated with enlightened values and is contrasted with crude nature. Not until the close of the 19th cent. was the term generally established in the social sciences and anthropology. There it is variously defined according to the interest and purpose of different schools; some concentrate on structures, others on the genesis or transmission of social heritages, others on the psychological forces at work, others essay a comparison, sometimes normative, of dominant themes. It seems desirable to preserve the older distinction, used in England and France, between culture and civilization, or at least to separate their frames of reference; the last, as its name implies, means civil intercourse under the protection of laws, though it is sometimes used of a nation with a developed political organization, which may be despotic. "Cultured" and "civilized" are in themselves morally neutral epithets, the second perhaps less than the first. It is possible to find a high civilization with a low culture, thus a completely industrialized country with an excess of verbalized social patterns; so conversely, a low civilization with a high culture, thus a group with but rudimentary, if any, political institutions which yet displays good social engineering and a rich symbolism in its corporate life. BIBLIOGRAPHY: A. L. Kroeber and C. Kluckholm, *Culture, A Critical Review of Concepts and Definitions* (1952).

[T. GILBY]

CULTURE, THEOLOGY OF. In a sense theology pure and simple and a theology of culture mean the same thing. For theology is a human concern and discipline on the relationships of man and his world to God. Culture is an integral part of that relationship, as it means both a set of established components and an always developing process. Vatican Council II generalizes this meaning of culture as "all those factors by which man refines and unfolds his manifold spiritual and bodily qualities" (VatII ChModWorld, n. 53). As literally equivalent to "cultivating," culture is man's humanization of his life and his world—as is clear from the narrower associations of the term with the expression, in all the forms of art, of the nobler experiences and aspirations of life. The theological positive evaluation of humanization, of a true humanism, rests in general on a doctrine of *creation and divine *government. For creation means God's investing the world with its own intrinsic and proper goodness; the properly human values are included, even supreme in the worth of creation. Thus to value the world and above all the world as humanized is to respond humanly to God's creation. That includes recognizing that just as the universe itself manifests variety in its imitation of divine goodness, so there is a plurality with rich diversity in human cultures. The ethnic, geographical, historical differences are to be reverenced and fostered. The heritage of the peoples of the earth are the distinctively human variety in God's creation. The contribution of individuals or of peoples to the human development of others is, further, the consciously pursued participation in the divine government that means particularly being the cause of the betterment of others. The teaching on man made to God's image indicates that this dignity of the human person is the reason for developing his spiritual and bodily qualities. That dignity also sets priorities, since it indicates the genuine hierarchy of human values: the necessary care for physical well-being is subordinated to spiritual betterment: accordingly the primary cultural values are those of mind, will, conscience, human brotherhood (*ibid.*, n. 61). The recognition of the primacy of the life of the spirit means a concern for the conditions of physical existence, of a life that makes possible an upright, moral way of living, and a share in the experiences of truth, beauty, goodness, according to the choice and capacity of each human being. That makes imperative the theological teaching on *social justice, the exclusion of every form of discrimination. Particularly with regard to education and the arts, the spiritual dignity of man calls for a proportionate place being given to the classical, humanistic tradition; sheer technology is insufficient. Theology has also the right to comment that the Incarnation gives a new, exalted meaning to culture. The humanization of the world has its divine ratification in Christ; part of the meaning of his coming is the restoration of all things in him (Eph 1.10); that is a divine assurance of human worth. Yet Christ's restoration is also redemptive; the humanism it authenticates is not earthbound, nor is it naively optimistic. The goals and values of culture are always subject to perversion because of the fact of sin. Theology recognizes sin's constant manifestation in the quest for progress, yet does not despair, because the healing of Christ makes human betterment possible; the heights to which humanity is raised in him gives hope to human striving. Christ's new commandment of charity gives every attempt to further the well-being of others a loftier meaning. Every truly human value genuinely belongs to human communion in love through Christ, and from that has both its new, immediate worth and its final significance.

[T. C. O'BRIEN]

CUM DATA, the decree issued (1929) by the Holy See, that barred married Ruthenian clergy from admission to North America, and from ordination in North America. It did not change previous regulations for Eastern rite clergy already married and living in America.

[R. C. EGAN]

CUM OCCASIONE, a bull of Innocent X issued May 31, 1653. It condemned five propositions of Cornelius *Jansen, four as heretical (D 2001–05). These predestinarian propositions (a summary of Jansen's *Augustinus* by Nicolas Cornet of the Sorbonne) minimize freedom and merit: saving grace is irresistible and not given to all. An appeal of Bp. Habert of Vabres for papal condemnation, drafted by St. Vincent de Paul, was signed by some 80 French bishops 11 bishops defended *Jansenism. A congregation of cardinals held 50 meetings (the Pope attended 10) and consulted the universities and leading theologians; condemnation followed. The Jansenists, led by A. *Arnauld, countered by denying that the propositions as stated were attributable to Jansen. BIBLIOGRAPHY: Pastor 30:239–280; H. Daniel-Rops, *Church in the Seventeenth Century* (tr. J. J. Buckingham, 1963) 349–353.

[W. DAVISH]

CUMDACH, a form of shrine or reliquary used by Irish clergy in the early Middle Ages for storing Gospel Books precious because of their scarcity. One of the earliest (*c.*1000) contained the Gospel Book of St. Molaise d. 563).

[M. J. DALY]

CUMMINGS, EDWARD ESTLIN (1894–1962), poet. C. was born in Cambridge, Mass. into a happy, cultivated family including besides his parents, two aunts, one uncle, and a grandmother. In this sphere of ethical and artistic literacy, C. was exposed to poetry, music, and art, as well as to healthy human development in the family circle. The classical bias of his education at Harvard merged later with his firsthand knowledge of the changes wrought by mechanization, experimentation, and discovery. He volunteered (World War I) with the American Red Cross in the Ambulance Corps in France, and was imprisoned for 3 months by French authorities for "disrespect." Drafted on his return to the U.S., he remained in the Army until the Armistice. After the war, he joined the many avant-garde figures in Paris (1920–23). After this period C. might be said to have embarked on an academic career. Henceforward he wrote his interesting if paradoxically simple poetry, and took up painting. One novel and a play emerged during these productive years. In an age that praised sometimes uncritically the innovative and the daring, C.'s real value as an artist was somehow submerged in overpraise of typographical oddities, coined words and phrases, or other conscious linguistic distortions. These preoccupations are now more readily recognized as techniques bearing the meaning of the poetry. This is not to deny C.'s craftsmanship, esp. his employment of verbal music and symbolic imagery. C., incidentally, had several art displays of his own works in both the U.S. and England (1931, 1944, 1949). Presently, he is perhaps in danger again of being overpraised for profundity or philosophic relationships with Swift, Blake, or Coleridge. C.'s theme of prevailing love and self-transcendence does indeed merit recognition as a Christian concept. There is vibrance as well as nostalgia in his optimistic reading of human potential.

C. wrote *Tulips and Chimneys* (1923). Other collections are *Collected Poems* (1938), *Poems* (1923–54). He wrote one novel, *The Enormous Room* (1922) based on his experiences in World War I. C. was awarded, in 1950, a Fellowship in the American Academy of Poets; in 1952, he was Charles Eliot Norton Professor at Harvard; and in 1957 received the Bollingen Prize in Poetry. BIBLIOGRAPHY: C. Norman, *Magic-Maker: E. E. Cummings* (1972); *E. E. Cummings: A Collection of Critical Essays* (ed. N. Friedman, 1972); G. Firmage, *E. E. Cummings: A Bibliography* (repr. 1974).

[R. M. FUNCHION]

CUMMINS, GEORGE DAVID (1822–76), founder of the Reformed Episcopal Church. Born in Smyrna, Del., C.

studied at Dickinson College (B.A., 1841; M.A., 1844) and was licensed to preach in 1842 by the Baltimore Conference of the Methodist Episcopal Church. He entered the Protestant Episcopal Church in 1845 and was ordained the same year. He served as rector of churches in Norfolk and Richmond, Va., Washington, D.C., and Baltimore, Md., before accepting a call to Trinity Church, Chicago, in 1863. Chosen in 1866 as assistant bishop of Kentucky, he strongly opposed the influence of the *Oxford movement in the Episcopal Church. His Society to Promote Evangelical Religion brought him into conflict with the *General Convention in 1868–69. He had the support of the Virginia Theological Seminary faculty and other influential low churchmen, who joined him in promoting an American branch of the *Evangelical Alliance as a counterbalance to the spread of Catholic doctrine and ritual within the Episcopal Church. His insistence on intercommunion with evangelical Protestant Churches and his belittling of Anglican orders led to formal charges against him. In Dec. 1873, with 20 other evangelicals, he established the Reformed Episcopal Church, but few Episcopalians followed him.

[R. K. MacMASTER]

CUMONT, FRANZ VALÉRY MARIE (1868–1947), Belgian historian of ancient religions, archeologist. C. examined a variety of Eastern Mediterranean religious beliefs and practices which contributed to the milieu of early Christianity. His pioneering works include *Textes et monuments figurés relatifs aux mystères de Mithra*, (2 v., 1894–99); *The Mysteries of Mithra* (1903); *Astrology and Religion among the Greeks and Romans* (1912); *After Life in Roman Paganism* (1922); *Les Religions orientales dans le paganisme romain* (4th ed. 1928); with J. Bidez, *Les Mages hellénisés* (2 v., 1938); *Lux perpetua* (1949). BIBLIOGRAPHY: N. Turci, EncCatt 4:1053.

[E. V. GALLAGHER]

CUNHA, EUCLIDES DA (1866–1909), Brazilian author whose *Os sertões* (1902; tr. S. Putnam, *Rebellion in the Backlands*, 1944) contains his observations and study of the religious fanatics who defied the Brazilian government in 1896–97 under the leadership of Antonio Conselhiero. The book discusses the complex racial problems of Brazil from what would, by today's standards, be called a racist point of view. BIBLIOGRAPHY: J. Pontes, NCE 4:534.

CUNIBERT OF COLOGNE, ST. (betw. 590 and 600–c.663), bishop. Born in the Moselle region of France, C. was consecrated bp. of Cologne in 623 and took part in the synods of Clichy and Reims. He is accredited with having founded charitable institutions, convents, and churches, among them St. Clement in Cologne. The latter was renamed St. Cunibert and houses the relics of the saint. BIBLIOGRAPHY: Butler 4:322; C. Marcora, BiblSanct 4:404–407.

[J. BLAIR]

CUNILIATI, FULGENZIO (1685–1759), Italian Dominican, author of *Universae theologiae moralis accurata complexio* (2 v., 1754), defending *probabiliorism, and of numerous devotional collections of meditations. He wrote under the pseudonym Mariano degli Amatori. An exemplary religious, he was esp. gifted as spiritual advisor and was vicar general of the Bl. James Salomoni Congregation.

[T. C. O'BRIEN]

CURATE (Lat. *curatus*, charged with, or entrusted with, the care of something), a term originally used to designate a priest to whom the cure (care) of souls was committed, i.e., a priest in charge of a parish. The cognate terms in French, Italian, and Spanish—*curé, curato, cura*—retain this meaning. In the English-speaking world, however, the term as popularly used came to be applied not to the principal priest of a parish but to a clergyman who assists the principal priest in the performance of his parochial duties. From pre-Reformation times the beneficed incumbent of a parish was often unable because of a plurality of benefices, or actual occupation in other matters, or the size of his parish, to perform personally all the offices for which his benefice made him responsible. His duties therefore had to be discharged with the help of a nonbeneficed clergyman whom he employed for that purpose, and it is the latter who came to be called the curate in English. Pluralism has been eradicated, and means other than benefices have been found to provide for the assignment and support of the clergy in their pastoral work, but the term curate continues in Anglican, and to a lesser extent in RC, usage to signify an assistant priest in a parish. In the RC Church in the U.S. a priest appointed to help the pastor of a parish is more commonly called an assistant or associate pastor.

[P. K. MEAGHER]

CURCI, CARLO MARIA (1810–91), Italian Jesuit polemicist. A Jesuit from 1826, C. became a teacher of Hebrew and Sacred Scripture. In 1849 he published the first of his works in defense of the temporal power of the papacy. In 1850 he founded the journal *Civiltà Cattolica* and became its first director and a frequent contributor. He also published several volumes of sermons and biblical exegesis. After the loss of the Papal States in 1870 C. espoused the view that the Pope should renounce all territorial claims and thus promote the re-Christianization of those alienated from the faith by the Church-State conflict. In 1877 he was dismissed from the Society, and his further works on the same subject were placed on the Index. C. spent the remaining years of his life in Florence, writing on the same theme but taking no active part in religious or political struggles. A few months before his death he submitted to the condemnation of his opinions and was readmitted to the Society. BIBLIOGRAPHY: E. Lucatello, NCE 4:535; O. Baumhauer, LTK 3:109.

CURÉ D'ARS, see VIANNEY, JEAN BAPTISTE MARIE, ST.

CURIA, a term taken from Medieval Latin (Fr., *cour*) to indicate the complexus of authorities, officials, and assistants charged with aiding a king or high official in the administration of his office. In the ecclesiastical sphere the pope, bishops of dioceses, and metropolitans have their curias, which embrace all the authorities, officials, and assistants who together constitute the pope's, bishop's, or metropolitan's entourage and assist in the administration of the affairs of the Church, metropolitanate, or see.

[P. K. MEAGHER]

CURIA, DIOCESAN, a body appointed by the diocesan bp. as assistants for the governance of the diocese; the vicar general, officialis, chancellor, promotor of justice, defender of the bond, synodal judges and examiners, pastor consultants, auditors, notaries (CIC, c. 363).

[T. C. O'BRIEN]

CURIA ROMANA (ROMAN CURIA), the aggregate of the congregations, secretariats, courts, special commissions, which assist the Roman Pontiff in the government of the RC Church. Its structure developed over the course of many centuries with the changing needs of the times and the increasing complexity of ecclesiastical administration. It assumed a form substantially like that it has today in 1588 under Pope Sixtus V. However, Vatican Council II made it apparent that changes and reorganization were necessary. A special commission of cardinals, headed by Card. F. Roberti was appointed to study the situation and recommend needed changes. In 1967 the pope issued an apostolic constitution *Regimini ecclesiae universae,* based chiefly on the recommendations of the Roberti commission, which put into effect the changes considered necessary.

The reorganized Roman Curia, in its initial state, consisted of the Secretariat of State, the function of which is to provide assistance to the pope in his care for the universal Church and in coordinating the work of the various congregations or departments of government. The former Secretariat of Extraordinary Ecclesiastical Affairs was replaced by the Council of *Public Affairs of the Church, which is concerned with the Holy See's dealing with governments. Initially in the reorganized curia there were 10 congregations: (1) the Congregation for the *Doctrine of the Faith, which replaced the Holy Office; (2) the Congregation for the *Oriental Churches; (3) the Congregation for *Bishops, which replaced the Consistorial Congregation; (4) the Congregation of the *Clergy, which was concerned with the pastoral ministry of priests and deacons and replaced the Congregation of the Council; (5) the Congregation for *Catholic Education, which replaced the Congregation for Seminaries and Universities; (6) the Congregation for the *Evangelization of Peoples, an alternative title for the *Propagation of the Faith; (7) the Congregation for *Religious and Secular Institutes; (8) the Congregation for

*Divine Worship, which succeeded the older Congregation of Rites in all matters except those pertaining to the processes of beatification and canonization of saints, which are now dealt with by a newly instituted congregation called (9) the Congregation for *Causes of the Saints; (10) the Congregation for the *Discipline of the Sacraments. In an apostolic constitution issued by Pope Paul VI on July 17, 1975, a further change was made. The Congregation for the Discipline of the Sacraments was merged into one with the Congregation for Divine Worship. The new congregation is called the Sacred Congregation for the Sacraments and Divine Worship. This merger became effective on August 1, 1975, and it reduces the number of existing congregations to nine. In this change the function of the former congregations fall into two sections, each headed by an undersecretary.

Three new secretariats of importance were established in the reorganization of the curia. Their concern is to promote relations with other Christian bodies (the Secretariat for *Christian Unity), with non-Christians (the Secretariat for *Non-Christians), and non-believers (the Secretariat for *Non-Believers).

The three courts or tribunals of the Holy See remain substantially unchanged: the *Roman Rota, the Apostolic *Penitentiary, and the Apostolic *Signatura, the Church's supreme court.

A number of special commissions have also been created to assist the congregations in dealing with special types of problems that fall within their competence. BIBLIOGRAPHY: J. Hennesey, NCE 16:111–112; J. J. Markham, NCE 4:539–540.

[P. K. MEAGHER]

CURIE, MARIE SKLODOWSKA (1867–1934), physicist. Born in Poland, the daughter of a professor of physics in Warsaw, C. came to Paris in 1891, attended the Sorbonne, and met scientists engaged in searching for sources of radioactivity and magnetism. Encouraged by discoveries of Roentgen's rays and Becquerels pitchblende, Marie and her husband Pierre sought the hidden element now known as radium. She and Pierre after tireless efforts and experiments discovered both polonium and radium (1898). In 1910 with André Debierne she isolated metallic radium. She twice earned the Nobel Prize: 1903 for physics and 1911 for chemistry. Her work was honored by many institutes including the Univ. of Paris and the Pasteur Institute. Her doctoral dissertation *Radio-active Substances* (1902) is considered a masterpiece of scientific discovery. BIBLIOGRAPHY: E. Curie, *Madame Curie* (1937); International Atomic Energy Agency, *Marie Sklodowska-Curie: Centenary Lectures* (pa. 1968); R. Reid, *Marie Curie* (1974, pa. 1975).

[R. M. FUNCHION]

CURIE, PIERRE (1859–1906), French scientist. After graduation from the Sorbonne, C. did research on the magnetism in iron and electric polarity. It was while engaged in such work at the Paris Municipal School of Physics and Chemistry that he met Marie Sklodowska, his future wife. With hers, his later investigations centered on discovering the hidden element in uranium. His association with Marie resulted in an almost mutual discovery of radium. In the meantime C. was offered a chair in physics at the Univ. of Geneva, an offer he rejected. Later he accepted such a chair at the Sorbonne. Like his wife, he shunned publicity and the commercial exploitation of their discovery. His sudden death in 1906 shocked and stunned Marie, who devoted her remaining years to scientific investigation so often encouraged by her husband. BIBLIOGRAPHY: M. Curie, *Pierre Curie* (1923).

[R. M. FUNCHION]

CURIOSITY: (1) the natural bent of the human mind to seek knowledge; (2) as a moral failure, an excessive indulgence in this natural propensity. St. Thomas Aquinas opposes such indulgence to true devotion to learning (studiousness). Absolutely speaking no knowledge is bad, since the mind is made to know. The inordinateness consists, rather, in the failure of the will to integrate the pursuit of knowledge into the whole, right moral direction of life. Thus curiosity as sinful means a search for inconsequential knowledge to the neglect of what must be learned in order to reach God or to fulfill the duties of state; or it means a study of creation that excludes reference to the creator; or an undisciplined inquisitiveness towards knowledge above one's capacities. BIBLIOGRAPHY: ThAq ST 2a2ae,167.

[T. C. O'BRIEN]

CURLEY, MICHAEL JOSEPH (1879–1947), abp., educator. Born in Westmeath, Ireland, C.'s clerical study began at Mungret College, Limerick, where he was recruited for the Church in Florida; from Propaganda he received the S.T.L. degree; ordained at the Lateran in 1904, he began pastoral work at DeLand, Florida. Consecrated ordinary of St. Augustine (1914) at a time of great RC population expansion there, he had to contend with racist harassment. He built many schools. Transferred to Baltimore as its 10th abp. in 1921, he built or expanded the schools and seminaries, serving meanwhile as chancellor of The Catholic Univ. of America. C. fostered the lay retreat movement and the Confraternity of the Laity, and had incorporated the Bureau of Catholic Charities. To govern both Baltimore and the newly created diocese cut off from it (1939), C. was installed as Abp. of Baltimore and Washington, D.C.

[M. R. BROWN]

CURRIER, CHARLES WARREN (1857–1918), bp., writer. Ordained (1880) a Redemptorist priest in Holland, C. came to the U.S. for reasons of health. After 9 years as a home missionary in the eastern U.S., recurrence of ill health caused him to seek dispensation from his vows as a Redemptorist, which was granted in 1891. He was attached to the Archdiocese of Baltimore thereafter, except for the period 1913–15 when he was bp. of the new see of Matanzas, Cuba. This post also he found necessary to resign because of his health. C. was a noted Hispanist and was active in the International Congresses of Americanists. He served as the official U.S. government representative at the congresses in Stuttgart (1904), in Buenos Aires (1910), and Mexico City (1910). Among his writings his best-known work is *History of Religious Orders* (1894). BIBLIOGRAPHY: DAB 4:602–603; M. J. Curley NCE 4:546.

[J. L. HALPIN]

CURSE, the utterance in words, whether spoken or unspoken, of a malediction or imprecation against another, expressing the desire that evil befall him. It is of its nature a grave sin against charity and justice. If the one who curses another expects or hopes that God will hear the imprecation and bring to pass the evil the curser desires, it also involves some sin against faith and against the virtue of religion because of the irreverence toward God that it implies. If the curse is uttered publicly or in the presence of the one cursed, the element of contumely also enters into the act. The notion that curses are of their nature effective is superstitious. Though cursing is per se a grave sin, it is often in concrete cases mitigated by circumstances, e.g., by the overwhelming force of passion from which it springs. Also it should be observed that some forms of expression which, if taken literally, would constitute a true curse, are not in common usage understood to imply malice.

[P. K. MEAGHER]

CURSE (IN THE BIBLE). To understand the significance of the curse in the OT it has to be realized, first, that the holiness of the divine presence is destructive to all it encounters that is in any way evil or alien to itself; second, that this holiness, in its destructive aspect, can be embodied in words and directed by the utterer against a person or object conceived to be dangerous or hostile to himself. The curse, then, is not an expression of anger or emotion, but something essentially sacred. Thus the solemn ritual cursing of the enemy before battle was a vital element in the holy war. The curses against the nations surrounding Judah in Amos 1.2–2.16 probably have the force of ritual imprecations embodying, as it were, the voice of Yahweh himself as he "roars from Zion and makes his voice heard from Jerusalem" (Amos 1.2). In some instances Yahweh himself utters the curse directly (e.g., Gen 3.14; 12.3 etc.). More often it is uttered by his client or representative. But in any case once uttered the destructive power of holiness which it unleashes into the world must take effect even though in some instances it may be turned back by Yahweh on the head of the utterer himself (e.g., Gen 12.3; 27.9). The destructive impact of the curse can be averted or countered by Yahweh's blessing, the embodiment and expression of his holiness in its creative aspects (cf. Num 23.8).

Of special interest and importance is the "hypothetical curse." If a given sin or offense is committed in the future, or has already been committed secretly in the past, then immediately and automatically the destructive force of the curse pronounced in the present will fall upon the perpetrator. Thus the covenant concludes with hypothetical curses of this kind that the assembled people invoke upon any of its members who break its laws (cf. Dt 7.11–26). Again in the ritual of the "waters of cursing" a woman suspected of adultery is made to swallow water into which the words of a written curse have been washed, mingled with dust from the floor of the tabernacle (cf. Num 5.12–31). This is essentially a form of judgment by *ordeal. If the curse takes effect then the woman has committed adultery; if not then she is innocent.

[D. J. BOURKE]

CURSILLO, a three-day program for achieving spiritual renewal. The name is from the Spanish *cursillo de cristianidad,* little course in Christianity. Bp. J. Hervas of Ciudad Real, Spain, assisted by several clergy and laymen, was chiefly instrumental in devising the program. It came into use in Spain following World War II and spread abroad soon thereafter. In the U.S. it was used first among the Spanish-speaking people of the Southwest, particularly Texas. Later it spread and by 1961 was being held in English.

In a normal cursillo some 40 people, men or women, gather under the direction of a team composed of both priests and laymen. The most frequent meeting time is from Thursday evening to Sunday evening. During the course of the 3 days the priest members of the team give five meditations and five talks known as drills; the lay members of the team give ten drills relating material covered by the priests to the life of laymen in the world, and members of the group then divide into smaller groups for discussion. A Mass highlights each day's program, and provision is made for other devotional exercises. The cursillo aims to convey through experience the importance of community life centered in Christ.

[T. EARLY]

CURSING, in common speech the protestive use of offensive or profane language; in moral theology, the calling down of evil on another person. Whether expressed in an optative or an imperative mood, cursing one's fellow man is sinful because it is an expression of hatred, while cursing things is a lapse, sometimes just silly, from the virtue of fortitude, which regulates irascibility. To curse God is a grievous sin of blasphemy, if sometimes extenuated by a lack of deliberation in an emergency reaction. Swearing is a chronic offense against good manners and debases the currency of emphatic language, exclamation, and expletive relief.

[T. GILBY]

CURSORES APOSTOLICI (Lat. for apostolic runners), functionaries attached to the Roman Curia whose duty it is to invite the persons expected to assist at consistories and other papal ceremonies, to serve as doorkeepers at a conclave, to post papal rescripts at the doors of major Roman basilicas, and to summon those specially invited to attend canonizations, the funerals of cardinals, and certain other solemnities.

[P. K. MEAGHER]

CURSUS, a device for prose rhythm, originally based on vowel quantity but later shifted to accent pattern. Cursus was devised by the Greek orators as a type of punctuation indicating the end of a clause or sentence. Cicero adapted the device to Latin usage and a number of Latin writers used the Ciceronian arrangement of prose. In the 4th cent. A.D. the use of stress replaced the length of syllable arrangement. The Fathers of the Church used the cursus in prayers, and the imperial and papal chanceries employed it. After some period of disuse the cursus was revived by Pope Urban II and what came to be known as the *Cursus Curiae Romanae* was adopted by the chanceries of Western Europe. Medieval writers in England often employed the cursus. Cranmer used it in his collects for the Book of Common Prayer.

[J. R. AHERNE]

CURTIS, ALFRED ALLEN (1831–1908), bishop. Ordained to the ministry in the Episcopal Church in 1859, C. was converted to Roman Catholicism and received into that Church by Card. Newman (1872). After his ordination as a Catholic priest (1874), C. served as secretary to Abp. Bayley and to his successor, Card. Gibbons. He helped to organize and was secretary at the Third Plenary Council of Baltimore (1884). Consecrated bp. of Wilmington (1886), he built 15 churches and founded parishes and parochial schools. Ill health forced him to resign, and he returned to Baltimore as vicar general to Card. Gibbons. BIBLIOGRAPHY: J. T. Ellis, *Life of James Cardinal Gibbons* (2 v., 1952).

[J. L. HALPIN]

CURTIUS, ERNST ROBERT (1886–1956), literary critic and philologist. He was trained in Romance studies at the Universities of Strasbourg, Berlin, and Heidelberg; his interest in medievalism was fostered by the positivist Gustav Gröber. He taught at Bonn, Marburg, and Heidelberg. His chief work, *Europäische Literatur und lateinisches Mittelalter* (1948, 1954, Eng., tr. W. R. Trask, 1953), deals with the survivals of the ancient world in European literature, through the Latin Middle Ages. BIBLIOGRAPHY: A. Adler, NCE 4:550; *Hispanic Review* 25 (1957) 24–25.

[F. D. LAZENBY]

CUSACK, THOMAS FRANCIS (1862–1918), bishop. Ordained in Troy, N.Y., in 1885, C. became auxiliary bp.

of New York in 1904 and bp. of Albany in 1915. His chief efforts were extended in a campaign to draw converts and in promoting missions for the faithful.

[J. R. AHERNE]

CUSHING, RICHARD (1895–1970), abp. of Boston, cardinal. A product of South Boston and the Irish community, he was ordained in 1921, named auxiliary to Card. O'Connell in 1939, and succeeded as abp. in 1944. Craggy in appearance and rough-hewn in character he was loved for his humanity and charity by all Bostonians, Catholic or otherwise. He was an early advocate of ecumenism, and his grasp of the importance of education led to an incredible expansion of Catholic schools from elementary to university level. Created a cardinal (1958), his contribution to a new Catholic attitude toward the Jews in Vatican Council II made him a worldwide figure. He founded the Missionary Society of St. James made up of diocesan priests who volunteered for work in Latin America. The Cardinal's last 15 years were marked by severe suffering, a fact that did not deter him from the vigorous pursuit of the good of the archdiocese. BIBLIOGRAPHY: J. H. Fenton *Salt of the Earth* (1965).

[J. R. AHERNE]

CUSHITES, see ETHIOPIANS.

CUSPINIAN, JOHANNES (Spieshaymer; 1473–1529), physician, diplomat, and poet. C. studied at Leipzig and at Vienna, where he earned a doctorate in medicine. He taught poetics and rhetoric at the Univ. of Vienna and became the leader of the humanistic circle there. In 1501 he was named rector of the university and was four times dean of the faculty of medicine. At the same time he carried out many diplomatic missions for the Habsburg emperors. It was he who arranged the marriage of the Habsburg children to the offspring of Ladislaus of Bohemia and Hungary. He also attempted to rally the Christian princes against the Turks after the Battle of Mohács (1526). He produced a number of histories which show a critical sense unusual for his times. BIBLIOGRAPHY: G. J. Donnelly, NCE 4:550.

[D. G. NUGENT]

CUSTODIA, a small opaque receptacle that can be completely closed. It is used for the reservation in the tabernacle of a large host consecrated for use in the monstrance.

[N. KOLLAR]

CUSTODIAN OF THE HOLY LAND and Guardian of Mount Zion, title of the superior of the Franciscan Friars Minor in Jerusalem, whose small community constitutes the hierarchical unit, *custode,* or Custody. From the 13th to mid-19th cent. the Franciscans were the only permanent representatives of the RC Church in Palestine; they suffered many hardships protecting the right of the Western Church to worship at the holy places according to the Latin rite.

The Custodian had episcopal jurisdiction (without the rank of bishop) over all Roman Catholics in Palestine until 1847, when Pope Pius IX restored the Latin patriarchate to Jerusalem because of the increase of Western pilgrims to the Holy Land. Today he still has episcopal privilege, but his principal duty is to enhance the international quality of the Custody of the Holy Land.

[H. P. ANNAS]

CUSTODY OF SENSES, a phrase used in ascetical literature for the controlled restraint of vagrant sensations—of the five external senses and of the internal senses of imagination and memory—in order to concentrate on the life of the spirit. Sometimes it leaves the impression of a cliché of professional jargon, or of a hobby notion; nevertheless it belongs to the classical tradition on the cultivation of prayer and recollection in the presence of God. BIBLIOGRAPHY: St. John of the Cross, *Ascent of Mt. Carmel,* 3.25; ThAq ST 1a2ae, 65.3.

[T. GILBY]

CUSTOM (through the Fr. from the Lat. *consuetudo*), in general, a habitual practice; in law and social science, a long-continued usage which by common consent has become a rule of conduct. The force of custom was well recognized by Roman Law, and the adoption of local customs originated a great portion of the English common law. In the legal and political development of the high Middle Ages it held a paramount place, but with the crystalization of the modern State and juridical Church in the late Middle Ages customary law came to be increasingly supplanted by statute law, even to be abrogated in effect by decree, and the requirement that it should meet with the approval, at least tacit, of the prince or supreme governor was more insistently emphasized.

General custom, according to Blackstone, is the common law properly so called; particular custom affects the inhabitants of a region. For it to have the force of law it must be reasonable and consonant with natural right, of long and continuous standing, peaceably enjoyed, certain, imperative and not optional, and consistent with other customs. In relation to positive law it falls into three types: according to a law *(secundum legem),* of which it is recognized the best interpreter; beside the law *(praeter legem),* to which it is supplementary in that it clears up a cognate matter; and against a law *(contra legem),* which either has not been effectively imposed, or has fallen into abeyance, or was never generally adopted and for sound reasons. As being extrajudicial in this last respect, custom, not surprisingly, came to be looked at somewhat askance by tidy-minded and centralizing officials, both ecclesiastical and civil. But the right was acknowledged by the Decretals of Gregory IX, and pragmatically accepted as late as the application of the disciplinary decrees of the Council of Trent. Finally it should be noted that the field of custom is as wide as that of law, namely the social community; hence the habits of an individual, or even the traditions of a family, do not establish a custom in the sense of this note.

[T. GILBY]

CUSTOM (CANON LAW), a term used in RC canon law to indicate a norm or rule of conduct that is unwritten in the sense that it stems from no formal enactment on the part of a competent legislator, but arises simply from usage or observance by a community over a period of time. Such observances may, under certain conditions, come to have the force of law. Different types of custom are distinguished in canon law. Some are said to be contrary to law (*contra legem*); others, to lie outside or to reach beyond the law (*praeter legem*); still others, to be according to law (*iuxta legem*). The most important condition for a custom to attain the force of law is the approval and consent of the competent legislator. This approval may be expressly granted, but if the legislator knows of the existence of the custom and does nothing to put a stop to it, he is understood to grant it his tacit approval. Except in cases of customs according to law, or in cases in which the legislator himself introduces the custom, or expressly gives approval to it, a prescriptive period of time must pass, varying in length according to the type of custom in question, before a usage or practice can acquire the force of law. For customs contrary to law, this period must be of at least 40 years duration, and if the particular law in question contains a clause forbidding customs to the contrary, the duration of the prescriptive period must be of at least 100 years. The legislator is not deemed to abrogate centenary or immemorial customs by a general prohibition of contrary custom unless he expressly declares his intention to do so. In establishing the existence of a custom, it must be shown not only that it was observed for the necessary prescriptive period, but also that it was adopted by the majority of the people in a community, esp. the more learned or prominent members of the community, and that they adopted it with the intention of binding themselves legally. BIBLIOGRAPHY: CIC cc. 25–30; L. A. Voegtle, NCE 4:551–553.

[P. K. MEAGHER]

CUSTOMARY, an authorized collection of rules, practices, and liturgical observances of a religious community, which are not detailed in its official rule or constitution.

[M. RILEY]

CUSTOS, in *Gregorian chant notation a small note written at the end of a line of music, or at the end of a section of music where a change of clef occurs, indicating the first pitch of the next line or section.

[A. DOHERTY]

CUTHBERT OF CANTERBURY, ST. (d. 758), abbot, abp. of Canterbury. He became a monk and abbot of Lyminge, was chosen bp. of Hereford in 736, and was elevated to the primatial see in 740. He carried on a notable correspondence with St. Boniface and presided over councils at Clovesho which enacted important canons for the English Church. He was the first abp. buried in the cathedral. BIBLIOGRAPHY: G. M. Fusconi, BiblSanct 4:411–413; B. Clograve, NCE 4:553.

[J. DRUSE]

CUTHBERT OF LINDISFARNE, ST. (d. 687), Anglo-Saxon abbot and bishop. A Lothian shepherd become monk at Melrose, he abandoned Irish for Roman usage and became prior at Lindisfarne. He lived as a hermit on Farne (676–685) until he reluctantly became bp. of Lindisfarne. His relics at Durham were the chief pilgrimage spot in N England. BIBLIOGRAPHY: *Two Lives of St. Cuthbert* (ed. B. Colgrave, 1940); A. Rimoldi and R. Aprile, BiblSanct 4:413–414.

[J. DRUSE]

CUTHBERT OF WEARMOUTH (d. *c*.775), Anglo-Saxon abbot. He became a monk at Jarrow in 718 where he was a pupil of Bede. He became abbot of Jarrow and Wearmouth *c*.750. C. is remembered for his correspondence with Cuthwine, Boniface, and Lull. BIBLIOGRAPHY: B. Colgrave, NCE 4:554.

[J. DRUSE]

CUTHBERT, FATHER (Lawrence Anthony Hess; 1866–1939), celebrated as the outstanding English Capuchin of the 20th century. C. was ordained in the Capuchin Order in 1889. He was provincial of the English province from 1922 to 1925 and served as principal of the Capuchin house of studies at Oxford from 1911 to 1930. Oxford gave him an honorary degree. C. was a prolific writer, principally on Franciscan themes. His best-known work is *Life of St. Francis of Assisi* (1912). Other works were *The Romanticism of St. Francis and Other Studies in the Genius of the Franciscans* (1915), *The Capuchins: A Contribution to the History of the Counter Reformation* (1929), and *The Mystery of the Redemption* (1939). From 1930 until his death, C. was president of the Capuchin Franciscan College of St. Lawrence in Assisi.

[J. R. AHERNE]

CUTHBURGA, ST. (d. *c*.725), Anglo-Saxon queen and abbess. Sister of King Ine of Wessex, she was married to Aldfrid, King of Northumbria and became mother of King Osred. She left her family to become a nun at Barking and then founded the monastery at Wimborne (possibly with her sister Tetta). BIBLIOGRAPHY: A. Rimoldi, BiblSanct 4:414–415; Butler 3:481–482.

[J. DRUSE]

CUXA, ABBEY OF, Cistercian monastery in the Pyrenees at Prades, France, former Benedictine monastery. In 878 the abbey buildings were destroyed by a landslide, following which Abbot Protase transferred the monks to the church of St. Germain in Cuxa. In later years the greed of noble families was aroused by the large amount of land owned by the monks. In 1473, King Louis XI introduced commendation. From 1592 until the Revolution Cuxa belonged to the cloistered Congregation of Taragon. The monks successfully opposed secularization but evaded the reforms recommended for French Benedictines by Pope Clement XIV (1772). The monks were dispersed by the Revolution (1790) and the abbey destroyed (1793). Cistercians restored monastic life at Cuxa in 1919. Remains of the old monastery include the church of St. Michael, an original specimen of Mozarabic art (10th and 11th cent.), one of two square towers (11th cent.), and nine cloisters arcaded with beautifully sculpted capitals (12th cent.), most of which are at The Cloisters of the Metropolitan Museum in New York City. BIBLIOGRAPHY: J. Daoust, NCE 4:554–555; Cottineau 1:937–938.

[A. P. DEEGAN]

CUZCO CATHEDRAL, PERU. Work was begun (1560) under Juan Antonio Veramendi of Spain, and in 1598 the Spaniard Francesca Becerre (who did Lima cathedral) submitted final plans. The cathedral, completed in 1654 except for the towers (c.1657), is of hall type with three naves of equal height and nonprojecting transepts without lantern. Of rectangular plan the interior—colossal and austere—relates to the Herreran classicism of the Escorial (1567), the hard reddish-brown Andean stone adding grandeur to the majestic space. The mid-17th cent. façade also of Andean stone is dominated by an elaborate main portal with two rusticated side portals and solid towers relieved by open belfries. An organ of Flemish construction (1600–25), gilded wooden screenwork, the altar in 18th-cent. French rococo, the retable of the Trinity, and a famous 16th-cent. image of *Christ of the Earthquakes* are noteworthy. BIBLIOGRAPHY: P. Kelemen, *Baroque and Rococo in Latin America* (1951).

[M. J. DALY]

CYBARD, ST., see EPARCHIUS, ST.

CYBELE, the great mother-goddess of Anatolia, worshiped in conjunction with her youthful lover Attis, whose annual death and resurrection were reflected in the changes of the seasons. In Greece, where her cult had spread by the 5th cent. B.C., C. was variously identified with Rhea, Ge, and Demeter. In Rome, where she was officially introduced in 205–204, she was known as the "Magna Mater," or Great Mother. Because of the cruel and orgiastic nature of her rites, her priesthood was not open to Roman citizens until the time of Claudius. The promise of immortality and the fascination of her ritual made her worship extremely popular throughout the Roman Empire. She was commonly portrayed as wearing a crown, carrying a drum or cymbals, and attended by lions. BIBLIOGRAPHY: K. Latte, *Römische Religionsgeschichte* (1960) 258–262.

[M. J. COSTELLOE]

CYCLADIC IDOLS, elegant, sophisticated standing nude female figures of marble buried in modest stone tombs of people on the Cycladic Islands (2600–1100 B.C.). The flat wedge forms, angular and abstract, showing arms folded across the chest, columnar neck and tilted oval shield face, featureless except for a ridgelike nose, are of a wide variety in scale and are marked by subtle nuances of organic form. They evidence an inexplicable refinement upon the heavy-bodied fertility goddesses characteristic of the Old Stone Age and indeed of earlier Cycladic periods.

[M. J. DALY]

CYDONES, DEMETRIUS (c.1324–97 or 98), Byzantine humanist, theologian, and statesman. Educated well in Thessalonica, he accompanied the Emperor John VI Cantacuzenus to Constantinople to serve in his administration. Later, under John V Palaeologus, he occupied the post of *mesazon* (equivalent to prime minister) and played an important role in the imperial government, particularly in the negotiations regarding union with Rome. A strong opponent of *Palamism, he became a Roman Catholic and accompanied John V to Rome in 1369. In connection with his administrative position he learned Latin and translated into Greek works of St. Thomas Aquinas, St. Augustine, and others, which became very influential in Byzantine theological circles. He wrote polemical and other works including four autobiographical apologies for his faith. Some 450 letters of his are extant and comprise an important source for the intellectual and political history of the period. BIBLIOGRAPHY: Beck 733–737.

[G. T. DENNIS]

CYDONES, PROCHOROS (d. 1368 or 69), Byzantine theologian. A brother of Demetrius *Cydones, Prochoros became a monk and priest on Mt. Athos. Under the influence of Western scholastic thought, he translated several Latin theological works into Greek and strenuously combatted the teachings of Gregory *Palamas. Because of this he was excommunicated by the Byzantine Church in 1368. BIBLIOGRAPHY: Beck 737–739; G. Mercati, "Notizie di Procoro e Demetrio Cidone," *Studi e Testi* 56 (1931).

[G. T. DENNIS]

CYLINDER SEALS, see SEALS, CYLINDER.

CYMBAL, percussion instrument used in temple worship (2 Chr 29.25). Structurally they were the same as modern cymbals; tonal variety was achieved by striking horizontally or vertically.

[F. J. MONTALBANO]

CYNEBURG, ST. (d. c.680), Anglo-Saxon queen and abbess. She was a daughter of Penda of Mercia and was married about 580 to Alcfrith of Deira. In later years she entered the religious life and founded the abbey at Castor.

She is named in a runic inscription on the Bewcastle Cross. BIBLIOGRAPHY: J. F. Alonso, BiblSanct 3:1256–57; Butler 1:500–501.

[J. DRUSE]

CYNEWULF, Old English Christian poet of East Anglia in the early 9th cent., known through his runic signatures in four poems: *The Fates of the Apostles, The Ascension (Christ II), Juliana,* and *Elene.* Among other poems formerly ascribed to him but not now considered his, though they show his influence, are *Christ I, Dream of the Rood,* and others. At the end of *Elene,* C. tells of his sinful youth, his conversion, and the gift of song granted to him. His work is marked by love of legendary lore connected with saints' lives and by an intricate use of vivid images and symbols. Thus, he sees Christ as a bright bird swooping to earth and his Ascension as a "leap" to God. Whether C. belongs to a tradition of sophisticated religious writing or founded such a tradition is uncertain. BIBLIOGRAPHY: C. W. Kennedy, *Poems of Cynewulf Translated into English Prose* (1910); C. Schaar, *Critical Studies in Cynewulf* (1949, repr. 1969).

[M. M. BARRY]

CYNICISM, the most durable and influential of the Minor Socratic groups or sects. The Cynics derive their name from the nickname of their founder Diogenes of Sinope, who because of his rejection of conventions and his squalid life was called "the Dog" *(kyōn).* In keeping with the individualism of their founder, the Cynics never formed an organized school in a strict sense. Hence it is often difficult to designate a given philosopher as a Cynic, as Cynic principles are often combined with elements taken from Stoicism, Platonism, and other schools of Greek philosophy. For the main tenets of the school, see DIOGENES OF SINOPE. The most important disciple of Diogenes, Crates of Thebes (*c.*365–285 B.C.), accompanied by his wife Hipparchia, led a wandering life, preaching voluntary poverty and independence, giving consolation to people in distress, and reconciling enemies. His poems were mostly recastings of earlier verse to which he gave a Cynic slant or content. Bion of Borysthenes (*c.*325–*c.*255 B.C.) and Menippus of Gadara (1st half of 3d cent. B.C.) wrote witty satires in which indulgent ridicule played an important part. They were the first to combine Cynicism and Hedonism. Cercidas of Megalopolis (*c.*290–*c.*220) attacked the evils of wealth and advocated a program of social reform based on Cynic principles.

Cynicism declined in the 2d and 1st cent. B.C. but enjoyed a vigorous revival under the Early Empire. Greek and Roman writers refer repeatedly to the Cynic beggar philosophers who swarmed throughout the East and West. A distinction was now made between the true Cynics and the depraved charlatans who brought disgrace upon the name. The true Cynics found themselves in close contact with the Stoics; and the diatribe, originally of Cynic origin, was used effectively as a literary vehicle by both Stoics and Cynics under the empire. The later Cynics reflect the eclectic tendencies of later Greek philosophers in general and exhibit Stoic, Platonic, and even Neoplatonic elements in their teachings. Among leading Cynics under the empire may be mentioned Demetrius (fl. under Nero), Dio Chrysostomus (*c.*40–after 112), Demonax of Cyprus (2d cent. A.D.), Peregrinus Proteus of Parium (*c.* A.D. 100–165), Oenomaus of Gadara (fl. *c.*120), and Sallustus (b. *c.*430 A.D.). The Cynic-Stoic diatribe early became a significant literary form, and the Cynic-Stoic *topoi* or commonplaces were adapted to Christian use by St. Basil, among others. BIBLIOGRAPHY: OCD 248; LexAW 1657–58; D. R. Dudley, *History of Cynicism* (1937); RAC 3:990–1009 s.v. "Diatribe."

[M. R. P. MCGUIRE]

CYPRIAN OF ANTIOCH, ST., legendary bp. and martyr. According to the story told of him he was a native Antiochian who traveled far in search of the secrets of the art of magic, which he used to evil purpose. He tried to seduce a Christian virgin, Justina, but was overcome by the power of Christ and was converted. Baptized, he later became bp. of Antioch, and Justina retired to a convent. During the persecution of Diocletian both were tortured and beheaded in Nicomedia. There is no record of a bp. of Antioch named Cyprian. The legend has no discernible basis in fact and may involve a confusion with the life of *Cyprian of Carthage. BIBLIOGRAPHY: Butler 3:652–654.

[R. B. ENO]

CYPRIAN OF CARTHAGE, ST. (d. 258), bp. of Carthage from 249, martyr. Born of wealthy parents, C. received an excellent education, and, according to St. Jerome, taught rhetoric before his conversion (*c.*246). Early in 250, at the outbreak of the Decian persecution, he withdrew from Carthage and governed his see through letters, a prudent course of action at the time but one which was misunderstood by some even in Rome. During this time he had to condemn the confessors in prison who were granting pardons to apostates without episcopal approval. Returning to Carthage at the end of the persecution (251), he took a middle course between the laxists and rigorists in his dealings with the lapsed. The following year, when a new persecution under Gallus seemed imminent, he permitted all those who had fallen to be reconciled with the Church and to receive communion so that they might be strengthened for the combat. Synods over which he presided in 255 and 256, following an African tradition, pronounced heretical baptisms invalid. This brought about a threat of excommunication from Pope St. Stephen. The intervention of Dionysius of Alexandria, the outbreak of the Valerian persecution, and the death of the Pope (August 2, 257), prevented its execution. This same month C. was exiled to Curubis. Returning to Carthage, he was condemned by the proconsul Galerius Maximus and beheaded after ordering that 25 gold pieces should be given to his executioner.

Though C. was neither an original nor very profound thinker, he was the most authoritative Latin writer before Augustine. The large number of extant MSS of his works show how widely he was read down through the Middle Ages. His writings, which are more of a moral and disciplinary than speculative nature, consist of 13 treatises and a collection of 81 letters, 16 of which are addressed to him. The *Ad Donatum* (246) is an account of his conversion. The *De habitu virginum* (249) contains advice for consecrated virgins on their manner of life. The *De lapsis* (251) prescribes the norms to be followed in reconciling apostates. The *De ecclesiae unitate* (251), his most original work, stresses the obligation of remaining within the Church: *Habere non potest Deum patrem qui ecclesiam non habet matrem*—"One cannot have God as a father who does not have the Church as a mother" (c. 6). The *De dominica oratione* (251–252) is an exposition of the Lord's Prayer; the *Ad Demetrianum* (252) an apology for the faith directed to a pagan. The *De mortalitate* (252–253) was written to console the people afflicted by a plague that was ravaging the empire. The *De opere et eleemosynis* (252–253) is a treatise on almsgiving. The *De bono patientiae* (256) and the *De zelo et livore* (256–257), both occasioned by the baptismal controversy, discuss respectively the virtue of patience and the vice of envy. The *Ad Fortunatum de exhortatione martyrii* (257), is a compilation of scriptural texts referring to martyrdom. The *Ad Quirinum (Testimoniorum libri III)* (c.248) is a similar collection of texts on the Jews and on moral virtues. The *Quod idola dii non sint* (c.246), of doubtful authenticity, contains a refutation of polytheism, a defense of the unity of God, and a treatise on Christ. The letters, which deal with a variety of pastoral problems over a period of years, are important for the history of the time.

Though Cyprian was mistaken in his opinions on the nature of the episcopacy and the conditions required for the validity of the sacraments, he is an important witness to numerous doctrines and practices of the early Church: infant baptism; the confession of sins, and public penance; the Mass as a memorial of the Last Supper making present the sacrifice upon the Cross; and the immediate admission of martyrs to the beatific vision. As may be seen in his writings, Cyprian was not only a statesman in his manner of ruling but he was also one of the most noble and attractive Fathers of the Church. BIBLIOGRAPHY: Altaner, 193–205.

[M. J. COSTELLOE]

CYPRIAN OF TOULON, ST. (d. betw. 543 and 549), bp. of Toulon, staunch opponent of Semi-Pelagianism. Disciple, friend, and supporter of Caesarius of Arles, he was principal author (among several collaborators) of the *Vita s. Caesarii,* one of the finest biographical efforts of the 6th cent. and much esteemed by modern critics of medieval hagiography. C.'s orthodoxy is evident in his letter of 530 to Bp. Maximus of Geneva. BIBLIOGRAPHY: G. M. Cook, NCE 4:566; G. M. Fusconi, BiblSanct 3:1280–81.

[G. M. COOK]

CYPRUS, predominantly Greek Orthodox island in E Mediterranean; also known as *Kittim in OT (Gen 10.4). Greeks began colonizing c.1400 B.C., and in Homer Aphrodite is identified with Paphos, the city of western Cyprus where she came out of the sea. Though the island was later dominated by many outsiders, including Phoenicia, Assyria, Egypt, Rome and Britain, the majority culture remains Greek. Jewish settlers in considerable numbers arrived under the Ptolemies, who ruled following the death of Alexander. According to Acts, some of the Cypriot Jews were among the earliest Christians, and in the persecution following Stephen's martyrdom some Christians fled to Cyprus (11.19–20); Barnabas, a native of the island (4.36), and Paul preached in Cypriot synagogues and before the Roman proconsul, Sergius Paulus, who "believed" (13.4–12); after separating from Paul, Barnabas visited Cyprus again with Mark (15.39). The Jews of Cyprus, along with those of Egypt and Cyrene, revolted against Rome betw. 115 and 117, and were expelled.

Bishops from Cyprus attended the Council of Nicea (325), and the Council of Ephesus (431) upheld the Cypriot Church's claims of independence against the authority asserted by Antioch. Among noted early ecclesiastics of Cyprus was St. Epiphanius (d. 403), a native of Palestine elected in 367 to the chief see of Cyprus, Constantia (Salamis). Following the division of the Roman Empire, Cyprus became subject to the Eastern emperors, and from the 7th to 10th cent. was fought over by Constantinople and Muslims. The end of Arab rule in the 10th cent. brought a period in which monasteries were built and became a dominant cultural force.

Richard I of England (Lion-Heart) conquered Cyprus in 1191 and turned it over to Guy de Lusignan, dispossessed king of Jerusalem. In 1196 a Latin hierarchy was imposed, and the Greek Cypriot Church became a rallying point for resistance to foreign domination. Cyprus was a trading center vital to the interests of merchants, and the Genoese gained influence for a time. But in 1464 King James II expelled them and then became allied in 1472 to Venice through marriage. Following his death the next year, Venice controlled Cyprus until the Turks took it in 1571.

Turkish rule brought an end to the Latin hierarchy, but the Greek Church was allowed to reorganize with three bishops and an archbishop (of Nicosia), an arrangement that continues today. The Turks recognized the Greek hierarchy as the responsible leaders of the Greek community, and the archbishop as the ethnarch, or leader of the people. When a revolt against Turkish rule broke out in Greece in 1821, the Turks suspected Cypriot bishops of supporting it, and they were all killed, along with other leading Cypriots.

Britain took control of Cyprus in 1878 and formally incorporated it into the British Empire in 1914. Among the Greek population a movement developed for union *(enosis)* with Greece. But the Turkish minority were vigorously opposed. Led by Makarios, abp. 1950–77, Greek Cypriots carried out a struggle against the British that led to establishment of Cyprus as a republic in 1960. An agreement specified that it would remain independent and that the Turkish minority would enjoy certain rights. Makarios was elected the first president and later reelected. In 1974 he was overthrown by forces directed from Greece and seeking *enosis*. But Turkey intervened with military force, and Makarios was restored to power, though the island was left in a divided state. BIBLIOGRAPHY: H. D. Purcell, *Cyprus* (1968).

[T. EARLY]

CYPRUS TREASURE, one of the richest examples of Byzantine silverwork is a series of nine silver plates from Cyprus with classical figures in repoussé depicting the life of David and bearing the control stamp of the Emperor Heraclius (610–629). Two plates are in the Museum in Nicosia, seven in the Metropolitan Museum of Art, New York. The complete series appeared in a new sequence in the Exhibition of Early Christian Art at the Metropolitan Museum of Art (1977).

[M. J. DALY]

CYRANO DE BERGERAC, SAVINIEN DE (1619–55), French writer whose life was romantically dramatized in E. Rostand's play (1897). C. retired from the army after being wounded at Arras (1641) and studied philosophy, becoming a *libertin* disciple of the epicurean Gassendi. His two burlesque novels of imaginary travel to the sun and moon, *Histoire comique des états et empires de la lune* (1656) and *Histoire comique des états et empires du soleil* (1662), express ideas that reflect the influence of Gassendi's empiricism, Cartesian rationalism, and pantheistic naturalism, making C. a forerunner of the 18th-cent. philosophes. He also wrote two plays: *Le Pédant joué* (c. 1645), which inspired *Molière; and the daring *La Mort d'Agrippine* (1654). It is thought that C. converted at the end of his life with the aid of the prayers of his relative, Mère Marguerite de Jésus (Catherine de Cyrano), prioress of the Daughters of the Cross, in whose convent he is buried. BIBLIOGRAPHY: R. Pintard, *Le Libertinage érudit dans la première moitié du XVIIᵉ siècle* (2 v., 1943).

[R. N. NICOLICH]

CYRENAIC SCHOOL, one of the *Minor Socratic Schools, founded by Aristippus of Cyrene (fl. c.425–355 B.C.). He taught that sensations alone give certain knowledge, that subjective sensations are the basis for practical conduct, and that the end of conduct is to obtain pleasurable sensations. Pleasure, accordingly, is the end of life, and this pleasure should be positive and present. This largely physical hedonism, however, which stresses the pleasure of the moment, is actually controlled by the judgment of the wise man, who weighs the choices of pleasure and looks to the future as well as to the present in this respect. His chief disciples were Theodorus the Atheist of Cyrene (c.330–270 B.C.), who maintained that individual acts of gratification are indifferent, that circumstances can justify acts like steal-

ing, and that there are no gods whatever; Hegesias of Cyrene (c.330–270 B.C.), who likewise taught indifference regarding individual acts of gratification, but emphasized a negative concept of life, namely, absence of pain and sorrow—which gave a justification for suicide; Anniceris of Cyrene (c.330–270 B.C.), who again stressed pleasure as the end of life, but a higher pleasure as reflected, for example, in love of family and country, and friendship. It is possible that *Euhemerus of Messane (c.340–260 B.C.) may have been Cyrenaic or that his agnosticism at least is to be traced to Cyrenaic influence. The Cyrenaic School disappeared with the deaths of the representatives mentioned. BIBLIOGRAPHY: Copleston 1:121–123; Ueberweg 1:170–178.

[M. R. P. MCGUIRE]

CYRENE, an ancient city of North Africa (now Shahhat, Libya). Founded by Greeks in the 7th cent. B.C., Cyrene became famous for medicine and Sophistic philosophy. It fell successively to Persia, Macedonia, Egypt, Rome, and Islam, and in more recent days to the Turks and briefly to the Italians. In the NT, men of Cyrene are mentioned several times: Simon helped Jesus carry his cross (Mt 27.32); Lucius announced to the gentiles the coming of Paul and Barnabas (Acts 11.19; 13.1); Jews from Cyrene were among those who heard Peter's first sermon (Acts 2.10). Jason of Cyrene wrote the account of the exploits of Judas Maccabee that underlies 2 Maccabees. The presence of a Christian community in Cyrene is attested from the mid-3d century. Recent investigations have unearthed important examples of Greek art and architecture. BIBLIOGRAPHY: A. Rose, *History of Ancient Cyrenaica* (1948); R. Goodchild, *Cyrene and Apollonia* (1959).

[M. J. SUELZER]

CYRIL OF ALEXANDRIA, ST. (c.382–444), bp. of *Alexandria, foremost adversary of *Nestorius, principal orthodox figure of the ecumenical Council of *Ephesus (431), defender of the *theotokos, patron saint of *monophysitism. Nestorius, bp. of Constantinople, had denied that Mary is the mother of God-as-such in terms that seemed to imply that she is not the mother of God at all and that Christ is two persons, one divine and one human. Cyril, a violent and arbitrary personage, as was Nestorius himself, armed with a papal demand that Nestorius retract, demanded in addition that Nestorius explicitly profess the opposite theology as couched in C.'s own *Twelve Anathematisms*. When Nestorius refused, C. had him deposed and his doctrine condemned at the Council of Ephesus.

C.'s celebrated Christological and Mariological formulae are "One nature, incarnate, of the Word of God," which Apollinaris had used to deny a human soul in Christ (see APOLLINARIANISM) but which for C. seems to have meant the orthodox unicity of Christ's person (C. thought the expression was *Athanasius'); "If Christ is God and Mary is his mother, then how is she not God's mother?''; and *''hypostatic union.'' After Ephesus C. negotiated with John, bp. of Antioch, a compromise *Antiochene Creed* which included the expressions ''union without mixture'' of Christ's divine and human natures, and ''consubstantial with his Father in his divinity, consubstantial with us in his humanity.'' The Christological position of *Antioch was akin to that of Nestorius and the Antiochene party had been Nestorius' allies, hence John had resented C.'s deposition of Nestorius at Ephesus.

Very shortly after C.'s death the Monophysites, claiming that by ''one nature'' C. had meant that Christ had no fully human nature, appropriated him as the great Doctor of their theological position and continue to regard him as such today. *ANATHEMAS OF CYRIL.

[R. R. BARR]

CYRIL OF CONSTANTINOPLE, ST. (*c.* 1138–1224), a Greek priest and hermit of Mt. Carmel. The tradition that he was a Carmelite prior general is incorrect. Two works, *Oraculum angelicum s. Cyrilli,* and *Epistola ad Eusebium* are attributed to him, but they belong rather to the Carmelite Philip Ribot, who wrote toward the end of the 14th century. BIBLIOGRAPHY: K. J. Egan, NCE 4:576; G. Mesters, LTK 6:710.

[M. R. P. MCGUIRE]

CYRIL CONTARIS (known also as Cyril of Beroea, d. 1640), pro-Catholic patriarch of Constantinople (1635–36, 1638–39). He was instrumental in the deposition of Patriarch Cyril Lucaris (1638) and the condemnation of his Calvinistic leanings throughout the Orthodox Church. Cyril Contaris secretly made a Catholic profession of faith in the hands of the Catholic Patriarchal Vicar Petricca (Dec. 1638). He was later deposed, exiled to Tunis, and strangled by Turkish agents. At one time there was some thought in Rome of initiating his cause of beatification as a martyr. BIBLIOGRAPHY: A. De Santis, *Un tentativo di unione nel sec. XVII* (1966).

[G. ELDAROV]

CYRIL OF JERUSALEM, ST. (*c.* 313–*c.* 386), bp. from 348, Doctor of the Church. Born, or at least educated, in Jerusalem, C. was ordained a priest by St. Maximus whom he succeeded as bp. of that city. Some obscurity veils the circumstances of C.'s succession, but he appears to have enjoyed at first the support of Acacius, the Arian metropolitan of Caesarea. Soon, however, sharp conflict arose between the two, partly because of a dispute of long standing over the comparative dignity of their respective sees, and partly because of C.'s insistent adherence to the Christological doctrine of Nicaea. Three times C. was deposed and banished from his see by the Arians. First, through the machinations of Acacius he was deposed in 357 by a council in his own city, but was restored the next year by the Council of Seleucia in which the Semi-Arian party had the upper hand. Again, in 360, Acacius, through the intervention of the Emperor, had him expelled, but 2 years later, under the amnesty of *Julian the Apostate, he was able to return. Finally, a decree of Valens in 367 banished all the bishops restored under Julian, and C. remained in exile until the death of Valens (378). He attended the Council of Constantinople I (381) and formally accepted the *homoousios (consubstantial) qualification which an inclination toward Semi-Arian doctrine had theretofore made him reluctant to admit. Deeply versed in the Scriptures and distinguished by his powers of theological synthesis, C. was also a most effective preacher. His extant works include a sermon on the Pool of Bethesda, a letter to the emperor Constantius, three fragments, and his *Cathecheses.* The last is his most famous work and is among the most important documents that have come down from Christian antiquity. It contains C.'s catechetical sermons, probably delivered in 348 and taken down by an auditor. They are divided into two groups. The first contains a procatechesis or introductory lecture and 18 sermons delivered during Lent to the catechumens who were to be baptized. The second is made up of five sermons, the so-called mystagogical catecheses, delivered to the newly baptized after Easter. It has been plausibly suggested that these last five sermons are the work of John, C.'s nephew and successor in the see of Jerusalem. Noteworthy doctrinal points of the catecheses are their insistence on the full divinity of the Son and on the Real Presence and the sacrificial aspects of the Eucharist. As a source for the history of doctrine and esp. of the liturgy, the catecheses are invaluable. Works: PG 33; Greek text and Eng. tr., ed. F. Cross, *St. Cyril of Jerusalem's Lectures on the Christian Sacraments: the Procatechesis and the Five Mystagogical Catecheses* (1951); Loeb 4 (ed. W. Telfer, 1956) 64–192. BIBLIOGRAPHY: Quasten 3:362–377; Butler 1:623–626.

[R. B. ENO]

CYRIL LUCARIS (1572–1638), **PATRIARCH OF CONSTANTINOPLE** from 1620). Having studied at Padua, Venice, and Geneva, where he was influenced by Calvinism, he became *syncellus to *Meletius Pegas, patriarch of Alexandria, whom he succeeded in 1602. C. opposed the Union of *Brest, issued a vernacular translation of the Bible, and expanded the educational system under his jurisdiction. He also presented the *Codex Alexandrinus to England *c.* 1625. In 1629, C. published his *Confessio fidei* which was a presentation of the Orthodox faith affirming such Reform tenets as: the superiority of Scripture over the Church, justification by faith, the depravity of the human will, and the recognition of only baptism and the Eucharist as sacraments. His thought dominated Greek theology during the 17th cent., but the *Confessio* was condemned by later synods. He was murdered by the Sultan's janissaries for political reasons. BIBLIOGRAPHY: C. Emereau, DTC 9.1:1003–19.

[F. T. RYAN]

CYRIL OF SCYTHOPOLIS (524–588), hagiographer. From his 20th year C. lived as a monk, first at the monastery of St. Euthymius, and then at the monastery of St. Sabas. There he wrote the lives of the famous Palestinian monks of the then recent past—SS. Euthymius, Sabas, John the Hesychast, Cyriacus, Theodosius, Theognius, and Abraham. These biographies are conspicuous for their accuracy and historical reliability in comparison with similar productions of antiquity. Works: PG 114:595–734; crit. ed. E. Schwartz, TU 49 (1939). BIBLIOGRAPHY: Altaner 257–258.

[R. B. ENO]

CYRIL OF TUROV, ST. (c.1130–82), ascetical writer and preacher. C.'s parents were people of substance in Turov (Turau), then the capital city of a principality practically independent of Kiev. He received a good education, probably from Greek teachers, from whom he acquired a rhetorical style in the Byzantine manner. He entered a monastery but soon went on to become an anchorite in the forest. He was living in this state when his reputation for sanctity caused the prince and people of Turov to bring him back to that city to be bp. in 1169. There he preached a number of celebrated sermons which are among the gems of ancient Russian literature. Although he was later called the Slavonic Chrysostom, in his own day and for some time afterwards his ascetical works were more appreciated. These are related to those of St. John Climacus and St. Theodore of Studius. They reveal in places the influence of the romance of Barlaam and Josaphat, composed by St. John Damascene on the basis of the Buddha's life. C.'s prayers have been highly praised by modern Russian writers on spirituality. BIBLIOGRAPHY: Butler 2:181; A. Koren, BiblSanct 3:1322–24.

[G. EVERY]

CYRIL AND METHODIUS, SS., the monastic names under which two brothers, Constantine (Cyril, 826–869) and Michael (Methodius, 815–885) are venerated as the apostles of the Slavs. They were born in Thessalonica and educated in Constantinople, where Cyril was a pupil of *Photius. He gave up a career at the imperial court, became a priest, and was named patriarchal librarian of Hagia Sophia. Methodius, after serving as governor of a Greco-Slav district, had become a monk on Mt. Olympus, where he was later joined by his brother. The two were among a delegation sent c.860 to the *Khazars who were undecided at the time whether to adopt Judaism, Islam, or Christianity. The account of the debate with the Khazars has been lost in both its Greek and Slavonic forms. On returning to Constantinople Cyril taught at the patriarchal academy while Methodius served as abbot of the monastery of Polychronion. In 862 Emperor Michael III, responding to an appeal of the Moravian Duke Ratislav, sent the two brothers to establish a native Church among the Slavic people. Prior to their mission, C. had developed a Slavonic

alphabet (see CYRILLIC ALPHABET) and had translated part of the Scriptures into the Slavonic tongue. They also drew up and introduced a Slavonic liturgy, a move that received papal approval despite opposition from Western clergy in Moravia. C. died in Rome shortly afterward and was buried in the church of San Clemente. After being consecrated bp., Methodius returned to Moravia, where he encountered further opposition from the Bavarian clergy and was actually imprisoned for 3 years. Undaunted by further harassment from ecclesiastical and political leaders, he continued his efforts to Slavicize the Church in his missionary field. After his death his disciples were driven from the country but this had the beneficial effect of spreading the work of Cyril and Methodius to the neighboring Bulgars, Bohemians, and southern Poles. BIBLIOGRAPHY: F. Dvornik, *Slavs: Their Early History and Civilization* (1956); V. Grumel, BiblSanct 3:1328–37.

[F. T. RYAN]

CYRILLIC ALPHABET. SS. Cyril and Methodius, setting out from Constantinople in the 9th cent. to evangelize the Slavs, translated the liturgy into the language of the people. Many points about their lives are controverted by scholars, but this much seems certain: to produce a language formed enough to sustain translation of the Greek, they gave it a full grammar and esp. a participial structure.

St. Cyril is credited with creating the Cyrillic alphabet for the Old Slavonic language by using Greek letters to represent sounds common to both languages, using Hebrew letters like *shin* to represent Slav sounds, e.g., *sh* (not in Greek), and making up new letters for sounds found neither in Greek nor in Hebrew.

The original Cyrillic alphabet consists of 42 letters. From this alphabet derive, by rounding out the ancient characters (as was done by Peter the Great for the Russian alphabet), the Russian, Ukrainian, Bulgarian, and Serbian forms of the Cyrillic alphabets.

[C. ENGLERT]

CYRINIUS, see QUIRINIUS.

CYRION (Kyrion), catholicos of Iberia (c.598–c.610). Iberia, which had been Monophysite, was reconciled with Rome after 519. The Armenian Church was still Monophysite when C. became catholicos but in 600 he came to reconciliation with Rome. In 608 or 609 the catholicos of Armenia excommunicated Cyrion and his Catholic followers.

[J. R. AHERNE]

CYRUS, KING OF PERSIA (559–530 B.C.), founder of the Persian Empire. After becoming king of Elam, he conquered Media (550), Lydia and Asia Minor (546), W India (545), and the Babylonian Empire, including Syria and Palestine (539). He based his government of conquered lands on a closely knit network of satraps, whose loyalty was ensured by the spying of world history's first secret police system. The first emperor to acknowledge and condone native cultural and religious traditions throughout his empire, he was proclaimed to be a savior and messiah by Israelite prophets of the Babylonian Exile and fulfilled their expectations by allowing the Jews to return to Palestine along with their Temple's treasures in 538. (See Is 41.2–4; 44.28; 45.1; 46.11; Ezra 1.1–11. He was killed in a battle against northern invaders in 530.

[J. F. FALLON]

CYRUS, MELCHITE PATRIARCH OF ALEXANDRIA (d. 641), promoter of the Monothelite heresy. Nothing better illustrates the confused overlapping of the interest of the Eastern Empire and the Eastern Church than the case of Cyrus of Alexandria. Emperor Heraclius wished to convert the Monophysites of Egypt and at the same time secure their support for his regime. With the help of Sergius, Patriarch of Constantinople, he persuaded C. to devise a new formula to explain the dual nature of Christ, a statement supposedly in keeping with the decree of the Council of Chalcedon. The new formula, called Monothelitism, was acceptable to the heretics but ultimately was denounced by the Third Ecumenical Council (680). Heraclius made C. patriarch of Alexandria in 630. When the Saracens threatened Alexandria, C. was entrusted with its defense. The city fell in 640 and he died within a year. BIBLIOGRAPHY: J. F. Sollier, CE 4:597–598.

[J. R. AHERNE]

CYRUS THE POET (fl. 446), prefect of Constantinople, bp. of Cotyaeum. C. was an Egyptian poet and philosopher who became prefect of Constantinople under the patronage of Empress Eudocia. In his capacity as city administrator he made extensive renovations and was compared to Constantine the Great who founded Constantinople. When Eudocia was forced to retire to Jerusalem, C. was dismissed. To escape execution he became a cleric and was appointed bp. of Cotyaeum where he exercised a prudent administration. Intrigue drove him from his see, and he came back to Constantinople as administrator of large property holdings.

[J. R. AHERNE]

CZECH CONFESSIONS, another name for the *Bohemian Confessions of 1535 and 1575.

CZECHOSLOVAK CHURCH (Církev Československá), a *national Church. An organization of priests presented to Benedict XV in 1919 a petition that included election of bps., democratization of church government, vernacular liturgy, and freedom from celibacy. When the petition was rejected by the Pope, a few rebelled, were excommunicated, and in 1920 formed the Czechoslovak Church. The first bp., Matthew Pavlek, obtained valid consecration but left the Church after struggling in vain against liberalizing tendencies. Thereafter apostolic succession was rejected. The Church took on a presbyterian

form of government, but with four unconsecrated bps., the bp. of Prague being patriarch. The first patriarch was Karl Farský, and under him liberal religious thought prevailed: the Scriptures were taken as but one of many witnesses to God's word; the critique of religious truth was man's reason; Christ was Son of God only in an ethical sense; original sin and other Christian dogmas were rejected. The Church did not maintain the numerical strength achieved during its early days when it was closely identified with Czech nationalism. Latest obtainable figures (1963) showed a membership of 750,000. Since 1948 the Church has sought the favor of the Communist regime. BIBLIOGRAPHY: Gründler 1.362–363; Latourette CRA 4:196–197; L. Nemec, *Church and State in Czechoslovakia, Historically, Juridically, and Theologically Documented* (1955) 124–130.

[T. C. O'BRIEN]

CZECHOSLOVAKIA, a country in central Europe, a land mainly of Czechs and Slovaks and of several other minorities, its territory comprising Bohemia, Moravia, Silesia, Slovakia, and Carpathian Ruthenia. (They were part of the Empire of Austria-Hungary until 1918 when the Republic of Czechoslovakia was formed.) Against a rich cultural and religious background, the infiltration of West Slavic tribes into the present territory reached its zenith by the 6th cent. and political identity was achieved in the 9th-cent. with the great Moravian Empire (846–906). Christianity came from both the West, when in 845 14 Czech tribes were baptized in Regensburg and from the East when in 863 brothers, SS. Cyril and Methodius, came from Byzantium to preach the gospel in the Slavic language in response to the request of Moravian Prince Rostislav. After the collapse of Great Moravia, Slovaks fell under the rule of Magyars, and a new political entity was formed in the 10th cent. in Bohemia, where Christianity continued to spread from the Latin West, while the Slavic liturgy survived. The victory of Christianity was sealed by the martyrdom of St. Ludmila (916) and her grandson, the young Duke St. Wenceslas I (929), followed by the erection of a bishopric in Prague (973) and by the renewal of the Moravian hierarchy with the establishment of the bishopric of Olomouc (1063). Bohemia and Moravia formed the Kingdom of the Czechs and were known as "historical lands of the Czechs Crown," which included also Upper and Lower Austria until 1635. Flourishing Christianity was reinforced by the creation of the archbishopric of Prague (1344), when Prague became the cultural center in the Empire through the establishment of Charles IV Univ., the first in central Europe.

By the 15th cent. the country was affected by the radical religious reform of Jan Hus. This spirit was received by Peter Chelčicky and the Unitas Fratrum (*Bohemia Brethren) was formed (1447) based on his teachings. The *Utraquist Church was established in 1436 and its equality with the Catholic Church was formally recognized by the *Compactata. Though Pope Pius II declared the Compactata invalid in 1462, the equal status of Utraquists was temporarily guaranteed by local laws. Gradually, under the pressure, some returned to the Catholic Church, others known as Neo-Utraquists, joined the Unitas Fratrum and those professing Lutheranism, in the Czech Confession (*Bohemian Confessions) of 1575. After the Battle of the White Mountain (1620), Catholicism was declared the sole state religion; the Brethren, led by Jan Amos Komensky (*Comenius), emigrated and the nation was re-Catholicized. In Slovakia, the Reformation was not utterly defeated as in the Czech lands. Here relations between Catholics and the Protestants were stabilized in 1606 by the Peace of Vienna and by the Peace of Linz in 1645; the Protestants were divided into Lutherans and Calvinists.

The Enlightenment brought religious tolerance to Czech lands owing to the Austrian Toleration Patent of 1781, and in still greater measure in Slovakia. The stormy year of 1848 marked the beginning of the transition to a constitutional state. The toleration enjoyed by most of the Churches was tacitly transformed into a liberal regime of "legal recognition" with the RC Church retaining its privileged status, formalized in the Concordat with the Holy See of 1855. However, the Concordat was de facto abolished by the Constitution of 1887. The spirit of liberalism was reflected also in legislation of the latter half of the 19th cent. that defined the status and operation of "recognized" Churches and religious societies in detail. Nonrecognized denominations were considered legally nonexistent. The conditions a religious denomination had to satisfy to obtain legal recognition were specified in Austrian Law No. 68 of 1874, which applied in the Czech lands, and on Hungarian Law No. 43 of 1895, which applied to Slovakia and Ruthenia. This was the situation by the time of the dissolution of the Austro-Hungarian Empire and creation of the Czechoslovak Republic in 1918.

With the establishment of Czechoslovak national independence, also, a national *Czechoslovak church came into existence in 1920 in addition to all churches and denominations accepted by the new State, in which the Czechoslovak constitution of Feb. 29, 1920, guaranteed all inhibitants of the Republic "full and absolute protection of life and liberty, without regard to their origin, nationality, language, race, or religion" (Art. 106). Thus, according to the census of Feb. 15, 1921, religious distribution in the Czechoslovak Republic was in detail the following:

Entire population	13,613,172
Roman Catholic	10,384,833
Without any belief	724,504
Greek Catholic	535,543
Augsburg Churches	526,206
Czechoslovak Church	525,333
Jews	353,925
Czech Brothers	234,100
Helvetians	209,502
Greek Orthodox	73,097
Old Catholic	20,255

Free Reformed	5,095
Hermhuter	4,044
Baptists	2,107
Methodists	1,461
Anglicans	459
American Orthodox	149
American Catholic	43
Salvation Army	16
Other religions	5,380

This reflects the religious pluralism that enjoyed complete freedom and tolerance in the Czechoslovak democracy. The integration was even more stabilized, when the Catholic majority was steadied by the *modus vivendi* of Feb. 2, 1928 between the Czechoslovak Republic and the Holy See. This integration lasted till 1939, when the Protectorate of Bohemia and Moravia was established following the Nazi occupation (1939–45), and the activity of all Churches was restricted.

After World War II (1945), the existence of the Czechoslovak Republic was restored with the loss of Carpathian Ruthenia to Russia, and religious freedom temporarily revived until the Communists seized power by their *Putsch* of Feb. 25, 1948. The country was termed the People's Republic; freedom was greatly restricted. Under a new law of May 9, 1948 freedom was nominally guaranteed, but in reality a total religious persecution was pursued by the Communist government. According to the Constitution of 1960 the country is called the Czechoslovak Socialist Republic, with religious freedom still much restricted.

The years 1967–68 witnessed a movement of liberation in the Communist regime in Czechoslovakia under Alexander Dubcek and its suppression by the invading Russians. In 1968, during this "thaw", the Slovak Byzantine rite Catholics approached the government, petitioning that they be exonerated from the false charges against them in 1948, and that their Church be allowed to reconstitute itself and resume normal life. It was decided between the government and the Catholics that a vote would be held in each parish and that those parishes in which a majority favored returning to the Catholic Church would be allowed to do so. On this basis, of the 246 parishes forced into schism in 1948, 204 have voted to resume their life as Byzantine-Slavonic rite Catholics. In 1972 the apostolates of nuns were limited to farms and mental hospitals; in 1973, although the government permitted the ordination of four bishops, severe restrictions which hampered future apostolic work were issued against the further education of seminarians and priests. The estimated Catholic population at that time was 10,935,000 out of a total population of 13,775,000 inhabitants in 1961. In 1974 Vatican and Czech officials resumed talks which, though still continuing, have had no noticeable results. In 1977 hopes for negotiations increased with the nomination of Bp. Francis Tomašek of Prague as cardinal. Church-State relations in Czechoslovakia, remain tense as ever, nonetheless, in spite of these sanguine expectations. BIBLIOGRAPHY: V. Busek and N.

Spulbec, *Czechoslovakia,* (tr. F. A. Praeger, 1957); L. Nemec, *Church and State in Czechoslovakia* (1955); *idem,* "Czechoslovak Heresy and Schism," *Transactions of American Philosophical Society* (1975); G. N. Shuster, *Religion behind the Iron Curtain* (1959); T. Zubek, *Church of Silence in Slovakia* (1956).

[L. NEMEC]

CZECHOSLOVAKIA, ORTHODOX CHURCH OF. A small group of Czech Orthodox received a bp. from the ecumenical patriarch in 1923, and 2 years later were joined by a larger group of Western Christians who had separated from Rome. The patriarch of Belgrade then provided them with a bishop. In 1951 the patriarch of Moscow acknowledged the autocephalous state of the Czechoslovakian Orthodox Church, which today includes about 250,000 faithful, under the care of the metropolitan of Prague and all Czechoslovakia. It includes three other dioceses: Olomouc-Brno, Michalovce, and Prešov, with seminaries in Prague and Prešov. The Byzantine Catholic eparchies of Michalovce and Prešov had been forcibly absorbed into Orthodoxy by 1950, but in 1968 parishes were given the option of remaining Orthodox or of rejoining the Byzantine Church in communion with Rome. A majority (204 of 246) voted to resume their life as Byzantine-Slavonic rite Catholics.

[T. BIRD]

CZENGER, CONFESSION OF, another name for the *Hungarian Confession (1557 or 58), adopted for the *Reformed Church by a synod at Czenger on the NE border of Hungary.

CZEPKO, DANIEL (1605–60), Protestant German poet, jurist, and historian. C. published his first German and Latin poems when he was 17. A member of the early Silesian school of poets, he is often referred to as a mystic,

but it is truer to say that his mystical poems represent a single stage in his religious development. He was susceptible to the gamut of baroque influences. In him rational speculation can be found alongside naive faith, worldliness, alongside emotional renunciation. His *600 Aphorisms of the Wise* influenced Angelus Silesius' *Cherubinischen Wandersmann* both in form and content. BIBLIOGRAPHY: F. W. Wentzlaff-Eggebert, RGG 1:1898.

CZERSKI, JOHANN (1815–93), cofounder of the German Catholic movement (*Deutschkatholizismus). Two years after his ordination as a priest, he left the Church and founded in 1844 a reform community of dissatisfied Roman Catholics. In 1846 he joined with Johann *Ronge in organizing the German Catholic movement. Ronge's more rationalistic ideas prevailed, and C. lost his position of leadership. He spent his remaining years as an obscure, itinerant preacher, eventually abandoning Christianity entirely.

[J. WILLKE]

CZESTOCHOWA, OUR LADY OF, a wooden icon of Mary and the Child traditionally believed to have been painted by St. Luke on a tablet made by St. Joseph for the Holy Family in Nazareth. Most likely the icon dates from the 9th cent. and is Greek or Greek-Italian in origin, with 13th-cent. overpaintings. In 1382, Prince Ladislaus Opolszyk brought the icon to Częstochowa from his castle in the Ukraine. Three cuts in the Virgin's right cheek are accredited to desecration by robbers in 1430. Until its restoration in 1925, only the smoke-blackened faces and hands of the Virgin and Child were visible. More than a million pilgrims a year visit the shrine in Częstochowa housed on the *Jasna Góra* (hill of light) in a basilica that is the most renowned shrine in Central Europe. BIBLIOGRAPHY: Z. Aradi, *Shrines of Our Lady around the World* (1954).

[J. BLAIR]

D

DABLON, CLAUDE (1619–97), superior of the Jesuit missions in New France. After ordination in France, D. was sent to Canada as a missionary in 1655. He worked among the Hurons in modern Ontario and became superior (1669) of the Jesuit missions in the Great Lakes area with headquarters at Sault Ste. Marie. In charge of all the French Jesuit missions in N America (1671–80; 1686–93), he was responsible for efforts to evangelize the Iroquois and the Illinois and other Western tribes. BIBLIOGRAPHY: T. J. Campbell, *Pioneer Priests of North America* (1908) 1:110–133.

[R. K. MacMASTER]

DABROWSKI, JOSEPH (1842–1903), missionary. Born in Poland, D. took part as a young man in the uprising of 1863 against Russian oppression and was obliged to flee Poland when the rebellion failed. After studies at the newly founded Polish College in Rome, he was ordained in 1869. D. then came to the U.S. to minister to Polish Catholics in Wisconsin. The need for bilingual Polish-American priests to care for the large group of Catholics in the area was answered by his establishment of SS. Cyril and Methodius Seminary in Detroit, which opened in 1887; he was its rector for 19 years. D. had to take action against 29 seminarians for open rebellion, and the experience so affected him that he died of a paralytic stroke within a few days. BIBLIOGRAPHY: F. T. Seroczynski, CE 16:32; J. V. Swastek, NCE 4:609.

[J. R. AHERNE]

DADA (French for "hobby horse"), the arbitrarily chosen name for the art movement that originated in 1915 in Zürich with Tristan Zara, Hugo Ball, Hülseneck, Jean Arp, Sophie Taüber, Marcel Janco, and Otto van Rees. At the same time Dada appeared in New York with Marcel Duchamp, Picabia, Man Ray, W. Arensberg, and Marius de Zayas in the Gallery Stieglitz. Other groups were formed later in Berlin (Hülseneck), Cologne (Max Ernst), and Paris (Bre-

ton). Dada, rooted in a feeling of powerlessness against a war-filled world and a consequent disillusionment with culture and civilization, broke with the past and in expressions negative, provocative, critical, alienating, and disturbing in art and literature, sought to shock the world into a realization of evils in society. Political and anarchic activities (*c.*1920) brought the Dada movement to a close as art moved into Surrealism. Modern abstract art and other contemporary art forms were highly stimulated by Data. BIBLIOGRAPHY: A. H. Barr and G. Hugnet, *Fantastic Art, Dada, Surrealism* (1947); R. Motherwell, *Dada Painters and Poets, An Anthology* (1951).

[P. HEFTING]

DADDI, BERNARDO (1290–1348), one of the leading Florentine painters of his day. Working in a Giottesque style, D. painted a triptych (1328) for the Church of Ognissanti, a *Madonna and Child with Saints* (1334), *The Vision of St. Bernard* (1335), *Three Dominican Saints* (Sta. Maria Novella, 1338), the splendid panel *Madonna and Child with Angels* at Or San Michele, Florence (for A. Orcagna's tabernacle), and a charming *Madonna and Child* in the Berenson Collection, Settignano. D.'s miniaturist style often shows affinity to the Sienese school. BIBLIOGRAPHY: O. Sirén, *Giotto and Some of His Followers* (1917); R. Offner, *Critical and Historical Corpus of Florentine Painting* (1930).

[M. J. DALY]

DADO, ST., see OUEN OF ROUEN, ST.

DAĒVAS AND AHURAS, terms applied to certain Persian divinities. The opposition between the two terms is similar to the opposition of *devas* and *asuras* in India, but with different values. In India the notion of *asura* deteriorated because of emphasis on its occult side, which led to the *asura*'s being regarded as evil or malevolent. The *asuras* in India accordingly were reduced to the rank of demons. In Iran, on the contrary, the *ahuras* were exalted into higher divine beings, while the *daēvas* suffered a corresponding decline. It is quite possible that Zoroaster was responsible for giving the higher value to the *ahuras*. As regards the *daēvas*, the *Avesta* employs the term in most cases as synonymous with non-*ahura*. The ancient gods are so designated in the more recent parts of the *Avesta*. *Daēvas* is employed also to designate demons who were never ancient gods at all. BIBLIOGRAPHY: J. Duchesne-Guillemin, NCE 4:611; *idem, La Religion de l'Iran ancien* (1962) 189–193.

[M. R. P. MCGUIRE]

DAFFARA, MARCOLINO LORENZO (1893–1952), Italian Dominican theologian. D. was prominent in the restoration of Thomism in Italy. His chief work is *Cursus manualis theologiae dogmaticae* (5 v., 1944–48), a soundly Thomistic manual of theology. D. also collaborated in the Italian translation of the *Summa theologiae*.

[T. C. O'BRIEN]

DAGOBERT II (d. 679), Merovingian king. Nephew of Dagobert I who had restored the royal authority in the kingdom of the Western Franks, he was exiled to an Irish monastery as a child. It was a period when chaos and savagery were endemic, and the mayors of the palace were steadily increasing their power over puppet kings. On the murder of his predecessor, D. was brought back to France, with the help of St. Wilfrid of York, and proclaimed king (676). Three years later he was murdered while hunting, because he was too energetic for the liking of some magnates. He was buried near Verdun and was honored in Lorraine as a saint and martyr. His tomb was destroyed by the Huguenots. BIBLIOGRAPHY: I. Daniele, BiblSanct 4:425.

[T. GILBY]

DAGON, Mesopotamian god of weather and vegetation. The Philistines introduced his cult in Palestine where he had temples in the cities of Gaza and Ashdod (Azotus). BIBLIOGRAPHY: G. Contenau, *Religions of the Ancient East* (tr. M. B. Loraine, 1958) 76–77.

[F. J. MONTALBANO]

DAGUESSEAU, FRANÇOIS, see AGUESSEAU, HENRI FRANÇOIS D'.

DAHLMANN, JOSEPH (1861–1930), German Jesuit Orientalist. After study in Holland, England, and Germany and extensive travel in the Orient, D. taught Indology and German literature at both the Catholic College of Tokyo (1913–30) and the Imperial Japanese University (1914–24). He wrote authoritatively on the early history of missions in the Far East and he also served as adviser on Far-Eastern affairs. BIBLIOGRAPHY: J. Flynn, NCE 4:611–612.

[M. J. SUELZER]

DAHSHUR, necropolis in the desert S of Saqqara, Middle Egypt, the location of two stone pyramids of the Pharoah

Snefru (4th dynasty, *mastabas, and brick pyramids of Amenemhet II and Senusret III originally encased in limestone and granite. Jewelry of the royal ladies of Dahshur were laid in symbolic arrangements around cartouches of the Pharoah. BIBLIOGRAPHY: T. de Morgan, *Fouilles à Dahchour*, 1895.

[M. J. DALY]

DAIBUTSU, see AMIDA BUDDHA.

DAIG, ST. (Daig mac Cairill; d. *c.* 587), Irish bishop. He was the founder of the church of Inishkeen, near the borders of Louth and Monaghan. Particulars in the AS (Aug. 3:656–662) concerning his life are not reliable. BIBLIOGRAPHY: P. Corish, BiblSanct 4:426; C. McGrath, NCE 4:613.

DAIMON, Gr., a divine power or being. (1) In Greek literature and philosophy (e.g., in Homer and Plato) the term came to mean beings midway between the gods and men, some good, some bad, and having influence on human destiny (see ThAq ST 1a.103, 6 ad 1); there was also a belief in a daimon for each individual (Plato, *Phaedo* 107D). (2) In biblical Greek the term came to mean an evil spirit. *DEMON; *DEVIL.

[T. C. O'BRIEN]

DAIN, MARIE ALPHONSE (1896–1964), Greek paleographer and Byzantinist. As director of studies of the École Pratique des Hautes Études in the division of history and philology, he exercised a marked influence on a number of students who became outstanding scholars in their own right. He made a special contribution to scholarship by his studies on the Greek military writers and in Greek paleography. He has well been described as a Christian humanist. As a soldier, he served his country with conspicuous bravery in World War I and as a member of the Resistance in World War II. BIBLIOGRAPHY: P. Courcelle, NCE 4:615–616; *Bulletin de l'Association Guillaume Budé*, 4th ser., 3 (1964) 297–305.

[M. R. P. MCGUIRE]

DALBERG, a noble family of the German Rhineland, members of which were important in ecclesiastical as well as in political and cultural history. Among them were:

Johann von Dalberg (1455–1503), bp. of Worms and chancellor of the Univ. of Heidelberg. Besides administering his diocese and serving the Emperor Frederick III on various diplomatic missions, he warmly supported the university, strengthening it academically and enlarging its library. He made the university and his diocese centers of the new humanism.

Wolfgang von Dalberg (1537–1601), elector and abp. of Mainz, chosen for the position because it was thought that his willingness to compromise might serve the interests of religious peace. In the earlier years of his episcopate, he strove to maintain a neutral position in the contention between Catholics and Protestants, but after the Council of Trent, under some pressure, he cooperated in the implementation of the reform measures enacted by the council.

Adolf von Dalberg (1678–1737), prince-abbot of Fulda, who aspired to restore Fulda to its ancient glory as a seat of learning. He combined existing Jesuit and Benedictine schools to form a university known as Alma Adolphina (1732). The foundation declined after the suppression of the Jesuits, and when the Benedictine monastery was secularized, it was abandoned.

Karl Theodor von Dalberg (1744–1817), bp. of Constance (1799), abp. of Mainz (1802), abp. of Regensburg (1806), president of the Confederation of the Rhine (1806), Grand Duke of Frankfort (1810). With the fall of Napoleon (1814), he lost the considerable secular power he had achieved by favor of the Emperor and thenceforth lived quietly at Regensburg. His *Febronian sympathies were well known, but the charge that he aimed at setting up a German national Church that would be largely independent of Rome is not clearly established. BIBLIOGRAPHY: G. J. Donnelly, NCE 4:616–617; A. Dru, *Contribution of German Catholicism* (1963) 39–40.

[D. G. NUGENT]

DALFINUS, ST., see AUNEMUND OF LYONS, ST.

DALGAIRNS, JOHN DOBREE (religious name Bernard; 1818–76), convert to Catholicism, Oratorian, writer. A native of Guernsey, D., while at Oxford, joined the *Oxford Movement. Retiring with *Newman to Littlemore, he was received into the Church by Bl. Dominic *Barberi (1845). Ordained a year later in France, D. joined the Oratory at Rome and served as preacher and confessor at the London Oratory. His most esteemed work was *The Holy Communion, Its Philosophy, Theology and Practice* (1861), a compendium of Catholic teaching and an attack upon lingering Jansenist excesses. D. wrote many historical, doctrinal studies and edited several translations of ascetical works. BIBLIOGRAPHY: Gillow BDEC 2:4–5 for a complete list of his writings; R. W. Church, *Oxford Movement* (1891) 206; W. Ward, *W. G. Ward and the Oxford Movement* (1889).

[T. C. O'BRIEN]

DALI, SALVADOR (1904–) Spanish painter, writer, supreme Surrealist of amazing technical skill evidenced in enigmatic, disturbing works rich in symbolic imagery. After study in Madrid, D. was attracted (1923) by the metaphysical and psychoanalytical aspects of De Chirico and Carrà. Showing works of precise draftsmanship at Barcelona (1925) and Madrid (1926), D. then visited Picasso (1928) in Paris where interest in surrealism and biomorphic shapes reoriented his works. D. paints a hallucinatory dream world (*Persistence of Memory,* 1931), of supremely

illusionistic forms in frightening juxtaposition, with distorted, grotesque shapes of deep meaning, or enigmatic shapes within shapes. Addressing himself to religious themes, D. painted a *Madonna, Crucifixion, The Sacrament of the Last Supper* (1955) with characteristic technical skill, modified and enriched by his metaphysical inferences in image and composition. BIBLIOGRAPHY: R. Descharnes, *World of Salvador Dali* (1962).

[M. J. DALY]

DALMATIA, predominantly Catholic region on the E shore of the Adriatic, now part of the Yugoslav republic of Croatia. The population is mostly Croatian but also includes Orthodox Serbs and a few Italians. Dalmatians were originally an Illyrian tribe, subjected to varying degrees of Roman domination from 228 B.C. and finally subdued by Augustus. Illyria is mentioned by Paul (Rom. 15.19), but the presence of Christianity there is not definite before the 3d century. The area was conquered by Ostrogoths in the 5th cent., but later taken by Justinian. The Croatians, a Slavic people, moved into the area *c.*614, converted to Christianity, and became oriented to the West. Zadar (Zara), capital of Dalmatia from the 7th cent. to 1918, is the seat of a Catholic archdiocese, distinctive for its use of the *Glagolitic liturgy. Through the Middle Ages, Dalmatia was subjected to many outside powers, but principally Croatia and Venice. In 1420 Croatia ceded control to Venice, though the Turks contested the area until 1699. In 1797, when the Venetian republic was dissolved, Dalmatia went to Austria. Briefly seized by France later, it was returned by the 1815 Congress of Vienna and remained under Austria until 1918. At the outbreak of World War I, the Allies secretly promised Dalmatia to Italy in return for assistance in the war. However, Dalmatia became a part of the federation later named Yugoslavia, though Italy retained Zadar and several islands. In World War II, Italy annexed Dalmatia but it returned to Yugoslavia after the war.

[T. EARLY]

DALMATIC, the outer liturgical garment worn by the deacon. In its present form it usually has wide short sleeves, is open at the sides, and reaches below the knees. This vestment was originally a garment of wool or linen that originated in the Greek province of Dalmatia. It was adopted by Romans of the upper class and became a distinctively clerical garment when it passed from secular use. Probably it was worn first only by the pope, but the privilege of wearing it was extended to deacons in Rome by the 4th century. By the 12th cent. it was distinctive of diaconal rank. The earlier dalmatic was usually white with two vertical red stripes (*clavi*) running the length of the garment in both front and rear, one over each shoulder. Sometimes in later dalmatics the *clavi* were joined together with a horizontal stripe. By the 12th cent. the color of the garment varied with the liturgical occasion on which it was worn. In modern times the dalmatic has often been indistinguishable in its style and design from the subdeacon's *tunicle, although it is desirable that the tunicle should have narrower sleeves and either have no *clavi*, or at least have its *clavi* unjoined. The dalmatic may be worn by the bishop under the chasuble when he pontificates. BIBLIOGRAPHY: H. Norris, *Church Vestments: Their Origin and Development* (1950).

[P. K. MEAGHER]

DALMATIUS OF CONSTANTINOPLE (5th cent.). After serving in the imperial army under Theodosius I, D. entered a monastery with his son Faustus *c*.384. When Isaac, the abbot, died, D. was elected successor and also was charged with directing the other monastic houses in Constantinople. When the results of the Council of Ephesus became known, D. left his monastery for the first time in 48 years to beg the Emperor's help in combatting heresy and procuring the condemnation of Nestorius. BIBLIOGRAPHY: V. Grumel, DHGE 14:27–28; K. Baus, LTK 3:130–131.

[P. K. MEAGHER]

DALMAU, LUIS (fl. 1428–59), Spanish painter sent by Alfonso V to Castile (1428), then to Flanders (1431) where Jan Van Eyck was completing the famous Ghent Altarpiece (1432). D.'s greatest extant work, *Enthroned Virgin and Child with Councilors* (1443–45) for the Town Hall chapel, Barcelona, a composition clearly adapted from the works of Van Eyck (with original portraits of the councilors) introduced the Flemish style into Spain. D. influenced his son Antonio (1450–99) and the anonymous Pedralbes and Gerona Masters.

[M. J. DALY]

D'ALTON, EDWARD ALFRED (1859–1941), Irish historian. Ordained in 1887, D. held several clerical titles. In his early writings he avoided controversy, but his later writings reveal partisanship. He contributed to the *Dublin Review* and wrote several articles for the *Catholic Encyclopedia*. His major work was *History of Ireland* to 1908 (3 v. 1903–10); to 1925 (3d ed., 8½ v., 1920–25).

[M. HIGGINS]

DALY, THOMAS AUGUSTINE (1871–1948), American journalist, poet. Always a Philadelphian, he began his career as a newspaperman on the *Philadelphia Record* in 1891. For 17 years he was general manager of the *Catholic Standard and Times* where much of his early verse first appeared. Daly specialized in dialect poetry, chiefly Italian dialect based on his knowledge of S Philadelphia. His best poetic work is to be found in *Selected Poems* (1936). D. was a poet of the immigrant, a writer of faith and humor, who showed deep sympathy for the people he portrayed.

[J. R. AHERNE]

DAMAGE, in moral theology, a loss, Lat. *damnum*, unjustly inflicted on another person. The term primarily refers to loss of property and as such is a title to *restitution over and above *theft; damage as such means a loss to the victim, but not a gain to the one inflicting it. The most obvious, and rampant, example of damage is vandalism. To give rise to the obligation of restitution the damage must be real and be the effect of a sinful act of *injury, i.e., of an act of injustice that is intended. Thus where an injurious act was intended but did not achieve its result, there would be no loss, and so no obligation to restitution. Where an action, without culpable *negligence, accidentally causes a loss to another, there is no moral obligation to restitution (although civil law might assess damages and there would then be a moral obligation to obey the law). In addition to damage in regard to property, there can also be personal damage, and chiefly as the result of *detraction or *calumny. Then the offender has the obligation to take steps to undo the damage to the victim's reputation.

[T. C. O'BRIEN]

DAMASCENE, DIMITRI SEMENOV RUDNEV (1737–95), Russian theologian, bishop. Born near Moscow, D. studied there and at Göttingen. Returning to Russia (1773), he became a monk and worked with Platon Levkhine, metropolitan of Moscow. In 1782 he was consecrated bp. of Sievsk and transferred the following year to Novgorod. His works include an edition of the Metropolitan Platon's works; a German translation of Nestorius's chronicle published at Göttingen, *Einleitung in die synchronistische Universalhistorie* (1771, pp. 979–1000); and an important index to Russian publications (1518–1785). BIBLIOGRAPHY: A. Palmieri, DTC 4:26–27; M. Jugie, *Catholicisme* 3:428–429.

[P. K. MEAGHER]

DAMASCIUS (*c*.458–after 533), rhetorician and Neoplatonic philosopher, and last scholarch of the Platonic Academy at Athens. On the speculative side he is important for questioning the possibility of human reason's attaining the truth. He held that all the terms employed in metaphysical speculation, unity, division, identity, difference, similarity, dissimilarity, first and second, cause and effect, procession and regression, are strictly analogies and cannot go beyond analogies. They do not represent actuality. For him speculation and truth are different spheres. On the other hand, he showed a marked enthusiasm for and belief in theurgy in theory and practice. When Justinian closed the philosophical schools of Athens in 529 A.D., he went to Persia but subsequently returned to Roman territory. BIBLIOGRAPHY: Copleston 1:481; P. Merlan, LexAW 686–687; Ueberweg 1:633–634; CHGMP 305–313.

[M. R. P. MCGUIRE]

DAMASCUS, a city in Syria, mentioned in both the OT and the NT. Lying E of Mt. Hermon and W of the vast Arabian desert, Damascus was an important commercial and military city. Its bountiful water supply created an ideal location for the capital of Syria and the hub of important land trade routes. Damascus was inhabited from ancient times and is mentioned in Amarna, Egyptian, and Assyrian documents from as early as the 15th-14th cent. B.C., at which time the Aramaeans occupied the territory and gave it its biblical name Aram. In the OT period David battled the Syrians and occupied the territory (2 Sam 8.5–6; 10.6–19). After Solomon, the Syrians participated in the successes and failures of the divided kingdom until Tiglath-Pileser III captured Damascus in 732 B.C. and exiled its citizens. In NT times Paul was blinded during his encounter with Christ near Damascus, was led to Judas's house on the street called Straight, and baptized. After the recovery of his sight, Paul preached the Gospel there until his life was threatened. Damascus was prosperous in the Christian era. It has been predominantly Muslim since 635. In the 1970s it had about 835,000 citizens. BIBLIOGRAPHY: EDB 480–481.

[S. MUSHOLT]

DAMASCUS, MARTYRS OF. Bl. Emmanuel Ruiz, Bl. Francis Masabki, and clerical and lay companions of the Maronite rite were murdered by marauding Mohammedans in Damascus, Syria, July 9, 1860. Religious freedom had been granted in Turkey by the Sultan in 1856, but the Mohammedans disapproved, and their unrest grew during the next few years, erupting into riots, marauding, and massacre in May 1860 before the furor spent itself. Thousands of Christians were murdered and many towns destroyed throughout Lebanon. Bl. Emmanuel and Bl. Francis were in a Franciscan monastery in Damascus when the riots broke out there. The monastery was stormed and most of the priests and many laymen were murdered. BIBLIOGRAPHY: A general account can be found in *Annals of the Propagation of the Faith* for 1860, 308–326; Butler 3:68–70.

DAMASCUS FRAGMENTS, Hebrew MSS describing the origins and way of life of a Hebrew sect. (Essenes) who settled near Damascus (or Qumran) in the 2d century B.C.. Two MSS were discovered at Cairo in 1896; nine others were found in Caves 4, 5, and 6 of Qumran. They are now known as the Damascus Document.

[F. J. MONTALBANO]

DAMASUS I, ST. (d. 384), POPE from 366. A Roman of Spanish ancestry, D. was a deacon under Liberius (352–366) whom he accompanied into exile. However, like many of the Roman clergy, D. on returning to Rome gave his loyalty to the antipope *Felix II, who was forced on the Church by the Emperor Constantius; but when Liberius came back to Rome, D. was reconciled with him. D.'s own election to the papacy was challenged by an opposing faction which chose Ursinus (Ursicinus), and much bloodshed resulted. The Emperor Valentinian recognized D. and exiled Ursinus. The schism continued, however, and some of its adherents laid serious accusations againt D., but he was exonerated by the Emperor and by an ecclesiastical court of

44 bishops. D. defended the Catholic faith with vigor. He deposed Arian bishops wherever possible and condemned *Apollinarianism and *Macedonianism (368 and 369). He took no part in the Council of Constantinople (381), which only achieved ecumenical status in its later acceptance by the Council of *Chalcedon. D. sided with St. Athanasius in his struggle against the Meletian schism at Antioch. He was the first pope to refer to the See of Rome as the Apostolic See and, in a Council of Rome (382), emphasized that the bp. of Rome's claims rested on St. Peter. He took a special interest in organizing the papal chancery and in the preservation of papal records and the acts of the martyrs. In his reign, Latin became the principal liturgical language of the Roman Church. He encouraged St. Jerome, his secretary, in the revision and translation that resulted in the Vulgate. It is thought that Jerome had a hand in the proclamation of the canon of the NT by the Roman Synod of 374. D. built many churches, including the original S. Lorenzo in Damaso, St. Sebastian, and a baptistery at the Vatican in honor of St. Peter. He promoted the restoration of the catacombs and composed many epitaphs for inscription on the burial monuments. He also wrote a number of short accounts of the martyrs and some hymns. The primacy of the Roman Church was greatly strengthened by imperial decrees in the reign of D., and, in 380, the Emperor Theodosius I proclaimed the religion of the Roman State to be that which St. Peter had preached and of which Damasus was the supreme head. The early papal decretals ascribed to the reign of Siricius (384–399) probably belong to the time of Damasus. He was interred in a small church of his own construction on the Via Ardeatina, the ruins of which were discovered in 1902–03. Works: PL 13:109. BIBLIOGRAPHY: M. R. P. McGuire, NCE 4:624–625; T. J. Shahan, CE 4:613–614; Butler 4:536–538.

[P. F. MULHERN]

DAMASUS II (before his election known as Poppo; d.1048), POPE for 3 weeks in 1048. D., a Bavarian, was made bp. of Brixen in the time of the Emperor Henry III. He was prominent in the reform synods of Sutri and Rome, which in 1046 had ruled against three claimants to the papacy. On the death of Clement II (Oct. 9, 1047), one of the deposed claimants, Benedict IX, seized Rome with the aid of his family, the counts of Tusculum. The Emperor Henry, in virtue of this title "Patrician of the Romans," named D. pope, who was then installed in office with the help of German troops. Three weeks later at Palestrina where he had gone to avoid the heat of Rome, he died. He was not accepted by the Romans, and his death has been variously attributed to malaria or poison. He is buried in St. Lawrence-outside-the-Walls. BIBLIOGRAPHY: V. Gellhaus, NCE 4:625–626; T. Oestreich, CE 4:614.

[P. F. MULHERN]

DAMBERGER, JOSEPH FERDINAND (1795–1859), Bavarian Jesuit, church historian. Ordained in 1818, D.

achieved some distinction as a preacher but gave up that career to enter the Jesuits in Switzerland (1837). He was professor of church history at Lucerne from 1845 until the expulsion of the Jesuits from Switzerland (1847) caused him to withdraw to Innsbruck and later to Regensburg. The remainder of his life he devoted to his monumental *Synchronistiche Geschichte der Kirche und Welt im Mittelalter* (15 v., 1850–63), the last volume of which was completed by D. Rattinger. It is a work of vast erudition, though ponderous in style, and sometimes partisan and uncritical in its method. BIBLIOGRAPHY: Sommervogel 2:1786–87; J. Brucher, DTC 4:36.

[T. C. O'BRIEN]

DAME (Lat. *domina,* mistress) in church usage, the title of a professed Benedictine, Cistercian, and Bridgettine nun.

DAMIAN, ST., MARTYR, see COSMAS AND DAMIAN, SS.

DAMIAN OF PAVIA, ST. (d. 697), theologian and bishop. He opposed the Monothelites at the Synod of Milan (680) and composed the letter sent to the Emperor Constantine IV, which was read at the sixth Ecumenical Council (Constantinople III). He acted as peacemaker between the Byzantine Emperor and the Lombards. BIBLIOGRAPHY: A. Amore, BiblSanct 4:445.

[J. E. LYNCH]

DAMIAN DEI FURCHERI, BL. (*c.*1400–84), Italian Dominican preacher. D. became a renowned orator and was influential in the reform movement current at the time in his order. He is known to have been at San Marco's in Florence in 1441. His writings include sermons and meditations. He was beatified in 1848. BIBLIOGRAPHY: Quétif-Échard 1:808; Butler 4:207; P. Simonelli, BiblSanct 5:1320–21; *Archivum Fratrum Praedicatorum* 31 (1961) 213–306.

[M. J. FINNEGAN]

DAMIEN, FATHER (Joseph de Veuster; 1840–89), Belgian missioner to the lepers. Ordained (1864) a priest of the community known as Fathers of the Sacred Heart of Jesus and Mary, D. served at various mission stations on Hawaii. Requesting permission to go to the leper colony on Molokai as its resident priest, he found conditions among the lepers there deplorable, physically and morally. He supplied rudimentary medical care and served the lepers by building shelters, digging their graves, creating a water supply and a whole new village. He also built a large shed to serve as a primitive hospital. In 1885 he contracted leprosy but continued his work as before. The coming of Joseph Dutton opened a new chapter in his life and gave the lepers a gifted friend. By his last year D. had three other priests and three Franciscan sisters. The prophecy that no sister would ever contract leprosy is still verified. His last days were filled with achievement in improving the life of the lepers. When he died, a worldwide tribute was paid him, and a new era

opened for the care of the lepers. BIBLIOGRAPHY: J. Farrow, *Damien the Leper* (1937); G. Daws, *Holy Man: Father Damien of Molokai* (1973).

[J. R. AHERNE]

DAMMARTIN (DAMPMARTIN) FAMILY, French family of architects and sculptors who served Church and nobility from the mid-14th to mid-15th century. **Drouet de (d. 1413),** was in the service of the Duke of Berry in Bourges (1368). For the Duke of Burgundy he directed (1383) the construction of the Chartreuse de Champmol in Dijon, executing the portal sculpture for Ste.-Chapelle, Dijon (1387). In 1396 D. returned to the court of the Duke of Berry. **Guy de (d. *c.*1398),** was in the service of Charles V. After 1370, he followed his brother Drouet to the court of Jean, Duke of Berry, and rebuilt (1388) the salon of the Palais Royal at Poitiers in rich late Gothic style after its destruction by the English. **Jean de (d. 1454),** architect, nephew of Guy, as supervisor at Le Mans Cathedral (1421) built the transept in Rayonnant Gothic style, and as master of works (1432) completed the nave and portal of the cathedral of Tours.

[M. J. DALY]

DAMNATION, a word sometimes used for the judgment of condemnation to hell that will be pronounced by Christ, the supreme judge, on the wicked at the end of the world (Mt 25.41–46). But the word itself is hardly used with this meaning in Sacred Scripture. As the objective result of a condemnatory action, damnation signifies the state of the damned, primarily of those condemned to eternal punishments. In this meaning it includes the pain of sense as well as the pain of loss. One speaks, for instance, of damnation to hell-fire, that is, to the extrinsic agent that inflicts an agony of suffering on the men and demons in hell. The word damnation itself is derived from the Latin *damnum* meaning injury and also loss, denoting deprivation of that which should have been possessed. In this root sense theologians speak of the damnation of unbaptized infants to Limbo. These souls do not suffer the pains of hell or any positive affliction, but they have lost that for which they were destined in the original plan of divine providence. In this sense they undergo damnation even though, owing to lack of knowledge of their true supernatural destiny, the vision of God, they do not suffer any positive pain because of their loss.

Though the terms damned and damnation are used in the strict sense of those condemned to the punishments of hell, they might in a limited way be applied to the souls in purgatory. Though this usage is rare, if found at all in Catholic speech and writings, it could be justified on the ground that these souls do positively suffer because of the temporary loss of God that they know to be due to their unforgiven venial faults and unremitted temporal punishment of serious sins committed in this mortal life.

Damnation, therefore, properly speaking means the eternal punishments of hell. Analogously it is used of the state of those who have died in original sin without personal faults. Both of these categories of men will forever be among the lost. Their state will always be characterized by the loss of the beatific vision. There is an essential difference however, and one of vast importance, between these two classes. In the one case there is the intensely vivid consciousness of the deprivation of the enjoyment of the infinite good for which they were made. In the other there is the calm enjoyment of the good things of creation and of God as the source of these created benefits, with blissful absence of awareness of the supernatural intuitive vision for which they had been destined. BIBLIOGRAPHY: E. G. Hardwick, NCE 4:627; 6:1005–07; A. Winklhofer, *Coming of His Kingdom* (tr. A. V. Littledale, 1963).

[T. J. MOTHERWAY]

D'AMOUR, O'NEIL CHARLES (1919–68), American priest and leading Catholic educator. Ordained in 1944, with an M. A. degree from The Catholic University of America in 1950, he became an ardent and eloquent protagonist of the need for Catholic school systems in the United States. D. held supervisory posts in the Diocese of Marquette, Wis., becoming in 1964 its superintendent of schools. He was chairman of the committee of superintendents responsible for Voice of the Community (1967) and lectured and wrote extensively on Catholic education.

[M. B. MURPHY]

DAN, son of Jacob and Bilhah, Rachel's maid (Gen 30.1–8). The tribe of Dan included Samson, but disappeared from history when conquered by Ben-hadad I of Syria (1 Kg 15.20).

[F. J. MONTALBANO]

DAN, CITY OF, northernmost city of Israel. It became the location of a schismatic sanctuary in the Northern Kingdom (1 Kg 12.28–29) and hence was denounced by Amos (8.14).

[F. J. MONTALBANO]

DANCE OF DEATH (*Danse macabre, Totentanz*), a mimed procession, expressing medieval concern with death and a warning "memento mori." The drama of Death (skeleton) leading young and old, high and lowly to their graves had wide currency in murals (*Les Innocents,* other cemeteries of Paris and Basle) and esp. prints (Holbein the Younger, 1538; A. Rethel, 1848). BIBLIOGRAPHY: J. M. Clark, *Dance of Death in the Middle Ages and the Renaissance* (1950).

[R. BERGMANN]

DANCE OF SIVA, see NATARĀJA.

DANCING, RELIGIOUS. Man has ever searched for more expressive forms of communication with the trans-cendent. Thus, religious dance has been found to supplement, even replace, speech. J. Huizinga and A. E. Jensen in *Myth and Cult among Primitive Peoples,* give a detailed history of religious dance among primitive peoples as far back as the upper paleolithic age. Throughout the East, sacred dancers were a prominent feature in religious worship; in Egypt, colleges of female dancers and singers were annexed to certain shrines. Many of these religious dances consisted of slow and stately processions through the streets of the city or around the altar. In the OT, dancing was an adjunct of worship, a practice probably borrowed from neighboring people. "Thus Miriam took a timbrel in her hand; and all the women went after her with timbrels and dances . . ." (Ex 15.20–21). And David on the recovery of the ark, "danced with all his might before the Lord" (2 Kg 6.14). It is also clear from many passages in the Psalms that dancing formed part of the liturgy in the temple (Ps 149.9; 150.4; Jer 20.4; Cant 7.1). In early Christian times dancing was a part of the celebration of the vigils of martyrs as the people thus expressed their joy in the church or at the martyr's tomb. Bishops frequently censured, not dancing itself, but the sometimes accompanying coarse and vulgar words or movements. In the Middle Ages the practice developed of combining more closely dance and formal worship, esp. during the chief liturgical seasons. Even until the present, dancing before the high altar in Seville cathedral takes place on the feasts of the Immaculate Conception, Corpus Christi, and in Shrovetide. Today there is renewed interest in liturgical dance, often a creative process of response to a scriptural theme with the use of music, gesture, and rhythmical movements. Still, for the most part, Christians of the 20th cent. are not as yet inclined to accept liturgical dancing, even after Vatican Council II. Proponents of it, however, point out the beauty of reverent movement that can animate and graphically express the words of Psalm or prayer, stimulate spiritual joy, and induce a closer union of God and worshiper. BIBLIOGRAPHY: A. Closs, NCE 4:629–630; M.-G. Wosien, *Sacred Dance* (1974); É. Bertaud, DSAM 3:21–37; E. Backman, *Religious Dance in the Christian Church and in Popular Medicine* (1952); D. A. Kister, "Dance and Theater in Christian Worship," *Worship* 45 (1971) 588–598.

[K. O'NEILL]

DANIEL (Hebrew, *dāniyyē'l* for *danî-'el,* "my judge is God"), the young Judahite described in the Book of Daniel (1.3–6). He was captured in Jerusalem in 605 B.C. and taken to the household of Nebuchadnezzar. He remained in Babylon until the 3d year of Cyrus (537 B.C.). Known only from the Book of Daniel he is remembered as the hero in the deuterocanonical chapter 13, who was blessed with wise judgment and favored with apocalyptic visions. In Ezra 8.2; Neh 10.6 there is a post-Exilic priest of Jerusalem of the same name. Still another D., whose name in Hebrew was *dān'el* ("God judges") and who lived in the days of Noah and Job is found in Ezek 14.14, 20; 28.3. The different spelling of his name indicates that he is probably Dan-el mentioned in Ugaritic literature. BIBLIOGRAPHY: EDB 483–484.

[A. P. HANLON]

DANIEL OF BELVEDERE, ST. (d. 1227), Franciscan missionary and martyr. D., provincial at the time of the Calabrian province, set out with six companions to preach the gospel to the Muslims of Morocco. Almost certainly none of the missionary party had any knowledge of Arabic. After spending a few days in a compound outside the city of Ceuta in the company of a group of Christian merchants, the missioners prepared themselves with prayer and entered the city where they straightway began to preach. They were arrested, imprisoned, and offered the option of embracing the Islamic faith. When they refused this, they were beheaded. BIBLIOGRAPHY: Butler 4:79–80; G. D. Gordini, BiblSanct 4:469–470.

[M. E. DUFFY]

DANIEL PALOMNIK (d. 1122), abbot, traveler, writer. This important Russian is known to have been in Constantinople and the Holy Land in 1106–07 and to have written a detailed and generally accurate description of the Holy Places in simple Russian. His work is contemporary with Russia's first chronicle by Nestor. D. was probably abbot of a monastery in the province of Chernigov in Little Russia; he became bp. of Suriev in 1115. His diary was widely copied (75 MSS are extant) and exists in two printed Russian texts; there are two translations of it in French and one in English. Although not the first Russian in the Holy Land, D. may have influenced subsequent travelers through his diary. Text, *The Pilgrimage of the Russian Abbot Daniel* (Eng. tr. C. W. Wilson, 1888); *Pélerinage en Terre Sainte de l'Igoumène Russe Daniel 1113–1115* (Fr. tr. A. de Noroff). BIBLIOGRAPHY: B. J. Comaskey, NCE 4:631; B. Leib, *Rome, Kiev et Byzance à la fin du XIe siècle* (1924) 276–285.

[S. WILLIAMS]

DANIEL THE STYLITE, ST. (409–493). Born at Maratha, near Samosata in Syria, D. entered a monastery at the age of 12. He was elected abbot of his monastery but declined and set off on a 5-year missionary journey, part of which was spent with *Simeon the Stylite. D. established a hermitage at Constantinople in an abandoned temple where he lived for 9 years. At the death of Simeon, D. became a Stylite and in the course of the next 13 years lived on three different pillars. He exercised a considerable influence on ecclesiastical and civil affairs in his time. BIBLIOGRAPHY: H. Delehaye, *Les Saints stylites* (1923); V. Laurent, DHGE 14:73; Butler 4:539–541.

[P. K. MEAGHER]

DANIEL, ANTHONY, ST. (1601–48), Jesuit missionary, martyr. He entered the Society at Rouen in 1621. Two years after his ordination (1630), he was sent to the mission of Cape Breton Island and transferred in 1633 to Quebec. He founded a school for Indian boys at Quebec in 1636 and spent his life traveling and preaching among the Indians until he was slain July 4, by an Iroquois war party near the present town of Hillsdale, Ont. For bibliog. see NORTH AMERICAN MARTYRS.

[P. K. MEAGHER]

DANIEL, GABRIEL (1649–1728) a Jesuit appointed historian of France by Louis XIV. He wrote *Histoire de France* in 17 volumes, a work judged to be the most complete and accurate history of France at that time (1713). D. also refuted the Jansenists; the vortex theory of Descartes; the "Provincial Letters" of Pascal. His published works include philosophical, theological, and historical treatises. BIBLIOGRAPHY: Sommervogel 2:1795–1815.

[K. O'NEILL]

DANIEL-ROPS, HENRI (pseudonym for Henri Petiot; 1901–65), French scholar. Educated in letters and law at the Univ. of Grenoble, he taught history in secondary schools from 1922–46 and wrote prolifically for 40 years. In addition to his numerous short stories, articles, and essays, he published about 70 books, 20 of them novels. Some of his works were translated into English. His first book, *Notre inquiétude* (1926), a series of essays, reveals an uneasiness among those who approached maturity before and after World War I. D. affirmed himself as a Catholic author with his best-known novel, *Morte où est ta victoire?* (*Death, Where Is Thy Victory?* , 1946), which was exceedingly popular and made into a motion picture. In 1937, *Tournant de la France* and *Ce qui meurt et ce qui naît,* two collections of essays, developed his conviction that the safeguard of the world is Christianity. His second and most famous novel, *L'Épée de feu,* maintains that suffering in the world has meaning only if one accepts the gospel message. He returned to his profession as a historian with *Le Peuple de la Bible* (1943), the first of 12 volumes on biblical and ecclesiastical history. The series, finished just before his death, made him world famous. He laid the groundwork for and became editor of the 150-volume *Twentieth Century Encyclopedia of Catholicism* (1958–71). In 1955 he was elected to the French Academy. BIBLIOGRAPHY: E. Jarry, NCE 4:632–633.

[S. A. HEENEY]

DANIEL, BOOK OF, in English Bibles the fourth of the prophetic books of the Old Testament. The Hebrew Bible places Daniel between Esther and Ezra in the last section of the Hebrew canon (the Writings); the Greek and Latin Bibles place the book among the prophets. The book takes its name from an unknown Jewish hero of the Babylonian Exile (587–538 B.C.) but was written during the time of the persecution of Antiochus IV Epiphanes (167–164 B.C.). It begins in Hebrew, shifts to Aramaic in 2.4b until 7.28; the remainder is in Hebrew, with the exception of the Greek fragments found in 3.24–90; 13–14. The Greek additions are not accepted as canonical by Jews and Protestants. Chapters 1–6 are midrashic narratives with a setting in Babylon just before and after Babylon's fall and illustrate the reward of those who were faithful to God. Chapters 7–12 record four apocalyptic visions that predict the final victory of God and his saints over the forces of evil. The book is noted for its doctrine on angels, the messianic kingdom, the resurrection, and eternal life. BIBLIOGRAPHY: R. E. Anderson, *Unfolding the Prophecies of Daniel* (pa. 1975).

[F. J. MONTALBANO]

DANIÉLOU, JEAN (1905–1974), theologian, historian of the early Church, cardinal. From a family o f intellectual prominence, D. early decided to join the Jesuits, though so distinguished a French Catholic as the novelist François Mauriac attempted to dissuade him because he feared such a move would inhibit his intellectual freedom. How wrong this fear was is evidenced by the entire career of this remarkable man. With de Lubac he brought out *Sources chrétiennes,* critical editions of the Fathers of the Church. He worked out a theology resting on the solid knowledge of the Fathers of the Church but highly sensitive to contemporary Catholic and non-Christian thought. The *Salvation of the Nations, Advent,* and *The Presence of God,* produced between 1949 and 1958, are masterpieces of spirituality and theology. His spiritual direction was wise and considerate and formed a large part of his labor. A *peritus* at Vatican Council II, he struck a position between extreme conservatism and the progressive position. In 1969 Pope Paul VI created him a cardinal. D. suffered the fate of all moderates: he was attacked from both sides. When he joined with others in defense of Paul VI at the time of *Humanae vitae*—with which he disagreed as a theologian—he parted company with the more extreme theologians. D. was always his own man. One has only to consult the masterwork completed in his last years, *A History of Early Christian Doctrine Before the Council of Nicaea,* to realize what a towering thinker he was. BIBLIOGRAPHY: G. Vallquist, "Jean Cardinal Daniélou," *The Month* 7 (1974).

[J. R. AHERNE]

DANNENMAYER, MATTHIAS (1744–1805), Catholic professor of church history at Freiburg from 1772, where his teaching was imbued with the Enlightenment spirit. Emperor Joseph II in 1786 brought him to the Univ. of Vienna. His *Institutiones historiae ecclesiasticae Novi Testamenti* (1788) became a prescribed textbook in all imperial schools of theology, despite its being condemned by ecclesiastical authorities for its bias in favor of Josephinism and Febronianism. BIBLIOGRAPHY: H. Rumpler, NCE 4:639.

[J. E. LYNCH]

D'ANNUNZIO, GABRIELE (1863–1938), Italian poet whose creative work and political views engendered such controversy. D. was nonetheless one of the great lyric poets of modern Italy. *Canto nuovo* (1882) demonstrates the qualities of pagan sensuousness, not to say decadence, which would mark his later work. A follower of Nietzsche, Wagner, the French Symbolists and English Pre-Raphaelites, he espoused amoral aestheticism in art and libertinism in life. His chief work, *Laudi del cielo, del mare, della terra e degli eroi* (1903–12) was a landmark in Italian poetry. The collection *Alcione,* a pastoral of simplicity and power, appeared in 1904. D. wrote also a number of novels and plays, the best known of the latter being *Francesca da Rimini* (1910). D. went from decadence to a mystical apprehension of the greatness of Italy and was at first an admirer of Fascism. In 1919 he led a group that seized Fiume and held it as an independent city until Dec. 1920. BIBLIOGRAPHY: T. Antonglini, *D'Annunzio* (1938, repr. 1975); C. Testore, EncCatt 4:1167–69.

[J. R. AHERNE]

DANTE ALIGHIERI (1265–1321), theological and philosophical poet, a man who represents, perhaps better than any other, the climax of the Middle Ages. Not only was he a poet, but he was also a philosopher, theologian, soldier, politician, traveler, and, in some sense, mystic as well. The factors behind his formation include: the political vitality of the Italian communes, the piety to be found in the religious orders, the apex of the development of Scholasticism in the universities, and the coming to flower of poetry in Provence and Sicily. He was born in Florence to a family of slight distinction and was baptized in the old baptistery of San Giovanni, later made famous by Ghiberti's portals. He studied the seven liberal arts with the Dominicans at Santa Maria Novella and was early familiar with Provençal poetry and the classics. At an early age he first saw his Beatrice, who became his poetic inspiration, although there seems to have been little objective relationship between the two. Her death, when D. was 25, touched off a spiritual crisis from which it took him several years to recover. He married *c.* 1294 and fathered four children, two of whom, including a daughter he named Beatrice, entered the religious life.

D. was a genius of extraordinary versatility. He wrote some music, tried his hand at painting, and served with distinction as a soldier. Politics played a critical part in his development. From as early as 1295 he was politically active. He held various civic offices and in 1300 was elected one of the six priors, the plural executive authority and highest office in the State. This led to another misfortune. He was a member of the Whites in what started as a local partisan struggle but became an international incident when Pope Boniface VIII sent Charles of Valois as arbitrator. D.'s faction lost; he himself was falsely charged with fraud and misappropriation of funds, was exiled from Florence in 1302, and sentenced to death *in absentia.* Thereafter he traveled widely, spent his last years in Ravenna, where he died and was buried. It was during these years of exile that he emerged as a great writer. After recovering from the crisis that followed Beatrice's death, he had written the *Vita nuova*, a work of prose and poetry that defies categorization although it may be roughly described as a kind of mystical, spiritual, poetic autobiography centering upon his love of Beatrice. During his exile other works followed—*De vulgare eloquentia* (1305), a plea for vernacular poetry; the *Convivio* (*c*.1306), a philosophical commentary; the *De monarchia* (*c*.1312), the creed of D.'s Ghibellinism; and the *Divina commedia*, the final cantos of which were finished just before his death.

The *Divina commedia*, originally called the *Comedy* because it begins in sorrow and concludes in joy, was his supreme masterpiece. It is a spiritual odyssey, profoundly religious from beginning to end. Its opening line, "In the middle of the journey of our life," is reminiscent of the liturgy's *Media vita in morte sumus*. D.'s journey was from the dark wood of this world through the still darker realm of sorrow (the *Inferno*), through the *Purgatorio*, and into the *Paradiso* and the beatific vision itself. In the first part he is guided by the poet Vergil, representing such things as the plenitude of the natural order and reason; at the gates of paradise his guide is Beatrice, representing the supernatural order of grace. It is now recognized that Dante was profoundly influenced by the thought of St. Thomas Aquinas, but the *Divina commedia* is more than religious in the narrow sense; it is a poetic compendium of medieval history, science, and culture. All this is welded into a whole of enduring beauty with superb architectonic skill. D. not only represents a lyrical synthesis of the Middle Ages: he laid deep foundations for the Christian humanism of the Renaissance. BIBLIOGRAPHY: T. Bergin, *Dante* (1965); P. Toynbee, *Dante Alighieri* (4th ed., 1910); É. Gilson, *Dante the Philosopher* (tr. D. Moore, 1949), a work based too largely on writings other than the *Divine Comedy;* G. G. Walsh, *Medieval Humanism* (1942) for an overview; E. Auerbach, *Dante, Poet of the Secular World* (tr. R. Manheim, pa. 1974).

[D. G. NUGENT]

DANTON, GEORGES JACQUES (1759–94), major figure in the French Revolution, who assured its success at a critical juncture, but who ultimately became its victim. He studied law in Paris after 1780 and in 1788 was elected to membership in the Estates-General, which met in May, 1789. His massive build, popular appeal, energetic determination, and inspired oratory brought him to prominence as the Revolution progressed in intensity. Already a leader of the radical Cordeliers' Club in 1791, he was elected to the Commune of Paris in December of that year and demanded increasingly radical measures. He was probably behind the storming of the Tuileries palace on August 10, 1792, which led to the overthrow of the monarchy 6 weeks later. Appointed minister of justice in the provisional government set up in its place, D. occupied himself chiefly with

questions of national defense during the dark days of August and September when the invading Prussian and Austrian armies threatened to overwhelm both France and its revolution. D. refused to despair: with brilliance, boldness, and the help of the *sans-culottes* of the capital, he succeeded in rallying French patriotism, in throwing out the invaders, and eventually in carrying the war abroad in an attempt to spread the revolutionary doctrines that had made victory possible. Thus, his influence was at its height when he was elected to the National Convention in September. During the next year, however, as the French army met with reverses, D. adopted a more moderate stance: he favored bringing the war to an end on the basis of negotiations rather than through a definitive victory; to this end, he opposed executing the King and Queen; in June 1793, he also tried to prevent the expulsion of the moderate Girondins from the Convention; in all this, he failed, his conciliatory program tending mainly to accentuate the differences between him and the majority of the Jacobins, esp. their emerging leader *Robespierre. Accusations (some apparently true) that he had taken bribes from royalists and other questionable sources could only compromise his cause. Replaced on the Committee of Public Safety on which he had served from April to July 1793, D. withdrew from Paris but returned later that fall. His attempt to abate the Terror, now in full swing, brought him into direct conflict with the Robespierre faction, which equated his indulgence, or opposition to revolutionary rigorism, with treason. Denounced by Saint-Just before the Committee, D. was arrested March 31, summarily tried by the Revolutionary Tribunal, then condemned by the Convention. Eloquent at his trial, he faced execution by the guillotine (April 5) with the courage he had shown throughout his life.

[E. M. GATES]

DANZAS, FERDINAND (religious name Antonin; 1817–88), Dominica collaborator in his order's restoration in France. While an art student in Italy, D. came under the influence of H. *Lacordaire and became a Dominican (1841). He worked with Lacordaire and succeeded him as provincial (1854–58), but in the divergence of views between Lacordaire and V. *Jandel he sided with the latter and became first provincial of the Lyons province (1862). Throughout his life he continued his interest in art; he was also coauthor with P. Balme of *Études sur les temps primitifs de l'ordre de S. Dominique* (5 v., 1873). BIBLIOGRAPHY: A. Duval, *Catholicisme* 3:464.

[T. C. O'BRIEN]

DAPHNI (CHURCH OF THE DORMITION) a domed Greek-cross-plan Byzantine monastery church founded near Athens *c*.1080. Its splendid mosaics (*Pantocrator* in the dome, *Nativity, Baptism, Transfiguration, Crucifixion* and *Dormition* in the W wall) were possibly executed by artists from Constantinople. Though Hellenistic in classical beauty and grace, and plastically realized in gradations of five or six tones of colors, the mosaics are rooted in a Macedonian-Comnenian style. At Daphni the severely iconic program of Byzantine mosaic cycles expanded most fully, showing fourteen scenes of the life of Christ and five of the life of the Virgin. BIBLIOGRAPHY: R. Krautheimer, *Early Christian and Byzantine Architecture* (1965); E. Diez and O. Demus, *Byzantine Mosaics in Greece* (1931).

[S. MURRAY]

DAQUIN (D'AQUIN), LOUIS CLAUDE (1694–1772), French organist who began his career at 12 at the Sainte Chapelle. He succeeded his teacher, Louis Marchand, at the convent of the Cordeliers and, in 1739, became organist of the Chapel Royal. He wrote harpsichord music, notably the famous "Le Coucou" organ pieces, noëls, motets, and fugues, which are mainly in manuscripts. BIBLIOGRAPHY: M. L. Pereyra, Grove DMM 2:595; *The International Cyclopedia of Music and Musicians* (ed. O. Thompson, 1964) 488.

[M. T. LEGGE]

DARBOY, GEORGES (1813–71), French ecclesiastic. Ordained in 1836, D. held posts such as professor of theology at Langres (1839–45); vicar-general of Paris (1852); prothonotary of St. Denis (1855); bp. of Nancy (1859). Named abp. of Paris (1863), he was a zealous and able administrator as well as author of numerous books. He became the advisor of Napoleon III in matters of Church and State; his pastoral letter of Lent 1864 refuted *Renan's Vie de Jesus;* he reconsecrated the restored Notre Dame. Staunchly Gallican in defense of the rights of the episcopate, with Bp. *Dupanloup he led opposition to the declaration of papal infallibility at Vatican I, as both inopportune and questionably grounded. He even tried to have Napoleon III intervene; left the council before the vote on the definition; when asked to do so by Rome, he subscribed to it, March 2, 1871. In April during the Commune uprising he was imprisoned, and on May 24 executed with a number of companions at La Roquette in Paris. Among his scholarly writings are translations of the works of *pseudo-Dionysius, and of the *Imitation of Christ* to which he added reflections of his own. Among his other works were *Les Femmes de la Bible* (1846–49) and *Les Saintes femmes* (1851).

[T. C. O'BRIEN]

DARBY, JOHN NELSON (1800–82), leading figure in the establishment of the *Plymouth Brethren. D., a grandson of the naval hero Lord Nelson, was graduated from Trinity College, Dublin (1819), and for a time was a lawyer. He was ordained in the Church of Ireland (1825) and served as a curate in Wicklow. Dissatisfied both with the state ties of the established Church and with the divisions among *Nonconformist Churches, he became attracted to those groups of like-minded Christians, calling themselves Brethren, Christians, Believers, or Saints, who sought to restore a simple primitive Christianity. Since the largest center of the movement was Plymouth, England, the adherents became known as Plymouth Brethren. D.'s ideas on *dispensationalism, the presence of Christ in the gathering of the devout, the Brethren's assurance of salvation, and the charismatic ministry of all in their communities made him a leader, so that the Plymouth Brethren were often called Darbyites. After a division among them in 1848 over association with non-Brethren, the name was particularly applied to the Exclusive Brethren as opposed to the Open Brethren. D. made evangelical journeys to continental Europe, the U.S., Canada, the West Indies, Australia, and New Zealand. The 32 volumes of his collected writings were published in London (1867–83). BIBLIOGRAPHY: DNB 5:493–494; O. T. Allis, *Prophecy and the Church* (1945); C. B. Bass, *Backgrounds to Dispensationalism . . .* (1960).

[W. J. WHALEN]

DARET, JACQUES (b. *c.*1404), Flemish painter. A native of Tournai apprenticed 1427 with Roger van der Weyden to the Master of Flémalle (Robert Campin), D. became Dean of the Guild of St. Luke (1432). He copied the Master of Flémalle's Dijon Nativity and painted (1435) a Visitation, Presentation, and Adoration of the Magi for the exterior of a carved wooden altar for the abbot of St. Vaast.

[M. J. DALY]

DARIA, ST., see CHRYSANTHUS AND DARIA, SS.

DARIUS I, THE GREAT (550–486 B.C.), **KING OF PERSIA** from 522. Son of Hystaspes, D. came to power after a period of unrest. Under his rule the empire reached from Iran to Libya, from Thrace to India. His campaigns near the Black Sea and the Danube led to the Ionian Revolt (499–493). The subsequent Persian expedition against Greece, well-known through the writings of Herodotus, was marked first by a Persian victory at Thermopylae; and then by Athenian victory at Marathon (490). D. confirmed the decree of Cyrus authorizing the rebuilding of the ruined Temple in Jerusalem. He promoted this work in the face of hostilities. The Temple was completed in his 6th year. Ezra-Nehemia and the oracles of Haggai and Zechariah present D. as a ruler tolerant of the religions of subject peoples.

[E. J. DILLON]

DARK AGES, a pejorative designation of a period in European history, the terminal dates of which depend on the interpreter. The Renaissance designation of a "middle age" *(medium aevum)* was a scornful dismissal of the period from the 6th to the 16th cent. as unbrightened by the pursuit of classical learning. Well into the 19th cent., a politically and religiously polemical reading of history made the Dark Ages and the Middle Ages coterminous. A fairer evaluation of the contributions of the 12th and 13th cent. in all areas of knowledge, in the arts, in education, set the Dark Ages back to the period from the 5th to the 11th cent. Even in this era, however, the history of Irish and Benedictine monasticism shows that the darkness was far from total. The designation may be most accurately applicable to the chaotic times of the barbarian invasions and following on the fall of Rome.

[T. C. O'BRIEN]

DARK NIGHT, see NIGHT OF THE SENSES; NIGHT OF THE SOUL.

DARKNESS (IN THE BIBLE), a theme joined with manifestations of divine power in biblical thought patterns that appear to have disparate mythological origins sometimes difficult to identify. Darkness is closely associated with God's own awesome presence (2 Sam 22.12); here the imagery refers to the storm clouds (cf. Hab 3.3). In other texts, darkness is more directly related to the failure of the heavenly bodies to shine because they have become paralyzed at the approach of the warrior God who fights for this people (Is 13.10; Joel 2.10; 2.2(?); probably also Jos 10.12–13a, later reinterpreted in v. 13b); or even fights against his people (Is 5.30; Jer 4.23). This darkness came to be applied to the beginning of a new world order (Mk 13.24; Acts 2.20), in which finally there would be no darkness (Zech 14.7; Rev 21.25) nor any need for the sun (Rev 22.5). It becomes difficult to distinguish such thought from a third context, the darkness of the original world chaos, which has the vestigial characteristics of an independent being (Gen 1.2; Is 45.19; Job 38.19) totally subject to God's creative activity (Gen 1.4–5; Ps 104.20; Dan 3.72; Is 45.7). This darkness appears closely related to that in the land of the dead (Job 10.21–22; Tob 4.10; Ps 86.13); both are in fact identified in a discussion of the ninth plague in Egypt (Wis 17.14; cf. Ex 10.22; Acts 13.11). The attempt to explain this plague and some other of the above texts through actual cosmic disturbances involving Venus and Mars has not won acceptance.

The separation from God implicit in this third context becomes clear hostility in the application of the symbol to moral evil, whether referring to the evil spirits (Eph 6.12), the punishment of the wicked (Mt 8.12; 2 Pet 2.17), or to the sinful world in general (Jn 1.5; Lk 22.53; Eph 4.18; 2 Cor 6.14; Rom 13.12; probably also Jn 3.2 and 13.30). The call of the sinner from the darkness of evil into light (Jn 12.46; Eph 5.8) is expressed in the miraculous healing of the blind (cf. Acts 26.18), probably according to the understanding of Jesus himself (Mt 6.23; Lk 7.22; cf. Is 42.7).

[P. J. KEARNEY]

DARTMOUTH COLLEGE CASE (*Trustees of Dartmouth College v. William H. Woodward*), U.S. Supreme Court case in 1819 significant primarily for the defense of contracts and also for the protection of private educational institutions. In 1816 the New Hampshire state legislature attempted to change Dartmouth College, a private school chartered by the British crown in 1769, into a state university. After a judgment by the New Hampshire state court adverse to the college, the case was appealed to the U.S. Supreme Court. The decision, written by Chief Justice John Marshall, interpreted the charter as a contract protected against impairment by the federal constitution and ruled against the state. Along with its great constitutional, legal, and commercial implications, the decision guaranteed the status of private educational institutions and resulted in a sharp increase in the number of private and denominational schools. Indirectly, it also hastened the establishment of state universities. BIBLIOGRAPHY: 4 Wheaton (U.S.), 518 (1819); H. J. Friendly, *Dartmouth College Case and the Public-Private Penumbra* (1969).

[J. C. WILLKE]

DARWIN, CHARLES ROBERT (1809–82), English naturalist and evolutionist. Finding neither medicine (at Edinburgh) nor divinity (at Cambridge) to his taste, D. pursued biological studies on his own. His research and writing culminated in his evolutionary theory presented in *The Origin of Species* (1859) and *The Descent of Man* (1871). D. proposed that all living things, including man, have developed from a few extremely simple forms by a gradual descent with modifications, accounting for the process by "natural selection." The publication of these works evoked great controversy because they appeared to undermine the theistic proof for the existence of God based on design. D. remained aloof from the controversies between radicals and reactionaries, rationalists and believers occasioned by the publication of his theories. His personal belief began with a vague deism or theism, progressed through a disbelief in Christianity to conclude, in his own words, in agnosticism. BIBLIOGRAPHY: G. R. DeBeer, *Charles Darwin* (1958).

[W. B. MAHONEY]

DASEIAN NOTATION, a system of music notation of the 9th and 10th cent. in which the tones of the scale were represented by signs derived from Greek prosodic accents. Used for monophonic melodies and *organum, it provided a means of notating pitch exactly when *neums did not yet do so. BIBLIOGRAPHY: W. Apel, *Notation of Polyphonic Music* (5th ed., 1953).

[P. MURPHY]

DASIUS, ST. (d. 303?), Roman soldier and martyr. According to legend, D., a soldier of the Durostorum garrison, was chosen "king of the Saturnalia," and as such was permitted to live with complete license for one month, after which he was to be sacrificed to Kronos. Considering that death was inevitable, D. declared himself a Christian and refused to take part in the Saturnalian preparations. Brought before the legate Bassus, he could not be induced to sacrifice to the gods and suffered death by beheading. A bibliography of the legend can be found in Butler 4:393.

[P. K. MEAGHER]

DATARY APOSTOLIC, a former office of the *Curia Romana, but suppressed by the 1967 apostolic constitution *Regimini ecclesiae universae,* which transferred its functions to the papal Secretariat of State. The name derived from its original responsibility, the dating of papal documents. The office was established in the 14th cent. for greater papal, central control over benefices and their revenues. The cardinal datary until the 19th cent. had a broad competence, not only over benefices, but in matters concerning marriage, religious life, and ecclesiastical penalties. The reform of the curia under Pius X by the apostolic constitution *Sapienti consilio,* June 29, 1908, which was incorporated into the CIC, greatly reduced the power of the datry.

[T. C. O'BRIEN]

DATING, RADIOCARBON, see RADIOCARBON DATING.

DAUBENTON, GUILLAUME (1648–1723), French Jesuit and confessor to Philip V, first Bourbon king of Spain. D.'s influence approached that of Card. *Alberoni, esp. since Philip treated every political question as a matter of conscience. In a period of absence from Spain (1705–15) caused by court intrigue, D. was in France where he took part in the promotion of stages for the bull *Unigenitus and also in the promotion of the cause of St. John Frances *Regis, whose biography he wrote (1716). BIBLIOGRAPHY: P. Mech, *Catholicisme* 3:474–475.

[T. C. O'BRIEN]

DAUCHER, ADOLF (*c.*1460–1523 or 1524), German sculptor in Ulm, then in Augsburg where he was associated with Hans Holbein the Elder as an exponent of Renaissance style. D.'s major work is the choir stalls in the Fuggerkapelle, Augsburg. BIBLIOGRAPHY: P. M. Holm, *Adolf Daucher und die Fuggerkapelle bei Sankt Anna in Augsburg* (1921).

[M. J. DALY]

DAUDET, LÉON (pseudonym, Rivarol; 1867–1942), leading French pamphleteer of his time. D. was the editor of *Action Française* and a member of the Goncourt Academy. He was a bitter opponent of the Catholic supporters of the Third Republic; he also led campaigns against Jews, anticlericals, Freemasonry, members of Parliament, and defeatists during World War I. D. published numerous articles dealing with medicine, psychology, politics, and literary criticism. His reminiscences are memorable for their lively style and skilled use of words. BIBLIOGRAPHY: J. Morienval, *Catholicisme* 3:475–478.

[K. O'NEILL]

DAUGHTERS OF ISABELLA, an organization founded in 1904 as a society for Catholic women, envisaged as a service agency for the interests of the Church and society and as a contributor to the religious, intellectual, and social development of its members. Founded in New Haven, Conn., as an auxiliary to a local council of the Knights of Columbus, the organization grew rapidly and spread throughout the U.S. and Canada and, in more recent times, the Philippines. By 1963 the society had 116,000 members.

Organized in local circles, state circles with national officers and a national board of directors, the Daughters of Isabella are engaged in work for children and youth, educational support through scholarships. A special program has been providing CCD instruction for men and women in the armed forces. The society has also given generous help to missionaries and refugees.

[J. R. AHERNE]

DAUMIER, HONORÉ (1808–79). French lithographer, painter, and sculptor. He studied under the painter and archeologist Alexandre Lenoir, mastered the newly discovered lithography technique, and entered the Paris Academy in 1828. D., resenting injustices against the poor, expressed his indignation in 4,000 lithographs in the satirical weeklies *Silhouette, La Caricature* (*Massacre of the Rue Transonain,* 1834), and *Le Charivari* through social satires in seven series, including his renowned *Men of Justice* (1845–49), which exposed the inhumanity of lawyers and judges. In expressive, agitated lines D., conscious of the dignity of man, is never pessimistic, often amusing, always poignant. He painted with a Rembrandt palette figures heroic as those of Michelangelo (*Uprising,* 1860; *Third Class Carriage,* 1862; *Christ and His Disciples; We Want Barabbas; The Kneeling Magdalen,* 1848). He made 45 terra-cotta busts of politicians (1830–32).

[M. J. DALY]

DAVENPORT, CHRISTOPHER AND JOHN, two brothers prominent in 17th-cent. ecclesiastical and political life.

Christopher (religious name, Franciscus a Sancta Clara, 1598–1680), Franciscan theologian. Born at Coventry, C., with his brother John, studied at Oxford (1613–15) and while there converted to Catholicism. He continued his studies, first at Douai and then at Ypres, where he joined the Franciscans (1617). He studied theology at Salamanca, then taught briefly at Douai before being appointed (1625) to restore the Recollects in England. He served as chaplain for Queen Henrietta Maria before the Civil War. In his devotion to the cause of reunion, he cultivated friendly relations with many Anglicans, one of whom, Jeremy *Taylor, came under suspicion because of the association. C. himself was forced into hiding during the Civil War, using the aliases Francis Hunt and Francis Coventry. With the *Restoration (1660) he again became court chaplain and converted Anne, Duchess of York. He wrote numerous philosophical, historical, theological, and pastoral treatises (collected in 2 v., Douai, 1665–67). His *Paraphrastica expositio articulorum confessionis Anglicanae*, published as an appendix to *Deus, natura, gratia* (1634), sought to show the compatibility of the *Thirty-Nine Articles with RC teaching; it was condemned in Spain but not in Rome. BIBLIOGRAPHY: H. Dauphin, DHGE 14:109–111; Gillow BDEC 2:24–28.

John (1597–1670), Puritan minister, a founder of New Haven Colony (Conn.). After studying with his brother Christopher at Oxford, J. was ordained in the C of E. While a vicar in London he adopted Puritan views. He left England, going first to Amsterdam (1633) and then to America (1637). With Theophilus Eaton (d. 1658) and others, he helped found the colony of New Haven. In 1667 because of religious (see HALFWAY COVENANT) and political disputes, J. left New Haven to become minister of the First Church in Boston. His works include *Power of Congregational Churches Asserted and Vindicated* (1672).

[T. C. O'BRIEN]

DAVENTRY PRIORY, former Cluniac monastery in Daventry, England, founded before 1109 by Hugh of Leicester with four canons and four Benedictine monks from the Abbey of La Charité-sur-Loire. Daventry prospered during the succeeding centuries until it was dissolved in 1525 and became, with other religious houses of little importance, part of Wolsey's College at Oxford, later known as Henry VIII College and finally, Christ Church.

[S. A. HEENEY]

DAVID, King of Israel (1000–961 B.C.). The son of Jesse of Bethlehem, he tended his father's flocks before he became Saul's armor-bearer and musician, playing the lyre to soothe the manic-depressive king. As David's popularity grew with his slaying of Goliath and victories over the Philistines, the jealous Saul repeatedly sought to kill him. D. fled to the wilderness of Judah and on to Philistine territory where he served as a Philistine mercenary at Geth, still managing to help his countrymen. At Saul's death, the southern tribes recognized D. as king, whereas the northern tribes recognized Ishbaal, Saul's son. At Ishbaal's death, 7 years later, D. was chosen king of Israel.

D.'s political acumen was shown in his steps to consolidate his kingdom. He captured Jerusalem, a neutral city between the northern and southern tribes and moved his capital there, building himself a palace and making the city the religious center of the nation by erecting an altar and bringing there the ark of the covenant. His plans to build a temple were discouraged by the prophet Nathan who promised in the name of Yahweh that the Davidic dynasty would be eternal. D. extended the Israelite empire from Sinai and the Gulf of Aqaba to S Syria through conquest of the Philistines, Edomites, Moabites and Ammonites. The court history (2 Sam 9–20; 1 Kg 1–2) recounts the glorious achievements of David, but it reports his human failures as well: his adultery with Bathsheba; his murder of her husband Uriah; his rebuke by the prophet Nathan; tragedy upon tragedy in the royal family, esp. the treason of his son Absalom. David still deserves honor as Israel's greatest king: great warrior, shrewd politician, a deeply religious man (in the less advanced moral code of that day), poet and musician, capable organizer, creator of a united Israel, the ideal king to whom future writers would compare all other kings. BIBLIOGRAPHY: J. M. Meyers, Inter DB 1:771–782; H. B. Gaubert, *David and the Foundation of Jerusalem* (1973).

[F. J. MONTALBANO]

DAVID I, ST. (c.1080–1153), king of Scotland from 1124. His reign marks Scotland's entrance into the mainstream of European political, social, and religious development. He founded royal burghs, established diocesan organizations independent of York, patronized new monastic orders, and supported Matilda against Stephen. BIBLIOGRAPHY: G. M. Fusconi, BiblSanct 4:516–518; Butler 2:383–384.

[R. W. HAYS]

DAVID OF AUGSBURG (c.1200–72), Franciscan ascetical-mystical theologian. D. served as a teacher at the studium generale in Madgeburg, master of novices in Regensburg (1235–50), visitator (1246) with Berthold of Regensburg, and inquisitor against the Waldensians. He was both a distinguished preacher and one of the greatest writers of his day. His teaching was practical. He preached perfect obedience and humility, warned against illusions, and laid greater stress on the active than the contemplative life. His principal Latin writings, *De reformatione hominis interioris*, *De compositione hominis exterioris*, and *De septem processibus religiosorum*, have been incorrectly attributed to SS. Bernard and Bonaventure. The authenticity of his *De inquisitione haereticorum* (ed. 1879) has been questioned. His writing influenced the Spanish Franciscan and German mystics of the 14th century. BIBLIOGRAPHY: M. Bihl, "Survey of Scholarship on David of Augsburg," AFH (1914) 7:765–769; (1925) 18:143–147; (1933) 26:527–531.

[M. B. MONAGHAN]

DAVID OF DINANT (d. after 1210), scholastic philosopher. Born perhaps in Dinant, Belgium, or Dinan, Brittany, he lectured at Paris c.1200 on Aristotle and taught a materialistic pantheism, identifying God with Aristotle's primary matter. The Council of Sens (1210) ordered all copies of his *Quaternuli* to be burnt, and he was exiled from France as a heretic. Only fragments of his writings survive, though much can be reconstructed from citations in Albert the Great and Thomas Aquinas, who dismisses D.'s position as "most stupid" (ThAq ST 1a, 3.8). BIBLIOGRAPHY: Gilson HCP 241–243; Copleston 2:184–185.

[T. EARLY]

DAVID DISHYPATOS, a 14th-cent. Byzantine polemicist and Hesychast probably born of the noble family of Dishypatoi in Thessalonica. Though little is known of his life, it is believed that he was a monk of the Lavra Monastery at Mount Athos and that he worked in close contact with Gregory Palamas during the Hesychastic movement. About 1347, at the request of Empress Anne of Savoy, he wrote a brief but important account of the controversy between Palamas and his opponents, Barlaam and Gregory Akindynos. Most of his writings are unedited. BIBLIOGRAPHY: V. Laurent, DHGE 14:115–116; E. Candal, EncCatt 4:1247; Beck 730–732.

[R. A. TODD]

DAVID OF HIMMEROD, BL. (c.1100–79), Cistercian monk and mystic. A native of Florence, D. studied in Paris, became a monk at Clairvaux (1131), and helped establish the abbey of Himmerod (Rhineland) in 1134. His vita, compiled some 25 years after his death (ed. A. Schneider, 1955), is one of the earliest examples of Cistercian hagiography and is remarkable for its departure from the older style of hagiography that stressed unusual events, striking phenomena, and miracles. Instead, D.'s *vita* dwells upon his activities that illustrate his virtues and the richness of his interior life. BIBLIOGRAPHY: J. Schanz, "David von Florenz," *Cistercienser Chronik* 73–75 (1966–68); M.-A. Dimier, BiblSanct 4:513–514; C. Hontoir, DSAM 3:44–46.

[L. J. LEKAI]

DAVID OF VÄSTMANLAND, ST. (d. c.1082), reputedly a Cluniac monk of Anglo-Saxon origin. He was sent to Sweden c.1020 as a missionary. He worked first in the S part of that country and later in Västmanland. D. is sometimes called David of Munkthorp from the name of the church built where he was accustomed to baptize. BIBLIOGRAPHY: Zimmermann 2:455, 458; A. L. Sibilia, BiblSanct 4:516.

DAVID OF WALES, ST. (Dewi; 6th cent.), patron saint of Wales. Called "the water-drinker" from his extreme asceticism, he typifies the golden age of Welsh monasticism. He studied under Paulinus of Wales, founded several monasteries, including St. Davids where he was the first bp., and presided at councils on ecclesiastical discipline at Llanddewi Brefi (c.560) and Caerleon (the "Synod of Victory," [569]). His trip to Jerusalem and consecration as metropolitan are legends associated with claims of primacy for the See of St. Davids by his biographer Rhygyfarch (d. 1099) and Bp. Bernard (1115–48). BIBLIOGRAPHY: A. Amore and A. M. Raggi, BiblSanct 4:514–515; Butler 1:449–451.

[R. W. HAYS]

DAVID, CHRISTIAN (1690–1751), evangelist and missionary of the *Moravian Church. Born in Moravia, D. had a deep religious experience at the age of 20, and after a period of uncertainty converted from Catholicism to *Pietism. He combined traveling at his carpenter's trade with evangelism. After meeting Count *Zinzendorf he was instrumental in the Count's opening his estates to Bohemian Brethren refugees and felled the first tree for the building of *Herrnhut in 1722. D. helped build settlements elsewhere in Germany and in Pennsylvania and served briefly as a missionary in Greenland. As a preacher he deeply impressed John *Wesley during the latter's visit to Herrnhut. BIBLIOGRAPHY: G. Hamilton, *History of the Moravian Church* (1967).

[J. R. WEINLICK]

DAVID, FRANZ (1510–79), Transylvanian Unitarian leader. Born in Koloszvár (Cluj), he studied in Wittenberg (1545–48) and returned to Hungary to become rector of a RC school. He became a Lutheran and superintendent of the Hungarian Lutheran Church (1557). After debates with the Calvinist leader, Peter Mélius, D. became a Calvinist and was superintendent of the Hungarian *Reformed Church (1564). Debates within the Reformed Church and D.'s own inquiring mind led him to question the doctrines of the Trinity and the divinity of Christ. With G. *Blandrata, he won many of the nobles over to Unitarianism. At a general synod in 1568, some Reformed ministers separated, under his leadership, forming the nucleus of a Unitarian church, of which he became bishop. His inquiries led him to reject the addressing of prayer to Christ. Since innovations in religion had been forbidden by royal decree, D. was arrested, tried, and died in prison. He is regarded as the founder of the Hungarian Unitarian Church. BIBLIOGRAPHY: E. M. Wilbur, *History of Unitarianism* (2 v., repr., 1965) 2:16–80.

[J. C. GODBEY]

DAVID, GERARD (1460–1523), early Netherlandish painter, probably trained in Haarlem, admitted to the painters' guild in Bruges in 1484. The last important master to paint in the style of Van Eyck and Van der Weyden, D. simplified their religious symbolism and emotional content. In such paintings as the *Baptism* altarpiece (Bruges) and the *Marriage at Cana* (Louvre) D.'s dignified and somewhat homely figures quietly reenact the miracles in a space rationalized by focal point perspective and devoid of multiple symbolic references. BIBLIOGRAPHY: E. Panofsky, *Early Netherlandish Painting* (2 v., 1953); M. Whinney, *Early Flemish Painting* (1968).

[S. N. BLUM]

DAVID, JOHN BAPTIST MARY (1761–1841), missionary and bishop ordained a Sulpician in 1785, his life was disrupted by the French Revolution, and he volunteered with Flaget for the American missions. When Flaget became first bp. of Bardstown, D. accompanied him, and the two men, against incredible odds, slowly built a diocese in the wilderness. D. founded the Sisters of Charity of

Nazareth who became a major influence in Kentucky. His plea against appointment as bp. of Philadelphia was heeded; he was named coadjutor bp. of Bardstown in 1819. D. was a prolific writer on devotional and catechetical subjects.

[J. R. AHERNE]

DAVIDSON, RANDALL THOMAS (1848–1930), abp. of Canterbury. The son of Scottish, Presbyterian parents, D. was educated at Trinity College, Oxford. He was resident chaplain to Abp. Tait (1877–82), married Tait's second daughter, and was his biographer (1891). Queen Victoria came to esteem him as a valued counselor and in 1883 appointed him dean of Windsor. He was bp. of Rochester (1891–95), then of Winchester (1895–1903), and was engaged in controversy over use of ritual in the Church of England. He was appointed abp. of Canterbury in 1903. In this office he was conciliatory and fair, striving to preserve the unity and the *comprehensiveness of the Church of England. He resisted disestablishment of the Church in Wales (1920), mediated in conflicts concerning *modernism, presided at the ecumenically important *Lambeth Conference of 1920, and encouraged the *Malines Conversations. He also spoke out for the Church on political and social issues. From 1906 onward he labored in the cause of a revision of the Book of Common Prayer; he was disappointed by the rejections (1927, 1928) of the *Revised Prayer Book. He resigned in 1928, and was elevated to a peerage as Baron Davidson of Lambeth. BIBLIOGRAPHY: G. K. A. Bell, *Randall Davidson* (2 v., 1935).

[T. GILBY]

DAVIES, WILLIAM (c. 1560–93), Welsh priest and martyr. After his ordination at Reims (1585), D. worked zealously for 8 years in Wales. He was arrested in 1592 at Holyhead, tried, and found guilty of having entered the realm as a priest, a charge he freely admitted. The death sentence was not pronounced immediately. He was given an opportunity to dispute with the Queen's Council and was subjected to months of imprisonment. Finally, offered the choice of abandoning his Catholicism or facing death, he chose the latter and was executed at Beaumaris. BIBLIOGRAPHY: J. H. Pollen, *Acts of English Martyrs* (1891) 96–126.

DAVIGNON, HENRI (1879–1964), Belgian writer. D. belonged to an aristocratic Catholic family of industrial magnates and political figures and studied at Louvain, where he edited the Catholic literary journal, *L'Escholier*. He wrote for the progressive Catholic review, *Durendal*, and edited the *Revue Générale* of Brussels (1919–37)), a publication founded by Card. Sterckx. Although he authored several plays, his fame rests on novels markedly influenced by Bourget and Barres and written with the psychological finesse of the Catholic moralist concerned with spiritual tensions of married couples. They include *Le Prix de la vie* (1909), *L'Ami français* (1923), and *Le Vieux Bon Dieu* (1927). *Un Plus grand amour* (1929) and his masterpiece, *Un Pénitent de Furnes* (1925), orchestrate universal Christian themes like vicarious suffering, Flemish devotions such as the public carrying of the penitential cross. D. treated the moral dilemma of the Catholic author confronting the problem of evil in essays like *Au service de l'idéal* (1912). He also wrote numerous essays and novels on various aspects of Belgian life, local history and customs, and linguistic heritage. BIBLIOGRAPHY: M. F. Inial, *Henri Davignon* (1948).

[G. E. GINGRAS]

DAVILA, FRANCISCO, see ÁVILA, FRANCISCO DE.

DÁVILA Y PADILLA, AGUSTÍN (1562–1604), Mexican historian, abp. of Santo Domingo from 1599. D. entered the Dominican Order in 1579 and was professed in 1580. An excellent scholar and outstanding orator, he held a number of posts in his order, including that of definitor of the general chapter in Rome and procurator before the courts of Madrid and Rome. His chief work, commissioned by the government, was the *Historia de la fundación de la provincia de Santiago de Méjico de la Orden de Predicadores* (1596). BIBLIOGRAPHY: M. R. Martin and G. Lovett, *Encyclopedia of Latin-American History* (1968) 116; E. Gómez Tagle, NCE 4:662.

[M. T. REILLY]

DAVIS, ANDREW JACKSON (1826–1910), Spiritualist leader. Born in Blooming Grove, N.Y., he had only a few months of schooling before he was apprenticed to a shoemaker as a child. In 1843 he met an itinerant lecturer on mesmerism and soon gained fame as a clairvoyant and faith healer. In 1845–47 he gave a series of lecutres while in a trance; they were transcribed and published as *Nature's Divine Revelations* (1847). His many books on occult subjects, notably *The Great Harmonia*, *The Philosophy of Spiritual Intercourse*, and *A Stellar Key to the Summer Land*, had a marked influence on the development of Spiritualist thought and provided much of its terminology. The Children's Progressive Lyceum, which he founded at Buffalo, N.Y., in 1863, as a Spiritualist "Sunday school," is regarded as the beginning of Spiritualism as a denomination.

[R. K. MACMASTER]

DAVIS, HENRY (1866–1952), English Jesuit moral theologian. He taught moral theology 1911–51, first at St. Beuno's College in Wales, then at Heythrop. Best known of his works was his *Moral and Pastoral Theology* (4 v., 1935), which was widely used as a manual in English-speaking countries. He also edited Suárez's *De legibus* (1944) and Gregory the Great's *Pastoral Care* (1950). BIBLIOGRAPHY: T. Corbishley, NCE 4:662–663.

[M. J. SUELZER]

DAWSON, CHRISTOPHER (1889–1970), English Catholic historian and writer. D.'s family background provided him with an early familiarity with the religious and social traditions of England's upper classes. He was educated at Winchester, most religious of the English public schools, and at Trinity College, Oxford, leaving there in 1911 to study economics with Prof. Gustave Cassel in Sweden. D. returned to Oxford for postgraduate studies in history and sociology, and became acquainted with the works of E. Troeltsch, who may be credited with influencing D. to center his lifelong interest on the relation between religion and culture. His contact with Catholic culture and hagiography and his impression of the unity existing between Catholic theology and Catholic life, led him to be received formally into the Catholic Church at St. Aloysius', Oxford, in 1914, two years before his marriage to Valery Mills. Only after many years of study did he publish in 1928 his first book, the beginning of an unabated output throughout his life. He became Lecturer at University College, Exeter (1930–1936), Forwood Lecturer in the philosophy of religion, Liverpool (1934), Gifford Lecturer in Edinburgh (1947 and 1948), and professor of RC Studies, Harvard Univ. (1958–1962). He was a general editor of *Essays in Order;* beginning in 1940 he was for many years editor of *Dublin Review.* There is a notable unity and continuity to his works; from such early works as: *The Making of Europe; Enquiries into Religion and Culture;* and such post-World War II works as: *Religion and Culture* (1948); *Religion and the Rise of Western Culture* (1950); *Understanding Europe* (1952); down to his last works: *The Crisis of Western Education* (1961); *The Dividing of Christendom* (1965); *The Formation of Christendom* (1967). He never had the audience of a Toynbee, Spengler, or Gibbon; he considered that the historian had too much still to learn from the painstaking methodology of anthropologists before undertaking vast syntheses. At odds with conventional wisdom, he would admit that Western man with his scientific methodology, esp. in anthropology, had done much to make even Eastern people, and other non-Western peoples, more aware of their own cultures; but he was convinced Western man had neglected similar investigations into his own culture, esp. into what he considered to be the foundations of Western culture, the so-called Dark Ages (A.D. 400–1000). To him religion is the energizing influence in all human activity. He believed that only a return to the spiritual traditions of Christianity would save Western civilization. He believed that the Church that created Europe could save Europe and the world; and that the West may still have the most vital contribution to make to a coming world order from its tradition of Christian mysticism and classical humanism, whose synthesis is the achievement of Catholic culture. BIBLIOGRAPHY: afterword by J. J. Mulloy in Dawson's, *The Dynamics of World History* (1956).

[E. J. DILLON]

DAY, DOROTHY (1897–), founder of the *Catholic Worker movement. A native of Brooklyn, N.Y., she grew up in California and Chicago, becoming interested in Marxism at the Univ. of Illinois. In 1916 she came to New York, where she wrote for Socialist and Communist periodicals. In 1927 she was received into the Catholic Church; her book *From Union Square to Rome* is an account of her conversion. On May Day, 1933, she inaugurated *The Catholic Worker,* a monthly newspaper devoted to social justice, with emphasis on voluntary poverty and the practice of the works of mercy. Her books include *The Long Loneliness* (1952), an autobiography, and *Loaves and Fishes* (1963), an account of life at the New York Catholic Worker house. BIBLIOGRAPHY: *America* 127 (1972) special issue; W. D. Miller, *Harsh and Dreadful Love: Dorothy Day and the Catholic Worker Movement* (1973).

[D. CODDINGTON]

DAY, GEORGE (1501–56), bp. of Chichester from 1543. D. was educated at Cambridge and served as chaplain to John Fisher and as vice-chancellor of Cambridge. In 1547 he showed his conservatism by upbraiding the Fellows of King's College for failure to say private Masses. During the reign of Edward VI he preached against the destruction of altars and lost his see as a result. When Mary Tudor became queen, he was released from prison and restored to his diocese. BIBLIOGRAPHY: J. E. Paul, NCE 4:663; DNB 14:231.

[M. J. SUELZER]

DAY-LEWIS, CECIL (1904–72), poet. Born in Ireland, son of a clergyman, he was educated at Sherbonne School and Oxford. A perceptive critic as well as poet, he belonged to the post-Eliot circle. With Auden, Spender, et al. he denied the romanticized vision of *The Waste Land* while admitting the existence of bleak desolation. *A Hope for Poetry* (1934) enunciates the conflict of loyalties facing modern man. To face current reality without losing lyric tone and universality became the dominant chord in *Beechen Vigil* (1925), *Country Comets* (1928), and *Transitional Poem* (1929). D.-L. also wrote under the pseudonym of Nicholas Blake a series of detective stories (*The Smiler with the Knife,* 1939) and edited several anthologies of poetry. He was named poet laureate by Queen Elizabeth in 1968. His *The Poetic Image* (1947) remains a useful work of contemporary criticism. BIBLIOGRAPHY: C. Dyment, *C. Day Lewis* (1955).

[R. M. FUNCHION]

DAY HOURS (HORAE DIURNAE), all the hours of the *Divine Office (since 1971 the Liturgy of the Hours) except *Matins. *DIURNAL.

DAY OF ATONEMENT (YOM KIPPUR), one of the best-known Jewish feasts, introduced in late OT times and continuing in modern Judaism as the prime day of expiation and penance. In the Hebrew of the OT the feast is called, *yom hakkippurim,* "the day of expiations," while in Acts

27.9 it is simply "The Fast." The feast is observed on the 10th day of the 7th month of Tishri (September–October). Its origin is probably late since it is not mentioned in preexilic or even early postexilic texts. When Ezekiel tells of the reconstructed temple liturgy, he includes a rite of atonement (Ezek 45.18–20), but the rite is not identical with that of this feast, and furthermore it was observed on the 1st and 7th day of the month. The references in the Pentateuch (Lev 16.1–34; 23.26–32; 25.9; Num 29.7–11) all come from the most recent source, the priestly tradition. It seems that the later temple worship after the exile was projected back into the desert period, although some elements of the feast certainly must have had a long history as independent rites of atonement within Israel.

The OT ritual is described in Lev 16.1–34. As it now stands the rite can be divided into three parts. First the high priest sacrificed a bull as a sin offering for his own sins and those of the Aaronite priesthood. It was during this ceremony that he entered the Holy of Holies—the only occasion in the year that this was done; he placed incense before the mercy seat and sprinkled the bull's blood on and before it. In later times two distinct entrances were involved, one with incense and the other with blood, although this is not clear from the text. Second, the high priest made another sin offering, this time a male goat for the sins of the people, and he again entered the Holy of Holies to sprinkle the mercy seat. With the blood of both the bull and the male goat the high priest then purified the Holy of Holies, the Tent of Meeting, and finally the altar by putting some of the blood on the horns of the altar. All this was done to cleanse them from the uncleannesses of the people. The third element involves the scapegoat. Toward the beginning of the ceremony, the high priest cast lots upon two male goats, one lot for the Lord and the other lot for Azazel. The goat upon which the lot for the Lord fell was used in the sin offering above, but the one for Azazel was presented alive before the Lord, while the high priest placed his hands upon its head and confessed over it all the iniquities of the people. The goat bore all the sins of Israel and was led away to perish in the wilderness. This last part of the ritual has parallels among the Babylonians. The meaning of Azazel is disputed. Some have translated it "for the precipice," and thus linked the name with the Rabbinical tradition that the goat was cast over a precipice. Parallelism with "for the Lord" seems to demand that "for Azazel" is the name of a devil dwelling in the wilderness. The ritual of the scapegoat was symbolic for the people's repentance.

It is generally agreed that this account in Lev ch. 16 is composite in nature, representing several strata of tradition. There are a number of doublets and the narrative does not flow smoothly. It is almost impossible to determine which elements of the feast made up the original rite. Verses 29–34 are later than the rest of ch. 16; they are similar to Lev 23.27–32 in which the date for the feast was set for the 10th of Tishri and other acts of penance were prescribed, in particular the very strict sabbath rest. With the destruction of the Temple and the end of Jewish sacrifices, the feast developed into an elaborate liturgy of prayers, hymns, biblical readings, and repeated confessions of sin. The synagogue services are almost continuous, beginning on the previous evening with a penitential service and the singing of the *Kol Nidre,* a formula of absolution from vows, and followed by four more services on the day itself. The evening before the feast is also the time for the festive meal before sundown, the lighting of the festival lamps, and the settling of debts and disputes to bring about reconciliation. The tone of the feast has remained strongly one of expiation, penance, and reconciliation. Various penitential acts are undertaken; the sabbath rest is very strict with no work, washing, or even marital intercourse. A fast of 24 hours is observed. Candles are burned in memory of the dead. BIBLIOGRAPHY: G. W. MacRae, NCE 1:1026–27; J. C. Rylaarsdam, InterDB T-1:313–316; De Vaux AncIsr 507–510.

[O. N. BUCHER]

DAY OF RECOLLECTION, a practice of setting aside specific days on which priests, religious, and/or laypeople come together for special prayer, conferences, discussions aimed at heightening their spiritual consciousness and promoting their spiritual development. It serves much the same purpose as a retreat, esp. for those who cannot spare the time for the more extended exercises.

[P. K. MEAGHER]

DAY OF THE LORD (Eschatolology), a term whose development in richness of meaning extended over a period of history from the conquest into NT times. In the wide sense it indicates a time when Yahweh will reveal his judgment or manifest his punitive justice through calamities. In the narrow sense it is an eschatological idea indicating the time of long-awaited salvation after judgment is passed on all things hostile to Yahweh. In a total view of history, the term designates Yahweh's solemn intervention in the course of history. Originally the phrase referred to military victory in favor of the people of God, a day of vindication for the oppressed people over an enemy through Yahweh's saving help. From this national and political meaning, the term came to have the more spiritual content of freeing men from the bondage of sin so that Yahweh might have complete dominion over his world. The prophet Amos was the first to confront the people concerning their naïve assumption that Yahweh would be with them at all costs. He informed them that the Day of the Lord for them would not be what they thought—a day of victory and glory—but rather a day of wrath and vengeance. The people must learn to keep the covenant with their Lord. Amos does not eschew completely the idea that the Day is one of salvation. Elsewhere he spoke of salvation for a remnant (5.4, 6, 14, 15) who would be faithful to the covenant. The prophets who followed Amos spoke of this Day in the same vein. In Is 2.6–22 the Day is one of annihilating judgment by the

Lord. He will vindicate his claim as the only God. Ezekiel makes the same claim for Yahweh (7.7). Joel sees the possibility of escape from the devastating Day through repentance alone (2.12–17). Note the reversion in this section (2.11) to the ancient idea of Yahweh as leader of warriors. Coupled with this archaic notion is Joel's emphasis on the salvation to come presented as a return to the primeval age. He sees this as introducing the definitive age of Yahweh's saving activity (4.17–21). Zechariah has the same twofold presentation—sinners suffering, the faithful triumphing. Jerusalem is destroyed, but Yahweh comes to rescue his faithful ones (14.1–5). There is also an emphasis on the paradise theme (14.6–8). The prophecy of Malachi sees the Day as one of purification for the just and of condemnation for the wicked (3.2–4, 19).

The NT borrows the same concept with its Christian overtones. Some of the writers use the term as does the OT to speak of a Day of judgment and purification in which the heavens and the earth will be cleansed and renewed to make a new world of love and justice (2 Pet 3). This Day is identified in 1 and 2 Th with the second coming of Christ. Thus the apocalyptic sections of the synoptics really speak of this Day as understood in Christian teaching. At this time the just will be further purified, the evil punished, and all things made anew by Christ for his Father. It is for this Day that all Christians must be prepared and waiting. It will come swiftly and make known all the works of men. BIBLIOGRAPHY: H. de Baar, *Bible on the Second Coming* (tr. F. van der Heijden, 1965); J. Bright, *Kingdom of God* (1953); L. Cerný, *Day of Yahweh and Some Relevant Problems* (1948).

[F. GAST]

DE ALEATORIBUS, a brief homily, formerly attributed to St. *Cyprian, inveighing against dice games and gambling in general as the invention of the devil. Harnack attributed the work to Pope *Victor I (189–199), but in more recent opinion it is commonly held to have been written in the mid-3d century. *De Aleatoribus* is also of interest to philology because it is written in popular Latin. BIBLIOGRAPHY: M. Pellegrino, EncCatt 4:1250.

[R. B. ENO]

DE ARTE ILLUMINANDI (On the Art of Illumination), an anonymous 14th cent. treatise on manuscript illumination probably by an Italian illuminator. The only extant version—a 14th cent. copy of the earlier original —considers pigments, gilding, binders and technique of application. BIBLIOGRAPHY: *Anonymous 14th Century Treatise, De Arte Illuminandi* (tr. and with introduction by D. V. Thompson and G. H. Hamilton, 1933).

[M. J. DALY]

DE FIDE, designation for articles of faith which the Church explicitly and authoritatively presents as revealed by God, so that their denial is heresy. Typical are the early creeds and some later professions of faith. Statements *de fide* may be formally defined by popes or ecumenical councils, or contained in the ordinary, universal teaching of the bishops (D 3011). As such, their content is true and establishes a norm of faith, but their expression is necessarily conditioned by the culture from which they proceed. Theologians agree that a truth that is formally implied in a revealed dogma, i.e., deducible by a strict logical process, may be declared *de fide*, and many such dogmas now proclaimed as God's word revealed in Scripture and tradition were not always clearly seen to be such (D 3886). A growing number of theologians today would also hold that propositions only virtually implied can be defined *de fide*. BIBLIOGRAPHY: C. Journet, *What Is Dogma?* (1964). *DOGMA; *MAGISTERIUM.

[W. DAVISH]

DE HAERETICO COMBURENDO, an act passed by Parliament in 1401 against the *Lollards. Those accused of heresy were to be tried by ecclesiastical courts and, if convicted, handed over to the civil power for execution by burning. Some see in this act the introduction of the *Inquisition in England. First repealed by Henry VIII and then reenacted by Mary Tudor, the act was finally revoked under Elizabeth I. BIBLIOGRAPHY: Bihlmeyer-Tüchle 2:437; K. B. McFarlane, *John Wycliffe and the Beginnings of English Nonconformity* (1953) 160–183.

[T. C. O'BRIEN]

DE MOTIONE OECUMENICA (On the Ecumenical Movement), the instruction issued by the RC Congregation of the Holy Office (now Congregation for the Doctrine of the Faith [Dec. 20, 1949]; AAS 42 [1950], 142–147) prescribing that bishops give prudent encouragement and direction to, while shielding the faithful from the dangers arising from, the *ecumenical movement. The document was a response to the growing desire among many persons outside the Church for the reunion of all who believe in Christ. In tone the instruction recalls the defensive documents of the Counter Reformation period. Its significance, however, lies in the cautious but positive first steps taken toward the opening of a new era of RC participation in the ecumenical movement. *DECREE ON ECUMENISM.

[R. A. MATZERATH]

DE PROFUNDIS, Psalm 130 (129 in Vulgate), so called from the first words in Latin (Out of the depths). One of the seven Penitential Psalms, it expresses the sorrow of an individual who laments his sins, but keeps his unbounded trust in God. It was probably written about the time of the Exile and expresses the hope of the anguished exiles. It belongs to the collection known as Gradual (going up) Psalms. As an expression of the attitude of the Israelites "coming up" (returning from exile), it served well as a song for the faithful to use on their "going up" in pilgrimage to Jerusalem. BIBLIOGRAPHY: A. Weiser, *Psalms, A Commentary* (tr. H. Hartwell, 1962) 772–776.

[F. J. MONTALBANO]

DE REBAPTISMATE, a theological treatise written *c.*256 by an unknown author in N Africa; it is a part of the controversy between Pope Stephen (254–257) and St. Cyprian (d. 258) over the rebaptism of heretics. The author distinguishes between baptism and the laying on of hands, considering the latter as the more important activity. The laying on of hands (confirmation) gives the Spirit, grants remission of sin, and effects salvation. On this basis, the importance of baptism is lessened, and the author argues against rebaptizing heretics if they received the laying on of hands. The tract has on occasion been attributed to Cyprian, but this is unrealistic, given its anti-Cyprianic tone. BIBLIOGRAPHY: J. N. D. Kelly, *Early Christian Doctrines* (4th ed., 1968) 210.

[B. ROSENDALL]

DE RECTA IN DEUM FIDE, a patristic theological text defending the orthodox faith against the doctrines of *Marcion and Bardesanes. Its author is unknown, although the work was incorrectly attributed to *Origen. It was probably written in Syria *c.*300 and is extant in its original Greek text and a Latin translation. Written in dialogue form, the text presents and refutes first Marcion's distinction between an OT and NT God and then the *Gnostic views of Bardesanes. BIBLIOGRAPHY: Quasten 2:146–147.

[T. M. MCFADDEN]

DE SACRAMENTIS, the Latin title given to a series of six sermons, probably delivered by St. Ambrose in 390 or 391. They were given on six successive days, from Tuesday of Easter week to the following Sunday, to the newly baptized, and contain an exact description of the rite of baptism, an ample explanation of the celebration of the Eucharist, and an excursus on the Lord's prayer. The authenticity of the treatise has been consistently challenged, but recent scholarship favors the opinion that *De Sacramentis* is a faithful recording of sermons delivered by Ambrose himself. According to this opinion, Ambrose's *De mysteriis* is a later, more brief and polished consideration of the same material. BIBLIOGRAPHY: *St. Ambrose on the Sacraments and on the Mysteries* (ed. J. H. Strawley, tr. J. Thompson, 1950).

[J. J. FLOOD]

DEACON (Gr. *diakonos,* servant, helper), one of the ranks or orders in the Christian ministry. Its institution has traditionally been traced to the Apostles' choice of seven disciples to see to the service of the poor (Acts 6.1–6). In NT times deacons preached and baptized under the direction of the presbyters or bishops. The first usage of the term makes it clear that its specifically Christian meaning was well known (Phil 1.1; 1 Tim 3.8). By the end of the 1st cent. the order formed a distinct, hierarchical rank in third place after bishops and priests, as is clearly mentioned by SS. Clement of Rome, Ignatius of Antioch, and Polycarp. In general, deacons assisted at the Eucharist and baptism, led the laity in prayers, chanted the gospel, and received the offerings from the people. Their original office of collecting and distributing alms gave them a certain importance and influence, so that the first deacon, or *archdeacon, often became the bishop's chief administrative officer. Deacons frequently served as counselors of the bishop and as diocesan functionaries and, owing to their experience and prominence, many of them were subsequently elected bishops. This was particularly true in the major sees, such as Rome, where they also functioned as papal legates. The number of Roman deacons was long restricted to seven, a situation regarded as being the origin of the seven cardinal deacons. But during the later Middle Ages the diaconate diminished considerably in importance, so that it generally became merely the final stage in preparing for the priesthood. The RC Church maintained the practice of ordaining as deacons only those who intended to become priests; they were bound by celibacy. Practically, their own function became participation in solemn liturgical ceremonies. Vatican Council II increased the number of these functions. The Council also decreed that the diaconate may be restored as a permanent and separate rank in the Latin Church and that married men may be ordained to this rank (Vat II Const Church 29). The diaconate is one of the three orders recognized in the Anglican Communion and is received as a step toward the priesthood. The deacon exercises liturgical functions similar to those of the RC deacon.

The Eastern Churches have retained the diaconate as a permanent and separate order, both in monasteries and among the parish clergy, in which case married men are ordained. The deacon's chief function is an important one, since he leads the prayers of the faithful.

Protestant usage of the term varies. John Calvin in the *Ecclesiastical Ordinances* for Geneva named four orders of ministry: pastors, teachers, elders, and deacons. In the *Reformed and Presbyterian Churches the deacons are laymen who continue the basic functions assigned to them by Calvin, administration of church goods and poor relief, as well as the care of the infirm. In the Lutheran tradition in the U.S. the deacon has similar functions. In Europe Lutheran deacons are full-time church workers caring for spiritual and social works of the Church; an assistant pastor may also be called deacon. In other Churches the deacon is usually a layman, or in some cases, a laywoman, chosen or appointed, sometimes for works of mercy or the temporal concerns of the local church, sometimes to assist the minister in his preaching and spiritual ministrations. BIBLIOGRAPHY: F. S. Weiser, *Serving Love: Chapters in the Early History of the Diaconate in American Lutheranism* (1960); E. P. Echlin, NCE 16:123–124, s. v. "Diaconate, Permanent."

[G. T. DENNIS]

DEACONESS, a woman officially designated to perform certain functions in the Church. The office apparently existed in apostolic times, although the terminology is not clear (Rom 16.1; 1 Tim 3.11). The term itself does not seem to have come into use until the 4th cent., which also saw a marked increase in the importance of the position, as it is described in the *Didascalia Apostolorum* and the *Apostolic Constitutions*. Apparently they were ordained by the *laying on of hands by the bishop. The deaconess was to devote herself to the care of the sick and the poor, to help instruct women, and keep them in order in church. Her most important function was to assist at the baptism of women, chiefly for the sake of propriety since baptism was generally performed by immersion. When adult baptism grew rarer, the office of deaconess decreased in importance and soon died out, although it lasted somewhat longer in the Eastern Church. The possibility of deaconesses in the RC Church is involved in contemporary discussions about the ordination of women.

In the 19th cent. several Protestant Churches revived the office in a modified form by establishing or approving communities of women who would devote themselves to hospitals and other charitable works. The first such community was founded in 1836 by T. Fliedner, pastor of a Lutheran and Reformed parish in Kaiserswerth, Germany. In their ceremony of dedication the new deaconesses promised to be obedient and faithful to their calling. The restoration of the office spread throughout Europe. The Anglican Church approved the order in 1861, and diocesan institutes modeled on Kaisersweth were established. The deaconess was ordained by the imposition of hands of the bishop. Four deaconesses from Kaiserswerth in 1849 came to staff what is now the Passavant Hospital, Pittsburgh, Pa.; the first American motherhouse for deaconesses was established in Philadelphia in 1890. Both of these foundations are Lutheran. Most of the Protestant denominations have adopted the office of deaconess in some form. The largest number, over 700, are in the Methodist Church, but there are many also in the Episcopal Church, the United Church of Christ, and in the United Church of Canada. BIBLIOGRAPHY: J. Forget, DTC 4:685–703; M. Winter, EncLuthCh 1:659–664; F. S. Weiser, *Serving Love: Chapters in the Early History of the Diaconate in American Lutheranism* (1960); *idem, Love's Response: A Story of Lutheran Deaconesses in America* (1962); J. M. Ford, NCE 16:116.

[G. T. DENNIS]

DEAD (IN THE BIBLE). The biblical notions on the condition of the dead evince a slow development. The ancient Hebrews held the same notions about life and death as the Canaanites among whom they lived. These notions were derived from observation of phenomena. They noted that life, a movement from within and the ability to accomplish things, ceased with man's last breath and that man's lifeless body crumbled to dust. Hence they looked upon a breathing man as a "living-being," or a "living soul," *nefesh,* con-stituted of God-given breath and God-molded dust (cf. Gen 2.7). A corpse, on the other hand, was considered a "dead soul" *(nefesh),* (cf. Num 6.6; Lev 21.11). The notion of a distinction between soul and body, therefore, was something unintelligible to the ancient Hebrew, and he did not look upon death as the separation of these two elements. Yet death was not regarded as an annihilation. As long as the body continued to exist and as long as the bones at least remained, the soul continued to exist, like a shade, in extreme weakness in the abode of the dead. (Is 14.9; 26.14,19; Ps 88.11). Hence the dead were called the "weak ones" (Heb refā'im; Job 26.5, Is 14.9; etc.). Sheol, sometimes called Abaddon or Hades (in LXX and NT), the abode of the dead, is at times scarcely distinguishable from the grave. It is the land of lifelessness, the land of silence and inactivity. The dead are bereft of all power and vitality, a "nothing" (Is 14.10). There pleasure (Sir 14.11–17), knowledge (Ec 9.5; Job 14.21f), and even prayer-adoration (Ps 6.5; 30.10; 115.17.) cease. Indeed the dead are said to exist no longer (Ps 39.13; Sir 17.28). All men, kings and slaves, saints and sinners, are indiscriminately gathered into a land of silence, oblivion, and hopelessness (Job 7.9–11; 14.7–22; 115.17; Num 16.33). Yet the very poetic books that paint such a hopeless picture of the dead also portray the dead in Sheol as arising to greet newcomers (Is 14.9–11) and seem to suggest some notion of feeling or consciousness on the part of the dead (Job 14.22). So the hope lingered that the dead not merely existed but actually continued to live. It would be impossible to explain Saul's consultation of the ghost of Samuel (1 Sam 28.8) without admitting some belief in afterlife for the dead.

The rise of an awareness of individual responsibility (cf. Ezek 14.12–20; 18.1–32; 33.10–20) and the realization that occasionally, at least, evil persons die unpunished led to the introduction of a notion of punishment after death. Thus Ezek 32.20f assigns enemy leaders to the deepest part of the pit (Sheol), the place reserved for those slaughtered and uncircumcised, a position of disgrace. This seems to be the starting point of the teaching of retribution for sins after death. The notion of disgrace transforms the worms of the grave, referred to in Is 14.11 as a blanket covering the corpse, into worms that do not die or cease eating and a fire that refuses to be put out (Is 66.24; Sir 7.17; Jdt 16.20–21; and Mk 9.48).

In the exile, meditation upon the life-giving function of the word of God as dramatized in the 37th ch. of Ezek seems to have fostered speculation that Yahweh's power extended also to the abode of the dead. This was confirmed by Is 7.11 where Yahweh is ready to work "a sign . . . coming . . . from the depths of Sheol." Furthermore, Is 53.8–12 spoke of the slaughtered Servant of Yahweh "dividing the spoil with the mighty." Granted that the Servant might be considered the remnant of Israel rather than an individual, the passage opened the door to speculation about resurrection from the dead. Indeed this thought of resurrection from the dead is clearly expressed in 2 Macc 7.14 and

Dan 12.1–3 amid the persecution of the suffering servants of Yahweh during the persecution of Antiochus IV, *c*.165 B.C. (cf. Is 25.8; 26.19).

Finally, under the influence of Grecian anthropology, through the Greek-speaking Jews of Alexandria, the notion of immortality was introduced in Wis 3.1–9. But an immortal soul existing independent of the body by which man is existentially man may be only a temporary condition if the afterlife is to be truly human. Hence resurrection of the body on the last day is demanded (cf. 1 Cor 15). In this framework, the Day of Yahweh gives way to a particular judgment at the moment of death, in and through which man is awarded rest and joy in the bosom of Abraham, paradise or heaven (Phil 1.23; Lk 16.22f; Lk 23.43) or punishment in the pit of flames. The general judgment on the last day, the Day of the Lord, becomes the occasion for the proclamation of Yahweh's victory and moment of the resurrection of the bodies of the dead to glory (1 Cor 15; 1 Thes 3.13–14; 2 Thes 1.7–8; Mt 25.31–32; Rev 21.2–5). Here more than in any other area of religious thought, the condescension, the humanization or adaptation of divine revelation to the cultural milieu of the recipients is seen. In this area, consequently, attention must be given to the date of the biblical testimony and the literary genre in which it is couched. BIBLIOGRAPHY: De Vaux AncIsr 56–61; T. Maertens, *Biblical Themes* (1964) D48, E7, F6, F12.

[J. A. PIERCE]

DEAD, ABSOLUTION OF THE, see ABSOLUTION OF THE DEAD.

DEAD, BOOK OF THE, see BOOK OF THE DEAD.

DEAD, CARE OF BODIES OF THE, the special reverent treatment required by religious custom and law in the disposal of the human body after death. Some special observance is practiced by almost all religions for reasons associated with the beliefs peculiar to each. Although for Christians burying the dead was not included among the works of mercy mentioned by Jesus in the eschatological discourse on the judgment (Mt 25.35–36), the special practices adopted at an early date are not without scriptural warrant. In the OT Tobit was praised by the angel (Tob 12.13) for this work (1.17–18; 2.3–5), and in the NT Jesus commended the woman who anointed him at Bethany, which he took as done to prepare him for burial (Mt 26.12). Two theological considerations support Christian practice in this matter: (1) the body as part of the human person is "the temple of the Holy Spirit" (1 Cor 6.19); and (2) concern for the decent disposal of the dead may witness to the core Christian belief in the resurrection of the dead to another life in Christ. Although the denial of fitting treatment to the bodies of the dead may be sinful, it is possible that sentimentality, vanity, and even greed on the part of those whose business it is to care for the dead may result in lavish expenditure and ridiculous pomp to the detriment of the living.

Ordinary Christian practice calls for burial in the earth or in a tomb. "Burial" at sea and *cremation (for Roman Catholics in permitted conditions) are generally considered acceptable. Roman Catholic church law neither prescribes nor prohibits embalming; the canons of the Code concern themselves in general with the funeral rites both in the church and cemetery. Autopsy is permissible to determine the cause of death or when it is mandatory in civil law (as in cases of possible homicide), or to further the progress of medical science, provided in the latter case the necessary permission is obtained and decent respect is shown not only for the feelings of survivors but also for the body itself as partaking in human dignity. Donation of parts of the body for transplantation is generally approved and indeed considered a laudable act of charity in some circumstances, provided that, in the case of absolutely necessary organs such as the heart, death is certain, and provided also that the necessary permission (of the donor before death, of his family after death) has been obtained. Aborted fetuses should be treated with the same respect, as should also major amputated members. BIBLIOGRAPHY: CIC index s.v. *Cadavera;* H. Köster, NCE 4:669–671; M. B. Walsh, NCE 4:671; St. Augustine, *Enchiridion* 109; *On Care for the Dead,* PL 40:595.

[C. NEELY]

DEAD, MASS FOR THE, the Eucharistic Sacrifice offered on behalf of a deceased person. From the early centuries of the Church, it has been customary to offer Mass for one who has died on the 3d day after his death. Originally this probably concluded a watch kept at the grave. In the West it later became common to celebrate Mass either at the grave or in the church on the occasion of the funeral itself. Masses were also offered on the 7th and 30th days after death and upon the anniversary of the death date. In the East the funeral Mass did not become part of the burial rite, but Masses were offered on the 3d, 9th, and 40th days after death and upon the anniversary day. Precedent was claimed for the Western practice of observing the 3d, 7th, and 30th days: Jesus rose on the 3d day; Joseph proclaimed 7 days of mourning for his father (Gen 50.10); for 30 days the Hebrew people mourned for Moses (Dt 34.8) and Aaron (Num 20.29). But other circumstances such as the desire to give Christian meaning to occasions observed by pagans could have been influential in determining those days. The liturgy of the burial rite and Masses for the dead originally reflected two themes: one of joy at the deceased's completion of his earthly pilgrimage and his union with Christ, and the other of hope that his survivors might help him to his rest by the suffrage of prayer and Eucharistic Sacrifice. The natural sadness of the occasion appears to have been deliberately muted by early Christians in order to affirm their faith in the resurrection and to disavow pagan attitudes toward the fact of death. But the occasion was inevitably associated with other thoughts, and in time some of these found expression in the liturgy—the consolation of the friends and relatives of the deceased, the reminding of those present of their own mortality and the awesome judgment that awaits the soul upon its separation from the body. This latter, and largely adventitious, theme became prominent in the later Middle Ages when the Dies Irae was introduced; black vestments and mournful music gave the whole ceremony a lugubrious solemnity. In the 15th and 16th cent. some reaction to this appeared as the Mass of the Angels, said in white vestments, began to be used at the funerals of children, but this mitigation of the gloomier rite provided a liturgy that still fell far short of expressing the true meaning of the occasion. Vatican Council II called for a revision of the burial rite in general and for a special Mass for the burial of children (Vat II SacLit 81–82). The adoption in 1919 of the 5th cent. Mozarabic preface for the dead was a sounder step toward the correction of the medieval view of this Mass. For the late revision of the burial rite and the Mass for the dead called for by Vat II Sac Lit 81–82, and in effect since 1971, see International Committee on English in the Liturgy, tr., *Rite of Funerals* (1971); also, *FUNERAL RITE. According to present legislation, the funeral Mass itself ranks as most important of the Masses celebrated for the dead, and this may be celebrated on any day with the exception of solemnities that are holy days of obligation, and the Sundays of the Advent, Lent, and Easter season. Other Masses for the dead are permitted on obligatory memorials (apart from Ash Wednesday and Holy Week), but only on these occasions: on first learning of a death, on the occasion of final burial, and on the first anniversary of death. Other Masses for the dead are permitted when votive Masses are permitted, but only if the Masses are actually applied to the dead. (*Sacramentary* of 1974, "General Instructions of the Roman Missal," ch. 8, nn. 336–337). BIBLIOGRAPHY: A. C. Rush, *Death and Burial in Christian Antiquity* (1941); *Reforming the Rites of Death* (*Concilium*, v. 32, ed. J. Wagner, 1968).

[N. KOLLAR; P. K. MEAGHER]

DEAD, PRAYERS FOR THE. From apostolic times the Church has cherished the belief that the souls of the departed can be helped by the prayers of the living. In this sense 2 Macc 12.39–45 is conclusive: after a battle, Judas had expiatory sacrifices offered for the slain Jewish soldiers, "that the sin they had committed [against the prescription of Dt 7.25] might be wholly blotted out". Patristically, this conviction has always been bound up with the doctrine of *purgatory; Clement of Alexandria in 208 recommended prayers for the dead (*Strom.* 7.12.18; PG 9:508). In 337 Constantine the Great died and prayers were offered for him by the Church (Eusebius, *Vita Constantini* 4.71; PG 20:1225). More specifically, it is the Eucharistic Sacrifice that was offered for the dead (Cyril of Jerusalem, *Catech.* 23.9; PG 33:1115) with the certainty that this is done "by a special dispensation of the Holy Spirit" (Chrysostom, Hom. 21 in Ac. 4; PG 60:170). Oriental liturgies, both Jacobite and Ethiopian, testify to the same

practice, and at the reunion Council of Florence (1439) the belief was firmly held by both sides, East and West (see D 1304). The doctrine was finally sanctioned by the Council of Trent in 1563 (D 1820), which, however, banned as superstitious the custom of offering for the dead a fixed number of Masses (see *Conc. trid.* 8:963); Gregorian Masses were not included in the ban.

The theological basis of the doctrine is the communion of saints, understood originally as a living communion in holy things rather than of holy persons. The living and the dead are all members of the same Church with the possibility of exercising a mutual salutary influence. If purgatory is but a momentary occurrence of intense purification accomplished either by the ''fire'' of the indwelling Spirit or by an encounter with the risen Christ, then in virtue of the prayers of the living Church God may perform this work of purification more briefly or less painfully than he would otherwise (Christological aspect of the question). Besides, the prayers of the living can have as their effect an increase in the voluntary acceptance, out of love permeated by unshakable hope, of the purifying sufferings imposed on the departed soul, this acceptance rendering the work of purification easier (anthropological aspect). Consequently, both the risen Christ and the soul can be influenced by the prayers of the living Church. The fact that this ecclesiastical supplication usually takes place after the person's death offers no special difficulty: God's foreknowledge applies these future prayers to the dying, whose purification is therefore affected by the Church's intercession. Purgatory and suffrages for the dead are essentially ecclesial realities. BIBLIOGRAPHY: E. Brisbois, "Durée du purgatoire et les suffrages pour les défunts," NRT 81 (1959) 838–845.

[A. M. BERMEJO]

DEAD, WORSHIP OF THE, the historically ambivalent forms of interaction with and commemoration of the dead found in most cultures and religions. Such interaction may be said to be positive when help is extended to the dead by providing an adequate tomb, effective rituals, food offerings, prayers, and the observance of mourning periods. It is negative when the dead, like other spirits, ghosts, and demons with whom they often merge, are considered a threat to the living. In this case rituals, offerings, prayers, and magical techniques are aimed at restraining the dead from acts of destruction and revenge. Often both attitudes coexist side by side. Worship of the dead was prevalent in those primitive societies which engaged in sun-worship since they believed that the sun carried the dead into the underworld at sunset and could restore them to the light at dawn. Its complexity seems to grow with both economical and social differentiation. In general it is less developed among gatherers and hunters. It becomes very complex among the sedentary cultures of planters, for whom the identity of the village, the fertility of the field, and their magico-religious interpretation are in many respects substantialized in the mystique of birth and death and the rituals that refer to them. Finally it culminates in archaic high cultures with their emphasis on social status as expressed in the burial customs such as existed in Ancient Egypt, China, America, and some of the ancient African kingdoms. In ancient Greece, food offerings were laid at a crossroad every month for Hecate, the goddess of the underworld, and for the ghosts of those who could not rest in their graves. In the OT, traces remain of sacrifices offered to or for the dead, and of the practice of furnishing them with food even though this was condemned by official Judaism (Dt 26.14). BIBLIOGRAPHY: W. Crooke, Hastings ERE 4:479–484; J. G. Frazer, *Belief in Immortality and the Worship of the Dead* (3 v., 1913–24); *idem, Fear of the Dead in Primitive Religion* (3 v., 1933–36); R. T. Christiansen, *Dead and the Living* (1946). *ANCESTOR WORSHIP.

[W. DUPRÉ]

DEAD SEA, a salt lake located at the S end of the Jordan valley, its N tip lying slightly less than 18 miles E of Jerusalem. The surface of the lake averages 1,274 feet lower than the Mediterranean, making it the lowest spot on the surface of the earth. The N part of the lake reaches a depth of 1,300 feet, but in much of the S part the depth is no greater than 3 feet. The lake is fed chiefly by the Jordan River; its waters have no access to the sea, being hemmed in by high mountains to the S, yet the volume of its waters is fairly constant because evaporation matches the intake of new waters. The water is extremely saline, far more than ocean water. Two small streams of the W shore form a fertile oasis, within which the community of Qumran lived in natural caves. There the Dead Sea Scrolls were discovered. Some believe the area in which the Dead Sea is located to have been the site of the ancient cities of Sodom and Gomorrah.

[P. K. MEAGHER]

DEAD SEA SCROLLS, MSS discovered in caves near *Qumran. The discovery occurred by accident when in 1947 a Ta'amireh Bedouin, wishing to flush one of his flock from a cave, threw a rock and heard the sound of breaking pottery. He had struck on the tall jars in which the Scrolls had been stored. His fellow tribesmen attempted to sell the first Scroll through an antiquities dealer in Bethlehem. Eventually six additional large Scrolls turned up from the same cave, and the identification was made only after certain mistakes and difficulties. Three of these Scrolls were purchased by F. L. Sukenik for the Hebrew Univ. and taken into what became the State of Israel just as the 1947 war broke out. Four other MSS were smuggled by Mar Samuel to the U.S., put up for sale, and purchased for the State of Israel. This put the seven major Scrolls in the possession of the Jewish State. Once the identification had been made and the probable antiquity of the Scrolls became known, the scroll-hunt was on. This resulted in countless finds, and every cave in the Qumran area was systematically combed by many archeologists, often preceded in their

work by Bedouins, who sold numerous fragments to antiquities dealers or often directly to R. de Vaux. Discoveries have since been made at least three other sites on the W side of the Dead Sea: Khirbet Mird, Wadi Murabba'at, and the famous hill-fortress, Masada. However, the discoveries at Mird and Murabba'at have nothing directly to do with Qumran material. The term "Dead Sea Scrolls" was given to the early MSS and has more or less remained; it is misleading, however, and the title used on the inventory volumes, *Discoveries in the Judaean Desert,* is much more exact. Prior to the 1967 Israel-Jordan war, the seven major Scrolls and the Masada fragments belonged to the State of Israel, while thousands of fragments from caves 2–11 (for the most part) were housed in the Jordanian Rockefeller Museum just outside and NE of the walled city of Jerusalem. Their present whereabouts (1977) is not generally known.

From Cave I there are the following major Scrolls, the first six in Hebrew: a complete Is MS; a second fragmentary Is MS; a sectarian commentary on Hab 1–2; the *Manual of Discipline,* giving a fairly good account of the rules of the *Qumran community; a number of thanksgiving hymns, very similar in style to some of the psalms; a document called *The War between the Sons of Light and the Sons of Darkness,* a description of something like an apocalyptic war; and a midrash in Aramaic on some parts of Gen, commonly called the *Genesis Apocryphon.* From the other caves countless fragments were found. These include parts of every book of the Hebrew Bible with the exception of Esther. Some of the apocrypha (called deuterocanonical books by RCs) are also represented in the finds, e.g., parts of Job and Sirach. Countless fragments of the pseudepigrapha (called by RCs apocrypha or apocryphal books) also turned up, e.g., Jubilees, Enoch, Testament of the Twelve Patriarchs, and the Damascus Document (the Zadokite Fragment, which had been found in Cairo in the late 19th century). This latter document is now thought to be from Qumran. A supplementary, and apparently later, *Rule of the Community* was also discovered, and there were a number of sectarian commentaries. One of the documents, the letters of which were hammered into copper, contains a list of treasure sites; few scholars took them seriously, though a former editor of Scroll material organized a party to excavate the sites he could identify. The project was without success and damaged some otherwise important archeological sites.

Since some of the MSS were biblical and their antiquity was a question of great importance, much attention was given to dating these Scrolls. This was done by epigraphy, by study of the type of pottery in which they were found, together with other archeological indications, and finally by use of the carbon 14 test on the linen wrappers that had been placed around each Scroll in Cave I. Most scholars rallied to the view that the Scrolls had been copied out prior to, or around, the time of Christ. The average date assigned was 33 A.D., with a possible variation of 100 years either way.

This would make the MSS about 1,000 years older than the oldest pre-Qumran Hebrew MSS of the Bible. In some cases considerable light has been thrown on the Hebrew text itself, on the Hebrew *Vorlage* used by the LXX translators, and on countless smaller questions regarding individual readings. The nonbiblical documents are extremely valuable for the insights they give us into the religious outlook during the so-called inter-Testamental period. Even the sectarian commentaries have some value, though the exegesis is often fanciful. In 1967 an important sectarian scroll was obtained by Israeli archeologist, Yigael Yadin; it is the largest scroll of all the Qumran finds and contains a divinely revealed description of the future ideal Temple and regulations for its governance. This *Temple Scroll*'s publication has been projected for 1977. Although much other material remains to be edited and published, the Dead Sea Scrolls have contributed greatly to our knowledge of the Bible. BIBLIOGRAPHY: F. M. Cross, *Ancient Library of Qumran and Modern Biblical Studies* (1961).

[I. HUNT]

DEADLY SINS, SEVEN, the ordinary English term for what Catholic theology calls the *capital sins. BIBLIOGRAPHY: OED 2:113; 3:62.

[U. VOLL]

DEAF, EDUCATION OF THE, rehabilitation of those suffering from partial or total hearing loss either from birth or acquired later by accident or illness. Not only the congenitally deaf and those whose hearing loss dates from early childhood, who are consequently unable to speak (deaf-mutes), but those also whose deafness was acquired after the age of 5 and who thus have normal speech or at least some language patterns, require special education. Since total and partial deafness renders oral communication difficult, for many centuries before and after Christ, those so afflicted were considered mentally retarded and uneducable. Although Ven. Bede (*c.*673–735) makes passing mention of the cure of a deaf-mute, it was not until the 16th cent. that a Spanish Benedictine monk, Pedro Ponce de León, devised a successful method of teaching deaf children to speak, read, write, and calculate. The first book on educating the deaf, by Juan Pablo Bonet, appeared in Madrid in 1620; and in 1769, Abbé Charles-Michel de l'Épée, originator of a systematic sign language, opened the first free school in Paris. De l'Épée's manual method strongly influenced T. H. Gallaudet, founder of the first U.S. public school for the deaf in Hartford, Conn., for whom Gallaudet College, Washington, D.C., is named. In the 20th cent., oralism, or lip-reading and speech training, largely replaced the manual method in public, private, and denominational institutions, counting among its professional advocates the Sisters of St. Joseph of Carondelet, St. Louis, Mo.; Alexander Graham Bell; Max A. Goldstein, founder of the Central Institute for the Deaf, St. Louis, Mo.; and Sarah Fuller, organizer of day schools for the deaf. The International Catholic Deaf Association (ICDA), concerned with the spiritual as well as physical needs of the deaf, coordinates the activities of priests, brothers, and laymen from its headquarters in Brooklyn, N.Y. BIBLIOGRAPHY: R. E. Bender, *Conquest of Deafness* (1960); E. H. Behrmann, "Hearing Impaired," *Catholic Special Education* (1971) 69–92; S. E. Ryan, *Role of the Sisters of St. Joseph in the Education of the Deaf* (1956).

[M. B. MURPHY]

DEAF ASSOCIATION, INTERNATIONAL CATHOLIC, see INTERNATIONAL CATHOLIC DEAF ASSOCIATION.

DEAN (Lat. *decem,* ten), an official who enjoys authority less than that of bp. or abbot. In monastic orders a dean was in charge of each 10 monks. The senior dean was in charge of the monastery in the absence of the abbot or provost. In cathedral chapters, the dean is in charge of the physical property and ritual. In the C of E cathedral deans exercise considerable authority apart from the bishop. In the RC Church, the chapter of the cathedral elects the dean, subject to the approval of the bishop. The dean of the College of Cardinals (since 1965 chosen by election) presides in the absence of the pope and at the coronation of a new pope. In institutions of higher learning the dean usually stands in second position to the president.

[J. R. AHERNE]

DEAN, RURAL (Vicar forane), in the RC Church the title of a priest appointed by the bishop to aid him in administering a portion or district in his diocese. Although similar forms of this office had existed in earlier centuries, in its present form it was established (1565) by St. Charles Borromeo in Milan, whence it spread to other parts of the world. The precise function of rural deans varies somewhat from place to place, but in general it involves the duty of supervising the activities of the diocesan clergy engaged in parish work within the boundaries of his deanery, visiting the different parishes, ascertaining the fidelity of the clergy in the fulfillment of their obligations, and reporting annually to the bishop upon the conditions he has found to exist in the different parishes of his jurisdiction. Current legislation concerning rural deans may be found in CIC c. 131; cc. 445–450 and in ClerSanct cc. 483–488.

[P. K. MEAGHER]

DEAN OF THE SACRED COLLEGE, see CARDINAL DEAN.

DE ANDREA, MIGUEL (1877–1960) bp., sociologist. Ordained in 1899 he was a pastoral figure and promoter of social justice all his life. Made a titular bp. in 1919 he was founder of the Argentine Popular Union and the House for Working Women. Proposed for abp. of Buenos Aires, he was passed over for reasons never made public, an omission that caused much friction in the Argentine Church. He worked ceaselessly for improved labor conditions, workmen's compensation, low-cost housing and other social projects. BIBLIOGRAPHY: A. Carranza, *Itinerario de monseñor de Andrea* (1957).

[J. R. AHERNE]

DEASE, MARY TERESA, MOTHER (1820–89), missionary; born in Dublin, Ireland. Following her profession in the Institute of the Blessed Virgin Mary at Rathfarnham, she became a pioneer missionary in 1847 to Toronto, Canada. Because of the ill effects of climate, poverty, and a sense of insecurity, three of the missionary sisters succumbed within two years of their arrival in Toronto. Mother Teresa became superior and took the responsibility of the first house founded in America. Later she was made superior general and lived to see her institute spread through many cities of Ontario and Illinois.

[R. A. TODD]

DEATH, HASTENING OF, the medico-moral problem concerning the natural moral obligation to preserve life and the proscription in the Decalogue, "Thou shalt not kill." Suicide or homicide are intrinsically immoral, actions contrary to both natural and divine law. The problem of an action hastening death, or correlatively omission of a course of action that prolongs life, arises most urgently in the case of a certainly terminal illness or an irreversible damage from injury. A patient, a patient's relatives, or the attending medical experts have as a general moral norm that no direct action to induce death is morally justifiable (see EUTHANASIA). In all cases suicide and homicide are infringements on God's supreme dominion over life, and on society's good which includes the respect and care for the life of every member. The thornier problem concerns rather the omission of procedures that prolong life, an omission, therefore, that hastens death. The generally recognized principle is simple to state: all concerned are obliged to take the ordinary means required to preserve life. The moral dilemma arises, however, in judging between the ordinary and the extraordinary. The measure of both is relative. The general community of laymen, the legal profession, and the medical profession—each has a different standard, thus an ethical or moral obligation that may differ accordingly. A medical procedure of proven effectiveness and ready availability may oblige a physician to its use in virtue of his professional oath. A judge may be obliged to define ordinary means of preserving life on the basis of legal precedent or on expert medical opinion. Such standards, however, may not be those to which a patient or a patient's family (in the case of unconsciousness or incapacity) must look for moral guidance. Medical procedures, simply because they are technologically sophisticated, may be extraordinary means, no matter how readily available. Medical means that are costly, therefore work serious hardship, may thereby be extraordinary. Medical procedures that do more than is required of a person to preserve his life may thereby be extraordinary. The meaning of life does include the quality of life; it means more than the physical fact of a heart beat or brain wave. From the Christian point of view, life is an imitation of Christ and the process of dying, a part of that life, as is the opportunity to accept death. A medical procedure that simply suspends the process and delays death by mere technology may also be an extraordinary means. The moral measure must ultimately be not technology but general, human consensus. Conflict of judgment and obligation may arise between professional and layman. The physician is radically assisting the patient to fulfill an obligation from God and before God; the patient's judgment should have precedence.

[T. C. O'BRIEN]

DEATH, THEOLOGY OF. The Paschal Mystery, Christ's Passion, death, and Resurrection, is the criterion of a Christian theology of death. Such a theology can recognize considerations abstractly antecedent to the concrete history of salvation. Thus death and physical deterioration are natural consequences of human nature's material composition, the union of soul with body. There is, as well, a possibility to demonstrate by philosophical reasoning the immortality of the *soul on the basis of its having a level of existence and activity transcending the bodily level. The soul's manner of separated existence and final, natural destiny can be speculated to be a state of imperfect survival (since the connatural condition of the soul is to be united with the body) and to be a state of reward or punishment corresponding to a person's relationship to the First Cause and Final End of all creation. There can also be a recognition that innate in human nature is a natural *desire to see God and correspondingly a natural dread of death not simply as a physical phenomenon, but as it looms in spite of philosophical arguments for immortality, as the absurd negation of personal existence, consciousness, and desire for transcendence. Christian theology, however, must see such considerations as abstractions, displaced by the concrete divine economy of salvation revealed in Jesus Christ. The Paschal Mystery reveals that dying and death are consequences of sin; they are in themselves not any longer natural consequences of materiality but divine punishments, punitive evils that occur because of sin that deprives human nature of grace, and of immortality as a gift consequent upon grace (ThAq ST 1a2ae, 85. 5 & 6; see ORIGINAL SIN). Punishment by definition is inflicted against the will of the one punished. In Christ because of his loving acceptance of his Passion and death, dying and death ceased to be purely punitive and became expiatory, atoning; this is his first victory over sin: his power to love the Father was the power to lay down the life that no one took from him, the power to lay it down and to take it up again (Jn 10.17–18). Christ's second victory over sin is his Resurrection, his humanity rising, no longer subject to suffering or death. Christ's way of dying and his Resurrection are the model and the source of the Christian's way of living and dying. The symbolism and effectiveness of baptism mean that the recipient becomes as one passing through Christ's own death and Resurrection (ThAq ST 3a, 69.2 & ad 1). Baptism makes Christ's death and Resurrection occur in and for the baptized; the person's living and dying are meant to express a personal ratification of that reality, a personal imitation of Christ. None of the evils to which human nature is subject in consequence of sin are purely punitive for the Christian who in faith and charity lives in imitation of Christ, appropriates the power of Christ to lay down his life and to take it up again. To be pure punishments these evils would be endured involuntarily, the will of the sufferer would be in rebellion against them. But by the power of Christ's death and Resurrection the Christian also accepts these ills with loving trust in the Father, and they become expiatory. Dying and death are not events outside the pattern of life, putting an absurd negation to life's hopes and concerns; they are part of each person's plan of salvation, even as they are part of Christ's way of saving. His acceptance of the Father's will merits his own Resurrection and enables the Christian who imitates him to merit a share in that Resurrection. The process of salvation will be complete when, passing through death in charity, each person attains the complete restoration of even bodily immortality in the final resurrection (ThAq ST 3a, 69.3). Theology can trace out such general lines that mark the mystery of death because of the Paschal Mystery. The way that those lines are traced in any individual's life is another issue. The mystery places before each person a need for faith in the particularity, the individualness of the Father's loving care for each. Ideally the process of death and dying should be an imitation of Christ continuous with a life lived in fulfillment of the Christ-like identity given in baptism. A life lived in sinful denial of that identity does not give promise of a final imitation of Christ. Yet the ways of the Father's care are of almost infinite variety. Deathbed conversions do occur. Conversely the ideal pattern of a Christian life does go awry; crises of faith and of hope loom to torment individuals. Whether in an instant or over a long, darkened period, the opportunity for personal and effective acceptance of dying and of death is given in the Father's mysterious ways; Christ's cry of abandonment preceded his final commendation of his spirit to the Father. The one certainty is that for every person the Paschal Mystery stands always as the power to die with Christ and to rise with him. BIBLIOGRAPHY: ThAq ST (Lat-Eng; v. 27, *Effects of Sin*, ed. T. C. O'Brien) app. 1.

[T. C. O'BRIEN]

DEATH OF GOD, a theme given prominence in modern thought by F. Nietzsche (1844–1900), for whom it was "an attempt at a diagnosis of contemporary civilization, not a metaphysical speculation about ultimate reality" (W. Kaufmann, *Nietzsche* [1956], 78). The concept had been used earlier, e.g., by Hegel; it is even found in primitive myths of dying and rising gods. In Christian theology the death of Christ is, from one standpoint, the death of God; but the doctrine of the Trinity safeguards against any thought that God ceased to exist. The phrase became the theme of a popular movement of *radical theology in the U.S. in the 1960s, particularly through the writings of T. Altizer and W. Hamilton. The concept did not achieve clear definition but seemed to express a conviction that God had ceased to be an effective force in modern life. This cessation was regarded by its advocates as an event of positive value, releasing man from religious and other structures of the past for a new freedom in the future. The idea was combined with a shift of emphasis from worshiping God to following Jesus and from faith to love. It was also connected with views derived from the prison writings of D. *Bonhoeffer (1906–45), including that of the "world come of age." It became almost a slogan for a time through publicity in the popular press but failed to gain significant support among theologians. BIBLIOGRAPHY: T. Altizer and W. Hamilton, *Radical Theology and the Death of God* (1966).

[T. EARLY]

DEATH AGONY, see AGONY OF DEATH.

DEATH-WISH, or instinct, a term in later Freudian literature for a desire conflicting with the more basic libidinal drive (Eros) and supposedly tending toward death (Thanatos). The explanatory hypothesis for the phenomenon argued that this aggressive instinct, externally directed, was the origin of violence (sadism), but when directed inward was suicidal (masochism). Freud attempted a justification of this rather limited and confused theory with generalizations on the tendency for living matter to return to an inanimate state. More germane to the observed phenomenon was another of his notions that organic response to stimuli seemed directed to their removal and are thus "fulfilled" in unconsciousness or the synthetic death of sleep. Suicidal or self-destructive tendencies are all too real; Freudian theory about them has been embarrassing to his disciples, since some of its elements are highly arguable and basically inconsistent with the essence of his general theory on human motivation. Therefore, while psychiatrists continue to encounter the self-punishing and self-hating impulses, most do not accept the death-wish as a valid account of the aggressive drive.

[M. E. STOCK]

DEBORAH (from the Heb. meaning "honeybee"), a feminine name in the Old Testament. (1) The nurse of Rebecca who died just below Bethel and was buried beneath the oak, which came to be called the Oak of Tears (Gen 24.59; 35.8). (2) A judge in Israel, the wife of Lappidoth who rendered decisions in disputes of Israelites, she, a prophetess, was chosen by Yahweh to summon Barak of Naphtali to wage a holy war against Sisera, the commander of Jabin's army. Barak refused to execute the orders of

Yahweh unless D. accompanied him into battle, so she marched with him. She chose the day of battle and assured Barak that Yahweh was marching ahead of him into battle. Israel annihilated the army of Sisera, but, in accord with D.'s prophecy, the general of the enemy host was slain by a woman, Jael (Jg ch. 4–5). BIBLIOGRAPHY: De Vaux AncIsr 261.

[J. A. PIERCE]

DEBORAH, CANTICLE OF, the fifth ch. of Jg, a very early and powerful piece of Hebrew poetry celebrating the victory of Yahweh in his holy war against the army of Jabin of Cedes which was commanded by Sisera. It is generally conceded that the poem is almost contemporary with the event (c.1100 B.C.). Though it is called the Canticle of Deborah, it almost certainly was not composed by her or sung by her alone. Both Deborah and Barak are directly addressed in the poem (v. 12). Deborah is hailed as a "mother in Israel," who summoned the almost weaponless Israelites to wage the holy war against the chariots of Sisera. Six of the ten northern tribes answered her summons and are honored in the canticle. The canticle with a haunting rhythm proclaims both the hospitality of Jael toward Sisera and her courage in slaying him by driving a tent peg through his temple. Throughout the canticle it is evident that the victory belongs to Yahweh, who gives strength to those who love him. BIBLIOGRAPHY: W. F. Albright, *Song of Deborah in the Light of Archaeology,* BASOR 62 (1936) 26–31, as well as ch. 4–5 of Jg.

[J. A. PIERCE]

DEBRUYNE, DONATIEN (1871–1935), textual critic. D. served on the Pontifical Vulgate Commission, was subprior of the Benedictine Abbey of Maredsous (1921–25), and an editor of the *Revue Bénédictine* (1921–35). He did extensive work in evaluating and cataloguing early Christian MSS, esp. the Vulgate and *Vetus Latina* versions of the Bible. BIBLIOGRAPHY: M. Strange, NCE 4:697–698.

[T. M. MCFADDEN]

DEBT, something owed *(debitum)* to another in *justice. The term has a general meaning in moral theology that is coextensive with all the forms of the virtue of justice; and a restricted meaning, corresponding to general English usage, in the area of commutative justice. The general meaning describes the moral object—an action or a thing—that justice requires a person to respect in his dealings with others. Such actions or things are owed because they belong to another, are the right of another (ThAq ST 2a2ae.57.1). Accordingly as the debt arises from the nature of things or from the determination of positive law or private contract, the debt honored by justice is either a natural debt or a legal debt (ThAq, *In Ethic.*VIII, lect.13). In a second sense, a "legal debt" is contrasted with a "moral debt" in order to distinguish justice in its narrowest sense, from virtues allied to it. Then legal debt stands for anything owed according to

an exactly determinable measure or equality. A moral debt is less determinate: either because it is not fully equitable, as with the virtues of *religion, filial *piety, respect for benefactors; or because it is not calculable, but shaped by circumstances and sensitivity to the demands of virtue and decency, as in the case of truthfulness, friendliness or generosity. In its narrow sense a debt means money or its equivalent owed to another in commutative justice. The debt may arise out of a contract or its equivalent; or on the basis of damage done, which the debtor must compensate. The debt must be discharged according to the exact amount owed; or in part if payment of the whole is impossible. Circumstances may at times allow deferment of payment, but the obligation remains; as long as it is unjustly not honored, the debtor is the unjust *possessor of what belongs to another. Civil law that may cancel debts or suspend them, does not necessarily cancel the moral obligation; *bankruptcy laws, however, are a special case. BIBLIOGRAPHY: ThAq ST (Lat-Eng v. 41, ed. T. C. O'Brien) app. 1.

[T. C. O'BRIEN]

DEBUSSY, CLAUDE ACHILLE (1882–1918), composer. Born in France, D. studied piano at the Paris Conservatory and for 3 years was in the entourage of Madame von Meck (the "beloved friend" of Tchaikovsky) as a pianist. After years of struggle to win the *Prix de Rome,* D. achieved success with *L'Enfant prodigue* in 1884. The influence of the Symbolist poets and Impressionist painters was profound on D. and he wrote music that matched their spirit. In Paris again (1887–88) he submitted to the Academy the haunting musical composition for voice and orchestra, *La Damoiselle élue,* based on Dante Rosetti's poem, *The Blessed Damozel.* In the work, much of D.'s innovative musical approach is foreshadowed. In 1894, appeared *Prélude à l'aprés-midi d'un faune,* inspired by a poem of Mallarmé. There followed perhaps D.'s most characteristic work, *Nocturnes: Nuages, Fêtes et Sirènes* that remain popular favorites today. His *Pélleas et Mélisande,* based on the play by Maeterlinck, and first performed in Paris in 1902, is not only a splendid creation but a sturdy survivor among operas performed. In 1903 D. completed *La Mer,* an orchestral composition revealing the epitome of Impressionism. Wagnerian influence is apparent in *Le Martyre de Saint-Sébastien* (based on G. D'Annunzio's "mystery" play). In his last years D. devoted his talents to a series of piano compositions (e.g., *Acute études* 1915) and three sonatas. D. was a man of volatile character and numerous love affairs; he made historic contributions to the development of music and had great influence on younger composers.

[J. R. AHERNE]

DECADE, a group or division of ten. In the religious sense, the most common meaning of decade is a 15th part of the Rosary consisting of the recitation of 1 Our Father and

10 Hail Marys during which one meditates on 1 of the 15 mysteries.

[M. T. REILLY]

DÉCADI, CULT OF, a patriotic cult observed every ten days in the calendar of the French Republic, an attempt to substitute the Christian Sunday for a naturalistic, nonreligious service. The *Décadi* was a ceremonial with bonfires, chants, and imprecations prescribed for certain feasts, as, for example, youth, age, knowledge. In 1797 the Second Directory promulgated the *Décadi* as the national official cult. Penal legislation insisted on the suspension of court and government business, schools, factories, and shops. On the *Décadi* alone could marriages be solemnized. Many bishops suffered imprisonment and death for resisting the suppression of Sunday observance and that of Christian marriage. Napoleon reopened the closed churches in 1799 and officially dissolved the cult in 1805.

[K. O'NEILL]

DECALOGUE, see COMMANDMENTS, TEN.

DECAPOLIS (Gr. *deka*, 10; *polis*, city), confederation of 10 predominantly Hellenistic cities and their environs which was part of the Roman Province of Syria organized by Pompey in 63 B.C. The original 10 were Abila, Canath, Damascus, Dion, Gadara, Gerasa, Hippos, Pella, Philadelphia, and Scythopolis. Pliny (5,18) enumerates Raphana among the ten and drops Abila. All but one of these cities were east of the Jordan river; only Scythopolis was west of the Jordan. Each of the cities, which enjoyed a good deal of autonomy, had its own local government. Although originally there were 10 cities in the confederation, there was some variance in the number at different periods before the disintegration of the Decapolis at the beginning of the 2d cent. of the Christian Era. The Decapolis and its cities are mentioned in the NT in Mt 4.25: "Large crowds followed him, coming from . . . the Decapolis . . ."; in Mk 5.20 in the cure of the man possessed by "legion" and again in Mk 7.31: "he went . . . right through the Decapolis region." BIBLIOGRAPHY: Abel GéogrPal 2:145ff.

[J. A. PIERCE]

DECEIT, the act, habit, or practice of taking advantage of the simplicity of others for fraudulent or dishonest purposes. It generally implies a deliberate intention to delude or to lead another into error from which the deceiver expects to derive some advantage to himself. Of its nature it stands opposed to the virtue of veracity, and also to justice and honesty when it is employed to gain unfair advantage over another in transaction.

[P. K. MEAGHER]

DECHAMPS, ÉTIENNE (1613–1701), anti-Jansenist controversialist. A native of Bourges and a Jesuit from 1630, D. taught at various schools but won renown rather as an anti-Jansenist than as a teacher. Under the pseudonym of Antoine Richard he published his *Defensio censurae s. facultatis parisiensis . . . seu Disputatio theologica de libero arbitrio* (1645). His most important work, *De haeresi janseniana . . .* (1654) was a justification of Innocent X's condemnation of the five propositions extracted from the *Augustinus (D 2001–05). In his *Quaestio facti . . .* (1659) he defended *probabalism against *Les Provinciales* of *Pascal, and took issue with P. *Quesnel. BIBLIOGRAPHY: Sommervogel 2:1863–69; J. Brucker, DTC 4:176–178.

[T. C. O'BRIEN]

DECHAMPS, VICTOR AUGUSTE (1810–83), Belgian Redemptorist, theologian, and churchman. He became a Redemptorist after his ordination (1835), taught in the congregation's scholasticate, 1836–40, the period in which he developed his "method of Providence" for apologetics. The method fixed as the motive of credibility the correlation between human need of the divine and the objective reality of the Church, with is marks of divine origin. After being active in Redemptorist government and apostolate, D. was named bp. of Namur (1865), then of Malines (1867). At Vatican Council I he was a prominent Infallibilist and contributor to the formulation of the constitution *De fide catholica*. A cardinal from 1875, he nominated D. *Mercier for the professorship of Thomistic studies at Louvain. On his apologetic method he published: *Entretiens sur la démonstration de la foi* (1856); *Lettres théologiques* (1861); *La Question religieuse* (2 v., 1861). BIBLIOGRAPHY: M. Becqué, *Le Cardinal Dechamps* (2 v., 1956).

[T. C. O'BRIEN]

DE CHIRICO, GIORGIO (1888–   ), metaphysical painter. Born of Italian parents in Greece, D. studied the Quattrocento masters in Italy (1905) and was influenced by Böcklin when in Munich (1909). Of visionary temperament C. painted in Florence (1910) unique and compelling panels juxtaposing elements of enigmatic relationship in haunting, airless, shadow-ridden spaces intensified by sharp perspectives which strongly influenced the surrealists and established C. as one of the most original artists of his time (*The Melancholy and Mystery of a Street*, 1914). After an impressive metaphysical period (1919–25). C.'s work was characterized by an uninspired academic performance. BIBLIOGRAPHY: J. T. Soby, *Giorgio de Chirico* (1955).

[M. J. DALY]

DECIUS, (C. Messius Quintus Traianus Decius; *c.*201–251), **ROMAN EMPEROR** from 249. Although D. was a native of Pannonia, he was of Etruscan descent and probably of a senatorial family. After being prefect of Rome, he was sent by the Emperor Philip the Arab to command the armies on the Danube. In the summer of 249 he was proclaimed emperor by his troops against his own wishes. He defeated Philip near Verona in September of that same year, was accepted by the senate, and assumed the surname of Trajan. He engaged in extensive road building, created a new financial office, and attempted to revive the old state religion, a measure that led to a general persecution of the Christians. He perished in a swamp after being defeated by the Goths near Abrittus in the Dobruja. BIBLIOGRAPHY: K. Wittig, PW 15:1244–84.

[M. J. COSTELLOE]

DECIUS, PERSECUTION OF. In Dec. 249 or Jan. 250, the Emperor Decius began the first general persecution of the Christians in the Roman Empire. Prior to this the persecutions had been of a local or sporadic character or had been directed at a particular class such as the catechumens. Decius' edict, which aimed at attaining a greater unity within the state and appeasing the neglected pagan gods, provided for the establishment of commissions throughout the empire before which all would have to present themselves and perform some sacrificial rite, the pouring out of a libation before, or offering of incense to, the statues of the gods, or the tasting of the flesh of sacrificed victims. Those who obeyed were given *libelli,* certificates indicating their compliance with the decree. Though the text of Decius' original edict is no longer extant, 43 of these *libelli* dating from June 12 to July 15, 250, have been discovered in Egypt. The first known victim of the persecution was Pope St. *Fabian, who was put to death in Jan. 250. Others who went into exile or were tortured or put to death at this time were St. *Cyprian of Carthage, *Dionysius of Alexandria, *Gregory Thaumaturgus, Alexander of Jerusalem, Babylus of Antioch, Origen, Pionius of Smyrna, and Carpus, Papylus, and Agathonice of Pergamum. The violence of the persecution after years of peace caught the Christians by surprise. Many complied with the imperial edict or obtained a certificate to that effect through bribery. The reconciliation of the lapsed created severe conflicts within the Church in Rome and Carthage and contributed to the *Novatian schism. BIBLIOGRAPHY: H. Leclercq, DACL 14:568; K. Gross, RAC 3:618–629.

[M. J. COSTELLOE]

DECLARATION, ROYAL, see ROYAL DECLARATION.

DECLARATION AND ADDRESS, a document of the Christian Association of Washington, Pa., "agreed upon and ordered to be printed," Sept. 7, 1809, stating the particular beliefs and early practices of the Churches variously known as Disciples of Christ, Christian Churches, the Christian Church, and Churches of Christ. The printed document has 56 pages of some 500 words each. The Declaration proposes "that we form ourselves into a religious association . . . for the sole purpose of promoting simple evangelical Christianity, free from all mixture of human opinions and inventions of men." The Address opens with the assertion that "the church of Christ on earth is essentially, intentionally and constitutionally one." Rejecting creeds as mere human formulas, it states further that "noth-

ing ought to be inculcated upon Christians as articles of faith, nor required of them as terms of communion but what is expressly taught and enjoined upon them in the word of God." An Appendix tries to make it clear that "we have no intention to interfere, either directly or indirectly, with the peace and order of the settled churches . . . or, by endeavouring to erect churches out of churches—to distract and divide congregations." The unity it advocated, at a moment when the leader of the Christian Association, T. *Campbell, had renounced the authority of his *presbytery and of the Pennsylvania Synod of the Seceder Presbyterian Church, was not achieved. The Association became the Brush Run Church in 1811. BIBLIOGRAPHY: W. E. Garrison and A. T. DeGroot, *Disciples of Christ: A History* (rev. ed., 1958) 145–161; Mayer RB 381–382; Schaff Creeds 1:931–933.

[H. E. SHORT]

DECLARATION OF BREDA, the assurances given by King Charles II of England at Breda in Holland, April 4–14, 1660, before the *Restoration; the granting of "liberty to tender consciences" was included.

[T. C. O'BRIEN]

DECLARATION OF FAITH AND ORDER (Congregational Union of England and Wales), a statement adopted at the second General Meeting of the Congregational Union of England and Wales in 1833. The *Declaration of the Faith, Church Order, and Discipline of the Congregational, or Independent Churches,* which arose from a paper to the constituting Meeting of the Union in 1832 and was circulated to the Churches, consisted of seven Preliminary Notes, twenty Principles of Religion, and thirteen Principles of Church Order and Discipline. Churches accepted the Declaration because it was not considered authoritative but simply a statement, for general information, of what was commonly believed and accepted among Congregationalists.

[R. F. G. CALDER]

DECLARATION OF NULLITY, the official pronouncement that a putative marriage was not a true, Christian marriage at all. The declaration is made by the Roman Rota or by a diocesan tribunal after thorough official investigation and interrogation. Grounds for a finding of nullity may be a defect that negated the ostensible matrimonial consent either because of the deceit or the incapacity of one or both of the parties; the existence of an undiscovered or undisclosed diriment (invalidating) impediment (see IMPEDIMENTS, MATRIMONIAL); the fact that the canonical form of marriage (i.e., contraction before an authorized priest and two witnesses) was not observed. A declaration of nullity is not the same procedure as the dissolution of a marriage. *PAULINE PRIVILEGE; *PETRINE PRIVILEGE.

[T. C. O'BRIEN]

DECLARATION OF RIGHTS (1689), a statement assented to by William III and Mary before their coronation. It guaranteed the continuation of the C of E, the fundamental liberties of Englishmen, and the rights of Parliament. This declaration was presented to William and Mary by a committee of the Convention Parliament, and after their assent had been secured, it was enacted as the Bill of Rights in 1689. Beginning with a catalogue of the misdeeds by which James "did endeavour to subvert and extirpate the Protestant religion and the laws and liberties of this kingdom," the Bill denied the right of the King to suspend, dispense, or execute laws without the consent of Parliament. It secured for Englishmen their personal liberties, the independence of the courts, the rights of habeas corpus and of jury trial, freedom of speech, and free elections; it also ensured frequent and regular Parliaments with freedom of debate for members. Provision was made for succession to the throne, first through the heirs of William and Mary; in case they had no issue, through Princess Anne of Denmark and her heirs; if she had no children, through any heirs William might have by future marriage. The Bill declared that any person in communication with the Church of Rome, or who "shall profess the popish religion, or shall marry a papist," should be excluded from the English throne. BIBLIOGRAPHY: H. Gee and W. J. Hardy, *Documents Illustrative of English Church History* (1921); G. Clark, *Later Stuarts, 1660–1714* (2d ed., 1955). *ROYAL DECLARATION.

[N. H. MARING]

DECLARATION OF THE RIGHTS OF MAN AND CITIZEN, Aug. 27, 1789, an idealistic manifesto of 17 points on man's rights regarded as "natural, inalienable, and sacred." Emanating from the National Constituent Assembly, France's representative body in the first phase of the Revolution, it was prefaced to the Constitution of 1791. Modified versions of the declaration were attached to subsequent constitutions of 1793 and 1795. In general the declaration proclaimed popular sovereignty and contract over the absolute state, characterized every citizen's political position, and emphasized freedom and responsibility, justice, authority, and legality, security, and sovereignty. Its wider significance endures in later movements for freedom and reform. The following principles are upheld: (1) equality as opposed to hereditary privilege; freedom of all men, although slavery still existed in French colonies; (2) the State has the responsibility of preserving man's rights of liberty, property, and security; (3) liberty is the freedom to act as long as one does not harm another person; (4) law expresses the nation's desire for everyone's general welfare; (5) all citizens are eligible for public office and employment; (6) freedom of opinion expressed in speech and press; (7) general taxation; (8) the desire for the guarantee of rights and the separation of political powers to preserve liberty; (9) right of resistance to oppression. Lacunae included freedom of petition, of assembly, of association, and rights to economic freedom, and religious organization. BIBLIOGRAPHY: G. Lefebvre, *Coming of the French Revolution* (tr. R. R. Palmer, 1947); J. H. Stewart, *Documentary History of the French Revolution* (1951); S. Kent, "Declaration of the Rights of Man and Citizen," *Great Expression of Human Rights* (ed. R. M. McIver, 1950) 145–181.

[R. J. MARAS]

DECLARATION OF THE SOVEREIGN, see ROYAL DECLARATION.

DECLARATION OF UTRECHT, an Old Catholic *doctrinal standard, issued (1889) in Germany by the Utrecht conference of the five bps. of Dutch, German, and Swiss Old Catholic Churches (see UNION OF UTRECHT). It is binding on all bps. and priests. Doctrinal principles are eight: (1) adherence to *Vincent of Lérin's rule of faith, where the threefold test of orthodoxy is *quod ubique, quod semper, quod ab omnibus creditum est:* thus acceptance of the first seven ecumenical councils; (2) rejection of the *infallibility and universal episcopate of the pope, because they contradict the ancient Church's faith, but acceptance of the bp. of Rome as *primus inter pares;* (3) rejection of the dogma of the Immaculate Conception because it is against Scripture and the tradition of the first centuries; (4) rejection of such modern papal pronouncements as *Unigenitus* (1713), *Auctorem fidei* (1794), and the *Syllabus of Errors* (1864); renewal of protests against the Roman Curia's errors and its attacks on *national Churches; (5) rejection of the Council of Trent's disciplinary decrees, and acceptance of its dogmatic decisions only if they harmonize with primitive church teaching. According to Bp. U. Küry, a Swiss Old Catholic, the last is the most significant point since the Dutch Church thereby "ceased to be in any sense Roman Catholic, and placed herself, with other Old Catholic Churches, alongside the Orthodox and Anglican Communions: she opened the way to future reunion of all nonpapal Catholic Churches, which her adherence to Trent had hitherto made impossible"; (6) acceptance of the eucharistic *Real Presence as a commemoration of the crucifixion, but without any mention of *transubstantiation; (7) hope for agreement between Christian Churches; (8) willingness to eliminate ecclesiastical abuses and the worldliness of the hierarchy. BIBLIOGRAPHY: U. Küry, *Die Altkatholische Kirche* (1966); C. B. Moss, *Old Catholic Movement* (1966).

DECLARATIONS OF INDULGENCE, proclamations (1660–88) by which the later Stuarts vainly sought to achieve religious toleration. Efforts to extend religious freedom were complicated by conflicting interests between the C of E and Dissenters, divided opinions among Dissenters, the contest between King and Parliament, and widespread fear of Roman Catholicism. In the Declaration of Breda (1660), Charles II had agreed to "declare a liberty to tender consciences," provided that Parliament enact appropriate laws. In fulfillment of this pledge, he issued a Declaration of Indulgence in 1660 but could not get approval of Commons; a similar Declaration, in 1662, was voided by Parliament. The *Act of Uniformity (1662) dampened hopes of all parties wishing broader tolerance; about 2,000 ministers were ejected from their livings. Charles issued another Declaration of Indulgence (1672) suspending all penal laws against Dissenters and *Recusants. Although many were released from prison and began to worship publicly, Parliament persuaded King Charles to withdraw his dispensation, and persecution was resumed. The opposition to toleration stemmed partly from determination to enforce religious uniformity and partly from the dilemma that toleration could not easily be granted to Protestants without including Catholics. A primary objection to the 1672 Declaration of Indulgence, however, grew out of the constitutional struggle then in progress between Parliament and the King. Pressure for the withdrawal of religious toleration was a challenge to the royal right to waive penalties prescribed by Parliament.

When James II succeeded to the throne (1685), he was determined that Catholics should have liberty. Unlike his brother, he was a devout Catholic and had the Mass said openly. He expected not only to remove political and religious disabilities but eventually to restore the Catholic faith in England. In 1687, he issued a Declaration of Indulgence. Expressing the wish that "all the people of our dominions were members of the Catholic Church," he declared that "the conscience ought not to be constrained nor people forced in matters of mere religion." The chief provisions of the Declaration were that: (1) the C of E should continue as before "by law established"; (2) penal laws for nonconformity were suspended; (3) private worship of all peaceable persons was permitted; and (4) pardon was granted to all "nonconformists and recusants" convicted for violations of laws regarding religion. James proceeded to appoint Catholics to posts in government, in military service, in the judiciary, and at Oxford. A year later, he reissued the Declaration, ordering bps. to see that it was read in all the churches; seven who refused to obey were imprisoned, tried for libel, and acquitted. The King's high-handed methods had alienated many, and his proceedings against the bps. brought a climax of feeling. When the birth of a son indicated the probable succession of RC rulers, political leaders decided that a dynastic change was needed; this was accomplished by the *Revolution of 1688. BIBLIOGRAPHY: F. Bate, *Declaration of Indulgence, 1672* (1908); H. Gee and W. J. Hardy, *Documents Illustrative of English Church History* (1921); D. Ogg, *England in the Reigns of James II and William III* (1955).

[N. H. MARING]

DECLARATORY ACTS (SCOTLAND), two statements, one of the United Presbyterian Church (1879), the other of the Free Church (1892), regarding the *Westminster Confession. Both Acts modified certain ar-

ticles of the Confession (esp. on atonement, election, human depravity, and the civil magistrate) and recognized liberty of opinion concerning nonessentials of the *Reformed faith. A small group, who thought any departure from the Confession an apostasy, seceded from the Free Church and became the Free Presbyterian Church. The Acts, however, permitted a broader freedom of theological inquiry than before and relieved ministers and officeholders of the Churches from committing themselves to principles inconsistent with liberty of conscience and the right of private judgment. BIBLIOGRAPHY: J. R. Fleming, *History of the Church of Scotland, 1875–1929* (1933) 306–308 (text).

[J. A. R. MACKENZIE]

DECLARATORY ARTICLES, see ARTICLES DECLARATORY (CHURCH OF SCOTLAND).

DECOLLATION OF ST. JOHN THE BAPTIST, the former liturgical title of the commemorative celebration of the martyrdom of St. John the Baptist as observed in Roman, Greek, and other Christian churches on August 29th. "Decollation" is simply the Anglicized form of the Latin *decollatio*, meaning decapitation. In the vernacular liturgy of the present time, the English Roman Catholics refer to the feast as the Passion of St. John the Baptist, while in the U.S. the present title is the Beheading of St. John the Baptist.

DE CONCILIO JANUARIUS VINCENT (1836–98), pastor, teacher, author. Born in Italy, he was ordained in Genoa (1860) for the diocese of Newark, N.J. He was first pastor of St. Michael's, Jersey City; taught at Seton Hall College; helped prepare the Catechism of the Third Council of Baltimore; and worked and wrote in the service of the religious needs of Italian immigrants. His published works include books on apologetics, theology, and Thomistic philosophy.

[T. C. O'BRIEN]

DECORATIONS, PAPAL, see PAPAL DECORATIONS.

DE COUCY, ROBERT (d. 1311), French Gothic architect, master of St. Nicaise, Reims (after 1263), who at Reims Cathedral (1290) effected the upper W façade and the labyrinth in the nave honoring previous Reims architects. BIBLIOGRAPHY: L. Demaison, *La Cathédral de Reims* (1954).

[M. J. DALY]

DE COURCY, HENRY (1820–61), French historian, correspondent in the U.S. for *L'Univers* (see L. *Veuillot). D.'s works, some written under the pseudonym C. de Laroche-Héron, chiefly concerned French interests. One, however, was translated by the American church historian, John Gilmary *Shea as *The Catholic Church in the United States*. The picture it presented reflected Veuillot's extreme *ultramontanism, was offensive to Protestants, and made a Francophile assessment of the American Church. The convert O. *Brownson in particular assailed D.'s views.

[T. C. O'BRIEN]

DECREE, in the theology of *predestination, a term to describe the act of God's will putting into effect the plan or economy of salvation. From the Lat. *discernere,* the term has the connotation of an ordered and discerning choice. It has at least a verbal affinity with the Vulgate text (e.g. of Eph 1.11), which speaks of predestination being *secundum propositum ejus quo operatur omnia secundum consilium voluntatis suae* (according to the purpose of him who accomplishes all things according to the counsel of his will). Traditional RC theology affirmed a positive decree of predestination, but not of reprobation; strict Calvinism equivalently maintained a positive decree predestining the elect and reprobating the nonelect. It may be questioned whether the classical discussions in causal categories reflect the meaning and intent of the Pauline doctrine of predestination. BIBLIOGRAPHY: J. Farelly, *Predestination, Grace, and Free Will* (1964). *ELECTION, DIVINE.

[T. C. O'BRIEN]

DECREE (CANON LAW), a formal pronouncement of the Holy See, having the force of a command or prohibition. The term has the connotation of being a decision binding either on the whole Church or on the addressee. In the ordinary workings of the Holy See a decree is issued usually by a congregation of the *Curia Romana with the pope's approval. Vatican Council II among its documents issued nine classified as decrees, four as dogmatic constitutions, three as declarations. *DOCUMENTS, PAPAL.

[T. C. O'BRIEN]

DECREE ON ECUMENISM *(Unitatis redintegratio),* the pastoral document of Vatican Council II that sets forth for all Roman Catholics the guidelines and methods by which they may respond to the grace of the Holy Spirit calling for "restoration of unity among all the followers of Christ" (Vat II Ecum 1). Adopted by a vote of 2,137 to 11 and promulgated Nov. 21, 1964, by Paul VI at the end of the third session, the document is the result of three earlier texts. On Dec. 1, 1962, the General Congregation of the Council decided to combine into a single schema: a document, *On the Unity of the Church,* composed by the Commission for the Eastern Churches; a chapter on ecumenism intended for the schema, *On the Church;* and a draft prepared by the *Secretariat for Promoting Christian Unity on general ecumenical principles. The comparatively short 24 sections or articles of the Decree (an introduction and three chapters) treat Catholic principles on ecumenism, the practice of ecumenism, and Churches and ecclesial communities separated from the Roman Apostolic See.

Recognizing that the present division among Christians "contradicts the will of Christ, scandalizes the world, and

damages that most holy cause, the preaching of the Gospel to every creature" *(ibid.,* 1), the Decree notes that among "our separated brethren" a movement for the restoration of unity "fostered by the grace of the Holy Spirit" has increased day by day. The chief advances made by the Decree on Ecumenism are the acceptance of this ecumenical movement and the encouragement given to Catholics to participate in it according to their Catholic principles. The Decree also makes an important contribution to the beginnings of a new *ecclesiology. For the first time in a RC ecclesiastical document, religious bodies tracing their origins from the Reformation are called Churches, with ecclesial gifts and sacred actions capable of giving birth to the life of grace and admission to the community of salvation *(ibid.,* 4). Calling "spiritual ecumenism" the soul of the ecumenical movement, the Decree lays down two objectives for the practice of worship in common *(communicatio in sacris):* to express the unity of the Church, which generally forbids common worship, and to obtain grace, which sometimes commends it *(ibid.,* 8). Among the guidelines offered for Catholic ecumenical activity, the first is to avoid expressions, judgments, and actions that do not represent the condition of our separated brethren with truth and fairness *(ibid.,* 4). Dialogue between experts is encouraged, as are cooperative works carried out for the "common good of humanity." It is hoped that, under the attentive guidance of the bishops, these ecumenical activities, together with common prayer and church renewal, will overcome the obstacles preventing "perfect ecclesiastical communion" *(ibid.,* 4). BIBLIOGRAPHY: L. Jaeger, *Stand on Ecumenism: The Council's Decree* (tr. H. Graef, 1965).

[R. MATZERATH]

DECRETALISTS, medieval jurists engaged in the compilation and exegesis of papal decretals. The work is distinct from that of the decretists, which centered on Gratian's *Decretum,* even though many jurists engaged in both. From the time of universal acceptance of the *Decretum* (c.1160) to the promulgation of Gregory IX's *Decretals* (1234), compilation and organization of papal legislation occupied the decretalists. The period following Gregory's *Decretals* saw the flourishing of canonical interpretative commentaries, *glossae, summae,* and other forms of exposition.

[T. C. O'BRIEN]

DECRETALS, letters *(epistolae* or *litterae decretales)* of papal decision on matters of discipline and teaching that indicate the growth in power of the medieval papacy and mark the development of canon law. Papal issuance of mandatory letters is clearly dated from at least the pontificate of Siricius (letter, 385, to Himerius, Bp. of Tarragona), but the practice has its greatest significance in the Middle Ages. Increase of papal power is evident in the marked increase in the number of decretals. Their meaning and status as law came to be more clearly defined: they are strictly speaking rescripts in response to questions submitted for papal decision. The *Decretum* of Gratian commented on their binding force; the strongest kind of statement of papal authority in dogmatic, moral, and disciplinary matters is given by *Huguccio's *Summa* (*c*.1190), in elaborating on the force of decretals. The growth and development of canon law are marked by the promulgation of decretal collections, esp. the *Decretals* of Gregory IX; the *Liber Sextus* of Boniface VIII; the *Clementinae* of Clement V; and two sets of *Extravagantes* that together composed the *Corpus Juris Canonici of 1582. In modern practice the term decretal usually is restricted to documents on canonization or dogmatic teaching.

[T. C. O'BRIEN]

DECRETISTS, medieval canonists occupied with the study of Gratian's *Decretum;* in a wider use the term applies to any jurist concerned with Church law *(decreta)* as distinct from civil laws *(leges).* The decretist period extends from the mid-12th cent. to 1234, the year of promulgation of Gregory IX's *Decretals.* Its first center was Bologna, but notable work was also done at Paris, Cologne, and Oxford. The earlier decretists glossed Gratian's text with simple annotations, marginal and interlinear; progress in the work, paralleling the *scholastic method in theology, led to the *quaestio* and *summa* method of exposition by running commentary. *Huguccio of Bologna's *Summa* (1188–90) is the prime example of this. The highest stage reached in this phase of canonical science is marked by the *apparatus* technique of closely organized and ordered glosses, as exemplified by the *apparatus* of Alanus Anglicus (1202); of Lawrence of Spain (1210–15); Joannes Teutonicus (1216).

[T. C. O'BRIEN]

DEDICATION OF CHURCHES, see CHURCHES, DEDICATION OF.

DEDICATION OF THE TEMPLE, FEAST OF, a feast known in Hebrew as *Hanŭkkah.* Its Greek title is *enkainia* meaning renewal or inauguration. The origin of the feast is given in 1 Macc 4.36–59, which recounts how on the 25th day of Kislev (Dec.), 164 B.C. exactly 3 years to the day after the desecration of the Temple by Antiochus Epiphanes with the Abomination of Desolation (1 Macc 1.54; Dan 9.27; 11.31), Judas Maccabee purified the sanctuary and dedicated it. The commemoration of this event as an annual feast was promulgated through a letter contained in 2 Macc 1–9, which was written in 124 B.C. The feast is referred to as the feast of Tabernacles in the month of Kislev. The reference to the feast of Tabernacles (which is observed on the 15th of Tishri usually Oct.) may indicate a deliberate attempt to associate the Maccabean feast of the dedication of the Temple with the first dedication of the Temple by Solomon on the feast of Tabernacles (1 Kg 8.2, 65) and the rededication of the altar of the Temple after the Exile on the same date (Ezra 3.4). It may also refer to a similarity of ritual. Both are joyful feasts in which palms are carried in procession. The feast was observed in NT times for it is mentioned in Jn 10.22 and is popularly observed even today. It survived the destruction of the Temple because of the ritual of lights, which is independent of the sanctuary. On the first night of the 8-day feast, a lamp is lit before each house, and on each of the following nights of the feast another lamp is lit until the last night of the feast. This feature is not explicitly mentioned in early notices of the feast, but a hint of it is given in the phrase "kindled the lamps" (2 Macc 1.8); and Josephus (*Ant.* 12; 7.7) calls it the Feast of Lights. He says *(ibid.)* that the lights symbolized the freedom that shone unexpectedly upon the Jews. Later writers interpret the lights as a symbol of the Law which is called light in Pr 6.23 and Ps 119.105. BIBLIOGRAPHY: De Vaux AncIsr 510–514.

[J. A. PIERCE]

DEED OF DECLARATION, a legal instrument created by John *Wesley in 1784 in England. It was necessitated because the Wesleyan Methodist meetinghouses and property were held in trust for Wesley, and for those whom he appointed, as premises to be freely used for preaching. Wesley wanted this provision extended on his death to the yearly conference of Methodist preachers. The term *conference needed legal definition. The Deed explained the words "yearly conference," declaring who are its members and how their succession was to be continued. Wesley chose 100 of his more than 200 preachers, thus creating, for legal purposes, a conference within the conference. With the union of all Methodist bodies in 1932, the legal 100 was retained only as an honorary residue of a few persons. BIBLIOGRAPHY: J. S. Simon, *John Wesley, the Last Phase* (1934) 208–219; L. Tyerman, *Life and Times of the Rev. John Wesley* (3d ed., 1876) 417–426.

[F. E. MASER]

DEER, ABBEY OF, Cistercian abbey founded in 1219 in Aberdeen, Scotland, by William Comyn with monks from Kinross. Abbot Robert, the first superior, was recalled to Kinross the following year, having been elected abbot there. The abbey did not flourish, and in 1267 there was still reason to complain of the poor, ramshackle buildings. By 1543 when its last abbot, Robert Keith, took office only 14 monks remained. Keith died in Paris (1551), evidently on his return from the general chapter at Cîteaux. His nephew, Robert Keith, succeeded him but abandoned Catholicism, having been affected by the English Reformation, and succeeded in having the goods of the abbey eventually settled upon him as Baron of Deer. Nothing remains of the abbey but the foundation. BIBLIOGRAPHY: W. D. Simpson, *Abbey of Deer* (1952); J. M. Canivez, DHGE 14:157–158.

[S. A. HEENEY]

DEER MANDALA, Japanese painting for the Kasuga Shintō shrine in Nara, evidencing the blend of Buddhism and Shintōism. Deer of the Kasuga shrine were long venerated as sacred guardians, and mandalas as magical diagrammatic paintings or carvings. In early examples the deer carried on its back a branch of the Sakaki tree supporting a mirror—sacred symbol in Shinto. In late Heian and Kamakura periods a synthesis between Buddhism and Shintoism was expressed in a new iconography, the Buddhist figure and Shinto gods (then considered manifestations of Buddhist deities) appearing within branches of the tree supported by the deer. BIBLIOGRAPHY: R. T. Paine and S. Soper, *Art and Architecture of Japan* (1955).

[M. J. DALY]

DEĒSIS (Gr., entreaty), in the Orthodox Church a tripartite icon showing Christ flanked on his right side by the holy Mother of God and on his left by John the Baptist. The side images face toward the central figure of the enthroned Christ and extend their hands toward him in a gesture of prayer and entreaty. Sometimes these attendant figures are extended by the addition of other saints, which usually include the Archangels Michael and Gabriel, the Apostles Peter and Paul and SS. Basil, John Chrysostom, Gregory of Nazianzus and Nicholas. The *deēsis* is usually found high on the iconostasis in the Byzantine tradition in the middle and above the Last Supper icon. Among the Greeks a small icon of the *deēsis* in triptych form is often placed on the altar when the priest is traveling and celebrates the Liturgy outside a church.

[A. J. JACOPIN]

DEFAMATION, the general term used in RC moral theology for an act that unjustly deprives another of his good name or reputation. The term includes both calumny, which takes away another's reputation by lies, and *detraction, which tells the truth but without necessity (as in the revelation of another's secret faults), whether these offenses are committed in their more blatant and obvious forms, or by exaggerations and insinuations that reflect discreditably on another. Defamation is considered a sin against both charity and justice, and when it does, or is seen as likely to do, notable harm, it is said to be a serious sin, but various circumstances such as the quality and character of both the defamer and the defamed, the publicity that may or may not attend the defamatory words; etc., may aggravate or diminish the gravity of the sin. As an offense against strict justice defamation gives rise to an obligation to repair the damage done so far as that is possible. BIBLIOGRAPHY: ThAq ST 2a2ae, 73.

[J. HENNESSEY]

DEFECTS, DISCLOSURE OF, see DEFAMATION.

DEFENDANTS. The virtue of justice regulates the conduct of those involved in court proceedings, thus of defendants in a civil or criminal suit. As a member of society, the defendant's actions should be regulated by the demands of *legal justice. In *commutative justice the defendant's par-

ticular obligation is not to do harm by his words; he is accordingly required to defend himself truthfully, according to the right rules of evidence. In the American system of laws this, of course, takes into account the principle of innocence being presumed until guilt is proved. No defendant in a criminal case is required to give self-incriminating evidence. A defendant may also remain silent or be prudently evasive in regard to truths he is not bound to reveal. Giving evidence under oath adds the obligation to avoid *perjury. BIBLIOGRAPHY: ThAq ST 2a2ae.69, 1–3.

[T. C. O'BRIEN]

DEFENDER OF THE BOND (Lat., *Defensor vinculi*), an office established by Benedict XIV in 1741 to deal with matters of procedural law in trials about the validity of marriage and holy orders. The title is held by a priest (a precedent established in 1883). The defender of the bond in ensuring that a challenge to the validity of marriage or of orders is sound is responsible for review of evidence, scrutiny of briefs, interrogation of witnesses, and maintenance of proper procedures in trial. There are other norms under which the defender acts that deal with the content of the litigation rather than with judicial procedure. An account of those norms and their application is found in the Code of Canon Law (CIC cc. 1993–98) and in texts of the Congregation for Divine Worship. The Oriental Church has a separate legislative set of norms and procedures.

[J. R. RIVELLO]

DEFENDER OF THE FAITH, a title conferred (1521) on Henry VIII by Pope Leo X in recognition of Henry's treatise *Assertio septem sacramentorum,* defending the doctrine of the seven sacraments against Martin Luther. In 1544, Parliament recognized the title as an official designation of English sovereigns, and it remains as such since that date. BIBLIOGRAPHY: ODCC 384.

[T. M. MCFADDEN]

DEFENESTRATION OF PRAGUE, an event, May 23, 1618, at the beginning of the Bohemian phase of the *Thirty Years' War: Protestants in revolt against the pro-Catholic policies of Ferdinand II hurled two of the ten imperial governors through a window of the palace at Prague; though they fell 50 feet, the two survived.

[T. C. O'BRIEN]

DEFENSE MECHANISM, a term used in *psychoanalysis to designate an unconscious mental reaction which serves to prevent the recognition and acknowledgment of frightening or painful facts (usually the existence of obscene or hostile urges) about ourselves. A person defends his conscious self from the need to admit unwelcome truths. In actual fact, people have many ways of defending themselves from the experience of unpleasant thoughts: they avoid thinking about their failures and shortcomings, daydream about pleasant things, rationalize guilt feelings, or pass faults off with jokes. The distinctive difference in strict defense mechanisms, although they operate somewhat like these other defensive measures, is that they take place unconsciously and are generally used to cope with the more violent and frightening thoughts prompted by sexual and aggressive drives. Since they operate unconsciously, a person only knows them if he can bring himself, or be brought by others, to acknowledge what he is defending against, and this generally requires sufficient maturity or personality strength to make the defenses no longer necessary. The importance of defense mechanisms in the moral and spiritual life lies in the fact that a person generally cannot overcome immature and irrational urges and feelings unless he recognizes them, and he cannot recognize them as long as he unconsciously defends himself against admitting them. The major defense mechanism recognized by psychoanalysis is *repression, i.e., the unconscious elimination of sexual or aggressive memories, wishes, fantasies, etc., from conscious awareness. Elimination from conscious awareness means that a person does not admit to himself the existence of these elements in himself and therefore does not articulate them, i.e., integrate them into his patterns of reasonable thinking, because they are too frightening. Repression therefore renders images and impulses literally "unthinkable." However, they tend to continue pressing for conscious recognition and succeed in gaining attention, often in disguise, in dreams, wit, parapraxes, and symptoms. Since fantasies and memories that become associated with repressed material also tend to be repressed, repression can eliminate large areas of experience from consciousness.

Repression is considered the most powerful defense mechanism; other mechanisms are brought into play to handle materials that escape repression. For example, by isolation one succeeds in repressing the emotional reaction connected with a fantasy while permitting the fantasy into consciousness. By denial, one can reject unwelcome memories and replace them with acceptable fantasies of a past that never actually occurred. By reaction formation a person can repress one aspect of an ambivalent (love-hate) relationship and operate as if only the other aspect were real. Projection is a mechanism by which undesirable qualities and reactions of one's own personality are attributed to other people. Introjection of or identification with another person is an unconscious mode of coping with fear of a person or mourning for the loss of a person. Undoing is a reaction by which a person by ritualistic actions compensates for evils of which he unconsciously believes himself guilty. Turning against oneself is making oneself the object of hostile and aggressive impulses which one dare not act out toward other people. Regression and sublimation also have defensive functions: by the former a person retreats from threatening situations into immature modes of behavior; the latter relieves the pressure of instinctual drives by releasing them on substitute, socially acceptable objects.

Listing the defense mechanisms and indicating their ef-

fect on emotions and thinking processes emphasizes the importance, for moral and spiritual theology, of understanding their operations. For instance, if sexual desires are heavily repressed instead of being accepted and controlled maturely, a person may be emotionally unable to achieve a happy marital status, or may enter a life of virginity or celibacy with inadequate appreciation of motivation. If difficulties arise in either state, an understanding of repression and its effects is virtually essential to an adequate moral or spiritual evaluation. Heavy sexual repression may also result in neurotic symptoms or abnormal sexual reactions which complicate moral judgments and inhibit spiritual growth. Similarly, to the extent that interpersonal relations are ambivalent, an understanding of the reaction formation process is essential to an understanding of why one person cannot genuinely love or trust or accept or forgive another, and the genuine moral and spiritual aspects of these relations do not emerge until the unconscious motivations are clarified. Many moral and spiritual problems dealing with relations to authority, obedience, depression, self-aggrandizement, sensitivity to criticism, need for affection and assurance, etc., cannot be resolved until a person understands the drives and emotions he fears and how he is defending himself against them. Some authors believe that moral and spiritual growth is effectively inhibited by the existence of extensive defense mechanisms; others believe that these, like other failings and weaknesses, can contribute to spiritual growth. Some authors also believe that only professional help in the form of *psychotherapy can remove these mechanisms; others believe that religion itself helps to resolve them. BIBLIOGRAPHY: M. Oraison, *Love or Constraint* (1959).

[M. E. STOCK]

DEFENSELESS MENNONITES, a name used by members of both the *Conference of the Evangelical Mennonite Church and of the *Evangelical Mennonite Brethren before adoption of the present titles. "Defenseless" is a reference to the Mennonite doctrine of *nonresistance.

[T. C. O'BRIEN]

DEFINITION, (1), in Aristotelian logic, the composite expression of what a thing is or what its name means; the first is called a real definition (from *res,* reality); the second, a nominal definition or definition by name. The second is useful for the clarifying of preliminaries to argumentation meant to discover the reality of the thing named. The real definition intends to express what the *definitum* is in itself. In its most nearly perfect form, the ideal that logic discusses, it is an essential definition (Aristotle, *Topics* 1.101b), consisting in the proximate genus and specifying difference of the thing defined. Such a definition is convertible with the things defined, truly makes it known, and, since it is composed of genus and difference, applies to every individual in a species, although not to the individual as such. Other forms of the real definition are: definition by some distinctive trait or property; by one or more of the *causes; or by some superficial and merely incidental quality. A composite expression, first mental then externalized, a definition is not a *proposition, but may be derived from inductive or deductive propositions. Thus a definition itself is not true or false, but adequate or inadequate. Once developed, a good definition can lead to further knowledge, and esp. as it functions in *demonstration (proof) as a middle term. The definitions that philosophy develops are few in relation to the countless species of things; most knowledge of nature is descriptive. (2) In theology, the word definition has one special use: a solemn statement of the teaching Church that a truth is divinely revealed and therefore to be believed with divine faith.

[T. C. O'BRIEN]

DEFINITION, DOGMATIC, a solemn and authoritative judgment of the Church in the area of doctrine. It is not identical with revelation or the original expression of it found in Scripture, but is a statement of faith held by the Church as a result of a living reflection on the revealed mysteries. Dogmatic definitions are solemnly promulgated in the name of the Church by the pope speaking *ex cathedra* or by an ecumenical council. Conciliar definitions have taken various forms: creeds and confessions of faith, as well as short canons and condemnations (anathemas) appended to doctrinal treatises. Though it is generally recognized that dogmatic definitions have a permanent value, it is also recognized that they can be improved upon and sometimes must be reformulated to meet new contingencies. Even while accepting the truth of a dogmatic definition, theologians must be concerned with its aptness, i.e., the degree to which the verbal formulation is adequate to the reality which is believed. BIBLIOGRAPHY: E. G. Hardwick, NCE 4:719–720; K. Rahner, *Theological Investigations* 5 (1966) 42–66. *MAGISTERIUM.

[B. L. MARTHALER]

DEFINITION, INFALLIBLE, in the RC Church, a solemn declaration by the Church witnessing to religious truth with divine assurance of certitude and of preservation from error. While most definitions are concerned with things that are divinely revealed, they can also be ideas or facts merely connected with revelation. Thus the Council of Trent defined as part of revelation that man merits before God when he freely cooperates with his grace. A century later Alexander VII defined, though not as formally revealed, that Jansen taught certain doctrines in his book *Augustinus,* including the idea that man does not need real internal freedom to merit in the present state of fallen nature. In both cases, however, the ultimate basis for acceptance of an infallible definition is Catholic belief in the Church's divine authorization to teach the truths of salvation without fear of misleading the faithful. Since definitions are binding in conscience on all the faithful, only the Church's highest teaching authority can validly define with infallible certainty.

This may be either an ecumenical council representing the Catholic hierarchy united with the bp. of Rome, or the pope when he speaks *ex cathedra* as successor of St. Peter and head of the Catholic Church. There must be on the part of council and pope the intention of making an irrevocable pronouncement that is universally binding on all believers; otherwise no definition is made. There should also be clear evidence of this intention; otherwise no strict obligation to believe with absolute certitude is imposed.

There are several ways of recognizing when something is defined. The fact may be conveyed directly with such formulas as "we define" or "let him be anathema" (if anyone holds the opposite). Or the duty of believing may be stated under penalty of exclusion from the Church or from salvation. Or the term heretical may be attached to the denial of the definition; or the contrary doctrine may be qualified as opposed to revelation or the Christian faith. While infallibly defined teaching is normally intended and identified as such when first proposed, the recognition of its definitive character may be deferred to a later date. A classic example is the condemnation of Semi-Pelagianism by a provincial council of Orange A.D. 529), confirmed 2 years later by Pope Boniface II. There are no simple categories of infallible definitions. Their variety defies classification. Yet four main types are commonly distinguished: (1) strictly dogmatic, e.g., the Real Presence of Christ in the Eucharist, (2) doctrinal-historical, e.g., identifying the canonical books of the Bible, (3) ritual, e.g., the matter and form of baptism, and (4) moral, e.g., the indissolubility of Christian marriage. For Roman Catholics, the Church's right to define spans the whole gamut of Christian tradition that stems from the Apostles. In the words of Vatican Council II, it "includes everything that contributes toward the holiness of life and increase in faith of the people of God" (Vat II DivRev, 8).

Although the term definition suggests delimitation and implies a certain finality of judgment, it does not exclude the possibility of new insights or even new definitions in a matter already defined. Quite the contrary. Christian tradition, which is the object of ecclesiastical definition, develops in the Church with the help of the Holy Spirit. There is growth not only in the understanding of the realities but also in the words that have been handed down. This occurs through prayer and study on the part of believers, through the Church's experience of what it teaches, and through the preaching of those who, as successors of the Apostles, have divine surety of preserving and proclaiming what God has revealed. "As the centuries succeed one another, the Church constantly moves forward toward the fulness of divine truth, until the words of God reach their complete fulfillment in her" (Vat II *ibid.*).

In one sense an infallible definition means an end (finis), but only to uncertainty about religious truth. In another sense it affirms a new beginning. Defined truth becomes the object of valid contemplation precisely because it is certainly true, and the ground for sound dogmatic progress because it gives a sure basis for theological investigation. BIBLIOGRAPHY: E. G. Hardwick, NCE 4:719–720; F. X. Lawlor, *ibid.* 7:496–498; C. Dillenschneider, *Le Sens de la foi et la progrès dogmatique du mystère marial* (1954).

[J. A. HARDON]

DEFINITOR, RELIGIOUS, a religious elected to participate officially in the government of the congregation; in some orders the definitor is an elected member of a general or provincial chapter or governing council. Definitions at a general or provincial chapter have legislative power over a whole religious institute or a province. Where counsellors have the title of definitor, their power is not legislative but consultative only.

[R. A. TODD]

DEFORIS, JEAN PIERRE (1732–94), Maurist theologian. D.'s fame derives from his edition of *Bossuet's works (18 v. of a planned 24; 1772–1790). He collaborated in the edition of the *Concilia Galliae* (1789) and in an attack upon Rousseau, *Réfutation d'un nouvel ouvrage de J. J. Rousseau intitulé: Émile* (1762). He was suspected both of Jansenist tendencies and of helping to compose the *Civil Constitution of the Clergy, but proved both charges false. During the terror he was imprisoned, and finally guillotined. BIBLIOGRAPHY: Hurter 5.1:305–306; B. Heurtebrize, DTC 4:230–231, with list of works and collaborations.

[P. K. MEAGHER]

DE GASPERI, ALCIDE (1881–1954), Italian statesman and principal founder of the postwar Christian Democratic party. Born in Austria-Hungary, he received his education in Habsburg schools, graduating from the Univ. of Vienna in 1905. He continued his work as journalist and parliamentarian after Italy's annexation of the Trentino from Austria-Hungary (1919) and was a leader of the Partito Popolare until its suppression by Mussolini. From 1929 to 1943 he worked in the Vatican Library. During World War II he revived the Partito Popolare under the name of the Christian Democratic Party. In Dec. 1945 he became the first Christian Democratic premier, retaining this post until July 1953. His ministries furthered agrarian and industrial reform, alliance with the West, and European unity. BIBLIOGRAPHY: E. A. Carrillo, *Alcide De Gasperi: The Long Apprenticeship* (1965); M. R. C. De Gasperi, *De Gasperi, Uomo solo* (1964).

[E. A. CARRILLO]

DE GAULLE, CHARLES (André Joseph Marie; 1890–1970), French general, statesman. A son of an ardently Catholic family, he was a graduate of the St. Cyr military academy and a professional soldier. His service in World War I drew the attention of Marshall Pétain who appointed him to his staff. In 1940 as Under Secretary of Defense and War he conferred with Prime Minister Winston Churchill in London. Upon his return to France, which had surrendered to the Third Reich, he refused to accept the surrender. In London he headed a French government in exile and the Free French Army from 1940 to 1944. After the liberation of France, he acted as chief of state of the provisional government.

Pushed aside by the new republic, he retired to his residence in Colombey-les-deux-Églises from which he was finally recalled in 1958 to form a new government. As premier he engineered acceptance of a new French constitution in the same year. Later as president of France and head of the Gaullist party, which was to dominate French politics for many years, his influence was enormous. His personal magnetism drew Frenchmen to a new ideal of French greatness. Irritating as he was to English and American leaders, he exhibited an almost mystical sense of French greatness and destiny. He saw the new France as a third force, aligned neither to the U.S. nor the Soviet Union. In his own country he was regarded variously as Charles le Grand or as a dictatorial impostor. It might be said that he revived the whole concept of *la gloire* which Bonaparte had impressed upon the French people. Whatever history may finally accord Charles de Gaulle, no one can subtract from his achievement in raising his beloved France from the abyss of defeat and disillusionment in 1940 to prestige as a world power in the 1960s. BIBLIOGRAPHY: R. C. Macrides *DeGaulle, Implacable Ally* (1966); A. Malraux, *Felled Oaks: Conversation with De Gaulle* (1972); F. Mauriac, *De Gaulle* (1964).

[J. R. AHERNE]

DEGRADATION, an ecclesiastical penalty by which an offender is deposed from ecclesiastical office and becomes disqualified to acquire or to discharge any offices, dignities, benefices, pensions, or positions in the Church, and also is deprived of whatever offices and benefits he already has. To this point, degradation does not differ from deposition, but unlike deposition, degradation adds the indignities of perpetual deprival of the right to wear ecclesiastical garb and reduction to lay status. Degradation is only imposed for offenses declared in law to be punishable with that penalty. The penalty may be imposed verbally or by edict, or by the solemn observance of the rite prescribed in the *Roman Pontifical*. These ceremonies are rarely used in modern times because one to be degraded is unlikely to cooperate willingly in the service. BIBLIOGRAPHY: CIC cc. 2303–05.

[P. K. MEAGHER]

DEGREES, THEOLOGICAL. In modern RC usage the primary theological degrees are those granted by the theology faculty of a pontifical university or by a theological faculty having pontifical status. They are: the *baccalaureatus* (S.T.B.), the *licentiatus* (S.T.L.), and the *doctoratus* or *laurea* (S.T.D.); the last two confer the right to teach theology. The D.D. appearing by custom in the U.S. after a bishop's name is the honorary title doctor of divinity. In the medieval universities the baccalaureate was an apprentice stage, during which the bachelor read and commented on the *Sentences* of Peter Lombard; the masterate constituted the recipient as a *magister,* having the right to teach and to resolve the scholastic debate, the **quaestio disputata.* In biblical studies the Pontifical Biblical Commission confers the degrees of baccalaureate, licentiate, and doctorate in Sacred Scripture. Pontifical faculties of canon law confer the J.C.B., J.C.L., and J.C.D.; baccalaureate, licentiate, and doctorate respectively (AAS 67 [1975] 153–158). Theological schools often distinguish between academic and professional or ministerial degrees. The first correspond to general usage, the graduate degrees being the M.A. and Ph.D. in theology. The nomenclature for professional degrees is in a transitional stage, but such designations as bachelor, master, or doctor in theology usually refer to a professional degree as does the doctorate in ministry (D. Min.). The masterate or doctorate in religious studies or religious education are other common academic degrees.

[T. C. O'BRIEN]

DE GROOT, JOHANNES VINCENTIUS (1848–1920), Dutch Dominican ecclesiologist, best known for his *Summa apologetica de ecclesia Christi* (1920). He became a Dominican in 1866. He helped establish a chair at the Univ. of Amsterdam in 1894, and became its first incumbent; his efforts furthered the pursuit and recognition of Thomistic studies. He was also active in the cause of securing the civil and religious liberties of Catholics in Holland.

[T. C. O'BRIEN]

DEHARBE, JOSEPH (1800–71), German Jesuit, author of a celebrated catechism. His chief life's work, parish missions and catechizing, began in Switzerland in 1840, and, because of Swiss persecution of the Jesuits, continued throughout Germany from 1842 until his death. His catechism (*Katholische Katechismus oder Lehrebegriff,* 1847 and 1848), stood as the official text for many dioceses in Germany, Austria-Hungary, and Switzerland until well into the 20th century. Translated into English, it was published in Cincinnati in 1869 and for many decades remained the most widely used of all catechisms. D. continually revised his catechism in the interest of simplification and clarity; he published several other works based on it.

[T. C. O'BRIEN]

DE HUECK, BARONESS CATHERINE KOLY-SCHINE (Mrs. Edward *Doherty; 1900–), founder of Friendship House and the Madonna House Apostolate in Canada. A native of Novgorod, she fled Russia after the 1917 Revolution and settled in Toronto, Canada, where she founded the first Friendship House in 1931. In 1947 she opened a Friendship House at Combermere, Ontario, from which Madonna House developed; she became director-general of the women's group. BIBLIOGRAPHY: C. De Hueck-Doherty, NCE 9:51; D. M. Cantwell, *ibid.,* 6:207–208.

[D. CODDINGTON]

DEI, MATTEO AND MILIANO (fl. 1439–55), Florentine goldsmiths. To Matteo is attributed a niello pax (*Coronation of the Virgin,* 1455, Florence). Miliano was commissioned with A. Pollaiuolo and Betto di Francesco Betti to make the silver cross for the altar of S. Giovanni in the Florentine Baptistery (1457–59).

[M. J. DALY]

DEI FILIUS, a dogmatic constitution promulgated by Vatican Council I, April 24, 1870. It has four chapters with their corresponding canons. The first deals with the nature of God the creator; the second vindicates man's power to know God by the natural light of human reason and explains in what sense divine revelation is nevertheless necessary; the third deals with the nature, reasonableness, object, necessity, and conditions of faith; the fourth explains the distinct but complementary functions of faith and reason. BIBLIOGRAPHY: D 3000–45; Eng. tr. J. F. Clarkson et al., *Church Teaches* (1955) 26–35, 47.

[J. H. ROHLING]

DEICOLUS OF LURE, ST. (*Dichul* in Irish; d. 625), Irish monk trained by St. Columbanus, who went to France with his master; spent 25 years at Luxeuil, from which he was expelled with his fellows by Queen Brunhilde (610). Illness forced him to stay behind the others in the Vosges Mountains. There he built a hermitage and was later joined by others. Out of this little foundation grew the great Abbey of Lure, where a monk wrote D.'s life some 300 years later. BIBLIOGRAPHY: G. Bataille, BiblSanct 4:536.

[R. T. MEYER]

DEIFICATION, making or being made like God, a descriptive term for transformation and regeneration through grace. The term is particularly related to the expression in 2 Pt 1.4, "becoming sharers of the divine nature." Among the Greek Fathers there are many variants on "divinization" (*theōsis; theopoiein*) that have enriched the theology of grace in the Eastern Church: Clement of Alexandria *Paedagogus* 3,1,1,1.PG 8,556; Athanasius, *Ad Serapionem* 1,24.PG 26,585; *Ep. De synodis* 51.PG 26,784; Basil, *Adv. Eunomium* 9,23. PG 32,109; Cyril of Alexandria, *Homil. Paschal.* 10,2. PG 77,617. Frequently such passages are careful to point out that through grace men become like God, but in distinction from a pantheistic sense, or from Christ's natural sonship. Augustine makes a similar qualification on *deificatos ex gratia* (*Enarrat. in Ps.,* Ps.18,49,2.PL 36,565). A particularly important use of deification is that of Pseudo-Dionysius who defines it as "a certain likening to and union with God, to the degree possible" (*De eccles.hierarch.* 4,1.PG 3,696). Enjoying quasi-apostolic authority, his works influenced theology and mysticism in the West. Thus the theme of likeness to the divine, both by God's governing and by communicating grace, is thematic in St. Thomas Aquinas (ThAq ST 1a.103,4; 1a2ae.110). In the mystical tradition, Jan van *Ruysbroeck, esp. in his *Spiritual Espousals,* makes deification the central idea; he clearly rejects a pantheistic absorption into God and develops the meaning of deification through the scriptural phrase, "the image of God." For a theological evaluation of the term, see GRACE, SUBSTANTIAL.

[T. C. O'BRIEN]

DEIMEL, ANTON (1865–1954), German Jesuit Sumerian scholar. D. held the chair of Assyriology at the Pontifical *Biblical Institute (1909–54); wrote numerous articles on the Bible and Oriental studies; edited and interpreted early Sumerian texts; and founded the series *Orientalia* (1920) and *Analecta Orientalia* (1931). He published the important *Sumerisches Lexikon* (4 v., 1925–50), the first extensive Sumerian lexicon. BIBLIOGRAPHY: J. A. Brinkman, NCE 4:721.

[T. M. MCFADDEN]

DEIR BARAMUS, 4th-cent. Coptic monastery in the Wadi el-Natrun, between Cairo and Alexandria, Egypt. The *qasr,* or tower of refuge, seems to be a prototype for other such structures in the area.

[M. J. DALY]

DEIR EL BAHARI (ART), site of great mortuary temple built (*c.*1485 B.C.) by Queen Hatshepsut (18th dynasty) in memory of her father. Aesthetically impressive and unique in the supreme harmony of its pillared facade with the vertical clefts of the cliffs' patterns, the three colonnaded terraces, dramatically rhythmic in the light and dark of the 16-sided chambered columns beautifully proportioned and spaced by the architect Senmut, were enhanced, Queen Hatshepsut states in the Annals, by exotic plants and animals. Of great historic and ethnic significance are the painted reliefs of trade recording the fauna and flora of Somaliland. At the same site is an earlier temple of the Pharaoh Mentuhotep (11th dynasty) combining the Old Kingdom pyramidal form with a hypostyle temple plan. A Coptic monastery at the top of the cliff overlooks the two mortuary temples. BIBLIOGRAPHY: L. Dabrowski, "Queen Hatshepsut's Temple at Deir el Bahari . . .", *Illustrated London News,* 245 (1964).

[M. J. DALY]

DEIR ES-SURIAN, Coptic monastery in the Wadi-el-Natrun containing from the 9th cent. the Church of el-'Adra with frescoes and fine stucco decoration, a refectory and *qasr* (tower of refuge).

[M. J. DALY]

DEISIS, see DEĒSIS.

DEISM, a theory of natural religion that, in its modern form, appeared first in the latter half of the 17th cent. in England. The deists were acute, if not profound, thinkers with a philosophy logically persuasive and, to a point, emotionally attractive. Goethe, who witnessed the deist phase of German thought, suggested that in an atmosphere saturated with Newtonian science and the cult of common sense, deism was a perfectly sensible religion to adopt. The English deists, with few exceptions, claimed that their crusades against miracles and priestcraft were undertaken solely for the sake of a pure, natural Christianity. Deism spread during the 18th cent. to Germany, with G. Lessing and H. S. Reimarus, and to France, where it left a lasting impression and attracted an influential and growing public. Voltaire was the outstanding spokesman and propagandist for a form of deism that, as designed, was intended to replace Christianity.

Deists recognize the existence of a God distinct from the world, possibly even a personal God, but deny that God exercises providential care of man or the universe. It is doubtful that their God is a creator; in any case he has left the world to itself, without intervening further in the course of nature or of human life. Deism requires a God to explain the order and reign of law in the world and, less certainly, the world's origin and continuance. The rationalists and empiricists of the late 17th and 18th cent. who rejected Christianity sought a basis in nature and in reason for belief in a Supreme Being that did not entail faith in traditional religious creeds. Deism is thus a form of rationalism, tinged with skepticism and in revolt against revealed religion. A law of nature is postulated—immanent and immutable —originally implanted by the author of nature, but its actual operation may be studied exhaustively without reference to its author.

Deism, called the "halfway house to atheism," restricts the scope and depth of man's relations to God, in which religion consists. For deism, a religion wholly in harmony with reason must confine itself to the fewest possible truths, all of which must be purely natural. No revelation is required to discover these truths; in any case a positive or revealed religion is impossible for deists, because it would presuppose on the part of the creator the suspension of his own natural laws. The source of the tragic history of so-called "revealed" religion is the uncritical reliance on authority and the absence of universally valid criteria of true religion. The deist demands, as a correlative to his concept of God, a purely "natural religion," freed from the shackles of dogmatic, ecclesiastical, and institutional Christianity. BIBLIOGRAPHY: L. Stephen, *English Thought in the Eighteenth Century* (v. 1, 1876); F. E. Manuel, *Eighteenth Century Confronts the Gods* (1959); P. Gay, *Deism: An Anthology* (pa. 1968).

[J. P. REID]

DEISS, LUCIEN (1921–), composer. A Holy Ghost Father of Chevilly-Larue, France, D. studied at Strasbourg,

Paris, and Rome and later became professor of Scripture and of dogmatic theology at the major seminary of his congregation. Author of numerous books on Scripture and liturgy, D. is well known, both in Europe and in America, as a composer of liturgical music adapted to modern needs. His numerous collections of biblical hymns and psalms and his many recordings reflect his aim to create a body of music that may function as the "handmaid of the liturgy."

[M. T. LEGGE]

DEITY, an abstract term for *God, signifying the divine nature considered in itself apart from the person who is that nature. In common parlance, it is often used equivalently for God.

[T. M. MCFADDEN]

DE KONINCK, CHARLES (1906–65), theologian and philosopher. Belgian-born but reared in childhood in Detroit, he returned to Belgium for his college work, after which he entered the Dominicans but was obliged to leave for reasons of health. He received his Ph.D. in Louvain (1934), became professor of philosophy at Laval Univ., Quebec, Canada, and served as dean of the philosophical faculty there (1939–56). Throughout his career he also taught at various times as visiting professor at other institutions. In philosophy, D. was an ardent Thomist, his work extending from scholarly textual commentaries to the treatment of contemporary problems. His tireless effort to apply Thomistic principles to modern life often excited controversy in academic circles. He is esp. remembered for his determined stand in defending the primacy of the common good against the view of those termed personalists, who championed the supremacy of the individual or private good. His best-known writings include: *Ego Sapientia. La sagesse qui est Marie* (1943); *De la primauté du bien commun* (1943); *Hollow Universe* (1960); *La piété du Fils; Études sur l' Assomption* (1954). As *theologus* to Card. M. Roy at Vatican Council II, he was the only layman to serve in that capacity.

[J. T. HICKEY]

DE LA BARRIÈRE, JEAN, see BARRIÈRE, JEAN DE LA.

DE LA CROIX, CHARLES (1792–1869), missionary. As a seminarian in Belgium, he resisted the bishop imposed on Ghent by Napoleon and was imprisoned. After the Empire had fallen, he resumed his studies and was ordained in 1818. Bp. Du Bourg recruited him for Missouri where he superintended the building of a seminary to train priests for Louisiana. He worked among the Catholics of Missouri and the Osage Indians and prepared the way for De Smet and other Jesuit missionaries, who were to work among the Indians. His last assignment was in lower Louisiana.

[J. R. AHERNE]

DELACROIX, EUGÈNE (1798–1863), French painter, brilliant master of the romantic school. D. was first success-ful in the Salon of 1822, showing the *Barque of Dante* based on the Inferno, Canto I, with borrowings from Michelangelo and Rubens. In luminous, sonorous color, dramatic dark and light, the literary, historic and exotic subjects of D.'s panels reflect an intense and exuberant technique that was a revolt against the coolly intellectual classicists (*Death of Sardanapalus,* 1827; *Liberty Leading the People,* 1831). From his African *Journal* D. introduced Oriental themes of Arabs, Turkish, and Algerian women in sumptuous color which led to numerous commissions for architectural decorations. Other famous paintings by D. are *Entry of the Crusaders into Constantinople* (1841), wall and ceiling murals in the Chapel of the Angels, St. Sulpice (1846–61), *Christ on the Sea of Galilee* (1853). Thousands of tonal and linear studies attest to D.'s powerfully expressive draftsmanship. Such later expressionists as Van Gogh and Picasso witness to D.'s strong, lasting influence. BIBLIOGRAPHY: *Journal of Eugène Delacroix* (tr. H. Wellington, 1951).

[M. J. DALY]

DELANOUE, JEANNE, BL. (1666–1736), French foundress. In 1704 she established the institute of the Sisters of St. Anne of Providence, which she governed until her death. St. Louis-Marie *Grignion de Montfort assisted at the first investiture. She was beatified in 1947. BIBLIOGRAPHY: L. Tricoire, *Catholicisme* 6:669–670.

[M. J. SUELZER]

DELANY, SELDEN PEABODY (1874–1935), priest-convert to Catholicism from Episcopalianism, author. Graduated from Harvard and Western Theological Seminary, he was ordained an Episcopalian priest and served in the parish ministry in Massachusetts and Wisconsin before becoming (1915) editor of the *American Church Monthly* and a curate at St. Mary the Virgin Church in New York City. He became pastor in 1930 but in the same year resigned and was received into the Catholic Church. After theological studies at the Beda in Rome he was ordained a Catholic priest in 1934. About 200 Episcopalians followed his example and were received into the Catholic Church. D. wrote an account of his conversion in *Why Rome?* (1930), relating that the doctrine of papal primacy had been the major obstacle to his conversion. He also published *Married Saints* (1935) and *Rome from Within* (1935).

[A. A. O'NEILL]

DE LA SALLE BROTHERS, see CHRISTIAN BROTHERS.

DE LA TAILLE, MAURICE (1872–1933), French Jesuit and theologian. D.'s most important work is *The Mystery of Faith,* an investigation into the theology of Eucharistic Sacrifice. Published in 1921 as a development of his studies of the Epistle to the Hebrews, this work received both wide approbation and strong opposition. D. claimed that Christ's sacrifice is composed of two complementary elements: an immolation on Calvary and many oblations, first at the Last Supper and subsequently in every Mass. These two elements complement each other so as to make the one sacrifice of Christ perennially present for us. The sacrificial aspect of the Mass, therefore, is not purely in the order of sign, but is really present at each eucharistic action insofar as Christ always continues to offer himself to the Father as a pleasing victim for sins. Contemporary theologians do not generally accept this theory, although its brilliance and significance in fostering a sounder theory of Eucharistic Sacrifice is consistently affirmed. BIBLIOGRAPHY: M. De La Taille, *Mystery of Faith* (2 v., tr. J. Carroll and P. J. Dalton, 1941–1950); *Hypostatic Union and Created Actuation by Uncreated Grace* (tr. C. Vollert, 1952); B. Leeming, "A Master Theologian: Father Maurice De La Taille," *Month* 163 (1934) 31–40.

[J. FLOOD]

DELATION, canonical term for reporting to ecclesiastical authority a doctrine or work evidencing unorthodoxy; it is a form of *denunciation.

[T. C. O'BRIEN]

DELATTE, PAUL HENRI OLIS (1848–1937), Benedictine, third abbot of *Solesmes. Ordained a secular priest in 1872, D. began a promising career in philosophy at Lille but gave it up to enter the novitiate at Solesmes (1883) where later he became abbot and superior general of the French congregation (1890). During his rule the Solesmes community endured the trial of expulsion from France and a period of exile on the Isle of Wight (1901–21). D. codified the Roman edition of the Gregorian chant and wrote a biography of P. *Guéranger (2 v., 1912), a commentary on the Rule of St. Benedict (1913), and a five-volume commentary on the NT (1922 and 1924). BIBLIOGRAPHY: H. Dauphin, DHGE 14:172–174.

[P. K. MEAGHER]

DELATTRE, LOUIS ALFRED (1850–1932), archeologist. Born at Déville-lès-Rouen, D. became a *White Father at Algiers in 1872. He was sent to Carthage and placed in charge of archeological excavations in that area. He made a number of important discoveries, among them the tomb of SS. Perpetua and Felicity and several very early Christian basilicas; and he also made other important contributions to scholarly knowledge of the early Church in Africa, e.g., his *Le Culte de la S. Vierge en Afrique d'après les monuments archéologiques* (1907). His publications and reports number more than 600; a list of the principal works may be found in P. Lesourd, *Les Pères Blancs* (1935). BIBLIOGRAPHY: G. Massot, *Catholicisme* 3:552–554; P. Gandolphe, DHGE 14:174–176.

[P. K. MEAGHER]

DELAWARE, a Middle Atlantic state, Del. was the first of the original thirteen states admitted to the Union in 1787. Following Spanish and Portuguese explorations in the 16th cent., the area was discovered by Henry Hudson in 1609 and given its name by Governor de la Warr of Virginia. The Dutch attempted the first settlement at Zwaanendael, now Lewes, in 1631. Indian attacks caused this effort to fail, and Swedes then settled at Christinahama, now Wilmington, in 1638. The colony again passed into Dutch hands before being taken by the British in 1664. Swedish Lutheranism and Dutch Reform Calvinism continued to develop even after England took control of Delaware. In the 18th cent. an influx of Scotch-Irish gave prominence to Presbyterians, while Methodist missionaries moved into the state after the American Revolution. Methodism became the major denomination in the 19th cent., a position it still occupies in the southern portion of the state. The first Catholic congregation had been organized at Coffee Run in 1772, and Catholic communities were thereafter served by Jesuit missionaries from Maryland. Franciscans, Benedictines, Sulpicians, and Augustinians subsequently labored in Delaware.

The Diocese of Wilmington was established in 1868 as a suffragan of the metropolitan See of Baltimore, Md. Thomas Andrew *Becker, the first bp., fostered institutional growth within the diocese until his transfer to Savannah, Ga., in 1886. Under his successor, Alfred Allen *Curtis, diocesan development by 1896 showed 30 priests, 22 parishes, 18 missions, 12 schools, and 3 orphanages. In the 20th cent. the long and notable episcopacy of John Edmond FitzMaurice (1925–60) resulted in numerous social services and schools, including Archmere, a Norbertine secondary school for boys and Padua, a Franciscan secondary school for girls. In 1976 Catholics numbered 116, 536 or 14.4% of the total population (807,533). Nine Catholic high schools enrolled more than 4,655 students, while 10,706 pupils attended 29 Catholic elementary schools in the state. BIBLIOGRAPHY: J. T. Scharf, *History of Delaware, 1609–1888* (1889); W. A. Powell, *History of Delaware* (1928); *Story of the Beginnings of the Catholic Faith in Delaware* (1960); D. W. Johnson et al, *Churches and Church Membership in the U.S.: 1971* (1974).

[J. L. MORRISON; R. M. PRESTON]

DELEGATION (CANON LAW), the granting of jurisdictional power to act for another. While delegation has its roots in Roman law, the fundamental canonical notion is contained in Rule 68 of the Rules of Law of Boniface VIII: one can do through another what one can do by oneself. The power of jurisdiction may be delegated by the law itself (e.g., CIC c. 209), or it may be expressly granted by an act of the superior to a particular person. Unless the law provides otherwise, one who has ordinary jurisdiction (i.e., jurisdiction attached to an office by the law itself) can delegate it in whole or in part to another (CIC c. 199.1). In general, the power of jurisdiction delegated by the Holy See can be subdelegated (CIC c. 199.2). One who has received delegated power is understood in law to have received all other powers necessary to exercise the jurisdiction he has received (CIC c. 200.1). BIBLIOGRAPHY: Bouscaren-Ellis-Korth 136–139; R. A. Kearney, *Principles of Delegation* (1929); L. Bender, *Potestas ordinaria et delegata* (1957).

[L. M. KNOX]

DELEGATION, APOSTOLIC, see APOSTOLIC DELEGATION.

DELEHAYE, HIPPOLYTE (1859–1941), Jesuit hagiographer. After studies at Tonghien and Louvain, D. joined the *Bollandists in 1887. Much of his special interest lay in the field of Greek hagiography. He was the best known of modern Bollandists and their president from 1912 until his death. Among his works are: *Sanctus* (1927); *Les Origines du culte des martyrs* (2d ed. 1933); *Legends of the Saints* (tr. D. Attwater, 1962), which contains a memoir on him and a bibliog. of his scientific works. BIBLIOGRAPHY: P. Peeters, AnalBoll 60 (1942) 1–52.

[R. B. ENO]

DELFINI, JOHN ANTHONY (1507–61), Italian Conventual Franciscan theologian and philosopher. He taught at Padua and Bologna, was provincial of the Bologna province from 1548, then from 1559 until 1561 was vicar general of his whole order. He also served, 1550–59, as an inquisitor for Bologna and Romagna. At the Council of Trent as a theological consultant he represented the Scotist view in the conciliar discussions. Most of his theological works date from the Tridentine period of his career; they include: *De potestate ecclesiastica* (1549), *Universale fere negotium de Ecclesia* (1552), *De tractandis in concilio oecumenico* (1561).

[T. C. O'BRIEN]

DELFT, MASTER OF (fl. 1490–1520), Netherlandish painter and designer of woodcut illustrations and named by Max Friedländer as master of a triptych in National Gallery, London. D.'s style is related to that of the Master of the *Virgo inter virgines*.

[M. J. DALY]

DELGADO, IGNACIO, BL. (1761–1838), Spanish Dominican and missionary to SE Asia. In 1790 D. became vicar apostolic of E Tonkin and was nominated bishop in 1794. During his 50-year apostolate he erected schools, convents, and churches, and increased the number of converts. He suffered a painful martyrdom; he was beatified by Leo XIII in 1900. BIBLIOGRAPHY: R. Bellotti, EncCatt 4:1359; S. M. Bertucci, BiblSanct 4:542–543.

[K. O'NEILL]

DELGADO, JOSÉ MATÍAS (1768–1833), Salvadoran priest and political leader. D. led the uprising against the colonial regime in 1811; he also led the resistance to the incorporation of El Salvador into the Mexican Empire (1822–23). President of the congress that drew up a constitution for the Central American Federation (1823), D. was the leader of the revolt that overthrew the first president of the federation, Manual José Arce (1829).

[M. T. REILLY]

D'ELIA, PASQUALE (1890–1963), Jesuit missionary and missiologist. Born in Italy, he studied theology at the Jesuit college in Woodstock, Md.; he taught theology in the Jesuit theologate, Shanghai (1921–34), and at the Gregorianum in Rome from 1934 onward. He published many articles on Jesuit missionary history in China and a noteworthy *History of the Catholic Church in China* (1956).

[T. C. O'BRIEN]

DELIBERATION, in psychology the process of weighing possible choices; in moral theology, the prelude to an effective decision for which a person is held responsible. A *human act in its technical meaning is one that proceeds from "deliberative will": the dual terms express both the cognitive and affective elements in *freedom. Deliberation implies some inner poise or balance, *indifferentia* as it is called, before opposite courses of action. This is only possible when the object or objects presented are less than the all-good. Even God comes to us in limited guise and as entailing unpleasant doing of duty. Consequently we can now deliberate about him before loving him; this would not be possible were he seen face to face. Then love would be fully voluntary, that is, spontaneous and fully knowing what it is about, but without the "hesitancy" which is a condition of deliberation and free choice. To the extent that they irrupt on this determinancy, factors such as threats, violence, or lust diminish deliberation. It is that phase in a complete human act occupied with the means to an end already intended, and is governed by that part of practical wisdom or prudence called *boulēsis*, or good counsel. ThAq ST 1a2ae, 14, (esp. in ed. Lat.-Eng., v. 17, ed. T. Gilby, 1970).

[T. GILBY]

DELICT, see CRIME (CANON LAW).

DE LISLE, AMBROSE LISLE MARCH PHILLIPS (1809–78), English philanthropist, writer. Born in Leicestershire of a well-known family of Huguenot descent, he became a convert to Roman Catholicism at the age of 15, a fact that shaped all the activities and interests of his life. Ill health forced him to leave Trinity College, Cambridge, after only 2 years, and in 1835 he settled with his wife at his estate at Gracedieu. He had already indicated an unusual interest in religious matters and now implemented this by bringing the congregation known as Rosminians to England, founding a monastery of Cistercian monks, and becoming a member of the Third Order of St. Dominic. Visionary and idealistic in his approach to religious matters, he became deeply involved in the movement for corporate union of the Church of England with Rome and founded the Association for Promoting the Unity of Christendom. Although the movement toward corporate reunion carried some weight at this time, it never reached the magnitude his enthusiastic imagination predicted for it. He consulted the Vatican about the movement, but soon discovered that neither the Old English Catholics at home nor the shrewd churchmen at Rome shared his indiscriminate vision. Even when he had been reprimanded, however, he continued loyal to the Vatican, promoting Roman Catholicism in England by his writing and personal influence. BIBLIOGRAPHY: E. S. Purcell, *Life and Letters of Ambrose Phillipps de Lisle* (2 v., 1900).

[I. MAHONEY]

DELISLE, LÉOPOLD VICTOR (1826–1910), director of the Bibliothèque Nationale in Paris, author on paleography, diplomatics, and medieval history. He esp. dedicated himself to the description and editing of MSS; his four-volume *Cabinet des manuscrits* (1868–81) in detailing the MSS collection of the Bibliothèque Nationale provides a concrete history of the book during the Middle Ages. Scholars investigating the historical development of the liturgy are particularly indebted to his work. BIBLIOGRAPHY: M. Noirot, *Catholicisme* 3:566.

[M. B. MONAGHAN]

DELITZSCH, FRANZ JULIUS (1813–90), German Lutheran, of Jewish descent, the leading Christian student of Judaica in his day. He was educated at the Univ. of Leipzig, taught there, and there founded the Institute for Jewish studies. His commentaries on Gen, Ps, and Is greatly influenced OT studies, esp. in England and America, where the higher criticism was late in gaining a foothold. D.'s abiding concern was to re-create for Christians the Jewish background of Jesus and the NT times. His son Friedrich (1850–1922) was the leading Assyriologist of his day and effectively demonstrated the dependence of many OT forms on Babylonian prototypes.

[E. J. DILLON]

DELITZSCH, FRIEDRICH (1850–1922), Orientalist and Sanskrit specialist. Son of the German theologian, Franz Delitzsch, D. taught at Leipzig where he had also received his doctorate. He developed a systematic, scientific approach in early Assyriology through his own treatises on Semitic languages and also through his work on Oriental and Sumerian geography. He is the author of an Assyrian dictionary, grammar, and several books in Assyrian literature. BIBLIOGRAPHY: J. Brinkman, NCE 4:736; F. Weissbach, *Reallexikon der Assyriologie* (ed. E. Ebeling and B. Meissner, 1938) 2:198.

[A. A. O'NEILL]

DELL, PETER, THE ELDER (*c.* 1480–1552), Franconian artist who studied with Riemenschneider and Hans Leinberger, executing most of the tomb monuments of his time. (Epigraph of Bishop von Bibra, Würzburg Cathedral).

[M. J. DALY]

DELLA CHIESA, BERNARDINO (1644–1721), missionary bp. in China. A Franciscan superior at Orvieto, he was consecrated bp. in 1680 and set out for China where he arrived in 1684. At the time there was a serious dissension among the religious missionaries in China, a number of whom were under excommunication because they refused to obey the directive of Rome that they work under the authority of the vicars apostolic. Della Chiesa lifted the censure. When Charles Maigrot was named administrator of the missions of China, he reimposed the decree of excommunication. The case was appealed to Rome which revoked the decree. Della Chiesa was named vicar apostolic of Fuchien and general administrator of all Chinese missions, becoming bp. of Peking in 1701. He was always loyal to the Holy See and a man of moderation; many of his problems stemmed from the incredibly slow communication with Rome. The dispute over adaptation of ritual to Chinese custom created a painful situation for him who had to condemn the practice, a decision approved by the Congregation for the Propagation of the Faith. His last years were spent in unhappy disputes with some missioners. BIBLIOGRAPHY: A. Van den Wyngaert, DHGE 8:787–788.

[J. R. AHERNE]

DELLA PORTA, GIACOMO, see PORTA, GIACOMO DELLA.

DELLA QUERCIA, JACOPO, see QUERCIA, JACOPO DELLA.

DELLA ROBBIA (LUCA, ANDREA, GIOVANNI), a family of sculptors in 15th- and 16th-cent. Florence esp. noted for their glazed and colored terracotta *tondo* or lunette reliefs. These consisted mostly of Madonna and Child with angels and saints, usually with the figures in white against a blue ground, framed in the distinctive "della Robbia wreath" of flowers, fruits, and classical moldings. **Luca** (1400–82), the most important, was regarded by Alberti as one of the founders of the Italian Renaissance. His major work is the marble *Singing Gallery* (1431–38; Florence, Cathedral Museum). **Andrea** (1435–1525), his nephew, continued the family workshop and is remembered for the roundels of children on the arcade of the Ospedale degli Innocenti, Florence (1463–66). **Giovanni** (1469–1529), most important of Andrea's five sons directed the workshop toward a more naturalistic and pictorial style. BIBLIOGRAPHY: J. Pope-Hennessy, *Italian Renaissance Sculpture* (1958); J. Brunetti, EncWA 4:295–302.

[L. A. LEITE]

DELLA ROVERE, an Italian family originating near Savona and influential in both political and ecclesiastical spheres from the mid-15th to the early 17th century. The first historically important Della Rovere was Francisco, who became Pope *Sixtus IV in 1471. During his pontificate he arranged marriages, benefices, and gave other aid to his relatives. He points up the growing secularization of the papacy. Francisco's nephew, Giuliano, became cardinal and later Pope *Julius II (1503–13), the most important of the family. Many others of the Della Roveres enjoyed high position outside the Church. Through marriage to the daughters of the Duke of Urbino and the king of Sicily, two Della Roveres, Giovanni and Leonardo, increased the prestige of the family.

[D. G. NUGENT]

DELLA SOMAGLIA, GIULIO MARIA (1744–1830), cardinal, secretary of state for Pope Leo XII. After being secretary to several Roman Congregations, he became a cardinal in 1795, took part in the Venice conclave (1800) that elected Pius VII, and negotiated that pope's return to Rome. He incurred the wrath of Napoleon I in 1810, was exiled and stripped of his benefices. After the Emperor's downfall, D. filled several papal offices, was bishop of Frascati (1814), then of Ostia and Velletri (1820). As secretary of state (1823–28), he shared in Leo XII's attempts to restrain the rising forces of republicanism. BIBLIOGRAPHY: E. E. Y. Hales, *Revolution and the Papacy* (1960).

[T. C. O'BRIEN]

DELLO JOIO, NORMAN (1913–   ), composer. Born in New York City the son of an organist and choirmaster, D. studied first with his father and with Pietro Yon, his godfather. Later, at Juilliard, he studied with Bernard Wagenaar and, at Yale, with Paul Hindemith, whose influence was the greatest force in his development as a composer. He taught composition at Sarah Lawrence College and at Mannes College, was a recipient of two Guggenheim Fellowships, and was a consultant for the Ford Foundation. He has lectured in colleges and written for music journals. D. has composed orchestral works, concertos, chamber and piano music, operas, dance music, film and television music, songs and music for chorus. He also has written Masses and other settings for the liturgy, one of his latest publications being *Mass in Honor of the Eucharist* composed for the 1976 Eucharistic Congress in Philadelphia. His works are simple and spontaneous in style and evidence the diverse elements of chant, of Italian grand opera, and of jazz, in which he was early steeped. Religious themes inspire many of his compositions, such as *A Psalm for David* (1950), *Lamentations of Soul* (1954), and *Meditations on Ecclesiastes* (1956). *Dictionary of Contemporary Music* (ed. J. Vinton; 1974) 180–181.

[M. T. LEGGE]

DELP, ALFRED (1907–45), a convert to Roman Catholicism in 1920. He entered the Society of Jesus and did his studies at Feldkirch, partly under the direction of Karl Rahner. From 1931 to 1934 he was a prefect in the Jesuit school in Feldkirch and then resumed his philosophical studies in Munich. In 1935 he went to Holland to study theology, was ordained to the priesthood in 1938, and in the following year began his association as a consultant in sociology for *Stimmen der Zeit*. It was in this latter role that he was discovered by Helmuth von Moltke, the leader of the German Resistance group which had its center at his estate, Kreisau, in Silesia. D. joined this group in the spring of 1942, developing with them plans for a post-war state based on principles of social justice. Because this presupposed the demise of Hitler as head of State, he was arrested with other members of the group, subjected to a farcical trial before the People's Court, and sentenced to death for "treason." He was hanged on Feb. 2, 1945. His writings from prison were published in 1956 as *Im Angesicht des Todes* and later translated into English as *Prison Meditations*. His other works include: *Tragische Existenz* (1935); *Der Mensch in die Geschichte* (1941); *Zur Erde entschlossen* (1949); *Der mächtige Gott* (1949); *Kämpfer, Beter, Zeuge, Briefe und Beiträge von Freunden* (1955); and *Der Mensch vor sich selbst* (1956). BIBLIOGRAPHY: G. van Room, *Neuordnung im Widerstand* (1967); E. Zeller, *Geist der Freiheit* (1963).

[M. A. GALLIN]

DELPHI (ART), city in central Greece, equidistant from the N shore of the Gulf of Corinth and the S face of Mt. Parnassus. In classical times the seat of the famed oracle, but for this article the most important remains are the ruins of the 7th-cent. temple of Athena Pronaia, one of the earliest Doric temples known, the Great Tholos (400 B.C.), of early Corinthian order, and the Temple of Apollo (c.360 B.C.). Along the Sacred Way are the famous Treasury of the Siphnians (525 B.C.), with its renowned sculptured frieze, and the Treasury of the Athenians (c.510–500 B.C.), together with numerous victory monuments. On the slope were the Lesche (assembly-halls) of the Cnidians with the famous murals of Polygnotos, a theater (4th cent. B.C.) and a stadium for Pythian games. The history of Greek art can be traced through these monuments at Delphi.

[M. J. DALY]

DELPHI, ORACLE OF, an oracle of Apollo and the principal oracle of ancient Greece. It was located at what was thought to be the center of the earth, marked by the sacred navel-stone, or *omphalos,* on the S slope of Mount Parnassus. The first oracles of the god were given through the interpretation of natural signs such as the song and flight of birds. Later they were uttered through the mouth of a frenzied virgin priestess, the Pythia. The oracle gave responses to questions of a religious and secular nature, to individuals and to official embassies, to Greeks and to foreigners. Frequently ambiguous and politically opportunistic, the oracle nevertheless played an important role in Greek colonization, giving advice on the choice of a site and patron deity, and in developing a more perfect moral sense among the Greeks by insisting that the intent with which an act was committed must be taken into account. Under the Roman emperors it gradually lost its influence and was finally abolished by Theodosius in 390 A.D. BIBLIOGRAPHY: H. W. Parke, *History of the Delphic Oracle* (1939).

[M. J. COSTELLOE]

DELPHINA OF SIGNE, BL. (*c.* 1283–1360), Franciscan tertiary. The daughter of noble parents, she married Elzéar of Sabran (*c.* 1300) with whom she shared a life of sanctity amidst the demands of public position. At the court of Robert of Naples, where Elzéar tutored Robert's son, D. became a close friend and spiritual guide to Queen Sancha. After Robert's death (1323), D. returned to Provence and devoted herself to prayer, penance, and works of mercy. BIBLIOGRAPHY: G. Bataille, BiblSanct 4:540–541; Butler 3:661–662.

[H. DRESSLER]

DELPHINUS OF BORDEAUX, ST. (late 4th cent.). D. took part in the fight against *Priscillianism. He held a synod at Bordeaux (385–386) to which were invited the Spanish leaders of the movement, among them Instantius. The synod upheld orthodox doctrine and deprived Instantius of his bishopric. D. corresponded with St. *Ambrose and was a close friend of St. *Paulinus of Nola, whom he baptized. Five extant letters testify to the friendship between the two (all written to D.; his letters to Paulinus are lost). BIBLIOGRAPHY: P. Fabre, *Essai sur la chronologie de l'oeuvre de S. Paulin de Nole* (1948) 57–65; *idem S. Paulin de Nole et l'amitié chrétienne* (1949) 252–261; R. Aubert, DHGE 14:185–187; Butler 4:605.

[P. K. MEAGHER]

DEL PRADO, NORBERTO (1852–1918), Spanish Dominican theologian. A member of the Province of the Holy Rosary of the Philippines, he taught moral theology, first at Santo Tomas in Manila (1887–91), then at the Univ. of Fribourg, Switzerland (1891–1918). His two outstanding works are: *De gratia et libero arbitrio* (3 v., 1907), an exhaustive presentation of the Dominican teaching on grace as authentically that of St. Thomas Aquinas; the *De veritate fundamentali philosophiae christianae,* which arrays all of St. Thomas's metaphysics under the aegis of the real distinction between *essence and existence.

[T. C. O'BRIEN]

DEL RIO, MARTIN ANTON (1551–1609), statesman, Jesuit theologian. A celebrated scholar and doctor of law (Salamanca), he served in numerous public capacities in the Low Countries. He entered the Society of Jesus in 1680 and in time held the chairs of philosophy, theology, and Scripture at a number of universities including Louvain and Salamanca. He was an extraordinary linguist with a knowledge of nine languages. His writings are voluminous and carefully composed. They cover humanistic studies, scriptural and theological works, and ascetical treatises. His most celebrated work on magic was well regarded and went through many editions.

[J. R. AHERNE]

DEL SARTO, ANDREA (1486–1530), Florentine Renaissance painter, who worked with Piero di Cosimo (1498–1508) and at the court of Francis I, Fontainebleau (1518–19). D.'s *Tobias Altar* (1511 Vienna) is characterized by the exaggerated *sfumato* and facial expression of Leonardo. A fresco, *Birth of the Virgin* (1514, Florence), shows the soft atmosphere, sweet expressions, and sentiment of D.'s mature style. A *Madonna and Child with Infant St. John* and *Madonna of the Harpies* (1517, Florence) evidence tendencies leading to the mannerism of Andrea's pupil Pontormo. BIBLIOGRAPHY: T. Shearman, *Andrea del Sarto,* (2 v., 1965).

[M. J. DALY]

DELUGE, the legendary flood (Gen 6–8) that covered the whole world. Such a universal catastrophe is found in some form in many ancient cultures, but the story of the flood as found in Genesis came into Canaanite folklore from Babylonian influence. When Israel entered Canaan the Israelites expropriated this legend along with so much else of Canaanite culture and wove it into the story of its own national origins. It was the *Yahwist, writing in the 10th cent. B.C., who first accomplished this feat; and though the Priestly editor (see ELOHIST) prefers the Priestly version of the story, he not only incorporates much of the Yahwist version, but is ultimately indebted to the Yahwist for the basic story. The Yahwist's account is based on the Babylonian myth preserved in the Gilgamesh Epic. According to the latter, the gods decided capriciously to send a flood upon the earth. One of the gods, Ea, resolved to save his favorite mortal, Utnapishtim. So without divulging the gods' intention, Ea commanded Utnapishtim to build a ship of prescribed dimensions. The fortunate mortal discerned the reason and complied. He then entered the ship with his family, his dependents, and a number of animals. A storm raged for 6 days, and all mankind was destroyed. On the 7th day Utnapishtim sent out in succession a dove, a swallow, and a raven. The first two returned; the raven did not. Then Utnapishtim released the animals, left the ship himself, and offered sacrifices whose pleasing aroma reached the gods. The significant differences between this version and the biblical conflation of the Yahwist and the Priestly account, are some theological touches. Thus, in Genesis the flood was not a capricious act of God, but punishment for wickedness. Noah found favor because of his righteousness. After the flood God makes a covenant with Noah promising never again to destroy all flesh, and gives the rainbow as the recurring sign of this covenant.

[E. J. DILLON]

DELUIL-MARTINY, MARIE de JÉSUS (1841–84), foundress of the Daughters of the Heart of Jesus. She was born in Marseilles, France, and baptized Marie Caroline Philomène. D. was educated by the Visitation nuns. She founded a congregation of contemplatives, whose apostolate was to make reparation to the Hearts of Jesus and Mary and also to pray for priests. During the lifetime of the foundress, the Institute spread throughout France and Belgium, and since then houses were established in four other European countries. BIBLIOGRAPHY: K. Hofmann, LTK 3:213; R. Garrigou-Lagrange, *La Vita interiore della Madre Maria di Gesù* (1939); A. DeBonhome, "Dévotions prohibées," DSAM 3:786–788.

[R. A. TODD]

DELUSION, a false belief, often grossly so, which a person holds tenaciously because it gratifies some pressing unconscious psychological need. He holds it so deeply that facts and logic ordinarily effective in correcting false beliefs of a person of similar experience and education are totally unavailing. When delusions are elaborated into intricate, coherent patterns of ideas, they are said to be systematized. Common types of delusion are of grandeur and of persecution. Delusions may be symptoms of organic diseases like cerebral arteriosclerosis and Addison's disease, or of psychic disturbance; they are the most characteristic symptoms of paranoid conditions. Often a person can have extensive delusions that do not interfere with a normal, productive life. They do not become dangerous until they focus as hostile ideas toward one or several persons. When the counselor or spiritual adviser observes delusions in a client or parishioner, he should realize the need for psychiatric assistance.

[M. E. STOCK]

DEMAN, THOMAS (1899–1954), French Dominican moral theologian. At the time of his early death from an undetected peritonitis, D. was eulogized by the great historian of moral theology, Dom O. Lottin, as "the best moralist of the age." D. became a Dominican in 1921, was ordained in 1927. He achieved eminence at the theology faculty of the Univ. of Fribourg, where he became *professor ordinarius* of moral theology in 1945 and was dean of the faculty, 1945–50. He was also devoted to preaching, to pastoral counseling, and to the spiritual direction of the Daughters of St. Catherine of Siena, a secular institute. By his research and writing D. made an immense contribution to the return of moral theology to its roots, evangelical inspiration, and positive direction. For him that meant in great measure retrieving the Christian insight characteristic of the moral thought of St. Thomas Aquinas, a treasure all but lost to the Church because of the dominance for 4 cent. of casuistry and *probabilism over the science of moral theology. D.'s massive monograph "Probabilisme" (DTC 13:417–619) laid bare with minute documentation and assessed with critical insight the distortion of the Christian

life, above all of its charity-motivated interiority, that probabilism caused. His volume *Prudence* in the *Somme théologique* (ed. *Revue des jeunes,* 1947) is the most authentic of all presentations of St. Thomas's view of the living of the Christian life. D. also contributed to the DSAM, wrote many thoughtful articles in theological journals, was director of the *Bullétin thomiste,* and editor of the section on moral philosophy for the RevScPhilTh 1930–39. His books include *Aux origines de la théologie morale* (1951), a conference given at Montreal; published posthumously was his *Le traitement scientifique de la morale chrétienne selon Saint Augustin* (1957). He left unpublished a work on the formation of the theology of grace in St. Thomas's works. All regretted that he did not live to achieve the major work towards which his research was always pointed, a full development of foundational principles of moral theology. It is equally regrettable that the work he did complete is not better known in this era of a renewal of moral theology.

[T. C. O'BRIEN]

DEMEESTER, MARIE LOUISE, MOTHER (1857–1928), foundress of the Missionary Sisters of St. Augustine, sometimes called the Missionary Canonesses of St. Augustine. A native of Roulers, Belgium, she was a member of a teaching order of the Canonesses of St. Augustine until 1897, when her desire to aid foreign missions was fulfilled through the founding of a new community devoted to education and charitable works. Houses were established in India, the Philippines, Africa, China, the Virgin Islands, and (1919) in the U.S. Her community, international in scope, maintained missions in 9 countries. BIBLIOGRAPHY: J. Calbrecht, NCE 4:744.

[R. A. TODD]

DEMETER, Greek goddess of agriculture, particularly of grain, the daughter of Kronos and Rhea, and the mother of Kore, or Persephone. According to the Homeric Hymn to D., Hades fell in love with Kore and carried her off to the Lower World. Setting out in search of her, D. came to Eleusis in the guise of an old woman but eventually revealed herself. Returning to Olympus, she was joined by her daughter for a portion of each year, and during this time she allowed the earth to bring forth its crops. This famous etiological myth was the basis for the worship of D. at Eleusis. Among the Romans she was identified with Ceres and her daughter with Proserpina. BIBLIOGRAPHY: M. Nilsson, *Geschichte der griechischen Religion* (2d ed., 1955) 1:456–481.

[M. J. COSTELLOE]

DEMETER OF CNIDUS, Hellenistic statue (c.350 B.C.). The seated figure, of massive proportions and enveloped in a heavy himation with rich folds, is of two kinds of marble; the head, of finer Parian stone, marked by the sadness of D.

grieving for her daughter in the underworld is in the style of the School of Scopas.

[M. J. DALY]

DEMETRACOPOULOS, ANDRONICUS (1826–72), Greek Orthodox archimandrite and scholar. A native of Kalavryta in the Peloponnesus, D. died in Leipzig, where from 1858 he was pastor to the Greek community. His work consists mainly of editions of previously unedited Byzantine texts, and of studies of literary and doctrinal history, especially bearing on the Schism. Though written from the Orthodox viewpoint, his works are scholarly and accurate in their basic information. BIBLIOGRAPHY: V. Laurent, DHGE 14:193–194; L. Petit, DTC 4:263; V. Grumel, *Catholicisme* 3:575.

[P. K. MEAGHER]

DEMETRIAN OF KHYTRI, ST. (d. *c*.911), bp. and national patron of Cyprus. After some 40 years as a monk, he was named bp. of Khytri in Cyprus. At the age of 80 he journeyed to Baghdad to ransom captives taken by the Arabs.

[G. T. DENNIS]

DEMETRIAS, ST. (b. *c*.398), a woman of patrician birth who fled to Carthage during Alaric's siege of Rome (410). She decided to receive the veil of a consecrated virgin (413) after hearing a sermon of St. Augustine. Many of her relatives and servants followed her example. Her mother received letters of congratulation from Pope Innocent I and Augustine, and D. herself received letters on virginity from Pelagius, Augustine, and Jerome (*Ep.* 130). During the pontificate of Leo I, she had the church of St. Stephen built on her estate on the Via Latina. BIBLIOGRAPHY: G. Bardy, DSAM 3:133–137.

[F. J. MURPHY]

DEMETRIUS, ST. (Sl., *Dmitry*), martyr, slain probably in Macedonia during the persecution of Maximian early in the 4th cent., known as the Great Martyr (Megalomartyr) in the Eastern Church. The legendary accounts of his life and his miracles became immensely popular. In the 5th cent. a great basilica, of which some mosaics remain, was built over his reputed tomb in Thessalonica and became the center of pilgrimages. Patron and protector of Thessalonica, he was honored with a cult that spread throughout the East, especially among the Slavs. He is also regarded as the patron of soldiers. BIBLIOGRAPHY: Butler 4:63; R. Janin, BiblSanct 4:556–564.

[G. T. DENNIS]

DEMETRIUS OF ALEXANDRIA, ST. (d. 231), bp. of Alexandria, possibly the 11th successor of St. Mark, but the first bp. of Alexandria (189–231) about whom anything is known. He was the patron of *Origen and defended him even after his self-mutilation. But when Origen was or-

dained without permission in Caesarea (*c*.230), D. held local synods which condemned him and deposed him from the priesthood. The catechetical school of Alexandria flourished during his episcopate. Jerome claims that D. sent Pantaenus to Yemen and Ethiopia, but this probably took place before he was bishop. The letters ascribed to him concerning the Easter controversy are not authentic. BIBLIOGRAPHY: A. Tessarolo, BiblSanct 4:552–553; Butler 4:67.

[F. J. MURPHY]

DEMETRIUS CYDONES, see CYDONES, DEMETRIUS.

DÉMIA, CHARLES (1637–89), French educator, priest of the archdiocese of Lyons, noted for his work in promoting diocesan schools in France, for his contribution to pedagogical methods, and for the foundation of the teaching order of the Sisters of St. Charles at Belley. BIBLIOGRAPHY: F. Rynois, *Un Grand homme, trop peu connu, Charles Démia* (1937).

DEMIURGE, a Greek term signifying originally "one who works for the people," "a craftsman." Plato employed the word in his *Timaeus* to designate the divine Craftsman who, following the unchangeable model of the ideas or forms, fashioned our present world. He is best regarded as a symbolic figure representing the operation of reason in the universe. In Plato, he is not identified with the Good, or as the creator or source of the ideas or forms, or as the world-soul. Such identifications, however, are found in Middle Platonism and in Neoplatonism. BIBLIOGRAPHY: Copleston 1:189–193, 247–252; W. Theiler, RAC 3 (1957) 694–711.

[M. R. P. MCGUIRE]

DEMOCRACY (med. Lat. *democratia*, William of Moerbeke's transliteration of the Gr. which comes from *demos*, the common people, and *kratos*, rule), government by the people, either directly, as in a small-town assembly, or through their elected representatives, as in some modern states. Disdained by Plato as encouraging insolence, anarchy, waste, impudence, and eventually tyranny (cf. *Republic* 563), and cautiously allowed by Aristotle as one element in a well-tempered polity (cf. *Politics* 3.5), it slowly, but not universally, lost its pejorative sense when the *demos* stood for free citizens in agreement about the laws, and when the Romans took the *populus* to mean all lawful people including the senate, not just the *plebs*, the populace or mass. Even under the most authoritarian emperors, the theory was that political power emanated from the people. This, too, was the theory of medieval times, feudal and post-feudal, with, however, the proviso that power lay under the sovereignty of God. It was obscured under the political absolutism of the Renaissance and Reformation, yet still persisted in schools of divinity and strengthened the great defenses of popular liberties from the 17th cent. onwards.

Two traditions then appear, the later, to be touched on first, has been historically associated with forces let loose by the French Revolution. The earlier, rooted in the teaching of the scholastic masters of the 16th cent., notably *Vitoria and *Suarez, is associated with the English revolution and less ambiguously with the American Revolution. Respect for law, natural and customary, is the touchstone of the difference between them, as Edmond *Burke was quick to notice. For a democracy that makes the general will an absolute (a general will constituted, unchecked by other factors, by what the majority decides) is, though Christians still may contrive to live under it, not acceptable to Christian thought; it is a form of mob-rule, even when, perhaps more ominously, the mob is not unwashed and not illiterate by modern standards. A constitutional democracy, however, that balances, as the canonists did, the "greater" part with the "saner" part, and that limits what the majority may do by protecting minority rights and encouraging free association, is probably the regime most in line with the Christian concern for freedom from arbitrary power, for the extension of a "responsible society," and for the rights of the politically weak and inarticulate. Moreover when, as has happened, "government of the people, by the people, for the people" is integrated in a system which also combines monarchy and aristocracy, that is the principles of unity and departmental probity, then, it seems, this comes nearest to the Christian ideals of a commonwealth.

Nevertheless, despite the fact that Christians have always been found who have thrown themselves wholeheartedly into political causes—for instance, throne and altar during the first half of the past century, or the proletarian revolution during the second half of the present—the great Christian theologians, wary of panaceas, have usually manifested a certain detachment from political forms, apart from their consistent condemnation of an invasive political tyranny. The Church, too, has showed itself content to work with any regime that makes a well-ordered and peaceful life possible for ordinary people. Democracy is a word with many emotive fringes, and it is well not to identify them, even the most generous, with the cause of Christianity. Neither to defend nor to attack political *egalitarianism, universal suffrage through the ballot-box, nor, for that matter, hereditary rank and privilege—is mandatory by the Gospel. BIBLIOGRAPHY: C. H. McIllwain, *Constitutionalism, Ancient and Modern* (1958); T. E. Utley and J. S. Maclure, *Documents of Modern Political Thought* (1957, repr. 1973); J. H. Hallowell, *Moral Foundation of Democracy* (1954); R. Niebuhr, *Children of Light and Children of Darkness* (1944), Vat II Church ModWorld 76.

[T. GILBY]

DEMOCRACY, CHRISTIAN, see CHRISTIAN DEMOCRACY.

DEMOCRITUS OF ABDERA, see LEUCIPPUS OF MILETUS AND DEMOCRITUS OF ABDERA.

DEMOGRAPHY, the discipline concerned with the quantitative aspects of human populations. A narrow definition of the field would include the measurement and analysis of the aggregate size, age, sex, and other aspects of human populations. The events which alter the structure of a population—fertility, mortality, and migration—have been the subjects of intensive analyses in the past 100 years, and sophisticated mathematical and statistical techniques now are employed by demographers in their formal work. Broadly, demography includes studies that focus on population structure and change in sociological, economic, or biological perspectives. Thus, a considerable amount of attention has been given to the assessment of the social and economic effects of different levels of human fertility. Closely allied to this type of analysis are so-called action programs in which demographers aid attempts to control the birth rate. In recent years, demographers have turned with greater frequency to the study of socio-psychological factors in human reproduction. Statistical studies of migration have grown more comprehensive and rigorous, while some progress has been made in assessing the sociological and economic impact of different forms of migration. The examination of death as a demographic event has been marked by methodological advances in the use of the life table, a statistical tool for the analysis of the effects of the age/death correlation on the structure of a hypothetical population. Better methods of data collection have been responsible in part for advances in epidemiology, the study of the distribution of morbidity in a population. BIBLIOGRAPHY: D. J. Bogue, *Principles of Demography* (1969); P. M. Hauser and O. D. Duncan, *Study of Population* (1959); D. Kirk et al., *International Encyclopedia of the Social Sciences* (1968) 12:342–388.

[G. W. DOWDALL]

DEMON, in Catholic theology, an evil spirit. In the Greek, from which the word was taken, it was used in reference to an inferior god or goddess, and in the plural, to the souls of men of the golden age who formed the connecting link between gods and men; only later does it mean an evil spirit or devil. The biblical notion seems to have affinities with the Mesopotamian belief that the lesser evils of life were attributable to the influence of demons whom the sorcerer could exorcise only when he knew their names; conversely good demons were guardian genii not unlike the cherubim. The OT severely prohibited magic and looked to Yahweh to protect the Jews from such evils (of demonic origin?) as are mentioned in Ps 91.5–6. In apocryphal books demons are described as fallen angels and identified with the fathers of the race of giants (Gen 6.1–4). Paul asserts that sacrifices offered to false gods are offered to demons (1 Cor 10.20–21) and ascribes false teaching to their influence (1 Tim 4.1). They are called "angels of the devil" (Mt 25.41) whose kingdom is hierarchically organized. This biblical imagery is sometimes taken as little more than a mythological personification of evil; however, H. Schlier in

Principalities and Powers in the New Testament (1961) 67–68, concludes: "the manifold principalities and powers which unfold the one satanic power are encountered as a kind of personal and powerful being [whose] power has been broken on the cross and in the resurrection." The Church has always taught the existence of personal evil spirits who have become so through their own will. BIBLIOGRAPHY: W. Foerster, Kittel TD 2:14–20.

[B. FORSHAW]

DEMONIAC, see DIABOLICAL POSSESSION; DIABOLICAL OBSESSION.

DEMONOLATRY, worship of demons. Belief in the power of demons to inflict evils of various kinds has sometimes led to attempts at winning their favor through rites and prayers. Strongly condemned by orthodox religion, the practice may express rebellion against God and a survival of pagan practices. It has had a revival in the late 20th century.

[T. EARLY]

DEMONOLOGY, the study of demons or evil spirits. From the standpoint of Christian theology demons were originally angels created by God but who fell through their rebellion and are now the angels of Satan. More philosophically they are defined as the principles of disorder in the universe. In addition to the orthodox teaching of the Church on the subject, popular superstition has developed a body of occult theory, which is also called demonology. From this superstition arose various practices supposed to secure the good will of demons and avoid their evil effects. General interest in demons reached a high point in the 16th and 17th centuries. They were visualized in literal fashion and extensively portrayed in works of art. Entering into association with demons was forbidden by the authorities and those who were thought to do so were punished for *witchcraft.

[T. EARLY]

DEMOTIC SCRIPT (Gr. *demotikos,* popular), term used since the time of Herodotus (5th cent. B.C.) for the Egyptian style of writing that, beginning in the 6th cent. B.C., succeeded the *hieratic script for nonreligious matters. BIBLIOGRAPHY: R. H. Pierce, *Three Demotic Papyri: in the Brooklyn Museum . . .* (1972).

[T. C. O'BRIEN]

DEMPSEY, MARY JOSEPH, SISTER (1856–1939) administrator. D. entered the Third Order Regular of St. Francis (1878). Appointed superintendent of St. Mary's Hospital, Rochester, Minn. (1892), she was influential in its growth and expansion. She participated in the organization of the Catholic Hospital Association of the U.S. and Canada. Her reputation in medicine was international. BIBLIOGRAPHY: H. Clapesattle, *Doctors Mayo* (1941).

[K. BATEMAN]

DEMPSEY, TIMOTHY (1867–1936), humanitarian. Born in Ireland, ordained there in 1891, D. came to the U.S. in the same year. St. Louis was to be the city where he would become famous. In 1906 he opened a hotel for workingmen, a low cost hostel for the down-and-out. D. followed this with a nursery for the day care of children (1910) and in 1911 a hotel for women, which provided the same desirable atmosphere for working women as did the hotel for men. His success in arbitrating labor disputes was phenomenal. His remarkable influence on the underworld led to the ending of a gang war which had rocked St. Louis. His free lunchroom at the height of the depression of the 1930s served millions of meals. In these years, D. added to his institutions a hostel for blacks, which gave free lodging to thousands. BIBLIOGRAPHY: H. J. McAuliffe, *Father Tim* (1944).

[J. R. AHERNE]

DEMPSTER, THOMAS (1570–1625), Scottish scholar who spent much of his active career abroad because his RC faith excluded him from teaching positions in Scotland and England worthy of his talents.

Of his works, the *Historia ecclesiastica gentis Scotorum* has kept D.'s name alive. It contains almost 1,300 biographies of saints and other notable people, to all of whom he attributed Scotch birth. Admittedly he borrowed from the historian Hector Boice. In spite of such methods, D. was important as a historian of contemporary events, for much of what he gathered is no longer available elsewhere. *De bello a christianis contra barbaros gesto* contributed most to his reputation as a scholar. D. also wrote on law, mythology, and cosmography; he composed poems and at least one tragedy. The only poem, however, that still enjoys some reputation is his *Musca*. His work on the whole is of mixed quality—some valuable, some trivial. BIBLIOGRAPHY: J. H. Baxter, DHGE 215–218; H. Bradley, DNB 785–790.

[S. A. HEENEY]

DEMYTHOLOGIZING, a method of biblical criticism developed and applied by R. Bultmann (1884–1976). This method of biblical criticism concerns itself with the cultural religious expressions or myths used by the biblical authors to convey their religious message, the kerygma or proclamation. Myth has a technical meaning—the human expression of religious experience. This definition does not concern itself with the truth or falsity of the myth. It simply defines the way religious man expresses his experience. This understanding of myth is valid whether the human expression be the etchings on the caves of Neanderthal man, or the biblical writing of the Old and New Testaments, or a religious proclamation today. Religious kerygma or proclamation is always clothed in the cultural concepts of the times. Demythologizing concerns itself with the kerygma of the Scriptures. For example, the NT is not a biography of Jesus. It is a theological interpretation of the life of Jesus clothed in the cultural religious expressions of the Greco-Hebrew world. The NT clouds over the Jesus of history to proclaim a Jesus of faith. What remains are faith expressions concerning Jesus. These faith expressions of religious experience are mythologies. Demythologizing seeks to place the mythologies in their cultural contexts in order to understand the basic biblical kerygma. There are many examples of mythological coloring in the NT. The Greek preexistent *Logos* myth colors the biblical interpretation of who Jesus is. The Mesopotamian Son of Man myth colors the interpretation of the Resurrection. The Gnostic myths color the interpretation of the redemptive value of the life and death of Jesus. What is suggested by these examples is that there were preexistent mythologies that assisted the early Christian communities to experience, conceptualize, and articulate their understanding of Jesus. They expressed their faith, their religious experience and understanding of Jesus by the linguistic tools available to them, namely, mythologies. Demythologizing the NT gives us an understanding of the theological insights of the first Christian communities by understanding their cultural religious expressions. By demythologizing biblical myths of the NT, the contemporary Christian confronts the basic and original mystery of Jesus Christ. Demythologizing is not a rejection of the mythological insights of the NT; it is an explanation of them. Bultmann's use of demythologizing is influenced by the philosophy of existentialism. After stripping the NT of its mythological expressions, Bultmann concluded to an existential kerygma by which Jesus summons man to a decision-making confrontation between God and the transitory world. The kergyma of the NT presents this confrontation to every generation of man. Bultmann errs in his use of demythologizing by rejecting the valid insights of the early Christian myths, and failing to see that the basic kerygma itself can never be expressed otherwise than by mythology.

Demythologizing is a valid method of biblical criticism. It should not be applied to the Scriptures alone. All religious expressions are mythological whether expressed by the Evangelists, the Fathers, the great Church Councils, or proclamations of religious leaders today. Demythologizing as a method opens up the continual evolution of man's religious expressions of faith in the face of God's mysteries. RC teaching, however, inisists on a fundamental deposit of faith which the Church rightly understands, faithfully preserves, and authentically transmits (see TEACHING AUTHORITY OF THE CHURCH). BIBLIOGRAPHY: R. Bultmann, *Kerygma and Myth* (ed. H. W. Bartsch (1961); M. Eliade, *Cosmos and History* (1959).

[W. J. DUGGAN]

DENARIUS, a Roman silver coin originally a tenth but later a sixteenth of an *as,* practically the size of a British sixpence. In the NT period it was the amount paid for a day's work (Mt 20:1–15).

[J. J. O'ROURKE]

DE NEVE, JOHN (1821–1898), administrator. Ordained in Belgium in 1847, he worked in the U.S. until 1859 when he was appointed rector of the American College of Louvain. An able administrator and fund-raiser, he was obliged to resign for reasons of health in 1871. Returning to the position of rector in 1881, he served for another ten years, placing the college on a sound footing economically and educationally. BIBLIOGRAPHY: J. D. Sauter, *American College of Louvain, 1857–1898* (1959).

[J. R. AHERNE]

DENIAL, in psychoanalysis a defense mechanism by which a person blocks out unwanted aspects of external reality by wish-fulfilling fantasy or play-acting behavior. For example, a child who actively fears his father imagines himself a soldier and plays at gunfighting to repudiate his weakness and physical helplessness. In extreme cases, denial becomes a psychotic mechanism, e.g., when a person refuses to admit the death of someone beloved and acts as if he were still alive. The use of denial by adults indicates at the very least an immature attitude toward reality.

[M. E. STOCK]

DENIFLE, HEINRICH SEUSE (1844–1905), Dominican church historian of Austrian birth. Called to Rome (1883) and appointed by Pope Leo XIII a papal archivist, D. became a collaborator in a new edition of the works of Thomas Aquinas. From 1899 on he devoted all his time to visiting Austrian and German archives and libraries to collect material for his work on Luther, which became his best-known writing. His major work was *Luther und Lutherthum* (1904–09). An important contribution to research on Luther is D.'s discovery of a copy of the hitherto unknown Luther commentary on the Epistle to the Romans. D.'s somewhat biased interpretation of Luther's character has been rejected by later RC historians. BIBLIOGRAPHY: R. Walsh, CE 4:719–721; A. Walz, LTK 3:227–228.

[K. BATEMAN]

DENIS, see also DIONYSIUS.

DENIS THE CARTHUSIAN (*c.* 1402–71), mystical writer, called *Doctor ecstaticus.* Born at Rychel in Belgium, he entered the Charterhouse at Roermond, Holland, in 1425, and there spent most of his life. His collected works (publ. in 44 v., 1895–1935) include commentaries on the Bible, on *Pseudo–Dionysius and *Boethius; and treatises on philosophy and on ecclesiastical reform. His principal work, *De contemplatione* (Opera, v. 41, 135–389), evidences the strong influence of the apophatic theology of Dionysius and of Jan van *Ruysbroek. Contemplative union, through the gift of wisdom, reaches a positive experience of God's perfection, but then must advance to the experience of negation, the deepening awareness of God's being unlike and beyond any perfection known. Some question D.'s originality, but modern scholarship has yielded greater appreciation of why his works were so highly esteemed and widely used. BIBLIOGRAPHY: A. Stoelen, DSAM 3:430–450.

[T. C. O'BRIEN]

DENIS OF PARIS, ST. (Denys, Dionysius; d. *c.*250), popularly regarded as the patron saint of France. According to *Gregory of Tours, D., together with Rusticus and Eleutherius, was sent from Rome to preach the faith in Paris where all three suffered martyrdom. Many legends grew up about D., many of which are traceable to his biography as written in the 9th cent. by Hilduin, abbot of St. Denis. At that time the writings of *Pseudo-Dionysius had only recently been introduced into France. Hilduin identified D. as the Dionysius of Athens converted by Paul and the supposed author of these writings. According to further embellishments introduced by Hilduin, D. was sent to Paris by Pope *Clement I and when, after many vain attempts to put him to death, his persecutors succeeded in decapitating him on Montmartre, he picked up his head and walked two miles to the site of the future abbey that was to bear his name; of which it has been said "C'est le premier pas qui compte."

[R. B. ENO]

DENIS, MAURICE (1870–1943), French painter and one of the most important theorists of his time. D. as a member of the *Nabis* defined their aesthetics (1890). Influenced by Gauguin's symbolism (1888), by synthetism and Art Nouveau, D. modelled more vigorously after an Italian trip (1895–97). Profoundly religious, D. sought to express through symbolism not the external world, but states of mind (*Ave Maria with Red Slippers*, 1898). He painted his most famous *Homage to Cézanne* in 1900. Gradually devoting himself exclusively to religious art, D. founded with G. Desvallieres the Ateliers de l'Art Sacré. BIBLIOGRAPHY: P. Jamot, *Maurice Denis* (1945).

[M. J. DALY]

DENK, HANS (Denck; *c.*1495–1527), advocate of a religion of inner experience. D. was a humanist and associate of J. *Oecolampadius. Through the influence of T. *Münzer in Nuremberg (1523) and then of B. *Hubmaier in Augsburg, D. became a leading preacher of Anabaptist views in Augsburg, Worms, Strassburg, and Basel. D.'s name is not bound simply to that movement, however. He opposed Protestant theories of predestination and RC teaching on the sacraments and the external Church in favor of individual inner mystical experience. Each was free to choose to live by Christ, the indwelling Word. D. published several short treatises that reflect the mysticism of the *Theologia Germanica, and he collaborated in translating the prophetic books of the Bible from Hebrew into German. Works: *Hans Denk, Schriften* (ed. G. Baring and W. Fellmann, 1955–60). BIBLIOGRAPHY: A. Coutts, *Hans Denk, c.1495–1527, Humanist and Heretic* (1927); J. F. G. Goet-

ters, RGG 2:82; R. M. Jones, *Spiritual Reformers in the 16th and 17th Centuries* (pa. 1959) 17–30.

[T. C. O'BRIEN]

DĒNKART, THE, "the Work of Religion," a kind of encyclopedia of Persian religion written in Pahlavi or Middle Persian (*c.*10th cent. A.D.). It is esp. important for its varied content, and in particular for its use of or references to lost books *(nasks)* of the Avesta. BIBLIOGRAPHY: J. Duchesne-Guillemin, *La Religion de l'Iran ancien* (1962).

[M. R. P. MCGUIRE]

DENMARK, predominantly Lutheran country of NW Europe; a constitutional monarchy. Christianity first reached Denmark through Frisian traders and the missionaries who followed them. The first known missionary to visit Denmark was *Willibrord (658–739). In the 9th cent., King Harold was baptized on a visit to Louis the Pious, who sent *Ansgar (Anskar) back with the king to evangelize the Danes. Abp. Adaldag of Bremen established the first Danish sees in 948. But general conversion followed the baptism *c.*960 of King Harold Bluetooth. Canute II (1018–35), who also ruled England and Norway, brought priests and bishops associated with the *Cluniac reform into the country. Canute IV (1080–86) strongly supported the Church, but his financial demands led to his murder by a mob. He was later venerated as patron saint of the country. The Danish Church, originally under Bremen-Hamburg, from 1104 had its own abp. at Lund, S Sweden, then forming part of Denmark. Church life flourished in the 12th and 13th cent., but the subsequent period saw a decline only partly halted under King Waldemar Atterday (1340–75) and his daughter Margaret (1387–1412). The latter united Norway and Sweden under the Danish throne, but Sweden gained independence in 1523 and acquired Norway in 1814, though Denmark retains Greenland. Frederick I (1523–33) supported the Reformation, and the selection of Christian II as king in 1534 guaranteed its lasting success in Denmark. Monasteries were dissolved, and the extensive church estates confiscated. In 1537 Luther's friend, J. *Bugenhagen, crowned Christian III and ordained superintendents, later called bps., the king had chosen to replace the Catholic bishops. A law of 1624 decreed death for any Catholic priest found at work in Denmark, and a 1683 law provided for confiscating property of converts to Catholicism. After a period of rationalism, N.F.S. *Grundtvig (1783–1872) led a revival of orthodox Lutheranism. In opposition, S. *Kierkegaard (1813–55) set forth an existentialist approach. Laws of 1849 and 1852 brought religious freedom and disestablishment, but the Lutheran Church retained state support. The RC presence in Denmark before these laws of religious freedom was largely confined to members of foreign embassies. In a country that is nominally 98 per cent Lutheran, Danish Catholics still are a minuscule group. But the prefecture apostolic of Denmark was created in 1869, raised to a vicariate apostolic in 1892; finally in 1953 the

Diocese of Copenhagen, which includes the Faroes and Greenland, was erected. The small Catholic community has continued to grow and has exhibited remarkable vitality, in the establishment of parishes, schools, hospitals, orphanages, and in the vigor and excellence of the apostolate of the press. The most famous Danish Catholic author is J. Jørgensen, who made Catholic life and history known to his compatriots. In 1976 the Catholic population was 26,355.

[T. EARLY]

DENN, PAUL (1847–1900), Jesuit martyr. In China (1898) under Emperor Ts'euhi, a reaction set in against reforms pressed upon China by the Western powers. About 5000 Catholics were victims of the Boxers, an organized band who attacked foreigners and Christians. Pope Pius XII beatified 56 of these (1956), of whom four were French Jesuit priests. D. was one of these. BIBLIOGRAPHY: H. Cordier, CE 9:746–48; Butler 3:59–62.

[K. BATEMAN]

DENOMINATION, in a broad sense a synonym for *sect or for any church body composed of local congregations united in belief and government. In the more precise typology of E. *Troeltsch, denomination stands between the "church type" and the "sect type," as a religious group accommodated to the prevailing culture, willingly accepting itself as one among many other denominations, stressing practical cooperation, and minimizing distinctive theological differences. The theological view underlying such a concept was at least implicit in the Reformers' refusal to identify the Church with a particular institution, but the 17th-cent. *Independents gave expression to the idea as a rationale for the existence of Christian unity under diverse doctrinal, organizational, and liturgical forms. The term itself came into use in the 18th-cent. revivals in England and the U.S.; John *Wesley, for example, stated: "From real Christians of whatever denomination I earnestly desire not to be distinguished at all" (*The Character of a Methodist*). Both the underlying idea and denominations themselves are particularly a feature of Christianity in the U.S., because of religious freedom and the separation of Church and State. BIBLIOGRAPHY: J. M. Yinger, *Religion, Individual, and Society* (1957); W. S. Hudson, "Denominationalism as a Basis for Ecumenicity," *Church History* 24 (1955) 32–50; S. Meade, *Lively Experiment* (1963) ch. 7. *VOLUNTARYISM.

[N. H. MARING]

DENOMINATIONAL SCHOOLS, private, church-related institutions operated by a religious denomination. Predating the public school by centuries, non-Catholic denominational schools trace their European origin to the 16th century. During the Reformation religious and political controversy led many Churches to establish schools to inculcate and support their particular religious tenets. In the U.S. the colonists, who had come to the New World seeking religious freedom, saw the school as a means of perpetuating their individual ideals. Thus there appeared schools operated by Quakers, Calvinists, Dutch Reformed, Presbyterians, and Lutherans. In later years, many Protestant Churches favored the public school, although a relatively small number continue to operate their own, among whom are Mennonites, Lutherans, Episcopalians, Baptists, Seventh Day Adventists, and Mormons. Jewish parents prefer the public school. Their special religious and cultural needs are attended to after school and in Sabbath classes. BIBLIOGRAPHY: N. Edward and H. G. Richey, *School in the American Social Order* (1963).

[M. B. MURPHY]

DENOMINATIONALISM, a term used in several senses: (1) a synonym for *sectarianism in all its senses; (2) a view of the Church that allows and even favors the coexistence of many differing church bodies (see DENOMINATION); (3) the theory and practice that joins many local churches in one ecclesiastical body, united by belief and government. Denominationalism in the third sense has often been opposed in the U.S. by those stressing *congregational polity or seeking to emphasize *voluntaryism. Such opposition has appeared in the Christian Churches and Independent Churches, in Pentecostalism, and among Baptists, e.g., the General Association of Regular Baptist Churches. *ANTIDENOMINATIONALISM.

[N. H. MARING]

DENS, PIERRE (1690–1775), Belgian theologian. Ordained in 1715 and granted a graduate degree from the University of Louvain in 1723, he became professor and, from 1735 until his death, president of the Mechelen diocesan seminary. From 1754 he was archpriest of the Mechelen canonry. He is remembered for the 14-vol., posthumous *Theologia ad usum seminariorum . . .,* a manual in question and answer form, prized for its practicality and continuing in use even in the early 20th century.

[T. C. O'BRIEN]

DENUNCIATION, making public the sin or crime of another. (1) In moral theology St. Thomas Aquinas connects denunciation with *fraternal correction, which, out of *charity, has the good of others, even the one denounced, as its concern; *accusation is rather a matter of justice, concerned with achieving just retribution for a crime (ST 2a2ae.68,1). The virtue of charity towards others may require that a public, known action be denounced as sinful, for the spiritual good of the accused, that he may correct his ways; or for others, that they may have no doubt about or attraction towards the condemned action (see SCANDAL). Where a sin is altogether secret and against oneself alone, the only obligation is to try to influence the one guilty to correct his ways. Where a sin is secret, but includes a possible danger to the physical or spiritual well-being of individuals or a group, there must be, where possible, an attempt at correcting the sin privately, and if that is not possible, a denunciation of the sin for the good of others (*ibid.* 33.7). (2) Canon law sets out the conditions where denunciation of a canonical crime is obligatory on the basis of law, office, or the common good (CIC cc. 1935–38); it requires denunciation of the sin of *solicitation (CIC cc. 904; 2368,2); it penalizes a false denunciation of solicitation (op. cit. cc. 894;2363). Special provision is made for denunciation of pernicious books (op. cit. c. 1397); and regarding nullity of marriage (op. cit. c. 1971).

[T. C. O'BRIEN]

DENZINGER, HEINRICH JOSEPH (1819–83), Belgian theologian, compiler and first editor of the *Enchiridion Symbolorum et Definitionum* (1854; 32d edition, A. Schönmetzer, ed., 1963). "Denzinger," its familiar appellation, is a handbook of excerpts from documents of the teaching Church from earliest times. D. published, as well, important studies in historical theology.

[T. C. O'BRIEN]

DEO GRATIAS (thanks be to God), the response given by the congregation after the Readings and at the Dismissal of the Latin Mass, and frequently in other ceremonies. Thanksgiving of praise to God was a familiar theme in Jewish prayer, and its continued Christian expression extends liturgical thanksgiving and praise into daily life. BIBLIOGRAPHY: J. H. Miller, *Fundamentals of the Liturgy* (1957).

[N. R. KRAMER]

DEOCHAR, ST. (Theotger; d. betw. 820 and 829), a monk of Fulda, later a disciple of Alcuin at Charlemagne's court and first abbot of the Benedictine foundation of Herrieden in Franconia. He was an authority on the Scriptures and the monastic life. BIBLIOGRAPHY: Zimmermann 2:283–285; L. Falkenstein, BiblSanct 4:569–570.

[B. F. SCHERER]

DÉODAT DE BASLY (1862–1937), Franciscan theologian. He joined the Friars Minor at Caen (1879) and was founder (1897) and lifelong resident of the friary at Le Havre. In Christology D. ascribed to *Duns Scotus the *assumptus homo* theme and set forth as a cardinal principle that Christ's place in God's plans is anterior to human need of redemption. The defense of D.'s teaching on the *assumptus homo* by P. Seiler led subsequently to controversy over the psychological unity of Christ (see OssRom, July 27, 1951; DTC, Tables 2647–48). D.'s writings included a theological epic, *La Christiade française* (1918–27); *L'Assumptus Homo* (1928); *Le Moi de Jésus Christ* (1929); *Scotus docens (France Franciscaine* 14, 1934). His *Capitalia opera* was to be a systematic textual exposition of the doctrine of Scotus; only 2 of 12 projected volumes were published (1909–11). BIBLIOGRAPHY: DTC, Tables 938–939.

[T. C. O'BRIEN]

DEODATO ORLANDI (fl. 1288–1301), Italian painter of Lucca mentioned in documents of 1288 and 1301 when he signed two Crucifixes and a polyptych, all three works evidencing the dissolution of the Byzantine style at that time.

[M. J. DALY]

DEODATUS OF BLOIS, ST., a hermit and cenobite of the early 6th century. His legend claims that he influenced King Clovis, the Frankish conqueror, by his prayers for military success, to become an orthodox, rather than an Arian, Christian.

[J. F. FALLON]

DEODATUS OF NEVERS, ST. (St. Dié; d. c.679), a monk, possibly of Irish origin, who was bp. of Nevers c.650. Led by his desire for solitude, he resigned his office and after various vicissitudes finally built a monastery at the confluence of the Fave and Meurthe Rivers in the Vosges Mountains in France. Known first as Jointures, it and the town that grew up around it were later called Saint-Dié in his honor. Its rule, basically that of St. Columbanus, was tempered somewhat by the Rule of St. Benedict. D.'s 11th-cent. vita mixes historical fact with legendary material. BIBLIOGRAPHY: Butler 2:584–585; R. Aubert, DHGE 14:435–436; G. Bataille, BiblSanct 4:572.

[P. K. MEAGHER]

DEODATUS OF NOLA, ST. (d. 473) the bp. of Nola who, according to his vita (either composed or copied in 1117), was archpriest of Nola while Paulinus was bishop. Entrusted with the administration of church revenue, he was accused before Valentinian III of diverting the revenue to his own use, and after suffering imprisonment and exile, was eventually released. Two years later he succeeded Paulinus as bishop. The inscription on his tomb, *Dilectus a Deo et hominibus in sacerdotium,* (Beloved by God and men for his priesthoood) has led Mallard (EncCatt 7:1913) to assert he was not bp. of Nola, only archpriest, but the Bollandist Papebroch interprets *sacerdotium* in the sense of *episcopatum,* and Lanzoni retains his name in the list of the bps. of Nola. BIBLIOGRAPHY: P. Burchi, BiblSanct 4:571–572.

[F. J. MURPHY]

DEOGRATIAS, SS. (1) **Deogratias** (d. 457), bp. of Carthage; consecrated c.454 at the request of Valentian III. D. was strong in his faith and gained respect of both pagans and Arians. By selling valuable gold and silver articles of the altar, he ransomed captive slaves, who were brought to Africa when Genseric sacked Rome. He also provided living quarters for them in two of the largest churches in Carthage. Some Arians were so embittered by his works of mercy that they threatened to take his life. After a short episcopate of about 3 years, he died and was deeply mourned by his subjects. (2) **Deogratias** (St. Felix of Cantalice, 1515–1587), a Capuchin lay brother; born of devout peasant parents at Cantalice in Apulia, Italy. He entered the Capuchin monastery of Città Ducale and was about 30 when he made solemn vows. In 1549, Felix was sent to Rome to fill the office of questor, whose daily duty was to beg for food and alms in support of the community. Although his post was difficult, he was delighted with the amount of inconvenience and mortification the work afforded him. His spirit of recollection was uninterrupted, and whatever befell him, the words *Deo gratias* were so frequently on his lips that Roman street-urchins called him Brother Deogratias. At the time of his death he received a vision of Our Lady. Felix was canonized by Clement XI in 1712. BIBLIOGRAPHY: M. da Alatri, BiblSanct 5:538–540; P. W. de Paris, *Catholicisme* 4:1153–54; Butler 2:344–345; for the first Deogratias, see Butler, 1:658–659; A. Amore, BiblSanct 4:573.

[R. A. TODD]

DEONTOLOGY (Gr. *deon,* duty, and *logos,* science), literally the science of duty or moral obligation. The term is thought to have been first used by J. *Bentham (1748–1832) to distinguish between what men ought to do and what they actually do, or between obligation and custom in human behavior. The word also appeared as the title of one of Bentham's later and incomplete works, published posthumously (1834). In current philosophical usage, deontology identifies any system of ethics in which duty is posed as the criterion of morality instead of such concepts as virtue, moral sentiment, reason, and practicality. In general, under such a view, certain acts are held to be morally obligatory regardless of their results in terms of human welfare or convenience. In the writings of RC moralists, and more particularly those of the continental European world, the word is used to designate a special ethics concerned with the duties of a particular profession. In theodicy the adjectival form has been applied to a particular form of argument for the existence of God, the deontological argument being that which proceeds from the recognition of duty inherent in the human conscience.

So far as the philosophical use is concerned, the ethics of I. *Kant (1724–1804) typifies deontology in its basic outlook. For Kant, the only acceptable ethical motivation is respect for the moral law. Although right conduct may ensue from less worthy inducements (e.g., prudence or charity), ideally one should act always out of deference for the law. Moreover, the precepts of the moral law have such universality of application and binding force that exceptions are inadmissible. Thus, any personal circumstance, convenience, or concession that is opposed to one's respect for the law in the actions that it dictates, must be sacrificed, even when the welfare of others is involved instead of one's own interests.

In the 20th cent., deontologism has been largely identified with an English school of ethics based principally in Oxford and concerned in great measure with the principle of right and moral obligation. Some of this school contend that right and good are not equitable since a greater good is sometimes the result of a wrong rather than a right action. Usually antiutilitarian, they tend to base their more positive positions upon a revived form of intuitionism, according to which one experiences rational insights or intutions of the right which are acceptable to reason as self-evident. Hence, assertions relative to moral rules or to duty in the concrete must be supported by intellectual intuitions rather than by considerations such as prudence, benevolence, or any emotional motive. Further topics of interest to members of this group concern such questions as whether man possesses rational insight with respect to the one right choice in a given situation, or merely one between conflicting obligations; or again, whether, when duties are in conflict, choice should be guided by more than mere opinion. BIBLIOGRAPHY: Kant's *Critique of Practical Reason* (1788; tr. L. W. Beck, 1949); W. D. Ross, *Right and the Good* (1930); E. F. Carritt, *Theory of Morals* (1928, repr. 1974); H. A. Prichard, *Duty and Ignorance of Fact,* British Academy Lecture (1932).

[J. T. HICKEY]

DEPLOIGE, SIMON ÉGIDE (1868–1927), moral and social philosopher who succeeded Card. *Mercier as director of the Institut Supérieur de Philosophie at Louvain. His theme as professor and as author of *Le Conflit de la morale et de la sociologie* (1911) was the compatibility of the moral teaching of St. Thomas Aquinas with the valid findings of sociology. D. was one of the chief collaborators in the reconstruction of the Louvain library after World War I. BIBLIOGRAPHY: DTC Tables 940; F. Renoirte, *Catholicisme* 3:636.

DEPORTATION (IN THE BIBLE), a method of pacification of conquered nations by forced migration of noble, warrior, and artisan classes to other areas of a world empire. Introduced by the Assyrian emperor Tiglath-Pileser III (8th cent. B.C.) for N Israel, it was used by Sargon II for S Israel (Fall of Samaria: 721 B.C.), and by the Babylonian conqueror of Judah, Nebuchadnezzar, in 597, 587, and 582 B.C. When the deported showed submission, they enjoyed certain freedoms in exile: property rights, religious and tribal assembly, limited travel, commercial enterprise, and permission to return home after Cyrus conquered Babylonia in 539 B.C. Many preferred to remain in Mesopotamia as merchants and money-lenders, yet retained the Jewish religion, culture, and identity, thus giving rise to the synagogue and the Diaspora.

[J. F. FALLON]

DEPOSING POWER, power of the pope to excommunicate and dethrone princes. In the Middle Ages it was generally accepted that the power of the Roman Pontiff was above that of all temporal sovereigns. Barbosa wrote, "There is nothing strange in attributing to the Roman Pontiff, as the vicar of him whose is the earth and the fullness thereof . . . and so to transfer sovereignties, break sceptres, and remove crowns." This theory weakened with the abolition of the feudal system. In addressing the Academy of Catholic Religion (1871), Pope Pius IX said, "No one now thinks any more of the right of deposing princes, which the Holy See formerly exercised; and the Supreme Pontiff even less than any one." The CIC of 1918 contains no word of any deposing power.

[M. T. REILLY]

DEPOSIT OF FAITH, the truths entrusted by God to the Christian community (1 Tim 6.20; 2 Tim 1.12, 14). Since Christian truths are not attained by philosophical deduction but by an acceptance of God's salvific acts in history, the deposit of faith necessarily encompasses these saving events and their divinely revealed meaning. Vatican Council I used the phrase in this sense and emphasized the Church's obligation to preserve and interpret the deposit of faith, neither adding to it nor subtracting anything from it. Thus the deposit of faith is distinct from the Church's formulation of doctrine. The Church must continually proclaim God's acts in history, but it does this with historically variable formulations (Vat II Ecum 6). Guarding the deposit left with the Church requires that its correct understanding be communicated in ever-changing contemporary language and thought patterns. BIBLIOGRAPHY: J. H. Newman, *Essay on the Development of Christian Doctrine* (ed. C. F. Harrold, 1949); C. Pozo, SacMund 2:98–102; P. F. Chirico, NCE 4:780–781. *DOCTRINE, DEVELOPMENT OF.

[T. M. MCFADDEN]

DEPOSITIO MARTYRUM, the oldest known list of Roman martyrs. Along with the Depositio Episcoporum, it forms the so-called Philocalian Calendar, which may be found in the Chronographer, a work attributed to Furius Dionysius Philocalus in 354. The two lists briefly indicate the name and the burial day of the month of the martyrs and popes of the early Christian Church up to 336. These *depositiones* provided information to the faithful of Rome regarding feasts of martyrs, which was needed for liturgical worship. Archeological findings have confirmed the authenticity of both lists, esp. the findings of the inscriptions of St. Fabian and Pope Callistus (d. 203). BIBLIOGRAPHY: H. Leclercq, DACL 10:2523–2619; R. Bryan, NCE 4:781.

[R. A. TODD]

DEPOSITION (CANON LAW) in canon law, *depositio* (CIC, c. 2298, n. 10), one of the vindicative penalties applicable only to clergy. The only worse penalties are perpetual deprival of the right to wear clerical garb (e.g., the cassock) and "degradation," perpetual deprival of clerical rank. Deposition includes *suspension from office and deprival of eligibility for offices, dignities, pension, or benefit in the Church; it does not free from the obligations of holy orders or exclude from clerical privileges (c. 2303,

§1). The penalty can only be inflicted for causes expressly stated in law (§3) and must be inflicted by the condemnatory sentence of a tribunal of five judges (c. 1576 §1, n. 2). A cleric so punished who does not give signs of correcting his ways can be perpetually deprived of the right to wear clerical garb and of all clerical privileges.

[T. C. O'BRIEN]

DEPRAVITY, see TOTAL DEPRAVITY.

DEPRESSION, (1) in a general sense, a term that may describe *sorrow or *despair through their effects, to cast the spirit down or to make it withdrawn because of the loss of some good, or the difficulty attendant on pursuing it. The moral control of this negative feeling is the concern of the virtues of *courage, *patience, *magnanimity. In the essential meaning of the life of grace, the theological virtues of *hope and *charity empower a person to aspire to and find joy in union with God. (2) In a clinical meaning for psychology, depression has two forms: the neurosis of depressive reaction; the psychoses of manic-depression or psychotic, depressive reaction. Besides having physiological symptoms, such depressions are marked by emotional dejection or despondency and a withdrawal from reality. Morally, any act resulting from pathological depression is inculpable; it points to the need of diagnosis and therapy.

[T. C. O'BRIEN]

DEPRÈS, JOSQUIN, see DESPREZ, JOSQUIN.

DERBE, a city in Lycaonia which in Roman times belonged to the province of Galatia. Paul and Barnabas preached the Gospel there after Paul was stoned at Lystra (Acts 14.19). Paul returned to Derbe on his second missionary journey (Acts 16.1). Gaius, one of his associates, was from Derbe (Acts 20.4). The location of Derbe was discovered in 1956 at a site 50 miles E of Lystra at modern Kerti Hüyük. BIBLIOGRAPHY: M. Ballance, "Site of Derbe: a New Inscription," *Anatolian Studies* 7 (1957) 147–151.

[S. MUSHOLT]

DERISION, an offense in words, gestures, writings, and other deeds, by which one sinfully causes shame or embarrassment to another because of his defects of soul or body, or even because of the circumstances of his life. Derision or mockery is closely related to contumely, although many theologians, e.g., St. Thomas Aquinas, distinguish the two. Contumely, like insult and detraction, is opposed to another's honor; derision is opposed to his serenity, causing embarrassment and fear of dishonor rather than dishonor itself. Other theologians see contumely and derision as specifically the same. The malice of derision depends on a number of factors. It is directly opposed to commutative justice, but may involve sins against piety, religion, etc., depending on the status of the one offended. The condition of the derider and the derided, the gravity of the matter, and other circumstances must be considered. At times derisive words or actions may be used without malice, as in correction or in friendly banter. BIBLIOGRAPHY: ThAq ST 2a2ae, 79.

[J. HENNESSEY]

DE ROSSI, GIOVANNI BATTISTA, see ROSSI, GIOVANNI BATTISTA DE.

DERVISHES, members of Sufi (see SUFISM) congregations; the term, of uncertain etymology, is often used in a more restricted sense as the equivalent of Arabic *faqîr,* a mendicant (see FAKIR). Most of the orders or congregations (Arab., *tarîqa,* pl., *turuq,* literally, way or path), particularly in Arabic-speaking areas, tend to be orthodox (among them the Qâdirîya, the largest and most widespread of all), though many depart widely in their teaching from normal Islamic doctrine, as e.g., the Bektashis. These emerged in the 13th cent. in opposition to the Mawlawîya and came to dominate the *Janissaries, who showed a positive disrespect for common Muslim practice, including the formal prayer (*salât,* see ISLAM); and taught a bizarre mixture of *Shiite and Christian doctrine in which *Ali holds the chief place in a trinity consisting of Ali, *Mohammed and Allâh (God). From the 13th cent., with the progressive decline of Islamic society and the almost universal corruption of government, and as established orthodoxy came to lose contact with the people, more and more persons turned to the Sufis for religious guidance until the orders, though condemned generally by most orthodox authorities, came to form the principal means through which popular religion was taught, practiced, and, most notably in black Africa, propagated. Each order traces its origins to some famous Sufi and through him to some early mystic and thence back into the entourage of the Prophet. The order is headed by a Sheikh ("master," in Persian, *pîr*), to whom supernatural powers and knowledge are commonly attributed and whose blessing *(baraka)* is felt to be particularly efficacious to him who receives it. The local head of the order, called the *muqaddam,* whose independence varies according to the organizational structure of the particular congregation, holds almost absolute authority over the individual members of the local house or cell which is called a *zâwiya* (a place of prayer and seclusion; for the derivation, see MOSQUE). or *ribât* (originally, in sense, a fortress on the borders from which dedicated ascetics carried on the *jihad, a member of which is called a *murâbit,* from which term is derived the French and English marabout, meaning a solitary Muslim ascetic). Initiation into an order is preceded by a period of postulancy *(irâda)* during which the candidate *(murîd)* is instructed by the master and introduced into the discipline of the order. Initiation is given in various degrees consisting, for those who continue to live in their own homes and to carry out their usual occupations, in the meticulous devotion to the common religious duties of all Muslims. For others who take upon themselves the rigid ascetic discipline of the Sufis, living as mendicants

either together in the house or alone, initiation is continued into the most advanced doctrines and techniques of the mystics. The members of an order, known as *ikhwân* (brothers), meet once a week (on Friday) or twice, to pray together and to carry out their special rituals. At such meetings, commonly referred to as *dhikr* (mentioning [of the name of God], see KORAN), the members of the *zâwiya* repeat aloud or silently a short prayer or ejaculation, a formula from the Koran, the name Allâh, or simply a single syllable. They are led by one who, accompanied frequently by music or dance, chants the formula over and over again at an ever-increasing cadence so as to induce an apparent state of ecstasy. It is from their peculiar dance during these reunions that the Mawlawîya received the name of Whirling Dervishes. There have been and are yet a great number of orders ranging from the Qâdirîya, which counts great numbers of members throughout Islam, to congregations of no more than local significance. The function of the individual congregation, again, shows many variations: some are primarily social clubs or lodges whose members meet socially for prayer once a week; others, particularly in the Middle Ages, have constituted the basis, tightly organized and highly disciplined, for the trade or craft guilds and other professional or military associations; others have played an important role, esp. in more backward areas, in operating schools; and some, finally, have had primarily political aims. In many cases an individual may belong to more than one order, depending upon the extent of the obligations that the rule of a specific order might impose upon him. The social importance of the orders, esp. in the periods when government in various areas of Islam was corrupt and oppressive, has been extremely great, for many of them cut across class and professional lines and their discipline, under the direction of the sheikhs and *muqaddams,* frequently gave them significant political power. BIBLIOGRAPHY: L. Massignon, EncIslam[1], s.v. Tarika; I. Friedlander, *Whirling Dervishes* (pa. 1975).

[R. M. FRANK]

DERZHAVIN, GAVRIL ROMANOVICH (1743–1816), leading Russian poet of the 18th century. His lyric poems, esp. the odes, reveal his preoccupation with Baroque themes *(vanitas vanitatum; carpe diem).* Though classical in form, they avoid the grandiose monumentalism of Lomonosov in favor of naturalness and vigor of expression. *Felitsa* (1783), in honor of Catherine the Great, exemplifies D.'s introduction of irony and a sometimes unadorned criticism into the ode of panegyric. His most famous ode, *Bog* (God, 1784), combines praise of God with a strongly humanistic expression of man's role in the universe. BIBLIOGRAPHY: A. V. Zapadov, *Derzhavin* (1958); J. V. Clardy, *G. R. Derzhavin* (1968).

[M. F. McCARTHY]

DE SANCTIS, GAETANO (1862–1935), Italian psychologist and psychiatrist, a Catholic pioneer in these fields, professor at the Univ. of Rome from 1905, director of its institute of experimental psychology.

[T. C. O'BRIEN]

DE SANCTIS, GAETANO (1870–1957), Italian historian. Educated at the Univ. of Rome, he later succeeded K. J. Beloch in its chair of Greek history. The Fascists removed him from this post, but in 1944 the chair was restored to him for life. In 1950 he also received a life appointment as senator of the Italian Republic. He had special interest in both economic and social problems and was active in archeological explorations in Crete and Cyrenaica. He is considered an outstanding authority in early Greek and Roman history, and *Storia dei Romani* (1907–64) is considered his greatest work. Other important writings include: *Attis, storia della Republica Ateniese* (1898); *Storia dei Greci* (1939); *Studi di storia della storiografia greca* (1951), and two volumes published after his death, *Vita e pensiero nell' età delle grandi conquiste* and *Dalla battaglia di Pidna alla caduta di Numanzia*. BIBLIOGRAPHY: A. Rostagni, *Rivista di filologia e di istruzione classica* 35 (1957) 113–116.

[R. A. TODD]

DESCANT (variant of *discant,* Lat. *discantus*), term used in the 19th cent. to describe the highest pitched instruments, e.g., *descant recorder;* the soprano clef; and ornamentation or variation in melody. In modern hymn-singing, it describes an obbligato part that soars above the tune. BIBLIOGRAPHY: S. Kenney, Apel HDMus 228.

[M. T. LEGGE]

DESCARTES, RENÉ (1596–1650), French philosopher and mathematician, the wellspring of modern philosophy. Educated at the Jesuit college of La Flèche, he acquired a knowledge of and a distaste for the Scholasticism of the later period. His genius was mathematical; indeed his invention of analytical geometry was a landmark in the history of mathematics. D. spent most of his mature life in Holland, a country offering greater intellectual freedom than France. Called to Sweden by Queen Christina as her personal tutor and philosopher in residence, he soon succumbed to the harsh climate. A believing, even devout, Catholic all his life, D. divorced his philosophical speculation from his faith. His was the spirit of his age: he was a rationalist in his serene conviction that the human mind can attain all truth; impatient, even scornful, of the past; alive to the power of the new mathematics and physics. He was preoccupied with methodology. Convinced of the power of the human mind, he thought that proper rules of reasoning could lead men to all knowledge, philosophical and scientific alike. D.'s method begins with a universal doubt, not skeptical but methodological in character. He wanted to put all knowledge to question: sense knowledge, the opinions of the past, even the truth of our intellectual knowledge. Now, if I doubt, I think. The way is thus prepared for the fundamental

intuition of an indubitable truth: *Cogito ergo sum,* "I think, therefore I am." From this insight, D. moves on to establish his criterion of truth. All ideas that are clear (present to and known by an attentive mind) and distinct (precise, different from all others, and embracing only those notes that belong to it alone) are true. The clear and distinct idea is indubitable, intuitive, infallible, and innate. It is the thinker's task to render his clear ideas distinct. The proper ordering of clear and distinct ideas in a chain of connections, each link of which is clearly and distinctly seen, leads to true and certain conclusions. D. gives 21 rules for such ordering.

One line of reasoning leads to God. D. rejects the traditional arguments from causality and offers an ontological one that is reminiscent of St. Anselm. Even our ideas must have a cause, he contends. We have an idea of God. But nothing less than God could possibly cause our idea of him. Therefore God exists. D. adds to Anselm's argument the note of causality. He was sharply criticized in his own time (by Hobbes and others) and since, primarily for his assumption that we can have a clear and distinct idea of God. Having established the existence of self by intuition and of God by demonstration, D. next sets out to prove the existence of the external world. He bases all other certitudes on that of God's existence. We have clear and distinct ideas of the external world. If the world did not exist, then God would be a deceiver, which is impossible. Faithful to an older mode of thought, D. held that whatever exists is either a substance or an attribute of a substance. Mind (or self), God, and matter are clearly not attributes, but substances. Substance is "a thing which so exists that it needs no other thing in order to exist." This definition applies in its full rigor only to God, but mind and matter can be so defined, for they need only God's concurrence to exist. A clear and distinct idea of a substance can be gained through knowledge of any of its attributes, but is best gained by recognition of its principal one. In the case of mind (self, soul) this attribute is thought. By thought D. understands all the facts of consciousness: idea, volitions, and emotions. The fundamental attribute of body is extension in three dimensions. All else that may be attributed to body presupposes extension. D.'s picture of the physical world is based on this notion of the essence of material things. With Galileo he denies the "secondary qualities" of bodies: color, taste, density; but going beyond Galileo, he reduces the primary qualities to the single one of extension. Body, then, is identified with space. A true and certain science of physics thus becomes possible, for space is the subject of geometrical knowledge, which is true and certain. Physics is the science of the local motion of bodies. God has created a certain quantity of motion in the universe, a quantity which remains constant. All events in the universe of matter come about through the transfer of motion from one body to another by impact. Final and formal causes—so important in medieval natural philosophy—disappear. So thoroughgoing is D.'s mechanical approach that for him even animals are but complicated automata. His philosophy of physics (but not his personal elaboration of detail) was to rule the thinking of scientists until the advent of quantum and relativistic theory at the dawn of the 20th century.

D.'s philosophy of man is consistent with his notions of matter and of God. We are endowed with free will, and know this by the clarity of our idea of it. This freedom is consistent with God's preordination, for God's power is infinite although we cannot know the mode of its operation. We are endowed with understanding as well, and understanding is the power by which we seek truth. Thought gives us by means of ideas, knowledge of the world outside us: a world made up of bodies, which are extended; and of minds, which are not. Sense perception gives us knowledge as well, through "adventitious" ideas of color, taste, and the like. The ideas that give true knowledge, however, are those created in us innately by God, or those achieved by a rigorous and methodical chain of analysis. Adventitious ideas may be fallacious. Man's nature, then, for D. is dualistic, since mind and body are distinct substances. The problem of their interaction and of the validity of our knowledge of the external world is insoluble in D.'s system except by the invocation of God's goodness and omnipotence. This dichotomy of soul and body poses the problem of "the ghost in the machine," which was to haunt later philosophers. D.'s influence cannot be overestimated. His new method of philosophizing and the problems he raised were to mark philosophy for the next century and a half. In particular his influence appears in the thought of British empiricism in Locke and Hume and in the continental rationalism of Spinoza and Leibnitz. Not until Kant began to reexamine the bases of thought was a new direction achieved. BIBLIOGRAPHY: É. Gilson, *Unity of Philosophical Experience* (1948); J. Maritain, *Dream of Descartes* (1944); *idem, Three Reformers* (1928, repr. 1970).

[W. B. MAHONEY]

DESCENT OF AMIDA, REIHOKAN, MOUNT KOYA (12th cent.). Japanese silk painting representing *Raigō*—the descent of Amida Buddha to receive the soul of the dying into the Western Paradise of eternal bliss. The Buddha, painted in gold, is surrounded by 31 devout bodhisattvas, richly dressed, some in deep devotion others playing celestial music.

[M. J. DALY]

DESCENT OF CHRIST INTO HELL, the fifth article of the Creed. It professes the descent of Christ to Sheol, the place of the dead. This doctrine has often been neglected, as supposedly linked with early mythological ideas of the afterlife or with medieval legends about the harrowing of hell; but recently it has been more widely discussed in the light of developments both in the theology of the Resurrection and in that of death. Three scriptural themes can be discerned here. (1) As firstborn of the dead, Christ holds the keys of death and Sheol (Rev 1.18; Col 1.18; 2 Tim 1.10). (2) As a true moral man, Christ truly died, truly suffered the dead-

ness to which all are subject (Acts 2.24–36; Rom 10.6–13; Eph 4.8–10). The Fathers emphasized this against the Apollinarist denial of a human soul in Christ. (3) Christ "in the spirit . . . went to preach to the spirits in prison," for "the dead had to be told the good news as well" (1 Pet 3.18–19; 4.6). Some Fathers saw this as an epiphany, a self-manifestation in which Christ proclaimed the good news that salvation was achieved. Others attributed to the descent a more directly soteriological function (see Mt 27.52).

St. Thomas Aquinas, recognizing the inseparability of revelation and redemption, harmonizes both patristic themes, ThAq ST 3a, 52. Christ's descent was an effective manifestation of the saving power of his humanity: it was for the dead what the sacraments are for the living, a means by which the dead were brought into contact with the redemptive mystery (ThAq ST 3a, 52.1 ad 2). For it was "in the spirit" that Christ, made "life-giving spirit" in his exaltation (1 Cor 15.45), went among the dead.

Many attendant problems still demand theological reflection. Did Christ descend only in his human soul or in his glorified humanity as a whole? Among the dead, who received the benefit of this saving visitation? What does this mystery contribute to our understanding of death itself? BIBLIOGRAPHY: E. Biser, TheolDig 8 (1960) 111–114; J. Galot, *ibid.* 13 (1965) 89–94; H. Vorgrimler, "Christ's Descent into Hell: Is It Important?" *Concilium* 1.2 (1966) 75–81, a survey article with full bibliog.

[R. L. STEWART]

DESCHAMPS, EUSTACHE (*c.* 1346–*c.* 1406), poet, satirist, and dramatist, possibly a nephew of Guillaume de *Machaut, by whom he was educated. Besides his extensive lyric work, he wrote an important treatise on versification and was in contact with important authors of his time. An officer of Charles V, he frequently used political and social material for his verse. His farces and *moralités* show considerable flair and a lively lyricism.

[J. P. WILLIMAN]

DESCHAMPS, JEAN AND PIERRE, architects of the latter 13th and early 14th cent. in S central France. Their work is an academic review of the northen Gothic of Amiens, St. Denis and Soissons. Jean began (*c.*1250) the building of the *chevet* chapels of Clermont-Ferrand (where he is buried), and they were completed by Pierre (his son?). Jean probably did the Limoges Cathedral (begun 1276), the *chevet* of Narbonne Cathedral (after 1286). Work at the Cathedrals of Toulouse and Rodez are less certainly attributed to the Deschamps.

[M. J. DALY]

DESCORT, a *lai* or *lay,* i.e., a form of medieval French poetry developed mainly in N France during the 13th cent. by the trouvères and ending with Machaut. Their texts consist of poems (usually addressed to the Virgin or a lady) of

60, 100, or more lines of varying length, meter, and rhyme.
BIBLIOGRAPHY: Apel HDMus 460.

[M. T. LEGGE]

DESECRATION, a form of *sacrilege, consisting in profanation or violation of the sacred. The sacred means any reality or person dedicated to the service or worship of God; irreverence towards it, then, is contrary to the virtue of *religion by which due reverence is shown to God. The seriousness of the sin corresponds to the sanctity of the person, place, or object violated. Thus abuse of a person consecrated to God is worse than one against a holy place or object. Profanation of the sacraments, and esp. of the Holy Eucharist, has a special malice (ThAq ST 2a2ae.99). Canon law attaches particular legislation to the violation of a blessed or consecrated church by the commission of murder in it, or violent shedding of blood, or indecent practices; and requires reconciliation of the building before its use for divine worship (CIC cc. 1172–77). Special penalties are attached to the sin of desecrating the Blessed Sacrament (*ibid.,* c. 2320); desecration of a cemetery is put on the same level as desecration of a church (*ibid.,* cc. 1207; 2329). Special penalties are attached to the violation of monastic cloisters; (*ibid.,* c. 2342); laying violent hands on the Roman Pontiff (*ibid.,* c. 2343); violating cadavers (*ibid.,* c. 2328).

[T. C. O'BRIEN]

DESERT (CARMELITE), remote places to which members of the Order of Carmel can withdraw at times for intense periods of prayer and contemplation. The Carmelites trace the practice back to the prophet Elias and the band who gathered around him in the solitude of Mount Carmel. This tradition was evoked with the 16th-cent. reforms when the contemplative orientation of the Carmelite life was reaffirmed. In modern times, these "deserts" have been reestablished in France and Spain. New experiments are beginning in the U.S., including shared deserts where the friars are joined by lay people and other religious who are seeking a deeper contemplative life.

[M. B. PENNINGTON]

DESERT FATHERS, early Christians who retired into the solitude of the Egyptian deserts to lead a life of prayer and mortification. This ascetical movement, which began about the mid-3d cent., flourished particularly in the 4th as a reaction to the secular triumphs of Christianity after it had obtained its freedom and the favor of the emperors. The first Desert Fathers were not philosophers but simple fellahin of the Nile Valley. Frequently opposed to any reconciliation of Christianity with Hellenistic culture, they came in time to appreciate the advantages of secular as well as sacred studies. From their pens came collections of the sayings of the Fathers, letters, sermons, ascetical treatises, biographies, monastic rules, and historical and theological essays of great value. The earliest Desert Fathers were anchorites or hermits and lived alone in their solitudes. Later they began to live a common life together as cenobites, thus laying the foundations for monasticism. Among the most renowned of the early hermits were Paul of Thebes (*c.*227–340) and Anthony of Egypt (*c.*250–356). Pachomius is regarded as the founder of cenobitism (*c.*290–346). The profound influence which the life of Anthony had upon Christians of the West is vividly portrayed by St. Augustine in his *Confessions* 8.6.13–15. BIBLIOGRAPHY: Quasten 3:146–189.

[M. J. COSTELLOE]

DESERT JOURNEY OF THE ISRAELITES, the wanderings of the Jewish people after the Exodus. They are recorded in three complex accounts underlying Ex, Num, and Deuteronomy. The details cannot be reconstructed with certainty. The various halting places number 40 (Num ch. 33), doubtless a conventional number; many of the places named cannot be surely identified. Certain stages in the journey are recognizable.

(1) *From Egypt to Sinai.* On leaving Rameses (Tanis-Avaris; Ex 12.37), the Israelites forded the Red (Reed) Sea around Lake Timsah, not many miles N of modern Suez (Ex 14.15–16). Then, although the "road to the land of the Philistines" led directly to the Promised Land (Ex 13.17), the Israelites turned S (probably because of permanent military posts maintained by the Egyptians to guard their frontier), and advanced into the desert of Shur (Ex 15.22). After stops at Marah, Elim (Ex 15.23–27), a place by the sea (Num 33.10), Rephidim (Ex 17.1), and a successful battle against the Amalekites, they gained the foot of Mt. Sinai (Ex 19.1). Along the way they had been sustained by manna and migratory quail (Ex ch. 16). (2) *Sinai.* Three months after leaving Egypt, Mt. Sinai (or Horeb), the traditional site of the "mountain of the Lord," was reached (Ex 19.1–3). Here at Jebel Musa, the 7,500-foot mountain at the S tip of the Sinai Peninsula, the covenant was struck between Yahweh and his people, and Israel received the law that made her a people (Ex 20.1–23.19). (3) *From Sinai to Kadesh.* Two years later, accompanied by the ark (Ex 25.10–22) and the tent (Ex 33.7–11), the Israelites took leave of Sinai. The trip to Kadesh-barnea, made over territory largely unexplored and uncharted to this day, required 11 days (Dt. 1.2). (4) *Kadesh.* The Israelites remained near this great oasis, located 50 miles S of Beersheba, for some 38 years. The delay in entering the Promised Land was a penalty for the complaints of Aaron and Miriam (Num ch. 12), the rebellion of Korah (Num ch. 16), and the murmuring at Meribah (Num ch. 20). From Kadesh, scouts were sent into Canaan (Num 13.1–32.8), and there was an abortive attempt to enter that land from the S (Num 14.39–45). Permission was sought to travel through Edom's territory on the King's Highway (Num 20.17), but the request was refused. (5) *From Kadesh to Jordan.* The Israelites therefore next marched in a SE direction to Mt. Hor and to the tip of the Gulf of Aqaba (Num 14.25; 20.22; 21.4). Then,

proceeding N along the Arabah, they kept to the W of unfriendly Edom until they reached the wadi Zered, where they turned E so as to circle Moab. Challenged by Sihon (Num 21.21–35), the wanderers achieved at Heshbon their first major military victory, at the expense of the Amorites. Not long afterwards they pitched their camp in the plains of Moab, near the Jordan opposite Jericho (Num 22.1; 33,48). BIBLIOGRAPHY: B. Anderson, *Understanding the Old Testament* (1966); L. Grollenberg, *Atlas of the Bible* (1956); J. Bright, *History of Israel* (1956, 2d ed., 1972); G. Wright, *Biblical Archaeology* (1963).

[R. T. A. MURPHY]

DESERTION, a sin against justice: the abandonment of one's spouse or minor children. Desertion by a husband or wife is a sin against the obligation of mutual conjugal support incurred by the marriage contract; in a sacramental marriage it also disfigures the union as reflecting the permanent and loving bond between Christ and the Church, his spouse. Desertion of a minor child offends against the natural law and its demands that parents attend to their child's physical, mental, and moral development. What usually is understood by desertion is physical abandonment and failure to give financial support; but morally, desertion can also be psychological: a total failure to show true marital or parental love and care.

[T. C. O'BRIEN]

DESGABETS, ROBERT (d. 1678), Benedictine theologian. D. became a monk at the abbey of Hautevillers near Reims (1636). As a professor of theology, he rejected scholasticism and devoted himself to Augustinian and patristic thought. At Paris from 1656 as procurator general, he came into contact with foremost Cartesians and adopted their physical, mechanistic theories. These he viewed as sufficient to explain the mystery of the Eucharist. His ideas were opposed by *Bossuet, *Pascal, and P. *Nicole. Censured by his superiors, D. retired to the small monastery of Breuil in Commercy (Dept. of the Meuse). BIBLIOGRAPHY: R. Heurtebrize, DTC 4:622–624; B. Romeyer, *Catholicisme* 3:667–668 with bibliog.

DESHAYES, GABRIEL (1767–1841), religious founder. Ordained in 1792, D. began his priestly life during the Reign of Terror in France. He lent himself to diverse apostolates in his zeal for souls: missions, retreats, catechetics, teaching, and a variety of social works (esp. for the blind and deaf). D. was eminently noted for his part in the foundation of religious communities. Among others, he established the Congregation of Sisters of Christian Instruction of St.-Gildas-des-Bois; then joined forces with J. de La Mennais to found the Brothers of Auray (1819). In 1820 he realized his desire to join the Company of Mary and was later elected superior general of the two institutes of St. Louis Grignion de Montfort, the Congregation of Mary and the Daughters of Wisdom. He collaborated also in founding

the Sisters of the Guardian Angel of Quillon and, in 1839, the Brothers of St. Francis of Assisi for agricultural schools. BIBLIOGRAPHY: L. Le Crom, *Catholicisme* 3:670–671; R. Aubert, DHGE 14:340–342.

[S. A. HEENEY]

DESHON, GEORGE (1823–1903), American missionary, author. D. was a graduate of the U.S. Military Academy at West Point and later a teacher there. After his conversion to Catholicism, he entered the Redemptorist Order and was assigned to the mission apostolate throughout the E states. Dispensed from his vows in 1858, he founded with Isaac Hecker and two other former Redemptorists the Society of Missionary Priests of St. Paul the Apostle (known as the Paulists) in New York City. In residence there till his death, D. contributed greatly to the growth of the community through his business ability and knowledge of engineering as well as by his deep spirituality. He was elected superior general in 1897. Shortly before he died he established the Paulist house in Chicago. He wrote for the *Catholic World* and published *Guide for Catholic Young Women* (1860) and *Parochial Sermons* (1901). BIBLIOGRAPHY: J. McSorley, *Father Hecker and His Friends* (2d ed. 1952, pa. 1972).

[S. A. HEENEY]

DESIDERATUS OF BOURGES, ST. (d. *c*.550), councilor and bishop. One of three saintly brothers born of devout parents of Soissons, D. served at the court of King Chlotar I and used his power to overcome the heresies of Nestorius and Eutyches. In 543 he became bp. of Bourges and was present at the Fifth Council of Orleans during the reign of Childebert I. During his 9-year episcopate he became known as a peacemaker. The church of St. Symphorien (St. Ursin) at Bourges is believed to have been founded by him. BIBLIOGRAPHY: G. Bataille, BiblSanct 4:578; Butler 2:251–252.

[R. A. TODD]

DESIDERIO DA SETTIGNANO (*c*.1430–64), Italian sculptor influenced by Donatello. D. competed (1461) for the commission of the Madonna della Tavola (cathedral, Orvieto), executed the great marble tomb of Carlo Marsuppini (d. 1453) in the church of Sta. Croce, Florence, the tabernacle of the Holy Sacrament (S. Lorenzo, 1461), many famed, exquisitely cut low reliefs (Madonnas; *Young St. John the Baptist),* and busts of children *(Infant John the Baptist).* Of great skill and strong design D.'s work ranged from delicate surface nuances to strong undercutting in diverse moods of ecstatic joy, charm, and melancholy *(St. Jerome,* National Gallery, Wash., D.C.). BIBLIOGRAPHY: C. Seymour, *Sculpture in Italy, 1400–1500,* 1966.

[M. J. DALY]

DESIDERIUS, KING OF THE LOMBARDS (756–774), last of the native Lombard kings. Father-in-law of Charlemagne, Carloman, Arichis of Beneventum, and Tassilo of Bavaria, he broke with Charlemagne who had repudiated his daughter and who favored the papacy toward which the Lombards were hostile. In 774 Charlemagne besieged Pavia, captured it, and deported D. to Frankland where he died in obscurity. BIBLIOGRAPHY: T. Hodgkin, *Italy and Her Invaders* (1892–99, repr. 1967) v. 7.

[A. CABANISS]

DESIDERIUS (DIDIER) OF CAHORS, ST. (Gangericus or Géry; d. 655?), bishop. Of wealthy Gallo-Roman stock, D. was educated at the Merovingian court school. He served as treasurer to Chlotar II and Dagobert I (618–630), then succeeded his brother Rusticus as bp. of Cahors. A number of his letters, to kings and bishops are extant. BIBLIOGRAPHY: Butler 4:348–349; G. Mathon, BiblSanct 4:580–581.

[G. M. COOK]

DESIDERIUS OF LANGRES, ST. (d. *c*.407 or 411), patron of the city of Saint-Dizier in France and third bp. of Langres. D.'s name appears in the records of the Councils of Sardique (343) and Cologne (346). He probably suffered martyrdom with many of his own people for whom he begged mercy of the invading Vandals in 407 or 411. Several churches in France were given his name. In the 7th cent., Warnacher wrote D.'s vita. BIBLIOGRAPHY: R. Aigrain, *Catholicisme* 3:753–754; R. Van Doren, DHGE 14:405; J.-C. Didier, BiblSanct 4:582–584.

[R. A. TODD]

DESIDERIUS RHODONENSIS, ST., Alsatian bishop and martyr, who on his return from a pilgrimage to Rome was killed along with his deacon companion, Raginfridus, by brigands near Belfort. D. was buried at the site of the murder and his tomb is located in a chapel later known as St.-Dizier-l'Évêque. This church, presented to the Abbey of Murbach by Count Everard of Alsace *c*.735, gives evidence of his cult in the 8th century. BIBLIOGRAPHY: R. Aigrain, *Catholicisme* 3:751–752; G. Bataille, BiblSanct 4:586–587.

[R. A. TODD]

DESIDERIUS OF VIENNE, ST. (d. 607 or 611), martyr. Bp. of Vienne from *c*.595, D. received letters from Pope St. Gregory I, one recommending Augustine of Canterbury, then on his way to evangelize England, to D.'s charity. D. was accused of paganism on the basis of his interest in the classics, a charge from which he was completely exonerated by Gregory. Through the machinations of Queen Brunhilde D. was deposed at a council held in Chalon-sur-Saône (602–603) but 4 years later was restored to his see. Because he continued to reprove the queen and her son Theodoric II for their profligate behavior, Brunhilde ordered his arrest and eventually had him assassinated in either 607 or 611. BIBLIOGRAPHY: J. C. Didier, BiblSanct 4:585–586; Butler 2:374–375.

[H. DRESSLER]

DESIRE FOR GOD, NATURAL, an innate, human disposition towards union with God. Besides apologetic and devotional connotations (Tertullian, *Apol*. I, 17, *O testimonium animae naturaliter christianae;* Augustine, *Confessions* I, 1, *Our heart is not at rest until it rests in thee.*), the theme has received a precise theological meaning. In the context of the abstract possibilities or capacities within man's natural being for the unmediated union with Father, Son, and Holy Spirit that grace in fact brings about, the desire for God means the innate tendency expressing such capacities. The abstraction is developed both to clarify the transcendence and gratuitousness of grace as it is actually given, and to establish that an immediate union with God is not, in Karl Barth's expression, a "violent miracle." Historically Catholic theology has discussed the theme against the background of St. Thomas Aquinas's argument that for the mind to perceive the being of God is not an impossibility, since there is an innate desire for such a direct contemplation (ThAq ST 1a.12,1; cf 1a2ae.2,8; 3,8). The general theological consensus is that there can be such a desire, actual and not merely implicit, but that it would be experienced as ineffectual. As to Aquinas, in discussing the recurrent phrase *homo capax Dei* (ThAq ST 1a.93,4; 1a2ae. 113,10; 2a2ae. 2, 3; 3a. 4,1 ad 2; 9, 2 ad 3; 23,1), he looks to the actual relationship to the divine that grace means in order to seek some understanding of its possibility, and not the converse (see 1a2ae.113, 10, citing Augustine, *De Trin.* XIV, 8). He points to the human mind's experience of the meaning of being and the will's orientation towards the value of the good as such a passive amenability to being raised up to union with God (see OBEDIENTIAL POTENCY); that the life of grace and blessedness are not an alien imposition (see ThAq ST 1a.12, 4 ad 3). The desire to contemplate the divine being is as possible, and as limited, as a metaphysics; the theoretical range of the human mind can reach the inference that the meaning of being involves dependence on a first cause. That same range prompts a surge toward the unique reality of that first cause, but at the same time the basis for a realization that the transcendence of that unique being surpasses the mind's power to comprehend. Theology can point to these abstract possibilities as an openness to the union with God that grace in its Trinitarian dispensation brings about; and also that in actuality any effective response of man to the divine is prompted by that grace alone (ThAq ST 1a2ae.89, 6). BIBLIOGRAPHY: W. R. O'Connor, *Eternal Quest* (1947).

[T. C. O'BRIEN]

DESIRE, MORALITY OF. The appetitive movement toward attaining some good concerns moral theology under three headings. (1) A psychological consideration of the make-up of man recognizes desire (*concupiscientia*) first of all as an emotion, a response of the sensory appetite towards attaining a sensually appealing object. Because it belongs to human nature, it is both good in itself and has its place within the components of living and acting humanly, even as the realities that serve man's physical life are goods, meant to contribute to his complete well-being. An analogous response of the will, the appetite following on intelligence, is also a form of desire. (See ThAq ST 1a2ae.30,1–3). The will itself is in fact the expression of the natural desire of human nature towards the true human good (*ibid.*, 1a.80, 1–2; 1a2ae.8,1; 10,1–2; 85,1–2; DESIRE TO SEE GOD, NATURAL). (2) A second psychological consideration required by moral evaluation concerns the voluntariness of a given action. Since voluntariness or *voluntarity implies the quality of issuing from within the appetites, desire as described above indicates voluntariness; but a surge of emotion that completely overcomes control is outside the realm of psychological voluntariness (*ibid.*, 6, 7; 10, 3). (3) As to the moral evaluation of acts as good or evil, desire relates to the meaning both of virtue and of sin. As to virtue, desire needs the control and moderation of moral virtue integrating the connatural orientation of emotion into the pursuit of the complete human good. Virtue so understood means habituation of appetitive movements to the control of reason and will. The specific response of desire to the enjoyable, to what appeals to the sensory side, left undirected, can hinder by excess or neglect the perception and intent of the true good; the virtue particularly required is *temperance. (See 1a2ae.58, 2; 59; 61.2; 65.1). The need for virtue and healing that derive from grace is further urged because of *original sin: its result is a less harmonious integration of emotion with reason and will, part of the condition theology came to designate as *concupiscence. As to the question of personal sin, even as desire, like all human emotions, can be the domain of virtue, so too it can be sinful, i.e., inasmuch as emotions are meant to be controlled humanly; the purely emotional response itself, however, cannot be a *mortal sin (*ibid.*, 74, 3–4). A desire of the emotional level or of the will itself that is deliberately and willingly entertained and is set upon a sinful action, unlike other purely inner sins, takes on the inordinateness of the outward action desired.

[T. C. O'BRIEN]

DESMAISIÈRES, MARÍA MIGUELA OF THE BL. SACRAMENT, ST. (1809–1865), foundress of the Handmaids of the Blessed Sacrament and of Charity. She was Viscountess of Jorbalán and, while quite young, was devoted to works of charity, esp. for cholera victims and wayward girls. D. founded a religious community (1859) to aid such unfortunate young women and remained superior until her death. She established seven houses throughout Europe, Japan, and Latin America, undaunted by evil tongues attacking her reputation. D. died a martyr to charity in a cholera epidemic and was canonized March 4, 1934. BIBLIOGRAPHY: I. Bastarrika, NCE 4:803–04.

[M. HIGGINS]

DESMARES, TOUSSAINT (1601–87), Oratorian, Jansenist. D. came early under *Saint-Cyran's influence, which his other preceptor, C. de *Condren, sought to combat. His Jansenist leanings became apparent in his preaching, and in 1648 he had to flee to Quimper. He was an emissary to Rome in the Jansenist cause (1653). After his expulsion from the Oratory, D. was given shelter by the Duke of Liancourt and was involved in the events that led to the first of *Pascal's *Lettres Provinciales* (1656). One of D.'s published works was *Les Saints Pères vengés par eux-mêmes* (1652). BIBLIOGRAPHY: A. Ingold, DTC 4:630; J. Orcibal, *Origines du jansénisme* (1947–48) 3:241.

DESMARETS (DES MARESTS) DE SAINT-SORLIN, JEAN (1595–1676), French writer, royal counselor, and first chancellor of the French Academy (1634–38). Winning Richelieu's favor, D. gained literary success with his comedy, *Les Visionnaires* (1637). Converting from *libertin* freethinking to devotion (*c*.1645), he wrote a Counter-Reformation epic in 26 *chants*, *Clovis ou la France chrétienne* (1654). Becoming an ardent anti-Jansenist, he attacked the Port-Royal nuns who refused to sign the "formulary" (1665), and played an important role in the burning of the madman, Simon Morin, who called himself the son of Christ. D.'s treatise, *De la comparaison de la langue et de la poésie française avec la grecque et la latine* (1670), in which he sided with the "moderns," began the literary "Quarrel of the Ancients and the Moderns." One of his three points of comparison was that Christian "marvels" (miracles) were superior to pagan "marvels." BIBLIOGRAPHY: Bremond 6:445–518.

[R. N. NICOLICH]

DE SMET, PIERRE JEAN (1801–1873), Jesuit missionary. Of powerful physique and winning personality, De S. left Belgium for the U.S. where he entered the Jesuits and was ordained (1827) in St. Louis. There he spent the succeeding 10 years. In 1838 he began his astounding career as a missionary to the Indians. His journeys on the missions as well as incredible voyages to collect money in support of them constitute one of the amazing chapters of mission history. From the midwest to Oregon he founded mission centers. He was known among the Indians as Blackrobe and was revered as no other white man. He was the supreme arbiter of conflicts among the Indians, most notably in 1868 when Sitting Bull and his braves were planning a major war against the whites; De S. succeeded in negotiating peace. BIBLIOGRAPHY: W. H. W. Fanning, CE 4:752–753.

[J. R. AHERNE]

DESOLATION, in the spiritual life, an experience of being alone; sometimes an element in spiritual *abandonment, part of the *purification of the spirit. The exemplar of this experience is Christ and his feeling on the cross of abandonment by the Father. St. John of the Cross, as well as other mystical writers, maintains that the night of the senses and the night of the soul include such an experience. It is true that the awareness of what union with God in beatitude means is often present in the spiritual life by way of negation or of the opposite. Just as blessedness is a constant, conscious fulfillment in being with God, the purification of the spirit can mean the sense of God's presence through the feeling of his absence. It is the effect of a contemplative perception of his infinite transcendence. Yet it remains a good and a gift because it brings with it, however painfully, the reality of the divine. It is not despair; it is a perception of the absence of God as he is real, not a loss of God as though he were nothingness.

[T. C. O'BRIEN]

DESPAIR, etymologically and in theological use, the opposite of *hope (sperare-desperare):* (1) the opposite of hope as an emotion or aspiration towards any good that is attainable, but with difficulty. Despair at this level is a withdrawal from trying to reach a goal, a succumbing before the difficulties and effort required. Despair includes the dejected attitudes connoted by "depression," "despondency," "discouragement." On a purely emotional level such feelings are simply a natural reaction to hardship. But they are meant to be controlled, since the many objects of human hope are true human values that should be pursued, not abandoned. To surrender to defeat because of arduousness or difficulty in doing the good is to fail in the pursuit of the ideal of virtue. These negative feelings towards the good are to be controlled by such virtues as *courage, *patience, *magnanimity. All involve steadfastness and positive striving for what is worthwhile; despair in general describes opposite attitudes. Among the vices exhibiting aspects of despair are those opposed to the hopeful virtues; *pusillanimity, lack of heart, most exactly describes despair as morally culpable. (2) Despair also names the sin and vice opposed, by falling short, to hope, the theological virtue. The terminology remains the same, but the realities intended are quite distinct from what belongs to the level of the moral virtues. The theological virtue of hope is the positive aspiration and fixed intent towards that union with Him that God promises; it is an expectation of fulfillment, guarded because of the transcendence of what God promises and human impotence, yet confident because of the Father's loving and powerful gift that does fulfill his promises. The motive of theological hope is not self-reliance, but the reality of the divine giving of grace that alone overcomes sin and makes salvation achievable. In that meaning of hope lies the sinfulness of despair. For the refusal to look for and to be positive in striving for salvation impugns the divine willingness to accomplish what the gift of grace means. The enormity of theological despair—it is numbered among the *sins against the Holy Spirit—is its destructive negation of the very meaning of grace; it subverts the basic condition of relationship to God as he is the Father who gives to those who are always prodigal sons. Because of its radical destructive force, it is the closest experience on earth to being in hell; in a sense the fixity of will in being cut

off from God is the essence of hell. Such a repudiation of God is not an easy sin to commit. The awareness of sinfulness, discouragement over personal failing, experience of the difficulties in the way of salvation are not theological despair. Christ's agony in the garden and abandonment on the cross are assurances that the way of salvation includes dark moments. But the peril in despair points out how necessary for the Christian life are the right understanding and the constant vitality of hope. BIBLIOGRAPHY: ThAq ST 2a2ae.20.

[T. C. O'BRIEN]

DES PÉRIERS, BONAVENTURE (1500?–1544?), French writer, freethinker. As an evangelical, D. defended Clement *Marot, suspected of Protestantism, against the attacks of François Sagon. He assisted Robert Olivetan and *Lefèvre d'Étaples in the preparation of their vernacular OT, and Étienne Dolet with his *Commentarii linguae latinae.* Made *valet-de-chambre* to Margaret of Angoulême, Queen of Navarre, protectress of Reformers, he participated in the freedom of discussion and thought at court, expressing his skepticism in his daring *Cymbalum mundi* (1537), suppressed by the government in 1538. BIBLIOGRAPHY: J. W. Hassell, *Sources and Analogues of the Nouvelles Récréations et Joyeux Devis of Bonaventure des Périers* (v. 2, 1969).

[R. N. NICOLICH]

DESPORTES, PHILIPPE (1546–1606), French court poet of King Henry III. In reward for his services the King bestowed upon him the abbeys of Tiron and Josaphat (1582) and other religious benefices. On Henry III's death (1589) he allied himself with the Holy League (for which he was attacked in the *Satire Ménippée*) before passing to the side of Henry IV (1594), from whom, however, he refused the archbishopric of Bordeaux. His *Premières oeuvres,* augmented in successive editions, include love sonnets, elegies, *chansons,* imitations of Ariosto, and *bergeries.* After his *Dernières amours* (1583) he almost completely abandoned secular for religious verse, in which he had begun to take an interest in 1575. His religious work includes his translation of the Psalms (1591, 1598, 1603), later used by St. Francis de Sales and Jean-Pierre Camus. D. was an important figure in the transition in French poetry from the Pléiade to the 17th century. BIBLIOGRAPHY: J. Lavaud, *Un Poète de cour aux temps des derniers Valois: Philippe Desportes* (1936); H. Hatzfeld, "Style of Philippe Desportes," *Symposium* 7 (1953) 262–273.

[R. N. NICOLICH]

DESPREZ (Des Prés, Des Prez, Deprès), **JOSQUIN** (*c.* 1450–1521), Flemish composer, student of Okeghem and later of Obrecht and Busnois. D. served in various Italian courts before entering the papal chapel (1486). In 1494 he entered the service of Louis XII and, at the end of his life, became a canon at the collegiate church of Condé.

D. wrote 3 books of Masses, over 100 motets, and many songs. His music is divided into two styles, in both of which he excelled. In the first, he experimented in the invention and solution of problems of contrapuntal technique. From these he was led to his later, freer, and purer style in which he showed a rare command of expressive melody. A. W. Ambros called him "the first musician who impresses us as having genius." BIBLIOGRAPHY: J. R. Milne, Grove DMM 4:666–669; N. Bridgman, "The Age of Ockeghem and Josquin," *Ars Nova and the Renaissance;* NOHM 3:262–270.

[M. T. LEGGE]

DESTINY. (1) Sometimes a synonym for final *end—the point to which one is directed or strives. The supernatural destiny of man is considered in theology in connection with *grace, *predestination, *providence, and *the supernatural. (2) Sometimes it is taken as a force moving human affairs to an appointed end and is equivalent to *fate. *DAIMON.

[T. C. O'BRIEN]

DESTINY, SUPERNATURAL, see SUPERNATURAL DESTINY.

DESURMONT, ACHILLE (1828–98), French Redemptorist ascetical writer. He held various positions of authority within his community in addition to being a pastor of a parish and a prolific writer. His works, *Rapporte de notre règle avec la fin de notre institute* (1854) and *La Charité sacerdotale* (1899) reflect the author as a religious, conscientious pastor of souls. His *Oeuvres complètes,* a compilation of his retreats, meditations, etc., stamp him the true missionary, the true disciple of St. Alphonsus Liguori. BIBLIOGRAPHY: P. Pourrat, *Catholicisme* 3:685–686; G. Liéven, DSAM 3:648–651.

[M. HIGGINS]

DESVALLIÈRES, GEORGES (1861–1950), painter, pioneer in modern French *Art Sacré* movement. He studied under *Moreau with *Rouault and *Matisse, and helped found the *Salon d'automne* (1903). Following tragic experiences in World War I, he painted shockingly expressionistic works, e.g., "Sacred Heart of the Trenches." With M. *Denis he founded the *Ateliers d'art sacré* (1919) and worked toward renewed spiritual significance in religious art. BIBLIOGRAPHY: P. Ladoué, "Peintre et apôtre: Georges Desvallières," *Convertis du XX.ᵉ siècle* (ed. F. Lelotte, 1953); R. J. Verostko, NCE 4:808–809.

[R. J. VEROSTKO]

DETACHMENT, a nonce word when used by spiritual authors for the action or result of untying or cutting our bonds with the world into which we are born unto corruption. All Christians are called to release themselves from the three concupiscences of which St. John speaks, the flesh, the eyes, and the pride of life (1 Jn 2.16); otherwise they cannot rise in the things of God. This freeing of the self from selfishness is compared by St. John of the Cross to the cutting of cords that bind a bird to earth and prevent its flight. The term is applied by an athletic asceticism to arduous, subtle, and sometimes recondite exercises for purifying our intentions. It sometimes goes with a bad philosophy and worse theology, as though detachment were a good in itself, a happy release from and disdain for earthly creatures, and not just a good for the sake of a higher attachment, namely to God and to creatures as his. BIBLIOGRAPHY: St. John of the Cross, *Ascent of Mt. Carmel,* bk 1, ch. 1.8; A. Royo and J. Aumann, *Theology of Christian Perfection* (1962) 319–323.

[T. GILBY]

DETERMINISM, in general a philosophic or scientific view that the universe, including the activities of man, operates in accordance with inexorable laws that admit the possibility neither of human free will nor the presence of a first and undetermined principle existing apart from the cosmos. In the history of thought, numerous versions of deterministic theory have arisen causing ambiguity of terminology. In the present context, the following principal forms of determinism are distinguished: physical, economic, psychological, and ethical.

Physical. Theories of physical determinism are as old as recorded philosophic thought so that the rise of modern science in the 17th and 18th cent. with its attendant deterministic attitude, simply tended to revise and elaborate similar thinking extending as far back as the Greek atomists of the 5th cent. B.C. Leucippus, the founder of the school, and Democritus who worked out its practical applications, maintained that material reality is constituted of three elements—the void, motion, and atoms, the last being minute, invisible particles that join in various combinations because of the presence of the void and the vortex motion of the universe which propels them. But this motion is irrational with no intelligence to direct it, and thus all nature is determined by the inflexible laws of matter and motion which alone guide it in its course. Epicurus (341–270 B.C.) and his disciples were quick to recognize the moral implications of this view, judging that man's behavior could now no longer be deemed free but was to be accounted for rather by the motion of atoms. Later Epicureans revised the original position to provide a limited role for free will and chance. More recent deterministic hypotheses have been linked with the scientific method of observation and experiment. These tend to stress the mathematical exactitude of mechanical laws active in nature and the blind necessity with which they operate. The materialistic doctrine of Thomas Hobbes (1588–1679) exemplifies the tendency in some quarters to interpret human nature in terms of the laws of physics. Denying the existence of a spiritual soul, Hobbes saw human conduct as nothing more than the behavior of matter. Whatever happens throughout the universe is causally determined by modifications in material particles, ruling out any possibility of voluntary acts proceeding from man as their undetermined source.

Economic. This form of deterministic doctrine has its origins largely in the writings of Karl Marx (1818–83), whose materialistic approach to history has come to be called the economic interpretation of history or economic determinism. In this account, all human activity is motivated by the economic inducement. The whole sweep of man's history is essentially a story of the production and exchange of goods and services, and these have been the foremost factors in conditioning man's entire existence. Once man survived with crude forms of subsistence, such as hunting and fishing, slowly learned agriculture, established farms and towns, developed crafts and skills, until at last there emerged the modern industrial colossus. But at each stage of economic evolution, there was a corresponding progress in the forms of culture or civilization. The degree or level of the latter is thus directly related to and dependent upon the prevailing economic system, so that all the elements of human life, be they religious, philosophical, political, aesthetic, ethical, etc., are determined ultimately by the existing economic milieu, and progress in direct ratio with it. From this contention follows Marx's theory of class struggle since out of the economic environment arises the class system. In his analysis, eventually the proletariat will rise against its masters, ending class strife with the emergence of a classless society.

Psychological. This species of determinism maintains the thesis that human conduct is completely conditioned and governed by factors external to the human agent over which he has little if any control, so that his behavior is virtually inevitable and unavoidable and could not in fact be other than it is. Hence, the life of the individual takes its shape from prenatal experience, the personality and compatibility of one's parents, home environment, body structure and nervous system, native endowments and predispositions. Theories of psychological determinism hold in common that the human will has no power of self-determination but is moved rather by extrinsic and coercive agencies. Hobbes, for instance, contended that voluntary human action is caused by alternating motives of desire and aversion which are reducible to physical forces. Hence, the immediate cause of a voluntary action is an act of will which is never free in the sense of being uncaused, for it is always caused by either desire or aversion. Many contemporary psychiatrists discount claims of human freedom made by philosophy, regarding the matter as subject to decision only by empirical investigation. *BEHAVIORISM.

Ethical. The tradition of Greek antiquity as represented by Socrates, Plato, and Aristotle sets forth a classic view in the area of ethical determinism. Socrates (*c.*470–399 B.C.) asserted that every man seemingly chooses whatever in his view is best for him, whereas Plato (427–347 B.C.) went further to say that the man who knows precisely what is

morally good can hardly elect to do anything else, so that the evil-doer must surely be involuntary in his action or ignorant of the good. For Plato, the knowledge of the morally good action and the doing of it are necessarily linked. Thus, virtue is identified with knowledge and vice with ignorance; if any man should seek evil, it must be because he is uninformed as to the real good. Since the human will is determined to incline toward the good, real, or apparent, all of man's voluntary actions are thus ethically determined. Far from limiting man's freedom, the greatest good confers the greatest freedom, whereas any good less than the highest determines man to a limitation of freedom, and he who pursues evil is pitiably enslaved. Aristotle (384–322 B.C.) tends to reject the ethical determinism of his predecessors on the grounds that man's appetites or desires are often at war with reason in coveting something evil when it is known to be evil. Many contemporary thinkers incline toward the same view because it seems to accord with human experience. BIBLIOGRAPHY: for physical determinism: C. Bailey, *Greek Atomists and Epicurus* (1928); *Body, Man and Citizen* (ed. R. Peters, 1962). For economic determinism: K. Marx, *Contribution to the Critique of Political Economy,* preface and translation by N. Stone (1904); *idem, Communist Manifesto* (ed. M. Eastman, 1932). For psychological determinism: J. Hosper, "What Means This Freedom," and P. Edwards, "Hard and Soft Determinism," in P. Nowell-Smith, *Ethics* (1954); A. J. Ayer, *Philosophical Essays* (1954), ch. 12. For ethical determinism: Plato's *Protagoras, Gorgias,* and *Hippias Minor;* Aristotle's *Nicomachean Ethics.*

[J. T. HICKEY]

DETMOLD, GROTTO OF THE HOLY SEPULCHER, 12th-cent. German rock-formed chapel near Detmold, Westphalia. The entrance relief *(Descent from the Cross, c.*1115) carved *in situ* 18 feet high, is a fine example of German Romanesque monumental sculpture. The stiff, angular, linear style recalls barbaric art, with no reference to French Romanesque of Burgundy or Languedoc, but evidencing the *retardataire* nature of German Romanesque. BIBLIOGRAPHY: E. Panofsky, *Die deutsche Plastik des XI. bis XIII. Jahrhunderts* (1924).

[M. J. DALY]

DE TORRES, BARTOLOMÉ, see TORRES, BARTOLOMÉ DE.

DETRACTION, the unjust damaging of a person's reputation by revealing some secret fault or defect of his, or by expressing one's own or another's suspicion of a person, without proportionate reason for doing so. It differs from calumny which damages a reputation by lying. The reputation in question is that general esteem which people have of fellow human beings so that they will deal with them socially in friendship or in business. Every man, since God created him as a social being, has the God-given right to the esteem necessary for social living unless he has forfeited or yielded it. Generally he forfeits this right only when he has done something or has some defect which renders him a peril to others in social dealings. The test of whether a given revelation or statement about another amounts to detraction is whether it will actually cause a lessening of the esteem mentioned above. If it is clear that it will cause no such loss of esteem, it will not be detraction. If it will cause such a loss, and there is no proportionate reason for allowing the loss to occur, it is detraction regardless of how the statement is made: whether as a fact, suspicion, conjecture, or as something heard from others. And what is stated need not be anything of which the person himself is responsible. For example, to reveal that a person was born out of wedlock can often damage the general esteem in which he is held. Since detraction is a violation of a strict right, it obliges the detractor to restitution of what he has damaged: that is, the general esteem in which the other person is held. This can often best be done by showing respect and honor in the presence of others to the person damaged. BIBLIOGRAPHY: K. B. Moore, NCE 4:815–816; J. J. Farraher, "Detractio et jus in famam," *Periodica* 41 (1952) 6–35.

[J. J. FARRAHER]

DEUS SCIENTIARUM DOMINUS, an apostolic constitution of Pope Pius XI (May 24, 1931) to foster higher standards in ecclesiastical studies by establishing uniformity of requirements in all institutes granting pontifical degrees. It set up norms for the direction of such institutes, for the qualifications of their personnel as well as their physical equipment and economic stability, for the minimum requirements for degrees and esp. for the doctorate. It became effective with the academic year 1932–33 and revoked all contrary prescriptions and privileges in force before that time. It has been superseded by post-Vatican II seminary programs.

[J. H. ROHLING]

DEUSDEDIT (ADEODATUS) I, ST. (d. 618), **POPE** from 615. A priest of the Roman church for 40 years, D. succeeded Boniface IV at a time when the civil government was in a state of near chaos in consequence of the Lombard invasions. During D.'s pontificate, the Emperor's representative, the exarch of Ravenna, was assassinated. D. remained loyal to the Emperor and welcomed the new exarch, who came to put down rebellion and to punish those responsible for his predecessor's murder. Earthquake, followed by a plague, added to the disorder of the time. Few authentic records are extant. D. was interred in Rome. BIBLIOGRAPHY: C. Sheedy, NCE 4:822; Butler 4:296; Mann 1:280–293.

[P. F. MULHERN]

DEUSDEDIT (ADEODATUS) II, ST. (d. 676), **POPE** from 672. A Roman and a monk of the Coelian Monastery, D. succeeded Vitalian in the papacy. Like his predecessor

he spent his pontificate defending the Church against the Monothelite interests, ecclesiastical and civil, of the East. With him began the custom of dating papal acts from the beginning of a pope's pontificate. He enlarged his former monastery on the Coelian. His two extant letters are a defense of monastic exemption (PL 87:1141–46). The Bollandists were able to discover no indication of an early cult, but his feast is noted in some martyrologies. BIBLIOGRAPHY: C. M. Aherne, NCE 1:128; Mann 1.2:17–19.

[P. F. MULHERN]

DEUSDEDIT OF CANTERBURY, sixth abp. of Canterbury. Successor to St. Honorius in 653, he was the first native Englishman to serve as primate. No further details of his life or ministry are extant.

[J. F. FALLON]

DEUSDEDIT OF MONTE CASSINO, ST., (d. 834), abbot and martyr. He was taken captive by Sicard of Benevento, who wished to confiscate the abbey properties and he died during his imprisonment. The location of his relics is not known. BIBLIOGRAPHY: AS (1780) Oct. 4:104; Mabillon, *Acta sanctorum ordinis S. Benedicti* 4:463; MGS 7:596; PL 173–1090.

[W. A. JURGENS]

DEUSDEDIT, COLLECTION OF, second major canonical work under Pope Gregory VII. Card. Deusdedit, a friend of Gregory VII, edited this collection of canons at the suggestion of the pope. The primary purpose of the work was to support the privileged status and universal rights and responsibilities of the Roman primacy as a basis for achieving the ends of the Reformation. It dealt with the RC Church's authority and temporalities, the Roman clergy, and the liturgy of the Church in its properties and personnel. Four tables of rubrics provide an index to facilitate its use. Deusdedit was also the editor of an important collection of Pope Gregory's correspondence. BIBLIOGRAPHY: J. J. Ryan, NCE 4:823; J. P. Kirsch, CE 6:760.

[M. T. LEGGE]

DEUTEROCANONICAL (literally "of the second canon"), a name used esp. by Catholics for the following books of the Greek Septuagint version of the Bible, not found in the Hebrew Scriptures, but received in the early Church: Tob, Jdt, Wis, Sir, Bar, 1–2 Macc, and certain additional parts of the book of Dan and Esther. They are listed among the *Apocrypha by Protestants. The terms deuterocanonical and protocanonical (the other books of the OT) were first applied in this sense by Sixtus of Siena (1520–69). The distinction does not refer to the existence of separate canons, but of a later date of universal acceptance in regard to the deuterocanonicals. The word is also infrequently used of those NT books about which there was hesitation or dispute in the early Church: Heb, Jas, 2 Pet,

2–3 Jn, Jude, Revelation. BIBLIOGRAPHY: O. Eissfeldt, *Old Testament, an Introduction* (1965) 571–637.

[C. BERNAS]

DEUTERONOMIC REFORMS, the name commonly given to a principally religious reform carried out by Josiah of Judah (640–609 B.C.) in the latter part of the 7th cent. B.C. It is so called because the reform measures, as reported in 2 Kg 23.1–24, are in remarkable agreement with the code of laws found in Deuteronomy. Josiah first renewed the covenant with Yahweh (2 Kg 23.1–3) whose stipulations had not been faithfully followed; Dt has several passages strongly urging the following of these covenant obligations (see 5.1–22). He then ordered the destruction of all objects of idolatry in the temple and of all shrines and places of worship outside Jerusalem (2 Kg 23.4–20); the prohibition of idolatry and provision for worship at a single sanctuary (Jerusalem) are a special emphasis of Dt (see 12.1–31). The king's celebration of the Passover (2 Kg 23.21–23) is in keeping with Dt 16.1–8. Finally, some of the language of 2 Kg 23 recalls the style of Deuteronomy. Because of these agreements scholars believe that Josiah followed the spirit and even the letter of a code of laws already existing and that the code was the core of the present book of Dt (some form of ch. 12–26). In 2 Kg 22.3–20 we read that, during the repair of the temple which has been neglected during the irreligious reigns of Manasseh (687–642) and Amon (642–640), a "book of the Law" (the core of Dt) was found by Hilkiah the high priest. It was taken to the king who reported the matter to the prophetess Huldah. She foretold destruction because of the failure to keep the commandments of Yahweh. But this would not take place before the king's death because of his reforming zeal. The reform itself, as described above, followed.

[E. H. MALY]

DEUTERONOMIST, the name given to the school of priests responsible for the development of the book of Dt; it can also refer to the unique theology of Deuteronomy. Levitical priests of the northern kingdom of Israel were probably responsible for the original formulation of the legal traditions of Deuteronomy. The priests of the temple of Jerusalem in Judah were responsible for the later, definitive development. The style of Dt is strongly exhortatory, suggesting composition in a period of religious crisis. The theology is marked by a covenant emphasis, the people being urged "today" to express their loyal love of Yahweh by keeping his commandments. Idolatry, particularly Canaanite, is denounced. A single place of worship (Jerusalem, though not mentioned, is intended) is permitted. The effective power of the liturgy in renewing Yahweh's saving acts is featured, and Israel's resulting joy and confidence in the Lord are described. All of this is presented in the form of discourses or homilies attributed to Moses in order to underline their authenticity. BIBLIOGRAPHY: EDB 560–563. *DOCUMENTARY THEORY.

[E. H. MALY]

DEUTERONOMY, BOOK OF, fifth book of the Pentateuch. The Greek word *deuteronomion* (literally "second law") is found in the Septuagint version of this book. In accord with the Hebrew text it is generally translated "a copy of (this) law." The word, applied to the entire book since the time of LXX, indicates its relationship to the preceding books of law (Ex-Lev). In a series of homilies attributed to Moses, the law of the covenant is repeated in a new, strongly exhortatory form. There are four major sections: (1) the journey from Horeb (Sinai) to Beth-peor, E of the Jordan, is recalled (1.1–4.43); (2) the covenant law is partially disclosed and obedience to it is urged (4.44–11.32); (3) the third discourse contains the core of the book, the so-called Deuteronomic code (12.1–26.19); and (4) concluding injunctions are given, with formulae of curses and blessings, a song of Moses, blessing of the tribes and details of Moses' death and burial (29.1–34.12).

The composition of Dt is extremely complex; only the broad outlines of its development are the object of general agreement. The northern kingdom of Israel was responsible for the first formulation of Dt's legal traditions, which were then taken to Jerusalem after the fall of the North in 721 B.C. A Jerusalem theology permeated the next stage of development, probably during the reign of Hezekiah (715–687 B.C.). The period of Manasseh and Amon followed (687–640 B.C.) during which idolatry flourished and the authentic traditions were ignored and neglected. During the reign of Josiah (640–609 B.C.) the high priest Hilkiah found a "book of the Law" while repairing the temple. Likely, it was some form of the Deuteronomic code (ch. 12–26) and was made the basis of a reform. During and after the Babylonian exile, later stages of the book's development occurred; scholars are still attempting to analyze these more accurately. Sometime during this same period the material contained in the canonical books of Jos–2 Kg was edited in the light of Dt's theology, and Dt itself was prefixed as the introduction to this so-called Deuteronomic history. It was later in the postexilic period, around the time of Ezra (latter part of 5th cent. B.C.), that Dt was separated from the following historical books and made a part of the preceding, and principally legal, books to form the Pentateuch.

[E. H. MALY]

DEUTERUS, earliest designation (9th cent.) for the second of the four basic modes. In the church modes, the Phyrgian or third mode was the *deuterus authenticus* and the Hypophrygian or fourth mode, the *deuterus plagius*. BIBLIOGRAPHY: R. C. Pian, Apel HDMus 165–166.

[M. T. LEGGE]

DEUTINGER, MARTIN (1815–64), German Catholic philosopher and theologian. A priest from 1837, D. taught philosophy at Freising (1842–46), Munich (1846–47), and Dillingen (1847–52). He then retired from teaching and from 1858 was university preacher in Munich. In an effort to reconcile revelation with the idealistic philosophy of his time, D. abandoned the Christian philosophical tradition and constructed a philosophy of his own based on an elaborate dialectic of trilogies. Although he had considerable power and depth of mind, his repudiation of all philosophies but his own left him with no enduring part in the philosophical dialogue of his time. Only his insights in the field of aesthetics can be said to have had any lasting influence. BIBLIOGRAPHY: F. P. Siegfried, CE 4:761–762; A. Scholz, LTK 3:264.

[M. J. SUELZER]

DEUTSCH-KATHOLISCHE KIRCHE, see DEUTSCH-KATHOLIZISMUS.

DEUTSCHE CHRISTEN, Christians in Germany under the Hitler regime who sought to form a Church conformed to Nazi ideology. *GERMAN CHRISTIANS.

DEUTSCHER RITTERORDEN, see TEUTONIC KNIGHTS.

DEUTSCHES REQUIEM, EINE, German Requiem, a choral work in seven movements by Johannes Brahms. Based on texts freely chosen from the Old and New Testaments, it is not a liturgical Requiem Mass.

[M. T. LEGGE]

DEUTSCHKATHOLIZISMUS, a German Catholic schismatic movement begun by Johann *Ronge and Johann *Czerski about 1845. Ronge, a priest from Breslau (Wroclaw), was degraded from the priesthood and excommunicated after his attack on the bp. of Trier for fostering veneration of the relic of the holy coat in 1844. After Ronge founded a reformed congregation at Breslau in 1845, he was joined by Czerski, also a degraded priest, in organizing a new body, the Deutsche-Katholische Kirche, which rejected, among other things, papal primacy, celibacy, indulgences, devotion to the saints, veneration of relics, and all the sacraments except baptism and the Lord's Supper. In the climate of liberalism and nationalism hostile to the dogmatic character and *ultramontane tendencies of the RC Church in Germany, Ronge's agitations won a widespread following, but his influence was short-lived. Within several years the new Church numbered 80,000 adherents with several hundred congregations. While ostensibly founded on Scripture, the new Church was heavily rationalistic and soon lost all vestiges of its RC background, as well as many followers who had hoped for genuine reform from within the RC Church. In 1850 most of the German Catholics united with the Protestant Free Congregations, and in 1859 many merged with the Friends of Light, an anti-Christian sect. A few German Catholic Churches retained their original identity and lingered into the 20th century. BIBLIOGRAPHY: G. Maron, RGG 2:112–113.

[J. WILLKE]

DEUTZ, ABBEY OF. Benedictine monastery across the Rhine from Cologne. It was founded (1002) by St. Heribert, abp. of Cologne, at the request of the dying King Otto III, who bequeathed it many national treasures. D. was absorbed (1491) by the reform group of Benedictines, the Bursfeld Congregation, and it continued to flourish until the secularization of 1803. St. Heribert is believed to be buried in the monastery chapel crypt, the only part of the once vast complex to survive in pristine condition.

DE VALERA, EAMON (1882–1975), father of modern Ireland. Born in New York of a Spanish father and Irish mother, De V. was taken to Ireland at the age of three. He became a teacher of mathematics at Maynooth. In 1913 he joined the Irish Volunteers and in the Easter Rebellion of 1916 was commandant of the forces at Boland's Mill. De V. was condemned to death with the other rebel leaders but was released from prison in 1917. He was elected Member of Parliament from East Clare in 1917 as a member of Sinn Fein. Arrested a second time, he escaped from Lincoln jail in February 1919 and was elected president of the provisional government of the republic. In the negotiations between his government and Britain, De V. and his cabinet proposed a united Ireland with external association with Britain. When the Irish delegation accepted the proposed Irish Free State, De V. rejected the compromise. In the civil war of 1922 he led the republicans against the Free Staters, was imprisoned, and released in 1924. In 1927 he founded the opposition party, *Fianna Fail,* and entered the Dail as its leader. The general election of 1932 made him president of the Council and Minister of External Affairs. In the succeeding 6 years he eliminated the constitutional ties with Britain. In 1937 the new constitution established the republic of Eire and De V. as its prime minister. Throughout World War II De V. maintained a policy of neutrality. In 1948 his government was defeated but came back into power in 1951 and again in 1957. In 1959 he was elected president of Ireland. Throughout the many changes in Irish politics, De V. manifested a hardy power of survival. No Irishman in the 20th cent. did more to create the modern Republic of Ireland. De V. was one of the most respected Catholic statesmen of his age and brought both revolutionary spirit and great wisdom of moderation to the Irish cause over a period of 60 years. BIBLIOGRAPHY: M. J. McManus, *DeValera* (1957).

[J. R. AHERNE]

DEVAS, CHARLES STANTON (1848–1906), English political economist. D. was converted to Catholicism before entering Oxford and took a conspicuous part in the campaign that opened the English universities to Catholics. He collaborated on the *Dublin Review* and furthered the Catholic social movement in England. In his social theory he strongly opposed the unnatural separation of economic science from morality. His chief writings are *Studies in*

Family Life (1886) and *Key to World Progress* (1906). BIBLIOGRAPHY: R. P. Walsh, NCE 4:826.

[M. J. SUELZER]

DÉVAY, MÁTYÁS, see BIRÓ, MÁTYÁS DÉVAI.

DEVELOPMENT OF DOCTRINE, see DOCTRINE, DEVELOPMENT OF.

DEVELOPMENTAL PSYCHOLOGY, the branch of psychology that investigates the typical stages or phases of mental and emotional growth as they are successively experienced from infancy to old age. The first major contribution to developmental psychology was *Freud's theory of psychosexual stages. Other important contributions are those of Gesell, Ilg, and Ames on personality development from infancy to late adolescence; J. Piaget on intellectual stages; H. Werner on comparative psychology of age groups; E. Erikson on stages of psychosocial growth, and various psychiatric studies on the climacteric and the onset of senility. Since religious thinking, feeling, and behavior are partly a function of a person's stage of general psychological development, studies of typical patterns of religious development are of this branch of psychology. BIBLIOGRAPHY: L. Stott, *Psychology of Human Development* (1974).

[M. E. STOCK]

DEVĪ, Hindu goddess and consort of Siva, identified with Pārvatī and Umā who is forbidding as Durgā and Kālī.

[M. J. DALY]

DEVIL, a term derived from the Gr. *diabolos,* meaning slanderer, refers in Christian usage primarily to Satan (the "accuser") and secondarily to all his followers, who are identified as fallen angels. There is only peripheral biblical reference to the fall of the angels (Jude 6; 2 Pet 2.4), whose sin is taken by later Judaism (e.g., Enoch) as angelic sin with women (Gen 6.1–2). Revelation 12.7–9, however, records the story of Michael's successful fight against the dragon and his angels and later identifies the dragon with the "primeval serpent and Satan" (20.2). Jude 9 refers to Michael's disputing with the devil about the corpse of Moses, but there is no biblical explanation of the fall of Satan. Hence the Thomist and Scotist explanations are based on theological reflection rather than on revelation: Aquinas taught that Satan by a single sin of pride desired supernatural bliss by his own powers, Scotus, that he became fixed in sin by a series of sins of excessive love of his own excellence.

There is much in the Bible about Satan and devils (or demons). Apart from Job (1.6; 2.7), where he is not an evil spirit but the heavenly prosecutor, Satan is generally represented as the occasion of man's fall (Gen 3) and of subsequent sins, esp. in the later writings (e.g., 1 Chr 21.1, *c.*3d cent. B.C.). In Christ's life, also, Satan and devils appear as

representing the kingdom of this world opposed to the kingdom of God which Christ is establishing (Mk 1.13—Christ's temptations; Mt 13.24–30—parable of weeds among wheat; and demoniacs Christ cured); and Christ prays to preserve his Disciples from Satan (Lk 22.31–32). But in fact Satan's power is broken; he has no power over Christ (Jn 14.30), and he is already condemned (Jn 16.11), he and his devils being assigned to eternal punishment (Mt 25.41). Catholic theology (apart from Origen's Neoplatonist belief in the devils' ultimate salvation) is united in repeating this teaching and in stating both that Satan and the devils are condemned for their personal sin and that they strive to lead men into sin and to harm the Church (Lateran IV, 1215; D 800). BIBLIOGRAPHY: J. H. Crehan, CDT 2:166–171; L. Cristiani, *Evidence of Satan in the Modern World* (pa. 1975).

[B. FORSHAW]

DEVIL AND SIN. The reality of the *devil is associated with the causing of sin (Eph 6, 12). Diabolical power to influence men towards evil, however, is subject to divine providence; Christ's victory includes his triumph over the power of Satan (ThAq ST 3a.49,2). Further, in kind the influence is limited to enticement; no being but God and the person acting can directly cause the will to make a choice; any other influence on choice is indirect and persuasive only (*ibid.* 1a.114; 1a2ae 80). The mysterious case of *diabolical possession is a special problem; it need not mean that the possessed person is a sinner.

[T. C. O'BRIEN]

DEVIL WORSHIP is the practice of offering homage to some personified force of evil hostile to God, which is conceived as having at least limited dominion over the world. As a belief it is usually based on the dualism of two counterbalancing and universal forces of good and evil, but may, as with the Yezidis of Armenia and the Caucasus, hold that Satan or Iblis will be ranged under God in the end. It takes various forms and includes practices, squalid and bizarre, sometimes intentionally sacrilegious or blasphemous on the part of Christian believers—they fall rather flat otherwise. But diabolism, in the sense of devil-dealing, is not necessarily devil worship, nor is it traffic with demons, black magic, and suchlike sorts of superstition. Some blood-curdling legends are not to be credulously entertained: the informed theologian will not judge Voodoo, for instance, as altogether benighted, and the Christian traveler will find the devil-worshiping villages in the foothills of the Caucasus composed of honorable folk, though out to propitiate a very present power. BIBLIOGRAPHY: M. D. Griffin, NCE 4:829.

[C. P. SVOBODA]

DEVIL'S ADVOCATE, popular name for the promoter general of the faith, an official of the Congregation of Rites (now the Sacred Congregation for the Causes of the Saints).

In beatification and *canonization proceedings, he confronts the advocates of the action with the Church's demand for proof. The office is first mentioned during the papacy of Leo X (1515–21).

[T. EARLY]

DEVINE, ARTHUR (1849–1919), Irish Passionist priest ordained in 1872. D. spent about 30 years as professor of theology in London. He also taught Scripture and canon law and was consultor to his provincial. His great interest in the Oxford Movement brought many Anglicans into the Church. D. supported the revival of Gaelic by often preaching in that tongue. He is the author of *Auxilium praedicatorum, A Short Gloss upon the Gospels, History of the Passion, A Manual of Ascetical Theology, The Sacraments Explained, The Creed Explained*, besides his contribution of articles to the *Catholic Encyclopedia* and to Catholic magazines.

[M. HIGGINS]

DEVOLUTION, RIGHT OF, the right of collation of an ecclesiastical benefice that another collator exercises by default of the ordinary collator. In the Middle Ages, 3 months normally were allowed for a vacancy; thus if the clergy of a cathedral church failed to elect a bishop within 3 months, the "power of electing" passed to their immediate ecclesiastical superior, who in turn had 3 months in which to act (Lateran Council IV c. 23:ConOecDekr 122). Only rarely did this right devolve to the Holy See. In present church law, however, all benefices that have not been filled within 6 months of vacancy pass out of the hands of the ordinary collators to the Holy See (CIC c. 1432.3). BIB-LIOGRAPHY: G. J. Ebers, *Das Devolutionsrecht vornehmlich nach katholischen Kirchenrecht* (1906); L. E. Boyle NCE 4:830–831.

[L. E. BOYLE]

DEVOTIO MODERNA (Lat., modern devotion), a school and trend of spirituality that originated in the circle around Gerard Groote (1340–84) and his disciple Florentius Radewijns (1350–1400), founder of the *Brethren of the Common Life and of the Canons Regular of Windesheim; it reached its highest expression in the *Imitation of Christ* of Thomas à Kempis (1380–1471). In addition to Groote, Radewijns, and à Kempis, other prominent authors of the school were Gerlac Peters (1378–1411), Henrik Mande (1360–1431), its greatest mystic, and Johannes Mauburnus (Mombaer, 1460–1501), whose *Rosetum exercitiorum* was practically an encyclopedia of the spirituality of the *Devotio moderna*. During the 15th cent. *Devotio moderna* spread into parts of Germany, France, Spain, and possibly Italy. Called "modern" in contrast to the speculative and scholastic spirituality of the "old" German mysticism of Meister *Eckhart, it eschewed speculation and made little place for learning. The questions posed by the *Imitation of Christ*, 1.1: "What does it profit you to talk learnedly of the

Trinity. . . ? Of what value is knowledge without the fear of God?" indicate the school's underestimation of culture, knowledge, and purely human values. Marked by a pronounced preference for affective spirituality, *Devotio moderna* drew inspiration from Cistercian, Carthusian, and Franciscan sources. Christocentric rather than theocentric, it cultivated devotion to the Eucharist, meditation on Christ the man, and the imitation of the virtues of Christ. Accordingly it encouraged devout reading of the Scriptures, circulated copies of the Bible, and promoted translation into the vernacular. This school of spirituality claimed that self-knowledge, the practice of the virtues, and the avoidance of vice lay at the root of perfection. Though not excluding mysticism, it insisted upon self-abnegation and effort of the will: "The more constraint you put upon yourself the more progress you will make; that is certain" (*ibid.*, 1.25). Born during the dark days of the *Great Western Schism, *Devotio moderna* lacked an appreciation of the Church and the hierarchy. It placed great stress on the inner life of the individual but had less regard for external works and ritual. Intention, reflection, and fervor were primary. To encourage these, it introduced method into meditation and the other exercises of life. Advocating solitude, silence, and retirement from the world, the disciples of this school manifested little concern for the apostolate.

While *Devotio moderna* itself was anti-intellectual, most of the humanists of northern Europe, notably Erasmus, were affected by its positive spirituality. This explains their preoccupation with religious interests and with reform. The emphases in this form of spirituality were also dispositive for Reformation teachings on the nature of the Christian life. *Devotio moderna* as a school of spirituality disappeared as the Reformation brought an end to its main centers; many of its teachings, however, were absorbed into Erasmian, Ignatian, Benedictine, Franciscan and Dominican systems of spirituality. BIBLIOGRAPHY: R. R. Post, *De moderne devotie* (2d ed., 1950); A. Hyma, *Christian Renaissance* (1925, 2d ed. 1965).

[W. A. HINNEBUSCH]

DEVOTION, from Lat. *devotio,* the action of being addicted for good or evil, then the condition of being attached to something good, and in Christian usage of being dedicated or vowed to God's service. In this sense it passes from ecclesiastical to Romantic languages and so appears in Middle English. Exactly defined by St. Thomas Aquinas as a ready willingness in giving oneself up to service in God's household, he considers it, not as a special virtue, but as a capital quality in the activity of the virtue of *religion, as cherishing or holding dear is that for charity. Its classical text is the *Introduction to the Devout Life* by St. Francis de Sales. It is not to be confused with "sensible devotion," though this indeed is something to be grateful for, and a certain joyousness *(laetitia)* is remarked as its proper effect. It may flourish amid "spiritual dryness," and we are to learn from the Parable of the Two Sons (Mt 21.28–31) that action rather than speech is the test of service. BIBLIOGRAPHY: ThAq ST 2a2ae, 82, esp. in ed. Lat.-Eng. v. 39, ed. K. O'Rourke).

[T. GILBY]

DEVOTIONS. In the singular, devotion means primarily the quality or condition of being devoted or given earnestly to God's worship and service, the essence of *religion taken as a virtue. By extension it is sometimes applied, esp. among Roman Catholics, to the sensible experience, generally vaguely pleasurable, that sometimes but not necessarily accompanies fervent prayer; thus, e.g., to pray with devotion may mean to pray with sensible warmth; to pray without devotion, to pray with no sense of warmth, or with a feeling of aridity. In the plural the word is often applied to practices, usually involving prayer or religious reflection, of a kind apt to arouse the quality of earnestness in God's service. Thus a manual of devotions is a book of prayer designed for private as distinguished from formal public or liturgical worship. In a similar sense, among Protestants, organizational meetings at a local church may be preceded by "devotions," i.e., a short period of devout reflection that usually includes a hymn, a Scripture reading, and a prayer. "Popular devotions," in RC usage, is a term covering a wide variety of optional prayers and practices, often peripheral to the central themes of Christian worship, that people find helpful as means of arousing devotion in the primary meaning of the term—e.g., the rosary, the way of the cross, such special services as novenas and triduums, and the invocation of special saints.

[P. K. MEAGHER]

DEVOUT HUMANISM, a designation made familiar by Abbé Henri Bremond in his *Histoire littéraire du sentiment religieux en France* (12 v., 1911–36), of the first volume of which the term is the title. Midway between the somewhat severe view of human corruption by original sin as espoused by St. Augustine and John Calvin, and the Pelagian and modern secularist exaggeration of natural goodness in human nature, devout humanism sought to find a description of man neither optimistic nor pessimistic. The theologian of devout humanism was a Louvain professor Lessius who influenced St. Francis de Sales' *Introduction to the Devout Life*. St. Jane Frances de Chantal, founder of the Visitation nuns, spread the doctrine in her community. In the 20th cent. such notable thinkers as Jacques Maritain, Christopher Dawson, Martin D'Arcy, and John Courtney Murray have been its exponents.

[J. R. AHERNE]

DE WETTE, WILHELM (1780–1849), Protestant theologian, exegete. D. taught (1810–1819) at Heidelberg and Berlin. His thinking was greatly influenced by Griesbach. In his early essays and critical works on the Bible, he attempted to discredit the narratives of the Pentateuch. Archaeological studies led him to believe revealed truths to be myths and mere poetic fantasies. Contemporary rationalists condemned him for his repudiation of cold reasoning; the Pietists rejected him for reducing to myths the stories of the birth, Resurrection, and Ascension of Christ. His commentary *Kurzgefasstes exegetisches Handbuch zum Neuen Testament,* established D.'s reputation and influence as a scholar. BIBLIOGRAPHY: ODCC 394–395; DB 5.2:2501–02.

[A. A. O'NEILL]

DEWEY, JOHN (1859–1952), American philosopher, psychologist, educator, and social reformer. D. taught at the universities of Minnesota (1888–89), Michigan (1889–94), Chicago (1894–1904), and Columbia (1904–30). His efforts in both philosophy and psychology were aimed principally at his all-pervasive concern—the reform of American educational methods that he sought to formalize in a psychology of learning emphasizing concepts such as activity, process and growth, the importance of experience in attaining maturity, and the cultivation of student interest. He also stressed the need for analyzing modern society to determine its goals and corresponding educational requirements. His philosophy, known as instrumentalism or experimentalism, is a version of the pragmatism first formulated by C. S. *Peirce and amplified by William *James. It seeks to apply its principles to social, ethical, and political situations in the concrete. In morals, it prescribes the method of valuation by which man is to resolve his choices between values by projecting the probable consequences of proposed actions. Such choices will be reasonable insofar as they are based upon an intelligent habit of conduct, and irrational when grounded in prejudice or ignorance. Thus the experimental approach of science holds true in ethics also, any notion of a fixed and immutable moral law rooted in the nature of man as rational, being rejected as part of an authoritarian past, not in keeping with the possibilities of more empirical standards. Similarly, a scientific knowledge of human conditions leads to the good society in which all citizens have opportunity for maximum growth and experience. BIBLIOGRAPHY: M. H. Thomas *John Dewey: A Centennial Bibliography,* (1962) for the most comprehensive bibliog. of D.'s works; R. Bernstein, *John Dewey* (1966); G. Geiger, *Dewey in Perspective* (1958); R. Roth, *John Dewey and Self-Realization* (1962); J. Boydston, *Checklist of Writing about John Dewey* (1974).

[J. T. HICKEY]

DE WULF, MAURICE (1867–1947), Belgian professor and historian of medieval philosophy. He studied at the Univ. of Louvain (1885–91) and upon receiving his doctorate (1893) was immediately appointed professor at the Institut Supérieur de Philosophie at Louvain where he remained until 1939. He taught medieval philosophy at Harvard (1920–27) and through this and other academic contacts contributed to the development of medieval studies in the U.S. His two more influential works were *Histoire de la* *philosophie médiévale* (1900) and *Histoire de la philosophie en Belgique* (1910).

[J. T. HICKEY]

DEXIOS, THEODORE (d. *c.* 1360), a Byzantine monk of anti-Palamite conviction. His spiritual father was Matthew of Ephesus, and he received his monastic habit from Nicephorus Gregoras. With Gregory Akindynos he engaged in propaganda aimed at overcoming Palamism in Thessalonika. He disdained the use of the dialectical method in theology. He produced a treatise against John VI Cantacuzenus and the synodal Tome of 1351. BIBLIOGRAPHY: Beck 330, 716, 729; M. Jugie, DTC 11.2:1804–05.

[R. A. TODD]

DEZA, DIEGO DE (*c.* 1444–1523), Dominican theologian, bishop, and inquisitor. As a prof. at Salamanca (1480), D. was a precursor of the 16th–cent. renewal of Thomism in Spain. From 1487 he was at the court of Ferdinand and Isabella, where he gave staunch support to the enterprise of Christopher Columbus. He was successively bp. of Zamora (1494), Salamanca (1494), Jaén (1498), Palencia (1500), and abp. of Seville (1504–23); at the time of his death he was abp. designate of Toledo. As grand inquisitor (1598–1607) his zeal did not stop short of cruelty. BIBLIOGRAPHY: M. Garcia, "Fray Diego de Deza, campeón de la doctrina de Santo Tomas," *Ciencia tomista* (1922) 188–198; S. E. Morison, *Admiral of the Ocean Sea* (1942).

DHARMA, Sanskrit word, from the root *d h r,* meaning to hold, uphold, or maintain, used with varying meanings in both *Hinduism and *Buddhism. Among the most important usages are the following: (1) an ordering principle of the universe; the ultimate basis or force accounting for the way things are, both physically (e.g., the order of the seasons) and morally (why some actions are right and others wrong); (2) the duty appropriate to one's caste or state in life ("Better to do one's own *dharma,* though devoid of merit, than to do another's, however well performed": *Bhagavad Gita* 3, 35; 18, 47); in this sense it constitutes the third of the four traditional goals or pursuits *(vargas)* of human life in Hinduism, beyond pleasure *(kama)* and wealth *(artha),* but surpassed by liberation *(moksa)*; (3) usually in its Pali form *(dhamma)* it refers to the teaching or doctrine of the Buddha—who pointed to "the way things truly are" (e.g., that the misery of human life is caused by possessiveness), as opposed to how they appear—and the way of life based on that teaching. In this last sense it is one of the three "jewels" or bases of Buddhism, as in the affirmation: "I take refuge in the Buddha, the *Samqha* (the community of monks and nuns), and the Dharma." BIBLIOGRAPHY: R. C. Zaehner, *Hinduism* (1966) 102–24 and *passim*; E. Conze, *Buddhist Thought in India* (1967) 92–106.

[D. P. EFROYMSON]

DHARMAÇAKRA, mudra or iconographic position of hands of the Buddha signifying teaching or turning the wheel *(çakra)* of the Law *(dharma).* The hands are against the chest, the right palm out, the left palm in, fingers counting off the Noble Eightfold Paths.

[M. J. DALY]

DHARMAPĀLA, defender *(pāla)* of the law *(dharma),* these Tantric divinities of Buddhism are ferocious but not malignant.

[M. J. DALY]

DHIMMI, a non-Muslim living within the confines of an Islamic state. Such a person was subject to Islamic law, but permitted to continue to practice his or her religion without interference on the condition that a poll-tax *(jizya)* was paid and that the religion of the Dhimmi was privately practiced, not propagated. The designation *dhimmi* derives from *Ahl al-dhimma* which means Protected Peoples. Though these aliens were officially protected, they were considered second-class citizens and forced to dress in a manner reflecting their social inferiority, to build their houses no taller than those of their Muslim neighbors, to yield to Muslims on the road, and to face the inevitable prejudices and dangers of a stigmatized people.

[R. J. LITZ]

DHŪ-NUWĀS MASRUK, the name given in Syriac sources to the pre-Islamic king of S Arabia who gained fame for his ferocious persecution of Christians. His Arabic name is Zur'at ben Tibbān As'ad. His actual name in S Arabian epigraphy was Yūsuf 'As'ar Yat'ar. During the persecution (*c.* 523–525) 14,000 Christians were slain, and 11,000 were taken prisoner. The origin of his hostility is uncertain, but is often attributed to alleged pro-Jewish feeling. It may have been, however, retaliation for the ill-conceived invasion of Yemen by the Christian king of Ethiopia, bent on converting Arabs to Christianity. To stop the persecution the Byzantine Emperor Justinian I (518–527) instigated the Ethiopian king to attempt another invasion, which the latter did with overwhelming force. Apparently, D. was assassinated and succeeded by a Christian king.

[E. J. DILLON]

DHYANA, a stage of yoga. In Hinduism dhyana is meditation or concentration of mind that leads to the final stage of contemplation, total absorption in the object in mind. BIBLIOGRAPHY: S. N. Dasgupta, *Hindu Mysticism* (1960).

[M. T. REILLY]

DIABELLI, ANTON (Antonio; 1781–1858), Austrian music publisher and composer of Italian descent. While studying for the priesthood, D. was a music pupil of Michael Haydn. In 1803, having given up training for the priesthood, he became associated with Joseph Haydn. Subsequently he became a popular teacher, composer, and arranger of pianoforte pieces, and later a publisher. His easy to sing Masses, esp. the *Landmessen,* are still popular in Austria. BIBLIOGRAPHY: C. F. Pohl, Grove DMM 2:683.

[M. T. LEGGE]

DIABOLICAL OBSESSION, the prolonged harassment of a person by the devil; the devil's "laying siege" (Lat., *obsidere*) to a person from the outside. The best-known case in the life of a modern saint (as distinct from the fathers of the Egyptian desert in the 3d and 4th cent., whose constant troubles from devils lack consistent historical basis) is the activity by which the devil *(le grappin)* made the life of St. John Vianney uncomfortable and his sleep sometimes impossible. These manifestations were to some extent similar to those of poltergeists in haunted houses. While completely accepting the possibility, the Church has always been skeptical of alleged instances of diabolical intervention in human affairs. Accordingly, it demands a rigorous examination of phenomena before accepting that causes other than natural ones are required as adequate explanation of them. In the case of the Curé d'Ars (John Vianney), a notable Catholic spiritual writer provides a natural explanation for these phenomena. The Church, however, by allowing ritual exorcisms of places and material objects as part of its blessing of them, acknowledges its readiness to use spiritual means to combat all possible diabolical manifestations. BIBLIOGRAPHY: F. Trochu, *Curé d'Ars* (tr. E. E. Graf, 1927); L. J. Elmer, NCE 4:838–839.

[B. FORSHAW]

DIABOLICAL POSSESSION, a condition in which a demon or evil spirit is in control of some of a person's faculties and activities. There is mention in the OT of something like possession in the affliction of Saul by an evil spirit (1 Sam 16.14; 18.10); soothsaying was understood to imply a kind of transitory possession (Lev 20.27; 1 Sam 28.7); and certain illnesses were attributed to the activity of evil spirits (Tob 3.8; 6.15; 8.3). The number of cases of possession referred to in the NT is astonishing when judged in the light of later ideas concerning the prevalence of this affliction. One explanation is that notion of possession played a great part in the thinking of the Jewish people among whom Jesus lived. They made much of the connection between sin and suffering (see Jn 9.2), and they attributed psychic disorders, as well as other kinds of sickness, to the direct action of evil spirits. Jesus' cures of these disorders could have been interpreted by the populace as an expulsion of demons, and Jesus simply made no attempt to teach them otherwise, any more than he corrected the many other false scientific notions they entertained. He thus accommodated his words and deeds to their popular beliefs, not only because the correction of errors of that kind was beyond the scope of his mission, but also because toleration of their errors was in this matter pedagogically useful inasmuch as it enabled him to direct their attention more effec-

tively to the truth he came to teach. His messianic mission involved in a special way the destruction of the kingdom of Satan and the establishment of the kingdom of God. In view of the attitudes of his contemporaries, the disciples included, these cures were dramatic indications of the real nature of his mission and of the reality of his power over the forces of evil, and esp. over sin and Satan. He made this point quite explicit when the Pharisees accused him of expelling demons by the power of Beelzebub, the prince of devils: "But if it is through the Spirit of God that I cast devils out, then know that the kingdom of God has overtaken you" (Mt 12.28).

In the popular belief of Christians of earlier times the possibility and the fact of diabolical possession and obsession were taken for granted. They have been regarded as afflictions rather than as sinful conditions, although in some cases they may exist in consequence of sin. Theologians have noted that a man's behavior, insofar as it is under the strict control of an evil spirit, cannot be accounted sinful, for his action is not human and free. Theologians also teach that an evil spirit cannot directly act on a man's will (because it is a spiritual faculty), but only on his physical being; it can cause feelings and imaginations that may tempt a man, but it cannot cause him to sin. In diabolical possession, as distinct from obsession, the evil spirit affects a person from inside his body, partially taking over the executive faculties (e.g., speech) with the result that it is not so much the possessed person who acts as the devil through him. Modern discoveries in the field of psychopathology have lessened the readiness of contemporary theologians to accept diabolical possession as a fact; even among those who acknowledge the fact, there is a disposition to think it a rare phenomenon. Thus J. de Tonquédec in his *Les Maladies nerveuses et les manifestations diaboliques* (1938) thought that 90% of cases of alleged possession were in fact pseudo-possession. The modern skeptic must explain as best he can certain famous instances of possession that have been recorded in history, e.g., the case of the nuns at Loudun, which was at its worst in 1635. BIBLIOGRAPHY: *Satan, a Symposium* (ed. W. Farrell, 1951).

[J. J. CASTELOT; B. FORSHAW]

DIABOLISM. The practice of communicating or having commerce with the devil, esp. when this is intended to do him homage or service, or includes working in alliance with him. Diabolism appears to derive from superstitious belief in the possibility of gaining temporary advantages from its practice or of avoiding misfortunes the devil might bring about.

[T. EARLY]

DIABOLUS IN MUSICA (Lat., the devil in music), medieval and Renaissance term for the musical interval of the *tritone, regarded as the most dissonant interval. Much space in theoretical treatises of that era was devoted to rules for handling or even avoiding the tritone.

[A. DOHERTY]

DIACONATE, PERMANENT. In the Churches with an episcopal polity the diaconate was until recently a step on the way to the priesthood and thus only temporary. It is reckoned as one of the sacramental holy orders, along with the presbyterate (priesthood) and the episcopacy. Vatican Council II (Vat II ConstCh, n. 29) called for restoration of the diaconate as a way of life in those areas of the Church where it would be useful. Many regional conferences of bps. acted on the new opportunity and there are now deacons working in many local Churches throughout the world, sometimes full-time, sometimes in their spare time. Some are married before being ordained and remain so, others have assumed celibacy along with the diaconate. In the U.S. Catholic deacons already number in the hundreds. The names deacon and diaconate refer directly to the principle of service *(diakonia)* which Christ established as the only legitimation of any office or function in the Church (Mk 10.43; cf. Vat II ConstCh, n. 24). Where the diaconate is no more than a stage on the path to the priesthood, its prerogatives are confined to certain liturgical acts, such as assisting the priest at high Mass. The Council reminded the Church that deacons could also be used regularly for baptizing, preaching, and administering communion, though not for saying Mass or hearing confessions in the sacramental sense. Beyond these "services," however, it recalled the broad field of activity in pastoral and charitable work that is the deacon's natural and practically unbounded sphere. The question of ordaining women as deaconesses, a custom widely attested to in ancient Christian tradition and fully acknowledged by the Eastern and Anglican Churches, is currently receiving renewed attention among Roman Catholics. BIBLIOGRAPHY: R. L. Rashke, *Deacon in Search of Identity* (1975); H. Vorgrimler, *Commentary on the Documents of Vatican II* (1967) 1:226–230; *International Bibliography on the Priesthood and the Ministry* (ed. A. Guitard and M. G. Bulteau, 1971–).

[P. MISNER]

DIACONIA, a hospice. From Apostolic times the function of deacons was both charitable and liturgical. In Rome and many other centers the city was divided into districts (called diaconia) for service to the poor, to widows, to the sick, and to visitors. The monks of the desert exercised the same function as did later monastic groups. The popes consistently provided care, esp. in times of famine, to the needy. The custom of providing for the poor, the sick, and pilgrims lasted well into the Middle Ages. BIBLIOGRAPHY: R. Veillard, *Recherches sur les origines de la Rome chrétienne* (1959).

[J. R. AHERNE]

DIACONICUM, see DIAKONIKON.

DIADOCHUS OF PHOTICE (d. *c.*486), bp. in Epirus and spiritual writer. According to Photius D. was among the opponents of the Monophysites at the Council of Chalcedon, but he is more important in history for his contribution to spiritual literature and his effective opposition to the *Messalian idealization of *apatheia.* His chief work, which has exercised an enduring influence in both East and West, is the *Capita centum gnostica,* a sort of spiritual guide or way of perfection. Marked by the influence of *Evagrius Ponticus, it treats of the virtues, and esp. of charity, in their relationship to perfection, of the difficulties of prayer and the states of desolation, of the twofold (natural and supernatural) image of God, of the practice of the presence of God, and the Jesus Prayer. Also attributed to D. are a sermon on the Ascension and a collection of questions and answers on the spiritual life under the title *The Vision of John the Baptist.* Works: PG 65:1141–1212; critical ed. of the *Capita centum,* (J. E. Weis-Liebersdorf, 1912); French tr. E. des Places, *Cent chapitres sur la perfection spirituelle. Vision. Sermon sur l'Ascension,* SC (1943). BIBLIOGRAPHY: E. des Places, DSAM 3:817–834; NCE 4:841–842; Altaner 391; Quasten 3:509.

[R. B. ENO]

DIAKONIKON, in the Eastern Churches a small room, classically apsidal in form, at the far end of the south aisle (as one faces east) in a Byzantine church, opening, however, not into the aisle but into the presbytery behind the iconostasis. It is traditionally cared for by deacons (hence the name). In it are kept vestments and sacred vessels (hence its other name, *skevophylakion,* from Gr. *skevophylax,* "guardian of the furnishings"). In former times the records and library of the church were also kept there. The *diakonikon* is also found in Armenian, East and West Syrian, and Coptic tradition; but the name, in the various languages concerned, is often applied to a sacristy whose place varies in modern churches.

[A. CODY]

DIALECTICAL AND HISTORICAL MATERIALISM, the version of Marxist thought elaborated by Soviet theoreticians, under the aegis of Josef *Stalin. Nature is a totality in which all objects and phenomena are organically linked with each other and reciprocally affect each other. All phenomena and every political, social, and economic situation must be analyzed not separately but as elements of the great entity. Nature is a state of motion in which things are constantly being born, developing, disintegrating, and disappearing. Dialectical thinking uncovers the profound truth that all development proceeds from a condition of insignificant, latent quantitative changes to rapid, sudden qualitative changes, a process both ineluctable and necessary. Natural events imply internal contradictions, negative and positive aspects, and the conflict between these comprises the internal content of the evolutionary process. In consequence, judgments of absolute value cannot be made (a canon violated flagrantly by Marxists); everything must be judged historically. There are no immutable systems or eternal principles; every regime is liable to replacement. Revolution is natural and irresistible—so also is class war. Historical materialism is the application of dialectical materialism to society. The principal forces determining the character of the social order are found in the method of obtaining the means of existence and of producing material goods. The key to the understanding and control of history is the discovery of the laws governing the development of methods of production. There can be no progression from one method to another except through the revolutionary overthrow of former relations of production. BIBLIOGRAPHY: G. A. Wetter, *Dialectical Materialism* (1959); V. Adoratsky, *Dialectical Materialism* (1934); M. M. Bober, *Karl Marx's Interpretation of History* (1948); R. T. De George, *Patterns of Soviet Thought; Origin and Development of Dialectical and Historical Materialism* (pa. 1970).

[J. P. REID]

DIALECTICAL THEOLOGY, see CRISIS THEOLOGY.

DIALECTICS, in a broad sense, any kind of rational procedure; in a strict sense, a rational procedure based on a particular view of reality, a view that sees reality as subject to continuous change, as moving from one pole to the other. This view requires from a mind that seeks to grasp reality as it really is, not to use the method of classical (Aristotelian) logic, made of abstract and fixed concepts, but the method of dialectics, which passes from a concept to its opposite. It is of this second meaning of dialectics that this article treats. For the origin of dialectics one must go back to Plato and to the Neoplatonists. In Plato it has only a logical function; in the Neoplatonists it has both a logical and an ontological function: it is the instrument used by the mind to investigate reality, and it is the way followed by everything that proceeds from the One. Dialectics receives its final shape from Hegel (d. 1831), who distinguishes in the movements of thought and of reality three moments: thesis, antithesis, and synthesis; in the first moment something is posited, or asserted; in the second what has been posited in the first is denied, whereas its opposite is posited; in the third both that which is posited and that which is denied are taken together and sublimated into a superior form.

Platonic dialectics was used by both the Church Fathers and the Scholastics, by some in a more, by others in a less, rigid form; and it was used more as an ontological paradigm than as a logical tool. The logical tool used by them in order to talk about God and his mysteries was analogy, an instrument perfectly coherent with their views on the relationship between nature and grace, a relationship of harmony, not of opposition. Protestant theologians, who have a dialectical conception of the relationship between nature and grace (they are conceived as two opposites that can never be reconciled, though they exist together in the Christian man, who is *simul justus et peccator),* have found in dialectics a very congenial tool for theological language. Although dialectics has been used by almost every Protestant theologian, it has become the distinctive character of two Protestant theological movements: the movement called *crisis or dialectical theology (K. Barth in *Römerbrief* and E. Brunner) and the movement called *radical theology, or death-of-God theology (T. Altizer). BIBLIOGRAPHY: T. J. J. Altizer, *Gospel of Christian Atheism* (1966); E. Brunner, *Theology of Crisis* (1931); H. U. von Balthasar, ''Analogie und Dialektik,'' DivThomF (1944) 171–216; *ibid.* (1945) 3–56; L. Malevez, ''Théologie dialectique, théologie catholique, et théologie naturelle,'' RechSR (1938) 385–429, 527–569.

[B. MONDIN]

DIALOGUE, in general, includes every form of meeting and communication between individuals, groups, and communities to bring about greater understanding and better human relations in an atmosphere of sincerity, integrity, respect for persons, and mutual confidence. Three fundamental types of religious dialogue may be distinguished: (1) encounter on the basis of simple human solidarity, with a view to drawing the participants out of their isolation and mutual mistrust; (2) encounter on the plane of action, which aims at establishing the conditions for collaboration toward fixed objectives, despite doctrinal differences; and (3) encounter on the plane of search for truth with respect to doctrinal questions in which the participants are personally involved. Dialogue differs from instruction, which is ordered essentially toward the doctrinal enlightenment of one of the participants, whereas dialogue consists in mutual give and take. It differs from polemic and controversy insofar as these are ordered principally to the defending of a position and to demonstrating the falsity of an adversary's position. Dialogue is not a simple confrontation because it seeks on both sides a *rapprochement* and deeper understanding. Finally, dialogue as such does not aim at persuading the other of the value of one's own position. Dialogue of Christians with other Christians of differing traditions, with those of non-Christian religions, and with unbelievers is a unique phenomenon of the present age. BIBLIOGRAPHY: J. Loew, ''Personal, Pastoral Contact with the Non-Believer,'' *Concilium* 23 (1967) 103–110; R. Kwant, *Encounter* (1963). *ECUMENISM.

[J. P. REID]

DIALOGUE, INTERFAITH, see INTERFAITH DIALOGUE.

DIALOGUE MASS, see MASS, DIALOGUE.

DIAMPER, SYNOD OF, a diocesan council of Syro-Indians of the Eastern Christian Church of Malabar that met in 1599 at Diamper (Udamperur), a see vacant after the death of its last Chaldean bishop. The abp. of Angamale, a see not at that time included in the Latin hierarchy, was suspected of heresy. Acting under the authority of two briefs from Rome of dubious legitimacy, Alexis de

Menezes, then abp. of the Latin See of Goa, convoked the council and presided over it. He dealt in a high-handed manner with the Malabarians, who were forced to Latinize their liturgical books and customs and submit to Latin bishops. This led to much discontent among the Malabarians, a circumstance that provoked schism and contributed to the establishment in 1653 of the Malabar Uniate Church. BIBLIOGRAPHY: ODCC 395–396; Attwater CCE (1947) 212–213; A. S. Atiya, *History of Eastern Christianity* (1967) 365–369.

[R. A. TODD]

DIANA OF THE EPHESIANS, an Asian mother-goddess mentioned in Acts 19.28 having nothing in common with the virgin hunting-goddess of Greece and Rome except the name. She was worshiped for centuries in a primitive sanctuary near the mouth of the Caÿster before the founding of Ephesus by Greek colonists *c*.1100 B.C. Eventually adopted by the Greeks, a succession of temples were erected in her honor outside the city, the last of which, built after 350 B.C., was one of the wonders of the ancient world. From Ephesus her worship spread throughout Asia Minor and to Greece, Rome, and even Gaul. She was usually represented as a female figure with multiple protrusions, which have usually been taken as breasts but may perhaps be large eggs. Her worship at Ephesus involved the service of eunuch priests and thousands of female slaves known as hierodules. BIBLIOGRAPHY: F. W. Beare, InterDB 1:242.

[M. J. COSTELLOE]

DIANA, ANTONINO (1585–1663), expert casuist and a trusted adviser of three popes. A Sicilian and a Theatine, D. published solutions to thousands of moral cases. In the less genial theological climate of the 18th cent. he was considered, as by St. Alphonus Liguori, to show leanings toward laxism.

[T. GILBY]

DIAPASON, Greek term for the octave. In French the word became synonymous with the tuning fork and its pitch—"diapason normal" is concert pitch. On the organ the term refers to the main foundation stop, the tone of which is peculiar to and characteristic of the instrument.

[M. T. LEGGE]

DIAPENTE, in music Greek name for the interval of the fifth. *Epidiapente* refers to a fifth above; *subdiapente,* to a fifth below.

[M. T. LEGGE]

DÍAS, BARTHOLOMEU (d. 1500), Portuguese courtier and naval officer. Seeking Prester John's kingdom for John II of Portugal, D. discovered the Cape of Good Hope, opened 1,260 miles of African coast, and (with De Covilhão) confirmed the Indies ocean route. After building Da Gama's fleet, he perished at sea returning from Cabral's

discovery of Brazil (1500). BIBLIOGRAPHY: I. B. Heffernan, NCE 4:851.

[R. I. BURNS]

DIASPORA (Gk., dispersion), members of any religious body living as a minority, whether in or outside their homeland, and maintaining contact with the central authorities of that body. The earliest use of the word is in the LXX, where it translates several Hebrew expressions. One implies the concept of Judaism as a sowing, a growth, and a longing to be gathered. The Jewish diaspora began with Assyrian and Babylonian deportations (722 and 597 B.C.). By NT times it had become so widespread that Alexandria alone contained a million Jews. Christians took over from Judaism the consciousness of living in a diaspora (see I Pet 2.11). The notion faded rapidly, however, when Christianity became the established religion. (Some 20th-cent. thinkers are convinced that Christianity is returning to its original diaspora status.) The term was revived in Germany about 100 years ago to designate Protestants living in RC lands and members of the RC Church living in Protestant lands. At times it applies to immigrant and mission congregations as well. Although the principle *cuius regio eius religio once established religious unity in German principalities, many factors gave rise to diaspora conditions: consolidation of Protestant and RC lands, boundary changes, the free passage of artists, students, etc., population shifts, the weakening of the principle of a state Church. The first recorded use of diaspora in the sense of a religious minority was probably that of the High Consistory of the Old Prussian Union in 1852. The term is used esp. in Lutheran literature. BIBLIOGRAPHY: F. Lau, EncLuthCh 1:700–704; B. Schulz and J. P. Michael, LTK 3:343–346.

[M. J. SUELZER]

DIASPORA, RUSSIAN, a collective term for the dispersed Russians who for one reason or another have left their homeland and have taken up residence and often citizenship in another country. The first wave of the diaspora was made up of poor people seeking a better livelihood and included also some sectarians fleeing religious persecution by the czarist government; the latest, of Russians, principally Orthodox, fleeing from the Communist regime. Between World Wars I and II there were large Russian enclaves in Manchuria and in various Chinese cities, such as Shanghai and Tsingtao. The Russian Orthodox community in Manchuria flourished with its own hierarchy, monastic communities, seminary, press, and other necessities for ecclesiastical life. Russians living in diaspora are now found in Japan, Iran, Istanbul, Yugoslavia, West Germany, France, Canada, the U.S., and in various Latin American countries. Whenever it has been possible, the Orthodox Church has tried to function and to fulfill the spiritual needs of its scattered Russian children. The intellectual center of the Russian Diaspora, as far as the Orthodox are concerned, is the Theological Institute of St. Sergius in Paris, which has trained priests for the parishes outside the Soviet Union and has produced some scholars of international repute in the ecclesiastical sciences. Offshoot of St. Sergius in the Western Hemisphere is St. Vladimir's Seminary in Tuckahoe, N. Y. Many of its present staff were trained at St. Sergius in Paris, and it serves much the same purpose as its mother institution, i.e., the training of priests for parish work and scholars who can effectively present Orthodoxy to the Western world, and defend it against its attackers. Like St. Sergius, St. Vladimir accepts students from all over the Orthodox world, and even some from the Monophysite Churches, i.e., the Armenian and the Ethiopian.

Ecclesiastically, the Russian Diaspora is split into at least three major jurisdictions, mirroring the experience of the Mother Church in the homeland in the early years of Communist domination. The Russian Orthodox Church outside Russia with some 22 bishops in various parts of the world, claims to be the largest body. The Orthodox of this jurisdiction venerate the family of Czar Nicholas II as martyrs for the Orthodox faith and try to keep together and functioning some semblance of the old Romanoff court with its numerous nobility. The American Russian Greek Catholic Orthodox Church, commonly known as the Metropolia, counts a larger number of adherents in the U.S. itself, and certainly represented the pre-World War I Russian Church in the U.S. by canonical continuity. The third group, based in Paris and dependent upon the ecumenical patriarch of Constantinople (Istanbul), is scarcely at all represented in the U.S., but claims adherents among the Russians in Western Europe. A smaller fourth group is directly under the patriarch of Moscow and emphasizes the patriotism of Russians in order to persuade them to return to its jurisdiction.

[A. WALKER]

DIASTEMATIC, in 11th-cent. musical notation "heighted" or intervallic neumes written on a staff, imagined or indicated, by one, two, or finally four lines.

[M. T. LEGGE]

DIATESSARON (Gr., by means of the four), a 2d-cent. harmony of the four Gospels by *Tatian in which the separate texts are interwoven so as to produce a single continuous narrative. The original language was more probably Greek than Syriac, although this is diputed. The Diatessaron became the standard text of the Gospels in the Syriacspeaking Church down to the 5th cent., when it was replaced by the *Peshitta with the four separate Gospels. Because Tatian became suspect of Encratite teaching, most of the copies of the text were destroyed. A 4th-cent. commentary by St. Ephrem has been preserved in an Armenian translation, and two relatively late Arabic translations have also survived. In the Latin Codex Fuldensis the order of the Diatessaron has been preserved, though the text is that of the *Vulgate. A medieval Dutch harmony of the Scriptures also has evidently been modelled upon it. In 1933 a 2d-cent.

Greek papyrus fragment of it was found. BIBLIOGRAPHY: B. Plooij, *Primitive Text of the Diatessaron. The Liège Manuscript of a Mediaeval Dutch Translation* (1923); C. Peters, *Das Diatesseron Tatians* (1939).

[D. J. BOURKE]

DIATESSARON (MUSIC), Greek name for the musical interval of the fourth. *Epidiatessaron* refers to a fourth above; *subdiatessaron,* to a fourth below.

[M. T. LEGGE]

DIATRIBE, by definition, a bitter, vilifying denunciation; by literary genre (Plato), a discourse. Itinerant preachers and teachers among the Cynics (fl. 3d cent. B.C.) used the style as a means of haranguing people in moral sermons. The diversity of their themes embraced such multiple aspects of life as wealth, disease, death, marriage, with the use of epigrams, scandalous stories, obscene jokes, poetic parodies, and similar material. Roman satire was a successor of the Cynic diatribe. In the hands of a Latin satirist such as Lucilius (*c.* 180–120 B.C.), the diatribe became literary. Its style is said to have "affected most of the preachers under the empire and undoubtedly exercised some influence on the homilies of the Greek Fathers." BIBLIOGRAPHY: OCD, 274–275.

[S. A. HEENEY]

DÍAZ, MANUEL (1574–1659), missioner, astronomer. A Jesuit, D. entered China in 1610 and spent almost 50 years there. He was vice-provincial of China for 18 years. His published works in Chinese include theological and astronomical writings. BIBLIOGRAPHY: G. H. Dunne, *Generations of Giants* (1962).

[J. R. AHERNE]

DÍAZ, PORFIRIO (1830–1915), Mexican statesman. Born in Oaxaca of a Spanish father and an Indian mother, D. studied for the priesthood but left to fight in the Mexican War (1846–48) against the U.S. Attracted by Benito *Juárez, he decided to add law and politics to his career in the army. He took part in the War of Reform (1858–60) and earned a generalcy in the war against the French (1861–67). D. gained the presidency of Mexico in 1880, a post he held with few interruptions for 30 years. He succeeded in greatly improving the material conditions of the country as a whole; but the imbalance of prosperity between rural and urban areas eventually aroused the active enmity of the peons. In 1911 after winning reelection for the seventh time, D. was forced to resign when a peasant rebellion incited by his election opponent, F. Madero, placed the latter in office. He went into exile in Paris, where he died 4 years later. BIBLIOGRAPHY: C. Beals, *Porfirio Díaz* (1932); J. C. Valades, *El porfirismo* (3 v., 1941–47); D. Hannay, *Díaz* (1917); repr. 1970).

[P. DAMBORIENA]

DÍAZ Y BARRETO, PASCUAL (1875–1936), bishop. A native of Mexico ordained in 1899, D. entered the Jesuits in 1903. After study in Europe he taught in Mexico for a number of years when he was named bp. of Tabasco (1923). The persecution that broke out in the 1920s drove him from Tabasco and in 1927 he was exiled by President Plutarco Calles. In 1929 he and Abp. Ruiz y Flores concluded a temporary arrangement with President Portes Gil in Mexico City. In the same year D. became abp. of Mexico City. As the persecution grew more violent his burden became so great that his health broke down and he died shortly thereafter. BIBLIOGRAPHY: E. J. Correa, *Pascual Díaz S. J. el Arzobispo Mártir* (1945).

[J. R. AHERNE]

DIBELIUS, MARTIN (1883–1947), German Protestant NT scholar, noted for work in *form criticism (Formgeschichte,* a term he coined). Born at Dresden, he studied at Neuchâtel, Leipzig, Berlin, and Tübingen, and taught at Berlin (1910–15) and Heidelberg (1915–47), where he died. Applying to the NT principles used by A. *Harnack in studying the history of religion and by H. *Gunkel in OT studies, he sought to trace the pre-literary gospel tradition by identifying literary forms within the Gospels and Acts and placing these units in the life situation of the early Church. See his *From Tradition to Gospel* (2d ed., 1933; tr. B. L. Wolff, 1972).

[T. EARLY]

DIBELIUS, OTTO (1880–1967), German Lutheran bishop. Born of a Prussian family of civil servants and churchmen, D. entered the ministry after a year of advanced study at the Univ. of Edinburgh. His practice of mingling freely with his parishioners and encouraging them to take an active part in the life of the Church set a precedent in Germany. In 1925 he became superintendent of the Kurmark church district, where he continued the policies he had initiated as a pastor. His first important publication as bishop, *The Century of the Church* (1927), urged ministers to lead the Church into all the concerns of public life. He applauded the separation of Church and State that resulted from the fall of the Reich in 1918—a sharp departure from Luther's view of the role of the State. In 1937 he preached against anti-Semitism, for which act he was suspended from office; but his resistance to Nazism continued despite threat of rearrest. After the collapse of Germany he joined Pastor *Niemöller in 1945 in signing the Stuttgart confession of guilt in the name of the German Protestant Churches. The same year he was appointed bp. of Berlin-Brandenburg. He was the first chairman of the executive council of the Evangelische Kirche in Deutschland (EKD), a federation of confessional Churches that he helped establish in 1948. D.'s devotional and historical writings attained the rank of best sellers, partly because of their conversational style.

BIBLIOGRAPHY: O. Dibelius, *In the Service of the Lord: An Autobiography* (tr. M. Ilford, 1964).

[M. J. SUELZER]

DIBON, Hebrew (OT) equivalent of modern Arabic Dhiban, a city in Jordan 40 miles S of Amman. The OT records that during the period of Israelite settlement (*c.* 1250 B.C.) Dibon became part of the tribal territory of Gad (Num 32.34; 33.45), and later of Reuben (Jos 13.9). David added it to his kingdom *c.* 975 B.C. (2 Sam 8.2). On the Moabite Stone, discovered at Dibon in 1868, Mesha, king of Moab, records his rebellion against Israel and his rebuilding of Qarhoh, which is probably Dibon. This text dates from *c.* 830 B.C., and seems to refer to the same rebellion as that described in 2 Kg 3.4–27. The prophetic curses in Is 15.2, 9, and Jer 48.18, 22, apparently reflect the ancient antagonism existing between Moab and Judah (Gen 19.30–38). BIBLIOGRAPHY: InterDB 1:840–841.

[T. CRANE]

DICCONSON, EDWARD (1670–1752), early vicar apostolic for the Northern district of the English mission, titular bp. of Malla. Until his appointment in 1740 he had taught theology, 1700–20, at the English College of Douai, then was assigned a pastoral ministry in the Midlands. In 1736 he was the agent in Rome for the English mission. As vicar apostolic he shared in obtaining from Benedict XIV the directives for administration of the English mission. BIBLIOGRAPHY: B. Hemphill, *Early Vicars Apostolic of England, 1685–1750* (1954).

[T. C. O'BRIEN]

DICKINSON, EMILY (1830–86), American poet; schooled at Mount Holyoke Female Seminary and Amherst Institute; recluse who left Amherst only twice in her mature life; shy, intense, eccentric but rich in friends who either occasioned or received her verse. Her correspondence fills three volumes and is the raw material of poetry. Aside from the poetry and the letters, she deliberately clothed herself in mystery, out of which came only unsatisfactory hints of three overpowering loves, only one, and that in later years, bringing her more than artistic fulfillment. Resolutely she refused to publish in her lifetime, only reluctantly permitting a handful of poems to appear in print. The decision was wise and far more subtle than a wish to shun publicity. Her verse departs radically from Victorian and 19th-cent. American models and would have been totally bewildering to her contemporaries. The gnomic, brief utterances condense a vision that sees the world, death, immortality in almost shocking clarity. Her poetic measure has a gait that at first disturbs but ultimately fascinates. D. was no simple soul voicing ingenuous impressions of life but a consummate artist with an instinctive grasp of the essentially poetic. Her more than 1700 separate poems constitute a staggering outpouring, largely the work of the period 1858–65. She said once "If fame belonged to me I could not escape her.'' From the first publication of the poems in 1890 to the present she has emerged as one of two distinctive voices in 19th-cent. American poetry, sharing that accolade and overwhelming influence with Walter Whitman. The recluse of Amherst in her unassuming way taught the world what poetry could be in its essence. BIBLIOGRAPHY: J. E. Walsh, *Hidden Life of Emily Dickinson* (1971); E. Wylder, *Emily Dickinson's Manuscripts* (1971); J. Cody, *Great Pain: The Inner Life of Emily Dickinson* (1971); R. Weisbuch, *Emily Dickinson's Poetry* (1975).

[J. R. AHERNE]

DICKINSON, JONATHAN (1688–1747), Presbyterian clergyman and educator. Born in Mass. and educated at Yale, he settled at Elizabethtown (now Elizabeth), N.J., where he preached regularly to six or seven congregations and exerted wide influence on the synod of Philadelphia. While he considered himself a strong Calvinist, he refused to support a strict subscription to the *Westminster Confession and was responsible for the compromise in the *Adopting Act of 1729. D. also participated in the *Great Awakening, and, when the "Old Side" Presbyterians opposed the revivalistic spirit and practices of the "New Side" clergymen, he helped form the synod of New York (1745). He assisted in founding the College of New Jersey, now Princeton University. Some of his theological writings, *Sermons and Tracts* (1793) and *True Scripture Doctrine Concerning Some Important Points in Christian Faith* (1841), extended his influence into the 19th century.

[J. H. SMYLIE]

DICTATUS PAPAE, a document composed by the pope himself, though the term has come to refer specifically to an entry in the Register of Gregory VII (1073–85) which asserts official papal supremacy in spiritual and temporal matters throughout Christendom. Nearly all of the 27 titles in Register II, 55a, deal with principles of ecclesiology with special emphasis upon the primacy of the Roman Church and the bp. of Rome in the universal Church. The pope's power to depose emperors and to free subjects from compromising allegiances to superiors are notable among the few titles pertaining to papal relations with secular princes. The *Dictatus* of Pope Gregory did not significantly affect subsequent developments in canon law.

[R. J. LITZ]

DICTINIUS (d. 5th cent.), bp. of Astorga. After certain Spanish bishops refused to accept communion with Galician Priscillianists according to the arrangement of St. Ambrose and Pope Siricius, Bp. Symposius consecrated his son D. bishop (c.396). Council Toledo I (400), which brought most Priscillianists back into communion, cited D. for teaching the existence of principles of good and evil, the *innascibilitas* of the Word, and the identity of Christ's divine and human natures. D.'s writings were widespread long after his retraction but have all disappeared; only his

Libra, refuted by St. Augustine for condoning a lie for reasons of religion, is known by name. Pope Leo I (447), a council of Braga (563), and a cult in Astorga attest to D.'s sainted memory. BIBLIOGRAPHY: C. M. Molas, DHGE 14:394–395.

[E. P. COLBERT]

DICTIONNAIRE HISTORIQUE ET CRITIQUE (1697), Pierre Bayle's most important and influential work. By means of long, critical notes to short texts presenting the generally accepted views on subjects dealing with history, philosophy, and religion, and by cross-references, Bayle cunningly showed the contradictory and conflicting evidence concerning the subjects he treated. He thus attacked traditional and orthodox concepts and influenced the *Encyclopédie* and other works of the *philosophes*.

[A. S. CRISAFULLI]

DIDACHE (the full title probably is: *The Lord's Instruction to the Gentiles through the Twelve Apostles),* a short Christian treatise of 16 chapters written in Greek. The author is unknown. According to some scholars the treatise, in its present form, was written not much later than the Pauline Epistles or the canonical Gospels; others, however, suggest the end of the 2d or the beginning of the 3d cent. as possible dates of composition. The Church of Antioch in Syria is currently considered the most likely place of origin. The contents are divided into three loosely connected parts. The first (ch. 1–6) gives a summary of Christian moral teaching introduced by the imagery of the two ways: one of life, the other of death. The second (ch. 7–10) forms a ritual section giving directives for baptism (the sole extant reference from this period for administering the sacrament by infusion), daily prayer, fasting, and the Eucharist. The third (ch. 11–15) deals with disciplinary regulations for the Christian community. The concluding section urges Christians to be ready for Christ's second coming which is regarded as imminent. Bryennios discovered the complete Greek text of this document and published a critical edition in 1883. BIBLIOGRAPHY: Quasten 1:29–39.

[H. DRESSLER]

DIDACUS OF ALCALÁ, ST. (Diego; d. 1463), Franciscan lay brother and ascetic. D. was sent from Córdoba, Spain, to the Canaries for missionary work (1441–49). In 1450 he was in Rome for the canonization of Bernardine of Siena and after 1456 in Alcalá, where he was revered for penances, miracles, and intuitive theology. He was canonized in 1588. BIBLIOGRAPHY: G. Bardy, *Catholicisme* 3:747.

[E. P. COLBERT]

DIDACUS OF AZEVEDO, BL. (Diego of Azebes; d. 1207), bishop. As prior of the cathedral chapter at Osma (Spain) D. worked in harmony with his subprior (St.) Dominic to transform their community into a chapter of

Canons Regular. D. became bp. of Osma (1201), sought unsuccessfully to resign his see (1205), and traveling through the S of France with Dominic encountered the disorder widespread there because of the Albigensian heresy. They began to engage in apostolic preaching; D. returned to Osma to seek support for the effort, while Dominic continued the work in the field. BIBLIOGRAPHY: Butler 4:327–328; G. Cappelluti, BiblSanct 4:609–610.

[M. E. DUFFY]

DIDASCALIA APOSTOLORUM, a treatise, originally written in Greek, of which the full title in English translation is *The Catholic Teaching of the 12 Apostles and Holy Disciples of our Savior*. It was composed in the first decade of the 3d cent. in Syria. A probable conjecture, based on internal evidence, is that the compiler was a converted Jewish physician. The work is modeled on the *Didache,* and in turn its first six books are the model and source for the *Apostolic Constitutions*. Despite its title the *Didascalia* is concerned throughout with practice rather than doctrine. The author is relatively lenient with respect to penitent sinners, probably in reaction to the rigorism of the Montanists and Novatians. The Syrian text was first published in 1854 and an incomplete Latin translation in 1900. Although the original Greek text is lost, some idea of it may be gathered from the *Apostolic Constitutions*. Text: *Didascalia et Constitutiones Apostolorum I* (ed. F. X. Funk, 1905) 1–384. Syriac-Eng. tr. with Latin fragments, *Didascalia Apostolorum* (ed. R. H. Connolly, 1929). Quasten 2:147–152.

[R. B. ENO]

DIDEROT, DENIS (1713–84), perhaps the most truly versatile of the 18th-cent. philosophes, an original thinker, brilliant, of boundless intellectual energy and overflowing with ideas. D. was chief editor and general promoter of the French *Encyclopedia,* for which he obtained the services of the outstanding luminaries of the day and to which he contributed a great number of articles. Beginning as a deist, he ended as a naturalistic pantheist, with a strong inclination to deny God entirely. D.'s writings on religious subjects took as their central problem man's place in a universe which seemed to be wholly material and ruled by blind chance. In his earlier works D. saw some value for morality in religion but eventually his antipathy towards the Christian religion hardened and became implacable. BIBLIOGRAPHY: J. Morley, *Diderot and the Encyclopedists* (2 v., 1878); A. M. Wilson, *Diderot* (2 v., 1957, 1972); *Diderot Studies* (ed. O. E. Fellows et al., 1949–52); L. G. Crocker, *Diderot, the Embattled Philosopher* (1954).

[J. P. REID]

DIDIER, ST., see DESIDERIUS, ST.

DIDON, HENRI MARTIN (1840–1900), French Dominican preacher, educator, and writer. An eloquent and original preacher, D. offended some by seeming too bold in his thinking, and after his 1880 Lenten course at La Trinité in Paris, mounting criticism caused the Dominican master general to send him to Corsica for a period of retirement. There he began his book, *Jésus Christ,* which appeared in 1891 and enjoyed a great success both in French and the other languages into which it was translated (Eng. tr. 1892; 6th ed. 1929). A series of conferences at the Madeleine was translated into English under the title *Belief in the Divinity of Jesus* (1894). Many other of his conferences were published and, after his death, much of his correspondence. BIBLIOGRAPHY: A. Duval, DHGE 14:411–415; A. L. McMahon, CE 4:782.

DIDYMUS THE BLIND (c.313–398), theologian of Alexandria. Blind from early childhood, D. was entrusted with the celebrated catechetical school at Alexandria, which he directed for many years, and was the last of its famous teachers. *Jerome and *Rufinus both attended his lectures during their stay in Egypt. Although D. was sound in his Christological and Trinitarian doctrine, the evident influence of *Origen upon his teaching brought him into theological disrepute. The council in Constantinople in 553 avoided including him, along with Origen, in its anathemas, but the Patriarch Eutychius, in the edict giving effect to the decree of the council, anathematized him; and later general councils (681 and 787) included him explicitly in the condemnations of the Origenists. For this reason, perhaps, most of his many works have been lost. Extant are: three books on the Holy Spirit that have survived in a Latin translation by Jerome (PL 39:1031–86); three books on the Trinity (PG 39:269–992); and a work against the Manichaeans (PG 39:1085–1110). A commentary on Zechariah was discovered among the Toura MSS in 1941 (SC, ed. L. Doutreleau, 1962) 83–85. BIBLIOGRAPHY: Quasten 3:84–100; J. Chapman, CE 4:784.

[R. B. ENO]

DIECKMANN, HERMANN (1880–1928), German Jesuit theologian. He taught at Valkenburg, Holland, from 1915 until his untimely death. His chief distinction was achieved in the field of fundamental theology, in which he stands out as one of the last and ablest representatives of the older polemical tradition in ecclesiology that was beginning to decline in favor even during his lifetime. BIBLIOGRAPHY: J. Beumer, NCE 4:861.

[M. J. SUELZER]

DIEDENHOFER, COUNCILS OF, see THIONVILLE, COUNCILS OF

DIEGO, ST., see DIDACUS OF ALCALÁ, ST.

DIEGO OF CADIZ, BL. (1743–1801), Spanish Franciscan. D. became a preacher and confessor of extraordinary power and influence among high and low. His devotion to the Trinity and continual emphasis on the mystery earned him the title "apostle of the Holy Trinity." He preached in large churches and in the streets to enormous crowds. He turned over all gifts to the poor. Pope Leo XIII beatified D. in 1894. BIBLIOGRAPHY: Butler 1:672–673; B. d'Arenzano, BiblSanct 4:610–612.

[J. R. AHERNE]

DIEGO OF ESTELLA (1524–78), Spanish mystic and theologian. A nephew of St. Francis Xavier, in 1552 D. joined the Friars Minor in Salamanca. D. was chosen court preacher and theological advisor to Philip II. He was censured by the Inquisition for his *Commentary on St. Luke,* but he died before the trial. His most noted writings are *Meditaciones devotísmas del amor de Dios* (translated into many languages) and *Libro de la vanidad del mundo.* BIBLIOGRAPHY: R. Aubert, DHGE 14:438–439; D. de Monleras, DSAM 4.2:1366–70.

[M. HIGGINS]

DIEHL, CHARLES (1859–1944), French Byzantinist. After advanced studies at the French School in Rome and Athens, D. began his career as teacher of history at Nancy and came to the Sorbonne in 1899. His mastery of the sources and their critical evaluation as well as his work in archeology and Byzantine art made him an authority in his field. In *Byzance, grandeur et décadence* (1919) he studied the rise and fall of the Byzantine Empire, its influence on its neighbors, and the heritage it bequeathed to Turkey, Russia, and the Balkans. BIBLIOGRAPHY: *Byzantion* (American Series 3, 1944–45) 17:414–423.

[H. DRESSLER]

DIEKAMP, FRANZ (1864–1943), theologian. D. taught at the Univ. of Münster and is noted for his contributions to patrology, the history of dogma, and speculative theology. He founded the *Theologische Revue* (1902), and edited the *Münsterische Beiträge zur Theologie.* His best known work is *Katholische Dogmatik nach den Grundsätzen des hl. Thomas* (3 v., 1912–14; new ed. by K. Jüssen, 1958–1962), a manual of Thomistic dogmatic theology. BIBLIOGRAPHY: K. Jüssen, NCE 4:862–863.

[T. M. MCFADDEN]

DIENTZENHOFER FAMILY (fl. 17th and 18th cent.), creators of a Bohemian baroque style influencing German baroque architecture. **Georg** (1643–89) settling in Prague, worked in Franconia designing the facade of St. Martin at Bamberg (1681–91) and a chapel near Waldsassen (1685–89). **Christoph** (1655–1722), leading Bohemian architect, designed St. Niklas, Prague (1703–11), and the Church of St. Margaret (1719–21) attached to the Benedictine monastery of Brevnov (Breunau), in the undulating style of Guarino Guarini (in Prague, 1679). **Kilian Ignaz** (1689–1751), son of Christoph, became a leading master of heavy, massive baroque in Prague (Villa Amerika, 1720;

Sulva Tarouca Palace 1749) with endless varieties of curvilinear design in numerous churches. **Johann** (1663–1726), brother of George and Christoph, shows the influence of Borromini at the Cathedral of Fulda (1704–12) and Bohemian curvilinear style in the Benedictine Abbey of Banz (1710–18). The magnificent Pommersfelden Castle (1711–18) for Lothar Franz von Schoenborn is dominated by D.'s Franconio-Bohemian style. BIBLIOGRAPHY: E. Hempel, *Baroque Art and Architecture in Central Europe* (1965).

[M. J. DALY]

DIEPENBROCK, MELCHIOR VON (1798–1853), prince bishop of Breslau, cardinal. A native of Westphalia, D. fought with the Prussian army in the 1814–15 war against France. Under the influence of the noted theologian John Michael Sailer he studied for the priesthood and was ordained in 1823. With Sailer he became part of a group at Ratisbon that labored for the reunion of all Christian Churches. Named prince bishop of Breslau, he reluctantly accepted and was consecrated in 1845. As secular ruler of the Austrian region of his diocese he introduced many reforms and exercised great charity. As bp. he fought the nationalist attempt to create a German national Church and rejected the attempt to subordinate the Church to the states of Prussia and Austria. In 1850 at the request of King Frederick William IV he was appointed chaplain of the Prussian army. That same year he was made a cardinal. D. was an unwavering advocate of the rights of the Church and a protagonist of a united Germany ruled by the Habsburgs. BIBLIOGRAPHY: H. Raab, DHGE 14:1509–11.

[J. R. AHERNE]

DIERINGER, FRANZ XAVER (1811–76), dogmatic theologian. After teaching in Freiburg and Speier, D. was appointed to the University of Bonn to provide an orthodox counterbalance to *Hermesianism. He restored the reputation of the theology faculty there, founded the periodical *Katholische Zeitschrift für Wissenschaft und Kunst* (since 1849 called *Katholische Vierteljahrschrift*), and wrote numerous scientific and popular dogmatic tracts. He opposed the definition of papal infallibility at Vatican Council I, but submitted upon its promulgation. BIBLIOGRAPHY: F. Lauchert, CE 4:786–787; A. Rock, NCE 4:863.

[T. M. MCFADDEN]

DIES FASTI, the Latin term for court days, i.e., days on which legal business could be transacted without fear of offending the gods. The days of the calendar were divided by the Romans into different classes (see CALENDAR), and the calendar was marked with notations such as *F(astus), C(omitiales),* and *N(efastus). Dies comitiales* were days on which it was lawful to summon the assembly and the senate; they could also be used as court days if the assembly did not meet. The calendars allowed for 192 such days in the year, but of this number some were eliminated because they fell on a market day, or the last day of the month, or during the time assigned to the seven seasons of public games, so that the average number of *dies comitiales* was reduced to 150 a year. *Dies nefasti,* designated by the college of pontifices, were days on which the court could not sit, nor the comitia assemble because of holidays, purifications, or other religious reasons. *Dies religiosi* were days which had been declared unlucky because of some disaster; on such days not only was it unlawful to transact any legal or political business, but it was unlucky to begin any important affair. BIBLIOGRAPHY: H. Rose, OCD 280; *idem, Primitive Culture in Italy* (1925).

[F. MURPHY]

DIES IRAE (day of wrath), opening words in the Sequence for the dead in the Mass. Not originally designed as a Sequence, it received final acceptance by Pius V in 1570. Its origin is usually ascribed to the 13th cent. but sometimes to the 12th. The tradition that it was written by *Thomas of Celano (fl. 1220–49) is now generally rejected. It is based on biblical passages such as Zeph 1.14–16, and describes the *Last Judgment in strong and vivid language. Some scholars see traces of classical and nonbiblical Jewish influence. Its great popularity is shown by its frequent translation into vernaculars. Its *Gregorian chant setting is perhaps the most famous of all chant melodies, and has been employed in numerous compositions by later composers, notably Berlioz and Liszt. In concert *requiems such as those by Mozart, Verdi, and Britten, the text has usually been given a large-scale dramatic setting, often in several sections.

[T. EARLY; A. DOHERTY]

DIESSBACH, NIKOLAUS JOSEPH ALBERT VON (1732–98), a soldier and a Jesuit, born of an aristocratic Calvinist family in Switzerland. He was converted to Catholicism in 1754 and ordained a Jesuit priest in 1764. D. was an exemplary religious, a zealous and learned educator of young clerics, sought after as a spiritual director. Above all, an apostle of the Word, he wrote various works of asceticism and apologetics. Worthy of note was a fearless written statement to Emperor Leopold II in which he strongly emphasized the dangers of Jansenism. D., together with Pio Brunone Lanteri, founder of the Oblates of the Virgin Mary, spread abroad the works of St. Alphonsus Liguori to counteract the insidious attacks of Jansenism on the Church. D. founded the association, Amicizia Cristiana, and used for the protection of the Church the same weapons of the press and secret meetings as were employed against it by the Freemasons. Both priests can be credited with helping to check the heresy of Jansenism. BIBLIOGRAPHY: A. P. Frutaz, EncCatt 4:1577–78; P. Bailly, DSAM 3:881–883.

[S. A. HEENEY]

DIETARY LAWS, laws laid down by priests or religious leaders, particularly in the religions of antiquity, which described clean and unclean foods, thus distinguishing what was acceptable for eating and what was rejected. The Israelites apparently had many such laws as a part of their religious traditions and heritage, but it remained for the great lawgiver Moses and later the priesthood to codify these laws and give them legal and moral force. A curious method for distinguishing those animals which are clean or unclean is found in Dt 14.4–8 and Lev 11.26–28. Clean was the animal "that parteth the hoof . . . and cheweth the cud." These included the ox, the sheep, the goat, the hart, the roe-buck, etc. Animals were unclean that did not part the hoof or did not chew the cud or that "go upon their paws". These included the camel, rock-badger, hare, swine, etc. Among the fish the clean were distinguished by fins and scales, but those which like the eel resembled reptiles were unclean. Birds of prey like the eagle, vulture, raven, owl, night-hawk, etc., were unclean because they were carnivorous and fed on carrion or filth. About 20 species were included in this category. Even creeping things were divided into clean and unclean: the weasel, the mouse, the tortoise, the chameleon, the mole, etc., falling into the unclean class. Additional prohibitions were established against the eating of blood or of the most delectable portion of the fat. The Israelites were taught that "the life of the flesh is in the blood" (Lev 17.11) and that God had "given it to you upon the altar to make an atonement for your souls." It was therefore not to be eaten but to be offered solely unto God. The choicest portions of the fat were also reserved for the Deity. The hip sinew was never eaten, possibly in recollection of the story that God had touched the hollow of Jacob's thigh when He wrestled with him at Peniel (Gen 32.32). Another prohibition forbade the boiling of a kid in its mother's milk. Many of the dietary laws antedate Moses, going back as far as the Deluge (Gen 9.4). By Moses' day they already had tribal authority based upon usage and custom. Moses and later the priesthood codified and greatly expanded the laws on the theory that God is holy and can tolerate only a people who are clean and have not defiled themselves with unclean food. The prohibitions now seem natural rather than arbitrary since herbivorous animals produce the most savory meat while carnivorous animals not only supply a less savory meat but live off carrion which was exceedingly offensive to the Israelites. Among Christians dietary laws fell into rapid disuse. St. Peter in Acts 10.9–43 was warned by God against them; and Paul, Apostle to the Gentiles, always staunchly opposed laying Jewish customs on Christian shoulders. In Acts 15.20 the only dietary law for the Christian is to abstain from things strangled and from blood. BIBLIOGRAPHY: EDB 572–573; S. I. Leven and E. A. Boyden, *Kosher Code of the Orthodox Jew* (1940, repr. 1975).

[F. E. MASER]

DIETRICH, see THEODORIC OF NIEHEIM.

DIETZ, PETER ERNEST (1878–1947), labor priest. Ordained in 1904, Dietz became a lifelong champion of labor, applying the principles of Pope Leo XIII's *Rerum Novarum* throughout his career. He stands with Father John A. Ryan as a powerful advocate for labor legislation and a declaration on the labor question by the American bishops. He founded the American Academy for Christian Democracy to prepare young women for social work. D. had great influence on the American Federation of Labor and originated the industrial council plan among the building trades in Cincinnati. Opposition by Catholic business men forced the closing of his Academy, and D. withdrew from public life and went to Milwaukee as a pastor. BIBLIOGRAPHY: M. H. Fox, *Peter E. Dietz, Labor Priest* (1953).

[J. R. AHERNE]

DÍEZ LAUREL, BARTHOLOMÉ. BL. (d. 1627), Franciscan martyr whose cause was grouped with that of 205 martyrs of Japan. His real name was Díaz Laruel, and apparently no reliable biography has yet been written. He was born in Puerto de Santa María, Spain and entered the Franciscans while a sailor on tour in Mexico in 1616. He left the order only to return again the following year. He was in Manila in 1618, where he learned and practiced medicine. In 1623 he went as a missionary to Japan, disguised as a physician; he was imprisoned and put to death at Nagasaki. He is esp. venerated in Mexico.

[E. J. DILLON]

DIFFERENTIAL PSYCHOLOGY, the branch of psychology investigating the range and patterns of the variations in human capacities and achievements as manifested in different individuals either as individuals or as representatives of different sexes, races, cultures, temperaments, etc. Probably the most famous product of differential psychology is the intelligence test, which establishes an individual's intelligence quotient (IQ), i.e., the ratio of his performance on tests as compared to the average performance of other individuals of his age. Since comparisons of people by sex, race, and nationality are often used for propaganda purposes in arguing political, social, and educational issues, and therefore arouse strong emotional reactions, the findings of differential psychology are often criticized for bias. The greatest problem in differential psychology is to isolate the effect of cultural influences from what is to be ascribed to basic human capacities. BIBLIOGRAPHY: A. L. Van Kaam, NCE 4:865; A. Anastasi, *Differential Psychology* (1958).

[M. E. STOCK]

DIFFINITOR, see DEFINITOR, RELIGIOUS.

DIGAMY, a term describing remarriage after the dissolution of a previous marriage by the death of one of the contracting parties. It differs from bigamy in this respect. Societal and cultural norms vary regarding such remarriage

as do the attitudes of various religions toward it. The tradition of the Catholic Church is one marked by reinterpretation of it both biblically and theologically and by a defense of it, esp. when threatened by such groups as the Montanists. BIBLIOGRAPHY: J. Van Paassen, NCE 4:867.

[J. R. RIVELLO]

DIGBY, EVERARD (1578–1606), courtier and conspirator. Both D. and his wife were converted to Catholicism by the Jesuit John Gerard (1599). He was knighted for supporting the cause of James, but later grew dissatisfied with the King for his failure to grant toleration to Catholics, and was drawn into conspiracy by Robert Catesby to strike a violent blow against the government. Whatever the true nature and purpose of the Gunpowder Plot may have been, D.'s part in it was to have been the organization of a revolt in the Midlands to follow upon the coup in London. D. was apprehended, stood trial in Westminster Hall, was condemned and executed. He protested openly that Father Gerard was ignorant of the plot. BIBLIOGRAPHY: R. Ross Williamson, *Gunpowder Plot* (1952); A. Jessopp, DNB 5:956–957.

[V. SAMPSON]

DIGBY, GEORGE (1612–77), Earl of Bristol. Born in Spain, where his father was ambassador, D. studied at Magdalen College, Oxford. He became a member of Parliament for Dorset and held various positions in the government when the Royalists were in power. In an exchange of letters with Sir Kenelm Digby, his kinsman, he attacked the RC Church which Kenelm defended. Although D. himself became a Catholic, he spoke in favor of the Test Act (1673), yet voted against it, justifying his position by declaring that he was a Catholic of the Church, not the court, of Rome. D. was personally exempted by act of Parliament from the obligation of taking the test. BIBLIOGRAPHY: Gillow BDEC.

[V. SAMPSON]

DIGBY, KENELM HENRY (c. 1797–1880), English writer. While studying at Trinity College, Cambridge, he became greatly interested in the Middle Ages, which led to his conversion to Roman Catholicism in 1825. His works include *The Broadstone of Honor or Rules for the Gentlemen of England* (1822), his first book, considered his best. His most learned work was *Mores Catholici or The Ages of Faith* (11 v., 1831–40).

[S. A. HEENEY]

DIGNITY OF MAN, theologically, the worth of the human being as the *image of God. That identity has been given its full ratification in the Incarnation, in which the human nature of Christ is united to the Word, and through which the grace of divine sonship is opened up to every human being. The "image of creation" in every person consists in the condition of being endowed with intelligence and with the capability for self-determination. That in fact means the capacity for reflectively responding to the thrust towards the goods and the goals that are in keeping with being a fully human person. It means the ability to appreciate and to put order into the goals of existence, and consciously to experience, as well, their deprivation. In such powers every human being is the equal of every other; because of them each is a person of worth. The power to perceive and to order the priorities in human existence is the essence of freedom, and that freedom is best described as freedom of conscience. For in its fullest sense freedom of conscience is the power to discern the good to be pursued in life and to decide on the best ways to achieve that good as a goal. The dignity of the person as expressed in free self-determination becomes the norm for his right equally to share in the opportunities that will allow for fulfillment in what is worthy of human dignity. That opportunity is ultimately, as well, the person's openness to grace. (See Vat II ChurchModWorld 12–17.)

[T. C. O'BRIEN]

DIKERION, a term used to designate a double candlestick used by a Byzantine bp. to bless the people. The two candles represent the dual nature of Christ.

DILLARD, VICTOR (1897–1945), Jesuit sociologist and hero of the French resistance. After military service in World War I, D. entered the Jesuits; he became a sociologist, in which capacity he visited the U.S., and was active in youth movements. In 1940 he returned to the army, escaping to Vichy after the French collapse, where he became an object of suspicion to the Gestapo. In 1943 he made his way to Germany to serve the forced laborers imported from France, was arrested for anti-Nazi activity, and died during his imprisonment at Dachau. In addition to many professional articles, D. published *Au Dieu inconnu* (1938), a book of meditations on the Holy Spirit for youth. BIBLIOGRAPHY: Contre-amiral Dillard, *La Vie et la mort de R. P. Dillard* (1947); "Le Père V. Dillard," *Études* (Oct. 1945) 84–101.

[T. C. O'BRIEN]

DILTHEY, WILHELM (1833–1911), German philosopher, noted particularly for studies in the philosophy of history and culture. The son of a Reformed pastor, D. studied at Berlin, taught there (1865), and at Basel (1867), Kiel (1868), and Breslau (1871) before returning to Berlin in 1882 as successor to R. H. *Lotze.

D. was primarily concerned with the nature of man's historical consciousness, and the difference between cultural studies such as history and religion and the natural sciences. His principal work was *Einleitung in die Geisteswissenschaften (Introduction to the Spiritual Sciences,* 1883). He wished to work out a critique of historical reason comparable to the critiques of I. *Kant and thereby to overcome positivism in the field of cultural philosophy. He saw all historical phenomena as an expression of man's life experience, which was inwardly understood before it was scientifically analyzed. Man's relation to history differs fundamentally, he held, from his relationship to the natural sciences.

D. has been widely influential among religious scholars, particularly through E. *Troeltsch. His theories have been employed by biblical scholars who interpreted biblical texts as expressions of life experience. The contemporary German philosopher M. *Heidegger has built much of his theory of human existence upon the work of Dilthey. BIBLIOGRAPHY: H. A. Hodges, *Philosophy of Wilhelm Dilthey* (1952, repr. 1974); R. A. Makkreel, *Dilthey, Philosopher of the Human Studies* (pa. 1975).

[T. EARLY]

DIMISSORIAL LETTERS, in CIC (cc. 958–964) a term deriving from Roman Law, a release authorizing the bp. receiving it to ordain a candidate for *holy orders. The release is required on the premise that an ordinand must have a canonical affiliation (see INCARDINATION AND EXCARDINATION). In the case of secular clergy the ordinand's affiliation is to his own diocese, and if his bp. is not to ordain him, the ordaining bp. must receive authorization. In the case of a religious, the affiliation is to the religious institute in which he has made perpetual profession: dimissorial letters on his behalf must be sent by the competent religious superior to the ordaining bishop. Dimissorial letters are given for each specific order to be received, ordinarily in writing and accompanied by testimonial letters on the ordinand's suitability for ordination.

[T. C. O'BRIEN]

DINKELSBÜHL, ST. GEORGE (1448–92), hall church in western Bavaria. One of the most beautiful examples of the late Gothic style in Germany, and most important work of Nikolaus Eseler the Elder. With its sister church, St. George in Nördlingen, it is a perfect hall-church form, the graceful piers of the long nave and aisles soaring to an intricate vaulting.

[M. J. DALY]

DINTILHAC, JORGE (1878–1947), priest of the Order of the Sacred Hearts. Three years after entering he made his final vows (1897). He continued his theological studies in Valparaiso (1901) and received his doctorate in theology at the Univ. of San Marcos in Lima (1902). Then began his fruitful teaching career in the Recoleta School in Lima. D. promoted the foundation of the Catholic Univ. of Peru (1918) and was its rector until his death. BIBLIOGRAPHY: A. Tauro, *Diccionario Enciclopédico del Perú* (ed. M. Baca, 1966) 1:486.

[M. T. REILLY]

DIO CASSIUS COCCEIANUS (*c.* 155–235), Roman historian and administrator. Born in Nicaea, Bithynia, the son of Cassius Apronianus, governor of Dalmatia and Cilicia, and grandson of the Greek orator and philosopher Dio Chrysostomus, D. moved to Rome after his father's death (180) where he entered upon a varied career of public service as senator, praetor, administrator in Pergamum and Smyrna, consul (211), proconsul of Africa, legate to Dalmatia and Pannonia, and consul a second time (229). His writings include a history of Rome in 80 books, from the arrival of Aeneas in Italy to the time of his second consulship (Books 37–54 are preserved complete; 17, 36, 55–60, 79–80 in part; 1–21 and 36–80 in epitome). The sources for the history are the early annals, the annals of the empire as used by Tacitus, the historians Polybius and Livy, memoirs, and for contemporary events his own authority. Annalistic in format, stylistically an imitation of Thucydides, the history emphasizes the political ramifications of events. Although it is noticeably inaccurate in its delineation of the institutions of Republican Rome and not incisive in its critical judgment of history, it is nevertheless a significant witness to the history of Imperial Rome during the lifetime of Dio. Text: *Dio's Roman History* (Loeb, tr. E. W. Carey, 9 v., 1914–1927). BIBLIOGRAPHY: G. T. Griffith, "The Greek Historians," *Fifty Years of Classical Scholarship* (ed. M. Platnauer, 1954) 175–192.

[F. MURPHY]

DIOCESE (Gr. *dioikēsis,* administrative unit), a territorial unit of the Church, governed by a bp. ruling in his own name and not as delegate of another. The diocese is an administrative division chiefly in the RC, Anglican, and Old Catholic Churches. Vatican II defines a diocese as "that portion of God's people which is entrusted to a bishop to be shepherded by him with the cooperation of the presbytery" (Vat II BpPastOff 11). While certainly not of divine institution, territorial division of the Church is attested to in the 1st century. An urban Christian community was organized under its bp., whose authority gradually expanded to cover the rural areas. These communities, or territorial divisions, were at first called simply churches (Gr. *ekklesiai),* then parishes *(paroikiai).* The term diocese, already used in the 4th cent., did not become the exclusive term to designate territorial divisions until the 13th century. In the Eastern Church a diocese meant a much larger administrative unit comprising several provinces, corresponding to usage of the term in civil administration. What is called a diocese in the Western Church, the Eastern Church calls an eparchy. The establishment and the boundaries of a diocese generally follow civil territorial divisions and are usually named after the city in which the bp. resides. The erection, changing of boundaries, and suppression of a diocese belong by right to the highest authority in a particular Church. In the RC Church this has come to be the prerogative of the pope. In the best interests of the faithful Vatican II decreed that an extensive revision of the present diocesan administration and boundaries be undertaken as soon as possible, but this has not yet been put into effect. The Council also laid down norms for such changes (Vat II BpPastOff 22–24). In the C of E, dioceses may be erected only by act of Parliament; in the Protestant Episcopal Church the determination of dioceses belongs to the *General Convention of the Church. In the Eastern Church it is determined by the patriarch (or his equivalent) with his synod. An archdiocese is essentially the same in structure as a diocese, except that its head, an archbishop, enjoys prestige of rank and ceremonial precedence.

[G. T. DENNIS]

DIOCLETIAN (Gaius Aurelius Valerius Diocletianus; *c.*247–316), **ROMAN EMPEROR** (284–305). Rising up from the ranks D. became commander of the imperial bodyguard and was proclaimed emperor by the army after the murder of Numerian. D. proved to be a bold and imaginative innovator and gave new life to the empire which had been subject to almost continuous anarchy during the earlier decades of the 3d century. In 285 he appointed Maximian as his assistant as ruler of the West with the title of Caesar, and in the following year raised him to the rank of Augustus. In 293, to further increase the stability of the government, he established the "Tetrarchy," appointing Galerius as Caesar to help rule in the East and Constantius Chlorus as another Caesar to assist Maximian in the West. On May 1, 305, because of his poor health he abdicated, forcing Maximian to follow his example. He returned to public life briefly in 308 when he helped Galerius reestablish the rule at Carnuntum. Diocletian reorganized the army, restored military discipline, revised the system of coinage and of taxation. In 301 he issued a famous edict in an attempt to curb inflation by setting a maximum on prices. To enhance the dignity of the imperial office he assumed the trappings of royalty and gave a religious foundation to his rule by claiming to be the representative of Jupiter, as Maximian was that of Hercules. His able and distinguished career was marred by a prolonged and savage persecution of the Christians. BIBLIOGRAPHY: W. Ensslin, PW 7 A.1:2419–95; R. Paribeni, EncCatt 4:1653–56.

[M. J. COSTELLOE]

DIOCLETIAN, ERA OF, an important period of political, social, economic, and religious reforms in the Roman Empire marking the transition from the Principate to the more absolutistic Dominate. The era is named after Gaius Aurelius Valerius Diocletianus (*c.*247–316); Roman emperor, 284–305. A Dalmation of humble birth, he rose to high rank in the military service and was chosen emperor by the army at Nicomedia to avenge the murder of Numerian. To bring to an end the disastrous civil wars of the 3d cent. and to obtain greater efficiency of administration, he associated Maximian as co-Augustus with himself in 286, giving him the rule of the West while reserving the East for himself. In 292 he made a further division of the empire through the appointment of two Caesars to help the Augusti—Constantius Chlorus in the West and Galerius in the East. The various provinces of the empire were divided and grouped into 12 dioceses. The legions were also reduced in size but increased in numbers. A new system of taxation was adopted, and an attempt was made to stop inflation with a famous Edict on Maximum Prices issued in 301. Conservative in religion, Diocletian insisted upon the sanctity of his own person as a kind of semi-divine ruler. On March 31, 296, he issued a severe edict against the Manichees, and in 303–304 he issued a series of four edicts against the Christians providing for the destruction of their churches, burning of their books, and the eventual imprisonment and execution of those who refused to apostatize. This persecution, known as "The Great Persecution," persisted for some years after Diocletian's abdication in 305 and was only officially ended with the "Edict of Milan" of 313. Diocletian erred seriously in his religious policy and has been criticized for his regimentation of society, insisting that every citizen should remain in the class into which he had been born. On the whole, however, his rule was one of enlightened public service. BIBLIOGRAPHY: Harold Mattingly, OCD, 283–284; M. Rostovtzeff, *History of the Ancient World* (1927, repr. 1971) 2:310–332.

[M. J. COSTELLOE]

DIOCLETIAN, ERA OF (CHRONOLOGY),

a term used in a system of reckoning dates from the accession of Diocletian. The use of this system was confined chiefly to Egypt. There this era began on Thôt 1 (Aug. 29), the beginning of the civil year in 284 A.D.. That its use was widespread is attested by the fact that dating according to this era is found not only in official documents but also in Greek papyri and on inscriptions. It continued in general use in Egypt till some time after the Arab conquest in 640. Since the beginning of this era coincided with the beginning of a 19-year lunar cycle, it proved a useful system for calculating the date of Easter. St. Athanasius, patriarch of Alexandria, dated his annual *Festal Letters* (PG 26:1360–) which announced the date of Easter to the bps. of Egypt in terms of the "year of Diocletian." In the course of time this era acquired another name. According to Eusebius (*Hist. eccl.* 8.8), countless numbers of men, women, and children died as martyrs during the Diocletian persecution in Egypt. Since it was assumed that the persecution began with the Emperor's accession, the era came to be known also as the Era of the Martyrs. Under this name it is still in use among the Abyssinians and the Copts as a system of dating. When Dionysius Exiguus extended the calculation for the dates for Easter down to 626, he abandoned the dating according to the Diocletian era. In replacing it with his *Anno Domini* reckoning, he miscalculated the date of Christ's birth by some 4 to 7 years later than the event. BIBLIOGRAPHY: W. Seston, RAC 3:1052; H. Lietzmann, *Zeitrechnung der römischen Kaiserzeit, des Mittelalters,* *und der Neuzeit* (1956) 11–12; V. Grumel, *La Chronologie* (1958) 36–40.

[H. DRESSLER]

DIOCLETIAN, PERSECUTION OF,

the persecution begun by the Emperors Diocletian and Galerius in 303 and which persisted until 311. It is known as "the Great Persecution." The first years of Diocletian's reign were marked by a spirit of tolerance, but this was changed for a number of different reasons: the refusal of Christians to take the military oath or participate in religious ceremonies, the violent anti-Christian polemic of such writers as Porphyry and Hierocles, his own policies of reform, and the promptings of his co-regent Galerius. In 297 Diocletian published an edict against the Manichees which set a pattern for his later attacks on Christianity. From 295 on there are records of various Christian soldiers and recruits being executed for failure to comply with military regulations having a religious connotation. The first general edict against the Christians, which was signed by the two Augusti and the two Caesars, was issued on Feb. 23, 303. This ordered the destruction of places of worship, the surrender of the Scriptures for burning, and the taking away of civil rights from Christians. A fire in the palace and uprisings in Melitene and Syria led to further repressive measures. A second edict of March 303, ordered the imprisonment of the clergy. A third edict of December 21, 303, granted freedom to clerics who would offer sacrifice and ordered the execution of those who refused to do so. A final edict issued in April, 304, was directed at all Christians. Failure to pour a libation or offer sacrifice was punished by condemnation to the mines or to death.

The decrees were carried out with varying degrees of intensity throughout the empire. There were numerous executions in Palestine and in Egypt, where on some days the number of victims in certain areas amounted to a hundred and more (Eusebius, *Eccl. Hist.* 8.9.3). In Italy and Africa the persecution was also violent, but it was less so in Britain and Gaul. Pope Marcellinus was executed in Rome in 304 and it was impossible to elect a successor to him until 307. Among others to die were Pamphilus of Caesarea, Lucian of Antioch, Peter of Alexandria, Methodius of Olympus, and Sylvanus of Gaza. Estimates as to the number of martyrs vary widely, running from 2,500 or 3,000 (Grégoire), which is certainly too low, to 50,000 (Hertling). In 311, Galerius, realizing the failure of the persecution and suffering from a mortal illness himself, promulgated an edict of toleration allowing the Christians "to again exist" and to worship in common. The defeat of Maxentius by Constantine in 312 and the so-called "Edict of Milan" of the following spring brought an end to the persecution, though it was renewed again in the East under Licinius when he clashed with Constantine in 321. Even after the establishment of peace for the Church, the persecution had its repercussions in the status of the *traditores,* those who had handed the Scriptures over to pagan authorities. In N Africa this problem was largely responsible for the Donatist schism. BIBLIOGRAPHY: W. Seston, RAC 3:1036–54; H. Grégoire, *Les Persécutions dans l'empire romain* (1951); L. Hertling, "Die Zahl der Märtyrer bis 313," Greg 25 (1944) 103–129.

[M. J. COSTELLOE]

DIODOROS OF TARSUS (d. before 394), bishop. After studying at Athens D. became a monk and was soon chosen superior of a monastery near Antioch, probably his native city. He is credited with introducing the use of alternate choirs in the singing of the Psalms. He was a leader among the theologians who supported the decisions of Nicaea and was exiled to Armenia in 372 by the emperor Valens because of his zeal for Nicaean orthodoxy. Elected bp. of Tarsus 6 years later, he attended the First Council of Constantinople (381) and with St. Pelagius was acclaimed by the emperor Theodosius as a norm of orthodoxy. The most noted among his pupils were *John Chrysostom and *Theodore of Mopsuestia; among his friends were SS. Basil, Meletius, and Flavian. In his exegesis he followed the Antiochene tradition of literal interpretation as opposed to the allegorizing interpretation of the Alexandrians. In his attack upon Apollinarianism he appears to have emphasized the completeness of the humanity of Christ to the point of asserting two hypostases, though what he said need not be understood in an unorthodox sense. The developments of D.'s thought by Theodore, the teacher of Nestorius, caused the Antiochenes to charge D. with some responsibility for the Nestorian heresy. He was attacked by Cyril as early as 438, and a synod at Constantinople in 499 anathematized him. Of his many writings—biblical commentaries; dogmatic, apologetic, and polemical treatises; works on natural science, esp. astronomy—only fragments remain. Works: PG 33:1561–1628. BIBLIOGRAPHY: Quasten 3:397–401.

[R. B. ENO]

DIOGENES OF APOLLONIA IN PHRYGIA (fl. c.440 or 430 B.C.), an eclectic philosopher, but predominantly in the Ionian tradition. Among his works, only one, *On Nature,* is known through the extant excerpts made by *Simplicius. He revived the doctrine of *Anaximines that Air was the origin of things, attributing to it mind and divinity, and making it the principle of soul and intelligence in all living beings. His preoccupation with Air occasioned the parody of his views in the *Clouds* of Aristophanes. Like *Anaxagoras he made the brain rather than the heart the organ of sensation and thought. His physiological ideas on generation, respiration, and blood were regarded as sufficiently important to receive full attention from *Aristotle. He regarded the earth as flat and round and the heavenly bodies as fiery hot pumice stones. His curious theory of magnetism is based on the analogy of breathing. However, the fantastic side of his views should not be exaggerated. Guthrie emphasizes that "he both developed and

popularized three doctrines, all interrelated: the idea of air as *archē*, the essential identity of microcosm and macrocosm (the human soul and the divine, omnipresent, controlling mind), and the teleological interpretation of nature" (Guthrie 381). BIBLIOGRAPHY: OCD 284; Guthrie 1:362–381.

[M. R. P. MCGUIRE]

DIOGENES OF SINOPE (c.400–c.325 B.C.), founder of Cynicism. Brought to Athens at an early age by his father, he lived in poverty and, either under the influence of the teachings of *Antisthenes of Athens (c.445–360 B.C.) or independently, he rejected all conventions. He held that happiness is attained by satisfying one's natural needs in the cheapest and easiest way possible, stressing self-sufficiency *(autarkeia),* training *(askēsis)* of the body to reduce its needs to the barest minimum, and shamelessness *(anaideia).* Because of his outlook and his squalid manner of life he was called "the Dog" *(kyōn),* and his followers came to be designated Cynics *(kynikoi).* He wrote dialogues and tragedies, but exercised his major influence by his personal life and conduct, becoming a legendary figure almost in his own lifetime. The Stoics, who owed much to him, exaggerated his association with Antisthenes in order to establish a connection between their teachings and the teachings of Socrates. BIBLIOGRAPHY: OCD 285; LexAW 743; D. R. Dudley, *History of Cynicism* (1937) 17–58; I. G. Kidd, EncPhil 2:284–285.

[M. R. P. MCGUIRE]

DIOGNETUS, EPISTLE TO, a Christian apology of unknown authorship and date, erroneously classified by custom among the writings of the *Apostolic Fathers. This work was cited by no ancient or medieval writer, and only a single MS copy of it, dating from the 13th or 14th cent., has ever been discovered. Addressed apparently to an inquiring pagan, it is like other apologies in its ridicule of idol worship and its exposition of the inadequacy of Jewish religion. In contrast it gives a sketch of Christian belief and indicates the dignity of the role of Christians in the world, for they are to the world as the soul is to the body. After an apparently incomplete exposition of the benefits of conversion, the work in the last two chapters (11–12) becomes florid and obscure and loses all the literary charm and limpidity of the earlier chapters. These final chapters, lacking connection with what precedes them, are generally conceded to belong to a different document. Unsuccessful efforts have been made to assign the letter to various known figures of antiquity, e.g., Justin Martyr, Lucian the Martyr, Quadratus, Pantaenus. Text: PG 2:1167–86; *Apostolic Fathers* (Loeb 2, tr. and ed. K. Lake, 1930) 348–373. BIBLIOGRAPHY: J. Chapman, CE 5:8–9.

[R. B. ENO]

DIONIGI DA PIACENZA (1637–95), a Capuchin missionary. D. labored in the Congo from 1667 to 1671, then went to Brazil. Later he was sent to missions in Asia Minor, Persia, Russian Georgia (where he served as proprefect), and finally in Venice where he died. D. wrote two books of his experiences, which were widely distributed and even translated into French and German during his lifetime. These works were incorporated in many collections of works on foreign travel.

[M. T. REILLY]

DIONYSIANA COLLECTIO, a collection of texts, for the most part rigorously executed. These texts were a protostep in preparation for the reconciliation of the Western and Eastern Churches—a long desired goal of Dionysius. The collection dates from the 6th cent. and includes texts of the various councils (including Nicaea) held in that period. It was probably prepared during the papacy of Pope Hormisdas (514–523). While the collection bears the name of Dionysius, it is not the only one so titled.

[J. R. RIVELLO]

DIONYSIUS, see also DENIS.

DIONYSIUS, ST. (d. 268), **POPE** from 259 or 260. D. won favorable attention in the East because of the part he took as a presbyter of the Roman Church under Pope St. Stephen I (254–257) in the *rebaptism controversy. His election as pope followed an extended vacancy in that office because of persecution. The edict of toleration of Gallienus (260) led to the restoration of the confiscated properties of the Church and D. put order into their administration. He summoned (c. 260) a synod to pass judgment on the disagreement in Alexandria on the relation of the Son to the Father and issued a letter condemning once more the doctrine of the neo-Sabellians (for whom the Trinity was a matter of names) as well as the Subordinationists (who represented the Son as a created being). He asked and received from Dionysius, bp. of Alexandria, an explanation of certain of his views that could be understood in an unorthodox sense. This intervention was cited by Julius in 340 as a precedent showing Roman supervision of other sees in matters of doctrine. Shortly before his death D. was advised by the Synod of Antioch that it had condemned Paul of Samosata. D. was buried in the papal crypt of the catacomb of Callistus. BIBLIOGRAPHY: E. G. Weltin, NCE 4:876; J. P. Kirsch, CE 5:9–10; Butler 4:618.

[P. F. MULHERN]

DIONYSIUS (Dionisi; c. 1440–1508), Russian painter second only to Rublev in the Moscow School. D. painted frescoes in the Borovski Monastery, Novgorod (1466–67) and in the Uspensky Cathedral of the Dormition, Moscow (1482). Eighty-seven icons (of which only 2 remain) are listed to him in the Volokolamski Monastery, Novgorod, where D. began the paintings in 1484. Frescoes in the Church of the Birth of the Virgin, Moscow, the only ones extant, are in light colors—unique in that period.

[M. J. DALY]

DIONYSIUS OF ALEXANDRIA, ST. (called The Great by Eusebius and Basil; d. c. 265), bp. from 247, whose eminence among the 3d-cent. bps. was exceeded only by that of St. Cyprian. Having read his way from paganism to Christianity, D. studied at the catechetical school at Alexandria, first under *Origen, then, after Origen's banishment, under Heraclas. When Heraclas became bp., D. succeeded him as head of the school and later also as bishop. During his episcopate the Church at Alexandria endured famine, plague, and repeated persecution. Though keenly intelligent and profoundly versed in the Scriptures, D. is better known for his effectiveness as a leader. It was largely through his influence that the bps. of the East rejected *Novatian's claims to the papacy. He engaged in controversy about the validity of baptism conferred by a heretic and vigorously combatted Sabellianism and the *Monarchianism of Paul of Samosata. He was himself accused by Pope Dionysius of teaching a form of tritheism, but exculpated himself by means of an explanatory letter. In his book *On the Promises* he refuted the attempt of Bp. Nepos of Arsinoe (Egypt) to undermine the allegorical interpretation of the Book of Revelation in the interests of a literalist *millenarianism. In this work D. expressed doubt about the Johannine authorship of Revelation. His writings, most of which were in the form of letters, have survived only in the fragments cited by Eusebius and Athanasius, who are the principal sources of what is known of his life. Works: PG 10:1233–1344; 1575–1602. BIBLIOGRAPHY: Quasten 2:101–109; J. Chapman, CE 5:11–13; Butler 4:364–366; Lex AW 753.

[R. B. ENO]

DIONYSIUS THE AREOPAGITE, see PSEUDO-DIONYSIUS.

DIONYSIUS OF CORINTH, ST. (d. c. 180), bishop. According to *Eusebius, D. wrote letters to the Churches of Athens, Sparta, Nicomedia, Gortyna, Amastris, Cnossos, and Rome. The letter to Rome thanks the Church there for its help and mentions that the letter of *Clement to the Church of Corinth was still read with honor at their Sunday worship. D. saw the various heresies in the Church as stemming from the influence of pagan philosophy. His letters and other writings are lost except for the fragments cited by Eusebius. BIBLIOGRAPHY: Quasten 1:280–282; Butler 2:52.

[R. B. ENO]

DIONYSIUS EXIGUUS (d. c. 526), a Scythian monk, canonist, compiler, and translator. Little is known of his life. The *Exiguus* (little) attached to his name appears to have been assumed by D. as a gesture of humility and bears no reference to his physical stature. He was brought up by Gothic monks and was well trained in Greek and Latin tongues. Pope Gelasius in 496 summoned him to Rome to classify the pontifical archives and to compile a collection of conciliar and papal decrees. He proceeded with this work during the pontificate of Pope Hormisdas (514–523). His collection of canon law was the first to gain wide acceptance and was in general use in Europe in the 7th and 8th centuries. As a chronologist D. was responsible for the acceptance of the date A.U.C. 753 as the year in which the Incarnation took place; this reckoning, though erroneous, is still in use. Works: PL 67:9–520. BIBLIOGRAPHY: J. Rambaud-Buchot, DDC 4:1131–52.

[R. A. TODD]

DIONYSIUS OF FOURNA, 18th-cent. Byzantine monk, author of the *Painter's Guide*—rules for style and technique, believed of earlier origin by some scholars. The *Painter's Guide* was edited in Greek by P. Keramaeus (St. Petersburg, 1909). BIBLIOGRAPHY: C. Diehl, *La Peinture byzantine* (1933).

[M. J. DALY]

DIONYSIUS OF THE NATIVITY, BL. (Pierre Berthelot; 1600–38), missionary and martyr. A professional navigator and cartographer, D. was captured by Dutch pirates and imprisoned at Java on his first expedition to the Indies. Later in Malacca he worked for the Portuguese, assuming command of a ship. Ordained a Discalced Carmelite (1638), he was assigned at the request of the Portuguese viceroy as chaplain to Sumatra where he and the lay brother, Bl. Redemptus of the Cross, were captured and martyred by the natives when they refused to apostatize. Leo XIII beatified them in 1900. BIBLIOGRAPHY: Butler 4:448–449; V. di S. Maria, BiblSanct 4:648–650.

[M. T. REILLY]

DIONYSUS, CULT OF, a religious phenomenon of the Greco-Roman world. In antiquity there were various myths and theories about the origins of Dionysus, a god associated sometimes with the cycle of vegetation and sometimes with phenomena of ecstasy or possession. His increasing and eventually exclusive connection with wine may represent a synthesis of both these aspects. Some sacrifices to him continued to be wineless. Though barely mentioned in Homer, D.'s name has been read in a Linear B text and was presumably known to the Mycenaean-Minoan world. Among the Thracians he was a divinity of nature in the wild; his votaries, often women *(maenads)*, sometimes called *bacchoi*, danced or roamed ecstatically through the countryside, tore animals to pieces and devoured them raw *(omophagia)*. It was a sacramental meal in which the power of the god (sometimes portrayed as an animal) entered the worshiper. Skins of animals were worn, and also masks. Mask and costume in festivals of D. were part of the origin of Greek (specifically Attic) drama. His worship spread

into Greece proper both from the N and from the E, where the Phrygians (a Thracian tribe) knew him also as a god of the underworld and as a child. At Delphi he shared honors with Apollo as a god of prophecy. At Thebes he was worshiped as offspring of Zeus and Semele. D. loomed large in Orphic speculation, was increasingly the center of "mysteries" in Hellenistic and Roman times, and attracted an extensive legend of distant conquests. Initiation into his mysteries apparently involved a happy afterlife, as is indicated by Dionysiac themes decorating sarcophagi. He was pictured at first as a bearded adult, later as a beardless youth. BIBLIOGRAPHY: W. K. C. Guthrie, *Greeks and Their Gods* (1950); M. P. Nilsson, *Dionysiac Mysteries of the Hellenistic and Roman Age* (1957); C. Kerenyi, *Dionysos: Archetypal Image of Indestructible Life* (tr. R. Manheim, 1975). *GREEK RELIGION, *MYSTERY RELIGIONS (GRECO-ORIENTAL).

[Z. STEWART]

DIOSCORIDES MANUSCRIPT, MS from Constantinople (512) whose full-page illuminations link Greco-Roman and Byzantine painting styles. The first folio, classical in style, shows portraits of physicians and of the author together with a miniature of the Byzantine princess Juliana Anicia for whom the MS was made, and illustrations of medicinal plants of Alexandria and Pergamon, which became the source of later herbals. The use of gold and of brilliant color mark the MS as Byzantine.

[M. J. DALY]

DIOSCORUS (d. 530), **POPE** for 22 days in 530, by some accounted an antipope, but his claim is incontestable unless it is admitted that a pope has a right to name his successor. An Alexandrian by birth, D. was adopted into the Roman clergy and occupied important positions. Under *Symmachus (498–514), he headed a mission to the Gothic court at Ravenna, and under *Felix IV (526–530) he was papal legate to the imperial court at Constantinople. He was the leader of the proimperial faction at the papal court during the reign of Felix and the latter, pro-Gothic, tried to insure continuity of his own policy by naming *Boniface his successor. The Roman clergy would not accept Boniface but elected D. Both claimants were consecrated the same day. The Church was saved from disunion by D.'s death less than a month after his consecration, and the Roman clergy then accepted Boniface. Despite the latter's attempt to discredit D.'s memory it now seems that he was the duly elected pope and that the reign of Boniface should date from his acceptance by the clergy after D.'s death. Agapetus I in 535 removed the anathema that Boniface had pronounced against Dicscorus. BIBLIOGRAPHY: T. Oestreich, CE 5:18; J. Chapin, NCE 4:878.

[P. F. MULHERN]

DIOCORUS (d. 454), **PATRIARCH OF ALEXANDRIA** (444–451). D. was successor to *Cyril of Alexandria, whose Christological views he supported, but upon becoming patriarch he took vigorous measures to exclude Cyril's relatives from their lucrative and responsible offices and to curb certain clerics whom Cyril had favored. He exerted great efforts to further the prestige of Alexandria at the expense of Constantinople and Antioch. Capitalizing on the authority of his predecessor and the Monophysite tendencies of the Egyptian monks, D. supported *Eutyches against the orthodox party and succeeded in having Flavian, the patriarch of Constantinople, deposed and the *Tome of Leo rejected at the so-called *Robber Council of Ephesus (449). However, after the death of Emperor Theodosius II in 450, the situation was reversed. The Tome of Leo was adopted by the Council of *Chalcedon and D. was banished to Paphlagonia. BIBLIOGRAPHY: Fliche-Martin 4:211–240; F. X. Murphy, NCE 4:879.

[R. B. ENO]

DIPHONA, Greek synonym for *bicinia,* i.e., 16th cent. vocal or instrumental compositions in two parts, without accompaniment. They are of great artistic value and educational significance. BIBLIOGRAPHY: Apel HDMus 94.

[M. T. LEGGE]

DIPLOMACY, PAPAL. The pope maintains formal diplomatic relations with most of the states of the world. In return these states accredit their own ambassadors (or ministers plenipotentiary) to the Holy See in Vatican City. This exchange is conducted under the rules of international law and practice. The nuncios or pro-nuncios, as the papal envoys are styled, enjoy full diplomatic privilege and immunity where they are stationed. In some countries with a long tradition of relations with the pope, such as France and Spain, the nuncio acts as ex officio dean of the diplomatic corps regardless of his length of service. The diplomatic corps accredited to the Vatican is entirely separate and distinct from that accredited to the Italian government. From 1940 to 1949 American representation consisted of the mission of Myron C. *Taylor who had the title of "Personal Representative of the President of the United States, with rank of ambassador." This somewhat ambiguous mission was terminated with the resignation of Taylor. Subsequently, liaison with the Vatican is maintained informally by a minor attaché of the U.S. embassy to Italy.

Papal diplomacy can also be applied, in a less proper sense, to the system by which the Holy See is represented in most countries by a Vatican official known as the apostolic delegate. Unlike the nuncio, he has no official status with the government of the country but concerns himself with only its bps., clergy, and faithful. At Vatican Council II the bps. asked the Pope to clarify the exact function of the apostolic delegate in relation to the local church leaders. The motu proprio *Sollicitudo omnium ecclesiarum* (1969), responding to this request, emphasized that the delegate has a mission only to help the local clergy and not to supplant the bps. in the exercise of their own responsibilities.

A new development in Vatican diplomacy is the growing participation of the Holy See in international diplomatic conferences for the drafting of conventions, particularly in the humanitarian and cultural field. Though nuncios and delegates are usually abps., the use of laymen for these conferences is becoming standard. The Holy See maintains permanent official observers at various international organizations, such as the United Nations and UNESCO. It is a formal member of some organizations of a purely technical nature, such as the International Telecommunications Union.

In the diplomatic world, the Holy See is unique; and its exact juridical status or personality is the subject of many theoretical studies. Between 1870 and 1929, the pope was without any recognized territorial sovereignty, but in that period the number of reciprocal diplomatic representations actually increased. The creation of the Vatican City State (1929) does not therefore entirely explain these activities. In those countries which have entered into a formal concordat with the Holy See, the nuncio has the mission of consulting with the government on Church-State matters regulated by that agreement. In non-concordat countries, considerations of foreign policy play a great role, particularly in recent years with the rise of the young states in the developing areas of the world. Improved relations with the Soviet Union and communist-style governments, along with vigorous peace initiatives on the part of the Holy See, have also given a new dimension to papal diplomacy. A significant indication of these changes was the unprecedented address by Pope Paul VI to the UN General Assembly in New York in 1965. Current papal contacts with Communist regimes is regarded by many Catholics both in and exiled from those states as a betrayal; Ukrainian Catholics in particular have been embittered by the Holy See's refusal to create a Ukrainian patriarchate outside Russia. BIBLIOGRAPHY: R. A. Graham, *Vatican Diplomacy* (1959); *idem,* NCE 4:881–884 with bibliog.

[R. A. GRAHAM]

DIPLOMATICS, ECCLESIASTICAL. Diplomatics is a term used to describe those studies that deal with public documents, charters, private and public records, and juridical and legal documents. Within the Church these critical studies deal with similar content. Ecclesiastical diplomatics primarily denotes papal documents, but the term applies as well to papers and documents of private individuals in the Church as well as to persons of rank. BIBLIOGRAPHY: W. M. Plochl, NCE 4:884–885; K. A. Fink, LTK 10:560–563.

[J. R. RIVELLO]

DIPPEL, JOHANN KONRAD (1673–1734), Lutheran theologian, alchemist, physician, and chemist credited with the invention of the dye called "Prussian blue." D. was born at Frankenstein, studied at Giessen, and became in his youth a staunch defender of Lutheran orthodoxy. But after a time, and through the influence of G. *Arnold, he turned to

Pietism. He began to teach that the Church had betrayed its ideals from Constantinian times, disparaged dogma in favor of piety and practical Christianity, and attacked the institutional Church. These views brought criticism and strong opposition; he wandered from one place to another until he was expelled successively from Germany, Denmark, Holland, and Sweden. In his last years he engaged in bitter polemics against the mysticism of Count *Zinzendorf. D.'s main works were: *Orthodoxia orthodoxorum* (1697), *Papismus Protestantium vapulans* (1698), and *Vera demonstratio evangelica* (1729).

[P. DAMBORIENA]

DIPTYCHS, from Gr. *diptukon,* a small folding tablet of wood or metal, with ornamental outside surfaces and inner surfaces bearing an inscription on wax or engraved. Their liturgical use, both in the East and the West, was connected with the practice of remembering in the Eucharistic Liturgy those whom the community honored or for whom they prayed: the martyrs, the deceased, those sharing in Christian communion; such names and also those of catechumens were recorded on the diptychs and read off by one of the liturgical ministers. The phrase "to strike someone from the diptychs" chiefly recalls the schism between East and West. In the East the practice of striking the pope's name became common with the Photian rebellion against Rome (see PHOTIUS); it was answered by papal excommunication of the patriarchs of Constantinople. (These hostile acts were repented mutually by Pope Paul VI and Athenagoras I of Constantinople at the closing of Vatican Council II, Dec. 7, 1965.) The actual liturgical use of the diptychs ceased in the West by the 12th cent. and in the East by the 14th.

[T. C. O'BRIEN]

DIPTYCHS, CONSULAR, see CONSULAR DIPTYCHS.

DIPYLON GATE, most important NW gate of Athens, double as the name implies, with 130′ courtyard. Through it passed the religious processions on the Sacred Way to Eleusis, and commercial traffic to the port of Piraeus. Outside the gate lay the chief cemetery, Cerameicus, from which the word ceramic derives.

[M. J. DALY]

DIPLYON VASE, large Geometric amphora (5′) from a tomb near the Dipylon Gate. One of a series, this masterpiece of the Geometric style (800–750 B.C.) shows a surface divided by horizontal bands painted with friezes of animals and various geometric motifs, with a focal scene of prothesis, where figures, abstract and decorative, are disposed in the serene order characteristic of Greek expression. BIBLIOGRAPHY: J. M. Davison, *Attic Geometric Workshops (Yale Classical Studies,* v. 16, 1961).

[M. J. DALY]

DIRECTANEUS. In psalmody, the term *psalmus directaneus* is a psalm to be sung to a psalm tone without antiphon. BIBLIOGRAPHY: Apel HDMus 702.

[M. T. LEGGE]

DIRECTION, SPIRITUAL, see SPIRITUAL DIRECTION.

DIRECTORY OF PUBLIC WORSHIP, see WESTMINSTER DIRECTORY FOR WORSHIP

DIRGE, in medieval times, the public recitation of *Matins and *Lauds from the *Office of the Dead. The term is taken from *dirige,* the first word of the first *antiphon at Matins. Later the word came to mean a burial hymn.

[T. M. MCFADDEN]

DIRIMENT IMPEDIMENT (Lat. *dirimo,* to bring to naught), an obstacle that renders a marriage *invalid, in distinction from a simple or "impeding" impediment that renders a marriage *illicit (CIC, c. 1036). *IMPEDIMENTS, MATRIMONIAL.

[T. C. O'BRIEN]

DI ROSA, MARIA CROCIFISSA, ST. (1813–55), foundress of the Handmaids of Charity. Urged by her father, D. engaged in a variety of good works, which later were guided by Faustino Pinzoni, her spiritual director. She cared for the sick during a cholera epidemic in Italy; in Brescia, she organized Sunday school groups, the first school for the deaf, the first home for the rehabilitation of girls, and encouraged the enactment of reforms to aid indigent women. Her chief accomplishment was the foundation (1840) of the religious congregation, the Handmaids of Charity. She befriended the Jesuits of the College of St. Christopher, the Daughters of the Sacred Heart, and the hospital in Brescia. D. was inspired by the sorrows of Christ to aid the sick and the poor.

[M. T. REILLY]

DISCALCED ORDERS (Lat., *dis-calceatus,* without foot covering), those religious orders which, in the reform movements of the 16th cent., adopted the practice of going without shoes to signify a spirit of poverty and penance. The reformed Carmelites specifically took their title from this: the Order of Discalced Carmelites. Other orders which adopted the practice were the Camaldolese, the Minims, some Augustinians, the Servites, the Feuillants, the Trinitarians, and the Reformed Mercedarians. Some of the newly founded congregations such as the Passionists also adopted the practice. The religious significance of going barefooted has foundations in the OT (Ex 3.5, 2 Sam 15.30, Is 20.2, 4) where it signified reverence, self-abasement, poverty, and supplication. Although it was a common practice among the monks of the East, Western monastic legislators provided for the use of such footgear by the monks as was commonly used in the region in which they lived. St. Francis of Assisi and his followers adopted the practice primarily in imitation of Christ and as an expression of poverty. While for Francis this meant actually going without anything at all on the feet, later both among the Franciscans and among other discalced, sandals were commonly worn. In modern times, shoes and socks have been used by discalced religious when outside their convents or monasteries. With the renewal inspired by Vatican Council II and adaptation to the needs and values of today the practice of going barefoot is being largely abandoned in Western countries.

[M. B. PENNINGTON]

DISCANT, in 12th to 15th-cent. music a type of polyphonic music in which a part was composed or improvised against the plainsong. As distinguished from *organum,* with which it had formerly been synonymous, it is a more elaborate setting, including melismas in the upper part. In modern times there has been a revival of discant in church music with the choir superimposing counterpoint on congregational melodies. BIBLIOGRAPHY: S. Kenney, Apel HDMus 236–237; A. Hughes Grove DMM 2:673.

[M. T. LEGGE]

DISCANTUS SUPRA LIBRUM, term usually applied to the elaborate methods of improvised harmonization on a single notated melody found "in the book," i.e., the book of Gregorian chant. BIBLIOGRAPHY: Apel HDMus 237–238.

[M. T. LEGGE]

DISCANTUS VISIBILIS, alternate name for a *sight,* i.e., a term in 15th–cent. English treatises indicating the range and permissible intervals of the voice parts added above a plainsong. BIBLIOGRAPHY: Apel HDMus, 775.

[M. T. LEGGE]

DISCERNMENT OF SPIRITS, a classical formula in ascetical theology to indicate the activity whereby a person comes to understand his own interior spiritual state and the phenomena (spiritual aridity, psychological motivations, inclinations to act, etc.) that manifest that state. The term is adopted from the NT, "Beloved, do not believe every spirit, but test the spirits to see whether they are of God" (1 Jn 4.1), and 1 Cor 12.10 where Paul speaks of the gift of distinguishing between spirits. These sections seem to proceed from Jewish belief at that time in good and evil spirits which regularly influenced human actions. This emphasis continued into the patristic period when the distinction between diabolical illusion and the promptings of the Holy Spirit was continually a matter of concern. In medieval times, however, discernment of spirits came to be synonymous with the virtue of prudence applied to questions of spiritual advancement more subtle than matters covered by ordinary norms of conduct. This orientation has continued until today, esp. in the Ignatian method of spirituality, although emphasis is placed upon experiential

insight rather than a totally speculative categorization of interior inclinations. BIBLIOGRAPHY: J. Pegon, DSAM 3:1222–1291; *idem,* NCE 4:893–895.

[T. M. MCFADDEN]

DISCIPLE (Lat. *discipulus,* "learner-pupil" and by extension "follower-adherent" of a teacher; an adequate translation of the Gr. *mathētēs* which occurs more than 250 times in the NT). In the singular it occurs seven times in the synoptic Gospels. The basic meaning, "pupil," is appropriate in Mt 10.24–25 and Lk 6.40 because of the clear contrast of the disciple with his teacher. Yet, in Mt, this passage lies in a section in which Jesus is instructing the newly appointed Apostles (10.5–11.1), whereas in Lk, it is placed within the Sermon on the Plain (6.17–49) where the identity and function of the disciples (followers) of Jesus are delineated. The meaning follower-adherent seems to be intended in the other occurrences (Mt 10.42; 27.57; Lk 14.26,27,33), where total commitment to Christ is stressed. The singular also occurs 16 times in Jn: twice to refer to one committed to Christ (9.28; 19.3) and 14 times in reference to "the other disciple" and "the disciple whom Jesus loved" who has been traditionally identified as John of Zebedee (Jn 18.15 [bis],16; 19.26,27 [four times]; 20.2, 3, 4, 8; 21.7, 20, 23, 24). In five occurrences in the Acts, it refers to individuals who follow the Christian way of life (Acts 9.10,26,36; 16.1; 21.16).

In the plural, the Gospels contain 13 clear references to the "disciples" of the Baptist (e.g., Mk 2.18; 6.29; Jn 1.35,37), three references to the "disciples" of the Pharisees (Mk 2.18; Mt 22.16) and one passage in which the Jewish leaders call themselves the "disciples" (followers) of Moses (Jn 9.28). The remaining occurrences of the term in the plural (*c.*200) refer to the "disciples" of Christ. Some of these are clearly identified, e.g.: Lk 6.17; 19.37 and Jn 6.66 refer to large groups of Christ's followers; Mt 10.1; 11.1 speak of "his twelve disciples (Apostles)"; Mt 28.16 speaks of "the eleven disciples (Apostles)"; Mt 17.6 speaks of the Peter and James and John as "disciples"; Jn 12.4 speaks of "one of his disciples, Judas"; Lk 10.1–17 refers to the 70 or 72 disciples who are sent forth to preach the Gospel with much the same instructions that the Apostles received in Mt 10.5–15 and Mk 6.7–11 (Lk seems to be indicating that others besides the Apostles have the duty of preaching the Gospel). Many feel that the remaining occurrences of the term disciples are somewhat ambiguous and can refer either to the followers of Christ in general or to the Apostles. Such a stand gives rise to at least one theological problem, with regard to the interpretation of Mt 18.18, where the disciples are given the power to bind and to loose. Although a recent study has proposed that Mt makes a precise distinction between "the disciples" (Gr. *hoi mathētai*) which ordinarily designates the Apostles and "his disciples" (*hoi mathētai autou*) which designates the followers of Christ in general. Previously a study of parallel passages and the context was the only means of discovering whether the reference was to the Apostles or the followers and this still remains the only means of determining the meaning of the term in Mk, Lk, and Jn who do not make the precise distinction made by Mt. In the Acts, beginning with 6.1 and continuing through 21.16, the term disciples is used 24 times to refer to Christians. This seems to have been a primitive usage which disappeared rather early. The term, Christian, which was first used in Antioch (Acts 11.26) supplanted it.

One must recognize a general tendency within the Gospels to form the spirit of the Apostles and confer the mission of the Apostles upon all Christians, with reservations regarding the authority and orders of the Apostles. Hence, the very ambiguity of the term disciple(s) seems somewhat functional. BIBLIOGRAPHY: E. R. Martinez, "Interpretation of 'Oi Mathētai' in Mt 18," CBQ 23 (1961) 281–292; R. Brown, *Gospel According to John* (Anchor Bible; 1966) 29.92–98.

[J. A. PIERCE]

DISCIPLES OF CHRIST, one of the names used by the followers of Alexander and Thomas *Campbell after 1830. In the early 20th cent. there was a division, with the conservative element taking the name Churches of Christ; the progressives, Disciples of Christ. The 1956 convention of the latter changed the name to Christian Churches, but Disciples of Christ remains the informal designation. *CHRISTIAN CHURCHES' (DISCIPLES OF CHRIST), INTERNATIONAL CONVENTION.

[N. H. MARING]

DISCIPLESHIP, derived from the NT "disciple," which is the Anglicized form of the Latin *discipulus,* by which the Vulgate translates *mathētēs* (learner or follower). In modern Protestant usage, the concept of discipleship stresses obedience to Jesus Christ. Instead of interpreting Christian life chiefly in terms of assent to doctrines, religious feelings, or participation in churchly activities, it implies that to be a Christian means to obey Christ in the totality of life. Thus the meaning of discipleship is akin to that underlying Thomas à Kempis's *Imitation of Christ.* Therein the writer explains his understanding of what it means to "follow His [Christ's] teachings and His manner of living" (1.1). The connection between the concept of the *Imitation* and discipleship is suggested by D. *Bonhoeffer in a work entitled in German *Nachfolge* (cf. German title of the *Imitation, Nachfolge Christi),* but which in English was translated *The Cost of Discipleship* (tr. R. H. Fuller, 1953). Asserting that "cheap grace" is grace without discipleship, he declared that faith is real only when it is expressed in obedience. Modern hymnals commonly have a section captioned "Discipleship," and parenthetically may note "Christian Life" as a synonym. Pastors often refer to preparatory classes for church membership as "discipleship classes," and publication houses publish discipleship materials for use in such classes.

Historically, there have been various conceptions of normative expressions of Christian life. The contemporary authority crisis has created problems for one who would set forth standards of individual or corporate Christian behavior. The inadequacy of traditional Protestant styles of Christian living has been described by E. Farley in *Requiem For A Lost Piety* (1966). A contemporary approach to Christian life is P. Hessart, *Christian Life* (1967). BIBLIOGRAPHY: F. H. Littell, "Discipline of Discipleship in the Free Church Tradition," *Mennonite Quarterly Review* 35 (1961) 111–119; J. A. Mackay, "Call To Discipleship," *Theology Today* 7 (1950) 217–227.

[N. H. MARING]

DISCIPLINE, a term referring to the way the life of Christians is to be ordered, particularly in the community life of the Church. In that sense it comprises the various elements of law and general procedure that the Churches have developed on the basis of Scripture and historical experience. The term discipline is also used for the summaries of such regulations, published under the title Book of Discipline. The book of discipline generally contains the requirements of the particular Church in regard to rights and responsibilities of officers and organizational units within the total church structure; procedures for ordaining clergy and assigning them to their individual places of service; rubrics by which the rites of the Church are to be conducted; acceptance and excommunication of members, and similar matters. Discipline is the Church's attempt to make *discipleship concrete. The Christian faith is viewed as a way of life in which believers are united in communities where they seek to obey the commands of Christ. In the past, it has often been asserted that a precise order of discipline could be derived from the NT, but the possibility of that is increasingly questioned. Emphasis is shifting, therefore, to an effort toward gaining from the NT an understanding of the basic purpose of the Church, with detailed regulations left for determination on the basis of their suitability for fulfilling that purpose.

The *Reformed tradition is noted for a special emphasis on discipline, and is sometimes interpreted as an attempt to make the strictly disciplined life of monastic communities the pattern for the whole Church. John Calvin asserted that the Church should regulate the religious and moral life of its members, and under his leadership the church in Geneva became famous for its strict discipline. Adapting Calvin's Geneva *Ordinances,* John *Knox published rules for reforming the Church in Scotland in First Book of Discipline (1560).

Discipline is often used with particular reference to that aspect of church government that involves correction of members for their failure to fulfill Church requirements. In the RC Church this aspect of discipline is exercised primarily by hierarchical authority, according to a complex system of penalties, e.g., excommunication, prescribed by canon law. In Protestant Churches this responsibility more often rests with the local congregation. In past generations an offender was often required to appear before a meeting of the congregation, which would consider his case and possibly excommunicate him if he were obstinate and did not show contrition. The procedure frequently led to an undue emphasis on minor matters, as well as a spirit of self-righteousness in those judging the conduct of their fellow Christians; general revulsion against such aspects, along with the spirit of a more tolerant age, has led to the virtual end of the practice. Many church leaders are seeking an alternative form of discipline, but none has been widely accepted.

[T. EARLY]

DISCIPLINE (METHODIST), a book containing the Constitution, General Rules, Articles of Religion, Government, and Ritual of the Methodist Church, as well as the decisions of the Judicial Council, the Social Creed, and Miscellaneous Resolutions of the *General Conference. The formal title is *Doctrines and Discipline of the Methodist Church.* In 1743 John Wesley wrote the General Rules for his *societies. Largely rules of conduct, they have been adopted by all Methodist bodies. In 1744 Wesley began calling yearly conferences of his preachers. Periodically he published cumulative summaries of the proceedings called "Large Minutes." When the Methodist Episcopal Church in America was organized in 1784 it adopted: (1) a Discipline based on Wesley's "Large Minutes" of 1780, (2) his Twenty-Four Articles of Religion, and (3) a *Ritual. The Articles of Religion were Wesley's abridgment of the *Thirty-Nine Articles of the Anglican Church. The Americans added a 25th Article: "Of the Rulers of the United States of America" (see TWENTY-FIVE ARTICLES OF RELIGION). The Ritual was Wesley's abridgment of the *Book of Common Prayer. In 1808 the Church adopted a Constitution. In time the Discipline was expanded to include these and other elements. With the merger that formed the Methodist Church in 1939, a new Discipline was adopted.

The Discipline may be revised quadrennially by the General Conference, which, among other restrictions, may not alter the General Rules or the Articles of Religion or abolish episcopacy. Methodist respect for the Discipline is seen in the book's "Episcopal Greetings," where it is referred to as "revelation of the Holy Spirit working in and through our people." BIBLIOGRAPHY: J. J. Tigert, *Constitutional History of American Episcopal Methodism* (1916); HistAmMeth 1.213–232; N. B. Harmon, *Organization of the Methodist Church* (2d rev. ed., 1962).

[F. E. MASER]

DISCIPLINE, THE, a whip to chastise the body as a penance. Originally used in a punishment prescribed by monastic rule, the use developed in the M Ages as a means of imitation of the scourging of Jesus (Mt 26.27); St. Peter Damian (d. 1072) particularly recommended the practice in his preaching and writing (*De laude flagellorum,* PL

145:679–686). Religious communities had a regular ritual with recitation of psalms—especially 50 (51) the *Miserere*—while the superior, celebrant, or the individual himself administered the whip to bared shoulders. While the earlier ascetics used thorn-branches, iron chains, or leather straps tipped with metal or bone, the instrument itself was gradually modified to strands of rope bound together and knotted at the ends. *Flagellation became a practice of penitential processions of the laity in the 13th cent. and lasted into the 19th cent. in Europe, and even to the 20th cent. in some places; but the instrument used was probably not a permanent part of home furniture as it was in a monastic cell. Suspicion of excesses, and even of sexual perversions such as sadism and masochism, along with modern moderation of penance, has caused the decline and practical disappearance of the discipline as ascetic equipment. BIBLIOGRAPHY: L. Gougaud, *Devotions and Ascetical Practices in the Middle Ages* (tr. G. C. Bateman, 1927).

[P. F. MULHERN]

DISCIPLINE, BOOK OF (PRESBYTERIAN), the title of two works on *polity. (1) The first, written largely by John Knox and approved by the General Assembly of the Church of Scotland in 1560, sets forth the "policy and discipline" by which the life of the Scottish nation was to be reformed. The chapters on the ministry, superintendents, and compulsory national education are esp. important, but the recommendations were never fully implemented, chiefly because the proposed educational system involved loss of revenue by the nobility. (2) A second Book of Discipline (1581) expounds the scheme of church government by which most Presbyterian Churches have been regulated. Written mainly by A. *Melville, the document distinguishes civil from ecclesiastical government and helped create a polity that secured cooperation between Church and State without confusing the jurisdiction proper to each. Church government ordinarily consists in the offices of minister, teacher, elder, and deacon. The powers of *presbytery, *synod, and *general assembly are also defined. See bibliog. for Church of Scotland.

DISCIPLINE, ECCLESIASTICAL, like discipline in general, it may be understood as (1) a set of rules governing conduct, or (2) the formation envisaged by such rules, or (3) the orderly conduct that ensues from the observance of such rules. At times the word is used in ways that fuse some or all of these meanings. Here both terms are significant: "discipline" focuses on the area of conduct in so far as it can be distinguished from the area of doctrine and belief; "ecclesiastical" reminds one that he is talking of a set of regulations not (for the most part) immediately enacted by God but by those who have governed in Christ's name within the apostolic succession. Currently the discipline as it affects the Latin Church (CIC c. 1) is embodied largely in the *Code of Canon Law, which took effect on May 19, 1918. Discipline can also be determined for particular areas by councils and episcopal conferences, and within the diocese by the bishop. In the Catholic view the right to establish discipline is found in the charge given by Our Lord to the Twelve and in the understanding of this charge within the Church from the time of the Apostles themselves. The maintenance of discipline presents continual and delicate problems, for discipline does not exist for its own sake. At times there may be too great a tendency in the Church as in other large and long-standing societies to retain disciplinary provisions that have outlived their usefulness, but it is clear too that discipline has changed, is in process of change, and will continue to change as the conditions of life change for the members of the Church. BIBLIOGRAPHY: E. Dublanchy, DTC 3.1:567–568; J. Gewiess, LTK 6:284–286.

[S. E. DONLON]

DISCIPLINE OF THE SACRAMENTS, CONGREGATION FOR THE, see SACRAMENTS AND DIVINE WORSHIP, SACRED CONGREGATION FOR THE.

DISCIPLINE OF THE SECRET *(disciplina arcani),* a custom in the early Christian church of concealing certain doctrines and religious practices from the catechumens and pagans as a safeguard against persecution and profanation. It was in use mostly during the first 5 cent. and was reflected in the custom of not admitting catechumens to the Mass of the Faithful in the Eucharistic Celebration. Symbolic reminders were the fish, the lamb, and the shepherd found in the ancient catacombs. Reference to the practice has been found in the writings of Tertullian, St. Cyprian, and Origen, as well as those of SS. Cyril and John Chrysostom in the East and SS. Ambrose and Augustine in the West. The custom was abandoned by the 6th cent., but a form of it has been in use in the African missions of the White Fathers. BIBLIOGRAPHY: F. Oppenheim, EncCatt 1:1793–97.

[R. A. TODD]

DISCORD, a fault here taken to mean a want of harmony or concord between persons when this results in a positive clash of wills likely to spill over into quarreling, antagonism, and strife. Moreover, it supposes that the harmony or concord that is wanting ought to be present. Thus it is not to be identified simply with difference of opinion, because unity of mind and judgment, except in certain essential matters, is not possible and is not per se an offense against Christian peace and concord. It becomes sinful when it involves a culpable disregard of the Christian's obligation to love God and to love his neighbor as himself. When this happens, it is more or less seriously sinful depending on the culpability of the cause from which it flows (e.g., vanity, perhaps, or obstinacy), or the seriousness of the strife and contention in which it debouches. BIBLIOGRAPHY: J. Fearon, NCE 4:896–897.

[P. K. MEAGHER]

DISCOURAGEMENT, a state of sadness and disheartenment in which one loses confidence in his efforts because of a real or imagined want of success in the fulfillment of his expectations. It falls short of despondency or despair, but it can be a serious obstacle to spiritual progress as well as a severe trial of soul. Sometimes a prolonged or profound discouragement may be the product of psycho-physical causes and can amount to a major or minor depressed phase in the manic-depressive cycle. In such cases the help of a psychiatrist and the use of the medicines or other treatment he may prescribe can be helpful. In other cases, the disheartenment may be the result of the unreasonable expectations of the afflicted person, or perhaps of the expectations imposed on him by family or friends. Sometimes the discouragement can be due to environmental or family situations that are not easily remedied. In such cases recourse to special prayer and the help of a sympathetic confessor or counselor may be valuable. Spiritual reading, esp. centered upon topics that tend to reinforce hope, such as the mercy and the love of God, is to be recommended. It should be noted that a state of discouragement, besides being sometime a spiritual obstacle, may also serve a good purpose, because, as is evident in the lives of many saints, it may serve as a preparation for a new step forward in the spiritual life. BIBLIOGRAPHY: W. Herbst, NCE 4:897.

[P. K. MEAGHER]

DISCRETIO SPIRITUUM, see DISCERNMENT OF SPIRITS.

DISCRETION. The Vulg *discretio* translates the Gr. NT *diakrisis,* the power of discernment of spirits, and between good and evil (1 Cor 12.10). In a general way discretion or discernment may be understood of the perceptiveness characteristic of the act and virtue of *prudence, i.e., its sensitivity to the requirements of virtue in each singular instance. More particularly, it may be taken for the wit to deal with exceptional cases (*gnomē* in St. Thomas's Lat. text, 2a2ae.51.4), and means judiciousness where ordinary rules of acting do not apply. As discretion is taken for discreteness, it describes a quality of the virtue of *truthfulness that observes proper reticence. But historically in spiritual theology, the discernment of spirits has a more specialized meaning. Its need and function are described in antiquity by *John Cassian and St. *John Climacus; in the Middle Ages by *Richard of St. Victor and St. *Bernard of Clairvaux, by Jean *Gerson and *Denis the Carthusian. It is prominent in St. *Ignatius of Loyola's rules for spiritual living, in the writings of Card. *Bona, G. B. *Scaramelli, and A. *Tanquerey. In general it means perceptiveness, the power to discriminate among the "spirits" of the soul, i.e., the movements toward good or evil. As a person progresses and may be more seriously subjected to temptation, judgment on the rightness and source of the soul's experiences requires special perceptiveness. The discernment of spirits, then, is particularly needed by a spiritual director; it presupposes study and prayer on his part, but esp. his own sensitivity to the guidance of the Holy Spirit. The *charismatic gift *discretio spirituum* in I Cor 12.10 empowers the recipient to know, for the good of others, the secrets of heart known only to God (ThAq ST 1a2ae. 111,4). This charism is recognized in the lives of many saints, e.g., SS. Philip Neri, John Vianney, and Rose of Lima.

[T. C. O'BRIEN]

DISCRIMINATION, here understood as the distinction made in favor of or against persons based on their group, class, race, nationality, religion, or sex, rather than upon their individual merits. It denies to persons what is their due according to civil law and/or the Christian law of love, and/or common human decency. It is an offense against civil law when the rights are transgressed in defiance of constitution or statutory law, and it is always an offense against Christian charity, more or less grave according to the importance of the good withheld from the person discriminated against, and the gravity of the harm that is done.

[P. K. MEAGHER]

DISCRIMINATION, ECONOMIC, the unjust denial of economic benefits, or opportunities. The injustice may be against *distributive justice, which requires that each member of a community receive what is due in proportion to his rank, contributions, or even his needs, according to the measure of the *common good. The injustice may violate *commutative justice, where, namely, some person is preferred and another deprived with regard to work, wages, or any economic advantage, solely for personal reasons, unrelated to the issue involved, i.e., race, sex, age. *ECONOMIC JUSTICE.

[T. C. O'BRIEN]

DISEASES SCROLL, 12th cent. Japanese *emaki,* now divided among many collections, which, together with the *emaki* of the Hungry Demons and Hells, reflects Buddhist teaching of the Six Roads of endless Reincarnation. The Diseases Scroll is treated by the artist with a touch of humor rather than with ugliness or sadism. BIBLIOGRAPHY: H. Okudaira, *Emake* (1962).

[M. J. DALY]

DISENTIS, ABBEY OF, Benedictine foundation of the 8th cent. in the upper Rhine valley, Switzerland. After a long history of apostolic and cultural service to the surrounding Rhaetian land, it became in the 18th cent., and remains, an important center for the Romansh languages, culture, and spirituality.

[J. F. FALLON]

DISESTABLISHMENT, a term referring generally to withdrawal of the legal status of an *established Church and particularly to a movement in England. In the 19th cent., English *Nonconformists won freedom from former disabilities and engaged in efforts to abolish establishment. Congregationalists, such as R. W. Dale and Edward Miall, were foremost in the sustained effort for disestablishment. In 1844, the British Anti-State Church Association (later the Liberation Society) was formed. As other rights were granted, however, opposition to establishment waned. Subsequently, some voices have been raised within the Church of England itself for disestablishment, particularly after the House of Commons rejected (1927–28) the proposed changes in the Book of Common Prayer long desired by many Anglicans (see REVISED PRAYER BOOK). More recently, prominent persons, such as Cyril Garbett, Abp. of York, have insisted upon more self-government for the Church, even if it means disestablishment. BIBLIOGRAPHY: H. Davies, *English Free Churches* (1952); C. Garbett, *Church and State in England* (1950).

[N. H. MARING]

DISHYPATOS, DAVID, see DAVID DISHYPATOS.

DISINTERESTED LOVE, historically, a controverted theme, associated with 17th-cent. *Quietism in Italy (see *MOLINOS, MIGUEL), and the later *amour pur* issue that divided F. *Fénelon and J. *Bossuet (see GUYON, J.). The Quietist or semi-Quietist meaning is that there is a love for God so pure and detached from self that it includes even equanimity about one's own eternal damnation. Historical considerations apart, simply as a concept, a love disinterested to the point of self-negation is incompatible with the meaning of *charity. St. Thomas Aquinas provides a way for theology to express that meaning by his description of the relationship between love and union. A union in being or likeness is the cause of love; love itself is an affective union of two persons with each other; the effect love seeks is a union of presence between the lovers that is consistent with their relationship (ThAq ST 1a2ae, 28.1 and ad 2). He accordingly describes charity, not as simple benevolence that can be one-sided, but as a friendship, because it is a mutual love, a love returning love (*ibid*, 65.5). God by his love communicates the likeness to the divine, i.e., sonship, that makes a mutual love between son and Father possible, and that tends to eternal presence with the Father (see DIVINE NATURE, PARTAKERS OF). The child loves the Father more than self in the sense that God is more than self; but the love cannot exist to the exclusion of self, for union is of two persons. Eternal blessedness with God is sought, but not as subordinating God to one's own happiness; the vision of God is beatific since it is union with God. The element of truth in the meaning of a disinterested love is that only God is capable of a total giving, a total generosity; in loving, the creature is fulfilled, no matter how generous the love, because the creature is not self-sufficient; even the giving is a receiving (see FINALITY, PRINCIPLE OF).

[T. C. O'BRIEN]

DISKOS (Gr., disk, plate), the plate used in the Byzantine Church to hold the bread that is offered and sanctified in the divine liturgy. Equivalent to the Roman paten, it too is made of gold or silver or at least gilded metal. It was originally a large tray or platter on which the deacon bore the consecrated bread, as can still be seen in many magnificent specimens of the 5th and 6th centuries. The modern *diskos* is rarely larger than about eight inches in diameter and has a rim and concave inner surface. The Russian style adds an attached base or foot to facilitate its carrying in procession, and this style is now usually found among the Greeks and other Byzantines. The flat, footless *diskos* is still used by some Orthodox, and among the Melkites and some other Eastern Catholics. The Ukrainian and Ruthenian Catholics at times simply use a Roman-style paten. The *diskos* is always placed to the left of the *poterion* (chalice) when on the table of preparation or the altar, and is never placed on top of the chalice as in the Roman rite. After the Holy Bread has been placed in the chalice the Ukrainian and Ruthenian Catholics use the *diskos* as a sort of communion plate, which is held by the priest along with the chalice to prevent particles from falling to the ground, a practice unknown in Orthodoxy. The Melkites, since they alone in the Byzantine Rite no longer use the spoon to distribute communion, leave the consecrated bread on the *diskos,* and the priest, holding both *diskos* and chalice in one hand if there is no deacon to assist, dips the bread (intinction) from the *diskos* into the chalice and then places it in the mouth of the communicant. The term *diskos* is also applied to any plate used to hold bread during a liturgical service.

[A. J. JACOPIN]

DISMAS, ST., the name most frequently given to the repentant thief who died with Christ on Calvary. The Gospels do not identify either of the thieves by name, but apocryphal literature invented a number of names for both. In the West the good thief has more commonly been called Dismas, the unrepentant thief Gestas. According to popular legend, Dismas was rewarded on Calvary because he had protected Our Lady and her Child at the time of the flight into Egypt. The cult of the good thief dates from the 9th or 10th cent. in the East, and from the 14th in the West. D. is venerated as patron of those in prison. BIBLIOGRAPHY: Butler 1:676–677. *GOOD THIEF.

DISMISSAL OF RELIGIOUS.

DISOBEDIENCE, CIVIL, see CIVIL DISOBEDIENCE.

DISPARITY OF CULT, the name given in RC canon law to a diriment impediment to marriage between a baptized RC and an unbaptized person. Unless a dispensation from this impediment is granted by competent authority, the impediment renders the marriage null and void, and illicit. The validity of the contract thus hinges upon valid re-ception of RC baptism by one of the parties prior to marriage, while the other remains unbaptized. In the early Church, marriages of the faithful with those who had not accepted the faith were forbidden. Although the displine has varied in the course of time in certain particulars, the present law as described in the Code of Canon Law provides that marriages attempted without dispensation from this impediment are null (CIC c. 1070, par. 1). There are obvious disadvantages to such marriages from a Catholic point of view, for they may easily lead to the breakdown of the marriage. The important question of mixed marriages received several times the attention of Vatican Council II, and it was seen that the discipline of the Church needed better formulation. The latest general rules governing these marriages are to be found in the *motu proprio* of Pope Paul VI, *Matrimonia mixta,* which was issued March 31, 1970 and became effective Oct. 1, 1970. There are set forth the conditions and consequences of a dispensation. The penalties decreed by CIC c. 2319 are all abrogated. A marriage between a Catholic and an unbaptized person is, if entered without a dispensation, invalid, and even when a dispensation has been granted, is probably not a sacrament, even for the Catholic party. The Church, however, in certain circumstances and for a just cause is prepared to dispense from the impediment, on condition that the Catholic party undertakes to avoid the danger of falling away from the faith, and sincerely promises to do all in his power to have all the children baptized and brought up in the RC Church. The *motu proprio* has put the onus firmly upon the Catholic partner. The canonical form must be observed for the validity of the marriage.

[A. FARRELL]

DISPENSATION, a word that may in religious use have different meanings: (1) a system or method of achieving salvation decreed by God in the form of a covenant—thus, e.g., we speak of New and Old Dispensations, just as we do of New and Old Covenants; (2) in RC canon law a provision whereby an ecclesiastical legislator, his successor, or those delegated to do so, may relax the binding power of a law in special circumstances or in particular cases so that in these circumstances or cases, individuals are not obliged to do what the law enjoins or to avoid what the law forbids. A dispensation is not an abrogation of the law itself, which remains intact and continues to bind those not dispensed from its observance. According to CIC c. 81, the power to grant dispensations from ecclesiastical laws, whether universal or territorial, belongs exclusively to the Roman Pontiff, though he may, with regard to particular laws, delegate others to grant dispensations. In diocesan statutes the ordinary of a diocese may dispense from their observance in particular cases or in special circumstances. Some laws are considered to be immediately of divine origin, and from the observance of these no dispensation is possible. (3) Dispensation is also a term used in reference to the administration of the sacraments. To dispense the Eucharist means to administer that sacrament.

[P. K. MEAGHER]

DISPENSATIONALISM, a system of Bible interpretation set in a framework of a particular type of *premillenarianism. Fundamental to the system is the concept "dispensation," defined as "a period of time during which man is tested in respect to his obedience to some specific revelation of the will of God" (New Scofield Reference Bible [1967] 3). "Dispensation" is an Anglicized form of the Latin equivalent of the Greek word *oikonomia,* which means administration, management, or economy, as of a household or business. The implication of the word for this system is that God has dealt with men at different periods on different terms. Seven dispensations are distinguished: (1) Innocence, during the Edenic covenant in which man was tested by the prohibition of eating of the tree of the knowledge of good and evil; (2) Conscience, after expulsion from the garden, the testing of men by a requirement to avoid all evil known by conscience; (3) Human government, during which men were in submission to laws made by fellowmen, and governments were given the right of capital punishment; (4) Promise, during the Abrahamic covenant, making unconditional promise of blessing through Abraham's seed; (5) Law, when Israel, though remaining under the Abrahamic covenant, was placed under a disciplinary system; (6) Church, the era beginning with the postresurrection outpouring of the Holy Spirit when salvation depends upon belief in the gospel of Jesus Christ; and (7) Kingdom, the millennium, the time when God's promises to Israel will be fulfilled as the faithful are restored to their land under the Davidic monarch, with Christ as king. This millennial kingdom involves only Israel and has nothing to do with the Church. At its close, Satan's final rebellion takes place; he is cast into the lake of fire, and Christ delivers the kingdom to the Father.

While focusing upon eschatology, dispensational premillenarianism involves the meaning and significance of the entire Bible. Its advocates emphasize their consistent literalism, including fulfillment of OT prophecies, a sharp discontinuity between Israel and the Church, and the removal of the Church from earth (pretribulation rapture) before the millennium. To some conservative Christians the entire system seems fantastic, and has been labeled a heresy. Its critics charge that its ideas are novel, its typology fanciful, and its hermeneutical principles arbitrary. Its proponents, however, consider "dispensational truth" the only valid approach to the Bible. Having roots in the *Plymouth Brethren movement, the ideas were given systematic form in the *Scofield Reference Bible first published in 1909 (rev. 1917 and 1967). L. S. Chafer published *Systematic Theology* (8 v., 1947), embodying the system, and Dallas Theological Seminary makes dispensationalism pivotal in its curriculum. Many *Bible schools have used the Scofield Bible as a text, and thousands of people have been so indoctrinated in the system as to make them suspicious of all who disagree. Hence, dispensationalism has been the source of divisiveness among conservative Christians. BIBLIOGRAPHY: For a positive view by a modern scholar, see C. C. Ryrie, *Dispensationalism Today* (1965, pa. 1975). For a critique by a former dispensationalist, see C. B. Bass, *Backgrounds to Dispensationalism* (1960).

[N. H. MARING]

DISPERSION OF THE APOSTLES, the feast—not universally observed—commemorating their departure on their missionary journeys. Through the endeavors of the Apostles to spread the gospel to all nations, God's will was carried out for the conversion of the world, substituting a new diaspora for the Jewish one. St. James mentions this (Jas 1.1); Peter (1 Pet 1.1) and Luke (Acts 2.1–11) speak about forming the new people of God in order to lead dispersed mankind back into the unity of faith. The children of God are gathered together by the sacrifice of Christ (Jn 11,52). BIBLIOGRAPHY: DBT 10.

[A. P. HANLON]

DISPUTATION OF LEIPZIG, theological debate, June 27–July 16, 1519, in which J. *Eck opposed first A. *Karlstadt and then Martin *Luther. A literary exchange between Eck and Karlstadt had already taken place over Luther's *Ninety-Five Theses. Once Luther intervened in the debates (from July 4), Eck, the experienced disputant, made the doctrinal authority of the Church the central issue and drew from Luther an unequivocal agreement with doctrines of Jan *Hus against papal authority. The Disputation marked the end of Luther's earlier hesitations; his direct antipapal assaults, *The Liberty of the Christian Man, To the Christian Nobility of the German Nation,* and *On the Babylonian Captivity of the Church,* all appeared in 1520, as did the bull *Exsurge Domine* excommunicating him. BIBLIOGRAPHY: R. Fife, *Revolt of Martin Luther* (1957) 327–394.

DISPUTATIONS, SCHOLASTIC, classroom debates, formerly used in seminary philosophic and theological courses, conducted in strict syllogistic form. The protagonist *(defendens)* proposed a thesis and a set of strict arguments establishing it; the antagonist *(objiciens)* argued against it syllogistically, and his arguments had to be met and countered in strict logical form. (see QUAESTIO DISPUTATA.)

[T. C. O'BRIEN]

DISSENT, THEOLOGY OF, the theological grounds for resisting lawful authority; the term as such is linked with the unrest of the 1960s, with movements of civil disobedience (see NONVIOLENT RESISTANCE), but the issues it denotes are perennial. There is a natural tension between individual *conscience, the immediate rule for a person's right moral choices (to be against conscience is the immediate index of sinfulness in an action) and the meaning of obedience, which entails accepting a superior's decision as the rule for right action (ThAq ST 2a2ae, 104.1 ad 1, ad 2, ad 3; 2 ad 3). One element for resolution of a crisis arising out of that tension is a right evaluation of obedience. Virtuous obedience is not outward compliance to rule; it is the inner choice to obey. That means the inner acceptance of the legitimacy of the authority commanding and the acceptance of a command as formative in the decision of conscience to obey. Disagreement of mind about the issue involved is perfectly compatible with a choice to obey. To obey while disagreeing is not to act against conscience, since the choice to obey implies honest acceptance of the authority of the superior. On the other hand an honestly and responsibly based conviction that to choose to obey would amount to choosing to sin precludes obeying. Such a conviction is involved in the meaning of conscientious objection to military service or to war. Two other concrete areas of life call for a theology of dissent. In the case of political dissent in civil society, actual resistance to law or to a political regime has to be guided by consideration of the general welfare of the community as a whole. Dissent is legitimate where there is injustice; it cannot, however, be expressed in courses of action more upsetting than is the injustice it seeks to remedy. Dissent within the Church is a second and complex issue. Vatican Council II affirmed that religious freedom is a right inherent in the dignity of the human person; that no one can be forced to act in a manner contrary to conscience nor be restrained from acting in accord with conscience; that no simply human power can command or prohibit the internal, voluntary, free acts that constitute the exercise of religion (VatII RelFreed, n.3). Within the life of the Church itself the Council also affirmed that "all the faithful, clerical and lay, possess a lawful freedom of inquiry and thought, and the freedom to express their mind humbly and courageously about those matters in which they enjoy competence" (VatII ChModWorld, n.62). With reference to the laity in particular, the Council stated that "every layman should openly reveal (to pastors) his needs and desires with that freedom and confidence which befits a son of God and a brother in Christ. An individual layman, by reason of the knowledge, competence, or outstanding ability which he may enjoy, is permitted and sometimes even obliged to express his opinion in things which concern the good of the Church. When occasions arise let this be done through the agencies set up by the Church for that purpose. Let it always be done in truth, in courage, and in prudence, with reverence and charity towards those who by reason of their sacred office represent the person of Christ" (VatII ConstCh, n.37). Theological or activist dissent in the Church cannot be legitimate in matters of faith itself, since faith rests on the believer's adherence and assent to God himself as the authenticator of matters of faith; such faith is engaged in matters solemnly proposed by the magisterium. Dissent can have place in lesser matters of doctrine and discipline. Because the Church is hierarchic, acceptance of membership

means acceptance of an obedience relationship to authority; speaking in 1977 on the revision of canon law Paul VI ruled out conscientious objection to church law, which would destroy ecclesiastical obedience. An attitude that pits a person or group against church authority as an adversary does not respect the implications of church membership or obedience. An attitude in authorities in the Church that is coercive and repressive does not respect the inner quality of religion itself nor that their office is to serve. The opportunity for dissent is often the opportunity for growth: to be fruitful thought and action need to be carried out in respect, in charity, and in giving proper proportion to the individual's place vis à vis the whole believing community.

[T. C. O'BRIEN]

DISSENTERS, a term applied broadly to a variety of English protesters. The name originated during the Restoration and was first used by the *Westminster Assembly (1643), referring to its *Independent members as "dissenting brethren." The term became common after 1662, when previous *Nonconformists were ejected from the established Church and called Dissenters. Nonconformist and Dissenter soon became interchangeable terms, replacing the earlier Puritan label, and were applied to all Protestants not communicants of the C of E. Logically Catholics should have been included in the appellation, but they were known as Recusants. Congregationalists, Baptists, and Presbyterians comprised the bulk of the Dissenters at first; Friends (Quakers) and Unitarians were small but influential minorities. Methodists, separately organized in 1791, during the 19th cent. became the largest Nonconformist Church. By 1900, the term *free Churches was replacing the designations Dissenter and Nonconformist. BIBLIOGRAPHY: E. Routley, *English Religious Dissent* (1960); B. R. White, *English Separatist Tradition: From the Marian Martyrs to the Pilgrim Fathers* (1971).

[N. H. MARING]

DISSIDENT, in a religious sense a term used of groups that reject the established Church. More commonly employed on the Continent, it is equivalent to dissenter, the more usual term in Britain. Even Churches that have official status in their own areas, such as some of the Orthodox Churches, have been considered dissidents by Roman Catholics. With growing secularism altering the status of all Churches, and the changed atmosphere of an ecumenical age, the term is less frequently employed.

[T. EARLY]

DISSIMULATION. (1) In moral theology, a concealment of the truth about oneself, esp. through a deed rather than through words. Its morality is evaluated on the basis of the meaning of the virtue of *truthfulness. That virtue includes reticence where reticence is called for and may include the rightness of concealing the truth. Lying or deceitful simulation are never morally right, but speaking or acting in a way that protects rightful privacy, another's good name, or professional secrecy, belong to the virtue of truthfulness. (2) In the discipline regulating the administration of the sacraments, dissimulation may be dictated in some instances. It is distinct from simulation of a sacrament, i.e., deceiving the would-be recipient. But, for example, a priest hearing confessions in a place visible to others might rightly simply bless a penitent whom he cannot absolve in order to prevent possible observers from the knowledge that absolution was refused.

[T. C. O'BRIEN]

DISSOCIATION, as understood in psychiatry, a term used to designate pathological phenomena characterized by failure to be integrated into the total pattern of perception, thought, memory, feeling, etc. One example is amnesia, in which a person is unable to recollect events from a certain period of his past; another is multiple personality, in which a person alternates between one personality pattern and another, and is often unaware of the fact. Dissociation implies severe mental and emotional stress. For the confessor, counsellor, spiritual director, etc., dissociation should be a sign of need for psychiatric treatment. Moral responsibility for actions performed in a genuinely dissociated state is practically nonexistent.

[M. E. STOCK]

DISSOLUTION OF MARRIAGE, see INDISSOLUBILITY OF MARRIAGE.

DISSOLUTION OF THE MONASTERIES, the gradual confiscation of the income and property of the English monasteries by Henry VIII. The religious houses had become unpopular both with the *New Learning of the 16th cent. and with Henry himself. Although many monasteries performed invaluable educational and charitable services, others were noted for intellectual lethargy and greed. But Henry's need for money, not the ideal of reform, moved him, through his agent T. *Cromwell, to suppress the monasteries. Two royal commissioners sent on a visitation of the monasteries wrote, in what became known as the "Black Book," a grossly exaggerated report of monastic simony and immorality. The report pointed out that the smaller monasteries were the most guilty, and in 1536 Parliament suppressed all monasteries with revenues below £1,200 a year, giving their incomes to the King. Obviously the incomes of the larger monasteries presented a continual temptation to Henry's greed—a temptation that was for the moment thwarted by the Pilgrimage of Grace, an uprising over the suppression of the smaller monasteries. By 1539, however, the strength of the King was so great that one after the other of the larger monasteries was forced to surrender, the Carthusians holding out the longest and providing a number of martyrs. Eventually even the shrine of St. Thomas at Canterbury was despoiled, and wagonloads of

gold, silver, precious stones, and costly vestments were taken to the King. Some of the funds from the suppression were used to establish new sees in England. BIBLIOGRAPHY: Hughes RE 1:36–89, 282–329.

[F. E. MASER]

DISTINCTIO, alternate term for *divisio,* the division, in Gregorian chant, of text and melody into sections, according to the sense of the words and the structure of the music. BIBLIOGRAPHY: O. Thompson, ed. *The International Cyclopedia of Music and Musicians,* 1964, p. 550.

[M. T. LEGGE]

DISTLER, HUGO (1908–42), German organist and composer. D. studied at the Leipzig Conservatory and subsequently held posts as organist and professor of music, notably at Stuttgart. He composed both sacred and secular choral works, chamber, organ, and piano music. His *Jahrkreis,* a collection of motets for amateur choirs, is an example of the contemporary idiom adapted to church usage. He is regarded as one of the most strongly individual personalities among the younger German church composers. BIBLIOGRAPHY: H. Strobel and K. Bartlett, Grove DMM 2:712–713.

[M. T. LEGGE]

DISTRACTION, in prayer, the alien images or thoughts, often affectively toned, that intrude on its attention or divert its intention. In the second case they stop the prayer; in the first case, esp. when they are not really wilful, though they may detract from the effect of spiritual refreshment, prayer still continues effectively and meritoriously. Talking with God is not, after all, the same thing as closely following a discussion or arguing a case, and though there is a disciplined art of mental prayer, there are schools and masters to bid us take it easily and without straining at it. Some fluctuation of attention does little to hold down the lifting of the mind to God. Distractions may arise from fatigue, bodily discomfort, being solicitous, like Martha, about many things. They are best treated by being "prayed through." BIBLIOGRAPHY: R. Vernay, DSAM 3:1347–63; ThAq ST 2a2ae, 83.13.

[T. GILBY]

DISTRIBUTISM, a social and political philosophy, articulate and active between 1910 and 1930, which attacked socialism on one side and big business on the other, and advocated the spread of private property and the devolution of responsibility for production. A key book is H. Belloc's *Servile State* (1912), and he and his friend, G. K. Chesterton, headed a campaign that banded together many able writers; their forum was known successively as *Eye Witness* (1911–13), *New Witness* (1912–23), *G. K.'s Weekly* (1925–38), and *Weekly Review* (1938–46). The Middle Ages were sometimes unduly romanticized, but there was a wealth of good writing, polemical, historical, poetical, and a zest that occasionally rose to the pitch of shrillness. The "Chester-Belloc" has proved to have more pride in ancestry than hope for posterity. Its argument has not been refuted but rather has gone by default in a world that increasingly centralizes the means of production and leaves power to the middleman of finance and consumption—promotion. As a protest movement Distributism did something to keep the public conscience alive to some of the drearier and remediable aspects of industrialized society, yet it became somewhat a scold and a sectary on the subjects of machinery and the party system, and, unconstructive and withdrawn from national processes, it distracted a generation of Christians from playing their full and proper part in the control of economic and political power. BIBLIOGRAPHY: J. M. Cleary, *Catholic Social Action in Britain, 1909–59* (1961); R. P. Walsh, NCE 4:912.

[T. GILBY]

DISTRIBUTIVE JUSTICE, see JUSTICE.

DISTRICT SUPERINTENDENT (METHODIST), an important administrative officer in the Methodist Church. He is a minister appointed by the bp. and supervises a number of churches (see CHARGE) within a geographical area or district of the *Annual Conference. The Conference determines the number of districts within its boundaries, and the bp. decides the boundaries of the districts after consultation with his district superintendents. The *Discipline carefully outlines the numerous duties of the district superintendent; chief among them are the duty to travel through his district to preach, to oversee the spiritual and temporal affairs of his churches, and to see that the Discipline is enforced and the program of the General Conference carried out. In the absence of the bp., during the intervals between Annual Conferences, the district superintendent may receive, change, or appoint preachers to the churches. The district superintendents of the Annual Conference make up the bp.'s cabinet. They represent the preachers on the cabinet and advise the bp. concerning preachers' appointments. They also act as a liaison between the bp. and the churches. The district superintendent serves on many important committees of the Conference, and his work, while not necessarily spectacular, is a source of strength to the Methodist organization. BIBLIOGRAPHY: N. B. Harmon, *Understanding the Methodist Church* (1955) 124; *Doctrines and Discipline of the Methodist Church* (1964).

[F. E. MASER]

DITTERS VON DITTERSDORF, KARL (1739–99), Austrian violinist and composer, pupil of König, Ziegler, and Bonno, a friend and contemporary of Gluck and Haydn. His activities centered aoround the princely houses of central Europe. He enjoyed an excellent reputation as a violinist and was a very popular composer, esp. of comic operas. In addition, he composed symphonies, concertos, operettas, several oratorios, cantatas, Masses, motets, and songs. His autobiography in English translation was published in 1896. BIBLIOGRAPHY: C. Pohl, Grove DMM 2:714–715.

[M. T. LEGGE]

DIURNAL, a book containing all the hours of the *Liturgy of the Hours except *matins. *DAY HOURS.

[N. KOLLAR]

DIVES (Lat., rich man), the name popularly given to the rich man who figures in a parable Jesus uttered about the right use of riches (Lk 16.19–31). The rich man died and was buried in Hades not because he was wealthy, but because while Lazarus, the poor man in the parable, had gone hungry, he had lived in luxury.

[R. T. A. MURPHY]

DIVINA COMMEDIA (Divine Comedy), the towering Christian epic composed by Dante Alighieri and completed *c.*1317 in Ravenna where Dante lived in exile. The work is comparable in scope to the Homeric and Virgilian epics. It sums up the thinking and knowledge of the entire period from the Fall of Rome to the Renaissance. Dante chose to write in Italian (and in so doing set Tuscan as the classic mode of Italian) though most literary and scholarly work was couched in Latin. Composed in *terza rima,* which Dante moulded, it consists of 100 cantos in three major sections: *Inferno, Purgatorio,* and *Paradiso.* In Dante's vision he is led by Virgil, representing human philosophy and human virtue, through hell, then purgatory. Beatrice, his lifelong love, leads him through the natural paradise to the true paradise illumined by the sight of God. Here St. Bernard becomes his guide who leads him to the Blessed Virgin. Through her he has a foretaste of the beatific vision where all knowing and loving are united in the Divine Essence. The *Divine Comedy* in vision and execution stands in the first rank of world literature. BIBLIOGRAPHY: É. Gilson, *Dante and Philosophy* (tr. D. Moore, 1949, repr. 1963); A. H. Gilbert, *Dante and His Comedy* (1963).

[J. R. AHERNE]

DIVINATION, the prediction of unknowable future events, or the uncovering of the occult, by arcane arts, sciences, and demonic compact. From ancient times seers and diviners, to inform clients about the future or the will of a provident divinity, used various mantic methods: oracular utterance, interpretation of portents and omens (augury), reading of the viscera of sacrificial animals, the use of lots (sorcery), the computation of celestial bodies (astrology), the invocation of the dead (necromancy), dream interpretation etc. In Mesopotamian culture divination was a revered function of priests. In early Israel, when one consulted God about the unknown, his priests and prophets used an *ephod* and sacred lots called *urim* and *thummim,* but divination of all sorts was explicitly prescribed (Dt 18.9–12). Saul's evocation of Samuel's ghost through the medium of Endor is recorded but not approved (1 Sam 28.3–25).

In the NT unclean spirits recognized the still secret identity of Jesus (Mk 1.23,24,34c; 3.11; 5.7), and a divining slave girl who had a mantic spirit identified Paul and his companions as "slaves of the most high God" (Acts 16.16–18). Divination may have been condemned under the terms for magical arts and cultic deception (Gal 5.20; Rev 21.8; 22.15).

Christian theology classifies divination as a species of superstition opposed to the virtue of religion, which gives due reverence to God. Its evil lies in presuming to foresee, foretell, or uncover something that God alone can know and reveal: one usurps divine power to make oneself be or appear divine. Legitimate prognostication interprets the projected effectiveness of observed causes, as in the arts and sciences of meteorology, astronomy, medicine, politics, etc., and involve no divination. Its further specific evil consists in the element of demonic assistance to do or know what is impossible for man, whether demons are expressly invoked or whether vain inquisitiveness about the unknowable subjects the unwary to demonic influence, deception, and involvement in the occult sciences to the detriment of the worship of God. The present widespread mania for the occult, for drug-induced psychedelic experience, and for astrology is a consequence of the rejection of belief in, and reverence for, God.

[J. F. FALLON]

DIVINE CHARITY, DAUGHTERS OF, a congregation founded by Mother Franziska Lechner in 1868 in Vienna, Austria, for the apostolates of education and social work. The sisters follow the Rule of St. Augustine and their constitutions have pontifical approval. The congregation in Europe and the U.S. is divided into provinces and independent houses governed by provincials and local superiors, all subject to the superior-general in Rome. The community's first foundation in the U.S. was a residence for business and professional women in New York City. As of 1975, professed members in the U.S. numbered more than 200 in three provinces: New York, Ohio, and Michigan. Nursing was added recently as a community apostolate.

[S. A. HEENEY]

DIVINE COMPASSION, SISTERS OF THE (RDC), a religious community founded in the Archdiocese of New York by Thomas S. Preston, vicar-general, and Mary Donnat Starr (Mother M. Veronica), the rule being approved (1886) by Abp. M. A. Corrigan of New York. Converts, both founders had been collaborators in operating the Association for Befriending Children and Young Girls and The House of the Holy Family. The object of the institute was the reformation of erring girls and the religious, mental, and industrial training of girls in moral danger from ignorance or harmful influences. In 1890 headquarters for the new community were moved to White Plains, New York. The institute founded there Good Counsel College (1923), a liberal arts college for women, and an academy; in New York City they conduct a commercial school, and in the diocese several other secondary and numerous elementary schools, a kindergarten, and a Montessori school. In 1976 of 216 members, 185 professed were in the diocese. BIBLIOGRAPHY: CE 5:52.

[M. T. REILLY]

DIVINE ELECTION, see ELECTION.

DIVINE ENERGIES, see ENERGIES, DIVINE.

DIVINE HEALING, a cardinal belief and practice in *Pentecostalism. Divine healing differs from the mental or metaphysical healing of *Christian Science, *New Thought, or *Spiritualism. Nor is it like *faith healing, in which a cure may come about simply through the internal belief of the sufferer. Divine healing is rather a gift or charisma (see Acts 4.30) from the power of the Holy Spirit to impart health to others. Healing is practiced through the laying on of hands (Mk 16.18), the observance of the prescriptions in James 5.14–18, and often with the use of anointed handkerchiefs or aprons (see Acts 19.12). With the exception of some extremists, most Pentecostals do not reject medical science; they rather see divine healing as a superior way to health. The basis for viewing healing as part of the *foursquare gospel is that bodily ills are a curse connected with sin, and that as Jesus atoned for all sin, so he delivers from all bodily infirmity. There are two types of Pentecostal healers: those who perform their task quietly, in chapels or private homes, in a ministry that is a blend of prayer, counseling, and the laying on of hands; and those professional healers who travel from city to city or from country to country to give healing sessions, often attended by huge crowds. Among the latter the best known is Oral *Roberts. There has been a great stress upon divine healing since World War II in Pentecostalism; it is also regarded as an essential means in the missionary enterprise. When the practice of divine healing does not effect a cure, some Pentecostal writers ascribe the failure to a lack of faith, or to sin; others, simply to the unsearchable wisdom of divine providence. BIBLIOGRAPHY: N. Bloch-Hoell, *Pentecostal Movement* (1964) 147–151; J. T. Nichol, *Pentecostalism* (1966) 15–17, 221–226; O. Roberts, *My Own Story* (1961).

[P. DAMBORIENA]

DIVINE INDWELLING, see INDWELLING, DIVINE.

DIVINE INTERVENTION, see INTERVENTION, DIVINE.

DIVINE LAW, see LAW, DIVINE.

DIVINE LOVE, ORATORY OF, a corps of social

apostles active in N Italy from the end of the 15th century. With the official name *Fraternità del divino amore sotto la protezione di San Girolamo,* the oratory was founded by the lawyer, Ettore Vernazza, and three other Genoese laymen, Giovanni Battista Salvago, Nicolò Grimaldi, and Benedetto Lomellino; St. *Catherine of Genoa was also active in its establishment. Its objective was personal holiness to be achieved by a fixed routine of prayer and ascetical practices, but particularly by works of Christian mercy such as attending the sick, caring for orphans, visiting criminals, and helping the poor. According to the rule, approved by Leo X in 1514, the number of members was not to exceed 36 laymen and 4 priests; to assure freedom in working with all social classes, their names were to be kept secret. Other oratories patterned after the Genoese foundation appeared in Florence, Milan, Rome and Naples. The Roman Oratory, dispersed at the sack of Rome (1527), produced several figures of Catholic reform, such as G. M. *Gilberti, St. *Cajetan (Gaetano da Thiene) and Gian Pietro Carafa (*Paul IV), cofounders of the Theatines, J. Sadoleto, L. *Lippomano, and G. *Contarini. BIBLIOGRAPHY: P. Paschini, *La beneficenza in Italia e le compagnie del divino amore* ... (1925³; E. D. McShane, NCE 4:915–916. *ORATORIANS.

[E. D. MCSHANE]

DIVINE NATURE, PARTAKER OF, a description of the recipient of habitual *grace, taken from 2 Pet 1.4 (see also Jn 15.4:17.22–23; Rom 8.14–17; 1 Jn 1.3). The mystery of divine grace was early understood to mean a divinization of the recipient, a participation in God's own life (St. Irenaeus, *Adv. Haer.* 5.9.1; PG 7.1144). Preciseness about the transformation as participation, however, came esp. from St. Thomas Aquinas. Living the life of grace and of glory means sharing in that knowing and loving that relate the divine persons to one another and express the divine nature. Accordingly, the life of grace and glory also has its basis in a new nature, an entitative identity, of which the grace-given knowing and loving are the connatural expression (ThAq ST 1a2ae, 110.2). The new being is described as a participation for two reasons: first, to assert the mysterious literalness of the transforming exaltation worked by God's love; second, to exclude any pantheistic implication: participation means that what God is in his own being he bestows in the form of a created, analogical likeness, as an accidental quality that gives the soul a new way of being, relating it directly to the divine (*ibid. ad* 2; see also GRACE, SUBSTANTIAL).

[T. C. O'BRIEN]

DIVINE OFFICE, see LITURGY OF THE HOURS.

DIVINE PERSON, one of the three subsistences in the Holy Trinity. That God is personal is a truth attainable to reason, for all the perfections implied in the concept of person are found in him in an infinite degree. But that God is three Persons is known only through revelation. Person is not a biblical term; nevertheless the NT witnesses to the personhood of Father, Son, and Spirit. The concept of person, as distinct from nature, is of Christian origin. The need for a clear conceptual expression of the mystery of the Trinity forced upon the mind of the Fathers of the Church this distinction unknown to the philosophies of their time. While in man's experience individual nature and person coincide in all cases, this is not true where the mystery of God is concerned. In the Christian tradition the elucidation of the two concepts went hand in hand with a clarification of the terminology. *Prosōpon* (Gr.; Lat., *persona*), which originally referred to the mask put on by an actor to incarnate the personage whose part he acted on the stage, evolved gradually toward the metaphysical notion of person; so did the Greek *hupostasis,* while its Latin counterpart, *substantia,* was pulled on the side of nature or substance.

When St. Thomas defined a person as an "individual with a rational nature" (ThAq ST 1a, 29.3ad 2), he was summing up the insights of centuries of Christian thinking and overcoming the last hesitations of his predecessors. As understood by him, the notion could be applied analogically to the Divine Persons, for Father, Son, and Spirit are three subjects subsisting in the divine nature. BIBLIOGRAPHY: A. M. Bermejo, NCE 11:170–171; M. J. Dorenkemper, *ibid.* 168–170; T. de Régnon, *Études de théologie positive sur la Sainte Trinité* (4 v., 1892–98).

[J. DUPUIS]

DIVINE PRAISES, a series of supplications blessing God, Jesus Christ, the Blessed Virgin, and St. Joseph. They were composed by Luigi Felici, SJ, in 1797 to counteract and make reparation for blasphemy. It is customary to recite these praises after Benediction of the Blessed Sacrament. Several popes have added to Felici's original list and attached indulgences to the prayer.

[T. M. MCFADDEN]

DIVINE PROVIDENCE OF ST. VINCENT DE PAUL, SISTERS OF, see SISTERS OF DIVINE PROVIDENCE OF RIBEAUVILLÉ.

DIVINE REDEEMER, SISTERS OF THE, a congregation founded in Alsace-Lorraine in 1849 by Mother Alphonse Marie Elizabeth Eppinger. In 1912 the community was established in the U.S.; the motherhouse is in Elizabeth, Pennsylvania. Apostolates include elementary and secondary education, nursing, care of the aged, and catechetics. In 1977 statistics showed a total of 124 professed sisters in the U.S.: Pennsylvania, Ohio, New York, and Minnesota; and 1107 in Europe: Hungary, Austria, and Czechoslovakia—a total membership of 1,231 sisters. The generalate is in Rome.

[S. A. HEENEY]

DIVINE RIGHT OF KINGS, see KINGS, DIVINE RIGHT OF.

DIVINE SAVIOR, SISTERS OF THE, a religious community founded (1888) in Rome, Italy, by Franziskus Maria Jordan and Baroness Theresia von Wüllenweber. The community enjoys pontifical status; the sisters are sometimes referred to as Salvatorians. It was founded as a response to the need for spreading the Gospel to all people, non-Catholic as well as Catholic. There is also an American foundation which was begun at the request of Abp. Frederick Katzer (1895) of Milwaukee, Wisconsin. The motherhouse is in Rome. In 1975 there were 1,738 members in 170 houses. BIBLIOGRAPHY: M. C. Van De Kamp, NCE 4:923.

[J. R. RIVELLO]

DIVINE WORD, SOCIETY OF THE, a RC clerical religious congregation founded in 1875 in Holland (Steyl). The society has spread to several continents. Prior to 1884 members took private vows as its founder Arnold Janssen prescribed. After the chapter of 1884, members made public vows. The main thrust of its work, i.e., mission to pagans, remains the same. The society maintains schools, engages in the training and education of clerics, concerns itself with scholarly work and publication, particularly in anthropology and its related disciplines, publishes its own quarterly, *Anthropos,* and maintains centers for the development of technical skills. All these activities are, as envisioned by the society, part of its charisma to preach the divine Word. It boasts the first Catholic foreign mission seminary in the U.S. (at Techny, Ill., in 1909) and a world famous ethnologist, Wilhelm Schmidt. In 1976, membership totaled 5,301 in 154 houses on all continents.

[J. R. RIVELLO]

DIVINI REDEMPTORIS, an encyclical letter of Pope Pius XI, addressing itself to the problem of atheistic communism. Published on the Feast of St. Joseph (March 19, 1937), the encyclical symbolizes a continuing papal concern for the Christian worker caught in the grips of economic depression, and faced with an invitation to find material prosperity through an economic system grounded in atheistic ideology. From this essentially pastoral impulse, the pope proceeds to give a comprehensive analysis of the theory and practice of communism. He declares the ideology to be "intrinsically evil" (No. 60) and the system to be "full of errors and sophisms, [one] which aims at upsetting the social order and at undermining the very foundation of Christian civilization" (No. 3). The Pontiff warns the Christian world against Communist efforts to collaborate with Christians on ostensibly good causes. He also reaffirms, as the Christian answer to the problem of atheistic communism, belief in God, the practice of detachment from material possessions, charity, and commutative and social justice. BIBLIOGRAPHY: Pope Pius XI, "On Atheistic Communism" *(Divini redemptoris), Catholic Mind* 35 (1937) 141–174.

[W. J. BYRON]

DIVINING ROD, a forked stick that is supposed to dip downward to signal the presence of water, metals, or minerals underground. Use of the device reflects probably a folkloric attribution of some natural property to the stick and not reliance on some demonic power, as in *divination.

[T. C. O'BRIEN]

DIVINITY. (1) From Lat. *divus,* a substantive meaning "god"; as an abstract term, the divine essence or nature, godhood; as a concrete term, the godhead, the divine being. In the NT the term occurs but once in the phrase, "the fullness of divinity" *(plērōma theotētos,* Col 2.9), the exegesis of which is disputed. In the Middle Ages the equivalent term *deitas,* gained some currency in that it translated *Theotēs,* used in a concrete sense by the widely quoted Pseudo-Dionysius (e.g., *On the Divine Names* 1). In theology the chief occurrences of *divinitas* or *deitas* are in connection with the *divine names, e.g., in pointing out that "God" and "divinity" refer to the identical reality but in different ways; and with the discussion of Christ's two natures. In philosophy of religion, "divinity" may denote the quality or sum of qualities that people attribute to the object of religious acts. (2) Theology as an academic discipline (esp. in Great Britain).

[T. C. O'BRIEN]

DIVINO AFFLANTE SPIRITU, an encyclical letter of Pope Pius XII (Sept. 30, 1943) concerning the study of Sacred Scripture. After summarizing the papal directives of the preceding decades, the encyclical sets down a program for greater progress in the study and understanding of the Bible in view of recent discoveries in archeology, ancient history, linguistics, and other sciences. It encourages scientific study of the Bible through the investigation of biblical texts in their original languages and insists upon the importance of textual criticism and a knowledge of the literary forms of ancient writers. Text: AAS 35 (1943) 297–326; Eng. Tr. in *Rome and the Study of Scripture* (5th ed., 1953) 79–107. BIBLIOGRAPHY: J. F. Whealon, NCE 4:925–926.

[J. H. ROHLING]

DIVINUM ILLUS MUNUS, *Leo XIII's encyclical (May 9, 1897) on the Holy Spirit, his invisible mission and presence in the soul as Sanctifier, his work as soul of the Church. BIBLIOGRAPHY: ASS (1896–97) 29:644–658.

[T. C. O'BRIEN]

DIVISIO, as a musical term, see DISTINCTIO.

DIVISION, in logic, a means of knowing by resolving a whole into its parts (Aristotle, *Prior Analytics* I,31; *Posterior Analytics* II,13; *Topics* VI,6). The elements in a division, then, are the whole, its member parts, and the basis according to which they are divided. The whole may be simply a term or word; and the parts, its various meanings; the division then is nominal. The whole may be a reality signified by the term; then the division is real (from *res,* thing). If the basis of a real division is a factor that does not essentially make up the whole, the division is accidental, e.g., dividing the whole "mankind" on the basis of color. An essential division either resolves a genus or generic class into its species (its so-called potential parts); or a quantitative whole into its integrating units. For logic, the essential division of a generic class into its specific parts is the most useful, esp. for determining a *definition of each part. A good, i.e., adequate, division must have a single and essential dividing factor; must be exhaustive; must be resolvable into parts less universal than the whole; and the parts must stand in mutual opposition.

[T. C. O'BRIEN]

DIVORCE (EASTERN CHURCHES). All the Eastern Orthodox Churches without exception regard the praise of permanency in marriage expressed by Jesus (Mt 19.3–10) as a moral ideal, but not as a legal prohibition of divorce. The Fathers, as Basil the Great, reluctantly recognized the need and the right of the Church to permit remarriage of divorced members. The original sole reason, adultery, was later extended to several other grounds on the presumption that they would anyway eventually lead to the termination of the marriage and to a relationship with another person. The only legal limitation in the Eastern Orthodox Church is the prohibition against a fourth marriage, which applies not only to divorced but also to widowed persons. The assertion of some Catholic historians that the Eastern Churches succumbed to the influence of the civil law, esp. in the Byzantine Empire, is unwarranted. The early Church in the East and in the West, while always emphasizing the ideal of permanency or relative indissolubility of Christian marriage, considered the legislation of Christian emperors permitting divorce as being a valid expression of the theological position of the Church. The espousal of absolute indissolubility in the Western Church goes back to the Carolingian renaissance of theology, while the Christian East retained its original practice of permitting the remarriage of divorced Christians. The Eastern Catholic Churches were obliged to accept the teaching and practice of the Roman Church at the time of their reunions. Abp. Elias Zoghby, Patriarchal Vicar of Egypt, proposed at Vatican Council II (Oct. 29, 1965) that the Catholic Church re-examine its position with respect to prohibition of the remarriage of divorced Catholics. He was seconded by the other bishops of the Melkite Patriarchate, esp. the late Patriarch Maximos IV. BIBLIOGRAPHY: V. J. Pospishil, *Divorce and Remarriage. Towards a New Catholic Teaching* (1967).

[V. J. POSPISHIL]

DIVORCED CATHOLICS. Traditionally the RC Church, unlike the Orthodox Church, has not recognized divorce and remarriage, but it has authorized marital separation in cases where one spouse has become a threat to the other's physical safety or spiritual well-being, or where one spouse has been injured by the infidelity of the other. There has also been the recognition that civil divorce is justifiable because of the civil effects of marriage and the need to protect the rights of the plaintiff; technically, although this is often not known or ignored, a Catholic seeking a civil divorce should have prior ecclesiastical permission to do so. The term "divorced Catholic" as such, therefore, does not mean a Catholic who is in any way separated from the Church or barred from the Church's sacramental life.

The term raises a pastoral problem, however, when it has the connotation of a Catholic who has obtained a civil divorce and entered into a second, civil marriage. (Even in this case, it should be noted, such a Catholic or any Catholic entering a civil marriage, is no longer excommunicated; the 19th-cent. excommunication incurred in the U.S. by any Catholic contracting a civil marriage was lifted, and retroactively, in 1977.) Because the Church does not admit the power of the State to annul a sacramental marriage, the civil divorce does not dissolve the divorced Catholic's earlier marriage; the second marriage is, therefore, not a valid marriage. The pastoral care of such remarried Catholics has always been a poignant issue; it has become a much more urgent and widespread one in contemporary society. In the U.S. it is fairly well established that 40% of all marriages end in divorce; it is also estimated that the same or a similarly high percentage is becoming true of Catholic marriages. When divorced Catholics remarry they can do so only in a civil ceremony. The pastoral issue is to find a way in which such Catholics who have remarried can be brought into full participation in the life and sacraments of the Church. (This current way of putting the question itself differs from an older one: the alternatives formerly were to renounce the second marriage partner or to live in the marriage as "brother and sister"; where neither alternative was acceptable the couple was "living in sin" and one troubled in conscience could only be encouraged to hold fast to faith and hope; some authors even objected to that much pastoral comforting as an encouragement of sin.)

By way of generalization (which is all that moral theology can propose) there are two basic approaches to the problem of the divorced and remarried Catholic. The one may be classified as the Tribunal Procedure; the other, as the Good-Conscience Procedure. The Tribunal Procedure means in effect a juridic process that will seek to establish that the previous marriage was not a true marriage, so that the second marriage can become a valid, Christian marriage. The spirit of pastoral renewal and reconciliation that has emerged in the Church since Vatican Council II has been nowhere more dramatically evident than in the theology and jurisprudence concerned with marriage. Simply at an administrative level many matrimonial cases that once had to be decided only in Rome and that often dragged on interminably are now within the competence of diocesan tribunals. Much more important is the reevaluation of grounds for annulment. Theology and canonical jurisprudence have both taken into account the contributions of the behavioral sciences in judging the meaning of marital consent; they have also raised their view of that consent above the level of seeing it merely as a contract which, if no obvious conditions were lacking, was unbreakable in law. The result is a reassessment of the essential constitutive of marriage, the free exchange of a *marital* consent by two persons capable of understanding and mature enough to give and accept such consent. With divorced and remarried Catholics in many cases it can be established that such an exchange has not occurred and that their first marriage never existed as a true marriage; a declaration of nullity is thus in order and the second marriage can be regularized. The divorced Catholic is thus enabled to resume full participation in the sacramental life of the Church. Clearly the tribunal procedure is the most satisfying solution both for the good order of the Christian community and for the conscience of those who benefit from it.

There are, however, divorced Catholics for whom there is no hope that the tribunal procedure will work or who have tried it without an annulment resulting. It is for them that the so-called Good-Conscience Procedure (sometimes called the Pastoral Solution) has been proposed. The proposal can have two meanings. The first is as an alternative that in fact rejects the need for the tribunal procedure. So understood the good-conscience course implies a rethinking of the theology of marriage and the question, particularly, of its *indissolubility. The implication is this: according to the existing law of the Church the divorced Catholic in a second marriage is still bound by the previous marriage bond; but in good conscience the person can come to the decision that the first marriage never was or ceased to be a true marriage. The person can, therefore, in good conscience consider the second to be the true marriage and can receive the sacraments. The good-conscience procedure can also mean, not rejection of the need for the tribunal procedure, but a recourse when that has failed or is clearly ruled out. The implication is not a denial of the perdurance of the first, sacramental marriage, but simply the conviction that while the situation is juridically unrectifiable, the person can still receive the sacraments. There has been some attempt to experiment with good-conscience procedures, but they have been repudiated by ecclesiastical authority. This "pastoral solution" certainly lacks the advantages of the tribunal procedure for the common good of the Church and the conscience of the individual, which is reassured by an official declaration of nullity.

The pastoral problem remains acute and is not completely solved by either approach indicated. The positive element present in today's Church, hovever, is pastoral concern. There are supportive groups of divorced and separated Catholics to assist and counsel persons whose marriages fail. A pastoral spirit is much more clearly the mark of chancery offices than heretofore. The Canon Law Society of America has become the leading force for an enlightened pastoral theology and a new understanding of church law. A greater sense throughout the Church of the need to be personally responsible in making decisions of conscience is a positive advance over a former extrinsecism. BIBLIOGRA-PHY: T. Tierney, "Marriage: What about the Conscience Solution?," *Emmanuel* 82 (1976) 42–45; S. Kelleher, *Divorce and Remarriage for Catholics*? (1973); idem, "The Laity, Divorce and Remarriage," *Commonweal* 102 (1975) 521–524; W. Bassett, "Divorce and Remarriage: The Catholic Search for a Pastoral Reconciliation," AER 162 (1970) 20–36, 92–105.

DIX, GREGORY (1901–52), Anglican Benedictine liturgist, distinguished for his appreciation of the religious and theological factors underlying liturgical development, as in his well-known *Shape of the Liturgy* (1944).

[N. KOLLAR]

DIX, OTTO (1891–1969), German painter. Educated at the Academies of Düsseldorf and Dresden, teacher at the Dresden Academy (1927), D. was dismissed by the Hitler regime (1933), his work being declared *entartete Kunst (degenerate art)*. Shocked by World War I and the consequent chaos in German society, D. painted cruel and cynical war scenes. His studies of urban life stressed the social injustice of his day. D.'s portraits and other works evidence an extreme realism with some Surrealistic elements. A veristic painter, he showed in his later works (some of religious subjects) a cool objectivity. After 1946 he used an Expressionistic technique. BIBLIOGRAPHY: Löffler, *Otto Dix* (1967).

[P. H. HEFTING]

DŁUBOSZ, JAN (Johannes Longinus; 1415–80), Polish priest and historian. D. served as secretary to the bp. of Krakow, Card. Olesnicki, as canon of the cathedral, and as Polish delegate to the Council of Basel. Although a student of humanism, he never became part of the movement. He died shortly after his appointment, but before his consecration, as abp. of Lvov. His multivolume historical work in classical Latin, *Annales seu chronicae inclyti regni poloniae*, persuaded Western European scholars of the richness of the Polish tradition. BIBLIOGRAPHY: P. Urban, DHGE 14:530.

[M. E. DUFFY]

DMITRY OF ROSTOV, ST. (1651–1709). Dmitry Tuptalo became a monk and in 1702 bp. of Rostov on the Don. He was an outspoken preacher and insisted on the Church's independence of state control. Much of his life was devoted to writing devotional and instructional works. His warm approach, esp. in his homilies, caused him to be greatly loved by his people.

[G. T. DENNIS]

DÖBLIN, ALFRED (1878–1957), a leading novelist of the expressionist school in Germany, a convert from

Judaism to Catholicism. His most important novel, *Berlin Alexanderplatz* (1929) was revolutionary in style and introduced a new epoch in narrative prose. BIBLIOGRAPHY: R. Links, *Döblin, Leben und Werk* (1965).

[I. MERKEL]

DOCETISM (Gr., *dokein,* to seem), a theological opinion which held that Jesus Christ had not a real but an apparent body or a celestial (ethereal) body and hence could no more than appear to suffer and die. The origins of Docetism are obscure; it seems to go back to early Greek thought, in particular to an exaggerated Neoplatonism. Some connect it with the Gnostic dualism that sought to keep God, as pure spirit, from direct contact with the impurities of matter. For many the bodily weakness of Christ while on earth and more particularly his ignominious death on the cross constituted an inevitable scandal: "the crucified Christ, to the Jews a scandal, to the pagans madness" (1 Cor 1:23). Ignatius of Antioch strenuously fought against Docetism, followed by Polycarp, Irenaeus, Serapion of Antioch, and Tertullian. The heresy was finally condemned at Chalcedon (451). BIBLIOGRAPHY: G. Bareille, DTC 4.2:1480–1501.

[P. FOSCOLOS]

DOCILITY, teachableness. (1) It is a part of the virtue of *prudence, making a person open to and desirous of the counsel of others in determining a morally right course of action (ThAq ST 2a2ae.49,3). The Gift of *counsel, connected with prudence, is docility to the special guidance of the Holy Spirit (*ibid.,* 52). (2) In a wider sense docility is a condition for learning. Aristotle remarks that a learner must first give credence to his teacher (*Sophistical Refutations* 2.161b3). The ideal way of learning is by personal discovery, but teaching is meant to ease the process. The end desired is that the student interiorize and assimilate true knowledge. The teacher functions as intermediary assisting the learner to reach that point (ThAq ST 1a.115,1; *De ver.* 11). Teachableness is a condition for learning to begin; it involves moral attitudes: the self-recognition proper to *humility; the virtue of *respect towards the teacher as a source of betterment (ThAq ST 2a2ae.103,4). Absence of docility by an intellectual egalitarianism renders the educational process impotent, and education as a human institution pointless. (3) Docility in matters of faith is amenability to the teaching office of the Church, and submits private judgment to the guidance assured by Christ to the believing community (Jn 16,13).

[T. C. O'BRIEN]

DOCTA IGNORANTIA, literally a learned or conscious ignorance, a phrase found in the writings of St. Augustine (*Epist.* 130.28; PL 35.505), but particularly associated with the epistemology of *Nicholas of Cusa. He developed the theme as part of his theory about man's ability to know God. The key to his theory is the resolution of all contradictories in the infinite, his *coincidentia oppositorum.* God is

the infinite; man can be aware of the finite and the opposition among finite things and concepts; he can be aware also of the principle of the resolution of contradictories. But he can only symbolize the infinite. Through these symbols he has some cognitive contact with the infinite to which they point, God; but that is necessarily also a lack of knowledge; thus it is a conscious ignorance. Cusa's theme was in contrast to the disregard by some scholastics of the negative side, the apophatic, as a necessary limit on all claims to knowledge about God. He is often hailed as a precursor to later epistemological skepticism.

[T. C. O'BRIEN]

DOCTOR (SCHOLASTIC TITLE), a title that derives from the Latin *docere* and indicates one who has the highest qualifications for teaching. In medieval universities the title meant freedom to teach without further examination. Originally limited to theology, law, and philosophy, since the 19th cent. the doctorate (Ph.D) has been conferred in all fields of knowledge.

[J. R. AHERNE]

DOCTOR OF THE CHURCH, an ecclesiastical writer who, because of the integrity of his faith, eminent learning, and holiness of life has been expressly honored with this title by the Church. In the early Church the "Doctors" (*didaskaloi, doctores, magistri probabiles*) were the recognized witnesses of the theology of their respective times. From the 8th cent. on, SS. Ambrose, Augustine, Jerome, and Gregory the Great have been regarded as the four great Doctors of the West, a status that was officially recognized by Boniface VIII in 1298. From the 9th cent., SS. John Chrysostom, Basil the Great, and Gregory of Nazianzus have been honored as the three great, or "ecumenical" Doctors in the East. To these St. Athanasius was later added. All four were recognized by Pius V in 1568 who had declared St. Thomas Aquinas Doctor in 1597. Since then 23 more saints have been declared to be Doctors of the Church. Their names and dates of recognition are as follows: Bonaventure (1588), Anselm (1720), Isidore of Seville (1722), Peter Chrysologus (1729), Leo the Great (1754), Peter Damian (1828), Bernard of Clairvaux (1830), Hilary of Poitiers (1851), Alphonsus Liguori (1871), Francis de Sales (1877), Cyril of Alexandria and Cyril of Jerusalem (1882), John Damascene (1890), Venerable Bede (1899), Ephrem the Syrian (1920), Peter Canisius (1925), John of the Cross (1926), Robert Bellarmine (1931), Albert the Great (1932), Anthony of Padua (1946), Lawrence of Brindisi (1959), Teresa of Avila (1970), and Catherine of Siena (1970). BIBLIOGRAPHY: E. Valton, DTC 4.2:1509–10; H. Rahner, LTK 6:229–231.

[M. J. COSTELLOE]

DOCTRINAL STANDARD, a statement used by a Church as its authoritative understanding of the Christian faith, and as a guide by which it is distinguished from other

Churches. Doctrinal standards are sometimes ranked in a hierarchy of importance, but all are generally considered subordinate to revealed truth as originally given in Christ and the Scriptures and are regarded as attempts to outline the fundamental truths of revelation. Normally individual members of the Church are expected to accept the standard, and clergy and teachers, to conform their teaching to it. Doctrinal standards acquire political importance where one Church is legally established or in some way favored and assent to its standards is required for those who would enjoy the privileges granted to the *established Church. Among some liberal groups opposition has arisen to any doctrinal standard as an unjust coercion of the individual conscience. Some *free Churches have rejected doctrinal standards, holding that the Bible is the sole and sufficient standard of belief; but they have nonetheless generally adopted covenants, declarations, or other statements defining their understanding of Christian doctrine.

Principal RC doctrinal standards have included creeds—notably the Apostles', the Nicene, and the Athanasian—and the doctrinal decisions of the popes and the *ecumenical councils. Among the Protestant Churches the variety of doctrinal standards is extensive. Doctrinal standards for Lutheranism are found in the *Book of Concord (1580), which contains the three ecumenical creeds, the *Augsburg Confession, Luther's Small Catechism (see CATECHISMS, LUTHER'S), and other confessions. The *Reformed Churches give less emphasis to confessions, but have been guided by such standards as the *Geneva Catechism (1545), the *Gallican Confession (1559), the *Belgic Confession (1561), and the *Heidelberg Catechism (1563). For the Presbyterian tradition stemming from England the *Westminster Confession has been primary. The Anglican standards are the *Book of Common Prayer and the *Thirty-Nine Articles.

In the rise of the ecumenical movement the discussion of doctrinal standards for a united Church has taken place particularly through the *Faith and Order movement, now a part of the *World Council of Churches. The World Council at its founding made an affirmation of faith in Christ as God and Savior the doctrinal standard for admission, but the desire of some Churches for a fuller statement led to a later expansion to include references to the Trinity and the Scriptures. Although some Christians insist that the Church should hold strictly to the doctrinal standards of the past, others consider it necessary to reexamine standards in the light of Scripture or modern knowledge or both. Those emphasizing historical relativity assert that the wording of a standard must be interpreted in the light of the historical period in which it was composed and that the expression of the same essential faith today may require different language.

[T. EARLY]

DOCTRINE, that which is taught. In classical Greek thought, the word *(didaskalía)* is common and means the teaching of a wise man or philosopher. Its meaning changes, however, in the Bible: in the plural it denotes the uncertain theories of men (Is 29.13), whereas the singular is always used to convey the sense of divine instruction (Rom 12.7). Thus Scripture establishes an opposition between the absolute and unequivocal revelation of God and the fleeting thoughts of men. Moreover in the NT, esp. in the *Pastoral Epistles, the word is connected with the historical revelation of God in Jesus (1 Tim 4.13; 2 Tim 3.16), and it becomes the Church's mission to proclaim that historical doctrine. Thus the Church's teaching office follows from the very nature of God's decisive intervention in time, and not from any absolutizing of human thought. The very meaning of the Christian community is to express, both in thought and in the life which flows from that thought, the doctrine revealed by God in Jesus. BIBLIOGRAPHY: K. H. Rengstorf, Kittel TD 2:160–165; M. E. Williams, NCE 4:939–940.

[T. M. MCFADDEN]

DOCTRINE, DEVELOPMENT OF, one of the most difficult problems of fundamental theology. It was the main issue in the modernist controversy and remains very much to the fore. Christianity has from the start recognized the historical and evolutive character of revelation. Therefore, although it is based on the assumption that the epoch of objective revelation in which the deposit of faith has been constituted *(traditio constitutiva)* came to an end, it has always been open to the idea that there may be a growth in the objective understanding of that tradition by the Church. That which is objectively revealed in a given epoch may not from the start be objectively understood in the fullness of its content. Objective understanding is contradistinguished from subjective understanding. The latter is a progress in the depth and firmness of realizing faith and is always personal. The former is a progress in the notional explication of the object of faith and is socio-historical. The Fathers of the Church generally spoke in such a way that the principle of development seemed to be a presupposition no less self-evident than the principle of immutability. The medieval theologians emphatically stated that truths, not explicitly contained in the creed, but implicit in it, and deduced from it by reasoning, may become part of the object of saving faith. In later scholastic theology different kinds of implicitness and consequently of explicating reasoning were distinguished, and the question was asked concerning their definability by the doctrinal authority of the Church. Those distinctions were often very subtle. The main distinction was that between formally implicit and virtually implicit statements. The former can be deduced from the formally explicit statements by a simple explanatory syllogism, which does not bring about any new knowledge. The deduction of the latter requires a true syllogism and produces new knowledge. On the basis of that distinction three main positions were held: (1) Only those statements that are formally implicit in the deposit of faith can be integrated in the creed

(Molina, Franzelin, and, in contemporary times, Schultes). (2) All propositions deduced in whatever way from one or two revealed premises can become objects of faith (Vázquez and recently Tuyaerts). (3) A further distinction has to be made in the virtually implicit. Virtual implicitness may be metaphysical, that is, of absolute necessity, as for instance that Christ, being a true man, had the capacity of laughing; or it may be physical or moral, as for instance that Christ had two lungs or that he actually exercised the faculty of laughing. Theological conclusions of the first kind are, those of the second kind are not, definable by the Church (Marín-Sola).

In the meantime the science of history had brought to light the real facts of the development of doctrine, and it gradually became clear that they could not be explained by any model of syllogistic operation. Moreover, different patterns of evolutionary explanation of nature and history were propagated by philosophers (Hegel, Schleiermacher) and scientists (Darwin) and were soon employed to explain the evolution of dogma. This led to the position of liberal theology. Liberal theology in all its forms started from the principle that faith has always to be revised in the light of the growing insights of reason and experience. It came to determine the immutable essence of Christianity in such a way that all doctrinal statements are excluded from it. The essence then consists either in the continuity of a religious experience that is available to all men and of which Christ has been the highest exemplary manifestation (Schleiermacher, Harnack, Tillich), or in the recurrent existential actualization of authentic life (life of love) under the impact of Christ, whose life and death reveal to men the love of God and the remission of sin (Bultmann). According to the radical position of liberal theology no doctrinal statement is unchangeable. Doctrines are necessary or inevitable objectifications of an experience that is beyond conceptual thought and plain language. They may point to the possibility of the essential experience and help men by the power of their symbolic reference. But they are linked up with a definite stage of cultural development and may pass away with it. They have only to be maintained as long and as far as they are helpful. In the Catholic Church ideas like these led to the crisis of modernism.

The scholastic attempts to explain the development of doctrine by the means of logical consequence, and the liberal theories of transformistic evolution are extreme opposites. According to the former, that which is revealed by God and assented to by the believer is conceived of as a set of propositions about God. The latter, on the contrary, exclude all propositional elements from revelation and faith. Is there no *via media* that preserves the propositional element of objective revelation but as dependent upon a beyond that is not propositional and does not simply belong to the past but is always at work in the life of the Church as a supernatural regulative power? Attempts in that direction were made by the German Catholic theologians of Tübingen (Drey, Möller, Kuhn), who tried to preserve the Catholic dogmatic position in a dialogue with the Romantic idealism of their time. But the most original and thorough theory to explain and justify the development of doctrine was worked out by John H. Newman in his *Essay on the Development of Christian Doctrine*. Newman's theory rests on a twofold analysis: of the way reason actually works and of the way ideas develop in society. The former leads to a distinction between real and notional apprehension: to one who has never experienced that which a word points to, the word means only a general notion; if, however, he has a personal experience of what is signified, then the word evokes a concrete reality. In the actual process of thinking a growth of the articulated notional expression of experience (breadth) may be combined with the growth of the personal grasp of reality (depth). The fecundity of the notional explanation depends upon the depth of the real apprehension, which in its turn becomes clearer to the mind in the process of explicitation. Newman calls "idea" the real insofar as it is present to the mind as a whole in a prereflective way, regulating the process of reflective thought, which unfolds its inexhaustible riches, bringing them together into a notional system. The relation between faith and theology is like that between real and notional apprehension. The object of faith is the reality of God and his saving work, present to the mind before and in the process of notional analysis. In the statements of the creed, worked out by the intellect, the believing person attains to the reality with which they are concerned. "Realizing is the life of true development." The presence of the inexhaustible mystery to the believing mind is the regulating power of dogmatic growth in the Church.

The second analysis brings to light the dialectical interplay of the various forces at work in the history of the Church and influencing the course of Christian consciousness. Like the individual person, so the Church "moves as a whole." From its very nature human thought, and esp. group-thought, is inclined to onesidedness. Onesided views easily provoke contrary views, equally onesided. The causes of those unbalanced tendencies are multiple, e.g., oppositions between philosophical schools, national jealousies, political interests, and personal tendencies. The dialectical interplay between them tends to divide and disturb the Church. Therefore a doctrinal authority, recognized by the community as a supreme court, which in certain situations and under certain circumstances would be infallible, is practically necessary to preserve the unity of the Church by discriminating between true developments and corruptions. The theory of Newman is called theological because both the source of development (the presence of saving reality to the believing mind) and its ultimate rule of truth (infallible authority) have a supernatural origin. The same theory was worked out in a strikingly similar way by M. Blondel and is now gradually being accepted in Catholic theology, under the combined influence of Newman and the rediscovery of the patristic and medieval theology of faith, esp. that of Aquinas. BIBLIOGRAPHY: J. H. Newman, *Essay* on the Development of Christian Doctrine (1968); T. Lynch, "Newman-Perrone Paper on Development," Greg (1935) 403–444; J. J. Byrne, "Notion of Doctrinal Development in the Anglican Writings of J. H. Newman," EphemThLov (1937) 230–286; J. H. Walgrave, Newman the Theologian (tr. A. V. Littledale, 1960); idem, NCE 4:940–944; O. Chadwick, From Bossuet to Newman (1957); V. F. Storr, Development of English Theology in the Nineteenth Century (1913); M. Blondel, "Histoire et dogme," (1904) in Les Premiers écrits de M. Blondel (1956) 149–228; E. O'Doherty, Doctrinal Progress and Its Laws (1924); F. Marín-Sola, L'Évolution homogène du dogme catholique (2 v., 1924); H. Hammans, Die neueren katholischen Erklärungen der Dogmentwicklung (1965); J. Pelikan, Christian Tradition: a History of the Development of Doctrine (Spirit of Eastern Christendom 2, 1974); idem, Development of Christian Doctrine: Some Historical Prolegomena (1969).

[J. H. WALGRAVE]

DOCTRINE IN THE CHURCH OF ENGLAND, the report in 1938 of a commission, set up in 1922 by the abps. of Canterbury and York, composed of members of the C of E holding moderate catholic, evangelical, and modernist positions. The report was documentary and not meant to be normative—an examination of belief actually held, not an authoritative declaration or a prescription of the limits of doctrinal variation. Its purpose was forgotten by some of its critics, though of course it did reflect contemporary persuasions.

DOCTRINE OF THE FAITH, CONGREGATION FOR THE, formerly known as the Holy Office, that congregation of the Curia Romana whose purpose is to assist the pope in the preservation and promotion of doctrines of *faith and morals. Although the pope is the head of the Congregation, its president is the cardinal secretary, and approximately 10 other cardinals also sit in its plenary sessions. Advising the Congregation is an international body of consultors and other experts (periti). The Congregation may issue on its authority three types of decrees. The first pertains only to specific cases, although these set important precedents. Secondly, disciplinary decrees binding on all subjects may proceed from the Congregation. Doctrinal decrees that, although not infallible or irreformable, require the assent of all may also be issued. Both disciplinary and doctrinal decrees are issued with the general approval of the papacy (in forma communi).

[R. A. ARONSTAM]

DOCTRINES AND COVENANTS, a book published in 1835 by Joseph *Smith, Jr., at Kirtland, Ohio. It records the divine revelations Smith claimed to have received. The work is a doctrinal source of major importance for the Mormons and is the first expression of their belief in a continuing revelation to their Church in the persons of its leaders. *LATTER-DAY SAINTS, CHURCH OF JESUS CHRIST OF.

[T. C. O'BRIEN]

DOCTRINES AND DISCIPLINE OF THE METHODIST CHURCH, see DISCIPLINE (METHODIST).

DOCUMENTARY THEORY, in biblical criticism, the thesis that the composition of the Pentateuch (and Jos) is traceable to four main documentary traditions. The four, with their code designation, in chronological order are: the *Yahwist (J c.870 B.C.), the *Elohist (E c.770 B.C.), the *Deuteronomist (D c.620 B.C.), and the *Priestly (P c.450 B.C.). Jean *Astruc in the 18th cent. distinguished the Yahwist and the Elohist elements in the Pentateuch. The theory was elaborated gradually: H. Hupfeld (d. 1866) more precisely assigned the basic documents; K. H. Graf (1815–69) determined a chronology; J. *Wellhausen was the most forceful and influential exponent of the whole position. He also allied the literary theory with an evolutionary interpretation of Israelite history and religion. This historical thesis of Wellhausen came to be rejected by biblical scholars, esp. because of archeological findings that illumined the religious history of the whole Near East. The literary thesis, of a plurality of documentary sources, is generally accepted by both Protestant and RC exegetes. The importance and application of the theory, however, have been greatly modified by the study of predocumentary *literary genres. BIBLIOGRAPHY: A. Weiser, Old Testament: Its Formation and Development (tr. D. M. Barton, 1961); L. Alonso-Schökel, Understanding Biblical Research (tr. P. J. McCord, 1963).

[T. C. O'BRIEN]

DOCUMENTS, PAPAL, the pronouncements of the Holy See, classified broadly into those issued by the pope and those issued by the *Curia Romana with the pope's approval. Those issued by the pope are subdivided into: apostolic constitutions, on points of grave doctrinal or disciplinary concern; the motu proprio, issued by the pope "on his own" in regard to a disciplinary issue of secondary importance; and letters: apostolic—on canonizations, episcopal appointments, establishment of a new diocese; pontifical—addressed to an individual on some specific occasion; encyclical—issued the whole hierarchy on social or theological matters; chirographi, i.e. written in the pope's own hand to a cardinal on some point of discipline. Oral pronouncements of the pope are called allocutions, and more significant ones are published in the Acta Apostolicae Sedis. Documents issued by the congregations of the Curia Romana are divided into *decrees, *rescripts, simple instructive replies, or, in the case of a juridical procedure, sentences. Other designations of papal documents are based on the material form, corresponding to the solemnity of their content, in which they are issued. Thus: the papal bull, is named from the leaden bulla, seal, attached with cords of silk to the parchment; the papal brief, is a parchment sealed with red wax stamped with the fisherman's ring; all other documents are issued simply as letters on paper stamped with the appropriate seals.

[T. C. O'BRIEN]

DODD, CHARLES, PSEUD., see TOOTELL, HUGH.

DODD, CHARLES HAROLD (1884–1973), NT professor and scholar. An ordained Congregationalist minister, he began his academic career at Oxford (1915), continued at Manchester (1930–35), and at Cambridge from 1935 was Norris-Hulse professor of divinity. Among his earlier publications is *The Epistle to the Romans* (1932) in the NT commentary edited by J. *Moffatt. D.'s most important contribution is his work on the Gospel of St. John, esp. its historicity, in *Interpretation of the Fourth Gospel* (1953); *The Historical Tradition in the Fourth Gospel* (1963). In biblical theology he published his theory of "realized eschatology" (see ESCHATOLOGISM) in *Parables of the Kingdom* (1938), *The Apostolic Preaching* (1936), *History and the Gospel* (1938). He was general ed. (1950–65), then codirector (1965–70) with Driver for the *New English Bible* (NT, 1961; OT and rev. NT, 1970). D. was a prominent ecumenist as well.

[T. C. O'BRIEN]

DODECACHORDON, a theoretical work of music published in 1547 by H. Glareanus (Heinrich Loris). Glareanus enlarged the traditional system of 8 church modes to 12, adding modes on A and on C with their plagals. The work is important also for its analyses of the works of Josquin and other 16th-cent. composers. BIBLIOGRAPHY: Apel HDMus, 239; P. Scholes, *Oxford Companion to Music* (1963) 651.

[M. T. LEGGE]

DODERER, HEIMITO VON (1896–1966), Austrian novelist, one of the great German narrators of the 20th century. He captured the atmosphere of decay in Viennese society after World War I in complex and voluminous novels. Born near Vienna, son of an architect, a descendant of N. Lenau, D. became an army officer at the age of 19. He fought in World War I, was captured at the Russian front, and spent 4 years in Siberia as prisoner of war. After his return he studied history at the Univ. of Vienna (Ph.D. 1925). After World War II, in which he also participated, he lived in Vienna as an independent writer. Works: *Die Strudlhofstiege* (1951), novel; *Die Dämonen* (1956), novel; *Grundlagen und Funktion des Romans* (1958), a literary essay on the novel,

[B. F. STEINBRUCKNER]

DODO OF ASCH, BL. (d. 1231), a Premonstratensian hermit. D. was reluctantly married several years before he became a Premonstratensian canon and his wife a nun. He was granted permission to live as a hermit in Bakkeveen where he practiced extraordinary austerities and received the gift of healing. He later transferred his hermitage to Asch where his reputation for sanctity and wonder-working drew many sick persons, who recovered at his hands. D. died at an advanced age as a result of injuries received from a falling wall. According to legend, his dead body bore the marks of the wounds of Christ. Many dismiss these marks, however, as having been caused by the accident. BIBLIOGRAPHY: Butler 1:706; N. Del Re, BiblSanct 4:670–671.

[M. B. MONAGHAN]

DOERING, MATTHIAS (*c.*1400–69), German Franciscan theologian. D. spent 5 years as a student in England. After teaching at Erfurt and heading his order's school there, he became provincial of the Saxony province (1427), which after 1432 was in obedience to the Council of Basel. In 1443 he was elected general of his order by supporters of the antipope Felix V. D. was a Scotist and was strongly influenced in his doctrine by Bonaventure. He was not the author of the *Confutatio primatus papae* that has been attributed to him.

[S. A. SCHULZ]

DOGMA, in Catholic theology a truth that the Church requires the faithful to accept as a doctrine revealed by God. In the early centuries, the term was used more frequently to describe a norm of Christian morality than to describe a principle of faith. Since the time of Cyril of Jerusalem and Gregory of Nyssa, the meaning of dogma as a truth of revelation began to prevail, and from at least the 17th cent. it has referred exclusively to an article of Catholic belief as distinct from a premise of ethical conduct. Two elements constitute a dogma. It is a truth immediately (formally) revealed by God in Scripture or tradition, whether explicitly (e.g., Christ's divinity) or implicitly (e.g., Mary's bodily assumption). It is also promulgated by the Church as a revealed truth. This can be done either solemnly by papal definition or the pronouncemnt of an ecumenical council or, more commonly, by the Church's ordinary and universal teaching authority. Speaking of this common method of making dogmas known in the Church, Vatican Council II explained that the bishops "proclaim Christ's doctrine infallibly whenever, even though dispersed throughout the world, but still maintaining the bond of communion among themselves and with the successor of Peter, and authentically teaching matters of faith and morals, they are in agreement on one position as definitively to be held" (Vat II ConstChurch 25). Consequently a dogma may be taught by the Church quite apart from an official definition. It is enough that its matter be somehow "contained in the word of God, written or handed down," and that its acceptance by all the faithful be "proposed by the Church as a divinely revealed object of belief, either in a solemn judgment or in its ordinary and universal teaching" (D 3011).

Viewed in this light, dogmas and defined teachings overlap, but they are not coextensive. Something may be defined, as when saints are canonized, without having been explicitly and (some would say) formally revealed. It is sufficient that the content of a definition be connected with revelation and that the Church's authority to define be divinely revealed. In this sense, not everything defined is technically a dogma. In its strict meaning, therefore, a dogma is the object of two kinds of faith, divine and Catholic. Divine faith is involved because in believing a dogma the person's motive is the word of God, who can neither deceive nor be deceived. Catholic faith is involved because the believer accepts the authority of the Church to teach infallibly what God has revealed. This twofold faith is closely related to the double aspect of every dogma as a union of revealed truth and its dogmatic expression. The revelation is from God and the formulation is from the Church, but under divine guidance. The two are inseparable. No doubt the terminology even of defined dogmas can be refined and improved as the Church gains new and deeper insight into the mysteries of faith. Any new terminology, however, is valid only under the aegis of the Church's magisterium. The Spirit of God which animates the Church thus insures that changes in the expression of the faith reflect an authentic development of doctrine. BIBLIOGRAPHY: E. Dublanchy, DTC 4.2:1574–1650; R. Latourelle, *Theology of Revelation* (1966) 249–314; A. Dulles, *Survival of Dogma,* (pa. 1973).

[J. A. HARDON]

DOGMATIC FACT, the designation whereby revealed truth is applied to doctrinal matters or to persons and events connected with doctrine. Thus the Church defines as dogmatic facts those factual statements so related to its faith as to be necessary for its proper explanation, acceptance, or defense. These facts may be historical, such as the legitimacy of a pope or an ecumenical council, or doctrinal, such as the unorthodox character of a given writing. Here ecclesiastical authority states the obvious, objective sense of the document and answers two questions: is this doctrine conformed to faith? is it contained in this work? For instance, the Council of Nicaea proclaimed as dogmatic fact that Arius's *Thalia* expressed heresy. BIBLIOGRAPHY: E. M. Burke, NCE 4:949–956.

[W. DAVISH]

DOGMATIC THEOLOGY, the theological science treating of religious, esp. Christian, dogma, the object of which is the whole of the divine revelation. As part of Christian, and esp. Catholic, theology, it is a scientific (i.e., reflexive, methodical, and systematic) finding, penetration, and presentation by the believer (i.e., in the light of faith) of all the divinely revealed salvational truths, or of the salvific self-revelation of the triadic God, which are witnessed to by the whole Church and are implicitly or explicitly proposed by the Church's teaching authority (magisterium). The subject matter of dogmatics is both essential and exisential: i.e., ''God's revelation, which forms the theme of dogmatic theology, affirms the *essential* relationship binding man and

his world to God, and at the same time God's saving deed done to man in salvific *history*'' (Rahner-Vorgrimler, 136). Therefore moral theology as the science of man's moral and supernatural conduct necessarily remains part of dogmatic theology with its salvific-historical structure. In dogmatics three principal elements can be distinguished: (1) the biblical, i.e., divinely inspired and written account of events of the divine revelation and the witness of the primitive Church to them; (2) the historical or positive, i.e., the description of the process of dogmatization of the biblical witness and the homogeneous evolution of dogma; and (3) the philosophical, speculative, or scholastic, i.e., the rational penetration of the dogma, and the presentation of different philosophies as terminological, conceptual, and structural foundations of dogmatization and systematization, or the critique and corrective of different cultures upon all subjective elements of dogmatics. German Lutheran theologian Georg Calixtus (1586–1656) seems to have been the first to use the term dogmatic theology. By the end of the 17th cent. it came into common use among Protestants and Catholics alike. BIBLIOGRAPHY: E. M. Burke, NCE 4:949–956; E. Dublanchy, DTC 4.2:1522–74; Y. M. J. Congar, *idem* 15.1:341–502; *Catholicisme* 3:949–951; *La Foi et la théologie* (1962); K. Rahner, LTK 3:446–454; G. Gloege, RGG 2:221–223.

[P. B. T. BILANIUK]

DOGMATISM, a term used to discredit as presumptuous any proposal of philosophical or religious truth as certain, absolute, or authoritative. In modern philosophical usage, the term has become widespread since Immanuel Kant claimed that existing systems of thought accepted their presuppositions uncritically. In a religious context, Christians are charged with dogmatism because they accept their tenets as revelation. Among the Churches those espousing authoritative creeds or official teaching have been accused of dogmatism by nonauthoritatarian or anticreedal Churches. Contemporary insistence upon the relativeness and inadequacy of all human concepts and language leads to the view that any theology claiming to be a valid formulation of divine revelation is dogmatism.

[T. C. O'BRIEN]

DOHERTY, EDWARD JOSEPH (1890–1975), journalist, author, and Melkite priest. D. became a journalist at the age of 15, writing for newspapers of Chicago and New York. Among his books are: *Tumbleweed, Splendor of Sorrow, Martin, King of Sinners,* and *I Cover God.* After the tragic death of his wife in 1939, he went to New York where he met the Baroness de Hueck. Together they revived the interracial apostolate of the Friendship House in Harlem. In 1943, they were married. Soon the work spread, and upon the invitation of the Bp. of Pembroke they cofounded what is now called Madonna House, located in Cambermere, Ontario, Canada. For more than 20 years they dedicated themselves to a life of love and service, embracing the vows of chastity, poverty, and obedience. In Nazareth, at the age of 79 D. was ordained a priest of the Melkite rite by Bp. Joseph Raya. BIBLIOGRAPHY: R. Pelton, "Psalm for a Just Man," *Restoration* 28 (1975) 6; C. DeHueck-Doherty, *Poustinia* (1975) 10–11.

[R. A. TODD]

DOLCI, CARLO (1616–86), Italian artist in Florence who painted extremely pious and excessively sweet Madonnas (*Madonna del Dito,* Rome) and allegorical figures (*Sincerity,* Vienna). His few portraits show some strength (*Claudia Felicitas* and *Self-Portrait,* both in the Uffizi).

[M. J. DALY]

DOLCINO, FRA (d. 1307), a medieval reformer who assumed leadership of the *Apostolici after the death of Gerard *Segarelli in 1300. D. possessed considerable executive talent and gave the sect some semblance of organization, reducing its doctrines to writing and adding a number of Joachimist concepts and some of his own apocalyptic prophecies (see JOACHIMISM). He prophesied the extermination of the cardinals and the pope and God's choosing a new pope. When the bps. of Novara and Vercelli took action against him, D. and 4,000 followers entrenched themselves in the Italian Alps. In 1305, Pope Clement V summoned a crusade against them because of their raids on the villages to obtain provisions. After 2 years of armed conflict they were finally subdued. D. and his spiritual sister, Marguerite of Trent, were captured and cruelly executed. BIBLIOGRAPHY: E. Anagnine, *Dolcino e il movimento ereticale all' inizio del Trecento* (1964); G. Mollat, NCE 4:957; J. M. Vidal, DHGE 3:1041–44, s. v. "Apostoliques."

[C. J. LYNCH]

DOLD, ALBAN (1882–1960), German Benedictine liturgist and historian. After serving as a military chaplain in World War I, D. became head of the Palimpsest Institute that was founded at Beuron in 1912. He perfected a method for the fluorescence-photography of palimpsests and founded the series *Texte und Arbeiten* for texts and liturgical studies, for which he himself edited 22 works. BIBLIOGRAPHY: V. Fiala, NCE 4:958.

[N. KOLLAR]

DOLET, ÉTIENNE (1504–46), French humanist and printer. D. was important in the French Renaissance for his contribution to Latinity, notably the *Commentarius linguae latinae* (2 v., 1535, 1538), and for promotion of the French language through his press. A rationalist from early years, he was three times arrested by the authorities and after the third was burned at Place Maumbert, Paris, as a lapsed heretic. The charges against him included esp. his denial of the immortality of the soul. A heretic in RC eyes, and despised by Calvin as a blasphemer, D. was not a Christian;

neither was he an atheist, but rather an early deist and freethinker. BIBLIOGRAPHY: H. Chamard, DictLetFranc 1:232–234; R. C. Christie, *Étienne Dolet; Martyr of the Renaissance* (1889); J. Lecler, DHGE 14:575–577.

[T. C. O'BRIEN]

DÖLGER, FRANZ JOSEPH (1879–1940), specialist in Christian antiquity. A native of Sulzbach, Germany, D. was ordained a priest in 1902 and received with highest honors a doctorate in theology from the Univ. of Würzburg 2 years later. As a professor at the Universities of Münster, Breslau, and Bonn, he showed his remarkable knowledge of classical and patristic literature. He is best known for his monumental study of the fish as a sacred religious symbol (5 v., 1910–43). BIBLIOGRAPHY: J. Quasten, CHR 27(1941) 112–114.

[H. DRESSLER]

DOLLFUSS, ENGELBERT (1892–1934), Austrian statesman. Educated in Vienna and Berlin, he served his country in various positions, including those of Christian Socialist leader (1929), Director of Railways (1930), Minister of Agriculture and Forestry (1931), and Chancellor (1932–34). During his chancellorship D.'s idea of Austrian independence conflicted with that of the German-directed National Socialist Party. After his efforts to collaborate with the Social Democrats failed, he determined to preserve Austrian independence by sacrificing democracy for a dictatorship. In March 1933 he suspended Parliament and ruled by emergency decree. He drew up a constitution based upon Pius XI's ideal of a corporate Christian state and promulgated it on May 1, 1934. Opposition by the Social Democrats and National Socialists culminated in strikes and riots, to which D. reacted by outlawing the Social Democratic Party and nationalizing all trade unions. Five months later the Nazis organized the Vienna *Putsch* and seized the chancellery; D. was assassinated by Austrian Nazis on July 25, 1934. BIBLIOGRAPHY: G. Brook-Shepherd, *Prelude to Infamy* (1969); S. B. Fay, "Dollfuss, Victim of Nazi Crime," *Current History* 40 (1934) 729–741; J. Wodka, NCE 4:958–959.

[M. A. WATHEN]

DÖLLINGER, JOHANNES JOSEF IGNAZ VON (1799–1890), church historian and controversialist. D. lived mainly in Bavaria. Born in Bamberg, he entered the Univ. of Würzburg at 16, and in 1820, the seminary at Bamberg; he was ordained in 1822. He was professor of church history and canon law at the lyceum in Aschaffenburg (1823–26) and at the Univ. of Munich (1826–72); in 1873 the King appointed him president of the Royal Bavarian Academy of Sciences. Because of his refusal to accept the declaration of Vatican Council I on papal infallibility, D., together with his friend and biographer J. *Friedrich, was excommunicated, April 1871. Though D. was instrumental in organizing the Old Catholic movement (see NUREMBERG DECLARATION), he never formally joined it. He attended Mass in RC churches, but did not receive the sacraments. All attempts to reconcile him with the RC Church were unsuccessful, and he received the last rites from Friedrich, now an Old Catholic priest. Until his open break with Rome, D. was prominent in the Catholic revival of Germany. He corresponded with, and in his travels visited, church leaders in France, Italy, and England. Something of an Anglophile, he admired Wiseman, wrote to Newman, and had a close friendship with his onetime pupil Lord Acton. The prestige he enjoyed among scholars and prelates in Europe and America made him valuable as a collaborator and formidable as an opponent.

His early fame resulted from historical studies; the first to win acclaim was *Die Lehre von der Eucharistie in den drei ersten Jahrhunderten* (1826). Perhaps his greatest opus is the study on the origins and consequences of the Reformation: *Die Reformation, ihre innere Entwicklung und ihre Wirkungen im Umfange des Lutherischen Bekenntnisses* (3 v., 1845–48). It was followed by a biography of Luther (1850; Eng. tr., 1853). Running through the last two works is the theme that the Reformation marked a break with the national traditions of the German people. Shortly before 1850 D. began to comment in writing and lectures on Church-State relations. In this period the papacy came more and more under his attention. He argued successfully that St. Hippolytus of Rome was the author of the newly discovered *Philosophoumena*. It was the basis for a study of the Roman Church A.D. 200–250, which D. published as *Hippolytus und Callistus* (1853; Eng. tr., 1876). About the same time he openly inveighed against the proclamation of the dogma of the Immaculate Conception (1854), primarily because of the manner in which it was done. He became increasingly distrustful of ultramontanes and critical of the Roman exercise of power. In 1861 he questioned the historical basis and usefulness of the Papal States in two published lectures: *Kirche und Kirchen, Papsttum und Kirchenstaat* (Eng. tr., 1862). D.'s loyalty to the pope was strained further in 1864, when Pius IX condemned some of his opinions in the *Syllabus of Errors* (cf. proposition 13; D 2913). Besides his numerous other scholarly and critical works, there are his pseudonymous writings. By intention polemical, the two best known were directed against Vatican I and the definition of papal infallibility. Using the pen name Janus, D. wrote a series of articles, later published in book form as *Der Papst und das Konzil* (1869; Eng. tr., 1870 and 1873). Many opposed the definition because they felt it inopportune, but D. opposed the doctrine itself, chiefly on historical grounds. During the council, he kept abreast of the proceedings with the help of well-placed contacts, Lord Acton among them. Under the pseudonym Quirinus, he attacked the conduct of the council, complaining that its leaders discriminated against those bps. who resisted the definition. These attacks appeared first as letters purporting to be from Rome and later in a volume, *Römische Briefe vom Konzil* (1870; Eng. tr., 1870).

All 20th-cent. critics are impressed with D.'s facility for languages, his encyclopedic learning, and the extent of his writings, but also see much of his work as derivative and his theological horizons as limited. His strengths and weaknesses indicate the possibilities and limitations of a purely historical approach to theology and doctrine. BIBLIOGRAPHY: S. Lösch, *Döllinger und Frankreich* (1955), with a list of D.'s writings, including Eng. translations; S. J. Tonsor, "Lord Acton on Döllinger's Historical Theology," *Journal of the History of Ideas* 20 (1959) 329–352; *idem*, NCE 4:959–960; J. J. Hennessey, *First Council of the Vatican: The American Experience* (1963).

[B. L. MARTHALER]

DOLORS OF OUR LADY, see SORROWS OF MARY.

D.O.M., abbreviation for *Deo, optimo, maximo* (to God, the best, the greatest), often a dedication inscription on monuments in imitation of a practice in classical antiquity. It is also found on the label of the liqueur called Bénédictine, which was first distilled by the monks of the Abbey of Fécamp in Normandy.

[T. C. O'BRIEN]

DOM, from the Latin *domnus* or *dominus*, a title of respect originally given to kings and emperors, popes, bishops, later to abbots and barons (10th cent.), and finally to knights. Is some monastic orders, esp. those following the Rule of St. Benedict, it has been given to all senior members of the community, or to all the solemnly professed; but among the Cistercians and others it has been reserved to the abbot. At the present time in the U.S. its use is being generally abandoned for the more simple title of father or brother.

DOMCHOR, choir of a German cathedral, Protestant or Roman Catholic.

DOME OF THE ROCK (erroneously called Mosque of Omar; 688–691), earliest surviving masterpiece of Muslim architecture. It was built in Jerusalem for the Umayyad caliph 'Abd al Malik on the site of the old Temples of Solomon and Herod over a bare rock, the *sakhra,* sacred site of Abraham's offering and Mohammed's "night journey to heaven." The octagonal structure with four portals is sheathed in marble and glazed tiles, its gilded wooden dome on a cylindrical drum marked interiorly by two ambulatories. The magnificent metal grille surrounding the domed space within was added by the Crusaders. Extremely rich encrustations in marble, mosaic, and bronze are Sassanian and Hellenistic in style while the archaic Kufic inscription is the first in Islam. The Dome of the Rock, though an eclectic blending, evidences a distinctly unique style. BIBLIOGRAPHY: O. Grabar, "Umayyad Dome of the Rock in Jerusalem," *Ars Orientalis* 3 (1959).

[M. J. DALY]

DOMENEC, MICHAEL (1816–78). Born in Spain, D. joined the Vincentians in Paris and completed his studies for the priesthood in the U.S., where he was ordained in 1839. After working in Philadelphia, Penna., for some years, he was consecrated bp. of Pittsburgh in 1860. Though involved in controversy over his seminary and the *Pittsburgh Catholic,* as well as beset by financial problems, his tenure saw a phenomenal growth in numbers of Catholics. A builder of parishes and schools, he brought to his diocese seven communities of nuns and three groups of religious men. At Vatican I he originally voted against the definition of papal infallibility but changed later. When a new diocese was formed from Pittsburgh, D. became its bishop. He resigned for poor health in 1877 and returned to Spain. BIBLIOGRAPHY: W. Purcell, *Catholic Pittsburgh's One Hundred Years* (1943).

[J. R. AHERNE]

DOMENECH, EMMANUEL (1828–86), French missionary, writer. D. began his studies for the priesthood, but interrupted them to go to St. Louis, Mo., as a volunteer for the missions of the Southwest. After completing his theology there and studying the needs of the missions, he went to S Texas. In the aftermath of the War with Mexico, lawlessness and widespread misery engulfed the region. D. became a powerful offsetting influence, and his impact was felt through the extensive territory. Forced by ill health to return to France, he was later assigned to the French forces sent to Mexico and acted as chaplain to Emperor Maximilian. Upon his return to France, D. devoted his remaining years to study and writing. Among his works are *Voyage dans les solitudes américaines* (1858), *Histoire du Mexique* (1868), and *Souvenier d'outre-mer* (1884). BIBLIOGRAPHY: J. Mooney, CE 5:102.

[J. R. AHERNE]

DOMENICA DA PARADISO (1473–1552), mystic. A native of Florence and controversial figure, who attempted religious life three times without success, D. claimed to see in a vision the Dominican habit and Blessed Columba Rieti going to heaven. In 1513 she founded a convent, where she remained, superior for life, and adopted the reform of Savonarola. Though some questions arise about her, the first steps toward canonization were taken in 1624. BIBLIOGRAPHY: H. Thurston, *Surprising Mystics* (1955).

[J. R. AHERNE]

DOMENICHINO (DOMENICO ZAMPIERI; 1581–1641), painter from Bologna, the student of L. Carracci. In Rome (1602) D. assisted A. Carracci in frescoes of the Farnese Gallery. D. moved toward a classical Raphael-esque space organization *(Communion of St. Jerome,* 1614, Rome). Criticized, he strove for the baroque dynamic, illusionistic effects of Michelangelo and Correggio: *Four Evangelists* (1624–25) in San Andrea della Valle, Rome,

and frescoes in the cathedral, Naples. He was considered a supreme 17th-cent. Italian classicist by Poussin. D.'s *Landscape with St. John Baptizing* (Cambridge) attests strongly to his influence upon Claude Lorraine. BIBLIOGRAPHY: D. Posner, "Domenichino and Lanfranco," *Essays in Honor of Walter Friedländer* (1965).

[M. J. DALY]

DOMENICO DI BARTOLO (*c.*1400–1447), Sienese painter showing the influence of Masaccio in a *Madonna of Humility with Musical Angels* (Siena, 1433). D. designed the pavement graffito of the *Emperor Sigismund Enthroned* for the Siena cathedral, a *Madonna and Child* (1437; Johnson Collection, Philadelphia, Pa.), and a polyptych, *Madonna and Child with Saints and Five Scenes from the Life of John the Baptist* (1438, Perugia). His frescoes (1441–44) in the Ospedale della Scala are monumental and most important as evidence of impressive innovations from Renaissance Florence in 15th-cent. Siena. BIBLIOGRAPHY: C. Brandi, *Quattrocentisti senesi* (1949).

[M. J. DALY]

DOMENICO DI MICHELINO (1417–91), Florentine painter, follower of Fra Angelico, known for his signed and dated fresco of Dante in the cathedral of Florence (1465).

[M. J. DALY]

DOMENICO VENEZIANO (*c.*1400–62), Italian painter documented in a letter (1438) to Piero di Cosimo de' *Medici requesting commissions. D. executed three frescoes at San Egidio, Florence, with Piero della Francesca (1439–45) and probably at the Casa Santa in Loreto (*c.*1440, all lost). Influences of Fra Angelico and Masaccio are indicated but uncertain. Attributed to D. are the Olivieri portraits (Isabella Stewart Gardner Museum, Boston; Metropolitan Museum, New York) and Madonnas (Berenson collection, Settignano; the National Gallery, Washington, D.C.). D.'s major work, the altarpeice in Sta. Lucia dei Magnoli (1440–45; Florence, Uffizi) shows D.'s contribution in color and treatment of space and the human figure. His last work, *SS. Francis and John the Baptist,* relates stylistically to Castagno. There is no reason to believe that D. introduced oil painting in Florence. His major contribution is a lyrical use of color with sculpturesque form. BIBLIOGRAPHY: L. Berti, *Catalogo della mostra di quattro maestri del primo Rinascimento* (1954).

[M. J. DALY]

DOMESDAY BOOK, a record of a survey of England made 1085–87 at the instigation of William the Conqueror. His agents went into all sections of the country and secured information about all parcels of land. The purpose is not known. It may have been for aid in taxation, but in any event it is admired as one of the outstanding administrative feats of the Middle Ages. The record is preserved in two volumes, which are at the Public Record Office in London.

It is considered immensely valuable for historians, including church historians for its record of parish churches and their finances.

[T. EARLY]

DOMESTIC PRELATE, see PAPAL CHAMBERLAIN.

DOMICILE, a more or less permanent place of residence which has certain effects in canon law, e.g., it subjects the resident to particular laws (CIC cc. 13) or determines the jurisdictional competency of a tribunal (CIC cc. 1561, 1964). Domicile is called voluntary if acquired by voluntary choice or by actual residence, legal if imposed by the law itself. Voluntary domicile is acquired by staying in a place with the intention of remaining permanently, or by actually staying in a place for 10 years. Three classes of persons have domiciles imposed on them by the law: (1) on a wife, the domicile of her husband, (2) on an insane person, the domicile of his guardian, (3) on a minor, the domicile of his parent or guardian (CIC cc. 92, 93). The place of domicile determines a person's proper pastor and proper ordinary. Domicile is lost by departure from the place with the intention of not returning (CIC c. 95). BIBLIOGRAPHY: Woywod-Smith 67–72; 888–892; J. M. Costello, *Domicile and Quasi-domicile* (1930); J. H. Hackett, *Concept of Public Order* (1959).

[L. M. KNOX]

DOMINATIONS (*kuriotetes*), one of the classes of supernatural beings, or angels, mentioned by St. Paul in Col 1.16 and Eph 1.21, the only places they are specifically spoken of in the New Testament. They are always referred to in the plural. BIBLIOGRAPHY: W. Foerster, Kittel TD 3:1096–97.

[E. A. WEIS]

DOMINATIVE POWER, in its primary canonical usage, the power of religious superiors to govern the subjects who are bound by vow to obey. The pleonastic qualifier "dominative" has as its reason the fact that in religious life the superior can command an act of obedience (not simply external compliance) because the subject is vowed to obedience in all that belongs to religious life according to the community's constitution. The special term is also used to distinguish this power from the power of jurisdiction, which in its proper sense is hierarchical, requiring sacred ordination and concerned with the public good of the whole Church as such. Since the religious institute has a kind of wholeness as a society, dominative power does have some resemblance to the power of jurisdiction. The term in a wider sense may describe the ruling power of a superior in any society that is not a complete, self-contained unit; then it means the power to require compliance with a command: e.g., the domestic power of parents in the family; the ruling power of a teacher in the school.

[T. C. O'BRIEN]

DOMINE (less correctly, Dominie), an informal title for a clergyman in the Netherlands and other countries where the Dutch Reformed Church in its various branches is located. It has been used in this way by other Protestant denominations, and also as a synonym for "minister." The Latin meaning of "lord" or "master" is not implied by the church use. The double connotation of reverence or respect and of affection characterizes it. While the term has been used by many church members into the mid-20th cent., Americans have generally discontinued its use on the ground that it does not fit the modern age.

[E. EENIGENBURG]

DOMINGUES, ALFONSO (fl. *c.*1380–1400), Portuguese architect at the monastery church of Batalha (1386), where a marked verticalism relates to English 14th-cent. Perpendicular style.

[M. J. DALY]

DOMINGUES, DOMINGO (fl. *c.*1300–1320), Portuguese architect of the early Gothic cloister of the Cistercian abbey at Alcobaça, begun in 1308. The two-storied cloister was completed in 1311 by Diogo Dias.

[M. J. DALY]

DOMINIC, ST. (*c.*1171–1221), founder of the *Dominicans. After elementary studies, D. studied the liberal arts and theology at the cathedral school of Palencia. He became a canon regular at the cathedral of Osma and was ordained priest *c.*1194. His primary characteristics were personal charm, compassion, strict asceticism, purity of life, contemplative prayer, and evangelical preaching. After visits to Denmark and Rome (1203–05), D. and his bishop began to evangelize the Albigenses of S France in 1206, developing a mode of apostolic preaching in poverty. At the same time, they founded a monastery for women converts. After the bp. died in 1207, D. gathered disciples and continued the mission. With episcopal consent, he founded (1215) the Order of Preachers, which was confirmed by Honorius III (1216) and entrusted with a general preaching mission. In 1217 D. sent friars to Spain and Paris. In 1218 he established a priory and his headquarters at Bologna. Encouraged by papal approval and support, he devoted his remaining years to organizing, extending, and visiting the houses of the order, and preaching in Lombardy. In early 1216, at a formative chapter, D. and the friars chose to live under the Rule of St. Augustine and drew up the first part of the Constitutions. Under D.'s presidency the first general chapter (1220) completed the Constitutions, regulating the order's government, academic program, preaching mission, and poverty. At the second chapter (1221), D. determined the areas for eight provinces in Europe and the Near East and sent friars to establish those not yet founded. With organizational skill, awareness of the needs of the Church, and the introduction of revolutionary innovations D. fashioned an order that blended the contemplative life of the monk with the active ministry of the evangelist. D. was canonized in 1234. BIBLIOGRAPHY: M. H. Vicaire, *St. Dominic and His Times* (tr. K. Pond, 1964); L. von Matt and M. H. Vicaire, *St. Dominic: A Pictorial Biography* (1957). *St. Dominic: Biographical Documents* (ed. C. Lehner, 1964).

[W. A. HINNEBUSCH]

DOMINIC OF ALQUESSA (d. 1301), Spanish Dominican theologian who studied and taught at Paris in the second half of the 13th cent. and then served as provincial of Spain for some years after 1297. He died in Saragossa at the beginning of the 14th century.

[L. E. BOYLE]

DOMINIC DE LA CALZADA, ST. (d. 1109), hermit. A Basque from Viloria (Burgos), he was rejected for the monastic life but was befriended and ordained by the papal legate, St. Gregory of Ostia. He pacified a wilderness on the pilgrimage route to Santiago de Compostela, constructing a road *(calzada)*, bridge, and hospice for the comfort and safety of pilgrims. BIBLIOGRAPHY: C. M. Molas, DHGE 14:609–610; J. F. Alonso, BiblSanct 4:682–683.

[R. I. BURNS]

DOMINIC OF FLANDERS (*c.*1425–79), Dominican, philosopher. Educated at Paris, he was already a professor of philosophy when he entered the Dominican Order at Bologna in 1461 while traveling in Italy. He taught at Bologna, where *Cajetan was among his students, and at Florence. In his commentaries on Aristotle, D. closely followed the thought of St. Thomas Aquinas, all of whose writings he knew thoroughly. The *Quaestiones . . . in duodecim metaphysicae libros Aristotelis* (1499) is noteworthy because of D.'s interpretation of St. Thomas on the nature and submect matter of metaphysics. BIBLIOGRAPHY: L. Mathieu, *Dominique de Flandre et sa métaphysique (Bibliothèque Thomiste* 24, 1942).

[T. C. O'BRIEN]

DOMINIC GUNDISALVI (Dominicus Gundissalinus; fl. *c.*1150–90), translator of the Arabian philosophers, author of several philosophical treatises. D.'s career was spent in Toledo, the center of the spread of Aristotelian and Arabian philosophy into 12th-cent. Western Europe. To this he contributed by his translations into Latin of Avicenna's *De anima* and *Metaphysica,* Algazel's, *Summa theoriae philosophia,* and Avicebron's *Fons vitae.* Gilson regards D.'s personal writings *(De divisione philosophiae, De processione mundi, De civitate, De immortalitate animae)* as initiating the expansion of philosophical interests, the attempt to combine non-Christian with Christian thought, and the methods of argumentation that were to be typical of the

13th cent. scholastics. BIBLIOGRAPHY: M. T. D'Alverny, NCE 4:966–967 with bibliog; Gilson HCP 235–239.

[T. C. O'BRIEN]

DOMINIC LORICATUS, ST. (d. 1060), Italian hermit and ascetic, called *Loricatus* (The Mailed) because of his practice of wearing a coat of mail next to his skin. Discovering as a young priest that his parents had procured his ordination by bribery, he refused to exercise his orders and retired to a hermitage at Montefeltro to live a life of extreme austerity. Some years later (*c.*1042) he entered the abbey of Fonte Avellana where *Peter Damian was abbot. The two shared the same devotion to penitential severity. It is to Peter Damian, who put D. in charge of a new foundation near San Severino, that we are principally indebted for what is known of D.'s life (PL 144:1012–24). BIBLIOGRAPHY: Butler 4:110–111; G. Cacciamani, BiblSanct 4:688.

[T. C. O'BRIEN]

DOMINIC OF THE MOTHER OF GOD, see BARBERI, DOMINIC, BL.

DOMINIC OF PRUSSIA (1384–1460), Carthusian spiritual writer. A native of E Prussia, he entered the Carthusians and is identified most with the monastery of Trier. Though he wrote a number of treatises, they remain unedited. *De contemptu mundi* is an autobiography. He is best known as the propagator of a rosary type of prayer consisting of 50 Hail Marys (without the Our Fathers) accompanied by meditations. He added 50 invocations to the Hail Marys, recalling mysteries of the lives of Christ or his Blessed Mother.

[J. R. AHERNE]

DOMINIC OF SILOS, ST. (d. 1073), Benedictine abbot who rebuilt and revived the monastery of Silos, Spain, in 1041 and made it a center of religious learning with Mozarabic influences. His cult drew pilgrims to Burgos from 1076 and long was a theme for popular literature. BIBLIOGRAPHY: B. Cignitti, BiblSanct 4:736–737.

[E. P. COLBERT]

DOMINIC OF SORA, ST. (951–1031), monk. Educated and ordained in the monastery of Foligno, D. divided his life between periods of contemplation as hermit or cenobite and periods of intense activity founding Benedictine monasteries throughout Italy. A wonderworker, he is still invoked for protection against thunderstorms. He died at his monastery of Sora in the Lazio compartimento in central Italy and is buried there. BIBLIOGRAPHY: F. Caraffa, BiblSanct 4:737–739; Butler 1:147.

[M. A. WINKELMANN]

DOMINICA IN ALBIS (short for *dominica in albis depositis* or *deponendis*), the Sunday after Easter, known also in English as *Low Sunday. It was so called because it was the day on which the newly baptized laid aside the white baptismal garments they had received at their baptism at the Easter Vigil service.

[P. K. MEAGHER]

DOMINICAL LETTER (Sunday Letter), the letter of the alphabet from A to G assigned to the Sundays in the liturgical calendar of any particular year. In the Church's calendar one of the seven letters A to G is assigned to each day of the week, beginning with A for Jan. 1. The series of letters is repeated successively throughout the year. The letter that coincides with the first Sunday of the year will be the dominical letter, i.e., the letter of the first and of all successive Sundays of the year. Thus in 1970 the dominical letter was D, since Jan. 1 fell upon a Thursday. In bissextile or leap years, there are two dominical letters, the first obtaining through January and February, the second through the rest of the year. Knowledge of the dominical letter was useful in determining the date of the month on which a Sunday of any year will fall, and in ascertaining the date of Easter. But where tables and calendars are readily available, its mention survives more as a curiosity than for its practical utility.

[P. K. MEAGHER]

DOMINICAN REPUBLIC, a republic located in the eastern portion of the Island of Santo Domingo in the Caribbean Sea, the western portion being occupied by the Republic of Haiti (19,332 sq mi; pop. est. 1975 4,469,300; ethnic distribution: white *c.*15%, Negro *c.* 15% mestizo (mulatto) 70%, according to the 1975 census). The island was discovered by Columbus in 1492 and named La Española (later, Hispaniola). The city of Santo Domingo, founded in 1496, was the first permanent settlement made by Europeans in the New World. As the native population was reduced by wars, epidemics, earthquakes, and ill-treatment, it was replaced by slaves from Africa. The first missionary was B. Buyl (Boyl), who arrived in 1493. He was followed by Dominicans (among whom was B. de Las Casas), Franciscans, Augustinians, Benedictines, and Jesuits. The University of Santo Domingo was founded in 1538, and in 1545 the city became the primatial see of the Americas. The importance and prosperity of the island declined after the conquest of Mexico and Peru. Many of the Spanish settlers left, and Dutch, French, and British buccaneers preyed upon the land. The colonial church was poor, and its clergy were too few and ill-trained to accomplish much. After the colony was ceded by Spain to France in 1795, it was conquered by the Haitians in 1801, retaken by the French in 1802, but it revolted and was restored to Spanish rule in 1808. In 1821 it cast off Spanish rule but fell again to the Haitians in 1822, who held it until they were expelled in 1844 and the Dominicans established an independent republic. Catholicism was made the state religion and agreement was reached concerning the nomination of bishops. The hierarchy was reestablished in 1848. The republic has been plagued with political and social unrest from the beginning and has known two long periods of tyrannous dictatorship (H. Heureaux, 1882–99; R. Trujillo Molina, 1930–61), a U.S. customs receivership (1905–41), and occupation by U.S. marines (1916–24). Trujillo favored the Church at first, apparently for his own ends. It was permitted to own property and was tax-exempt. Religious instruction was given in the schools; divorce was sanctioned only for non-Catholics. But the last years of the regime brought it into conflict with the hierarchy, which issued a strong pastoral letter demanding freedom for the people. This led to the expulsion of U.S. and Canadian priests. More recently the religious situation has improved, and there has been an influx of priests and religious from N America and Europe. Education is developing. The Univ. of Santo Domingo, after being closed 1801–15 because of the political situation, was reopened in 1815 as a lay institution, but Catholic higher education was resumed in 1962 with the foundation of the Universidad Católica ''Madre y Maestra'' at Santiago de los Caballeros. The Dominican Republic has one archdiocese (Santo Domingo), three suffragan sees (Santiago de los Caballeros, La Vega, and Higüey) and one prelacy *nullius* (San Juan de la Maguana). About 30% of the baptized Catholics, who make up 93.6% of the population (1975), practice their faith. There are 98 diocesan and 381 religious priests, and of the latter more than half are foreigners. The scarcity of priests is the greatest obstacle to the development of Catholic life and accounts for the religious ignorance and superstition that exists among the people. Methodists, Episcopalians, Adventists, Pentecostals, and Jehovah's Witnesses are represented among the Protestant denominations active in the country.

[P. DAMBORIENA]

DOMINICAN RITE. Because of the scholarly nature of their apostolate, the Dominicans early felt the need of a Mass rite short enough to permit suitable time for study and preaching and at the same time one that could be used uniformly in their many European convents. Thus in 1220 the Dominicans constructed their own rite from available sources. For 25 years they used this rite until the liturgical revolution sweeping Rome caused the Dominicans to revise their original rite. The new one was marked by beauty and simplicity; other religious orders and dioceses adopted it as their own. A few of the characteristics of the Dominican rite include the following: the water and wine were put into the chalice at the beginning of Mass; the Gloria and Credo were read from the Missal; the host and chalice were offered up in a single oblation and with a single prayer. The Mass of the Friars Preachers survived 7 centuries with only minor changes, but little if anything remains of it after the publication of the *Novus Ordo Missae.* BIBLIOGRAPHY: W. R. Bonniwell, *History of the Dominican Liturgy* (1945).

[K. O'NEILL]

DOMINICAN SPIRITUALITY, the type of spirituality characteristic of the Dominican tradition; it can be described as Christological, theocentric, contemplative, and evangelical. St. Dominic went beyond what was common in monastic institutions of his time to make Dominican spirituality apostolic. Consecrated by the vows, sustained by the common life, pivoting around the choral litrugy, and continuing in individual prayer, the spiritual life of the Dominican reaches out to souls, atones for sins, testifies by word and example, and begs that the Spirit may come into the hearts of those who hear the Word. Dominic himself sought to live the rule of the Apostles in its totality. He prayed frequently and specially to God for the gift of true charity to enable him to work for and win the salvation of men. Holiness for his sons consists in imitating the poor Christ of the Gospel, the preacher who taught the Apostles and sent them out to preach. Dominicans are to "go forth as men wanting their own salvation and that of others . . . as men of the Gospel following in the footsteps of their Savior, speaking with God or about God among themselves and with their neighbor" *(Constitutiones antiquae OP)*. Ideally they are preoccupied with truth, search for it, pray it, live it, preach it. Gazing upon the Word Incarnate, they seek to understand the meaning of Jesus and to penetrate the truths he revealed. They proclaim the Gospel so that the people may be saved and the God who saves may be glorified.

Dominican concern for truth sanctifies their study and places it at the heart of their spirituality. Dominic admonished and exhorted the friars often by word and by letter to study constantly the Old and the New Testaments. Albert the Great linked the spiritual life, study, and the apostolate: "The method for one who teaches things divine is to gain by grace the truth of the divine doctrine he must hand on to others, because in every theological undertaking one ought to start off with prayer. . . ." Dominican apostolic effort is rooted in a community that tells its members: "Before all things else, dear brethren, love God and then your neighbor" *(Rule of St. Augustine)*. In 1233 Jordan of Saxony recommended one thing only to the friars: ". . . have a constant mutual charity among yourselves, for it cannot be that Jesus will appear to those who have cut themselves off from the community: Thomas, because he was not with the others when Jesus came, did not merit to see him." Love for Christ Crucified who is preached, for his Heart, his Blood, his Holy Name, his Eucharist, for his mysteries studied and proclaimed, for his Mother and the history of salvation that is enshrined in her Rosary are the themes of Dominican devotion. BIBLIOGRAPHY: W. A. Hinnebusch, *Dominican Spirituality, Principles and Practice* (1965); P. Regamey, "Principles of Dominican Spirituality," *Some Schools of Catholic Spirituality* (ed. J. Gautier, 1959) 76–109.

[W. A. HINNEBUSCH]

DOMINICANS (Order of Friars Preachers, Blackfriars), an order founded by St. Dominic in 1215 to combat vice and error, and confirmed by Honorius III in 1216. The order's preaching mission motivated its life, intellectual concerns, and activities. The order has three branches: the first order of priests and brothers; the second order of cloistered nuns, and the third order, which has two parts: religious living in community who engage in educational, social, and charitable work, or who serve in foreign missions; and tertiaries, lay men and women who live according to the Dominican spirit. The habit consists of a white tunic, scapular hood, a black mantle, and a rosary.

Dominican life is both contemplative and apostolic. It stresses a solemn choir service (see DOMINICAN RITE), active community living, and an asceticism of silence, fasting and abstinence from meat (now mitigated). Dominic resolved the tension between this contemplative regime and preaching with revolutionary innovations: (1) substitution of study for manual labor and meditative reading; (2) a broad power of dispensation from ascetical and liturgical duties to be used when these impeded apostolic work or scholarly activity; (3) exclusion of parish work; (4) a strict poverty that limited even corporate possessions; (5) abandonment of monastic stability; (6) an interpretation of Rule and Constitutions that did not see them as binding under sin; (7) a democratic government. The order supplemented the Rule of St. Augustine (adopted 1216) with Constitutions drawn up in 1216 and 1221. Departments of government check and balance one another. Strong superiors (master general, provincials, and priors) have limited terms and are elected by, and are responsible to, chapters: general, provincial, and prioral. Triennial general chapters (annual until 1370) of provincials and/or elected delegates, have the power, and have used it throughout the order's history, to change the law or details of Dominican life and work.

Medieval Period, 1216–1500. The order's preoccupation with truth, esp. theological, stems from its purpose: preaching and the salvation of souls. Dominic laid the foundations for a rounded academic system. It was elaborated in final detail in 1259 by five masters, among them Albert the Great and Thomas Aquinas. From priory schools of philosophy and theology, the system moved upward to provincial schools of philosophy and theology, to general houses of study at university level. The latter were usually incorporated into one of the universities. Each province had a general house of studies after 1300. The order held two chairs of theology at the Univ. of Paris by 1230, one at Oxford by 1248.

Preachers by profession, Dominicans settled in cities and towns, built large, spacious churches, preached twice on Sundays and daily in Advent and Lent, and sent out itinerant preachers. To cover each priory's territory systematically, they divided it into districts and erected preaching homes in remote places. John of Vicenza, Venturino of Bergamo, Vincent Ferrer, and Manfred of Vercelli preached over wide areas. Girolamo Savonarola preached moral, political, and social reform in Florence. The friars formed libraries of theological and scriptural commentaries, sermon collections, preaching manuals, and source materials such as the *Summa for Preachers* of John Bromyard and the *Golden Legend* of James of Voragine. Dominicans engaged in many apostolates. They served as papal and royal emissaries, papal penitentiaries and reform agents, crusade preachers, inquisitors, masters of the Sacred Palace, and confessors for kings and nobles. There have been four Dominican popes, 69 cardinals, and more than 1,000 bishops. The spiritual direction of the order's nuns produced the 14th-cent. mystical movement inspired by Meister Eckhart, Henry Suso, and John Tauler, and represented by Margaret Ebner, Christine Ebner, and Elsbeth Stagel. The friars founded confraternities for the laity, e.g., Marian, Holy Name, Rosary, and worked among the Beguines.

The foreign missions, a major Dominican work, were a legacy from St. Dominic. In the Middle Ages the friars went into Morocco, unconverted Slavic lands, Russia, Syria, Mesopotamia, Asia, and India. The Congregation of Pilgrim Friars (*c*.1300) worked in S Russia and S Asia. Raymond of Peñafort (d. 1275) founded oriental language schools in Spain for Dominican missionaries. Thomas Aquinas and Raymond Martini wrote treatises to guide friars working among Jews and pagans. William of Tripoli and Ricoldo of Montecroce made Europe's first studies of the Muslim religion. Others wrote descriptions of Palestine, notably Felix Fabri.

Disciplinary decline began about 1300 and affected every area of Dominican activity. It accelerated after 1349 because of the unwise recruiting that followed the Black Death, scarcity of vocations, difficulties with poverty, and prevalent wars and plagues. In 1389 Raymond of Capua began a reform that achieved considerable success during the next 100 years.

Modern Period, 1500–1850. From the reform came new life in the 16th century. A Thomistic revival was led by Francisco de Vitoria (pioneer in international law, d. 1546), and Thomas de Vio (Cajetan). Dominican studies were broadened and adapted to the age of Humanism and Protestantism. The order opened colleges in Rome, Salamanca, Valladolid, and 12 colleges and universities in the Americas and the Philippines (e.g., Santo Domingo, 1538; Santo Tomás in Manila, 1645). Controversies with Protestants and with Catholic theologians (grace, Immaculate Conception, probabilism) occupied Dominican scholars. About 130 of the order's bishops and theologians, among whom were Melchior Cano and Domingo de Soto, took part in the Council of Trent. Santes Pagnini and Sixtus of Siena pioneered in biblical science; Michael le Quien, in oriental studies, Francis Combefis, in patristics, Noel Alexandre, in history, Nicholas Coeffeteau, in linguistics. Though Turkish advance weakened the Hungarian province and the rise of Protestantism destroyed three provinces and crippled 14 others, the order founded 11 new provinces in the Americas and Asia. The Philippine province (1592) staffed missions throughout the Far East.

The administration of the order suffered from religious and political upheavals. Few chapters could convene, and it was hard to have access to the master general. The spirit of the Enlightenment dampened enthusiasm, weakened discipline, and impeded recruiting. The French Revolution and the suppression of religious orders in Latin countries and Russia almost destroyed the order during the years 1789–1850 (see statistics below).

Contemporary Period, 1850–1968. The *Risorgimento, the *Kulturkampf, the expulsion of religious orders from France in 1903, the Spanish Civil War (1936–39), caused the order fresh setbacks. But steady progress began in 1843 when H. Lacordaire restored the Dominicans to France. V. Jandel, master general (1850–72), revived the government, reorganized the provinces, renewed religious life, and restored studies. Traditional activities—parish missions, retreats, theological education, foreign missions—were expanded. Lacordaire, L. Monsabré (d. 1907), V. McNabb (d. 1943), and in the U.S., C. H. McKenna (d. 1917) and H. I. Smith (d. 1957) were noted pulpit orators. Dominicans were in 40 mission fields in 1968. England after 1900 became a vigorous province; French Dominicans went into Scandinavian countries and were dominant in the Worker-Priest Movement.

New intellectual activities developed. The order founded the theological faculty of the Univ. of Fribourg (1890), reorganized the Angelicum (1908, since 1963 the Univ. of St. Thomas, Rome), opened St. Stephen's Biblical School in Jerusalem (founded 1890, by J. M. Lagrange). In the 20th cent. institutes were established for the study of Eastern Christian Churches in Paris and Constantinople, for Islamic studies in Cairo. Dominicans from the U.S. established the *Instituto Boliviana de Estudio y Acción Sociales* in Bolivia.

Dominicans in the U.S. The most vigorous Dominican growth in the 20th cent. has occurred in the U.S. (first province, 1804; 80 friars, 1876). Work was centered in parish missions, closed retreats, foreign missions (Peru, Bolivia, Nigeria, China, Pakistan, Kenya, Mexico), Newman Apostolate, college and university teaching (Providence College, 1919), spiritual institutes, and dramatics. G. Hartke founded the Speech and Drama Department at The Catholic University of America, Wash., D.C.; U. Nagle, playwright, and T. Carey organized Blackfriars Theater off Broadway. Dominicans publish *The Thomist, Cross and Crown, Dominicana*. W. Farrell (d. 1951) pioneered in introducing theology courses for the laity into the college curricula.

Statistics: Divided into eight provinces in 1221, the order had 22 by 1500, 45 provinces and 4 congregations by 1720, and 39 provinces in 1968. There were 13,000 friars in 1256, more than 20,000 before 1348. During the next 200 years membership declined. In the 18th cent. there were 13,894 friars (11 overseas provinces not reporting). By 1850 the roster had dropped to 3,000. In 1976 there were 7,776 friars (U.S., 1,194). BIBLIOGRAPHY: A. M.

Walz, *Compendium historiae Ordinis Praedicatorum* (2d ed., 1948); W. A. Hinnebusch, *Early English Friars Preachers* (1951); *idem, History of the Dominican Order* (1966) v. 1; *idem, Dominicans: A Short History* (pa. 1975).

[W. A. HINNEBUSCH]

DOMINICANS (SISTERS), religious originating in St. *Dominic's foundation of Notre Dame, Prouille, France in 1206; the conventual women of the third order; cloistered nuns constitute the Dominican Second Order. Affiliated with the Order of Preachers, along with Dominican spirituality they share the *Constitutions,* variously adapted, and the Rule of St. Augustine. They number some 35,317 in 3,722 houses throughout the world. The *Annuario Pontificio* (1976) shows in Europe foundations in Italy (San Sisto, Rome [1219] believed their true origin); in Czechoslovakia, Yugoslavia, Dalmatia; in France, Germany, Holland, Poland, Portugal, Spain (on the Continent there are 18,882 in 1,813 houses). They flourish on Malta (229 in 20 houses), in Ireland (762 in 38 houses), and England (511 in 34 houses); in Iraq (173 in 18 houses); in Africa (1,759 in 129 houses); in Australia (479 in 37 houses); New Zealand (148 in 14 houses); and the Philippines (252 in 40 houses). As in the Old World, zeal for *Veritas* distinguished friar, nun, and tertiary, so in the New the mission spirit made place for the Dominican family. In South America the tertiary *Rose of Lima was the Americas' first saint; Dominicans are today (943 in 112 houses) in the Argentine, Colombia, and Venezuela; as well as in Mexico (366 in 37 houses). In Canada, the main foundation (416 in 26 houses) is at Montreal; in the U.S., where conventuals have had their greatest growth there are some 9,984 in 1,326 houses; of some 30 foundations 17 are of pontifical rank. In Kentucky the first congregation was established (1822), named for St. *Catherine, Dominican tertiary of Siena and now Doctor of the Church; presently they are in 10 dioceses, as well as in Ponce, Puerto Rico. From Kentucky stem the earliest foundations: St. Mary of the Springs, Ohio (1830); Nashville, Tenn. (1860); Jacksonville, Ill. (1873; now at Springfield); Houston, Texas (1882; now at Galveston); these formed others. Before the mid-19th cent., independent of these arose Sinsinawa, Wis. (1849) and San Rafael, Calif. (1850). Missions spread coast to coast and in turn made other foundations. Indigenous ones arose, notably in New York; of diocesan groups several were founded by RC converts: Sparkhill (1876), Glens Falls (1883), and that for sick poor at Ossining (1879). Of pontifical rank is that at Hawthorne (1896) for the care of those with incurable cancer. As seed for other communities Dominicans came from Belgium, France, Germany, Ireland, Italy, Portugal, Spain; some from troubled Czechoslovakia (1923) and Poland (1929) found refuge in America. From the U.S., Dominicans have gone to numerous mission lands, esp. the *Maryknoll missioners (1912). Dominicans teach on all levels, care for the sick, and engage in other works. There are several communities of cloistered nuns esp. dedicated to adoration of the Eucharist and the perpetual Rosary. There are also monasteries of the Dominican Second Order in cities of the U.S.; they follow strictly the monastic observances and choral liturgical life of the order. Unlike many European monasteries, these are not under the jurisdiction of the master general of the Dominicans but of the local bishop. BIBLIOGRAPHY: W. A. Hinnebusch, *History of the Dominican Order* (1966); *idem, Dominicans: A Short History* (pa. 1975).

[M. R. BROWN]

DOMINICI, JOHN, BL., see JOHN DOMINICI, BL.

DOMINICUS GERMANUS (1588–1670), Franciscan missionary, lexicographer, and Orientalist. Born in Silesia, he made his profession as a Franciscan in 1624, studied Arabic and Oriental languages in Rome, studied and taught Arabic in Palestine, where he produced an Arabic grammar in 1636, and compiled an Arabic-Latin-Italian dictionary in 1639 (widely used until the 19th cent.). He also collaborated on the Arabic Bible published in 1671 and taught Arabic at El Escorial, Spain, where he went at the invitation of Philip IV in 1652. He stayed there until his death. While there he produced a Latin version of the Koran, considered the best translation of its day.

[E. J. DILLON]

DOMINION (Lat. *dominium;* cf. the cognate domain from the French), originally a Roman law notion, and accordingly treated here as the juridical power of disposing of and using an object as one freely wills; further implications in moral theology are touched on under other headings such as right, duty, ownership, and private property. God alone has supreme and total dominion, yet properly speaking he is not a juridical person, for he transcends all such categories. Consequently if we speak of human beings possessing full dominion, this is in no absolute or unlimited sense, but only within a legal frame of reference. There is no suggestion that we can dispose of objects merely according to our whim, unless they be products of our fancy or fun, and bagatelles: it would take a dull dog indeed to range these under strict justice.

Dominion is proper to human persons whether considered as individuals or as banded together in an association for some worthy cause or as comprising the whole political community—thus private dominion, corporate dominion, and State dominion. Human dominion is divided into full dominion *(plenum),* which is over the object and the benefits flowing from it, and includes possession, use, and disposal, and partial dominion *(semi-plenum),* which may include one or two of these but not all three, and where also the use may be restricted by law or agreement to one or several but not every form.

The objects, called goods, of human dominion fall into two general classes, those internal and those external to us. On mixed goods, part internal, part external, it is enough to notice that they are imponderables, of proper pride in a work of art you have produced, and of the credit and reputation arising from it; you can prize them as your own, and expect authority to protect you against being pirated.

Internal goods are a man's own limbs, health, and life. Over these he has no full dominion, for he does not belong to himself but to God. Yet though he acts as a trustee, divine law may enjoin him to risk the loss of these goods for the sake of a higher good. Nor has one man or any human group direct dominion over the innocent life of another, who, however, may lose his rights proportionately to the injustice of his aggression or of his menace to the common welfare. A system of *slavery, also, which permits some men to be regarded as chattels and beasts, even if they were carefully cared for, would be wrong on this count; a perpetual dominion over the services of another, however, must be judged on other counts.

External goods are the nonhuman things we consume, use, or enjoy; here in principle man has full dominion. How far this can be individual dominion will be ruled by the consideration that some blessings are for all to share in common, such as air, light, the sea, and the mountains. That lawful authority in the name of the common good has the right to control individual dominion and check its exercise is universally allowed; where to draw the line is a political decision which varies from country to country; legislation in this matter binds in conscience unless flagrantly contrary to natural decencies. It may be remarked that the defense of private dominion by the classical moralists fixes on the benefits of individual administration but attacks individual consumption to the exclusion of others in need. Here, also, it may be remarked that no individual or group or even State is endowed with such dominion as for the sake of short-term advantage to pollute or gravely and permanently ravage the world in which God has put us; in this matter we are already facing the need for the enforcement of supranational law.

Four titles to dominion may be enumerated: first, *occupancy of what does not belong to another together with the intention of possessing it; to this may be reduced the *finding of what has been abandoned by another; second, *accession, or the increment gained by what is already owned; third, *prescription, which comes from continuous possession which has been legalized; fourth, *contract, or the transference of property by treaty. All titles are variously ruled by custom and civil law. Dominion achieved by conquest, like booty and the spoils of war, should ideally be ruled by international law; usually, however, the brute fact has to wait the passage of years before it can be made to look respectable.

[T. GILBY]

DOMINIS, MARCANTONIO DE (1566–1624), RC abp. of Spalato (Split, Yugoslavia), who for a time joined the Church of England. D. was first a Jesuit but left the Society in 1596. He was made bp. of Zengy (1600), then (1602) abp. of Spalato and primate of Dalmatia, at that time part of the Republic of Venice. During a political dispute between Venice and the papacy, he resigned, made his way to England (1616), became an Anglican, and was made Dean of Windsor (1617). His *De republica ecclesiastica* (1617–22) rejected the primacy of the pope and advocated equality of bps. in governing the Church. He also published P. *Sarpi's *Istoria del Concilio Tridentino* (1619). His participation in the consecration of G. Montaigne as bp. of Lincoln is an act important to the historical succession of *Anglican orders. Returning to Rome and the RC Church under Pope Gregory XV (1621), D. published an attack on the C of E and a retraction of his earlier writings in *Sui reditus ex Anglia consilium* (1623). He became suspect to the Inquisition, however, was imprisoned, and died in Castel Sant' Angelo. For views on the Trinity found among his papers he was condemned posthumously as a relapsed heretic, his body disinterred and burned along with his writings.

[T. C. O'BRIEN]

DOMINUS AC REDEMPTOR, the papal brief, signed June 9, 1773 but dated July 21, by which Clement XIV suppressed the Society of Jesus, in order to come to terms with Portugal and the Bourbon houses of France, Spain, Naples, and Parma. In those places the brief (not a solemn bull) was welcomed; its promulgation was forbidden in Prussia and Russia; in Austria Jesuits were permitted to continue in their houses as secular priests. By force of the brief, 11,000 members ceased to exist as Jesuits. The letter cited papal precedents for the suppression of an order; and gave as its reasons that the society was a hindrance to the peace of the Church and no longer fruitfully a contributor to her life. There is an unsubstantiated report that Clement revoked the brief in 1774. The suppression continued until 1814 when Pius VII revoked *Dominus ac Redemptor* and fully restored the society by the apostolic constitution, *Sollicitudo omnium ecclesiarum*.

[T. C. O'BRIEN]

DOMINUS VOBISCUM (Latin for the Lord be or is with you), a formula in use in the Western Church in the Latin Mass and elsewhere in the liturgy as a greeting, invitation, and blessing. The words are spoken as a means of drawing the attention of the congregation to what is about to follow, generally a prayer or the reading of the Gospel. The phrase has biblical precedent (Ruth 2.4; cf. Mt 28.20; 18.20) and appears to have been in common use at least as early as the 3d cent. for it is mentioned in the *Apostolic Tradition* of Hippolytus (d. 253). The response, "*et cum spiritu tuo*" (literally, and with your spirit"), was in the past generally interpreted to mean simply "and also with you," as it is now translated in the English liturgy. Some, however, saw in it a reference to the Holy Spirit as given in Holy Orders.

BIBLIOGRAPHY: J. A. Jungmann, *Mass of the Roman Rite* (tr. F. Brunner, 1950) 1:361–365.

[P. K. MEAGHER]

DOMITIAN (Titus Flavius; 51–96 A.D.). **ROMAN EMPEROR** from 81. The second son of Vespasian, D. spent his youth in relative obscurity and although he was made consul, exercised no real authority during the reigns of his father and brother Titus. Of a proud and somber intelligence, he became embittered by this long repression. Becoming emperor in 81, he set about a renewal of religion and morality, erecting a number of imposing temples, executing delinquent Vestals, and checking unnatural vice. Alarmed by a conspiracy in 88, he began a ruthless suppression of all opposition. His reign of terror was ended when he was assassinated by Stephanus, a freedman of Flavius Clemens, his cousin who had been consul in 95, but who had been put to death at the Emperor's command. BIBLIOGRAPHY: S. Gsell, *Essai sur le règne de l'empereur Domitien* (1894).

[M. J. COSTELLOE]

DOMITIAN OF ANCYRA (6th cent.), bishop. An Eastern monk and advocate of the heresy Origenism, D. became a friend of Emperor Justinian I and was made bp. of Ancyra in Galatia. About 545 he wrote a work *On the Origenian Controversy* directed to Pope Vergilius I, in which he acknowledged the deception of his fellow Origenists. BIBLIOGRAPHY: E. Venables, DCB 1:875.

[J. R. AHERNE]

DOMITIAN OF MAASTRICHT, ST. (d. 560), bp., patron of Huy, Belgium. As bp. of Tongeren (Tongres, later Maastricht) he attended the Councils at Clermont (535) and Orléans (549). He preached in Aquitaine and evangelized the Meuse River valley. Tradition holds he slew a monster that poisoned the drinking water at Huy. BIBLIOGRAPHY: W. Lampen, BiblSanct 4:758–759.

[N. F. GAUGHAN]

DOMITILLA, FLAVIA, ST. (1st cent.), martyr. She was associated in hagiography with SS. Nereus and Achilleus, but little certain is known of her. Eusebius writes that she was the great-niece of the Emperor Domitian who exiled her, because of her Christian faith, to the island of Pontia where she was eventually burned to death for refusing to acknowledge idols. BIBLIOGRAPHY: Butler 2:284–285.

[J. R. AHERNE]

DOMITILLA CATACOMB, ROME, with the Catacomb of Priscilla, the most ancient and largest of early Christian catacombs, near the Via Ardeatina, originating in late 1st or early 2d cent. as the burial ground for Domitilla, wife of a martyred Roman consul. This catacomb is renowned for its wall paintings.

[M. J. DALY]

DOMNOLUS OF LE MANS, ST. (d. 581), first abbot of Saint-Laurent in Paris, bp. of Le Mans from 559. He is lauded by Gregory of Tours in his *Historia Francorum* (6.9; 9.39) as one of the saintliest men of his time. BIBLIOGRAPHY: G. Bataille, BiblSanct 4:770; R. Aigrain, *Catholicisme* 3:1012–13.

DOMNUS OF ANTIOCH, the name of two bps. of Antioch. (1) **Domnus, bp. of Antioch** (268–271). The son of Bp. Demetrianos of Antioch, who was taken prisoner by the Persians, D. was an opponent of *Paul of Samosata, who had replaced Demetrianos as bishop. A council at Antioch in 268 chose D. as legitimate bishop. He was a man of known orthodoxy and piety and an adherent of the party that favored the Roman Empire. Paul of Samosata, of the anti-Roman party, refused to vacate the see. D. was bp. for only 3 years and died before the decree of Aurelian declaring him the rightful bp. was issued. (2) **Domnus, patriarch of Antioch,** 441–449. Nephew and successor to John of Antioch, he presided over his see in the troubled doctrinal times of the Eastern Church in the mid-5th century. Influenced by *Theodoret of Cyr, D. led the Syrian Church. The powerful monastic groups of which Eutyches was leader and theologian did everything possible to discredit D. and his adviser Theodoret at the imperial court. D. wrote to the Emperor accusing Eutyches of denying the humanity of Christ. Constantinople retaliated by demanding the deposition of a metropolitan recently appointed by D. From Alexandria came a new attack by the Patriarch Dioscorus. Emperor Theodosius II called for an ecumenical council to judge Eutyches. Pope Leo I sent legates and documents supporting the doctrine of D. and Theodoret. The council met at Ephesus in 449, presided over by Dioscorus of Alexandria, who ruthlessly engineered Eutyches' vindication and D.'s deposition. Pope Leo refused to accept this *atricinuim, the Robber Synod, as he called it, and with the cooperation of the new Empress Pulcheria, a council was called at Chalcedon in 451 to undo the Robber Synod's damage. The deposed D. returned to his monastery in Jerusalem and there spent his remaining days. BIBLIOGRAPHY: L. Duchesne, *Early History of the Christian Church* (1911) v. 3 *passim;* Fliche-Martin 4:208–236.

[J. R. AHERNE]

DON JUAN DE AUSTRIA, see JOHN OF AUSTRIA.

DON JUAN LEGEND. With the exception of the story of Faust, no other legendary tale has run through as many versions or found more musical settings than the legend of Don Juan. Since there are more than 500 versions of the story, with wide variations of treatment, it is difficult to isolate the essential elements of the legend. The most common seems to have taken form in a morality play, *El Burlador de Sevilla* by Tirso de Molina (written between 1613 and 1630). In the play a womanizing Don Juan kills the father of one of his victims, Dona Ana, in a duel. Later

Don Juan invites the statue of the Commander to dinner. The statue accepts, kills Don Juan, and thrusts him into hell. The French playwright Molière wrote a version noted for its psychological insights into the motives of Don Juan. The most famous telling of all is Mozart's opera *Don Giovanni,* regarded as perhaps the greatest of all operas. The German writer E. T. A. Hoffmann gave a new direction to the tale. In his Romantic interpretation, Don Juan is not fickle but seeking the ideal woman. He becomes a rebel against God and society. Pushkin and de Musset both follow Hoffmann. Lord Byron tells a story with little regard for its traditional form. A celebrated version is performed in Spain and in South America on All Souls' Day. In it Don Juan is redeemed by a good woman and saved from damnation. G. B. Shaw made Don Juan someone pursued by women and ravished by them. Musical treatments of the legend have been composed by Mozart, Richard Strauss, Gluck, and Lalo. BIBLIOGRAPHY: A. E. Singer *Bibliography of the Don Juan Theme: Versions and Criticism* (West Va. Univ. Bull. ser. 54, 10:1; 1954).

[J. R. AHERNE]

DONAHOE, PATRICK (1811–1901), American Catholic journalist. In 1833 D. became associated with the *Jesuit,* a paper founded by the bp. of Boston for Irish immigrants. Its name was changed in 1836 to *Boston Pilot,* and by 1838 D. was its sole owner. Three serious fires in his plant at a time when he was overextended in loans brought him to bankruptcy, but he had satisfied his creditors and recovered the paper by 1890. BIBLIOGRAPHY: F. J. Lally, NCE 4:998.

[M. J. SUELZER]

DONAT, JOSEF (1868–1946), German Jesuit philosopher. Ordained in 1895, D. taught at the Univ. of Innsbruck for 35 years, serving for a time as its rector. His great work was *Summa philosophiae Christianae* (1910), which was distinguished for its blend of philosophy and science. His work *The Freedom of Science* (1914) was a study of the nature of science and freedom and a defense of the Catholic Church in its posture toward each. Another perceptive study is *Über Psychoanalyse und Individual-Psychologie* (1932). BIBLIOGRAPHY: A. Moschetti, EncFil 1:1715–16.

[J. R. AHERNE]

DONATELLO (Donato de Niccolò di Betto Bardi; 1386–1466), sculptor of Florence, one of the most influential figures in the establishment of Renaissance art. He studied with Ghiberti, was a lifelong friend of Brunelleschi, and twice journeyed to Rome to study the antiquities there. His works are distinguished by their vital realism, their exploration of perspective effects, and, in heroic subjects, by the grandness of their pathos. His colossal equestrian monument, the Gattamelata (Erasmo da Narni), in front of San Antonio (Padua) is the first free-standing equestrian monument of the modern age. It celebrates in an appropriately somber style, which recalls the greatness of Roman art at its best, the awesome dignity of a war lord. The large majority of his works represent Christian subjects. They are animated by a keen sense for the drama of the life of the Savior and the heroic aspects of sainthood, and are deeply moving. In several statues his realism deliberately startles or shocks the viewer (*Prophet,* called Il Zuccone; the youthful David in the nude; Judith in the act of beheading Holofernes; Mary Magdalen grown old and haggard), but only (though this is debated in some cases) to make visible in the contrast, the splendor of the souls inhabiting these figures. His last years were spent in designing two bronze pulpits for San Lorenzo, elaborate works of great spirituality. His best works are seen in Florence, Padua, and Siena. BIBLIOGRAPHY: H. W. Janson, *Sculpture of Donatello* (1963).

[P. P. FEHL]

DONATI, a class of *conversi* sometimes found in monasteries from the early Middle Ages. They did not become full-fledged monks but were permitted to reside in the monastery and to share in its life. This privilege was generally granted them in consideration of their benefactions or services to the community. Modern religious communities sometimes offer hospitality to individuals for similar reasons, and often they are called *donati.* They live with the community and participate in its life and activity but without making a formal novitiate or taking vows; sometimes as *tertiaries they are permitted to wear the habit.

[J. C. WILLKE]

DONATION OF ADRIAN, a name for the *Laudabiliter,* alleged bull of *Adrian IV.

DONATION OF CONSTANTINE, known also as the *Constitutum Constantini,* a document forged probably in the mid-8th cent., purporting to be a constitutional grant made by Emperor Constantine I to Pope Sylvester I. It is thought to have emanated from the papal chancery, headed at that time by Christophorus. The document draws heavily from the *Legenda s. Sylvestri,* an apocryphal work. Constantine tells the story of his conversion and of the cleansing of his leprosy. In return he decreed the supremacy of the successors of St. Peter over the whole Christian Church and conferred upon the pope imperial power, dignity, emblems, the Lateran Palace, and the right to rulership over Rome, the whole of Italy, and the Western regions. The purpose the forgery was primarily intended to serve is not beyond dispute. Possibly it was originally aimed at strengthening the position of the Roman See in the challenges against its primacy made by patriarchal sees in the East, esp. those connected with the Iconoclast troubles then rife in the East. Others claim that its immediate objective was to gain the support of Pepin on behalf of the papacy in its struggles with the Lombards in Italy, for which purpose Pope

Stephen II visited the Frankish court in 754. At any rate, the document was used for more than 200 years against adversaries of the Holy See in both East and West. The first serious questions raised about the document were put forward by lawyers, not on the issue of its authenticity, but on the grounds of the questionable legitimacy of such an extraordinary grant. After the time of Innocent III (r. 1198–1216), theologians and lawyers felt free to question the document, but it was not until the 15th cent. that it was proved to be a forgery by the independent studies of Laurentius Valla and Nicholas of Cusa. BIBLIOGRAPHY: W. Ullman, *Growth of Papal Government in the Middle Ages* (2d ed. 1962) 74–86; *Church and State through the Centuries* (ed. S. Z. Ehler and J. B. Morrel, 1954) 16–22.

[P. K. MEAGHER]

DONATION OF PEPIN, the gift to Pope Stephen II by Pepin the Short of the former Byzantine possessions in Italy, the exarchate of Ravenna and the Duchy of Rome —these forming the basis of the *States of the Church. According to the *Liber Pontificalis,* it was made when the two met at the Council of *Quiercy in 754. Stephen turned to Pepin for protection against the Lombards after appealing in vain to the Emperor in the East. When the Lombard King Desiderius later attacked the Roman territory, Stephen III appealed to Charlemagne, who defeated the Lombards (781 and 787) and confirmed the donation of Pepin, adding some additional lands.

[T. EARLY]

DONATISTS, members of a predominantly North African schism who broke away from the Church in 312 and received their name from their leader, *Donatus, who was consecrated bishop in 315 and died in exile c.355. Despite vigorous efforts on the part of Roman, Vandal, and Byzantine rulers to suppress it, Donatism persisted in North Africa into Muslim times. The immediate cause of the schism was the election of a successor to Mensurius as bp. of Carthage in 311. Without waiting for the arrival of their Numidian confreres, the assembled bps. proceeded to elect Caecilian, Mensurius's archdeacon, as his successor. This offended the absent bps., particularly Secundus, Bp. of Tigisis, a see that had for 40 years enjoyed the right of consecrating the bp. of Carthage. Under the presidency of Secundus 70 bps. met in Carthage and declared the consecration of Caecilian invalid on the grounds that he had been consecrated by Felix of Aptunga, a *traditor,* i.e., one who had handed over the Scriptures to the pagans during Diocletian's persecution. This council then elected Majorinus bishop. The bitter disputes that rose from this schism at Carthage required the intervention of the Emperor; Constantine I asked Pope Miltiades to settle the issues. In a council held at Rome on Oct. 2, 313, the bps. of Italy and Gaul decided in favor of Caecilian. Majorinus appealed the decision to the Emperor. A second council convoked in Arles on Aug. 1, 314, reaffirmed the decision.

Another appeal met with no more success. A synod held in Milan on Nov. 10, 316, declared that Caecilian was lawfully elected, validly consecrated, and in just possession of the See of Carthage. In the meantime Majorinus had died. Donatus, his successor, proved an able and energetic leader; in 317 he was banished by Constantius to Gaul or Spain along with other Donatist bps. for encouraging the *Circumcellions, Donatist terrorists, who were plundering the provinces. When Julian the Apostate became emperor in 361, these exiles were allowed to return to Africa, where the schism flourished for another 30 years.

After Parmenian, Donatus's successor, died in 391, the movement was weakened by internal schisms and dissensions. Continued Donatist attacks on the Catholics prompted the bps. assembled in a council at Carthage in 404 to ask Emperor Honorius to include the Donatists in the laws against heretics. On Feb. 12, 405, he issued an edict denouncing the Donatists as heretics for their practice of rebaptism and ordering them to restore the churches taken from the Catholics. When the Donatists petitioned for withdrawal of the edict, the imperial tribune Marcellinus at a large council held at Carthage in June 411, decided in favor of the Catholics. Further imperial decrees were issued against the Donatists in 412, 414, and 428.

The remarkable success of Donatism in the face of vigorous opposition may be attributed to political, social, and religious factors. The Donatists claimed to be the champions of the slaves and oppressed natives in the face of the Roman landlords. Their simple and uncomplicated doctrine, stressing the sanctity and the exclusiveness of their Church, appealed to a fanatical strain in the populace who looked upon themselves as a society of saints, though the Catholics regarded them as cruel and ruthless adversaries. Their errors were combatted by Optatus of Milevis and in particular by St. Augustine. The Donatist controversies led to the clarification of a number of important questions, e.g., the efficacy of the sacraments *ex opere operato;* the nature of the Church, of schism, and of heresy; and the relations between Church and State and of heretics to a Christian state. BIBLIOGRAPHY: W. H. C. Frend, *Donatist Church* (1952); G. Bareille, DTC 4:2:1701–27; A. Pincherle, EncCatt 4:1851–55.

[M. J. COSTELLOE]

DONATUS (d. c.355), bp. of Casae Nigrae in Numidia and later Donatist bp. of Carthage. At the end of the persecution under Diocletian, D. headed the party opposed to the election of Caecilian to succeed Mensurius as bp. of Carthage. Attacking Caecilian and his supporters as *traditores* (see TRADITOR), he, with other Numidian bps., elected Marjorinus as metropolitan. This marked the beginning of the Donatist schism (312). The following year D. himself became schismatic bp. of Carthage and head of the party that came to bear his name. He was a man of eloquence and strong personality, accused by St. Augustine of arrogance and impiety. BIBLIOGRAPHY: W. H. C. Frend, *Donatist Church* (1952). *DONATISTS.

[R. B. ENO]

DONATUS OF BESANÇON, ST. (*c.*590–*c.*660), a monk of Luxeuil of noble birth who became bp. of Besançon *c.*626. He is remembered esp. for having founded at Besançon two monasteries during his active episcopate. One was for men; it became known as the Abbey of St. Paul, and for it he composed a rule that combined elements from the rules of SS. Benedict and Columbanus. This is not certainly identifiable with the text reproduced by St. Benedict of Aniane in his *Codex regularum.* The other monastery was for women; it was called *Jussanum* or Jussamoutier. His rule for it, besides depending on the two sources he had used for his rule for men, shows the influence of the rule of St. Caesarius of Arles. Its text is reproduced in PL 87:273–298. BIBLIOGRAPHY: J. Marilier, BiblSanct 4:785–786; R. Aigrain, *Catholicisme* 3:1015–17.

DONATUS THE GRAMMARIAN, the most renowned Roman grammarian of the 4th cent. and St. Jerome's teacher. His chief contribution and most famous work is *Donati ars grammatica tribus libris comprehensa.* Other writings exist only in fragments or as introductions such as the prefaces to five of the six plays of Terence. D.'s name became synonymous with the study of grammar, and his text served as a popular schoolbook of the Middle Ages and a basic guide for subsequent studies from his day to modern times. BIBLIOGRAPHY: OCD 297.

[S. A. HEENEY]

DONDERS, PETER (1809–1887), Netherland Redemptorist missionary. D. labored with great success, first among the blacks, and then extended his apostolate to the Indians in Saramaca. Most of his life was spent in the care of lepers in Batavia, Surinam (Netherlands Guiana). Because of his heroic charity and deep spirituality, his cause for beatification was begun in 1900. BIBLIOGRAPHY: K. Kronenburg, *Apostle of the Lepers* (1930); J. Magnier, CE 5:129–130.

[K. O'NEILL]

DONGAN, THOMAS (1634–1715), colonial official. Born in Ireland, he attained the rank of colonel in the army, serving in England and France. Charles II appointed him lieutenant governor (1677–80) of Tangiers. In 1682 he was chosen by James, Duke of York and recent (1672) convert to Catholicism, to govern his American colony. New York's Catholic governor arrived in the colony (1683) accompanied by an English Jesuit, who was later joined by four other members of the Society. D. was chief sponsor of a bill (1683) containing a guarantee of religious freedom. But the downfall (1688) of James II brought renewed persecution of Catholics in England and colonial America, and D. was forced to flee New York. He returned to England

(1691) but died without recovering his confiscated lands. BIBLIOGRAPHY: T. P. Phelan, *Thomas Dongan, Colonial Governor of New York 1683–88* (1933).

[M. CARTHY]

DONIZETTI, GAETANO (1796–1848), Italian opera composer. D.'s works were performed and well received all over Europe. At a time when opera was, above all, an exhibition of vocal tone and technique, he satisfied the demand of capable singers for a medium to express their virtuosity. Of his works, *Lucia di Lammermoor, Don Pasquale,* and *L'Elisir d'amore* are still regularly performed. During a visit to Vienna, D. composed a *Miserere* and an *Ave Maria* for the court chapel. Both are in strict style and were well received by the German critics. BIBLIOGRAPHY: H. Edwards, Grove DMM 2:733–736.

[M. T. LEGGE]

DONNE, JOHN (1572–1631), English poet and divine. Related on his mother's side to Thomas More, D. grew up in the so-called Old Faith. His uncle, Jasper Heywood, a member of the Jesuit mission, was exiled in 1584. D.'s only brother, Henry, died in Newgate (1593), imprisoned there for sheltering a priest. His mother, Elizabeth Heywood Donne, still an adherent of the Old Faith, was living with D. in the deanery of St. Paul's at the time of her death. In her books of private devotion D. may have familiarized himself with forms of meditation, which helped to shape his *Holy Sonnets* (principally 1609), and with the mysteries of the rosary and the offices of the breviary, which influenced the *La Corona* sonnets (1607). D. attended Oxford and possibly also Cambridge, studied at the Inns of Court, and took part in Essex's expeditions to Cadiz (1596) and the Azores (1597). By 1598 D. had written the verse *Satires,* the *Elegies,* and a number of the *Songs and Sonnets.* In that year he became secretary to the Lord Keeper, Sir Thomas Egerton, and therefore presumably had conformed at least nominally to the Established Church. His secret marriage in 1601 to Anne More, Lady Egerton's niece, cut short a promising career ("John Donne, Anne Donne, Undone"). Living in poverty, surrounded by a growing family, the road to secular preferment blocked, D. finally yielded to King James's insistence and was ordained in 1615. There seems no reason to doubt the sincerity of his religious convictions. In 1621 James nominated him Dean of St. Paul's.

Izaak Walton's *Life* (1640) initiated the Jack Donne–John Donne conversion motif in Donne biography. Twentieth-century scholars have established the greater continuity of his life. He was a theologically traditional young gallant as well as later, a witty preacher and Dean of Paul's; a master of commanding phraseology in his *Devotions* ("Send not to know for whom the bell tolls") no less than in his love poems ("For Godsake hold your tongue, and let me love"). D.'s "rediscovery" after Grierson's edition of the *Poems* (1912) and his espousal by T. S. Eliot and others have been of major importance to 20th-cent.

poetry. Text: *Poems* (ed. H. J. C. Grierson, 2 v., 1912); *Devotions upon Emergent Occasions* (ed. J. Sparrow, 1923); *Divine Poems* (ed. H. L. Gardner, 1952); *Sermons* (eds. G. R. Potter and E. M. Simpson, 10 v., 1953–62); *Anniversaries* (ed. F. Manley, 1963); *Elegies and the Songs and Sonnets* (ed. H. L. Gardner, 1965). BIBLIOGRAPHY: R. C. Bald, *John Donne: A Life* (ed. W. Milgate, 1970); G. H. Carrithers, *Donne at Sermons* (1972); D. Cathcart, *Doubling Conscience: Donne and the Poetry of Moral Argument* (1975).

[M. S. CONLAN]

DONUS (d. 678), **POPE** from 676. Little is known of him except that he was requested by Emperor *Constantine IV Pogonatus to send delegates to a theological conference to prepare the way for a general council needed to deal with the persistence of *Monothelitism. He is credited with the restoration of several churches and disbanded the Syrian Nestorian monks of a Roman monastery who were stirring up trouble by their preaching. During his reign the schism begun by Maurus, abp. of Ravenna, who was seeking to make his see autocephalous, was brought to an end. BIBLIOGRAPHY: C. M. Aherne, NCE 4:1010; Mann 1.2:20; T. Oestreich, CE 5:133.

[P. F. MULHERN]

DOOLEY, THOMAS ANTHONY (1927–1961), physician, humanitarian, a doctor in the U.S. Navy Reserve. D.'s life is that of a contemporary saint. His two great ideals were to bring modern medicine to Southeast Asia and to show democracy as a force for good superior to communism. While in the navy he worked with Vietnamese refugees in Saigon. From this came the book *Deliver Us from Evil* in 1955. A year later D. resigned from the Navy to take a medical team to Laos. He worked there with enormous success until an injury sustained in the jungle forced him to return to the U.S. where he died at the age of 34. He is also author of *Edge of Tomorrow* (1958), *The Night They Burned the Mountain* (1960), and *Dr. Tom Dooley—My Story* (1960). The impact of D. as medical savior to thousands and as a totally winning personality made him a folk-hero. BIBLIOGRAPHY: T. Gallagher, *Give Joy to My Youth* (1965).

[J. R. AHERNE]

DOOR OF DEATH, see MANZÙ, GIACOMO.

DOORKEEPER, (OSTIARIUS, PORTER), the lowest of the minor orders. Instituted *c.*250, the order was formally abolished by Paul VI in 1972. The duties of the porter were "to ring the bells, open the church and sacristy, and open the book for the preacher" (Pontificale). In the early Church the porter had to guard the doors against intruders' disturbing the service; the porter was responsible always that religious decorum be maintained for sacred worship.

[K. O'NEILL]

DOORS, CHURCH. Impressive in monumental concepts, church doors of wood and metal in varied themes reflect iconographic and stylistic changes throughout the ages. The wooden doors of St. Sabina on the Aventine in Rome (*c.*432) with Oriental stylistic elements in 28 panels of the OT and NT show one of the earliest examples of the Crucifixion. Metal doors inlaid with niello, silver and gold (Amalfi, Monte Cassino, St. Paul-outside-the-Walls in Rome) show faces in thin silver plate with delicately engraved features. At St. Michele in Gargano the silver line flowing through the bronze, adding sublimity to the moving figures, reflects Byzantine MSS; at Trani there is a debt to Byzantine ivories. The sculptured forms on bronze doors for Abp. Bernward of Hildesheim at the cathedral of St. Michael (1015) derive from Carolingian and Ottonian miniatures, the three-dimensional heads relating also to Limoges enamels of the period. Gothic stone portals were followed by L. Ghiberti's Renaissance masterpieces for the Baptistery of the cathedral of Florence, the gilded bronze *Gates of Paradise* (1425–52) complementing the earlier doors of Gothic style by A. Pisano and L. Ghiberti. Bronze doors at Marienthal, Germany (1950), the innovative enameled aluminum doors at *Notre-Dame-du-Haut, Ronchamp, by Le Corbusier (1954–55), wooden doors of the cathedral at Ibadan, Nigeria, by Lamidi Fakeye (1956), and the famous *Doors of Death* for St. Peter's, Rome, by Giacomo Manzù (1964) are outstanding examples of 20th-cent. church doors. BIBLIOGRAPHY: H. Leisinger, *Romanesque Bronzes: Church Portals in Mediaeval Europe* (1956); A. Goldschmidt, *Die deutschen Bronzetüren des frühen Mittelalters,* (1926).

[M. J. DALY]

DOORS, HOLY, special entrance doors to the four major basilicas in Rome: St. Peter, St. Paul-outside-the-Walls, St. John Lateran, and St. Mary Major. These doorways are walled up except during a *Holy Year when they are opened by the pope and three cardinals in simultaneous ceremonies. BIBLIOGRAPHY: J. J. Gavigan, NCE 7:108–109.

[N. R. KRAMER]

DÖPFNER, JULIUS (1915–76), German abp, card. from 1958, leader at Vatican Council II. He was born in Hausen, N Bavaria, studied in Rome, and was ordained there in 1939. Named bp. of Würzburg in 1948, he was the youngest European bp. at that time. He won fame as bp. of Berlin, from 1957, for his forthright protests against East Germany's infringement of religious freedom; his attacks on the policy brought a government ban on his traveling outside Berlin itself. Against his own wishes he was transferred from Berlin to become abp. of Munich-Preising in 1961. At Vatican Council II Paul VI in 1963 appointed D. one of the four cardinal moderators, and he became identified as a leader of the progressive conciliar fathers, pitted, at least by the press, against the conservatives and their leader Card. Ottaviani. All through his episcopate D. fostered in word and action the cause of ecumenism in Germany. The last great effort of his life was directed against making abortion on demand legal in Germany.

[T. C. O'BRIEN]

DORATIUS, see DOUJAT, JOANNES.

DORCHESTER, ABBEY OF, former monastery of the Canons Regular of St. Augustine. Dorchester was in 634 the see of St. Birinus, sent by Pope Honorius I as bishop. The abbey was founded *c.*1140 by Alexander, bp. of Lincoln, for the Augustinian Canons and dedicated to SS. Peter, Paul, and Birinus. Because of the wealth of lands and tithes of the former bishopric, the abbey was richly endowed. The first abbot was probably Alured, elected in 1146; the last, John Mershe, elected in 1533. A year later he with five of his canons subscribed to the king's supremacy. Henry VIII reserved part of the abbey for a college dedicated to the Holy Trinity. His successor, however, dissolved it within a year. The abbey site and precincts have since passed through various hands. The church, built entirely by the Augustinian Canons during 2 cent., completed *c.*1330, is famous for its beauty and for the belief that the bones of St. Birinus rest there.

[K. O'NEILL]

DORDRECHT, SYNOD OF, see DORT, SYNOD OF.

DORDRECHT CONFESSION OF FAITH, an Anabaptist formula, accepted by some Mennonite Churches in the United States. The author was Adriaan Corenlisz, of the Flemish Mennonite Church at Dordrecht (Dort) in Holland; the Confession was accepted chiefly as a platform for union and cooperation between Flemish and Frisian Mennonite groups. There are 18 articles, expressing, beside general Christian beliefs, *believer's baptism, *footwashing, *avoidance (i.e., ostracism of the excommunicated), *nonresistance, and the prohibition of oaths. Mennonites traditionally have not imposed creedal formulas on the conscience of the individual; the Dordrecht Confession has been used as a catechetical instrument. Text: J. C. Wenger, *Doctrines of the Mennonites* (1952) 78–86. BIBLIOGRAPHY: J. C. Wenger, MennEnc 2:92–93.

[T. C. O'BRIEN]

DORÉ, GUSTAVE PAUL G. (1832–1883), French artist, painter, and sculptor, acclaimed in the 19th cent. for drawings, book illustrations, and caricatures. He is less appreciated today, but his works are still prized by a small number of collectors. In Paris (1847) D. executed weekly lithograph caricatures for *Journal pour rire.* Woodcuts for Rabelais' *Gargantua* (1854) and Balzac's *Droll Stories* (1855) made D. famous and were followed by others for Dante's *Inferno* (1861) and Cervantes' *Don Quixote* (1865). D. was not so successful in painting and sculpture,

his fantastic images being best suited to expression in black and white. After 1862 he made sketches that were transferred photographically to blocks, effecting dramatic illustrations for his most ambitious and successful project—an illustrated Bible (1865). BIBLIOGRAPHY: J. Valmy-Baysse, *Gustave Doré* (1930).

[M. J. DALY]

DORIA, ANDREA (1466 or 1468–1560), influential Italian statesman and admiral. D. began his career in the guards of Innocent III, then moved to the Neapolitan army of Alphonso of Aragon. Eventually he turned from land to sea service and became an independent naval power by financing his own fleet. D. was commander of the galleys of France under Francis I and those of Clement VII. He alternately fought for France and for Emperor Charles V. Absolute head of the naval forces of Austria, D. directed the struggle against the Turks and Barbary pirates. He was one of the most powerful men of the 16th century. Eminently successful in many and varied campaigns, he ultimately became the one-man ruler of Genoa, drawing up a constitution, which, though aristocratic, honored republican institutions and endured with only minor changes until 1798. BIBLIOGRAPHY: R. C. Anderson, *Naval Wars in the Levant, 1559–1853* (1952).

[S. A. HEENEY]

DORIAN (also *primus modus,* first mode), the *mode or scale beginning on D. Its *plagal form is termed hypodorian (*secundus tonus,* second mode).

[A. DOHERTY]

DORLAND, PETER (DORLANDUS; 1454–1507), Belgian Carthusian. A biography discovered by P. H. J. J. Scholtens in the Bibliothèque Nationale, Paris, *Vita venerabilis domini ac patris Petri Dorlandi carthusiensis* . . . states that his birthplace was the Walloon village of Walcourt (in Namur province). He studied at the Univ. of Louvain and became a Carthusian monk at Zeelhem *c.* 1475. His apostolic life as a preacher was very active. He worked esp. among poets and had a lifelong devotion to St. Genesius, patron of actors. He spent his last years in patient suffering. D. was a prolific writer, having produced some 60 works in Latin. Most celebrated is his *Viola animae,* a dialogue between our Blessed Lady and a servant of God; it is of greater literary value than many of his other works. His pious writings include sermons, poetry, hymns, and prayers. According to many scholars he wrote the medieval morality play, *Everyman* (*Elckerlyc* in Flemish; *Jedermann* in German). BIBLIOGRAPHY: R. Aubert, DHGE 14:682; S. Autore, DTC 4.2:1782–85.

[S. A. HEENEY]

DORMITION OF THE VIRGIN, a phrase used to refer to Mary's death. Although it is never mentioned in Scripture, a body of legends concerning Mary's death gradually arose in Christian apocryphal literature. These legends are called the *Transitus Mariae* Literature, and the earliest dates back to the second half of the 5th century. Although highly imaginative, they reveal a strong early Christian desire to discover everything possible about Mary's death, and a belief that something quite extraordinary attended that event. The apocrypha go into great detail. An angel, usually Gabriel, but sometimes even Christ himself, appears to Mary and foretells her death. The Apostles are miraculously brought in from great distances to be at her bedside and to receive her blessing. Christ appears and takes her soul to heaven while the Apostles carry her body to the valley of Josaphat for burial. Hostile men plan to burn her body, but the Holy Spirit intervenes and she is buried by the Apostles. After 3 days (sometimes longer), the Apostles open the tomb and find that Mary's body is gone. It is revealed to them that she has been taken up to heaven, body and soul. These legends show the antiquity of the Christian belief in the Assumption of Mary. Early in the 5th cent. a feast in honor of Mary's "rest," stressing the extraordinary circumstances surrounding her death, was celebrated on August 15th in Jerusalem. By the end of the 6th cent., Emperor Maurice (582–602) decreed that the Feast of Mary's Dormition be celebrated on August 15th throughout the Byzantine Empire. Rome adopted the feast in the 7th cent. and eventually changed its title from Dormition to the Assumption. BIBLIOGRAPHY: W. Burghardt, "The Testimony of the Patristic Age Concerning Mary's Death," *Marian Studies* 8 (1957) 58–59; D. F. Hickey, NCE 4:1017; R. H. Chabot, "Feasts in Honor of Our Lady," Carol Mariol 3:22–52. *ASSUMPTION OF MARY.

[T. R. HEATH]

DOROTHEANS, Congregation of the Sisters of St. Dorothy, founded (1834) in Quinto, Italy, by Bl. Paola *Frassinetti. The congregation has houses in Europe, N and S America, Africa, and China. In 1975 they numbered 2,241; their generalate is in Rome. The Dorotheans, whose rule is an adaptation of that of St. Ignatius, are dedicated to education, care of orphans, and to retreat work.

[J. R. RIVELLO]

DOROTHEUS OF ANTIOCH (fl. *c*.300), exegete. The little that is known of him is derived from *Eusebius (*Eccl. hist.* 7.32), who reports that he met D., a deacon, during the episcopacy of Cyril of Antioch (281–303). He was very learned in Hebrew and scriptural exegesis. He was a contemporary of *Lucian of Antioch, the teacher of *Arius, but there is nothing to show any doctrinal influence or collaboration between them. BIBLIOGRAPHY: L. Abramowski, DHGE 14:685–686; Quasten 2:144.

[R. B. ENO]

DOROTHEUS OF GAZA, 6th-cent. monk, founder of a monastery near Gaza, Egypt, *c*.435. He was notable for his inspiring sermons on such topics as the duties of monks,

humility, and fear of God. Twenty-four sermons are extant, as well as letters and explanations of some passages of St. Gregory of Nazianzus. D.'s works earned enduring esteem in monastic circles for profoundness of doctrine and accuracy of psychological observations. BIBLIOGRAPHY: G. Bardy, *Catholicisme* 3:1039–40.

[S. A. HEENEY]

DOROTHEUS OF MYTILENE (d. *c*.1444), Greek bp. who took a prominent part in the *Union of Florence. In his own See of Mytilene, D. had vigorously opposed the Latin patriarch. Even as he arrived with the emperor's entourage for the Council of Ferrara-Florence, he was anti-Roman. Yet he changed and came to work actively for a union based on the recognition of papal supremacy, but one that would preserve a pure Byzantine liturgy. Recent studies show him to be the likely author of the surviving portions of the Greek acts of the Council of Florence. BIBLIOGRAPHY: J. Gill, "*Quae supersunt actorum graecorum Concilii Florentini*" in *Concilum Florentinum. Documenta et Scriptores* (ser. B, v. 5, 1953); *Council of Florence* (1959) *passim*; V. Laurent, DHGE 14:689–690.

[T. C. O'BRIEN]

DOROTHEUS OF TYRUS (fl. mid-5th cent.), bp. of Tyrus (Tyre?). He was among the bps. of his province who, after the Council of Chalcedon, signed a letter to the Emperor Leo (*c*.457) requesting his approval for the council. He cannot therefore be identified with a doubtful Dorotheus of Tyre mentioned by a 9th-cent. chronicler as martyred under Julian (362). BIBLIOGRAPHY: G. Bardy, *Catholicisme* 3:1040–41; K. Baus, LTK 3:525.

[R. B. ENO]

DOROTHY, ST. (4th cent.), martyr. According to St. Aldhelm, quoting from the *Passio* concerning her, D. was tortured by Fabricius, governor of Caesarea in Cappadocia, for refusing to marry and to worship idols. Her representation during the Middle Ages holding a basket with three apples and three roses derives from the legend stating that as she was being led to execution the young lawyer Theophilus jeeringly asked her to send him apples and roses from the garden to which she was going. An angel appeared with a basket containing three apples and three roses; Theophilus was converted and became a martyr. D.'s body is believed to repose in the church bearing her name in Rome.

DORT, SYNOD OF (Dordrecht, near Rotterdam), an assembly of the *Reformed Church, convened to deal with *Arminianism. It met in 154 sessions, Nov. 1618–May 1619. The States General of Holland convoked the meeting to settle the long conflict between *Remonstrants and Contra-Remonstrants; 27 representatives from Reformed Churches of Switzerland, the Palatinate, England, and Scotland attended. In part because of political considerations, the Arminians, represented chiefly by S.

*Episcopius, were from the beginning treated as defendants on trial; many weeks passed before they were even admitted to the sessions. Their teaching was condemned, and many of their leaders were imprisoned or banished. Against the Arminians' *Remonstrance,* the five doctrinal chapters of the Synod, called the Canons of Dort, asserted unconditional divine *election and *reprobation; the *limited atonement of Christ; the *total depravity of men; *irresistible grace; and the *assurance of salvation or perseverance of the elect. The Canons of Dort were accepted as a doctrinal standard by the Reformed Church in Holland and by the *Reformed Church in America. They were given recognition, but less formal acceptance, by Reformed Churches elsewhere. BIBLIOGRAPHY: Mayer RB 225–226; Schaff Creeds 1:509–523; 3:550–597. *CALVINISM.

[T. C. O'BRIEN]

DOSIO, DORASTANTE MARIA (fl. 1650), Italian sculptor and silversmith who, while active in Bologna, created the bronze statue of Pope Alexander VII (1660) and worked in the Church of S. Giacomo Maggiore.

[M. J. DALY]

DOSITHEUS, ST. (d. *c.* 530). Reared a pagan, D. went to visit Jerusalem while still a youth. In Gethsemane, he was moved by a painting of those suffering in hell, and a mysterious old woman answered his question of how to avoid their fate by telling him to fast and pray. Following the counsel of friends, he became a monk near Gaza under Abbot Seridos, who entrusted him to the special guidance of Dorotheus of Gaza. D. was made infirmarian and taught to exercise extreme humility, obedience, and renunciation. After 5 years, he contracted tuberculosis; dying, he was promised heaven by Dorotheus, who assured the skeptical other monks that D. had reached a high level of sanctity, not through external austerity, but through the denial of self-will. BIBLIOGRAPHY: Butler 1:403–404; G. Bardy, *Catholicisme* 3:1041; PG 88:1611.

[P. K. MEAGHER]

DOSITHEUS OF JERUSALEM (1641–1707), **PATRIARCH OF JERUSALEM** from 1669, noted for his anti-Catholicism. During his long patriarchate he fought against Protestants and Catholics, sustained the Greek fraternity of the Holy Sepulcher, and developed the Hellenic influence in the Middle East, and esp. in Russia. He collected and published ancient and modern anti-Latin texts, the most important of which are his own books: *Acts of Faith* and *History of the Patriarchs of Jerusalem.* His own *Confession of Faith* is called by the Russians the *Letter of the Patriarchs* because it was sent in the name of all the patriarchs to the council united by Peter the Great. BIBLIOGRAPHY: A. Palmieri, DTC 4:1788–1800; A. Fortescue, CE 8:366 s.v. "Jerusalem."

[P. FOSCOLOS]

DOSITHEUS OF SAMARIA, founder of a Samaritan sect, Dositheans, that observed strict Levitical purity; some were vegetarians, some celibates. The sect is included in lists of Hegesippus and Hippolytus. D. is variously dated from the 3d cent. B.C. to the 1st cent. A.D. Some scholars see evidence of two men (and two sects) by that name, one pre-Christian and taking the Sadducean view of the resurrection and one post-Christian taking the Pharisees' view. Information in the Jewish, Samaritan, patristic, and Arabic sources does not give a clear picture.

[T. EARLY]

DOSITHEUS, APOCALYPSE OF, see APOCRYPHA (NEW TESTAMENT), 17.

DOSSAL (DORSAL), a reredos-like curtain hung behind the altar or suspended from the canopy. Before the change of the altar's position this curtain, with two others, one at each side, was hung from rods fastened on the wall or rested on four pillars erected at each end of the altar. Often the pillars were surmounted by angels holding candelabra, lighted on festive occasions.

[K. O'NEILL]

DOSSO, GIOVANNI LUTERI (*c.* 1490–1542), Italian painter of the Ferrarese school, executing mythologies (with Titian) and religious works (*Madonna and Three Saints, St. George, St. Jerome, Holy Family*) in sketchy, dry brush strokes and acid color. D.'s romantic landscapes and heavy figures gesture in pastoral overtones to Giorgione (note the detail from Giorgione's *Fête Champêtre* in the background of D.'s *Circe*). D. was assisted by his brother Battista (fl. 1517–53), a weaker painter from Raphael's *bottega.* BIBLIOGRAPHY: R. Longhi, *Officina ferrarese* (1934) 5:135–151.

[M. J. DALY]

DOSTOYEVSKY, FEODOR MIKHAILOVICH (1821–81), Russian novelist. This eminent writer, a member of the impoverished nobility, was gently reared by his mother. Through her he learned the religious experiences that colored his life and works. On the other hand, his severe and often harsh father created guilt feelings and traumatic shock in D.'s otherwise gentle nature. Both parents were Russian Orthodox, a fact that supplied the warp for the tapestry of D.'s novels. Though trained at a school of military engineering and commissioned in the army, his nature was uncongenial to military life. The humanities, esp. the works of Dickens and Balzac, steadily absorbed his interest. Ill health, seizures of epilepsy, and shattered nerves, consequent of 4 years of Siberian imprisonment, influenced his writings. D.'s human emphasis, his concern for the struggle between good and evil, was neither humanistic nor traditionally Christian. He was preoccupied with the struggle between the God-man and the man-God. This theme permeated his novels, e.g., *The Idiot* (1868),

The Brothers Karamazov (1869–70), and *The Possessed* (1871). His knowledge of psychology and his philosophic insights, added to his strong narrative style and character analyses, make him one of the giants of the literary world. It should be remembered that D.'s power lies mainly in his ideas which are so great and vast that his exquisite artistry is often overshadowed. D. was twice married. After an additional period of military service near the Siberian border had expired, he married a young widow. This marriage was ill-fated and a guilt complex stirred up the ever present threat of epilepsy. After the death of this wife from tuberculosis, he married Anna Snitkina, his stenographer. Her understanding and love at this period (1867) enabled him to pursue his writing. These novels are all marked with concern for the human soul and with the final solution to man's problems: the humility and love of Christ. D. has been said to be one of the most profound Christian writers. Other works by D. are *Notes from the Underground* (1864); *Crime and Punishment* (1866); *The Gambler* (1967); *The Eternal Husband* (1870); and *A Raw Youth* (1875). BIBLIOGRAPHY: A. Gide, *Dostoevsky* (Eng. tr. 1925, pa. 1961); D. I. Fanger, *Dostoevsky and Romantic Realism* (1965); K. A. Peace, *Dostoevsky, an Examination of the Major Novels* (pa. 1975); A. Gibson, *Religion of Dostoevsky* (1974).

[R. M. FUNCHION]

DOSWALD, HILARY JOSEPH (1877–1951), American Carmelite prior general. Ordained a Calced Carmelite in 1900, D. helped found and was principal of Mt. Carmel High School in Chicago. Named assistant general in 1925, he was elected prior general in 1931, in which capacity he served for 16 years. At the same time he served as consultant to the Congregation for the Sacraments in Rome. His tenure as prior general saw a dramatic increase in world membership for the order and increased missionary activity in Indonesia and Rhodesia. Under his direction were published *Life in Carmel* (1934) and *The Carmelite Directory of the Spiritual Life* (1951).

[J. R. AHERNE]

DOUAI (DOUAY), center of English Catholic refuge after Elizabeth became queen in 1558. Then a city of Flanders, Spanish Netherlands, it is now in N France. W. *Allen established a college there in 1568 to train English priests, many of whom were executed after returning to England. Because of wars in the Netherlands, the college operated in Reims 1578–93. Douai also became important as a publishing center for English Catholic literature. The English Catholic translation of the Bible was begun there and completed in Reims. Irish and Scottish seminaries, along with English Franciscan and Benedictine houses of study, were established in Douai. At the French Revolution, most of the English religious institutions had to leave. Catholics by that time could work in England, and the training of English

clergy was continued at Crook Hall (later at Ushaw) and St. Edmund's, Old Hall.

[T. EARLY]

DOUAY BIBLE, the name of the English Bible produced at the English College, founded in 1568 at Douai, formerly Douay (Belgium), by exiled RC Oxonian scholars William Allen, Gregory Martin, Richard Bristow, and William Reynolds. The college was moved in 1578 to Reims. The Douay version, chiefly the work of Martin, was from the Latin Vulgate. The NT appeared in 1582; the OT, completed earlier, was not published until 1609–10, the delay being due to lack of funds and possibly to the appearance of the editions of Sixtus and Clement (1590, 1592), which may have necessitated changes and revisions. Often criticized for being overly literal, the Douay Version was a remarkable achievement under the circumstances. BIBLIOGRAPHY: H. Pope, *English Versions of the Bible* (1952); P. Levi, *English Bible, 1584–1859* (1974) ch. 8.

[R. T. A. MURPHY]

DOUBLE, a liturgical term formerly used to indicate the importance of a feast in the church calendar. Since 1960 this mode of ranking a feast has been obsolete.

[N. KOLLAR]

DOUBLE CHORUS, a choir arranged in two equal and complete bodies which, by its responsive effects and in other ways, makes use of the independent character of the two groups.

[M. T. LEGGE]

DOUBLE EFFECT, PRINCIPLE OF, a moral principle rising from reflection on common experience. A motorist uses the lug wrench and jack to change a flat tire; he does not want dirt or blisters on his hands but he must put up with them. The principle extends into questions of right and wrong. A medical student wants to learn about sexual matters; he does not want the arousal of passion that may accompany his learning. To do good we frequently have to put up with unwanted, inevitable evils that follow. But on the following conditions: that the action itself is good or at least morally neutral; that the good effect is intended and the evil merely permitted; that the good outweighs the evil; that the evil effect must not be the means of producing the good effect. If it were, the action itself would be evil since evil would flow directly from it. "We ought not do evil that good may come." (Rom 3.8). A man cannot take his own life. Still, Christ said: "No greater love has any man than this, that he should give up his life for his friends." (John 15.13). How can a man "give up" his life without taking it? A soldier falls on a live grenade and is instantly killed. Is that suicide? Directly, no. It is the morally neutral act of smothering the grenade, which becomes good from the intention of saving the lives of the others. Death may follow inevitably but as such neither is it intended nor is it the means of saving his comrades. Other cases can be thought of, more complex and less tractable. Sometimes the distinctions may look somewhat thin. Nevertheless, like surgery, when applied with delicacy and a due sense of proportion, and not on occasion as a substitute or to the exclusion of other principles, they are valid and serviceable within the limits of casuistry. BIBLIOGRAPHY: J. Mangan, "Historical Analysis of the Principle of the Double Effect" *ThSt* 10 (1949) 40–61; F. J. Connell, *Outlines of Moral Theology* (2d ed., 1964) 22–24; *idem*, NCE 4, 1020–22.

[T. R. HEATH]

DOUBLE JUSTICE *(duplex justitia)*, the notion, first advanced by J. Gropper (1503–59), a RC theologian at Cologne, as an attempt by certain pre-Tridentine and esp. RC theologians to reach a compromise on the doctrine of *justification. As the formula itself suggests, its proponents sought to find a *via media* between *forensic justification and the view that identified the process of justification with the actual forgiveness of sins and the inner renewal of the soul through the infusion of grace. While acknowledging a personal inherent justice (righteousness), defenders of the double-justice theory contended that such justice remains essentially incomplete and therefore insufficient for man to reach eternal life. Accordingly, it must be completed by an imputation of the justice and merits of Christ in virtue of man's incorporation into the mystical body by faith and hope in Christ its head. Defenders of this view, mainly Augustinians, claimed support for their position from St. Paul and from the writings of Augustine, though the doctrine was largely inspired by a notion of *concupiscence that had been introduced into this school in the 14th cent. by Gregory of Rimini (see AUGUSTINIANISM). Thus according to G. Seripando (1492–1563), who championed the double-justice theory at the Council of Trent, concupiscence remains even after baptism as a dynamic source of sin and as a positive hindrance to the complete observance of the commandments. Since such a state is displeasing to God, and therefore somehow sinful, the justice of Christ must be applied to all members of his mystical body to supply what is wanting to their personal justice so that they can reach eternal life. Although the Council of Trent in formulating the decree on justification (D 1520–83) rejected, without condemning, double justice, the doctrine nevertheless occasioned an examination in detail at Trent of the whole question of justification. BIBLIOGRAPHY: Jedin Trent 2:253–261.

[R. P. RUSSELL]

DOUBLE MONASTERY, the arrangement whereby communities of monks and nuns shared proximate or the same conventual buildings and worshiped together in the same church. In early monasticism, it was common in both the West and East in order to assure the necessary spiritual direction, economic assistance, and security against attack. Although interdicted by Justinian (*Novellae* 123.36) in 546 and new foundations forbidden by the Council of Nicaea II (787), the popes were ambivalent in regard to it (e.g., at the beginning of the 12th cent., Paschal II opposed it, while Callistus II approved). It was favored by some of the leaders of the monastic revival of the 11th and 12th cent., and was practiced at several religious houses (notably the Convent of *Fontevrault) in the Middle Ages. The *Bridgitines and *Gilbertines were founded as orders of double monasteries, and the former continued the practice in Poland until *c.*1850 and elsewhere in Europe until the 15th century. BIBLIOGRAPHY: S. Hilpisch, *Die Doppelklöster* (1928); E. Jombart, DDC 3:972–974; Bihlmeyer-Tüchle 1:362.

[M. B. PENNINGTON]

DOUBLE PREDESTINATION, the teaching that God predestines some men to certain salvation and reprobates others to damnation (see REPROBATION). There are two forms: *supralapsarianism holds that there is an effective twofold divine plan of salvation and damnation anterior to God's foreknowledge of the Fall; *infralapsarianism, or sublapsarianism, holds that the plan is subsequent to foreknowledge of the Fall. Infralapsarianism is found in St. Augustine, and became the more common teaching of Churches in the Reformed tradition after the Synod of *Dort. Supralapsarianism was made explicit in *Calvinism by Theodore *Beza. In both forms, double predestination implies the positive reprobation of some to damnation. In this sense it is rejected by RC and Lutheran doctrinal standards and by *Arminianism. *PREDESTINATION.

[T. C. O'BRIEN]

DOUBLE TRUTH, THEORY OF, a philosophical position according to which there can coexist two truths, one for faith and one for reason, both true yet contradictory. It is not established that such doctrine was ever actually held by a particular thinker, though individuals and groups have been alleged to have held it during the Middle Ages. In the universities of 13th-cent. Europe, ancient Greek philosophy and science were being introduced to Western thought in Latin translation, accompanied by Arabic and Hebrew commentaries, esp. those of *Averroës (*c.*1126–*c.*1198), whose interpretations of Aristotle's works were in open opposition to Christian dogma. For instance, Averroës rendered Aristotle to hold the impossibility of personal immortality, the eternity of the world, and the noncontingency of existence, and since both Aristotle and Averroës were regarded as authoritative sources in philosophy by the faculties of medieval universities, their works received wide currency. Thus, a sharp difference arose in the West as between Christian theology and Averroistic philosophy, and it was in these circumstances that Christian disciples of Averroës, called Latin Averroists, were accused of maintaining the double truth and of having found a basis for that doctrine in the writings of Averroës himself. *Siger of Brabant, is perhaps the most notable case in point.

Because of the possible peril to Christian orthodoxy, the reading of Arabic commentary was forbidden in 1210, and in 1231 at the Univ. of Paris was permitted only subject to censorship. Moreover, the German theologian, *Albert the Great, issued a condemnatory treatise against the Averroists, whereas the Italian scholar, *Thomas Aquinas, promulgated his tractate *De unitate intellectus contra Averroistas c.*1269 in opposition to the Averroistic doctrine of monopsychism. Finally, É. *Tempier, abp. of Paris, condemned unorthodox philosophic doctrines in 1277, making specific reference to those who seemed to speak of the possibility of contradictories being simultaneously true.

History favors the view that no medieval thinker really professed such a position, since those who thought they found religion and reason to be at odds either adopted wholly the Averroistic interpretation of Aristotle as did John of Jandum, or asserted the supremacy of faith as did Siger of Brabant. It therefore seems that only insofar as some refused to side one way or the other, that they were accused of ambiguity or the theory of the double truth.

Averroës himself wrote a tractate *On the Harmony between Religion and Philosophy* (text tr. G. Hourani, 1961), in which he strove to emphasize that there is but one truth to which there are several avenues of approach depending upon the capabilities of the individual, the philosophic approach being reserved to only a few. In sum, the doctrine of the double truth cannot be explicitly attributed to any medieval thinker or to Averroës or to Aristotle as interpreted by Averroës, on the basis of evidence now extant. BIBLIOGRAPHY: F. van Steenberghen, *Aristotle in The West,* (tr. L. Johnston, rev. ed., 1955); *Siger de Brabant et l'averroïsme latin au XIIIe siècle,* (ed. P. Mandonnet, 2d ed., 2 v., 1908–11); A. Maurer, *Medieval Philosophy* (1962).

[J. T. HICKEY]

DOUBT, MORAL, an inability to decide about a course of moral action. (1) Antecedent doubt precedes an actual moral choice. It may regard two morally good courses; its resolution does not require deciding in favor of the objectively better; choice of a lesser good is not thereby morally defective. Doubt may also concern the rightness or wrongness of an action (or its *omission) and so regards a morally good or evil choice. In matters regulated by positive law, the doubt may concern the meaning of the law *(dubium juris),* or its present applicability *(dubium facti).* Since the objective of a morally good choice is the good-as-meant, and of the morally bad choice, the lack-of-good-as-meant (T. Gilby, see bibliog.), it is clear that a person cannot make a good moral choice without resolving doubt; a moral choice cannot just happen to be good because it was in fact not bad. The extrinsicism of *Probabilism approached moral doubt differently (see MORALITY, SYSTEMS OF). The state of indeterminateness in the will regarding

moral choices, is narrowed by laws imposed. Doubt, therefore, concerns what is legally permissible; whether it may be resolved in favor of liberty or of law. A person may not act in disregard of the doubt; he may decide in favor of liberty, as long as there is at least a probable opinion supportive, even if there is another opinion against. (2) Consequent doubt occurs after an action, and engages the examination of *conscience. To resolve such a doubt, moral theology has developed its so-called *Reflex Principles. BIBLIOGRAPHY: ThAq ST (Lat-Eng, v. 18, ed. T. Gilby) App. 10, "The Form of Moral Good."

[T. C. O'BRIEN]

DOUBT IN MATTERS OF FAITH, a suspension of judgment about the truth or falsehood of a statement or belief. A doubtful mind fluctuates between two contradictory or conflicting points of view, hesitant to accept either of them because decisive, objective evidence is lacking. The crises of doubt that may occur in matters of faith may vary considerably according to the stages of life. They may arise from the nature of faith itself. Always wrapped in obscurity, the certitude of faith is not so convincing as to preclude the psychological possibility of doubt. Or they may be traceable to a gap between a revealed truth and the biblical evidence supporting it. Finally, they may be due to a mental attitude that is not humble, open, and docile to the word of God. Stemming from these causes are the various kinds of doubt, namely, practical and theoretical, negative and positive, prudent and imprudent, natural and methodical, culpable and inculpable. The methodical doubt developed by the philosopher René Descartes (1596–1650) made its way into theology in the form of Georg Hermes's positive doubt (1775–1831). Hermes taught that positive doubt is usable as a basis for all theological inquiry. Pope Gregory XVI condemned his opinion in the brief *Dum acerbissimas* (D 2738–40), and Vatican Council I denied the right of anyone to suspend the assent of faith (D 3014, 3036). The Cartesian doubt, however, does not cancel that methodical test of faith which leads to a deepening or refinement of it. A suspension of judgment may be called for in the case of opinion that still needs verification, and is altogether compatible with a life of faith and assent to religious authority. Such doubt can spur investigation into the rational grounds of belief and inspire prayer for enlightenment and strength. BIBLIOGRAPHY: R. Guardini, *Life of Faith* (tr. J. Chapin, 1961); O. A. Rabut, *Faith and Doubt* (tr. B. and W. Whitman, 1967).

[J. FICHTNER]

DOUBTFUL FAITH, see POSSESSOR IN GOOD, BAD, OR DOUBTFUL FAITH.

DOUCELINE OF THE MIDI, ST., (*c.*1214–74), Béguine, known also as Donolina, Dulcelina, and Donzeline. She founded a house of *Béguines, pious women who accepted the ideals of St. Francis but without constituting themselves a religious order, first at Hyères, then a second and larger house at Marseilles, and a third foundation at Aix. BIBLIOGRAPHY: J. Daoust, NCE 4:1025.

[V. L. BULLOUGH]

DOUGHERTY, DENNIS (1865–1951), American cardinal. Ordained in 1890, D. taught at St. Charles Borromeo, the seminary of the archdiocese of Philadelphia. In 1903 he was named bp. of Nueva Segovia in the Philippines and subsequently became bp. of Jaro. When the Aglipay schismatics seized church property, the shrewd and patient contesting by D. led to the restoration of the properties. After 2 years as bp. of Buffalo, he was appointed abp. of Philadelphia, beginning a 33-year tenure which was to have profound influence on that metropolitan see. In 1922 he became the first cardinal archbishop of Philadelphia. D. typified the building prelates of the first half of the 20th cent., responsible for an astounding program that added 115 new parishes and 145 new parochial schools. His awareness of the importance of Catholic schools created in his archdiocese the most impressive Catholic educational establishment in the world. In addition to elementary schools, he built, or encouraged communities to build, 53 high schools. Four colleges were opened with his support. A strong administrator and firm leader, D. made Philadelphia unique among the dioceses of America.

[J. R. AHERNE]

DOUJAT, JOHANNES (1609–88), French historian and canonist. After practicing law in Toulouse and Paris, D. became professor of law at the Univ. of Paris (1655) and later dean. He is chiefly remembered for his contributions to the history of church law.

DOUKHOBORS (Dukhbors; Russ., spirit-wrestlers), members of a communal, mystical movement that originated in 18th-cent. Russia as a protest against the State and the Russian Orthodox Church. Rejecting the doctrine of the Trinity and the authority of the Bible, these peasants, who originally called themselves Christians of the Universal Brotherhood, taught that Christ was simply a man and reappears periodically in chosen men; that the soul is mortal and undergoes metempsychosis; and that those led by the Spirit are incapable of sin (see ANTINOMIANISM). Because of their opposition to government, private property, schools, war, and oaths, Doukhobors were periodically persecuted by the tsars and expelled by the Cossacks from their villages. With the assistance of L. Tolstoy and of English and American Quakers about 7,000 immigrated to W Canada (1898–99). They developed communal farms and became prosperous, but were plagued by a succession of dissolute leaders and by schisms. One of the leaders, Peter Vasilivich Verigin, who claimed that Christ was reincarnated in him, was killed by a time bomb in 1924. Under the leadership of his son about 18,000 Doukhobors, mostly residents of Saskatchewan, seem to have abandoned the original communal ideals and

many socially objectionable practices. A radical group in the movement, the 1,500 Sons of Freedom in British Columbia, however, have been charged with 800 acts of violence including bombing, arson, and other acts of destruction; one of their means of protest has been picketing in the nude. BIBLIOGRAPHY: *Doukhobors of British Columbia* (ed. H. B. Hawthorn, 1955); S. Holt, *Terror in the Name of God* (1964); G. Woodcock and I. Avakumovic, *Doukhobors* (1968).

[W. J. WHALEN]

DOURA-EUROPOS, see DURA-EUROPOS.

DOVE, a symbol adopted by Christians from very early times. The form of a dove was used as a symbol of the Holy Spirit personally or in his works and also of the Christian soul as indwelt by the Holy Spirit, freed, and entered into glory. As a symbol of martyrdom, the dove indicated the action of the Holy Spirit in the gift of fortitude necessary for the martyr's endurance of pain. In iconography the dove appears in representations of the Annunciation, Christ's baptism, the Ascension, and Pentecost. The symbol occurs most often in early representations of baptism.

[K. O'NEILL]

DOVER PRIORY, originally a Benedictine priory later used by Eadbald, King of Kent, c. 619 for secular canons. These alternated with canons regular and monks from Canterbury during its long history. Besides precious objects and other wealth, the monastery owned a well-stocked library with a detailed catalogue drawn up in 1389 and with additions made in the 15th century. Valuable MSS, belonging to Dover and still extant, include an Irish psaltery of the 10th cent. and the celebrated Bible of Dover, famous for its illuminations. A relic of the monastic buildings still survives: the refectory, incorporated in the present college of Dover (constructed in 1841). Also to be seen is a fresco of the 12th cent. representing the Last Supper. BIBLIOGRAPHY: H. Dauphin, DHGE 14:751–754; Knowles-Hadcock 64.

[S. A. HEENEY]

DOWDALL, GEORGE (1487–1558), abp. of Armagh, a member of the *Crutched Friars, and prior of their monastery at Ardee until its suppression in 1539. He acknowledged Henry VIII's Act of Supremacy, was appointed abp. of Armagh by the King, but opposed the subsequent introduction of Protestantism into Ireland. When this proved ineffectual, D. resigned, renounced his schism, and was later appointed (1553) by Julius III to the see of Armagh, thus taking over by papal appointment the primatial see of which he had been schismatical archbishop. During the reign of Queen Mary, he worked to eradicate any vestiges of Protestantism in Ireland. BIBLIOGRAPHY: A. Coleman, CE 5:145; J. Hurley, NCE 4:1027; DNB 15:384.

[T. M. MCFADDEN]

DOWDALL, JAMES (d. *c.*1599), Irish martyr. D. was a merchant who was driven onto the coast of Devonshire when sailing from France to Ireland. He was arrested, refused to acknowledge the spiritual supremacy of the crown, was convicted of treason, and hanged at Exeter. BIBLIOGRAPHY: D. Murphy, *Our Martyrs* (1896).

DOWIE, JOHN ALEXANDER (1847–1907), evangelist, faith healer, and founder of the *Christian Catholic Church. Taken from Edinburgh, Scotland, to Australia by his parents, D. returned to study at the Univ. of Edinburgh; in 1870 he was ordained as pastor of a Congregational church near Sydney. He became a full-time evangelist in 1878 and in 1888 left Australia to preach in the United States. He established his headquarters at Chicago in 1890. Faith healing, his main concentration, won him followers. As a preacher he was vituperative and slangy in crusading against liquor and tobacco and frankly sensationalist in his approach to evangelism. In 1896 he established the Christian Catholic Church and in 1901 opened Zion City, Ill., for his followers. D. proclaimed himself the Prophet Elijah in 1901, and in 1904 was anointed as the First Apostle. He was deposed as unfit to rule Zion City and the Church in 1906 and devoted his remaining days to lawsuits to recover his property rights.

DOWIEITES, followers of John Alexander *Dowie. *CHRISTIAN CATHOLIC CHURCH.

DOWLING, AUSTIN (1868–1930), American bishop. A quiet, unassuming but able administrator, D. was ordained in 1891 for the diocese of Providence, Rhode Island. As editor of the *Providence Visitor,* he made the paper nationally known. Named first bp. of Des Moines, he demonstrated the strong belief in Catholic education that was to characterize his whole career. He was appointed abp. of St. Paul in 1920 to succeed the famous Abp. Ireland. In St. Paul his achievements in promoting Catholic education and encouraging Catholics to take active roles in community and civic affairs were outstanding. His *Occasional Sermons and Other Addresses* (ed. J. T. McNicholas) were published in 1940.

[J. R. AHERNE]

DOWRY, OUR LADY'S, the title of a book written by Thomas E. Bridgett (1875), based on historical and literary sources, honoring the Mother of God as patroness of England because of the great devotion to her among the people during the Middle Ages.

[S. I. HIGGINS]

DOWRY, in Canon Law, a term referring to a sum of money deposited at the time of entrance to a community of women. It is largely restricted to postulants entering a cloistered community. The dowry must be invested and its principal left untouched. At the death of the religious, the principal reverts to the order. If a religious leaves she must be given the dowry principal.

[J. R. AHERNE]

DOWSON, ERNEST (1867–1900), English poet. The short, sad life of D. is symbolic of the strange school called *fin de siècle,* the Decadents, who thought that in the light of the sordid historical experience of the 19th cent., they should exalt the sensory and despise the pragmatic; Oscar Wilde was the prime example. D. was torn between the decadent and the religious and wrote classic poems celebrating each. The remorse that follows sensual indulgence, the fleeting nature of mortality, and the permanence of religious experience are characteristic of his poetry. The influence of Catholicism is apparent in all his work. His principal works are *Verses* (1896) and *Pierrot of the Minute,* a play (1897). BIBLIOGRAPHY: M. Longaker, *Ernest Dowson* (1944, 3d ed., 1967); V. Platt, *Ernest Dowson 1888–1897* (1914, repr. 1973).

[J. R. AHERNE]

DOXOLOGY (Gr., *doksē,* glory and *logos,* word), a liturgical formula of praise having several meanings. (1) Generically: an acclamation expressly attributing glory to God. Christian doxologies appear in the NT and in the Apostolic Fathers. The earliest doxologies are addressed to the Father or to the Son, but soon began to attribute glory to the Father through the Son, then became almost invariably Trinitarian, with glory being given to the Father *through* the Son *and* the Holy Spirit, or *through* the Son *in* the Holy Spirit. When the Arians began to give a subordinationist sense to the formulas using the preposition *through,* their orthodox opponents began to place all three persons of the Trinity on the same level, using formulas giving glory either "to the Father *with* the Son and Holy Spirit" (popular in Egypt in the 4th cent.) or "to the Father *and* the Son and Holy Spirit" (the 4th-cent. Syrian formula which was eventually adopted throughout the universal Church. (2) Specifically: (a) the Minor Doxology: "Glory to (the) Father and (the) Son and (the) Holy Spirit, now and forever and unto the ages of ages." The second phrase, in the tradition of the Syriac-speaking Churches, is "from everlasting and to everlasting" to which the West Syrians add "and unto the ages of ages"; the Latin Church added "as it was in the beginning" to the second phrase. In all ancient Churches the Minor Doxology is used esp. at the end of a Psalm or of a series of Psalms. (b) the Major Doxology, or *Gloria in excelsis,* extant in several recensions, one of which is found already in Book 8 of the Apostolic Constitutions. In the West it is recited or sung at the beginning of the Roman Mass while in Byzantine practice it is sung a little before, viz., at the end of the morning Office *(orthros)* when the Divine Liturgy follows. In the present Byzantine liturgy, it is retained on other days, but only recited. In both East and West Syrian tradition it also terminates the morning Office, although in the present West Syrian and Maronite structures of the Office, it actually terminates an old morning Office found now at the end of the night Office. In Byzantine terminology the word *doxologia* refers properly to the Major Doxology. BIBLIOGRAPHY: DACL 4:1525–36; J. A. Jungmann, LTK 3:535–536; B. Capelle, "Le Texte du Gloria in excelsis," RHE 44 (1949) 439–457.

[A. CODY]

DOXOLOGY (BIBLICAL). A doxology (Gr. *doksē,* glory and *logos,* word) is a short acclamation of thankful praise to God. It may stand as an independent unit or it may be part of a larger hymn of praise. In the OT, a frequent form is "Blessed be Yahweh . . . (1 Sam 25.39; 2 Sam 18.28; 1 Kg 1.48; 5.7; 8.56; etc.). It is not certain whether the verb "be," which makes the doxology a wish, is more appropriate than the verb "is," which would make the doxology a confession, since the Hebrew omits the verb. An exceptional explicit optative form *yehi . . . baruk* (may he be . . . blessed) occurs in 1 Kg 10.9 and 2 Chr 9.8. The acclamation may be expressed by numerous verbs: sing *(shir),* praise *(halăl),* give thanks to *(yadah),* and sing a Psalm *(zimmer).* The doxology may be expressed as a personal acclamation, e.g., Ps 9.1 "I thank you Yahweh . . . I sing praise to your name," or as a call for others to join in praise, e.g., the form *halleluyah* (praise Yahweh) which is found both at the beginning of Psalms (e.g., Ps 105–107; 111–114; etc.) and at the end of Psalms (e.g., Ps 150:6), or as a simple confession or wish as indicated above. Frequently the reason or the occasion for the ascription of praise to God is expressed by a clause introduced by a relative pronoun (e.g., Ps 66.20, "Blessed be God who neither . . . nor . . .") or by a clause introduced by a causal preposition (e.g., Ps 118.29, "Give thanks to Yahweh, *for* he is good"). Occasionally an explicit notice that the praise is to be eternal is added (e.g., Ps 106.48 "Blessed be Yahweh . . . from all eternity and forever"). When the doxology is found in a liturgical setting, in a Psalm or hymn, the worshipers might be urged to make the praise of Yahweh their own by answering "Amen" (e.g., Ps 89.51b; 106.48; 1 Chr 16.36).

The oldest doxology in the OT is the refrain of the Song of Moses (Ex 15.1,21). The Song of Moses is an expansive explicitation of the original doxology into a psalm of thanksgiving which dates from the time of the Judges. The Canticle of Deborah (Jg ch. 5) also is an amplification of an original spontaneous doxology. These two examples indicate both the spontaneous nature of doxologies and the tendency for later generations to amplify and explicitate the original. A doxology such as "Give glory to Yahweh forever" (Ps 104.31) is a rare and late type. For the ancients the glory of Yahweh is his presence in power in wondrous salvific acts on behalf of his chosen people (see 1 Chr 16.23 where "proclaim Yahweh's salvation" means tell of his glory or tell of his marvels). God's glory, too, is the indication of his presence by means of light (Ex 16.7,10; 24.16–17; 1 Kg 8.10.11, cf. also Is 60.1–3). Finally, God's

glory is also his reputation for loyalty and compassion, which he has earned through his salvific deeds (see Ex 14.4,17, where "I shall win glory for myself" means the Egyptians shall learn that I am Yahweh; the meaning of the name is demonstrated in the Exodus miracle and defined in Ex 34.6–8). Hence glory was conceived as an attribute or property of God rather than something that was attributed to him by man. The ancient doxology, in victory or deliverance, was "Blessed be Yahweh" (Gen 9.26; 24.27; Ex 18.10; 1 Sam 25.32). This was transferred to the liturgy and is now found both at the beginning and end of Psalms (Ps 103.1; 144.1; 66.20; 68.35b). The *halăl* and *yadah* forms are liturgical in origin and are found only in the Psalms (Ps 105.1; 106.1 and 117 for *halleluyah* forms; Ps 7.18; 118.29 for *yadah* forms). The angelic doxology of Is 6.3 is declarative, acknowledging God's reputation for holiness. Psalm 117 because of its brevity might rightly be considered a doxology, but Ps 150 and Dan 3.57–88 are more appropriately considered strings of doxologies.

The NT continues the usage of the OT. Thus 2 Cor 1.3 "Blessed be the God and Father . . . ." See also Eph 1.3 and 1 Pet 1.3 which are also similar to the ancient Hebrew form that omitted the verb. This type of doxology is likewise found as a parenthetical insertion (2 Cor 11.31); and it is found at the end of sentences in a declarative relative form, e.g., Rom 1.25, "the creator, who is blessed forever. Amen." Both the Benedictus (Lk 1:68–69) and the Magnificat (Lk 1.46–47) are expanded or greater doxologies similar to thanksgiving Psalms. The angelic doxology: "Glory to God in the highest" (Lk 2.14) also follows the rare OT usage. An optative form of this type occurs at the end of the sentence in Rom 16.27. More effusive forms appear later, e.g., "To the Eternal King, the undying, invisible and only God, be honor and glory forever and ever. Amen" (1 Tim 1.17). See also Jude 24 where "glory, majesty, authority and power" are proclaimed of God and Rev 7:12, which lists "glory, wisdom and thanksgiving, and honor and power and strength."

But what is peculiar to the NT doxologies is that Jesus, the Christ, is the subject of such doxologies; see Rom 9.5; Heb 13.21 "Jesus Christ, to whom be glory forever and ever. Amen." The series of doxologies in Rev 4.11; 5.12 and 5.13–14 are most significant in Christology because they indisputably argue for the divinity of Christ. The doxology attached to the Our Father by the Eastern Churches and the AV has been justly omitted by the RSV. The "Glory be" said after each Psalm in the recitation of the Divine Office also is nonbiblical. BIBLIOGRAPHY: EDB 589–590.

[J. A. PIERCE]

DOXOPATRES, NEILOS (Nilus the Archimandrite; fl. 12th cent.), Byzantine historian and theologian. At the court of Roger II in Sicily D. wrote (1142–43) a history of the origins and progress of the five Eastern patriarchates and of the patriarchs of Constantinople. He also wrote glosses on St. Athanasius and a theological treatise on the divine plan of salvation (*oikonomia*).

[T. C. O'BRIEN]

DOYLE, JAMES WARREN (1786–1834), Irish bp. and patriot. In 1800 he entered the Augustinian seminary in New Ross, was professed in 1806. His studies at the Univ. of Coimbra, Portugal, were interrupted by the Napoleonic invasion. Doyle joined the British forces as a volunteer and apparently made a deep impression on both the British and the Portuguese, for he was offered a diplomatic post with the latter when the French were defeated. He returned to New Ross and was ordained in 1809. In 1813 he took the chair of rhetoric at Carlow College. In 1819 D. was chosen bp. of Kildare and Leighlin, and brought the diocese the firmness of authority that it had long lacked. For the rest of his life D. was in the forefront of those who fought for social reform and the cause of Ireland. Under the initials "J.K.L." (James of Kildare and Leighlin) he became a foremost champion of the Catholic Church and the Irish. He published *A Vindication of the Religious and Civil Principles of the Irish Catholics* (1824) and *Letters on the State of Ireland* (1824–25). Both works had tremendous readership and influence. Summoned to report to Commons and Lords on the condition of Ireland, he earned the admiration of the Duke of Wellington and many others. He was a consistent advocate of reform legislation for the poor. D. died at age 50, worn out by a vigorous public life on behalf of Ireland. With Daniel O'Connell, and not less influential, he is one of the great figures in 19th-cent. Irish history.

[J. R. AHERNE]

DOYLE, WILLIAM (1873–1917), Irish Jesuit ascetic, retreat master, parish missioner to the urban poor, British army chaplain, killed while ministering to soldiers on the battlefield of Ypres in World War I.

[K. O'NEILL]

DRACHMA, (Gr. *drachmē*), a silver Greek coin whose weight and value steadily depreciated (from 0.14 ounces to 0.125 ounces). In NT times a drachma was equivalent to a 10th part of a Roman as. Four drachmas or a tetra-drachma were equal to a shekel. In Lk 15.8 a woman who lost a drachma is pictured as sweeping the entire house to find it. A drachma was roughly a day's wage. BIBLIOGRAPHY: De Vaux AncIsr 207–208; Orchard 760d.

[J. A. PIERCE]

DRACONTIUS, BLOSSIUS AEMILIUS (*c.*450–after 496), Christian Latin poet and lawyer in Carthage. His secular works include: a collection of short hexameter poems of little artistic value, entitled *Romulea,* comprising rhetorical exercises, nuptial songs, and mythological epyllia (free will and destiny); probably the once-anonymous *Orestis tragoedia.* His Christian poems include a short elegiac poem in 158 distichs, *Satisfactio ad Gunthamundum regem,*

written in prison and addressed to the Vandal king, begging forgiveness for having eulogized a foreign emperor, thought to be Zenon; and *De laudibus Dei,* his chief work, displaying greater poetic powers. BIBLIOGRAPHY: J. Duvernet, DHGE, 1960, 14:774–781.

[S. A. HEENEY]

DRAFT, see CONSCRIPTION.

DRAGHI, ANTONIO (1635–1700), Italian composer and director of the imperial chapel at Vienna. In addition to the main body of his work, *c.*175 operas, he composed over 40 oratorios, two Masses, a Stabat Mater, and some hymns. Most of his scores are preserved in MS in the National Library in Vienna.

[M. T. LEGGE]

DRAGON, in the Bible and other Near Eastern literature a symbol of the forces of evil. It is identified with Rahab in the poetic parallelism of Is 51.9. The primeval monster overcome by Yahweh is elsewhere called Leviathan (Ps 74.13–14), sea monster (Job 7.12), and Bashan (Ps 68.22). It was generally associated with the waters (Ezek 29.3), in allusion to the chaos that God had to conquer in forming the earth (Gen 1.9). The dragon also became an eschatological symbol of the evil God would destroy to accomplish the new creation (Is 27.1; Rev 20.2). The "great red dragon" of Rev is identified with the devil and Satan (12.3, 9).

[T. EARLY]

DRAMA, LITURGICAL, see LITURGICAL DRAMA.

DRAMA, MEDIEVAL, a representation of sacred narrative (biblical, saintly, or allegorical) by actors using dialogue, gesture, costume, and musical accompaniment. The medieval drama was independent of the ancient Greco-Roman theatrical tradition and also of the barbarian ritual drama connected with vegetation festivals. It originated as a paraliturgical embellishment of the Mass and the Divine Office, but was distinct from them, although a theory has been proposed that the Mass itself was regarded as ritual drama in the early Middle Ages. During the 9th cent. insertions called *tropes were added to the official liturgy of the Church, esp. at the Introit of the Mass, in France, Germany, and Spain. About a century later, dramatic dialogue and action were introduced into the chanting of these tropes, the earliest recorded one being the *Quem quaeritis* conversation between the Angel and the three Marys at the tomb on Easter morning. These simple dramas were in Latin, the actors were the members of the monastic or cathedral choirs, and the performances were held in the church itself. Most of the 10th-cent. plays were produced at the end of the Matins office on Easter morning. As long as Latin remained the language of these plays they continued as indoor productions closely associated with the ecclesiastical celebration of a few great feasts. In the later Middle

Ages vernacular versions were made of the Latin texts, and from about the middle of the 14th-cent. cycles of French, German, and English plays were composed, gradually covering the entire biblical span from Creation to the Last Judgment. These mystery cycles, as they were called, were performed out of doors, either on stationary platforms (often in arena theaters) or mounted on a series of pageant wagons drawn through the streets of a town. These enterprises were the responsibility of craft guilds in the British Isles and of semiprofessional lay confraternities on the Continent.

The texts of the Latin plays and most probably of their vernacular counterparts, were composed by clerical authors, often by the precentor (choirmaster) of a monastic community. The words were sung to the rhythms of Gregorian chant, as long as Latin was used, and were closely related to passages of the Divine Office and ultimately to the Latin Vulgate Bible. The embellishment of the plays with verse and rhetorical figures kept pace with the parallel growth of artistry in medieval Latin lyric poetry practiced in the monasteries and other centers of learning. Even in the vernacular mysteries, the academic quality of many theological passages scattered through the texts argues for continued clerical authorship. The vernacular plays were not secularized, even in very late survivals of the medieval tradition. Comic characters and incidents were regularly introduced, sometimes in bold parody of the sacred elements, but the dominant spirit of most texts remained reverent and profoundly religious. The vernacular plays were recited, not sung, but the prevailing lyricism and the formalized dignity of their movement retained the features of their ecclesiastical and learned origins. BIBLIOGRAPHY: C. J. Stratman, *Bibliography of Medieval Drama* (1954); E. C. Dunn, NCE 4:1039–48; R. Axton, *European Drama of the Early Middle Ages* (1975); D. Bevington, *Medieval Drama* (1975).

[E. C. DUNN]

DRAŠĆOVIĆ, GEORGE DE TRAKOSĆAN (1525–87), Croatian bp. and church reformer. As bp. of Pecs he attended the Council of Trent, where he represented the Hungarian Church; sensitive to the spirit of the Reformation, he advocated concession of the chalice to the laity at communion and the abolition of clerical celibacy. He later served as bp. of Zagreb (1563–78), Kalocsa (1572–78), and Győr (1578–87). He strove to improve the discipline and education of the clergy and wrote polemical works against Calvinism. He was named cardinal in 1585. In political affairs D. as viceroy led the defense against Turkish invasion; he was royal governor and imperial chancellor for Hungary (1578–85). BIBLIOGRAPHY: K. St. Draganović, LTK 3–542–543.

[T. C. O'BRIEN]

DRAVIDIANS, peoples whose language belongs to a group of languages of S India, which includes Kanarese, Malayalam, Tamil, Telugu, and uncultivated tongues like Kodaga and Tulu. While the name can refer either to the peoples or the language group, there is no ethnic connotation in the reference. One interpretation suggests the ancient Dravidians were tied to the Cretans; they migrated eastward from the Mediterranean, settling in both Sumeria and India, bringing with them a relatively advanced civilization. The Dravidians profoundly influenced the navigational skills, the architectural structures and styles, communal village system, agricultural and irrigational practices, warfare, dress, and many personal habits of later Aryan and Indo-Aryan inhabitants of the subcontinent. Many of the members of the Hindu pantheon are of Dravidic origin. Their non-Aryan language also influenced the evolution of later Indo-Aryan languages as well as Vedic and Sanskrit. A Dravidian "movement" has, in recent years been hostile to what are perceived as foreign elements (Sanskrit, Brahman ideals, caste classifications), and has emphasized the importance and worth of ancient classics written in Tamil. BIBLIOGRAPHY: A. L. Basham, *Wonder That Was India* (1959); R. L. Hardgrave, *Dravidian Movement* (1968).

[R. J. LITZ]

DREAM OF GERONTIUS, THE, a theological lyric and dramatic poem by John Henry Newman (1801–90). Published in 1865, it is in the tradition of the poetry of death, but not the merely elegiac or memorial type like "Adonais" or "In Memoriam," or "Elegy in a Country Churchyard," etc. These are yearning and somber; *The Dream* recalls *The Divine Comedy* and *Paradise Lost* more nearly in mood and meaning. Though it evokes such comparison or contrasts, it is a poem that merits distinction because of its dramatic expression of personal reflections on death. The intensely personal note pervading a universal inevitability of death supplies for the seeming deficiencies that critics will easily note. *The Dream* is brief (some 900 lines); it is personal; it carries Newman's thoughts and beliefs through a sure handling of appropriate forms. Blank verse carries much of Newman's musical, clear, appropriate phrases and words. The first 150 lines describe Gerontius before his death, not cowardly but fearful, asking prayers for his soul. The next and longer division describes and records Gerontius's thoughts and feelings as he awakes and relates with poetic clarity St. Catherine of Genoa's consoling doctrine on purgatory. *The Dream* is a product of one who lived long, perhaps a lifetime, with the thought of death. It is a manifesto of faith, wisdom, and trust temperately threaded with fear. So powerful was *The Dream* in its contemporary setting that it elicited praise from such dissonant voices as Swinburne and Kingsley, as well as more friendly critics. E. Elgar set it to music.

[R. M. FUNCHION]

DREAM OF THE ROOD, THE, one of the finest religious lyrics in the English language, in 8th-cent. W Saxon dialect in the Vercelli Book. It uses the dream-vision, a literary genre magnificently employed in the Middle Ages. The dreamer sees the Rood (Cross) covered with gleaming jewels, which change to drops of blood. The Cross tells the dreamer the story of Christ's Crucifixion in terms of an English warrior describing the death of his lord. The Cross (the thane) cannot take revenge for his master's death but must assist the champion who fearlessly embraces him. The poem is dramatic and full of fine contrasts between darkness and brightness, death and life, suffering and redemption. The tone is of great sincerity and faith. Two lines from it resemble verses cut on the Rothwell cross in Scotland (early 8th century). BIBLIOGRAPHY: L. C. Wrenn, NCE 5:372.

[M. B. BARRY]

DREAMS, psychological activities of fantasy, thought, urge, and feeling that occur during sleep. Historically, the significance of dreams has been variously estimated. Scripture describes dreams as vehicles of divine communication, and the belief still persists that they have a prophetic function. Ancient and medieval physicians were interested in their patients' dreams as a means of gaining insight into their maladies. Some psychologists have believed dreams to be random and casual phenomena having no significance. In 1900 Sigmund *Freud published *The Interpretation of Dreams,* which was the beginning of psychoanalysis and of an intense interest in dreams as disguised expressions of unconscious thought and wish fulfillment. Contemporary research on dreams reveals the facts that everyone normally dreams several times every night and in regular patterns, and that this dream activity is necessary for mental and emotional health. It seems that in dreams people often act out situations that are heavily charged with emotions like yearnings, fears, and frustrations, and that these fantasy experiences in sleep enable them to handle their feelings more adequately when they are awake. There is no moral responsibility in dreams as such since the capacity to judge and decide realistically is prevented by sleep. BIBLIOGRAPHY: A. M. Cuk, NCE 4:1053–56; R. Fleiss, *Revival of Interest in the Dream* (1973); C. J. Jung, *Dreams* (tr. H. F. Hull, pa. 1973).

[M. E. STOCK]

DREAMS (IN THE BIBLE). All the dreams narrated in the Bible occur in those sections that seem by their literary forms to derive from popular folklore or legend. They occur throughout the biblical era, from the patriarchal age (Gen 20.3–7) to that of the Apostles (Acts 9.10–16; 10.10–16; 16.9). With a few minor exceptions, biblical dreams, like those in the ancient Orient in general, are vehicles chosen by God (as others are by pagan gods) whereby he communicates directly with individual persons. Some dreams contain a clear message (Gen 20.3–7; 28.12; 31.10–13, 24; 46.1–4; 1 Sam 3.11–14; 1 Kg 3.5; 2 Chr 1.3–12; Job 4.12–21; 33.15–16; Wis 18.17–19; Mt 1.20; 2.12, 19, 22; 27.19; Acts 16.9). Others are symbolic but nevertheless sufficiently obvious that the meaning is readily ascertain-

able (Jg 7.13; Est 10.4–9; Dan ch. 7; 2 Macc 15.11–16; Acts 10.10–16; 11.5–10; 16.9). Other dreams, because of their obscurity, are unintelligible to the dreamer and require interpretation by a person particularly qualified (Gen 40.41–42; Dan ch. 2 and 4. In both of these cases the ability to interpret dreams is a sign of special divine favor; by exercising this charism the interpreters Joseph and Daniel show the power of Israel's God in the sight of the pagans. Early legislation forbids, among other pagan practices, ascribing dreams to gods other than Yahweh, the God of Israel (Dt 13.2–6; Lev 19.26), and false prophecy, whereby prophets claim falsely the authority to speak in Yahweh's name (Num 12.6). Jeremiah (23.23–32; 27.9; 29.8) and Zech (10.2) denounce such illicit pretensions to prophetic charism. Joel (2.28; Heb text 3.1) equates the gift of dreams with that of prophecy, to be given to all in the messianic age; St. Peter quotes this on Pentecost as realized in Christianity (Acts 2.17). Sirach recommends this ability to discern true dreams from false as one of the marks of the truly wise (Sir 34.1–7; cf. Ec 5.3, 7; Is 29.8). BIBLIOGRAPHY: M. R. E. Masterman, NCE 4:1056; EDB 593; InterDB 868.

[T. CRANE]

DREIKÖNIGENSCHREIN (Shrine of the Three Kings), gilded copper and silver reliquary in the treasury of the cathedral at Cologne, begun by the renowned Nicholas of Verdun in 1181, with additions in 1198 and 1220. In the form of a Romanesque basilica with precise miniature reproductions of the choir sculptures of the cathedral, it is probably one of the most important reliquary shrines of the Middle Ages.

[M. J. DALY]

DRESS, CLERICAL. Distinctive clerical dress is a relatively recent phenomenon. Until the end of the persecutions in the 4th cent., even liturgical vestments did not exist. Throughout the ancient and medieval periods, clerics were expected to wear conservative and simple attire that followed the custom of their countries, and this was the recommendation of the Council of Trent (1545–63). Only since the 17th cent. has it become customary for clerics to wear black. Clerical garb was required for priests in the U.S. only at the Third Plenary Council of Baltimore in 1884, which ordered clerics to wear collars and cassocks at home and in church. Outside, the collar and a long coat of black or other dark color were required. Although these instructions are still in effect, American custom now permits clerics other conservative attire. The Code of Canon Law simply prescribes (c. 136) that clerics should wear appropriate ecclesiastical clothing which fits the customs of the country and the requirements of the local ordinary.

[R. A. ARONSTAM]

DREVON, VICTOR (1820–80), French Jesuit, promoter of devotion to the Sacred Heart. D. founded a society for communions of reparation, which, at his death, he committed to the *Apostleship of Prayer. He also developed Paray-le-Monial as a devotional center and worked actively for the establishment of the feast of the Sacred Heart in the universal Church. BIBLIOGRAPHY: P. de Vregille, *Catholicisme* 3:1084–85.

DREXEL, FRANCIS ANTHONY (1824–85), banker, philanthropist. Senior member of the celebrated financial firm Drexel and Company, founded by his father, D. was a man of integrity and great charity. Throughout his life and in his will he showed himself a trustee of wealth rather than a proprietor. Father of Mother Katharine Drexel, foundress of the Sisters of the Blessed Sacrament, he trained his children in the tradition of generosity that he espoused. BIBLIOGRAPHY: J. F. Loughlin, CE 5:159.

[J. R. AHERNE]

DREXEL (DREXELIUS), JEREMIAS (1581–1638), Jesuit educator, writer, court preacher in Munich (1615–38). A convert from Lutheranism who entered the Jesuit order in 1598, D. later became professor of rhetoric in Munich and Augsburg and at the Jesuit seminary in Dillingen. His ascetical works include *De aeternitate considerationes* (1620) and *Heliotropum* (1627). BIBLIOGRAPHY: P. Bailly, DSAM 3:1714–17; P. Praz, *Studies in Seventeenth-Century Imagery* (1947) 2:49–50.

[M. F. MCCARTHY]

DREXEL, KATHARINE (1858–1955), religious foundress and missioner to blacks and Indians. A daughter of the distinguished Philadelphia Drexel family, Katharine inherited a large fortune. Heeding the call of the Third Council of Baltimore, she determined to use all of it to support missions to the Indians and blacks. At the suggestion of Leo XIII she founded the Sisters of the Blessed Sacrament for Indians and Colored People, using a Drexel home for the motherhouse. From 1891 until her death she devoted great energy and a fortune of $12 million to the work in the South, Middle West, and Northeast. In New Orleans she established Xavier University in 1915. Pope Pius XII called her apostolate "a glorious page in the annals of the Church." BIBLIOGRAPHY: K. Burton, *Golden Door: The Life of Katharine Drexel* (1957).

[J. R. AHERNE]

DREY, JOHANN SEBASTIAN VON (1777–1853), German theologian. Ordained in 1801, D. became professor of theology and apologetics at the Univ. of Ellwangen. When that university was transferred to Tübingen (1817), he became one of its founders and taught there until 1846. In 1819 he founded the *Tübinger theologische Quartalschrift,* which still flourishes. D., an influential figure in his time, contributed much to the history of theological thought. In his publications he championed reform, "inspired by the idea of the organic unity of theology and of the romantic conception of historical continuity" (Congar).

These ideas he expounded in his *Einleitung in das Studium der Theologie* (1819). He is chiefly remembered for his introduction of the historical method into theology and for his contribution to the establishment of apologetics as an autonomous science. Among his more notable writings are *Apologetik* (3 v., 1838–47) and *Origo et vicissitudines exomologeseos* (1815). BIBLIOGRAPHY: S. Cipriani, DE 1:911; Y. Congar, *Catholicisme* 3:1085–86.

[F. D. LAZENBY]

DREYER, BENEDICTUS (fl. 1510–55), German woodcarver, chief master of late Gothic sculpture in Lübeck. His masterpiece, *St. Michael* (*c.* 1515; Marienkirch, Lübeck) is characterized by D.'s painter-like technique and restrained ornamentation.

[M. J. DALY]

DREYFUS, ALFRED (1859–1935), French Jewish army officer, convicted of treason (passing military secrets to the Germans) in 1894, vindicated in 1906. The famous Dreyfus Case, which aroused intense political and racial passions, and divided France into left and right factions, also involved the Church. Clemenceau and the other Dreyfusards attributed D.'s conviction to Jesuit plotting. There was a strong tide of anticlericalism led by Pres. Waldeck-Rousseau, manifested by antireligious laws carried out under Justin Combes. BIBLIOGRAPHY: M. Thomas, *L'Affaire sans Dreyfus* (1961).

DRISCOLL, JAMES F. (1859–1922), seminary professor and editor. He was ordained in 1887 and joined the Sulpicians. Most of his career was spent in teaching theology, Scripture, and Semitic languages at the seminary of the Archdiocese of New York in Dunwoodie. From 1902 to 1909 D. served as rector of the seminary, becoming a priest of the archdiocese when the Sulpicians left Dunwoodie in 1906. In that period he edited a bimonthly periodical, the *New York Review,* which maintained a high level of scholarship in its 3-year existence. After resigning as rector, D. was pastor in New York City and in New Rochelle. BIBLIOGRAPHY: A. J. Scanlan, *St. Joseph's Seminary, Dunwoodie, New York, 1896–1921* (1922).

[J. R. AHERNE]

DRIVER, SAMUEL ROLLES (1846–1914), English OT and Hebrew scholar. D. was regius professor of Hebrew at Oxford and canon of Christ Church (1883–1914). His scholarship and numerous publications did much to establish the critical study of the OT in England. He wrote commentaries on nearly half of the OT books and an extensively used *Introduction to the Literature of the OT*. BIBLIOGRAPHY: ODCC 422; B. Verostko, NCE 4:1063.

[T. M. MCFADDEN]

DROGO OF METZ, (801–855), son of Charlemagne by the concubine Regina. Allegedly involved in revolt against Louis I, he was forcibly tonsured in 818. In 823 Louis designated him bp. of Metz, and from then on D. was his most reliable friend. Made papal vicar for Frankland after Louis' death, he lived quietly on his own lands. BIBLIOGRAPHY: H. Leclercq, DACL, 4.2:1540–49.

[A. CABANISS]

DRÔLERIES, fanciful, witty, amusing, and sometimes satiric forms adorning the margins of Gothic illuminated MSS, combining men and animals in a juxtaposition of acutely observed scenes of everyday life and religious themes in a playful freedom comparable to that of the jester.

[M. J. DALY]

DROSTE-HÜLSHOFF, ANNETTE ELISABETH VON (1797–1848), Germany's greatest lyric poetess. The two volumes of her *Gedichte* (1838, 1844) contain poems of astonishing vigor, impelling rhythm, colorful verbal imagery, classic concern for form, and realistic attention to detail. Love for her native Westphalia, visionary fancy, and psychological impressionism characterize her narrative poems, of which *Die Schlacht im Loener Bruch* (1837) is perhaps the best, and the realistic prose sketches of the *Bilder aus Westfalen* (1845). Her fervent Catholic faith, strong in the midst of doubt, inspired the cycle of liturgical poems begun as early as 1818, but published posthumously as *Das geistliche Jahr* (1852), which have been called the most significant religious poetry of the 19th century. The novella *Die Judenbuche* (1842) is at once a masterpiece of realistic prose and a genuine example of *Heimatdichtung* (literature of the homeland). BIBLIOGRAPHY: M. Mare, *Annette von Droste Hülshoff* (1965).

[M. F. MCCARTHY]

DROSTE ZU VISCHERING, CLEMENS AUGUSTE VON (1773–1845), abp. of Cologne. In opposition to the Prussian government, D. as administrator of the Univ. of Münster had insisted on the RC character of the Univ. and esp. on episcopal control of the theological faculty. In response, the university was closed and the faculty suspended. D. retired, leading a charitable and ascetic life and directing the Clemens Sisters he had founded (1808). D. was loyal and deeply religious, but the inflexibility of his temperament caused him grief in matters of faith and reason. Not only did he renew the Church-State conflict on several occasions by his intransigency, but also he antagonized the academic world by his rejection of a scientific approach to theology. BIBLIOGRAPHY: W. Müller, DHGE 14:815–820.

[M. R. BROWN]

DROUIN, HYACINTHE RENÉ (*c.* 1680–1740), Dominican theologian. After completing his doctoral studies at the Sorbonne, D. taught at Saint-Jacques and was regent at Saint-Honoré. In 1719 he was named professor of theology at the Univ. of Caen, where conflict with the Jesuits caused him to be banished by Louis XV. At the invitation of the King of Sardinia, D. transferred to the Univ. of Chambéry in 1722. The last decade of his life he spent in retirement at Ivrée. His main treatise is *De re sacramentaria contra perduelles haereticos*. BIBLIOGRAPHY: Quétif-Échard 3:696–699; A. Walz, LTK 3:578.

DRUG ADDICTION, a pathological condition that as such diminishes or altogether removes moral responsibility for either the use of narcotics or for actions consequent upon it. The condition, however, can be imputable in its origin: the voluntary use of drugs known to lead to addiction. The immorality of drugtaking consists in unnecessarily risking health of body and mind, as well as impairing moral judgment, by the use of substances known to be harmful and addictive. Unlike intoxicants, addictive drugs are not commonly used in harmless moderation; alcoholism is not a necessary, predictable consequence of the use of intoxicants; addiction is generally such a predictable consequence of the use of narcotic drugs. Addiction, however, that is a consequence of the legitimate, therapeutic, and prescribed use, e.g., of morphine, may be morally blameless. Whatever the origin of the condition, an addict has an objectively serious obligation to undergo treatment and seek rehabilitation, physical and mental.

[T. C. O'BRIEN]

DRUG PEDDLING, trafficking in addictive narcotics. Whatever the medical or legal definition of the drugs in question, catering to or inducing addiction is immoral on many counts. It is a sin of *scandal, gravely threatening moral and physical harm to another. It is a sin against *justice, directly injuring the health of another person. It is a form of *extortion, preying on the addiction of another. It offends against *legal justice, not just by flouting a particular law, but by doing grave damage to the well-being of society.

[T. C. O'BRIEN]

DRUIDS AND DRUIDISM, terms referring to the order of priesthood, bards, and prophets of both sexes in ancient Britain and Gaul. Though they formed a closed order, rank was not hereditary. As custodians of religion and culture, Druids were exempt from military and other duties. Female Druids were esp. revered as seers. Although Druids had their own mode of writing, their secret lore of religion, law, healing, mathematics, astronomy, and natural phenomena was relayed exclusively by word of mouth. For this reason, most of their religion is still shrouded in mystery and is the subject of scholarly debate. According to tradition, their rites were performed on mountains and in oak forests. (The term Druid itself has been explained as deriving from roots meaning "of the oak tree" and "those who know.") Some hills in France are still known as "Druid mountains"; the oldest Christian shrine in the Alsace, "Our Lady of the Oak Tree," is a former druidic place of worship, and a piece of the original oak tree still forms part of it. The dolmens and megaliths in Britain and Gaul, scattered throughout the rest of Europe and even in Asia Minor and Africa, are believed to have been connected with their accurate time measurements, based on astronomical observation. Druids divined on the basis of the movements of celestial bodies, the flights of birds, interpreting dreams, examining sacrificial animals, etc. They administered justice annually over the collected tribes. Some scholars believe that criminals were burned or sacrificed; others deny this theory. Even after the Roman emperors Julius Caesar, Augustus, and Claudius broke their political power and deprived them of their privileges, some of the population retained faith in the Druids' divination and magic. On the Isle of Man and in Wales the bards survived as an order until the subjugation of these territories by the English. In recent years, there has been a great revival of interest in the subject. BIBLIOGRAPHY: N. K. Chadwick, *Druids* (1966); S. Piggott, *Druids* (1968); D. Wright, *Druidism: The Ancient Faith of Britain* (1924, repr. 1974). *CELTIC RELIGION; TREE WORSHIP.

[D. H. BRUNAUER]

DRUMGOOLE, JOHN CHRISTOPHER (1816–88), priest social worker. At the age of 8 he was brought from Ireland to America where he was forced to leave school early to support his widowed mother. He worked in New York City until 1865 when he began study for the priesthood and was ordained 4 years later. His concern for the thousands of homeless children in New York, many of whom were Catholic, led him to found schools and homes, including the Mission of the Immaculate Virgin (1881), set up first in Manhattan and later at Mt. Loretto, Staten Island. He helped to get state legislation requiring child placement to be in homes and institutions of their own religion. BIBLIOGRAPHY: K. Burton, *Children's Shepherd: The Story of John Christopher Drumgoole* (1954).

[M. F. CARTHY]

DRUMONT, ÉDOUARD ADOLPHE (1844–1917), writer, polemicist. Born in Paris, D. began his career as a journalist. Influenced by other writers, notably Henri Lasserre, D. became a literary critic of some importance. But his most famous contribution was his work *La France juive,* a collection of private reflections and research on the role of the Jews throughout history. Polemical, anti-Semitic, and lacking in a solid theoretical base, the work nevertheless catapulted D. into the heart of Catholic social thought in 19th-cent. France. BIBLIOGRAPHY: J. Morienval, *Catholicisme* 3:1129–30.

[M. HIGGINS]

DRUNKENNESS, a sin or *vice contrary to temperance, and specifically, to *sobriety. *Gluttony describes any excess in consumption of food or drink (ThAq ST 2a2ae.148,1), but the drinking of intoxicants needs a special control because of their effect, the upsetting of the right balance of moral judgment, i.e., the narcotic effect of al-

cohol (*ibid.* 149, 1–2). The state of intoxication means being *non compos mentis;* it is the punitive consequence, not the sin of drunkenness itself which consists rather in a culpable action that leads to intoxication (*ibid.* 150,1). The drinking may be inculpable if a person has no experience of his capacity for alcohol, or merely venially sinful if the drinker does not avert to the onset of intoxication. Drunkenness is mortally sinful when it occurs with awareness or with intent to become drunk. The sinfulness consists in subjecting self to the impairment or loss of moral judgment; an accessory disorder may be risking health without just cause. Acts committed because of intoxication, while in themselves not voluntary, may be so in their cause: the intent to drink to excess with foreseeable consequences (*ibid.* 3,4). *Alcoholism is not the sin of drunkenness, but a pathological addiction, since alcohol is a drug. (see DRUG ADDICTION) BIBLIOGRAPHY: P. K. Meagher, NCE 4:1069–70.

[T. C. O'BRIEN]

DRUSES (Arab., *Durûz,* sing., *Durzî*), a religious sect living in the mountains of Syria and Lebanon. The name is taken from that of Moḥammed ibn Ismâ'îl al-Darazî, the first person publicly to proclaim the divinity of the *Fatimid Caliph al-Ḥâkim. The basic doctrine of the sect was formulated by Hamza Ibn 'Alî, who took over leadership of the movement from *c.*1017 A.D. (the first year of the Druse era). In this doctrine, which rejects completely *Ismaili teaching as well as that of orthodox *Islam, al-Ḥâkim is considered the incarnation of God and Hamza that of the Universal Mind. With the disappearance of al-Ḥâkim and Hamza in 1021, leadership passed to al-Muqtanâ, who acted as their representative, maintaining contact with Hamza for a number of years and compiling a collection of letters, some of them by al-Ḥâkim and Hamza, known as the *Rasâ'îl al-hikma,* which represent the Druse scriptures. The community, which was quickly suppressed in Egypt, spread to Syria where they yet await the glorious return of al-Ḥâkim and Hamza. BIBLIOGRAPHY: M. G. S. Hodgson and M. T. Gökbilgin, EncIslam², S.V. "*Durûz.*"

[R. M. FRANK]

DRUTHMAR, ST. (d. 1056). Benedictine abbot of the Westphalian monastery of Corvey in the early 11th cent. who effected a monastic reform. His cult began very soon after his death.

[J. F. FALLON]

DRUŻBICKI, GASPAR (1590–1662), Polish Jesuit ascetical writer and preacher. After some years of teaching D. served as novice master for 7 years, then as rector successively at Jesuit colleges in Kalisz, Ostrog, and Posen, and was twice provincial of the Polish Jesuits. He wrote voluminously in Latin and Polish on the religious life and composed meditations. Little of this was published during his lifetime. Many of his treatises are available in German and English translations. BIBLIOGRAPHY: W. J. Fulco, NCE 4:1070–71.

[M. J. SUELZER]

DRYBURGH, MONASTERY OF. Premonstratensian, Scottish foundation of the mid-12th cent. on the site of an ancient Celtic monastery. Wars between Scotland and England in the 14th and 15th cent. caused repeated damage to its buildings until only the church was left. The ruins are now a national monument of Scotland; tomb of Sir Walter Scott is at Dryburgh.

[J. F. FALLON]

DRYDEN, JOHN (1631–1700), English poet, satirist, dramatist, critic. Born in Northamptonshire, D. was brought up in a Puritan environment and educated at Cambridge. His first poem was on the death of Cromwell (1659); in 1660, *Astraea Redux* celebrated the return of Charles II. In 1663 D. married Lady Howard and turned playwright for a livelihood, averaging almost a play a year, 1663–81. The political, literary, and social life of London involved him in quarrels and feuds that gave rise to political and personal satires such as *Absalom and Achitophel, The Medall,* and *MacFlecknoe.* A Tory in politics, he defended the C of E in *Religio Laici* (1682), but on the death of Charles II and the accession of the Catholic James II, he became a Catholic, affirming his position in *The Hind and the Panther* (1687). A charge of insincerity and of currying court favor has been constantly repeated. However, in 1934 L. I. Bredvold (*The Intellectual Milieu of John Dryden*) demonstrated that D., always of skeptical mind and distrustful of man's own power to attain truth, was early anxious to find an absolute authority in Church and State, and that, hence, his change to Catholicism in 1686 was but a logical outgrowth of earlier thought. After the Protestant Revolution of 1688, he lost offices and turned to writing again for a living: plays, odes, translations. BIBLIOGRAPHY: M. Van Doren, *Poetry of John Dryden* (1931, rev. 1946); B. Schilling, *Dryden and the Conservative Myth* (1961); G. Cronin, Jr., NCE 4:1071–73; J. D. Garrison, *Dryden and the Tradition of Panegyric* (1975).

[N. MALTMAN]

DUALISM, an interpretation of reality or some aspect of it in terms of two ultimate principles. It is distinguished from *monism, which reduces reality to one principle, and pluralism, which asserts that reality is too varied for reduction to one or two principles.

At the beginning of Western philosophy, Thales and other Ionians sought to interpret the universe in terms of a single principle, an approach that reached its absolute form in Parmenides, who denied change. But Parmenides also taught a kind of dualism, for he distinguished things as they truly are from things as they appear. Plato taught a dualism of ideas and phenomenal reality, and Aristotle had dualism of form and matter, soul and body, and immaterial and material substance. But for Plato and Aristotle one can assert an ultimate unity in the ultimate causality of the ideas and the unmoved mover.

Epistemological dualism has been important in modern philosophy since Descartes set forth his dualism of thought and extension. For him the material world *(res extensa)* and the mental world *(res cogitans)* formed a dualism. Similarly Kant later distinguished between phenomena and noumena, the latter unknowable. A major effort has been made in later philosophy to bridge the epistemological dualism.

Dualism of a different kind arises in consequence of the problem of good and evil. To religious thinkers it has appeared important to affirm God as the one ultimate source of all things, yet that position can appear to make God responsible for evil. Zoroastrianism asserted that God was not responsible for evil, but that a second ultimate principle existed as its source. Manichaeism followed this dualistic approach, but was rejected by Christianity as a heresy. It held that the material world was under the control of Satan, and that for the sake of salvation man must escape his physical existence. This contradicted the Christian doctrine of the ultimate goodness of the creation. In the realm of personal ethics this can issue in either of two unsatisfactory moral positions, namely, either an extreme asceticism based upon contempt for the body, or an antinomianism based on indifference to what the body does because it is under Satan's control. Christian theology has taught that God is the creator of both soul and body, that man as a unified person must serve God in all that he does.

Other dualisms have been important in the history of Christian thought, such as that of nature and grace. Roman Catholic theology has held that grace perfects nature and adds to it, but that both have their source in God. Protestant theology has generally made the contrast between sin and grace. Medieval Christian philosophy emphasized a dualism of essence and existence, with the two having their unity in God whose essence is identical with his existence. The doctrine of Christ's nature as both human and divine is sometimes called a dualism. Here, too, orthodox theology insists upon an ultimate unity of the two natures in the one person. BIBLIOGRAPHY: A. O. Lovejoy, *Revolt against Dualism* (2d ed., 1960).

[T. EARLY]

DU BARTAS, GUILLAUME DE SALLUSTE (1544–90), French Huguenot poet. In the service of Henry IV he was sent on diplomatic missions, notably to James I of England. Entering late into the wars of religion, he composed a *Cantique de la Victoire à Ivry* (1590) but is best known for his *La Semaine* (1576), a biblical epic on creation, which expresses his Protestant fervor nurtured on biblical antiquity. Although criticized for its mannerist style, it was well received abroad with more than 30 editions and 6 translations, the English one, which influenced Milton, by Sir Philip Sydney. *La Seconde semaine* (1584, unfinished), was to be a continuation of Du B.'s history of humanity. Of lesser importance are his *Uranie, Le Triomphe de la foi,* and his first biblical epic, *Judith,* published in his early collection entitled *La Muse chrétienne* (1574). He was much admired by Goethe. BIBLIOGRAPHY: G. Pelissier, *La Vie et les oeuvres de Du Bartas* (1883); B. Braunrot, *Imagination poétique chez Du Bartas* (1974).

[R. N. NICOLICH]

DU BELLAY, JEAN (1492–1560), cardinal, religious reformer whose diplomatic service for the French Church promoted peace, church reform, and conciliation. D. made several diplomatic missions for Francis I to England, Rome, and the German states. He was successively bp. of Bayonne (1526), Paris (1532), Bordeaux (1545), and cardinal bishop of Ostia (1555). Included among his letters and published works are several volumes of poetry.

[K. O'NEILL]

DU BELLAY, JOACHIM (1527–60), French Renaissance poet and humanist. With *Ronsard, Du B. was one of the founders of the *Pléïade group of French Renaissance poets and wrote its literary manifesto defending the possibilities of the national language, *La Défense et illustration de la langue française* (1549). Hoping to advance under the patronage of his cousin, the diplomat Card. Jean Du Bellay, he prepared early for his service and accompanied his cousin to Rome as secretary (1553). His nostalgia and disillusionment upon observing Roman decadence, including the papal court, are expressed in his collections of poetry, esp. *Les Antiquités de Rome* and *Les Regrets* (both pub. 1558). His poems, esp. sonnets in the collection *L'Olive* (1549 and 1550), often reveal Christian Neoplatonist inspiration. BIBLIOGRAPHY: G. Dickinson, *Du Bellay in Rome* (1960); R. V. Merrill, *Platonism of Joachim du Bellay* (1925); A. W. Satterthwaite, *Spenser, Ronsard, and Du Bellay* (1960, repr. 1971).

[R. N. NICOLICH]

DUBLANCHY, EDMOND (1858–1938), theological writer. Born in France, he was ordained (1881) as a member of the Society of Mary at Armagh in Ireland and taught in several countries of the world, the U.S. included. He is known mainly because of his contributions to the DTC and for several theological volumes evidencing his fidelity to Thomas Aquinas. BIBLIOGRAPHY: S. Duffy and T. Gilbride, "Portrait of a Theologian, Edmond Dublanchy," AER 136 (1957) 155–166.

[T. C. O'BRIEN]

DUBOIS, GUILLAUME (1656–1723), French cardinal and prime minister under Louis XV. Educated at a monastery in Brive-la-Gaillarde in the Limousin and at the college of St. Michel in Paris, he became tutor to Philippe, later Duke of Orléans, but then Duke of Chartres. Subsequently D. arranged the marriage of Philippe with his cousin, Mlle. de Blois, the natural but legitimated daughter of Louis

XIV, thus ingratiating himself with the Sun King. As secretary to the Duke, D. was sent to London in 1698 as part of the French Embassy, but was recalled for intriguing. His ambitions found their full scope only after the death of the old king in 1715, when the Duke of Orléans became regent for the young Louis XV. He was made a councillor of state, after which his influence in national affairs steadily increased. D. directed his principal efforts to maintaining the peace established by the Treaty of Utrecht and to countering the expansionist aims of Spain. To this end he brought both England and the Netherlands into the Triple Alliance (1717), a grouping that was joined by Austria in 1718, and, by means of military intervention in Spain in 1719, forced Charles V to dismiss his chief minister, Card. Alberoni. In 1720 D. succeeded in obtaining from the regent the lucrative archbishopric of Cambrai and the following year, in recompense for bribes expended and his support of the anti-Jansenist papal bull *Unigenitus,* he was made cardinal by Innocent XIII. With his election to the Académie Française and his appointment as prime minister in 1722, D. reached the height of his power and influence. This position he maintained even after Louis XV reached his majority in 1723, but the same year died from surgery. D. was assuredly unscrupulous and venal (and by his enemies accused of debauchery and corruption as well); yet in spite of personal weaknesses, his policy of peace with the rest of Europe was a boon, providing a welcome respite to France after years of unprofitable wars.

[E. M. GATES]

DUBOIS, JOHN (1764–1842), bp. of New York. In 1791 he fled the Revolution in his native France, where he had been ordained (1787) after study at the College of Louis-le-Grand and St. Magloire Seminary in Paris. Arriving in the U.S., he did missionary work in Virginia, Maryland, and Pennsylvania. The school he founded (1807) at Emmitsburg, Md., became Mt. St. Mary's College and Seminary and, until 1826, D. and the institution were affiliated with the *Sulpicians. He was appointed third bp. of New York and consecrated (1826) in Baltimore. His unpopularity among New York's predominantly Irish community hampered his efforts to provide schools, churches, and other needed institutions. Nevertheless, despite outbreaks of lay *trusteeism within the Church and nativist attacks from without, D. tripled the number of priests for his growing Catholic population and increased the number of churches fourfold. By 1839 ill health forced him to turn over diocesan management to his coadjutor, John *Hughes. BIBLIOGRAPHY: C. G. Herbermann, "Rt. Rev. John Dubois, D.D." *Records and studies of the U.S. Catholic Historical Society of New York*[1] (1899) 278–355; M. Carthy, *Old St. Patrick's, New York's First Cathedral* (1947).

[M. CARTHY]

DUBOIS, LOUIS ERNEST (1856–1929), cardinal

archbishop of Paris from 1920. He had been bp. of Verdun (1901–09), abp. of Bourges (1909), and of Rouen (1916) before his appointment to Paris; he was created cardinal in 1916. He was esteemed by the Holy See for his staunch defense of the Church against the secularizing policies of the French government in 1905; but after World War I he was also sent to represent France on missions to the Near East, Poland, Austria, the U.S., and Canada. As abp. of Paris D. created many agencies promoting the liturgical and educational life of the Church; he favored the trade union movement and Catholic Action, but was bitterly opposed to *Action Française.

[T. C. O'BRIEN]

DUBOIS, PIERRE (c. 1250–c. 1321), French lawyer and political pamphleteer who attacked papal power in many tracts written to win public support for his ideas. He argued that the peace of Europe as well as the expansion of Christianity depended upon strong royal (i.e., French) leadership, rather than the pope's. His *Recovery of the Holy Land* (ed. and tr. W. I. Brandt) was published in 1956. BIBLIOGRAPHY: J. R. Strayer, NCE 4:1080.

[V. L. BULLOUGH]

DU BOS, CHARLES (1882–1939), French critic who explored European literature from a theological and metaphysical point of view. Of affluent Anglo-French parentage, he was educated in France and at Oxford (1900–01), where he began the pursuit of English literature that led to major criticism on Byron, Pater, Shelley, and James. After studying in Germany, Italy, and Holland (1902–07), he followed a literary career. D. was reared a Catholic, but his faith progressively weakened after 1908; a reading of Butler's *Way of All Flesh* in 1918 destroyed his spiritual equilibrium. There ensued a 9-year religious exile marked by spiritual tension and ascent, sensitively recounted in his *Journal intime* (9 v., 1946–61). Following his return to Catholicism (1927), an increasing religious fervor informed his critical writings, and he helped found *Vigile* Z1930), a journal having pronounced Catholic tendencies. He gave a series of private courses on wide-ranging literary subjects (1922–26) and lectured at the Pontigny international seminars (1923). Works focusing on spiritual problems in literature include *Le Dialogue avec André Gide* (1929); *Du spirituel dans l'ordre littéraire* (1930 to 1967); *François Mauriac et le problème du romancier catholique* (1933); *What is Literature?* (1938), four lectures delivered at St. Mary's College, Notre Dame, Indiana, where he taught (1937–39); *Goethe* (1949); and many essays in criticism collected as *Approximations* (7 v., 1922–37), particularly those in later volumes. In poor health, D. wrote a meditation on Christian suffering, *Dialogues avec la souffrance* (1941). BIBLIOGRAPHY: A. P. Bertucci, *Charles du Bos and English Literature* (1949); M. A. Gouhier, *Charles du Bos* (1951); C. Dedeyan, *Le Cosmopolitisme*

littéraire de Charles du Bos (1965); C. J. Mertens, *E.Fmotion et critique chez Charles du Bos* (1967).

[G. E. GINGRAS]

DU BOSE, WILLIAM PORCHER (1836–1918), American Episcopal theologian. He studied at The Citadel, Charleston, S.C., and the Univ. of Virginia, and after military service in the Civil War was ordained (1866). He accepted a call to the Univ. of the South in Sewanee, Tenn., in 1871 as chaplain and professor of ethics, lecturing on Aristotle. In 1873 he formed the department of theology and in 1894 became its dean. His thought was influenced by both the *Oxford movement and the *Mercersburg theology. He held that the Church is the life incorporate and corporate in Jesus Christ and that the sacraments were acts of God's incorporation of man into Christ, not expressions of faith. He also held that man cannot interpret Scriptures apart from the mind of the Church. His principal works are *The Soteriology of the New Testament* (1899); *The Gospel in the Gospels* (1906), a study of the apostolic faith; *The Gospel According to St. Paul* (1907), which stresses the principle of authority; and *The Reason of Life* (1911). BIBLIOGRAPHY: Smith-Jamison 1:298–303.

[R. K. MacMASTER]

DUBOURG, LOUIS WILLIAM VALENTINE (1766–1833), bp., educator. D., driven from France by the French Revolution, joined the Sulpicians in Baltimore (1794). Bp. Carroll named him president of Georgetown College (1796) and in 1803 he became the first president of St. Mary's College, Baltimore. He was appointed bp. of New Orleans in 1812, but the documents of appointment could not be transmitted because Pope Pius VII was captive of Napoleon. Carroll named D. administrator apostolic of New Orleans. The area was in sad shape with few priests and many of these resentful of his coming. He played an important role in supporting the American effort against the British attack in 1815. His major effort later was to recruit priests in Europe for his diocese. Consecrated bp. in 1815, he was successful in bringing both priests and religious to New Orleans. He established a college for boys and an academy for girls, brought a colony of Jesuits to Missouri for work on the Indian missions, and developed parishes throughout his territory. An imprudent series of recommended promotions brought him into disfavor among his clergy, and he resigned his see. He died as abp. of Besançon in France. BIBLIOGRAPHY: C. M. Chambon, CE 5:178–179.

[J. R. AHERNE]

DUBRICIUS, ST. (Dyfrig; 6th cent.), bp. in Wales. Although there is much legendary material concerning D., nothing certain is known of him except that he was an important personage in the Church in Wales in the 6th century. Legend claims that he was born near Hereford, that he founded a monastery at Henllan and another later at Moccas. He is variously credited with being bp. of Llandaff or abp. of Caerleon. According to Geoffrey of Monmouth, as abp. of Caerleon he crowned King Arthur at Colchester. It is said that in his last years he resigned his see and lived as a hermit on the isle of Bardsey. BIBLIOGRAPHY: S. Brechter, LTK 3:591–592; Butler 4:340–341.

[R. B. ENO]

DU CANGE, CHARLES DU FRESNE (1610–88), scholar and philologist, "the Muratori of France." He studied at Amiens and Orléans, became treasurer at Amiens in 1645, and lived in Paris after 1668. He was noted for editions of ancient French and Byzantine historians, chroniclers, and documentary collections. His chief fame lies in his *Glossarium ad scriptores mediae et infimae Latinitatis* (3 v., 1678; extended to 10 v. by Benedictines; repr. 1954) and *Glossarium . . . Graecitatis* (2 v., 1688; repr. 1943), both of which are essential for the study of medieval Latin and Greek. BIBLIOGRAPHY: R. Chalumeau, *Catholicisme* 3:1142; J. Grisar, LTK 3:591–592.

[F. D. LAZENBY]

DUCAS (fl. mid-15th cent.), Byzantine historian. His work, which has come down to us without title, after a preliminary survey of the world-chronicle type, covers in detail the period from 1341 to the conquest of Lesbos by the Turks in 1462. D. is the most indispensable and objective of the last Byzantine historians. Unlike the majority of his Byzantine contemporaries, he was a supporter of union with Rome. He had long been in intimate contact as a diplomat with the Genoese and was well informed on Western affairs pertaining to Byzantium. He wrote in the popular Greek language, and his style is characterized by warmth and a gift for vivid description. His work was soon translated into Italian. BIBLIOGRAPHY: H. Hunger, LTK 3:598; Ostrogorsky 416–418.

[M. R. P. MCGUIRE]

DUCAS, DEMETRIUS (d. 1527?), Byzantine humanist in Spain. From Crete he came to Venice, and later to Spain, where he became the pioneer in Greek studies. In 1508 he was associated with Aldus Manutius in Venice and was the chief editor of the Aldine *Rhetores Graeci*. After the publication (1509) of the Aldine *editio princeps* of Plutarch's *Moralia*, which he supervised, he apparently went to Spain, for in 1513 he was installed at the new Univ. of Alcalá and in the employ of Card. Ximénez. He was the chief editor of the Greek NT in Ximénez' Polyglot Bible. At Alcalá he published at his own expense two books, the first to be printed in Greek in the Iberian peninsula. In 1526 he was in Rome and edited there the Greek liturgies of SS. Basil and Chrysostom. He taught at the Univ. of Rome, but there is no trace of him after 1527. BIBLIOGRAPHY: D. J. Geanakoplos, NCE 4:1087; *idem, Greek Scholars in Venice: Studies in the Dissemination of Greek Learning from Byzantium to Western Europe* (1962) 223–255.

[M. R. P. MCGUIRE]

DUCCIO DE BUONINSEGNA (*c.* 1255–*c.* 1319), first and greatest painter in the early 14th century. Recorded are D.'s paintings on 12 chests (1278) and covers for the official registers of the city of Siena. He painted an altarpiece for the Palazzo Pubblico, Siena (1302, lost); *Madonna and Child Enthroned with Angels* (Uffizi) known as the Rucellai Madonna, first attributed by Vasari to Cimabue, but determined in the 20th cent. as D.'s. A work of masterly linear design, its Byzantine background shows a new sense of immediacy and space. D.'s major work is the *Maestà* altarpiece (1308), which was transferred from his studio to the cathedral in solemn procession (1311). The front carried the Madonna and Child surrounded by saints and angels, together with scenes of the childhood of Christ and the life of the Virgin; the back showed 26 scenes from the life of Christ between the baptism and the Ascension. Removed from the high altar (1506), by 1881 its panels had been destroyed or dispersed to London, Washington, D.C., Philadelphia, and New York. D.'s color and composition set the course of Sienese painting for 150 years. An innovator with decorative delicacy and the liveliness of Gothic France and Burgundy, D. created a new Sienese school through his transformation of the Byzantine tradition. BIBLIOGRAPHY: E. Carli, *Duccio di Buoninsegna* (1962).

[M. J. DALY]

DUCHAUSSOIS, PIERRE JEAN BAPTISTE (1878–1940), missionary and mission historian. A native of France, D. entered the Oblates of Mary Immaculate in 1897 and was sent to Canada (1903) where he taught at Ottawa until assigned to missionary work in Alberta (1913). At the request of the vicar apostolic of Mackenzie, D. prepared a history of the missions in N Canada, *Aux glaces polaires* (1920), a work of considerable repute in the field of mission literature (Eng. *Mid Snow and Ice,* 1923). He preached on behalf of the missions in France (1922) and went to Ceylon (1924), where his investigation of the situation of the missions led to his *Sous les feux de Ceylan* (1929). He also made a study-tour of the missions of South Africa (1932–35). BIBLIOGRAPHY: Y. Guéguen, *Catholicisme* 3:1143–44.

DUCHESNE, ANDRÉ (Quercitanus; 1584–1640), sometimes called the "Father of French History." His writings include scholarly works on various aspects of French royal and ecclesiastical history, collections of documents pertinent to Cluniac history and French historians, and critical editions. Living before the Maurists and the Bollandists, he anticipated their spirit of scholarship in productivity and methodology. A collection of his writings, including 121

MSS, is in the Bibliothèque nationale. BIBLIOGRAPHY: J. Daoust, NCE 4:1087–88.

[J. J. SMITH]

DUCHESNE, LOUIS (1843–1922), French church historian. As a student in Rome, D.'s interest in history and archeology of the ancient Church was awakened by G. B. de Rossi. After preparing himself by advanced studies in Paris, he became a member of the French archeological school in Rome and was employed in scholarly expeditions and research in Greece and Asia Minor. He was appointed to the chair of ecclesiastical history at the Catholic Institute of Paris, but was able to remain in that position for only 8 years because his critical approach to the history of the Church, esp. the beginnings of the Church in Gaul, and his sardonic wit made him many enemies. Thus in 1885, he became a professor of the École des Hautes Études in Paris. From 1895, until his death, he was director of the French archeological school in Rome, and from 1910, a member of the French Academy. His principal works comprise a critical ed. of and commentary on the *Liber Pontificalis* (1886–92); *Les Fastes épiscopaux de l'ancienne Gaule* (1894–1915); and *L'Histoire ancienne de l'Église* (3 v., 1906–10; tr. 3 v., 1909–1924), a work placed on the Index during the *Modernist controversy. With the passing of time, D.'s scholarly research and insights into the early history of the Church have been justified and sustained. BIBLIOGRAPHY: P. Frutaz, EncCatt 4:1960–65; F. X. Murphy, NCE 4:1088; C. Vogel, LTK 3:593.

[R. B. ENO]

DUCHESNE, ROSE PHILIPPINE, BL. (1769–1852), religious, teacher, pioneer. Endowed with strong will, great energy, and zeal, D. was an early member of the Society of the Sacred Heart in France. Sent to the U.S. by the foundress, Mother Barat, she participated in the founding of a boarding school for daughters of pioneers near St. Louis and in opening the first free school west of the Mississippi, as well as the first Catholic school for Indians in the U.S. D. founded a convent in St. Louis and a mission school for Indians in Kansas when she was 70 years old. The Historical Society of Missouri named her in 1918 the outstanding pioneer woman of the state. She was declared blessed in 1940 by Pius XII. BIBLIOGRAPHY: C. M. Lowth, CE 5:182; C. Vens, BiblSanct 4:847; Butler 4:378–381.

[J. R. AHERNE]

DUDLEY PRIORY, a former Cluniac monastery in Worcestershire, England. It developed in 1170 from Wenlock Priory (established *c.*1079). These were among the few Cluniac foundations in England, where Cluny had little impact on monasticism. Dudley Priory, long in ruins, has been restored as a historical monument.

[T. C. O'BRIEN]

DUDON, PAUL (1859–1941), French Jesuit and religious historian. A Jesuit from 1880, D. studied in Spain, taught at Bordeaux and Montpellier, and for 35 years was a collaborator on the review *Études,* producing many learned articles on the religious history of 19th-cent. France. Three of his books are especially noteworthy: *Lamennais et le Saint Siège, 1820–1834* (1911); *Le Quiétiste espagnol, M. Molinos* (1920); and *Saint Ignace de Loyola* (1934; tr. W. J. Young, 1949). BIBLIOGRAPHY: R. Brouillard, *Catholicisme* 3:1146–47, bibliog; J. Brodrick, *Origin of the Jesuits* (pa. 1960, repr. 1971).

[T. C. O'BRIEN]

DUE PROCESS OF LAW (U.S.). (1) In American civil law the phrase connotes particularly the Fifth and Fourteenth Amendments to the U.S. Constitution that forbid the deprival of life, liberty, or property without due process of law. While civil jurisprudence regarding the implications of due process is complicated, some points are clear. It amounts to a protection against government interference with personal rights and liberties. The U.S. Supreme Court's interpretations of the constitutional amendments make explicit some of the elements of due process. It demands counsel for the accused even at state expense; the presence of counsel at any interrogation of one accused; it excludes confessions of guilt extracted by force or pressure and any evidence attained by illegal means; it requires that trial transcripts be made available, even at public expense, to the accused. Guaranteed in general are those elements that protect the principle of the presumption of innocence until guilt has been proved and of keeping the government and its officials from violating rights that are viewed as more fundamental and universally recognized than civil law itself (see RIGHT AND RIGHTS: CIVIL RIGHTS). (2) In the Church the phrase has come to connote a movement towards establishing similar principles and procedures against administrative arbitrariness. The CIC, as it has been interpreted, puts outside the competence of ecclesiastical courts the exercise of administrative authority. Hitherto where there has been a grievance against the decision of an administrator the sole recourse was appeal to the next highest administrative authority. Contemporary concern for justice has created an atmosphere in which such a situation has come to be regarded as out of keeping with even the decrees of Vatican Council II, with their emphasis on the Church as a community, on the dignity of the person, and on freedom of conscience. Some notoriety has been created by the refusal of the theologian Hans Küng to accept unilateral decisions of the Roman Curia, without allowing him counsel, access to evidence, or confrontation of his accusers. The 1967 Synod of Bishops recommended that there be a revision of church administrative procedures and a papal commission was set up in 1971 to such an end. In the U.S. the National Conference of Catholic Bishops published in 1972 *On Due Process,* which was based on the procedures recommended by the Canon Law Society of America. Much of the conception of such procedures reflects American civil law. With the issuance in 1973 of a draft of the penal law to be incorporated into a new Code of Canon Law, part of the response and criticism centered on the issue of due process in the Church (see PENAL POWER OF THE CHURCH).

[T. C. O'BRIEN]

DUELING, a prearranged conflict with deadly weapons, between two private persons. It is both intrinsically sinful and proscribed by ecclesiastical law. Its immorality consists in putting one's own life in jeopardy without just reason, and in unjust aggression without the mitigation of self-defense. Those who are involved, as seconds or otherwise, are cooperators in sin. From the Council of Valence in 855 through the Middle Ages to the Council of Trent all forms of dueling have been forbidden, often under pain of ex-communication. The duel of honor, beginning in the 15th cent., was esp. condemned. Ecclesiastical proscription and penalties were incorporated into the CIC (cc. 1240–41, 2351).

[T. C. O'BRIEN]

DUFAY, GUILLAUME (*c.*1400–74), Burgundian composer. D. began his career as a chorister in the cathedral at Cambrai, with which city he had his most enduring association. He sang in the papal choir and then took his M.A. degree at the Sorbonne. He was appointed canon of Cambrai, Bruges, and other cathedrals. With Dunstable and Binchois he ranks as one of the greatest composers of that time and as the transitional figure between the Gothic tradition and that of the great Flemish school of polyphonic music. Upon a solid foundation of the French *ars nova,* he received and assimilated Italian and English influence. While the major portion of his compositions are sacred music (Masses, Magnificats, and motets), he also wrote French and Italian chansons.

[M. T. LEGGE]

DUFF, ALEXANDER (1806–78), first missionary of the Church of Scotland to India; he labored there from 1830–49, after 1843 as a member of the Free Church. From 1856–64 he again was in India, working on the foundation of the Univ. of Calcutta. Because of ill health he spent the remainder of his life in Scotland, but took a keen interest in the missions, esp. in S Africa.

[M. HIGGINS]

DUFFY, FRANCIS PATRICK (1871–1932), army chaplain. A Canadian by birth, D. immigrated to New York and was ordained in 1896. A popular seminary teacher and dynamic pastor, D. became chaplain of the Fighting 69th Regiment and shared its colorful and heroic career in World War I. His tough-minded humanity, his humor, and his complete dedication to every soldier in the regiment made him one of the most loved figures of the age. D. was honored by presidents, governors, and generals but always retained the common touch.

[J. R. AHERNE]

DUFOURCQ, ALBERT (1872–1952), French religious historian, professor of medieval history at the Univ. of Bordeaux (1900–38). His masterwork, *L'Avenir du christianisme* (4 v., 1908–36) is a history of the Church, and the title indicates his special insistence upon viewing the Church's past as a preparation for its future. The work reflects his deep Catholicism and his genuine insights into the meaning of Christianity. Two later works, *Le Christianisme antique* (1939) and *Le Christianisme moderne* (1949) amount to a resumé of *L'Avenir.* BIBLIOGRAPHY: G. Bardy, *Catholicisme* 3:1153–54.

DU FRESNE, CHARLES, see DU CANGE, CHARLES DU FRESNE.

DUGDALE, WILLIAM (1605–86), antiquarian. His best-known work is his *Monasticon Anglicanum* (3 v., 1655–73). He also published *Antiquities of Warwickshire* (1656) and *History of St. Paul's Cathedral in London* (1658)—both fine examples of English local historical writing—and *Baronage of England* (1675–76), the first important work on that subject. BIBLIOGRAPHY: D. C. Douglas, *English Scholars* (1939) 31–59; F. Espinasse, DNB 6:136–142.

DUGLIOLI, HELENA, BL. (1472–1520), widow. She was venerated by the people of Bologna for her life of prayer and mortification, both in her 30 years of married life and during her widowhood. Her cult was confirmed when Pope Leo XII beatified her in 1828. BIBLIOGRAPHY: Butler 3:627.

[K. O'NEILL]

DU HAMEL, JEAN BAPTISTE (1624–1706), French philosopher and theologian. A member of the Congregation of the Oratory D. wrote several works on science and natural philosophy and is best known for his comparative studies of Cartesianism and Scholasticism, in *De consensu veteris et novae philosophiae* (1663). He also published texts for seminary use in philosophy and theology. For 30 years he was Secretary of the French Academy of Sciences.

[J. R. RIVELLO]

DUHEM, PIERRE (1861–1916), physicist and historian of science. He taught at Lille and Rennes before becoming professor of theoretical physics at Bordeaux (1895). In 1913, he was elected to the Académie des Sciences but failed to gain a professorship at the Sorbonne, as much for his difficult disposition as for his Catholicism and his politics. His mind was set against the atomic theory, and he refused to work from models. He contributed significantly to thermodynamics, hydrodynamics, and the theory of elasticity; and to both science and philosophy by his analysis and historical investigations. He emphasized the continuity of scientific progress and gave special attention to the science of the Middle Ages esp. in the classic work he inaugurated, *Le Système du monde* (10 v. 1913–17, repr. 1954–59).

[H. JACK]

DU HOUX, JEANNE (1616–77), French religious of the Visitation. D. was forced in her youth to marry, but at her husband's early death she entered the Colombier Convent of the Visitation. In general, her religious life was oriented toward the mystical. Also, she carried the Salesian stamp of simplicity while other aspects of her spirituality were closer to the school of Bérulle. BIBLIOGRAPHY: E. Catta, DSAM 3:1769–73.

[K. O'NEILL]

DUHR, BERNHARD (1852–1930), German Jesuit. D. labored in Vienna, the Netherlands, and Munich as a Jesuit archivist. An authority on Jesuit history, esp. on the period from 1550 to 1800, he worked with objectivity and frankness. His most widely read book is *Jesuiten-Febeln,* and his most scholarly work is a six-volume history of the Jesuits in Germanic lands previous to their suppression. Intellectual pursuits did not prevent him from helping the poor. During World War I he set up programs with private American funds and personally worked among the poor. BIBLIOGRAPHY: P. Bailly, *Catholicisme* 3:1159.

[M. HIGGINS]

DUKHOBORS, see DOUKHOBORS.

DULIA, from Gr. *douleia* (slavery), a term most commonly used to distinguish the worship due to saints from the adoration *(latria)* owed to God alone (the special veneration of Mary is *hyperdulia*). St. Thomas Aquinas (ThAq ST 2a2ae, 103) adds to this meaning two others, in which dulia names a *virtue allied to *justice. First, it is a name applicable to any virtue prompting respect, service, honor towards those who have a right to receive them. Secondly, in a sense used by St. Augustine, it described the specific virtue that prompted respectful service of slave toward master, serf toward lord.

[T. C. O'BRIEN]

DUM ACERBISSIMAS, an apostolic letter of Gregory XVI (Sept. 26, 1835) censuring some of the views of Georg *Hermes (d. 1831), mainly his teaching that positive doubt is the basis of all theological investigation and that reason is the supreme norm and sole medium by which man can attain supernatural truths. The letter also states that at the direction of the Pope, competent theologians had carefully examined his works and, since they found that his books contained serious errors in some 20 listed areas of theology, it was necessary to prohibit and condemn them. BIBLIOGRAPHY: D 2738–40.

[J. H. ROHLING]

DUMAS, ALEXANDRE *(Père* and *Fils),* French dramatists and novelists. **Dumas** *père* (1802–70) created the French Romantic theater with his most enduring play *Henri III et sa cour* in 1829. Turning to the novel he used the same melodramatic techniques as in the plays. The novels were enormously popular, esp. the trilogy on the Three Musketeers and *The Count of Monte Cristo.* Though a journeyman of the novel, he managed to fascinate generations of readers. His "love stories" were once on the Index, but many of his novels were recommended on a list approved by Pope Benedict XV. **Dumas** *fils* (1824–95) was also a dramatist and novelist. His novel *La Dame aux Camélias* became a successful play, motion picture, and opera. As a dramatist he became a moralist, creating stories to argue his views on moral questions. He was a phenomenon of the bourgeois society of France in the 19th century. BIBLIOGRAPHY: A. Crisafulli, NCE 4:1097–98.

[J. R. AHERNE]

DUMMERMUTH, ANTONINUS (1841–1918), Belgian Dominican theologian, regent of studies for 30 years at the studium of Louvain. His weighty counterblast to an attack on physical premotion was popularly referred to as "the bomb." BIBLIOGRAPHY: A. D'Amato, EncCatt 4:1979–80.

[T. GILBY]

DUMONT, HENRI (1610–84), Belgian organist and composer. After studying and singing at Notre Dame church at Maestricht, and at Liège, he became organist, choirmaster, and a canon at Maestricht. His works include Masses, motets, chansons, and organ preludes.

[M. T. LEGGE]

DUMOUTET, ÉDOUARD EUGÈNE PAUL (1895–1943), French theologian. D. entered the Sulpician seminary at Issy in 1914 but soon left to serve in World War I. He was seriously wounded three times but survived to be ordained in 1921 and named auxiliary vicar of St. Marcel. In 1925 he became secretary of the *Revue apologètique* and its editor in 1939. He was made a doctor of theology at the Univ. of Strasbourg in 1926 and then served as professor of history at Issy until his death. D. was an authority on the cult of the Eucharist and published many monographs on its history. He also produced numerous articles on contemporary literature, art, and apologetics. BIBLIOGRAPHY: J. Trinquet, *Catholicisme* 3:1170.

DUNBOYNE ESTABLISHMENT, endowed three-year course of studies for graduate students at St. Patrick's College, Maynooth, Ireland. It is named for Lord Dunboyne who in 1800 gave property in Meath to fund the endowment; as John Butler, bp. of Cork, he had apostatized in 1786 upon inheriting the title of Lord Dunboyne; the endowment was a sign of his repentance.

[K. O'NEILL]

DUNDRENNAN, ABBEY OF, former Cistercian monastery, Kirkcudbrightshire, Scotland, founded in 1142 as a daughter house of Rievaulx. From it Mary Queen of Scots left Scotland in 1568. The abbey is now in ruins; it passed into the hands of the Crown in 1587.

[T. C. O'BRIEN]

DUNFERMLINE, ABBEY OF, monastery in Fife, Scotland, founded by Queen Margaret in 1074 and richly endowed by her and her sons. Under David I it became a Benedictine abbey with monks from Canterbury (1089). The bodies of Queen Margaret, her family, and other members of Scottish royalty are buried there. Though pillaged and desecrated during the Reformation, the abbey church is still in use. BIBLIOGRAPHY: D. O. Hunter-Blair, CE 5:190; H. Dauphin, DHGE 14:1044–47.

[K. O'NEILL]

DUNGAL. Various early Irish monks and educators bore this name. The most famous was D. of Saint-Denis (d. after 827), who communicated astronomic data to Charlemagne and was an adamant enemy of iconoclasm. BIBLIOGRAPHY: T. P. Halton, NCE 4:1100.

[J. F. FALLON]

DUNIN, MARTIN VON (1774–1842), Polish priest and educator. Ordained in 1797, D. became canon and chancellor in 1815. Later as educational advisor to the Prussian government, he came into open conflict concerning the education of children of mixed marriages and was condemned to jail. Eventually King Friedrich Wilhelm IV, sympathetic to his Polish subjects, allowed D. to return to his see. BIBLIOGRAPHY: S. Furlani, EncCatt 4:1982.

[M. HIGGINS]

DUNKERS (Dunkards, Tunkers; Ger. *tunken,* dip, immerse), originally a Pennsylvania Dutch nickname for the German Baptist Brethren (see BRETHREN CHURCHES), based on their practice of *trine immersion. *CONSERVATIVE DUNKERS; *OLD ORDER DUNKERS; *PROGRESSIVE DUNKERS.

[T. C. O'BRIEN]

DUNNE, M. FREDERIC (1874–1948), Trappist abbot. A native of Georgia, D. entered the Trappist monastery at Gethsemani, Kentucky, at the age of twenty. Within a short time he was called on to rescue a school for boys operated by the Trappists but now rocked by financial scandal. Elected abbot, he took office when the epidemic of Spanish influenza was decimating the monastery. The grim events

of history in the 1930s and 1940s brought an unprecedented number of candidates to Gethsemani. D. saw the opportunity to spread Trappist influence in new foundations. Under his direction monasteries were established and supplied from Gethsemani in Georgia, Utah, and New Mexico. D.'s impact on his own abbey was one of renewed austerity as he moved closer to the 12th-cent. spirit of his order. BIBLIOGRAPHY: T. Merton, *Waters of Siloe* (1949).

[J. R. AHERNE]

DUNNE, PETER MASTEN (1889–1957), Jesuit historian. A Californian by birth and through his career, D. was a teacher and mission historian. His specialty was the Jesuit mission effort in northern Mexico, Arizona, and Lower California. Among his manifold scholarly works are *Pioneer Blackrobes on the West Coast, Black Robes in Lower California,* and the biography, *Andrés Perez de Rihas.* BIBLIOGRAPHY: *Americas* 14 (1957) 92–93.

[J. R. AHERNE]

DUNS SCOTUS, JOHN (*c.* 1266–1308), theologian. Born in Scotland where he entered the Franciscans, he was educated at Oxford and Paris where he later taught, as he did at Cambridge and Cologne. D.S. is now assuming his rightful place as one of the greatest scholastics as historical studies and the critical edition of his work, begun in 1950, clear his name of unwarranted blame, uncritical praise, and falsely attributed writings. Original as it is, D.S.'s theology is in the tradition of Augustine, Bonaventure, and the Franciscan school of Oxford. His philosophical views reflect Avicenna more than Aristotle, and all his work is marked by exquisite metaphysical analysis. Key philosophical notions include his formal distinction (*actualis formalis a parte rei),* the univocity of being (though he insists on the essential difference in the modes of finite and infinite being), and the primacy of will over intellect. In D.S.'s theology the Incarnation is seen as the supreme created manifestation of the love of the Triune God, decreed from all eternity even apart from man's need for redemption. His Marian theology is seminal. Mary is linked to her Son in the eternal decrees. Almost alone in the Paris of his day, he taught the Immaculate Conception: Mary is preserved from sin, as she is redeemed, by the merits of Jesus Christ. BIBLIOGRAPHY: A. B. Wolter, EncPhil 2:427–436.

[W. B. MAHONEY]

DUNSANY, EDWARD J. M. D. PLUNKETT (1878–1957), playwright. Briefly associated with the Abbey Theater in Dublin, D. left his Irish colleagues and their Celtic myths to establish a weird mythology of his own. Influenced by the Belgian symbolic playwright Maeterlinck, he shows also the impact of William Blake. Not always easily comprehensible, D. often achieved an atmosphere of romantic terror and beauty. Among his collected works, the best are *Time and the Gods* (1906), *The Book of Wonder* (1912), and *The Charwoman's Shadow*

(1926). To savor D. at his best, readers should consult the play *A Night at an Inn*. BIBLIOGRAPHY: E. H. Bierstadt, *Dunsany the Dramatist* (1919).

[J. R. AHERNE]

DUNSTABLE, JOHN (*c.*1390–1453), English composer. He was considered by his contemporaries to be one of the greatest musicians of his day, which fame persisted even when scarcely any of his works were known, a state which continued until the early 20th century. Recent scholarship has made his music accessible again, and M. *Bukofzer has edited D.'s complete (known) works (*Musica Britannica* 8; 1954). His travels to the continent are among the few known facts of his life; the result was an interchange of ideas. The influence of smooth English harmony is seen in the works of 15th cent. French composers such as *Dufay and *Binchois, while D.'s compositions make use of continental techniques of *isorhythm and *counterpoint. D. wrote a number of fine *motets and was an early and important contributor to the development of the cyclic Mass.

[P. MURPHY]

DUNSTAN OF CANTERBURY, ST. (*c.*910–988), archbishop. D. was the greatest Englishman and the leading ecclesiastical reformer of his day. Born of a noble family and elected abbot of Glastonbury (940), he was exiled by King Edwig. His sojourn abroad brought him into contact with the continental reform movement. Recalled by King Edgar (957) and made successively bp. of Worcester and London and in 960 abp. of Canterbury, he and SS. Ethelwold and Oswald regenerated the English Benedictine houses. BIBLIOGRAPHY: *Memorials of Saint Dunstan* (ed. W. Stubbs, 1874); E. S. Duckett, *St. Dunstan of Canterbury* (1955); Knowles MOE *passim;* Butler 2:349–351.

[J. L. GRASSI]

DU PAC DE BELLEGARDE, GABRIEL (1717–89), French Jansenist historian, defender of the schismatic Church of Utrecht. As historian he obtained many documents for the archives of the *Ancienne Clérésie* at Utrecht; among his published works are: *Mémoires historiques sur l'affaire de la bulle Unigenitus dans les Pays-Bas* (4 v., 755) and *Histoire abrégée de l'Église métropolitaine d'Utrecht* (1765).

[K. O'NEILL]

DUPANLOUP, FÉLIX ANTOINE PHILIBERT (1802–78), French churchman. Ordained in 1825 and consecrated bp. of Orléans in 1849, D. was active in both religious and political affairs. Although a Conservative and Legitimist, he advocated a policy of moderation and restrained cooperation with the governments of Louis Philippe, Louis Napoleon, and the Third Republic. As a religious leader he founded the renowned Catéchismes de l'Assomption and the Académie de St-Hyacinthe, aided in the conversion of Talleyrand, introduced the cause of

Jeanne d'Arc's beatification, and championed the Holy See during the wars of Italian unification. He participated actively in the political life of France. As a member of a commission to draft an education bill, he was instrumental in the enactment of the Falloux Law (1850), which permitted authorized religious associations to establish primary and secondary schools as well as institutions of higher learning. An acknowledged scholar and writer, he was elected to the French Academy (1854), founded the Catholic daily, *L'Ami de la religion,* wrote educational, historical, and religious pamphlets. But in church history D. will be remembered both for his success in quieting the uproar occasioned by Pius IX's *Syllabus of Errors (1864) and his maladroit efforts at Vatican Council I to block the definition of papal infallibility. His *Observations Sur l'infallibilité* on the eve of the Council and his pressure tactics during it only intensified the efforts of the ultramontanist forces. BIBLIOGRAPHY: E. Faguet, *Mgr. Dupanloup* (1914); R. Aubert, NCE 4:1109–09.

[D. R. PENN]

DUPERRON, JACQUES DAVY (1556–1618), French card. and writer. Born in Switzerland of an exiled Norman family that had converted to Calvinism, D. eventually became a Catholic in France and was named lector to Henry III. He took orders in 1591. After supporting for a time the claim of Card. de Bourbon to the throne, he passed to the side of Henry IV, who named him bp. of Evreux (1591). D. is primarily remembered for his role in the conversion of Henry IV to Catholicism and for negotiating in Rome his absolution (1594–95). A brilliant speaker and preacher, he made numerous conversions in his diocese and defended Catholicism against Philippe Du Plessis-Mornay and, reportedly, Agrippa d'Aubigné at the Fontainebleau conference between Catholics and Huguenots (1600). Made cardinal (1604) and sent to Rome as ambassador, he participated in the conclaves that elected Leo XI as well as Paul V, whom he advised against involvement in the contemporary controversies on grace. Named abp. of Sens (1606) and member of the Regency Council (1610), he defended Robert Bellarmine and the ultramontane position, strongly opposing in the Estates General of 1614 the third estate's formulary denying the papal right to depose kings, for which he was attacked by James I of England. His religious, diplomatic, and literary works include: *Traité du Saint-Sacrement* (1612); *Réfutation des objections tirées des passages de saint Augustin contre l'Eucharistie* (1624); a funeral oration for Ronsard (1586); and *Les Délices de poésie françoise* (1620 and 1627). It has been said that D. was the first Catholic author to write on matters of religion in the vernacular. BIBLIOGRAPHY: C. Constantin, DTC 4.2:1953–60.

[R. N. NICOLICH]

DUPIN, LOUIS ELLIES (1657–1719), Jansenist theologian. D. received a doctorate in theology from the Sorbonne in 1684 and taught philosophy at the Collège

Royal until 1703. His most ambitious work, begun in 1686 and continued under varying titles until 1714, is the *Nouvelle bibliothèque des auteurs ecclésiastiques*. It proposed to give for each author a biography; a list, chronology, and outline of his works; an evaluation of the style and content; a list of editions. The work was attacked both for historical and theological errors and finally condemned. BIBLIOGRAPHY: A. Dodin, DSAM 3:1825–31; J. Carreyre, DTC 12.2:2111–15.

[H. DRESSLER]

DUPLESSIS-MORNAY, PHILIPPE (1549–1623), French statesman and Huguenot leader. He became a Protestant with his mother *c.* 1559 after his father's death. He was a man of high intelligence and became a spokesman for the Huguenot cause. He escaped the *St. Bartholomew's Day Massacre and became a minister for Henry of Navarre, until the latter accepted Catholicism in order to become Henry IV (1593) of France. D. was governor of Saumur from 1589 and in 1599 established a theology school that became a thriving center for Reformed studies. He himself engaged in debate with Catholics on theological issues. His writings in defense of the Huguenots were published as his *Mémoires et correspondence* (12 v., 1824–25). He was devoted to the cause of tolerance and freedom from religious oppression.

[T. C. O'BRIEN]

DUPLICATION, a term with two meanings in RC liturgy. (1) It designates the celebrant's repetition of Mass texts primarily meant for the whole congregation, choir, or *schola cantorum*. This practice arose by the 9th cent. at the latest when the spoken began often to replace the sung form of Mass. The document Vat II SacLit (28) abrogates any earlier law requiring duplication and stipulates that each person should perform only those acts that the nature of the liturgy requires of him. (2) The term is also used to signify the celebration of two Masses on the same day by the same priest. Duplication in this sense is more commonly called *bination in the U.S.

DUPLUM, in the music of the school of Notre Dame *(Ars antiqua),* the part above the tenor in an *organum* or *clausula.*

DUPRÉ, MARCEL (1886–1971), French organist and composer. Born into a family of musicians, D. began playing publicly at 10 years of age. He studied at the Paris Conservatory under F. A. *Guilmant and C. M. *Widor. He succeeded the latter as organist at Saint-Sulpice and later became director of the Paris Conservatory. A brilliant performer, he conducted numerous concert tours. As a performer and teacher, he probably exercised a greater influence than any other organist of his day. In the field of improvisation he had few, if any, rivals, and in composition he showed also a masterly facility. He composed chiefly

organ music of concert or symphonic, rather than liturgical, style but also produced choral, orchestral, and pianoforte music.

[M. T. LEGGE]

DURA-EUROPOS, a Mesopotamian border city established by Seleucus I on the Euphrates *c.* 300 B.C., now Salahiyeh in SE Syria. "Europos" was added to the early name of the settlement, referring to the place of origin of Seleucus or of members of the city's Macedonian garrison. An important caravan center, Dura-Europos fell to the Parthians *c.* 100 B.C. Rome took it briefly in A.D. 116, reestablished it in 165 as a fortress against the Persians, but lost it again before 260. Excavations furnish important evidence about the meeting of Hellenic and Oriental culture—the Iranian reaction to the hellenizing Seleucids. The chief discoveries include a private home converted *c.* 232 into a Christian assembly. Other finds are the remains of an acropolis, military installations, a synagogue, and temples to numerous divinities. Wall paintings of these buildings are remarkable for a stiff, schematized Greco-Iranian style showing Palmyrene gods in Iranian dress, scenes of sacrifice before the Greek temple of Zeus Theos, and salvation themes of Christ; the synagogue frescoes are valuable evidence of a departure from the Jewish prohibition against pictorial religious art. BIBLIOGRAPHY: M. Rostovzeff, *Dura-Europos and Its Art* (1938); Yale University, *Excavations at Dura-Europos* (ser. beginning 1929); *ibid.,* *Final Reports* (1943–59).

[M. J. SUELZER]

DURÁN, NARCISO (1776–1846), Franciscan friar. A zealous missionary of courage and cultivation, D. worked chiefly at Mission San José in N California. He compiled a Choir Book containing Masses and hymns written with simplified settings and notation systems for the instruction of the Indians. In 1824 he was elected to the first of three separate terms as *presidente* of missions. He was elected again in 1831 during the period of the secularization and sale of the missions, exhibiting great personal bravery in resisting the excesses of the Spanish military, who on their part tried to have him exiled. The Mexican government, however, allowed him to retire to Santa Barbara, whence he was called for his third term as president, serving until his death. BIBLIOGRAPHY: Z. Engelhardt, *Missions and Missionaries of California* (1912) 3:295 *passim*.

[M. T. LEGGE]

DURAND, ALFRED (1858–1928), French Jesuit biblical scholar. After studying Semitic languages in Rome and Paris, D. taught at the Jesuit house in Lyons-Fourvière (1897–1923). He translated and commented upon the Gospels of Matthew and John for the *Verbum Salutis* series; contributed numerous articles to French periodicals and reference works; and wrote the articles "Inspiration of the Bible" and "New Testament" for the *Catholic Encyclo-*

pedia. BIBLIOGRAPHY: A. Condamin, DBSuppl 2:448–450; B. F. Sargent, NCE 4:1114.

[T. M. MCFADDEN]

DURANDUS OF AURILLAC (fl. 1330–34), a Dominican who was among the theologians opposing (1333) Pope *John XXII's opinion on the state of the blessed, and to whom was attributed, probably erroneously, a work against *Durandus of Saint-Pourçain.

[T. C. O'BRIEN]

DURANDUS OF SAINT-POURÇAIN (*c.* 1275–1334), Dominican theologian who took positions opposed to those of St. Thomas Aquinas on human cognition, the efficacy of grace, the causality of the sacraments, and transubstantiation. He taught at Paris and at the papal court in Avignon before being consecrated a bishop (1317). His controverted teaching, much of it condemned by Dominican authorities for its anti-Thomism, appeared in his commentary on Peter Lombard's *Sentences* (1st ed. in 1307–08; revisions in 1310–13, 1317–27). Sometimes classified as a nominalist, D. rather was an independent thinker whose work remained a subject of controversy in the schools for several centuries. BIBLIOGRAPHY: J. Weisheipl, NCE 4:1114–16; Gilson, HCP 473–476.

[T. C. O'BRIEN]

DURANDUS OF TROARN (betw. 1005 and 1020–1088 or 1089), French Benedictine monk, scholar, abbot. He was probably a monk at Fontenelle under his uncle Abbot Gerard, and later studied at Rouen and Fécamp. He is best remembered for his treatise, *De corpore et sanguine Christi* (PL 149:1375–1424, 424). This work, strongly influenced by *Paschasius Radbertus (d. 859) and primarily intended for the edification of souls, is one of the earliest replies to the eucharistic teaching of Berengarius. Through the analysis of scriptural and patristic texts, D. propounded the Ambrosian doctrine of the conversion of the bread and wine into the identical body and blood of Christ. He later wrote a eucharistic poem some of which is still extant.

DURANDUS, WILLIAM (*c.* 1230–96), called "Speculator," outstanding canon lawyer, and encyclopaedic writer. His best-known works are the *Speculum Juris* (Mirror of the Law), indispensable for canonists until the Renaissance, and a compendium of the liturgy, the *Rationale divinorum officiorum,* which was immensely popular (the first nonscriptural text printed) until the Council of Trent. His *Rationale . . .* is one of the principal sources for the understanding of symbolism in Christian art. D. also wrote a legal manual, the *Repertorium juris,* and his *Pontificale* became the authoritative, episcopal liturgical guide. He served several popes, chiefly as a civil governor; he refused the archbishopric of Ravenna in favor of the See of Mende, where he wrote his last works. A nephew of the same name succeeded him, Durandus *Junior,* or Durandel-

lus, who later defended positions of Aquinas against Durandus of Saint-Pourçain. BIBLIOGRAPHY: L. Falletti, DDC 5:1014–75.

[J. P. WILLIMAN]

DURANTE, FRANCESCO (1684–1755), Italian composer and teacher, student of Scarlatti and Pitoni. D. held posts in various conservatories. His pupils included Pergolesi, Piccini, Paesiello, and Traetta. During D.'s lifetime, his reputation as a composer was great, and his MSS are found in many important libraries of Europe. His music, mainly for the Church, is a mixture of the flowing melodic character of the Neapolitan school and the contrapuntal characteristic of the Roman school. D.'s works include three oratorios, Masses, motets, cantatas, and duets.

[M. T. LEGGE]

DURANTE, OTTAVIO (fl. 17th cent.), monodic composer of the Roman school of early Baroque music. His *Arie devote* (Rome 1608) was inspired by the secular monodies of Caccini's *Nuove musiche.* D.'s compositions evidence the entrance of vocal virtuosity into the domain of religious song.

[M. T. LEGGE]

DURANTI, WILLIAM, THE YOUNGER (d. 1330), nephew of William D. the Elder, also bp. of Mende, from 1296. He was a member of the commission that investigated the Knights *Templar, 1308–11; at the Council of Vienne (1312), at which they were suppressed, D. spoke in defense of episcopal rights and against papal usurpation. He was for a time in disfavor at the papal court, but in 1329 he was entrusted by Pope John XXII with organizing a crusade. D. died, while engaged in this enterprise, on the Island of Cyprus.

[T. C. O'BRIEN]

DURBIN, ELISHA JOHN (1800–87), missionary. A native of Kentucky, D. was ordained in Bardstown in 1822 and embarked thence on a career as a missionary which was to cover 60 years. Bp. Flaget appointed him as pastor for an area in W Kentucky comprising one-third of the state. D. moved through his vast territory incessantly, founding churches and missions and reaching families scattered over an 11,000 square-mile area. At the age of 84 he could no longer sustain the rigors of his missionary activity and retired. His career earned him the title "Apostle of Western Kentucky." BIBLIOGRAPHY: L. G. Deppen, CE 5:209.

[J. R. AHERNE]

DÜRER, ALBRECHT (1471–1528), greatest and most famous German Renaissance master painter, printmaker, and brilliant humanist, learned and charming conversationalist—a genius companying with the most distinguished men of his day. Trained as craftsman by his father and M. Wolgemut, D. in early works shows a remarkable precocity (*Self-Portrait,* 1484). Works from the *Wanderschaft,* often unsigned, reveal the considerable influence of M. Schongauer and the Master of the Housebook. During visits to Venice D., impressed by Pollaiuolo, Bellini, and Mantegna, made detailed studies of nature, water color sketches of travels. Again in Germany, he wrote scientific treatises on anatomy, responding to the social upheavals of his time in the great woodcut series of the *Apocalypse* (1498), the *Large Passion,* and the *Life of the Virgin.* D. identified himself at this period in a self-portrait as the *Man of Sorrows* (1500). The engraving *Adam and Eve,* the painted Paumgärtner Alter, and the *Adoration of the Magi* (all 1504) embrace the ideals of form of the Italian Renaissance. D.'s mature period shows a synthesis of late Gothic and Renaissance styles in the master painting *Feast of the Rose Garlands* and "master" engravings—*Knight, Death and the Devil* (1513), *St. Jerome in His Study* (1514), and *Melancholia* (1514)—inspired by Christian piety but expressing the humanist dilemma of the artist participating at once in both active and contemplative life. Following the disasters of the Peasants' War (1525) and the intense religious concerns of the Reformation, D.'s last painting the *Four Apostles* (1526) is the noblest synthesis of Italian ideals in all northern painting. BIBLIOGRAPHY: E. Panofsky, *Albrecht Dürer: Life and Art* (1955); M. Brion, *Dürer, His Life and Work* (tr. J. Cleugh, 1960).

[M. J. DALY]

DURESS, in moral matters, fear, force, or undue pressure that may diminish the voluntarity of an action or take it away altogether. *FEAR; *FORCE AND MORAL RESPONSIBILITY.

[T. C. O'BRIEN]

DURET, GEORGES (1887–1943), French philosopher and educator. D. was ordained in 1912 after study at Poitiers and became professor of rhetoric and philosophy in the same city and edited a little review, *Notes for the Catholic Professors of France.* He published numerous articles and was influential as university chaplain in Poitiers. In World War II he opposed the German occupation of France and became known as the theologian of the resistance. He was arrested by the Germans in 1942 and died the following year in a concentration camp at Wolfenbüttel. BIBLIOGRAPHY: J. Charier, *Catholicisme* 3:1202.

[M. J. SUELZER]

DURHAM CATHEDRAL, Romanesque cathedral in N England grouped with castle and monastery on a rock, begun in 1093, with additions (choir stalls) as late as 1665. The 12th-cent. interior of overwhelming power and exquisite Anglo-Norman proportions is thought by some to predate St. Ambrogio, Milan, in rib-vaulting. The innovative feature of transverse arches is in essence a flying buttress. The post-Romanesque Chapel of the Nine Altars with the great Joseph window (*c.* 1280–90) introduced English Decorated style of foliage and figure capitals relating to the Lincoln Angel Choir. Notable are the Neville Screen (1372–80), the stalls and parclose screens carved by John Clement, and Bp. Hatfield's throne and monument (1381). South of the cathedral are the cloisters (12th cent.) and refectory, and to the W a dormitory of impressive splendor (1398–1404). BIBLIOGRAPHY: N. Pevsner, *Buildings of England* (1953) v. 9.

[M. J. DALY]

DURHAM, RITE OF, liturgical forms preserved in the *Rituale ecclesiae Dunelmensis,* or the Durham collectarium, a ritual book containing mostly collects and chapters for the day hours. It is a 10th-cent. Latin service book with Anglo-Saxon interlinear and is considered important for preserving material from the Anglo-Saxon Church. Though long in the possession of Durham Cathedral, it is thought by scholars to have been produced elsewhere. It is called the Ritual of King Alfrid, referring perhaps to the Alfrid who succeeded his brother Ecgfrid in 685, and therefore may have been transcribed from a book owned by him.

[T. EARLY]

DURKHEIM, ÉMILE (1858–1917), French sociologist. One of the fathers of modern sociology, D. was a professor at the universities of Bordeaux and Paris. Sociology, in D.'s formulation, was the study of social facts, patterns of activity external to an individual that nevertheless exercise coercive power over him. Society cannot be understood in psychological terms, for it constitutes a reality *sui generis,* qualitatively different from the individuals who compose it. Consequently, D. argued that sociology should be a separate science with its own distinctive subject matter and methodology. Deeply interested in the question of social order, D. saw two major forms of social solidarity, mechanical and organic. The first type characterized societies in which most members carry out similar activities, with deviance punished by repressive laws. Organic solidarity is found in a society in which the interdependence of dissimilar activities is an important feature. A study of variations in suicide rates extended his investigation of the group's influences in the individual. D. noted that anomie, a confusion of or breakdown in social norms, was linked with an increase in suicide. In his study of primitive religion, he asserted that religious belief and ritual, just as many such cultural items, arise out of the solidarity of the group. Drawing upon ethnographic accounts of primitive religion, he argued that primitive man held essentially the same attitude toward both society and the sacred. Thus, religion and social solidarity are each necessary for the other. BIBLIOGRAPHY: T. Parsons, *International Encyclopedia of the Social Sciences* (1968) 4:311–320; H. S. Hughes, *Consciousness and Society* (1958); A. Giddens, *Capitalism and Modern Social Theory* (1971); D. LaCapra, *Emile Durkheim* (1972). *RELIGION (IN PRIMITIVE CULTURE).

[G. W. DOWDALL]

DÜRR, LORENZ (1886–1939), German biblical exegete. D. received a doctorate in theology at Würzburg, studied Oriental languages in Berlin, and taught OT at the universities of Bonn, Braunsberg, Freising, and Regensburg. He published several scholarly works, many relating the OT to the larger cultural milieu from which it sprang. BIBLIOGRAPHY: R. Mayer, LTK 3:615–616; M. Rehm, NCE 4:1123.

[T. M. MCFADDEN]

DU SOLLIER, JEAN BAPTISTE (1669–1740), Belgian Jesuit, scholar, and Bollandist. Associated with the *Museum Bollandianum* from 1702, D. became its director in 1709. The *Acta Sanctorum* from June 5 to August 3 were produced under his editorship. These contain (June 6) D.'s elaborate edition of the *Martyrology of *Usuard* later reprinted by Migne (PL 123–124). BIBLIOGRAPHY: Sommervogel 1:1247–49; J. Peeters, *L'Oeuvre des Bollandistes* (1949).

DUSSAUD, RENÉ ÉLIE PIERRE (1868–1958), French Oriental scholar. Born at Neuilly, D. studied Oriental languages, becoming curator of Oriental antiquities at the Louvre, and later, curator general of the museum (1928–38). He worked in philology, epigraphy, archeology, and the comparative history of religions. A list of his works to 1938 may be found in *Mélanges syriens offerts à M. René Dussaud* (2 v., 1939) 1:v-xvi. BIBLIOGRAPHY: J. Trinquet, *Catholicisme* 3:1208.

[P. K. MEAGHER]

DUTHOIT, EUGÈNE (1869–1944), French Catholic actionist and a leading representative of Catholic social thought. D. graduated at the Catholic Univ. of Lille, where he became a professor and dean of his faculty. He established there the *E.Fcole des sciences sociales et politiques* (1894) and the *École des missionnaires du travail* (1932). He took an important part as professor and director in the work of the *Semaines sociales*. In addition to his scientific writings (see J. Folliet, *Catholicisme* 3:1208–09), D., a devout Franciscan tertiary who died with a reputation for sanctity, he wrote a small work of interest in the field of spirituality, *La Sanctification des heures*. BIBLIOGRAPHY: *Hommage à E. Duthoit,* a special issue of *La Chronique sociale de France,* July-Aug. 1944.

[P. K. MEAGHER]

DUTTON, JOSEPH (1843–1931), missionary. Dashing cavalry officer in the Civil War, romantic, monk, and servant to the lepers of Molakai, D. was a remarkable character. ter. After a tragic marriage he found his way to Catholicism and entered the Trappist monastery in Kentucky. Chancing upon an article on Father Damien and his work among the lepers, he left the monastery and went to Molakai. Steadfastly refusing to be advanced to the priesthood, Brother Joseph gave Damien the help he needed as the priest's strength waned through the advanced stages of leprosy. D. remained on Molakai after Damien's death, giving a total of 44 years to the service of the leper colony. BIBLIOGRAPHY: J. Farrow, *Damien the Leper* (1937).

[J. R. AHERNE]

DUTY (IMPOSTS), charges levied on imported goods. As such it is an indirect tax on the person importing them, and the moral obligation at issue comes under the general heading of *taxation. "Going through customs," as distinct from engaging in smuggling, raises the specific issue of an obligation to declare goods being brought in from abroad. Their nondeclaration could be justified by considering customs duties to be an instance of penal law, i.e., one that obliges morally to payment of penalty, but not to what the law enjoins; but the idea of purely penal laws has few defenders. The obligation to pay customs duties, therefore, when they are levied by just laws, is in keeping with commutative justice, which respects a debt owed; and distributive justice, which concerns contributing to the public good that just taxes are meant to serve. Falsifying customs declarations themselves is a form of *lying. These points being recognized, however, the ordinary traveller has some leeway, since the enforcement of the laws is usually flexible and tolerant of slight excesses over the legal limit of exemption from duties.

[T. C. O'BRIEN]

DU VAIR, GUILLAUME (1556–1621), French bishop. After serving as a civil magistrate he was ordained and made bp. of Marseilles (1603) and Lisieux (1617). He was active in Huguenot controversies and in the conversion and accession of Henry IV. A brilliant speaker, he wrote a treatise on French eloquence (1595) that influenced the pulpit oratory of the 17th century. He also produced translations of some ancient philosophers and published several series of meditations. BIBLIOGRAPHY: A. M. Bozzone, DE 1:922.

[M. J. SUELZER]

DUVAL, JEAN (BERNARD OF ST. THERESA; 1597–1669), Discalced Carmelite, bp, minister of state under Louis XIV from 1647. D. had been bp. of Baghdad and vicar apostolic for Persia since 1638, but returned to Paris in 1642 and established a seminary for missionaries to the Near East. He compiled Turkish and Persian dictionaries for use of the missioners. In the French court he was adviser to the king on church affairs.

[T. C. O'BRIEN]

DUVAL-ARNOULD, LOUIS (1863–1942), French Catholic lawyer and social actionist. At an early age D. joined the St. Vincent de Paul Society and was actively engaged in its work throughout his life. Through political economics he became interested in social studies and took a prominent part as professor and director in the *Semaines sociales*. After World War I, in which he achieved military distinction, he was a member of the Chamber of Deputies. His major works are *Apprentis et jeunes ouvriers* (1885);

Études d'histoire du droit d'après Sidoine Apollinaire (1885); and *Étienne Dolet* (1898). BIBLIOGRAPHY: V. Bucaille, *Catholicisme* 3:1211–12.

[P. K. MEAGHER]

DUVENECK, FRANK (1848–1919), American painter, etcher, sculptor. Born in Cincinnati, Ohio, during the 1860s, he decorated Catholic churches in Kentucky, Ohio, Pennsylvania, and Canada. In Munich (1870–72) he mastered the loose, vigorous brushwork and heavy, dark palette of that school, painting characteristic unpretentious American themes (*Whistling Boy,* 1872). An important teacher in Munich (1878), Italy (1879), and Cincinnati (1888), D., elected to the National Academy of Design (1906), strongly influenced R. Henri and his group (1908). D. painted murals for St. Mary's Cathedral, Covington, Ky. (1909–10). BIBLIOGRAPHY: N. Heermann, *Frank Duveneck* (1918).

[M. J. DALY]

DUVERGIER DE HAURANNE, JEAN, see SAINT-CYRAN, ABBÉ DE.

DVIN (DOVIN, DWIN), SYNODS OF, synods or councils of the Armenian Church held in Dvin, then the residence of the *Catholicos. Apart from the electoral synods of 604 and 607, these synods are known to have been held: (1) Under the Catholicos Babgen in 505 or 506 (rather than at Vagharshapat in 491), attended by the bps. of Armenia, Georgia, and Albania. The synod did not reject the Council of Chalcedon directly, but there is good reason for suspecting that in condemning "Nestorian" errors they meant to include the doctrines of the Chalcedonian faction. Doctrinal agreement was expressed with "the Romans," i.e., the Byzantines, who at that moment had the conciliatory *Henoticon* of the Emperor Zeno, with its un-Chalcedonian nuances, as the statement of their official doctrinal position. An extra-synodal letter of the same time, however, signed by the Catholicos, the bp. of Taron, as well as by certain Armenian secular princes and the Persian civil commissary (the *marzpan*), expressly and favorably mentioned Zeno's *Henoticon* and condemned Chalcedon. (2) Under Nerses II in 555 (rather than 551 or 552), with the Council of Chalcedon and the Tome of Pope Leo anathematized for having spoken of "two natures and two persons [*sic*] of Christ" (*dems,* i.e., faces, *prosōpa*). It was in this synod that the Church of Armenia took an officially and schismatically Monophysite position, aligning itself with the aphthartodocetist Monophysitism of Julian of Halicarnassus rather than with the opposite Monophysite doctrine of Severus of Antioch, which was also condemned. Communion with the Dyophysite Churches of Constantinople and Jerusalem (called "Nestorian"!) was rejected in favor of communion with the Syrian Monophysites. The addition of Peter the Fuller's "who was crucified for us" to the Trisagion was officially prescribed. (3) Under Abraham I in 608 or 609, in which the Church of Georgia with its Catholicos Kyrion I was excommunicated for accepting the doctrine of Chalce-

don, thus marking the definitive rupture between the Churches of Armenia and Georgia. (4) Under Nerses III in 649, at the request of the Byzantine Emperor Constans II, in the hope of establishing reunion between the Churches of Constantinople and Armenia, but the synod merely rejected Chalcedon once again. (5) Under John IV of Odzoun, *c.*719, reiterating a Monophysite position and occupying itself with liturgical legislation. BIBLIOGRAPHY: C. Toumanoff, "Christian Caucasia between Byzantium and Iran: New Light from Old Sources," *Traditio* 10 (1954) 109–189; J. Mécérian, *Histoire et institutions de l'Église arménienne* (1965) 64–71, 81, 90.

[A. CODY]

DVOŘÁK, ANTONÍN (1841–1904), Czech composer. Born into a family of modest means, D. studied at the Organ School, later Prague Conservatory, to which he returned as professor and director. His reputation as a composer grew and spread gradually throughout Europe, England, and America. From 1892 to 1895 he was director of the National Conservatory of Music in New York City; his *New World Symphony* and other American works derive from this period. Drawing on the rich treasure of Czech folk music, he became, with Smetana, founder of the Czech school of national music. His compositions, which include operas, chamber music, symphonies, overtures, oratorios, pianoforte music, and songs, manifest a notable mastery of instrumentation, great charm, purity of style, a wealth of lovely melody, and particularly in his sacred music, a religious fervor and nobility of expression. Chief among his sacred compositions are the oratorios *Stabat Mater* and *St. Ludmilla,* his *Requiem,* the *149th Psalm,* and a *Te Deum.*

[M. T. LEGGE]

DVOŘÁK, MAX RAUDNITZ (1874–1921), member of the Vienna school of art history who founded the *Geistesgeschichte,* a method in which the evolution of art is conceived as an evolution of the spirit, and art forms are explained as expressions of the ruling religious and intellectual ideas of a culture. BIBLIOGRAPHY: O. Benesch, *Neue Österreichische Biographie 1815–1918* 10 (1957) 189–198.

[L. A. LEITE]

DVORNIK, FRANCIS (1893–1975), Byzantine and Slavic scholar, historian, ecumenist. He was born in the village of Chomýž, Czechoslovakia, studied at the theological faculty, Olomouc, was ordained in 1916, and in 1920 was awarded the doctorate in theology. At the Sorbonne, Paris, 1920–26, he developed his scholarly concentration on Byzantine literature, languages, and history under the guidance of Professor Charles Diehl; as a resident in the home of F. *Portal he absorbed the principles of ecumenism, a cause to which he applied his scholarship throughout his life. D. completed and brilliantly defended his major thesis, *Les Slaves, Byzance, et Rome en IXᵉ siècle;* he became the first Czech in centuries to become a Sorbonne *Docteur ès Lettres;* his thesis won an award from the French Academy in 1927. He returned to his native land to become, in 1928, professor of church history in the theological faculty of the Charles University, Prague. He was elevated to the rank of *ordinarius* (full professor) in 1933 because of his work, *Les Légendes de Constantin et de Méthode vues de Byzance*, which vindicated the historical value of the *legenda* of SS. Cyril and Methodius. His "Le deuxième schisme de Photios, une mystification historique," *Byzantion* (1933) proved that there was no second Photian schism. As an ecumenist during this period he participated in the periodic Congresses of Velehrad on religious reunion of all Slavs, delivering lectures on aspects of Byzantine church history. In 1935 he became dean of the theology faculty at Charles University (Prague). But the Nazi occupation in 1939 led to the disruption of university life and to D.'s exile, first in France (1939–40), then in England (1940–47). He continued his research at the British Museum and in 1943 completed his masterwork on Photius, published first in French, then in English as *The Photian Schism, History and Legend* (1948; he published a new ed. in 1970, with revised preface and updated bibliography). D.'s work completely vindicated Photius and astounded historians and churchmen alike. In 1945 D. was Birkbeck lecturer at Cambridge; he received an honorary doctorate from the Univ. of London, was elected a fellow of the British Academy, and an honorary member of the Royal Historical Society. Invited by Harvard University in 1948 to become professor of Byzantine history at Dumbarton Oaks Institute of Byzantine Studies, Washington, D.C., D. spent the remaining 30 years of his life in fruitful research and universally acclaimed publication. The following are among his 35 published books: *The Making of Central and Eastern Europe* (1949); *The Idea of Apostolicity at Byzantium* (1958); *The Legend of St. Andrew* (1958); *Early Christian and Byzantine Political Philosophy: Origins and Background* (1966); *Byzantine Missions among the Slavs* (1970); *Origins of Intelligence Services* (1974). He also published numerous monographs and some 200 articles in learned journals. His historical scholarship and ecumenical principles achieved a convergence of the political, cultural, historical, and ecclesiological elements required for an understanding between East and West, and so contributed significantly to the possibility of church reunion. In his lifetime he was recognized as a unique authority, honored by knighthood in the French Legion of Honor, by numerous degrees and awards as historian and theologian. At his death, during a visit to his native Chomýž, he was eulogized as a scholar, Byzantologist, Slavist, medievalist, Czech and church historian, theologian, unionist, and ecumenist. BIBLIOGRAPHY: B. Dupuy, "L'Oeuvre de Msgr. François Dvornik," *Istina* 21 (1976): 154–165; H. G. Lunt, ed., *Harvard Slavic Studies* 2 (1954): 1–390; L. Nemec, "The Festive Profile of Francis Dvornik, the Scholar, the Historian and the Ecumenist," *Catholic Historical Review* 59 (1973): 185–224; *idem*, ed., "80th Birthday of F. Dvornik," Proměny (1973): 1–112 (multilingual Festschrift);

idem, "Francis Dvornik–a Master of Historical Synthesis (1977); S. der Nersessian, "Francis Dvornik," *Dumbarton Oak Papers* 27(1973) 1–10.

[L. NEMEC]

DWENGER, JOSEPH GERHARD (1837–1893), bishop. An orphan at age 12, D. became a member of the Congregation of the Most Precious Blood and was ordained in Cincinnati in 1859. He founded and was president of his congregation's seminary in Ohio. Named first bp. of Fort Wayne, he gave himself to the care of orphans and the vigorous expansion of parochial schools with a zeal that drew national attention.

[J. R. AHERNE]

DWIGHT, TIMOTHY (1752–1817), Congregationalist minister, eighth president of Yale. He was born at Northampton, Mass., the grandson of Jonathan *Edwards. D. graduated from Yale (1769) and entered the ministry 5 years later. He was a chaplain in the Continental Army, pastor at Greenfield Hill, Conn. (1783), and principal of a boys' school there. As president of Yale (1795–1817) he became the leader of the *Second Great Awakening, against the inroads of *deism, teaching and preaching the *New England theology of Edwards, in a revival of evangelical faith. His teaching was published posthumously as *Theology Explained and Defended* (5 v., 1818–19). He also wrote the hymn "I Love Thy Kingdom Lord." BIBLIOGRAPHY: life by C. E. Cunningham (1942); K. Silverman, *Timothy Dwight* (1969).

[T. C. O'BRIEN]

DYMPNA, ST. (7th cent.?), legendary martyr. Her cult began with the discovery in Gheel, near Antwerp, in the early 13th cent. of the body of a woman and the body of a man in two ancient sarcophagi. On the occasion of the elevation of the woman's remains, a number of epileptics and insane were reported to be cured. She was called Dympna and came to be accepted as patroness of the mentally afflicted. The story told of her is without historical foundation and appears to have been drawn from folklore. According to it she was the daughter of a pagan English or Irish king who tried to seduce her after her mother's death. On the advice of her confessor, Gerebernus (the name given to the man whose body was found near hers), she fled with him to Gheel on the Continent. There she was overtaken by her father; when she continued to refuse him, he took her life and that of Gerebernus as well. The story, coupled with D.'s role as protectress of the insane, can easily be seen by post-Freudian critics as a recognition in folklore of the prevalence of incest fantasy in certain forms of insanity. BIBLIOGRAPHY: Butler 2:320–321; J. Henning, LTK 3:618.

[R. B. ENO]

DYNAMISM, the notion that all natural phenomena manifest the action and interaction of physical or psychic forces;

that forces rather than rigid atoms constitute the matter of the universe; that it is the activity of unextended forces which provides the appearance of spatial extension. The perspective of dynamism is more compatible with models of physical action and reaction that are more abstract and non-intuitive (in the manner of contemporary atomic and physical theory or natural systems like Leibniz's monadology) than with mechanism and mechanistic sensory models of matter, particularly the hard indivisible atomic bits of Democritus and subsequent materialists. In ancient philosophy both Aristotle and Plato opposed Democritean materialism with theories of dynamism (Gr. *dynamis,* power). Plato maintained that a soul is the motive force of a body and that ever-shifting matter and shapes, which he called a receptacle, provide the universe with dynamic flux. Consistent with his idea of a Prime Mover and soul, Aristotle's doctrine of form and matter combining in substantial nature accounted for dynamic activity that was not solely material in cause. Leibniz's ontology which proposed monads (formal rather than material atoms which were simple, unextended, and resistant to internal change by external forces) presented a dynamistic view of the world that was flawed by his notion that human perception produces qualities of motion, homogeneity, extension. R. G. *Boscovich, European Jesuit mathematician, physicist, theorist and philosopher, was the first to present a formal natural philosophy of dynamism. Boscovich's greatest work, *A Theory of Natural Philosophy Reduced to a Single Law of the Actions Existing in Nature* (1758, 1763; tr. J. M. Child, 1922), presented his idea that permanent and similar point-centers (*puncta*) of forces without spatial extension (volume), interacting with other point-centers, more accurately describes the fundamental structure and phenomena of nature than the classical materialist view, which retained the mass and volume of finite rigid atoms. The contrast is that between a hard billiard ball and a force field with a point focus defining it, dynamic interactions are the interactions of forces rather than collisions, and extension is defined as the equilibrium of attractive and repulsive forces between two *puncta.* Boscovich thus freed scientific imagination and speculation from the conventions of a strict atomistic, materialistic world view. Later dynamism reflected the influence of Boscovich and Leibniz, whose monads in certain ways anticipated Boscovich's *puncta.* Kant's natural philosophy was dynamistic but his pointlike atoms were heterogeneous after Leibniz, not identical in the way of Boscovich. Schopenhauer's unified cosmic Will, when differentiated into distinct dynamic centers of will by Hartmann, Bahnsen, and Nietzsche, continued the philosophical and metaphysical elaborations of dynamism, while scientists, mostly in France and England, such as A. Ampere, M. Faraday and others, continued to develop the physical and scientific aspects of dynamism. J. C. Maxwell, whose theories were critical of Boscovich, described the point of view of his own electromagnetic field theories as ''Boscovichian.'' The recent discovery of distinct radii (thus, volumes) of subatomic particles and the awareness of the time-consuming nature of physical interactions of forces has subverted fundamental aspects of dynamism, but retains much of its generally abstract outlook.

[R. J. LITZ]

DYO KENTEMATA, in *Byzantine chant notation, one of the *somata,* or signs, indicating a note one scale-step higher than the previous note. It is used only in combination with other signs. Although written as two *kentema* signs, it does not indicate a doubled *kentema.*

[A. DOHERTY]

DYOPHYSITE (Gr., of two natures), one who maintains the Chalcedonian doctrine that full deity and full humanity exist in the person of Jesus Christ as two natures united without confusion or change. The Council of Chalcedon (451) condemned the monophysite doctrine of Eutyches, which held that the substantial union of the Logos with the humanity formed one nature only *(physis)* in which the humanity was completely absorbed by the divinity.

[P. FOSCOLOS]

DYOTHELETISM (Gk. *duo-thelēma,* two wills), the theory that Christ had both a human and divine will. It was held in opposition to *monotheletism, a Christological heresy condemned by the Council of Constantinople III (680–681). The council declared that since Christ had a human and divine nature, he thereby possessed two wills that were free but never in conflict. BIBLIOGRAPHY: G. Owens, NCE 9:1067–68. *THEODORE I, POPE; *MAXIMUS THE CONFESSOR, ST. .

[T. M. MCFADDEN]

DYSON, ROBERT (1895–1959), American Jesuit scripture scholar. After studies at the Biblical Institute in Rome, he served as professor there for 20 years. He collaborated with Alexander Jones in writing *Kingdom of Promise* (1947) and contributed articles to *Catholic Commentary on Holy Scripture* (1953). BIBLIOGRAPHY: F. L. Moriarty, NCE 4:1113–14.

[M. J. SUELZER]

DYSTELEOLOGY, a term coined by E. Häckel and used in both philosophy and the natural sciences to convey the notion of purposelessness in nature, or a denial of final causality, as opposed to teleology which views all beings as directed toward a specific end in accordance with an overall design or purpose. Dysteleology tends to consider the threatening or unfavorable appearances, particularly of life, such as malfunctioning organs, disease, nonfunctional structures, and death, pointing to them as arguments against the operation of purpose. In contrast, teleology stresses the absolute need for final causality or purpose in the universe.

[J. T. HICKEY]

E

EADMER OF CANTERBURY (d. 1130), theologian, historian. E. was chaplain, constant companion, and biographer of St. Anselm of Canterbury (d. 1109). He wrote *Vita s. Anselmi, Historia novorum* and an important treatise on the Immaculate Conception. For a study of his works as a whole and relations with Anselm see R. W. Southern, *St. Anselm and His Biographer* (1963).

[J. L. GRASSI]

EAKINS, THOMAS COWPERTHWAITE (1844–1916), greatest American realist painter of the 19th cent., sculptor, teacher, and accomplished linguist, E. studied in Philadelphia, Pa. (1861–66) at the Pennsylvania Academy of the Fine Arts and Jefferson Medical College, and in Paris with J. Gérôme and L. Bonnat (1866–69). After a trip to Spain (1869–70) E., inspired by Valásquez, Ribera, and Rembrandt, returned to Philadelphia where he spent his life. Distinguished teacher and director of the Pennsylvania Academy of the Fine Arts (1876–86) the "rebel" E. resigned because of difficulties with a too conservative governing board. Dedicated to "right," honest, uncompromising, scientifically-true statements, E.'s work shows a passionate concern with people and character. They show strong anatomic forms, enhanced by a marvelous light (*Max Schmitt in a Single Scull,* 1871, with the tiny self-portrait of the artist—a trained athlete—an interest which drew E. later to studies of the "instantaneous photograph" of motion—forerunner of the motion picture). A powerful *Crucifixion* (1880) and magnificent medical school portraits: *The Gross Clinic* (1875) of Jefferson College, earlier blindly rejected as revolting, and *The Agnew Clinic* (1889) of the Univ. of Pa. Medical College (1889) followed. E. left a record of his time in incisive portraits: Walt Whitman (1887–88) and other friends with distinguished notables of his day, including a gallery of Catholic notables, among them: Card. Sebastian Martinelli (1902) and Mgr. Diomede Falconio (1905) Apostolic Delegates; Abp. James F. Wood, Phila., Abp. William H. Elder, Cincinnati, Rt. Rev. Denis J.

Dougherty, Rev. Philip R. McDevitt (later Bishop of Harrisburg), Very Rev. J. Fedigan, OSA, Villanova, Pa., Msgr. James P. Turner, Rt. Rev. Msgr. Patrick J. Garvey, and the Honorable James A. Flaherty, Supreme Knight of Columbus. E.'s works seen now in the Louvre, the Metropolitan Museum, N.Y., the National Gallery of Art, and the Hirshhorn, Washington, D.C., the Philadelphia Museum of Art, the Whitney Phillips, the Corcoran, the Pennsylvania Academy of the Fine Arts, and St. Charles Seminary are tributes to the monumental power and deep sensitivity of a genius neglected in his time. BIBLIOGRAPHY: L. Goodrich, *Thomas Eakins: His Life and Work* (1933); F. Porter, *Thomas Eakins* (1959); M. Domit, *Sculpture of Thomas Eakins* (1969).

[M. J. DALY]

EALDRED (Aldred; d. 1069), Anglo-Saxon bp. of Worcester (1046) and abp. of York (1060). Warrior-bishop, ecclesiastical reformer, royal adviser and ambassador, E. was a power in Church and State. He crowned William the Conqueror and Matilda and administered Hereford and Ramsbury while bp. of Worcester. BIBLIOGRAPHY: W. A. Chaney, NCE 5:1.

[W. A. CHANEY]

EALH-WINE, see ALCUIN.

EALING ABBEY, Benedictine abbey of St. Benedict located in Ealing, a London borough. At the request of H. E. *Vaughan monks of Downside established a parish and school (1895) and later (1916) a priory. Even though it was raised to abbatial status (1955) it still retains the structure of parish.

[J. R. RIVELLO]

EARLS BARTON, church in Northamptonshire, central England, unique in that the tower space forms the body of the church, with a small projecting chancel. Built in the early 11th cent., the ornate tower of Saxon proportions with horizontal emphasis shows a surface network of stone strips and arcades derived from timber prototypes.

[M. J. DALY]

EARLY MONASTICISM. The first appearance of Christian monasticism can be traced to St. *Anthony who retired to the Egyptian desert in the 3d cent. to live a solitary life. He drew several disciples who imitated his austerity and evangelical dedication thus making Lower Egypt an eremitical center. In Upper Egypt St. *Pachomius (c.290–346) shifted the monastic way of life from the eremitic to the cenobitic by grouping his disciples under one roof near Tabennisi. This foundation gave rise to many others, and the number of monks increased to several thousand. From Egypt the monastic life spread to the Sinai Peninsula whose most outstanding example was St. *John Climacus, author of the ascetic work the *Ladder of Paradise*. Palestine, Syria, and Asia Minor quickly grew into monastic centers; but it was in Cappadocia that monasticism truly began to develop under more specified lines. St. *Basil the Great (fl. 4th cent.), having seen monastic life throughout Syria and Palestine, brought the cenobitic form to its full development through his rules (see ST. BASIL, RULE OF). This is not a detailed rule but lays down the general ideals and practices for monks living in common under a superior. This rule or *typikon* became the basis for all Orthodox monasticism. In Constantinople monasticism was established at the end of the 4th cent. and rapidly expanded. St. *Theodore of Studius (759–826) developed the Monastery of *Studius into the leading monastic center in the East and combined asceticism with literary endeavors. In 963 St. *Athanasius the Athonite founded the cenobitic monastery of *Laura on Mt. *Athos, which became a monastic federation. The mystical revival of the 11th cent. was primarily the work of *Simeon the New Theologian. The emphasis on quiet and elaborate ascetic practices gave rise to the movement known as *Hesychasm which grew under Gregory Palamas and ultimately brought about great controversy. Throughout the history of the Eastern Church the monks played a great role in influencing the populace on civil, theological, and ecclesiastical matters, e.g., *Iconoclasm, *Monophysitism.

[F. T. RYAN]

EARTH, BLESSED, earth blessed and sometimes placed in small quantity into the coffin at private services for the dead; sometimes it is scattered on the coffin as it is lowered into the grave. Sprinkling the coffin with holy water has been derived from this practice. The term also refers to the blessed ground or cemetery plot in which a Roman Catholic should be buried.

[T. M. MCFADDEN]

EARTH ART, a solution to the problem of "sculpture-site" growing out of Minimal or Primary Art, in which contemporary works of great scale had commanded and often overwhelmed their Environment. To attain this unity of the reality of sculpture with the reality of site artists sought a solution in earth itself—manipulating with giant equipment (dredges, cranes)—quantities of soil and rock in varied terrains to produce a new sculpture form of complete unity or entity with site. *Spiral Jetty* (1970) by Robert Smithson (1938–73), a vast curve of earth and rock in Great Salt Lake, Utah, is such a reciprocal correspondence of site and material. This manipulation of giant forces to reshape the masses of nature in "earth-art" is but a magnification of the timeless disposition of physical materials in new relationships by which the artist continuously reshapes his world.

[M. J. DALY]

EARTH-MOTHER. The concept of the earth as the mother of all things is found among many primitive peoples and in the religions of pagan antiquity. Traces of such worship may perhaps be found in the female figurines fashioned from ivory, stone, and clay by different tribes in Europe during the Late Stone Age. Female idols of the 4th millennium B.C. found in Asia Minor are at least partially connected with the worship of a nature goddess that appears under various guises in historical times. Prominent among these later developments were Cybele, the great mother-goddess of Anatolia, worshiped with her youthful consort Attis, the Dea Syria worshiped at Hierapolis, the Magna Mater Idaea or "Great Mother of Mt. Ida," and the Artemis of the Ephesians. In Mesopotamia the goddess Ishtar was considered to be the mistress of life. "Earth" is mentioned in an early list of gods from Asshur; and in the mythological poems from Ras Shamra, "Lady Earth" is one of the brides of Baal. Female statuettes from Crete holding snakes in their hands would indicate that the Minoans worshiped an earth-mother, probably borrowed from Asia Minor. There is no noticeable worship of the earth in Homer, the poet of the Greek aristocracy, but it plays a considerable part in the poetry of Hesiod, the champion of the poor peasants, where Gaia ("Earth") is represented as the Mother of the Titans and Giants. The later separation of Demeter, the goddess of grain, and Rhea, the mother of Zeus, from Gaia provided the Greeks wih nobler and more personal objects of nature worship. At Rome the earth was worshiped in primitive times under the title of Tellus Mater ("Earth-Mother"), the consort of Jupiter, the Sky-God. Later this worship was associated with other divinities with analogous attributes such as Flora, Dea Dia, and above all Ceres, the equivalent of the Greek Demeter. In 268 B.C. a temple to Tellus Mater was erected at Rome by the consul Publius Sempronius. BIBLIOGRAPHY: F. Altheim, *Terra Mater* (1931); C. D'Onofrio, EncCatt 11:2013–14; J. MacCullough, Hastings ERE 5:130–131; M. Eliade, *Patterns in Comparative Religion* (tr. R. Sheed, 1958) 239–247.

[M. J. COSTELLOE]

EASBY CROSS (8th or 9th cent.), an Anglo-Saxon carved stone standing cross from Easby, Yorkshire, fragments of which include compositions showing a group of Apostles, Christ in Majesty, and decorative vine scrolls, in a delicate style akin to Carolingian ivories. It is now in the Victoria and Albert Museum.

[R. L. S. BRUCE-MITFORD]

EAST, a direction that has had special symbolical significance in pagan religions as well as among Christians. Christ had lived to the E of the later center of Christendom, and according to common belief his second coming also was to be from that direction. The symbolism was reinforced by the familiar references to Christ under the figures of Light and the Sun (of righteousness, salvation, resurrection). This symbolism led to the custom of facing toward the East in prayer and of building churches on an East-West axis. BIBLIOGRAPHY: G. Cope, *Dictionary of Liturgy and Worship* (ed. J. G. Davies, 1972) 315–316. *ORIENTATION.

[N. KOLLAR]

EAST, OF ALL THE, a titular qualification used by several Eastern patriarchs, Catholic and Orthodox who hold the title of Antioch and therefore traditionally claim ecclesiastical supremacy over all the ancient Roman prefecture of the East (Palestine, Syria, Asia Minor, and the territories E to Persia). The control of Antioch over this area was recognized by two councils, namely, of Nicaea (325) and the first of Constantinople (381). Today the term is purely honorific.

[A. J. JACOPIN]

EAST SYRIAN CHURCH, the church of Mesopotamia, E of the Roman-Persian frontier, which became Nestorian in the 5th century. Its own members call it "the (Apostolic) Church of the East," or often today in Western languages, "the Assyrian Church." The origins of Christianity in the region are lost in legend. There were already many Christians in Mesopotamia when the Sassanid dynasty came to the Persian throne (224), and the Church continued to develop despite its persecution by earlier Sassanids (especially Shapur II) and its subjection to later ones, all Zoroastrians. By 410 there were 30 episcopal sees in Mesopotamia, with 6 others in Persia (Iran) and the region of the Persian Gulf, under the primacy of the metropolitan, or catholicos, of Seleucia-Ctesiphon. Culturally, the Church was less influenced by Hellenism, more by Judaism, than was the early West Syrian Church. Close documentation of this Church's movement into schism is lacking. It has been supposed that it declared its independence of the patriarchal jurisdiction of Antioch in the Synod of Markabta in 424 and that it became schismatically Nestorian shortly after the Council of Ephesus. That it was ever really subject to Antioch, however, has been questioned recently; and although Nestorian doctrine was prevalent in the region soon after

Ephesus, the Church as a whole does not seem to have taken an officially schismatic stand before the synod held in 486 under the catholicos Acacius.

Seleucia-Ctesiphon fell to the Muslims in 637. Real persecution of Nestorians by Muslims was only sporadic, and the total loss of Christianity in the area W of the Persian Gulf was partially compensated by conversions from Zoroastrianism, which had lost its advantage as the state religion. In N Mesopotamia the West Syrian Church gained many converts from Nestorianism. Nestorian missions were begun among the Altaic and Iranian peoples of Central Asia, and outposts were even to be found in India and China. The catholicos was given a certain delegated civil authority over the Nestorian community, a fact that led to the transfer of his residence from Seleucia-Ctesiphon to Baghdad and Samarra, residences of the Abbasid caliphate. Gradual attrition among the Mesopotamian Syrians continued to be compensated by conversions, esp. in Central Asia, and when the Nestorian Church had reached its greatest expansion in the 13th cent. an Öngüt Mongol, Mar Yahballâhâ III (1245–1317), was elected catholicos in Baghdad, by then under Mongol domination. From that point, the East Syrian Church began its rapid descent. By the end of the 14th cent. the Ming dynasty had wiped out the Church in China, as had the militant Islam of new Mongols like Tamerlane in Central Asia and even in vast areas of Mesopotamia. Turks and Kurds continued the work of the Mongols, and by the 16th cent. the East Syrian Church was an impoverished remnant found around Baghdad and in the mountainous parts of the triangle formed by Mossul, Lake Van, and Lake Urmia. The rest of its history to the present day is one of bare survival, of union of individuals and groups with Rome, and since the 19th cent. of American Protestant and Russian Orthodox proselytism and of Anglican aid. The Nestorians suffered mass murder by Turks and Kurds in the turmoil following World War I, and there are only around 75,000 of them left today. Their catholicos, Mar Ishai Shim'ûn XXI, having been expelled from Iraq in 1933 for refusing to pledge allegiance to the King, the catholicos now lives officially in Chicago, governing the Church in Iraq through a patriarchal vicar in Harir. BIBLIOGRAPHY: A. J. Maclean and W. H. Browne, *Catholicos of the East and His People* (1892); A. Fortescue, *Lesser Eastern Churches* (1913) 17–159; E. Tisserant, "Nestorienne (L'Église)", DTC 11:157–323; Attwater CCE 2:170–177. *Nestorian Collection of Christological Texts* (ed. L. Abramowski and A. E. Goodman, 2 v., 1971) *CHALDEAN RITE.

[A. CODY]

EAST SYRIAN LITURGY, the liturgical rites and practices of the ancient Church of Mesopotamia, used today by the Nestorian Church, the Catholic Chaldean Church and, with considerable Latinizing alteration, by the Syro-Malabars of South India. The liturgical language, even until very recently among the Syro-Malabars, continues to be classical Syriac, the readings being in Arabic or vernacular Syriac (Soureth). The liturgy's roots are presumably found in the liturgical practice of Edessa in the late 4th cent., hence with some Syro-Antiochene elements difficult to specify with certainty. The isolation of the Church at the extreme Eastern limits of Christendom after the schism in the 5th cent. led to a development quite independent of the liturgies of the Greco-Persian frontier. It reached a stable form rather early in its essentials by the time of the liturgical organization under the catholicos Ishô'yahb III (c.647–657), although new compositions and minor structural changes continued to be made. For the Eucharistic Sacrifice three anaphoras are used: those of "the apostles" (Addai and Mari), of "Mar Nestorius" (called "the second anaphora" by the Chaldeans), and "of Mar Theodore" (of Mopsuestia, the "third anaphora" of the Chaldeans). The authenticity of the ascriptions is in every case dubious. The most frequently used of the three is that of the apostles, which has attracted the attention of liturgists because its MS tradition shows no words of institution. The other two are prescribed for certain fixed times of the year. Nestorians do not reserve the Eucharist, but they do have the unique practice of adding to each batch of dough for Eucharistic bread a portion reserved from the preceding batch, as well as a portion of *malkā. Communion is given under both species, separately. Nestorians in modern times hold that there are five sacraments (rites in which a *mysterion* is communicated): baptism, Eucharist, laying-on-of-hands (holy orders), consecration of chrism, and burial. Older lists include matrimony, the consecration of monks, and the consecration of altars. Auricular confession is not practiced by Nestorians, and there is no evidence that the anointing of the sick was ever a part of their tradition. There is doubt about the theological notion of confirmation in the East Syrian Church, the old MSS of the baptismal ritual (none older than 16th cent.) indicating that the Holy Spirit has already been given in baptism itself. The Chaldeans today have a rite of confirmation in which the form is a translation into Syriac of the Latin form—a phenomenon evident elsewhere too in the Chaldean ritual.

The canonical hours consist of Vespers, the Night Office, and the Morning Office, with Compline and Sext in Lent. It can be argued that remnants of Compline and the day hours are to be found incorporated into Vespers and the Morning Office. Unlike the West Syrian office, that of the East Syrians has retained the lengthy psalmody, although in practice the quantities indicated are rarely, if ever, said in their totality. In Nestorian churches the Eucharistic Sacrifice is not frequent, but Vespers and the Morning Office, with the parish as a whole participating, are a daily occurrence. The liturgical year begins with the Sunday nearest the 1st of Dec. (Sunday of Advent or "of the Annunciation") and continues in cycles of basically seven weeks each. BIBLIOGRAPHY: G. P. Badger, *Nestorians and Their Rituals* (2 v., 1852); H. W. Codrington, ECQ 2 (1937) 79–83, 138–152, 202–209; *Nestorian Church,*

Liturgy and Ritual: The Liturgy of the Holy Apostles Addai and Mari (repr. 1970).

[A. CODY]

EASTER, a word of uncertain origin, said by Bede (*De ratione temporum* 1.5) to be derived from the Anglo-Saxon Eastre, the name of the old Teutonic goddess of spring, but claimed by others to come from the Old German word for dawn, a name given to the Christian festival because of a faulty translation of the plural *albae* used in certain Latin phrases associated with the paschal feast. Easter is the annual celebration of Christ's Resurrection; it is the oldest and the greatest Christian feast. After a prolonged controversy the date for its celebration was fixed for the first Sunday after the first full moon after the vernal equinox, but uniformity of observance on that day was not established in Western Europe until the 8th century. As the annual observance of the Resurrection its celebration extends throughout the Easter season, which lasts until the feast of Pentecost, a period of 50 days. However, every Sunday in the year is regarded by the Church as a continuation of Easter. Every week, on the day which she called the Lord's day, she keeps the memory of His Resurrection" (Vat II ConstSacLit 102). In the early Church it was the custom to baptize catechumens at the *Easter Vigil, and the Mass formulas still in use can be understood only within this baptismal context. BIBLIOGRAPHY: *Maison-Dieu* 67 (1961) 21–32; N. M. Denis-Boulet, *Christian Calendar* (tr. P. Hepburne-Scott, 1960); E. Johnson, NCE 5:6–8; X. Leon-Dufour, *Resurrection and the Message of Easter* (1975).

[N. KOLLAR]

EASTER, DATE OF. In the Christian Churches of the West, Easter Sunday is observed on the first Sunday after the full moon following the vernal equinox (March 21st) as established by the Council of Nicaea I (325) and in accord with the Gregorian calendar promulgated in 1582. Many of the Eastern Churches, however, did not accept the Gregorian calendar because it was a Roman reform. They base their calculation of Easter on the Julian calendar but maintain the Nicene stipulation that it must fall after the Passover. According to Western custom, Easter may fall between March 22d and April 25th, but Eastern computations date the feast between April 4th and May 8th inclusively. *Vatican Council II expressed a willingness to adopt an immovable date for Easter provided other Christian bodies were in agreement. BIBLIOGRAPHY: P. Archer, *Christian Calendar and the Gregorian Reform* (1941); Vat II SacLit, Appendix 1.

[F. T. RYAN]

EASTER CONTROVERSY, a series of disputes concerning the date of Easter lasting from the 2d to the 8th centuries. The 2d-cent. Roman practice of observing Easter on the Sunday following Passover conflicted with the Quartodecimans' observance on the 14th day of *Nisan, common to Asia Minor, and Pope Victor I attempted to solve this by imposing Roman usage *c*.190. The controversy continued between the Antiochene and Alexandrian schools because of divergent methods of calculating the "Paschal Moon", but the Council of Nicaea (325) favored the Alexandrian practice establishing Easter as the Sunday following the full moon after the vernal equinox. This decision, however, did not prevent other divergencies. Rome and Alexandria employed different methods of computation, but another step in uniformity was made through the calendar of *Dionysius Exiguus. In spite of his inaccuracies in dating the Christian era, the system he established remains in use. The Celtic calendar was also at variance with Roman custom, and controversy arose when St. *Augustine of Canterbury arrived in the British Isles with Roman missionaries in 597. The Roman calendar was finally enforced by Abp. Theodore of Canterbury and uniformity achieved by the end of the 8th century. BIBLIOGRAPHY: B. Krushch, *Der 84-jährige Oestercyclus mit 12-jährigen Saltus* (1879); G. Fritz, DTC 11.2:1948–70; J. Ford, NCE 5:8–9.

[F. T. RYAN]

EASTER CUSTOMS AND FOLKLORE. The abundant popular customs of Easter stem not only from its Christian festivity, with Jewish influence, but also from its celebration in early spring. Many lively traditional songs and dances, as well as Easter hymns and carols, are also rooted in pre-Christian vernal folklore. Traditional Easter foods have Christian significance (Easter lamb, cakes, pastries), but some were also regarded as fertility foods (Easter rabbit, eggs) or as reserved for festive occasions (Easter ham). The wearing of new, colorful spring clothing came to express the new life in Christ, often in an Easter walk or parade preceded by a decorated crucifix or the Easter candle, symbolic of the Risen Christ. Joyful communion with him is expressed in the daylong ringing of church bells, the lighting of lamps and decorated candles with the Easter fire, special personal greetings in Christ, and by kindness to the poor, strangers, and the imprisoned. *Easter plays figured prominently in medieval celebrations of the feast. BIBLIOGRAPHY: F. X. Weiser, *Handbook of Christian Feasts and Customs* (1958); id., *Easter Book* (1954).

[N. R. KRAMER]

EASTER CYCLE, the liturgical season embracing the period of preparation for Easter, beginning with *Septuagesima and extending through *Lent and *Holy Week; the celebration of Easter itself; and the prolongation of the Easter celebration through Pentecost and its octave. With the promulgation of the revised liturgical calendar in 1969, fulfilling the directives of Vatican Council II's call for such a revision, the season now embraces a period of 50 days from Easter Sunday to Pentecost. In its earliest observance Easter itself was the celebration of the whole of the paschal mystery, including Christ's death, Resurrection,

Ascension, and the sending of the Spirit; but gradually specific aspects of the mystery began to be given special attention on distinct days. Thus Holy Thursday, commemorating the Last Supper, and Good Friday, commemorating Christ's death, were celebrated from the 4th cent.; there were 50 days of celebration after Easter from the mid-3d cent.; the Ascension and Pentecost Sunday began to be observed in the 4th century. Since the 4th cent. Easter has had an octave, which was originally intended to serve the needs of the newly baptized who during that week wore the white baptismal robes and assembled daily for catechesis and the celebration of the Eucharist. The revised Sacramentary (1970) characterizes each liturgical season in part by the scriptural readings and Mass prayers assigned to each of them. During the Easter season the readings are from the Acts of the Apostles, chronicling the Resurrection and the original proclamation of Christ by the Apostles, and from the Gospel of John. The Mass prayers reflect the purpose and meaning of the season. BIBLIOGRAPHY: *Maison-Dieu* 67 (1961) 21–32; N. M. Denis-Boulet, *Christian Calendar* (tr. P. Hepburne Scott, 1960); E. Johnson, NCE 5:6–8.

[N. KOLLAR]

EASTER DUTY, the obligation of Roman Catholics to receive the *Eucharist at least once a year during Easter time. The computation of that time varies from country to country; in the U.S. it extends from the first Sunday in Lent to Trinity Sunday. The obligation does not extend to confession which, strictly speaking, is obligatory only for those in mortal sin.

[T. M. MCFADDEN]

EASTER EGGS, eggs decorated in various colors which are exchanged among Christians on Easter Sunday. They are a symbol of joy, of the rock-tomb from which Christ emerged, and of spring itself. The original custom may be based upon ancient fertility cults (Indo-European), the eggs' association with spring (Persia), or the custom of abstaining from eggs during Lent (early Christians). BIBLIOGRAPHY: J. Newall, *Eggs at Easter: Folklore Study* (1971).

[N. KOLLAR]

EASTER ISLAND, easternmost Polynesian island, renowned for distinctive huge volcanic stone carvings of heads and figures. Thirty feet high, these "cult" forms, solemn and monumental, probably do not antedate the 15th century. Driftwood has been used for recent skeleton-like ancestor figures.

[M. J. DALY]

EASTER LITANY (MORAVIAN), the liturgical service used by the Moravian Church at its Easter sunrise service. Believing that the Resurrection is the victorious climax of the Christian faith, the Moravians at the time of Count

*Zinzendorf thought it appropriate to use Easter as a time to express their fundamental beliefs. Accordingly, they prepared a litany that, in lieu of a formal creed, became their most authoritative statement of faith. It dates from 1749 and was originally composed in German. It is used not as a formula to be subscribed to but as an act of worship. Trinitarian in emphasis, it explicitly acknowledges the activity of each person of the Godhead. It embodies many Pauline texts, the Lord's Prayer, and phrases from the ancient creeds. There is evidence of Lutheran influence, and some of its phrases are direct quotations from Luther's *Catechisms, especially in regard to man's absolute dependence upon God for salvation through Christ. Other emphases are the blood atonement, baptism, the Lord's Supper, eternal life, and fellowship between the Church on earth and the Church triumphant. The Litany begins in the church building and concludes at the cemetery, which Moravians commonly call God's Acre. BIBLIOGRAPHY: Schaff Creeds 3:799–806; W. H. Allen, *Who Are the Moravians?* (1966).

[J. R. WEINLICK]

EASTER PLAY (LUDUS PASCHALIS), the fully elaborated drama of the Resurrection, consisting of three major scenes: the visit of the three Marys to the empty tomb, the race of Peter and John to the sepulcher, and the meeting of Christ by Mary Magdalene. There might also be minor incidents like the setting of a guard at the tomb or the Marys' purchase of ointments. This complex and artistically mature play is at least 2 cent. later than the first dramatizations of the *Quem quaeritis* trope. Its highly lyrical quality is demonstrated in the stanzas of lament sung by each of the Marys on the way to the tomb, but there is also dramatic action as Peter and John hasten to the sepulcher. Skillful use is made of *Victimae paschali*, the well-known sequence from the Easter Mass, as the Apostles encounter the women and question them. The drama's climax occurs at Mary Magdalene's recognition of Christ and the reversal of her sorrowful mood into ecstatic joy. BIBLIOGRAPHY: S. W. Miller, *Devotional Dramas for Easter* (pa. 1967).

[E. C. DUNN]

EASTER VIGIL, a name commonly given to the restoration on the night of Holy Saturday of the celebration of Christ's paschal mystery. It is a time of watching for the coming of Christ, and a celebration the sacraments of initiation of baptism, confirmation, and the Eucharist. The ceremonies are all related to the Resurrection and the initiation or renewal in grave there of Easter these themes. The blessing of the new fire, symbolic of the Resurrection, originated in Gaul (*c.*8th century). As the spark leaps from the stone to give light to the darkness, so Christ came forth from the tomb to give the light to the world. The *paschal candle, in use from the 5th cent., is symbolic of the risen Christ. From the 7th cent. the celebrant has made an incision in the stem of the candle in the form of a cross, with an alpha

above and an omega below, and in its arms (or on a parchment affixed to the candle) are inscribed the numbers of the current year. From the 10th cent. it has been customary to insert five grains of incense to represent the five wounds of Christ. The *Exsultet,* sung at the blessing of the candle, is in the form of an ancient eucharistic prayer. Its theme is the victory of Christ over death, sin, hell, and darkness. The reading of the lessons is the oldest part of the vigil, going back to the 6th century. The lessons center prophetically upon baptism and are in effect a commentary on its rite. There have been three basic forms of the lessons: (1) the classic Gregorian, so called because of the "classical" manner in which the orations summarize the 4 lessons; (2) the ancient Gelasian, with 10 lessons; (3) the stable Gelasian, with 12 lessons. Each of these basic forms has been used in the Easter Vigil. There are now 4 lessons, which together with their orations show the baptized as part of the new creation (Gen 1.1–2; 2), a new Exodus (Ex 14.24–15.1), a continuation of the Messianic people (Is 4.2–6), and as a person still capable of sin (Dt 3.22–30).

The Litany that begins after the lessons is a processional Litany found in the service as early as the 8th century. It is interrupted for the blessing of the *baptismal water and the renewal of the *baptismal promises. It continues while the altar is prepared for Mass. The Eucharist celebrated as the culmination of the Vigil service is both the fruit of the Christian's entry into Christ's Passover through baptism and the deepening of his paschal life through communion.

The Vigil was traditionally celebrated on the night of Holy Saturday and continued through the night to the dawn of Easter. By the 12th cent. in the West the Vigil, already beginning to be anticipated, was celebrated at noon, and by the time of the Missal of Pius V it was celebrated in the early hours of Holy Saturday. The restoration of the traditional custom of observance, never lost in the Eastern Church, was begun by Pius XII in 1951 and was definitely established in the Holy Week Ordinal of 1955, calls for the ceremonies to begin after sundown, preferably at a time that makes possible the celebration of mass at midnight.

BIBLIOGRAPHY: J. G. Davies, *Holy Week: A Short History* (1963); H. A. Schmidt, *Hebdomeda Sancta* (2 v., 1956–57); L. Bouyer, *Paschal Mystery: Meditations on the Last Three Days of Holy Week* (1950); W. J. O'Shea, NCE 2:9–12; A. McCormack, "Paschal Vigil," *Christian Initiation* (1969).

[N. KOLLAR]

EASTER WATER, the water which is blessed during the Easter Vigil service, and subsequently placed in the baptismal font or distributed to the faithful. This water has long had popular devotional usage as a sacramental means toward sanctifying all life in the Risen Christ. It reflects ancient fertility rites of sprinkling young men and women, animals and crops with life-giving water in the Spring. BIBLIOGRAPHY: F. X. Weiser, *Easter Book* (1954); *Handbook of Christian Feasts and Customs* (1958).

EASTERN CHURCHES, those that developed in the Eastern half of the Roman Empire. Subsequent to its political division, made first by Diocletian (293) and again by the sons of Theodosius I, namely Arcadius in the East (395) and Honorius in the West, the ecclesiastical division into Eastern and Western Churches was affected as well. The boundary ran between Italy and Greece, more precisely along the Sava, Drina, and Zeta rivers down to the city of Budva and to the Adriatic Sea. All lands W of the line belonged to the Latin or Western Church, while lands to the East belonged to Eastern Churches. Viewed in retrospect, the circumstance that a patriarchate was central in administration of the early Church gave the pentarchy—Rome, Alexandria, Antioch, Constantinople, Jerusalem—its importance. Originally at the Council of Nicaea (325) there were the first three patriarchates. Further conciliar legislation formed the two others, Constantinople in 381 (Constantinople I) and 431 (Ephesus) and Jerusalem in 451 (Chalcedon). Since these councils a division was delineated so that Western Christendom is identified with the Roman patriarchate and all Churches that have broken away from it. All the others, with schismatical bodies formed from them, make up the Eastern half.

All Eastern Churches evolved from the Patriarchates of Constantinople, Alexandria, and Antioch, and the Churches of Persia and Armenia, which developed outside the Roman Empire. All the daughter Churches dependent on these three Eastern Patriarchates embraced the rite and came under the jurisdiction of their mother Churches, namely the Byzantine, Alexandrian, and Antiochene (Syrian) rites respectively. The fourth of the original Churches and rites developed in Persia. Christianity reached this region by the 2d century. The ecclesiastical center of the Persian Church was the city of Seleucia-Ctesiphon. The bp. of this see *c.*400 obtained the primacy over all of Persia, taking the title of catholicos instead of patriarch. Christianity was always the religion of the minority and the hostile relations between the Persians and the Byzantine emperors made contact with the Churches within the Byzantine Empire both difficult and dangerous. Under the circumstances and esp. because of severe persecutions, the Persian bps. declared themselves an autonomous Church. The Persian rulers were tolerant to Nestorian Christians because they were a persecuted group within the Byzantine Empire. The Persian Church was the source of the East Syrian rite used by Chaldean Catholics, Malabars, and the Assyrian Nestorians of Iraq and India.

The Armenian Church came into existence owing to the fact that, according to tradition, St. Bartholomew became the Apostle of Armenia. The Church was established toward the end of the 3d cent. from the Church of Caesarea of Cappadocia. St. Gregory the Illuminator converted King Tiridates of Armenia along with the mass of the population (*c.*295). Christianity became the national religion, and from the 5th cent. the national language was used in the Armenian liturgy, which had evolved from the Antiochene rite.

A variety of differences developed: in rites, whether rites

be understood as the liturgical uses in the celebration of the Eucharist, the administration of the sacraments, fasting, etc.; or in a broader sense as the laws and discipline of a local Church (CIC *c.*798). But since various Eastern Churches (Catholic and non-Catholic) frequently use the same liturgical rite and people of the same ethnic or national group belong to different rites, a distinction must be made between the various Eastern liturgical rites and the various Eastern Churches or communions. There are five Eastern rites: the Alexandrian (Copts and Ethiopians); the Antiochene (West Syrians, Maronites, and Malankarese); the Chaldean (the Syro-Chaldeans and Malabarites); the Armenian; and the Byzantine, which has the most numerous branches (the Greeks, Melchites, Bulgarians, Russians and Serbians, Ruthenians, Ukrainians, Russian Old Believers, Romanians, Georgians, Albanians, Hungarians, Japanese, Chinese, Africans in Uganda, in Italy in the monastery of Grottoferrata near Rome, and among the Italo-Albanians). The Eastern rites are marked by their venerable antiquity, by the pomp, splendour, and spirit of piety in their ceremonies.

Of decisive importance for the Eastern Churches were the three great divisions brought about by Nestorianism, Monophysitism, and the controversies between Old and New Rome, i.e., between Rome and Byzantium (Constantinople). Hence the turning-points were the ecumenical councils at Ephesus (431) and Chalcedon (451) and the schism of Michael Cerularius in the year 1054, from which the decisive break between East and West is usually dated. In the history of the attempts at reunion by Rome and unions that were actually effected through the centuries, the union with the Maronites (1181) was a lasting one. The reunions brought about by the Councils of Lyons II (1274) and Florence (1438 or 1439–45) with the Greeks and other Orientals did not last. The major reunions of recent times are of the Uniates of Brest-Litovsk (1595) with the Ruthenians (Ukrainians and White Russians) and those of Alba-Julia (1697). There have been small groups of Uniate Albanians since the latter half of the 15th cent. in S Italy; of Uniate Serbians in Croatia since the end of the 16th cent.; and also later of Uniate groups among the Bulgarians and the Greeks. Greater success in the Near East attended the efforts of the Latin religious orders under the protection of Western powers. But even here there was a series of divisions and reunions. The unions with the Chaldeans, Syrians, Melchites, Armenians, and Copts are important. In India, the Portuguese brought about a measure of union with the Christians of Malabar (Diamper, 1599). Since 1930 many other Malabar Christians have accepted the union (the Malankarese). More understanding and a special ecumenical spirit toward all these Churches was established by Vatican Council II (1962–65).

The often used term ''Eastern Church,'' then, is frequently inexact. In fact, the local Eastern Churches or Eastern communions do not form a unity. They comprise five more or less united groups: the Nestorians, the Monophysites, the Orthodox, the Catholic Uniates, and the Protestants. Of the once very numerous group of Nestorians, who in the Middle Ages penetrated as far as India, China, and Mongolia, there are now only about 70,000, mainly in Iraq, with about 5,000 in India. The Monophysites are considerably stronger (some 14 million all told. Opponents of the definitions of Chalcedon, they are for this reason more recently called the "non-Chalcedonian Orthodox." They include the Copts and Ethiopians, the West Syrians (mainly in India), and Armenians. Strongest of all the Eastern groups are the Orthodox. They include the ancient patriarchates of Constantinople, Alexandria, Antioch, and Jerusalem (altogether about 2 million). Numerically the strongest Orthodox Churches, however, are those in Greece (8 million) and in the countries like Russia, Romania, Yugoslavia, and Bulgaria (about 80 million). The number of exiled Russian Orthodox organized into four different communities (the Moscow patriarchate, the Paris hierarchy, and two hierarchies in the U.S.) may be around 1 million.

In general, each Eastern rite includes a Catholic group united with Rome (Uniates). The Maronites, Italo-Albanians, Slovaks, and Malabar Christians are all Catholic, while the Georgians, Esthonians, Latvians, Finns, Japanese, and Chinese have no Catholic Uniate counterparts. There are also Eastern Christians in various countries who have gone over to Protestantism (the Mar Thoma Christians in India; the Nestorians who went over to Presbyterianism in the U.S.A.; the Ukrainians who became Congregationalists in Canada). There are also Protestant missions in the Near East.

The religious mixture and crossovers are understandable in view of the effects on people of frequent changes of localities and of social, historical, political, and economic pressures. All these influences brought on various structural changes as well. The original structure and meaning of patriarchates changed. Political changes created autocephalous units and numerous new patriarchates in the Churches separated from Rome besides those already mentioned: the Coptic and the Ethiopian (since 1959); those of the Monophysites of Antioch (Jacobites; the Jacobites of India have a catholicate); and of the Nestorians. There are two catholicates and two patriarchates of the Armenians; one catholicate of the Orthodox Georgians; the patriarchates among the Orthodox in Russia, Serbia, Romania, and Bulgaria are more recent. The Orthodox Church of Greece is autocephalous (with the abp. of Athens at the head), as are those of Cyprus, Albania, Poland, and Czechoslovakia. For the Catholics of the Eastern Churches there are six patriarchates, namely the Coptic, Syrian, Maronite, Melchite, Armenian and Chaldean, and one archbishop major with patriarchal rights among the Ukrainians. There are metropolitans for the Catholic Ethiopian Church (1), the Malankarese (1) and the Malabar Christians (2), the Catholic Romanians (1), and the Ukrainians (3). The remaining Catholics of the Eastern Church are directly under the Apostolic See (with the exception of the two groups in

Yugoslavia and Hungary who are subject to a Latin bishop). Other structural changes occurred as emigrants from Eastern Europe moved to such countries as the U.S., Canada, Latin America, Australia. The people demanded new independent ecclesiastical units and new links among those units based on old loyalties and new jurisdictions.

The nature of Eastern Churches is reflected in their doctrinal differences, outgrowth of the Trinitarian and Christological controversies (esp. those of Arianism, Nestorianism, Monophysitism and Monothelitism) concerning the Trinity (see FILIOQUE) and the nature and person of Christ. They emphasize pneumatology, unleavened (azyme) bread, liturgical rite and customs, national traditions and feeling; they evidence an intense conservatism and a tradition of Eastern piety impressive in its asceticism and mysticism.

The rupture between East and West came about, not at certain specific dates, but gradually; it was brought about in good faith, against the desire of both sides, the result of conjunctures of historical circumstances rather than of ill will. The Eastern Churches have no consciousness of having broken with their own past or with apostolic tradition, or of having denied anything whatever in it. The epithets "schismatic" and "heretic" are deeply resented by the Eastern Churches; and Rome in official pronouncements and documents refers now always to the separated Eastern brothers simply as dissidents. In 1927 Pius XI set out once for all what should be the Catholic attitude to the non-Catholic Eastern Christians: not an attitude of patronage or pity or superiority, much less of contempt or hostility, but one of love and esteem. "Catholics," he said, "are sometimes lacking in a right appreciation of their separated brethren and are even wanting in brotherly love, because they do not know enough about them. People do not realize how much faith, goodness, and Christianity there are in these bodies now separated from the age-long Catholic truth. Pieces broken from gold-bearing rock themselves bear gold. The ancient Christian bodies of the East keep so venerable a holiness that they deserve not only respect but complete sympathy." The Catholic Church has always considered itself to be the one Church of Christ and hence has continually worked for reunion after each schism. This is evident from the long history of the attempts at union and their partial success. But the attitude of the Catholic Church toward the Christian East has not always been the same; it has changed in keeping with the times. There have been alternating periods of great understanding and also deep estrangement. Undoubtedly, sympathy and concern for the separated Eastern Churches received a decided impulse from John XXIII, and from the Council convoked by him, a feature of which was the new ecumenical movement in the Catholic Church. Yet this did not happen all of a sudden, but was prepared by a series of papal letters and measures undertaken by Pius IX, Leo XIII, Benedict XV, and esp. Pius XI. A movement interested in the Eastern Churches has long existed in Germany, France, and elsewhere. Pius

XI made the Benedictine monastery of Amay-sur-Meuse in Belgium, later Chevetogne, a center of the movement. Benedict XV founded the Pontifical Oriental Institute in Rome, which was then greatly helped by Pius XI, whose encyclical *Rerum orientalium* of Sept. 8, 1928 recommended study of the Eastern Churches and esp. of their theology. Scholarly and informative periodicals have been published for years by the Benedictines, Augustinians, Assumptionists, Dominicans, Jesuits, and other orders to further the knowledge of the Christian East.

Vatican II not only promulgated a special Decree on the Eastern Catholic Churches, but also included in this decree (art. 24–29) and in the Decree on Ecumenism (in Part I of the third chapter: art. 13–18) a special reference to the Eastern Churches separated from Rome. These decrees express great esteem for the institutions, liturgy, and traditions of the Eastern Churches. The first decree speaks of the local Eastern Churches, of the preservation of their spiritual heritage, of the venerable institution of the patriarchate (all Catholic Eastern patriarchs are equal in dignity; their rights and privileges are stressed); it speaks also of the sacramental discipline, the celebration of feasts, of contact and intercommunion with the separated Eastern Churches (the practice with regard to *communicatio in sacris* is modified; (see Vat II Ecum., art. 8). In the same decree the elements that unite East and West are stressed. This change of attitude is being reciprocated also by many Eastern Churches, and thus hope for reunion is increased. It is right and proper that the Westerners should value the rights and usages and traditions and glorious history of their own, while they should also value those of Eastern Churches by accepting them as part of the whole which is to come BIBLIOGRAPHY: Attwater CCE; E. Benz, *Eastern Orthodox Church. Its Thought and Life* (1964); S. Bulgakov, *Orthodox Church* (1935); F. E. Brightman, *Liturgies Eastern and Western* (v. 1, 1896); F. Dvornik, *Idea of Apostolicity in Byzantium and the Legend of the Apostle Andrew* (1958); *idem, Photian Schism: History and Legend* (1948); L. M. Duchesne, *Churches Separated from Rome* (tr. A. H. Mathew, 1907); A. Fortescue, *Lesser Eastern Churches* (1913); *Uniate Eastern Churches* (ed. G. D. Smith, 1923), M. Gordillo, *Compendium theologiae orientalis* (3d. ed., 1950); *idem, Theologia orientalium cum latinorum comparata* (OrChrAnal 158, 1960); F. Heiler, *Urkirche und Ostkirche* (1937); R. Janin, *Les Églises orientales et les rites orientaux* (1955); M. Jugie, *Theologia dogmatica Christianorum ab Ecclesia Catholica dissidentium* (5 v., 1926–35); I. H. Dalmais, *Eastern Liturgies* (tr. D. Attwater, 1960); B. J. Kidd, Churches of Eastern Christendom (1927); A. King, *Rites of Eastern Christendom* (2 v., 1950); N. Ladomerszky, *Theologia orientalis* (1953); V. Lossky, *Mystical Theology of the Eastern Church* (1957); J. Meyendorff, *Orthodox Church* (1962); L. Nemec, "Ruthenian Uniate Church in its Historical Perspective," *Church History* 37 (1968) 1–24; H. Musset, *Histoire du christianisme spécialement en Orient* (3 v., 1948–49); F. J. McGarrigle et al., *Eastern Branches of the Catholic Church* (1938); P. Rondot, *Les Chrétiens d'Orient* (1955); N. Zernov, *Eastern Christendom* (1961); G. P. Badger, *Nestorians and Their Rituals* (2 v., 1852); L. E. Browne, *Eclipse of Christianity in Asia* (1933); H. C. Luke, *Mosul and Its Minorities* (1925); E. R. Hardy, *Christian Egypt* (1952); W. A. Wigram, *Separation of the Monophysites* (1923); D. L. O'Leary, *Ethiopian Church* (SPCK, 1936); T. E. Dowling, *Armenian Church* (SPCK, 1910, repr. 1955); M. Ormanian, *Church in Armenia* (ed. T. Poladian, tr. G. M. Gregory, 1955); B. Schultze, SacMund 120–135.

[L. NEMEC]

EASTERN ORTHODOX CHURCH. The second largest Christian communion in the world today, the Eastern Orthodox Church (also designated as the Greek Orthodox or the Orthodox Catholic Church) has a following which is variously estimated at between 100 and 250 million; exact figures are unavailable for Eastern European countries. Encompassing the majority of the Christian population in the Middle East, the Balkans, and the Soviet Union, it has more recently expanded, either through immigration or missionary activity, to America, Western Europe, East Africa, and the Far East.

As Apostles of Jesus preached throughout the Eastern Mediterranean world, communities or local Churches were established in most urban centers of the area, which were then under the control of the Roman Empire. In 324, Emperor Constantine transferred the imperial capital from Rome to Byzantium on the Bosphorus. The city was renamed "Constantinople-New Rome" and soon became not only the political capital of the Empire, but also the center of the Eastern Christian civilization. A leading role to be exercised by the bp. of Constantinople among his colleagues was sanctioned by the Councils of Constantinople (381) and Chalcedon (451). In the 6th cent., he assumed the title of "ecumenical patriarch" and occupied the second position after Rome in a system where five patriarchs— Rome, Constantinople, Alexandria, Antioch, Jerusalem— were considered as the main centers of the Christian world. Their role was decisive in the solution of doctrinal controversies which were debated at the Councils of Nicaea I (325), Constantiniple I (381), Ephesus (331), Chalcedon (451), Constantinople II (553), Constantinople III (680), and Nicaea II (787). These seven councils are the ones recognized as ecumenical by the Orthodox Church today.

Starting with the 9th cent., the Church of Constantinople undertook a major missionary expansion among the Slavic nations of Eastern Europe. Following the tradition of earlier missionaries, the Greeks SS. Cyril and Methodius, during their mission in Moravia, translated Scripture and the liturgy into the vernacular language of the Slavs. In 864 Bulgaria was converted to Christianity, followed, in 988, by Russia. In the Balkans, independent (autocephalous) Churches were soon created in Bulgaria and Serbia, while Russia assumed ecclesiastical independence only in 1448 and became a patriarchate in 1589. The establishment of new independent Slavic Churches followed a pattern that went back to the 5th cent., when, in addition to the patriarchates mentioned above, autocephalous Churches existed in Cyprus and Georgia.

Controversies on points of doctrine and discipline began between East and West in the early Middle Ages. The unilateral interpolation into the Creed of the word *filioque (procession of the Holy Spirit from the Father *and the Son*), which first occurred in Spain and was eventually adopted by the entire Latin West, was the source of bitter polemics, along with the issue of clergy celibacy and some liturgical practices. The solution of these problems became more difficult with the Gregorian reform in the West, which affirmed strict papal centralization and presupposed that the pope was the ultimate criterion of doctrine and discipline in the Church. The Christian East refused to recognize this form of papal supremacy. The date of 1054, generally quoted as the date of the schism between Rome and Constantinople, represents, in fact, only an incident in a long process of estrangement, which was exacerbated with the sack of Constantinople by the Crusaders (1204). Eventually, the estrangement became so deep that attempts at reunion (Councils of Lyons, 1274, and Florence, 1439) ended in failures.

The Muslim Turks captured Constantinople in 1453 and established their control over the entire Middle East and Balkan peninsula. For centuries Orthodox Christianity in those areas was reduced to mere survival. In Russia, meanwhile, Eastern Orthodoxy received the support of a mighty empire. Although tightly controlled by the tsars—in 1721, Peter the Great suppressed the patriarchate of Moscow and established instead the Holy Synod—the Russian Church continued the missionary tradition of the Byzantines throughout Asia, in Japan, and on the American continent. In 1917, on the eve of the revolution, the Moscow patriarchate was reestablished and the Church succeeded in surviving the bloody persecutions that followed the Communist takeover. The gradual disintegration of the Turkish empire in the 19th cent. led to the reestablishment of Greek, Slavic, and Romanian Churches in the Balkans, but the patriarchate of Constantinople, still on Turkish territory, saw its direct power and influence greatly reduced.

Today, the Orthodox Church consists of 14 independent or autocephalous Churches, united in faith, sacraments, and canon law. These churches include the patriarchates of Constantinople, Alexandria, Antioch, Jerusalem, Russia, Georgia, Serbia, Romania, and Bulgaria, and the autocephalous Churches of Cyprus, Greece, Poland, Czechoslovakia, and America. All recognize the honorary primacy of the ecumenical patriarch of Constantinople. The autonomous Churches of Finland, Crete, and Japan maintain token administrative ties with the patriarchates of Constantinople and Moscow respectively. In America, side by side with the autocephalous local Church, dioceses organized on an ethnic basis remain dependent upon mother Churches abroad (the largest of these in the Greek Archdiocese).

In its official doctrine, the Eastern Orthodox Church maintains the claim that it is the original, undivided Catholic Church of Christ and rejects the doctrinal definitions adopted in Western Catholicism since the schism (decrees of the Council of Trent, Immaculate Conception of Mary, papal infallibility). It holds Scripture and tradition as the highest expressions of Christian truth and considers that the most authoritative voice of tradition is the ecumenical council. On the other hand, it recognizes that history has known councils pretending to ecumenicity, which were eventually rejected by the Church. In the last resort, therefore, the expression of the Holy Spirit in the common consciousness of the entire Church remains for the Orthodox the ultimate guardian of the truth. Bishops—individually, or in council—are responsible for preserving the truth without depriving the entire people of God of very real responsibility. In addition to the doctrine of the seven councils, the doctrines defined by several councils of the late Byzantine period (particularly 1351) are also recognized as authoritative by the Orthodox Church, together with the statements and writings of all those who, at all times, expressed consistently the teaching of Scripture and the Fathers of the Church.

The decrees of Vatican Council II and the various gestures that followed that council, changed the atmosphere of relations between Orthodoxy and Roman Catholicism. Without formally eliminating the differences, they made further understanding much easier. The various Eastern Orthodox Churches are also actively participating in ecumenical encounters with other Christian bodies, maintaining that Christian union is possible not through absorption of one body by another, but through common and committed acceptance of the one saving truth of Christ. BIBLIOGRAPHY: J. Meyendorff, *Orthodox Church* (1964); *idem, Byzantine Theology–Historical Trends and Doctrinal Themes* (1976); T. Ware, *Orthodox Church* (1970).

[J. MEYENDORFF]

EASTERN RITES, the generic name sometimes given to the liturgical families of Eastern Christendom, usually with reference to the Catholic (Uniate) Churches as distinguished from the Orthodox, who differ primarily in not being in communion with Rome. With the exception of the Maronites, who are Catholic, each of these has both a Catholic and an Orthodox form. The root of the differentiation between Eastern and Western Christianity lies in the political division of the Roman Empire in the early centuries of the Christian era. Eastern Christianity was centered in Antioch in Syria and Alexandria in Egypt; these are the sources of the various Eastern liturgical families.

Antiochene Type. The first Greek influences on Christianity probably occurred in Antioch. Apart from possible NT fragments and the 3d-cent. *Didascalia Apostolorum*, there is no information on early liturgical developments here. Today's Liturgy of Saint James is a fusion of the primitive Antioch rite and the 4th-cent. Jerusalem rite. In the 5th cent. the liturgy of West Syria split into the Monophysite (Syrian

Jacobite) rite, using Syriac, and the Melkite, using Greek and faithful to the Council of Chalcedon. Melkites came under Constantinopolitan influence and in the 12th cent. adopted the Byzantine rite. Today's Maronites and Malankars, as well as the Syrian Jacobites and Syrian Uniates, follow a West Syrian liturgy. The East Syrian family originated outside the Empire, probably centered in Edessa, and remained more Semitic and Jewish, although there are only later Greek translations extant. It is represented today by the Nestorians, Chaldeans, and Malabars (a group of the latter, the Malankars, adopted a West Syrian liturgy). Constantinople, founded in the 4th cent., seems to have been most influenced liturgically by Antioch; liturgies derived from it are generally typed as Greco-Antiochene. Its Byzantine rite is today the most important of the Eastern rites. Translated into Slavonic, it became the liturgy of the Slavic peoples and of Russia. Apart from the Byzantine proper, there is the Ruthenian heavily Latinized, and the Melkite, originally West Syrian. While the origins of the Armenian rite are obscure, it is usually classified with the Greco-Antiochene families of Byzantium; it contains elements from many rites but has been particularly influenced by Byzantium and Rome.

Alexandrian Type. Generally conservative and close to the Roman rite, the Liturgy of Saint Mark in its development parallels that of West Syria: the Egyptian rite became Monophysite and adopted the Coptic vernacular. The Ethiopian rite, derived from the Coptic with Syrian elements, is unique in being heavily Africanized using dance, handclapping, and music close to the American Negro spirituals. BIBLIOGRAPHY: D. Attwater, *The Christian Churches of the East* (2v., 1961–62); I.H., Dalmais, *Eastern Liturgies* (1960); A. King, *Rites of Eastern Christendom* (2v., 1950).

[J. DALLEN]

EASTERN SCHISM, see SCHISM, EAST-WEST.

EASTERN THEOLOGY, the theology of the Eastern Churches. Its tradition of thought, roots in special cultural areas, milieu, and general mentality account for its distinctive quality. Although Eastern theology takes its point of departure from the same transcendent reality as Western theology, it is complementary because of the diversity of its conceptualization and formulation. Eastern theology today is gradually rediscovering its proper genius. Among the outstanding characteristics of this theology is its mystical bent, or integration with the spiritual life of man. The Greek Fathers conceived theology as the loftiest degree of the spiritual life, consisting of a quasi-experimental knowledge (contemplation) of the Trinity. Hence it is Trinitarian, having the Trinity for its origin, center, and eschatological goal. Because it is prone to accentuate the role of faith and is distrustful of reason and philosophy, it is an experiential theology. The same attitude led *Pseudo-Dionysius to develop a negative or apophatic theological method acknowledging reason's limitations.

BIBLIOGRAPHY: V. Lossky, *Mystical Theology of the Eastern Church* (tr. Members of the Fellowship of St. Alban, 1957); J. Meyendorff, *Orthodox Church* (tr. J. Chapin, 1962); idem, *Byzantine Theology* (1974). *WESTERN THEOLOGY; *EASTERN ORTHODOX CHURCH.

[J. FICHTNER]

EASTON, BURTON SCOTT (1877–1950), biblical scholar. Born in Connecticut and educated at the Univ. of Göttingen, the Univ. of Pennsylvania, and the Philadelphia Divinity School, he was ordained to the priesthood in the Protestant Episcopal Church in 1905. E. was professor of NT at Nashotah House in Nashotah, Wis. (1905–11), Western Theological Seminary in Chicago (1911–19), and the General Theological Seminary in New York City (1919–48). His major work, done in the field of NT criticism, is represented by *The Gospel according to St. Luke, A Critical and Exegetical Commentary* (1926); *The Gospel before the Gospels* (1928); *Christ in the Gospels* (1930); *The Purpose of Acts* (1936); *What Jesus Taught* (1938); and a *Commentary on the Pastoral Epistles* (1947). He was for a number of years associate editor of the *Anglican Theological Review* (for his biog. and bibliog. see v. 35, 147–161). He was chosen by the Library of Congress to catalogue the Migne edition of the Greek and Latin Fathers.

[H. H. GRAHAM]

EBBA, SS., the name of two saints. (1) **Ebba** (d. 683), daughter of Ethelfrid, King of Northumbria. She was veiled a nun at Coldingham by Finan, and was a friend to both Adamnan and Wilfrid. (2) **Ebba,** abbess of Coldingham who was martyred by the Danes after she had multilated her face to escape rape. BIBLIOGRAPHY: Butler 3:402; G. M. Fusconi, BiblSanct 4:886–887.

[J. DRUSE]

EBBO OF REIMS (c.775–851), abp. of Reims, bp. of Hildesheim. His mother was nurse of Louis I, who treated him as foster brother. After serving in Aquitaine, E. accompanied Louis to the imperial household, wielding great influence. As abp. of Reims he was Louis' envoy to Denmark. Strangely, he joined the unsuccessful revolt against the Emperor. Deposed (834), confined at Fulda, he was reinstated when Lothair acceded (840), but Charles the Bald banished him after the battle of Fontenoy and Sergius II degraded him. He then fled to Louis the German. In time elevated as bp. of Hildesheim, he still struggled against Hincmar, his successor at Reims, but died before vindication. BIBLIOGRAPHY: É. Lesne, *La Hiérarchie épiscopale en Gaule et en Germanie* (1905); J. Daoust, NCE 5:26.

[A. CABANISS]

EBBO OF SENS, ST. (d. 735), archbishop. A count of Tonnerre, E. abandoned the world for monasticism, was made abbot of his monastery (704), followed his uncle Goéric as bp. of Sens (c.709), had the military skill to repel Muslim attacks (c.725–731). He then retired into solitude, returning to Sens on Sundays to celebrate Mass and to preach. BIBLIOGRAPHY: GallChrist 12:12–13; P. Viard, BiblSanct 4:887–888.

[A. CABANISS]

EBBO, GOSPEL BOOK OF (816–833 A.D.), Carolingian illuminated MS belonging to Abp. Ebbo of Reims. Remarkable among illuminated MSS that are the finest achievement of the Carolingian Renaissance, the Ebbo Gospel Book from the famous Reims scriptorium is a masterpiece of the Palace School style of vibrant energy expressed in quick strokes in a linear impressionism, as opposed to the monumental, classical style of the Ada School characterized by solid color and gold. In the Ebbo Gospel Book medieval man is caught in the "divine frenzy" of inspiration—the drapery swirls, the hills heave, vegetation is tossed by a whirlwind; even the classical acanthus border pattern is freed in flamboyant rhythm. The dynamic line that distinguished the Gospel Book of Ebbo is related to the intertwining of the Irish MSS, and forerunner of the famous Utrecht Psalter (c. 820–832 A.D.), the most extraordinary of Carolingian MSS in energetic pen drawing. The Gospel Book of Ebbo is in the Municipal Library, Epernay, France.

[M. J. DALY]

EBENDORFER, THOMAS (1388–1464) Austrian historiographer, theologian, and diplomat. After receiving his doctorate in theology at the Univ. of Vienna, E. became a canon in St. Stephen's Cathedral. He wrote a report of the Council of Basel, a *Chronicle of the Emperors,* and an *Austrian Chronicle.* Although lacking in the humanistic spirit, his histories are notable for realistic detail and the use of nonliterary sources. Most of his philosophical, theological, and occasional works remain unedited. BIBLIOGRAPHY: M. M. Zykan, NCE 5:27.

[M. J. FINNEGAN]

EBERBACH, ABBEY OF, abbey near Wiesbaden, Germany, which was established (1116) by Adalbert, abp. of Mainz. It is believed that Achard built the church (consecrated 1186) which first served the Augustinian Canons Regular and later became a Cistercian foundation (1135). The abbey flourished during the 12th and 13th centuries. From its scriptorium come many codices at the Bodleian Library, Oxford, and the British Museum. Since its secularization in 1803 it has served as prison and sanatarium, and today is a museum. Most of its medieval buildings still stand.

[J. R. RIVELLO]

EBERHARD OF EINSIEDELN, BL. (d. 958), abbot. He resigned in 934 as provost of the cathedral of Strasbourg in order to join the hermits at Einsiedeln (Switzerland); he endowed and became first abbot of the Benedictine monastery that supplanted the hermitage. During the famine of 942, the monastery under his direction gave generously to

relieve the starving populace. BIBLIOGRAPHY: Butler 3:330.

[M. F. MCCARTHY]

EBERHARD OF ROHRDORF, BL. (Ever[h]ard; c.1160–1245), abbot. Of noble birth, E. entered the Cistercian monastery at Salem in the diocese of Constance in 1180, was elected abbot in 1191, and resigned because of age in 1240. The abbey prospered under his rule and greatly expanded its holdings. Without failing in his staunch loyalty to the Hohenstaufen, E. enjoyed the respect and confidence of popes such as Innocent III, Honorius III, and Gregory IX and was able to act effectively as a mediator and arbiter in negotiations between kings and emperors (Henry VI, Philip of Swabia, Frederick II) and the Holy See. At his abbey many conferences were held and important documents drawn up. BIBLIOGRAPHY: M. A. Dimier, DHGE 14:1291–93; M. Standaert, BiblSanct 5:383–384.

[S. WILLIAMS]

EBERHARD (EVERARD) OF TÜNTENHAUSEN, ST. (dates unknown), Bavarian shepherd. Veneration of E., who was never canonized, is first mentioned in 1428. He is the patron of shepherds and of domestic animals. In the 18th cent. his cult was approved as immemorial, the faithful invoking him for the cure of sick cattle and for good weather. BIBLIOGRAPHY: D. Andreini, NCE 5:28; N. Del Re, BiblSanct 5:388.

[M. J. FINNEGAN]

EBERLIN, JOHANNES (of Günzburg; 1470–1533), early Lutheran religious and social pamphleteer. E. was ordained in 1489, then became a Franciscan, and from 1516 a preacher at Tübingen and Ulm until he embraced Lutheranism (1521). He went to Switzerland where he published a series of pamphlets attacking Catholic practices, the religious orders, and celibacy, and advocating radical political and social change. After his return to Germany (1522), the cautions of Luther and P. *Melanchthon and the violence of the *Anabaptist movement caused E. to temper his social writings. He sought to quell the fury of the *Peasants' War. His last post was as court preacher at Wertheim. BIBLIOGRAPHY: G. Bebermeyer, RGG 2:297; F. Zoepfl, LTK 3:632.

[T. C. O'BRIEN]

EBIONITES, sect of Jewish Christians who rejected St. Paul's teaching and maintained allegiance to the Mosaic Law. Known only from scattered references in early Christian writers, the sect apparently arose in the 1st cent. and continued until the 4th, chiefly in Syria and Transjordan, but also in Egypt and Rome. They accepted Jesus as the Messiah, but held an adoptionist Christology. The term is from a Heb. word meaning poor ones. Holding their goods in common, they were vegetarian and practiced various ritual ablutions, climaxed with baptism. BIBLIOGRAPHY: H. J.

Schoepp, *Jewish Christianity: Factional Disputes in the Early Church* (tr. R. Douglas, 1969). *APOCRYPHA (NT) 18.

[T. EARLY]

EBIONITES, GOSPEL OF THE, see APOCRYPHA (NEW TESTAMENT), 18.

EBLA (TELL MARDIKH), Syria, site covering 140 acres of archaeological discoveries of rare importance esp. to biblical studies. Since 1964 a corps of Italian archeologists has worked at the dig (*c*.34 miles S of Aleppo and 75 miles E of ancient Ugarit) under the direction of Dr. Paolo Matthiae. In 1973 they discovered the 3d-millennium palace of the Eblaite kingdom, and in 1975 laid open the royal archives, which housed some 15,000 unusually large clay cuneiform tablets (now in the Aleppo Museum). Fashioned in the Sumerian style of the Early Bronze Age, most are in Sumerian, but those in the language of the Eblaites (presently designated as Old Canaanite) have been deciphered by means of a bilingual "key" tablet. These records reveal an Ebla of the time (*c*.2400–2250 B.C.) when the kingdoms of both Sumer-Akkad and Egypt flourished. Discoveries are expected to highlight the background of Genesis. At Ebla emerge from the tablets familiar OT names: Abraham and Esau, Saul and David (first occurrence of the name David outside the Hebrew Scriptures), Salem (identified as Jerusalem), Sodom, and Gomorrah. Reports of Tell Mardikh are being channeled through the Albright Institute of Archeological Research. (see W. F. *ALBRIGHT). BIBLIOGRAPHY: W. Wifall, Jr., "Preliminary Report on Ebla," *Biblical Theology Bulletin 7* (1977) 2:89–91.

[M. R. BROWN]

EBNER-ESCHENBACH, MARIE VON (1830–1916), Austrian novelist whose representation of the aristocratic culture of the late Austro-Hungarian Empire showed a consciousness of the social problems of her times. She spent her childhood in her father's castle in the Moravian countryside, where she learned to observe the social tensions between nobles and peasants. Her realistic portraits of both aristocracy and peasantry reveal sensitivity and kindness devoid of criticism. *Das Gemeindekind* (1887), a moving short novel about the child of a vagabond, and *Aus Spätherbsttagen* (1901) are counted among her best work. A number of her short stories are collected in *Dorf- und Schlossgeschichten* (1883). BIBLIOGRAPHY: S. R. Doyle, *Catholic Atmosphere in Marie von Ebner-Eschenbach* (1936, repr. 1970).

[B. F. STEINBRUCKNER]

EBRACH, ABBEY OF, Cistercian monastery in Germany (Upper Franconia) founded in 1127 from Morimond. After extensive devastation in the 16th and 17th cent., the abbey was rebuilt in magnificent Baroque, although the early Gothic church was preserved. Ebrach was suppressed in 1803. In 1851 the buildings were converted into a prison, except for the church which is used by the parish. BIBLIOGRAPHY: A. Schneider, NCE 5:29.

[L. J. LEKAI]

EBRULF, ST., see ÉVROUL, ST.

ECBATANA, Greek rendering of the old Persian *Hagmatana,* the present-day city of Hamadan, *c*.120 miles W of Teheran, Iran. Herodotus (I.96–98) attributes the founding of Ecbatana to Deioces the Mede, *c*.700 B.C. It was the Median capital until Cyrus the Great (550–530 B.C.) captured it; thereafter, it was the favorite summer residence of the Persian Achaemenid kings. Ezra 6.2 describes the finding at Ecbatana of a copy of the decree of Cyrus (538 B.C.) authorizing the reconstruction of the Temple of Jerusalem. The reputed tombs of Esther and Mordecai at Ecbatana are of dubious authenticity. The city is mentioned in passing in the tales of Judith (Jdt 1.1) and Tobit (Tob 3.7; 6.5). BIBLIOGRAPHY: InterDB 6.

[T. CRANE]

ECCARD, JOHANN GEORG, see ECKHART, JOHANN GEORG VON.

ECCE LIGNUM (Lat., Behold the wood), the versicle now chanted three times in the vernacular as the priest unveils a large crucifix on *Good Friday: "Behold the wood of the Cross on which has hung the salvation of the world." The people respond, "Come let us adore." Adoration is thus paid to Christ Crucified on the liturgical anniversary of his death. BIBLIOGRAPHY: J. Gaillard, *Holy Week and Eastern* (tr. W. Busch, 1954).

[N. R. KRAMER]

ECCLESIA (Lat. transliteration of Gr. *ekklēsia*). In secular use *ekklēsia* was a civic assembly, the word derived from *ekkalein,* to call out, summon. In biblical usage, e.g., in LXX, it referred to the assembly called by God out of the world to be his people. The NT writers, e.g., St. Paul, use *ekklēsia* to designate local assemblies of Christians, such as the Church of God gathered at Corinth (1 Cor 1.2). A more universal reference is plain, however, in St. Paul's Christological Epistles (Ephesians, Colossians) as he speaks of Christ as the head of his body which is the *ekklēsia,* the entire assembly of those who believe in him as Lord (Eph 1.22–23). The term *ekklēsia* is also employed in reference to the internal structure of the assembly (Mt 16.18; 18.17). Thus in the NT the word signifies the assembly of the people called and chosen by God, through and in Jesus Christ, in whom the ministry of the assembly exists. The *ekklēsia* is an assembly with an internal order of interdependence, for the sake of its world mission. The term, as well as its biblical meaning, is prominent in current ecumenical discussion on the nature of the Church. BIB-

LIOGRAPHY: K. L. Schmidt, Kittel TD 3:501–536. *CHURCH (NT); *ECCLESIOLOGY.

[M. B. SCHEPERS]

ECCLESIA DISCENS (Lat., the learning Church), a phrase used esp. by 19th cent. RC theologians to designate the body of the faithful who accept the authoritative teachings of the hierarchy (see ECCLESIA DOCENS). This designation accorded with the 19th- and early 20th-cent. emphasis on the monarchical structure of the Church, which allowed for a sharp dichotomy between the rulers and the ruled, the teachers and the taught. In this view the ordinary faithful who constitute the *ecclesia discens* are expected to give an assent of faith to the infallible teachings of the Church and an assent of religious obedience in matters subject to authoritative but noninfallible pronouncement. Contemporary ecclesiology stresses that any consensus of what the Church believes and teaches must take the beliefs of the faithful into account. The faithful are generally understood to exercise a check on orthodoxy insofar as they enjoy a sort of reflex infallibility in assimilating the teachings of their pastors. Theologians refer to it as passive infallibility or infallibility in believing. BIBLIOGRAPHY: J. G. Hagen, CE 13:603–605; J. H. Newman, *On Consulting the Faithful in Matters of Doctrine* (1961); *Election and Consensus in the Church* (*Concilium* 77, ed. G. Alberigo and A. Weiler, 1972). *MAGISTERIUM.

[B. MARTHALER]

ECCLESIA DOCENS (Lat., the teaching Church), the popes and bps. as holders of the teaching office in the Church. The phrase grew up in 19th-cent. ecclesiology as the correlative of *ecclesia discens*. Contemporary theologians have largely abandoned the term, preferring the broader concept *magisterium*. *Ecclesia docens* focuses on the instructional aspects of teaching and does not stress the kerygmatic and pastoral witness of the Church. Juxtaposed to the *ecclesia discens*, it seems to restrict the teaching role of the Church to a function within the Christian community without taking into account the right and responsibility it has to teach all nations, Christian and non-Christian. Contemporary ecclesiology prefers to stress the idea that the Church *en bloc* is magisterial vis-à-vis the world, just as the entire Christian community, constituted of bps. and faithful alike, is the *ecclesia discens*. BIBLIOGRAPHY: J. R. Lerch, NCE 13:959–965.

[B. MARTHALER]

ECCLESIA REFORMATA SED SEMPER REFORMANDA (Lat. the Church reformed but always in need of reform), a phrase used to bring out the Church's constant need for renewal. The saying belongs in a special way to the Churches of Calvinist and Lutheran origin. Through the *reformanda* aphorism, these Churches remind themselves that even though they once carried out the 16th-cent. Reformation, they have to strive continually to improve church institutions by measuring them against the Gospel. The phrase seems to have arisen among the Huguenots and to have been adopted from them by early Dutch Pietists. Recently it has been taken up by H. Küng and applied to the RC Church. A similar wording was used by Vat II Ecum 6, "Christ summons the Church . . . to that continual reformation of which she always has need." BIBLIOGRAPHY: Y. Congar, *Vraie et fausse réforme dans l'Église* (1968); H. Küng, *Council, Reform and Reunion* (tr. C. Hastings, 1961); RGG 5:884; R. Brown, *Spirit of Protestantism* (1965) 44–49; 166–167; J. Pelikan, *Christian Tradition: A History of the Development of Doctrine* (v. 1, 1975). *REFORM AND THE CHURCH.

[P. MISNER]

ECCLESIASTES, BOOK OF, part of OT wisdom literature. The title is a Greek equivalent for the Hebrew title *Qoheleth,* the pen name of the author, meaning "leader of the assembly," i.e., teacher or preacher. The central concerns of this book (dating from *c.*250 and only by a literary convention in Ch. 1–2 ascribed to Solomon) are these: the transitory nature of all human happiness, the limitations to which all human achievements are subject; and the ultimate futility of trying to overcome these limitations, to alter the inexorable course of life in the world, or to understand God's ways. It is impossible to measure or evaluate these ways of his by any abstract norms such as the human reason is capable of evolving. Good and bad alike are advancing inexorably to the common fate of death, and who knows what lies beyond that?

The author develops these basic themes in a series of loose dialogues with himself in which he puts now one point of view, now another, until he arrives at the conclusion that the only course open to a wise man is to accept things as they are, for all the impossibility of perceiving any coherent meaning or rightness in them, and to seek such limited enjoyment as is open to him in this world, though always with prudence and moderation, while firmly upholding the ultimate justice of God and his laws. "I know that there is nothing better for them than to be happy and enjoy themselves as long as they live; also that it is God's gift to man that everyone should eat and drink and take pleasure in all his toil" (3.13).

While retaining his ultimate hold upon Jewish tradition, this author appears to have been open to some degree of foreign influence from circles in which, broadly speaking, the same problems were being discussed. Given the dialogue style of the book, there is no need to ascribe the different, and partially irreconcilable points of view presented in it to different authors. BIBLIOGRAPHY: A. Barucq, *L'Ecclésiaste* (1968); H. Ranston, *Ecclesiastes and the Early Greek Wisdom Literature* (1923); R. Gordis, *Qohelet, The Man and His World* (1951); *idem, Wisdom of Ecclesiastes* (1955); H. L. Ginsberg, *Studies in Koheleth* (1950); R. Murphy, JBC 1:534–540.

[D. J. BOURKE]

ECCLESIASTICAL COURTS, see TRIBUNALS, EC-CLESIASTICAL.

ECCLESIASTICAL DISCIPLINE, see DISCIPLINE, EC-CLESIASTICAL.

ECCLESIASTICISM, a term normally used in a derogatory sense referring to a supposed excessive devotion to the Church as an institution, to the neglect of the Church's ministry. Those who stress the needs of the world and the obligation of the Church to give both spiritual enrichment and humanitarian service use the term in criticism of churchmen who seem to them concerned primarily with increasing the worldly power of the Church in dominating society. Ecclesiasticism implies a greater regard for an institution than for persons, specifically that institution through which the churchman gains his own power and honor. Critics of ecclesiasticism have interpreted the Church as a relatively unstructured community united by spiritual ties rather than by hierarchy and law, and their opposition to established or institutional Churches has often led them to separate and form new Churches, which in turn tend to develop the features of ecclesiastical organization. Ecclesiasticism also refers to undue concern for the externals of church life and practice as expressed in formalism and ritualism to the neglect of the inner life of love and faith. The term is also used in reference to an emphasis on the role of the Church in salvation and therefore tends to be associated with *sacerdotalism and *sacramentalism; in this sense it is sometimes used in the polemics of low churchmen against high churchmen.

[T. EARLY]

ECCLESIASTICUS, title given to the book of Sirach in the Latin Church from the 3d century. The title *Liber Ecclesiasticus* (Church Book) is explained either because the Church so frequently used this book or because, unlike the Palestinian synagogues, the Church recognized it as part of the biblical canon. *SIRACH.

[T. C. O'BRIEN]

ECCLESIOLOGICAL SIGNIFICANCE OF THE WORLD COUNCIL OF CHURCHES, a statement of the Central Committee of the World Council of Churches (WCC), meeting July 9–15, 1950, in Toronto, commended for "study and comment in the churches." This title became the subtitle in the published text of the statement, "The Church, the Churches, and the WCC." Designed to clarify the WCC's view of its own nature and to correct some misinterpretations, it denied that the WCC is a super-church or that it is to be identified with the *Una Sancta,* stating that a member Church is not required to view all conceptions of the Church as equally valid. "Membership does not imply that each Church must regard the other member Churches as Churches in the true and full sense of the word." For the text and dicussion concerning

it, see *Minutes and Reports of the Third Meeting of the Central Committee.*

[T. EARLY]

ECCLESIOLOGY, the branch of theology that assembles, analyzes, systematically correlates, and proposes what is to be found in the sources of revelation with regard to the Church.

New Testament and Church Fathers. Although ecclesiology did not appear as a distinct branch of theology until the Reformation, reflections on the nature of the Church are to be found in the NT and the earliest patristic traditions. The Pauline doctrine of the mystical body of Christ, e.g., exposes a definite theological insight into the nature of salvation and the communal relationship established thereby.

Among the earliest Church Fathers (Clement of Rome, Polycarp, Ignatius of Antioch), the Church was seen as the new Israel, composed of the divinely chosen members of Christ. The distinction between the Church as visible and invisible was not yet used. Irenaeus speaks of the Church as the great body of Christ in which the Spirit works and insures its key characteristics, esp. its possession of the truth. Clement of Alexandria and Origen stress the universal reality of the Church as the gathering of all the elect ruled by the Word, even those not present in the visible society of believers. Another thought occurs in Cyprian: the Church is an indivisible visible unity, universal but gathered around the local bishop with whom the believer must maintain dogmatic and eucharistic solidarity. The doctrine of the Eastern Church, esp. after the Council of Nicaea, was contained within its Christology, that union in the life of Christ binds all Christians together.

Augustine of Hippo played an important role in the development of ecclesiology. He used the Pauline image of the Church as the mystical body of Christ, and underlined the significance of its unity of belief and charity. Augustine also distinguished between the Church's perfect essence and its imperfect embodiment. It is perfect in essence because constituted by Christ who establishes its holy people; it is imperfect in embodiment insofar as it is a visible congregation of sinners.

The Scholastic Period. The basic insights of the Fathers continued into the scholastic period, in which the Church was viewed as a union, accomplished through the Spirit's gift of love, between God and man. This union or life of grace which incorporates itself in the Church is seen as social, i.e., it establishes a lateral communion among believers as well as a relationship to the Trinity. This lateral communion is so significant that separation from the pope, as the vicar of Christ, is a schismatic separation from Christ himself.

However, the medieval canonists (James of Viterbo, Giles of Rome, John of Paris) introduced a considerably different point of view. They stressed the legal and institutional structures of the Church, minimized its communal aspects in favor of the hierarchical, and pressed for a kind of papal theocracy.

Roman Catholic Ecclesiology in the Post-Reformation Period. As a consequence of the Reformation the attention of RC theologians began to focus almost exclusively on the visible aspects of the Church. Robert Bellarmine in particular championed the Church as the kingdom of God on earth—a kingdom, however, which emphasized the qualities of a sovereign state rather than those of the biblical kingdom of God. For the next 3 cent., this was the dominant ecclesiology. At the time of Vatican I, the majority of bishops refused to call the Church the mystical body because that term was too vague and might appear to favor the notion of an invisible Church. Polemical considerations limited their view of ecclesiology to what was contained in the customary treatises *De ecclesia* and manuals of apologetics.

But a new attitude began to emerge during the 19th century. J. A. *Möhler at the Univ. of Tübingen rejected the juridic ecclesiology of an institutionalized Church, and affirmed a community of believers brought together in love by the Spirit, a community which all ecclesiastical office was designed to serve. M. Scheeben sought to arrive at an adequate concept of the Church through a synthesis of its juridic and pneumatic aspects. Accordingly, the Church is seen as a mystery in its very being, organization, and activity. It is not a work of man, but of God. The Church is like Christ whose visible human reality did not totally express the depths of his divine being.

This ecclesiological synthesis of the juridic and spiritual, continued into contemporary theology by K. Adam, H. de Lubac, É. Mersch, and S. Tromp, formed the basis for Pius XII's encyclical *Mystici corporis* (1943). The encyclical denies an asocial concept of grace as well as any dichotomy between the visible RC Church and the mystical body of Christ on earth. Vatican II's *Dogmatic Constitution on the Church* advances this basic approach and incorporates several other theological developments. The Church is presented as the pilgrim people of God, already established as a community by faith and baptism. The dignity and function of the laity are stressed, as well as the collegial relationship between the pope and the bishops of the world. More stress is also put in contemporary ecclesiology on the human reality of the Church in relation to the Church as a divine institution. The weakness and fallibility of its individual members, as well as the errors of the past are more explicitly recognized. More attention is now given to the unity of the whole Church in relation to its hierarchical structure, and also to local and regional Churches.

Ecclesiology in the Protestant Tradition. Protestantism revolted substantially against the hierarchical, juridical view of the Church that had been developed by the medieval canonists. It saw the Church as an invisible society solely dependent upon its unique mediator, Christ. The concept of hierarchical authority was repudiated and the *priesthood of all believers was affirmed in such a way as to deny any power of *orders beyond that bestowed by baptism. One consequence of this position was that it retarded the development of an ecclesiology properly so called. The insights into Christianity within the Protestant tradition do not contribute to a consideration of the Church apart from the broader issues of soteriology. The refusal to acknowledge any intermediary between God and man predisposes Protestant theology to view church structures and organization as the product of human enterprise, necessary only for good order in preaching the word and distributing the sacrament.

The reality of ''Church'' is, of course, recognized in Protestantism, but the Church is seen as the fellowship in which all the Christians of a place are united in their life and worship. As such, the Church stands in the same relationship to God as redeemed man. Its holiness is that of the pardoned sinner. Its glory is derived totally from Christ's saving action. The Church is not an institution but a brotherhood, not divinely determined in a particular type of polity or episcopal tradition. It is a community of persons seeking the Spirit's guidance to forge those forms through which the word may be effectively proclaimed. This word alone has authority.

The cardinal principle of Protestant ecclesiology is, in K. *Barth's terminology, actualism. The worship community is entirely under the influence of an always new action of the Lord who is not limited to specific sacramental rites. The essential nature of the Church stands in antithesis to all law. BIBLIOGRAPHY: S. Jàki, *Les Tendances nouvelles de l'ecclésiologie* (1957); H. Küng, *Church* (tr. R. and R. Ockenden, 1967); G. Weigel, ''Catholic Ecclesiology in Our Time,'' *Christianity Divided* (ed. D. Callahan et al., 1961); K. Rahner, *Shape of the Church to Come* (1974).

[T. M. MCFADDEN]

ECCLESTON, SAMUEL (1801–51), American bishop. A convert to Roman Catholicism (1812) while attending St. Mary's College, Baltimore, E. entered St. Mary's Seminary (1819) and was ordained in 1825. After further theological studies at Issy, France, he returned to St. Mary's College as vice-president (1827) and 2 years later became president. Named coadjutor of Baltimore he succeeded to that see in 1834. During his term of office many new churches were erected (the cathedral, funded largely by his own means, neared completion), St. Charles College opened (1849), and five provincial councils were held at Baltimore. E. brought Redemptorists from Germany to care for the German Catholics in Baltimore. The Brothers of the Christian Schools opened (1846) the Calvert Hall School in Baltimore, their first foundation in the United States.

[M. B. MONAGHAN]

ECGBERT, see EGBERT.

ÉCHARD, JACQUES (1644–1724), French Dominican bibliographer, who was given the responsibility (1698) for the uncompleted Dominican bibliography of J. *Quétif, *Scriptores Ordinis Praedicatorium* (3 v., 1719–21). The work was brought further along, up to 1750, and there is a modern revision of 13th- and 14th-cent. entries, since the work still remains a rich mine on its subject. E. was sympathetic to the Jansenists and an *appellant in 1717 against *Unigenitus. BIBLIOGRAPHY: Quétif-Échard 3:369–375.

[J. R. RIVELLO]

ECHAVE IBIA, BALTASAR DE.

ECHMIADZIN, CATHOLICATE OF. After political reasons had caused the see of the legitimate catholicos of the Armenian Church to be changed many times, it was finally (1293) located at Sis, Cilicia (Turkey). In 1441 the Armenian hierarchy assembled at Sis elected Gregory Mousapekian patriarch. However, a dissident group of bps. from N Armenia protested and would approve the election only on condition that Gregory would transfer his see to Echmiadzin. This Gregory refused to do. The dissidents then elected a catholicos of their own, with whom began the catholicate of Echmiadzin. Although its origins were canonically questionable, this catholicate grew in influence until it became recognized as the center of the Armenian (Gregorian) Church. Its catholicos is in theory the highest-ranking prelate among the Armenians. He alone is entitled to consecrate bps. and bless the holy chrism. Even Sis came to accept his authority. At times favorable relations existed between Echmiadzin and Rome. The see of Echmiadzin suffered many persecutions, esp. from the Persians, part of whose policy it was to try to detach the Armenians from their spiritual capital. After 1828 when the Russians took over, the Czar tried in vain to Russify the Armenian Church, but he did succeed in influencing the elections of the catholicos. After World War II the freedom of the Armenians was partly restored, esp. after 1945 when a Russian citizen became catholicos. He was allowed to establish his see in Echmiadzin's old monastery, where he has a seminary and a printing press. He exercises jurisdiction not only over Armenians in the Soviet Union but also over many in Europe, Persia, and America. BIBLIOGRAPHY: L. Arpee, *History of Armenian Christianity* (1946); E. F. Fortesque, *Armenian Church: Founded by Saint Gregory the Illuminator* (1872, repr. 1970).

[J. MEIJER]

ECHMIADZIN, ST. HRIPSIME, Armenian church, cube of heavy masonry (61 A.D.) with a central dome. Four arms ending in apses have niches at the angles between them. Square sacristies complete the rectangular plan.

[M. J. DALY]

ECHMIADZIN CATHEDRAL, religious center of the Armenian Church in SW Russia. (c.480). The present building (1000 A.D.) is a square central-plan with 4 niches

(*exedrae*) added to each side. There are 9 bays determined by 4 central piers supporting the dome.

[M. J. DALY]

ECHTER VON MESPELBRUNN, JULIUS (1545–1617), Counter-Reformation prince bishop of Würzburg, Germany from 1573. He established a seminary according to the Tridentine decrees, made the Jesuit college a university, built churches, and brought back 100,000 people to Catholicism, partly, it is thought, by political pressure.

[T. C. O'BRIEN]

ECHTERNACH ABBEY, Benedictine monastery located in Luxembourg, founded c.700 by St. Willibrord on the site of what had been from 689 an almshouse for monks. In the 8th cent. it was a center from which Irish-Anglo Saxon culture spread; in the 10th cent. it became part of the *Cluniac reform. The monastery was suppressed in 1797 during the French Revolution. The 11th-cent. church was damaged during World War II, but has been restored. The crypt of the Carolingian church is still intact, and the remains of the Merovingian abbey church were unearthed in 1949.

[J. R. RIVELLO]

ECHTERNACH GOSPELS (c.690 A.D.), Gospel Book written in Northumbria in very fine Anglo-Saxon majuscule script. Its decoration, including Evangelist symbols, of the highest order in the Hiberno-Saxon style, shows strong similarity to the Ardagh Chalice. The MS is now in Bibliothèque Nationale, Paris.

[R. L. S. BRUCE-MITFORD]

ECK, JOHANN (1486–1543), German theologian, RC opponent of Luther. He was born Johann Maier at Eck in Swabia, and as a student in 1505 took the surname Eckius, or Eccius. He studied law, philosophy, and theology at Heidelberg, Tübingen, Cologne, and Freiburg, and was ordained at Strassburg in 1508. Professor of theology at Ingolstadt (1510–43), he also served as dean, pro-rector, and rector. Friendly at first to Luther, he perceived in the *Ninety-Five Theses the revolutionary character of Luther's position. His annotations on 30 of the theses, which he marked with an obelisk, were circulated (1518) as *Obelischi;* Luther answered with *Asterisci.* The famous *Disputation of Leipzig (1519) began with E.'s bettering *Karlstadt in debate; when Luther himself became the disputant, E.'s tactics brought out the Reformer's attack on the doctrinal authority of Rome; it was a decisive stage in Luther's break with the old Church. E. went to Rome, where he was charged with publishing in Germany the bull excommunicating Luther, *Exsurge Domine* (1520), which he had helped to draft. He also was a coauthor of the *Confutatio,* the RC reply to the *Augsburg Confession (1530), and was generally regarded as the chief RC spokesman against the doctrine of the Reformers. His more than 100 works, most of them in Latin, include *Enchiridion locorum communium adversus Lutheranos* (1525), which went into 90 editions. BIBLIOGRAPHY: R. Fife, *Revolt of Martin Luther* (1957) 327–394.

[M. J. SUELZER]

ECKART, ANSELM VON (1721–1809), German Jesuit victim of anti-Jesuit persecution in the era of the suppression of the society. Sent as a missionary to Brazil in 1753, he with his companions was arrested in 1759 by order of the Portuguese minister S. *Pombal, sent back to Lisbon in chains, and there imprisoned for 18 years. On release he resumed his Jesuit life in Poland where the bull suppressing the society had been barred from promulgation. E.'s memoirs of persecution and imprisonment were published.

[T. C. O'BRIEN]

ECKBERT OF SCHÖNAU (*c.* 1130–84), Benedictine abbot and theologian. After studies in Paris, E. became a canon at Bonn and in 1155 entered the Abbey of Schönau. Rainald, abp. of Cologne, selected him to debate the doctrines of the Cathari. E.'s *Sermones contra Catharos* are considered an effective refutation of the heresy, which he continued to attack even after his election as abbot of Schönau. His writings include *Stimulus amoris* (attributed to Bernard of Clairvaux and to Anselm of Canterbury); *Soliloquium seu meditationes* (also attributed to Anselm); and an account of the revelations of his sister Elizabeth of Schönau. BIBLIOGRAPHY: B. J. Comaskey, NCE 5:38.

[M. J. FINNEGAN]

ECKHART, JOHANN GEORG VON (1664–1730), German scholar, historian. He held a professorship at Helmstedt before entering the service of the royal house of Hanover, 1714–23. He then left for Cologne, where he became a Catholic. He served as archivist for the prince bishop of Würzburg, wrote a history of that see, as well as a *Corpus historicum medii aevi* (2 v., 1723) and other works.

[T. C. O'BRIEN]

ECKHART, MEISTER (*c.* 1260–1327 or 1328), Dominican theologian and mystic. A native of Thuringia, E. became a Dominican at Erfurt, was at Paris in 1277 studying the arts, and before 1280 began to study theology at Cologne. At Paris during 1293–94 he commented on the Sentences of Peter Lombard. He held office as prior of Erfurt (1294–*c.* 1300), and as vicar provincial of Thuringia (1294–98). At this time he published the ascetical instructions he had given to the young friars at Erfurt as *Reden der Unterscheidung.* He graduated as master of theology and lectured as regent at Paris (1302–03). He served (1303–11) as provincial of the Dominican province of Saxony and was appointed (1307) vicar general of the province of Bohemia. He held (1311–13) a second regency in theology at Paris. His *Quaestiones Parisienses* and commentaries on the Scriptures derive from his two regencies. He lectured (1313–22) in theology at Strassburg, where he became active as a preacher and spiritual director. He also served as vicar of the Dominican nuns in Alsace and Switzerland. At Strassburg he wrote two German works, *Das Buch der göttlichen Tröstung* and *Von dem edeln Menschen* (together called the *Liber benedictus*), and began an encyclopedic *Opus tripartitum* that would have dealt with a wide range of philosophical, theological, and biblical subjects.

E. ran into serious difficulties about his doctrine when the Abp. of Cologne initiated a process against him, based on two sets of propositions extracted chiefly from his sermons. Eckhart defended himself vigorously, esp. in a "Justificative Report," and contested the jurisdiction of the Cologne tribunal. Submitting in advance to the ultimate decision and protesting his faith, he appealed to the Pope, Jan. 1327. Hoping to defend himself personally, he set out for Avignon, but died before the case was concluded. On Mar. 27, 1328, John XXII condemned 28 of his propositions according to their obvious sense: 17 as heretical or erroneous, and 11 as unobjectionable if properly explained. E. had no heretical intent. His difficulties were caused by the abstruse nature of the matter he dealt with, his not-always-careful phraseology, his use of a developing vernacular, and his clash with the Franciscans and the partisans of Louis of Bavaria. He also suffered from the suspicions directed toward various heterodox groups. The Cologne and Avignon processes can be criticized for not checking propositions taken from E's sermons against his formal writings. Yet it is hard to defend the condemned propositions, and nearly all of them occur in his writings.

E. drew his teaching from many sources as well as from his own experience. His mysticism, speculative in character, was trinitarian and transcendental. He taught the absolute transcendence and unknowability of God, and total detachment in order to find the unity and image of God. He sought to verbalize the interior spiritual process by which a person, through a radical self-stripping, achieves union with God in the inmost depth of the soul. Though Eckhart's works were seldom copied after his condemnation, his teaching survived indirectly through such writers as John Tauler, Henry Suso, Jan van Ruysbroeck, and others in Germany, Switzerland, and the Low Countries. Editions: *Die deutschen und lateinische Werke* (ed. Deutsche Forschungsgemeinschaft, 1936); Latin works (ed. J. Koch et al., v. 1, 1964; v. 4, 1956; v. 5–6, in progress; German works (ed. J. Quint, v. 1, 1958; v. 2, 1971; v. 3, 1976; v. 5, 1963; v. 4 in progress); *Meister Eckhart: An Introduction to the Study of His Works with an Anthology of His Sermons* (ed. and tr. J. M. Clark, 1957); *Meister Eckhart, Selected Treatises and Sermons . . . from Latin and German* (ed. and tr. J. M. Clark and J. V. Skinner, 1958); *Meister Eckhart: A Modern Translation* (ed. and tr. R. B. Blakney, 1941; pa 1957). BIBLIOGRAPHY: J. M. Clark, *Great German Mystics* (1949); J. Ancelet-Hustache, *Meister Eckhart and the Rhineland Mystics* (tr. H. Graef, 1958).

[W. A. HINNEBUSCH]

ECKHEL, JOSEPH HILARIUS VON (1737–98), Austrian Jesuit historian and numismatist. When his career was brought to a premature end by illness, E. began the systematic study of archeology and numismatics. After the suppression of the Jesuits in 1773, he was made director of the numismatic section of the Imperial Museum at Vienna and 3 years later a professor at the University. His *Doctrina nummorum veterum* (8 v., 1792–98) is considered the pioneering work in the science of numismatics. BIBLIOGRAPHY: F. de Sa, NCE 5:40.

[R. B. ENO]

ECLECTICISM, a term used in Greco-Roman philosophy to indicate the practice of selecting elements from different philosophical schools or systems. *Carneades, the founder of the New Academy, already revealed eclectic tendencies, esp. in ethics, but eclecticism became a typical feature of ancient philosophy only from the end of 2d cent. B.C. Antiochus of Ascalon (fl. early 1st cent. B.C.), an Academic and a teacher of Cicero (in 79–78), did not hesitate to declare that there was no essential difference between the old teachings of the Academy, Peripatetics, and Stoics. *Panaetius and *Posidonius, the founders of Middle Stoicism, incorporated important Platonic and Aristotelian elements into their systems, and the later Aristotelianism, Neopythagoreanism, and esp. Neoplatonism exhibit a marked adoption and fusion of doctrines taken from earlier or contemporary schools. Individuals, as well as schools, are frequently characterized as eclectic, as, for example, Cicero, who took his epistemology largely from the New Academy and his ethics chiefly from the Stoics. Potamon of Alexandria (late 1st cent. B.C.) founded an Eclectic School as such, but it had little influence and soon disappeared. BIBLIOGRAPHY: Copleston 1:421 ff. and 442; S. Sambursky, LexAW 795; Ueberweg 1:32, 34, 410, 486, 565.

[M. R. P. MCGUIRE]

ÉCOLE BIBLIQUE (École Pratique d'Études Bibliques), school of advanced biblical studies, opened by M. J. *Lagrange in 1890 at Jerusalem on the site of the martyrdom of St. Stephen. From the first the school, staffed by French and Canadian Dominicans, has been characterized by its policy of bold and positive employment of all resources of modern science in investigating the literal meaning of the Scriptures and exploring all aspects of their historical and geographical background. The findings of the professors and others as recorded in the *Revue Biblique,* and also in the great series of commentaries and studies known as the *Études Bibliques,* have consistently demonstrated the soundness and orthodoxy of this approach. The school is famous for its contributions not only in the fields of biblical history and exegesis, but also in those of biblical anthropology, geography, and above all archeology. Numerous large-scale excavations have been conducted, the most famous of which is that of the sectarian settlement of *Qumran. In 1920 the French government formally recognized the school under the title *École Française*

Archéologique de Jérusalem. Among the professors of the school have been F.-M. *Abel, P.*Benoit, L.-H. *Vincent, and R. de *Vaux. BIBLIOGRAPHY: F.-M. Braun, *Work of Père Lagrange* (tr. R. T. A. Murphy, 1963).

[D. J. BOURKE]

ECOLOGY, in the primary sense the science of how organisms relate to their environment; but in ethical discussion the term is used particularly in relationship to questions of human responsibility for care of the material universe. A marked increase in public attention to these questions has been a notable feature of the 1970s. In the wake of growing concern over damage to the environment and the danger of future damage on a still greater scale, religious leaders have given increased attention to the theological basis for ecological responsibility. Some critics assert that biblical teaching regarding the dominion of man over creation (Gen 1.26–28) has contributed to abuse of the created order. And they have charged theologians with giving too uncritical support as man has sought to ''subdue'' the world. The human drive to master nature has been welcomed as it advanced medical care, reduced oppressive labor, and widened human opportunity. But to some degree attitudes have reversed with the spreading awareness of environmental pollution, the threat of nuclear destruction, and the dehumanizing effect of unlimited technology applied to the human person. Other interpreters contend that the Bible offers strong support for ecological concerns. The Genesis creation account includes the affirmation that God looked on everything he had made and pronounced it ''very good'' (1.31). The teaching that the earth is a product of divine creation carries the implication that man does not own it but stands in the relationship of steward or caretaker (Gen 2.15). The biblical doctrine of creation also makes man a part of the created order, a being formed out of the dust of the ground, and one who will return to dust. Man's spirit makes him something more than dust, but he nonetheless remains a creature. In the Christian doctrine of Incarnation, a new emphasis on the importance of the physical and earthly is given. God reveals himself within the earthly context and through a child born of woman. The eucharistic elements of bread and wine also tie Christian faith to the physical world. And Christian eschatology envisions a redeemed creation (Rom 8.21; Rev. 21.1). Some writers emphasize the need for considering ecology in connection with the issues of *social justice. Otherwise, they warn, privileged groups will promote environmental preservation in a way that leaves oppressed groups in poverty. God's lordship over the creation is interpreted to mean not only that man has a responsibility of stewardship but also that the creation should be so maintained as to serve the needs of all. The ecology issue has reopened many traditional theological questions from a new perspective—relation of man to nature, desacralization of nature, sacramentalism, acceptance of poverty as a way of life, etc. BIBLIOGRAPHY: T. Derr, *Ecology and Human Need* (1975).

[T. EARLY]

ÉCONOME (Gr. *oikonomos*, manager), in canon law the person entrusted with the management of finances in an ecclesiastical institution; in English usually called a bursar, treasurer, or procurator. Such an official must be appointed, e.g., in seminaries (CIC, *c.* 1358); in religious houses *the économe* must be someone other than the superior (*ibid.*, c. 516, nn. 2 and 3). The Oriental Code of Canon Law restored the ancient office of diocesan *oikonomos*, but the same office does not exist in the Latin Church.

[R. ARONSTAM]

ECONOMIC JUSTICE, that form of *social justice necessary because economic factors have a major impact on human social relationships. Papal social encyclicals, *Rerum novarum, Quadragesimo anno, Mater et magistra, Pacem in terris,* have sought to remedy social abuses arising both from the classic economic theories that chartered unrestrained capitalism, and the totalitarian control of economics and people practiced in the name of Marxism. Pius XI gave the term social justice its final and definitive acceptance in Catholic moral theology and social philosophy. Social justice requires the respect of those governing and those governed in a human society for the common good. This consists in the complex of benefits that the individual cannot achieve on his own, that is therefore the reason human society exists, and that makes possible for the members a proportionate share in the greatest possible good. A major element in this common good is the availability and fair distribution of the material goods necessary for life, and one in keeping with human dignity. Economic justice, then, is an essential function of social justice, and means the positive will of all involved in the economic process to respect the requirements of the common good in its economic aspects. A malaise between the concept of economics in its historical connotations, beginning with Adam Smith, and of justice must be acknowledged. The theories from which European and American economic processes have developed are theories of self-interest and profit that exclude or at best treat as a by-product equitable distribution of economic goods. There is nothing in the meaning of economics, however, that excludes justice (see ECONOMICS). A theory of economic justice does not pretend to be a theory of economics. A sound moral philosophy or theology accepts the necessity and relative autonomy of economic systems, the validity of economic analysis carried out on the basis of its own principles and leading to its proper conclusions about the effective administration of limited economic goods—natural resources, capital, labor. But a system or science of economics does not deal in absolutes: it must look to an extrinsic norm, an ethical norm, so that economic policy, formulated by either the private or the public sector, accepts the common good as a measure. Social legislation and the power of labor unions have achieved a de facto measure of justice in economic life. But the meaning of economic justice requires more than mere legal imposition of economic reforms; and more than the effectiveness of unions as private, vested interests; more, too, than confidence in the absoluteness of the law of supply and demand, or the salvific power of competition. Economic justice is the positive will to respect the contributions of all and the rightful share of all in the economic benefits included in the common good. "It is impossible for one man to enjoy extreme wealth without someone else suffering extreme want" (ThAq ST 2a2ae, 118.1 ad 2).

[T. C. O'BRIEN]

ECONOMICS, the art and sciences governing the exploitation of material resources for the proportionate benefit of both producers and consumers and of regulating distribution and the means of exchange. From the Gr. *oikonomia*, household management (a household meant a much more considerable establishment than the present family of a couple and their children), hence the treatise attributed to Aristotle, the *Economics*. The term had been widened by the 19th cent. to what was called Political Economy, and is now known simply as Economics. It contains many and conflicting schools of thought. As such it should be as morally neutral as the method of running a transport system or planning the drains; in fact, however, its implications in matters of *social justice are always immediate, for rights and duties are always involved in ownership, and not rarely urgent, for *homo economicus* becomes a victimizer or a victim, more often the latter, if he is taken as comprehending the entire individual subject to allegedly iron laws of supply and demand, and not as a useful myth or scientific abstraction. It is here that Christian philosophy takes a stand, and calls for the subordination of economics to ethics. BIBLIOGRAPHY: O. H. Taylor, *History of Economic Thought*, 1960.

[T. GILBY]

ECONOMY, DIVINE (Gr, *oikonomia*; Eph 3.9, cf. 1 Cor 2.7–8), the eternal and intellectual plan of the triadic God concerning the order of nature and of grace, which is revealed and executed by his acts of creation (theological and cosmological aspects), sanctification and divinization by the Holy Spirit (pneumatological aspect), self-revelation through the history of salvation (historical and ecclesiological aspects), and consummation, i.e., final and eternal fulfillment through a participation in his inner life and love (eschatological aspect). Strictly speaking the divine economy denotes the economy of salvation in which the fruits of Redemption are applied by God as the primary cause and through the creatures as secondary agents (e.g., Church, priest, sacrament). Essentially it is the mystery of Christ, the only mediator between God and the extradivine reality. Oriental Christianity understands *oikonomia* of the Church as a benign application of its canonical power. BIBLIOGRAPHY: M. R. E. Mastermann, NCE 5:86; W. Koester and J. Ratzinger, LTK 5: 76–80; R. Schnackenburg et al., *ibid.* 5:148–157; K. Rahner, *ibid.* 5:165–168.

[P. B. T. BILANIUK]

ECSTASY (IN THE BIBLE), a word of Greek origin meaning a displacement. Biblically, it refers to a psychic displacement by which someone is so controlled by the spirit of God that his mental faculties and some normal functions are held wholly or partly in suspension because of an intense emotional or mystical experience that absorbs all consciousness. B. Anderson states that ecstasy arises, not from mere emotional rapture, but from the spirit of Yahweh which falls upon a person, takes control of the center of the self, and makes him an instrument of the divine will. Some OT ecstatic prophets used musical instruments, singing, and dancing in liturgical rhythm to induce a trance-like state through natural means (1 Sam 10.5); Elisha (2 Kg 3.15) speaks about the employment of minstrels. In Is 28.7 false prophets are accused of using intoxicants to cause ecstasy. Not all ecstasy in the OT was brought about by natural means. Just as covenant, law, and kingship had their beginnings outside of Israel and acquired a spiritual aspect in Israel because they were used as instruments for the revelation of God's will, so too, prophetic ecstasies were often granted directly through divine influence without the use of any natural means to produce them as in the inaugural visions of isaiah, Jeremiah, and Ezekiel (Is 6.1–13; Jer 2.2–9; Ezek ch. 1. and 2), and in the visions of Amos (7.1–9; 8.1–3; 9.1–8). "Ecstasy" in the OT is often used to express that the spirit of the Lord came upon someone (Num 11.25; 24.2, 1 Sam 10.6; 19.20, 2 Kgs 3.15, Ezek 3.14; 11.24), or that one was "led forth" by the spirit (Ezek 11.24; 37.1).

Only ecstasies granted directly by God are mentioned in the NT, as with the prayer of St. Peter at Joppa (Acts 10.10; 11.5) and of St. Paul (Acts 22.17). The gift of *tongues as a type of ecstatic prayer is noted also in Acts 2.1–13; 10.44–46; 1 Cor 14.1–33. BIBLIOGRAPHY: B. Anderson, *Understanding the OT Testament* (1966) 191.

[A. P. HANLON]

ECSTASY (IN CHRISTIAN MYSTICISM), a temporary alienation from the senses and a detachment from the sensible world as a result of a person's intimate union with God. It admits of two types: prophetic ecstasy, which is a charism or *gratia gratis data* which accompanies an illumination of the intellect by God with a view to transmitting a message to others, and mystical or contemplative ecstasy, which is a phenomenon concomitant to the prayer of ecstatic union, a degree of infused contemplation. In both types of ecstasy, the reason for the alienation of the senses, (as it is usually exlained) is the same, namely, the illumination from God, affecting the intellect and will, is of such intensity that the physical powers and external senses are too weak to withstand it. If the mystic passes on to the higher prayers of nion in the contemplative state, ecstasy disappears as a concomitant phenomenon because the passive purgation of the senses has made it possible for the physical powers to respond to the divine operations. Ecstasy admits of varying degrees of alienation: suspension of the external senses alone, suspension of the external and inter-

nal senses, and total suspension of all powers in the direct contemplation of the divine essence (cf. ThAq ST 2a2ae, 175. 3 ad 1). According to St. Teresa of Avila, gentle and delightful ecstasy is called simple; the violent and painful variety is flight of the spirit or rapture (cf. St. Teresa, *Interior Castle,* ch. 4–6). Ecstasy produces definite effects on the body and soul of the recipient. The principal bodily effects are insensibility to all external stimuli, lessening of the heat of the body, retardation of bodily function, immobility of the body, and sometimes levitation. The effect on the soul of the ecstatic is that it receives a new energy for the works of virtue, sometimes to the point of heroism (cf. St. Francis de Sales, *Treatise on the Love of God,* 8.6). BIBLIOGRAPHY: St. Teresa of Avila, *Life,* (tr. E. Allison Peers, 1946); *Interior Castle* (tr. E. Allison Peers, 1946); St. John of the Cross, *Dark Night* (tr. E. Allison Peers, 1953); J. G. Arintero, *Mystical Evolution in the Development and Vitality of the Church* (tr. J. Aumann, 2 v., 1949–51); A. F. Poulain, *Graces of Interior Prayer* (tr. L. L. Yorke Smith, 1950); A. L. Saudreau, *Degrees of The Spiritual Life* (tr. B. Camm, 2 v., 1907); J. Maréchal, *Studies in the Psychology of the Mystics* (tr. A. Thorold, 1927); A. Royo, *Theology of Christian Perfection* (tr. and ed. J. Aumann, 1962); R. Omez, *Psychical Phenomena* (tr. R. Haynes, 1958).

[J. AUMANN]

ECSTATIC UNION, a state of alienation from the senses and all external stimuli produced by the intimacy of a soul's union with God. As a concomitant phenomenon of the prayer of union, ecstatic union is truly mystical; as a type of contemplative prayer, it is also known as the conforming union or the spiritual espousal. BIBLIOGRAPHY: A. Royo, *Theology of Christian Perfection* (tr. and ed. J. Aumann, 1962); J. G. Arintero, *Mystical Evolution in the Development and Vitality of the Church* (tr. J. Aumann, 2 v., 1949–51); idem, *Stages in Prayer* (tr. K. Pond, 1957); Card. Lercaro, *Practice of Mental Prayer* (tr. T. F. Lindsay, 1957).

[J. AUMANN]

ECTENE, in the Eastern Church a litany-like prayer of the liturgy. It is made up of short petitions answered by the congregation with "Kyrie eleison."

ECTHESIS, a term used esp. to designate the symbol of faith issued by the Byzantine Emperor Heraclius (610–641). It was actually drawn up by the Patriarch Sergius of Constantinople in 638, and was definitely Monothelite in character. It was soon condemned by Pope John IV (640–642). After much opposition, it was rescinded by the Emperor Constans II (641–668) and replaced in 648 by the *Typus* prepared with the advice of the Patriarch Paul of Constantinople. BIBLIOGRAPHY: P. Stephanov, LTK 3:791–792; Fliche-Martin 4:131–134.

[M. R. P. MCGUIRE]

ECTOPIC PREGNANCY, one that is abnormal, life threatening, and so poses the moral issue of indirect *abortion. Termed "ectopic" because outside (Gr. *ek*) the normal place *(topos)*, the womb, such a pregnancy is usually tubal, but may be one described as secondary abdominal, ovarian, or cervical. Each may be life threatening in varying degrees, to be determined medically. The moral rightness of surgical intervention to save the mother from bleeding or other pathological conditions, even though loss of the fetus may be an attendant side effect, is determined on the basis of the moral principle of *double effect. For moral views that hold abortion to be a woman's absolute, personal right no special moral dilemma arises regarding any pregnancy, normal or abnormal. BIBLIOGRAPHY: T. J. O'Donnell, *Morals and Medicine* (1959); *idem*, NCE 5:88–89.

[T. C. O'BRIEN]

ECUADOR, predominantly Catholic republic of NW South America. The population is mostly Indian or mestizo, with only a minority of European descent. The first Europeans entered Ecuador, then under Inca rule, with Pizarro en route to conquer Peru. His lieutenant, Benalcazar, took Ecuador in 1533. The ancient Indian capital of Quito, which became the Spanish administrative center, gave its name to the region till 1830. Franciscans accompanied the conquerors and began evangelization, aided later by other religious orders. Outstanding churches were built in Quito, a bishopric from 1545, and the city became a center of religious art, noted for its paintings and polychrome wood sculpture. Bolívar's victory in 1822 ended Spanish rule, though Ecuador was under Colombia until 1830. Church-State relations became a persistent issue in the newly independent country. President G. Garcia Morena (1861–65; 1869–75) gave the Catholic Church a dominant position in education and civil affairs, and under an 1869 constitution only Catholics could be full citizens. In reaction, separation of Church and State was decreed in 1906, and relations with the Vatican broken until 1937.

[T. EARLY]

ECUMENICAL COUNCILS (EASTERN THEORIES), see PHOTIAN SYNOD OF 879–880.

ECUMENICAL COUNCILS (Gr. *oikoumenē,* the whole inhabited world), councils that represent the whole Church in doctrinal or disciplinary matters of common concern. The dogmatic Constitution on the Church *Lumen Gentium,* issued by Vatican Council II, says, "A council is never ecumenical unless it is confirmed or at least accepted as such by the successor of Peter. It is the prerogative of the Roman Pontiff to convoke these councils, to preside over them, and to confirm them" (Vat II ConstCh 22). Papal confirmation may be *post factum,* because there have been ecumenical councils not convoked by the Pope (e.g., Nicaea) and not presided over by him (e.g., Constance).

Although there is no official listing of ecumenical councils, all Churches in the East and West recognize seven: Nicaea (A.D. 325); Constantinople I (381); Ephesus (431); Chalcedon (451); Constantinople II (553); Constantinople III (680–681); and Nicaea II (787). Contemporary RC authors generally list another 14: Constantinople IV (869–870); Lateran I (1123); Lateran II (1139); Lateran III (1179); Lateran IV (1215); Lyons I (1245); Lyons II (1274); Vienne (1311–12); Constance (1414–18); Ferrara-Florence (1438–39); Lateran V (1512–17); Trent (1545–63); Vatican I (1869–70); and Vatican II (1962–66). This list, exclusive of the two Vatican councils, seems to have been popularized by Caesar *Baronius late in the 16th century. Even RC scholars have serious reservations about the ecumenicity of some: Constantinople IV was first counted as ecumenical by the canonists of Pope Gregory VII (1073–85). The first three Lateran councils (1123, 1139 and 1179) are more properly called "general councils"; they came to be considered ecumenical only in the late Middle Ages, even though their organizers did not recognize them as such.

Historians and canonists have until recently said more about ecumenical councils than theologians. With the modern evolution of ecclesiology, dogmatic questions about the nature of ecumenical councils have attracted attention. According to Hans Küng, the Church itself is an ecumenical council of divine convocation; the historical councils, of human convocation, are representations of the Church. As a corollary, Küng also questions the exclusively episcopal make-up of modern councils. Another view, enunciated by Joseph Ratzinger, Hubert Jedin, and others, holds that the council represents only one particular aspect of the Church. Its structure is determined more by the constitution of the episcopal college than by the membership of the Church. Karl Rahner attempts to synthesize the views of Küng and Ratzinger. In summary—and this holds for Protestant views as well—it seems that any conciliar theory is determined by an ecclesiology. BIBLIOGRAPHY: F. Dvornik, *Ecumenical Councils* (1961); H. Jedin, *Ecumenical Councils of the Catholic Church* (1959); G. Baum, "Nature of Ecumenical Councils," *Ecumerist* (Oct., 1962) 4–6.

[B. L. MARTHALER]

ECUMENICAL CREEDS, *creeds so called because of universal or widespread acceptance or use. The *Nicene, *Athanasian, and *Apostles' Creeds have received this designation. Only the Nicene (Niceno-Constantinopolitan) Creed can be called ecumenical in the full sense, since it has been professed and used liturgically in both East and West. The RC Church has employed the three creeds in teaching and liturgy. The Reformation Churches for the most part have accorded recognition to these creeds, but the Apostles' Creed has had widest use. The Lutheran Churches (in the *Formula of Concord) and the C of E (in the *Thirty-Nine Articles) have explicitly adopted the three as doctrinal standards; the Protestant Episcopal Church omitted the

Athanasian Creed from its adaptation of the Articles and the Book of Common Prayer. Those who designate these creeds as ecumenical regard them as a possible basis for Christian unity. The epithet "ecumenical," however, is not acceptable to all, not even to some who acknowledge the creeds in question.

[F. E. MASER]

ECUMENICAL MOVEMENT, the process toward a greater expression of unity and cooperation among all Christians. "The 'ecumenical movement' means those activities and enterprises which, according to various needs of the Church and opportune occasions, are started and organized for the fostering of unity among Christians" (Vat II Ecum 4). By extension the phrase is also applied to efforts toward greater understanding and cooperation between Christians and persons of other religions.

Development. The 1910 *Edinburgh Conference is generally taken to mark the beginning of the movement in its modern form. At this conference representatives of 159 missionary societies agreed that the historically rooted denominational divisions of Europe and N America were generally irrelevant to the missionary task and that competitive *denominationalism was harmful. Remote antecedents of the movement include attempts to heal the schism between East and West, as in the Councils of Lyons (1274) and Florence (1439), and various unity efforts following the Reformation. In the 19th cent., prior to Edinburgh, many unity efforts had been made. In 1846 the *Evangelical Alliance was formed in London. Ecumenical cooperation in mission work had existed since the organization of the *London Missionary Society (1795). Some confessional bodies had created worldwide organizations: Lambeth Conference (1867), Alliance of Reformed Churches (1875), World Methodist Council (1891), Baptist World Alliance (1905), and others. Organizations such as the YMCA (1844) provided for ecumenical cooperation in particular projects.

Ecumenical, from the Greek *oikoumenē,* literally has a geographical reference: that which pertains to the whole inhabited world. Thus, church councils regarded as authoritative for the whole world (beginning with Nicaea I in 325) were called ecumenical councils. During World Wars I and II ecumenical leaders emphasized this aspect in the desire to transcend the national divisions of wartime. Also they have emphasized that the ecumenical nature of the Church requires a missionary concern for the whole world. Since, however, Christians of different nations sometimes have such differences that they are not in communion with each other, and since Christians within a particular nation are often divided among various denominations, the movement has involved interconfessional as well as international relationships. Following Edinburgh the movement developed along three lines, marked particularly by international conferences. The *Life and Work movement, seeking practical cooperation of the Churches for a stronger

witness in the secular order, held the Stockholm (1925) and Oxford (1937) Conferences. The slogan for Life and Work was "doctrine divides, service unites." The expression "ecumenical movement" is thought to have been first used by A. Deissmann in an address concluding the Stockholm Conference. Abp. N. *Söderblom was a key leader in this movement. A second line of development was the *Faith and Order movement, designed to discuss the doctrinal divisions that Life and Work minimized. Faith and Order met at the Lausanne (1927) and Edinburgh (1937) Conferences; Bp. C. H. *Brent was a leader in this movement. Participants in the two movements, often the same persons, came to feel that the two could not properly be separated. At the Oxford and Edinburgh Conferences (1937) plans were laid that led to merger, and to formation of the World Council of Churches (WCC) at the Amsterdam Assembly (1948). A third line of development was through the *International Missionary Council (IMC), organized in 1921, which sponsored a series of ecumenical conferences on missions: Jerusalem (1928), Madras (1938), Whitby (1947), Willingen (1952), and Accra (1957). In 1961 the IMC merged with the WCC at the New Delhi Assembly, bringing together two major concerns of the ecumenical movement: unity of all Churches of the world and mission to all people of the world. While this development was taking place on the international level, corresponding ecumenical efforts were made on national, regional, and local levels. Biblical and theological scholarship was becoming more ecumenical, and the Christian youth movement was developing along ecumenical lines. Also, members of different confessions were brought together by their common efforts to resist Nazism and to build a better world order.

Roman Catholic Participation. The RC Church did not participate in the ecumenical movement in the beginning, although some of its members worked along similar lines. Catholics in Germany participated in Una Sancta following World War I; the Malines Conversations between RCs and Anglicans were held (1921–26), and in the U.S. Fr. Paul (Lewis T. Wattson) of the Society of the Atonement founded the Week of Prayer for Christian Unity. After the Stockholm and Lausanne Conferences, however, Pius XI declared in 1928, "The Apostolic See can by no means take part in these assemblies nor is it in any way lawful for Catholics to give such enterprises their encouragement and support. If they did so, they would be giving countenance to a false Christianity quite alien to the one Church of Christ" (*Mortalium Animos*). Catholics were invited to attend the 1948 Amsterdam Assembly, but they were forbidden by the Holy Office (now Congregation for the Doctrine of the Faith) in the *monitum, Cum compertum,* issued June 5, 1948. In 1949, however, the Holy Office issued the Instruction *Ecclesia Catholica,* which gave recognition to the movement and set guidelines for Catholic participation under certain restricted conditions. The way for greater Catholic participation was opened with the establishment by Fr. J. G. M. Willebrands in 1952 of the Catholic Conference for Ecumenical Problems, and involvement progressed rapidly during the pontificate of John XXIII. When Pope John called for an ecumenical council, he took account of both senses of the term. It was an ecumenical council of the RC Church in that it was constituted by the hierarchy from all parts of the world, but observers from other Churches were invited to attend, giving it also a character to some degree ecumenical in the interconfessional sense, though only Catholics were full participants. Also, under Pope John RC observers first attended a WCC assembly (New Delhi, 1961). Through the efforts of John XXIII and Paul VI and the actions of Vatican II (1962–65) the ecumenical movement received full RC acceptance. The Secretariat for Promoting Christian Unity was established in 1960 and prepared the Decree on Ecumenism adopted by Vatican Council II in 1964. The decree stated, "This sacred Synod, therefore, exhorts all the Catholic faithful to recognize the signs of the times and to participate skillfully in the work of ecumenism" (4). It also acknowledged that divisions between Catholics and non-Catholics have been caused by faults on both sides. While in Rome for the Council, the bps. of the U.S. established a Commission for Ecumenical Affairs, which has its headquarters in Washington, D.C.

Ecumenical Leadership. Leaders of the ecumenical movement have sought to overcome the divisions caused by doctrinal differences without falling into *indifferentism. They have sought doctrinal unity through emphasis on biblical categories and terminology and through *interfaith dialogue to overcome misunderstandings. They have also sought to develop a greater sense of unity through cooperative work in missions, evangelism, and humanitarian service. The ecumenical movement as expressed in the WCC has involved most of the Protestant and Orthodox Churches of the world, though some conservative groups have chosen not to participate. These have feared that participation would result in compromise of doctrinal conviction and that the movement might result in a centralized, authoritarian organization that would endanger freedom. In the U.S. the Lutheran Church—Missouri Synod, and several smaller conservative bodies have refused to participate. Liberal groups, such as Unitarians, have also remained outside the WCC, because they do not meet its membership requirement of belief in Jesus Christ as God and Savior. Among conservatives the movement has found some expression apart from the WCC. These conservatives, while approving ecumenical cooperation, have objected to the WCC because it includes some groups they consider unorthodox and because they object to positions taken by WCC leadership on various social questions. Some conservatives support ecumenical activity that involves closer cooperation with other conservatives but with no goal of organic union. Some favor ecumenical cooperation with all Christians on such limited projects as evangelistic campaigns and Bible distribution. Some conservatives have organized the World Evangelical Fellowship (1951); the *International Council of Christian Churches has been organized (1948) under the leadership of Carl McIntire.

The ecumenical movement has been expressed also in a number of denominational mergers, including the United Church of Canada (1925), the Church of South India (1947), and in the U.S. the United Church of Christ (1957) and the United Methodist Church (1968). In 1960 E. C. Blake, then stated clerk of the United Presbyterian Church and later general secretary of the WCC, proposed a merger of certain of the main Churches of U.S. Protestantism; this proposal led to the *Consultation on Church Union which, if successful, would mean a historic step toward Christian unity.

Motivation. The ecumenical movement has been motivated in part by the increasing difficulties felt by the Churches in witnessing to the modern world. It is believed that a united Church would make a stronger impact, witnessing to the power of Christ to overcome the divisions among men and bringing a unity of effort to bear on the problems involved in preaching the gospel under modern conditions. The movement has given special emphasis to the words of Jesus' prayer: "that they may all be one; even as thou, Father, art in me, and I in thee, that they also may be in us, so that the world may believe that thou hast sent me" (Jn 17.21). The movement has recognized that Christian divisions are caused not only by doctrinal disagreement but also by differences of nationality, race, culture, social class, and institutional loyalty. To overcome these factors it stresses fraternal charity, sometimes called the ecumenical spirit. Leaders of the ecumenical movement have also stressed the importance of Church renewal, of *aggiornamento. They have taught that the need of the Church is not merely for organizational unity but for an inward renewal of the life of all Churches that would make them more effective in their service of Christ. The goal is for each Church to gain greater unity with Christ and thereby to grow toward greater unity with other Churches.

BIBLIOGRAPHY: G. Baum, *Catholic Quest for Christian Unity* (1965); *Documents on Christian Unity* (ed. G. K. Bell, 4 v., 1924–58); R. M. Brown, *Ecumenical Revolution* (1967); B. Leeming, *Vatican Council and Christian Unity* (1966); J. Mackay, *Ecumenics* (1964); J. T. McNeill, *Unitive Protestanism* (1930); N. Goodall, *Ecumenical Progress: A Decade of Change 1961–1971* (1972); Reports of WCC Assemblies (ed. W. A. Visser 't Hooft); "Decree on Ecumenism," *Documents of Vatican II* (ed. W. M. Abbott, 1966).

[T. EARLY]

ECUMENICAL PATRIARCH, a title of the Greek Orthodox patriarch of Constantinople, first used by Patriarch *John the Faster in 588, over the objections of Popes Pelagius II and Gregory I the Great—thereafter a point of conflict between East and West. In the East the title was first defended as meaning only that the patriarch of Constantinople had jurisdiction throughout the whole Byzantine Empire (see EASTERN SCHISM); the popes objected to it as implying an encroachment on Rome's universal primacy.

The meetings and exchanges between Popes *John XXIII and *Paul VI with Patriarch Athenagoras I were hopeful signs of ending hostility; the mutual disowning, at the end of Vatican Council II, Dec. 7, 1965, of past recriminations was esp. important.

[T. C. O'BRIEN]

ECUMENISM, concern for the realization of greater unity among Christians. By extension the term is sometimes used in reference to closer relationships between Christians and persons of other religions. It is distinguished from *evangelism and *proselytism in whch one communion tries to win converts from another. In the 20th cent. the historic interest of Christians in unity has received renewed impetus, as is seen in the ecumenical movement leading to such developments as the World Council of Churches and the unity efforts of Vatican Council II. Ecumenism stresses Jesus' prayer: "that they may all be one; even as thou, Father, art in me, and I in thee, that they also may be in us, so that the world may believe that thou hast sent me" (Jn 17.21), as well as other biblical passages that speak of the unity of Christians in the Church. It holds that unity is given by Christ and therefore is intrinsic to a true expression of the Christian faith; it is also motivated by the desire to bring a more effective witness to the world ("that the world may believe"). The Churches have felt increasing difficulty in reaching the modern world, and it is thought that a united Church would better witness to the power of Christ to overcome divisions among men, and that a pooling of resources would enable Christians to make a greater impact. Opponents of ecumenism, however, warn of the danger of weakening the Christian message through doctrinal compromise.

Some ecumenists have sought unity on the basis of a lowest common denominator of belief, the few beliefs upon which everyone could now agree. The principal leaders of the movement hold that the distinctives of the different Churches should not be disregarded; they do not hold that unity requires uniformity in thought and church life; instead they seek, through cooperative activity and *interfaith dialogue, to develop deeper mutual understanding and to enable each tradition to contribute its distinctive values to the total Christian community. Ecumenism demands not a belief that one system of doctrine or *church order is as valid as another but a willingness on the part of all Churches to recognize that they do not have a monopoly upon truth and virtue, that other Churches are not totally in error and sin. Since divisions among Christians are due not only to doctrinal differences but also to national, cultural, racial, and personal antagonisms, ecumenism calls for the spirit of brotherly love in removing these sources of division.

Ecumenism is generally associated with church renewal, or *aggiornamento. Organizational unity is considered inadequate unless Christians are united with Christ; conversely as Christians draw closer to Christ, they will draw closer to each other. Ecumenism, therefore, is not a search for some scheme upon which all may compromise, but a mutual search for the form of church life which will best express the will of Christ. See bibliog. for Ecumenical Movement.

[T. EARLY]

EDDINGTON, ARTHUR STANLEY (1882–1944), British astrophysicist, professor of astronomy and experimental philosophy at Cambridge from 1913, and director of the Cambridge Observatory from 1914. His observations contributed to the verification of Einstein's theory of relativity, and his fluent exposition of the development of astronomical science and theory won him a wide reputation. An active Quaker all his life, E. held that science and religion were distinct but not opposed; to him the spiritual nature of man was a thing unaccountable by science but deserving of recognition by scientists. BIBLIOGRAPHY: A. V. Douglas, *Life of Authur Stanley Eddington* (1956).

EDDY, MARY BAKER (1821–1910), founder of the *Church of Christ, Scientist. She was a chronic invalid, unhappily married and separated from her husband, when in 1862 she first became acquainted with the doctrines of Phineas *Quimby, a Maine faith healer. By 1866 she had developed her own faith-healing system and in 1875 published *Science and Health*. She taught that Christian Science is the wisdom of the Eternal Mind, revealed through Jesus Christ, who taught the power of Mind (Truth, God) to overcome illusions of sin, sickness, and death. In 1876 she formed the Christian Science Association, chartered in 1879 as the Church of Christ, Scientist. Her *Journal of Christian Science* (begun 1883) contributed to the growth of her following. After 1889 Mrs. Eddy lived in seclusion in Concord, N.H., but continued to direct Christian Science and to revise and enlarge her book. In 1892 she formed the First Church of Christ, Scientist, in Boston, giving the Mother Church authority over the entire movement. Alert to the end, she established the *Christian Science Monitor* in 1906, primarily to meet attacks on her movement in *McClure's Magazine* and other popular journals. Whether wholly original or not, Mrs. Eddy's system brought consolation to many and became a worldwide religion within her lifetime. BIBLIOGRAPHY: E. F. Dakin, *Mrs. Eddy* (1930); N. Beasley, *Cross and the Crown* (1942); R. Peel, *Mary Baker Eddy* (2 v., 1971–72); G. Pickering, *Creative Malady* (1974).

[R. K. MacMASTER]

EDEN, GARDEN OF (from Sumerian *edin*, prairie, steppe, through Akkadian *edinu*, and Heb. '*ēden* which introduces the idea of delight), the terrestrial paradise or place of blessedness and immortality presented in Gen 2.8, 10, 15. In the Garden of Eden dwelt in *original justice

Adam and Eve, in the time when their yet unvitiated senses savored fully Yahweh's garden (Gen 13.10; cf. Is. 51.3). Our first parents who "were in Eden, in the garden of God" (Ezek 28.13) were banished after the Fall of man (Gen 3.23–24). Scripture presents the Garden of Eden specifically "in the east," where God planted a garden by a river and there placed man, whom he had created (Gen 1.26–29). Eden is mentioned as very fertile and with magnificent trees (Gen 2.8–9; cf. Ezek 31.9, 16, 18); from it issued four rivers: Pishon, Gihon, Tigris, Euphrates (Gen 2.10–14). With but the inadequate geographical orientation of the writer of Genesis, many, to no avail, have sought to pinpoint the site, some in Armenia where both Tigris and Euphrates have their source. Hebrew folklore offers no specific site, nor in Near Eastern literature of the ancients is there a parallel to the Garden of Eden.

[M. R. BROWN]

EDES, ELLA B. (1832–1916), American journalist. Born in New England, E. became a convert to Catholicism in 1852. She went to live in Rome (c.1866), where she became (1870) Roman correspondent for newspapers such as the *Tablet* (London), the *New York Herald,* and many others. For her role in church conflicts, see R. F. McNamara, NCE 5:102.

EDESSA, CHRONICLE OF (A.D. 540), a Syrian chronicle covering largely a period from the 3d to the 6th centuries. Written by a cleric of Edessa who was orthodox but tinged with Nestorianism, it gives valuable sidelights on general history. The work is contained in a MS of the *Codex Vaticanus.*

[J. R. AHERNE]

EDESSA, SCHOOL OF, the theological thought and teaching of the Early Church in Syria and Mesopotamia. When in 363 the Emperor Jovian ceded Nisibis to the Persians, Ephrem the Syrian transferred his theological school from Nisibis to Edessa, a Mesopotamian city, which became a center of Oriental Christian culture and theological activity. The school exercised a great influence on the Church, and many of its students became bps. in Persia. It contributed to the acceptance of Nestorianism in the Persian Church. The theology of Theodore of Mopsuestia predominated and, in general, Antiochene theology was the standard at Edessa, which led to conflict with proponents of Alexandrian theology. After the Council of Chalcedon (451), the school, which had made Nestorianism its official teaching, was closed, and its members settled in Nisibis. BIBLIOGRAPHY: E. R. Hayes, *L'École d'Edesse* (1930); A. Van Roey, DHGE 14:1430–32.

[P. FOSCOLOS]

EDFU, in Upper Egypt on the W bank of the Nile, site of the famous well-preserved pylon Temple of Horus (237–57

B.C.). The girdle wall carved with religious scenes in the late style shows small figurines with smooth fulsome modelling, carries four flagstaffs in pylons beyond which is a colonnaded portico with a carving of scenes of Ptolemy IX (146–117 B.C.) engaged in cult rites—all leading to the impressive hypostyle hall with clerestory. A large sanctuary for the sacred boat is surrounded by an impressive ambulatory. The cylindrical well outside the girdle wall is a Nilometer. West of the temple are cultural finds of successive Islamic, Coptic, Greco-Roman, and Egyptian stratification.

[M. J. DALY]

EDGAR THE PEACEFUL (943–975), King of England from 959. Generous to the Church, E. encouraged ecclesiastical reform and monastic revival, supporting Dunstan of Canterbury, Ethelwold of Winchester, and Oswald of York. His reign brought order and peace and his liturgical coronation at Bath (973) was followed by homage from British and Scottish kings. BIBLIOGRAPHY: W. Hunt, DNB 6:365–370.

[W. A. CHANEY]

EDGEWORTH, MARIA (1767–1849), described sometimes as an Irish and sometimes as an English novelist. Born in Oxfordshire, she went with her father in 1782 to Ireland, which became her home and where she died in Edgeworthtown, County Longford. Variously, too, has she been evaluated as a novelist: lionized in her own lifetime, achieving a reading audience on three continents; at the turn of the century, allegedly unread or misread and misrepresented by critics repeating the errors of other critics; latterly she has been more intensively and comprehensively read and studied by scholars, to her credit. Contemporary criticism of the best minds of her time rated her highly, even extravagantly so. She is credited with leading the way in the English novel by producing the prototype of the saga, using four generations of the Rackrent family in her short novel *Castle Rackrent* (1800). She was also a pioneer in using a character narrator to unfold her story. *Castle Rackrent, The Absentee,* and *Ormond* are usually considered her best works. E. also wrote works on education in which she and her father, Richard Lovell Edgeworth, shared a keen interest. BIBLIOGRAPHY: J. Newcomer, *Maria Edgeworth the Novelist* (1967); M. D. Hawthorne, *Doubt and Dogma in Maria Edgeworth* (1967).

[S. A. HEENEY]

EDGEWORTH DE FERMONT, HENRY ESSEX.

EDICT OF MILAN, see MILAN, EDICT OF.

EDICT OF NANTES, an act of toleration for the French *Huguenots; the best known of the numerous treaties passed during the *Wars of Religion, but not the most remarkable. Issued by Henry IV on April 13, 1598, it was an intricate compendium of older documents; it lacked the clarity of the treaty of Beaulieu ("Peace of Monsieur," 1576). The Edict comprised the Edict proper consisting of 92 articles; 56 secret and private articles; 2 commissions (*brevets*) bearing on guarantees given to the Huguenots; and additional secret articles. It was predominantly concerned with judicial guarantees. It stipulated freedom of conscience but only limited freedom of worship: the Huguenot nobility was allowed to have *Reformed worship, as were the citizens of some 200 towns. It granted civil equality; promised subsidies for the maintenance of Huguenot pastors, schools, and troops; and guaranteed the fair administration of justice (special chambers to include one Huguenot judge each), the maintenance of garrisons for another 8 years, and the right to hold synods and provincial political councils. Although the Edict initiated a period of peace, it did not solve the underlying religious problems: it was a temporary measure that was defective because it was too rigid and failed to accommodate future changes. After the death of Henry IV (1610) the Huguenots were increasingly persecuted; by the Edict of Alais in 1629 they lost all civil rights, although nominally retaining religious freedom. This also was taken away when Louis XIV revoked the Edict of Nantes in 1685. See bibliog. for Huguenots.

[W. J. STANKIEWICZ]

EDICT OF RESTITUTION (1629), a decree of the Holy Roman Emperor, Ferdinand II, aimed at strengthening Habsburg power and restoring Catholic supremacy. At a high point of imperial fortunes during the Thirty Years' War, the Emperor was emboldened to issue this edict without consultation of the Imperial Diet. It called for restitution of all church properties taken over since the Convention of Passau (1552); outlawed all Protestants except Lutherans of the Augsburg Confession; and reinstated the principle *cuius regio eius religio*. Relentless enforcement displaced thousands of persons from their homes. The edict was the occasion for the decisive intervention the next year of *Gustavus II Adolphus on the Protestant side.

[T. C. O'BRIEN]

EDIFICATION, the "building up" metaphor for the process of perfecting the life of the Church. The Gospels use the idea, Jesus describing himself as the cornerstone of the building that God builds (Mt 21.42; Mk 12.10; Lk 20.17; cf. Ps 118.22); but the term is esp. prominent in St. Paul. He speaks of the building up of Christ's body and the growth of the temple of God (Eph 2.21; 4.12, 16). The idea includes the Father's activity as builder (1 Cor 3.10); Christ as foundation and source (Eph 4.10–16); the function of the ministers in the Church (Eph 2.20; 4.11); the significance of the *charismatic gifts bestowed on the members (1 Cor 14.12; Eph 4.16). The community life of the Church is a process of building up, in which the members assist and strengthen one another (Eph 4.16; Rom 1.11–12; 2 Cor 2.3; Phil 1.19). The very purpose of the Church itself is that Christians be "built together to become a dwelling place for God in the Spirit" (Eph 2.21–22). In devotional literature the term was taken to mean good example; it became trite and moralistic, to the detriment of the rich meaning it has in Scripture.

[T. C. O'BRIEN]

EDIGNA, BL. (d. 1109), virgin. Legendary sources state that she was a French princess who fled to Puch in Bavaria to remain a virgin. Her dwelling was a hollow linden tree from which, after her death, holy oil flowed. When an attempt was made to sell the oil, the flow stopped. Her cult survives at Puch, where she is venerated as patroness against theft. BIBLIOGRAPHY: J. C. Moore, NCE 5 (1967) 106.

[M. S. TANEY]

EDINBURGH CONFERENCES, two meetings held in Edinburgh that had great bearing on the *ecumenical movement: (1) that held in 1910, attended by 1,200 delegates of many denominations, at which the International Missionary Council was formed; (2) the second world conference of the *Faith and Order movement, held at Edinburgh, Aug. 3–18, 1937. The subjects considered were grace, the Church and the word of God, the communion of saints, the ministry of the Church and sacraments, and the unity of the Church in life and worship. Like the Lausanne Conference, this one failed to elicit any agreement on the number of sacraments or on the nature and transmission of the Church's ministry. The communion of saints was defined as representing the Church, the Body of Christ, in heaven and on earth. The conference agreed on a statement on grace (never approved, however, by the Churches represented). Grace was viewed as the expression of the loving-kindness of God toward man, manifested in the Church through the word and the sacraments; justification and sanctification were seen as inseparable aspects of grace, which, however, did not override human responsibility, but required a response by faith. The Conference, coming immediately after the Oxford Conference of the *Life and Work movement, voted a merger of the two movements in a proposed *World Council of Churches. BIBLIOGRAPHY: *Second World Conference on Faith and Order* (ed. L. Hodgson, 1938).

[D. CODDINGTON]

EDINOVERTSY (Russ., Fellow- or United-believers). A group of Old Believers begun in Russia in 1801, which entered into union with the Orthodox Church. They were subject to the local synodal Orthodox bps. until 1918, when the diocese of Okhtensk was established for them.

[T. BIRD]

EDMUND THE MARTYR, ST. (*c*.841–870), King of East Anglia from 855. E. was defeated and killed by the Danes; according to tradition, he was shot with arrows and beheaded for refusing to compromise Christianity or the welfare of his people. His body, buried at Hoxne, was translated to Bury, the center of his popular cult. BIBLIOGRAPHY: J. Dolan, BiblSanct 4:917–918; Butler 4:394–396; B. Houghton, *St. Edmund, King and Martyr: the Story of the Former Patron Saint of England* (1974).

[W. A. CHANEY]

EDMUND (RICH) OF ABINGDON, ST. (*c.*1170–1240), abp. of Canterbury, theologian. He attended school at Paris and Oxford, taught at Oxford, where he was among the first to introduce the new logic of Aristotle, preached the crusade for Gregory IX in 1227, and was elected to the see of Canterbury in 1233. He had a stormy and litigious episcopate, finding it neccessary to oppose encroachments by the crown on the one hand and the policies of Card. Otto, the papal legate, on the other. He died in voluntary exile at the Cistercian Abbey of Pontigny that had given shelter to St. Thomas Becket. His canonization (1246) followed shortly after his death. BIBLIOGRAPHY: Butler 4:355–358; J. Dolan, BiblSanct 4:920–921; M. R. Newbolt, *Edmund rich, Archbishop and Saint* (1928).

[J. L. GRASSI]

EDOM, a region S of the Dead Sea, extending to the Gulf of 'Aqaba; according to Gen 36.9, the hill country of Seir. The name, meaning red, derives from the color of the red sandstone of the region; Gen 25.30 associates it with the red food for which Esau, from whom the *Edomites descended, traded his birthright. The land was rich in copper. The Israelites had to pass through Edom on the way to Canaan (Num 20.20–21; Dt 2.4–6). In Jer 49.7 Edom is spoken of as the haven of wisdom.

[A. P. HANLON]

EDOMITES, the Semitic tribe that inhabited *Edom from *c.*1300 B.C.; described by Gen 36.10 as descendants of Esau and so related to the Israelites; in NT times they were called Idumeans. They are listed as nomads in the Egyptian records of Merneptah, *c.*1225 B.C. and of Rameses III, 1187 B.C. The Israelites were for generations at war with them (Gen 25.30; 32.4–9; 1 Chr 1.35–54). The OT also records that David conquered them (2 Sam 8.13–14) and that they remained subjected under Solomon (1 Kg 11.14–22). At a later period, because of their hostility to Juda, they were the objects of threatened punishment in Is 34.5–7; 63.1–6; Lam 4.21; Ezek 25.12–14.

[A. P. HANLON]

EDUCATE, RIGHT TO, a right to which claims are made on behalf of three institutions—family, Church, and State. No necessary conflict exists among these claims; in their more reasonable presentation, they are complementary rather than mutually exclusive. As to the family's right, Pius XI declared in *Divini illius magistri* "the family holds directly from the creator the mission and hence the right to educate." This right is conceived to be natural, inalienable,

anterior to any civil right, and inseparable from parents' obligation to educate their children, and consequently the violation of this right by any power whatever is an injustice. This was recognized by the U.S. Supreme Court in the *Oregon School case (1925), which declared: "The child is not the mere creature of the State; those who nurture and direct his destiny have the right, coupled with the high duty, to recognize and prepare him for additional duties." It was affirmed also by Vat II ChrEduc: "Parents must be recognized as the primary and principal educators" (no. 3). As to the Church's right to educate, Vatican Council II claimed: " . . . the office of educating belongs by a unique title to the Church, not merely because she deserves recognition as a human society capable of educating, but most of all because she has the responsibility of announcing the way of salvation to all men, of communicating the life of Christ to those who believe, and of assisting them with ceaseless concern so that they may grow into the fullness of that same life" (*loc. cit.*). The State's right and concern, acknowledged also by Vatican Council II, derives from its own particular end and object, i.e., the common welfare in the temporal order. BIBLIOGRAPHY: Pope Pius XI, *On Christian Education of Youth* (1929). *CHURCH AND STATE.

[M. B. MURPHY]

EDUCATION, CHRISTIAN. The beginnings of Christian education derived from the teaching mission of the Church heeding the injunction of Christ to the Apostles, "Go and make disciples of all nations." The earliest form was the program of instruction designed for catechumens. A second stimulus was the program designed for the education of the clergy, largely to aid them in understanding Sacred Scripture and the liturgy. This emphasis on sacred learning, even in the 2d cent., was not exclusive of secular learning, though the Church did not provide schools of general education. With the collapse of the Roman Empire monastic schools took the place of imperial schools. The educational apparatus through the Middle Ages and the founding of the universities centered on education for Christian living. With the Reformation Christian education grew more and more apologetic, in the sense of defensive of the faith. The separation of Catholic schools from the public institutions accelerated in the post-Reformation era, largely as the major work of the Jesuits and other communities of men and women founded specifically to conduct schools. The culmination of this movement came in the U.S. in the 19th cent. with the establishment of the parochial school system, academies and colleges. Cathedral schools, monastic educational institutions, the catechetical programs throughout the centuries, or the system of Catholic schools largely a product of American Catholicism, all rest on the principle that Christian education centers on instruction in Christian living.

In the 19th cent., Pope Leo XIII affirmed the rights of the family and the Church with respect to the education of children and youth and emphasized the obligation of the popes as teachers of mankind. Education as Pope Leo envisaged it was to be conceived as the pursuit of Christian wisdom, relying on the Scriptures, the Fathers, and Catholic philosophers and theologians, particularly St. Thomas Aquinas. The rise of totalitarianism in Italy and Germany in the 20th cent. occasioned the pivotal statement on Christian education by Pope Pius XI, *The Christian Education of Youth* (1929). It asserted the right of the family and the Church as antecedent to that of the State in the matter of education of the young. The encyclical stressed the education of the whole person, something the state cannot provide. Though Pius XI, for his purposes, passes over the intellectual aspect of education, he did so in the light of its primary message required by the times. Both Pius XII and John XXIII have reaffirmed the position of the encyclical on education. Vatican Council II, while reiterating the tradional emphasis of the Church on education for the moral formation of students, departs from the past in underlining the intellectual nature of formal education and goes farther to assert that the Christian is to receive an education which will enable him to live in the modern world, not separate himself from it. This point marks a break with preconciliar approaches. If the Christian is to be prepared for his place in the modern world, then his education must be of the highest quality intellectually.

Developments in the post-Vatican II era include an increased role of the laity in Catholic education, the growth of religious instruction, largely by laymen and laywomen, in parish units of the Confraternity of Christian Doctrine, (CCD), and a new emphasis on adult education. The decline in numbers of religious available for work in Catholic schools and the increasing financial burden of maintaining parochial schools have given major importance to the CCD. Preparation of teachers for instructing the young in religion has necessitated a new emphasis on adult education. Parents and other adults must themselves know and live the Christianity they teach. The often bewildering shifts of emphasis for those educated before the changes introduced by Vatican II require a program of updating. Essentially CCD attempts to convey to parents as well as children the way to apply the teachings of the faith to living in the modern world. There is stress also on involvement in prayer, liturgy, and the sacramental life. The CCD movement has had a mixed success and is constantly being reviewed to increase its effectiveness. It is no exaggeration to state that the strength of the parish CCD depends on the Christian awareness of the parish community itself.

A sign of the new approach of the Church to education on all levels is found in the change of the name of a major Roman congregation from the ''Congregation for Seminaries'' to the ''Congregation for Catholic Education.'' An important document issued by the Congregation in 1977 affirms the special character of Catholic schools as witness to the abiding centrality of the Gospels and an antidote to materialism. The consistent position of the Church over the centuries has been that education is a human right and that religious education is part of its God-given teaching mission.

[J. R. AHERNE]

EDUCATION, EARLY CHRISTIAN (1st to 5th centuries). The earliest centers of Christian education were catechetical in purpose, intended for the education of neophytes. The Scriptures, the articles of faith, liturgy, and the music of the liturgy constituted the curriculum. The training of clerics introduced new elements as the cathedral schools taught philosophy, the liberal arts, and language in addition to Scripture. Great teachers of Alexandria included Clement of Alexandria, Hippolytus, and Origen. The cathedral school was an outgrowth of the apostolic rule of community living where the bp. and his clergy lived a common life. Such centers as Rome, Antioch, and Alexandria provided educational centers for training clerics. St. Augustine in his see of Hippo, North Africa, established a quasi-monastic community which undertook the education of clergy, in the late 5th century. With the rise of monasticism in both East and West there was an early effort to educate nonclerics. St. Basil and St. Pachomius were among the first to give directions for the education of Christian children. Cassiodorus, in the 5th cent., emerges as the most significant founder of a monastic school, composing a genuinely liberal curriculum, and writing a number of texts in education. The fall of the Roman Empire destroyed the imperial schools of the West and it remained for the cathedral and monastic schools to carry on the tradition of education.

[J. R. AHERNE]

EDUCATION, MEDIEVAL. The history of education in the early and late Middle Ages developed out of the political and social history of its time and was essentially the work of the Church, the one constant agency that survived between the fall of Rome and the Renaissance. When the civilization of the late Roman empire was disrupted by the massive barbarian invasions, education all but stopped. The empire of *Charlemagne (r. 771–814) began to create the stability necessary for learning to flourish. At his death the empire suffered division and upheaval. Under Otto I, the Holy Roman Empire restored stability in the 10th century. The feudal era, in spite of its decentralization of political power and the centuries of bitter struggle between papacy and empire, saw an evolution that culminated in the universities, the high point of medieval education.

In the early Middle Ages, the need to educate clergy and to instruct the faithful led the Church to legislate the creation of schools. Children were taught in the catechetical schools, and cathedral or episcopal schools were established to prepare candidates for the priesthood. But in the early development of medieval learning the monastic schools were the dominant factor. They preserved learning in MS collection and copying; they alone taught literature; they provided the libraries of the time and produced the scholars.

Equally important was the monastic function of teaching agriculture and craftsmanship. Not inconsiderable was the cultural impact of churches and monasteries upon the evolution of new forms of art and architecture. As more of the ancient classics were acquired and a theory of education was more defined, the program of education preparatory for philosophy and theology comprised what were termed the seven liberal arts, grouped as the trivium (grammar, rhetoric, and dialectic) and the quadrivium (arithmetic, geometry, astronomy, and music). The chief centers of learning taught all of the seven arts. As articulated by one of the dominant medieval educational guides, *Hugh of St. Victor's *Didascalicon,* under these seven were arranged every branch of human knowledge that would make the student achieve wisdom and the restoration of the image of God in his being. Hugh also organized the "mechanical arts," which he called *adulterinae,* i.e., imitative, and which comprised all the skills needed to maintain bodily life. An important feature of this program was the conception of education as a retrieval of the learning of the past and the importance of "texts," the authoritative works of antiquity. The progress in education was marked by the interaction of reading *(lectio)* of these texts and their analysis through the use of logic (the *disputatio*).

Among the leaders in education Charlemagne was a key figure by his establishment of schools and encouragement of scholars. In England, Alfred the Great (r. 871–901) performed a similar function. Among scholars Boethius (480–524) is regarded as the father of medieval learning because of his *Consolations of Philosophy* and his translations of Aristotle. *Cassiodorus (490–585) by his *Institutiones divinarum et humanarum lectionum* set the pattern of literary study for centuries. Isidore of Seville (570–636) provided a mine of information, not always accurate, in his encyclopedic *Etymologies.* Alcuin was brought to France by Charlemagne and became the Emperor's chief educational advisor. His most important book, *On Grammar,* included an introduction to educational methodology. Alcuin showed the necessity of secular learning as companion to religious knowledge. The Monastery of Tours, of which he was abbot, became the center of learning in France. In this early period Rhabanus Maurus was of equal importance. From the 11th cent. the history of medieval education becomes the history of scholasticism as that connotes the method of reading-debate *(lectio-disputatio)* that characterized not only theology but philosophy, law, and medicine (see SCHOLASTICISM). It was the abuse of this method and the neglect of humane letters that led to the rejection of the medieval ideals by the humanists *(ibid.).*

But a prime expression and theater of the intellectual interest represented by scholasticism was the medieval university, which emerged in the late 12th and early 13th centuries. The fully developed university provided four schools: arts (philosophy), law, medicine, and theology. Characteristics of the university structure were democratic

government, clustering in large centers of population, and privileged status. While the universities remained under church jurisdiction they enjoyed considerable freedom, esp. from political interference. The modern degree system and the very ideal of a university, the *universitas studiorum,* were created by the medieval institution. Celebrated early universities were Bologna (1158), Paris (1180), Naples (1224), Salamanca (1230), and Oxford (1214). The Muslim universities of Spain (e.g., at Córdoba) made rich contributions to medicine, mathematics, and philosophy. The newer modes of educational institutions, chantry schools, (really parochial schools), guild schools, originally founded by the crafts, and later developing into municipal schools, supported by the towns, replaced the cathedral school and marked the passing of educational direction to agencies apart from the Church. BIBLIOGRAPHY: P. Monroe, *Brief Course in the History of Education* (1907); P. Eby and C. Arrowwood, *History and Philosophy of Education, Ancient and Medieval* (1940); H. Rashdall, *Universities of Europe in the Middle Ages* (ed. F. M. Powicke and A. B. Emden, 3 v., 1936); Hugh of St. Victor, *Didascalicon* (tr. J. Taylor; repr. 1961).

[J. R. AHERNE]

EDUCATION, RELIGIOUS, see RELIGIOUS EDUCATION.

EDUCATION OF THE DEAF, see DEAF, EDUCATION OF THE.

EDWARD THE CONFESSOR, ST. (1004–66), King of England from 1042. Though outwardly peaceful, E.'s reign was marked by quarrels of native and foreign factions, with his powerful father-in-law, Earl Godwin, and his family dominating much of it. Edward was pious and chaste, if weak and indolent. He refounded Westminster Abbey (1065) and was canonized in 1161. BIBLIOGRAPHY: H. Inskip, BiblSanct 4:921–925; Butler 4:100–103; F. Barlow, *Edward the Confessor* (1970).

[W. A. CHANEY]

EDWARD THE ELDER (d. 924), King of England from 899. King Alfred's elder son, E. successfully continued his father's wars against the Vikings, building many fortified settlements, and gaining control south of the Humber. He absorbed Mercia and increased the number of dioceses in S England. BIBLIOGRAPHY: F. Stenton, *Anglo-Saxon England* (1947) 315–335, 432–433, 706.

[W. A. CHANEY]

EDWARD THE MARTYR, ST. (c.963–978), King of England from 975. E.'s brief reign was marked by antimonastic reaction to the policies of his father, King Edgar. A faction supporting E.'s younger stepbrother Ethelred assassinated E. at Corfe. Miracles were soon attributed to him, and Ethelred helped establish his cult. BIBLIOGRAPHY: H. Inskip, BiblSanct 4:926–927; Butler 1:627–628.

[W. A. CHANEY]

EDWARD I (1239–1307), King of England from 1272. Son of Henry III, E., esp. before 1295, was one of England's ablest, most successful monarchs, the "English Justinian." He used parliaments (including the "Model Parliament," 1295) to strengthen royal policies and authority. His administrative reorganization and the series of great statutes between 1275 and 1290 (Westminster, Gloucester, Mortmain, *Quia emptores, Quo warranto,* etc.) are landmarks of jurisprudence which consolidated and reformed governmental institutions. E. conquered and fortified Wales, quarreled with France over Gascony, and stirred Scotland to rebellion under Wallace and Bruce. Ecclesiastical taxation strained relations with the papacy and abps. of Canterbury. BIBLIOGRAPHY: F. M. Powicke, *Thirteenth Century* (1962); *idem, King Henry III and the Lord Edward* (2 v., 1947).

[W. A. CHANEY]

EDWARD II (1284–1327), King of England from 1307. Weak and dependent upon unpopular favorites, E. was in continual conflict with his barons, whose ordinances (1311) and parliaments limited royal power. The Scots defeated him at Bannockburn (1314), further weakening his position. E. was dethroned and murdered by baronial opponents. BIBLIOGRAPHY: H. Johnstone, *Edward of Carnarvon* (1946); J. R. Maddicott: *Thomas of Lancaster, 1307–1322: A Study in the Reign of Edward 2nd* (1970).

[W. A. CHANEY]

EDWARD III (1312–77), King of England from 1327. Able and chivalrous, E. warred successfully in Scotland and France, where his claims opened up the Hundred Years' War. Opposition to foreign clergy caused the antipapal statutes of Provisors (1351) and Praemunire (1353). BIBLIOGRAPHY: M. McKisack, *Fourteenth Century* (1959); J. Mackinnon, *History of Edward the Third: 1327–1377* (1900; repr. 1974).

[W. A. CHANEY]

EDWARD VI (1537–53), King of England from 1547. Son of *Henry VIII and Jane Seymour, the boy was little more than 9 years old when he ascended the throne. His disposition was studious, his learning precocious. His religious feelings were intense, and his persuasions were those of his favorite preacher, Hugh *Latimer. His policies were steered in a Calvinist direction by an Erastian government, at first by Protector Somerset and later by Northumberland, who shrugged off the contention of the Catholic leaders that the royal supremacy should be in abeyance. J. *Knox and continental Reformers, notably M. *Bucer, *Peter Martyr Vermigli, and B. *Ochino, flocked in, and the King was hailed as the English Josiah. During his short reign the progress of the Reformation was marked by the imposition of the first *Book of Common Prayer (1549); a new *Anglican Ordinal (1550); a more Calvinist revision of the BCP (1552); and by the *Forty-Two Articles of Religion (1553). He showed signs of Tudor obstinacy and seemed indifferent to natural affection, laconically assenting to the execution of his uncles and priggishly promoting the persecution of his sister, Mary; yet when he died, of a rapid consumption, his will disclosed how completely he had been manipulated by the ambition of the Dudleys. BIBLIOGRAPHY: J. D. Martin, *Earlier Tudors* (1925); Hughes RE; W. K. Jordan, *Chronicle and Political Papers of King Edward the Sixth* (Folger Documents, 1966).

[T. GILBY]

EDWARDINE ARTICLES, alternate name for the *Forty-Two Articles promulgated for the Church of England in 1533 during the reign of Edward VI.

EDWARDS, JONATHAN (1703–58), eminent American Congregationalist theologian and preacher in the *Great Awakening. Born at East Windsor, Conn., E. entered Yale in 1716, graduating in 1720. His boyhood interest in matters scientific and spiritual flourished at Yale under the stimulus of reading Isaac Newton and John Locke. E.'s life and thought were dominated by a crucial religious experience by which he came to a "delightful conviction" of the sovereign majesty, power, and beauty of God. He was to rehearse this theme severely in the sermons of the Great Awakening period. In a gentler vein he cast the same conviction into a virtually Neoplatonic form in his late treatises. After briefly holding a pastorate in a Presbyterian church in New York (1722), he returned to Yale as a tutor (1724). He married Sarah Pierrepont, of New Haven, in 1727, the year he was called to be the associate pastor of the Northampton, Mass., church with his maternal grandfather Solomon Stoddard, whom he succeeded 2 years later. His evangelical preaching led to vigorous revivals in his parish and elsewhere in New England. Misunderstandings with his church members concerning the qualifications of those presenting themselves for church membership brought on a bitter controversy that led to his dismissal in 1750. The following year, burdened with a large family and virtually disgraced, he accepted the frontier mission post at Stockbridge, Massachusetts. He remained there until Jan., 1758, when he removed to Princeton to become president of the College of New Jersey (now Princeton Univ.), but he died of a smallpox inoculation on March 22.

As an evangelist E.'s reputation rests on the sermons preached during the Great Awakening, many of which detailed the horrors of divine punishment as well as the glories of salvation. As a philosopher and theologian his fame rests upon a series of treatises written in his Stockbridge days. *Concerning the Religious Affections* (1746) is a discriminating examination of true and false emotions and provides his most sustained defense of the role of genuine religious affections in the Great Awakening. His acute attack upon *Arminianism concerning freedom of the will is contained in his treatise *A Careful and Strict Enquiry into . . . Freedom of Will* (1754), wherein he argues logically against freedom of choice and defends a causality of will exempt from compulsion. *The Great Christian Doctrine of Original Sin* (1758) propounds the theory that men unfailingly fall into sin. Both treatises fit well within the framework of Calvinism. Among his posthumous writings, *The Nature of True Virtue* expands his early notes on excellence, where true virtue is interpreted as the cordial and benevolent consent of intelligent beings with Ultimate Being or Being in General. His essentially neoplatonic vision of reality is expressed in *The End for Which God Created the World*. In that work the purpose of divine creation is interpreted as the emanation of the divine being for its own sake. E.'s influence was to continue in the thought of Joseph Bellamy and Samuel Hopkins, who set in motion the theological movement known as the *New England theology. E.'s thought exhibits many contrasts. He consciously defended the *Five Points of Calvinism, yet preached also the need and value of personal religious experience in conversion. He was as biblical as any Puritan, yet steeped in the philosophy of the *Enlightenment. He was an evangelical preacher, but also a profound speculative theologian. The intense study of his writings begun in the 1950s has not yet yielded a complete or definitive evaluation. Modern editions of E.'s works include: *Freedom of the Will* (ed. P. Ramsey, 1957); *Religious Affections* (ed. J. E. Smith, 1959); *Works* (ed. E. Williams and E. Parsons, 10 v., 1847; repr. 1968); *Jonathan Edwards: His Life and Diary* (ed. D. Brainerd, 1968). BIBLIOGRAPHY: D. J. Elwood, *Philosophical Theology of Jonathan Edwards* (1960); O. E. Winslow, *Jonathan Edwards* (1941); P. Miller, *Jonathan Edwards* (1949); C. Cherry, *Theology of Jonathan Edwards* (1966); *Theology in America* (ed. S. E. Ahlstrom, 1967) 149–192.

[C. A. HOLBROOK]

EDWARDS, THOMAS (1599–1647), Puritan polemicist. Both as university preacher at Cambridge and afterwards at London, E. fiercely advocated Presbyterianism against both Episcopalians and Independents; he was often suspended and silenced. After the triumph of the Puritan cause, he turned against the many new sects in the Commonwealth with a violent work, *Gangraena* (1646). He died in Holland. BIBLIOGRAPHY: DNBConc 1:390.

[R. B. ENO]

EDWIN, KING OF NORTHUMBRIA, ST. (*c.*585–633). His history is testified to in the *Anglo-Saxon Chronicle* and in Bede's *Historia ecclesiastica*. He was son of King Deira, upon whose death, E. was banished. He fled to Wales, but later returned to England and, with the help of Redwald, king of East Anglia, recovered his throne. Not yet a Christian, E. sought and won the hand of Ethelburga,

daughter of St. Ethelbert, king of Kent, on condition that she be permitted to practice her faith. She took St. Paulinus with her as a chaplain, and he eventually prevailed upon E. to be baptized. He died in battle and has enjoyed some veneration in England as a martyr, but has apparently never had a liturgical cultus. BIBLIOGRAPHY: Butler 4:94–95.

[P. K. MEAGHER]

EEDEN, FREDERIK WILLEM VAN (1860–1932), Dutch physician, remembered in Holland chiefly as a poet, but abroad for his ideas of social reform. He founded a model farming community in Holland which failed after a few years; later he worked to establish the Van Eeden Colony in North Carolina. In 1922 he became a convert to Roman Catholicism. BIBLIOGRAPHY: J. I. Mendels, NCE 5:184.

EFFICACIOUS GRACE, see GRACE, EFFICACIOUS.

EFFICIENT CAUSE, also called agent cause, the active producer of a being or an activity; the agent or mover in the process from potentiality to actuality. *PRINCIPAL CAUSE; *INSTRUMENTAL CAUSE.

[T. C. O'BRIEN]

EGALITARIANISM (from French *égal*, equal). Equality, which may be expressed by an arithmetical equation or a geometrical proportion, is a mathematical relation of quantities implying matter, and consequently the application of the notion to forms which are alike, though legitimate, is analogical. With this qualification in mind, we address ourselves to human equality.

Four types may be distinguished for neatness in discussion: natural, social, political, and theological equality. First, natural equality is the sameness of essential characteristics shared by all members of a species. This, together with its proper implications, cannot be contested; all human beings form one specific class, as may be proved from cross-racial breeding—miscegenation is a sociological, not a biological term. It does not take you very far, for Aristotle who stressed the unity of the species also equably accepted that some men are born to be slaves, and the Stoics who stressed individual responsibility and were the precursors of political equality also tended to push this condition back into a Golden Age.

Second, social equality is present only in a classless society in which cultural, occupational, family, racial, and religious differences are not such as to alter, in kind or in any marked degree, the mutual acceptance of various members of the group.

Third, political equality spells the denial of privilege before the law, which is applied to all without discrimination, together with acceptance of the right of all adults to participate in or at least to influence the business of government.

Fourth, theological equality is implied in the universal

law of charity or friendship; it includes all the inferences to be drawn from St. Paul's declaration, "There is neither Jew nor Greek, neither slave nor freeman, neither male nor female. For you are all one in Christ" (Gal 3.28). This, too, is not under discussion, which leaves us to consider the second and third types, namely social and political equality.

A moment's reflection will rule out any question here of an arithmetical equality. It is neither self-evident, nor a gospel imperative, nor seriously advocated by anybody. What may be desired, however, is a geometrical equality of opportunities proportioned to personal abilities and needs and of rights not obstructed by conventions fixing persons unchangeably in a class, and one perhaps denied the full responsibility of citizenship. Social and political equality are not identical, and do not necessarily co-exist; the first may be proposed under a dictatorship; the second can flourish in a community conscious of its class-structures. Socialist theory treats social equality as a means toward achieving political equality; American democracy is cited as favoring the reverse process. The dialectic of ideas might suggest that both types of equality will almost automatically support the cause of human liberty; this, however, is not borne out by the dialectic of history.

The assumption, common to Hobbes and Locke —otherwise very different thinkers—of a tacit covenant or compact underlying the construction of political groups was followed by much liberal egalitarianism. Rousseau appealed to a classless state of pure and ideal nature. That "all men are created equal," asserted as politically axiomatic by the Declaration of Independence, should be understood in the light of the unanimous feeling for the social equality of whites which then prevailed in the American colonies. By the principle, "From each according to his capacity, to each according to his needs," Marxism is not to be classed as an egalitarian system. Equality before the law, of individuals in the State and of States among one another, is now the general theory: it was supported by *Mater et Magistra* (1961) and *Pacem in Terris* (1963). Equal rights movements in favor of women and black peoples have met with political success, but their economic and social aims have yet to be achieved.

[T. GILBY]

EGAN, MAURICE FRANCIS (1852–1924), American writer and diplomat. E. was a journalist and editor (*Freeman's Journal,* 1880–88), professor at the Univ. of Notre Dame (1888–96), and at The Catholic Univ. of America (1896–1907). He wrote, among many other works, the *Sexton Maginnis Stories, The Ghost of Hamlet* (1892), and *Studies in Literature* (1899). While in Washington his counsel was sought by government officials and in 1907 he was appointed minister to Denmark by Theodore Roosevelt, a post he held until 1918. In this capacity he is credited with improving relations between Denmark and the U.S. and between the U.S. and the RC

Church. BIBLIOGRAPHY: M. F. Egan, *Recollections of a Happy Life* (1924).

[M. B. MONAGHAN]

EGAN, MICHAEL (1761–1814), bishop. An Irish Franciscan who served his order in Rome and Ireland before undertaking missionary work in Lancaster (1802), and Philadelphia (1803), Pa., where he became its first bishop (1808). His administration was plagued by *trusteeism instigated by two priests, William *Harold and his uncle James Harold. BIBLIOGRAPHY: M. I. J. Griffin, *History of Rev. Michael Egan, First Bishop of Philadelphia* (1893); R. E. Quigley, *History of the Archdiocese of Philadelphia* (ed. J. F. Connelly, 1976).

[M. CARTHY]

EGBERT (d. 839), King of Wessex from 802. By his conquest of Mercia and the submission of Northumbria, East Anglia, and other realms, E. was the first Anglo-Saxon monarch to rule, directly or through subkings, over all England. He defeated a Cornish-Viking alliance (838) and allied Wessex with the Church of Canterbury. BIBLIOGRAPHY: B. W. Scholz, NCE 5:189 (bibliog.)

[W. A. CHANEY]

EGBERT OF IONA (639–729). English by birth, E. studied in Ireland. During a plague he vowed to go to Germany as a missionary, but a vision prompted him to send others instead. E. was instrumental in converting the Irish monks to the observance of the same Easter date as continental Europe. BIBLIOGRAPHY: E. I. Watkin, BiblSanct 4:952.

[R. T. MEYER]

EGBERT OF LIÈGE (b. *c.*972), poet, rhetorician, teacher; author of *Fecunda ratis (The Laden Ship, c.*1020), a collection of extracts from biblical, classical, patristic, and German vernacular sources. It is in two parts: shorter extracts in the *Prora distincta,* longer ones in the *Puppis aerata.* BIBLIOGRAPHY: F. J. E. Raby, *History of Secular Latin Poetry in the Middle Ages* (1934) 1:399–401.

[M. F. MCCARTHY]

EGBERT (ECGBERT) OF YORK (d. 766), archbishop. Of Northumbrian royal descent, E. was appointed bp. of York (732), but, on Bede's advice, secured the pallium (735) as first abp. of York after Paulinus. He founded its famous cathedral school and wrote a treatise, *De iure sacerdotali,* and probably contributed to certain other works that have been attributed to him. BIBLIOGRAPHY: R. Van Doren, BiblSanct 4:953–954.

[W. A. CHANEY]

EGEDE, HANS (1686–1758), Norwegian Lutheran missionary. In 1717 he began to raise funds for a mission to Greenland and was able to set out in 1721 with his wife, who was also a missionary. He returned to Copenhagen in 1736 to found a seminary for missionaries to Greenland, while his son took over his work among the Eskimos. BIBLIOGRAPHY: J. M. Jensen, EncLuthCh 1:768.

[M. J. SUELZER]

EGIDIO MARIA OF ST. JOSEPH, BL. (Francesco Pontillo; 1729–1812), Franciscan lay brother. Born near Taranto in Apulia, Italy, E. was a ropemaker from his early youth and, after his father's death, became at the age of 18 the support of the family. In 1754 he entered the Discalced Friars Minor of St. Peter of Alcantara at Naples. From 1759 until his death he lived at the friary of San Pasquale a Chiaia in Naples; there, as cook, porter, and alms gatherer, he served the sick and esp. the lazzaroni. His life was notable for devotion to the Eucharist, to Mary and Joseph, and for his care of those in need, who loved him. He was beatified in 1888. BIBLIOGRAPHY: Butler 1:275; M. da Alatri, BiblSanct 4:966–967.

[M. B. MONAGHAN]

EGINO, BL. (d. 1120), Benedictine abbot of St. Ulrich and Afra in Augsburg. Because he opposed the imperial party, he was banished from Augsburg. He was able to return in 1106, and in 1109 he was elected abbot of his monastery. After a final break with the simoniacal Bp. Hermann of Augsburg, he had to flee from Augsburg and went to Rome, where in 1120 he was received with honor by Pope Callistus II. On his return journey, he died at the Camaldolese monastery of San Michele and was buried there. BIBLIOGRAPHY: M. R. P. McGuire, NCE 5:191; Zimmermann 2:456, 459; DHGE 15:17–18.

[M. R. P. MCGUIRE]

EGMOND (EGMONT), ABBEY OF, famous Benedictine abbey in N Holland. It was founded in the 10th cent. by Count Dirk of Holland, at first for nuns, then for monks. It was the most important abbey of the country, the source of much of Holland's history. In 1251 it received the right of the pontificalia. By 1561 the abbey was incorporated into the *mensa episcopalis* of Haarlem. The Calvinists entirely destroyed the place in 1573; but the monks of the Solesmes Congregation restored it in 1935, and it became an abbey again by 1950. There is also a convent of Benedictine Sisters there. BIBLIOGRAPHY: A. Koch, DHGE 15:23–27.

[F. N. BACKMUND]

EGMONT, LAMORAL OF (1522–68), Flemish patriot, general, statesman, son of John IV of Egmont. After his elder brother's death E. inherited title to the principality of Gâvre and three baronies. A favorite of Emperor Charles V, he married Sabina of Bavaria (1544) who bore him 11 children. He distinguished himself in the army and in the diplomatic service. In the latter sphere he contributed notably to the negotiations leading to the marriage of the future Philip II of Spain with Mary Tudor of England. When Philip succeeded to the Spanish crown, a new policy regarding the Low Countries was adopted. Philip was determined to increase Spanish domination in that region, and the regent, his half-sister Margaret of Parma, at the instigation of Card. de Granville, in an effort to promote this policy aroused great popular opposition. William of Orange favored toleration in the current religious conflicts, and E. (though he remained a RC until his death) and Count Horn (Hoorn), another popular figure in the politics of the Low Countries, agreed with him. E. went to Spain in an effort to persuade Philip that the States General be convoked to settle the issue, but Philip rejected the proposal, and instead sent the Duke of Avila to see to the strict enforcement of the royal will. With the failure of E.'s mission, William of Orange went into exile. E. and Count Horn were arrested and after a travesty of a trial were condemned by the "Council of Blood." They were beheaded in 1568. Goethe wrote a poetic drama about E., for which the incidental music was composed by Beethoven.

[P. K. MEAGHER]

EGO, the Lat. pronoun "I", in epistemology the conscious, thinking subject as opposed to the object or nonego. The derivatives egoism and egotism have a moral inflection. The first regards self-interest as the foundation of morality, and is contrasted with altruism. The second designates an obtrusive self-reference. As a key technical term the word ego was used by Freud to refer to a basic structure of the human psyche to be distinguished from what he termed the id and the superego. The id covers the instinctual drives and the mental contents and functions connected with them; the superego, the unconscious moral norms and prohibitions and ideals; the ego, perceptions of reality, organized and logical thinking in relation to reality, affective reactions and control of the muscular system by which adaptive behavior is executed.

The infant is born with the id, but the ego develops gradually through the years. The primary function of the ego is to ascertain the most effective modes of discharging instinctual drive energy, i.e., to ascertain the activities that are appropriate and will bring no punishment. In this sense the ego is said to be in the service of the id, and may be defined as the part of the psyche that develops reality orientation in order better to effect satisfying release of drive energy. If the ego's task were simply this, life would be relatively easy. But early infantile experiences operate to produce the superego, which contains norms of behavior and produces guilt feelings when they are violated. This restricts the choices open to the ego. It is obliged to check or defend itself against id impulses which are incompatible with the real situation or contrary to superego norms, and these measures can be painful, maladaptive, and fatiguing. If a person's instinctual drives are constitutionally stronger than normal and/or his superego restrictions are numerous and rigid, the ego is caught in a difficult situation which generally deteriorates into a neurotic condition.

Freud conceived the ego as developing out of and essentially dependent on the id. He likened it to "a man on horseback, who has to hold in check the superior strength of the horse; with this difference, that the rider tries to do so with his own strength while the ego uses borrowed [id] forces." In the past 30 years, psychoanalysis has studied ego functioning more thoroughly (Freud's own work was id-centered) and has developed the concept of a conflict-free ego sphere and autonomous ego development, i.e., independent of energy from the id. BIBLIOGRAPHY: S. Freud, *Ego and the Id* (1923); H. Hartmann, *Ego Psychology and the Problem of Adaptation* (1958); E. F. Edinger, *Ego and Archetype: Individuation and the Religious Function of the Psyche* (1972).

EGOISM, a philosophical classification applied to any system of ethics or moral philosophy that makes the individual's pleasure or pain, approval or disapproval the measure of moral good or of moral evil. In the history of philosophy the term is associated particularly with the ethical system proposed by Thomas *Hobbes, whose primary moral postulate is that for each individual the natural and reasonable course is to seek his own pleasure or preservation. Hobbes surrounds that with variations of the golden rule, as ways that men surrender full exercise of the self-interest precept in order to make life in society possible. Many other ethical systems can be classified as egoist: that of ancient and Renaissance Epicureans; of P. *Gassendi and the philosophers of the *Enlightenment; of F. *Nietzsche. Any form of egoism has as presuppositions, explicit or implicit, the denial of a provident God, of any identifiable and achievable human good and end that measures human actions; the rejection of the naturalness of man's life in society with other men. As a moral philosophy egoism ignores the wisdom in classical ethical theories that hold justice to be a positive and voluntary respect for the rights of others, and as such to be supreme among natural virtues. If egoism has no particularly distinguished, contemporary philosopher as exponent, its postulate permeates contemporary life: in literature, in hedonism, and in the commitment to moral anarchy espoused by the countercultists in the name of "love."

[T. C. O'BRIEN]

EGRES, ABBEY OF, Cistercian monastery in central Hungary. Founded in 1179 by King Béla III with monks from Pontigny, it was richly endowed by King Andrew II (1205–35) who was buried there with his second wife, Jolanta. The abbey was devastated by Tartars in 1241; gradual decline until 1514 led to its suppression. BIBLIOGRAPHY: M. Csáky, NCE 5:194–195.

[L. J. LEKAI]

EGYPT, (United Arab Republic since 1961), a country occupying the Nile valley from the Mediterranean Sea south to the Nubian desert of Sudan. Continually inhabited from

3100 B.C. to the present, Egypt was an independent kingdom until 1085 B.C. when it succumbed to a series of invaders culminating in the conquest of Alexander the Great (332 B.C.). It became independent again under the Ptolemies until it was made a Roman province (30 B.C.). Under Graeco-Roman domination, the indigenous population was reduced to serfdom. The Graeco-Romans had their cultural center at Alexandria, and Greek landlords lived in cities along the Nile, principally at Ptolemais and Antinoë. The Coptic-speaking fellahin were converted to Christianity between 250 and 300, probably before their Graeco-Roman overlords. Their Christianity was simple and intense, and by the time of the Council of Chalcedon (451) it had become mixed with a strong sense of national self-determination and a positive hatred for anything Greek. Thus, when Patriarch Dioscurus opposed Constantinople and Rome at Chalcedon and chose Monophysitism, the majority of Egyptian Christians supported him. A minority, the Melkites (King's men), kept up ties with the Greek and Roman Churches. In 567 Emperor Justin II was forced to recognize the Monophysite patriarch of *Alexandria. In 640 Arabs invaded Egypt and were welcomed as deliverers from further Graeco-Roman harassment. Islam at best tolerated Egyptian Christianity, and at worst tried to wipe it out. Promise of social, political, and economic opportunities along with periodic bloody persecutions impelled the majority of Christians to embrace Islam. Christianity was gradually reduced to a heroic minority and remains so today. Christian Egypt at its height made significant contributions to Christianity. In Alexandria the catechetical school, founded to combat Gnosticism and prepare converts for baptism, grew into an influential theological academy. The number of eminent Egyptian Fathers of the Church attests to its scope and competence. Another far-reaching contribution was Egyptian monasticism. Beginning in the 3d cent. with individual hermits and anchoritic communities establishing themselves in the desert around Thebes (the Thebaid), it developed into a network of highly organized monastic communities. Their rules and spiritual writings spread to the whole Christian world and in some degree influenced all later monasticism. This reputation also made Egypt a goal for pilgrims from Europe and Asia. Egyptian Christians themselves traveled widely, and there is evidence of their influence in W Europe. This is esp. true of Ireland where the example of Egyptian monasticism helped to form a Christianity dominated by monastic communities similar to those of the Thebaid. BIBLIOGRAPHY: H. I. Bell, *Egypt from Alexander the Great to the Arab Conquest* (1948); *Legacy of Egypt* (ed. S. R. K. Glanville, 1942); E. R. Hardy, *Christian Egypt* (1952).

[D. W. JOHNSON]

EGYPT, EARLY CHURCH IN. Though there is no direct evidence for the existence of Christianity in Egypt in the 1st cent., the prominent position which the land occupied in the Greco-Roman world and the large numbers of

Jews living there are adequate reasons for believing that it was an early object of Christian missionary activities. The tradition that the Church at Alexandria was founded by St. Mark is hardly credible, since it is not mentioned by Clement or Origen and first appears in Eusebius (*Eccl. Hist.* 2.16.1). Even less likely is the contention of Salomon Reinach and a few others that a letter of the Emperor Claudius to the Alexandrines (contained in a papyrus in the British Museun) refers to the presence of Christians in their city. On the other hand, since there were Jews from "Egypt and the parts of Libya about Cyrene" (Acts 2:10) who heard the Apostles preaching in tongues on the first Christian Pentecost, it is possible that they were converted and brought the new faith back with them to Egypt when they returned home.

Fragments of four Christian papyri, one possibly dating back to the second decade of the 2d cent. and four others that are probably of Christian origin bear testimony to what must have been a considerable number of Christians in Egypt in the 2d century. That not all were orthodox is evidenced by St. Irenaeus's condemnations of the Gnostic heresies preached at Alexandria by Valentinus and Basilides. During the second half of the 2d cent. a catechetical school was erected at Alexandria to counteract heresies and to provide Christians with a means for acquiring a higher education, which was otherwise only available at the pagan university in the Museum. The first director of this school was Pantaenus, a Samaritan who had received a Greek philosophical education. The second was Clement of Alexandria, probably a native of Athens converted to Christianity in early middle age, who combined an ardent admiration for Greek culture with a genuine piety. The third was Origen, a native of Alexandria, an indefatigable worker, a great exegete, and despite some errors in doctrine certainly one of the most learned Christians of the early Church. The first known bishop in Egypt was Demetrius of Alexandria (189–231), and he seems to have been the first to consecrate other bishops outside the capital.

During the first centuries the Christians of Egypt were subjected to a number of cruel persecutions, particularly under the Emperors Septimius Severus, Decius, and Diocletian. The sufferings of these times have been well described by Eusebius in his *Ecclesiastical History*. During these persecutions many Christians fled into the desert. Later, many Christians voluntarily retired there in order to lead a life of prayer and penance. The first to adopt this type of asceticism is generally believed to have been Paul of Thebes (d. *c*.341). More famous, however, is St. *Anthony, who died at the age of 105 (in 356). Under Anthony the purely eremetical life began to give way to one in common. Regular monastic institutions, however, with a definite rule trace their origins to *Pachomius (d. *c*.346). The monasteries of Egypt soon became famous and were visited by pilgrims such as St. Jerome, Rufinus, John Cassian, Palladius, and Evagrius. Admiration for this form of life soon caused it to spread to the West.

The most famous of Alexandrian bishops was St. *Athanasius (295–373). A native of Alexandria, he took part in the Council of Nicaea as deacon and secretary of his bp. Alexander, whom he succeeded in 328. During the 4th and 5th cent. the patriarchs of Alexandria were involved in numerous controversies. Theophilus of Alexandria brought about the condemnation of St. John Chrysostom at the Synod of the Oak (403). St. Cyril acted as the delegate of Pope Celestine at the Council of Ephesus (431) and excommunicated Nestorius. At the Robber Synod of Ephesus in 449 Dioscorus tried to rehabilitate Eutyches. During the 6th and 7th cent. Egypt became the center of the Monophysitic controversies, which so weakened and divided the country that it fell first to Persians (617) and later to Arab followers of Mohammed (642). BIBLIOGRAPHY: M. C. Hilferty, NCE 5:224–227; DACL 4.2:2401–2571; H. I. Bell, *Cults and Creeds in Graeco-Roman Egypt* (1953), 78–105.

[M. J. COSTELLOE]

EGYPTIAN CHURCH ORDER, another name for what is substantially a translation of the *Apostolic Tradition* of Hippolytus of Rome. This document has been called Egyptian because it first became known to modern scholars through Ethiopic and Coptic manuscripts. Although it had great influence in the liturgical and canonical life of the Eastern Churches, it also throws new light on the early formation of the Roman liturgy. The document was written *c*.215. The first part deals with the hierarchy. After setting forth rules for the election and consecration of bps., there is a Eucharistic Liturgy to be celebrated on that occasion. More rules follow concerning he ordinations of the lower clergy. The second part deals with the laity, their Christian education, the sacraments and rules for Christian behavior. The third section contains general ecclesiastical observances including the Sunday Eucharist and rules for fasting. The conservative tone of the document seems to indicate an attempt to preserve older usages in the face of change. BIBLIOGRAPHY: Quasten 2:180–194; J. Quasten, NCE 5:227–228.

[D. W. JOHNSON]

EGYPTIAN RELIGION. The religion of the ancient Egyptians presents a bewildering complexity in the realm of religious thought, relieved only by a certain unity of religious practice. On closer inspection, complexity is seen to result from the way the Egyptians themselves handled the problem of development from an early stage, in which small areas had their local gods, to a stage in which a united Egypt ordered and classified the gods, each now with functions proper to him alone, in a national pantheon, the role and functions of the various gods continuing to change and blend through the centuries. Of all the Egyptian religious writings, none was normative in the sense that the Bible or the Koran are normative, yet various traditions were spontaneously maintained through all the change. Genuine

Egyptian religion reflected the peaceful nature of the people. The gods were not bloodthirsty, the cult, as such, was not ecstatic or orgiastic. Throughout its history there was always a difference between official religion, popular folk-religion, and the religion of the occult. Furthermore, the Egyptian pharaoh was himself a god and retained this divine character to the days of the Ptolemies. A particular phenomenon is the spread of Egyptian religion in the Greco-Roman world: here the syncretism of the times took old Egyptian divinities, rituals, cultic organization, only to confuse the divinities with those of other provenance (e.g., Osiris with Serapis from Sinope), infusing the rites with Hellenistic piety, reinterpreting them as Hellenistic mysteries or as philosophical cults.

The primitive local gods seem to have had animal forms for the most part; their human behavior led to typically Egyptian representation of such gods in human form with the original animal head or a symbolic part thereof. Some gods, apparently abstract in origin, were always represented in human form. The nature of the gods was expounded by myth; either by the cosmogonic myths produced by the learned activity of clerical circles, or by the popular myths, full of often earthy narrative color, telling of the vicissitudes of well-known divinities. The popular myths, esp. those of the Osirian cycle, were subject to constant variation and development, according to the shifting trends of popular preference and the creative imagination of men in different times and places. The more learned cosmogonic myths, once established, tended to remain stable. The latter type fixed the hierarchical relation of gods to one another; such relations, being constructed on the natures of the various divinities concerned, constituted a kind of Egyptian theodicy. The earliest systems were those of: (1) Heliopolis, which, reckoning with an Ennead of nine gods and goddesses, explained the origins and perdurance of the universe, admitted select gods into the Ennead's prominence, and gave supremacy to Re (the Sun) as absolute first principle, and (2) Hermopolis, which reckoned with an Ogdoad of four abstract, divine couples at the origins of the world, with Re himself created by them. The slightly later Memphitic system placed the Memphitic god Ptah at the head of the primordial gods of the Ogdoad. The rise of Thebes to hegemony *c*. 2000 B.C. led to a Theban construction placing Amon at the head of the pantheon, but the prevailing solar trend of Egyptian religion brought about a blending of Amon and Re. In the 14th cent. B.C., the solar cult itself took a radical turn, when Amenophis IV (Akhenaten) introduced a cult in which the solar disk itself *(aten),* devoid of all human or animal traits, was worshiped, to the practical exclusion of other gods and the explicit exclusion of the national cult of Amon. The *aten* cult was a joyous and lofty one, free of most magic and myth, celebrating the life of the universe emanating from the solar disk, but it hardly survived Akhenaten himself. Egyptologists still debate questions of primitive animism or fetishism, and of monotheism, henotheism, and transcendence in Egyptian religion. The *aten* cult was monotheistic, but it was neither typical nor successful. The universal character of Re or Amon-Re and syncretistic conceptions of fluid interchange of attributes among gods (esp. in the 1st millennium B.C.) may indicate a certain monotheistic sense, but partisan theological construction was also at work in such matters.

As elsewhere in the Ancient Near East, the earthly house of a god was the temple. The vast temple complexes of the New Kingdom (latter 2d millennium) and the Ptolemaic period (after 304 B.C.) show a plan in which a gate led through the massive frontal pylons into a large open court surrounded by porticoes, where the ordinary people gathered on festive occasions. Beyond this was a dim hall with a roof supported by multiple columns (hypostyle hall) where certain rites were performed in the presence of a privileged few. Further beyond, in darkness, were the god's living quarters, with the shrine containing the divine statue. The statue was not simply identified with the god: it was vitalized by magic rites which brought about its occupancy by the god's *ba,* a vital force that enabled its possessor to move about and to take on various aspects. The daily ritual comprised rites based materially on the services performed for a king by his courtiers—a morning wakening, washing, perfuming, incensing, clothing, and the offering of food thrice daily. The words to be spoken and the ritual directives, however, endowed the actions with a sense of recalling and reenacting events in Egyptian mythology, a sense which was even more pronounced in festive liturgies with their mythological drama and mimes celebrating events in the lives of the gods. Sacrificial offerings (vegetables, fruit, bread, meat, as food for the god), are also shown by ritual words and symbolic actions to have been permeated with mythological and magical concepts. Holocaust, absent in early times in ordinary worship, appeared in the New Kingdom and became common in later periods. Expiatory motives did not develop in Egyptian sacrifice.

Certain elements evident in the cult of a god recur in Egyptian rites having to to do with the care of the dead. Offerings of food to the dead were made to the accompaniment of ritual words and gestures analogous to those accompanying offerings of food to a god. In both cases, moreover, a statue of the dead person or of the god was magically animated to enable him to receive his food, and in both cases mythology of the Osirian cycle exerted a certain influence in ritual symbolism. As a result, modern authors have often spoken of a "cult" of the dead. More accurately, however, "sacrifice" in Egypt was essentially the votive offering of food to a god, not "sacrifice" in the usual sense; the mortuary rites now in question are also essentially food-offerings, not sacrifices; their occasional, and never normal, interpretation in late Egyptian religion as sacrifices to the dead arose from the identification of the dead with the divine Osiris. The Egyptians tended to look upon a prolongation of eating and other earthly satisfactions as the ideal of life after death, although both the solar religion of the 3d millennium and the Osirian ideals of the 2d millennium and later contained notions of beatitude in the divine regions, or of a kind of undetermined resurrection in imitation of Osiris. Even ideas of immortality were qualified. The individual could live after death through his immaterial *ba* and *ka,* but this was to some extent contingent upon conservation of his material body (hence the use of funerary statues as a substitute material reference for the *ba* and *ka,* and the development of mummification): if the body were destroyed, the immaterial powers had no more reference to this world and had to resign themselves to a kind of limbo existence.

Related to life after death is the Egyptian religious basis for morality. Already in the early 3d millennium the Pyramid Texts speak of a kind of judgment of a dead king by Re, but the criterion of good behavior at that time was little more than conformity to one's position in the highly-structured Egyptian society. From the end of Dynasty VI (*c.* 2200) on, an idea of wrong as an offense against individuals in a cosmic order appears clearly, along with the notion of divine displeasure at such an offense and of divine punishment. A morality based on justice developed, and if a man hoped to "see the face of all the gods" and enjoy good things in the afterlife, he would have to be free from guilt incurred by offenses against the gods, his fellow men, and himself. Otherwise he would be excluded from the kingdom of Osiris, not see the sun, go hungry and thirsty, be devoured by a monster. The common people turned to magic as a means of assuring admission to the presence of the gods even if actual moral behavior were found wanting; although in the Greco-Roman period, when magic was rampant, there is evidence of the notion that a man's actions alone determine his fate, that magic is of no avail in avoiding punishment for evil. Indeed, it was in the 1st millennium B.C., when theology had lost itself in sterile and puerile speculations, and popular piety was little more than trusting expectation of favors from the gods, that a few lofty minds achieved the highest moral ideals in the history of Egyptian religion, e.g., the Wisdom of Amen-em-Ope. BIBLIOGRAPHY: A. Erman, *Die Religion der Ägypter* (1934); H. Frankfort, *Ancient Egyptian Religion* (1948); J. Vandier, *La Religion égyptienne* (2d ed., 1949); J. Černý, *Ancient Egyptian Religion* (1952); H. Bonnet, *Reallexikon der ägyptischen Religionsgeschichte* (1952); S. Morenz, *Ägyptische Religion* (1960); J. Vergote, NCE 5:207–213; *Ancient Near Eastern Texts relating to the Old Testament* (tr. J. A. Wilson, ed. J. B. Pritchard, 2d ed., 1955) 3–36, 325–330, 365–381, 412–424, 431–433, 441–449.

[A. CODY]

EGYPTIANS, GOSPEL ACCORDING TO THE, see APOCRYPHA (NEW TESTAMENT), 19.

EHRHARD, ALBERT (1862–1940), German Church historian, patrologist, and Byzantinist. In his career as teacher of Church history, E. held professorships at the Univ. of Würzburg, Vienna, Freiburg, Strassburg and Bonn. His particular interest lay in the hagiographic and homiletic literature of the Greek Church. His works on the history of the Church set a new high standard for historical criticism. He was accused of revealing Modernist tendencies in his more strictly theological works, and this made him an object of suspicion to some during the early years of the 20th century. BIBLIOGRAPHY: J. Quasten, NCE 5:229–230; F. Loidl, LTK 3:719.

[R. B. ENO]

EHRLE, FRANZ (1845–1934), German Jesuit, prefect of the Vatican Library, medievalist, cardinal. Except for the years of World War I, E. spent his life after 1880 in Rome. He was responsible for the enrichment of the Vatican Library, improvement of its facilities for consultation, and for the care and use of manuscripts. The many MSS that he discovered, edited, and published with accompanying studies contributed vastly to the history of scholasticism. His own published works were listed in the "Album" attached to the *Miscellanea Francisci Ehrle* (5 v. 1924), a collection of studies and texts honoring him on his 80th birthday. BIBLIOGRAPHY: A. Pelzer, DHGE 15:65–69.

[T. C. O'BRIEN]

EICHENDORFF, JOSEPH VON (1788–1857), German Romantic poet. The intrinsic musicality of his poems, their mystic dreaminess and sensuous beauty, the recurrent themes of *Wanderlust* and *Heimatliebe* make Eichendorff's the greatest lyric poetry of German Romanticism (*Gedichte,* 1837). The affinity of his poems to the folksong and the simple piety that inspires them make them perennially popular. E. also composed plays, novels, narrative poems, novelle, and critical works (e.g., *Über die ethische und religiöse Bedeutung der neueren romantischen Poesie in Deutschland,* 1847). The novella *Aus dem Leben eines Taugenichts* (1826) is a masterpiece of romantic fiction. BIBLIOGRAPHY: W. Kosch, *Deutsches Literatur-Lexikon* (1963) 78; H. Tucker, Jr., NCE 5:230; L. R. Radner, *Eichendorff: The Spiritual Geometer* (1971).

[M. F. MCCARTHY]

EICHSTÄTT, MONASTERIES OF. The founder of the diocese, St. Boniface, established a Benedictine monastery adjacent to the cathedral, for only a short time. The *monasterium Scotorum* of the Holy Cross was a branch of the Irish Benedictines of St. James in Ratisbon; it had provosts instead of abbots. Their apostolate was to give lodging to pilgrims going to the Holy Land. When the abbey was closed in 1500, the revenues were given to the seminary, the monastery itself to the Capuchins (1623), in whose care it remains today.

At the venerated tomb of St. Walburga, an Anglo-Saxon princess, there was founded a community of canonesses in the 9th cent.; by 1035 Benedictine nuns occupied St. Walburga's. In the Middle Ages it was reserved to nobility. Though suppressed in 1809, it was restored in 1835 and has flourished since. From there came the first Benedictine nuns to the U.S., who have founded, since 1850, 22 dependent houses.

In a now incorporated suburb of Eichstätt stands the former abbey of Rebdorf, founded 1153 by Emperor Frederick Barbarossa for Canons Regular of St. Augustine. It attached itself in 1454 to the Windesheim Congregation and became a seat of humanist learning. Prior Kilian Leib (1503–53) was a notable humanist. Though suppressed in 1806, it was restored in 1958 by the Fathers of the Sacred Hearts. BIBLIOGRAPHY: N. Backmund, NCE 5:230–231.

[F. N. BACKMUND]

EIGHTEEN BENEDICTIONS, English form of the Hebrew name of the prayer called *shemoneh esreh.*

EIMERIC OF CAMPO (d. 1460), Dutch theologian and philosopher. E. taught at Paris, Diest, Cologne, and Louvain, where he was rector six times between 1435 and 1460. He supported the adherents of St. Albert the Great against the Thomists of Cologne in several works. BIBLIOGRAPHY: S. Cipriani, DE 2:950–951.

[M. J. SUELZER]

EINFÜHLUNG (EMPATHY), a term coined by Edward Titchener in 1909 for a German aesthetic theory and referring to the artist's projection of self into the objects studied. Franz Marc of the Blaue Reiter group is an exponent of this theory, seeking an inner harmony between himself and the animals he painted (*Blue Horses,* 1911).

[M. J. DALY]

EINHARD (Eginhard; *c.*770–840), Frankish historian. Educated first at Fulda, and then at the palace school at Aachen under *Alcuin, E. became one of Charlemagne's most trusted advisers and friends. He continued as counselor under Louis I, who rewarded him with the estates of Michelstadt and Seligenstadt. His *Life of Charlemagne,* the most remarkable achievement in medieval biography, was modeled on the *Vitae* of Suetonius, esp. the *Vita Augusti*; it departed from contemporary annalistic methods, and presented instead an intimate and personal portrait of Charlemagne in his character and reign. His *Translatio SS. Marcellini et Petri* (an account of the bringing of the martyrs' relics to Seligenstadt) and his surviving letters are valuable historical sources for the time. Works: *Life of Charlemagne* (tr. S. E. Turner, 1960); *History of the Translation of the Blessed Martyrs of Christ* (tr. B. Wendell, 1926); *Epistolae* (ed. K. Hampe, MGH Ep. 1899) 5:105–145. BIBLIOGRAPHY: E. S. Duckett, *Carolingian Portraits: A Study in the Ninth Century* (1962); R. E. Sullivan, NCE 5:232.

[M. S. TANEY]

EINSIEDELN, ABBEY OF, dedicated to Our Lady of the Hermits and located in the Swiss canton of Schwyz.

Eberhard, first abbot (934–958), united in a Benedictine community Benno and other companions who, like Eberhard, had settled as hermits in the place where St. Meinrad (slain in 861) had lived as a hermit for about 25 years. The abbey enjoyed the benefactions of royal houses—the Ottos and the dukes of Swabia. Duke Herman of Swabia had the first cloister buildings erected. Between 1029 and 1577, the abbey was destroyed by fire five times. Political struggles and wars were also disastrous for the abbey, but periodically buildings were restored and constructed. The present Baroque convent was erected in 1704–08; the church, in 1719–26, last restored in 1943. A popular place of pilgrimage since the 13th cent. and the first Swiss place of pilgrimage, it remains still a great attraction for tourists. In the mid-19th cent. daughter houses were founded in the U.S.: St. Meinrad, New Subiaco, Richardton; and in 1948, the Priory of Los Toldos, Argentina. BIBLIOGRAPHY: R. Henggeler DHGE 15:95–97.

[S. A. HEENEY]

EINSTEIN, ALBERT (1879–1955), German-born physicist whose theories of the photoelectric effect, quanta, and of general and special relativity were fundamental in the 20th cent. revolution in the physical sciences and natural philosophy. After study at the Polytechnic in Zurich, E. worked for 7 years at Berne as an examiner in the Swiss Patent Office. In 1905 he received his doctorate from the Univ. of Zurich for a dissertation relating to Brownian motion, "A New Determination of Molecular Dimensions." E. taught at Zurich (1909), Prague (1911), Zurich (1912), and in 1914 he was director of the Kaiser Wilhelm Institute for Physics at Berlin. After 1919 when his predictions on the deviation of light passing close to the sun, based on his theory of general relativity, were proven correct, his fame spread rapidly. He used his prominence to support pacifism, Zionism, the Hebrew Univ. in Jerusalem, and the League of Nation's Committee on Intellectual Cooperation. He left Germany when Hitler came to power, emigrating to the Institute for Advanced Study at Princeton, and became an American citizen in 1940. His fear that Germany might be developing weapons using nuclear fission led E. to warn the U.S. Government, a warning that prompted the Manhattan project for atomic weapons. Throughout his life, E.'s opposition to war and nuclear arms continued. His famous comment on indeterminacy at the subatomic level, "God does not play dice," must be understood more scientifically and philosophically than theologically; E. could not tolerate the notion that at its most fundamental levels of organization the universe was governed by chance.

[R. J. LITZ]

EISENGREIN, MARTIN (1535–78), German theologian, preacher, controversialist, friend and collaborator of Peter Canisius and Johann Eck. E. abandoned Lutheranism and became a Catholic in 1558. After his ordination to the Catholic priesthood in 1560 he strove by his preaching to counteract Protestant propaganda. BIBLIOGRA-PHY: B. L. Marthaler, NCE 5:235.

[M. J. SUELZER]

EISENGREIN, WILHELM (1543–84), nephew of Martin, chiefly remembered for his attacks, in four separate works, upon Flacius' *Centuries of Magdeburg*. BIBLIOGRAPHY: A. Brück, LTK 3:777–778.

[M. J. SUELZER]

EISENHOFER, LUDWIG (1871–1941), German liturgist. His first important work was his thorough revision (1912) of V. *Talhofer's *Handbuch der katholischen Liturgik* (2 v., 1883–93). Later he produced a *Handbuch* of his own under the same title (2 v., 1932–33), a work of lasting merit for its application of sound historical method to the study of liturgical development and literature. BIBLIOGRAPHY: E. Jerg, LTK 3:778.

[N. KOLLAR]

EJACULATION, see ASPIRATION (EJACULATION).

EKD, see EVANGELICAL CHURCH IN GERMANY.

EKKEHARD. There are four Ekkehards, all monks at the Abbey of Sankt Gallen, Switzerland, from the 10th to the 11th cent., and connected with the famous school at the Abbey.

Ekkehard I (*c*.910–973), born of a noble family, designated by Abbot Craloh (942–958) of Sankt Gall as his successor. After Craloh's death, the monks elected E., but awaiting imperial confirmation, he was lamed by a fall from his horse. He renounced his office in favor of Burkhard I (958–971) and continued as dean. He is supposed to be the author of "Waltharius," a Latin version of German folksaga, but this is challenged.

Ekkehard II, The Courtier ("Patatinus"), b. beginning of 10th cent., d. 990. Nephew and pupil of Ekkehard I, he taught in the inner and outer school of Sankt Gall, read Latin (Virgil) to the Duchess Hadwig of Swabia, and through her gained access to the Court of Emperor Otto I, introducing Sankt Gall into the Ottonian Renaissance. Later, the monk was appointed canon of Mainz. He is the hero of a novel by J. V. von Scheffel (1919).

Ekkehard III, Scholar, also nephew of Ekkehard I, preceded Notker Labeo (*c*.950–1022). He was chaplain to the Duchess Hadwig, and aided the foundation of the monastery of Stein-on-the-Rhine in 966. He was dean at the monastic school for more than 30 years. There is no record of his writings.

Ekkehard IV, Teacher (980–1061). Born in Alsace, E. studied under Notker Labeo, and succeeded him as director of the Cathedral School at Mainz, where he found favor with Emperor Conrad III. At Sankt Gall, E. continued the ancient monastery chronicle, "Casus s. Galli," begun by

Ratpert. Not a very good historian, E. still created a valuable source book for contemporary events. He was also skilled in music. BIBLIOGRAPHY: J. K. Bostock, *Handbook on Old High German Literature* (1955); H. F. Haefele, LTK 3:780–781; T. de Morembert, DHGE 14:1382–84.

[N. F. GAUGHAN]

EKPHŌNĒSIS (Gr., exclamation), the exclamation in a loud voice of the conclusion of a prayer which has been said in a low voice or silently so that the people may associate themselves with that prayer by their *Amen*. The usual Byzantine *ekphōnēsis* is in the form of a doxology.

[J. FRANCAVILLA]

EKRON (ACCARON), the name of one of the five principal Philistine cities listed in Jos 13.3. In 1 Macc 10.89 it is named Accaron. The data of Jg 1.18 (MT; but contradicted in LXX) and 1 Sam 7.14 (cf. also Jos 15.45; 19.43) that Ekron was occupied by Israel during these periods seem incorrect. For a time the captured ark was kept in Ekron, but the outbreak of plague in the city caused its removal to Beth Shemesh (1 Sam 5.10–6.16). After the slaying of Goliath the Philistines retreated to Ekron to escape a complete rout by Israel (1 Sam 17.52). The city figures in the denunciations of the prophets (Jer 25.20; Am 1.8; Zeph 2.4; Zech 9.5,7). It also appears in an inscription of the Egyptian Pharoah Shishak (935–914 B.C.) as one of the cities captured by him as well as in the inscriptions of the Assyrian King Sennacherib (705–681 B.C.) who restored Padi, King of Ekron, to his throne when disloyal elements in the city turned Padi over to Hezekiah, King of Judah, for imprisonment.

[C. P. CEROKE]

EL-GOD, generic name for the divinity in the ancient Semitic world and title of the supreme god of the Ugaritic pantheon. The name served as a vehicle for God's manifestation of himself to the Hebrew patriarchs (Gen 16.13; 21.33). The terms *Elohim* and *Eloah* also occur, as well as a number of composite forms. See Gen 14.22; 17.1; 21.33; 28.19; 33.20; Ex 6.3; Ps 18.3. BIBLIOGRAPHY: De Vaux AncIsr 289–294, 310, 374.

[C. BERNAS]

ELAM, state located on the slopes of the Iranian Plateau toward the Tigris-Euphrates valley, with its capital at Susa. It was listed in the table of the nations (Gen 10.22) and mentioned by Isaiah (11.11; 21.2; 22.6), Jeremiah (49.34–39), and Ezekiel (32.24). Elamites were among the groups present in Jerusalem at Pentecost (Acts 2.9). After a fluctuating history of dominance and decline from the 3d millennium B.C., Elam was destroyed by Ashurbanipal *c*.645 B.C., and it was later dominated by the Medes and then the Persians.

[T. EARLY]

ELAPHRON, in Middle Byzantine musical notation, a descending third.

ELATH, see ASIONGABER.

ELBEL, BENJAMIN (1690–1756), Franciscan theologian and casuist. A Bavarian, and a member of the Order of Friars Minor Recollect, he published a text for moral theology, *Theologia moralis decalogalis* (1731), that was reissued even into the 20th century. The work embodied the moral principles of *probabilism, and illustrated their application to concrete cases of conscience. BIBLIOGRAPHY: T. Deman, DTC 13:563 s.v. "Probabilisme."

[T. C. O'BRIEN]

ELCHASAITES, see ELKESAITES.

ELDAD HA-DANI, Jewish merchant and traveler of the 9th cent. A.D. On visits to Babylonia and Kairwan *c.* 880 and Spain in 883 he reported that an independent Jewish state existed in E Africa, inhabited by the so-called ten lost tribes. The existence of the *Falashas in Ethiopia indicates his report may have had some basis in fact. His stories perhaps influenced the legend of Prester John. An English translation of *The Tales of Eldad the Danite* appeared in 1855.

[T. EARLY]

ELDER, GEORGE (1793–1838), American educator. He attended Mount St. Mary's College, Emmitsburg, Md., and in 1816 entered St. Charles Seminary, Baltimore. Ordained in 1819 at the first ordination ceremony in the cathedral of Bardstown, Ky., he was assigned as an assistant at the cathedral. At the request of Bp. Flaget he founded St. Joseph's College for boys, which became one of the largest educational institutions in the entire West. In 1827 he was given charge of the disquieted parish of St. Pius in Scotts County. As one of the editors of the *Catholic Advocate,* the first Catholic weekly in Louisville, he became known for his articles on education, and for his provocative series, "Letters to Brother Jonathan." In 1830 he returned to St. Joseph's College as president; he remained there until his death, caused by fighting the fire that destroyed the main college building.

[C. KEENAN]

ELDER, WILLIAM HENRY (1819–1904), American archbishop. After graduating from Mount St. Mary's College, Emmitsburg, Md. in 1837, he entered the seminary and was ordained in Rome in 1846. He taught theology at Mount St. Mary's and was its president before becoming bp. of Natchez, Miss., in 1857. During the Civil War he was loyal to the Confederacy and in 1864 was convicted for refusing to honor the request of the Union Brig. General Tuttle that a special prayer for Pres. Lincoln be included in

the Mass. During the yellow fever epidemic of 1878 E.'s services to his people were heroic. In 1880 he became coadjutor bp. of Cincinnati, Ohio, and in 1883 succeeded to the see as archbishop. During his tenure the archdiocese was in severe financial straits and litigation was in progress over its funds; still E. established St. Gregory's, a preparatory seminary, and reopened Mount St. Mary's Seminary; established new parishes and schools; and convened provincial councils and diocesan synods to improve church discipline.

[C. KEENAN]

ELDER, an Eng. translation in preference to "priest," of the Gr. *presbuteros* and the Lat. equivalent *presbyter* to designate one who holds a certain office in a Church. The elder is esp., but not exclusively, characteristic of Presbyterianism. In the *Reformed Churches generally the ministry includes presbyters who preach and administer the sacraments (teaching elders) and presbyters who assist ministers of the Word in pastoral care and in the government of the Church (ruling elders). For the ruling elder, John *Calvin used the terms *senior, seigneur,* and *ancien;* he distinguished the elder as a second order from the ministers of the word and sacraments, whom he called variously bishops, presbyters, pastors, or ministers. Presbyterian use of elder ordinarily refers to the ruling elder. The elder is a layman, or in many Reformed Churches a laywoman, representing the people in the *church session and the *presbytery. Ordination to the office is by a minister, and for life, although in practice an elder may serve only for a term of years, then retire until reelected. In the Churches of God in North America (General Eldership) the term is used in much the same way. In Methodism the ministry is held to consist of the orders of deacon and elder, the second being the higher. A minister is elected elder by the Annual Conference, and is ordained by a bishop and other elders. The office is still thought to consist essentially in the power to administer the sacraments; while deacons and, in certain cases, lay preachers may exercise this power, only the elder can do so everywhere in the Church. In the Church of Jesus Christ of Latter-day Saints (Mormons) elder is the lowest of the order of the Melkisedek priesthood.

The term elder has also a more general use in Churches that do not accept the idea of a sacred ministry or ordination, and play down any distinction between clergy and laity. Elder or deacon then signifies anyone who officiates at worship or has a function in the governing of a Church. Such is the usage in the Christian Churches (Disciples of Christ).

[J. A. R. MACKENZIE]

ELDERS, in the OT period prior to the monarchy, the rulers of the tribes; later the rulers or authoritative persons in various localities were so designated, and with the priestly representatives formed the Sanhedrin of Jerusalem.

In the NT rulers of local Churches are so called (1 Tim 5.17); they formed a college (1 Tim 4.14) at least in some Churches. BIBLIOGRAPHY: J. J. O'Rourke, 11:745–746 s.v. "Presbyter."

[J. J. O'ROURKE]

ELDRAD, ST. (d. *c.*845), abbot of Novalese, a Benedictine monastery in Piedmont, whose many MSS made it a cultural center. He ruled the monastery for 20 years and provided lodging for pilgrims crossing the Alps into Italy. King Lothair made a gift to the monastery in 825 and in 827 E. negotiated successfully with Count Boso of Turin. BIBLIOGRAPHY: V. G. Gremigni, BiblSanct 4:982–985.

[J. E. LYNCH]

ELEAN-ERETRIAN SCHOOL, one of the *Minor Socratic Schools, named after Phaedo of Elis, disciple of Socrates and the Phaedo of Plato's dialogues, and Menedemus of Eretria (339–265 B.C.). Phaedo is said to have written dialogues distinguished for their wit and charm, partly under the influence of Socrates himself and partly under that of the *Megarian School. Menedemus, while continuing the tradition of Phaedo, adopted also the philosophical method and teachings of the Megarians. BIBLIOGRAPHY: OCD 557, 673; Ueberweg 1:158–159.

[M. R. P. MCGUIRE]

ELEANOR OF AQUITAINE (*c.*1122–1204), Duchess of Aquitaine, Queen of France (1137–52), Queen of England (1154–1204). Heiress of William X of Aquitaine, E.'s unsuccessful marriage to Louis VII of France, whom she accompanied on the Second Crusade, was annulled for consanguinity. Married (1152) to Henry II of England (1154–89), E. supported their sons in rebellion against Henry, who imprisoned her for years. Restored to power, she backed King Richard against his brother John, and, later, King John against her grandson Arthur. A patron of troubadour culture, E. died at Fontevrault (1204). BIBLIOGRAPHY: A. Kelly, *Eleanor of Aquitaine and the Four Kings* (1950); *Patron and Politician* (ed. W. W. Kibler, Symposia in the Arts and the Humanities, ser. no. 3, 1975).

[W. A. CHANEY]

ELEATICS, THE, a school of Early Greek philosophy founded by *Parmenides (*c.*515–*c.*445 B.C.) and continued by *Zeno (*c.*490–after 440 B.C.) and Melissus (fl. 540). Recent critical studies have shown that *Xenophanes of Colophon (*c.*570–475 B.C.), the traditional founder of this school, should not be considered an Eleatic in the strict sense. The school represented an uncompromising monism. BIBLIOGRAPHY: Guthrie 1:401–402; 2:1–118.

[M. R. P. MCGUIRE]

ELECTION, DIVINE. Biblical notions of election were aimed at imparting awareness of God's loyal love, so that the chosen might respond with due fidelity. Christian theological attempts to describe God's election of individuals to grace and glory were developments of postbiblical academics.

In the OT lowly men were recorded as chosen for greatness by God so that hope would be enkindled in those who paid attention to sacred history (Abraham, Gen 12–22 *passim*; Jacob-Israel, 25.21–26; Joseph ch. 37; Samuel, 1 Sam 3; David, 1 Sam 16.1–13; etc.). Israel as a people were chosen to be and act as sacred, cultic servants of the unique God (Ex 19.3–8). God's motives were love for them and fidelity to their ancestors; their response was to be loving, obedient loyalty (Dt 7.1–11; 4.32–40). After many refusals to live up to his election, they had to be punished, even with destruction (Am 3.2). Eventually, for a remnant of Judah, a new election, like a new creation, was proclaimed in Second Isaiah; its purpose was to bear witness to men about God's uniqueness (Is 41.8–10; 42.1–9; 43.1–15, etc.). Echoes of this theme appeared in Jeremiah and Ezekiel (Jer ch. 30–33; Ezek ch. 37). After the exile the cycle of election, rejection, and new election became the pattern for future hopes and the motivation for reforms (Neh 9.6–37; Est ch. 14–21, *New America Bible*). Election, then, was a didactic vehicle for exhorting the chosen to respond to God's gratuitous love.

In the NT Paul's notion of election had much the same purpose. He affirmed that Christians as a body were the beneficiaries of God's eternal decree uniting them to him in and through Jesus Christ (Rom ch. 8; Eph 1.3–14). He solved the problem of the partial rejection of the Jews by citing their refusal to believe in their new election that came through the Messiah's redemptive death for them (Rom 9.30–33). He offered no clear answer why God chose some and rejected others: this was God's problem, and, on the whole, although he should have shown his power and anger by destroying so many "vessels set for destruction," he did not do so in order to show his mercy to "those whom He called" (Rom 9.19–24). Thus by his election theology, Paul aimed at provoking Christians to a reflective acceptance of their sacred identity as God's beloved so that they might continue their mandatory growth in Christ from a position of strength rather than from the weakness of mere human striving to please God.

The theology of John's Gospel connected election with his main concern, the transmission of true faith-knowledge by mission and witness. Examples are: John the Baptist's witness (Jn 1.6,7,15,19–36; 3.26–36; 5.33–36); the disciples' vocation to faith and witness (1.14, "we have seen his glory: . . .", 38–2.11); the Samaritans (4.25–42); the Twelve (6.70; 13.12–21; 15.1–16, etc.); Jesus, God's Elect, was sent to baptize with the Holy Spirit of Truth (1.33,34; 7.37–39; 10.31–38; 16.7–15; cf. Is 42.1–9). The overall purpose of John's use of election for witnessing was to evoke and/or strengthen true faith (19.35; 20.30,31; 21.15–17,24).

The Synoptic Gospels match John's election themes (Lk 6.13; 9.57–62, and parallels; 10.1–3). Luke continued the themes in Acts (Acts 1.2,8,15–26; 9.15; 15.7). Also, in Luke Jesus was God's chosen one who must be believed (Lk 9.35; cf. 23.35). In a saying of Jesus, proper to Luke, the phrase, "the elect," was used to teach confident and persistent prayer (18.7,8). The NT did, however, clearly refer to a divine election to final salvation: in the eschatological preaching of Jesus (Mk 13.20,22,27, and parallels; Mt 22.14, the only place in the NT where God's call and election were clearly distinguished); in a theological comment of Luke (Acts 13.48, cf. 2.39); and in apocalyptic literature (Rev 2.7; 3.5; 13.8; 17.8; 20.12,15; 21.27; cf. Mal 3.16 and Dan 12.1). Yet, in all these texts, the intentions of the authors were not to delve into the reasons for God's election, but merely to state it as a goal that would motivate the faithful to continued confidence and loyalty in God's loving choice. The NT literature, therefore, since it came from people with faith in God's unique saving act in Christ and was directed to those who had at least a rudimentary faith in the same mystery, used concepts of divine election for the pragmatic purposes of fostering growth in the Christian life and of stimulating more intense missionary effort.

The Fathers of the Church, esp. St. Augustine, formed a theology of election and predestination that examined as its subject matter God's preferential selection of individuals for eternal salvation. Notions of divine election thus became constitutive of the dogmas, and dogmatic tracts, centering about the mystery of predestination, in contrast to the useful tools they had been in biblical times for preaching and teaching.

Theologically, election is related to *predestination, but both words are not to be taken as synonyms, though some early Fathers of the Church have used them interchangeably. Since the predestination of certain individuals to eternal salvation presupposes that God first wishes their salvation, theological speculation places the divine act of election prior to that of predestination (ThAq ST 1a, 23.4). Hence, election is that sovereign free act of God, prior to predestination, in which he resolves out of his love to offer an individual eternal salvation together with its concomitant graces and the aids requisite to attain this final glory, without doing away with man's personal decision and fidelity in this matter, but rather in granting these. In *Reformed theology, and esp. in Calvin's *Institutes of the Christian Religion,* election is the divine choice—rooted in God's sovereignty—whereby he adopts some to salvation and denies it to others (3.21.1). Calvin conceived election as having two degrees: the first is a general election, as that of a total nation, but one that is not firm and effectual since some individuals within the collectivity may be rejected, e.g., Ishmael and Esau. The second is the firm, effectual, and irrevocable election of individuals whereby God not only offers salvation but by his irresistible grace so assigns it that the certainty of its effect is not in doubt (3.21.6–7). This election flows exclusively from the divine sovereignty, and is not dependent upon the foreknowledge God has of man's good works, or of his faith; man is chosen by God to

be holy, he is not chosen because he wills to be holy (3.22.3). BIBLIOGRAPHY: J. Farrelly, *Predestination, Grace and Free Will* (1964); G. C. Berkouwer, *Divine Election* (1960); R. Shank, *Elect in the Son: A Study of the Doctrine of Election* (1970); A. W. Pink, *Doctrines of Election and Justification* (1974). *PREDESTINATION.

[J. F. FALLON; J. TYLENDA]

ELECTION (CANON LAW), one of the procedures by which the law provides for filling an ecclesiastical *office. Election confers the right on the one elected to receive an office, but not title to the office itself until any necessary *confirmation by competent authority and actual acceptance of the office. As to the electoral process, CIC cc. 16–178 sets forth the general requirements. All eligible voters of an electoral college must be summoned within 3 months of an occurring vacancy; if more than one-third of those having the right to elect are not called, any ensuing election is invalid. Balloting must be secret (see SCRUTINY) free from lay influence or any forms of coercion, and the ballots must designate the voter's choice unambiguously. No elector may vote for himself. As a general principle on electoral colleges c. 101 § 1, n. 1 provides that a majority is necessary to elect a candidate on the first or second ballot, but a plurality suffices on the third; but the number of ballotings varies according to the legitimate constitutions of religious communities. Election of religious superiors is regulated by cc. 506–507. Failure to observe the proper procedures, or the deliberate election of an unworthy candidate invalidates an election and may cause forfeiture of the right to elect, provision for the office being left to appointment by competent authority. *POSTULATION.

[R. ARONSTAM]

ELECTION OF POPES. In the first centuries of Christianity, the pope or bp. of Rome was chosen by the clergy and faithful of that city. The choice became restricted to the higher clergy because of the interference of the Roman emperors, however; and in 1179 Alexander III formally limited the right of election to the cardinals, establishing at the same time the rule of a two-thirds majority for a valid election. The procedures for papal elections have been modified as a result of various experiences and abuses, such as outside political pressures and excessively long conclaves. In modern times, papal elections have been held in Rome, except for the conclave that elected Pius VII in Venice. In the 19th cent., several conclaves were held in the Quirinal palace, then the main papal residence, but since 1846 all conclaves have taken place in the Sistine chapel of the Vatican Palace. The papal conclave, according to existing canons, must open within 15 or at most 18 days after the pope's death. A card. elector may be accompanied by an assistant, perhaps two if his health should require. Radios, telephones, telegraph, and presumably tape-recorders are forbidden. All participants are held to secrecy as to the course of the voting, even after the conclave, unless the newly elected pontiff should decide otherwise. Balloting takes place twice each day, with two votes taken on each occasion. Cardinals are prohibited from making any preconclave agreement or promises, and any such promises, if made, are declared null and void. However, this does not prevent the cardinals in conclave or beforehand from consulting one another and in particular with leading candidates for the papacy. The result of the balloting is indicated to those outside the conclave by black or white (at the time of election) smoke which emerges from a chimney built into the chapel. When the candidate receiving the two-thirds vote formally accepts the decision of the cardinals, he becomes from that minute bp. of Rome, i.e., pope, though the coronation takes place only later. BIBLIOGRAPHY: H. Scharp, *How the Catholic Church is Governed* (tr. A. Derrick, 1960) 45–61; A. Swift, NCE 11:572–574.

[R. A. GRAHAM]

ELECTORS, IMPERIAL, an electoral body empowered to choose emperors of the Holy Roman Empire. Frequent disagreement over the method of election and the person elected led Emperor Charles IV to issue the Golden Bull of 1356; it resolved the controversial issue, remained unaltered until the 17th cent., and lasted until the end of the empire in 1806. The document constituted seven electors: the abps. of Mainz, Trier, and Cologne; the count palatine of the Rhine; the duke of Saxony; the margrave of Brandenburg; the king of Bohemia. Their position gave them great power within their own territories, and preeminence in the empire. The secular electorates were hereditary, passing to the first-born son.

[C. KEENAN]

ELEMENTARY AND SECONDARY EDUCATION ACT (ESEA), an act proposed by President Lyndon B. Johnson and approved by Congress in 1965. ESEA, administered by the Bureau of Elementary and Secondary Education, authorizes the use of federal funds to: (1) strengthen elementary and secondary education programs for children in low-income areas; (2) provide additional library resources, textbooks, and other instructional material; (3) finance supplementary educational centers and services; (4) broaden areas of cooperative research; and (5) strengthen state departments of education. The act, a practical application of Johnson's antipoverty program, designed to meet the needs of all deprived children, authorizes funds for the education of all children from poor families whether in public or private (parochial) schools. In its provision for private schools, ESEA has met with some opposition on the grounds that it is a violation of the principle of separation of Church and State as expressed in the First Amendment to the Constitution.

[M. B. MURPHY]

ELEMENTS OF EXISTENCE, in Buddhist thought, the five "aggregates" or "heaps" (Sanskrit: *Skandhas;* Pali: *khandas*) of constituents that make up what appears as the individual personality or self. They are usually listed as: form (*rupa:* materiality; the physical aspect of things); feelings; perceptions; impulses; consciousness. The purpose of the analysis is to do away with the (false) conception that beneath these elements there is any real "self" (according to the Buddhist doctrine of *anatta,* or "no-self"), and thus to eliminate that "selfishness" or "self-centeredness" (*tanha:* craving; grasping) which is the root of all suffering. Further psychological and epistemological analysis emphasizes the subjectivity and untrustworthiness of the latter four of the five constituents (i.e., feelings, perceptions, impulses, and consciousness) by referring them to the 18 "elements" *(dhatu)* which affect them: the sense-organs, their objects, and the resultant perceptions or "consciousnesses." BIBLIOGRAPHY: E. Conze, *Buddhist Thought in India* (1967) 107–16; K. N. Jayatilleke, *Early Buddhist Theory of Knowledge* (1963).

[D. P. EFROYMSON]

ELEMENTS OF THIS WORLD, the basic constituents of the physical world: earth, fire, air, and water. The elements are a staple of Greek philosophy, taken over by the Greek Christian writers; as when, for example, the author of 2 Pet 3.10, 12 describes the Day of the Lord that comes unexpectedly as a thief in the night as the Day when the elements will be consumed in fire to make way for a new heaven and a new earth, a home for justice. Jewish apocalyptic combined the idea of elements with symbols derived from Persian mythology, so that the "elements of the world" denotes the spiritual powers behind the physical elements. Thus the seer of Revelations describes the angels to whom authority has been given over land and sea, wind and fire. Paul, (Gal 4; Col 2) describes man as subject to these powers in his infancy, before becoming joined to Christ the Head. Christ frees us from slavery to the elements of the universe by the gift of the spirit of sonship by which we call God "Abba" (familiar form for Father). Paul warns the Galatians not to be induced by someone's false show of knowledge back into service of those beings that are by nature no gods, the mean and beggarly elements of the universe.

[E. J. DILLON]

ELEOUSA MADONNA, type of Byzantine Madonna and Child revealing warm "maternal love" (*eleousa*) in contrast to the formal, hieratic, Hodegetria type Madonna of Byzantine style.

[M. J. DALY]

ELEPHANTA, island in the harbor of Bombay noted for Hindu rock-cut cave temples dedicated to the god Siva, created in the mid-7th cent. as a last great architectural-sculptural achievement in W India (desecrated in the 16th century). Derived from Ellora with unusual triple portals affording light, the two sanctuaries to Siva open toward the Himalayas. Most magnificent of three monumental panels is the 23-feet high *trimurti* or three-faced bust of Siva Maheśvara (Great Lord) expressing the transcendent essence of creation as the divine generative and destructive principles in the cycle of life. BIBLIOGRAPHY: S. Kramrisch, *Hindu Temple* (1947); H. R. Zimmer, *Art of Indian Asia* (1955).

[M. J. DALY]

ELEPHANTINE PAPYRI, a collection of Aramaic papyri discovered on the island of Elephantine in the upper Nile near modern Assuan. Elephantine is the Greek name for the Egyptian Yeb, which before 5th cent. B.C. had been colonized by Jews of unknown provenance, some of whom at least served as Egyptian military mercenaries at that frontier post. The group was certainly there before the Persian conquest of 525 B.C., though the exact date of arrival is unknown. It may have been connected with the dispersions mentioned in Jer chs. 41–44, though some scholars would place it as much as a cent. earlier. The documents first began to come to light in 1893 and were published in the years 1903–53. They record both public and private affairs: lawsuits, loans, house-transfers, matters of inheritance, marriage, slavery and manumission, etc. No parts of the OT were discovered, but fragments of the story of Ahikar have come to light, while the language of the papyri has clarified the Aramaic sections of Ezra (4.8–6.18; 7.12–26). Important information is contained on the religious beliefs of these Jews, who had built an altar and temple to Yahweh, who was worshiped under the titles Yeho or Yahu. The possible polytheistic nature of their religion—perhaps indicating their origin near Bethel—is suggested by the names of several other divinities, though W. F. Albright explains them as hypostatized aspects of Yahweh. The temple was destroyed through Egyptian enmity in 410 B.C., but was rebuilt after appeals to the authorities in Palestine; the names of the latter have provided additional evidence for a possible ministry of Ezra subsequent to that of Nehemiah. The last text dates from 399 B.C. and the final fate of the colony is unknown, though Egyptian national interests may well have played a part in its suppression not long afterwards. BIBLIOGRAPHY: E. Kraeling, "New Light on the Elephantine Colony," *Biblical Archaeologist Reader* (ed. G. Wright and D. Freedman, 1961) 128–144; G. Driver, *Aramaic Documents of the Fifth Century B.C.* (1954); W. F. Albright, *From the Stone Age to Christianity* (2d ed. 1957) 373; B. Porten, *Archives from Elephantine* (1968).

[C. BERNAS]

ELERT, WERNER (1885–1954), German Lutheran historical and systematic theologian, professor at Erlangen from 1923. He is best known for his *Morphologie des Luthertums* (2 v., 1951), an authoritative study of the distinctive theological teaching of Luther and of Lutheranism, esp. as expressed in the Lutheran confessions. E. was particularly attached to Luther's theme of Law and Gospel and their dialectical tension. The theme's application to ethics E. brought out in his *Das Christliche Ethos* (1949). He was an opponent of Barth's crisis theology.

[T. C. O'BRIEN]

ELEUSINIAN MYSTERIES, Attic rites of Eleusis, famed religious rites of antiquity. Enacted annually in the agricultural community was the myth of Demeter and Kore (Persephone): the descent of Pluto who stole the daughter away to his dark kingdom, and the triumph of the mother's love that assured Kore's periodic return. Culminating point was the *hierophant's* holding up an ear of wheat, fruit of the union of heaven and earth. The agricultural theme stirred the people's religious sense deeply. Not until the early 7th cent. B.C. did the cult become a mystery; the decisive change was in representation of the rites as a "priceless secret." The seasonal worship was adopted into the Athenian state religion, but the rite was still under care of the ancient families, Eumolpides and Kerykes, save for the *hierophant* (priest) designated by Athens. Preliminary rites were held then in Athens, with the September Boedromion ritual, and continued at Eleusis. By the 3d cent. B.C. the rites were refashioned and, fused with the Egyptian mysteries, spread widely. Hellenes of classic times recognized the symbolic mystic value. *Aristotle thought it not so much a matter of learning something as of experiencing the rites. Aristophanes indicates, as does Andocides, the moral impression made on many. Prevailing was the conviction that *mystai* who joined in the rites would have a more pleasant hereafter, as indicated in the so-called Homeric *Hymn to Demeter*. J. G. *Frazer in his *Golden Bough* aroused Christian interest. L. Bouyer denies that the rites foreshadow the Christ event, but holds that they prepared for Christianity by causing men to realize that salvation eludes the old solutions. *Clement of Alexandria in *Protrepticus* records the formula for the rite in which, when a pagan, he may have participated. Emperor *Theodosius the Great forbade celebration of the mysteries, and Alaric I destroyed their sanctuary (395 A.D.). BIBLIOGRAPHY: L. Bouyer, *Rite and Man* (tr. M. J. Costelloe, 1963); P. F. Foucart, *Les mystères d'Eleusis* (1914; repr. 1975).

[M. R. BROWN]

ELEUTHERIUS, ST. (d. 189), **POPE** from 175. According to the *Liber Pontificalis* E. was of Greek origin and ruled the Church in the reign of Emperor Commodus, a period of relative calm. *Montanism was beginning to cause a stir in Asia Minor. *Eusebius reports that *Irenaeus came to Rome from Lyons with a letter from the faithful there written apparently in a spirit of appeasement. What action E. took, if any, is unknown. Tertullian's report that the bp. of Rome was on the point of sending out a letter conceding the authenticity of the prophetic claims of the Montanists but then withdrew what he had written probably refers not to E. but to Victor, his successor in 189. The story told by Bede that King Lucius of Britain asked E. for missionaries seems to be based simply upon legend. BIB-LIOGRAPHY: Butler 2:423; A. Amore, EncCatt 5:226.

[R. B. ENO]

ELEUTHERIUS OF TOURNAI, ST. (456?–531?), bishop. Although what is reported of E. in the *Life of St. Medard* (PL 88:534–539) and in his own alleged autobiography (AS February 3:180) is not credited by scholars, the fact of his existence and episcopate seems incontestable. He was probably the first bp. of Tournai. Certain writings have been erroneously attributed to him (PL 65). BIBLIOGRAPHY: Butler 1:381; P. Villette, BiblSanct 4:1012.

[G. M. COOK]

ELEVATION, the lifting up of the Host for all to see after the Consecration at Mass. This practice, introduced in the Western Church in the late 12th and 13th cent., was prescribed by Eudes de Sully, abp. of Paris (d. 1208) and was observed generally throughout Europe by 1240. Its introduction has been variously ascribed to: (1) popular detestation of the denial of the Real Presence by *Berengarius (d. c.1088), an unlikely hypothesis when the date of Berengarius' death is considered; (2) a desire to signalize the moment when adoration of the consecrated Host could legitimately begin and so put a stop to the practice of those who began to adore when the priest took the bread into his hands before the consecration (see W. J. O'Shea, NCE 5:266); (3) a gesture of protest against the view of Peter Cantor that the consecration of the bread did not take place till after the words of consecration had been pronounced over the wine (see H. Thurston, CE 5:380). Whatever the immediate inspiration for the introduction of the practice may have been, it is certain that it responded to the popular desire to look upon the consecrated Host that had grown up with the intensification of the devotion to the Real Presence. The Elevation of the chalice developed more slowly and was not generally prescribed before the Missal of Pius V (1570). Today, according to the *Roman Missal* (1974), a bell may be rung before the Consecration as a signal to the people, and depending on local custom, it may also be rung at each Elevation. It advocates that the faithful consume the Hosts consecrated at the celebration of the Mass in which they participate.

[P. K. MEAGHER]

ELEVATION OF MAN, as understood in RC theology, the raising of the human creature, perhaps at the time of his creation, perhaps at a later moment, to a state in which it is possible to reach the vision of God. Man has a natural openness (obediential potency) to, or even, according to St. Thomas Aquinas, a natural desire for, this supernatural goal, even though he cannot attain it by his unaided powers, but only when he is raised to the order of grace, a higher order of being and activity than is proper to him simply because he is man. God planned this elevation, and the carrying of this plan into effect is the history of salvation. In

the first stage man was placed by his Creator in paradise (Gen ch. 2), in a state of more than natural happiness and familiarity with God, the state of original justice that was meant for all mankind. But man sinned, thereby forfeiting the special gifts he had from God and falling into a state of sinfulness and of moral and physical misery. The Fall, however, did not mean the end of the elevation of man. A savior was promised from the start (Gen 3.15) and throughout the OT. Christ came to restore fallen man and did so through His death and resurrection. The restoration entails, for all who are reborn in Christ through baptism of water or of desire, the life of grace, an anticipation of life eternal and a pledge of the return of the lost gifts of God at the fulfillment of salvation history. The redemption is a higher manner of elevation: it means incorporation into Christ and participation by the children of God in the Trinitarian relationships. BIBLIOGRAPHY: ThAq ST 1a, 94–102; C. Journet, *Meaning of Grace* (tr. A. V. Littledale, 1960); G. Colombo "Il problema del soprannaturale negli ultimi cinquant'anni," *Problemi et orientamenti di teologia dommatica* (2 v., 1957); J. P. Kenny, NCE 5:266–269; W. M. Principe, NCE 14:736–738.

[P. DE LETTER]

ELEVEN THOUSAND VIRGINS OF COLOGNE. A late 4th cent. Cologne inscription mentions a church honoring a group of virgin martyrs. A 9th-cent. legend names Ursula as leader and the number as 11 or 11,000. "Relics" discovered in the 12th cent. led to further elaboration. A feast (October 21) added to the Roman calendar in the 14th century was removed in 1969 because of lack of historical authentication.

[J. DALLEN]

ELFLEDA, ST. (d. c.714), Northumbrian princess. Dedicated to God as an infant because of her father's wartime vow, she grew up in the convent of St. Hilda, whom she succeeded, in her teens, as the second abbess of Whitby. She was instrumental in lessening the opposition in her family, and in England generally, to the reforms of St. Wilfrid and to his legitimate claims to his see at York. She aided in persuading her admired friend St. Cuthbert to receive episcopal consecration. Because of her royal connections her beneficial impact extended far beyond the confines of her monastery. BIBLIOGRAPHY: E. I. Watkin, BiblSanct 4:1019; Butler 1:278–279.

[J. F. FALLON]

ELFRIEDE, ST., see ETHELDRITA, ST.

ELGAR, EDWARD (1857–1934), English composer. He received his first musical training from his father, organist at St. George RC Church, Worcester: E. succeeded his father there in 1885. He wrote the music for Queen Victoria's diamond jubilee (1897). Two years later he wrote his *Enigma Variations,* a musical portrait of his friends and of himself. E.'s most famous religious composition, *The *Dream of Gerontius* (1900), is an oratorio, the music set to the poem by J. H. Newman; the work reveals the deep spirituality of E.'s own musical genius. Other religious works are the two oratorios *The Apostles* (1903) and *The Kingdom* (1906). He is also remembered for his concert overture, *Cockaigne; Falstaff,* a tone poem; and chamber music, two symphonies, a concerto for violin and one for cello. Of the famous five *Pomp and Circumstance Marches,* the first was written in 1901, the last in 1930. E. was knighted in 1904, received the Order of Merit in 1911; he was named Master of the King's Music in 1924. BIBLIOGRAPHY: D. McVeagh, *Edward Elgar: His Life and Music* (1955).

[L. MCBRIDE]

ELGIN MARBLES, monumental Greek sculptures from the Parthenon and Erechtheum collected by Lord Thomas Bruce Elgin (British ambassador to the Ottoman court at Constantinople) with permission from the Turkish government (1801) following their reckless destruction in the previous century. These precious fragments of the Parthenon pediments, metopes, and frieze cover the essential stylistic developments in Greek sculptural expression: the famous Panathenaic processional frieze from the E, N, and S walls; from the E pediment the *Dionysos (Herakles?)* formerly known as *Theseus* (prototype of the Adam of the Sistine ceiling), the *Three Fates* and heads of horses; from the W pediment—the colossal—*Poseidon.* One of the monumental caryatids from the Erechtheum, and a few architectural members and other details complete the treasure. The marbles were purchased from the earl of Elgin's collection by the British government in 1816 and have been since then the pride of the British Museum, London. BIBLIOGRAPHY: A. H. Smith, "Lord Elgin and His Collection," *Journal of Hellenic Studies,* 36 (1916).

[M. J. DALY]

ELI (HELI). (1) Ancestor of Joseph, virginal father of Jesus and husband of Mary. Luke writes of Jesus: "being—so it was supposed—the son of Joseph, son of Heli, son of Matthat, . . ." (3.23–24). In his first chapter Matthew (the one other Evangelist who traces the genealogy of Jesus) names Jacob as father of "Joseph, the husband of Mary" (16) and "son of David" (20). Exegetes have pondered the difficulty, some holding that E. was grandfather of Joseph. Augustine accepted the explanation of 3d-cent. Julius Africanus that Joseph was fruit of a *levirate marriage, natural son of Jacob but legal son of E.; this circumstance, moreover, foreshadows and accents the role of Joseph himself in the messianic story: legal but not physical father of Jesus. (2) OT personage, last of the judges and high priest of the sanctuary of Shiloh, who met Hannah at prayer, and later with her child brought for sanctuary service (1 Sam 1.9–17, 24–28). E.(1) and his son Joseph with Mary and Jesus, and Elizabeth, Zacharias, and

John, can be discerned in ambivalent features of the prophet's messianic web as in: E.(2)'s misjudgment of Hannah in her petition for a child (1 Sam 1.12–18); the dedication of Samuel to the Lord (1 Sam 1.24–28); and immediately following (c) Hannah's thanksgiving that was to be caught up in the Virgin Mary's Magnificat (cf. 1 Sam 2.1–10; Lk 1.46–55).

[M. R. BROWN]

ELI, ELI, a popular Yiddish folk song written in the Ahavoh Rabboh mode by Jacob Koppel in 1896. It depicts the sad fate of the Jewish people in its opening cry, "My God, my God, why hast Thou forsaken me" (Ps 22.2). It shows the determination of the Jews to remain faithful to God as it closes with, "Hear, O Israel, the Lord our God, the Lord is One." (Deut. 6.4). It became popular in the Jewish concert theatre through the efforts of the Cantor Joseph Rosenblatt (1880–1933), who sang it as an encore in many of his concerts. There are many arrangements of the song for voice and piano. Mischa Elman has recorded a violin transcription of the melody under the title, "Hebraic Melodies." BIBLIOGRAPHY: "Collected Writings of A. W. Binder," *Studies in Jewish Music* (ed. I. Heskes, 1971).

[L. MCBRIDE]

ELI, ELI, LAMA SABACHTHANI, the opening words of Ps 22 attributed to Jesus on the cross in Mt 27.46 and Mk 15.34. The JB translates them, "My God, my God, why have you deserted me?" Mark has the spelling *Eloi, Eloi.* Either version could easily have been mistaken for Elijah which is what the bystanders thought they heard Jesus call out.

[M. A. MCNAMARA]

ELIADE, MIRCEA (1907–), eminent contemporary scholar of comparative religion. Born in Rumania, E. studied at the universities of Bucharest and Calcutta; taught at Bucharest and the Sorbonne; and lectured widely through Europe and the United States. He is presently professor of history of religion at the Univ. of Chicago. E. stands in direct opposition to the merely positivistic study of religious phenomena which seeks to explain religion solely in sociological, economic or linguistic categories. Religion is considered on its own terms as man's perennial effort to live within a sacred sphere. Primitive religion is not regarded as the product of irrational fears and superstitions, but an effort to maintain a relationship with the foundations of reality. E. regards much of contemporary alienation as a failure to perceive the significance of religion in the structure of human life. Among his numerous books and articles are *Patterns in Comparative Religion* (1963); *Sacred and the Profane* (1961); *Cosmos and History: The Myth of the Eternal Return* (1954); *Images and Symbols* (1961); *Myths, Dreams, and Mysteries: The Encounter between Contemporary Faiths and Archaic Realities* (1960); and with J. M. Kitagawa, *History of Religions: Essays in Methodology*

(1959). BIBLIOGRAPHY: J. M. Kitagawa, *Myth and Symbols: Studies in Honor of Mircea Eliade* (1969).

[T. M. MCFADDEN]

ELIA, see ELIJAH.

ELIAS, ST. (430–518), **PATRIARCH OF JERUSALEM,** 494–516, anti-Monophysite polemicist. A monk who had fled from Egypt to Jerusalem, E. was proclaimed patriarch because of Chalcedonian orthodoxy. All through his life as patriarch he was staunchly opposed to Monophysite teaching and was persecuted because of this. He refused to have any part in *Severus of Antioch's condemnation of the *Tome* of Pope St. *Leo I; as a result he was driven into exile by the soldiers of Emperor Anastasius I.

[T. C. O'BRIEN]

ELIAS BAR SHINĀYĀ, (975–*c.*1049), Nestorian metropolitan, author. E. served as bp. of Beit-Nûhadra in 1002 and was later appointed metropolitan of Nisibis. He is best known for his literary works, among which his greatest contributions are his treatises on canon and civil law, his Syriac grammar, and a Syriac-Arabic dictionary. He wrote books based on Nestorian thought as well as a variety of dissertations and pastoral letters. His most famous book *Chronography,* a history of the Church from A.D. 25 to 1018, is valued for its otherwise lost historical sources. BIBLIOGRAPHY: E. Delly, *La Théologie d'Elie bar-Sénaya* (1957).

[C. KEENAN]

ELIAS OF CORTONA (*c.*1180–1253), Italian Franciscan lay brother and minister general. He was one of the earliest companions and a close friend of St. Francis of Assisi who appointed him first provincial of Syria and later his vicar. After Francis' death he assumed full control of the order, planned and raised funds for the construction of the basilica at Assisi as a monument and tomb for the saint. Elected general in 1232, he had a term marked by strife and intrigue between the factions favoring strict or relaxed observance of the rule. Deposed in 1239 by the chapter presided over by Pope Gregory IX for his despotism and scandalous life, he allied himself with the Emperor Frederick II, was excommunicated and expelled from the order, but before his death was reconciled with the Church. BIBLIOGRAPHY: R. B. Brooke, *Early Franciscan Government* (1959).

[D. A. MCGUCKIN]

ELIAS EKDIKOS, 12th-cent. Greek theologian. He retained the name Ekdikos, meaning defender, from the ecclesiastical office he held. He was the author of a Greek work on the ascetic life, *Didactic Anthologion,* extant in the Imperial Library of Vienna, and in the King's Library at Paris. In this his most important work, he presents a systematic treatment of Byzantine spiritual theology. Drawing heavily from biblical imagery, he delineates the search for

Christian perfection. E. flourished during an important period of Byzantine theology and was particularly influenced by Simon the Younger. BIBLIOGRAPHY: J. Meyendorff, *Byzantine Theology* (1974).

[D. MCGONAGLE]

ELIAS OF ENNA, ST. (*c.*823–903), Sicilian monk and hermit, a principal in the establishment of Byzantine monasticism in S Italy. After an adventurous life he became a monk on Mt. Sinai, lived as a hermit in Sicily and Greece, then founded an influential monastery in Calabria. BIBLIOGRAPHY: G. Rossi Taibbi, *Vita di S. Elia il Giovane* (1962).

[G. T. DENNIS]

ELIAS OF REGGIO, ST. (var. Spelaiotes, Speleotus, the Cavedweller; *c.*865–*c.*960), southern Italian, lived as monk and hermit in a cave near Melicuccà, Calabria, where a group of disciples gathered about him. BIBLIOGRAPHY: AS Sept. 3:843–888; F. Russo, EncCatt 5:237.

[G. T. DENNIS]

ELIAS OF THESSALONIKA, ST. (Elias the Younger, 823–903), monk. According to his 10th-cent. vita, he led an unsteady life, and was twice kidnapped by Arab pirates. He became a monk in Jerusalem, but left to continue his wanderings until he settled in Calabria (S Italy), where he joined a local monastic community. He died at Thessalonika on his way to Constantinople where Emperor Leo VI was to meet with him. BIBLIOGRAPHY: F. Russo, BiblSanct 4:1043–45.

[J. MADEY]

ELIGIUS OF NOYON-TOURNAI, ST. (*c.*588–660), bishop. E. completed his apprenticeship as goldsmith and his artistic gift was recognized by King Chlotar II, who appointed him master of the mint. He also served King Dagobert I. E. founded the monastery of Solignac in Limousin and nunneries at Paris and Noyon. In 641 he was chosen bp. of Noyon and Tournai. He preached the gospel in all of the territories under his care and concentrated on the conversion of infidels in his diocese. E. promoted the cultus of local saints and is responsible for the making of many reliquaries. During the 8th cent. his own cult existed and he became the patron saint of metalworkers. BIBLIOGRAPHY: Butler 4:455–458; P. Villette, BiblSanct 4:1064–69.

[C. KEENAN]

ELIJAH (ELIAS), Hebrew prophet of 9th cent. B.C. (1 Kg ch. 17–2 Kg ch. 2). He was a Tishbite, from Tishbe in Gilead, and worked primarily in the northern kingdom, where he was the champion of Yahweh against the Baalism promoted by Jezebel (1 Kg 16.31). The Elijah cycle contains numerous miracle stories: he was fed by the ravens (1 Kg 17.6), provided for the widow of Zarephath during the famine (17.8–16), restored the widow's son to life (17.17–24), called fire from heaven to devour the sacrifice on Mt. Carmel (18.20–40), twice called down fire to kill 50 messengers of Ahaziah (2 Kg 1.9–12), struck the Jordan with his mantle and caused the water to part (2.8), and at the end of his life instead of dying "went up by a whirlwind into heaven" (2.11). His denunciation of Ahab for the murder of Naboth puts E. in continuity with the ethical tradition in Israelite prophecy, in the line with Nathan, who preceded him (2 Sam 12), and Amos, who followed. Fleeing from Jezebel, E. went to Horeb (Sinai), where he heard God, not in the wind, earthquake, or fire, but in a "still small voice" (1 Kg 19.12). Following instructions received there, he cast his mantle on Elisha to designate him as his successor, and anointed Hazael to be king over Syria and Jehu to succeed Ahab in Israel. His translation to heaven led to an expectation of his return (Mal 4.5), which some saw fulfilled in John the Baptist (Mt 11.14; Jn 1.21) and Jesus (Mt 16.14). He appeared with Moses at the Transfiguration (Mt 17.3). These references to the NT indicate the perdurance of Jewish belief in Elijah's second coming as a messianic sign. The replies indicate that Christians understood the sign to be accomplished in Jesus.

In Jewish tradition at the Passover *seder* a cup of wine is poured for Elijah, and in the circumcision ceremony a chair is set aside for him, as symbols of his concern for the welfare of the Jewish people.

[T. EARLY]

ELIJAH (SECOND COMING OF). The assumption of Elijah into heaven in a fiery chariot (2 Kg 2.11–12) led to a belief that he had not died and that he would return to earth. Isaiah 40.3 spoke of a voice crying in the wilderness urging men to prepare a way for the coming of Yahweh. Malachi 3.1 spoke of the same messenger and identified him as Elijah (3.23–24), a preacher of reform. Sirach 48.10 ff testifies to the enduring expectation of the prophet's return. The Gospels (cf. Mt 16.14; 17.10–11; 27.47–49) indicate the existence of an intense expectation of the coming of Elijah at the time of Christ. There seems to be an expectation of both a prophet and Elijah, since the Baptist is asked both if he is the prophet and then if he is Elijah (Jn 1.21–22). Evidence from Qumran has confirmed this twofold expectation. The prophet (cf. Dt. 18.15,18) is apparently a new Moses who will introduce the eternal messianic kingdom by renewing the miracles of the Exodus. Elijah, on the other hand, is the reformer who precedes the Day of Yahweh, the final judgment (cf. Mt 3.6–12, note v. 11 which states that the one to follow "baptizes with fire"—the fire of judgment). In Mt 11.10,14 Christ identifies the Baptist as the expected Elijah. Hence the "baptism of fire" was reinterpreted in terms of Pentecost. BIBLIOGRAPHY: R. Brown, "Messianism of Qumrân," CBQ 19 (1957) 53–82; J. C. Fenton, *Gospel of St. Matthew* (Pelican Gospel Commentaries, 1964).

[J. A. PIERCE]

ELIM, the second encampment of the Israelites after their passage over the Red Sea in their journey from Egypt to Caanan. Here they found palm trees, oaks, tamarisks, acacias, and 12 abundant springs of water. It is usually identified with the oasis of Wādi Gharandel on the W shore of the Sinai Peninsula between Marah and the Desert of Sin, where it empties into the Gulf of Suez. BIBLIOGRAPHY: EDB 649.

[A. P. HANLON]

ELIN OF SKÖVDE, ST., see HELEN OF SKÖVDE, ST.

ELIOT, JOHN (1604–1690), Puritan preacher and "Apostle to the Indians." Born in Hertfordshire, England, and educated at Cambridge, in 1631 he migrated to New England, where he was pastor at Roxbury, Mass., for about 60 years. Besides serving as pastor, he was a missionary to Indian tribes of that area. Having learned the Algonquin language, he prepared a grammar, translated the Bible into that tongue, established a school to train native leaders, and organized his converts into 14 segregated Indian towns. During King Philip's War, the "praying Indians" were scattered, and the number of towns was reduced to four which gradually disappeared. Eliot was the author of several books, besides those in and about Indian languages: *The Christian Commonwealth* (1659); *Communion of Churches* (1665); and *The Harmony of the Gospels* (1678). With Thomas Weld and Richard Mather, he prepared *The Bay Psalm Book* of 1640. BIBLIOGRAPHY: O. E. Winslow, *John Eliot, Apostle to the Indians* (1968, repr. 1972).

[N. H. MARING]

ELIOT, T. S. (full name Thomas Stearns Eliot; 1888–1965), Anglo-American poet, critic, dramatist, editor of *Criterion,* a London quarterly (1922–39). E. was the youngest child of Henry Ware Eliot and Charlotte Stearns, grandson of William Greenleaf Eliot, Unitarian minister and social worker, the founder of Washington University, St. Louis. He was educated at Harvard, the Sorbonne, Merton College, Oxford, became a British citizen and an Anglo-Catholic (1927).

E.'s early poetry is detached, ironic, sophisticated, showing the plight of modern man frustrated and enfeebled by loss of cultural and religious values. *The Waste Land* (1922), a major work, reveals the chaotic fragmentation of human life in Western civilization. His religious peoms culminate in *Ash Wednesday* (1930) and *Four Quartets* (1935–42). His essays show increasing reliance upon religious authority and tradition. E.'s interest in solving the conflict between material and spiritual reality limited his dramatic breadth, but his power, integrity, and poetic craftsmanship are universally acknowledged. He was awarded the Order of Merit and the Nobel Prize in 1948. The chief influences on his religious and literary growth are family background of Puritan morality, French symbolist poets, philosophy under Babbitt, Santayana, and Bergson, interest in Elizabethan and Jacobean drama, and Dante. His style is erudite and complex. His dominant concern after his conversion was Christian theology as a support for collapsing civilization. His later works show impressive spiritual strength in their suggestion of the importance for man today of the Christian mysteries of the Incarnation and the indwelling of the Holy Spirit. Works: *Collected Poems, 1909–1962* (1963); *Selected Essays, 1917–1932* (1950); *Murder in the Cathedral* (1935); *Family Reunion* (1939); *The Cocktail Party* (1950); *The Confidential Clerk* (1954); *The Elder Statesman* (1959); *The Use of Poetry and the Use of Criticism* (1933); *The Idea of a Christian Society* (1940). BIBLIOGRAPHY: D. C. Gallup, *T. S. Eliot: A Bibliography* (1953, repr. 1969); H. Kenner, *The Invisible Poet* (1959); N. Frye, *T. S. Eliot* (1963); S. Bergsten, *Time and Eternity: a Study of the Structure and Symbolism of T. S. Eliot's Four Quartets* (1960); H. Howarth, *Notes on Some Figures behind T. S. Eliot* (1964); *T. S. Eliot: The Man and His Work* (ed. A. Tate, 1966).

[M. B. BARRY]

ELIPANDUS OF TOLEDO (d. after 800–[807?]), archbishop. He was the chief proponent of the 8th-cent. heresy of adoptionism which claimed that there are two distinct persons in Christ. He was condemned by Pope Adrian. At a council convened in Frankfurt (794) by Charlemagne, the heresy itself was formally condemned. E. remained in his see despite his condemnation. BIBLIOGRAPHY: C. M. Aherne, NCE 5:278.

[F. G. O'BRIEN]

ELISABETH, see ELIZABETH.

ELISHA (Elisae; Eliseus), the successor to *Elijah in his prophetic mission in the northern kingdom. E. was the leader of a band of devotees known as the "sons of the prophets," and figures primarily as a wonder-worker. Thus the "Elisha cycle" (2 Kg ch. 2–13) consists largely of a series of loosely connected miracle stories, and there seems to be some intention to represent him as a greater wonder-worker even than Elijah.

[D. J. BOURKE]

ELIZABETH, ST., wife of Zachary (Lk. 1.5) and mother of John the Baptist (Lk 1.57–60). She was related to Mary the Mother of Jesus in some vague way (Lk 1.36). Like many great women of the OT—Sarah, Rebekah, Rachel—she had been sterile for a long time. The Angel Gabriel appeared to Zachary in the Temple, promising that a son would be born to the couple (Lk 1.13), a son who would be "great before the Lord" and "filled with the Holy Spirit, even from his mother's womb" (Lk 1.15). Six months later, Mary went to Elizabeth to offer assistance. At Mary's approach, the infant in Elizabeth's womb leapt for joy (Lk 1.41) and Elizabeth cried out "Blessed art thou among women and blessed is the fruit of thy womb" (Lk

1.42). Elizabeth has been represented in art from the 5th cent. chiefly in the Visitation scene.

[J. E. LYNCH]

ELIZABETH I (1542—1603), **QUEEN OF ENGLAND** from 1558. This article is confined to the steps whereby E. made final the Church of England's break with Rome. During the reign of her half-sister Mary Tudor (1553–58), E. conformed at least outwardly to the old Catholic faith. Upon her accession, however, she was out of sympathy both with her RC subjects and with the radical Protestants who wished to place greater authority in the hands of the clergy. Her intent was to make the English sovereign and Parliament absolute in matter of doctrine and discipline. This she effected by two enactments of Parliament: the *Act of Supremacy (1559) and the *Act of Uniformity (1559). The former designated her the only "supreme governor . . . as well in all spiritual or ecclesiastical things or causes, as temporal." This title she preferred to that of supreme head of the Church used by Henry VIII, since by it she avoided offending Catholics, who looked on the pope as their chief, and the Puritans, who admitted only Christ as their head. E. moved completely to the side of the Protestants when her cousin Mary Stuart, Queen of Scotland, made herself leader of the Catholics in England and attempted to gain the English throne. As a result, Pius V in the bull *Regnans in excelsis* excommunicated and deposed E. in 1570. This act, however, really strengthened her position at home and abroad. The C of E came to be identified with English nationalism. In 1571 Parliament made it high treason to state that E. was a heretic and should be deposed. In the last decades of the century E. put through further legislation against Catholics. The worst parts of the penal codes were, however, dictated by new causes: the threat of foreign invasion and the remarkable success of missionary priests in England. During E.'s reign the C of E took on a form uniquely English. It retained much of Catholic tradition, though less than the Queen would have wished; but it subjected all things spirtual to the power of the realm. At the end of E.'s life only about 200,000 Catholics remained, along with a smaller number of staunch Puritans. Both groups could claim many martyrs; and succeeding monarchs inherited a host of religious problems. BIBLIOGRAPHY: H. J. Grimm, *Reformation Era* (1965) 464–479.

[M. J. SUELZER]

ELIZABETH OF HUNGARY (THURINGIA), ST. (1207-31), Franciscan tertiary. The daughter of King Andrew II of Hungary, E. was betrothed in infancy to Louis IV, son of the landgrave of Thuringia. In 1211 she was sent to Thuringia to be reared in her adopted country. At 14 she married Louis, who as landgrave encouraged her in her charitable works. After his death in Frederick II's Crusade, was directed by the austere Master Conrad. The hostility of her husband's family and of the townspeople compelled her to take refuge with her uncle, bp. of Bamberg. Having provided for her three children, she became a Franciscan tertiary. She was canonized in 1235. BIBLIOGRAPHY: Butler 4:386–389; E. Pásztor et al., BiblSanct 4:1110–23.

[M. J. FINNEGAN]

ELIZABETH OF PORTUGAL, ST. (c. 1271–1336), Queen. Daughter of Peter III of Aragon, grandniece of St. Elizabeth of Hungary, long-suffering wife of the immoral King Denis of Portugal (from 1282), in widowhood she became a Franciscan tertiary at Coimbra. ''The Peacemaker's'' holy life was signalized by devotion to the poor and included dramatic battlefield interventions. BIBLIOGRAPHY: L. Chierotti, BiblSanct 4:1096–98; Butler 2:578–580.

[R. I. BURNS]

ELIZABETH OF SCHÖNAU, ST. (1129–64), Benedictine nun. She was a severe ascetic and had many visions and revelations centering around the Passion and Resurrection. Many of the writings credited to her come from her brother Egbert, the abbot of the male Benedictines of Schönau abbey near Bonn, Germany. E. added greatly to the Ursuline legends by reporting her own visions of the vicissitudes of St. Ursula and her companions. BIBLIOGRAPHY: Butler 2:578–580; N. del Re, BiblSanct 11:730–732.

[J. F. FALLON]

ELIZABETH OF THE TRINITY (Elizabeth Catez; 1880–1906), French Carmelite mystic. At the age of 14, E. vowed virginity and entered the Carmel at Dijon when she was 21 years old. Here she placed great emphasis on the indwelling of the Blessed Trinity and strove constantly to be ever aware of this divine presence. From her readings in St. Paul, she discovered her mission to be an apostle dedicated to the praise of the Trinity. By her practice of inner silence and the exercise of faith and love through acts of fidelity to God's will, she became like her model, the Word. She composed a prayer to the Trinity and near her life's end two retreats entitled *How to Find Heaven upon Earth,* and *Last Retreat on the Praise of Glory.* Several attacks of a severe stomach ailment brought her the realization of her early death. She increased her devotion to Mary, the Gate of Heaven, and completely surrendered herself to be conformed to the death of Christ. The cause for her beatification began in 1963. BIBLIOGRAPHY: M. Philipon, *Spiritual Doctrine of Sister Elizabeth of the Trinity* (1947); H. von Balthasar, *Elizabeth of Dijon: An Interpretation of Her Spiritual Mission* (tr., A. Littledale, 1956).

[M. B. MONAGHAN]

ELIZALDE, MIGUEL DE (1618–78), Spanish moral theologian. A Jesuit from 1635, he taught in colleges of the Society at Valladolid, Salamanca, Rome, and Naples. His apologetic theory, published in 1668, that the possibility of

revelation is rationally demonstrable, won belated but strong acceptance in the 19th century. In moral theology he stood against *probabilism, then the majority moral system advocated in the Society. Deman (see bibliog.) points to E.'s work as a resource that could have returned moral theology to its ancient and healthier inspiration, esp. because it stressed the key influence of charity on the formation of right moral judgments. Permission to publish his antiprobabilist ideas was refused in 1669 during the generalate of J. P. *Oliva, but under the encouragement of the Jesuit Card. P.S. *Pallavicino, E. did publish them in his *De recta doctrina morum in quatuor libris* . . . (1670), under the pseudonym Antonio Calladei; a second edition in expanded form and under his own name appeared posthumously (1684). The work aroused the strong opposition of many Jesuits. BIBLIOGRAPHY: T. Deman, DTC 13:524, 527–530 s.v. ''Probabilisme.''

[T. C. O'BRIEN]

ELKESAITES (ELCHASAITES), A Judaeo-Christian sect that began in the 1st cent. and existed in Palestine and Syria. The name is of Syrian origin, from *Elxsai* or *Elkesai.* Whether this was the name of a real person or an esoteric symbol is uncertain. Neither is it clear that in the beginning the Elkesaites were Christian at all. Nothing is known of them except through the *Philosophoumena* of Hippolytus, which reports the preaching of Alcibiades, who brought the *Book of Elkesai* to Rome (c. 200). By this time their doctrine was a mixture of Jewish, Christian, astrological, magical, and Gnostic elements. They practiced circumcision, placed great emphasis on religious ablutions (including repeated baptisms), took a mitigated view of penance, rejected virginity and continence, made marriage mandatory for all, insisted on God's oneness, and denied the divinity of Christ and of the Holy Spirit. BIBLIOGRAPHY: G. Bareille, DTC 4:2233–39 (Elcésaites).

[T. C. O'BRIEN]

ELLARD, GERALD (1894–1963), American Jesuit liturgist. His studies at the Univ. of Munich led to his doctoral dissertation, *Ordination Anointings in the Western Church before 1000 A.D.* (1933), considered the first scholarly work done by an American in the history of the liturgy. His writings and lectures made him a leading figure in the *Liturgical Movement in the U.S. He was one of the original associate editors of *Orate Fratres* (later, *Worship*) to which he contributed many articles. Among his influential books were: *Christian Life and Worship* (1933), *Men at Work and Worship* (1940), and *Mass in Transition* (1956). BIBLIOGRAPHY: E. A. Diederich, YBLS 4 (1963) 3–21; *Liturgy for the People: Essays in Honor of Gerald Ellard* (ed. W. J. Leonard, 1963); L. Klein, ''Gerald Ellard, Pioneer of Renewal,'' *America* 128 (1973) 492–493.

[N. KOLLAR]

ELLENBORG, NIKOLAUS (1481–1543), German Benedictine of Ottobeuren, humanist. He pursued study of philosophy and medicine at Heidelberg and other universities, entered the Benedictine order in 1504 and was ordained in 1507. He served as novice master and prior. His endeavors to raise monastic scholarship in ancient and medieval learning, as well as his treatises and correspondence, earned him the reputation of humanist.

[J. R. RIVELLO]

ELLINGTON, EDWARD KENNEDY (DUKE; 1899–1975), American jazz musician and composer. Born in Washington, D.C., he began his piano study when he was 7 years old. Ten years later he made his first professional appearance as a jazz pianist and after 2 years formed a band. After many performances in Harlem, he became one of the most celebrated figures of American jazz. He united his musical talents, his excellence, and his elegance in a way that went beyond the usual meaning of jazz and constantly rejected the word jazz in connection with his work. Nevertheless, E.'s genius as a composer and orchestrator who could capture in permanent written form the spontaneity and mobility of true jazz are what place him in the first rank of American musicians.

E. was the first to lengthen his jazz compositions from the usual chorus of 12 to 30 bars. His first great try at an extended composition came in 1943 when he composed *Black, Brown, and Beige,* which ran for 50 minutes and which he introduced at one of his concerts in Carnegie Hall. His first sacred concert in 1965 revealed a new musical field. The composition starting with "In the beginning God . . ." was developed in typical Ellington style. It included his full orchestra, three choirs, a dancer, and several guests. E. considered it one of the most important things he had ever done.

[L. MCBRIDE]

ELLIOTT, WALTER (1842–1928), Paulist preacher, biographer of I. *Hecker. Attracted by Hecker's preaching, E. gave up his law practice in Detroit and became a Paulist, being ordained in 1872. He accomplished much as a preacher, founder of the Paulist house at The Catholic Univ. of America, organizer of preaching bands for the convert apostolate, and author. His name, however, chiefly recalls in general American church history the controversy called *Americanism. E. was the companion of Hecker during the Paulist founder's final years and from their conversations published a biography, first serially in the *Catholic World* (v. 51–53, 1890–91), then in book form as *The Life of Father Hecker* (1891). A French translation, or perhaps mistranslation, and the discussion it provoked were the immediate occasion of the Americanism issue. E.'s other publications include: *Missions to Non-Catholics* (1893); *Life of Christ* (1902); *Manual of Missions* (1922); he also translated from German the sermons of John Tauler

(1910). BIBLIOGRAPHY: J. McSorley, *Father Hecker and His Friends* (1953).

[T. C. O'BRIEN]

ELLIS, PHILIP (Michael; 1652–1726), English Benedictine, vicar apostolic, bishop, A convert to Catholicism in his youth, he left England and became a Benedictine (1670) at St. Gregory's, Douai, taking the name Michael. On his return to work in the apostolate after ordination, James II made him one of the royal chaplains. In this period of the King's pro-Catholic leanings there was actually a Benedictine community of 14 monks at St. James, London. Innocent XI appointed E. one of the four first vicars apostolic for England, E. being assigned to the W district and consecrated a titular bp. in May 1688. He never visited his territory, however, because with the Glorious Revolution he was briefly imprisoned in November of 1688. Shortly released he went to Rome and there, associated with Card. Howard, represented the interests of James II for a time. Unable to return to England, he resigned his vicariate in 1705, and Clement XI appointed him bp. of Segni in the Papal States. E. spent the remainder of his life there, where he built a diocesan seminary and bequeathed his property to it. He was buried in the seminary church. BIBLIOGRAPHY: J. A. Williams, "Bishops Gifford and Ellis and the Western Vicariate, 1688–1715," *JEcclHist* 15 (1964) 218–228.

ELLORA (ELURA), Indian village 18 miles NW of Aurangābād, the site of 34 rock-cut shrines (caves) of Buddhist, Hindu, and Jain religions. Caves I to XII of Mahāyāna Buddhism are the oldest (5th–7th cent.), cave X the Viśvakarma chaitya hall is the last of its type, relating to those at Ajantā. Hindu Brahmanical caves XIII to XXIX (7th–9th cent.) are unusual in the impressive Kailāsa temple to Siva, cave XVI, which was cast as a free-standing monolithic block. The Jain caves XXX–XXXIV (9th and 10th cent.) follow the Hindu temples in form. BIBLIOGRAPHY: R. S. Gupte and B. D. Mahjan, *Ajantā, Ellora, and Aurangābād Caves,* (1962).

[M. J. DALY]

ELLWANGEN, ABBEY OF, Benedictine abbey, founded *c.*764 at Ellwangen, Württemberg. It was established for supporting the Carolingian Franks against the Bavarians, recitation of the divine office, and clearing the German forests. In 817 it became an imperial abbey, in 979, was given papal protection, and in 1460, became an exempt collegiate church. The Jesuit St. Peter Canisius, was influential in keeping the region Catholic during the Reformation. The monastery was dissolved in the secularization of 1802–03. The old abbey church was the model for the cathedral at Worms.

[S. A. HEENEY]

ELMO, ST., a legendary martyr who reputedly died in the

first years of the 4th century. He is also known as Erasmus, Rasmus, Ermo, and Telmo. He is said to have been bp. of Formia. Many tales have been told of him though few have any basis in reality. He was identified as one of the Fourteen Holy Helpers. He was once venerated as patron of mariners, and the blue lights that sometimes appear at mastheads before and after storms became known as St. Elmo's Fire. However, when Bl. *Peter Gonzalez was adopted as patron of Portuguese sailors, he became for them the true St. Elmo. BIBLIOGRAPHY: Butler 2:453–454; AS June 1:211–219; A. Balducci, BiblSanct 4:1288–90.

[P. K. MEAGHER]

ELOHIM (Heb. *ĕlohim,* plural form of EL *(ĕl,* God). The term is used in the OT for pagan gods (Ex 18.11: Ps 86.8); idols (Ex 20.23); superhuman creatures (e.g., the "sons of God," Gen 6.1–4; Ps 29.1; Job 1.6; 38.7); angels (Ps 138.1); rulers or judges (Ps 82.1, 6); but in the main (more than 2000 times) refers to Yahweh, the "God" of Israel. Plural in form, when used of God Elohim appears with but few exceptions with singular verbs, as in Akkadian *(ilani)* and the Amarna Letters *(ilaniya).* The plural form is not indicative of a primitive polytheism, but is generally considered to be a plural of majesty which, when applied to God, implies that he comprehends all deity in himself. BIBLIOGRAPHY: DeVaux, AncIsr; O. Eissfeldt, *Old Testament, an Introduction* (3d ed., 1965).

[R. T. A. MURPHY]

ELOHIST TRADITION, the name given to the supposed writer or writers of the second oldest of the four main Pentateuchal sources. The name was chosen because of the author's penchant for using *Elohim as a divine name; another source (the Yahwist, or J), uses Yahweh. Other characteristics of Elohist tradition are, e.g., the use of Amorite for Canaanite, Horeb for Sinai; a measured style; an exacting but universalistic moral code; a solicitude for the divine transcendence. Elohist tradition is generally held to be of northern, Yahwist of southern origin. It contains no primitive history, but begins with the story of Abraham. At one time it was customary to date Elohist tradition very late, i.e., after the Exile; archaeology, however, has brought to light numerous extrabiblical parallels in laws and customs which show that many biblical practices and standards existed long before the dates usually assigned to the "sources." A close analysis of the Pentateuchal narratives discloses details and points of view which are older than and quite dissimilar to those in vogue when the documents or sources were supposedly written. Conclusions based on such evidence reflect a new caution in assigning dates to Elohist tradition, and indeed, in regard to the very existence of a separate source. It is better to speak of an Elohistic tradition than of a single author, and, while assigning a date shortly after the 9th cent. B.C. to this tradition, to allow an indeterminate period of time extending to Moses and even beyond, for the events themselves. BIBLIOGRAPHY: W. F. Albright, *From the Stone Age to Christianity* (2d ed., 1957); O. Eissfeldt, *Old Testament, an Introduction* (3d ed., 1965).

[R. T. A. MURPHY]

ELPHINSTONE, WILLIAM (*c.* 1431–1514), Scottish ecclesiastic and statesman. E. was educated at Glasgow Univ. where he became rector (1474), and in canon and civil law at Paris and Orleans; he became bp. of Ross (1481) and was translated to the see of Aberdeen (1483). He served James III as chancellor (1488) and conducted diplomatic missions for him and James IV. E. founded the Univ. of Aberdeen (1495), sponsored legal and liturgical reforms, and introduced printing into Scotland (1507). BIBLIOGRAPHY: L. Macfarlane, NCE 5:288.

[R. W. HAYS]

EL SALVADOR, the smallest and most densely populated of the Central American republics, bordered by Guatemala, Honduras, and the Pacific Ocean (8,260 sq. mi.; pop. [est. census 1971] 3,587,917; ethnic distribution, mestizo 85%, Indian 10%, white 5%), The population is more than 61% rural; the illiteracy rate is 50%. Pedro Alvarado, sent by Cortés, entered the territory in 1524 and in a short time its conquest was completed. It became part of the captaincy general of Guatemala in 1542. Its cultural and economic life during the colonial period is somewhat obscure. Independence from Spain was declared in 1821, and El Salvador avoided absorption into Iturbide's empire but from 1823 until 1839 was a member of the Central American Federation. Since the dissolution of the confederation El Salvador has had a succession of short-lived governments and a history of continuous and bitter strife between Conservatives and Liberals, the former generally favoring the Church, and the latter opposed to it. The leftist regime of 1960 was overthrown by Col. Julio Rivera, who was elected president in 1962 and again in 1967. During colonial times the Church in El Salvador was closely connected with that of Guatemala, and the country had no bp. of its own until 1842. The early evangelization was carried out chiefly by Franciscans, Dominicans, and Mercedarians. The constitution of 1841 gave official recognition only to the Catholic religion. Systematic attacks upon the Church began in 1871 and legislative measures against it were enacted. Freedom was extended to all religions; religious instruction was forbidden in the schools; the cemeteries were secularized; the state claimed full jurisdiction in matters of marriage and divorce; and legal restrictions were imposed on the Church limiting its right to acquire property. The Church's legal situation took a turn for the better in more recent times. The constitution of 1950 recognized the juridic personality of the Church; that of 1962, although it retained the separation of Church and State, permits the teaching of religion in schools. The Church enjoys at present a considerable freedom of action. San Salvador was made an archbishopric in 1913, and there are now four suffragan sees, Santa Ana (1913), San Miguel (1913), San Vincente (1943), and Santiago de María (1954). Candidates for the priesthood are trained at the interdiocesan seminary in San Salvador. There are not enough priests, sisters, and active laymen to give sorely needed religious instruction to the masses of baptized Christians, despite the considerable help that is provided by religious of various orders and congregations. As elsewhere in Central America, vigorous social action is a necessary part of the apostolate and some impressive steps in this direction have been taken. Protestant denominations (Central American Mission, American Baptist Missionary Society, Adventists, Jehovah's Witnesses, and Pentecostals) have gained adherents. Over 3,487,900 members make up the Catholic community, which includes 220 parishes and 394 priests (1975). In the early 1970s the Protestant community numbered some 57,700 members and had about 625 pastors. BIBLIOGRAPHY: J. R. Vega, NCE 12:1037; L. Lamadrid, NCE 5:288–289.

[P. DAMBORIENA]

ETTENBERG RELIQUARY.

ELVIRA, COUNCIL OF, held near Granada *c*.306, and attended by 19 Hispanic bishops. The acts, oldest and most complete Church code extant, throw light on Spanish Christianity some years before Priscillianism; 14 of the 18 rigorist canons were repeated at the Councils of Arles, Nicaea I, and Sardica. Some canons were taken into penitentials, but the acts do not appear in collections until the *Hispana collectio c*.666. Disciplinary rather than dogmatic, Elvira dealt with the sacraments and sought to keep Christians away from the scandals of pagan society and customs. Marriage to pagans, Jews, and heretics was forbidden, but no notion of invalidity appears. PL 84:301–310.

[E. P. COLBERT]

ELY, ANCIENT SEE AND ABBEY OF. The see was created in 1109 when Henry I and St. *Anselm of Canterbury separated the ''Isle of Ely'' (so called because it is surrounded by the fens) from the Diocese of Lincoln. The abbot was made bp.; the monks, the cathedral chapter. The Isle of Ely was a marriage gift to St. Ethelreda in 649; on her husband's death she founded in 673 a double monastery, which she ruled until her death in 679. The monastery continued and was a pilgrimage shrine until it was razed by the Danes in 870. It was restored in 970 as a Benedictine abbey by King Edgar and Ethelwold, bp. of Winchester. The location of the monastery made it an important stronghold; the bps. of Ely became influential rulers in their own territory and held important offices in the kingdom. At the time of the *dissolution of the monasteries the monastic community was suppressed (1539). The abbot became dean of the cathedral chapter, some of the monks, canons. The last RC bp. was Thomas Thirlby (1554–59). The see,

which includes Cambridgeshire, remained important in the C of E; a grammar school founded in 1541 continues, as does a theological college founded in 1876.

[T. C. O'BRIEN]

ELY CATHEDRAL, English Romanesque cathedral begun in 1083, with additions toward the W end (tower and porch) in the 12th cent., a Lady Chapel in English Decorated style, and a lierne rib choir. The octagon crossing (1323–30), considered a work of genius, was probably the idea of Alan of Walsingham, with timber work and lantern designs by William Hurle.

[M. J. DALY]

ELY, RICHARD THEODORE (1854–1943), social economist who influenced the *Social Gospel movement. Most of his professorial career was spent at the Univ. of Wisconsin. By his writings, e.g., *The Labor Movement in America* (1886) and *Social Aspects of Christianity* (1886), and by his association with the Church Social Union and the American Economic Association, E. promoted the theme that in Christian ethical teaching lies the solution to the problems of society. His ideas were accepted by many ministers, among them Washington Gladden and Lyman *Abbott.

[M. A. GARDNER, JR.]

ELYON, Hebrew adjective meaning lofty, most high; a title assigned to El, the chief god of the Canaanite pantheon, and the god of Melchizedek (Gen 14.18); later applied to Yahweh, God of Israel, (e.g., Ps 83.19; 97.9). BIBLIOGRAPHY: EDB 654–655.

[T. CRANE]

ELYOT, THOMAS (*c*.1490–1546), English scholar and diplomat. A friend of Sir Thomas More, he nevertheless aided the plans of Henry VIII, helped towards the divorce from Catherine of Aragon, and served the commission on monasteries, profiting personally from confiscated church lands. His *Boke Named the Governor,* 1531, was the first book on education written and printed in English. He insists on the usefulness of a ''liberal education'' for all who govern. The *Boke* was highly valued in his own time and is of importance still in the educational controversies of today. His *Dictionary,* 1538, was a model for later dictionaries. BIBLIOGRAPHY: S. E. Lehmberg, *Sir Thomas Elyot: Tudor Humanist* (1960).

[M. B. BARRY]

ELYSIAN FIELDS, also known as Elysium, or the Isles of the Blest, a place to which, according to classical mythology, certain favorites of the gods were taken without experiencing death. There, free from toil and entertained with wine, music, and dancing, they lived a life of perfect moral and physical bliss. This concept of the afterlife was probably a survival from pre-Hellenic times. Later, when men became more concerned with the fate of the dead, the Elysian Fields were transferred from the ends of the world or islands in the ocean to the Lower World, which was more consonant with the Homeric and general Greek view of the abode of the departed. BIBLIOGRAPHY: F. R. Walton, OCD 19–20, s.v. "After-Life."

[M. J. COSTELLOE]

ELZÉAR OF SABRAN, ST. (1286–1323), Provençal knight, later count of Ariano, Italy. E. was the husband of Bl. Delphina of Signe and godfather of Urban V, who formally recognized his holiness in 1369; he was canonized by Gregory XI in 1571. E. had an active career as military leader, diplomat, and counselor of Duke Charles of Calabria. He was revered during his life as a model of Christian charity. His remains were later transferred to the cathedral of Apt. BIBLIOGRAPHY: L. Hardick, NCE 5:291; A. Balducci, BiblSanct 4:1155–57.

[J. E. WRIGLEY]

EMANATIONISM, the pantheistic theory that all things come into existence as a necessary outpouring or radiation of the being of God. It is distinguished from the orthodox Christian doctrine that God created the universe out of nothing *(ex nihilo)* by a free act of will, and from evolutionary theories of higher levels developing from lower, since emanation is the descent from the higher to the lower.

Although adumbrations of the theory appear in various ancient religious and philosophical writings, it is classically expressed in *Neoplatonism, esp. by *Plotinus (*c*.205–270). He taught that by a process of overflow, in which the being of God was not diminished or changed, mind *(nous)* came from the One (God), soul from mind, and then particular forms and matter. Each step was a further removal from the perfection of God, so matter was judged lowest in perfection. The theory explained the imperfections of the world by its distance from God, in contrast with the Christian doctrine that the world was originally good.

Emanationism was also a feature of *Gnosticism, which in some cases posited a large number of emanations, and creation of the world by a lower, imperfect being. A consequence of the theory was that man's plight was understood as his involvement in the material world, rather than as his sin. Redemption, consequently, was seen as escape from the material world and reascent to God. In opposition to the Gnostics, Plotinus asserted that the world is not to be considered evil, even though it is the last emanation *(Enneads* 2,9). *Pseudo-Dionysius and *John Scotus Erigena made use of emanationism in their writings, and through them it influenced Christian theology, but was modified by the doctrine of creation. It has also influenced Jewish and Muslim thought. It was expressly condemned by Vatican Council I (D 3024).

[T. EARLY]

EMANCIPATION, CATHOLIC, see CATHOLIC EMANCIPATION.

EMANCIPATION, JEWISH, the restoration of citizenship that were lost to most Jewish communities during the Middle Ages. In the course of the 18th and 19th cent., many countries gradually restored equal rights to the Jewish people. During the 18th cent. the Declaration of Independence helped to qualify Jewish emancipation in the colonies of North America. Full equality in individual states was not realized until the 19th century. Through the Declaration of the Rights of Man (1789), the Jews of France were liberated, and by 1831 Judaism was officially recognized. Thereafter, French influence for equality spread through Italy, Holland, and Germany. During the Nazi regime, Germany retracted Jewish rights, there and in occupied Europe. It was not until the overthrow of the Nazis that equality was restored. Now, with some notable exceptions, the Jews share the same political and civil rights as citizens in almost all countries of the world. BIBLIOGRAPHY: Albert Mimmi, *Liberation of the Jews* (tr. 1973); J. Jehouda, *Five Stages of Jewish Emancipation* (1966).

[C. KEENAN]

EMARD, JOSEPH MÉDARD (1853–1927), Canadian abp. of Ottawa. Educated at the seminary of Montreal, he was a professor and vice-chancellor of Laval Univ., Quebec, before his consecration (1892) as bp. of Valleyfield. He was appointed abp. of Ottawa in 1922. Identified with French Canadian aspirations, by judicious handling of the school question (1913) and the conscription issue during World War I he became popular with other segments of the Canadian population.

[R. K. MacMASTER]

EMATH, see HAMATH.

EMBALMING (EARLY CHURCH). As part of the preparation of the corpse for burial there was frequent use of oils, prefumes, and spices, esp. myrrh. The practice is mentioned by early Christian writers, St. Augustine among them. In some burial rituals, according to Pseudo-Dionysius, there was a liturgical anointing to parallel at the end of life the baptismal anointing. The care both to prepare and to bury the body was a Christian continuation of the Jewish custom; cremation was the custom of pagan Rome that by the 5th cent. Christian burial had supplanted. The Christian care for the dead body was, of course, inspired by belief in the body's being "the temple of the Holy Spirit" and destined to share in Christ's Resurrection. The modern method of embalming is simply a hygienic measure, neither connected with Christian burial nor in fact practiced in many places. *Cremation has come to be permitted in the RC Church; objection to it was based on the anti-Christian motivation of those who first introduced it in 19th-cent.

Europe. Part of their advocacy was to reject the Christian meaning of death and faith in the Resurrection.

[T. C. O'BRIEN]

EMBER DAYS, the Monday, Wednesday, and Friday of four weeks (Ember Weeks) of the year, each of which coincides approximately with the beginning of a season. These days fall in the third week of Advent, the first week of Lent, the octave of Pentecost, and the week after the feast of the Triumph of the Cross (Sept. 14). The religious observance of these days has both a festive and a penitential character, with the latter predominating. In the RC Church these were days of mandatory fast and abstinence, but the decree *Poenitemini* (Feb. 1966) withdrew the obligation attached to that observance. The BCP includes these days among those on which fasting and abstinence are required by the Church. The keeping of the Ember Days goes back to the early Church, but their origin and purpose in the beginning are uncertain. It is possible to find analogous observances among both Jews and pagans. The *Liber pontificalis* attributes the establishment of the observance to Pope Callistus I (d. *c*.223), but this is unreliable authority for an event of that time. Three seasonal fasts of summer, fall, and winter were observed in the time of Leo I (d. 461), who preached on the subject. There is no clear evidence of the emergence of the spring Ember Days as something distinct from the Lenten fast until the 7th century. By the 9th cent. the observance had spread throughout Europe, but it was not until the matter was settled by Gregory VII in 1078 that the weeks in which the observance fell were definitely fixed. Since the 6th cent. at least, Ember Saturdays have been observed as days for ordination and continue to be among the days preferred for that purpose (CIC c. 1006.2). The conjunction of the time of prayer and fasting with that of ordination has led some to believe that the chief significance of the observance is supplication on behalf of the clergy and the ordinands in particular. The themes of the liturgy, however, do not support this view; they reflect the thoughts and feelings appropriate to the liturgical season in which the days fall. The Ember Days have not been suppressed in the new liturgy. They remain as days on which the Church gives public thanks to God and prays for man's needs. However, adaptations of time and manner of observance in different regions have been left to the determination of episcopal conferences. The Masses for these days are to be chosen from the votive Masses (*Sacramentary* of 1974, "General Norms for the Liturgical Year and the Calendar" nn. 45–47). BIBLIOGRAPHY: T. Maertens, *Feast in Honor of Yahweh* (1965); N. M. Denis-Boulet, *Christian Calendar* (1960); R. E. McNally, NCE 5:296–298; G. Morin, L'Origine des Quatre-Temps," RevBén 14 (1897) 337–346.

[N. KOLLAR]

EMBLEM BOOKS, collections of pictures designed for moral edification through allegorical interpretation. Usually each emblem was accompanied by an explanatory motto and a poetic or prose text as commentary. The 16th and 17th cent. saw the heyday of emblem books (beginning in 1531 with the *Emblemata* of Andrea Alciati), although their immediate origin can be seen in the block books of the 15th cent. and the block prints of that and earlier cent. wherein a maximum of illustration and a minimum of text were presented for the edification of the less literate. Often printers' devices were emblems, e.g., Plantin's "hand and compass" with *labore et constantia*. The symbolism derives both from medieval legends and classical history and romance, for emblem theory can be traced through Horace's *ut pictura poesis* back to Simonides and is closely linked with literary theory. Three English emblem books for Catholic meditation and devotion made illegal appearances in 17th-cent. England, of which *Partheneia Sacra* (1633) by the Jesuit Henry Hawkins is best known. Although emblem books still appeared in the 19th cent., their period of greatness culminates in the 17th-cent. works of John Bunyan. BIBLIOGRAPHY: R. J. Clements, *Picta Poesis: Literary and Humanistic Theory in Renaissance Emblem Books* (1960); R. Freeman, *English Emblem Books* (1966).

[F. J. WITTY]

EMBOLISM, liturgical term (Gr. *embolē,* inserting) applied in the Roman liturgy to the "Deliver us . . ." prayer between the last petition and the doxology of the Our Father. In some Eastern liturgies the embolisms are attached to the last two petitions.

[T. C. O'BRIEN]

EMBRIACHI, 15th-cent. Venetian family of master sculptors of reliefs in ivory and bone, series of which were incorporated into altarpieces and chests. Their most impressive work is an altarpiece at the Certosa in Pavia.

[M. J. DALY]

EMBRYOTOMY, the dismembering and sometimes evisceration of the fetus to effect delivery, there should be no moral objection since this is not *abortion in the moral sense. The term, however, now covers what has become a commonplace procedure in this age of abortion on demand: the crushing or suctioning of the living fetus to remove it. Since this involves a direct, death-dealing attack on the human life, it cannot be justified; one may not do evil that good may result. On Aug. 19, 1889, the Holy Office, in answer to a rather complicated set of questions, stated that the decree of May 28, 1884, (which condemned *craniotomy) applied to "every surgical procedure that is a direct killing of the fetus or the pregnant mother." This clearly includes embryotomy. When the procedure does not involve a direct killing of the fetus but is rather performed to save its life, e.g., cleidotomy, division of the clavicles to collapse the shoulder girdle, it is permissible if no less radical procedures are available.

[J. R. CONNERY]

EMBURY, PHILIP (1728–73), founder of Wesley Chapel, John Street, New York City, in 1768 (see METHODIST EPISCOPAL CHURCH). His parents were German Lutherans who had emigrated from the Palatinate to Ireland in 1709. He was converted under John *Wesley in 1752, becoming a local preacher, and immigrated to Colonial America in 1760. In 1766, inspired by his cousin Barbara Heck, who asserted that the immigrants, grown careless about religion, would "all go to Hell together," E. began preaching in his own home. He formed a Methodist *society that was given impetus by an ardent Methodist Thomas *Webb. A carpenter himself, E. supervised the building of Wesley Chapel (now a Methodist Colonial Shrine) and dedicated it Oct. 30, 1768. With other German Methodists he went (1770) to Camden, near Troy, New York. There and at Ashgrove, N.Y., where he is buried, he established Methodist societies. BIBLIOGRAPHY: HistAmMeth 1:76–78; N. Bangs, *History of the Methodist Episcopal Church* (1839) 1:47–48; S. Seaman, *Annals of New York Methodism* (1892) 1–50.

[F. E. MASER]

EMEBERT (ABLEBERT) OF CAMBRAI, ST. (fl. 627–645), the fifth or sixth occupant of the see of Cambrai-Arras after St. Vedast. Though he has enjoyed a liturgical cult in Cambrai, little or nothing is known of him. BIBLIOGRAPHY: AS January 1:1077–80.

EMERIC OF HUNGARY, ST. (1007–31), known as Imre in Hungarian, prince. One of several children of St. Stephen I, King of Hungary, and Blessed Gisela, he was educated by the Benedictine bishop, St. Gerard of Csanád. Though he made a vow of chastity, he was married for political reasons to a foreign princess c. 1026 and died in a hunting accident. He was canonized in 1083 and is popular in Poland and in Hungary. With the 20th cent. revival of his cult, he is honored as the patron saint of Hungarian youth. BIBLIOGRAPHY: Butler 4:266.

[M. S. TANEY]

EMERSON, RALPH WALDO (1803–82), American essayist and philosopher. The son of a Unitarian minister, E. studied at Harvard and prepared for the Unitarian ministry at Harvard Divinity School. After receiving approval to preach in 1826, he was ordained at the Second Church in Boston, which he served as minister until 1832. He resigned his ministry because he believed the observance of the Lord's Supper had no valid authority. He did, however, continue to preach. During a trip to Europe in 1833, he met S. T. Coleridge and Thomas Carlyle; he became a close friend of Carlyle. On his return he settled in Concord, Massachusetts. Thereafter he lectured on literature and philosophy, attaining eminence in American life. Among his many notable lectures were "The American Scholar," delivered before the Phi Beta Kappa Society at Cambridge in 1837, and "An Address Delivered before the Senior Class" of Harvard Divinity School in 1838. The latter address significantly modified the future of American Unitarianism through its influence on Theodore *Parker and others. Emerson's philosophy is inseparably related to transcendentalism as a religious idealism combining rationalism and intuitionism. An early work, *Essays* (1841), stressed the concept of the "Oversoul," portraying the immediate presence of God's spirit in nature and in man. Works: complete edition (ed. E. W. Emerson, 12 v., 1903–06); *Journals* (ed. E. W. Emerson and W. E. Forbes, 10 v., 1909–14); *Letters* (ed. R. L. Rusk, 6 v., 1939). BIBLIOGRAPHY: G. W. Cooke, *Bibliography of Ralph Waldo Emerson* (1900); F. O. Mathiessen, *American Renaissance* (1941); R. L. Rusk, *Life of Ralph Waldo Emerson* (1949); S. E. Whicher, *Freedom and Fate* (1953); P. Miller, *Transcendentalists* (1950).

[J. C. GODBEY]

ÉMERY, JACQUES ANDRÉ (1732–1811), French Sulpician, church leader in Revolutionary and Napoleonic era. Ordained in 1758, he spent his years as seminary professor and superior until being elected Sulpician superior general in 1782. The great challenges of his life began with the French Revolution. With the hierarchy in disarray, E. became the counselor of the French priests and their support in the confusion and turmoil they faced. He led in the refusal to accept the *Civil Constitution of the Clergy, but in issues that did not involve essential Catholic teaching, he showed the clergy how to accommodate to the demands of the changing regimes. He was vicar-general of Paris and, coming under suspicion, was imprisoned for over a year, during which he was pastor to his fellow prisoners. After the Revolution he was able to restore the life and work of the Sulpicians and to reopen their seminaries. Under Napoleon, E. was a leader in winning acceptance of the Concordat of 1801. When the Emperor violated its terms and conflict with Pius VII began, E. assisted the cause of the Pope. He refused to sign the findings of the commission to which Napoleon had appointed him in the hope of resolving the conflict with Rome. In one of his last acts, a month before his death, he withstood Napoleon face to face and maintained his support of Pius VII. BIBLIOGRAPHY: J. Leflon, *Monsieur Émery* (2 v., 1945–46).

[T. C. O'BRIEN]

EMESA, cult center of the Syrian sun god, Helio-Baal, city of Roman Emperor Heliogabalus (218–222) and later a Christian archbishopric. After the Arab conquest, its name was changed to Homs or Hims.

[T. EARLY]

EMIDIUS OF ANCONA, ST. (var. Emygdius; d. c.304), bp. and martyr. According to late and unreliable legend, E., a native of Trier, came to Rome with three companions, where he was consecrated bp. by Pope Marcellus I (307–09) and sent to evangelize the territory of

Ascoli Piceno. There he made many converts and suffered martyrdom under Diocletian (284–305). E. is honored esp. in central Italy and is invoked against earthquakes. BIBLIOGRAPHY: Butler 3:292–293; U. Fasola, DHGE 15:445.

[R. B. ENO]

ÉMIGRÉS, approximately 150,000 displaced persons who deliberately left France during the French Revolution, hoping to return when stability, and, perhaps, monarchy were restored. The reasons for departure were varied: disgust and disdain, economic stability, fear and terror, revolution and persecution, war and invasion. The people who departed came from all strata of society. The elite elements—the clergy (c.32,597 in number), most of them deportees by the Law of Aug. 26, 1792, and including almost 100% of the privileged higher clergy; the privileged nobility including royalty (c.21,624), among the first to leave; and military (more than 7,513 officers and 2,237 soldiers and sailors)—departed prior to Sept. 1792. Thus the departure of the first two Estates made probable the victory of the bourgeoisie, the monarchy's overthrow, and the rise of Jacobin nationalism and republicanism. Numerous fugitive bourgeoisie, workers, and peasants later became émigrés, largely after 1792 when the king fell from power. The laws on émigrés (1792–94) were important in swelling their number because they offered no hope of reconciliation toward those who had fled. King Louis XVI and Queen Marie Antoinette attempted flight but failed to reach refuge beyond the E frontier. Other distinguished royalty included the Count of Artois, the King's brother and leader of the counter-revolution; the Duke of Chartres, later King Louis Philippe; Dukes Choiseul, de la Rochefoucauld-Liancourt, and Princes Condé and Conti. Among the clergy were Cardinal de Rohan and Bishop Talleyrand; military defectors were prominent, counting such first-line generals as Lafayette, Dumouriez, Pichegru, and the grand Carnot; politicians, e.g., Mounier and Barère, were important. Despite the above array, the significance of the émigrés is numerical and categorical, not individual and personal. Also their enormous properties were confiscated by the state; under the empire and the restored monarchy, compensation for property losses became a major issue. Most of the émigrés remained in Europe. Court Artois maintained headquarters in Coblenz and Turin. Some came to the U.S., 600 settling in Gallipolis, Ohio; others scattered to Africa, even Asia, and S America. The majority of émigrés returned to France after June 1794, and the Great Terror; subsequent laws, including amnesties in 1795, 1800, and 1802, ended the period of exile. BIBLIOGRAPHY: D. Greer, *Incidence of the Emigration during the French Revolution* (1951); M. Ragon, *La Législation sur les émigrés, 1789–1825* (1904); M. Weiner, *French Exiles* (1961; repr. 1975).

[R. J. MARAS]

EMILIA. Historic region in north-central Italy, earlier an area of Etruscan colonization, with evidences of Roman civilization (3d cent. B.C.) at Rimini on the *Via Aemilia*; early Christian and Byzantine works in Ravenna; Romanesque cathedrals in Ferrara, Modena, Parma, Piacenza; and Gothic building at Bologna. Ferrara was an important Renaissance center (15th cent.) and the Bolognese Academy under the Carracci determined the dramatic 17th-cent. Italian baroque style.

[M. J. DALY]

EMILIANI, JEROME, ST. (1481–1537), religious founder. A wealthy commander in the Ventian army in his young manhood, he turned to God, after he had been miraculously freed from a cruel imprisonment, and became a priest. The rest of his life was spent in caring for the poor, the sick, and for abandoned children. He founded a congregation dedicated mainly to the education of destitute youth at Somascha in N Italy in 1532. While ministering to the sick, he became infected and died. He was canonized in 1767 and declared patron of orphans in 1928. His congregation, the Somaschi, though small, still carries on his work in Italy. BIBLIOGRAPHY: Butler 3:150–151; N. Del Re, Bibl-Sanct 6:1143–48.

[J. F. FALLON]

EMINENT DOMAIN, from Lat. *eminere,* to project, hence to be principal, and *dominium,* ownership. The right of eminent domain is a law-term, which applies either to foreign or domestic relations. It is defined for the first case as the lordship of an independent sovereign over territories by virtue of which no other sovereign can exercise any jurisdiction in them. For the second case, as the inherent power of the sovereign to control for public use in case of necessity all private property, esp. land. Its application will vary according to the maintenance or diminution, by force or agreement, of State independence; according to constitutional settlement as to where the effective organ of sovereignty lies; and according to contractual rights guaranteed by the State respecting the disposal of property. The justice of the claim of public authority to such a right, to be exercised within the limits and under the conditions prescribed by law, cannot be seriously questioned.

[T. GILBY]

EMINENTLY, a scholastic term qualifying the higher mode of existence that certain created predicates, e.g., goodness, truth, justice, have as they are attributed to the divine being. *NAMES OF GOD.

[T. C. O'BRIEN]

EMIPORON (*Yemiporon, Emiphoron*), the Armenian equivalent of the Byzantine *omophorion,* whose Western counterpart is the pallium. The Armenian bp., however, wears it over the *shourtchar,* the Byzantine *sakkos* not being used by the Armenians. It is taken off at the beginning of the Offertory.

[A. CODY]

EMMANUEL (Heb. *'immanu'el:* "God is with us"). the symbolic name which the maiden (Heb. *'ălmah* rather than *betulah,* virgin, presupposed by the LXX *parthenos*) will give her child (Is 7.14). Many interpreters identify the child-who-is-a-sign with Hezekiah, the son of Ahaz and heir to the throne of Judah. They see in his birth and accession to the throne of David God's fidelity to the oracle of Nathan which promises that the throne of David will be established forever (2 Sam 7.12–16). This opinion seems to be confirmed in Is 8.8 where the land of Judah is called "your country, O Emmanuel," and in 8.10 where there is an insistence that the Syro-Ephraimite plans and efforts to overthrow the throne of David (7.6) will be frustrated by Yahweh. Furthermore, the prophet, because of the characteristic prophetic lack of historical perspective, seemed to view the sufferings that the nation would undergo during the childhood of Emmanuel (7.15–25) as the birth-pangs of the Messianic Age, which this successor of David would introduce (Is 9.1–7; 11.1–9). Because the prophecy was not fulfilled in Hezekiah, it was felt that the powerful word of God (cf. Is 56.10–11) could not be frustrated and hence would eventually be fulfilled. The expectation, therefore, of the birth of Emmanuel, the son of David, who would introduce the Messianic Era, survived. Matthew saw the fulfillment of the prophecy in the birth of Christ (Mt 1.22–25). Indeed, he saw the entire life of Christ and particularly the activity of the risen, exalted Christ within His Church, the new Israel, the Kingdom of God, as a literal fulfillment of the prophecy (cf. Mt 28.20 where Christ who is God says: "And know that I am with you always"). Other interpreters have understood Isaiah's wife as the maiden and his child as the sign. Some too have understood it as referring directly to Christ, a view which seems to make the "sign" irrelevant to those to whom it was given. BIBLIOGRAPHY: B. Vawter, *Conscience of Israel* (1961, repr. 1969) 177–191; S. Porubcan, "The Word 'ôt in Is. 7.14," CBQ 22 (1960) 144–159.

[J. A. PIERCE]

EMMANUEL, BL. (d. 1298), canonist, bishop. Professor of canon law in Paris in the 1270s, he later (1290?) was archdeacon, then bp. of Cremona, Italy. He was forced by political pressure to resign in 1295 and retired to the Dutch Cistercian abbey of Adwert (Aduard), where later he was venerated as blessed. BIBLIOGRAPHY: A. Rimoldi, Bibl-Sanct 4:1158.

[L. J. LEKAI]

EMMANUEL PROPHECY, the fulfillment text of Mt 1.22, 23, which culminates Matthew's account of Jesus Christ's divine generation from the virgin, Mary (Mt 1.18–25). Its intent is to proclaim Jesus' identity with God (God is with us) as the most profound fulfillment of a vague OT prophecy of Is 7.14, a doctrine that is confirmed by Mt 28.18–20, where the resurrected Jesus asserts divine power (v 18), equality with the Father and the Holy Spirit (v 19), and continued presence with his disciples (v 20). The two texts form an inclusion that brackets the Gospel and is constitutive of Matthean incarnational theology. That such profound Christian meaning was not directly intended by the Isaian sign is patent. Isaiah was indicating, through prophetic knowledge and symbol, the conception and birth of a son from a young woman, not necessarily a virgin, whom he and his audience knew—whether she was a wife of Achaz is unclear. This son would be named Immanuel (*sic* in Is 7.14), thus symbolizing God's presence as the protector of Judah and the Davidic dynasty. David's realm, in a much reduced state, would be delivered from the besieging kings of Israel and Syria before the youth reached maturity (within 13 years or less, Is 7.15,16). Many interpreters of Isaiah think this son was to be Hezechiah, a pious Davidic king, who put his faith in Isaiah's principle, "God is with us", in glaring contrast to his father Achaz. Matthew's use of such a vague prophecy for such a specifically Christian teaching indicates how deeply below the surface of the OT early Christian prophetic insight delved in its pondering over the mystery of Jesus.

[J. F. FALLON]

EMMAUS (Gr. *Emmaous,* from the Heb. *Hammah,* meaning hot spring). (1) A town in Judea, identified with 'Amwas, 19 miles WNW of Jerusalem, where Judas Maccabee won a victory over Gorgias in 166 B.C. (1 Macc 3.40,57; 4.3). It was later fortified by Bacchides (1 Macc 9.50). In Byzantine times it was called Nicopolis. (2) The town in which the risen Christ manifested himself to the two disciples at supper by the breaking of the bread (Lk 24.13–35). The present identity and location of the town is disputed because of a variant reading in v. 13 of the account. The stronger reading, supported by Vaticanus, is "60 stadia" (*c.*7 miles), but other MSS read "160 stadia." The hasty return to Jerusalem (v. 33) argues for the shorter distance. But Eusebius and Jerome favored 'Amwas, mentioned above, as the site. A Byzantine basilica was built there to commemorate the event. The site has been rejected by others because of its distance from Jerusalem. El Qubebe, a town about 60 stadia (7 miles) W of Jerusalem has been accepted as the site by the Franciscans, who built a church there because of traditions dating from the 12th century. Qalniyeh, a town 5 miles W of Jerusalem, which claims to be the Emmaus mentioned by Josephus, shows ruins dating drom the time of Christ but lacks traditional support. BIBLIOGRAPHY: Orchard 774a; R. T. Murphy, "Gospel of Easter Monday," CBQ 6 (1944) 131–141.

[J. A. PIERCE]

EMMAUS MOVEMENT, named after Emmaus near Paris, a shelter for the poor initiated by the French priest and social worker Abbé Pierre (Henri Antoine Groués; b. 1912, Lyons) in 1949. Impatient with the slow progress of the French Assembly in promoting legislation on behalf of the homeless after World War II, Abbé Pierre organized ragpicker-housebuilder communities, constructing some 50 emergency villages near Paris. Radio appeals supported his program and spread his ideas of mutual assistance nationally and internationally. The Institute for Research into the Misery of the World (IRAMM) was founded in Geneva (1957), as well as other related groups of social action. It published a periodical: *Faim et Soif* (Paris 1954–), and had headquarters in Paris (32, rue de Bourdonnais). BIBLIOGRAPHY: *Abbé Pierre Speaks,* speeches collected by L. C. Repland (tr. C. Hastings and G. Lamb, 1956); *Man Is Your Brother: Television Talks and Sermons* (tr. R. Matthews, 1958); B. Simon, *Ragman's City* (tr. S. Cunliffe-Owen, 1957).

[J. FANG]

EMMERAM, ST. (d. *c.*660) martyr, patron of the monastery of St. Emmeram (formerly St. George). According to Bp. Arbeo (Aribo) of Freising (*c.*772), whose account is, however, unreliable, Emmeram was bp. of Poitiers, then preacher to the Slavs in Bavaria, and was murdered on a false accusation at Regensburg by members of the household of Duke Theodo. BIBLIOGRAPHY: G. Jacquemet, *Catholicisme* 4:60–61; R. Van Doren, BiblSanct 4:1200.

[M. F. MCCARTHY]

EMMERICH, ANNE CATHERINE (1774–1824), Westphalian mystic, stigmatic, and Augustinian nun. Forced to leave the cloister of Agnetenberg at the suppression of religious houses in 1812, she found shelter in Dülmen, where many people sought her out for their edification. The report made in 1813 to the vicar general of the diocese concerning the five wounds observed in her body led to a canonical inquiry. The investigations of canonists and theologians over a period of years failed to establish any evidence of fraud or deceit. In 1818 E. was visited by the poet C. *Brentano, to whom she related the contents of her alleged visions. His publication of these in the two books, *The Dolorous Passion of Our Lord and Savior Jesus Christ* and *The Life of the Blessed Virgin Mary* provoked controversy. BIBLIOGRAPHY: S. Back, *Wounded by Love* (tr. T. A. Rattler, 1971).

[M. R. BROWN]

EMOTION, understood as more or less synonymous with *feeling, affect, passion, etc., a psychological response in the order of attraction, repulsion, aggression, withdrawal, etc. Emotion is broadly involved in all human activity and is a factor to be reckoned with in the spheres of religion and morality. Contemporary psychologists frequently distinguish emotion from drive, considering the former to comprise feeling tones, the latter, urges toward objects, but in common language, emotion can signify either. Emotion involves an object perceived or imagined to which an organism, human or animal, reacts with some kind of excitement which is both psychological and physical. The scholastic tradition following Aristotle generally distinguishes eleven broad categories of basic emotions or passions, understanding the more delicately nuanced and variously identified emotions of actual experience to be derivatives from, or combinations of, the Aristotelian types. Six of Aristotle's emotions are activities of the concupiscible appetite, which responds to simple pleasure or pain: these are love, desire, and joy for pleasures anticipated or experienced, and dislike, aversion, and sorrow for pains foreseen or felt. In the irascible appetite, which responds to challenges and dangers, there are basic passions of hope, boldness, fear, despair, and anger. Contemporary psychologists divide emotions in different ways; one system, e.g., distinguishes emotions as they are progressively differentiated in the development of an infant. At birth, an infant exhibits only generalized excitement, but by the 3d month, distress feelings are distinct from delight feelings. By the 24th month, distress has differentiated into fear, disgust, anger, and jealousy, while delight has become joy, elation, and affection.

Generally speaking, people seek situations that arouse emotions that are agreeable and stimulating and avoid situations that are distressing and depressing. However, even emotions generally considered distressing, like fear, anger, and sorrow, are pleasurable in small, controlled quantities, and so people seek out challenging and competitive situations, enjoy tragic dramas, etc. Moreover, any emotion can become disagreeable if it is too intense. Hence, the optimum in emotional life seems to be a rich experience of generally pleasurable emotions with occasional peaks which do not last long enough to become distressing, along with a sprinkling of stress emotions. When emotional life threatens to become too violent, people tend to withdraw from the external situations that arouse them and repress the memories or fantasies that disrupt mental peace from within. As a consequence, they have a less realistic orientation towards the world and the people in it and less insight into their own psychological needs and wants, and this hampers their growth in personality, moral character, and religious maturity. When emotional life becomes depressing and frustrating, people tend to turn to more intense forms of stimulation or intoxication, e.g., sexual activity, drugs, and alcohol, and personal risks and dangers as antidotes and reliefs, and this also threatens personal, moral, and religious development. A third general area of emotional disturbance is the development of generalized attitudes of hostility as a result of continual frustrations and repression of resentments. In the 20th cent., the area of personal emotional needs and problems has been given greater scientific and clinical attention, which has resulted in the development of the relatively new field of *psychotherapy. The basic theories and techniques of psychotherapy have become the professional tools of psychiatrists and psychological counselors and a necessary part of the equipment of many clergymen, confessors, spiritual directors, and advisers. BIBLIOGRAPHY: W. J. Devlin, *Psychodynamics of Personality Development* (1964); E. Paci, *Function of the Sciences and the Meaning of Man* (tr. P. Piccone and J. Hansen, 1972).

[M. STOCK]

EMOTIONAL DISORDERS, *personality disorders that primarily affect feelings and urges and only in severe cases disrupt thinking and behavior. The severe forms, usually involving unresolved, unconscious emotional conflicts, are called neuroses. The almost universal symptom of neurosis is anxiety, i.e., the unfocused feeling of impending disaster that arises from the stress of unconscious conflict and the threat of being overwhelmed by instinctual urges. Such free-floating anxiety, rising to the point of panic in certain situations, is the principal symptom of simple anxiety neuroses. Dissociative neurotic reactions involve, in addition, some disruption of normal cognitive and behavior patterns, e.g., amnesia, somnambulism, temporary alterations of personality, mental stupor, or confusion. The conversion reactions, which include hysterical reactions, involve psychologically caused paralyses, anesthesias, losses of sight and hearing, muscular contractions, visceral disturbances, etc. Phobic reactions are violent fears attaching to ordinarily innocuous objects, e.g., fears of dirt, animals, high places, open places, closed places, etc. Obsessive-compulsive reactions are neuroses in which anxiety is controlled by persistently repetitive thoughts and ritualistic acts. Any of these neuroses can be experienced in various degrees of intensity; besides them there are emotional disorders which, while not so disruptive, nevertheless more or less seriously hamper a person's productivity, personal relations, and peace of mind. For instance, ambivalent (love-hate) relationships between parents and children, spouses, brothers and sisters, work-colleagues, etc. (wherever a personal bond exists beween people who are in close daily contact) lead to constant quarreling, insults to personal dignity, recriminations, jockeying for position, and eventually bitterness, unforgivingness, and deep hostility. An excessive need for achievement leads to intense competitiveness and overwork; these produce fatigue and tension, which in turn hamper effectiveness and threaten achievement, a situation that provokes harder efforts in a vicious spiral. Other forms of more or less uncontrollable urges and affects include sexual obsessions often accompanied by fear of sexuality in general, depressions in middle age in the case of men who feel they have not achieved enough and women who feel they are not loved. Some people also get into a vicious circle of self-spiting and self-deprecation as a reaction to insults and indignities to which they fear to retaliate openly, and since these reactions are usually inefficacious, their rage and urge to punish themselves increase.

Smothered or repressed fears and guilts also generate anxieties; unavoidable frustrations generate bitter envies and jealousies.

Often several conflicts are found in one disturbed individual. The untangling of all these self-defeating emotional conflicts usually requires outside help, i.e., the therapeutic counseling of psychologist, clergyman, confessor, or spiritual director. The basis of the cure, even of serious disorders like neuroses, is the quality and strength of the trust which the counselee can elicit for his counselor, on the strength of which he can relax his defensiveness and begin to accept himself with his urges and needs, his place in the world, the needs of others, etc. Resolution of the conflicts involves some understanding of their origins, and a deconditioning of the reaction patterns that have been formed. Since this is often painful, the counselee must also be provided with motivations (if they are lacking or insufficient) and general moral and psychological support and encouragement. Often changes in environment and situation are helpful. Antidepressant and tranquillizing drugs may be of great use to help emotionally disordered people through their more difficult periods. BIBLIOGRAPHY: F. J. Braceland and M. Stock, *Modern Psychiatry: A Handbook for Believers* (1963).

[M. STOCK]

EMOTIONALISM, here understood as an excessive emphasis upon emotions in religion. With the rise of revivalism in the 18th cent., emotionalism became a controversial factor in mainstream American Protestantism. Earlier Puritans had stressed inward experience as a sign of regeneration, but this experience did not commonly include a loss of emotional control. The *Great Awakening, however, introduced a type of preaching that often induced anxiety, crying aloud, shouting in exultation, etc. Many ministers deplored such displays of feeling; e.g., Charles *Chauncy preached a sermon *Enthusiasm Described and Cautioned Against* (1742). Jonathan *Edwards discouraged visible manifestations of emotions, but in his *Treatise on the Religious Affections* (1746), he defended "feelings" as essential to religion. He asserted that a moving religious experience might cause bodily manifestations but also warned that such phenomena could be delusions of Satan. The early *camp meetings were marked by shouting, weeping, and peculiar physical behavior. The "new measures" of Charles G. *Finney tended to play on the emotions, but Finney disapproved of emotional exhibitions. Later in the 19th cent, the revival meetings of Dwight L. *Moody and other professional evangelists were less demonstrative. Nevertheless, most revivalists used music, stories, and methods calculated to stir emotions to lead people to conversions. In the 20th cent. Billy *Sunday was criticized for his use of sensational methods; the revivals of Billy *Graham are much more moderate and controlled. Today there is little evidence of emotionalism in most Protestant services, but in *Pentecostalism *glossolalia (tongues-speaking), and other outward manifestations are regarded as evidence of the Holy Spirit's presence. Debates continue over the line between appeals to emotions that are essential to the religious experience of human beings and "emotionalism." BIBLIOGRAPHY: H. S. Smith et al., *American Christianity: A Historical Interpretation with Representative Documents* (2 v., 1960–63); H. N. Wright, *Christian Use of Emotional Power* (1974).

[N. H. MARING]

EMPEDOCLES OF ACRAGAS (*c*.492–*c*.432 B.C.), one of the most influential of the Presocratics. His two poems *On Nature* and *Purifications* are preserved only in scattered fragments in later writers. He attempted to reconcile the fact of existence of change and motion with the principle of Parmenides that Being—which Parmenides regarded as material—neither comes into being nor passes away. He conceived of the All as a spherical *plenum*. He maintained that there are four eternal kinds of matter —earth, air, fire, and water—which he called the "roots of things," thus laying the foundation for the doctrine of the four elements. Objects come into being through the mingling of the elements, but the elements themselves remain forever unchanged. The mingling and separating of these elements are an eternal process and are produced by the impulses of Love and Hate, or Harmony and Discord. These impulses are regarded as physical or material forces. The world-process is circular and has four stages which are repeated forever. He borrowed the doctrine of transmigration from Pythagoras without apparently perceiving its inconsistency with his own cosmology. He explained sense-perception in terms of effluences. All things are constantly giving off effluences, and when the pores of the sense-organs are of the proper size, the effluences enter and perception results. His theory of vision and effluences was adopted by both Plato and Aristotle, and his doctrine on particles was the starting point for the atomic theory of *Leucippus and Democritus. He believed that the blood around the heart is the organ of thought. He was the teacher of Gorgias, the founder of rhetoric, and is said to have been a wonder-worker and to have contributed to the development of medicine as a science. BIBLIOGRAPHY: A. Porteus, OCD 314; O. Gigon, LexAW 808–809; Copleston 1:61–65; Guthrie 2:122–265.

[M. R. P. MCGUIRE]

EMPHYTEUSIS, a means in the late Roman empire whereby uncultivated public lands were leased for long terms for a fixed annual rent. Justinian (529) merged the concept with that of perpeual right, making the lessee a proprietor. In 594 Justinian also granted to ecclesiastical bodies the faculty of entering into emphyteutic contracts, thus allowing the Church a way around imperial laws on the inalienable nature of church property. As employed by the Church, these contracts played a large part in developing virgin areas, and often made the holding of property possible for people without means. Much of the property thus developed eventually passed out of the hands of the Church into those of the lessees, often because Church authorities failed to assert their basic dominion on the death of a lessee. Emphyteutic contracts still have an important place in Italian law and are allowed in a limited form in France. With some modifications, the 1918 Code of Canon Law continued the medieval usage (CIC cc. 1540, 1542). BIBLIOGRAPHY: E. Levy, *West Roman Vulgar Law: The Law of Property* (1951).

[L. E. BOYLE]

EMPIRICISM, the doctrine that all human knowledge is rooted in experience. As a philosophical position, empiricism was associated with the British 17th- and 18th-cent. philosophers, Locke, Berkeley, and Hume. Too often, however, experience has not been consulted for what it actually does disclose; it was used, instead, merely to illustrate foregone conclusions about what it must reveal if it is to meet the requirements of some rationalist program. Experience has suffered not only from the stigma of being subjective, in the sense of being unreliable as a guide or standard, but it has been hedged in by various a priori demands. Instead of attending to the more difficult matter of finding appropriate languages in which to express the full range of experience, dogmatic empiricism tries to fit all experience into a pre-existent universe of discourse.

The basic roots of religion in experience can only be understood if experience is seen as an encounter with an objective world in the dual sense that the encounter is something objective and that what is encountered transcends the subjectivity of the individual and of any collection of individuals. A narrow empiricism can so diminish the scope of authentic experience as to rule out the very possibility of a meaningful knowledge of God, rooted in experience and illuminating it. BIBLIOGRAPHY: J. E. Smith, *Experience and God* (1968); H. D. Lewis, *Our Experience of God* (1959).

[J. P. REID]

EMPLOYEES. Most authors tend to define an employee as one who is paid for his services on the basis of a wage contract. By that description, the vast majority of persons paid for their time and talent fall under the rubric of employee, and that number shows every sign of increasing as the quality of required skills becomes more and more specialized and the corporate nature of practically all industries continues to increase. The legal, ethical, and moral concepts that have approached the problem of employment from the premise of a one-to-one relationship are rapidly becoming outmoded, but a satisfactory set of alternatives does not yet appear to be available. A clear example of the limitation of ethical and moral practices can be seen in the fact that to date no clear set of principles has been set down as to the nature, role, rights, and obligations of labor unions and those who deal with them. Much of the writing on this topic still concerns itself with the obligations of the individual member of the organization.

For the present, there seem to be two classes of problems

relating to employment: those dealing with low skill employees, and those relating to high wage, high skill employees. The traditional ethical approach to labor problems finds more application to the lower end of the employment scale. It is here that the employee finds himself in the one-to-one relationship to his employer. Even here, however, there is a tendency toward corporate forms of organization such as can be seen in the rapidly expanding service industries. Among the problems confronting the employee at that level is the need to endow such occupations with the dignity commensurate with expectations of society and human needs; the need to raise wages so that low skills will not necessarily imply a meager existence in an affluent society and yet not raise them to such a level that only a few will be able to afford the services; the need to insure proper working conditions so that those who are employed in the low wage/low skill industries will not be taken advantage of since they are the employees who have the least bargaining power in society.

At the other end of the scale where high skills and high wages are found there is an equally pressing need to define and protect the rights of the worker. The highly competitive nature of many such occupations does not eliminate the need of the worker to be able to provide for his family presently and in the future. Ethical treatments that speak of the worker's obligation to be on time, not to be wasteful of time at work and so on, seem to have little application to the many skilled workers who operate under a great deal of psychological pressure. Should the predictions of many be fulfilled—in an automated society only the very highly skilled need work—then the need to be legally, ethically, and morally clear and precise in the matter of rights and obligations for said workers, will become intense. BIBLIOGRAPHY: J. S. Auerbach, *Labor and Liberty; the La Follette Committee* (1966); J. F. Cronin, *Social Principles and Economic Life* (1960); H. M. Vollmer, *Employee Rights and the Employment Relationship* (1960); W. Anthony et al., *Social Responsibility of Business* (pa., 1973).

[N. L. CHOATE]

EMPLOYERS. A consideration of the issues confronting an employer begins with a distinction between managers and proprietors, both of whom are employers. The term manager refers to one who has a limited control over production rates, methods of production and distribution, and to whom a number of subordinates are responsible. It is in the limitation of his control and responsibilities and the nature of the corporate structure in which he is involved that the manager is distinguished from the proprietor. The proprietor owns and controls the means of production, has access to the necessary resources, and his profit is the primary criterion of effectiveness.

There are three dimensions to the issues of management: (1) the lateral competition among professional managers for advancement and its rewards, which comprises a segment of the competition among firms for technical expertise and managerial skills; (2) the management of subordinates in a just and humane fashion often complicated by an absence of the manager's control over policies, wage scales, and working conditions which affect employees directly responsible to manager; (3) the problem of the responsibility of managers to the public, managers who are often anonymous and invisible to the administrator in larger corporations.

Issues confronting the employer who is also proprietor tend to derive from the nature of small businesses in a large scale society. Among such businesses, those operating on low volume, high profit appear to be faring better than those attempting high volume and low profit. In either case there exist three problem areas in the employer relationship: (1) the difficulty in attracting able personnel in a low-wage industry where the decline in loyalty to the employer and service to the customer is widely recognized; (2) the diffusion of responsibilities among manufacturers and distributors, which is problematic to the proprietor as it is to the customer; (3) the absence of legal and ethical concepts that clearly recognize a distinction between corporate and entrepreneurial employers.

The response to the issues of management and proprietorship must be distinct. For the question of the corporate employer, there needs to be policies and legislation that restrict the power of the corporation and clarify the nature and locus of internal and external responsibilities. At the same time, the role of the manager should be expanded to include the capability to resolve unjust or uncomplimentary conditions afflicting subordinates. The needs of the proprietor are for conditions that protect and support the existence of small businesses while providing high quality service and fair working conditions for employees. That need is particularly acute at a time when members of minority groups look to that avenue as a means of escape and when the contributions of small businesses to the life and vitality of urban neighborhoods are among the requirements for stabilizing and humanizing the cities. BIBLIOGRAPHY: E. M. Baake, *Mutual Survival: The Goals of Union and Management* (1946, repr. 1966); R. J. Daiute, *Scientific Management and Human Relations* (1964). L. Preston and J. Post, *Private Management and Public Policy: Principle of Public Responsibility* (1975).

[N. L. CHOATE]

EMPLOYMENT, SOCIAL ISSUES OF, There are two dimensions to the social issues of employment: the relationship between employer and employee and the relationship of these two to the society in which they live. The fact of employment should contribute to the gain of employer, employee, and all who are affected by that employment. It is obvious that this is not always the case, as when prejudicial discrimination is practiced in employment, and managers instruct their workers to engage in activities that are damaging to the environment in which their fellows live or that result in a decline in the quality of goods or services. A frequent response is that all disclaim the matter as not being within their concern. The result tends to be broader and broader government controls which must be exercised in the interest of the commonweal.

There is a pressing need to redefine the concept of employment, since in a corporate society the vast majority of people are employees who can be thought of as managers and production workers. If in such a society, legal and ethical assumptions continue to reflect the entrepreneurial society, the location of responsibilities becomes illusive and wrongs can go uncorrected for that reason. This situation becomes acute in a society devoted to private property where ownership tends to be the criterion of responsibility.

The development of new technologies esp. in the processing of information creates a series of problems in employment which are yet to be solved. For the production worker, the rapid processing of large amounts of information tends to increase the pressure to work faster and to decrease the creativity that can be exercised. For the manager, information processing tends to broaden the significance of decisions for all concerned. The overall direction is toward producing more with a relatively smaller number of highly skilled managers and producers. The resulting labor surplus could conceivably be absorbed by the rapidly expanding service industries, but these tend to be low-wage, low-prestige jobs which often do not constitute desirable employment.

The issues of a just wage, job security, and a fair day's work for a fair wage have not yet been solved in the best interest of all. It continues to be true that many who are classified as poor are employed, and not infrequently by industries that could well afford to pay more reasonable wages. While labor unions have greatly assisted the question of job security, only one-third of all nonagricultural employees are in unions and the remainder continue to be subject to layoffs, dismissals, and recessions. The question of job security as it relates to managers must also be considered since they are often the first to be fired when the market fluctuates or there is a reorganization in the interests of efficiency. Managerial positions tend to be highly competitive, and the question arises as to the humane solution to the problem of those who lose in the competition, and those who win and are then subject to the pressures of the performance expected.

Labor unions often manifest slight recognition that their obligations extend beyond the self-interest of the individual members. In response a tendency has emerged to attempt to limit the influence of unions, and yet there is little evidence to indicate that capitalism would use its increased influence for the general welfare. There is a serious need for labor and management to recognize the broader consequences of their activities.

All that has been learned from industrial psychology and sociology also comprises a contemporary issue in employment. Whether that knowledge will be used for good or ill depends greatly on the social responsibility of managers and the recognition of its impact by employees.

The general decline in the quality of goods and services indicates a need on the part of both managers and producers to recognize their obligation to the public they serve and the firms employing them.

In general, employment has evolved from the small scale entrepreneurial condition to a large scale corporate condition, and that transition has generated a series of problems yet to be solved. BIBLIOGRAPHY: W. G. Bennis, *Changing Organizations* (1966); *Labor and the National Economy*, eds. W. Bowen and O. Ashenfelter (Problems of the American Economy Series, rev. ed. 1975); E. Schmidt, *Union Power and the Public Interest* (Principles of Freedom Series, 1973); *Participation by Employers and Workers' Organizations in Economic and Social Planning: A General Introduction* (Intl. Labour Office, 1971).

[N. L. CHOATE]

EMS, CONGRESS OF, the meeting held by the deputies of the prince archbishops of Trier, Mainz, Cologne, and Salzburg at Bad Ems from July 25 to Aug. 25, 1786. It culminated a long history of disputes between those German metropolitans and the papacy; the immediate reason for the conference was their fear that the establishment of a nunciature in Munich (1785) would lead to greater papal influence over their suffragans. The Congress agreed on a common program, the *Punctation of Ems (Emser Punktation)*, that would restrict papal powers regarding faculties, appeals, dispensations, taxes, and decrees. The Punctation revealed the influence of *Febronianism on church polity among German ecclesiastical leaders. The program failed to win imperial or significant episcopal support and was soon abandoned. BIBLIOGRAPHY: H. Holborn, *History of Modern Germany, 1648–1840* (1964).

[J. K. ZEENDER]

EMSER, HIERONYMUS (1478–1527), polemicist against Martin *Luther. E. studied at Tübingen and Basel and developed strong interests in church reform according to humanist and Erasmian ideas. From c. 1505 he was secretary to George, Duke of Saxony, whom he represented at Rome to plead for the canonization of Benno, Bp. of Meissen. E.'s biography of Benno (1512) is unreliable. Hearing Luther at the *Disputation of Leipzig (1519), E. turned against the Reformer's theology, and the two became literary adversaries. E. was ill-fitted theologically for the task, but the exchange was popular and vitriolic. After Luther's translation of the NT appeared (1522), E. attempted to reply with his own translation; what he produced, however, was largely Luther's translation corrected to match the Vulgate text. The Emser Bible went through numerous editions under RC auspices (16th–18th cent.). E. also engaged in controversy with *Karlstadt over images and with H. *Zwingli on the Mass. BIBLIOGRAPHY: E. Iserloh, LTK 3:855–856; F. Lau, RGG 2:462.

[E. D. MCSHANE]

EMYGDIUS OF ANCONA, ST., see EMIDIUS OF ANCONA, ST.

ENACIM, see ANAKIM.

ENARXIS (Gr., beginning), a term applied in the Byzantine Church to: (1) the beginning of any ceremony or ecclesiastical office; and (2) the section of the liturgy between the preparation of the gifts *(prothesis)* and the little entrance consisting of three diaconal litanies followed by a variable antiphon sung by the choir and/or people. The celebrant meanwhile silently recites the antiphon at the altar. This foreliturgy which precedes the liturgy of the word was inserted about the 9th century.

[R. K. GOLINI]

ENCAENIA, Gr. term for the feast of the dedication of a temple or church, specifically the rededication of the Temple in Jerusalem after desecration by Antiochus Epiphanes; also applied to the commemoration (Sept. 13) by the Byzantine Church of the dedication of the Basilica of the Resurrection built by Emperor Constantine in Jerusalem in the year 355.

[J. R. AHERNE]

ENCHIRIDION (Gr., something that one can or must have in hand) in general usage a handbook or manual, a concise treatise (see OED 3:146). St. Augustine wrote an *Enchiridion ad Laurentium* (423–424, in PL 41:229–290) on faith, hope, and charity. The term enchiridion appears frequently as a title in the writings of the Reformers, Luther, Melanchthon, and others, and indicates the intention to popularize contents; it was also used for collections of hymns. The Cambridge Platonist H. *More was the author of an *Enchiridion eticum* (1677, tr. E. Southwell, *An Account of Virtue,* 1690), based on Aristotle's *Nicomachean Ethics*; it was a popular work.

The series of enchiridia published by Herder is intended to provide collections of ecclesiastical and historical texts in a form convenient for study. Universally used is H. *Denzinger's *Enchiridion symbolorum* (1854, 32d ed. A Schönmetzer, 1963), a collection of doctrinal statements of the Magisterium. The *Enchiridion fontium historiae ecclesiasticae antiquae* by K. Kirch (6th ed. L. Ueding, 1947) gives early Church history sources. M. J. Rouët de Journel compiled both the *Enchiridion patristicum* (21st ed., 1960), a doctrinal anthology of the Fathers, and the *Enchiridion asceticum* (4th ed., 1947), ascetical writings of the Fathers. Other enchiridia published in Rome are the *Enchiridion biblicum* (4th ed., 1961); the *Enchiridion clericorum* (1975), a vastly improved edition of the 1938 original on the education of the clergy; and the *Enchiridion documentorum instaurationis liturgicae, 1963–73* (1976), on documents of the liturgical renewal.

[J. FANG]

ENCHIRIDION MILITIS CHRISTIANI, moral treatise of Desiderius *Erasmus (*The Handbook of the Militant Christian,* tr. Dolan, 1962), intended to promote spiritual reform in the Church. In its polemical parts Erasmus deplores ceremony as a hindrance to Christian life, and heaps scorn on monks and friars, their observances, and the very fabric of their religious life. In its positive proposals the work reflects both the author's personal background in the piety of the *Devotio moderna, and his humanist exaltation of learning. The Christian life is above all inward and spiritual; the craft of Christian living can be learned and a regimen developed that will overcome ignorance and weakness. The discourse has a patristic and biblical base, but the Christianity proposed is a purely ethical code, with little place given to the supernatural or to dogma. Popular and widely read, the book brought financial security to Erasmus. Some modern assessments classify it not only as literarily inferior to his more celebrated *Praise of Folly,* but as platitudinous, and in line with his pallid failure to face the issues of the Reformation. Others praise the work as part of the middle-ground he pointed to, between the extremes that divided Christians of a more doctrinal bent.

[T. C. O'BRIEN]

ENCLOSURE, a synonym, in British use esp., for the monastic or conventual *cloister.

ENCOLPION (Gr., something worn on the breast; Sl., *panagia*), a term with two meanings in Eastern Churches. (1) It is applied to a medallion worn around the neck by bps.; such medallions have a painted or enameled icon of Christ or the Mother of God framed in an often elaborate and jeweled setting. A crown appears over the holy image, and there is usually a pendant jewel beneath. Although the Russians generally speak of the encolpion as the panagia, this term is more correctly used only of an encolpion bearing the image of the Mother of God. It is rarely found in its early shape of a boxlike reliquary. It is the distinctive symbol of a bp. and may be used only by one of episcopal rank; in addition to the encolpion he usually wears the pectoral cross. Some bps. wear two encolpia, but this is properly a prerogative of the patriarch. When two encolpia are worn, the cross is placed in the middle with the image of Christ to the right and that of the Theotokos to the left. (2) The term also designates a type of popular prayer book containing the ordinary of the Sunday offices as well as frequently used prayers collected for the convenience of the faithful. It was sometimes carried about the neck in an ornamented metal cover suspended by a chain, and perhaps the name derives from this custom.

[A. J. JACOPIN]

ENCOMIENDA-DOCTRINA SYSTEM, in Spanish America, a trusteeship of no fixed duration by which a group of Indians were "commended" by the Spanish crown to the Spanish conquistadors, designated encomenderos, who then had the right to exact labor or tribute from the Indians. In return, the encomenderos were obliged to provide them with instruction in Christianity and in European social, cultural, and economic ideas. The development of the *doctrina,* an area set apart on the estate followed: land containing a church, a rectory, a school, a hospital, and a workshop. A priest, in the earlier period a member of a religious order, was the *doctrinero* (teacher). Compulsory attendance of the Indians at the *doctrina* for large group instruction led to the establishment of nearby Indian villages called pueblos, numbering about 9,000 in S America by 1574 with about 6 million inhabitants. This system, though a step toward establishing a stable economy, gave rise to many abuses, ill-treatment of the natives, and rank exploitation by the conquistadors. Laws were soon issued to protect the Indians and to promote their political and religious welfare. Much clerical opposition to the abuses arose, esp. on the part of the great Dominican Bartolomé de *Las Casas, who devoted over 50 years of his life to the Indians. He and other Dominicans persuaded Emperor Charles V to promulgate the famous New Laws (1542) for revocation of the right of Spaniards to service and tribute from the Indians. Though proved to be unenforceable, they led to a series of later laws alleviating the conditions. The encomienda endured as an institution until the 18th century. The *doctrina* eventually became an Indian parish under the care of the diocesan clergy. Religious orders then opened missions to care for the pagan Indians of the frontier. BIBLIOGRAPHY: L. Simpson, *Encomienda in New Spain* (1929, repr. 1966); L. Hanke, *Spanish Struggle for Justice in the Conquest of America* (1949, pa. 1966); S. de Madariaga, *Rise of the Spanish American Empire,* (1947, repr. 1975).

[M. B. MONAGHAN]

ENCOUNTER, a concept that in contemporary theology is particularly associated with Emil *Brunner (1889–1966), for whom the source of religious truth was God's personal act of meeting with man. Somewhat dependent upon existentialism and upon M. *Buber's *I and Thou* (1923), encounter stresses the personal nature of God and the personal quality of his dealings with men. The divine-human relationship of encounter is contrasted with that view which understands man's knowledge of God as a matter of propositional knowledge, given through objective revelation in the Bible, in creeds or the dogmatic teaching of the Church, or developed through reasoning (as in *natural theology). Those who stress encounter understand the knowledge of God either wholly or in major part as personal relationship rather than objective knowledge. They understand revelation as God's decision to reveal himself as a person, rather than information about himself, speaking to man and demanding a personal response from man. This approach is also in contrast to *subjectivism in which knowledge of God is something man already possesses on the basis of his own nature.

Those who stress this personal encounter also understand the response demanded from man to be personal, a decision to repent and to act in accordance with the command of God. This is in contrast with the view that would understand man's proper response to be primarily the intellectual acceptance of propositional statements, or, by subjectivists,

the full realization of his own nature. Belief is understood by those who stress encounter as an attitude that is revealed in personal obedience, rather than in acceptance of doctrinal statements about God and his nature. The emphasis upon encounter is a reaction against both the objectivity of othodoxy and its emphasis on right belief and against the subjectivity of *Pietism and its emphasis upon inner feelings. Encounter seeks to correlate in the manner of *dialectical theology the objectivity of the word of God and the subjectivity of faith, maintaining the fully personal character of both.

In the views of 20th-cent. theologians who emphasize encounter, doctrine, although not disparaged, is understood as secondary to the divine-human encounter. From the primary relationship of the encounter, doctrine emerges as man's attempt to understand and express what has happened, and therefore has an auxiliary role. Scripture and sacraments are also interpreted in this dialectical way, not as objective in the sense that one might impersonally handle and control the truth of God or his grace or as superfluous externals, but as means through which the personal encounter of God with man takes place. BIBLIOGRAPHY: E. Brunner, *Divine-Human Encounter* (1938).

[E. EARLY]

ENCRATITES, a name applied to various Gnostic sects by Irenaeus, Clement of Alexandria, Hippolytus, and others. The sects so named were dualistic, forbade use of wine or meat, and proscribed sexual intercourse in marriage. The emperors Constantine and Theodosius outlawed these sects.

[T. C. O'BRIEN]

ENCYCLICAL (Gr., *en-kyklos,* a circular), a highly stylized letter from the pope to his brother bps. and often to the faithful, although John XXIII and Paul VI have addressed encyclicals to "all men of good will." It has been a literary genre frequently used by popes, esp. since Benedict XIV (1740–58). They are usually known by the opening words, e.g., *Pacem in terris.* The encyclical is addressed to a wider audience than a *motu proprio,* but is less formal and solemn than an *apostolic constitution or a papal bull. It is characteristic of encyclicals to deal with current social and religious issues, and they are generally regarded as vehicles for maintaining a unity of faith and morals. They might be compared with authoritative policy statements issued by civil governments. In the 20th cent. there have been two significant controversies about the weight encyclicals have in the RC Church. In 1950, Pius XII took a position in *Humani generis* that was repeated by Vatican Council II: "In writing such letters the popes do not exercise the supreme power of their teaching authority." (ConstChurch 25). Pius XII added that when an encyclical takes a stand on a controverted subject, it "can no longer be regarded as a matter for free debate among theologians," but this sentence was deleted in the Council's final draft. The second controversy centered around Paul VI's encyclical

Humanae vitae, the possibility of a Catholic's forming his conscience in a way contradictory to encyclical instruction, and the relationship between national councils of bps. and papal teaching. The consensus today is that no generalization may be made about the teaching authority of encyclicals. Each must be judged on its individual merits. BIBLIOGRAPHY: G. K. Malone, NCE 5:332–333; A. Fremantle, *Papal Encyclicals in Their Historical Context* (1956); P. Nau, *Une Source doctrinale: les encycliques* (1952); J. Salaverry, SacMund 2:228–230. *MAGISTERIUM.

[B. L. MARTHALER]

ENCYCLICAL OF ANTHIMUS VII

ENCYCLICAL OF ANTHIMUS VII (1895), a denunciatory document written by the Patriarch of Constantinople in response to the ecumenical appeal of Pope Leo XIII's *Praeclara gratulationis* (1894). This Byzantine encyclical is one of the Symbolic Books whose statements and definitions, while authoritative, do not have infallible status. In this document Anthimus issued a long list of denunciations against the innovations of Latin Catholics. It restated doctrinal opposition previously stressed in the Encyclical of the Four Oriental Patriarchs (1848) by another patriarch of Constantinople, Constantius I: papism, baptism by aspersion, communion under one kind, the use of unleavened bread. Anthimus added new grievances with his attack on the idea of the fire of purgatory, immediate retribution, the newly defined dogmas of the Immaculate Conception (1854) and the primacy and infallibility of the pope (1870).

[M. B. MONAGHAN]

ENCYCLICAL OF THE FOUR PATRIARCHS

ENCYCLICAL OF THE FOUR PATRIARCHS (1848), a reply of the Orthodox patriarchs of Constantinople, Alexandria, Antioch, and Jerusalem to Pope Pius IX's appeal of January 1848 "To the Orientals" in which he called for their reunion with Rome. An attitude of mutual mistrust between the Catholic and Orthodox Churches prevailed at that time. The four patriarchs wrote a common letter, signed also by 29 metropolitans, addressing it to all the Orthodox faithful as an encyclical letter. In it they defined papism as a heresy and expressed the hope that the Pope would himself be converted and return to the true Catholic, Apostolic, and Orthodox Church. This encyclical of 1848 was given wide publicity and still remains an important authoritative statement of the Orthodox Church. BIBLIOGRAPHY: Greek text in I. N. Karmiris, *Ta dogmatika kai symvolika mnemeia tēs Orthodoxou Katholikēs Ekklēsias* (2 v., 1953) 905–995.

[P. FOSCOLOS]

ENCYCLOPEDISTS

ENCYCLOPEDISTS, the contributors to the *Encyclopédie* (35 v., 1751–80), the "reasoned Dictionary of the Sciences, the Arts, and the Crafts," an epitome of 18th cent. thought and reflection produced under the leadership of *Diderot and D'*Alembert. The *Encyclopedia's* stated purpose was to set forth the order and connection of the branches of human knowledge: history, science, philosophy, morality, and the arts and crafts. These volumes became a potent weapon in the *lutte philosophique* against what Voltaire called "The infamous," i.e., Christianity. The strategy called for much dissembling rather than an open, direct assault. D'Alembert wrote: "No doubt we have had articles in theology and metaphysics, but with theologians for censors and a privilege (which might be revoked), I defy you to make them any better" (letter, July 21, 1757). Diderot's policy was to "respect national prejudices but to overthrow the edifice of the mind and scatter to the wind an unprofitable heap of dust," by which he referred to Christian beliefs and institutions. The way of undeceiving men, he insisted, operates promptly on minds of the right stamp and without any troublesome consequences, secretly and without disturbance, on minds of every description. The *Encyclopedia's* greatest influence stemmed, undoubtedly, not so much from whatever blows it delivered to traditional religion as from its new and massive emphasis on the power of man and of man's reason, and on the dignity of man and his glorious prospects, implicit in that emphasis. The 11 volumes of copperplates were graphic expression of the new confidence in man's ability, through science and technology, to create a truly rational and humane social and economic order by his own main effort.

The religious and theological articles were written by fairly orthodox abbés, although, as D'Alembert remarked: "The first theologian was excommunicated, the second expatriated, the third died, and the fourth is l'Abbé Morellet." Publication of the several volumes was interrupted on more than one occasion, as authorities found fault with items or insinuations touching on the majesty of the state or the sacredness of established religious orthodoxy. Persecution was petty and annoying rather than truly serious and disruptive. The Jesuits were implacable enemies as were the members of the Parlement of Paris who condemned the whole *Encyclopedia* enterprise in 1759 and had the printing privilege withdrawn. Contributors to the *Encyclopedia* included practically every famous thinker in France of the time, from Montesquieu to Condorcet. Voltaire wrote on literary subjects, Buffon on Nature; Holbach translated German pieces on physical science; Rousseau wrote on music and political economy, Quesnay on taxes and grains; d'Alembert's pieces were on mathematics and Cartesianism while Diderot's contributions covered a wide range. BIBLIOGRAPHY: N. N. Schargo, *History of the Encyclopédie* (1947); J. E. Barker, *Diderot's Treatment of the Christian Religion in the Encyclopédie* (1947); A. M. Wilson, *Diderot: The Testing Years, 1713–59* (1957); *idem*, EncPhil 2:505–508; R. Z. Lauer, NCE 5:334–335.

[J. P. REID]

END (Lat. *finis*, Gr. *telos*), that for the sake of which something is, or, more precisely, acts. The first of the four Aristotelian causes: the *why* (final cause), a producer (efficient cause), puts a shape (formal cause), into matter (material cause). The notion is taken from natural and metaphysical philosophy into moral philosophy, and there, particularly for *eudaemonism, as supplying the motivation for human acts, it is treated as the capital determinant of right or wrong.

There is a radical ontological thrust—appetite, tendency, desire, urge, drive—in every being for some end or fulfillment in what is good for it. Some go so far as to call it a love, though to others this may seem too anthropomorphic a word; at least it dramatizes the profound finality that runs throughout the whole universe. Moral purpose is a special manifestation of this. A teleological reading of ethics is more customary in the Latin than in the German tradition, which, influenced by Kant, tends to treat duty as an absolute. This at least has the merit of correcting a utilitarianism that reduces the ultimate end to a good-for-man. BIBLIOGRAPHY: J. Maritain, *Preface to Metaphysics* (1962); J. J. Warren, NCE 5:335–338; ThAq ST 1a2ae, 1 ad 5 (esp. in ed. Lat-Eng, v. 16, ed. T. Gilby) appendices. *CHOICE; *HUMAN ACT; *INTENTION.

[T. R. HEATH]

END, MEANS. Among the objectives of moral actions, some are intended as ends, whether ultimate or intermediate; some are chosen as leading to an intended end (see END; INTENTION; CHOICE). The second, called usually by St. Thomas Aquinas, *ea quae sunt ad finem,* may be described as "means." The term has the disadvantage of classifying a whole set of objects of moral choice as pure utilities, whereas some are true or pleasurable goods in themselves; some are objectively evil; some are morally neutral; only the last are sheerly and exclusively "means" (see ABSOLUTES, MORAL). The couplet, ends-means, does have the advantage of pointing to one relationship between the objects of intention and the objects of choice. A morally right end invests the moral act with its first moral goodness. The same end is the measure that makes possible an object of choice as such: choice settles on that object because it has value in reference to the intended end. But the rightly intended end can only be a measure and determinant of the good in any means; because the end is intended as good, it can only be attained by what is conformed to that good. The end cannot, then, in the words of the moral aphorism, justify the means. To choose a means that in itself is morally wrong is in effect to cease intention of the end as good; a morally vitiated choice cannot be prompted by the intention of the end as good. The moral good is integrally "the-good-as-meant"; the morally vitiated object is "the-lack-of-good-as-meant" (Gilby). An erroneous exaggeration of intention, such as was attributed to Peter *Abelard, is erroneous not simply because it ignores all moral determinants in favor of subjectivism; it is erroneous because the intention of end as good cannot give rise to a choice of what conflicts with the good; the intention itself becomes vitiated where choice falls on an immoral means.

The end-means relationship also has a historical connotation. B. *Pascal and the Jansenists attributed to the Jesuit moralists a defense of "the end justifies the means." The calumny was often repeated, and is implied in the pejorative term, "jesuitical." It even led to the German Jesuits' challenging anyone to produce a single Jesuit moral treatise that made such an affirmation, and to a court case (1903) in which they were upheld. BIBLIOGRAPHY: ThAq St (Lat-Eng v. 18, ed. T. Gilby, *Principles of Morality* 1966) app. 121–179, esp. 167.

[T. C. O'BRIEN]

END OF THE WORLD, the completion in all of creation of the transforming self-communication of God for which it was created. According to Christian tradition this process of completion was focused in the resurrection of Christ and will be finalized in him in his parousia when, as Risen Lord, he will be revealed to all as the central meaning and the climax of the process manifested in him (Col 1.16–17). The purpose of statements in Scripture dealing with the end of the world is not to forecast or to describe the termination of the physical universe, although the apocalyptic language in which such statements are couched give that impression. They depict graphically (e.g., 1 Th 4.16; 2 Pet 3.10; Rev 21.1) the final period of world history when the powers of evil will make their supreme struggle against God and will be finally defeated and when, as the author of 2 Pet says, "the earth and all that it contains will be burnt up" (3.10). But the affirmation of the writers, whatever the assumptions betrayed in such graphic statements, is about a religious truth concerned with the judgment of God upon his creation. As the Christian reads history, God has revealed himself through Christ as being in control of a process of the created world toward a finality known by him. The control of that process which has been distorted by the free failings of men is being restored through Christ. The imperfect condition in which good and evil coexist is in process toward a state of perfection that is the end of the world as man presently experiences it and the beginning of what Revelation calls "a new heaven and a new earth" (21.1), the new messianic age, a time of fulfillment. Because that new age inaugurated by Christ has begun, the end of the world has already begun. BIBLIOGRAPHY: M. E. Williams, NCE 5:338–343; A. Winklhofer, *Coming of His Kingdom* (tr. A. V. Littledale, 1963).

[J. CORDOUE]

ENDOWMENTS, among Mormons the name for the secret temple rites in which only Mormons in good standing participate. Among these is the celebration of Mormon celestial marriages.

[T. C. O'BRIEN]

ENDS, KINDS OF, a division covering the different uses of the term end as it occurs in theological discussion. The basis for the division is not constant throughout and the headings may overlap. (1) End in intention and in execution. The first is the goal an agent has in mind in operating; it is the originating cause of his act. The second is goal as this is achieved in fact. (2) Objective end and subjective end. The first *(finis qui)* is the reality intended, a thing, e.g., food, but more deeply, a person; God most of all. Here may be included the person or persons for whom the act is done *(finis cui),* sometimes, though not altogether happily, at least for Thomist nomenclature, called the "altruistic" end. The second *(finis quo)* is the operation by which the objective end is reached or possessed. Thus eating *(finis quo)* food *(finis qui);* seeing and loving *(finis quo)* God *(finis qui).* (3) The end according to internal and to external finality. The first is the fulfillment of a thing or a nature considered in itself. The second is its integration in a working pattern of heterogeneous things or natures. Why do mosquitoes bite? The answer is easier in terms of the former than of the latter. (4) The purpose of the deed and the purpose of the doer. The first *(*finis operis)* is that on which an act of its type or kind is set, e.g., almsdeeds to relieve the needy. The second *(*finis operantis)* is a personal motive communicated to the deed, e.g., almsdeeds out of ostentatiousness. This is sometimes called an ulterior end, and, as peripheral to a given type of act, is numbered among its moral circumstances as "why" *(cur),* from what motive. (5) Proximate end and ultimate end. This applies to a teleological series in subordination, which may allow of intermediate ends. The first may be desired in itself, yet nevertheless leads to something other. The second promises nothing beyond itself. The frame of reference adopted may be particular, e.g., ultimate in some series of acts, as the obtaining of an academic degree is the various activities involved in fulfilling the requirements; or it may be universal, i.e., seen as ultimate for the whole of life, as is the ultimate end with which moral theology is concerned. Here two points are important: first, our ultimate end, which is God, is not to be treated as an ulterior end; our love for him is not an exterior attachment to our love of other things. Second, and connected, an end as such, even though proximate or intermediate, is a good in itself, even though not from or for itself, and is to be distinguished from a mere means, which as such is good only as useful for something else. These points are essential in a pluralist metaphysics and theology of creation. The above divisions do not pretend to exhaust the endless variety and crisscross of intentions and motives in human life. BIBLIOGRAPHY: ThAq ST 1a2ae, 1 ad 5 (esp. in ed. Lat-Eng, v. 17, ed. T. Gilby).

[T. GILBY]

ENDURA, in *Cathari teaching, sacred suicide, the highest act of virtue, liberating man's spirit from matter.

[T. C. O'BRIEN]

ENERGIES, DIVINE, in Byzantine theology the term describing the presence and action of God-in-self-revelation, or God-outside-himself, as opposed to the es-

sence of God-in-himself. The distinction between the divine energies and the divine essence of God, although constant in the Eastern patristic tradition, was formulated with greatest precision by St. *Gregory Palamas (d. 1359). According to Gregory, whose doctrine was officially adopted by the Orthodox Church, the essence of God is absolutely unknowable and totally incomprehensible to creaturely understanding. Both in this age of God's kingdom, as well as in the ages to come, man, as well as the angelic powers, can never know the essence of God. Nevertheless, God is known by creatures. Even in this world the knowledge of God is possible for men, and union with divine reality is given. This is so because of the divine energies of God through which he himself becomes accessible to creatures both in this age, through Christ and the Holy Spirit, as well as in the kingdom to come.

The divine energies emanate equally and by nature from the three persons of the Trinity, Father, Son and Holy Spirit. Even if there were no world or no man to receive them or to be in union with them, the divine energies would exist, flowing from the essence of God. Through these divine, uncreated energies God is revealed, while at the same time, so to speak, he preserves the total unknowability of his essential being which, inasmuch as he is God, remains always and forever beyond any creaturely comprehension. The divine energies are substantial and natural, i.e., they are of the substance and nature of God. They are eternal, uncreated, and inseparable from the Godhead. They are countless in number, and, unlike the divine essence, they are communicable, distinguishable, separable, namable, and accessible to men. Thus, they are not created entities, symbolic manifestations or fabricated signs of God's presence. They are the presence of God himself. When a man is in union with God and has a knowledge of him through the divine energies, it is indeed God himself who is met and is known, and nothing less. Through the divine energies, God creates and redeems the world. Through the energies, he grants to creatures the deifying life in union with himself and his own divine and uncreated nature. Therefore, in and through the divine energies, the essential unknowability of God is preserved, while the genuine communion which he desires for all creation with himself is made possible. In theological literature, synonyms for the divine energies are divine actions, operations, emanations, outpourings, manifestations, powers. BIBLIOGRAPHY: V. Lossky, *Mystical Theology of the Eastern Church* (1957, repr. 1973).

[T. HOPKO]

ENERGUMEN, literally, one who is agitated; a term used in the early Church for a person thought to be possessed by the devil and in need of *exorcism.

[T. C. O'BRIEN]

ENGAGEMENT, a mutual agreement to marry. Engagement is usually informal, i.e., a simple promise in which the couple express their commitment to each other and intention to marry. Solemn engagement is a formal contract, signed by the couple and either the pastor, local ordinary or two witnesses; it is not binding in conscience although damages may be sought by the injured party if the contract is broken without sufficient reason (CIC, c. 1017). There is no official rite for engagement, but certain ceremonies have been formulated (cf., *The Book of Catholic Worship*, prepared by the U.S. Liturgical Conference, pp. 746–748). Engaged couples continue to be bound by the norms of premarital chastity.

[T. M. MCFADDEN]

ENGEL, HANS LUDWIG (d. 1674), Austrian Benedictine of Melk, professor of canon law and from 1669 vice chancellor of the Univ. of Salzburg; author of *Collegium universi juris canonici* (1671–74) and of other canonical works.

[T. C. O'BRIEN]

ENGELBERG, ABBEY OF, Benedictine Swiss abbey founded (1120) near Zurich by Baron Conrad of Sellenburen. Both Pope Callistus II and Emperor Henry V, as well as succeeding popes and rulers, bestowed many privileges upon the abbey. Eventually, it became a kind of miniature ecclesiastical state and remained so until the French Revolution. Accordingly its abbotts possessed broad jurisdiction in spiritual matters and supreme authority in temporal matters over numerous villages and towns. Most of these rights were lost in the French Revolution. In the interim the abbey suffered destruction by fires, local wars, loss of members from the plague, and effects of the Reformation. Under competent abbots, however, it survived and has flourished in subsequent years. New buildings were erected to replace those destroyed. The abbey has been notable for a cultural expansion that it initiated; for its great school of printing and copying and the production of exquisite silver-gilt work; for its magnificent library reported to have included 20,000 volumes and 200 MSS, plundered by the French in 1798. Forty MSS are extant. In the 19th cent., freed from the pressures of temporal government, the monks became better able to devote themselves to community religious renewal; to the apostolate of education by establishing a boarding school; to the missions; the establishment of convents for women; and to the foundation of Conception Abbey, in Conception, Mo. in 1873 (then called New Engelberg). BIBLIOGRAPHY: G. Heer, DHGE 15:462–466.

[S. A. HEENEY]

ENGELBERT OF ADMONT (*c*.1250–1331), abbot and scholar. E. became a Benedictine *c*.1267 at the Abbey of Admont on the Enns River in central Austria. His studies in the cathedral school of St. Vitus at Prague (1271–74) were interrupted by war. From 1278 to 1287 he studied at Padua. In 1288 E. was elected abbot of Sankt Peter in Salzburg, and in 1298, abbot of Admont as the compromise candidate of the archduke of Austria and the abp. of Salzburg. During his 30-year abbacy he maintained the rights of the monastery and produced a number of theological, scientific, political, and historical works. Portions of his writings remain unpublished. BIBLIOGRAPHY: B. J. Comaskey, NCE 5:350.

[M. J. FINNEGAN]

ENGELBERT I OF COLOGNE, ST. (*c*.1185–1225), archbishop. Engelbert supported Philip of Swabia (d. 1208) against Otto IV, participated in the Albigensian Crusade (1212), was abp. of Cologne (1217–25), and became administrator of Germany and guardian of the future Henry VII in 1220. As bp. he was unpopular for his strict views. He was never officially canonized, but his cult was established Nov. 7, 1617. The *Vita* by Caesarius of Heisterbach (1226) has historical value. BIBLIOGRAPHY: M. F. McCarthy, NCE 5:350.

[M. F. MCCARTHY]

ENGELHARDT, ZEPHYRIN (1851–1934), Franciscan missionary, historian. Born in Germany, E. migrated the following year to the U.S. with his parents, who settled in Kentucky. In 1873 he entered the Franciscan Order and was ordained in 1878. Then for many years he worked as a missionary among the Indians. His career as a historian began in 1892 when he was assigned to write a history of the Franciscans in the United States. Most of his life after 1900 was devoted to travel and scholarly research for newspaper and magazine articles and for his most ambitious work, the four-volume series, *Missions and Missionaries of California* (1908–15), still a standard authority. BIBLIOGRAPHY: J. Kirsch, "Historians of the Padres," *America* 29 (1923) 376–377; F. B. Steck, "Father Zephyrin Engelhardt" *Commonweal* 20 (1934) 236–238.

[S. A. HEENEY]

ENGELS, FRIEDRICH (1820–95), German philosopher, collaborator and supporter for many years of Karl *Marx. He passed intellectually from Hegelianism, with Christian sympathies, through Feuerbachian antireligious humanism, to socialist materialism and communism. E.'s thinking is often at a deeper theoretical level than that of Marx, i.e., directed to metaphysical and epistemological problems rather than exclusively to questions of historical interpretation, political economy, and class struggle. E. set great store by dialectics, a concept inherited from Hegel, which he tried to apply in a materialist sense to the understanding of human and social origins and development. By defining matter as infinitely, endlessly in motion, E. argued for the necessity of revolution and inevitable progress. He worked with Marx very closely in many of the seminal works of *Marxism, including *Holy Family* (1845), *German Ideology* (1846), and the *Communist Manifesto* (1848), for which he submitted an outline. His own chief writings are *Ludwig Feuerbach and the Outcome of Classical German Philosophy*, *Anti-Dühring*, and *Dialec-*

tics of Nature (unfinished). BIBLIOGRAPHY: G. Meyer, *Friedrich Engels* (1935); K. Kantsky, *Friedrich Engels* (1908); S. Marcus, *Engels, Manchester and the Working Class* (1974); F. Engels, *Engels on Capital,* (1974). G. W. F. *HEGEL; L. A. *FEUERBACH.

[J. P. REID]

ENGELSBRÜDER, see ANGELIC BRETHREN.

ENGLAND, JOHN (1786–1842), missionary bp., scholar, and controversial writer. He studied in a school of the Church of Ireland (1792–1800), and, the Catholic Relief Bill of 1793 permitting, studied law for two years. He was ordained in Cork (1808) and was a tireless worker in numerous apostolates before coming to America. First bp. of Charleston, S.C., he was consecrated in Cork (1820) and shortly after drew up a model constitution for his See. Charleston diocese, with 4,000 to 8,000 Catholics and two resident priests embraced the Carolinas and Georgia. To reach his scattered flock, E. launched the *U.S. Catholic Miscellany* (1822), a pioneer RC newspaper; opened at Vauxhall, St. John Seminary; and established a school for blacks, both of which schools failed for lack of support. In Charleston he received teaching sisters, the Dames de la Retraite (1834–37) from Philadelphia, as well as Irish Ursulines to conduct an academy. He introduced the Brothers of San Marino as nurses and founded (1829) the Sisters of Charity of Our Lady of Mercy to teach the poor and to aid in the periodic scourges of yellow fever. He was the first RC priest to address Congress (1826). After lecturing in Ireland (1841), he arrived in Philadelphia in broken health but gave, nonetheless, 21 lectures en route to Charleston. He died shortly after, respected by Catholics and Protestants, who appreciated the vigor of his intelligence and the charity of his life. The *Miscellany* had recorded, since his MS *Diurnal* (1820–23), his missionary journeys. E. also left a catechism controverting the anti-Catholic one influenced by J. Blanko *White, a pioneer vernacular missal (1843), and his *Letters on Slavery* (1844). Against strong opposition he had urged the convening of the First Provincial Council of Baltimore (1829) and contributed significantly to those of 1833, 1837, and 1840. He is credited with writing their decrees. BIBLIOGRAPHY: P. K. Guilday, *Life and Times of John England* (2 v., 1927, repr. 1969); J. L. O'Brien, *John England, Bishop of Charleston: The Apostle to Democracy* (1934).

[M. R. BROWN]

ENGLAND, CHRISTIANITY IN. There were British bps. at the Council of Arles (314), which argues that Christianity was already well-rooted in Roman Britain. St. Alban is venerated as its protomartyr; his death is traditionally associated with the persecution under Diocletian, though some historians place it under Severus. With the departure of the Romans and the Anglo-Saxon invasions, the Christian communities retreated to the West, and it was to a heathen land that Pope St. Gregory the Great sent the Roman mission (597) under St. Augustine of Canterbury. Steadily the work of evangelization moved north where it met the tide of Celtic Christianity which had ebbed and was now flowing back, a movement associated with St. Aidan of Iona and Lindisfarne. The inevitable clash, of cultures, discipline, and ritual, was composed at the Synod of Whitby (663) in a Roman sense, largely through the efforts of St. Wilfrid of York. Soon the country was entirely Christianized, and the Anglo-Saxon Church became illustrious for its saints and scholars, and not least for its missionaries, who, together with the Celtic monks, recovered Middle Europe for the Church and made possible the Carolingian renaissance. The achievement was cruelly ravaged during the second Dark Ages, yet it was not long before the Danes were assimilated and converted, and a renewed prosperity was well under way when with conquest by the Normans (1066), descendants of the Northmen, the Church in England was integrated with the Hildebrandine reforms.

So it lasted until the Reformation, relatively peaceful, for the land was never fought over by foreign armies; it reached its greatest distinction in theology at Oxford in the 13th cent., and in devout and humane letters later, built most of its present churches, and combined a staunch loyalty to the Roman See (even if for political reasons during the Avignon Schism) with a sturdy opposition to its financial extortions and political pretensions.

Many causes contributed to the separation from Rome which began under Henry VIII and was protested against by only one bp., St. John Fisher; the others were better trained to minister to the State than to their flocks. Among the religious factors that perpetuated it not least was the respectability accorded a married clergy, which set up centers of support in every village throughout the realm. Final legal effect was given it in the Elizabethan settlement (1559). Queen Elizabeth herself was no religious zealot who wished to break with the past; but she knew her people and knew that her political advantage lay in her balance between the new Protestantism and the old Catholicism supported by the *tercios* of Spain. The papal bull that released her subjects from their allegiance put a weapon in the hands of her government; Catholics could now be treated as malignants and charged with treason. They fought a long fight, and served the Stuarts with devotion; by the end of the 18th cent. they had shrunk to an inconsiderable minority of the country gentry and their dependents. To their fortunes we shall return.

From English Protestantism itself two main streams have broadened out and taken various channels, through some of which it now shows signs of petering out. The first is that of the Established Church; its representatives have always claimed continuity with the past, and though they admit to being "catholic and reformed," in England they are often irked when called Protestant. Indeed Elizabeth's *via media* has transcended its historical occasions and produced an ecclesiastical polity which may command the admiration of a not uncritical outsider. True, it has not been persecuted and had to fight for its existence, except during the years of the Commonwealth, so that it can afford to be mellow and humane; true it has not always been free from a sort of well-bred insolence which goes with people of standing; true also that at times its bishops were so many chaplains to Whigs in the ascendancy, all of which may be but so many reflections of national characteristics. Nevertheless its "comprehensiveness" expresses a rare value. This may be represented as a reluctance to force issues that have disrupted other bodies, less fairly as embodying a spirit of compromise, though it may seem like this to men of Hibernian or Gallic religious cultures: in reality it seems to spring from a living identity at once consistent and resilient, a secret for biological success.

The second stream is that of the *Puritans, who became Congregationalists, Baptists, Presbyterians; once called Dissenters, later Nonconformists. They are now, together with the Methodists, who rose in the 18th cent., collectively referred to as the Free Churches. Their piety has run like a vein through literature; they have been a strong force in social reforms; from the first they were always prepared to translate their religious convictions into political action. They still maintain a fund of social enthusiasm, but virtual Unitarianism now spreads into them, as it did in the beginning, and it is doubtful whether effective preaching of the Incarnation can be generally expected of them.

In the last 150 years the Catholics have enjoyed their "second spring" and from Irish immigration and the effects of the Oxford Movement have notably increased in number, from less than one-thirtieth to more than one-tenth of the population. Their hierarchy was restored in 1850. They have their difficulties in these days of declining formal religious observance and of the restatement of religious culture, but redundant churches and chapels are not among them. Relations between the different confessions are now more cordial and open than they were, and though at first sight the C of E, the nominal religion of the majority, might seem and deserve to be, the bridge between Protestants and Catholics, it is arguable that the keypoint will be occupied by that body.

[T. GILBY]

ENGLAND, CHURCH OF, see CHURCH OF ENGLAND.

ENGLISH COLLEGE IN ROME (*Venerabile Collegio Inglese*), one of the oldest national seminaries, formally instituted in 1579 by Gregory XIII to supply priests for the English mission. Its site had been an English hospice dating from 1362; clerical students from the English College, Douai, had begun to reside there in 1577. Of its early graduates 42 were martyred in England. Staffed by the Jesuits, Robert *Persons being its most distinguished early rector (1597), the college was taken over by English diocesan clergy after suppression of the Society in 1773. In the 19th cent. Card. *Wiseman was one of the college's rec-

tors. Students do their courses at the Gregorian University. The Beda, another English ecclesiastical college in Rome, founded in 1852 for converted Anglican priests and graduate students, has been a separate establishment since 1917.

[T. C. O'BRIEN]

ENGLISH LADIES, see LORETTO, LADIES OF.

ENGLISH MARTYRS, see MARTYRS OF ENGLAND AND WALES.

ENGLISH MYSTICS, a classification that includes the four great English mystical writers of 14th-cent. England, Richard *Rolle de Hampole, Walter *Hilton, the unknown author of the *Cloud of Unknowing, and *Julian of Norwich, with their associates and the authors of a few similar minor works. As a group they are unequaled anywhere in contemporary Europe in the force and purity of their doctrine and in their direct style of writing, and individually they rank with the outstanding German and Flemish mystics of the time. The beginning of this flowering of English mysticism can be traced to Bede of Jarrow (8th cent.), whose homilies and commentaries contain much mystical teaching firmly grounded on the traditions of the Church and Holy Scripture and are marked by great affective devotion to the Passion of Christ and to the Blessed Virgin. After the Norman Conquest the tradition of mystical and devotional prayer was carried on by many writers, of whom *Anselm of Canterbury and *Aelred of Rievaulx are outstanding. In the 13th cent. the *Ancren Riwle* served as a guide to the solitary, contemplative life and is valuable as an account of the life of enclosed solitaries among whom mysticism flourished. Mysticism reached its height in 14th cent. England, developing in the midst of the unrest and suffering brought on by the Black Death, constant wars, and the corruption of the Church, the distress and turmoil of the times serving, perhaps, to beget an atmosphere sympathetic to solitary endeavor and personal mystical prayer. The four great writers of this period, although their sources are scriptural, patristic, and scholastic, are English to the core; they are unsurpassed in their use of words redolent of English life as well as in their deep devotion to Christ and his mother. They clearly influenced the life and thought of contemporaneous England and of the centuries that followed, until the dissolution of the monasteries in the 16th cent. and the destruction of an organized life of contemplation and solitude brought the mystical movement to a close.

BIBLIOGRAPHY: E. Colledge, NCE 10:180–181; *Medieval Mystics of England* (ed. E. Colledge, 1961); D. Knowles, *English Mystical Tradition* (1961); G. E. Hollingworth, *English Mystics* (1973).

[M. J. BARRY]

ENKOLPION, see ENCOLPION.

ENLIGHTENMENT (Ger. *Aufklärung*), the complex cultural movement of 18th-cent. Europe. The relationship of the Enlightenment to religion has been widely misrepresented, largely by a failure to admit fully its claims to distance from the Christian world. It was essentially the use of powerful new ideas to influence a social situation, to reconstruct an entire culture, to provide intellectual justification for the practical efforts of practical men. Yet the *lumières*, as they liked to call themselves, were hardly practical; nor were most of them influential on men of affairs. Hume and Gibbon in Britain, Lessing and Kant in Germany, and the host of philosophers—Voltaire, Rousseau, Helvetius, Holbach, Diderot, d'Alembert, and the rest—mounted an attack that undermined effectively both an obsolete socio-political order and the religious attachments by which the old regime sought to preserve itself and clothe itself with a sacred authority. C. L. Becker's thesis (*The Heavenly City of the Eighteenth Century Philosophers*, 1932) that Enlightenment was a derivative, vulgarized restatement of traditional Christian values, a secularized faith, hope, and charity, is largely discredited as a distortion. Religion, which meant Christianity, was essentially and radically challenged by a vigorous, hostile secularism. Cassirer is surely mistaken in describing Enlightenment as fundamentally religious.

The philosophes, or spokesmen of Enlightenment, claimed that Christians had assimilated and debased pagan virtues while they had incorporated and intensified pagan vices. The rationalist version of Christianity, worked up in the 16th and esp. the 17th cent., was absorbed by the philosophes and employed in the campaign against all organized religion. The men of Enlightenment were the natural heirs of "Christian" stoicism and skepticism, which had undermined the very reasonableness of religion. Deists and later apologists would strive mightily to reestablish this reasonableness, but the gap between reason and religion was exposed as unbridgeable and the philosophes undertook to demonstrate this by every means available.

Among British deists and German *Aufklärer* there was an overt and not unimportant religious component, but most French philosophes, and unbelievers like Gibbon and Hume, had a profoundly anti-Christian animus. The argument began, logically and chronologically, with the deists discarding all that was mysterious and miraculous about Christianity. There is, subsequently, no single strain of Enlightenment antireligious argument, but rather a number of elaborations. By mid-century Christianity was socially vulnerable to secularization. Yet the age of Enlightenment was still a religious age (Enlightenment itself was, then, a countercurrent), even in the midst of a barrage of philosophic propaganda. There took place, rather, a subtle shift of attention in which religious institutions and explanations were slowly displaced from the center to the periphery of life. Europeans in great numbers suffered the opposite attractions of inherited beliefs and a newly fashionable unbelief. The receptive public for philosophic thinking increased year by year as antireligious propaganda became more seductive and plausible. The movement was probably less a response of this specifically anti-Christian campaign than the expression of a grave crisis in religious confidence. Internecine squabbles, between and within religious denominations, were symptomatic of a general spiritual malaise. A bland piety, a self-satisfied reasonableness, the facile conviction that the Churches must, after all, move with the times, all these concessions to worldliness embodied the treason of the clerks. In Britain the Church's pursuit of social acceptability and political advantage pointed in the direction of the drift of the times.

In the German states the religious situation was less parlous but more complicated. Fratricidal war, alternating with a tolerance based on indifference, veiled the real enemy. Religion went on the defensive, dissipating into a vague religiosity or a worldly piety. In France the Church was extremely wealthy and powerful, yet the clergy marched on the way of self-destruction. The progress of philosophy was only a part of a cultural evolution. By the 18th cent. unbelievers and believers alike had lost much of the key to the symbolic language of Christianity, which was still medieval. The loss of religious fervor was widespread. In the face of mounting secularization the higher clergy were largely indifferent, the lower clergy powerless. The absurd state of religion, established yet impotent to stem the advance of godlessness, was ironically underlined by the empty and ostentatious piety of such immoral men as Louis XV. Curiously, the Churches turned modern with a vengeance, appealing constantly to reasonableness and fiercely rejecting *enthusiasm. Apologists prettified the image of God, and preachers emphasized the naturalness and ease of a Christian life accommodated to men's feeling and ambition. By the 1760s, when Enlightenment was everywhere on the offensive and laments about atheism multiplied, a frightened orthodoxy responded in panic. Often the contest between believers and philosophes had the unreal aspect of a contest decided in advance. Christians paid a heavy price for fraternizing with the enemy. The *lumières* appropriated the results of Christian labors, esp. the fruits of historical erudition, for secular and eventually for antireligious purposes. In return, Christians took every measure to suppress and harass the progress of philosophy. Anticlericalism and skepticism became political and on the eve of revolution joined forces with a naturalistic world view. The century of Enlightenment ended with religious interests seriously undermined and antireligion proposed as the ultimate remedy for the spiritual malady of the age. BIBLIOGRAPHY: P. Gay, *Enlightenment: An Interpretation* (1966); J. H. Overton and F. Relton, *English Church, 1714–1800* (1906); E. Cassirer, *Philosophy of the Enlightenment* (1960) ch. 4; R. R. Palmer, *Catholics and Unbelievers in Eighteenth Century France* (1939); *Enlightenment* (ed. F. E. Manuel, pa. 1965); *Enlightenment: A Comprehensive Anthology,* (ed. P. Gay, 1973).

[J. P. REID]

ENLIGHTENMENT (BAPTISMAL), the faith-effect of the sacrament of baptism viewed as a confirmation of the recipient in his knowledge of the mysteries of God. Baptism opens the eyes of the soul and brings new sight or enlightenment of the mysteries of faith to the recipient. Christ's healing of the man born blind in which the healing waters (of baptism) are linked to the granting of sight (enlightenment) provides a scriptural basis for this theme (John 9). Among the Fathers, Clement of Alexandria, esp. in his *Paedagogus,* developed the idea of Christian enlightenment. He distinguished it from Gnostic ideas of enlightenment which brought about a final perfection; Christian enlightenment was an ongoing process, the nurturing and perfection of faith. The liturgies of baptism and of the Easter Vigil also reflect the idea of a Christian enlightenment through baptism. BIBLIOGRAPHY: A. G. Martimort, *The Signs of the New Covenant* (2d ed. rev. 1963) 131–132; J. Lebreton and J. Zeiller, *Heresy and Orthodoxy* (1945) 333–335.

[B. ROSENDALL]

ENLIL, a divinity in the Mesopotamian pantheon; originally a god of wind or air, then a mountain god, then the god of earth (more accurately, of *terra firma* as distinct from the cosmic ocean) and a member of the great cosmic triad along with Anu and Enki, or Ea. Evidence suggests that he even tended to rival Anu for supremacy in the pantheon, but he normally remained second in rank. Enlil was the god who presided over the government and ordering of the earth, upheld earthly laws, and punished those guilty of breaking them. These functions help to explain why the national gods of both Babylonia (Marduk) and Assyria (Ashur) were called "the Enlil of the gods" and why in the Babylonian creation epic *(Enuma Elish)* it was Enlil who named Marduk "Lord of the Lands." BIBLIOGRAPHY: E. Dhorme, *Les Religions de Babylonie et d'Assyrie* (1945) 26–31.

[A. CODY]

ENMITY, hostility or ill will existing in an individual or group toward another individual or group. It may be one-sided or mutual. It may be directed toward the person of an adversary, or toward the frustration and defeat of activities conceived to be evil. The term is sometimes applied in an extended sense to the attitude of mutual conflict existing between competitors or rivals, e.g., in sports, politics, or business, who attack each other's legitimately assailable claim to superiority or privilege. Hostility or ill will aimed at the person of another is forbidden to the Christian by the law of love; if he is faithful to the gospel precept obliging him to love his enemies (Mt 5.43–44), he may be the object, but can never be the subject, of enmity of this kind. He may, however, and in some cases must, resist and seek to overcome the evil purposes of an unjust adversary. He may also engage in rivalry and competition, provided he can do so within the limits prescribed by charity and justice. Unlawful enmity is a form of *hatred, and its malice is estimated accordingly. BIBLIOGRAPHY: J. E. Fallon, NCE 5:443–444.

[P. K. MEAGHER]

ENNODIUS, MAGNUS FELIX (*c.*473–521), ecclesiastical writer, bp. of Pavia from *c.*513. Born at Arles, E. spent his early years in N Italy, probably at Milan. He was ordained deacon in 493 in Pavia by St. Epiphanius, whose life he later wrote, and then went to Milan where he served his uncle, Bp. Laurentius, as secretary, taught rhetoric, and produced his writings. Twice Pope *Hormisdas sent him as a member of a mission seeking to end the *Acacian schism. In addition to the life of Anthony of Lérins, a panegyric on King Theodoric, a defense of Symmachus, and a number of hymns and poems that are without conspicuous literary merit. He is honored in Pavia as a saint. Works: PL 63:13–364; critical ed., W. Hartel, CSEL (1882). BIBLIOGRAPHY: Butler 3:126–127; J. Fontaine, RAC 5:398–421.

[R. B. ENO]

ENOCH (Henoch), a person who appears in the genealogy of Seth as the son of Jared and the father of Methuselah. His chief significance for later generations was that he "walked with God," and at the end of his life "God took him," (Gen 5.24). From this brief and enigmatic statement has grown the major apocryphal work known as the Apocalypse of Henoch. *APOCRYPHA, OT.

[D. J. BOURKE]

ENOCH, BOOKS OF, two different apocalyptic works, normally referred to as Ethiopic Enoch (1 Enoch) and Slavonic Enoch (2 Enoch).

(1) **Ethiopic Enoch.** This work was accepted by some in the early Church as Scripture. It is quoted in Jude 14, and by some scholars is regarded as having a strong influence on NT literature. The only complete extant version of this originally Aramaic or Hebrew work is the Ethiopic one, accepted as canonical in the Abyssinian Church. It is made up of various writings, several of which would previously have existed as independent compilations. In some cases these are designated by special titles derived from 37.1, 72.1, 108.1. Again in some passages, esp. ch. 106–108, Noah rather than Enoch is the central figure. The earliest of these writings cannot be older than the 2d cent. B.C., though whether they reflect the circumstances of the Maccabean wars (168–142 B.C.) is a much disputed point. But none of them appear to envisage Rome as a possible danger to Judah or Jerusalem, which suggests that, with the possible exception of the "Similitudes of Enoch," the latest of them must have been written well before Pompey's invasion of 63 B.C..

In content ch. 1–5 are an introductory discourse of Enoch announcing the approaching world judgment. Chapters 6–36 form an angelological section recounting the fall of the angels, the rise of the giants, and containing two narratives, partially parallel, of Enoch's visionary journeys through the earth and the underworld. Chapters 37–71, the "Similitudes of Enoch," describe the dwelling-place of the just, the activities of the angels, the Messiah and his judgment, and the judgment and salvation wrought by the Son of Man. Chapters 72–82, the "Book of the Stars," are an astronomical section dealing with the movements of the sun, moon, and stars, and the method of calculating the divisions of the calendar and the points of the compass. Chapters 83–90 are a historical section describing visions of the flood and the history of the human race from Adam to the coming of the Messiah. Chapters 91–105 are a haggadic or didactic book containing Enoch's admonitions to his children and an "apocalypse of weeks" (93.1–14 and 91.12–17, in that order) in which the history of the world down to the last judgment and the messianic age is depicted in ten weeks or stages. The conclusion contains descriptions of the wonders and portents attendant upon the birth of Noah and a final exhortation to his descendants.

Since the discovery at Qumran of literary and other relics of an Essene sect, a connection with the Book of Enoch has been greatly emphasized. In particular the figure of Enoch himself is held to be significantly close to the Teacher of Righteousness in the Essene writings. Again, there are grounds for believing that the solar calendar of 364 days as calculated in Enoch may have been used at Qumran. The most important and the most controversial part of the discussion, however, is concentrated upon the "Similitudes of Enoch." Is this originally independent composition the work of a pre-Christian Jew or of a Judaeo-Christian of the 1st or 2d cent. A.D. who interpolated it into the preexisting compilation of Enoch in order to impart a Christian character to the whole? It is universally recognized that the Similitudes stands apart from the rest in point of style and doctrine. The central figure is designated as the "elect" and Son of Man (a term employed 14 times). He has been chosen and "hidden" apart by the "Lord of spirits" from before the creation (48.3–6; 46.3) to be judge even over the angels (61.8 ff.), the revealer of all hidden treasures (46.3). He is set on the throne of glory by the Lord of spirits, and the spirit of righteousness is poured out on him. He separates the sinners from the just, and the words of his mouth slay the wicked (62.2). But he is also a savior figure, a staff that supports the just, a light to the nations, the hope of the oppressed (48.4). He will sit down to table with the saved (62.14).

It has been held to be particularly significant that although abundant fragments from MSS of the rest of Enoch have been found at Qumran, no single fragment of the Similitudes has appeared. This, though admittedly an argument *ex silentio*, does appear to lend color to the view that the Similitudes are a later Christian interpolation in a substantially pre-Christian work.

(2) **Slavonic Enoch.** This quite different work, also known as the *Book of the Secrets of Enoch*, is a Slavonic translation of a Greek original probably written before 70 A.D. by a Jewish author. In its existing form, however, it has been adapted and reworked by Christians, probably as late as the 7th cent. A.D.. Dependent at many points on Ethiopic Enoch, it consists mainly of an account of Enoch's journey through the seven heavens (ch. 3–21). A second part (ch. 22–38) consists of a divine revelation of human history from Adam to the Flood. Finally the work records Enoch's admonitions to his children, his ascension into heaven, and a survey of his life.

Like Ethiopic Enoch, Slavonic Enoch evinces a highly developed sense of morality and an awareness of the afterlife as a time of punishment or reward for present steadfastness in virtue. Special emphasis is laid upon the social virtues. It, too, reflects a highly developed angelology, but there is a notable absence of allusions to the Messiah and his coming. BIBLIOGRAPHY: R. H. Charles, *Book of Enoch* (1912); C. Martin, *Le Livre d'Hénoch* (1906); A. Vaillant, *Le Livre des secrets d'Hénoch* (1952) [Slavonic]; L. Gry, *Les Paraboles d'Hénoch et leur messianisme* (1906); S. Mowinckel, *He That Cometh* (tr. G. Anderson, 1956), 346–455 [The Son of Man]; E. B. Szekeley, *Teaching of the Essenes from Enoch to the Dead Sea Scrolls* (1957).

[D. J. BOURKE]

ENRYAKUJI, Japanese Buddhist temple built between 782 and 805 at Mt. Hiei, NE of Kyoto, and monastery headquarters of the Tendai sect, which developed into a great complex. The present hall structure is the reconstruction of 1640. Since then it has been repaired regularly every 30 or 40 years, as is the Japanese custom.

[M. J. DALY]

ENTELECHY, a transliteration of the Gr. *entelecheia,* used by Aristotle for the actuality of a potentiality, and translated *actus* by the Latin scholastics. They also use this term for the actuating principle in a composite substance, e.g., soul in living body, and for active power or activity. *Leibniz speaks of his simple substances or monads as entelechies with respect to lower groups.

[T. GILBY]

ENTHRONEMENT FEAST, New Year's festival supposed by some scholars to have been celebrated during the Feast of Tents in pre-Exilic Jerusalem, commemorating the kingship of Yahweh. Scandinavian OT scholars have been the most noted exponents of the theory, which is based primarily on certain Psalms and deductions from parallel ceremonies among other Near Eastern peoples. The theory relies on such Psalms as 47, 93, and 96–99, in which the kingship of Yahweh is celebrated. The royal Psalms, such as 2 and 18, are also used in reconstructing the ceremony. It is thought to have included a re-enactment of Yahweh's primordial victory over chaos and a procession of the ark, Yahweh's throne. Many biblical scholars reject the reasons given to prove the existence of this feast. BIBLIOGRAPHY: J. J. Castelot, JBC 2:732–733.

[T. EARLY]

ENTHRONIZATION, also called installation, a ceremony in which a bp.-elect by seating himself on the episcopal throne in his cathedral and receiving the obeisance of his clergy, signals his taking possession of his diocese. No formal ceremony is prescribed for taking possession of the diocese; it is accomplished canonically by the bp.'s presenting his apostolic letters of appointment to the diocesan chapter or consultors. This presentation must be made within 4 months of his appointment and only after such presentation may the bp.-elect exercise jurisdiction in the diocese (CIC, cc. 333, 334).

[T. C. O'BRIEN]

ENTHUSIASM, a claim to unmediated union with God; also the kind of religious life that tends to result from belief in such union. Enthusiasm has been a primary source of many of the forms, some of them extravagant, that Christianity has taken. The term *entheos,* possessed by a god, was used by the Greeks to refer to divine possession, as by Apollo or Dionysius, and in Plato poetic inspiration is called a kind of enthusiasm. The English word became prominent during the 17th and 18th cent. as a term of reproach applied to those who claimed such direct and individual union with God as to give them an immediate and certain knowledge of their relationship to God and of his will. The term has been applied to such groups as Montanists, Cathari, Fraticelli, Convulsionaries, Quakers, and Methodists. In the Reformation era Luther used the equivalent *Schwärmerei* of the Anabaptists. During the *Great Awakening, George *Whitefield was denounced by the president and faculty of Harvard as an enthusiast, as "one that acts either according to Dreams, or some sudden impulses and impressions upon his mind, which he fondly imagines to be from the Spirit of God, perswading and inclining him thereby to such and such actions, tho' he hath no proof that such perswasions or impressions are from the Holy Spirit."

Modern authors use several criteria to classify and criticize manifestations of enthusiasm: the claim to immediate revelations that leads to a disregard for historical revelation as contained in Scripture and tradition; the claim to personal direction by the Spirit of God leading to rebellion against both civil authority and the disciplines of the Church; the claim to certainty of salvation through the direct action of God fostering a disregard for the sacraments and other forms of worship; the presumed direct knowledge of the will of God leading to *antinomianism and pride; and the emphasis upon the felt working of the Spirit resulting in unhealthy emotionalism and contempt for reason. Those charged with enthusiasm, however, reply that the examples

of inspiration and unusual workings of the Spirit that are found in the Bible support the validity of such phenomena in the present and that a personal and direct contact with God is essential if Christian faith is to be a living reality.

In general, enthusiasm may be considered a reaction to formalistic religion, and is often marked by ecstatic or charismatic emphases, such as *glossolalia. It also often engenders a sense of impending crisis with expectations of the end of the world, i.e., *millenarianism. To some extent it is associated with *revivalism and the crisis experience in which a person has immediate assurance of his conversion and of the forgiveness and salvation that he has surely received. BIBLIOGRAPHY: KnoxEnth; E. Troeltsch, *Social Teachings of the Christian Churches* (tr. O. Wyon, 2 v., 1956); L. McCann, NCE 5:446–449.

[T. EARLY]

ENTIRE SANCTIFICATION (holiness, second blessing, second work of grace), the form of *perfectionism taught in *Holiness Churches and, with less emphasis, in *Pentecostalism. The doctrine is an interpretation and extension of John Wesley's idea of *Christian perfection. In *A Plain Account of Christian Perfection,* Wesley, departing from the Reformation adage *homo simul justus et peccator* (man is at once righteous and a sinner), taught a grace of sanctification that is distinct from justification: by justification God saves a person from sins already committed; by sanctification God "extirpates man's sinful nature." The idea of sanctification, *Arminian in its basis, was prominent in 19th-cent. American *revivalism; C. *Finney taught that the sanctified "habitually live without sin or fall into it at intervals so few and far between that, in strong language, it may be said that they do not sin" (see OBERLIN THEOLOGY). During the revivalistic Holiness Movement, esp. after the Civil War, Wesley's teaching was given an interpretation regarded by Methodist authorities as extreme. Sanctification or perfection came not to mean a gradual process of attainment through the actions of Christian living, but an instantaneous endowment with sinlessness through the power of the Holy Spirit.

This sanctification is called entire because, while justification takes away or covers the guilt of voluntary, sinful actions, sanctification fills man with a holiness that takes away "inbred sin," the roots of sin, and the abiding tendencies left by original sin (see CONCUPISCENCE). Certain Holiness writers seem to explain entire sanctification as the indwelling of Christ in the sanctified. Some Pentecostals have viewed it as prerequisite to the *baptism with the Holy Spirit; Spirit baptism, however, not entire sanctification, is the core of Pentecostalism. This second blessing is achieved without the help of sacraments or of any ecclesial mediation. Although there is no time assigned in man's life to receive it, the general expectation is that it should happen during the revival services of the Churches. Entire sanctification may grow progressively throughout a person's life; although the possibility of loss of this grace is admitted, stress is laid upon its conferring assurance of salvation. One consequence of the teaching is a strict, often puritanical, moral code, the observance of which is viewed as an expression of freedom from interior inclination to what is sinful or frivolous. BIBLIOGRAPHY: Mayer RB 311–314 and bibliog.; N. Bloch-Hoell, *Pentecostal Movement* (1964) 122–129.

[T. C. O'BRIEN]

ENTRANCE, GREAT, in the Eastern Churches originally a procession in which the clergy moved from the nave into the sanctuary for the Liturgy of the Faithful. In the Byzantine and Armenian liturgies it has evolved into the procession in the early part of the Liturgy of the Faithful. The priest and deacon, accompanied by the lesser ministers, carry the bread and wine from the table of *prothesis* down the side aisle, then up the center of the nave and into the sanctuary, where the gifts are laid on the altar. The West Syrian liturgy has prayers deriving from the primitive entrance of the clergy, but has no procession. The accompanying *troparion* in the Byzantine liturgy is today almost always the *cheroubikon;* the Armenians sing a variable *srbasatzouthiun* (hagiody or hagiology) referring, like the *cheroubikon,* to the angelic hosts. BIBLIOGRAPHY: J. J. Jungmann, *Public Worship: A Survey* (tr. C. Howell, 1957).

[A. CODY]

ENTRANCE, LITTLE, in the Eastern Churches originally the entrance of the clergy into the church for the beginning of the liturgy. Today, in the Byzantine liturgy, it has been transformed into a short procession in which the priest, the deacon carrying the gospel book, and the lesser ministers come from the north door of the iconostasis and move directly to the central door, through which the priest and deacon enter the sanctuary, where the deacon places the book on the altar. In the Armenian and West Syrian liturgies the remnant of the ancient procession simply moves in a circle once around the altar. In the Coptic liturgy the priest enters the sanctuary and incenses the clergy (who are to be in the apse) and the altar. The Syrians and Copts do not carry the Gospel book.

[A. CODY]

ENUMA ELISH, ancient Babylonian myth of creation, so titled from the opening words of the Akkadic text ("When on high . . ."). Discovered in fragmentary form on clay tablets in various places in Mesopotamia, the Akkadic original has been reconstructed and deciphered almost in its entirety. The narrative describes the emergence of the gods (theogony) and the creation of the universe (cosmogony) from the primordial seas and mists; after a series of conflicts, Marduk emerges as victor and reigns supreme as head of the pantheon and lord of creation.

The obvious exaltation of Marduk, as well as some other elements of style and language and some local allusions,

indicate that at least in this form the narrative derives from the old Babylonian period, perhaps around the time of Hammurabi (1728–1686 B.C.). However, it contains other elements that seem to derive from the 3d millennium B.C. Variant readings have been discovered that exalt Assur instead of Marduk, thus indicating an attempt to adapt the tale to Assyrian conditions. Still other factors suggest a West Semitic origin, perhaps Syrian or Phoenician. However, scholars at present are still inclined to favor its Babylonian provenance.

Although scholars once concluded that some elements of the OT were derived from the Enuma Elish, present opinion is that both borrow freely from the universal oral patrimony of the ancient Orient and its characteristic mythopoeic form of thought and language. Similarities are evident in such biblical themes as creation, the conflict between Yahweh and the other gods, Yahweh's conquest of the sea monster. Compare, e.g., Gen 1.26; Is 27.1; 51.9–10; Ps 89.10–12; Job 26.12–13. BIBLIOGRAPHY: J. A. Brinkman, NCE 5:449–451.

[T. CRANE]

ENVY, sadness caused by another's blessings or good fortune. Sometimes confused with jealousy, which wants some good to be one's exclusive possession, envy begrudges another the good that is his possession. Envy is expressly reprobated in Scripture (Acts 7.9; 1 Cor 13.4; Gal 5.26). It reveals a mean and unpleasant want of benevolence toward others and inhibits joy in their well-being and mercy in their suffering, all of which belong to the virtue of charity. It is reckoned among the *capital sins. BIBLIOGRAPHY: ThAq ST 2a2ae, 36.

EOBAN, ST. (d. 754), Anglo-Saxon missionary and bp. in the Netherlands. Messenger and amanuensis of St. Boniface, he was sent to England and to the Pope. As *chorbishop he shared Boniface's work among the Frisians. He is listed as bp. of Utrecht and was martyred with Boniface at Dokkum. BIBLIOGRAPHY: C. M. Fischer, DHGE 15:516; J. F. Alonso, BiblSanct 4:1249–50.

[J. L. DRUSE]

ÉON DE L'ÉTOILE (fl. 12th cent.), a fanatic Breton preacher. E. was an uneducated layman who took the first words of the liturgical formula for exorcism, *per eum qui venturus est iudicare vivos et mortuos* (through him who is to come to judge the living and the dead), to be a reference to his own name. He proclaimed therefore that he was the Son of God, commissioned to judge the world. He organized followers, sometimes called Breton Heretics, who lived in the forest, engaging in immoral practices and emerging to pillage homes, monasteries, and churches. E. was cited before a provincial council at Reims in 1148 and was confined to prison as a madman.

[T. C. O'BRIEN]

EPACT, the excess of the solar year over the lunar, calculated as the number of days of the moon's age on January 1st. It has been used to fix the date of Easter since the introduction of the Gregorian Calendar in 1582. *COMPUTUS.

[J. R. AHERNE]

EPANOKAMILAFKION (Gr., "over the kamilafkion"; Sl. *parakemelavka*), a black veil used in Eastern Churches. It is attached to and covers the kamilafkion; it falls behind, over the wearer's shoulders and down the back. It is used by bps., dignitaries, and priest-monks. The veil is split at both sides near the bottom and so produces two long, pendantlike sections which, according to legend, were introduced by St. John Chrysostom to pull over his shoulders in order to hide his scarred face. A white veil is worn by the patriarch of Moscow and Russian metropolitans.

[A. J. JACOPIN]

EPARCHIUS, ST. (numerous variants of the name occur, e.g., Cybar[d], Cibar[d], Ybar[d]; 504–581 [or 558]), a recluse, who had a considerable cult in Angoulême in the 6th cent., according to *Gregory of Tours. Gregory and a 9th-cent. vita credit him with extraordinary virtue and many miracles, the most dramatic of which was his saving the life of a man who had been hanged. A basilica was built above the saint's tomb, and connected with it there was a monastery (Saint-Cybard) built probably during the reign of Pepin I of Aquitaine (817–838). BIBLIOGRAPHY: R. Aigrain, *Catholicisme* 3:392–394; J. Joussain, BiblSanct 3:1249–1252.

[G. M. COOK]

ÉPÉE, CHARLES MICHEL DE L' (1712–89), founder of systematic education of deaf-mutes. Born at Versailles, É. entered the seminary but was refused orders because of his Jansenist tendencies. He went to Troyes and was ordained by Bossuet (1738). An outbreak of anti-Bossuet sentiment caused É. to move to Paris (1743), where he became a lawyer. Later (1753), he became interested in the education of two deaf-mute girls and eventually developed a successful teaching method based on sign language, finger-spelling and lipreading, which he described in his *Institution des sourds et muets par la voie des signes méthodiques* (1776). By 1780 he had about 80 students, and his school received a royal pension that was continued by the citizen government after the Revolution. BIBLIOGRAPHY: P. Oleron, *Les Sourds-muets* (1950); T. de Morembert, DHGE 15:550–52.

EPHESIANS, LETTER TO THE, 10th book in the NT canon, ascribed without hesitation to St. Paul by early Christian tradition. However, since the turn of the 19th cent., some scholars have doubted or denied the Pauline authorship of Ephesians. The evidence they have developed, when considered cumulatively, carries real weight: some 40 words in the epistle are not found in other Pauline letters; its style is at times somewhat obscure, has occasional sentences of unusual length, and lacks the verve characteristic of Paul; some 73 of its verses reflect borrowings from Colossians, and others appear to be dependent on passages in Romans, First and Second Corinthians, Galatians, Philippians, and First and Second Thessalonians. In addition, the conception of Satan, of mystery, of eschatology, and perhaps of marriage does not mirror the ideas on these subjects in other epistles of Paul. This evidence from language, style, and theological thought convinces some scholars that Ephesians is a pseudonymous work, non-Pauline in origin, to be dated 80–100 A.D. Other scholars believe that this evidence does not warrant the complete denial of Pauline authorship. In their judgment its Christology and its presentation of the doctrine of justification through faith (1.3–23; 2.1–10) have sufficient affinity with the thought of Paul to require his actual role in its composition. In this opinion, the Apostle entrusted the epistle's composition to an amanuensis, who reflected Paul's influence but who retained much of his own individuality.

The destination of the epistle is as puzzling as its authorship. Although the MS tradition preponderantly supports the superscription, "To the Ephesians," a number of early significant MSS read simply, "to the saints and faithful who are in Christ Jesus" (Vaticanus, Sinaiticus, P46 in addition to MSS known to Basil and Origen). This evidence would not in itself be decisive against Ephesus as the epistle's destination were it not also for the fact that not a single member of the Ephesian community is greeted or mentioned in it. Since it was Paul's practice to extend such personal greetings in his letters and since he was well-acquainted with this community (cf. Acts 19.1–20.1), it hardly seems plausible that he omitted mention of certain of its members in a letter addressed to it. This uncertainty over the epistle's destination has occasioned a number of conjectures: it is the epistle to the Laodiceans, alluded to in Col 4.16 (Marcion); it is Paul's last message to the Church; it was prepared by an anonymous author as an introduction to the Pauline *corpus,* or possibly as a Christian philosophy of history; finally, it was a circular letter, written at the same time as the other epistles of the captivity, Colossians and Philemon, and directed to the communities of the province of Asia. All of these explanations are open to serious objection, the least vulnerable being the theory of the circular letter. The fact is that Col 4.16 does not speak of a letter to Laodicea but simply says that the Colossians should read the letter that was sent there. Conceivably, this letter could be Ephesians, carried among the various communities of the Lycus valley to bear upon the same religious problems Paul dealt with in Colossians. It is unnecessary to suppose, with some modern scholars, that a blank was left in this circular letter to be filled in with the name of specific communities. The address of Ephesians can easily be understood to mean "to those who are holy and faithful in Christ Jesus." While this opinion does not admit of stronger substantiation, it remains a plausible explanation of the original purpose of Ephesians. The epistle is clearly divided into doctrinal and moral sections (1.3–3.21; 4.1–6.20). Its doctrine expresses the mystery of God's eternal plan of Redemption in Christ, in whom all history is to receive its final fulfillment (1.3–14), now revealed through Christian faith (1.11–14). It prays for deeper Christian perception of this mystery that has been especially illuminated by the Resurrection and Ascension of Jesus (1.15–22). It reflects upon the spiritual transformation worked in the Christian through the power of Jesus' Resurrection and Christian baptism (2.1–10) and upon the unity achieved in the Church between Jew and gentile (2.11–22). It dwells upon the apostolic mission of Paul to the gentiles (3.1–13), concluding with a prayer for the Christian perception of the cosmic significance of Christ (3.14–21). Its moral exhortation bears upon fraternal love in the community, acknowledgment and use of charismatic gifts, on sensuality and deceit, the relationship of husband and wife, the rearing of children, and the care and role of slaves. BIBLIOGRAPHY: D. Guthrie, *New Testament Introduction* (1961); Wikenhauser NTI; P. Feine et al., *Einleitung in das Neue Testament* (1964); F. W. Beare, *Introduction and Exegesis of Ephesians,* InterB.

[C. P. CEROKE]

EPHESUS, city in Western Asia Minor. Founded by Ionian Greeks in the 11th cent. B.C., it came successively under Athenian, Macedonian, and Roman rule. Ephesus was the Roman capital of Asia Minor (to 287) and, owing to its excellent location, an important and prosperous maritime city. It possessed the famous Temple of Diana, one of the seven wonders of the ancient world, and was a center of magical practice. The Church was established there early and was visited by St. Paul, to whom is generally attributed an epistle to its members. It is the place where St. John is reputed to have written his Gospel and he may also have been buried there. An impressive basilica was built over his supposed tomb. According to one tradition, the Dormition or Assumption of the Virgin Mary occurred on a hill near the city. In the early history of the Church, Ephesus played a prominent role, and its bp. exercised authority over much of Asia Minor. It was the site of the ecumenical council (431) which condemned Nestorianism as well as of the Robber-Synod of 449. With the ascendancy of the see of Constantinople, however, Ephesus declined in importance. Early in the 14th cent. it was occupied by the Turks and is now a mere village located near the extensive ruins of the ancient city. In the Middle Ages it was called Haghios Theologos after St. John the Theologian (Evangelist), which the Latins corrupted to Altoluogo; the Turkish form of the name was Ayasuluk, but it is now called Selçuk. BIBLIOGRAPHY: PW 5.2:2773–2822; H. Leclercq, DACL 5.1:118–142; R. Janin, DHGE 15:554–561.

[P. FOSCOLOS]

EPHESUS, COUNCIL OF (431), third ecumenical council, which condemned Nestorianism as heretical. *Nestorius, patriarch of Constantinople (428–431), espoused an *Antiochene Christology, the unnuanced exposition of which led to the council. Nestorius insisted that, even after the Incarnation, the Word could not suffer or change; that Christ was a true man who lived a genuine human life; that there were not two persons in Christ but that Christ's concrete individuality *(prosōpon)* was different from the *prosōpon* of the Word or the *prosōpon* of his humanity. For Nestorius, it was ambiguous to speak of Mary as the God-bearer *(*Theotokos)*; *Christotokos* was more precise. He was opposed by *Cyril of Alexandria who insisted upon a hypostatic union to explain the Incarnation and, in the course of the controversy, presented Nestorius' position as denying the unity of persons in Christ. Cyril induced Pope Celestine to condemn Nestorius (430) and drew up 12 anathemas which he appended to the papal letters of condemnation. Nestorius refused to submit and prevailed upon Emperor Theodosius II to convoke a council at Ephesus. But Cyril, when the arrival of the Antiochene bps. was delayed, held a synod of 61 like-minded bps. who anathematized Nestorius. When the Antiochene group arrived, they held a new synod, deposed Cyril, and condemned the anathemas. The papal legates, however, supported Cyril and declared his synod the true Council of Ephesus. The council's major achievement was to reiterate the Church's acceptance of the Nicene Creed and to recognize Cyril's *Second Letter to Nestorius* as its authoritative interpretation. BIBLIOGRAPHY: J. N. D. Kelly, *Early Christian Doctrines* (2d ed., 1960); Quasten 3:116–142. *NESTORIANISM.

[R. R. BARR]

EPHESUS, ROBBER SYNOD OF (Lat., *Latrocinium*), the name given by Pope Leo I (and current since) to the council that met at Ephesus in 449. The abbot Eutyches, who held a form of the Monophysite doctrine, had been deposed by his bp., Flavian of Constantinople, and had appealed to Dioscorus, bp. of Alexandria, who prevailed upon Emperor Theodosius II to summon a council to rehabilitate Eutyches, depose Flavian, and "reaffirm the Orthodox faith" against the Nestorians. Invited by Theodosius, Pope Leo I sent three legates with his *Tome to Flavian* (June 13, 449) in which he exposed in detail the Catholic doctrine on the Incarnation. The council was entirely dominated by Dioscorus. Eutyches was acquitted of heresy and reinstated, Flavian and other bps. deposed. The letter from the Pope had not been read, and in its place the Acts of the Synod of Constantinople which had condemned Eutyches were read; all opposition was suppressed by intimidation or actual violence. Flavian died of physical injuries soon afterwards. Leo I refused to recognize the council, excommunicated Dioscorus, and demanded a new and greater council. Two years later the Council of Chalcedon reversed the acts of Ephesus by deposing Dioscorus, condemning Eutychianism, and defining the dogma of the Incarnation along the lines of Leo's *Tome*. BIBLIOGRAPHY: G. Bardy, Fliche-Martin, 4:220–226; P. Camelot, Grill-Bacht Konz 1:213–242; H. Bacht, *ibid.* 2:197–231.

[P. FOSCOLOS]

EPHOD, a kind of linen apron worn by priests or ministers at a sanctuary (1 Sam 2.18; 2 Sam 6.14). A second type of ephod, which was carried, was used in consulting the Lord (1 Sam 2.28). The high priest wore over his tunic and cloak a third type, a colorful kind of breastplate (Ex 28.6) distinct, however, from the pouch in which the *Urim and Thummim were contained. Under Gideon the ephod became a cult object (Jg 8.27), and Micah made it an idol (17.5). The ephod was not used as an instrument of divinization after David (1 Sam 23.9; 30.7; cf. Hos 3.4).

[R. T. A. MURPHY]

EPHODI, PSEUD., see DURAN, PROFIAT.

EPHPHETA (Aramaic, be thou opened), the word used by Jesus in effecting the cure of the deaf-mute in the region of the Decapolis. This was a rather unique miracle that seems to have been worked in stages (Mk 7.31–37).

[J. A. PIERCE]

EPHRAIM (a name meaning "he has made me fruitful"), the second son of Joseph (Gen 41.52), who with Manasseh, his brother, comprised the "house of Joseph." As a strong, aggressive tribe, Ephraim occupied the hill country that linked Shechem to Bethel (Jos 16.4–10; 1 Chr 7.28). The periodic disputes that broke out between Ephraim and Manasseh (Jg 7.24–8.3) and with Gilead (Jg 12.1–6), illustrate Ephraim's persistent claim to primacy in the North. Among the prophets, Isaiah, Jeremiah, Ezekiel, and Hosea referred to the N kingdom as Ephraim. The town of that name, which Jesus visited shortly before the Passover (Jn 11.54), is identified with Taiyibeh (about 6 miles E of Bethel).

[R. T. A. MURPHY]

EPHRATA (EPHRATHAH), Hebrew adjective meaning fruitful, the name of two towns in biblical Palestine, one in the territory of Judah, the other in that of Benjamin. Ephrata of Judah became identified with Bethlehem, home of David (1 Sam 17.12; Mic 5.1–2). The founder of Bethlehem was a descendant of Ephrath, wife of Caleb (1 Chr 2.19). Ephrata of Benjamin, where Rachel died at the birth of Benjamin (Gen 35.16–20), is identified by Jeremiah (31.15) with Rama in the land of Benjamin, about 7 miles N of Jerusalem. The reference to Bethlehem as the site of Rachel's tomb (1 Sam 10.2) is probably inexact.

[T. CRANE]

EPHRATA COMMUNITY, a communal body founded (1732–34) by Johann Conrad *Beissel, who established the groups in the wilderness of Lancaster Co., Pennsylvania. The community was known as Ephrata, and the village, restored, is now a state historical possession (1968). Practices of Ephrata featured celibacy, Sabbatarianism, and the use of monastic names, apparel, cells, and regimen. Authority for customs, practices, and doctrine were alleged to have been received by Beissel in mystical trances and inspiration. The community was industrious, excelling in farming, milling, printing, and calligraphic art. The worship was mystical, characterized by long sermons, devout prayer vigils, and highly stylized vocal music. The society lasted less than 100 years because of internal dissension and lack of leadership. The Seventh Day Baptists, however, trace their origins to Beissel's foundation.

[A. T. RONK]

EPHREM THE SYRIAN, ST. (*c.*306–373), classical ecclesiastical writer of the Syrian Church, exegete, Doctor of the Church. Born in Nisibis in Mesopotamia of Christian parents, E. was not baptized until he was a young man. According to some reports he attended the Council of Nicaea with St. James of Nisibis. He was ordained a deacon (*c.*338), but did not advance to the priesthood so far as is known. When Nisibis was ceded to the Persians, E. migrated to Edessa, which remained within the Roman Empire, where he wrote most of his works and taught in the famous school there, probably founded by him. Although E. was a most prolific writer, much of his work has been lost, and much has survived only in translation. He wrote in Syriac, but his works were soon translated into Greek, Latin, and Armenian. Among his important prose writings are his Scriptural commentaries, including one on Tatian's Diatessaron. He wrote antiheretical treatises against *Bardesanes, *Marcion, Mani, the Gnostics, the Arians, and Julian. He has been called the "Harp of the Holy Spirit" because of his poetical writings and hymns, many of which were incorporated into the Syrian liturgy, but the quality of his poetry, as translated into other tongues and without the original rhythms, is not greatly appreciated by Western readers. The 77 *Carmina Nisibena,* four of which are missing, are important for the information they provide on contemporary events. His sermons deal mainly with practical problems rather than with the doctrinal controversies then current. After the publication of the Assemani edition of his works, E. was much cited by theologians for the witness he bore to thought of the Syrian Church on disputed topics such as the sinlessness of Mary, the veneration of the saints, purgatory, the primacy of Peter, and the Real Presence. Benedict XV proclaimed him a Doctor of the Church in 1920. Works: J. and S. *Assemani, eds., 6 v., three Syriac and three Greek (1732–46); crit. ed. of the commentary on the Diatessaron with Lat. tr. L. Leloir, CSCO 137 and 145; Fr. tr. ed. L. Leloir, SC 121 (1966); Eng. tr. of selections, NPNFC (ser. 2, v. 13.2, ed. J. Gwynn, 1898). BIBLIOGRAPHY: Altaner 401–405; PSO 52–77; E. Beck et al., DSAM 4:788–822; Butler 2:574–577.

[R. B. ENO]

EPIC, a long narrative poem elevated in style and heroic in mood, recounting the exploits of a single individual having some national significance. Epics may be divided into primitive or oral, and literary. The former, composed for recitation, were limited in style and content by the restrictions of a listening audience. The latter, written to be read, allowed more flexibility of language and subject matter, but were also influenced by the ancient traditions of oral epic. Among the most ancient epics are those of Sumer dating from the 3d millennium B.C., which were later taken over and elaborated by the Babylonians and Assyrians. The most famous of these is the story of Gilgamesh, a kind of demigod like Hercules. European epic begins with the *Iliad* and the *Odyssey*; though they are the product of a long tradition of oral composition, these two poems are among the world's great literary masterpieces. In the drawing of character, tragic power, elaboration of plot, and perfection of style they far surpass other primitive or oral epics such as the *chansons de geste* in Old French, *Beowulf* in Old English, and the *Nibelungenlied* in Middle High German. Greek literary epic is represented by the *Argonautica* of Apollonius of Rhodes. Latin epic of this type had its origins in the translation of Homer's *Odyssey* by Livius Andronicus and the composition of the *Bellum Punicum* by Gnaeus Naevius and the *Annales* by Quintus Ennius. It reached its perfection in Virgil's *Aeneid*. During the Renaissance there was a revival of the literary epic as of other genres. Among the epics of this period are the *Africa* of Petrarch, the *Orlando Furioso* of Lodovico Ariosto, the *Gerusalemme Liberata* of Torquato Tasso, and the *Lusiads* of Luiz de Camões. To these may perhaps also be added by extension the *Divina Commedia* of Dante Alighieri, the *Faerie Queene* of Edmund Spenser, and the *Paradise Lost* of John Milton. One of the most popular of modern epics is the *Dreizehnlinden* of Friedrich Wilhelm Weber, which has appeared in numerous editions and versions since it was first published in 1878. BIBLIOGRAPHY: C. M. Bowra, *From Virgil to Milton* (1945); W. P. Ker, *Epic and Romance* (1897).

[M. J. COSTELLOE]

EPICLESIS, from the Gr. verb *epikaleo,* to call upon, invoke, and used in a liturgical meaning for any invocation of God's name in blessing or consecrating; but specifically, and with concrete historical connotations, a part of the Eucharistic Liturgy. The General Instructions of the *Roman Missal* of 1970, n. 55 (translated in the *Sacramentary* of 1974) state that there occurs in the Eucharistic Prayers the "Epiclesis, whereby through the invocations proper [to each Eucharistic Prayer] the Church pleads that gifts offered by men to be consecrated may become the Body and Blood of Christ and that being changed to be received in Communion they may be for the salvation of all who share in them." The wording bears implicit witness to a history of controversy about the epiclesis. First of all the Instruction makes clear that the Latin Church and in particular the

Roman rite accepts the epiclesis as part of the Eucharistic Liturgy, a fact that in East-West polemics was denied by some Latin theologians. The Instruction also makes clear that the epiclesis has its two historic meanings and two phrases in the liturgy; it forms part of the consecrating prayers and after the Consecration expresses a prayer for the sanctification of those who share in the Eucharist. Concretely in the four *Eucharistic Prayers, the old Roman Canon and the three new ones, formulated since Vatican Council II, there is an invocation of divine power before the words of institution and consecration, accompanied by imposition of hands over the gifts, that the gifts offered may become the Body and Blood of Christ; after the Consecration there is the prayer (oblation) that those who share in Christ's Body and Blood may share in the fruits of salvation. In both instances only the old Roman Canon, Eucharistic Prayer I, does not explicitly mention the Holy Spirit. This omission in Prayer I reflects the gradual suppression of the epiclesis in the West, and is in part the reason why some Latin theologians denied that there was any epiclesis at all in the Eucharistic Liturgy. The point of controversy was the epiclesis as entering into the consecration, a development which, while not traceable beyond the 4th cent., fixed this consecratory epiclesis in the Eastern liturgies. Greek patristic writers supported the liturgical practice because it emphasized the divinity of the Holy Spirit and his association as sanctifier in the saving works of the Father and the Son. With the schism between East and West extreme positions were taken on both sides: some Greek theologians insisting that the consecration consisted in the epiclesis alone; some Latin theologians insisting that the consecration consisted exclusively in the Lord's words of institution and rejecting the epiclesis entirely; (see D 1320, 1325, 3556). The reform of the liturgy evidenced in the new *Roman Missal* has the ecumenical value of putting such polemic opposition aside, and the theological advantage of paralleling in the Eucharistic Liturgy the action of each of the Divine Persons in the Incarnation and in a way appropriate to each. In the Eucharistic Consecration and fruitfulness the work of Father, Son, and Holy Spirit is integral and interrelated just as they are in themselves and in the economy of salvation. BIBLIOGRAPHY: G. A. Maloney, NCE 5:465–466, for the pre-Vatican Council II state of the issue.

[T. C. O'BRIEN]

EPICTETUS OF HIERAPOLIS (A.D. 5–c.120), late Stoic philosopher. He was a slave of Epaphroditus, a freedman who held a secretarial office under Nero and Domitian. His master allowed him to attend the lectures of the Stoic philosopher Musonius and eventually gave him his freedom. E. taught philosophy at Rome until all philosophers were banished by Domitian in 89. He settled at Nicopolis in Epirus and taught there for the rest of his life. The future consul and historian Flavius Arrianus was his pupil *c.*110. Twenty years later (*c.* 130), he compiled the lectures and discourses of his teacher in two collections, the *Diatribai* (8 bks.) and *Homiliai* (12 bks.). Arrianus later prepared an *Encheiridion* or summary of the more significant thoughts and teachings of Epictetus (4 bks.). Four books of the *Diatribai* and the *Encheiridion* are extant.

E. is eminently practical in his outlook, exhibiting little interest in theoretical questions, and he is deeply religious. All men have a capacity for virtue, and God has given every man the means for becoming happy. However, some formal philosophical training or education is necessary, for man must learn to distinguish between what is in his power, and what is not. Honor, wealth, good health, avoidance of calamities are not in his power, but through self-education he can attain what is truly in his own power, namely, right judgment and right will. For moral progress, he advocates a daily examination of conscience, which will lead to the eradication of bad habits and their replacement by good. Man must not be discouraged by moral failures, but must persevere. Cleanliness of body is recommended as the first duty toward one's self. Special emphasis is placed on the virtues of simplicity, temperance, modesty, chastity, truthfulness, and loyalty. The Cynics are praised as preachers of truth and for their indifference to external goods, but E. does not approve their rejection of the amenities of civilization. E. is profoundly human as well as profoundly religious throughout his works. He has a genuine love for the masses, which is inspired in part by his personal experience as a slave, but which is motivated, above all, by his warm and personal faith in the all-seeing Providence of a good and benevolent God.

E. exercised a marked influence on Marcus Aurelius and on later pagans. His influence on Christian thought from the Early Christian writers to the end of the 18th cent. was considerable and has been investigated systematically in the articles by Jagu, Spanneut, and Julien-Eymard d'Angers listed below. BIBLIOGRAPHY: K. von Fritz, OCD 324; LexAW 830–831; Copleston 1:431–435; M. Spanneut, RAC 5:499–681; A. Jagu, et al., DSAM 4.1:822–854.

[M. R. P. MCGUIRE]

EPICUREANISM, after Stoicism, probably the most popular philosophical school from *c.* 300 B.C. to *c.* 200 A.D., after which it began to decline. It practically disappeared in the course of the 4th century. Its founder, Epicurus of Samos (342–271 B.C.), followed the lectures of a Platonist Pamphilus at Samos, and subsequently those of Nausiphanes, an Atomist, at Teos. He settled permanently at Athens in 307 and opened his school in his own garden, which he bequeathed to his followers—hence the designation of his system as the Philosophy of the Garden. He was given divine honors even before his death. Of his voluminous works the great majority are extant only in fragments. He defines philosophy as the means for obtaining happiness through discussion and reasoning. He divides philosophy into canonic or logic, physics, and ethics. He is primarily concerned with the acquisition of happiness in terms of the present life—the only life he recognizes. He is interested in logic and physics only insofar as they support his ethical teaching. Mathematics, dialectic, and rhetoric are rejected from formal consideration.

Canonic or Logic. All knowledge is based on sense-knowledge. Perception (*aisthēsis*), the basic criterion of truth, is effected through the penetration of the sense organs by images (*eidola*). Such perception is always true. Concepts (*prolepseis*) or memory images are the second criterion, and feelings (*pathē*), the third: "the criteria of truth are the senses, and the preconceptions, and the passions."

Physics (metaphysics, theology, cosmology, psychology). The Democritean physics is adopted in its essential features, because Epicurus regarded it as best suited to serve the practical end of freeing men from fear of the gods and of suffering after death. The universe and all in it is explained in terms of the atomic theory. Nothing comes from nothing and nothing passes into nothingness. Atoms and the void exist from eternity, and a declination of the atoms is postulated to bring about the collision of the atoms to form bodies and to explain freedom of the will. The earth and all the visible stars constitute one world, but there are many other worlds. The stars, however, are not animate and divination and astrology are rejected. The gods exist but live in a blissful state in the intermundial regions; they take no part in the affairs of men or the world. They are to be honored but not to be feared. True piety is identified with right thought. There is no relation between the evils of human life and a divine guidance of the universe. The soul is composed of smooth or round atoms, and it possesses a rational part—as is evident from the emotions of fear and joy—and an irrational part. The latter is the principle of life that permeates the whole body. At death the atoms constituting the soul are separated and all perception ceases: "death is the privation of perception."

Ethics (personal ethics or conduct, politics, and philosophy of law). The ethical teaching of Epicurus is based chiefly on that of the Cynics. Pleasure is the highest good, but is to be understood as the pleasure of motion, and esp. as the serenity of soul that comes of the absence of pain (*ataraxia*). Bodily pain is allayed or outweighed by mental pleasure. Simple living, approaching the ascetic, is emphasized, and the virtues of simplicity, moderation, temperance, and cheerfulness are constantly stressed. Insight (*phronēsis*) is regarded as the highest virtue, enabling the wise man (*phronimos*) to apply right measure (*summetrēsis*) in respect to pleasure and pain. Injustice is not intrinsically bad but is to be avoided because of the fear of incurring the punishments normally imposed for unjust acts. The selfish and egocentric features of Epicurean ethics are counterbalanced by the emphasis on friendship and generosity—the cultivation of true friendship being one of the most characteristic marks of the Epicurean school. Political life is, ordinarily, to be avoided by the wise man as disturbing tranquillity of soul. Civil society is explained as originating in a kind of social contract.

Abuse of the tenets of Epicureanism, esp. among the

Romans, has given it a bad name, but even in its ideal form it must be described as a materialistic, hedonistic, escapist philosophy that justified withdrawal not only from the troubles of the world but also from one's responsibility to society. Unlike other systems of ancient philosophy, there are no appreciable changes in Epicureanism throughout its history. Among the more significant Epicurean philosophers were Metrodorus of Lampsacus (331–278 B.C.); Hermarchus of Mytilene (c.325–250 B.C.); Philodemus of Gadara (c.110–c.40 B.C.); and esp. the great Roman poet Lucretius (94–55 B.C.). BIBLIOGRAPHY: C. O. Brink, OCD 324–325; Copleston 1:401–412; C. Bailey, *Greek Atomists and Epicurus* (1928); A. J. Festugière, *Epicurus and His Gods* (1956); W. Schmid, "Epikur," RAC 5 (1962) 681–819, with excellent treatment of Epicurus in Christian writers, 774–816, and copious bibliog. 816–819.

[M. R. P. MCGUIRE]

EPIDAURUS, THOLOS OF (360–320 B.C.), the most beautiful circular building in Greece, 66 feet in diameter, having a peristyle of 26 Doric columns, a circular cella with 14 free-standing Corinthian columns carrying an innovative frieze entablature, a floor paved with black and white slabs, and a subterranean labyrinth probably for the snake cult of Aesculapius. Fragments of the Tholos are housed in the Archeological Museum, Epidaurus.

[M. J. DALY]

EPIGONATION (Gr. for thigh; Sl. *palitza; nabedrennik),* Byzantine liturgical vestment common to bishops, archimandrites, and other dignitaries. It is a stiffened square of embroidery suspended by one of the angles and hanging at the right side to symbolize the sword of justice. The Slavs have developed the *epigonation* into two distinct vestments, the *palitza* which is the *epigonation* proper, and the *nabedrennik* which is rectangular and suspended by two corners and appears somewhat like a bag. Among the Melchites it is used by all dignitaries, and Orthodox parish priests who are confessors usually are considered to have the right to the *epigonation*. In the Western Church its use has survived only in the papal regalia and is called the *subcinctorium*.

[A. J. JACOPIN]

EPIGRAPHY, CHRISTIAN, the science dealing with ancient Christian inscriptions, i.e., with writings or copies of writings no longer extant, on hard materials such as stone, metal, bone, and plaster originated before the close of the 7th century. In addition to Christian inscriptions in various Eastern languages, there are still in existence some 10,000 in Greek and 40,000 in Latin. Of these the largest number, c.2,000 in Greek and 18,000 in Latin, come from Rome. The earliest dated inscription from Rome is a Latin text on the sarcophagus of Marcus Aurelius Prosenes, a former official of the imperial household, who "was taken up to God" during the consulships of Praesens and Extricatus (217). The earliest definitely dated Greek inscription from the same city is that of Pope Pontianus in the Crypt of the Popes in the Catacomb of Callistus. Though the date is not given on the inscription, it must come from the time of his death in 235. Where no consular or era dates are given upon inscriptions, their dates may be conjectured from the style of writing employed, the language and formulae used, and particularly by surrounding archeological remains if the inscriptions are found *in situ*.

Written as a rule in the common spoken language, Koine Greek or Vulgar Latin, Christian inscriptions are an invaluable source of information with respect to the names, marital and civil status, and beliefs of relatively unknown early Christians, whose names are of various types, some derived from pagan and mythological sources (Diogenes, Hermes), others from Scripture (Susanna, Maria), others of a specifically Christian origin (Anastasia, Redempta), others chosen out of a spirit of humility (Stercorius, Sceleratus), and still others that were simply nicknames added to their given names (Anna Gaudiosa *sive* Africa). Many give the ages of individuals at the time of their marriage and death. A wide variety of occupations such as physician, baker, merchant, dyer, teacher, and even charioteer are noted. More significant are explicit or implicit expressions of faith in the efficacy of prayers and the sacraments, particularly baptism and the Eucharist, and of hope in attaining everlasting life. Of these one of the most interesting is that of Abercius, bp. of Hieropolis, dating from before 216 A.D., discovered in Asia Minor in 1883 and now in the Lateran Museum in Rome. In it he describes his pilgrimage as "a pupil of a chaste Shepherd" to Rome, where he saw a people "having a resplendent seal," that is, baptized. A somewhat similar Greek inscription is the epitaph of Pectorius from Autun. Undoubtedly some of the most important inscriptions that have come down from early Christian times are the simple graffiti of pious pilgrims such as those found on the walls of the triclia beneath the nave of St. Sebastian's on the Via Appia and on the little monument above the tomb of St. Peter beneath the high altar of his basilica. Ancient Christian monuments with inscriptions are also frequently adorned with various symbols such as an anchor or a fish, but these belong more properly to the science of iconography. BIBLIOGRAPHY: L. Jalabert, et al., DACL 7.1:623–1089; F. Grossi Gondi, *Trattato di epigrafia cristiana latina e greca* (1920); M. R. P. McGuire, NCE 5:470–475.

[M. J. COSTELLOE]

EPIGRAPHY, HEBREW, properly, the study of ancient Hebrew inscriptions on hard material, stone, metal, etc., but by many extended to include ancient Hebrew writing in ink on soft material, papyrus, leather or parchment. Since Hebrew and Phoenician were essentially the same language and used the same script, Hebrew epigraphy includes study of Phoenician inscriptions. Besides those on coins and seals, the most famous pre-Exilic inscriptions are: the Gezer calendar (10th cent. B.C.); the Mesha stele from Moab (late 9th cent.), which shows the Moabites and Israelites used the same language; the Siloam inscription (700

B.C.) in Jerusalem's water tunnel excavated by Hezekiah's orders (2 Kgs 20.20); the tomb inscription from the slopes of the Kidron valley near the town of Siloam. Other writings in the Phoenician script have been found on *ostraca from Samaria (7th cent.) and Lachish (c.589 B.C.). Post-Exilic inscriptions and writings appear in the square Aramaic script adopted from the Mesopotamians and familiar from the Hebrew Bible. The old script remained in use, however, among conservative Hebrew elements, such as the Qumran sectarians and the followers of Bar-Cochba (c.125 A.D.).

[J. F. FALLON]

EPIKEIA, from the Greek, a quality of justice tempered by ease and equity. Hence one too great a gentleman to stand stiffly on his own rights was said to be *epiekes.* It enters Justinian's codification of Roman Law with its Christian regard for liberty, its preference for clemency over harshness, benignity over severity, equity over rigidity of right. The Bible applies the term to the loving-kindness of divine justice and of Christ's rule, which to theology is rooted in God's mercy (cf. ThAq ST 21.4). In moral theology it is a special type of the virtue of justice called into play when one is faced with a situation where carrying out the ordinary laws would produce an injustice. Some of the more juridically minded authors seem to admit it almost apologetically as a fringe-virtue to justice, and out of kindliness allow that on occasion it may reverse their presumption in favor of law rather than liberty. St. Thomas, however, stands for an older tradition closer to that of the English common law, and treats it as neither a component element in justice (an integral part), nor an adjunct to it (a virtual part), but as the highest kind of justice. Some confusion may arise here because the same term *legalis* can stand for both "lawful" (literally in the fullest sense) and legalistic. Thus when legal justice means the general justice serving the common good, which is the purpose of all law, then *epikeia* is seen as its most ample expression; but when it means keeping to the words of a law, then *epikeia* is contrasted with it. Yet it is not an escape from law, but, directed by prudence and in particular by *gnome,* a recourse to higher law. It should be distinguished from exemption, an authoritative declaration that the law does not apply; from interpretation, a manifestation of the authentic meaning of a law; and from dispensation, a relaxation of a law for particular benefit. *Epikeia* applies only to positive law, for there are no exceptions at the heart of natural law. Both in philosophy and in theology, the *jus naturale* is the *jus aequum,* and its precepts as such are moral and equitable, not the stereotypes of a code. BIBLIOGRAPHY: ThAq ST (Lat-Eng, v. 41, ed. T. C. O'Brien).

[T. GILBY]

EPIMACHUS, ST., see GORDIAN AND EPIMACHUS, SS.

EPIMANIKIA (Gr., sleeve or glove; Sl. *narukavniki, porutchi*), in the Eastern Churches, an ornamental cuff worn over the sleeves of the *sticharion* at the wrists by bps., priests, and sometimes deacons. They are usually marked with a cross in the middle. Their origin is uncertain; possibly it can be linked with the Roman *maniple, or they may be an adaptation of imperial gauntlets or gloves. They made their appearance in the 11th cent. and by the 12th their use was common to bps. and priests. Of all the Eastern Churches, only the Chaldean makes no use of them.

[A. J. JACOPIN]

EPIPHANES (d. c.130), Gnostic, son of Carpocrates, E. was a child prodigy: dying at the age of 17 he yet left a work, *On Justice,* that contains much of his father's thought; parts are quoted in Clement of Alexandria's *Stromata* 3(2,5–9). According to E.'s work ignorance and passion, in disturbing the equality of men and the community of goods, have introduced evil into the world; the idea of private property forms no part of the divine plan, but is of human invention. E. also concluded that all laws should be suppressed; there should be community of property and even of wives. A temple was dedicated to his honor on the island of Cephalonia.

[T. C. O'BRIEN]

EPIPHANIUS (fl. 6th cent.), **PATRIARCH OF CONSTANTINOPLE** (520–535). E. collaborated with the Emperors *Justin and *Justinian in fostering better relations with the papacy after the *Acacian Schism (482–519). Soon after his election he sent a profession of faith to Pope *Hormisdas, clearly showing his adherence to the orthodox doctrine of *Chalcedon. He maintained close relations with Rome, where he was always highly regarded. BIBLIOGRAPHY: Fliche-Martin 4:423–432.

[P. K. MEAGHER]

EPIPHANIUS OF CONSTANTIA, ST. (Salamis; c.310–403), bp. and metropolitan of Cyprus from 367, staunch assailant of heresy. A native of Palestine, E. founded a monastery and became its superior. After being made bp. he moved about much in the cause of orthodoxy. His principal work *Panarion* (cf. Augustine, *De haer.*) is an account and rebuttal of all heresies that had existed up to that time, including some whose real existence is open to doubt. His *Ancoratus* provides what is perhaps the earliest version of the Nicene-Constantinopolitan Creed. In his readiness to suspect heresy everywhere, he took a narrow, rigid, and partisan position in the first Origenistic controversy (see ORIGENISM). He attacked Origen as the fountainhead of all heresies, going to Palestine c.394 to join forces with St. Jerome in denouncing *John, bp. of Jerusalem, as an Origenist. He preached against John in his own city, ordained Jerome's brother without John's permission, and generally sought to stir up the people against their bishop. On a mission to Constantinople on behalf of *Theophilus of Alexandria, he discovered that he was being used against *John Chrysostom. He withdrew from the city immediately but died on his journey back to Cyprus.

Works: PG 41–43. BIBLIOGRAPHY: Quasten 3:384–396; Butler 2:285–287.

[R. B. ENO]

EPIPHANIUS OF PAVIA, ST. (*c*.438–*c*.496), bishop. E. was one of the most influential Italian bps. during the period of the collapse of the Western Empire. Bishop of Pavia from the early age of 28, he was greatly esteemed for his sanctity and the greatness of his charity toward all. Through his influence with rulers, he attempted to mitigate the burdens and sufferings of the people. Toward the end of his life he undertook an arduous journey to Lyons to negotiate with King Gundobard of the Burgundians for the release of 6,000 prisoners from Italy. He finally died from exhaustion brought about by his errands of mercy. BIBLIOGRAPHY: Butler 1:139; B. Kotting, LTK 3:947.

[R. B. ENO]

EPIPHANIUS THE HAGIOPOLITE, possibly a monk of Jerusalem who, before 785, wrote a valued description of Jerusalem and the holy places. It can be found in PG 120:260–272.

EPIPHANY, the feast celebrated on Jan. 6 or (in the U.S.) a Sunday betw. Jan. 2 and 8. In the East the dominant festal theme has been that of the baptism of Jesus; in the West, that of the adoration of the Magi. This celebration has various levels of meaning as a consequence of the feast's complex history. The word epiphany (sometimes theophany), signifying a manifestation of divinity, was used of the benevolent appearances of God as recorded in both Old and New Testaments. St. Paul uses the term in reference to both first and second comings of Christ. The term sometimes signifies a miraculous manifestation of divine power, and later was also applied to events of great significance in the life of royalty. There is evidence that a feast of the baptism of Christ was celebrated by certain Gnostics in Alexandria in the 3d cent., and a little later by orthodox Christians of that city. The feast was probably introduced to take the place of an Egyptian celebration of the birth of light at the winter solstice and/or the renewal of the Nile's waters. In the East the feast has had four themes: the birth of Christ, the baptism of Christ, the adoration of the Magi, and the miracle of Cana. From the second half of the 4th cent. the feast was observed at Rome, and about the same time the East began to celebrate the Western Christmas feast of Dec. 25. As the East adopted the Christmas celebration, its Epiphany feast became more and more the solemn commemoration of Christ's baptism in the Jordan. The Eastern custom of blessing the water and performing baptisms on this day emphasizes Jan. 6 as a baptismal feast. In the West the emphasis of the feast shifted from Augustine's concept of it as the manifestation of Christ to the gentiles to the medieval celebration of the feast of the three kings, since it was supposed that the Magi were kings and three in number. The vigil and octave of the Epiphany were abolished in 1956, and the former octave day became the Commemoration of the Baptism of Our Lord in the Western Church. The new calendar and Missal of 1969 changed the Feast of the Baptism to the first Sunday after Epiphany, and where the Epiphany itself is not observed as a holy day of obligation (a status the day enjoys according to the general law [CIC c. 1247.1] of the RC Church), it is celebrated on the first Sunday after the octave of Christmas, i.e., the Sunday that falls between Jan. 2 and Jan. 8, inclusive. In the U.S. the feast is not observed as a holy day of obligation, hence is to be celebrated on the Sunday after the Solemnity of Mary, Mother of God. BIBLIOGRAPHY: A. Strittmatter, "Christmas and the Epiphany: Origins and Antecedents," *Thought* 17 (1942) 600–626; C. F. Allison and W. H. Kelber, *Epiphany* (pa. 1975).

[N. KOLLAR]

EPISCOPACY, a term referring to the office of bishop (Gr., *episcopos*), i.e., the office itself or period of tenure in it (episcopate); a body of bps. in a Church or geographical region; or that form of *polity according to which the Church is governed by episcopal authority. In the last sense episcopacy is in opposition to both the presbyterian and congregational forms of polity. *HISTORIC EPISCOPATE.

EPISCOPAL CEREMONY AND VESTURE. The Roman liturgy in its fullest form is seen in papal ceremonies and in episcopal ceremonies when the bishop presides in his cathedral with pontificals (episcopal vestments and insignia). In general, pontificals are an expression of the bishop's pastoral office and authority. The use of pontificals has at times been extended to non-episcopal prelates (e.g., prothonotaries apostolic) but is now reserved to bishops or to prelates with jurisdiciton. Episcopal ceremonies were previously regulated by the *Caeremoniale Episcoporum* of Clement VIII (1600), were much simplified in 1968, and are contained in the *Pontificale Romanum,* also extensively revised since Vatican II in favor of greater simplicity. Apart from the Mass, the most important episcopal ceremonies are the sacraments of confirmation (at which priests may preside in certain circumstances) and of orders or ordination and special blessings (especially of oils, churches, altars, and chalices).

Items of most importance are the following. The *throne* is a chair on a dais, often with a canopy, from which the bishop presides; the throne in his cathedral is termed the *cathedra* and the faldstool is a folding chair or portable throne used when the bp. is outside the cathedral or not seated on the throne. The miter is a hat made of two flat pieces of similar size coming to a point and joined at the bottom by a circle setting on the bishop's head, with two flaps called "fanons" suspended from the back; the *zuchetto* or skullcap is generally worn under it. The crozier (crosier) or shepherd's staff, dating at least to the 6th cent., is a sign of pastoral office and of authority and jurisdiction. The ring is likewise a symbol of pastoral office, as is the pectoral cross, worn from a chain around the neck. Other items of vesture sometimes worn are the *mozzetta,* a shoulder cape; the *mantelleta,* a cape with openings for the arms; and the *cappa magna,* a large shoulder cape with hood and train.

Now optional are buskins (silk stockings) and sandals; the rochet, a linen tunic, basically a short alb; the morse, an ornamental clasp; the dalmatic, the deacon's vestment, worn under the bishop's chasuble. Now abolished are the *bugia,* a candlestick placed or held near the book from which the bishop is reading; the tunic, the subdeacon's vestment formerly worn under the bishop's other vestments; the gremial, a veil or apron placed over the bishop's knees when seated. Except for his wearing pontificals, the bishop's celebration of Mass is little different from another, although the ceremonies were formerly more elaborate. Perhaps the most obvious remaining difference is that the bishop gives a blessing with three signs of the cross rather than only one.

[J. DALLEN]

EPISCOPAL CHURCH, an alternate, official title for the *Protestant Episcopal Church, approved by the *General Convention of the Church in 1967.

EPISCOPAL CHURCH IN SCOTLAND, an autocephalous province of the *Anglican Communion with a membership of about 100,000, in 7 dioceses. The *Primus is one of the diocesan bps. elected by his fellows as the Church's presiding officer. Political tensions between the English and Scots were paralleled in ecclesiastical matters long before the Reformation. In the 16th cent. the Lutheran and Reformed elements in continental Protestantism found their way quickly into Scotland. Despite English countermeasures, by 1560 the reformed *Church of Scotland had been firmly grounded, Presbyterian in polity and Calvinist in doctrine. A century of bitter political and ecclesiastical contest followed, but the outcome of that tangled history was the establishment, in 1690, of the (Presbyterian) Church of Scotland as the national Church. The minority who chose to retain *episcopacy following the 1690 settlement continued a fragile and threadbare existence. Suspect because of their Jacobite sympathies, harassed by hostile political forces in England, disendowed, and often penalized for their continuing tradition of Catholic worship and doctrine, the tiny community survived the harsh tests of 18th-cent. Scottish history. In 1764 the Church produced its own liturgy, restoring the oblation and invocation (epiclesis) to the canon. In 1784 the first bishop-elect of the newly free Protestant Episcopal Church in the U.S., Samuel *Seabury, was consecrated by the Scottish bps. in Aberdeen, since it was then legally impossible for the C of E to give episcopal orders to other than its own clergy. In gratitude for the gift of the episcopate, the Episcopal Church of the U.S. agreed to base its eucharistic liturgy on that of the Scottish Church, thus strengthening a significant second liturgical tradition within Anglicanism. BIBLIOGRAPHY: S. Neill, *Anglicanism* (pa. 1958).

[S. F. BAYNE]

EPISCOPAL CONFERENCES, associations of bishops of a large area (generally of one country) holding periodical (generally annual) meetings to discuss matters of common concern and to exercise jointly their pastoral function. Such conferences, organized during the past cent. in nearly all sections of the Church, are one of the most important institutions through which the Catholic episcopacy carries out its mission. They have been sanctioned and regulated by Vatican Council II. In Vat II BpPastOff 36–38, the Council declares that since such conferences (which it distinguishes from the traditional provincial and plenary councils) have given abundant proof of their usefulness, it is highly desirable that they be organized in all parts of the world. The Council then indicates those who belong to these regional associations, and directs that the conferences are by their own statutes to set up permanent organs or commissions for more effective activity.

In regard to the right of the conferences to enact legislation binding throughout their region, the Council declares that decisions reached by conferences and approved subsequently by the Holy See bind juridically in those cases only that are prescribed by common law or determined by special mandate of the Holy See. It may be noted that one important area in which the conferences have been enabled to legislate is that of liturgy, the public worship of the Church. BIBLIOGRAPHY: É. Guerry, "Pastoral," *La Documentation catholique* 61, no. 1419 (1964).

[S. E. DONLON]

EPISCOPAL CROWN, see CROWN, EPISCOPAL.

EPISCOPAL SCHOOLS, see CATHEDRAL SCHOOLS.

EPISCOPAL STAFF, see STAFF, EPISCOPAL; and see CROZIER.

EPISCOPAL THRONE, see THRONE, EPISCOPAL.

EPISCOPALIAN, a member of the *Protestant Episcopal Church; also used inaccurately sometimes as a synonym for Anglican; one who holds that episcopacy is the true form of *polity in the Church.

EPISCOPALISM, a view of the Church that maintains that supreme teaching and governing authority is vested immediately in the body of bps., as successors of the Apostles. RC, Eastern, Anglican, and Old Catholic Churches are agreed in this teaching as it differs from Presbyterianism, Congregationalism, *collegialism, or *territorialism. Episcopalism historically, however, has also meant a denial of the personal primacy of the pope, maintaining that he is simply *primus inter pares* (see CONCILIARISM; FEBRONIANISM; GALLICANISM). By the dogmatic definition of papal infallibility of Vatican Council I the RC Church differs from other Churches in rejecting this sense of episcopalism; Vatican Council II explains RC teaching on the body of bps. in discussing their *collegiality (Vat II ConstCh 18–29).

[T. C. O'BRIEN]

EPISCOPATE (Gr. *episcopos,* bishop), the office itself or the tenure of a bp.; the body of bps. in a Church or region. The term, however, frequently refers to the office or order of bp. as an institution in the Church, esp. in the phrase, recurrent in ecumenical discussions, *historic episcopate. Many Churches, whether or not they recognize *apostolic succession or the office of bp. as a sacred order, maintain that the episcopate has from NT times been an essential of the Christian Church. Others, esp. in the traditions of Presbyterianism or Congregationalism, disagree. *LAMBETH QUADRILATERAL; *ECUMENISM; *CONSULTATION ON CHURCH UNION.

[T. C. O'BRIEN]

EPISCOPI VAGANTES (Lat., literally, wandering bishops), in the ancient and early medieval Church, a designation for bps. who were itinerant for various reasons, missionary or otherwise; in modern times, bps. who have secured, but through irregular or fraudulent means, valid episcopal orders, or, having obtained them regularly, have then broken off relations with the body that ordained them and have become more or less unaffiliated. While often assuming grandiose titles and jurisdictions, these bps., not being in communion with any historic Christian ecclesial body, usually have at most only a small, personal following. Two prominent modern *episcopi vagantes* who in turn were the source of a much larger number of other episcopal ordinations in the 20th cent. were Arnold Harris Mathew (d. 1919) and Joseph R. Vilatte (d. 1929). These two, together with Leon Chechemian, an alleged Armenian bp., consecrated a considerable number of other free bps. for such small groups as the American Catholic Church, the African Orthodox Church, the Liberal Catholic Church, and even organizations of theosophical tendencies. Eastern Orthodoxy does not recognize the validity of orders of the numerous prelates claiming affiliation with, or canonical descent from, Orthodox or other Eastern hierarchs. BIBLIOGRAPHY: H. R. T. Brandreth, *Episcopi Vagantes and the Anglican Church* (2d ed., 1961); P. Anson, *Bishops at Large* (1964).

[R. B. ENO]

EPISCOPIUS, SIMON (Bishop; 1583–1643), Arminian theologian. E., a native of Amsterdam, studied at the Univ. of Leiden under both J. *Arminius and F. *Gomarus and in 1612 succeeded the latter in the chair of theology. He was the principal spokesman for the *Remonstrants at the Synod of *Dort and protested against the prejudgment of their case. He was banished by the Synod and during the time of his exile composed (1622) a *Confessio,* a doctrinal statement of *Arminianism. After the death of the enemy of the Remonstrants, Prince Maurice of Nassau (1625), E. was able to return to Holland and in 1634 became rector and professor at the college of the Remonstrants in Amsterdam. In his *Institutiones theologicae* (4 v., 1650–51) E. did what Arminius had not done, namely, presented a systematic exposition and defense of Arminianism. Broad and tolerant in his views, E. minimized the importance of speculative dogmas and insisted rather on the practical aspect of Christianity, stressing man's responsibility to such an extent that he was accused of *Pelagianism. Like most Arminians at the time, he was also, probably without foundation, accused of *Socinianism. BIBLIOGRAPHY: Bihlmeyer-Tüchle 3:202; W. F. Dankbaar, RGG 2:531–532; H. C. Rogge, EncRelKnow 4:159–160.

[T. C. O'BRIEN]

EPISTEMOLOGY, from Gr. *epistēmē,* science, and *logos,* a study or rationale; thus an inquiry about knowledge. (1) In a classically strict acceptance of the term, epistemology is the study of the conditions that make scientific knowledge possible (see Aristotle, *Posterior Analytics,* on the conditions necessary for *epistēmē,* knowledge with certitude deriving from probative argumentation, i.e., demonstration). In this sense epistemology can be seen as the logic proper to each kind of science: the determination of its own principles, methodology, and limitations. Thus there is a distinct epistemology for theoretical and for moral philosophy; for philosophy and theology; for the physical sciences (philosophy of science). (2) Historically and by usage, however, epistemology has come to mean the study of the validity and truth value of knowledge, and of the grounds for its certitude. It is equivalent to a critique of knowledge, and so is also called criteriology (Gr. *krisō,* to judge); or gnosiology (Gr. *gnōsis,* knowledge). The development of modern philosophy, esp. from R. *Descartes on, transformed the meaning of philosophy so that it was pursued largely as a knowledge about knowing; reality and fact became the exclusive province of the physical sciences. Principal landmarks in the process were Descartes' own vindication of certitude by the clarity of pure ideas; *empiricism (see J. LOCKE; D. HUME), limiting justifiable knowledge to the sum of sense data; and above all the critical, transcendental method of I. *Kant, who limited all transphenomenal elements in judgment to a priori, mental categories. Since Kant, the impossibility of a valid metaphysics has simply been taken for granted by most philosophers; among exceptions with a realistic and ontological intent are *existentialism, *phenomenology, process philosophy (see A. N. WHITEHEAD); some forms of spiritualism and vitalism (see H. BERGSON; M. BLONDEL). Catholic, scholastic philosophy, because of the consequences for theology of philosophical agnosticism, empiricism, and subjectivism, has sought to develop an epistemology that would defend a moderate and metaphysical realism: No unanimity has developed on the nature of such an epistemology, its place in philosophy, or its method. Some of the epistemologies proposed have conceded a great deal to the Kantian critique (see TRANSCENDENTAL THOMISM). The philosophical thought of St. Thomas

Aquinas points up certain fundamentals about the epistemological problem. As a study about knowing, it is a reflective process, presupposing the experience of direct knowledge. That experience is not of a pure mental phenomenon; it is the experience of knowing something, not the experience simply of knowing. The rejection of the validity of knowledge presupposes that the object of knowing is the mental idea; this assumption of psychological immanentism creates the impossible dilemma of vindicating the representational fidelity or correspondence of idea to thing; it totally misses the meaning of abstraction and the intentionality of knowledge (ThAq ST 1a, 85.2). The act of knowing on which epistemology centers is the compositive act of judgment (expressible in a declarative sentence). Judgment is essentially the mind's assertion of its own conformity to what is known, to the real. But that does not mean the assertion of the compatibility of predicate with subject, as the compatibility, logically, of two terms; much less is it the attribution of the predicate ''existence'' to a subject (see ESSENCE AND EXISTENCE). ''The mind's composition is a sign of the identity of the things combined'' (*ibid*. 5 ad 3; see also 13.12 & ad 3; 14.14). In its composite act of judging, the mind refers itself to the total existent (signified as subject) known to be existing according to that partial aspect the mind grasps (signified as predicate). The existential reference of judgment is the very reason why there can be falsity. But this description of judgment opens the way for the reflective act that is unmistakably self-vindicating. That is the experience of being, not being as something, but of something as being (see *ibid*. 1a2ae, 94.2; 1a, 79.8). BIBLIOGRAPHY: L. Régis, *Epistemology* (tr. I. Byrne, 1959); ThAq ST (Lat-Eng; v. 31, ed. T. C. O'Brien) 195–201.

[T. C. O'BRIEN]

EPISTLE (Gr. *epistolē*), designation for the literary form of several NT writings. These are usually official communications of instruction or correction to a Church or a group of Churches, written by an Apostle or sent under his authority. Since the work of A. Deissmann, a distinction between the Epistle and the Letter has been accepted by most biblical scholars. According to this distinction, the Epistle is a doctrinal pronouncement, a kind of public manifesto; the Letter, more personal, concrete, addressed to a particular situation. The Pauline writings that are considered to be more in the form of Epistles in the strict sense are Rom, Eph, and the *Pastoral Letters; the other Pauline writings are regarded as Letters. Other Epistles are Heb, Jas, 1 and 2 Pet, 1 Jn, and Jude. The distinction is not applied in cut-and-dried fashion but does have bearing on biblical exegesis. In English versions of the Bible, the term Letter has been universally substituted in the title of these NT writings. In style the writings in question are an adaptation of ancient epistolary conventions, and thus consist in an opening formula of greeting, an expression of thanks, the message, and a concluding greeting. BIBLIOGRAPHY: A. Deissmann, *Bible Studies* (1907) 3–59; C. L. Mitton, *Formation of the Pauline Corpus of Letters* (1955); J. A. Fitzmyer, JBC 2:223–226.

[T. C. O'BRIEN]

EPISTLE SONATA, *Sonata da Chiesa,* the church sonata frequently heard in church ceremonies during the 17th and 18th cent., before or after the reading of the Epistle. It consisted usually of four movements that were abstract and serious in mood, a slow introduction, a quick fugal movement, a slow expressive movement and another quick movement. The Epistle Sonata was a feature of the service at the Salzburg Cathedral. Mozart composed several for organ and two violins; sometimes he added other stringed or wind instruments.

[L. MCBRIDE]

EPISTOLA APOSTOLORUM, an apocryphal work, dating from the mid-2d cent., purporting to be a letter from all the Apostles to the whole Church. The original Greek text, written probably in Asia Minor or Egypt, is lost. There is a complete Ethiopic translation. The contents claim to be revelations from Christ to his disciples from the Resurrection to the Ascension. In addition to the NT, the sources for the work are the *Apocalypse of Peter,* the *Epistle of Barnabas,* and the *Shepherd of Hermas.* BIBLIOGRAPHY: M. R. James, *Apocryphal New Testament* (1945) 485–503; Quasten 1:150–153.

[H. DRESSLER]

EPISTOLAE OBSCURORUM VIRORUM (Letters of Obscure Men), a satire against the enemies of J. *Reuchlin. The title plays on that of the *Epistolae clarorum virorum* (Letters of Renowned Men), a short collection of testimonials published by Reuchlin in his own behalf (1514). The *Epistolae obscurorum virorum* contains more than 100 letters; the first series, by Johannes Crotus Rubianus (1486–1540), appeared in 1515; the second series, by Ulrich von Hutten (1488–1523), in 1517. The letters are written to Ortwin *Gratius, humanist of the anti-Reuchlin party, purporting to be from scholastics and clerics, for whom fantastic names were invented. Parodying a barbarous scholastic Latin, the biting shafts of the letters made the personal lives and intellectual aridity of churchmen who were resisting the *New Learning the laughingstock of the humanist world. The *Epistolae* were a sign of a cultural environment favorable to the Reformation. BIBLIOGRAPHY: F. G. Stokes, *Epistolae obscurorum virorum: The Latin Text with an English Rendering, Notes and Historical Introduction* (1909).

EPITAPHION (Gr. for tomb; Sl., *plaschenitsa*), in Byzantine liturgy a term having two meanings: (1) The bier decorated with flowers used in the Good Friday liturgy to represent the tomb of Christ. (2) The embroidered or painted shroud placed on the bier. There are two forms in current use: one showing only the body of the dead Christ; the other showing the body as well as the attendant figures of Mary, John, Joseph of Arimathea, Nicodemus, and the holy women. In Greek usage the icon of the body of Christ is actually removed from the cross on Good Friday and placed on top of the epitaphion to be carried in solemn procession through the church and is later put aside so as to leave only the embroidered shroud to represent the deposition. The Slavs do not remove the icon but simply carry the embroidered epitaphion. For the veneration of the faithful, the epitaphion is placed under a domed canopy. After the solemn funeral of Christ on Good Friday, the Greeks carry the epitaphion to the altar where it remains the entire Easter season. The Slavs usually put it on the altar on Holy Saturday. The antimension and gospel book are placed on it and the liturgy is celebrated on top of it. The Catholic Melkites do not make great use of the epitaphion, but carry in procession a flower-decorated box or coffin in which is deposited the image of the crucified.

[A. J. JACOPIN]

EPITHALAMIUM, a marriage poem or song honoring bride and groom, and sung usually by a chorus at the wedding ceremony. Psalm 45 is a royal wedding song, believed by some to have been written for the marriage of Solomon, but by others to have purely mystical meaning. Sometimes composers of organ music have given the title to any wedding piece.

[L. MCBRIDE]

EPITOME, an abridgment or concise summary, a term used as a title for many collections of both Roman law and medieval canon law (e.g., *Epitome Hadriani*; *Epitome Juliani*). The *Epitomes* or *Epitomae* is part of the *Pseudo-Clementinae,* early Christian writings falsely ascribed to Clement of Rome. An equivalent medieval term is *micrologus.*

[T. C. O'BRIEN]

EPITRACHELION (Gr. for "on the neck"; Sl., *epitrachie*) the priestly *stole in the Byzantine Church. It is composed of a long band of silk or brocade about five inches wide and passed around the neck and falling in front in two pendants almost to the floor. At intervals, buttons or sewing hold the two pendants together. The epitrachelion may be ornamented with embroidery and fringes; usually six crosses are spaced in pairs on the front with a small one at the neck. It has preserved a longer appearance than the more usual Roman stole. The monastic form of the epitrachelion is a single broad band passed over the head and hanging in one piece in front, somewhat like a scapular. The Byzantine epitrachelion is the model for the stole in the Coptic, Ethiopian, Syrian, and Armenian Churches. The

stole is worn whenever the priest fulfills a liturgical function. BIBLIOGRAPHY: *Handbook of American Orthodoxy* (1972) 182–183.

[A. J. JACOPIN]

EPPING, JOSEPH (1835–94), German Jesuit, mathematician and astronomer. He became a Jesuit in 1859 and during most of his life taught in Holland at the seminaries of Blijenbeck and Exaeten. He became known esp. for his work on Babylonian astronomy, collaborating with the Assyriologist J. N. *Strassmaier. They published numerous studies, including a volume of *Stimmen aus Maria-Laach* (v. 21, 1881) and contributions to the *Zeitschrift für Assyriologie*. E. also wrote *Astronomisches aus Babylon* (1889).

[T. EARLY]

EPPINGER, ELIZABETH (1814–67), religious foundress. E. was born in Niederbronn, Alsace; she received little formal education and was burdened with poor health. By the age of 32 because of visions and revelations she was called the "Ecstatic of Niederbronn," and was sought out as a counselor. In 1848 E. made private vows on the advice of her confessor Rev. Jean Reichard and the following year, with his assistance, founded the Congregation of the Daughters of the Divine Redeemer. She became Mother Marie Alphonse and was first mother general. The community was devoted to the care of the sick poor in their homes and to other poor people. Later its apostolates included the education of youth, the care of orphans, the aged, and the infirm in institutions. The community prospered under E.'s direction, spread to Germany, Austria, Hungary, and the United States. Her beatification process has been begun.

[M. B. MONAGHAN]

EPSTEIN, JACOB (1880–1959), British sculptor, illustrator, water colorist. He was born in New York City, where he studied at the Art Student League under Geo. Grey Barnard. E. worked in Paris (1902–06), then went to England, becoming a British citizen. His early innovative style scandalized many and some works were destroyed. E. met Brancusi and Modigliani in Paris in 1912. Returning to England, E. did a statue of *Christ* (1917) and other religious subjects of great power: *Visitation* (1926), *Madonna and Child* (1927), *Genesis* (1931), *Behold the Man* (1935). Whereas his work in stone is strongly blocked, E.'s bronze surfaces are dramatically textured. His famous *Social Consciousness* (Philadelphia Museum of Art) attains a classical serenity within a stark Gothic linearism in a work of great emotional significance. E. executed numerous probing portraits (*Conrad, Einstein, Robeson*). Having overcome unbelievably adverse criticism, E. raised the sights of British sculpture and so made possible a Henry Moore and a Barbara Hepworth. BIBLIOGRAPHY: J. Epstein, *Let There Be Sculpture* (1940).

[M. J. DALY]

EPTADIUS, ST. (fl. early 6th cent.), monastic founder. Sketchy details of his life indicate that he was from the region of the present-day department of Nièvre, ordained priest by St. Flavian of Autun because of a reputation for sanctity and works of mercy. Clovis wished to make E. bp. of Auxerre, but the saint went into hiding until Clovis relented. A small community gathered around E. and out of it developed the monastery known later—according to a 9th-cent. charter from Charles the Bald—as St. Eptadius of Cervon.

[T. C. O'BRIEN]

EPWORTH LEAGUE, a Methodist youth organization. Various organizations for youth existed in the Methodist Episcopal Church when, May 14–15, 1889, their representatives met in Cleveland to form a single organization, the Epworth League, its name commemorating the birthplace of John Wesley. In 1890 it published its official periodical, the *Epworth Herald,* and in 1892 the *General Conference approved the new organization. It had four departments: Spiritual Work; Mercy and Help; World Evangelism; and Literary and Social. The members pledged to ''take some active part'' in the Church. It served as a link between the Sunday school and the adult church and as a training ground for church leadership. It was also adopted by the Methodist Episcopal Church, South, and the Methodist Church of Canada. In 1944 the Epworth League was succeeded by the Methodist Youth Fellowship. BIBLIOGRAPHY: HistAmMeth 2:645–646.

[F. E. MASER]

EQUAL JOB OPPORTUNITY. Discrimination resulting in unequal job opportunities exists when decisions relating to hiring or advancement are based on any factors other than the objective facts of the employers' needs and the employees' qualifications.

While there has been considerable improvement since the adoption of the Fair Employment Practices in the 1960s, there continues to exist a great deal of inequality in employment. The major thrust of discrimination originates in racial distinctions, but there also exist inequalities based on age, sex, ethnic origin, and educational level. Fair Employment Practices have greatly aided in the solution to the problem, but there is a clear need for a more vigorous prosecution of these laws, for stronger laws, and aggressive watchdog commissions. In many cases, violations go unnoticed, and institutionalized or informal means of discrimination go unchecked. An active application of the existing laws would not entirely solve the problem, although the absence of racial discrimination does necessarily result in active recruitment among minority groups.

Many employers demand qualifications beyond the actual requirements of the task. The aptitude tests used by employers can also be unfair in not actually testing the aptitudes but rather testing familiarity with terms and concepts related to social class. Some labor unions have been guilty of unequal practices while others have adopted a strict policy of equal employment, but the role of the unions is less important than that of management since only one-third of nonagricultural employees are union members.

Equal job opportunity for all requires strong and active Fair Employment Practices' commissions, affirmed by employers in adopting internal and external policies of equal opportunity, active recruitment, and periodic evaluation of progress toward the desired objective. BIBLIOGRAPHY: A. Ferman, *The Negro and Equal Employment Opportunities* (1968); P. H. Norgren, *Toward Fair Employment* (1964). G. M. Von Furstenberg et al., *Patterns of Racial Discrimination* (2 v., 1974).

[N. L. CHOATE]

EQUALITY, as a moral concept, the value and measure of rightness that *justice respects. This virtue, in its various forms, regards what belongs to another person, i.e., an action or object that precisely matches the other's right to it. The equality may be arithmetic—quantitatively determinable, as in a purchase; or geometric—proportionate to the other person's status, needs, or merits. Because justice observes equality as its norm and measure, in any relationship between persons that justice regulates an equality proper to the interaction characterizes the condition existing between the two parties; the recipient is to be respected impartially and exactly. Issues of justice arise with respect to natural equality, political equality, and social equality, accordingly as the rights involved derive from nature, positive law, or the structure of a society. A theistic moral philosophy presupposes that all men are equal in terms or rights connected with their God-given common nature and dignity as persons. What founds and constitutes political and social equality, however, has depended historically on political and social systems, and their underlying theories. The ''all men are created equal'' of the American Declaration of Independence is an idea deriving from the social theory of J. J. *Rousseau, proposing that absolute social equality is the ideal and natural condition of man. The American system intends to achieve social equality through political equality, i.e., equality before the law, excluding discrimination and special privilege. The social quality intended is not that of the classless society, but one in which every citizen can receive what belongs to him in virtue of his being a citizen, and in proportion to his abilities, efforts, and needs. This is equality of opportunity; it cannot guarantee equality of results. Political equality, founded in positive law, is ideally a guarantee of civil rights that excludes discrimination based on wealth, race, sex, age, religion or any other privilege. Violations of political equality can be wrong morally on two accounts. Since just, positive laws are a norm for determining moral good or evil, discrimination can be morally wrong because it is contrary to a just law. Whether it is a moral evil consisting in violation of a specific form of justice is a further issue. Civil rights are guaranteed by civil law; whether a particular civil right is consonant with natural rights, civil law neither establishes nor guarantees. A philosophy or theology of justice has to provide guidance for moral judgment regarding such issues as the right to employment, to equal housing, the rights of women to abortion, the rights of homosexuals. In determining the basis for such rights a distinction must be made: in the American political system the sole appeal is to the principle of equality before the law; that is not equivalent or tantamount to establishing that an alleged right has its basis in moral justice.

[T. C. O'BRIEN]

EQUALITY IN THE CHURCH. "If by the will of Christ some are made teachers, dispensers of mysteries, and shepherds on behalf of others, yet all share a true equality with regard to the dignity and the activity common to all the faithful for the building up of the body of Christ" (VatII ConstCh 32). The equality in dignity this conciliar ideal affirms is the new being in which all share from their rebirth in Christ, the same filial grace and vocation to holiness, and share together as a community in one faith, one hope of salvation, one undivided charity (ibid.). On this ground inequality based on race, nationality, social condition, or sex is excluded (ibid.; see Gal 3.28; Col 3.11). The activity in which all equally share is the apostolate as inherent in the Christian's vocation (see VatII ApostLaity 2). There is diversity in the way that activity is carried out, but the diversity of offices has a common basis, the baptism by which all share in the priestly, prophetic, and kingly identity from Christ; the exercise of this identity has a unity of purpose, and it has an ideal characteristic, not of lordship but of service (VatII ConstCh 32). Specifically this equality in service is divided into the hierarchic offices imposed by holy orders, to teach, to sanctify, and to govern; and the active cooperation of those such offices serve, both to strengthen the ministry of their ordained pastors and to carry out by their own services and charisms the purposes of the hierarchic offices (see LAY APOSTOLATE). These are the ideals inherent in the very nature of the Church and conform to the scriptural imaging of that nature. The conciliar statement and explicitation of this ideal is a step forward from both a juridic ecclesiology (in which the Church's formal nature was identified with the hierarchy) and from a juridic exercise of authority that was often enough autocratic. Signs of a change in the actual realization of the ideal are: the synod of bishops; priests' senates; parish councils; renewal of religious life on more participatory lines; the consultation of the laity by the hierarchy; the draft of the reformulation of the law of the Church; and in general an atmosphere of marked cooperative service in the carrying out of the life and activity of the Church. Yet the change does not altogether match the proposed ideals. Voices continue to be raised in the Church asking, for example, for a more com-

plete acceptance of the principle of due process in any sort of juridic procedure. There is the vexed issue of the ordination of women to the priesthood, rejected in a document (issued Jan. 27, 1977) of the Congregation for the Doctrine of the Faith with explicit endorsement of Paul VI. The document claims that denial of ordination does not discriminate against women, because equality in the Church does not mean identity of function; and because sacred ordination is in no case a right. As the Church is a living community of believers there is always tension between the ideal and its achievement. The clear perception and affirmation of the ideal, however, is a positive and continuing support in the life process of the pilgrim Church to the expression of its ideals.

[T. C. O'BRIEN]

EQUIPROBABILISM, an effort to keep a golden mean between the moral systems of *probabiliorism on the one hand, with its severity esp. in the climate of Jansenist rigorism, and on the other, *probabilism, esp. in its lax exaggerations. The name most associated with this system, although not its originator, is St. Alphonsus Liguori who, as an equitable and well-equipped lawyer, had an aversion to an excessive polarization of either law or liberty. When the two are confronted, the fundamental *reflex principle applied by equiprobabilism is: possession has the benefit of the doubt. This means that when opposing opinions are roughly equal in probability, it is morally permissible to take the opinion in favor of liberty when the doubt is on the existence of the law, but the law continues to bind when the only doubt is about its cessation. BIBLIOGRAPHY: J. F. Connell, NCE 5:502.

[C. WILLIAMS]

EQUITY, a term relating to *justice and having several senses in moral theology (equity in English common law refers to a system of laws based on decisions made in equity, rather than on the basis of statute law). (1) St. Thomas Aquinas uses *aequitas* to translate the Gr. *epieikeia* (ThAq ST 2a2ae, 120.1); following Aristotle (Ethics V, 10.1138a2), he sees this as a higher form of justice: it regards the equitable, the truly just, where observing the written law would defeat the very purpose of the law, service to the public, common good (ThAq ST 2a2ae, 120.1). The use of equity as synonymous with *epieikeia* continued in later moral theology but with a different meaning: it is the presumed benign intent of the law-giver, allowing exception where observance of the law would be a hardship. (2) Equity is used also to mean moderation in asserting personal rights and pertains to the virtue of cordiality or friendliness (ibid. 80; 114). (3) Equity can also be taken as a rule or norm that justice observes. Roman law recognized equity as a guide for judges to moderate the hardships written law could work in some particular case (ibid. 60.5 ad2);

equity also can be the equivalent of *equality, the balance or standard that all forms of justice respect.

[T. C. O'BRIEN]

EQUIVOCATION (Lat. *equivocatio: equi,* equal, and *vocare,* to call; Gr. *homōnumia),* double-meaning, or the use of the same term for different concepts, which may be for logic the occasion of fallacy and for moral science, of misleading another.

(1) Ideas are rendered into images and in the communication of discourse are ordinarily spoken out or written down. In fact there are other and more gestured forms of rational dialogue also open to error and deception, but it will be convenient here to keep to speech and script. Fallacies may arise when one and the same term is used with different meanings, e.g., ''charity,'' or with different implications, or as when one and the same sentence is variously accented. Talking at cross-purposes abounds in human conversation, and it is the function of preliminary definition to rule this out. To be more technical, it may be said that every single argument that draws a conclusion from four key terms in its two premises, or that uses the middle term in its two premises, or that uses the middle term with a double meaning, falls into the fallacy of equivocation.

However, some concepts, and these the best, are too rich and supple to be worked with as plain and fixed meanings, thus ''beauty'' when applied to a racehorse and a Haydn finale, or the values we recognize in human life and praise in God. They are said to be equivocal by design, *aequivoca a consilio,* or analogical, for though they are applied to objects that simply speaking are different, there is yet some likeness between them which allows them to be named in common. The likeness is not purely verbal, as with *aequivoca a casu* which just chance to have a common name. Notice that here equivocation is possible only with terms, not ideas. A benign ambiguity with ideas, however, allows of metaphor and its sublimation into *analogy by philosophical science. Natural philosophers contrast ''equivocal causes,'' which are of a nature higher than that of their effects and are principal causes, with ''univocal causes'' which are of the same nature and amount only to instrumental and partial causal antecedents.

(2) Equivocation enters into moral science with the question of truthfulness, a social virtue that is breached by talking or acting a *lie. This in its fullness carries the intention to deceive, but is present whenever it can mislead another about something he has a right to know. However, there are many circumstances in which an interlocutor may have no right to what is in one's mind—indeed rights, including his own, may be infringed if one divulges it. Both common decency and polite society recommend some verbal economy in hiding the truth from unjust intrusion, and the casuists allowed some degree of equivocation, or amphibology as it is called. Their distinctions were somewhat over-delicate to an allegedly more blunt Anglo-Saxonism, as in Charles Kingsley, but in truth all cultures have their own characteristic reticences, and indeed evasions, which are not lies to anybody of good sense. *LYING; *MENTAL RESERVATION.

[T. GILBY]

ERA, CHRISTIAN, that period of time from the birth of Christ. As a means of reckoning for chronological purposes, it was first used by *Dionysius Exiguus in the 6th cent. and gradually spread throughout Europe. It was in common use by the beginning of the 8th century. *CALENDAR.

[T. M. MCFADDEN]

ERAS, HISTORICAL, see CALENDAR.

ERASMUS, DESIDERIUS (1467–1536), greatest of the humanists through his personal and literary influence. Desiderius is a latinization of Erasmus, the name he adopted as the Greek form of Herasmus, his baptismal name. Born at Rotterdam (thus the designation Roterodammensis or Roterodamus), he was probably the son of a priest; during his studies at Deventer with the *Brethren of the Common Life his humanistic interests began. He entered a monastery of Augustinian Canons Regular at Steyn near Gouda in 1486, and was ordained in 1492. Shortly thereafter he received permission to leave the monastery, and he never returned; a papal brief of 1517 terminated his canonical affiliation. At Paris in 1495, repelled by scholastic theology, he cultivated literary interests. He visited England in 1499, where J. *Colet directed his interests to Greek and the New Testament. He returned to France in 1500, made a second visit to England, 1505–06, then spent 3 years, 1506–09, in Italy. While in England again, 1511–1514, he was Lady Margaret Professor of Greek and theology at Cambridge and completed his *Novum instrumentum,* the first published edition (Basel, 1516) of the Greek NT, with Latin translation and notes. The edition was the basis for many vernacular translations of the time and a landmark in scriptural studies. From 1514 to 1521, E. moved from place to place in Belgium and Holland, then settled at Basel with the printer John Froben, until the city accepted the Reformation in 1529. His last residence was at Freiburg, but he died at Basel while on a visit.

Erasmus is the very epitome of the strength and weakness of Renaissance humanism as an active force in the affairs of men. His intellectual inspiration is Roman rather than Greek; among the Fathers his guide was not the philosophical and mystical Augustine but the literary and urbane Jerome (he edited the works of Jerome, 9 v., 1516–18, as well as those of Augustine and other Fathers). E. typifies the fatal indifference and hostility of the entire humanist movement to the speculative or scientific imagination. He ridiculed concern with natural science as a distraction from the humane wisdom of life. From the Florentine Platonists he borrowed, not their metaphysics but their practical program, a universal and tolerant ethical religion, stripped of theological sophistication and directed solely to conduct. The guiding idea throughout all his subtle but mordant attacks on the religious institutionalism around him is that simple moral teaching is the true lesson of the Gospels and the genuine "philosophy of Christ." He prided himself on being the Christianizer of the Renaissance and the humanizer of Christianity.

Erasmus was distressed by the Church's elaborate theological and sacramental structure, and in his *Enchiridion militis christiani* (1503; tr. J. P. Dolan, *Handbook of the Militant Christian*, 1962) and other works he advocated a simple, humane, and undogmatic Christian religion. He appeals frequently to the Sermon on the Mount and insists that Christ called for a life, not a debate; a transformation rather than a process of reasoning. He could not see the human function of external rites and ceremonies, but he reserved his bitterest barbs for the monastic ideal, its essence and not merely its perversions and corruptions (esp. in his *Encomium Moriae* 1509; tr. H. H. Hudson, *Praise of Folly*, 1941). His exalted conception of human dignity and worth, man's power and freedom, lacked the philosophical acumen to give it systematic grounding. His most pretentious theoretical essay, a defense of man's freedom under grace, against Luther, reveals a lack of speculative power *(Diatribe de libero arbitrio,* 1524; Luther's reply is the *De servo arbitrio,* 1525; both works in E. F. Winter, tr., *Discourse on Free Will,* 1961). E.'s writings directly contributed to the religious revolution. He himself at first cautiously welcomed the reform attempts of Luther, but he came to be repelled by what he regarded as excesses and intemperate language. Retiring from the battle between defenders of RC orthodoxy and the Protestant Reformers, E. was assailed by both. He continued to employ his rhetorical skill in behalf of a tolerant, humane, cosmopolitan culture. He looked backward, to the Bible and classical antiquity; his spiritual legacy is that of a witty, charming, mediating conservative; but his own program was too vague to achieve the peace and unity he sought. BIBLIOGRAPHY: P. Smith, *Erasmus: A Study of His Life, Ideals, and Place in History* (1923); J. Huizinga, *Erasmus* (1924); M. P. Gilmore, NCE 5:508–511, with bibliog.

[J. P. REID]

ERASTIANISM, control of ecclesiastical affairs by the State. Deriving from Thomas Erastus (1524–83), the term is often applied to situations unrelated to his views. Opposing the introduction of Genevan theocratic discipline, Erastus, a Swiss professor at Heidelberg (1558–80), taught that in a Christian state all coercive power, even excommunication, belongs to civil magistrates. More a type of Church-State relationship than a precise system, Erastianism in many variations has existed in Lutheran states, England, and elsewhere. *Reformed Churches sought to subordinate the State to the Church, but in practice Reformed countries often were Erastian. Thomas Hobbes, in *Leviathan* (1651), developed an Erastian system in an extreme form. It should be noted that all Churches have tried to exclude certain areas from State domination, but under any Erastian system such distinctions are difficult to maintain. BIBLIOGRAPHY: J. N. Figgis, "Erastus and the Erastians," *Divine Right of Kings* (1914); M. Dunster, *Erastus* (1975).

[N. H. MARING]

ERCHEMPERT, a 9th cent. monk of Monte Cassino; after the abbey's destruction in 884 he lived at Capua. He is the author of a *Historia Langobardorum Beneventanorum,* covering the period 774–889 (MGHSrerLang 234–264); a metrical *Martyrologium* (ed. of A. M. Amelli in *Spicilegium Casinense* 1 [1893]); and of other works not now extant. BIBLIOGRAPHY: L. Spätling, EncCatt 5:477–478; Manitius 1:709ff.

[W. A. JURGENS]

ERCONWALD OF LONDON, ST. (d. *c.*693), Anglo-Saxon bp. and monastic founder. He converted his patrimony into abbeys, over one of which he presided as abbot, and the other, for women, was put under the direction of his sister, St. Ethelburga. Consecrated bp. of London by St. Theodore (675), he worked to reconcile Theodore with St. Wilfrid. He retired and died at Barking, and his relics were enshrined at St. Paul's, London. BIBLIOGRAPHY: Bede, *Ecclesiastical History,* 4.6:11; Butler 2:299–300.

[J. DRUSE]

ERDESWICKE, SAMPSON (d. 1603), English *recusant, author of a *Survey of Staffordshire,* squire of the family estate at Shandon.

ERDINGTON, ABBEY OF, former Benedictine abbey in the diocese of Birmingham, England, founded (1876) as a priory of the German abbey of Beuron. The small community from Germany—four priests and one lay brother—settled in the rectory provided by D. H. Haigh, who had built the church. Construction was soon undertaken and a first wing occupied in 1880. English vocations were few, and it was not until 1896 that Erdington became an abbey, dedicated to St. Thomas of Canterbury. Again, before World War I, the abbot of Beuron sent additional monks. Because the British government decided to intern German aliens, most of the monks had to leave Erdington. As a compromise, the abp. of Birmingham replaced the superior with one of English birth until 1919. A decision was made to sell Erdington as soon as some religious community would be interested in acquiring it. Twenty-eight monks returned to Germany, the abbot and eleven others staying. With permission from Rome the Redemptorists bought Erdington in 1922. Dom Höckelmann restored St. Martin's Abbey in Württemberg, Germany, to which the Erdington community was transferred. The English professed monks joined various English and Belgian abbeys. BIBLIOGRAPHY: H. Dauphin, DHGE 15:688–689.

[S. A. HEENEY]

ERECHTHEUM (ERECHTHEON), an Ionic temple on the Acropolis hill at Athens (begun in 421 B.C., continued in 409 B.C.), built of Pentelic marble in a complicated plan. It was constructed on two levels to fit the topography of the site, has three diverse porticoes, and the central doorway of the N porch offers the finest examples of Greek design. The renowned Caryatid Porch or Porch of the Maidens on the S side is named for its six ideally noble, serene statues supporting the roof.

[M. J. DALY]

EREMITANI, CHURCH OF THE, church built in Padua for the Augustinians in the 13th century. After devastating bombing (1944) there remain only fragments of the glorious frescoes of the legend of St. James painted 1448–55 by the master A. Mantegna, whose historically authentic classical references, bold perspective and solidly modeled forms raised N Italian painting to an excellence equal to the greatest art of 15th-cent. Florence. BIBLIOGRAPHY: A. Mantegna, *Mantegna* . . . (ed. E. Tietze-Conrat, 1955).

[M. J. DALY]

ERFURT, CATHEDRAL OF. The cathedral, founded in 752 by St. Boniface in the chief city of Thuringia—a center of Gothic panel painting—is largely late Gothic, with notable 12th-cent. candlestick, an impressive Gothic altarpiece, and stained glass windows. The Expressionistic quality of German Gothic Sculpture is seen in the *Foolish Virgins* of the NW portal (*c.* 1360):

[M. J. DALY]

ERFURT, UNIVERSITY OF, a medieval university, the oldest of its kind in Germany, and a center of Franciscan scholarship. Originating supposedly in the four 13th-cent. collegiate schools or *universitas studentium* in the archdiocese of Mainz, the univ., through the Erfurt schools, in 1362 first presented its petition to Urban V for recognition as a *studium generale,* although it is thought to have had only two faculties—civil law and theology—of the four required. Despite Charles IV's support, the petition went unheeded until the Avignon antipope, Clement VII, in 1379 issued a bull of foundation, authorizing the faculties of grammar, logic, philosophy, and medicine, but not canon law, and named the abp. of Mainz as chancellor. Urban VI in 1387 issued a second bull with privileges similar to those of Paris. By the 15th cent. Erfurt had a larger enrollment than any other German university, a fact attributed in part to the fame of its school of jurisprudence, to its participation in the nominalist and realist controversies, and to the presence of the forerunner of the Reformation, John of Wesel. Indeed, the university's willingness to examine and discuss novel theories led to its sobriquet, *novorum omnium portus.* One of its later students was Martin Luther. After the Reformation, although it granted no degrees, Erfurt continued as a Catholic univ. until Gustavus Adolphus II of Sweden (1631–49) established the faculty of Protestant theology. With the annexation of Erfurt to Prussia in 1816, the univ. was suppressed. BIBLIOGRAPHY: H. Rashdall, *Universities of Europe in the Middle Ages* (ed. F. M. Powicke and A. B. Emden (3 v., 1936).

[M. B. MURPHY]

ERHARD, ST. (fl. 7th cent.), probably a monk who became a regional bp. and the founder of seven monasteries. E. was buried in the monastery of Niedermünster. Pope Leo IX exhumed his relics Oct. 8, 1052. BIBLIOGRAPHY: R. Bauerreiss, LTK 3:988–89; H. Dressler NCE 5:513–14.

[H. DRESSLER]

ERIC IX JEDVARDSSON, KING OF SWEDEN, ST. (d. *c.* 1160). According to legend, he was a good king who worked unceasingly for the welfare of his people but was slain by a Dane in a dispute over his right to the throne. Though he was never formally canonized, numerous paintings, sculptures, and hymns commemorate him as well as coins bearing his image. The cathedral of Uppsala supposedly houses his relics.

[F. G. O'BRIEN]

ERKEMBODO, ST. (d. 734), Benedictine, fourth abbot of Saint Bertin. E. acquired a reputation as a liturgist. He maintained amicable relations with Carolingian rulers Chilperic II and Theodoric IV. In 720 he became the fifth bp. of Thérouanne. He was buried in the church of Saint-Omer and is the object of a cult which still continues. BIBLIOGRAPHY: L. van der Essen, *Étude critique . . . des saints mérovingiens de l'ancienne Belgique* (1907).

[B. F. SCHERER]

ERLANGEN SCHOOL, the 19th-cent. theological movement initiated at the Univ. of Erlangen in Germany. The attempt to combine both *Pietism and Lutheran orthodoxy with elements of F. *Schleiermacher's thought was its direct concern. An emphasis on biblical interpretation that developed an early theory of *salvation history, however, is the principal lasting importance of the Erlangen School. BIBLIOGRAPHY: D. Ritschl, NCE 5:515–516.

[T. C. O'BRIEN]

ERLEMBALD, ST. (d. 1075), an 11th-cent. reform leader in Milan. A member of the aristocratic Cotta family, E. led the reform party against the antireform forces of Abp. Guido Velate. He was killed in a street battle against the antireform forces; in 1095 his relics were enshrined in the Church of St. Dionysius. BIBLIOGRAPHY: PL 143:1485–1504; MGHS 20:48; A. Rimoldi, BiblSanct 5:3–6.

[W. A. JURGENS]

ERMELINDE, ST. (d. end of 6th cent.). Apart from legend, it is recorded that E. lived as an ascetic and hermit at Beauvechain, then at Meldaert, Belgium, where she is buried in a chapel built in her honor. A legendary vita has her connected with the Carolingian Pepin I, a member of a rich family of Brabant, and foundress of a monastery at Chaumont. BIBLIOGRAPHY: *The Book of Saints* (comp. Benedictine Monks of St. Augustine's Abbey, Ramsgate, 1966); M. De Somer, BiblSanct 5:6–7.

[M. E. DUFFY]

ERMENBURGA, ST. (d. *c.*695) Anglo-Saxon queen and abbess. A Kentish princess, she was married to a Mercian prince. Her brothers were killed in a dynastic struggle and Egbert I of Kent gave her as compensation lands in Thanet. After her husband's death, she founded an abbey there, in which she was succeeded as abbess by her daughter, St. Mildred. BIBLIOGRAPHY: J. Stéphan, BiblSanct 5:32–33.

[J. DRUSE]

ERMENRICH OF PASSAU, (*c.*814–874), Benedictine, bp. of Passau. Sent to Bulgaria by Louis the German in 867, he tried to counteract the influence of SS. Cyril and Methodius. E. is perhaps to be identified with Ermenrich of Ellwangen, whose letter (sent between 850 and 855) to Grimald, Abbot of Sankt Gallen, contains valuable information about the monastic schools of the time. BIBLIOGRAPHY: W. Fink, DHGE 15:759–761; W. Wattenbach, *Deutschlands Geschichtsquellen im Mittelalter* (1893) 1:282–284.

[M. F. MCCARTHY]

ERMIN, ST. (d. 737), monk, abbot, bishop. Of noble birth, E. was ordained priest and then appointed chaplain to Bp. Madelgar of Laon. After serving in that capacity he turned to Benedictine monasticism and succeeded Ursmar as abbot and bp. of Lobbes, *c.*711. BIBLIOGRAPHY: P. Villete, BiblSanct 5:60.

[A. CABANISS]

ERMINFRID, ST. (7th cent.), a Frankish noble at the court of Clotaire II where his brother Waldalen was chancellor. He entered the abbey of Luxueil in 627. Inheriting an empty church at Islia, E. reestablished monastic life there, subordinate to Luxueil. He died at an advanced age and was buried at Cusance. BIBLIOGRAPHY: V. Turck, LTK 3:1031; J. Marilier, BiblSanct 5:48.

[J. DRUSE]

ERMINOLD OF PRUFENING, BL. (d. 1121), Benedictine abbot. As a youth he entered the monastery of Hirsau under Abbot William. After taking part in the unsuccessful attempt to reform the Abbey of Lorsch (1106–07), he was appointed by Bp. Otto of Bamberg to be abbot of the new foundation at Prufening. E. introduced strict Cluniac reform measures there, which so enraged the monks that one of them finally murdered him. His relics are buried in a

catafalque that is recognized as an outstanding example of early German Gothic art. The artist is the "Erminold Master," so called from his connection with the catafalque. BIBLIOGRAPHY: A. M. Zimmerman, BiblSanct 5:61.

[M. S. TANEY]

ERMONI, VINCENZO (1858–1910), church historian. E. was a Vincentian from 1878 until 1907, when he left the congregation in the course of the Modernist crisis. His chief field of scholarly interest was the history of the early Church. He produced 14 pamphlets in the series *Science et Religion* (1903–07) and made important contributions to the DTC. He also wrote a life of John Damascene. BIBLIOGRAPHY: J. J. Twomey, LTK 3:1035.

[M. J. SUELZER]

ERNEST OF PARDUBICE (PARDUBITZ), BL. (*c.*1297–1364), abp. of Prague from 1344. After studies at Prague, Bologna, and Padua, E. was ordained, named canon, then dean of St. Vitus Cathedral; he was elected bp. (1343) and first abp. of Prague. Organizer and reformer as well as scholar, he acted through his diocesan synod to improve administrative procedures, to reform the moral standards of clergy and laity, to found a new cathedral and two monasteries, and also the Charles Univ. of Prague (1348). BIBLIOGRAPHY: S. H. Thomson, "Learning at the Court of Charles IV," *Speculum* 25 (1950) 1–20; I. Pole, BiblSanct 5:69–70.

[M. E. DUFFY]

ERNEST OF ZWIEFALTEN, ST. (d. 1148), abbot and martyr. After 5 years spent as abbot of Zwiefalten, Swabia, E. abdicated because of disorders in the monastery. Following a pilgrimage to the Holy Land he was, according to legend, tortured by the Saracens in Mecca. He is venerated as a martyr in Zwiefalten, but his cult is not officially recognized. BIBLIOGRAPHY: G. Spahr, NCE 5:518; R. Henggeler, BiblSanct 5:70.

[M. J. FINNEGAN]

EROS, the Greek god of love, frequently associated with, but distinct from, Pothos (Longing) and Himeros (Desire). Homer uses the word *eros* for the strong physical attraction Paris feels for Helen, and Zeus for Hera; it causes the limbs of the suitors of Penelope to tremble; but Homer does not personify this emotion as a god. In Hesiod and other later writers, particularly those influenced by the Orphic cosmogonies, E. is represented as a primeval god, the son of Chaos, or Night, or the Luminous Day, or Heaven, or Earth, or Uranus, or Chronos, or some other deity. In still later mythology he becomes the son of Aphrodite by Zeus or Ares or Hermes, and the brother of Anteros, the god of mutual love, described at times as his opponent. Because of his ability to affect the minds of both men and gods, Eros is represented by the lyric poets and upon the vases of the 6th and 7th cent. B.C. as cunning and cruel, striking his victims with an ax or whip, and at other times as fickle, playful, and confusing. He is young and beautiful, warm and sweet (Alcman), or bittersweet (Sappho). Euripides was the first to equip him with a bow and arrow and to postulate the existence of a plurality of such divinities, the Erotes, later taken over by the Romans as Amores, or Cupidines. In archaic art, Eros is represented as a beautiful winged youth, but with the passage of time he becomes younger and younger until, in the Hellenistic Age, he degenerates into a kind of mischievous child. A similar decline may be noted in the emotion that he personifies. Earlier writers looked upon Eros as the unifying power that brings order out of chaos, the source of human and divine love, the patron of youthful affection that binds citizens together and inspires them to noble deeds; but later authors associate him primarily with sensual passion.

Thespiae in Boeotia and Parion on the Hellespont were the two chief centers of his worship. In the former city he was originally worshiped under the form of an aniconic image, a red stone. Later, in the 4th cent., statues made by Praxiteles and Lysippus were erected at Thespiae in his honor; but these did not replace his earlier symbol. Every 4th year the Thespians held a festival known as the Erotidia with games and musical contests as a part of his worship, and this continued down into Roman times. Like the worship of Eros at Thespiae, his worship at Parion was ancient, antedating the period of Ionic colonization. At Athens Eros was the object of a joint cult with Aphrodite on the north slope of the Acropolis. His feast there was celebrated in the spring, in the month of Munichion.

As the god of both male and female love, Eros was a constant source of inspiration for both classical and Hellenistic sculptors. Among his most famous representations are a high relief at the center of the Boston Triptych, the Eros of Centocelle, now in the Vatican Museum, and numerous copies of an original statue attributed to Lysippus portraying the god as a boy stringing his bow. Eros's love for a human maiden is depicted in a number of paintings and statues and narrated in a long passage in the *Metamorphoses* of Apuleius (4.28–6.24). Among his attributes are the rose, hare, goat, and cock. He is one of the few pagan gods carried over into Christian iconography. BIBLIOGRAPHY: A. Furtwängler, *Lexikon der griechische und römische Mythologie*. 1.1:1339–72; F. M. A. Hanfmann, OCD 338–339.

[M. J. COSTELLOE]

EROTIC LITERATURE, literature in which sex, love, and marriage are the dominant theme or one of the major emphases (so called from the Greek god of love, Eros). These elements are legitimate, both artistically and morally, in a great percentage of all literature (witness such a work as *Romeo and Juliet*), and are indeed necessary in most creative works that deal with the relationships between man and woman. Most of such works do not ignore the spiritual elements that give significance to human drives. When the sex elements are treated in their purely physical dimensions, however, with tacit and sometimes even explicit denial of the spiritual, and even more when the physical elements are sensationalized for shock value, legitimate erotic literature can slither into obscenity and pornography. Though literary obscenity and pornography may be hard to define, their existence is recognized in the laws of all modern civilized countries, which propose means for controlling them by various kinds of censorship. Properly erotic literature can be and frequently is great literature; it should be maintained that obscenity and pornography so debase the nature of literature that it ceases to be worthy of the name. BIBLIOGRAPHY: N. St. John-Stevas, *Obscenity and the Law* (1956); H. C. Gardiner, NCE 5:518–519; A. Mordell, *Erotic Motive in Literature* (1919; repr. 1975).

[H. C. GARDINER]

ÉROULT, see ÉVROUL.

ERRÁZURIZ, CRESCENTE (1839–1931), Chilean churchman and historian, known also as Fray Raimundo Errázuriz. Of an aristocratic family, E. first entered the Dominican Order and then became a diocesan priest. He taught at the seminary and at the Catholic Univ. of Chile, founded several periodicals, and became the author of a valuable historical work, *Los orígenes de la Iglesia chilena* (1873). In 1917 he was named abp. of Santiago. E. fought against the Church-State separation decreed by the government, but after its promulgation he accepted the *fait accompli*. As head of the Chilean Church, he remained a staunch adversary of communism, which was then gaining adherents in the country, and advocated wholeheartedly the social reforms that were being initiated. BIBLIOGRAPHY: J. L. Mecham, *Church and State in Latin America* (1966).

[P. DAMBORIENA]

ERRINGTON, GEORGE (1804–86), coadjutor bp. to Card. Nicholas *Wiseman. Ordained (1827) in Rome, E. was vice-rector of the English College there while Wiseman was rector. When the latter returned as a bp. to England, E. returned with him and headed St. Mary's College, Oscott, for 4 years, then engaged in pastoral work. With the restoration of the hierarchy in England he became first bp. of Plymouth. In 1855 he went to London as coadjutor to Wiseman with the right of succession. E. was too inflexible for the easygoing Wiseman and in 1860 was removed by Pius IX. E. thereafter refused two important sees. He participated in Vatican Council I (1869–70). His last years were spent directing the studies of theological students at St. Paul's College in the diocese of Clafton. E. was a scholar and man of rigid integrity.

[J. R. AHERNE]

ERROR, in philosophical psychology or epistemology, a false judgment, judgment being taken as the mental assertion of conformity between a reality as known and the reality as existent. Where the conformity is according to fact there is truth; where it is not according to fact there is error. In its proper sense error can exist only in affirmation or denial: thus a judgment limited to one aspect of a thing is not rendered erroneous by there being more to the thing. Further, distortions in the prior, more passive or receptive phases of knowing—i.e., sense knowledge or the mind's apprehension prior to judgment—may lead to, but are not themselves error. *ERROR (IN FAITH AND THEOLOGY); *ERROR (IN MORAL JUDGMENT).

[T. C. O'BRIEN]

ERROR (IN FAITH OR THEOLOGY). Error in general is the falsity of a judgment or proposition when measured against reality or fact; it is the act of mind accepting the false as true or rejecting the true as false. It is said to be philosophical when it concerns matters purely within the domain of reason; it is opposed to faith or theology when it is contrary to a truth contained explicitly or implicitly in divine revelation. Sometimes the term is used in distinction to formal *heresy to imply an inculpable deviation from revealed truth. At other times it is used to qualify the denial of truth or the affirmation of falsity (with or without some degree of fault) when the pertinence of the opposing truth to the body of revealed doctrine has not been established beyond doubt (e.g., not established by official definition). In this case, error admits of varying degrees in accordance with the degree to which the truth it opposes approaches more or less nearly to the status of a clearly revealed doctrine of faith. Finally, the term has been used since the time of Pope Clement XI to attach a note of censure to propositions opposed in some way to faith and morals. In this sense various types of error are distinguished, according to the kind of truth to which a proposition appears opposed —divine faith, ecclesiastical faith, common Catholic teaching—and to established theological conclusions (theological error properly so called). *CONSCIENCE; *IGNORANCE; *ERROR (IN MORAL JUDGMENT).

[P. K. MEAGHER]

ERROR (IN MORAL JUDGMENT), in moral theology, a false moral judgment, arising out of moral *ignorance, and classified as culpable or not on the same grounds. In every sin there is in fact an error: the disordered moral choice is based on an evaluation of the deficient, apparent good, for the genuine good. Error in the antecedent moral judgment is an objective lack of conformity with the good as measured by reference to the rightly ordered will. The distortion here derives from the coloring or pressure affecting moral judgment because of the bent of appetite.

[T. C. O'BRIEN]

ERROR, TOLERATION OF, forebearance from repressing or correcting false doctrine. The term has historical connotations: the position that safeguarding the one true Christian faith belongs to the protection of the public good, and that therefore heretics must be restrained (see INQUISITION; ThAq ST 2a2ae, 10.7 ad 11; 11.3). Toleration, however, is the course to be followed either in a de facto pluralistic situation, or where repression of error would be more disturbing to peace and good order than the error itself. Since Vat II RelFreed, the positive value of liberty of conscience and religion has received a recognition that seems to make pointless the positions associated with "toleration of error." In a more practical and pastoral sense, this phrase suggests suspension of doctrinal differences in the interest of positive charity among Christians. It also describes the confessor's prudential restraint from correcting a sincerely erroneous conscience out of care for the penitent's simpleness or weakness.

[T. C. O'BRIEN]

ERROR COMMUNIS, a term in canon law, occurring in CIC c. 209 and referring to a mistaken supposition shared by most people in a region or involved in a situation. The canon refers to the matter of *jurisdiction: in a case where it is generally but mistakenly thought that a priest, e.g., a confessor, has jurisdiction the "Church supplies" the jurisdiction that is in fact lacking.

[T. C. O'BRIEN]

ERTHAL, VON, family name of two brothers, both bps., who held opposite views on the relationship of Church and State. **Friedrich Karl Joseph** (1719–1802) was prince bishop of Mainz from 1774, primate of Germany and imperial chancellor (1774–1802). Worldly and attached to the ideas of the *Enlightenment, he supported subjection of Church to State and was a leader at the Congress of *Ems. The French Revolution led to loss of his positions and his expulsion from Mainz. **Franz Ludwig** (1730–95) was bp. of Würzburg and Bamberg from 1779. He remained loyal to Rome, was an exemplary pastor, zealous for church discipline and priestly spirituality, and opposed *Febronianism. He was the author of *Principles of Government,* a challenge to the views adopted by his brother.

[T. C. O'BRIEN]

ERZBERGER, MATTHIAS (1875–1921), longtime leader of the Center Party in Germany. He took part in the founding of the Christian Trade Union in Mainz and was always associated with movements promoting social justice. E. was a critic of the German colonial policy in Africa in the early years of the 20th cent. but later veered toward an annexationist position. He initiated the Peace Resolution in the Reichstag in 1917 and in 1918 joined the cabinet of Prince Max of Baden, heading the Armistice delegation to Versailles. He served as Reich minister for finance 1919–20. He was assassinated by a fanatic nationalist. BIBLIOGRAPHY: G. Binder, *Irrtum und Widerstand* (1968).

[M. A. GALLIN]

ESARHADDON, king of Assyria and Babylonia (681–669 B.C.). His name in Akkadian means: "Ashur (the god of Assyria) has given a brother" (for a lost son). He was the son of Sennacherib and the father of Ashurbanipal. Sennacherib, as recounted in Kings and in Isaiah, withdrew his siege of Jerusalem, and at home was murdered by two of his own sons. The two sons fled to Ararat, and the other son E. succeeded to the throne. Unlike other Assyrian kings E. was well disposed toward the Babylonians and well received by them. He penetrated deep into Persia, defeating the Cimmerians and the Medes, allying himself with the Scythians. Rather than waste time fighting in Palestine and Syria, he concentrated on subduing Egypt, which was continually inciting its former vassals to rebellion. The Assyrian army forced Pharaoh to retreat into Upper Egypt. Memphis was conquered, and E. tried ruling Egypt through a combination of native puppets and Assyrian advisers. But this did not work out well for long. E. died of some illness on his way to Egypt to put down a rebellion.

[E. J. DILLON]

ESAU, elder twin of Jacob and son of Isaac and Rebekah (Gen 25.20–26). He was considered the ancestor of the Edomites (Gen 36.1), as Jacob was of the Israelites. Esau sold his rights of primogeniture to Jacob (Gen 25.27–34), and by deceit Jacob got the blessing from his father that the elder son normally would have received (Gen ch. 27). Esau forgave Jacob, however, when Jacob returned 20 years later after fleeing Esau's wrath (Gen ch. 28–33). Paul used the story of Esau and Jacob to show that God's mercy is given apart from any human worth (Rom 9.10–16; see also Mal 1.2–3; Heb 12.16, where a different interpretation is given).

[T. EARLY]

ESCALANTE, JUAN ANTONIO (1633–70), Spanish painter. E. studied under Francisco de Guevara and was influenced by Venetian works. Painting in a baroque manner with brilliant ease and varied palette, E. in his *Annunciation* (1663) and *Dream of St. Joseph* (1665) shows idealism of form and delicacy of touch. Under the influence of Rubens, he painted *the Conversion of St. Paul* in a more robust style.

[M. J. DALY]

ESCAPE OF PRISONERS, here understood as the act of persons legally held for trial or imprisoned as punishment for crime, who break away from the confinement imposed upon them. Since the detention of such persons is intended for the protection of the community, and, if they are convicted, as fit punishment for crime, their escape appears to involve some moral problem. The obligation of maintaining such persons in custody falls on the civil authorities, and guards would certainly fail in their duty by aiding, directly or indirectly, a break from prison. But a man undergoing punishment is under no obligation to cooperate, and moralists generally agree that he may take his chances provided he inflicts no injustice on another, does not break his word, and is ready to face the consequences of failure.

ESCARRE, AURELIO MARÍA (1908–68), abbot of Montserrat in Spain. He became a Benedictine at Montserrat in 1923, was ordained in 1933. He escaped to Italy when many of the monks were massacred during the Spanish Civil War. In 1941 he was returned to the abbey as coadjutor abbot, and 2 years later became abbot. E. led his community back from the demoralization of war and made Montserrat a center of scholarship and liturgy as well as of the study and cultivation of Catalán culture and language. In the 1960's Dom Aurelio became a leading spokesman for human liberties and social justice. His open criticism of the Spanish government led to his resignation as abbot in 1965.

[T. C. O'BRIEN]

ESCH, NICHOLAS VAN (Eschius; 1507–78), ascetical and mystical theologian in the tradition of the *Brothers of the Common Life, esp. notable for his encouragement of *lay spirituality. He was educated by the Brothers in Flanders and at the Univ. of Louvain. Ordained in 1530, he became a tutor at Cologne; St. *Peter Canisius was among his pupils. Kept by weak health from becoming a Carthusian, E. was appointed chaplain to the beguinage of Diest. He devoted himself to writing on the spiritual life. Among his works, many of them first published in Flemish, then translated, are: *Margarita evangelica* (1545); *Isagoge seu introductio in vitam universam* (1563); *Templum animae* (1563); *Exercitia theologiae mysticae* (1563); and the posthumously published collection, *Exercitia spiritualia . . .* (1612). He also translated into Latin some of Tauler's German writings.

[T. C. O'BRIEN]

ESCHATOLOGICAL ETHICS, moral preaching charged with *eschatos,* the furthest, or news of the "last things," death, judgment, heaven, hell, the end of time, the second coming of Christ. Judaic teaching held that history was moving toward an end when men would be brought suddenly to salvation or condemnation. This was the background for the Christian teaching. Early Christians believed that the end had already come, that is, in the life, death and esp. in the Resurrection of Christ, esp. the crucial event of history. Some thought that the last events were imminent. But as time went on, a cooling of the NT eschatological temperature took place, and expectation of Christ's coming moved to a quieter hope. And through the centuries, Christian eschatology staged the drama in the death of each individual.

Three stages can be discerned in eschatological ethics. First, the attitude towards life and the manner of living of Christians who expected the end at once. "Our time is growing short. Those who have wives should live as though they had none . . . And those who have to deal with the world should not become engrossed in it. I say this because the world as we know it is passing away." (1 Cor 7.29–30). Second, when the sense of impending doom lifted, Christians grew aware of the gift given them in the power and promises of Christ and began to live their lives accordingly (cf. esp. Heb 11). Finally, and now more prevalently, it means how each Christian should stand and live, in view of the fact that each will die soon enough and come before judgment, and that "we have here no lasting home." (Heb 13.14). BIBLIOGRAPHY: R. Schnackenburg, *Moral Teaching of the New Testament* (1967) 186–196.

[T. R. HEATH]

ESCHATOLOGICAL THEOLOGY, the theology named for its orientation to eschatology, the doctrine concerning the final outcome of the universe and humanity. As a result of the revival of biblical studies, it is one of the emphases that have characterized theology in the first half of the 20th century. The term was widely used by the historians of religion when they spoke of the beliefs of the Egyptians, Babylonians, Persians, Greeks, Romans, etc.; it is also used for the tract *De novissimis—novissima* (the Latin equivalent of the Greek *ta eschata*). Among RC eschatologists are L. Bouyer, L. Cerfaux, R. Guardini, J. Daniélou; among Protestants, A. Schweitzer, P. Tillich, R. Niebuhr, D. H. Dodd, and R. Bultmann. Generally speaking, they feel that Christianity is carried along toward the future and the coming of Christ by a powerful dynamism, though some think the future bodes ill for the universe. Others hold that human progress can be turned into good or evil, depending upon the use Christians make of it. BIBLIOGRAPHY: F. Martin and M. E. Williams, NCE 5:524–538; J. Moltmann, *Theology of Hope* (tr. J. W. Leitch, 1967). *INCARNATIONAL THEOLOGY.

[J. FICHTNER]

ESCHATOLOGISM, the interpretation of the Jesus of the Gospels as proclaiming the imminent *eschaton,* the end time when the kingdom of God is to be established on earth. The term primarily categorizes the unrealized eschatology first proposed by J. *Weiss, father of 19th-cent. *form-criticism, and then expounded by Albert *Schweitzer. The premise of the theory is that the Gospels do not afford knowledge of the historical Jesus, but only of the thought of the early Christians about him, and about their own response to his message. That message shows that Jesus fits into the setting of Jewish apocalyptic myth at his period as one who became gradually conscious of his messianic and apocalyptic mission. The message proclaiming the imminence of the kingdom is world-negating; the proclamation being unfulfilled; future Christians can still learn both its world negation and the world affirmation contained in Jesus' ethic of love. Christian dogmas of Incarnation and atonement simply have nothing to do with the Gospel. Another, opposite view of the eschatological interpretation is the so-called realized eschatology of C. *Dodd. This sees Jesus as in fact bringing about the kingdom of God by his

preaching and its effect, and as providing the example for every Christian to make the kingdom continually present. The eschatological myth also has prominence in the thought of R. *Bultmann: the eschatological, unfulfilled content of the NT is a primary example of the need to demythologize in order to reach the existential *kerygma underlying the myth. BIBLIOGRAPHY: J. Macquarrie, *Twentieth-Century Religious Thinkers* (1963) 144–147, 363–364.

[T. C. O'BRIEN]

ESCHATOLOGY. The term is composed of two Greek words, *eschata* (the last things) and *logos* (science). Eschatology is, then, the science of the last things. In Christian theology until the end of the 19th cent., eschatology was considered as that part of systematic theology that deals with death, particular judgment, heaven and hell, as being the last events to happen to a human life. Since then scholars concerned with Jewish and Christian theologies began to distinguish between social and individual eschatology. Kaufmann Kohler wrote in the *Jewish Encyclopedia* (1903) that "Jewish eschatology deals primarily and principally with the final destiny of the Jewish nation and the world in general, and only secondarily with the future of the individual; the main concern of Hebrew legislator, prophet, and apocalyptic writer being Israel as the people of God and the victory of his truth and justice on earth." The biblical writer speaks of the "last days," or "the day of the Lord" as decisive moments in history during which an extraordinary complex of events will happen to terminate an era and inaugurate a new one (Gen 49.1; Dt 32.20; Am 5.20). Commonly, the new era was expected to be a messianic one full of justice and truth (Is 9.1–10). Eschatological events multiply in *apocalyptic and *apocryphal literature. There the cosmic elements play a decisive role in calculating history in terms of periods with the conviction that the end is imminent. That end was also thought to bring about, through some revolutionary changes, the disparately expected kingdom of God (Dn 7.13–14). For the futurist eschatological school such as appears in Johannes Weiss, Albert Schweitzer, M. Werner, etc., Jesus had the apocalyptic attitude of his contemporaries and he thought of himself as having the burden to bring about the coming of the kingdom of God in power. Peter's confession (Mt 16.16), they claim, is a confirmation of their theory. Charles H. Dodd in his "realized eschatology" sees in the earthly ministry of Christ the perfect fulfillment of the messianic hope. In imitating his obedience Christians can make the kingdom come for themselves and attain its fruition. After a serious study of a large number of eschatological passages in the NT, the majority of Christian scholars hold today a moderate eschatology: the fulfillment of the kingdom of God is accomplished in two stages: (1) through Christ's Passion and his victorious Resurrection shared sacramentally with his followers; this is the consumed stage; and (2) in a future stage of perfect fulfillment at the time of the *Parousia when he will reappear in glory to judge mankind and to inaugurate the other-worldly, irenic phase of the kingdom. Contemporary Protestant scholars such as George B. Caird (Oxford) still insist on individual eschatology, while their Catholic colleagues tend toward an integration theory: "Man," writes Michael E. Williams (NCE 5:536d), "can reach his fulfillment as individual only within the framework of society, and society is moving toward the final completion of God's saving plan." BIBLIOGRAPHY: *Background of the NT and its Eschatology,* eds. William D. Davies and D. Daube (1956); R. W. Gleason, *World to Come* (1958).

[J. R. GHANEM]

ESCOBAR, ANDRÉS DE (1366 or 67–1439 or 40), Benedictine canonist and theologian. Abbot of Randulf in the Diocese of Braga, he entered service in the papal curia in 1397 and remained there most of his life. He attended the Councils of Constance, Basel, and Ferrara-Florence. In 1408 he was named bp. of Cività in Sardinia and in 1422 of Ajaccio in Corsica, but he was never a residential bishop. E. is mainly important for his canonico-moral writings on penance, for his works on church reform and on reunion with the Greeks, against whom he defended papal primacy and infallibility in his *De graecis errantibus* (1437).

[T. C. O'BRIEN]

ESCOBAR, MARINA DE, VEN. (1554–1633), Spanish foundress, mystic. Born of an intellectual and pious family, E. early demonstrated rare powers of reflection. In 1587 she dedicated her life to God. In 1615, with the help of her director, Ven. Luis de La Puente, she adapted the constitutions of St. Bridget for a foundation of the Bridgettines (also called Brigettines of Recollection) in Spain. During the last 30 years of her life, she was bedridden. At the insistence of her spiritual directors, she wrote notes about her mystical experiences. As a kind of autobiography, they were published, first in two parts after her death; then in 1766, as a whole: *Vida maravillosa de la Venerable Virgen Doña Marina de Escobar.*

[S. A. HEENEY]

ESCOBEDO, BARTOLOMÉ (d. before 1563), Spanish singer and composer, member of the papal choir. In 1556, by commission, E. composed a six-part *Missa Philippus Rex Hispaniae* to mark the coronation of Philip II of Spain. Other works include the Mass, *Ad te levavi,* preserved in the Sistine Chapel, and five motets for four or five voices. BIBLIOGRAPHY: NOHM 4.

[A. M. MACK]

ESCORIAL, EL (San Lorenzo de El Escorial), monastery located near Madrid, Spain. A candidate (among others) for the title "eighth wonder of the world" El Escorial was built in the years 1563–84, at the instance of Philip II in thanksgiving for the military victory of St. Quentin (St. Lawrence Day, August 10, 1557). Though the chief architect was Francesco Paciotto, an Italian engineer, Philip himself imposed much of his own spirit on the edifice. The brilliant engineer Juan de Herrera who supervised most of the work expedited the construction. Built in the shape of a gridiron (honoring the martyring instrument of St. Lawrence) the monastery provides a geometric design, solid, vast, and severe. Its inner courts are seven, each with fountain. The cloister enclosures are decorated with unusual murals. The basilica alone is an impressive building, its altar poised at the top of an incredible set of steps. (According to tradition, Philip could view the Mass from his residence 3 miles distant). A unique feature of El Escorial is the pantheon, burial place of Emperor Charles V and succeeding kings, princes, queens, and royal children. Don John of Austria, illegitimate son of Charles V, is also buried here The pantheon is a series of chapels, marvelous in the glory of marble.

Originally given to the Hieronymite Order (now extinct) the monastery since 1885 has been Augustinian. It contains a magnificent collection of oil paintings by such masters as Titian, Velasquez, and Tintoretto, and a library containing thousands of rare books as well as one of the finest collections of Arabic MSS in the world. The Augustinians conduct a university there; both they and the Hieronymites created a tradition of scholarship in the monastery.

[J. R. AHERNE]

ESCRIVÁ DE BALAGUER, JOSÉ MARÍA (1902–75), Spanish priest, founder of *Opus Dei. E. was ordained in Saragossa (1925). He founded (1928) *Opus Dei as an association of the faithful dedicated to leading an intense Christian life while performing ordinary duties of secular or professional occupations. A woman's branch was founded in 1930, and the Sacerdotal Society of the Holy Cross and Opus Dei received papal approbation in 1950. E. worked for 47 years in his apostolate, inspiring the members by his exemplary teachings and spiritual life. He was president general of Opus Dei until his death. His body was placed in the crypt of the Oratory of Our Lady of Peace in Rome. BIBLIOGRAPHY: J. Escrivá De Balaguer, *La Constitución apostólica "Provida Mater Ecclesia" y el Opus Dei* (1949).

[R. A. TODD]

ESDRAELON, PLAIN OF, also Valley of Jezreel, area in N Palestine, settled by Israelites during the Judges period (*c.*1200–1020 B.C.; cf. Jg 6.33–37). Hosea refers to the area's fertility (Hos 2.21–23) and to the bloody purge that King Jehu of Israel effected nearby in 842 B.C. (Hos 1.4–5; 2 Kg 9–10). BIBLIOGRAPHY: EDB 1160–61.

[T. CRANE]

ESDRAS, BOOKS OF, two unrelated OT apocrypha. (1) 1 Esdras is a historical work that parallels material in the canonical Book of *Ezra and Nehemiah. Esdras is a Greek and Latin form of Ezra; the Books of Ezra and Nehemiah in the Vulgate are entitled I Esdras and II Esdras; the Esdras apocrypha are designated III Esdras and IV Esdras. Scholars identify I Esdras as the original LXX text of what became canonical Ezra. This text was regarded as Scripture by many in the early cent. but was rejected as apocryphal by St. Jerome because it did not correspond to the text of Ezra-Nehemiah in the Hebrew Bible. (2) 2 Esdras is an apocalyptic work in three parts, distinct in origin and subject matter. Chapters 1–2, of 2d-cent. Christian origin, speak of God turning from the Jews to the Gentiles, and of the Church. The words of the *Requiem aeternam* in the liturgy are derived from 2.34–35. The second section, ch. 3–14 is Jewish, *c.*100–120 A.D. and is also called the *Apocalypse of Ezra* because of the seven visions of Ezra on the persecution of Israel that it recounts. The third part, ch. 15–17, is a Christian epilogue of the 3d century. BIBLIOGRAPHY: R. Brown, JBC 2:541–542.

[T. C. O'BRIEN]

ESDRAS-NEHEMIAH, BOOKS OF, see EZRA-NEHEMIAH, BOOK OF.

ESELER, NICLAUS, THE ELDER (fl. 1439–92), leading S German architect who definitively developed the late Gothic Hallenkirche (hall church) with ambulatory. His principal churches are St. Michael in Schwäbisch Hall, St. George in Nördlingen, and St. George in Dinkelsbühl. E.'s son Niclaus the Younger continued his father's work.

[M. J. DALY]

ESKIL. Two venerable men associated with Scandinavia bore this name: (1) Eskil, abp. of Lund, Bl. (*c.*1100–81), sometimes said to have been of Danish origin, but he appears to have been born in what is now Sweden itself, at a time when it was under Danish jurisdiction. He spent much of his youth abroad at Hildesheim where he studied, and at Clairvaux where he became a friend of St. Bernard. He was made bp. of Roshilde in Denmark (1132) and abp. of Lund (1137). In 1156 he was created primate of Sweden and served as papal legate for the establishment of the archiepiscopal see of Uppsala. He retired from his see in 1177 and spent the remainder of his life as a monk at Clairvaux. BIBLIOGRAPHY: AS April 1:856. (2) Eskil, St. (d. *c.*1038, earlier the date 1080 was usually given), bp. and martyr. He is sometimes said to have been bp. of Strängnäs, but that see was not founded until 1245. E. was probably of English origin, a relative of St. Sigfrid; he accompanied the latter on a missionary journey to Sweden, probably serving as a missionary bishop. E. worked with considerable success but stirred the wrath of the pagan ministry. When he humiliated them in an attempt to offer sacrifice, the king had him stoned to death. Strangely, E. is not mentioned in the Roman Martyrology, though he has been venerated in the Northland as one of their most celebrated martyrs. BIBLIOGRAPHY: Butler 2:533–534; A. L. Sibilia, BiblSanct 5:92–95.

ESKÎMŌ (Syriac, from the Gr. *schima;* in Arab. *iskîm*), the monastic habit. The term is used today esp. of the black, close-fitting monastic hood, decorated with white crosses, also called *qûbʿûnō* or *kûssîtō*, with which the head of a Jacobite or Syro-Malankara bp., or of a Jacobite monk, is always covered. It is sometimes exchanged by a Jacobite for one having the crosses in gold thread when he is the Eucharistic celebrant. A solid black *eskîmō*, adorned only by a metal cross on the forehead, is worn (only at Mass) by Syrian Catholic bishops.

ESMEIN, ADHÉMAR (1848–1913), French jurist and historian of law. E. received his doctorate in 1875 and taught at Douai and Paris. Early in his career he became interested in the history of law, a subject upon which he produced several definitive works. His *Mariage en droit canonique* (1891) is his masterwork in the field of canon law. BIBLIOGRAPHY: L. Charvet, DDC 5:454–457.

ESOTERICISM, restriction of religious doctrine or ritual participation to initiates; also the cultivation of occult doctrines or practices. The word derives from the Gr. *esōterō*, comparative of *esō*, within. Esotericism was first connected with the Greek mysteries, then with a distinction between the teachings given by philosophers to the many and those given to an inner circle. As a religious or quasi-religious phenomenon, it is present in the case of the secret fraternal orders and in such religio-philosophic systems as *theosophy, *spiritualism, and *anthroposophy. Certain esoteric aspects may be seen in early Christianity, with the distinction between the Mass of catechumens, open to all, and the Mass of the faithful, restricted to the baptized. The mysteries of the NT, however, are not items of esoterica, but are proclaimed as the wonders of God's gracious action saving man. Esotericism may be rooted in a primitive fascination with the magical. It does represent an attitude that sacred things are profaned by the presence of unbelievers or that the benefits bestowed by sacred things are rightly restricted to committed disciples.

[T. EARLY]

ESP, see EXTRASENSORY PERCEPTION

ESPADA Y LANDA, JUAN JOSÉ DÍAZ (1756–1832), bishop of Havana. A Spaniard, Espada was a canon of the cathedral in Villafranca del Vierzo and was for a time inquisitor of Majorca. Named bp. of Cuba, he was consecrated in Havana (1802). E. constructed a vast cemetery in Havana and abolished the custom of burial in the churches. His career of 30 years as bp. saw accomplished tighter ecclesiastical organization, expansion of social institutions and public works, as well as reform of university and lower education.

[J. R. AHERNE]

ESPARZA ARTIEDA, MARTINO (1609–89), Spanish Jesuit and theologian who taught at Valladolid, Salamanca, and Rome. He is known principally for his defense of *probabilism. He was one of the five censors of a work of Tirso *Gonzalez and is thought to have been the one who formulated the decision of the group. His chief work was his *Cursus theologicus* (1666). BIBLIOGRAPHY: Hurter 4:358–359; Sommervogel 3:449–452.

[P. K. MEAGHER]

ESPEN, ZEGER BERNHARD VAN (1646–1728), Flemish jurist and canonist. Ordained in 1673 he became professor at the Collège Adrien VI, Louvain. A partisan of Jansenism, he had to leave Louvain in 1628 because of his defense of the election of C. Steenhoven as abp. of Utrecht (see UTRECHT, SCHISM OF); he died shortly afterward. His works include: *Jus ecclesiasticum* (2 v., 1700), highly regarded, though put on the Index in 1704; *Pro Jansenius: De censuris ecclesiasticis* (1709); *De promulgatione legum ecclesiasticarum* (1721). He also wrote many tractates against the bull *Unigenitus* and on the formulary imposed on the Jansenists in 1665. His works were put on the Index *in globo* in 1732.

[T. C. O'BRIEN]

ESPENCE, CLAUDE TOGNIEL DE (1511–71), theologian; from 1540 rector of the Sorbonne. In 1547 he represented Henry II of France at the Council of Trent. He strove, without success, at the colloquy at Poissy (1561) to bring moderation to the doctrinal disputes between the Protestant and Catholic parties. E. published several works on teachings controverted during the Reformation period, esp. notably on the Eucharist and on predestination.

[T. C. O'BRIEN]

ESPINAR, ALONSO DE (d. 1513), Franciscan missioner. A Spaniard, E. accompanied the expedition of Nicolas de Ovando to Santo Domingo in 1500, establishing a friary in the capital city. Drawn into the controversy (1511) covering the Spanish treatment of the Indians, he opposed the radical views of his fellow religious, including Bartolomé de *las Casas, and was one of three royal commissioners who prepared the moderate Ordinance of Burgos (1512–13). While returning to Santo Domingo from Spain with eight Franciscans he had recruited, he died at sea. BIBLIOGRAPHY: L. G. Canedo, DHGE 15:972–973.

[J. R. AHERNE]

ESPINOSA, ISIDRO FÉLIX DE (1679–1755), Franciscan missioner and historian. A native of Qaerétaro, Mexico, E. became a Franciscan and was ordained in 1703. He worked in the missions of the N Rio Grande. An explorer of the interior of Mexico, he became its historian and later led a group of Franciscan missioners into that region. From 1722 on he devoted himself to historical chronology of the Franciscan missions. Two works deserve special mention:

Crónica de la Provincia franciscana de Michoacán (1899) and *Crónica . . . de todos los colegios de Propaganda Fide de esta Nueva-España de misioneros franciscanos . . .* (1746). BIBLIOGRAPHY: L. G. Canedo, DHGE 15:992–993.

[J. R. AHERNE]

ESPIS, a town in the diocese of Montauban, France, site of alleged apparitions of the Bl. Virgin in 1946. After investigation of the supposed miracles, visions, and revelations, Bp. Théas forbade priests and religious to participate in pious acts connected with the events (1947). Bp. de Courrèges extended this prohibition to all the faithful (1950) (1950) and declared that the events at Espis showed no evidence of supernatural origin and that any and all acts of cult, public or private, were forbidden under pain of excommunication. BIBLIOGRAPHY: G. Jacquemet, *Catholicisme* 4:463.

ESPOUSAL, see BREACH OF PROMISE.

ESPRIT, monthly review founded in 1932 by Emmanuel Mounier (1905–50), and soon the most effective publication for the French Catholic Left. Against the dehumanization of industrial society and the abuses of capitalism, *Esprit* championed the gospel social teaching and the doctrine of personalism—the supreme dignity of each human achieved through participation in a living community. It became more important after the Liberation when it insisted on dialogue with unbelievers and Communists. A bridge to non-Catholic opinion, it defended new apostolic forms (e.g., priest-workers) and a Christian humanism that saw all creation dignified by the Incarnation. Occasional special numbers (e.g., May–June 1948 on Marxism) were particularly valuable. BIBLIOGRAPHY: C. Moix, *La Pensée d'Emmanuel Mounier* (1960).

[J. N. MOODY]

ESQUIÚ, MAMERTO (1826–83), Franciscan bishop. An Argentinian, E. was vowed by his parents to the Franciscans and entered the novitiate at the age of 15. Ordained in 1849 he began a career as a confessor and as a preacher whose classical eloquence made him famous. Called the "orator of the Constitution" he was vice-president of the committee that devised a provincial constitution for Catamarca. To escape the bishopric, he volunteered for the missions of Bolivia, where his apostolate included founding the journal *El Cruzado* in 1868. Upon the death of the abp. of Buenos Aires, E. was nominated to succeed him by the Argentine Senate. Again he fled, this time first to Peru, then to Ecuador. He was assigned by the superior general to reform the Franciscan houses in Argentina. A member of the provincial parliament, E. was again proposed for bp. this time of Córdoba. He was unable to decline and in 1880 was consecrated. His brief episcopate was marked by zealous visitation of his diocese and the charity and simplicity of his character. In 1923 his cause for beatification was begun and was introduced in 1946 at Rome. BIBLIOGRAPHY: R. Aubert, DHGE 15:998–999.

[J. R. AHERNE]

ESROM, ABBEY OF, important Cistercian abbey in Denmark. It was founded by Abp. Lund of Eskil, a friend and admirer of St. Bernard, to whom he offered a rich property for the establishment of a daughterhouse of Clairvaux. The foundation dates from 1151, when Pope Eugene III granted it a bull of protection. It received the approval of other popes, bishops, and kings, who accorded it generous gifts and privileges. Esrom prospered and established in less than 50 years six daughterhouses, two of which—Soro and Colbaz—founded two and three others respectively. By the 14th cent. Esrom was affiliated with 12 abbeys. By the end of the 15th cent., however, the abbey had declined both spiritually and temporally. It was suppressed after the Diet of Copenhagen (1530). After the Danish Reformation (1536), all abbeys and religious houses were dissolved. Some ruins of Esrom abbey and church remain. BIBLIOGRAPHY: M. A. Dimier, DHGE 15:1000–02.

[S. A. HEENEY]

ESSEN MINSTER. Begun during the time of the Abbesses Matilda (971–1011) and Theophano (1039–58), the structure boasts a beautiful W façade, with a central tower flanked by two small stair towers preceded by a forecourt. The W choir is copied from Charlemagne's *Palatine Chapel at Aachen. A 10th-cent. crypt at the E end was extended (mid-11th cent.) as the funerary chapel of Theophano. The early church was rebuilt as a rib-vaulted hall church (*c.* 1275). A remarkable treasury includes a *Virgin and Child* in gilded lindenwood (973–982), a processional cross of Matilda in gold, copper, jewels, and enamel (on wood), and a precious Gospel Book of Theophano with a cover of gold *repoussé* plaques and jewels framing an Ottonian ivory. BIBLIOGRAPHY: H. Jantzen, *Ottonische Kunst* (1959).

[M. J. DALY]

ESSENCE, from Lat. *essentia,* an abstract form deriving from the verb *esse, to be* (ThAq ST 1a,29.1 ad 4), and used in several senses. (1) In scholastic philosophy the meaning of essence is seen from the following: "In reference to being *(ens),* essence means something common to all the natures by reason of which diverse beings belong to diverse genera and species, e.g., 'humanity' is the essence of man" (*idem, De ente et essentia* 1). St. Thomas indicates that, with slight nuances, "quiddity" referring to a definition of what *(quid),* a thing, is; "form," the distinctive element, and "nature," the principle of activity, have the same referent as "essence." The last term, however, is used to indicate that through it and in it, a being has its actuality, *esse (ibid.).* He further indicates that since *substance alone properly is a being (an *accident having being only as

modifications of a substance), essence belongs most properly to a substance. Substance however, is also taken as "second substance," i.e., as a universal category; and then substance and essence are used interchangeably to indicate what, in any being, the constitutive and distinctive element is. In the discussion of the distinction between *essence and existence, "essence" stands for the existent subject. Finally, the term is also transferred to signify any constitutive element. (2) In Lat. theology *essentia* was used in several contexts to translate the Gr. *ousia,* instead of *substantia* (see ThAq ST 1a,29.2; cf 1 ad 4). Thus, Trinitarian theology discusses the one essence of the three divine persons, the term being equivalent to "nature" (*ibid.* 39.1). In the discussion of the Incarnation, "nature" is used to mean essence (*ibid.* 3a,2.1). A second notable use of *essentia* derives from the translation of the works of *Pseudo–Dionysius made by *John Scotus Erigena; where the Gr. has *ousia,* the translation uses *essentia.* The term describes the angels, spiritual substances, who are pure essences, not having a material component. In theological anthropology and in the discussion of grace and the virtues, the distinction is made between the essence of the human soul and its powers or faculties (*ibid.* 1a,77.1; 1a2ae,56; 110.2–4).

[T. C. O'BRIEN]

ESSENCE AND EXISTENCE, the potentiality-actuality composition in all beings other than God; "in every substance but God the substance and its *esse* are really distinct" (ThAq CG 2.52). The "really distinct" means distinctness (though not separability) in the existent, and not just that a possible essence is conceivable apart from existence. St. Thomas Aquinas seldom uses the term *existentia;* the term itself can suggest that the actuality of a being is mere factuality, as though there were real essences, some of which adventitiously receive a further predicate, "existence." The composition of essence and *esse* means rather that in an actual existent, *esse* is the ultimate and integrating actuality of the being that is. The being exists as the subject actualized, thus as the potentiality in reference to its actuality, *esse,* and as such as other than, not identical with, its own actuality. The term *essence in this context stands, not for abstract meaning, or defining element, but the subject, and most properly, the substance as that the actuality of which is *to be, esse.* "The whole substance is the 'that which is' and the *esse* the 'that by which' the substance is termed a being *(ens)*" (*ibid.* 54). The composition means, then, not a conjunction of essence and *esse* so that a third thing (ens) results, but the being *(ens)* is a composite reality, one actualized by something other than itself. In that composite *ens,* "although the *esse* is diverse from its essence, that does not mean that *esse* is something supplementary in the way an accident is; rather the *esse* is, as it were, constituted through the principles of the essence" (*idem, In metaphysic.* IV, lect. 2). The intent of that statement can be understood only on the basis of the one proper and universal reason for the real distinction: that God is the absolute being, not an actualized subject, but the being identical with his own actuality. There can be but one such being; any other must have its being derived from the absolute being; and its mode of being must be contracted and limited. The causing of other beings, then, is the causing of limited subjects in which the limiting mode is proportionately actualized. The proof for the real distinction, then, is not based on external contingency—that what exists need not or at some point will not exist; the proof rather is the necessarily composite metaphysical structure of all beings other than God, the Being. For St. Thomas, reality is not made up of two "instantiations" of being, the created and the uncreated; rather there is the Being and the beings. The facts from which the proofs for the *existence of God begin are manifestations of the ontologically radical potentiality-actuality structure of all beings; their terminal points can lead to a further conclusion that the first cause is absolute *esse*. From there a necessary turnabout follows: every other being is a participated and limited being; that entails the real distinction; the dependence on the uniquely proper divine causality of *esse* for continuance in existence; and the subordination of the whole system of created causes to the indispensable influence of the first cause. BIBLIOGRAPHY: THAq ST Eng-Lat, Vol. 8, T. Gilby, ed., Appendix 1, "Derived Existence"; Vol. 14, T. C. O'Brien, ed., Appendix 1, "*Esse*, the Proper Effect of God Alone."

[T. C. O'BRIEN]

ESSENES (a name probably deriving ultimately from the Aram. plural *hasin* [the holy, pious], corresponding to Heb. *hasidim*, and represented in Gr. as *Essēnoi* or *Essaioi*), a Jewish-Palestinian ascetical sect. Though not mentioned in the Bible, they are described by Flavius Josephus, by Philo the Jew, and by Pliny the Elder, and also by some ecclesiastical writers. Their main residence was said to be at Engedi (today a productive Israeli agricultural site) on the W shore of the Dead Sea. They apparently arose *c.*150 B.C. during the Maccabean era and still existed when Josephus wrote. According to the writers mentioned above, they practiced poverty, held their property in common, were celibate (although Josephus states that one group of them could marry), were devoted to prayer, reading, self-support (involving farming), and frequent ritual baths. They venerated Moses, believed in the angels, and in the immortality of the soul, which they conceived to be an emanation from some higher substance, they separated themselves from worship at Jerusalem (which they looked upon as corrupt), and did not offer animal sacrifice. Their doctrine was similar to that of the Pharisees. Josephus thought that they were fatalists. Their complete doctrine was communicated only to the fully initiated and approved members. While usually classified as Jews, they seem to have admitted at some time outside doctrinal influences such as Zoroastrian dualism. They had their own liturgical (solar) calendar (which may have been followed by other Jews as well), and they dis-

sociated themselves from official Judaism. Most scholars incline to the view that the community at Qumran was Essene. The description given by Josephus in most respects parallels the self-description found in the Qumran documents. Unlike Josephus, the Qumran documents are not clear about celibacy, though the fact that women were buried at Qumran is not of great importance in the discussion. Animal sacrifices may have been offered at Qumran. They did have priests. Similarities far outweigh the dissimilarities, and some allowance must be made for imperfect reporting by Josephus and Philo regarding a sect bound by rules of secrecy and separation. They transcribed numerous biblical and non-biblical documents, many of which were found at Qumran. The Essenes/Qumranites are important as a late-Jewish, pre-Christian religious movement, with their expectation of a Davidic as well as an Aaronic (priestly) Messiah. They may have had some indirect influence on Christianity. BIBLIOGRAPHY: R. E. Brown, NCE 5:552–553; M. Black, *Scrolls and Christian Origins* (1962).

[I. HUNT]

ESTABLISHED CHURCH, in general any Church the doctrines, worship, and discipline of which are supported by law; but the term has special reference to England. The C of E does not trace its establishment to a specific statute. The Canons of 1603 mention "the Church of England by law established," and thereafter the term appears in Parliamentary Acts, but these references are simply recognition of an already existing condition. The essence of establishment is incorporation of church law in the law of the realm, and such had been the case from Anglo-Saxon times. Nowhere carefully defined, the nature of the establishment has gradually developed by custom and through a long series of legislative measures, such as the adoption of the *Book of Common Prayer, the *Thirty-Nine Articles, and disciplinary measures. Symbolized in the coronation of the king by the abp. of Canterbury, the relation of Church and State is one of interdependence. In the House of Lords, two abps. and 24 bps. have opportunity to inform that body on ecclesiastical matters and to influence political and social legislation. The sentences of ecclesiastical courts are enforced by the state. Although the state does not provide financial support of the clergy, it shares oversight of endowments and income. As representatives of the Church, clergymen have considerable prestige and influence upon the public mind. Special prayers are offered in behalf of king and Parliament, judicial and executive agencies, and the nation as a whole. A system of parishes includes the entire populace; neither sparsely settled areas nor congested cities are without the ministry of the Church. The influence of the priest pervades every community, as his services are available to all persons in a parish in baptism, confirmation, matrimony, and burial. With its close connection to the state, the C of E has a specific responsibility to inform the consciences of people as to the moral obligation to express justice and love in law and judicial acts.

Benefits that accrue to the established Church also make it vulnerable to a state control adverse to its interests. Appointment of bps. and deans of cathedrals and other church patronage are rights of the Crown, and all clergy declare allegiance to the king and his successors. The Church may not alter its doctrinal formulas as its Book of Common Prayer without Parliament's approval, and a secular court is the highest appellate court in deciding ecclesiastical cases. New dioceses or parishes require the consent of an agency responsible to Parliament. The resources of the Church are also under the administration of the state, largely through the Church Commissioners, a body of laymen and clergymen appointed by Parliament. While the Church enjoys a large measure of freedom, there is always potential for conflict of interest and for interference with doctrines and use of endowments, especially since today Parliament is composed largely of non-Anglicans. A serious controversy arose in 1928, when a revision of the *Book of Common Prayer was voted down by the House of Commons. BIBLIOGRAPHY: C. Garbett, *Church and State in England* (1950). *STATE CHURCH; *NATIONAL CHURCH.

[N. H. MARING]

ESTAING, CHARLES HECTOR D' (1729–94), French admiral who participated in the American Revolution. E.'s military career began with his appointment as colonel of a regiment at the age of 16. He fought against the British in the Seven Years War and was twice imprisoned. Returning to France, he was named lieutenant general in the Navy (1763) and by 1777 was made vice admiral. He assumed command of a French fleet assigned to aid the American colonies against the British (1778), but his naval efforts met with only a few successes. He returned to France by 1780, wounded and a failure, with his leadership in question. He served well the American cause by convincing Lafayette to urge the French government to send Rochambeau's expeditionary force to America. In 1787 E. entered the political arena upon his election to the Assembly of Notables. He was appointed commandant of the National Guard in 1789 and admiral of the National Assembly in 1792. Because of his equivocal stand in the French Revolution—loyalty to the King and sympathy with some reform—he was arrested, tried, and executed on April 28, 1794. He was the author of the poems "Le Rêve" and "Les Thermopyles," and also of a book on the colonies.

[M. B. MONAGHAN]

ESTANG, LUC (1911–   ), pseudonym of Lucien Bastard, French novelist, essayist, and poet. He experienced in his early years of want in Paris a period of religious crisis, the aftermath of which was a mature commitment to Christianity. E. has achieved wide fame for his novels, particularly the controversial trilogy *Charges d'âmes* (1949–54). BIBLIOGRAPHY: P. Cogny, *Sept romanciers au-delá du*

roman (1963); W. Fowlie, "Postwar French Poets," *Poetry* 80 (1952) 311–371.

[G. E. GINGRAS]

ESTE, an Italian family of princely status that ruled in Ferrara from the 13th to the 17th century. Its possessions also included Modena and Reggio. The family name originated in the 10th cent. when Emperor Otto gave Marchese Oberto the fief of Este. **Azzo VI** (1193–1212) was the first Este to establish practical authority in Ferrara. The family produced several famous Renaissance cardinals and great political leaders. **Ippolito I** (1479–1520) conducted successful military campaigns against the League of Cambrai (1509) and was a generous patron of the arts. Leonardo da Vinci was his friend, and Ariosto dedicated his *Orlando Furioso* to him. **Ippolito II** (d. 1572) represented French interests in Italy as cardinal-protector of France and aspired to the tiara. He also was much interested in the arts and built the famous Villa d'Este at Tivoli. BIBLIOGRAPHY: E. P. Colbert, NCE 5:554–556.

[D. NUGENT]

ESTERRI D'ANEU, SANTA MARÍA, 11th-cent. basilica in Lérida, Spain, renowned for the monumental Catalonian apsidal fresco by the Master of Pedret (fl. *c.* 1130), showing the Virgin and Child enthroned, adored by the Magi, and attended by the archangels Michael and Gabriel. Similar frescoes in Lombardy point to N Italian and earlier Byzantine sources. Technique and innovative iconography in the accompanying figures of Elijah and Isaiah with seraphim establish the fresco as a 12th-cent. work. (The apsidal fresco of the same subject from S. Juan de Tredós by the Master of Pedret is in The Cloisters, New York.)

[M. J. DALY]

ESTHER, BOOK OF. This book of the OT is a novel relating how the Jewish people in Persia were saved when threatened with annihilation by their enemies, and how they revenged themselves upon those same enemies by annihilating them instead. All this was achieved through the influence of a single virtuous daughter of Israel, Esther, who became the most favored and dutiful queen of Ahasuerus, king of Persia, and used her position to win his favor on behalf of her people. Her uncle Mordecai had been condemned to be hanged by the king's vizier Haman for refusing to betray his religious principles; but through Esther's influence, Haman was hanged on the very gibbet he had prepared for his victim, and Mordecai received his viziership instead. Thus the essential message of Esther is, first, that those who attempt to lay violent hands upon the Jews will instead fall victim to that fate; and second, that this can be achieved through a single dutiful daughter of Israel who is irresistibly charming to the foreign potentate. The story seems to have been written some time in the 2d cent. B.C., and to have had a number of additions made from a variant recension to render it more explicitly religious in tone. These additions are deuterocanonical, and therefore not included in the canon of non-Catholic Bibles. BIBLIOGRAPHY: A. Barucq, *Judith, Esther* (2d ed. 1959); T. Gaster, *Purim and Hannukah in Eastern and Western Traditions* (1950); H. Gunkel, *Esther* (1916).

[D. J. BOURKE]

ESTIENNE (Lat. Stephanus), French family of printers and humanists founded by **Henry E. (c.1460–1520),** who established his printing press in Paris near the Sorbonne (c.1504). Henry's second son, **Robert (1503–59),** continued the family tradition (1526). Having already collaborated in the printing of a Latin edition of the NT and the Psalms (1522–23), he published a complete Bible in Latin (1527–28) and his *Dictionarium seu linguae latinae thesaurus* (1531). Appointed royal printer of Hebrew and Latin (1539), and then of Greek (1540), he published numerous classics and early Christian writers as well as the first Greek NT with critical apparatus (1550). Opposed, however, by the Sorbonne theologians, who suspected his liberalism of heresy and who obtained a ban on his series of Latin Bibles (1547), Robert moved to Geneva (1550) after consulting with Calvin and converted to the Reformed religion. Among the works Robert printed in Geneva were a Latin-Greek NT (1551) with the division of the text into verses that is still standard, a concordance of the Bible (1555), works of Calvin, and a reply to his own Sorbonne accusers, *Ad censuras theologorum parisiensium responsio* (1552).

Charles (c.1504–64), Robert's younger brother, who remained a Catholic, took control of the E. Paris press on his brother's departure for Geneva and succeeded him as royal printer. He is, however, better known as an author, and his many works include an anatomical study. **Henry (1531–98),** Robert's eldest son, an accomplished Hellenist, traveled through Europe searching for Greek MSS before joining his father in Geneva. His numerous publications include many first printed editions of classical texts, the result of his research, such as the works of Anacreon (1554) and Aeschylus's *Agamemnon* (1557), as well as his *Thesaurus graecae linguae* (1572), probably his most famous work, a masterpiece of lexicography. His French writings include: *Traité de la conformité du langage français avec le grec* (1565), which asserts the merits of the French language; *Apologie pour Hérodote* (1566), a satire on ecclesiastical customs that displeased the Geneva authorities, who had him arrested; *Deux dialogues du nouveau langage françois, italianizé et autrement desguizé* (1578), a defense of French against Italianizing influences, which again displeased the Geneva Council; and his *Précellence du langage françois* (1579), also in praise of the national language, published in Paris while he was visiting King Henry III. On his return to Geneva (1580) he was imprisoned, so that (after 1583) he spent little time in that city. He died in Lyons, France.

Paul (1566–c.1627), Henry's eldest son, succeeded his father, publishing among other works Sophocles's *Tragedies.* Banished (until 1619) from Geneva for participation in a Savoy conspiracy, he disappeared after selling the family press (1627). Antoine (1592–1674), Paul's son, became French royal printer after abjuring Calvinism. Robert (1530–c.1571), second son of the first Robert, having remained a Catholic after his father's departure for Geneva, reestablished the family Paris press (1556) and succeeded his uncle Charles as royal printer. BIBLIOGRAPHY: E. T. Armstrong, *Robert Étienne, Royal Printer: An Historical Study of the Elder Stephanus* (1954); H. Clément, *Henri Estienne et son oeuvre française* (1898).

[R. N. NICOLICH]

ESTIMATIVE POWER, in scholastic accounts of the knowing powers, an internal sense having as object what is physically beneficial or harmful; thus the equivalent of instinct. At the level of animal life this power is called the *sensus insensati,* i.e., it apprehends what is not apprehended by the external senses, a physical object as good or bad. This apprehension is rooted in the natural appetite for self-preservation; the knowledge is "affective," corresponding to the bent of appetite (see ThAq ST 1a, 78.4). The explanation is important to an understanding of a similar kind of intellectual power, *synderesis, whose acts are the rudimentary apprehensions of moral good or evil. In man the estimative power is also called the "cognitive" or discursive power and even "particular reason"; the meaning is that this internal sense in man has a further function, the disposing of sensory apprehensions for the mind's apprehension of *universals (ibid.). BIBLIOGRAPHY: G. Klubertanz, *Discursive Power* (1952).

[T. C. O'BRIEN]

ESTIUS, GULIELMUS (Wilhelm Hessels van Est; (1542–1613), exegete. A native of Gorkum (Gorinchem) in Holland, E. studied at Utrecht and then at Louvain, where for 10 years he studied philosophy, theology, and Scripture, and for another 10 years taught philosophy. In 1582 he became a professor and in 1595 chancellor of the Univ. of Douai. There he replaced (1594) the *Sentences* of *Peter Lombard with the text of St. Thomas in the theological courses. E. wrote a history of the *Gorkum martyrs (*Historia martyrum Gorcomiensium,* AS July 2:754–847), one of whom (Nicholas Pieck) was his uncle. His most important work was published posthumously, a commentary on the Pauline and Catholic Epistles (Douai, 1614–15, best ed. Mainz, 7 v., 1858–60). It combined careful and sensible exegesis with great patristic learning, the primary concern always being to arrive at the literal meaning of the text. He was involved in a controversy over M. *Baius, whom he supported against *Lessius, and was much esteemed for his piety, humility, and compassion for the poor. BIBLIOGRAPHY: H.-M. Feret, *Catholicisme* 4:522–523; J. Ferrer,

Pecado original y justificación en la doctrina de Gulielmus Estius (1960); L. Salembier, DTC 5:871–878.

[R. B. ENO]

ESTONIA republic of the Soviet Union; northernmost of the three Baltic republics. A Finno-Ugrian people, Estonians were settled in the area by the 11th cent. After various unsuccessful attempts to introduce Christianity in Livonia, German name for the area now covered by Estonia and Latvia, Bp. Albert arrived in 1199 and began forced conversion. He dedicated the country to Mary and it became known as the "Land of the Virgin." He established his see at Riga in 1201, and the following year founded the Knights (or Brothers) of the Sword, an order that then moved to conquer the Estonians. Conquest was completed with the help of Danish King Waldamar II, who arrived in 1219 and founded Tallinn, now the capital. In 1237 the Knights became a branch of the *Teutonic Order, with rule over Livonia. During the Reformation, Lutheranism gradually prevailed in Estonia. On the dissolution of the Knights in 1561, Poland gained Livonia, but surrendered it to Sweden in 1629. Peter I of Russia took the area in 1721. Following the Russian Revolution of 1917, Estonia became independent, but it was retaken by the Soviet Union during World War II. A strong national consciousness has continued to resist Russian cultural domination.

[T. EARLY]

ESTONIA, ORTHODOX CHURCH OF, a Church founded in 1923. It was recognized by the Patriarchate of Constantinople as an autocephalous metropolia consisting of three dioceses, later reduced to two, Tallin and Narva. It existed independently from 1923 to 1944, with a brief period of Russian control in 1941, but it was absorbed into the Patriarchate of Moscow in 1944 and is now a simple diocese. In 1968 an American citizen, Father Sergius Samon, was elected bp. for Estonian Orthodox exiles in Australia, Canada, Europe, and the U.S.; he is subject to the Patriarchate of Constantinople. BIBLIOGRAPHY: *Handbook of American Orthodoxy* (1972) 2, 35.

[T. BIRD]

ESTOUTEVILLE, GUILLAUME D' (*c.*1412–83), cardinal, diplomat. An active figure in papal diplomacy, he played a significant role in papal dealings with France and was employed (1451) in a papally sponsored attempt to end the Hundred Years' War. BIBLIOGRAPHY: Pastor 3,4 *passim.*

[J. MULDOON]

ÉTAMPES, NOTRE-DAME-DU-FORT (1125), French Gothic church in a palace complex. The jamb statues of the S portal (*c.*1150) show remarkable affinity to figures of the W portals at Chartres and St. Denis.

[M. J. DALY]

ETERNAL LIFE, the gratuitous share in the plenitude of being proper to God, which can be experienced in this life but is ordered to completion in heaven. An idea of life after death developed in the latest books of the OT where it is conceived of as a resurrection of the body. In the NT it is variously understood. The Synoptics see it as fulfillment after death rather than as a presently shared reality. Paul understands it as life of the Spirit communicated by the risen Jesus which is shared as a present reality (Rom 6.4) to be fulfilled in the resurrection of the Christian. John writes of it as life that is conferred in the resurrection of the Christian who keeps the commandments of God (12.50) and has faith in Jesus (3.15), in whom are the words of eternal life (6.68) and in whom believers live forever though they die (11.25–27). Christian tradition, therefore, understands that one shares divine life in this world in union with the risen Lord, a life that grows toward complete manifestation in the whole man, soul and glorified body, at the resurrection of the flesh. Catholic theology has understood that this deeper sharing may be experienced, though incompletely, immediately at death in a personal love relationship with God. BIBLIOGRAPHY: R. L. Stewart and P. M. Coyle, NCE 8:738–744 s.v. "Life." *BEATIFIC VISION.

[J. CORDOUE]

ETERNAL PUNISHMENT, the suffering endured after death in a state of finality called *hell by those who have freely alienated themselves from God during life. Extrabiblical Jewish writings refer to *Gehenna which punishes with eternal fire but is not certainly a place of eternal punishment, since annihilation of the wicked and release following a period of punishment are expressed possibilities. In the NT, the eternity of punishment is alluded to in various ways. Mark speaks of the fire of Gehenna as unquenchable (9.3); and Matthew, of an eternal force (18.8). In John the punishment is exclusion from eternal life (5.29; 8.24) while Paul refers to the eternal destruction of the impious (2 Th 1.9). The eternity of punishment has found expression in tradition (D 411) against the background of *apocatastasis, the doctrine of universalism which holds that ultimately all men will be saved because of God's mercy. Not all contemporary theologians are satisfied with the attempts made in the past to show that an eternity of punishment is compatible with the mercy of God. It seems important to stress the self-judgment involved in the punishment rather than to see it as an extrinsic condemnation inflicted by God. It is the logical consequence of the working out of man's free, alienating actions in life. BIBLIOGRAPHY: T. McDermott, "Hell," *New Blackfriars* 48 (1967) 186–197; A. Winklhofer, *Coming of His Kingdom* (tr. A. V. Littledale, 1963).

[J. CORDOUE]

ETERNITY. (1) Its full and proper meaning is the *eternity of God. (2) Applied to the life of the blessed, eternity is the changelessness of their share in a *beatific vision and rest in God (ThAq ST 1a, 10.3). (3) Applied to the damned, it is their interminable state of punishment (*ibid.*, ad 2). (4) Applied to the origin and duration of the created universe, eternity is the opposite of a beginning in *time. St. Thomas Aquinas opposed the traditionalists among his contemporaries in affirming that a temporal beginning of creation is not demonstrable by philosophy; an eternally existing, yet created universe is not impossible or contradictory (*ibid.*, 46.2). Classic Greek philosophy presupposed the world to be an eternal, total system, which included the function of prime causes, and with which philosophical explanation deals. Aristotle in particular held for the eternity of matter and movement. BIBLIOGRAPHY: ThAq ST (Lat-Eng v. 14, ed. T. C. O'Brien, Appendix 1 "The Use of Aristotle").

[T. C. O'BRIEN]

ETERNITY OF GOD, in the classical definition of *Boethius, the interminable, unchangeable, and perfect possession of life. Neither the OT nor NT contains this philosophical concept, but speaks of time in terms totally relative to human experience. Eternity is thought of as endless duration, as an unlimited expanse of time, not as other than time. Within this conceptual framework, however, God is certainly regarded as eternal. God exists before creation, and from age to age (Ps 90.2); creation changes but God remains the same (Ps 102.26–28); to him a thousand years are but a day (Ps 90.4; 2 Pet 3.8); and in his constant will to bring salvation, he is called eternal (Rom 16.26). He is the Alpha and Omega (Rev 1.8), the beginning and the end (Rev 21.6). In addition to the aspect of duration, therefore, Scripture combines the notion of God's faithfulness with that of eternity.

Speculative theology, however, has continually tried to explain eternity as wholly other than time. Time is not contained in eternity as a second is contained in a minute. Eternity transcends the changing order of created being and stands as one moment: to speak of God as eternal is to speak of him as unchangeable. There is no division or measure to God, no successive states. God is substantial eternity, since eternity is a necessary attribute of his perfect essence (ThAq ST 1a, 10). It is this divine eternity that bestows meaning on created time and supplies its direction. This concept of time and eternity, which has reappeared in contemporary RC theology after much mishandling in the nominalist and decadent scholastic period, is essential to a correct understanding of God's "foreknowledge" and man's future free actions. It is not that God, existing at this point of time, foresees what we will do at some future date. Rather God, to whom all things are present in an eternal now, knows what for us is future in the single moment of his unchangeable existence. BIBLIOGRAPHY: F. H. Brabant, *Time and Eternity in Christian Thought* (1937); A. Darlap and J. de Finance, SacMund 2:249–252.

[T. M. MCFADDEN]

ETHELBERT, KING OF EAST ANGLIA, ST. (d.794), martyr, son of King Ethelred of East Anglia, whom he succeeded. He was involved in the perennial struggles among the kingdoms of the heptarchy; he was seized by Offa II of Mercia and beheaded. Legend alleges a romantic attachment to Offa's daughter. His relics at Hereford became a great shrine. BIBLIOGRAPHY: M. R. James "Two Lives of St. Ethelbert," EHR (1917) 32:214–244; G. D. Gordini, BiblSanct 5:116; Butler 2:358–359.

[J. L. DRUSE]

ETHELBERT, KING OF KENT, ST. (d.616), Bretwalda and lawgiver. E. became king of Kent in 560 and later exercised authority over all England as Bretwalda. Married to the Frankish Christian princess Bertha, he permitted St. Augustine to enter and evangelize Kent in 596. He became a Christian, founded several churches including St. Paul's in London, and influenced other Anglo-Saxon monarchs to become Christian. He issued in 604 the first Anglo-Saxon code of laws, which bears his name. Through him, Frankish influence was maintained in S E England, the Roman ideas began to return, and the primatial See of the Anglo-Saxon Church was set in his capitol, Canterbury. BIBLIOGRAPHY: J. L. Druse NCE 5:566; Butler 1:414–415; N. Del Re, BiblSanct 5:116–118.

[J. L. DRUSE]

ETHELBERT OF YORK (d. *c.*781), abp. of York. Relative, protégé, and successor of Abp. Egbert, E. directed the famous school of York, where Alcuin was his pupil. As abp. (consecrated 767), he rebuilt the minster and increased its great library. After retiring, E. dedicated the completed cathedral shortly before his own burial in it. BIBLIOGRAPHY: H. Dauphin, DHGE 15:1158–59.

[W. A. CHANEY]

ETHELBURGA, SS. Three holy women bore this name. (1) **Ethelburga of Kent,** also called Tata, and E. of Lyminge (from the name of a monastery she founded in Kent; d. *c.*647), daughter of King Ethelbert of Kent. She married Edwin, pagan king of Northumbria. St. Paulinus accompanied her as chaplain and together they worked to promote the conversion of her husband and his people. Edwin accepted baptism, and after his death E. returned to Kent where she founded the monastery which she governed as abbess until her death. See AS September 3:206; October 6:6, 112–113; Butler 2:35; F. Caraffa, BiblSanct 5:120; Bede, *Historia ecclesiastica* 2:9–. (2) **Ethelburga of Barking** (d. *c.*678), abbess of Barking. She was trained in the religious life by St. Hildelitha, who was brought from France to help with the foundation. See Bede, *Historia ecclesiastica* 4:6–9; Butler 4:95–96; E. I. Watkin, BiblSanct 5:118. (3) **Ethelburga of Faremoutiers,** whom some martyrologies call E. of Auberge (d. 695), daughter of

Anna, king of East Anglia. She went with her half sister, St. Sethrida, to France where they were received into the monastery of Faremoutiers-en-Brie. See Butler 3:34; Bede, *Historia ecclesiastica* 3:8; P. Burchi, BiblSanct 5:118–119.

[P. K. MEAGHER]

ETHELDRITA, ST. (Aelfthryth, Alfreda, Elfthryta; d. after 833). The daughter of King Offa of Mercia (d. 796), she was, according to tradition, betrothed to King Ethelbert of East Anglia, whom Offa killed (794). She apparently lived for years as a recluse at Crowland. BIBLIOGRAPHY: L. Boyle, BiblSanct 5:120–121.

[W. A. CHANEY]

ETHELHARD OF CANTERBURY (Aethelheard; d. 805), abp. of Canterbury. Mercian influence in E.'s elevation as abp. (792) provoked Kentish opposition, and E. was exiled. By 803 he was vindicated through papal and Mercian cooperation. The Mercian archbishopric of Lichfield was abolished, and the ecclesiastical unity of S England under Canterbury was reasserted.

[W. A. CHANEY]

ETHELNOTH OF CANTERBURY, ST. (Aethelnoth, "the Good"; d. 1038), abp. of Canterbury. He was a monk of Glastonbury and dean of Christ Church, Canterbury, before he became abp. (1020). A principal advisor to King Canute, E. strengthened Canterbury's influence by royal grants and relic-collecting. BIBLIOGRAPHY: G. D. Gordini, BiblSanct 5:123; Butler 4:222–223.

[W. A. CHANEY]

ETHELREDA, ST. (d. 679), Queen of Northumbria, abbess of Ely. A princess of East Anglia, married twice for diplomatic reasons, she maintained her virginity and founded the Abbey of Ely. Her shrine there became a principal pilgrimage place, and the later form of her name (Audrey) gave rise to the English word "tawdry" from the cheap souvenirs sold to pilgrims to the shrine. BIBLIOGRAPHY: Bede, *Historia ecclesiastica* 4:3; J. Stephan, BiblSanct 5:121–122.

[J. L. DRUSE]

ETHELWOLD OF WINCHESTER, ST. (d. 984), leader of English monastic revival. As bp. of Winchester (963), E. substituted monks for worldly clerics at the Old and New Minsters. Teacher, builder, and royal adviser, he restored and founded monasteries, stimulated art and music, and prepared the *Regularis concordia.* BIBLIOGRAPHY: E. J. Walkin, BiblSanct 5:129–130; Butler 3:240–241.

[W. A. CHANEY]

ETHERIA (Aetheria; Egeria; fl. early 5th cent.), a noblewoman (probably an abbess or a nun) of N Spain or S Gaul, who made a pilgrimage to the holy places in Palestine in the early 5th century. The chronicle of her travels, known as the *Peregrinatio Aetheriae,* has survived in an 11th-cent. MS discovered in 1884. This work is of general historical and philological interest (it is written in a curious vulgar Latin), but it is esp. valued by liturgists for its description of the liturgical services she witnessed in Jerusalem and its vicinity. Text: (ed. and Fr. tr. H. Pétré, 1948; Eng. tr. M. L. McClure and C. L. Feltoe, 1919).

[P. K. MEAGHER]

ETHICAL CULTURE MOVEMENT, ethical humanism originating with the founding of the New York Society for Ethical Culture, May 15, 1876, by F. *Adler. Although most of the approximately 100 original members were Jewish, later many of Christian background were added. Societies were organized in other cities, and in 1889 a federation, the American Ethical Union, was formed; in 1970 it included 30 societies, with some 7,000 members. A corresponding movement began in England in 1887 under the leadership of S. Coit (1857–1944), an American, and the English Ethical Union was formed in 1896. A Berlin society was organized in 1892, and the first meeting of the International Ethical Movement was held in Germany in 1893. In 1952 the American Ethical Union joined ethical unions and other humanist organizations of several countries to form the International Humanist and Ethical Union, with headquarters in Utrecht. The movement makes no metaphysical or theological affirmations, though it generally holds that the moral law is grounded in objective reality. Societies have weekly meetings, normally on Sundays, without prayer or ritual, but with music, reading, and an address. They also conduct forums, clubs, youth groups, and other programs. The movement has supported a wide variety of liberal social causes and has been influential beyond its numbers because of the high intelligence level of much of its membership. BIBLIOGRAPHY: H. Blackham, *Ethical Movement during Seventy Years* (1946); D. Muzzey, *Ethics as a Religion* (2d ed., 1951); F. Adler, *Creed and Deed* (1877, repr. 1972).

[T. EARLY]

ETHICAL FORMALISM, a generic description of any theory of morality tending to stress the formal aspects of the moral act, usually at the expense of the material ones. The formal considerations are the moral law itself and the intention or motivation of the agent in acting, whereas the material considerations are the content of the act, i.e., what it is that is done and the consequences of what is done. Formalist ethics generally tends to hold that the subjective element in the moral act, i.e., the reason for its performance, is the principal determinant of the character of the act as morally good or evil, though many variations of the position exist, each with its own context, as found in thinkers such as J. J. *Rousseau, J. *Herbart, I. *Kant, and J. *Royce. Kant's moral philosophy is commonly regarded as the prototype of formalism because it represents a quest for ethical principles determining what is inherently right or wrong, regardless of circumstances, and capable of recognition immediately as true and binding upon an agent. These moral laws are prior to experience; they are grounded in a sense of duty arising from man's rational nature. The moral code functioning in man is nothing other than the human will governed by reason. The good will of the agent, i.e., a dutiful will that acts out of deference for the principle of duty, and on that basis alone, is central in morality. If a man acts thus for a good motive, his act is morally good irrespective of the consequences, for the latter do not determine the moral quality of the action.

[J. T. HICKEY]

ETHICS, from Gr. *ēthē,* which Cicero translated as mores, manners, customs, character, disposition. (1) Ethics may refer to a code of conduct regulating a profession—thus medical ethics, legal ethics. (2) Ethics also means moral philosophy, the meaning of which has varied nearly infinitely in the course of history (see ETHICS, HISTORY OF). Within the context of Christian educational programs, ethics, qualified as "Christian ethics," is sometimes used rather than the name "moral theology"; the usage in part reflects history, the difference between Catholic and Protestant ideas of the subject matter of theology and, indeed, of man's moral life in reference to grace. In another usage, the force of "ethics" as distinct from moral theology is that it builds a science of morals on a purely philosophical base, excluding or abstracting from revelation and faith. The disadvantage of such a usage is that moral theology may come to be thought of as ethics with a slight addition of such considerations as grace, theological virtue, and other "supplementary" notions; it is even sometimes alleged that there is no essential distinction between "morality" and "Christian morality." In fact, the method, content, and norms of moral theology are altogether differentiated from a philosophical ethics, simply because moral theology begins with the givenness of the relationship to God in grace, and its norms of moral good and evil depend on the measure and meaning of *charity.

[T. C. O'BRIEN]

ETHICS, EXISTENTIAL, see EXISTENTIAL ETHICS

ETHICS, HISTORY OF. "Ethics" is here used for that branch of rational inquiry which considers how human beings ought to behave, and if possible to give the reason why. The following division into periods is somewhat arbitrarily adopted: (1) Greek; (2) Hellenist and Roman; (3) Medieval; (4) Post-Renaissance; (5) Post-Kantian; and (6) Contemporary. This cursory account will probably be more useful if it attempts to trace the genealogy of ideas operative in the English-speaking world than if it is tightly packed with select names and dates: the resulting simplification will, of course, have to be taken with more than a grain of salt.

Greek. The story beings, though not abruptly, with the dialectic of *Socrates (5th cent. B.C.), found in the early dialogues of *Plato; it moves into the conflicts between the conventions traditional in the contemporary aristocracy and the criticisms of them by the *Sophists, and delicately draws the teeth of both parties. Plato's own dialectic, which appears in his later works, is toward the pure form of the Good; it shows a distrust of bodily pleasure, holds that moral evil is due to ignorance or madness, and advocates rules by an intellectual elite. His disciple, *Aristotle, inherited some of his temper and principles, but was a scientist by training and an empirical philosopher by taste: he treats the Good as the causal end shaping action, including moral action, and relates this to the happiness of a moral agent. These two have proved the giants for all subsequent ethical discussions; they anticipate the contrast between nonnaturalistic theories that separate values and facts and naturalistic theories that bring them together; also between a purely cognitive evaluation of moral virtue and an allowance for an affective element.

Hellenist and Roman. After them the interest shifted from theoretical to practical ethics. The main issue lay between the *Epicureans and the *Stoics, those who proposed respectively an enjoyable or an invulnerable way of living. On both sides there was a refinement on crude beginnings. The hearty *hedonism of the *Cyrenaics developed into the enlightened appreciation of the Epicureans; the savage insensibility of the *Cynics into the public-spirited imperturbability of the Stoics. And in practice there was little to choose between the *ataraxia* of the former and the *apatheia* of the latter. Yet here again we have some anticipation of the later conflict between the ethical utilitarianism of those who hold that action is right when it is beneficial and the ethical formalism of those who hold that right is a value for its own sake and nothing else.

Medieval. So heterogeneous are the elements of ethical thinking at this period that an attempt at a summary would be baffled but for the unity secured by a descensive theology springing from divine Revelation. Here the influence of St. *Augustine is capital. Already *Plotinus had opened a metaphysical and mystical way of escape from mere moralism into the blessedness of union with the fount of being. Neoplatonism was to run for centuries as a main stream in Judaic, Christian, and Islamic thought. St. Augustine was above all a theologian; for him the reign of grace, manifested in divine charity, transcended the measures proposed by moral philosophers, which at most could make the present life fairly tolerable and prepare us for salvation. His doctrine of the *Eternal Law is Neoplatonist, and of its derivation into *Natural Law, which is very much to the mind of the Stoics, together with his emphasis on obedience to divine authority, has strongly characterized Christian ethics ever since. Insofar as other Latin Fathers have an ethical philosophy it is Stoic in its presuppositions and temper, not least in its distrust of pleasure.

A significant contribution was made by *Abelard's insistence that morality was a quality of personal intention; this was to provide a providential corrective to an over-rigid application of *positive law, and of Roman canon law in particular. A revolution, so quiet that even now it is not generally appreciated, took place in Christian ethical philosophy with St. *Thomas Aquinas. He rediscovered Aristotelianism, was the first to construct a scientific frame of reference for moral theology, and founded a tradition, centered round *eudemonism, of not confining morality to an enclave but of treating it in open relation to all other matters of human interest. The tradition, however, soon narrowed to a school, and the general picture of late *Scholasticism is not one of integration.

Post-Renaissance. Henceforth the history of ethical philosophy proceeds with scarcely more than a perfunctory acknowledgment of the theology of Revelation. Though such labels should be used with care, the contrasts sounded by Aristotelianism, Epicureanism, and Thomism on one side, and Platonism, Stoicism, and Augustinianism on the other, continue to echo. In general terms the alternatives were that moral meanings are inferred from the premoral and expect the postmoral and that they are special objects of intuition. For the first we may cite *Hobbes, who grounded ethics on objective laws of biology and psychology; *Spinoza, who derived humane precepts from the instinct of self-preservation; *Locke, who evaluated them as likely to produce pleasure or reduce pain; *Hume, who related them to sentiments of approbation. For the second we may cite the Cambridge Platonists, for whom an immutable moral order was as readily cognizable as were the relations of numbers; or Joseph *Butler, who noted the special and ineducible qualities of the concept of duty; and the *Common Sense Intuitionism of Thomas Reid and Richard Price.

Post-Kantian. Ethical philosophy has never been the same since *Kant, and still labors to repair the gap he drove between the laws of nature and causal determinism, which were matters of theoretical and descriptive judgment, and the laws of freedom and the ethical principles, which were matters of practical and prescriptive judgment. With his constructive criticism of the workings of pure reason went an exaltation of moral obligation irrespective of consequences. Yet after him *Utilitarianism was to reach its greatest strength, in *Bentham, James *Mill, above all in John Stuart *Mill, its classical exponent, to dominate British and American ethical philosophy, and to find a complement in *Pragmatism. In Germany, however, a more transcendental idealism held the field, with a marked emphasis on the affirmation of the will, for *Fichte the absolute will, for *Hegel the embodiment of the Nation's will. Suitably modulated, Hegelianism came into England through J. H. Green and F. H. Bradley, and into America through Josiah Royce: in effect it was turned upside down by Karl Marx, who, in subjecting the realization of mind and will to a socio-economic historical dialectic, might be considered a utilitarian rather than an idealist.

Contemporary. Such terms, and others, like objectivism, subjectivism, relativism, naturalism, cognitivism, noncognitivism, hedonism, formalism, and so forth, are subject to so many permutations in the acute though often minute inquiries of recent years that they are better avoided, even as jotted headings from this brief glance. A great debate sprang from G. E. Moore's attack (*Ethics*, 1912) on the so-called naturalistic fallacy of identifying good as an empirical property. His utilitarianism was attacked in turn by H. L. Prichard and by W. D. Ross (*The Right and the Good,* 1930), who pointed out, and thereby came close to Kant, that no "ought" proposition can be elicited from a proposition not containing an "ought." The effect of these criticisms has been widespread, but how decisive they have proved is a matter of debate: naturalistic theories sturdily survived, notably in America, e.g., R. B. Perry and J. Dewey (*Theory of Valuation,* 1939). The effect of sociological and anthropological studies has been to show the varieties of moral experience and to question the validity of universal standards (E. Westermarck, *Ethical Relativity,* 1932). *Existentialism, which lays its stress on commitment, not meaning, on a "loving conflict," not agreement, advocates a morality beyond reason and the world of "essences." To a linguistic philosopher this is a dramatization of a logical point, that most of our ethical generalizations in fact are not verifiable on rational grounds. There are signs that the analysis of the logic of moral reasoning is losing its interest; it is possible that phenomenological descriptions of the content of moral forms may restore some sort of order to a discipline that at present is scattered all over the place.

BIBLIOGRAPHY: H. Sidgwick, *Outlines of the History of Ethics* (5th ed., 1902); C. D. Broad, *Five Types of Ethical Theory* (1930); C. C. Stevenson, *Ethics and Language* (1945); T. E. Hill, *Contemporary Ethical Theories* (1950); F. C. Copleston, *Aquinas* (1955); C. C. Brinton, *History of Western Morals* (1959).

[T. GILBY]

ETHICS, PROTESTANT CHRISTIAN, see PROTESTANT CHRISTIAN ETHICS.

ETHICS AND RELIGION. When the terms are antithetically presented, as not uncommonly, ethics covers the norms of rational behavior in this world expressed in good sense, justice, courage, and moderation, whereas religion is set on an object out of this world altogether and making demands not subject to individual or collective needs. There are several variations on the theme: thus the Marxist treatment of religion as the opium of the people deadening them to social abuses; thus the colonialist and tourist prejudice that the natives though devoutly religious are not very ethical; thus too the suspicion that mystics, like artists, claim immunity from the ordinary decencies, such as washing and paying their debts. There is sociological confirmation, for it seems that churchgoing and public-spirit observances are often in inverse ratio, and that believing communities and civically respectable communities smell rather different; the first have their charm, but if there is an epidemic, it is more likely to be put down to divine anger than to neglect of the drains.

Much of the conflict is incidental or lies in the emotive fringes of the terms; nevertheless there is a perennial tension between the claims of justice and of charity, and as a sober moralism will hesitate to applaud extravagance so a religion worthy of the name which declares truths about the divinity will not reduce its teaching to a code of human conduct. An ethical philosophy which proclaims that moral good is supreme and categorically imperative will require, within its system, religion to conform to its standards; so conversely a theology which identifies its entire content with religion will cast ethics in a subordinate role. In fact classical Catholic moral theory has its own grammar which may serve to elucidate the subject.

Ethics or morals concern *human acts, and these enter into the Christian life; this, however, points beyond them to God's revelation of himself as far surpassing a mere integrator of our moral universe. The fundamental truths of faith are about him, not about us, and consequently there is much more than ethics in Christianity. Moreover our activity as Christians is not confined to ethical practices, for these are ruled by the *moral virtues, which direct us toward God but of themselves reach no further than observing a human and gracious mode of living, whereas the *theological virtues of faith, hope, and charity break out of the creaturely environment and rest on God himself.

If all this is comprehended in the term religion, then of course ethics will be a part of it, minor though indispensable. The term, however, has a proper and more specific sense, namely that moral virtue, allied to the moral virtue of justice which renders to God what is his due, namely *our* service and worship. This falls under the rule of morals and ethics and must observe the mean of moral virtue between too little and too much, in this case between the vicious extremes of religiosity and irreligion, of which the first can take antisocial forms and justly incur the reproaches suggested in the opening paragraph. *RELIGION AND MORALITY.

[T. GILBY]

ETHICS IN PRIMITIVE SOCIETIES, rules or principles governing behaviour in small-scale communities. Rarely formulated in abstract systems, ethical norms are usually elicited by specific actions. Those norms relate differently to other social rules and customs, social organization, and religious beliefs in each society. Though Tylor's evolutionist characterization of primitive religions as devoid of ethical content has been rightly abandoned, no single characterization of primitive ethics can be advanced in its place. Blatantly antisocial actions (e.g., murder, incest, theft) are widely discouraged between members of the same group, but may be free from sanctions when perpetrated against outsiders. Moral rules often shade imperceptibly into other areas, making it difficult for the observer to disengage an ethical system intact. For example, the African Nuer category of "faults" includes some actions that would generally be recognized as moral transgressions (e.g., incest, adultery) but also others that seem outside the ethical realm (rules about eating, cow-milking, etc.); actions are grouped together because they merit the same punishment. When unifying ethical principles are to be discovered, they tend to stress the unity, solidarity, and equality of the group. The African Dinka concept of *cieng* envisions an ideal social order in which people are united in full concord and the expectations of the community are harmoniously balanced. For the Dinka, the harmonious life is the moral life. Similarly, the moral life among the Tangu of New Guinea pivots on the twin values of amity and equivalence. Tangu see themselves as bound together in a web of mutual obligations which come into play most frequently in the exchange of foodstuffs. Whoever produces less is suspected of contempt for the primary communal values; whoever produces more is suspected of arrogant self-aggrandizement. Since perfect equivalence, which replicates the divine status of being unobliged, is a chimerical goal, Tangu often resort to a formal, public airing of grievances, which is the accepted means for finding and maintaining moral equilibrium, restoring overt amity, and accommodating the current distribution of power. The values of amity and equivalence determine the rhythms of Tangu life and define the moral actor. Although any event can be seen as precipitating a moral issue, the activity of sorcerers poses an extreme threat to the moral and social order in many communities. They are thought to be inverse humans, strangers or, outsiders who give no indication of entering into reciprocal relations; their actions indicate that they operate outside the acknowledged moral order. Accordingly, suspicions of sorcery force a close evaluation of the web of moral obligations by all involved. In such situations, the diviner functions as a social diagnostician and upholder of the prevailing morality, who, by careful questioning and inference, elicits the essentials of the situation from his clients and seeks to articulate an acceptable course of action which will rectify the disturbed social relations. Suspicions of sorcery subside as moral harmony returns. As Victor Turner notes, diviners "play a vital role in upholding tribal morality [since] moral law is most vividly made known through its breach." As an alien in the midst of a society, the sorcerer provokes a clearer articulation of moral notions. The alien *par excellence,* the European, can also provoke a moral crisis in tribal societies. For Tangu, the Europeans' clear superiority in the production of foodstuffs and other goods (often without apparent labor) and their foreign moral assumptions pose the question of the measure of the moral actor most acutely. How can Tangu consider themselves moral beings if they have no hope of entering into equivalent relations? Although a variety of related problems and values—cash economy, urbanization and increased social mobility, literacy, different systems of education and medicine, etc.—are involved in the meeting of tribal and Western cultures; the abandonment, readjustment, or accelerated development of traditional moral rules and principles is often a part of the larger enterprise of coming to grips with new horizons of human possibilities. BIBLIOGRAPHY: E. Norbeck, *Religion in Primitive Society* (1961) ch. 10; K. Burridge, *Tangu Traditions* (1969); idem, *Mambu* (1960); E. E. Evans-Pritchard, *Nuer Religion* (1956); idem, *Witchcraft, Oracles, and Magic among the Azande* (1937); V. Turner, *Revelation and Divination in Ndembu Ritual* (1975); M. Fortes, *Oedipus and Job in West African Religion* (1958).

[E. V. GALLAGHER]

ETHIOPIA, ancient Christian kingdom in NE Africa between the Sudan and the Red Sea. The population is racially mixed with Negro, Hamitic, and south Semitic peoples represented. The Semitic group is culturally dominant. They trace their ancestry back to Makeda, the biblical queen of Sheba, and her son Menelik, the legendary founder of the royal dynasty. It is certain that the south Semitic people were settled in Ethiopia by the time Christianity arrived in the person of St. *Frumentius (c.320). The king, 'Ezana, embraced Christianity and made it the official religion of his kingdom, which centered around Aksum. This early period was one of relative stability for Ethiopia. In the late 5th cent. the *Nine Saints, probably Syrian monks, arrived and did extensive missionary work. It is not certain whether they were Monophysites. Ethiopia had close ties with the Coptic Church of Egypt, and sometime after Chalcedon it became Monophysite. The Arab invasion of NE Africa left Ethiopia isolated and eventually surrounded by Islam. At this point Ethiopian history becomes a blank until 1286. Around 920, a Jewish dynasty seems to have gained control of the country and persecuted Christianity. In 1268, the old dynasty was restored with the help of abbot Takla Hâymanôt who secured large landholdings for the Church. The prerogative of the Coptic Church of Egypt to appoint the bishop (*abuna*) of the Ethiopian Church dates from the 13th cent. and is based on a pseudo-canon of Nicaea. Also at this time political power shifted to the S away from Aksum. In the 14th cent., conflicts arose between the monasteries and the clergy who lived at court. They were not settled until the second half of the 15th cent. when the monasteries gained autonomy. From 1520 to 1551, Ethiopia was subjected to a Muslim invasion under Ahmed Gran during which Aksum was destroyed. The King asked for aid from the Portuguese who had first visited Ethiopia in 1487. In 1543, Gran was defeated and killed near Lake Tana. From 1557 to 1635, Ethiopia experienced foreign influence and ''missionary'' efforts at the hands of the Jesuits. Their tactlessness and the imperialistic inclinations of the Portuguese resulted in Ethiopian distrust of Europeans and strengthened the ties of the Church with Alexandrian Christianity. Ethiopia moved through the 19th and into the 20th cent. in a state of semifeudalism. In 1930, with the accession of Emperor Haile Selassie I, and in spite of Italian occupation (1935–41), Ethiopia began an era of reform and modernization in both State and national Church. The overthrow in 1974 of the Emperor caused a series of royalist revolts in

Feb. 1975. A military government is in effective power, though still diverted by sporadic outbreaks of unrest outside the capital city. BIBLIOGRAPHY: D. Mathew, *Ethiopia* (1947, repr. 1974); A. H. Jones and E. Monroe, *History of Ethiopia* (1955).

[D. W. JOHNSON]

ETHIOPIAN ART, an exclusively Christian art that extends from the conversion of the Aksumite kingdom (4th cent.) to the present day. Unfortunately, almost nothing exists from the 4th to the 16th cent. because of the destructive invasion of Ahmed Gran (1528–40). The steles at *Aksum (4th cent.) and the rock-hewn churches at Lalibela (early 13th cent.) survive as examples of early and medieval, uniquely Ethiopian architecture. Painting flourished from the 16th to the 18th cent., after which its quality and skill deteriorated. King Fasilidas II (1632–67) established a school of painting at Gondor, which set the characteristic Ethiopian style. Colorful murals, a chief means of religious instruction, covered the walls of churches and the cubicle cell in their centers that contained the sanctuary. They follow strict rules of symbolic expression in colors, in the stance and facial expressions of the figures, and in clothing. A whole range of subjects is expected to be displayed, including the Trinity, the life of Jesus and Mary, legends of the saints and of the founding of the monarchy. BIBLIOGRAPHY: *Larousse Encyclopedia of Byzantine and Medieval Art* (1963) 78–81.

[D. W. JOHNSON]

ETHIOPIAN CHRISTIAN LITERATURE, in the narrow sense, the literature of Ethiopia written in *Geez. Since the latter part of the 19th cent. when Amharic replaced Geez as the literary language, there has arisen a promising secular literature. Prior to this Ethiopian literature was for the most part Christian, so bound together was the life of Church and country. The value of Ethiopic literature lies chiefly in what it provides of texts that would otherwise be totally or in large part unknown. From the time of St. Frumentius, Greek and Coptic works were translated into Geez, and often only the Geez text has survived. Of the works composed in Geez, most are unoriginal and rely heavily on Greek and Coptic works as models, especially on the Bible. The Bible was translated in the earliest period of Ethiopian Christianity, and it contains several non-canonical books, notably Enoch and Jubilees. A collection of patristic sayings, the *Qerlos,* the rules of St. Pachomius, and some liturgical services belong to the early period. Both literature and history went through a dark age from *c.*650 to the late 13th century. During this interval the Arabs had captured Egypt and done extensive damage to the Coptic Mother Church. The second literary period opens with the revision of the Bible and the translation of new liturgical works. Most translations were now made from Arabic, since both Greek and Coptic had died out in Egypt. Apocrypha, legends of the saints, hymn collections, and a historical romance, the *Kebra Nagast* (The Glory of the Kings), dealing with the history of the Ethiopian dynasty, date from this time. Also in the second period, the *Sinodos,* a book of canon law, and the *Didascalia,* a general work on Church life and structure, were both translated. The so-called Golden Age of Ethiopian literature covers the 15th and the first half of the 16th century. Polemics against superstition and magic appear under the patronage of King Zar'a Yâ'qob, and generate a rich counter-literature expounding superstition and magic. The first regular chronicles were written, hymnology was extensively enriched, and more translations were made, notably the *Universal History* of George the Egyptian. After this third period general literary decay follows. Exceptions were the only two original philosophers of Ethiopia, Zar'a Yâ'qob and his disciple Walda Ḥeywat who together produced the *Enquiries.* A translation of Abu Isḥaq ibn al 'Assal's *Nomocanons* gave Ethiopia its ecclesiastical and civil law code, the *Fetha Nagast* (The Law of the Kings), which is still the official law code of Ethiopia. BIBLIOGRAPHY: J. M. Harden, *Introduction to Ethiopic Christian Literature* (1926).

[D. W. JOHNSON]

ETHIOPIAN CHURCH. From the time of St. Frumentius (d. *c.*380) until the present, the Church of Ethiopia has maintained close ties with the Coptic Church of Egypt. In the 13th cent. the Coptic patriarch assumed the right to consecrate a Coptic bp. as head *(abuna)* of the Ethiopian Church. He based his claims on the fact that St. *Athanasius had consecrated St. *Frumentius and on a pseudo-canon of Nicaea, an 8th cent. forgery. This situation prevailed until 1950 when Emperor Haile Selassie I secured autonomy for the Ethiopian Church. In place of the Coptic *abuna* there is now a katholikos-patriarch, a native Ethiopian, who resides at Addis Ababa. He acknowledges the primacy of Alexandria but is otherwise independent. The bps. under his jurisdiction do not seem to have well-defined sees as yet. The clergy, which makes up as much as one-third of the male population, is divided into two main groups, the parish clergy and the monks. Priests and lay clerks *(dabtaras)* make up the parish clergy. The latter are usually more literate than the priests and supervise the liturgical services. The monks, a mobile and theologically more sophisticated group, are respected by the people and are the real spiritual leaders. Steps are being taken to improve the training of the clergy, but abuses such as mass ordinations and a hereditary caste system make the effort difficult. Sometime after the Council of Chalcedon (451), the Ethiopian Church became *Monophysite. Just how well Monophysitism was originally understood and when it became an operative factor in Ethiopian theology are uncertain. It is known that in 1654, a Christological controversy arose which centered on Acts 10.38: "God anointed Jesus of Nazareth with the Holy Spirit and with power." Two schools used this text to explain the relationship of Jesus' divinity to His humanity, one by asserting that there is simply one divine nature in Christ and that the humanity is a mere phantasm, the other asserting the elevation of the humanity to divinity through the anointing. The issue is far from lucid, and in 1879 King John IV simply declared that the Ethiopian Church was Monophysite according to the tradition of the northern monasteries who held that the two parties were proposing essentially the same doctrine.

Peculiar to Ethiopian Christianity are certain Judaizing tendencies such as the observance of the Sabbath and the distinction between clean and unclean foods. The Virgin Mary is held in high esteem, sometimes to the point of divinization. Isolation and illiteracy are probably responsible for the widespread superstition and magical practices and the importance attached to demons. Ethiopians were represented at the Council of Florence, and, in the person of some kings, the primacy of Rome has been acknowledged. But the clergy, under its Coptic *abuna,* rejected the union of Florence. Catholic missions have been active in Ethiopia since the 15th cent., but only a small minority of Ethiopians are Catholic, chiefly in Eritrea. A 1973 estimate sets the Ethiopian population at 26,080,000. Of these a little over half of 1% belong to the Ethiopian Church. BIBLIOGRAPHY: Attwater CCE; A. A. King, *Rites of Eastern Christendom* (2 v., 1950); de L. O'Leary, *Ethiopic Church* (1936).

[D. W. JOHNSON]

ETHIOPIAN CHURCH MUSIC, sacred music of the Coptic Rite, reputedly invented by St. Jarēd. According to old accounts, this music is based upon three modes, *'ezel, 'arārāj,* and *ge'ez,* believed by later scholars to be diatonic or perhaps pentatonic. The melodies, highly melismatic and familiar, form the basis of the Lauds of Our Lady, the Divine Office, and the Mass. Collections of psalms and hymns in praise of the Virgin Mary probably date from the 7th cent., the great age of Ethiopian religious poetry. Equivalent to the antiphonary of the Roman Church is the book called the *Mawā Sèet.* Two priests, Azaj Gera and Azaj Ragueb, are credited with the introduction of Ethiopian notation, a system combining letters and signs. This double system could have evolved from the dual influence of the Syrians and the Copts. In performance, the hymns are played in various rhythms, sometimes unaccompanied and unmeasured; they are also rhythmically accompanied by stamping sticks, the sistra, and the drums.

[A. M. MACK]

ETHIOPIAN LITURGY, the liturgical rites of the Church of Ethiopia. From the time of the introduction of Christianity into Ethiopia, the liturgy of that country has been dependent on the liturgy of the Church of Alexandria and its developments. The final form of the Ethiopian Eucharistic Liturgy is essentially that of the Coptic Church translated into *Geez, a dead language after the 16th cent., and not replaced in the liturgy with a subsequent vernacular. The vestments are typical of the Eastern Church, except for a short cape *(lanka)* with five pendants worn over the *phelonion*. The Eucharistic Liturgy is customarily celebrated barefoot. It begins with the preparation. The leavened bread, stamped with 13 squares and baked on the day of the Liturgy, is carried to the altar in a basket. The offerings are prepared on a wooden board *(tabot),* and the paten and chalice are covered with veils. After the *enarxis, there follow the proanaphòra and *anaphora, almost identical with those of the Coptic Church. There are 14 anaphoras, that of the *Apostles being the most commonly used. Communion is received under both kinds, either by intinction or separately. It is seldom received by the laity. The words of institution, ''This bread is my body'' and ''This chalice is my blood,'' are peculiar to the Ethiopian liturgy. Aside from the eucharistic rite, drums and liturgical dances are used extensively. In outdoor processions the priests walk under embroidered umbrellas accompanied by attendants carrying elaborately carved processional crosses. Baptism by triple immersion is similar to Coptic usage. Confirmation and anointing of the sick are no longer practiced. Penance is brief with a general accusation followed by absolution, and it is generally administered only at the time of death. The lengthy Ethiopian Divine Office consists mainly of Psalms and dates from the 14th century. Manuscript texts, inconsistent usage, and general carelessness in the performance of liturgical rites make it difficult to state what is actually done liturgically throughout Ethiopia. Most of the clergy are illiterate or poorly educated and sometimes barely know the rites. They are usually assisted by the lay clerks *(dabtaras)* who are better educated. The Catholic Ethiopian clergy are better educated, and they have had printed texts of the Eucharistic Liturgy available to them since 1945. The Divine Office was printed for the Catholics in 1952. BIBLIOGRAPHY: A. A. King, *Rites of Eastern Christendom* (2 v., 1947); S. A. Mercer, *Ethiopic Liturgy* (1915, repr. 1970).

[D. W. JOHNSON]

ETHIOPIANS (Cushites), people living in the area S of Egypt. Biblical usage of the terms, which were generally interchangeable, was vague since little was known of the area. Genesis names Cush as a son of Ham (10.6). The area, also known as Nubia, became independent of Egypt *c.*1000 B.C. with a capital at Napata, near modern Jebel Barkal. Napata dominated Egypt during the 25th (Ethiopian) dynasty (715–663 B.C.). Among the Ethiopians mentioned in the Bible was Ebe-melech, a eunuch who rescued Jeremiah (Jer 38.7–13; 39.15–18). His conversion (Acts 8.26–39) was an important step in the spread of the gospel in Ethiopia.

[T. EARLY]

ETHNARCH (Gr. for ruler of the nation or people; Turk., *millet-bashi),* a title given to the patriarch of Constantinople or the major abp. of a Christian Church under Turkish rule. After his election the patriarch received, in exchange for a substantial sum, the *berat from the sultan approving him

as ecclesiastical and civil head of the Christians in the Ottoman Empire with the duty of collecting taxes from them and with a specified civil jurisdiction.

[G. T. DENNIS]

ÉTIENNE, see ESTIENNE.

ETIMASIA, Byzantine style Last Judgment scene in which an empty throne replaces Christ as Judge. This throne, with a cross on its back and on the seat an open *Evangeliar and a purple mantle, symbolizes by its emptiness the invisible divine nature and power of Christ.

[M. J. DALY]

ETIOLOGY (in the Bible), an explanation, often in story form, for the origin or cause (Gr. *aitia*) of a personal or place name, custom, institution found in the Bible. This explanation may at times possess genuine historical value, but is often based on popular etymologies or folklore. BIBLIOGRAPHY: Gen 2.3, 23–24; 3.20; 16.14; 19.26, 32.32; Ex 12.11–12; Jos 4.19–24; 5.8–9, etc. BIBLIOGRAPHY: O. Eissfeldt, *Old Testament: An Introduction* (tr. P. Ackroyd, 1965) 32–56.

[C. BERNAS]

ETRUSCAN RELIGION. Knowledge of the origins and evolution of Etruscan religion, like knowledge of the Etruscans themselves, is quite limited, being derived from passing observations in Roman authors, from a number of largely unintelligible inscriptions, and from archeological remains. Its composite nature is indicated, however, by the dedication of single temples to a trinity of gods, a practice that probably had its antecedents in Anatolia, by the art of foretelling the future from the examination of animal livers, which may be traced to Babylonia, and by the inclusion of Greek and Italic deities among the objects of its worship. The Etruscans believed that their religion had been revealed to them by Tages, the grandson of Jupiter, and by the nymph Vegoia (Begoe). This primitive revelation was later codified in a series of books known as the *libri haruspicini,* which set forth the rules for divination through the examination of entrails of victims; the *libri fulgurales,* which dealt with the interpretation of lightning flashes; the *libri rituales,* which gave norms to be observed in the founding of cities, the erection of altars and temples, and the organization of armies; and, finally, the *libri Acheruntici,* which were concerned with death and the afterlife. Among the most prominent gods were Tinia (Jupiter), Uni (Juno), and Menrva (Minerva), a triad later adopted by the Romans. The many elaborate Etruscan tombs still extant reveal their great preoccupation with death. The frescoes of the earlier tombs represent the next world as one of joy and happiness. During the 4th cent. B.C., however, under the pressures of military defeat and political decline, this concept was gradually replaced by one of fear and sadness. The whole life of the Etruscans, both public and private, seems to have been dominated by their religious beliefs. Unlike the later Greeks and Romans, they never succeeded in separating the sacred from the secular. BIBLIOGRAPHY: A. Grenier, *Les religions étrusque et romaine* (1948); R. Bloch, *Etruscans* (1958); E. Richardson, *Etruscans: Their Art and Civilization* (1964); M. Pallotino, *Etruscans* (rev. ed. 1975).

[M. J. COSTELLOE]

ETSI PASTORALIS, an encyclical of Pope Benedict XIV in 1742 which recognizes and confirms the privileges of the *Italo-Greeks. While reiterating papal approval of their rites, customs, and traditions, he placed them under the jurisdiction of the local Latin bps. and obliged them to follow the Latin rite in a few instances (the Gregorian Calendar, commemoration of the pope and local ordinary in the liturgy, and the observance of Latin holy days as well as fast and abstinence).

[E. EL-HAYEK]

ETT, KASPAR (1788–1847), student of J. Schlett and J. Gratz, and court organist of St. Michael's, Munich. He revived and performed older sacred works from the 16th through the 18th centuries. He also used these works as models for his own compositions, which include Masses, a Requiem, a *Miserere,* and a *Stabat Mater.* Although most of his compositions are unpublished, his MSS are preserved in the Munich library.

[A. M. MACK]

ETYMOLOGIAE, the *Etymologiarum libri XX* of *Isidore of Seville, completed and edited after his death by his disciple, Brauli of Saragossa. The prototype of medieval encyclopedias, the work ranges over the whole field of knowledge available to the author. Derived from Isidore's readings of Latin authors, the etymologies, often fanciful, became a stock part of the medieval schoolmen's lexicon.

[T. C. O'BRIEN]

EUBEL, KONRAD, (1842–1923), conventual Franciscan, historian. E. was a penitentiary at St. Peter's in Rome for 20 years, during which time he developed his *Hierarchia catholica medii aevi,* a chronological listing of the popes, cardinals, and bishops of all Christianity according to the alphabetical order of the Latin names of the dioceses.

[J. J. SMITH]

EUBULIA, from the Gr. *eboulia,* good counsel, the moral virtue of being well advised. A virtual part *(pars potentialis)* of the virtue of prudence, it directs the mind-will process of reflection and deliberation which precedes the practical judgment of choice *(electio, liberum arbitrium).*

[T. GILBY]

EUCHARIST, the common meal instituted by Jesus Christ "on the night when he was betrayed" (1 Cor 11.23) and celebrated by Christians as a sign and a means of his presence. Christian devotion and theology have long pondered its meaning, and from their thought has come a great variety of eucharistic doctrines, practices, and emphases. Some of these are so central as to require inclusion in any catalogue of eucharistic teaching, however brief it may be. By the very circumstances of its institution, as recounted in Mt 26.26–28, Mk 14.22–24, Lk 22.17–20, and Cor 11.23–25, the Eucharist necessarily involves an act of remembrance. Stories such as that of the disciples on the way to Emmaus (Lk 24.30–31) suggest that the very repetition of the ritual act of breaking the bread and sharing the cup was a means of calling him to mind and of sustaining the memory of his saving words and deeds. The institution of the Christian Eucharist is set into the framework of the commemoration of the Jewish Passover, where the remembrance and recital of the acts of God in the Exodus from Egypt linked the Israelite of the present with the events by which the covenant between God and Israel was established. Similarly, eating and drinking "in remembrance of me" are a link between the Christian believer and the days of Christ on earth. Although the development of more elaborate forms of Christian ritual has sometimes tended to obscure this, the gestures and actions of the celebration are also intended to serve this memorial purpose. Especially the participation in the bread and in the cup evokes in the Christian memory the life, death, and Resurrection of Jesus Christ, permitting Christians to become contemporary to those events, as men "before whose eyes Jesus Christ was publicly portrayed as crucified" (Gal 3.1).

No less prominent in any account of the meaning of the Eucharist is its social character. In many religions—and, for that matter, in the common life of many cultures —eating and drinking together have made men into a community (see the etymology of the word symposium). Some forms of Christian piety, both Protestant and RC, have tended to obscure this communal nature of the Eucharist by their concentration upon the benefits given to the individual through his private and personal devotion. But the NT, esp. 1 Cor. 10–11, is too explicit in its teaching to permit this individualism to stand. The relation between the Eucharist and Christian community is, however, a bilateral one. On the one hand, there is a degree of unity in faith and doctrine that seems to be presupposed by the Eucharist, such that a lesser degree would make a sharing in the communion impossible for many Christians. On the other hand, the Eucharist not only symbolizes but also effects a unity, including a unity of faith and doctrine. This bilateral relationship makes esp. difficult and painful the problem of *intercommunion between Christians of differing denominational traditions, and the problem has been a prominent issue for discussion in the modern ecumenical movement.

The problem of the nature of the eucharistic presence is, for many traditions, related to the problem of intercommunion; for it is on the doctrine of the presence that many Christians diverge. The first theological controversy over the presence did not come until the 9th cent., and the history of the question before that time does not present a clear line of doctrinal development. But most Christians appear to have believed that Jesus Christ was present in some special sense and in some unique way. He was present in the celebrating community, but he was also present in the eucharistic elements, which were regularly called the body and blood of Christ. The doctrine of *transubstantiation is the form taken by the doctrine of the *Real Presence in the Latin West; it is intended to be not a speculative doctrine of metaphysics but a dogma of faith in the intention of Christ as expressed in the institution of the Eucharist. The belief in the presence of the body and blood of Christ also forms the basis for the many forms of eucharistic devotion outside the framework of the community's celebration. If he is present, he may be addressed in prayer.

The doctrine of the Real Presence is also the dogmatic basis for the sacrificial interpretation of the Eucharist. Christians are agreed that Christ, as the eternal High Priest, "entered once for all into the Holy Place, taking not the blood of goats and calves but his own blood, thus securing an eternal redemption" (Heb 11.12), and that therefore the sacrifice of Calvary neither needs to be nor can be repeated. But the idea of Christians offering themselves as a sacrifice at the Eucharist is an ancient one. It is based on the union between the sacrifice of the believer and the sacrifice of Christ on Calvary, in the name of which one comes to the altar. Thus we plead the merits of the one sacrifice of Christ, offering up ourselves to God in union with the body and blood that were sacrificed on the Cross and that are present in the Eucharistic Celebration. Some theologians, esp. in the later Middle Ages, spoke of the "repetition of Calvary" less carefully than sound theology would have dictated, and various forms of folk devotion have followed this example. But in the public teaching of the Church the absolute uniqueness of the sacrifice of Christ has remained uppermost.

This brief list does not exhaust even those eucharistic themes that have been prominent in Christian language. A widespread idea has been the teaching that the Eucharist contained and conveyed a "drug of immortality," which enabled the physical nature of man to participate in the eternal life of God. The symbolic interpretation of the Eucharist has been important even to those theologians who have insisted that it be seen as more than a symbol, and in some forms of Protestant sacramental theology this interpretation has tended to become central. Much of the meaning of the Eucharist in all the traditions has been expressed not in theology, but in the liturgy, to which theology has sought to conform, with greater or lesser success. BIBLIOGRAPHY: A. Vonier, *Key to the Doctrine of the Eucharist* (1960); Y. Briloth, *Eucharistic Faith and Practice, Evangelical and Catholic* (1934); *Intercommunion* (ed. D. Baillie and J. Marsh, 1952).

[J. PELIKAN]

EUCHARIST (SACRAMENT). From the time of Trent, Catholic theologians have distinguished between the Eucharist as sacrament and the Eucharist as sacrifice, seemingly unmindful that the Eucharistic Sacrifice is itself a sacrament, or symbolic action, which makes visibly present and operative Christ's unique sacrifice on Calvary and his continuing intercession in heaven. For this reason one must distinguish instead the two basic phases or aspects of the single sacrament of the Eucharist: the symbolic action or sacrifice and the real and abiding presence of Christ that results. The question of *transubstantiation is considered in a special article.

Eucharistic Sacrifice. The liturgy of the Eucharist is essentially the same as the rite of the Last Supper, in which Christ first offered his body and blood to the Father by way of an expiatory sacrifice before he gave himself to the Apostles to be their food and drink. This sacrificial oblation within the context of a religious meal is clearly indicated not only in the Antiochene tradition of Paul (1 Cor 11.23–25) and, probably, of Luke (22.14–20), but in the Palestinian or Jerusalem tradition of Mark (14.22–24) and of Matthew (26.26–28). Both traditions speak of Christ's blood as "blood of the (new) covenant, which is being shed for the many," a reference which would recall irresistibly to the mind of a Jew the Sinai convenant, also sealed in the blood of sacrifice (cf. Ex 24.8). Accordingly, the Last Supper was not simply a religious meal commemorating the Jewish Passover. Within the context of that meal, Jesus instituted a rite of sacrifice that, to cite Trent, represented "the sacrifice in blood to be accomplished but once on the altar of the cross" (D 1741). In stressing the representative or symbolic character of the Last Supper sacrifice and the Eucharistic Sacrifice that Jesus commanded to be celebrated in memory of him, the Fathers of Trent hoped to answer the objection raised by the Reformers that the Mass could not be a sacrifice for the simple reason that "Christ was offered but once to bear the sins of the many" (Heb 9.28). The Catholic reply, admittedly obscured by many post-Tridentine theologians who tended to exaggerate the reality of Christ's immolation in the Mass, is basically that of St. Thomas Aquinas, confirmed by Trent. To the question "Whether Christ is immolated in this sacrament?" St.Thomas replies: "The celebration of this sacrament . . . is a kind of representative image of Christ's Passion, which is his true immolation" (ThAq ST 3a, 83). To prove, however, the effectiveness of the Eucharist as a representative or sacrament-sacrifice, Thomas cites the prayer over the gifts for the 9th Sunday after Pentecost: "Whenever the commemoration of this sacrifice is celebrated, the work of our redemption is enacted" (*ibid.*).

The Real Presence. Although Catholic teaching regards the Eucharistic Sacrifice as a symbolic or mystical immolation of Christ as victim, the reality of the oblation on the part of Christ, and of those who offer themselves with him, is assured by Trent's teaching that Christ is "truly, really, and substantially" contained in the sacrament of the Eucharist" (D 1636). The decisive word here is substantially. Catholic theologians agree that Christ is truly present and operative in all the sacraments, and Reformed theologians admit with Calvin that Christ is dynamically present to the recipient of the sacrament of the Lord's Supper. But it is only in the Eucharist, according to Catholic teaching, that the whole reality of the risen Christ is corporeally (substantially) present, not only at the moment when he is received but as long as the sacramental sign of consecrated bread and wine remains. True, this bodily presence of Christ in the sacrament is different from the presence of other bodies to their material surroundings. Using the analogy of the vitalizing presence of the soul, which is wholly present to the human body at every point, Catholic theologians explain the manner in which the totality of Christ is wholly present to every part and particle of the sacrament before reception, and the manner in which, during holy communion, the lifegiving body of Christ, united to the Spirit, vitalizes the recipient, making him one with himself and with the members of his mystical body in a fellowship of life and of love.

Meal of Fellowship. In recent years, there has been a renewed interest in the Eucharist as a fellowship or community meal in which the participants joyfully await the coming of the risen Lord into their midst. Without subscribing to the view that the Eucharistic Liturgy should be patterned on the post-Resurrection meals that the Lord took with his Disciples, Catholic theologians stress the fact that the Eucharist is a memorial *(anamnesis)* not only of the Passion and death but also of the glorious Resurrection of Our Lord and Savior, and that in partaking of the risen Lord, Christians receive the pledge and earnest of their own glorious resurrection. Again, the bond of Christian fellowship is not any gathering at which food is served. The focal point of unity is the consecrated cup and bread. "The cup of blessing that we bless, is it not a participation in the blood of Christ? The bread which we break, is it not a participation in the body of Christ? Because there is one bread, we who are many are one body, for we all partake of the one bread" (1 Cor 10.16–17). BIBLIOGRAPHY: E. Masure, *Sacrifice of the Mystical Body* (tr. A. Thorold, 1954); P. Palmer, *Sacraments and Worship* (*Sources of Christian Theology* 1, 1955); J. M. Powers, *Eucharistic Theology* (1967); W. F. Dewan, NCE 5:599–609; E. J. Kilmartin, *ibid.* 5:609–615.

[P. PALMER]

EUCHARIST (WORSHIP AND CUSTODY). The custody and worship of the Eucharist derive from the belief that the Eucharist is a permanent sacrament in which the presence of Christ remains under the appearances of bread and wine after the celebration of the liturgy. The practice varies among the Christian Churches, depending upon their theology concerning the *Real Presence and the spiritual significance of the elements after the Eucharistic Sacrifice has been completed. Patristic writings testify to the prac-

tice of keeping the Eucharist (almost always under the species of bread) in private homes to facilitate reception of communion. Historically, the primary reason for reserving the host outside of Mass is the administration of *Viaticum, and only secondarily the distribution of Communion outside of Mass and the adoration of Christ present in the Eucharist. Prior to the 16th cent. the Eucharist was reserved in an *ambry or some movable vessel such as a *pyx placed near or hanging above the altar, but today the *tabernacle has become the usual place for reservation. The tabernacle must be a secure structure placed in a prominent place such as a centrally located chapel or in the middle of the main altar. The Eucharist may be reserved in only one tabernacle in a church.

The earliest evidence of permanent exposition of the Eucharist dates from the end of the 14th cent. in Germany. At that time, the *monstrance appears as a vessel to expose the host for the adoration of the faithful. The practice of exposing the Eucharist for adoration received greater emphasis after the Council of Trent. Exposition during Mass and Vespers, and *Benediction of the Blessed Sacrament date from this period. In the 16th cent. the *Forty Hours Devotion became popular in Rome and was officially approved by Pope Clement VIII (1592). As a RC reaction against Protestant eucharistic practices, this devotion spread throughout Europe and gave rise to other specifically RC observances such as nocturnal *adoration and various perpetual adoration societies. Reservation of the Eucharist is also practiced in some churches of the Anglican Communion. The liturgical renewal deriving from Vatican Council II wishes that these devotions not be separated from the full mystery of the Eucharist, but that such worship direct men's minds to the offering of the Eucharist at Mass and its reception in communion. BIBLIOGRAPHY: *Eucharist Today* (ed. R. Tartre, 1967); J. Powers, *Eucharistic Theology* (1967).

[J. J. FLOOD]

EUCHARISTIC ADORATION, the worship of *latria, due only to God, which is directed to the Eucharist because of the belief that Jesus Christ, the God-man, is in some way present in the bread and wine. The practice of eucharistic adoration, therefore, necessarily depends upon a comprehensive eucharistic theology, and would not be found in those Christian Churches which deny the *Real Presence. Because of RC belief that Christ is completely and substantially present under the appearances of bread and wine, the Eucharist is adored not only during Mass but also outside Mass when the Host is reserved for *Viaticum and for the adoration of the faithful.

The Church's belief in Christ's enduring presence in the Eucharist is derived from his words in instituting the sacrament which bespeak a presence related to his sacrifice: "This is my body, which is being given for you" (Lk 22.19); "This is my blood of the new covenant, which is being shed for the multitude" (Mk 14.24). The body and blood of Christ must be present in this sacrificial state so that subsequently they can be given for eating and drinking. Christ affirms the reality of his eucharistic presence in itself. This presence is established with reference to communion, but communion does not absorb this presence completely or give it its total justification. Christ's words of institution, although not explicitly an invitation to eucharistic adoration, do not imply that eucharistic adoration is alien to his thought and will. To adore the Eucharist is to worship the Christ who is present in his sacrifice as food to be eaten.

The Church's liturgical norms pertaining to the Eucharist, esp. those norms deriving from the liturgical renewal of Vatican Council II, emphasize that adoration of the Eucharist at *Forty Hours Devotions, *Benediction, Holy Hours, etc., direct the minds of the faithful to the totality of the eucharistic mystery: Christ truly present in a sacrificial state that permits men to receive him in a sacramental meal. BIBLIOGRAPHY: *Eucharist Today* (ed. R. Tartre, 1967); J. Delorme et al., *Eucharist in the New Testament* (1965). *EUCHARIST (WORSHIP AND CUSTODY).

[J. J. FLOOD]

EUCHARISTIC CONGRESSES, assemblies of the clergy, religious, and laity held for the purpose of increasing understanding of devotion to the Holy Eucharist. They have been international, as well as national, regional or local, in scope and include both educational (lectures, seminars, etc.) and inspirational (liturgical observances and public ceremonies) activities. Marie Tamisier (1834–1910) first promoted local meetings in France to foster eucharistic devotion and dedication to Christian ideals. Philibert Vrau, in cooperation with Msgr. Louis Gaston de Ségur and with the approval of Pope Leo XIII, organized the first international congress at Lille in 1881. Since then international congresses have been held in Europe, North and South America, Africa, Australia, and Asia. Pope Paul VI attended the 38th International Congress held at Bombay and the 39th International Congress in Bogotá. The 40th International Congress took place at Melbourne in 1973 and the 41st at Philadelphia, Pennsylvania, in 1976. National congresses have been held in Spain, Italy, France, and the U.S., and regional or local congresses have been held in many countries. BIBLIOGRAPHY: J. C. Willke, NCE 5:617–618.

[J. C. WILLKE]

EUCHARISTIC CONTROVERSIES, debates among Christians concerning the proper understanding of the Eucharist, particularly the question of how Christ is present in the sacrament. Amidst all the terminological difficulties and shifts in meaning throughout centuries of controversy, it is possible to discover two extreme positions: an exaggerated materialism in which the eucharistic body of Christ in no way differs from the body of Christ which suffered upon the cross, and an exaggerated symbolism in which Christ's eucharistic presence is only a representative reminder of the God-man.

The first notable controversy occurred in the 9th cent. when *Paschasius Radbertus, Benedictine abbot of Corbie, wrote *On the Body and Blood of the Lord* (831). Following *Isidore of Seville, he defined a sacrament as a liturgical rite in which the external visible action brings about an internal and invisible effect. Paschasius asserted that Christ is bodily, literally present in the elements (bread and wine) used in the Eucharist, although he does employ the word figure to refer to that which remains visible (bread and wine) and truth to that which is invisible (the body of Christ). Thus he writes, "And since He willed to remain, though under the figure of bread and wine, we must believe that after the consecration these are nothing else at all but the flesh and blood of Christ. . . . (This flesh) is in no way at all distinct from that which was born of Mary . . ." (1.2). Radbertus' opinion was challenged by *Ratramnus, also a monk of Corbie, who asserted that the elements are not changed and that the Eucharist should be considered a symbol (figure) rather than a direct expression of the reality (truth) which is Christ's body. He distinguished the body of Christ in the sacrament from the flesh that was born, crucified, and buried. Ratramnus' opinion was supported by Rabanus Maurus (c.776–856), abp. of Mainz, who formulated a more balanced position than either the extreme realism of Radbertus or the symbolism of Ratramnus.

The controversy revived in the 11th cent. when *Berengar of Tours, attempting to defend the theories of Ratramnus, became the first medieval theologian to challenge the doctrine that bread and wine are changed into the substance of Christ's body and blood. When he was attacked by *Lanfranc, later abp. of Canterbury, Berengar insisted that he was following Augustine by teaching that the word sacrament signifies visible and material reality, and that the senses directly perceive not only the appearances of any object but also its essence. Thus the sense perception of bread and wine, even after the consecration, proves that the essence of the bread and wine remain and that the body of Christ is present only through the believer's faith. The Sixth Council of Rome (1079) condemned Berengar and made a significant advance in eucharistic theology by abandoning the figure/truth dichotomy and upholding both reality (Christ's body actually present) and symbol (the sign of bread and wine) in the sacrament. This advance received a more precise exposition at Lateran Council IV (1215), which condemned the Albigensians' Manichaean rejection of the eucharistic bread's becoming the body of Christ. The council's statement is the first official use of the term transubstantiation, "Jesus Christ himself is at once priest and sacrifice, whose body and blood are truly contained in the sacrament of the altar under the species of bread and wine, bread having been transubstantized into his body, wine into his blood" (D 802). In the 13th cent. St. Thomas, developing the orthodox doctrine in terms drawn from Aristotelian philosophy, held that while the elements remained the same in appearance, taste, etc. (accidents), their substance was changed into the body and blood of

Christ. Nevertheless, later Reformation controversies were foreshadowed in the 14th and 15th cent. by John *Wycliffe and Jan *Hus, the first of whom closely followed Berengar. The Council of Constance (1414–18) condemned the eucharistic theories of both theologians.

Controversy over the Eucharist was a major feature of the Reformation. In the *Marburg Articles (1529) Luther and Zwingli were unable to resolve their differences over the interpretation of Christ's statement, "This is my body" (Mk 14.22), though both denied transubstantiation. Zwingli contended that the elements are only signs, whereas Luther held that Christ is present with them, a doctrine sometimes called consubstantiation. Thus Luther writes, "To hold that real bread and real wine, and not merely their accidents, are present on the altar, would be much more probable and require fewer superfluous miracles. . . ." (Babylonian Captivity of the Church, ed. T. Tappert, 381). Calvin, occupying a middle ground between Luther's realism and Zwingli's symbolism, taught what has been called a virtualism: "The reality signified Christ offers and sets forth to all who sit down together at the spiritual banquet, although the faithful alone receive it with profit. . . . We may be confident that when we have received the symbol of the body, the body itself is no less given to us" (Institutes 17.10). The C of E's Book of Common Prayer allowed varying interpretations, and historically Anglicanism has embraced both Catholic and Reformed doctrines. There is still some controversy concerning *Cranmer's teachings, significant insofar as he was the first to give doctrinal direction to the English Reformation, but he appears to have been Zwinglian in his eucharistic theology. Contemporary sacramental and ecumenical theology have stressed the philosophical variations that gave rise to the Reformation differences, and there has been some convergence on the part of RC and Protestant theology on Real Presence and the Eucharist as sacrament and sacrifice. Generally speaking, RC theology has restored the symbolic aspect of Christ's presence while Protestant theology has, in some cases, abandoned any explanation that would interpret the Eucharist as merely a commemorative meal. BIBLIOGRAPHY: *Lutherans and Catholics in Dialogue* 3 (ed. National Committee of Lutheran World Federation and Bishops' Committee for Ecumenical and Interreligious Affairs, 1967); *Sources of Christian Theology* 1 (ed. P. Palmer, 1955); C. E. Sheedy, *Eucharistic Controversy of the Eleventh Century* (1947).

[T. EARLY]

EUCHARISTIC ELEMENTS, the bread and wine which, according to RC theology, are changed into the body and blood of Christ at Mass. After the consecration, the elements remain in their outward appearance, but they become the sacramental sign of Christ's body and blood, which have replaced the underlying reality of bread and wine. This eucharistic *transubstantiation imposes a new significance and finality upon the elements because of the new reality that they contain: the reality of Christ, whole and entire. These elements now signify not bread and wine, but Christ's body and blood. Their purpose is no longer physical nourishment with natural food, but spiritual nourishment. When the eucharistic elements decompose, Christ's eucharistic presence, which they manifested, ceases to exist. BIBLIOGRAPHY: J. Powers, *Eucharistic Theology* (1967, repr. 1972); C. O'Neill, *New Approaches to the Eucharist* (1967).

[J. J. FLOOD]

EUCHARISTIC FAST, the period of time prior to receiving the Eucharist during which the faithful must abstain from solid and liquid food. The Church had enjoined a fast (CIC c. 858) from all solids and liquids beginning at midnight prior to receiving communion, but its provisions were revised by Pius XII in the apostolic constitution *Christus Dominus* (1953) and later in the motu proprio *Sacram communionem* (1957). Paul VI further modified (1964) these earlier decrees so that the present requirement is a fast of 1 hour from solid and liquid foods including alcoholic beverages. This fast does not apply to water or medicines. The fast is to be calculated from the moment of receiving communion and does not oblige those receiving the Eucharist as Viaticum. The origins of the eucharistic fast are quite early; St. Augustine mentions it as an almost universal practice by the 4th century. The Council of Constance (1418) declared that the Eucharist may be received only by those fasting. BIBLIOGRAPHY: N. Halligan, *Administration of the Sacraments* (1962); A. Carr, "How Long before Communion for Alcoholic Beverage?" HPR 65 (1965) 434–435.

[J. J. FLOOD]

EUCHARISTIC HEART OF JESUS, a title associated with the adoration of Christ in the Eucharist fostered by devotion to the Sacred Heart. Devotion to the Sacred Heart, esp. in its development from the revelations to Margaret Mary *Alacoque, has always been closely related to adoration and reception of the Eucharist. Christ's divine and incarnate love for mankind, symbolized by his human heart, is most clearly manifested in his sacrificial death on Calvary and in the Eucharist, which sacramentally prolongs this sacrifice and its benefits to mankind. The Eucharist makes Christ's Sacred Heart sacramentally present to the believer. Since the Sacred Heart is an integral part of Christ's humanity, which is totally present in the Eucharist, the reception of the Eucharist entails sacramental contact with the Sacred Heart, the font of God's incarnate love for men. BIBLIOGRAPHY: Pius XII, "Encyclical on the Sacred Heart *Haurietis Aquas*" *Catholic Mind* 54 (1956) 435–469; D. Von Hildebrand, *Sacred Heart* (1965). *SACRED HEART, DEVOTION TO; *HAURIETIS AQUAS.

[J. J. FLOOD]

EUCHARISTIC MISSIONARIES OF ST. DOMINIC, an American congregation of religious women, founded as the Missionary Servants of the Holy Eucharist in 1927 at Amite, Louisiana, by Catherine Bostick (as Mother Catharine, the first superior general) and Zoe Grouchy (Mother Margaret). Members are involved mostly in parish work and staff diocesan offices of the Confraternity of Christian Doctrine. In 1956 Abp. Joseph Rummel sponsored their affiliation with the Order of Preachers. Their spiritual exercises emphasize the Liturgy of the Eucharist and the Liturgy of the Hours. The community works mainly in Louisiana, but has one foundation in Tucson, Arizona.

[C. KEENAN]

EUCHARISTIC PRAYERS (REVISED ROMAN MASS).

In keeping with Vatican Council II's proposal that revisions be made in the rite of the Mass (Vat II SacLit 50), three Eucharistic Prayers were prepared to supplement the single Canon that had been used in the Roman rite in the West since the 4th century. The Latin text of the new prayers was approved by the Congregation of Rites on May 23, 1968, and their use authorized from Aug. 15, 1968, although in many countries there was a delay because of the time needed to prepare suitable vernacular translations. They were approved and confirmed by Pope Paul VI in his constitution on the Roman Missal (April 3, 1969), when he also made two slight changes in the words of consecration in the Roman Canon to bring them into conformity with those of the new Eucharistic Prayers.

"Eucharist," as the Mass is frequently called, means thanksgiving; hence a eucharistic prayer is a prayer of thanksgiving. From the synoptic accounts of the institution of the Eucharist (Mt 26.26–28; Mk 14.22–24; Lk 22.19–20), we know that Christ pronounced a blessing of thanks *(eucharistēsas)* and praise *(eulogēsas)* over the bread and wine before changing them into his body and blood. Blessings of this type known as *berakim* appear frequently in the OT (e.g., Gen 24.27; Ex 18.10–11; Psalms, *passim*) and were of particular importance at a ritualistic meal (cf. *Manual of Discipline of the Qumran Community*, 5.5–6). It was within the framework of a traditional Jewish prayer that Christ instituted the Eucharistic Sacrifice of the New Law and taught his Apostles how to continue this memorial of his death. Since the Jewish blessing could include praise and thanks to God not only for his immediate gifts but also for his saving deeds in the history of his people, it allowed for much improvisation and free composition.

In the early Church, the bp., the one who presided at the Eucharistic Sacrifice, must have prayed freely within a kind of general framework. A lack of talent or preparation for such extempore liturgies gradually led to the introduction of fixed forms of prayer, which were already being introduced in the early 3d cent. (Hippolytus, *Apostolic Tradition* 10.3–5). Fixed formulas came to be adopted in the 4th cent., giving rise to five main types of eucharistic prayer, or anaphora—Roman, Egyptian, Antiochene (West Syrian), East Syrian, and Gallico-Spanish. In all these there is an essential nucleus consisting of a hymn of praise and thanksgiving (later separated in the Roman rite from the Canon as the Preface), an account of the Last Supper, the words of consecration, and a prayer for the Church and all those partaking in the sacrificial meal. Other elements were sometimes added such as the *Sanctus,* commemorations of the saints, and various intercessions. Though the Oriental rites had a number of anaphoras, the text of each was fixed. In contrast to this the Roman rite settled upon a single Canon which allowed for slight variations at the *Hanc igitur* and before the words of consecration on a few of the greatest feasts. This sameness was in part relieved by the option of a large number of different Prefaces. But in time the number of these was reduced, and the ideological separation of the Preface from the rest of the Canon in the Middle Ages only emphasized its singularity.

The three new Eucharistic Prayers have been adopted for obvious pastoral reasons. The Mass is at once a hymn of praise and of thanksgiving, a sacrifice, and a banquet, and no single text, regardless of how perfect it might be, could express all the richness of its significance.

Though noble in style and stressing the sacrificial character of the Eucharist, the Roman Canon is less unified than some of the other traditional anaphoras because of additions made in the 5th and 6th centuries. It is also less instructive in that it does not present an account of the whole history of salvation as is found in many Eastern anaphoras, nor does it mention the role of the Holy Spirit in transforming the bread and wine into the body and blood of Christ and in uniting into one body those who through communion partake of the sacrifice. The new Eucharistic Prayers by offering alternatives should obviate the monotony which can come from the repeated hearing of a prayer, esp. when it is in the vernacular; but even more important, they should help the people to enter more fully into the mysteries of salvation.

The new anaphoras are all based upon traditional forms and expressions and, though each has its own particular style and character, all follow the same structural pattern. They are all introduced by a dialogue between celebrant and people. This is followed by the Eucharistic Prayer proper in the following order: (1) *Preface.* In the name of the entire people of God, the priest praises the Father and thanks him through his Son, Jesus Christ, for the work of salvation or some aspect of it in keeping with the spirit of the day or feast being celebrated. (2) *Acclamation.* United with the angels in heaven the priest and people sing or recite the *Sanctus-Benedictus.* (3) *Epiclesis.* God's power is invoked so that through the working of the Holy Spirit the gifts that are offered may become the Body and Blood of Christ. (4) *Institution narrative.* Through the words of Scripture the Last Supper is renewed and the bread and wine changed into Christ's body and blood. (5) *Acclamation.* The expression *mysterium fidei,* which somehow became inserted into the formula for the consecration of the wine, has been detached from its former context and made to serve as a cue for one of a number of brief acclamations on the part of the people (6) *Anamnesis*. In this prayer the Church recalls the saving work of Christ's death, Resurrection, and Ascension as he commanded. (7) *Epiclesis*. After an offering to the Father of the consecrated bread and wine, the Church, and in particular the assembled congregation, prays that the Holy Spirit may transform those who communicate in the offerings so that they enter more fully into the mystery of Christ's death and Resurrection and be more closely united with each other. (8) *Intercessions*. These make it clear that the sacrifice is being offered for the Church and all its members, both living and dead. (9) *Final Doxology*. This prayer of praise and adoration of the Father through the Son in the unity of the Holy Spirit concludes all the Eucharistic Prayers, and the congregation with a final Amen expresses its approval.

Though the three new Eucharistic Prayers all follow this same general pattern, they are markedly different in length, style, and emphasis. The second Eucharistic Prayer (the first is the old Roman Canon) is based essentially on the early 3d-cent. Roman anaphora contained in the *Apostolic Tradition* of Hippolytus. Obscure phrases have been clarified and the more complex simplified or omitted. The *Sanctus* has been introduced, intercessions added, and the final doxology altered. This anaphora is marked by its simplicity and brevity and is particularly appropriate for ferial days, for children's Masses, and for Masses for small groups. Like the following anaphora, it has a special prayer that may be added in Masses for the dead.

The third Eucharistic Prayer is longer and richer than the second. It emphasizes the theology of sacrifice and the Holy Spirit. The prayer immediately after the *Sanctus* includes a passage from the prophet Malachy (1.11) having reference to the sacrifice of the New Law. The anamnesis, like those of many Oriental anaphoras, makes a specific mention of Christ's second coming. It is particularly suited for Sundays, as an alternative for the Roman Canon, and for the major feasts.

The fourth Eucharistic Prayer, still longer than the third, follows the pattern of many anaphoras of the Eastern Church, showing forth the fulfillment of the divine plan for the human race in Christ. It has a fixed Preface and contains a wealth of scriptural allusions. It may be used when there is no special Preface required by the liturgy of the day and is particularly appropriate for congregations that have a fuller knowledge and deeper appreciation of Scripture.

All three of the new Eucharistic Prayers have greater clarity and unity than the Roman Canon. Through their use, along with the new Prefaces (which are expected to be increased to a total of 70), the people of God should acquire a deeper appreciation of the treasures of their faith and an enrichment of their own spiritual lives. Nevertheless some criticism has been leveled against them, e.g., that they appeal more to liturgical historians than to ordinary laymen, that they are not original enough, and that they do not express the needs and desires of modern man. But the ceaseless search for relevance is a common delusion and can hardly be expected in the old and ever new memorial of the Sacrifice of Calvary. The Latin style of the new anaphoras is adequate, though not particularly distinguished. There is some dissatisfaction with the approved English version, i.e., unnecessary liberties have been taken with the texts; compound sentences are often reduced to simple with a consequent loss of logical connection; individual words are not faithfully rendered, scriptural references are distorted so as to be at times unrecognizable, and the whole is cast in a kind of basic English that lacks the eloquence and even poetry of the originals. It is to be noted that since 1975 Eucharistic Prayers for Masses of Reconciliation and for children's Liturgies have been made available. BIBLIOGRAPHY: C. Vagaggini, *Canon of the Mass and Liturgical Reform* (1967); P. Coughlan, *New Eucharistic Prayers* (1968); *Order of Mass: English Translation Approved by the National Conference of Catholic Bishops and Confirmed by the Apostolic See* (1970); M. J. Costelloe, "New Eucharistic Prayers," HPR 70 (1969) 171–179.

[M. J. COSTELLOE]

EUCHERIUS OF LYONS, ST. (d. *c.*455), bp. After placing his two sons (both of whom were later honored as saints) in the monastery of Lérins, E. himself became a monk there and *c.*434 was chosen bp. of Lyons. Though he was held in great esteem in his day, little is known of his episcopal activity except that he was present at the first Council of *Orange (441). He wrote two exegetical treatises, two small works on the monastic life, and an account of the Theban Legion. Works: PL 50:685–1214; crit. ed. CSEL 31 (1894), ed. K. Wotke. BIBLIOGRAPHY: Altaner 541; Butler 4:353–354.

[R. B. ENO]

EUCHERIUS OF ORLÉANS, ST. (d. 743), bishop. Scion of Merovingian nobility, he became a monk at Jumièges (*c.*709–714). Against his will he was made bp. of Orléans (*c.*716–721). Because of family hostility to the emerging Carolingians, he was banished by Charles Martel to Cologne (737), but was later permitted to retire to Saint-Trond. BIBLIOGRAPHY: R. Wasselynck, BiblSanct 5:140–141.

[A. CABANISS]

EUCHOLOGION (Gr., prayer book), the Byzantine liturgical book that contains the texts and rubrics of the three Divine Liturgies (St. John Chrysostom, St. Basil, the Presanctified Gifts) as well as the ritual for the sacraments, the Office of the Dead, the ordinary of the Divine Office, prayers for the sick, blessings, sacramentals, and other prayers. It is the service book for bishop, priest, and deacon and as such is a sort of combination of the Latin Missal, Ritual, and Pontifical. The complete Euchologion is called the Great Euchologion to distinguish it from the abridged Lesser Euchologion and the Liturgikon, which contains only the texts of the three liturgies. The earliest extant MSS of the Euchologion date from the 8th and 9th cent. and its printed texts from the 16th. BIBLIOGRAPHY: G. V. Shann, *Manual of Prayers of the Holy Orthodox Church* (1969).

[A. J. JACOPIN]

EUDAEMON-JOANNES, ANDREAS (1560–1625), Jesuit controversialist. A descendant of the Palaeologi emperors, E. was born on Crete. As a youth he went to Italy where he joined the Jesuits in 1581. He was accorded numerous honors by Urban VIII and selected to accompany the Pope's nephew, Card. Barberini, on a legation to France (1625). He died shortly after their return to Rome. E. wrote several treatises in defense of Robert Bellarmine against the attacks of L. Daneau (Daneaus; d. 1595), John *Barclay, and Lancelot *Andrewes. BIBLIOGRAPHY: J. Boucher, DTC 5:1465–66; Sommervogel 3:482–486; Hurter 3:705–706.

EUDAEMONISM, a basic ethical position which, in contrast to *deontologism, sees human activity as properly motivated when it is directed toward the attainment of happiness. Eudaemonism gives primary consideration to the goodness of ethically satisfactory action, whereas deontologism stresses rather its rightness.

Happiness may be variously understood, and there are accordingly different types of eudaemonism. Aristotle, who is usually cited as typifying the eudaemonistic approach in antiquity, contended that *eudaimonia,* as the principal good attainable by man, is a continuing life activity wherein the powers of the soul are exercised in accordance with their highest and most excellent capacities. Thus, for Aristotle, *eudaimonia* (literally, the state of being under the protection of a benign spirit) is a well-being closely identified with well-living, esp. in the exercise of the highest activities of which man is capable as man. These activities are realized above all in the life of speculative wisdom or contemplation of the most exalted truth and in the practice of the moral virtues.

Epicurus, on the other hand, represents a radically different type of eudaemonism; he held that the principal human good consists in pleasure and the absence of pain, the view later adopted by the English Utilitarians (e.g., J. Bentham and J. S. Mill) who interpreted *eudaimonia* as happiness and happiness as pleasure.

In modern ethical thought there has been an effort to distinguish between happiness and pleasure, and many agree with Aristotle that pleasure is not the constituent but rather an accompaniment of the well-being and well-living that is happiness.

[J. T. HICKEY]

EUDES OF ROSNY (d. after 1272), Franciscan theologian. From 1244 to 1272 E. studied and taught at the Univ. of Paris, from which he received a master's degree in theology in 1257. As a student he signed a condemnation of the Talmud in 1248. He was appointed to examine the rule written by Bl. Isabelle for the Poor Clares and to help investigate the election of an abbess of Saint-Pierre-aux-Nonnains. He probably succeeded *Bonaventure as master-regent. Some writings are attributed to him: a commentary on the first book of the *Sentences* and a few sermons. BIBLIOGRAPHY: A. Teetaert, DTC 14:1–3.

[J. E. WRIGLEY]

EUDES, JOHN, ST. (1601–80), founder of the Congregation of Jesus and Mary (Eudists), parish missionary, liturgist. At the Jesuit college at Caen from 1615, E. entered the Oratory of P. de *Bérulle (1623); was ordained priest (1625); became superior of Caen Oratory. He founded, with M. Lamy and Visitation nuns, the Sisters of Our Lady of Charity of the Refuge (1641) from whom the Sisters of the Good Shepherd derive. For 20 years as an Oratorian, E. devoted himself with great success to preaching parish missions; from the experience he became deeply convinced of the need to provide excellent training for priests destined for the parish ministry. He proposed to found and staff such seminaries, and at first had Oratorian approval. When this was withdrawn, he made the painful decision to leave the Oratory. In 1643 he founded his own Congregation of Jesus and Mary, a society of common life for secular priests. Their work was to be the staffing of seminaries to prepare effective diocesan priests. The congregation founded seminaries at Caen (1644), Coutances (1650), Lisieux (1653), Rouen (1658) Évreux (1667), and Rennes (1670). E. was esp. gratified to be asked for Évreux by Bp. H. de Maupas, who not only gave the house but was the first bp. to approve E.'s Office of the Sacred Heart (1670). Earliest celebration of the feast was in the congregation's seminary. E. composed Offices and Masses to honor the Holy Hearts of Jesus and Mary. Besides *Constitutions* for his congregations, E. wrote works of devotion (*Oeuvres complètes,* 12 v., 1905–11). His lay societies flourished: the Confraternity of the Sacred Heart and the Society of the Admirable Heart of Mary. Pius X beatified E. (1909), naming him apostle of liturgical devotion to the Sacred Heart; Pius XI canonized him in 1925. BIBLIOGRAPHY: D. Sargent, *Their Hearts Be Praised* (1949); C. B. duChesnay, BiblSanct 6:994–996; Butler 3:353–354.

[M. R. BROWN]

EUDISTS (Congregation of Jesus and Mary), a society of secular priests and some brothers living a community life, without vows, founded in France (1643) by St. John *Eudes. Its purpose was primarily to establish seminaries to train diocesan priests and preachers for parochial missions. The French Revolution caused the dissolution of the congregation (1790), which at that time operated 13 seminaries, 3 minor seminaries, 4 colleges, and 3 parishes. Though its apostolates expanded under the leadership of eminent superiors general when the congregation was revived after the Revolution, it still maintained seminaries and education as its chief work. In 1976 the congregation numbered 590 members in 67 houses spread throughout France, South America, the U.S., Canada, and Africa. BIBLIOGRAPHY: C. B. duChesnay, DHGE 15:1331–35; G. Hamon, EncCatt 4:296–298; G. DeSauvigny, NCE 5:623–624.

[S. A. HEENEY]

EUDOCIA, BYZANTINE EMPRESS, wife of Arcadius, Eastern Roman emperor from 383 to 408. She was the daughter of Bautho, a Frankish chieftain who had been Roman consul (385). Her marriage (395) was arranged as a part of a political court intrigue by the eunuch Eutropius, but she soon became independent and the true power behind her ineffectual husband. Having been scolded in an intemperate manner in a sermon on the frivolity of her court by St. John Chrysostom, the patriarch of Constantinople, she brought about his deposition by a synod under Theophilus of Alexandria (403) and his first and second exile. Shortly afterwards E. died after a miscarriage (404). Among her five children were Theodosius II and Pulcheria, who was regent for her minor brother.

[V. J. POSPISHIL]

EUDOCIA (EUDOXIA) AELIA, BYZANTINE EMPRESS (d. *c*.460), wife of the Eastern Roman emperor Theodosius II (408 to 450). Athenais, her original name, the daughter of Leontius, a pagan philosopher, was introduced to Theodosius through Pulcheria, his sister. Having accepted Christianity, she married him (421). Their daughter Licinia Eudoxia married later the Western emperor Valentinian III. Having fallen out with Pulcheria, E. went to live permanently in Jerusalem (443), which she embellished with several churches and whose fortifications she restored. A learned woman, she quoted Homer, wrote a poetic paraphrase of a part of Holy Scripture, a life of Christ in hexameters, the lives of several saints. She was for a time sympathetic to Monophysitism, probably less for its theological content and more out of sympathy for the social and ethnic tendencies in the Near East expressed in the Monophysitic movement. Byzantine writers depicted her as the Athenian pagan who, after having been at the pinnacle of secular power, ended her life as mystic at the tomb of Christ.

[V. J. POSPISHIL]

EUDORUS OF ALEXANDRIA (fl. *c*.25 B.C.), an eclectic philosopher who, combining Platonic and Neopythagorean concepts, maintained that the one *(hen)* and the undetermined dyad *(aoristos duas)* are the first principles. But above both he postulated a higher "One," thus teaching a monistic doctrine that definitely pointed the way to the monism of Plotinus. BIBLIOGRAPHY: P. Merlan, LexAW 907–908; CHGMP 81.

[M. R. P. MCGUIRE]

EUDOXIUS (*c*.300–*c*.370), an influential Arian bp. who took part in many of the Arian councils of the 4th century.

He was born at Arabissos in Lesser Armenia and may have studied under Lucian of Antioch. Elected Arian bp. of Germanicia sometime after 330, E. became bp. of Antioch in 358 after the death of Leontius, and bp. of Constantinople in 360 after the deposition of Macedonius. An able and ambitious cleric and a radical Anomoean in doctrine, he was a powerful adversary of orthodoxy until his death. A few fragments of his treatise on the Incarnation are still extant. BIBLIOGRAPHY: L. Euding, LTK 3:1171; M. Spanneut, DHGE 15:1337–40.

[M. J. COSTELLOE]

EUGENDUS OF CONDAT, ST. (Oyand, Oyen; *c*.449–510), abbot. According to a biography attributed to a disciple, Eugendus as a child was entrusted to SS. Romanus and Lupicinus, founders of Condat (today, Saint-Claude), of which he later became abbot. E. rebuilt the monastery after its destruction by fire, taking advantage of the occasion to change its Eastern semi-eremitical, to a more communal, pattern of life. He encouraged education and reading and was esteemed for his humility and learning. BIBLIOGRAPHY: Butler 1:5–6; J. Manilier, BiblSanct 5:179–180.

[G. M. COOK]

EUGENE I, ST. (d. 657), **POPE.** *Martin I was still alive in the Crimea, the prisoner of Emperor *Constans II, when E. was elected. The legitimacy of his pontificate before Martin's death (655) is not clearly established, even though Martin addressed a letter to him (654). Possibly against his own conciliatory temperament, E. was influenced by the Roman people and clergy to take a hard stand against *Monothelitism and to reject a synodal letter from the patriarch of Constantinople, Peter, which echoed the *Typos of Constans. Only the need to defend against the Arabs kept the emperor from treating E. as he had Martin. *Wilfred of York probably visited Rome during E.'s pontificate.

[R. B. ENO]

EUGENE II (d. 827), **POPE** from 824. Of a noble family, E. was cardinal priest of Santa Sabina, and the choice fell to him as a compromise candidate in the bitter election following St. Paschal I's death. The proimperial nobles whom Paschal had exiled were reinstated by Eugene. The Frankish coemperor, Lothair I, met E. in Rome and won from him his acceptance of the Constitution of Lothair *(Constitutio Romana),* which in effect established the emperor as temporal overlord of the pope. This gave the lay nobility of Rome a voice in the election of the pope and established a series of checks, by way of permanent commissioners, on the government of the Papal States. Each pope in his election and before consecration was to take an oath of loyalty to this Constitution of Lothair. E. accepted, apparently without protest, the regulations of this new law and in a Roman synod (826) promulgated the articles about the papal election. The same synod enacted a group of canons aimed at ecclesiastical reform, and E. seems to have assumed the initiative in some other matters. He commissioned St. *Ansgar as successor of Abbo of Rheims in the mission to Scandinavia. The attempt of the Frankish rulers, at the request of the Greek Emperor, to promote a new mission to Constantinople for discussions of the iconoclast issues, seems to have met with a nullifying silence on E.'s part. BIBLIOGRAPHY: Mann 2.1:156–182; H. K. Mann, CE 5:598–599.

[P. F. MULHERN]

EUGENE III, BL. (Bernard of Pisa, d. 1153), **POPE** from 1145. He was a Cistercian monk, a devoted disciple of St. Bernard of Clairvaux (the saint addressed his *De consideratione* to him), and abbot of SS. Vincent and Anastatius. Elected pope during troubled times in Rome, E. fled to the abbey of Farfa where he was consecrated bishop. In 1145 he inaugurated the Second Crusade with the bull *Quantum praedecessores* which granted a plenary indulgence, protection of family and property, and a moratorium on interest for debts to those who participated. St. Bernard was later commissioned to preach this crusade. Two weeks later the pope returned to Rome, but because of the strife fomented by Arnold of Brescia, he was forced to seek refuge. The following March he canonized Emperor Henry II. Early in 1147 E. began his travels in France. Among the important synods at which he presided was the one convened at Paris, which condemned the errors of Gilbert de la Porrée. With his activities for ecclesiastical and monastic reform, he combined the spirit of prayer. Pope Pius IX formally approved the veneration of Eugene III in 1872. BIBLIOGRAPHY: Butler 3:43–45; I. Danieli, BiblSanct 5:196–201.

[H. DRESSLER]

EUGENE IV (Gabriele Condulmaro; *c.*1383–1447), **POPE** from 1431. Of a wealthy Venetian family, he became a monk and then successively bp. of Siena (1407), cardinal (1408), and pope (1431), taking upon his election the name Eugene IV. As pope he faced a twofold task: the restoration of unity in the Western Church, still precarious since the Great Schism that ended in 1417, and the achieving of union with the Greek Church. Political and financial complications hindered him in his efforts to deal with the first problem, but more annoying was the obstinacy of the Council of *Basel. Negotiations with the Greeks dragged on interminably. Finally both problems were confronted together at the Council of *Florence and were there, to a certain extent, solved. Despite enormous difficulties E.'s courage and perseverance defeated the conciliarists at Basel, and his sincerity, ardor for union, and willingness to make concessions ensured the success, temporary though it was, of the Council of Florence. BIBLIOGRAPHY: J. Gill, *Eugene IV, Pope of Christian Union* (1961).

[G. T. DENNIS]

EUGENE OF TOLEDO (or of Deuil), **ST.** According to a Frankish account (*c.*850) that confuses an evangelist of Toledo whose existence is uncertain with a saint of Deuil whose name is not known, Dionysius (the Areopagite) of Paris made E. a bishop and sent him from Arles to Toledo *c.*100; later, on a visit to Paris, E. followed Dionysius in martyrdom; 300 years later his body was discovered near Deuil. Relics went to St. Denis in the late 9th cent. and from there to Toledo in 1156 and 1565. Until 1148, however, Spain knew only two by the name of Eugene who were bps. of Toledo. Both were scholarly monks. The first (636–646) is known through Ildefonsus; the second (646–657) reformed church music and left an important anthology of Latin poetry and a revision of Dracontius, which was popular until 1800. BIBLIOGRAPHY: Butler 4:329–330; AnalBoll 83 (1965) 329–349; 84 (1966) 59–76.

[E. P. COLBERT]

EUGENIA, ST. (d. 735), abbess of Hohenberg (Mont-Ste. Odile) in Alsace (*c.*720–*c.*735). She seems to have been the daughter of Duke Adalbert of Alsace and the niece of St. Odilia (foundress and first abbess of Hohenberg), whom she succeeded as abbess. Her grave was plundered by the Swedes during the Thirty Years' War. BIBLIOGRAPHY: A. M. Zimmerman, BiblSanct. 5:180.

[M. F. MCCARTHY]

EUGENICS (Gr. *eugenēs,* well-born) a term coined by F. *Galton (1883) to signify a branch of biology. As a pure science it explores the inborn factors of living organisms, and specifically of human organisms; as an applied science it promotes the breeding of the genetically fit. Over the former we need not delay; it has long been recognized that hereditary as well as environmental factors shape the individual, and Galton, impressed by the Darwinian theory of natural selection, viz., that variants in a species better adapted to their environment survive in the struggle for existence, set himself to study the hereditary materials contributed by parents. These are numerous and various, but the most thoroughly studied is the complete set of genes provided by the two germs, the seed and the egg: the functional interactions are complex, but it has been shown that some undesirable variations have a genetic basis.

As an applied science eugenics raises questions of theology and social morality. Galton founded the Laboratory of National Eugenics in 1904, which has inspired active education societies for "Rassenhygiene" all over the world. Much field work has been done, and the literature is voluminous, on the influence of "tainted" heredity on disease, mental deficiency, and crime. An energetic campaign has been conducted against "random mating" and, not without success in some countries, for the introduction of sterilization laws. However, the movement has now lost some of its steam; its disgraceful and widespread application by the Nazis is remembered, and we ask ourselves who is to decide which is the ideal type to breed to. Then again biological science has grown more wary about a simplification of one dominant factor, and through what is called euthenics (Gr. *eutheneia,* well-provisioning) goes more deeply into environmental factors and promotes the remedies of social medicine.

Some of the methods of eugenics cannot be theologically endorsed, e.g., *sterilization; others are not practical politics, e.g., *segregation. As for its aims one feels more sympathy when they are stated negatively rather than positively. For, with all respect for the total and Christian view of suffering, who would not avoid the effects of breeding from some types of bad stock? All the same, with due respect for the humane views of geneticists, theology will hesitate to be limited to their identification of good stock. The reserves expressed by medical science about narrowing the breeding-pool are enlarged by theological science into a wider scene; it catches a glimpse of St. Peter's vision on the house-top at Joppa (Acts 10.9). A minor parable of the reasons is found in dog-lovers, e.g., those who want a working-dog and have their doubts about show-breeding.

[T. GILBY]

EUGENIUS VULGARIUS (fl. 900), poet and grammarian. Ordained priest, perhaps by Pope Formosus (d. 896), he defended (907) the validity of holy orders conferred by the discredited pontiff in *De causa Formosiana libellus*. This work angered Pope Sergius III (904–911), to whom he later surrendered. His poems and letters are found in MGH Poetae 4:412–440. BIBLIOGRAPHY: Raby SLP 1:286–289.

[G. E. CONWAY]

EUGIPPIUS OF LUCULLANUM (450?–after 533), abbot and disciple of Severinus, the apostle of Noricum. In 492 he and his companions took the body of Severinus to Castellum Lucullanum near Naples. There they erected a tomb and built a monastery. E. composed for his monks a rule that is no longer extant. He wrote (c.511) a life of Severinus, valuable as the sole extant source for the history of Noricum in his generation. The collection he made of 348 excerpts from the writings of Augustine is important for the textual criticism of that author. BIBLIOGRAPHY: J. Lenzenweger, LTK 3:1179.

[M. J. SUELZER]

EUGNOSTOS, LETTER OF, see APOCRYPHA (NEW TESTAMENT), 20.

EUHEMERUS OF MESSENE, (fl. 300 B.C.) a Greek mythographer renowned for his *Sacred Record* in which he gave a rationalistic explanation of the origins of religion. In this novel he claimed that he had made a visit to the island of Panchaia in the Indian Ocean and had found there in a temple a column recording the deeds of Uranus, Kronos, and Zeus. From this he concluded that the gods had originally been kings and heroes who had been rewarded for their good deeds by being divinized. Though his work seems to have had little effect upon the Greeks, a Latin translation of it by Ennius contributed to the spread of skepticism in Rome. Christian apologists such as Clement of Alexandria, Minucius Felix, Lactantius, and St. Augustine appealed to Euhemerus in their refutations of pagan religions and practices. In the last cent. the term euhemerism was coined to describe anthropological theories about the origins of religion. BIBLIOGRAPHY: Jacoby, PW 6:952–971.

[M. J. COSTELLOE]

EULALIA OF MÉRIDA, ST. (d. c.304), virgin and voluntary martyr; her passion is similar to that of St. Agnes. Prudentius praised her in a hymn, and her cult spread throughout the West. From c.600 the Mozarabic liturgy honors a Eulalia (of Barcelona) with a similar passion, but claims that the second is a double of the first are contested. One of the oldest known works in French is a Cantilena of St. Eulalia. BIBLIOGRAPHY: Butler 4:530–531.

[E. P. COLBERT]

EULALIUS (d. 423), antipope. After the death of Pope Zosimus in 418, the archdeacon E. was chosen as successor by a group of clergy gathered at the Lateran Basilica; at the Basilica of Theodora another group elected Boniface, an elderly priest. Both were installed on Sunday, Dec. 29, Boniface at St. Peter's and E. at the Lateran. E. was rejected the following Easter for provoking riots. The Emperor Honorius in 419 decreed that in future a papal election must be virtually unanimous.

[T. EARLY]

EULOGIUS, ST. (d. 607), **PATRIARCH OF ALEXANDRIA** from 581. He had been a monk at Antioch. Pope St. Gregory the Great's letter to him (they had met in Constantinople c.582) attests E.'s denying that Christ in any way lacked knowledge (D 474–476). He was also an adherent to the Christology of the Council of Chalcedon and his anti-Monophysite writings have come down through Photius (PG 103, 934–955); he also was an opponent of Novatianism (PG 103, 532–536).

[T. C. O'BRIEN]

EULOGIUS OF CÓRDOBA, ST. (d. 859), martyr. A holy and learned priest who carried on the zeal of his teacher Esperaindeo for a revival of Latin letters in Muslim Córdoba, E. defended the martyrs of Córdoba in three closely related works that constitute a treatise on voluntary martyrdom. His death marked the end of the martyrdoms. In 884 his relics were taken to Oviedo and in 1737 in part were returned to Córdoba. The single MS of his works was lost after the edition in 1574. BIBLIOGRAPHY: E. P. Colbert, *Martyrs of Córdoba, 850–859* (1962).

[E. P. COLBERT]

EULOGIUS GEORGIEWSKI (1868–1946), metropolitan and founder of the Russian Orthodox Church of Western Europe. After a period of imprisonment in Russia following the Revolution, E., already an abp., emigrated to Paris in 1920 and founded a theological seminary with funds provided by the YMCA. In 1931 he placed himself and 75 Russian Orthodox congregations under the patriarch of Constantinople; but in 1945 he was willing to reestablish fellowship with the Moscow patriarchate. Though chosen as exarch for Western Europe, he was refused approval by Constantinople. BIBLIOGRAPHY: H. Schaeder, RGG 2:732.

[M. J. SUELZER]

EULOGY (Gr., fair speech or language): (1) the form given to biographies of the saints in antiquity, imitative of the classic rhetoric of the *encomium* or *laudatio funebris,* and stressing the virtues and deeds of the saint; (2) the panegyric preached at the funeral liturgy—in some regions for all funerals, in others only at funerals of clergy. The new (1969) funeral rites, General Instruction n. 45, forbid any kind of funeral eulogy "in the homily of rite celebrated without Mass; the homily at a funeral Mass may include thanks to God for his gifts to the deceased (n. 41); (3) the Gr. *eulogia* (blessing), the blessing of bread, or the blessed bread itself, for catechumens after the Eucharist.

[T. C. O'BRIEN]

EUNAPIUS OF SARDES (*c*.345–414), sophist of Neoplatonic outlook and sympathies. He was a pupil of Chrysanthius, a member of the Pergamene School. He was an intense admirer of the Emperor Julian and hostile to Christianity. His *Lives of the Sophists* is a valuable, if highly stylized source, for the intellectual life of the 4th cent., and in particular for the Pergamene School of Neoplatonism. BIBLIOGRAPHY: W. Spoerri, LexAW 914–915; Ueberweg 1:621.

[M. R. P. MCGUIRE]

EUNOMIUS OF CONSTANTINOPLE (*c*.335–*c*.394), bp. of Cyzicus, heresiarch. As a student and later, secretary, of the Arian Aetius in Alexandria, E. learned the art of dialectic. He was ordained deacon in 358 and in 360 was promoted to the bishopric of Cyzicus in Mysia by his friend, Eudoxius of Constantinople. He was forced to resign his see for openly professing extreme Arian (*Anomoean) views and became, upon the death of Aetius, the leader of the radical Arian party. He traveled much throughout the East promoting his heretical opinions. The orthodox emperors attempted to repress his activities. His last years were spent at his home in Cappadocia. Although most of his works were burned by imperial order after his death, his position can be seen in the replies of his adversaries, Basil, Gregory of Nyssa, and Apollinaris. Using the methods of Greek philosophy and dialectic, he fought against the Nicaean doctrine of consubstantiality and taught in its place a form of subordinationism. Surviving fragments of his writings can be found in PG 30:835–868. BIBLIOGRAPHY: Quasten 3:306–309.

[R. B. ENO]

EUNUCH (Heb. *saris*), used in Dt (23.1) for an emasculated man. Although employed as guardians of the royal harem (hence the Gr. term *eunouchos,* chamberlain), eunuchs were excluded from public worship because no blemished creature was permitted in the Lord's service (Lev 21.20; 22.24), and also perhaps because self-mutilation was practiced in honor of certain oriental deities. Faithful observance of the Sabbath and the covenant might, however, cancel out this impediment (Is 56.4–5). Not all eunuchs were castrated men, and many *sarisim* held offices of considerable importance, both at court (Gen 37.36; 39.1: 40.2, 7; 1 Sam 8.15; 1 Kg 22.9; 2 Kg 8.6; Dan 1.3; Est 1.10, 12; 6.2; Jer 34.19) and in the army (Jer 39.3, 13; 2 Kg 18.17; 25.19; 1 Chr 28.1). The Ethiopian eunuch baptized by Philip (Acts 8.26–39) was treasurer of his queen. Faced with Christ's recommendation of deliberate virginity or continence (Mt 19.12), Origen took the advice literally (Eusebius, *Hist. eccl.* 6:8.1), but subsequently regretted his drastic action. Christ's words about the eunuch implied a perpetual resolve, or a condition that would not be changed.

[R. T. A. MURPHY]

EUOUAE, an *aide-mémoire* from the vowels in *saeculorum. Amen,* the concluding words of the doxology in liturgical books of the Roman rite. Appearing at the end of Introits, and responsories of the Breviary the letters are marked with the notes ending the doxology so as to lead into the resumption of the Introit or responsory verse. Because of a similarity in spelling the device has been erroneously confused with *Evoe,* ancient Greek word expressing the frenzied joy of the bacchanalia.

[A. M. MACK]

EUPHEMIA, ST. (d. *c*.303), martyred at Chalcedon under Diocletian. Her tortures are described in a late and unreliable *passio.* Historically certain, however, is the fact that a basilica was erected in her honor; this became a center of pilgrimage and in 451 was the site of the ecumenical council. Her cult was widespread in the West as well as in the East, and stories of her miracles multiplied. BIBLIOGRAPHY: Butler 3:567–568; G. Lucchesi, BiblSanct 5:154–160.

[R. B. ENO]

EUPHEMITES, non-Christian ascetics of Mesopotamia. Epiphanius (*Penar.* 80; cf. Augustine, *Haer.* 57) mentions them along with the Euchites and Messalians. All existed in the same region and had some similar practices, but the Euphemites were pagans. BIBLIOGRAPHY: É. Amann, DTC 10:792–795.

[L. MÜLLER]

EUPHRASIA, ST. (*c*.380–410), virgin. E.'s father, Antigonus, a wealthy senator of Constantinople and a relative of Emperor Theodosius I, died while she was still an infant. The emperor took her in wardship and betrothed her to the son of another senator, but at the age of 7 she was taken by her mother to Egypt, where she felt drawn to the life she observed in a convent near the place where her mother settled. She was permitted to live with the nuns. At the age of 12, she notified the Emperor Arcadius that she did not wish to marry and gave him her fortune to be used for the poor. She lived on in the convent as an exemplary religious, dying at the age of 30. BIBLIOGRAPHY: Butler 1:581–583; G. Lucchesi, BiblSanct 5:233–235.

[R. B. ENO]

EUPHROSYNE OF ALEXANDRIA, ST., a legendary personage, supposedly of the 5th century. Named in the Roman Martyrology and an object of some devotion in the East, E.'s real existence is considered doubtful. Her story is not unlike that told of several other legendary saints. When her father affianced her to a wealthy young man, she is supposed to have fled to a monastery disguised as a man and calling herself Smaragdus. As a ''monk'' she established a reputation for sanctity that grew with the years and finally reached the ears of her father who still grieved at her loss. He sought her counsel, and she, unrecognized, had numerous conferences with him, finally revealing her sex and identity only with approaching death. When she died her father took her place in the monastery. BIBLIOGRAPHY: Butler 1:4; P. Bertocchi, BiblSanct 5:175–176.

EUROPÄISMUS, a concept used by Ernest *Troeltsch in his attempt to reconcile the existence of absolute values with the emergence of changing cultural orders. The result of this reconciliation is the development of a synthesis, *Europäismus,* between the purely historicist view of man, with its dangers of extreme relativism, and the historical view of man, grounded in the acceptance of an essential unchanging nature of man. Such a view made it possible to speak about Christian ethics and eternal values, yet Troeltsch never fully accounted for ethics.

[J. R. RIVELLO]

EUSEBIA OF HAMAY, ST. (c.627–c.680), Benedictine abbess. Daughter of St. Adalbald and St. Rictrude, at the age of 9 she joined the Abbey of Hamay, ruled by her grandmother, Gertrude. When Gertrude died in 640, E.'s mother placed her in the office as abbess, even though she was only 12. Later, Rictrude, who herself was governing the Abbey of Marciennes, called E. and her community there. But the move was not lasting, and soon E. was allowed to take her nuns back to Hamay. There she ruled with great wisdom and prudence until her death at the age of 40. She is honored in the French, Belgian, and Benedictine liturgical calendars. BIBLIOGRAPHY: G. Bardy, *Catholicisme,* 4:710–711; M. De Somer, BiblSanct 5:243–245.

[N. F. GAUGHAN]

EUSEBIA OF SAINT-CYR, ST. Benedictine abbess of St.-Cyr, Marseilles, who lived between the 7th and the 9th cent. The legend of her martyrdom and disfigurement, and that of 40 of her nuns, probably arose from her having been buried in a tomb (belonging to someone else much earlier) whose sculptured likeness had been mutilated simply by time and temperature. BIBLIOGRAPHY: G. Bardy, *Catholicisme,* 5:710; P. Burchi, BiblSanct 5:245–246.

[J. F. FALLON]

EUSEBIAN CANONS, a systematic arrangement devised by *Eusebius of Caesarea to enable the reader of the NT to find passages in other Gospels parallel to a particular passage from one Gospel. He divided the Gospels into small numbered sections and then prepared a table of 10 columns, each column representing different possibilities of parallel coverage (e.g., column 1 listed passages common to the four Gospels; col. 2, those common to the Synoptics, col. 3, those common to Mt, Lk, and Jn, and so on). A number against a section of the text referred the reader to the appropriate column (or canon) where the parallel passages were listed. The system was much used down to the 13th cent., and tables were commonly found in MSS of the Gospels. Eusebius explained the system in a letter to Carpianus (PG 22:1275–92) and mentions that he conceived it as an improvement upon the Sections of Ammonius of Alexandria, which were built upon the text of Matthew. BIBLIOGRAPHY: Quasten 3:335–336.

[R. B. ENO]

EUSEBIO DI SAN GIORGIO (1467 or 1470–1540?), one of the greatest painters of the School of Perugia, E., a pupil of Perugino, was equally influenced by Pinturicchio—as seen in his *Adoration of the Magi* (1505). He shows Raphaelesque qualities in the later altarpiece *Madonna and Saints* (1512).

[M. J. DALY]

EUSEBIUS, ST. (d. 311), **POPE** from c.309. Successor in the papacy to Marcellus, E. had to deal with the dissension in the Roman Church regarding the treatment of those who had apostatized during the persecution of Diocletian (see LAPSI). Heraclius was the leader of a group of *lapsi* who were demanding immediate reconciliation without penance. The strife between the two groups caused such commotion that the Emperor Maxentius exiled both Heraclius and E., who died shortly thereafter in Sicily. His veneration as a martyr is based upon his death in exile. BIBLIOGRAPHY: Butler 3:340; J. P. Kirsch, CE 5:615–616; I. Daniele, BiblSanct 5:246–248.

[R. B. ENO]

EUSEBIUS OF CAESAREA (c.260–c.339), bp. of Caesarea, Palestine, from c.313, ecclesiastical writer, apologete, ''Father of Church History.'' An adult convert, he became a member of a circle of scholars in the tradition of Origen under his teacher Pamphilius; E. referred to himself as "Eusebius Pamphilii." The first principal event of his own life was his witnessing of church persecutions (303–313), during which time he was an exile and fugitive, possibly even a prisoner, in Egypt. Next came his participation in the Arian controversies. He was fiercely against *Sabellianism and favored Arius; for this he was put under sentence of excommunication by a council at Antioch (c.324), pending a final decision by what was to become the Council of Nicaea I. At Nicaea he proposed the creed of Caesarea as testimony of his orthodoxy; the creed formulated by the Council, however, was more precise than E.'s, esp. in its inclusion of the *homoousios, a term he opposed. He did accept the Council's creed, however, but remained ill-disposed toward Nicene teaching and accused some of its defenders of Sabellianism. Finally, and above all, there is E.'s lifetime of writing. Even before the period of persecution he had produced scriptural studies, apologetics, and historical works. His biblical writing included editing texts, commentaries—largely allegorical—on Isaiah and Psalms, the Onomasticon, on biblical topography, the Gospel Questions and solutions, and a General Elementary Introduction, a compendium of Christian teaching. As Christian apologies E. composed the Praeparatio evangelica, against pagans and the philosophers; and Demonstratio evangelica, on the fulfillment of OT belief and prophecy by the Gospels. In history his Chronicles (to the year 303), the Martyrs of Palestine on the persecutions he had witnessed, and his panegyric Life of Constantine are all valuable sources. But his title, "Father of Church History," rests above all on the Ecclesiastical History. Originally it consisted of seven books, covering from the Apostolic Age to 303; by 323 he had expanded it to ten books, covering the periods of persecution, then of peace, during his own lifetime. He merited his title because his History is the first such work, because it is a compilation of rich documents, and because the work became a mine of information for subsequent centuries. Mainly, of course, the History is that of the Eastern Church. An Eng. tr. by K. Lake and J. E. L. Oulton is part of the Loeb Classical Library (2 v., 1926–32). BIBLIOGRAPHY: D. C. Wallace-Hadrill, Eusebius of Caesarea (1960).

[T. C. O'BRIEN]

EUSEBIUS OF CREMONA, ST. (d. after 420), associate of St. *Jerome. In his youth E. was a schoolmate of Jerome in Rome. Later he accompanied Jerome to the Holy Land (c.385) and lived in the same monastery with him. Back in Rome toward the end of the cent., he was one of the circle of Jerome's friends and supporters. In the first Origenist controversy, he supported Jerome against Rufinus, possibly with some want of scruple as to means. At least Rufinus accused him of stealing his translation of *Origen's De principiis to send to Jerome, and of changing part of it for the worse. E.'s feud with Rufinus continued for years. The report on the death of Jerome attributed to E. is really a medieval composition. BIBLIOGRAPHY: Butler

1:485–486; A. Frutaz, LTK 3:199–1200; A. Rimoldi, Bibl-Sanct 5:253–254.

[R. B. ENO]

EUSEBIUS OF DORYLAEUM (5th cent.), bp. and defender of the faith. E.'s attack upon Nestorius, made while he was still a layman, was instrumental in bringing about the latter's condemnation at Ephesus (431). Later as bp., when the errors of his friend *Eutyches became apparent, E. denounced him at a local council in Constantinople (448). By the intervention of *Dioscorus, the fate of Eutyches was delayed, and E. himself was persecuted at the *Latrocinium (449). At Chalcedon E. was vindicated when the heresy of Eutyches was condemned and Dioscorus punished. BIBLIOGRAPHY: C. Bareille, DTC 5:1532–37.

[P. K. MEAGHER]

EUSEBIUS OF EMESA (c.300–c.359), semi-Arian bishop. A native of Edessa, E. studied in Antioch and Alexandria. A disciple of *Eusebius of Caesarea, he also became a friend of George of Laodicea, a defender of Arius, during his student days in Alexandria. Shortly before his election to the see of Emesa, the Arian Synod of Antioch (340) offered him the see of Alexandria to replace Athanasius then in exile for the second time, but he wisely declined. The Christians of Emesa did not welcome him despite his knowledge of Syriac, and he was able to take possession of his diocese only after a special intervention by the patriarch of Antioch. Notwithstanding his associations, E. was more of an *Origenist than an Arian. He defended the full divinity of Christ, yet still insisted upon the superiority of the Father. Of his writings only about 30 of his homilies are extant in addition to fragments of others. Works: PG 861:509–562. BIBLIOGRAPHY: Quasten 3:348–351.

[R. B. ENO]

EUSEBIUS OF NICOMEDIA (d. c.342), Arian bishop. E. played a leading role in the beginnings of the Arian controversy. Like *Arius, he had been a pupil of *Lucian of Antioch. When Arius was condemned at Alexandria, he appealed to E., who used all the influence within his power as bp. of the important See of Nicomedia to help him. Though E. subscribed to the Creed at the Council of *Nicaea, he became the leader of the extreme wing of Arianism. He was exiled briefly (326–328) in Gaul but was recalled by *Constantine at the request of the Empress. Henceforth he was in high favor with the Emperor, whom he baptized on his deathbed (337), and with his successor, Constantius. By means of this favor, E. was able to bring about the temporary triumph of the Arian party and the deposition of *Athanasius. He was translated c.339 to the see of Constantinople. BIBLIOGRAPHY: Quasten 3:190–193.

[R. B. ENO]

EUSEBIUS OF SAMOSATA, ST. (d. c.380), bp. from 361, zealous defender of the Nicaean faith during the Arian ascendancy under the Emperors Constantius and Valens. He helped to elect the orthodox Meletius bp. of Antioch and refused to surrender the acts of the electing synod when the Arians tried to depose Meletius. In 370 he exerted his influence on behalf of *Basil in a disputed election for the See of Caesarea. During the reign of the Arian Emperor Valens, he traveled about Syria and Palestine to encourage the orthodox to resist. For his pains he was banished to Thrace in 374, but returned 4 years later at the death of the Emperor. He was killed by a tile thrown by an Arian woman in the town of Dolikha. BIBLIOGRAPHY: Butler 2:607–608.

[R. B. ENO]

EUSEBIUS OF VERCELLI, ST. (d. 371), bp. from 340. A native of Sardinia, educated in Rome, E. on becoming bp. lived in a quasi-monastic manner with some of his clergy, thus introducing in the West a way of life later developed by the *Canons Regular. Besides being conspicuous for his pastoral zeal, E. was a leading figure in the struggle against *Arianism and was exiled to Scythopolis in Palestine by the Emperor Constantius in 355 when he refused to condemn *Athanasius at the Synod of Milan. Under the amnesty granted by *Julian the Apostate, E. was permitted to leave his place of exile, where he had suffered grievously, and took part in the Council of Alexandria; later he went on to Antioch where he became involved, but creditably, in the trouble that led *Lucifer of Cagliari into schism. Back in Italy he met and joined forces with *Hilary of Poitiers in measures against Arianizing influences. Three of his letters are extant, but his translation of the *Commentary on the Psalms* of Eusebius of Caesarea has been lost. Works: PL 12:947–972. BIBLIOGRAPHY: Butler 4:569–571; Altaner 429; E. Crovella, BiblSanct 5:263–270.

[R. B. ENO]

EUSTACE OF LUXUEIL, ST. (c.560–629), abbot of the Abbey of Luxueil in France, and successor to St. *Columban, c.612). He was a preacher both in the region of the monastery and as a missionary to Bavaria, c.617. E.'s rule was marred by the need to censure one of the monks, Agrestius, who was preaching the doctrines of the *Three Chapters condemned at the Council of Constantinople II. Agrestius also complained of the harshness of discipline at Luxueil; the more moderate Rule of St. Benedict was adopted by E.'s successor as abbot. E.'s cult, at the Abbey of Vergaville, Lorraine, to which his remains were transferred c.966, continued down to the French Revolution. BIBLIOGRAPHY: P. Viard, BiblSanct 5:294–295; G. Böing, LTK 3:1202.

[T. C. O'BRIEN]

EUSTACE, MAURICE (d. 1587), Irish Jesuit martyr. E. was educated at Douai and entered the Jesuit novitiate at Bruges. After returning to Ireland at the request of his father, he was accused of being a Jesuit, convicted, and hanged.

[V. SAMPSON]

EUSTACHE DE ST. PAUL ASSELINE (1573–1640), *Feuillant theologian and a leading figure in the revival of French spirituality in the 17th century. E. received his doctorate at the Sorbonne (1604) and entered the Feuillants at Paris the following year. Besides filling various administrative positions of importance in his own order, he gave assistance to other religious communities in the work of reform. He was acquainted with Francis de Sales, Bérulle, and Marie de l'Incarnation. He was respected at Port-Royal, though he was in no way involved in the *Jansenism of that community, and even advocated a frequency of communion not usual at that time. His spiritual writings show the influence of the *Imitation of Christ,* Louis of Granada, and SS. Ignatius of Loyola, Teresa of Avila, and Francis de Sales. They lack something of the literary floweriness that was admired at the time, but are doctrinally solid and full of helpful spiritual counsel. For his writings see M. Standaert, DSAM 4:1701–05.

EUSTACHIO, FRA (1473–1555), Italian Dominican, miniature painter of the High Renaissance style. Influenced by Fra Bartolommeo, E. is admired more for classical border patterns than for figures. His work may be seen in Florence at the library of S. Marco and in the cathedral.

[M. J. DALY]

EUSTATHIUS OF ANTIOCH, ST. (d. c.336) bp. 324–330. As a leading opponent of Arianism and of Origenism, E. played a prominent role at the Council of Nicaea. In a conflict with *Eusebius of Caesarea he was accused of *Sabellianism and banished by Constantine to Thrace in 330. Conflicting views of E. see him on the one hand as a pillar of orthodoxy, or on the other as a connecting link between the heresies of *Paul of Samosata and *Nestorius. He desired to show that Jesus was fully man as well as fully God against those who maintained that the Logos had assumed a human body without a human soul. However, in this attempt he coined phrases like "the God-bearing man" which were to loom large in the prehistory of Nestorianism. Because of the association of his name with those of *Theodore of Mopsuestia and *Nestorius, many of his writings were destroyed. His treatise (against *Origen) on the witch of Endor is the only complete work extant. Of the others, only fragments have survived. Works: PG 17:609–1066. BIBLIOGRAPHY: Quasten 3:302–306; R. V. Sellers, *Eustathius of Antioch* (1928).

[R. B. ENO]

EUSTATHIUS OF SEBASTE in Pontus (c.300–c.377), bp. from c.356. Probably the son of the Arian Bp. Eulalius of Sebaste, E. studied under Arius at Alexandria. He was impressed by Egyptian monasticism and introduced it to Asia Minor. His own asceticism was admired by his friend, Basil, but some of his followers carried their ascetic practices to excesses similar to those later found among the *Messalians. His doctrinal positions were vacillating and unclear. He attended the councils of the period; as the delegate of the Council of Lampsacus to the Pope (365) he signed the Nicene Creed in Rome, despite his disapproval of the term *homoousios* because it was unscriptural. With Basil of Ancyra, he defended a moderate position against the extreme Arians. In his last years, he was a proponent of the *Macedonian heresy which denied the divinity of the Holy Spirit. BIBLIOGRAPHY: W. Hafner, LTK 3:1203–04.

[R. B. ENO]

EUSTATHIUS OF THESSALONICA (*c*.1115–94), theologian and humanist, metropolitan of Thessalonica from 1175, A man of broad culture, E. taught rhetoric in Constantinople before being promoted to the episcopate. Among his writings are commentaries on Homer, Pindar, and the geographic epic of Dionysius Periegete. As metropolitan he worked zealously for reform, esp. of monastic life. His works on religious topics can be found in PG 135–136; they reveal his ideas of Christian virtue and ascetical practice. His loftiness of style and content seem to have dulled his appeal to those for whom he wrote, for there is little to show that his works were widely read. Nevertheless, they are valuable evidence on the spirituality of his time. BIBLIOGRAPHY: J. Darrouzès, DSAM 4:1712–14.

[P. K. MEAGHER]

EUSTOCHIA CALAFATO, BL., (1434–86), a Poor Clare at Sta. Maria di Basicò. In 1457 Callistus III permitted her to found a community under the Franciscan Observants. Established first at S. Maria Accomandata (1458), the community was transferred to Monte Vergine (1463). Her spirituality was characterized by her devotion to poverty, personal penance, and to the Passion. Pius VI confirmed her cult in 1782. BIBLIOGRAPHY: Wadding Ann 14:577–589; G. Morabito, 3:660–662.

[J. J. SMITH]

EUSTOCHIA OF PADUA, BL. (1444–69), Benedictine nun. Daughter of a nun, at a time when scandals were rife in society and in the cloister, she was educated in the convent of San Prosdocimo. Her mother's community having been replaced by one of stricter observance, she was later reluctantly admitted to the new one. Naturally of gentle and docile disposition, she after a time seemed to suffer diabolical possession. Suspected of being a witch, she was denied profession; however, through the intercession of her confessor, she took vows after 4 years. E. ultimately became a revered member of the community. After her death miracles were ascribed to her. When her body was exhumed for relocation, it was discovered incorrupt. BIB-

LIOGRAPHY: I. Daniele, BiblSanct 5:305–306; Butler 1:325–327.

[C. KEENAN]

EUSTOCHIUM, ST. (*c*.370–*c*.419), Roman virgin, daughter of St. Paula of Rome. Both desired to live according to the spirituality of the Egyptian desert fathers, remaining at the same time in their home. While in Rome, St. Jerome became their spiritual director (382–385). They followed him as he journeyed toward Egypt and finally settled in Bethlehem, founding there three communities of women. The supervision of these was assumed by E. after Paula's death in 404. Jerome dedicated some of his writing to E. and Paula, notably in better-known epistles and in his eulogy. BIBLIOGRAPHY: F. Caraffa, BiblSanct 5:302–304; Butler 3:665–666.

[A. A. O'NEILL]

EUSTRATIADES SOPHRONIOS (1872–1947), Turkish-born metropolitan of Leontopolis, scholar. While serving as a deacon at St. George Orthodox church in Vienna, he earned his doctorate. Moving to Alexandria at the invitation of the patriarch Photius, he was ordained priest and bp., and made metropolitan of Leontopolis. There he devoted himself to writing for the reviews of the patriarchate. After resigning his see in 1914 because of the climate, he spent several years cataloguing Greek MSS in some minor monasteries of Mount Athos and in various archives of Thessalonica. His editions are not critical but provide much useful material for the study of Byzantine and post-Byzantine literature and church history. BIBLIOGRAPHY: V. Grumel, *Catholicisme* 4:724.

[M. J. SUELZER]

EUTHANASIA, termination of human life in case of incurable illness for the sake of ending misery. Also called mercy killing, it is prompted by desire to end suffering in those thought to be in such a state that their mental faculties are gone beyond recall or that they are totally obsessed by pain that cannot be alleviated. It is advocated by some as an act of mercy to hasten a death that is close and unavoidable when the suffering is extreme. Recent campaigns have sought to gain legal sanction for the practice. Euthanasia is also sometimes advocated for extreme cases of mental deficiency, particularly if combined with much physical malformation. It has been opposed on the grounds that the prohibition of the direct taking of innocent life is an absolute moral requirement that cannot be set aside, that no human authority can so usurp a power that belongs to God alone, that his love and mercy tracks down all human agony, that legal authorization is a social and political danger, and that euthanasia is radically against the spirit of medical science and art. It is conceded, however, that there is no obligation to keep a body alive "officiously," as it is said, that is, by artificial animation when all mental life is gone or by what by informed estimation is reckoned an ''extraordinary'' operation. BIBLIOGRAPHY: J. P. Kenny, *Principles of Medical Ethics* (2 ed., 1962).

[T. GILBY]

EUTHYMIUS I (*c*.834–917), **PATRIARCH OF CONSTANTINOPLE** from 907–912. He was the abbot of St. Theodora in Constantinople and in 886 became the confessor of Emperor Leo VI, the Wise. He became patriarch when Leo deposed the Patriarch Nicholas I Mysticus for refusing to sanction the emperor's fourth marriage, to his mistress Zoe. E. accepted only after being certain that a dispensation had been granted by the four other patriarchs for the marriage. When Leo died, Nicholas was restored and E. was banished; the two were reconciled, however, before E.'s death. He was renowned as a preacher, but few of his sermons are extant; a history of the first seven ecumenical councils once ascribed to him was probably composed 5 cent. later by Euthymius II. E. has been revered as a saint in the Greek Church since the 10th century.

[A. A. O'NEILL]

EUTHYMIUS THE GREAT, ST. (377–473). Born at Melitene in Armenia of Greek-speaking parents, E. received a good education under the direction of the bp. and was given supervisory charge of the monks of the diocese. This proved too busy a life for his liking, and he made his way to the holy places, where he joined a community of hermits at Pharan, not far from Jerusalem. With one of them, whose name was Theoctistus, he established another monastery of the same kind, first in the desolate region close to the Dead Sea, and later, when disciples came to join them, near the road from Jericho to Jerusalem. A church was built for them and consecrated by the Patriarch Juvenal in 428, and as a result of miracles of healing, the monastery became celebrated and influential. This was a cause of embarrassment to Euthymius, who retired for most of the week into the wilderness but made himself available for counsel on Saturdays and Sundays. His influence contributed to the general acceptance of the Council of Chalcedon in the holy places and in Palestine. Among his disciples was St. Sabbas, whose laura later surpassed his own in reputation, though the monastery of St. Euthymius long continued to be a place for pilgrim monks and a Christianizing influence among the Bedouins. BIBLIOGRAPHY: A. J. Festugière, *Les Moins d'Orient*, 3.1 (1962); Butler 1:130–132; V. Grumel, BiblSanct 5:329–333.

[G. EVERY]

EUTHYMIUS SAĪFI (*c*.1648–1725), Syrian Catholic Melchite abp. and reunionist. While still externally in schism, he was named abp. of Sidon and Tyre in 1683, but the next year he sent a profession of faith to Rome. In 1701 he was appointed administrator for all Catholic Melchites in the patriarchate of Antioch. In a very hostile environment he was an ardent promoter of union with Rome and wrote a book in Arabic on union, which was translated into Latin,

Liber sideris fulgentis inter ambos polos universae Ecclesiae (2d ed., 1863). He also founded a congregation of monks in 1708. BIBLIOGRAPHY: C. Karalevskij, DHGE 3:645–647 s. v. ''Antioch.''

[G. T. DENNIS]

EUTHYMIUS OF SARDES (d. 834), opponent of *iconoclasm. A native of Lycaonia (Asia Minor), after studies in Alexandria, he returned to become monk, priest, and finally metropolitan of Sardes. He participated in the council of Nicaea II in 787. Being an iconodule, he was exiled by the iconoclast emperor Leo V, and suffered torture under Michael II, was executed at the order of Theophilus. E. was befriended by St. Theodore Studites, three of whose letters to E. are extant.

[J. MADEY]

EUTHYMIUS ZIGABENUS, 12th-cent. Byzantine theologian, exegete, and monk from the environs of Constantinople. Little is known of his life. He is the author of *Panoplia Dogmatike,* purporting to be a refutation of all heresies, and written at the request of Emperor Alexius Comnenus. It consists mostly of a compilation of earlier treatments of the subject. His exegetical works rely heavily on John Chrysostom and other earlier biblical commentators.

[E. J. DILLON]

EUTRAPELIA, from the Greek meaning a well-turned, ready, and agreeable wit, occasionally used in a bad sense, but introduced by Aristotle as the moral virtue of moderation in taking recreation. It strikes a mean between ribaldry (*bomolochia*) and boorishness (*agroikia*). The need of relaxation was well recognized by John Cassian, and St. Thomas Aquinas treats the finding of solace in games and jokes, so long as they are not indecent, dissipating, nor outside their due occasions, as a function of the virtue of modesty, which is allied to temperance, and therefore among the endowments of divine grace. The sobersides, of course, were more inclined to deprecate superfluity than insufficiency in this matter, yet they taught that it was against the good life to show oneself dour, uncouth, a wet-blanket, or a spoil-sport, and even admitted a place for comic nonsense. Their principles still apply, although the growth of sport in the modern world has brought in new problems, some of them threats to *eutrapelia* itself, such as commercialism, professionalism, and a somewhat hysterical competitiveness. It should be noticed that the fun and amusement the moralists consider is restricted to the field of the temperate moral virtues; the deeper psychology of play should be read in terms of St. Augustine on enjoyment (*frui*) and of St. Thomas Aquinas on delight (*delectatio*) as the healthy response to an end in itself, even a nonultimate end. BIBLIOGRAPHY: ThAq ST, 1a2ae, questions 31–34; 2a2ae, 168.

[T. GILBY]

EUTROPIUS. Isidore of Seville and John Biclarensis give data about a bp. E. of Valencia in Spain (c.590–c.610). By 580 he was abbot of a monastery near Cuenca founded c.570 by refugee monks from Africa; he defended his rule in a letter to a Bp. Peter; E.'s collection of excerpts from Cassian on capital sins is also extant (PL 80:9–20). With Leander, E. supervised the Council of Toledo III (589) at which the Visigoths became Catholic. Gennadius mentions an ascetic priest E. to whom four extant spiritual works (395–415) are attributed (J. Madoz, *Estudios eclesiásticos* 16 [1942] 27–54). The late-15th-cent. St. E. of Orange was, according to a contemporary vita, a thaumaturge and ascetic. The poet Fortunatus says that a St. E. was the first bp. of Saintes, Gregory of Tours adding that he was a 1st-cent. martyr. BIBLIOGRAPHY: R. Aubert et al., DHGE 16:78–86.

[E. P. COLBERT]

EUTYCHES (371?–455), founder of *Monophysitism, the heretical doctrine that Christ has no human nature, but only the divine nature. As superior of hundreds of monks and influential friend of the imperial court at Constantinople, he propagated the doctrine that the personal unity of the incarnate Word entails a mixture of his natures, with the infinite divine nature completely absorbing the finite human one.

[R. R. BARR]

EUTYCHIAN, ST. (d. 283), **POPE** from 275. Nothing is known of this pope, successor to St. Felix. The *Liber pontificalis* says that he was a Tuscan. Because he ruled during the peaceful period before the persecution of Diocletian, the statement of the Roman Martyrology that he died a martyr, and the assertion of the *Liber pontificalis* that he buried many martyrs with his own hands are unreliable. The same is to be said of the anachronistic report that he established the custom of blessing the produce of the fields. In the 19th cent. fragments of his epitaph were found in the catacomb of Callistus. BIBLIOGRAPHY: Butler 4:516; A. Amore, EncCatt 5:871.

[R. B. ENO]

EUTYCHIANS, followers of *Eutyches who claimed that there is one nature in Christ. The name refers not only to mid-5th-cent. monks at Constantinople whose leader was Eutyches, but to all those in later years holding teachings attributed to him, e.g., *Sergius Grammaticus and *Julian of Halicarnassus. Unlike the more powerful *Monophysites, few Eutychians registered opposition to the Council of *Chalcedon. They shared the intellectual and theological limitations of their founder and were too literal, upholding the position of St. Cyril of Alexandria against the Nestorians. Among the Monophysites, *Severus of Antioch was the most outspoken critic of the later Eutychianism. BIBLIOGRAPHY: Daniélou-Marrou 361–368.

[F. H. BRIGHAM]

EUTYCHIOS OF ALEXANDRIA (877–940), **PATRIARCH OF ALEXANDRIA** from 933, Melchite historian and theologian. His tenure as patriarch was marked by controversy between him and his flock. His writings roused the ire of Maronites and Jacobites, and later figured in the 17th-cent. English theological dispute over whether there was any difference between priests and bps. in the Alexandrian tradition. His *Annals* purports to be a religious and profane history of the world from the beginning to his own time. Its special value is in the factual information it gives, not available elsewhere, about the Muslim Caliphates and the Egyptian Church. An important theological treatise on the divine economy, given among the works of St. *Athanasius in PG 111:907–1156, almost certainly was written by E. in Arabic, *Kitāb al-Burhān* (Book of Demonstration); he also wrote a work on the angels, and a dialogue between a Christian and a heretic.

[E. J. DILLON]

EUTYCHÌUS, PATRIARCH OF CONSTANTINOPLE (512–582). Born in Phrygia, E. entered monastic life at Amasia and was sent to Constantinople as a legate of the bp. (552). He so impressed Justinian that he was appointed to succeed Mennas as patriarch of Constantinople (552). Articulate in the controversy of the Three Chapters, E. presided at the 5th Ecumenical Council (Constantinople 553) but was sent into exile at Amasia by the Emperor Justinian whose sympathy with the Aphthartodocetae error he opposed (565). He was reinstated as patriarch by Justin II after the death of Patriarch John III Scholasticus (577). Of his writings, fragments of an important sermon on the Eucharist and a letter to Pope Vigilius survive (PG 86.2.2391–2406). BIBLIOGRAPHY: R. Janin, DHGE 16:94–95.

[F. H. BRIGHAM]

EUZOIUS OF CAESAREA (d. 376), a deacon of Alexandria and follower of Arius who was condemned with him by the synod of Egypt and Libya (318, 319 or 323) and again by the Council of Nicaea (325). E. attended the Arian council of Jerusalem (335) and became bp. of Antioch (360) after Meletius had abandoned Arianism. He baptized the dying Emperor Constantius (361) and placed the Arian Lucius upon the episcopal throne at Alexandria (373). He died 5 years before Arianism was effectively checked by the Council of Constantinople (381). BIBLIOGRAPHY: M. Spanneut, DHGE 16:98–101.

[M. J. COSTELLOE]

EVAGRIUS OF PONTUS (346–399), extremely influential Origenist, first monk to become a great author, founder of an ascetical, spirit-flesh tradition which endured to the mid-20th cent., father of the three-step ascetical-mystical theory of virtue, contemplation, union. A native of Pontus in Asia Minor, E. was ordained a deacon by *Gregory of Nazianzus and achieved great success as a preacher in Constantinople. In 382 he fled the world to join the monks of the Nitrian Mts., where he gained his livelihood copying MSS and became the disciple and friend of Macarius of Egypt. Because he was condemned posthumously (Constantinople, 553) with *Origen and Didymus the Blind for his Origenism (E. had attempted to reduce Origen's doubtful teachings to ascetical practice), few of E.'s writings are extant, as is so often the case with an allegedly heterodox author, whose works were usually destroyed or not recopied and thus allowed to perish. A fair number remain in translation or under false names, and many more should be discovered as MS research progresses. BIBLIOGRAPHY: Quasten 3:169–176; A. and C. Guillaumont, DSAM 4.2:1731–44.

[R. R. BARR]

EVANGELARIUM, a book containing passages from the Gospels to be read at Mass on Sundays, feasts, etc., in the Eastern and Western Churches. It was generally used by the deacon at high Mass, but has now been replaced by full lectionaries containing all the scriptural excerpts for various occasions. BIBLIOGRAPHY: J. H. Miller, *Fundamentals of the Liturgy* (1959).

[N. R. KRAMER]

EVANGELIAR, MS with texts primarily from the four Gospels, the illuminated or illustrated pages of which are important as exquisite examples and determinants in the development of art through the ages. The imagery of many sculptured portals is derived from such MS pages. The Ada Gospels (c.800, Trier) is an important example.

[M. J. DALY]

EVANGELICAL (Gr. *euangelion,* gospel), a term whose meaning must be determined by the context. During the Reformation, Protestants distinguished themselves from Catholics by the term "evangelical," believing that they had recovered the gospel in their doctrine of justification by faith. In Prussia the union of Lutheran and *Reformed Churches was called the Evangelical Church, and the Protestant Church of Germany today is known as the Evangelical Church of Germany. In parts of Europe Evangelical may signify Lutheran as distinct from Reformed Churches. The 18th-cent. Wesleyan revivals in England were known as the evangelical revivals, and a *Low-Church party within the C of E but influenced by the Methodist movement were also called evangelicals. In the U.S. the term may refer to those who stress *evangelism and personal religious experience, biblical authority, human sinfulness, the atonement of Christ, and the necessity of a new birth (see NEW EVANGELICALISM). It may also simply signify Protestant in contrast to RC or Orthodox. BIBLIOGRAPHY: K. S. Latourette, *History of Christianity* (1953, repr. 1975). *EVANGELICALISM.

[N. H. MARING]

EVANGELICAL ALLIANCE, an interdenominational organization founded in 1846 to associate and concentrate the strength of enlightened Protestantism against the encroachments of popery and Puseyism (see OXFORD MOVEMENT) and to protect the interests of scriptural Christianity. The organizing meeting in London was attended not only by English but by American and continental churchmen. The question of slavery in the U.S. was an early disruptive factor; German participation was diverted with the formation of the Evangelische Bund. Nevertheless the Alliance flourished and established an admirable record of aiding persecuted Protestant minorities and of ecumenical activity. The American branch of the Evangelical Alliance was formally organized after the Civil War, predominantly by Presbyterian and *Reformed groups. Doctrinal positions were conservative; the early leader was Philip *Schaff. In the late 19th cent. the *Social Gospel was prominent in the activities of the Alliance. The Alliance was replaced by 1908 by the Federal Council of Churches, for which it had prepared the way. The World Evangelical Alliance continues to exist, with headquarters in London, but its activities are largely confined to British Protestant interests. BIBLIOGRAPHY: *History of the Ecumenical Movement, 1517–1948* (ed. R. Rouse and S. C. Neil, 1967).

[T. GILBY]

EVANGELICAL AND REFORMED CHURCH, since 1959 part of the *United Church of Christ, a denomination formed in 1934 through the merger of the Reformed Church in the United States and the Evangelical Synod of North America. This union reflected the similarities in background and teaching of the participants. Polity in both Churches was along the lines of Presbyterianism. By 1959 the Evangelical and Reformed Church had c.800,000 members and a flourishing program of education (eight colleges, three seminaries) and of home and foreign missions.

The Reformed Church in the U.S. was first a *synod dependent on the Reformed Church in Holland, organized by M. *Schlatter at Philadelphia in 1747. Members were immigrants to Pennsylvania from the *Reformed tradition in Switzerland and the German Palatinate. In 1793 this synod declared itself independent as the German Reformed Church; in 1863 German was dropped from the title. Growth was principally in Pennsylvania and Ohio; in 1924 a majority of the Hungarian Reformed united with the Church (see HUNGARIAN REFORMED CHURCH IN AMERICA). The major problem experienced by the Church was the 19th-cent. incursion of *revivalism, which diminished the stature of the *Heidelberg Catechism and in turn the historical confessional identity of the Church. The *Mercersburg theology, an interpretive re-emphasis on the Catechism, was a reaction that led to a *high-church vs. *broad-church polarization among members. The Catechism did regain its place as the doctrinal standard and was recognized as having a place in church life. At the same time a liberal attitude toward doctrine and worship and attention to "deeds not creeds" characterized the spirit of the Church. At the time of the 1934 merger, there were c.350,000 members in the U.S. and missions in China, Japan, and Iraq. *REFORMED CHURCH IN THE U.S.

The Evangelical Synod of North America had as its background the Evangelical Church proclaimed in Prussia in 1817 as the state Church by King Frederick William III. This Church united Reformed and Lutheran Churches on the basis of F. *Schleiermacher's theory that confessions of faith were irrelevant. The first organization in the U.S. was at St. Louis in 1840, the German Evangelical Church Union of the West; the present name was adopted in 1877 after other similar German synods in the eastern and midwestern states joined the Missouri group. The Heidelberg and Luther's *Catechisms, as well as the *Augsburg Confession, were accepted as doctrinal standards, but liberty of conscience toward them was proclaimed. Greater stress was put upon purity of life and a practical, social Christianity than upon doctrine. Membership at the time of the merger was about 280,000.

[T. C. O'BRIEN]

EVANGELICAL CHURCH IN GERMANY, a federation of Lutheran, Reformed, and United Churches of Germany. Formed in 1918 at Eisenach, the Evangelische Kirche in Deutschland (EKD) supersedes two other attempts at reorganization made after the collapse of the monarchy in 1918: the Deutscher Evangelischer Kirchenbund (1922) and the Deutsche Evangelische Kirche (1933), which had been rendered powerless by the Nazis. The EKD does not interfere with the confessional affiliation of its members, but it does emphasize their common foundation in the message of Jesus as contained in the Scriptures. The chief agencies are a synod and an executive council. Deliberations are limited to such common interests as missions, social service, ecumenism, and relations with the Federal and East German governments. Of the 27 member Churches, 13 are Lutheran 12 are United, and 2 are Reformed. BIBLIOGRAPHY: J. Beckmann and G. Wasse, RGG 2:779–785.

[M. J. SUELZER]

EVANGELICAL COUNSELS, see COUNSELS, EVANGELICAL.

EVANGELICAL FRIENDS ALLIANCE, an association of the Ohio, Kansas, Oregon, and Rocky Mountain Yearly Meetings of the Religious Society of Friends formed in 1965 for the purpose of providing closer fellowship and common action. Belonging to the *Gurneyite tradition, the member yearly *meetings subscribe to the main tenets of evangelical Protestantism (the Bible as the rule of faith, Jesus' vicarious atonement, salvation and forgiveness of sin, the Church as a visible and eschatological reality), but

Quaker belief on inward spiritual experience is also preserved. Alliance members are active in evangelism at home and abroad. In 1966 there were about 30,000 members. BIBLIOGRAPHY: *American Quakers Today* (ed. E. B. Bronner, 1966).

[J. C. WILLKE]

EVANGELICAL LUTHERAN CHURCHES, ASSOCIATION OF (AELC), body formed by congregations withdrawing from the Lutheran Church—Missouri Synod. It was organized Dec. 3, 1976, in Chicago by representatives of about 150 congregations grouped in five regional synods. Formation of the AELC resulted from conflict within the Missouri Synod that had drawn national attention. Though the conflict came to involve issues of church government and personal antagonisms, it stemmed from a dispute over use of historical-critical methods of biblical interpretation at the Synod's Concordia Seminary in St. Louis. AELC members came from defenders of these methods. Since most of them were not theological liberals, they were known as the moderates, in distinction from the conservatives led by Synod President J. A. O. Preus. Schism was set in motion after moderates from Concordia formed a rival school, Concordia Seminary-in-Exile (Seminex), at St. Louis in 1974, and some district presidents insisted on ordaining its uncertified graduates. At the Synod's biennial convention in 1975, a majority of delegates supported conservative positions, and in 1976 Preus removed defiant district presidents from office. Meanwhile, moderates had formed Evangelical Lutherans in Mission, which served as their primary instrument of cooperative activity until formal separation was effected with establishment of the AELC. Founders stressed their commitment to Lutheran unity and their desire to avoid setting up a new church that would be a permanent, separate entity.

[T. EARLY]

EVANGELICAL UNITED BRETHREN CHURCH, a Church formed in 1946 in Johnstown, Pa., by the union between the Evangelical Church and the Church of the United Brethren in Christ. These two denominations both were American-born, emerging from German-speaking forebears in Pennsylvania and Maryland; both were products of the *Second Great Awakening—espousing *Arminianism in theology and emphasizing conversion coupled with an individual sanctification ethic that expressed their *Pietism. Both adopted a polity patterned after that of American Methodism—with powers delegated from the *General Conference (national) to the local conference (congregational) through the annual conference, which possessed certain presbyterial features. In both denominations pastors were stationed annually by the bishops in conjunction with the annual conference superintendents; both denominations were small. The 441,566 United Brethren and the 263,536 Evangelicals were clustered in the town and country areas of Pennsylvania, Indiana, Illinois, and Ohio.

The Church of the United Brethren in Christ was formed when revivalist preachers of several Protestant denominations began in 1800 to gather annually to promote extension of their Pietism among German settlers in America. Philip W. *Otterbein (1726–1813), a German Reformed pastor in Baltimore and a friend of F. *Asbury, Methodist bp., and Martin Boehm, a Mennonite lay preacher, were the early leaders. A reluctance to move beyond the nonsectarian, voluntary societal pattern was gradually overcome under the leadership of Christian Newcomer (1749–1830), whose organizational efforts resulted in 1816 in the first General Conference of delegates in Mount Pleasant, Pa., which adopted a *Discipline* containing an elemental confession of faith and rules providing for an itinerant ministry. Further constitutional development in 1841 was preceded by the appearance in 1834 of the *Religious Telescope,* the denominational paper, and followed by the opening of Otterbein College, Westerville, Ohio (1847), the founding of the first missionary society (1853), and opening of the first theological seminary (1871). In 1889 the expanding denomination suffered schism: it revised its Articles of Faith and Constitution, and dissident conservatives who preferred the Constitution of 1841, which prohibited membership in secret societies, withdrew to organize the United Brethren in Christ, Old Constitution. During the 20th cent. the original body manifested a growing unitive spirit, attempting two unsuccessful transconfessional unions, joining the Federal and World Councils of Churches, and cooperating with other denominations on the foreign field in China, Japan, the Philippines, Puerto Rico, Ecuador, and to some extent, Sierra Leone. Home missions were located in New Mexico and Florida among Spanish-speaking people.

The Evangelical Church was begun through the evangelistic, itinerant preaching of Jacob *Albright, a Pennsylvania Lutheran farmer whose conversion experience and spiritual concern impelled him to preach. Albright ministered independently, organizing his first classes in 1800 and holding the first annual conference of his preachers in 1807. In 1809 a *Discipline* containing Articles of Faith very similar to those of the Methodist Episcopal Church was adopted. At the first General Conference, held in 1816, the name Die Evangelische Gemeinschaft (Evangelical Association) was adopted. The German-language ministry predominated until World War I. Growth was augmented by the appearance of the church papers, *Der Christliche Botschafter* (1836) and the *Evangelical Messenger* (1848); the creation of a missionary society (1839); and the opening of North Central College, Naperville, Ill. (1861), and a theological seminary (1876). An unfortunate division occurred (1891–94) because theological differences over the doctrine of sanctification turned into a personality duel between two bishops. While three-fifths of the membership of the Evangelical Association remained in the continuing body, the remaining two-fifths seceded in 1894

to organize the United Evangelical Church. This rupture was healed in 1922 when, with the exception of several thousand United Evangelicals who preferred to organize the Evangelical Congregational Church, the two groups reunited to create the Evangelical Church. At the time of the union of 1946, this body supported missions in Japan, China, Germany, Switzerland, and Nigeria, and U.S. missions among Wisconsin Italians and Kentucky mountaineers.

Divided into seven episcopal areas, with headquarters in Dayton, Ohio, the Evangelical United Brethren Church supported seven colleges and three seminaries. In 1962 it revised its Confession of Faith. It was a member of the National and World Councils of Churches and also of the *Consultation on Church Union. The long and amiable relationship sustained by its predecessor bodies with the Methodist Church lent considerable logic to its 1968 union with that body, which created the *United Methodist Church. BIBLIOGRAPHY: P. H. Eller, *These Evangelical United Brethren* (1950); R. Albright, *History of the Evangelical United Brethren Church* (1925); *Book of Ritual of the Evangelical United Brethren Church* (1955).

[K. J. STEIN]

EVANGELICALISM, a term with a variety of applications. It may be taken as a synonym for Protestantism, in keeping with the Reformers' reference to themselves as *evangelical Christians. In the U.S. evangelicalism sometimes means the *revivalism that became a characteristic of American Protestants in the 19th century. Stressing religious experience and the need for decisive individual conversion, evangelicalism in this sense tended to ignore *confessions of faith, *ecclesiology, and sacramental theology, as well as other aspects of systematic theology, and brought criticism from J. Nevins (see MERCERSBERG THEOLOGY), H. *Bushnell, and others. The term is also used in opposition to liberalism and *modernism to designate conservative Christianity within all denominations. Since the early 1950s many theological conservatives (e.g., H. J. Ockenga, E. J. Carness, C. F. H. *Henry) have expressed dissatisfaction with the lack of social concern, the dearth of scholarship, and the limited scope of interest in theological subject matter of the fundamentalists; they have become known as the New Evangelicals and their movement as New Evangelicalism (see FUNDAMENTALISM). Early associated with Fuller Theological Seminary, Pasadena, Calif., and with the fortnightly *Christianity Today,* New Evangelicals have produced a number of scholarly works and have had a wide influence in American Protestantism. Differences exist within the New Evangelicalism, but it is characterized by stress upon the authority (and inerrancy) of the Bible, *evangelism, and the necessity of individual conversion, the need for comprehensive and competent theological scholarship, and some expressions of Christian social concern. Holding to traditional doctrines, it emphasizes the lost condition of sinful men, the efficacy of the atoning death of Christ, and the grace of God, which justifies men who go to him in faith and repentance. BIBLIOGRAPHY: R. Quebedeaux, *Young Evangelicals* (1974); *Evangelicals* (ed. D. F. Wells and J. D. Woodbridge, 1975); *Chicago Declaration* (ed. R. Sider, 1974); B. L. Ramm, *Evangelical Heritage* (1973).

[N. H. MARING]

EVANGELICALS OF THE AUGSBURG CONFESSION, often used as an official designation for Lutherans in European countries.*AUGSBURG CONFESSION.

EVANGELIENBUCH (*Liber evangeliorum* or *Krist*), a life of Christ in five books based on pericopes; the first rhymed poem in German literature; composed in the South Rhenish Franconian (Old High German) dialect of Alsace between 865 and 871 by *Otfried of Weissenburg. Its narrative sections are followed by didactic and allegorical interpretations (*mystice, spiritualiter, moraliter*), which are important sources of our knowledge of 9th-cent. Christian theology. For text, see O. Erdman, 4th ed. rev. L. Wolff, 1962 (*Altdeutsche Textbibliothek*, 49); BIBLIOGRAPHY: W. Kosch, *Deutsches Literatur-Lexikon* (1963) 307.

[M. F. MCCARTHY]

EVANGELISCHE MICHAELSBRUDERSCHAFT (Lutheran Confraternity of Michael), a German Protestant movement founded in Marburg in 1931 as an outgrowth of the *Berneuchen circle. It aims for renewal of the Protestant Church through the Eucharist and through spirituality and retreats, and has also become prominent through its ecumenical efforts in the *Una Sancta movement. BIBLIOGRAPHY: R. Mumm, LTK 7:402–403; M. J. Taylor, *Protestant Liturgical Renewal* (1963).

EVANGELISM, a term meaning proclaiming the gospel. Although the word "evangelism" does not appear in the NT, *euangelion* (gospel) and related words do, and the idea of proclaiming the gospel and winning converts to the Christian faith is present. Evangelism has been basic to the Church's mission, but methods of evangelizing have varied widely. Person-to-person witnessing by early Christians, debating in synagogues, spontaneous addresses to informal assemblies, winning a tribe by converting its leader, and catechetical instruction for inquirers were among the early forms. Renewed emphasis upon personal religious commitment led to the Methodist revivals in England and the *Great Awakening in the U.S., where *revivalism became the chief means of evangelism for nearly 2 centuries. As the effectiveness of mass evangelism declined and *secularism increased, new methods of reaching those alienated from the Churches have been sought. The World and National Councils of Churches have departments of evangelism, as does nearly every denomination. In 1967, a worldwide meeting in Berlin considered the theology and methodology of evangelism. Considerable controversy has been evoked

since mid-20th cent. by the question as to whether ministering to men's material and social needs is an essential part of evangelism or simply an aftereffect. According to a widely accepted definition, evangelism is "the presentation of the good news of God in Jesus Christ, so that men are brought, through the power of the Holy Spirit, to put their trust in God; accept Jesus Christ as their Savior from the guilt and power of sin; follow and serve Him as their Lord in the fellowship of the Church and in the vocations of the common life." BIBLIOGRAPHY: *One Race, One Gospel, One Task* (ed. C. F. H. Henry and W. S. Mooneyham, 2 v., 1967); *Report of New Delhi Assembly* (ed. W. A. Visser 't Hooft, 1962); M. Green, *Evangelism in the Early Church* (1970); C. F. H. Henry, *Fundamentals of the Faith* (pa. 1975).

[N. H. MARING]

EVANGELIST, a proclaimer of the Gospel (*evangelion*). The term was applied to Philip (Acts 21.8), who preached the Gospel in Samaria (Acts 8). A spiritual gift, it is listed after apostles and prophets (Eph 4.11). Timothy had to "do the work of an evangelist" (2 Tim 4.5). The word was used later of the authors of the four canonical Gospels. BIBLIOGRAPHY: M. J. Hunt, NCE 5:650–654.

[A. VIARD]

EVANGELISTS, ICONOGRAPHY OF THE. The four apocalyptic "beasts" symbolizing the Evangelists Matthew, Mark, Luke, and John, derive from Ezekiel's vision (by the River Chebar) "four living creatures each having the face of a man in front, the face of a lion to the right, the face of an ox to the left, and the face of an eagle at the back . . . a wheel of the chariot of Yahweh by each of them. Above them . . . upon the throne a figure having the glory of the Lord." (Ezek 1.6–30). Honorius of Autun (*Cant. cant.* PL 172:462) determines the symbolic quadriga of Aminadab in the window at St. Denis carrying the ark, Aaron's rod, and the tables of the Law of the Old Covenant, while from the ark rises the crucified Christ upheld by God the Father, and near the wheels (as in Ezekiel's vision) the four symbolic beasts (Evangelists) draw the triumphal chariot of the New Covenant to the ends of the earth. John (Rev 4) writes "I saw a throne and round the throne, on each side of the throne are four living creatures . . . a lion, . . . an ox, . . . a man, . . . a flying eagle glorifying the One on the throne." These animals relate to Assyrian *karibu* (Cherubim, Ex 25.18), the composite man-lion-eagle-ox beasts guarding palaces and temples of Babylon. Rabanus Maurus (Ezek 1; PL 110:515) states that in the primitive church, the four mystic creatures carried three distinct meanings: (1) Matthew is man, his geneological table establishing Christ as man; Mark is the lion that sleeps with its eyes open (symbol of Divinity in the tomb) and rouses its cubs to life 3 days after their birth, (symbolizing the Resurrection); Luke is the ox of sacrifice, that of Zechariah in the Old Law, and of Christ in the New Law; John, is the eagle that flies into the sun, as John leads us

to the divinity of Christ. (2) The four beasts signify Christ, as man in his nativity, ox in his death, lion in his Resurrection, and eagle in his Ascension. In the 10th-cent. Evangeliarum of Otto, Gospels are marked by paintings of these episodes in the life of Christ, and cathedrals juxtapose these historic incidents and symbols in glass and stone. (3) The four beasts further signify virtues necessary for salvation: the Christian must be a man, a reasonable animal; the ox signifies his sacrifice of wordly pleasures; the lion, his courage and the eagle, his contemplation of eternity. Pagan and Christian bestiaries are inextricably interwoven in these animals: the lion from Pliny, (*Hist. nat.*, 8.17); the eagle from the *Bestiaire* of Pierre le Picard (*Arsenal* MS 3516, 198. Honorius's *Speculum ecclesiae* borrows freely from these ancient bestiaries. The symbolic beasts, ubiquitous in the tympana of Romanesque churches, appear also in gospel pages, book covers, and enamels. At lecterns carrying the four symbols, the book was placed upon the specific beast signifying the Evanglist read, though more often the eagle alone supported the gospel book. BIBLIOGRAPHY: E. Mâle, *Gothic Image* (1958).

EVANGELIZATION, in the broad sense of the term, all missionary action having conversion to Christianity as a goal; in a more restricted sense, the second phase of missionary catechesis in which the basic Christian message is presented to the prospective Christian (see CATECHESIS, MISSIONARY). This basic message or kerygma embraces the Christian doctrine of God's love for man, revelation, sin, and esp. salvation through Christ. This stage of evangelization does not engage in apologetical arguments, but seeks to relate the person of Christ to the concrete, existential needs of the nonbeliever. Thus a basic principle of this kerygmatic approach is to keep Christ constantly in focus, since he is the heart of the Gospel message and the key to any further elaboration of Christian doctrine. It is at this stage that the individual responds by his initial act of faith, accepting Christ and the invitation to share in the riches of divine adoption. In many instances evangelization must be preceded by pre-evangelization, a process of predisposing the individual so that faith becomes a viable option for him. Once the Good News has been announced and has been initially accepted, the prospective Christian becomes a catechumen and enters a period of more complete and systematic instruction as an immediate preparation for baptism. BIBLIOGRAPHY: J. A. Jungmann, *Good News Yesterday and Today* (1962); J. Hofinger, *Art of Teaching Christian Doctrine* (1957); Paul VI, *Evangeli nuntiandi (Exhortation on Evangelization*, Dec. 1975). *CATECHETICS.

[L. J. LUZBETAK]

EVANGELIZATION OF PEOPLES OR PROPAGATION OF THE FAITH, CONGREGATION FOR THE (formerly the Congregation for the Propagation of the Faith), one of the nine sacred congregations of the *Curia Romana. The history of the congregation begins with a commission of cardinals instituted by St. Pius V in 1568 for the missions in the East Indies and among the Italo-Greeks and for ecclesiastical affairs in the Protestant territories of Europe. A temporary congregation was formed in 1573 by Gregory XIII for the conversion of infidels. This commission was modified by Clement VIII, but ceased to exist after some years of activity. Then in 1622, a more stable congregation was erected by Gregory XV and confirmed by the apostolic constitution, *Inscrutabili divinae.* It was established in part to commission missionaries who would be subject to the Holy See and so to achieve a control that was impossible where the *patronato real* was exercised. The Congregation has competence over most persons and affairs of the Church in mission territories. In 1967, at the time of the constitution *Regimini ecclesiae universae,* the congregation received the name of the Congregation for the Evangelization of Peoples or for the Propagation of the Faith. Its objective is to proclaim the Gospel, form communities of faith, and encourage sacramental life among believers. The Congregation seeks to promote a process that will result eventually in self-supporting local Churches, with indigenous ministerial personnel.

[R. A. TODD]

EVANS, PHILIP, ST. (1645–79), Welsh Jesuit martyr. E. was educated at Saint-Omer, entered the Jesuits (1665), and was ordained at Liège (1675). He was sent to work in South Wales where the authorities overlooked his activities for a time, but when the persecution stiffened after the discovery of the Titus Oates Plot (1678), a price was put on his head and he was captured. He refused the Oath of Allegiance, was found guilty of having unlawfully entered the country as a priest, and was executed at Gallows Field, Cardiff. He was beatified in 1929 and canonized in 1970.

EVANSTON ASSEMBLY, second general assembly of the World Council of Churches (Aug. 1954), at Evanston, Ill.; its theme was "Christ the Hope of the World." The preliminary report was debated at length: the more orthodox European view saw the ultimate hope for the unity of the Churches in the second coming of Christ; the more activist American approach emphasized the unity already existing and the good that Christians can do here and now. The major document was "The Christian Hope." Subsidiary themes of the assembly were: our oneness in Christ and our disunity as Churches; the mission of the Church to those outside her life; the responsible society in a world perspective; Christians in the struggle for world community; the Church amid racial and ethnic tensions; and the Christian in his vocation.

EVARISTUS, ST. (d. 105), **POPE** from 97. Nothing is known of this, the fourth, successor of St. Peter and the immediate successor of St. *Clement I. According to the *Liber Pontificalis,* he was the son of a Hellenist Jew of Bethlehem. In the same source it is stated that he divided the city into seven parishes ("titles") with a priest assigned to each; also that he appointed seven deacons for the city.

This is an obvious anachronism. There is no evidence to support an old tradition that E. died a martyr. BIBLIOGRAPHY: Butler 4:204; I. Daniele, BiblSanct 5:372–373.

[R. B. ENO]

EVE, like *Adam, Eve (Heb. *hăwwah,* she causes to be) in Genesis ch. 2 and 3 is not a proper name but a noun descriptive of woman's role as the one from whom all mankind derives existence. This name is given her by the man (Gen 3.20). The Priestly account merely mentions the fact of woman's creation together with that of man (1.27), but the Yahwist account (2.18–25) is a full pictorial representation of her origin: by passing over all animals (whose nature Adam grasps, as his ability to name them indicates to the Hebrew mentality) he realizes their unsuitability to be his partner; God thereupon forms woman from his rib. Clearly the author's purpose here is primarily to state that woman has the same nature as man and as such is a suitable marital partner for him, and that her dignity is equal to his.

Does the writer furthermore teach the physical origin of woman from man? The Biblical Commission decree of 1909 was usually interpreted in this sense, and ingenious efforts were made to explain how this could be so, the least fantastic being that the woman was the man's daughter (cf. P. G. Fothergill, CDT 2.260–261). However, it is now generally admitted that Gen 2.21–22 is a picturesque way of presenting woman's equality with man, their attraction to each other, and the true nature of marriage —notwithstanding Paul's argument from the wording of Gen 2.22 in 1 Cor 11.9. Even though one holds that woman's subordination to man is taught in Genesis, he need not admit that the physical origin of Eve from Adam is any more taught by Paul than the parentlessness of Melchisedech in Heb 7.2–3. Science, of course, takes it for granted that the evolutionary process would apply to both sexes.

Genesis goes on to recount the Fall: the woman succumbs to the serpent's temptation, then tempts the man herself; both fall and accordingly are driven out of paradise, the woman cursed by God to endure henceforth the pains of childbirth. The primary theological reference of this narrative is to Mary as the antitype of Eve, as Christ was of Adam. Traditional theology, while admiring the psychological perceptiveness shown in this narrative, never gave to Eve an essential place in the theological elaboration of original sin: the human race inherited it precisely as descended from Adam. Early patristic tradition saw in Eve's subordinate position to Adam a type of Mary's subordinate position to Christ; it went on to postulate a similar contribution (subordinate and nonessential) from Mary in reversing this state of mankind. This reversal was thought to be aptly symbolized by the reversal of Eve's Latin name *(Eva)* by the greeting *(Ave)* that introduced God's invitation to Mary to become the mother of the Savior (Lk 1.28). Exegetically Gen 3.15 does not offer positive confirmation of this role of

the second Eve. In the Vulgate the subject of the verb *conteret* should not be she (i.e., Eve) but it (i.e., the woman's seed; i.e., the human race through Christ, its prime representative). Even the actual meaning of *conteret* does not indicate a clear victory of the woman's seed. BIBLIOGRAPHY: E. H. Peters and T. R. Heath, NCE 4:655–657; J. L. McKenzie, *Two-Edged Sword* (1956); C. Vollert, *Theology of Mary* (1965) 134–138.

[B. FORSHAW]

EVE, GOSPEL OF, an apocryphal work mentioned by Epiphanius, who ascribes it to the Gnostics. From the only certain surviving quotation we can deduce that it was apocalyptic in character and related to two central figures, of whom one was extremely tall and the other stunted, standing together on a mountain. The tall figure addresses the visionary and declares that he is identical with him, using characteristically Gnostic terms to express the idea that there is solidarity and collaboration between the Savior and the saved. BIBLIOGRAPHY: E. Hennecke, *New Testament Apocrypha* (ed., tr. W. Schneemelcher, 1963) 1:241–253.

[D. J. BOURKE]

EVE OF LIÈGE, BL. (d. after 1264) is described in an account, chiefly autobiographical, in AS April 1:433–475 *(Vita Julianae).* *Juliana of Liège, her intimate friend, probably inspired E. to become a recluse in a cell by St. Martin's Church (Liège). E. influenced theologians, and *Urban IV in the brief *Scimus, O filia* praised her share in establishing the feast of *Corpus Christi.

[J. E. WRIGLEY]

EVELYN, JOHN (1620–1706), English author. Of particular historical value is his *Diary,* which covers the years 1641–97. It remained in MS until 1818. E. supported the royalist party and was abroad 1643–47. For the years 1647–49, he maintained a correspondence in cipher with his father-in-law, Sir Richard Browne, who was in Paris in the interest of King Charles I. He lived on his family estate during the years of the Commonwealth. He was one of the founders of the Royal Society (1662). A devout adherent of the C of E, he opposed both the profligacy of the court of Charles II as well as the leniency of James II toward Catholicism. He wrote many papers on politics, religion, science, gardening, and the culture of trees. BIBLIOGRAPHY: F. Higham, *John Evelyn, Esquire: An Anglican Layman of the 17th Century* (pa. 1968); B. Saunders, *John Evelyn and His Times* (1971).

[M. M. BARRY]

EVENSONG (OE *aefensang,* song at nightfall), name given in medieval England to the canonical hour of Vespers and in the C of E applied to the office of Evening Prayer. With the Reformation, RC use of the English word became obsolescent. The BCP used Evensong (1549), replaced it

(1552) by Evening Prayer (a composite of Vespers and Compline, based on the medieval *Sarum Rite), and then restored the name (1662).

[M. R. BROWN]

EVERARD (EBERHARD, EVRARDUS) THE GERMAN (d. 13th cent.), poet, formerly identified with Evrard of Bethune. After studying in Paris and Orléans, E. taught at Bremen and Cologne. His long didactic poem *Laborintus* is valued by historians of culture and by students of language. It contains much information on 13th-cent. curricula.

[M. J. FINNEGAN]

EVERARD OF TÜNTENHAUSEN, see EBERHARD OF TÜNTENHAUSEN, ST.

EVERARD OF YPRES (fl. 12th cent.), Belgian canonist. Born at Ypres (Flanders), E. received his education mostly at Paris in the liberal arts and theology. He was a pupil of and loyally devoted to Gilbert of Poitiers. E. also was trained in canon law and used his knowledge as attendant to Card. Hyacinth (later Pope Celestine III), in 1162–63. His canon law writings show influences of John of Faenza and Rufinus. He entered the Cistercian Order after 1185. E. wrote a *Summula* (handbook) of canon law, mostly a series of questions and answers. There is also a Latin dialogue between *Ratius and Everard,* which, although supposedly fictional, betrays autobiographical positions and criticizes Bernard of Clairvaux as well as some aspects of monastic life. E. was probably a teacher and was well acquainted with the classical poets. He spent his last years, and probably died, at Clairvaux. BIBLIOGRAPHY: N. Haring, "The Cistercian Everard of Ypres," Med St 17 (1955) 143–172.

[N. F. GAUGHAN]

EVERGISLUS, ST. (d. before 594), bp. of Cologne. The information provided by St. Gregory of Tours is much to be preferred to the unreliable 11th-cent. vita. Contrary to the report of the latter, he seems not to have died a violent death. His relics are now in the parish church of St. Peter in Cologne. BIBLIOGRAPHY: AS Oct. 10:650–661; AnalBoll 6 (1887) 193–198.

[W. A. JURGENS]

EVERYMAN, an English morality play *c.*1500, generally believed to be a derivation from a Dutch play about the same date, *Elckerlijk.* Its conciseness shows its superiority over most of the moral plays which begin with the birth of Mankind and follow his career through life in a struggle between good and evil. A brief prologue announces the theme; then God dispatches his servant Death to summon Everyman to his reckoning. Everyman, not at all prepared, begs for delay and tries to bribe the messenger. Failing this he is granted the right to ask his companions to go with him.

Each of these sharply defined characters—Fellowship, Kindred, Cousin, and Goods—gives an excuse and refuses to go. There are humor and irony in their comments. Goods points out bluntly that Everyman should have realized that Goods is for this life only and not for eternity. This scene is good theology and exciting theater. Everyman then attempts to achieve salvation through Good Deeds, who is lying weak and cold and barely able to speak. Good Deeds sends him to Knowledge, then to Confession, and lastly to Priesthood. Finally Good Deeds is strengthened and able to accompany Everyman to the grave. Here Beauty, Strength, Discretion, Five Wits, and Knowledge leave him in turn as Everyman enters the grave. An angel receives Everyman's soul.

Everyman occupies a distinguished place in English drama because of its universality of theme and grandeur of allegory combined with characterization that is very human. The style is clear and "speaks" well; dialogue is direct and keeps to the central point—the final outcome of man's conduct in life. *Everyman* is still good theater. BIBLIOGRAPHY: E. K. Chambers, *Medieval Stage* (1920); H. Craig, *English Religious Drama of the Middle Ages* (1955); L. V. Ryan, "Doctrine and Dramatic Structure in *Everyman,*" *Speculum* 32 (1957) 722–735.

[M. M. BARRY]

EVESHAM, ABBEY OF, former Benedictine abbey in Worcestershire, England, founded (*c.*701) by St. Egwin, on a site given by Ethelred, king of Mercia, designated, according to legend, by the Blessed Virgin. Few facts about it are known between 701 and 941, but considered authentic are privileges granted by Pope Constantine (708–715) and various land grants by kings. Because of antimonasticism in 976, the monks were dispersed but later restored by Bp. Adulf (992–1002). During the Norman Conquest, the abbey became a haven for refugees. Severely affected by the 14th-cent. Black Death and subsequent decline, it flourished under Abbot Litchfield (1514–39), who was forced to resign by Cromwell and was replaced by an abbot who ceded Evesham to the King in 1539. Only ruins remain. BIBLIOGRAPHY: D. L. Bethell, DHGE 16:128–132; Knowles MOE *passim.*

[S. A. HEENEY]

EVIDENCE, APOLOGETIC, the signs God provided to attest and guarantee his self-revelation, the divinity of Jesus, and the divine origin of his Church. Its purpose is to show the believer and nonbeliever the rationale of the act of faith. It can be classified into external (miracle, prophecy) and internal (the sublimity and harmony of doctrine, its appeal to human aspirations, the life of the Church). The type of evidence largely determines the apologetical method, e.g., historical, psychological. Rationalists, existential phenomenologists, historians, however, question the probative force of such evidence. Though not without loopholes, it is adequate if taken in the light of faith. BIB-

LIOGRAPHY: A. Dulles, *Apologetics and the Biblical Christ* (*Woodstock Papers* 6, 1963).

[J. FICHTNER]

EVIL, the privative lack of some good; *privation of a good, as both the condition and the process of being deprived. Deriving from *Plotinus, this description means to counter a *dualism positing a primal, absolute good, source of all good, and a primal absolute evil, source of all evil (see GNOSTICISM; MANICHAEISM). To categorize evil as privation is not to deny its reality or force. Experientially and ontologically, evil is the evil of, to, or for something, refers, therefore, to an existent, thus to a good, and itself exists because this subject exists as lacking something it should have (see FINALITY, PRINCIPLE OF).

Philosophy and the Problem of Evil. On the basis of the privative character of evil, philosophy measures it by reference to the good that, in keeping with its kind of being, a subject lacks. Thus absence of a good not appropriate—e.g., of intelligence in brute animals—is not an evil. Another measure takes into account a lack in a subject as a single entity and then as a member of a larger whole: thus the evil of death for one member is in fact a good for the whole species, or for a higher species. A further assessment separates the nonvolitional and the volitional subject to classify evil as either physical (natural) or moral (human). Human evils are further divided into fault and punishment according to their relation to a person's will. Lack of the good proper to acting humanly is voluntary; fault is a moral choice lacking right order. A loss of good that goes against will is the evil of punishment for fault. All these qualifications have bearing on the ultimate philosophical issue, the origin of evil. A theistic philosophy is committed to the position that the First Cause is an absolutely good and provident being, not, therefore, a malign, direct cause of evil. The condition of metaphysical limitation, creatureliness, is not an evil, since only to the uncaused does it belong to be absolutely unlimited. The passing away of material beings is not evil, but the natural consequence of materiality; it does not entail causing evil but ordering all things and ultimately to the total good of the whole universe. The distinction between natural and human evils suggests, further, that to suffer evil is the reflective experience of loss and pain; the cruelties in the subhuman world of nature are particular physical evils, but not suffering. With regard to the human suffering of evil, the experience that the loss of a lesser good may mean gaining a higher one rightly recognizes priorities in the makeup of human good. The origin of fault or sin rests in the condition of peccability: having to reach a good and a goal, the intelligent creature is not a rule unto itself, but defectible, and thus sometimes defective in its choices (ThAq ST 1a, 63.1). Punishment, on the other hand, as an evil to its victim, is a deprival justly inflicted for fault. Such are the elements traditionally brought to face the origin of evil.

*Process thought makes a departure, a God suffering evil in and with all other beings in his "consequent nature."

Christian Theology. Theology has inherited, and notably since Augustine, the use of philosophical categories to cope with the problem of evil. Prior by right and decisive as criterion, however, in its assessment of evil is the revealed mystery of salvation. The Genesis account of creation was written to account for present physical and moral evils retrospectively: God created the world good, but human sin introduced evil; the same theme is in St. Paul's declaration that by one man sin and death entered into the world, and that all have ratified that sin by their own (Rom 5.12). But concomitantly the biblical message is one of salvation. The concern and direction of theology, therefore, center on human evil, sin and penalty. Christ is the only absolutely sure divine answer to human agonizing over evil. Christ alone reveals God the loving Father; philosophy has, in fact, no grounds for questioning how a loving God can allow evil; it does not know a loving God, but only qualities of a First Cause inferrable from effects. Theology cannot expect from philosophical categories to vindicate the divine fatherhood revealed by Christ. His revelation is not a cosmological account pointing out a beneficent First Cause, but a witnessing to a loving Father, communicating himself in person, drawing man into the interpersonal union of love (see CHARITY). That is the divine answer to sin and punishment, the *exhaustive* division, in the view of faith, of human evil (ThAq ST 1a, 48.5; *De malo* 1.4). Christ gives sin its Christian meaning as the prodigal's wilful separation from the Father. The divine response is pardon and reconciliation, so that no one need be willingly separated; the divine self-communication embraces the problem of sinfulness by a pardoning grace making the sinner lovable and able to love in return. Theology must point to human defectibility as the cause of sin; ask also why God permits it; but decisive for its speculations is Christ's message of reconciling grace. Christ conquers, as well, the evils of punishment. He transforms merely afflictive punishment, contrary to the victim's will, into expiation—the voluntary acceptance in love of all the evils besetting mankind. For the Christian joined to Christ, no suffering need be sheer punishment, but through a sharing in Christ's grace can be transformed into willing imitation of the Passion that leads to the Resurrection, the final triumph over evil. BIBLIOGRAPHY: ThAq ST (Lat-Eng; v. 27, ed. T. C. O'Brien, Appendix 1, "Guilt and Punishment"; Appendix 2, "Mortal Sin").

[T. C. O'BRIEN]

EVIL EYE, an ancient and almost universal superstitious belief in a baneful influence exercised by a glance from the eye. Among the classical Greeks this was known as *baskania*; among the Latins as *fascinum*. In modern German it is called *böser Blick,* and in the Neapolitan dialect, *jettatura*. In more colloquial terms it is known as *mauvais oeil* in French and *malocchio* in Italian, Spanish, and Portuguese.

Though the evil eye may be found in such animals as the fox and the snake, it is more common to human beings. It may be attributed to a person because of some natural defect such as a squint or hunchback, or simply because of presumed malice. Various remedies have been and still are employed to counteract the influence of the evil eye such as spitting upon the ground or doing something ridiculous or indecent to neutralize its power. The ancient Romans frequently wore amulets for this purpose. They could be made of gold, an incorruptible metal, or of coral, which would catch the evil influence on its sharp spines, or they could be made to resemble male or female sex organs and enclosed in a little case. When worn about the neck these were supposed to attract (fascinate) the evil eye and thus nullify its effects. BIBLIOGRAPHY: F. T. Elworthy, Hastings ERE 5:608–615; *idem, Evil Eye* (pa. 1970).

[M. J. COSTELLOE]

EVIL-MERODACH, KING OF BABYLON (Akkadian, *Awīl-Marduk;* in Heb. *'ĕwīl-merōdak,* a caustic play on words whereby Man of Marduk became Blessed [i.e., cursed] Fool). Son of Nebuchadnezzar II, Evil-merodach ascended the throne of Babylon in 562 B.C., only to be murdered in 559 by his brother-in-law, Neriglissar. The Bible mentions him briefly, noting that he had set Jehoiachin, former King of Juda, free from an imprisonment that had lasted 37 years (2 Kg 25.27; Jer 52.31).

EVITERNITY, a word that translates the medieval abstract Lat. *aeviternitas,* for *aevum,* an age, sometimes of never-ending time (Gr. *aion;* cf. cognate English term "for aye"). Found in 16th- and 17th-cent. usage, the term is now obsolete; it was confused both with everlasting time and eternity. Dr. Johnson was near the mark: "Eviternal," he declared briskly, "eternal in a limited sense, duration not infinitely, but indefinitely long." Meditating on Boethius, *De consolatione philosophiae,* the scholastics saw an intermediate duration between eternity and time; the first, the perfect possession altogether and all at once of boundless life, was God's alone; the second was for things subject to continuous flux in matter, and measured according to a before and after both in their being and in their changes of quantity and place. Spiritual creatures are not in this frame of reference, nor is the hypothetical order of indestructible heavenly bodies put forward by the Aristotelian cosmology. These last can be neglected. There remain spiritual substances. They are not creatures of time, but everlasting, and their duration is not strictly temporal, though it might be extrinsically denominated by our time; and the measurable changes in activity and quality to which they were subject was accorded the special name of *aevum,* which may be rendered for ever, for all ages, for aeons. BIBLIOGRAPHY: ThAq ST 1a, 10.4 and 5 (esp. in ed. Lat-Eng; v. 2, ed. T. McDermott, 1964), appendix 16 (by T. Gilby) 227–229.

[T. GILBY]

EVODIUS OF ANTIOCH, ST. (d. 564), considered by *Eusebius the first bp. of Antioch and by Origen as the successor of St. Peter. He is wrongly noted as the first to use the name Christian. His name does not appear in the early martyrology but was introduced later. E. is sometimes erroneously confused with the Evodias in Phil 4:2. Little historically is in fact known about E.'s life, works, or death. BIBLIOGRAPHY: R. Aubert, DHGE 16:133.

[M. HIGGINS]

EVOLUTION (from the Latin *evolvere,* to unroll, as a scroll, to unfold what has been wrapped up). In its modern sense, as applying to the development of organic beings from a rudimentary to a more mature condition, it was first used by Charles Bonnet in 1762 who looked to the evolution of a preexistent form in the germ rather than to fecundation from outside. His view, however, is now called the theory of preformation, and evolution refers to theories of the 19th cent. and after, which are historical consequences of Jean Baptiste Lamarck (1744–1829) and Charles Darwin (1809–82). Both were concerned with the origin of species; the customary opinion at that time, associated with a fundamentalist reading of Scripture, was a separate creation for each. Instead they postulated a common ancestry and explained the differentiations, the first by an adaptive response of innate aptitudes, the second by the process of natural selection; both postulated the inheritance of acquired characteristics.

Mechanism was to prevail over vitalism, at least as the majority view in scientific circles; yet it is important to distinguish between the philosophical and religious agnosticism of Darwin and the confident materialism of Ernest Haekel (1834–1919) who ruled out all question of a planning intelligence. Evolution has now been extended from biology and takes in most of the anthropological sciences, cultural, social, psychological, ethical, and sometimes theological. It is often rather a loaded term, and to speak, as Newman did, of development might have been better. The idea of a gradual emergence of higher forms from lower is as old as the hills; it is found in many cosmogonies and is present in St. Augustine's doctrine of *rationes seminales,* and as for the production of new characteristics plant and animal breeders have been doing that for centuries. What is new is a whole evolutionary philosophy.

Supported by widespread and detailed observation, and by the convergence of results in different fields of inquiry, evolution is now fairly generally accepted as established and as having passed from a condition of a mere hypothesis. Nevertheless, there are some guiding, even warning, principles still to be noticed. One concerns the distinction between the particular sciences and a more synoptic science from which theology cannot be excluded; another, that between a descriptive and a normative science. We take them in turn.

First, a particular science observes and assembles its facts (which, of course, are not things in the round but a selection of abstracts defined by its instruments of measurement), relates them by its laws which are cast into mathematical notation, and elucidates these by imposing a hypothesis, sometimes by calling on a neighboring science; this is regarded as good, rather than true, if it seems to put the field into clear and reasonable shape. And so the discourse goes spiraling up, as more and more facts are discovered and exploited, and the laws and hypotheses are trimmed and streamlined. Eventually a stage is reached that is sufficiently comprehensive to be called a theory, in the Greek and contemplative sense of the word. That seems to have been the case with evolution.

Notice, however, that particular sciences, or groups of particular sciences, can draw conclusions only within their own media, outside of which they are purely recommendatory. For instance, a biological science may show that specific variations are results from environmental factors; it may even think of these as randoms within its proper field of reference, but it acts *ultra vires* once it starts to pass judgments in philosophical terms, and treat them as "effects" due only to "chance" and excluding the "causality" of divine providence. They have to be careful of their language, as have the philosophers and theologians as well, defining their terms accurately, lest teleology spell the miraculous intervention of a *deus ex machina,* and the dialogue between the two sides lapse into a dispute at cross-purposes, like that celebrated failure of communication between Thomas Huxley and Bp. Samuel Wilberforce at Oxford in 1960, from which the man of science, not the divine, emerged in fitter shape.

Next, the distinction between a descriptive and a normative science bears on the present question because of the tendency, not so marked at present as it was, to think of evolution as inevitably for the better. More complex pieces of mechanism are regarded as superior to the simpler, more intricate urban cultures as preferable to the more primitively agricultural; the railroad engineer may not agree, nor the commuter, nevertheless the opposite has almost become axiomatic. All of us, and scientists not least, are incurably ethical. Yet whatever may be said about prehistoric times, human history scarcely shows a steady line of development in one direction so that we can make an optimistic value judgment. *Candide* is very much a text for our times. The truth of the matter seems to be that gains in one area are often offset by losses in another.

Then also we have to allow for the freaks who break out of the evolutionary process. We admire them as seers, prophets, and saints. In this connection the philosophy of emergent evolution may be noticed, which attempts to correct the mechanistic, determinist, and preformationist theories of evolution by insisting on the discontinuity of some changes with what went before: it introduces a distinction between resultant properties which are wholly determined by physical causality and are repetitive and predictable, and emergent properties which are novel and unpredictable.

The only history to which the Christian faith is committed is the history of God's dealings with his one people, which begins with Genesis and still continues. The only rational truths it will always maintain are those necessarily implied in its message, for instance that God creates and sustains the whole universe and that he rules it with his loving providence. It would not be at all perturbed if scientists were satisfied they were managing to produce "living" from "dead" matter. It would look critically at any claim to produce a human being, but even that it could tolerate, so long as the qualification indicated above was observed; though the special causality of God in the creation of a new human being was not acknowledged, neither was it ruled out.

Considerable attention has been directed in the past few years to the synthesis of scientific, philosophical, and theological thinking on the subject of evolution attempted by *Teilhard de Chardin. Evolution, as he saw it, is a process in space and time that generates new levels of more complex organization. All observable phenomena of the universe are involved in this process, particularly the phenomenon of man. But evolution is not only a process in which the material or quantified aspects of matter have moved from the simple to the more complex; it is also a process in which primitive psychism has moved to more intense consciousness. Man presently climaxes the process of evolution as the most complex expression of cellular structures and the most intensely conscious. Moving backward and downward in space and time along the axis of the more to the less complex, man is found to share the stem of his origin with the other primates. This was a common lemuroid stock which was itself one of the many directions the mammalia pursued in the upward course of their development. Further down the ladder of evolution the mammals arose from the amphibia, whose immediate ancestors were the fish which the chordates invested with primitive nervous systems and centers of interpretation. The chordates themselves represent a specific direction taken by some metazoa over against the direction toward arthropodic kingdoms. Metazoa came into existence through aggregations of protozoa or one-celled animals. Protozoa are bacterial-like organisms with sentient characteristics. Bacteria, the immediate ancestors of protozoa, have their origins in the carbon compounds of protein.

In the process of evolution, a critical stage is set with the complex union of amino acids containing carbon, nitrogen, hydrogen, and oxygen. These are the building blocks of all life. Primitive living cells have their origins in the molecular arrangement of amino acids. Some great pressure or intense heat was required to cause the amino acids to issue in the first living cells. Life has its origins in the warm seas' teaming with protein matter. The sphere of hydrogen and oxygen that covered the earth's surface was preceded by the less complex molecular layers of rock that form the earth's crust. Before the layer of rock, the various molecular structures of metal were in process of forming the earth's core.

The descent of man's complexity backward and downward into the more simple molecular structures of the earth constitutes the process of anthropogenesis in reverse. The atoms that crystalized to form the earth probably had their origin from our sun, which itself came into being by a condensation of cosmic dust.

Science can go back only to the point of describing the primal world stuff as cosmic dust or untold trillions of tiny subatomic particles of matter or energy. It is within the framework of faith that we understand God to be the creator of the primordial world stuff. Created in space and time, the cosmic dust moves forward and upward toward more complex levels of organization. Teilhard de Chardin was convinced that the primitive psychism of cosmic dust was moving forward and upward in more intense forms of consciousness. Matter in process of complexification and consciousness has reached such an intense level of organization in man that he is capable of discovering God buried deeply within the process. Revelation constitutes that part of evolution in which man has concerned himself with the unfolding of God's presence in man's universe. BIBLIOGRAPHY: P. Teilhard de Chardin, *Phenomenon of Man* (tr. B. Wall, 1959); H. J. Birx, *Pierre Teilhard de Chardin's Philosophy of Evolution* (1972).

[T. GILBY; W. J. DUGGAN]

EVOLUTIONARY ETHICS, originally the extension into moral science of theories, biological and metabiological, that new species were produced through the accumulative effect of small genetic variations over a long period of time and, it was usually held, apart from any initial purpose or guiding intelligence. The view was popularized by Herbert Spencer, challenged by Thomas Huxley (who noted that ethics, notably in the matter of protecting the weak, can cut across the struggle for survival), and modified by Julian Huxley (who stressed our deliberate shaping of the process and thereby made it more than the operation of blind mechanisms). At present evolutionary ethics, which in many cases amounts to *ethical relativism, though the consequence is not necessary, reflects the temper of current religious philosophies (see TEILHARD DE CHARDIN).

Among the questions to be asked are the following. Can it be assumed that evolution is always for the better? Does adaptation to more evolved conditions as such express a value? Is there any evidence in the history of ethics or, which is more important, of Christian moral teaching for specific changes? That there has been development (possibly a less loaded term than evolution) goes without saying, but like that of dogma it has been homogeneous, not heterogeneous. Does not the notion of freedom, central to ethics, sharply contrast with the inevitable unwindings of potentialities? Finally it may be remarked that the evidence for the different and even contrary forms of conduct prescribed by human groups to meet their environments, offered by historical and comparative anthropology and sociology, is all very well in their own proper medium, but

that the differences appear less striking when they are evaluated according to the analogies of a steadily philosophical science of morals. BIBLIOGRAPHY: M. Ginsberg, *Evolution and Progress* (1961).

[T. GILBY]

EVOVAE, see EUOUAE.

EVRARD OF BETHUNE (fl. 12th cent.). One fact known of him is that he wrote a major work, the *Antihaeresis,* which outlined the fundamental beliefs of the Cathari in order to refute them. This could have been written only during the last half of the 12th cent. or at the latest at the beginning of the 13th. Another of his books, the *Graecismus,* which is a versified Latin grammar, was widely used in the Middle Ages. E. showed literary knowledge of early medieval Latin authors, but his writing is mediocre and his thought undistinguished.

[F. G. O'BRIEN]

EVRE, ST., see APER OF TOUL, ST.

ÉVREUX, CATHEDRAL OF NOTRE DAME, early Romanesque structure destroyed by fire in the 12th cent., the choir and chapels rebuilt by Bp. Mathieu des Essarts (1299–1310) with additions in 14th and 15th cent. and finally consecrated in 1548. Famous 14th-cent. stained glass related to the Rouen school in elegant design was given by Bp. Jean du Prat (1328–34) and Geoffroi Fae (1335–40). Later, glass related to the Paris school of realism was presented by Bp. Bernard Cariti and Guillaume de Centiers. The choir surpasses the nave in height and in the airiness and elegant proportions of its clerestory. On the exterior the openwork spire at the crossing and the flamboyant Gothic N transept are noteworthy. BIBLIOGRAPHY: M. Aubert, *Gothic Cathedrals of France* (1959).

[M. J. DALY]

ÉVROUL, ST. (Éroult, Ebrulf; d. 596?), abbot. After some years as a high official at the Merovingian court, he separated from his wife, gave his wealth to the poor, and devoted himself to prayer and penance in the forest of Ouche in Normandy. A community formed around him from which came the monastery of Saint-Évroult. He also founded 15 other monasteries. BIBLIOGRAPHY: P. Viard, BiblSanct 4:893–894; Butler 4:639–640.

[G. M. COOK]

ÉVROUL, (EBRULF) OF SAINT-FUSCIEN-AU-BOIS, ST. (d. *c.*600), abbot. The bp. of Beauvais ordained E. to the priesthood because of his holy life. According to report, the monks of St.-Fuscien-au-Bois chose him as abbot for the same reason. His cult began shortly after his death. BIBLIOGRAPHY: T. De Morembert, DHGE

16:220–21; H. Dressler, NCE 5:698; P. Viard, BiblSanct 4:892–893.

[H. DRESSLER]

EWALD, SS., (d. *c*.690). According to St. Bede there were two brothers, priests of the English nation, named Ewald. Because of the color of their hair one was called Black Ewald, the other White Ewald. Both died as martyrs in their efforts to convert the Saxons. BIBLIOGRAPHY: E. Hegel, *Kirchliche Vergangenheit im Bistum Essen* (1960) 13–14; Butler 4:17.

[H. DRESSLER]

EWALD, GEORG HEINRICH AUGUST (1803–75), German Protestant biblical scholar. At Göttingen he taught philosophy, OT exegesis, and languages from 1824 to 1837; then philosophy and theology at Tübingen till 1848 when he returned to Göttingen. In 1867 he was forced into retirement because of his opposition to Prussian domination. He was called the founder of the historico-comparative method in the science of Semitic languages. Among his numerous scholarly works were a Hebrew grammar (1827; 8th ed., 1870) and a history of Israel (3 v., 1843–59; 3d ed., 7 v., 1864–69). Though he supported critical analysis of the Bible, he opposed the radicalism of F. C. *Baur and the *Tübingen School.

[T. EARLY]

EX CATHEDRA, a phrase used by St. Cyprian *(ex cathedra Petri)* and applied by Melchior Cano to the authority of the Roman See ("See" is from the Lat. *sedes*, meaning seat or chair). The expression was inserted by Vatican Council I in its definition of the Roman pontiff's infallibility. To be infallible, a pope's definition must be *ex cathedra*, which means that it must meet the following conditions: (1) It must be issued by the pope in his office as universal pastor and teacher of all Christians. (2) It must determine a doctrine concerned with faith or morals. (3) It must be imposed as an object of unconditional and binding assent for all Catholics. Definitions that meet these conditions are declared by the Council to be "of themselves, and not by the Church's consensus, irreformable" (D 3074).

[M. GARCIA]

EX OMNIBUS AFFLICTIONIBUS, the bull of Pius V, Oct. 1, 1567, censuring certain propositions ascribed to Michel du Bay (*Baius), and sent to the faculty of theology at Louvain, where Baius was a professor. Because of his ambiguous response, the censure was renewed by Gregory XIII in *Provisionis nostrae*, Jan. 25, 1580, to which Baius submitted. In 1642 *Ex omnibus afflictionibus* was renewed against *Jansenism by Urban VIII's, *In eminenti*, and the long-standing dispute over interpretation of Pius V's original censure became heated (see COMMA PIANUM). The propositions condemned (D 1901–79) jeopardized the meaning of the supernatural, and exaggerated the sinfulness of fallen

human nature; and were censured as heretical, erroneous, rash, suspect, and offensive to pious ears (D 1980).

[T. C. O'BRIEN]

EX OPERE OPERANTIS, a technical term used in RC sacramental theology in reference to the efficacy of a sacrament as measured by the dispositions of the minister (i.e., its efficacy in virtue of the one performing the rite) as distinguished from its efficacy as measured by the objective value of the act itself *(*ex opere operato)*, i.e., its efficacy in virtue of the rite performed. Originally the term was used in reference to the faith and probity of the minister of the sacrament, but in later theology it usually refers to the dispositions of the recipient of the sacrament. According to RC teaching, the grace of the sacrament is dependent in part on the dispositions of the recipient, but not at all on the dispositions of the minister. BIBLIOGRAPHY: B. J. Leeming, *Principles of Sacramental Theology* (1956).

[P. F. PALMER]

EX OPERE OPERATO, literally, "in virtue of the work [i.e., rite] performed," a technical term used in RC sacramental theology in reference to the objective efficacy of a sacrament as the action of Christ, as distinguished from efficacy that may be attributed to it from the dispositions of the minister or of the recipient *(*ex opere operantis)*. At the Council of Trent the expression was used in opposition to the view of the Reformers that the sole purpose of the sacrament is to foster or nourish faith or confidence in God's mercy, by which faith man is alone justified. Thus, "If anyone shall say that the sacraments of the new law do not confer grace *ex opere operato*, let him be anathema" (D 1608). BIBLIOGRAPHY: B. J. Leeming, *Principles of Sacramental Theology* (1956).

[P. F. PALMER]

EX VOTO (Lat. by reason of a vow), an offering made out of gratitude for a favor received or to fulfill a pledge made when the favor was prayed for. The votive (vigil) lamps or candles seen in churches are examples. The plaques, silver hearts, or other ornaments on the walls of shrines, esp. in Latin countries, are *ex voto* offerings.

[T. C. O'BRIEN]

EXALTATION OF JESUS. The creeds of the Church (D 10, 44, 72, 150, 502, 681) profess that Jesus "sits at the right hand of the Father" in his glorified human nature. The exaltation as the term of Christ's Resurrection-Ascension means that in his person has been realized and manifested the eschatological state of apocalyptic expectation, that Jesus possesses eternal life in the presence of God not merely as participant but as source. As the mystery of Resurrection-Ascension signifies that Jesus has transcended history and man's historical experience, so also does the exaltation of Jesus belong to the meta-historical order and as such, knowledge of this mystery comes through divine revelation. In its earliest Christology the Christian community crystallized its experience of Jesus' divine vindication in the words of Ps 110.1: "The Lord says to my lord: 'Sit at my right hand, till I make your enemies your footstool.'" (Acts 2.33–36; 5.31). Psalm 110 was a song in praise of a princely, hence a messianic figure to whom God had given power at his enthronement. In doing so, the Lord had designated him as son from the dawning (Ps 110.3). This royal figure also possessed priestly power after the manner of the king-priest of ancient Salem, Melchizedek (Ps 110.4). Through its use of this psalm in a manner not unlike that found in the *Qumran Pesharim (Commentaries), the Christian community expressed its conviction of Jesus' exaltation as Lord (*Mar*) and its expectation of his imminent return in glory and judgment (*Maranatha,* cf. 1 Cor 16.22). This same conviction is further reflected in the Pauline tradition (Rom 8.34; Eph 1.20; Col 3.1). Quite early in the Christology, Ps 110 was linked, possibly through the influence of Ps 8.4, 6, with Dan 7.13, which speaks of a Son of Man's coming to dominion, glory, and greatness, the reward promised to the suffering Maccabean martyrs. The Church had already identified Jesus with the Son of Man in the light of its Resurrection experience or based upon Jesus' own use of the expression. The clearest trace of the linkage of Ps 110.1 with Dan 7.13 is to be found in Stephen's vision (Acts 7.55–56): "Behold, I see the heavens opened and the Son of Man standing at the right hand of God." Not only did the early Church relate Jesus' exaltation with the *parousia but also connected this mystery with his Passion and the forgiveness of sins. As part of the apologetic to Jews for a crucified Messiah, the Crucifixion was interpreted in the light of Zech 12.10ff (e.g., Jn 19.37). Furthermore, the community linked Zech 12.10ff with Dan 7.13 to assert that the exalted one whose crucifixion effects the forgiveness of sins (Zech 13.1) is the Son of Man who comes in judgment (e.g., Rev 1.7). In other terms, the servant Christology, whose basis may indeed go back to Jesus himself, also explicitated this relationship of the exaltation to the Passion and the forgiveness of sins. Jesus has fulfilled the prophecy of Is 52.13–53.12 through suffering for sinners (Acts 8.32; Rom 4.25; Mk 14.24; 1 Pet 2.21–25) and through his exaltation (Acts 3.13). In Phil 2.6–11, the most significant Pauline statement of Jesus' exaltation, there is contained an early and a higher Christology than that expressed in Acts. This clarifies the relationship conceived by the Church between Jesus' exaltation and his divine preexistence and drives home the all-embracing cosmic character of that exaltation. The hymn confesses the Lordship of Christ in terms of his divine equality with God before the Incarnation, his obedient humiliation leading to death, and his exaltation as universal Lord, the culmination of his divine *kenosis* (see KENOTIC THEORIES), before whom every knee in the celestial, terrestrial, and infernal spheres should bend. The emphasis on the preexistence affirms that the early Church viewed Jesus' exaltation as a glorious return to the heavenly

world whence he had come. The NT gives further evidence of other early homologies containing all or part of the Christology and structure contained in Phil 2.6–11 with various consequences of the exaltation being highlighted, e.g., 1 Tim 3.16; Col 1.15–20; Eph 2.14–16; 1 Pet 3.18–19, 22; Heb 1:3.

The exaltation of Jesus in Paul's theology is not presented as a feature of purely academic interest, but has a distinctly "for us" character. Thus in Epistles where he links it with the parousia (1 Thess 1.10; 2 Thess 1.7), Paul's intention is to exhort Christians to constancy in their faith. Similarly, the Apostle's use of the homology found in Phil 2.6–11 is in a context of exhorting his readers to a life of love and forbearance. Confronted with an incipient *gnosticism which questioned whether the reign of the exalted Christ extended to the realm of the spirits, the Pauline tradition categorically repeated what had already been stated about Christ's triumph over the heavenly powers (1 Cor 15.24–27; Phil 2.10), affirming that his exaltation had been accomplished through the cross (Col 2.15), confirms Jesus as Head of his body, the Church (Col 1.18), and extends over all celestial powers (Eph 1.20ff). Christ in fact has taken possession of the universe which he "fills" (Eph 4.10) as well as "recapitulates" (Eph 1.10). The Pastoral Letters consistently affirm the Pauline teaching, maintaining the cosmic dimension of the exaltation (1 Tim 3.16). The Gospel tradition historicizes the exalted state of Jesus by presenting the divine glory as manifest in his earthly life, revealing itself at his birth, baptism, Transfiguration, in his words and miracles. Among the Synoptics, Mark relates the exaltation to the Crucifixion and esp. to the soon to return Son of Man. Through the climactic conclusion to his Gospel in 28.16–20 in which the glorified Son of Man asserts his presence within the Church until the end of the age, Matthew emphasizes the link between Christ and the ongoing life of the Church. While his emphasis on the Ascension makes the exaltation an act of the Church's sacred past, Luke's theology of the Holy Spirit in both his Gospel and the Acts underscores the continuing effect of the exaltation for both the time of the Church and the life of the individual. Of all the Gospels, John's makes the closest connection between the exalted glory of Jesus and his life in its various aspects: the preexistence, the person and activity of Jesus as revealer, his presence in the life of the Church through "another Paraclete," his union with the Father, and even the parousia. In such a theological vision, the fourth Evangelist quite naturally dramatizes the essential link between the passion and the exaltation by describing Jesus on the cross as having already entered the process of glorification (Jn 3.13–15; 12.32–33). The Resurrection in John is dramatized so that it is obviously part of the Ascension. Jesus is lifted up on the cross; he is raised up from the dead; he goes up to the Father—all as part of one action and one hour. In Hebrews, Jesus goes directly to the Father from the cross, passing through the heavens (4.14) into the heavenly sanctuary where, as high priest at God's right hand (1.3; 8.1; 10.12f; 12.2) above the angels (1:4–13; 2:7ff), he makes intercession for men (9:24). The Catholic Epistles likewise depict Jesus "at the right hand of God" (1 Pet 3.22) and as "an advocate with the Father (1 Jn 2.1)." The same belief also underlies the images of the final victory of the exalted Jesus in Revelation (Rev 3.21; 5.1–7, 7.17). BIBLIOGRAPHY: P. Benoit, *Exégèse et théologie* (2 v., 1961) 1:365–368; 2:76–88; E. Schweizer, *Lordship and Discipleship,* 1960); N. Perrin, *Modern Pilgrimage in NT Christology* 1974).

[T. J. RYAN]

EXALTATION OF THE CROSS. The feast of the Exaltation of the Precious and Lifegiving Cross, celebrated in the Byzantine Church on September 14, commemorates the finding of the Holy Cross, the dedication in 335 of the Basilica of the Resurrection on the site of the Holy Sepulcher and the recovery in 629 by the Emperor Heraclius of the relics of the Cross that had been carried off by the Sassanid Persians in 614. The liturgical rite for this feast, which is also celebrated again on the third Sunday of Lent, includes a special Morning office. The *cross is placed on a tray garlanded with flowers and basil leaves and is borne in solemn procession from the altar three times around the church to the tetrapodion and then five times it is solemnly elevated and adored with the great metany. Between each raising or "exaltation" the choir chants the "Lord have mercy" one hundred times. The Divine Liturgy is then celebrated. In the Western Church the feast is now known as the Triumph of the Cross.

[A. J. JACOPIN]

EXAMEN, also called particular examen, an examination of conscience directed toward overcoming specific predominant faults or imperfections with a view to overcoming their hindrance of spiritual progress. In religious rules the examen has often been a programmed element in community prayer.

[T. C. O'BRIEN]

EXAMINATION OF CONSCIENCE, see CONSCIENCE, EXAMINATION OF.

EXAMINERS, SYNODAL, diocesan officials appointed, according to canon law (CIC, c. 387–389), by the diocesan synod to scrutinize the theological knowledge of all candidates for the office of parish pastor (*ibid.,* 459, §3, n.3). They also advise the bp. in cases of judicial procedures taken against clerics, although he is not bound by their counsel. If he so desires, the bp. may use the examiners also to test candidates for ordination, or priests requesting the faculty to preach or hear confessions.

[R. ARONSTAM]

EXCALCEATI (Lat., unshod), a group of superstitious people, classified by Filaster (*Haer.* 81; cf. Augustine *Haer.* 68) as heretics. They went about barefoot because,

according to their interpretation of Ex 3.5, Jos 5.16, and Is 20.2, the wearing of shoes was sinful.

[L. MÜLLER]

EXCARDINATION, see INCARDINATION AND EXCARDINATION.

EXCELLENCE, eminence consequent upon some good quality, advantage, or status. Ontological excellence corresponds to fullness in being, therefore in ontological goodness; thus the divine excellence is the absoluteness of the divine goodness. In moral theology the excellence of other persons engages the virtue of *respect that regards the debt of honoring those who are in some way superior. Those in legitimate authority by that fact have a superiority that requires subordinates to give the honor due to a superior's status. In the case of the actual exercise of governing power, the subordinate also owes obedience (ThAq ST 2a2ae, 102.3). There is, as well, reason to give honor to those having any sort of excellence (*ibid.* 103.2 and ad 3, on Phil. 2.3). Excellence, or pretended excellence, is also the basis for classifying types of *pride, as this sin is an inordinate estimate of one's superiority: its basis is either an exaggeration of self-worth or claiming credit for what is a gift of nature or grace; or contempt for the excellence in others (*ibid.* 162.4).

[T. C. O'BRIEN]

EXCLAUSTRATION (from the Lat. *extra claustrum,* i.e., outside the cloister), permission given to a religious to leave his religious community temporarily for a serious reason (CIC c. 638). Such a person remains a religious, and thus continues to be bound by his vows and such other obligations of the religious life as can be observed outside the cloister (CIC c. 639). An exclaustrated religious is subject to the bp. of the place where he is staying rather than to his proper religious superior. Exclaustration is granted by indult of the Holy See to members of pontifical institutes, and by the local ordinary to members of diocesan institutes. *Exclaustration ad nutum Sanctae Sedis* (at the will of the Holy See) is not requested by the religious, but is imposed by the Holy See for the good of the institute or of the individual religious. BIBLIOGRAPHY: Woywod-Smith 348–352.

[L. M. KNOX]

EXCLUSION, RIGHT OF (Jus exclusionis), a veto prerogative claimed by rulers of Catholic States (France, Spain, Austria) to exclude, explicitly and by name, an eligible person from election to the papacy. The first exercise of this presumed but never officially recognized privilege was in the 16th cent. and the last time in 1903 by Austrians against Card. *Rampolla. Pius X annulled the right in his *Commissum nobis* (1904) and *Vacante Sede Apostolica* (1904).

[R. J. LITZ]

EXCOMMUNICATION, the most severe *censure prescribed by the CIC. Its purpose is not to punish a delinquent Catholic, but rather to encourage his speedy repentance. Only a baptized Christian who is subject to the laws of the Church can be excommunicated, and only for a morally serious, actual violation of that law, and only when he contumaciously refuses correction. The CIC enumerates those cases in which excommunication can be applied; in some, the sentence of excommunication follows automatically upon the criminal action (*latae sententiae*), in others, a competent judge must impose the sentence (*ferendae sententiae*). Excommunication cannot remove the delinquent from the Church nor can it obliterate the effects of his baptism. It does, however, severely limit his association with the Christian community. Unless the Holy See has decreed an excommunicate as *vitandus,* to be shunned by all the faithful, he may attend divine services, but can take no active part. The excommunicate is forbidden to participate in all of the sacraments including the Eucharist, and if he is named in a published decree, he is barred from the sacramentals as well. He receives no benefit from the indulgences and public prayers of the Church, although individuals may continue to pray for him privately. Legitimate ecclesiastical acts are forbidden to the excommunicate, since it is clearly inappropriate and may involve public scandal for the official actions of the Church to be carried out by a delinquent. Sponsoring at baptism, officiating in ecclesiastical courts, and the administration of church property are examples of ecclesiastical acts from which the excommunicate is excluded. The excommunicate may not receive any income from an ecclesiastical office or church property. He may not participate in any ecclesiastical election, nor be elected to any church dignity nor promoted to holy orders. A person who dies excommunicate may be granted Christian burial unless his publicly unrepentant life would render this scandalous, or unless a decree of excommunication has been published against him. If Christian burial is allowed, publicly announced masses may be offered for him; but if Christian burial is refused, only private, unannounced masses are to be offered.

While these determinations of the CIC for the most part remain in force, there is no doubt that the whole penal law of the Church will be radically changed once the present process of revision has been completed. *PENAL POWER OF THE CHURCH.

[R. A. ARONSTAM]

EXCUSE, in moral theology on the binding force of laws, a cause that exempts a person from observing the law. Such an excuse may be an objective, absolute inability to fulfill the law, or a relative or circumstantial inability (a so-called moral inability). Where the first kind of excuse is present, no law binds. Where it is a question of a moral inability, i.e., the person could observe the law only with great difficulty and inconvenience, man-made laws (called positive laws) need not be observed. Such a difficulty, however,

does not excuse from fulfilling what is prescribed or refraining from what is forbidden by natural law. The notion of excusing causes is also applied to the obligation of *restitution arising from sins against justice, where, e.g., the dire need of the one obligated amounts to an absolute inability to repay. In the area of canonical *censures, a complete unawareness that a penalty is attached to a certain sin excuses from incurrence of the censure, even where a person is guilty of the sin.

[T. C. O'BRIEN]

EXEAT (CANON LAW), (Lat., let him depart) letter of perpetual and absolute *excardination required by canon law (CIC c. 112) before a cleric may be permanently attached to a diocese other than his own. BIBLIOGRAPHY: J. T. McBride, *Incardination and Excardination of Seculars* (1941).

[L. M. KNOX]

EXEGESIS, BIBLICAL, the concrete explanation of Sacred Scripture, using the principles of hermeneutics. Exegesis had its beginnings within the OT itself, when earlier texts were "re-read," glossed upon, or edited to make them relevant to a new situation, e.g., Wis 11-19. Much of this exegesis went to make up a literature about the Bible and formed a basis for the rabbinic teaching of the Talmud and Midrashim during the Christian era. The NT in its turn explained the OT in the light of the Christ-event, which happened "according to the Scriptures" (see 1 Cor 15.3; 10.1–13; 2 Cor 3.5–18; Gal 4.21–31; Heb 7.1–10, etc.). In the early Christian centuries a predominantly allegorical type of exegesis was pursued by the school of Alexandria, while the rival school of Antioch favored a more literal mode of interpretation. The patristic age in general is noted for its intense study of the Bible, with emphasis on moral values, though the preliminaries of textual criticism, etc., were by no means neglected. Little original work was produced during the Dark Ages, but with the rise of Scholasticism, precise definition and categorization became standard exegetical tools. With the coming of humanism and the Reformation, new avenues of approach to the Bible were opened, which have endured to the present day. Some have led to a confirmed dogmatic stance, others to a rationalistic attitude, others still to an extreme conservatism and fundamentalism. Among Catholics, the immediate post-Reformation period was one of fruitful activity, but with the rise of rationalism and later of Modernism, a conservative reaction set in that was only overcome with the publication of the encyclical *Divino afflante Spiritu* of Pius XII in 1943 and subsequent ecclesiastical documents. BIBLIOGRAPHY: C. Dodd, *According to the Scriptures* (1952); L. Alonso Schökel, *Inspired Word* (1965, repr. 1972); B. Smalley, *Study of the Bible in the Middle Ages* (1952, repr. 1964); *Peake's Commentary on the Bible* (ed. M. Black and H. H. Rowley, 1962).

[C. BERNAS]

EXEGETE, a person technically proficient in the practice of biblical interpretation. Many biblical figures were exegetes in the true sense, explaining and interpreting the Scriptures to their contemporaries—thus Ezra, the unknown author of the book of Wisdom, Peter, Paul, James, John, etc. Hillel, Aqiba, and Rashi are only a few of the many illustrious Jewish teachers of the Christian era, while Origen, Jerome, Augustine, and Gregory the Great are among the greatest Christian interpreters of the patristic age. St. Bernard and other monastic authors carried on their traditions, and many of the scholastics, as St. Thomas Aquinas, were skilled exegetes as well as great speculative theologians. Luther, Calvin, and other Reformers contributed much to scriptural studies, while Richard Simon among Catholics of the post-Reformation period showed himself a forerunner of the present scientific era of biblical investigation. Research and discoveries in the fields of philology, textual and literary criticism, history and archeology over the past century and a half have greatly influenced and aided the work of exegetes and have led to a renewed understanding and appreciation of the Word of God. BIBLIOGRAPHY: Robert Tricot 1:678–780; L. A. Schökel, *Understanding Biblical Research* (tr. P. McCord, 1963).

[C. BERNAS]

EXEKIAS (fl. *c.*550–525 B.C.), Attic vase painter and greatest master of black-figured ware. His work emphasized psychological tension rather than action, with a restrained dignity. The amphora of Achilles and Ajax playing draughts (Vatican Museum) is a famous and distinctive work.

[M. J. DALY]

EXEMPLAR CAUSE, the idea in the mind of an intelligent, *efficient cause, according to which an effect has its design, order, or constitution. The influence of the exemplar determines the inner form of an effect, but the exemplar does not enter into the makeup of the effect itself and so is designated as an extrinsic *formal cause. *IDEAS, DIVINE.

[T. C. O'BRIEN]

EXEMPLARISM, as a general classification, a term applicable to any philosophy or theology that posits an ideal model, exemplar, and source for the reality and knowledge of the various kinds of existents. Prominent instances in the history of philosophy are *Plato's separated ideas; *Philo's *logos* and intermediate intelligences as exemplars; *Plotinus and the Neoplatonists, positing a necessarily emanating Intelligence and World Soul; the Stoics' "seed-bearing reasons" *(logoi spermatikoi);* the *natura creans creata* of *John Scotus Eriugena; the exemplary idea proposed by the School of *Chartres as the solution to the problem of universals. Any Christian theology can be classified as exemplarist in its explanation of creation if it affirms that God is the exemplar cause of all things; that the divine *ideas are the intelligible expression of all the kinds of created being (see EXEMPLARITY OF GOD).

Exemplarism has, however, a specific historical connotation: its meaning in the teaching of SS. Augustine and Bonaventure and its conjunction in their theory with divine illumination. Augustine's exemplarism is already clearly contained in his proof for God's existence as required because of the mind's experience of immutable truths *(De divers. quaest.* 83. PL 40, 38; *De lib. arbit.* 2.3–15. PL 32, 1243–63; *Confess.* 7.10.16. PL 32, 742). From the Prologue of John, Augustine understands the Word to be the complete expression of the subsistent divine being and truth; in the Word are hierarchically contained the ideas of all created being; the Word is the exemplar and source, both of all created ideas in the angelic and human mind, and of all created beings in their gradated perfections. The human mind's attainment of truth depends on its being illumined by the Word, not through innate ideas or direct vision of the divine, but by a continuing fontal and regulative presence, sustaining the mind's true knowledge. Because of this, illumination on the mind's own ideas is truly representative of the ideas in the Word; truth can be eternal and immutable in no other way. (See *De Gen. ad litt.* 12.30. PL 34,479; *Epist.* 120.2. PL 33,453; *De Trin.* 12.15. PL 42,1011). Bonaventure, intending to adhere closely to Augustine and to use Aristotle only as a subsidiary resource, makes exemplarism central in his teaching. He repeats Augustine on the divine ideas in the Word; sees creation as their "radiation," constituting all things in their being and kind. In the mind's journey toward God it may consider traces of the divine through causality, but attains full truth only in knowing all things, and particularly the image of God in itself, in the light of the divine ideas. For this it needs the presence of divine light, illumining and empowering it to grasp all things as reflecting subsistent, eternal truth. The process of contemplation so begun reaches perfection through divine revelation.

[T. C. O'BRIEN]

EXEMPLARITY OF GOD, the doctrine that God is the model or exemplar according to which all created being was fashioned. Before he is able to act, an agent must have in his mind a plan of what he is to do; this is particularly true of the makers of artifacts. All creation, therefore, as made by God corresponds to a plan or exemplar of God. Beyond this, because God is in fact the creator on whom everything totally depends, all things are participations of his perfection. The exemplarity of God includes a double relationship of all things to God insofar as they are both fashioned after his plan and are participations of his perfection. This idea, derived from Neoplatonism, was prominent in medieval Augustinianism. BIBLIOGRAPHY: A. Ampe, DSAM 4:1870–78; C. J. Chereso, NCE 5:715.

[B. FORSHAW]

EXEMPLUM, a moralized anecdote presented generally within a sermon to illustrate the theme. Narrative and human interest in these stories appealed strongly to medieval congregations, and collections of tales for the use of clerics were common. These stories were often repeated but were varied with bits of local color and contemporary setting. English literature owes much to the medieval sermon for opening a world of legend and romance, of life and death, mystery and adventure. "Preaching, and in especial the provision made for it in the way of collecting and preserving illustrative matter of all kinds, became the vehicle by which much of the lighter thought and imagination of antiquity—classical, oriental, and early medieval—passed over into the thinking and writing of the modern world." (G. R. Owst, *Literature and Pulpit in Medieval England* [1961] 207).

[M. M. BARRY]

EXEMPTION, a concession granted to a person or group of persons that removes them from the authority of the normal canonical superior. The need for such a privilege arose when, in the course of the 5th cent., conflicts began between young monastic communities seeking to define their way of life under the direction of their abbot and the local bp. who was responsible for the pastoral care of all within his diocese. Bishops were generally reluctant to allow abbots freedom in governing even the internal affairs of the monastery. Monastic exemption from episcopal authority was infrequent before the 10th cent. when, along with immunity from lay intervention, it became an important part of the charter of the house of *Cluny in Burgundy. Cluniac monasteries spread quickly over Europe; older monasteries demanded and received exemptions at this time, and newer orders made an exemption from episcopal authority a cornerstone of their programs. The Council of Trent in the 16th cent. sought to arrest this tendency by restoring religious jurisdiction over many religious communities. The distinction between exempt and nonexempt orders is less important today as the governing structures of religious orders have become increasingly similar and as the role of the bp. has been enlarged to cover all pastoral activities within his diocese.

[R. ARONSTAM]

EXEQUATUR AND PLACET, rights that civil authorities have or claim to have over the life of the Church within the area of their sovereignty. They had their origins in the system of lay proprietorship of the early Middle Ages, but were frequently abused in the increasingly secularized states of the 19th cent. and have been now totally rejected by the Church (see D 1829; CIC, c. 2333). The *placet* (literally, "it is pleasing") indicates a broad range of powers, e.g., to regulate the movements of bps. or to prevent the excommunication of a government's subjects, while the *exequatur* (literally, "let it be done") indicates the specific power to permit or prevent the reception of papal decisions and statements within the area of the jurisdiction of the civil authority.

[R. ARONSTAM]

EXEQUIES (also OBSEQUIES), general term for funeral rites or burial ceremonies, derived from the Latin word for funeral procession.

EXETER CATHEDRAL (cathedral of St. Peter), 13th-cent. edifice in SW England with two Norman transept towers and Norman walls. It is notable for its glazing, nave vaulting, a richly carved rood screen, a minstrel gallery with musician angels, choir stalls still carrying misericords by John of Glastonbury, and an exquisite wood-carved bp.'s throne by Thomas de Winton (1313–17). The cathedral is an example of the personal style of the unknown Master of Exeter, combining luxurious French Decorated style with English proportions, making Exeter one of the most unusual of English cathedrals.

[M. J. DALY]

EXHIBITIONISM, immoderate self-display. (1) In a wide sense it is acting in a way that draws attention to self; morally it may be an expression of *vain-glory; it may also be contrary to the virtue of proper decorum (*modestia*) in externals, the good manners that restrain vulgar display or outrageous fashions (ThAq ST 2a2ae,168.1;169.1); it may also be opposed to the virtue of *truthfulness as this excludes any false display of qualities one lacks (*ibid*.112.1 & 2;113.2). (2) Sexual exhibitionism is usually considered to be a perverted compulsion towards indecent exposure, which may be more pathological than immoral. It is possible that some extremes of undress in style combine elements of exhibitionism in both its meanings.

[T. C. O'BRIEN]

EXILARCH (Aramaic, *resh galuta*), lay leader of the Jewish community in Babylon (Parthia). The origins of the office are not clear, but it certainly existed by 140 A.D. or before, and probably as early as the 70s of the 1st cent., when the destruction of Jerusalem (and the demise of its leadership role) together with the needs of the Parthian regime, seem to have led to a measure of self-government for the Jewish community. Tension between exilarch and rabbinate appears in the 3d cent., probably accounting for the exilarch's claim of Davidic descent. Divisions in Judaism (e.g., Rabbanites vs. *Karaites) led to decline in the status of the exilarchate in the Arab period (9th century). BIBLIOGRAPHY: J. Neusner, *History of the Jews in Babylonia,* (5 v., 1965–69); *Encyclopedia Judaica* 6 (1971) 1023–34.

[D. P. EFROYMSON]

EXILE OF ISRAEL, the period from the first deportation of the Jews to Babylonia in 598 or 597 B.C. until their return to Jerusalem after the edict of Cyrus in 538 (Ezra 6.3–5), or even to the completion of the new temple in 515. When Jer 25.12 speaks of a duration of 70 years, 70 must be taken as a round number.

It was an ancient practice in the Near East to remove conquered nations from their own land and settle them in other parts of the empire. Such deportations affected mainly noble and wealthy families, landowners, artisans, and soldiers in order to deprive the land of leadership and to break the national identity. Thus Tiglath-pileser III of Assyria removed portions of the population in 733 (2 Kg 15.29) and, after the fall of Samaria, Sargon, according to his own indication, deported 27,290. This Assyrian deportation gave rise to the question of the "Ten Lost Tribes."

The exact number of people deported by Nebuchadnezzar cannot be established. Jeremiah mentions three deportations in the years 598 or 597, 587, and 582 respectively and lists the corresponding numbers of the deported as 3,023, 832, and 745, a total of 4,600 (Jer 52.28–30). The author of 2 Kg 24.14, 16 speaks of 8,000 or 10,000 deported in 598 or 597; he mentions the second deportation without giving any number (2 Kg 25.11) and says nothing about a third deportation. The total number must have been considerable; and Ezra 2.64–65 gives the number of those who returned (between 537 and 428) as about 50,000.

The deportees were settled in S Mesopotamia (cf. Ezek 3.15; 11.1). Their lot was one of servitude, and they were forced to supply labor for Nebuchadnezzar's building projects. But many could live in their own settlements (Ezek 3.15; Ezra 2.59; 8.17) under their own elders (Ezek 8.1; 14.1; 20.1), build houses, engage in agriculture (Jer 29.5–6), and enter business in the "city of merchants" (Ezek 17.4; Bar 1.5).

The exile put Israel's faith on trial. Some accepted idolatry and participated in pagan worship (Ezek 14.3; 20.31). Many remained true to their faith, shook off their initial despondency, and gained a clearer grasp of Yahweh's unicity and universality. Jeremiah from Jerusalem, and Ezekial, and Deutero-Isaiah in Babylonia helped them to see God's activity and plan in defeat, exile, and eventual restoration. With new fervor they observed the ancient traditions and laws, the circumcision, the Sabbath, ritual cleanness. There must have been also considerable Priestly literary activity. It has been suggested that most of the historical books of the OT were collected and edited, and that the codification of the Law as it appears in the Pentateuch was begun during the exile. And probably the synagogue made its first appearance in exile, a substitute for the worship of the temple. BIBLIOGRAPHY: J. Bright, *History of Israel*, (1959, 2d ed., 1972) 323–355.

[F. BUCK]

EXIMENIS, FRANCISCO (*c.* 1340–1409), Catalan Franciscan. After studies in Cologne, Paris, Oxford, and Rome, he taught theology at Toulouse and Barcelona. In Valencia (1383–1408) he took part in royal affairs and wrote extensively in Catalan for the laity and in Latin for the clergy. Four books (2,600 chapters) of a proposed popular encyclopedia for Christians and a devotional life of Christ (influenced by *Ludolf of Saxony and synthesizing Scotist thought) were very popular; a work on angels influenced by Pseudo-Dionysius is important, as is one on contemplation. E. cites *Joachim of Fiore and *Ubertino of Casale often; in the Schism he sided with Benedict XIII, who named him patriarch of Jerusalem (1408). BIBLIOGRAPHY: I. Vaquez, DHGE 16:252–255.

[E. P. COLBERT]

EXIMIAM TUAM, a brief of Pius IX (June 15, 1857) dealing with the doctrinal errors of Anton *Günther. The Sacred Congregation of the Index had prohibited nine of his works as infected by Hegelianism. (Jan. 8, 1857). In a letter to Pius IX, Günther himself promptly submitted, but since his views had been rejected only in summary fashion, his followers thought that some of his opinions could still be held. Their view was disapproved by Pius IX in *Eximiam tuam*, in which he listed the individual errors. BIBLIOGRAPHY: D 2828–31.

[J. H. ROHLING]

EXINANITION (Lat. *exinanitio;* Gr. *kenōsis),* an emptying, renunciation, or putting aside of glory or of dignity. The notion is applied to Christ by St. Paul (Phil 2.6–11) quoting, and perhaps editing, a Palestinian hymn. Although there is no uniformity about the details of the exegesis, the Fathers of the Church generally recognize this text as an indication of (1) the divinity of Christ (indeed the preexistence of Christ seems to be Paul's starting point); (2) his real and complete humanity; and (3) his personal unity. Thus the hymn speaks of Christ's preexistence (v. 6–7a); the self-emptying of Christ, who willed not to manifest his glory but to adopt the status of a suffering and mortal creature (v. 7b-8); and the exaltation that comes to Christ (v. 9–11). Catholic theology has uniformly rejected all kenotic theories that explain this passage in terms of diminution or setting aside, even temporarily, of divinity (see Pius XII, *Sempiternus Rex,* AAS 43 [1951], 637 ff.). Such theories were popular with some Protestants, esp. in Reformation times and again in the 19th century. BIBLIOGRAPHY: P. Henry, DBSuppl 5:7–161; A. Grillmeier, *Christ in Christian Tradition* (tr. J. S. Bowden, 1965) 19–23; J. Ternus, "Chalkedon und die Entwicklung der protestantischen Theologie," *Das Konzil von Chalkedon* (ed. A. Grillmeier and H. Bacht, 1954) 3:531–611.

[J. HENNESSEY]

EXISTENCE, see ESSENCE AND EXISTENCE.

EXISTENCE OF GOD. The claim that man, through normal use of his natural faculties, can arrive at the conviction of the reality of some sort of supreme being, is not held by all. Theists maintain that there is a supreme being, the ground of all beings and values, naturally knowable to man, with valid although incomplete knowledge. Deism emphasizes the transcendence of a supreme being, holding that God and the world are irrevocably distinct and not mutually concerned. Pantheism emphasizes the immanence of a supreme being, identifying God with the entire universe. Agnosticism suspends judgment alleging that there is insufficient ground for affirming or denying the existence of a supreme being. Atheism denies the existence of God. Among those who hold the existence of a supreme being, ontologists assert that there is innate, intuitive, immediate knowledge of the first being. Traditionalists, because of their exaggerated notion of the effects of original sin, hold that supernatural revelation is necessary for any knowledge of God. Monotheism, held by Christians, Jews, and Muslims, is a theory that conciliates both transcendence and immanence of God. Kantians deny the ability of speculative reason to affirm or deny the existence of God as more than a postulate of practical reason. Some argue both the need and the possibility of demonstrating his existence.

If something is self-evident, it needs no proof. However, something might be self-evident in itself and not to man in general or only to the learned. Because God is absolutely intelligible, his existence is self-evident in itself, but not to man who is incapable of complete understanding of God's nature. Consequently, demonstration, a way of proof giving certain knowledge, is needed. Operating causally and through the use of a middle term, the relationship between subject and predicate is established. If the definition that serves as middle term is based on causes, from that which is prior absolutely, an a priori argument is established. If the middle term is a nominal definition, the argument —proceeding from what is prior relatively—proceeds from effect to cause and establishes an a posteriori proof. Because effects are better known than causes, demonstration of God's existence proceeds from what is relatively prior to man. The middle term is a nominal definition from observed facts of experience. God can be known through an inductive process begun by sensory contact with the real world and followed by intellectual reflection. Not the most perfect knowledge results; however, there is valid and cogent demonstration that serves as a rational basis for revealed truth.

Of the a priori proofs for the existence of God, one is of historical and current significance. The ontological argument, first formulated explicitly by St. Anselm in the *Proslogion* calls God ". . . a being other than which nothing greater can be conceived." Anselm continues that it is great to exist in the mind; it is greater to exist also in reality. Hence, if God is the greatest being, his existence must be at once mental and real. This attempt to present a single argument for a believer seeking to understand his faith met with immediate opposition by Gaunlon of Marmoutier, who protested that it moved illicitly from the logical to the real order and that it assumed an unproved definition. Anselm responded that, since the argument concerns the only neces-

sary Being, there is no ground for positing an illicit move. The argument was rejected by St. Thomas Aquinas because not all men define God in this manner and because it failed to prove his extramental existence. Alexander of Hales, Bonaventure, and Duns Scotus accepted it. Descartes adopted it in his own form, adding a distinction between the positively infinite and the merely indefinite, and asserting that it is necessary to explain how imperfect finite man can have the idea of an infinite, perfect being. Kant rejected it by denying existence as a mere attribute of being because properties of being presuppose existence. On the contemporary scene, the argument is still debated and restated in a variety of ways.

The traditional Thomistic a posteriori demonstrations for the existence of God proceed inductively from effect to cause. Since the realities of sensory experience are limited, composed of act and potency, contingent, possessing varying degrees of perfection and evidence purposiveness, the principle of causality runs as a common feature of the five demonstrations. Although each is treated as effects of a cause, each arrives at a cause distinctly. The arguments as proposed demonstrate not the nature, but the existence, of a cause. Since being is the proper effect of God, the demonstrations establish God as the unique cause of dependent beings. The first four ways are sometimes called the cosmological argument; the fifth, the teleological argument.

Motion or change is the reduction of something from potency to act; nothing can be reduced from potency to act except by something already in act. The force of the argument lies in the fact that motion itself is an incomplete act, a dependent actuality requiring an outside agent for its realization. This causality is necessary for every movement. Without ignoring the reality of secondary causes, it is argued that if there is no original source of motion, itself unmoved, there could be no intermediate or proximate motion. Hence, an unmoved mover is posited to explain motion in the experienced world.

In Laws X, Plato makes much of the same argument. Plato accepted the validity of causality and rejected the possibility of an infinite series of per se movers. In the *Laws,* and without recourse to myths, Plato discussed formally the existence and goodness of God. His arguments to establish God's existence begin with the most universal characteristic of things: motion and change. Aristotle concludes the *Physics* with a demonstration of the existence of a first unmoved mover. He combines the transcendence of Plato with the immanence of cosmic principles. Assuming the validity of the causal principle and rejecting an infinite regress in movers, Aristotle concluded to an unchanging initiator of change. For him, however, there are many cosmic movers and the world's motions are eternal.

Efficient Causality. The world of sense shows a subordination of efficient causes. Every effect must have a cause, for if a thing were to cause itself, it would have to exist prior to its own existence to cause itself to be. In efficient causality also, it is impossible to have an infinite regression, for none is intelligible (in the order of per se efficient causes) unless there is a first in the series, or a cause outside of the series. The proof from causality is vehemently opposed by Hume who presents a skeptical analysis of cause, maintaining that there is no universal principle of causality that is defensible. Habit answers for the customary connections made between temporally sequential events. He asserts that cause itself cannot be explained by the senses nor validly admitted by the intellect. As a consequence, God cannot be proved satisfactorily by reason, but can be accepted in faith. Kant likewise rejects the argument as worthless because of his rigid limiting of the mind to dealing only with phenomena. While Kant denies speculative reason the power to reach God, he grants this to the practical reason in the moral realm. Leibniz will accept the proof from causality, adding to it his notion of sufficient reason. He asserts that this truth of fact is the only one of its kind capable of demonstration. Since truths of fact affirm real existence, they fall under sufficient reason. Leibniz also accepts Anselm's ontological argument. He has two series of proofs: an a posteriori proof, wherein God imposes himself as sufficient reason for contingent beings, and an a priori proof in which the necessity of God is that of the eternal truths that the mind sees as necessary in themselves. Descartes' acceptance of the principle of causality is evidenced as the underlying assumption of his *Meditations*. The theism of Descartes has two basic considerations: the unqualified acceptance of causality and the adherence of the perfect being as the only adequate object of understanding and, therefore, the natural good of rational beings. He regards the culmination of science as the knowledge of God. Descartes acknowledges a notion of God as infinite and perfect, and of himself as finite and imperfect in being and in action. Since the lesser cannot produce the greater, he argues that man cannot receive these notions from himself. God is then posited as the cause of these ideas. He follows this a posteriori argument with an a priori proof that is, in essence, a restatement of Anselm's argument.

Contingency. This indicates that natural things are generated and corrupted, i.e., that it is possible for them to be and possible for them not to be. Contingent beings are by nature dependent, limited, and need grounding in a necessary being. Necessity implies the lack of potency not-to-be. Since nothing can be the cause of its own necessity, and since infinite regress is contradictory, there is needed a being of intrinsic necessity, with no extrinsic dependence to account for its necessity but which is able to cause necessity in others. Kant rejects the argument from necessity and contingency. Experience shows the existence of a limited, dependent being, needing an absolutely necessary being to explain them. He questions if this necessity is identical with the perfection of a supreme being. Because of the ontological vein of the argument, Kant rejects it as he does all metaphysics. At best he calls this a speculative possibility, not a proof.

Grades of Perfection. Differences of perfection are noted in the beings of experience. More and less are predicated of things against some maximum standard which is the cause of all in that state. This argument considers those perfections admitting of more or less, not of absolute perfections. This is the dimension of the transcendentals: perfections without limitations in themselves but found in limited ways in participating beings. Transcendental perfections, i.e., those that contain no limitation or imperfection, are received from exemplary and efficient causes. The cause of participated perfection is the operating efficient cause, the source of all perfections.

Teleological argument. This holds that man observes that things lacking intelligence act nearly always in the same way to obtain the best end for the given species. Beings that lack intelligence cannot move toward an end consistently unless there is some sort of intelligent direction given. Intelligence is needed to perceive ends and means and the relationships between them. Therefore, the necessity of an agent for the direction of the cosmic collectivity of non-intelligent beings concludes to the existence of a Supreme Intelligence. This demonstration is also used in terms of value. Plato had concluded from the existence of order in the universe to the divine mind as its intelligent ground. Aristotle taught a cosmic teleological synthesis. Kant denied that there is sufficient evidence to say that there is an existing directing mind: he taught that just as good an argument could be made for a plurality of minds. Kant's difficulties included the beings who do not achieve their ends, evil, pain. Darwin's survival-of-the-fittest theory seems to mandate death, defeat, and pain as necessary to evolution. Guyay and Russell assert that nature is indifferent, with no directing force. These and subsequent findings of science might call for a restatement of the problem.

Moral Argument. Modern philosophy advances other arguments for the existence of God. One of the strongest is based on moral obligation and conscience. Men know the desirability of doing good and avoiding evil. Not to act in this way results in guilt and remorse. While education and environment develop conscience, it is the common experience of all men that they must be "good." It is also man's experience that there is no law without a lawgiver; no effective law without sanction. Therefore, there must be a supreme lawgiver and one capable of rewarding and punishing man, if not in this life, then in another. Kant sees this, basically, as the only acceptable proof for the existence of God. He totally abandoned the possibility of an intellectual attainment of God; for him, the only acceptable proof argued from the order of morality and moral obligation. Man must act from a sense of duty; man's happiness is proportioned directly to his virtue, i.e., to the fulfillment of duty. But man is essentially incapable of granting himself happiness consequent upon moral living. God is needed to effect the harmony of happiness and virtue. Belief in God belongs to the sphere of practical reason which holds ascendancy over the speculative.

Pascal opts for the existence of God by encouraging man

to consider the matter in terms of a wager. If there is no God, and man wagers that there is no God, he may win the wager and lose nothing else; if he wagers that there is a God (and there is not), he may lose the wager and nothing else. On the other hand, if there is God and man wagers that there is God, he wins the wager and eternity; if he wagers there is no God (and there is), he loses the wager and eternity. From a purely gambling point of view, it is better to wager for God than not.

Contemporary thought. In contemporary philosophy, Bergson rejects the classical proofs, claiming that man knows God through a direct mystical intuition; Husserl's phenomenology cites God as the supreme value attained by man through emotional acts; Marcel allows for the discovery of God through the realization of the self; Sartre grounds all value in man's freedom, divorcing both man and his freedom from a nonexistent God.

Other arguments include the universal concern of all men for happiness which is not achieved in this life: the fact that men in all ages and cultures have worshipped (and it would be difficult to explain away this universal behavior as illusory or mistaken); the agreement of all mankind to religious experience; the testimony of mystics whose witness throughout the centuries is impressive. If man is not to discount the corporate experience of the human race, religious experience of the ages cannot be ignored. While any of the arguments might fail to be convincing or satisfactory, taken in totality and in the light of the convergent lines of thought, they present matter for reflection. Given the universe as known, given human experience as known, modern man has to find which of the proposed hypotheses best explains these matters. *GOD, PROOFS FOR THE EXISTENCE OF.

[M. HALPIN]

EXISTENTIAL ETHICS, a term sometimes used to designate Jean-Paul Sartre's application of his philosophy of existentialism to the field of human action, based on the premise that there is no God, no universal moral law, no set of luminous values to guide a man in his personal choice, and no universally given human nature: man is thrown into existence and must out of his freedom forge his essence. More generally it refers to a theory proposed by Karl Rahner as a complement to scholastic ethics, which, he contends, does not take adequate notice of the concrete, the individual, the personal. Objective ethical norms are valuable and necessary for proper Christian decision, but they are not enough to bring a man to decide what to do in every case. Existential ethics attempts to fill in this lacuna of law by developing a doctrine of the concreteness of God's call at a given moment, and the concreteness of the man's response to that call, in a kind of covenant morality brought down to the individual person, based on an I-Thou relationship with the personal God. Crucial to the theory, too, is the "art" of discerning the Spirit of God in this or that situation. The role of the virtue of prudence and of the gifts of

the Holy Spirit was neglected in the manuals of scholastic ethics, and here lies the value of this emphasis on the individual and the personal impact of God's call. The dialogue between the old and new continues, and it has been broadened with the appearance of many ethical theories, chiefly from outside the RC tradition, the main thrust of which is existential. BIBLIOGRAPHY: J.-P. Sartre, *Existentialism* (tr. B. Frechtman, 1947); J. McGlynn and J. Toner, *Modern Ethical Theories* (1961) 93–114; K. Rahner, *Theological Investigations* 2 (1964) 217–234; ThAq ST 1a2ae, 18–21 (esp. in ed. Lat-Eng, v. 18, Appendices, ed. T. Gilby); W. A. Wallace, "Existential Ethics: a Thomistic Appraisal," *Thomist* 27 (1963) 493–515.

[T. R. HEATH]

EXISTENTIAL METAPHYSICS, an important orientation of contemporary Thomism, centered on the thesis that the object of metaphysical science is radically existential. Developed by such eminent thinkers as J. Maritain, C. Fabro, L. B. Geiger, and, above all, É. Gilson, existential metaphysics stands in conscious opposition to the Wolff-influenced essentialism of much of modern Thomism. Stressing the view of the Angelic Doctor that "existence is the act of all forms and natures" and the "perfection of all perfections," existential metaphysics effectively avoids the awkward equation, inherent in an essentialist ontology, of being and essence. But it also avoids the opposite extreme of the essence-less existentialism of J. P. Sartre; for Gilson as for St. Thomas, no more is there existence without essence than there is essence without existence. Recognition of the primary of existence in the metaphysics of Aquinas is now as widespread as it is of major importance. The Gilsonian school, however, goes further. It is true that St. Thomas understood that God, in revealing His name to be "He Who Is" (Ex. 3.14), meant precisely *ipsum esse,* existence itself. But Gilson's positions that God thereby revealed to metaphysics the nature of its object, that Thomistic philosophy cannot be separated from Thomistic theology, and that the ultimate object of metaphysics coincides with that of theology, with all the presuppositions and consequences entailed, remain quite controverted. BIBLIOGRAPHY: É. Gilson, *Being and Some Philosophers* (2d ed., 1952); J. Maritain, *Preface to Metaphysics: Seven Lectures on Being* (1939); T. C. O'Brien, *Metaphysics and the Existence of God* (1960).

[R. E. HENNESSEY]

EXISTENTIAL PHENOMENOLOGY, the second and more realistic phase of the phenomenological movement, succeeding the idealism of Edmund Husserl's transcendental phenomenology, and dominating contemporary continental philosophy.

The foundations of existential phenomenology are those of the preceding phenomenology, the doctrine of the intentionality of consciousness and the method of phenomenological description. Consciousness is intentional in that it necessarily refers to an object not an element of, but lying beyond itself. The method calls for absolute neutrality in approaching the object, "bracketing" or suspending all presuppositions, even those of existence or non-existence, so as to deal with only the meaning or essence of the phenomenon.

But yet there are major differences. Existential phenomenology repudiates both Husserl's disengaged transcendental ego, to whom all else can be made objective, and his phenomenological rationalism or essentialism. It sees instead an engaged ego, "being-in-the-world," constituted by its being in the world, and constituting the meanings or essences of that world.

While sharing these basics, the perspectives of such prominent thinkers as M. Heidegger and J. P. Sartre, M. Merleau Ponty, and Gabriel Marcel manifest wide diversities concerning the being of man and God.

[R. E. HENNESSEY]

EXISTENTIAL PSYCHOLOGY,

a distinct approach to the study of man which endeavors to integrate the richness, variety, and complexity of human phenomena (treated by many other psychological schools in terms of many different constructs) into one systematic frame of reference. The integrating concept is existence, i.e., man should discover he is a being who "ex-sists," or stands out, as a body with other bodies in the world. The method of existential psychology is phenomenological, i.e., the concrete description or expression of raw experience in ways that elucidate its fundamental meaning for the individual. Existential psychology (like existential and phenomenological philosophy from which it is derived) exerts considerable influence on contemporary moral theology and philosophy. BIBLIOGRAPHY: A. L. Van Kaam, NCE 5:728–729; T. C. Greening, *Existential Humanistic Psychology* (pa. 1971).

[M. E. STOCK]

EXISTENTIAL THEOLOGY,

the manner of theologizing that uses existentialist philosophy as a hermeneutic, i.e., as a principle of interpretation of revelation. Contemporary existentialism traces its inspiration to S. *Kierkegaard (1813–55). Its best-known religious exponents have been M. *Buber, P. *Tillich, G. Marcel, and R. Bultmann. It expresses a rejection of a Christianity as a body of doctrines to be understood and explained, and looks to revelation as an answer to the question of human existence whereby the gospel can help man to achieve real selfhood through the active realization of his existence. As wholly transcendent, God cannot become an object of thought or analysis, but is known only as encountered in the personal decision of faith. The gospel speaks of the human existence to be realized. The Scriptures must be demythologized, or stripped of antiquated symbolic categories, so that they may call contemporary man to his proper situation. Since the Scriptures serve only to make known the historical character of man's own existence, it is unnecessary to inquire into the historical truth of the gospel events. Faith in turn is not response but an existential understanding of self in its existence and in its relations to God and the world. The practical expression of faith is obedience, in which man attains his authentic being. The existentialist approach has been criticized principally for ignoring the importance of the historical events for the gospel narratives. The existentialist hermeneutic seems unable to accommodate all the streams of scriptural thought and, by choosing to ignore all but one, seems to distort the gospel. BIBLIOGRAPHY: J. Macquarrie, *Existentialist Theology* (1955).

[E. F. MALONE]

EXISTENTIALISM,

a term applied to certain philosophical doctrines traceable to Kierkegaard's attack on the abstract idealism of Hegel in the 1840s. In the 20th cent. existentialism designates a concern with the primacy of existence over essence, with the existing human person as central, and a generally phenomenological approach to the problems of life and philosophy. As such, it has become a label affixed rather indiscriminately to thinkers who may share very little in the way of philosophical conclusions but whose overall frame of reference provokes an intense analysis of the above-cited major themes.

It is a common conviction of existentialists that there is no knowledge independent of a knowing subject, that knowledge is not an end in itself but proceeds from, and terminates in, the question, what does this mean to *me,* the knower, the existing thinker? Abstract, conceptual truth must be transferred to the concrete inwardness of a spiritual life. Alienation is a recurrent motif: man is surrounded by a world of utter insecurity in which he experiences the finiteness of his existence. The most intensely shattering experience is that of nothingness, which strikingly reveals his temporality. All existentialists stress the creative possibility of anguish, a theme first philosophically elaborated in S. *Kierkegaard's *The Concept of Dread* (1884). Boredom, ennui, despair, and melancholy are degrees and modes of anguish and can be authentic or unauthentic, i.e., they can force man to decision or drive him to distraction in pleasure-seeking. For Heidegger the greatest value of existential despair is that it manifest man to himself most luminously.

For the existentialist, authentic humanity can only be realized in and by the solitary individual; the world is at best a kind of testing-ground of honesty, the matter for one's process of self-realization. Nevertheless, authentic existence cannot do without the world and the other, for human existence is essentially being in a situation. Limit situations, as Jaspers describes them, are those in which man faces the many cliffs and abysses that cannot be bridged by any exertion of human thinking. But authentic man sees in death the decisive motivating power that spurs him to the highest existential resolve. Death is the final existential link with the dimension of futurity, conclusively implementing the individual's past and present.

Kierkegaard and G. *Marcel are Christians who are usually included in the ranks of existentialists; J.-P. *Sartre and *Nietzsche are unquestionably atheistic; M. Heidegger and K. Jaspers are complex and somewhat obscure on the religious question. For a Christian existentialism, the realization of the eternal in the temporality of human existence is possible only in the religiously committed personality. If God is omitted or bracketed (as with Heidegger) or flatly denied (as with Nietzsche and Sartre), there remains only the yawning abyss of nothingness, a void that cannot be filled because he who alone could fill it is refused admission. Christian theologians, both Catholic and Protestant, have found considerable enlightenment in the thinking of existentialists, particularly in the latter's focusing on themes of personal inwardness and responsibility and of the necessity of coming to terms in utter sincerity with the demands of truth. BIBLIOGRAPHY: J. Collins, *Existentialists* (1952); *Christianity and The Existentialists,* (ed. C. Michalson, 1956); D. Roberts, *Existentialism and Christian Belief* (1957); R. Harper, *Existential Experience* (pa. 1972).

[J. P. REID]

EXODUS, BOOK OF, the 2d book of the Bible and the Pentateuch (Torah), containing sacred and catechetical stories of: God's deliverance of Israel from slavery in Egypt (Ex 1.1–12.36); the journey to Sinai (Ex 12.37–18.27); the covenant between God and Israel (19.1–24.18); the instructions about the Dwelling and their fulfillment (24.1–31.18; 35.1–40.38); the breaking of the covenant with its renewal (32.1–34.35). The work is a collection of ancient, religious folk traditions that began with Moses in the 13th cent. B.C. when nomadic tribes of Aramaeans were gradually forming the confederation called "the Sons of Israel." Through the eras of Israel's history, the conquest of Canaan and the establishment of stable monarchy under King David (c.1220–980 B.C.), the divided kingdoms of Judah and Israel (940–721), Judah alone (721–587), the Exile (587–539), and the Restoration (539–c.400 B.C.), the oral and written traditions about the Exodus kept developing in many Yahwistic sanctuaries as part of the liturgical and cultural growth of the Israelite folk. Written collections were already being formed from David's time (1000 B.C.) in the cultic centers of the northern tribes and in Judah. Exodus's final edition appeared at least 8 cent. after the events it commemorates in epic fashion, and only after the pact with God had been revoked for Israel in general, and had been renewed with a faithful, monotheistic remnant made up mostly of Judeans (Jews). Its last revision was the work of priestly scribes who were the dominant force in the ethnarchy of post-exilic Judah and the inheritors and preservers of all the traditions before them. Their redaction left the ancient materials essentially intact but stitched together, despite the resultant clashing connections, dislocations, and duplications. The finished product shows indications of three major traditions: the Yahwist, from Judah's heritage; the Elohist, probably originating in the northern tribes; and the Priestly, itself not simply editorial but drawing on ancient traditions.

For the Jewish religion Exodus describes God's greatest saving acts, the remembrance of which was relived every year at the three major feasts, Passover, Pentecost, and Booths (Tabernacle). The plague stories and God's contest with Pharaoh display God's concern for his people, his ubiquitous power over creation, and his government of human history. The Passover traditions weave together separate nomadic and agricultural, springtime liturgies and connect them with the hurried escape from the Egyptians and the marvelous passage of the sea of reeds. The march through the desert with its signs and wonders, along with the recalcitrance and infidelities of the people, epitomizes Israel's unfaithful relations with the faithful God, who wants their exclusive love and worship. The alliance that God freely and graciously instigates and completes exalts the people above all others and establishes them as the separated, holy ones who will guard his revelation of himself for its deliverance to the rest of men. The rules of the covenant, especially the Ten Commandments, set up the essential religious, moral, and liturgical life for Jews henceforth. The traditions about the portable desert sanctuary celebrate Israel's holiness, for, indeed, the Holy God dwells in their midst. Yet, again, the long story of Israel's rejections of God and his having constantly to call them back to their original submission to him is underlined by the episode of the golden calf (ch. 32), Moses' intercession on their behalf, and the Alliance's renewal (ch. 34). All the basic themes of the Yahwistic religion are there, the ones that had to be emphasized over and over again through Yahweh's prophets down the long ages. Now, in the 4th cent. B.C., when Exodus was in circulation and being read, Jews all over the world in the diaspora could relive the salvation and election that made them a special, divinely guided people, still searching for the true promised land.

[J. F. FALLON]

EXODUS FROM EGYPT, Israel's departure from Egypt, one of the most important events in the history of this people (Ex 1–15). According to Ex 12.40–41, the Israelites lived in Egypt 430 years; Gen 15.13 and Acts 7.6 give the round number of 400 years. It was probably during the period of the Hyksos (1720–1570 B.C.), who were Semites, when Joseph and the first Israelites went to Egypt. A later Pharaoh, fearful of the rapidly increasing Hebrew population, enslaved them. In this situation Yahweh sent Moses to demand the release of Israel, his people. After a long series of plagues, the Pharaoh finally let them go. When he repented and sent a force of chariots to recapture the Israelites, the Egyptian forces were overwhelmed at the Red Sea.

Earlier in the 20th cent., scholars such as J. W. Jack, J.

Garstang, W. J. Phythian-Adams thought the Exodus occurred in the 15th cent. B.C. during the reign of Thutmose III (1490–1435). This view agreed with the statement of 1 Kg 6.1 that the Exodus took place 480 years before the founding of Solomon's temple. More recently, however, the late date which places the Exodus in the reign of Ramses II (1290–24) has been generally accepted (cf. H. H. Rowley, W. F. Albright, etc.). Egyptian history and archeological evidence of the destruction of Canaanite cities such as Lachish, Debir, Eglon, Hazor *c.*1220 favor this late date.

According to Ex 12.37, 600,000 men, not counting children and women, journeyed forth, a figure that would make the total number of the emigrating throng impossibly large. It has been suggested to read "family" instead of "thousand" *('eleph),* which would reduce the number to 600 families.

Although many place-names are given in the Book of Exodus, the exact route of the Exodus and the precise place of the crossing of the sea cannot be determined. The crossing may have occurred in the area of Lake Timsah and the Bitter Lakes. The sea crossed is traditionally held to have been the Red Sea, but the Hebrew term *yam suph* properly means "Reed Sea," suggesting a marshy area such as is found in the vicinity of those lakes. Without denying the historical and wondrous nature of the event, it can be presumed that epical embellishments have been added to the account in order to further enhance God's glory.

The Exodus marked the beginning of Israel's existence as a nation and made the people conscious that Yahweh was their Savior and the Lord of history. There are many passages throughout the OT that express Israel's "Exodus-faith" (e.g., Dt 26.5–11; Jos 24.1–13; Am 3.1–2; 9.7; Hos 11.1; Mic 6.3–5; Jer 2.6; Pss 78.11–14; 105.23–42; 106.6–12). The story was kept alive in the Passover Festival. And when the Israelites were in Exile, they looked upon the Exodus as a pledge of their own deliverance (e.g., Is 43.16–19; 51.9–11). BIBLIOGRAPHY: H. Cazelles, "Les Localisations de l'Exode et la critique littéraire," RevBibl 62 (1955) 321–365; G. Hebert, *When Israel Came out of Egypt* (1961).

[F. BUCK]

EXOMOLOGESIS, Gr. term for confession, found in the *Didache, in Tertullian and Cyprian writing on penance, in references both to the whole penitential rite and to the public or private confession of sins.

[T. C. O'BRIEN]

EXORCISM, the liberation by prayer and symbolic action of persons, places, or things from harassment, infestation, possession, or obsession by evil spirits. Exorcism was practiced by primitive Christians in imitation of Christ and his first disciples. Little is known of the circumstances that called for resort to exorcism or of the procedures that were used in the primitive Church. The earliest exorcisms of which there is satisfactory record are those incorporated *c.*200 into the ritual for use during the catechumenate. These have survived in synthesized form in the minor exorcisms of the new baptismal rites approved for children (1969) and adults (1972). They were originally introduced because the adult catechumen was on the point of forswearing his allegiance to the pagan gods, generally identified in popular Christian consciousness with evil spirits, and had need to be protected against their anger. When infant baptism became the common practice these exorcisms lost much of their relevance, and in their survival are probably best explained as a symbolic anticipation of the general deliverance from evil that will come to the baptizand through baptism. Other liturgical exorcisms of ancient origin are used in the blessing or consecration of churches and objects such as salt, water, oils, altars, sacred vessels, and bells. When a special ritual for the exorcism of possessed persons began to be used is unknown. Such rites were multiplied and became elaborate during the Middle Ages when spiritual beings, good and evil, were commonly thought to intervene frequently in human affairs. The rules to be observed in exorcism and the rite to be observed, as these are set forth in current *Roman Ritual,* have been purged of many fanciful notions of possession prevalent in earlier times, and priests are cautioned against believing too readily that a person is possessed by an evil spirit. The exorcism of those possessed or molested by evil spirits is not common in the modern Church. It is still provided for by a church law, however. The solemn exorcism of a possessed person may be undertaken only by a priest who has obtained special and express permission from his ordinary (CIC c. 1151.1); a simple exorcism, aimed at imposing restraint on the activity of evil spirits (e.g., in some locality or community), rather than at the liberation of a possessed or obsessed individual, may be performed by priests enjoying a general authorization from their ordinary (See P. T. Weller, *The Roman Ritual* [1964] 659–662). The exorcisms connected with baptism and with certain blessings and consecrations may be legitimately performed by the authorized ministers of those rites. BIBLIOGRAPHY: Abbo, 2:423–426; E. J. Gratsch, NCE 5:748–749; L. J. Elmer, NCE 5:749–750; *Rites of the Catholic Church* (1976)54–59, 200–202.

[P. K. MEAGHER]

EXORCIST, one of the four minor orders suppressed in the Latin Church by Paul VI's *motu proprio, Ministeria quaedam,* Aug. 15, 1972 (AAS 64:529–540). Its survival as a minor order before that time was purely symbolic and a formality, since the recipient never exercised the order; *exorcism is reserved by church law to a specially authorized priest.

[T. C. O'BRIEN]

EXPECTANCIES, a descriptive term referring to benefices to be conferred in fulfillment of a legally binding promise of succession, on the anticipation of their becoming vacant. This practice was known as early as the 12th cent., the Holy See pledging through *litterae expectativae* to grant a benefice not yet vacant. Such expectative letters might be either determinate or indeterminate, according to whether or not a particular benefice was specified. The practice was condemned by Lateran Council III, by Pope Boniface VIII, and by the Council of Trent. The present CIC voids all such promises, while protecting the right of the Holy See to appoint coadjutor bishops with the right of succession. BIBLIOGRAPHY: F. X. Wernz, *Ius decretalium* 2 (6 v., 1898–1905) 315; G. E. Lynch, *Coadjutors and Auxiliaries of Bishops* (1947).

[W. A. JURGENS]

EXPECTANT CHURCH, see CHURCH SUFFERING.

EXPEDITUS, ST., name for personage frequently invoked as patron in an emergency; also identified erroneously as leader of "the Thundering Legion." H. Delahaye credits E.'s relatively late popularity to the strong attraction that a play on words exerts on the choice of a patron (hence Expeditus will expedite fulfillment of a petition). The Expeditus legend has found its way into literature. BIBLIOGRAPHY: J.-M. Sauguet, BiblSanct 5:95–96; Butler 2:128–129; L. Sheppard, *Saints Who Never Were* (1969) 66–68.

[M. R. BROWN]

EXPERIENCE, RELIGION OF, a phrase used to classify the various interpretations of Christianity that make the affective response in the believer, rather than the authority of Bible or Church, to be the *rule of faith. (see ENTHUSIASM). In the history of Protestantism emphasis on experience lies at the origin of such groups as Anabaptists, Quakers, Moravians, and Methodists. *Pietism, *revivalism, the *Holiness movement, and *Pentecostalism all have stressed the experience of the individual believer. None of these forms of Christianity has opposed the authority of the Bible; some have been fundamentalists; some have even acknowledged the authority of *confessions of faith. Each, however, in varying ways, has given primacy to the experienced word of God within the believer, presupposing a correspondence between this experience and the content of the biblical message because of the one divine source. In this sense "religion of experience" has been contrasted with "religion of authority," which is the interpretation of Christianity made by exponents of orthodoxy. The exponents of orthodoxy see faith as authenticated by scriptural texts or by authoritative interpretation of these texts, whether by theologians (e.g., in Lutheran *orthodoxy) or by teaching authority or *magisterium (in the RC Church).

Beginning in the 19th cent. *liberal theology explicitly placed experience as the basis for religious belief. The teaching of F. *Schleiermacher was widely accepted: that all religion, Christianity being its highest form, is based on the feeling of absolute dependence, and religious doctrines are a projection of man's affective states. This approach was strengthened by the development of the psychology of religion; e.g., in William James's *Varieties of Religious Experience* (1902) religious beliefs and practices were examined to determine their basis in the inner life of man. By an appeal to human experience as the basis for belief, liberal theologians sought to make religion compatible with science and philosophy, or at least to make religion immune from attack by turning for vindication to the subjective rather than to biblical text or church dogma. A similar trend was thought to be present in RC *Modernism, which met with papal condemnation. From the end of World War I the place of experience in the life of faith has received continuing attention. Karl *Barth led in the reaction to liberal theology and in the rejection of its appeal to human experience, asserting the transcendence of God and his objective saving word. Exponents of orthodoxy have continued to warn against subjectivism and to defend the essential relationship of Christian faith to the historical events of Jesus' life and, in some cases, to the classic Protestant confessions of faith or to RC dogmatic definitions. *Existential theology, *experience theology, *kerygmatic theology, and the demythologizing of the *Bultmann School, however, all may be viewed as renewed assertions of the primacy of personal response. Some RC theologians seek to narrow the separation between authority and experience by pointing out that tradition, or the living understanding of revelation, comes from both the ordinary and the charismatic experience of the whole Christian community, including its head and its members.

In RC teaching the virtue of faith is understood to be a direct, personal response to God; the teaching authority of the Church simply declares what has been revealed and its meaning. The theology of St. Thomas Aquinas, inspired by NT teaching on the Holy Spirit, makes the gifts of the Holy Spirit, which are essentially experiential, indispensable to living faith and to salvation (ThAq ST 1a2ae, 68.1 & 2). The Reformation principle *sola scriptura* was originally understood as an appeal not to a written text but to the word of God made living in the believer by the experience of faith. Often the opposition to religion of authorship has been a reaction to an objectification and externalization of faith and grace that have disregarded their essentially personal nature. BIBLIOGRAPHY: J. E. Smith, *Experience and God* (1968).

[T. C. O'BRIEN]

EXPERIENCE, RELIGIOUS, man's awareness of his relationship to the sacred or holy. It is an act or a group of acts which gives man understanding of himself with reference to God. There have been widely different interpretations of religious experience within religious thought and Christianity in particular. A strongly personal, existential, and nonrationalistic interpretation is characteristic of the 16th-cent. Reformation, 19th-cent. pietism (see KIER-

KEGAARD, SOREN). Within the philosophy of H. *Bergson and W. *James, religious experience is largely the product of subjective utility and psychological well-being. But many religious thinkers refuse to limit religious experience to mere feelings or subjectivity. It is real and actual since man is aware that he has been confronted by or has entered into communion with One who is transcendental, the Absolute. Since God is absolute mystery he is incomprehensible, but man still has some understanding of Him and the ideas that he has will necessarily play an important part in his interpretation of any religious experience. It is more than the projection of personal ideas and concepts concerning God, for in a valid and authentic religious experience one passively experiences God in the sense of having received a gift or blessing. It is the most personal of all experiences since it summons a man to take a position towards God and the world of moral and religious values. Man is aware that he is called to exercise his radical and most fundamental freedom since God is the ground and ultimate meaning of his life. The experience of the holy may be more or less clear, but since there are many different degrees and levels in the human personality, man is aware of and responds to God in varying degrees. In a man's basic moral choices, it sometimes happens that he is more directly conscious of making a decision to embrace one moral value, such as telling the truth here and now, but at a deeper level of his personality he knows that he is open to the whole world of moral and religious values, and hence to their Author. In higher mystical experiences a man is much more directly aware of his relationship to God. Since religion is a personal matter but not limited to man's own personal satisfaction, it must remain open to adoration, thanksgiving, and prayer to God in unison with others. Thus religious experiences may and to a certain degree must remain open to the community of men. BIBLIOGRAPHY: J. Mouroux, *Christian Experience* (1954); W. James, *Varieties of Religious Experience* (1958); N. Smart, *Religious Experience of Mankind* (1969); R. Haughton, *Theology of Experience* (1972). *EXPERIENCE, RELIGION OF; EXPERIENCE, RELIGIOUS.

[M. GRIFFIN]

EXPERIENCE THEOLOGY, a methodological approach originating in the 19th cent. that viewed the theological enterprise as descriptive of religious experience. Its principal exponents, F. *Schleiermacher, R. Otto, and J. W. Oman, held that the data of theology are not revelation but experience of faith, which is a personal awareness of the divine encounter. Statements of dogma are the reflective articulation of the understanding implicit in the variety of religious sentiments. Subjectivism is tempered by the judgment and acceptance by the Christian community of religious attitudes, which become current but changeable tradition. Scripture is similarly valued as stimulating and regulating the individual and group experience. Experience theology sought to introduce a vitality into theology by

reacting against the contemporary conceptualist orthodoxy and rationalism. Experience theology has been criticized for its practical identification of religious experience with revelation and the resultant inability to evaluate the saving act of God in men. BIBLIOGRAPHY: J. Macquarrie, *Twentieth-Century Religious Thought* (1963) 211–225. *LIBERAL THEOLOGY.

[E. F. MALONE]

EXPERIMENTAL PSYCHOLOGY, the branch of psychology that employs methods consistent with objective, controlled observation. As a distinct kind of psychology it dates from the establishment of the first psychological laboratory by W. Wundt in 1879. It restricts itself to data that can be objectively described and (usually) measured quantitatively and by instruments in order to insure freedom from subjective bias and the replicability of its procedures by other experimenters. In its basic form, the variables in a situation are controlled so that the interrelations of two or a few can be clearly observed. Wherever it is applicable, experimental psychology yields exact knowledge of the phenomena under investigation. It does not supply causal connections between phenomena and is not applicable to great areas of human behavior.

[M. E. STOCK]

EXPERIMENTALISM (EDUCATION), a term designating John Dewey's instrumental or pragmatic educational philosophy, which holds that experimental scientific techniques are the only valid evaluating tools of ideals, values, beliefs, and practices. Essentially empirical in origin, experimentalism—or instrumentalism, as Dewey preferred to call it—rejects the absolute and unchangeable in the social and moral order, and values ideas and concepts only for their instrumental role in problem-solving. It views man as a biological organism continuous with nature, devoid of any spiritual or transcendental quality, and thriving only in a thoroughly democratic way of life in which the democratic ideal serves as the unique criterion of behavior. Experimentalism's impact on education is best seen in the progressive educational movement initiated by Dewey at his Laboratory School in Chicago (1896–1904) and implemented by his followers at the experimental school at the State Univ. of Iowa (1915), at Lincoln School, Teachers College, Columbia Univ. (1917), and at Dalton, Mass., and Winnetka, Ill. (1919). Later progressive ideas were widely accepted in elementary schools in the U.S. and abroad. Defining education as growth leading to more growth with no determined goals, experimentalism emphasizes learning by doing through the pupils' purposeful activity, concern for individual differences in interest and potential, and freedom of expression and action. Experimentalism insists that education is life, not a preparation for life; and since it rejects any spiritual or supernatural dimension, many religious leaders have viewed it with suspicion and consider it opposed to a Christian philosophy of education.

BIBLIOGRAPHY: M. C. Baker, *Foundations of John Dewey's Educational Theories* (1955).

[M. B. MURPHY]

EXPERIMENTATION, MEDICAL. The use of human subjects in the testing of unproven medications or medical procedures represents a form of medical experimentation that invites closest moral scrutiny. If done primarily in an effort to serve the best interests of the subject's own health, experimentation may be justified provided that the risk entailed does not notably outweigh the advantages reasonably expected, and that proper consent of the patient is obtained or legitimately presumed. Such would clearly be the case, e.g., in emergency situations wherein no proven remedy is available and one's only hope lies in measures whose efficacy is less than certain. Because the subject of the experiment perhaps may benefit therefrom, justification for the procedure can readily be found in the moral principle of *totality.

Less easy to justify is any form of experimentation that promises no medical benefit for its subject but is calculated to serve only the altruistic interests of science and ultimately the common good. As understood by most theologians, the principle of totality is not relevant to this situation, and recourse must be had elsewhere if experimentation of this kind is to be vindicated in any circumstances. Accordingly, those who within limits defend this form of experimentation ordinarily do so by appealing to the principle of fraternal love and maintain that one may, out of love for fellow man, consent to do for another what one may legitimately do for himself.

Although it is impossible to define exactly the limits beyond which one may not licitly go in this matter, several helpful norms can be suggested. (1) No one may legitimately agree to an experiment that would entail his certain death, with the possible exception of a criminal condemned to death; (2) when risk of death or bodily harm is foreseen as insignificant, no willing subject need hesitate to submit to medical experimentation; (3) in the remainder of cases, which would represent the majority of practical possibilities in civilized society, it seems safe to say that, for a proportionately serious reason, one may for the benefit of others permit himself to be a subject in an experiment that is not likely to do grave and permanent damage to bodily integrity or seriously endanger life. It is assumed that in any such case the procedure will previously have been adequately tested in animals, that the results give valid grounds for believing that its benefits for humans will be proportionate to its risks, and that all reasonable precautions are taken to protect from unforeseen and unintended harm any who submit to the experiment. Under no circumstances may experimentation of this kind be conducted without the informed consent of the subject. BIBLIOGRAPHY: J. J. Lynch NCE 5:756; AAS 44 (1952) 779–789.

[J. J. LYNCH]

EXPIATION, a word, coming into Christian usage from the OT, that translates the Hebrew *kippĕr,* whence the great Jewish liturgical feast of Yom Kippur is named (Lev ch. 16). The modern use of the word expiation has tended to confuse it with a chastisement, or punitive reparation, for sin. It is sometimes associated with the image of an angry God, who is placated by the sinner's punishment. In the OT to expiate means to purify, that is, to take a person, place, or thing and make it pleasing instead of displeasing to God. Expiation supposes the existence of a sin and works to destroy it. But as sin is seen to be the rebellious alienation of man from God, expiation has the effect of effacing the sin while reuniting man with God.

Expiation was expressed by the great ritual of the Day of Atonement. The high priest went beyond the veil of the holy of holies bearing the blood of a bull and a ram which he poured on the cover of the ark (the *kapporeth,* which is translated as mercy seat, or propitiatory), the place where the glory of God dwelt. Thus he signified the people's union (or quest for restored union) with God. There is nothing here of constraining God by cultic action to be propitious. The expiation is an expression of willingness to be purified. It has authentic value to the extent that the gesture coincides with the people's inner disposition, their repentance, and readiness to accept God's gift of pardon. There is a gradual shift of emphasis until expiation comes to be seen as God's gift rather than as man's work.

The redemptive work of Christ is conceived against this background in Heb 7.25 and 9.4. Risen and entering into his Father's presence, he offers the expiation that brings man pardon, interceding for man as did the high priest. Paul also sees Jesus' dying as the expiation (Rom 3.25). The blood of the new covenant, Christ's own, is poured over his flesh, which is simultaneously a *kapporeth,* where the glory of God dwells bodily, and the man in whom are all others, thus signifying the definitive union that is henceforth available to all through the pardon of their sins. BIBLIOGRAPHY: K. W. Bolle, NCE 5:758–762; Kittel TD 3:301–322; DBT. *ATONEMENT: *RECONCILIATION; *REPARATION.

[C. REGAN]

EXPILLY, LOUIS ALEXANDRE (1742–94), constitutional bp. during the French Revolution. As a partisan of the revolutionaries in the Estates General from 1789, he attacked the rights of the clergy to hold property and was an author of the Civil Constitution of the Clergy, and one of the first to subscribe to it. In 1790 he was chosen constitutional bp. of Finistère, had himself consecrated at Paris and installed at Quimper. In April 1791 a letter of Pius VI voided E.'s nomination, declared his consecration illicit, and forbade E. to exercise episcopal functions. The Pope's letter E. ignored. In 1793 the political faction he supported fell from favor, and he was executed at Brest in June 1794. BIBLIOGRAPHY: J. Leflon, *Catholicisme* 4:965–967.

[T. C. O'BRIEN]

EXPOSITION, the exhibition of the consecrated Host for the veneration of the faithful. In public exposition the Host is visible in a monstrance; when the Host remains enclosed in a pyx or ciborium and only the tabernacle door is opened, exposition is said to be private. The practice was one of a number of eucharistic devotions that arose in the 12th and 13th centuries. The way appears to have been prepared for this practice by the elevation of the Host at Mass to satisfy the desire of the people to look upon the consecrated bread. Although the Church condemned certain abuses connected with the desire to see the Host, exposition continued to be approved as a legitimate practice (see D 1656). The institution of the Feast of Corpus Christi in the 13th cent., which occasioned many practices of eucharistic piety, also influenced the introduction of exposition. The "stations" or pauses in the eucharistic procession on that feast provided a brief exposition before the blessing with the monstrance was given. Exposition during the octave of Corpus Christi, even during Mass, was permitted. The modern movement toward liturgical reform, emphasizing the dynamic action of the Mass rather than the more static adoration of the consecrated species, has led to disparagement of the practice in some quarters. Nevertheless, the Sacred Congregation of Rites in its *Instruction on Eucharistic Worship* (May 25, 1967) declares it a valuable practice which "stimulates the faithful to an awareness of the marvelous presence of Christ and is an invitation to spiritual communion with Him" (no. 60). However, the *Instruction* insists that exposition should be conducted in such a manner that it is seen in its relation to the Mass, and that nothing in the decoration should obscure the intention of Christ in instituting the Eucharist (*ibid.*). Furthermore, it is now forbidden to celebrate Mass before the Blessed Sacrament exposed (*ibid.* no. 61). BIBLIOGRAPHY: E. Dumoutet, *Le Désir de voir l'hostie* (1926); Podhradsky, 89–90.

[E. R. FALARDEAU]

EXPRESSIONISM. In art a term referring to any emotionally motivated or oriented statement which may show: (1) traditional form in non-descriptive, symbolic, or interpretative color and agitated technique, (2) forms misshapen, violently distorted, or fantastically imagined, or (3) the complete elimination of representational elements in "non-objective" shapes presenting free, spontaneous records of hand and medium, and further enriched and intensified by affirmations of the emotional property of color.

The 20th-cent. Expressionist movement is identified with the works of two German groups: *The Bridge (Die Brücke)* organized by E. Kirchner in Dresden in 1905, including Heckel, Schmidt-Rotluff, Nolde, and others; and the *Blue Rider (Der Blaue Reiter),* led by W. Kandinsky in Munich in 1911, among whom were Marc, Jawlensky, and Macke. The late Gothic woodcuts of Dürer and Schöngauer and the grotesque distortions of Grünewald were forerunners of the forceful contemporary German Expressionist prints of E.

Kirchner and E. Nolde; works of Max Beckmann in strong color and line expressed the subhuman and depraved passions of a postwar world in the *Neue-Sachlichkeit.* The "Fauves" (Wild Beasts) of Paris (1905)—preceded by the frenzied statements of Van Gogh, the erotic subconscious images of Munch and the fantastic horrors of Ensor—communicated emotions through unexpected shapes, intense and shocking color, and tempestuous techniques, as in Rouault's grave social and religious records, and the sheer anguish of Soutine. Kandinsky of the Blue Rider group finally gave free play to the hand in spontaneous improvisations, the shapes determined by the psyche alone, liberating unconscious imagery in non-objective abstract forms leading to Abstract-Expressionism. The contribution of Expressionism rivalled the influence of cubism as an abiding force in 20th-century art.

Among many Expressionist works of religious significance are G. Rouault's *Men of Justice* (1913), *The Passion* (1943), *The Miserere* Series (published 1948), E. Nolde's *Last Supper* (1909), *Christ among the Children* (1910), *Dance around the Golden Calf* (1910), *The Prophet* (1912), *St. Mary of Egypt* (1912); K. Kollwitz's modern Dance of Death among the starving mothers and children of postwar Germany. BIBLIOGRAPHY: W. Kandinsky, *Concerning the Spiritual in Art,* (1947), M. Brion, *Kandinsky* (1961), B. S. Myers, *The German Expresssionists: A Generation in Revolt* (1963).

[M. J. DALY]

EXPULSION OF PENITENTS, a feature of the penitential discipline of the early Church whereby sinners after a confession of their sins were then temporarily excluded from all ecclesial participation for a period of public satisfaction, only after which were they granted absolution and reconciled with the Church. During the period of satisfaction, the sinner belonged to a special class *(ordo paenitentium)* with inferior status in the Church. A variety of penitential works were also imposed: fastings, vigils, the wearing of sackcloth and ashes, and the giving of alms, all intended to symbolize the penitent's separation from the sheep of Christ's flock. The length of the period of satisfaction varied greatly and was determined by the bishop. Expulsion of penitents continued until about the 6th cent. when church discipline changed, allowing reception of the sacrament of penance more than once. The practice was, in effect, an early example of liturgical excommunication. BIBLIOGRAPHY: J. Miller, *Fundamentals of the Liturgy* (1959) 458–462.

[B. ROSENDALL

EXSUFFLATION, see INSUFFLATION.

EXSULTET, the name, taken from the opening word of its Latin version, the Great Easter Song or hymn of praise sung in connection with the blessing and offering of the paschal candle in the Easter Vigil service. The hymn is a proclamation and praise of the wonders of God, esp. that of Christ's Resurrection, which occurred on this night. The author is uncertain, although St. Ambrose (d. 397) and St. Augustine (d. 431) are frequently suggested.

[B. C. ROSENDALL]

EXSULTET ROLLS, illuminated scroll MSS peculiar to S Italy in the 11th and 12th centuries. On these long parchment strips, containing the *Exsultet,* the hymn chanted by the deacon at the lighting of the Paschal Candle, appropriate subjects were depicted in inverted positions so that the congregation might see them upright, as the MSS was unrolled forward over the lectern by the deacon as he advanced through the text. Most rolls show Byzantine influence and have close connection with Monte Cassino. BIBLIOGRAPHY: M. Avery, *Exsultet-Rolls of South Italy* (1936).

[R. C. MARKS]

EXSUPERANTIUS, ST., see FELIX, REGULA, AND EX-SUPERANTIUS, SS.

EXSURGE DOMINE, the initial bull of excommunication issued against Martin *Luther by Leo X, June 15, 1520. Luther was given 60 days to make submission; he did not, and sentence of excommunication was rendered in the bull *Decet Romanum Pontificem,* Jan 3, 1521. This culminated the canonical process that had begun in Rome in June 1518 as a result of Luther's *Ninety-Five Theses but had dragged on until the appointment of a commission headed by Card. Cajetan and Pietro Accolti in Feb. 1520. The commission prepared, with the aid of J. *Eck, a text of 41 propositions drawn from Luther's writings on indulgences, the efficacy of the sacraments, and the primacy of papal authority. Cajetan had wished a specific condemnatory qualification attached to each proposition, but the commission followed Eck's proposal and condemned the ensemble as "heretical, scandalous, offensive to the faithful, misleading and erring from Catholic truth" (D 1451–92). *Exsurge Domine* incorporated the propositions and the condemnation. As official promulgator of the bull, Eck met with little success. The German bps. thought it inopportune politically, and it ran counter to their own attachment to *conciliarism. Throughout Germany, many regarded Luther as the champion of their grievances against Rome and of their hope for reform of the Church. On Dec. 10, 1520, at Wittenberg, Luther burned the bull together with a copy of the canon law of the Church. BIBLIOGRAPHY: Jedin Trent 1:172–182.

[T. C. O'BRIEN]

EXTENSION SOCIETY, CATHOLIC CHURCH, agency established in 1905 to support mission work in areas of the U.S. where the Catholic Church was weak. It was founded by a Canadian-born priest, later bp., working in Detroit, F. C. *Kelley, who served as president for 19

years. In 1910 Pius X raised it to pontifical status. Its activities include assistance to needy priests and seminarians, aid in construction of churches, and operation of a lay missionary volunteer program. It operates under a board that includes bps., priests and lay members. Headquarters are in Chicago, from which *Extension Magazine* is published.

[T. EARLY]

EXTERN SISTERS, women religious in simple vows who live within a monastery of nuns, but outside the papal cloister. As members of the religious family, they care for the external necessities of the monastery and provide contact with the outside world, performing such tasks as answering the door, shopping, etc. They customarily wear a habit different from that of the cloistered sister. Present norms for the discipline of extern sisters are found in the 1961 Instruction of the Sacred Congregation of Religious (AAS 53–371). BIBLIOGRAPHY: D. W. Bonner, *Extern Sisters in Monasteries of Nuns* (1963).

[L. M. KNOX]

EXTORTION, the unjust exacting of money or other things of monetary value, by trickery or intimidation. Since such tactics imply coercion, extortion is like *robbery: in practice it may also differ from robbery in that the victim is duped into an apparent consent to the loss incurred. The term in a restricted sense describes such practices by public officials. In a wider use it applies to blackmail, kidnapping, or confidence games. Morally it is against justice, and its seriousness depends on the loss and damages to the physical or moral person victimized.

[T. C. O'BRIEN]

EXTRA ECCLESIAM NULLA SALUS, a Latin expression literally meaning outside the Church there is no salvation. Patristic in origin (see, e.g., Cyprian, EnchPatr. 557; Origen, *ibid.* 537) and often found in magisterial statements (e.g., D 469, 792), it conveys a central message of the Gospel: the Church is the sacramental prolongation or continuation of Christ's saving mission in the world.

Seen in light of the solidarity in Christ of mankind through the Incarnation and in light of the universality of God's saving intention in Christ, the expression portrays the fact that the Church itself exists, at least initially, far beyond its visible boundaries. Those who are outside the Church in this sense are those who reject the saving grace of Christ, his call to faith and love.

This is not to say that the Church in its initial or anonymous presence does not long for fullness of expression in a genuine community of salvation, one in faith, one in baptism and sacraments, one in divinely founded ministry.

To think of the visible elements of Church as unimportant or optional to those who recognize them is the error of indifferentism. On the other hand, to condemn those inculpably outside the visible boundaries of the Catholic Church was the error of the Feeneyites. BIBLIOGRAPHY: Vat

II ConstChurch 13–17; D 3866–73; R. Hasseveldt, DTC, *Tables générales* 1:1119–21; E. Dublanchy, *ibid.* 4.2:2155–75; M. Eminyan, NCE 5:768; M. -J. le Guillou, SacMund 1:326–327; Y. M. J. Congar, *Sainte église (Unam sanctam* 41, 1963) 417–432.

[J. F. GALLAGHER]

EXTRAORDINARY AFFAIRS OF THE CHURCH, CONGREGATION FOR, see PUBLIC AFFAIRS OF THE CHURCH, COUNCIL OF.

EXTRAORDINARY MINISTERS OF THE EUCHARIST.

An instruction of the Congregation for the Discipline of the Sacraments (now the Congregation for Divine Worship and the Sacraments), issued June 29, 1973, and designed to facilitate reception of the Eucharist, among its provisions authorized certain unordained (thus not "ordinary" ministers) persons in the Church to administer holy communion (AAS 65 [1973] 265–267). The authorization of individuals (not a class of people) is placed in the hands of the diocesan bishop or his delegate. The administration may take place either within the Mass or outside of Mass; in the second case the instruction has particularly in view both communion for the sick and *viaticum. Authorization may be given for a single occasion, for a defined period of time, or permanently. The Congregation also issued a rite called a *mandatum* for the giving of this authorization. The circumstances in which extraordinary ministers may be designated are outlined: the scarcity of ordained ministers in a place or impediments to their functioning, e.g., illness or the press of minsterial obligations; such a number of communicants at Mass as would unduly protract the service; the spiritual needs of the sick who are confined to their homes or in hospital. The instruction requires that for designation as an extraordinary minister, a person must be suitable. In general that means, of course, that the person be a good Catholic and one whose appointment would not cause raised eyebrows. A gradation of preference, however, is also given: e.g., a *reader, a major seminarian, a religious man or woman, a catechist, one of the lay faithful (*christifidelis*), man or woman. In religious houses having an oratory the superior or a vicar of the superior may be appointed. Extraordinary ministers may be communion to themselves.

[T. C. O'BRIEN]

EXTRASENSORY PERCEPTION (ESP),

psychological phenomena of knowledge gained through means that are paranormal in that they are not sensory. They are grouped under the heading of psi-functions of the mind, under which three main types of ESP phenomena are investigated, namely: *telepathy, *clairvoyance, and *premonition. Many different tests have been devised; one, conducted by Dr. J. B. Rhine of Duke University, employs a "sender" and a "receiver," These two attempt to exchange varying types of information—usually the sequence of symbols in a shuffled deck of special ESP cards. The results of their exchanges are subjected to statistical analysis and compared to probability expectations. The results of such scientific research satisfies parapsychologists that all men enjoy some faculty of extrasensory perception and that this cannot be relegated to the realm of the occult. However, no test has yet identified the most proficient perceivers or suggested how ESP powers might be developed. BIBLIOGRAPHY: C. D. Broad, *Lectures on Psychical Research* (1962); S. G. Soal and F. Bateman, *Modern Experiments in Telepathy* (1954); R. Haynes, *Hidden Springs: An Enquiry into Extra-Sensory Perception* (1973, pa. rev. ed. 1974).

[C. P. SVOBODA]

EXTRAVAGANTES

(Lat., circulating outside), a term first applied to papal *decretals not included in Gratian's *Decretum (extra Decretum vagantes);* then to those issued after the *Decretals of Gregory IX (1234); then to those subsequent to the *Liber Sextus of Boniface VIII. The *extravagantes* included in the *Corpus Juris Canonici of 1582 were two earlier collections (the *Extravagantes* of John XXII, and the so-called *Extravagantes communes),* but the Corpus did not give them the status of authentic collections.

[T. C. O'BRIEN]

EXTREME UNCTION, see ANOINTING OF THE SICK.

EXTRINSICISM,

the view that considers peripheral, external, nonconstitutive, or adventitious factors paramount in philosophical or theological analysis. As applied particularly in theology, extrinsicism refers to the penchant of some writers to emphasize juridical or legal aspects of a problem rather than ontological or existential ones. Extrinsicists are taken with the intentional order more than with the real, with plans and decrees more than with natures and essences, with facticity more than with existence. They do not constitute a formal school of theology as such, nor do they propose their ideas in the form of an exclusive and all-embracing system. Instead, they seem to manifest an eclecticism and at times a seeming arbitrariness in the application of their principle. Classical is the case of Luther on justification as it has been interpreted by Catholic theologians. The repentant sinner is not changed ontologically, but by means of faith the justice of Christ is imputed to him. He is *simul justus et peccator.* Essentially he is still a sinner deserving of punishment. But because of the obsequy of his faith, God's eyes focus no longer on the "form of servitude" that is in him but on Christ's "form of sovereignty" that cloaks him. Another instance of extrinsicism is seen in Scotus's doctrine that grace and (mortal) sinfulness are not from a metaphysical standpoint mutually exclusive. They are opposed only because of a divine decree. St. Thomas Aquinas, on the other hand, rejects extrinsicism in this case. Grace and sin are as mutually exclusive as cold and heat. In the area of moral theology probabilists require extrinsic probability, i.e., the support of qualified experts before an opinion established by less than conclusive arguments can become a norm for action. Use is made of such extrinsicism by all moral theologians. Since the time of Cajetan, theologians have relied largely on a principle of what some may call extrinsicism to maintain a clear-cut distinction between the natural and supernatural orders. The supernatural order is that established by a totally gratuitous divine decree, there being nothing in nature corresponding to it except an obediential potency. With his explanation of the natural desire for the beatific vision, H. de Lubac crystallized a movement away from this position. More recently, K. Rahner's introduction of a supernatural existential has polarized elements of the question in such a way as definitely to exclude a purely extrinsicist solution. BIBLIOGRAPHY: H. de Lubac, *Mystery of the Supernatural* (1967).

[C. R. MEYER]

EXUPÉRIEN, FRÈRE (Adrien Mas; 1829–1905), French educator, a Christian Brother from 1847. He became director of novices in Paris in 1859. With Canon H. Chaumont he founded (1882) a youth organization under the patronage of St. Benedict Joseph Labre to foster piety, self-sacrifice, and apostolic interest among young people. E.'s cause was introduced at Rome in 1934. BIBLIOGRAPHY: F. Frédien, *Catholicisme* 4:1017–18; T. Napione, Bibl-Sanct 5:112–113.

[P. K. MEAGHER]

EXUPERIUS, ST. (Exsuperius; d. *c.*412), bp. of Toulouse from *c.*404, one of the eminent bps. of early Gaul. He encouraged the development of monasticism, giving liberally to the monks as far off as Palestine, Egypt, and Libya. His generosity received a tribute from St. Jerome, who dedicated to him his commentary on Zechariah. He was equally generous with the poor of his own diocese who had suffered much from the barbarian invasions; to relieve their necessities he went as far as to sell the sacred vessels. In response to an inquiry he made of Innocent I concerning the canon of the Scriptures, the Pope sent him a letter (Feb. 405), listing the books then received as canonical in Rome, which are identical with those of the Catholic canon today, including the deuterocanonical books. BIBLIOGRAPHY: Butler 3:664–665; L. A. Kelly, CE 5:731; G. Bareille, DTC 5:2022–27.

[R. B. ENO]

EYBLER, JOSEPH (1765–1846; from 1834 Edler von), Austrian composer. He received his early training at the boys' seminary of Vienna under Albrechtsberger. A friend of Haydn and Mozart, E. nursed Mozart in his last illness. He held several positions both as conductor and composer: choirmaster of the Carmelite Church; vice-"Hofkapellmeister"; tutor to the children of Empress Maria Theresa; and, in 1824, first court Kapellmeister. Although he composed symphonies, quartets, sonatas, songs, etc., he is more importantly remembered for his sacred music: 32 Masses, 1 Requiem, 7 Te Deums, 30 Offertories, and 2 oratorios.

[A. M. MACK]

EYCK, HUBERT (d. 1426) and **JAN VAN** (d. 1441), painters of the early Flemish school and brother-collaborators on the Ghent altarpiece (St.-Bavon), completed in 1432 if the Latin quatrain crediting Hubert with the beginning and Jan with the completion of the polyptych, appearing on the frame of the lower central panel (*Adoration of the Lamb*) of the altarpiece, may be believed. The polyptych is obviously the work of at least two artists and on the basis of the more primitive part assigned to Hubert, certain other paintings are attributed to him (*Three Marys at the Sepulcher,* Rotterdam, Boymans-Van Beuningen Mus.; *Friedsam Annunciation,* New York, Metropolitan Mus.). Jan is documented as having been *varlet de chambre* to John of Bavaria (1422–24) and Philip the Good of Burgundy (1425–). It is evident, from a simple examination of his paintings (Arnolfini marriage group, 1434; *Madonna with the Canon van der Paele,* 1436), that he had developed oil painting into the most subtle and brilliant medium for the rendering of light effects and details of the figure unsurpassed to this day. BIBLIOGRAPHY: M. J. Friedländer, *Early Netherlandish Painting I* (1967); E. Panofsky, *Early Netherlandish Painting I* (1958) 178–246; C. D. Cuttler *Northern Painting,* (1968).

[L. A. LEITE]

EYMARD, PIERRE JULIEN, ST. (1811–68), founder of the Blessed Sacrament Fathers and Brothers, a congregation devoted to promoting devotion to the Eucharist. Born at La Mure d'Isère near Grenoble, France, E. was a secular priest and Marist Father before founding his congregation. He exemplified the apostolic side of his congregation by promoting the instruction of poor adults for their first communion and by fostering frequent preaching. He stipulated that each member of his society make an hour of meditation before the Blessed Sacrament solemnly exposed every eighth hour, championed the Roman rite in opposition to those promoting neo-Gallican rites prevalent in 19th-cent. France, and encouraged frequent communion. E. was associated with others noted for their zeal for spreading devotion to the Eucharist, e.g., Hermann Cohen (Forty Hours), Mlle. Tamisier (Eucharistic Congresses), Theodoline Dubouche (foundress of the Sisters of Marie Reparatrice). The congregation in 1976 numbered *c.*1300 religious in 116 houses spanning every continent. E. is well known as the author of a series of ascetical writings on the Eucharist gleaned from his personal notes, conferences, and sermons, edited posthumously by Albert Tesnière, SSS, one of his early disciples. BIBLIOGRAPHY: F. Trochu, *Le Bienheureux Pierre-Julien Eymard* (1949); L. Saint-Pierre, "*L'Heure*" *du Cénacle dans la vie et les oeuvres de Pierre-Julien Eymard* (1968).

[E. R. FALARDEAU]

EYRE, THOMAS (1718–1810), first president of Ushaw College, the seminary near Durham for the northern dioceses of England. Ordained at Douai, then a professor there, from 1775 to 1795 he worked on the Stella Mission, Newcastle. During this period he gathered materials for his unrealized project of completing Dodd's *Church History*. In 1794 E. became president of Crook Hall, Durham, established because the French Revolution forced the closing of the English College, Douai; he remained president of the seminary when it was transferred to Ushaw.

[M. HIGGINS]

EYSTON, CHARLES (1667–1721), English Catholic, author of the antiquarian pamphlet, "A Little Monument to the Once Famous Abbey and Borough of Glastonbury"; it was first published in T. Hearne's *History and Antiquities of Glastonbury* (1722).

[T. C. O'BRIEN]

EYZAGUIRRE, JOSÉ IGNACIO VÍCTOR (1817–75), Chilean clergyman, historian, and politician. Ordained to the priesthood, E. soon became well known as an orator, taught at the Catholic Univ. of Chile, and took active part in politics as senator and vice-president of the congress. In 1850 he published his *Historia eclesiástica, política y literaria de Chile,* which won him fame at home and abroad. Forced to leave the country for political reasons, he traveled in Europe, sent important reports to the Vatican, and established contact with its officials. In Rome he helped found the *Collegio Pio Latino Americano* for the training of esp.-gifted seminarians. In South America he carried out several missions entrusted to him by the papacy. BIBLIOGRAPHY: *Diccionario enciclopedia hispanoamericana* 7:1243; C. Silva Cotopa, *Monseñor José Ignacio Víctor Eyzaguirre* (1919).

[P. DAMBORIENA]

EZECHIA, see HEZEKIAH.

EZEKIEL (Heb. *yeḥĕzke'l,* may El [God] strengthen), the son of Buzi (Ezek 1.3), of a priestly family. He grew up in Jerusalem, was familiar with the Temple, and must have known Jeremiah. During the first deportation to Babylonia in 598 or 597 B.C., he was brought with others (2 Kg 24.11–16) to Tel-abib (Ezek 1.1; 3.15), near Nippur. He had his own house (Ezek 3.24; 8.1); he was married, but his wife died *c.*587 (Ezek 24.18). His prophetic mission began 5 years after his captivity (Ezek 1.2). Fourteen dates, scattered between Ezek 1.2 and 29.17, extend his ministry from 593 or 592 until 571. In visionary trances, but not in reality, he visited Jerusalem several times (Ezek 8.1–11, 25; 40.1–48).

As priest and "watchman" (Ezek 3.17; 33.2), he is concerned for the spiritual welfare of his flock and prepares them for his prophetical message of restoration. He differs from other prophets by his frequent visions and trances and

his many symbolical actions. His eloquence, his masterful use of allegory, his powerful and imaginative expressions won him many hearers (Ezek 33.30–33) who admired his art, if not his message. BIBLIOGRAPHY: E. Sellin and G. Fohrer, "Ezekiel" *Introduction to the OT* (1968) 403–418; J. Dheilly, *Prophets* (tr. R. Attwater, 1960) 46–130.

[F. BUCK]

EZEKIEL (EZECHIEL), BOOK OF, a prophetical book of the OT. There are indications (e.g., Ezek 2.4–7; 3.4–7; 11.21; 20.1–2; 24.19–24; 33.30–33) that Ezekiel proclaimed his message orally. But unlike other prophets, he himself seems to have written down his sayings. And sometimes he wrote his inspirations first and proclaimed them later (cf. 3.16b–21). His book, composed of individual sayings and collections, was not assembled by the prophet himself, but by a later editor. The Hebrew text is poorly preserved. But fragments, detached from the Ezekiel scroll found in cave 11 at Qumran, show that already in the 1st cent. B.C. the Hebrew text was fixed in a form very similar to our Masoretic text. The book falls into three sections: (1) Chapters 1–24 contain his call and prophecies of doom against Judah and Jerusalem, uttered before 586 B.C. (2) Chapters 25–32 are oracles against foreign nations, arranged, with the exception of Egypt, in geographical and chronological order. (3) Chapters 33–48 contain prophecies of restoration. The first half (33–39) describes the new covenant, the resurrection of the people, and the downfall of Gog. The second half (40–48) gives the great vision of the new kingdom of God with the program for the new organization of the temple, the city, and the land. Ezekiel fights against Israel's idolatry (6; 8–10), which is ingratitude and adultery (16; 23). Each one is responsible for himself (18). God is one and omnipresent (1–3), Lord of all nations (25–32), of death and life (37); he acts for his glory (20.9, 22; 36.20–22). He promises restoration (34.11–15; 36. 24–26), a new and everlasting covenant (37.26). Yahweh will give a new spirit and a new heart (36.26–27). And a new David (34.23–30), a "prince," will rule (cf. 44.2; 45.16,22 ff.). BIBLIOGRAPHY: H. H. Rowley, "Book of Ezechiel in Modern Study," *Bulletin of John Rylands Library* 36 (1953–54) 146–190; W. Zimmerli, *Ezechiel* (1965).

[F. BUCK]

EZIONGEBER, see ASIONGABER.

EZNIK OF KOLB (fl. 5th cent.), early Armenian Christian writer. E. was one of the scholars who helped *Mesrob, originator of the Armenian alphabet, translate much of Christian Greek and Syriac literature into the vernacular and to revise the Armenian version of the Bible. Later he became bp. of Bagrevand and wrote a "Confutation of the Sects" (*c.*441–448) in four books against the pagan materialists, the Persian magi, the Greek philosophers, and the followers of *Marcion. BIBLIOGRAPHY: Altaner 411.

[R. B. ENO]

EZRA, a priest (Ezra 7.11; 10.10) who traced his descent from Aaron through Zadok (Ezra 8.2; 1 Chr 5.24–41) and a scribe (Ezra 7.6, 12.21), a title which is explained as "a secretary for Jewish affairs in the Persian government." He was well versed in the law of Moses (Ezra 7.6,10,14). Ezra was commissioned by the Persian King Artaxerxes to go to Jerusalem to undertake certain reforms to purify and strengthen the ancient faith of Israel. Although Ezra 7.7–9 gives certain indications, the time of E.'s arrival is very much in dispute; there were three kings of Persia called Artaxerxes. The 7th year of Artaxerxes I, i.e., 458 B.C., is too early, and the 7th year of Artaxerxes II, i.e., 397 B.C., is too late. A solution, preferred by many, presupposes a faulty textual transmission and reads the 37th year of Artaxerxes I, i.e., 428 B.C. Ezra arrived in Jerusalem, leading a group of over 1,250 Jews (Ezra 7.7; 8.1–20). He began his reform by reading the law to the people (Neh 8.1–12) and dealt with the problems of mixed marriages (Ezra 10.1–44). The Feast of Tabernacles was celebrated (Neh 8.13–18), and the people concluded a great covenant with God, pledging themselves to live according to the law (Neh 9.1–10.40). Although Ezra is not mentioned in Sirach's lists of worthy men (Sir 49.13) nor in the NT, Josephus and the Talmud praise him highly. BIBLIOGRAPHY: J. Bright, *History of Israel* (1959) 362–386; J. M. Myers, "Ezra-Nehemiah" in the *Anchor Bible* (1965); C. C. Torrey, *Ezra Studies* (rev. ed. 1970).

[F. BUCK]

EZRA (ZORAH), ST. GEORGE (A.D. 516), in S Syria a church planned as an octagon inscribed in a square, with circular ambulatory around a central higher octagonal arcade which once supported a dome. It is an early example of such famous Justinian types as S. Vitale, Ravenna, A.D. 526–547, though it is now greatly altered.

[M. J. DALY]

EZRA-NEHEMIAH, BOOKS OF. Originally forming a single complex with 1 and 2 Chr, these two books should be treated as one for purposes of interpretation. The same author who composed Chronicles, discreetly ignoring the 50 years of exile, resumes his story at the point where Cyrus issues his decree in 538 B.C. and describes the reorganization of the people, the rebuilding and repeopling of the city and Temple, and the expulsion of aliens who threaten to corrupt the purity of the people and their religion. Though the background history is obscure and disputed, it seems increasingly probable that several of the events recorded actually occurred in a different order, and that the actual sequence should be reconstructed somewhat as follows: (1) The first expedition of returning Jewish exiles arrives from Babylon under Sheshbazzar (a scion of the Davidic house,

replaced shortly afterwards by his nephew Zerubbabel) and Joshua the high priest. The rebuilding of the city and Temple is undertaken but abandoned until 520 owing to the fierce opposition of Samaritans and others. (2) Encouraged by the prophets Haggai and Zechariah, the Jews resume and complete the rebuilding of the Temple (520–515), and the Passover is celebrated there once more (Ezra 1–6). (3) Nehemiah, a highly placed Jewish official at the court of Artaxerxes I, having received permission c.445 to rebuild the walls of Jerusalem, journeys there and in spite of menaces and intrigues on the part of the aliens, succeeds in his aim. Nehemiah then organizes the repopulation of Jerusalem and persuades the Jews to remit oppressive debts when these are owed by their fellow Jews (Neh 1–7). In the course of a second visit (shortly after 432) Nehemiah corrects a number of abuses, expelling foreigners who have meanwhile infiltrated even the temple precincts, and have been causing foreign wives to be divorced. He also makes it obligatory for the community to provide for the support of the Levites and to observe the Sabbath. These measures are ratified by a compact (Neh 9.38–10.40). (4) Ezra is likewise authorized by Artaxerxes II to carry out reforms among his own people. At the feast of Tabernacles he solemnly reads and reimposes the law of Moses (in this case probably represented by the "Priestly" source of the Pentateuch), and the people pledge themselves to abide by it, and in particular to avoid foreign marriages and to divorce and expel all foreign wives. The rights and privileges of the Levites and temple personnel are once more reasserted (Ezra ch. 7–10, Neh ch. 8). The whole compilation is pervaded by a sense of the vital importance of reconstituting and preserving the community as the people of Yahweh and guarding it from corruption by foreign influences. BIBLIOGRAPHY: L. W. Batten, *Ezra and Nehemiah* (1949); K. Galling, *Ezra-Nehemiah* (1954); A. Gelin, *Les Livres d'Esdras et de Néhémie* (2d ed., 1960); S. Mowinckel, *Studien zu dem Buche Ezra-Nehemia* I-II (1964); G. Wright, *Date of Esra's Coming to Jerusalem* (1947); C. C. Torrey, *Chronicler's History of Israel, Chronicles–Ezra-Nehemiah, Restored to Its Original Form* (1954); J. Bright, *History of Israel* (1959) 356–386; H. Cazelles, "La Mission d'Esdras," VT 4 (1954) 113–140; A. Albright, *Biblical Period from Abraham to Ezra* (1963) 90–96.

[D. J. BOURKE]

EZZELINO (III) DA ROMANO, faction chief and tyrant of Verona, Vicenza, and Padua (1194–1259). Son of Ezzelino II (the Monk) and Adelaide of Mangona, E. was a descendant of Ezzelino I, a German knight who settled in Italy in the 11th century. E. married the natural daughter of Emperor Frederic II and became a staunch supporter of imperial policy and leader of the Ghibelline faction in 1232. Receiving support from German troopers, he took control of the March of Verona, and later Vicenza and Padua, leading to years of despotism, ferocious enmity to faction rivals, and cruelty streaked with sadism and insanity, so vicious that he was accused of heresy. In time, his support from the ''popolani'' of Padua was so weakened that when Pope Alexander II proclaimed a crusade against him under Philip of Ravenna, Padua was easily freed June, 1256. E. struck back at Brescia and defeated Philip in 1258, but this led to a league of Guelf-Ghibelline neighbors against him. E. was captured in the battle of Cassano, and committed suicide October 1, 1259. BIBLIOGRAPHY: L. Simeoni, EncIt (1949) 14:692–693.

[N. F. GAUGHAN]

EZZOLIED (or *Ezzos Gesang),* a medieval German poem about the creation, fall, and redemption of mankind. It was composed *c.*1060 by the Bamberg Canon Ezzo at the request of Bp. Gunther of Bamberg (1057–65). There are two MSS, neither of them the original (see K. A. Barack, *Ezzos Gesang von den Wundern Christi und Notkers Memento Mori,* ed. in facsimile, 1879): the 11th-cent. Strassburg MS (A) has only the first seven strophes; the 12th-cent. Vorau MS (B) has the complete text, but revised and enlarged. BIBLIOGRAPHY: M. O'C. Walshe, *Medieval German Literature* (1962) 37–39, 372–373; H. de Boor and R. Newald, *Geschichte der deutschen Literatur* (1960) 145–147 and *passim.*

[M. F. MCCARTHY]

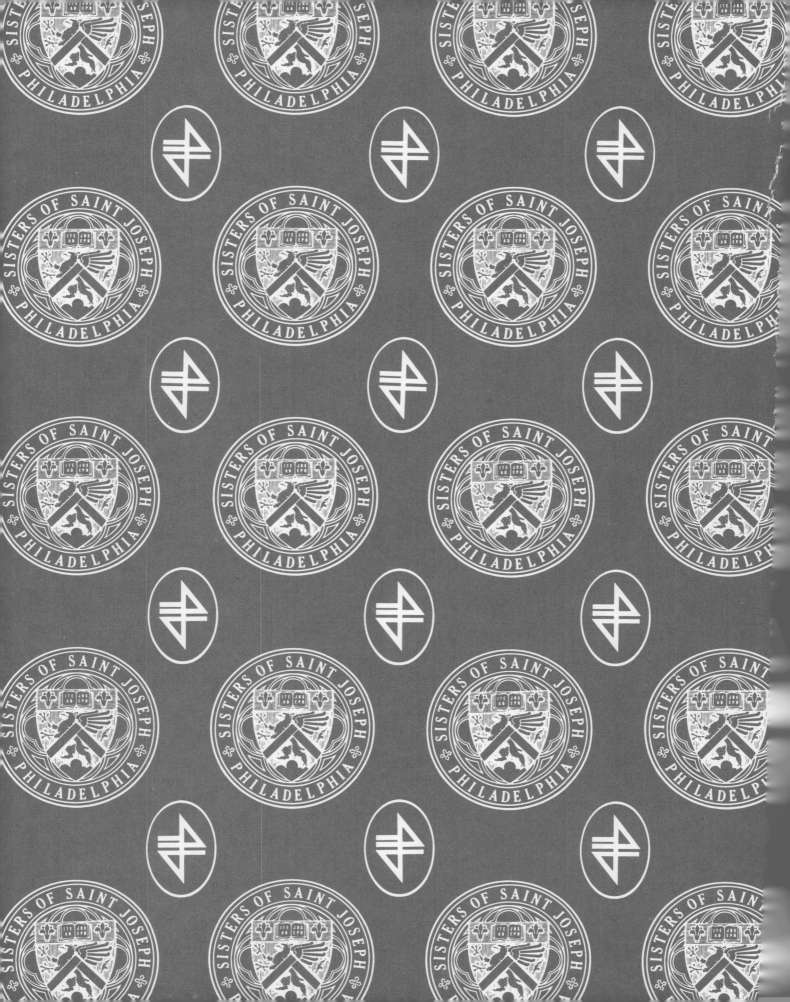